W9-AZM-452

12/27/99

Max Johnson

463 - Franklin Stone

LANGENSCHEIDT'S
NEW COLLEGE
MERRIAM-WEBSTER
ENGLISH DICTIONARY

Langenscheidt's New College Merriam-Webster

English Dictionary

LANGENSCHEIDT

NEW YORK · BERLIN · MUNICH

© 1996 Merriam-Webster, Inc. Springfield, Massachusets, U.S.A.
© 1998 Langenscheidt KG, Berlin and Munich
Printed in Germany

Contents

Preface

In 1898 an abridged dictionary titled Webster's Collegiate Dictionary took the place, in the Merriam-Webster line, of an earlier book titled Webster's National Pictorial Dictionary. The new book was based upon the 1890 edition of the Merriam-Webster Unabridged, and it aimed, its editors said, "to present the most essential parts of Webster's International Dictionary, in a compact and convenient form, suited to the general reader and especially to the college student." The change cannot have seemed momentous to the people involved; nonetheless, it inaugurated a series of editions that has continued for nearly a hundred years. The book you hold, Merriam-Webster's Collegiate Dictionary, Tenth Edition, is the very latest in that series. Its title is new, and its contents have undergone the most searching and extensive sort of review and modification over the two-year course of work, but it remains rooted as firmly as ever in the Merriam-Webster tradition of excellence in the making of dictionaries.

A word must be said about the new title, which breaks with tradition in beginning not with Webster's but with Merriam-Webster's. During the time that our Collegiate Dictionary has been in existence, we have seen the proliferation of dictionaries from other publishers bearing the designation Webster's in their titles. In 1982 we changed the name of our company from the G. & C. Merriam Company that it had borne since its inception in 1831 to Merriam-Webster, Incorporated. Events of the succeeding decade have brought us to believe that we must now place even greater emphasis on the Merriam-Webster combination, which is uniquely ours. The new title of a very prominent dictionary in our line reflects this belief.

Although Merriam-Webster's Collegiate Dictionary, Tenth Edition, may lack a familiar ring, this dictionary like all earlier editions is meant to serve the general public as its chief source of information about the words of our language. Its title may suggest a special appropriateness for the student, but those who work in offices and those who read, think, and write at home will equally find it a trustworthy guide to the English of our day.

The ever-expanding vocabulary of our language exerts inexorable pressure on the contents of any dictionary. Words and senses are born at a far greater rate than that at which they die out. The 1600 pages of this Collegiate make it the most comprehensive ever published. And its treatment of words is as nearly exhaustive as the compass of an abridged work permits. As in all Merriam-Webster dictionaries, the information given is based on the collection of 14,500,000 citations maintained in the offices of this company. These citations show words used in a wide range of printed sources, and the collection is constantly being augmented through the efforts of the editorial staff. Thus, the user of the dictionary may be confident that entries in the Collegiate are based on current as well as older material. The citation files hold 4,500,000 more examples than were available to the editors of Webster's Third New International Dictionary, published in 1961, and 1,500,000 more than the editors of the Ninth Edition had at their disposal. The editors of this edition also had available to them for the first time a machine-readable corpus of over 20,000,000 words of text drawn from the wide and constantly changing range of publications that supply the paper slips in the citation files.

Those entries known to be trademarks or service marks are so labeled and are treated in accordance with a formula approved by the United States Trademark Association. No entry in this dictionary, however, should be regarded as affecting the validity of any trademark or service mark.

The best features of the vocabulary section in the last edition have been retained, reviewed, and improved for this one. Over a hundred additional pictorial illustrations are present, and many of them were drawn especially for this book in order to supplement and clarify definitions. To the synonym paragraphs brief verbal illustrations have consistently been added to assist with the understanding of the discrimination offered. Usage paragraphs, which appeared for the first time in the Ninth Edition, are here again, augmented in number and extensively revised in the light of the research and thought that produced Webster's Dictionary of English Usage about halfway between these editions. The dates of first use provided at most main entries, also new to the last edition, have proved to be very popular with users of the Collegiate. For the Tenth Edition, thousands of these dates have been pushed back in time, anywhere from a single year to several centuries from published materials not available ten years ago, from the continuing investigations of our own editors, and from the contributions of hundreds of interested readers.

The front matter of this book establishes a context for understanding what this dictionary is and how it came to be, as well as how it may be used most effectively. The Explanatory Notes address themselves to the latter topic. They answer the user's questions about the conventions, devices, and techniques by which the editors have been able to compress mountains of information about English words into little more than 1400 pages. All users of the dictionary are urged to read this section through and then consult it for special information as they need to. The brief essay on our language as it is recorded in Merriam-Webster dictionaries, and this Collegiate in particular, is meant to satisfy an interest in lexicography often expressed in the correspondence which our editors receive. The Guide to Pronunciation serves both to show how the pronunciations in this book are arrived at and to explain the mechanics of the respelling system in which they are set down.

The back matter retains five sections from the last edition of the Collegiate. These are Abbreviations and Symbols for Chemical Elements, Foreign Words and Phrases that occur frequently in English texts but have not become part of the English vocabulary; thousands of proper names brought together under the separate headings Biographical Names and Geographical Names; a gathering of important Signs and Symbols that cannot readily be alphabetized; and a Handbook of Style in which various stylistic conventions (as of punctuation and capitalization) are summarized and exemplified. All the sections are expanded in this edition.

Looking at a copy of that long-ago first Collegiate Dictionary, one is struck by how different it is, as a physical book and as a work of reference, from the present edition. The board covers are heavy, the margins of the page are wide, and the type is relatively large; at the same time it holds only about 1100 pages and only about half the number of vocabulary entries of this Tenth Edition. At that time the Merriam-Webster citation file was no more than in its infancy. Yet the editors of that book created it with the same careful, serious attention that the present editors have brought to their work.

The publishers said of their original Collegiate Dictionary, "For the book as a whole we venture to claim that in its class and for its purpose it has no superior and no equal." The trained, experienced, permanent staff of Merriam-Webster, Incorporated, who worked on this Tenth Edition and whose names are given on the facing page, have no less confidence in what they have created. They offer it to people everywhere who need information about the vocabulary of English, in the assurance that it will prove a reliable companion.

Frederick C. Mish
Editor in Chief

Editorial Staff

Editor in Chief
Frederick C. Mish

Executive Editor
John M. Morse

Director of Defining
E. Ward Gilman

Senior Editor, Operations
Madeline L. Novak

Senior Editors
Robert D. Copeland · James G. Lowe
· Roger W. Pease, Jr. · Stephen J. Perrault

Associate Editors
Michael G. Belanger · Paul F. Cappellano
· Joanne M. Despres · Kathleen M. Doherty
· James L. Rader · Brian M. Sietsema

Assistant Editors
Susan L. Brady · Jennifer N. Cislo
· Jennifer S. Goss · Peter D. Haraty
· Amy K. Harris · Daniel J. Hopkins
· Alexandra C. Horowitz · René P. Houle
· Rachel King · Deborah S. Morris
· Brett P. Palmer · Michael D. Roundy
· Maria A. Sansalone · Joan I. Swartz
· Jennifer B. Tufts · Linda Picard Wood

Editorial Assistants
Donna L. Rickerby · Katherine C. Sietsema

Product Development Editor
Mark A. Stevens

Librarian
Francine A. Roberts

Departmental Secretary
Georgette B. Boucher

Head of Typing Room
Gloria J. Afflitto

Senior Clerk
Ruth W. Gaines

Clerks and Typists
Demetra C. Doolin · Mary M. Dunn
· Florence A. Fowler · Patricia M. Jensen
· Ella L. Johnson · Marjorie C. Kochanowicz
· Veronica P. McLymont

Editorial Contributors
Cynthia S. Ashby · Sharon Goldstein
· Eileen M. Haraty

Merriam-Webster, Incorporated
Joseph J. Esposito, President
Thomas E. Stanley, Senior Vice President and Publisher

angle brackets *PAGE 18a*	
binomial *PAGE 21a*	
boldface colon *PAGE 19a*	
called also *PAGE 18a*	
capitalization label *PAGE 15a*	
centered dots *PAGES 10a, 11a*	
cognate cross-reference *PAGES 21a, 22a*	
cutback inflected forms *PAGES 13a, 14a*	
date *PAGE 17a*	
defined run-on entry *PAGE 11a*	
definition *PAGE 19a*	
directional cross-reference *PAGE 21a*	
equal variant *PAGE 11a*	
etymology *PAGES 15a,16a*	
functional label *PAGE 13a*	
guide phrase *PAGE 18a*	
homographs *PAGE 10a*	
illustrative quotation *PAGE 18a*	
inflected forms *PAGES 13a, 14a*	
inflectional cross-reference *PAGES 21a, 22a*	
list of undefined words *PAGE 22a*	
lowercase *PAGE 15a*	
main entry *PAGE 10a*	
often attrib *PAGE 15a*	

²**pet** *adj* (1584) **1 :** kept or treated as a pet **2 :** expressing fondness or endearment ⟨a ~ name⟩ **3 :** FAVORITE ⟨a ~ project⟩

pharaoh ant *n* (ca. 1947) **:** a little red ant ⟨*Monomorium pharaonis*⟩ that is a common household pest

phar·ma·cy \'fär-mə-sē\ *n, pl* **-cies** [LL *pharmacia* administration of drugs, fr. Gk *pharmakeia*, fr. *pharmakeuein* to administer drugs, fr. *pharmakon* magic charm, poison, drug] (1651) **1 :** the art, practice, or profession of preparing, preserving, compounding, and dispensing medical drugs **2 a :** a place where medicines are compounded or dispensed **b :** DRUGSTORE **3 :** PHARMACOPOEIA 2

phase–contrast microscope *n* (1947) **:** a microscope that translates differences in phase of the light transmitted through or reflected by the object into differences of intensity in the image — called also *phase microscope*

Phi·lis·tine \'fi-lə-‚stēn; fə-'lis-tən, -‚tēn; 'fi-lə-stən\ *n* (14c) **1 :** a native or inhabitant of ancient Philistia **2** *often not cap* **a :** a person who is guided by materialism and is usu. disdainful of intellectual or artistic values **b :** one uninformed in a special area of knowledge — **philistine** *adj, often cap* — **phi·lis·tin·ism** \-lə-‚stē-‚ni-zəm; -'lis-tə-, -‚tē-, -lə-stə-\ *n, often cap*

pic·tur·esque \‚pik-chə-'resk\ *adj* [F & It; F *pittoresque*, fr. It *pittoresco*, fr. *pittore* painter, fr. L *pictor*, fr. *pingere*] (1703) **1 a :** resembling a picture **: suggesting a painted scene b :** charming or quaint in appearance **2 :** evoking mental images : VIVID **syn** see GRAPHIC — **pic·tur·esque·ly** *adv* — **pic·tur·esque·ness** *n*
pie var of PI

²**pillory** *vt* **-ried; -ry·ing** (ca. 1600) **1 :** to set in a pillory as punishment **2 :** to expose to public contempt, ridicule, or scorn

pin·fold \-‚fōld\ *n* [ME, fr. OE *pundfald*, fr. *pund-* enclosure + *fald* fold] (13c) **1 :** ²POUND 1a **2 :** a place of restraint

pins and needles *n pl* (1813) **:** a pricking tingling sensation in a limb growing numb or recovering from numbness — on pins and needles **: in a nervous or jumpy state of anticipation

pi·ra·nha \pə-'rä-nə; -'ran-və, -'ran-\ *n* [Pg. fr. Tupi *pirāva*, fr. *pira* fish + *āva* tooth] (1869) **:** any of various usu. small So. American characin fishes (genus *Serrasalmo*) having very sharp teeth and including some that may attack and inflict dangerous wounds upon humans and large animals — called also *caribe*

pis·til \'pis-t'l\ *n* [NL *pistillum*, fr. L, pestle — more at PESTLE] (1749) **:** a single carpel or group of fused carpels usu. differentiated into an ovary, style, and stigma — see FLOWER illustration

pla·gal \'plā-gəl\ *adj* [ML *plagalis*, ultim. fr. Gk *plagios* oblique, sideways, fr. *plagos* side; akin to L *plaga* net, region, Gk *pelagos* sea] (1597) **1** *of a church mode* **:** having the keynote on the 4th scale step — compare AUTHENTIC 4a **2** *of a cadence* **:** progressing from the subdominant chord to the tonic — compare AUTHENTIC 4b

plagu·ey *or* **plaguy** \'plā-gē, plē-\ *adj* (1615) **:** causing irritation or annoyance : TROUBLESOME — **plaguey** *adv* — **plagu·i·ly** \-gə-lē\ *adv*
plead \'plēd\ *vb* **plead·ed** \'plē-dəd\ *or* **pled** *also* **plead** \'pled\; **plead·ing** [ME *plaiden* to institute a lawsuit, fr. MF *plaidier*, fr. *plaid* plea] *vi* (13c) **1 :** to argue a case or cause in a court of law **2 a :** to make an allegation in an action or other legal proceeding; *esp* **:** to answer the previous pleading of the other party by denying facts therein stated or by alleging new facts **b :** to conduct pleadings **3 :** to make a plea of a specified nature ⟨~ not guilty⟩ **4 a :** to argue for or against a claim **b :** to entreat or appeal earnestly **~** *vt* **1 :** to maintain (as a case or cause) in a court of law or other tribunal **2 :** to allege in or by way of a legal plea **3 :** to offer as a plea usu. in defense, apology, or excuse — **plead·able** \'plē-də-bəl\ *adj* — **plead·er** *n* — **plead·ing·ly** \'plē-diŋ-lē\ *adv*

plo·ver \'plə-vər, 'plō-\ *n, pl* **plover** *or* **plovers** [ME, fr. MF, fr. (assumed) VL *pluviarius*, fr. L *pluvia* rain — more at PLUVIAL] (14c) **1 :** any of a family (Charadriidae) of shore-inhabiting birds that differ from the sandpipers in having a short hard-tipped bill and usu. a stouter more compact build **2 :** any of various birds (as a turnstone or sandpiper) related to the plovers

¹**plu·vi·al** \'plü-vē-əl\ *adj* [L *pluvialis*, fr. *pluvia* rain, fr. fem. of *pluvius* rainy, fr. *pluere* to rain — more at FLOW] (ca. 1656) **1 a :** of or relating to rain **b :** characterized by abundant rain **2** *of a geologic change* **:** resulting from the action of rain

¹**point·ed** \'pȯin-tad\ *adj* (14c) **1 a :** having a point **b :** being an arch with a pointed crown; *also* **:** marked by the use of a pointed arch ⟨~ architecture⟩ **2 a :** being to the point : PERTINENT **b :** aimed at a particular person or group **3 :** CONSPICUOUS, MARKED ⟨~ indifference⟩ — **point·ed·ly** *adv* — **point·ed·ness** *n*
²**pointed** *adj* [short for *appointed*] (1523) *obs* **:** SET, FIXED
poise *vb* **poised; pois·ing** [ME, to weigh, ponder, fr. MF *pois-*, stem of *peser*, fr. L *pensare* — more at PENSIVE] *vt* (1598) **1 a :** BALANCE; *esp* **:** to hold or carry in equilibrium ⟨carried a water jar *poised* on her head⟩ **b :** to hold supported or suspended without motion in a steady position ⟨*poised* her fork and gave her guest a knowing look —Louis Bromfield⟩ **2 :** to hold or carry (the head) in a particular way **3 :** to put into readiness : BRACE **~** *vi* **1 :** to become drawn up into readiness **2 :** HOVER

²**pole** *vb* **poled; pol·ing** *vt* (1573) **1 :** to act upon with a pole **2 :** to impel or push with a pole **~** *vi* **1 :** to propel a boat with a pole **2 :** to use ski poles to gain speed

poleis *pl of* POLIS
post- *prefix* [ME, fr. L, fr. *post*; akin to Lith *pas* at, Gk *apo* away from — more at OF] **1 a :** after **:** subsequent **:** later ⟨*post*date⟩ **b :** behind **:** following after ⟨*post*lude⟩ ⟨*post*consonantal⟩ **2 a :** subsequent to **:** later than ⟨*post*operative⟩ **b :** posterior to ⟨*post*orbital⟩

post-abor·tion	post-Ein·stein·ian	post-mat·ing
post-ac·ci·dent	post-election	post-me·di·e·val
post-ad·o·les·cent	post-em·bry·o·nal	post-mid·night
post-am·pu·ta·tion	post-em·bry·on·ic	post-neo·na·tal

po·sy \'pō-zē\ *n, pl* **posies** [alter. of *poesy*] (1533) **1 :** a brief sentiment, motto, or legend **2 a :** BOUQUET, NOSEGAY **b :** FLOWER
po·tas·si·um \pə-'ta-sē-əm\ *n, often attrib* [NL, fr. *potassa* potash, fr. E *potash*] (ca. 1807) **:** a silver-white soft light low-melting univalent metallic element of the alkali metal group that occurs abundantly in nature esp. combined in minerals — see ELEMENT table

Explanatory Chart

po·ten·tate \'pōt-ᵊn-ˌtāt\ n (15c) : RULER, SOVEREIGN; *broadly* : one who wields great power or sway

pot·herb \'pät-ˌərb, -ˌhərb\ n (1538) : a usu. leafy herb that is cooked for use as greens; *also* : one (as mint) used to season food

pot lik·ker \-'li-kər\ *Southern & Midland var of* POT LIQUOR

pot·sherd \'pät-ˌshärd\ n [ME *pot-sherd*, fr. *pot* + *sherd* shard] (14c) : a pottery fragment

pouf *also* **pouffe** \'püf\ n [F *pouf*, something inflated, of imit. origin] (1817) **1** : PUFF 3b(3) **2** : a bouffant or fluffy part of a garment or accessory **3** : OTTOMAN — **poufed** *or* **pouffed** \'püft\ *adj*

poult \'pōlt\ n [ME *polet, pulte* young fowl — more at PULLET] (15c) : a young fowl; *esp* : a young turkey

pow·dery \'pau̇-də-rē\ *adj* (15c) **1 a** : resembling or consisting of powder ⟨~ snow⟩ **b** : easily reduced to powder : CRUMBLING **2** : covered with or as if with powder

prexy \'prek-sē\ *also* **prex** \'preks\ n, pl **prex·ies** *also* **prex·es** [*prexy* fr. *prex*, by shortening & alter. fr. *president*] (1871) *slang* : PRESIDENT — used chiefly of a college president

proph·et \'prä-fət\ n [ME *prophete*, fr. OF, fr. L *propheta*, fr. Gk *prophētēs*, fr. *pro* for + *phanai* to speak — more at FOR, BAN] (12c) **1** : one who utters divinely inspired revelations; *specif, often cap* : the writer of one of the prophetic books of the Old Testament **2** : one gifted with more than ordinary spiritual and moral insight; *esp* : an inspired poet **3** : one who foretells future events : PREDICTOR **4** : an effective or leading spokesman for a cause, doctrine, or group **5** *Christian Science* **a** : a spiritual seer **b** : disappearance of material sense before the conscious facts of spiritual Truth — **proph·et·hood** \-ˌhud\ n

pro·pose \prə-'pōz\ *vb* **pro·posed; pro·pos·ing** [ME, fr. MF *proposer*, fr. L *proponere* (perf. indic. *proposui*) — more at PROPOUND] *vi* (14c) **1** : to form or put forward a plan or intention ⟨man ~s, but God disposes⟩ **2** *obs* : to engage in talk or discussion **3** : to make an offer of marriage ⟨~⟩ ~ *vt* **1 a** : to set before the mind (as for discussion, imitation, or action) ⟨~ a plan for settling the dispute⟩ **b** : to set before someone and esp. oneself as an aim or intent ⟨*proposed* to spend the summer in Italy⟩ **2 a** : to set forth for acceptance or rejection ⟨~ terms for peace⟩ ⟨~ a topic for debate⟩ **b** : to recommend to fill a place or vacancy : NOMINATE ⟨~ them for membership⟩ **c** : to offer as a toast ⟨~ the happiness of the couple⟩ — **pro·pos·er** n

¹pros·pect \'prä-ˌspekt\ n [ME, fr. L *prospectus* view, prospect, fr. *prospicere* to look forward, exercise foresight, fr. *pro-* forward + *specere* to look — more at PRO-, SPY] (15c) **1** : EXPOSURE 3b **2 a** (1) : an extensive view (2) : a mental consideration : SURVEY **b** : a place that commands an extensive view : LOOKOUT **c** : something extended to the view : SCENE **d** *archaic* : a sketch or picture of a scene **3** *obs* : ASPECT **4 a** : the act of looking forward : ANTICIPATION **b** : a mental picture of something to come : VISION **c** : something that is awaited or expected : POSSIBILITY **d** *pl* (1) : financial expectations (2) : CHANCES **5** : a place showing signs of containing a mineral deposit **6 a** : a potential buyer or customer **b** : a likely candidate — **in prospect** : possible or likely for the future

syn PROSPECT, OUTLOOK, ANTICIPATION, FORETASTE mean an advance realization of something to come. PROSPECT implies expectation of a particular event, condition, or development of definite interest or concern ⟨the *prospect* of a quiet weekend⟩. OUTLOOK suggests a forecasting of the future ⟨a favorable *outlook* for the economy⟩. ANTICIPATION implies a prospect or outlook that involves advance suffering or enjoyment of what is foreseen ⟨the *anticipation* of her arrival⟩. FORETASTE implies an actual though brief or partial experience of something forthcoming ⟨the frost was a *foretaste* of winter⟩.

¹pros·trate \'prä-ˌstrāt\ *adj* [ME *prostrat*, fr. L *prostratus*, pp. of *prosternere*, fr. *pro-* before + *sternere* to spread out, throw down — more at STREW] (14c) **1** : stretched out with face on the ground in adoration or submission; *also* : lying flat **2** : completely overcome and lacking vitality, will, or power to rise ⟨was ~ from the heat⟩ **3** : trailing on the ground : PROCUMBENT ⟨~ shrub⟩ **syn** *see* PRONE

pro·ten·sive \-'ten(t)-siv\ *adj* [L *protensus*, pp. of *protendere*] (1671) **1** *archaic* : having continuance in time **2** *archaic* : having lengthwise extent or extensiveness — **pro·ten·sive·ly** *adv*

Protestant ethic n (1926) : an ethic that stresses the virtue of hard work, thrift, and self-discipline

prove \'prüv\ *vb* **proved; proved** *or* **prov·en** \'prü-vən, *Brit also* 'prō-\; **prov·ing** \'prü-vin\ [ME, fr. OF *prover*, fr. L *probare* to test, approve, prove, fr. *probus* good, honest, fr. *pro-* for, in favor + *-bus* (akin to OE *bēon* to be) — more at PRO-, BE] *vt* (13c) **1** *archaic* : to learn or find out by experience **2 a** : to test the truth, validity, or genuineness of ⟨the exception ~s the rule⟩ ⟨~ a will at probate⟩ **b** : to test the worth or quality of; *specif* : to compare against a standard — sometimes used with *up* or *out* **c** : to check the correctness of (as an arithmetic result) **3 a** : to establish the existence, truth, or validity of (as by evidence or logic) ⟨~ a theorem⟩ ⟨the charges were never *proved* in court⟩ **b** : to demonstrate as having a particular quality or worth ⟨the vaccine has been *proven* effective after years of tests⟩ ⟨*proved* herself a great actress⟩ **4** : to show (oneself) to be worthy or capable ⟨eager to ~ myself in the new job⟩ ~ *vi* : to turn out esp. after trial or test ⟨the new drug *proved* effective⟩ — **prov·able** \'prü-və-bəl\ *adj* — **prov·able·ness** n — **prov·ably** \-blē\ *adv* — **prov·er** \'prü-vər\ n

usage The past participle *proven*, orig. the past participle of *preve*, a Middle English variant of *prove* that survived in Scotland, has gradually worked its way into standard English over the past three and a half centuries. It seems to have first become established in legal use and to have come only slowly into literary use. Tennyson was one of its earliest frequent users, prob. for metrical reasons. It was disapproved by 19th century grammarians, one of whom included it in a list of "words that are not words." Surveys made some 30 or 40 years ago indicated that *proved* was about four times as frequent as *proven*. But our evidence from the last 10 or 15 years shows this no longer to be the case. As a past participle *proven* is now about as frequent as *proved* in all contexts. As an attributive adjective ⟨*proved* or *proven* gas reserves⟩ *proven* is much more common than *proved*.

provided *conj* [ME, pp. of *providen* to provide] (15c) : on condition that : with the understanding : IF **usage** *see* PROVIDING

punch up *vt* (ca. 1959) : to give energy or forcefulness to ⟨jokes added to *punch up* a speech⟩

Label	Reference
primary stress	PAGE 12a
pronunciation	PAGES 12a, 13a
regional label	PAGES 17a, 18a
secondary stress	PAGE 12a
secondary variant	PAGE 11a
sense divider	PAGE 19a
sense letter	PAGE 19a
sense number	PAGE 19a
stylistic label	PAGES 17a, 18a
subject label	PAGE 18a
swung dash (boldface)	PAGE 13a
swung dash (lightface)	PAGE 18a
synonymous cross-reference	PAGES 21a, 22a
synonym paragraph	PAGE 22a
syn see	PAGE 22a
temporal label	PAGE 17a
undefined run-on entry	PAGE 11a
uppercase	PAGE 15a
usage note	PAGES 18a, 19a
usage paragraph	PAGE 19a
usage see	PAGE 19a
verbal illustration	PAGE 18a

Explanatory Notes

Entries

MAIN ENTRIES

A boldface letter or a combination of such letters, including punctuation marks and diacritics where needed, that is set flush with the left-hand margin of each column of type is a main entry or entry word. The main entry may consist of letters set solid, of letters joined by a hyphen or a diagonal, or of letters separated by one or more spaces:

> **¹alone** . . . *adj*
>
> **au·to–da–fé** . . . *n*
>
> **and/or** . . . *conj*
>
> **automatic pilot** . . . *n*

The material in lightface type that follows each main entry on the same line and on succeeding indented lines explains and justifies its inclusion in the dictionary.

Variation in the styling of compound words in English is frequent and widespread. It is often completely acceptable to choose freely among open, hyphenated, and closed alternatives (as *lifestyle, life-style,* or *life style*). However, to show all the stylings that are found for English compounds would require space that can be better used for other information. So this dictionary limits itself to a single styling for a compound:

> **peace·mak·er**
>
> **pell–mell**
>
> **boom box**

When a compound is widely used and one styling predominates, that styling is shown. When a compound is uncommon or when the evidence indicates that two or three stylings are approximately equal in frequency, the styling shown is based on the analogy of parallel compounds.

ORDER OF MAIN ENTRIES

The main entries follow one another in alphabetical order letter by letter without regard to intervening spaces or hyphens: *battle royal* follows *battlement* and *earth-shattering* follows *earthshaking*. Those containing an Arabic numeral are alphabetized as if the numeral were spelled out: *3-D* comes between *three-color* and *three-decker*. Those that often begin with the abbreviation *St.* in common usage have the abbreviation spelled out: *Saint Anthony's fire*.

Full words come before parts of words made up of the same letters. Solid compounds come first and are followed by hyphenated compounds and then open compounds. Lowercase entries come before entries that begin with a capital letter:

> **semi** . . . *n*
>
> **semi-** . . . *prefix*
>
> **take·out** . . . *n*
>
> **take–out** . . . *adj*
>
> **take out** . . . *vt*
>
> **tim·o·thy** . . . *n*
>
> **Tim·o·thy** . . . *n*

HOMOGRAPHS

When one main entry has exactly the same written form as another, the two are distinguished by superscript numerals preceding each word:

> **¹melt** . . . *vb* **¹pine** . . . *n*
>
> **²melt** *n* **²pine** *vi*

Sometimes such homographs are related: the two entries *melt* are derived from the same root. Sometimes there is no relationship: the two entries *pine* are unrelated beyond the accident of spelling. The order of homographs is usually historical: the one first used in English is entered first. A homograph derived from an earlier homograph by functional shift, however, follows its parent immediately, with the result that occasionally one homograph appears ahead of another that is older in usage. For example, of the three entries *kennel* the second (a verb) is derived from the first (a noun). Even though the unrelated third entry *kennel* was used in English many years before the second, it follows the two related entries.

GUIDE WORDS

A pair of guide words is printed at the top of each page. The entries that fall alphabetically between the guide words are found on that page.

It is important to remember that alphabetical order rather than position of an entry on the page determines the selection of guide words. The first guide word is the alphabetically first entry on the page. The second guide word is usually the alphabetically last entry on the page:

> **academe • accessible**

The entry need not be a main entry. Another boldface word—a variant, an inflected form, or a defined or undefined run-on—may be selected as a guide word. For this reason the last printed main entry on a page is not always the last entry alphabetically:

> **ace • achromatize**

On the page where these guide words are used, *achromatic lens* is the last printed entry, but *achromatize,* a derivative word run on at *achromatic,* is the last entry alphabetically and so has been chosen as the second guide word.

All guide words must themselves be in alphabetical order from page to page throughout the dictionary; thus, the alphabetically last entry on a page is not used if it follows alphabetically the first guide word on the next page:

> **alençon • alignment**

On the page where these guide words are found, *alinement,* a variant at the entry *alignment,* is the last entry alphabetically, but it is not used as the second guide word because it follows alphabetically the entry *alike,* which is the first guide word on the next page. To use *alinement* would violate the alphabetical order of guide words from page to page, and so the entry *alignment* is the second guide word instead.

END-OF-LINE DIVISION

The centered dots within entry words indicate division points at which a hyphen may be put at the end of a line of print or writing. Thus the noun *pos·si·bil·i·ty* may be ended on one line with:

> pos-
> possi-
> possibil-
> possibili-

and continued on the next with:

> sibility
> bility
> ity
> ty

Centered dots are not shown after a single initial letter or before a single terminal letter because printers seldom cut off a single letter:

> **aswirl** . . . *adj*
>
> **mouthy** . . . *adj*
>
> **idea** . . . *n*

Nor are they shown at second and succeeding homographs unless these differ among themselves:

> ¹**re·form** . . . *vb*   ¹**min·ute** . . . *n*
>
> ²**reform** *n*   ²**minute** *vt*
>
> ³**reform** *adj*   ³**mi·nute** . . . *adj*

There are acceptable alternative end-of-line divisions just as there are acceptable variant spellings and pronunciations. It is, for example, all but impossible to produce a convincing argument that either of the divisions *aus·ter·i·ty, au·ster·i·ty* is better than the other. But space cannot be taken for entries like *aus·ter·i·ty or au·ster·i·ty*, and *au·s·ter·i·ty* would likely be confusing to many. No more than one division is, therefore, shown for an entry in this dictionary.

Many words have two or more common pronunciation variants, and the same end-of-line division is not always appropriate for each of them. The division *pi·an·ist*, for example, best fits the variant \pē-'a-nist\ whereas the division *pi·a·nist* best fits the variant \'pē-ə-nist\. In instances like this, the division falling farther to the left is used, regardless of the order of the pronunciations:

> **pi·a·nist** \pē-'a-nist, 'pē-ə-nist\

A double hyphen at the end of a line in this dictionary (as in the definition at *abstract expressionism*) stands for a hyphen that belongs at that point in a hyphenated word and that is retained when the word is written as a unit on one line.

VARIANTS

When a main entry is followed by the word *or* and another spelling, the two spellings are equal variants. Both are standard, and either one may be used according to personal inclination:

> **ocher** *or* **ochre**

If two variants joined by *or* are out of alphabetical order, they remain equal variants. The one printed first is, however, slightly more common than the second:

> **plow** *or* **plough**

When another spelling is joined to the main entry by the word *also*, the spelling after *also* is a secondary variant and occurs less frequently than the first:

> **can·cel·la·tion** *also* **can·cel·ation**

Secondary variants belong to standard usage and may be used according to personal inclination. If there are two secondary variants, the second is joined to the first by *or*. Once the word *also* is used to signal a secondary variant, all following variants are joined by *or*:

> ¹**Shake·spear·ean** *or* **Shake·spear·ian** *also* **Shak·sper·ean** *or* **Shak·sper·ian**

Variants whose spelling places them alphabetically more than a column away from the main entry are entered at their own alphabetical places and usually not at the main entry:

> ¹**jibe** . . . *var of* GIBE
>
> ³**rime, rimester** *var of* RHYME, RHYMESTER

Variants having a usage label appear only at their own alphabetical places:

> **metre** . . . *chiefly Brit var of* METER
>
> **agin** . . . *dial var of* AGAINST

RUN-ON ENTRIES

A main entry may be followed by one or more derivatives or by a homograph with a different functional label. These are run-on entries. Each is introduced by a lightface dash and each has a functional label. They are not defined, however, since their meanings are readily derivable from the meaning of the root word:

> **slay** . . . *vb* . . . — **slay·er** *n*
>
> **spir·it·ed** . . . *adj* . . . — **spir·it·ed·ly** *adv* — **spir·it·ed·ness** *n*
>
> **stac·ca·to** . . . *adj* . . . — **staccato** *adv* — **staccato** *n*

A main entry may be followed by one or more phrases containing the entry word or an inflected form of it. These are also run-on entries. Each is introduced by a lightface dash but there is no functional label. They are, however, defined since their meanings are more than the sum of the meanings of their elements:

> **hole** . . . *n* . . . — **in the hole :** . . .
>
> ¹**live** . . . *vb* . . . — **live it up :** . . .

Defined phrases of this sort are run on at the entry constituting the first major element in the phrase. The first major element is ordinarily a verb or a noun, but when these are absent another part of speech may serve instead:

> ¹**but** . . . *conj* . . . — **but what :** . . .

When there are variants, however, the run-on appears at the entry constituting the first major invariable element in the phrase:

> ¹**clock** . . . *n* . . . — **kill the clock** *or* **run out the clock :** . . .
>
> ¹**hand** . . . *n* . . . — **on all hands** *or* **on every hand :** . . .

A run-on entry is an independent entry with respect to function and status. Labels at the main entry do not apply unless they are repeated.

Attention is called to the definition of *vocabulary entry* in this book. The term *dictionary entry* includes all vocabulary entries as well as all boldface entries in the separate sections of the back matter headed "Abbreviations and Symbols for Chemical Elements," "Foreign Words and Phrases," "Biographical Names," and "Geographical Names."

Pronunciation

Pronunciation is indicated between a pair of reversed virgules \\ following the entry word. The symbols used are listed in the chart printed inside the back cover of this dictionary and on the page facing the first page of the dictionary proper. An abbreviated list appears at the bottom of the second column of each right-hand page of the vocabulary. Explanations of the symbols are given in the Guide to Pronunciation.

SYLLABLES

A hyphen is used in the pronunciation to show syllabic division. These hyphens sometimes coincide with the centered dots in the entry word that indicate end-of-line division; sometimes they do not:

> ab·sen·tee \\,ab-sən-'tē\\
>
> ¹met·ric \\'me-trik\\

STRESS

A high-set mark \\'\\ indicates primary (strongest) stress or accent; a low-set mark \\,\\ indicates secondary (medium) stress or accent:

> heart·beat \\'härt-,bēt \\

The stress mark stands at the beginning of the syllable that receives the stress.

Stress marks are an indication of the relative prominence of the syllables in a word. In running speech the primary stress can vary in English words for several contextual and semantic reasons. Because the variation is so great, this book shows the primary stress of a word in its pronunciation as a single word out of context.

VARIANT PRONUNCIATIONS

The presence of variant pronunciations indicates that not all educated speakers pronounce words the same way. A second-place variant is not to be regarded as less acceptable than the pronunciation that is given first. It may, in fact, be used by as many educated speakers as the first variant, but the requirements of the printed page make one precede the other:

> apri·cot \\'a-prə-,kät, 'ā-\\
>
> for·eign \\'fȯr-ən, 'fär-\\

A variant that is appreciably less common than the preceding variant is preceded by the word *also* :

> ¹al·loy \\'a-,lȯi *also* ə-'lȯi\\

A variant preceded by *sometimes* is even less common, though it does occur in educated speech:

> in·vei·gle \\in-'vā-gəl *sometimes* -'vē-\\

Sometimes a regional label precedes a variant:

> ¹great \\'grāt, *Southern also* 'gre(ə)t\\

The label *dial* precedes a variant that is noteworthy or common in a dialect or dialects of American English, but that is not considered to be a standard pronunciation:

> ask \\'ask, 'ȧsk; *dial* 'aks\\

The symbol \\÷\\ is placed before a pronunciation variant that occurs in educated speech but that is considered by some to be unacceptable:

> cu·po·la \\'kyü-pə-lə, ÷-,lō\\

This symbol refers only to the immediately following variant and not to subsequent variants separated from it by a comma or a semicolon.

PARENTHESES IN PRONUNCIATIONS

Symbols enclosed by parentheses represent elements that are present in the pronunciation of some speakers but are absent from the pronunciation of other speakers, or elements that are present in some but absent from other utterances of the same speaker:

> ¹twin·kle \\'twiŋ-kəl\\ *vb* . . . twin·kling\\-k(ə-)liŋ\\
>
> sat·is·fac·to·ry \\,sa-təs-'fak-t(ə-)rē\\
>
> re·sponse \\ri-'spän(t)s\\

Thus, the parentheses at *twinkling* mean that there are some who pronounce the \\ə\\ between \\k\\ and \\l\\ and others who do not pronounce it.

PARTIAL AND ABSENT PRONUNCIATIONS

When a main entry has less than a full pronunciation, the missing part is to be supplied from a pronunciation in a preceding entry or within the same pair of reversed virgules:

> cham·pi·on·ship \\-,ship\\
>
> Ma·dei·ra \\mə-'dir-ə, -'der-\\

The pronunciation of the first three syllables of *championship* is found at the main entry *champion* :

> ¹cham·pi·on \\'cham-pē-ən\\

The hyphens before and after \\'der\\ in the pronunciation of *Madeira* indicate that both the first and the last parts of the pronunciation are to be taken from the immediately preceding pronunciation.

Partial pronunciations are usually shown when two or more variants have a part in common. When a variation of stress is involved, a partial pronunciation may be terminated at the stress mark which stands at the beginning of a syllable not shown:

> di·verse \\dī-'vərs, də-', 'dī-,\\
>
> an·cho·vy \\'an-,chō-vē, an-'\\

In general, no pronunciation is indicated for open compounds consisting of two or more English words that have own-place entry:

> witch doctor *n*

A pronunciation is shown, however, for any element of an open compound that does not have entry at its own alphabetical place:

> Oc·cam's razor \\'ä-kəmz-\\
>
> sieve of Er·a·tos·the·nes \\-,er-ə-'täs-thə-,nēz\\

Only the first entry in a sequence of numbered homographs is given a pronunciation if their pronunciations are the same:

> ¹re·ward \\ri-'wȯrd\\
>
> ²reward

Pronunciations are shown for obsolete words only if they occur in Shakespeare:

clois·tress \\'klȯi-strəs\\ *n . . . obs*

The pronunciation of unpronounced derivatives and compounds run on at a main entry is a combination of the pronunciation at the main entry and the pronunciation of the suffix or final element as given at its alphabetical place in the vocabulary:

— **oval·ness** *n*

— **shot in the dark**

Thus, the pronunciation of *ovalness* is the sum of the pronunciations given at *oval* and *-ness*; that of *shot in the dark*, the sum of the pronunciation of the four elements that make up the phrase.

Functional Labels

An italic label indicating a part of speech or some other functional classification follows the pronunciation or, if no pronunciation is given, the main entry. The eight traditional parts of speech are indicated as follows:

¹bold . . . *adj*	**bo·le·ro** . . . *n*
hand·some·ly . . . *adv*	**²under** . . . *prep*
¹but . . . *conj*	**some·one** . . . *pron*
oops . . . *interj*	**¹shrink** . . . *vb*

If a verb is both transitive and intransitive, the labels *vt* and *vi* introduce the subdivisions:

flat·ten . . . *vb* . . . *vt* . . . ~ *vi*

A boldface swung dash ~ is used to stand for the main entry (as *mortify*) and separate the subdivisions of the verb. If there is no subdivision, *vt* or *vi* takes the place of *vb*:

²fleece *vt*

ap·per·tain . . . *vi*

Labeling a verb as transitive, however, does not preclude occasional intransitive use (as in absolute constructions).

Other italicized labels used to indicate functional classifications that are not traditional parts of speech are:

poly- *comb form*	**-itis** *n suffix*
-logy . . . *n comb form*	**-ize** *vb suffix*
-if·er·ous *adj comb form*	**Ly·cra** . . . *trademark*
super- *prefix*	**-nd** *symbol*
Gram·my . . . *service mark*	**¹may** . . . *verbal auxiliary*
¹-ic *adj suffix*	**gid·dap** . . . *vb imper*
²-ward *or* **-wards** *adv suffix*	**me·thinks** . . . *vb impersonal*

NC–17 . . . *certification mark*

Two functional labels are sometimes combined:

zilch . . . *adj or n*

afloat . . . *adj or adv*

Inflected Forms

In comparison with some other languages English does not have many inflected forms. Of those which it has, several are inflected forms of words belonging to small, closed groups (as the personal pronouns or the demonstratives). These forms can readily be found at their own alphabetical places with a full entry (as *whom*, the objective case form of *who*) or with a cross-reference in small capital letters to another entry (as *those*, the plural form of *that*).

Most other inflected forms, however, are covered explicitly or by implication at the main entry for the base form. These are the plurals of nouns, the principal parts of verbs (the past tense, the past participle when it differs from the past tense, and the present participle), and the comparative and superlative forms of adjectives and adverbs. In general, it may be said that when these inflected forms are created in a manner considered regular in English (as by adding *-s* or *-es* to nouns, *-ed* and *-ing* to verbs, and *-er* and *-est* to adjectives and adverbs) and when it seems that there is nothing about the formation likely to give the dictionary user doubts, the inflected form is not shown in order to save space for information more likely to be sought. Inflected forms are also not shown at undefined run-ons or at some entries bearing a limiting label:

gour·mand . . . *n* . . . — **gour·man·dize** . . . *vi*

¹fem·i·nine . . . *adj* . . . — **fem·i·nine·ness** . . . *n*

²lake *n* . . . — **laky** . . . *adj*

²cote . . . *vt* . . . *obs* : to pass by

crouse . . . *adj* . . . *chiefly Scot* : BRISK, LIVELY

On the other hand, if the inflected form is created in an irregular way or if the dictionary user is likely to have doubts about it (even though it is formed regularly), the inflected form is shown in boldface, either in full or cut back to a convenient and easily recognizable point. Full details about the kinds of entries at which inflected forms are shown and the kinds at which they are not shown are given in the three following sections.

NOUNS

The plurals of nouns are shown in this dictionary when suffixation brings about a change of final *-y* to *-i-*, when the noun ends in a consonant plus *-o* or in *-ey*, when the noun ends in *-oo*, when the noun has an irregular plural or a zero plural or a foreign plural, when the noun is a compound that pluralizes any element but the last, when a final consonant is doubled, when the noun has variant plurals, and when it is believed that the dictionary user might have reasonable doubts about the spelling of the plural or when the plural is spelled in a way contrary to expectations:

²spy *n, pl* **spies**

si·lo . . . *n, pl* **silos**

¹ro·deo . . . *n, pl* **ro·de·os**

²shampoo *n, pl* **shampoos**

¹mouse . . . *n, pl* **mice**

moose . . . *n, pl* **moose**

cri·te·ri·on . . . *n, pl* **-ria**

son–in–law . . . *n, pl* **sons–in–law**

¹quiz . . . *n, pl* **quiz·zes**

¹fish . . . *n, pl* **fish** *or* **fish·es**

cor·gi . . . *n, pl* **corgis**

³dry *n, pl* **drys**

Cutback inflected forms are used when the noun has three or more syllables:

ame·ni·ty . . . *n, pl* -ties

The plurals of nouns are usually not shown when the base word is unchanged by suffixation, when the noun is a compound whose second element is readily recognizable as a regular free form entered at its own place, or when the noun is unlikely to occur in the plural:

¹night . . . *n*

²crunch *n*

fore·foot . . . *n*

mo·nog·a·my . . . *n*

Nouns that are plural in form and that regularly occur in plural construction are labeled *n pl*:

munch·ies . . . *n pl*

Nouns that are plural in form but that are not always construed as plurals are appropriately labeled:

ro·bot·ics . . . *n pl but sing in constr*

two bits *n pl but sing or pl in constr*

A noun that is singular in construction takes a singular verb when it is used as a subject; a noun that is plural in construction takes a plural verb when it is used as a subject.

VERBS

The principal parts of verbs are shown in this dictionary when suffixation brings about a doubling of a final consonant or an elision of a final -*e* or a change of final -*y* to -*i*-, when final -*c* changes to -*ck* in suffixation, when the verb ends in -*ey*, when the inflection is irregular, when there are variant inflected forms, and when it is believed that the dictionary user might have reasonable doubts about the spelling of an inflected form or when the inflected form is spelled in a way contrary to expectations:

²snag *vt* snagged; snag·ging

¹move . . . *vb* moved; mov·ing

¹cry . . . *vb* cried; cry·ing

²frolic *vi* frol·icked; frol·ick·ing

¹sur·vey . . . *vb* sur·veyed; sur·vey·ing

¹drive . . . *vb* drove . . . ; driv·en . . . ; driv·ing

²bus *vb* bused *or* bussed; bus·ing *or* bus·sing

²visa *vt* vi·saed . . . ; vi·sa·ing

²chagrin *vt* cha·grined . . . ; cha·grin·ing

The principal parts of a regularly inflected verb are shown when it is desirable to indicate the pronunciation of one of the inflected forms:

learn . . . *vb* learned \ˈlərnd, ˈlərnt\; learn·ing

rip·en . . . *vb* rip·ened; rip·en·ing \ˈrī-pə-niŋ, ˈrīp-niŋ \

Cutback inflected forms are often used when the verb has three or more syllables, when it is a disyllable that ends in -*l* and has variant spellings, and when it is a compound whose second element is readily recognized as an irregular verb:

elim·i·nate . . . *vt* -nat·ed; -nat·ing

³quarrel *vi* -reled *or* -relled; -rel·ing *or* -rel·ling

¹re·take . . . *vt* -took . . . ; -tak·en . . . ; -tak·ing

The principal parts of verbs are usually not shown when the base word is unchanged by suffixation or when the verb is a compound whose second element is readily recognizable as a regular free form entered at its own place:

¹jump . . . *vb*

pre·judge . . . *vt*

Another inflected form of English verbs is the third person singular of the present tense, which is regularly formed by the addition of -*s* or -*es* to the base form of the verb. This inflected form is not shown except at a handful of entries (as *have* and *do*) for which it is in some way anomalous.

ADJECTIVES & ADVERBS

The comparative and superlative forms of adjectives and adverbs are shown in this dictionary when suffixation brings about a doubling of a final consonant or an elision of a final -*e* or a change of final -*y* to -*i*-, when the word ends in -*ey*, when the inflection is irregular, and when there are variant inflected forms:

¹red . . . *adj* red·der; red·dest

¹tame . . . *adj* tam·er; tam·est

¹kind·ly . . . *adj* kind·li·er; -est

¹ear·ly . . . *adv* ear·li·er; -est

dic·ey . . . *adj* dic·i·er; -est

¹good . . . *adj* bet·ter . . . ; best

¹bad . . . *adj* worse . . . ; worst

¹far . . . *adv* far·ther . . . *or* fur·ther . . . ; far·thest *or* fur·thest

The superlative forms of adjectives and adverbs of two or more syllables are usually cut back:

³fancy *adj* fan·ci·er; -est

¹ear·ly . . . *adv* ear·li·er; -est

The comparative and superlative forms of regularly inflected adjectives and adverbs are shown when it is desirable to indicate the pronunciation of the inflected forms:

¹young . . . *adj* youn·ger \ˈyəŋ-gər \; youn·gest \ˈyəŋ-gəst \

The inclusion of inflected forms in -*er* and -*est* at adjective and adverb entries means nothing more about the use of *more* and *most* with these adjectives and adverbs than that their comparative and superlative degrees may be expressed in either way; *lazier* or *more lazy; laziest* or *most lazy*.

At a few adjective entries only the superlative form is shown:

³mere . . . *adj, superlative* mer·est

The absence of the comparative form indicates that there is no evidence of its use.

The comparative and superlative forms of adjectives and adverbs are not shown when the base word is unchanged by suffixation or when the word is a compound whose second element is readily recognizable as a regular free form entered at its own place:

¹near . . . *adv*

un·wary . . . *adj*

The comparative and superlative forms of adverbs are not shown when they are identical with the inflected forms of a preceding adjective homograph:

¹hot . . . *adj* hot·ter; hot·test

²hot *adv*

Capitalization

Most entries in this dictionary begin with a lowercase letter. A few of these have an italicized label *often cap*, which indicates that the word is as likely to be capitalized as not, that it is as acceptable with an uppercase initial as it is with one in lowercase. Some entries begin with an uppercase letter, which indicates that the word is usually capitalized. The absence of an initial capital or of an *often cap* label indicates that the word is not ordinarily capitalized:

> **lunk·head** . . . *n*
>
> **gar·gan·tuan** . . . *adj, often cap*
>
> **Mo·hawk** . . . *n*

The capitalization of entries that are open or hyphenated compounds is similarly indicated by the form of the entry or by an italicized label:

> **obstacle course** *n*
>
> **neo-Dar·win·ian** . . . *adj, often cap N*
>
> **off–off–Broadway** *n, often cap both Os*
>
> **un–Amer·i·can** . . . *adj*
>
> **Dutch oven** *n*
>
> **Old Glory** *n*

A word that is capitalized in some senses and lowercase in others shows variations from the form of the main entry by the use of italicized labels at the appropriate senses:

> **re·nais·sance** . . . *n* . . . **1** *cap* . . . **2** *often cap*
>
> **Shet·land** . . . *n* . . . **2** *often not cap*
>
> **Trin·i·ty** . . . *n* . . . **2** *not cap*

Attributive Nouns

The italicized label *often attrib* placed after the functional label *n* indicates that the noun is often used as an adjective equivalent in attributive position before another noun:

> **gold** . . . *n, often attrib*
>
> **busi·ness** . . . *n, often attrib*

Examples of the attributive use of these nouns are *gold chain* and *business ethics.*

While any noun may occasionally be used attributively, the label *often attrib* is limited to those having broad attributive use. This label is not used when an adjective homograph (as *iron* or *paper*) is entered. And it is not used at open compounds (as *X ray*) that may be used attributively with an inserted hyphen (as in *X-ray therapy*).

Etymology

The matter in boldface square brackets preceding the definition is the etymology. Meanings given in roman type within these brackets are not definitions of the entry, but are meanings of the Middle English, Old English, or non-English words within the brackets.

The etymology traces a vocabulary entry as far back as possible in English (as to Old English), tells from what language

and in what form it came into English, and (except in the case of such words outside the general vocabulary of English as *bascule* and *zloty*) traces the pre-English source as far back as possible if the source is an Indo-European language. These etyma are printed in italics.

OLD, MIDDLE, AND MODERN ENGLISH

The etymology usually gives the Middle English and the Old English forms of words in the following style:

> **¹nap** . . . *vi* . . . [ME *nappen,* fr. OE *hnappian* . . .]
>
> **¹old** . . . *adj* [ME, fr. OE *eald* . . .]

An etymology in which a word is traced back to Middle English but not to Old English indicates that the word is found in Middle English but not in those texts that have survived from the Old English period:

¹slab . . . *n* [ME *slabbe*]

¹stale . . . *adj* . . . [ME, aged (of ale), not fresh; akin to MD *stel* stale]

An etymology in which a word is traced back directly to Old English with no intervening mention of Middle English indicates that the word has not survived continuously from Old English times to the present. Rather, it died out after the Old English period and has been revived in modern times:

> **ge·mot** . . . *n* [OE *gemōt* . . .]
>
> **thegn** . . . *n* [OE . . .]

An etymology is not usually given for a word created in English by the combination of existing constituents or by functional shift. This indicates that the identity of the constituents is expected to be self-evident to the user.

book·shelf . . . *n* . . . : an open shelf for holding books

¹fire·proof . . . *adj* . . . : proof against or resistant to fire

off–put·ting . . . *adj* . . . : that puts off : REPELLENT, DISCONCERTING

penal code *n* . . . : a code of laws concerning crimes and offenses and their punishment

³stalk *n* . . . **1** : the act of stalking

In the case of a family of words obviously related to a common English word but differing from it by containing various easily recognizable suffixes, an etymology is usually given only at the base word, even though some of the derivatives may have been formed in a language other than English:

¹equal . . . *adj* [ME, fr. L *aequalis,* fr. *aequus* level, equal] . . . **1 a** (1) : of the same measure, quantity, amount, or number as another

equal·i·ty . . . *n* . . . **1** : the quality or state of being equal

equal·ize . . . *vt* . . . **1** : to make equal

While *equalize* was formed in Modern English, *equality* was actually borrowed into Middle English (via Middle French) from Latin *aequalitas.*

LANGUAGES OTHER THAN ENGLISH

The etymology gives the language from which words borrowed into English have come. It also gives the form or a transliteration of the word in that language if the form differs from that in English:

¹mar·ble . . . *n* [ME, fr. OF *marbre,* fr. L *marmor,* fr. Gk *marmaros*]

pome·gran·ate . . . *n* [ME *poumgrenet,* fr. MF *pomme grenate,* lit., seedy apple]

souk . . . *n* [Ar *sūq* market]

In a few cases the expression "ultim. fr." replaces the more usual "fr." This expression indicates that one or more intermediate steps have been omitted in tracing the derivation of the form preceding the expression from the form following it:

tri·lo·bite . . . *n* [ultim. fr. Gk *trilobos* three-lobed, fr. *tri-* + *lobos* lobe]

Words cited from certain American Indian languages and from some other languages that are infrequently printed have been rendered with the phonetic symbols used by scholars of those languages. These symbols include the following: a raised dot to the right of a vowel letter to mark vowel length; a hook below a vowel letter to mark nasality; an apostrophe over a consonant letter to mark glottal release; a superscript *w* to the right of a consonant letter to mark labialization; the symbol ɔ to render \ȯ\; the symbol *i* to render a high central vowel; the Greek letters β, δ, and γ to render voiced labial, dental, and velar fricatives; the symbol *x* to render \k̲\; the symbol ʔ to render a global stop; and the symbol λ (crossed lambda) for a voiceless lateral affricate. Examples of these symbols can be found at etymologies for the words *Athabascan, babassu, coho, geoduck, muskellunge, obeah, potlatch,* and *sego lily.*

WORDS OF UNKNOWN ORIGIN

When the source of a word appearing as a main entry is unknown, the expression "origin unknown" is usually used. Only in exceptional circumstances (as with some ethnic names) does the absence of an etymology mean that it has not been possible to furnish an informative etymology. More often, it means that no etymology is believed to be necessary. This is the case, for instance, with most of the entries identified as variants and with many derivatives.

ETYMOLOGIES OF TECHNICAL WORDS

Much of the technical vocabulary of the sciences and other specialized studies consists of words or word elements that are current in two or more languages, with only such slight modifications as are necessary to adapt them to the structure of the individual language in each case. Many words and word elements of this kind have become sufficiently a part of the general vocabulary of English as to require entry in an abridged dictionary. Because of the vast extent of the relevant published material in many languages and in many scientific and other specialized fields, it is impracticable to ascertain the language of origin of every such term. Yet it would not be accurate to formulate a statement about the origin of any such term in a way that could be interpreted as implying that it was coined in English. Accordingly, whenever a term that is entered in this dictionary belongs recognizably to this class of internationally current terms and whenever no positive evidence is at hand to show that it was coined in English, the etymology recognizes its international status and the possibility that it originated elsewhere than in English by use of the label ISV (for International Scientific Vocabulary):

mega·watt . . . *n* [ISV]

phy·lo·ge·net·ic . . . *adj* [ISV, fr. NL *phylogenesis* . . .]

¹-ol *n suffix* [ISV, fr. *alcohol*]

COMPRESSION OF INFORMATION

An etymology giving the name of a language (including ME or OE) and not giving the foreign (or Middle English or Old English) form indicates that this form is the same as that of the entry word:

ka·pok . . . *n* [Malay]

¹po·grom . . . *n* [Yiddish, fr. Russ . . .]

¹dumb . . . *adj* [ME, fr. OE . . .]

An etymology giving the name of a language (including ME or OE) and the form in that language but not giving the foreign (or Middle English or Old English) meaning indicates that this meaning is the same as that expressed in the first definition in the entry:

¹wea·ry . . . *adj* . . . [ME *wery,* fr. OE *wērig* . . .] . . . **1 :** exhausted in strength . . .

When a word from a foreign language (or Middle English or Old English) is a key element in the etymologies of several related entries that are found close together, the meaning of the word is usually given at only one of the entries:

ve·lo·ce . . . *adv or adj* [It, fr. L *veloc-, velox*]

ve·loc·i·pede . . . *n* [F *vélocipède,* fr. L *veloc-, velox* + *ped-, pes* foot — more at FOOT]

ve·loc·i·ty . . . *n* . . . [MF *velocité,* fr. L *velocitat-, velocitas,* fr. *veloc-, velox* quick; prob. akin to L *vegēre* to enliven — more at WAKE]

When an etymology includes the expression "by alter." and the altered form is not cited, the form is the term given in small capital letters as the definition:

crit·ter . . . *n* [by alter.] . . . **:** CREATURE

When the origin of a word is traced to the name of a person or place not further identified, additional information may be found in the Biographical Names or Geographical Names section in the back matter:

far·ad . . . *n* [Michael *Faraday*]

jodh·pur . . . *n* [*Jodhpur,* India]

RELATED WORDS

When a word of Indo-European origin has been traced back to the earliest language in which it is attested, words descended from the same Indo-European base in other languages (especially Old High German, Latin, Greek, and Sanskrit) are usually given:

na·vel . . . *n* [ME, fr. OE *nafela;* akin to OHG *nabalo* navel, L *umbilicus,* Gk *omphalos*]

¹wind . . . *n* . . . [ME, fr. OE; akin to OHG *wint* wind, L *ventus,* Gk *aēnai* to blow, Skt *vāti* it blows]

Sometimes, however, to avoid space-consuming repetition, the expression "more at" directs the user to another entry where the cognates are given:

ho·ly . . . *adj* . . . [ME, fr. OE *hālig;* akin to OE *hāl* whole — more at WHOLE]

Besides the use of "akin to" to denote relatedness, some etymologies make special use of "akin to" as part of a longer formula "of — origin; akin to —." This formula indicates that a word was borrowed from some language belonging to a group of languages whose name is inserted in the blank before the word *origin,* that it is impossible to say that the word in question is a borrowing of a particular attested word in a particular language of the source group, and that the form cited in the blank after the expression *akin to* is related to the word in question as attested within the source group:

ba·nana . . . *n* . . . [Sp or Pg; Sp, fr. Pg, of African origin; akin to Wolof *banäna* banana]

²brier *n* [F *bruyère* heath, fr. MF *bruiere,* fr. (assumed) VL *brucaria,* fr. LL *brucus* heather, of Celt origin; akin to OIr *froech* heather; akin to Gk *ereikē* heather]

This last example shows the two contrasting uses of "akin to." The word cited immediately after "of Celt origin; akin to" is an attested Celtic word descended from the same etymon as the unattested Celtic source of the Latin word. The word cited after the second "akin to" is evidence that the Celtic etymon has deeper relations within Indo-European.

Dates

At most main entries a date will be found enclosed in parentheses immediately preceding the boldface colon or number that introduces the first sense:

som·bre·ro . . . *n* . . . [Sp, fr. *sombra* shade] (1599) : a high-crowned hat of felt or straw with a very wide brim worn esp. in the Southwest and Mexico

This is the date of the earliest recorded use in English, as far as it could be determined, of the sense which the date precedes. Several caveats are appropriate at this point. First, a few classes of main entries that are not complete words (as prefixes, suffixes, and combining forms) or are not generic words (as trademarks and names of figures from mythology) are not given dates. Second, the date given applies only to the first sense of the word entered in this dictionary and not necessarily to the word's very earliest meaning in English. Many words, especially those with long histories, have obsolete, archaic, or uncommon senses that are not entered in this dictionary, and such senses have been excluded from consideration in determining the date:

¹slur . . . *n* [obs. E dial. *slur* thin mud, fr. ME *sloor*; akin to MHG *slier* mud] (1609) **1 a** : an insulting or disparaging remark or innuendo : ASPERSION

The 1609 date is for a sense of *slur* synonymous with *aspersion*. *Slur* also has an obsolete sense, "thin mud," that was recorded as early as the fifteenth century; but since this sense is not entered, it is ignored for purposes of dating. Third, the printed date should not be taken to mark the very first time that the word—or even the sense—was used in English. Many words were certainly in spoken use for decades or even longer before they passed into the written language. The date is for the earliest written or printed use that the editors have been able to discover. This fact means further that any date is subject to change as evidence of still earlier use may emerge, and many dates given now can confidently be expected to yield to others in future printings and editions.

A date will appear in one of three different styles:

put·tee . . . . *n* [Hindi *paṭṭī* strip of cloth, fr. Skt *paṭṭikā*] (1886) **1** : a cloth strip wrapped around the leg from ankle to knee

¹moon·light . . . *n* (14c) : the light of the moon

¹thrall . . . *n* [ME *thral*, fr. OE *thræl*, fr. ON *thræll*] (bef. 12c) **1 a** : a servant slave : BONOMAN; *also* : SERF

The style that names a year (as 1886) is the one used for the period from the sixteenth century to the present. The style that names only a century (as 14c) is the one used for the period from the twelfth century through the fifteenth century, a span that roughly approximates the period of Middle English. The style (bef. 12c) is used for the period before the twelfth century back to the earliest records of English, a span that approximates the period of Old English. Words first attested after 1500 can usually be dated to a single year because the precise dates of publication of modern printed texts are known. If a word must be dated from a modern text of uncertain chronology, it will be assigned the latest possible date of the text's publication prefixed by the abbreviation *ca.* (for *circa*). For words from the Old and Middle English periods the examples of use on which the dates depend very often occur in manuscripts which are themselves of uncertain date and which may record a text whose date of composition is highly conjectural. To date words from these periods by year would frequently give a quite misleading impression of the state of our knowledge, and so the broader formulas involving centuries are used instead.

Each date reflects a particular instance of the use of a word, most often within a continuous text. In cases where the earliest appearance of a word dated by year is not from continuous text but from a source (as a dictionary or glossary) that de-

fines or explains the word instead of simply using it, the year is preceded by *ca.*:

magnesium sulfate *n* (ca. 1890) : a sulfate of magnesium . . .

In such instances, *ca.* indicates that while the source providing the date attests that the word was in use in the relevant sense at that time, it does not offer an example of the normal use of the word and thus gives no better than an approximate date for such use. For the example above no use has so far been found that is earlier than its appearance (spelled *magnesium sulphate*) as an entry in Webster's International Dictionary, published in 1890, so the date is given with the qualifying abbreviation.

Usage

USAGE LABELS

Three types of status labels are used in this dictionary—temporal, regional, and stylistic—to signal that a word or a sense of a word is not part of the standard vocabulary of English.

The temporal label *obs* for "obsolete" means that there is no evidence of use since 1755:

¹per·du . . . *n* . . . *obs*

gov·ern·ment . . . *n* . . . **2** *obs*

The label *obs* is a comment on the word being defined. When a thing, as distinguished from the word used to designate it, is obsolete, appropriate orientation is usually given in the definition:

¹cat·a·pult . . . *n* . . . **1** : an ancient military device for hurling missiles

far·thin·gale . . . *n* . . . : a support (as of hoops) worn esp. in the 16th century beneath a skirt to expand it at the hipline

The temporal label *archaic* means that a word or sense once in common use is found today only sporadically or in special contexts:

¹goody . . . *n* . . . *archaic*

lon·gi·tude . . . *n* . . . **2** *archaic*

A word or sense limited in use to a specific region of the U.S. has a regional label. Some regional labels correspond loosely to areas defined in Hans Kurath's *Word Geography of the Eastern United States*. The adverb *chiefly* precedes a label when the word has some currency outside the specified region, and a double label is used to indicate considerable currency in each of two specific regions:

pung . . . *n* . . . *NewEng*

ban·quette . . . *n* . . . **1** . . . **b** *Southern*

³pas·tor . . . *n* . . . *chiefly Southwest*

do·gie . . . *n* . . . *chiefly West*

gal·lery . . . *n* . . . **2** . . . **b** *Southern & Midland*

¹pot·latch . . . *n* . . . **2** *Northwest*

smear·case . . . *n* . . . *chiefly Midland*

crul·ler . . . *n* . . . **2** *Northern & Midland*

Words current in all regions of the U.S. have no label.

A word or sense limited in use to one of the other countries of the English-speaking world has an appropriate regional label:

cutty sark . . . *n* . . . *chiefly Scot*

lar·ri·kin . . . *n* . . . *chiefly Austral*

in·da·ba . . . *n* . . . *chiefly SoAfr*

spal·peen . . . *n* . . . *chiefly Irish*

¹bon·net . . . *n* . . . **2 a** *Brit*

book off *vi* . . . *Canad*

¹din·kum . . . *adj* . . . *Austral & NewZeal*

gar·ron . . . *n* . . . *Scot & Irish*

The label *dial* for "dialect" indicates that the pattern of use of a word or sense is too complex for summary labeling: it usually includes several regional varieties of American English or of American and British English:

least·ways . . . *adv* . . . *dial*

The label *dial Brit* indicates currency in several dialects of the Commonwealth; *dial Eng* indicates currency in one or more provincial dialects of England:

bo·gle . . . *n* . . . *dial Brit*

¹hob . . . *n* . . . **1** *dial Eng*

The stylistic label *slang* is used with words or senses that are especially appropriate in contexts of extreme informality, that usually have a currency not limited to a particular region or area of interest, and that are composed typically of short-ened or altered forms or extravagant or facetious figures of speech:

⁴barb *n* . . . *slang* : BARBITURATE

²skin·ny *n* . . . *slang* : inside information : DOPE

main squeeze *n* . . . *slang* : one's principal romantic partner

There is no satisfactory objective test for slang, especially with reference to a word out of context. No word, in fact, is invariably slang, and many standard words can be given slang applications.

The stylistic label *nonstand* for "nonstandard" is used for a few words or senses that are disapproved by many but that have some currency in reputable contexts:

learn . . . *vb* . . . **2 a** *nonstand*

ir·re·gard·less . . . *adv* . . . *nonstand*

The stylistic label *substand* for "substandard" is used for those words or senses that conform to a widespread pattern of usage that differs in choice of word or form from that of the prestige group of the community:

is . . . *pres 3d sing of* BE, *dial pres 1st & 2nd sing of* BE, *substand pres pl of* BE

A subject label or guide phrase is sometimes used to indicate the specific application of a word or sense:

knock·about . . . *adj* . . . **3** *of a sailing vessel*

²break *n* . . . **5** . . . **d** *mining*

²up *adj* . . . **5** *of a quark*

In general, however, subject orientation is given in the definition:

Di·do . . . *n* . . . : a legendary queen of Carthage in Virgil's *Aeneid* who kills herself when Aeneas leaves her

je·té . . . *n* . . . : a springing jump in ballet made from one foot to the other in any direction

ILLUSTRATIONS OF USAGE

Definitions are sometimes followed by verbal illustrations that show a typical use of the word in context. These illustrations are enclosed in angle brackets, and the word being illustrated is usually replaced by a lightface swung dash. The swung dash stands for the boldface entry word, and it may be followed by an italicized suffix:

¹key . . . *n* . . . **3 a** . . . < the ~ to a riddle >

nary . . . *adj* . . . < ~ a person wanted to go >

²plummet *vi* . . . **2** . . . < prices ~ed >

weak . . . *adj* . . . **4** . . . **b** . . . (2) . . . < history was my ~est sub-ject >

The swung dash is not used when the form of the boldface entry word is changed in suffixation, and it is not used for open compounds:

¹true . . . *adj* . . . **8** . . . < in the *truest* sense >

turn off *vt* . . . **4** . . . < *turn* the water *off* >

Illustrative quotations are also used to show words in typical contexts:

con·flict·ed . . . *adj* . . . < this unhappy and ~ modern woman — John Updike >

Omissions in quotations are indicated by suspension points:

alien·ation . . . *n* . . . < ~ . . . from the values of one's society and family —S.L. Halleck >

USAGE NOTES

Definitions are sometimes followed by usage notes that give supplementary information about such matters as idiom, syntax, semantic relationship, and status. A usage note is introduced by a lightface dash:

²cry *n* . . . **11** : . . . — usu. used in the phrase *a far cry*

²drum . . . *vt* . . . **2** : . . . — usu. used with *out*

¹so . . . *adv* . . . **1 a** : . . . — often used as a substitute for a preceding clause

¹sfor·zan·do . . . *adj or adv* . . . : . . . — used as a direction in music

grin·go . . . *n* . . . : . . . — often used disparagingly

pissed . . . *adj* . . . **1** . . . : . . . — sometimes considered vulgar

hajji . . . *n* . . . : . . . — often used as a title

Two or more usage notes are separated by a semicolon:

²thine *pron* . . . : that which belongs to thee — used without a following noun as a pronoun equivalent in meaning to the adjective *thy*; used esp. in ecclesiastical or literary language and still surviving in the speech of Friends esp. among themselves

Sometimes a usage note calls attention to one or more terms with the same denotation as the main entry:

water moccasin *n* . . . **1** : a venomous semiaquatic pit viper (*Agkistrodon piscivorus*) chiefly of the southeastern U.S. that is closely related to the copperhead — called also *cottonmouth, cottonmouth moccasin*

The called-also terms are shown in italic type. If such a term falls alphabetically more than a column away from the main entry, it is entered at its own place with the sole definition being a synonymous cross-reference to the entry where it appears in the usage note:

cotton·mouth . . . *n* . . . : WATER MOCCASIN

cottonmouth moccasin *n* . . . : WATER MOCCASIN

Sometimes a usage note is used in place of a definition. Some function words (as conjunctions and prepositions) have little or no semantic content; most interjections express feelings but are otherwise untranslatable into meaning; and some other words (as oaths and honorific titles) are more amenable to comment than to definition:

¹**of** . . . *prep* . . . **1** — used as a function word to indicate a point of reckoning

¹**oyez** . . . *vb imper* . . . — used by a court or public crier to gain attention before a proclamation

¹**or** . . . *conj* . . . **1** — used as a function word to indicate an alternative

gol·ly . . . *interj* . . . — used as a mild oath or to express surprise

sir . . . *n* . . . **2 a** — used as a usu. respectful form of address

USAGE PARAGRAPHS

Brief usage paragraphs have been placed at a number of entries for terms that are considered to present problems of confused or disputed usage. A usage paragraph typically summarizes the historical background of the item and its associated body of opinion, compares these with available evidence of current usage, and often adds a few words of suitable advice for the dictionary user.

Each paragraph is signaled by an indented boldface italic *usage*. Where appropriate, discussion is keyed by sense number to the definition of the meaning in question. Most paragraphs incorporate appropriate verbal illustrations and illustrative quotations to clarify and exemplify the points being made:

ag·gra·vate . . . *vt* . . . **1** *obs* **a** : to make heavy : BURDEN **b** : INCREASE **2** : to make worse, more serious, or more severe : intensify unpleasantly < problems have been *aggravated* by neglect > **3 a** : to rouse to displeasure or anger by usu. persistent and often petty goading **b** : to produce inflammation in
   usage Although *aggravate* has been used in sense 3a since the 17th century, it has been the object of disapproval only since about 1870. It is used in expository prose < when his silly conceit . . . about his not-very-good early work has begun to *aggravate* us —William Styron > but seems to be more common in speech and casual writing < a good profession for him, because bus drivers get *aggravated* —Jackie Gleason (interview, 1986) > < & now this letter comes to *aggravate* me a thousand times worse —Mark Twain (letter, 1864) >. Sense 2 is far more common than sense 3a in published prose. Such is not the case, however, with *aggravation* and *aggravating*. *Aggravation* is used in sense 3 somewhat more than in its earlier senses; *aggravating* has practically no use other than to express annoyance.

When a second word is also discussed in a paragraph, the main entry for that word is followed by a run-on *usage* see — which refers to the entry where the paragraph may be found:

     ²**af·fect** . . . *vb* . . . **usage** see EFFECT

Definitions

DIVISION OF SENSES

A boldface colon is used in this dictionary to introduce a definition:

¹**coo·per** . . . *n* . . . : one that makes or repairs wooden casks or tubs

It is also used to separate two or more definitions of a single sense:

un·cage . . . *vt* . . . : to release from or as if from a cage : free from restraint

Boldface Arabic numerals separate the senses of a word that has more than one sense:

²**savage** *n* . . . **1** : a person belonging to a primitive society **2** : a brutal person **3** : a rude or unmannerly person

Boldface lowercase letters separate the subsenses of a word:

¹**grand** . . . *adj* . . . **5 a** : LAVISH. SUMPTUOUS . . . **b** : marked by a regal form and dignity **c** : fine or imposing in appearance or impression **d** : LOFTY, SUBLIME

Lightface numerals in parentheses indicate a further division of subsenses:

take out . . . *vt* . . . **1 a** (1) : DEDUCT, SEPARATE (2) : EXCLUDE, OMIT (3) : WITHDRAW, WITHHOLD

A lightface colon following a definition and immediately preceding two or more subsenses indicates that the subsenses are subsumed by the preceding definition:

²**crunch** *n* . . . **3** : a tight or critical situation: as **a** : a critical point in the buildup of pressure between opposing elements . . . **b** : a severe economic squeeze . . . **c** : SHORTAGE

se·quoia . . . *n* . . . either of two huge coniferous California trees of the bald cypress family that may reach a height of over 300 feet (90 meters): **a** : BIG TREE **b** : REDWOOD 3a

The word *as* may or may not follow the lightface colon. Its presence (as at ²*crunch*) indicates that the following subsenses are typical or significant examples. Its absence (as at *sequoia*) indicates that the subsenses which follow are exhaustive.

The system of separating the various senses of a word by numerals and letters is a lexical convenience. It reflects something of their semantic relationship, but it does not evaluate senses or set up a hierarchy of importance among them.

Sometimes a particular semantic relationship between senses is suggested by the use of one of four italic sense dividers: *esp*, *specif*, *also*, or *broadly*.

The sense divider *esp* (for *especially*) is used to introduce the most common meaning subsumed in the more general preceding definition:

²**slick** *adj* . . . **3 a** : characterized by subtlety or nimble wit : CLEVER; *esp* : WILY

The sense divider *specif* (for *specifically*) is used to introduce a common but highly restricted meaning subsumed in the more general preceding definition:

     pon·tiff . . . *n* . . . **2** : BISHOP; *specif* : POPE

The sense divider *also* is used to introduce a meaning that is closely related to but may be considered less important than the preceding sense:

chi·na . . . *n* . . . **1** : PORCELAIN; *also* : vitreous porcelain wares (as dishes, vases, or ornaments) for domestic use

The sense divider *broadly* is used to introduce an extended or wider meaning of the preceding definition:

flot·sam . . . *n* . . . **1** : floating wreckage of a ship or its cargo; *broadly* : floating debris

ORDER OF SENSES

The order of senses within an entry is historical: the sense known to have been first used in English is entered first. This is not to be taken to mean, however, that each sense of a multisense word developed from the immediately preceding sense. It is altogether possible that sense 1 of a word has given rise to sense 2 and sense 2 to sense 3, but frequently sense 2 and sense 3 may have arisen independently of one another from sense 1.

When a numbered sense is further subdivided into lettered subsenses, the inclusion of particular subsenses within a sense is based upon their semantic relationship to one another, but their order is likewise historical: subsense 1a is earlier than 1b, 1b is earlier than 1c, and so forth. Divisions of subsenses indicated by lightface numerals in parentheses are also in historical order with respect to one another. Subsenses may be out of historical order, however, with respect to the broader numbered senses:

¹job . . . *n* . . . (ca. 1627) **1 a :** a piece of work; *esp* : a small miscellaneous piece of work undertaken on order at a stated rate **b :** the object or material on which work is being done **c :** something produced by or as if by work <do a better ∼ next time> **d :** an example of a usu. specified type : ITEM <this ∼ is round-necked and sleeveless —Lois Long> **2 a :** something done for private advantage <suspected the whole incident was a put-up ∼ > **b :** a criminal enterprise; *specif:* ROBBERY **c :** a damaging or destructive bit of work <did a ∼ on him> **3 a** (1) : something that has to be done : TASK (2) : an undertaking requiring unusual exertion <it was a real ∼ to talk over that noise> **b :** a specific duty, role, or function **c :** a regular remunerative position **d** *chiefly Brit* : state of affairs — used with *bad* or *good* <it was a good ∼ you didn't hit the old man —E. L. Thomas>

At *job* the date indicates that the earliest unit of meaning, sense 1a, was born in the seventeenth century, and it is readily apparent how the following subsenses are linked to it and to each other by the idea of work. Even subsense 1d is so linked, because while it does not apply exclusively to manufactured items, it often does so, as the illustrative quotation suggests. Yet 1d did not exist before the 1920s, while 2a and 3a (1) both belong to the seventeenth century, although they are later than 1a. Even the very last subsense, 3d, is earlier than 1d, as it is found in the works of Dickens.

Historical order also determines whether transitive or intransitive senses are given first at verbs which have both kinds. If the earliest sense is transitive, all the transitive senses precede all the intransitive senses.

OMISSION OF A SENSE

Occasionally the dictionary user, having turned to an entry, may not find a particular sense that was expected or hoped for. This usually means no more than that the editors judged the sense insufficiently common or otherwise important to include in a dictionary of this scope. Such a sense will frequently be found at the appropriate entry in a dictionary (as Webster's Third New International Dictionary) that has room for less common words and meanings. One special case is worth noting, however.

At times it would be possible to include the definition of a meaning at more than one entry (as at a simple verb and a verb-adverb collocation or at a verb and an adjective derived from a participle of that verb). To save space for other information such double coverage is avoided, and the meaning is generally defined only at the base form. For the derivative term the meaning is then considered to be essentially self-explanatory and is not defined. For example *cast off* has a sense "to get rid of" in such typical contexts as "cast off all restraint," and so has the simple verb *cast* in contexts like "cast all restraint to the winds." This meaning is defined as sense 1e(2) of *cast* and is omitted from the entry *cast off*, where the dictionary user will find a number of senses that cannot be considered self-explanatory in relation to the entries for *cast* and *off*. Likewise, the entry for the adjective *picked* gives only one sense—"CHOICE, PRIME"—which is not the meaning of *picked* in such a context as "the picked fruit lay stacked in boxes awaiting shipment." A definition suitable for this use is not given at *picked* because one is given at the first homograph *pick*, the verb from which the adjective *picked* is derived, as sense 3a—"to gather by plucking."

INFORMATION AT INDIVIDUAL SENSES

Information coming between the entry word and the first definition of a multisense word applies to all senses and subsenses. Information applicable only to some senses or subsenses is given between the appropriate boldface numeral or letter and the symbolic colon. A variety of kinds of information is offered in this way:

²palm *n* . . . **3** [L *palmus*, fr. *palma*]

²rally *n* . . . **4** *also* ral·lye

¹disk *or* disc . . . *n* . . . **4** . . . **b** *usu disc*

cru·ci·fix·ion . . . *n* . . . **1 a** *cap*

¹tile . . . *n* . . . **1** *pl* tiles *or* tile a . . .

del·i·ca·tes·sen . . . *n pl* . . . **1** . . . **2** *sing, pl* delicatessens

fix·ing . . . *n* . . . **2** *pl*

²die . . . *n, pl* dice . . . *or* dies . . . **1** *pl* dice . . . **2** *pl* dies . . . **3** *pl* dies

¹folk . . . *n, pl* folk *or* folks . . . **4** *folks pl*

At *palm* the subetymology indicates that the third sense, while ultimately derived from the same source (Latin *palma*) as the other senses of the word, has a different immediate etymon (Latin *palmus*), from which it receives its meaning. At *rally* one is told that in the fourth sense the word has a variant spelling not used for other senses and that this variant is a secondary or less common one. At *disk* the italic label of sense 4b indicates that, while the spelling *disk* is overall somewhat the more common (since it precedes *disc* out of alphabetical order at the beginning of the entry), *disc* is the usual spelling for this particular sense. At *crucifixion* the label *cap* points out the one meaning of the word in which it is capitalized. At the first homograph *tile* no plural is shown at the beginning of the entry because the usual plural, *tiles,* is regular. The subsenses of sense 1, however, have a zero plural as well as the usual one, and so both plurals appear in boldface at sense 1. At *delicatessen* the situation is different: the entry as a whole is labeled a plural noun, but sense 2 is used as a singular. In this sense *delicatessen* can take the plural ending *-s* when needed, a fact that is indicated by the appearance of the plural in boldface at the sense. At *fixing* the italic abbreviation simply means that when used in this sense the word is always written in its plural form, *fixings.* At the second homograph *die* the actual distribution of the variant plurals can be given sense by sense in italic type because both variants are shown in boldface earlier in the entry. At the first homograph *folk* a singular noun is shown with variant plurals of nearly equal frequency, when all senses are taken into account. The fourth sense, however, is unique in being always plural in form and construction. The form of the plural for this sense is *folks,* as shown, and the placement of the form before the label instead of after it (as at the senses of *die*) means that this sense is always plural.

When an italicized label or guide phrase follows a boldface numeral, the label or phrase applies only to that specific numbered sense and its subsenses. It does not apply to any other boldface numbered senses:

¹boot . . . *n* . . . **1** *archaic* . . . **2** *chiefly dial* . . . **3** *obs* . . .

¹fa·vor . . . *n* . . . **2** *archaic* a . . . **b** (1) . . . (2) . . . **3**

At *boot* the *archaic* label applies only to sense 1, the *chiefly dial* label only to sense 2, and the *obs* label only to sense 3. At *favor* the *archaic* label applies to all the subsenses of sense 2 but not to sense 3.

When an italicized label or guide phrase follows a boldface letter, the label or phrase applies only to that specific lettered sense and its subsenses. It does not apply to any other boldface lettered senses:

²stour *n* . . . **1 a** *archaic* . . . **b** *dial Brit*

The *archaic* label applies to sense 1a but not to sense 1b. The *dial Brit* label applies to sense 1b but not to sense 1a.

When an italicized label or guide phrase follows a parenthesized numeral, the label or phrase applies only to that specific numbered sense:

in·car·na·tion . . . *n* . . . **1a** (1) . . . (2) *cap*

The *cap* label applies to sense 1a(2) and to no other subsenses of the word.

Names of Plants & Animals

The entries that define the common or vernacular names (as *peach* and *lion*) of plants and animals or sometimes a related term (as *streptomycin*), if a common name is rare or does not exist, employ in part the formal, codified, New Latin vocabulary of biological systematics. This vocabulary has been developed and used by biologists in accordance with international codes of botanical and zoological nomenclature for the purpose of identifying and indicating the relationships of plants and animals. This system of names classifies organisms into a hierarchy of groups—taxa—with each kind of organism having one—and only one—correct name and belonging to one—and only one—taxon at each level of classification in the hierarchy.

This contrasts with the system of common or vernacular names which is determined by popular usage and in which one organism may have several names (as *mountain lion, cougar,* and *painter*), different organisms may have the same name (as *dolphin*), and there may be variation in meaning or overlapping of the categories denoted by the names (as *whale, dolphin,* and *porpoise*).

The fundamental taxon is the genus. It includes a group of closely related kinds of plants (as *Prunus,* which includes the wild and cultivated cherries, apricots, peaches, and almonds) or animals (as *Canis,* which includes domestic dogs, coyotes, jackals, and wolves). The genus name is a capitalized singular noun.

The unique name of each kind of organism or species—the binomial or species name—consists of a singular capitalized genus name combined with an uncapitalized specific epithet. The name for a variety or subspecies—the trinomial, variety name, or subspecies name—adds a similar varietal or subspecific epithet. The cultivated cabbage (*Brassica oleracea capitata*), the cauliflower (*Brassica oleracea botrytis*), and brussels sprouts (*Brassica oleracea gemmifera*) belong to the same species (*Brassica oleracea*) of cole.

Names of taxa higher than the genus (as family, order, and class) are capitalized plural nouns that are often used with singular verbs and that are not abbreviated in normal use. No two genera of animals in good standing are permitted to have the same name, nor are any two genera of plants in good standing. Since the botanical and zoological codes are independent, however, a plant genus and an animal genus may have the same name. Thus, a number of cabbage butterflies (as *Pieris rapae*) are placed in a genus of animals with the same name as the plant genus to which the Japanese andromeda (*Pieris japonica*) belongs. Although no two higher taxa of plants are permitted to have the same name, the rules of zoological nomenclature do not apply to taxa above the family so that rarely some widely separated groups may receive the same taxonomic name (as the ordinal name Decapoda in the entry *decapod*) from different specialists.

The taxonomic names of biological nomenclature used in this dictionary are enclosed in parentheses and usually come immediately after the primary orienting noun. Genus names as well as binomials and trinomials are italicized, but names of taxa above the genus are not italicized:

¹bee·tle . . . *n* . . . **1** : any of an order (Coleoptera) of insects having four wings of which the outer pair are modified into stiff elytra that protect the inner pair when at rest

rob·in . . . *n* . . . **1 a** : a small chiefly European thrush (*Erithacus rubecula*) resembling a warbler and having a brownish olive back and orangish face and breast **b** : any of various Old World songbirds that are related to or resemble the European robin **2** : a large No. American thrush (*Turdus migratorius*) with olivaceous to slate gray upperparts, blackish head and tail, black and whitish streaked throat, and dull reddish breast and underparts

strep·to·my·cin . . . *n* . . . : an antibiotic organic base $C_{21}H_{39}N_7O_{12}$ produced by a soil actinomycete (*Streptomyces griseus*), active against many bacteria, and used esp. in the treatment of infections (as tuberculosis) by gram-negative bacteria

Sometimes two or more different New Latin names can be found used in current literature for the same organism or group. This happens when older monographs and field guides are kept in print after name changes occur, when there are legitimate differences of opinion about the validity of names, and when the rules of priority do not apply or are not applied. To help the reader in recognizing an organism or group, some entries in this dictionary give two taxonomic names connected by "syn." for synonym:

li·on . . . *n* . . . **1 a** . . . : a large heavily-built social cat (*Panthera leo* syn. *Leo leo*) of open or rocky areas chiefly of sub-Saharan Africa . . .

Taxonomic names are used in this dictionary to provide precise technical identifications through which defined terms may be pursued in technical writings. Because of their specialized nature taxonomic names do not have separate entry. However, many common names are derived directly from the names of taxa and especially genera with little or no modification. It is particularly important to distinguish between a common name and the genus name from which it is derived without a change in spelling, as these names appear in print. The common name (as clostridium or drosophila) is not usually capitalized or italicized but does have a plural (as clostridia or drosophilas) which often has an ending different from that of the singular. In contrast the genus name (as *Clostridium* or *Drosophila*) is capitalized and italicized but never takes a plural. A common name in plural form (as coleoptera) may sometimes be spelled like the name of a taxon, but it is not usually capitalized.

The entries defining the names of plants and animals are usually oriented to higher taxa by other vernaculars (as by *alga* at *seaweed* or *thrush* at *robin*) or by technical adjectives (as by *composite* at *daisy, leguminous* at *pea,* or *oscine* at *warbler*) so that the name of a higher taxon may often be found by consulting an entry defining a more inclusive common name or a term related to it. Among the higher plants, except for the composites and legumes and a few tropical groups, such orientation is by a vernacular family name linked at the corresponding taxonomic entry to its technical equivalent:

²rose . . . *n* . . . **1 a** : any of a genus (*Rosa* of the family Rosaceae, the rose family) of usu. prickly shrubs with pinnate leaves and showy flowers . . .

ap·ple . . . *n, often attrib* . . . **1** : the fleshy usu. rounded and red, yellow, or green edible pome fruit of a tree (genus *Malus*) of the rose family; *also* : an apple tree

A genus name may be abbreviated to its initial letter when it is used more than once in senses not separated by a boldface number:

nas·tur·tium . . . *n* . . . : any of a genus (*Tropaeolum* of the family Tropaeolaceae, the nasturtium family) of herbs of Central and So. America with showy spurred flowers and pungent seeds; *esp* : either of two widely cultivated ornamentals (*T. majus* and *T. minus*)

Cross-Reference

Four different kinds of cross-references are used in this dictionary: directional, synonymous, cognate, and inflectional. In each instance the cross-reference is readily recognized by the lightface small capitals in which it is printed.

A cross-reference following a lightface dash and beginning with *see* or *compare* is a directional cross-reference. It directs the dictionary user to look elsewhere for further information. A *compare* cross-reference is regularly appended to a definition; a *see* cross-reference may stand alone:

wel·ter·weight . . . *n* . . . — compare LIGHTWEIGHT, MIDDLE-WEIGHT

¹ri·al . . . *n* . . . — see MONEY table

A cross-reference immediately following a boldface colon is a synonymous cross-reference. It may stand alone as the only definitional matter for an entry or for a sense or subsense of an entry; it may follow an analytical definition; it may be one of two synonymous cross-references separated by a comma:

gar·ban·zo . . . *n* . . . : CHICKPEA

¹ne·glect . . . *vt* . . . **1** : to give little attention or respect to : DISRE-GARD

²main *adj* . . . **1** : CHIEF, PRINCIPAL

A synonymous cross-reference indicates that a definition at the entry cross-referred to can be substituted as a definition for the entry or the sense or subsense in which the cross-reference appears.

A cross-reference following an italic *var of* is a cognate cross-reference:

kaf·tan *var of* CAFTAN

Sometimes a cognate cross-reference has a limiting label preceding *var of* as a specific indication that the variant is not standard English:

haul·ier . . . *Brit var of* HAULER

²hist . . . *dial var of* HOIST

sher·ris . . . *archaic var of* SHERRY

A cross-reference following an italic label that identifies an entry as an inflected form of a noun, of an adjective or adverb, or of a verb is an inflectional cross-reference. Inflectional cross-references appear only when the inflected form falls at least a column away from the entry cross-referred to:

calves *pl of* CALF

³wound . . . *past and past part of* WIND

When guidance seems needed as to which one of several homographs or which sense of a multisense word is being referred to, a superscript numeral may precede the cross-reference or a sense number may follow it or both:

¹toss . . . *vt* . . . **3** . . . **c** : MATCH 5a

Synonyms

Brief paragraphs discriminating words of closely associated meaning from one another have been placed at a number of entries. They are signaled by an indented boldface italic *syn*. Each paragraph begins with a list of the words to be discussed in it, followed by a concise statement of the element of meaning that the words have in common. The discriminations themselves are amplified with verbal illustrations:

²answer *vb* . . .
syn ANSWER, RESPOND, REPLY, REJOIN, RETORT mean to say, write, or do something in return. ANSWER implies the satisfying of a question, demand, call, or need <*answered* all the questions>. RESPOND may suggest an immediate or quick reaction <*responded* eagerly to a call for volunteers>. REPLY implies making a return commensurate with the original question or demand <an invitation that requires you to *reply*>. REJOIN often implies sharpness or quickness in answering <"who asked you?" she *rejoined*>. RETORT suggests responding to an explicit charge or criticism by way of retaliation <he *retorted* to the attack with biting sarcasm>.

When a word is included in a synonym paragraph, the main entry for that word is followed by a run-on *syn* see—which refers to the entry where the synonym paragraph appears:

²respond *vb* . . . *syn* see ANSWER

When a word is a main entry at which there is a synonym paragraph and is also included in another paragraph elsewhere, the paragraph at the main entry is followed by a run-on *syn* see in addition—which refers to the entry where the other paragraph may be found:

¹nat·u·ral . . . *adj* . . .
syn NATURAL, INGENUOUS, NAIVE, UNSOPHISTICATED, ARTLESS mean free from pretension or calculation . . . *syn* see in addition REGULAR

¹reg·u·lar . . . *adj* . . .
syn REGULAR, NORMAL, TYPICAL, NATURAL mean being of the sort or kind that is expected as usual, ordinary, or average . . .

Combining Forms, Prefixes & Suffixes

An entry that begins or ends with a hyphen is a word element that forms part of an English compound:

mega- *or* **meg-** *comb form* . . . **1** . . . **b** . . . <*mega*hit>

-logy *n comb form* . . . **1** . . . <phrase*ology*>

-lyze *vb comb form* . . . <electro*lyze*>

-like *adj comb form* . . . <bell-*like*> <lady*like*>

pre- *prefix* . . . **1 a** (1) . . . <*pre*historic>

¹-ory . . . *n suffix* . . . **1** . . . <observat*ory*>

¹-ic *adj suffix* . . . **2 a** . . . <alderman*ic*>

²-ly *adv suffix* . . . **1 a** . . . <slow*ly*>

-ize *vb suffix* . . . **2 a** . . . <crystall*ize*>

Combining forms, prefixes, and suffixes are entered in this dictionary for three reasons: to make easier the writing of etymologies of words in which these word elements occur over and over again; to make understandable the meaning of many undefined run-ons which for reasons of space would be omitted if they had to be given etymologies and definitions; and to make recognizable the meaningful elements of new words that are not well enough established in the language to warrant dictionary entry.

Lists of Undefined Words

Lists of undefined words occur after the entries of these prefixes and combining forms:

anti-	multi-	re-
co-	non-	self-
counter-	out-	sub-
hyper-	over-	super-
inter-	post-	ultra-
mis-	pre-	un-

These words are not defined because they are self-explanatory; their meanings are simply the sum of a meaning of the prefix or combining form and a meaning of the root word. Centered dots are shown to save the dictionary user the trouble of consulting another entry. The lists are not exhaustive of all the words that might be, or actually have been, formed with these prefixes and combining forms. The dictionary has room for only the most common or important examples.

The English Language in the Dictionary

In the offices where Merriam-Webster's Collegiate Dictionary, Tenth Edition was edited, several thousand letters are received each year. The topics they articulate are enormously varied. Some letters merely ask for a particular bit of information about the English language that has been sought but not found in the dictionary. A few others are in hot pursuit of a special interest. Still others, their writers having come to think of the dictionary as an all-purpose reference book, ask questions about many other subjects besides words. A surprising number of correspondents, however, express considerable curiosity about how their dictionary—that formidably long and closely printed work with its many special abbreviations, symbols, and devices and its multitude of uses—came to be just the book it is.

They may ask quite directly such questions as how words make it into the dictionary or what it is that lexicographers do when they are editing or reediting a dictionary. But even questions of a very different sort on the surface may unwittingly reveal much the same interest. "Why did you fail to include word x in your book?" and "Why don't you still use the system of transcribing pronunciations with which I grew up instead of the present one with its 'up-side down e'?" may be in part expressions of annoyance at what is seen (not always accurately) as the dictionary's failure to do its job, but they are just as truly demands to know how dictionary editors make the decision to exclude some words from a given dictionary or to revise a long-standing feature of earlier editions. What follows is an effort to present a brief overview of the English language and its history and to provide brief and necessarily somewhat general answers to a few of the questions that users of this dictionary probably have about it, the processes that went into its making, and its relation to that fascinating and sometimes maddening marvel which we call the English language.

Language is the object of study of the academic discipline known as linguistics. Although the roots of linguistic science are found in earlier centuries, it is in most respects a modern creation, and the understanding of language that it offers us differs in a number of fundamental ways from the conceptions of language held by thinkers of the ancient and medieval worlds, the Renaissance, or the Enlightenment. This understanding does not differ, however, in every way. The use of language is still seen by linguists as a peculiarly human activity. We often use the word *language* to refer to the limited stock of movements or utterances by which some animals communicate a limited number of messages, but in doing so we recognize that we are speaking of something different in kind from our own language. Moreover, modern definitions of language are just as likely as earlier definitions to emphasize its functional aspect: language enables human beings, at least those who share a particular language, to communicate with each other by stating ideas, expressing feelings, and exchanging information.

Modern definitions of language, though, are more likely than older ones to stress some other aspects. One is the arbitrary nature of the relationship between the conventional sounds or other signs which serve as the vehicle of language and the meaning being conveyed by them. A few naive souls may believe that domestic swine are called pigs because their habits are so dirty, but it is clear to most that no inherent or necessary connection exists between the sequence of sounds \p\ plus \i\ plus \g\ and "any of various stout-bodied short-legged omnivorous mammals (family Suidae) with a thick bristly skin and a long mobile snout." A similarly naive Frenchman or German could insist with neither more nor less reason that *cochon* or *Schwein* is the word that naturally expresses the essential piggishness of the animal.

A linguistically oriented definition would also be likely to emphasize the systematic nature of language. Were it not for highly organized systems operating within any natural language, it could hardly be the subtle and effective tool of communication that it is. These systems are enormously complex both in themselves and in their mutual interaction, so complex indeed that no language has yet had its workings fully described; yet, paradoxically, and fortunately for the human race, any child with a normal ability to learn can, within a very few years, master at least the essentials of these systems for any one language with which it is in daily contact (or even two languages if the child's environment is bilingual). It is uncertain whether this is so because, as some linguists believe, at a profound level of structure the details that make English so different from other languages are unimportant and the systems of all languages are largely the same, but the fact that we learn our native language almost effortlessly up to a certain basic level of control is hardly to be denied.

The Systems of Language

The major systems that make up the broad comprehensive system of language itself are four in number: lexicon, grammar, semantics, and phonology. The one that dictionary editors and dictionary users are most directly concerned with is the vocabulary or *lexicon*, the collection of words and word elements which we put together in various ways to form larger units of discourse: phrases, clauses, sentences, paragraphs, and so forth. All languages have a lexicon, and all lexicons are governed by rules that permit some kinds of word formation, make others dubious, and render still others clearly impossible. In English we might say *versatileness* without hesitation if we needed such a word and could not for the moment think of *versatility*, even though the former is not normally part of our everyday working vocabulary; but *versatilize* might give us pause, and *nessversatile* we would simply never utter. The size of the lexicon varies considerably from language to language. The language of an isolated people, for example, may be perfectly adequate with a relatively small and fixed vocabulary, since it has no need of the coinages attendant upon modern technology, while English and other major languages have enormous stocks of words, to which they add year by year at a great rate. Since the dictionary is concentrated upon the lexicon, our discussion of the other systems of language, as it proceeds, will be largely concerned with how they are related to the lexicon and thus are important within the dictionary.

The grammatical system of language governs the way in which words are put together to form the larger units of discourse mentioned earlier. Grammar, of course, varies a great deal from language to language just as the lexicon does: in English, word order is a dominant factor in determining meaning, while the use of inflectional endings to mark the grammatical function of individual words within a sentence plays a clearly subordinate role, though important in some ways (as in indicating the number of a noun, the case of a personal pronoun, or the tense of a verb). Other languages show markedly different patterns, such as Latin with its elaborate set of paradigms for nouns, verbs, adjectives, and pronouns and its highly flexible word order. The semantic system of a language has to do with meanings and thus with the relation between the conventionalized symbols that constitute language and the external reality about which we need to communicate through language. The phonological system of a language is what allows a speaker of that language to transform a grammatical unit embodying a meaning into a flow of uttered sounds that can be heard and interpreted (accurately, if all goes well) by another speaker of the language. This system is always very tightly organized. The inventory of basic meaningful units of sound within a language (called *phonemes* by linguists) is never very large compared with the number of words and word elements in the lexicon; most speakers of English get by with about 40. Phonemes are identified by the fact that in some pairs of words they create a contrast that signals a difference in meaning: we consider the vowel sounds of *trip* and *trap* to be different phonemes because the difference in vowel sounds is the sole determinant of their being distinct words. Their consonant sounds are identical. Similarly, the initial consonant sounds of *pull* and *bull, tie* and *die,* and *come* and *gum* are contrasting phonemes. On the other hand, the sound at the beginning of *pit* and at the end of *tip* are phonetically quite different, but as they do not contrast meaningfully we do not perceive them as distinct phonemes. The combinations of these phonemes permitted in a given language are severely restricted, as are the ways in which speech sounds occur in conjunction with other significant elements of the phonological system such as stress (force or intensity) and intonation (the rise and fall in pitch of the voice as it moves through an utterance). In English, for example, it is possible for the consonants \str\ to occur in succession, but only at the beginning of a word (as in *strict*) or in the middle (as in *monstrous*), not at the end, and the sequence \pgr\ cannot occur at either the beginning or the end of a word but may occur in the middle (as in *upgrade*).

Variation and Change in Language

All of the systems of language are constantly in operation, and in a given language at a given time they may seem almost to be monolithic or at least to have sufficient identity that it makes sense, for example, to talk of *the* grammar of English. And, indeed, how could it be otherwise? Language would be a far more imperfect tool of communication than it is if the speakers of a language were not functioning within a system sufficiently unified to permit almost constant mutual intelligibility. Yet the impression of unity which we receive when we take a broad descriptive look at a single language at a particular time (taking a *synchronic* point of view, as linguists say) is more than a little misleading because it has failed to take account of the enormous variation that exists within the language.

Each of us speaks a distinctive form of English that is not identical in every particular with the form spoken by anyone else; linguists call this individual variety of a language an *idiolect.* Those whose idiolects share certain features of vocabulary, grammar, and phonology that are distinctively different from corresponding features shared by others who live in a different geographical area or belong to a different social group or who differ in some other way that affects their language are said to speak a *dialect* of the language. Researchers have identified a number of different geographical dialect areas within the United States, rather clearly marked on the

Eastern seaboard but progressively less well defined as one moves west; yet, the dialects of American English do not differ overall very greatly from one another; some dialects of Great Britain are more strikingly divergent in phonology, for example, than are any two dialects within this country, and some dialects of other languages approach the condition of mutual unintelligibility that is often taken to divide separate dialects from separate languages.

Nor is variation in language by any means confined to matters of idiolect or dialect. Variation may also be related to the several functional varieties of a language that people take up and discard as their roles and relationships change from moment to moment throughout the day. Such variation can involve vocabulary, pronunciation, and even grammar. A worker who queries one colleague concerning the whereabouts of another with "Seen John?" from which both the auxiliary verb *have* and the subject *you* have been deleted may not put the question in the same casual way to a superior.

If variation is one of the most prominent aspects of language as one considers it today, the inescapable fact that emerges from considering language historically (taking a *diachronic* point of view, as linguists say) is change. No living language stands still, however much we might wish at times that it would. Change over the short run is most readily noticed in the lexicon, as a comparison of successive editions of any modern dictionary will show; in grammar and phonology the forces of change typically operate much more slowly. Still, the cumulative effect of changes that are imperceptible as they occur can be impressive when measured across the centuries. The English of one's great-great-grandfather might not sound so very different from one's own. Perhaps it might seem a bit stiff and formal, a bit old-fashioned in its vocabulary, but the differences would not be dramatic. If we could somehow listen to an English-speaker of King Alfred's time, however, we would hear what all but a few scholars of historical English would take to be a foreign tongue.

The History of English

The history of English is conventionally, if perhaps too neatly, divided into three periods usually called Old English (or Anglo-Saxon), Middle English, and Modern English. The earliest period begins with the migration of certain Germanic tribes from the continent to Britain in the fifth century A.D., though no records of their language survive from before the seventh century, and it continues until the end of the eleventh century or a bit later. By that time Latin, Old Norse (the language of the Viking invaders), and especially the Anglo-Norman French of the dominant class after the Norman Conquest in 1066 had begun to have a substantial impact on the lexicon, and the well-developed inflectional system that typifies the grammar of Old English had begun to break down. The following brief sample of Old English prose illustrates several of the significant ways in which change has so transformed English that we must look carefully to find points of resemblance between the language of the tenth century and our own. It is taken from Aelfric's "Homily on St. Gregory the Great" and concerns the famous story of how that pope came to send missionaries to convert the Anglo-Saxons to Christianity after seeing Anglo-Saxon boys for sale as slaves in Rome:

Eft he axode, hu ðære ðeode nama wære þe hi of comon. Him wæs geandwyrd, þæt hi Angle genemnode wæron. þa cwæð he, "Rihtlice hi sind Angle gehatene, for ðan ðe hi engla wlite habbað, and swilcum gedafenað þæt hi on heofonum engla geferan beon."

A few of these words will be recognized as identical in spelling with their modern equivalents—*he, of, him, for, and, on*—and the resemblance of a few others to familiar words may be guessed—*nama* to *name, comon* to *come, wære* to *were, wæs* to *was*—but only those who have made a special study of Old English will be able to read the passage with understanding. The sense of it is as follows: "Again he [St. Gregory] asked what might be the name of the people from which they came. It was answered to him that they were named Angles. Then he said, 'Rightly are they called Angles because they have the beauty of angels, and it is fitting that such as they should be angels' companions in heaven.'" Some of the words in the original have survived in altered form, including *axode (asked), hu (how), rihtlice (rightly), engla (angels), habbað (have), swilcum (such), heofonum (heaven),* and *beon (be).* Others, however, have vanished from our lexicon, mostly without a trace, including several that were quite common words in Old English: *eft* "again," *ðeode* "people, nation," *cwœð* "said, spoke," *gehatene* "called, named," *wlite* "appearance, beauty," and *geferan* "companions." Recognition of some words is naturally hindered by the presence of two special characters, þ, called "thorn," and ð, called "edh," which served in Old English to represent the sounds now spelled with *th.*

Other points worth noting include the fact that the pronoun system did not yet, in the late tenth century, include the third person plural forms beginning with *th-: hi* appears where we would use *they.* Several aspects of word order will also strike the reader as oddly unlike ours. Subject and verb are inverted after an adverb—*þa cwœð he* "Then said he"—a phenomenon not unknown in modern English but now restricted to a few adverbs such as *never* and requiring the presence of an auxiliary verb like *do* or *have.* In subordinate clauses the main verb must be last, and so an object or a preposition may precede it in a way no longer natural: *þe hi of comon* "which they from came," *for ðan ðe hi engla wlite habbað* "because they angels' beauty have."

Perhaps the most distinctive difference between Old and Modern English reflected in Aelfric's sentences is the elaborate system of inflections, of which we now have only remnants. Nouns, adjectives, and even the definite article are inflected for gender, case, and number: *ðære ðeode* "(of) the people" is feminine, genitive, and singular, *Angle* "Angles" is masculine, accusative, and plural, and *swilcum* "such" is masculine, dative, and plural. The system of inflections for verbs was also more elaborate than ours: for example, *habbað* "have" ends with the *-að* suffix characteristic of plural present indicative verbs. In addition, there were two imperative forms, four subjunctive forms (two for the present tense and two for the preterit, or past, tense), and several others which we no longer have. Even where Modern English retains a particular category of inflection, the form has often changed. Old English present participles ended in *-ende* not *-ing,* and past participles bore a prefix *ge-* (as *geandwyrd* "answered" above).

The period of Middle English extends roughly from the twelfth century through the fifteenth. The influence of French (and Latin, often by way of French) upon the lexicon continued throughout this period, the loss of some inflections and the reduction of others (often to a final unstressed vowel spelled *-e*) accelerated, and many changes took place within the phonological and grammatical systems of the language. A typical prose passage, especially one from the later part of the period, will not have such a foreign look to us as Aelfric's prose has; but it will not be mistaken for contemporary writing either. The following brief passage is drawn from a work of the late fourteenth century called *Mandeville's Travels.* It is fiction in the guise of travel literature, and, though it purports to be from the pen of an English knight, it was originally written in French and later translated into Latin and English. In this extract Mandeville describes the land of Bactria, apparently not an altogether inviting place, as it is inhabited by "full yuele [evil] folk and full cruell."

In þat lond ben trees þat beren wolle, as þogh it were of scheep; whereof men maken clothes, and all þing þat may ben made of wolle. In þat contree ben many ipotaynes, þat dwellen som tyme in the water, and somtyme on the lond: and þei ben half man and half hors, as I haue seyd before; and þei eten men, whan þei may take hem. And þere ben ryueres and watres þat ben fulle byttere, þree sithes more þan is the water of the see. In þat contré ben many griffounes, more plentee þan in ony other contree. Sum men seyn þat þei han the body vpward as an egle, and benethe as a lyoun: and treuly þei seyn soth þat þei ben of þat schapp. But o griffoun hath the body more gret, and is more strong, þanne eight lyouns, of suche lyouns as ben o this half; and more gret and strongere þan an hundred egles, suche as we han amonges vs. For o griffoun þere wil bere fleynge to his nest a gret hors, ʒif he may fynde him at the poynt, or two oxen ʒoked togidere, as þei gon at the plowgh.

The spelling is often peculiar by modern standards and even inconsistent within these few sentences (*contré* and *contree, o* [*griffoun*] and *a* [*gret hors*], *þanne* and *þan,* for example). Moreover, there is in addition to thorn another old character ʒ, "yogh," to make difficulty. It can represent several sounds but here may be thought of as equivalent to *y.* Even the older spellings (including those where *u* stands for *v* or vice versa) are recognizable, however, and there are only a few words like *ipotaynes* "hippopotamuses" and *sithes* "times" that have dropped out of the language altogether. We may notice a few words and phrases that have meanings no longer common such as *byttere* "salty," *o this half* "on this side of the world," and *at the poynt* "to hand," and the effect of the centuries-long dominance of French on the vocabulary is evident in many familiar words which could not have occurred in Aelfric's writing even if his subject had allowed them, words like *contree, ryueres, plentee, egle,* and *lyoun.*

In general word order is now very close to that of our time, though we notice constructions like *hath the body more gret* and *three sithes more þan is the water of the see.* We also notice that present tense verbs still receive a plural inflection as in *beren, dwellen, han,* and *ben* and that while nominative *þei* has replaced Aelfric's *hi* in the third person plural, the form for objects is still *hem.* All the same, the number of inflections for nouns, adjectives, and verbs has been greatly reduced, and in most respects Mandeville is closer to Modern than to Old English.

The period of Modern English extends from the sixteenth century to our own day. The early part of this period saw the completion of a revolution in the phonology of English that had begun in late Middle English and that effectively redistributed the occurrence of the vowel phonemes to something approximating their present pattern. (Mandeville's English would have sounded even less familiar to us than it looks.) Other important early developments include the stabilizing effect on spelling of the printing press and the beginning of the direct influence of Latin and, to a lesser extent, Greek on the lexicon. Later, as English came into contact with other cultures around the world and distinctive dialects of English developed in the many areas which Britain had colonized, numerous other languages made small but interesting contributions to our word-stock.

The historical aspect of English really encompasses more than the three stages of development just under consideration. English has what might be called a prehistory as well. As we have seen, our language did not simply spring into existence; it was brought from the Continent by Germanic tribes who had no form of writing and hence left no records. Philologists know that they must have spoken a dialect of a language that can be called West Germanic and that other dialects of this unknown language must have included the ancestors of such languages as German, Dutch, Low German, and Frisian. They know this because of certain systematic similarities which these languages share with each other but do not share with, say, Danish. However, they have had somehow to reconstruct what that language was like in its lexicon, phonology, grammar, and semantics as best they can through sophisticated techniques of comparison developed chiefly during the last century. Similarly, because ancient and modern languages like Old Norse and Gothic or Icelandic and Norwegian have points in common with Old English and Old High German or Dutch and English that they do not share with French or Russian, it is clear that there was an earlier unrecorded language that can be called simply Germanic and that must be reconstructed in the same way. Still earlier, Germanic was just a dialect (the ancestors of Greek, Latin, and Sanskrit were three other such dialects) of a language conventionally designated Indo-European, and thus English is just one relatively young member of an ancient family of languages whose descendants cover a fair portion of the globe. (For more detail on the Indo-European languages and their relationships, see the table having that title in the dictionary.)

The Dictionary and the Systems of English

By far the largest part of this volume is called "A Dictionary of the English Language" and so is naturally concerned with the systems of English that we have cursorily surveyed in their synchronic and diachronic aspects. In fact, information related to all four systems is given at most entries in the dictionary, as well as information related to what could reasonably be considered a fifth system of English and many other (though not all) languages—writing. The writing system provides an alternative to speech that permits long-distance transmission and visual reception of a communication and also enables a record to be kept for much longer than human memory can keep it. The writing system of Modern English allows for considerable variation, as is shown by the persistence of variant spellings like *veranda* and *verandah* or *judgment* and *judgement* and by the fact that many compound words have solid, hyphenated, and open stylings all in common use concurrently (as *decision maker, decision-maker,* and *decisionmaker*). At the same time, however, it tends to be a force for standardization and unification because recorded language creates a precedent for future language use and provides a basis on which language use can be taught to the younger members of a community. This conservative effect is one reason why spelling reformers have so far met with but modest success in their efforts.

We may now begin to look at the ways in which the specific systems of our language are treated in the dictionary and at the processes of lexicography which produce the information about these systems that the dictionary user encounters. A dictionary is necessarily and obviously concerned with the lexicon above all, and the information it can convey about the language systems is confined to the level of the word or short phrase. The result is that no dictionary of English, however good it may be, can provide all of the information about the English language that one might wish to have at one time or another. Thus, for example, details about such important aspects of phonology as the patterns of sentence stress and sentence intonation cannot be accommodated in a work of reference organized in terms of words, nor can grammatical topics such as word order in subordinate clauses or the structural relation of interrogative to declarative sentences.

The History of English in the Dictionary

A similar limitation applies to the treatment of the historical aspect of English; yet, Merriam-Webster's Collegiate Dictionary, Tenth Edition is able to offer a good deal of historical information about words. What we earlier called the prehistory of English is encountered in the etymologies that appear in square brackets ahead of the definitional material at many entries. An etymology tells us what is known of an English

word before it became the word we enter in the dictionary; that is, if the word was created in English the etymology shows, to whatever extent is not already obvious from the shape of the word, what materials were used to form it, and if the word was borrowed into English the etymology traces the steps of the borrowing process backward from the point at which the word entered English to the earliest recorded ancestral language. Where it is most relevant, note is made of one or several words from other languages that are related ("akin") to the entry word but are not in the direct line of borrowing. Thus, a word like Aelfric's *heofon* (ignoring for the moment the dative plural inflection *-um* that it bears in the passage we looked at earlier) appears as part of this dictionary's etymology for the modern word *heaven:* [ME *heven,* fr. OE *heofon;* akin to OHG *himil* heaven]. Since *heaven* is a native English word, it has only two recorded ancestors, Middle English *heven* and Old English *heofon.* Beyond those forms lie only the hypothetical, reconstructed forms of West Germanic, Germanic, and Indo-European. In this case one related West Germanic word is shown, Old High German *himil,* which is the parent of Modern German *Himmel* but only a second cousin of our English word. Similarly Mandeville's *contree* appears as the first element in the etymology of its modern descendant *country:* [ME *contree,* fr. OF *contrée,* fr. ML *contrata,* fr. L *contra* against, on the opposite side]. Here we see that our word can be traced back through three nouns of Middle English, Old French, and Medieval Latin (all of which had the same basic meaning as the Modern English noun and so are not glossed) to a Latin preposition (which has a different meaning and so is glossed). The two etymological patterns are, as we would expect from what we know of the history of the English vocabulary, among the most common and are repeated with differing details at entry after entry throughout the book. Of course, borrowings that have occurred within the Modern English period are more various, and we find such exotic language names as Nahuatl (at *chocolate*), Taino (at *²barbecue*), Tagalog (at *boondocks*), Malay (at *¹amok*), and Kimbundu (at *banjo*) as well as the more familiar Russian (at *troika*), Italian (at *¹ballot*), Arabic (at *mullah*), Spanish (at *¹macho*), and Japanese (at *tycoon*).

An etymologist must know a good deal about the history of English and also about the relationships of sound and meaning and their changes over time that underlie the reconstruction of the Indo-European family, but even that considerable learning is not enough to do all that must be done to provide etymologies of English words in a dictionary such as this. A knowledge is also needed of the various processes by which words are created within Modern English: among the most important processes are shortening, or clipping (see *¹prom*), functional shift (as the noun *commute* from the verb *commute*), back-formation (see *grid*), combination of initial letters (see *radar*), transfer of personal or place names (see *silhouette* and *denim*), imitation of sounds (see *¹whiz*), folk etymology (see *Jerusalem artichoke*), and blending of two words (see *motel*). Also available to one who feels the need for a new word to name a new thing or express a new idea is the very considerable store of prefixes, suffixes, and combining forms that already exist in English. Some of these are native and others are borrowed from French, but the largest number have been taken directly from Latin or Greek, and they have been combined in many different ways often without any special regard for matching two elements from the same original language. The combination of these word elements has produced many scientific and technical terms of Modern English. Once in a while a word is created spontaneously out of the creative play of sheer imagination. (For examples of the latter sort of creation see the etymologies of *boondoggle* and *googol* in the dictionary. Such invention is common, as Merriam-Webster editors know from their mail, which frequently includes requests from coiners that their brand-new words be entered in the dictionary. Very few coinages of this kind ever come into common enough use to justify dictionary entry, however.)

An etymologist working on a new edition of the Collegiate Dictionary must review the etymologies at existing main entries and prepare such etymologies as are required for the main entries being added to the new edition. In the course of the former activity adjustments must sometimes be made either to incorporate a useful piece of information that has previously been overlooked or to revise the account of the word's origin in the light of new evidence. Such evidence may be unearthed by the etymologist or may be the product of published research by scholars of historical linguistics and others. In writing new etymologies this editor must, of course, be alive to the possible languages from which a new term may have been borrowed and to the possible ways in which one may have been created. New scientific and technical terms sometimes pose special difficulties. While they are most often formed from familiar word elements, occasionally a case like *methotrexate* presents itself in which one part (here *-trexate*) resists identification.

When all attempts to provide a satisfactory etymology have failed, the editor has recourse to the formula "origin unknown." This formula seldom means that the editor is unaware of various speculations about the origin of the term but instead usually means that no single theory conceived by the etymologist or proposed by others is well enough backed by evidence to include in a serious work of reference, even when qualified by "probably" or "perhaps." Thus, our editors frequently have to explain to correspondents that the dictionary fails to state that the origin of *posh* is in the initial letters of the phrase "port out, starboard home"—supposedly a shipping term for the cooler accommodations on steamships plying between Britain and India from the mid-nineteenth century on—not because the story is unknown to us but because no evidence to support it has yet been produced. Some evidence exists that casts strong doubt on it; the word is not known earlier than 1918 (in a source unrelated to shipping), and the acronymic explanation does not appear until 1935. It therefore seems reasonable to consider the acronymic explanation a modern invention and assign *posh* the etymology [origin unknown]. The etymologist must sift such theories, often several conflicting theories of greater or lesser likelihood, and try to evaluate the evidence conservatively but fairly in arriving at the soundest possible etymology that the available information permits. Occasionally time will prove the result to be somewhat (or even quite) mistaken, and the etymology will need to be replaced by something better. This can happen even when the etymologist felt quite certain of the original etymology, and it is just one reason why dictionaries must be reedited from time to time if they are to remain reliable.

Historical information about words is also provided by the date appearing in parentheses just before the first or only definition at most main entries. The date given is for the earliest recorded use known to our editors of the first entered sense of that entry. In most cases the date is also, in effect, for the earliest use of the word itself that we know of. Some words, however, had early senses that later passed from common use without gaining special literary importance, and these senses are omitted from this dictionary. Because it would be misleading to give a date for a sense that the dictionary does not show, the date is always for the first sense actually defined at the entry. Because the senses of any word having more than one are always presented in historical order, with the one known to have been used first given first, the date serves as a link between the prehistory of the word shown in the etymology and its later recorded history of semantic development within the language as reflected in the order of definitions.

Evidence for the dates has come from a number of sources. Especially for words that have been a part of the language since before this century, the most important sources have been the major historical dictionaries of English. These works include for each sense dated examples of use from one or several authors including the earliest one available to the editors. Chief among these dictionaries is the majestic twenty-volume Oxford English Dictionary, Second Edition. Also of great importance have been the Middle English Dictionary, A Dictionary of American English, A Dictionary of Americanisms, The Scottish National Dictionary, and A Dictionary of the Older Scottish Tongue. Other dictionaries and studies that include dated quotations and have proved helpful in particular cases include Hobson-Jobson (a glossary of Anglo-Indian terms), The Stanford Dictionary of Anglicised Words and Phrases, Bailey's Early Modern English, Schäfer's Early Modern English Lexicography, Wright's English Dialect Dictionary, Cassidy and Le Page's Dictionary of Jamaican English, Branford's Dictionary of South African English, Avis's Dictionary of Canadianisms on Historical Principles, Cassidy's Dictionary of American Regional English, Wentworth's American Dialect Dictionary, Wentworth and Flexner's Dictionary of American Slang, and the several editions of The Barnhart Dictionary of New English. The Century Dictionary and Cyclopedia and the successive editions of Merriam-Webster's unabridged dictionaries and their supplements of new words have also provided much assistance, for while these dictionaries do not incorporate dated quotations, an entry in one or another of them is sometimes earlier than any example of the word from running text that we have been able to find.

The other major source of dates, especially for the period from 1890 to the present, is the Merriam-Webster file of examples of words used in context, which are called citations. More will be said of this collection later. Here it need only be noted that among the more than 14,500,000 slips which the file contains frequently appear one or more examples of a given word that are earlier than any quoted in other sources. And, of course, our citations have been essential to the dating of a considerable number of entries not included in any of the dictionaries mentioned above. The date of 1949 at *classical conditioning* is a case of the first sort, the earliest example in a reference source being from 1964, while the date of 1979 at *elevator music* is of the second sort. Some of the older books in our editorial library and in other libraries to which our editors have access have occasionally supplemented the resources of the citation file in supplying dates.

Almost from the appearance of the first volume of The Oxford English Dictionary, scholars have been discovering earlier dates for particular words and senses by examining works not searched for examples by the dictionary's readers or by reading some works a second time and publishing the results of their findings in various journals. Many hundreds of entries in this dictionary include a date derived from one of these articles, and while far too many scholars and other interested students have participated in this work for a listing here to be practical, some collective acknowledgment of our debt to them is necessary. The date of 1676 at *menagerie* may be cited as an example of one derived from a source of this kind; the quotation discovered by this scholar is 36 years older than the earliest example that had previously been found.

The style of the date is determined by the period of English to which the sense being dated belongs: for entries from Old English we indicate simply that the example is from the period before the twelfth century (bef. 12c); for those from Middle English we indicate their century, as (14c); for those from Modern English we give a single year, as (1742).

Some caution needs to be exercised in interpreting the significance of a date. It is never meant to indicate the exact point at which a word entered the language. For one thing, words have often been in spoken use for many years before they come to be written down. For another, many texts from the earlier periods in which they might have been written down have not survived. Then, too, not all surviving texts, even for the earlier periods, have been read to collect examples for any historical dictionary, and obviously for the modern era only a very small sample of all published material has been examined in that way. One can perhaps with some justification think of the date as indicating a time by which one can be sure that the word was in use, but it will be safest simply to remember that the date actually belongs to the earliest occurrence known to the editors of this dictionary of the first entered sense of the word.

Leaving the historical aspect of English aside now, we may consider how information about the systems of English as they presently exist is recorded in this dictionary. The phonological system needs little more than a mention here. Its role in this dictionary is discussed in some detail in the "Guide to Pronunciation," which immediately follows this section, as is the way in which the pronunciations shown in the dictionary have been determined.

Semantics in the Dictionary

In turning to consider the coverage of the semantic system in the dictionary, we face several difficult problems. If one function of a dictionary is more important than its many others, surely that function is to define the meaning of words. But while definition is central to the dictionary and quite obviously is involved with semantics, for the most part it deals with individual words in isolation from other words and thus ignores, to a considerable extent, the systematic, relational side of English semantics. Another problem is that although we know quite a lot about the system of English phonology and a good deal (though less) about the grammatical system, our understanding of the semantic system is very imperfect, and much of what we do know about it does not come very obviously into play in a dictionary. Still, we will have a glimpse of this system when we consider the dictionary treatment of synonyms, and in the meantime there is much to be said about the defining of words. Perhaps the first thing that we need to remind ourselves of is that when we speak of the meaning of a word we are employing an artificial, if highly useful, convention. Meaning does not truly reside within the word but in the minds of those who hear or read it. This fact alone guarantees that meaning will be to a great degree amorphous; no two people have had exactly the same experience with what a word refers to and so the meaning of the word will be slightly or greatly different for each of us. It is obvious, then, that a dictionary which set itself the task of defining the meanings of words in their entirety would be a foolhardy enterprise. So dictionary editors invoke the traditional distinction between *denotation*—the direct and specific part of meaning which is sometimes indicated as the total of all the referents of a word and is shared by all or most people who use the word—and *connotation*—the more personal associations and shades of meaning that gather about a word as a result of individual experience and which may not be widely shared. The dictionary concerns itself essentially with the denotations of words.

For the editors of this dictionary the defining process began long before they actually sat down to examine critically the definitions of the last edition and to formulate trial definitions. It began with an activity that is called in our offices "reading and marking." Ordinarily each editor spends a portion of the working day reading a variety of newspapers, magazines, and books, looking for anything that might be useful to a definer of English words. Because both time and staff are limited and the scope of English seems nearly unlimited, changes in subject matter, geographical area covered, and individual publications must be made from time to time in a way carefully calculated to ensure the breadth and depth as well as the continuity of our coverage of the vocabulary of English. An editor who is reading and marking will, of course, be looking for examples of new words and for unusual applications of familiar words that suggest the possible emergence of a new meaning but will also be concerned to provide evidence of the current status of variant spellings, inflected forms, and the stylings of compound words, to collect examples that may be quotable as illustrations of typical use in the dictionary, and to record many other useful kinds of information. In each instance the reader will underline the word or phrase that is of interest and mark off as much context as is considered helpful in clarifying the meaning. This example of a word used in context is called a *citation* of the word. Ideally the editor would like all citations to illuminate the meaning of the word, but some passages will remain obscure no matter how far they extend, and sometimes one must mark a citation simply for the occurrence of the word or meaning (especially when it is new), trusting that the reading-and-marking process will yield more helpful examples in the long run. In the case of ephemeral words, of course, this may never happen, but truly ephemeral words will not need to be defined for a dictionary. At this early stage of the dictionary-making process, editors do not make judgments about the likelihood of a word's establishing itself in the language. If a possible citation has even the barest potential to be useful at a later time, it is marked.

These samples of words in bracketed context are put onto 3 $\times$ 5 slips of paper, and the citation slips are placed in alphabetical order in rows of filing cabinets. (In recent years new citations have also been preserved in machine-readable form.) The slips will be used, as needed, by the editors in their roles as writers of definitions and certain other parts of dictionary entries. The editors engaged in this tenth edition of the Collegiate reviewed every one of the nearly million and a half citations that had been gathered since the ninth edition was prepared in the early 1980s. When necessary, they also drew upon the additional resources of what are called the "consolidated" files, those that contain all the citations (over thirteen million) that had been accumulated in our offices since the late nineteenth century and had been used in the editing of the many dictionaries this company published before the present one.

The actual defining process begins with a number of special assignments called "group defining projects," which may range from a small set of words like those for the days of the week or the letters of the English alphabet (for which parallel, formulaic definitions are required) to the vocabulary of a large subject area such as music or anthropology. When these assignments have been completed, defining proceeds alphabetically, with the editors responsible for the terminology of the life sciences or the physical sciences and related technologies working independently of the editors responsible for defining the general vocabulary.

If you were a definer, you would typically be working at a given moment with a group of citations covering a relatively short segment of the alphabet, *gri-* to *gro-*, for example, and with the entries of the dictionary being reedited that fall within the same segment. Your job would be to determine, under the guidance of the citations, which existing entries could remain in the new edition essentially unchanged because their usage showed no significant alteration, which entries needed to be revised either by modification of existing definitions or by the addition of new ones, which old entries were expendable for the new edition, and what new entries should be added to keep coverage of the lexicon up-to-date. You would begin by reading and sorting out the citation slips, first by grammatical function, in the case of a word like *groom* that is both noun and verb, and then by meaning within each part of speech. For each group of citations that was covered by an adequate existing definition, you would need only to indicate that you had examined them and would do nothing to the definition. For definitions needing adjustment, you would indicate the change to be made. In many cases, you would have some citations left over that were not covered by an existing definition, and it would then be your job to determine whether that segment of meaning was perhaps relatively uncommon and not backed by a sufficient range and number of citations and so not needed for the dictionary or whether in fact it was a sense that dictionary users are entitled to find suitably defined when they come looking for it. In the former case you would reject the citations, and eventually they would find their way back to the files to await review for another dictionary (by which time perhaps the citational backing would be stronger and a definition needed). In the latter case the responsibility to frame the kind of definition that will adequately convey that particular segment of meaning to the dictionary user would be yours.

In writing that definition, you could follow any of a number of paths marked out by the instructions given to each definer. These include both the general policies and practices that govern all Merriam-Webster dictionaries and the more specific directions and prohibitions contained in the "style file," as it is called, for this particular dictionary.

The kind of definition that you would write in most cases is called an analytical definition. It consists in its purest form of the statement of a class to which the term being defined is assigned and a number of characteristics which differentiate the individual from other members of the class. For example, the first sense of *grove* is defined in this Collegiate as "a small wood without underbrush," assigning a grove to the more general class of woods and using "small" and "without underbrush" to indicate in what ways a grove is unlike other kinds of woods. Another possibility would be for you to define a synonym, as is done at the sixth sense of the noun *grip*, where the definition is "STAGEHAND." Defining by synonym tends to be inexact because even true synonyms do not have just the same meaning and is perhaps most useful in cases like the one just mentioned where one kind of referent has two or more names, a situation that occurs frequently with the common names of plants and animals. For this reason we link any synonym definition to an analytical definition by making the synonym a cross-reference (in small capital letters) to another entry where an analytical definition suitable for both words is given: at *stagehand* is the definition "a stage worker who handles scenery, properties, or lights," which is also a good definition of the sixth sense of *grip*.

Within these basic defining patterns many variations are permitted. Some analytical definitions may justifiably be truncated by the use of a related word within the definition in order to save precious space for more entries. For example, *grievance committee* can be defined as "a committee formed by a labor union or by employer and employees jointly to discuss and where possible to eliminate grievances" because the second sense of *grievance* is "a cause of distress (as an unsatisfactory working condition) felt to afford reason for complaint or resistance," and so the definition of *grievance committee* need not give that information a second time.

It is also possible to add a synonymous cross-reference to an analytical definition and thereby incorporate at little cost of space a second version of the meaning that looks at it from a slightly different aspect. It is possible, as in the definition of *grievance* just cited, to add a parenthetical element that specifies one or several of the typical referents of the word or that indicates the sole or a typical object of a transitive verb. One may begin an adjective definition with one of a wide variety of formulas but others are forbidden. It is clear already that definers' instructions are elaborately detailed, and it would be tedious to rehearse them here. Their purpose is to assist in developing the definer's native talent so that the definitions that he or she writes are consistently good ones. What is a good definition? Many qualities could be mentioned, and probably different definers would rank the relative importance of those on any list differently; but all definers want a sufficient range and number of their definitions to be objective in reflecting what the word means as it is actually used rather than what the definer or someone else thinks it ought to mean,

and they want their definitions to be accurate, clear, informative, and concise. In short, they want their definitions to have the qualities that users have in mind when they call a dictionary they admire "authoritative."

In the course of your defining, you would have an opportunity fairly often to make another kind of decision: whether to include or omit a new candidate for main entry. Let us take as an example the word *greenmail*, which is one of many entries new to this edition of the Collegiate Dictionary. If you had been the definer who handled that word, you would have been faced with a group of over three dozen citations to read covering a span of nine years, with the greatest concentration in the five years from 1984 to 1988 but continuing to the present. They would include extracts from such publications as *The New York Times, TV Guide, Newsweek, Art in America, The Boston Globe, The New Yorker, Fortune, The Christian Science Monitor, Vogue, The Wall Street Journal,* and *Harper's.* In reading the citations you would notice that while they varied in many details of context, they seemed to be describing a single kind of situation in the corporate world but that *greenmail* itself might refer either to the practice as a whole or (much less often) to the money paid to buy back the stock. You might then have produced the following definition incorporating those two meanings: "the practice of buying enough of a company's stock to threaten a hostile takeover and reselling it to the company at a price above market value; *also*: the money paid for such stock."

The number and time span of the citations and the variety of the sources would already have told you that this was a very strong, and perhaps even an essential, candidate for entry in the new edition. There is no magic number of citations that guarantees entry and no particular span of years that must be reached. To a great extent the judgment made here must rest on your insight and experience as a definer who has seen the citational backing for many words, who has most likely defined words for other Merriam-Webster dictionaries in the past, and who thus has some sense of the relative importance and degree of establishment of new entries within the lexicon and of their likely staying power.

You would have noticed that in addition to the evidence for the noun *greenmail* there were also nine citations for *greenmail* used as a verb and nineteen for an agent noun *greenmailer.* Seeing both that they were less important than the noun (though also well backed by citations) and that their meanings were easy to infer from the meaning of the main entry word, you would have added them to your new main entry as undefined run-ons.

To take one further example of a somewhat different kind, if you had been the life-sciences definer responsible for handling the term *magnetic resonance imaging,* you would have read 30 citations. Many of these would have been from sources such as *The Journal of the American Medical Association* and *Science News,* likely to be seen chiefly by people with specialized interests; but you would also have seen examples from *Sports Illustrated, Discover, The New York Times,* and *Business Week.* In other words, the term is likely to be encountered by people with general interests and, given its nature, will probably be looked up in a dictionary fairly often. Such considerations would have led you to propose entry for the term and with a much higher priority than if the citational backing had been nearly all technical.

It is worth noting briefly that in the course of your work as a definer you would have been concerned with what the citations reveal about a word in addition to its meaning. The definer is initially responsible for most of the framework of the entry including not only spelling variants and run-ons but also inflected forms, usage notes, verbal illustrations, and temporal, regional, stylistic, and subject labels.

The other important part of the entries in this dictionary that is concerned with English semantics is the synonym paragraph. These paragraphs are not written by each individual definer as particular entries are encountered but are rather the special assignment of usually one editor, who decides which words will be included in a single paragraph and at which entry the paragraph will be placed. The synonym editor has a number of responsibilities in addition to the actual writing or revising of the synonym paragraph. Each entry for a term discussed in a paragraph must be checked to ensure that the definition of a given sense is fully consonant with its treatment in the paragraph, and the editor has the authority to make small adjustments of definitions so that no discrepancies which might puzzle a user remain.

Like the definer, this editor must read citations very carefully to see that the opening statement of the core meaning shared by the synonyms includes neither too much nor too little, that each discrimination of one word from the others is accurate, and that typical examples are chosen as a basis on which to frame verbal illustrations. It is particularly in these paragraphs that the dictionary user comes into contact with the systematic side of English semantics because here the concern is with the relationship of meanings instead of the meanings themselves as discrete entities. For example, the synonym paragraph at *splendid* in this dictionary states that *splendid, resplendent, gorgeous, glorious, sublime,* and *superb* mean "extraordinarily or transcendently impressive." This statement of meaning is at once too broad and too narrow to be a good definition for any of the words; it trims away the particular elements of meaning that make each word distinctive (the most important of which are stated in the following discussion). It does, however, give us an accurate notion of the point at which these words come into a precise semantic relationship with each other.

Grammar and Usage in the Dictionary

The last of the four systems of English whose reflection we may see, at least briefly and occasionally, in the dictionary is the grammatical system. As we saw earlier, this system involves chiefly the relationship between words as they form more complex units rather than individual words themselves. A descriptive grammar of English is a very different kind of book from a dictionary. Nevertheless, virtually every entry in this dictionary contains at least one piece of information about its grammatical nature and the kinds of relationships it can enter into, namely, the functional label which typically indicates the part of speech of the entry or, in the case of terminal word elements, the part of speech of the words that they form. If an entry is labeled *adv*, we know that it can describe the action of a verb but cannot itself be the main verb of a sentence, while an entry labeled *n* cannot link the subject of a sentence with a predicate adjective but can be the subject. Other parts of the entry also give us information that is grammatical in nature. One sort of information is offered by the boldface inflected forms that are shown at every entry for which they are irregular exceptions to the ordinary patterns of English inflection or may present some other sort of problem to the dictionary user. Another is offered by the undefined run-on entries. They illustrate the complex patterns by which one word or a number of words can be derived from a single base by means of affixation or functional shift. Certain kinds of usage notes following or standing in place of definitions also present grammatical information. Typical of the former kind of usage note is the one given at sense 3c of *boy*, "often used interjectionally to express intensity of feeling," and the one given at sense 2b of the verb ³*conk*, "usu. used with *off* or *out*." Typical of the latter are the several usage notes at the entry for the preposition *for*, "used as a function word to indicate duration of time or extent of space" at sense 9, for example.

Usage is a concept that embraces many aspects of and attitudes toward language. Grammar is certainly only a small part of what goes to make up usage, though some people use one term for the other, as when they label what is really a controversial point of usage a grammatical error. Usage guidance is offered in this dictionary in many ways; it would be little exaggeration to say that any information a user seeks and finds in this book can offer some guidance as to usage. But usage information is chiefly conveyed through three devices: usage notes; temporal, regional, and stylistic labels; and usage paragraphs. The first two are developed by definers from their examination of citations, including sometimes (and particularly in the case of the labels) citations found in historical, dialect, and slang dictionaries as well as those in Merriam-Webster's citation file. The usage paragraphs like the synonym paragraphs are the result of a special project chiefly in the hands of one editor with assistance from several others. The editors attempted to select particular problems of confused or disputed usage that would be of broad general interest and could be treated at individual entries in the dictionary. The great majority of them involve words that have traditionally been points of dispute (a few of these are now probably more traditional than truly the subjects of heated dispute), but some are relatively new items for this kind of consideration. Several paragraphs deal with pronunciation, a subject rarely treated in books about usage.

The editors who wrote the paragraphs used several kinds of material: books describing one or another aspect of the history of usage as a problem in English; books and articles ruling on particular points of usage, whether the product of one person or a group; historical and other dictionaries; and above all citations of usage itself from our file. In digesting this mass of information and presenting it in a very brief compass, the editors have typically combined information on the history of the controversy, the current state of expressed opinion, illustrations of both old and modern use (often quoted), and practical advice. These paragraphs have profited greatly from the extensive research in the same materials that was carried out in the course of work on Webster's Dictionary of English Usage.

It has been close to 250 years since Dr. Johnson published his great dictionary and well over 150 years since Noah Webster's American Dictionary of the English Language appeared. Even the more modest Collegiate series will be approaching its hundredth birthday in just a few years. It seems clear that the long tradition of English dictionaries is not likely to wither and die. Indeed, dictionaries are likely to become, if anything, even more important to the general public in the future, at least as long as the vocabulary of English continues the rapid growth which began earlier in this century and which seems now to intensify year by year. As long as they are edited with a proper regard for the right of the dictionary user to have accurate information about what English words actually mean and how they are actually used, those dictionaries will continue to serve a useful purpose and to be needed. Though they are incomplete as descriptions of the systems of English and are edited by fallible humans whose best intentions sometimes fall short of the mark, such dictionaries will continue to form, as the best dictionaries have always done, a helpful bridge between what we know about language and how we use it. Movement across such a bridge is, of course, in both directions: our use of language furnishes the basis for our knowledge of it, but our knowledge of it also helps us to use it more effectively.

Guide to Pronunciation

Pronunciation is not an intrinsic component of the dictionary. For some languages, such as Spanish, Swahili, and Serbo-Croatian, the correspondence between orthography and pronunciation is so close that a dictionary need only spell a word correctly to indicate its pronunciation. Modern English, however, displays no such consistency in sound and spelling, and so a dictionary of English must devote considerable attention to the pronunciation of the language. The English lexicon contains numerous eye rhymes such as *love, move,* and *rove,* words which do not sound alike despite their similar spellings. On the other hand, it also contains rhyming words such as *breeze, cheese, ease, frieze,* and *sleaze* whose rhymes are all spelled differently.

This grand mismatch between words that look alike and words that sound alike does at least serve to record something of the history of the English-speaking peoples and their language. Spelling often indicates whether a word comes down from the native Anglo-Saxon word stock or was adopted in successive ages from the speech of a missionary monk chanting Latin, a seafaring Viking dickering in Old Norse, a Norman nobleman giving orders in French, or a young immigrant to turn-of-the-century America. For example, the sound \sh\ is spelled as *sh* in native English *shore,* as *ch* in the French loan *champagne,* as *sk* in one pronunciation of the Norwegian loan *ski,* as *si* in the Renaissance Latin loan *emulsion,* and as *sch* in the recent Yiddish loan *schlepp.* English vowels present different complexities of sound and spelling, due in large part to the fact that William Caxton introduced printing to England in A.D. 1476, many decades before the sound change known as the Great Vowel Shift had run its course. With the rise of printing came an increasingly fixed set of spelling conventions, but the conventionalized spellings soon lost their connection to pronunciation as the vowel shift continued. The stressed vowels of *sane* and *sanity* are therefore identical in spelling though now quite different in quality. For the trained observer the vagaries of English orthography contain a wealth of linguistic history; for most others, however, this disparity between sound and spelling is just a continual nuisance at school or work.

Readers often turn to the dictionary wanting to learn the exact pronunciation of a word, only to discover that the word may have several pronunciations, as is the case for *deity, economic, envelope,* and *greasy,* among many others. The inclusion of variant pronunciations disappoints those who want their dictionary to list one "correct" pronunciation. In truth, though, there can be no objective standard for correct pronunciation other than the usage of thoughtful and, in particular, educated speakers of English. Among such speakers one hears much variation in pronunciation.

Dictionaries of English before the modern era usually ignored pronunciation variants, instead indicating a single pronunciation by marking the entry word with diacritics to indicate stress and letter values. These systems were cumbersome, however, and reflected the dialectal biases of the editors more than the facts about how a word was actually spoken. Lexicographers came eventually to recognize the need for separate respellings which could record the entire range of accepted variants along with appropriate notes about dialectal distribution or usage.

This dictionary records many types of variation in pronunciation. Distinctions between British and American speech are frequently noted, as are differences among the three major dialect areas of the U.S.—Northern, Southern, and Midland. Words that have distinctive pronunciations in Canada, such as *decal* and *khaki,* have those pronunciations duly noted. Pronunciations peculiar to certain spheres of activity are also represented, as for example the variants of *athwart* and *tackle* heard in nautical use. Finally, a wide range of unpredictable variations are included, such as the pronunciation of *economic* with either \e\ or \ē\. Unpredictable variations frequently cut across the boundaries of geographical dialects, sometimes running along the lines of social class, ethnicity, or gender instead. In fine, this dictionary attempts to include—either explicitly or by implication—all pronunciation variants of a word that are used by educated speakers of the English language.

The pronunciations in this dictionary are informed chiefly by the Merriam-Webster pronunciation file. This file contains citations that are transcriptions of words used by native speakers of English in the course of utterances heard in speeches, interviews, and conversations. In this extensive collection of 3 × 5 slips of paper, one finds the pronunciations of a host of people: politicians, professors, curators, artists, musicians, doctors, engineers, preachers, activists, journalists, and many others. The Merriam-Webster pronunciation editors have been collecting these citations from live speech and from radio, television, and shortwave broadcasts since the 1930s. It is primarily on the basis of this large and growing file that questions of usage and acceptability in pronunciation are answered. All of the pronunciations recorded in this book can be documented as falling within the range of generally acceptable variation, unless they are accompanied by a restricting usage note or symbol or a regional label.

No system of indicating pronunciation is self-explanatory. The following discussion sets out the signification and use of the pronunciation symbols in this book, with special attention to those areas where experience has shown that dictionary users may have questions. More detailed information can be found in the Guide to Pronunciation in Webster's Third New International Dictionary. The order of symbols discussed below is the same as the order on the page of Pronunciation Symbols, with the exception that the symbols which are not letter characters are here listed first. Those characters which have corresponding symbols in the International Phonetic Alphabet (IPA) are shown with their IPA equivalents.

\ \ All pronunciation information is printed between reversed virgules. Pronunciation symbols are printed in roman type and all other information, such as labels and notes, is printed in italics.

\ˈ\ A high-set stress mark precedes a syllable with primary (strongest) stress; a low-set mark precedes a syllable with secondary (medium) stress; a third level of weak stress requires no mark at all: \\'pen-mən-ˌship\\.

Since the nineteenth century the International Phonetics Association has recommended that stress marks precede the stressed syllable, and linguists worldwide have adopted this practice on the basic principle that before a syllable can be uttered the speaker must know what degree of stress to give it. In accordance with the practice of French phoneticians, no stress marks are shown in the transcription of words borrowed from French whose pronunciations have not been anglicized, as at *ancien régime* and *émeute*.

\\ - \\ Hyphens are used to separate syllables in pronunciation transcriptions. In actual speech, of course, there is no pause between the syllables of a word. The placement of hyphens is based on phonetic principles, such as vowel length, nasalization, variation due to the position of a consonant in a syllable, and other nuances of the spoken word. The syllable breaks shown in this book reflect the careful pronunciation of a single word out of context. Syllabication tends to change in rapid or running speech: a consonant at the end of a syllable may shift into a following syllable, and unstressed vowels may be elided. The numerous variations in pronunciation that a word may have in running speech are of interest to phoneticians but are well outside the scope of a dictionary of general English.

The centered dots in boldface entry words indicate potential end-of-line division points and not syllabication. These division points are determined by considerations of both morphology and pronunciation, among others. A detailed discussion of end-of-line division is contained in the article on Division in Boldface Entry Words in Webster's Third New International Dictionary. In this book a consistent approach has been pursued, both toward word division based on traditional formulas and toward syllabication based on phonetic principles. As a result, the hyphens indicating syllable breaks and the centered dots indicating end-of-line division often do not fall in the same places.

\\( )\\ Parentheses are used in pronunciations to indicate that whatever is symbolized between them is present in some utterances but not in others; thus *factory* \\'fak-t(ə-)rē\\ is pronounced both \\'fak-tə-rē\\ and \\'fak-trē\\, *industry* \\'in-(ˌ)dəs-trē\\ is pronounced both \\'in-dəs-trē\\ and \\'in-ˌdəs-trē\\. In some phonetic environments, as in *fence* \\'fen(t)s\\ and *boil* \\'bȯi(ə)l\\, it may be difficult to determine whether the sound shown in parentheses is or is not present in a given utterance; even the usage of a single speaker may vary considerably.

\\ , ; \\ Variant pronunciations are separated by commas; groups of variants are separated by semicolons. The order of variants does not mean that the first is in any way preferable to or more acceptable than the others. All of the variants in this book, except those restricted by a regional or usage label, are widely used in acceptable educated speech. If evidence reveals that a particular variant is used more frequently than another, the former will be given first. This should not, however, prejudice anyone against the second or subsequent variants. In many cases the numerical distribution of variants is equal but one of them, of course, must be printed first.

\\ ÷ \\ The obelus, or division sign, is placed before a pronunciation variant that occurs in educated speech but that is considered by some to be questionable or unacceptable. This symbol is used sparingly and primarily for variants that have been objected to over a period of time in print by commentators on usage, in schools by teachers, or in correspondence that has come to the Merriam-Webster editorial department. In most cases the objection is based on orthographic or etymological arguments. For instance, the second variant of *cupola* \\'kyü-pə-lə, ÷-ˌlō\\, though used frequently in speech, is objected to because *a* is very rarely pronounced \\ō\\ in English. The pronunciations \\'fe-byə-ˌwer-ē\\ and \\'fe-bə-ˌwer-ē\\ (indicated simultaneously by the use of parentheses) are similarly marked at the entry for *February* \\ ÷'fe-b(y)ə-ˌwer-ē, 'fe-brə-\\, even though they are the most frequently heard pronunciations, because some people insist that both *r*'s should be pronounced. The obelus applies only to that portion of the transcription which it immediately precedes and not to any other variants following.

\\ ə \\ in unstressed syllables as in **banana, collide, abut** (IPA [ə]). This neutral vowel, called *schwa*, may be represented orthographically by any of the letters *a, e, i, o, u, y*, and by many combinations of letters. In running speech unstressed vowels are regularly pronounced as \\ə\\ in American and British speech. Unstressed \\ə\\ often intrudes between a stressed vowel and a following \\l\\ or \\r\\ though it is not represented in the spelling, as in *eel* \\'ē(ə)l\\ and *sour* \\'saủ(-ə)r\\.

\\ 'ə, ˌə \\ in stressed syllables as in **humdrum, abut.** (IPA [ʌ]).

\\ ᵊ \\ immediately preceding \\l\\, \\n\\, \\m\\, \\ŋ\\, as in **battle, cotton,** and one pronunciation of **open** \\'ō-pᵊm\\ and of **and** \\ᵊŋ\\ as in one pronunciation of the phrase *lock and key* \\ˌläk-ᵊŋ-'kē\\. The symbol \\ᵊ\\ preceding these consonants does not itself represent a sound. It signifies instead that the following consonant is syllabic; that is, the consonant itself forms the nucleus of a syllable that does not contain a vowel.

In the pronunciation of some French or French-derived words \\ᵊ\\ is placed immediately after \\l\\, \\m\\, \\r\\ to indicate one nonsyllabic pronunciation of these consonants, as in the French words table "table," prisme "prism," and titre "title," each of which in isolation and in some contexts is a one-syllable word.

\\ ər \\ as in **further, merger, bird** (IPA [ɜ, ɚ]). (See the section on \\r\\.) The anglicized pronunciation of the vowel \\œ\\ is represented in this book as \\ə(r)\\. (See the section on \\œ\\.)

\\ 'ər-, 'ə-r \\ as in two different pronunciations of *hurry*. Most U.S. speakers pronounce \\'hər-ē\\ with the \\ər\\ representing the same sounds as in *bird* \\'bərd\\. Usually in metropolitan New York and southern England and frequently in New England and the southeastern U.S. the vowel is much the same as the vowel of *hum* followed by a syllable-initial variety of \\r\\. This pronunciation of *hurry* is represented as \\'hə-rē\\ in this book. Both types of pronunciation are shown for words composed of a single meaningful unit (or *morpheme*) as in *current, hurry,* and *worry*. In words such as *furry, stirring,* and *purring* in which a vowel or vowel-initial suffix is added to a word ending in *r* or *rr* (as *fur, stir,* and *purr*), the second type of pronunciation outlined above is heard only occasionally and is not shown in this dictionary.

\a\ as in mat, map, mad, gag, snap, patch (IPA [æ]). Some variation in this vowel is occasioned by the consonant that follows it; thus, for some speakers *map, mad,* and *gag* have noticeably different vowel sounds. There is a very small number of words otherwise identical in pronunciation that these speakers may distinguish solely by variation of this vowel, as in the two words *can* (put into cans; be able) in the sentence "Let's can what we can." However, this distinction is sufficiently infrequent that the traditional practice of using a single symbol is followed in this book.

\ā\ as in day, fade, date, aorta, drape, cape (IPA [e, eɪ, ei]). In most English speech this is actually a diphthong. In lowland South Carolina, in coastal Georgia and Florida, and occasionally elsewhere \ā\ is pronounced as a monophthong. As a diphthong \ā\ has a first element \e\ or monophthongal \ā\ and a second element \i\.

\ä\ as in bother, cot, and, with most American speakers, father, cart (IPA [ɑ]). The symbol \ä\ represents the vowel of *cot, cod,* and the stressed vowel of *collar* in the speech of those who pronounce this vowel differently from the vowel in *caught, cawed,* and *caller,* represented by \ȯ\. In U.S. speech \ä\ is pronounced with little or no rounding of the lips, and it is fairly long in duration, especially before voiced consonants. In southern England \ä\ is usually accompanied by some lip rounding and is relatively short in duration. The vowel \ȯ\ generally has appreciable lip rounding. Some U.S. speakers (a perhaps growing minority) do not distinguish between *cot—caught, cod—cawed,* and *collar—caller,* usually because they lack or have less lip rounding in the words transcribed with \ȯ\. Though the symbols \ä\ and \ȯ\ are used throughout this book to distinguish the members of the above pairs and similar words, the speakers who rhyme these pairs will automatically reproduce a sound that is consistent with their own speech.

In words such as *card* and *cart* most U.S. speakers have a sequence of sounds that we transcribe as \är\. Most speakers who do not pronounce \r\ before another consonant or a pause, however, do not rhyme *card* with either *cod* or *cawed* and do not rhyme *cart* with either *cot* or *caught*. The pronunciation of *card* and *cart* by such speakers, although not shown in this dictionary, would be transcribed as \'kȧd\ and \'kȧt\. Speakers of r-dropping dialects will automatically substitute \ȧ\ for the transcribed \är\. (See the sections on \ȧ\ and \r\.)

\ȧ\ as in father as pronounced by those who do not rhyme it with *bother* (IPA [a, ɐ]). The pronunciation of this vowel varies regionally. In eastern New England and southern England it is generally pronounced farther forward in the mouth than \ä\ but not as far forward as \a\. In New York City and the southeastern U.S. it may have much the same quality as \ä\ but somewhat greater duration.

In areas in which \r\ is not pronounced before another consonant or a pause, \ȧ\ occurs for the sequence transcribed in this book as \är\. (See the sections on \ä\ and \r\.) In these areas \ȧ\ also occurs with varying frequency in a small group of words in which *a* in the spelling is followed by a consonant letter other than *r* and is not preceded by *w* or *wh*, as in *father, calm, palm,* and *tomato* but not in *watch, what,* or *swap* (though \ȧ\ does sometimes occur in *waft*). Especially in southern England and, less consistently, in eastern New England \ȧ\ occurs in certain words in which \a\ is the usual American vowel and in most of which the vowel is followed by \f\, \th\, \s\, or by \n\ and another consonant, as in the words *after, bath, mask,* and *slant.*

The symbol \ȧ\ is also used in the transcription of some foreign-derived words and names. This vowel, as in French *patte* "paw" and *chat* "cat," is intermediate between \a\ and \ä\ and is similar in quality to the \ȧ\ heard in eastern New England.

\au̇\ as in now, loud, out (IPA [aʊ, au]). The initial element of this diphthong may vary from \a\ to \ȧ\ or \ä\, the first being more common in Southern and south Midland speech than elsewhere. In coastal areas of the southern U.S. and in parts of Canada this diphthong is often realized as \əu̇\ when immediately preceding a voiceless consonant, as in the noun *house* and in *out.*

\b\ as in baby, rib (IPA [b]).

\ch\ as in chin, nature \'nā-chər\ (IPA [tʃ]). Actually, this sound is \t\ + \sh\. The distinction between the phrases *why choose* and *white shoes* is maintained by a difference in the syllabication of the \t\ and the \sh\ in each case and the consequent use of different varieties (or *allophones*) of \t\.

\d\ as in did, adder (IPA [d]). (See the section on \t\ below for a discussion of the flap allophone of \d\.)

\e\ as in bet, bed, peck (IPA [ɛ]). In Southern and Midland dialects this vowel before nasal consonants often has a raised articulation that approximates \i\, so that *pen* has nearly the pronunciation \'pin\.

\'ē, ˌē\ in stressed syllables as in beat, nosebleed, evenly, easy (IPA [i]).

\ē\ in unstressed syllables, as in easy, mealy (IPA [i, ɪ, ᵻ]). Though the fact is not shown in this book, some dialects such as southern British and southern U.S. often, if not usually, pronounce \i\ instead of unstressed \ē\.

\f\ as in fifty, cuff (IPA [f]).

\g\ as in go, big, gift (IPA [g]).

\h\ as in hat, ahead (IPA [h]).

\hw\ as in whale as pronounced by those who do not have the same pronunciation for both *whale* and *wail*. Most U.S. speakers distinguish these two words as \'hwā(ə)l\ and \'wā(ə)l\ respectively, though frequently in the U.S. and usually in southern England \'wā(ə)l\ is used for both. Some linguists consider \hw\ to be a single sound, a voiceless \w\ (IPA [ʍ]).

\i\ as in tip, banish, active (IPA [ɪ]).

\ ī \ as in site, side, buy, tripe (IPA [aɪ, ai, ɑɪ, ɑi]). Actually, this sound is a diphthong, usually composed of \ä\ + \i\ or \a\ + \i\. In Southern speech, especially before a pause or voiced consonant, as in *shy* and *five*, the second element \i\ may not be pronounced (IPA [a:]). Chiefly in eastern Virginia, coastal South Carolina, and parts of Canada the diphthong is approximately \'ə\ + \i\ before voiceless consonants, as in *nice* and *write* (IPA [ʌɪ]).

\ j \ as in job, gem, edge, join, judge. Actually, this sound is \d\ + \zh\ (IPA [dʒ]). Assuming the anglicization of *Jeanne d'Arc* as \zhän-'därk\, the distinction between the sentences *They betray John Dark* and *They betrayed Jeanne d'Arc* is maintained by a difference in the syllabication of the \d\ and the \zh\ in each case and the consequent use of different varieties (or *allophones*) of \d\.

\ k \ as in kin, cook, ache (IPA [k]).

\ k̲ \ as in German ich "I," Buch "book," and one pronunciation of English loch. Actually, there are two distinct sounds in German; the \k̲\ in *ich* (IPA [ç]) is pronounced toward the front of the mouth and the \k̲\ in *Buch* is pronounced toward the back (IPA [x]). In English, however, no two words otherwise identical are distinguished by these two varieties of \k̲\, and therefore only a single symbol is necessary.

\ l \ as in lily, pool (IPA [l, ɫ]). In words such as *battle* and *fiddle* the \l\ is a syllabic consonant (IPA [l̩]). (See the section on \ə\ above.)

\ m \ as in murmur, dim, nymph (IPA [m]). In pronunciation variants of some words, such as *open* and *happen*, \m\ is a syllabic consonant (IPA [m̩]). (See the section on \ə\ above.)

\ n \ as in no, own (IPA [n]). In words such as *cotton* and *sudden*, the \n\ is a syllabic consonant (IPA [n̩]). (See the section on \ə\ above.)

\ ⁿ \ indicates that a preceding vowel or diphthong is pronounced with the nasal passages open, as in French *un bon vin blanc* \œⁿ-bōⁿ-vaⁿ-bläⁿ\ "a good white wine."

\ ŋ \ as in sing \'siŋ\, singer \'siŋ-ər\, finger \'fiŋ-gər\, ink \'iŋk\ (IPA [ŋ]). In some rare contexts \ŋ\ may be a syllabic consonant (IPA [ŋ̍]). (See the section on \ə\ above.)

\ ō \ as in bone, know, beau (IPA [o, ou, oʊ]). Especially in positions of emphasis, such as when it is word final or when as primary stress, \ō\ tends to become diphthongal, moving from \ō\ toward a second element \u̇\. In southern England and in some U.S. speech, particularly in the Philadelphia area and in the Pennsylvania-Ohio-West Virginia border area, the first element is often approximately \ə\. In coastal South Carolina, Georgia, and Florida stressed \ō\ is often monophthongal when final, but when a consonant follows it is often a diphthong moving from \ō\ to \ə\. In this book the symbol \ō\ represents all of the above variants. As an unstressed vowel before another vowel, \ō\ is often pronounced as a schwa with slight lip rounding that is separated from the following vowel by the glide \w\, as in *following* \'fä-lə-wiŋ\. This reduced variant is not usually shown at individual entries.

\ ȯ \ as in saw, all, gnaw, caught (IPA [ɔ]). (See the section on \ä\.)

\ œ \ as in French boeuf "beef," German Hölle "hell" (IPA [œ]). This vowel, which occurs only in foreign-derived terms and names, can be approximated by attempting to pronounce the vowel \e\ with the lips moderately rounded as for the vowel \u̇\. This vowel is often anglicized as the \ər\ of *bird* by those who do not "drop their r's" or as the corresponding vowel of *bird* used by those who do (see the section on \r\). Where this anglicization is shown, it is represented as \ə(r)\.

\ œ̄ \ as in French feu "fire," German Höhle "hole" (IPA [ø]). This vowel, which occurs primarily in foreign-derived terms and names, can be approximated by attempting to pronounce a monophthongal vowel \ā\ with the lips fully rounded as for the vowel \ü\. This vowel also occurs in Scots and thus is used in the pronunciation of *guidwillie*, mainly restricted to Scotland.

\ ȯi \ as in coin, destroy (IPA [ɔɪ, ɔi]). In some Southern speech, especially before a consonant in the same word, the second element may disappear or be replaced by \ə\. Some utterances of *drawing* and *sawing* have a sequence of vowel sounds identical to that in *coin*, but because *drawing* and *sawing* are analyzed by many as two-syllable words they are transcribed with a parenthesized hyphen: \'drȯ(-)iŋ\, \'sȯ(-)iŋ\.

\ p \ as in pepper, lip (IPA [p]).

\ r \ as in red, rarity, car, beard. What is transcribed here as \r\ in reality represents several distinct sounds. Before a stressed vowel \r\ denotes a continuant produced with the tongue tip slightly behind the teethridge (IPA [ɹ]). This sound is usually voiceless when it follows a voiceless stop, as in *pray, tree,* and *cram*. After a vowel in the same syllable \r\ is most often a semivowel characterized by retroflexion of the tongue tip. The sequences \ar\, \är\, \er\, \ir\, \ȯr\, \u̇r\, and \ər\ may then be considered diphthongs. In some speech the retroflexion of the \r\ occurs throughout the articulation of the vowel, but in other cases the first vowel glides into a retroflex articulation. In the latter cases a brief transition vowel is sometimes heard; this variable and nondistinctive glide is not transcribed in this book, but is considered implicit in the symbol \r\.

In Received Pronunciation \r\ is sometimes pronounced as a flap (IPA [ɾ]) in the same contexts in which \t\ and \d\ occur as flaps in American English. (See the section on \t\ below.) Occasionally the flap may be heard after consonants, as in *bright* and *grow*. In other dialects of British English, particularly Scots, \r\ may be pronounced as an alveolar trill (IPA [r]) or as a uvular trill (IPA [R]). In some dialects, especially those of the southeastern U.S., eastern New England, New York City, and southern England, \r\ is not pronounced after a vowel in the same syllable. This is often, if somewhat misleadingly, referred to as r-dropping. In these dialects *r* is pronounced as a nonsyllabic \ə\ when it occurs in these positions or there may be no sound corresponding to the *r*; thus *beard, corn,* and *assured* may be pronounced as \'biəd\, \'kȯən\, and \ə-'shu̇əd\ or, usually with some lengthening of the vowel sound, as \'bid\, \'kȯn\, and \ə-'shu̇d\. In *car, card,* and *cart* those who do not pronounce \r\ generally have a vowel which we would transcribe as \ȧ\, usually pronounced with some lengthening and without a following \ə\. (See the sections on \ä\ and \å\.) The stressed vowel of *bird* and *hurt* in r-dropping speech is similar to the vowel used by r-keepers in the same words but without the simultaneous raising of the center and/or tip of the tongue. In the U.S. most speakers of r-dropping dialects will pronounce \r\ before consonants in some words or in some contexts. Because it is determined by the phonetic context, r-dropping is not explicitly represented in this dictionary; speakers of r-dropping dialects will automatically substitute the sounds appropriate to their own speech.

\s\   as in source, less (IPA [s]).

\sh\   as in shy, mission, machine, special (IPA [ʃ]). Actually, this is a single sound, not two. When the two sounds \s\ and \h\ occur in sequence, they are separated by a hyphen in this book, as in *grasshopper* \'gras-ˌhä-pər\.

\t\   as in tie, attack, late, later, latter (IPA [t]). In some contexts, as when a stressed or unstressed vowel precedes and an unstressed vowel or \əl\ follows, the sound represented by *t* or *tt* is pronounced in most American speech as a voiced flap produced by the tongue tip tapping the teethridge (IPA [ɾ]). In similar contexts the sound represented by *d* or *dd* has the same pronunciation. Thus, the pairs *ladder* and *latter*, *leader* and *liter*, *parody* and *parity* are often homophones. At the end of a syllable \t\ often has an incomplete articulation with no release, or it is accompanied or replaced by a glottal closure. When \t\ occurs before the syllabic consonant \ᵊn\ as in *button* \'bə-t°n\, the glottal allophone is often heard. This may reflect a syllabication of \t\ with the preceding stressed syllable (i.e. \'bət-ᵊn\).

\th\   as in thin, ether (IPA [θ]). Actually, this is a single sound, not two. When the two sounds \t\ and \h\ occur in sequence they are separated by a hyphen in this book, as in *knighthood* \'nīt-ˌhud\. In some dialects of American English this sound is regularly replaced by \f\.

\th\   as in then, either, this (IPA [ð]). Actually, this is a single sound, not two. The difference between \th\ and \th\ is that the former is pronounced without and the latter with vibration of the vocal cords.

\ü\   as in rule, youth, union \'yün-yən\, few \'fyü\ (IPA [u]). As an unstressed vowel before another vowel, \ü\ is often pronounced as a schwa with slight lip rounding that is separated from the following vowel by the glide \w\, as *valuing* \'val-yə-wiŋ\. This reduced variant is not usually shown at individual entries. Younger speakers of American English often use a more centralized and less rounded pronunciation of \ü\ in certain words (as *news* and

musician), both in stressed and especially in unstressed syllables.

\u̇\   as in pull, wood, book, curable \'kyu̇r-ə-bəl\, fury \'fyu̇r-ē\ (IPA [ʊ]).

\ue\   as in German füllen "to fill," hübsch "handsome" (IPA [ʏ]). This vowel, which occurs only in foreign-derived terms and names, can be approximated by attempting to pronounce the vowel \i\ with the lips moderately rounded as for the vowel \u̇\.

\ūe\   as in French rue "street," German fühlen "to feel" (IPA [y]). This vowel, which occurs only in foreign-derived terms and names, can be approximated by attempting to pronounce the vowel \ē\ with the lips fully rounded as for the vowel \ü\.

\v\   as in vivid, invite (IPA [v]).

\w\   as in we, away (IPA [w]).

\y\   as in yard, young, cue \'kyü\, curable \'kyu̇r-ə-bəl\, few \'fyü\, fury \'fyu̇r-ē\, union \'yün-yən\ (IPA [j]). The sequences \lyü\, \syü\, and \zyü\ in the same syllable, as in *lewd*, *suit*, and *presume*, are common in southern British speech but are rare in American speech and only \lü\, \sü\, and \zü\ are shown in this dictionary. A sequence of \h\ and \y\ as in *hue* and *huge* is pronounced by some speakers as a \k\ articulated toward the front of the mouth (IPA [ç]).

In English \y\ does not occur at the end of a syllable after a vowel. In a few words of French origin whose pronunciation has not been anglicized, a postvocalic \y\ is transcribed, as in *mille-feuille* \mēl-fœy\ and in *rouille* \'rü-ē, rüy\. The sound represented is the consonantal \y\ of *yard*.

\ʸ\   indicates that during the articulation of the preceding consonant the tongue has substantially the position it has for the articulation of the \y\ of *yard*, as in French *digne* \dēnʸ\ "worthy." Thus \ʸ\ does not itself represent a sound but rather modifies the preceding symbol.

\z\   as in zone, raise (IPA [z]).

\zh\   as in vision, azure \'a-zhər\ (IPA [ʒ]). Actually, this is a single sound, not two. When the two sounds \z\ and \h\ occur in sequence, they are separated by a hyphen in this book, as in *hogshead* \'hogz-ˌhed, 'hägz-\.

Abbreviations in This Work

For a list of standard abbreviations in common use, see the section Abbreviations and Symbols for Chemical Elements in the back matter.

Abbr.	Meaning
A.&M.	Agricultural and Mechanical
ab	about
abbr	abbreviation
abl	ablative
Acad	Academy
acc	accusative
act	active
A.D.	anno Domini
adj	adjective
adv	adverb
AF	Anglo-French
AFB	Air Force Base
Afrik	Afrikaans
Agric	Agriculture
Alb	Albanian
alter	alteration
Am	America, American
Amer	American
AmerF	American French
AmerInd	American Indian
AmerSp	American Spanish
anc	ancient, anciently
ant	antonym
anthropol	anthropologist, anthropology
aor	aorist
Ar	Arabic
Arab	Arabian
Aram	Aramaic
archaeol	archaeologist
Arm	Armenian
art	article
astron	astronomer, astronomy
attrib	attributive, attributively
atty	attorney
aug	augmentative
Austral	Australian
Av	Avestan
AV	Authorized Version
b	born
bacteriol	bacteriologist
B.C.	before Christ, British Columbia
bef	before
Belg	Belgian
Beng	Bengali
bet	between
bib	biblical
biochem	biochemist
biol	biologist
Braz	Brazilian
BrazPg	Brazilian Portuguese
Bret	Breton
Brit	Britain, British
bro	brother
Bulg	Bulgarian
c	century
C	centigrade, College
ca	circa
Canad	Canadian
CanF	Canadian French
cap	capital, capitalized
Catal	Catalan
caus	causative
Celt	Celtic
cen	central
cent	century
chem	chemist
Chin	Chinese
comb	combining
Comm	Community
compar	comparative
Confed	Confederate
conj	conjugation, conjunction
constr	construction
contr	contraction
Copt	Coptic
Corn	Cornish
criminol	criminologist
d	died
D	Dutch
Dan	Daniel, Danish
dat	dative
dau	daughter
def	definite
deriv	derivative
dial	dialect
dim	diminutive
disc	discovered
Dor	Doric
dram	dramatist
Du	Dutch
DV	Douay Version
e	eastern
E	east, eastern, English
econ	economist
Ed	Education
educ	educator
Egypt	Egyptian
emp	emperor
Eng	England, English
equiv	equivalent
esp	especially
est	estimated
ethnol	ethnologist
exc	except
F	Fahrenheit, French
fem	feminine
Finn	Finnish
fl	flourished
Flem	Flemish
fr	from
Fr	France, French
freq	frequentative
Fris	Frisian
ft	feet
fut	future
G	German
Gael	Gaelic
gen	general, genitive
Ger	German
Gk	Greek
Gmc	Germanic
Goth	Gothic
gov	governor
govt	government
Gr Brit	Great Britain
Heb	Hebrew
hist	historian
Hitt	Hittite
Hung	Hungarian
Icel	Icelandic
IE	Indo-European
imit	imitative
imper	imperative
incho	inchoative
indef	indefinite
indic	indicative
infin	infinitive
Inst	Institute
instr	instrumental
intens	intensive
interj	interjection
interrog	interrogative
Ir	Irish
irreg	irregular
Is	island
ISV	International Scientific Vocabulary
It, Ital	Italian
ital	italic
Jav	Javanese
Jp	Japanese
L	Latin
LaF	Louisiana French
lat	latitude
Lat	Latin
LG	Low German
LGk	Late Greek
LHeb	Late Hebrew
lit	literally, literary
Lith	Lithuanian
LL	Late Latin
long	longitude
m	meters
manuf	manufacturer
masc	masculine
math	mathematician
MBret	Middle Breton
MD	Middle Dutch
ME	Middle English
Mech	Mechanical
Med	Medical
Mex	Mexican, Mexico
MexSp	Mexican Spanish
MF	Middle French
MGk	Middle Greek
MHG	Middle High German
mi	miles
mil	military
min	minister
MIr	Middle Irish
ML	Medieval Latin
MLG	Middle Low German
modif	modification
MPer	Middle Persian
MS	manuscript
mt	mountain
Mt	Mount
MW	Middle Welsh
n	northern, noun
N	north, northern
naut	nautical
NE	northeast

36a

neut	neuter	*pers*	person	*Shak*	Shakespeare
NewEng	New England	*Pg*	Portuguese	*sing*	singular
NewZeal	New Zealand	*philos*	philosopher	*Skt*	Sanskrit
NGk	New Greek	*PhilSp*	Philippine Spanish	*Slav*	Slavic
NHeb	New Hebrew	*physiol*	physiologist	*So*	South
NL	New Latin	*pl*	plural	*SoAfr*	South Africa,
No	North	*Pol*	Polish		South African
nom	nominative	*polit*	political, politician	*sociol*	sociologist
nonstand	nonstandard	*pop*	population	*Sp, Span*	Spanish
Norw	Norwegian	*Port*	Portuguese	*specif*	specifically
nov	novelist	*pp*	past participle	*spp*	species
n pl	noun plural	*prec*	preceding	*St*	Saint
NZ	New Zealand	*prep*	preposition	*Ste*	Sainte
obs	obsolete	*pres*	present, president	*subj*	subjunctive
occas	occasionally	*prob*	probably	*subsp*	subspecies
OCS	Old Church Slavonic	*pron*	pronoun,	*substand*	substandard
OE	Old English		pronunciation	*superl*	superlative
OF	Old French	*pronunc*	pronunciation	*Sw, Swed*	Swedish
OFris	Old Frisian	*Prov*	Provençal	*syn*	synonym, synonymy
OHG	Old High German	*prp*	present participle	*Syr*	Syriac
OIr	Old Irish	*Pruss*	Prussian	*Tag*	Tagalog
OIt	Old Italian	*pseud*	pseudonym	*Tech*	Technology
OL	Old Latin	*psychol*	psychologist	*theol*	theologian
ON	Old Norse	*R.C.*	Roman Catholic	*Theol*	Theological
ONF	Old North French	*redupl*	reduplication	*Toch*	Tocharian
OPer	Old Persian	*refl*	reflexive	*trans*	translation
OPg	Old Portuguese	*rel*	relative	*treas*	treasury
OProv	Old Provençal	*resp*	respectively	*Turk*	Turkish
OPruss	Old Prussian	*rev*	revolution	*U*	University
orig	original, originally	*Rom*	Roman, Romanian	*ultim*	ultimately
ORuss	Old Russian	*RSV*	Revised Standard Version	*usu*	usually
OS	Old Saxon	*Russ*	Russian	*var*	variant, variety
OSp	Old Spanish	*S*	south, southern	*v, vb*	verb
OW	Old Welsh	*Sc*	Scottish, Scots	*vi*	verb intransitive
PaG	Pennsylvania German	*Scand*	Scandinavian	*VL*	Vulgar Latin
part	participle	*ScGael*	Scottish Gaelic	*voc*	vocative
pass	passive	*Sch*	School	*vt*	verb transitive
Per, Pers	Persian	*Scot*	Scotland, Scottish	*W*	Welsh, west, western
perf	perfect	*secy*	secretary	*WGmc*	West Germanic
perh	perhaps	*Sem*	Seminary, Semitic	*zool*	zoologist

Pronunciation Symbols

For more information see the Guide to Pronunciation.

ə .... banana, collide, abut

ˈə, ˌə .... humdrum, abut

ə .... immediately preceding \l\, \n\, \m\, \ŋ\, as in battle, mitten, eaten, and sometimes open \ˈō-pᵊm\, lock and key \-ᵊŋ-\; immediately following \l\, \m\, \r\, as often in French table, prisme, titre

ər .... further, merger, bird

ˈər-, ˈə-r .... as in two different pronunciations of hurry \ˈhər-ē, ˈhə-rē\

a .... mat, map, mad, gag, snap, patch

ā .... day, fade, date, aorta, drape, cape

ä .... bother, cot, and, with most American speakers, father, cart

à .... father as pronounced by speakers who do not rhyme it with bother; French patte

aù .... now, loud, out

b .... baby, rib

ch .... chin, nature \ˈnā-chər\

d .... did, adder

e .... bet, bed, peck

ˈē, ˌē .... beat, nosebleed, evenly, easy

ē .... easy, mealy

f .... fifty, cuff

g .... go, big, gift

h .... hat, ahead

hw .... whale as pronounced by those who do not have the same pronunciation for both whale and wail

i .... tip, banish, active

ī .... site, side, buy, tripe

j .... job, gem, edge, join, judge

k .... kin, cook, ache

k̲ .... German ich, Buch; one pronunciation of loch

l .... lily, pool

m .... murmur, dim, nymph

n .... no, own

ⁿ .... indicates that a preceding vowel or diphthong is pronounced with the nasal passages open, as in French un bon vin blanc \œ̃ⁿ -bōⁿ -vaⁿ -bläⁿ\

ŋ .... sing \ˈsiŋ\, singer \ˈsiŋ-ər\, finger \ˈfiŋ-gər\, ink \ˈiŋk\

ō .... bone, know, beau

ȯ .... saw, all, gnaw, caught

œ .... French boeuf, German Hölle

œ̄ .... French feu, German Höhle

ȯi .... coin, destroy

p .... pepper, lip

r .... red, car, rarity

s .... source, less

sh .... as in shy, mission, machine, special (actually, this is a single sound, not two); with a hyphen between, two sounds as in grasshopper \ˈgras-ˌhä-pər\

t .... tie, attack, late, later, latter

th .... as in thin, ether (actually, this is a single sound, not two); with a hyphen between, two sounds as in knighthood \ˈnīt-ˌhùd\

t̲h̲ .... then, either, this (actually, this is a single sound, not two)

ü .... rule, youth, union \ˈyün-yən\, few \ˈfyü\

ù .... pull, wood, book, curable \ˈkyùr-ə-bəl\, fury \ˈfyùr-ē\

ue .... German füllen, hübsch

ūe .... French rue, German fühlen

v .... vivid, give

w .... we, away

y .... yard, young, cue \ˈkyü\, mute \ˈmyüt\, union \ˈyün-yən\

ʸ .... indicates that during the articulation of the sound represented by the preceding character the front of the tongue has substantially the position it has for the articulation of the first sound of yard, as in French digne \dēnʸ\

z .... zone, raise

zh .... as in vision, azure \ˈa-zhər\ (actually, this is a single sound, not two); with a hyphen between, two sounds as in hogshead \ˈhȯgz-ˌhed, ˈhägz-\

\ .... slant line used in pairs to mark the beginning and end of a transcription: \ˈpen\

ˈ .... mark preceding a syllable with primary (strongest) stress: \ˈpen-mən-ˌship\

ˌ .... mark preceding a syllable with secondary (medium) stress: \ˈpen-mən-ˌship\

- .... mark of syllable division

() .... indicate that what is symbolized between is present in some utterances but not in others: factory \ˈfak-t(ə-)rē\

÷ .... indicates that many regard as unacceptable the pronunciation variant immediately following: cupola \ˈkyü-pə-lə, ÷-ˌlō\

38a

A Dictionary of
the English Language

¹a \'ā\ *n, pl* **a's** *or* **as** \'āz\ *often cap, often attrib* (bef. 12c) **1 a** : the 1st letter of the English alphabet **b** : a graphic representation of this letter **c** : a speech counterpart of orthographic *a* **2** : the 6th tone of a C-major scale **3** : a graphic device for reproducing the letter *a* **4** : one designated *a* esp. as the 1st in order or class **5 a** : a grade rating a student's work as superior in quality **b** : one graded or rated with an A **6** : something shaped like the letter A

²a \ə, (')ā, *Canad* 'a\ *indefinite article* [ME, fr. OE *ān* one — more at ONE] (bef. 12c) **1** — used as a function word before singular nouns when the referent is unspecified ⟨*a* man overboard⟩ and before number collectives and some numbers ⟨*a* dozen⟩ **2** : the same ⟨birds of *a* feather⟩ ⟨swords all of *a* length⟩ **3 a** — used as a function word before a singular noun followed by a restrictive modifier ⟨*a* man who was here yesterday⟩ **b** : ANY ⟨*a* man who is sick can't work⟩ **c** — used as a function word before a mass noun to denote a particular type or instance ⟨*a* bronze made in ancient times⟩ ⟨glucose is *a* simple sugar⟩ **d** — used as a function word before a proper noun representing an example or type ⟨the attractions of *a* Boston or *a* Cleveland⟩ **4** — used as a function word with nouns to form adverbial phrases of quantity, amount, or degree ⟨felt *a* little tired⟩
usage In speech and writing *a* is used before a consonant sound ⟨*a* door⟩ ⟨*a* human⟩. Before a vowel sound *an* is usual ⟨*an* icicle⟩ ⟨*an* honor⟩ but esp. in speech *a* is used occasionally, more often in some dialects than in others ⟨*a* apple⟩ ⟨*a* obligation⟩. Before a consonant sound represented by a vowel letter *a* is usual ⟨*a* one⟩ ⟨*a* union⟩ but *an* also occurs though less frequently now than formerly ⟨*an* unique⟩ ⟨such *an* one⟩. Before unstressed or weakly stressed syllables with initial *h* both *a* and *an* are used in writing ⟨*a* historic⟩ ⟨*an* historic⟩ but in speech *an* is more frequent whether \h\ is pronounced or not. In the King James Version of the Old Testament and occasionally in writing and speech *an* is used before *h* in a stressed syllable ⟨*an* huntress⟩ ⟨*an* hundred⟩ ⟨children are *an* heritage of the Lord —Ps 127:3(AV)⟩.

³a \ə\ *also* (')ā\ *prep* [ME, fr. OE *a-, an, on*] (bef. 12c) **1** *chiefly dial* : ON, IN, AT **2** : in, to, or for each ⟨twice *a* week⟩ ⟨five dollars *a* dozen⟩
usage see ²A

⁴a \ə, (,)ā\ *vb* [ME, contr. of *have*] (14c) *archaic* : HAVE ⟨I might *a* had husbands afore now —John Bunyan⟩

⁵a \ə\ *prep* [ME, by contr.] (15c) : OF — often attached to the preceding word ⟨kinda⟩ ⟨lotta⟩

¹a- \ə\ *prefix* [ME, fr. OE] **1** : on : in : at ⟨abed⟩ **2** : in (such) a state or condition ⟨afire⟩ **3** : in (such) a manner ⟨aloud⟩ **4** : in the act or process of ⟨gone *a*-hunting⟩ ⟨atingle⟩

²a- \(')ā *also* (')a *or* (')ā\ *or* **an-** \(')an\ *prefix* [L & Gk; L, fr. Gk — more at UN-] : not : without ⟨asexual⟩ — *a-* before consonants other than *h* and sometimes even before *h*, *an-* before vowels and usu. before *h* ⟨achromatic⟩ ⟨ahistorical⟩ ⟨anastigmatic⟩ ⟨anhydrous⟩

-a- *comb form* [ISV] : replacing carbon esp. in a ring ⟨aza-⟩

-a \ə\ *n suffix* [NL, fr. *-a* (as in *magnesia*)] : OXIDE ⟨silica⟩

aah \'ä, *often prolonged and/or followed by* ə\ *vi* (1953) : to exclaim in amazement, joy, or surprise ⟨one finds oneself oohing and ~ing over the exciting new TV commercials —Walter Goodman⟩ — **aah** *n*

aard·vark \'ärd-,värk\ *n* [obs. Afrik. fr. Afrik *aard* earth + *vark* pig] (1827) : a large burrowing nocturnal ungulate mammal (*Orycteropus afer*) of sub-Saharan Africa that has a long snout, extensile tongue, powerful claws, large ears, and heavy tail and feeds esp. on termites and ants

aard·wolf \-,wùlf\ *n* [Afrik, fr. *aard* + *wolf*] (1833) : a maned striped nocturnal mammal (*Proteles cristatus*) of southern and eastern Africa that resembles the related hyenas and feeds chiefly on insects and esp. termites

aardvark

Aar·on \'ar-ən, 'er-\ *n* [LL, fr. Gk *Aarōn*, fr. Heb *Ahărōn*] : a brother of Moses and high priest of the Hebrews

Aa·ron·ic \a-'rä-nik, e-\ *adj* (ca. 1828) **1** : of or stemming from Aaron **2** : of or relating to the lower order of the Mormon priesthood

ab \'ab\ *n* (1983) : an abdominal muscle — usu. used in pl.

Ab \'äb, 'äv, 'óv\ *n* [Heb *Abh*] (ca. 1771) : the 11th month of the civil year or the 5th month of the ecclesiastical year in the Jewish calendar — see MONTH table

ab- \(,)ab, əb\ *prefix* [ME, fr. OF & L; OF, fr. L *ab-, abs-, a-*, fr. *ab, a-* more at OF] : from : away : off ⟨abaxial⟩

aba \ə-'bä, ä-'bä\ *n* [Ar *'abā'*] (1811) **1** : a loose sleeveless outer garment worn as traditional dress by men in the Middle East **2** : a fabric woven from the hair of camels or goats

ab·a·ca \,a-bə-'kä, 'a-bə-,\ *n* [Sp *abacá*, fr. Tag *abaká*] (ca. 1818) **1** : a strong fiber obtained from the leafstalk of a banana (*Musa textilis*) native to the Philippines — called also *Manila hemp* **2** : the plant that yields abaca

aback \ə-'bak\ *adv* (bef. 12c) **1** *archaic* : BACKWARD, BACK **2** : in a position to catch the wind upon the forward surface of a square sail **3** : by surprise ⟨was taken ~ by her sharp retort⟩

abac·te·ri·al \,ā-bak-'tir-ē-əl\ *adj* (ca. 1935) : not caused by or characterized by the presence of bacteria ⟨~ prostatitis⟩

aba·cus \'a-bə-kəs, ə-'ba-\ *n, pl* **aba·ci** \'a-bə-,sī, -,kē; ə-'ba-,kī\ *or* **aba·cus·es** [L, fr. Gk *abak-, abax*, lit., slab] (14c) **1** : an instrument for performing calculations by sliding counters along rods or in grooves **2** : a slab that forms the uppermost member or division of the capital of a column

¹abaft \ə-'baft\ *prep* [¹a- + *baft* (aft)] (1594) : to the rear of; *specif* : toward the stern from

²abaft *adv* (1628) : toward or at the stern : AFT

ab·a·lo·ne \,a-bə-'lō-nē, 'a-bə-,\ *n* [AmerSp *abulón*, fr. Rumsen (American Indian language of Monterey Bay, Calif.) *aulon*] (1850) : any of a genus (*Haliotis*) of edible rock-clinging gastropod mollusks that have a flattened shell slightly spiral in form, lined with mother-of-pearl, and with a row of apertures along its outer edge

¹aban·don \ə-'ban-dən\ *vt* [ME *abandounen*, fr. MF *abandoner*, fr. *abandon*, n., surrender, fr. *a bandon* in one's power] (14c) **1 a** : to give up to the control or influence of another person or agent **b** : to give up with the intent of never again claiming a right or interest in **2** : to withdraw from often in the face of danger or encroachment ⟨~ ship⟩ **3** : to withdraw protection, support, or help from **4** : to give (oneself) over unrestrainedly **5 a** : to cease from maintaining, practicing, or using ⟨~ed their native language⟩ **b** : to cease intending or attempting to perform ⟨~ed the escape⟩ — **aban·don·er** *n* — **aban·don·ment** \-dən-mənt\ *n*
syn ABANDON, DESERT, FORSAKE mean to leave without intending to return. ABANDON suggests that the thing or person left may be helpless without protection ⟨*abandoned* children⟩. DESERT implies that the object left may be weakened but not destroyed by one's absence ⟨a *deserted* town⟩. FORSAKE suggests an action more likely to bring impoverishment or bereavement to that which is forsaken than its exposure to physical dangers ⟨a *forsaken* lover⟩. *syn* see in addition RELINQUISH

²abandon *n* (1822) : a thorough yielding to natural impulses; *esp* : ENTHUSIASM, EXUBERANCE ⟨with reckless ~⟩

aban·doned \ə-'ban-dənd\ *adj* (14c) **1** : wholly free from restraint **2** : given up : FORSAKEN

à bas \ä-'bä\ [F] (ca. 1897) : down with ⟨*à bas* the profiteers⟩

abase \ə-'bās\ *vt* **abased; abas·ing** [ME *abassen*, fr. MF *abaisser*, fr. *a-* (fr. L *ad-*) + (assumed) VL *bassiare* to lower] (15c) **1** *archaic* : to lower physically **2** : to lower in rank, office, prestige, or esteem — **abase·ment** \-'bās-mənt\ *n*

abash \ə-'bash\ *vt* [ME *abaishen*, fr. (assumed) MF *abaiss-, abair* to astonish, alter. of MF *esbair*, fr. *ex-* + *baer* to yawn — more at ABEYANCE] (14c) : to destroy the self-possession or self-confidence of : DISCONCERT *syn* see EMBARRASS — **abash·ment** \-mənt\ *n*

abate \ə-'bāt\ *vb* **abat·ed; abat·ing** [ME, fr. OF *abattre* to beat down — more at REBATE] *vt* (13c) **1 a** : to put an end to ⟨~ a nuisance⟩ **b** : NULLIFY ⟨~ a writ⟩ **2 a** : to reduce in degree or intensity : MODERATE **b** : to reduce in value or amount : make less esp. by way of relief ⟨~ a tax⟩ **3** : DEDUCT, OMIT ⟨~ part of the price⟩ **4 a** : to beat down or cut away so as to leave a figure in relief **b** *obs* : BLUNT **5** : DEPRIVE ~ *vi* **1** : to decrease in force or intensity **2 a** : to become defeated or become null or void **b** : to decrease in amount or value — **abat·er** *n*
syn ABATE, SUBSIDE, WANE, EBB mean to die down in force or intensity. ABATE stresses the idea of progressive diminishing ⟨the storm *abated*⟩. SUBSIDE implies the ceasing of turbulence or agitation ⟨the protests *subsided* after a few days⟩. WANE suggests the fading or weakening of something good or impressive ⟨*waning* enthusiasm⟩. EBB suggests the receding of something (as the tide) that commonly comes and goes ⟨the *ebbing* of daylight⟩. *syn* see in addition DECREASE

\ə\ abut \ᵊ\ kitten, F table \ər\ further \a\ ash \ā\ ace \ä\ mop, mar
\aù\ out \ch\ chin \e\ bet \ē\ easy \g\ go \i\ hit \ī\ ice \j\ job
\ŋ\ sing \ō\ go \ò\ law \òi\ boy \th\ thin \ṯh\ the \ü\ loot \ù\ foot
\y\ yet \zh\ vision \á, k̲, ⁿ, œ, œ̄, ʉ, ʉ̄, ʸ\ *see* Guide to Pronunciation

abate·ment \ə-'bāt-mənt\ n (14c) **1** : the act or process of abating : the state of being abated **2** : an amount abated; *esp* : a deduction from the full amount of a tax

ab·a·tis \'a-bə-ˌtē, 'a-bə-təs\ n, pl **ab·a·tis** \'a-bə-ˌtēz\ or **ab·a·tis·es** \'a-bə-tə-səz\ [F, fr. *abattre*] (1766) : a defensive obstacle formed by felled trees with sharpened branches facing the enemy

ab·at·toir \'a-bə-ˌtwär, -ˌtwȯr, -ˌtȯr\ n [F, fr. *abattre*] (1820) : SLAUGHTERHOUSE

ab·ax·i·al \(ˌ)a-'bak-sē-əl\ adj (1857) : situated out of or directed away from the axis 〈the ~ or lower surface of a leaf〉

ab·ba·cy \'a-bə-sē\ n, pl **-cies** [ME *abbatie*, fr. LL *abbatia*] (15c) : the office, dignity, jurisdiction, or tenure of an abbot

Ab·bas·id \ə-'ba-səd, 'a-bə-səd\ n (1788) : a member of a dynasty of caliphs (750–1258) ruling the Islamic empire esp. from their capital Baghdad and claiming descent from Abbas the uncle of Muhammad

ab·ba·tial \ə-'bā-shəl, a-\ adj (ca. 1642) : of or relating to an abbot, abbey, or abbess

ab·bé \a-'bā, 'a-ˌbā\ n [F, fr. LL *abbat-*, *abbas*] (1530) : a member of the French secular clergy in major or minor orders — used as a title

ab·bess \'a-bəs\ n [ME *abbesse*, fr. OF, fr. LL *abbatissa*, fem. of *abbat-*, *abbas*] (13c) : a woman who is the superior of a convent of nuns

Abbe·vil·li·an \ˌab-'vi-lē-ən, ˌa-bə-\ adj [*Abbeville*, France] (ca. 1934) : of or relating to an early Lower Paleolithic culture of Europe characterized by bifacial stone hand axes

ab·bey \'a-bē\ n, pl **abbeys** [ME, fr. OF *abaïe*, fr. LL *abbatia* abbey, fr. *abbat-*, *abbas*] (13c) **1 a** : a monastery ruled by an abbot **b** : a convent ruled by an abbess **2** : an abbey church

ab·bot \'a-bət\ n [ME *abbod*, fr. OE, fr. LL *abbat-*, *abbas*, fr. LGk *abbas*, fr. Aram *abbā* father] (bef. 12c) : the superior of a monastery for men

ab·bre·vi·ate \ə-'brē-vē-ˌāt\ vt **-at·ed; -at·ing** [ME, fr. LL *abbreviatus*, pp. of *abbreviare* — more at ABRIDGE] (15c) : to make briefer; esp : to reduce to a shorter form intended to stand for the whole *syn* see SHORTEN — **ab·bre·vi·a·tor** \-ˌā-tər\ n

ab·bre·vi·a·tion \ə-ˌbrē-vē-'ā-shən\ n (15c) **1** : the act or result of abbreviating : ABRIDGMENT **2** : a shortened form of a written word or phrase used in place of the whole 〈*amt* is an ~ for *amount*〉

ABC \ˌā-(ˌ)bē-'sē\ n, pl **ABC's** or **ABCs** \-'sēz\ (13c) **1** : ALPHABET — usu. used in pl. **2 a** : the rudiments of reading, writing, and spelling — usu. used in pl. **b** : the rudiments of a subject

ABD \ˌā-(ˌ)bē-'dē\ n, pl **ABDs** also **ABD's** [all but dissertation] (1965) : a doctoral candidate who has completed required courses and examinations but not a dissertation

Ab·di·as \ab-'dī-əs\ n [LL, fr. Gk] : OBADIAH

ab·di·cate \'ab-di-ˌkāt\ vb **-cat·ed; -cat·ing** [L *abdicatus*, pp. of *abdicare*, fr. *ab-* + *dicare* to proclaim — more at DICTION] vt (1541) **1** : to cast off : DISCARD **2** : to relinquish (as sovereign power) formally 〈~ a throne〉 ~ vi : to renounce a throne, high office, dignity, or function — **ab·di·ca·ble** \-kə-bəl\ adj — **ab·di·ca·tion** \ˌab-di-'kā-shən\ n — **ab·di·ca·tor** \'ab-di-ˌkā-tər\ n

syn ABDICATE, RENOUNCE, RESIGN mean to give up a position with no possibility of resuming it. ABDICATE implies a giving up of sovereign power or sometimes an evading of responsibility such as that of a parent 〈*abdicated* the throne〉. RENOUNCE may replace it but often implies additionally a sacrifice for a greater end 〈*renounced* her inheritance by marrying a commoner〉. RESIGN applies to the giving up of an unexpired office or trust 〈*resigned* from the board〉.

ab·do·men \'ab-də-mən, -ˌdō-; əb-'dō-mən, ab-\ n [MF & L; MF, fr. L] (1615) **1** : the part of the body between the thorax and the pelvis; *also* : the cavity of this part of the trunk containing the chief viscera **2** : the posterior section of the body behind the thorax in an arthropod — see INSECT illustration — **ab·dom·i·nal** \ab-'dä-mə-nᵊl, əb-, -'däm-nᵊl\ adj — **ab·dom·i·nal·ly** \-ē\ adv

ab·du·cens nerve \ab-'dü-ˌsenz-, -'dyü-\ n [NL *abducent-*, *abducens*, L, prp. of *abducere*] (1947) : either of the 6th pair of cranial nerves that are motor nerves supplying the rectus on the outer and lateral side of each eye — called also *abducens*

ab·du·cent nerve \ab-'dü-sᵊnt-, -'dyü-\ n (1875) : ABDUCENS NERVE

ab·duct \ab-'dəkt, əb-\ vt [L *abductus*, pp. of *abducere*, lit., to lead away, fr. *ab-* + *ducere* to lead — more at TOW] (1834) **1** : to carry off (as a person) by force **2** : to draw or spread away (as a limb or the fingers) from a position near or parallel to the median axis of the body or from the axis of a limb — **ab·duc·tor** \-'dək-tər\ n

ab·duc·tion \ab-'dək-shən, əb-\ n (1666) **1** : the action of abducting : the condition of being abducted **2** : the unlawful carrying away of a woman for marriage or intercourse

abeam \ə-'bēm\ adv or adj (ca. 1836) : off to the side of a ship or plane esp. at a right angle to the middle of the ship or plane's length

¹abe·ce·dar·i·an \ˌā-bē-(ˌ)sē-'der-ē-ən\ n [ME *abecedary*, fr. ML *abecedarium* alphabet, fr. LL, neut. of *abecedarius* of the alphabet, fr. the letters *a* + *b* + *c* + *d*] (1603) : one learning the rudiments of something (as the alphabet)

²abecedarian adj (1665) **1 a** : of or relating to the alphabet **b** : alphabetically arranged **2** : RUDIMENTARY

abed \ə-'bed\ adv or adj (13c) : in bed

Abel \'ā-bəl\ n [LL, fr. Gk, fr. Heb *Hebhel*] : a son of Adam and Eve killed by his brother Cain

abe·lia \ə-'bēl-yə\ n [NL, fr. Clarke *Abel* †1826 Eng. botanist] (ca. 1899) : any of a genus (*Abelia*) of shrubs of Asian or Mexican origin having opposite leaves and white, red, or pink flowers

abe·li·an \ə-'bē-lē-ən\ adj, often cap [Niels *Abel* †1829 Norw. mathematician] (ca. 1909) : COMMUTATIVE 2 〈~ group〉 〈~ ring〉

Abe·na·ki \ˌa-bə-'nä-kē\ n, pl **Abenaki** or **Abenakis** (1721) **1** : a member of a group of American Indian peoples of northern New England and adjoining parts of Quebec **2** : either of the two Algonquian languages spoken by the Abenaki peoples

Ab·er·deen An·gus \ˌa-bər-ˌdēn-'aŋ-gəs\ n [*Aberdeen & Angus*, counties in Scotland] (1862) : ANGUS

¹ab·er·rant \a-'ber-ənt, ə-; 'a-bə-rənt, -ˌber-ənt\ adj [L *aberrant-*, *aberrans*, prp. of *aberrare* to go astray, fr. *ab-* + *errare* to wander, err] (ca. 1780) **1** : straying from the right or normal way **2** : deviating from the usual or natural type : ATYPICAL — **ab·er·rance** \-ən(t)s\ n — **ab·er·ran·cy** \-ən(t)-sē\ n — **ab·er·rant·ly** adv

²aberrant n (1938) **1** : an aberrant group, individual, or structure **2** : a person whose behavior departs substantially from the standard

ab·er·rat·ed \'a-bə-ˌrā-təd\ adj [L *aberratus*, pp. of *aberrare*] (1893) : ABERRANT

ab·er·ra·tion \ˌa-bə-'rā-shən\ n [L *aberrare*] (1594) **1** : the fact or an instance of being aberrant esp. from a moral standard or normal state **2** : failure of a mirror, refracting surface, or lens to produce exact point-to-point correspondence between an object and its image **3** : unsoundness or disorder of the mind **4** : a small periodic change of apparent position in celestial bodies due to the combined effect of the motion of light and the motion of the observer **5** : an aberrant individual — **ab·er·ra·tion·al** \-shnəl, -shə-nᵊl\ adj

abet \ə-'bet\ vt **abet·ted; abet·ting** [ME *abetten*, fr. MF *abeter*, fr. OF, fr. *a-* (fr. L *ad-*) + *beter* to bait, of Gmc origin; akin to OE *bǣtan* to bait] (14c) **1** : FORWARD **2** : to assist or support in the achievement of a purpose 〈*abetted* the thief in his getaway〉 *syn* see INCITE — **abet·ment** \-mənt\ n — **abet·tor** or **abet·ter** \-'be-tər\ n

abey·ance \ə-'bā-ən(t)s\ n [MF *abeance* expectation, fr. *abaer* to desire, fr. *a-* + *baer* to yawn, fr. ML *batare*] (1660) **1** : temporary inactivity : SUSPENSION **2** : a lapse in succession during which there is no person in whom a title is vested

abey·ant \-ənt\ adj [back-formation fr. *abeyance*] (ca. 1859) : being in abeyance

ab·hor \əb-'hȯr, ab-\ vt **ab·horred; ab·hor·ring** [ME *abhorren*, fr. L *abhorrēre*, fr. *ab-* + *horrēre* to shudder — more at HORROR] (15c) : to regard with extreme repugnance : LOATHE *syn* see HATE — **ab·hor·rer** \-'hȯr-ər\ n

ab·hor·rence \əb-'hȯr-ən(t)s, -'här-\ n (1660) **1 a** : the act or state of abhorring **b** : the feeling of one who abhors **2** : one that is abhorred

ab·hor·rent \-ənt\ adj [L *abhorrent-*, *abhorrens*, prp. of *abhorrēre*] (1599) **1** *archaic* : strongly opposed **b** : feeling or showing abhorrence **2** : not agreeable : CONTRARY 〈a notion ~ to their philosophy〉 **3** : being so repugnant as to stir up positive antagonism 〈acts ~ to every right-minded person〉 — **ab·hor·rent·ly** adv

Abib \ä-'vēv\ n [Heb *Ābhībh*, lit., ear of grain] (1535) : the 1st month of the ancient Hebrew calendar corresponding to Nisan — see MONTH table

abid·ance \ə-'bī-dᵊn(t)s\ n (1647) **1** : an act or state of abiding : CONTINUANCE **2** : COMPLIANCE 〈~ by the rules〉

abide \ə-'bīd\ vb **abode** \-'bōd\ or **abid·ed; abid·ing** [ME, fr. OE *ābidan*, fr. *ā-*, perfective prefix + *bīdan* to bide; akin to OHG *ir-*, perfective prefix] vt (bef. 12c) **1** : to wait for : AWAIT **2 a** : to endure without yielding : WITHSTAND **b** : to bear patiently : TOLERATE 〈cannot ~ such bigots〉 **3** : to accept without objection 〈will ~ your decision〉 ~ vi **1** : to remain stable or fixed in a state **2** : to continue in a place : SOJOURN *syn* see BEAR, CONTINUE — **abid·er** n — **abide by** **1** : to conform to **2** : to acquiesce in

abid·ing \ə-'bī-diŋ\ adj (14c) : ENDURING, CONTINUING 〈an ~ interest in nature〉 — **abid·ing·ly** adv

ab·i·gail \'a-bə-ˌgāl\ n [*Abigail*, servant in *The Scornful Lady*, a play by Francis Beaumont & John Fletcher] (1671) : a lady's personal maid

abil·i·ty \ə-'bi-lə-tē\ n, pl **-ties** [ME *abilite*, fr. MF *habilité*, fr. L *habilitat-*, *habilitas*, fr. *habilis* apt, skillful — more at ABLE] (14c) **1 a** : the quality or state of being able 〈~ of the soil to hold water〉; *esp* : physical, mental, or legal power to perform **b** : competence in doing : SKILL **2** : natural aptitude or acquired proficiency 〈children whose *abilities* warrant higher education〉

-ability *also* **-ibility** n suffix [ME *-abilite*, *-ibilite*, fr. MF *-abilité*, *-ibilité*, fr. L *-abilitas*, *-ibilitas*, fr. *-abilis*, *-ibilis* *-able* + *-tas* -ty] : capacity, fitness, or tendency to act or be acted on in a (specified) way 〈agglutin*ability*〉

ab in·i·tio \ˌab-ə-'ni-shē-ˌō\ adv [L] (1599) : from the beginning

abio·gen·e·sis \ˌā-ˌbī-ō-'je-nə-səs\ n [NL, fr. ²*a-* + *bio-* + L *genesis*] (1870) : the supposed spontaneous origination of living organisms directly from lifeless matter — **abio·ge·nist** \ˌā-(ˌ)bī-'ä-jə-nist\ n

abio·gen·ic \ˌā-ˌbī-ō-'je-nik\ adj (1891) : not produced by the action of living organisms 〈~ synthesis of amino acids〉

abi·o·log·i·cal \ˌā-ˌbī-ə-'lä-ji-kəl\ adj (1868) : not biological; esp : not involving or produced by organisms 〈~ synthesis of amino acids〉

abi·ot·ic \ˌā-(ˌ)bī-'ä-tik\ adj (ca. 1893) : not biotic : ABIOLOGICAL 〈the ~ environment〉 — **abi·ot·i·cal·ly** \-ti-k(ə-)lē\ adv

ab·ject \'ab-ˌjekt\ adj [ME, fr. L *abjectus*, fr. pp. of *abicere* to cast off, fr. *ab-* + *jacere* to throw — more at JET] (15c) **1** : sunk to or existing in a low state or condition 〈to lowest pitch of ~ fortune thou art fallen —John Milton〉 **2 a** : cast down in spirit : SERVILE, SPIRITLESS 〈a man made ~ by suffering〉 **b** : showing utter hopelessness or resignation 〈~ surrender〉 **3** : expressing or offered in a humble and often ingratiating spirit 〈~ flattery〉 〈an ~ apology〉 *syn* see MEAN — **ab·ject·ly** \'ab-ˌjekt-lē, ab-\ adv — **ab·ject·ness** \-ˌjek(t)-nəs, -'jek(t)-\ n

ab·jec·tion \ab-'jek-shən\ n (14c) **1** : a low or downcast state : DEGRADATION **2** : the act of making abject : HUMBLING, REJECTION 〈I protest . . . this vile ~ of youth to age —G. B. Shaw〉

ab·ju·ra·tion \ˌab-jə-'rā-shən\ n (15c) **1** : the act or process of abjuring : an oath of abjuring

ab·jure \ab-'jùr\ vt **ab·jured; ab·jur·ing** [ME, fr. MF or L; MF *abjurer*, fr. L *abjurare*, fr. *ab-* + *jurare* to swear — more at JURY] (15c) **1 a** : to renounce upon oath **b** : to reject solemnly **2** : to abstain from : AVOID 〈~ extravagance〉 — **ab·jur·er** n

syn ABJURE, RENOUNCE, FORSWEAR, RECANT, RETRACT mean to withdraw one's word or professed belief. ABJURE implies a firm and final rejecting or abandoning often made under oath 〈*abjured* the errors of his former faith〉. RENOUNCE often equals ABJURE but may carry the meaning of disclaim or disown 〈*renounced* abstract art and turned to portrait painting〉. FORSWEAR may add to ABJURE an implication of perjury or betrayal 〈I cannot *forswear* my principles〉. RECANT stresses the withdrawing or denying of something professed or taught 〈if they *recant* they will be spared〉. RETRACT applies to the withdrawing of a promise, an offer, or an accusation 〈the newspaper had to *retract* its allegations against the mayor〉.

ab·late \a-'blāt\ vb **ab·lat·ed; ab·lat·ing** [L *ablatus* (pp. of *auferre* to remove), fr. *ab-* + *latus*, pp. of *ferre* — more at UKASE, BEAR, TOLERATE] vt (1542) : to remove esp. by cutting, abrading, or evaporating ~ vi : to become ablated; *esp* : VAPORIZE 1

ab·la·tion \a-'blā-shən\ n (15c) : the process of ablating: as **a** : surgical removal **b** : loss of a part (as ice from a glacier or the outside of a nose cone) by melting or vaporization

¹**ab·la·tive** \'ab-lə-tiv\ adj (15c) : of, relating to, or constituting a grammatical case expressing typically the relations of separation and source and also frequently such relations as cause or instrument — **ablative** n

²**ab·la·tive** \a-'blā-tiv\ adj (ca. 1569) **1** : of or relating to ablation **2** : tending to ablate ⟨~ material on a nose cone⟩ — **ab·la·tive·ly** adv

ablative absolute \'a-blə-tiv-\ n (ca. 1828) : a construction in Latin in which a noun or pronoun and its adjunct both in the ablative case form together an adverbial phrase expressing generally the time, cause, or an attendant circumstance of an action

ab·laut \'ä-blaút, 'a-; 'äp-,laút\ n [G, fr. ab away from + Laut sound] (1849) : a systematic variation of vowels in the same root or affix or in related roots or affixes esp. in the Indo-European languages that is usu. paralleled by differences in use or meaning (as in sing, sang, sung, song)

ablaze \a-'blāz\ adj or adv (1801) **1** : being on fire **2** : radiant with light or emotion ⟨his face all ~ with excitement —Bram Stoker⟩

able \'ā-bəl\ adj **abler** \-b(ə-)lər\; **ablest** \-b(ə-)ləst\ [ME, MF, fr. L habilis apt, fr. habēre to have — more at HABIT] (14c) **1 a** : having sufficient power, skill, or resources to accomplish an object **b** : susceptible to action or treatment **2** : marked by intelligence, knowledge, skill, or competence — **ably** \-b(ə-)lē\ adv

-able also **-ible** adj suffix [ME, fr. OF, fr. L -abilis, -ibilis, fr. -a-, -i-, verb stem vowels + -bilis capable or worthy of] **1** : capable of, fit for, or worthy of (being so acted upon or toward) — chiefly in adjectives derived from verbs ⟨break*able*⟩ ⟨collect*ible*⟩ **2** : tending, given, or liable to ⟨agree*able*⟩ ⟨perish*able*⟩ — **-ably** adv suffix

able–bod·ied \,ā-bəl-'bä-dēd\ adj (ca. 1622) : having a sound strong body

able–bodied seaman n (ca. 1909) : ABLE SEAMAN

able seaman n (1702) : an experienced deck-department seaman qualified to perform routine duties at sea

abloom \a-'blüm\ adj (1855) : abounding with blooms : BLOOMING ⟨parks ~ with roses⟩

ab·lut·ed \a-'blü-təd, a-\ adj [back-formation fr. ablution] (1650) : washed clean

ab·lu·tion \a-'blü-shən, a-\ n [ME, fr. MF or L; MF, fr. L ablution-, ablutio, fr. abluere to wash away, fr. ab- + luere to wash; akin to L lavere to wash — more at LYE] (1533) **1 a** : the washing of one's body or part of it (as in a religious rite) **b** pl : the act or action of bathing **2** pl, Brit : a building housing bathing and toilet facilities on a military base — **ab·lu·tion·ary** \-shə-,ner-ē\ adj

ABM \,ā-(,)bē-'em\ n, pl **ABM's** or **ABMs** \-'emz\ (1963) : ANTIBALLISTIC MISSILE

Ab·na·ki \ab-'nä-kē\ var of ABENAKI

ab·ne·gate \'ab-ni-,gāt\ vt **-gat·ed; -gat·ing** [back-formation fr. abnegation] (1623) **1** : DENY, RENOUNCE ⟨abnegated their God⟩ **2** : SURRENDER, RELINQUISH ⟨abnegated her powers⟩ — **ab·ne·ga·tor** \-,gā-tər\ n

ab·ne·ga·tion \,ab-ni-'gā-shən\ n [LL abnegation-, abnegatio, fr. L abnegare to refute, fr. ab- + negare to deny — more at NEGATE] (14c) : DENIAL; esp : SELF-DENIAL

¹**ab·nor·mal** \(,)ab-'nór-məl, əb-\ adj [alter. of F anormal, fr. ML anormalis, fr. L a- + LL normalis normal] (ca. 1836) : deviating from the normal or average : UNUSUAL, EXCEPTIONAL ⟨~ behavior⟩ — **ab·nor·mal·ly** \-mə-lē\ adv

²**abnormal** n (1912) : an abnormal person

ab·nor·mal·i·ty \,ab-nər-'ma-lə-tē, -(,)nór-\ n, pl **-ties** (1854) **1** : the quality or state of being abnormal **2** : something abnormal

abnormal psychology n (ca. 1903) : a branch of psychology concerned with mental and emotional disorders (as neuroses, psychoses, and mental deficiency) and with certain incompletely understood normal phenomena (as dreams and hypnosis)

abo \'a-(,)bō\ n, pl **ab·os** (1908) Austral : ABORIGINE — often used disparagingly

¹**aboard** \a-'bōrd, -'bórd\ adv or adj (14c) **1** : ALONGSIDE **2 a** : on, onto, or within a vehicle (as a car or ship) **b** : in or into a group, association, or organization ⟨her second promotion since coming ~⟩ **3** baseball : on base

²**aboard** prep (15c) : ON, ONTO, WITHIN ⟨go ~ ship⟩ ⟨~ a plane⟩

ABO blood group \,ā-(,)bē-'ō-\ n (1949) : any of the four blood groups A, B, AB, and O comprising the ABO system

abode \a-'bōd\ n [ME abod, fr. abiden to abide] (13c) **1** obs : WAIT, DELAY **2** : a temporary stay : SOJOURN **3** : the place where one abides : HOME

aboil \a-'bói(a)l\ adj or adv (1810) **1** : being at the boiling point : BOILING **2** : intensely excited or stirred up ⟨the meeting was ~ with controversy⟩

abol·ish \a-'bä-lish\ vt [ME abolisshen, fr. MF aboliss-, stem of abolir, fr. L abolēre; prob. akin to adolescere to grow up — more at ADULT] (15c) **1** : to end the observance or effect of : ANNUL **2** : DESTROY — **abol·ish·able** \-li-shə-bəl\ adj — **abol·ish·er** n — **abol·ish·ment** \-mənt\ n

ab·o·li·tion \,a-bə-'li-sh'n\ n [MF, fr. L abolition-, abolitio, fr. abolēre] (1529) **1** : the act of abolishing : the state of being abolished **2** : the abolishing of slavery — **ab·o·li·tion·ary** \-li-sh'n-,er-ē\ adj

ab·o·li·tion·ism \-li-sh'n-,i-zəm\ n (1808) : principles or measures fostering abolition esp. of slavery — **ab·o·li·tion·ist** \-ist\ n or adj

ab·oma·sum \,a-bō-'mā-səm\ n, pl **-sa** \-sə\ [NL, fr. L ab- + omasum ox's tripe] (ca. 1706) : the fourth compartment of the ruminant stomach that follows the omasum and has a true digestive function — compare RUMEN, RETICULUM — **ab·oma·sal** \-səl\ adj

A–bomb \'ā-,bäm\ n (1945) : ATOMIC BOMB 1

abom·i·na·ble \a-'bäm-nə-bəl, -'bä-mə-\ adj (14c) **1** : worthy of or causing disgust or hatred : DETESTABLE ⟨the ~ treatment of the poor⟩ **2** : quite disagreeable or unpleasant ⟨~ weather⟩ — **abom·i·na·bly** \-blē\ adv

abominable snow·man \-'snō-mən, -,man\ n, often cap A&S (1921) : a mysterious creature with human or apelike characteristics reported to exist in the high Himalayas — called also yeti

abom·i·nate \a-'bä-mə-,nāt\ vt **-nat·ed; -nat·ing** [L abominatus, pp. of abominari, lit., to deprecate as an ill omen, fr. ab- + omin-, omen, omen] (1644) : to hate or loathe intensely : ABHOR **syn** see HATE — **abom·i·na·tor** \-,nā-tər\ n

abom·i·na·tion \a-,bä-mə-'nā-shən\ n (14c) **1** : something abominable **2** : extreme disgust and hatred : LOATHING

ab·oral \(,)a-'bór-əl, -'bór-\ adj (1857) : situated opposite to or away from the mouth ⟨a sea urchin's ~ surface⟩ — **ab·oral·ly** \-ə-lē\ adv

¹**ab·orig·i·nal** \,a-bə-'rij-nəl, -'rij-ə-n°l\ adj (1667) **1** : being the first or earliest known of its kind present in a region ⟨~ forests⟩ ⟨~ rocks⟩ **2 a** : of or relating to aborigines **b** often cap : of or relating to the indigenous peoples of Australia **syn** see NATIVE — **ab·orig·i·nal·ly** adv

²**aboriginal** n (1767) **1** : ABORIGINE 1 **2** often cap : ABORIGINE 2

ab·orig·i·ne \,a-bə-'rij-ə-(,)nē, -'ri-jə-\ n [L aborigines, pl., fr. ab origine from the beginning] (1533) **1** : an aboriginal inhabitant esp. as contrasted with an invading or colonizing people **2** often cap : a member of any of the indigenous peoples of Australia

¹**aborn·ing** \a-'bór-niŋ\ adv [¹a- + E dial. borning (birth)] (1916) : while being born or produced ⟨a resolution that died ~⟩

²**aborning** adj (1943) : being born or produced ⟨the ~ fiasco⟩

¹**abort** \a-'bórt\ vb [L abortus, pp. of aboriri to miscarry, fr. ab- + oriri to rise, be born — more at ORIENT] vi (1580) **1** : to bring forth prematurely or stillborn offspring **2** : to become checked in development so as to degenerate or remain rudimentary ~ vt **1 a** : to induce the abortion of or give birth to prematurely **b** : to terminate the pregnancy of before term **2 a** : to terminate prematurely : CANCEL ⟨~ a project⟩ ⟨~ a spaceflight⟩ **b** : to stop in the early stages ⟨~ a disease⟩ — **abort·er** n

²**abort** n (1944) : the premature termination of a flight (as of an aircraft or spacecraft), a mission, or an action or procedure relating to a flight ⟨a launch ~⟩

abor·ti·fa·cient \a-,bór-tə-'fā-shənt\ n (1873) : an agent (as a drug) that induces abortion — **abortifacient** adj

abor·tion \a-'bór-shən\ n (1547) **1** : the termination of a pregnancy after, accompanied by, resulting in, or closely followed by the death of the embryo or fetus: as **a** : spontaneous expulsion of a human fetus during the first 12 weeks of gestation — compare MISCARRIAGE **b** : induced expulsion of a human fetus **c** : expulsion of a fetus by a domestic animal often due to infection at any time before completion of pregnancy — compare CONTAGIOUS ABORTION **2** : MONSTROSITY **3** : arrest of development (as of a part or process) resulting in imperfection; also : a result of such arrest

abor·tion·ist \-sh(ə-)nist\ n (1871) : one who induces abortions

abor·tive \a-'bór-tiv\ adj (14c) **1** obs : prematurely born **2** : FRUITLESS, UNSUCCESSFUL **3** : imperfectly formed or developed **4** : tending to cut short — **abor·tive·ly** adv — **abor·tive·ness** n

ABO system \,ā-(,)bē-'ō-\ n (1944) : the basic system of antigens of human blood behaving in heredity as an allelic unit to produce any of the ABO blood groups

abound \a-'baúnd\ vi [ME, fr. MF abonder, fr. L abundare, fr. ab- + unda wave — more at WATER] (14c) **1** : to be present in large numbers or in great quantity : be prevalent **2** : to be copiously supplied ⟨life ~ed in mysteries —Norman Mailer⟩ ⟨institutions ~ with evidence of his success —Johns Hopkins Mag.⟩

¹**about** \a-'baút\ adv [ME, fr. OE abūtan, fr. ¹a- + būtan outside — more at BUT] (bef. 12c) **1 a** : reasonably close to ⟨a year ago⟩ **b** : ALMOST ⟨~ starved⟩ **c** : on the verge of — usu. used with be and a following infinitive ⟨is ~ to join the army⟩; used with a negative to express intention or determination ⟨not ~ to quit⟩ **2** : on all sides : AROUND **3 a** : in rotation **b** : around the outside **4** : HERE AND THERE **5** : in the vicinity : NEAR **6** : in succession : ALTERNATELY ⟨turn ~ is fair play⟩ **7** : in the opposite direction ⟨face ~⟩ ⟨the other way ~⟩

²**about** prep (bef. 12c) **1** : in a circle around : on every side of : AROUND **2 a** : in the immediate neighborhood of : NEAR **b** : on or near the person of **c** : in the makeup of ⟨a mature wisdom ~ him⟩ **d** : at the command of ⟨has his wits ~ him⟩ **3** : engaged in ⟨act as if they know what they're ~ —T. S. Matthews⟩ **4 a** : with regard to : CONCERNING **b** : concerned with **c** : fundamentally concerned with or directed toward ⟨poker is ~ money —David Mamet⟩ **5** : over or in different parts of

³**about** adj (1815) **1** : moving from place to place; specif : being out of bed **2** : AROUND 2

about–face \a-'baút-'fās\ n [fr. the imper. phrase about face] (1861) **1** : a 180° turn to the right from the position of attention **2** : a reversal of direction **3** : a reversal of attitude, behavior, or point of view — **about–face** vi

about–turn \-'tərn\ n (1893) Brit : ABOUT-FACE

¹**above** \a-'bəv\ adv [ME, fr. OE abufan, fr. a- + bufan above, fr. be- + ufan above; akin to OE ofer over] (bef. 12c) **1 a** : in the sky : OVERHEAD **b** : in or to heaven **2 a** : in or to a higher place **b** : higher on the same page or on a preceding page **c** : UPSTAIRS **d** : above zero ⟨10 degrees ~⟩ **3** : in or to a higher rank or number ⟨30 and ~⟩ **4** archaic : in addition : BESIDES **5** : UPSTAGE

²**above** prep (bef. 12c) **1** : in or to a higher place than : OVER **2 a** : superior to (as in rank, quality, or degree) **b** : out of reach of **c** : in preference to **d** : too proud or honorable to stoop to **3** : exceeding in number, quantity, or size : more than **4** : as distinct from and in addition to ⟨heard the whistle ~ the roar of the crowd⟩

³**above** n, pl **above** (13c) **1 a** : something that is above **b** : a person whose name is written above **2 a** : a higher authority **b** : HEAVEN **usage** Although still objected to by some, the use of above as a noun in sense 1a ⟨none of the above⟩ ⟨the above is Theseus's opinion —William Blake⟩ and as an adjective ⟨without the above reserve —O. W. Holmes †1935⟩ has been brought up on the above words —Viscount Montgomery⟩ has been long established as standard.

⁴**above** adj (1604) : written or discussed higher on the same page or on a preceding page **usage** see ³ABOVE

\ə\ abut \ᵊ\ kitten, F table \ər\ further \a\ ash \ā\ ace \ä\ mop, mar
\aú\ out \ch\ chin \e\ bet \ē\ easy \g\ go \i\ hit \ī\ ice \j\ job
\ŋ\ sing \ō\ go \ó\ law \ói\ boy \th\ thin \th̶\ the \ü\ loot \ú\ foot
\y\ yet \zh\ vision \à, k̲, ⁿ, œ, œ̄, ᵫ, ᵫ̄, ʸ\ see Guide to Pronunciation

above all *adv* (14c) : before every other consideration : ESPECIALLY

¹**above-board** \ə-'bəv-,bȯrd, -,bȯrd\ *adv* [fr. the difficulty of cheating at cards when the hands are above the table] (1594) : in a straightforward manner : OPENLY

²**aboveboard** *adj* (1648) : free from all traces of deceit or duplicity

above-ground \ə-'bəv-,grau̇nd\ *adj* (1878) 1 : located or occurring on or above the surface of the ground 2 : existing, produced, or published by or within the establishment 〈~ movies〉

ab ovo \ab-'ō-(,)vō\ *adv* [L, lit., from the egg] (ca. 1586) : from the beginning

ab·ra·ca·dab·ra \,a-brə-kə-'da-brə\ *n* [LL] (1565) 1 : a magical charm or incantation 2 : unintelligible language

abrade \ə-'brād\ *vb* **abrad·ed; abrad·ing** [L *abradere* to scrape off, fr. *ab-* + *radere* to scrape — more at RODENT] *vt* (1677) 1 a : to rub or wear away esp. by friction : ERODE b : to irritate or roughen by rubbing 2 : to wear down in spirit : IRRITATE, WEARY ~ *vi* : to undergo abrasion — **abrad·able** \-'brā-də-bəl\ *adj* — **abrad·er** *n*

Abra·ham \'ā-brə-,ham\ *n* [LL, fr. Gk *Abraam*, fr. Heb *'Abhrāhām*] : an Old Testament patriarch regarded by Jews as the founder of the Hebrew people through his son Isaac and by Muslims as the founder of the Arab peoples through his son Ishmael

abra·sion \ə-'brā-zhən\ *n* [ML *abrasion-, abrasio*, fr. L *abradere*] (ca. 1656) 1 a : a wearing, grinding, or rubbing away by friction b : IRRITATION 2 : an abraded area of the skin or mucous membrane

¹**abra·sive** \ə-'brā-siv, -ziv\ *n* (1853) : a substance (as emery or pumice) used for abrading, smoothing, or polishing

²**abrasive** *adj* (1875) 1 : tending to abrade 2 : causing irritation 〈~ manners〉 — **abra·sive·ly** *adv* — **abra·sive·ness** *n*

ab·re·ac·tion \,a-brē-'ak-shən\ *n* [part trans. of G *Abreagierung* catharsis, fr. *ab* off, away (fr. OHG *aba*) + *Reagierung* reaction, fr. L *reagere* to react — more at OF, REACT] (1912) : the expression and emotional discharge of unconscious material (as a repressed idea or emotion) by verbalization esp. in the presence of a therapist — **ab·re·act** \-'akt\ *vb*

abreast \ə-'brest\ *adv or adj* (15c) 1 : beside one another with bodies in line 〈columns of men five ~〉 2 : up to a particular standard or level esp. of knowledge of recent developments 〈keeps ~ of the latest trends〉

abridge \ə-'brij\ *vt* **abridged; abridg·ing** [ME *abregen*, fr. MF *abregier*, fr. LL *abbreviare*, fr. L *ad-* + *brevis* short — more at BRIEF] (14c) 1 a *archaic* : DEPRIVE b : to reduce in scope : DIMINISH 〈attempts to ~ the right of free speech〉 2 : to shorten in duration or extent 〈modern transportation that ~s distance〉 3 : to shorten by omission of words without sacrifice of sense : CONDENSE *syn* see SHORTEN — **abridg·er** *n*

abridg·ment *or* **abridge·ment** \ə-'brij-mənt\ *n* (15c) 1 : the action of abridging : the state of being abridged 2 : a shortened form of a work retaining the general sense and unity of the original

abroach \ə-'brōch\ *adv or adj* (14c) 1 : in a condition for letting out a liquid (as wine) 〈a cask set ~〉 2 : in action or agitation : ASTIR 〈mischiefs that I set ~—Shak.〉

abroad \ə-'brȯd\ *adv or adj* (13c) 1 : over a wide area : WIDELY 2 : away from one's home 3 : beyond the boundaries of one's country 4 : in wide circulation : ABOUT 5 : wide of the mark : ASTRAY

ab·ro·gate \'a-brə-,gāt\ *vt* **-gat·ed; -gat·ing** [L *abrogatus*, pp. of *abrogare*, fr. *ab-* + *rogare* to ask, propose a law — more at RIGHT] (1526) 1 : to abolish by authoritative action : ANNUL 2 : to treat as nonexistent 〈*abrogating* their responsibilities〉 *syn* see NULLIFY — **ab·ro·ga·tion** \,a-brə-'gā-shən\ *n*

abrupt \ə-'brəpt\ *adj* [L *abruptus*, fr. pp. of *abrumpere* to break off, fr. *ab-* + *rumpere* to break — more at REAVE] (1591) 1 a : characterized by or involving action or change without preparation or warning : UNEXPECTED 〈came to an ~ stop〉 〈an ~ turn to the left〉 〈an ~ decision to retire〉 b : unceremoniously curt 〈an ~ manner〉 c : lacking smoothness or continuity 〈an ~ transition〉 2 : giving the impression of being cut or broken off; *esp* : involving a sudden steep rise or drop 〈~ hills〉 〈a high ~ bank bounded the stream〉 *syn* see PRECIPITATE, STEEP — **abrupt·ly** \ə-'brəp(t)-lē\ *adv* — **abrupt·ness** \ə-'brəp(t)-nəs\ *n*

abrup·tion \ə-'brəp-shən\ *n* (1606) : a sudden breaking off or away

ABS \,ā-(,)bē-'es\ *n* [acrylonitrile-butadiene-styrene] (1966) : a tough rigid plastic used esp. for automobile parts and building materials

ab·scess \'ab-,ses\ *n, pl* **ab·scess·es** \-,se-səz, -,sēz; -sə-səz\ [L *abscessus*, lit., act of going away, fr. *abscedere* to go away, fr. *abs-, ab-* + *cedere* to go] (1615) : a localized collection of pus surrounded by inflamed tissue — **ab·scessed** \-,sest\ *adj*

ab·scise \ab-'sīz\ *vb* **ab·scised; ab·scis·ing** [L *abscisus*, pp. of *abscidere*, fr. *abs-* + *caedere* to cut] *vt* (1612) : to cut off by abscission ~ *vi* : to separate by abscission

ab·scis·ic acid \ab-'si-zik-, -sik-\ *n* [*abscision* (var. of *abscission*) + *-ic*] (1968) : a plant hormone $C_{15}H_{20}O_4$ that is a sesquiterpene widespread in nature and that typically promotes leaf abscission and dormancy and has an inhibitory effect on cell elongation

ab·scis·in \'ab-sə-sən, ab-'si-s⁀ⁿ\ *n* [*abscision* + *-in*] (1961) : ABSCISIC ACID

ab·scis·sa \ab-'si-sə\ *n, pl* **abscissas** *also* **ab·scis·sae** \-'si-(,)sē\ [NL, fr. L, fem. of *abscissus*, pp. of *abscindere* to cut off, fr. *ab-* + *scindere* to cut — more at SHED] (1694) : the horizontal coordinate of a point in a plane Cartesian coordinate system obtained by measuring parallel to the x-axis — compare ORDINATE

ab·scis·sion \ab-'si-zhən\ *n* [L *abscission-, abscissio*, fr. *abscindere*] (15c) 1 : the act or process of cutting off : REMOVAL 2 : the natural separation of flowers, fruit, or leaves from plants at a special separation layer

ab·scond \ab-'skänd, əb-\ *vi* [L *abscondere* to hide away, fr. *abs-* + *condere* to store up, conceal — more at CONDIMENT] (ca. 1578) : to depart secretly and hide oneself — **ab·scond·er** *n*

ab·seil \'ab-,sāl, -,sīl\ *vi* [G *abseilen*, fr. *ab* down, off + *Seil* rope] (1941) *chiefly Brit* : RAPPEL

[diagram with y-axis vertical and x-axis horizontal, showing point P and A, labeled]
P ——|—— **A**
AP abscissa of point **P**

ab·sence \'ab-sən(t)s\ *n* (14c) 1 : the state of being absent 2 : the period of time that one is absent 3 : WANT, LACK 〈an ~ of detail〉 4 : inattention to present surroundings or occurrences 〈~ of mind〉

¹**ab·sent** \'ab-sənt\ *adj* [ME, fr. MF, fr. L *absent-, absens*, prp. of *abesse* to be absent, fr. *ab-* + *esse* to be — more at IS] (14c) 1 : not present or attending : MISSING 2 : not existing : LACKING 〈danger in a situation where power is ~—M. H. Trytten〉 3 : INATTENTIVE, PREOCCUPIED — **ab·sent·ly** *adv*

²**ab·sent** \ab-'sent, 'ab-\ *vt* (15c) : to keep (oneself) away

³**ab·sent** \'ab-sənt\ *prep* (1945) : in the absence of : WITHOUT

ab·sen·tee \,ab-sən-'tē\ *n* (1605) : one that is absent: as a : a proprietor that lives away from his or her estate or business b : one missing from work or school — **absentee** *adj*

absentee ballot *n* (1932) : a ballot submitted (as by mail) in advance of an election by a voter who is unable to be present at the polls

ab·sen·tee·ism \,ab-sən-'tē-,i-zəm\ *n* (1829) 1 : prolonged absence of an owner from his or her property 2 : chronic absence (as from work or school); *also* : the rate of such absence

ab·sent-mind·ed \,ab-sənt-'mīn-dəd\ *adj* (1854) 1 : lost in thought and unaware of one's surroundings or actions : PREOCCUPIED; *also* : given to absence of mind 2 : indicative of or resulting from preoccupation or absence of mind — **ab·sent-mind·ed·ly** *adv* — **ab·sent-mind·ed·ness** *n*

absent without leave *adj* (ca. 1919) : absent without authority from one's place of duty in the armed forces

ab·sinthe *also* **ab·sinth** \'ab-(,)sin(t)th\ *n* [F *absinthe*, fr. L *absinthium*, fr. Gk *apsinthion*] (1612) 1 : WORMWOOD 1; *esp* : a common European wormwood (*Artemisia absinthium*) 2 : a green liqueur flavored with wormwood or a substitute, anise, and other aromatics

ab·so·lute \'ab-sə-,lüt, ,ab-sə-'\ *adj* [ME *absolut*, fr. L *absolutus*, fr. pp. of *absolvere* to set free, absolve] (14c) 1 a : free from imperfection : PERFECT b : free or relatively free from mixture : PURE 〈~ alcohol〉 c : OUTRIGHT, UNMITIGATED 〈an ~ lie〉 2 : being, governed by, or characteristic of a ruler or authority completely free from constitutional or other restraint 3 a : standing apart from a normal or usual syntactical relation with other words or sentence elements 〈the ~ construction *this being the case* in the sentence "this being the case, let us go"〉 b *of an adjective or possessive pronoun* : standing alone without a modified substantive 〈*blind* in "help the blind" and *ours* in "your work and ours" are ~〉 c *of a verb* : having no object in the particular construction under consideration though normally transitive 〈*kill* in "if looks could kill" is an ~ verb〉 4 : having no restriction, exception, or qualification 〈an ~ requirement〉 〈~ freedom〉 5 : POSITIVE, UNQUESTIONABLE 〈~ proof〉 6 : independent of arbitrary standards of measurement b : relating to or derived in the simplest manner from the fundamental units of length, mass, and time 〈~ electric units〉 c : relating to, measured on, or being a temperature scale based on absolute zero 〈~ temperature〉; *specif* : KELVIN 〈10° ~〉 7 : FUNDAMENTAL, ULTIMATE 〈~ knowledge〉 8 : perfectly embodying the nature of a thing 〈~ justice〉 9 : being self-sufficient and free of external references or relationships 〈an ~ term in logic〉 〈~ music〉 10 : being the true distance from an aircraft to the earth's surface 〈~ altitude〉 — **absolute** *n* — **ab·so·lute·ness** *n*

absolute ceiling *n* (ca. 1920) : the maximum height above sea level at which a particular airplane can maintain horizontal flight under standard air conditions — called also *ceiling*

absolute convergence *n* (ca. 1909) : convergence of a mathematical series when the absolute values of the terms are taken

absolute humidity *n* (1867) : the amount of water vapor present in a unit volume of air — compare RELATIVE HUMIDITY

ab·so·lute·ly \'ab-sə-,lüt-lē, ,ab-sə-'\ *adv* (14c) 1 : in an absolute manner or condition — often used as an intensive 〈~ brilliant〉 2 : with respect to absolute values 〈an ~ convergent series〉

absolute magnitude *n* (1902) : the intrinsic luminosity of a celestial body (as a star) if viewed from a distance of 10 parsecs — compare APPARENT MAGNITUDE

absolute pitch *n* (1864) 1 : the position of a tone in a standard scale independently determined by its rate of vibration 2 : the ability to recognize or sing a given isolated note

absolute space *n* (ca. 1889) : SPACE 4b

absolute value *n* (1907) 1 : a nonnegative number equal in numerical value to a given real number 2 : the positive square root of the sum of the squares of the real and imaginary parts of a complex number

absolute zero *n* (1848) : a theoretical temperature characterized by complete absence of heat and equivalent to exactly $-273.15°C$ or $-459.67°F$

ab·so·lu·tion \,ab-sə-'lü-shən\ *n* (13c) : the act of absolving; *specif* : a remission of sins pronounced by a priest (as in the sacrament of reconciliation)

ab·so·lut·ism \'ab-sə-,lü-,ti-zəm\ *n* (1830) 1 a : a political theory that absolute power should be vested in one or more rulers b : government by an absolute ruler or authority : DESPOTISM 2 : advocacy of a rule by absolute standards or principles 3 : an absolute standard or principle — **ab·so·lut·ist** \-,lü-tist\ *n or adj* — **ab·so·lu·tis·tic** \,ab-sə-(,)lü-'tis-tik\ *adj*

ab·so·lu·tive \,ab-sə-'lü-tiv\ *adj* (1952) : of, being, or relating to an inflectional morpheme that typically marks the subject of an intransitive verb or the direct object of a transitive verb in an ergative language

ab·so·lut·ize \'ab-sə-,lü-,tīz\ *vt* **-ized; -iz·ing** (1919) : to make absolute : convert into an absolute

ab·solve \əb-'zälv, -'sälv, -'zȯlv, -'sȯlv *also without l*\ *vt* **ab·solved; ab·solv·ing** [ME, fr. L *absolvere*, fr. *ab-* + *solvere* to loosen — more at SOLVE] (15c) 1 : to set free from an obligation or the consequences of guilt 2 : to remit (a sin) by absolution *syn* see EXCULPATE — **ab·solv·er** *n*

ab·sorb \əb-'sȯrb, -'zȯrb\ *vt* [MF *absorber*, fr. L *absorbēre*, fr. *ab-* + *sorbēre* to suck up; akin to Lith *surbti* to sip, Gk *rophein* to gulp down] (15c) 1 : to take in and make part of an existent whole 〈the capacity of China to ~ invaders〉 2 a : to suck up or take up 〈a sponge ~s water〉 〈charcoal ~s gas〉 〈plant roots ~ water〉 b : to take in : ACQUIRE, LEARN 〈convictions ~ed in youth —M. R. Cohen〉 c : USE UP, CONSUME 〈the fever ~ed her strength〉 3 : to engage or engross wholly 〈~ed in thought〉 4 a (1) : to receive without recoil or echo 〈provided with a sound-*absorbing* surface〉 (2) : ENDURE, SUSTAIN 〈~ing hardships⟩ (3) : ASSUME, BEAR ⟨the expenses were ~ed by the company⟩ **b** : to transform (radiant energy) into a different form usu. with a resulting rise in temperature ⟨the earth ~s the sun's rays⟩ — **ab·sorb·abil·i·ty** \əb-ˌsȯr-bə-ˈbi-lə-tē, -ˌzȯr-\ n — **ab·sorb·able** \əb-ˈsȯr-bə-bəl, -ˈzȯr-\ adj — **ab·sorb·er** n

ab·sor·bance \əb-ˈsȯr-bən(t)s, -ˈzȯr-\ n (1947) : the ability of a layer of a substance to absorb radiation expressed mathematically as the negative common logarithm of transmittance

ab·sor·ben·cy \əb-ˈsȯr-bən(t)-sē, -ˈzȯr-\ n, pl **-cies** (1859) **1** : the quality or state of being absorbent **2** or **ab·sor·ban·cy** : ABSORBANCE

ab·sor·bent also **ab·sor·bant** \-bənt\ adj [L absorbent-, absorbens, prp. of absorbēre] (1718) : able to absorb ⟨as ~ as a sponge⟩ — **absorbent** also **absorbant** n

ab·sorb·ing adj (1876) : fully taking one's attention : ENGROSSING ⟨an ~ novel⟩ — **ab·sorb·ing·ly** \-biŋ-lē\ adv

ab·sorp·tance \əb-ˈsȯrp-tən(t)s, -ˈzȯrp-\ n [absorption + -ance] (ca. 1931) : the ratio of the radiant energy absorbed by a body to that incident upon it

ab·sorp·tion \əb-ˈsȯrp-shən, -ˈzȯrp-\ n [F & L; F, fr. L absorption-, absorptio, fr. absorbēre] (1741) **1 a** : the process of absorbing or of being absorbed — compare ADSORPTION **b** : interception of radiant energy or sound waves **2** : entire occupation of the mind ⟨~ in his work⟩ — **ab·sorp·tive** \-tiv\ adj

absorption band n (1867) : a dark band in an absorption spectrum

absorption line n (ca. 1889) : a dark line in an absorption spectrum

absorption spectrum n (1879) : an electromagnetic spectrum in which a decrease in intensity of radiation at specific wavelengths or ranges of wavelengths characteristic of an absorbing substance is manifested esp. as a pattern of dark lines or bands

ab·sorp·tiv·i·ty \əb-ˌsȯrp-ˈti-və-tē, -ˌzȯrp-\ n, pl **-ties** (ca. 1859) : the property of a body that determines the fraction of incident radiation absorbed by the body

ab·stain \əb-ˈstān, ab-\ vi [ME absteinen, fr. MF abstenir, fr. L abstinēre, fr. abs-, ab- + tenēre to hold — more at THIN] (14c) : to refrain deliberately and often with an effort of self-denial from an action or practice — **ab·stain·er** n

ab·ste·mi·ous \ab-ˈstē-mē-əs\ adj [L abstemius, fr. abs- + -temius; akin to L temetum intoxicating drink] (1609) : marked by restraint esp. in the consumption of food or alcohol; also : reflecting such restraint ⟨an ~ diet⟩ — **ab·ste·mi·ous·ly** adv — **ab·ste·mi·ous·ness** n

ab·sten·tion \əb-ˈsten(t)-shən, ab-\ n [LL abstention-, abstentio, fr. L abstinēre] (1521) : the act or practice of abstaining — **ab·sten·tious** \-shəs\ adj

ab·sti·nence \ˈab-stə-nən(t)s\ n [ME, fr. MF, fr. L abstinentia, fr. abstinent-, abstinens, prp. of abstinēre] (14c) **1** : voluntary forbearance esp. from indulgence of an appetite or craving or from eating some foods : ABSTENTION **2** : habitual abstaining from intoxicating beverages — **ab·sti·nent** \-nənt\ adj — **ab·sti·nent·ly** adv

¹ab·stract \ab-ˈstrakt, ˈab-\ adj [ML abstractus, fr. L, pp. of abstrahere to drag away, fr. abs-, ab- + trahere to pull, draw] (14c) **1 a** : disassociated from any specific instance ⟨~ entity⟩ **b** : difficult to understand : ABSTRUSE ⟨~ problems⟩ **c** : insufficiently factual : FORMAL ⟨possessed only an ~ right⟩ **2** : expressing a quality apart from an object ⟨the word poem is concrete, poetry is ~⟩ **3 a** : dealing with a subject in its abstract aspects : THEORETICAL ⟨~ science⟩ **b** : IMPERSONAL, DETACHED ⟨the ~ compassion of a surgeon —Time⟩ **4** : having only intrinsic form with little or no attempt at pictorial representation or narrative content ⟨~ painting⟩ — **ab·stract·ly** \ab-ˈstrak(t)-lē, ˈab-\ adv — **ab·stract·ness** \-ˈstrak(t)-nəs, ˈab-\ n

²ab·stract \ˈab-ˌstrakt, in sense 2 also ab-ˈ\ n [ME, fr. L abstractus] (15c) **1** : a summary of points (as of a writing) usu. presented in skeletal form; also : something that summarizes or concentrates the essentials of a larger thing or several things **2** : an abstract thing or state **3** : ABSTRACTION 4a

³ab·stract \ab-ˈstrakt, ˈab-, in sense 3 usu ˈab-\ vt (1542) **1** : REMOVE, SEPARATE **2** : to consider apart from application to or association with a particular instance **3** : to make an abstract of : SUMMARIZE **4** : to draw away the attention of **5** : STEAL, PURLOIN ~ vi : to make an abstraction — **ab·stract·able** \-ˈstrak-tə-bəl, -ˌstrak-\ adj — **ab·strac·tor** or **ab·stract·er** \-tər\ n

ab·stract·ed \ab-ˈstrak-təd, ˈab-\ adj (1643) **1** : PREOCCUPIED, ABSENT-MINDED ⟨the ~ look of a professor⟩ **2** : ABSTRACT 4 ⟨~ geometric shapes⟩ — **ab·stract·ed·ly** adv — **ab·stract·ed·ness** n

abstract expressionism n (1951) : an artistic movement of the mid-20th century comprising diverse styles and techniques and emphasizing esp. an artist's liberty to convey attitudes and emotions through non-traditional and usu. nonrepresentational means — **abstract expressionist** n or adj

ab·strac·tion \ab-ˈstrak-shən, əb-\ n (1549) **1 a** : the act or process of abstracting : the state of being abstracted **b** : an abstract idea or term **2** : absence of mind or preoccupation **3** : abstract quality or character **4 a** : an abstract composition or creation in art **b** : ABSTRACTIONISM — **ab·strac·tion·al** \-shnəl, -shə-nᵊl\ adj — **ab·strac·tive** \ab-ˈstrak-tiv, ˈab-\ adj

ab·strac·tion·ism \ab-ˈstrak-shə-ˌni-zəm, əb-\ n (1926) : the principles or practice of creating abstract art — **ab·strac·tion·ist** \-sh(ə-)nist\ adj or n

abstract of title (1858) : a summary statement of the successive conveyances and other facts on which a title to a piece of land rests

ab·struse \əb-ˈstrüs, ab-\ adj [L abstrusus, fr. pp. of abstrudere to conceal, fr. abs-, ab- + trudere to push — more at THREAT] (1599) : difficult to comprehend : RECONDITE ⟨the ~ calculations of mathematicians⟩ — **ab·struse·ly** adv — **ab·struse·ness** n

ab·stru·si·ty \-ˈstrü-sə-tē\ n, pl **-ties** (1646) **1** : the quality or state of being abstruse : ABSTRUSENESS **2** : something that is abstruse

¹ab·surd \əb-ˈsərd, -ˈzərd\ adj [MF absurde, fr. L absurdus, fr. ab- + surdus deaf, stupid] (1557) **1** : ridiculously unreasonable, unsound, or incongruous **2** : having no rational or orderly relationship to human life : MEANINGLESS; also : lacking order or value **3** : dealing with the absurd or with absurdism — **ab·surd·ly** adv — **ab·surd·ness** n

²absurd n (1946) : the state or condition in which human beings exist in an irrational and meaningless universe and in which human life has no ultimate meaning — usu. used with the

ab·surd·ism \əb-ˈsər-ˌdi-zəm, -ˈzər-\ n (1946) : a philosophy based on

the belief that the universe is irrational and meaningless and that the search for order brings the individual into conflict with the universe — compare EXISTENTIALISM — **ab·surd·ist** \-dist\ n or adj

ab·sur·di·ty \əb-ˈsər-də-tē, -ˈzər-\ n, pl **-ties** (1528) **1** : the quality or state of being absurd : ABSURDNESS **2** : something that is absurd

abub·ble \ə-ˈbə-bəl\ adj (ca. 1869) **1** : being in the process of bubbling **2** : being in a state of agitated activity or motion : ASTIR

abuild·ing \ə-ˈbil-diŋ\ adj (1535) : being in the process of building or of being built

abu·lia \ā-ˈbü-lē-ə, -ˈbyü-, ə-\ n [NL, fr. ²a- + Gk boulē will] (ca. 1864) : abnormal lack of ability to act or to make decisions — **abu·lic** \-lik\ adj

abun·dance \ə-ˈbən-dən(t)s\ n (14c) **1** : an ample quantity : PROFUSION **2** : AFFLUENCE, WEALTH **3** : relative degree of plentifulness ⟨low ~s of uranium and thorium —H. C. Urey⟩

abun·dant \-dənt\ adj [ME, fr. MF, fr. L abundant-, abundans, prp. of abundare to abound] (14c) **1 a** : marked by great plenty (as of resources) ⟨a fair and ~ land⟩ **b** : amply supplied ⟨an area ~ with bird life⟩ **2** : occurring in abundance : AMPLE ⟨~ rainfall⟩ syn see PLENTIFUL — **abun·dant·ly** adv

¹abuse \ə-ˈbyüs\ n [ME, fr. MF abus, fr. L abusus, fr. abuti to consume, fr. ab- + uti to use] (15c) **1** : a corrupt practice or custom **2** : improper or excessive use or treatment : MISUSE ⟨drug ~⟩ **3** obs : a deceitful act : DECEPTION **4** : language that condemns or vilifies usu. unjustly, intemperately, and angrily **5** : physical maltreatment
syn ABUSE, VITUPERATION, INVECTIVE, OBLOQUY, BILLINGSGATE mean vehemently expressed condemnation or disapproval. ABUSE, the most general term, usu. implies the anger of the speaker and stresses the harshness of the language ⟨scathing verbal abuse⟩. VITUPERATION implies fluent and sustained abuse ⟨a torrent of vituperation⟩. INVECTIVE implies a comparable vehemence but suggests greater verbal and rhetorical skill and may apply to a public denunciation ⟨blistering political invective⟩. OBLOQUY suggests defamation and consequent shame and disgrace ⟨subjected to obloquy and derision⟩. BILLINGSGATE implies practiced fluency and variety of profane or obscene abuse ⟨directed a stream of billingsgate at the cabdriver⟩.

²abuse \ə-ˈbyüz\ vt abused; abus·ing (15c) **1** : to put to a wrong or improper use ⟨~ a privilege⟩ **2** obs : DECEIVE **3** : to use so as to injure or damage : MALTREAT **4** : to attack in words : REVILE — **abus·able** \-ˈbyü-zə-bəl\ adj — **abus·er** n

abu·sive \ə-ˈbyü-siv, -ziv\ adj (1583) **1** : characterized by wrong or improper use or action; esp : CORRUPT ⟨~ financial practices⟩ **2 a** : using harsh insulting language : characterized by or serving for abuse **b** : physically injurious ⟨~ behavior⟩ — **abu·sive·ly** adv — **abu·sive·ness** n

abut \ə-ˈbət\ vb abut·ted; abut·ting [ME abutten, partly fr. OF aboter to border on, fr. a- (fr. L ad-) + bout blow, end, fr. boter to strike; partly fr. OF abuter to come to an end, fr. a- + but end, aim — more at ¹BUTT, ⁴BUTT] vi (15c) **1** : to touch along a border or with a projecting part ⟨land ~s on the road⟩ **2 a** : to terminate at a point of contact **b** : to lean for support ~ vt **1** : to border on **2** : to cause to abut

abu·ti·lon \ə-ˈbyü-tᵊl-ˌän, -tᵊl-ən\ n [NL, genus name, fr. Ar awbūtīlūn abutilon] (ca. 1578) : any of a genus (Abutilon) of plants of the mallow family often having lobed leaves and solitary bell-shaped flowers

abut·ment \ə-ˈbət-mənt\ n (1644) **1** : the place at which abutting occurs **2** : the part of a structure (as an arch or a bridge) that directly receives thrust or pressure

abut·tals \ə-ˈbə-tᵊlz\ n pl (1630) : the boundaries of lands with respect to adjacent lands

abut·ter \ə-ˈbə-tər\ n (1673) : one that abuts; specif : the owner of a contiguous property

abut·ting adj (1599) : that abuts or serves as an abutment : ADJOINING, BORDERING

abuzz \ə-ˈbəz\ adj (1859) : filled or resounding with or as if with a buzzing sound ⟨a lake ~ with outboards⟩ ⟨a town ~ with excitement⟩

aby or **abye** \ə-ˈbī\ vt [ME abien, fr. OE ābycgan, fr. ā- + bycgan to buy — more at ABIDE, BUY] (bef. 12c) archaic : to suffer a penalty for

abysm \ə-ˈbi-zəm\ n [ME abime, fr. MF abisme, modif. of LL abyssus] (14c) : ABYSS ⟨the dark backward and ~ of time —Shak.⟩

abys·mal \ə-ˈbiz-məl, a-\ adj (ca. 1656) **1 a** : having immense or fathomless extension downward, backward, or inward ⟨an ~ cliff⟩ **b** : immeasurably great : PROFOUND ⟨~ ignorance⟩ **c** : immeasurably low or wretched ⟨~ living conditions of the poor⟩ **2** : ABYSSAL — **abys·mal·ly** \-mə-lē\ adv

abyss \ə-ˈbis, a- also ˈa-(ˌ)bis\ n [ME abissus, fr. LL abyssus, fr. Gk abyssos, fr. abyssos, adj., bottomless, fr. a- + byssos depth; perh. akin to Gk bathys deep] (14c) **1** : the bottomless gulf, pit, or chaos of the old cosmogonies **2 a** : an immeasurably deep gulf or great space **b** : intellectual or moral depths

abys·sal \ə-ˈbi-səl\ adj (1691) **1** : UNFATHOMABLE a **2** : of or relating to the bottom waters of the ocean depths

abyssal plain n (1954) : any of the great flat areas of ocean floor

Ab·ys·sin·i·an cat \ˌa-bə-ˈsi-nē-ən-, -ˈsin-yən-\ n [Abyssinia, kingdom in Africa] (1876) : any of a breed of small slender cats of African origin with short brownish hair ticked with bands of darker color

ac- — see AD-

-ac n suffix [NL -acus, fr. Gk -akos, var. of -ikos -ic after stems ending in -i-] : one affected with ⟨hemophiliac⟩

aca·cia \ə-ˈkā-shə\ n [NL, genus name, fr. L, acacia tree, fr. Gk akakia] (14c) **1** : GUM ARABIC **2** : any of a large genus (Acacia) of leguminous shrubs and trees

Abyssinian cat

\ə\ abut \ᵊ\ kitten, F table \ər\ further \a\ ash \ā\ ace \ä\ mop, mar
\aú\ out \ch\ chin \e\ bet \ē\ easy \g\ go \i\ hit \ī\ ice \j\ job
\ŋ\ sing \ō\ go \ȯ\ law \ȯi\ boy \th\ thin \t͟h\ the \ü\ loot \ú\ foot
\y\ yet \zh\ vision \á, k̲, ⁿ, œ, ōͤ, œ, ūͤ, ⁿ\ see Guide to Pronunciation

of warm regions with leaves pinnate or reduced to phyllodes and white or yellow flower clusters

ac·a·deme \'a-kə-ˌdēm, ˌa-kə-'\ *n* [L *Academus* (in the phrase *inter silvas Academi* among the groves of Academus), fr. Gk *Akadēmos* — more at ACADEMY] (1588) **1 a** : a place of instruction : SCHOOL **b** : the academic life, community, or world ⟨in the halls of ∼⟩ **2** : ACADEMIC; *esp* : PEDANT

ac·a·de·mia \ˌa-kə-'dē-mē-ə\ *n* [NL, fr. L, academy] (1946) : ACADEME 1b

¹ac·a·dem·ic \ˌa-kə-'de-mik\ *n* (1587) **1** : a member of an institution of learning **2** : one who is academic in background, outlook, or methods **3** *pl* : academic subjects

²academic *also* **ac·a·dem·i·cal** \-mi-kəl\ *adj* (1588) **1 a** : of, relating to, or associated with an academy or school esp. of higher learning **b** : of or relating to performance in academic courses ⟨∼ excellence⟩ **c** : very learned but inexperienced in practical matters ⟨∼ thinkers⟩ **d** : based on formal study esp. in an institution of higher learning **2** : of or relating to literary or artistic rather than technical or professional studies **3 a** : THEORETICAL, SPECULATIVE ⟨an ∼ question⟩ **b** : having no practical or useful significance **4** : conforming to the traditions or rules of a school (as of literature or art) or an official academy : CONVENTIONAL — **ac·a·dem·i·cal·ly** \-mi-k(ə-)lē\ *adv*

academic freedom *n* (1901) : freedom to teach or to learn without interference (as by government officials)

ac·a·de·mi·cian \ˌa-kə-də-'mi-shən, ə-ˌka-də-\ *n* (1748) **1 a** : a member of an academy for promoting science, art, or literature **b** : a follower of an artistic or philosophical tradition or a promoter of its ideas **2** : ACADEMIC

ac·a·dem·i·cism \ˌa-kə-'de-mə-ˌsi-zəm\ *also* **acad·e·mism** \ə-'ka-də-ˌmi-zəm\ *n* (1610) **1** : the doctrines of Plato's Academy; *specif* : the skeptical doctrines of the later Academy holding that nothing can be known — compare PYRRHONISM **2** : a formal academic quality (as in art or music) **3** : purely speculative thoughts and attitudes

academic year *n* (ca. 1934) : the annual period of sessions of an educational institution usu. beginning in September and ending in June

acad·e·my \ə-'ka-də-mē\ *n, pl* **-mies** [L *academia*, fr. Gk *Akadēmeia*, fr. *Akadēmeia*, gymnasium where Plato taught, fr. *Akadēmos* Attic mythological hero] (1549) **1 a** : a school usu. above the elementary level; *esp* : a private high school **b** : a high school or college in which special subjects or skills are taught **c** : higher education — used with *the* ⟨the functions of the ∼ in modern society⟩ **2** *cap* **a** : the school for advanced education founded by Plato **b** : the philosophical doctrines associated with Plato's Academy **3** : a society of learned persons organized to advance art, science, or literature **4** : a body of established opinion widely accepted as authoritative in a particular field

Aca·di·an \ə-'kā-dē-ən, a-\ *n* (1705) **1** : a native or inhabitant of Acadia **2** : a descendant of the French-speaking inhabitants of Acadia expelled after the French loss of the colony in 1755; *esp* : CAJUN — **Acadian** *adj*

acan·tho·ceph·a·lan \ə-ˌkan(t)-thə-'se-fə-lən\ *n* [ultim. fr. Gk *akantha* thorn, spine + *kephalē* head — more at CEPHALIC] (ca. 1909) : SPINY-HEADED WORM — **acanthocephalan** *adj*

acan·thus \ə-'kan(t)-thəs\ *n, pl* **acanthus** [NL, genus name, fr. Gk *akanthos*, an acanthus, fr. *akantha* thorn] (1616) **1** : any of a genus (*Acanthus* of the family Acanthaceae, the acanthus family) of prickly herbs of the Mediterranean region **2** : an ornamentation (as in a Corinthian capital) representing or suggesting the leaves of the acanthus

acanthus 2

a cap·pel·la *also* **a ca·pel·la** \ˌä-kə-'pe-lə\ *adv or adj* [It *a cappella* in chapel style] (ca. 1864) : without instrumental accompaniment

ac·a·ri·a·sis \ˌa-kə-'rī-ə-səs\ *n* (1828) : infestation with or disease caused by mites

acar·i·cide \ə-'kar-ə-ˌsīd\ *n* [*acarus* + -*i*- + -*cide*] (ca. 1879) : a pesticide that kills mites and ticks — **acar·i·cid·al** \ə-ˌkar-ə-'sī-d°l\ *adj*

ac·a·rid \'a-kə-rəd\ *n* (1881) : any of an order (Acarina) of arachnids including the mites and ticks; *esp* : a typical mite (family Acaridae) — **acarid** *adj*

ac·a·rus \'a-kə-rəs\ *n, pl* **-ri** \-ˌrī\ [NL, genus name, fr. Gk *akari*, a mite] (1658) : MITE; *esp* : one of a formerly extensive genus (*Acarus*)

acat·a·lec·tic \(ˌ)ā-ˌka-tə-'lek-tik\ *adj* [LL *acatalecticus*, fr. *acatalectus*, fr. Gk *akatalēktos*, fr. *a-* + *katalēgein* to leave off — more at CATALECTIC] (1589) : not catalectic ⟨∼ verse⟩ — **acatalectic** *n*

acau·les·cent \ˌā-kȯ-'le-s°nt\ *adj* [*a-* + L *caulis* stem — more at HOLE] (1854) : having no stem or appearing to have none

ac·cede \ak-'sēd, ik-\ *vi* **ac·ced·ed; ac·ced·ing** [ME, fr. L *accedere* to go to, be added, fr. *ad-* + *cedere* to go] (15c) **1 a** : to become a party (as to an agreement) **b** : to express approval or give consent : give in to a request or demand **2** *archaic* : APPROACH **3** : to enter upon an office or position *syn* see ASSENT

¹ac·ce·le·ran·do \(ˌ)ä-ˌche-lə-'rän-(ˌ)dō; ik-ˌse-, (ˌ)ak-\ *adv or adj* [It, lit., accelerating, fr. L *accelerandum*, gerund of *accelerare*] (ca. 1842) : gradually faster — used as a direction in music

²accelerando *n, pl* **-dos** (1889) : a gradual increase in tempo

ac·cel·er·ant \ik-'se-lə-rənt, ak-\ *n* (1916) : a substance used to accelerate a process (as the spreading of a fire)

ac·cel·er·ate \-lə-ˌrāt\ *vb* **-at·ed; -at·ing** [L *acceleratus*, pp. of *accelerare*, fr. *ad-* + *celer* swift — more at HOLD] *vt* (ca. 1530) **1** : to bring about at an earlier time **2** : to cause to move faster; *also* : to cause to undergo acceleration **3** : to hasten the progress or development of **b** : INCREASE ⟨∼ food production⟩ **4 a** : to enable (a student) to complete a course in less than usual time **b** : to speed up (as a course of study) ∼ *vi* **1 a** : to move faster : gain speed **b** : GROW, INCREASE ⟨inflation was *accelerating*⟩ **2** : to follow an accelerated educational program — **ac·cel·er·at·ing·ly** \-ˌrā-tiŋ-lē\ *adv*

ac·cel·er·a·tion \ik-ˌse-lə-'rā-shən, (ˌ)ak-\ *n* (1531) **1** : the act or process of accelerating : the state of being accelerated **2** : the rate of change of velocity with respect to time; *broadly* : change of velocity

acceleration of gravity (ca. 1889) : the acceleration of a body in free fall under the influence of earth's gravity expressed as the rate of increase of velocity per unit of time and assigned the standard value of 980.665 centimeters per second per second

acceleration principle *n* (ca. 1941) : a theory in economics: an increase or decrease in income induces a corresponding but magnified change in investment

ac·cel·er·a·tive \ik-'se-lə-ˌrā-tiv, ak-\ *adj* (1751) : of, relating to, or tending to cause acceleration : ACCELERATING

ac·cel·er·a·tor \ik-'se-lə-ˌrā-tər, ak-\ *n* (1611) : one that accelerates: as **a** : a muscle or nerve that speeds the performance of an action **b** : a device (as a pedal) for controlling the speed of a motor vehicle engine **c** : a substance that speeds a chemical reaction **d** : an apparatus for imparting high velocities to charged particles (as electrons)

ac·cel·er·om·e·ter \ik-ˌse-lə-'rä-mə-tər, ak-\ *n* [ISV *acceleration* + -*o*- + -*meter*] (ca. 1890) : an instrument for measuring acceleration or for detecting and measuring vibrations

¹ac·cent \'ak-ˌsent, ak-\ [MF *accenter*, fr. *accent* intonation, fr. L *accentus*, fr. *ad-* + *cantus* song — more at CHANT] *vt* (1530) **1 a** : to pronounce with accent : STRESS **b** : to mark with a written or printed accent **2** : to give prominence to : make more prominent

²ac·cent \'ak-ˌsent, *chiefly Brit* -sənt\ *n* (1538) **1** : a distinctive manner of expression: as **a** : an individual's distinctive or characteristic inflection, tone, or choice of words — usu. used in pl. **b** : a way of speaking typical of a particular group of people and esp. of the natives or residents of a region **2** : an articulative effort giving prominence to one syllable over adjacent syllables; *also* : the prominence thus given a syllable **3** : rhythmically significant stress on the syllables of a verse usu. at regular intervals **4** *archaic* : UTTERANCE **5 a** : a mark (as ˌ, ´, ^) used in writing or printing to indicate a specific sound value, stress, or pitch, to distinguish words otherwise identically spelled, or to indicate that an ordinarily mute vowel should be pronounced **b** : an accented letter **6 a** : greater stress given to one musical tone than to its neighbors **b** : ACCENT MARK 2 **7 a** : emphasis laid on a part of an artistic design or composition **b** : an emphasized detail or area; *esp* : a small detail in sharp contrast with its surroundings **c** : a substance or object used for emphasis **8** : a mark placed to the right of a letter or number and usu. slightly above it: as **a** : a double prime **b** : PRIME **9** : special concern or attention : EMPHASIS ⟨an ∼ on youth⟩ — **ac·cent·less** \-ləs\ *adj*

accent mark *n* (ca. 1889) **1** : ACCENT 5a, 8 **2 a** : a symbol used to indicate musical stress **b** : a mark placed after a letter designating a note of music to indicate in which octave the note occurs

ac·cen·tu·al \ak-'sen(t)-shə(-wə)l, ik-\ *adj* [L *accentus*] (1610) : of, relating to, or characterized by accent; *specif* : based on accent rather than on quantity or syllabic recurrence ⟨∼ poetry⟩ — **ac·cen·tu·al·ly** *adv*

ac·cen·tu·ate \ik-'sen(t)-shə-ˌwāt, ak-\ *vt* **-at·ed; -at·ing** [ML *accentuatus*, pp. of *accentuare*, fr. L *accentus*] (ca. 1731) : ACCENT, EMPHASIZE; *also* : INTENSIFY ⟨∼s the feeling of despair⟩ — **ac·cen·tu·a·tion** \ik-ˌsen(t)-shə-'wā-shən, (ˌ)ak-\ *n*

ac·cept \ik-'sept, ak- *also* ek-\ *vb* [ME, fr. MF *accepter*, fr. L *acceptare*, freq. of *accipere* to receive, fr. *ad-* + *capere* to take — more at HEAVE] *vt* (14c) **1 a** : to receive willingly ⟨∼ a gift⟩ **b** : to be able or designed to take or hold (something applied or added) ⟨a surface that will not ∼ ink⟩ **2** : to give admittance or approval to ⟨∼ her as one of the group⟩ **3 a** : to endure without protest or reaction ⟨∼ poor living conditions⟩ **b** : to regard as proper, normal, or inevitable ⟨the idea is widely ∼ed⟩ **c** : to recognize as true : BELIEVE ⟨refused to ∼ the explanation⟩ **4 a** : to make a favorable response to ⟨∼ an offer⟩ **b** : to agree to undertake (a responsibility) ⟨∼ a job⟩ **5** : to assume an obligation to pay; *also* : to take in payment ⟨we don't ∼ personal checks⟩ **6** : to receive (a legislative report) officially ∼ *vi* : to receive favorably something offered — usu. used with *of* — **ac·cept·ing·ly** \-'sep-tiŋ-lē\ *adv* — **ac·cept·ing·ness** \-tiŋ-nəs\ *n*

ac·cept·able \ik-'sep-tə-bəl, ak- *also* ek-\ *adj* (14c) **1** : capable of or worthy of being accepted ⟨no compromise would be ∼⟩ **2 a** : WELCOME, PLEASING ⟨compliments are always ∼⟩ **b** : barely satisfactory or adequate ⟨performances varied from excellent to ∼⟩ — **ac·cept·abil·i·ty** \ik-ˌsep-tə-'bi-lə-tē, (ˌ)ak-, ek-\ *n* — **ac·cept·able·ness** \ik-'sep-tə-bəl-nəs, ak-\ *n* — **ac·cept·ably** \-blē\ *adv*

ac·cep·tance \ik-'sep-tən(t)s, ak-\ *n* (1574) **1** : an agreeing either expressly or by conduct to the act or offer of another so that a contract is concluded and the parties become legally bound **2** : the quality or state of being accepted or acceptable **3** : the act of accepting : the fact of being accepted : APPROVAL **4 a** : the act of accepting a time draft or bill of exchange for payment when due according to the specified terms **b** : an accepted draft or bill of exchange **5** : ACCEPTATION 2

ac·cep·tant \-tənt\ *adj* (1851) : willing to accept : RECEPTIVE

ac·cep·ta·tion \ˌak-ˌsep-'tā-shən\ *n* (15c) **1** : ACCEPTANCE; *esp* : favorable reception or approval **2** : a generally accepted meaning of a word or understanding of a concept

ac·cept·ed *adj* (15c) : generally approved or used — **ac·cept·ed·ly** *adv*

ac·cept·er \ik-'sep-tər, ak-\ *n* (1585) **1** : one that accepts **2** : ACCEPTOR 2

ac·cep·tive \ak-'sep-tiv\ *adj* (1596) **1** : ACCEPTABLE **2** : RECEPTIVE

ac·cep·tor \ik-'sep-tər, ak-\ *n* (14c) **1** : ACCEPTER 1 **2** : one that accepts an order or a bill of exchange **3** : an atom, molecule, or subatomic particle capable of receiving another entity (as an electron) esp. to form a compound — compare DONOR 3a

¹ac·cess \'ak-ˌses *also* ik-'ses\ *n* [ME, fr. MF & L; MF *acces* arrival, fr. L *accessus* approach, fr. *accedere* to approach — more at ACCEDE] (14c) **1 a** : ONSET 2 **b** : a fit of intense feeling : OUTBURST **2 a** : permission, liberty, or ability to enter, approach, communicate with, or pass to and from **b** : freedom or ability to obtain or make use of **c** : a way or means of access **3** : the act or an instance of accessing **3** : an increase by addition ⟨a sudden ∼ of wealth⟩

²access *vt* (1962) : to get at : gain access to ⟨∼ed the computer by phone⟩

ac·ces·si·ble \ik-'se-sə-bəl, ak-, ek-\ *adj* (15c) **1** : providing access **2 a** : capable of being reached ⟨∼ by rail⟩; *also* : being within reach ⟨fashions at ∼ prices⟩ **b** : easy to speak or deal with ⟨∼ people⟩ **3** : capable of being influenced : OPEN **4** : capable of being used or seen : AVAILABLE **5** : capable of being understood or appreciated ⟨the author's most ~ stories⟩ ⟨an ~ film⟩ — **ac·ces·si·bil·i·ty** \-,se-sə-'bi-lə-tē\ *n* — **ac·ces·si·ble·ness** \-'se-sə-bəl-nəs\ *n* — **ac·ces·si·bly** \-blē\ *adv*

¹**ac·ces·sion** \ik-'se-shən, ak-\ *n* (1588) **1 a :** increase by something added **b :** acquisition of additional property (as by growth or increase of existing property) **2 :** something added : ACQUISITION **3 :** the act of assenting or agreeing **4 a :** the act of becoming joined : ADHER-ENCE **b :** the act by which one nation becomes party to an agreement already in force between other powers **5 a :** an act of coming near or to : APPROACH, ADMITTANCE **b :** the act of coming to high office or a position of honor or power **6 :** a sudden fit or outburst : ACCESS — **ac·ces·sion·al** \-'sesh-nəl, -'se-shə-n°l\ *adj*

²**accession** *vt* (1892) : to record in order of acquisition

ac·ces·so·ri·al \ak-sə-'sōr-ē-əl, -'sȯr-\ *adj* (1726) **1 :** of or relating to an accessory ⟨~ liability⟩ **2 :** of, relating to, or constituting an accession : SUPPLEMENTARY ⟨~ services⟩

ac·ces·so·rise *Brit var of* ACCESSORIZE

ac·ces·so·rize \ik-'se-sə-,rīz, ak-\ *vb* **-rized; -riz·ing** *vt* (1939) : to furnish with accessories ~ *vi* : to wear clothing accessories

¹**ac·ces·so·ry** *also* **ac·ces·sa·ry** \ik-'se-sə-rē, ak-, ek-, -'ses-rē, *also* ə-'se-\ *n, pl* **-ries** (15c) **1 a :** a person not actually or constructively present but contributing as an assistant or instigator to the commission of an offense — called also *accessory before the fact* **b :** a person who knowing that a crime has been committed aids or shelters the offender with intent to defeat justice — called also *accessory after the fact* **2 a :** a thing of secondary or subordinate importance : ADJUNCT **b :** an object or device not essential in itself but adding to the beauty, convenience, or effectiveness of something else ⟨auto *accessories*⟩ ⟨clothing *accessories*⟩

²**accessory** *adj* (1607) **1 :** assisting as a subordinate; *esp* : contributing to a crime but not as the chief agent **2 :** aiding or contributing in a secondary way : SUPPLEMENTARY **3 :** present in a minor amount and not essential as a constituent ⟨an ~ mineral in a rock⟩

accessory fruit *n* (ca. 1900) : a fruit (as the apple) of which a conspicuous part consists of tissue other than that of the ripened ovary

accessory nerve *n* (ca. 1842) : either of a pair of motor nerves that are the 11th cranial nerves of higher vertebrates, arise from the medulla and the upper part of the spinal cord, and supply chiefly the pharynx and muscles of the upper chest, back, and shoulders

access time *n* (1950) : the time lag between the time stored information (as in a computer) is requested and the time it is delivered

ac·ciac·ca·tu·ra \(,)ä-,chä-kə-'tür-ə\ *n* [It, lit., crushing] (ca. 1819) : a discordant note sounded with a principal note or chord and immediately released

ac·ci·dence \'ak-sə-dən(t)s, -,den(t)s\ *n* [ME, fr. MF, fr. L *accidentia* inflections of words, nonessential qualities, pl. of *accident-, accidens,* n.] (15c) : a part of grammar that deals with inflections

ac·ci·dent \'ak-sə-dənt, -,dent; 'aks-dənt\ *n* [ME, fr. MF, fr. L *acci-dent-, accidens* nonessential quality, chance, fr. prp. of *accidere* to happen, fr. *ad-* + *cadere* to fall — more at CHANCE] (14c) **1 a :** an unforeseen and unplanned event or circumstance **b :** lack of intention or necessity : CHANCE ⟨met by ~ rather than by design⟩ **2 a :** an unfortunate event resulting esp. from carelessness or ignorance **b :** an unexpected and medically important bodily event esp. when injurious ⟨a cerebrovascular ~⟩ **c :** an unexpected happening causing loss or injury which is not due to any fault or misconduct on the part of the person injured but for which legal relief may be sought **3 :** a nonessential property or quality of an entity or circumstance ⟨the ~ of nationality⟩

¹**ac·ci·den·tal** \,ak-sə-'den-t°l\ *adj* (14c) **1 :** arising from extrinsic causes : INCIDENTAL, NONESSENTIAL **2 :** occurring unexpectedly or by chance **b :** happening without intent or through carelessness and often with unfortunate results — **ac·ci·den·tal·ly** \-'dent-lē, -'den-t°l-ē\ *also* **ac·ci·dent·ly** \-'dent-lē\ *adv* — **ac·ci·den·tal·ness** \-'den-t°l-nəs\ *n*

syn ACCIDENTAL, FORTUITOUS, CASUAL, CONTINGENT mean not amenable to planning or prediction. ACCIDENTAL stresses chance ⟨any resemblance to actual persons is entirely *accidental*⟩. FORTUITOUS so strongly suggests chance that it often connotes entire absence of cause ⟨a series of *fortuitous* events⟩. CASUAL stresses lack of real or apparent premeditation or intent ⟨a *casual* encounter with a stranger⟩. CONTINGENT suggests possibility of happening but stresses uncertainty and dependence on other future events for existence or occurrence ⟨the *contingent* effects of the proposed law⟩.

²**accidental** *n* (1651) **1 :** a nonessential property **2 a :** a note foreign to a key indicated by a signature **b :** a prefixed sign indicating an accidental

accident insurance *n* (1866) : insurance against loss through accidental bodily injury to the insured

accident–prone *adj* (1926) **1 :** having a greater than average number of accidents **2 :** having personality traits that predispose to accidents

ac·ci·die \'ak-sə-dē\ *n* (13c) : ACEDIA

ac·cip·i·ter \ak-'si-pə-tər, ik-\ *n* [NL, genus name, fr. L, hawk] (ca. 1828) : any of a genus (*Accipiter*) of medium-sized forest-inhabiting hawks that have short broad wings and a long tail and a characteristic flight pattern of several quick flaps and a glide — **ac·cip·i·trine** \-'si-pə-,trīn\ *adj or n*

¹**ac·claim** \ə-'klām\ *vb* [L *acclamare,* lit., to shout at, fr. *ad-* + *clamare* to shout — more at CLAIM] *vt* (1633) **1 :** APPLAUD, PRAISE **2 :** to declare by acclamation ~ *vi* : to shout praise or applause — **ac·claim·er** *n*

²**acclaim** *n* (1667) : the act of acclaiming **2 :** PRAISE, APPLAUSE

ac·cla·ma·tion \,a-klə-'mā-shən\ *n* [L *acclamation-, acclamatio,* fr. *acclamare*] (1585) **1 :** a loud eager expression of approval, praise, or assent **2 :** an overwhelming affirmative vote by cheers, shouts, or applause rather than by ballot

ac·cli·mate \'a-klə-,māt; ə-'klī-mət, -,māt\ *vb* **-mat·ed; -mat·ing** [F *acclimater,* fr. *a-* (fr. L *ad-*) + *climat* climate] (1792) : ACCLIMATIZE

ac·cli·ma·tion \,a-klə-'mā-shən, -,klī-\ *n* (1826) : ACCLIMATIZATION; *esp* : physiological adjustment by an organism to environmental change

ac·cli·ma·tise *Brit var of* ACCLIMATIZE

ac·cli·ma·ti·za·tion \ə-,klī-mə-tə-'zā-shən\ *n* (1830) : the process or result of acclimatizing

ac·cli·ma·tize \ə-'klī-mə-,tīz\ *vb* **-tized; -tiz·ing** *vt* (1836) : to adapt to a new temperature, altitude, climate, environment, or situation ~ *vi* : to become acclimatized — **ac·cli·ma·tiz·er** *n*

ac·cliv·i·ty \ə-'kli-və-tē, a-\ *n, pl* **-ties** [L *acclivitas,* fr. *acclivis* ascending, fr. *ad-* + *clivus* slope — more at DECLIVITY] (1614) : an ascending slope (as of a hill)

ac·co·lade \'a-kə-,lād, -,läd\ *n* [F, fr. *accoler* to embrace, fr. (assumed) VL *accollare,* fr. L *ad-* + *collum* neck — more at COLLAR] (1623) **1 a :** a ceremonial embrace **b :** a ceremony or salute conferring knighthood **2 a :** a mark of acknowledgment : AWARD **b :** an expression of praise **3 :** a brace or a line used in music to join two or more staffs carrying simultaneous parts

ac·com·mo·date \ə-'kä-mə-,dāt\ *vb* **-dat·ed; -dat·ing** [L *accommo-datus,* pp. of *accommodare,* fr. *ad-* + *commodare* to make fit, fr. *commodus* suitable — more at COMMODE] *vt* (1550) **1 :** to make fit, suitable, or congruous **2 :** to bring into agreement or concord : REC-ONCILE **3 :** to provide with something desired, needed, or suited (as a helpful service, a loan, or lodgings) **4 a :** to make room for **b :** to hold without crowding or inconvenience **5 :** to give consideration to : allow for ⟨~ the special interests of various groups⟩ ~ *vi* : to adapt oneself; *also* : to undergo visual accommodation **syn** see ADAPT, CON-TAIN — **ac·com·mo·da·tive** \-,dā-tiv\ *adj* — **ac·com·mo·da·tive-ness** *n*

ac·com·mo·dat·ing *adj* (1775) : HELPFUL, OBLIGING — **ac·com·mo-dat·ing·ly** \-,dā-tiŋ-lē\ *adv*

ac·com·mo·da·tion \ə-,kä-mə-'dā-shən\ *n* (1603) **1 :** something supplied for convenience or to satisfy a need: as **a :** lodging, food, and services or traveling space and related services — usu. used in pl. ⟨tourist ~s on the boat⟩ ⟨overnight ~s⟩ **b :** a public conveyance (as a train) that stops at all or nearly all points **c :** LOAN **2 :** the act of accommodating : the state of being accommodated: as **a :** the providing of what is needed or desired for convenience **b :** ADAPTATION, ADJUSTMENT **c :** a reconciliation of differences : SETTLEMENT **d :** the automatic adjustment of the eye for seeing at different distances effected chiefly by changes in the convexity of the crystalline lens; *also* : the range over which such adjustment is possible — **ac·com·mo·da-tion·al** \-shnəl, -shə-n°l\ *adj*

¹**ac·com·mo·da·tion·ist** \-'dā-sh(ə-)nist\ *n* (1964) : a black who adapts to the ideals or attitudes of whites ⟨making Uncle Toms, compromisers, and ~s . . . thoroughly ashamed —Ossie Davis⟩

²**accommodationist** (1964) : favoring or practicing accommodation or compromise

accommodation ladder *n* (1769) : a light ladder or stairway hung over the side of a ship for ascending from or descending to small boats

ac·com·mo·da·tor \ə-'kä-mə-,dā-tər\ *n* (ca. 1630) : one that accommodates; *esp* : a part-time or special-occasion domestic worker

ac·com·pa·ni·ment \ə-'kəm-pə-nē-mənt, -'kəmp-nē-\ *n* (ca. 1744) **1 :** an instrumental or vocal part designed to support or complement a melody **2 :** an addition (as an ornament) intended to give completeness or symmetry : COMPLEMENT **b :** an accompanying situation or occurrence : CONCOMITANT

ac·com·pa·nist \ə-'kəmp-nist, -'kəm-pə-\ *n* (ca. 1828) : one (as a pianist) who plays an accompaniment

ac·com·pa·ny \ə-'kəmp-nē, -'kämp-; -'kəm-pə-, -'käm-\ *vb* **-nied; -ny-ing** [ME *accompanien,* fr. MF *accompaignier,* fr. a- (fr. L *ad-*) + *compaing* companion — more at COMPANION] *vt* (15c) **1 :** to go with as an associate or companion **2 :** to perform an accompaniment to or for **3 a :** to cause to be in association ⟨*accompanied* their advice with a warning⟩ **b :** to be in association with ⟨the pictures that ~ the text⟩ ~ *vi* : to perform an accompaniment

ac·com·plice \ə-'käm-pləs, -'kəm-\ *n* [alter. (fr. incorrect division of *a complice*) of *complice*] (1589) : one associated with another esp. in wrongdoing

ac·com·plish \ə-'käm-plish, -'kəm-\ *vt* [ME *accomplisshen,* fr. MF *acompliss-,* stem of *accomplir,* fr. (assumed) VL *accomplēre,* fr. L *ad-* + *complēre* to fill up — more at COMPLETE] (14c) **1 :** to bring about (a result) by effort ⟨have much to ~ today⟩ ⟨regretted that he had never ~ed a marriage to her —Francis Hackett⟩ **2 :** to bring to completion : FULFILL ⟨we can ~ the job in an hour⟩ **3 :** to succeed in reaching (a stage in a progression) ⟨would starve before ~ing half the distance —W. H. Hudson †1922⟩ **4** *archaic* **a :** to equip thoroughly **b :** PER-FECT **syn** see PERFORM — **ac·com·plish·able** \-pli-shə-bəl\ *adj* — **ac·com·plish·er** *n*

ac·com·plished *adj* (15c) **1 a :** proficient as the result of practice or training ⟨an ~ dancer⟩ **b :** having many social accomplishments **2 :** established beyond doubt or dispute ⟨an ~ fact⟩

ac·com·plish·ment \ə-'käm-plish-mənt, -'kəm-\ *n* (15c) **1 :** the act of accomplishing : COMPLETION **2 :** something that has been accomplished : ACHIEVEMENT **3 a :** a quality or ability equipping one for society **b :** a special skill or ability acquired by training or practice

¹**ac·cord** \ə-'kȯrd\ *vb* [ME, fr. OF *acorder,* fr. (assumed) VL *accordare,* fr. L *ad-* + *cord-, cor* heart — more at HEART] *vt* (12c) **1 :** to bring into agreement : RECONCILE **2 :** to grant or give esp. as appropriate, due, or earned ~ *vi* **1** *archaic* : to arrive at an agreement **2** *obs* : to give consent **3 :** to be consistent or in harmony : AGREE **syn** see GRANT

²**accord** *n* [ME, fr. OF *acort,* fr. *acorder*] (14c) **1 a :** AGREEMENT, CONFORMITY ⟨acted in ~ with the company's policy⟩ **b :** a formal reaching of agreement : COMPACT, TREATY **2 :** balanced interrelationship : HARMONY **3** *obs* : ASSENT **4 :** voluntary or spontaneous impulse to act ⟨gave generously of their own ~⟩

ac·cor·dance \ə-'kȯr-d°n(t)s\ *n* (14c) **1 :** AGREEMENT, CONFORMITY ⟨in ~ with a rule⟩ **2 :** the act of granting

ac·cor·dant \-d°nt\ *adj* (14c) **1 :** CONSONANT, AGREEING **2 :** HARMONI-OUS, CORRESPONDENT — **ac·cor·dant·ly** *adv*

according as *conj* (1500) **1 :** in accord with the way in which **2 a :** depending on how **b :** depending on whether : IF

\ə\ abut \°\ kitten, F table \ər\ further \a\ ash \ā\ ace \ä\ mop, mar \aů\ out \ch\ chin \e\ bet \ē\ easy \g\ go \i\ hit \ī\ ice \j\ job \ŋ\ sing \ō\ go \ȯ\ law \ȯi\ boy \th\ thin \th\ the \ü\ loot \ů\ foot \y\ yet \zh\ vision \ä, k̲, ⁿ, œ, œ̄, ue, ūe, ʸ\ *see* Guide to Pronunciation

ac·cord·ing·ly \ə-'kȯr-diŋ-lē\ *adv* (14c) **1** : in accordance : CORRESPONDINGLY **2** : CONSEQUENTLY, SO

according to *prep* (14c) **1** : in conformity with **2** : as stated or attested by **3** : depending on

¹ac·cor·di·on \ə-'kȯr-dē-ən\ *n* [G *Akkordion*, fr. *Akkord* chord, fr. OF *acort*, fr. OF *acort*] (1831) : a portable keyboard wind instrument in which the wind is forced past free reeds by means of a hand-operated bellows — **ac·cor·di·on·ist** \-dē-ə-nist\ *n*

accordion

²accordion *adj* (1885) : folding or creased or hinged to fold like an accordion ⟨an ~ pleat⟩ ⟨an ~ door⟩

ac·cost \ə-'kȯst, -'käst\ *vt* [MF *accoster*, ultim. fr. L *ad-* + *costa* rib, side — more at COAST] (1612) : to approach and speak to often in a challenging or aggressive way

ac·couche·ment \ä,a-küsh-'män, ə-'küsh-\ *n* [F] (1803) : the time or act of giving birth

ac·cou·cheur \ä,a-kü-'shər\ *n* [F] (1759) : one that assists at a birth; *esp* : OBSTETRICIAN

¹ac·count \ə-'kaunt\ *n* (14c) **1** *archaic* : RECKONING, COMPUTATION **2 a** : a record of debit and credit entries to cover transactions involving a particular item or a particular person or concern **b** : a statement of transactions during a fiscal period and the resulting balance **3 a** : a statement explaining one's conduct **b** : a statement or exposition of reasons, causes, or motives ⟨no satisfactory ~ of these phenomena⟩ **c** : a reason for an action : BASIS ⟨on that ~ I must refuse⟩ **4 a** : a formal business arrangement providing for regular dealings or services (as banking, advertising, or store credit) and involving the establishment and maintenance of an account; *also* : CLIENT, CUSTOMER **b** : money deposited in a bank account and subject to withdrawal by the depositor **5 a** : VALUE, IMPORTANCE ⟨it's of no ~ to me⟩ **b** : ESTEEM ⟨stood high in their ~⟩ **6** : ADVANTAGE ⟨turned her wit to good ~⟩ **7 a** : careful thought : CONSIDERATION ⟨have to take many things into ~⟩ **b** : a usu. mental record : TRACK ⟨keep ~ of all you do⟩ **8** : a description of facts, conditions, or events : REPORT, NARRATIVE ⟨the newspaper ~ of the fire⟩ ⟨by all ~s they're well-off⟩; *also* : PERFORMANCE ⟨a straightforward ~ of the sonata⟩ — **on account** : with the price charged to one's account — **on account of** : for the sake of : by reason of — **on no account** : under no circumstances — **on one's own account 1** : on one's own behalf **2** : at one's own risk **3** : by oneself : on one's own

²account *vb* [ME, fr. MF *acompter*, fr. *a-* (fr. L *ad-*) + *compter* to count] *vt* (14c) **1** : to think of as : CONSIDER ⟨~s himself lucky⟩ **2** : to probe into : ANALYZE ~ *vi* **1** : to furnish a justifying analysis or explanation — used with *for* ⟨couldn't ~ for the loss⟩ **2 a** : to be the sole or primary factor — used with *for* ⟨the pitcher ~ed for all three putouts⟩ **b** : to bring about the capture, death, or destruction of something ⟨~ed for two rabbits⟩

ac·count·abil·i·ty \ə-,kaun-tə-'bi-lə-tē\ *n* (1794) : the quality or state of being accountable; *esp* : an obligation or willingness to accept responsibility or to account for one's actions ⟨public officials lacking ~⟩

ac·count·able \ə-'kaun-tə-bəl\ *adj* (14c) **1** : subject to giving an account : ANSWERABLE **2** : capable of being accounted for : EXPLAINABLE *syn* see RESPONSIBLE — **ac·count·able·ness** \-'kaun-tə-bəl-nəs\ *n* — **ac·count·ably** \-blē\ *adv*

ac·coun·tan·cy \ə-'kaun-t³n(t)-sē\ *n* (1854) : the profession or practice of accounting

¹ac·coun·tant \ə-'kaun-t³nt\ *n* (15c) **1** : one that gives an account or is accountable **2** : one who is skilled in the practice of accounting or who is in charge of public or private accounts — **ac·coun·tant·ship** \-t³n(t),ship\ *n*

²accountant *adj* (15c) *obs* : ACCOUNTABLE, ANSWERABLE ⟨I stand ~ for as great a sin —Shak.⟩

account executive *n* (1931) : a business executive (as in an advertising agency) responsible for dealing with a client's account

ac·count·ing \ə-'kaun-tiŋ\ *n* (ca. 1716) **1** : the system of recording and summarizing business and financial transactions and analyzing, verifying, and reporting the results; *also* : the principles and procedures of accounting **2 a** : work done in accounting or by accountants **b** : an instance of applied accounting or of the settling or presenting of accounts

account payable *n, pl* **accounts payable** (ca. 1936) : the balance due to a creditor on a current account

account receivable *n, pl* **accounts receivable** (1936) : a balance due from a debtor on a current account

ac·cou·tre *or* **ac·cou·ter** \ə-'kü-tər\ *vt* -**cou·tred** *or* -**cou·tered**; -**cou·tring** *or* -**cou·ter·ing** \-'kü-tə-riŋ, -'kü-triŋ\ [F *accoutrer*, fr. MF *acoustrer*, fr. *a-* + *costure* seam, fr. (assumed) VL *consutura* — more at COUTURE] (1596) : to provide with equipment or furnishings : OUTFIT *syn* see FURNISH

ac·cou·tre·ment *or* **ac·cou·ter·ment** \ə-'kü-trə-mənt, -'kü-tər-mənt\ *n* (1549) **1 a** : EQUIPMENT, TRAPPINGS; *specif* : a soldier's outfit usu. not including clothes and weapons — usu. used in pl. **b** : an accessory item of clothing or equipment — usu. used in pl. **2** *archaic* : the act of accoutring **3** : an identifying and often superficial characteristic or device — usu. used in pl. ⟨~s of power that define our diplomacy — Elizabeth Drew⟩

ac·cred·it \ə-'kre-dət\ *vt* [L *accreditus*, pp. of *accredere* to give credence to, fr. *ad-* + *credere* to believe — more at CREED] (1535) **1 a** : to give official authorization to or approval of: **a** : to provide with credentials; *esp* : to send (an envoy) with letters of authorization **b** : to recognize or vouch for as conforming with a standard **c** : to recognize (an educational institution) as maintaining standards that qualify the graduates for admission to higher or more specialized institutions or for professional practice **2** : to consider or recognize as outstanding **3** : ATTRIBUTE, CREDIT *syn* see APPROVE — **ac·cred·i·table** \-də-tə-bəl\ *adj* — **ac·cred·i·ta·tion** \ə-,kre-də-'tā-shən, -'dā-\ *n*

ac·crete \ə-'krēt\ *vb* **ac·cret·ed; ac·cret·ing** [back-formation fr. *accretion*] *vi* (1784) : to grow or become attached by accretion ~ *vt* : to cause to adhere or become attached; *also* : ACCUMULATE

ac·cre·tion \ə-'krē-shən\ *n* [L *accretion-, accretio*, fr. *accrescere* — more at ACCRUE] (1615) **1** : the process of growth or enlargement by a gradual buildup: as **a** : increase by external addition or accumulation (as by adhesion of external parts or particles) **b** : the increase of land by the action of natural forces **2** : a product of accretion; *esp* : an extraneous addition ⟨~s of grime⟩ — **ac·cre·tion·ary** \-shə-,ner-ē\ *adj* — **ac·cre·tive** \ə-'krē-tiv\ *adj*

¹ac·cru·al \ə-'krü-əl\ *n* (1880) **1** : the action or process of accruing **2** : something that accrues or has accrued

²accrual *n* (1917) : being a method of accounting that recognizes income when earned and expenses when incurred regardless of when cash is received or disbursed

ac·crue \ə-'krü\ *vb* **ac·crued; ac·cru·ing** [ME *acreuen*, prob. fr. MF *acreue* increase, fr. *acreistre* to increase, fr. L *accrescere*, fr. *ad-* + *crescere* to grow — more at CRESCENT] *vi* (15c) **1** : to come into existence as a legally enforceable claim **2** **a** : to come about as a natural growth, increase, or advantage ⟨the wisdom that ~s with age⟩ **b** : to come as a direct result of some state or action ⟨rewards due to the feminine will ~ to me —Germaine Greer⟩ **3** : to accumulate or be added periodically ⟨interest ~s on a daily basis⟩ ~ *vt* : to accumulate or have due after a period of time ⟨~ vacation time⟩ — **ac·cru·able** \-'krü-ə-bəl\ *adj*

ac·cul·tur·ate \ə-'kəl-chə-,rāt, a-\ *vt* -**at·ed; -at·ing** [back-formation fr. *acculturation*] (1930) : to change through acculturation

ac·cul·tur·a·tion \ə-,kəl-chə-'rā-shən, a-\ *n* (1880) **1** : cultural modification of an individual, group, or people by adapting to or borrowing traits from another culture; *also* : a merging of cultures as a result of prolonged contact **2** : the process by which a human being acquires the culture of a particular society from infancy — **ac·cul·tur·a·tion·al** \-shnəl, -shə-n³l\ *adj* — **ac·cul·tur·a·tive** \ə-'kəl-chə-,rā-tiv, a-\ *adj*

ac·cu·mu·late \ə-'kyü-m(y)ə-,lāt\ *vb* -**lat·ed; -lat·ing** [L *accumulatus*, pp. of *accumulare*, fr. *ad-* + *cumulare* to heap up — more at CUMULATE] *vt* (15c) : to gather or pile up esp. little by little : AMASS ⟨~ a fortune⟩ ~ *vi* : to increase gradually in quantity or number

ac·cu·mu·la·tion \ə-,kyü-m(y)ə-'lā-shən\ *n* (15c) **1** : something that has accumulated or has been accumulated **2** : the action or process of accumulating : the state of being or having accumulated **3** : increase or growth by addition esp. when continuous or repeated ⟨~ of interest⟩

ac·cu·mu·la·tive \ə-'kyü-m(y)ə-,lā-tiv, -lə-\ *adj* (ca. 1651) **1** : CUMULATIVE ⟨an age of rapid and ~ change⟩ **2** : tending or given to accumulation — **ac·cu·mu·la·tive·ly** *adv* — **ac·cu·mu·la·tive·ness** *n*

ac·cu·mu·la·tor \ə-'kyü-m(y)ə-,lā-tər\ *n* (1748) : one that accumulates: as **a** : a device (as in a hydraulic system) in which a fluid is collected and esp. in which it is kept under pressure as a means of storing energy **b** *Brit* : STORAGE BATTERY **c** : a part (as in a computer) where numbers are totaled or stored

ac·cu·ra·cy \'a-kyə-rə-sē, -k(ə)rə-\ *n, pl* -**cies** (1662) **1** : freedom from mistake or error : CORRECTNESS **2 a** : conformity to truth or to a standard or model : EXACTNESS **b** : degree of conformity of a measure to a standard or a true value — compare PRECISION 2a

ac·cu·rate \'a-kyə-rət, 'a-k(ə)rət\ *adj* [L *accuratus*, fr. pp. of *accurare* to take care of, fr. *ad-* + *cura* care] (1596) **1** : free from error esp. as the result of care ⟨an ~ diagnosis⟩ **2** : conforming exactly to truth or to a standard : EXACT ⟨providing ~ color⟩ **3** : able to give an accurate result ⟨an ~ gauge⟩ *syn* see CORRECT — **ac·cu·rate·ly** \'a-kyə-rət-lē, 'a-k(ə)-rət-, 'a-k(y)ərt-\ *adv* — **ac·cu·rate·ness** \-kyə-rət-nəs, -k(ə)rət-nəs\ *n*

ac·cursed \ə-'kərst, -'kər-səd\ *or* **ac·curst** \ə-'kərst\ *adj* [ME *acursed*, fr. pp. of *acursen* to consign to destruction with a curse, fr. *a-* (fr. OE *ā*, perfective prefix) + *cursen* to curse — more at ABIDE] (13c) **1** : lying under or as if under a curse **2** : DAMNABLE — **ac·curs·ed·ly** \-'kər-səd-lē\ *adv* — **ac·curs·ed·ness** \-'kər-səd-nəs\ *n*

ac·cus·al \ə-'kyü-zəl\ *n* (1594) : ACCUSATION

ac·cu·sa·tion \,a-kyə-'zā-shən, -(,)kyü-\ *n* (14c) **1** : the act of accusing : the state or fact of being accused **2** : a charge of wrongdoing

¹ac·cu·sa·tive \ə-'kyü-zə-tiv\ *adj* [ME, fr. MF or L; MF *accusatif*, fr. L *accusativus*, fr. *accusatus*, pp. of *accusare*] (15c) **1** : of, relating to, or being the grammatical case that marks the direct object of a verb or the object of any of several prepositions **2** : ACCUSATORY

²accusative *n* (ca. 1620) : the accusative case of a language : a form in the accusative case

ac·cu·sa·to·ry \ə-'kyü-zə-,tōr-ē, -,tȯr-\ *adj* (14c) : containing or expressing accusation : ACCUSING

ac·cuse \ə-'kyüz\ *vb* **ac·cused; ac·cus·ing** [ME, fr. OF *acuser*, fr. L *accusare* to call to account, fr. *ad-* + *causa* lawsuit] *vt* (14c) **1** : to charge with a fault or offense : BLAME **2** : to charge with an offense judicially or by a public process ~ *vi* : to bring an accusation — **ac·cus·er** \ə-'kyü-zər\ *n* — **ac·cus·ing·ly** \-'kyü-ziŋ-lē\ *adv*

ac·cused *n, pl* **accused** (1593) : one charged with an offense; *esp* : the defendant in a criminal case

ac·cus·tom \ə-'kəs-təm\ *vt* [ME, fr. MF *acostumer*, fr. *a-* (fr. L *ad-*) + *costume* custom] (15c) : to make familiar with something through use or experience — **ac·cus·tom·a·tion** \-,kəs-tə-'mā-shən\ *n*

ac·cus·tomed \ə-'kəs-təmd\ *adj* (15c) **1** : often used or practiced : CUSTOMARY ⟨her ~ cheerfulness⟩ **2** : adapted to existing conditions ⟨eyes ~ to the dark⟩ **3** : being in the habit or custom ⟨~ to making decisions⟩ *syn* see USUAL — **ac·cus·tomed·ness** \-təm(d)-nəs\ *n*

AC/DC \'ā-(,)sē-'dē-(,)sē\ *adj* [fr. the likening of a bisexual person to an electrical appliance which can operate on either alternating or direct current] (ca. 1960) : BISEXUAL 1b

¹ace \'ās\ *n* [ME *as*, fr. MF, fr. L, unit, a copper coin] (14c) **1 a** : a die face marked with one spot **b** : a playing card marked in its center with one pip **c** : a domino end marked with one spot **2** : a very small amount or degree : PARTICLE **3** : a point scored esp. on a service (as in tennis or handball) that an opponent fails to touch **4** : a golf score of one stroke on a hole; *also* : a hole made in one stroke **5** : a combat pilot who has brought down at least five enemy airplanes **6** : one that excels at something — **ace in the hole 1** : an ace dealt face down to a player (as in stud poker) and not exposed until the showdown **2** : an effective and decisive argument or resource held in reserve — **within an ace of** : on the point of : very near to ⟨came *within an ace of* winning⟩

²**ace** vt **aced; ac·ing** (1923) **1 :** to score an ace against (an opponent) **2 :** to make (a hole in golf) in one stroke **3 :** to gain a decisive advantage over — DEFEAT — usu. used with *out* **4 :** to earn a high grade on (as an examination); *specif* : to get an A on

³**ace** adj (1926) : of first or high rank or quality

-**aceae** n pl suffix [NL, fr. L, fem. pl. of -aceus -aceous] : plants of the nature of ⟨Rosaceae⟩ — in names of families of plants

ace·dia \ə-'sē-dē-ə\ n [LL, fr. Gk akēdeia, fr. a- + kēdos care, grief — more at HATE] (1607) : APATHY, BOREDOM

ACE inhibitor \ˌā-(ˌ)sē-'ē-; 'ās-\ n [angiotensin converting enzyme] (1985) : any of a group of antihypertensive drugs (as captopril) that relax arteries and promote renal excretion of salt and water by inhibiting the activity of angiotensin converting enzyme

Acel·da·ma \ə-'sel-də-mə\ n [Gk Akeldama, fr. Aram ḥăqēl dĕmā, lit., field of blood] : the potter's field bought with the money Judas had been paid for betraying Christ

acel·lu·lar \(ˌ)ā-'sel-yə-lər\ adj (1940) **1 :** containing no cells ⟨∼ vaccines⟩ **2 :** not divided into cells : consisting of a single complex cell — used esp. of protozoa and ciliates

acen·tric \(ˌ)ā-'sen-trik\ adj (1937) : lacking a centromere ⟨∼ chromosomes⟩

-**aceous** adj suffix [L -aceus] **1 a :** characterized by : full of ⟨setaceous⟩ **b :** consisting of ⟨diatomaceous⟩ : having the nature or form of ⟨tuffaceous⟩ **2 a :** of or relating to a group of animals typified by (such) a form ⟨cetaceous⟩ or characterized by (such) a feature ⟨crustaceous⟩ **b :** of or relating to a plant family ⟨solanaceous⟩

aceph·a·lous \(ˌ)ā-'se-fə-ləs, ə-'se-\ adj [Gk akephalos, fr. a- + kephalē head — more at CEPHALIC] (ca. 1731) **1 :** lacking a head or having the head reduced **2 :** lacking a governing head or chief

ace·quia \ə-'sā-kē-ə, ä-\ n [Sp, fr. Ar as-sāqiyah the irrigation stream] (1844) Southwest : an irrigation ditch or canal

acerb \ə-'sərb, a-\ adj [F or L; F acerbe, fr. L acerbus; akin to L acer sharp — more at EDGE] (1622) : ACERBIC

ac·er·bate \'a-sər-ˌbāt\ vt -**bat·ed; -bat·ing** (ca. 1731) : IRRITATE, EXASPERATE

acer·bic \ə-'sər-bik, a-\ adj (1865) : acid in temper, mood, or tone — **acer·bi·cal·ly** \-bi-k(ə-)lē\ adv

acer·bi·ty \-bə-tē\ n, pl -**ties** (1572) : the quality of being acerbic

ac·er·o·la \ˌa-sə-'rō-lə\ n [AmerSp, fr. Sp, fruit of a shrub (Crataegus azarolus), fr. Ar az-zuʿrūr] (1945) : any of various West Indian shrubs (genus Malpighia) with mildly acid cherrylike fruits very rich in vitamin C

acet- or **aceto-** comb form [F & L; F acét-, fr. L acet-, fr. acetum vinegar; akin to acēre to be sour, acer sharp — more at EDGE] : acetic acid : acetic ⟨acetyl⟩

ac·e·tab·u·lum \ˌa-sə-'ta-byə-ləm\ n, pl -**lums** or -**la** \-lə\ [L, lit., vinegar cup, fr. acetum vinegar] (1661) **1 :** a ventral sucker of a trematode **2 :** the cup-shaped socket in the hipbone — **ac·e·tab·u·lar** \-lər\ adj

ac·e·tal \'a-sə-ˌtal\ n [G Azetal, fr. acet- acet- + Alkohol alcohol] (1853) : any of various compounds characterized by the grouping C(OR)₂ and obtained esp. by heating aldehydes or ketones with alcohols

ac·et·al·de·hyde \ˌa-sə-'tal-də-ˌhīd\ n [ISV] (1877) : a colorless volatile water-soluble liquid aldehyde C₂H₄O used chiefly in organic synthesis

acet·amide \ə-'se-tə-ˌmīd, ˌa-sə-'ta-ˌmīd\ n [ISV] (1873) : a white crystalline amide C₂H₅NO of acetic acid used esp. as a solvent and in organic synthesis

acet·amin·o·phen \ə-ˌsē-tə-'mi-nə-fən, ˌa-sə-tə-\ n [acet- + amino + phenol] (1958) : a crystalline compound C₈H₉NO₂ that is a hydroxy derivative of acetanilide and is used in chemical synthesis and in medicine to relieve pain and fever

ac·et·an·i·lide \ˌa-sə-'ta-nə-ˌlīd, -ləd\ n [ISV] (ca. 1864) : a white crystalline compound C₈H₉NO that is derived from aniline and acetic acid and is used esp. to relieve pain or fever

ac·e·tate \'a-sə-ˌtāt\ n (1827) **1 :** a salt or ester of acetic acid **2 :** CELLULOSE ACETATE; also : something (as a textile fiber) made from cellulose acetate **3 :** a phonograph recording disk made of an acetate or coated with cellulose acetate

ac·et·azol·amide \ˌa-sə-tə-'zō-lə-ˌmīd, -'zä-, -məd\ n [acet- + azole + amide] (1954) : a diuretic drug C₄H₆N₄O₃S₂ used esp. in the treatment of edema associated with congestive heart failure and of glaucoma

ace·tic acid \ə-ˌsē-tik-\ n [prob. fr. F acétique, fr. L acetum vinegar] (1808) : a colorless pungent liquid acid C₂H₄O₂ that is the chief acid of vinegar and that is used esp. in synthesis (as of plastics)

acetic anhydride n (1876) : a colorless liquid C₄H₆O₃ with a pungent odor used in organic synthesis (as of cellulose acetate and aspirin)

ace·ti·fy \ə-'sē-tə-ˌfī, -'se-\ vt -**fied; -fy·ing** (ca. 1828) : to turn into acetic acid or vinegar — **ace·ti·fi·ca·tion** \ə-ˌse-tə-fə-'kā-shən, -ˌsē-\ n

ace·to·ace·tic acid \ˌa-sə-(ˌ)tō-ə-ˌsē-tik-, ə-ˌsē-tō-\ n [part trans. of G Azetessigsäure, fr. azet- acet- + Essigsäure acetic acid] (ca. 1900) : an unstable acid C₄H₆O₃ that is a ketone body found in abnormal quantities in the blood and urine in some conditions (as diabetes)

ac·e·tone \'a-sə-ˌtōn\ n [G Azeton, fr. L acetum] (ca. 1839) : a volatile fragrant flammable liquid ketone C₃H₆O used chiefly as a solvent and in organic synthesis and found in abnormal quantities in diabetic urine — **ac·e·ton·ic** \ˌa-sə-'tä-nik\ adj

ace·to·ni·trile \ə-ˌsē-tō-'nī-trəl, ˌa-sə-tō-, -ˌtrīl\ n (ca. 1869) : the colorless liquid nitrile CH₃CN of acetic acid used chiefly in organic synthesis and as a solvent

ace·to·phe·net·i·din \ˌa-sə-(ˌ)tō-fə-'ne-tə-dən, ə-ˌsē-tō-\ n [ISV] (1910) : PHENACETIN

ace·tous \'a-sə-təs, ə-'sē-təs\ adj (1778) : relating to or producing vinegar ⟨∼ fermentation⟩; also : SOUR, VINEGARY

ace·tyl \ə-'sē-tᵊl, 'a-sə-; 'a-sə-ˌtēl\ n (ca. 1864) : the radical CH₃CO— of acetic acid — often used in combination

acet·y·late \ə-'se-tᵊl-ˌāt\ vt -**lat·ed; -lat·ing** (ca. 1900) : to introduce the acetyl radical into (a compound) — **acet·y·la·tion** \-ˌse-tᵊl-'ā-shən\ n — **acet·y·la·tive** \-'set-ᵊl-ˌā-tiv\ adj

ace·tyl·cho·line \ə-ˌse-tᵊl-'kō-ˌlēn, -ˌsē-; 'a-sə-ˌtēl-\ n [ISV] (1906) : a neurotransmitter C₇H₁₇NO₃ released at autonomic synapses and neu-

romuscular junctions and formed enzymatically in the tissues from choline

ace·tyl·cho·lin·es·ter·ase \-ˌkō-lə-'nes-tə-ˌrās, -ˌrāz\ n (1947) : an enzyme that occurs esp. in some nerve endings and in the blood and promotes the hydrolysis of acetylcholine

acetyl CoA \-ˌkō-'ā\ n (ca. 1959) : ACETYL COENZYME A

acetyl coenzyme A n (1952) : a compound C₂₅H₃₈N₇O₁₇P₃S formed as an intermediate in metabolism and active as a coenzyme in biological acetylations

acet·y·lene \ə-'se-tᵊl-ən, -tᵊl-ˌēn\ n (1864) : a colorless gaseous hydrocarbon HC≡CH used chiefly in organic synthesis and as a fuel (as in welding and soldering) — **acet·y·le·nic** \ə-ˌse-tᵊl-'e-nik, -'e-nik\ adj

ace·tyl·sal·ic·y·late \ə-ˌse-tᵊl-sə-'li-sə-ˌlāt\ n (ca. 1960) : a salt or ester of acetylsalicylic acid

ace·tyl·sal·i·cyl·ic acid \ə-ˌse-tᵊl-ˌsa-lə-ˌsi-lik-\ n [ISV] (1897) : ASPIRIN 1

ac·ey–deuc·ey also **ac·ey–deu·cy** \ˌā-sē-'dü-sē, -'dyü-\ n (1925) : a variation of backgammon in which a throw of a 1-2 wins extra turns

¹**Achae·an** \ə-'kē-ən\ or **Achai·an** \-'kī-ən, -'kā-ən\ adj (1567) : of, relating to, or characteristic of Achaea; broadly : of or relating to Greece

²**Achaean** or **Achaian** n (1607) : a native or inhabitant of Achaea; broadly : GREEK

Ach·ae·me·ni·an \ˌa-kə-'mē-nē-ən\ adj (1717) : of or relating to the Achaemenids

Achae·me·nid \ə-'kē-mə-nəd\ n, pl -**menids** also -**men·i·dae** \ˌa-kə-'me-nə-ˌdē\ [Gk Achaimenides, fr. Achaimenes, 7th cent. B.C. Pers. king, founder of the dynasty + -ides (patronymic suffix)] (1889) : a member of the ruling house of ancient Persia generally considered historically important from the assumption of power by Cyrus the Great (559 B.C.) to the overthrow of Darius III (330 B.C.)

acha·la·sia \ˌā-kə-'lā-zh(ē-)ə\ n [NL, fr. a- + Gk chalasis slackening + NL -ia] (1914) : failure of a ring of muscle (as the anal sphincter or one of the esophagus) to relax

Acha·tes \ə-'kā-tēz\ n [L] : a faithful companion of Aeneas in Virgil's Aeneid

¹**ache** \'āk\ vi **ached; ach·ing** [ME aken, fr. OE acan] (bef. 12c) **1 a :** to suffer a usu. dull persistent pain **b :** to become distressed or disturbed (as with anxiety or regret) **c :** to feel compassion **2 :** to experience a painful eagerness or yearning

²**ache** n (bef. 12c) **1 :** a usu. dull persistent pain **2 :** a condition marked by aching

achene \ā-'kēn\ n [NL achaenium, fr. a- + Gk chainein to yawn — more at YAWN] (1855) : a small dry indehiscent one-seeded fruit (as of a sunflower) developing from a simple ovary and usu. having a thin pericarp attached to the seed at only one point

Ach·er·on \'a-kə-ˌrän, -rən\ n [Gk Acheron] : a river in Hades

Acheu·le·an or **Acheu·li·an** \ə-'shü-lē-ən\ adj [F acheuléen, fr. St. Acheul, near Amiens, France] (ca. 1909) : of or relating to a Lower Paleolithic culture typified by bifacial tools with round cutting edges

à che·val \ˌä-shə-'väl\ adv [F, lit., on horseback] (1832) **1 :** with a leg on each side : ASTRIDE **2 :** in such a way as to be played or chanced simultaneously on two numbers or events (as in roulette)

achieve \ə-'chēv\ vb **achieved; achiev·ing** [ME acheven, fr. MF achever to finish, fr. a- (fr. L ad-) + chief end, head — more at CHIEF] vt (14c) **1 :** to carry out successfully : ACCOMPLISH ⟨∼ a gradual increase in production⟩ **2 :** to get or attain as the result of exertion : REACH ⟨achieved a high degree of skill⟩ ⟨achieved greatness⟩ ∼ vi : to attain a desired end or aim : become successful **syn** see PERFORM — **achiev·able** \-'chē-və-bəl\ adj — **achiev·er** n

achieved adj (1918) : brought to or marked by a high degree of development or refinement : FINISHED ⟨fully ∼ poems⟩

achieve·ment \ə-'chēv-mənt\ n (15c) **1 :** the act of achieving : ACCOMPLISHMENT **2 a :** a result gained by effort **b :** a great or heroic deed **3 :** the quality and quantity of a student's work **syn** see FEAT

Achil·les \ə-'ki-lēz\ n [L, fr. Gk Achilleus] : the greatest warrior among the Greeks at Troy and slayer of Hector

Achilles' heel n [fr. the story that Achilles was vulnerable only in the heel] (1864) : a vulnerable point

Achilles tendon n (ca. 1879) : the strong tendon joining the muscles in the calf of the leg to the bone of the heel

ach·ing \'ā-kiŋ\ adj (13c) **1 :** that aches ⟨an ∼ back⟩ **2 :** causing or reflecting distress, deep emotion, or longing ⟨∼ country ballads⟩ — **ach·ing·ly** adv

achlor·hy·dria \ˌā-ˌklòr-'hi-drē-ə, -ˌklòr-\ n [NL, fr. a- + ISV chlor- + hydr- + NL -ia] (1898) : absence of hydrochloric acid from the gastric juice — **achlor·hy·dric** \-'hi-drik, -'hī-\ adj

achon·drite \(ˌ)ā-'kän-ˌdrīt\ n (ca. 1904) : a stony meteorite without rounded grains — **achon·drit·ic** \ˌā-ˌkän-'dri-tik\ adj

achon·dro·pla·sia \ˌā-ˌkän-drə-'plā-zh(ē-)ə\ n [NL, fr. a- + chondr- + -plasia] (ca. 1893) : a genetic disorder disturbing normal growth of cartilage, resulting in a form of dwarfism characterized by a usu. normal torso and shortened limbs, and usu. inherited as an autosomal dominant — **achon·dro·plas·tic** \-'plas-tik\ adj

ach·ro·mat \'a-krə-ˌmat\ n (1900) : ACHROMATIC LENS

ach·ro·mat·ic \ˌa-krə-'ma-tik, (ˌ)ā-\ adj (1766) **1 :** refracting light without dispersing it into its constituent colors : giving images practically free from extraneous colors ⟨an ∼ telescope⟩ **2 :** not readily colored by the usual staining agents **3 :** possessing no hue : being or involving black, gray, or white : NEUTRAL ⟨∼ visual sensations⟩ **4 :** being without accidentals or modulation : DIATONIC — **ach·ro·mat·i·cal·ly** \-ti-k(ə-)lē\ adv — **achro·ma·tism** \(ˌ)ā-'krō-mə-ˌti-zəm, a-\ n — **achro·ma·tize** \(ˌ)ā-'krō-mə-ˌtīz, a-\ vt

achromatic lens n (ca. 1864) : a lens made by combining lenses of different glasses having different focal powers so that the light emerging from the lens forms an image practically free from unwanted colors

---

\ə\ abut \ᵊ\ kitten, F table \ər\ further \a\ ash \ā\ ace \ä\ mop, mar \aú\ out \ch\ chin \e\ bet \ē\ easy \g\ go \i\ hit \ī\ ice \j\ job \ŋ\ sing \ō\ go \ò\ law \òi\ boy \th\ thin \t͟h\ the \ü\ loot \ u̇\ foot \y\ yet \zh\ vision \á, k̲, ⁿ, œ, œ̄, ᵫ, ᵫ̄, ᵊ\ see Guide to Pronunciation

achy \'ā-kē\ *adj* **ach·i·er; ach·i·est** (1875) : afflicted with aches — **ach·i·ness** *n*

acic·u·lar \ə-'si-kyə-lər\ *adj* [LL *acicula* (dim. of L *acus* needle) + E *-ar* — more at ACUTE] (1794) : shaped like a needle ⟨∼ leaves⟩ ⟨∼ crystals⟩

¹ac·id \'a-səd\ *adj* [F or L; F *acide*, fr. L *acidus*, fr. *acēre* to be sour — more at ACET-] (1626) **1 a** : sour, sharp, or biting to the taste **b** : sharp, biting, or sour in manner, disposition, or nature ⟨an ∼ individual⟩ **c** : sharply clear, discerning, or pointed ⟨an ∼ wit⟩ **d** : piercingly intense and often jarring ⟨∼ yellow⟩ **2 a** : of, relating to, or being an acid; *also* : having the reactions or characteristics of an acid ⟨∼ soil⟩ ⟨an ∼ solution⟩ **b** *of salts and esters* : derived by partial exchange of replaceable hydrogen ⟨∼ sodium carbonate NaHCO₃⟩ **c** : containing or involving the use of an acid (as in manufacture) **d** : marked by or resulting from an abnormally high concentration of acid ⟨∼ indigestion⟩ **3** : relating to or made by a process (as in making steel) in which the furnace is lined with acidic material and an acidic slag is used **4** : rich in silica ⟨∼ rocks⟩ — **ac·id·ly** *adv* — **ac·id·ness** *n*

²acid *n* (1696) **1** : a sour substance; *specif* : any of various typically water-soluble and sour compounds that in solution are capable of reacting with a base to form a salt, redden litmus, and have a pH less than 7, that are hydrogen-containing molecules or ions able to give up a proton to a base, or that are substances able to accept an unshared pair of electrons from a base **2** : something incisive, biting, or sarcastic ⟨a social satire dripping with ∼⟩ **3** : LSD — **ac·idy** \'a-sə-dē\ *adj*

ac·id-fast \'a-səd-,fast\ *adj* (1903) : not easily decolorized by acids

ac·id-head \-,hed\ *n* (1966) : an individual who uses LSD

acid·ic \ə-'si-dik, a-\ *adj* (1880) **1** : acid-forming **2** : ACID

acid·i·fi·er \ə-'si-də-,fī(-ə)r, a-\ *n* (ca. 1828) : one that acidifies; *esp* : a substance used to increase soil acidity

acid·i·fy \-,fī\ *vt* **-fied; -fy·ing** (1797) **1** : to make acid **2** : to convert into an acid — **acid·i·fi·ca·tion** \-,si-də-fə-'kā-shən\ *n*

acid·i·met·ric \ə-,si-də-'me-trik\ *adj* (1900) : of or relating to the precise determination of the amount of acid present in a solution — **ac·i·dim·e·ter** \,a-sə-'di-mə-tər\ *n* — **ac·i·dim·e·try** \-'di-mə-trē\ *n*

acid·i·ty \ə-'si-də-tē, a-\ *n, pl* **-ties** (1620) **1** : the quality, state, or degree of being acid **2** : the state of being excessively acid

acid·o·phil \ə-'si-də-,fil, a-\ *also* **acid·o·phile** \-,fīl\ *n* (ca. 1900) : a substance, tissue, or organism that stains readily with acid stains — **acidophil** *also* **acidophile** *adj*

ac·i·do·phil·ic \ə-,si-də-'fi-lik\ *adj* (ca. 1900) **1** : staining readily with acid stains : ACIDOPHIL **2** : preferring or thriving in a relatively acid environment

ac·i·doph·i·lus milk \,a-sə-'dä-f(ə-)ləs-\ *n* [NL *Lactobacillus acidophilus*, lit., acidophilic lactobacillus] (1921) : milk fermented by any of several bacteria and used therapeutically to change the intestinal flora

ac·i·do·sis \,a-sə-'dō-səs\ *n* [NL] (1900) : an abnormal condition characterized by reduced alkalinity of the blood and other body tissues — **ac·i·dot·ic** \-'dä-tik\ *adj*

acid phosphatase *n* (1949) : a phosphatase (as the phosphomonoesterase from the prostate gland) optimally active in acid medium

acid precipitation *n* (1979) : precipitation (as rain or snow) having increased acidity caused by environmental factors (as atmospheric pollutants)

acid rain *n* (1858) : acid precipitation in the form of rain

acid rock *n* (1966) : rock music with lyrics and sound relating to or suggestive of drug-induced experiences

acid test *n* (1912) : a severe or crucial test

acid·u·late \ə-'si-jə-,lāt\ *vt* **-lat·ed; -lat·ing** [L *acidulus*] (1732) : to make acid or slightly acid — **acid·u·la·tion** \-,si-jə-'lā-shən\ *n*

acid·u·lent \ə-'si-jə-lənt\ *adj* [F *acidulant*, fr. prp. of *aciduler* to acidulate, fr. L *acidulus*] (1834) : ACIDULOUS

acid·u·lous \ə-'si-jə-ləs\ *adj* [L *acidulus*, fr. *acidus*] (1769) : somewhat acid or harsh in taste or manner

ac·i·nar \'a-sə-nər, -,när\ *adj* (1936) : of, relating to, or comprising an acinus ⟨pancreatic ∼ cells⟩

ac·i·nus \'a-sə-nəs\ *n, pl* **-ni** \-,nī\ [NL, fr. L, berry, berry seed] (ca. 1751) : any of the small sacs terminating the ducts of some exocrine glands and lined with secretory cells — **ac·i·nous** \-nəs\ *adj*

ack–ack \'ak-,ak\ *n* [Brit. signalmen's former telephone pron. of *AA*, abbr. of *antiaircraft*] (1926) : an antiaircraft gun; *also* : antiaircraft fire

ackee *var of* AKEE

ac·knowl·edge \ik-'nä-lij, ak-\ *vt* **-edged; -edg·ing** [*ac-* (as in *accord*) + *knowledge*] (15c) **1** : to recognize the rights, authority, or status of **2** : to disclose knowledge of or agreement with **3 a** : to express gratitude or obligation for **b** : to take notice of **c** : to make known the receipt of **4** : to recognize as genuine or valid ⟨∼ a debt⟩

syn ACKNOWLEDGE, ADMIT, OWN, AVOW, CONFESS mean to disclose against one's will or inclination. ACKNOWLEDGE implies the disclosing of something that has been or might be concealed ⟨*acknowledged* an earlier peccadillo⟩. ADMIT implies reluctance to disclose, grant, or concede and refers usu. to facts rather than their implications ⟨*admitted* the project was over budget⟩. OWN implies acknowledging something in close relation to oneself ⟨must *own* I know little about computers⟩. AVOW implies boldly declaring, often in the face of hostility, what one might be expected to be silent about ⟨*avowed* that he was a revolutionary⟩. CONFESS may apply to an admission of a weakness, failure, omission, or guilt ⟨*confessed* a weakness for sweets⟩.

ac·knowl·edged \-lijd\ *adj* (1598) : generally recognized, accepted, or admitted — **ac·knowl·edged·ly** \-lijd-lē, -li-jəd-\ *adv*

ac·knowl·edg·ment *or* **ac·knowl·edge·ment** \ik-'nä-lij-mənt, ak-\ *n* (1594) **1 a** : the act of acknowledging **b** : recognition or favorable notice of an act or achievement **2** : a thing done or given in recognition of something received **3** : a declaration or avowal of one's act or of a fact to give it legal validity

ac·me \'ak-mē\ *n* [Gk *akmē* point, highest point — more at EDGE] (1620) : the highest point or stage; *also* : one that represents perfection of the thing expressed *syn* see SUMMIT

ac·ne \'ak-nē\ *n* [Gk *aknē* eruption of the face, MS var. of *akmē*, lit., point] (ca. 1828) : a disorder of the skin caused by inflammation of the skin glands and hair follicles; *specif* : a form found chiefly in adolescents and marked by pimples esp. on the face — **ac·ned** \-nēd\ *adj*

acock \ə-'käk\ *adj or adv* (1846) : being in a cocked position

acoe·lo·mate \(,)ā-'sē-lə-,māt\ *n* (ca. 1889) : an invertebrate lacking a coelom; *esp* : one belonging to the group comprising the flatworms and nemerteans and characterized by bilateral symmetry and a digestive cavity that is the only internal cavity — **acoelomate** *adj*

acold \ə-'kōld\ *adj* (14c) *archaic* : COLD, CHILLED ⟨the owl, for all his feathers, was ∼ —John Keats⟩

ac·o·lyte \'a-kə-,līt\ *n* [ME, fr. MF & ML; MF, fr. ML *acoluthus*, fr. MGk *akolouthos*, fr. Gk, adj., following, fr. *a-, ha-* together (akin to Gk *homos* same) + *keleuthos* path] (14c) **1** : one who assists the clergyman in a liturgical service by performing minor duties **2** : one who attends or assists : FOLLOWER

ac·o·nite \'a-kə-,nīt\ *n* [MF or L; fr. L *aconitum*, fr. Gk *akoniton*] (1578) **1** : MONKSHOOD **2** : the dried tuberous root of a common monkshood (*Aconitum napellus*) formerly used as a sedative and anodyne

acorn \'ā-,korn, -,korn\ *n* [ME *akern*, fr. OE *æcern*; akin to OE *æcer* field, MHG *ackeran* acorns collectively, OIr *áirne* sloe, Lith *uoga* berry] (bef. 12c) : the nut of the oak usu. seated in or surrounded by a hard woody cupule of indurated bracts

acorn squash *n* (1937) : an acorn-shaped dark green winter squash with a ridged surface and sweet yellow to orange flesh

acorn worm *n* (ca. 1889) : any of a class (Enteropneusta) of burrowing wormlike marine animals having an acorn-shaped proboscis and classified with the hemichordates

acous·tic \ə-'kü-stik\ *or* **acous·ti·cal** \-sti-kəl\ *adj* [Gk *akoustikos* of hearing, fr. *akouein* to hear — more at HEAR] (1605) **1** : of or relating to the sense or organs of hearing, to sound, or to the science of sounds ⟨∼ apparatus of the ear⟩ ⟨∼ energy⟩: as **a** : deadening or absorbing sound ⟨∼ tile⟩ **b** : operated by or utilizing sound waves **2** : of, relating to, or being a musical instrument whose sound is not electronically modified — **acous·ti·cal·ly** \-k(ə-)lē\ *adv*

acorn squash

ac·ous·ti·cian \,a-,kü-'sti-shən, ə-,kü-\ *n* (1859) : a specialist in acoustics

acous·tics \ə-'kü-stiks\ *n pl* (1683) **1** *sing in constr* : a science that deals with the production, control, transmission, reception, and effects of sound **2** *also* **acoustic** : the qualities that determine the ability of an enclosure (as an auditorium) to reflect sound waves in such a way as to produce distinct hearing

ac·quaint \ə-'kwānt\ *vt* [ME, fr. OF *acointier*, fr. *acointe* familiar, fr. L *accognitus*, pp. of *accognoscere* to recognize, fr. *ad-* + *cognoscere* to know — more at COGNITION] (14c) **1** : to cause to know personally ⟨was ∼ed with the mayor⟩ **2** : to make familiar : cause to know firsthand *syn* see INFORM

ac·quain·tance \ə-'kwān-t³n(t)s\ *n* (14c) **1 a** : the state of being acquainted **b** : personal knowledge : FAMILIARITY **2 a** : the persons with whom one is acquainted ⟨should auld ∼ be forgot —Robert Burns⟩ **b** : a person whom one knows but who is not a particularly close friend — **ac·quain·tance·ship** \-,ship\ *n*

ac·qui·esce \,a-kwē-'es\ *vi* **-esced; -esc·ing** [F *acquiescer*, fr. L *acquiescere*, fr. *ad-* + *quiescere* to be quiet — more at QUIESCENT] (ca. 1620) : to accept, comply, or submit tacitly or passively — often used with *in* and sometimes with *to* *syn* see ASSENT

ac·qui·es·cence \-'es-³n(t)s\ *n* (1612) **1** : the act of acquiescing : the state of being acquiescent **2** : an instance of acquiescing

ac·qui·es·cent \-'e-s³nt\ *adj* [L *acquiescent-, acquiescens*, prp. of *acquiescere*] (1753) : inclined to acquiesce — **ac·qui·es·cent·ly** *adv*

ac·quir·able \ə-'kwīr-ə-bəl\ *adj* (1646) : capable of being acquired

ac·quire \ə-'kwīr\ *vt* **ac·quired; ac·quir·ing** [ME *aqueren*, fr. MF *aquerre*, fr. L *acquirere*, fr. *ad-* + *quaerere* to seek, obtain] (15c) **1** : to get as one's own: **a** : to come into possession or control of often by unspecified means **b** : to come to have as a new or added characteristic, trait, or ability (as by sustained effort or natural selection) ⟨∼ fluency in French⟩ ⟨bacteria that ∼ tolerance to antibiotics⟩ **2** : to locate and hold (a desired object) in a detector ⟨∼ a target by radar⟩

acquired immune deficiency syndrome *n* (1982) : AIDS

acquired immunodeficiency syndrome *n* (1982) : AIDS

acquired taste *n* (1858) : one that is not easily or immediately liked or appreciated

ac·quire·ment \ə-'kwīr-mənt\ *n* (1630) **1** : a skill of mind or body usu. resulting from continued endeavor **2** : the act of acquiring

ac·qui·si·tion \,a-kwə-'zi-shən\ *n* [ME *acquisicioun*, fr. MF or L; MF *acquisition*, fr. L *acquisition-, acquisitio*, fr. *acquirere*] (14c) **1** : the act of acquiring **2** : something acquired or gained — **ac·qui·si·tion·al** \-shnəl, -shə-n³l\ *adj* — **ac·quis·i·tor** \ə-'kwi-zə-tər\ *n*

ac·quis·i·tive \ə-'kwi-zə-tiv\ *adj* (1846) : strongly desirous of acquiring and possessing *syn* see COVETOUS — **ac·quis·i·tive·ly** *adv* — **ac·quis·i·tive·ness** *n*

ac·quit \ə-'kwit\ *vt* **ac·quit·ted; ac·quit·ting** [ME *aquiten*, fr. OF *aquiter*, fr. *a-* (fr. L *ad-*) + *quite* free of — more at QUIT] (13c) **1 a** *archaic* : to pay off (as a claim or debt) **b** *obs* : REPAY, REQUITE **2** : to discharge completely (as from an obligation or accusation) ⟨the court *acquitted* the prisoner⟩ **3** : to conduct (oneself) usu. satisfactorily esp. under stress ⟨the recruits *acquitted* themselves like veterans⟩ *syn* see BEHAVE, EXCULPATE — **ac·quit·ter** *n*

ac·quit·tal \ə-'kwi-t³l\ *n* (15c) : a setting free from the charge of an offense by verdict, sentence, or other legal process

ac·quit·tance \ə-'kwi-t³n(t)s\ *n* (14c) : a document evidencing a discharge from an obligation; *esp* : a receipt in full

acr- *or* **acro-** *comb form* [MF or Gk; MF *acro-*, fr. Gk *akr-, akro-*, fr. *akros* topmost, extreme; akin to Gk *akmē* point — more at EDGE] **1** : beginning : end : tip ⟨acronym⟩ **2 a** : top : peak : summit ⟨acropetal⟩ **b** : height ⟨acrophobia⟩

acre \'ā-kər\ *n* [ME, fr. OE *æcer*; akin to OHG *ackar* field, L *ager*, Gk *agros*, and perh. to L *agere* to drive — more at AGENT] (bef. 12c) **1 a** *archaic* : a field esp. of arable land or pastureland **b** *pl* : LANDS, ESTATE **2** : any of various units of area; *specif* : a unit in the U.S. and England equal to 43,560 square feet (4047 square meters) — see WEIGHT table **3** : a broad expanse or great quantity ⟨∼s of free publicity⟩

acre·age \'ā-k(ə-)rij\ *n* (1859) : area in acres : ACRES

acre–foot \'ā-kər-'fŭt\ *n* (1900) : the volume (as of irrigation water) that would cover one acre to a depth of one foot

acre–inch \'ā-kər-'inch\ *n* (ca. 1909) : one twelfth of an acre-foot

ac·rid \'a-krəd\ *adj* [modif. of L *acr-, acer* sharp — more at EDGE] (1712) **1** : sharp and harsh or unpleasantly pungent in taste or odor : IRRITATING **2** : deeply or violently bitter : ACRIMONIOUS ⟨an ~ denunciation⟩ *syn* see CAUSTIC — **acrid·i·ty** \a-'kri-də-tē, ə-\ *n* — **ac·rid·ly** \'a-krəd-lē\ *adv* — **ac·rid·ness** *n*

ac·ri·dine \'a-krə-,dēn\ *n* (ca. 1877) : a colorless crystalline compound $C_{13}H_9N$ occurring in coal tar and important as the parent compound of dyes and pharmaceuticals

acridine orange *n* (ca. 1909) : a basic orange dye structurally related to acridine and used esp. to stain nucleic acids

ac·ri·fla·vine \,a-krə-'flā-,vēn, -vən\ *n* [*acridine* + *flavine*] (1917) : a yellow dye $C_{14}H_{14}N_3Cl$ used as an antiseptic esp. for wounds

Ac·ri·lan \'a-krə-,lan, -lən\ *trademark* — used for an acrylic fiber

ac·ri·mo·ni·ous \,a-krə-'mō-nē-əs\ *adj* (1775) : caustic, biting, or rancorous esp. in feeling, language, or manner ⟨an ~ dispute⟩ — **ac·ri·mo·ni·ous·ly** *adv* — **ac·ri·mo·ni·ous·ness** *n*

ac·ri·mo·ny \'a-krə-,mō-nē\ *n, pl* **-nies** [MF or L; MF *acrimonie,* fr. L *acrimonia,* fr. *acr-, acer*] (1542) : harsh or biting sharpness esp. of words, manner, or disposition

ac·ri·tarch \'a-kri-,tärk\ *n* [Gk *akritos* uncertain (fr. *a-* + *kritos,* verbal of *krinein* to decide) + *archē* beginning — more at CERTAIN, ARCH-] (1963) : any of a group of fossil one-celled marine planktonic organisms of uncertain and possibly various taxonomic affinities held to represent the earliest known eukaryotes

ac·ro·bat \'a-krə-,bat\ *n* [F & Gk; F *acrobate,* fr. Gk *akrobatēs,* fr. *akros* + *bainein* to go — more at COME] (1825) **1** : one that performs gymnastic feats requiring skillful control of the body **2 a** : one skillful at exercises of intellectual or artistic dexterity **b** : one adept at swiftly changing or adapting a position or viewpoint ⟨a political ~⟩ — **ac·ro·bat·ic** \,a-krə-'ba-tik\ *adj* — **ac·ro·bat·i·cal·ly** \-ti-k(ə-)lē\ *adv*

ac·ro·bat·ics \,a-krə-'ba-tiks\ *n pl but sing or pl in constr* (1882) **1** : the art, performance, or activity of an acrobat **2 a** : a spectacular, showy, or startling performance or demonstration involving great agility or complexity

ac·ro·cen·tric \,a-krō-'sen-trik\ *adj* (1945) : having the centromere situated so that one chromosomal arm is much shorter than the other — **acrocentric** *n*

ac·ro·lect \'a-krə-,lekt\ *n* [*acr-* + *-lect* (as in *dialect*)] (1964) : the language variety of a speech community closest to the standard or prestige form of a language

acro·le·in \ə-'krō-lē-ən\ *n* [ISV *acr-* (fr. L *acr-, acer*) + L *olēre* to smell — more at ODOR] (ca. 1857) : a colorless irritant pungent liquid aldehyde C_3H_4O used chiefly in organic synthesis

ac·ro·meg·a·ly \,a-krō-'me-gə-lē\ *n* [ISV] (1889) : chronic hyperpituitarism marked by progressive enlargement of hands, feet, and face — **ac·ro·me·gal·ic** \-'ga-lik\ *adj or n*

ac·ro·nym \'a-krə-,nim\ *n* [*acr-* + *-onym*] (1943) : a word (as *radar* or *snafu*) formed from the initial letter or letters of each of the successive parts or major parts of a compound term — **ac·ro·nym·ic** \,a-krə-'ni-mik\ *adj* — **ac·ro·nym·i·cal·ly** \-mi-k(ə-)lē\ *adv*

acrop·e·tal \ə-'krä-pə-t'l, a-\ *adj* [*acr-* + *-petal* (as in *centripetal*)] (1875) : proceeding from the base toward the apex or from below upward ⟨~ development of floral buds⟩ — **acrop·e·tal·ly** \-t'l-ē\ *adv*

ac·ro·pho·bia \,a-krə-'fō-bē-ə\ *n* [NL] (ca. 1892) : abnormal dread of being at a great height — **ac·ro·phobe** \'a-krə-,fōb\ *n*

acrop·o·lis \ə-'krä-pə-ləs\ *n* [Gk *akropolis,* fr. *akr-* acr- + *polis* city — more at POLICE] (1662) : the upper fortified part of an ancient Greek city (as Athens); *also* : a usu. fortified height of a city or district elsewhere (as in Central America)

ac·ro·some \'a-krə-,sōm\ *n* [ISV] (1899) : an anterior prolongation of a spermatozoon that releases egg-penetrating enzymes — **ac·ro·so·mal** \,a-krə-'sō-məl\ *adj*

¹across \ə-'krós, *chiefly dial* -'króst\ *adv* [ME *acros,* fr. AF *an crois,* fr. *an* in (fr. L *in*) + *crois* cross, fr. L *crux*] (14c) **1** : in a position reaching from one side to the other : CROSSWISE **2** : to or on the opposite side **3** : so as to be understandable, acceptable, or successful ⟨get an argument ~⟩

²across *prep* (1591) **1 a** : from one side to the opposite side of : OVER, THROUGH ⟨swam ~ the river⟩ **b** : on the opposite side of ⟨lives ~ the street from us⟩ **2** : so as to intersect or pass through at an angle ⟨sawed ~ the grain of the wood⟩ **3** : so as to find or meet ⟨came ~ your football in the hall closet⟩ **4** : THROUGHOUT ⟨obvious interest ~ the nation —Robert Goralski⟩ **b** : so as to include or take into consideration all classes or categories ⟨~ differences, they insist, there can be no rational dialogue —Huston Smith⟩

³across *adj* (1646) : being in a crossed position

across–the–board *adj* (1945) **1** : placed to win if a competitor wins, places, or shows ⟨an ~ racing bet⟩ **2** : embracing or affecting all classes or categories : BLANKET ⟨an ~ price increase⟩

acros·tic \ə-'krós-tik, -'kräs-\ *n* [MF & Gk; MF *acrostiche,* fr. Gk *akrostichis,* fr. *akr-* acr- + *stichos* line; akin to *steichein* to go — more at STAIR] (1530) **1** : a composition usu. in verse in which sets of letters (as the initial or final letters of the lines) taken in order form a word or phrase or a regular sequence of letters of the alphabet **2** : ACRONYM — **acrostic** *also* **acros·ti·cal** \-ti-kəl\ *adj* — **acros·ti·cal·ly** \-ti-k(ə-)lē\ *adv*

ac·ryl·am·ide \,a-kr'l-'a-,mīd, ə-'kri-lə-\ *n* [*acrylic* + *amide*] (1946) : an amide C_3H_5NO that is derived from acrylic acid, that polymerizes readily, and that is used in the manufacture of synthetic textile fibers

ac·ry·late \'a-krə-,lāt\ *n* (1873) : a salt or ester of acrylic acid **2** : ACRYLIC RESIN

¹acryl·ic \ə-'kri-lik\ *adj* [ISV *acrolein* + *-yl* + ¹*-ic*] (1855) **1** : of or relating to acrylic acid or its derivatives ⟨~ polymers⟩ **2** : made or consisting of an acrylic ⟨an ~ window⟩

²acrylic *n* (1942) **1 a** : ACRYLIC RESIN **b** : a paint in which the vehicle is an acrylic resin **c** : a painting done in an acrylic resin **2** : ACRYLIC FIBER

acrylic acid *n* (ca. 1855) : an unsaturated liquid acid $C_3H_4O_2$ that polymerizes readily to form useful products (as constituents for varnishes and lacquers)

acrylic fiber *n* (1951) : a quick-drying synthetic textile fiber made by polymerization of acrylonitrile usu. with other monomers

acrylic resin *n* (1936) : a glassy thermoplastic made by polymerizing acrylic or methacrylic acid or a derivative of either and used for cast and molded parts or as coatings and adhesives

ac·ry·lo·ni·trile \,a-krə-lō-'nī-trəl, -,trēl\ *n* (1893) : a colorless volatile flammable liquid nitrile C_3H_3N used chiefly in organic synthesis and for polymerization

¹act \'akt\ *n* [ME, partly fr. L *actus* doing, act, fr. *agere* to drive, do; partly fr. L *actum* thing done, record, fr. neut. of *actus,* pp. of *agere* — more at AGENT] (14c) **1 a** : the doing of a thing : DEED **b** : something done voluntarily **2** : a state of real existence rather than possibility **3** : the formal product of a legislative body : STATUTE; *also* : a decision or determination of a sovereign, a legislative council, or a court of justice **4** : the process of doing : ACTION ⟨caught in the ~⟩ **5** *often cap* : a formal record of something done or transacted **6** : one of the principal divisions of a theatrical work (as a play or opera) **7 a** : one of successive parts or performances (as in a variety show or circus) **b** : the performer or performers in such an act **c** : a performance or presentation identified with a particular individual or group **d** : the sum of a person's actions or effects that serve to create an impression or set an example ⟨a hard ~ to follow⟩ **8** : a display of affected behavior : PRETENSE

²act *vt* (1594) **1 a** : to represent or perform by action esp. on the stage **b** : FEIGN, SIMULATE **c** : IMPERSONATE **2** *obs* : ACTUATE, ANIMATE **3** : to play the part of as if in a play ⟨~ the man of the world⟩ **4** : to behave in a manner suitable to ⟨~ your age⟩ **~** *vi* **1 a** : to perform on the stage **b** : to behave as if performing on the stage : PRETEND **2** : to take action : MOVE ⟨think before ~ing⟩ ⟨~ed favorably on the recommendation⟩ **3** : to conduct oneself : BEHAVE ⟨~ like a fool⟩ **4** : to perform a specified function : SERVE ⟨trees ~ing as a windbreak⟩ **5** : to produce an effect : WORK ⟨wait for a medicine to ~⟩ **6** *of a play* : to be capable of being performed ⟨the play ~s well⟩ **7** : to give a decision or award ⟨adjourned without ~ing on the bill⟩ — **act·abil·i·ty** \,ak-tə-'bi-lə-tē\ *n* — **act·able** \'ak-tə-bəl\ *adj*

Ac·tae·on \ak-'tē-ən\ *n* [L, fr. Gk *Aktaiōn*] : a hunter turned into a stag and killed by his own hounds for having seen Artemis bathing

ACTH \,ā-(,)sē-(,)tē-'āch\ *n* [*adrenocorticotropic hormone*] (1944) : a protein hormone of the anterior lobe of the pituitary gland that stimulates the adrenal cortex — called also *adrenocorticotropic hormone*

ac·tin \'ak-tən\ *n* [ISV, fr. L *actus*] (1942) : a cellular protein found esp. in microfilaments (as those comprising myofibrils) and active in muscular contraction, cellular movement, and maintenance of cell shape

actin- *or* **actini-** *or* **actino-** *comb form* [NL, ray, fr. Gk *aktin-, aktino-,* fr. *aktin-, aktis;* perh. akin to OE *ūhte* morning twilight, L *noct-, nox* night — more at NIGHT] **1** : having a radiate form ⟨*actinolite*⟩ **2** : actinic radiation (as X rays) ⟨*actinometer*⟩

¹act·ing \'ak-tiŋ\ *n* (1664) : the art or practice of representing a character on a stage or before cameras

²acting *adj* (1797) **1** : holding a temporary rank or position : performing services temporarily ⟨~ president⟩ **2 a** : suitable for stage performance ⟨an ~ play⟩ **b** : prepared with directions for actors ⟨an ~ text of a play⟩

ac·tin·i·an \ak-'ti-nē-ən\ *n* [NL *actinia,* fr. Gk *aktin-, aktis*] (1888) : SEA ANEMONE

ac·tin·ic \ak-'ti-nik\ *adj* (1844) : of, relating to, resulting from, or exhibiting actinism — **ac·tin·i·cal·ly** \-ni-k(ə-)lē\ *adv*

ac·ti·nide \'ak-tə-,nīd\ *n* [ISV] (1945) : any of the members of the series of elements that begins with actinium or thorium and ends with lawrencium — see PERIODIC TABLE table

ac·ti·nism \'ak-tə-,ni-zəm\ *n* (1844) : the property of radiant energy esp. in the visible and ultraviolet spectral regions by which chemical changes are produced

ac·tin·i·um \ak-'ti-nē-əm\ *n* [NL] (1900) : a radioactive trivalent metallic element that resembles lanthanum in chemical properties and that is found esp. in pitchblende — see ELEMENT table

ac·tin·o·lite \ak-'ti-n'l-,īt\ *n* (ca. 1828) : a bright or grayish green amphibole occurring in fibrous, radiate, or columnar forms

ac·ti·nom·e·ter \,ak-tə-'nä-mə-tər\ *n* (1833) : any of various instruments for measuring the intensity of incident radiation; *esp* : one in which the intensity of radiation is measured by the speed of a photochemical reaction — **ac·ti·no·me·tric** \-nō-'me-trik\ *adj* — **ac·ti·nom·e·try** \-'nä-mə-trē\ *n*

ac·ti·no·mor·phic \,ak-tə-(,)ti-nō-'mór-fik, -tə-nō-; ak-,ti-nō-\ *adj* [ISV] (1900) : being radially symmetrical and capable of division by any longitudinal plane into essentially symmetrical halves ⟨an ~ tulip flower⟩ — **ac·ti·no·mor·phy** \'ak-tə-nō-,mór-fē, ak-,ti-nō-\ *n*

ac·ti·no·my·ces \,ak-,ti-nō-'mī-,sēz, -nō-mēz\ *n, pl* **actinomyces** [NL, genus name, fr. *actin-* + Gk *mykēt-, mykēs* fungus; akin to Gk *myxa* mucus — more at MUCUS] (1882) : any of a genus (*Actinomyces*) of filamentous or rod-shaped bacteria that includes usu. commensal and sometimes pathogenic forms inhabiting mucosal surfaces esp. of the oral cavity of warm-blooded vertebrates

ac·ti·no·my·cete \-'mī-,sēt, -mī-'sēt\ *n* [ultim. fr. Gk *aktin-, aktis* + *mykēt-, mykēs*] (1911) : any of an order (Actinomycetales) of filamentous or rod-shaped bacteria (as the actinomyces and streptomyces) — **ac·ti·no·my·ce·tous** \-mī-'sē-təs\ *adj*

ac·ti·no·my·cin \-'mī-s'n\ *n* (1940) : any of various red or yellow-red mostly toxic polypeptide antibiotics isolated from soil bacteria (esp. *Streptomyces antibioticus*); *specif* : one used to inhibit DNA or RNA synthesis

ac·ti·no·my·co·sis \-mī-'kō-səs\ *n* [NL] (1882) : infection with or disease caused by actinomycetes; *esp* : a chronic disease of cattle, swine, and humans characterized by hard granulomatous masses usu. in the mouth and jaw — **ac·ti·no·my·cot·ic** \-'kä-tik\ *adj*

\ə\ abut \'ə\ kitten, F table \ər\ further \a\ ash \ā\ ace \ä\ mop, mar
\aú\ out \ch\ chin \e\ bet \ē\ easy \g\ go \i\ hit \ī\ ice \j\ job
\ŋ\ sing \ō\ go \ó\ law \ói\ boy \th\ thin \t͟h\ the \ü\ loot \ú\ foot
\y\ yet \zh\ vision \à, k̲, ⁿ, œ, œ̄, ue, ūe, ᵞ\ see Guide to Pronunciation

ac·ti·non \'ak-tə-ˌnän\ n [NL, fr. *actinium*] (1926) : a gaseous radioactive isotope of radon that has a half-life of about 4 seconds

ac·tion \'ak-shən\ n (14c) **1** : the initiating of a proceeding in a court of justice by which one demands or enforces one's right; *also* : the proceeding itself **2** : the bringing about of an alteration by force or through a natural agency **3** : the manner or method of performing: **a** : the deportment of an actor or speaker or his expression by means of attitude, voice, and gesture **b** : the style of movement of the feet and legs (as of a horse) **c** : a function of the body or one of its parts **4** : an act of will **5 a** : a thing done : DEED **b** : the accomplishment of a thing usu. over a period of time, in stages, or with the possibility of repetition **c** *pl* : BEHAVIOR, CONDUCT ⟨unscrupulous ∼s⟩ **d** : INITIATIVE, ENTERPRISE ⟨a man of ∼⟩ **6 a** (1) : an engagement between troops or ships (2) : combat in war ⟨gallantry in ∼⟩ **b** (1) : an event or series of events forming a literary composition (2) : the unfolding of the events of a drama or work of fiction : PLOT (3) : the movement of incidents in a plot **c** : the combination of circumstances that constitute the subject matter of a painting or sculpture **7 a** : an operating mechanism **b** : the manner in which a machine or instrument operates **8 a** : the price movement and trading volume of a commodity, security, or market **b** : the process of betting including the offering and acceptance of a bet and determination of a winner **c** : an opportunity for financial gain ⟨a piece of the ∼⟩ **9** : the most vigorous, productive, or exciting activity in a particular field, area, or group ⟨they itch to go where the ∼ is —D. J. Henahan⟩

ac·tion·able \'ak-sh(ə-)nə-bəl\ adj (1591) : subject to or affording ground for an action or suit at law — **ac·tion·ably** \-blē\ adv

ac·tion·less \'ak-shən-ləs\ adj (ca. 1817) : marked by inaction : IMMOBILE

action painting n (1952) : abstract expressionism marked esp. by the use of spontaneous techniques (as dribbling, splattering, or smearing) — **action painter** n

action potential n (1926) : a momentary change in electrical potential (as between the inside of a nerve cell and the extracellular medium) that occurs when a cell or tissue has been activated by a stimulus

ac·ti·vate \'ak-tə-ˌvāt\ vb **-vat·ed; -vat·ing** vt (1626) **1** : to make active or more active: as **a** (1) : to make (as molecules) reactive or more reactive (2) : to convert (as a provitamin) into a biologically active derivative **b** : to make (a substance) radioactive **c** : to treat (as carbon or alumina) so as to improve adsorptive properties **d** (1) : to set up or formally institute (as a military unit) with the necessary personnel and equipment (2) : to put (an individual or unit) on active duty ∼ vi : to become active — **ac·ti·va·tion** \ˌak-tə-'vā-shən\ n — **ac·ti·va·tor** \'ak-tə-ˌvā-tər\ n

activated carbon n (1921) : a highly adsorbent powdered or granular carbon made usu. by carbonization and chemical activation and used chiefly for purifying by adsorption — called also *activated charcoal*

activation analysis n (1949) : NEUTRON ACTIVATION ANALYSIS

activation energy n (1940) : the minimum amount of energy required to convert a normal stable molecule into a reactive molecule

ac·tive \'ak-tiv\ adj [ME, fr. MF or L; MF *actif*, fr. L *activus*, fr. *actus*, pp. of *agere* to drive, do — more at AGENT] (14c) **1** : characterized by action rather than by contemplation or speculation **2** : producing or involving action or movement **3 a** *of a verb form or voice* : asserting that the person or thing represented by the grammatical subject performs the action represented by the verb ⟨*hits* in "he hits the ball" is ∼⟩ **b** : expressing action as distinct from mere existence or state **4** : quick in physical movement : LIVELY **5** : marked by vigorous activity : BUSY ⟨the stock market was ∼⟩ **6** : requiring vigorous action or exertion ⟨∼ sports⟩ **7** : having practical operation or results : EFFECTIVE ⟨an ∼ law⟩ **8 a** : disposed to action : ENERGETIC ⟨took an ∼ interest⟩ **b** : engaged in an action or activity ⟨an ∼ club member⟩ **c** *of a volcano* : currently erupting or likely to erupt — compare DORMANT 2a, EXTINCT 1b **d** : characterized by emission of large amounts of electromagnetic energy ⟨an ∼ galactic nucleus⟩ **9** : engaged in full-time service esp. in the armed forces ⟨∼ duty⟩ **10** : marked by present operation, transaction, movement, or use ⟨∼ account⟩ **11 a** : capable of acting or reacting : reacting readily ⟨∼ nitrogen⟩ **b** : tending to progress or to cause degeneration ⟨∼ tuberculosis⟩ **c** *of an electronic circuit element* : capable of controlling voltages or currents **d** (1) : requiring the expenditure of energy ⟨∼ calcium ion uptake⟩ (2) : functioning by the emission of radiant energy ⟨radar is an ∼ sensor⟩ **12** : still eligible to win the pot in poker **13** : moving down the line : visiting in the set — used of couples in contredanses or square dances — **active·ly** adv — **ac·tive·ness** n

active immunity n (ca. 1903) : usu. long-lasting immunity that is acquired through production of antibodies within the organism in response to the presence of antigens — compare PASSIVE IMMUNITY

active transport n (1963) : movement of a chemical substance by the expenditure of energy through a gradient (as across a cell membrane) in concentration or electrical potential and opposite to the direction of normal diffusion

ac·tiv·ism \'ak-ti-ˌvi-zəm\ n (1915) : a doctrine or practice that emphasizes direct vigorous action esp. in support of or opposition to one side of a controversial issue — **ac·tiv·ist** \-vist\ n or adj — **ac·tiv·is·tic** \ˌak-ti-'vis-tik\ adj

ac·tiv·i·ty \ak-'ti-və-tē\ n, pl **-ties** (1530) **1** : the quality or state of being active **2** : vigorous or energetic action : LIVELINESS **3** : natural or normal function: as **a** : a process (as digestion) that an organism carries on or participates in by virtue of being alive **b** : a similar process actually or potentially involving mental function; *specif* : an educational procedure designed to stimulate learning by firsthand experience **4** : an active force **5 a** : a pursuit in which a person is active **b** : a form of organized, supervised, often extracurricular recreation **6** : an organizational unit for performing a specific function; *also* : its function or duties

act of God (ca. 1859) : an extraordinary interruption by a natural cause (as a flood or earthquake) of the usual course of events that experience, prescience, or care cannot reasonably foresee or prevent

ac·to·my·o·sin \ˌak-tə-'mī-ə-sən\ n [ISV *actin* + -o- + *myosin*] (1942) : a viscous contractile complex of actin and myosin concerned together with ATP in muscular contraction

ac·tor \'ak-tər *also* -ˌtȯr\ n (15c) **1** : one that acts : DOER **2 a** : one who represents a character in a dramatic production **b** : a theatrical

performer **c** : one that behaves as if acting a part **3** : one that takes part in any affair — **ac·tor·ish** \-tə-rish\ adj

act out vt (1611) **1 a** : to represent in action ⟨children *act out* what they read⟩ **b** : to translate into action ⟨unwilling to *act out* their beliefs⟩ **2** : to express (as an impulse or a fantasy) directly in overt behavior without modification to comply with social norms

ac·tress \'ak-trəs\ n (1676) : a woman who is an actor — **ac·tressy** \-trə-sē\ adj

Acts \'akts\ n pl but sing in constr : a book in the New Testament narrating the beginnings of the Christian Church — called also *Acts of the Apostles*; see BIBLE table

ac·tu·al \'ak-ch(ə-w)əl, -sh(ə-w)əl\ adj [ME *actuel*, fr. MF, fr. LL *actualis*, fr. L *actus* act] (14c) **1** obs : ACTIVE **2 a** : existing in act and not merely potentially **b** : existing in fact or reality ⟨∼ and imagined conditions⟩ **c** : not false or apparent ⟨∼ costs⟩ **3** : existing or occurring at the time : CURRENT ⟨caught in the ∼ commission of a crime⟩

actual cash value n (ca. 1946) : money equal to the cost of replacing lost, stolen, or damaged property after depreciation

ac·tu·al·i·ty \ˌak-chə-'wa-lə-tē, ˌak-shə-\ n, pl **-ties** (1652) **1** : the quality or state of being actual **2** : something that is actual : FACT, REALITY ⟨possible risks which have been seized upon as *actualities* —T. S. Eliot⟩

ac·tu·al·ize \'ak-ch(ə-w)ə-ˌlīz, -sh(ə-w)ə-ˌlīz\ vb **-ized; -iz·ing** vt (1701) : to make actual : REALIZE ∼ vi : to become actual — **ac·tu·al·iza·tion** \ˌak-ch(ə-w)ə-lə-'zā-shən, -sh(ə-w)ə-lə-\ n

ac·tu·al·ly \'ak-ch(ə-w)ə-lē, -sh(ə-w)ə-lē; 'aksh-lē, 'aks-\ adv (15c) **1** : in act or in fact : REALLY ⟨nominally but not ∼ independent —Karl Loewenstein⟩ ⟨don't know how old they ∼ are⟩ ⟨∼, they just arrived⟩ **2** : in point of fact : in truth — used to suggest something unexpected ⟨I have ∼ been invited⟩ ⟨he could ∼ read the Greek⟩

ac·tu·ar·i·al \ˌak-chə-'wer-ē-əl, -shə-\ adj (1869) **1** : of or relating to actuaries **2** : relating to statistical calculation esp. of life expectancy — **ac·tu·ar·i·al·ly** \-ē-ə-lē\ adv

ac·tu·ary \'ak-chə-ˌwer-ē, -shə-\ n, pl **-ar·ies** [L *actuarius* shorthand writer, alter. of *actarius*, fr. *actum* record — more at ACT] (1553) **1** obs : CLERK, REGISTRAR **2** : one who calculates insurance and annuity premiums, reserves, and dividends

ac·tu·ate \'ak-chə-ˌwāt, -shə-\ vt **-at·ed; -at·ing** [ML *actuatus*, pp. of *actuare* to execute, fr. L *actus* act] (1645) **1** : to put into mechanical action or motion **2** : to move to action *syn* see MOVE — **ac·tu·a·tion** \ˌak-chə-'wā-shən, -shə-\ n

ac·tu·a·tor \'ak-chə-ˌwā-tər, -shə-\ n (ca. 1864) : one that actuates; *specif* : a mechanical device for moving or controlling something

act up vi (1903) **1** : to act in a way different from that which is normal or expected: as **a** : to behave in an unruly, recalcitrant, or capricious manner **b** : SHOW OFF **c** : to function improperly ⟨this typewriter is *acting up* again⟩ **2** : to become active or acute after being quiescent ⟨her rheumatism started to *act up*⟩

acu·ity \ə-'kyü-ə-tē, a-\ n, pl **-ities** [MF *acuité*, fr. LL *acuitat-, acuitas*, fr. L *acuere*] (1543) : keenness of perception : SHARPNESS

acu·le·ate \ə-'kyü-lē-ət\ adj [L *aculeatus* having stings, fr. *aculeus* sting, fr. *acus*] (1875) : relating to or being hymenopterans (as bees, ants, and many wasps) of a division (Aculeata) typically having the ovipositor modified into a sting

acu·men \ə-'kyü-mən, 'a-kyə-mən\ n [L *acumin-, acumen*, lit., point, fr. *acuere*] (ca. 1580) : keenness and depth of perception, discernment, or discrimination esp. in practical matters : SHREWDNESS *syn* see DISCERNMENT

acu·mi·nate \ə-'kyü-mə-nət\ adj (1646) : tapering to a slender point

acu·pres·sure \'a-kyə-ˌpre-shər, 'a-kə-\ n (1958) : SHIATSU

acu·punc·ture \'a-kyə-ˌpən(k)-chər\ n [L *acus* + E *puncture*] (1684) : an orig. Chinese practice of puncturing the body (as with needles) at specific points to cure disease or relieve pain (as in surgery) — **acu·punc·tur·ist** \-ˌpən(k)-chə-rist\ n

acute \ə-'kyüt\ adj **acut·er; acut·est** [L *acutus*, pp. of *acuere* to sharpen, fr. *acus* needle; akin to L *acer* sharp — more at EDGE] (14c) **1 a** (1) : characterized by sharpness or severity ⟨∼ pain⟩ (2) : having a sudden onset, sharp rise, and short course ⟨∼ disease⟩ **b** : lasting a short time ⟨∼ experiments⟩ **2** : ending in a sharp point: as **a** : being or forming an angle measuring less than 90 degrees ⟨∼ angle⟩ **b** : composed of acute angles ⟨∼ triangle⟩ **3 a** *of an accent mark* : having the form **b** : marked with an acute accent **c** : of the variety indicated by an acute accent **4 a** : marked by keen discernment or intellectual perception esp. of subtle distinctions : PENETRATING ⟨an ∼ thinker⟩ **b** : responsive to slight impressions or stimuli ⟨∼ hearing⟩ **5** : felt, perceived, or experienced intensely ⟨∼ distress⟩ **6** : seriously demanding urgent attention — **acute·ly** adv — **acute·ness** n

syn ACUTE, CRITICAL, CRUCIAL mean of uncertain outcome. ACUTE stresses intensification of conditions leading to a culmination or breaking point ⟨an *acute* housing shortage⟩. CRITICAL adds to ACUTE implications of imminent change, of attendant suspense, and of decisiveness in the outcome ⟨the war has entered a *critical* phase⟩. CRUCIAL suggests a dividing of the ways and often a test or trial involving the determination of a future course or direction ⟨a *crucial* vote⟩. *syn* see in addition SHARP

acy·clic \(ˌ)ā-'sī-klik, -'si-\ adj (1878) : not cyclic: as **a** : not disposed in whorls or cycles **b** : having an open-chain structure : ALIPHATIC ⟨an ∼ compound⟩

acy·clo·vir \(ˌ)ā-'sī-klō-ˌvir\ n [²a- + *cycl-* + *virus*] (1979) : a cyclic nucleoside $C_8H_{11}N_5O_3$ used esp. to treat the symptoms of the genital form of herpes simplex

ac·yl \'a-səl\ n, often attrib [ISV, fr. *acid*] (1899) : a radical RCO- derived usu. from an organic acid by removal of the hydroxyl from all acid groups — often used in combination

ac·yl·ate \'a-sə-ˌlāt\ vt **-at·ed; -at·ing** (1907) : to introduce an acyl group into — **ac·yl·a·tion** \ˌa-sə-'lā-shən\ n

¹ad \'ad\ n, often attrib (1841) **1** : ADVERTISEMENT 2 **2** : ADVERTISING

²ad n (1947) : ADVANTAGE 4

ad- or **ac-** or **af-** or **ag-** or **al-** or **ap-** or **as-** or **at-** prefix [ME, fr. MF, OF & L; MF, fr. OF, fr. L, fr. *ad* — more at AT] **1** : to : toward — usu. *ac-* before *c, k,* or *q* ⟨acculturation⟩ and *af-* before *f* ⟨affluent⟩ and *ag-* before *g* ⟨aggradation⟩ and *al-* before *l* ⟨alliteration⟩ and *ap-* before *p* ⟨apportion⟩ and *as-* before *s* ⟨assuasive⟩ and *at-* before *t* ⟨attune⟩ and *ad-* before other sounds but sometimes *ad-* even before one of the listed consonants ⟨adsorb⟩ **2** : near : adjacent to — in this sense always in the form ad- ⟨adrenal⟩

¹-ad \,ad, əd\ *adv suffix* [L *ad*] : in the direction of : toward ⟨cephal*ad*⟩

²-ad *n suffix* [prob. fr. NL *-ad-*, *-as*, fr. Gk. suffix denoting descent from or connection with] : member of a botanical group ⟨bromel*iad*⟩

Ada \'ä-də\ *trademark* — used for a structured computer programming language

ad·age \'a-dij\ *n* [MF, fr. L *adagium*, fr. ad- + *-agium* (akin to *aio* I say); akin to Gk *ē* he said] (1548) : a saying often in metaphorical form that embodies a common observation

¹ada·gio \ə-'dä-j(ē-,)ō, ä-,-zh(ē-,)ō\ *adv or adj* [It, fr. ad to + *agio* ease] (1724) : at a slow tempo — used chiefly as a direction in music

²adagio *n, pl* **-gios** (1754) **1** : a musical composition or movement in adagio tempo **2** : a ballet duet by a man and woman or a mixed trio displaying difficult feats of balance, lifting, or spinning

¹Ad·am \'a-dəm\ *n* [ME, fr. LL, fr. Gk, fr. Heb *Ādhām*] **1** : the first man and father by Eve of Cain and Abel **2** : the unregenerate nature of man — used esp. in the phrase *the old Adam* — **Adam·ic** \ə-'da-mik\ *or* **Adam·i·cal** \-mi-kəl\ *adj*

²Adam *adj* [Robert *Adam* & James *Adam*] (1872) : of, relating to, or being an 18th century decorative style (as of furniture) characterized by straight lines, surface decoration, and conventional designs (as festooned garlands and medallions)

ad·a·mance \'a-də-mən(t)s\ *n* (1954) : ADAMANCY

ad·a·man·cy \-mən(t)-sē\ *n* [²*adamant* + *-cy*] (1937) : OBSTINACY

adam–and–eve \,a-də-mən-'(d)ēv\ *n* (1807) : PUTTYROOT

¹ad·a·mant \'a-də-mont, -,mant\ *n* [ME, fr. MF, fr. L *adamant-*, *adamas* hardest metal, diamond, fr. Gk] (14c) **1** : a stone (as a diamond) formerly believed to be of impenetrable hardness **2** : an unbreakable or extremely hard substance

²adamant *adj* (1923) : unshakable or immovable esp. in opposition : UNYIELDING **syn** see INFLEXIBLE — **ad·a·mant·ly** *adv*

ad·a·man·tine \,a-də-'man-,tēn, -,tīn, -'man-t²n\ *adj* [ME, fr. L *adamantinus*, fr. Gk *adamantinos*, fr. *adamant-*, *adamas*] (13c) **1** : made of or having the quality of adamant **2** : rigidly firm : UNYIELDING **3** : resembling the diamond in hardness or luster

Adam's apple *n* (ca. 1775) : the projection in the front of the neck formed by the largest cartilage of the larynx

Adam's needle *n* (ca. 1760) : an often cultivated yucca (*Yucca filamentosa*) of coastal pine barrens of the eastern U.S. with a basal rosette of sharp-tipped leaves having loose threads along the margins

adapt \ə-'dapt, a-\ *vb* [F or L; F *adapter*, fr. L *adaptare*, fr. ad- + *aptare* to fit, fr. *aptus* apt, fit] *vt* (15c) : to make fit (as for a specific or new use or situation) often by modification ~ *vi* : to become adapted — **adapt·ed·ness** *n*

syn ADAPT, ADJUST, ACCOMMODATE, CONFORM, RECONCILE mean to bring one thing into correspondence with another. ADAPT implies a modification according to changing circumstances ⟨*adapted* themselves to the warmer climate⟩. ADJUST suggests bringing into a close and exact correspondence or harmony such as exists between parts of a mechanism ⟨*adjusted* the budget to allow for inflation⟩. ACCOMMODATE may suggest yielding or compromising to effect a correspondence ⟨*accommodated* his political beliefs in order to win⟩. CONFORM applies to bringing into accordance with a pattern, example, or principle ⟨refused to *conform* to society's idea of morality⟩. RECONCILE implies the demonstration of the underlying compatibility of things that seem to be incompatible ⟨tried to *reconcile* what they said with what I knew⟩.

adapt·able \ə-'dap-tə-bəl, a-\ *adj* (1800) : capable of being adapted : SUITABLE **syn** see PLASTIC — **adapt·abil·i·ty** \-,dap-tə-'bi-lə-tē\ *n*

ad·ap·ta·tion \,a-,dap-'tā-shən, -dəp-\ *n* (1610) **1** : the act or process of adapting : the state of being adapted **2** : adjustment to environmental conditions: as **a** : adjustment of a sense organ to the intensity or quality of stimulation **b** : modification of an organism or its parts that makes it more fit for existence under the conditions of its environment **3** : something that is adapted; *specif* : a composition rewritten into a new form — **ad·ap·ta·tion·al** \-shnəl, -shə-n²l\ *adj* — **ad·ap·ta·tion·al·ly** *adv*

adapt·er *also* **adap·tor** \ə-'dap-tər, a-\ *n* (1801) **1** : one that adapts **2 a** : a device for connecting two parts (as of different diameters) of an apparatus **b** : an attachment for adapting apparatus for uses not orig. intended

adap·tion \ə-'dap-shən, a-\ *n* (1704) : ADAPTATION

adap·tive \ə-'dap-tiv, a-\ *adj* (1824) : showing or having a capacity for or tendency toward adaptation — **adap·tive·ly** *adv* — **adap·tive·ness** *n* — **adap·tiv·i·ty** \,a-,dap-'ti-və-tē\ *n*

adaptive radiation *n* (1902) : evolutionary diversification of a generalized ancestral form with production of a number of adaptively specialized forms

Adar \ä-'där, 'ä-\ *n* [ME, fr. Heb *Ădhār*] (14c) : the 6th month of the civil year or the 12th month of the ecclesiastical year in the Jewish calendar — see MONTH table

Adar She·ni \ä-,där-shä-'nē\ *n* [Heb *Ădhār Shēnī* second Adar] (ca. 1901) : VEADAR

ad·ax·i·al \(,)a-'dak-sē-əl\ *adj* (ca. 1900) : situated on the same side as or facing the axis (as of an organ) ⟨the ~ or upper surface of a leaf⟩

add \'ad\ *vb* [ME, fr. L *addere*, fr. ad- + *-dere* to put — more at DO] *vt* (14c) **1** : to join or unite so as to bring about an increase or improvement ⟨~s 60 acres to his land⟩ ⟨wine ~s a creative touch to cooking⟩ **2** : to say further : APPEND **3** : to combine (numbers) into an equivalent simple quantity or number **4** : to include as a member of a group ⟨don't forget to ~ me in⟩ ~ *vi* **1 a** : to perform addition **b** : to come together or unite by addition **2 a** : to serve as an addition ⟨the movie will ~ to his fame⟩ **b** : to make an addition ⟨~ed to her savings⟩ — **add·able** *or* **add·ible** \'a-də-bəl\ *adj*

ad·dax \'a-,daks\ *n, pl* **ad·dax·es** [L] (1693) : a large light-colored Saharan antelope (*Addax nasomaculatus*) that has long spiralling horns

ad·dend \'a-,dend, ə-'dend\ *n* [short for *addendum*] (1674) : a number to be added to another

ad·den·dum \ə-'den-dəm\ *n, pl* **-den·da** \-'den-də\ [L, neut. of *addendus*, gerundive of *addere*] (1684) **1** : a thing added : ADDITION **2** : a supplement to a book — often used in pl. but sing. in constr.

¹ad·der \'a-dər\ *n* [ME, alter. (by false division of *a naddre*) of *naddre*, fr. OE *nǣdre*; akin to OHG *nātara* adder, L *natrix* water snake] (14c)

1 : the common venomous viper (*Vipera berus*) of Europe; *broadly* : a terrestrial viper (family Viperidae) **2** : any of several No. American snakes (as the hognose snakes) that are harmless but are popularly believed to be venomous

adder 1

²add·er \'a-dər\ *n* (1580) : one that adds; *esp* : a device (as in a computer) that performs addition

ad·der's–tongue \'a-dərz-,təŋ\ *n* (1578) **1** : any of a genus (*Ophioglossum*, family Ophioglossaceae) of small ferns having a spore-bearing stalk resembling a serpent's tongue **2** : DOGTOOTH VIOLET

¹ad·dict \ə-'dikt\ *vt* [L *addictus*, pp. of *addicere* to favor, fr. ad- + *dicere* to say — more at DICTION] (1534) **1** : to devote or surrender (oneself) to something habitually or obsessively ⟨~ed to gambling⟩ **2** : to cause addiction to a substance in

²ad·dict \'a-,(,)dikt\ *n* (1909) **1** : one who is addicted to a substance **2** : DEVOTEE ⟨a detective novel ~⟩

ad·dic·tion \ə-'dik-shən, a-\ *n* (1599) **1** : the quality or state of being addicted ⟨~ to reading⟩ **2** : compulsive need for and use of a habit-forming substance (as heroin, nicotine, or alcohol) characterized by tolerance and by well-defined physiological symptoms upon withdrawal; *broadly* : persistent compulsive use of a substance known by the user to be harmful

ad·dic·tive \-'dik-tiv\ *adj* (1939) : causing or characterized by addiction

Ad·di·son's disease \'a-də-sənz-\ *n* [Thomas *Addison* †1860 Eng. physician] (ca. 1856) : a destructive disease marked by deficient adrenocortical secretion and characterized by extreme weakness, loss of weight, low blood pressure, gastrointestinal disturbances, and brownish pigmentation of the skin and mucous membranes

ad·di·tion \ə-'di-shən, a-\ *n* [ME, fr. MF, fr. L *addition-*, *additio*, fr. *aădere*] (14c) **1** : a part added (as to a building or residential section) **2** : the result of adding : INCREASE **3** : the act or process of adding; *esp* : the operation of combining numbers so as to obtain an equivalent simple quantity **4** : direct chemical combination of substances into a single product — **in addition** : ²BESIDES, ALSO — **in addition to** : combined or associated with : ¹BESIDES 2

ad·di·tion·al \-'dish-nəl, -'di-shə-n²l\ *adj* (1646) : existing by way of addition : ADDED

ad·di·tion·al·ly \-'dish-nə-lē, -'di-shən-lē, 'di-shə-n²l-ē\ *adv* (ca. 1665) : in or by way of addition : FURTHERMORE

¹ad·di·tive \'a-də-tiv\ *adj* (1699) **1** : of, relating to, or characterized by addition **2** : produced by addition **3** : characterized by, being, or producing effects (as drug responses or gene products) that when the causative factors act together are the sum of their individual effects — **ad·di·tive·ly** *adv* — **ad·di·tiv·i·ty** \,a-də-'ti-və-tē\ *n*

²additive *n* (1945) : a substance added to another in relatively small amounts to effect a desired change in properties ⟨food ~s⟩

additive identity *n* (1960) : an identity element (as 0 in the group of whole numbers under the operation of addition) that in a given mathematical system leaves unchanged any element to which it is added

additive inverse *n* (1958) : a number that when added to a given number gives zero ⟨the *additive inverse* of 4 is −4⟩ — compare OPPOSITE 3

¹ad·dle \'a-d²l\ *adj* [ME *adel* filth, fr. OE *adela*; akin to MLG *adele* liquid manure] (1592) **1** *of an egg* : ROTTEN **2** : CONFUSED

²addle *vb* **ad·dled; ad·dling** \'a-d²l-iŋ, 'a-d²l-iŋ\ *vt* (ca. 1712) **1** : to throw into confusion : CONFOUND ~ *vi* **1** : to become rotten : SPOIL **2** : to become confused

ad·dle·pat·ed \'a-d²l-,pā-təd\ *adj* (1630) **1** : being mixed up : CONFUSED **2** : ECCENTRIC

¹add–on *n* (1946) : something added on: as **a** : a sum or amount added on **b** : something (as an accessory or added feature) that enhances the thing it is added to

²add–on \'a-,dän, -,dȯn\ *adj* (1955) **1** : being or able to be added on **2** : able to be added to ⟨~ certificates of deposit⟩

¹ad·dress \ə-'dres, a- *also* 'a-,dres\ *vb* [ME *adressen*, fr. MF *adresser*, fr. a- (fr. L ad-) + *dresser* to arrange — more at DRESS] (14c) **1** *archaic* **a** : DIRECT, AIM **b** : to direct to go : SEND **2 a** : to direct the efforts or attention of (oneself) ⟨will ~ himself to the problem⟩ **b** : to deal with : TREAT ⟨intrigued by the chance to ~ important issues —I. L. Horowitz⟩ **3** *archaic* : to make ready; *esp* : DRESS **4** : to communicate directly ⟨~es his thanks to his host⟩ **b** : to speak or write directly to; *esp* : to deliver a formal speech to **5 a** : to mark directions for delivery on ⟨~ a letter⟩ **b** : to consign to the care of another (as an agent or factor) **6** : to greet by a prescribed form **7** : to adjust the club preparatory to hitting (a golf ball) **8** : to identify (as a peripheral or memory location) by an address or a name for information transfer ~ *vi, obs* : to direct one's speech or attentions — **ad·dress·er** *n*

²ad·dress \ə-'dres, *for 5 & 7 & 4 also* 'a-,dres\ *n* (1539) **1** : dutiful and courteous attention esp. in courtship — usu. used in pl. **2 a** : readiness and capability for dealing (as with a person or problem) skillfully and smoothly : ADROITNESS **b** *obs* : a making ready; *also* : a state of preparedness **3 a** : manner of bearing oneself ⟨a man of rude ~⟩ **b** : manner of speaking or singing : DELIVERY **4** : a formal communication; *esp* : a prepared speech delivered to a special audience or on a special occasion **5 a** : a place where a person or organization may be communicated with **b** : directions for delivery on the outside of an object (as a letter or package) **c** : the designation of place of delivery placed between the heading and salutation on a business letter **6** : a preparatory position of the player and club in golf **7** : a location (as in the memory of a computer) where particular information is stored; *also* : the digits that identify such a location **syn** see TACT

ad·dress·able \ə-'dre-sə-bəl\ *adj* (1953) **1** : able to be addressed : di-

\ə\ abut \²\ kitten, F table \ər\ further \a\ ash \ā\ ace \ä\ mop, mar \aȯ\ out \ch\ chin \e\ bet \ē\ easy \g\ go \i\ hit \ī\ ice \j\ job \ŋ\ sing \ō\ go \ȯ\ law \ȯi\ boy \th\ thin \th\ the \ü\ loot \ u̇\ foot \y\ yet \zh\ vision \à, k̲, ⁿ, œ, œ̄, ue, ūe, ᵇ\ *see* Guide to Pronunciation

rectly accessible ⟨∼ registers in a computer⟩ **2** : of or relating to a subscription television system that uses decoders addressable by the system operator — **ad·dress·abil·i·ty** \ə-ˌdre-sə-'bi-lə-tē\ n
ad·dress·ee \ˌa-ˌdre-'sē, ə-ˌdre-'sē\ n (1810) : one to whom something is addressed
ad·duce \ə-'düs also -'dyüs\ vt **ad·duced; ad·duc·ing** [L adducere, lit., to lead to, fr. ad- + ducere to lead — more at TOW] (15c) : to offer as example, reason, or proof in discussion or analysis — **ad·duc·er** n
¹**ad·duct** \ə-'dəkt, a-\ vt [L adductus, pp. of adducere] (ca. 1839) : to draw (as a limb) toward or past the median axis of the body; also : to bring together (similar parts) ⟨∼ the fingers⟩ — **ad·duc·tive** \-'dək-tiv\ adj
²**ad·duct** \'a-ˌdəkt\ n [G Addukt, fr. L adductus] (1941) : a chemical addition product
ad·duc·tion \ə-'dək-shən, a-\ n (14c) **1** : the action of adducting : the state of being adducted **2** : the act or action of adducing
ad·duc·tor \-'dək-tər\ n [NL, fr. L, one that draws to, fr. adductus] (1615) **1** : a muscle that draws a part toward the median line of the body or toward the axis of an extremity **2** : a muscle that closes the valves of a bivalve mollusk
add up vi (1850) **1 a** : to come to the expected total ⟨the bill doesn't add up⟩ **b** : to form an intelligible pattern : make sense ⟨her story just doesn't add up⟩ **2 a** : AMOUNT 1b — used with to ⟨the play adds up to a lot of laughs⟩ **b** : to amount to a lot ⟨just a little each time, but it all adds up⟩ ∼ vt : to form an opinion of ⟨added him up at a glance⟩
-ade n suffix [ME, fr. MF, fr. OProv -ada, fr. LL -ata, fr. L, fem. of -atus -ate] **1** : act : action ⟨blockade⟩ **2** : product; esp : sweet drink ⟨limeade⟩
Adé·lie penguin \ə-'dā-lē-\ n [Adélie Coast, Antarctica] (1907) : a small antarctic penguin (Pygoscelis adeliae) — called also Adélie
-adelphous adj comb form [prob. fr. NL -adelphus, fr. Gk adelphos brother, fr. ha-, a- together (akin to homos same) + delphys womb — more at SAME, DOLPHIN] : having (such or so many) stamen fascicles ⟨monadelphous⟩
aden- or **adeno-** comb form [NL, fr. Gk, fr. aden, adēn; akin to L inguen groin] : gland ⟨adenine⟩ : adenoid ⟨adenovirus⟩
ad·e·nine \'a-dᵊn-ˌēn\ n [ISV, fr. its presence in glandular tissue] (1885) : a purine base C₅H₅N₅ that codes hereditary information in the genetic code in DNA and RNA — compare CYTOSINE, GUANINE, THYMINE, URACIL

Adélie penguin

ad·e·ni·tis \ˌa-dᵊn-'ī-təs\ n [NL] (ca. 1848) : inflammation of a gland; esp : LYMPHADENITIS
ad·e·no·car·ci·no·ma \ˌa-dᵊn-(ˌ)ō-ˌkär-sᵊn-'ō-mə\ n [NL] (ca. 1889) : a malignant tumor originating in glandular epithelium — **ad·e·no·car·ci·no·ma·tous** \-mə-təs\ adj
ad·e·no·hy·poph·y·sis \ˌa-dᵊn-ˌō-hī-'pä-fə-səs\ n, pl **-y·ses** \-fə-ˌsēz\ [NL] (1935) : the anterior glandular lobe of the pituitary gland — **ad·e·no·hy·poph·y·se·al** \-(ˌ)hi-ˌpä-fə-'sē-əl\ or **ad·e·no·hy·po·phys·i·al** \-ˌhī-pə-'fi-zē-əl\ adj
¹**ad·e·noid** \'a-dᵊn-ˌōid, 'ad-ˌnōid\ n [Gk adenoeidēs glandular, fr. adēn] (ca. 1890) : an enlarged mass of lymphoid tissue at the back of the pharynx characteristically obstructing breathing — usu. used in pl.
²**adenoid** adj (ca. 1947) **1** : of or relating to the adenoids **2** : relating to, affected with, or associated with abnormally enlarged adenoids ⟨a severe ∼ condition⟩ ⟨∼ facies⟩
ad·e·noi·dal \ˌa-dᵊn-'ōi-dᵊl\ adj (1919) : exhibiting the characteristics (as snoring, mouth breathing, and voice nasality) of one affected with abnormally enlarged adenoids : ADENOID ⟨an ∼ tenor⟩ — not usu. used technically
ad·e·no·ma \ˌa-dᵊn-'ō-mə\ n, pl **-mas** also **-ma·ta** \-mə-tə\ [NL adenomat-, adenoma] (1870) : a benign tumor of a glandular structure or of glandular origin — **ad·e·no·ma·tous** \-mə-təs\ adj
aden·o·sine \ə-'de-nə-ˌsēn, -sən\ n [ISV, blend of adenine and ribose] (ca. 1909) : a nucleoside C₁₀H₁₃N₅O₄ that is a constituent of RNA yielding adenine and ribose on hydrolysis
adenosine diphosphate n (1938) : ADP
adenosine mo·no·phos·phate \-ˌmä-nə-'fäs-ˌfāt, -ˌmō-\ n (1950) : AMP
adenosine 3′,5′–monophosphate \-ˌthrē-ˌfiv-\ n (1970) : CYCLIC AMP
adenosine tri·phos·pha·tase \-trī-'fäs-fə-ˌtās, -ˌtāz\ n (1943) : ATPASE
adenosine tri·phos·phate \-tri-'fäs-ˌfāt\ n (1938) : ATP
ad·e·no·vi·rus \ˌa-dᵊn-ō-'vī-rəs\ n (1956) : any of a group of DNA-containing viruses orig. identified in human adenoid tissue, causing respiratory diseases (as catarrh), and including some capable of inducing malignant tumors in experimental animals — **ad·e·no·vi·ral** \-rəl\ adj
ad·e·nyl·ate cy·clase \ə-ˌde-nᵊl-ət-'sī-ˌklās, -ˌāt-, -ˌklāz; ˌa-dᵊn-ˌi-lāt-, -ə-ˌlāt-\ n (1968) : an enzyme that catalyzes the formation of cyclic AMP from ATP
ad·e·nyl cyclase \'a-dᵊn-ˌil-\ n [adenine + -yl] (1968) : ADENYLATE CYCLASE
ad·e·nyl·ic acid \'a-dᵊn-ˌi-lik-\ n (1894) : AMP
¹**ad·ept** \'a-ˌdept, ə-'dept, a-\ n [NL adeptus alchemist who has attained the knowledge of how to change base metals into gold, fr. L, pp. of adipisci to attain, fr. ad- + apisci to reach — more at APT] (1709) : a highly skilled or well-trained individual : EXPERT ⟨an ∼ at chess⟩
²**adept** \ə-'dept also 'a-ˌdept\ adj (ca. 1691) : thoroughly proficient : EXPERT **syn** see PROFICIENT — **adept·ly** \ə-'dep-(t)lē, a-\ adv — **adept·ness** \-'dep(t)-nəs\ n
ad·e·qua·cy \'a-di-kwə-sē\ n, pl **-cies** (1808) : the quality or state of being adequate
ad·e·quate \-kwət\ adj [L adaequatus, pp. of adaequare to make equal, fr. ad- + aequare to equal — more at EQUABLE] (ca. 1617) **1** : sufficient for a specific requirement ⟨∼ taxation of goods⟩; also : barely sufficient or satisfactory ⟨her first performance was merely ∼⟩ **2** : lawfully and reasonably sufficient **syn** see SUFFICIENT — **ad·e·quate·ly** adv — **ad·e·quate·ness** n
ad eun·dem \ˌa-dē-'ən-dəm\ or **ad eundem gra·dum** \-'grä-dəm\ adv or adj [NL ad eundem gradum] (1711) : to, in, or of the same rank —

used esp. of the honorary granting of academic standing or a degree by a university to one whose actual work was done elsewhere
¹**à deux** \(ˌ)ä-'də(r), (ˌ)ä-dœ\ adj [F] (1886) : involving two people esp. in private ⟨a cozy evening à deux⟩
²**à deux** adv (1927) : privately or intimately with only two present ⟨dined à deux⟩
ad·here \ad-'hir, əd-\ vb **ad·hered; ad·her·ing** [MF or L; MF adhérer, fr. L adhaerēre, fr. ad- + haerēre to stick] vi **1** : to give support or maintain loyalty **2** obs : ACCORD **3** : to hold fast or stick by or as if by gluing, suction, grasping, or fusing **4** : to bind oneself to observance ∼ vt : to cause to stick fast **syn** see STICK
ad·her·ence \-'hir-ən(t)s\ n (1531) **1** : the act, action, or quality of adhering **2** : steady or faithful attachment : FIDELITY
¹**ad·her·ent** \ad-'hir-ənt, əd-\ adj [ME, fr. MF or L; MF adhérent, fr. L adhaerent-, adhaerens, prp. of adhaerēre] (15c) **1** : able or tending to adhere **2** : connected or associated with esp. by contract **3** : ADNATE — **ad·her·ent·ly** adv
²**adherent** n (15c) : one that adheres: as **a** : a follower of a leader, party, or profession **b** : a believer in or advocate esp. of a particular idea or church **syn** see FOLLOWER
ad·he·sion \ad-'hē-zhən, əd-\ n [F or L; F adhésion, fr. L adhaesion-, adhaesio, fr. adhaerēre] (1624) **1** : steady or firm attachment : ADHERENCE **2** : the action or state of adhering **3** : the abnormal union of separate tissue surfaces by new fibrous tissue resulting from an inflammatory process; also : the newly formed uniting tissue **4** : agreement to join ⟨∼ of all nations to a copyright convention⟩ **5** : the molecular attraction exerted between the surfaces of bodies in contact — **ad·he·sion·al** \-'hēzh-nəl, -'hē-zhə-nᵊl\ adj
¹**ad·he·sive** \-'hē-siv, -ziv\ adj (1670) **1** : tending to remain in association or memory **2** : tending to adhere or cause adherence **3** : prepared for adhering — **ad·he·sive·ly** adv — **ad·he·sive·ness** n
²**adhesive** n (1912) **1 a** : an adhesive substance (as glue or cement) **2** : a postage stamp with a gummed back
adhesive binding n (1955) : PERFECT BINDING — **ad·he·sive–bound** \-ˌbaúnd\ adj
adhesive tape n (1928) : tape coated on one side with an adhesive mixture; esp : one used for covering wounds
¹**ad hoc** \'ad-'häk, -'hōk, 'äd-'hōk\ adv [L, for this] (1659) : for the particular end or case at hand without consideration of wider application
²**ad hoc** adj (1879) **1 a** : concerned with a particular end or purpose ⟨an ad hoc investigating committee⟩ **b** : formed or used for specific or immediate problems or needs ⟨ad hoc solutions⟩ **2** : fashioned from whatever is immediately available : IMPROVISED ⟨large ad hoc parades and demonstrations —Nat Hentoff⟩
¹**ad ho·mi·nem** \(')ad-'hä-mə-ˌnem, -nəm\ adj [NL, lit., to the person] (1598) **1** : appealing to feelings or prejudices rather than intellect **2** : marked by an attack on an opponent's character rather than by an answer to the contentions made
²**ad hominem** adv (1962) : in an ad hominem manner ⟨was arguing ad hominem⟩
adi·a·bat·ic \ˌa-dē-ə-'ba-tik, ˌā-ˌdī-ə-\ adj [Gk adiabatos impassable, fr. a- + diabatos passable, fr. diabainein to go across, fr. dia- + bainein to go — more at COME] (1870) : occurring without loss or gain of heat ⟨∼ expansion of a body of air⟩ — **adi·a·bat·i·cal·ly** \-ti-k(ə-)lē\ adv
adieu \ə-'dü, a-, -'dyü\ n, pl **adieus** or **adieux** \-'düz, -'dyüz\ [ME, fr. MF, fr. a (fr. L ad) + Dieu God, fr. L Deus — more at DEITY] (14c) : FAREWELL — often used interjectionally
ad in·fi·ni·tum \ˌad-ˌin-fə-'nī-təm also ˌäd-\ adv or adj [L] (1610) : without end or limit
¹**ad in·ter·im** \'ad-'in-tə-rəm, -ˌrim also 'äd-\ adv [L] (1787) : for the intervening time : TEMPORARILY
²**ad interim** adj (1818) : made or serving ad interim
adi·os \ˌä-dē-'ōs, ˌa-\ interj [Sp adiós, fr. a (fr. L ad) + Dios God, fr. L Deus] (1837) — used to express farewell
adip- or **adipo-** comb form [L adip-, adeps, prob. fr. Gk aleipha fat, oil, fr. aleiphein to rub with oil — more at ALIPHATIC] : fat ⟨adipocyte⟩
adip·ic acid \ə-'di-pik-\ n [ISV] (1877) : a white crystalline dicarboxylic acid C₆H₁₀O₄ formed by oxidation of various fats and also made synthetically for use esp. in the manufacture of nylon
ad·i·po·cyte \'a-di-pō-ˌsīt\ n (1959) : FAT CELL
ad·i·pose \'a-də-ˌpōs\ adj [NL adiposus, fr. L adip-, adeps] (1743) : of or relating to animal fat; broadly : FAT — **ad·i·pos·i·ty** \ˌa-də-'pä-sə-tē\ n
adipose tissue n (1854) : connective tissue in which fat is stored and which has the cells distended by droplets of fat
ad·it \'a-dət\ n [L aditus approach, fr. adire to go to, fr. ad- + ire to go — more at ISSUE] (1602) : a nearly horizontal passage from the surface in a mine
ad·ja·cen·cy \ə-'jā-sᵊn(t)-sē\ n, pl **-cies** (1646) **1** : something that is adjacent **2** : the quality or state of being adjacent : CONTIGUITY
ad·ja·cent \ə-'jā-sᵊnt\ adj [ME, fr. MF or L; MF, fr. L adjacent-, adjacens, prp. of adjacēre to lie near, fr. ad- + jacēre to lie; akin to L jacere to throw — more at JET] (15c) **1 a** : not distant : NEARBY ⟨the city and ∼ suburbs⟩ **b** : having a common endpoint or border ⟨∼ lots⟩ ⟨∼ sides of a triangle⟩ **c** : immediately preceding or following **2** of two angles : having the vertex and one side in common — **ad·ja·cent·ly** adv
syn ADJACENT, ADJOINING, CONTIGUOUS, JUXTAPOSED mean being in close proximity. ADJACENT may or may not imply contact but always implies absence of anything of the same kind in between ⟨a house with an adjacent garage⟩. ADJOINING definitely implies meeting and touching at some point or line ⟨had adjoining rooms at the hotel⟩. CONTIGUOUS implies having contact on all or most of one side ⟨offices in all 48 contiguous states⟩. JUXTAPOSED means placed side by side so as to permit comparison and contrast ⟨a skyscraper juxtaposed to a church⟩.
ad·jec·ti·val \ˌa-jik-'tī-vəl\ adj (1797) **1** : ADJECTIVE **2** : characterized by the use of adjectives — **ad·jec·ti·val·ly** \-və-lē\ adv
¹**ad·jec·tive** \'a-jik-tiv also 'a-jik-ˌtīv\ adj [ME, fr. MF or LL; MF adjectif, fr. LL adjectivus, fr. L adjectus, pp. of adjicere to throw to, fr. ad- + jacere to throw — more at JET] (14c) **1** : of, relating to, or functioning as an adjective ⟨an ∼ clause⟩ **2** : not standing by itself : DEPENDENT

3 : requiring or employing a mordant ⟨~ dyes⟩ **4** : PROCEDURAL ⟨~ law⟩ — **ad·jec·tive·ly** *adv*

²**adjective** *n* (14c) : a word belonging to one of the major form classes in any of numerous languages and typically serving as a modifier of a noun to denote a quality of the thing named, to indicate its quantity or extent, or to specify a thing as distinct from something else

ad·join \ə-'jȯin, a-\ *vb* [ME, fr. MF *adjoindre*, fr. L *adjungere*, fr. *ad-* + *jungere* to join — more at YOKE] *vt* (14c) **1** : to add or attach by joining **2** : to lie next to or in contact with ~ *vi* : to be close to or in contact with one another

ad·join·ing *adj* (15c) : touching or bounding at a point or line **syn** see ADJACENT

ad·joint \'a-jȯint\ *n* [F, fr. pp. of *adjoindre* to adjoin] (1907) : the transpose of a matrix in which each element is replaced by its cofactor

ad·journ \ə-'jərn\ *vb* [ME *ajournen*, fr. MF *ajourner*, fr. *a-* (fr. L *ad-*) + *jour* day — more at JOURNEY] *vt* (15c) **1** : to suspend indefinitely or until a later stated time ~ *vi* **1** : to suspend a session indefinitely or to another time or place **2** : to move to another place

ad·journ·ment \-mənt\ *n* (1607) **1** : the act of adjourning **2** : the state or interval of being adjourned

ad·judge \ə-'jəj\ *vt* **ad·judged; ad·judg·ing** [ME *ajugen*, fr. MF *ajugier*, fr. L *adjudicare*, fr. *ad-* + *judicare* to judge — more at JUDGE] (14c) **1 a** : to decide or rule upon as a judge : ADJUDICATE **b** : to pronounce judicially : RULE **2** *archaic* : SENTENCE, CONDEMN **3** : to hold or pronounce to be : DEEM ⟨~ the book a success⟩ **4** : to award or grant judicially in a case of controversy

ad·ju·di·cate \ə-'jü-di-ˌkāt\ *vb* **-cat·ed; -cat·ing** *vt* (1775) : to settle judicially ~ *vi* : to act as judge — **ad·ju·di·ca·tive** \-ˌkā-tiv, -kə-\ *adj* — **ad·ju·di·ca·tor** \-ˌkā-tər\ *n*

ad·ju·di·ca·tion \ə-ˌjü-di-'kā-shən\ *n* [F or LL; F, fr. LL *adjudicatio*, fr. L *adjudicare*] (1691) **1** : the act or process of adjudicating **2 a** : a judicial decision or sentence **b** : a decree in bankruptcy — **ad·ju·di·ca·to·ry** \-'jü-di-kə-ˌtȯr-ē, -ˌtȯr-\ *adj*

¹**ad·junct** \'a-ˌjəŋ(k)t\ *n* [L *adjunctum*, fr. neut. of *adjunctus*, pp. of *adjungere*] (1588) **1** : something joined or added to another thing but not essentially a part of it **2 a** : a word or word group that qualifies or completes the meaning of another word or other words and is not itself a main structural element in its sentence **b** : an adverb or adverbial (as *heartily* in "Most children eat heartily" or *at noon* in "We will leave at noon") attached to the verb of a clause to express a relation of time, place, frequency, degree, or manner — compare DISJUNCT **2 3** : an associate or assistant of another — **ad·junc·tive** \ə-'jəŋ(k)-tiv, a-\ *adj*

²**adjunct** *adj* (1595) **1** : added or joined as an accompanying object or circumstance **2** : attached in a subordinate or temporary capacity to a staff ⟨an ~ psychiatrist⟩ — **ad·junct·ly** \'a-ˌjəŋ(k)-tlē, -ˌjəŋ-klē\ *adv*

ad·junc·tion \a-'jəŋ(k)-shən\ *n* (1618) : the act or process of adjoining

ad·ju·ra·tion \ˌa-jə-'rā-shən\ *n* (1611) **1** : a solemn oath **2** : an earnest urging or advising — **ad·jur·a·to·ry** \ə-'jur-ə-ˌtȯr-ē, -ˌtȯr-\ *adj*

ad·jure \ə-'jur\ *vt* **ad·jured; ad·jur·ing** [ME, fr. MF & L; MF *ajurer*, fr. L *adjurare*, fr. *ad-* + *jurare* to swear — more at JURY] (14c) **1** : to command solemnly under or as if under oath or penalty of a curse **2** : to urge or advise earnestly **syn** see BEG

ad·just \ə-'jəst\ *vb* [ME *ajusten*, fr. MF *ajuster* to gauge, adjust, fr. *a-* (fr. L *ad-*) + *juste* right, exact — more at JUST] *vt* (14c) **1 a** : to bring to a more satisfactory state: (1) : SETTLE, RESOLVE (2) : RECTIFY **b** : to make correspondent or conformable : ADAPT **c** : to bring the parts of to a true or more effective relative position ⟨~ a carburetor⟩ **2** : to reduce to a system : REGULATE **3** : to determine the amount to be paid under an insurance policy in settlement of a loss) ~ *vi* **1** : to adapt or conform oneself (as to new conditions) **2** : to achieve mental and behavioral balance between one's own needs and the demands of others **syn** see ADAPT — **ad·just·abil·i·ty** \-ˌjəs-tə-'bi-lə-tē\ *n* — **ad·just·able** \-'jəs-tə-bəl\ *adj* — **ad·jus·tive** \-'jəs-tiv\ *adj*

adjustable rate mortgage *n* (1981) : a mortgage having an interest rate which is usu. initially lower than that of a mortgage with a fixed rate but is adjusted periodically according to the cost of funds to the lender

ad·just·ed *adj* (ca. 1674) **1** : accommodated to suit a particular set of circumstances or requirements **2** : having achieved an often specified and usu. harmonious relationship with the environment or with other individuals ⟨a well-*adjusted* schoolchild⟩

ad·just·er *also* **ad·jus·tor** \ə-'jəs-tər\ *n* (1673) : one that adjusts; *esp* : an insurance agent who investigates personal or property damage and makes estimates for effecting settlements

ad·just·ment \ə-'jəs(t)-mənt\ *n* (1644) **1** : the act or process of adjusting **2** : a settlement of a claim or debt in a case in which the amount involved is uncertain or full payment is not made **3** : the state of being adjusted **4** : a means (as a mechanism) by which things are adjusted one to another **5** : a correction or modification to reflect actual conditions — **ad·just·men·tal** \ə-ˌjəs(t)-'men-tᵊl, ˌa-jəs(t)-\ *adj*

ad·ju·tan·cy \'a-jə-tən(t)-sē\ *n* (1775) : the office or rank of an adjutant

ad·ju·tant \'a-jə-tənt\ *n* [L *adjutant-, adjutans*, prp. of *adjutare* to help — more at AID] (1539) **1** : a staff officer in the army, air force, or marine corps who assists the commanding officer and is responsible esp. for correspondence **2** : one who helps : ASSISTANT

adjutant general *n, pl* **adjutants general** (1645) **1** : the chief administrative officer of an army who is responsible esp. for the administration and preservation of personnel records **2** : the chief administrative officer of a major military unit (as a division or corps)

¹**ad·ju·vant** \'a-jə-vənt\ *adj* [F or L; F, fr. L *adjuvant-, adjuvans*, prp. of *adjuvare* to aid — more at AID] (1574) **1** : serving to aid or contribute : AUXILIARY **2** : assisting in the prevention, amelioration, or cure of disease ⟨~ chemotherapy following surgery⟩

²**adjuvant** *n* (1609) : one that helps or facilitates: as **a** : an ingredient (as in a prescription or a solution) that modifies the action of the principal ingredient **b** : something (as a drug or method) that enhances the effectiveness of medical treatment **c** : a substance enhancing the immune response to an antigen

Ad·le·ri·an \ad-'lir-ē-ən, ad-\ *adj* [Alfred *Adler*] (1924) : of, relating to, or being a theory and technique of psychotherapy emphasizing the importance of feelings of inferiority, a will to power, and overcompensation in neurotic processes

¹**ad–lib** \'ad-'lib\ *vb* **ad–libbed; ad–lib·bing** [*ad lib*] *vt* (1919) : to deliver spontaneously ~ *vi* : to improvise esp. lines or a speech — **ad–lib** *n*

²**ad–lib** *adj* (1935) : spoken, composed, or performed without preparation

ad lib *adv* [NL *ad libitum*] (ca. 1811) **1** : in accordance with one's wishes **2** : without restraint or limit

¹**ad li·bi·tum** \(ˌ)ad-'li-bə-təm\ *adv* [NL, in accordance with desire] (1610) : AD LIB ⟨rats fed *ad libitum*⟩

²**ad libitum** *adj* (ca. 1801) : omissible according to a performer's wishes — used as a direction in music; compare OBBLIGATO

ad·man \'ad-ˌman\ *n* (1909) : a person who writes, solicits, or places advertisements

ad·mass \'ad-ˌmas\ *n, often attrib* [*advertising* + *mass*] (1955) *chiefly Brit* : mass-media advertising; *also* : the society influenced by it

ad·mea·sure \ad-'me-zhər, -'mā-\ *vt* **-sured; -sur·ing** [ME *amesuren*, fr. MF *amesurer*, fr. *a-* (fr. L *ad-*) + *mesurer* to measure] (1641) : to determine the proper share of : APPORTION

ad·mea·sure·ment \-'me-zhər-mənt, -'mā-\ *n* (1523) **1** : determination and apportionment of shares **2** : determination or comparison of dimensions **3** : DIMENSIONS, SIZE

Ad·me·tus \ad-'mē-təs\ *n* [L, fr. Gk *Admētos*] : a king of Pherae who is saved by Apollo from his fated death when his wife Alcestis offers to die in his place

ad·min·is·ter \ad-'mi-nə-stər\ *vb* **-is·tered; -is·ter·ing** \-st(ə-)riŋ\ [ME *administren*, fr. MF *administrer*, fr. L *administrare*, fr. *ad-* + *ministrare* to serve, fr. *minister* servant — more at MINISTER] *vt* (14c) **1** : to manage or supervise the execution, use, or conduct of ⟨~ a trust fund⟩ **2 a** : to mete out : DISPENSE ⟨~ punishment⟩ **b** : to give ritually ⟨~ the last rites⟩ **c** : to give remedially ⟨~ a dose of medicine⟩ ~ *vi* **1** : to perform the office of administrator **2** : to furnish a benefit : MINISTER ⟨~ to an ailing friend⟩ **3** : to manage affairs — **ad·min·is·tra·ble** \-strə-bəl\ *adj* — **ad·min·is·trant** \-strənt\ *n*

ad·min·is·trate \-ˌstrāt\ *vb* **-trat·ed; -trat·ing** [L *administratus*, pp. of *administrare*] (ca. 1617) : ADMINISTER

ad·min·is·tra·tion \ad-ˌmi-nə-'strā-shən, (ˌ)ad-\ *n* (14c) **1** : performance of executive duties : MANAGEMENT **2** : the act or process of administering **3** : the execution of public affairs as distinguished from policy-making **4 a** : a body of persons who administer **b** *often cap* : a group constituting the political executive in a presidential government **c** : a governmental agency or board **5** : the term of office of an administrative officer or body

ad·min·is·tra·tive \ad-'mi-nə-ˌstrā-tiv, -strə-\ *adj* (ca. 1731) : of or relating to administration or an administration : EXECUTIVE — **ad·min·is·tra·tive·ly** *adv*

administrative county *n* (1949) : a British local administrative unit often not coincident with an older county

administrative law *n* (1896) : law dealing with the establishment, duties, and powers of and available remedies against authorized agencies in the executive branch of the government

ad·min·is·tra·tor \ad-'mi-nə-ˌstrā-tər, -ˌstrā-ˌtȯr\ *n* (15c) **1** : a person legally vested with the right of administration of an estate **2 a** : one that administers esp. business, school, or governmental affairs **b** : a priest appointed to administer a diocese or parish temporarily

ad·min·is·tra·trix \-ˌmi-nə-'strā-triks\ *n, pl* **-tra·tri·ces** \-'strā-trə-ˌsēz\ [NL] (ca. 1623) : a woman administrator esp. of an estate

ad·mi·ra·ble \'ad-m(ə-)rə-bəl\ *adj* (15c) **1** : deserving the highest esteem : EXCELLENT **2** *obs* : exciting wonder : SURPRISING — **ad·mi·ra·bil·i·ty** \ˌad-m(ə-)rə-'bi-lə-tē\ *n* — **ad·mi·ra·ble·ness** \'ad-m(ə-)rə-bəl-nəs\ *n* — **ad·mi·ra·bly** \-blē\ *adv*

ad·mi·ral \'ad-m(ə-)rəl\ *n* [ME, fr. MF *amiral* admiral & ML *admiralis* emir, *admirallus* admiral, fr. Ar *amir-al-* commander of the (as in *amir-al-bahr* commander of the sea)] (15c) **1** *archaic* : the commander in chief of a navy **2 a** : FLAG OFFICER **b** : a commissioned officer in the navy or coast guard who ranks above a vice admiral and whose insignia is four stars — compare GENERAL **3** *archaic* : FLAGSHIP **4** : any of several brightly colored butterflies (family Nymphalidae)

admiral of the fleet (1660) : the highest-ranking officer of the British navy

ad·mi·ral·ty \'ad-m(ə-)rəl-tē\ *n* (15c) **1** *cap* : the executive department or officers formerly having general authority over British naval affairs **2** : the court having jurisdiction over questions of maritime law; *also* : the system of law administered by admiralty courts

ad·mi·ra·tion \ˌad-mə-'rā-shən\ *n* (15c) **1** *archaic* : WONDER **2** : an object of esteem **3** : delighted or astonished approbation

ad·mire \ad-'mīr\ *vb* **ad·mired; ad·mir·ing** [MF *admirer*, fr. L *admirari*, fr. *ad-* + *mirari* to wonder, fr. *mirus* astonishing] (1579) **1** *archaic* : to marvel at **2** : to regard with admiration ~ *vi, dial* : to like very much ⟨I would ~ to know why not —A. H. Lewis⟩ **syn** see REGARD — **ad·mir·er** *n* — **ad·mir·ing·ly** \-'mīr-iŋ-lē\ *adv*

ad·mis·si·ble \ad-'mi-sə-bəl, ad-\ *adj* [F, fr. ML *admissibilis*, fr. L *admissus*, pp. of *admittere*] (ca. 1611) **1** : capable of being allowed or conceded : PERMISSIBLE ⟨evidence legally ~ in court⟩ **2** : capable or worthy of being admitted ⟨~ to the university⟩ — **ad·mis·si·bil·i·ty** \-ˌmi-sə-'bi-lə-tē\ *n*

ad·mis·sion \ad-'mi-shən, ad-\ *n* (15c) **1 a** : the act or process of admitting **b** : the state or privilege of being admitted **c** : a fee paid at or for admission **2 a** : the granting of an argument or position not fully proved **b** : acknowledgment that a fact or statement is true **syn** see ADMITTANCE — **ad·mis·sive** \-'mi-siv\ *adj*

ad·mit \ad-'mit, ad-\ *vb* **ad·mit·ted; ad·mit·ting** [ME *admitten*, fr. L *admittere*, fr. *ad-* + *mittere* to send] *vt* (15c) **1** : to allow scope for : PERMIT ⟨~s no possibility of misunderstanding⟩ **b** : to concede as true or valid ⟨*admitted* making a mistake⟩ **2** : to allow entry (as to a place, fellowship, or privilege) ⟨an open window had *admitted* rain⟩ ⟨*admitted* to the club⟩ ~ *vi* **1** : to give entrance or access **2 a** : AL-

\ə\ abut \ᵊ\ kitten, F table \ər\ further \a\ ash \ā\ ace \ä\ mop, mar \au̇\ out \ch\ chin \e\ bet \ē\ easy \g\ go \i\ hit \ī\ ice \j\ job \ŋ\ sing \ō\ go \ȯ\ law \ȯi\ boy \th\ thin \t̲h̲\ the \ü\ loot \u̇\ foot \y\ yet \zh\ vision \a, k, ⁿ, œ, œ̄, ᵫ, ᵫ̄, ᵞ\ see Guide to Pronunciation

LOW, PERMIT 〈~s of two interpretations〉 **b** : to make acknowledgment — used with *to* **syn** see ACKNOWLEDGE

ad·mit·tance \əd-'mi-t³n(t)s, ad-\ *n* (1536) **1** : permission to enter (as a place or office) : ENTRANCE **2** : the reciprocal of the impedance of a circuit

 syn ADMITTANCE, ADMISSION mean permitted entrance. ADMITTANCE is usu. applied to mere physical entrance to a locality or a building 〈members must show their cards upon *admittance* to the club〉. ADMISSION applies to entrance or formal acceptance (as into a club) that carries with it rights, privileges, standing, or membership 〈two recommendations are required for *admission* to the club〉.

ad·mit·ted·ly \əd-'mi-təd-lē, ad-\ *adv* (1804) **1** : as has been or must be admitted 〈an ~ inadequate treatment〉 **2** : it must be admitted 〈~, we took a chance〉

ad·mix \ad-'miks\ *vt* [back-formation fr. obs. *admixt* mingled (with), fr. ME, fr. L *admixtus*] (1533) : to mix in

ad·mix·ture \ad-'miks-chər\ *n* [L *admixtus*, pp. of *admiscēre* to mix with, fr. *ad-* + *miscēre* to mix — more at MIX] (1605) **1 a** : the action of mixing **b** : the fact of being mixed **2 a** : something added by mixing **b** : a product of mixing : MIXTURE

ad·mon·ish \ad-'mä-nish\ *vt* [ME *admonesten*, fr. MF *admonester*, fr. (assumed) VL *admonestare*, alter. of L *admonēre* to warn, fr. *ad-* + *monēre* to warn — more at MIND] (14c) **1** : to indicate duties or obligations to **b** : to express warning or disapproval to esp. in a gentle, earnest, or solicitous manner **2** : to give friendly earnest advice or encouragement to **syn** see REPROVE — **ad·mon·ish·er** *n* — **ad·mon·ish·ing·ly** \-ni-shiŋ-lē\ *adv* — **ad·mon·ish·ment** \-mənt\ *n*

ad·mo·ni·tion \ad-mə-'ni-shən\ *n* [ME *amonicioun*, fr. MF *amonition*, fr. L *admonition-, admonitio*, fr. *admonēre*] (14c) **1** : gentle or friendly reproof **2** : counsel or warning against fault or oversight

ad·mon·i·to·ry \ad-'mä-nə-ˌtōr-ē, -ˌtȯr-\ *adj* (1594) : expressing admonition : WARNING — **ad·mon·i·to·ri·ly** \-ˌmä-nə-'tōr-ə-lē, -ˌtȯr-\ *adv*

ad·nate \'ad-ˌnāt\ *adj* [L *adnatus, adgnatus*, pp. of *adgnasci* to be born in addition, grow later — more at AGNATE] (1661) : grown to a usu. unlike part esp. along a margin 〈a calyx ~ to the ovary〉 — **ad·na·tion** \ad-'nā-shən\ *n*

ad nau·se·am \ad-'nȯ-zē-əm *also* -ˌam\ *adv* [L] (1647) : to a sickening or excessive degree

ad·nexa \ad-'nek-sə\ *n pl* [NL, fr. L *annexa*, neut. pl. of *annexus*, pp. of *annectere* to bind to — more at ANNEX] (1899) : conjoined, subordinate, or associated anatomic parts — **ad·nex·al** \-səl\ *adj*

ado \ə-'dü\ *n* [ME, fr. *at do*, fr. *at* + *don, do* to do] (14c) **1** : fussy bustling excitement : TO-DO **2** : time-wasting bother over trivial details 〈wrote the paper without further ~〉 **3** : TROUBLE, DIFFICULTY

ado·be \ə-'dō-bē\ *n* [Sp, fr. Ar *aṭ-ṭūb* the brick, fr. Copt *tōbe* brick] (1748) **1** : a brick or building material of sun-dried earth and straw **2** : a structure made of adobe bricks **3** : a heavy clay used in making adobe bricks; *broadly* : alluvial or playa clay in desert or arid regions — **ado·be·like** \-ˌlīk\ *adj*

ado·bo \ə-'dō-bō, ä-'thō-bō\ *n, pl* **-bos** [Sp] (ca. 1951) : a Philippine dish of fish or meat marinated in a sauce usu. containing vinegar and garlic, browned in fat, and simmered in the marinade

ad·o·les·cence \ˌa-d³l-'e-s³n(t)s\ *n* (15c) **1** : the state or process of growing up **2** : the period of life from puberty to maturity terminating legally at the age of majority **3** : a stage of development (as of a language or culture) prior to maturity

¹ad·o·les·cent \-s³nt\ *n* [F, fr. L *adolescent-, adolescens*, prp. of *adolescere* to grow up — more at ADULT] (15c) : one that is in the state of adolescence

²adolescent *adj* (1785) **1** : of, relating to, or being in adolescence **2** : emotionally or intellectually immature — **ad·o·les·cent·ly** *adv*

Ado·nai \ˌä-də-'nȯi, -'ni\ *n* [Heb *ʼădhōnāy*] (14c) — used as a name of the God of the Hebrews

Ado·nis \ə-'dä-nəs, -'dō-\ *n* [L, fr. Gk *Adōnis*] **1** : a youth loved by Aphrodite who is killed at hunting by a wild boar and restored to Aphrodite from Hades for a part of each year **2** : a very handsome young man

adopt \ə-'däpt\ *vt* [ME, fr. MF or L; MF *adopter*, fr. L *adoptare*, fr. *ad-* + *optare* to choose] (1500) **1** : to take by choice into a relationship; *esp* : to take voluntarily (a child of other parents) as one's own child **2** : to take up and practice or use 〈~ed a moderate tone〉 **3** : to accept formally and put into effect 〈~ a constitutional amendment〉 **4** : to choose (a textbook) for required study in a course — **adopt·abil·i·ty** \-ˌdäp-tə-'bi-lə-tē\ *n* — **adopt·able** \-'däp-tə-bəl\ *adj* — **adopt·er** *n*

 syn ADOPT, EMBRACE, ESPOUSE mean to take an opinion, policy, or practice as one's own. ADOPT implies accepting something created by another or foreign to one's nature 〈forced to *adopt* new policies〉. EMBRACE implies a ready or happy acceptance 〈*embraced* the customs of their new homeland〉. ESPOUSE implies an implication of close attachment to a cause and a sharing of its fortunes 〈*espoused* the cause of women's rights〉.

adopt·ee \ə-ˌdäp-'tē\ *n* (1892) : one that is adopted

adop·tion \ə-'däp-shən\ *n* (14c) : the act of adopting : state of being adopted

adop·tion·ism *or* **adop·tian·ism** \-shə-ˌni-zəm\ *n, often cap* (1874) : the doctrine that Jesus of Nazareth became the Son of God by adoption — **adop·tion·ist** \-sh(ə-)nist\ *n, often cap*

adop·tive \ə-'däp-tiv\ *adj* (15c) **1** : made or acquired by adoption 〈the ~ father〉 **2** : tending to adopt **3** : of or relating to adoption — **adop·tive·ly** *adv*

ador·able \ə-'dȯr-ə-bəl, -'dȯr-\ *adj* (1611) **1** : worthy of being adored **2** : extremely charming 〈an ~ child〉 — **ador·abil·i·ty** \-ˌdȯr-ə-'bi-lə-tē, -ˌdȯr-\ *n* — **ador·able·ness** \-'dȯr-ə-bəl-nəs, -'dȯr-\ *n* — **ador·ably** \-blē\ *adv*

ad·o·ra·tion \ˌa-də-'rā-shən\ *n* (1528) : the act of adoring : the state of being adored

adore \ə-'dȯr, -'dȯr\ *vt* **adored; ador·ing** [ME *adouren*, fr. MF *adorer*, fr. L *adorare*, fr. *ad-* + *orare* to speak, pray — more at ORATION] (14c)

1 : to worship or honor as a deity or as divine **2** : to regard with loving admiration and devotion 〈*adored* his daughter〉 **3** : to be extremely fond of 〈~s pecan pie〉 **syn** see REVERE — **ador·er** *n* — **ador·ing·ly** *adv*

adorn \ə-'dȯrn\ *vt* [ME, fr. MF *adorner*, fr. L *adornare*, fr. *ad-* + *ornare* to furnish — more at ORNATE] (14c) **1** : to enhance the appearance of esp. with beautiful objects **2** : to enliven or decorate as if with ornaments 〈people of fashion who ~ed the Court〉

 syn ADORN, DECORATE, ORNAMENT, EMBELLISH, BEAUTIFY, DECK, GARNISH mean to enhance the appearance of something by adding something unessential. ADORN implies an enhancing by something beautiful in itself 〈a diamond necklace *adorned* her neck〉. DECORATE suggests relieving plainness or monotony by adding beauty of color or design 〈*decorate* a birthday cake〉. ORNAMENT and EMBELLISH imply the adding of something extraneous, ORNAMENT stressing the heightening or setting off of the original 〈a white house *ornamented* with green shutters〉, EMBELLISH often stressing the adding of superfluous or adventitious ornament 〈*embellish* a page with floral borders〉. BEAUTIFY adds to EMBELLISH a suggestion of counterbalancing plainness or ugliness 〈will *beautify* the grounds with flower beds〉. DECK implies the addition of something that contributes to gaiety, splendor, or showiness 〈a house all *decked* out for Christmas〉. GARNISH suggests decorating with a small final touch and is used esp. in referring to the serving of food 〈an entrée *garnished* with parsley〉.

adorn·ment \-mənt\ *n* (14c) **1** : the action of adorning : the state of being adorned **2** : something that adorns

ADP \ˌā-(ˌ)dē-'pē\ *n* [*a*denosine *d*i*p*hosphate] (1944) : an ester of adenosine that is reversibly converted to ATP for the storing of energy by the addition of a high-energy phosphate group — called also *adenosine diphosphate*

ad rem \(ˌ)ad-'rem\ *adv or adj* [L, to the thing] (1599) : to the point or purpose : RELEVANTLY

adren- *or* **adreno-** *comb form* [*adrenal*] **1** : adrenal glands 〈*adreno*cortical〉 **2** : adrenaline 〈*adren*ergic〉

¹ad·re·nal \ə-'drē-n³l\ *adj* [*ad-* + *renal*] (1875) : of, relating to, or derived from the adrenal glands or their secretions 〈~ steroids〉

²adrenal *n* (1882) : ADRENAL GLAND

ad·re·nal·ec·to·my \ə-ˌdrē-n³l-'ek-tə-mē\ *n* (ca. 1910) : surgical removal of one or both adrenal glands — **ad·re·nal·ec·to·mized** \-ˌmīzd\ *adj*

adrenal gland *n* (1875) : either of a pair of complex endocrine organs near the anterior medial border of the kidney consisting of a mesodermal cortex that produces glucocorticoid, mineralocorticoid, and androgenic hormones and an ectodermal medulla that produces epinephrine and norepinephrine — called also *adrenal, suprarenal gland*

Adren·a·lin \ə-'dre-n³l-ən\ *trademark* — used for a preparation of levorotatory epinephrine

adren·a·line \ə-'dre-n³l-ən\ *n* (1901) : EPINEPHRINE — often used in nontechnical contexts 〈the fans were jubilant, raucous, their ~ running high —W. P. Kinsella〉

ad·ren·er·gic \ˌa-drə-'nər-jik\ *adj* [*adren-* + *ergic*] (1934) **1** : liberating or activated by adrenaline or a substance like adrenaline 〈an ~ nerve〉 **2** : resembling adrenaline esp. in physiological action 〈~ drugs〉 — **ad·ren·er·gi·cal·ly** \-ji-k(ə-)lē\ *adv*

ad·re·no·chrome \ə-'drē-nō-ˌkrōm\ *n* (ca. 1913) : a red-colored mixture of quinones derived from epinephrine by oxidation

ad·re·no·cor·ti·cal \ə-ˌdrē-nō-'kȯr-ti-kəl\ *adj* (1936) : of, relating to, or derived from the cortex of the adrenal glands

ad·re·no·cor·ti·co·ste·roid \-ˌkȯr-ti-kō-'stir-ˌȯid *also* -'ster-\ *n* (1960) : a steroid obtained from, resembling, or having physiological effects like those of the adrenal cortex

ad·re·no·cor·ti·co·trop·ic \ə-ˌdrē-nō-ˌkȯr-ti-kō-'trō-pik\ *also* **ad·re·no·cor·ti·co·tro·phic** \-'trō-fik\ *adj* (1936) : acting on or stimulating the adrenal cortex 〈~ activity〉

adrenocorticotropic hormone *n* (1937) : ACTH

ad·re·no·cor·ti·co·tro·pin \-'trō-pən\ *also* **ad·re·no·cor·ti·co·tro·phin** \-'trō-fən\ *n* (1952) : ACTH

Adria·my·cin \ˌā-drē-ə-'mī-s³n, ˌa-drē-\ *trademark* — used for a preparation of the hydrochloride of doxorubicin

adrift \ə-'drift\ *adv or adj* (1624) **1** : without motive power and without anchor or mooring **2** : without ties, guidance, or security **3** : free from restraint or support

adroit \ə-'drȯit\ *adj* [F, fr. OF, fr. *a-* (fr. L *ad-*) + *droit* right, droit] (1652) **1** : having or showing skill, cleverness, or resourcefulness in handling situations 〈an ~ leader〉 **syn** see CLEVER, DEXTEROUS — **adroit·ly** *adv* — **adroit·ness** *n*

ad·sci·ti·tious \ˌad-sə-'ti-shəs\ *adj* [L *adscitus*, fr. pp. of *adsciscere* to admit, adopt, fr. *ad-* + *sciscere* to get to know, fr. *scire* to know — more at SCIENCE] (1620) : derived or acquired from something extrinsic : ADVENTITIOUS

ad·sorb \ad-'sȯrb, -'zȯrb\ *vb* [*ad-* + *absorb*] *vt* (1882) : to take up and hold by adsorption ~ *vi* : to become adsorbed — **ad·sorb·able** \-'sȯr-bə-bəl, -'zȯr-\ *adj* — **ad·sorb·er** \-'sȯr-bər, -'zȯr-\ *n*

ad·sor·bate \ad-'sȯr-bət, -'zȯr-, -ˌbāt\ *n* (1928) : an adsorbed substance

ad·sor·bent \-bənt\ *n* (1917) : a usu. solid substance that adsorbs another substance — **adsorbent** *adj*

ad·sorp·tion \ad-'sȯrp-shən, -'zȯrp-\ *n* [*ad-* + absorption] (1882) : the adhesion in an extremely thin layer of molecules (as of gases, solutes, or liquids) to the surfaces of solid bodies or liquids with which they are in contact — compare ABSORPTION — **ad·sorp·tive** \-'sȯrp-tiv, -'zȯrp-\ *adj*

ad·u·lar·ia \ˌa-jə-'lar-ē-ə, ˌa-dyə-, -'ler-\ *n* [It, fr. F *adulaire*, fr. *Adula*, Swiss mountain group] (1798) : a transparent or translucent orthoclase

ad·u·late \'a-jə-ˌlāt, 'a-dyə-; 'a-d³l-ˌāt\ *vt* **-lat·ed; -lat·ing** [back-formation fr. *adulation*, fr. ME, fr. MF, fr. L *adulation-, adulatio*, fr. *adulari* to fawn on (of dogs), flatter] (1777) : to flatter or admire excessively or slavishly — **ad·u·la·tion** \ˌa-jə-'lā-shən, ˌa-dyə-; ˌa-d³l-'ā-\ *n* — **ad·u·la·tor** \'a-jə-ˌlā-tər, 'a-dyə-; 'a-d³l-ˌā-\ *n* — **ad·u·la·to·ry** \-lə-ˌtōr-ē, -ˌtȯr-\ *adj*

¹adult \ə-'dəlt, 'a-ˌdəlt\ *adj* [L *adultus*, pp. of *adolescere* to grow up, fr. *ad-* + *-olescere* (fr. *alescere* to grow) — more at OLD] (1531) **1** : fully developed and mature : GROWN-UP **2** : of, relating to, intended for, or befitting adults 〈an ~ approach to a problem〉 **3** : dealing in or with explicitly sexual material ⟨∼ bookstores⟩ ⟨∼ movies⟩ — **adult·hood** \ə-ˈdəlt-ˌhu̇d\ *n* — **adult·ly** \ə-ˈdəlt-lē, ˈa-ˌdəlt-\ *adv* — **adult·ness** \ə-ˈdəlt-nəs, ˈa-ˌdəlt-\ *n*

²**adult** *n* (1658) : one that is adult; *esp* : a human being after an age (as 21) specified by law — **adult·like** \ə-ˈdəlt-ˌlīk\ *adj*

adult education *n* (1851) : CONTINUING EDUCATION

adul·ter·ant \ə-ˈdəl-t(ə-)rənt\ *n* (ca. 1755) : an adulterating substance or agent — **adulterant** *adj*

¹**adul·ter·ate** \ə-ˈdəl-tə-ˌrāt\ *vt* **-at·ed; -at·ing** [L *adulteratus*, pp. of *adulterare*, fr. *ad-* + *alter* other — more at ELSE] (1531) : to corrupt, debase, or make impure by the addition of a foreign or inferior substance or element; *esp* : to prepare for sale by replacing more valuable with less valuable or inert ingredients — **adul·ter·a·tor** \-ˌrā-tər\ *n*

²**adul·ter·ate** \ə-ˈdəl-t(ə-)rət\ *adj* (1590) **1** : tainted with adultery : ADULTEROUS **2** : being adulterated : SPURIOUS

adul·ter·a·tion \ə-ˌdəl-tə-ˈrā-shən\ *n* (1506) **1** : the process of adulterating : the condition of being adulterated **2** : an adulterated product

adul·ter·er \ə-ˈdəl-tər-ər\ *n* (1513) : a person who commits adultery; *esp* : a man who commits adultery

adul·ter·ess \ə-ˈdəl-t(ə-)rəs\ *n* (1611) : a woman who commits adultery

adul·ter·ine \ə-ˈdəl-tə-ˌrīn, -ˌrēn\ *adj* (1542) **1 a** : marked by adulteration : SPURIOUS **b** : ILLEGAL **2** : born of adultery

adul·ter·ous \ə-ˈdəl-t(ə-)rəs\ *adj* (1606) : relating to, characterized by, or given to adultery — **adul·ter·ous·ly** *adv*

adul·tery \ə-ˈdəl-t(ə-)rē\ *n*, *pl* **-ter·ies** [ME, alter. of *avoutrie*, fr. MF, fr. L *adulterium*, fr. *adulter* adulterer, back-formation fr. *adulterare*] (15c) : voluntary sexual intercourse between a married man and someone other than his wife or between a married woman and someone other than her husband; *also* : an act of adultery

ad·um·brate \ˈa-dəm-ˌbrāt, a-ˈdəm-\ *vt* **-brat·ed; -brat·ing** [L *adumbratus*, pp. of *adumbrare*, fr. *ad-* + *umbra* shadow — more at UMBRAGE] (1581) **1** : to foreshadow vaguely : INTIMATE **2 a** : to give a sketchy representation or outline of **b** : to suggest or disclose partially **3** : OVERSHADOW, OBSCURE — **ad·um·bra·tion** \ˌa-(ˌ)dəm-ˈbrā-shən\ *n* — **ad·um·bra·tive** \a-ˈdəm-brə-tiv\ *adj* — **ad·um·bra·tive·ly** *adv*

adust \ə-ˈdəst\ *adj* [ME, fr. L *adustus*, pp. of *adurere* to set fire to, fr. *ad-* + *urere* to burn — more at EMBER] (15c) **1** : SCORCHED, BURNED **2** *archaic* : of a sunburned appearance **3** *archaic* : of a gloomy appearance or disposition

ad va·lo·rem \ˌad-və-ˈlōr-əm, -ˈlȯr-\ *adj* [L, according to the value] (1698) : imposed at a rate percent of value ⟨*ad valorem* tax on goods⟩

¹**ad·vance** \əd-ˈvan(t)s\ *vb* **ad·vanced; ad·vanc·ing** [ME *advauncen*, fr. OF *avancier*, fr. (assumed) VL *abantiare*, fr. LL *abante* in front, fr. L *ab-* + *ante* before — more at ANTE] *vt* (15c) **1** : to accelerate the growth or progress of **2** : to bring or move forward **3** : to raise to a higher rank **4** *archaic* : to lift up : RAISE **5 a** : to bring forward in time; *esp* : to make earlier ⟨∼ the date of the meeting⟩ **b** : to place later in time **6** : to bring forward for notice, consideration, or acceptance : PROPOSE **7** : to supply or furnish in expectation of repayment **8** : to raise in rate : INCREASE ⟨∼ the rent⟩ ∼ *vi* **1** : to move forward : PROCEED **2** : to make progress : INCREASE ⟨∼ in age⟩ **3** : to rise in rank, position, or importance **4** : to rise in rate or price — **ad·vanc·er** *n*

syn ADVANCE, PROMOTE, FORWARD, FURTHER mean to help (someone or something) to move ahead. ADVANCE stresses effective assisting in hastening a process or bringing about a desired end ⟨*advance* the cause of peace⟩. PROMOTE suggests an encouraging or fostering and may denote an increase in status or rank ⟨a campaign to *promote* better health⟩. FORWARD implies an impetus forcing something ahead ⟨a wage increase would *forward* productivity⟩. FURTHER suggests a removing of obstacles in the way of a desired advance ⟨used the marriage to *further* his career⟩.

²**advance** *n* (1668) **1** : a moving forward **2 a** : progress in development ⟨mistaking material ∼ for spiritual enrichment —H. J. Laski⟩ **b** : a progressive step : IMPROVEMENT ⟨an ∼ in medical technique⟩ **3 a** : a rise in price, value, or amount **4** : a first step or approach made ⟨her attitude discouraged all ∼s⟩ **5** : a provision of something (as money or goods) before a return is received; *also* : the money or goods supplied — **in advance** : before a deadline or an anticipated event — **in advance of** : AHEAD OF

³**advance** *adj* (1701) **1** : made, sent, or furnished ahead of time ⟨∼ sales⟩ **2** : going or situated before ⟨an ∼ party of soldiers⟩

ad·vanced *adj* (1534) **1** : far on in time or course ⟨a man ∼ in years⟩ **2 a** : being beyond others in progress or ideas ⟨tastes a bit too ∼ for the times⟩ **b** : being beyond the elementary or introductory ⟨∼ chemistry⟩ **c** : greatly developed beyond an initial stage ⟨the most ∼ scientific methods⟩ ⟨∼ weapons systems⟩

advanced degree *n* (1928) : a university degree (as a master's or doctor's degree) higher than a bachelor's

Advanced level *n* (1947) : A LEVEL

advance man *n* (1906) : an employee who makes arrangements and handles publicity in advance of an appearance or engagement by the employer (as a political candidate or a circus)

ad·vance·ment \əd-ˈvan(t)s-mənt\ *n* (1599) **1** : the action of advancing : the state of being advanced : **a** : promotion or elevation to a higher rank or position **b** : progression to a higher stage of development **2** : an improved feature : IMPROVEMENT

¹**ad·van·tage** \əd-ˈvan-tij\ *n* [ME *avantage*, fr. MF, fr. *avant* before, fr. LL *abante*] (1523) **1** : superiority of position or condition ⟨higher ground gave the enemy the ∼⟩ **2** : a factor or circumstance of benefit to its possessor ⟨lacked the ∼s of an education⟩ **3 a** : BENEFIT, GAIN; *esp* : benefit resulting from some course of action ⟨a mistake which turned out to our ∼⟩ **b** *obs* : INTEREST 2a **4** : the first point won in tennis after deuce — **to advantage** : so as to produce a favorable impression or effect

²**advantage** *vt* **-taged; -tag·ing** (1549) : to give an advantage to : BENEFIT

ad·van·ta·geous \ˌad-ˌvan-ˈtā-jəs, -vən-\ *adj* (1598) : giving an advantage : FAVORABLE — **ad·van·ta·geous·ly** *adv* — **ad·van·ta·geous·ness** *n*

ad·vec·tion \ad-ˈvek-shən\ *n* [L *advection-, advectio* act of bringing, fr. *advehere* to carry to, fr. *ad-* + *vehere* to carry — more at WAY] (1910)

: the usu. horizontal movement of a mass of fluid (as air or an ocean current); *also* : transport (as of pollutants or plankton) by such movement — **ad·vect** \-ˈvekt\ *vt* — **ad·vec·tive** \-ˈvek-tiv\ *adj*

Ad·vent \ˈad-ˌvent, *chiefly Brit* -vənt\ *n* [ME, fr. ML *adventus*, fr. L, arrival, fr. *advenire*] (12c) **1** : the period beginning four Sundays before Christmas and observed by some Christians as a season of prayer and fasting **2 a** : the coming of Christ at the Incarnation **b** : SECOND COMING **3** *not cap* : a coming into being or use ⟨the ∼ of spring⟩ ⟨the ∼ of pasteurization⟩ ⟨the ∼ of personal computers⟩

Ad·vent·ism \ˈad-ˌven-ˌti-zəm\ *n* (1874) **1** : the doctrine that the second coming of Christ and the end of the world are near at hand **2** : the principles and practices of Seventh-Day Adventists — **Ad·vent·ist** \ˈad-ˌven-tist, ad-ˈ, ˈad-\, *adj or n*

ad·ven·ti·tia \ˌad-vən-ˈti-shə, -(ˌ)ven-\ *n* [NL, alter. of L *adventicia*, neut. pl. of *adventicius* coming from outside, fr. *adventus*, pp.] (1876) : an external chiefly connective tissue covering of an organ; *esp* : the external coat of a blood vessel — **ad·ven·ti·tial** \-shəl\ *adj*

ad·ven·ti·tious \ˌad-(ˌ)ven-ˈti-shəs, -vən-\ *adj* [L *adventicius*] (1603) **1** : coming from another source and not inherent or innate **2** : arising or occurring sporadically or in other than the usual location ⟨∼ roots⟩ — **ad·ven·ti·tious·ly** *adv*

ad·ven·tive \ad-ˈven-tiv\ *adj* (ca. 1859) **1** : introduced but not fully naturalized **2** : ADVENTITIOUS 2 — **adventive** *n*

Advent Sunday *n* (15c) : the first Sunday in Advent

¹**ad·ven·ture** \əd-ˈven-chər\ *n* [ME *aventure*, fr. OF, fr. (assumed) VL *adventura*, fr. L *adventus*, pp. of *advenire* to arrive, fr. *ad-* + *venire* to come — more at COME] (14c) **1 a** : an undertaking usu. involving danger and unknown risks **b** : the encountering of risks ⟨the spirit of ∼⟩ **2** : an exciting or remarkable experience ⟨an ∼ in exotic dining⟩ **3** : an enterprise involving financial risk

²**adventure** *vb* **ad·ven·tured; ad·ven·tur·ing** \-ˈven-ch(ə-)riŋ\ *vt* (14c) **1** : to expose to danger or loss : VENTURE **2** : to venture upon : TRY ∼ *vi* **1** : to proceed despite risk **2** : to take the risk

ad·ven·tur·er \əd-ˈven-ch(ə-)rər\ *n* (1593) **1** : one that adventures: as **a** : SOLDIER OF FORTUNE **b** : one that engages in risky commercial enterprises for profit **2** : one who seeks unmerited wealth or position esp. by playing on the credulity or prejudice of others

ad·ven·ture·some \əd-ˈven-chər-səm\ *adj* (ca. 1731) : inclined to take risks : VENTURESOME — **ad·ven·ture·some·ness** *n*

ad·ven·tur·ess \əd-ˈven-ch(ə-)rəs\ *n* (1754) : a female adventurer; *esp* : one who seeks position or livelihood by questionable means

ad·ven·tur·ism \əd-ˈven-chə-ˌri-zəm\ *n* (1932) : improvisation or experimentation (as in politics or military or foreign affairs) in the absence or in defiance of accepted plans or principles — **ad·ven·tur·ist** \-ˈven-ch(ə-)rist\ *n* — **ad·ven·tur·is·tic** \-ˌven-chə-ˈris-tik\ *adj*

ad·ven·tur·ous \əd-ˈven-ch(ə-)rəs\ *adj* (14c) **1** : disposed to seek adventure or to cope with the new and unknown ⟨an ∼ explorer⟩ **b** : INNOVATIVE ⟨an ∼ artistic style⟩ **2** : characterized by unknown dangers and risks ⟨an ∼ journey⟩ — **ad·ven·tur·ous·ly** *adv* — **ad·ven·tur·ous·ness** *n*

syn ADVENTUROUS, VENTURESOME, DARING, DAREDEVIL, RASH, RECKLESS, FOOLHARDY mean exposing oneself to danger more than required by good sense. ADVENTUROUS implies a willingness to accept risks but not necessarily imprudence ⟨*adventurous* pioneers⟩. VENTURESOME implies a jaunty eagerness for perilous undertakings ⟨*venturesome* stunt pilots⟩. DARING heightens the implication of fearlessness in courting danger ⟨*daring* mountain climbers⟩. DAREDEVIL stresses ostentation in daring ⟨*daredevil* motorcyclists⟩. RASH suggests imprudence and lack of forethought ⟨a *rash* decision⟩. RECKLESS implies heedlessness of probable consequences ⟨a *reckless* driver⟩. FOOLHARDY suggests a recklessness that is inconsistent with good sense ⟨only a *foolhardy* sailor would venture into this storm⟩.

¹**ad·verb** \ˈad-ˌvərb\ *n* [ME *adverbe*, fr. MF, fr. L *adverbium*, fr. *ad-* + *verbum* word — more at WORD] (14c) : a word belonging to one of the major form classes in any of numerous languages, typically serving as a modifier of a verb, an adjective, another adverb, a preposition, a phrase, a clause, or a sentence, expressing some relation of manner or quality, place, time, degree, number, cause, opposition, affirmation, or denial, and in English also serving to connect and to express comment on clause content — compare ADJUNCT, CONJUNCT, DISJUNCT

²**adverb** *adj* (1879) : ADVERBIAL

ad·ver·bi·al \ad-ˈvər-bē-əl\ *adj* (1611) : of, relating to, or having the function of an adverb — **adverbial** *n* — **ad·ver·bi·al·ly** \-ə-lē\ *adv*

ad ver·bum \ˈad-ˈvər-bəm\ *adv* [L] (ca. 1580) : to a word : VERBATIM

ad·ver·sar·i·al \ˌad-və(r)-ˈser-ē-əl\ *adj* (1926) : of, relating to, or characteristic of an adversary : adversary procedures : ADVERSARY

¹**ad·ver·sary** \ˈad-və(r)-ˌser-ē\ *n, pl* **-sar·ies** (14c) : one that contends with, opposes, or resists : ENEMY — **ad·ver·sari·ness** *n*

²**adversary** *adj* (14c) **1** : of, relating to, or involving an adversary **2** : having or involving antagonistic parties or opposing interests ⟨divorce can be an ∼ proceeding⟩

ad·ver·sa·tive \əd-ˈvər-sə-tiv, ad-\ *adj* (15c) : expressing antithesis, opposition, or adverse circumstance ⟨the ∼ conjunction *but*⟩ — **ad·versative** *n* — **ad·ver·sa·tive·ly** *adv*

ad·verse \ad-ˈvərs, ˈad-ˌ\ *adj* [ME, fr. MF *advers*, fr. L *adversus*, pp. of *advertere*] (14c) **1** : acting against or in a contrary direction : HOSTILE ⟨hindered by ∼ winds⟩ **2 a** : opposed to one's interests ⟨an ∼ verdict⟩ ⟨heard testimony ∼ to their position⟩; *esp* : UNFAVORABLE ⟨∼ criticism⟩ **b** : causing harm : HARMFUL ⟨∼ drug effects⟩ **3** *archaic* : opposite in position — **ad·verse·ly** *adv* — **ad·verse·ness** *n*

ad·ver·si·ty \ad-ˈvər-sə-tē\ *n, pl* **-ties** (13c) **1** : a state or condition contrary to one of well-being **2** : an instance of adversity *syn* see MISFORTUNE

¹**ad·vert** \ad-ˈvərt\ *vi* [ME *adverten*, fr. MF & L; MF *advertir*, fr. L *advertere*, fr. *ad-* + *vertere* to turn — more at WORTH] (15c) **1** : to turn the mind or attention — used with *to* ⟨∼ed to the speaker⟩ **2** : to

\ə\ abut \ᵊ\ kitten, F table \ər\ further \a\ ash \ā\ ace \ä\ mop, mar \au̇\ out \ch\ chin \e\ bet \ē\ easy \g\ go \i\ hit \ī\ ice \j\ job \ŋ\ sing \ō\ go \ȯ\ law \ȯi\ boy \th\ thin \t͟h\ the \ü\ loot \u̇\ foot \y\ yet \zh\ vision \à, k̲, ⁿ, œ, œ̄, ᴜᴇ, ᵫ̄, ᶦ\ see Guide to Pronunciation call attention in the course of speaking or writing : make reference — used with *to* ⟨~*ed* to foreign-language sources⟩

²**ad·vert** \'ad-,vərt\ *n* (1860) *chiefly Brit* : ADVERTISEMENT

ad·ver·tence \ad-'vər-t²n(t)s\ *n* (14c) **1** : the action or process of adverting : ATTENTION **2** : ADVERTENCY 1

ad·ver·ten·cy \-t²n(t)-sē\ *n, pl* **-cies** (1646) **1** : the quality or state of being advertent : HEEDFULNESS **2** : ADVERTENCE 1

ad·ver·tent \-t²nt\ *adj* [L *advertent-, advertens,* prp. of *advertere*] (1671) : giving attention : HEEDFUL — **ad·ver·tent·ly** *adv*

ad·ver·tise \'ad-vər-,tīz\ *vb* **-tised; -tis·ing** [ME, fr. MF *advertiss-,* stem of *advertir*] *vt* (15c) **1** : to make something known to : NOTIFY **2 a** : to make publicly and generally known ⟨*advertising* their readiness to make concessions⟩ **b** : to announce publicly esp. by a printed notice or a broadcast **c** : to call public attention to esp. by emphasizing desirable qualities so as to arouse a desire to buy or patronize : PROMOTE ~ *vi* : to issue or sponsor advertising ⟨~ for a secretary⟩ — **ad·ver·tis·er** *n*

ad·ver·tise·ment \,ad-vər-'tīz-mənt; əd-'vər-təz-mənt, -tə-smənt\ *n* (15c) **1** : the act or process of advertising **2** : a public notice; *esp* : one published in the press or broadcast over the air

ad·ver·tis·ing *n* (1762) **1** : the action of calling something to the attention of the public esp. by paid announcements **2** : ADVERTISEMENTS ⟨the magazine contains much ~⟩ **3** : the business of preparing advertisements for publication or broadcast

ad·ver·tize, ad·ver·tize·ment *Brit var of* ADVERTISE, ADVERTISEMENT

ad·ver·to·ri·al \,ad-vər-'tōr-ē-əl, -'tor-\ *n* [blend of *advertisement* and *editorial*] (1946) : an advertisement that imitates editorial format

ad·vice \əd-'vīs\ *n* [ME, fr. MF *avis* opinion, prob. fr. the phrase *ce m'est a vis* that appears to me, part trans. of L *mihi visum est* it seemed so to me, I decided] (14c) **1** : recommendation regarding a decision or course of conduct : COUNSEL ⟨he shall have power, by and with the ~ and consent of the Senate, to make treaties —*U.S. Constitution*⟩ **2** : information or notice given — usu. used in pl. **3** : an official notice concerning a business transaction

ad·vis·able \əd-'vī-zə-bəl\ *adj* (1582) : fit to be advised or done : PRUDENT *syn* see EXPEDIENT **2** : the act or process of advising — **ad·vis·abil·i·ty** \-,vī-zə-'bi-lə-tē\ *n* — **ad·vis·able·ness** \-'vī-zə-bəl-nəs\ *n* — **ad·vis·ably** \-blē\ *adv*

ad·vise \əd-'vīz\ *vb* **ad·vised; ad·vis·ing** [ME, fr. MF *aviser,* fr. *avis*] *vt* (14c) **1 a** : to give advice to : COUNSEL ⟨~ her to try a drier climate⟩ **b** : CAUTION, WARN ⟨~ them of the consequences⟩ **c** : RECOMMEND ⟨~ prudence⟩ **2** : to give information or notice to : INFORM ⟨~ them of their rights⟩ ~ *vi* **1** : to give advice ⟨~ on legal matters⟩ **2** : to take counsel : CONSULT ⟨~ with your parents⟩ — **ad·vis·er** *also* **ad·vi·sor** \-'vī-zər\ *n*

ad·vised \əd-'vīzd\ *adj* (14c) : thought out : CONSIDERED — often used in combination ⟨ill-*advised* plans⟩ — **ad·vis·ed·ly** \-'vī-zəd-lē\ *adv*

ad·vis·ee \əd-,vī-'zē\ *n* (1824) : one that is advised

ad·vise·ment \əd-'vīz-mənt\ *n* (14c) **1** : careful consideration : DELIBERATION **2** : the act or process of advising (as a college student)

¹**ad·vi·so·ry** \əd-'vī-zə-rē, -'vī-zə-\ *adj* (1778) **1** : having or exercising power to advise **2** : containing or giving advice

²**advisory** *n, pl* **-ries** (1936) : a report giving information (as on the weather) and often recommending action to be taken

ad·vo·ca·cy \'ad-və-kə-sē\ *n* (15c) : the act or process of advocating or supporting a cause or proposal

advocacy journalism *n* (1970) : journalism that advocates a cause or expresses a viewpoint — **advocacy journalist** *n*

¹**ad·vo·cate** \'ad-və-kət, -,kāt\ *n* [ME *advocat,* fr. MF, fr. L *advocatus,* fr. pp. of *advocare* to summon, fr. *ad- + vocare* to call, fr. *voc-, vox* voice — more at VOICE] (14c) **1** : one that pleads the cause of another; *specif* : one that pleads the cause of another before a tribunal or judicial court **2** : one that defends or maintains a cause or proposal

²**ad·vo·cate** \-,kāt\ *vt* **-cat·ed; -cat·ing** (1599) : to plead in favor of *syn* see SUPPORT — **ad·vo·ca·tion** \,ad-və-'kā-shən\ *n* — **ad·vo·ca·tive** \'ad-və-,kā-tiv\ *adj* — **ad·vo·ca·tor** \-,kā-tər\ *n*

ad·vow·son \əd-'vau̇-z²n\ *n* [ME, fr. OF *avoueson,* fr. ML *advocation-, advocatio,* fr. L, act of calling, fr. *advocare*] (14c) : the right in English law of presenting a nominee to an ecclesiastical benefice

ady·nam·ic \,ā-(,)dī-'na-mik, ,a-də-'na-\ *adj* [Gk *adynamia* lack of strength, fr. *a- + dynamis* power, fr. *dynasthai* to be able] (1829) : characterized by or causing a loss of strength or function ⟨~ ileus⟩

ad·y·tum \'a-də-təm\ *n, pl* **-ta** \-tə\ [L, fr. Gk *adyton,* neut. of *adytos* not to be entered, fr. *a- + dyein* to enter] (1611) : the innermost sanctuary in an ancient temple open only to priests : SANCTUM

adze *also* **adz** \'adz\ *n* [ME *adese,* fr. OE *adesa*] (bef. 12c) : a cutting tool that has a thin arched blade set at right angles to the handle and is used chiefly for shaping wood

ad·zu·ki bean \ad-'zü-kē-\ *n* [Jp *azuki*] (1795) : an annual bushy leguminous plant (*Vignis angularis* syn. *Phaseolus angularis*) widely grown in Japan and China for its seeds which are used as food and to produce a flour; *also* : its seed — called also *adzuki*

ae \'ā\ *adj* [ME (northern dial.) *a,* alter. of *an*] (1737) *chiefly Scot* : ONE

Ae·a·cus \'ē-ə-kəs\ *n* [L, fr. Gk *Aiakos*] : a son of Zeus who is given the Myrmidons as followers and becomes on his death a judge of the underworld

ae·cio·spore \'ē-shə-,spȯr, 'ē-sə-, -,spȯr\ *n* (1905) : one of the spores arranged within an aecium in a series like a chain

ae·ci·um \'ē-shē-əm, 'ē-sē-\ *n, pl* **-cia** \-shē-ə, -sē-\ [NL, fr. Gk *aikia* outrage, assault, fr. *aikēs, aeikēs* unseemly, fr. *a- + -eikēs,* fr. *eikenai* to seem] (1905) : the fruiting body of a rust fungus in which the first binucleate spores are usu. produced — **ae·cial** \-sh(ē-)əl\ *adj*

ae·des \ā-'ē-(,)dēz\ *n, pl* **aedes** [NL, genus name, fr. Gk *aēdēs* unpleasant, fr. *a- + ēdos* pleasure; akin to Gk *hēdys* sweet — more at SWEET] (ca. 1909) : any of a genus (*Aedes*) of mosquitoes including the vector of yellow fever, dengue, and other diseases — **ae·dine** \'ē-,dīn\ *adj*

ae·dile \'ē-,dīl, 'ē-d²l\ *n* [L *aedilis,* fr. *aedes* temple — more at EDIFY] (1540) : an official in ancient Rome in charge of public works and games, police, and the grain supply

Ae·ge·an \i-'jē-ən\ *adj* [L *Aegaeus,* fr. Gk *Aigaios*] (1550) **1** : of or relating to the arm of the Mediterranean Sea east of Greece **2** : of or relating to the chiefly Bronze Age civilization of the islands of the Aegean Sea and the countries adjacent to it

ae·gis \'ē-jəs\ *also* 'ā-\ *n* [L, fr. Gk *aigis,* lit., goatskin, fr. *aig-, aix* goat; akin to Arm *ayc* goat] (1611) **1** : a shield or breastplate emblematic of majesty that was associated with Zeus and Athena **2 a** : PROTECTION ⟨under the ~ of the constitution⟩ **b** : controlling or conditioning influence ⟨many American mothers, under the ~ of benevolent permissiveness . . . actually neglect their children —*Time*⟩ **3 a** : AUSPICES, SPONSORSHIP ⟨under the ~ of the museum⟩ **b** : control or guidance esp. by an individual, group, or system ⟨acted under the court's ~⟩

Ae·gis·thus \i-'jis-thəs\ *n* [L, fr. Gk *Aigisthos*] : a lover of Clytemnestra slain with her by her son Orestes

-aemia *chiefly Brit var of* -EMIA

Ae·ne·as \i-'nē-əs\ *n* [L, fr. Gk *Aineias*] : a son of Anchises and Aphrodite, defender of Troy, and hero of Virgil's *Aeneid*

Ae·ne·o·lith·ic \ā-,nē-ə-ō-'li-thik\ *adj* [L *aeneus* of copper or bronze, fr. *aes* copper, bronze — more at ORE] (1901) : of or relating to a transitional period between the Neolithic and Bronze ages in which some copper was used

¹**ae·o·lian** \ē-'ō-lē-ən, ē-'ōl-yən\ *adj* (1605) **1** *often cap* : of or relating to Aeolus **2** : giving forth or marked by a moaning or sighing sound or musical tone produced by or as if by the wind

²**aeolian** *var of* EOLIAN

¹**Ae·o·lian** \ē-'ō-lē-ən, ā-, -'ōl-yən\ *adj* (1589) : of or relating to Aeolis or its inhabitants

²**Aeolian** *n* (ca. 1889) **1** : a member of a group of Greek peoples of Thessaly and Boeotia that colonized Lesbos and the adjacent coast of Asia Minor **2** : AEOLIC

aeolian harp *n* (1791) : a box-shaped musical instrument having stretched strings usu. tuned in unison on which the wind produces varying harmonics over the same fundamental tone

¹**Ae·ol·ic** \ē-'ä-lik\ *adj* (1674) : AEOLIAN

²**Aeolic** *n* (1902) : a group of ancient Greek dialects used by the Aeolians

Ae·o·lus \'ē-ə-ləs\ *n* [L, fr. Gk *Aiolos*] : the Greek god of the winds

ae·on *or* **eon** \'ē-ən, 'ē-,än\ *n* [L, fr. Gk *aiōn* — more at AYE] (1647) **1** : an immeasurably or indefinitely long period of time : AGE **2 a** *usu* **eon** : a very large division of geologic time usu. longer than an era **b** : a unit of geologic time equal to one billion years

ae·o·ni·an \ē-'ō-nē-ən\ *or* **ae·on·ic** \-'ä-nik\ *adj* (1765) : lasting for an immeasurably or indefinitely long period of time

ae·py·or·nis \,ē-pē-'ȯr-nəs\ *n* [NL, genus name, fr. Gk *aipys* high + *ornis* bird — more at ERNE] (1851) : any of a genus (genus *Aepyornis* or order Aepyornithiformes) of gigantic ratite birds known only from remains found in Madagascar — called also *elephant bird*

aer- *or* **aero-** *comb form* [ME *aero-,* fr. MF, fr. L, fr. Gk *aer-, aero-,* fr. *aēr*] **1 a** : air : atmosphere ⟨*aerate*⟩ ⟨*aerobiology*⟩ **b** : air and ⟨*aerospace*⟩ **2** : gas ⟨*aerosol*⟩ **3** : aviation ⟨*aerodrome*⟩

aer·ate \'a(-ə)r-,āt, 'e(-ə)r-\ *vt* **aer·at·ed; aer·at·ing** (1794) **1** : to supply (the blood) with oxygen by respiration **2** : to supply or impregnate (as the soil or a liquid) with air **3 a** *Brit* : CARBONATE 2 **b** : to make light or sparkling — **aer·a·tion** \,a(-ə)r-'ā-shən, ,e(-ə)r-\ *n*

aer·a·tor \'a(-ə)r-,ā-tər, 'e(-ə)r-\ *n* (1861) : one that aerates; *esp* : an apparatus for aerating something (as sewage)

aer·en·chy·ma \,ar-'eŋ-kə-mə, ,er-\ *n* [NL] (ca. 1893) : the spongy modified cork tissue of many aquatic plants that facilitates gaseous exchange and maintains buoyancy

¹**ae·ri·al** \'ar-ē-əl, 'er-; ā-'ir-ē-əl\ *adj* [L *aerius,* fr. Gk *aerios,* fr. *aēr*] (1604) **1 a** : of, relating to, or occurring in the air or atmosphere **b** : existing or growing in the air rather than in the ground or in water **c** : high in the air ⟨~ spires⟩ **d** : operating or operated overhead on elevated cables or rails ⟨an ~ tram⟩ **2** : suggestive of air: as **a** : lacking substance **b** : FANCIFUL, ETHEREAL ⟨visions of ~ joy —P. B. Shelley⟩ **3 a** : of or relating to aircraft ⟨~ navigation⟩ **b** : designed for use in, taken from, or operating from or against aircraft **c** : effected by means of aircraft ⟨~ transportation⟩ **4** : of, relating to, or gained by the forward pass in football — **ae·ri·al·ly** \-ə-lē\ *adv*

²**aer·i·al** \'ar-ē-əl, 'er-\ *n* (1902) **1** : ANTENNA 2 **2** : FORWARD PASS

ae·ri·al·ist \'ar-ē-ə-list, 'er-, ā-'ir-\ *n* (1905) : one that performs feats in the air or above the ground esp. on the trapeze

aerial ladder *n* (1904) : a mechanically operated extensible ladder usu. mounted on a fire truck

aerial perspective *n* (1720) : the expression of space in painting by gradation of color and distinctness

ae·rie \'ar-ē, 'er-, 'ir-, ā-(ə)-rē\ *n* [ML *aerea,* fr. OF *aire,* prob. fr. (assumed) VL *agrum* origin, nest, lair, fr. L *ager* field — more at ACRE] (1581) **1** : the nest of a bird on a cliff or a mountaintop **2** *obs* : a brood of birds of prey **3** : an elevated often secluded dwelling, structure, or position

aero \'a(-ə)r-(,)ō, 'e(-ə)r-\ *adj* [*aero-*] (1874) : of or relating to aircraft or aeronautics ⟨an ~ engine⟩

aer·o·bat·ics \,ar-ə-'ba-tiks, ,er-\ *n pl but sing or pl in constr* [*aer- + acrobatics*] (ca. 1911) : spectacular flying feats and maneuvers (as rolls and dives) — **aer·o·bat·ic** \-tik\ *adj*

aer·obe \'a(-ə)r-,ōb, 'e(-ə)r-\ *n* [F *aérobie,* fr. *aéro-* aer- + *-bie* (fr. Gk *-bion,* fr. *bios* life) — more at QUICK] (1886) : an organism (as a bacterium) that lives only in the presence of oxygen

aer·o·bic \,a(-ə)r-'ō-bik, ,e(-ə)r-\ *adj* (1884) **1** : living, active, or occurring only in the presence of oxygen ⟨~ respiration⟩ **2** : of, relating to, or induced by aerobes **3** : involving, utilizing, or used in aerobics ⟨an ~ workout⟩ ⟨~ fitness⟩ — **aer·o·bi·cal·ly** \-bi-k(ə-)lē\ *adv*

aer·o·bics \-biks\ *n pl* (1967) **1** *sing or pl in constr* : a system of physical conditioning involving exercises (as running, walking, swimming, or calisthenics) strenuously performed so as to cause marked temporary increase in respiration and heart rate **2** : aerobic exercises

aero·bi·ol·o·gy \,ar-ō-bī-'ä-lə-jē\ *n* [*aer- + biology*] (ca. 1937) : the science dealing with the occurrence, transportation, and effects of airborne materials (as viruses, pollen, or pollutants) — **aero·bi·o·log·i·cal** \-,bī-ə-'lä-ji-kəl\ *adj*

aero·bi·o·sis \,ar-ō-bī-'ō-səs, ,er-, -bē-\ *n, pl* **-o·ses** \-,sēz\ [NL] (ca. 1900) : life in the presence of air or oxygen

aero·brake \'ar-ō-,brāk, 'er-\ *vt* (1965) : to decelerate (as a spacecraft) by passage through a planetary atmosphere

aero·drome \'ar-ə-,drōm, 'er-\ *n* (1908) *chiefly Brit* : AIRFIELD

aero·dy·nam·i·cist \,ar-ō-dī-'na-mə-sist, ,er-\ *n* (1926) : one who specializes in aerodynamics

aero·dy·nam·ics \-'na-miks\ *n pl but sing or pl in constr* (ca. 1837) : a branch of dynamics that deals with the motion of air and other gaseous fluids and with the forces acting on bodies in motion relative to such fluids — **aero·dy·nam·ic** \-mik\ *also* **aero·dy·nam·i·cal** \-mi-kəl\ *adj* — **aero·dy·nam·i·cal·ly** \-mi-k(ə-)lē\ *adv*

aero·dyne \'ar-ə-,dīn, 'er-\ *n* [*aerodynamic*] (ca. 1906) : a heavier-than-air aircraft (as an airplane, helicopter, or glider) — compare AEROSTAT

aero·elas·tic·i·ty \,ar-ō-,ē-,las-'ti-sə-tē, ,er-, -i-,las-\ *n* (1935) : distortion (as from bending or flexing) in a structure (as an airplane wing or a building) caused by aerodynamic forces — **aero·elas·tic** \-'las-tik\ *adj*

aero·em·bo·lism \,ar-ō-'em-bə-,li-zəm, ,er-\ *n* (ca. 1939) : a condition equivalent to bends caused by rapid ascent to high altitudes and resulting exposure to rapidly lowered air pressure

aero·foil \'ar-ə-,fȯil, 'er-\ *n* (1907) *chiefly Brit* : AIRFOIL

aero·gram *or* **aero·gramme** \'ar-ə-,gram, 'er-\ *n* (1899) : AIR LETTER 2

aer·og·ra·pher's mate \,a-'rä-grə-farz-, ,e-\ *n* (ca. 1952) : a navy petty officer specializing in meteorology

aer·o·lite \'ar-ə-,līt, 'er-\ *n* (ca. 1815) : a stony meteorite

aero·mag·net·ic \,ar-ō-mag-'ne-tik, ,er-\ *adj* (1948) : of, relating to, or derived from a study of the earth's magnetic field esp. from the air ⟨an ~ survey⟩

aero·me·chan·ics \-mə-'ka-niks\ *n pl but sing or pl in constr* (ca. 1909) : mechanics that deals with the equilibrium and motion of gases and of solid bodies immersed in them

aero·med·i·cine \-'me-də-sən\ *n* (1942) : a branch of medicine that deals with the diseases and disturbances arising from flying and the associated physiological and psychological problems — **aero·med·i·cal** \-'me-di-kəl\ *adj*

aer·om·e·ter \,a(-ə)r-'ä-mə-tər, ,e(-ə)r-\ *n* [prob. fr. F *aéromètre*, fr. *aér-* + *-mètre* -meter] (1794) : an instrument for ascertaining the weight or density of air or other gases

aero·naut \'ar-ə-,nȯt, 'er-, -,nät\ *n* [F *aéronaute*, fr. *aér-* aer- + Gk *nautēs* sailor — more at NAUTICAL] (1784) : one that operates or travels in an airship or balloon

aero·nau·tics \,ar-ə-'nȯ-tiks, ,er-, -'nä-\ *n pl but sing in constr* (ca. 1824) **1** : a science dealing with the operation of aircraft **2** : the art or science of flight — **aero·nau·ti·cal** \-ti-kəl\ *also* **aero·nau·tic** \-tik\ *adj* — **aero·nau·ti·cal·ly** \-ti-k(ə-)lē\ *adv*

aer·on·o·my \,a(-ə)r-'ä-nə-mē, ,e(-ə)r-\ *n* (1957) : a science that deals with the physics and chemistry of the upper atmosphere of planets — **aer·on·o·mer** \-mər\ *n* — **aer·o·nom·ic** \,ar-ə-'nä-mik, ,er-\ *or* **aer·o·nom·i·cal** \-mi-kəl\ *adj* — **aer·on·o·mist** \,a(-ə)r-'ä-nə-mist, ,e(-ə)r-\ *n*

aero·plane \'ar-ə-,plān, 'er-\ *n* [F *aéroplane*, fr. *aéro-* aer- + *-plane*, prob. fr. fem. of *plan* flat, level, fr. L *planus* — more at FLOOR] (1873) *chiefly Brit* : AIRPLANE

aero·sol \'ar-ə-,säl, 'er-, -,sȯl\ *n* (1923) **1** : a suspension of fine solid or liquid particles in gas ⟨smoke, fog, and mist are ~s⟩ **2** : a substance (as an insecticide or cosmetic) dispensed from a pressurized container esp. as an aerosol; *also* : the container for this

aero·sol·ize \-,sä-,līz, -,sȯ-, -sə-\ *vt* **-ized; -iz·ing** (1944) : to disperse as an aerosol — **aero·sol·iza·tion** \,ar-ə-,sä-lə-'zā-shən, -,sȯ-, -sə-\ *n*

¹aero·space \'ar-ō-,spās, 'er-\ *n* (ca. 1958) **1** : space comprising the earth's atmosphere and the space beyond **2** : a physical science that deals with aerospace **3** : the aerospace industry

²aerospace *adj* (1958) : of or relating to aerospace, to vehicles used in aerospace or the manufacture of such vehicles, or to travel in aerospace ⟨~ research⟩ ⟨~ profits⟩ ⟨~ medicine⟩

aerospace plane *n* (1960) : an airplane designed to be able to reach low earth orbit

aero·stat \-,stat\ *n* [F *aérostat*, fr. *aér-* + *-stat*] (1784) : a lighter-than-air aircraft (as a balloon or blimp) — compare AERODYNE

aero·stat·ics \,ar-ō-'sta-tiks, ,er-\ *n pl but sing or pl in constr* [modif. of NL *aerostatica*, fr. *aer-* + *statica* statics] (1784) : a branch of statics that deals with the equilibrium of gaseous fluids and of solid bodies immersed in them

aero·ther·mo·dy·nam·ics \-,thər-mə-(,)dī-'na-miks\ *n pl but sing or pl in constr* (1949) : the thermodynamics of gases and esp. of air — **aero·ther·mo·dy·nam·ic** \-mik\ *adj*

¹aery \'ar-ē, 'er-ē, 'ä-ə-rē\ *adj* **aer·i·er; -est** [L *aerius* — more at AERIAL] (1652) : having an aerial quality : ETHEREAL ⟨~ visions⟩ — **aer·i·ly** \'ar-ə-lē, 'er-\ *adv*

²aery *like* AERIE\ *var of* AERIE

Aes·cu·la·pi·an \,es-k(y)ə-'lā-pē-ən\ *adj* [*Aesculapius*, Greco-Roman god of medicine, fr. L, fr. Gk *Asklēpios*] (1605) : of or relating to Aesculapius or the healing art

Ae·sir \'ā-,zir, -,sir\ *n pl* [ON *Æsir*, pl. of *āss* god] : the principal race of Norse gods

Ae·so·pi·an \ē-'sō-pē-ən, -'sä-\ *also* **Ae·sop·ic** \-'sä-pik\ *adj* (1728) **1** : of, relating to, or characteristic of Aesop or his fables **2** : conveying an innocent meaning to an outsider but a hidden meaning to a member of a conspiracy or underground movement ⟨~ language⟩

aes·thete \'es-,thēt, *Brit usu* 'ēs-\ *n* [back-formation fr. *aesthetic*] (1881) : one having or affecting sensitivity to the beautiful esp. in art

¹aes·thet·ic \es-'the-tik, is-, *Brit usu* ēs-\ *or* **aes·thet·i·cal** \-ti-kəl\ *adj* [G *ästhetisch*, fr. NL *aestheticus*, fr. Gk *aisthētikos* of sense perception, fr. *aisthanesthai* to perceive — more at AUDIBLE] (1798) **1 a** : of, relating to, or dealing with aesthetics or the beautiful ⟨~ theories⟩ **b** : ARTISTIC ⟨a work of ~ value⟩ **c** : pleasing in appearance : ATTRACTIVE ⟨easy-to-use keyboards, clear graphics, and other ergonomic and ~ features —Mark Mehler⟩ **2** : appreciative of, responsive to, or zealous about the beautiful; *also* : responsive to or appreciative of what is pleasurable to the senses — **aes·thet·i·cal·ly** \-ti-k(ə-)lē\ *adv*

²aesthetic *n* (1822) **1** *pl but sing or pl in constr* : a branch of philosophy dealing with the nature of beauty, art, and taste and with the creation and appreciation of beauty **2** : a particular theory or conception of beauty or art : a particular taste for or approach to what is pleasing to the senses and esp. sight ⟨modernist ~s⟩ ⟨staging new ballets which reflected the ~ of the new nation —Mary Clarke & Clement Crisp⟩ **3** *pl* : a pleasing appearance or effect : BEAUTY ⟨appreciated the ~s of the gemstones⟩

aesthetic distance *n* (1938) : the frame of reference that an artist creates by the use of technical devices in and around the work of art to differentiate it psychologically from reality

aes·the·ti·cian \,es-thə-'ti-shən\ *n* (1829) : a specialist in aesthetics

aes·thet·i·cism \es-'the-tə-,si-zəm, is-\ *n* (1855) **1** : a doctrine that the principles of beauty are basic to other and esp. moral principles **2** : devotion to or emphasis on beauty or the cultivation of the arts

aes·thet·i·cize \-,sīz\ *vt* **-cized; -cizing** (1864) : to make aesthetic

aes·ti·val \'es-tə-vəl\ *var of* ESTIVAL

aes·ti·va·tion *var of* ESTIVATE, ESTIVATION

aether *var of* ETHER 2a

ae·ti·ol·o·gy *chiefly Brit var of* ETIOLOGY

af- — see AD-

¹afar \ə-'fär\ *adv* [ME *afer*, fr. *on fer* at a distance and *of fer* from a distance] (14c) : from, to, or at a great distance ⟨roamed ~⟩

²afar *n* (14c) : a great distance ⟨saw him from ~⟩

afeard *or* **afeared** \ə-'fird\ *adj* [ME *afered*, fr. OE *āfǣred*, pp. of *āfǣran* to frighten, fr. *ā-*, perfective prefix + *fǣran* to frighten — more at ABIDE, FEAR] (bef. 12c) *dial* : AFRAID

afe·brile \(,)ā-'fe-,bril *also* -'fē-\ *adj* (1875) : not marked by fever

af·fa·ble \'a-fə-bəl\ *adj* [MF, fr. L *affabilis*, fr. *affari* to speak to, fr. *ad-* + *fari* to speak — more at BAN] (15c) **1** : being pleasant and at ease in talking to others **2** : characterized by ease and friendliness **syn** see GRACIOUS — **af·fa·bil·i·ty** \,a-fə-'bi-lə-tē\ *n* — **af·fa·bly** \-blē\ *adv*

af·fair \ə-'far, -'fer\ *n* [ME & MF; ME *affaire*, fr. MF, fr. *a faire* to do] (14c) **1** *a pl* : commercial, professional, public, or personal business **b** : MATTER, CONCERN **2** : a procedure, action, or occasion only vaguely specified; *also* : an object or collection of objects only vaguely specified ⟨their house was a 2-story ~⟩ **3** *also* **af·faire a** : a romantic or passionate attachment typically of limited duration : LIAISON 2b **b** : a matter occasioning public anxiety, controversy, or scandal : CASE

¹af·fect \ə-,fekt\ *n* [ME, fr. L *affectus*, fr. *afficere*] (14c) **1** *obs* : FEELING, AFFECTION **2** : the conscious subjective aspect of an emotion considered apart from bodily changes **usage** see EFFECT

²af·fect \ə-'fekt, a-\ *vb* [ME, fr. MF & L; MF *affecter*, fr. L *affectare*, freq. of *afficere* to influence, fr. *ad-* + *facere* to do — more at DO] *vt* (15c) **1** *archaic* : to aim at **2** *archaic* : to have affection for **b** : to be given to : FANCY ⟨~ flashy clothes⟩ **3** : to make a display of liking or using : CULTIVATE ⟨~ a worldly manner⟩ **4** : to put on a pretense of : FEIGN ⟨~ indifference, though deeply hurt⟩ **5** : to tend toward ⟨drops of water ~ roundness⟩ **6** : FREQUENT ~ *vi, obs* : INCLINE 2 **syn** see ASSUME **usage** see EFFECT

³affect *vt* [ME, fr. *affectus*, pp. of *afficere*] (15c) : to produce an effect upon: as **a** : to produce a material influence upon or alteration in ⟨paralysis ~ed his limbs⟩ **b** : to act upon (as a person or a person's mind or feelings) so as to effect a response : INFLUENCE **usage** see EFFECT — **af·fect·abil·i·ty** \-,fek-tə-'bi-lə-tē\ *n* — **af·fect·able** \-'fek-tə-bəl\ *adj*

syn AFFECT, INFLUENCE, TOUCH, IMPRESS, STRIKE, SWAY mean to produce or have an effect upon. AFFECT implies the action of a stimulus that can produce a response or reaction ⟨the sight *affected* her to tears⟩. INFLUENCE implies a force that brings about a change (as in nature or behavior) ⟨our beliefs are *influenced* by our upbringing⟩ ⟨a drug that *influences* growth rates⟩. TOUCH may carry a vivid suggestion of close contact and may connote stirring, arousing, or harming ⟨plants *touched* by frost⟩ ⟨his emotions were *touched* by her distress⟩. IMPRESS stresses the depth and persistence of the effect ⟨only one of the plans *impressed* him⟩. STRIKE, similar to but weaker than *impress*, may convey the notion of sudden sharp perception or appreciation ⟨*struck* by the solemnity of the occasion⟩. SWAY implies the acting of influences that are not resisted or are irresistible, with resulting change in character or course of action ⟨politicians who are *swayed* by popular opinion⟩.

af·fec·ta·tion \,a-,fek-'tā-shən\ *n* (1548) **1 a** : the act of taking on or displaying an attitude or mode of behavior not natural to oneself or not genuinely felt **b** : speech or conduct not natural to oneself : ARTIFICIALITY **2** *obs* : a striving after **syn** see POSE

af·fect·ed \ə-'fek-təd, a-\ *adj* (1587) **1** : INCLINED, DISPOSED ⟨was well ~ toward her⟩ **2 a** : given to affectation : assumed artificially or falsely : PRETENDED ⟨an ~ interest in art⟩ — **af·fect·ed·ly** *adv* — **af·fect·ed·ness** *n*

af·fect·ing \ə-'fek-tiŋ, a-\ *adj* (1720) : evoking a strong emotional response **syn** see MOVING — **af·fect·ing·ly** \-tiŋ-lē\ *adv*

af·fec·tion \ə-'fek-shən\ *n* [ME, fr. OF *affection*, fr. L *affection-, affectio*, fr. *afficere*] (13c) **1** : a moderate feeling or emotion **2** : tender attachment : FONDNESS ⟨she had a deep ~ for her parents⟩ **3 a** (1) : a bodily condition (2) : DISEASE, MALADY **b** : ATTRIBUTE ⟨shape and weight are ~s of bodies⟩ **4** *obs* : PARTIALITY, PREJUDICE **5** : the feeling aspect (as in pleasure) of consciousness **6 a** : PROPENSITY, DISPOSITION **b** *archaic* : AFFECTATION 1 **7** : the action of affecting : the state of being affected **syn** see FEELING — **af·fec·tion·less** \-ləs\ *adj*

af·fec·tion·al \ə-'fek-shnəl, -shə-n[']l\ *adj* (1859) : of or relating to the affections — **af·fec·tion·al·ly** *adv*

af·fec·tion·ate \ə-'fek-sh(ə-)nət\ *adj* (15c) **1** *obs* : INCLINED, DISPOSED **2** : having affection or warm regard : LOVING **3** : proceeding from affection : TENDER ⟨~ care⟩ — **af·fec·tion·ate·ly** *adv*

af·fec·tioned \-shənd\ *adj* (1555) *archaic* : having a tendency, disposition, or inclination : DISPOSED

af·fec·tive \a-'fek-tiv\ *adj* (1623) **1** : relating to, arising from, or influencing feelings or emotions : EMOTIONAL ⟨~ disorders⟩ **2** : expressing emotion ⟨~ language⟩ — **af·fec·tive·ly** *adv* — **af·fec·tiv·i·ty** \,a-,fek-'ti-və-tē\ *n*

af·fect·less \'a-,fekt-ləs, a-'fekt-\ *adj* (1967) : showing or expressing no emotion; *also* : UNFEELING ⟨a ruthless ~ society⟩ — **af·fect·less·ness** *n*

af·fen·pin·scher \'a-fən-,pin-chər\ *n* [G, fr. *Affe* ape + *Pinscher*, a breed of hunting dog] (1903) : any of a breed of toy dogs with a wiry

---

\ə\ abut \ᵊ\ kitten, F table \ər\ further \a\ ash \ā\ ace \ä\ mop, mar

\aů\ out \ch\ chin \e\ bet \ē\ easy \g\ go \i\ hit \ī\ ice \j\ job

\ŋ\ sing \ō\ go \ȯ\ law \ȯi\ boy \th\ thin \t͟h\ the \ü\ loot \ů\ foot

\y\ yet \zh\ vision \á, k̲, ⁿ, œ, œ̄, ɯ, ɯ̄, ʸ\ see Guide to Pronunciation black, red, tan, or gray coat, erect ears, large round eyes, and bushy eyebrows, chin tuft, and mustache

¹af·fer·ent \'a-fə-rənt, -ˌfer-ənt\ *adj* [L *afferent-, afferens*, prp. of *afferre* to bring to, fr. *ad-* + *ferre* to bear — more at BEAR] (ca. 1847) : bearing or conducting inward; *specif* : conveying impulses toward a nerve center (as the brain or spinal cord) — compare EFFERENT — **af·fer·ent·ly** *adv*

²afferent *n* (1949) : an afferent anatomical part (as a nerve)

¹af·fi·ance \ə-'fī-ən(t)s\ *n* [ME, fr. MF, fr. *affier* to pledge, trust, fr. ML *affidare* to pledge, fr. L *ad-* (assumed) VL *fidare* to trust — more at FIANCÉ] (14c) *archaic* : TRUST, CONFIDENCE

²affiance *vt* **-anced; -anc·ing** (1555) : to solemnly promise (oneself or another) in marriage : BETROTH

af·fi·ant \ə-'fī-ənt\ *n* [MF, fr. prp. of *affier*] (1807) : one that swears to an affidavit; *broadly* : DEPONENT

af·fi·cio·na·do *var of* AFICIONADO

af·fi·da·vit \ˌa-fə-'dā-vət\ *n* [ML, he has made an oath, fr. *affidare*] (1593) : a sworn statement in writing made esp. under oath or on affirmation before an authorized magistrate or officer

¹af·fil·i·ate \ə-'fi-lē-ˌāt\ *vb* **-at·ed; -at·ing** [ML *affiliatus*, pp. of *affiliare* to adopt as a son, fr. L *ad-* + *filius* son — more at FEMININE] *vt* (1761) **1 a :** to bring or receive into close connection as a member or branch **b :** to associate as a member ⟨~*s* herself with the local club⟩ **2 :** to trace the origin of — *vi* : to connect or associate oneself : COMBINE — **af·fil·i·a·tion** \-ˌfi-lē-'ā-shən\ *n*

²af·fil·i·ate \ə-'fi-lē-ət, -ˌāt\ *n* (1879) : an affiliated person or organization

af·fil·i·at·ed \-lē-ˌā-təd\ *adj* (1795) : closely associated with another typically in a dependent or subordinate position ⟨the university and its ~ medical school⟩

¹af·fine \a-'fīn, ə-\ *n* [MF *affin*, fr. L *affinis*, fr. *affinis* related] (ca. 1509) : a relative by marriage : IN-LAW

²affine *adj* [L *affinis*, adj.] (1918) : of, relating to, or being a transformation (as a translation, a rotation, or a uniform stretching) that carries straight lines into straight lines and parallel lines into parallel lines but may alter distance between points and angles between lines ⟨~ geometry⟩ — **af·fine·ly** *adv*

af·fined \a-'fīnd, ə-\ *adj* (1597) **1 :** joined in a close relationship : CONNECTED **2 :** bound by obligation

af·fin·i·ty \ə-'fi-nə-tē\ *n, pl* **-ties** [ME *affinite*, fr. MF or L; MF *affinité*, fr. L *affinitas*, fr. *affinis* bordering on, related by marriage, fr. *ad-* + *finis* end, border] (14c) **1 :** relationship by marriage **2 a :** sympathy marked by community of interest : KINSHIP **b** (1) **:** an attraction to or liking for something ⟨people with an ~ to darkness —Mark Twain⟩ ⟨pork and fennel have a natural ~ for each other —Abby Mandel⟩ (2) **:** an attractive force between substances or particles that causes them to enter into and remain in chemical combination **c :** a person esp. of the opposite sex having a particular attraction for one **3 a :** likeness based on relationship or causal connection ⟨found an ~ between the teller of a tale and the craftsman —Mary McCarthy⟩ ⟨this investigation, with *affinities* to a case history, a psychoanalysis, a detective story —Oliver Sachs⟩ **b :** a relation between biological groups involving resemblance in structural plan and indicating a common origin *syn* see ATTRACTION

affinity chromatography *n* (1970) : chromatography in which a macromolecule (as a protein) is isolated and purified by passing it in solution through a column treated with a substance having a ligand for which the macromolecule has an affinity that causes it to be retained on the column

affinity group *n* (1970) : a group of people having a common interest or goal or acting together for a specific purpose (as for a chartered tour)

af·firm \ə-'fərm\ *vb* [ME *affermen*, fr. MF *afermer*, fr. L *affirmare*, fr. *ad-* + *firmare* to make firm, fr. *firmus* firm — more at FIRM] *vt* (14c) **1 a :** VALIDATE, CONFIRM **b :** to state positively **2 :** to assert (as a judgment or decree) as valid or confirmed **3 :** to express dedication to ~ *vi* **1 :** to testify or declare by affirmation as distinguished from swearing an oath **2 :** to uphold a judgment or decree of a lower court *syn* see ASSERT — **af·firm·able** \ə-'fər-mə-bəl\ *adj* — **af·fir·mance** \ə-'fər-mən(t)s\ *n*

af·fir·ma·tion \ˌa-fər-'mā-shən\ *n* (15c) **1 a :** the act of affirming **b :** something affirmed : a positive assertion **2 :** a solemn declaration made under the penalties of perjury by a person who conscientiously declines taking an oath

¹af·fir·ma·tive \ə-'fər-mə-tiv\ *adj* (15c) **1 :** asserting a predicate of a subject **2 :** asserting that the fact is so **3 :** POSITIVE ⟨~ approach⟩ **4 :** favoring or supporting a proposition or motion — **af·fir·ma·tive·ly** *adv*

²affirmative *n* (15c) **1 :** an expression (as the word *yes*) of affirmation or assent **2 :** an affirmative proposition **3 :** the side that upholds the proposition stated in a debate

affirmative action *n* (1965) : an active effort to improve the employment or educational opportunities of members of minority groups and women

¹af·fix \ə-'fiks, a-\ *vt* [L *affixus*, pp. of *affigere* to fasten to, fr. *ad-* + *figere* to fasten — more at FIX] (1533) **1 :** to attach physically ⟨~ a stamp to a letter⟩ **2 :** to attach in any way : ADD, APPEND ⟨~ a signature to a document⟩ **3 :** IMPRESS ⟨~*ed* my seal⟩ *syn* see FASTEN — **af·fix·able** \-'fik-sə-bəl\ *adj* — **af·fix·a·tion** \ˌa-ˌfik-'sā-shən\ *n* — **af·fix·ment** \ə-'fik-smənt, a-\ *n*

²af·fix \'a-ˌfiks\ *n* (1612) **1 :** one or more sounds or letters occurring as a bound form attached to the beginning or end of a word, base, or phrase or inserted within a word or base and serving to produce a derivative word or an inflectional form **2 :** APPENDAGE — **af·fix·al** \-ˌfik-səl\ *or* **af·fix·i·al** \ə-'fik-sē-əl\ *adj*

af·fla·tus \ə-'flā-təs, a-\ *n* [L, act of blowing or breathing on, fr. *afflare* to blow on, fr. *ad-* + *flare* to blow — more at BLOW] (1660) : a divine imparting of knowledge or power : INSPIRATION

af·flict \ə-'flikt\ *vt* [ME, fr. L *afflictus*, pp. of *affligere* to cast down, fr. *ad-* + *fligere* to strike — more at PROFLIGATE] (14c) **1 obs a :** HUMBLE **b :** OVERTHROW **2 a :** to distress so severely as to cause persistent suffering or anguish **b :** TROUBLE, INJURE

syn AFFLICT, TRY, TORMENT, TORTURE, RACK mean to inflict on a person something that is hard to bear. AFFLICT is a general term and applies to the causing of pain or suffering or of acute annoyance, embarrassment, or any distress ⟨ills that *afflict* the elderly⟩. TRY suggests imposing something that strains the powers of endurance or of self-control ⟨children often *try* their parents' patience⟩. TORMENT suggests persecution or the repeated inflicting of suffering or annoyance ⟨a horse *tormented* by flies⟩. TORTURE adds the implication of causing unbearable pain or suffering ⟨*tortured* by a sense of guilt⟩. RACK stresses straining or wrenching ⟨a body *racked* by pain⟩.

af·flic·tion \ə-'flik-shən\ *n* (14c) **1 :** the state of being afflicted **2 :** the cause of persistent pain or distress **3 :** great suffering

af·flic·tive \ə-'flik-tiv\ *adj* (ca. 1611) : causing affliction : DISTRESSING, TROUBLESOME — **af·flic·tive·ly** *adv*

af·flu·ence \'a-ˌflü-ən(t)s *also* a-'flü- *or* ə-\ *n* (14c) **1 a :** an abundant flow or supply : PROFUSION **b :** abundance of property : WEALTH **2 :** a flowing to or toward a point : INFLUX

af·flu·en·cy \-ən(t)-sē\ *n, pl* **-cies** (1664) : AFFLUENCE

¹af·flu·ent \-ənt\ *adj* [ME, fr. MF, fr. L *affluent-, affluens*, prp. of *affluere* to flow to, flow abundantly, fr. *ad-* + *fluere* to flow — more at FLUID] (15c) **1 :** flowing in abundance ⟨~ streams⟩ ⟨~ creativity⟩ **2 :** having a generously sufficient and typically increasing supply of material possessions ⟨our ~ society⟩ *syn* see RICH — **af·flu·ent·ly** *adv*

²affluent *n* (1828) **1 :** a tributary stream **2 :** an affluent person

af·ford \ə-'fōrd, -'fȯrd\ *vt* [ME *aforthen*, fr. OE *geforthian* to carry out, fr. *ge-*, perfective prefix + *forthian* to carry out, fr. *forth* — more at CO-, FORTH] (14c) **1 a :** to manage to bear without serious detriment ⟨you can't ~ to neglect your health⟩ **b :** to be able to bear the cost of ⟨can't ~ to be out of work long⟩ ⟨able to ~ a new car⟩ **2 :** to make available, give forth, or provide naturally or inevitably ⟨the sun ~*s* warmth to the earth⟩ ⟨the roof ~*ed* a fine view⟩ *syn* see GIVE — **af·ford·abil·i·ty** \-ˌfȯr-də-'bi-lə-tē, -ˌfȯr-\ *n* — **af·ford·able** \-'fȯr-də-bəl, -'fȯr-\ *adj* — **af·ford·ably** \-blē\ *adv*

af·for·es·ta·tion \(ˌ)a-ˌfȯr-ə-'stā-shən, ə-, -ˌfär-\ *n* [ML *afforestation-, afforestatio*, fr. *afforestare* to put under forest laws, fr. L *ad-* + ML *foresta, forestis* forest] (1615) : the act or process of establishing a forest esp. on land not previously forested — **af·for·est** \a-'fȯr-əst, -'fär-\ *vt*

¹af·fray \ə-'frā\ *n* [ME, fr. MF, fr. *affreer* to startle] (14c) : FRAY, BRAWL

²affray *vt* [ME *affraien*, fr. MF *affreer*] (14c) *archaic* : STARTLE, FRIGHTEN

af·fri·cate \'a-fri-kət\ *n* [prob. fr. G *Affrikata*, fr. L *africata*, fem. of *africatus*, pp. of *africare* to rub against, fr. *ad-* + *fricare* to rub — more at FRICTION] (1880) : a stop and its immediately following release into a fricative that are considered to constitute a single phoneme (as the \t\ and \sh\ of \ch\ in *choose*) — **af·fric·a·tive** \a-'fri-kə-tiv, ə-\ *n or adj*

¹af·fright \ə-'frīt\ *vt* [ME *afyrht, afright* frightened, fr. OE *āfyrht*, pp. of *āfyrhtan* to frighten, fr. *ā-*, perfective prefix + *fyrhtan* to fear; akin to OE *fyrhto* fright — more at ABIDE, FRIGHT] (bef. 12c) : FRIGHTEN, ALARM

²affright *n* (1596) : sudden and great fear : TERROR

¹af·front \ə-'frənt\ *vt* [ME *afronten*, fr. MF *afronter* to defy, fr. (assumed) VL *affrontare*, fr. L *ad-* + *front-, frons* forehead] (14c) **1 a :** to insult esp. to the face by behavior or language **b :** to cause offense to ⟨a system of law about both family and marriage that ~*ed* lay society —J. H. Mundy⟩ **2 a :** to face in defiance : CONFRONT ⟨~ death⟩ **b** *obs* **:** to encounter face-to-face **3 :** to appear directly before *syn* see OFFEND

²affront *n* (1533) **1** *obs* **:** a hostile encounter **2 :** a deliberate offense : INSULT ⟨an ~ to his dignity⟩

af·fu·sion \a-'fyü-zhən\ *n* [LL *affusion-, affusio*, fr. L *affundere* to pour on, fr. *ad-* + *fundere* to pour — more at FOUND] (1615) : an act of pouring a liquid on (as in baptism)

Af·ghan \'af-ˌgan *also* -gən\ *n* [Per *afghān* Pashtun] (1767) **1 a** (1) **:** PASHTUN (2) **:** PASHTO **b :** a native or inhabitant of Afghanistan **2** *not cap* **:** a blanket or shawl of colored wool knitted or crocheted in strips or squares **3** *not cap* **:** a Turkoman carpet of large size and long pile woven in geometric designs **4 :** AFGHAN HOUND — **Afghan** *adj*

Afghan hound *n* (1925) : any of a breed of tall slim swift hunting dogs of Near Eastern origin with a coat of silky thick hair and a long silky topknot

af·ghani \af-'ga-nē, -'gä-\ *n* [Per *afghānī*, lit., of the Pashtuns] (1927) — see MONEY table

afi·cio·na·da \ə-ˌfi-sh(ē-)ə-'nä-də, -fē-, -sē-ə-, -ˌdä\ *n* [Sp, fem. of *aficionado*] (1952) : a female aficionado

afi·cio·na·do \-'nä-(ˌ)dō\ *n, pl* **-dos** [Sp, fr. pp. of *aficionar* to inspire affection, fr. *afición* affection, fr. L *affection-, affectio* — more at AFFECTION] (1845) : a person who likes, knows about, and appreciates a usu. fervently pursued interest or activity : DEVOTEE ⟨~*s* of the bullfight⟩ ⟨movie ~*s*⟩

afield \ə-'fē(ə)ld\ *adv or adj* (bef. 12c) **1 :** to, in, or on the field ⟨was weak at bat but strong ~⟩ **2 :** away from home : ABROAD **3 :** out of the way : ASTRAY ⟨irrelevant remarks that carried us far ~⟩

afire \ə-'fīr\ *adv or adj* (13c) : being on fire : BLAZING

aflame \ə-'flām\ *adj or adv* (1555) : AFIRE

af·la·tox·in \ˌa-flə-'täk-sən\ *n* [NL *Aspergillus flavus*, species of mold + E *toxin*] (1962) : any of several carcinogenic mycotoxins that are produced esp. in stored agricultural crops (as peanuts) by molds (as *Aspergillus flavus*)

afloat \ə-'flōt\ *adj or adv* [ME *aflot*, fr. OE *on flot*, fr. *on* + *flot*, fr. *flot* deep water, sea; akin to OE *flēotan* to float — more at FLEET] (bef. 12c) **1 a :** borne on or as if on the water **b :** being at sea **2 :** free of difficulties : SELF-SUFFICIENT ⟨the inheritance kept them ~ for years⟩ **3 a :** circulating about ⟨nasty stories were ~⟩ **b :** ADRIFT

aflut·ter \ə-'flə-tər\ *adj* (1830) **1 :** being in a flutter : FLUTTERING **2 :** nervously excited **3 :** filled with or marked by the presence of fluttering things ⟨roofs ~ with flags⟩

afoot \ə-'fu̇t\ *adv or adj* (13c) **1 :** on foot **2 :** in the process of development : UNDER WAY ⟨something out of the ordinary was ~ —Hamilton Basso⟩

afore \ə-'fōr, -'fȯr\ *adv or conj or prep* [ME, fr. OE *onforan*, fr. *on* + *foran* before — more at BEFORE] (bef. 12c) *chiefly dial* : BEFORE

afore·men·tioned \-'men(t)-shənd\ *adj* (1587) : mentioned previously

afore·said \-ˌsed\ *adj* (14c) : said or named before or above

afore·thought \-ˌthȯt\ *adj* (1581) : previously in mind : PREMEDI-
TATED, DELIBERATE ⟨with malice ∼⟩
a for·ti·o·ri \ˌä-ˌfȯr-shē-'ȯr-ˌī, ˌä-ˌfȯr-shē-'ȯr-ē, -ˌfȯr-tē-, -'ȯr-\ *adv* [NL,
lit., from the stronger (argument)] (1588) : with greater reason or more
convincing force — used in drawing a conclusion that is inferred to be
even more certain than another ⟨the man of prejudice is, *a fortiori*, a
man of limited mental vision⟩
afoul of \ə-'faú-ləv\ *prep* (1824) **1 :** in or into conflict with **2 :** in or
into collision or entanglement with
Afr- *or* **Afro-** *comb form* [L *Afr-*, *Afer*] : African ⟨*Afro*-American⟩
: African and ⟨*Afro*-Asiatic⟩
afraid \ə-'frād, *Southern also* ə-'fred\ *adj* [ME *affraied*, fr. pp. of *affraien* to frighten — more at AFFRAY] (14c) **1 :** filled with fear or apprehension ⟨∼ of machines⟩ ⟨∼ for his job⟩ **2 :** filled with concern or
regret over an unwanted situation ⟨I'm ∼ I won't be able to go⟩ **3
:** having a dislike for something ⟨∼ of hard work⟩ *syn* see FEARFUL
A–frame \'ā-ˌfrām\ *n* (ca. 1909) **1 :** a support structure shaped like
the letter A **2 :** a building typically having triangular front and rear
walls and a roof reaching to the ground
afreet *or* **afrit** \'a-ˌfrēt, ə-'frēt\ *n* [Ar *'ifrīt*] (1786) : a powerful evil
jinni, demon, or monstrous giant in Arabic mythology
afresh \ə-'fresh\ *adv* (15c) : from a fresh beginning : ANEW, AGAIN
¹Af·ri·can \'a-fri-kən *also* 'ä-\ *n* (bef. 12c) **1 :** a native or inhabitant of
Africa **2 :** a person esp. a black person of African ancestry
²African *adj* (1564) : of, relating to, or characteristic of the continent
of Africa or its people — **Af·ri·can·ness** \-kə(n)-nəs\ *n*
Af·ri·ca·na \ˌa-fri-'ka-nə, -'kä-, -'kā- *also* ˌä-\ *n pl* (1908) : materials (as
books, documents, or artifacts) relating to African history and culture
Af·ri·can–Amer·i·can \ˌa-fri-kə-nə-'mer-ə-kən *also* ˌä-\ *n* (1984)
: AFRO-AMERICAN — **African–American** *adj*
African buffalo *n* (1902) : CAPE BUFFALO
African daisy *n* (ca. 1889) : any of a genus (*Arctotis*) of widely culti-
vated composite herbs
Af·ri·can·der *or* **Af·ri·kan·der** \ˌa-fri-'kan-dər\ *n* [Afrik *Afrikaner*,
Afrikaander, lit., Afrikaner] (1852) : any of a breed of tall red large-
horned humped southern African cattle used chiefly for meat or draft
African elephant *n* (1607) : ELEPHANT 1a
Af·ri·can·ise *Brit var of* AFRICANIZE
Af·ri·can·ism \'a-fri-kə-ˌni-zəm *also* 'ä-\ *n* (1641) **1 :** a characteristic
feature (as a custom or belief) of African culture **2 :** a characteristic
feature of an African language occurring in a non-African language **3
:** allegiance to the traditions, interests, or ideals of Africa
Af·ri·can·ist \-nist\ *n* (1895) : a specialist in African languages or
cultures
Af·ri·can·ize \-ˌnīz\ *vt* **-ized; -iz·ing** (1853) **1 :** to cause to acquire a
distinctively African trait **2 :** to bring under the influence, control, or
cultural or civil supremacy of Africans and esp. black Africans — **Af-
ri·can·iza·tion** \ˌa-fri-kə-nə-'zā-shən *also* ˌä-\ *n*
Africanized bee *n* (1974) : a honeybee that originated in Brazil as an
accidental hybrid between an aggressive African subspecies (*Apis mellifera scutellata*) and previously established European honeybees and
has spread to Mexico and the southernmost U.S. by breeding with
local bees producing populations retaining most of the African bee's
traits — called also *Africanized honeybee, killer bee*
African mahogany *n* (1842) : MAHOGANY 1b
African violet *n* (1902) : any of several tropical African gesneriads
(esp. *Saintpaulia ionantha*) widely grown as houseplants for their velvety fleshy leaves and showy purple, pink, or white flowers
¹Af·ri·kaans \ˌa-fri-'kän(t)s, ˌä-, -'känz, 'a-fri-ˌ, 'ä-\ *n* [Afrik, fr. *afrikaans*, adj., African, fr. obs. Afrik *afrikanisch*, fr. L *africanus*] (1908)
: a language developed from 17th century Dutch that is one of the
official languages of the Republic of So. Africa
²Afrikaans *adj* (1923) : of or relating to Afrikaners or Afrikaans
Af·ri·ka·ner \ˌa-fri-'kä-nər\ *n*, *often attrib* [Afrik, lit., African, fr. L
africanus] (1824) : a South African of European descent whose native
language is Afrikaans — **Af·ri·ka·ner·dom** \-dəm\ *n*
¹Af·ro \'a-(ˌ)frō\ *adj* [prob. fr. *Afro-American*] (1938) : characterized by
or being a hairstyle of tight curls in a full evenly rounded shape
²Afro *n*, *pl* **Afros** (1968) : an Afro hairstyle
Af·ro–Amer·i·can \ˌa-frō-ə-'mer-ə-kən\ *n* (1853)
: an American of African and esp. of black African descent — **Afro–American** *adj*
Af·ro–Asi·at·ic \ˌa-frō-ˌā-zhē-'a-tik, -zē- *also*
-shē-\ *adj* (1953) : of, relating to, or being a family
of languages widely distributed over southwestern
Asia and Africa comprising the Semitic, Egyptian,
Berber, Cushitic, and Chadic subfamilies
Af·ro·cen·tric \ˌa-frō-'sen-trik\ *adj* (1966) : centered on or derived from Africa or the Africans —
Af·ro·cen·trism \-ˌtri-zəm\ *n*
¹aft \'aft\ *adv* [ME *afte* back, fr. OE *æftan* from
behind, behind; akin to OE *æfter*] (1628) : near,
toward, or in the stern of a ship or the tail of an
aircraft : ABAFT ⟨called all hands ∼⟩
²aft *adj* (1816) : REARWARD, AFTER 2 ⟨the ∼ decks⟩

Afro

³aft *Scot var of* OFT
¹af·ter \'af-tər\ *adv* [ME, fr. OE *æfter*; akin to OHG *aftar* after, and
prob. to OE *of* off] (bef. 12c) : following in time or place : AFTERWARD,
BEHIND, LATER ⟨we arrived shortly ∼⟩ ⟨returned 20 years ∼⟩
²after *prep* (bef. 12c) **1 a :** behind in place **b** (1) : subsequent to in
time or order (2) : subsequent to and in view of ⟨∼ all our advice⟩ **2**
— used as a function word to indicate the object of a stated or implied
action ⟨go ∼ gold⟩ ⟨was asking ∼ you⟩ **3 :** so as to resemble: as **a
:** in accordance with **b :** with the name of or a name derived from
that of **c :** in the characteristic manner of **d :** in imitation of
³after *conj* (bef. 12c) : subsequently to the time when
⁴after *adj* (bef. 12c) **1 :** later in time ⟨in ∼ years⟩ **2 :** located toward
the rear and esp. toward the stern of a ship or tail of an aircraft
⁵af·ter \'äf-tər\ *verbal auxiliary* (1800) *chiefly Irish* — used with a present participle to indicate action completed and esp. just completed ⟨the
poor old man is ∼ dying on me —J. M. Synge⟩
⁶after *n* (ca. 1902) : AFTERNOON
after all *adv* (1846) **1 :** in spite of considerations or expectations to
the contrary : NEVERTHELESS ⟨decided to take the train *after all*⟩ ⟨didn't

rain *after all*⟩ **2** — used as a sentence modifier to emphasize something to be taken into consideration ⟨literature which is *after all* only a
special department of reading —W. W. Watt⟩
af·ter·birth \'af-tər-ˌbərth\ *n* (1587) : the placenta and fetal membranes that are expelled after delivery
af·ter·burn·er \-ˌbər-nər\ *n* (1947) **1 :** a device incorporated into the
tail pipe of a turbojet engine for injecting fuel into the hot exhaust
gases and burning it to provide extra thrust **2 :** a device for burning
or catalytically destroying unburned or partially burned carbon compounds in exhaust (as from an automobile)
af·ter·care \-ˌker, -ˌkar\ *n* (1894) : the care, treatment, help, or supervision given to persons discharged from an institution (as a hospital)
af·ter·clap \-ˌklap\ *n* (14c) : an unexpected damaging or unsettling
event following a supposedly closed affair
af·ter·deck \-ˌdek\ *n* (1897) : the part of a deck abaft amidships
af·ter·ef·fect \'af-tə-rə-ˌfekt\ *n* (1817) : an effect that follows its cause
after an interval
af·ter·glow \'af-tər-ˌglō\ *n* (1871) **1 :** a reflection of past splendor,
success, or emotion **2 :** a glow remaining where a light has disappeared
af·ter·hours \ˌaf-tər-'aú(-ə)rz\ *adj* (1929) : engaged in or operating
after a legal or conventional closing time ⟨∼ drinking⟩ ⟨an ∼ club⟩
af·ter·im·age \'af-tər-ˌi-mij\ *n* (1874) **1 :** a usu. visual sensation occurring after stimulation by its external cause has ceased
af·ter·life \'af-tər-ˌlīf\ *n* (ca. 1593) **1 :** an existence after death **2 :** a
later period in one's life
af·ter·mar·ket \-ˌmär-kət\ *n* (1940) **1 :** the market for parts and accessories used in the repair or enhancement of a product (as an automobile) **2 :** a secondary market available after sales in the original
market are finished ⟨a movie in the videocassette ∼⟩
af·ter·math \-ˌmath\ *n* [⁴*after* + *math* (mowing, crop)] (1523) **1 :** a
second-growth crop — called also *rowen* **2 :** CONSEQUENCE, RESULT
⟨stricken with guilt as an ∼ of the accident⟩ **3 :** the period immediately following a usu. ruinous event ⟨in the ∼ of the war⟩
af·ter·most \-ˌmōst\ *adj* (1773) : farthest aft
af·ter·noon \ˌaf-tər-'nün\ *n* (13c) **1 :** the part of day between noon
and sunset **2 :** a relatively late period (as of time or life) ⟨in the ∼ of
the 19th century⟩ — **afternoon** *adj*
af·ter·noons \-'nünz\ *adv* (1896) : in the afternoon repeatedly : on any
afternoon
af·ter·piece \'af-tər-ˌpēs\ *n* (1779) : a short usu. comic entertainment
performed after a play
af·ters \'af-tərz\ *n pl* (ca. 1909) *Brit* : DESSERT
af·ter·shave \'af-tər-ˌshāv\ *n* (1946) : a usu. scented lotion for use on
the face after shaving
af·ter·shock \-ˌshäk\ *n* (1894) **1 :** a minor shock following the main
shock of an earthquake **2 :** an aftereffect of a distressing or traumatic
event
af·ter·taste \-ˌtāst\ *n* (ca. 1798) : persistence of a sensation (as of flavor or an emotion) after the stimulating agent or experience has gone
af·ter–tax \-'taks\ *adj* (1954) : remaining after payment of taxes and
esp. of income tax ⟨an ∼ profit⟩
af·ter·thought \-ˌthȯt\ *n* (ca. 1661) **1 :** an idea occurring later **2 :** a
part, feature, or device not thought of originally
af·ter·time \-ˌtīm\ *n* (1597) : FUTURE
af·ter·ward \'af-tə(r)-wərd\ *or* **af·ter·wards** \-wərdz\ *adv* (13c) : at a
later or succeeding time : SUBSEQUENTLY, THEREAFTER
af·ter·word \-ˌwərd\ *n* (1890) : EPILOGUE 1
af·ter·world \-ˌwərld\ *n* (1596) : a future world : a world after death
ag \'ag\ *adj* (ca. 1918) : of or relating to agriculture ⟨∼ schools⟩
ag- — see AD-
Aga·da \ə-'gä-də, -'gȯ-\ *var of* HAGGADAH
again \ə-'gen, -'gin, -'gān\ *adv* [ME, alter. of *againes*, fr.
again] (13c) **1 a :** in opposition or hostility to **b :** contrary to ⟨∼
the law⟩ **c :** in competition with **d :** as a basis for disapproval of
⟨had nothing ∼ him⟩ **2 a :** directly opposite : FACING **b** *obs* : exposed to **3 :** compared or contrasted with **4 a :** in preparation or
provision for **b :** as a defense or protection from **5 a :** in the direction of and into contact with **b :** in contact with **6 :** in a direction
opposite to the motion or course of : counter to **7 a :** as a counterbalance to **b :** in exchange for **c :** as a charge on **8 :** before the
background of
²against *conj* (14c) *archaic* : in preparation for the time when ⟨throw
on another log of wood ∼ father comes home —Charles Dickens⟩
Ag·a·mem·non \ˌa-gə-'mem-ˌnän, -nən\ *n* [L, fr. Gk *Agamemnōn*] : a
king of Mycenae and leader of the Greeks in the Trojan War
aga·mete \(ˌ)ā-'ga-ˌmēt *also* -gə-'mēt\ *n* [ISV, fr. Gk *agametos* unmar-
ried, fr. *a-* + *gamein* to marry, fr. *gamos* marriage] (ca. 1920) : an
asexual reproductive cell (as a spore)
agam·ic \(ˌ)ā-'ga-mik\ *adj* [Gk *agamos* unmarried, fr. *a-* + *gamos*]
(1850) : ASEXUAL, PARTHENOGENETIC
agam·ma·glob·u·lin·emia \ˌā-ˌga-mə-ˌglä-byə-lə-'nē-mē-ə\ *n* [NL, fr.
a- + ISV *gamma globulin* + NL *-emia*] (ca. 1952) : a condition in
which the body forms few or no gamma globulins or antibodies —
agam·ma·glob·u·lin·emic \-'nē-mik\ *adj*
aga·mo·sper·my \(ˌ)ā-'ga-mə-ˌspər-mē, 'a-gə-mō-ˌspər-\ *n* [Gk *agamos*
+ E *-spermy*] (1944) : APOGAMY; *specif* : apogamy in which sexual
union is not completed and the embryo is produced from the innermost
layer of the integument of the female gametophyte

\ə\ abut \'ə\ kitten, F table \ər\ further \a\ ash \ā\ ace \ä\ mop, mar
\aú\ out \ch\ chin \e\ bet \ē\ easy \g\ go \i\ hit \ī\ ice \j\ job
\ŋ\ sing \ō\ go \ȯ\ law \ȯi\ boy \th\ thin \th̲\ the \ü\ loot \ù\ foot
\y\ yet \zh\ vision \à, k̲, ⁿ, œ, œ̄, œ, ē̄, ᵊ\ see Guide to Pronunciation

ag·a·pan·thus \\,a-gə-'pan(t)-thəs\ *n, pl* **-thus** *also* **-thuses** [NL, genus name, fr. Gk *agapē* + *anthos* flower — more at ANTHOLOGY] (ca. 1789) : any of several African plants (genus *Agapanthus*) of the lily family cultivated for their umbels of showy blue or purple flowers

¹**aga·pe** \ä-'gä-(,)pā, 'ä-gə-,pā\ *n* [LL, fr. Gk *agapē*, lit., love] (1607) 1 : LOVE FEAST 2 : LOVE 4a

²**agape** \ə-'gāp *also* -'gap\ *adj or adv* (1667) 1 : wide open : GAPING 2 : being in a state of wonder

agar \'ä-gər\ *n* [Malay *agar-agar*] (1889) 1 : a gelatinous colloidal extractive of a red alga (as of the genera *Gelidium, Gracilaria,* and *Eucheuma*) used esp. in culture media or as a gelling and stabilizing agent in foods 2 : a culture medium containing agar

agar–agar \,ä-gər-'ä-gər\ *n* [Malay] (1820) : AGAR

aga·ric \'a-gər-ik, ə-'gar-ik\ *n* [L *agaricum*, a fungus, fr. Gk *agarikon*] (15c) 1 : the dried fruiting body of a fungus (*Fomes officinalis* syn. *Polyporus officinalis*) formerly used in medicine 2 : any of a family (Agaricaceae) of fungi with the sporophore usu. resembling an umbrella and with numerous gills on the underside of the cap

aga·rose \'a-gə-,rōs, 'ä-, -,rōz\ *n* (1964) : a polysaccharide obtained from agar and used esp. as a supporting medium in gel electrophoresis

ag·ate \'a-gət\ *n, often attrib* [MF, fr. L *achates*, fr. Gk *achatēs*] (1570) 1 : a fine-grained variegated chalcedony having its colors arranged in stripes, blended in clouds, or showing mosslike forms 2 : something made of or fitted with agate: as **a** : a drawplate used by gold-wire drawers **b** : a playing marble of agate 3 : a size of type approximately 5½ point

agate line *n* (ca. 1935) : a space one column wide and ¹/₁₄ inch deep used as a unit of measurement in classified advertising

agate ware *n* (1857) 1 : pottery veined and mottled to resemble agate 2 : an enameled iron or steel ware for household utensils

aga·ve \ə-'gä-vē\ *n* [NL *Agave*, genus name, fr. L, a daughter of Cadmus, fr. Gk *Agauē*] (ca. 1797) : any of a genus (*Agave* of the family Agavaceae, the agave family) of plants having spiny-margined leaves and flowers in tall spreading panicles and including some cultivated for their fiber or sap or for ornament

agaze \ə-'gāz\ *adj* (ca. 1902) : engaged in the act of gazing

¹**age** \'āj\ *n* [ME, fr. OF *aage*, fr. (assumed) VL *aetaticum,* fr. L *aetat-, aetas,* fr. *aevum* lifetime — more at AYE] (13c) 1 **a** : the time of life at which some particular qualification, power, or capacity arises or rests ⟨the voting ~ is 18⟩; *specif* : MAJORITY **b** : one of the stages of life **c** : the length of an existence extending from the beginning to any given time ⟨a boy 10 years of ~⟩ **d** : LIFETIME **e** : an advanced stage of life 2 : a period of time dominated by a central figure or prominent feature ⟨the ~ of Pericles⟩: as **a** : a period in history or human progress ⟨the ~ of reptiles⟩ ⟨the ~ of exploration⟩ **b** : a cultural period marked by the prominence of a particular item ⟨entering the atomic ~⟩ **c** : a division of geologic time that is usu. shorter than an epoch 3 **a** : the period contemporary with a person's lifetime or with his or her active life **b** : a long time — usu. used in pl. ⟨haven't seen him in ~s⟩ **c** : GENERATION 4 : an individual's development measured in terms of the years requisite for like development of an average individual *syn* see PERIOD

²**age** *vb* **aged; ag·ing** *or* **age·ing** *vi* (14c) 1 : to become old : show the effects or the characteristics of increasing age 2 : to acquire a desirable quality (as mellowness or ripeness) by standing undisturbed for some time ⟨letting cheese ~⟩ ~ *vt* 1 : to cause to become old 2 : to bring to a state fit for use or to maturity — **ag·er** \'ā-jər\ *n*

-age *n suffix* [ME, fr. OF, fr. L *-aticum*] 1 : aggregate : collection ⟨track*age*⟩ 2 **a** : action : process ⟨haul*age*⟩ **b** : cumulative result of ⟨break*age*⟩ **c** : rate of ⟨dos*age*⟩ 3 : house or place of ⟨orphan*age*⟩ 4 : state : rank ⟨peon*age*⟩ 5 : charge ⟨post*age*⟩

aged \'ā-jəd, 'ājd; 'ājd *for 1b*\ *adj* (15c) 1 : grown old: as **a** : of an advanced age **b** : having attained a specified age ⟨a man ~ 40 years⟩ 2 : typical of old age — **ag·ed·ness** \'ā-jəd-nəs\ *n*

age–group \'āj-,grüp\ *n* (1904) : a segment of a population that is of approximately the same age or is within a specified range of ages

age·ism *also* **ag·ism** \'ā-(,)ji-zəm\ *n* (1969) : prejudice or discrimination against a particular age-group and esp. the elderly — **age·ist** *also* **ag·ist** \-jist\ *adj*

age·less \'āj-ləs\ *adj* (1651) 1 : not growing old or showing the effects of age 2 : TIMELESS, ETERNAL ⟨~ truths⟩ — **age·less·ly** *adv* — **age·less·ness** *n*

age·long \'āj-,lȯŋ\ *adj* (1810) : lasting for an age : EVERLASTING

age–mate \-,māt\ *n* (1583) : one who is of about the same age as another

agen·cy \'ā-jən(t)-sē\ *n, pl* **-cies** (1658) 1 : the capacity, condition, or state of acting or of exerting power : OPERATION 2 : a person or thing through which power is exerted or an end is achieved : INSTRUMENTALITY ⟨communicated through the ~ of the ambassador⟩ 3 **a** : the office or function of an agent **b** : the relationship between a principal and his agent 4 : an establishment engaged in doing business for another ⟨an advertising ~⟩ 5 : an administrative division (as of a government) ⟨the ~ for consumer protection⟩

agency shop *n* (ca. 1946) : a shop in which the union serves as the agent for and receives dues and assessments from all employees in the bargaining unit regardless of union membership

agen·da \ə-'jen-də\ *n* [L, neut. pl. of *agendum,* gerundive of *agere*] (1871) 1 : a list or outline of things to be considered or done ⟨~s of faculty meetings⟩ 2 : an underlying often ideological plan or program ⟨a political ~⟩ — **agen·da·less** \-də-ləs\ *adj*

agen·dum \-dəm\ *n, pl* **-da** \-də\ *or* **-dums** [L] (ca. 1847) 1 : AGENDA 2 : an item on an agenda

agen·e·sis \(,)ā-'je-nə-səs\ *n* [NL] (ca. 1879) : lack or failure of development (as of a body part)

agent \'ā-jənt\ *n* [ME, fr. ML *agent-, agens,* fr. L, prp. of *agere* to drive, lead, act, do; akin to ON *aka* to travel in a vehicle, Gk *agein* to drive, lead] (15c) 1 : one that acts or exerts power 2 **a** : something that produces or is capable of producing an effect : an active or efficient cause **b** : a chemically, physically, or biologically active principle 3 : a means or instrument by which a guiding intelligence achieves a result 4 : one who is authorized to act for or in the place of another: as **a** : a representative, emissary, or official of a government ⟨crown ~⟩ ⟨federal ~⟩ **b** : one engaged in undercover activities (as espionage) : SPY ⟨secret ~⟩ **c** : a business representative (as of an athlete or entertainer) ⟨a theatrical ~⟩

agent–general *n, pl* **agents–general** (1833) : a chief agent; *specif* : the representative in England of a British dominion

agent·ing \'ā-jən-tiŋ\ *n* (1681) : the business or activities of an agent

Agent Orange *n* [so called fr. the identifying color stripe on its container] (1970) : an herbicide widely used as a defoliant in the Vietnam War that is composed of 2,4-D and 2,4,5-T and contains dioxin as a contaminant

agent pro·vo·ca·teur \,ä-,zhän-prō-,vä-kə-'tər, 'ä-jənt-\ *n, pl* **agents provocateurs** \,ä-,zhän-prō-,vä-kə-'tər, 'ä-jən(t)s-prō-\ [F, lit., provoking agent] (1877) : one employed to associate with suspected persons and by pretending sympathy with their aims to incite them to some incriminating action

agent·ry \'ā-jən-trē\ *n, pl* **-ries** (1925) : the office, duties, or activities of an agent

age of consent (1504) : the age at which one is legally competent to give consent esp. to marriage or to sexual intercourse

age of reason (ca. 1794) 1 : a period characterized by a prevailing belief in the use of reason; *esp* : the 18th century in England and France 2 : the time of life when one begins to be able to distinguish right from wrong

age–old \'ā-'jōld\ *adj* (1904) : having existed for ages : ANCIENT

ag·er·a·tum \,a-jə-'rā-təm\ *n, pl* **-tum** *also* **-tums** [NL, genus name, fr. Gk *agēratos* ageless, fr. *a-* + *gēras* old age — more at GERONT-] (1866) : any of a genus (*Ageratum*) of tropical American composite herbs often cultivated for their small showy heads of blue or white flowers; *also* : a related blue-flowered plant (*Eupatorium coelestinum*)

Ag·ga·dah \ə-'gä-də, -'gȯ\ *var of* HAGGADAH

Ag·ge·us \a-'gē-əs\ *n* [LL *Aggaeus,* fr. Gk *Aggaios,* fr. Heb *Ḥaggai*] : HAGGAI

¹**ag·gie** \'a-gē\ *n, often cap* [agricultural + *-ie*] (1902) : an agricultural school or college; *also* : a student at such an institution

²**aggie** *n* [agate + *-ie*] (1915) : a playing marble; *specif* : AGATE 2b

ag·gior·na·men·to \ə-,jȯr-nə-'men-(,)tō\ *n, pl* **-tos** [It, fr. *aggiornare* to bring up to date, fr. *a* to (fr. L *ad-*) + *giorno* day, fr. LL *diurnum* day — more at JOURNEY] (1963) : a bringing up to date : MODERNIZATION ⟨dedicated to the ~ of the church⟩

¹**ag·glom·er·ate** \ə-'glä-mə-,rāt\ *vt* **-at·ed; -at·ing** [L *agglomeratus,* pp. of *agglomerare* to heap up, join, fr. *ad-* + *glomer-, glomus* ball — more at CLAM] (1684) : to gather into a ball, mass, or cluster

²**ag·glom·er·ate** \-rət\ *adj* (1828) : gathered into a ball, mass, or cluster; *specif* : clustered or growing together but not coherent ⟨an ~ flower head⟩

³**ag·glom·er·ate** \-rət\ *n* (1830) 1 : a rock composed of volcanic fragments of various sizes and degrees of angularity 2 : a jumbled mass or collection : AGGLOMERATION

ag·glom·er·a·tion \ə-,glä-mə-'rā-shən\ *n* (1774) 1 : the action or process of collecting in a mass 2 : a heap or cluster of usu. disparate elements ⟨urban ~s knit together by the new railways —*Times Lit. Supp.*⟩ — **ag·glom·er·a·tive** \ə-'glä-mə-,rā-tiv\ *adj*

ag·glu·ti·na·bil·i·ty \ə-,glü-t⁵n-ə-'bi-lə-tē\ *n* (1901) : capacity (as of red blood cells) to be agglutinated — **ag·glu·ti·na·ble** \ə-'glü-t⁵n-ə-bəl\ *adj*

¹**ag·glu·ti·nate** \ə-'glü-t⁵n-,āt\ *vb* **-nat·ed; -nat·ing** [L *agglutinatus,* pp. of *agglutinare* to glue to, fr. *ad-* + *glutinare* to glue, fr. *glutin-, gluten* glue — more at CLAY] *vt* (1586) 1 : to cause to adhere : FASTEN 2 : to combine into a compound : attach to a base as an affix 3 : to cause to undergo agglutination ~ *vi* : to unite or combine into a group or mass 2 : to form words by agglutination

²**ag·glu·ti·nate** \-t⁵n-ət, -t⁵n-,āt\ *n* (1952) : a clump of agglutinated material (as blood cells or mineral particles in soil)

ag·glu·ti·na·tion \ə-,glü-t⁵n-'ā-shən\ *n* (1541) 1 : the action or process of agglutinating 2 : a mass or group formed by the union of separate elements 3 : the formation of derivational or inflectional words by putting together constituents of which each expresses a single definite meaning 4 : a reaction in which particles (as red blood cells or bacteria) suspended in a liquid collect into clumps and which occurs esp. as a serologic response to a specific antibody

ag·glu·ti·na·tive \ə-'glü-t⁵n-,ā-tiv, -ə-tiv\ *adj* (1634) 1 : ADHESIVE 2 : characterized by linguistic agglutination

ag·glu·ti·nin \ə-'glü-t⁵n-ən\ *n* [ISV *agglutin*ation + *-in*] (1902) : a substance (as an antibody) producing agglutination

ag·glu·ti·no·gen \ə-'glü-t⁵n-ə-jən\ *n* [*agglutin*in + *-o-* + *-gen*] (1904) : an antigen whose presence results in the formation of an agglutinin — **ag·glu·ti·no·gen·ic** \-,glü-t⁵n-ə-'je-nik\ *adj*

ag·gra·da·tion \,a-grə-'dā-shən\ *n* [*ad-* + *gradation*] (1898) : a modification of the earth's surface in the direction of uniformity of grade by deposition

ag·gran·dise *Brit var of* AGGRANDIZE

ag·gran·dize \ə-'gran-,dīz *also* 'a-grən-\ *vt* **-dized; -diz·ing** [F *agrandiss-,* stem of *agrandir,* fr. *a-* (fr. L *ad-*) + *grandir* to increase, fr. L *grandire,* fr. *grandis* great] (1634) 1 : to make great or greater : INCREASE, ENLARGE 2 : to make appear great or greater : praise highly 3 : to enhance the power, wealth, position, or reputation of ⟨exploited the situation to ~ himself⟩ — **ag·gran·dize·ment** \ə-'gran-dəz-mənt, -,dīz- *also* ,a-grən-'dīz-\ *n* — **ag·gran·diz·er** \ə-'gran-,dī-zər *also* 'a-grən-\ *n*

ag·gra·vate \'a-grə-,vāt\ *vt* **-vat·ed; -vat·ing** [L *aggravatus,* pp. of *aggravare* to make heavier, fr. *ad-* + *gravare* to burden, fr. *gravis* heavy — more at GRIEVE] (1530) 1 *obs* **a** : to make heavy : BURDEN **b** : INCREASE 2 : to make worse, more serious, or more severe : intensify unpleasantly ⟨problems have been *aggravated* by neglect⟩ 3 **a** : to rouse to displeasure or anger by usu. persistent and often petty goading **b** : to produce inflammation in

usage Although *aggravate* has been used in sense 3a since the 17th century, it has been the object of disapproval only since about 1870. It is used in expository prose ⟨when his silly conceit . . . about his not-very-good early work has begun to *aggravate* us —William Styron⟩

but seems to be more common in speech and casual writing ⟨a good profession for him, because bus drivers get *aggravated* —Jackie Gleason (interview, 1986)⟩ ⟨& now this letter comes to *aggravate* me a thousand times worse —Mark Twain (letter, 1864)⟩. Sense 2 is far more common than sense 3a in published prose. Such is not the case, however, with *aggravation* and *aggravating*. *Aggravation* is used in sense 3 somewhat more than in its earlier senses; *aggravating* has practically no use other than to express annoyance.

aggravated assault *n* (1925) : an assault that is more serious than a common assault: as **a** : an assault combined with an intent to commit a crime **b** : any of various assaults so defined by statute

aggravating *adj* (1775) : arousing displeasure, impatience, or anger
usage see AGGRAVATE

ag·gra·va·tion \ˌa-grə-'vā-shən\ *n* (ca. 1555) **1** : an act or circumstance that intensifies or makes worse **2** : the act, action, or result of aggravating; *esp* : an increasing in seriousness or severity **3** : IRRITATION, PROVOCATION **usage** see AGGRAVATE

¹ag·gre·gate \'a-gri-gət\ *adj* [ME *aggregat*, fr. L *aggregatus*, pp. of *aggregare* to add to, fr. *ad-* + *greg-*, *grex* flock] (15c) : formed by the collection of units or particles into a body, mass, or amount : COLLECTIVE: as **a** (1) : clustered in a dense mass or head ⟨an ~ flower⟩ (2) : formed from several separate ovaries of a single flower ⟨~ fruit⟩ **b** : composed of mineral crystals of one or more kinds or of mineral rock fragments **c** : taking all units as a whole ⟨~ sales⟩ — **ag·gre·gate·ly** *adv* — **ag·gre·gate·ness** *n*

²ag·gre·gate \-ˌgāt\ *vt* **-gat·ed; -gat·ing** (15c) **1** : to collect or gather into a mass or whole **2** : to amount in the aggregate to : TOTAL

³ag·gre·gate \-gət\ *n* (15c) **1** : a mass or body of units or parts somewhat loosely associated with one another **2** : the whole sum or amount : SUM TOTAL **3 a** : an aggregate rock **b** : any of several hard inert materials (as sand, gravel, or slag) used for mixing with a cementing material to form concrete, mortar, or plaster **c** : a clustered mass of individual soil particles varied in shape, ranging in size from a microscopic granule to a small crumb, and considered the basic structural unit of soil **4** : SET 21 **5** : MONETARY AGGREGATE — **in the aggregate** : considered as a whole : COLLECTIVELY ⟨dividends for the year amounted *in the aggregate* to 25 million dollars⟩

ag·gre·ga·tion \ˌa-gri-'gā-shən\ *n* (1547) **1** : a group, body, or mass composed of many distinct parts or individuals **2 a** : the collecting of units or parts into a mass or whole **b** : the condition of being so collected — **ag·gre·ga·tion·al** \-shnəl, -shə-nᵊl\ *adj*

ag·gre·ga·tive \'a-gri-ˌgā-tiv\ *adj* (1644) **1** : of or relating to an aggregate **2** : tending to aggregate — **ag·gre·ga·tive·ly** *adv*

ag·gress \ə-'gres\ *vi* (ca. 1714) : to commit aggression : act aggressively

ag·gres·sion \ə-'gre-shən\ *n* [L *aggression-, aggressio* attack, fr. *aggredi* to attack, fr. *ad-* + *gradi* to step, go — more at GRADE] (1611) **1** : a forceful action or procedure (as an unprovoked attack) esp. when intended to dominate or master **2** : the practice of making attacks or encroachments; *esp* : unprovoked violation by one country of the territorial integrity of another **3** : hostile, injurious, or destructive behavior or outlook esp. when caused by frustration

ag·gres·sive \ə-'gre-siv\ *adj* (1824) **1 a** : tending toward or exhibiting aggression ⟨~ behavior⟩ **b** : marked by combative readiness ⟨an ~ fighter⟩ **2 a** : marked by obtrusive energy **b** : marked by driving forceful energy or initiative : ENTERPRISING ⟨an ~ salesman⟩ **3** : strong or emphatic in effect or intent ⟨~ colors⟩ ⟨~ flavors⟩ **4** : more severe, intensive, or comprehensive than usual esp. in dosage or extent ⟨~ chemotherapy⟩ — **ag·gres·sive·ly** *adv* — **ag·gres·sive·ness** *n* — **ag·gres·siv·i·ty** \ˌa-ˌgre-'si-və-tē\ *n*

syn AGGRESSIVE, MILITANT, ASSERTIVE, SELF-ASSERTIVE mean obtrusively energetic esp. in pursuing particular goals. AGGRESSIVE implies a disposition to dominate often in disregard of others' rights or in determined and energetic pursuit of one's ends ⟨was taught to be *aggressive* in his business dealings⟩. MILITANT also implies a fighting disposition but suggests not self-seeking but devotion to a cause, movement, or principle ⟨*militant* protesters held a rally against racism⟩. ASSERTIVE suggests bold self-confidence in expression of opinion ⟨the more *assertive* speakers dominated the forum⟩. SELF-ASSERTIVE connotes forwardness or brash self-confidence ⟨a *self-assertive* young executive climbing the corporate ladder⟩.

ag·gres·sor \ə-'gre-sər\ *n* (1646) : one that commits or practices aggression

ag·grieve \ə-'grēv\ *vt* **ag·grieved; ag·griev·ing** [ME *agreven*, fr. MF *agrever*, fr. L *aggravare* to make heavier] (14c) **1** : to give pain or trouble to : DISTRESS **2** : to inflict injury on **syn** see WRONG

ag·grieved \ə-'grēvd\ *adj* (14c) **1** : troubled or distressed in spirit **2 a** : suffering from an infringement or denial of legal rights ⟨~ minority groups⟩ **b** : showing or expressing grief, injury, or offense ⟨an ~ plea⟩ — **ag·griev·ed·ly** \-'grē-vəd-lē\ *adv*

ag·grieve·ment \ə-'grēv-mənt\ *n* (1847) : the quality or state of being aggrieved

ag·gro \'a-(ˌ)grō\ *n, pl* **aggros** [prob. *aggravation* + ¹*-o*] (1969) **1** *Brit* : deliberately aggressive, provoking, or violent behavior **2** *Brit* : EXASPERATION, IRRITATION

aghast \ə-'gast\ *adj* [ME *agast*, fr. pp. of *agasten* to frighten, fr. *a-* (perfective prefix) + *gasten* to frighten — more at ABIDE, GAST] (13c) : struck with terror, amazement, or horror : SHOCKED

ag·ile \'a-jəl, -ˌjīl\ *adj* [MF, fr. L *agilis*, fr. *agere* to drive, act — more at AGENT] (1581) **1** : marked by ready ability to move with quick easy grace **2** : having a quick resourceful and adaptable character ⟨an ~ mind⟩ — **ag·ile·ly** \-jə(l)-lē, -ˌjī(l)-lē\ *adv*

agil·i·ty \ə-'ji-lə-tē\ *n, pl* **-ties** (15c) : the quality or state of being agile : NIMBLENESS, DEXTERITY ⟨played with increasing ~⟩

agin \ə-'gin\ *dial var of* AGAINST

aging *pres part of* AGE

ag·ism *var of* AGEISM

ag·i·tate \'a-jə-ˌtāt\ *vb* **-tat·ed; -tat·ing** [L *agitatus*, pp. of *agitare*, freq. of *agere* to drive — more at AGENT] *vt* (15c) **1 a** *obs* : to give motion to **b** : to move with an irregular, rapid, or violent action ⟨the storm *agitated* the sea⟩ **2** : to excite and often trouble the mind or feelings of : DISTURB **3 a** : to discuss excitedly and earnestly **b** : to stir up public discussion of ~ *vi* : to attempt to arouse public feeling ⟨*agitated* for better schools⟩ **syn** see SHAKE, DISCOMPOSE — **ag·i·tat·ed·ly**

adv — **ag·i·ta·tion** \ˌa-jə-'tā-shən\ *n* — **ag·i·ta·tion·al** \-shnəl, -shə-nᵊl\ *adj*

ag·i·ta·tive \'a-jə-ˌtā-tiv\ *adj* (1687) : causing or tending to cause agitation

ag·i·ta·to \ˌa-jə-'tä-(ˌ)tō\ *adv or adj* [It, lit., agitated, fr. L *agitatus*] (ca. 1801) : in a restless and agitated manner — used as a direction in music

ag·i·ta·tor \'a-jə-ˌtā-tər\ *n* (ca. 1734) : one that agitates: as **a** : one who stirs up public feeling on controversial issues ⟨political ~s⟩ **b** : a device or an apparatus for stirring or shaking

ag·it·prop \'a-jət-ˌpräp\ *n* [Russ, fr. *agitatsiya* agitation + *prop*aganda] (1935) : PROPAGANDA; *esp* : political propaganda promulgated chiefly in literature, drama, music, or art — **agitprop** *adj*

Aglaia \ə-'glī-ə, -'glä-ə\ *n* [L, fr. Gk] : one of the three Graces

aglare \ə-'glar, -'gler\ *adj* (1872) : GLARING ⟨his eyes ~ with fury⟩

agleam \ə-'glēm\ *adj* (1870) : gleaming esp. with reflected light

ag·let \'a-glət\ *n* [ME, fr. MF *aguillette, aiguillette*, dim. of *aguille, aiguille* needle, fr. LL *acicula, acucula* ornamental pin, dim. of L *acus* needle, pin — more at ACUTE] (15c) **1** : the plain or ornamental tag covering the ends of a lace or point **2** : any of various ornamental studs, cords, or pins worn on clothing

agley \ə-'glā, -'glē, -'glī\ *adv* [Sc, fr. *¹a-* + *gley* to squint] (1785) *chiefly Scot* : AWRY, WRONG ⟨the best-laid schemes o' mice an' men gang aft ~ —Robert Burns⟩

aglit·ter \ə-'gli-tər\ *adj* (1865) : glittering esp. with reflected light

aglow \ə-'glō\ *adj* (1817) : glowing esp. with warmth or excitement

agly·cone \a-'glī-ˌkōn\ *also* **agly·con** \-ˌkän\ *n* [ISV *a-* (fr. Gk *ha-, a-* together) + *glyc-* + *-one, -on*] (1925) : an organic compound (as a phenol or alcohol) combined with the sugar portion of a glycoside

¹ag·nate \'ag-ˌnāt\ *n* [L *agnatus*, fr. pp. of *agnasci* to be born in addition to, fr. *ad-* + *nasci* to be born — more at NATION] (1534) **1** : a relative whose kinship is traceable exclusively through males **2** : a paternal kinsman

²agnate *adj* (1782) **1** : ALLIED, AKIN **2** : related through male descent or on the father's side — **ag·nat·ic** \ag-'na-tik\ *adj*

Ag·ne·an \'äg-nē-ən\ *n* [*Agni*, ancient kingdom in Turkestan] (1939) : TOCHARIAN A

ag·nize \ag-'nīz\ *vt* **ag·nized; ag·niz·ing** [L *agnoscere* to acknowledge (fr. *ad-* + *noscere* to know) + E *-ize* (as in *recognize*) — more at KNOW] (1535) *archaic* : RECOGNIZE, ACKNOWLEDGE

ag·no·men \ag-'nō-mən\ *n, pl* **-nom·i·na** \-'nä-mə-nə\ *or* **-no·mens** [L, irreg. fr. *ad-* + *nomen* name — more at NAME] (1665) : an additional cognomen given to a person by the ancient Romans (as in honor of some achievement)

ag·no·sia \ag-'nō-zhə, -shə\ *n* [NL, fr. Gk *agnōsia* ignorance, fr. *a-* + *gnōsis* knowledge, fr. *gignōskein*] (ca. 1900) : loss or diminution of the ability to recognize familiar objects or stimuli usu. as a result of brain damage

¹ag·nos·tic \ag-'näs-tik, əg-\ *n* [Gk *agnōstos* unknown, unknowable, fr. *a-* + *gnōstos* known, fr. *gignōskein* to know — more at KNOW] (1869) : a person who holds the view that any ultimate reality (as God) is unknown and prob. unknowable; *broadly* : one who is not committed to believing in either the existence or the nonexistence of God or a god — **ag·nos·ti·cism** \-tə-ˌsi-zəm\ *n*

²agnostic *adj* (1873) **1** : of, relating to, or being an agnostic or the beliefs of agnostics **2** : NONCOMMITTAL, UNDOGMATIC

Ag·nus Dei \ˌäg-ˌnús-'dā(-ˌē), -ˌnüs-; ˌän-yüs-; ˌag-nəs-\ *n* [ME, fr. LL, lamb of God; fr. its opening words] (14c) **1** : a liturgical prayer addressed to Christ as Savior **2** : an image of a lamb often with a halo and a banner and cross used as a symbol of Christ

ago \ə-'gō\ *adj or adv* [ME *agon, ago*, fr. pp. of *agon* to pass away, fr. OE *āgān*, fr. *ā-* (perfective prefix) + *gān* to go — more at ABIDE, GO] (14c) : earlier than the present time ⟨10 years ~⟩

agog \ə-'gäg\ *adj* [MF *en gogues* in mirth] (1559) : full of intense interest or excitement : EAGER ⟨kids all ~ over new toys⟩

¹a-go-go \ä-'gō-(ˌ)gō, ə-\ *n* [*Whisky à Gogo*, café and discotheque in Paris, France, from F *à gogo* galore, fr. MF] (1965) : a nightclub for dancing to pop music : DISCO

²a-go-go *adj* (1965) **1** : GO-GO 1 **2** : being in a whirl of motion **3** : being up-to-date — often used postpositively

-agogue *n comb form* [F & NL; F, fr. LL *-agogus* promoting the expulsion of, fr. Gk *-agōgos*, fr. *agein* to lead; NL *-agogon*, fr. Gk, neut. of *-agōgos* — more at AGENT] : substance that promotes the secretion or expulsion of ⟨emmen*agogue*⟩

agon \'ä-ˌgän, ä-'gōn\ *n* [Gk *agōn*] (1600) : CONTEST, CONFLICT; *esp* : the dramatic conflict between the chief characters in a literary work

ag·o·nal \'a-gə-nᵊl\ *adj* (1901) : of, relating to, or associated with agony and esp. the death agony

agone \ə-'gòn *also* -'gän\ *adj or adv* (14c) *archaic* : AGO

ag·o·nise, agonised, agonising *Brit var of* AGONIZE, AGONIZED, AGONIZING

ag·o·nist \'a-gə-nist\ *n* [LL *agonista* competitor, fr. Gk *agōnistēs*, fr. *agōnizesthai* to contend, fr. *agōn*] (ca. 1623) **1** : one that is engaged in a struggle **2** [fr. *antagonist*] **a** : a muscle that is controlled by the action of an antagonist with which it is paired **b** : a chemical substance capable of combining with a receptor on a cell and initiating a reaction or activity — compare ANTAGONIST 2b

ag·o·nis·tic \ˌa-gə-'nis-tik\ *adj* (1648) **1** : of or relating to the athletic contests of ancient Greece **2** : ARGUMENTATIVE **3** : striving for effect : STRAINED **4** : of, relating to, or being aggressive or defensive social interaction (as fighting, fleeing, or submitting) between individuals usu. of the same species — **ag·o·nis·ti·cal·ly** \-ti-k(ə-)lē\ *adv*

Agnus Dei

\ə\ abut \ᵊ\ kitten, F table \ər\ further \a\ ash \ā\ ace \ä\ mop, mar \aú\ out \ch\ chin \e\ bet \ē\ easy \g\ go \i\ hit \ī\ ice \j\ job \ŋ\ sing \ō\ go \ò\ law \òi\ boy \th\ thin \th̲\ the \ü\ loot \ú\ foot \y\ yet \zh\ vision \á, k̲, ⁿ, œ, œ̄, ᵫ, ᵫ̄, ᶦ\ *see* Guide to Pronunciation

ag·o·nize \'a-gə-ˌnīz\ *vb* **-nized; -niz·ing** *vt* (1583) : to cause to suffer agony : TORTURE ~ *vi* **1** : to suffer agony, torture, or anguish ⟨~s over every decision⟩ **2** : STRUGGLE
agonized *adj* (1583) : characterized by, suffering, or expressing agony
agonizing *adj* (1593) : causing agony : PAINFUL — **ag·o·niz·ing·ly** *adv*
ag·o·ny \'a-gə-nē\ *n, pl* **-nies** [ME *agonie*, fr. LL *agonia*, fr. Gk *agōnia* struggle, anguish, fr. *agōn* gathering, contest for a prize, fr. *agein* to lead, celebrate — more at AGENT] (14c) **1 a** : intense pain of mind or body : ANGUISH, TORTURE **b** : the struggle that precedes death **2 a** : a violent struggle or contest **3** : a strong sudden display (as of joy or delight) : OUTBURST *syn* see DISTRESS
agony column *n* (1863) : a newspaper column of personal advertisements relating esp. to missing relatives or friends
¹ag·o·ra \'a-gə-rə\ *n, pl* **-ras** *or* **-rae** \-ˌrē, -ˌrī\ [Gk, fr. *ageirein* to gather] (1589) : a gathering place; *esp* : the marketplace in ancient Greece
²ago·ra \ˌä-gə-'rä\ *n, pl* **ago·rot** \-'rōt\ [NHeb *ăgōrāh*, fr. Heb, a small coin] (1963) — see *shekel* at MONEY table
ag·o·ra·pho·bia \ˌa-g(ə-)rə-'fō-bē-ə\ *n* [NL, fr. Gk *agora* + NL *-phobia*] (1873) : abnormal fear of being helpless in an embarrassing or unescapable situation that is characterized esp. by the avoidance of open or public places — **ag·o·ra·phobe** \'a-g(ə-)rə-ˌfōb\ *n* — **ag·o·ra·pho·bic** \-'fō-bik\ *adj or n*
agou·ti \ə-'gü-tē\ *n* [F, fr. Sp. *agutí*, fr. Tupi] (1625) **1** : any of a genus (*Dasyprocta*) of tropical American rodents about the size of a rabbit **2** : a grizzled color of fur resulting from the barring of each hair in several alternate dark and light bands
agrafe *or* **agraffe** \ə-'graf\ *n* [F *agrafe*] (1643) : a hook-and-loop fastening; *esp* : an ornamental clasp used on armor or costumes
agran·u·lo·cyte \(ˌ)ā-'gran-yə-lō-ˌsīt\ *n* (ca. 1923) : a white blood cell without cytoplasmic granules
agran·u·lo·cy·to·sis \-ˌā-ˌgran-yə-lō-ˌsī-'tō-səs\ *n, pl* **-to·ses** \-'tō-ˌsēz\ [NL] (1927) : an acute febrile condition marked by severe decrease in blood granulocytes and often associated with the use of certain drugs
ag·ra·pha \'a-grə-fə\ *n pl* [Gk, neut. pl. of *agraphos* unwritten, fr. *a-* + *graphein* to write — more at CARVE] (1890) : sayings of Jesus not in the canonical gospels but found in other New Testament or early Christian writings
agraph·ia \(ˌ)ā-'gra-fē-ə\ *n* [NL, fr. ²*a-* + Gk *graphein* to write] (1871) : the pathologic loss of the ability to write
¹agrar·i·an \ə-'grer-ē-ən, -'grar-\ *adj* [L *agrarius*, fr. *agr-, ager* field — more at ACRE] (1618) **1** : of or relating to fields or lands or their tenure **2 a** : of, relating to, or characteristic of farmers or their way of life **b** : organized or designed to promote agricultural interests ⟨an ~ political party⟩ ⟨~ reforms⟩
²agrarian *n* (1818) : a member of an agrarian party or movement
agrar·i·an·ism \-ē-ə-ˌni-zəm\ *n* (1830) : a social or political movement designed to bring about land reforms or to improve the economic status of the farmer
agree \ə-'grē\ *vb* **agreed; agree·ing** [ME, fr. MF *agreer*, fr. *a gre* at will, fr. *a* (fr. L *ad*) + *gre* will, pleasure, fr. L *gratum*, neut. of *gratus* pleasing, agreeable — more at GRACE] *vi* (15c) **1** : ADMIT, CONCEDE ⟨~s that he is right⟩ **2** *chiefly Brit* : to settle on by common consent : ARRANGE ⟨I agreed rental terms with him —Eric Bennett⟩ ~ *vi* **1** : to accept or concede something (as the views or wishes of another) ⟨~ to a plan⟩ **2 a** : to achieve or be in harmony (as of opinion, feeling, or purpose) ⟨we ~ in our taste in music⟩ **b** : to get along together **c** : to come to terms **3 a** : to be similar : CORRESPOND ⟨both copies ~⟩ **b** : to be consistent ⟨the story ~s with the facts⟩ **4** : to be fitting, pleasing, or healthful : SUIT ⟨this climate ~s with him⟩ **5** : to have an inflectional form denoting identity or other regular correspondence in a grammatical category (as gender, number, case, or person)
syn AGREE, CONCUR, COINCIDE mean to come into or be in harmony regarding a matter of opinion. AGREE implies complete accord usually attained by discussion and adjustment of differences ⟨on some points we all can *agree*⟩. CONCUR tends to suggest cooperative thinking or acting toward an end but sometimes implies no more than approval (as of a decision reached by others) ⟨if my wife *concurs*, it's a deal⟩. COINCIDE, used more often of opinions, judgments, wishes, or interests than of people, implies an agreement amounting to identity ⟨their wishes *coincide* exactly with my desire⟩. *syn* see in addition ASSENT
agree·able \ə-'grē-ə-bəl\ *adj* (14c) **1** : pleasing to the mind or senses esp. as according well with one's tastes or needs ⟨an ~ companion⟩ ⟨an ~ change⟩ **2** : ready or willing to agree or consent **3** : being in harmony : CONSONANT — **agree·abil·i·ty** \ə-ˌgrē-ə-'bi-lə-tē\ *n* — **agree·able·ness** \ə-'grē-ə-bəl-nəs\ *n* — **agree·ably** \-blē\ *adv*
agree·ment \ə-'grē-mənt\ *n* (15c) **1 a** : the act or fact of agreeing **b** : harmony of opinion, action, or character : CONCORD **2 a** : an arrangement as to a course of action **b** : COMPACT, TREATY **3 a** : a contract duly executed and legally binding **b** : the language or instrument embodying such an agreement
ag·ri·busi·ness \'a-grə-ˌbiz-nəs, -nəz\ *n* [*agriculture* + *business*] (ca. 1955) : an industry engaged in the producing operations of a farm, the manufacture and distribution of farm equipment and supplies, and the processing, storage, and distribution of farm commodities
ag·ri·busi·ness·man \ˌa-grə-'biz-nəs-ˌman, -mən, -ˌnaz-\ *n* (1961) : a person who works in or manages an agribusiness
ag·ri·cul·tur·al \ˌa-gri-'kəl-ch(ə-)rəl\ *adj* (1776) : of, relating to, used in, or concerned with agriculture — **ag·ri·cul·tur·al·ly** *adv*
ag·ri·cul·ture \'a-gri-ˌkəl-chər\ *n* [ME, fr. MF, fr. L *agricultura*, fr. *ager* field + *cultura* cultivation — more at ACRE, CULTURE] (15c) : the science, art, or practice of cultivating the soil, producing crops, and raising livestock and in varying degrees the preparation and marketing of the resulting products : FARMING — **ag·ri·cul·tur·ist** \ˌa-gri-'kəl-ch(ə-)rist\ *or* **ag·ri·cul·tur·al·ist** \-ch(ə-)rə-list\ *n*
ag·ri·mo·ny \'a-grə-ˌmō-nē\ *n, pl* **-nies** [ME, fr. MF & L; MF *aigremoine*, fr. L *agrimonia*, MS var. of *argemonia*, fr. Gk *argemōnē*] (14c) : any of a genus (*Agrimonia* and esp. *A. eupatoria*) of herbs of the rose family having compound leaves, slender spikes of small yellow flowers, and fruits like burs
agro- *comb form* [F, fr. Gk, fr. *agros* field — more at ACRE] **1** : of or belonging to fields or soil : agricultural ⟨*agro*chemical⟩ **2** : agricultural and ⟨*agro*-industrial⟩

ag·ro·chem·i·cal \ˌa-grō-'ke-mi-kəl\ *also* **ag·ri·chem·i·cal** \ˌa-gri-\ *n* (1956) : an agricultural chemical (as an herbicide or an insecticide)
ag·ro·for·est·ry \ˌa-grō-'fòr-ə-strē, -'fär-\ *n* (1977) : land management for the simultaneous production of food, crops, and trees; *also* : the science of agroforestry — **ag·ro·for·est·er** \-stər\ *n*
ag·ro·in·dus·tri·al \ˌa-grō-in-'dəs-trē-əl\ *adj* (1940) : of or relating to production (as of power for industry and water for irrigation) for both industrial and agricultural purposes
agron·o·my \ə-'grä-nə-mē\ *n* [prob. fr. F *agronomie*, fr. *agro-* + *-nomie* -nomy] (1814) : a branch of agriculture dealing with field-crop production and soil management — **ag·ro·nom·ic** \ˌa-grə-'nä-mik\ *adj* — **ag·ro·nom·i·cal·ly** \-mi-k(ə-)lē\ *adv* — **agron·o·mist** \ə-'grä-nə-mist\ *n*
aground \ə-'graünd\ *adv or adj* (14c) **1** : on the ground ⟨planes aloft and ~⟩ **2** : on or onto the shore or the bottom of a body of water ⟨a ship run ~⟩
ague \'ā-(ˌ)gyü\ *n* [ME, fr. MF *aguë*, fr. ML (*febris*) *acuta*, lit., sharp fever, fr. L, fem. of *acutus* sharp — more at ACUTE] (14c) **1** : a fever (as malaria) marked by paroxysms of chills, fever, and sweating that recur at regular intervals **2** : a fit of shivering : CHILL — **agu·ish** \'ā-ˌgyü-ish\ *adj*
ah \'ä\ *interj* [ME] (13c) — used to express delight, relief, regret, or contempt
aha \ä-'hä\ *interj* [ME] (14c) — used to express surprise, triumph, or derision
ahead \ə-'hed\ *adv or adj* (1596) **1 a** : in a forward direction or position : FORWARD **b** : in front **2** : in, into, or for the future ⟨plan ~⟩ **3** : in or toward a more advantageous position ⟨helped others to get ~⟩ **4** : at or to an earlier time : in advance ⟨make payments ~⟩
ahead of *prep* (1748) **1** : in front or advance of **2** : in excess of
ahem \a-'hem\ *interj* [imit.] (1763) — used esp. to attract attention
ahim·sa \ə-'him-ˌsä\ *n* [Skt *ahimsā* noninjury] (1875) : the Hindu and Buddhist doctrine of refraining from harming any living being
ahis·tor·i·cal \ˌā-his-'tòr-i-kəl, -'tär-\ *or* **ahis·tor·ic** \-ik\ *adj* (1945) : not concerned with or related to history, historical development, or tradition ⟨the ~ attitudes of the radicals⟩
ahold \ə-'hōld\ *n* [prob. fr. the phrase *a hold*] (1872) : HOLD ⟨if you could get ~ of a representative —Norman Mailer⟩
A horizon \'ā-\ *n* (1936) : the uppermost dark-colored layer of a soil consisting largely of partly disintegrated organic debris
ahoy \ə-'hòi\ *interj* [*a-* (as in *aha*) + *hoy*] (1751) — used in hailing ⟨ship ~⟩
Ah·ri·man \'är-i-mən, -ˌmän\ *n* [Per, modif. of Av *aṅrō mainyuš* hostile spirit] : Ahura Mazda's antagonist who is a spirit of darkness and evil in Zoroastrianism
Ahu·ra Maz·da \ə-ˌhür-ə-'maz-də, ä-ˌhür-\ *n* [Av *Ahuramazda*, lit., wise god] : the Supreme Being represented as a deity of goodness and light in Zoroastrianism
Ai·as \'ī-əs\ *n* [Gk] : AJAX
ai·blins \'ā-blənz\ *adv* [*able* + *-lings, -lins* -lings] (ca. 1605) *chiefly Scot* : PERHAPS
¹aid \'ād\ *vb* [ME *eyden*, fr. MF *aider*, fr. L *adjutare*, freq. of *adjuvare*, fr. *ad-* + *juvare* to help] *vt* (15c) : to provide with what is useful or necessary in achieving an end ~ *vi* : to give assistance — **aid·er** *n*
²aid *n* (15c) **1** : a subsidy granted to the king by the English parliament until the 18th century for an extraordinary purpose **2 a** : the act of helping **b** : help given : ASSISTANCE; *specif* : tangible means of assistance (as money or supplies) **3 a** : an assisting person or group — compare AIDE **b** : something by which assistance is given : an assisting device ⟨an ~ to understanding⟩ ⟨a visual ~⟩; *esp* : HEARING AID **4** : a tribute paid by a vassal to his lord
aide \'ād\ *n* [short for *aide-de-camp*] (1777) : a person who acts as an assistant; *specif* : a military officer acting as assistant to a superior
aide–de–camp \ˌād-di-'kamp, -'käⁿ\ *n, pl* **aides–de–camp** \ˌād(z)-di-\ [F *aide de camp*, lit., camp assistant] (1670) : a military aid; *also* : a civilian aide usu. to an executive
aide–mé·moire \ˌād-mäm-'wär\ *n, pl* **aide–mémoire** [F, fr. *aider* to aid + *mémoire* memory] (1846) **1** : an aid to the memory; *esp* : a mnemonic device **2** : a written summary or outline of important items of a proposed agreement or diplomatic communication
aid·man \'ād-ˌman\ *n* (1944) : an army medical corpsman attached to a field unit
AIDS \'ādz\ *n* [acquired immunodeficiency syndrome] (1982) : a disease of the human immune system that is caused by infection with HIV, that is characterized cytologically esp. by severe reduction in the numbers of helper T cells, that in modern industrialized nations occurs esp. in homosexual and bisexual men and in intravenous users of illicit drugs, that is commonly transmitted in blood and bodily secretions (as semen), and that renders the subject highly vulnerable to life-threatening conditions (as Pneumocystis carinii pneumonia) and to some that become life-threatening (as Kaposi's sarcoma)
AIDS–related complex *n* (1984) : a group of symptoms (as fever, weight loss, and lymphadenopathy) that is associated with the presence of antibodies to HIV and is followed by the development of AIDS in a certain proportion of cases
AIDS virus *n* (1985) : HIV
ai·grette \ā-'gret, 'ā-\ *n* [F, plume, egret, fr. MF — more at EGRET] (1630) **1** : a spray of feathers (as of the egret) for the head **2** : a spray of gems worn on a hat or in the hair
ai·guille \ā-'gwē(ə)l, -'gwē\ *n* [F, lit., needle — more at AGLET] (1816) : a sharp-pointed pinnacle of rock
ai·guil·lette \ˌā-gwi-'let\ *n* [F — more at AGLET] (1816) : AGLET; *specif* : a shoulder cord worn by designated military aides — compare FOURRAGÈRE
ai·ki·do \ˌī-ki-'dō, ī-'kē-(ˌ)dō\ *n* [Jp *aikidō*, fr. *ai-* match, coordinate + *ki* breath, spirit + *dō* art, way] (1956) : a Japanese art of self-defense employing locks and holds and utilizing the principle of nonresistance to cause an opponent's own momentum to work against him
¹ail \'ā(ə)l\ *vb* [ME *eilen*, fr. OE *eglan*; akin to Goth *agljan* to harm] *vt* (bef. 12c) : to cause physical or emotional pain, discomfort, or trouble to ~ *vi* : to have something the matter; *esp* : to suffer ill health
²ail *n* (13c) : AILMENT
ai·lan·thus \ā-'lan(t)-thəs\ *n* [NL, fr. Ambonese *ai lanito*, lit., tree (of) heaven] (1807) : any of a small Asian genus (*Ailanthus* of the family

Simaroubaceae, the ailanthus family) of chiefly tropical trees and shrubs with bitter bark, pinnate leaves, and terminal panicles of ill-scented greenish flowers

ai·le·ron \'ā-lə-ˌrän\ *n* [F, fr. dim. of *aile* wing — more at AISLE] (1909) : a movable airfoil at the trailing edge of an airplane wing that is used for imparting a rolling motion esp. in banking for turns — see AIRPLANE illustration

ail·ment \'āl(ə)l-mənt\ *n* (ca. 1706) **1** : a bodily disorder or chronic disease **2** : UNREST, UNEASINESS

ai·lu·ro·phile \ī-'lur-ə-ˌfīl, ā-\ *n* [Gk *ailouros* cat] (1927) : a cat fancier : a lover of cats

ai·lu·ro·phobe \-ˌfōb\ *n* (1905) : a person who hates or fears cats

¹aim \'ām\ *vb* [ME, fr. MF *aesmer* & *esmer*; MF *aesmer*, fr. OF, fr. *a-* (fr. L *ad-*) + *esmer* to estimate, fr. L *aestimare*] *vi* (14c) **1** : to direct a course; *specif* : to point a weapon at an object **2** : ASPIRE, INTEND ⟨~s to reform the government⟩ ~ *vt* **1** *obs* : GUESS, CONJECTURE **2** *a* : POINT **b** : to direct to or toward a specified object or goal ⟨a program ~ed at reducing pollution⟩

²aim *n* (14c) **1** *obs* : MARK, TARGET **2** **a** : the pointing of a weapon at a mark **b** : the ability to hit a target **c** : a weapon's accuracy or effectiveness **3** *obs* **a** : CONJECTURE, GUESS **b** : the directing of effort toward a goal **4** : a clearly directed intent or purpose *syn* see INTENTION — **aim·less** \-ləs\ *adj* — **aim·less·ly** *adv* — **aim·less·ness** *n*

ain \'ān\ *adj* [prob. fr. ON *eiginn*] (1721) *Scot* : OWN

ain't \'ānt\ [contr. of *are not*] (1778) **1** : am not : are not : is not **2** : have not : has not **3** : do not : does not : did not — used in some varieties of Black English

   usage Although widely disapproved as nonstandard and more common in the habitual speech of the less educated, *ain't* in senses 1 and 2 is flourishing in American English. It is used in both speech and writing to catch attention and to gain emphasis ⟨the wackiness of news, once so deliciously amusing, *ain't* funny anymore —Richard Schickel⟩ ⟨I am telling you—there *ain't* going to be any blackmail —R. M. Nixon⟩. It is used esp. in journalistic prose as part of a consistently informal style ⟨the creative process *ain't* easy —Mike Royko⟩. This informal *ain't* is commonly distinguished from habitual *ain't* by its frequent occurrence in fixed constructions and phrases ⟨well—class it *ain't* —Cleveland Amory⟩ ⟨for money? say it *ain't* so, Jimmy! —Andy Rooney⟩ ⟨you *ain't* seen nothing yet⟩ ⟨that *ain't* hay⟩ ⟨two out of three *ain't* bad⟩ ⟨if it *ain't* broke, don't fix it⟩. In fiction *ain't* is used for purposes of characterization; in familiar correspondence it tends to be the mark of a warm personal friendship. It is also used for metrical reasons in popular songs ⟨*Ain't* She Sweet⟩ ⟨It *Ain't* Necessarily So⟩. Our evidence shows British use to be much the same as American.

Ai·nu \'ī-(ˌ)nü\ *n, pl* **Ainu** *or* **Ainus** [Ainu *aynu* person] (1819) **1** : a member of an indigenous people of the Japanese archipelago, the Kuril Islands, and part of Sakhalin Island **2** : the language of the Ainu people

ai·o·li \(ˌ)ī-'ō-lē, (ˌ)ä-\ *n* [Prov, fr. *ai* garlic + *oli* oil] (ca. 1900) : a sauce made of crushed garlic, egg yolks, olive oil, and lemon juice and sometimes potato : garlic mayonnaise

¹air \'ar, 'er\ *n, often attrib* [ME, fr. MF, fr. L *aer*, fr. Gk *aēr*] (14c) **1** **a** *archaic* : BREATH **b** : the mixture of invisible odorless tasteless gases (as nitrogen and oxygen) that surrounds the earth **c** : a light breeze **2** **a** : empty space **b** : NOTHINGNESS ⟨vanished into thin ~⟩ **c** : a sudden severance of relations ⟨she gave me the ~⟩ **3** ⟨prob. trans. of It *aria*⟩ **a** : TUNE, MELODY **b** *Elizabethan & Jacobean music* : an accompanied song or melody in usu. strophic form **c** : the chief voice part or melody in choral music **4** **a** : outward appearance of a thing ⟨an ~ of luxury⟩ **b** : a surrounding or pervading influence : ATMOSPHERE ⟨an ~ of mystery⟩ **c** : the look, appearance, or bearing of a person esp. as expressive of some personal quality or emotion : DEMEANOR ⟨an ~ of dignity⟩ **d** : an artificial or affected manner ⟨put on ~s⟩ **5** : public utterance ⟨give ~ to his opinion⟩ **6** : COMPRESSED AIR **7 a** (1) : AIRCRAFT ⟨go by ~⟩ (2) : AVIATION ⟨~ safety⟩ ⟨~ rights⟩ (3) : AIR FORCE ⟨~ headquarters⟩ **b** : the medium of transmission of radio waves; *also* : RADIO, TELEVISION ⟨went on the ~⟩ **8** : a football offense utilizing primarily the forward pass ⟨trailing by 20 points, the team took to the ~⟩ **9** : an air-conditioning system *syn* see POSE — **air·less** \-ləs\ *adj* — **air·less·ness** *n* — **in the air** : in wide circulation : ABOUT — **up in the air** : not yet settled

²air *vt* (1530) **1** : to expose to the air for drying, purifying, or refreshing : VENTILATE — often used with *out* **2** : to expose to public view or bring to public notice **3** : to transmit by radio or television ⟨~ a program⟩ ~ *vi* **1** : to become exposed to the open air **2** : to become broadcast ⟨the program ~s daily⟩ *syn* see EXPRESS

air bag *n* (1969) : an automobile safety device consisting of a bag designed to inflate automatically in front of an occupant in case of collision

air ball *n* (1981) : a missed shot in basketball that fails to touch the rim and backboard

air base *n* (1915) : a military base intended chiefly for the operation of aircraft

air bladder *n* (1731) : a sac containing gas and esp. air; *esp* : a hydrostatic organ present in most fishes that serves as an accessory respiratory organ

air·boat \'ar-ˌbōt, 'er-\ *n* (1946) : a shallow-draft boat driven by an airplane propeller and steered by an airplane rudder

air·borne \-ˌbōrn, -ˌbȯrn\ *adj* (1641) **1** : done or being in the air : being off the ground : as **a** : carried through the air (as by an aircraft) **b** : supported esp. by aerodynamic forces or propelled through the air by force **2** : trained for deployment by air and esp. by parachute

air brake *n* (1871) **1** : a brake operated by a piston driven by compressed air **2** : a surface that may be projected into the airstream for increasing drag and lowering the speed of an airplane

¹air·brush \-ˌbrəsh\ *n* (ca. 1889) : an atomizer for applying by compressed air a fine spray (as of paint or liquid color)

²airbrush *vt* (1938) : to paint, treat, or alter with an airbrush

air·burst \-ˌbərst\ *n* (1917) : the burst of a shell or bomb in the air

air·bus \-ˌbəs\ *n* (1945) : a short-range or medium-range subsonic jet passenger airplane

air chief marshal *n* (1919) : a commissioned officer in the British air force who ranks with a general in the army

air commodore *n* (1919) : a commissioned officer in the British air force who ranks with a brigadier in the army

air–con·di·tion \ˌar-kən-'di-shən, ˌer-\ *vt* [back-formation fr. *air conditioning*] (1933) : to equip (as a building) with an apparatus for washing air and controlling its humidity and temperature; *also* : to subject (air) to these processes — **air con·di·tion·er** \-'di-sh(ə-)nər\ *n* — **air–con·di·tion·ing** \-'di-sh(ə-)niŋ\ *n*

air·craft \'ar-ˌkraft, 'er-\ *n, pl* **aircraft** *often attrib* (1850) : a vehicle (as an airplane or balloon) for traveling through the air

aircraft carrier *n* (1919) : a warship with a flight deck on which airplanes can be launched and landed

air·crew \'ar-ˌkrü, 'er-\ *n* (1921) : the crew manning an airplane

air–cush·ion vehicle *n* (ca. 1962) : HOVERCRAFT

air dam *n* (1965) : a device attached to the underside of the front of an automobile to improve stability, aerodynamic performance, and engine cooling by redirecting the flow of air

air·date \-ˌdāt\ *n* (1971) : the scheduled date of a broadcast

air·drome \'ar-ˌdrōm, 'er-\ *n* [alter. of *aerodrome*] (1917) : AIRPORT

air·drop \-ˌdräp\ *n* (ca. 1945) : delivery of cargo or personnel by parachute from an airplane in flight — **air–drop** *vt* — **air–drop·pa·ble** \-ˌdrä-pə-bəl\ *adj*

air–dry \-'drī\ *adj* (1856) : dry to such a degree that no further moisture is given up on exposure to air

Aire·dale terrier \'ar-ˌdāl-, ˌer-\ *n* [*Airedale*, valley of the Aire river, England] (1880) : any of a breed of large terriers with a hard, wiry, black-and-tan coat — called also *Airedale*

air·er \'ar-ər, 'er-\ *n* (ca. 1847) *Brit* : a frame on which clothes are aired or dried

air·fare \'ar-ˌfar, 'er-ˌfer\ *n* (1918) : fare for travel by airplane

air·field \-ˌfēld\ *n* (1927) : an area of land from which aircraft operate: as **a** : AIRPORT **b** : AIR BASE

air·flow \-ˌflō\ *n* (ca. 1911) : a flow of air; *specif* : the motion of air (as around parts of an airplane in flight) relative to the surface of a body immersed in it

air·foil \-ˌfȯil\ *n* (ca. 1922) : a body (as an airplane wing or propeller blade) designed to provide a desired reaction force when in motion relative to the surrounding air

air force *n* (1917) **1** : the military organization of a nation for air warfare **2** : a unit of the U.S. Air Force higher than a division and lower than a command

air·frame \-ˌfrām\ *n* (1931) : the structure of an aircraft, rocket vehicle, or missile without the power plant

air·freight \-'frāt\ *n* (1929) : freight transport by air in volume; *also* : the charge for this service — **airfreight** *vt*

air·glow \-ˌglō\ *n* (ca. 1950) : light that is observed esp. during the night, that originates in the high atmosphere of a planet (as the earth), and that is associated with photochemical reactions of gases caused by solar radiation

air gun *n* (ca. 1753) **1** : a gun from which a projectile is propelled by compressed air **2** : any of various hand tools that work by compressed air; *esp* : AIRBRUSH

¹air·head \-ˌhed\ *n* [*air* + *-head* (as in *beachhead*)] (ca. 1944) : an area in hostile territory secured usu. by airborne troops for further use in bringing in troops and materiel by air

²airhead *n* (1972) : a mindless or stupid person — **air·head·ed** \-ˌhe-dəd\ *adj*

air·hole \-ˌhōl\ *n* (1766) : a hole to admit or discharge air

air·ing \'ar-iŋ, 'er-\ *n* (ca. 1606) **1** : exposure to air or heat for drying or freshening **2** : exposure to or exercise in the open air esp. to promote health or fitness **3** : exposure to public view or notice **4** : a radio or television broadcast

air lane *n* (ca. 1910) : a path customarily followed by airplanes

air letter *n* (1920) **1** : an airmail letter **2** : a sheet of airmail stationery that can be folded and sealed with the message inside and the address outside

air·lift \'ar-ˌlift, 'er-\ *n* (1945) : a system of transporting cargo or passengers by aircraft usu. to or from an otherwise inaccessible area — **airlift** *vt*

air·line \-ˌlīn\ *n* (1910) : an air transportation system including its equipment, routes, operating personnel, and management

air line *n* (1813) : a straight line through the air between two points

air·lin·er \-ˌlī-nər\ *n* (1908) : an airplane operated by an airline

air lock *n* (1857) **1** : an intermediate chamber with two airtight doors or openings to permit passage between two dissimilar spaces (as two places of unequal atmospheric pressure) **2** : a stoppage of flow caused by air being in a part where liquid ought to circulate

air·mail \'ar-ˌmā(ə)l, 'er-\ *n* (1913) : the system of transporting mail by aircraft; *also* : the mail thus transported — **airmail** *vt*

air·man \-mən\ *n* (1873) **1** : a civilian or military pilot, aviator, or aviation technician **2** : an enlisted man in the air force: as **a** : an enlisted man of one of the three ranks below sergeant **b** : an enlisted man ranking above an airman basic and below an airman first class

airman basic *n* (ca. 1961) : an enlisted man of the lowest rank in the air force

airman first class *n* (1952) : an enlisted man in the air force ranking above an airman and below a sergeant

air·man·ship \'ar-mən-ˌship, 'er-\ *n* (1908) : skill in piloting or navigating airplanes

air marshal *n* (1919) : a commissioned officer in the British air force who ranks with a lieutenant general in the army

air mass *n* (1893) : a body of air extending hundreds or thousands of miles horizontally and sometimes as high as the stratosphere and maintaining as it travels nearly uniform conditions of temperature and humidity at any given level

air mattress *n* (1926) : MATTRESS 1b

Air Medal *n* (1942) : a U.S. military decoration awarded for meritorious achievement while participating in an aerial flight

\ə\ abut \ᵊ\ kitten, F table \ər\ further \a\ ash \ā\ ace \ä\ mop, mar
\aú\ out \ch\ chin \e\ bet \ē\ easy \g\ go \i\ hit \ī\ ice \j\ job
\ŋ\ sing \ō\ go \ȯ\ law \ȯi\ boy \th\ thin \t͟h\ the \ü\ loot \ú\ foot
\y\ yet \zh\ vision \á, k̲, ⁿ, œ, œ̄, ue, ūe, ᵊ\ see Guide to Pronunciation

air mile *n* (1919) : a mile in air travel
air–mind·ed \'ar-'mīn-dəd, 'er-\ *adj* (1924) : interested in aviation or in air travel — **air–mind·ed·ness** *n*
air·mo·bile \-,mō-bəl, -,bēl, -,bil\ *adj* (1965) : of, relating to, or being a military unit whose members are transported to combat areas usu. by helicopter
air·park \-,pärk\ *n* (1929) : a small airport usu. near an industrial area
air piracy *n* (1948) : the hijacking of a flying airplane : SKYJACKING
air·plane \'ar-,plān, 'er-\ *n* [alter. of *aeroplane*] (1907) : a powered heavier-than-air aircraft that has fixed wings from which it derives most of its lift

airplane: *1* weather radar, *2* cockpit, *3* jet engine, *4* engine pod, *5* pylon, *6* wing, *7* vertical stabilizer, *8* rudder, *9, 10* tabs, *11* elevator, *12* horizontal stabilizer, *13* inboard flap, *14* inboard spoiler, *15, 16* tabs, *17* aileron, *18* outboard flap, *19* outboard spoiler, *20* sound suppressor, *21* thrust reverser, *22* cabin air intake, *23* fuselage, *24* nose landing gear

air plant *n* (1841)   **1** : EPIPHYTE   **2** : BRYOPHYLLUM
air·play \-,plā\ *n* (1966) : the playing of a musical recording on the air by a radio station
air pocket *n* (1912) : a condition of the atmosphere (as a local down current) that causes an airplane to drop suddenly
air police *n* (1944) : the military police of an air force
air·port \'ar-,pōrt, 'er-, -,pȯrt\ *n* (1919) : a place from which aircraft operate that usu. has paved runways and maintenance facilities and often serves as a terminal
air·post \-'pōst\ *n* (ca. 1927) : AIRMAIL
air·pow·er \-,paú(-ə)r\ *n* (1908) : the military strength of a nation's air force
air pump *n* (1660) : a pump for exhausting air from a closed space or for compressing air or forcing it through other apparatus
air raid *n* (1914) : an attack by armed airplanes on a surface target — usu. hyphened when used attributively ⟨*air-raid* shelter⟩
air rifle *n* (1886) : a rifle whose projectile (as a BB or pellet) is propelled by compressed air or carbon dioxide
air right *n* (1922) : a property right to the space above a surface area or object
air sac *n* (ca. 1828)   **1** : one of the air-filled spaces in the body of a bird connected with the air passages of the lungs   **2** : ALVEOLUS 1b   **3** : a thin-walled dilation of a trachea occurring in many insects
air·screw \'ar-,skrü, 'er-\ *n* (1894) *chiefly Brit* : an airplane propeller
air·ship \-,ship\ *n* (1819) : a lighter-than-air aircraft having propulsion and steering systems
air show *n* (1950) : an exhibition of aircraft and aviation skills
air·sick \-,sik\ *adj* (1785) : affected with motion sickness associated with flying — **air·sick·ness** *n*
air·space \-,spās\ *n* (1911) : the space lying above the earth or above a certain area of land or water; *esp* : the space lying above a nation and coming under its jurisdiction
air·speed \-,spēd\ *n* (ca. 1909) : the speed (as of an airplane) with relation to the air — compare GROUND SPEED
air·stream \-,strēm\ *n* (1869) : a current of air; *specif* : AIRFLOW
air·strip \-,strip\ *n* (1942) : a runway without normal air base or airport facilities
¹airt \'ärt, 'ert\ *n* [ME *art*, fr. ScGael *àirt*] (15c) *chiefly Scot* : compass point : DIRECTION
²airt *vt* (ca. 1782) *chiefly Scot* : DIRECT, GUIDE
air taxi *n* (1920) : a small commercial airplane used for short flights between localities not served by scheduled airlines
air·tight \'ar-,tīt, 'er-\ *adj* (1760)   **1** : impermeable to air or nearly so   **2 a** : having no noticeable weakness, flaw, or loophole ⟨an ~ argument⟩   **b** : permitting no opportunity for an opponent to score ⟨an ~ defense⟩ — **air·tight·ness** *n*
air·time \-,tīm\ *n* (1942)   **1** : the time at which a radio or television broadcast is scheduled to begin   **2** : the time or any part thereof that a radio or television station is on the air
air–to–air \,ar-tə-²(w)ar, ,er-tə-²(w)er\ *adj* (1941) : launched from one airplane in flight at another ⟨~ missiles⟩; *also* : involving aircraft in flight ⟨~ combat⟩
air vice-marshal *n* (1919) : a commissioned officer in the British air force who ranks with a major general in the army
air·wave \'ar-,wāv, 'er-\ *adj* (1944) : of, created for, or heard on the airwaves
air·waves \-,wāvz\ *n pl* (1928) : the medium of radio and television transmission — not used technically
air·way \-,wā\ *n* (1849)   **1** : a passage for a current of air (as in a mine or to the lungs)   **2** : a designated route along which airplanes fly from airport to airport; *esp* : such a route equipped with navigational aids   **3** : AIRLINE   **4** : a channel of a designated radio frequency for broadcasting or other radio communication
air·wor·thy \-,wər-thē\ *adj* (1829) : fit for operation in the air ⟨an ~ airplane⟩ — **air·wor·thi·ness** *n*
airy \'ar-ē, 'er-\ *adj* **air·i·er; -est** (14c)   **1 a** : of or relating to air : ATMOSPHERIC   **b** : high in the air : LOFTY ⟨~ perches⟩   **c** : performed

in air : AERIAL ⟨~ leaps⟩   **2** : UNREAL, ILLUSORY ⟨~ romances⟩   **3 a** : being light and graceful in movement or manner : SPRIGHTLY, VIVACIOUS   **b** : ETHEREAL   **4 a** : open to the free circulation of air   **b** : having openings or spaces ⟨~ lacework⟩   **5** : AFFECTED, PROUD ⟨~ condescension⟩ — **air·i·ly** \'ar-ə-lē, 'er-\ *adv* — **air·i·ness** \-ē-nəs\ *n*
airy–fairy \-'far-ē, -'fer-ē\ *adj* (1869)   **1** *chiefly Brit* : DELICATE, FAIRYLIKE   **2** *chiefly Brit* : lacking substance or purpose ⟨in . . . an ~, unserious, insufficiently careful fashion —*Times Lit. Supp.*⟩
aisle \'ī(ə)l\ *n* [ME *ile*, alter. of *ele*, fr. MF, wing, fr. L *ala*; akin to OE *eaxl* shoulder, L *axis* axletree — more at AXIS] (15c)   **1** : the side of a church nave separated by piers from the nave proper   **2 a** : a passage (as in a theater or railroad passenger car) separating sections of seats   **b** : a passage (as in a store or warehouse) for inside traffic
aisle·way \-,wā\ *n* (1926) : AISLE 2b
ait \'āt\ *n* [ME *eyt*, alter. of OE *īggoth*, fr. *īg* island — more at ISLAND] (bef. 12c) *Brit* : a little island
aitch \'āch\ *n* [F *hache*, fr. (assumed) VL *hacca*] (ca. 1580) : the letter *h*
aitch·bone \'āch-,bōn\ *n* [ME *hachbon*, alter. (resulting from incorrect division of *a nachebon*) of (assumed) ME *nachebon*, fr. ME *nache* buttock (fr. MF, fr. LL *natica*, fr. L *natis*) + *bon* bone] (15c)   **1** : the hipbone esp. of cattle   **2** : the cut of beef containing the aitchbone
ajar \ə-'jär\ *adj or adv* [earlier *on char*, fr. *on* + *char* turn — more at CHARE] (15c) : slightly open ⟨a door ~⟩
Ajax \'ā-,jaks\ *n* [L, fr. Gk *Aias*]   **1** : a Greek hero in the Trojan War who kills himself because the armor of Achilles is awarded to Odysseus   **2** : a fleet-footed Greek hero in the Trojan War
aju·ga \ə-'jə-gə\ *n*, **-ga** *or* **-gas** [NL, fr. ²*a-* + L *jugum* yoke — more at YOKE] (ca. 1899) : ¹BUGLE
Akan \'ä-,kän\ *n, pl* **Akan** *or* **Akans** (1694)   **1** : a member of any of the Akan-speaking peoples (as the Ashanti)   **2** : a Kwa language of southern Ghana and the southeast Ivory Coast
akee \'a-,kē, a-'kē\ *n* [origin unknown] (1794) : the fleshy fruit of an African tree (*Blighia sapida*) of the soapberry family grown in the Caribbean area, Florida, and Hawaii that is edible when ripe but has a toxic pink raphe attaching the aril to the seed and toxic arils when immature or overripe; *also* : the tree
AK–47 \,ā-,kā-,fōr-tē-'se-v°n, -,för-\ *n* [Russ *avtomat Kalashnikova 1947* Kalashnikov automatic rifle of 1947] (1968) : a Soviet-designed 7.62 mm (.30 cal.) gas-operated magazine-fed rifle for automatic or semiautomatic fire
akim·bo \ə-'kim-(,)bō\ *adj or adv* [ME *in kenebowe*] (15c)   **1** : having the hand on the hip and the elbow turned outward   **2** : set in a bent position ⟨a tailor sitting with legs ~⟩
akin \ə-'kin\ *adj* (1586)   **1** : related by blood : descended from a common ancestor or prototype   **2** : essentially similar, related, or compatible
Aki·ta \ə-'kē-tə, ä-\ *n* [fr. *Akita*, Japan] (1928) : any of a breed of large muscular dogs of Japanese origin
Ak·ka·di·an \ə-'kä-dē-ən\ *n* (ca. 1855)   **1** : an extinct Semitic language of ancient Mesopotamia   **2** : a Semitic inhabitant of central Mesopotamia before 2000 B.C. — **Akkadian** *adj*
ak·va·vit \'ä-kwə-,vēt, 'äk-və-\ *var of* AQUAVIT
al- — see AD-
¹-al *adj suffix* [ME, fr. OF & L; OF, fr. L *-alis*] : of, relating to, or characterized by ⟨direction*al*⟩ ⟨fiction*al*⟩
²-al *n suffix* [ME *-aille*, fr. OF, fr. L *-alia*, neut. pl. of *-alis*] : action : process ⟨rehears*al*⟩
³-al *n suffix* [F, fr. *alcool* alcohol, fr. ML *alcohol*] : aldehyde ⟨furfur*al*⟩
ala \'ā-lə\ *n, pl* **alae** \-,lē\ [L — more at AISLE] (1738) : a wing or a winglike anatomic process or part — **alar** \'ā-lər\ *adj* — **ala·ry** \-lə-rē\ *adj*
à la *also* **a la** \,ä-(,)lä, ,ä-lə, ,a-lə\ *prep* [F *à la*] (1589) : in the manner of
al·a·bas·ter \'a-lə-,bas-tər\ *n* [ME *alabastre*, fr. MF, fr. L *alabaster* vase of alabaster, fr. Gk *alabastros*] (14c)   **1** : a compact fine-textured usu. white and translucent gypsum often carved into vases and ornaments   **2** : a hard compact calcite or aragonite that is translucent and sometimes banded — **alabaster** *or* **al·a·bas·trine** \,a-lə-'bas-trən\ *adj*
à la carte *also* **a la carte** \,ä-lə-'kärt, ,a-lə-\ *adv or adj* [F, by the bill of fare] (1826) : according to a menu that prices each item separately
alack \ə-'lak\ *interj* [ME] (15c) — used to express sorrow or regret
alac·ri·ty \ə-'la-krə-tē\ *n* [L *alacritas*, fr. *alacr-, alacer* lively, eager] (15c) : promptness in response : cheerful readiness ⟨accepted the invitation with ~⟩ — **alac·ri·tous** \-krə-təs\ *adj*
Alad·din \ə-'la-d°n\ *n* : a youth in the *Arabian Nights' Entertainments* who comes into possession of a magic lamp
à la grecque \,ä-lə-'grek, ,a-lə-\ *adj, often cap G* [F, in the Greek manner] (ca. 1925) : served in a sauce made of olive oil, lemon juice, and several seasonings (as fennel, coriander, sage, and thyme)
à la king \,ä-lə-'kiŋ, ,a-lə-\ *adj* (1919) : served in a cream sauce with mushrooms and pimiento or green peppers ⟨chicken *à la king*⟩
al·a·me·da \,a-lə-'mē-də, -'mā-\ *n* [Sp, fr. *álamo* poplar] (1797) : a public promenade bordered with trees
à la mode *also* **a la mode** \,ä-lə-'mōd, ,a-lə-\ *adj* [F, according to the fashion] (1650)   **1** : FASHIONABLE, STYLISH   **2** : topped with ice cream
al·a·nine \'a-lə-,nēn\ *n* [G *Alanin*, irreg. fr. *Aldehyd* aldehyde] (ca. 1879) : a simple nonessential crystalline amino acid $C_3H_7NO_2$
al·a·nyl \'a-lə-,nil\ *n* [ISV *alanine* + *-yl*] (ca. 1928) : an acyl radical of alanine
¹alarm \ə-'lärm\ *also* **ala·rum** \ə-'lär-əm, -'lar-, *Brit also* -'ler-\ *n* [ME *alarme, alarom*, fr. MF *alarme*, fr. OIt *all'arme*, lit., to the arms] (14c)   **1** *usu* **alarum**, *archaic* : a call to arms ⟨the angry trumpet sounds *alarum* —Shak.⟩   **2** : a signal (as a loud noise or flashing light) that warns or alerts; *also* : a device that signals ⟨set the ~ to wake me at seven⟩   **3** : sudden sharp apprehension and fear resulting from the perception of imminent danger   **4** : a warning notice   *syn* see FEAR
²alarm *also* **alarum** *vt* (1605)   **1** : DISTURB, EXCITE   **2** : to give warning to   **3** : to strike with fear — **alarm·ing·ly** \-'lär-miŋ-lē\ *adv*
alarm clock *n* (1697) : a clock that can be set to sound an alarm at a desired time
alarm·ism \ə-'lär-,mi-zəm\ *n* (1867) : the often unwarranted exciting of fears or warning of danger — **alarm·ist** \-mist\ *n or adj*
alarm reaction *n* (1936) : the initial reaction of an organism (as increased hormonal activity) to stress
alarums and excursions *n pl* (1592)   **1** : martial sounds and the

movement of soldiers across the stage — used as a stage direction in Elizabethan drama **2** : clamor, excitement, and feverish or disordered activity

alas \ə-'las\ *interj* [ME, fr. OF, fr. *a* ah + *las* weary, fr. L *lassus* — more at LASSITUDE] (13c) — used to express unhappiness, pity, or concern

Alas·kan malamute \ə-'las-kən-\ *n* (1938) : any of a breed of powerful heavy-coated deep-chested dogs of Alaskan origin that have erect ears, heavily cushioned feet, and a plumy tail

Alas·ka time \-'las-kə-\ *n* (1945) : the time of the 9th time zone west of Greenwich that includes most of Alaska

¹alate \'ā-ˌlāt\ *adj* [L *alatus*, fr. *ala*] (1668) : having wings or a winglike part

²alate *n* (1941) : a winged insect (as an aphid) of a kind having winged and wingless forms

alb \'alb\ *n* [ME *albe*, fr. OE, fr. ML *alba*, fr. L, fem. of *albus* white; akin to Gk *alphos* white leprous spot] (bef. 12c) : a full-length white linen ecclesiastical vestment with long sleeves that is gathered at the waist with a cincture

al·ba·core \'al-bə-ˌkōr, -ˌkȯr\ *n, pl* **-core** *or* **-cores** [Pg *albacor*, fr. Ar *al-bakūrah* the albacore] (1579) : a large pelagic tuna (*Thunnus alalunga*) with long pectoral fins that is a source of canned tuna; *broadly* : any of various tunas (as a bonito)

albacore

Al·ba·nian \al-'bā-nē-ən, -nyən *also* ȯl-\ *n* (1579) **1** : a native or inhabitant of Albania **2** : the Indo-European language of the Albanian people — see INDO-EUROPEAN LANGUAGES table — **Albanian** *adj*

al·ba·tross \'al-bə-ˌtrȯs, -ˌträs\ *n, pl* **-tross** *or* **-tross·es** [prob. alter. of obs. *alcatrace* frigate bird, fr. Sp or Pg *alcatraz* pelican, fr. Ar *al-ghaṭṭās*, a kind of sea eagle] (1672) **1** : any of a family (Diomedeidae) of large web-footed seabirds that have long slender wings, are excellent gliders, and include the largest seabirds **2 a** : something that causes persistent deep concern or anxiety **b** : something that greatly hinders accomplishment : ENCUMBRANCE

al·be·do \al-'bē-(ˌ)dō\ *n, pl* **-dos** [LL, whiteness, fr. L *albus*] (ca. 1859) : reflective power; *specif* : the fraction of incident radiation (as light) that is reflected by a surface or body (as the moon or a cloud)

al·be·it \ȯl-'bē-ət, al-\ *conj* [ME, lit., all though it be] (14c) : conceding the fact that : even though

Al·bi·gen·ses \ˌal-bə-'jen-ˌsēz\ *n pl* [ML, pl. of *Albigensis*, lit., inhabitant of Albi, fr. *Albiga* (Albi), France] (1625) : members of a Catharistic sect of southern France flourishing primarily in the 12th and 13th centuries — **Al·bi·gen·sian** \-'jen(t)-shən, -'jen(t)-sē-ən\ *adj or n* — **Al·bi·gen·sian·ism** \-shə-ˌni-zəm, -sē-ə-ˌ\ *n*

al·bi·nism \'al-bə-ˌni-zəm, al-'bī-\ *n* (1836) : the condition of an albino — **al·bi·nis·tic** \ˌal-bə-'nis-tik\ *adj*

al·bi·no \al-'bī-(ˌ)nō\ *n, pl* **-nos** [Pg, fr. Sp, fr. *albo* white, fr. L *albus*] (1777) : an organism exhibiting deficient pigmentation; *esp* : a human being or nonhuman mammal that is congenitally deficient in pigment and usu. has a milky or translucent skin, white or colorless hair, and eyes with pink or blue iris and deep-red pupil

al·bi·not·ic \ˌal-bə-'nä-tik\ *adj* [*albino* + *-tic* (as in *melanotic*)] (1872) **1** : of, relating to, or affected with albinism **2** : tending toward albinism

Al·bi·on \'al-bē-ən\ *n* [L] (bef. 12c) **1** : Great Britain **2** : England

al·bite \'al-ˌbīt\ *n* [Sw *albit*, fr. L *albus*] (ca. 1843) : a triclinic usu. white feldspar consisting of a sodium aluminum silicate — **al·bit·ic** \al-'bit-ik\ *adj*

al·bum \'al-bəm\ *n* [L, a white tablet, fr. neut. of *albus*] (1612) **1 a** : a book with blank pages used for making a collection (as of autographs, stamps, or photographs) **b** : a paperboard container for a phonograph record : JACKET **c** : one or more recordings (as on tape or disc) produced as a single unit ⟨a 2-record ∼⟩ **2** : a collection usu. in book form of literary selections, musical compositions, or pictures : ANTHOLOGY

al·bu·men \al-'byü-mən; 'al-byü-, -byə-\ *n* [LL, fr. *albus*] (1599) **1** : the white of an egg — see EGG illustration **2** : ALBUMIN

al·bu·min \al-'byü-mən; 'al-byü-, -byə-\ *n* [ISV *albumen* + *-in*] (1869) : any of numerous simple heat-coagulable water-soluble proteins that occur in blood plasma or serum, muscle, the whites of eggs, milk, and other animal substances and in many plant tissues and fluids

al·bu·min·ous \al-'byü-mə-nəs\ *adj* (1791) : relating to, containing, or having the properties of albumin or albumen

al·bu·min·uria \(ˌ)al-ˌbyü-mə-'nür-ē-ə, -'nyür-\ *n* [NL] (ca. 1842) : the presence of albumin in the urine often symptomatic of kidney disease — **al·bu·min·uric** \-'nür-ik, -'nyür-\ *adj*

al·ca·ic \al-'kā-ik\ *adj, often cap* [LL *Alcaicus* of Alcaeus, fr. Gk *Alkaïkos*, fr. *Alkaios* Alcaeus, *fl ab* 600 B.C. Greek poet] (ca. 1637) : relating to or written in a verse or strophe marked by complicated variation of a dominant iambic pattern — **alcaic** *n, often cap*

al·cai·de *or* **al·cay·de** \al-'kī-dē\ *n* [Sp *alcaide*, fr. Ar *al-qā'id* the captain] (1502) : a commander of a castle or fortress (as among Spaniards, Portuguese, or Moors)

al·cal·de \al-'käl-dē\ *n* [Sp, fr. Ar *al-qāḍī* the judge] (1565) : the chief administrative and judicial officer of a Spanish town

al·ca·zar \al-'kä-zər, -'ka-\ *n* [Sp *alcázar*, fr. Ar *al-qaṣr* the castle] (ca. 1615) : a Spanish fortress or palace

Al·ces·tis \al-'ses-təs\ *n* [L, fr. Gk *Alkēstis*] : the wife of Admetus who dies for her husband and is restored to him by Hercules

al·che·mist \'al-kə-mist\ *n* (15c) : a person who studies or practices alchemy — **al·che·mis·tic** \ˌal-kə-'mis-tik\ *also* **al·che·mis·ti·cal** \-ti-kəl\ *adj*

al·che·mize \'al-kə-ˌmīz\ *vt* **-mized; -miz·ing** (1597) : to change by alchemy : TRANSMUTE

al·che·my \'al-kə-mē\ *n* [ME *alkamie*, *alquemie*, fr. MF or ML; MF *alquemie*, fr. ML *alchymia*, fr. Ar *al-kīmiyā*', fr. *al* the + *kīmiyā*' alchemy, fr. LGk *chēmeia*] (14c) **1** : a medieval chemical science and speculative philosophy aiming to achieve the transmutation of the base metals into gold, the discovery of a universal cure for disease, and the discovery of a means of indefinitely prolonging life **2** : a power or

process of transforming something common into something special **3** : an inexplicable or mysterious transmuting — **al·chem·i·cal** \-mi-kəl\ *also* **al·chem·ic** \al-'ke-mik\ *adj* — **al·chem·i·cal·ly** \-mi-k(ə-)lē\ *adv*

Alc·me·ne \alk-'mē-nē\ *n* [Gk *Alkmēnē*] : the mother of Hercules by Zeus in the form of her husband Amphitryon

al·co·hol \'al-kə-ˌhȯl\ *n* [NL, fr. ML, powdered antimony, fr. OSp, fr. Ar *al-kuḥul* the powdered antimony, fr. *kuḥl* kohl] (1672) **1 a** : ethanol esp. when considered as the intoxicating agent in fermented and distilled liquors **b** : drink (as whiskey or beer) containing ethanol **c** : a mixture of ethanol and water that is usu. 95 percent ethanol **2** : any of various compounds that are analogous to ethanol in constitution and that are hydroxyl derivatives of hydrocarbons

¹al·co·hol·ic \ˌal-kə-'hȯ-lik, -'hä-\ *adj* (1790) **1 a** : of, relating to, or caused by alcohol **b** : containing alcohol **2** : affected with alcoholism — **al·co·hol·i·cal·ly** \-li-k(ə-)lē\ *adv*

²alcoholic *n* (ca. 1890) : a person affected with alcoholism

al·co·hol·ism \'al-kə-ˌhȯ-ˌli-zəm, -kə-hə-\ *n* (1860) **1** : continued excessive or compulsive use of alcoholic drinks **2** : poisoning by alcohol; *esp* : a complex chronic psychological and nutritional disorder associated with excessive and usu. compulsive drinking

Al·co·ran \ˌal-kə-'ran\ *n* [ME, fr. MF or ML; MF & ML, fr. Ar *al-qur'ān*, lit., the reading] (14c) *archaic* : KORAN

al·cove \'al-ˌkōv\ *n* [F *alcôve*, fr. Sp *alcoba*, fr. Ar *al-qubbah* the arch] (1676) **1 a** : a small recessed section of a room : NOOK **b** : an arched opening (as in a wall) : NICHE **2** : SUMMERHOUSE 2 — **al·coved** \-ˌkōvd\ *adj*

al·cy·o·nar·ian \ˌal-sē-ə-'nar-ē-ən\ *n* [ultim. fr. Gk *alkyoneion*, a zoophyte, fr. neut. of *alkyoneios* of a kingfisher, fr. *alkyon* kingfisher; fr. its resemblance to a kingfisher's nest] (1878) : any of a subclass (Alcyonaria) of colonial anthozoans (as the sea pen) having polyps with eight branched tentacles and eight septa

Al·cy·o·ne \al-'sī-ə-(ˌ)nē\ *n* [L, fr. Gk *Alkyonē*] : the brightest star in the Pleiades

Al·deb·a·ran \al-'de-bə-rən\ *n* [Ar *al-dabarān*, lit., the follower] : a red star of the first magnitude that is seen in the eye of Taurus and is the brightest star in the Hyades

al·de·hyde \'al-də-ˌhīd\ *n* [G *Aldehyd*, fr. NL *al. dehyd.*, abbr. of *alcohol dehydrogenatum* dehydrogenated alcohol] (ca. 1846) : ACETALDEHYDE; *broadly* : any of various highly reactive compounds typified by acetaldehyde and characterized by the group CHO — **al·de·hy·dic** \ˌal-də-'hī-dik\ *adj*

al den·te \al-'den-(ˌ)tā, äl-\ *adj* [It; lit., to the tooth] (1935) : cooked just enough to retain a somewhat firm texture

al·der \'ȯl-dər\ *n* [ME, fr. OE *alor*; akin to OHG *elira* alder, L *alnus*] (bef. 12c) : any of a genus (*Alnus*) of toothed-leaved trees or shrubs of the birch family that have catkins which become woody, that grow in moist ground, and that have wood used in turnery

al·der·man \'ȯl-dər-mən\ *n* [ME, fr. OE *ealdorman*, fr. *ealdor* parent (fr. *eald* old) + *man* — more at OLD] (bef. 12c) **1** : a person governing a kingdom, district, or shire as viceroy for an Anglo-Saxon king **2 a** : a magistrate formerly ranking next below the mayor in an English or Irish city or borough **b** : a high-ranking member of a borough or county council in Ireland or formerly in England chosen by elected members **3** : a member of a city legislative body — **al·der·man·ic** \ˌȯl-dər-'ma-nik\ *adj*

al·der·wom·an \'ȯl-dər-ˌwù-mən\ *n* [*alder-* (as in *alderman*) + *woman*] (1768) : a female member of a city legislative body

al·dol \'al-ˌdȯl, -ˌdōl\ *n* [ISV *aldehyde* + *-ol*] (1874) : a colorless beta-hydroxy aldehyde $C_4H_8O_2$ used esp. in organic synthesis; *broadly* : any of various similar aldehydes — **al·dol·iza·tion** \ˌal-ˌdō-lə-'zā-shən, -ˌdȯ-\ *n*

al·dol·ase \'al-də-ˌlās, -ˌlāz\ *n* [*aldol* + *-ase*] (1940) : a crystalline enzyme that occurs widely in living systems and catalyzes reversibly the cleavage of a phosphorylated fructose into triose sugars

al·dose \'al-ˌdōs, -ˌdōz\ *n* [ISV *aldehyde* + *-ose*] (1894) : a sugar containing one aldehyde group per molecule

al·do·ste·rone \al-'däs-tə-ˌrōn, ˌal-dō-'ster-ˌōn, -'stir-; 'al-dō-stə-ˌrōn\ *n* [*aldehyde* + *-o-* + *-sterone*] (1954) : a steroid hormone $C_{21}H_{28}O_5$ of the adrenal cortex that functions in the regulation of the salt and water balance of the body

al·do·ste·ron·ism \al-'däs-tə-rə-ˌni-zəm; ˌal-dō-'ster-(ˌ)rō-, -'stir-; ˌal-dō-stə-'rō-\ *n* (1955) : a condition that is characterized by excessive secretion of aldosterone and typically by loss of body potassium, muscular weakness, and elevated blood pressure

al·drin \'ȯl-drən, 'al-\ *n* [Kurt *Alder* †1958 G chemist + E ¹-*in*] (1949) : an exceedingly poisonous cyclodiene insecticide $C_{12}H_8Cl_6$

ale \'ā(ə)l\ *n* [ME, fr. OE *ealu*; akin to ON *ǫl* ale, Lith *alus*] (bef. 12c) **1** : an alcoholic beverage brewed esp. by rapid fermentation from an infusion of malt with the addition of hops **2** : an English country festival at which ale is the principal beverage

ale·a·tor·ic \ˌā-lē-ə-'tȯr-ik, -'tär-\ *adj* [L *aleatorius*] (1961) : characterized by chance or indeterminate elements ⟨∼ music⟩

ale·a·to·ry \'ā-lē-ə-ˌtȯr-ē, -ˌtȯr-\ *adj* [L *aleatorius* of a gambler, fr. *aleator* gambler, fr. *alea* a dice game] (1693) **1** : depending on an uncertain event or contingency as to both profit and loss ⟨an ∼ contract⟩ **2** : relating to luck and esp. to bad luck **3** : ALEATORIC

alee \ə-'lē\ *adv* (14c) : on or toward the lee — compare AWEATHER

ale·house \'ā(ə)l-ˌhau̇s\ *n* (bef. 12c) : a place where ale is sold to be drunk on the premises

Al·e·man·nic \ˌa-lə-'ma-nik\ *n* [LL *alemanni*, of Gmc origin; akin to Goth *alamans* totality of people] (ca. 1797) : the group of dialects of German spoken in Alsace, Switzerland, and southwestern Germany

alem·bic \ə-'lem-bik\ *n* [ME, fr. MF & ML; MF *alambic* & ML *alembicum*, fr. Ar *al-anbīq*, fr. *al* the + *anbīq* still, fr. LGk *ambik-*, *ambix* alembic, fr. Gk, cap of a still] (14c) **1** : an apparatus used in distillation **2** : something that refines or transmutes as if by distillation

\ə\ abut \ᵊ\ kitten, F table \ər\ further \a\ ash \ā\ ace \ä\ mop, mar \au̇\ out \ch\ chin \e\ bet \ē\ easy \g\ go \i\ hit \ī\ ice \j\ job \ŋ\ sing \ō\ go \ȯ\ law \ȯi\ boy \th\ thin \ṯẖ\ the \ü\ loot \u̇\ foot \y\ yet \zh\ vision \à, ḵ, ⁿ, œ, œ̄, ᵫ, ᵫ̄, ᵛ\ *see* Guide to Pronunciation

⟨philosophy . . . filtered through the ∼ of Plato's mind —B. T. Shropshire⟩

alen·çon \ə-'len-ˌsän, -'len(t)-sən\ *n, often cap* [*Alençon*, France] (1865) : a delicate needlepoint lace

aleph \'ä-ˌlef, -ləf\ *n* [Heb *āleph*, prob. fr. *eleph* ox] (14c) : the 1st letter of the Hebrew alphabet — see ALPHABET table

aleph–null \-'nəl\ *n* (ca. 1909) : the number of elements in the set of all integers which is the smallest transfinite cardinal number

alembic 1

¹**alert** \ə-'lərt\ *adj* [It *all'erta*, lit., on the ascent] (1618) **1 a :** watchful and prompt to meet danger or emergency **b :** quick to perceive and act **2 :** ACTIVE, BRISK *syn* see WATCHFUL, INTELLIGENT — **alert·ly** *adv* — **alert·ness** *n*

²**alert** *n* (1796) **1 :** the state of readiness of those warned by an alert **2 :** an alarm or other signal of danger **3 :** the period during which an alert is in effect — **on the alert :** on the lookout esp. for danger or opportunity

³**alert** *vt* (ca. 1868) **1 :** to call to a state of readiness : WARN **2 :** to make aware of ⟨∼ed the public to the dangers of pesticides⟩

-ales *n pl suffix* [NL, fr. L, pl. of *-alis* -al] : plants consisting of or related to — in the names of orders of plants ⟨Conifer*ales*⟩

al·eu·rone \'al-yə-ˌrōn\ *n* [G *Aleuron*, fr. Gk, flour; akin to Arm *atam* I grind] (1869) : protein matter in the form of minute granules or grains occurring in seeds in endosperm or in a special peripheral layer

Aleut \ə-ˈlüt, 'a-lē-ˌ; ə-'lüt\ *n* [Russ] (1780) **1 :** a member of a people of the Aleutian and Shumagin islands and the western part of Alaska Peninsula **2 :** the language of the Aleuts

A level *n* (1951) **1 :** the second of three standardized British examinations in a secondary school subject used as a qualification for university entrance; *also* : successful completion of an A-level examination in a particular subject — called also *Advanced level*; compare O LEVEL, S LEVEL **2 a :** the level of education required to pass an A-level examination **b :** a course leading to an A-level examination

al·e·vin \'a-lə-vən\ *n* [F, fr. OF, fr. *alever* to lift up, rear (offspring), fr. L *allevare*, fr. *ad-* + *levare* to raise — more at LEVER] (1868) : a young fish; *esp* : a newly hatched salmon when still attached to the yolk sac

¹**ale·wife** \'āl-ˌwīf, -ˌwif\ *n* (15c) : a woman who keeps an alehouse

²**alewife** *n* [perh. alter. of obs. *allowes*, a kind of shad, fr. F *alose* shad, fr. OF, fr. LL *alausa*] (1633) : a clupeid food fish (*Alosa pseudoharengus*) very abundant along the Atlantic coast; *also* : any of several related fishes (as the menhaden)

al·ex·an·der \ˌa-lig-'zan-dər, -ˈe-\ *n, often cap* (1928) : an iced cocktail made from crème de cacao, sweet cream, and gin or brandy

Al·ex·an·dri·an \ˌa-lig-'zan-drē-ən, -ˈe-\ *adj* (ca. 1860) **1 :** of or relating to Alexander the Great **2 :** HELLENISTIC

al·ex·an·drine \-'zan-ˌdrēn, -drən, -ˌdrīn\ *n, often cap* [MF *alexandrin*, adj., fr. *Alexandre* Alexander the Great; fr. its use in a poem on Alexander] (1667) : a line of verse of 12 syllables consisting regularly of 6 iambs with a caesura after the 3d iamb — **alexandrine** *adj*

al·ex·an·drite \-'zan-ˌdrīt\ *n* [G *Alexandrit*, fr. *Alexander I* Russ. emperor] (ca. 1880) : a grass-green chrysoberyl that shows a red color by transmitted or artificial light

alex·ia \ə-'lek-sē-ə\ *n* [NL, fr. *a-* + Gk *lexis* speech, fr. *legein* to speak — more at LEGEND] (1878) : aphasia marked by loss of ability to read

Al·fa \'al-fə\ (1952) : a communications code word for the letter *a*

al·fal·fa \al-'fal-fə\ *n* [Sp, modif. of Ar dial. *al-faṣfaṣah* the alfalfa] (1845) : a deep-rooted European leguminous plant (*Medicago sativa*) widely grown for hay and forage

alfalfa weevil *n* (1912) : a small dark brown European weevil (*Hypera postica*) that is now a widespread pest of alfalfa in No. America

al·fil·a·ria \ˌal-fi-lə-'rē-ə\ *n* [AmerSp *alfilerillo*, fr. Sp, dim. of *alfiler* pin, modif. of Ar *al-khilāl* the thorn] (1868) : a European weed (*Erodium cicutarium*) of the geranium family grown for forage in the western U.S.

al·for·ja \al-'för-(ˌ)hä\ *n* [Sp, fr. Ar *al-khurj*] (1611) *West* : SADDLEBAG

al·fres·co \al-'fres-(ˌ)kō\ *adj or adv* [It] (1753) : taking place or located in the open air : OUTDOOR, OUTDOORS ⟨an ∼ lunch⟩ ⟨an ∼ restaurant⟩

al·ga \'al-gə\ *n, pl* **al·gae** \'al-(ˌ)jē\ *also* **algas** [L, seaweed] (1551) : a plant or plantlike organism of any of several phyla, divisions, or classes of chiefly aquatic usu. chlorophyll-containing nonvascular organisms of polyphyletic origin that usu. include the green, yellow-green, brown, and red algae in the eukaryotes and the blue-green algae in the prokaryotes — **al·gal** \-gəl\ *adj*

al·ga·ro·ba *also* **al·gar·ro·ba** \ˌal-gə-'rō-bə\ *n* [Sp *algarroba*, fr. Ar *al-kharrūbah* the carob] (1577) **1 :** CAROB 1 **2** [MexSp, fr. Sp]: MESQUITE; *also* : its pods

al·ge·bra \'al-jə-brə\ *n* [ML, fr. Ar *al-jabr*, lit., the reduction] (1551) **1 :** a generalization of arithmetic in which letters representing numbers are combined according to the rules of arithmetic **2 :** any of various systems or branches of mathematics or logic concerned with the properties and relationships of abstract entities as complex numbers, matrices, sets, vectors, groups, rings, or fields) manipulated in symbolic form under operations often analogous to those of arithmetic — compare BOOLEAN ALGEBRA — **al·ge·bra·ist** \-ˌbrā-ist\ *n*

al·ge·bra·ic \ˌal-jə-'brā-ik\ *adj* (1662) **1 :** relating to, involving, or according to the laws of algebra **2 :** involving only a finite number of repetitions of addition, subtraction, multiplication, division, extraction of roots, and raising to powers ⟨∼ equation⟩ — compare TRANSCENDENTAL — **al·ge·bra·i·cal·ly** \-'brā-ə-k(ə-)lē\ *adv*

algebraic number *n* (1904) : a root of an algebraic equation with rational coefficients

-algia *n comb form* [Gk, fr. *algos* pain] : pain ⟨neur*algia*⟩

al·gi·cide *or* **al·gae·cide** \'al-jə-ˌsīd\ *n* (1904) : an agent used to kill algae — **al·gi·cid·al** \ˌal-jə-'sī-dᵊl\ *adj*

al·gid \'al-jəd\ *adj* [L *algidus*, fr. *algēre* to feel cold] (ca. 1623) : COLD

al·gin \'al-jən\ *n* (1883) : any of various colloidal substances (as an alginate or alginic acid) derived from marine brown algae and used esp. as emulsifiers or thickeners

al·gi·nate \'al-jə-ˌnāt\ *n* (ca. 1909) : a salt or ester of alginic acid

al·gin·ic acid \(ˌ)al-'ji-nik-\ *n* [ISV *algin* + ¹*-ic*] (1885) : an insoluble colloidal acid ($C_6H_8O_6$)$_n$ that in the form of its salts is a constituent of the cell walls of brown algae

Al·gol \'al-ˌgäl, -ˌgȯl\ *n* [Ar *al-ghūl*, lit., the ghoul] : a binary star in the constellation Perseus whose larger member orbits and eclipses the smaller brighter star causing periodic variation in brightness

AL·GOL *or* **Al·gol** \'al-ˌgäl, -ˌgȯl\ *n* [*algorithmic language*] (1959) : an algebraic computer programming language used esp. in mathematical and scientific applications

al·go·lag·nia \ˌal-gō-'lag-nē-ə\ *n* [NL, fr. Gk *algos* pain + Gk *lagneia* lust, from *lagnos* lustful — more at SLACK] (ca. 1900) : a perversion (as sadism or masochism) characterized by pleasure and esp. sexual gratification in inflicting or suffering pain — **al·go·lag·ni·ac** \-'lag-nē-ˌak\ *n*

al·gol·o·gy \al-'gäl-ə-jē\ *n* (1849) : the study or science of algae — called also *phycology* — **al·go·log·i·cal** \ˌal-gə-'lä-ji-kəl\ *adj* — **al·gol·o·gist** \al-'gäl-ə-jist\ *n*

Al·gon·qui·an \al-'gän-kwē-ən, -'gän-\ *or* **Al·gon·quin** \-kwən\ *or* **Al·gon·ki·an** \-'gän-kē-ən\ *also* **Al·gon·kin** \-'gän-kən\ *n* [CanF *Algonquin*] (1625) **1** *usu Algonquin* **a :** an American Indian people of the Ottawa river valley **b :** the dialect of Ojibwa spoken by these people **2** *usu Algonquian* **a :** a family of American Indian languages spoken by peoples from Labrador to Carolina and westward into the Great Plains **b :** a member of the peoples speaking Algonquian languages

al·go·rithm \'al-gə-ˌri-thəm\ *n* [alter. of ME *algorisme*, fr. OF & ML; OF, fr. ML *algorismus*, fr. Ar *al-khuwārizmi*, fr. *al-Khuwārizmi* fl A.D. 825 Arab mathematician] (ca. 1894) : a procedure for solving a mathematical problem (as of finding the greatest common divisor) in a finite number of steps that frequently involves repetition of an operation; *broadly* : a step-by-step procedure for solving a problem or accomplishing some end esp. by a computer — **al·go·rith·mic** \ˌal-gə-'rith-mik\ *adj* — **al·go·rith·mi·cal·ly** \-mi-k(ə-)lē\ *adv*

Al·ham·bra \al-'ham-brə\ *n* [Sp, fr. Ar *al-ḥamrā'* the red house] (1612) : the palace of the Moorish kings at Granada, Spain

¹**alias** \'ā-lē-əs, 'āl-yəs\ *adv* [L, otherwise, fr. *alius* other — more at ELSE] (15c) : otherwise called : otherwise known as

²**alias** *n* (1605) : an assumed or additional name

Ali Ba·ba \ˌa-lē-'bä-bə, ˌä-lē-\ *n* : a woodcutter in the *Arabian Nights' Entertainments* who enters the cave of the Forty Thieves by using the password *Sesame*

¹**al·i·bi** \'a-lə-ˌbī\ *n* [L, elsewhere, fr. *alius*] (1743) **1 :** the plea of having been at the time of the commission of an act elsewhere than at the place of commission; *also* : the fact or state of having been elsewhere at the time **2 :** an excuse usu. intended to avert blame or punishment (as for failure or negligence) *syn* see APOLOGY

²**alibi** *vb* **-bied; -bi·ing** *vt* (1909) : to exonerate by an alibi : furnish an excuse for ∼ *vi* : to offer an excuse

Al·ice–in–Won·der·land \ˌa-lə-sən-'wən-dər-ˌland\ *adj* [fr. *Alice's Adventures in Wonderland* (1865) by Lewis Carroll] (1925) : suitable to a world of fantasy or illusion : UNREAL

ali·cy·clic \ˌa-lə-'sī-klik, -'si-klik\ *adj* [ISV *aliphatic* + *cyclic*] (1891) : of, relating to, or being an organic compound that contains a ring but is not aromatic — compare ALIPHATIC

al·i·dade \'a-lə-ˌdād\ *n* [ME *allidatha*, fr. ML *alhidada*, fr. Ar *al-'idādah* the revolving radius of a circle] (15c) : a rule equipped with simple or telescopic sights and used for determination of direction: as **a :** a part of an astrolabe **b :** a part of a surveying instrument consisting of the telescope and its attachments

¹**alien** \'ā-lē-ən, 'āl-yən\ *adj* [ME, fr. MF, fr. L *alienus*, fr. *alius*] (14c) **1 a :** belonging or relating to another person, place, or thing : STRANGE **b :** relating, belonging, or owing allegiance to another country or government : FOREIGN **2 :** differing in nature or character typically to the point of incompatibility *syn* see EXTRINSIC — **alien·ly** *adv* — **alien·ness** \-lē-ən-nəs, -yən-nəs\ *n*

²**alien** *n* (14c) **1 :** a person of another family, race, or nation **2 :** a foreign-born resident who has not been naturalized and is still a subject or citizen of a foreign country; *broadly* : a foreign-born citizen **3 :** EXTRATERRESTRIAL

³**alien** *vt* (14c) **1 :** ALIENATE, ESTRANGE **2 :** to make over (as property)

alien·able \'āl-yə-nə-bəl, 'ā-lē-ə-nə-\ *adj* (1611) : transferable to another's ownership — **alien·abil·i·ty** \ˌāl-yə-nə-'bi-lə-tē, ˌā-lē-ə-nə-\ *n*

alien·age \'āl-yə-nij, 'ā-lē-ə-nij\ *n* (1809) : the status of an alien

alien·ate \'ā-lē-ə-ˌnāt, 'āl-yə-\ *vt* **-at·ed; -at·ing** (ca. 1509) **1 :** to make unfriendly, hostile, or indifferent where attachment formerly existed **2 :** to convey or transfer (as property or a right) usu. by a specific act rather than the due course of law **3 :** to cause to be withdrawn or diverted *syn* see ESTRANGE — **alien·ator** \-ˌnā-tər\ *n*

alien·ation \ˌā-lē-ə-'nā-shən, ˌāl-yə-\ *n* (14c) **1 :** a withdrawing or separation of a person or a person's affections from an object or position of former attachment : ESTRANGEMENT ⟨∼ . . . from the values of one's society and family —S. L. Halleck⟩ **2 :** a conveyance of property to another

alien·ee \-'nē\ *n* (1531) : one to whom property is transferred

alien·ism \'ā-lē-ə-ˌni-zəm, 'āl-yə-\ *n* (1808) : ALIENAGE

alien·ist \-nist\ *n* [F *aliéniste*, fr. *aliéné* insane, fr. L *alienatus*, pp. of *alienare* to estrange, fr. *alienus*] (1864) : PSYCHIATRIST

alien·or \ˌā-lē-ə-'nȯr, ˌāl-yə-\ *n* (ca. 1552) : one who transfers property to another

¹**alight** \ə-'līt\ *vi* **alight·ed** *also* **alit** \ə-'lit\; **alight·ing** [ME, fr. OE *ālihtan*, fr. *ā-* (perfective prefix) + *lihtan* to alight — more at ABIDE, LIGHT] (bef. 12c) **1 :** to come down from something (as a vehicle): as **a :** DISMOUNT **b :** DEPLANE **2 :** to descend from or as if from the air and come to rest : LAND, SETTLE **3** *archaic* : to come by chance — **alight·ment** *n*

²**alight** *adj* (15c) **1** *chiefly Brit* : being on fire **2 :** lighted up

align *also* **aline** \ə-'līn\ *vb* [F *aligner*, fr. OF, fr. *a-* (fr. L *ad-*) + *ligne* line, fr. L *linea*] *vt* (ca. 1693) **1 :** to bring into line or alignment **2 :** to array on the side of or against a party or cause ∼ *vi* **1 :** to get or fall into line **2 :** to be in or come into precise adjustment or correct relative position — **align·er** *n*

align·ment *also* **aline·ment** \ə-'līn-mənt\ *n* (1790) **1 :** the act of aligning or state of being aligned; *esp* : the proper positioning or state of adjustment of parts (as of a mechanical or electronic device) in relation to each other **2 a :** a forming in line : the line thus formed **3 :** the ground plan (as of a railroad or highway) in distinction from the profile **4** : an arrangement of groups or forces in relation to one another ⟨new ~s within the political party⟩

¹**alike** \ə-'līk\ *adv* (14c) : in the same manner, form, or degree : EQUALLY ⟨was denounced by teachers and students ~⟩

²**alike** *adj* [ME ilik, ilich (fr. OE gelic) & alik, alter. of OE onlīc, fr. on + līc body — more at LIKE] (15c) : exhibiting close resemblance without being identical ⟨~ in their beliefs⟩ — **alike·ness** *n*

¹**al·i·ment** \'a-lə-mənt\ *n* [ME, fr. L alimentum, fr. alere to nourish — more at OLD] (15c) : FOOD, NUTRIMENT; *also* : SUSTENANCE ⟨there was nothing there of conversational ~ —Kingsley Amis⟩

²**al·i·ment** \-,ment\ *vt* (15c) : to give aliment to : NOURISH, SUSTAIN

al·i·men·ta·ry \,a-lə-'men-t(ə-)rē\ *adj* (1615) **1** : of or relating to nourishment or nutrition **2** : furnishing sustenance or maintenance

alimentary canal *n* (1764) : the tubular passage that extends from mouth to anus and functions in digestion and absorption of food and elimination of residual waste

al·i·men·ta·tion \,a-lə-mən-'tā-shən, -,men-\ *n* (ca. 1656) : the act or process of affording nutriment or nourishment ⟨intravenous ~⟩

al·i·mo·ny \'a-lə-,mō-nē\ *n, pl* **-nies** [L alimonia sustenance, fr. alere] (1656) **1** : an allowance made to one spouse by the other for support pending or after legal separation or divorce **2** : the means of living : MAINTENANCE

A–line \'ā-,līn\ *adj* (1964) : having a flared bottom and a close-fitting top — used of a garment ⟨an ~ skirt⟩

al·i·phat·ic \,a-lə-'fa-tik\ *adj* [ISV, fr. Gk aleiphat-, aleiphar oil, fr. aleiphein to smear; perh. akin to Gk lipos fat — more at LEAVE] (1889) : of, relating to, or being an organic compound having an open-chain structure (as an alkane) — compare ALICYCLIC, AROMATIC 2

al·i·quot \'a-lə-,kwät, -,kwət\ *adj* [ML aliquotus, fr. L aliquot some, several, fr. alius other + quot how many — more at ELSE, QUOTE] (1570) **1** : contained an exact number of times in something else — used of a divisor or part ⟨5 is an ~ part of 15⟩ ⟨an ~ portion of a solution⟩ **2** : FRACTIONAL ⟨an ~ part of invested capital⟩ — **aliquot** *n*

A–list \'ā-,list\ *n* (1980) : a list or group of individuals of the highest level of society, excellence, or eminence

alit·er·a·cy \,ā-'li-tər-ə-,sē, ə-'\ *n* (1984) : the quality or state of being able to read but uninterested in doing so — **alit·er·ate** \-'li-tər-ət\ *adj or n*

alive \ə-'līv\ *adj* [ME, fr. OE on life, fr. on + līf life] (bef. 12c) **1** : having life : not dead or inanimate **2** : still in existence, force, or operation : ACTIVE ⟨kept hope ~⟩ **3** : knowing or realizing the existence of : SENSITIVE ⟨~ to the danger⟩ **4** : marked by alertness, energy, or briskness **5** : marked by much life, animation, or activity : SWARMING ⟨streets ~ with traffic⟩ **6** — used as an intensive following the noun ⟨the proudest boy ~⟩ **syn** see AWARE — **alive·ness** *n*

ali·yah *or* **ali·ya** \ä-'lē-(,)yä, ,ä-lē-'yä\ *n* [NHeb 'aliyāh, fr. Heb, ascent] (ca. 1934) : the immigration of Jews to Israel

aliz·a·rin \ə-'li-zə-rən\ *n* [prob. fr. F alizarine] (ca. 1835) **1** : an orange or red crystalline compound $C_{14}H_8O_4$ formerly prepared from madder and now made synthetically and used esp. to dye Turkey reds and in making red pigments **2** : any of various acid, mordant, and solvent dyes derived like alizarin proper from anthraquinone

al·ka·hest \'al-kə-,hest\ *n* [NL alchahest] (1641) : the universal solvent believed by alchemists to exist — **al·ka·hes·tic** \,al-kə-'hes-tik\ *adj*

al·ka·li \'al-kə-,lī\ *n, pl* **-lies** *or* **-lis** [ME, fr. ML, fr. Ar al-qili the ashes of the plant saltwort] (14c) **1** : a soluble salt obtained from the ashes of plants and consisting largely of potassium or sodium carbonate; *broadly* : a substance (as a hydroxide or carbonate of an alkali metal) having marked basic properties — compare BASE 7a **2** : ALKALI METAL **3** : a soluble salt or a mixture of soluble salts present in some soils of arid regions in quantity detrimental to agriculture

alkali metal *n* (ca. 1885) : any of the univalent mostly basic metals of group I of the periodic table comprising lithium, sodium, potassium, rubidium, cesium, and francium — see PERIODIC TABLE table

al·ka·lim·e·ter \,al-kə-'li-mə-tər\ *n* [F alcalimètre, fr. alcali alkali + -mètre -meter] (ca. 1828) : an apparatus for measuring the strength or the amount of alkali in a mixture or solution — **al·ka·lim·e·try** \-'lim-ə-trē\ *n*

al·ka·line \'al-kə-lən, -,līn\ *adj* (1677) : of, relating to, containing, or having the properties of an alkali or alkali metal : BASIC; *esp, of a solution* : having a pH of more than 7 — **al·ka·lin·i·ty** \,al-kə-'li-nə-tē\ *n*

alkaline battery *n* (1941) : a long-lived dry cell that has an alkaline electrolyte which decreases corrosion of the cell — called also *alkaline cell*

alkaline earth metal *n* (ca. 1903) : any of the bivalent strongly basic metals of group II of the periodic table comprising beryllium, magnesium, calcium, strontium, barium, and radium — called also *alkaline earth*; see PERIODIC TABLE table

alkaline phosphatase *n* (1949) : any of the phosphatases that are optimally active in alkaline medium and occur in esp. high concentrations in bone, the liver, the kidneys, and the placenta

al·ka·lin·ize \'al-kə-lə-,nīz\ *vt* **-ized; -iz·ing** (1800) : to make alkaline — **al·ka·lin·iza·tion** \,al-kə-lə-nə-'zā-shən, -lə-nə-\ *n*

al·ka·loid \'al-kə-,lòid\ *n* (ca. 1831) : any of numerous usu. colorless, complex, and bitter organic bases (as morphine or codeine) containing nitrogen and usu. oxygen that occur esp. in seed plants — **al·ka·loi·dal** \,al-kə-'lòi-d²l\ *adj*

al·ka·lo·sis \,al-kə-'lō-səs\ *n* (1911) : an abnormal condition of increased alkalinity of the blood and tissues — **al·ka·lot·ic** \-'lä-tik\ *adj*

al·kane \'al-,kān\ *n* [alkyl + -ane] (1899) : any of numerous saturated hydrocarbons; *specif* : any of a series of open-chain hydrocarbons C_nH_{2n+2} (as methane and ethane) — called also *paraffin*

al·ka·net \'al-kə-,net\ *n* [ME, fr. OSp alcaneta, dim. of alcana henna shrub, fr. ML alchanna, fr. Ar al-ḥinnā' the henna] (14c) **1 a** : a European plant (Alkanna tinctoria) of the borage family; *also* : its root **b** : a red dyestuff prepared from the root **2** : a plant (Anchusa officinalis) of the borage family with delicate usu. blue flowers

al·kene \'al-,kēn\ *n* [ISV alkyl + -ene] (1899) : any of numerous unsaturated hydrocarbons having one double bond; *specif* : any of a series of open-chain hydrocarbons C_nH_{2n} (as ethylene)

alk·ox·ide \al-'käk-,sīd, -səd\ *n* [alkyl + oxide] (ca. 1889) : a basic salt derived from an alcohol by the replacement of the hydroxyl hydrogen with a metal

alk·oxy \'al-,käk-sē\ *adj* [ISV alkyl + oxygen] (ca. 1925) : of, relating to, or containing a univalent radical composed of an alkyl group united with oxygen — often used in combination

al·kyd \'al-kəd\ *n* [blend of alkyl and acid] (1929) **1** : any of numerous synthetic resins that are used esp. for protective coatings and in paint **2** : a paint in which the vehicle is an alkyd resin

¹**al·kyl** \'al-kəl\ *adj* (1882) : having a monovalent organic group and esp. one C_nH_{2n+1} (as methyl) derived from an alkane (as methane)

²**alkyl** *n* [prob. fr. G, fr. Alkohol alcohol] (1952) : a compound of one or more alkyl groups with a metal ⟨mercury ~s⟩

alkylating agent *n* (1900) : a substance that causes replacement of hydrogen by an alkyl group esp. in a biologically important molecule; *specif* : one with mutagenic activity that inhibits cell division and growth and is used to treat some cancers

al·kyl·ation \,al-kə-'lā-shən\ *n* (1900) : the act or process of introducing one or more alkyl groups into a compound (as to increase octane number in a motor fuel) — **al·kyl·ate** \'al-kə-,lāt\ *vt*

al·kyne \'al-,kīn\ *n* [alkyl + -yne, alter. of -ine] (ca. 1909) : any of a series of open-chain hydrocarbons C_nH_{2n-2} (as acetylene) having one triple bond

¹**all** \'òl\ *adj* [ME all, al, fr. OE eall; akin to OHG all all] (bef. 12c) **1 a** : the whole amount or quantity of ⟨needed ~ the courage they had⟩ ⟨sat up ~ night⟩ **b** : as much as possible ⟨spoke in ~ seriousness⟩ **2** : every member or individual component of ⟨~ men will go⟩ ⟨~ five children were present⟩ **3** : the whole number or sum of ⟨~ the angles of a triangle are equal to two right angles⟩ **4** : EVERY ⟨~ manner of hardship⟩ **5** : any whatever ⟨beyond ~ doubt⟩ **6** : nothing but ⟨~ attention⟩ **b** : having or seeming to have (some physical feature) in conspicuous excess or prominence ⟨~ legs⟩ **c** : paying full attention with ⟨~ ears⟩ **7** *dial* : used up : entirely consumed — used esp. of food and drink **8** : being more than one person or thing ⟨who ~ is coming⟩ **syn** see WHOLE — **all the** : as much of . . . as : as much of a . . . as ⟨all the home I ever had⟩

²**all** *adv* (bef. 12c) **1 a** : WHOLLY, QUITE ⟨sat ~ alone⟩ — often used as an intensive ⟨~ out of proportion⟩ ⟨~ over the yard⟩ **b** : selected as the best (as at a sport) within an area or organization — used in combination ⟨all-league halfback⟩ **2** *obs* : ONLY, EXCLUSIVELY **3** *archaic* : JUST **4** : so much ⟨~ the better for it⟩ **5** : for each side : APIECE ⟨the score is two ~⟩

³**all** *pron* (bef. 12c) **1** : the whole number, quantity, or amount : TOTALITY ⟨~ that I have⟩ ⟨~ of us⟩ ⟨~ of the books⟩ **2** : EVERYBODY, EVERYTHING ⟨gave equal attention to ~⟩ ⟨that is ~⟩ — **all in all** : on the whole : GENERALLY ⟨all in all, things might have been worse⟩ — **and all** : and everything else esp. of a kind suggested by a previous context ⟨cards to fill out with . . . numbers and all —Sally Quinn⟩

⁴**all** *n* (1593) : the whole of one's possessions, resources, or energy ⟨gave his ~ for the cause⟩

all– *or* **allo–** *comb form* [Gk, fr. allos other — more at ELSE] **1** : other : different : atypical ⟨allogamous⟩ ⟨allotropy⟩ **2** *allo-* : isomeric form or variety of (a specified chemical compound) ⟨allopurinol⟩ **3** *allo-* : being one of a group whose members together constitute a structural unit esp. of a language ⟨allophone⟩

¹**al·la breve** \,ä-lə-'brev, ,ä-lā-'bre-(,)vä\ *n* [It, lit., according to the breve] (ca. 1740) : the sign marking a piece or passage to be played alla breve; *also* : a passage so marked

²**alla breve** *adv or adj* (ca. 1823) : in duple or quadruple time with the beat represented by the half note

Al·lah \'ä-lə, 'a-lə, 'ä-,lä, ä-'lä\ *n* [Ar allāh] (1584) : GOD 1a — used in Islam

alla breve

all along *adv* (1670) : all the time ⟨knew the truth all along⟩

¹**all–Amer·i·can** \,ò-lə-'mer-ə-kən\ *adj* (1888) **1 a** *also* **all–Amer·i·ca** : selected (as by a poll of journalists) as one of the best in the U.S. in a particular category at a particular time ⟨an ~ quarterback⟩ **b** : having only all-American participants ⟨an ~ basketball team⟩ **2** : composed wholly of American elements **3** : representative or typical of the U.S. or its ideals ⟨an ~ boy⟩ ⟨her ~ optimism⟩ **4** : of or relating to the American nations as a group

²**all–American** *n* (1920) : one (as an athlete) that is voted all-American

al·lan·to·in \ə-'lan-tə-wən\ *n* [prob. fr. G, fr. NL allantois + G -in] (ca. 1845) : a crystalline oxidation product $C_4H_6N_4O_3$ of uric acid used to promote healing of local wounds and infections

al·lan·to·is \ə-'lan-tə-wəs\ *n, pl* **al·lan·to·ides** \,a-lən-'tō-ə-,dēz, ,a-,lan-\ [NL, ultim. fr. Gk allant-, allas sausage] (1646) : a vascular fetal membrane of reptiles, birds, and mammals that is formed as a pouch from the hindgut and that in placental mammals is intimately associated with the chorion in formation of the placenta — **al·lan·to·ic** \,a-lən-'tō-ik, ,a-,lan-\ *adj*

al·lar·gan·do \,ä-lär-'gän-(,)dō\ *adj or adv* [It, widening, verbal of allargare to widen, fr. al- (fr. L ad-) + largare to widen] (ca. 1893) : becoming gradually slower and more stately — used as a direction in music

all–around \,ò-lə-'raund\ *adj* (1867) **1** : considered in or encompassing all aspects : COMPREHENSIVE ⟨the best ~ performance so far⟩ **2** : competent in many fields ⟨an ~ performer⟩ **3** : having general utility or merit

al·lay \ə-'lā, ə-\ *vb* [ME aleyen, fr. OE ālecgan, fr. ā- (perfective prefix) + lecgan to lay — more at ABIDE, LAY] *vt* (14c) **1** : to subdue or reduce in intensity or severity : ALLEVIATE ⟨expect a breeze to ~ the heat⟩ **2** : to make quiet : CALM ~ *vi, obs* : to diminish in strength : SUBSIDE **syn** see RELIEVE

all but *adv* (1593) : very nearly : ALMOST ⟨would be all but impossible⟩

all clear *n* (1902) : a signal that a danger has passed

all–day \'òl-'dā\ *adj* (ca. 1870) : lasting for, occupying, or appearing throughout an entire day ⟨an ~ trip⟩

---

al·lée \ä-'lā, a-\ *n* [F, fr. MF *alee* — more at ALLEY] (1759) : a walkway lined with trees or tall shrubs

al·le·ga·tion \ˌa-li-'gā-shən\ *n* (15c) **1** : the act of alleging **2** : a positive assertion; *specif* : a statement by a party to a legal action of what the party undertakes to prove **3** : an assertion unsupported and by implication regarded as unsupportable ⟨vague ∼s of misconduct⟩

al·lege \ə-'lej\ *vt* al·leged; al·leg·ing [ME *alleggen*, fr. MF *alleguer*, fr. L *allegare* to dispatch, cite, fr. *ad-* + *legare* to depute — more at LEGATE] (14c) **1** *archaic* : to adduce or bring forward as a source or authority **2** : to assert without proof or before proving ⟨the newspaper ∼s the mayor's guilt⟩ **3** : to bring forward as a reason or excuse

al·leged \ə-'lejd, -'le-jəd\ *adj* (1509) **1** : asserted to be true or to exist ⟨an ∼ miracle⟩ **2** : questionably true or of a specified kind : SUPPOSED, SO-CALLED ⟨bought an ∼ antique vase⟩ **3** : accused but not proven or convicted ⟨an ∼ gangster⟩ — al·leg·ed·ly \-'le-jəd-lē\ *adv*

Al·le·ghe·ny spurge \ˌa-lə-ˌgā-nē- also -ˌge-nē-\ *n* [*Allegheny* Mountains, U.S.A.] (ca. 1936) : a low herb or subshrub (*Pachysandra procumbens*) of the box family widely grown as a ground cover

al·le·giance \ə-'lē-jən(t)s\ *n* [ME *allegeaunce*, modif. of MF *ligeance*, fr. OF, fr. *lige* liege] (14c) **1 a** : the obligation of a feudal vassal to his liege lord **b** (1) : the fidelity owed by a subject or citizen to a sovereign or government (2) : the obligation of an alien to the government under which the alien resides **2** : devotion or loyalty to a person, group, or cause *syn* see FIDELITY — al·le·giant \-jənt\ *adj*

al·le·gor·i·cal \ˌa-lə-'gòr-i-kəl, -'gär-\ *adj* (1528) **1** : of, relating to, or having the characteristics of allegory **2** : having hidden spiritual meaning that transcends the literal sense of a sacred text — al·le·gor·i·cal·ly \-k(ə-)lē\ *adv* — al·le·gor·i·cal·ness \-kəl-nəs\ *n*

al·le·go·rise *Brit var of* ALLEGORIZE

al·le·go·rist \ˌa-lə-ˌgòr-əst, -ˌgär-\ *n* (1684) : a creator of allegory

al·le·go·ri·za·tion \ˌa-lə-ˌgòr-ə-'zā-shən, -ˌgór-, -gər-\ *n* (1847) : allegorical representation or interpretation

al·le·go·rize \'a-lə-ˌgòr-ˌīz, -ˌgór-, -gər-\ *vb* -rized; -riz·ing *vi* (1581) **1** : to give allegorical explanations **2** : to compose or use allegory ∼ *vt* **1** : to treat or explain as an allegory **2** : to make into allegory — al·le·go·riz·er *n*

al·le·go·ry \'a-lə-ˌgòr-ē, -ˌgór-\ *n*, *pl* -ries [ME *allegorie*, fr. L *allegoria*, fr. Gk *allēgoria*, fr. *allēgorein* to speak figuratively, fr. *allos* other + *-ēgorein* to speak publicly, fr. *agora* assembly — more at ELSE, AGORA] (14c) **1** : the expression by means of symbolic fictional figures and actions of truths or generalizations about human existence; *also* : an instance (as in a story or painting) of such expression **2** : a symbolic representation : EMBLEM 2

¹al·le·gret·to \ˌa-lə-'gre-(ˌ)tō, ˌä-lə-\ *adv or adj* [It, dim. of *allegro*] (ca. 1740) : faster than andante but not so fast as allegro — used as a direction in music

²allegretto *n*, *pl* -tos (ca. 1846) : a musical composition or movement in allegretto tempo

¹al·le·gro \ə-'le-(ˌ)grō, -'lā-\ *n*, *pl* -gros (1683) : a musical composition or movement in allegro tempo

²allegro *adv or adj* [It, merry, fr. (assumed) VL *alecrus* lively, alter. of L *alacr-*, *alacer*] (ca. 1721) : at a brisk lively tempo — used as a direction in music

al·lele \ə-'lē(ə)l\ *n* [G *Allel*, short for *Allelomorph*] (1928) **1** : any of the alternative forms of a gene that may occur at a given locus **2** : either of a pair of alternative Mendelian characters (as smooth and wrinkled seed in the pea) — al·le·lic \-'lē-lik, -'le-\ *adj* — al·lel·ism \-'lē(ə)ˌli-zəm, -'le-\ *n*

allelo- *comb form* [Gk *allēlon* of each other, fr. *allos...allos* one ... the other, fr. *allos* other — more at ELSE] **1** : alternative ⟨allelomorph⟩ **2** : reciprocal ⟨allelopathy⟩

al·le·lo·morph \ə-'lē-lə-ˌmórf, -'le-lə-\ *n* (1902) : ALLELE — al·le·lo·mor·phic \-ˌlē-lə-'mór-fik, -le-lə-\ *adj* — al·le·lo·mor·phism \ə-'lē-lə-ˌmór-ˌfi-zəm, -'le-lə-\ *n*

al·le·lop·a·thy \ˌa-lə-'lä-pə-thē, -'le-lə-; *also* ˌā-lə-'lä-pə-thē\ *n* [ISV] (1948) : the suppression of growth of one plant species by another due to the release of toxic substances — al·le·lo·path·ic \ə-ˌlē-lə-'pa-thik, -ˌlə-lə-\ *adj*

al·le·lu·ia \ˌa-lə-'lü-yə\ *interj* [ME, fr. LL, fr. Gk *allēlouia*, fr. Heb *halălūyāh* praise ye Jehovah] (14c) : HALLELUJAH

al·le·mande \'a-lə-ˌmän(d), -mən, -ˌmänd, *1a & 2 also* ˌa-lə-'\ *n*, *often cap* [F, fr. fem. of *allemand* German] (1685) **1** : a musical composition or movement (as in a baroque suite) in moderate tempo and duple or quadruple time **2 a** : a 17th and 18th century court dance developed in France from a German folk dance **b** : a dance step with arms interlaced

al·l-em·brac·ing \ˌò-lim-'brā-siŋ\ *adj* (ca. 1649) : COMPLETE, SWEEPING

Al·len wrench \'a-lən-\ *n* [*Allen* Manufacturing Co., Hartford, Conn.] (1943) : an L-shaped hexagonal metal bar either end of which fits the socket of a screw or bolt

al·ler·gen \'a-lər-jən\ *n* [ISV *allergy* + *-gen*] (1910) : a substance that induces allergy — al·ler·gen·ic \ˌa-lər-'je-nik\ *adj* — al·ler·ge·nic·i·ty \ˌa-lər-jə-'ni-sə-tē\ *n*

al·ler·gic \ə-'lər-jik\ *adj* (1911) **1** : of, relating to, inducing, or affected by allergy **2** : having an aversion ⟨∼ to work⟩

al·ler·gist \'a-lər-jist\ *n* (1928) : a specialist in allergy

al·ler·gy \'a-lər-jē\ *n*, *pl* -gies [G *Allergie*, fr. *all-* + Gk *ergon* work — more at WORK] (1910) **1** : altered bodily reactivity (as hypersensitivity) to an antigen in response to a first exposure ⟨a bee venom ∼ so severe that a second sting may be fatal⟩ **2** : exaggerated or pathological reaction (as by sneezing, respiratory embarrassment, itching, or skin rashes) to substances, situations, or physical states that are without comparable effect on the average individual **3** : medical practice concerned with allergies **4** : a feeling of antipathy or repugnance

al·le·thrin \'a-lə-thrən\ *n* [*allyl* + *pyrethrin*] (1950) : a light yellow viscous oily synthetic insecticide $C_{19}H_{26}O_3$ used esp. in household aerosols

al·le·vi·ate \ə-'lē-vē-ˌāt\ *vt* -at·ed; -at·ing [LL *alleviatus*, pp. of *alleviare*, fr. L *ad-* + *levis* light — more at LIGHT] (15c) : RELIEVE, LESSEN: as **a** : to make (as suffering) more bearable ⟨her sympathy *alleviated* his distress⟩ **b** : to partially remove or correct *syn* see RELIEVE — al·le·vi·a·tion \ə-ˌlē-vē-'ā-shən\ *n* — al·le·vi·a·tor \-'lē-vē-ˌā-tər\ *n*

¹al·ley \'a-lē\ *n*, *pl* alleys [ME, fr. MF *alee*, fr. OF, fr. *aler* to go] (14c) **1** : a garden or park walk bordered by trees or bushes **2 a** (1) : a

grassed enclosure for bowling or skittles (2) : a hardwood lane for bowling; *also* : a room or building housing a group of such lanes **b** : the space on each side of a tennis doubles court between the sideline and the service sideline **c** : an area in a baseball outfield between two outfielders when they are in normal positions **3** : a narrow street; *esp* : a thoroughfare through the middle of a block giving access to the rear of lots or buildings — up one's alley *also* down one's alley : suited to one's own tastes or abilities

²alley *n*, *pl* alleys [by shortening and alter. fr. *alabaster*] (1720) : a playing marble; *esp* : one of superior quality

al·ley–oop \ˌa-lē-'yüp\ *n* [alter. of *allez-oop*, cry of a circus acrobat about to leap, prob. fr. F *allez*, 2d pers. pl. imper. of *aller* to go + E *-oop*, perh. alter. of *up*] (1967) : a basketball play in which a leaping player catches a pass above the basket and immediately dunks the ball; *also* : the usu. looping pass thrown on such a play

al·ley·way \'a-lē-ˌwā\ *n* (1788) **1** : a narrow passageway **2** : ALLEY 3

All Fools' Day *n* (1712) : APRIL FOOLS' DAY

all fours *n pl* (1563) **1 a** : all four legs of a quadruped **b** : the two legs and two arms of a person when used to support the body **2** *sing in constr* : any of various card games in which points are scored for the high trump, low trump, jack of trumps, and game

all get–out \ˌòl-'get-ˌaùt, -'git-\ *n* (1884) : the utmost conceivable degree — used in comparisons to suggest something superlative ⟨is handsome as *all get-out* and has a deft way with the ladies —John McCarten⟩

all hail *interj* (14c) — used to express greeting, welcome, or acclamation

All·hal·lows \òl-'ha-(ˌ)lōz, -laz\ *n*, *pl* Allhallows [short for *All Hallows' Day*] (1503) : ALL SAINTS' DAY

al·li·a·ceous \ˌa-lē-'ā-shəs\ *adj* [L *allium* garlic] (1792) : resembling garlic or onion esp. in smell or taste

al·li·ance \ə-'lī-ən(t)s\ *n* (13c) **1 a** : the state of being allied : the action of allying **b** : a bond or connection between families, states, parties, or individuals ⟨a closer ∼ between government and industry⟩ **2** : an association to further the common interests of the members; *specif* : a confederation of nations by treaty **3** : union by relationship in qualities : AFFINITY **4** : a treaty of alliance

al·lied \ə-'līd, 'a-ˌlīd\ *adj* (14c) **1** : having or being in close association : CONNECTED ⟨a strong personal pride ∼ with the utmost probity⟩ ⟨two families ∼ by marriage⟩ **2** : joined in alliance by compact or treaty; *specif, cap* : of or relating to the nations united against Germany and its allies in World War I or those united against the Axis powers in World War II **3 a** : related esp. by common properties or qualities ⟨heraldry and ∼ subjects⟩ **b** : related genetically

allies *pl of* ALLY

al·li·ga·tor \'a-lə-ˌgā-tər\ *n* [Sp *el lagarto* the lizard, fr. *el* the (fr. L *ille* that) + *lagarto* lizard, fr. (assumed) VL *lacartus*, fr. L *lacertus, lacerta* — more at LIZARD] (1579) **1 a** : either of two crocodilians (genus *Alligator*) having broad heads not tapering to the snout and a special pocket in the upper jaw for reception of the enlarged lower fourth tooth **b** : CROCODILIAN **2** : leather made from alligator hide

alligator clip *n* (ca. 1941) : a spring-loaded clip that has jaws resembling an alligator's and is used for making temporary electrical connections

alligator pear *n* [by folk etymology fr. Sp *aguacate* — more at AVOCADO] (1763) : AVOCADO

alligator snapper *n* (1884) : a snapping turtle (*Macrochelys temminckii*) of the rivers of the Gulf states that may reach nearly 150 pounds (68 kilograms) in weight and 5 feet (1.5 meters) in length

alligator clip

all–im·por·tant \ˌò-lim-'pór-t°nt, -tənt\ *adj* (1839) : of very great or greatest importance ⟨an ∼ question⟩

all–in \ˌò-'lin\ *adj* (1890) **1** *chiefly Brit* : ALL-INCLUSIVE **2** *chiefly Brit* : being almost without restrictions ⟨∼ wrestling⟩

all in *adj* (1903) : TIRED, EXHAUSTED ⟨after a day of wood-splitting he was *all in*⟩

all–in·clu·sive \ˌò-lin-'klü-siv, -ziv\ *adj* (ca. 1855) : including everything ⟨a broader and more nearly ∼ view⟩ — all–in·clu·sive·ness *n*

al·lit·er·ate \ə-'li-tə-ˌrāt\ *vb* -at·ed; -at·ing [back-formation fr. *alliteration*] *vi* (1816) **1** : to form an alliteration **2** : to write or speak alliteratively ∼ *vt* : to arrange or place so as to make alliteration ⟨∼ syllables in a sentence⟩

al·lit·er·a·tion \ə-ˌli-tə-'rā-shən\ *n* [*ad-* + L *littera* letter] (ca. 1656) : the repetition of usu. initial consonant sounds in two or more neighboring words or syllables (as wild and woolly, *thr*eatening *thr*ongs) — called also *head rhyme, initial rhyme*

al·lit·er·a·tive \ə-'li-tə-ˌrā-tiv, -tə-rā-tiv\ *adj* (1764) : of, relating to, or marked by alliteration — al·lit·er·a·tive·ly *adv*

al·li·um \'a-lē-əm\ *n* [NL, genus name, fr. L, garlic] (1807) : any of a large genus (*Allium*) of bulbous herbs of the lily family including the onion, garlic, chive, leek, and shallot

all–night \'òl-'nīt\ *adj* (1888) **1** : lasting throughout the night ⟨an ∼ poker game⟩ **2** : open throughout the night ⟨an ∼ diner⟩

all–night·er \'òl-'nī-tər\ *n* (1967) : something that lasts all night; *specif* : an all-night study session

allo- — see ALL-

al·lo·an·ti·body \ˌa-lō-'an-ti-ˌbä-dē\ *n* (1964) : an antibody produced following introduction of an alloantigen into the system of an individual of a species lacking that particular antigen — called also *isoantibody*

al·lo·an·ti·gen \ˌa-lō-'an-ti-jən\ *n* (1964) : an antigen present only in some individuals (as of a particular blood group) of a species and capable of inducing the production of an isoantibody by individuals which lack it — called also *isoantigen*

al·lo·ca·ble \'a-lə-kə-bəl\ *adj* (1916) : capable of being allocated

al·lo·cate \'a-lə-ˌkāt\ *vt* -cat·ed; -cat·ing [ML *allocatus*, pp. of *allocare*, fr. L *ad-* + *locare* to place, fr. *locus* place — more at STALL] (ca. 1641) **1** : to apportion for a specific purpose or to particular persons or things : DISTRIBUTE ⟨∼ tasks among human and automated components⟩ **2** : to set apart or earmark : DESIGNATE ⟨∼ a section of the building for special research purposes⟩ — al·lo·cat·a·ble \-ˌkā-tə-bəl\ *adj* — al·lo·ca·tion \ˌa-lə-'kā-shən\ *n* — al·lo·ca·tor \'a-lə-ˌkā-tər\ *n*

al·lo·cu·tion \ˌa-lə-ˈkyü-shən\ *n* [L *allocution-, allocutio,* fr. *alloqui* to speak to, fr. *ad-* + *loqui* to speak] (1615) : a formal speech; *esp* : an authoritative or hortatory address

all of *adv* (1829) : FULLY ⟨she's *all of* 20 years old⟩

al·log·a·mous \ə-ˈlä-gə-məs\ *adj* (ca. 1890) : reproducing by cross-fertilization — **al·log·a·my** \-mē\ *n*

al·lo·ge·ne·ic \ˌa-lō-jə-ˈnē-ik\ *also* **al·lo·gen·ic** \-ˈje-nik\ *adj* [*all-* + *-geneic* (as in *syngeneic*)] (1961) : involving, derived from, or being individuals of the same species that are sufficiently unlike genetically to interact antigenically

al·lo·graft \ˈa-lə-ˌgraft\ *n* (1961) : a homograft between allogeneic individuals — **allograft** *vt*

al·lo·graph \ˈa-lə-ˌgraf\ *n* (1951) **1** : a letter of an alphabet in a particular shape (as A or a) **2** : a letter or combination of letters that is one of several ways of representing one phoneme (as *pp* in *hopping* representing the phoneme \p\) — **al·lo·graph·ic** \ˌa-lə-ˈgra-fik\ *adj*

al·lom·e·try \ə-ˈlä-mə-trē\ *n* (1936) : relative growth of a part in relation to an entire organism or to a standard; *also* : the measure and study of such growth — **al·lo·met·ric** \ˌa-lə-ˈme-trik\ *adj*

allomorph *n* [*allo-* + *morpheme*] (1945) : one of a set of forms that a morpheme may take in different contexts ⟨the *-s* of *cats,* the *-en* of *oxen,* and the zero suffix of *sheep* are *~s* of the English plural morpheme⟩ — **al·lo·mor·phic** \ˌa-lə-ˈmȯr-fik\ *adj* — **al·lo·mor·phism** \ˈa-lə-ˌmȯr-ˌfi-zəm\ *n*

al·longe \a-ˈlōⁿzh\ *n* [F, lit., lengthening] (ca. 1859) : RIDER 2a

al·lo·pat·ric \ˌa-lə-ˈpa-trik\ *adj* [*all-* + Gk *patra* fatherland, fr. *patēr* father — more at FATHER] (1942) : occurring in different geographical areas or in isolation ⟨*~* speciation⟩ — compare SYMPATRIC — **al·lo·pat·ri·cal·ly** \-tri-k(ə-)lē\ *adv* — **al·lop·a·try** \ə-ˈlä-pə-trē\ *n*

al·lo·phane \ˈa-lə-ˌfān\ *n* [Gk *allophanēs* appearing otherwise, fr. *all-* + *phainesthai* to appear, middle voice of *phainein* to show — more at FANCY] (ca. 1821) : an amorphous translucent mineral of various colors often occurring in incrustations or stalactite forms and consisting of a hydrous aluminum silicate

al·lo·phone \ˈa-lə-ˌfōn\ *n* [*allo-* + *phone*] (1938) : one of two or more variants of the same phoneme ⟨the aspirated \p\ of *pin* and the unaspirated \p\ of *spin* are *~s* of the phoneme \p\⟩ — **al·lo·phon·ic** \ˌa-lə-ˈfä-nik\ *adj*

al·lo·poly·ploid \ˌa-lō-ˈpä-li-ˌplȯid\ *n* (1928) : a polyploid individual or strain having a chromosome set composed of two or more chromosome sets derived more or less complete from different species — **al·lopolyploid** *adj* — **al·lo·poly·ploi·dy** \-ˌplȯi-dē\ *n*

al·lo·pu·ri·nol \ˌa-lō-ˈpyu̇r-ə-ˌnȯl, -ˌnōl\ *n* [*all-* + *purine* + [1-*ol*] (1964) : a drug $C_5H_4N_4O$ used to promote excretion of uric acid

all–or–none \ˌȯl-ər-ˈnən\ *adj* (1900) : marked either by entire or complete operation or effect or by none at all ⟨*~* response of a nerve cell⟩

all–or–noth·ing \-ˈnə-thiŋ\ *adj* (1765) **1** : ALL-OR-NONE **2 a** : accepting no less than everything ⟨he's an *~* perfectionist⟩ **b** : risking everything ⟨an *~* combat strategy⟩

al·lo·sau·rus \ˌa-lə-ˈsȯr-əs\ *n* [NL, fr. Gk *all-* + *sauros* lizard] (1899) : any of a genus (*Allosaurus*) of huge carnivorous No. American theropod dinosaurs of the Upper Jurassic period

al·lo·ste·ric \ˌa-lō-ˈster-ik, -ˈstir-\ *adj* [*all-* + *steric*] (1962) : of, relating to, or being a change in the shape and activity of a protein (as an enzyme) that results from combination with another substance at a point other than the chemically active site — **al·lo·ste·ri·cal·ly** \-i-k(ə-)lē\ *adv* — **al·lo·ste·ry** \ˈa-lō-ˌster-ē, -ˌstir-\ *n*

al·lot \ə-ˈlät\ *vt* **al·lot·ted; al·lot·ting** [ME *alloten,* fr. MF *aloter,* fr. *a-* (fr. L *ad-*) + *lot,* of Gmc origin; akin to OE *hlot* lot] (15c) **1** : to assign as a share or portion ⟨*~* 10 minutes for the speech⟩ **2** : to distribute by or as if by lot ⟨*~* seats to the press⟩ — **al·lot·ter** *n*

al·lo·te·tra·ploid \ˌa-lō-ˈte-trə-ˌplȯid\ *n* (1930) : AMPHIDIPLOID — **al·lo·te·tra·ploi·dy** \-ˌplȯi-dē\ *n*

al·lot·ment \ə-ˈlät-mənt\ *n* (1574) **1** : the act of allotting — APPORTIONMENT **2** : something that is allotted; *esp, chiefly Brit* : a plot of land let to an individual for cultivation

al·lo·trope \ˈa-lə-ˌtrōp\ *n* [ISV, back-formation fr. *allotropy*] (ca. 1889) : a form showing allotropy

al·lot·ro·py \ə-ˈlä-trə-pē\ *n, pl* **-pies** (1850) : the existence of a substance and esp. an element in two or more different forms (as of crystals) usu. in the same phase — **al·lo·trop·ic** \ˌa-lə-ˈträ-pik\ *adj*

all' ot·ta·va \ˌa-lə-ˈtä-və, ˌä-lō-\ *adv or adj* [It, at the octave] (ca. 1823) : OTTAVA

al·lot·tee \ˌə-ˌlä-ˈtē\ *n* (1846) : one to whom an allotment is made

al·lo·type \ˈa-lə-ˌtīp\ *n* (1960) : an alloantigen that is part of a plasma protein (as an antibody) — **al·lo·typ·ic** \ˌa-lə-ˈti-pik\ *adj* — **al·lo·typ·i·cal·ly** \-pi-k(ə-)lē\ *adv* — **al·lo·typy** \ˈa-lə-ˌti-pē\ *n*

all–out \ˈȯl-ˈaut\ *adj* (1908) **1** : made with maximum effort : THOROUGHGOING ⟨an *~* effort to win the contest⟩ **2** : FULL-BLOWN 2

all out *adv* (1895) : with full determination or enthusiasm : with maximum effort — used chiefly in the phrase *go all out*

[1]**all-over** \ˈȯ-ˌlō-vər\ *adj* (1859) : covering the whole extent or surface ⟨a sweater with an *~* pattern⟩

[2]**allover** *n* (1838) **1** : an embroidered, printed, or lace fabric with a design covering most of the surface **2** : a pattern or design in which a single unit is repeated so as to cover an entire surface

all over *adv* (1577) **1** : over the whole extent ⟨decorated *all over* with a flower pattern⟩ **2** : EVERYWHERE ⟨looked *all over* for the book⟩ **3** : in every respect : THOROUGHLY ⟨she is her mother *all over*⟩

al·low \ə-ˈlau̇\ *vb* [ME, fr. MF *alouer* to place, (fr. ML *allocare*) & *allouer* to approve, fr. L *allaudare* to extol, fr. *ad-* + *laudare* to praise — more at ALLOCATE] *vt* (14c) **1 a** : to assign as a share or suitable amount (as of time or money) ⟨*~* an hour for lunch⟩ **b** : to reckon as a deduction or an addition ⟨*~* a gallon for leakage⟩ **2 a** *chiefly Southern & Midland* : to be of the opinion : THINK **b** *dial* : SAY, STATE **c** : to express an opinion — usu. used with *as how* or *that* **3** *chiefly Southern & Midland* : INTEND, PLAN **4** : ADMIT, CONCEDE ⟨must *~* that money causes problems in marriage⟩ **5 a** : PERMIT ⟨doesn't *~* people to smoke in his home⟩ **b** : to forbear or neglect to restrain or prevent ⟨*~* the dog to roam⟩ ~ *vi* **1** : to make a possibility : ADMIT — used with *of* ⟨evidence that *~s* of only one conclusion⟩ **2** : to give consideration to circumstances or contingencies — used with *for* ⟨*~* for expansion⟩

al·low·able \ə-ˈlau̇-ə-bəl\ *adj* (15c) : PERMISSIBLE — **al·low·ably** \-blē\ *adv*

[1]**al·low·ance** \ə-ˈlau̇-ən(t)s\ *n* (14c) **1 a** : a share or portion allotted or granted **b** : a sum granted as a reimbursement or bounty or for expenses ⟨salary includes cost-of-living *~*⟩; *esp* : a sum regularly provided for personal or household expenses ⟨each child has an *~*⟩ **c** : a fixed or available amount ⟨provide an *~* of time for recreation⟩ **d** : a reduction from a list price or stated price ⟨a trade-in *~*⟩ **2** : an imposed handicap (as in a horse race) **3** : an allowed dimensional difference between mating parts of a machine **4** : the act of allowing : PERMISSION **5** : a taking into account of mitigating circumstances or contingencies

[2]**allowance** *vt* **-anced; -anc·ing** (ca. 1828) **1** *archaic* : to put on a fixed allowance (as of food and drink) **2** *archaic* : to supply in a fixed or regular quantity

al·low·ed·ly \ə-ˈlau̇-əd-lē\ *adv* (1602) : by allowance : ADMITTEDLY

al·lox·an \ə-ˈläk-sən\ *n* [G, fr. *Allantoin* + *Oxalsäure* oxalic acid + *-an*] (1853) : a crystalline compound $C_4H_2N_2O_4$ causing diabetes mellitus when injected into experimental animals

[1]**al·loy** \ˈa-ˌlȯi *also* ə-ˈlȯi\ *n* [F *aloi,* fr. OF *alei,* fr. *aleir* to combine, fr. L *alligare* to bind — more at ALLY] (1604) **1** : the degree of mixture with base metals : FINENESS **2** : a substance composed of two or more metals or of a metal and a nonmetal intimately united usu. by being fused together and dissolving in each other when molten; *also* : the state of union of the components **3 a** : an admixture that lessens value **b** : an impairing alien element **4** : a compound, mixture, or union of different things ⟨an ethnic *~* of many peoples⟩ **5** *archaic* : a metal mixed with a more valuable metal to give durability or some other desired quality

[2]**alloy** \ə-ˈlȯi *also* ˈa-ˌlȯi\ *vt* (1661) **1 a** : TEMPER, MODERATE **b** : to impair or debase by admixture **2** : to reduce the purity of by mixing with a less valuable metal **3** : to mix so as to form an alloy ~ *vi* : to lend itself to being alloyed ⟨iron *~s* well⟩

all–pow·er·ful \ˈȯl-ˈpau̇(-ə)r-fəl\ *adj* (1667) : having complete or sole power

all–pur·pose \-ˈpər-pəs\ *adj* (1928) : suited for many purposes or uses

[1]**all right** *adj* (1701) **1** : SATISFACTORY, AGREEABLE ⟨whatever you decide is *all right* with me⟩ **2** : SAFE, WELL ⟨he was ill but he's *all right* now⟩ **3** : GOOD, PLEASING — often used as a generalized term of approval ⟨an *all right* guy⟩ *usage* see ALRIGHT

[2]**all right** *adv* (1837) **1** : very well ⟨*all right,* let's go⟩ **2** : beyond doubt : CERTAINLY ⟨she has pneumonia *all right*⟩ **3** : well enough : SATISFACTORILY ⟨does *all right* in school⟩ *usage* see ALRIGHT

all–round \ˈȯl-ˈrau̇nd\ *var of* ALL-AROUND

all–round·er \ˈȯl-ˈrau̇n-dər\ *n* (1875) *Brit* : one that is all-around

All Saints' Day *n* (ca. 1798) : November 1 observed in Western liturgical churches as a Christian feast in honor of all the saints

All Souls' Day *n* (14c) : November 2 observed in some Christian churches as a day of prayer for the souls of the faithful departed

all·spice \ˈȯl-ˌspīs\ *n* (1621) **1** : the berry of a West Indian tree (*Pimenta dioica*) of the myrtle family; *also* : the allspice tree **2** : a mildly pungent and aromatic spice prepared from allspice berries

[1]**all–star** \ˈȯl-ˌstär\ *adj* (1889) : composed wholly or chiefly of stars or of outstanding performers or participants ⟨an *~* cast⟩

[2]**all–star** *n* (ca. 1934) : a member of an all-star team

all that *adv* (1945) : to an indicated or suggested extent or degree : SO ⟨didn't take his threats *all that* seriously⟩

all–time \ˈȯl-ˌtīm\ *adj* (1914) **1** : FULL-TIME 1 **2** : being for or of all time up to and including the present; *esp* : exceeding all others of all time ⟨an *~* best-seller⟩

all told *adv* (1850) : with everything taken into account : in all

al·lude \ə-ˈlüd\ *vi* **al·lud·ed; al·lud·ing** [L *alludere,* lit., to play with, fr. *ad-* + *ludere* to play — more at LUDICROUS] (1533) : to make indirect reference; *broadly* : REFER

[1]**al·lure** \ə-ˈlu̇r\ *vt* **al·lured; al·lur·ing** [ME *aluren,* fr. MF *alurer,* fr. OF, fr. *a-* (fr. L *ad-*) + *loire* lure — more at LURE] (15c) : to entice by charm or attraction *syn* see ATTRACT — **al·lure·ment** \-ˈlu̇r-mənt\ *n* — **al·lur·ing·ly** *adv*

[2]**allure** *n* (1548) : power of attraction or fascination : CHARM

al·lu·sion \ə-ˈlü-zhən\ *n* [LL *allusion-, allusio,* fr. L *alludere*] (1548) **1** : an implied or indirect reference esp. in literature; *also* : the use of such references **2** : the act of alluding or hinting at — **al·lu·sive** \-ˈlü-siv, -ziv\ *adj* — **al·lu·sive·ly** *adv* — **al·lu·sive·ness** *n*

[1]**al·lu·vi·al** \ə-ˈlü-vē-əl\ *adj* (1802) : relating to, composed of, or found in alluvium ⟨*~* soil⟩ ⟨*~* diamonds⟩

[2]**alluvial** *n* (1866) : an alluvial deposit

alluvial fan *n* (1873) : the alluvial deposit of a stream where it issues from a gorge upon a plain or of a tributary stream at its junction with the main stream

al·lu·vi·on \ə-ˈlü-vē-ən\ *n* [L *alluvion-, alluvio,* fr. *alluere* to flow past, deposit (of water), fr. *ad-* + *lavere* to wash — more at LYE] (1536) **1** : the wash or flow of water against a shore **2** : FLOOD, INUNDATION **3** : ALLUVIUM **4** : an accession to land by the gradual addition of matter (as by deposit of alluvium) that then belongs to the owner of the land to which it is added; *also* : the land so added

alluvial fan

al·lu·vi·um \-vē-əm\ *n, pl* **-vi·ums** *or* **-via** \-vē-ə\ [ML, alter. of L *alluvio*] (ca. 1656) : clay, silt, sand, gravel, or similar detrital deposited by running water

[1]**al·ly** \ə-ˈlī, ˈa-ˌlī\ *vb* **al·lied; al·ly·ing** [ME *allien,* fr OF *alier,* fr. L *alligare* to bind to, fr. *ad-* + *ligare* to bind — more at LIGATURE] *vt*

\ə\ abut \ᵊ\ kitten, F table \ər\ further \a\ ash \ā\ ace \ä\ mop, mar \au̇\ out \ch\ chin \e\ bet \ē\ easy \g\ go \i\ hit \ī\ ice \j\ job \ŋ\ sing \ō\ go \ȯ\ law \ȯi\ boy \th\ thin \ṯh\ the \ü\ loot \u̇\ foot \y\ yet \zh\ vision \a̠, k̲, ⁿ, œ, œ̄, ᵫ, ᵫ̄, ᵊ\ *see* Guide to Pronunciation

(14c) **1** : to unite or form a connection between : ASSOCIATE ⟨allied himself with a wealthy family by marriage⟩ **2** : to connect or form a relation between ⟨as by likeness or compatibility⟩ : RELATE ∼ vi : to form or enter into an alliance

²**al·ly** \'a-,lī, ə-'lī\ n, pl **allies** (1598) **1** : a sovereign or state associated with another by treaty or league **2** : a plant or animal linked to another by genetic or taxonomic proximity **3** : one that is associated with another as a helper : AUXILIARY

-ally adv suffix [¹-al + -ly] : ²-LY ⟨terrifically⟩ — in adverbs formed from adjectives in -ic with no alternative form in -ical

al·lyl \'a-ləl\ adj [ISV, fr. L allium garlic] (1854) : being or containing the unsaturated univalent group C₃H₅—

al·lyl·ic \ə-'li-lik, a-\ adj (1857) : involving or characteristic of an allyl group

al·ma·gest \'al-mə-,jest\ n [ME almageste, fr. MF & ML, fr. Ar al=majusti, the Arabic version of Ptolemy's astronomy treatise, fr. al the + Gk megistē (syntaxis), lit., greatest (composition)] (14c) : any of several early medieval treatises on a branch of knowledge

al·ma ma·ter \,al-mə-'mä-tər\ n [L, fostering mother] (1696) **1** : a school, college, or university which one has attended or from which one has graduated **2** : the song or hymn of a school, college, or university

al·ma·nac \'ȯl-mə-,nak, 'al-\ n [ME almenak, fr. ML almanach, prob. fr. Ar al-manākh the almanac] (14c) **1** : a publication containing astronomical and meteorological data for a given year and often including a miscellany of other information **2** : a usu. annual publication containing statistical, tabular, and general information

al·man·dine \'al-mən-,dēn, -,dīn\ n [ME alemaundine, fr. MF alemandine, alter. of alabandine, fr. ML alabandina, fr. Alabanda, ancient city in Asia Minor] (15c) : ALMANDITE

al·man·dite \'al-mən-,dīt\ n [alter. of almandine] (ca. 1868) : a deep red garnet consisting of an iron aluminum silicate

¹**al·mighty** \ȯl-'mī-tē\ adj [ME, fr. OE ealmihtig, fr. eall all + mihtig mighty] (bef. 12c) **1** often cap : having absolute power over all ⟨Almighty God⟩ **2** : relatively unlimited in power **3** : great in magnitude or seriousness — **al·mighti·ness** n

²**almighty** adv (1833) : to a great degree : EXTREMELY ⟨although he did not precisely starve, he was ∼ hungry —W. A. Swanberg⟩

Almighty n (bef. 12c) : GOD 1 — used with the

al·mond \'ä-mənd, 'a-, 'äl-, 'al-\ n [ME almande, fr. MF, fr. LL amandula, alter. of L amygdala, fr. Gk amygdalē] (14c) **1 a** : the drupaceous fruit of a small tree (Prunus dulcis syn. P. amygdalus) of the rose family with flowers and young fruit resembling those of the peach; esp : its ellipsoidal edible kernel used as a nut **b** : any of several similar fruits **2** : a tree that produces almonds

al·mond–eyed \-,īd\ adj (1870) : having narrow slant almond-shaped eyes

al·mo·ner \'al-mə-nər, 'ä-mə-\ n [ME almoiner, fr. MF almosnier, fr. almosne alms, fr. LL eleemosyna] (15c) **1** : one who distributes alms **2** Brit : a social-service worker in a hospital

¹**al·most** \'ȯl-,mōst, ȯl-'\ adv [ME, fr. OE ealmǣst, fr. eall + mǣst most] (bef. 12c) : very nearly but not exactly or entirely

²**almost** adj (1709) : very near but not quite ⟨an ∼ failure⟩

alms \'ä(l)mz, NewEng also 'ämz\ n, pl **alms** [ME almesse, almes, fr. OE ælmesse, ælmes, fr. LL eleemosyna alms, fr. Gk eleēmosynē pity, alms, fr. eleēmōn merciful, fr. eleos pity] (bef. 12c) **1** archaic : CHARITY **2** : something (as money or food) given freely to relieve the poor — **alms·giv·er** \-,gi-vər\ n — **alms·giv·ing** \-,gi-viŋ\ n

alms·house \-,haus\ n (14c) **1** Brit : a privately financed home for the poor **2** : POORHOUSE

alms·man \-mən\ n (bef. 12c) : a recipient of alms

al·ni·co \'al-ni-,kō\ n [aluminum + nickel + cobalt] (1935) : a powerful permanent-magnet alloy containing iron, nickel, aluminum, and one or more of the elements cobalt, copper, and titanium

al·oe \'a-(,)lō\ n [ME, fr. L, fr. L, dried juice of aloe leaves, fr. Gk aloē] (bef. 12c) **1** pl : the fragrant wood of an East Indian tree (Aquilaria agallocha) of the mezereon family **2 a** : any of a large genus (Aloe) of succulent chiefly southern African plants of the lily family with basal leaves and spicate flowers **b** : the dried juice of the leaves of various aloes used esp. formerly as a purgative — usu. used in pl. but sing. in constr.

aloe vera \-'ver-ə, -'vir-\ n [NL, species name, fr. Aloe + L vera, fem. of verus true — more at VERY] (ca. 1936) : an aloe (Aloe barbadensis syn. A. vera) whose leaves furnish an emollient extract used esp. in cosmetics and skin creams; also : such a preparation

¹**aloft** \ə-'lȯft\ adv [ME, fr. ON ā lopt, fr. ā on, in + lopt air — more at ON, LOFT] (13c) **1** : at or to a great height **2** : in the air; esp : in flight ⟨as in an airplane⟩ ⟨meals served ∼⟩ **3** : at, on, or to the masthead or the higher rigging

²**aloft** prep (14c) : on top of : ABOVE ⟨bright signs ∼ hotels⟩

alog·i·cal \(,)ā-'lä-ji-kəl\ adj (1694) : being outside the bounds of that to which logic can apply — **alog·i·cal·ly** \-k(ə-)lē\ adv

alo·ha \ə-'lō-,(h)ä, ä-, -(h)ə\ interj [Hawaiian, fr. aloha love] (1820) — used as a greeting or farewell

aloha shirt n (1940) : HAWAIIAN SHIRT

¹**alone** \ə-'lōn\ adj [ME, fr. al all + one one] (13c) **1** : separated from others : ISOLATED **2** : exclusive of anyone or anything else : ONLY **3 a** : considered without reference to any other ⟨the children ∼ would eat that much⟩ **b** : INCOMPARABLE, UNIQUE ⟨∼ among their contemporaries in this respect⟩ — **alone·ness** \-'lōn-nəs\ n

syn ALONE, SOLITARY, LONELY, LONESOME, LONE, FORLORN, DESOLATE mean isolated from others. ALONE stresses the objective fact of being by oneself with slighter notion of emotional involvement than most of the remaining terms ⟨everyone needs to be alone sometimes⟩. SOLITARY may indicate isolation as a chosen course ⟨glorying in the calm of her solitary life⟩ but more often it suggests sadness and a sense of loss ⟨left solitary by the death of his wife⟩. LONELY adds to SOLITARY a suggestion of longing for companionship ⟨felt lonely and forsaken⟩. LONESOME heightens the suggestion of sadness and poignancy ⟨an only child often leads a lonesome life⟩. LONE may replace LONELY or LONESOME but typically is as objective as ALONE ⟨a lone robin pecking at the lawn⟩. FORLORN stresses dejection, woe, and listlessness at separation from one held dear ⟨a forlorn lost child⟩. DESOLATE implies inconsolable grief at loss or bereavement ⟨desolate after her brother's death⟩.

²**alone** adv (13c) **1** : SOLELY, EXCLUSIVELY **2** : without aid or support

¹**along** \ə-'lȯŋ\ prep [ME, fr. OE andlang, fr. and- against + lang long — more at ANTE-] (bef. 12c) **1** : in a line parallel with the length or direction of **2** : in the course of **3** : in accordance with : IN

²**along** adv (14c) **1** : FORWARD, ON ⟨move ∼⟩ **2** : from one to another ⟨word was passed ∼⟩ **3 a** : in company : as a companion ⟨brought his wife ∼⟩ — often used with with ⟨walked to school ∼ with her friends⟩ **b** : in association — used with with ⟨work ∼ with colleagues⟩ **4 a** : sometime within a specified or implied extent of time — usu. used with about ⟨∼ about July 17⟩ **b** : at or to an advanced point ⟨plans are far ∼⟩ **5** : in addition : ALSO — often used with with ⟨a bill came ∼ with the package⟩ **6 a** : at hand : as a necessary or useful item ⟨brought an extra one ∼⟩ ⟨had his gun ∼⟩ **7** : on hand : THERE ⟨tell him I'll be ∼ to see him⟩

along of prep [ME ilong on, fr. OE gelang on, fr. ge-, associative prefix + lang — more at CO-] (bef. 12c) dial : BECAUSE OF

along·shore \ə-'lȯŋ-'shōr, -'shȯr\ adv or adj (1779) : along the shore or coast ⟨walked ∼⟩ ⟨∼ currents⟩

¹**along·side** \-'sīd\ adv (1707) **1** : along the side : in parallel position **2** : at the side : close by ⟨a guard with a prisoner ∼⟩

²**alongside** prep (1793) **1 a** : along the side of **b** : BESIDE 1 **2 a** : in company with ⟨men she has been working —Richard Halloran⟩ **b** : in addition to ⟨a special category ∼ the awards it annually presents —Horizon⟩

alongside of prep (1781) : ALONGSIDE

¹**aloof** \ə-'lüf\ adv [obs. aloof to windward, fr. ¹a- + louf, luf luff] (ca. 1540) : at a distance

²**aloof** adj (1608) : removed or distant either physically or emotionally ⟨the ∼ composer neither worried nor cared about public opinion —Mary Jane Matz⟩ ⟨he stood ∼ from worldly success —John Buchan⟩ **syn** see INDIFFERENT — **aloof·ly** adv — **aloof·ness** n

al·o·pe·cia \,a-lə-'pē-sh(ē-)ə\ n [ME allopicia, fr. L alopecia, fr. Gk alōpekia, fr. alōpek-, alōpēx fox; akin to Arm alues fox, Skt lopāśa] (14c) : loss of hair, wool, or feathers : BALDNESS — **al·o·pe·cic** \-'pē-sik\ adj

aloud \ə-'laud\ adv [ME, fr. ¹a- + loud] (13c) **1** archaic : in a loud manner : LOUDLY **2** : with the speaking voice

alow \ə-'lō\ adv [ME, fr. ¹a- + low] (13c) : BELOW ⟨∼ in the ship's hold⟩

alp \'alp\ n [back-formation fr. Alps, mountain system of Europe] (15c) **1** : a high rugged mountain **2** : something suggesting an alp in height, size, or ruggedness

al·paca \al-'pa-kə\ n [Sp, fr. Aymara allpaqa] (1811) **1** : a domesticated mammal (Lama pacos) esp. of Peru that is prob. descended from the guanaco **2 a** : wool of the alpaca **b** (1) : a thin cloth made of or containing this wool (2) : a rayon or cotton imitation of this cloth

al·pen·glow \'al-pən-,glō\ n [part trans. of G Alpenglühen, fr. Alpen Alps + Glühen glow] (1871) : a reddish glow seen near sunset or sunrise on the summits of mountains

al·pen·horn \'al-pən-,hȯrn\ or **alp·horn** \'alp-,hȯrn\ n [G, fr. Alpen + Horn horn] (1864) : a straight wooden horn 5 to 14 feet (about 1.5 to 4.3 meters) in length used chiefly by Swiss herdsmen

al·pen·stock \'al-pən-,stäk\ n [G, fr. Alpen + Stock staff] (1829) : a long iron-pointed staff used in mountain climbing

¹**al·pha** \'al-fə\ n [ME, fr. L, fr. Gk, of Sem origin; akin to Heb āleph aleph] (13c) **1** : the 1st letter of the Greek alphabet — see ALPHABET table **2** : something that is first : BEGINNING **3** : ALPHA WAVE **4** : ALPHA PARTICLE

²**alpha** adj (1863) **1** : closest in the structure of an organic molecule to a particular group or atom — symbol α ⟨α-substitution⟩ **2** : socially dominant esp. in a group of animals **3** : ALPHABETIC

al·pha–ad·ren·er·gic \'al-fə-,a-drə-'nər-jik\ adj (1966) : of, relating to, or being an alpha-receptor ⟨∼ blocking action⟩

alpha and omega n [fr. the fact that alpha and omega are respectively the first and last letters of the Greek alphabet] (1526) **1** : the beginning and ending **2** : the principal element

al·pha·bet \'al-fə-,bet, -bət\ n [ME alphabete, fr. LL alphabetum, fr. Gk alphabētos, fr. alpha + bēta beta] (1513) **1 a** : a set of letters or other characters with which one or more languages are written esp. if arranged in a customary order **b** : a system of signs or signals that serve as equivalents for letters **2** : RUDIMENTS, ELEMENTS

al·pha·bet·ic \,al-fə-'be-tik\ or **al·pha·bet·i·cal** \-ti-kəl\ adj (1567) **1** : arranged in the order of the letters of the alphabet **2** : of, relating to, or employing an alphabet — **al·pha·bet·i·cal·ly** \-ti-k(ə-)lē\ adv

al·pha·bet·iza·tion \,al-fə-,be-tə-'zā-shən\ n (1889) **1** : the act or process of alphabetizing **2** : an alphabetically arranged series, list, or file

al·pha·bet·ize \'al-fə-bə-,tīz\ vt **-ized; -iz·ing** (1796) **1** : to arrange alphabetically **2** : to furnish with an alphabet — **al·pha·bet·iz·er** n

alphabet soup n (1934) : a hodgepodge esp. of initials (as of the names of organizations)

al·pha–fe·to·pro·tein \,al-fə-,fē-tō-'prō-,tēn, -'prō-tē-ən\ n (1968) : a fetal blood protein present abnormally in adults with some cancers (as of the liver) and normally in the amniotic fluid of pregnant women with high or low levels tending to be associated with certain birth defects (as spina bifida or Down's syndrome)

alpha globulin n [ISV] (1923) : any of several globulins of plasma or serum that have at alkaline pH the greatest electrophoretic mobility next to albumin — compare BETA GLOBULIN, GAMMA GLOBULIN

al·pha–he·lix \,al-fə-'hē-liks\ n (1955) : the coiled structural arrangement of many proteins consisting of a single chain of amino acids stabilized by hydrogen bonds — **al·pha–he·li·cal** \-'he-li-kəl, -'hē-li-\ adj

alpha iron n (1902) : the form of iron stable below 910°C

al·pha·mer·ic \,al-fə-'mer-ik\ adj [alphabetic + numeric] (ca. 1952) : ALPHANUMERIC

al·pha·nu·mer·ic \-,nü-'mer-ik, -,nyü-\ also **al·pha·nu·mer·i·cal** \-i-kəl\ adj [alphabetic + numeric, numerical] (1950) **1** : consisting of both letters and numbers and often other symbols (as punctuation marks and mathematical symbols) ⟨an ∼ code⟩; also : being a character in an alphanumeric system **2** : capable of using or displaying alphanumeric characters — **al·pha·nu·mer·i·cal·ly** \-i-k(ə-)lē\ adv — **al·pha·nu·mer·ics** \-iks\ n pl

alpha particle n (1903) : a positively charged nuclear particle identical with the nucleus of a helium atom that consists of two protons and two

ALPHABET TABLE

Showing the letters of five non-Roman alphabets and the transliterations used in the etymologies

HEBREW[1,4]

Letter	Name	Translit.
א	aleph	' [2]
ב	beth	b, bh
ג	gimel	g, gh
ד	daleth	d, dh
ה	he	h
ו	waw	w
ז	zayin	z
ח	heth	ḥ
ט	teth	ṭ
י	yod	y
כ ך	kaph	k, kh
ל	lamed	l
מ ם	mem	m
נ ן	nun	n
ס	samekh	s
ע	ayin	'
פ ף	pe	p, ph
צ ץ	sadhe	ṣ
ק	qoph	q
ר	resh	r
שׂ	sin	ś
שׁ	shin	sh
ת	taw	t, th

ARABIC[3,4]

Alone	Joined prec.	Joined both	Joined foll.	Name	Translit.
ا	ـا			alif	[5]
ب	ب	ﺒ	ﺑ	bā	b
ت	ت	ﺘ	ﺗ	tā	t
ث	ث	ﺜ	ﺛ	thā	th
ج	ج	ﺠ	ﺟ	jīm	j
ح	ح	ﺤ	ﺣ	ḥā	ḥ
خ	خ	ﺨ	ﺧ	khā	kh
د	ـد			dāl	d
ذ	ـذ			dhāl	dh
ر	ـر			rā	r
ز	ـز			zāy	z
س	س	ﺴ	ﺳ	sīn	s
ش	ش	ﺸ	ﺷ	shīn	sh
ص	ص	ﺼ	ﺻ	ṣād	ṣ
ض	ض	ﻀ	ﺿ	ḍād	ḍ
ط	ط	ﻄ	ﻃ	ṭā	ṭ
ظ	ظ	ﻈ	ﻇ	ẓā	ẓ
ع	ع	ﻌ	ﻋ	'ayn	'
غ	غ	ﻐ	ﻏ	ghayn	gh
ف	ف	ﻔ	ﻓ	fā	f
ق	ق	ﻘ	ﻗ	qāf	q
ك	ك	ﻜ	ﻛ	kāf	k
ل	ل	ﻠ	ﻟ	lām	l
م	م	ﻤ	ﻣ	mīm	m
ن	ن	ﻨ	ﻧ	nūn	n
ه	ه	ﻬ	ﻫ	hā	h [6]
و	ـو			wāw	w
ي	ي	ﻴ	ﻳ	yā	y

GREEK[7]

Letter	Name	Translit.
A α	alpha	a
B β	beta	b
Γ γ	gamma	g, n
Δ δ	delta	d
E ε	epsilon	e
Z ζ	zeta	z
H η	eta	ē
Θ θ	theta	th
I ι	iota	i
K κ	kappa	k
Λ λ	lambda	l
M μ	mu	m
N ν	nu	n
Ξ ξ	xi	x
O o	omicron	o
Π π	pi	p
P ρ	rho	r, rh
Σ σ s	sigma	s
T τ	tau	t
Υ υ	upsilon	y, u
Φ φ	phi	ph
X χ	chi	ch
Ψ ψ	psi	ps
Ω ω	omega	ō

RUSSIAN[8]

Letter	Translit.
А а	a
Б б	b
В в	v
Г г	g
Д д	d
Е е	e
Ж ж	zh
З з	z
И и Й й	i, ĭ
К к	k
Л л	l
М м	m
Н н	n
О о	o
П п	p
Р р	r
С с	s
Т т	t
У у	u
Ф ф	f
Х х	kh
Ц ц	ts
Ч ч	ch
Ш ш	sh
Щ щ	shch
Ъ ъ	" [9]
Ы ы	y
Ь ь	' [10]
Э э	e
Ю ю	yu
Я я	ya

SANSKRIT[11]

Letter	Translit.	Letter	Translit.
अ	a	ञ	ñ
आ	ā	ट	ṭ
इ	i	ठ	ṭh
ई	ī	ड	ḍ
उ	u	ढ	ḍh
ऊ	ū	ण	ṇ
ऋ	ṛ	त	t
ॠ	ṝ	थ	th
ऌ	ḷ	द	d
ॡ	ḹ	ध	dh
ए	e	न	n
ऐ	ai	प	p
ओ	o	फ	ph
औ	au	ब	b
ं	ṃ	भ	bh
ः	ḥ	म	m
क	k	य	y
ख	kh	र	r
ग	g	ल	l
घ	gh	व	v
ङ	ṅ	श	ś
च	c	ष	ṣ
छ	ch	स	s
ज	j	ह	h
झ	jh		

1 See ALEPH, BETH, etc., in the vocabulary. Where two forms of a letter are given, the one at the right is the form used at the end of a word. 2 Not represented in transliteration when initial. 3 The left column shows the form of each Arabic letter that is used when it stands alone, the second column its form when it is joined to the preceding letter, the third column its form when it is joined to both the preceding and the following letter, and the right column its form when it is joined to the following letter only. In the names of the Arabic letters, ā, ī, and ū respectively are pronounced like a in *father*, i in *machine*, u in *rude*. 4 Hebrew and Arabic are written from right to left. The Hebrew and Arabic letters are all primarily consonants; a few of them are also used secondarily to represent certain vowels, but full indication of vowels, when provided at all, is by means of a system of dots or strokes adjacent to the consonantal characters. 5 Alif represents no sound in itself, but is used principally as an indicator of the presence of a glottal stop (transliterated ' medially and finally; not represented in transliteration when initial) and as the sign of a long a. 6 When ة has two dots above it (ة), it is called *tā marbūta* and, if it immediately precedes a vowel, is transliterated *t* instead of *h*. 7 See ALPHA, BETA, GAMMA, etc., in the vocabulary. The letter gamma is transliterated *n* only before velars; the letter upsilon is transliterated *u* only as the final element in diphthongs. 8 See CYRILLIC in the vocabulary. 9 This sign indicates that the immediately preceding consonant is not palatalized even though immediately followed by a palatal vowel. 10 This sign indicates that the immediately preceding consonant is palatalized even though not immediately followed by a palatal vowel. 11 The alphabet shown here is the Devanagari. When vowels are combined with preceding consonants they are indicated by various strokes or hooks instead of by the signs here given, or, in the case of short a, not written at all. Thus the character क represents *ka*; the character का, *kā*; the character कि, *ki*; the character की, *kī*; the character कु, *ku*; the character कू, *kū*; the character कृ, *kṛ*; the character कॄ, *kṝ*; the character के, *ke*; the character कै, *kai*; the character को, *ko*; the character कौ, *kau*; and the character क्, *k* without any following vowel. There are also many compound characters representing combinations of two or more consonants.

neutrons and is ejected at high speed in certain radioactive transformations — called also *alpha, alpha ray*

alpha privative *n* (1590) : the prefix *a-* or *an-* expressing negation in Greek and in English

al·pha–re·cep·tor \'al-fə-ri-₁sep-tər\ *n* (1961) : any of a group of receptors postulated to exist on nerve cell membranes of the sympathetic nervous system to explain the specificity of certain adrenergic agents in affecting only some sympathetic activities (as vasoconstriction, relaxation of intestinal muscle, and contraction of most smooth muscle)

alpha wave *n* (1936) : an electrical rhythm of the brain with a frequency of 8 to 13 cycles per second that is often associated with a state of wakeful relaxation — called also *alpha, alpha rhythm*

Al·phe·us \al-'fē-əs\ *n* [L, fr. Gk *Alpheios*] : a Greek river-god who pursues the nymph Arethusa and is finally united with her

al·pine \'al-₁pīn\ *n* (ca. 1828) **1** : a plant native to alpine or boreal regions that is often grown for ornament **2** *cap* : a person possessing Alpine physical characteristics

Alpine *adj* (15c) **1** *often not cap* : of, relating to, or resembling the Alps or any mountains **2** *often not cap* : of, relating to, or growing in the biogeographic zone including the elevated slopes above timberline **3** : of or relating to a physical type characterized by a broad head, stockiness, medium height, and brown hair or eyes often regarded as constituting a branch of the Caucasian race **4** : of or relating to competitive ski events consisting of slalom and downhill racing — compare NORDIC

al·pin·ism \'al-pə-₁ni-zəm\ *n, often cap* (1884) : mountain climbing in the Alps or other high mountains — **al·pin·ist** \-nist\ *n*

al·ready \ȯl-'re-dē, 'ȯl-₁\ *adv* [ME *al redy*, fr. *al redy*, adj., wholly ready, fr. *al* all + *redy* ready] (14c) **1** : prior to a specified or implied past, present, or future time : by this time : PREVIOUSLY ⟨he had ∼ left when I called⟩ **2** — used as an intensive ⟨all right ∼⟩ ⟨enough ∼⟩

al·right \(₁)ȯl-'rīt, 'ȯl-₁\ *adv or adj* (1887) : ALL RIGHT
usage The one-word spelling *alright* appeared some 75 years after *all right* itself had reappeared from a 400-year-long absence. Since the early 20th century some critics have insisted *alright* is wrong, but it has its defenders and its users. It is less frequent than *all right* but remains in common use esp. in journalistic and business publications. It is quite common in fictional dialogue, and is used occas. in other writing ⟨the first two years of medical school were *alright* —Gertrude Stein⟩.

Al·sa·tian \al-'sā-shən\ *n* [ML *Alsatia* Alsace] (1917) : GERMAN SHEPHERD

al·sike clover \'al-₁sak-, -₁sīk-\ *n* [*Alsike*, Sweden] (1852) : a European perennial clover (*Trifolium hybridum*) much used as a forage plant

al·so \'ȯl(t)-(₁)sō, 'ȯ-\ *adv* [ME, fr. OE *eallswā*, fr. *eall* all + *swā* so — more at SO] (bef. 12c) **1** : LIKEWISE 1 **2** : in addition : BESIDES, TOO

al·so–ran \-₁ran\ *n* (1896) **1** : a horse or dog that finishes out of the money in a race **2** : a contestant that does not win **3** : one that is of little importance esp. competitively ⟨was just an ∼ in the scramble for . . . privileges —C. A. Buss⟩

Al·ta·ic \al-'tā-ik\ *adj* (ca. 1828) **1** : of or relating to the Altai Mountains **2** : of, relating to, or constituting the Turkic, Tungusic, and Mongolian language families collectively

Al·tair \al-'tīr, -'tar, -'ter, 'al-₁\ *n* [Ar *al-ṭā'ir*, lit., the flier] : the brightest star in the constellation Aquila

al·tar \'ȯl-tər\ *n, often attrib* [ME *alter*, fr. OE *altar*, fr. L *altare*; prob. akin to L *adolēre* to burn up] (bef. 12c) **1** : a usu. raised structure or place on which sacrifices are offered or incense is burned in worship **2** : a table on which the eucharistic elements are consecrated or which serves as a center of worship or ritual

altar boy *n* (1772) : a boy who assists the celebrant in a liturgical service

altar call *n* (1946) : an appeal by an evangelist to worshipers to come forward to signify their decision to commit their lives to Christ

altar of repose *often cap A&R* (ca. 1872) : REPOSITORY 2

al·tar·piece \'ȯl-tər-₁pēs\ *n* (1644) : a work of art that decorates the space above and behind an altar

altar rail *n* (1860) : a railing in front of an altar separating the chancel from the body of the church

altar stone *n* (14c) : a stone slab with a compartment containing the relics of martyrs that forms an essential part of a Roman Catholic altar

alt·az·i·muth \(₁)al-'taz-məth, -'ta-zə-\ *n, often attrib* [ISV *altitude* + *azimuth*] (1860) : a telescope mounted so that it can swing horizontally and vertically; *also* : any of several other similarly mounted instruments

al·ter \'ȯl-tər\ *vb* **al·tered; al·ter·ing** \-t(ə-)riŋ\ [ME, fr. MF *alterer*, fr. ML *alterare*, fr. L *alter* other (of two); akin to L *alius* other — more at ELSE] *vt* (14c) **1** : to make different without changing into something else **2** : CASTRATE, SPAY ∼ *vi* : to become different **syn** see CHANGE — **al·ter·abil·i·ty** \₁ȯl-t(ə-)rə-'bi-lə-tē\ *n* — **al·ter·able** \'ȯl-t(ə-)rə-bəl\ *adj* — **al·ter·ably** \-blē\ *adv* — **al·ter·er** \-tər-ər\ *n*

al·ter·ation \₁ȯl-tə-'rā-shən\ *n* (14c) **1** : the act or process of altering : the state of being altered **2** : the result of altering : MODIFICATION

al·ter·cate \'ȯl-tər-₁kāt\ *vi* **-cat·ed; -cat·ing** [L *altercatus*, pp. of *altercari*, fr. *alter*] (1530) : to dispute angrily or noisily : WRANGLE

al·ter·ca·tion \₁ȯl-tər-'kā-shən\ *n* (14c) : a noisy heated angry dispute; *also* : noisy controversy

alter ego \₁ȯl-tər-'ē-(₁)gō *also* -'e-(₁)gō\ *n* [L, lit., second I] (1537) : a second self: as **a** : a trusted friend **b** : the opposite side of a personality **c** : COUNTERPART 3

¹al·ter·nate *US & Canad* 'ȯl-tər-nət *also* 'al-; *chiefly Brit* ȯl-'tər-\ *adj* [L *alternatus*, pp. of *alternare*, fr. *alternus* alternate, fr. *alter*] (1513) **1** : occurring or succeeding by turns ⟨a day of ∼ sunshine and rain⟩ **2 a** : arranged first on one side and then on the other at different levels or points along an axial line ⟨∼ leaves⟩ — compare OPPOSITE **b** : arranged one above or alongside the other **3** : every other : every second ⟨he works on ∼ days⟩ **4** : constituting an alternative ⟨took the ∼ route home⟩ **5** : ALTERNATIVE 3 — **al·ter·nate·ly** *adv*

²al·ter·nate \'ȯl-tər-₁nāt *also* 'al-\ *vb* **-nat·ed; -nat·ing** *vt* (1599) **1** : to perform by turns or in succession **2** : to cause to alternate ∼ *vi* : to change from one to another repeatedly ⟨rain *alternated* with sun⟩

³al·ter·nate *same as* 1\ *n* (1717) **1** : ALTERNATIVE **2** : one that substitutes for or alternates with another

alternate angle *n* (1660) : one of a pair of angles with different verti-

alternate interior angles
a, a', b, b'; alternate exterior angles *c, c', d, d'*

ces and on opposite sides of a transversal at its intersection with two other lines: **a** : one of a pair of angles inside the two intersected lines — called also *alternate interior angle* **b** : one of a pair of angles outside the two intersected lines — called also *alternate exterior angle*

alternating current *n* (1839) : an electric current that reverses its direction at regularly recurring intervals — abbr. *AC*

alternating group *n* (1904) : a permutation group whose elements comprise those permutations of *n* objects which can be formed from the original order by making consecutively an even number of interchanges of pairs of objects

alternating series *n* (ca. 1909) : a mathematical series in which consecutive terms are alternatively positive and negative

al·ter·na·tion \₁ȯl-tər-'nā-shən *also* ₁al-\ *n* (15c) **1 a** : the act or process of alternating or causing to alternate **b** : alternating occurrence : SUCCESSION **2** : INCLUSIVE DISJUNCTION **3** : the occurrence of different allomorphs or allophones

alternation of generations (1858) : the occurrence of two or more forms differently produced in the life cycle of a plant or animal usu. involving the regular alternation of a sexual with an asexual generation

¹al·ter·na·tive \ȯl-'tər-nə-tiv, al-\ *adj* (1540) **1** : ALTERNATE 1 **2** : offering or expressing a choice ⟨several ∼ plans⟩ **3** : existing or functioning outside the established cultural, social, or economic system ⟨∼ newspaper⟩ ⟨∼ lifestyles⟩; *also* : different from the usual or conventional ⟨∼ fuels⟩ — **al·ter·na·tive·ly** *adv* — **al·ter·na·tive·ness** *n*

²alternative *n* (1624) **1 a** : a proposition or situation offering a choice between two or more things only one of which may be chosen **b** : an opportunity for deciding between two or more courses or propositions **2 a** : one of two or more things, courses, or propositions to be chosen **b** : something which can be chosen instead ⟨the only ∼ to intervention⟩ **syn** see CHOICE

alternative school *n* (1972) : an elementary or secondary school with a nontraditional curriculum

al·ter·na·tor \'ȯl-tər-₁nā-tər *also* 'al-\ *n* (1892) : an electric generator for producing alternating current

alt·horn \'alt-₁hȯrn\ *n* [G, fr. *alt* alto + *Horn* horn] (1859) : an alto saxhorn

al·though *also* **al·tho** \ȯl-'thō\ *conj* [ME *although*, fr. *al* all + *though*] (14c) : in spite of the fact that : even though

al·tim·e·ter \al-'ti-mə-tər, 'al-tə-₁mē-tər\ *n* [L *altus* + E *-meter*] (ca. 1828) : an instrument for measuring altitude; *esp* : an aneroid barometer designed to register changes in atmospheric pressure accompanying changes in altitude — **al·tim·e·try** \al-'ti-mə-trē\ *n*

al·ti·pla·no \₁al-ti-'plä-(₁)nō\ *n, pl* **-nos** [AmerSp, fr. L *altus* + *planum* plain] (1919) : a high plateau or plain : TABLELAND

al·ti·tude \'al-tə-₁tüd *also* -₁tyüd\ *n* [ME, fr. L *altitudo* height, depth, fr. *altus* high, deep — more at OLD] (14c) **1 a** : the angular elevation of a celestial object above the horizon **b** : the vertical elevation of an object above a surface (as sea level or land) of a planet or natural satellite **c** (1) : a perpendicular line segment from a vertex of a geometric figure (as a triangle or a pyramid) to the opposite side or the opposite side extended or from a side or face to a parallel side or face or the side or face extended (2) : the length of an altitude **2** : a high level (as of quality or feeling) ⟨the ∼s of his anger⟩ **3 a** : vertical distance or extent **b** : position at a height **c** : an elevated region : EMINENCE — usu. used in pl. **syn** see HEIGHT — **al·ti·tu·di·nal** \₁al-tə-'tü-d³n-əl, -'tyü-\ *adj* — **al·ti·tu·di·nous** \-d³n-əs\ *adj*

altitude sickness *n* (1920) : the effects (as nosebleed or nausea) of oxygen deficiency in the blood and tissues developed in rarefied air at high altitudes

¹al·to \'al-(₁)tō\ *n, pl* **altos** [It, lit., high, fr. L *altus*] (ca. 1724) **1 a** : COUNTERTENOR **b** : CONTRALTO **2** : the second highest voice part in a 4-part chorus **b** : a member of a family of instruments having a range lower than that of the treble or soprano; *esp* : an alto saxophone

²alto *adj* (ca. 1724) : relating to or having the range or part of an alto

al·to·cu·mu·lus \₁al-tō-'kyü-myə-ləs\ *n, pl* **-li** \-₁lī, -₁lē\ [NL, fr. L *altus* + NL *-o-* + *cumulus*] (1894) : a fleecy cloud formation consisting of large whitish globular cloudlets with shaded portions — see CLOUD illustration

¹al·to·geth·er \₁ȯl-tə-'ge-thər\ *adv* [ME *altogedere*, fr. *al* all + *togedere* together] (13c) **1** : WHOLLY, COMPLETELY ⟨an ∼ different problem⟩ ⟨stopped crying ∼⟩ **2** : in all : ALL TOLD ⟨spent a hundred dollars ∼⟩ **3** : on the whole : in the main ⟨∼ their efforts were successful⟩

²altogether *n* (1894) : NUDE — used with *the* ⟨posed in the ∼⟩

al·to–re·lie·vo *or* **al·to–ri·lie·vo** \₁al-(₁)tō-ri-'lē-(₁)vō, ₁äl-(₁)tō-rēl-'yä-(₁)vō\ *n, pl* **alto–relievos** *or* **alto–ri·lie·vi** \-vē, -₁vē\ *also* \₁äl-(₁)tō-rēl-'yä-(₁)vē\ [It *altorilievo*] (1664) **1** : HIGH RELIEF **2** : a sculpture in high relief

al·to·stra·tus \₁al-tō-'strā-təs, -'stra-\ *n, pl* **-ti** \-₁tī\ [NL, fr. L *altus* + NL *-o-* + *stratus*] (1894) : a cloud formation similar to cirrostratus but darker and at a lower level — see CLOUD illustration

al·tri·cial \al-'tri-shəl\ *adj* [L *altric-, altrix*, fem. of *altor* one who nourishes, fr. *alere* to nourish — more at OLD] (1872) : being hatched or born or having young that are hatched or born in a very immature and helpless condition so as to require care for some time ⟨∼ birds⟩ — compare PRECOCIAL

al·tru·ism \'al-trü-₁i-zəm\ [F *altruisme*, fr. *autrui* other people, fr. OF, oblique case form of *autre* other, fr. L *alter*] (1853) **1** : unselfish regard for or devotion to the welfare of others **2** : behavior by an animal that is not beneficial to or may be harmful to itself but that benefits others of its species — **al·tru·ist** \-trü-ist\ *n* — **al·tru·is·tic** \₁al-trü-'is-tik\ *adj* — **al·tru·is·ti·cal·ly** \-ti-k(ə-)lē\ *adv*

al·u·la \'al-yə-lə\ *n, pl* **-lae** \-₁lē, -₁lī\ [NL, fr. L, dim. of *ala* wing — more at AISLE] (1772) : the process of a bird's wing corresponding to the thumb and bearing a few short quills — called also *bastard wing*

¹al·um \'a-ləm\ *n* [ME, fr. MF *alum, alun*, fr. L *alumen*] (14c) **1** : a potassium aluminum sulfate KAl(SO₄)₂·12H₂O or an ammonium aluminum sulfate NH₄Al(SO₄)₂·12H₂O used esp. as an emetic and as an astringent and styptic **2** : any of various double salts isomorphous with potassium aluminum sulfate **3** : ALUMINUM SULFATE

²alum \ə-'ləm\ *n* [by shortening] (1930) : ALUMNUS, ALUMNA

alu·mi·na \ə-'lü-mə-nə\ *n* [NL, fr. L *alumin-, alumen* alum] (1801) : aluminum oxide Al₂O₃ occuring native as corundum and in hydrated forms (as in bauxite)

alu·mi·nate \-nət\ *n* (1841) : a compound of alumina with a metallic oxide

al·u·min·i·um \ˌal-yə-'mi-nē-əm\ *n* [NL, fr. *alumina*] (1812) *chiefly Brit* : ALUMINUM

alu·mi·nize \ə-'lü-mə-ˌnīz\ *vt* **-nized; -niz·ing** (1934) : to treat or coat with aluminum

alu·mi·no·sil·i·cate \ə-ˌlü-mə-nō-'si-lə-ˌkāt, -'si-li-kət\ *n* [L *alumin-, alumen* + *-o-* + ISV *silicate*] (1907) : a combined silicate and aluminate

alu·mi·nous \ə-'lü-mə-nəs\ *adj* (15c) : of, relating to, or containing alum or aluminum

alu·mi·num \ə-'lü-mə-nəm\ *n, often attrib* [NL, fr. *alumina*] (1812) : a bluish silver-white malleable ductile light trivalent metallic element that has good electrical and thermal conductivity, high reflectivity, and resistance to oxidation and is the most abundant metal in the earth's crust where it always occurs in combination — see ELEMENT table

aluminum sulfate *n* (1873) : a white salt Al₂(SO₄)₃ usu. made by treating bauxite with sulfuric acid and used in making paper, in water purification, and in tanning

alum·na \ə-'ləm-nə\ *n, pl* **-nae** \-(ˌ)nē *also* -ˌnī\ [L, fem. of *alumnus*] (1879) **1** : a girl or woman who has attended or has graduated from a particular school, college, or university **2** : a girl or woman who is a former member, employee, contributor, or inmate

alum·nus \ə-'ləm-nəs\ *n, pl* **-ni** \-ˌnī\ [L, foster son, pupil, fr. *alere* to nourish — more at OLD] (1645) **1** : one who has attended or has graduated from a particular school, college, or university **2** : one who is a former member, employee, contributor, or inmate

al·um·root \'a-ləm-ˌrüt, -ˌrut\ *n* (1813) : any of a genus (*Heuchera*) of No. American herbs of the saxifrage family having basal rounded or lobed toothed leaves; *esp* : one (*H. americana*) of eastern No. America

al·u·nite \'al-yə-ˌnīt, 'a-lə-\ *n* [F, fr. *alun* alum] (1868) : a mineral that consists of a hydrous potassium aluminum sulfate and occurs in massive form or in rhombohedral crystals

al·ve·o·lar \al-'vē-(ə-)lər\ *adj* (1799) **1** : of, relating to, resembling, or having alveoli; *esp* : of, relating to, or constituting the part of the jaws where the teeth arise, the air-containing cells of the lungs, or glands with secretory cells about a central space **2** : articulated with the tip of the tongue touching or near the teethridge — **al·ve·o·lar·ly** *adv*

al·ve·o·late \-lət\ *adj* (ca. 1823) : pitted like a honeycomb ⟨~ pollen⟩

al·ve·o·lus \al-'vē-ə-ləs\ *n, pl* **-li** \-ˌlī, -(ˌ)lē\ [NL, fr. L, dim. of *alveus* cavity, hollow, fr. *alvus* belly, beehive; akin to Lith *aulys* beehive, Gk *aulos* tube, flute] (ca. 1706) **1** : a small cavity or pit: as **a** : a socket for a tooth **b** : an air-containing cell of the lungs **c** : an acinus of a compound gland **d** : a cell or compartment of a honeycomb **2** : TEETHRIDGE

al·way \'ȯl-(ˌ)wā\ *adv* [ME *alwey, alneway*, fr. OE *ealne weg*, lit., all the way, fr. *ealne* (acc. of *eall* all) + *weg* (acc.) way — more at WAY] (14c) *archaic* : ALWAYS

al·ways \'ȯl-wēz, -wəz, -(ˌ)wāz *also* 'ȯ-\ *adv* [ME *alwayes*, fr. *alwey*] (14c) **1** : at all times : INVARIABLY **2** : FOREVER, PERPETUALLY **3** : at any rate : in any event ⟨as a last resort one can ~ work⟩

Al·yce clover \'a-ləs-\ *n* [prob. by folk etymology fr. NL *Alysicarpus*, genus name, fr. Gk *halysis* chain + *karpos* fruit] (1941) : a low spreading annual Old World legume (*Alysicarpus vaginalis*) used in the southern U.S. as a cover crop and for hay and forage

alys·sum \'ȯl-ə-səm also ə-'li-səm\ *n* [NL, fr. Gk *alysson*, plant believed to cure rabies, fr. neut. of *alyssos* curing rabies, fr. *a-* + *lyssa* rabies] (1548) **1** : any of a genus (*Alyssum*) of Old World herbs of the mustard family with small usu. yellow racemose flowers **2** : SWEET ALYSSUM

Alz·hei·mer's disease \'älts-ˌhī-mərz-, 'alts-\ *n* [Alois *Alzheimer* †1915 Ger. physician] (1912) : a degenerative disease of the central nervous system characterized esp. by premature senile mental deterioration — called also *Alzheimer's*

am [ME, fr. OE *eom;* akin to ON *em* am, L *sum*, Gk *eimi*] *pres 1st sing of* BE

AM \'ā-ˌem\ *n, often attrib* [*amplitude modulation*] (1940) : a broadcasting system using amplitude modulation; *also* : a radio receiver of such a system

ama \'ä-(ˌ)mä\ *n, pl* **amas** *or* **ama** [Jp] (1946) : a Japanese diver esp. for pearls

amah \'ä-(ˌ)mä\ *n* [Pg *ama* wet nurse, fr. ML *amma*] (1839) : an Oriental female servant; *esp* : a Chinese nurse

amain \ə-'mān\ *adv* (1540) **1** : with all one's might ⟨attacking a huge rack of beef with a cleaver, she flailed away ~ —Jay Jacobs⟩ **2** *archaic* **a** : at full speed **b** : in great haste **3** *archaic* : to a high degree : EXCEEDINGLY ⟨they whom I favour thrive in wealth ~ —John Milton⟩

Am·a·le·kite \'a-mə-ˌle-ˌkīt, ə-'ma-lə-ˌkīt\ *n* [Heb *'Ămālēqī*, fr. *'Ămālēq* Amalek, grandson of Esau] (1560) : a member of an ancient nomadic people living south of Canaan

amal·gam \ə-'mal-gəm\ *n* [ME *amalgame*, fr. MF, fr. ML *amalgama*] (15c) **1** : an alloy of mercury with another metal that is solid or liquid at room temperature according to the proportion of mercury present and is used esp. in making tooth cements **2** : a mixture of different elements : COMBINATION

amal·gam·ate \-gə-ˌmāt\ *vt* **-at·ed; -at·ing** (1617) **1** : to unite in or as if in an amalgam; *esp* : to merge into a single body **syn** see MIX — **amal·gam·ator** \-ˌmā-tər\ *n*

amal·gam·ation \ə-ˌmal-gə-'mā-shən\ *n* (1612) **1 a** : the action or process of amalgamating : UNITING **b** : the state of being amalgamated **2** : the result of amalgamating : AMALGAM **3** : CONSOLIDATION, MERGER ⟨~ of two corporations⟩

aman·dine \ˌä-ˌmän-'dēn\ *adj* [F] (1945) : prepared or served with almonds

am·a·ni·ta \ˌa-mə-'nī-tə, -'nē-\ *n* [NL, genus name, fr. Gk *amanitai*, pl., a kind of fungus] (1899) : any of a genus (*Amanita*) of white=

amanita

spored fungi that typically have a volva and an annulus about the stipe and that includes some deadly poisonous forms

am·a·ni·tin \-'nī-t⁹n, -'nē-\ *n* [*amanita* + *-in*] (ca. 1847) : a highly toxic peptide that is produced by the death cap and that selectively inhibits mammalian RNA polymerase

aman·ta·dine \ə-'man-tə-ˌdēn\ *n* [ISV *amantad-* (alter. of *adamantane*, C₁₀H₁₆) + *amine*] (1964) : a drug used esp. as the hydrochloride C₁₀H₁₇N·HCl to prevent infection (as by an influenza virus) by interfering with virus penetration into host cells

aman·u·en·sis \ə-ˌman-yə-'wen(t)-səs\ *n, pl* **-en·ses** \-(ˌ)sēz\ [L, fr. (*servus*) *a manu* slave with secretarial duties] (1619) : one employed to write from dictation or to copy manuscript

am·a·ranth \'a-mə-ˌran(t)th\ *n* [L *amarantus*, a flower, fr. Gk *amaranton*, fr. neut. of *amarantos* unfading, fr. *a-* + *marainein* to waste away] (1548) **1** : any of a large genus (*Amaranthus* of the family Amaranthaceae, the amaranth family) of coarse herbs including forms cultivated as food crops and various pigweeds **2** : a flower that never fades **3** : a red azo dye

am·a·ran·thine \ˌa-mə-'ran(t)-thən, -'ran-ˌthīn\ *adj* (1667) **1 a** : of or relating to an amaranth **b** : UNDYING **2** : of the color amaranth

am·a·ret·to \ˌa-mə-'re-(ˌ)tō, ˌä-\ *n* [It, dim. of *amaro* bitter, fr. L *amarus*] (1945) **1 am·a·ret·ti** \-(ˌ)tē\ *pl* : macaroons made with bitter almonds **2** *often cap* : an almond-flavored liqueur

am·a·ryl·lis \ˌa-mə-'ri-ləs\ *n* [NL, genus name, prob. fr. L, name of a shepherdess in Virgil's *Eclogues*] (ca. 1794) : an autumn-flowering So. African bulbous plant (*Amaryllis belladonna* of the family Amaryllidaceae, the amaryllis family) widely grown for its deep red to whitish umbellate flowers; *also* : a plant of any of several related genera (as *Hippeastrum* or *Sprekelia*)

amass \ə-'mas\ *vb* [MF *amasser*, fr. OF, fr. *a-* (fr. L *ad-*) + *masser* to gather into a mass, fr. *masse* mass] *vt* (15c) **1** : to collect for oneself : ACCUMULATE ⟨~ a great fortune⟩ **2** : to collect into a mass : GATHER ⟨must select rather than simply ~ details⟩ ~ *vi* : to come together : ASSEMBLE — **amass·er** — **amass·ment** \-mənt\ *n*

am·a·teur \'a-mə-(ˌ)tər, -ˌtür, -ˌtyür, -ˌchür, -chər\ *n, often attrib* [F, fr. L *amator* lover, fr. *amare* to love] (1784) **1** : DEVOTEE, ADMIRER **2** : one who engages in a pursuit, study, science, or sport as a pastime rather than as a profession **3** : one lacking in experience and competence in an art or science — **am·a·teur·ish** \ˌa-mə-'tər-ish, -'t(y)ür-, -'chür-, -'chər-\ *adj* — **am·a·teur·ish·ly** *adv* — **am·a·teur·ish·ness** \-nəs\ *n* — **am·a·teur·ism** \'a-mə-ˌtər-ˌi-zəm, -ˌt(y)ür-, -ˌchür-; -ˌtə-ˌri-, -ˌchə-ˌri-\ *n*

syn AMATEUR, DILETTANTE, DABBLER, TYRO mean a person who follows a pursuit without attaining proficiency or professional status. AMATEUR often applies to one practicing an art without mastery of its essentials ⟨a painting obviously done by an *amateur*⟩; in sports it may also suggest not so much lack of skill but avoidance of direct remuneration ⟨remained an *amateur* despite lucrative offers⟩. DILETTANTE may apply to the lover of an art rather than its skilled practitioner but usu. implies elegant trifling in the arts and an absence of serious commitment ⟨had no patience for *dilettantes*⟩. DABBLER suggests desultory habits of work and lack of persistence ⟨a *dabbler* who started novels but never finished them⟩. TYRO implies inexperience often combined with audacity with resulting crudeness or blundering ⟨shows talent but is still a mere *tyro*⟩.

Ama·ti \ä-'mä-tē, ə-\ *n, pl* **Amatis** (1833) : a violin made by a member of the Amati family of Cremona

am·a·tive \'a-mə-tiv\ *adj* [ML *amativus*, fr. L *amatus*, pp. of *amare*] (1636) : AMOROUS **1** — **am·a·tive·ly** *adv* — **am·a·tive·ness** *n*

am·a·to·ry \'a-mə-ˌtȯr-ē, -ˌtȯr-\ *adj* (1599) : of, relating to, or expressing sexual love

am·au·ro·sis \ˌa-mȯ-'rō-səs\ *n, pl* **-ro·ses** \-ˌsēz\ [NL, fr. Gk *amaurōsis*, lit., dimming, fr. *amauroun* to dim, fr. *amauros* dim] (ca. 1657) : partial or complete loss of sight occurring esp. without an externally perceptible change in the eye — **am·au·rot·ic** \-'rä-tik\ *adj*

amaurotic idiocy *n* (1896) : any of several resessive genetic conditions characterized by the accumulation of lipid-containing cells in the viscera and nervous system, mental retardation, and impaired vision or blindness; *esp* : TAY-SACHS DISEASE

¹amaze \ə-'māz\ *vb* **amazed; amaz·ing** [ME *amasen*, fr. OE *āmasian*, fr. *ā-* (perfective prefix) + (assumed) *masian* to confuse — more at ABIDE] *vt* (bef. 12c) **1** *obs* : BEWILDER, PERPLEX **2** : to fill with wonder : ASTOUND ~ *vi* : to show or cause astonishment **syn** see SURPRISE — **amaz·ed·ly** \-'mā-zəd-lē\ *adv*

²amaze *n* (15c) : AMAZEMENT

amaze·ment \ə-'māz-mənt\ *n* (1595) **1** *obs* : CONSTERNATION, BEWILDERMENT **2** : the quality or state of being amazed **3** : something that amazes

amaz·ing·ly \ə-'mā-ziŋ-lē\ *adv* (1673) **1** : to an amazing degree ⟨~ low prices⟩ **2** : what is amazing ⟨~ the runnerup was only two seconds behind —Jim Doherty⟩

am·a·zon \'a-mə-ˌzän, -zən\ *n* [ME, fr. L, fr. Gk *Amazōn*] (14c) **1** *cap* : a member of a race of female warriors of Greek mythology **2** : a tall strong often masculine woman

Am·a·zo·nian \ˌa-mə-'zō-nē-ən, -nyən\ *adj* (1594) **1** : relating to, resembling, or befitting an Amazon or an amazon **2** : of or relating to the Amazon River or its valley

am·a·zon·ite \'a-mə-zə-ˌnīt\ *n* [*Amazon* River] (ca. 1879) : an apple=green or bluish-green microcline

am·a·zon·stone \-zən-ˌstōn\ *n* (1836) : AMAZONITE

am·bage \'am-bij\ *n, pl* **am·ba·ges** \am-'bā-(ˌ)jēz, 'am-bi-jəz\ [back-formation fr. ME *ambages*, fr. MF or L; MF, fr. L, fr. *ambi-* + *agere* to drive — more at AGENT] (14c) **1** *archaic* : AMBIGUITY, CIRCUMLOCUTION — usu. used in pl. **2** *archaic* : indirect ways or proceedings

am·bas·sa·dor \am-'ba-sə-dər, əm-, im-, -ˌdȯr, -'bas-dər\ *n* [ME *ambassadour*, fr. MF *ambassadeur*, ultim. of Gmc origin; akin to OHG *ambaht* service] (14c) **1** : an official envoy; *esp* : a diplomatic agent of

\ə\ abut \'ʰ\ kitten, F table \ər\ further \a\ ash \ā\ ace \ä\ mop, mar \au̇\ out \ch\ chin \e\ bet \ē\ easy \g\ go \i\ hit \ī\ ice \j\ job \ŋ\ sing \ō\ go \ȯ\ law \ȯi\ boy \th\ thin \t͟h\ the \ü\ loot \u̇\ foot \y\ yet \zh\ vision \ä, ᴷ, ⁿ, œ, œ̄, ᵫ, ᵫ̄, �\ *see* Guide to Pronunciation the highest rank accredited to a foreign government or sovereign as the resident representative of his own government or sovereign or appointed for a special and often temporary diplomatic assignment **2 a** : an authorized representative or messenger **b** : an unofficial representative 〈traveling abroad as ∼s of goodwill〉 — **am·bas·sa·do·ri·al** \-ˌba-sə-'dōr-ē-əl, -'dȯr-\ *adj* — **am·bas·sa·dor·ship** \-'ba-sə-dər-ˌship\ *n*

ambassador–at–large *n, pl* **ambassadors–at–large** (1908) : a minister of the highest rank not accredited to a particular foreign government or sovereign

am·bas·sa·dress \am-'ba-sə-drəs, əm-, im-\ *n* (1594) **1** : a woman who is an ambassador **2** : the wife of an ambassador

am·beer \'am-ˌbir\ *n* [prob. alter. of *amber*; fr. its color] (1848) *chiefly Southern & southern Midland* : TOBACCO JUICE

¹**am·ber** \'am-bər\ *n* [ME *ambre*, fr. MF, fr. ML *ambra*, fr. Ar *'anbar* ambergris] (14c) **1** : a hard yellowish to brownish translucent fossil resin that takes a fine polish and is used chiefly in making ornamental objects (as beads) **2** : a variable color averaging a dark orange yellow

²**amber** *adj* (15c) **1** : consisting of amber; resembling amber; *esp* : having the color amber

am·ber·gris \'am-bər-ˌgris, -ˌgrē(s)\ *n* [ME *ambregris*, fr. MF *ambre gris*, fr. *ambre* + *gris* gray — more at GRIZZLE] (15c) : a waxy substance found floating in or on the shores of tropical waters, believed to originate in the intestines of the sperm whale, and used in perfumery as a fixative

am·ber·i·na \ˌam-bə-'rē-nə\ *n* [fr. *Amberina*, a trademark] (1885) : a late 19th century American clear glassware of a graduated color that shades from ruby to amber

am·ber·jack \-ˌjak\ *n* [fr. its color] (ca. 1893) : any of several carangid fishes (genus *Seriola*); *esp* : a large vigorous sport fish (*S. dumerili*) of the western Atlantic

ambi- *prefix* [L *ambi-*, *amb-* both, around; akin to L *ambo* both, Gk *amphō* both, *amphi* around — more at BY] : both 〈*ambi*valence〉

am·bi·dex·ter·i·ty \ˌam-bi-(ˌ)dek-'ster-ə-tē\ *n* (1593) : the quality or state of being ambidextrous

am·bi·dex·trous \ˌam-bi-'dek-strəs\ *adj* [LL *ambidexter*, fr. L *ambi-* + *dexter* right-hand — more at DEXTER] (1646) **1** : using both hands with equal ease **2** : unusually skillful : VERSATILE **3** : characterized by duplicity : DOUBLE-DEALING — **am·bi·dex·trous·ly** *adv*

am·bi·ence *or* **am·bi·ance** \'am-bē-ən(t)s, 'äm-bē-än(t)s; äⁿ-byäⁿs\ *n* [F *ambiance*, fr. *ambiant* ambient] (1889) : a feeling or mood associated with a particular place, person, or thing : ATMOSPHERE

am·bi·ent \'am-bē-ənt\ *adj* [L *ambient-*, *ambiens*, prp. of *ambire* to go around, fr. *ambi-* + *ire* to go — more at ISSUE] (1596) : existing or present on all sides : ENCOMPASSING

²**ambient** *n* (1624) : an encompassing atmosphere : ENVIRONMENT

am·bi·gu·i·ty \ˌam-bə-'gyü-ə-tē\ *n, pl* **-ties** (15c) **1 a** : the quality or state of being ambiguous esp. in meaning **b** : an ambiguous word or expression **2** : UNCERTAINTY

am·big·u·ous \am-'bi-gyə-wəs\ *adj* [L *ambiguus*, fr. *ambigere* to be undecided, fr. *ambi-* + *agere* to drive — more at AGENT] (1528) **1 a** : doubtful or uncertain esp. from obscurity or indistinctness 〈eyes of an ∼ color〉 **b** : INEXPLICABLE **2** : capable of being understood in two or more possible senses or ways *syn* see OBSCURE — **am·big·u·ous·ly** *adv* — **am·big·u·ous·ness** *n*

am·bi·sex·u·al \ˌam-bi-'sek-sh(ə-)wəl, -'sek-shəl\ *adj* (1939) : BISEXUAL — **ambisexual** *n* — **am·bi·sex·u·al·i·ty** \-ˌsek-shə-'wa-lə-tē\ *n*

am·bit \'am-bət\ *n* [ME, fr. L *ambitus*, fr. *ambire*] (1597) **1** : CIRCUIT, COMPASS **2** : the bounds or limits of a place or district **3** : a sphere of action, expression, or influence : SCOPE

¹**am·bi·tion** \am-'bi-shən\ *n* [ME, fr. MF or L; MF, fr. L *ambition-*, *ambitio*, lit., act of soliciting for votes, fr. *ambire*] (14c) **1 a** : an ardent desire for rank, fame, or power **b** : desire to achieve a particular end **2** : the object of ambition **3** : a desire for activity or exertion 〈felt sick and had no ∼〉 — **am·bi·tion·less** \-ləs\ *adj*

syn AMBITION, ASPIRATION, PRETENSION mean strong desire for advancement. AMBITION applies to the desire for personal advancement or preferment and may suggest equally a praiseworthy or an inordinate desire 〈driven by *ambition*〉. ASPIRATION implies a striving after something higher than oneself and usu. implies that the striver is thereby ennobled 〈an *aspiration* to become president someday〉. PRETENSION suggests ardent desire for recognition of accomplishment often without actual possession of the necessary ability and therefore may imply presumption 〈has literary *pretensions*〉.

²**ambition** *vt* (1664) : to have as one's ambition : DESIRE

am·bi·tious \am-'bi-shəs\ *adj* (14c) **1 a** : having or controlled by ambition **b** : having a desire to achieve a particular goal : ASPIRING **2** : resulting from, characterized by, or showing ambition — **am·bi·tious·ly** *adv* — **am·bi·tious·ness** *n*

am·biv·a·lence \am-'bi-və-lən(t)s\ *n* [ISV] (1918) **1** : simultaneous and contradictory attitudes or feelings (as attraction and repulsion) toward an object, person, or action **2 a** : continual fluctuation (as between one thing and its opposite) **b** : uncertainty as to which approach to follow — **am·biv·a·lent** \-lənt\ *adj* — **am·biv·a·lent·ly** *adv*

am·bi·ver·sion \ˌam-bi-'vər-zhən, -shən\ *n* [*ambi-* + *-version* (as in *introversion*)] (1927) : the personality configuration of an ambivert

am·bi·vert \'am-bi-ˌvərt\ *n* [*ambi-* + *-vert* (as in *introvert*)] (1927) : a person having characteristics of both extrovert and introvert

¹**am·ble** \'am-bəl\ *vi* **am·bled**; **am·bling** \-b(ə-)liŋ\ [ME, fr. MF *ambler*, fr. L *ambulare* to walk, fr. *ambi-* + *-ulare* (verb base akin to MW *el* he may go, Gk *ēlythe* he went) — more at ELASTIC] (14c) : to go at or as if at an amble : SAUNTER — **am·bler** \-b(ə-)lər\ *n*

²**amble** *n* (14c) **1 a** : an easy gait of a horse in which the legs on the same side of the body move together **b** : ⁷RACK b **2** : an easy gait **3** : a leisurely walk

am·blyg·o·nite \am-'bli-gə-ˌnīt\ *n* [G *Amblygonit*, fr. Gk *amblygōnios* obtuse-angled, fr. *amblys* blunt, dull + *gōnia* angle — more at MOLLIFY, -GON] (ca. 1828) : a mineral that consists of basic lithium aluminum phosphate commonly containing sodium and fluorine and occurs in white cleavable masses

am·bly·opia \ˌam-blē-'ō-pē-ə\ *n* [NL, fr. Gk *amblyōpia*, fr. *amblys* + *-ōpia* -opia] (ca. 1706) : dimness of sight esp. in one eye without apparent change in the eye structures — called also *lazy eye* — **am·bly·opic** \-'ō-pik, -'ä-pik\ *adj*

Am·boi·nese \ˌam-ˌbȯi-'nēz, -'nēs, am-'bȯi-\ *or* **Am·bo·nese** \ˌam-bə-'nēz, -'nēs\ *n, pl* **Amboinese** *or* **Ambonese** (ca. 1864) **1** : a native or inhabitant of Ambon **2** : the group of closely related Austronesian languages spoken on Ambon — **Amboinese** *or* **Ambonese** *adj*

am·boy·na *or* **am·boi·na** \am-'bȯi-nə\ *n* [*Amboina*, Moluccas, Indonesia] (ca. 1859) : a mottled curly-grained wood of a leguminous tree (*Pterocarpus indicus*) of southeastern Asia

am·bro·sia \am-'brō-zh(ē-)ə\ *n* [L, fr. Gk, lit., immortality, fr. *ambrotos* immortal, fr. *a-* + *-mbrotos* (akin to *brotos* mortal) — more at MURDER] (15c) **1 a** : the food of the Greek and Roman gods **b** : the ointment or perfume of the gods **2** : something extremely pleasing to taste or smell **3** : a dessert made of oranges and shredded coconut — **am·bro·sial** \-zh(ē-)əl\ *adj* — **am·bro·sial·ly** \-zh(ē-)ə-lē\ *adv*

ambrosia beetle *n* (ca. 1900) : any of various small wood-boring beetles (family Scolytidae) that cultivate a fungus on which they feed and raise their larvae

am·bro·type \'am-brə-ˌtīp\ *n* [Gk *ambrotos* + E *type*] (1858) : a positive picture made of a photographic negative on glass backed by a dark surface

am·bry \'am-brē; 'äm-rē, 'ȯm-\ *n, pl* **ambries** [ME *almery*, fr. MF *almarie*, *armarie*, fr. L *armarium*, fr. *arma* weapons — more at ARM] (14c) **1** *dial chiefly Brit* : PANTRY **2** : a recess in a church wall (as for holding sacramental vessels)

ambs·ace \'äm-ˌzās\ *n* [ME *ambes as*, fr. OF, fr. *ambes* both + *aces*] (13c) *archaic* : the lowest throw at dice; *also* : something worthless or unlucky

am·bu·la·cral \ˌam-byə-'la-krəl, -'lā-\ *adj* (1836) : of, relating to, or being any of the radial areas of echinoderms along which run the principal nerves, blood vessels, and elements of the water-vascular system 〈∼ grooves〉

am·bu·la·crum \-krəm\ *n, pl* **-cra** \-krə\ [NL, fr. L, alley, fr. *ambulare* to walk — more at AMBLE] (1837) : an ambulacral area or part

am·bu·lance \'am-byə-lən(t)s, -bə- *also* -ˌlan(t)s\ *n* [F, fr. (*hôpital*) *ambulant*, lit., ambulant field hospital, fr. *ambulant* itinerant, fr. L *ambulant-*, *ambulans*, prp. of *ambulare*] (1809) : a vehicle equipped for transporting the injured or sick

ambulance chaser *n* (1897) : a lawyer or lawyer's agent who incites accident victims to sue for damages — **ambulance chasing** *n*

am·bu·lant \'am-byə-lənt\ *adj* (1619) : moving about : AMBULATORY

am·bu·late \-ˌlāt\ *vi* **-lat·ed**; **-lat·ing** [L *ambulatus*, pp. of *ambulare*] (ca. 1623) : to move from place to place : WALK — **am·bu·la·tion** \ˌam-byə-'lā-shən\ *n*

¹**am·bu·la·to·ry** \'am-byə-lə-ˌtōr-ē, -ˌtȯr-\ *adj* (1622) **1** : of, relating to, or adapted to walking; *also* : occurring during a walk **2** : moving from place to place : ITINERANT **3** : capable of being altered 〈a will is ∼ until the testator's death〉 **4 a** : able to walk about and not bedridden **b** : performed on or involving an ambulatory patient or an outpatient 〈∼ medical care〉 〈an ∼ electrocardiogram〉 — **am·bu·la·to·ri·ly** \ˌam-byə-lə-'tōr-ə-lē, -'tȯr-\ *adv*

²**ambulatory** *n, pl* **-ries** (ca. 1616) : a sheltered place (as in a cloister or church) for walking

am·bus·cade \'am-bə-ˌskād, ˌam-bə-'\ *n* [MF *embuscade*, modif. of OIt *imboscata*, fr. *imboscare* to place in ambush, fr. *in* (fr. L) + *bosco* forest, of Gmc origin; akin to OHG *busc* forest — more at IN, BUSH] (ca. 1588) : AMBUSH — **ambuscade** *vb* — **am·bus·cad·er** *n*

¹**am·bush** \'am-ˌbush\ *vb* [ME *embushen*, fr. MF *embuschier*, fr. *en* in (fr. L *in*) + *busche* stick of firewood] *vt* (14c) **1** : to station in ambush **2** : to attack from an ambush : WAYLAY ∼ *vi* : to lie in wait : LURK — **am·bush·er** *n* — **am·bush·ment** \-mənt\ *n*

²**ambush** *n* (15c) **1** : a trap in which concealed persons lie in wait to attack by surprise **2** : the persons stationed in ambush; *also* : their concealed position **3** : an attack esp. from an ambush

ame·ba, ame·boid *var of* AMOEBA, AMOEBOID

am·e·bi·a·sis \ˌa-mi-'bī-ə-səs\ *n, pl* **-a·ses** \-ˌsēz\ (1905) : infection with or disease caused by amoebas (esp. *Entamoeba histolytica*)

ame·bic dysentery \ə-'mē-bik-\ *n* (1891) : acute human intestinal amebiasis caused by an amoeba (*Entamoeba histolytica*) and marked by dysentery, gripes, and erosion of the intestinal wall

ame·bo·cyte *var of* AMOEBOCYTE

ameer *var of* EMIR

ame·lio·rate \ə-'mēl-yə-ˌrāt, -'mē-lē-ə-\ *vb* **-rat·ed**; **-rat·ing** [alter. of *meliorate*] (1767) : to make better or more tolerable ∼ *vi* : to grow better *syn* see IMPROVE — **ame·lio·ra·tion** \-ˌmēl-yə-'rā-shən, -ˌmē-lē-ə-\ *n* — **ame·lio·ra·tive** \-'mēl-yə-ˌrā-tiv, -'mē-lē-ə-\ *adj* — **ame·lio·ra·tor** \-ˌrā-tər\ *n*

am·e·lo·blast \'a-mə-lō-ˌblast\ *n* [obs. *amel* enamel (ME, ultim. fr. OF *esmail*) + *-o-* + *-blast* — more at ENAMEL] (1882) : one of a group of columnar cells that produce and deposit enamel on the surface of a developing vertebrate tooth

amen \(')ä-'men, (')ā-; 'ä- *when sung*\ *interj* [ME, fr. OE, fr. LL, fr. Gk *amēn*, fr. Heb *āmēn*] (bef. 12c) — used to express solemn ratification (as of an expression of faith) or hearty approval (as of an assertion)

ame·na·ble \ə-'mē-nə-bəl, -'me-\ *adj* [prob. fr. (assumed) AF, fr. MF *amener* to lead up, fr. OF, fr. *a-* (fr. L *ad-*) + *mener* to lead, fr. LL *minare* to drive, fr. L *minari* to threaten — more at MOUNT] (1596) **1** : liable to be brought to account : ANSWERABLE 〈citizens ∼ to the law〉 **2 a** : capable of submission (as to judgment or test) : SUITED 〈the data is ∼ to analysis〉 **b** : readily brought to yield, submit, or cooperate **c** : WILLING 1 〈was ∼ to spending more time at home〉 *syn* see RESPONSIBLE, OBEDIENT — **ame·na·bil·i·ty** \-ˌmē-nə-'bil-ət-ē, -ˌme-\ *n* — **ame·na·bly** \-'mē-nə-blē, -'me-\ *adv*

amen corner \'ā-ˌmen-\ *n* (1860) : a conspicuous corner in a church occupied by fervent worshipers

amend \ə-'mend\ *vb* [ME, fr. OF *amender*, modif. of L *emendare*, fr. *e*, *ex* out + *menda* fault; akin to L *mendax* lying, *mendicus* beggar, and perh. to Skt *mindā* physical defect] *vt* (13c) **1** : to put right; *esp* : to make emendations in (as a text) **2** : to change or modify for the better : IMPROVE 〈∼ the situation〉 **b** : to alter esp. in phraseology; *esp* : to alter formally by modification, deletion, or addition 〈∼ the constitution〉 ∼ *vi* : to reform oneself *syn* see CORRECT — **amend·able** \-'men-də-bəl\ *adj* — **amend·er** *n*

amen·da·to·ry \ə-'men-də-ˌtōr-ē, -ˌtȯr-\ *adj* [*amend* + *-atory* (as in *emendatory*)] (ca. 1828) : CORRECTIVE

amend·ment \ə-'men(d)-mənt\ *n* (13c) **1** : the act of amending

: CORRECTION **2** : a material (as compost or sand) that aids plant growth indirectly by improving the condition of the soil **3 a** : the process of amending by parliamentary or constitutional procedure **b** : an alteration proposed or effected by this process ⟨the 18th ∼⟩

amends \ə-'men(d)z\ *n pl but sing or pl in constr* [ME *amendes*, fr. MF, pl. of *amende* reparation, fr. *amender*] (14c) : compensation for a loss or injury : RECOMPENSE ⟨make ∼⟩

ame·ni·ty \ə-'me-nə-tē, -'mē-\ *n, pl* **-ties** [ME *amenite*, fr. L *amoenitat-, amoenitas*, fr. *amoenus* pleasant] (14c) **1 a** : the quality of being pleasant or agreeable **b** (1) : the attractiveness and value of real estate or of a residential structure (2) : a feature conducive to such attractiveness and value **2** : something (as a conventional social gesture) that conduces to smoothness or pleasantness of social relationships **3** : something that conduces to comfort, convenience, or enjoyment

amen·or·rhea \ˌā-ˌme-nə-'rē-ə, ˌä-\ *n* [NL, fr. *a-* + Gk *mēn* month + NL *-o-* + *-rrhea* — more at MOON] (1804) : abnormal absence or suppression of menses — **amen·or·rhe·ic** \-'rē-ik\ *adj*

ament \'a-mənt, 'ā-\ *n* [NL *amentum*, fr. L, thong, strap] (1791) : CATKIN — **amen·tif·er·ous** \ˌa-mən-'ti-f(ə-)rəs\ *adj*

amen·tia \(ˌ)ā-'men(t)-sh(ē-)ə, (ˌ)ä-\ *n* [NL, fr. L, madness, fr. *ament-, amens* mad, fr. *a-* (fr. *ab-*) + *ment-, mens* mind — more at MIND] (14c) : MENTAL RETARDATION; *specif* : a condition of lack of development of intellectual capacity

Am·er·asian \ˌa-mə-'rā-zhən, -shən\ *n* [*American* + *Asian*] (1953) : a person of mixed American and Asian descent; *esp* : one fathered by an American and esp. an American serviceman in Asia

amerce \ə-'mərs\ *vt* **amerced; amerc·ing** [ME *amercien*, fr. AF *amercier*, fr. OF *a merci* at (one's) mercy] (15c) : to punish by a fine whose amount is fixed by the court; *broadly* : PUNISH — **amerce·ment** \-'mər-smənt\ *n* — **amer·cia·ble** \'-mər-sē-ə-bəl, -'mər-shə-bəl\ *adj*

¹**Amer·i·can** \ə-'mer-ə-kən, -'mər-, -'mar-, -i-kən\ *n* (1578) **1** : an American Indian of No. America or So. America **2** : a native or inhabitant of No. America or So. America **3** : a citizen of the U.S. **4** : AMERICAN ENGLISH

²**American** *adj* (1598) **1** : of or relating to America **2** : of or relating to the U.S. or its possessions or original territory — **Amer·i·can·ness** \-kə(n)-nəs\ *n*

Amer·i·ca·na \ə-ˌmer-ə-'kä-nə, -ˌmor-, -ˌmar-, -'ka-nə\ *n pl* (1841) **1** : materials concerning or characteristic of America, its civilization, or its culture; *broadly* : things typical of America **2** : American culture

American chameleon *n* (1881) : a lizard (*Anolis carolinensis*) of the southeastern U.S. that can vary its skin color from green to brown and is often kept as a pet

American cheese *n* (1804) : a process cheese made from American cheddar

American dog tick *n* (1927) : a common No. American ixodid tick (*Dermacentor variabilis*) esp. of dogs and humans that is an important vector of Rocky Mountain spotted fever and tularemia — called also *dog tick*

American dream *n, often cap D* (1931) : an American social ideal that stresses egalitarianism and esp. material prosperity

American eel *n* (ca. 1949) : a yellow to greenish-brown eel (*Anguilla rostrata*) that is lighter below, has 103 to 111 vertebrae, is found in fresh and coastal waters along the Atlantic coasts of No. America, and is held to spawn in or near the Sargasso Sea

American elm *n* (1813) : a large elm (*Ulmus americana*) with gradually spreading branches and pendulous branchlets that is common in eastern No. America

American English *n* (1806) : the English language as spoken in the U.S. — used esp. with the implication that it is clearly distinguishable from British English yet not so divergent as to be a separate language

Amer·i·ca·nese \ə-ˌmer-ə-kə-'nēz, -ˌmor-, -ˌmar-, -i-kə-, -'nēs\ *n* (1882) : AMERICAN ENGLISH

American foxhound *n* (ca. 1891) : any of an American breed of foxhounds smaller than the English foxhound but with longer ears and a short glossy coat usu. of black, tan, and white

American Indian *n* (1732) : a member of any of the aboriginal peoples of the western hemisphere except usu. the Eskimos; *esp* : an American Indian of North America and esp. the U.S.

Amer·i·can·isa·tion, Amer·i·can·ise *Brit var of* AMERICANIZATION, AMERICANIZE

Amer·i·can·ism \ə-'mer-ə-kə-ˌni-zəm, -'mər-, -'mar-\ *n* (1781) **1** : a characteristic feature of American English esp. as contrasted with British English **2** : attachment or allegiance to the traditions, interests, or ideals of the U.S. **3 a** : a custom or trait peculiar to America **b** : the political principles and practices essential to American culture

Amer·i·can·ist \-kə-nist\ *n* (1881) **1** : a specialist in American culture or history **2** : a specialist in the languages or cultures of the aboriginal inhabitants of America

Amer·i·can·iza·tion \ə-ˌmer-ə-kə-nə-'zā-shən, -ˌmor-, -ˌmar-\ *n* (1858) **1** : the act or process of Americanizing **2** : instruction of foreigners (as immigrants) in English and in U.S. history, government, and culture

Amer·i·can·ize \ə-'mer-ə-kə-ˌnīz, -'mər-, -'mar-\ *vb* **-ized; -iz·ing** *vt* (1797) **1** : to cause to acquire or conform to American characteristics **2** : to bring (as an area) under the political, cultural, or commercial influence of the U.S. ∼ *vi* : to acquire or conform to American traits

American pit bull terrier *n* (1950) : any of a breed of dogs developed to combine the traits of terriers and bulldogs that have extremely powerful jaws and great strength and tenacity — called also *pit bull terrier*

American plan *n* (1856) : a hotel plan whereby the daily rates cover the costs of the room and three meals — compare EUROPEAN PLAN

American saddlebred *n* (1948) : any of a breed of 3-gaited or 5-gaited saddle horses developed chiefly in Kentucky from Thoroughbreds and smooth-gaited stock — called also *American saddle horse*

American shorthair *n* (1974) : any of a breed of cats with a usu. solid-colored or tabby coat; *broadly* : SHORTHAIR

American Sign Language *n* (1960) : a sign language for the deaf in which meaning is conveyed by a system of articulated hand gestures and their placement relative to the upper body

American Staffordshire terrier *n* (1971) : a strong stocky terrier of a breed orig. developed for dogfighting

American Standard Version *n* (1901) : an American version of the Bible based on the Revised Version and published in 1901 — called also *American Revised Version*

American trotter *n* (1894) : STANDARDBRED

American water spaniel *n* (1947) : any of a breed of medium-sized spaniels of American origin that have a thick curly chocolate or liver-colored coat

am·er·i·ci·um \ˌa-mə-'ri-shē-əm, -sē-\ *n* [NL, fr. *America* + NL *-ium*] (1946) : a radioactive metallic element produced by bombardment of plutonium with high-energy neutrons — see ELEMENT table

Am·er·in·di·an \ˌa-mə-'rin-dē-ən\ *n* [*American* + *Indian*] (ca. 1898) : AMERICAN INDIAN — **Am·er·ind** \'a-mə-ˌrind\ *n or adj* — **Amerin·dian** *adj*

Ame·slan \'a-məs-ˌlan, 'am-ˌslan\ *n* (1972) : AMERICAN SIGN LANGUAGE

Ames test \'āmz-\ *n* [Bruce N. *Ames* b1928 Am. biochemist] (1977) : a test for identifying potential carcinogens by studying their mutagenic effect on bacteria

am·e·thyst \'a-mə-thəst, -(ˌ)thist\ *n* [ME *amatiste*, fr. OF & L; OF, fr. L *amethystus*, fr. Gk *amethystos*, lit., remedy against drunkenness, fr. *a-* + *methyein* to be drunk, fr. *methy* wine — more at MEAD] (13c) **1 a** : a clear purple or bluish violet variety of crystallized quartz that is much used as a jeweler's stone **b** : a deep purple variety of corundum **2** : a moderate purple — **am·e·thys·tine** \ˌa-mə-'this-tən\ *adj*

am·e·tro·pia \ˌa-mə-'trō-pē-ə\ *n* [NL, fr. Gk *ametros* without measure (fr. *a-* + *metron* measure) + NL *-opia* — more at MEASURE] (1875) : an abnormal refractive condition (as myopia, hyperopia, or astigmatism) of the eye in which images fail to focus upon the retina — **am·e·tro·pic** \-'trō-pik, -'trä-\ *adj*

Am·har·ic \am-'har-ik; 'am-ˌhär-, äm-\ *n* (1813) : a Semitic language that is the official language of Ethiopia — **Amharic** *adj*

ami·a·ble \'ā-mē-ə-bəl\ *adj* [ME, fr. MF, fr. LL *amicabilis* friendly, fr. L *amicus* friend; akin to L *amare* to love] (14c) **1** *archaic* : PLEASING, ADMIRABLE **2 a** : generally agreeable ⟨an ∼ comedy⟩ **b** : being friendly, sociable, and congenial — **ami·a·bil·i·ty** \ˌā-mē-ə-'bi-lə-tē\ *n* — **ami·a·ble·ness** \'ā-mē-ə-bəl-nəs\ *n* — **ami·a·bly** \-blē\ *adv*

syn AMIABLE, GOOD-NATURED, OBLIGING, COMPLAISANT mean having the desire or disposition to please. AMIABLE implies having qualities that make one liked and easy to deal with ⟨an *amiable* teacher not easily annoyed⟩. GOOD-NATURED implies cheerfulness or helpfulness and sometimes a willingness to be imposed upon ⟨a *good-natured* girl who was always willing to pitch in⟩. OBLIGING stresses a friendly readiness to be helpful ⟨our *obliging* innkeeper found us a bigger room⟩. COMPLAISANT often implies passivity or a yielding to others because of weakness ⟨was too *complaisant* to protest a decision he thought unfair⟩.

am·i·ca·ble \'a-mi-kə-bəl\ *adj* [ME, fr. LL *amicabilis*] (15c) : characterized by friendly goodwill : PEACEABLE — **am·i·ca·bil·i·ty** \ˌa-mi-kə-'bi-lə-tē\ *n* — **am·i·ca·ble·ness** \'a-mi-kə-bəl-nəs\ *n* — **am·i·ca·bly** \-blē\ *adv*

syn AMICABLE, NEIGHBORLY, FRIENDLY mean exhibiting goodwill and an absence of antagonism. AMICABLE implies a state of peace and a desire on the part of the parties not to quarrel ⟨maintained *amicable* relations⟩. NEIGHBORLY implies a disposition to live on good terms with others and to be helpful on principle ⟨*neighborly* concern⟩. FRIENDLY stresses cordiality and often warmth or intimacy of personal relations ⟨sought *friendly* advice⟩.

am·ice \'a-məs\ *n* [ME *amis*, prob. fr. MF, pl. of *amit*, fr. ML *amictus*, fr. L, cloak, fr. *amicire* to wrap around, fr. *am-, amb-* around + *jacere* to throw — more at AMBI-, JET] (13c) : a liturgical vestment made of an oblong piece of cloth usu. of white linen and worn about the neck and shoulders and partly under the alb

ami·cus \ə-'mē-kəs, -'mī-\ *n, pl* **ami·ci** \-'mē-ˌkē, -'mi-ˌsī\ (1951) : AMICUS CURIAE

amicus cu·ri·ae \-'kyür-ē-ˌī, -'kür-, -i-ˌē\ *n, pl* **amici curiae** [NL, lit., friend of the court] (1612) : one (as a professional person or organization) that is not a party to a particular litigation but that is permitted by the court to advise it in respect to some matter of law that directly affects the case in question

amid \ə-'mid\ *or* **amidst** \-'midst, -'mitst\ *prep* [*amid* fr. ME *amidde*, fr. OE *onmiddan*, fr. *on* + *middan*, dat. of *midde* mid; *amidst* fr. ME *amiddes*, fr. *amidde* + *-es -s*] (bef. 12c) **1** : in or into the middle of : surrounded by : AMONG **2 a** : DURING **b** : with the accompaniment of ⟨resigned ∼ rumors of misconduct⟩

am·i·dase \'a-mə-ˌdās, -ˌdāz\ *n* [ISV] (1921) : an enzyme that hydrolyzes acid amides usu. with the liberation of ammonia

am·ide \'a-ˌmid, -məd\ *n* [ISV, fr. NL *ammonia*] (ca. 1847) **1** : an inorganic compound derived from ammonia by replacement of an atom of hydrogen with another element (as a metal) **2** : an organic compound derived from ammonia or an amine by replacement of ammonical hydrogen with an acyl group — compare AMINE, IMIDE

ami·do \ə-'mē-(ˌ)dō, 'a-mə-ˌdō\ *adj* [ISV *amide* + *-o-*] (1877) : relating to or containing an organic amide group — often used in combination

am·i·dol \'a-mə-ˌdol, -ˌdōl\ *n* [G, fr. *Amidol*, a trademark] (1892) : a colorless crystalline salt $C_6H_8N_2O·2HCl$ used chiefly as a photographic developer

amid·ships \ə-'mid-ˌships\ *adv* (1692) **1** : in or toward the part of a ship midway between bow and stern **2** : in or toward the middle

ami·go \ə-'mē-(ˌ)gō, ä-\ *n, pl* **-gos** [Sp, fr. L *amicus* — more at AMIABLE] (1837) : FRIEND

amine \ə-'mēn, 'a-ˌmēn\ *n* [ISV, fr. NL *ammonia*] (1863) : any of a class of organic compounds derived from ammonia by replacement of hydrogen with one or more alkyl groups — compare AMIDE 2

ami·no \ə-'mē-(ˌ)nō\ *adj* [ISV *amine* + *-o-*] (1904) : relating to, being, or containing an amine group — often used in combination

amino acid *n* (1898) : an amphoteric organic acid containing the amino group NH_2; *esp* : any of the alpha-amino acids that are the chief

---

\ə\ abut \ˀ\ kitten, F table \ər\ further \a\ ash \ā\ ace \ä\ mop, mar \aú\ out \ch\ chin \e\ bet \ē\ easy \g\ go \i\ hit \ī\ ice \j\ job \ŋ\ sing \ō\ go \ó\ law \ói\ boy \th\ thin \t̲h̲\ the \ü\ loot \ů\ foot \y\ yet \zh\ vision \ä, k̲, ⁿ, œ, œ̄, ue, ū̄, ᵛ\ *see* Guide to Pronunciation components of proteins and are synthesized by living cells or are obtained as essential components of the diet

ami·no·ac·id·uria \ə-,mē-nō-,a-sə-'dur-ē-ə,-'dyur-\ *n* [NL] (ca. 1923) : a condition in which one or more amino acids are excreted in excessive amounts

ami·no·ben·zo·ic acid \ə-,mē-nō-ben-'zō-ik-\ *n* [ISV] (1904) : any of three crystalline derivatives $C_7H_7NO_2$ of benzoic acid; *esp* : PARAAMINOBENZOIC ACID

ami·no·pep·ti·dase \ə-,mē-nō-'pep-tə-,dās, -,dāz\ *n* (1943) : an enzyme that hydrolyzes peptides by acting on the peptide bond next to a terminal amino acid containing a free amino group

ami·i·noph·yl·line \,a-mə-'nä-fə-lən\ *n* [*amino* + *theophylline*] (1934) : a theophylline derivative $C_{16}H_{24}N_{10}O_4$ used esp. to stimulate the heart in congestive heart failure and to dilate the air passages in respiratory disorders

am·i·nop·ter·in \,a-mə-'näp-tə-rən\ *n* [*amino* + *pter*oylglutamic acid + *-in*] (1948) : a derivative of glutamic acid $C_{19}H_{20}N_8O_5$ used esp. as a rodenticide

ami·no·py·rine \ə-,mē-nō-'pīr-,ēn\ *n* [ISV, fr. *amino* + *anti*pyrine] (ca. 1936) : a crystalline compound $C_{13}H_{17}N_3O$ formerly used to relieve pain and fever but now largely abandoned for this purpose because of the occurrence of fatal agranulocytosis as a side effect in some users

ami·no·sal·i·cyl·ic acid \ə-,mē-nō-,sa-lə-'si-lik-\ *n* (1925) : any of four isomeric derivatives $C_7H_7NO_3$ of salicylic acid that have a single amino group; *esp* : PARA-AMINOSALICYLIC ACID

ami·no·trans·fer·ase \-'tran(t)s-fə-,räs, -,rāz\ *n* (ca. 1965) : TRANSAMINASE

amir *var of* EMIR

Amish \'ä-mish, 'a-, 'ā-\ *adj* [prob. fr. G *amisch*, fr. Jacob *Amman* or *Amen fl* 1693 Swiss Mennonite bishop] (1844) : of or relating to a strict sect of Mennonite followers of Amman that settled in America chiefly in the 18th century — **Amish** *n*

¹**amiss** \ə-'mis\ *adv* (13c) **1 a** : in a mistaken way : WRONGLY ⟨if you think he's guilty, you judge ~⟩ **b** : ASTRAY ⟨something had gone ~⟩ **2** : in a faulty way : IMPERFECTLY

²**amiss** *adj* (14c) **1** : not being in accordance with right order **2** : FAULTY, IMPERFECT **3** : out of place in given circumstances — usu. used with a negative ⟨a few remarks may not be ~ here⟩

ami·to·sis \,ā-mī-'tō-səs\ *n* [NL, fr. ²*a-* + *mitosis*] (1894) : cell division by simple cleavage of the nucleus and division of the cytoplasm without spindle formation or appearance of chromosomes — **ami·tot·ic** \-'tä-tik\ *adj* — **ami·tot·i·cal·ly** \-ti-k(ə-)lē\ *adv*

am·i·trip·ty·line \,a-mə-'trip-tə-,lēn\ *n* [*amino* + *trypto*phan + *-yl* + ²*-ine*] (1961) : a tricyclic antidepressant drug $C_{20}H_{23}N$

am·i·trole \'a-mə-,trōl\ *n* [*amino* + *triazole*] (ca. 1960) : a systemic herbicide $C_2H_4N_4$ used in areas other than food croplands

am·i·ty \'a-mə-tē\ *n, pl* **-ties** [ME *amite*, fr. MF *amité*, fr. ML *amicitas*, fr. L *amicus* friend — more at AMIABLE] (15c) : FRIENDSHIP; *esp* : friendly relations between nations

am·me·ter \'a-,mē-tər\ *n* [*ampere* + *-meter*] (1882) : an instrument for measuring electric current in amperes

am·mine \'a-,mēn, a-'mēn\ *n* [ISV *ammonia* + ²*-ine*] (1897) **1** : a molecule of ammonia as it exists in a coordination complex ⟨hex*ammine*-cobalt chloride $Co(NH_3)_6Cl_3$⟩ **2** : a compound that contains an ammine

am·mo \'a-(,)mō\ *n* [by shortening & alter.] (1911) : AMMUNITION

am·mo·nia \ə-'mō-nyə\ *n* [NL, fr. L *sal ammoniacus* sal ammoniac, lit., salt of Ammon, fr. Gk *ammōniakos* of Ammon, fr. *Ammōn* Ammon, Amen, an Egyptian god near one of whose temples it was prepared] (ca. 1799) **1** : a pungent colorless gaseous alkaline compound of nitrogen and hydrogen NH_3 that is very soluble in water and can easily be condensed to a liquid by cold and pressure **2** : AMMONIA WATER

am·mo·ni·ac \ə-'mō-nē-,ak\ *n* [ME & L; ME, fr. L *ammoniacum*, fr. Gk *ammōniakon*, fr. neut. of *ammōniakos* of Ammon] (15c) : the aromatic gum resin of a Persian herb (*Dorema ammoniacum*) of the carrot family used as an expectorant and stimulant and in plasters

am·mo·ni·a·cal \,a-mə-'nī-ə-kəl\ *also* **am·mo·ni·ac** \ə-'mō-nē-,ak\ *adj* (1798) : of, relating to, containing, or having the properties of ammonia

am·mo·ni·ate \ə-'mō-nē-,āt\ *vt* **-at·ed; -at·ing** (ca. 1928) **1** : to combine or impregnate with ammonia or an ammonium compound **2** : to subject to ammonification — **am·mo·ni·a·tion** \-,mō-nē-'ā-shən\ *n*

ammonia water *n* (ca. 1928) : a water solution of ammonia

am·mo·ni·fi·ca·tion \ə-,mä-nə-fə-'kā-shən, -,mō-nə-\ *n* (1886) **1** : the act or process of ammoniating **2** : decomposition with production of ammonia or ammonium compounds esp. by the action of bacteria on nitrogenous organic matter — **am·mo·ni·fy** \-,fī\ *vb*

am·mo·nite \'a-mə-,nīt\ *n* [NL *ammonites*, fr. L *cornu Ammonis*, lit., horn of Ammon] (1758) : any of a subclass (Ammonoidea) of extinct cephalopods with flat spiral shells that were esp. abundant in the Mesozoic age — **am·mo·nit·ic** \,a-mə-'ni-tik\ *adj*

Am·mon·ite \'a-mə-,nīt\ *n* [LL *Ammonites*, fr. Heb *'Ammōn* Ammon (son of Lot), descendant of Ammon] (1537) : a member of a Semitic people who in Old Testament times lived east of the Jordan between the Jabbok and the Arnon — **Ammonite** *adj*

am·mo·ni·um \ə-'mō-nē-əm\ *n* [NL, fr. *ammonia*] (1808) : an ion NH_4^+ derived from ammonia by combination with a hydrogen ion and known in compounds (as salts) that resemble in properties the compounds of the alkali metals

ammonium carbonate *n* (ca. 1881) : a carbonate of ammonium; *specif* : the commercial mixture of the bicarbonate and carbamate used esp. in smelling salts

ammonium chloride *n* (1869) : a white crystalline volatile salt NH_4Cl that is used in dry cells and as an expectorant — called also *sal ammoniac*

ammonium cyanate *n* (ca. 1881) : an inorganic white crystalline salt NH_4CNO that can be converted into organic urea

[illustration caption] ammonite

ammonium hydroxide *n* (1904) : a weakly basic compound NH_4OH that is formed when ammonia dissolves in water and that exists only in solution

ammonium nitrate *n* (ca. 1881) : a colorless crystalline salt NH_4NO_3 used in explosives and fertilizers and in veterinary medicine

ammonium phosphate *n* (ca. 1881) : a phosphate of ammonium; *esp* : DIAMMONIUM PHOSPHATE

ammonium sulfate *n* (ca. 1881) : a colorless crystalline salt $(NH_4)_2SO_4$ used chiefly as a fertilizer

am·mo·noid \'a-mə-,noid\ *n* (1884) : AMMONITE

am·mu·ni·tion \,am-yə-'ni-shən\ *n* [obs. F *amunition*, fr. MF, alter. of *munition*] (ca. 1626) **1 a** : the projectiles with their fuses, propelling charges, or primers fired from guns **b** : CARTRIDGES **c** : explosive military items (as grenades or bombs) **2** : material for use in attacking or defending a position ⟨~ for the defense lawyers⟩

am·ne·sia \am-'nē-zhə\ *n* [NL, fr. Gk *amnēsia* forgetfulness, alter. of *amnēstia*] (1786) **1** : loss of memory due usu. to brain injury, shock, fatigue, repression, or illness **2** : a gap in one's memory **3** : the selective overlooking or ignoring of those events or acts that are not favorable or useful to one's purpose or position — **am·ne·si·ac** \-zhē-,ak, -zē-\ *or* **am·ne·sic** \-zik, -sik\ *adj or n*

am·nes·ty \'am-nə-stē\ *n, pl* **-ties** [Gk *amnēstia* forgetfulness, fr. *amnēstos* forgotten, fr. *a-* + *mnasthai* to remember — more at MIND] (1580) : the act of an authority (as a government) by which pardon is granted to a large group of individuals — **amnesty** *vt*

am·nio·cen·te·sis \,am-nē-ō-(,)sen-'tē-səs\ *n, pl* **-te·ses** \-,sēz\ [NL, fr. *amnion* + *centesis* puncture, fr. Gk *kentēsis*, fr. *kentein* to prick — more at CENTER] (1957) : the surgical insertion of a hollow needle through the abdominal wall and into the uterus to obtain amniotic fluid esp. for the determination of fetal sex or chromosomal abnormality

am·ni·on \'am-nē-,än, -ən\ *n, pl* **amnions** *or* **am·nia** \-nē-ə\ [NL, fr. Gk, caul, fr. *amnos* lamb — more at YEAN] (1667) **1** : a thin membrane forming a closed sac about the embryos of reptiles, birds, and mammals and containing a serous fluid in which the embryo is immersed **2** : a membrane analogous to the amnion and occurring in various invertebrates — **am·ni·ot·ic** \,am-nē-'ä-tik\ *adj*

am·ni·ote \'am-nē-,ōt\ *n* [NL *Amniota*, fr. *amnion*] (ca. 1909) : any of a group (Amniota) of vertebrates that undergo embryonic development within an amnion and include the birds, reptiles, and mammals — **amniote** *adj*

amniotic fluid *n* (1855) : the serous fluid in which the embryo is suspended within the amnion

amniotic sac *n* (ca. 1881) : AMNION

amo·bar·bi·tal \,a-mō-'bär-bə-,tól\ *n* [*amyl* + *-o-* + *barbital*] (1949) : a barbiturate $C_{11}H_{18}N_2O_3$ used as a hypnotic and sedative; *also* : its sodium salt

amoe·ba \ə-'mē-bə\ *n, pl* **-bas** *or* **-bae** \-(,)bē\ [NL, genus name, fr. Gk *amoibē* change, fr. *ameibein* to change — more at MIGRATE] (1855) : any of a large genus (*Amoeba*) of naked rhizopod protozoans with lobed and never anastomosing pseudopodia, without permanent organelles or supporting structures, and of wide distribution in fresh and salt water and moist terrestrial environments; *broadly* : a naked rhizopod or other amoeboid protozoan — **amoe·bic** \-bik\ *adj*

am·oe·bi·a·sis *var of* AMEBIASIS

amoe·bo·cyte \ə-'mē-bə-,sīt\ *n* (1892) : a cell (as a phagocyte) having amoeboid form or movements

amoe·boid \ə-'mē-,bóid\ *adj* (1856) : resembling an amoeba specif. in moving or changing in shape by means of protoplasmic flow

amoeba: *1* pseudopodium, *2* nucleus, *3* contractile vacuole, *4* food vacuole

¹**amok** \ə-'mək, -'mäk\ *n* [Malay *amok*] (1665) : a murderous frenzy that occurs chiefly among Malays

²**amok** *adv* (1672) **1** : in a murderously frenzied state **2 a** : in a violently raging manner ⟨a virus that had run ~⟩ **b** : in an undisciplined, uncontrolled, or faulty manner ⟨films ... about computers run ~ —*People*⟩

³**amok** *adj* (1944) : possessed with or motivated by a murderous or violently uncontrollable frenzy

amo·le \ə-'mō-lē\ *n* [AmerSp, fr. Nahuatl *ahmōlli* soap] (1831) : a plant part (as a root) possessing detergent properties and serving as a substitute for soap; *also* : a plant (as a yucca or agave) so used

among \ə-'məŋ\ *also* **amongst** \-'məŋ(k)st\ *prep* [*among* fr. ME, fr. OE *on gemonge*, fr. *on* + *gemonge*, dat. of *gemong* crowd, fr. *ge-* (associative prefix) + *-mong* (akin to OE *mengan* to mix); *amongst* fr. ME *amonges*, fr. *among* + *-es -s* — more at CO-, MINGLE] (bef. 12c) **1** : in or through the midst of : surrounded by **2** : in the company or association with ⟨living ~ artists⟩ **3** : by or through the aggregate of ⟨discontent ~ the poor⟩ **4** : in the number or class of ⟨wittiest ~ poets⟩ ⟨~ other things she was president of her college class⟩ **5** : in shares to each of ⟨divided ~ the heirs⟩ **6 a** : through the reciprocal acts of ⟨quarrel ~ themselves⟩ **b** : through the joint action of ⟨made a fortune ~ themselves⟩ *usage* see BETWEEN

amon·til·la·do \ə-,män-tə-'lä-(,)dō, -ti(l)-'yä-(,)thō\ *n, pl* **-dos** [Sp, lit., done in the manner of *Montilla*, town in Andalusia] (1825) : a medium dry sherry

amor·al \(,)ā-'mor-əl, (,)a-, -'mär-\ *adj* (1882) **1 a** : being neither moral nor immoral; *specif* : lying outside the sphere to which moral judgments apply ⟨science as such is completely ~ —W. S. Thompson⟩ **b** : lacking moral sensibility ⟨infants are ~⟩ **2** : being outside or beyond the moral order or a particular code of morals ⟨~ customs⟩ — **amor·al·ism** \-ə-,li-zəm\ *n* — **amor·al·i·ty** \,ā-mə-'ra-lə-tē, ,a-, -(,)mó-\ *n* — **amor·al·ly** \(,)ā-'mor-ə-lē, (,)a-, -'mär-\ *adv*

amo·ret·to \,a-mə-'re-(,)tō, ,ä-\ *n, pl* **-ti** \-(,)tē\ *or* **-tos** [It, dim. of *amore* love, cupid, fr. L *amor*] (1622) : CUPID, CHERUB 2

am·or·ist \'a-mə-rist\ *n* (1581) **1** : a devotee of love and esp. sexual love : GALLANT **2** : one that writes about romantic love — **am·or·is·tic** \,a-mə-'ris-tik\ *adj*

Am·o·rite \'a-mə-,rīt\ n [Heb *Ĕmōrī*] (1535) : a member of one of various Semitic peoples living in Mesopotamia, Syria, and Palestine during the 3d and 2d millennia B.C. — **Amorite** adj

am·o·rous \'a-mə-rəs, 'am-rəs\ adj [ME, fr. MF, fr. ML amorosus, fr. L amor love, fr. amare to love] (14c) **1** : strongly moved by love and esp. sexual love ⟨~ women⟩ **2** : being in love : ENAMORED — usu. used with of ⟨~ of the girl⟩ **3 a** : indicative of love ⟨received ~ glances from her partner⟩ **b** : of or relating to love ⟨an ~ novel⟩ — **am·o·rous·ly** adv — **am·o·rous·ness** n

amor·phous \ə-'mór-fəs\ adj [Gk amorphos, fr. a- + morphē form] (ca. 1731) **1 a** : having no definite form : SHAPELESS ⟨an ~ cloud mass⟩ **b** : being without definite character or nature : UNCLASSIFIABLE ⟨an ~ segment of society⟩ **c** : lacking organization or unity ⟨an ~ style⟩ **2** : having no real or apparent crystalline form : UNCRYSTALLIZED ⟨an ~ mineral⟩ — **amor·phous·ly** adv — **amor·phous·ness** n

amort \ə-'mórt\ adj [short for all-a-mort, by folk etymology fr. MF à la mort to the death] (1590) archaic : being at the point of death

am·or·ti·za·tion \,a-mər-tə-'zā-shən also ə-,mór-\ n (ca. 1859) **1** : the act or process of amortizing **2** : the result of amortizing

am·or·tize \'a-mər-,tīz also ə-'mór-\ vt -tized; -tiz·ing [ME amortisen to deaden, alienate in mortmain, modif. of MF amortiss-, stem of amortir, fr. (assumed) VL admortire to deaden, fr. L ad- + mort-, mors death — more at MURDER] (1882) **1** : to provide for the gradual extinguishment of (as a mortgage) usu. by contribution to a sinking fund at the time of each periodic interest payment **2** : to amortize an expenditure for ⟨~ intangibles⟩ ⟨~ the new factory⟩ — **am·or·tiz·able** \-,tī-zə-bəl\ adj

Amos \'ā-məs\ n [Heb *Āmōs*] **1** : a Hebrew prophet of the 8th century B.C. **2** : a prophetic book of canonical Jewish and Christian Scripture — see BIBLE table

am·o·site \'a-mə-,sīt, -,zīt\ n [Amosa (fr. Asbestos Mines of South Africa) + ¹-ite] (ca. 1918) : an iron-rich amphibole that is a variety of asbestos

¹amount \ə-'maúnt\ vi [ME, fr. MF amonter, fr. amont upward, fr. a- (fr. L ad-) + mont mountain — more at MOUNT] (14c) **1 a** : to be equivalent ⟨acts that ~ to treason⟩ **b** : to reach in kind or quality ⟨wants her son to ~ to something⟩ ⟨doesn't ~ to much⟩ **2** : to reach a total : add up ⟨the bill ~s to $10⟩

²amount n (1710) **1 a** : the total number or quantity : AGGREGATE **b** : the quantity at hand or under consideration ⟨has an enormous ~ of energy⟩ **2** : the whole effect, significance, or import **3** : a principal sum and the interest on it

usage Number is regularly used with count nouns ⟨a large number of mistakes⟩ ⟨any number of times⟩ while amount is mainly used with mass nouns ⟨annual amount of rainfall⟩ ⟨a substantial amount of money⟩. The use of amount with count nouns has been frequently criticized; it usu. occurs when the number of things is thought of as a mass or collection ⟨glad to furnish any amount of black pebbles —New Yorker⟩ ⟨a substantial amount of film offers —Lily Tomlin⟩ or when money is involved ⟨a substantial amount of loans —E. R. Black⟩.

amour \ə-'múr, ä-, a-\ n [ME, love, affection, fr. MF, fr. OProv amor, fr. L, fr. amare to love] (14c) : a usu. illicit love affair; also : LOVER

amour pro·pre \,ä-,múr-'prōpr², ,ä-, -'própr²\ n [F amour-propre, lit., love of oneself] (1775) : SELF-ESTEEM

amox·i·cil·lin \ə-,mäk-sē-'si-lən\ n [amino + ox- + penicillin] (1973) : a semisynthetic penicillin C₁₆H₁₉N₃O₅S derived from ampicillin

amox·y·cil·lin Brit var of AMOXICILLIN

Amoy \a-'mòi, ä-\ n (1904) : the dialect of Chinese spoken in and near Amoy in southeastern China

amp \'amp\ n [by shortening] (1886) **1** : AMPERE **2** : AMPLIFIER; also : a unit consisting of an electronic amplifier and a loudspeaker

AMP \,ā-,em-'pē\ n [adenosine monophosphate] (1951) : a mononucleotide of adenine C₁₀H₁₂N₅O₃H₂PO₄ that was orig. isolated from mammalian muscle and is reversibly convertible to ADP and ATP in metabolic reactions — called also adenosine monophosphate, adenylic acid; compare CYCLIC AMP

am·per·age \'am-p(ə-)rij, -,pir-ij\ n (1893) : the strength of a current of electricity expressed in amperes

am·pere \'am-,pir also -,per\ n [André-Marie Ampère] (1881) **1** : the practical meter-kilogram-second unit of electric current that is equivalent to a flow of one coulomb per second or to the steady current produced by one volt applied across a resistance of one ohm **2** : the base unit of electric current in the International System of Units that is equal to a constant current which when maintained in two straight parallel conductors of infinite length and negligible circular sections one meter apart in a vacuum produces between the conductors a force equal to 2 × 10⁻⁷ newton per meter of length

ampere·hour n (1885) : a unit quantity of electricity equal to the quantity carried past any point of a circuit in one hour by a steady current of one ampere

ampere·turn n (1884) : the meter-kilogram-second unit of magnetomotive force equal to the magnetomotive force around a path that links with one turn of wire carrying an electric current of one ampere

am·per·o·met·ric \,am-pir-ə-'me-trik\ adj [ampere + -o- + -metric] (1940) : relating to or being a chemical titration in which the measurement of the electric current flowing under an applied potential difference between two electrodes in a solution is used for detecting the end point

am·per·sand \'am-pər-,sand\ n [alter. of and (&) per se and, lit., (the character) & by itself (is the word) and] (1835) : a character typically & standing for the word and

am·phet·amine \am-'fe-tə-,mēn, -mən\ n [ISV alpha + methyl + phen- + ethyl + amine] (1938) : a racemic compound C₉H₁₃N or one of its derivatives (as dextroamphetamine or methamphetamine) frequently abused as a stimulant of the central nervous system but used clinically esp. as the sulfate or hydrochloride salt to treat hyperactive children and the symptoms of narcolepsy and as a short-term appetite suppressant in dieting

amphi- or **amph-** prefix [L amphi- around, on both sides, fr. Gk amphi-, amph-, fr. amphi — more at AMBI-] : on both sides : of both kinds : both ⟨amphibrach⟩ ⟨amphidiploid⟩

am·phib·ia \am-'fi-bē-ə\ n pl (1607) : AMPHIBIANS

am·phib·i·an \-bē-ən\ n [ultim. fr. Gk amphibion amphibious being, fr. neut. of amphibios] (1835) **1** : an amphibious organism; esp : any of a class (Amphibia) of cold-blooded vertebrates (as frogs, toads, or salamanders) intermediate in many characters between fishes and reptiles and having gilled aquatic larvae and air-breathing adults **2** : an airplane designed to take off from and land on either land or water — **amphibian** adj

am·phib·i·ous \am-'fi-bē-əs\ adj [Gk amphibios, lit., living a double life, fr. amphi- + bios mode of life — more at QUICK] (1643) **1** : combining two characteristics **2 a** : relating to or adapted for both land and water ⟨~ vehicles⟩ **b** : executed by coordinated action of land, sea, and air forces organized for invasion; also : trained or organized for such action ⟨~ forces⟩ **3** : able to live both on land and in water ⟨~ plants⟩ — **am·phib·i·ous·ly** adv — **am·phib·i·ous·ness** n

am·phi·bole \'am(p)-fə-,bōl\ n [F, fr. LL amphibolus, fr. Gk amphibolos ambiguous, fr. amphiballein to throw round, doubt, fr. amphi- + ballein to throw — more at DEVIL] (ca. 1823) **1** : HORNBLENDE **2** : any of a group of complex silicate minerals with like crystal structures that contain calcium, sodium, magnesium, aluminum, and iron ions or a combination of them

am·phib·o·lite \am-'fi-bə-,līt\ n (1833) : a usu. metamorphic rock consisting essentially of amphibole

am·phi·bol·o·gy \,am(p)-fə-'bä-lə-jē\ n, pl -gies [ME amphibologie, fr. LL amphibologia, alter. of L amphibolia, fr. Gk, fr. amphibolos] (14c) : a sentence or phrase (as "nothing is good enough for you") susceptible of more than one interpretation

am·phib·o·ly \am-'fi-bə-lē\ n, pl -lies [LL amphibolia] (ca. 1588) : AMPHIBOLOGY

am·phi·brach \'am(p)-fə-,brak\ n [L amphibrachys, fr. Gk, lit., short at both ends, fr. amphi- + brachys short — more at BRIEF] (1589) : a metrical foot consisting of a long syllable between two short syllables in quantitative verse or of a stressed syllable between two unstressed syllables in accentual verse ⟨romantic is an accentual ~⟩ — **am·phi·brach·ic** \,am(p)-fə-'bra-kik\ adj

am·phic·ty·o·ny \am-'fik-tē-ə-nē\ n, pl -nies [Gk amphiktyonia] (1835) : an association of neighboring states in ancient Greece to defend a common religious center; broadly : an association of neighboring states for their common interest — **am·phic·ty·on·ic** \(,)am-,fik-tē-'ä-nik\ adj

am·phi·dip·loid \,am(p)-fi-'di-,plòid\ n (1930) : an interspecific hybrid having a complete diploid chromosome set from each parent form — called also allotetraploid — **amphidiploid** adj — **am·phi·dip·loi·dy** \-,plòi-dē\ n

am·phim·a·cer \am-'fi-mə-sər\ n [L amphimacrus, fr. Gk amphimakros, lit., long at both ends, fr. amphi- + makros long — more at MEAGER] (1589) : a metrical foot consisting of a short syllable between two long syllables in quantitative verse or of an unstressed syllable between two stressed syllables in accentual verse ⟨twenty-two is an accentual ~⟩

am·phi·mix·is \,am(p)-fi-'mik-səs\ n, pl -mix·es \-,sēz\ [NL, fr. amphi- + Gk mixis mingling, fr. mignynai to mix — more at MIX] (1893) : the union of gametes in sexual reproduction

Am·phi·on \am-'fī-ən\ n [L, fr. Gk Amphiōn] : a musician of Greek mythology who builds the walls of Thebes by charming the stones into place with his lyre

am·phi·ox·us \,am(p)-fē-'äk-səs\ n, pl -oxi \-,sī\ or -ox·us·es [NL, fr. amphi- + Gk oxys sharp] (1847) : any of a genus (Branchiostoma) of lancelets; broadly : LANCELET

am·phi·path·ic \,am(p)-fə-'pa-thik\ adj [amphi- + -pathic (as in empathic)] (1945) : AMPHIPHILIC

am·phi·phil·ic \-'fi-lik\ adj (1950) : of, relating to, or being a compound (as a surfactant) consisting of molecules having a polar water-soluble group attached to a water-insoluble hydrocarbon chain; also : being a molecule of such a compound — **am·phi·phile** \'am(p)-fə-,fīl\ n

am·phi·ploid \'am(p)-fi-,plòid\ adj (1945) of an interspecific hybrid : having at least one complete diploid set of chromosomes derived from each parent species — **amphiploid** n — **am·phi·ploi·dy** \-,plòi-dē\ n

am·phi·pod \-,päd\ n [ultim. fr. Gk amphi- + pod-, pous foot — more at FOOT] (1835) : any of a large order (Amphipoda) of small crustaceans (as the beach flea) with a laterally compressed body — **amphipod** adj

am·phi·pro·style \,am(p)-fi-'prō-,stīl\ adj [L amphiprostylos, fr. Gk, fr. amphi- + prostylos having pillars in front, fr. pro- + stylos pillar — more at STEER] (1850) : having columns at each end only ⟨an ~ building⟩ — **amphiprostyle** n

am·phis·bae·na \,am(p)-fəs-'bē-nə\ n [L, fr. Gk amphisbaina, fr. amphis on both sides (fr. amphi around) + bainein to walk, go — more at BY, COME] (14c) : a serpent in classical mythology having a head at each end and capable of moving in either direction — **am·phis·bae·nic** \-nik\ adj

am·phi·the·ater \'am(p)-fə-,thē-ə-tər also 'am-pə-,thē-\ n [L amphitheatrum, fr. Gk amphitheatron, fr. amphi- + theatron theater] (14c) **1** : an oval or circular building with rising tiers of seats ranged about an open space and used in ancient Rome esp. for contests and spectacles **2 a** : a very large auditorium **b** : a room with a gallery from which doctors and students may observe surgical operations **c** : a rising gallery in a modern theater **d** : a flat or gently sloping area surrounded by abrupt slopes **3** : a place of public games or contests — **am·phi·the·at·ric** \,am(p)-fə-thē-'a-trik also ,am-pə-thē-\ or **am·phi·the·at·ri·cal** \-tri-kəl\ adj — **am·phi·the·at·ri·cal·ly** \-tri-k(ə-)lē\ adv

Am·phit·ry·on \am-'fi-trē-ən\ n [Gk Amphitryōn] : the husband of Alcmene

am·pho·ra \'am(p)-fə-rə\ n, pl -rae \-,rē, -,rī\ or -ras [L, modif. of Gk amphoreus, amphiphoreus, fr. amphi- + phoreus bearer, fr. pherein to bear — more at BEAR] (14c) **1** : an ancient Greek jar or vase with a large oval body, narrow cylindrical neck, and two handles that rise

\ə\ abut \ᵊ\ kitten, F table \ər\ further \a\ ash \ā\ ace \ä\ mop, mar \aú\ out \ch\ chin \e\ bet \ē\ easy \g\ go \i\ hit \ī\ ice \j\ job \ŋ\ sing \ō\ go \ó\ law \ói\ boy \th\ thin \th̲\ the \ü\ loot \ú\ foot \y\ yet \zh\ vision \ȧ, k̲, ⁿ, œ, œ̄, ue, ūe, ᵌ\ see Guide to Pronunciation

almost to the level of the mouth **2** : a 2=
handled vessel shaped like an amphora

am·pho·ter·ic \,am(p)-fə-'ter-ik\ *adj* [ISV, fr.
Gk *amphoteros* each of two, fr. *amphō* both
— more at AMBI-] (ca. 1849) : partly one and
partly the other; *specif* : capable of reacting
chemically either as an acid or as a base

am·pho·ter·i·cin B \,am(p)-fə-'ter-ə-sən-'bē\
n [*amphoteric* + [1]-*in*] (1955) : an antifungal
antibiotic obtained from a soil actinomycete
(*Streptomyces nodosus*) and used esp. to treat
systemic fungal infections

am·pi·cil·lin \,am-pə-'si-lən\ *n* [*amino* +
penicillin] (1961) : a penicillin $C_{16}H_{19}N_3O_4S$
that is effective against gram-negative and
gram-positive bacteria and is used to treat
various infections of the urinary, respiratory,
and intestinal tracts

am·ple \'am-pəl\ *adj* **am·pler** \-p(ə-)lər\;
am·plest \-p(ə-)ləst\ [MF, fr. L *amplus*]
(15c) **1** : generous or more than adequate in
size, scope, or capacity ⟨there was room for an ∼ garden⟩ **2** : generously sufficient to satisfy a requirement or need ⟨they had ∼ money for
the trip⟩ **3** : BUXOM, PORTLY ⟨an ∼ figure⟩ *syn* see SPACIOUS, PLENTI-
FUL — **am·ple·ness** \-pəl-nəs\ *n* — **am·ply** \-plē\ *adv*

am·plex·us \am-'plek-səs\ *n* [NL, fr. L, embrace, fr. *amplecti* to embrace, fr. *am-*, *amb-* around + *plectere* to braid — more at AMBI-, PLY]
(ca. 1927) : the mating embrace of a frog or toad during which eggs are
shed into the water and there fertilized

am·pli·dyne \'am-plə-,dīn\ *n* [*ampli*fier + Gk *dyna*mis power — more
at DYNAMIC] (1940) : a direct-current generator that precisely controls
a large power output whenever a small power input is varied in the field
winding of the generator

am·pli·fi·ca·tion \,am-plə-fə-'kā-shən\ *n* (1546) **1 a** : an act, example, or product of amplifying **b** : a usu. massive replication esp. of a
gene or DNA sequence (as in a polymerase chain reaction) **2 a** : the
particulars by which a statement is expanded **b** : an expanded statement

am·pli·fi·er \'am-plə-,fī(-ə)r\ *n* (1542) : one that amplifies; *specif* : an
electronic device (as in a stereo system) for amplifying voltage, current,
or power

am·pli·fy \-,fī\ *vb* **-fied; -fy·ing** [ME *amplifien*, fr. MF *amplifier*, fr. L
amplificare, fr. *amplus*] *vt* (15c) **1** : to expand (as a statement) by the
use of detail or illustration or by closer analysis **2 a** : to make larger
or greater (as in amount, importance, or intensity) : INCREASE **b** : to
increase the strength or amount of; *esp* : to make louder **c** : to cause
(a gene or DNA sequence) to undergo amplification ∼ *vi* : to expand
one's remarks or ideas *syn* see EXPAND

am·pli·tude \-,tüd, -,tyüd\ *n* (1542) **1** : the quality or state of being
ample : FULLNESS **2** : the extent or range of a quality, property, process, or phenomenon: as **a** : the extent of a vibratory movement (as of
a pendulum) measured from the mean position to an extreme **b** : the
maximum departure of the value of an alternating current or wave from
the average value **3** : ARGUMENT 6b

amplitude modulation *n* (1921) : modulation of the amplitude of a
radio carrier wave in accordance with the strength of the audio or other
signal; *also* : a broadcasting system using such modulation — compare
FREQUENCY MODULATION

am·poule or **am·pule** also **am·pul** \'am-,pyü(ə)l, -,pül\ *n* [ME *ampulle*
flask, fr. OE & OF; OE *ampulle* & OF *ampoule*, fr. L *ampulla*] (1886)
1 : a hermetically sealed small bulbous glass vessel that is used to hold
a solution for hypodermic injection **2** : a vial resembling an ampoule

am·pul·la \am-'pu̇l-ə, 'am-,pyü-lə\ *n, pl* **-lae** \-(,)lē, -,lī\ [ME, fr. OE,
fr. L, dim. of *amphora*] (bef. 12c) **1** : a glass or earthenware flask with
a globular body and two handles used esp. by the ancient Romans to
hold ointment, perfume, or wine **2** : a saccular anatomic swelling or
pouch — **am·pul·la·ry** \am-'pu̇-lər-ē, 'am-pyə-,ler-ē\ *adj*

am·pu·tate \'am-pyə-,tāt\ *vt* **-tat·ed; -tat·ing** [L *amputatus*, pp. of
amputare, fr. *am-*, *amb-* around + *putare* to cut, prune — more at
AMBI-] (1638) : to remove by or as if by cutting; *esp* : to cut (as a limb)
from the body — **am·pu·ta·tion** \,am-pyə-'tā-shən\ *n*

am·pu·tee \,am-pyə-'tē\ *n* (1910) : one that has had a limb amputated

am·trac or **am·track** \'am-,trak\ *n* [*amphibious* + *tractor*] (1944) : a
flat-bottomed military vehicle that moves on tracks on land or water

amuck \ə-'mək\ *var of* AMOK

am·u·let \'am-yə-lət\ *n* [L *amuletum*] (1584) : a charm (as an ornament) often inscribed with a magic incantation or symbol to protect
the wearer against evil (as disease or witchcraft) or to aid him

amuse \ə-'myüz\ *vb* **amused; amus·ing** [MF *amuser*, fr. OF, fr. *a-* (fr.
L *ad-*) + *muser* to muse] *vt* (15c) **1 a** *archaic* : to divert the attention
of so as to deceive **b** *obs* : to occupy the attention of : ABSORB **c** *obs*
: DISTRACT, BEWILDER **2 a** : to entertain or occupy in a light, playful,
or pleasant manner ⟨∼ the child with a story⟩ **b** : to appeal to the
sense of humor of ⟨the joke doesn't ∼ me⟩ ∼ *vi, obs* : MUSE — **amus-
ed·ly** \-'myü-zəd-lē\ *adv* — **amus·er** *n* — **amus·ive** \ə-'myü-zəv,
-səv\ *adj*

syn AMUSE, DIVERT, ENTERTAIN mean to pass or cause to pass the time
pleasantly. AMUSE suggests that one's attention is engaged lightly or
frivolously ⟨*amuse* yourselves while I prepare dinner⟩. DIVERT implies
the distracting of the attention from worry or routine occupation esp.
by something funny ⟨a light comedy to *divert* the tired businessman⟩.
ENTERTAIN suggests supplying amusement or diversion by specially
prepared or contrived methods ⟨a magician *entertaining* children at a
party⟩.

amuse·ment \ə-'myüz-mənt\ *n* (1603) **1** : a means of amusing or
entertaining ⟨what are her favorite ∼s⟩ **2** : the condition of being
amused ⟨his ∼ knew no bounds⟩ **3** : pleasurable diversion : ENTER-
TAINMENT ⟨plays the piano for ∼⟩

amusement park *n* (1909) : a commercially operated park having
various devices for entertainment (as a merry-go-round and roller
coaster) and usu. booths for the sale of food and drink

amus·ing \ə-'myü-ziŋ\ *adj* (1712) : giving amusement : DIVERTING —
amus·ing·ly \-ziŋ-lē\ *adv* — **amus·ing·ness** *n*

amyg·da·la \ə-'mig-də-lə\ *n, pl* **-lae** \-,lē, -,lī\ [NL, fr. L, almond, fr.

amphora 1

Gk *amygdalē*] (ca. 1860) : the one of the four basal ganglia in each
cerebral hemisphere that is part of the limbic system and consists of an
almond-shaped mass of gray matter in the anterior extremity of the
temporal lobe — called also *amygdaloid nucleus*

amyg·da·lin \-lən\ *n* [L *amygdala*] (1651) : a white crystalline cyano-
genetic glucoside $C_{20}H_{27}NO_{11}$ found esp. in the seeds of the apricot,
peach, and bitter almond

amyg·da·loid \-,lȯid\ *adj* [Gk *amygdaloeidēs*, fr. *amygdalē*] (1836) **1**
: almond-shaped **2** : of, relating to, or affecting an amygdala

amyg·da·loi·dal \ə-,mig-də-'lȯi-d°l\ *adj* (1813) : of, being, or containing small cavities in igneous rock that are filled with deposits of different minerals (as chalcedony or calcite) — **amyg·da·loid** \ə-'mig-də-
,lȯid\ *n*

am·yl \'a-məl\ *n* [L *amylum* + E -*yl*] (1850) : a univalent hydrocarbon
radical C_5H_{11} — that occurs in various isomeric forms and is derived
from pentane

amyl- or **amylo-** *comb form* [L *amylum*, fr. Gk *amylon*, fr. neut. of
amylos unmilled (of grain), fr. *a-* + *mylē* mill — more at MEAL]
: starch ⟨*amylo*plast⟩

amyl acetate *n* (ca. 1881) : BANANA OIL

amyl alcohol *n* (1863) : any of eight isomeric alcohols $C_5H_{12}O$ used
esp. as solvents and in making esters; *also* : a commercially produced
mixture of amyl alcohols used esp. as a solvent

am·y·lase \'a-mə-,lās, -,lāz\ *n* (1893) : any of a group of enzymes (as
amylopsin) that catalyze the hydrolysis of starch and glycogen or their
intermediate hydrolysis products

amyl nitrite *n* (ca. 1881) : a pale yellow pungent flammable liquid
ester $C_5H_{11}NO_2$ of commercial amyl alcohol and nitrous acid — compare POPPER 2

am·y·loid \-,lȯid\ *n* (1872) : a waxy translucent substance consisting of
protein in combination with polysaccharides that is deposited in some
animal organs and tissues under abnormal conditions (as Alzheimer's
disease) — **amyloid** *adj*

am·y·loid·osis \,a-mə-,lȯi-'dō-səs\ *n* [NL] (ca. 1900) : a disorder characterized by the deposition of amyloid in bodily organs and tissues

am·y·lo·lyt·ic \,a-mə-lō-'li-tik\ *adj* [NL *amylolysis*, fr. *amyl-* + -*lysis*]
(1876) : characterized by or capable of the enzymatic splitting of
starch into soluble products (∼ enzymes) ⟨∼ activity⟩

am·y·lo·pec·tin \,a-mə-lō-'pek-tən\ *n* (1905) : a component of starch
that has a high molecular weight and branched structure and does not
tend to gel in aqueous solutions

am·y·lo·plast \'a-mə-(,)lō-,plast\ *n* (1886) : a colorless plastid that
forms and stores starch

am·y·lop·sin \,a-mə-'läp-sən\ *n* [*amyl-* + -*psin* (as in *trypsin*)] (ca.
1881) : the amylase of the pancreatic juice

am·y·lose \'a-mə-,lōs, -,lōz\ *n* (1877) : a component of starch characterized by its straight chains of glucose units

amyo·to·nia \,ā-,mī-ə-'tō-nē-ə\ *n* [NL] (ca. 1919) : deficiency of muscle tone

amyo·tro·phic lateral sclerosis \,ā-,mī-ə-'trō-fik-, -'trä-\ *n* [[2]*a-* +
my- + -*trophic*] (ca. 1889) : a rare progressive degenerative fatal disease affecting the spinal cord, usu. beginning in middle age, and characterized esp. by increasing and spreading muscular weakness — called
also *Lou Gehrig's disease*

Am·y·tal \'a-mə-,tȯl\ *trademark* — used for amobarbital

[1]an \ən, (')an\ *indefinite article* [ME, fr. OE *ān* one — more at ONE]
(bef. 12c) : [2]A *usage* see [2]A

[2]an \ən, an\ *prep* (bef. 12c) : [3]A 2 *usage* see [2]A

[3]an or **an'** *conj* (12c) **1** ⟨*see* AND⟩ : AND **2** \'an\ *archaic* : IF

an- — see [2]A-

[1]-an or **-ian** also **-ean** *n suffix* [-*an* & -*ian* fr. ME -*an*, -*ian*, fr. OF & L;
OF -*ien*, fr. L -*ianus*, fr. -*i-* + -*anus*, fr. -*anus*, adj. suffix; -*ean* fr. such
words as *Mediterranean, European*] **1** : one that is of or relating to
⟨*American*⟩ ⟨*Boston*ian⟩ **2** : one skilled in or specializing in ⟨phoneti-
cian⟩

[2]-an or **-ian** also **-ean** *adj suffix* **1** : of or belonging to ⟨*American*⟩
⟨*Florid*ian⟩ **2** : characteristic of : resembling ⟨*Mozart*ean⟩

[3]-an *n suffix* [ISV -*an*, -*ane*, alter. of -*ene*, -*ine*, & -*one*] **1** : unsaturated
organic compound ⟨*furan*⟩ **2** : anhydride of a carbohydrate ⟨*dextr*an⟩

[1]ana \'a-nə\ *adv* [ME, fr. ML, fr. Gk, at the rate of, lit., up] (14c) : of
each an equal quantity — used in prescriptions

[2]ana \'a-nə, 'ä-, 'ā-\ *n, pl* **ana** or **anas** [-*ana*] (ca. 1751) **1** : a collection
of the memorable sayings of a person **2** : a collection of anecdotes or
interesting information about a person or a place

ana- or **an-** *prefix* [L, fr. Gk, up, back, again, fr. *ana* up — more at ON]
1 : up : upward ⟨*ana*bolism⟩ **2** : back : backward ⟨*ana*tropous⟩

-ana or **-iana** *n pl suffix* [NL, fr. L, neut. pl. of -*anus* -an & -*ianus* -ian]
: collected items of information esp. anecdotal or bibliographical concerning ⟨*Americana*⟩

ana·bap·tism \,a-nə-'bap-,ti-zəm\ *n* [NL *anabaptismus*, fr. LGk *ana-
baptismos* rebaptism, fr. *anabaptizein* to rebaptize, fr. Gk *ana-* again +
baptizein to baptize] (1577) **1** *cap* **a** : the doctrine or practices of the
Anabaptists **b** : the Anabaptist movement **2** : the baptism of one
previously baptized

Ana·bap·tist \-'bap-tist\ *n* (1532) : a Protestant sectarian of a radical
movement arising in the 16th century and advocating the baptism and
church membership of adult believers only, nonresistance, and the
separation of church and state — **Anabaptist** *adj*

anab·a·sis \ə-'na-bə-səs\ *n, pl* **-a·ses** \-,sēz\ [Gk, inland march, fr.
anabainein to go up or inland, fr. *ana-* + *bainein* to go — more at
COME] (ca. 1706) **1** : a going or marching up : ADVANCE; *esp* : a military advance **2** [fr. the retreat of Greek mercenaries in Asia Minor
described in the *Anabasis* of Xenophon] : a difficult and dangerous
military retreat

an·a·bat·ic \,a-nə-'ba-tik\ *adj* [Gk *anabatos*, verbal of *anabainein*]
(1853) : moving upward : RISING ⟨an ∼ wind⟩

anabolic steroid *n* (1961) : any of a group of usu. synthetic hormones
that increase constructive metabolism and are sometimes abused by
athletes in training to increase temporarily the size of their muscles

anab·o·lism \ə-'na-bə-,li-zəm\ *n* [ISV *ana-* + metab*olism*] (1886) : the
constructive part of metabolism concerned esp. with macromolecular
synthesis — compare CATABOLISM — **an·a·bol·ic** \,a-nə-'bä-lik\ *adj*

anach·ro·nism \ə-'na-krə-,ni-zəm\ *n* [prob. fr. MGk *anachronismos*, fr.
anachronizesthai to be an anachronism, fr. LGk *anachronizein* to be

late, fr. Gk *ana-* + *chronos* time] (ca. 1646)   **1 :** an error in chronology; *esp* **:** a chronological misplacing of persons, events, objects, or customs in regard to each other   **2 :** a person or a thing that is chronologically out of place; *esp* **:** one from a former age that is incongruous in the present — **anach·ro·nis·tic** \ə-,na-krə-'nis-tik\ *also* **ana·chron·ic** \,a-nə-'krä-nik\ *adj* — **anach·ro·nis·ti·cal·ly** \ə-,na-krə-'nis-ti-k(ə-)lē\ *adv* — **anach·ro·nous** \ə-'na-krə-nəs\ *adj* — **anach·ro·nous·ly** *adv*

an·a·clit·ic \,a-nə-'kli-tik\ *adj* [Gk *anaklitos*, verbal of *anaklinein* to lean upon, fr. *ana-* + *klinein* to lean — more at LEAN] (1922) **:** of, relating to, or characterized by the direction of love toward an object (as the mother) that satisfies nonsexual needs (as hunger)

an·a·co·lu·thon \,a-nə-kə-'lü-,thän\ *n, pl* **-tha** \-thə\ *also* **-thons** [LL, fr. LGk *anakolouthon* inconsistency in logic, fr. Gk, neut. of *anakolouthos* inconsistent, fr. *an-* + *akolouthos* following, fr. *ha-, a-* together + *keleuthos* path] (ca. 1706) **:** syntactical inconsistency or incoherence within a sentence; *esp* **:** a shift in an unfinished sentence from one syntactic construction to another (as in "you really ought—well, do it your own way") — **an·a·co·lu·thic** \-thik\ *adj* — **an·a·co·lu·thi·cal·ly** \-thi-k(ə-)lē\ *adv*

an·a·con·da \,a-nə-'kän-də\ *n* [prob. modif. of Sinhalese *henakandayā*, a slender green snake] (1768) **:** a large semiaquatic constricting snake (*Eunectes murinus*) of the boa family of tropical So. America that may reach a length of 30 feet (9.1 meters); *broadly* **:** any of the large constricting snakes

anaconda

anac·re·on·tic \ə-,na-krē-'än-tik\ *n* (1656) **:** a poem in the manner of Anacreon; *esp* **:** a drinking song or light lyric

Anacreontic *adj* [L *anacreonticus*, fr. *Anacreont-*, *Anacreon* Anacreon, fr. Gk *Anakreont-*, *Anakreōn*] (1611)   **1 :** of, relating to, or resembling the poetry of Anacreon   **2 :** convivial or amatory in tone or theme

an·a·cru·sis \,a-nə-'krü-səs\ *n, pl* **-cru·ses** \-,sēz\ [NL, fr. Gk *anakrousis* beginning of a song, fr. *anakrouein* to begin a song, fr. *ana-* + *krouein* to strike; akin to Lith *kraušyti* to strike] (1830)   **1 :** one or more syllables at the beginning of a line of poetry that are regarded as preliminary to and not a part of the metrical pattern   **2 :** UPBEAT; *specif* **:** one or more notes or tones preceding the first downbeat of a musical phrase

an·a·dama bread \,a-nə-'da-mə-\ *n* [origin unknown] (1954) **:** a leavened bread made with flour, cornmeal, and molasses

an·a·dem \'a-nə-,dem\ *n* [L *anadema*, fr. Gk *anadēma*, fr. *anadein* to wreathe, fr. *ana-* + *dein* to bind — more at DIADEM] (1604) *archaic* **:** a wreath for the head : GARLAND

ana·di·plo·sis \,a-nə-də-'plō-səs, ,a-nə-(,)dī-'plō-\ *n, pl* **-plo·ses** \-,sēz\ [LL, fr. Gk *anadiplōsis*, lit., repetition, fr. *anadiploun* to double, fr. *ana-* + *diploun* to double — more at DIPLOMA] (ca. 1550) **:** repetition of a prominent and usu. the last word in one phrase or clause at the beginning of the next (as in "rely on his honor—honor such as his?")

anad·ro·mous \ə-'na-drə-məs\ *adj* [Gk *anadromos* running upward, fr. *anadramein* to run upward, fr. *ana-* + *dramein* to run — more at DROMEDARY] (ca. 1753) **:** ascending rivers from the sea for breeding ⟨shad are ~⟩ — compare CATADROMOUS

anae·mia, anae·mic *chiefly Brit var of* ANEMIA, ANEMIC

an·aer·obe \'a-nə-,rōb; (,)an-'a(-ə)r-,ōb, -'e(-ə)r-\ *n* [ISV] (1884) **:** an anaerobic organism

an·aer·o·bic \,a-nə-'rō-bik; ,an-,a(-ə)-, -,e(-ə)-\ *adj* (ca. 1881)   **1 a :** living, active, occurring, or existing in the absence of free oxygen ⟨~ respiration⟩   **b :** of, relating to, or being activity in which the body incurs an oxygen debt ⟨~ exercise⟩   **2 :** relating to or induced by anaerobes — **an·aer·o·bi·cal·ly** \-bi-k(ə-)lē\ *adv*

an·aero·bi·o·sis \,a-nə-rō-(,)bī-'ō-səs, -bē-; ,an-,a(-ə)-, -,e(-ə)-\ *n, pl* **-o·ses** \-'ō-,sēz\ [NL] (ca. 1889) **:** life in the absence of air or free oxygen

an·aes·the·sia, an·aes·thet·ic *chiefly Brit var of* ANESTHESIA, ANESTHETIC

ana·gen·e·sis \,a-nə-'je-nə-səs\ *n* [NL] (1889) **:** evolutionary change producing a single lineage in which one taxon replaces another without branching — compare CLADOGENESIS

ana·glyph \'a-nə-,glif\ *n* [LL *anaglyphus* embossed, fr. Gk *anaglyphos*, fr. *anaglyphein* to emboss, fr. *ana-* + *glyphein* to carve — more at CLEAVE] (1651)   **1 :** a sculptured, chased, or embossed ornament worked in low relief   **2 :** a stereoscopic motion or still picture in which the right component of a composite image usu. red in color is superposed on the left component in a contrasting color to produce a three-dimensional effect when viewed through correspondingly colored filters in the form of spectacles — **ana·glyph·ic** \,a-nə-'gli-fik\ *adj*

an·ag·no·ri·sis \,a-,nag-'nór-ə-səs, *n, pl* **-ri·ses** \-,sēz\ [Gk *anagnōrisis*, fr. *anagnōrizein* to recognize, fr. *ana-* + *gnōrizein* to make known; akin to Gk *gnōrimos* well-known, *gignōskein* to come to know — more at KNOW] (ca. 1800) **:** the point in the plot esp. of a tragedy at which the protagonist recognizes his or her or some other character's true identity or discovers the true nature of his or her own situation

an·a·go·ge *or* **an·a·go·gy** \'a-nə-,gō-jē\ *n, pl* **-ges** *or* **-gies** [LL *anagoge*, fr. LGk *anagōgē*, fr. Gk, reference, fr. *anagein* to refer, fr. *ana-* + *agein* to lead — more at AGENT] (15c) **:** interpretation of a word, passage, or text (as of Scripture or poetry) that finds beyond the literal, allegorical, and moral senses a fourth and ultimate spiritual or mystical sense — **an·a·gog·ic** \,a-nə-'gä-jik\ *or* **an·a·gog·i·cal** \-ji-kəl\ *adj* — **an·a·gog·i·cal·ly** \-ji-k(ə-)lē\ *adv*

¹**an·a·gram** \'a-nə-,gram\ *n* [prob. fr. MF *anagramme*, fr. NL *anagramma*, modif. of Gk *anagrammatismos*, fr. *anagrammatizein* to transpose letters, fr. *ana-* + *grammat-, gramma* letter — more at GRAM] (1589)   **1 :** a word or phrase made by transposing the letters of another word or phrase   **2** *pl but sing in constr* **:** a game in which words are formed by rearranging the letters of other words or by arranging letters taken (as from a stock of cards or blocks) at random — **an·a·gram·mat·ic** \,a-nə-grə-'ma-tik\ *also* **an·a·gram·mat·i·cal** \-ti-kəl\ *adj* — **an·a·gram·mat·i·cal·ly** \-ti-k(ə-)lē\ *adv*

²**anagram** *vt* **-grammed; -gram·ming** (1630)   **1 :** ANAGRAMMATIZE   **2 :** to rearrange (the letters of a text) in order to discover a hidden message

an·a·gram·ma·tize \,a-nə-'gra-mə-,tīz\ *vt* **-tized; -tiz·ing** (1588) **:** to transpose (as letters in a word) so as to form an anagram — **an·a·gram·ma·ti·za·tion** \-,gra-mə-tə-'zā-shən\ *n*

anal \'ā-nᵊl\ *adj* (1769)   **1 :** of, relating to, or situated near the anus ⟨~ fin⟩   **2 a :** of, relating to, characterized by, or being the stage of psychosexual development in psychoanalytic theory during which the child is concerned esp. with its feces   **b :** of, relating to, characterized by, or being personality traits (as parsimony, meticulousness, and ill humor) considered typical of fixation at the anal stage of development ⟨~ disposition⟩ ⟨~ neatness⟩ — **anal·ly** \-nᵊl-ē\ *adv*

anal·cime \ə-'nal-,sēm\ *n* [F, fr. Gk *analkimos* weak, fr. *an-* + *alkimos* strong, fr. *alkē* strength] (1803) **:** a white or slightly colored mineral that consists of hydrated silicate of sodium and aluminum and occurs in various igneous rocks in massive form or in crystals

anal·cite \ə-'nal-,sīt\ *n* (1868) **:** ANALCIME

an·a·lects \'a-nᵊl-,ek(t)s\ *also* **an·a·lec·ta** \,a-nᵊl-'ek-tə\ *n pl* [NL *analecta*, fr. Gk *analekta*, neut. pl. of *analektos*, verbal of *analegein* to collect, fr. *ana-* + *legein* to gather — more at LEGEND] (1652) **:** selected miscellaneous written passages

an·a·lem·ma \,a-nə-'le-mə\ *n* [L, sundial on a pedestal, fr. Gk *analēmma*, lofty structure, sundial, fr. *analambanein* to take up, restore, fr. *ana-* + *lambanein* to take — more at LATCH] (1832) **:** a plot or graph of the position of the sun in the sky at a certain time of day (as noon) at one locale measured at regular intervals throughout the year that has the shape of a figure 8; *also* **:** a scale (as on a globe or sundial) based on such a plot that shows the sun's position for each day of the year or that allows local mean time to be determined — **an·a·lem·mat·ic** \,a-nə-le-'ma-tik, -lə-\ *adj*

an·a·lep·tic \,a-nᵊl-'lep-tik\ *n* [Gk *analēptikos*, fr. *analambanein*] (1671) **:** a drug that stimulates the central nervous system — **analeptic** *adj*

an·al·ge·sia \,a-nᵊl-'jē-zh(ē-)ə, -zē-ə\ *n* [NL, fr. Gk *analgēsia*, fr. *an-* + *algēsis* sense of pain, fr. *algein* to suffer pain, fr. *algos* pain] (ca. 1706) **:** insensibility to pain without loss of consciousness — **an·al·ge·sic** \-'jē-zik, -sik\ *adj or n* — **an·al·get·ic** \-'je-tik\ *adj or n*

anal·i·ty \ā-'na-lə-tē\ *n, pl* **-ties** (1939) **:** the psychological state or quality of being anal

an·a·log \'a-nᵊl-,óg, -,äg\ *adj* (1948)   **1 :** of, relating to, or being an analogue   **2 a :** of, relating to, or being a mechanism in which data is represented by continuously variable physical quantities   **b :** of or relating to an analog computer   **c :** being a timepiece having hour and minute hands

analog computer *n* (1948) **:** a computer that operates with numbers represented by directly measurable quantities (as voltages or rotations) — compare DIGITAL COMPUTER, HYBRID COMPUTER

an·a·log·i·cal \,a-nᵊl-'ä-ji-kəl\ *also* **an·a·log·ic** \-jik\ *adj* (1609)   **1 :** of, relating to, or based on analogy   **2 :** expressing or implying analogy — **an·a·log·i·cal·ly** \-ji-k(ə-)lē\ *adv*

anal·o·gist \ə-'na-lə-jist\ *n* (ca. 1828) **:** one who searches for or reasons from analogies

anal·o·gize \-,jīz\ *vb* **-gized; -giz·ing** *vi* (1655) **:** to use or exhibit analogy ~ *vt* **:** to compare by analogy

anal·o·gous \ə-'na-lə-gəs\ *adj* [L *analogus*, fr. Gk *analogos*, lit., proportionate, fr. *ana-* + *logos* reason, ratio, fr. *legein* to gather, speak — more at LEGEND] (1646)   **1 :** showing an analogy or a likeness that permits one to draw an analogy   **2 :** being or related to as an analogue *syn* see SIMILAR — **anal·o·gous·ly** *adv* — **anal·o·gous·ness** *n*

¹**an·a·logue** *or* **an·a·log** \'a-nᵊl-,óg, -,äg\ *n* [F *analogue*, fr. *analogue* analogous, fr. Gk *analogos*] (1826)   **1 :** something that is analogous or similar to something else   **2 :** an organ similar in function to an organ of another animal or plant but different in structure and origin   **3** *usu* **analog :** a chemical compound that is structurally similar to another but differs slightly in composition (as in the replacement of one atom by an atom of a different element or in the presence of a particular functional group)   **4 :** a food product made by combining a less expensive food (as soybeans or whitefish) with additives to give the appearance and taste of a more expensive food (as beef or crab)

²**an·a·logue** *chiefly Brit var of* ANALOG

anal·o·gy \ə-'na-lə-jē\ *n, pl* **-gies** (15c)   **1 :** inference that if two or more things agree with one another in some respects they will prob. agree in others   **2 a :** resemblance in some particulars between things otherwise unlike : SIMILARITY   **b :** comparison based on such resemblance   **3 :** correspondence between the members of pairs or sets of linguistic forms that serves as a basis for the creation of another form   **4 :** correspondence in function between anatomical parts of different structure and origin — compare HOMOLOGY *syn* see LIKENESS

an·al·pha·bet \(,)an-'al-fə-,bet, -bət\ *n* [Gk *analphabētos* not knowing the alphabet, fr. *an-* + *alphabētos* alphabet] (ca. 1889) **:** one who cannot read : ILLITERATE — **an·al·pha·bet·ic** \,an-,al-fə-'be-tik\ *adj or n* — **an·al·pha·bet·ism** \(,)an-'al-fə-bə-,ti-zəm\ *n*

anal·y·sand \ə-'na-lə-,sand\ *n* [*analyse* + *-and* (as in *multiplicand*)] (1917) **:** one who is undergoing psychoanalysis

an·a·lyse *chiefly Brit var of* ANALYZE

anal·y·sis \ə-'na-lə-səs\ *n, pl* **-y·ses** \-,sēz\ [NL, fr. Gk, fr. *analyein* to break up, fr. *ana-* + *lyein* to loosen — more at LOSE] (1581)   **1 :** separation of a whole into its component parts   **2 a :** the identification or separation of ingredients of a substance   **b :** a statement of the constituents of a mixture   **3 a :** proof of a mathematical proposition by assuming the result and deducing a valid statement by a series of reversible steps   **b** (1) **:** a branch of mathematics concerned mainly with functions and limits   (2) **:** CALCULUS 1b   **4 a :** an examination of a complex, its elements, and their relations   **b :** a statement of such an analysis   **5 a :** a method in philosophy of resolving complex expressions into simpler or more basic ones   **b :** clarification of an expression by an elucidation of its use in discourse   **6 :** the use of function words

\ə\ abut \ᵊ\ kitten, F table \ər\ further \a\ ash \ā\ ace \ä\ mop, mar
\aú\ out \ch\ chin \e\ bet \ē\ easy \g\ go \i\ hit \ī\ ice \j\ job
\ŋ\ sing \ō\ go \ó\ law \ói\ boy \th\ thin \th̲\ the \ü\ loot \ú\ foot
\y\ yet \zh\ vision \ä, k̲, ⁿ, œ, œ̄, ue, ūe, ᵒ\ *see* Guide to Pronunciation

instead of inflectional forms as a characteristic device of a language   **7** : PSYCHOANALYSIS

analysis of variance (ca. 1939) : analysis of variation in an experimental outcome and esp. of a statistical variance in order to determine the contributions of given factors or variables to the variance

analysis si·tus \-'sī-təs, -'sē-, -,tüs\ *n* [NL, lit., analysis of situation] (ca. 1909) : TOPOLOGY 2a(1)

an·a·lyst \'a-nᵊl-əst\ *n* [F *analyste*, fr. *analyse* analysis] (1656)   **1** : a person who analyzes or who is skilled in analysis   **2** : PSYCHOANALYST

an·a·lyt·ic \,a-nᵊl-'i-tik\ *or* **an·a·lyt·i·cal** \-ti-kəl\ *adj* [LL *analyticus*, fr. Gk *analytikos*, fr. *analyein*] (1601)   **1** : of or relating to analysis or analytics; *esp* : separating something into component parts or constituent elements   **2** : being a proposition (as "no bachelor is married") whose truth is evident from the meaning of the words it contains — compare SYNTHETIC   **3** : skilled in or using analysis esp. in thinking or reasoning ⟨a keenly ~ person⟩   **4** : characterized by analysis rather than inflection ⟨~ languages⟩   **5** : PSYCHOANALYTIC   **6** : treated or treatable by or using the methods of algebra and calculus   **7 a** *of a function of a real variable* : capable of being expanded in a Taylor's series in powers of *x − h* in some neighborhood of the point *h*   **b** *of a function of a complex variable* : differentiable at every point in some neighborhood of a given point or points — **an·a·lyt·i·cal·ly** \-ti-k(ə-)lē\ *adv* — **an·a·lyt·ic·i·ty** \,a-nᵊl-ə-'ti-sə-tē\ *n*

analytic geometry *n* (ca. 1886) : the study of geometric properties by means of algebraic operations upon symbols defined in terms of a coordinate system — called also *coordinate geometry*

analytic philosophy *n* (1936) : a philosophical movement that seeks the solution of philosophical problems in the analysis of propositions or sentences — called also *philosophical analysis*; compare ORDINARY=LANGUAGE PHILOSOPHY

an·a·lyt·ics \,a-nᵊl-'i-tiks\ *n pl but sing or pl in constr* (ca. 1590) : the method of logical analysis

an·a·ly·za·tion \,a-nᵊl-ə-'zā-shən\ *n* (1742) : ANALYSIS

an·a·lyze \'a-nᵊl-,īz\ *vt* **-lyzed; -lyz·ing** [prob. irreg. fr. *analysis*] (1587)   **1** : to study or determine the nature and relationship of the parts of by analysis ⟨~ a traffic pattern⟩   **2** : to subject to scientific or grammatical analysis   **3** : PSYCHOANALYZE — **an·a·lyz·abil·i·ty** \,a-nᵊl-,ī-zə-'bi-lə-tē\ *n* — **an·a·lyz·able** \'a-nᵊl-,ī-zə-bəl\ *adj* — **an·a·lyz·er** \-,ī-zər\ *n*

syn ANALYZE, DISSECT, BREAK DOWN mean to divide a complex whole into its parts or elements. ANALYZE suggests separating or distinguishing the component parts of something (as a substance, a process, a situation) so as to discover its true nature or inner relationships ⟨*analyzed* the problem of the trade deficit⟩. DISSECT suggests a searching analysis by laying bare parts or pieces for individual scrutiny ⟨commentators *dissected* every word of the President's statement⟩. BREAK DOWN implies a reducing to simpler parts or divisions ⟨*break down* the budget⟩.

an·am·ne·sis \,a-,nam-'nē-səs\ *n, pl* **-ne·ses** \-,sēz\ [NL, fr. Gk *anamnēsis*, fr. *anamimnēskesthai* to remember, fr. *ana-* + *mimnēskesthai* to remember — more at MIND] (ca. 1593)   **1** : a recalling to mind : REMINISCENCE   **2** : a preliminary case history of a medical or psychiatric patient

an·am·nes·tic \-'nes-tik\ *adj* [Gk *anamnēstikos* easily recalled, fr. *anamimnēskesthai*] (ca. 1753)   **1** : of or relating to an anamnesis   **2** : of or relating to a secondary response to an immunogenic substance after serum antibodies can no longer be detected in the blood

ana·mor·phic \,a-nə-'mor-fik\ *adj* [NL *anamorphosis* distorted optical image] (ca. 1925) : producing, relating to, or marked by intentional distortion (as by unequal magnification along perpendicular axes) of an image ⟨an ~ lens⟩

An·a·ni·as \,a-nə-'nī-əs\ *n* [Gk, prob. fr. Heb *Ḥānanyāh*]   **1** : an early Christian struck dead for lying   **2** : LIAR

an·a·pest \'a-nə-,pest\ *n* [L *anapaestus*, fr. Gk *anapaistos*, lit., struck back (a dactyl reversed), fr. *ana-* + *-paistos*, verbal of *paiein* to strike] (ca. 1678) : a metrical foot consisting of two short syllables followed by one long syllable or of two unstressed syllables followed by one stressed syllable (as *unabridged*) — **an·a·pes·tic** \,a-nə-'pes-tik\ *adj or n*

ana·phase \'a-nə-,fāz\ *n* [ISV] (1887) : the stage of mitosis and meiosis in which the chromosomes move toward the poles of the spindle — **ana·pha·sic** \,a-nə-'fā-zik\ *adj*

ana·phor \'a-nə-,for\ *n, pl* **anaphors** *also* **anaph·o·ra** \ə-'na-f(ə-)rə\ [back-formation fr. *anaphoric*] (1975) : a word or phrase with an anaphoric function

anaph·o·ra \ə-'na-f(ə-)rə\ *n* [LL, fr. LGk, fr. Gk, act of carrying back, reference, fr. *anapherein* to carry back, refer, fr. *ana-* + *pherein* to carry — more at BEAR] (ca. 1589)   **1** : repetition of a word or expression at the beginning of successive phrases, clauses, sentences, or verses esp. for rhetorical or poetic effect ⟨Lincoln's "we cannot dedicate—we cannot consecrate—we cannot hallow—this ground" is an example of ~⟩ — compare EPISTROPHE   **2** : use of a grammatical substitute (as a pronoun or a pro-verb) to refer to the denotation of a preceding word or group of words; *also* : the relation between a grammatical substitute and its antecedent

an·a·phor·ic \,a-nə-'for-ik, -'fär-\ *adj* (1904) : of or relating to anaphora ⟨an ~ usage⟩; *esp* : being a word or phrase that takes its reference from another word or phrase and esp. from a preceding word or phrase — compare CATAPHORIC — **ana·phor·i·cal·ly** \-i-k(ə-)lē\ *adv*

an·aph·ro·di·si·ac \,a-,na-frə-'dē-zē-,ak, -zhē-, -'di-zē-\ *adj* (1823) : inhibiting or discouraging sexual desire — **anaphrodisiac** *n*

ana·phy·lac·tic \,a-nə-fə-'lak-tik\ *adj* (1907) : of, relating to, affected by, or causing anaphylaxis or anaphylactic shock — **ana·phy·lac·ti·cal·ly** \-ti-k(ə-)lē\ *adv* — **ana·phy·lac·toid** \-'lak-,toid\ *adj*

anaphylactic shock *n* (1910) : an often severe and sometimes fatal systemic reaction in a susceptible individual upon exposure to a specific antigen (as wasp venom or penicillin) after previous sensitization that is characterized esp. by respiratory symptoms, fainting, itching, and urticaria

ana·phy·lax·is \-'lak-səs\ *n, pl* **-lax·es** \-,sēz\ [NL, fr. *ana-* + *prophylaxis*] (1907)   **1** : hypersensitivity (as to foreign proteins or drugs) resulting from sensitization following prior contact with the causative agent : ANAPHYLACTIC SHOCK

an·a·pla·sia \,a-nə-'plā-zh(ē-)ə\ *n* [NL] (ca. 1909) : reversion of cells to a more primitive or undifferentiated form — **an·a·plas·tic** \-'plas-tik\ *adj*

an·a·plas·mo·sis \,a-nə-,plaz-'mō-səs\ *n, pl* **-mo·ses** \-,sēz\ [NL, fr. *Anaplasma*, genus name, fr. *ana-* + *plasma* (protoplasm)] (1920) : a tick-borne disease of cattle and sheep caused by a bacterium (*Anaplasma marginale*) and characterized esp. by anemia without blood= tinged urine and by jaundice

an·arch \'a-,närk\ *n* [back-formation fr. *anarchy*] (1667) : a leader or advocate of revolt or anarchy

an·ar·chic \a-'när-kik, ə-\ *also* **an·ar·chi·cal** \-ki-kəl\ *adj* (1649)   **1 a** : of, relating to, or advocating anarchy   **b** : likely to bring about anarchy ⟨~ violence⟩   **2** : lacking order, regularity, or definiteness ⟨~ art forms⟩ — **an·ar·chi·cal·ly** \-k(ə-)lē\ *adv*

an·ar·chism \'a-nər-,ki-zəm, -,när-\ *n* (1642)   **1** : a political theory holding all forms of governmental authority to be unnecessary and undesirable and advocating a society based on voluntary cooperation and free association of individuals and groups   **2** : the advocacy or practice of anarchistic principles

an·ar·chist \'a-nər-kist, -,när-\ *n* (1678)   **1** : one who rebels against any authority, established order, or ruling power   **2** : one who believes in, advocates, or promotes anarchism or anarchy; *esp* : one who uses violent means to overthrow the established order — **anarchist** *or* **an·ar·chis·tic** \,a-nər-'kis-tik, -,(,)när-\ *adj*

an·ar·cho–syn·di·cal·ism \a-,när-kō-'sin-di-kə-,li-zəm, ,a-nər-kō-\ *n* (ca. 1928) : SYNDICALISM — **an·ar·cho–syn·di·cal·ist** \-kə-list\ *n or adj*

an·ar·chy \'a-nər-kē, -,när-\ *n* [ML *anarchia*, fr. Gk, fr. *anarchos* having no ruler, fr. *an-* + *archos* ruler — more at ARCH-] (1539)   **1 a** : absence of government   **b** : a state of lawlessness or political disorder due to the absence of governmental authority   **c** : a utopian society of individuals who enjoy complete freedom without government   **2 a** : absence or denial of any authority or established order   **b** : absence of order : DISORDER ⟨not manicured plots but a wild ~ of nature — Israel Shenker⟩   **3** : ANARCHISM

ana·sar·ca \,a-nə-'sär-kə\ *n* [NL, fr. *ana-* + Gk *sark-, sarx* flesh — more at SARCASM] (14c) : generalized edema with accumulation of serum in the connective tissue — **ana·sar·cous** \-kəs\ *adj*

An·a·sa·zi \,ä-nə-'sä-zē\ *n, pl* **Anasazi** [Navajo *anaasází*, lit., enemy ancestors] (1938) : a prehistoric American Indian inhabitant of the canyons of northern Arizona and New Mexico and southwestern Colorado

an·as·tig·mat \a-'nas-tig-,mat, ,a-nə-'stig-\ *n* [G, back-formation fr. *anastigmatisch* anastigmatic] (1890) : an anastigmatic lens

an·a·stig·mat·ic \,a-nə-(,)stig-'ma-tik, ,a-,nas-tig-\ *adj* [ISV] (1890) : not astigmatic — used esp. of lenses that are able to form approximately point images of object points

anas·to·mose \ə-'nas-tə-,mōz, -,mōs\ *vb* **-mosed; -mos·ing** [prob. back-formation fr. *anastomosis*] *vt* (1697) : to connect or join by anastomosis ~ *vi* : to communicate by anastomosis

anas·to·mo·sis \ə-,nas-tə-'mō-səs\ *n, pl* **-mo·ses** \-,sēz\ [LL, fr. Gk *anastomōsis*, fr. *anastomoun* to provide with an outlet, fr. *ana-* + *stoma* mouth, opening — more at STOMACH] (1541)   **1** : the union of parts or branches (as of streams, blood vessels, or leaf veins) so as to intercommunicate : INOSCULATION   **2** : a product of anastomosis : NETWORK — **anas·to·mot·ic** \-'mä-tik\ *adj*

anas·tro·phe \ə-'nas-trə-(,)fē\ *n* [ML, fr. Gk *anastrophē*, lit., turning back, fr. *anastrephein* to turn back, fr. *ana-* + *strephein* to turn] (ca. 1550) : inversion of the usual syntactical order of words for rhetorical effect — compare HYSTERON PROTERON

an·a·tase \'a-nə-,tās, -,tāz\ *n* [F, fr. Gk *anatasis* extension, fr. *anateinein* to extend, fr. *ana-* + *teinein* to stretch — more at THIN] (ca. 1828) : a tetragonal form of titanium dioxide used esp. as a white pigment

anath·e·ma \ə-'na-thə-mə\ *n* [LL *anathemat-, anathema*, fr. Gk, thing devoted to evil, curse, fr. *anatithenai* to set up, dedicate, fr. *ana-* + *tithenai* to place, set — more at DO] (1526)   **1 a** : one that is cursed by ecclesiastical authority   **b** : someone or something intensely disliked or loathed — usu. used as a predicate nominative ⟨this notion was ~ to most of his countrymen —S. J. Gould⟩   **2 a** : a ban or curse solemnly pronounced by ecclesiastical authority and accompanied by excommunication   **b** : the denunciation of something as accursed   **c** : a vigorous denunciation : CURSE

anath·e·ma·tize \-,tīz\ *vt* **-tized; -tiz·ing** (1566) : to pronounce an anathema upon   **syn** see EXECRATE

An·a·to·lian \,a-nə-'tō-lē-ən, -'tōl-yən\ *n* (1590)   **1** : a native or inhabitant of Anatolia and specif. of the western plateau lands of Turkey in Asia   **2** : a branch of the Indo-European language family that includes a group of extinct languages of ancient Anatolia — see INDO-EUROPEAN LANGUAGES table — **Anatolian** *adj*

anat·o·mise *Brit var of* ANATOMIZE

anat·o·mist \ə-'na-tə-mist\ *n* (1543)   **1** : a student of anatomy; *esp* : one skilled in dissection   **2** : one who analyzes minutely and critically ⟨an ~ of urban society⟩

anat·o·mize \-,mīz\ *vt* **-mized; -miz·ing** (15c)   **1** : to cut in pieces in order to display or examine the structure and use of the parts : DISSECT   **2** : ANALYZE

anat·o·my \ə-'na-tə-mē\ *n, pl* **-mies** [LL *anatomia* dissection, fr. Gk *anatomē*, fr. *anatemnein* to dissect, fr. *ana-* + *temnein* to cut] (14c)   **1** : a branch of morphology that deals with the structure of organisms   **2** : a treatise on anatomic science or art   **3** : the art of separating the parts of an organism in order to ascertain their position, relations, structure, and function : DISSECTION   **4** *obs* : a body dissected or to be dissected   **5** : structural makeup esp. of an organism or any of its parts   **6** : a separating or dividing into parts for detailed examination : ANALYSIS   **7 a** (1) : SKELETON (2) : MUMMY   **b** : the human body — **an·a·tom·ic** \,a-nə-'tä-mik\ *or* **an·a·tom·i·cal** \-mi-kəl\ *adj* — **an·a·tom·i·cal·ly** \-mi-k(ə-)lē\ *adv*

anat·ro·pous \ə-'na-trə-pəs\ *adj* (ca. 1846) : having or being an ovule inverted so that the micropyle is bent down to the funiculus to which the body of the ovule is united

-ance *n suffix* [ME, fr. OF, fr. L *-antia*, fr. *-ant-, -ans* -ant + *-ia* -y]   **1** : action or process ⟨further*ance*⟩ : instance of an action or process ⟨perform*ance*⟩   **2** : quality or state : instance of a quality or state ⟨protuber*ance*⟩   **3** : amount or degree ⟨conduct*ance*⟩

an·ces·tor \'an-,ses-tər *also* -səs-\ *n* [ME *ancestre,* fr. OF, fr. L *antecessor* predecessor, fr. *antecedere* to go before, fr. *ante-* + *cedere* to go — more at CEDE] (13c) **1 a** : one from whom a person is descended and who is usu. more remote in the line of descent than a grandparent **b** : FOREFATHER **2 1** : FORERUNNER, PROTOTYPE **3** : a progenitor of a more recent or existing species or group
ancestor worship *n* (1854) : the custom of venerating deceased ancestors who are considered still a part of the family and whose spirits are believed to have the power to intervene in the affairs of the living
an·ces·tral \an-'ses-trəl\ *adj* (15c) : of, relating to, or inherited from an ancestor ⟨~ estates⟩ — **an·ces·tral·ly** \-trə-lē\ *adv*
an·ces·tress \'an-,ses-trəs\ *n* (1580) : a female ancestor
an·ces·try \'an-,ses-trē\ *n* (14c) **1** : line of descent : LINEAGE; *esp* : honorable, noble, or aristocratic descent **2** : persons initiating or comprising a line of descent : ANCESTORS
An·chi·ses \an-'kī-(,)sēz, aŋ-\ *n* [L, fr. Gk *Anchisēs*] : the father of Aeneas rescued by his son from the burning city of Troy
¹an·chor \'aŋ-kər\ *n, often attrib* [ME *ancre,* fr. OE *ancor,* fr. L *anchora,* fr. Gk *ankyra;* akin to OE *anga* hook — more at ANGLE] (bef. 12c) **1** : a device usu. of metal attached to a ship or boat by a cable and cast overboard to hold it in a particular place by means of a fluke that digs into the bottom **2** : a reliable or principal support : MAINSTAY **3** : something that serves to hold an object firmly **4** : an object shaped like a ship's anchor **5** : an anchorman or anchorwoman **6** : the member of a team (as a relay team) that competes last **7** : a large business (as a department store) that attracts customers and other businesses to a shopping center or mall — **an·chor·less** \-ləs\ *adj* — **at anchor** : being anchored

anchor 1: *A* yachtsman's: *1* ring, *2* stock, *3* shank, *4* bill, *5* fluke, *6* arm, *7* throat, *8* crown; *B* grapnel; *C* mushroom

²anchor *vb* **an·chored; an·chor·ing** \-k(ə-)riŋ\ *vt* (13c) **1** : to hold in place in the water by an anchor **2** : to secure firmly : FIX **3** : to act or serve as an anchor for ⟨it is she who is ~ing the rebuilding campaign —G. D. Boone⟩ ⟨~ing the evening news⟩ ~ *vi* **1** : to cast anchor **2** : to become fixed
an·chor·age \'aŋ-k(ə-)rij\ *n* (15c) **1 a** : a place where vessels anchor : a place suitable for anchoring **b** : the act of anchoring : the condition of being anchored **2** : a means of securing : a source of reassurance ⟨this ~ of Christian hope —T. O. Wedel⟩ **3** : something that provides a secure hold
an·cho·ress \'aŋ-k(ə-)rəs\ *or* **an·cress** \-krəs\ *n* [ME *ankeresse,* fr. *anker* hermit, fr. OE *ancor,* fr. OIr *anchara,* fr. LL *anachoreta*] (14c) : a woman who is an anchorite
an·cho·rite \'aŋ-kə-,rīt\ *also* **an·cho·ret** \-,ret\ *n* [ME, fr. ML *anchorita,* alter. of LL *anachoreta,* fr. LGk *anachōrētēs,* fr. Gk *anachōrein* to withdraw, fr. *ana-* + *chōrein* to make room, fr. *chōros* place] (15c) — **an·cho·rit·ic** \,aŋ-kə-'ri-tik\ *adj* — **an·cho·rit·i·cal·ly** \-ti-k(ə-)lē\ *adv*
an·chor·man \'aŋ-kər-,man\ *n* (1911) **1** : one who is last: as **a** : the member of a team who competes last ⟨the ~ on a relay team⟩ **b** : one who has the lowest scholastic standing in a graduating class **2** : a broadcaster (as on a news program) who introduces reports by other broadcasters and usu. reads the news **3** : MODERATOR 2c
an·chor·peo·ple \-,pē-pəl\ *n pl* (1973) : ANCHORPERSONS
an·chor·per·son \-,pər-sⁿn\ *n* (1973) : an anchorman or anchorwoman
an·chor·wom·an \-,wu̇-mən\ *n* (1973) : a woman who anchors a broadcast
an·cho·ve·ta *also* **an·cho·vet·ta** \,an-chō-'ve-tə\ *n* [Sp *anchoveta,* dim. of *anchova*] (1940) : a small anchovy (*Cetengraulis mysticetus*) of the Pacific coast of No. America
an·cho·vy \'an-,chō-vē, an-'\ *n, pl* **-vies** *or* **-vy** [Sp *anchova*] (1596) : any of a family (Engraulidae) of small fishes resembling herrings; *esp* : a common Mediterranean fish (*Engraulis encrasicholus*) used esp. in appetizers, as a garnish, and for making sauces and relishes
an·cien ré·gime \äⁿs-yaⁿ-rā-'zhēm\ *n* [F, lit., old regime] (1794) **1** : the political and social system of France before the Revolution of 1789 **2** : a system or mode no longer prevailing
¹an·cient \'ān(t)-shənt, 'āŋ(k)-shənt\ *adj* [ME *ancien,* fr. MF, (assumed) VL *anteanus,* fr. L *ante* before — more at ANTE-] (14c) **1** : having had an existence of many years **2** : of or relating to a remote period, to a time early in history, or to those living in such a period or time; *esp* : of or relating to the historical period beginning with the earliest known civilizations and extending to the fall of the western Roman Empire in A.D. 476 **3** : having the qualities of age or long existence: **a** : VENERABLE **b** : OLD-FASHIONED, ANTIQUE *syn* see OLD — **an·cient·ness** *n*
²ancient *n* (1502) **1** : an aged living being ⟨a penniless ~⟩ **2** : one who lived in ancient times **a** *pl* : the civilized people of antiquity; *esp* : those of the classical nations **b** : one of the classical authors ⟨Plutarch and other ~s⟩ **3** : an ancient coin
³ancient *n* [alter. of *ensign*] (1554) **1** *archaic* : ENSIGN, STANDARD, FLAG **2** *obs* : the bearer of an ensign

ancient history *n* (1595) **1** : the history of ancient times **2** : knowledge or information that is widespread and has lost its initial freshness or importance : common knowledge
an·cient·ly *adv* (1502) : in ancient times : long ago
an·cient·ry \-shən-trē\ *n* (1580) : ANTIQUITY, ANCIENTNESS
an·cil·la \an-'si-lə\ *n, pl* **-lae** \-(,)lē\ [L, female servant] (1902) : an aid to achieving or mastering something else
an·cil·lary \'an(t)-sə-,ler-ē, *esp Brit* an-'si-lə-rē\ *adj* (1667) **1** : SUBORDINATE, SUBSIDIARY ⟨the main factory and its ~ plants⟩ **2** : AUXILIARY, SUPPLEMENTARY ⟨the need for ~ evidence⟩ — **ancillary** *n*
an·con \'aŋ-,kän\ *n, pl* **an·co·nes** \aŋ-'kō-nēz\ [L, fr. Gk *ankōn* elbow; akin to OE *anga* hook — more at ANGLE] (ca. 1706) : a bracket, elbow, or console used as an architectural support
-ancy *n suffix* [L *-antia* — more at -ANCE] : quality or state ⟨piquancy⟩
an·cy·lo·sto·mi·a·sis \,aŋ-ki-,lō-stə-'mī-ə-səs, ,an(t)-sə-\ *n, pl* **-a·ses** \-,sēz\ [NL, fr. *Ancylostoma,* genus of hookworms, fr. Gk *ankylos* hooked (akin to OE *anga* hook) + *stoma* mouth — more at ANGLE, STOMACH] (1887) : infestation with or disease caused by hookworms; *esp* : a lethargic anemic state in humans due to blood loss from hookworms feeding in the small intestine
and \ən(d), (')an(d) *after* t, d, s *or* z, *often* ᵊn *after* p or b, *sometimes* ⁿŋ *after* k *or* g\ *conj* [ME, fr. OE; akin to OHG *unti* and] (bef. 12c) **1** — used as a function word to indicate connection or addition esp. of items within the same class or type; used to join sentence elements of the same grammatical rank or function **2 a** — used as a function word to express logical modification, consequence, antithesis, or supplementary explanation **b** — used as a function word to join one finite verb (as *go, come, try*) to another so that together they are logically equivalent to an infinitive of purpose ⟨come ~ see me⟩ **3** *obs* : IF **4** — used in logic to form a conjunction — **and so forth** \ən-'sō-,fȯrth, -,fȯrth\ **1** : and others or more of the same or similar kind **2** : further in the same or similar manner **3** : and the rest **4** : and other things — **and so on** \ən-'sō-,ȯn, -,än\ *:* and so forth
AND \'and\ *n* (1949) : a logical operator that requires both of two inputs to be present or two conditions to be met for an output to be made or a statement to be executed
An·da·lu·sian \,an-də-'lü-zhən\ *n* [*Andalusia,* Spain] (1966) : any of a breed of horses of Spanish origin that have a high-stepping gait
an·da·lu·site \,an-də-'lü-,sīt\ *n* [F *andalousite,* fr. *Andalousie* Andalusia, region in Spain] (ca. 1828) : a mineral consisting of a silicate of aluminum usu. in thick orthorhombic prisms of various colors
¹an·dan·te \än-'dän-(,)tā, -'dän-tē; an-'dän-tē\ *adv or adj* [It, lit., going, prp. of *andare* to go] (1724) : moderately slow — usu. used as a direction in music
²andante *n* (1784) : a musical composition or movement in andante tempo
¹an·dan·ti·no \,än-,dän-'tē-(,)nō\ *adv or adj* [It, dim. of *andante*] (1819) : slightly faster than andante — used as a direction in music
²andantino *n, pl* **-nos** (1845) : a musical composition or movement in andantino tempo
an·des·ite \'an-di-,zīt\ *n* [G *Andesit,* fr. *Andes*] (1850) : an extrusive usu. dark grayish rock consisting essentially of oligoclase or feldspar — **an·des·it·ic** \,an-di-'zi-tik\ *adj*
and how *adv* (1865) — used to emphasize the preceding idea ⟨having a great time—*and how!*⟩
and·iron \'an-,dī(-ə)rn\ *n* [ME *aundiren,* modif. of MF *andier*] (14c) : either of a pair of metal supports for firewood used on a hearth and made of a horizontal bar mounted on short legs with usu. a vertical shaft surmounting the front end
and/or \'an-,dȯr\ *conj* (1853) — used as a function word to indicate that two words or expressions are to be taken together or individually ⟨language comprehension *and/or* production —David Crystal⟩
an·dou·ille \än-'dü-ē, ,än-dü-'ē\ *n* [F, fr. OF *andoille,* fr. (assumed) VL *inductilia,* neut. pl. of *inductilis* made by insertion, fr. L *inductus,* pp. of *inducere* to insert, bring in — more at INDUCE] (1605) : a highly spiced smoked pork sausage
an·douil·lette \,än-dü-'yet\ *n* [F, dim. of *andouille*] (1611) : a fresh pork sausage made with pork or chitterlings
andr- *or* **andro-** *comb form* [L, fr. Gk, fr. *andr-, anēr;* akin to Oscan *ner-* man, Skt *nar-* man, strength] **1** : male human being ⟨*andro*centric⟩ **2** : male ⟨*andro*ecium⟩
an·dra·dite \'an-'drä-,dīt, 'an-drə-,dīt\ *n* [José B. de *Andrada* e Silva †1838 Brazilian geologist] (1868) : a garnet of any of various colors ranging from yellow and green to brown and black
an·dro·cen·tric \,an-drə-'sen-trik\ *adj* (1903) : dominated by or emphasizing masculine interests or a masculine point of view
An·dro·cles \'an-drə-,klēz\ *n* [L, fr. Gk *Androklēs*] : a fabled Roman slave spared in the arena by a lion from whose foot he had years before extracted a thorn
an·droe·ci·um \an-'drē-shē-əm, -sē-əm\ *n, pl* **-cia** \-shē-ə, -sē-ə\ [NL, fr. *andr-* + Gk *oikion,* dim. of *oikos* house — more at VICINITY] (ca. 1839) : the aggregate of stamens in the flower of a seed plant
an·dro·gen \'an-drə-jən\ *n* [ISV] (1936) : a male sex hormone (as testosterone) — **an·dro·gen·ic** \,an-drə-'je-nik\ *adj*
an·dro·gen·e·sis \,an-drō-'je-nə-səs\ *n* [NL] (ca. 1900) : development of an embryo containing only paternal chromosomes due to failure of the egg to participate in fertilization — **an·dro·ge·net·ic** \-jə-'ne-tik\ *adj*
an·dro·gyne \'an-drə-,jīn\ *n* [MF, fr. L *androgynus*] (1552) : one that is androgynous
an·drog·y·nous \an-'drä-jə-nəs\ *adj* [L *androgynus* hermaphrodite, fr. Gk *androgynos,* fr. *andr-* + *gynē* woman — more at QUEEN] (1651) **1** : having the characteristics or nature of both male and female **2 a** : neither specifically feminine nor masculine ⟨the ~ pronoun *them*⟩ **b** : suitable to or for either sex ⟨~ clothing⟩ **3** : having traditional male and female roles obscured or reversed ⟨an ~ marriage⟩ — **an·drog·y·ny** \-nē\ *n*

\ə\ abut \ᵊ\ kitten, F table \ər\ further \a\ ash \ā\ ace \ä\ mop, mar
\au̇\ out \ch\ chin \e\ bet \ē\ easy \g\ go \i\ hit \ī\ ice \j\ job
\ŋ\ sing \ō\ go \ȯ\ law \ȯi\ boy \th\ thin \t̲h̲\ the \ü\ loot \u̇\ foot
\y\ yet \zh\ vision \á, k̲, ⁿ, œ, œ̄, ᵫ, ᵬ, ᵊ\ *see* Guide to Pronunciation

an·droid \'an-ˌdroid\ n [LGk *androeidēs* manlike, fr. Gk *andr-* + *-oeidēs* -oid] (ca. 1751) : a mobile robot usu. with a human form

An·drom·a·che \an-'drä-mə-(ˌ)kē\ n [L, fr. Gk *Andromachē*] : the wife of Hector

an·drom·e·da \an-'drä-mə-də\ n [NL *Andromeda*, genus name, fr. L] (ca. 1760) : any of several evergreen shrubs (genera *Pieris* and *Andromeda*) of the heath family; *esp* : JAPANESE ANDROMEDA

An·drom·e·da \an-'drä-mə-də\ n [L, fr. Gk *Andromedē*] **1** : an Ethiopian princess of Greek mythology rescued from a monster by her future husband Perseus **2** [L (gen. *Andromedae*)] : a northern constellation directly south of Cassiopeia between Pegasus and Perseus

an·dros·ter·one \an-'dräs-tə-ˌrōn\ n [ISV] (1934) : an androgenic hormone that is a hydroxy ketone $C_{19}H_{30}O_2$ found in human male and female urine

ane \'ān\ adj or n or pron (bef. 12c) chiefly Scot : ONE

-ane n suffix [ISV *-an*, *-ane*, alter. of *-ene*, *-ine*, & *-one*] **1** : ³-AN 1 〈furane〉 **2** : saturated hydrocarbon 〈alkane〉 〈methane〉

an·ec·dot·age \'a-nik-ˌdō-tij\ n (1823) **1** : the telling of anecdotes; *also* : ANECDOTES **2** : garrulous old age

an·ec·dot·al \ˌa-nik-'dō-t²l\ adj (1836) **1 a** : of, relating to, or consisting of anecdotes 〈an ~ biography〉 **b** : ANECDOTIC 2 〈my ~ uncle〉 **2** : based on or consisting of reports or observations of usu. unscientific observers 〈~ evidence〉 **3** : of, relating to, or being the depiction of a scene suggesting a story 〈~ painting〉 〈~ detail〉 — **an·ec·dot·al·ly** \-t²l-ē\ adv

an·ec·dot·al·ist \ˌa-nik-'dō-t²l-ist\ or **an·ec·dot·ist** \ˌa-nik-ˌdō-tist\ n (1837) : one who is given to or is skilled in telling anecdotes — **an·ec·dot·al·ism** \-t²l-ˌi-zəm\ n

an·ec·dote \'a-nik-ˌdōt\ n, pl **anecdotes** also **an·ec·dota** \ˌa-nik-'dō-tə\ [F, fr. Gk *anekdota* unpublished items, fr. neut. pl. of *anekdotos* unpublished, fr. *a-* + *ekdidonai* to publish, fr. *ex* out + *didonai* to give — more at EX-, DATE] (ca. 1721) : a usu. short narrative of an interesting, amusing, or biographical incident

an·ec·dot·ic \ˌa-nik-'dä-tik\ or **an·ec·dot·i·cal** \-'dä-ti-kəl\ adj (ca. 1744) **1** : ANECDOTAL 1a **2** : given to or skilled in telling anecdotes — **an·ec·dot·i·cal·ly** \-'dä-ti-k(ə-)lē\ adv

an·echo·ic \ˌa-ni-'kō-ik\ adj (1946) : free from echoes and reverberations 〈an ~ chamber〉

an·elas·tic \ˌa-n²l-'as-tik\ adj (1947) : relating to the property of a substance in which there is no definite relation between stress and strain — **an·elas·tic·i·ty** \-n²l-ˌas-'ti-sə-tē, -'tis-tē\ n

anem- or **anemo-** comb form [Gk, fr. *anemos* — more at ANIMATE] : wind 〈anemometer〉

ane·mia \ə-'nē-mē-ə\ n [NL, fr. Gk *anaimia* bloodlessness, fr. *a-* + *-aimia* -emia] (1824) **1 a** : a condition in which the blood is deficient in red blood cells, in hemoglobin, or in total volume **b** : ISCHEMIA **2** : lack of vitality

ane·mic \ə-'nē-mik\ adj (1858) **1** : relating to or affected with anemia **2 a** : lacking force, vitality, or spirit 〈an ~ rendition of the song〉 〈~ efforts at enforcement〉 **b** : lacking interest or savor : INSIPID 〈~ wines〉 **c** : lacking in substance or quantity 〈~ returns on an investment〉 〈~ attendance〉 — **ane·mi·cal·ly** \-mi-k(ə-)lē\ adv

anemo·graph \ə-'ne-mə-ˌgraf\ n (1865) : a recording anemometer

an·e·mom·e·ter \ˌa-nə-'mä-mə-tər\ n (ca. 1751) : an instrument for measuring and indicating the force or speed of the wind

an·e·mom·e·try \ˌa-nə-'mä-mə-trē\ n (1847) : the process of ascertaining the force, speed, and direction of wind or an airflow

anem·o·ne \ə-'ne-mə-nē\ n [L, fr. Gk *anemōnē*] (1548) **1** : any of a large genus (*Anemone*) of the buttercup family having lobed or divided leaves and showy flowers without petals but with conspicuous often colored sepals — called also *windflower* **2** : SEA ANEMONE

an·e·moph·i·lous \ˌa-nə-'mä-fə-ləs\ adj (1874) : pollinated by wind

an·en·ceph·a·ly \ˌan-(ˌ)en-'se-fə-lē\ n, pl **-lies** [²a- + *encephal-* + ²-y] (ca. 1889) : congenital absence of all or a major part of the brain — **an·en·ce·phal·ic** \-ˌen(t)-sə-'fa-lik\ adj

anent \ə-'nent\ prep [ME *onevent*, *anent*, fr. OE *on efen* alongside, fr. *on* + *efen* even] (13c) : ABOUT, CONCERNING

an·er·oid \'a-nə-ˌroid\ adj [F *anéroïde*, fr. Gk *a-* + LGk *nēron* water, fr. Gk, neut. of *nearos*, *nēros* fresh; akin to Gk *neos* new — more at NEW] (ca. 1848) : using no liquid; *specif* : operating by the effect of outside air pressure on a diaphragm forming one wall of an evacuated container 〈~ barometer〉

an·es·the·sia \ˌa-nəs-'thē-zhə\ n [NL, fr. Gk *anaisthēsia* insensibility, fr. *a-* + *aisthēsis* perception, fr. *aisthanesthai* to perceive — more at AUDIBLE] (ca. 1721) : loss of sensation with or without loss of consciousness

an·es·the·si·ol·o·gist \-ˌthē-zē-'ä-lə-jist\ n (1942) : ANESTHETIST; *specif* : a physician specializing in anesthesiology

an·es·the·si·ol·o·gy \-jē\ n (ca. 1914) : a branch of medical science dealing with anesthesia and anesthetics

¹an·es·thet·ic \ˌa-nəs-'the-tik\ adj (1846) **1** : of, relating to, or capable of producing anesthesia **2** : lacking awareness or sensitivity 〈unmoved and quite ~ to his presence —S. J. Perelman〉 — **an·es·thet·i·cal·ly** \-ti-k(ə-)lē\ adv

²anesthetic n (1848) **1** : a substance that produces anesthesia **2** : something that brings relief : PALLIATIVE

anes·the·tist \ə-'nes-thə-tist, Brit -'nēs-\ n (1882) : one who administers anesthetics

anes·the·tize \-thə-ˌtīz\ vt **-tized; -tiz·ing** (1848) : to subject to anesthesia

an·es·trous \(ˌ)an-'es-trəs\ adj (ca. 1909) **1** : not exhibiting estrus **2** : of or relating to anestrus

an·es·trus \-trəs\ n [NL] (1927) : the period of sexual quiescence between two periods of sexual activity in cyclically breeding mammals

an·eu·ploid \'an-yü-ˌploid\ adj (1926) : having or being a chromosome number that is not an exact multiple of the usu. haploid number — compare EUPLOID — **aneuploid** n — **an·eu·ploi·dy** \-ˌploi-dē\ n

an·eu·rysm also **an·eu·rism** \'an-yə-ˌri-zəm\ n [Gk *aneurysma*, fr. *aneurynein* to dilate, fr. *ana-* + *eurynein* to stretch, fr. *eurys* wide — more at EURY-] (15c) : an abnormal blood-filled dilatation of a blood vessel and esp. an artery resulting from disease of the vessel wall — **an·eu·rys·mal** \ˌan-yə-'riz-məl\ adj

anew \ə-'nü, -'nyü\ adv [ME *of newe*, fr. OE *of nīwe*, fr. *of* + *nīwe* new] (bef. 12c) **1** : for an additional time : AFRESH **2** : in a new or different form

an·frac·tu·os·i·ty \(ˌ)an-ˌfrak-chə-'wä-sə-tē, -shə-\ n, pl **-ties** (1596) **1** : the quality or state of being anfractuous **2** : a winding channel or course; *esp* : an intricate path or process (as of the mind)

an·frac·tu·ous \an-'frak-chə-wəs, -shə-\ adj [F *anfractueux*, fr. LL *anfractuosus*, fr. L *anfractus* coil, bend, fr. *an-* (fr. *ambi-* around) + *-fractus*, fr. *frangere* to break — more at AMBI-, BREAK] (1621) : full of windings and intricate turnings : TORTUOUS

an·gel \'ān-jəl\ n [ME, fr. OE *engel* & OF *angele*; both fr. LL *angelus*, fr. Gk *angelos*, lit., messenger] (bef. 12c) **1 a** : a spiritual being superior to man in power and intelligence; *esp* : one in the lowest rank in the celestial hierarchy **b** pl : an order of angels — see CELESTIAL HIERARCHY **2** : an attendant spirit or guardian **3** : a white-robed winged figure of human form in fine art **4** : MESSENGER, HARBINGER 〈~ of death〉 **5** : a person like an angel (as in looks or behavior) **6** *Christian Science* : inspiration from God **7** : one (as a backer of a theatrical venture) that aids or supports with money or influence **8** : ANGELFISH — **an·gel·ic** \an-'je-lik\ or **an·gel·i·cal** \-li-kəl\ adj — **an·gel·i·cal·ly** \-li-k(ə-)lē\ adv

angel dust n (1973) : PHENCYCLIDINE

An·ge·le·no \ˌan-jə-'lē-(ˌ)nō\ n, pl **-nos** [AmSp *angeleño*, fr. Los *Angeles*, Calif.] (1888) : a native or resident of Los Angeles, Calif.

an·gel·fish \'ān-jəl-ˌfish\ n (1668) **1** : any of several compressed bright-colored bony fishes (family Pomacanthidae) of warm seas **2** : SCALARE

angel food cake n (1920) : a usu. white sponge cake made of flour, sugar, and whites of eggs

angel–hair pasta \'an-jəl-ˌher-, -ˌhar-\ n (1981) : pasta smaller in diameter than vermicelli

an·gel·i·ca \an-'je-li-kə\ n [NL, genus name, fr. ML, fr. LL, fem. of *angelicus* angelic, fr. LGk *angelikos*, fr. Gk, of a messenger, fr. *angelos*] (1527) **1 a** : any of a genus (*Angelica*) of herbs of the carrot family; *esp* : a Eurasian biennial or perennial (*A. archangelica*) whose roots and fruit yield a flavoring oil **b** : a confection prepared from angelica **2** cap : a sweet fortified wine produced in California

angelica tree n (1785) : HERCULES'-CLUB 1

an·gel·ol·o·gy \ˌān-jə-'lä-lə-jē\ n, often cap (ca. 1828) : the theological doctrine of angels or its study — **an·gel·ol·o·gist** \-jist\ n

An·ge·lus \'an-jə-ləs\ n [ML, fr. LL, angel; fr. the first word of the opening versicle] (1658) **1** : a devotion of the Western church that commemorates the Incarnation and is said in the morning, at noon, and in the evening **2** : a bell announcing the time for the Angelus

¹anger vb **an·gered; an·ger·ing** \-g(ə-)riŋ\ vt (13c) : to make angry ~ vi : to become angry

²anger \'an-gər\ n [ME, affliction, anger, fr. ON *angr* grief; akin to OE *enge* narrow, L *angere* to strangle, Gk *anchein*] (14c) **1** : a strong feeling of displeasure and usu. of antagonism **2** : RAGE 2 — **an·ger·less** \-ləs\ adj

syn ANGER, IRE, RAGE, FURY, INDIGNATION, WRATH mean an intense emotional state induced by displeasure. ANGER, the most general term, names the reaction but in itself conveys nothing about intensity or justification or manifestation of the emotional state 〈tried to hide his *anger*〉. IRE, more frequent in literary contexts, may suggest greater intensity than *anger*, often with an evident display of feeling 〈cheeks flushed dark with *ire*〉. RAGE suggests loss of self-control from violence of emotion 〈screaming with *rage*〉. FURY is overmastering destructive rage that can verge on madness 〈in her *fury* she accused everyone around her of betrayal〉. INDIGNATION stresses righteous anger at what one considers unfair, mean, or shameful 〈a refusal to listen that caused general *indignation*〉. WRATH is likely to suggest a desire or intent to revenge or punish 〈rose in his *wrath* and struck his tormentor to the floor〉.

An·ge·vin \'an-jə-vən\ adj [F, fr. OF, fr. ML *andegavinus*, fr. *Andegavia* Anjou] (1769) : of, relating to, or characteristic of Anjou or the Plantagenets — **Angevin** n

angi- or **angio-** comb form [NL, fr. Gk *angei-*, *angeio-*, fr. *angeion* vessel, blood vessel, dim. of *angos* vessel] **1** : blood or lymph vessel : blood vessels and 〈angioma〉 〈angiocardiography〉 **2** : pericarp 〈angiosperm〉

an·gi·na \an-'jī-nə, *Can* an-jə-\ n [L, throat inflammation, fr. Gk *anchonē* strangling, fr. *anchein* to strangle] (1578) : a disease marked by spasmodic attacks of intense suffocative pain: as **a** : a severe inflammatory or ulcerated condition of the mouth or throat **b** : ANGINA PECTORIS — **an·gi·nal** \an-'jī-n²l, 'an-jə-\ adj

angina pec·to·ris \-'pek-t(ə-)rəs\ n [NL, lit., angina of the chest] (1744) : a disease marked by brief paroxysmal attacks of chest pain precipitated by deficient oxygenation of the heart muscles

an·gio·car·di·og·ra·phy \ˌan-jē-ō-ˌkär-dē-'ä-grə-fē\ n (1938) : the roentgenographic visualization of the heart and its blood vessels after injection of a radiopaque substance — **an·gio·car·dio·graph·ic** \-dē-ə-'graf-ik\ adj

an·gio·gen·e·sis \ˌan-jē-ō-'je-nə-səs\ n [NL] (1899) : the formation and differentiation of blood vessels — **an·gio·gen·ic** \-'je-nik\ adj

an·gio·gram \'an-jē-ə-ˌgram\ n (1933) : a roentgenogram made by angiography

an·gi·og·ra·phy \ˌan-jē-'ä-grə-fē\ n (1933) : the roentgenographic visualization of the blood vessels after injection of a radiopaque substance — **an·gio·graph·ic** \ˌan-jē-ə-'gra-fik\ adj

an·gi·o·ma \ˌan-jē-'ō-mə\ n [NL] (1871) : a tumor composed chiefly of blood vessels or lymph vessels — **an·gi·o·ma·tous** \-mə-təs\ adj

an·gio·plas·ty \'an-jē-ə-ˌplas-tē\ n, pl **-ties** (ca. 1919) : surgical repair of a blood vessel; *esp* : BALLOON ANGIOPLASTY

an·gio·sperm \'an-jē-ə-ˌspərm\ n [ultim. fr. NL *angi-* + Gk *sperma* seed — more at SPERM] (ca. 1828) : any of a class (Angiospermae) or division (Magnoliophyta) of vascular plants (as magnolias, grasses, oaks, roses, and daisies) that have the ovules and seeds enclosed in an ovary, form the embryo and endosperm by double fertilization, and typically have each flower surrounded by a perianth composed of two sets of floral envelopes comprising the calyx and corolla — called also *flowering plant* — **an·gio·sper·mous** \ˌan-jē-ə-'spər-məs\ adj

an·gio·ten·sin \ˌan-jē-ō-'ten(t)-sən\ n [angi- + hypertension + -in] (ca. 1961) : either of two forms of a kinin of which one has marked vaso-

constrictive action; *also* : a synthetic amide derivative of the physiologically active form used to treat some forms of hypotension
angiotensin converting enzyme *n* (1970) : a proteolytic enzyme that converts the physiologically inactive form of angiotensin to the active vasoconstrictive form
¹**an·gle** \'aŋ-gəl\ *n* [ME, fr. MF, fr. L *angulus*] (14c) **1** : a corner whether constituting a projecting part or a partially enclosed space ⟨they sheltered in an ∼ of the building⟩ **2 a** : the figure formed by two lines extending from the same point; *also* : DIHEDRAL ANGLE **b** : a measure of an angle or of the amount of turning necessary to bring one line or plane into coincidence with or parallel to another **3 a** : the precise viewpoint from which something is observed or considered; *also* : the aspect seen from such an angle **b** (1) : a special approach, point of attack, or technique for accomplishing an objective (2) : an often improper or illicit method of obtaining advantage ⟨he always had an ∼ to beat the other fellow⟩ **4** : a sharply divergent course ⟨the road went off at an ∼⟩ **5** : a position to the side of an opponent in football from which a player may block his opponent more effectively or without penalty — usu. used in the phrases *get an angle* or *have an angle* — **an·gled** \-gəld\ *adj*
²**angle** *vb* **an·gled; an·gling** \-g(ə-)liŋ\ *vi* (1741) : to turn or proceed at an angle ∼ *vt* **1** : to turn, move, or direct at an angle **2** : to present (as a news story) from a particular or prejudiced point of view : SLANT
³**angle** *vi* **an·gled; an·gling** \-g(ə-)liŋ\ [ME *angelen*, fr. *angel* fishhook, fr. OE, fr. *anga* hook; akin to OHG *ango* hook, L *uncus*, Gk *onkos* barbed means, *ankos* glen] (15c) **1** : to fish with a hook **2** : to use artful means to attain an objective ⟨*angled* for an invitation⟩
An·gle \'aŋ-gəl\ *n* [L *Angli*, pl., of Gmc origin; akin to OE *Engle* Angles] (bef. 12c) : a member of a Germanic people that invaded England along with the Saxons and Jutes in the 5th century A.D. and merged with them to form the Anglo-Saxon peoples
angle bracket *n* (ca. 1956) : BRACKET 3b
angle iron *n* (ca. 1853) **1** : an iron cleat for joining parts of a structure at an angle **2** : a piece of structural steel rolled with an L-shaped section
angle of attack (1908) : the acute angle between the direction of the relative wind and the chord of an airfoil
angle of depression (1790) : the angle formed by the line of sight and the horizontal plane for an object below the horizontal
angle of elevation (ca. 1737) : the angle formed by the line of sight and the horizontal plane for an object above the horizontal
angle of incidence (1628) : the angle that a line (as a ray of light) falling on a surface or interface makes with the normal drawn at the point of incidence — see CRITICAL ANGLE illustration
angle of reflection (1638) : the angle between a reflected ray and the normal drawn at the point of incidence to a reflecting surface
angle of refraction (ca. 1737) : the angle between a refracted ray and the normal drawn at the point of incidence to the interface at which refraction occurs
an·gler \'aŋ-glər\ *n* (15c) **1** : one that angles **2** : ANGLERFISH
an·gler·fish \-,fish\ *n* (ca. 1889) : any of several pediculate fishes (as the goosefishes); *esp* : MONKFISH
angle shot *n* (ca. 1922) : a picture taken with the camera pointed at an angle from the horizontal
an·gle·site \'aŋ-gəl-,sīt, -glə-\ *n* [F *anglésite*, fr. *Anglesey* Island, Wales] (ca. 1841) : a mineral consisting of lead sulfate formed by the oxidation of galena
an·gle·worm \'aŋ-gəl-,wərm\ *n* (1832) : EARTHWORM
An·gli·an \'aŋ-glē-ən\ *n* (1726) **1** : a member of the Angles **2** : the Old English dialects of Mercia and Northumbria — **Anglian** *adj*
An·gli·can \'aŋ-gli-kən\ *adj* [ML *anglicanus*, fr. *anglicus* English, fr. L *Angli* Angles] (1635) **1** : of or relating to the established episcopal Church of England and churches of similar faith and order in communion with it **2** : of or relating to England or the English nation — **Anglican** *n* — **An·gli·can·ism** \-kə-,ni-zəm\ *n*
an·gli·ce \'aŋ-glə-(,)sē\ *adv, often cap* [ML, adv. of *anglicus*] (1602) : in English; *esp* : in readily understood English ⟨the city of Napoli, ∼ Naples⟩
an·gli·cise *often cap, var of* ANGLICIZE
an·gli·cism \'aŋ-glə-,si-zəm\ *n, often cap* [ML *anglicus* English] (1642) **1** : a characteristic feature of English occurring in another language **2** : adherence or attachment to English customs or ideas
An·gli·cist \'aŋ-glə-sist\ *n* (1930) : a specialist in English linguistics
an·gli·cize \'aŋ-glə-,sīz\ *vt* **-cized; -ciz·ing** *often cap* (1710) **1** : to make English in quality or characteristics **2** : to adapt (a foreign word or phrase) to English usage; *esp* : to borrow into English without alteration of form or spelling and with or without change in pronunciation — **an·gli·ci·za·tion** \,aŋ-glə-sə-'zā-shən\ *n, often cap*
an·gling \'aŋ-gliŋ\ *n* (15c) : the action of one who angles; *esp* : the action or sport of fishing with hook and line
An·glist \'aŋ-glist\ *n* (1888) : ANGLICIST
An·glo \'aŋ-(,)glō\ *n, pl* **Anglos** [in sense 2, fr. AmerSp, short for Sp *angloamericano* Anglo-American] (1800) **1** : ANGLO-AMERICAN **2** : a white inhabitant of the U.S. of non-Hispanic descent — **Anglo** *adj*
An·glo- *comb form* [NL, fr. LL *Angli*] **1** \'aŋ-(,)glō, -glō\ : English ⟨*Anglo*-Norman⟩ **2** \-(,)glō\ : English and ⟨*Anglo*-Japanese⟩
An·glo-Amer·i·can \,aŋ-glō-ə-'mer-ə-kən\ *n* (ca. 1782) : a North American whose native language is English; *esp* : an inhabitant of the U.S. of English origin or descent — **Anglo-American** *adj*
An·glo-Cath·o·lic \-'kath-lik, -'ka-thə-\ *adj* (1838) : of or relating to a High Church movement in Anglicanism emphasizing its continuity with historic Catholicism and fostering Catholic dogmatic and liturgical traditions — **Anglo-Catholic** *n* — **An·glo-Ca·thol·i·cism** \-kə-'thä-lə-,si-zəm\ *n*
An·glo-French \-'french\ *n* (ca. 1884) : the French language used in medieval England
An·glo·ma·nia \-'mā-nē-ə, -,nyə\ *n* (1787) : an absorbing or pervasive interest in England or things English
An·glo-Nor·man \-'nȯr-mən\ *n* (1735) **1** : any of the Normans living in England after the Norman conquest of 1066 **2** : the form of Anglo-French used by Anglo-Normans — **Anglo-Norman** *adj*
An·glo·phile \'aŋ-glə-,fīl\ *also* **An·glo·phil** \-,fil\ *n* [F, fr. anglo- + -phile] (1883) : one who greatly admires or favors England and things English — **Anglophile** *or* **An·glo·phil·ic** \,aŋ-glə-'fi-lik\ *adj*

An·glo·phil·ia \,aŋ-glə-'fi-lē-ə\ *n* (1896) : unusual admiration or partiality for England, English ways, or things English — **An·glo·phil·i·ac** \-lē-,ak\ *adj*
An·glo·phobe \'aŋ-glə-,fōb\ *n* [prob. fr. F, fr. anglo- + -phobe] (1866) : one who is averse to or dislikes England and things English — **An·glo·pho·bia** \,aŋ-glə-'fō-bē-ə\ *n* — **An·glo·pho·bic** \-bik\ *adj*
an·glo·phone \'aŋ-glə-,fōn\ *adj, often cap* (1965) : consisting of or belonging to an English-speaking population esp. in a country where two or more languages are spoken — **Anglophone** *n*
An·glo-Sax·on \,aŋ-glō-'sak-sən\ *n* [NL *Anglo-Saxones*, pl., alter. of ML *Angli Saxones*, fr. L *Angli* Angles + LL *Saxones* Saxons] (bef. 12c) **1** : a member of the Germanic peoples conquering England in the 5th century A.D. and forming the ruling class until the Norman conquest — compare ANGLE, JUTE, SAXON **2 a** : ENGLISHMAN; *specif* : a person descended from the Anglo-Saxons **b** : a white gentile of an English-speaking nation **3** : OLD ENGLISH 1 **4** : direct plain English; *esp* : English using words considered crude or vulgar — **Anglo-Saxon** *adj*
an·go·ra \aŋ-'gȯr-ə, an-, -'gȯr-\ *n* (1852) **1** : the hair of the Angora rabbit or Angora goat — called also *angora wool* **2** : a yarn of Angora rabbit hair used esp. for knitting **3** *cap* **a** : ANGORA CAT **b** : ANGORA GOAT **c** : ANGORA RABBIT
Angora cat *n* [*Angora* (Ankara), Turkey] (1819) : a long-haired domestic cat; *specif* : any of a breed that differs from the Persian in having a narrower head and slighter body
Angora goat *n* (1833) : any of a breed or variety of the domestic goat raised for its long silky hair which is the true mohair
Angora rabbit *n* (1849) : any of a breed of long-haired usu. white rabbits with red eyes that is raised for fine wool
an·gry \'aŋ-grē\ *adj* **an·gri·er; -est** (14c) **1** : feeling or showing anger : WRATHFUL **2 a** : indicative of or proceeding from anger ⟨∼ words⟩ **b** : seeming to show anger or to threaten in an angry manner ⟨an ∼ sky⟩ **3** : painfully inflamed ⟨an ∼ rash⟩ — **an·gri·ly** \-grə-lē\ *adv* — **an·gri·ness** \-grē-nəs\ *n*

Angora rabbit

angry young man *n* (1941) **1** : an outspoken critic of or protester against an economic condition or social injustice **2** : one of a group of mid-20th century British authors whose works express the bitterness of the lower classes toward the established sociopolitical system and toward the mediocrity and hypocrisy of the middle and upper classes
angst \'äŋ(k)st, 'aŋ(k)st\ *n* [Dan & G; Dan, fr. G] (ca. 1942) : a feeling of anxiety, apprehension, or insecurity
ang·strom \'aŋ-strəm *also* 'ȯŋ-\ *n* [Anders J. *Ångström*] (1892) : a unit of length equal to one ten-billionth of a meter
¹**an·guish** \'aŋ-gwish\ *n* [ME *angwisshe*, fr. OF *angoisse*, fr. L *angustiae*, pl., straits, distress, fr. *angustus* narrow; akin to OE *enge* narrow — more at ANGER] (13c) : extreme pain, distress, or anxiety **syn** see SORROW
²**anguish** *vi* (14c) : to suffer anguish ∼ *vt* : to cause to suffer anguish
an·guished *adj* (14c) **1** : suffering anguish : TORMENTED ⟨the ∼ martyrs⟩ **2** : expressing anguish : AGONIZED ⟨∼ cries⟩
an·gu·lar \'aŋ-gyə-lər\ *adj* [MF or L; MF *angulaire*, fr. L *angularis*, fr. *angulus* angle] (15c) **1 a** : forming an angle : sharp-cornered **b** : having one or more angles **2** : measured by an angle ⟨∼ distance⟩ **3 a** : stiff in character or manner : lacking smoothness or grace **b** : lean and having prominent bone structure — **an·gu·lar·ly** *adv*
angular acceleration *n* (1883) : the rate of change per unit time of angular velocity
an·gu·lar·i·ty \,aŋ-gyə-'lar-ə-tē\ *n, pl* **-ties** (1642) **1** : the quality of being angular **2** *pl* : angular outlines or characteristics
angular momentum *n* (1870) : a vector quantity that is a measure of the rotational momentum of a rotating body or system, that is equal in classical physics to the product of the angular velocity of the body and system and its moment of inertia with respect to the rotation axis, and that is directed along the rotation axis
angular velocity *n* (1819) : the rate of rotation around an axis usu. expressed in radians or revolutions per second or per minute
an·gu·la·tion \,aŋ-gyə-'lā-shən\ *n* (1869) **1** : the action of making angular **2** : an angular position, formation, or shape
An·gus \'aŋ-gəs\ *n* [*Angus*, county in Scotland] (1842) : any of a breed of usu. black hornless beef cattle originating in Scotland
an·he·do·nia \,an-(,)hē-'dō-nē-ə, -,nyə\ *n* [NL, fr. ²a- + Gk *hēdonē* pleasure — more at HEDONISM] (1897) : a psychological condition characterized by inability to experience pleasure in normally pleasurable acts — **an·he·don·ic** \-'dä-nik\ *adj*
an·hin·ga \an-'hiŋ-gə\ *n* [Pg, fr. Tupi] (1769) : any of a genus (*Anhinga*) of fish-eating birds related to the cormorants but distinguished by a longer neck and sharply pointed rather than hooked bill; *esp* : one (*A. anhinga*) occurring from the southern U.S. to Argentina
an·hy·dride \an-'hī-,drīd\ *n* (1863) : a compound derived from another (as an acid) by removal of the elements of water
an·hy·drite \-,drīt\ *n* [Gk *Anhydrit*, fr. Gk *anydros*] (ca. 1823) : a mineral consisting of an anhydrous calcium sulfate that is usu. massive and white or slightly colored
an·hy·drous \-drəs\ *adj* [Gk *anydros*, fr. *a-* + *hydōr* water — more at WATER] (1819) : free from water and esp. water of crystallization
ani \'ä-'nē\ *n* [Sp *aní*, or Pg *ani*, fr. Tupi *aní*] (ca. 1823) : any of a genus (*Crotophaga*) of black cuckoos of the warmer parts of America
anile \'ā-,nīl, 'ä-\ *adj* [L *anilis*, fr. *anus* old woman] (1652) : of or resembling a doddering old woman; *esp* : SENILE — **anil·i·ty** \a-'ni-lə-tē, ā-, ə-\ *n*
an·i·line \'a-nᵊl-ən\ *n* [G *Anilin*, fr. *Anil* indigo, fr. F, fr. Pg, fr. Ar *an-*

\ə\ abut \ᵊ\ kitten, F table \ər\ further \a\ ash \ā\ ace \ä\ mop, mar \aů\ out \ch\ chin \e\ bet \ē\ easy \g\ go \i\ hit \ī\ ice \j\ job \ŋ\ sing \ō\ go \ȯ\ law \ȯi\ boy \th\ thin \t̲h̲\ the \ü\ loot \ů\ foot \y\ yet \zh\ vision \à, ᵏ, ⁿ, œ, œ̄, ᵫ, ᵫ̄, ᶫ\ *see* Guide to Pronunciation *nil* the indigo plant, fr. Skt *nīlī* indigo, fr. fem. of *nila* dark blue] (1850) : an oily liquid poisonous amine $C_6H_5NH_2$ obtained esp. by the reduction of nitrobenzene and used chiefly in organic synthesis (as of dyes)

aniline dye *n* (1864) : a dye made by the use of aniline or one chemically related to such a dye; *broadly* : a synthetic organic dye

ani·lin·gus \ˌā-ni-ˈliŋ-gəs\ *or* **ani·linc·tus** \-ˈliŋ(k)-təs\ *n* [NL, fr. *anus* + -*i*- + -*lingus, -linctus* (as in *cunnilingus, cunnilinctus*)] (1949) : erotic stimulation achieved by contact between mouth and anus

an·i·ma \ˈa-nə-mə\ *n* [NL, fr. L, soul] (1923) : an individual's true inner self that in the analytic psychology of C. G. Jung reflects archetypal ideals of conduct; *also* : an inner feminine part of the male personality — compare ANIMUS, PERSONA

an·i·mad·ver·sion \ˌa-nə-ˌmad-ˈvər-zhən, -məd-, -ˈvər-shən\ *n* [L *animadversion-, animadversio,* fr. *animadvertere*] (1599) 1 : a critical and usu. censorious remark — often used with *on* 2 : adverse criticism

an·i·mad·vert \-ˈvərt\ *vb* [L *animadvertere* to pay attention to, censure, fr. *animum advertere,* lit., to turn the mind to] *vt* (15c) *archaic* : NOTICE, OBSERVE ~ *vi* : to make an animadversion

¹**an·i·mal** \ˈa-nə-məl\ *n* [L, fr. *animale,* neut. of *animalis* animate, fr. *anima* soul — more at ANIMATE] (14c) 1 : any of a kingdom (Animalia) of living things including many-celled organisms and often many of the single-celled ones (as protozoans) that typically differ from plants in having cells without cellulose walls, in lacking chlorophyll and the capacity for photosynthesis, in requiring more complex food materials (as proteins), in being organized to a greater degree of complexity, and in having the capacity for spontaneous movement and rapid motor responses to stimulation 2 a : one of the lower animals as distinguished from human beings b : MAMMAL; *broadly* : VERTEBRATE 3 : a human being considered chiefly as physical or nonrational; *also* : this nature 4 : an individual with a particular interest or aptitude (a political ~) 5 : MATTER, THING (the theater . . . is an entirely different ~ —Arthur Miller); *also* : CREATURE 1c — **an·i·mal·like** \-mə(l)-ˌlīk\ *adj*

²**animal** *adj* (1615) 1 : of, relating to, resembling, or derived from animals 2 a : of or relating to the physical or sentient as contrasted with the intellectual or rational b : SENSUAL, FLESHLY 3 : of or relating to the animal pole of an egg or to the part from which ectoderm normally develops *syn* see CARNAL — **an·i·mal·ly** \-mə-lē\ *adv*

animal control *n* (1957) : an office or department responsible for enforcing ordinances relating to the control, impoundment, and disposition of animals

animal cracker *n* (1898) : a small cookie in the shape of an animal

an·i·mal·cule \ˌa-nə-ˈmal-(ˌ)kyü(ə)l\ *also* **an·i·mal·cu·lum** \-ˈmal-kyə-ləm\ *n, pl* **-cules** *also* **-cu·la** \-kyə-lə\ [NL *animalculum,* dim. of L *animal*] (1662) : a minute usu. microscopic organism

animal heat *n* (1779) : heat produced in the body of a living animal by functional chemical and physical activities

animal husbandry *n* (1919) : a branch of agriculture concerned with the production and care of domestic animals

an·i·mal·ier \ˌa-nə-mə-ˈlir\ *n* [F, fr. *animal* animal, fr. L] (1912) : a sculptor or painter of animal subjects

an·i·mal·ism \ˈa-nə-mə-ˌli-zəm\ *n* (1831) : ANIMALITY — **an·i·mal·is·tic** \ˌa-nə-mə-ˈlis-tik\ *adj*

an·i·mal·i·ty \ˌa-nə-ˈma-lə-tē\ *n* (1615) 1 : qualities associated with animals: a : VITALITY b : a natural unrestrained unreasoned response to physical drives or stimuli 2 : the animal nature of human beings

an·i·mal·ize \ˈa-nə-mə-ˌlīz\ *vt* -**ized**; -**iz·ing** (1741) 1 : to represent in animal form 2 : to cause to be or act like an animal — **an·i·mal·iza·tion** \ˌa-nə-mə-lə-ˈzā-shən\ *n*

animal kingdom *n* (1776) : a basic group of natural objects that includes all living and extinct animals — compare MINERAL KINGDOM, PLANT KINGDOM

animal magnetism *n* (1784) 1 : a mysterious force claimed by Mesmer to enable him to hypnotize patients 2 : a magnetic charm or appeal; *esp* : SEX APPEAL

animal model *n* (1976) : an animal sufficiently like humans in its anatomy, physiology, or response to a pathogen to be used in medical research in order to obtain results that can be extrapolated to human medicine

animal pole *n* (1887) : the point on the surface of an egg that is diametrically opposite to the vegetal pole and usu. marks the most active part of the protoplasm or the part containing least yolk

animal rights *n pl but sing in constr* (1879) : fair and humane treatment of animals — often used attributively

animal spirits *n pl* (1543) 1 *sometimes* **animal spirit** *obs* : the nervous energy that is the source of physical sensation and movement 2 : vivacity arising from physical health and energy

animal starch *n* (ca. 1860) : GLYCOGEN

¹**an·i·mate** \ˈa-nə-mət\ *adj* [ME, fr. L *animatus,* pp. of *animare* to give life to, fr. *anima* breath, soul; akin to OE *ōthian* to breathe, L *animus* spirit, Gk *anemos* wind, Skt *aniti* he breathes] (15c) 1 : possessing or characterized by life : ALIVE 2 : full of life : ANIMATED 3 : of or relating to animal life as opposed to plant life 4 : referring to a living thing (an ~ noun) — **an·i·mate·ly** *adv* — **an·i·mate·ness** *n*

²**an·i·mate** \-ˌmāt\ *vt* -**mat·ed**; -**mat·ing** (15c) 1 : to give spirit and support to : ENCOURAGE 2 a : to give life to b : to give vigor and zest to 3 : to move to action 4 a : to make or design in such a way as to create apparently spontaneous lifelike movement b : to produce in the form of an animated cartoon *syn* see QUICKEN

an·i·mat·ed \-ˌmā-təd\ *adj* (1534) 1 : endowed with life or the qualities of life : ALIVE (viruses that can behave as ~ bodies or inert crystals) b : full of movement and activity c : full of vigor and spirit : LIVELY (an ~ discussion) 2 : having the appearance of something alive 3 : made in the form of an animated cartoon *syn* see LIVELY — **an·i·mat·ed·ly** *adv*

animated cartoon *n* (1915) 1 : a motion picture made from a series of drawings simulating motion by means of slight progressive changes in the drawings 2 : ANIMATION 2a

an·i·ma·tion \ˌa-nə-ˈmā-shən\ *n* (1597) 1 : the act of animating : the state of being animate or animated 2 a : a motion picture made by photographing successive positions of inanimate objects (as puppets or mechanical parts) b : ANIMATED CARTOON 1 3 : the preparation of animated cartoons

an·i·ma·to \ˌä-nə-ˈmä-(ˌ)tō, ˌa-\ *adv or adj* [It, fr. L *animatus*] (ca. 1724) : with animation — used as a direction in music

an·i·ma·tor \ˈa-nə-ˌmā-tər\ *n* (1611) 1 : one that animates (the prime ~ of the movement) 2 : an artist who creates drawings for an animated cartoon

an·i·mism \ˈa-nə-ˌmi-zəm\ *n* [G *Animismus,* fr. L *anima* soul] (1832) 1 : a doctrine that the vital principle of organic development is immaterial spirit 2 : attribution of conscious life to objects in and phenomena of nature or to inanimate objects 3 : belief in the existence of spirits separable from bodies — **an·i·mist** \-mist\ *n* — **an·i·mis·tic** \ˌa-nə-ˈmis-tik\ *adj*

an·i·mos·i·ty \ˌa-nə-ˈmä-sə-tē\ *n, pl* -**ties** [ME *animosite,* fr. MF or LL; MF *animosité,* fr. LL *animositat-, animositas,* fr. L *animosus* spirited, fr. *animus*] (1605) : ill will or resentment tending toward active hostility : an antagonistic attitude *syn* see ENMITY

an·i·mus \ˈa-nə-məs\ *n* [L, spirit, mind, courage, anger] (1816) 1 : basic attitude or governing spirit : DISPOSITION, INTENTION 2 : a usu. prejudiced and often spiteful or malevolent ill will 3 : an inner masculine part of the female personality in the analytic psychology of C. G. Jung — compare ANIMA — *syn* see ENMITY

an·ion \ˈa-ˌnī-ən\ *n* [Gk, neut. of *aniōn,* prp. of *anienai* to go up, fr. *ana-* + *ienai* to go — more at ISSUE] (1834) : the ion in an electrolyzed solution that migrates to the anode; *broadly* : a negatively charged ion

an·ion·ic \ˌa-(ˌ)nī-ˈä-nik\ *adj* (ca. 1920) 1 : of or relating to anions 2 : characterized by an active and esp. surface-active anion

anis- *or* **aniso-** *comb form* [NL, fr. Gk, fr. *anisos,* fr. *a-* + *isos* equal] : unequal (anisotropic)

an·ise \ˈa-nəs\ *n* [ME *anis,* fr. MF, fr. L *anisum,* fr. Gk *annēson, anison*] (14c) : an herb (*Pimpinella anisum*) of the carrot family having carminative and aromatic seeds; *also* : ANISEED

ani·seed \ˈa-nə(s)-ˌsēd\ *n* [ME *anis seed,* fr. *anis* + *seed*] (14c) : the seed of anise often used as a flavoring in liqueurs and in cooking

an·is·ei·ko·nia \ˌa-ˌnī-ˌsī-ˈkō-nē-ə\ *n* [NL, fr. *anis-* + Gk *eikōn* image — more at ICON] (1934) : a defect of binocular vision in which the two retinal images of an object differ in size — **an·is·ei·kon·ic** \-ˈkä-nik\ *adj*

an·is·ette \ˌa-nə-ˈset, -ˈzet\ *n* [F, fr. *anis*] (1837) : a usu. colorless sweet liqueur flavored with aniseed

an·isog·a·mous \ˌa-(ˌ)nī-ˈsä-gə-məs\ *adj* (1891) : characterized by fusion of heterogamous gametes or of individuals that usu. differ chiefly in size (~ reproduction) — **an·isog·a·my** \-ˈsä-gə-mē\ *n*

an·iso·me·tro·pia \ˌa-ˌnī-sə-mə-ˈtrō-pē-ə\ *n* [NL, fr. Gk *anisometros* of unequal measure (fr. *anis-* + *metron* measure) + NL *-opia* — more at MEASURE] (ca. 1880) : unequal refractive power in the two eyes — **an·iso·me·tro·pic** \-ˈträ-pik, -ˈtrō-\ *adj*

an·iso·trop·ic \ˌa-ˌnī-sə-ˈträ-pik\ *adj* (1879) : exhibiting properties with different values when measured in different directions (an ~ crystal) — **an·iso·trop·i·cal·ly** \-pi-k(ə-)lē\ *adv* — **an·isot·ro·py** \-(ˌ)nī-ˈsä-trə-pē\ *also* **an·isot·ro·pism** \-ˌpi-zəm\ *n*

an·ker·ite \ˈaŋ-kə-ˌrīt\ *n* [G *Ankerit,* fr. M. J. *Anker* †1843 Austrian mineralogist] (ca. 1843) : a dolomitic iron-containing mineral

ankh \ˈäŋk\ *n* [Egypt '*nh* live] (1888) : a cross having a loop for its upper vertical arm and serving esp. in ancient Egypt as an emblem of life

an·kle \ˈaŋ-kəl\ *n* [ME *ankel,* fr. OE *anclēow;* akin to OHG *anchlāo* ankle] (bef. 12c) 1 : the joint between the foot and the leg; *also* : the region of this joint 2 : the joint between the cannon bone and pastern (as in the horse)

an·kle·bone \ˈaŋ-kəl-ˌbōn, ˌaŋ-kəl-\ *n* (14c) : ²TALUS 1

an·klet \ˈaŋ-klət\ *n* (1819) 1 : something (as an ornament) worn around the ankle 2 : a short sock reaching slightly above the ankle

ankh

an·ky·lo·saur \ˈaŋ-kə-lō-ˌsȯr\ *n* [NL *Ankylosauria,* fr. *Ankylosaurus*] (1949) : any of a suborder (Ankylosauria) of herbivorous Cretaceous dinosaurs having a long low-lying thickset body covered dorsally with bony plates

an·ky·lo·sau·rus \ˌaŋ-kə-lō-ˈsȯr-əs\ *n* [NL, genus name, fr. Gk *ankylos* + *sauros* lizard] (1908) : any of a No. American genus (*Ankylosaurus*) of large ankylosaurs having a bony club at the end of the tail

an·ky·lose \ˈaŋ-ki-ˌlōs, -ˌlōz\ *vb* -**losed**; -**los·ing** [back-formation fr. *ankylosis*] *vt* (1787) : to unite or stiffen by ankylosis ~ *vi* : to undergo ankylosis

an·ky·lo·sis \ˌaŋ-ki-ˈlō-səs\ *n, pl* -**lo·ses** \-ˌsēz\ [NL, fr. Gk *ankylōsis,* fr. *ankyloun* to make crooked, fr. *ankylos* crooked — more at ANGLE] (1713) 1 : stiffness or fixation of a joint by disease or surgery 2 : union of separate bones or hard parts to form a single bone or part — **an·ky·lot·ic** \-ˈlä-tik\ *adj*

an·ky·lo·sto·mi·a·sis \ˌaŋ-ki-lō-stə-ˈmī-ə-səs\ *var of* ANCYLOSTOMIASIS

an·la·ge \ˈän-ˌlä-gə\ *n, pl* -**gen** \-gən\ *also* -**ges** \-gəz\ [G, lit., act of laying on] (1892) : the foundation of a subsequent development; *esp* : PRIMORDIUM

an·na \ˈä-nə\ *n* [Hindi *ānā*] (1708) 1 : a former monetary unit of Burma, India, and Pakistan equal to ¹/₁₆ rupee 2 : a coin representing one anna

an·nal·ist \ˈa-nᵊl-ist\ *n* (ca. 1611) : a writer of annals : CHRONICLER — **an·nal·is·tic** \ˌa-nᵊl-ˈis-tik\ *adj*

an·nals \ˈa-nᵊlz\ *n pl* [L *annales,* fr. pl. of *annalis* yearly — more at ANNUAL] (1542) 1 : a record of events arranged in yearly sequence 2 : historical records : CHRONICLES 3 : records of the activities of an organization

An·nam·ese \ˌa-nə-ˈmēz, -ˈmēs\ *n, pl* **Annamese** [*Annam,* region of Vietnam] (1826) 1 *or* **An·nam·ite** \ˈa-nə-ˌmīt\ : a native or inhabitant of Annam 2 : VIETNAMESE 2 — **Annamese** *adj* — **Annamite** *adj*

an·nat·to \ə-ˈnä-(ˌ)tō\ *n* [Carib *annoto* tree producing annatto] (1629) : a yellowish red dyestuff made from the pulp around the seeds of a tropical tree (*Bixa orellana,* family Bixaceae); *also* : the tree that yields annatto

an·neal \ə-ˈnē(ə)l\ *vb* [ME *anelen* to set on fire, fr. OE *onǣlan,* fr. *on* + *ǣlan* to set on fire, burn, fr. *āl* fire; akin to OE *ǣled* fire, ON *eldr*] *vt* (1664) 1 a : to heat and then cool (as steel or glass) usu. for softening and making less brittle; *also* : to cool slowly usu. in a furnace b : to heat and then cool (nucleic acid) in order to separate strands and induce combination at lower temperature esp. with complementary strands of a different species   **2** : STRENGTHEN, TOUGHEN   ~ *vi* : to be capable of combining with complementary nucleic acid by a process of heating and cooling

an·ne·lid \'a-n^ə-l-əd, 'a-nə-,lid\ *n* [ultim. fr. L *anellus* little ring — more at ANNULET] (1834) : any of a phylum (Annelida) of usu. elongated segmented coelomate invertebrates (as earthworms, various marine worms, and leeches) — **annelid** *adj* — **an·nel·i·dan** \ə-'ne-lə-dᵊn, a-\ *adj or n*

¹an·nex \ə-'neks, 'a-,neks\ *vt* [ME, fr. MF *annexer*, fr. OF, fr. *annexe* joined, fr. L *annexus*, pp. of *annectere* to bind to, fr. *ad-* + *nectere* to bind] (14c)   **1** : to attach as a quality, consequence, or condition   **2** *archaic* : to join together materially : UNITE   **3** : to add to something earlier, larger, or more important   **4** : to incorporate (a country or other territory) within the domain of a state   **5** : to obtain or take for oneself — **an·nex·ation** \,a-,nek-'sā-shən\ *n* — **an·nex·ation·al** \-shnəl, -shə-nᵊl\ *adj* — **an·nex·ation·ist** \-sh(ə-)nist\ *n*

²an·nex \'a-,neks, -niks\ *n* (1501) : something annexed as an expansion or supplement: as   **a** : an added stipulation or statement : APPENDIX   **b** : a subsidiary or supplementary structure : WING

an·nexe \'a-,neks, -niks\ *chiefly Brit var of* ²ANNEX

An·nie Oak·ley \,a-nē-'ō-klē\ *n, pl* **Annie Oakleys** [*Annie Oakley* †1926 Am. markswoman; fr. the resemblance of a punched pass to a playing card with bullet holes through the spots] (ca. 1910) : a free ticket

an·ni·hi·late \ə-'nī-ə-,lāt\ *vb* **-lat·ed; -lat·ing** [LL *annihilatus*, pp. of *annihilare* to reduce to nothing, fr. L *ad-* + *nihil* nothing — more at NIL] *vt* (1525)   **1 a** : to cause to be of no effect : NULLIFY   **b** : to destroy the substance or force of   **2** : to regard as of no consequence   **3** : to cause to cease to exist; *esp* : KILL   **4 a** : to destroy a considerable part of ⟨bombs *annihilated* the city⟩   **b** : to vanquish completely : ROUT ⟨*annihilated* the visitors 56–0⟩ — ~ *vi, of a particle and its antiparticle* : to vanish or cease to exist by coming together and changing into other forms of energy (as radiation or particles) — **an·ni·hi·la·tion** \-,nī-ə-'lā-shən\ *n* — **an·ni·hi·la·tor** \-,lā-tər\ *n* — **an·ni·hi·la·to·ry** \-'nī-ə-lə-,tōr-ē, -,tór-\ *adj*

an·ni·ver·sa·ry \,a-nə-'vərs-rē, -'vər-sə-\ *n, pl* **-ries** [ME *anniversarie*, fr. ML *anniversarium*, fr. L, neut. of *anniversarius* returning annually, fr. *annus* year + *versus*, pp. of *vertere* to turn — more at ANNUAL, WORTH] (13c)   **1** : the annual recurrence of a date marking a notable event   **2** : the celebration of an anniversary

an·no Do·mi·ni \,a-(,)nō-'dä-mə-nē, -'dō-, -,nī\ *adv, often cap A* [ML, in the year of the Lord] (1530) — used to indicate that a time division falls within the Christian era

an·no he·gi·rae \-hi-'ji-(,)rē, -'he-jə-,rē\ *adv, often cap A&H* [NL, in the year of the Hegira] (ca. 1889) — used to indicate that a time division falls within the Islamic era

an·no·tate \'a-nə-,tāt\ *vb* **-tat·ed; -tat·ing** [L *annotatus*, pp. of *annotare*, fr. *ad-* + *notare* to mark — more at NOTE] *vi* (1733) : to make or furnish critical or explanatory notes or comment   ~ *vt* : to make or furnish annotations for (as a literary work or subject) — **an·no·ta·tive** \-,tā-tiv\ *adj* — **an·no·ta·tor** \-,tā-tər\ *n*

an·no·ta·tion \,a-nə-'tā-shən\ *n* (15c)   **1** : a note added by way of comment or explanation   **2** : the act of annotating

an·nounce \ə-'naún(t)s\ *vb* **-nounced; -nounc·ing** [ME, fr. MF *annoncer*, fr. L *annuntiare*, fr. *ad-* + *nuntiare* to report, fr. *nuntius* messenger] *vt* (15c)   **1** : to make known publicly : PROCLAIM ⟨*announced* the appointment⟩   **2 a** : to give notice of the arrival, presence, or readiness of ⟨~ dinner⟩   **b** : to indicate beforehand : FORETELL   **3** : to serve as an announcer of ~ *vi* : to serve as an announcer   **2 a** : to declare one's candidacy   **b** : to declare oneself politically — used with *for* or *against*   *syn* see DECLARE

an·nounce·ment \ə-'naún(t)-smənt\ *n* (1798)   **1** : the act of announcing or of being announced   **2** : a public notification or declaration   **3** : a piece of formal stationery designed for a social or business announcement

an·nounc·er \ə-'naún(t)-sər\ *n* (ca. 1611) : one that announces: as   **a** : a person who introduces television or radio programs, makes commercial announcements, or gives station identification   **b** : a person who describes and comments on the action in a broadcast sports event

an·noy \ə-'nói\ *vb* [ME *anoien*, fr. MF *enuier*, fr. LL *inodiare* to make loathsome, fr. L *in* + *odium* hatred — more at ODIUM] *vt* (13c)   **1** : to disturb or irritate esp. by repeated acts   **2** : to harass esp. by quick brief attacks   ~ *vi* : to cause annoyance — **an·noy·er** *n*
   syn ANNOY, VEX, IRK, BOTHER mean to upset a person's composure. ANNOY implies a wearing on the nerves by persistent petty unpleasantness ⟨their constant complaining *annoys* us⟩. VEX implies greater provocation and stronger disturbance and usu. connotes anger but sometimes perplexity or anxiety ⟨*vexed* by her teenager's failure to pick up his room⟩. IRK stresses difficulty in enduring and the resulting weariness or impatience of spirit ⟨careless waste *irks* the boss⟩. BOTHER suggests interference with comfort or peace of mind ⟨don't *bother* me while I'm reading⟩.   *syn* see in addition WORRY

an·noy·ance \ə-'nói-ən(t)s\ *n* (14c)   **1** : the act of annoying or of being annoyed   **2** : the state or feeling of being annoyed : VEXATION   **3** : a source of vexation or irritation : NUISANCE

an·noy·ing *adj* (14c) : causing vexation : IRRITATING — **an·noy·ing·ly** \-iŋ-lē\ *adv*

¹an·nu·al \'an-yə(-wə)l\ *adj* [ME, fr. MF & LL; MF *annuel*, fr. LL *annualis*, blend of L *annuus* yearly (fr. *annus* year) and L *annalis* yearly (fr. *annus* year); prob. akin to Goth *athnam* (dat. pl.) years, Skt *atati* he walks, goes] (14c)   **1** : covering the period of a year ⟨~ rainfall⟩   **2** : occurring or happening every year or once a year : YEARLY ⟨an ~ reunion⟩   **3** : completing the life cycle in one growing season — **an·nu·al·ly** *adv*

²annual *n* (14c)   **1** : an event that occurs yearly   **2** : a publication appearing yearly   **3** : something that lasts one year or season; *specif* : an annual plant

an·nu·al·ize \'an-yə-(-wə)-,līz\ *vt* **-ized; -iz·ing** (1918) : to calculate or adjust to reflect a rate based on a full year ⟨quarterly returns yielding at an *annualized* rate of 7 percent⟩

annual ring *n* (ca. 1879) : the layer of wood produced by a single year's growth of a woody plant

an·nu·itant \ə-'nü-ət-ənt, -'nyü-\ *n* (1720) : a beneficiary of an annuity

an·nu·ity \ə-'nü-ə-tē, -'nyü-\ *n, pl* **-ities** [ME *annuite*, fr. MF *annuité*,

fr. ML *annuitat-, annuitas,* fr. L *annuus* yearly] (15c)   **1** : a sum of money payable yearly or at other regular intervals   **2** : the right to receive an annuity   **3** : a contract or agreement providing for the payment of an annuity

an·nul \ə-'nəl\ *vt* **an·nulled; an·nul·ling** [ME *annullen*, fr. MF *annuller*, fr. LL *annullare*, fr. L *ad-* + *nullus* not any — more at NULL] (15c)   **1** : to reduce to nothing : OBLITERATE   **2** : to make ineffective or inoperative : NEUTRALIZE ⟨~ the drug's effect⟩   **3** : to declare or make legally invalid or void ⟨wants the marriage *annulled*⟩   *syn* see NULLIFY

an·nu·lar \'an-yə-lər\ *adj* [MF or ML; MF *annulaire*, fr. ML *anularis,* fr. L *anulus*] (1571) : of, relating to, or forming a ring ⟨an ~ skin lesion⟩

annular eclipse *n* (1771) : an eclipse in which a thin outer ring of the sun's disk is not covered by the apparently smaller dark disk of the moon

an·nu·late \'an-yə-lət, -,lāt\ *adj* (ca. 1823) : furnished with or composed of rings : RINGED

an·nu·la·tion \,an-yə-'lā-shən\ *n* (1829) : a ringlike anatomical structure

an·nu·let \'an-yə-lət\ *n* [modif. of MF *annelet,* dim. of *anel,* fr. L *anellus,* dim. of *anulus*] (1598)   **1** : a little ring   **2** : a small architectural molding or ridge forming a ring

an·nul·ment \ə-'nəl-mənt\ *n* (15c)   **1** : the act of annulling : the state of being annulled   **2** : a judicial pronouncement declaring a marriage invalid

an·nu·lus \'an-yə-ləs\ *n, pl* **-li** \-,lī, -(,)lē\ *also* **-lus·es** [ML, L *anulus* finger ring, fr. *anus* ring — more at ANUS] (1563)   **1** : RING   **2** : a part, structure, or marking resembling a ring: as   **a** : a line of cells around a fern sporangium that ruptures the sporangium by contracting   **b** : a growth ring (as on the scale of a fish) that is used in estimating age

an·nun·ci·ate \ə-'nən(t)-sē-,āt\ *vt* **-at·ed; -at·ing** (ca. 1536) : ANNOUNCE

an·nun·ci·a·tion \ə-,nən(t)-sē-'ā-shən\ *n* [ME *annunciacioun,* fr. MF *anunciation,* fr. LL *annuntiation-, annuntiatio,* fr. L *annuntiare* — more at ANNOUNCE] (14c)   **1** *cap* : March 25 observed as a church festival in commemoration of the announcement of the Incarnation to the Virgin Mary   **2** : the act of announcing or of being announced : ANNOUNCEMENT

an·nun·ci·a·tor \ə-'nən(t)-sē-,ā-tər\ *n* (ca. 1753) : one that annunciates; *specif* : a usu. electrically controlled signal board or indicator — **an·nun·ci·a·to·ry** \-sē-ə-,tōr-ē, -,tór-\ *adj*

an·nus mi·ra·bi·lis \,a-nəs-mə-'rä-bə-ləs, ,ä-\ *n, pl* **an·ni mi·ra·bi·les** \'a-,nī-mə-'rä-bə-,lāz, 'ä-(,)nē-mə-'rä-bə-,läs\ [NL, lit., wonderful year] (1660) : a remarkable or notable year

an·ode \'a-,nōd\ *n* [Gk *anodos* way up, fr. *ana-* + *hodos* way] (1834)   **1** : the electrode of an electrochemical cell at which oxidation occurs: as   **a** : the positive terminal of an electrolytic cell   **b** : the negative terminal of a galvanic cell   **2** : the electron-collecting electrode of an electron tube — compare CATHODE — **an·od·ic** \a-'nä-dik\ *also* **an·od·al** \-'nō-dᵊl\ *adj* — **an·od·i·cal·ly** \-di-k(ə-)lē\ *also* **an·od·al·ly** \-dᵊl-ē\ *adv*

an·od·ize \'a-nə-,dīz\ *vt* **-ized; -iz·ing** (1931) : to subject (a metal) to electrolytic action as the anode of a cell in order to coat with a protective or decorative film — **an·od·iza·tion** \,a-,nō-də-'zā-shən, ,a-nə-\ *n*

¹an·o·dyne \'a-nə-,dīn\ *adj* [L *anodynos,* fr. Gk *anōdynos, a-* + *odynē* pain; prob. akin to OE *etan* to eat] (1543)   **1** : serving to assuage pain   **2** : not likely to offend or arouse tensions : INNOCUOUS

²anodyne *n* (ca. 1550)   **1** : something that soothes, calms, or comforts ⟨the ~ of bridge, a comfortable book, or sport —Harrison Smith⟩   **2** : a drug that allays pain

anoint \ə-'nóint\ *vt* [ME, fr. MF *enoint,* pp. of *enoindre,* fr. L *inunguere,* fr. *in-* + *unguere* to smear — more at OINTMENT] (14c)   **1** : to smear or rub with oil or an oily substance   **2 a** : to apply oil to as a sacred rite esp. for consecration   **b** : to choose by or as if by divine election; *also* : to designate as if by a ritual anointment — **anoint·er** *n* — **anoint·ment** \-mənt\ *n*

anointing of the sick (ca. 1884) : EXTREME UNCTION

ano·le \ə-'nō-lē\ *n* [prob. fr. F *anolis,* fr. Arawak of the Lesser Antilles] (ca. 1753): any of a genus (*Anolis* of the family Iguanidae) of arboreal American lizards (as the American chameleon) that have a brightly colored dewlap and the ability to change color

anom·a·lous \ə-'nä-mə-ləs\ *adj* [LL *anomalus,* fr. Gk *anōmalos,* lit., uneven, fr. *a-* + *homalos* even, fr. *homos* same — more at SAME] (1655)   **1** : inconsistent with or deviating from what is usual, normal, or expected : IRREGULAR, UNUSUAL   **2 a** : of uncertain nature or classification   **b** : marked by incongruity or contradiction : PARADOXICAL   *syn* see IRREGULAR — **anom·a·lous·ly** *adv* — **anom·a·lous·ness** *n*

anom·a·ly \ə-'nä-mə-lē\ *n, pl* **-lies** (1603)   **1** : the angular distance of a planet from its perihelion as seen from the sun   **2** : deviation from the common rule : IRREGULARITY   **3** : something different, abnormal, peculiar, or not easily classified

an·o·mie *also* **an·o·my** \'a-nə-mē\ *n* [F *anomie,* fr. MF, fr. Gk *anomia* lawlessness, fr. *anomos* lawless, fr. *a-* + *nomos* law, fr. *nemein* to distribute — more at NIMBLE] (1933) : social instability resulting from a breakdown of standards and values; *also* : personal unrest, alienation, and uncertainty that comes from a lack of purpose or ideals — **ano·mic** \a-'nä-mik, -'nō-\ *adj*

anon \ə-'nän\ *adv* [ME, fr. OE *on ān,* fr. *on* in + *ān* one — more at ON, ONE] (bef. 12c)   **1** *archaic* : at once : IMMEDIATELY   **2** : SOON, PRESENTLY   **3** : after a while : LATER

an·o·nym \'a-nə-,nim\ *n* (1812)   **1** : one who is anonymous   **2** : PSEUDONYM

an·o·nym·i·ty \,a-nə-'ni-mə-tē\ *n, pl* **-ties** (1820)   **1** : the quality or state of being anonymous   **2** : one that is anonymous

anon·y·mous \ə-'nä-nə-məs\ *adj* [LL *anonymus,* fr. Gk *anōnymos,* fr. *a-* + *onyma* name — more at NAME] (1631)   **1** : not named or identified ⟨an ~ author⟩ ⟨they wish to remain ~⟩   **2** : of unknown author-

\ə\ abut \ᵊ\ kitten, F table \ər\ further \a\ ash \ā\ ace \ä\ mop, mar \aú\ out \ch\ chin \e\ bet \ē\ easy \g\ go \i\ hit \ī\ ice \j\ job \ŋ\ sing \ō\ go \ó\ law \ói\ boy \th\ thin \t̲h̲\ the \ü\ loot \ú\ foot \y\ yet \zh\ vision \a, k, ⁿ, œ, œ̄, ᵫ, ᵫ̄, ᵊ\ *see* Guide to Pronunciation ship or origin ⟨an ∼ tip⟩ **3** : lacking individuality, distinction, or recognizability ⟨the ∼ faces in the crowd⟩ ⟨the gray ∼ streets —William Styron⟩ — **anon·y·mous·ly** adv — **anon·y·mous·ness** n

anoph·e·les \ə-'nä-fə-ˌlēz\ n [NL, genus name, fr. Gk anōphelēs useless, fr. a- + ophelos advantage, help; akin to Gk ophellein to increase, Arm aweli more] (1899) : any of a genus (Anopheles) of mosquitoes that includes all mosquitoes which transmit malaria to humans — **anoph·e·line** \-ˌlīn\ adj or n

an·o·rak \'a-nə-ˌrak\ n [Dan, fr. Inuit (Greenland) annoraaq] (1922) : a usu. pullover hooded jacket long enough to cover the hips

¹an·o·rec·tic \ˌa-nə-'rek-tik\ also **an·o·ret·ic** \-'re-tik\ adj [Gk anorektos, fr. a- + oregein to reach after — more at RIGHT] (ca. 1894) **1 a** : lacking appetite **b** : ANOREXIC 2 **2** : causing loss of appetite

²anorectic also **anoretic** n (ca. 1957) **1** : an anorectic agent **2** : AN-OREXIC

an·orex·ia \ˌa-nə-'rek-sē-ə, -'rek-shə\ n [NL, fr. Gk, fr. a- + orexis appetite, fr. oregein] (1598) **1** : loss of appetite esp. when prolonged **2** : ANOREXIA NERVOSA

anorexia ner·vo·sa \-(ˌ)nər-'vō-sə, -zə\ n [NL, nervous anorexia] (1873) : a serious disorder in eating behavior primarily of young women in their teens and early twenties that is characterized esp. by a pathological fear of weight gain leading to faulty eating patterns, malnutrition, and usu. excessive weight loss

¹an·orex·ic \-'rek-sik\ adj (ca. 1907) **1** : ANORECTIC **2** : affected with or as if with anorexia nervosa

²anorexic n (1912) : a person affected with anorexia nervosa

an·orex·i·gen·ic \ˌa-nə-ˌrek-sə-'ge-nik\ adj (1948) : ANORECTIC 2

an·or·thite \ə-'nór-ˌthīt\ n [F, fr. a- + Gk orthos straight] (1833) : a white, grayish, or reddish feldspar occurring in many igneous rocks — **an·or·thit·ic** \ˌa-nór-'thi-tik\ adj

an·or·tho·site \ə-'nór-thə-ˌsīt\ n [F anorthose, a feldspar, fr. a- + Gk orthos — more at ORTH-] (1863) : a granular plutonic igneous rock composed almost exclusively of a soda-lime feldspar (as labradorite) — **an·or·tho·si·tic** \-ˌnór-thə-'si-tik\ adj

an·os·mia \a-'näz-mē-ə\ n [NL, fr. a- + Gk osmē smell — more at ODOR] (ca. 1811) : loss or impairment of the sense of smell — **an·os·mic** \-mik\ adj

¹an·oth·er \ə-'nə-thər also a- or ā-\ adj (12c) **1** : different or distinct from the one first considered ⟨the same scene viewed from ∼ angle⟩ **2** : some other ⟨do it ∼ time⟩ **3** : being one more in addition to one or more of the same kind ⟨have ∼ piece of pie⟩

²another pron (13c) **1** : an additional one of the same kind : one more **2** : one that is different from the first or present one **3** : one of a group of unspecified or indefinite things ⟨in one way or ∼⟩

anoth·er–guess \ə-'nə-thər-ˌges\ adj [alter. of anothergates, fr. ¹another + gate] (1644) archaic : of another sort

an·ovu·la·to·ry \(ˌ)an-'äv-yə-lə-ˌtōr-ē, -'öv-, -ˌtor-\ adj (1934) **1** : not involving or accompanied by ovulation ⟨∼ bleeding⟩ **2** : suppressing ovulation

an·ox·emia \ˌa-ˌnäk-'sē-mē-ə\ n [NL] (ca. 1881) : a condition of subnormal oxygenation of the arterial blood — **an·ox·emic** \-mik\ adj

an·ox·ia \a-'näk-sē-ə\ n [NL] (1931) : hypoxia esp. of such severity as to result in permanent damage

an·ox·ic \(ˌ)a-'näk-sik\ adj (1920) **1** : of, relating to, or affected with anoxia **2** : greatly deficient in oxygen : OXYGENLESS ⟨∼ water⟩

an·ser·ine \'an(t)-sə-ˌrīn\ adj [L anserinus, fr. anser goose — more at GOOSE] (ca. 1828) : of, relating to, or resembling a goose

¹an·swer \'an(t)-sər\ n [ME, fr. OE andswaru (akin to ON andsvar answer); akin to OE and- against, swerian to swear — more at ANTE-] (bef. 12c) **1 a** : something spoken or written in reply to a question **b** : a correct response **2** : a reply to a legal charge or suit : PLEA; also : DEFENSE **3** : something done in response or reaction ⟨his only ∼ was to walk out⟩ **4** : a solution of a problem **5** : one that imitates, matches, or corresponds to another ⟨television's ∼ to the news magazines⟩

²answer vb **an·swered; an·swer·ing** \'an(t)s-riŋ, 'an(t)-sə-\ vi (bef. 12c) **1** : to speak or write in reply **2 a** : to be or make oneself responsible or accountable **b** : to make amends : ATONE **3** : to be in conformity or correspondence ⟨∼ed to the description⟩ **4** : to act in response to an action performed elsewhere by another **5** : to be adequate : SERVE ∼ vt **1 a** : to speak or write in reply to **b** : to say or write by way of reply **2** : to reply in rebuttal, justification, or explanation **3 a** : to correspond to ⟨∼s the description⟩ **b** : to be adequate or usable for : FULFILL **4** obs : to atone for **5** : to act in response to ⟨∼ed the call to arms⟩ **6** : to offer a solution for; esp : SOLVE — **an·swer·er** \'an(t)-sər-ər\ n

syn ANSWER, RESPOND, REPLY, REJOIN, RETORT mean to say, write, or do something in return. ANSWER implies the satisfying of a question, demand, call, or need ⟨answered all the questions⟩. RESPOND may suggest an immediate or quick reaction ⟨responded eagerly to a call for volunteers⟩. REPLY implies making a return commensurate with the original question or demand ⟨an invitation that requires you to reply⟩. REJOIN often implies sharpness or quickness in answering ⟨"who asked you?" she rejoined⟩. RETORT suggests responding to an explicit charge or criticism by way of retaliation ⟨he retorted to the attack with biting sarcasm⟩.

an·swer·able \'an(t)s-rə-bəl, 'an(t)-sə-\ adj (1536) **1** archaic : SUITABLE, ADEQUATE **2** : liable to be called to account : RESPONSIBLE **3** archaic : CORRESPONDING, SIMILAR **4** : capable of being refuted **syn** see RESPONSIBLE

answering machine n (1961) : a machine that receives telephone calls by playing a recorded message and usu. by recording messages from callers

answering service n (1941) : a commercial service that answers telephone calls for its clients

ant \'ant\ n [ME ante, emete, fr. OE æmette; akin to OHG āmeiza ant] (bef. 12c) : any of a family (Formicidae) of colonial hymenopterous insects with a complex social organization and various castes performing special duties — **ants in one's pants** : impatience for action or activity : RESTLESSNESS

ant- — see ANTI-

¹-ant n suffix [ME, fr. OF, fr. -ant, prp. suffix, fr. L -ant-, -ans, prp. suffix of first conjugation, fr. -a- (stem vowel of first conjugation) + -nt-, -ns, prp. suffix; akin to OE -nde, prp. suffix, Gk -nt-, -n, part. suf-

fix] **1 a** : one that performs (a specified action) : personal or impersonal agent ⟨claimant⟩ ⟨coolant⟩ **b** : thing that promotes (a specified action or process) ⟨expectorant⟩ **2** : one connected with ⟨annuitant⟩ **3** : thing acted upon (in a specified manner) ⟨inhalant⟩

²-ant adj suffix **1** : performing (a specified action) or being (in a specified condition) ⟨somnambulant⟩ **2** : promoting (a specified action or process) ⟨expectorant⟩

an·ta \'an-tə\ n, pl **antas** or **an·tae** \-ˌtē, -ˌtī\ [L; akin to ON ǫnd anteroom] (1598) : a pier produced by thickening a wall at its termination

ant·ac·id \(ˌ)ant-'a-səd, 'an-ˌta-\ n (1732) : an agent that counteracts or neutralizes acidity — **antacid** adj

A anta

An·tae·an \an-'tē-ən\ adj [Antaeus, a giant overcome by Hercules] (1921) **1** : MAMMOTH **2** : having superhuman strength

an·tag·o·nism \an-'ta-gə-ˌni-zəm\ n (ca. 1828) **1 a** : opposition of a conflicting force, tendency, or principle ⟨the ∼ of democracy to dictatorship⟩ **b** : actively expressed opposition or hostility ⟨∼ between factions⟩ **2** : opposition in physiological action; esp : interaction of two or more substances such that the action of any one of them on living cells or tissues is lessened **syn** see ENMITY

an·tag·o·nist \-nist\ n (1594) **1** : one that contends with or opposes another : ADVERSARY, OPPONENT **2** : an agent of physiological antagonism: as **a** : a muscle that contracts with and limits the action of an agonist with which it is paired — called also antagonistic muscle **b** : a chemical that acts within the body to reduce the physiological activity of another chemical substance (as an opiate); esp : one that opposes the action on the nervous system of a drug or a substance occurring naturally in the body by combining with and blocking its nervous receptor — compare AGONIST 2b

an·tag·o·nis·tic \(ˌ)an-ˌta-gə-'nis-tik\ adj (1632) : marked by or resulting from antagonism — **an·tag·o·nis·ti·cal·ly** \-ti-k(ə-)lē\ adv

an·tag·o·nize \an-'ta-gə-ˌnīz\ vt **-nized; -niz·ing** [Gk antagōnizesthai, fr. anti- + agōnizesthai to struggle, fr. agōn contest — more at AGONY] (ca. 1742) **1** : to act in opposition to : COUNTERACT **2** : to incur or provoke the hostility of

ant·arc·tic \(ˌ)an-'tärk-tik, -'är-tik\ adj, often cap [ME antartik, fr. L antarcticus, fr. Gk antarktikos, fr. anti- + arktikos arctic] (14c) : of or relating to the south pole or to the region near it

antarctic circle n, often cap A&C (1556) : the parallel of latitude that is approximately 66½ degrees south of the equator and that circumscribes the southern frigid zone

An·tar·es \an-'tar-(ˌ)ēz, -'ter-\ n [Gk Antarēs] : a giant red star of very low density that is the brightest star in Scorpio

ant·bear \'ant-ˌbar, -ˌber\ n (ca. 1889) : AARDVARK

ant cow n (1875) : an aphid from which ants obtain honeydew

¹an·te \'an-tē\ n [ante-] (1838) **1** : a poker stake usu. put up before the deal to build the pot ⟨the dealer called for a dollar ∼⟩ **2** : COST, PRICE ⟨these improvements would raise the ∼⟩

²ante vb **an·ted; an·te·ing** vt (1845) : to put up (an ante); also : PAY, PRODUCE — often used with up ∼ vi : PAY UP — often used with up

ante- prefix [ME, fr. L, fr. ante before, in front; akin to OE and- against, Gk anti before, against — more at END] **1 a** : prior : earlier ⟨antedate⟩ **b** : anterior : forward ⟨antecommon⟩ **2 a** : prior to : earlier than ⟨antediluvian⟩ **b** : in front of ⟨antechoir⟩

ant·eat·er \'ant-ˌē-tər\ n (1764) : any of several mammals that feed largely or entirely on ants or termites: as **a** : any of a family (Myrmecophagidae) of New World edentates with a long narrow snout, a long tongue, and large salivary glands that includes the giant anteater and tamandua **b** : PANGOLIN **c** : ECHIDNA **d** : AARDVARK

an·te·bel·lum \ˌan-ti-'be-ləm\ adj [L ante bellum before the war] (ca. 1847) : existing before a war; esp : existing before the Civil War

an·te·cede \ˌan-tə-'sēd\ vt **-ced·ed; -ced·ing** [L antecedere] (1624) : PRECEDE

an·te·ced·ence \-'sē-dᵊn(t)s\ n (1651) : PRIORITY, PRECEDENCE

¹an·te·ced·ent \ˌan-tə-'sē-dᵊnt\ n [ME, fr. ML & L; ML antecedent-, antecedens, fr. L, what precedes, fr. neut. of antecedent-, antecedens, prp. of antecedere to go before, fr. ante- + cedere to go] (14c) **1 a** : a substantive word, phrase, or clause whose denotation is referred to by a pronoun (as John in "Mary saw John and called to him"); broadly : a word or phrase replaced by a substitute **2** : the conditional element in a proposition (as if A in "if A, then B") **3** : the first term of a mathematical ratio **4 a** : a preceding event, condition, or cause **b** pl : the significant events, conditions, and traits of one's earlier life **5 a** : PREDECESSOR; esp : a model or stimulus for later developments **b** pl : ANCESTORS, PARENTS

²antecedent adj (14c) : PRIOR **syn** see PRECEDING — **an·te·ced·ent·ly** adv

an·te·ces·sor \ˌan-ti-'se-sər\ n [ME antecessour, fr. L antecessor — more at ANCESTOR] (14c) : one that goes before : PREDECESSOR

an·te·cham·ber \'an-ti-ˌchām-bər\ n [F antichambre, fr. MF, fr. It anticamera (fr. L ante-) + MF chambre room] (ca. 1656) : ANTEROOM

an·te·chap·el \-ˌcha-pəl\ n (1703) : a vestibule or anteroom to a chapel or church

an·te·choir \'an-ti-ˌkwī(-ə)r\ n (ca. 1889) : a space enclosed or reserved for the clergy and choristers at the entrance to a choir

¹an·te·date \'an-ti-ˌdāt\ n (15c) : a date assigned to an event or document earlier than the actual date of the event or document

²an·te·date \'an-ti-ˌdāt, ˌan-ti-'\ vt (1572) **1 a** : to date as of a time prior to that of execution **b** : to assign a date prior to that of actual occurrence **2** archaic : ANTICIPATE **3** : to precede in time

an·te·di·lu·vi·an \ˌan-ti-də-'lü-vē-ən, -(ˌ)dī-\ adj [ante- + L diluvium flood — more at DELUGE] (1646) **1** : of or relating to the period before the flood described in the Bible **2** : made, evolved, or developed a long time ago ⟨an ∼ automobile⟩ — **antediluvian** n

an·te·fix \'an-ti-ˌfiks\ n, pl **-fix·ae** \-ˌfik-ˌsē\ or **-fix·es** \-ˌfik-səz\ [L antefixum, fr. neut. of antefixus, pp. of antefigere to fasten before, fr. ante- + figere to fasten — more at FIX] (1832) : an ornament at the eaves of a classical building concealing the ends of the joint tiles of the roof

an·te·lope \'an-tᵊl-ˌōp\ n, pl **-lope** or **-lopes** [ME, fabulous heraldic

an·te·lope beast, prob. fr. MF *antelop* savage animal with sawlike horns, fr. ML *anthalopus*, fr. LGk *antholop-*, *antholops*] (15c) **1 a :** any of various ruminant mammals (family Bovidae) chiefly of Africa and southwest Asia that differ from the true oxen esp. in lighter racier build and horns directed upward and backward **b :** PRONGHORN **2 :** leather from antelope hide

an·te me·ri·di·em \,an-ti-mə-'ri-dē-əm, -dē-,em\ *adj* [L] (1563) : being before noon — abbr. *a.m.*

an·te·mor·tem \-'mòr-təm\ *adj* [L *ante mortem*] (1883) : preceding death

an·te·na·tal \-'nā-t³l\ *adj* (1817) : PRENATAL ⟨∼ diagnosis of birth defects⟩ — **an·te·na·tal·ly** \-ē\ *adv*

an·ten·na \an-'te-nə\ *n, pl* **-nae** \-(,)nē\ *or* **-nas** [ML, fr. L, sail yard] (1646) **1** *pl* **-nae :** one of a pair of slender movable segmented sensory organs on the head of insects, myriapods, and crustaceans — see IN-SECT illustration **2 :** a usu. metallic device (as a rod or wire) for radiating or receiving radio waves **3** *antennae pl* **:** a special sensitivity or receptiveness ⟨his political *antennae* proved to be shrewder than ever —Erich Segal⟩ — **an·ten·nal** \-'te-n³l\ *adj*

an·ten·nule \an-'ten-(,)yü(ə)l\ *n* (1845) : a small antenna or similar appendage — **an·ten·nu·lar** \-'ten-yə-lər\ *adj*

an·te·nup·tial \,an-ti-'nəp-shəl, -chəl; ÷-shə-wəl, ÷-chə-\ *adj* (1818) : PRENUPTIAL

an·te·pen·di·um \,an-ti-'pen-dē-əm\ *n, pl* **-di·ums** *or* **-dia** \-dē-ə\ [ML, fr. L *ante-* + *pendēre* to hang — more at PENDANT] (ca. 1696) : a hanging for the front of an altar, pulpit, or lectern

an·te·pe·nult \,an-ti-'pē-,nəlt, -pi-\ *also* **an·te·pen·ul·ti·ma** \-pi-'nəl-tə-mə\ *n* [LL *antepaenultima*, fem. of *antepaenultimus* preceding the next to last, fr. L *ante-* + *paenultimus* penultimate] (1581) : the third syllable of a word counting from the end (as *cu* in *accumulate*) — **an·te·pen·ul·ti·mate** \-pi-'nəl-tə-mət\ *adj or n*

an·te·post \'an-ti-,pōst\ *adj* (1902) *Brit* : relating to or being wagers on a horse race made esp. before the day of the race

an·te·ri·or \an-'tir-ē-ər\ *adj* [L, compar. of *ante* before — more at ANTE-] (1541) **1 a :** situated before or toward the front **b :** situated near or toward the head or part most nearly corresponding to a head **2 :** coming before in time or development *syn* see PRECEDING — **an·te·ri·or·ly** *adv*

an·te·room \'an-ti-,rüm, -,rùm\ *n* (1762) : an outer room that leads to another room and that is often used as a waiting room

anth- — see ANTI-

an·thel·min·tic \,ant-,hel-'min-tik, ,an-,thel-\ *adj* [*anti-* + Gk *helminth-*, *helmis* worm] (1684) : expelling or destroying parasitic worms esp. of the intestine — **anthelmintic** *n*

an·them \'an(t)-thəm\ *n* [ME *antem*, fr. OE *antefn*, fr. LL *antiphona*, fr. LGk *antiphōna*, pl. of *antiphōnon*, fr. Gk, neut. of *antiphōnos* responsive, fr. *anti-* + *phōnē* sound — more at BAN] (bef. 12c) **1 :** a psalm or hymn sung antiphonally or responsively **b :** a sacred vocal composition with words usu. from the Scriptures **2 :** a song or hymn of praise or gladness

an·the·mi·on \an-'thē-mē-ən\ *n, pl* **-mia** \-mē-ə\ [Gk, fr. dim. of *anthemon* flower, fr. *anthos* — more at ANTHOLOGY] (1865) : a flat ornament of floral form (as in relief sculpture or in painting)

an·ther \'an(t)-thər\ *n* [NL *anthera*, fr. L, medicine made fr. flowers, fr. Gk *anthēra*, fr. fem. of *anthēros* flowery, fr. *anthos*] (ca. 1706) : the part of a stamen that produces and contains pollen and is usu. borne on a stalk — see FLOWER illustration — **an·ther·al** \-thə-rəl\ *adj*

an·ther·id·i·um \,an(t)-thə-'ri-dē-əm\ *n, pl* **-id·ia** \-dē-ə\ [NL, fr. *anthera*] (1854) : the male reproductive organ of some cryptogamous plants — **an·ther·id·i·al** \-dē-əl\ *adj*

an·the·sis \an-'thē-səs\ *n* [NL, fr. Gk *anthēsis* bloom, fr. *anthein* to flower, fr. *anthos*] (ca. 1823) : the action or period of opening of a flower

ant·hill \'ant-,hil\ *n* (14c) : a mound of debris thrown up by ants or termites in digging their nest

an·tho·cy·a·nin \,an(t)-thə-'sī-ə-nən\ *also* **an·tho·cy·an** \-'sī-ən, -,an\ *n* [Gk *anthos* + *kyanos* dark blue] (1839) : any of various soluble glycoside pigments producing blue to red coloring in flowers and plants

an·thol·o·gist \an-'thä-lə-jist\ *n* (1805) : a compiler of an anthology

an·thol·o·gize \-,jīz\ *vt* **-gized; -giz·ing** (1892) : to compile, publish, or include in an anthology — **an·thol·o·giz·er** \-,jī-zər\ *n*

an·thol·o·gy \an-'thä-lə-jē\ *n, pl* **-gies** [NL *anthologia* collection of epigrams, fr. MGk, fr. Gk, flower gathering, fr. *anthos* flower + *logia* collecting, fr. *legein* to gather; akin to Skt *andha* herb — more at LEGEND] (1640) **1 :** a collection of selected literary pieces or passages or works of art or music **2 :** ASSORTMENT ⟨an ∼ of threadbare clichés of . . . bistro cuisine —Jay Jacobs⟩ — **an·tho·log·i·cal** \,an(t)-thə-'lä-ji-kəl\ *adj*

an·thoph·i·lous \an-'thä-fə-ləs\ *adj* [ISV, fr. Gk *anthos* + E *-philous*] (1883) : feeding upon or living among flowers ⟨∼ insects⟩

an·tho·phyl·lite \,an(t)-thə-'fi-,līt, (,)an-'thä-fə-\ *n* [G *Anthophyllit*, fr. NL *anthophyllum*, fr. Gk *anthos* + *phyllon* leaf — more at BLADE] (ca. 1828) : an orthorhombic mineral of the amphibole group that is essentially a silicate of magnesium and iron and is usu. lamellar or fibrous and when fibrous is one of the less common forms of asbestos

an·tho·zo·an \,an(t)-thə-'zō-ən\ *n* [ultim. fr. Gk *anthos* + *zōion* animal; akin to Gk *zōē* life — more at QUICK] (ca. 1889) : any of a class (Anthozoa) of marine coelenterates (as the corals and sea anemones) having polyps with radial partitions — **anthozoan** *adj*

an·thra·cene \'an(t)-thrə-,sēn\ *n* (1863) : a crystalline aromatic hydrocarbon $C_{14}H_{10}$ obtained from coal-tar distillation

an·thra·cite \'an(t)-thrə-,sīt\ *n* [Gk *anthrakitis*, fr. *anthrak-*, *anthrax* coal] (1812) : a hard natural coal of high luster differing from bituminous coal in containing little volatile matter and in burning very cleanly — called also *hard coal* — **an·thra·cit·ic** \,an(t)-thrə-'si-tik\ *adj*

an·thrac·nose \an-'thrak-,nōs\ *n* [F, fr. Gk *anthrak-*, *anthrax* + *nosos* disease] (1886) : any of numerous destructive plant diseases caused by imperfect fungi and characterized esp. by necrotic lesions

an·thra·ni·late \an-'thra-n³l-,āt, ,an-thrə-'ni-,lāt\ *n* (1921) : a salt or ester of anthranilic acid

an·thra·nil·ic acid \,an(t)-thrə-'ni-lik-\ *n* [ISV *anthracene* + *aniline*] (1881) : a crystalline acid $NH_2C_6H_4COOH$ used as an intermediate in the manufacture of dyes (as indigo), pharmaceuticals, and perfumes

an·thra·qui·none \,an(t)-thrə-kwi-'nōn, -'kwi-,nōn\ *n* [prob. fr. F, fr. *anthracene* + *quinone*] (1869) : a yellow crystalline ketone $C_{14}H_8O_2$ often derived from anthracene and used esp. in the manufacture of dyes

an·thrax \'an-,thraks\ *n* [ME *antrax* carbuncle, fr. L *anthrax*, fr. Gk, coal, carbuncle] (1876) : an infectious disease of warm-blooded animals (as cattle and sheep) caused by a spore-forming bacterium (*Bacillus anthracis*), transmissible to humans esp. by the handling of infected products (as wool), and characterized by external ulcerating nodules or by lesions in the lungs

anthrop- *or* **anthropo-** *comb form* [L *anthropo-*, fr. Gk *anthrōp-*, *anthrōpo-*, fr. *anthrōpos*] : human being ⟨*anthropogenic*⟩

an·throp·ic \an-'thrä-pik\ *or* **an·throp·i·cal** \-pi-kəl\ *adj* [Gk *anthrōpikos*, fr. *anthrōpos*] (ca. 1806) : of or relating to human beings or the period of their existence on earth

anthropic principle *n* (1974) : either of two principles in cosmology: **a :** conditions that are observed in the universe must allow the observer to exist — called also *weak anthropic principle* **b :** the universe must have properties that make inevitable the existence of intelligent life — called also *strong anthropic principle*

an·thro·po·cen·tric \,an(t)-thrə-pə-'sen-trik\ *adj* (1863) **1 :** considering human beings as the most significant entity of the universe **2 :** interpreting or regarding the world in terms of human values and experiences — **an·thro·po·cen·tri·cal·ly** \-tri-k(ə-)lē\ *adv* — **an·thro·po·cen·tric·i·ty** \-pō-(,)sen-'tri-sə-tē\ *n* — **an·thro·po·cen·trism** \-'sen-,tri-zəm\ *n*

an·thro·po·gen·ic \-pə-'je-nik\ *adj* (1923) : of, relating to, or resulting from the influence of human beings on nature ⟨∼ pollutants⟩

an·thro·poid \'an(t)-thrə-,pòid\ *n* [Gk *anthrōpoeidēs* resembling a human, fr. *anthrōpos*] (1832) **1 :** APE 1b **2 :** a person resembling an ape ⟨the howling ∼s of the Hookworm Belt —H. L. Mencken⟩ — **anthropoid** *adj*

anthropoid ape *n* (ca. 1837) : APE 1b

an·thro·pol·o·gy \,an(t)-thrə-'pä-lə-jē\ *n* [NL *anthropologia*, fr. *anthrop-* + *-logia* -logy] (1593) **1 :** the science of human beings; *esp* : the study of human beings in relation to distribution, origin, classification, and relationship of races, physical character, environmental and social relations, and culture **2 :** theology dealing with the origin, nature, and destiny of human beings — **an·thro·po·log·i·cal** \-pə-'lä-ji-kəl\ *adj* — **an·thro·po·log·i·cal·ly** \-ji-k(ə-)lē\ *adv* — **an·thro·pol·o·gist** \,an(t)-thrə-'pä-lə-jist\ *n*

an·thro·pom·e·try \,an(t)-thrə-'pä-mə-trē\ *n* [F *anthropométrie*, fr. *anthrop-* + *-métrie* -metry] (ca. 1839) : the study of human body measurements esp. on a comparative basis — **an·thro·po·met·ric** \-pə-'me-trik\ *adj*

an·thro·po·morph \'an(t)-thrə-pə-,mòrf\ *n* (1894) : a stylized human figure (as in prehistoric art)

an·thro·po·mor·phic \,an(t)-thrə-pə-'mòr-fik\ *adj* [LL *anthropomorphus* of human form, fr. Gk *anthrōpomorphos*, fr. *anthrōp-* + *-morphos* -morphous] (1827) **1 :** described or thought of as having a human form or human attributes ⟨∼ deities⟩ **2 :** ascribing human characteristics to nonhuman things ⟨∼ supernaturalism⟩ — **an·thro·po·mor·phi·cal·ly** \-fi-k(ə-)lē\ *adv*

an·thro·po·mor·phism \-,fi-zəm\ *n* (1753) : an interpretation of what is not human or personal in terms of human or personal characteristics : HUMANIZATION — **an·thro·po·mor·phist** \-fist\ *n*

an·thro·po·mor·phize \-,fīz\ *vb* **-phized; -phiz·ing** (1845) : to attribute human form or personality to ∼ *vi* : to attribute human form or personality to things not human — **an·thro·po·mor·phi·za·tion** \-,mòr-fə-'zā-shən\ *n*

an·thro·po·pa·thism \,an(t)-thrə-'pä-pə-,thi-zəm, -pō-'pa-,thi-\ *n* [LGk *anthrōpopatheia* humanity, fr. Gk *anthrōpopathēs* having human feelings, fr. *anthrōp-* + *pathos* experience — more at PATHOS] (1847) : the ascription of human feelings to something not human

an·thro·poph·a·gous \,an(t)-thrə-'pä-fə-gəs\ *adj* (ca. 1828) : feeding on human flesh — **an·thro·poph·a·gy** \-fə-jē\ *n*

an·thro·poph·a·gus \-fə-gəs\ *n, pl* **-a·gi** \-fə-,gī, -,jī, -,gē\ [L, fr. Gk *anthrōpophagos*, fr. *anthrōp-* + *-phagos* -phagous] (1552) : MAN-EATER, CANNIBAL

an·thro·pos·o·phy \,an(t)-thrə-'pä-sə-fē\ *n* (1916) : a 20th century religious system growing out of theosophy and centering on human development

an·thur·i·um \an-'thùr-ē-əm, -'thyùr-\ *n* [NL, fr. Gk *anthos* flower + *oura* tail — more at ANTHOLOGY, ASS] (ca. 1839) : any of a genus (*Anthurium*) of tropical American plants of the arum family with large often highly colored leaves, a cylindrical spadix, and a colored spathe

¹an·ti \'an-,tī, 'an-tē\ *n, pl* **antis** [*anti-*] (1788) : one that is opposed

²anti (1857) : OPPOSED

³anti *prep* (1953) : opposed to : AGAINST

anti- *or* **ant-** *or* **anth-** *prefix* [*anti-* fr. ME, fr. MF & L; MF, fr. L, against, fr. Gk, fr. *anti*; *ant-* fr. ME, fr. L, against, fr. Gk, fr. *anti*; *anth-* fr. L, against, fr. Gk, fr. *anti* — more at ANTE-] **1 a :** of the same kind but situated opposite, exerting energy in the opposite direction, or pursuing an opposite policy ⟨*anticlinal*⟩ **b :** one that is opposite in kind to ⟨*anticlimax*⟩ **2 a :** opposing or hostile to in opinion, sympathy, or practice ⟨*anti*-Semite⟩ **b :** opposing in effect or activity ⟨*antiacid*⟩ **3 :** serving to prevent, cure, or alleviate ⟨*antianxiety*⟩ **4 :** combating or defending against ⟨*antiaircraft*⟩ ⟨*antimissile*⟩

an·ti·ac·a·dem·ic	an·ti·al·ler·gen·ic	an·ti·au·thor·i·tar·i·an
an·ti–ac·ne	an·ti·ane·mia	an·ti·au·thor·i·tar·i·an·ism
an·ti·ad·min·is·tra·tion	an·ti·apart·heid	an·ti·au·thor·i·ty
an·ti·ag·gres·sion	an·ti·aph·ro·di·si·ac	an·ti·back·lash
an·ti·ag·ing	an·ti·aris·to·crat·ic	an·ti·bi·as
an·ti–AIDS	an·ti·ar·thrit·ic	an·ti·bill·board
an·ti·al·co·hol	an·ti·ar·thri·tis	an·ti–Bol·she·vik
an·ti·al·co·hol·ism	an·ti·as·sim·i·la·tion	an·ti·boss
an·ti·alien	an·ti·asth·ma	an·ti·bour·geois

\ə\ abut \'ə\ kitten, F table \ər\ further \a\ ash \ā\ ace \ä\ mop, mar
\aú\ out \ch\ chin \e\ bet \ē\ easy \g\ go \i\ hit \ī\ ice \j\ job
\ŋ\ sing \ō\ go \ò\ law \òi\ boy \th\ thin \t̶h̶\ the \ü\ loot \ù\ foot
\y\ yet \zh\ vision \à, k, ⁿ, œ, œ̄, ᵫ, ᵫ̄, ʸ\ see Guide to Pronunciation

an·ti·boy·cott
an·ti–Brit·ish
an·ti·bug
an·ti·bu·reau·crat·ic
an·ti·bur·glar
an·ti·bur·glary
an·ti·cak·ing
an·ti·cap·i·tal·ism
an·ti·cap·i·tal·ist
an·ti·car·cin·o·gen
an·ti·car·ci·no·gen·ic
an·ti·car·ies
an·ti·Cath·o·lic
an·ti·Ca·thol·i·cism
an·ti·cel·lu·lite
an·ti·cen·sor·ship
an·ti·cho·les·ter·ol
an·ti·Chris·tian
an·ti·Chris·tian·i·ty
an·ti·church
an·ti·cig·a·rette
an·ti·city
an·ti·clas·si·cal
an·ti·cling
an·ti·clot·ting
an·ti·cold
an·ti·col·li·sion
an·ti·co·lo·nial
an·ti·co·lo·nial·ism
an·ti·co·lo·nial·ist
an·ti·com·mer·cial
an·ti·com·mer·cial·ism
an·ti·com·mu·nism
an·ti·com·mu·nist
an·ti·con·glom·er·ate
an·ti·con·ser·va·tion
an·ti·con·ser·va·tion·ist
an·ti·con·sum·er
an·ti·con·ven·tion·al
an·ti·cor·po·rate
an·ti·cor·ro·sion
an·ti·cor·ro·sive
an·ti·cor·rup·tion
an·ti·coun·ter·feit·ing
an·ti·crack
an·ti·cre·ative
an·ti·crime
an·ti·cru·el·ty
an·ti·cult
an·ti·cul·tur·al
an·ti·dan·druff
an·ti–Dar·win·i·an
an·ti–Dar·win·ism
an·ti·def·a·ma·tion
an·ti·de·pres·sion
an·ti·de·seg·re·ga·tion
an·ti·de·sert·i·fi·ca·tion
an·ti·des·ic·cant
an·ti·de·vel·op·ment
an·ti·di·a·bet·ic
an·ti·di·ar·rhe·al
an·ti·di·lu·tion
an·ti·dis·crim·i·na·tion
an·ti·dog·mat·ic
an·ti·draft
an·ti·eco·nom·ic
an·ti·ed·u·ca·tion·al
an·ti·egal·i·tar·i·an
an·ti·elite
an·ti·elit·ism
an·ti·elit·ist
an·ti·emet·ic
an·ti–En·glish
an·ti·en·tro·pic
an·ti·ep·i·lep·sy
an·ti·ep·i·lep·tic
an·ti·erot·ic
an·ti·es·tab·lish·ment
an·ti·es·tro·gen
an·ti·evo·lu·tion
an·ti·evo·lu·tion·ary
an·ti·evo·lu·tion·ism
an·ti·evo·lu·tion·ist
an·ti·fam·i·ly
an·ti·fas·cism
an·ti·fas·cist
an·ti·fash·ion
an·ti·fash·ion·able
an·ti·fa·tigue
an·ti·fe·male
an·ti·fem·i·nine
an·ti·fem·i·nism
an·ti·fem·i·nist
an·ti·fil·i·bus·ter
an·ti·flu
an·ti·foam
an·ti·foam·ing
an·ti·fog·ging
an·ti·fore·clo·sure
an·ti·for·eign
an·ti·for·eign·er
an·ti·for·mal·ist
an·ti·fraud
an·ti–French

an·ti·fric·tion
an·ti·fur
an·ti·gam·bling
an·ti·gay
an·ti–Ger·man
an·ti·glare
an·ti·gov·ern·ment
an·ti·growth
an·ti·guer·ril·la
an·ti·gun
an·ti·her·pes
an·ti·hi·er·ar·chi·cal
an·ti·hi·jack
an·ti·his·tor·i·cism
an·ti·ho·mo·sex·u·al
an·ti·hu·man·ism
an·ti·hu·man·is·tic
an·ti·hu·man·i·tar·i·an
an·ti·hunt·er
an·ti·hunt·ing
an·ti·hys·ter·ic
an·ti·ic·ing
an·ti·ideo·log·i·cal
an·ti·im·pe·ri·al·ism
an·ti·im·pe·ri·al·ist
an·ti·in·cum·bent
an·ti·in·fec·tive
an·ti·in·fla·tion
an·ti·in·fla·tion·ary
an·ti·in·sti·tu·tion·al
an·ti·in·te·gra·tion
an·ti·in·tru·sion
an·ti–Ital·ian
an·ti·jam
an·ti·jam·ming
an·ti–Jap·a·nese
an·ti–Jew·ish
an·ti·kick·back
an·ti·knock
an·ti·la·bor
an·ti·leak
an·ti·lep·ro·sy
an·ti·lib·er·al
an·ti·lib·er·al·ism
an·ti·lib·er·tar·i·an
an·ti·lit·er·ate
an·ti·lit·ter
an·ti·lit·ter·ing
an·ti·log·i·cal
an·ti·lynch·ing
an·ti·ma·cho
an·ti·ma·lar·ia
an·ti·male
an·ti·man
an·ti·man·age·ment
an·ti·mar·i·jua·na
an·ti·mar·ket
an·ti·ma·te·ri·al·ism
an·ti·ma·te·ri·al·ist
an·ti·mech·a·nist
an·ti·merg·er
an·ti·meta·bol·ic
an·ti·meta·phys·i·cal
an·ti·mil·i·ta·rism
an·ti·mil·i·ta·rist
an·ti·mil·i·tary
an·ti·mis·ce·ge·na·tion
an·ti·mis·sile
an·ti·mod·ern
an·ti·mod·ern·ist
an·ti·mo·nar·chi·cal
an·ti·mo·nar·chist
an·ti·mo·nop·o·list
an·ti·mo·nop·o·ly
an·ti·mos·qui·to
an·ti·mu·si·cal
an·ti·nar·ra·tive
an·ti·na·tion·al
an·ti·na·tion·al·ist
an·ti·nat·u·ral
an·ti·na·ture
an·ti·nau·sea
an·ti–Na·zi
an·ti–Ne·gro
an·ti·nep·o·tism
an·ti·noise
an·ti·obe·si·ty
an·ti·ob·scen·i·ty
an·ti·or·ga·ni·za·tion
an·ti·pa·pal
an·ti·par·ty
an·ti·pes·ti·cide
an·ti·pi·ra·cy
an·ti·plague
an·ti·plaque
an·ti·plea·sure
an·ti·poach·ing
an·ti·po·lice
an·ti·po·lit·i·cal
an·ti·pol·i·tics
an·ti·pop·u·lar
an·ti·porn
an·ti·por·no·graph·ic
an·ti·por·nog·ra·phy

an·ti·pot
an·ti·pov·er·ty
an·ti·pred·a·tor
an·ti·press
an·ti·prof·i·teer·ing
an·ti·pro·gres·sive
an·ti·pros·ti·tu·tion
an·ti·pru·rit·ic
an·ti·ra·bies
an·ti·rac·ism
an·ti·rac·ist
an·ti·rack·e·teer·ing
an·ti·ra·dar
an·ti·rad·i·cal
an·ti·rad·i·cal·ism
an·ti·rape
an·ti·ra·tio·nal
an·ti·ra·tio·nal·ism
an·ti·ra·tio·nal·ist
an·ti·ra·tio·nal·i·ty
an·ti·re·al·ism
an·ti·re·al·ist
an·ti·re·ces·sion
an·ti·re·ces·sion·ary
an·ti·red
an·ti·re·duc·tion·ism
an·ti·re·duc·tion·ist
an·ti·re·flec·tion
an·ti·re·flec·tive
an·ti·re·form
an·ti·reg·u·la·to·ry
an·ti·re·li·gion
an·ti·re·li·gious
an·ti·rev·o·lu·tion·ary
an·ti·rit·u·al·ism
an·ti·rock
an·ti·roll
an·ti·ro·man·tic
an·ti·ro·man·ti·cism
an·ti·roy·al·ist
an·ti–Rus·sian
an·ti·rust
an·ti·sat·el·lite
an·ti·schizo·phre·nia
an·ti·schizo·phren·ic
an·ti·sci·ence
an·ti·sci·en·tif·ic
an·ti·se·cre·cy
an·ti·seg·re·ga·tion
an·ti·sei·zure
an·ti·sen·ti·men·tal
an·ti·sep·a·rat·ist
an·ti·sex
an·ti·sex·ist
an·ti·sex·u·al
an·ti·sex·u·al·i·ty
an·ti·shark
an·ti·ship
an·ti·shock
an·ti·shop·lift·ing
an·ti·skid
an·ti·slav·ery
an·ti·sleep
an·ti·slip
an·ti·smog
an·ti·smoke
an·ti·smok·er
an·ti·smok·ing
an·ti·smug·gling
an·ti·smut
an·ti·so·cial·ist
an·ti–So·vi·et
an·ti–So·vi·et·ism
an·ti·spec·u·la·tion
an·ti·spec·u·la·tive
an·ti·spend·ing
an·ti–Sta·lin·ist
an·ti·state
an·ti·stick
an·ti·sto·ry
an·ti·stress
an·ti·strike
an·ti·stu·dent
an·ti·sub·ma·rine
an·ti·sub·si·dy
an·ti·sub·ver·sion
an·ti·sub·ver·sive
an·ti·sui·cide
an·ti·syph·i·lit·ic
an·ti·take·over
an·ti·tank
an·ti·tar·nish
an·ti·tax
an·ti·tech·no·log·i·cal
an·ti·tech·nol·o·gy
an·ti·ter·ror·ism
an·ti·ter·ror·ist
an·ti·theft
an·ti·the·o·ret·i·cal
an·ti·to·bac·co
an·ti·to·tal·i·tar·i·an
an·ti·tra·di·tion·al

an·ti·tu·ber·cu·lar
an·ti·tu·ber·cu·lo·sis
an·ti·tu·ber·cu·lous
an·ti·tu·mor
an·ti·tu·mor·al
an·ti·ty·phoid
an·ti·ul·cer
an·ti·un·em·ploy·ment
an·ti·union

an·ti·uni·ver·si·ty
an·ti·ur·ban
an·ti·vi·o·lence
an·ti·vi·ral
an·ti·vi·rus
an·ti·vivi·sec·tion
an·ti·vivi·sec·tion·ist
an·ti·war

an·ti·wear
an·ti·wel·fare
an·ti–West
an·ti–West·ern
an·ti·whal·ing
an·ti·wom·an
an·ti·wrin·kle
an·ti–Zi·on·ist

an·ti·abor·tion \,an-tē-ə-'bôr-shən, ,an-,tī-\ *adj* (1971) : opposed to abortion ⟨~ lobbyists⟩ — **an·ti·abor·tion·ist** \-sh(ə-)nist\ *n*

an·ti·air \,an-tē-'ar, -'er-, -,tī-\ *adj* (1925) : ANTIAIRCRAFT

¹an·ti·air·craft \-'ar-,kraft, -'er-\ *adj* (1914) : designed for or concerned with defense against air attack

²antiaircraft *n* (1926) : antiaircraft guns or their fire

an·ti–Amer·i·can \-ə-'mer-ə-kən, -'mər-, -'mar-, -i-kən\ *adj* (1773) : opposed or hostile to the people or the government policies of the U.S. — **an·ti–Amer·i·can·ism** \-kə,ni-zəm\ *n*

an·ti·anx·i·ety \-(,)aŋ-'zī-ə-tē\ *adj* (1962) : tending to prevent or relieve anxiety ⟨~ drugs⟩

an·ti·ar·rhyth·mic \,an-tē-(,)ā-'rith-mik, ,an-,tī-\ *adj* (1954) : tending to prevent or relieve cardiac arrhythmia ⟨an ~ agent⟩

an·ti·art \-'ärt\ *n* (1937) : art based on premises antithetical to traditional or popular art forms; *specif* : DADA

an·ti·aux·in \-'ôk-sən\ *n* (1949) : a plant substance that opposes or suppresses the natural effect of an auxin

an·ti·bac·te·ri·al \,an-ti-bak-'tir-ē-əl, ,an-,tī-\ *adj* (ca. 1897) : directed or effective against bacteria — **antibacterial** *n*

an·ti·bal·lis·tic missile \,an-ti-bə-'lis-tik-, ,an-,tī-\ *n* (ca. 1959) : a missile for intercepting and destroying ballistic missiles

an·ti·bi·o·sis \-bī-'ō-səs, -bē-\ *n* [NL] (1899) : antagonistic association between organisms to the detriment of one of them or between one organism and a metabolic product of another

¹an·ti·bi·ot·ic \,an-ti-bī-'ä-tik, -,tī-; ,an-ti-bē-\ *adj* (1894) 1 : tending to prevent, inhibit, or destroy life 2 : of or relating to antibiotics or to antibiosis — **an·ti·bi·ot·i·cal·ly** \-ti-k(ə-)lē\ *adv*

²antibiotic *n* (1943) : a substance produced by or a semisynthetic substance derived from a microorganism and able in dilute solution to inhibit or kill another microorganism

an·ti·black \-'blak\ *adj* (1952) : opposed or hostile to black people — **an·ti·black·ism** \-'bla-,ki-zəm\ *n*

an·ti·body \,an-ti-,bä-dē\ *n* (1900) : any of a large number of proteins of high molecular weight that are produced normally by specialized B cells after stimulation by an antigen and act specifically against the antigen in an immune response, that are produced abnormally by some cancer cells, and that typically consist of four subunits including two heavy chains and two light chains — called also *immunoglobulin*

an·ti·busi·ness \,an-ti-'biz-nəs, ,an-ti-, -nəz\ *adj* (1938) : antagonistic toward business and esp. big business

an·ti·bus·ing \-'bə-siŋ\ *adj* (ca. 1969) : opposed to the busing of schoolchildren ⟨~ parents⟩ ⟨~ campaign⟩

¹an·tic \'an-tik\ *n* [It *antico* ancient thing or person, fr. *antico* ancient, fr. L *antiquus* — more at ANTIQUE] (1529) 1 : an attention-drawing often wildly playful or funny act or action : CAPER ⟨childish ~s⟩ 2 *archaic* : a performer of a grotesque or ludicrous part : BUFFOON

²antic *adj* (1548) 1 *archaic* : GROTESQUE, BIZARRE 2 **a** : characterized by clownish extravagance or absurdity **b** : whimsically gay : FROLICSOME — **an·ti·cal·ly** \-ti-k(ə-)lē\ *adv*

an·ti·can·cer \,an-,tī-'kan(t)-sər, ,an-ti-\ *adj* (1926) : used against or tending to arrest cancer ⟨~ drugs⟩ ⟨~ activity⟩ ⟨~ effects⟩

an·ti·cho·lin·er·gic \-,kō-lə-'nər-jik\ *adj* (1942) : opposing or blocking the physiologic action of acetylcholine — **anticholinergic** *n*

an·ti·cho·lin·es·ter·ase \-'nes-tə-,rās, -,rāz\ *n* (1942) : a substance (as neostigmine) that inhibits a cholinesterase by combination with it

An·ti·christ \'an-ti-,krīst, -,tī-\ *n* [ME *anticrist*, fr. OE & LL; OE *antecrist*, fr. LL *Antichristus*, fr. Gk *Antichristos*, fr. *anti-* + *Christos* Christ] (bef. 12c) 1 : one who denies or opposes Christ; *specif* : a great antagonist expected to fill the world with wickedness but to be conquered forever by Christ at his second coming 2 : a false Christ

an·tic·i·pant \an-'ti-sə-pənt\ *adj* (1626) : EXPECTANT, ANTICIPATING — usu. used with *of* — **anticipant** *n*

an·tic·i·pate \an-'ti-sə-,pāt\ *vb* -pat·ed; -pat·ing [L *anticipatus*, pp. of *anticipare*, fr. *ante-* + *-cipare* (fr. *capere* to take) — more at HEAVE] *vt* (1532) 1 : to give advance thought, discussion, or treatment to 2 : to meet (an obligation) before a due date 3 : to foresee and deal with in advance : FORESTALL 4 : to use or expend in advance of actual possession 5 : to act before (another) often so as to check or counter 6 : to look forward to as certain : EXPECT ~ *vi* : to speak or write in knowledge or expectation of later matter *syn* see FORESEE, PREVENT — **an·tic·i·pat·able** \-,pā-tə-bəl\ *adj* — **an·tic·i·pa·tor** \-,pā-tər\ *n*

an·tic·i·pa·tion \(,)an-,ti-sə-'pā-shən\ *n* (14c) 1 **a** : a prior action that takes into account or forestalls a later action **b** : the act of looking forward; *esp* : pleasurable expectation 2 : the use of money before it is available 3 **a** : visualization of a future event or state **b** : an object or form that anticipates a later type 4 : the early sounding of one or more tones of a succeeding chord to form a temporary dissonance — compare SUSPENSION *syn* see PROSPECT

an·tic·i·pa·to·ry \an-'ti-sə-pə-,tōr-ē, -,tōr-\ *adj* (1669) : characterized by anticipation : ANTICIPATING

an·ti·cler·i·cal \,an-ti-'kler-i-kəl, ,an-,tī-\ *adj* (1845) : opposed to clericalism or to the interference or influence of the clergy in secular affairs — **anticlerical** *n* — **an·ti·cler·i·cal·ism** \-kə,li-zəm\ *n*

an·ti·cli·mac·tic \,an-ti-klī-'mak-tik, -klə-\ *also* an·ti·cli·mac·ti·cal \-ti-kəl\ *adj* (1898) : of, relating to, or marked by anticlimax — **an·ti·cli·mac·ti·cal·ly** \-ti-k(ə-)lē\ *adv*

an·ti·cli·max \,an-ti-'klī-,maks\ *n* (1710) 1 : the usu. sudden transition in discourse from a significant idea to a trivial or ludicrous idea; *also* : an instance of this transition 2 : an event (as at the end of a series) that is strikingly less important than what has preceded it

an·ti·cli·nal \,an-ti-'klī-n°l\ *adj* [*anti-* + Gk *klinein* to lean — more at LEAN] (1882) : occurring at right angles to the surface or circumference of a plant organ ⟨an ~ pattern of cell walls⟩

an·ti·cline \'an-ti-ˌklīn\ *n* (ca. 1861) : an arch of stratified rock in which the layers bend downward in opposite directions from the crest — compare SYNCLINE

cross section of strata showing anticline

an·ti·clock·wise \ˌan-ti-'kläk-ˌwīz, ˌan-ˌtī-\ *adj or adv* (1898) *chiefly Brit* : COUNTERCLOCKWISE

an·ti·co·ag·u·lant \-kō-'a-gyə-lənt\ *n* (ca. 1905) : a substance that hinders the clotting of blood — **anticoagulant** *adj*

an·ti·co·don \-'kō-ˌdän\ *n* (1965) : a triplet of nucleotide bases in transfer RNA that identifies the amino acid carried and binds to a complementary codon in messenger RNA during protein synthesis at a ribosome

an·ti·com·pet·i·tive \-kəm-'pe-tə-tiv\ *adj* (1952) : tending to reduce or discourage competition

an·ti·con·vul·sant \-kən-'vəl-sənt\ *also* **an·ti·con·vul·sive** \-siv\ *adj* (1734) : used or tending to control or to prevent convulsions (as in epilepsy) — **anticonvulsant** *also* **anticonvulsive** *n*

an·ti·cy·clone \ˌan-ti-'sī-ˌklōn\ *n* (1877) **1** : a system of winds that rotates about a center of high atmospheric pressure clockwise in the northern hemisphere and counterclockwise in the southern, that usu. advances at 20 to 30 miles (about 30 to 50 kilometers) per hour, and that usu. has a diameter of 1500 to 2500 miles (2400 to 4000 kilometers) **2** : HIGH 2 — **an·ti·cy·clon·ic** \-sī-'klä-nik\ *adj*

an·ti·dem·o·crat·ic \ˌan-ti-ˌde-mə-'kra-tik, ˌan-ˌtī-\ *adj* (1837) : opposed or hostile to the theories or policies of democracy

¹**an·ti·de·pres·sant** \-di-'pre-sᵊnt\ *adj* (1961) : used or tending to relieve or prevent psychic depression

²**antidepressant** *n* (1962) : an antidepressant drug — compare TRICYCLIC ANTIDEPRESSANT

an·ti·de·riv·a·tive \-di-'ri-və-tiv\ *n* (ca. 1942) : INDEFINITE INTEGRAL

an·ti·di·uret·ic hormone \ˌan-ti-dī-yù-'re-tik-\ *n* (1942) : VASOPRESSIN

an·ti·dot·al \ˌan-ti-'dō-tᵊl\ *adj* (1646) : of, relating to, or acting as an antidote — **an·ti·dot·al·ly** \-'tᵊl-ē\ *adv*

an·ti·dote \'an-ti-ˌdōt\ *n* [ME *antidot*, fr. L *antidotum*, fr. Gk *antidotos*, fr. fem. of *antidotos* given as an antidote, fr. *antididonai* to give as an antidote, fr. *anti-* + *didonai* to give — more at DATE] (15c) **1** : a remedy to counteract the effects of poison **2** : something that relieves, prevents, or counteracts ⟨an ~ to the mechanization of our society⟩ — **antidote** *vt*

an·ti·dro·mic \ˌan-ti-'drä-mik\ *adj* [*anti-* + Gk *dromos* racecourse, running — more at DROMEDARY] (ca. 1927) : proceeding or conducting in a direction opposite to the usual one — used esp. of a nerve impulse or fiber — **an·ti·drom·i·cal·ly** \-mi-k(ə-)lē\ *adv*

an·ti·drug \ˌan-ˌtī-ˌdrəg, ˌan-ti-\ *adj* (1970) : acting against or opposing illicit drugs or their use ⟨~ activist⟩ ⟨~ program⟩

an·ti·dump·ing \ˌan-ti-'dəm-piŋ, ˌan-ˌtī-\ *adj* (1915) : designed to discourage the importation and sale of foreign goods at prices well below domestic prices ⟨~ tariffs⟩

an·ti·elec·tron \ˌan-tē-ə-'lek-ˌträn, ˌan-ˌtī-\ *n* (1931) : POSITRON

an·ti·fed·er·al·ist \ˌan-ti-'fe-d(ə-)rə-list, ˌan-ˌtī-\ *n, often cap A&F* (1787) : a member of the group that opposed the adoption of the U.S. Constitution

an·ti·fer·ro·mag·net·ic \-ˌfer-ō-mag-'ne-tik\ *adj* (1936) : FERRIMAGNETIC — **an·ti·fer·ro·mag·net** \-'mag-nət\ *n* — **an·ti·fer·ro·mag·net·i·cal·ly** \-mag-'ne-ti-k(ə-)lē\ *adv* — **an·ti·fer·ro·mag·net·ism** \-'mag-nə-ˌti-zəm\ *n*

an·ti·fer·til·i·ty \-fər-'ti-lə-tē\ *adj* (1953) : capable of or tending to reduce or destroy fertility : CONTRACEPTIVE ⟨~ agents⟩

an·ti·flu·o·ri·da·tion·ist \-ˌflúr-ə-'dā-sh(ə-)nist, -ˌflȯr-, -ˌflȯr-\ *n* (1961) : a person opposed to the fluoridation of public water supplies

an·ti·foul·ing \-'faú-liŋ\ *adj* (1895) : intended to prevent fouling of underwater structures (as the bottoms of ships) ⟨~ paint⟩

an·ti·freeze \'an-ti-ˌfrēz\ *n* (1924) : a substance added to a liquid (as the water in an automobile engine) to lower its freezing point

an·ti·fun·gal \ˌan-ti-'fəŋ-gəl, ˌan-ˌtī-\ *adj* (1945) : destroying fungi; *also* : inhibiting the growth of fungi — **antifungal** *n*

an·ti·gen \'an-ti-jən, -jen\ *n* [G, fr. F *antigène*, fr. *anticorps* antibody + *-gène* -gen] (1908) : a usu. protein or carbohydrate substance (as a toxin or enzyme) capable of stimulating an immune response — **an·ti·gen·ic** \ˌan-ti-'je-nik\ *adj* — **an·ti·gen·i·cal·ly** \-ni-k(ə-)lē\ *adv* — **an·ti·ge·nic·i·ty** \-jə-'ni-sə-tē\ *n*

antigenic determinant *n* (1950) : EPITOPE

an·ti·glob·u·lin \ˌan-ti-'glä-byə-lən, ˌan-ˌtī-\ *n* (ca. 1909) : an antibody that combines with and precipitates globulin

An·tig·o·ne \an-'ti-gə-(ˌ)nē\ *n* [Gk *Antigonē*] : a daughter of Oedipus and Jocasta who buries her brother Polynices' body against the order of her uncle Creon

¹**an·ti·grav·i·ty** \ˌan-ti-'gra-və-tē, ˌan-ˌtī-\ *adj* (1944) : reducing, canceling, or protecting against the effect of gravity

²**antigravity** *n* (1949) : a hypothetical effect resulting from cancellation or reduction of a gravitational field

an·ti·he·mo·phil·ic factor \ˌhē-mə-'fi-lik-\ *n* (1947) : FACTOR VIII

an·ti·he·ro \'an-ti-ˌhē-(ˌ)rō, 'an-ˌtī-, -ˌhir-(ˌ)\ *n* (1714) : a protagonist or notable figure who is conspicuously lacking in heroic qualities — **an·ti·he·ro·ic** \ˌan-ti-hi-'rō-ik, ˌan-ˌtī-\ *adj*

an·ti·her·o·ine \ˌan-ti-'her-ə-wən, ˌan-ˌtī-\ *n* (1907) : a female antihero

an·ti·his·ta·mine \-'his-tə-ˌmēn, -mən\ *n* (1946) : any of various compounds that counteract histamine in the body and that are used for treating allergic reactions (as hay fever) and cold symptoms — **antihistamine** *adj* — **an·ti·his·ta·min·ic** \-ˌhis-tə-'mi-nik\ *adj or n*

an·ti·hu·man \-'hyü-mən, -'yü-\ *adj* (1854) **1** : acting or being against humanity **2** : reacting strongly with human antigens

an·ti·hy·per·ten·sive \-ˌhī-pər-'ten(t)-siv\ *n* (ca. 1957) : a substance that is effective against high blood pressure — **antihypertensive** *adj*

an·ti·id·io·type \ˌan-tē-'i-dē-ə-ˌtīp, ˌan-ˌtī-\ *n* (1975) : an antibody that treats another antibody as an antigen and suppresses its immunoreactivity — **an·ti·id·io·typ·ic** \-ˌi-dē-ə-'ti-pik\ *adj*

an·ti·in·flam·ma·to·ry \-in-'fla-mə-ˌtȯr-ē\ *adj* (ca. 1957) : counteracting inflammation — **anti-inflammatory** *n*

an·ti·in·tel·lec·tu·al \-ˌin-tᵊl-'ek-ch(ə-w)əl, -'ek-shwəl\ *adj* (1936) : opposing or hostile to intellectuals or to an intellectual view or approach — **anti-intellectual** *n* — **an·ti·in·tel·lec·tu·al·ism** \-'ek-chə-(wə)-ˌli-zəm, -'ek-shwə-\ *n*

an·ti·leu·ke·mic \-lü-'kē-mik\ *adj* (1951) : counteracting the effects of leukemia

an·ti·life \-'līf\ *adj* (1929) : antagonistic or antithetical to life or to normal human values

an·ti·lock \'an-ˌtī-ˌläk, 'an-ti-\ *adj* (1974) : being a braking system for a motor vehicle designed to keep the wheels from locking by electronically controlled pulsed application of the brake for each wheel

an·ti·log \'an-ti-ˌlȯg, 'an-ˌtī-, -ˌläg\ *n* (1910) : ANTILOGARITHM

an·ti·log·a·rithm \ˌan-ti-'lȯ-gə-ˌri-thəm, ˌan-ˌtī-, -'lä-\ *n* (1675) : the number corresponding to a given logarithm

an·ti·ma·cas·sar \ˌan-ti-mə-'ka-sər\ *n* [*anti-* + *Macassar* (*oil*) (a hairdressing)] (1852) : a cover to protect the back or arms of furniture

an·ti·mag·net·ic \ˌan-ti-mag-'ne-tik, ˌan-ˌtī-\ *adj* (1946) *of a watch* : having a balance unit composed of alloys that will not remain magnetized

an·ti·ma·lar·i·al \-mə-'ler-ē-əl\ *adj* (ca. 1893) : serving to prevent, check, or cure malaria — **antimalarial** *n*

an·ti·mat·ter \'an-ti-ˌma-tər, 'an-ˌtī-\ *n* (1950) : matter composed of antiparticles

an·ti·me·tab·o·lite \ˌan-ti-mə-'ta-bə-ˌlīt, ˌan-ˌtī-\ *n* (1945) : a substance that replaces or inhibits an organism's utilization of a metabolite

an·ti·mi·cro·bi·al \ˌan-ti-mī-'krō-bē-əl\ *adj* (ca. 1910) : destroying or inhibiting the growth of microorganisms — **antimicrobial** *n*

an·ti·mis·sile missile \ˌan-ti-'mi-səl-, ˌan-ˌtī-; *chiefly Brit* ˌan-ti-'mi-ˌsīl-\ *n* (ca. 1956) : ANTIBALLISTIC MISSILE

an·ti·mi·tot·ic \ˌan-ti-mī-'tä-tik, ˌan-ˌtī-\ *adj* (1970) : inhibiting or disrupting mitosis ⟨~ agents⟩ ⟨~ activity⟩ — **antimitotic** *n*

an·ti·mo·ni·al \ˌan-tə-'mō-nē-əl\ *adj* (1605) : of, relating to, or containing antimony — **antimonial** *n*

an·ti·mo·nide \'an-ti-mə-ˌnid\ *n* (1863) : a binary compound of antimony with a more positive element

an·ti·mo·ny \'an-tə-ˌmō-nē\ *n* [ME *antimonie*, fr. ML *antimonium*] (15c) **1** : STIBNITE **2** : a trivalent and pentavalent metalloid element that is commonly metallic silvery white, crystalline, and brittle and that is used esp. as a constituent of alloys and semiconductors — see ELEMENT table

an·ti·my·cin A \ˌan-ti-'mī-sᵊn-ˌä\ *n* [*anti-* + *-mycin*] (1949) : a crystalline antibiotic $C_{28}H_{40}N_2O_9$ used esp. as a fungicide, insecticide, and miticide — called also *antimycin*

an·ti·neo·plas·tic \ˌan-ti-ˌnē-ə-'plas-tik, ˌan-ˌtī-\ *adj* (1954) : inhibiting or preventing the growth and spread of neoplasms or malignant cells

an·ti·neu·tri·no \-nü-'trē-(ˌ)nō, -nyü-\ *n* (1934) : the antiparticle of the neutrino

an·ti·neu·tron \-'nü-ˌträn, -'nyü-\ *n* (1942) : the antiparticle of the neutron

ant·ing \'an-tiŋ\ *n* (1936) : bird behavior in which ants are rubbed on the feathers to obtain chemicals (as formic acid) from the ants

an·ti·node \'an-ti-ˌnōd, 'an-ˌtī-\ *n* [ISV] (1882) : a region of maximum amplitude situated between adjacent nodes in a vibrating body — **an·ti·nod·al** \ˌan-ti-'nō-dᵊl, ˌan-ˌtī-\ *adj*

an·ti·no·mi·an \ˌan-ti-'nō-mē-ən\ *n* [ML *antinomus*, fr. L *anti-* + Gk *nomos* law] (1645) **1** : one who holds that under the gospel dispensation of grace the moral law is of no use or obligation because faith alone is necessary to salvation **2** : one who rejects a socially established morality — **antinomian** *adj* — **an·ti·no·mi·an·ism** \-mē-ə-ˌni-zəm\ *n*

an·tin·o·my \an-'ti-nə-mē\ *n, pl* **-mies** [G *Antinomie*, fr. L *antinomia* conflict of laws, fr. Gk, fr. *anti-* + *nomos* law — more at NIMBLE] (1592) **1** : a contradiction between two apparently equally valid principles or between inferences correctly drawn from such principles **2** : a fundamental and apparently unresolvable conflict or contradiction ⟨*antinomies* of beauty and evil, freedom and slavery —Stephen Holden⟩ — **an·ti·nom·ic** \ˌan-ti-'nä-mik\ *adj*

an·ti·nov·el \'an-ti-ˌnä-vəl, 'an-ˌtī-\ *n* (1958) : a work of fiction that lacks most or all of the traditional features of the novel — **an·ti·nov·el·ist** \-ˌnäv-list, -ˌnä-və-\ *n*

an·ti·nu·cle·ar \ˌan-ti-'nü-klē-ər, ˌan-ˌtī-, -'nyü-, ÷-kyə-lər\ *adj* (1958) **1** : tending to react with cell nuclei or their components (as DNA) ⟨~ antibodies⟩ **2** : opposing the use or production of nuclear power plants

an·ti·nu·cle·on \-'n(y)ü-klē-ˌän\ *n* (1946) : the antiparticle of a nucleon

an·ti·nuke \-'nük, -'nyük\ *adj* (1975) : ANTINUCLEAR 2

an·ti·ox·i·dant \ˌan-tē-'äk-sə-dənt, ˌan-ˌtī-\ *n* (1926) : a substance that inhibits oxidation or reactions promoted by oxygen or peroxides — **antioxidant** *adj*

an·ti·ozon·ant \-'ō-(ˌ)zō-nənt\ *n* (1954) : a substance that opposes ozonization or protects against it

an·ti·par·al·lel \ˌan-ti-'par-ə-ˌlel, ˌan-ˌtī-, -ˌləl\ *adj* (ca. 1660) : parallel but oppositely directed or oriented ⟨~ electron spins⟩ ⟨two ~ chains of nucleotides comprise DNA⟩

an·ti·par·a·sit·ic \ˌan-ti-ˌpar-ə-'si-tik, ˌan-ˌtī-\ *adj* (ca. 1860) : acting against parasites

an·ti·par·ti·cle \'an-ti-ˌpär-ti-kəl, 'an-ˌtī-\ *n* (1934) : a subatomic particle identical to another subatomic particle in mass but opposite to it in electric and magnetic properties (as sign of charge) that when brought together with its counterpart produces mutual annihilation; *esp* : a subatomic particle not found in ordinary matter

an·ti·pas·to \ˌan-ti-'pas-(ˌ)tō, ˌän-ti-, -'päs-\ *n, pl* **-ti** \-(ˌ)tē\ [It, fr. *anti-* (fr. L *ante-*) + *pasto* food, fr. L *pastus*, fr. *pascere* to feed — more at FOOD] (1590) : any of various typically Italian hors d'oeuvres; *also* : a plate of these served esp. as the first course of a meal

an·ti·pa·thet·ic \ˌan-ti-pə-'the-tik, (ˌ)an-ˌti-pə-\ *adj* (1640) **1** : having a natural aversion; *also* : not sympathetic : HOSTILE **2** : arousing antipathy ⟨mountains . . . are ~ to me —Havelock Ellis⟩ — **an·ti·pa·thet·i·cal·ly** \-ti-k(ə-)lē\ *adv*

\ə\ abut \ᵊ\ kitten, F table \ər\ further \a\ ash \ā\ ace \ä\ mop, mar \aú\ out \ch\ chin \e\ bet \ē\ easy \g\ go \i\ hit \ī\ ice \j\ job \ŋ\ sing \ō\ go \ȯ\ law \ȯi\ boy \th\ thin \t̲h̲\ the \ü\ loot \ú\ foot \y\ yet \zh\ vision \à, k̲, ⁿ, œ, ōē, ue, ūē, ᵊ\ *see* Guide to Pronunciation

an·tip·a·thy \an-'ti-pə-thē\ *n, pl* **-thies** [L *antipathia,* fr. Gk *antipatheia,* fr. *antipathēs* of opposite feelings, fr. *anti-* + *pathos* experience — more at PATHOS] (1601) **1** *obs* : opposition in feeling **2** : settled aversion or dislike : DISTASTE **3** : an object of aversion *syn* see ENMITY

an·ti·per·son·nel \ˌan-ti-ˌpər-s²n-'el, ˌan-ˌtī-\ *adj* (1939) : designed for use against military personnel ⟨an ~ mine⟩

an·ti·per·spi·rant \-'pər-sp(ə-)rənt\ *n* (1943) : a preparation used to check perspiration

an·ti·phlo·gis·tic \-flə-'jis-tik\ *adj* (1769) : ANTI-INFLAMMATORY

an·ti·phon \'an-tə-fən, -ˌfän\ *n* [ME *antiphone,* fr. MF, fr. LL *antiphona* — more at ANTHEM] (15c) **1** : a psalm, anthem, or verse sung responsively **2** : a verse usu. from Scripture said or sung before and after a canticle, psalm, or psalm verse as part of the liturgy

¹an·tiph·o·nal \an-'ti-fə-n²l\ *n* (1537) : ANTIPHONARY

²antiphonal *adj* (1719) : of, relating to, or suggesting an antiphon or antiphony — **an·tiph·o·nal·ly** \-n²l-ē\ *adv*

an·tiph·o·nary \an-'ti-fə-ˌner-ē\ *n, pl* **-nar·ies** (15c) **1** : a book containing a collection of antiphons **2** : a book containing the choral parts of the Divine Office

an·tiph·o·ny \an-'ti-fə-nē\ *n, pl* **-nies** (1592) : responsive alternation between two groups esp. of singers

an·tiph·ra·sis \an-'ti-frə-səs\ *n, pl* **-ra·ses** \-ˌsēz\ [LL, fr. Gk, fr. *anti-* + *phrasis* diction — more at PHRASE] (1533) : the usu. ironic or humorous use of words in senses opposite to the generally accepted meanings (as in "this giant of 3 feet 4 inches")

¹an·tip·o·dal \an-'ti-pə-d²l\ *adj* (1646) **1** : of or relating to the antipodes; *specif* : situated at the opposite side of the earth or moon ⟨an ~ meridian⟩ ⟨an ~ continent⟩ **2** : diametrically opposite ⟨an ~ point on a sphere⟩ **3** : entirely opposed ⟨a system ~ to democracy⟩

²antipodal *n* (1919) : any of three cells in the female gametophyte of most angiosperms that are grouped at the end of the embryo sac farthest from the micropyle — called also *antipodal cell*

an·ti·pode \'an-ti-ˌpōd\ *n, pl* **an·tip·o·des** \an-'ti-pə-ˌdēz\ [ME *antipodes,* pl., persons dwelling at opposite points on the globe, fr. L, fr. Gk, fr. pl. of *antipod-, antipous* with feet opposite, fr. *anti-* + *pod-, pous* foot — more at FOOT] (1549) **1** : the parts of the earth diametrically opposite — usu. used in pl.; often used of Australia and New Zealand **2** : the exact opposite or contrary — **an·tip·o·de·an** \ˌ(ˌ)an-ˌti-pə-'dē-ən\ *adj or n*

an·ti·po·et·ic \ˌan-ti-pō-'e-tik, ˌan-ˌtī-\ *adj* (1847) : of, relating to, or characterized by opposition to traditional poetic technique or style

an·ti·pol·lu·tion \-pə-'lü-shən\ *adj* (1924) : designed to prevent, reduce, or eliminate pollution ⟨~ laws⟩ — **antipollution** *n*

an·ti·pope \'an-ti-ˌpōp\ *n* [ME *antepope,* fr. MF *antipape,* fr. ML *antipapa,* fr. *anti-* + *papa* pope] (15c) : one elected or claiming to be pope in opposition to the pope canonically chosen

an·ti·pro·ton \ˌan-ti-'prō-ˌtän, ˌan-ˌtī-\ *n* (1940) : the antiparticle of the proton

an·ti·psy·chot·ic \ˌan-ti-sī-'kä-tik\ *n* (1966) : NEUROLEPTIC — **antipsychotic** *adj*

an·ti·py·ret·ic \-pī-'re-tik\ *n* (ca. 1681) : an agent that reduces fever — **antipyretic** *adj*

an·ti·py·rine \-'pīr-ˌēn\ *n* [fr. *Antipyrine,* a trademark] (1884) : an analgesic and antipyretic $C_{11}H_{12}N_2O$ formerly widely used but now largely replaced in oral use by less toxic substances (as aspirin)

¹an·ti·quar·i·an \ˌan-tə-'kwer-ē-ən\ *n* (1610) : one who collects or studies antiquities

²antiquarian *adj* (1771) **1** : of or relating to antiquarians or antiquities **2** : dealing in old or rare books — **an·ti·quar·i·an·ism** \-ē-ə-ˌni-zəm\ *n*

an·ti·quark \'an-ti-ˌkwärk, 'an-ˌtī-\ *n* (1964) : the antiparticle of the quark

an·ti·quary \'an-tə-ˌkwer-ē\ *n, pl* **-quar·ies** (1586) : ANTIQUARIAN

an·ti·quate \'an-tə-ˌkwāt\ *vt* **-quat·ed; -quat·ing** [LL *antiquatus,* pp. of *antiquare,* fr. L *antiquus*] (1596) : to make old or obsolete — **an·ti·qua·tion** \ˌan-tə-'kwā-shən\ *n*

an·ti·quat·ed *adj* (1623) **1** : OBSOLETE ⟨an ~ calendar⟩ **2** : outmoded or discredited by reason of age : being out of style or fashion ⟨~ methods of farming⟩ **3** : advanced in age *syn* see OLD

¹an·tique \(ˌ)an-'tēk\ *n* (1530) **1** : a relic or object of ancient times **2 a** : a work of art, piece of furniture, or decorative object made at an earlier period and according to various customs laws at least 100 years ago **b** : a manufactured product (as an automobile) from an earlier period

²an·tique \(ˌ)an-'tēk, *in verse often* 'an-tik\ *adj* [MF, fr. L *antiquus,* fr. *ante* before — more at ANTE-] (1534) **1** : existing since or belonging to earlier times : ANCIENT ⟨~ trade routes to the Orient⟩ **2 a** : being in the style or fashion of former times ⟨~ manners and graces⟩ **b** : made in or representative of the work of an earlier period ⟨~ mirrors⟩; *also* : being an antique **3** : selling or exhibiting antiques ⟨an ~ show⟩ *syn* see OLD

³an·tique \(ˌ)an-'tēk\ *vb* **-tiqued; -tiqu·ing** *vt* (1923) : to finish or refinish in antique style : give an appearance of age to ~ *vi* : to shop around for antiques — **an·tiqu·er** \-'tē-kər\ *n*

an·tiq·ui·ty \an-'ti-kwə-tē\ *n, pl* **-ties** (13c) **1** : ancient times; *esp* : those before the Middle Ages **2** : the quality of being ancient **3** *pl* **a** : relics or monuments (as coins, statues, or buildings) of ancient times **b** : matters relating to the life or culture of ancient times **4** : the people of ancient times

an·ti·ra·chit·ic \ˌan-ti-rə-'ki-tik, ˌan-ˌtī-\ *adj* (ca. 1860) : used or tending to prevent the development of rickets ⟨an ~ vitamin⟩

an·ti·re·jec·tion \ˌan-ti-ri-'jek-shən, ˌan-ˌtī-\ *adj* (1968) : used or tending to prevent organ transplant rejection ⟨~ drugs⟩ ⟨~ treatment⟩

an·ti·rheu·mat·ic \ˌan-ti-rù-'ma-tik, ˌan-ˌtī-\ *adj* (1817) : alleviating or preventing rheumatism ⟨~ therapy⟩ ⟨~ drugs⟩ — **antirheumatic** *n*

an·ti·roll bar \'an-ˌtī-ˌrōl-\ *n* (1951) : SWAY BAR

an·tir·rhi·num \ˌan-tə-'rī-nəm\ *n* [NL, genus name, fr. L, snapdragon, fr. Gk *antirrhinon,* fr. *anti-* like (fr. *anti* against, equivalent to) + *rhin-, rhis* nose — more at ANTI-] (1548) : SNAPDRAGON

antis *pl of* ANTI

an·ti·scor·bu·tic \ˌan-ti-skȯr-'byü-tik, ˌan-ˌtī-\ *adj* (1725) : counteracting scurvy ⟨the ~ vitamin is vitamin C⟩ — **antiscorbutic** *n*

an·ti–Sem·i·tism \ˌan-ti-'se-mə-ˌti-zəm, ˌan-ˌtī-\ *n* (1882) : hostility toward or discrimination against Jews as a religious, ethnic, or racial group — **an·ti–Se·mit·ic** \-sə-'mi-tik\ *adj* — **an·ti–Sem·ite** \-'se-ˌmīt\ *n*

an·ti·sense \'an-ˌtī-ˌsen(t)s, 'an-ˌtī-\ *adj* [*anti-* + *nonsense*] (1984) : having a complementary sequence to a segment of genetic material (as mRNA) and serving to inhibit gene function ⟨~ nucleotides⟩ ⟨~ RNA⟩ — compare MISSENSE, NONSENSE

an·ti·sep·sis \ˌan-tə-'sep-səs\ *n* (1875) : the inhibiting of the growth and multiplication of microorganisms by antiseptic means

¹an·ti·sep·tic \ˌan-tə-'sep-tik\ *adj* [*anti-* + Gk *sēptikos* putrefying, septic] (1751) **1 a** : opposing sepsis, putrefaction, or decay; *esp* : preventing or arresting the growth of microorganisms (as on living tissue) **b** : acting or protecting like an antiseptic **2** : relating to or characterized by the use of antiseptics **3 a** : scrupulously clean : ASEPTIC **b** : extremely neat or orderly; *esp* : neat to the point of being bare or uninteresting **c** : free from what is held to be contaminating **4** : coldly impersonal ⟨an ~ greeting⟩ — **an·ti·sep·ti·cal·ly** \-ti-k(ə-)lē\ *adv*

²antiseptic *n* (1751) : a substance that checks the growth or action of microorganisms esp. in or on living tissue; *also* : GERMICIDE

an·ti·se·rum \'an-ti-ˌsir-əm, 'an-ˌtī-, -ˌser-\ *n* [ISV] (1901) : a serum containing antibodies

an·ti·so·cial \ˌan-ti-'sō-shəl, ˌan-ˌtī-\ *adj* (1797) **1** : averse to the society of others : UNSOCIABLE **2** : hostile or harmful to organized society; *esp* : being or marked by behavior deviating sharply from the social norm — **an·ti·so·cial·ly** \-shə-lē\ *adv*

an·ti·so·lar \-'sō-lər\ *adj* (ca. 1890) : being or having a direction away from the sun ⟨the ~ point⟩

an·ti·spas·mod·ic \-spaz-'mä-dik\ *adj* (1763) : capable of preventing or relieving spasms or convulsions — **antispasmodic** *n*

an·ti·stat \-'stat\ *or* **an·ti·stat·ic** \-'sta-tik\ *adj* (1952) : reducing, removing, or preventing the buildup of static electricity

an·tis·tro·phe \an-'tis-trə-(ˌ)fē\ *n* [LL, fr. Gk *antistrophē,* fr. *anti-* + *strophē* strophe] (ca. 1550) **1 a** : the repetition of words in reversed order **b** : the repetition of a word or phrase at the end of successive clauses **2 a** : a returning movement in Greek choral dance exactly answering to a previous strophe **b** : the part of a choral song delivered during the antistrophe — **an·ti·stroph·ic** \ˌan-tə-'strä-fik\ *adj* — **an·ti·stroph·i·cal·ly** \-fi-k(ə-)lē\ *adv*

an·ti·sym·met·ric \-sə-'me-trik\ *adj* (1923) : relating to or being a relation (as "is a subset of") that implies equality of any two quantities for which it holds in both directions ⟨the relation *R* is ~ if *aRb* and *bRa* implies *a* = *b*⟩

an·tith·e·sis \an-'ti-thə-səs\ *n, pl* **-e·ses** \-ˌsēz\ [LL, fr. Gk, lit., opposition, fr. *antitithenai* to oppose, fr. *anti-* + *tithenai* to set — more at DO] (1529) **1 a** (1) : the rhetorical contrast of ideas by means of parallel arrangements of words, clauses, or sentences (as in "action, not words" or "they promised freedom and provided slavery") (2) : OPPOSITION, CONTRAST ⟨the ~ of prose and verse⟩ **b** (1) : the second of two opposing constituents of an antithesis (2) : the direct opposite **2** : the second stage of a dialectic process

an·ti·thet·i·cal \ˌan-tə-'the-ti-kəl\ *also* **an·ti·thet·ic** \-'the-tik\ *adj* (1583) **1** : constituting or marked by antithesis **2** : being in direct and unequivocal opposition *syn* see OPPOSITE — **an·ti·thet·i·cal·ly** \-ti-k(ə-)lē\ *adv*

an·ti·throm·bin \ˌan-ti-'thräm-bən, ˌan-ˌtī-\ *n* (ca. 1911) : any of a group of substances that inhibit blood clotting by inactivating thrombin

an·ti·thy·roid \ˌan-ti-'thī-ˌrȯid\ *adj* (1908) : able to counteract excessive thyroid activity ⟨~ drugs⟩

an·ti·tox·ic \-'täk-sik\ *adj* (ca. 1890) **1** : counteracting toxins **2** : being or containing antitoxins ⟨~ serum⟩

an·ti·tox·in \ˌan-ti-'täk-sən\ *n* [ISV] (ca. 1890) : an antibody that is capable of neutralizing the specific toxin (as a specific causative agent of disease) that stimulated its production in the body and is produced in animals for medical purposes by injection of a toxin or toxoid with the resulting serum being used to counteract the toxin in other individuals; *also* : an antiserum containing antitoxins

an·ti·trades \'an-ti-ˌtrādz, 'an-ˌtī-\ *n pl* (1875) : the westerly winds above the trade winds

an·ti·trust \ˌan-ti-'trəst, ˌan-ˌtī-\ *adj* (1890) : of, relating to, or being legislation against or opposition to trusts or combinations; *specif* : consisting of laws to protect trade and commerce from unlawful restraints and monopolies or unfair business practices

an·ti·trust·er \-'trəs-tər\ *n* (1947) : one who advocates or enforces antitrust provisions of the law

an·ti·tus·sive \-'tə-siv\ *adj* (ca. 1909) : a cough suppressant — **antitussive** *adj*

an·ti–uto·pia \ˌan-ti-yù-'tō-pē-ə, ˌan-ˌtī-\ *n* (1966) **1** : DYSTOPIA 1 **2** : a work describing an anti-utopia — **an·ti–uto·pi·an** \-pē-ən\ *adj or n*

an·ti·ven·in \ˌan-ti-'ve-nən, ˌan-ˌtī-\ *n* [ISV] (1895) : an antitoxin to a venom; *also* : an antiserum containing such antitoxin

an·ti·vi·ta·min \ˌan-ti-'vī-tə-mən, *Brit usu* -ˌvi-\ *n* (1927) : a substance that makes a vitamin metabolically ineffective

an·ti·white \ˌan-ti-'hwīt, ˌan-ˌtī-, -'wīt\ *adj* (1906) : opposed or hostile to people belonging to a light-skinned race

ant·ler \'ant-lər\ *n* [ME *aunteler,* fr. MF *antoillier,* fr. (assumed) VL *anteoculare,* fr. neut. of *anteocularis* located before the eye, fr. L *ante-* + *oculus* eye — more at EYE] (14c) : one of the paired deciduous solid bone processes that arise from the frontal bone on the head of an animal of the deer family; *also* : a branch of an antler — **ant·lered** \-lərd\ *adj*

ant lion *n* (1815) : any of various neuropterous insects (as of the genus *Myrmeleon*) having a long-jawed larva that digs a conical pit in which it lies in wait to catch insects (as ants) on which it feeds

An·to·ni·an \an-'tō-nē-ən\ *n* [L *Antonius* Anthony] (ca. 1907) : a member of one of

ant lion: *1* larva, *2* adult

several monastic communities (as the Armenian Antonians) that follow a rule devised by St. Anthony

an·ton·o·ma·sia \,an-tə-nō-'mā-zh(ē-)ə, (,)an-,tä-nə-\ *n* [L, use of an epithet for a proper name, fr. Gk, fr. *antonomazein* to call by a new name, fr. *anti-* + *onomazein* to name, fr. *onoma* name — more at NAME] (ca. 1550) : the use of a proper name to designate a member of a class (as a *Solomon* for a *wise ruler*); *also* : the use of an epithet or title in place of a proper name (as *the Bard* for *Shakespeare*)

an·to·nym \'an-tə-,nim\ *n* (1870) : a word of opposite meaning ⟨the usual ∼ of *good* is *bad*⟩ — **an·ton·ym·ic** \,an-tə-'ni-mik\ *adj* — **an·ton·y·mous** \an-'tä-nə-məs\ *adj* — **an·ton·y·my** \-mē\ *n*

an·tre \'an-tər\ *n* [F, fr. L *antrum*] (1604) : CAVE 1

an·trum \'an-trəm\ *n, pl* **an·tra** \-trə\ [LL, fr. L, cave, fr. Gk *antron;* akin to Arm *ayr* cave] (ca. 1751) : the cavity of a hollow organ or a sinus — **an·tral** \-trəl\ *adj*

ant·sy \'ant-sē\ *adj* (1838) **1** : impatient of restraint; *esp* : FIDGETY **2** : NERVOUS, APPREHENSIVE

Anu·bis \ə-'nü-bəs, -'nyü-\ *n* [L, fr. Gk *Anoubis,* fr. Egypt *inpw*] : a jackal-headed god in Egyptian mythology who leads the dead to judgment

an·uran \ə-'nyùr-ən, a-, -'nùr-\ *adj or n* [ultim. fr. Gk *a-* + *oura* tail — more at ASS] (1900) : any of an order (Anura) of amphibians comprising the frogs, toads, and tree toads all of which lack a tail in the adult stage and have long strong hind limbs suited to leaping and swimming — **anuran** *adj*

an·uria \ə-'nyùr-ē-ə, a-, -'nùr-\ *n* [NL] (1838) : absence or defective excretion of urine — **an·uric** \-'nyùr-ik, -'nùr-\ *adj*

anus \'ā-nəs\ *n* [L, ring, anus; perh. akin to OIr *ánne* ring] (15c) : the posterior opening of the alimentary canal

an·vil \'an-vəl\ *n* [ME *anfilt,* fr. OE; akin to OHG *anafalz* anvil; akin to L *pellere* to beat — more at FELT] (bef. 12c) **1** : a heavy usu. steel-faced iron block on which metal is shaped (as by hand hammering) **2** : INCUS

anx·i·ety \aŋ-'zī-ə-tē\ *n, pl* **-eties** [L *anxietas,* fr. *anxius*] (ca. 1525) **1 a** : painful or apprehensive uneasiness of mind usu. over an impending or anticipated ill **b** : fearful concern or interest ∼ : a cause of anxiety **2** : an abnormal and overwhelming sense of apprehension and fear often marked by physiological signs (as sweating, tension, and increased pulse), by doubt concerning the reality and nature of the threat, and by self-doubt about one's capacity to cope with it *syn see* CARE

anx·i·o·lyt·ic \aŋ-zē-ō-'li-tik, ,aŋ(k)-sē-\ *n* [*anxiety* + *-o-* + *-lytic*] (1965) : a drug that relieves anxiety — **anxiolytic** *adj*

anx·ious \'aŋ(k)-shəs\ *adj* [L *anxius;* akin to L *angere* to strangle, distress — more at ANGER] (ca. 1616) **1** : characterized by extreme uneasiness of mind or brooding fear about some contingency : WORRIED **2** : characterized by, resulting from, or causing anxiety : WORRYING **3** : ardently or earnestly wishing *syn see* EAGER — **anx·ious·ly** *adv* — **anx·ious·ness** *n*

¹any \'e-nē\ *adj* [ME, fr. OE *ænig;* akin to OHG *einag* any, OE *ān* one — more at ONE] (bef. 12c) **1** : one or some indiscriminately of whatever kind: **a** : one or another taken at random ⟨ask ∼ man you meet⟩ **b** : EVERY — used to indicate one selected without restriction ⟨∼ child would know that⟩ **2** : one, some, or all indiscriminately of whatever quantity: **a** : one or more — used to indicate an undetermined number or amount ⟨have you ∼ money⟩ **b** : ALL — used to indicate a maximum or whole ⟨needs ∼ help he can get⟩ **c** : a or some without reference to quantity or extent ⟨grateful for ∼ favor at all⟩ **3 a** : unmeasured or unlimited in amount, number, or extent ⟨∼ quantity you desire⟩ **b** : appreciably large or extended ⟨could not endure it ∼ length of time⟩

²any *pron, sing or pl in constr* (bef. 12c) **1** : any person or persons : ANYONE **2 a** : any thing or things **b** : any part, quantity, or number

³any *adv* (14c) : to any extent or degree : AT ALL ⟨was never ∼ good⟩

any·body \-,bä-dē, -bə-\ *pron* (14c) : any person : ANYONE

any·how \-,hau\ *adv* (1690) **1** : in any manner whatever **b** : in a haphazard manner **2 a** : at any rate **b** : in any event

any·more \,e-nē-'mōr, -'mòr\ *adv* (14c) **1** : any longer ⟨I was not moving ∼ with my feet —Anaïs Nin⟩ **2** : at the present time : NOW ⟨hardly a day passes without rain ∼⟩

usage Although both *anymore* and *any more* are found in written use, in the 20th century *anymore* is the more common styling. *Anymore* is regularly used in negative ⟨no one can be natural *anymore* —May Sarton⟩, interrogative ⟨do you read much *anymore*?⟩, and conditional ⟨if you do that *anymore*, I'll leave⟩ contexts and in certain positive constructions ⟨the Washington's is too sophisticated to believe *anymore* in solutions —Russell Baker⟩. In many regions of the U.S. the use of *anymore* in sense 2 is quite common in positive constructions, esp. in speech ⟨everybody's cool *anymore* —Bill White⟩ ⟨every time we leave the house *anymore*, I play a game called "Stump the House-breaker" —Erma Bombeck⟩. The positive use appears to have been of Midland origin, but it is now reported to be widespread in all speech areas of the U.S. except New England.

any·one \'e-nē-(,)wən\ *pron* (1536) : any person at all

any·place \-,plās\ *adv* (1916) : in any place : ANYWHERE

¹any·thing \-,thiŋ\ *pron* (bef. 12c) : any thing whatever : any such thing

²anything *adv* (bef. 12c) : AT ALL

any·time \'e-nē-,tīm\ *adv* (1926) : at any time whatever

any·way \-,wā\ *adv* (13c) **1** : ANYWISE **2** : in any case : ANYHOW

any·ways \-,wāz\ *adv* (13c) **1 a** *archaic* : ANYWISE **b** *dial* : to any degree at all **2** *chiefly dial* : ANYHOW, ANYWAY

¹any·where \-,(h)wer, -,(h)war, -(h)wər\ *adv* (14c) **1** : at, in, or to any place or point **2** : to any extent : AT ALL **3** — used as a function word to indicate limits of variation ⟨∼ from 40 to 60 students⟩

²anywhere *n* (1924) : any place

any·wheres \-,(h)werz, -,(h)warz, -(h)wərz\ *adv* (1775) *chiefly dial* : ANYWHERE

any·wise \'e-nē-,wīz\ *adv* (13c) : in any way whatever : AT ALL

An·zac \'an-,zak\ *n* [Australian and New Zealand Army Corps] (1915) : a soldier from Australia or New Zealand

A–OK \,ā-(,)ō-'kā\ *adv or adj* (1959) : very definitely OK

A1 \'ā-'wən\ *adj* (1837) **1** : having the highest possible classification — used of a ship **2** : of the finest quality : FIRST-RATE

ao·rist \'ā-ə-rəst, 'e-ə-\ *n* [LL & Gk; LL *aoristos,* fr. Gk, fr. *aoristos* undefined, fr. *a-* + *horistos* definable, fr. *horizein* to define — more at HORIZON] (1581) : an inflectional form of a verb typically denoting simple occurrence of an action without reference to its completeness, duration, or repetition — **aorist** *or* **ao·ris·tic** \,ā-ə-'ris-tik, ,e-ə-\ *adj* — **ao·ris·ti·cal·ly** \-ti-k(ə-)lē\ *adv*

aor·ta \ā-'òr-tə\ *n, pl* **-tas** *or* **-tae** \-tē\ [NL, fr. Gk *aortē,* fr. *aeirein* to lift] (1543) : the great arterial trunk that carries blood from the heart to be distributed by branch arteries through the body — see HEART illustration — **aor·tic** \-'òr-tik\ *adj*

aortic arch *n* (1903) : one of the arterial branches in vertebrate embryos that exist in a series of pairs with one on each side of the embryo, connect the ventral arterial system lying anterior to the heart to the dorsal arterial system above the alimentary tract, and persist in adult fishes but are reduced or much modified in the adult of higher forms

aor·tog·ra·phy \,ā-,òr-'tä-grə-fē\ *n* (ca. 1935) : arteriography of the aorta — **aor·to·graph·ic** \(,)ā-,òr-tə-'gra-fik\ *adj*

aou·dad \'aù-,dad, 'ä-ü-\ *n* [F, fr. Berber *audad*] (1861) : a wild bovine (*Ammotragus lervia*) of No. Africa that is closely related to goats and sheep and has been introduced into the southwestern U.S.

à ou·trance \,ä-,ü-'träns\ *adv* [F] (1883) : to the limit : UNSPARINGLY

¹ap- — see AD-

²ap- — see APO-

apace \ə-'pās\ *adv* [ME, prob. fr. MF *à pas* on step] (14c) **1** : at a quick pace : SWIFTLY **2** : ABREAST — used with *of or* with

Apache \ə-'pa-chē, *in sense 3* ə-'pash\ *n, pl* **Apache** *or* **Apach·es** \-'pa-chēz; -'pash, -'pa-shəz\ [AmerSp, perh. fr. Zuni *ʔapačŭ* Navajo, Apachean] (1745) **1** : a member of a group of American Indian peoples of the southwestern U.S. **2** : any of the Athabascan languages of the Apache people **3** *not cap* [F, fr. *Apache* Apache Indian] : **a** : a member of a gang of criminals esp. in Paris : RUFFIAN — **Apach·e·an** \ə-'pa-chē-ən\ *adj or n*

ap·a·nage *var of* APPANAGE

apa·re·jo \,a-pə-'rā-(,)hō\ *n, pl* **-jos** [AmerSp] (1844) : a packsaddle of stuffed leather or canvas

¹apart \ə-'pärt\ *adv* [ME, fr. MF *à part,* lit., to the side] (14c) **1 a** : at a little distance ⟨tried to keep ∼ from the family squabbles⟩ **b** : away from one another in space or time ⟨towns 20 miles ∼⟩ **2** : as a separate unit : INDEPENDENTLY ⟨viewed ∼, his arguments were unsound⟩ **b** : so as to separate one from another ⟨found it hard to tell the twins ∼⟩ **3** : excluded from consideration : ASIDE ⟨a few blemishes ∼, the novel is excellent⟩ **4** : in or into two or more parts : to pieces ⟨coming ∼ at the seams⟩

²apart *adj* (1786) **1** : SEPARATE, ISOLATED **2** : holding different opinions : DIVIDED — **apart·ness** *n*

apart from *prep* (1833) : other than : BESIDES

apart·heid \ə-'pär-,tāt, -,tīt\ *n* [Afrik, fr. D, fr. *apart* apart + *-heid* -hood] (1947) **1** : racial segregation; *specif* : a policy of segregation and political and economic discrimination against non-European groups in the Republic of So. Africa **2** : SEPARATION, SEGREGATION ⟨I favor ∼ of smokers —L. E. Bellin⟩ ⟨sexual ∼⟩

apart·ment \ə-'pärt-mənt\ *n* [F *appartement,* fr. It *appartamento*] (1641) **1** : a room or set of rooms fitted esp. with housekeeping facilities and usu. leased as a dwelling **2** : a building containing several individual apartments — **apart·men·tal** \ə-,pärt-'men-tᵊl\ *adj*

apartment hotel *n* (1909) : a hotel containing apartments as well as accommodations for transients

apartment house *n* (1874) : a building containing separate residential apartments — called also *apartment building*

ap·a·thet·ic \,a-pə-'the-tik\ *adj* (1744) **1** : having or showing little or no feeling or emotion : SPIRITLESS **2** : having little or no interest or concern : INDIFFERENT *syn see* IMPASSIVE — **ap·a·thet·i·cal·ly** \-ti-k(ə-)lē\ *adv*

ap·a·thy \'a-pə-thē\ *n* [Gk *apatheia,* fr. *apathēs* without feeling, fr. *a-* + *pathos* emotion — more at PATHOS] (1603) **1** : lack of feeling or emotion : IMPASSIVENESS **2** : lack of interest or concern : INDIFFERENCE

ap·a·tite \'a-pə-,tīt\ *n* [G *Apatit,* fr. Gk *apatē* deceit] (1803) : any of a group of calcium phosphate minerals occurring variously as hexagonal crystals, as granular masses, or in fine-grained masses as the chief constituent of phosphate rock and of bones and teeth; *esp* : calcium phosphate fluoride

apato·sau·rus \ə-,pa-tə-'sòr-əs\ *n* [NL, fr. Gk *apatē* + *sauros* lizard] (ca. 1899) : BRONTOSAURUS

¹ape \'āp\ *n* [ME, fr. OE *apa;* akin to OHG *affo* ape] (bef. 12c) **1 a** : MONKEY; *esp* : one of the larger tailless or short-tailed Old World forms **b** : any of two families (Pongidae and Hylobatidae) of large tailless semierect primates (as the chimpanzee, gorilla, orangutan, or gibbon) — called also *anthropoid, anthropoid ape* **2 a** : MIMIC **b** : a large uncouth person — **ape·like** \'āp-,līk\ *adj*

²ape *vt* **aped; ap·ing** (1632) : to copy closely but often clumsily and ineptly *syn see* COPY — **ap·er** *n*

³ape *adj* (ca. 1955) : being beyond restraint : CRAZY, WILD — usu. used in the phrase *go ape*

apeak \ə-'pēk\ *adj or adv* [alter. of earlier *apike,* prob. fr. F *à pic* vertically] (1596) : being in a vertical position ⟨with oars ∼⟩

ape–man \'āp-,man, -'man\ *n* (1879) : a primate (as an australopithecine) intermediate in character between Homo sapiens and the higher apes

aper·çu \ä-per-süe, ,a-pər-'sü\ *n, pl* **aperçus** \-süe(z), -'süz\ [F, fr. *aperçu,* pp. of *apercevoir* to perceive, fr. OF *aperceivre,* fr. *a-* (fr. L *ad-*) + *perceivre* to perceive — more at PERCEIVE] (1828) **1** : a brief survey or sketch : OUTLINE **2** : an immediate impression; *esp* : INSIGHT 2

ape·ri·ent \ə-'pir-ē-ənt\ *adj* [L *aperient-, aperiens,* prp. of *aperire*] (1626) : gently moving the bowels : LAXATIVE — **aperient** *n*

\ə\ abut \ᵊ\ kitten, F table \ər\ further \a\ ash \ā\ ace \ä\ mop, mar \aù\ out \ch\ chin \e\ bet \ē\ easy \g\ go \i\ hit \ī\ ice \j\ job \ŋ\ sing \ō\ go \ò\ law \òi\ boy \th\ thin \t̲h̲\ the \ü\ loot \ù\ foot \y\ yet \zh\ vision \à, k̲, ⁿ, œ, œ̄, ue, uē, ᵞ\ *see* Guide to Pronunciation

ape·ri·od·ic \ˌā-ˌpir-ē-'ä-dik\ *adj* (1879) **1** : of irregular occurrence ⟨∼ floods⟩ **2** : not having periodic vibrations : not oscillatory — **ape·ri·od·i·cal·ly** \-di-k(ə-)lē\ *adv* — **ape·ri·o·dic·i·ty** \-ē-ə-'di-sə-tē\ *n*

aper·i·tif \ə-ˌper-ə-'tēf, a-\ \ä-pər-(ə-)'tēf\ *n* [F *apéritif* aperient, aperitif, fr. MF *aperitif*, adj., aperient, fr. ML *aperitivus*, irreg. fr. L *aperire*] (1894) : an alcoholic drink taken before a meal as an appetizer

ap·er·ture \'ap-ə(r)-ˌchùr, -chər, -ˌtyùr, -ˌtùr\ *n* [ME, fr. L *apertura*, fr. *apertus*, pp. of *aperire* to open] (15c) **1** : an opening or open space : HOLE **2 a** : the opening in a photographic lens that admits the light **b** : the diameter of the stop in an optical system that determines the diameter of the bundle of rays traversing the instrument **c** : the diameter of the objective lens or mirror of a telescope

apet·al·ous \(ˌ)ā-'pe-tʰl-əs\ *adj* (ca. 1706) : having no petals

apex \'ā-ˌpeks\ *n, pl* **apex·es** *or* **api·ces** \-ˌsēz, 'a-\ [L] (1601) **1 a** : the uppermost point : VERTEX ⟨the ∼ of a mountain⟩ **b** : the narrowed or pointed end : TIP ⟨the ∼ of the tongue⟩ **2** : the highest or culminating point ⟨the ∼ of his career⟩ *syn* see SUMMIT

Ap·gar score \'ap-ˌgär-\ *n* [Virginia *Apgar* †1974 Am. anesthesiologist] (1962) : an index used to evaluate the condition of a newborn infant based on a rating of 0, 1, or 2 for each of the five characteristics of color, heart rate, response to stimulation of the sole of the foot, muscle tone, and respiration with 10 being a perfect score

aphaer·e·sis *or* **apher·e·sis** \ə-'fer-ə-səs\ *n, pl* **-e·ses** \-ˌsēz\ [LL, fr. Gk *aphairesis*, lit., taking off, fr. *aphairein* to take away, fr. *apo* + *hairein* to take] (ca. 1550) : the loss of one or more sounds or letters at the beginning of a word (as in *round* for *around* and *coon* for *raccoon*) — **aph·ae·ret·ic** \ˌa-fə-'re-tik\ *adj*

aph·a·nite \'a-fə-ˌnit\ *n* [F, fr. Gk *aphanēs* invisible, fr. a- + *phainesthai* to appear — more at PHENOMENON] (ca. 1828) : a dark rock of such close texture that its separate grains are invisible to the naked eye — **aph·a·nit·ic** \ˌa-fə-'ni-tik\ *adj*

apha·sia \ə-'fā-zh(ē-)ə\ *n* [NL, fr. Gk, fr. a- + *-phasia*] (1867) : loss or impairment of the power to use or comprehend words usu. resulting from brain damage — **apha·sic** \-zik\ *n or adj*

aph·elion \a-'fēl-yən\ *n, pl* **-elia** \-yə\ [NL, fr. *apo-* + Gk *hēlios* sun — more at SOLAR] (1656) : the point in the path of a celestial body (as a planet) that is farthest from the sun — compare PERIHELION

aph·e·sis \a-fə-səs\ *n, pl* **-e·ses** \-ˌsēz\ [NL, fr. Gk, release, fr. *aphienai* to let go, fr. *apo-* + *hienai* to send — more at JET] (1880) : aphaeresis consisting of the loss of a short unaccented vowel (as in *lone* for *alone*) — **aphet·ic** \ə-'fe-tik\ *adj* — **aphet·i·cal·ly** \-ti-k(ə-)lē\ *adv*

aphid \'ā-fəd *also* ā-fəd\ *n* (1884) : any of numerous very small sluggish homopterous insects (superfamily Aphidoidea) that suck the juices of plants

aphid lion *n* (1949) : any of several insect larvae (as a lacewing or ladybug larva) that feed on aphids — called also *aphis lion*

aphis \'ā-fəs *also* 'a-fəs\ *n, pl* **aphi·des** \-fə-ˌdēz, 'a-fə-\ [NL *Aphid-, Aphis*, genus name] (1771) : any of a genus (*Aphis*) of aphids; *broadly* : APHID

apho·nia \(ˌ)ā-'fō-nē-ə\ *n* [NL, fr. Gk *aphōnia*, fr. *aphōnos* voiceless, fr. a- + *phōnē* sound — more at BAN] (1778) : loss of voice and of all but whispered speech — **apho·nic** \-'fä-nik, -'fō-\ *adj*

aph·o·rism \'a-fə-ˌri-zəm\ *n* [MF *aphorisme*, fr. LL *aphorismus*, fr. Gk *aphorismos* definition, aphorism, fr. *aphorizein* to define, fr. *apo-* + *horizein* to bound — more at HORIZON] (1528) **1** : a concise statement of a principle **2** : a terse formulation of a truth or sentiment : ADAGE — **aph·o·rist** \-rist\ *n* — **aph·o·ris·tic** \ˌa-fə-'ris-tik\ *adj* — **aph·o·ris·ti·cal·ly** \-ti-k(ə-)lē\ *adv*

aph·o·rize \'a-fə-ˌriz\ *vi* **-rized; -riz·ing** (1669) : to write or speak in or as if in aphorisms

apho·tic \(ˌ)ā-'fō-tik\ *adj* (ca. 1900) : being the deep zone of an ocean or lake receiving too little light to permit photosynthesis

aph·ro·di·si·ac \ˌa-frə-'dē-zē-ˌak, -'di-zē-\ [Gk *aphrodisiakos* sexual, gem with aphrodisiac properties, fr. *aphrodisia* heterosexual pleasures, fr. neut. pl. of *aphrodisios* of Aphrodite, fr. *Aphroditē*] (1719) **1** : an agent (as a food or drug) that arouses or is held to arouse sexual desire **2** : something that excites — **aphrodisiac** *also* **aph·ro·di·si·a·cal** \ˌa-frə-di-'sī-ə-kəl, -'zī-\ *adj*

Aph·ro·di·te \ˌa-frə-'di-tē\ *n* [Gk *Aphroditē*] : the Greek goddess of love and beauty — compare VENUS

api·ar·i·an \ˌā-pē-'er-ē-ən\ *adj* (1801) : of or relating to beekeeping or bees

api·a·rist \'ā-pē-ə-rist, -ˌpē-er-ist\ *n* (1816) : BEEKEEPER

api·ary \'ā-pē-ˌer-ē\ *n, pl* **-ar·ies** [L *apiarium*, fr. *apis* bee] (1654) : a place where bees are kept; *esp* : a collection of hives or colonies of bees kept for their honey

api·cal \'ā-pi-kəl *also* 'a-pi-\ *adj* [prob. fr. NL *apicalis*, fr. L *apic-, apex*] (1828) **1** : of, relating to, or situated at an apex **2** : of, relating to, or formed with the tip of the tongue ⟨*n, l*, and *r* are ∼ consonants⟩ — **api·cal·ly** \-k(ə-)lē\ *adv*

apical dominance *n* (1947) : inhibition of the growth of lateral buds by the terminal bud of a shoot

apical meristem *n* (ca. 1934) : a meristem at the apex of a root or shoot that is responsible for increase in length

apic·u·late \a-'pik-yə-lət, ā-\ *adj* [NL *apiculus*, dim. of L *apic-, apex*] (1830) : ending abruptly in a small distinct point ⟨an ∼ leaf⟩

api·cul·ture \'ā-pə-ˌkəl-chər\ *n* [prob. fr. F, fr. L *apis* bee + F *culture*] (1864) : the keeping of bees esp. on a large scale — **api·cul·tur·al** \ˌā-pə-'kəl-ch(ə-)rəl\ *adj* — **api·cul·tur·ist** \-ch(ə-)rist\ *n*

apiece \ə-'pēs\ *adv* (15c) : for each one : INDIVIDUALLY

Apis \'ā-pəs\ *n* [L, fr. Gk, fr. Egypt *ḥp*] : a sacred bull worshiped by the ancient Egyptians

ap·ish \'ā-pish\ *adj* (1532) : resembling an ape: as **a** : extremely silly or affected **b** : given to slavish imitation — **ap·ish·ly** *adv* — **ap·ish·ness** *n*

APL \ˌā-(ˌ)pē-'el\ *n* [*a programming language*] (1966) : a computer programming language designed esp. for the concise representation of algorithms

ap·la·nat·ic \ˌa-plə-'na-tik\ *adj* [a- + Gk *planasthai* to wander — more at PLANET] (1794) : free from or corrected for spherical aberration ⟨an ∼ lens⟩

aplas·tic anemia \(ˌ)ā-ˌplas-tik-\ *n* (1928) : anemia that is characterized by defective function of the blood-forming organs (as the bone marrow) and is caused by toxic agents (as chemicals or X rays) or is idiopathic in origin

¹aplen·ty \ə-'plen-tē\ *adj* (1830) : being in plenty or abundance — used postpositively ⟨money ∼ for all his needs⟩

²aplenty *adv* (1846) **1** : in abundance : PLENTIFULLY **2** : very much : EXTREMELY ⟨scared ∼⟩

ap·lite \'a-ˌplit\ *n* [prob. fr. G *Aplit*, fr. Gk *haploos* simple — more at HAPL-] (1879) : a fine-grained light-colored granite consisting almost entirely of quartz and feldspar — **ap·lit·ic** \a-'pli-tik\ *adj*

aplomb \ə-'pläm, -'pləm\ *n* [F, lit., perpendicularity, fr. MF, fr. *a plomb*, lit., according to the plummet] (1828) : complete and confident composure or self-assurance : POISE *syn* see CONFIDENCE

ap·nea \'ap-nē-ə\ *n* [NL, fr. a- + *-pnea*] (ca. 1719) **1** : transient cessation of respiration **2** : ASPHYXIA — **ap·ne·ic** \-nē-ik\ *adj*

ap·noea *chiefly Brit var of* APNEA

apo- *or* **ap-** *prefix* [ME, fr. MF & L; MF, fr. L, fr. Gk, fr. *apo* — more at OF] **1** : away from : off ⟨aphelion⟩ **2** : detached : separate ⟨apogamy⟩ **3** : formed from : related to ⟨apomorphine⟩

apoc·a·lypse \ə-'pä-kə-ˌlips\ *n* [ME, revelation, Revelation, fr. LL *apocalypsis*, fr. Gk *apokalypsis*, fr. *apokalyptein* to uncover, fr. *apo-* + *kalyptein* to cover — more at HELL] (13c) **1 a** : one of the Jewish and Christian writings of 200 B.C. to A.D. 150 marked by pseudonymity, symbolic imagery, and the expectation of an imminent cosmic cataclysm in which God destroys the ruling powers of evil and raises the righteous to life in a messianic kingdom **b** *cap* : REVELATION 3 **2 a** : something viewed as a prophetic revelation **b** : ARMAGEDDON

apoc·a·lyp·tic \ə-ˌpä-kə-'lip-tik\ *also* **apoc·a·lyp·ti·cal** \-ti-kəl\ *adj* (1663) **1** : of, relating to, or resembling an apocalypse **2** : forecasting the ultimate destiny of the world : PROPHETIC **3** : foreboding imminent disaster or final doom : TERRIBLE **4** : wildly unrestrained : GRANDIOSE **5** : ultimately decisive : CLIMACTIC — **apoc·a·lyp·ti·cal·ly** \-ti-k(ə-)lē\ *adv*

apoc·a·lyp·ti·cism \-tə-ˌsi-zəm\ *or* **apoc·a·lyp·tism** \ə-'pä-kə-ˌlip-ˌti-zəm\ *n* (1884) : apocalyptic expectation; *esp* : a doctrine concerning an imminent end of the world and an ensuing general resurrection and final judgment

apoc·a·lyp·tist \ə-'pä-kə-ˌlip-tist\ *n* (1835) : the writer of an apocalypse

apo·chro·mat·ic \ˌa-pə-krō-'ma-tik\ *adj* [ISV] (1887) : free from chromatic and spherical aberration ⟨an ∼ lens⟩

apoc·o·pe \ə-'pä-kə-(ˌ)pē\ *n* [LL, fr. Gk *apokopē*, lit., cutting off, fr. *apokoptein* to cut off, fr. *apo-* + *koptein* to cut — more at CAPON] (ca. 1550) : the loss of one or more sounds or letters at the end of a word (as in *sing* from Old English *singan*)

apo·crine \'a-pə-krən, -ˌkrīn, -ˌkrēn\ *adj* [ISV *apo-* + Gk *krinein* to separate — more at CERTAIN] (1926) : producing a fluid secretion by pinching off one end of the secretory cell while leaving the rest intact ⟨an ∼ gland⟩; *also* : produced by an apocrine gland

apoc·ry·pha \ə-'pä-krə-fə\ *n pl but sing or pl in constr* [ML, fr. LL, neut. pl. of *apocryphus* secret, not canonical, fr. Gk *apokryphos* obscure, fr. *apokryptein* to hide away, fr. *apo-* + *kryptein* to hide — more at CRYPT] (14c) **1** : writings or statements of dubious authenticity **2** *cap* **a** : books included in the Septuagint and Vulgate but excluded from the Jewish and Protestant canons of the Old Testament — see BIBLE table **b** : early Christian writings not included in the New Testament

apoc·ry·phal \-fəl\ *adj* (1590) **1** : of doubtful authenticity : SPURIOUS **2** *often cap* : of or resembling the Apocrypha *syn* see FICTITIOUS — **apoc·ry·phal·ly** \-fə-lē\ *adv* — **apoc·ry·phal·ness** *n*

apo·dic·tic \ˌa-pə-'dik-tik\ *also* **apo·deic·tic** \-'dik-tik\ *adj* [L *apodicticus*, fr. Gk *apodeiktikos*, fr. *apodeiknynai* to demonstrate, fr. *apo-* + *deiknynai* to show — more at DICTION] (ca. 1645) : expressing or of the nature of necessary truth or absolute certainty — **apo·dic·ti·cal·ly** \-ti-k(ə-)lē\ *adv*

apod·o·sis \ə-'pä-də-səs\ *n, pl* **-o·ses** \-ˌsēz\ [NL, fr. Gk, fr. *apodidonai* to give back, deliver, fr. *apo-* + *didonai* to give — more at DATE] (ca. 1638) : the main clause of a conditional sentence — compare PROTASIS

apo·en·zyme \ˌa-pō-'en-ˌzīm\ *n* [ISV] (1936) : a protein that forms an active enzyme system by combination with a coenzyme and determines the specificity of this system for a substrate

apog·a·my \ə-'pä-gə-mē\ *n* [ISV] (ca. 1878) : development of a sporophyte from a gametophyte without fertilization — **apog·a·mous** \ə-'pä-gə-məs\ *adj*

apo·gee \'a-pə-(ˌ)jē\ *n* [F *apogée*, fr. NL *apogaeum*, fr. Gk *apogaion*, fr. neut. of *apogeios, apogaios* far from the earth, fr. *apo-* + *gē, gaia* earth] (1594) **1** : the point in the orbit of an object (as a satellite) orbiting the earth that is at the greatest distance from the center of the earth; *also* : the point farthest from a planet or a satellite (as the moon) reached by an object orbiting it — compare PERIGEE **2** : the farthest or highest point : CULMINATION ⟨Aegean civilization reached its ∼ in Crete⟩ — **apo·ge·an** \ˌa-pə-'jē-ən\ *adj*

apogee 1

apo·li·po·pro·tein \ˌa-pō-ˌli-pō-'prō-ˌtēn, -ˌli-, -ˌtē-ən\ *n* (1970) : a protein that combines with a lipid to form a lipoprotein

apo·lit·i·cal \ˌā-pə-'li-ti-kəl\ *adj* (1935) **1** : having no interest or involvement in political affairs; *also* : having an aversion to politics or political affairs **2** : having no political significance — **apo·lit·i·cal·ly** \-k(ə-)lē\ *adv*

Ap·ol·lin·i·an \ˌa-pə-'li-nē-ən\ *adj* (1924) : APOLLONIAN

Apol·lo \ə-'pä-(ˌ)lō\ *n* [L *Apollin-, Apollo*, fr. Gk *Apollōn*] : the Greek and Roman god of sunlight, prophecy, music, and poetry

Ap·ol·lo·ni·an \ˌa-pə-'lō-nē-ən\ *adj* (1663) **1** : of, relating to, or resembling the god Apollo **2** : harmonious, measured, ordered, or balanced in character — compare DIONYSIAN

Apol·lyon \ə-'päl-yən, -'pä-lē-ən\ *n* [Gk *Apollyōn*] : the angel of the bottomless pit in the Book of Revelation

¹apol·o·get·ic \ə-ˌpä-lə-'je-tik\ *n* (15c) : APOLOGETICS 1

²apologetic *adj* [Gk *apologetikos*, fr. *apologeisthai* to defend, fr. *apo-* + *logos* speech] (1649) **1 a** : offered in defense or vindication ⟨the ∼ writings of the early Christians⟩ **b** : offered by way of excuse or apology ⟨an ∼ smile⟩ **2** : regretfully acknowledging fault or failure : CON-

TRITE ⟨was ∼ about his mistake⟩ — **apol·o·get·i·cal·ly** \-ti-k(ə-)lē\ *adv*

apol·o·get·ics \-tiks\ *n pl but sing or pl in constr* (ca. 1733) **1** : systematic argumentative discourse in defense (as of a doctrine) **2** : a branch of theology devoted to the defense of the divine origin and authority of Christianity

ap·o·lo·gia \ˌa-pə-ˈlō-j(ē-)ə\ *n* [LL] (1784) : a defense esp. of one's opinions, position, or actions ⟨the finest ∼ or explanation of what drives a man to devote his life to pure mathematics —*Brit. Book News*⟩ **syn** see APOLOGY

apol·o·gise *Brit var of* APOLOGIZE

apol·o·gist \ə-ˈpä-lə-jist\ *n* (1640) : one who speaks or writes in defense of someone or something

apol·o·gize \-ˌjīz\ *vi* **-gized; -giz·ing** (1597) : to make an apology — **apol·o·giz·er** *n*

ap·o·logue \ˈa-pə-ˌlóg, -ˌläg\ *n* [F, fr. L *apologus*, fr. Gk *apologos*, fr. *apo-* + *logos* speech, narrative] (ca. 1555) : an allegorical narrative usu. intended to convey a moral

apol·o·gy \ə-ˈpä-lə-jē\ *n, pl* **-gies** [MF or LL; MF *apologie*, fr. LL *apologia*, fr. Gk, fr. *apo-* + *logos* speech — more at LEGEND] (1533) **1 a** : a formal justification : DEFENSE **b** : EXCUSE 2a **2** : an admission of error or discourtesy accompanied by an expression of regret **3** : a poor substitute : MAKESHIFT

syn APOLOGY, APOLOGIA, EXCUSE, PLEA, PRETEXT, ALIBI mean matter offered in explanation or defense. APOLOGY usu. applies to an expression of regret for a mistake or wrong with implied admission of guilt or fault and with or without reference to palliating circumstances ⟨said by way of *apology* that he would have met them if he could⟩. APOLOGIA implies not admission of guilt or regret but a desire to make clear the grounds for some course, belief, or position ⟨his speech was an *apologia* for his foreign policy⟩. EXCUSE implies an intent to avoid or remove blame or censure ⟨used illness as an *excuse* for missing the meeting⟩. PLEA stresses argument or appeal for understanding or sympathy or mercy ⟨her usual *plea* that she was nearsighted⟩. PRETEXT suggests subterfuge and the offering of false reasons or motives in excuse or explanation ⟨used any *pretext* to get out of work⟩. ALIBI implies a desire to shift blame or evade punishment and imputes plausibility rather than truth to the explanation offered ⟨his *alibi* failed to stand scrutiny⟩.

apo·lune \ˈa-pə-ˌlün\ *n* [*apo-* + L *luna* moon — more at LUNAR] (ca. 1968) : the point in the path of a body orbiting the moon that is farthest from the center of the moon — compare PERILUNE

apo·mict \ˈa-pə-ˌmikt\ *n* [prob. back-formation fr. ISV *apomictic*, fr. *apo-* + Gk *mignynai* to mix — more at MIX] (ca. 1938) : one produced or reproducing by apomixis — **apo·mic·tic** \ˌa-pə-ˈmik-tik\ *adj* — **apo·mic·ti·cal·ly** \-ti-k(ə-)lē\ *adv*

apo·mix·is \ˌa-pə-ˈmik-səs\ *n, pl* **-mix·es** \-ˌsēz\ [NL, fr. *apo-* + Gk *mixis* act of mixing, fr. *mignynai*] (1913) : reproduction (as apogamy or parthenogenesis) involving specialized generative tissues but not dependent on fertilization

apo·mor·phine \ˌa-pə-ˈmȯr-ˌfēn\ *n* [ISV] (1888) : a crystalline morphine derivative $C_{17}H_{17}NO_2$ that is a dopamine agonist and is administered as the hydrochloride for its powerful emetic action

apo·neu·ro·sis \ˌa-pə-nu̇-ˈrō-səs, -nyu̇-\ *n* [NL, fr. Gk *aponeurōsis*, fr. *aponeurousthai* to pass into a tendon, fr. *apo-* + *neuron* sinew — more at NERVE] (1676) : a broad flat sheet of dense fibrous collagenous connective tissue that covers, invests, and forms the terminations and attachments of various muscles — **apo·neu·rot·ic** \-ˈrä-tik\ *adj*

ap·o·phthegm \ˈa-pə-ˌthem\ *var of* APOTHEGM

apo·phyl·lite \ˌa-pə-ˈfi-ˌlīt, ə-ˈpä-fə-ˌlīt\ *n* [F, fr. *apo-* + Gk *phyllon* leaf — more at BLADE] (1810) : a mineral composed of a hydrous potassium calcium silicate that is related to the zeolites and is usu. found in transparent square prisms or white or grayish masses

apoph·y·sis \ə-ˈpä-fə-səs\ *n, pl* **-y·ses** \-ˌsēz\ [NL, fr. Gk, fr. *apo-* + *phyein* to bring forth — more at BE] (1646) : an expanded or projecting part esp. of an organism — **apoph·y·se·al** \-ˌpä-fə-ˈsē-əl\ *adj*

ap·o·plec·tic \ˌa-pə-ˈplek-tik\ *adj* [F or LL; F *apoplectique*, fr. LL *apoplecticus*, fr. Gk *apoplēktikos*, fr. *apoplēssein*] (1611) **1** : of, relating to, or causing stroke **2** : affected with, inclined to, or showing symptoms of stroke **3** : of a kind to cause or apparently cause stroke ⟨an ∼ rage⟩; *also* : greatly excited or angered — **apo·plec·ti·cal·ly** \-ti-k(ə-)lē\ *adv*

ap·o·plexy \ˈa-pə-ˌplek-sē\ *n* [ME *apoplexie*, fr. MF & LL; MF, fr. LL *apoplexia*, fr. Gk *apoplēxia*, fr. *apoplēssein* to cripple by a stroke, fr. *apo-* + *plēssein* to strike — more at PLAINT] (15c) : STROKE 5

aport \ə-ˈpȯrt, -ˈpȯrt\ *adv* (1627) : on or toward the left side of a ship ⟨put the helm hard ∼⟩

apo·se·mat·ic \ˌa-pə-si-ˈma-tik\ *adj* (1890) : being conspicuous and serving to warn ⟨∼ coloration⟩ — **apo·se·mat·i·cal·ly** \-ti-k(ə-)lē\ *adv*

ap·o·si·o·pe·sis \ˌa-pə-ˌsī-ə-ˈpē-səs\ *n, pl* **-pe·ses** \-ˌsēz\ [LL, fr. Gk *aposiōpēsis*, fr. *aposiōpan* to be fully silent, fr. *apo-* + *siōpan* to be silent, fr. *siōpē* silence] (1578) : the leaving of a thought incomplete usu. by a sudden breaking off (as in "his behavior was—but I blush to mention that") — **ap·o·si·o·pet·ic** \-ˈpe-tik\ *adj*

apos·po·ry \ˈa-pə-ˌspȯr-ē, -ˌspȯr-; ə-ˈpäs-pə-rē\ *n* (1884) : production of gametophytes directly from diploid cells of the sporophytes without spore formation (as in certain ferns and mosses) — **apos·po·rous** \ˈa-pə-ˌspȯr-əs, -ˌspȯr-; ə-ˈpäs-pə-rəs\ *adj*

apos·ta·sy \ə-ˈpäs-tə-sē\ *n, pl* **-sies** [ME *apostasie*, fr. LL *apostasia*, fr. Gk, lit., revolt, fr. *aphistasthai* to revolt, fr. *apo-* + *histasthai* to stand — more at STAND] (14c) **1** : renunciation of a religious faith **2** : abandonment of a previous loyalty : DEFECTION

apos·tate \ə-ˈpäs-ˌtāt, -tət\ *n* (14c) : one who commits apostasy — **apostate** *adj*

apos·ta·tise *Brit var of* APOSTATIZE

apos·ta·tize \ə-ˈpäs-tə-ˌtīz\ *vi* **-tized; -tiz·ing** (1611) : to commit apostasy

a pos·te·ri·o·ri \ˌä-(ˌ)pō-ˌstir-ē-ˈȯr-ē, -ˌster-; ˌä-(ˌ)pō-ˌstir-ē-ˈȯr-ˌī, -(ˌ)pō-, -ˈȯr-ē; -ˈȯr-\ *adj* [L, lit., from the latter] (1588) **1** : INDUCTIVE **2** : relating to or derived by reasoning from observed facts — compare A PRIORI — **a posteriori** *adv*

apos·tle \ə-ˈpä-səl\ *n* [ME, fr. OF & OE; OF *apostle* & OE *apostol*, both fr. LL *apostolus*, fr. Gk *apostolos*, fr. *apostellein* to send away, fr. *apo-* +

stellein to send] (bef. 12c) **1** : one sent on a mission: as **a** : one of an authoritative New Testament group sent out to preach the gospel and made up esp. of Christ's 12 original disciples and Paul **b** : the first prominent Christian missionary to a region or group **2 a** : a person who initiates a great moral reform or who first advocates an important belief or system **b** : an ardent supporter : ADHERENT ⟨an ∼ of liberty⟩ **3** : the highest ecclesiastical official in some church organizations **4** : one of a Mormon administrative council of 12 men — **apos·tle·ship** \-ˌship\ *n*

Apostles' Creed *n* (ca. 1658) : a Christian statement of belief ascribed to the Twelve Apostles and used esp. in public worship

apos·to·late \ə-ˈpäs-tə-ˌlāt, -lət\ *n* [LL *apostolatus*, fr. *apostolus*] (14c) **1** : the office or mission of an apostle **2** : an association of persons dedicated to the propagation of a religion or a doctrine

ap·os·tol·ic \ˌa-pə-ˈstä-lik\ *adj* (13c) **1 a** : of or relating to an apostle **b** : of, relating to, or conforming to the teachings of the New Testament apostles **2 a** : of or relating to a succession of spiritual authority from the apostles held (as by Roman Catholics, Anglicans, and Eastern Orthodox) to be perpetuated by successive ordinations of bishops and to be necessary for valid sacraments and orders **b** : PAPAL — **apos·to·lic·i·ty** \ə-ˌpäs-tə-ˈli-sə-tē\ *n*

apostolic delegate *n* (ca. 1907) : an ecclesiastical representative of the Holy See to the Catholic hierarchy of another country

Apostolic Father *n* (1828) : a church father of the first or second century A.D.

¹apos·tro·phe \ə-ˈpäs-trə-(ˌ)fē\ *n* [L, fr. Gk *apostrophē*, lit., act of turning away, fr. *apostrephein* to turn away, fr. *apo-* + *strephein* to turn] (1533) : the addressing of a usu. absent person or a usu. personified thing rhetorically ⟨Carlyle's "O Liberty, what things are done in thy name!" is an example of ∼⟩ — **ap·os·troph·ic** \ˌa-pə-ˈsträ-fik\ *adj*

²apostrophe *n* [MF & LL; MF, fr. LL *apostrophus*, fr. Gk *apostrophos*, fr. *apostrophos* turned away, fr. *apostrephein*] (1727) : a mark ' used to indicate the omission of letters or figures, the possessive case, or the plural of letters or figures — **apostrophic** *adj*

apos·tro·phise *Brit var of* APOSTROPHIZE

apos·tro·phize \ə-ˈpäs-trə-ˌfīz\ *vb* **-phized; -phiz·ing** *vt* (1718) : to address by or in apostrophe ∼ *vi* : to make use of apostrophe

apothecaries' measure *n* (ca. 1900) : a system of liquid units of measure used chiefly by pharmacists

apothecaries' weight *n* (1765) : a system of weights used chiefly by pharmacists — see WEIGHT table

apoth·e·cary \ə-ˈpä-thə-ˌker-ē\ *n, pl* **-car·ies** [ME *apothecarie*, fr. ML *apothecarius*, fr. LL, shopkeeper, fr. L *apotheca* storehouse, fr. Gk *apothēkē*, fr. *apotithenai* to put away, fr. *apo-* + *tithenai* to put — more at DO] (14c) **1** : one who prepares and sells drugs or compounds for medicinal purposes **2** : PHARMACY

apo·the·ci·um \ˌa-pə-ˈthē-shē-əm, -sē-\ *n, pl* **-cia** \-shē-ə, -sē-\ [NL, fr. L *apotheca*] (1830) : a spore-bearing structure in many lichens and fungi consisting of a discoid or cupped body bearing asci on the exposed flat or concave surface — **apo·the·cial** \-sh(ē-)əl, -sē-əl\ *adj*

ap·o·thegm \ˈa-pə-ˌthem\ *n* [Gk *apophthegmat-, apophthegma*, fr. *apophthengesthai* to speak out, fr. *apo-* + *phthengesthai* to utter] (ca. 1587) : a short, pithy, and instructive saying or formulation : APHORISM — **apo·theg·mat·ic** \ˌa-pə-theg-ˈma-tik\ *adj*

ap·o·them \ˈa-pə-ˌthem\ *n* [ISV *apo-* + *-them* (fr. Gk *thema* something laid down, theme)] (ca. 1856) : the perpendicular from the center of a regular polygon to one of the sides

apo·the·o·sis \ə-ˌpä-thē-ˈō-səs, ˌa-pə-ˈthē-ə-səs\ *n, pl* **-o·ses** \-ˌsēz\ [LL, fr. Gk *apotheōsis*, fr. *apotheoun* to deify, fr. *apo-* + *theos* god] (ca. 1580) **1** : elevation to divine status : DEIFICATION **2** : the perfect example : QUINTESSENCE ⟨this is the literary ∼ of the shaggy dog story —Thomas Sutcliffe⟩ — **apo·the·o·size** \ə-ˈpä-thē-ə-ˌsīz, ə-ˈpä-thē-ə-\ *vt*

apo·tro·pa·ic \ˌa-pə-trō-ˈpā-ik\ *adj* [Gk *apotropaios*, fr. *apotrepein* to avert, fr. *apo-* + *trepein* to turn] (1883) : designed to avert evil ⟨an ∼ ritual⟩ — **apo·tro·pa·i·cal·ly** \-ˈpā-ə-k(ə-)lē\ *adv*

Ap·pa·la·chian \ˌa-pə-ˈlā-ch(ē-)ən, -ˈla-, -ˈchən\ *n* (1888) : a white native or resident of the Appalachian mountain area

Appalachian dulcimer *n* (1962) : DULCIMER 2

ap·pall *also* **ap·pal** \ə-ˈpȯl\ *vb* **ap·palled; ap·pall·ing** [ME, fr. MF *apalir*, fr. OF, fr. *a-* (fr. L *ad-*) + *palir* to grow pale, fr. L *pallescere*, incho. of *pallēre* to be pale — more at FALLOW] *vi* (14c) *obs* : WEAKEN, FAIL ∼ *vt* : to overcome with consternation, shock, or dismay **syn** see DISMAY

ap·pall·ing *adj* (1817) : inspiring horror, dismay, or disgust ⟨living under ∼ conditions⟩ — **ap·pall·ing·ly** *adv*

Ap·pa·loo·sa \ˌa-pə-ˈlü-sə\ *n* [origin unknown] (1947) : any of a breed of rugged saddle horses developed in western No. America and usu. having a white or solid-colored coat with small spots

ap·pa·nage \ˈa-pə-nij\ *n* [F *apanage*, fr. OF, fr. *apaner* to provide for a younger offspring, fr. ML *appanare*, fr. L *ad-* + *panis* bread — more at FOOD] (1602) **1 a** : a grant (as of land or revenue) made by a sovereign or a legislative body to a dependent member of the royal family or a principal vassal **b** : a property or privilege appropriated to or by a person as something due **2** : a rightful endowment or adjunct

Appaloosa

ap·pa·rat \ˈa-pə-ˌrat, ä-pə-ˈrät\ *n* [Russ] (1941) : APPARATUS 2

ap·pa·rat·chik \ˌä-pə-ˈrä(t)-chik\ *n, pl* **-chiks** *also* **-chi·ki** \-chi-kē\ [Russ, fr. *apparat*] (1941) **1** : a member of a Communist apparat **2** : an official blindly devoted to superiors or to the organization

ap·pa·ra·tus \ˌa-pə-ˈra-təs, -ˈrä-\ *n, pl* **-tus·es** *or* **-tus** [L, fr. *apparare* to prepare, fr. *ad-* + *parare* to prepare — more at PARE] (ca. 1628) **1 a**

\ə\ abut \ᵊ\ kitten, F table \ər\ further \a\ ash \ā\ ace \ä\ mop, mar \au̇\ out \ch\ chin \e\ bet \ē\ easy \g\ go \i\ hit \ī\ ice \j\ job \ŋ\ sing \ō\ go \ȯ\ law \ȯi\ boy \th\ thin \t͟h\ the \ü\ loot \u̇\ foot \y\ yet \zh\ vision \á, k̲, ⁿ, œ, œ̄, ᵫ, ᵫ̄, ᵊ\ *see* Guide to Pronunciation

: a set of materials or equipment designed for a particular use   **b** : a group of anatomical or cytological parts functioning together ⟨mitotic ~⟩   **c** : an instrument or appliance designed for a specific operation   **2** : the functional processes by means of which a systematized activity is carried out: as   **a** : the machinery of government   **b** : the organization of a political party or an underground movement

¹ap·par·el \ə-'par-əl\ *vt* **-eled** *or* **-elled; -el·ing** *or* **-el·ling** [ME *appareillen*, fr. MF *apareillier* to prepare, fr. (assumed) VL *appariculare*, fr. L *apparare*] (14c)   **1** : to put clothes on : DRESS   **2** : ADORN, EMBELLISH

²apparel *n* (14c)   **1** : the equipment (as sails and rigging) of a ship   **2** : personal attire : CLOTHING   **3** : something that clothes or adorns ⟨the bright ~ of spring⟩

ap·par·ent \ə-'par-ənt, -'per-\ *adj* [ME, fr. MF *aparent*, fr. L *apparent-, apparens*, prp. of *apparēre* to appear] (14c)   **1** : open to view : VISIBLE   **2** : clear or manifest to the understanding   **3** : appearing as actual to the eye or mind   **4** : having an indefeasible right to succeed to a title or estate   **5** : manifest to the senses or mind as real or true on the basis of evidence that may or may not be factually valid ⟨the air of spontaneity is perhaps more ~ than real —J. R. Sutherland⟩ — **ap·par·ent·ness** \-'par-ənt-nəs, -'per-\ *n*
syn APPARENT, ILLUSORY, SEEMING, OSTENSIBLE mean not actually being what appearance indicates. APPARENT suggests appearance to unaided senses that is not or may not be borne out by more rigorous examination or greater knowledge ⟨the *apparent* cause of the accident⟩. ILLUSORY implies a false impression based on deceptive resemblance or faulty observation, or influenced by emotions that prevent a clear view ⟨an *illusory* sense of security⟩. SEEMING implies a character in the thing observed that gives it the appearance, sometimes through intent, of something else ⟨the *seeming* simplicity of the story⟩. OSTENSIBLE suggests a discrepancy between an openly declared or naturally implied aim or reason and the true one ⟨the *ostensible* reason for their visit⟩.
syn see in addition EVIDENT

ap·par·ent·ly \-lē\ *adv* (1566) : it seems apparent ⟨the window had ~ been forced open⟩ ⟨~, we're supposed to wait here⟩
apparent magnitude *n* (1875) : the luminosity of a celestial body (as a star) as observed from the earth — compare ABSOLUTE MAGNITUDE
apparent time *n* (1694) : the time of day indicated by the hour angle of the sun or by a sundial
ap·pa·ri·tion \ˌa-pə-'ri-shən\ *n* [ME *apparicioun*, fr. LL *apparition-, apparitio* appearance, fr. L *apparēre*] (15c)   **1 a** : an unusual or unexpected sight : PHENOMENON   **b** : a ghostly figure   **2** : the act of becoming visible : APPEARANCE — **ap·pa·ri·tion·al** \-'rish-nəl, -'ri-shə-nᵊl\ *adj*
ap·par·i·tor \ə-'par-ə-tər\ *n* [L, fr. *apparēre*] (15c) : an official formerly sent to carry out the orders of a magistrate, judge, or court
¹ap·peal \ə-'pē(ə)l\ *n* (13c)   **1** : a legal proceeding by which a case is brought before a higher court for review of the decision of a lower court   **2** : a criminal accusation   **3 a** : an application (as to a recognized authority) for corroboration, vindication, or decision   **b** : an earnest plea : ENTREATY   **4** : the power of arousing a sympathetic response : ATTRACTION ⟨movies had a great ~ for him⟩
²appeal *vb* [ME *appelen* to accuse, appeal, fr. MF *apeler*, fr. L *appellare*, fr. *appellere* to drive to, fr. *ad-* + *pellere* to drive — more at FELT] *vt* (14c)   **1** : to charge with a crime : ACCUSE   **2** : to take proceedings to have (a lower court's decision) reviewed in a higher court ~ *vi*   **1** : to take a lower court's decision to a higher court for review   **2** : to call upon another for corroboration, vindication, or decision   **3** : to make an earnest request   **4** : to arouse a sympathetic response — **ap·peal·abil·i·ty** \-ˌpē-lə-'bi-lə-tē\ *n* — **ap·peal·able** \-'pē-lə-bəl\ *adj* — **ap·peal·er** *n*
ap·peal·ing \ə-'pē-liŋ\ *adj* (1813)   **1** : marked by earnest entreaty : IMPLORING   **2** : having appeal : PLEASING — **ap·peal·ing·ly** \-liŋ-lē\ *adv*
ap·pear \ə-'pir\ *vi* [ME *apperen*, fr. OF *aparoir*, fr. L *apparēre*, fr. *ad-* + *parēre* to show oneself] (13c)   **1 a** : to be or come in sight ⟨the sun ~s on the horizon⟩   **b** : to show up ⟨~s promptly at eight each day⟩   **2** : to come formally before an authoritative body ⟨must ~ in court today⟩   **3** : to have an outward aspect : SEEM ⟨~s happy enough⟩   **4** : to become evident or manifest ⟨there ~s to be evidence to the contrary⟩   **5** : to come into public view ⟨first ~ed on a television variety show⟩ ⟨the book ~ed in print a few years ago⟩   **6** : to come into existence ⟨hominids ~ed late in the evolutionary chain⟩
ap·pear·ance \ə-'pir-ən(t)s\ *n* (14c)   **1 a** : external show : SEMBLANCE ⟨although hostile, he preserved an ~ of neutrality⟩   **b** : outward aspect : LOOK ⟨had a fierce ~⟩   **c** *pl* : outward indication ⟨trying to keep up ~s⟩   **2 a** : a sense impression or aspect of a thing ⟨the blue of distant hills is only an ~⟩   **b** : the world of sensible phenomena   **3 a** : the act, action, or process of appearing   **b** : the presentation of oneself in court as a party to an action often through the representation of an attorney   **4 a** : something that appears : PHENOMENON   **b** : an instance of appearing : OCCURRENCE
ap·pease \ə-'pēz\ *vt* **ap·peased; ap·peas·ing** [ME *appesen*, fr. MF *apaisier*, fr. *a-* (fr. L *ad-*) + *pais* peace — more at PEACE] (14c)   **1** : to bring to a state of peace or quiet : CALM   **2** : to cause to subside : ALLAY ⟨*appeased* my hunger⟩   **3** : PACIFY, CONCILIATE; *esp* : to buy off (an aggressor) by concessions usu. at the sacrifice of principles **syn** see PACIFY — **ap·peas·able** \-'pē-zə-bəl\ *adj* — **ap·pease·ment** \-'pēz-mənt\ *n* — **ap·peas·er** *n*
¹ap·pel·lant \ə-'pe-lənt\ *adj* (14c) : of or relating to an appeal : APPELLATE
²appellant *n* (15c) : one that appeals; *specif* : one that appeals from a judicial decision or decree
ap·pel·late \ə-'pe-lət\ *adj* [L *appellatus*, pp. of *appellare*] (1768) : of, relating to, or recognizing appeals; *specif* : having the power to review the judgment of another tribunal ⟨an ~ court⟩
ap·pel·la·tion \ˌa-pə-'lā-shən\ *n* (15c)   **1** : an identifying name or title : DESIGNATION   **2** *archaic* : the act of calling by a name   **3** : a geographical name (as of a region, village or vineyard) under which a winegrower is authorized to identify and market wine
ap·pel·la·tive \ə-'pe-lə-tiv\ *adj* (15c)   **1** : of or relating to a common noun   **2** : of, relating to, or inclined to the giving of names — **ap·pel·la·tive** *n* — **ap·pel·la·tive·ly** *adv*
ap·pel·lee \ˌa-pə-'lē\ *n* (1531) : one against whom an appeal is taken

ap·pend \ə-'pend\ *vt* [ME, fr. MF *appendre*, fr. LL *appendere*, fr. L, to weigh, fr. *ad-* + *pendere* to weigh — more at PENDANT] (14c)   **1** : ATTACH, AFFIX   **2** : to add as a supplement or appendix (as in a book)
ap·pend·age \ə-'pen-dij\ *n* (1649)   **1** : an adjunct to something larger or more important : APPURTENANCE   **2** : a subordinate or derivative body part; *esp* : a limb or analogous part (as a seta)   **3** : a dependent or subordinate person
ap·pen·dant \ə-'pen-dənt\ *adj* (15c)   **1** : belonging as a right by prescription — used of annexed land in English law   **2** : associated as an attendant circumstance   **3** : attached as an appendage ⟨a seal ~ to a document⟩ — **appendant** *n*
ap·pen·dec·to·my \ˌa-pən-'dek-tə-mē, ˌa-ˌpen-\ *n, pl* **-mies** [L *appendic-, appendix* + E *-ectomy*] (ca. 1895) : surgical removal of the vermiform appendix
ap·pen·di·cec·to·my \ə-ˌpen-də-'sek-tə-mē\ *n, pl* **-mies** (1894) *Brit* : APPENDECTOMY
ap·pen·di·ci·tis \ə-ˌpen-də-'sī-təs\ *n* [NL] (1886) : inflammation of the vermiform appendix
ap·pen·dic·u·lar \ˌa-pən-'di-kyə-lər\ *adj* (1651) : of or relating to an appendage and esp. a limb ⟨the ~ skeleton⟩
ap·pen·dix \ə-'pen-diks\ *n, pl* **-dix·es** *or* **-di·ces** \-də-ˌsēz\ [L *appendic-, appendix*, fr. *appendere*] (1542)   **1 a** : APPENDAGE   **b** : supplementary material usu. attached at the end of a piece of writing   **2** : a bodily outgrowth or process; *specif* : VERMIFORM APPENDIX
ap·per·ceive \ˌa-pər-'sēv\ *vt* **-ceived; -ceiv·ing** [F *apercevoir*] (1876) : to have apperception of
ap·per·cep·tion \-'sep-shən\ *n* [F *aperception*, fr. *apercevoir*, fr. MF *aperceivre*, fr. a- (fr. L *ad-*) + *perceive* to perceive] (1753)   **1** : introspective self-consciousness   **2** : mental perception; *esp* : the process of understanding something perceived in terms of previous experience — **ap·per·cep·tive** \-'sep-tiv\ *adj*
ap·per·tain \ˌa-pər-'tān\ *vi* [ME *apperteinen*, fr. MF *apartenir*, fr. LL *appertinēre*, fr. L *ad-* + *pertinēre* to belong — more at PERTAIN] (14c) : to belong or be connected as a rightful part or attribute : PERTAIN
ap·pe·tence \'a-pə-tən(t)s\ *n* (1610) : APPETENCY
ap·pe·ten·cy \-tən(t)-sē\ *n, pl* **-cies** [L *appetentia*, fr. *appetent-, appetens*, prp. of *appetere*] (1631) : a fixed and strong desire : APPETITE —
ap·pe·tent \-tənt\ *adj*
ap·pe·tis·er, ap·pe·tis·ing *Brit var of* APPETIZER, APPETIZING
ap·pe·tite \'a-pə-ˌtīt\ *n* [ME *apetit*, fr. MF, fr. L *appetitus*, fr. *appetere* to strive after, fr. *ad-* + *petere* to go to — more at FEATHER] (14c)   **1** : any of the instinctive desires necessary to keep up organic life; *esp* : the desire to eat   **2 a** : an inherent craving ⟨an insatiable ~ for work⟩   **b** : TASTE, PREFERENCE ⟨the cultural ~s of the time —J. D. Hart⟩ — **ap·pe·ti·tive** \-ˌtī-tiv\ *adj*
ap·pe·tiz·er \'a-pə-ˌtī-zər\ *n* (1859) : a food or drink that stimulates the appetite and is usu. served before a meal
ap·pe·tiz·ing \-ˌtī-ziŋ\ *adj* (1653) : appealing to the appetite esp. in appearance or aroma; *also* : appealing to one's taste ⟨an ~ display of merchandise⟩ **syn** see PALATABLE — **ap·pe·tiz·ing·ly** \-ziŋ-lē\ *adv*
ap·plaud \ə-'plȯd\ *vb* [ME, fr. MF or L; MF *applaudir*, fr. L *applaudere*, fr. *ad-* + *plaudere* to applaud] *vi* (15c) : to express approval esp. by clapping the hands ~ *vt*   **1** : to express approval of : PRAISE ⟨~ her efforts to lose weight⟩   **2** : to show approval of esp. by clapping the hands — **ap·plaud·able** \-'plȯd-ə-bəl\ *adj* — **ap·plaud·ably** \-blē\ *adv* — **ap·plaud·er** *n*
ap·plause \ə-'plȯz\ *n* [ML *applausus*, fr. L, beating of wings, fr. *applaudere*] (15c)   **1** : marked commendation : ACCLAIM ⟨the kind of ~ every really creative writer wants —Robert Tallant⟩   **2** : approval publicly expressed (as by clapping the hands)
ap·ple \'a-pəl\ *n, often attrib* [ME *appel*, fr. OE *æppel*; akin to OHG *apful* apple, OIr *ubull*, OCS *ablŭko*] (bef. 12c)   **1** : the fleshy usu. rounded and red, yellow, or green edible pome fruit of a tree (genus *Malus*) of the rose family; *also* : an apple tree   **2** : a fruit or other vegetable production suggestive of an apple — compare OAK APPLE — **apple of one's eye** : one that is highly cherished ⟨his daughter is the *apple of his eye*⟩
apple butter *n* (ca. 1774) : a thick brown spread made by cooking apples with sugar and spices usu. in cider
ap·ple·cart \-ˌkärt\ *n* (1788) : a plan, system, situation, or undertaking that may be disrupted or terminated ⟨upset the ~⟩
ap·ple–cheeked \'a-pəl-ˌchēkt\ *adj* (1864) : having cheeks the color of red apples
ap·ple·jack \-ˌjak\ *n* (1816) : brandy distilled from hard cider; *also* : an alcoholic beverage traditionally made by freezing hard cider and siphoning off the concentrated liquor
ap·ple–knock·er \-ˌnä-kər\ *n* (1919) : RUSTIC
apple maggot *n* (1867) : a dipteran fly (*Rhagoletis pomonella*) whose larva burrows in and feeds esp. on apples
ap·ple–pie \'a-pəl-ˌpī\ *adj* (1780)   **1** : EXCELLENT, PERFECT ⟨~ order⟩   **2** : of, relating to, or characterized by traditionally American values (as honesty or simplicity) ⟨is the epitome of ~ wholesomeness⟩
ap·ple–pol·ish \'a-pəl-ˌpä-lish\ *vb* [fr. the traditional practice of schoolchildren bringing a shiny apple as a gift to their teacher] *vi* (1935) : to attempt to ingratiate oneself : TOADY ~ *vt* : to curry favor with (as by flattery) — **ap·ple–pol·ish·er** *n*
ap·ple·sauce \-ˌsȯs\ *n* (1739)   **1** : a relish or dessert made of apples stewed to a pulp and sweetened   **2** *slang* : BUNKUM, NONSENSE
apple scab *n* (ca. 1899) : a disease of apple trees caused by a fungus (*Venturia inaequalis*) producing dark blotches or lesions on the leaves, fruit, and sometimes the young twigs
ap·pli·ance \ə-'plī-ən(t)s\ *n* (1561)   **1** : an act of applying   **2 a** : a piece of equipment for adapting a tool or machine to a special purpose : ATTACHMENT   **b** : an instrument or device designed for a particular use; *specif* : a household or office device (as a stove, fan, or refrigerator) operated by gas or electric current   **c** *Brit* : FIRE ENGINE   **3** *obs* : COMPLIANCE **syn** see IMPLEMENT
ap·pli·ca·ble \'a-pli-kə-bəl *also* ə-'pli-kə-\ *adj* (1660) : capable of or suitable for being applied : APPROPRIATE ⟨statutes ~ to the case⟩ **syn** see RELEVANT — **ap·pli·ca·bil·i·ty** \ˌa-pli-kə-'bi-lə-tē *also* ə-ˌpli-kə-\ *n*
ap·pli·cant \'a-pli-kənt\ *n* (ca. 1782) : one who applies ⟨a job ~⟩
ap·pli·ca·tion \ˌa-plə-'kā-shən\ *n* [ME *applicacioun*, fr. L *application-, applicatio* inclination, fr. *applicare*] (15c)   **1** : an act of applying: **a** (1) : an act of putting to use ⟨~ of new techniques⟩   (2) : a use to

which something is put 〈new ~s for old remedies〉 (3) : a program (as a word processor or a spreadsheet) that performs one of the important tasks for which a computer is used **b** : an act of administering or superposing 〈~ of paint to a house〉 **c** : assiduous attention 〈succeeds by ~ to her studies〉 **2 a** : REQUEST, PETITION 〈an ~ for financial aid〉 **b** : a form used in making a request **3** : the practical inference to be derived from a discourse (as a moral tale) **4** : a medicated or protective layer or material 〈an oily ~ for dry skin〉 **5** : capacity for practical use 〈words of varied ~〉

ap·pli·ca·tive \'a-plə-ˌkā-tiv, ə-'pli-kə-\ *adj* (1638) **1** : APPLICABLE, PRACTICAL **2** : put to use : APPLIED — **ap·pli·ca·tive·ly** *adv*

ap·pli·ca·tor \'a-plə-ˌkā-tər\ *n* (1659) : one that applies; *specif* : a device for applying a substance (as medicine or polish)

ap·pli·ca·to·ry \'a-pli-kə-ˌtōr-ē, -ˌtor-, ə-'pli-kə-\ *adj* (1649) : capable of being applied

ap·plied \ə-'plīd\ *adj* (1656) **1** : put to practical use 〈~ art〉; *esp* : applying general principles to solve definite problems 〈~ sciences〉 **2** : working in an applied science 〈an ~ physicist〉

¹**ap·pli·qué** \ˌa-plə-'kā\ *n* [F, pp. of *appliquer* to put on, fr. L *applicare*] (1801) : a cutout decoration fastened to a larger piece of material

²**appliqué** *vt* **-quéd; -qué·ing** (1881) : to apply (as a decoration or ornament) to a larger surface : OVERLAY

ap·ply \ə-'plī\ *vb* **ap·plied; ap·ply·ing** [ME *applien*, fr. MF *aplier*, fr. L *applicare*, fr. *ad-* + *plicare* to fold — more at PLY] *vt* (14c) **1 a** : to put to use esp. for some practical purpose 〈*applies* pressure to get what he wants〉 **b** : to bring into action 〈~ the brakes〉 **c** : to lay or spread on 〈~ varnish〉 **d** : to put into operation or effect 〈~ a law〉 **2** : to employ diligently or with close attention 〈should ~ yourself to your work〉 ~ *vi* **1** : to have relevance or a valid connection 〈this rule *applies* to freshmen only〉 **2** : to make an appeal or request esp. in the form of a written application 〈~ for a job〉 — **ap·pli·er** \-'plī(-ə)r\ *n*

ap·pog·gia·tu·ra \ə-ˌpä-jə-'tùr-ə\ *n* [It, lit., support] (1753) : an embellishing note or tone preceding an essential melodic note or tone and usu. written as a note of smaller size

ap·point \ə-'pȯint\ *vb* [ME, fr. MF *apointier* to arrange, fr. *a-* (fr. L *ad-*) + *point* point] *vt* (14c) **1 a** : to fix or set officially 〈~ a trial date〉 **b** : to name officially 〈will ~ her director of the program〉 **c** *archaic* : ARRANGE **d** : to determine the disposition of (an estate) to someone by virtue of a power of appointment **2** : to provide with complete and usu. appropriate or elegant furnishings or equipment ~ *vi* : to exercise a power of appointment *syn* see FURNISH

ap·poin·tee \ə-ˌpȯin-'tē, ˌa-\ *n* (1768) **1** : one who is appointed **2** : one to whom an estate is appointed

ap·point·ive \ə-'pȯin-tiv\ *adj* (1881) : of, relating to, or filled by appointment 〈an ~ office〉

ap·point·ment \ə-'pȯint-mənt\ *n* (15c) **1 a** : an act of appointing : DESIGNATION **b** : the designation by virtue of a vested power of a person to enjoy an estate **2** : an arrangement for a meeting : ENGAGEMENT **3** : EQUIPMENT, FURNISHINGS — usu. used in pl. **4** : a nonelective office or position 〈holds an academic ~〉

ap·por·tion \ə-'pōr-shən, -'pȯr-\ *vt* **-tioned; -tion·ing** \-sh(ə-)niŋ\ [MF *apportionner*, fr. *a-* (fr. L *ad-*) + *portionner* to portion] (1574) : to divide and share out according to a plan; *esp* : to make a proportionate division or distribution of — **ap·por·tion·able** \-shə-nə-bəl\ *adj*

ap·por·tion·ment \-shən-mənt\ *n* (1579) : an act or result of apportioning; *esp* : the apportioning of representatives or taxes among the states according to U.S. law

ap·pose \a-'pōz\ *vt* **ap·posed; ap·pos·ing** [MF *aposer*, fr. OF, fr. *a-* + *poser* to put — more at POSE] (1596) **1** *archaic* : to put before : apply (one thing) to another **2** : to place in juxtaposition or proximity

ap·po·site \'a-pə-zət\ *adj* [L *appositus*, fr. pp. of *apponere* to place near, fr. *ad-* + *ponere* to put — more at POSITION] (1621) : highly pertinent or appropriate : APT *syn* see RELEVANT — **ap·po·site·ly** *adv* — **ap·po·site·ness** *n*

ap·po·si·tion \ˌa-pə-'zi-shən\ *n* (15c) **1 a** : a grammatical construction in which two usu. adjacent nouns having the same referent stand in the same syntactical relation to the rest of a sentence (as *the poet* and *Burns* in "a biography of the poet Burns") **b** : the relation of one of such a pair of nouns or noun equivalents to the other **2 a** : an act or instance of apposing; *specif* : the deposition of successive layers upon those already present (as in cell walls) **b** : the state of being apposed — **ap·po·si·tion·al** \-'zish-nəl, -'zi-shə-nᵊl\ *adj*

ap·pos·i·tive \ə-'pä-zə-tiv, a-\ *adj* (1693) : of, relating to, or standing in grammatical apposition — **appositive** *n* — **ap·pos·i·tive·ly** *adv*

ap·prais·al \ə-'prā-zəl\ *n* (1817) : an act or instance of appraising; *esp* : a valuation of property by the estimate of an authorized person

ap·praise \ə-'prāz\ *vt* **ap·praised; ap·prais·ing** [ME *appreisen*, fr. MF *aprisier* to apprize] (15c) **1** : to set a value on : estimate the amount of **2** : to evaluate the worth, significance, or status of; *esp* : to give an expert judgment of the value or merit of *syn* see ESTIMATE — **ap·prais·ee** \ə-ˌprā-'zē\ *n* — **ap·praise·ment** \-'prāz-mənt\ *n* — **ap·prais·er** *n* — **ap·prais·ing·ly** \-'prā-ziŋ-lē\ *adv* — **ap·prais·ive** \-'prā-ziv\ *adj*

ap·pre·cia·ble \ə-'prē-shə-bəl, -'pri-shə-bəl\ *adj* (1818) : capable of being perceived or measured *syn* see PERCEPTIBLE — **ap·pre·cia·bly** \-blē\ *adv*

ap·pre·ci·ate \ə-'prē-shē-ˌāt, -'pri- *also* -'prē-sē-\ *vb* **-at·ed; -at·ing** [LL *appretiatus*, pp. of *appretiare*, fr. L *ad-* + *pretium* price — more at PRICE] *vt* (1655) **1 a** : to grasp the nature, worth, quality, or significance of 〈~ the difference between right and wrong〉 **b** : to value or admire highly 〈~s our work〉 **c** : to judge with heightened perception or understanding : be fully aware of 〈must see it to ~ it〉 **d** : to recognize with gratitude 〈certainly ~s your kindness〉 **2** : to increase the value of ~ *vi* : to increase in number or value — **ap·pre·ci·a·tor** \-ˌā-tər\ *n* — **ap·pre·cia·to·ry** \-'prē-shə-ˌtōr-ē, -'pri-shə-, -ˌtor-\ *adj* *syn* APPRECIATE, VALUE, PRIZE, TREASURE, CHERISH mean to hold in high estimation. APPRECIATE often connotes sufficient understanding to enjoy or admire a thing's excellence 〈*appreciates* fine wine〉. VALUE implies rating a thing highly for its intrinsic worth 〈*values* our friendship〉. PRIZE implies taking a deep pride in something one possesses 〈Americans *prize* their freedom〉. TREASURE emphasizes jealously safeguarding something considered precious 〈a *treasured* memento〉. CHERISH implies a special love and care for something 〈*cherishes* her children above all〉. *syn* see in addition UNDERSTAND

ap·pre·ci·a·tion \ə-ˌprē-shē-'ā-shən, -ˌpri- *also* -ˌprē-sē-\ *n* (1604) **1 a** : JUDGMENT, EVALUATION; *esp* : a favorable critical estimate **b** : sensitive awareness; *esp* : recognition of aesthetic values **c** : an expression of admiration, approval, or gratitude **2** : increase in value

ap·pre·cia·tive \ə-'prē-shə-tiv, -'pri- *also* -'prē-shē-,ā-\ *adj* (ca. 1698) : having or showing appreciation — **ap·pre·cia·tive·ly** *adv* — **ap·pre·cia·tive·ness** *n*

ap·pre·hend \ˌa-pri-'hend\ *vb* [ME, fr. L *apprehendere*, lit., to seize, fr. *ad-* + *prehendere* to seize — more at GET] *vt* (15c) **1** : ARREST, SEIZE 〈~ a thief〉 **2 a** : to become aware of : PERCEIVE **b** : to anticipate esp. with anxiety, dread, or fear **3** : to grasp with the understanding : recognize the meaning of ~ *vi* : UNDERSTAND, GRASP

ap·pre·hen·si·ble \ˌa-pri-'hen(t)-sə-bəl\ *adj* (ca. 1631) : capable of being apprehended — **ap·pre·hen·si·bly** \-blē\ *adv*

ap·pre·hen·sion \ˌa-pri-'hen(t)-shən\ *n* [ME, fr. LL *apprehension-, apprehensio*, fr. L *apprehendere*] (14c) **1 a** : the act or power of perceiving or comprehending 〈a person of dull ~〉 **b** : the result of apprehending mentally : CONCEPTION 〈according to popular ~〉 **2** : seizure by legal process : ARREST **3** : suspicion or fear esp. of future evil : FOREBODING

ap·pre·hen·sive \-'hen(t)-siv\ *adj* (14c) **1** : capable of apprehending or quick to do so : DISCERNING **2** : having apprehension : COGNIZANT **3** : viewing the future with anxiety or alarm *syn* see FEARFUL — **ap·pre·hen·sive·ly** *adv* — **ap·pre·hen·sive·ness** *n*

¹**ap·pren·tice** \ə-'pren-təs\ *n* [ME *aprentis*, fr. MF, fr. OF, fr. *aprendre* to learn, fr. L *apprendere, apprehendere*] (14c) **1 a** : one bound by indenture to serve another for a prescribed period with a view to learning an art or trade **b** : one who is learning by practical experience under skilled workers a trade, art, or calling **2** : an inexperienced person : NOVICE 〈an ~ in cooking〉 — **ap·pren·tice·ship** \-tə(sh)-ˌship, -təs-ˌship\ *n*

²**apprentice** *vb* **-ticed; -tic·ing** *vt* (1596) : to set at work as an apprentice; *esp* : to bind to an apprenticeship by contract or indenture ~ *vi* : to serve as an apprentice

ap·pressed \a-'prest\ *adj* [L *appressus*, pp. of *apprimere* to press to, fr. *ad-* + *premere* to press — more at PRESS] (1791) : pressed close to or lying flat against something 〈leaves ~ against the stem〉

ap·pres·so·ri·um \ˌa-pre-'sōr-ē-əm, -'sȯr-\ *n, pl* **-ria** \-ē-ə\ [NL, fr. L *apprimere*] (1897) : the flattened thickened tip of a hyphal branch by which some parasitic fungi are attached to their host

ap·prise \ə-'prīz\ *vt* **ap·prised; ap·pris·ing** [F *appris*, pp. of *apprendre* to learn, teach, fr. OF *aprendre*] (1694) : to give notice to : TELL *syn* see INFORM

ap·prize \ə-'prīz\ *vt* **ap·prized; ap·priz·ing** [ME *apprisen*, fr. MF *aprisier*, fr. OF, fr. *a-* (fr. L *ad-*) + *prisier* to appraise — more at PRIZE] (14c) : VALUE, APPRECIATE

¹**ap·proach** \ə-'prōch\ *vb* [ME *approchen*, fr. OF *aprochier*, fr. LL *appropiare*, fr. L *ad-* + *prope* near; akin to L *pro* before — more at FOR] *vt* (13c) **1 a** : to draw closer to : NEAR **b** : to come very near to : be almost the same as 〈his mathematics ~es mysticism —Theodore Sturgeon〉 〈as the quantity *x* ~es zero〉 **2 a** : to make advances to esp. in order to create a desired result 〈was ~ed by several Broadway producers〉 **b** : to take preliminary steps toward accomplishment or full knowledge or experience of 〈~ the subject with an open mind〉 ~ *vi* **1** : to draw nearer **2** : to make an approach in golf

²**approach** *n* (15c) **1 a** : an act or instance of approaching 〈the ~ of summer〉 **b** : APPROXIMATION 〈in this book he makes his closest ~ to greatness〉 **2 a** : the taking of preliminary steps toward a particular purpose 〈experimenting with new lines of ~〉 **b** : a particular manner of taking such steps 〈a highly individual ~ to language〉 **3** : a means of access : AVENUE **4 a** : a golf shot from the fairway toward the green **b** : the steps taken by a bowler before he delivers the ball; *also* : the part of the alley behind the foul line from which the bowler delivers the ball **5** : the descent of an aircraft toward a landing place

ap·proach·able \ə-'prō-chə-bəl\ *adj* (1571) : capable of being approached : ACCESSIBLE; *specif* : easy to meet or deal with — **ap·proach·abil·i·ty** \-ˌprō-chə-'bi-lə-tē\ *n*

ap·pro·bate \'a-prə-ˌbāt\ *vt* **-bat·ed; -bat·ing** [ME, fr. L *approbatus*, pp. of *approbare* — more at APPROVE] (15c) : APPROVE, SANCTION — **ap·pro·ba·to·ry** \'a-prə-bə-ˌtōr-ē, ə-'prō-bə-, -ˌtȯr-\ *adj*

ap·pro·ba·tion \ˌa-prə-'bā-shən\ *n* (14c) **1** *obs* : PROOF **2 a** : an act of approving formally or officially **b** : COMMENDATION, PRAISE

¹**ap·pro·pri·ate** \ə-'prō-prē-ˌāt\ *vt* **-at·ed; -at·ing** [ME, fr. LL *appropriatus*, pp. of *appropriare*, fr. L *ad-* + *proprius* own] (15c) **1** : to take exclusive possession of : ANNEX 〈no one should ~ a common benefit〉 **2** : to set apart for or assign to a particular purpose or use 〈~ money for the research program〉 **3** : to take or make use of without authority or right — **ap·pro·pri·able** \-prē-ə-bəl\ *adj* — **ap·pro·pri·a·tor** \-ˌprē-ˌā-tər\ *n*

²**ap·pro·pri·ate** \ə-'prō-prē-ət\ *adj* (15c) : especially suitable or compatible : FITTING *syn* see FIT — **ap·pro·pri·ate·ly** *adv* — **ap·pro·pri·ate·ness** *n*

ap·pro·pri·a·tion \ə-ˌprō-prē-'ā-shən\ *n* (14c) **1** : an act or instance of appropriating **2** : something that has been appropriated; *specif* : money set aside by formal action for a specific use — **ap·pro·pri·a·tive** \-'prō-prē-ˌā-tiv\ *adj*

ap·prov·able \ə-'prü-və-bəl\ *adj* (15c) : capable or worthy of being approved — **ap·prov·ably** \-blē\ *adv*

ap·prov·al \ə-'prü-vəl\ *n* (1616) : an act or instance of approving : APPROBATION — **on approval** : subject to a prospective buyer's acceptance or refusal 〈stamps sent to collectors *on approval*〉

ap·prove \ə-'prüv\ *vb* **ap·proved; ap·prov·ing** [ME, fr. MF *aprover*, fr. L *approbare*, fr. *ad-* + *probare* to prove — more at PROVE] *vt* (14c) **1** *obs* : PROVE, ATTEST **2** : to have or express a favorable opinion of 〈couldn't ~ such conduct〉 **3 a** : to accept as satisfactory 〈hopes she will ~ the date of the meeting〉 **b** : to give formal or official sanction to : RATIFY 〈Congress *approved* the proposed budget〉 ~ *vi* : to take a

---

\ə\ abut \ᵊ\ kitten, F table \ər\ further \a\ ash \ā\ ace \ä\ mop, mar \aù\ out \ch\ chin \e\ bet \ē\ easy \g\ go \i\ hit \ī\ ice \j\ job \ŋ\ sing \ō\ go \ȯ\ law \ȯi\ boy \th\ thin \t͟h\ the \ü\ loot \ù\ foot \y\ yet \zh\ vision \à, ᴋ, ⁿ, œ, œ̄, ᴜᴇ, ᵫ, ᵒ, ʸ\ see Guide to Pronunciation

favorable view ⟨doesn't ∼ of fighting⟩ — **ap·prov·ing·ly** \-'prü-viŋ-lē\ *adv*
syn APPROVE, ENDORSE, SANCTION, ACCREDIT, CERTIFY mean to have or express a favorable opinion of. APPROVE often implies no more than this but may suggest considerable esteem or admiration ⟨the parents *approve* of the marriage⟩. ENDORSE suggests an explicit statement of support ⟨publicly *endorsed* her for Senator⟩. SANCTION implies both approval and authorization ⟨the President *sanctioned* covert operations⟩. ACCREDIT and CERTIFY usu. imply official endorsement attesting to conformity to set standards ⟨the board voted to *accredit* the college⟩ ⟨must be *certified* to teach⟩.
approved school *n* (1932) *Brit* : a school for juvenile delinquents
¹**ap·prox·i·mate** \ə-'präk-sə-mət\ *adj* [LL *approximatus*, pp. of *approximare* to come near, fr. L *ad-* + *proximare* to come near — more at PROXIMATE] (15c) **1** : located close together ⟨∼ leaves⟩ **2** : nearly correct or exact ⟨an ∼ solution⟩ — **ap·prox·i·mate·ly** *adv*
²**ap·prox·i·mate** \-ˌmāt\ *vb* **-mat·ed; -mat·ing** *vt* (15c) **1 a** : to bring near or close **b** : to bring (cut edges of tissue) together **2** : to come near or to be close to in position, value, or characteristics ⟨a child tries to ∼ his parents' speech⟩ ∼ *vi* : to come close — usu. used with *to*
ap·prox·i·ma·tion \ə-ˌpräk-sə-'mā-shən\ *n* (15c) **1** : the act or process of drawing together **2** : the quality or state of being close or near ⟨an ∼ to the truth⟩ ⟨an ∼ of justice⟩ **3** : something that is approximate; *esp* : a mathematical quantity that is close in value to but not the same as a desired quantity — **ap·prox·i·ma·tive** \-'präk-sə-ˌmā-tiv\ *adj*
ap·pur·te·nance \ə-'pərt-nən(t)s, -'pər-t⁾n-ən(t)s\ *n* (14c) **1** : an incidental right (as a right-of-way) attached to a principal property right and passing in possession with it **2** : a subordinate part or adjunct ⟨the ∼ of wealth is fashion and ceremony —Shak.⟩ **3** *pl* : accessory objects : APPARATUS
ap·pur·te·nant \ə-'pərt-nənt, -'pər-t⁾n-ənt\ *adj* [ME *apertenant*, fr. MF, fr. OF, prp. of *apartenir* to belong — more at APPERTAIN] (14c) **1** : constituting a legal accompaniment **2** : AUXILIARY, ACCESSORY — **appurtenant** *n*
aprax·ia \(ˌ)ā-'prak-sē-ə\ *n* [NL, fr. Gk, inaction, fr. *a-* + *praxis* action, fr. *prassein* to do — more at PRACTICAL] (ca. 1881) : loss or impairment of the ability to execute complex coordinated movements without impairment of the muscles or senses — **aprac·tic** \-'prak-tik\ *or* **aprax·ic** \-'prak-sik\ *adj*
après \(ˌ)ä-'prā, 'ä-ˌprā; 'a-ˌ\ *prep* [F *après-*, fr. *après* after] (1967) : AFTER ⟨∼ tennis⟩ — usu. used in combination ⟨*après*-theater party⟩
après-ski \ˌä-ˌprā-'skē, ˌa-\ *n*, *often attrib* [F *après* after + *ski* ski, skiing] (1951) : social activity (as at a ski lodge) after a day's skiing
apri·cot \'a-prə-ˌkät, 'ā-\ *n*, *often attrib* [alter. of earlier *abrecock*, ultim. fr. Ar *al-birqūq* the apricot, ultim. fr. L (*persicum*) *praecox*, lit., early ripening (peach) — more at PRECOCIOUS] (1551) **1 a** : the oval orange-colored fruit of a temperate-zone tree (*Prunus armeniaca*) resembling the related peach and plum in flavor **b** : a tree that bears apricots **2** : a variable color averaging a moderate orange
April \'ā-prəl\ *n* [ME, fr. OF & L; OF *avrill*, fr. L *Aprilis*] (bef. 12c) : the 4th month of the Gregorian calendar
April fool *n* (1687) : the butt of a joke or trick played on April Fools' Day; *also* : such a joke or trick
April Fools' Day *n* (1854) : April 1 characteristically marked by the playing of practical jokes
a pri·o·ri \ˌä-prē-'ōr-ē, ˌa-; ˌā-(ˌ)prī-'ōr-ˌī, -ˌprē-'ōr-ē; -'ȯr-\ *adj* [L, lit., from the former] (1652) **1 a** : DEDUCTIVE **b** : relating to or derived by reasoning from self-evident propositions — compare A POSTERIORI **c** : presupposed by experience **2 a** : being without examination or analysis : PRESUMPTIVE **b** : formed or conceived beforehand — **a priori** *adv* — **apri·or·i·ty** \-'ȯr-ə-tē\ *n*
apron \'ā-prən, -pərn\ *n*, *often attrib* [ME, alter. (resulting fr. false division of *a napron*) of *napron*, fr. MF *naperon*, dim. of *nape* cloth, modif. of L *mappa* napkin] (15c) **1** : a garment usu. of cloth, plastic, or leather usu. tied around the waist and used to protect clothing or adorn a costume **2** : something that suggests or resembles an apron in shape, position, or use: as **a** : the lower member under the sill of the interior casing of a window **b** : an upward or downward vertical extension of a bathroom fixture (as a sink or tub) **c** : an endless belt for carrying material **d** : an extensive fan-shaped deposit of detritus **e** : the part of the stage in front of the proscenium arch **f** : the area along the waterfront edge of a pier or wharf **g** : a shield (as of concrete or gravel) to protect against erosion (as of a waterway) by water **h** : the extensive paved part of an airport immediately adjacent to the terminal area or hangars — **aproned** \-prənd, -pərnd\ *adj*
apron string *n* (1542) : the string of an apron — usu. used in pl. as a symbol of dominance or complete control ⟨though 40 years old he was still tied to his mother's *apron strings*⟩
¹**ap·ro·pos** \ˌa-prə-'pō, 'a-prə-ˌ\ *adv* [F *à propos*, lit., to the purpose] (1668) **1** : at an opportune time : SEASONABLY **2** : BY THE WAY
²**apropos** *adj* (1686) : being both relevant and opportune *syn* see RELEVANT
³**apropos** *prep* (1910) : APROPOS OF
apropos of *prep* (1746) : with regard to : CONCERNING
apro·tic \(ˌ)ā-'prō-tik\ *adj* [²*a-* + *proton* + ¹*-ic*] (1931) *of a solvent* : incapable of acting as a proton donor
apse \'aps\ *n* [ML & L; ML *apsis*, fr. L] (1822) **1** : APSIS 1 **2** : a projecting part of a building (as a church) that is usu. semicircular in plan and vaulted
ap·si·dal \'ap-sə-d⁾l\ *adj* (1846) : of or relating to an apse or apsis
ap·sis \'ap-səs\ *n*, *pl* **ap·si·des** \-sə-ˌdēz\ [NL *apsid-, apsis*, fr. L, arch, orbit, fr. Gk *hapsid-, hapsis*, fr. *haptein* to fasten] (1658) **1** : the point in an astronomical orbit at which the distance of the body from the center of attraction is either greatest or least **2** : APSE 2
apt \'apt\ *adj* [ME, fr. L *aptus*, lit., fastened, fr. pp. of *apere* to fasten; akin to L *apisci* to grasp, obtain, *apud* near, Hitt *hap-* to attach] (14c) **1** : unusually fitted or qualified : READY ⟨proved an ∼ tool in the hands of the conspirators⟩ **2 a** : having a tendency : LIKELY ⟨plants ∼ to suffer from drought⟩ **b** : ordinarily disposed : INCLINED ⟨∼ to accept what is plausible as true⟩ **3** : suited to a purpose; *esp* : being to the point ⟨an ∼ quotation⟩ **4** : keenly intelligent and responsive

syn see FIT, QUICK   *usage* see LIABLE — **apt·ly** \'ap(t)-lē\ *adv* — **apt·ness** \'ap(t)-nəs\ *n*
ap·ter·ous \'ap-tə-rəs\ *adj* [Gk *apteros*, fr. *a-* + *pteron* wing — more at FEATHER] (1775) : lacking wings ⟨∼ insects⟩
ap·ter·yx \'ap-tə-riks\ *n* [NL, fr. *a-* + Gk *pteryx* wing; akin to Gk *pteron*] (1813) : KIWI
ap·ti·tude \'ap-tə-ˌtüd, -ˌtyüd\ *n* [ME, fr. ML *aptitudo*, fr. LL, fitness, fr. L *aptus*] (15c) **1 a** : INCLINATION, TENDENCY **b** : a natural ability : TALENT **2** : capacity for learning : APTNESS **3** : general suitability *syn* see GIFT — **ap·ti·tu·di·nal** \ˌap-tə-'tüd-d⁾n-əl, -'tyü-\ *adj* — **ap·ti·tu·di·nal·ly** *adv*
aptitude test *n* (1923) : a standardized test designed to predict an individual's ability to learn certain skills
ap·y·rase \'a-pə-ˌrās, -ˌrāz\ *n* [adenosine + *pyrophosphate* + *-ase*] (1945) : any of several enzymes that hydrolyze ATP with the liberation of phosphate and energy
aqua \'ä-kwə *also* 'a-\ *n* [L — more at ISLAND] (14c) **1** *pl* **aquae** \'ä-ˌkwī *also* 'a-(ˌ)kwē\ : WATER; *esp* : WATER 5a(2) **2** *pl* **aquas** : a light greenish blue color
aqua·cade \'ä-kwə-ˌkād, 'a-\ *n* [*Aquacade*, a water spectacle orig. at Cleveland, Ohio] (1937) : a water spectacle that consists usu. of exhibitions of swimming and diving with musical accompaniment
aqua·cul·ture *also* **aqui·cul·ture** \'ä-kwə-ˌkəl-chər, 'a-\ *n* [L *aqua* + E *-culture* (as in *agriculture*)] (1867) : the cultivation of the natural produce of water (as fish or shellfish) — **aqua·cul·tur·al** \ˌä-kwə-'kəl-ch(ə-)rəl, ˌa-\ *adj* — **aqua·cul·tur·ist** \-'ch(ə-)rist\ *n*
aqua for·tis \'ä-kwə-'fȯr-təs, 'a-\ *n* [NL *aqua fortis*, lit., strong water] (15c) : NITRIC ACID
Aqua–Lung \'ä-kwə-ˌləŋ, 'a-\ *trademark* — used for an underwater breathing apparatus
aqua·ma·rine \ˌä-kwə-mə-'rēn, ˌa-\ *n* [NL *aqua marina*, fr. L, sea water] (1677) **1** : a transparent beryl that is blue, blue-green, or green in color **2** : a pale blue to light greenish blue
aqua·naut \'ä-kwə-ˌnȯt, 'a-, -ˌnät\ *n* [L *aqua* + E *-naut* (as in *aeronaut*)] (1881) : a scuba diver who lives and operates both inside and outside an underwater shelter for an extended period
¹**aqua·plane** \'ä-kwə-ˌplān, 'a-\ *n* (1914) : a board towed behind a speeding motorboat and ridden by a person standing on it — **aqua·plan·er** *n*
²**aquaplane** *vi* (ca. 1923) **1** : to ride on an aquaplane **2** *Brit* : HYDROPLANE
aqua re·gia \-'rē-j(ē-)ə\ *n* [NL, lit., royal water] (1610) : a mixture of nitric and hydrochloric acids that dissolves gold or platinum
aqua·relle \ˌä-kwə-'rel, ˌa-\ *n* [F, fr. obs. It *acquarella* (now *acquerello*), fr. *acqua* water, fr. L *aqua*] (1869) : a drawing usu. in transparent watercolor — **aqua·rell·ist** \-'re-list\ *n*
Aquar·i·an \ə-'kwar-ē-ən, -'kwer-\ *n* (1911) : AQUARIUS 2b — **Aquarian** *adj*
aquar·ist \ə-'kwar-ist, -'kwer-\ *n* (ca. 1893) : a person who keeps or maintains an aquarium
aquar·i·um \ə-'kwar-ē-əm, -'kwer-\ *n*, *pl* **-i·ums** *or* **-ia** \-ē-ə\ [prob. alter. of *aquatic vivarium*] (ca. 1847) **1** : a container (as a glass tank) or an artificial pond in which living aquatic animals or plants are kept **2** : an establishment where aquatic collections of living organisms are kept and exhibited
Aquar·i·us \-ē-əs\ *n* [L (gen. *Aquarii*), lit., water carrier] **1** : a constellation south of Pegasus pictured as a man pouring water **2 a** : the 11th sign of the zodiac in astrology — see ZODIAC table **b** : one born under the sign of Aquarius
¹**aquat·ic** \ə-'kwä-tik, -'kwa-\ *adj* (1642) **1** : growing or living in or frequenting water ⟨∼ mosquito larvae⟩ **2** : taking place in or on water ⟨∼ sports⟩ — **aquat·i·cal·ly** \-ti-k(ə-)lē\ *adv*
²**aquatic** *n* (ca. 1600) **1** : an aquatic animal or plant **2** *pl but sing or pl in constr* : water sports
aqua·tint \'a-kwə-ˌtint, 'ä-\ *n* [It *acqua tinta* dyed water] (1782) : a method of etching a printing plate so that tones similar to watercolor washes can be reproduced; *also* : a print made from a plate so etched — **aquatint** *vt* — **aqua·tint·ist** \-ˌtin-tist\ *n*
aqua·vit \'ä-kwə-ˌvēt, 'ä-\ *n* [Sw, Dan, & Norw *akvavit*, fr. ML *aqua vitae*] (1890) : a clear Scandinavian liquor flavored with caraway seeds
aqua vi·tae \ˌa-kwə-'vī-tē, ˌä-\ *n* [ME, fr. ML, lit., water of life] (15c) : a strong alcoholic liquor (as brandy)
aq·ue·duct \'a-kwə-ˌdəkt\ *n* [L *aquaeductus*, fr. *aquae* (gen. of *aqua*) + *ductus* act of leading — more at DUCT] (1538) **1 a** : a conduit for water; *esp* : one for carrying a large quantity of flowing water **b** : a structure for conveying a canal over a river or hollow **2** : a canal or passage in a part or organ
aque·ous \'ā-kwē-əs, 'a-\ *adj* [ML *aqueus*, fr. L *aqua*] (1646) **1 a** : of, relating to, or resembling water **b** : made from, with, or by water **2** : of or relating to the aqueous humor
aqueous humor *n* (1643) : a transparent fluid occupying the space between the crystalline lens and the cornea of the eye
aqui·fer \'a-kwə-fər, 'ä-\ *n* [NL, fr. L *aqua* + *-fer*] (1901) : a water-bearing stratum of permeable rock, sand, or gravel — **aquif·er·ous** \a-'kwi-fə-rəs, ä-\ *adj*
Aq·ui·la \'a-kwə-lə *also* ə-'kwi-lə\ *n* [L (gen. *Aquilae*), lit., eagle] : a constellation in the northern hemisphere represented by the figure of an eagle
aq·ui·le·gia \ˌa-kwə-'lē-j(ē-)ə\ *n* [NL] (1871) : COLUMBINE
aq·ui·line \'a-kwə-ˌlīn, -lən\ *adj* [L *aquilinus*, fr. *aquila* eagle] (1646) **1** : curving like an eagle's beak ⟨an ∼ nose⟩ **2** : of, relating to, or resembling an eagle — **aq·ui·lin·i·ty** \ˌa-kwə-'li-nə-tē\ *n*
aquiv·er \ə-'kwi-vər\ *adj* (1883) : marked by trembling or quivering ⟨all ∼ with excitement⟩
ar \'är\ *n* [ME] (14c) : the letter *r*
-ar *adj suffix* [ME, fr. L *-aris*, alter. of *-alis* -al] : of or relating to ⟨molecul*ar*⟩ : being ⟨spectacul*ar*⟩ : resembling ⟨oracul*ar*⟩
Ar·ab \'ar-əb, 'er-; *dial also* 'ā-ˌrab\ *n* [ME, fr. L *Arabus, Arabs*, fr. Gk *Arab-, Araps*] (14c) **1 a** : a member of the Semitic people of the Arabian peninsula **b** : a member of an Arabic-speaking people **2** : ARABIAN HORSE — **Arab** *adj*
¹**ar·a·besque** \ˌar-ə-'besk\ *adj* [F, fr. It *arabesco* Arabian in fashion, fr. *arabo* Arab, fr. L *Arabus*] (ca. 1656) : of, relating to, or being in the style of arabesque or an arabesque

²**arabesque** *n* (1786)   **1** : an ornament or style that employs flower, foliage, or fruit and sometimes animal and figural outlines to produce an intricate pattern of interlaced lines   **2** : a posture in ballet in which the body is bent forward from the hip on one leg with one arm extended forward and the other arm and leg backward   **3** : an elaborate or intricate pattern ⟨richly pierced by an ∼ of wormholes —John Chase⟩ ⟨as lawyers . . . perform their procedural ∼*s* —Daniel Okrent⟩

¹**Ara·bi·an** \ə-ˈrā-bē-ən\ *n* (14c)   **1** : a native or inhabitant of Arabia   **2** : ARABIAN HORSE

²**Arabian** *adj* (14c) : ARABIC 1

Arabian horse *n* (1737) : any of a breed of swift compact horses developed in Arabia and usu. having gray or chestnut silky hair

¹**Ar·a·bic** \ˈar-ə-bik\ *n* (14c) : a Semitic language orig. of the Arabs of the Hejaz and Nejd that is now the prevailing speech of a wide region of southwestern Asia and northern Africa

²**Arabic** *adj* (1526)   **1** : of, relating to, or characteristic of Arabia or the Arabs   **2** : of, relating to, or constituting Arabic   **3** : expressed in or utilizing Arabic numerals

arab·i·ca \ə-ˈra-bə-kə\ *n, often attrib* [NL, specific epithet of *Coffea arabica*, fr. L, fem. of *Arabicus* Arabian] (1922)   **1** : an evergreen shrub or tree (*Coffea arabica*) yielding seeds that produce a high-quality coffee and form a large portion of the coffee of commerce   **2** : the seeds of arabica

Arabic alphabet *n* (1841) : an alphabet of 28 letters derived from the Aramaic alphabet which is used for writing Arabic and also with adaptations for other languages of the Islamic world

arab·i·cize \ə-ˈra-bə-ˌsīz\ *vt* **-cized; -ciz·ing** *often cap* (1872)   **1** : to adapt (a language or elements of a language) to the phonetic or structural pattern of Arabic   **2** : ARABIZE 1 — **arab·i·ci·za·tion** \ə-ˌra-bə-sə-ˈzā-shən\ *n*

Arabic numeral *n* (ca. 1847) : any of the number symbols 0, 1, 2, 3, 4, 5, 6, 7, 8, 9 — see NUMBER table

arab·i·nose \ə-ˈra-bə-ˌnōs, -ˌnōz\ *n* [ISV *arabin* (the solid principle in gum arabic, fr. *gum arabic* + ¹-*in*) + -*ose*] (ca. 1884) : a white crystalline aldose sugar $C_5H_{10}O_5$ occurring esp. in vegetable gums

ara·bi·no·side \ar-ə-ˈbi-nə-ˌsīd, ə-ˈra-bə-nō-ˌsīd\ *n* (1927) : a glycoside that yields arabinose on hydrolysis

Ar·ab·ise *Brit var of* ARABIZE

Ar·ab·ism \ˈar-ə-ˌbi-zəm\ *n* (1614)   **1** : a characteristic feature of Arabic occurring in another language   **2** : devotion to Arab interests, culture, aspirations, or ideals

Ar·ab·ist \ˈar-ə-bist\ *n* (1753)   **1** : a specialist in the Arabic language or in Arabic culture   **2** : a person who favors Arab interests and positions in international affairs

Ar·ab·ize \ˈar-ə-ˌbīz\ *vt* **-ized; -iz·ing** (1883)   **1 a** : to cause to acquire Arabic customs, manners, speech, or outlook   **b** : to modify (a population) by intermarriage with Arabs   **2** : ARABICIZE 1 — **Ar·ab·i·za·tion** \ˌar-ə-bə-ˈzā-shən\ *n*

¹**ar·a·ble** \ˈar-ə-bəl\ *adj* [MF or L; MF, fr. L *arabilis*, fr. *arare* to plow; akin to OE *erian* to plow, Gk *aroun*] (15c)   **1** : fit for or used for the growing of crops   **2** *Brit* : engaged in, produced by, or being the cultivation of arable land — **ar·a·bil·i·ty** \ˌar-ə-ˈbi-lə-tē\ *n*

²**arable** *n* (1576) *chiefly Brit* : land fit or used for the growing of crops; *also* : a plot of such land ⟨the village ∼ of Anglo-Saxon times⟩

ar·a·chi·don·ic acid \ˌar-ə-kə-ˈdä-nik-\ *n* [NL *Arachid-*, *Arachis* + E -*onic* (as in *gluconic acid*)] (1913) : a liquid unsaturated fatty acid $C_{20}H_{32}O_2$ that occurs in most animal fats, is a precursor of prostaglandins, and is considered essential in animal nutrition

ar·a·chis oil \ˈar-ə-kəs-\ *n* [NL *Arachis*, genus that includes the peanut, fr. Gk *arakis*, dim. of *arakos*, a legume] (ca. 1889) : PEANUT OIL

arach·nid \ə-ˈrak-nəd, -ˌnid\ *n* [NL *Arachnid-*, fr. Gk *arachnē* spider] (1869) : any of a class (Arachnida) of arthropods comprising chiefly terrestrial invertebrates, including the spiders, scorpions, mites, and ticks, and having a segmented body divided into two regions of which the anterior bears four pairs of legs but no antennae — **arachnid** *adj*

¹**arach·noid** \ə-ˈrak-ˌnȯid\ *adj* (1789)   **1** : of or relating to a thin membrane of the brain and spinal cord that lies between the dura mater and the pia mater   **2** : covered with or composed of soft loose hairs or fibers

²**arachnoid** *n* [NL *arachnoides*, fr. Gk *arachnoeidēs*, like a cobweb, fr. *arachnē* spider, spider's web] (ca. 1847) : an arachnoid membrane

³**arachnoid** *adj* [NL *Arachnida* + E -*oid*] (1852) : resembling or related to the arachnids

ara·go·nite \ə-ˈra-gə-ˌnīt, ˈar-ə-gə-\ *n* [G *Aragonit*, fr. *Aragon*, Spain] (1803) : a mineral similar to calcite in consisting of calcium carbonate but differing from calcite in its orthorhombic crystallization, greater density, and less distinct cleavage — **ara·go·nit·ic** \ə-ˌra-gə-ˈni-tik, ˌar-ə-gə-\ *adj*

ar·ak *var of* ARRACK

Ar·a·mae·an \ˌar-ə-ˈmē-ən\ *n* [L *Aramaeus*, fr. Gk *Aramaios*, fr. Heb *ʾĀrām* Aram, ancient name for Syria] (1839)   **1** : ARAMAIC 2 : a member of a Semitic people of the second millennium B.C. in Syria and upper Mesopotamia — **Aramaean** *adj*

Ar·a·ma·ic \ˌar-ə-ˈmā-ik\ *n* (1882) : a Semitic language known since the ninth century B.C. as the speech of the Aramaeans and later used extensively in southwest Asia as a commercial and governmental language and adopted as their customary speech by various non-Aramaean peoples including the Jews after the Babylonian exile

Aramaic alphabet *n* (1925)   **1** : an extinct North Semitic alphabet dating from the ninth century B.C. which was for several centuries the commercial alphabet of southwest Asia and the parent of other alphabets (as Syriac and Arabic)   **2** : the square Hebrew alphabet as distinguished from the early Hebrew alphabet

ar·a·mid \ˈar-ə-məd, -ˌmid\ *n* [*aromatic poly*amide] (1972) : any of a group of lightweight but very strong heat-resistant synthetic aromatic polyamide materials that are fashioned into fibers, filaments, or sheets and used esp. in textiles and plastics

Arap·a·ho *or* **Arap·a·hoe** \ə-ˈra-pə-ˌhō\ *n, pl* **-ho** *or* **-hos** *or* **-hoe** *or* **-hoes** (1812)   **1** : a member of an American Indian people of the plains region ranging from Saskatchewan and Manitoba to New Mexico and Texas   **2** : the Algonquian language of the Arapaho people

Arau·ca·ni·an \ˌar-ȯ-ˈkā-nē-ən, -ˌō-ˈkä-\ *also* **Arau·can** \ə-ˈraů-kən\ *n* [Sp *araucano*, fr. *Arauco*, former province in Chile] (1809)   **1** : a member of a group of Indian peoples of south central Chile and adja-

cent regions of Argentina   **2** : the language of the Araucanian people that constitutes an independent language family — **Araucanian** *adj*

ar·au·car·ia \ˌar-ˌȯ-ˈkar-ē-ə\ *n* [NL, fr. *Arauco*] (1809) : any of a genus (*Araucaria* of the family Araucariaceae, the araucaria family) of So. American or Australian coniferous trees that resemble pines and are often grown as ornamentals — **ar·au·car·i·an** \-ē-ən\ *adj*

Ar·a·wak \ˈar-ə-ˌwäk, -ˌwak\ *n, pl* **Arawak** *or* **Arawaks** (1769)   **1** : a member of an Indian people of the Arawakan group now living chiefly along the coast of Guyana   **2** : the language of the Arawak people

Ar·a·wak·an \ˌar-ə-ˈwä-kən, -ˈwa-\ *n, pl* **Arawakan** *or* **Arawakans** (1901)   **1** : a member of a group of Indian peoples of South America and the West Indies   **2** : the language family of the Arawakan peoples

arb \ˈärb\ *n* (1979) : ARBITRAGEUR

ar·ba·lest *or* **ar·ba·list** \ˈär-bə-list\ *n* [ME *arblast*, fr. OE, fr. OF *arbaleste*, fr. LL *arcuballista*, fr. L *arcus* bow + *ballista* — more at ARROW] (bef. 12c) : a crossbow esp. of medieval times

ar·bi·ter \ˈär-bə-tər\ *n* [ME *arbitre*, fr. MF, fr. L *arbitr-, arbiter*] (14c)   **1** : a person with power to decide a dispute : JUDGE   **2** : a person or agency having absolute power of deciding

arbiter el·e·gan·ti·a·rum \-ˌe-lə-ˌgan-shē-ˈar-əm, -ˈer-\ *n* [L, lit., arbiter of refinements] (1818) : a person who prescribes, rules on, or is a recognized authority on matters of social behavior and taste

ar·bi·tra·ble \ˈär-bə-trə-bəl, är-ˈbi-\ *adj* (1531) : subject to decision by arbitration

¹**ar·bi·trage** \ˈär-bə-ˌträzh\ *n* [F, fr. MF, arbitration, fr. OF, fr. *arbitrer* to render judgment, fr. L *arbitrari*, fr. *arbitr-, arbiter*] (1875)   **1** : the nearly simultaneous purchase and sale of securities or foreign exchange in different markets in order to profit from price discrepancies   **2** : the purchase of the stock of a takeover target esp. with a view to selling it profitably to the raider

²**arbitrage** *vi* **-traged; -trag·ing** (1900) : to engage in arbitrage

ar·bi·tra·geur \ˌär-bə-(ˌ)trä-ˈzhər\ *or* **ar·bi·trag·er** \ˈär-bə-ˌträ-zhər\ *n* [F *arbitrageur*, fr. *arbitrage*] (1870) : one that practices arbitrage

ar·bi·tral \ˈär-bə-trəl\ *adj* (1609) : of or relating to arbiters or arbitration

ar·bit·ra·ment \är-ˈbi-trə-mənt\ *n* [ME, fr. MF *arbitrement*, fr. *arbitrer*] (15c)   **1** *archaic* : the right or power of deciding   **2** : the settling of a dispute by an arbiter   **3** : the judgment given by an arbitrator

ar·bi·trary \ˈär-bə-ˌtrer-ē\ *adj* (15c)   **1** : depending on individual discretion (as of a judge) and not fixed by law ⟨the manner of punishment is ∼⟩   **2 a** : not restrained or limited in the exercise of power : ruling by absolute authority ⟨an ∼ government⟩   **b** : marked by or resulting from the unrestrained and often tyrannical exercise of power ⟨protection from ∼ arrest and detention⟩   **3 a** : based on or determined by individual preference or convenience rather than by necessity or the intrinsic nature of something ⟨an ∼ standard⟩ ⟨take any ∼ positive number⟩ ⟨∼ division of historical studies into watertight compartments —A. J. Toynbee⟩   **b** : existing or coming about seemingly at random or by chance or as a capricious and unreasonable act of will ⟨when a task is not seen in a meaningful context it is experienced as being ∼ —Nehemiah Jordan⟩ — **ar·bi·trari·ly** \ˌär-bə-ˈtrer-ə-lē\ *adv* — **ar·bi·trar·i·ness** \ˈär-bə-ˌtrer-ē-nəs\ *n*

ar·bi·trate \ˈär-bə-ˌtrāt\ *vb* **-trat·ed; -trat·ing** *vt* (1592)   **1** *archaic* : DECIDE, DETERMINE   **2** : to act as arbiter upon   **3** : to submit or refer for decision to an arbiter ⟨agreed to ∼ their differences⟩ ∼ *vi* : to act as arbitrator — **ar·bi·tra·tive** \-ˌträ-tiv\ *adj*

ar·bi·tra·tion \ˌär-bə-ˈträ-shən\ *n* (15c) : the action of arbitrating; *esp* : the hearing and determination of a case in controversy by an arbiter — **ar·bi·tra·tion·al** \-sh(ə)nəl\ *adj*

ar·bi·tra·tor \ˈär-bə-ˌträ-tər\ *n* (15c) : one that arbitrates : ARBITER

¹**ar·bor** \ˈär-bər\ *n* [ME *erber* plot of grass, arbor, fr. MF *herbier* plot of grass, fr. *herbe* herb, grass] (14c) : a shelter of vines or branches or of latticework covered with climbing shrubs or vines

²**arbor** *n* [L, tree, shaft] (1659)   **1** : a spindle or axle of a wheel   **2** : a main shaft or beam   **3** : a shaft on which a revolving cutting tool is mounted   **4** : a spindle on a cutting machine that holds the work to be cut

arbor- *or* **arbori-** *comb form* [L *arbor*] : tree ⟨*arbori*culture⟩

Arbor Day *n* [L *arbor* tree] (1872) : a day designated for planting trees

ar·bo·re·al \är-ˈbȯr-ē-əl, -ˈbȯr-\ *adj* [L *arboreus* of a tree, fr. *arbor*] (ca. 1667)   **1** : of, relating to, or resembling a tree   **2** : inhabiting or frequenting trees ⟨∼ monkeys⟩ — **ar·bo·re·al·ly** \-ə-lē\ *adv*

ar·bo·re·ous \-ē-əs\ *adj* (1657) : ARBOREAL ⟨an ∼ palm⟩

ar·bo·res·cent \ˌär-bə-ˈre-sᵊnt\ *adj* (1675) : resembling a tree in properties, growth, structure, or appearance — **ar·bo·res·cence** \-sᵊn(t)s\ *n*

ar·bo·re·tum \ˌär-bə-rə-ˈrē-təm\ *n, pl* **-retums** *or* **-re·ta** \-ˈrē-tə\ [NL, fr. L, plantation of trees, fr. *arbor*] (1838) : a place where trees, shrubs, and herbaceous plants are cultivated for scientific and educational purposes

ar·bor·i·cul·ture \ˈär-bər-ə-ˌkəl-chər, är-ˈbȯr-ə-\ *n* [*arbori-* + -*culture* (as in *agriculture*)] (1828) : the cultivation of trees and shrubs esp. for ornamental purposes — **ar·bor·i·cul·tur·al** \ˌär-bər-ə-ˈkəl-chər-əl, är-ˌbȯr-ə-\ *adj*

ar·bor·ist \ˈär-bə-rist\ *n* (1578) : a specialist in the care and maintenance of trees

ar·bor·i·za·tion \ˌär-bə-rə-ˈzā-shən\ *n* (1794) : formation of or into an arborescent figure or arrangement; *also* : such a figure or arrangement (as a dendritic process of a nerve cell)

ar·bor·ize \ˈär-bə-ˌrīz\ *vi* **-ized; -iz·ing** (1847) : to branch freely and repeatedly

ar·bor·vi·tae \ˌär-bər-ˈvī-tē\ *n* [NL *arbor vitae*, lit., tree of life] (1646) : any of various evergreen trees and shrubs (esp. genus *Thuja*) of the cypress family that usu. have closely overlapping or compressed scale leaves and are often grown for ornament and in hedges

ar·bour *chiefly Brit var of* ARBOR

\ə\ abut \ᵊ\ kitten, F table \ər\ further \a\ ash \ā\ ace \ä\ mop, mar \aů\ out \ch\ chin \e\ bet \ē\ easy \g\ go \i\ hit \ī\ ice \j\ job \ŋ\ sing \ō\ go \ȯ\ law \ȯi\ boy \th\ thin \t͟h\ the \ü\ loot \ů\ foot \y\ yet \zh\ vision \ä, k̲, ⁿ, œ, œ̄, ŭe, ̄ē, ᵊ\ *see* Guide to Pronunciation

ar·bo·vi·rus \\'är-bə-'vī-rəs\ *n* [*arthropod-borne virus*] (1957) : any of various RNA viruses (as the causative agents of encephalitis, yellow fever, and dengue) transmitted by arthropods

ar·bu·tus \är-'byü-təs\ *n* [NL, fr. L, strawberry tree] (1548) **1** : any of a genus (*Arbutus*) of shrubs and trees of the heath family with white or pink flowers and red or orange berries **2** : a creeping plant (*Epigaea repens*) of the heath family that occurs in eastern No. America and bears fragrant pink or white flowers in early spring

¹arc \\'ärk\ *n* [ME *ark*, fr. MF *arc* bow, fr. L *arcus* bow, arc — more at ARROW] (14c) **1** : the apparent path described above and below the horizon by a celestial body (as the sun) **2** : something arched or curved **3** : a sustained luminous discharge of electricity across a gap in a circuit or between electrodes; *also* : ARC LAMP **4** : a continuous portion (as of a circle or ellipse) of a curved line **5** : degree measurement on the circumference of a circle — used esp. in the phrase *of arc* ⟨11 minutes 3 seconds of ~⟩

²arc *vi* **arced** \\'ärkt\; **arc·ing** \\'är-kiŋ\ (1893) **1** : to form an electric arc **2** : to follow an arc-shaped course ⟨the missile ~*ed* across the sky⟩

³arc *adj* [*arc sine* arc or angle (corresponding to the) sine (of so many degrees)] (ca. 1949) : INVERSE 2 — used with the trigonometric functions and hyperbolic functions

ar·cade \är-'kād\ *n* [F, fr. It *arcata*, fr. *arco* arch, fr. L *arcus*] (1725) **1** : a long arched building or gallery **2** : an arched covered passageway or avenue (as between shops) **3** : a series of arches with their columns or piers **4** : an amusement center having coin-operated games

ar·cad·ed \-'kä-dəd\ *adj* (1805) : having, formed in, or decorated with arches or arcades ⟨~ streets⟩ ⟨an ~ bowl⟩

ar·ca·dia \är-'kā-dē-ə\ *n*, *often cap* [*Arcadia*, region of ancient Greece frequently chosen as background for pastoral poetry] (ca. 1890) : a region or scene of simple pleasure and quiet

ar·ca·di·an \är-'kā-dē-ən\ *adj*, *often cap* (1589) **1** : idyllically pastoral; *esp* : idyllically innocent, simple, or untroubled **2 a** : of or relating to Arcadia or the Arcadians **b** : of or relating to Arcadia

Ar·ca·di·an \är-'kā-dē-ən\ *n* (1590) **1** *often not cap* : a person who lives a simple quiet life **2** : a native or inhabitant of Arcadia **3** : the dialect of ancient Greek used in Arcadia

ar·cad·ing \är-'kā-diŋ\ *n* (1849) : a series of arches or arcades used in the construction or decoration esp. of a building

Ar·ca·dy \\'är-kə-dē\ *n* (14c) : ARCADIA

ar·cane \är-'kān\ *adj* [L *arcanus*] (1547) : known or knowable only to the initiate : SECRET ⟨the ~ rites of a mystery cult⟩; *broadly* : MYSTERIOUS, OBSCURE ⟨the technical consultant's ~ explanations⟩

ar·ca·num \är-'kā-nəm\ *n*, *pl* **-na** \-nə\ [L, fr. neut. of *arcanus* secret, fr. *arca* chest — more at ARK] (15c) **1** : mysterious knowledge, language, or information accessible only by the initiate — usu. used in pl. **2** : ELIXIR 1

arc·co·sine \\(ˌ)är(k)-'kō-ˌsīn\ *n* (ca. 1884) : the inverse function to the cosine ⟨if *y* is the cosine of θ, then θ is the ~ of *y*⟩

¹arch \\'ärch\ *n* [ME *arche*, fr. MF, fr. (assumed) VL *arca*, fr. L *arcus* — more at ARROW] (14c) **1** : a typically curved structural member spanning an opening and serving as a support (as for the wall or other weight above the opening) **2 a** : something resembling an arch in form or function; *esp* : either of two vaulted portions of the bony structure of the foot that impart elasticity to it **b** : a curvature having the form of an arch **3** : ARCHWAY

arch 1: *1* round: *imp* impost, *sp* springer, *v* voussoir, *k* keystone, *ext* extrados, *int* intrados; *2* horseshoe; *3* lancet; *4* ogee; *5* trefoil; *6* basket-handle; *7* Tudor

²arch *vt* (15c) **1** : to cover or provide with an arch **2** : to form into an arch ~ *vi* **1** : to form an arch **2** : to take an arch-shaped course

³arch *adj* ['ärch-] (1547) **1** : PRINCIPAL, CHIEF ⟨your ~ opponent⟩ **2 a** : MISCHIEVOUS, SAUCY **b** : marked by a deliberate and often forced irony, brashness, or impudence — **arch·ly** *adv* — **arch·ness** *n*

¹arch- *prefix* [ME *arche-*, *arch-*, fr. OE & OF; OE *arce-*, fr. LL *arch-* & L *archi-*; OF *arch-*, fr. LL *arch-* & L *archi-*, fr. Gk *arch-*, *archi-*, fr. *archein* to begin, rule; akin to Gk *archē* beginning, rule, *archos* ruler] **1** : chief : principal ⟨*arch*fiend⟩ **2** : extreme : most fully embodying the qualities of the kind ⟨*arch*conservative⟩

²arch- — see ARCHI.

¹-arch *n comb form* [ME *-arche*, fr. OF & LL & L; OF *-arche*, fr. LL *-archa*, fr. L *-arches*, *-archus*, fr. Gk *-archēs*, *-archos*, fr. *archein*] : ruler : leader ⟨matri*arch*⟩

²-arch *adj comb form* [prob. fr. G, fr. Gk *archē* beginning] : having (such) an arche or (so many) points of origin ⟨end*arch*⟩

archae- *or* **archaeo-** *also* **archeo-** *comb form* [Gk *archaio-*, fr. *archaios* ancient, fr. *archē* beginning] : ancient : primitive ⟨*archae*opteryx⟩ ⟨*Ar*cheozoic⟩

ar·chae·bac·te·ri·um \ˌär-kē-ˌbak-'tir-ē-əm\ *n* [NL] (1977) : any of a class (Archaeobacteria) or a separate kingdom (Archaebacteria) of primitive bacteria including methane-producing forms, some red halophilic forms, and others of harsh hot acidic environments

ar·chaeo·as·tron·o·my \ˌär-kē-(ˌ)ō-ə-'strä-nə-mē\ *n* (1971) : the study of the astronomy of ancient cultures

ar·chae·ol·o·gy *or* **ar·che·ol·o·gy** \ˌär-kē-'ä-lə-jē\ *n* [F *archéologie*, fr. LL *archaeologia* antiquarian lore, fr. Gk *archaiologia*, fr. *archaio-* + *-logia* -logy] (1837) **1** : the scientific study of material remains (as fossil relics, artifacts, and monuments) of past human life and activities **2** : remains of the culture of a people : ANTIQUITIES — **ar·chae·o·log·i·**

cal \ˌär-kē-ə-'lä-ji-kəl\ *adj* — **ar·chae·o·log·i·cal·ly** \-k(ə-)lē\ *adv* — **ar·chae·ol·o·gist** \ˌär-kē-'ä-lə-jist\ *n*

ar·chae·op·ter·yx \ˌär-kē-'äp-tə-riks\ *n* [NL, fr. *archae-* + Gk *pteryx* wing; akin to Gk *pteron* wing — more at FEATHER] (1859) : a primitive crow-sized bird (genus *Archaeopteryx*) of the Upper Jurassic period of Europe having reptilian characteristics (as teeth and a long bony tail)

ar·cha·ic \är-'kā-ik\ *adj* [F or Gk; F *archaïque*, fr. Gk *archaïkos*, fr. *archaios*] (1832) **1** : having the characteristics of the language of the past and surviving chiefly in specialized uses **2** : of, relating to, or characteristic of an earlier or more primitive time : ANTIQUATED ⟨~ legal traditions⟩ **3** *cap* : of or belonging to the early or formative phases of a culture or a period of artistic development; *esp* : of or belonging to the period leading up to the classical period of Greek culture **4** : surviving from an earlier period; *specif* : typical of a previously dominant evolutionary stage **5** *cap* : of or relating to the period from about 8000 B.C. to 1000 B.C. and the North American cultures of that time *syn* see OLD — **ar·cha·i·cal·ly** \-i-k(ə-)lē\ *adv*

archaic smile *n* (1889) : an expression that resembles a smile and is characteristic of early Greek sculpture

ar·cha·ism \\'är-kē-ˌi-zəm, -(ˌ)kā-ˌi-\ *n* [NL *archaïsmus*, fr. Gk *archaïsmos*, fr. *archaios*] (1643) **1** : the use of archaic diction or style **2** : an instance of archaic usage **3** : something archaic; *esp* : something (as a practice or custom) that is outmoded or old-fashioned — **ar·cha·ist** \-ist\ *n* — **ar·cha·is·tic** \ˌär-kē-'is-tik, -(ˌ)kā-\ *adj* — **ar·cha·ize** \\'är-kē-ˌīz, -(ˌ)kā-\ *vb*

arch·an·gel \\'är-ˌkān-jəl\ *n* [ME, fr. OF or LL; OF *archangele*, fr. LL *archangelus*, fr. Gk *archangelos*, fr. *archi-* + *angelos* angel] (12c) **1** : a chief angel **2** *pl* : an order of angels — see CELESTIAL HIERARCHY — **arch·an·gel·ic** \ˌär-(ˌ)kan-'je-lik\ *adj*

arch·bish·op \\(ˌ)är(k)-'bi-shəp\ *n* [ME, fr. OE, fr. LL *archiepiscopus*, fr. LGk *archiepiskopos*, fr. *archi-* + *episkopos* bishop — more at BISHOP] (bef. 12c) : a bishop at the head of an ecclesiastical province or one of equivalent honorary rank

arch·bish·op·ric \-shə-(ˌ)prik\ *n* (bef. 12c) **1** : the see or province over which an archbishop exercises authority **2** : the jurisdiction or office of an archbishop

arch·con·ser·va·tive \\(ˌ)ärch-kən-'sər-və-tiv\ *n* (1934) : an extreme conservative — **archconservative** *adj*

arch·dea·con \\(ˌ)ärch-'dē-kən\ *n* [ME *archedeken*, fr. OE *arcediacon*, fr. LL *archidiaconus*, fr. LGk *archidiakonos*, fr. Gk *archi-* + *diakonos* deacon] (bef. 12c) : a clergyman having the duty of assisting a diocesan bishop in ceremonial functions or administrative work

arch·dea·con·ry \-kən-rē\ *n*, *pl* **-ries** (1779) : the district or residence of an archdeacon

arch·di·o·cese \\(ˌ)ärch-'dī-ə-səs, -ˌsēz, -ˌsēs\ *n*, *pl* **-ces·es** \-'dī-ə-ˌsēz, -ˌsē-zəz, -sə-səz, -sə-ˌsēz\ (1844) : the diocese of an archbishop — **arch·di·oc·e·san** \ˌärch-dī-'ä-sə-sən\ *adj*

arch·du·cal \\(ˌ)ärch-'dü-kəl, -'dyü-\ *adj* [F *archiducal*, fr. *archiduc*] (1665) : of or relating to an archduke or archduchy

arch·duch·ess \-'də-chəs\ *n* [F *archiduchesse*, fem. of *archiduc* archduke, fr. MF *archeduc*] (1618) **1** : the wife or widow of an archduke **2** : a woman having in her own right a rank equal to that of an archduke

arch·duchy \-'də-chē\ *n* [F *archiduché*, fr. MF *archeduché*, fr. *archeduc* archduke, fr. MF *archeduc*] (1680) : the territory of an archduke or archduchess

arch·duke \-'dük, -'dyük\ *n* [MF *archeduc*, fr. *arche-* arch- + *duc* duke] (ca. 1530) **1** : a sovereign prince **2** : a prince of the imperial family of Austria — **arch·duke·dom** \-dəm\ *n*

Ar·che·an *or* **Ar·chae·an** \är-'kē-ən\ *adj* [Gk *archaios*] (1872) **1** : of, relating to, or being the earliest eon of geological history or the corresponding system of rocks — see GEOLOGIC TIME table **2** : PRECAMBRIAN — **Archean** *n*

ar·che·go·ni·al \ˌär-ki-'gō-nē-əl\ *adj* (1865) : of or relating to an archegonium; *also* : ARCHEGONIATE

¹ar·che·go·ni·ate \-nē-ət\ *adj* (ca. 1888) : bearing archegonia

²archegoniate *n* (ca. 1903) : a plant (as a moss, fern, horsetail, or club moss) that bears archegonia

ar·che·go·ni·um \-nē-əm\ *n*, *pl* **-nia** \-nē-ə\ [NL, fr. Gk *archegonos* originator, fr. *archein* to begin + *gonos* procreation; akin to Gk *gignesthai* to be born — more at ARCH-, KIN] (1854) : the flask-shaped female sex organ of bryophytes, lower vascular plants (as ferns), and some gymnosperms

arch·en·e·my \\(ˌ)ärch-'e-nə-mē\ *n*, *pl* **-mies** (1550) : a principal enemy

arch·en·ter·on \är-'ken-tə-ˌrän, -rən\ *n* [NL] (1877) : the cavity of a gastrula forming a primitive or primary gut

Ar·cheo·zo·ic *also* **Ar·chaeo·zo·ic** \ˌär-kē-ə-'zō-ik\ *adj* (1872) : ARCHEAN 1 — **Archeozoic** *n*

ar·cher \\'är-chər\ *n* [ME, fr. OF, fr. LL *arcarius*, alter. of *arcuarius*, fr. *arcuarius* of a bow, fr. L *arcus* bow — more at ARROW] (14c) **1** : a person who uses a bow and arrow **2** *cap* : SAGITTARIUS

ar·cher·fish \\'är-chər-ˌfish\ *n* (ca. 1889) : a small East Indian fish (*Toxotes jaculator*) that catches insects by stunning them with water ejected from its mouth; *also* : any of various related fish of similar habits

ar·chery \\'är-chə-rē\ *n* (15c) **1** : the art, practice, or skill of shooting with bow and arrow **2** : an archer's weapons **3** : a body of archers

ar·che·spo·ri·um \ˌär-ki-'spōr-ē-əm, -'spór-\ *n*, *pl* **-ria** \-ē-ə\ [NL, fr. *arche-* (as in *archegonium*) + *-sporium* (fr. *spora* spore)] (ca. 1889) : the cell or group of cells from which spore mother cells develop — **ar·che·spo·ri·al** \ˌär-ki-'spōr-ē-əl, -'spór-\ *adj*

ar·che·type \\'är-ki-ˌtīp\ *n* [L *archetypum*, fr. Gk *archetypon*, fr. neut. of *archetypos* archetypal, fr. *archein* + *typos* type] (1545) **1** : the original pattern or model of which all things of the same type are representations or copies : PROTOTYPE; *also* : a perfect example **2** : IDEA 1a **3** : an inherited idea or mode of thought in the psychology of C. G. Jung that is derived from the experience of the race and is present in the unconscious of the individual — **ar·che·typ·al** \ˌär-ki-'tī-pəl\ *also* **ar·che·typ·i·cal** \-'ti-pi-kəl\ *adj* — **ar·che·typ·al·ly** \-pə-lē\ *adv*

arch·fiend \\(ˌ)ärch-'fēnd\ *n* (1667) : a chief fiend; *esp* : SATAN

archi- *or* **arch-** *prefix* [F or L; F *archi-*, fr. L, fr. Gk — more at ARCH-] : primitive : original : primary ⟨*archi*enteron⟩

ar·chi·di·ac·o·nal \ˌär-ki-dī-'a-kə-nᵊl\ *adj* [LL *archidiaconus* archdeacon] (15c) : of or relating to an archdeacon

ar·chi·epis·co·pal \,är-kē-ə-'pis-kə-pəl\ *adj* [ML *archiepiscopalis,* fr. LL *archiepiscopus* archbishop — more at ARCHBISHOP] (1611) : of or relating to an archbishop — **ar·chi·epis·co·pal·ly** \-p(ə-)lē\ *adv*
ar·chi·epis·co·pate \-pət, -,pāt\ *n* (1792) : ARCHBISHOPRIC
ar·chil \'är-chəl\ *n* [ME *orchell*] (15c) **1** : a violet dye obtained from lichens (genera *Roccella* and *Lecanora*) **2** : a lichen that yields archil
ar·chi·man·drite \,är-kə-'man-,drīt\ *n* [LL *archimandrites,* fr. LGk *archimandritēs,* fr. Gk *archi-* + LGk *mandra* monastery, fr. Gk, fold, pen] (1591) : a dignitary in an Eastern church ranking below a bishop; *specif* : the superior of a large monastery or group of monasteries
Ar·chi·me·des' screw \,är-kə-'mē-dēz-\ *n* [*Archimedes*] (ca. 1859) : a device made of a tube bent spirally around an axis or a broad-threaded screw encased by a cylinder and used to raise water

Archimedes' screw

ar·chi·pe·lag·ic \,är-kə-pə-'la-jik, ,är-chə-\ *adj* (1841) : of, relating to, or located in an archipelago
ar·chi·pel·a·go \,är-kə-'pe-lə-,gō, ,är-chə-\ *n, pl* **-goes** *or* **-gos** [*Archipelago* Aegean Sea, fr. It *Arcipelago,* lit., chief sea, fr. *arci-* (fr. L *archi-*) + Gk *pelagos* sea — more at PLAGAL] (1502) **1** : an expanse of water with many scattered islands **2** : a group of islands
ar·chi·tect \'är-kə-,tekt\ *n* [MF *architecte,* fr. L *architectus,* fr. Gk *architektōn* master builder, fr. *archi-* + *tektōn* builder, carpenter — more at TECHNICAL] (1563) **1** : a person who designs buildings and advises in their construction **2** : a person who designs and guides a plan or undertaking ⟨the ~ of American foreign policy⟩
ar·chi·tec·ton·ic \,är-kə-,tek-'tä-nik\ *adj* [L *architectonicus,* fr. Gk *architektonikos,* fr. *architektōn*] (1645) **1** : of, relating to, or according with the principles of architecture : ARCHITECTURAL **2** : having an organized and unified structure that suggests an architectural design — **ar·chi·tec·ton·i·cal·ly** \-ni-k(ə-)lē\ *adv*
ar·chi·tec·ton·ics \-'tä-niks\ *n pl but sing or pl in constr, also* **ar·chi·tec·ton·ic** \-nik\ (1660) **1** : the science of architecture **2 a** : the unifying structural design of something **b** : the system of structure
ar·chi·tec·tur·al \,är-kə-'tek-chə-rəl, -'tek-shrəl\ *adj* (ca. 1794) **1** : of or relating to architecture : conforming to the rules of architecture **2** : having or conceived of as having a single unified overall design, form, or structure — **ar·chi·tec·tur·al·ly** *adv*
ar·chi·tec·ture \'är-kə-,tek-chər\ *n* (1555) **1** : the art or science of building; *specif* : the art or practice of designing and building structures and esp. habitable ones **2 a** : formation or construction as or as if as the result of conscious act ⟨the ~ of the garden⟩ **b** : a unifying or coherent form or structure ⟨the novel lacks ~⟩ **3** : architectural product or work **4** : a method or style of building **5** : the manner in which the components of a computer or computer system are organized and integrated
ar·chi·trave \'är-kə-,trāv\ *n* [MF, fr. OIt, fr. *archi-* + *trave* beam, fr. L *trab-, trabs* — more at THORP] (1563) **1** : the lowest division of an entablature resting in classical architecture immediately on the capital of the column — see ENTABLATURE illustration **2** : the molding around a rectangular opening (as a door)
ar·chi·val \är-'kī-vəl\ *adj* (ca. 1828) : of, relating to, contained in, or constituting archives
1ar·chive \'är-,kīv\ *n* [F & L; F, fr. L *archivum,* fr. Gk *archeion* government house (in pl., official documents), fr. *archē* rule, government — more at ARCH] (1603) : a place in which public records or historical documents are preserved; *also* : the material preserved — often used in pl.
2archive *vt* **ar·chived; ar·chiv·ing** (1926) : to file or collect (as records or documents) in or as if in an archive
ar·chi·vist \'är-kə-vist, -,kī-\ *n* (1753) : a person in charge of archives
ar·chi·volt \'är-kə-,vōlt\ *n* [It *archivolto,* fr. ML *archivoltum*] (ca. 1731) : an ornamental molding around an arch corresponding to an architrave
ar·chon \'är-,kän, -kən\ *n* [L, fr. Gk *archōn,* fr. prp. of *archein*] (1579) **1** : a chief magistrate in ancient Athens **2** : a presiding officer
ar·cho·saur \'är-kə-,sor\ *n* [NL *Archosauria,* fr. Gk *archōn* + *sauros* lizard] (1933) : any of a subclass (Archosauria) of reptiles comprising the dinosaurs, pterosaurs, and crocodilians — **ar·cho·sau·ri·an** \,är-kə-'sor-ē-ən\ *adj*
arch·priest \(,)ärch-'prēst\ *n* (14c) : a priest of preeminent rank
arch·way \'ärch-,wā\ *n* (1802) : a way or passage under an arch; *also* : an arch over a passage
-archy *n comb form, pl* **-archies** [ME *-archie,* fr. MF, fr. L *-archia,* fr. Gk, fr. *archein* to rule — more at ARCH-] : rule : government ⟨squirearchy⟩
arc lamp *n* (1882) : an electric lamp that produces light by an arc made when a current passes between two incandescent electrodes surrounded by gas — called also *arc light*
ar·co \'är-(,)kō\ *adv or adj* [It, fr. *arco* bow, fr. L *arcus* — more at ARROW] (1806) : with the bow — usu. used as a direction in music for players of stringed instruments; compare PIZZICATO
arc·sine \'ärk-'sīn\ *n* (ca. 1909) : the inverse function to the sine ⟨if *y* is the sine of θ, then θ is the ~ of *y*⟩
arc·tan·gent \(,)ärk-'tan-jənt\ *n* (ca. 1909) : the inverse function to the tangent ⟨if *y* is the tangent of θ, then θ is the ~ of *y*⟩
1arc·tic \'ärk-tik, 'är-tik\ *adj* [ME *artik,* fr. L *arcticus,* fr. Gk *arktikos,* fr. *arktos* bear, Ursa Major, north; akin to L *ursus* bear, Skt *ṛkṣa*] (14c) **1** *often cap* : of or relating to the north pole or the region near it **2 a** : a bitter cold : FRIGID ⟨an ~ smile⟩ **b** : cold in temper or mood ⟨an ~ smile⟩ — **arc·ti·cal·ly** \-ti-k(ə-)lē\ *adv*
2arc·tic \'är-tik, 'ärk-tik\ *n* (1867) : a rubber overshoe reaching to the ankle or above
arctic char *n* (ca. 1902) : a Holarctic char (*Salvelinus alpinus*) of arctic waters occurring in freshwater or anadromous populations
arctic circle *n, often cap A&C* (1834) : the parallel of latitude that is approximately 66½ degrees north of the equator and that circumscribes the northern frigid zone
arctic fox *n* (1772) : a small migratory Holarctic fox (*Alopex lagopus*) esp. of coastal arctic and alpine tundra

arctic tern *n* (1844) : a Holarctic tern (*Sterna paradisaea*) that breeds in arctic regions and migrates to southern Africa and So. America
Arc·tu·rus \ärk-'tur-əs, -'tyur-\ *n* [L, fr. Gk *Arktouros,* lit., bear watcher] : a giant fixed star of the first magnitude in Boötes
ar·cu·ate \'är-kyə-wət, -,wāt\ *adj* [L *arcuatus,* pp. of *arcuare* to bend like a bow, fr. *arcus* bow] (1626) : curved like a bow ⟨an ~ cloud⟩ — **ar·cu·ate·ly** *adv*
-ard *also* **-art** *n suffix* [ME, fr. OF, of Gmc origin; akin to OHG *-hart* (in personal names such as *Gērhart* Gerard), OE *heard* hard] : one that is characterized by performing some action, possessing some quality, or being associated with some thing esp. conspicuously or excessively ⟨braggart⟩ ⟨dullard⟩ ⟨pollard⟩
ar·den·cy \'är-d°n(t)-sē\ *n* (1549) : the quality or state of being ardent
ar·dent \'är-d°nt\ *adj* [ME, fr. MF, fr. L *ardent-, ardens,* prp. of *ardēre* to burn, fr. *ardor*] (14c) **1** : characterized by warmth of feeling typically expressed in eager zealous support or activity **2** : FIERY, HOT ⟨an ~ sun⟩ **3** : SHINING, GLOWING ⟨~ eyes⟩ *syn* see IMPASSIONED — **ar·dent·ly** *adv*
ardent spirits *n pl* (1833) : strong distilled liquors
ar·dor \'är-dər\ *n* [ME, fr. MF & L; MF, fr. L *ardor* burning, heat, ardor, fr. *aridus* dry — more at ARID] (14c) **1 a** : an often restless or transitory warmth of feeling ⟨the sudden ~s of youth⟩ **b** : extreme vigor or energy : INTENSITY **c** : ZEAL **d** : LOYALTY **2** : sexual excitement *syn* see PASSION
ar·dour *chiefly Brit var of* ARDOR
ar·du·ous \'är-jə-wəs, -dyü-wəs\ *adj* [L *arduus* high, steep, difficult; akin to OIr *ard* high] (1538) **1 a** : hard to accomplish or achieve : DIFFICULT ⟨years of ~ training⟩ **b** : marked by great labor or effort : STRENUOUS ⟨a life of ~ toil —A. C. Cole⟩ **2** : hard to climb : STEEP *syn* see HARD — **ar·du·ous·ly** *adv* — **ar·du·ous·ness** *n*
1are \ər, (,)är\ [ME, fr. OE *earun;* akin to ON *eru, erum* are, OE *is* is] *pres 2d sing or pres pl of* BE
2are \'är, 'er, 'är\ *n* [F, fr. L *area*] (ca. 1819) — see METRIC SYSTEM table
ar·ea \'ar-ē-ə, 'er-;\ 'ä-rē-ə\ *n* [L, open space, threshing floor; perh. akin to L *arēre* to be dry — more at ARID] (1538) **1** : a level piece of ground **2** : the surface included within a set of lines; *specif* : the number of unit squares equal in measure to the surface — see METRIC SYSTEM table, WEIGHT table **3** : the scope of a concept, operation, or activity : FIELD ⟨the whole ~ of foreign policy⟩ **4** : AREAWAY ⟨went down the steps into the ~ of a house —James Joyce⟩ **5** : a particular extent of space or surface or one serving a special function: as **a** : a part of the surface of the body **b** : a geographic region **6** : a part of the cerebral cortex having a particular function — **ar·e·al** \-ē-əl\ *adj* — **ar·e·al·ly** \-ə-lē\ *adv*
area code *n* (1961) : a 3-digit number that identifies each telephone service area in a country (as the U.S. or Canada)
ar·ea·way \'ar-ē-ə-,wä, 'er-;\ 'ä-rē-\ *n* (1899) : a sunken space affording access, air, and light to a basement
are·ca \ə-'rē-kə, 'ar-i-kə\ *n* [NL, fr. Pg, fr. Malayalam *aṭaykka*] (1510) : any of several tropical Asian palms (*Areca* or related genera) esp : BETEL PALM
arec·o·line \ə-'re-kə-,lēn\ *n* [ISV *areca* + ¹*-ol* + ²*-ine*] (1899) : a toxic parasympathomimetic alkaloid $C_8H_{13}NO_2$ that is used as a veterinary anthelmintic and occurs naturally in betel nuts
are·na \ə-'rē-nə\ *n* [L *harena, arena* sand, sandy place] (1600) **1** : an area in a Roman amphitheater for gladiatorial combats **2 a** : an enclosed area used for public entertainment **b** : a building containing an arena **3 a** : a sphere of interest, activity, or competition ⟨the political ~⟩ **b** : a place or situation for controversy ⟨in the public ~⟩
ar·e·na·ceous \,ar-ə-'nā-shəs\ *adj* [L *arenaceus,* fr. *arena*] (1646) **1** : resembling, made of, or containing sand or sandy particles **2** : growing in sandy places
arena theater *n* (1943) : THEATER-IN-THE-ROUND
ar·e·nic·o·lous \,ar-ə-'ni-kə-ləs\ *adj* [L *arena* + E *-i-* + *-colous*] (ca. 1859) : living, burrowing, or growing in sand
aren't \'ärnt, 'är-ənt\ (1810) **1** : are not **2** : am not — used in questions
ar·eo·cen·tric \,ar-ē-ō-'sen-trik\ *adj* [Gk *Areios* of Ares, fr. *Arēs*] (1877) : having or relating to the planet Mars as a center
are·o·la \ə-'rē-ə-lə\ *n, pl* **-lae** \-,lē\ *or* **-las** [NL, fr. L, small open space, dim. of *area*] (1664) : a small area between things or about something; *esp* : a colored ring (as about the nipple, a vesicle, or a pustule) — **are·o·lar** \-lər\ *adj* — **are·o·late** \-lət\ *adj*
ar·e·ole \'ar-ē-,ōl\ *n* (ca. 1934) : a small pit or cavity
Ar·e·op·a·gite \,ar-ē-'ä-pə-,gīt, -,jīt\ *n* (14c) : a member of the Areopagus — **Ar·e·op·a·git·ic** \-,ä-pə-'ji-tik\ *adj*
Ar·e·op·a·gus \,ar-ē-'ä-pə-gəs\ *n* [L, fr. Gk *Areios pagos,* fr. *Areios pagos* (lit., hill of Ares), a hill in Athens where the tribunal met] (1586) : the supreme tribunal of Athens
Ar·es \'ar-(,)ēz, 'er-\ *n* [Gk *Arēs*] : the Greek god of war — compare MARS
arête \ə-'rāt\ *n* [F, lit., fish bone, fr. LL *arista,* fr. L, beard of grain] (1838) : a sharp-crested ridge in rugged mountains
Ar·e·thu·sa \,ar-ə-'thü-zə, -'thyü-\ *n* [L, fr. Gk *Arethousa*] : a wood nymph who is changed into a spring while fleeing the advances of the river-god Alpheus
ar·ga·li \'är-gə-lē\ *n* [Mongolian] (ca. 1774) : a large wild sheep (*Ovis ammon*) of Asia that is noted for its large horns
Ar·gand diagram \'är-,gän-, -'gän-\ *n* [Jean Robert *Argand* †1825 Swiss mathematician] (1908) : a system of rectangular coordinates in which the complex number *x* + *iy* is represented by the point whose coordinates are *x* and *y*
ar·gent \'är-jənt\ *n* [ME, fr. MF & L; MF, fr. L *argentum;* akin to Gk *argyros* silver, *argos* white, Skt *rajata* whitish, silvery] (15c) **1** *archaic* : the metal silver; *also* : WHITENESS **2** : the heraldic color silver or white — **argent** *adj*
ar·gen·tif·er·ous \,är-jən-'ti-f(ə-)rəs\ *adj* (1801) : containing silver

---

¹ar·gen·tine \'är-jən-₁tīn, -₁tēn\ *adj* (15c) : SILVER, SILVERY

²argentine *n* (1577) : SILVER; *also* : any of various similar materials

ar·gen·tite \'är-jən-₁tīt\ *n* (ca. 1837) : native silver sulfide having a metallic luster and dark lead-gray color and constituting a valuable ore of silver

ar·gil \'är-jəl\ *n* [ME, fr. L *argilla,* fr. Gk *argillos;* akin to Gk *argos* white] (14c) : CLAY; *esp* : POTTER'S CLAY

ar·gil·la·ceous \₁är-jə-'lā-shəs\ *adj* (ca. 1731) : of, relating to, or containing clay or clay minerals : CLAYEY

ar·gil·lite \'är-jə₁līt\ *n* (1795) : a compact argillaceous rock cemented by silica and having no slaty cleavage

ar·gi·nase \'är-jə-₁nās, -₁nāz\ *n* [ISV] (1904) : a crystalline enzyme that converts naturally occurring arginine into ornithine and urea

ar·gi·nine \'är-jə-₁nēn\ *n* [G *Arginin*] (1886) : a crystalline basic amino acid $C_6H_{14}N_4O_2$ derived from guanidine

Ar·give \'är-₁jiv, -₁gīv\ *adj* [L *Argivus,* fr. Gk *Argeios,* lit., of Argos, fr. *Argos* city-state of ancient Greece] (1598) : of or relating to the Greeks or Greece and esp. the Achaean city of Argos or the surrounding territory of Argolis — **Argive** *n*

ar·gle–bar·gle \₁är-gəl-'bär-gəl\ *n* [redupl. of Sc & E *argle,* alter. of *argue*] (1872) *chiefly Brit* : ARGY-BARGY

Ar·go \'är-(₁)gō\ *n* [L (gen. *Argus*), fr. Gk *Argō*] : a large constellation in the southern hemisphere lying principally between Canis Major and the Southern Cross

ar·gol \'är-₁gól\ *n* [ME *argoile,* fr. AF *argoil*] (14c) : crude tartar deposited in wine casks during aging

ar·gon \'är-₁gän\ *n* [Gk, neut. of *argos* idle, lazy, fr. *a-* + *ergon* work; fr. its relative inertness — more at WORK] (1894) : a colorless odorless inert gaseous element found in the air and in volcanic gases and used esp. in welding, lasers, and electric bulbs — see ELEMENT table

ar·go·naut \'är-jə-₁nót, -₁nät\ *n* [L *Argonautes,* fr. Gk *Argonautēs,* fr. *Argō,* ship in which the Argonauts sailed + *nautēs* sailor — more at NAUTICAL] (14c) **1** *a cap* : any of a band of heroes sailing with Jason in quest of the Golden Fleece **b** : an adventurer engaged in a quest **2** : PAPER NAUTILUS

ar·go·sy \'är-gə-sē\ *n, pl* **-sies** [modif. of It *ragusea* Ragusan vessel, fr. *Ragusa,* Dalmatia (now Dubrovnik, Croatia)] (1587) **1** : a large ship; *esp* : a large merchant ship ⟨three of your *argosies* are . . . come to harbor —Shak.⟩ **2** : a fleet of ships **3** : a rich supply ⟨an ~ of railway folklore —F. P. Donovan⟩

ar·got \'är-gət, -(₁)gō\ *n* [F] (1860) : an often more or less secret vocabulary and idiom peculiar to a particular group ⟨shoved into a taxi by a porter whose ~ I couldn't understand —Allen Tate⟩

ar·gu·able \'är-gyü-ə-bəl\ *adj* (ca. 1611) **1** : open to argument, dispute, or question **2** : that can be plausibly or convincingly argued

ar·gu·ably \'är-gyü-(ə-)blē\ *adv* (1890) : it can be argued ⟨the word is ~ useful⟩ ⟨~ the busiest airport in the world⟩

ar·gue \'är-(₁)gyü\ *vb* **ar·gued; ar·gu·ing** [ME, fr. MF *arguer* to accuse, reason & L *arguere* to demonstrate, prove; MF *arguer,* fr. L *argutare* to prate, freq. of *arguere;* akin to Hitt *arkuwai-* to plead, respond] *vi* (14c) **1** : to give reasons for or against something : REASON **2** : to contend or disagree in words : DISPUTE ~ *vt* **1** : to give evidence of : INDICATE **2** : to consider the pros and cons of : DISCUSS **3** : to prove or try to prove by giving reasons : MAINTAIN **4** : to persuade by giving reasons : INDUCE *syn* see DISCUSS — **ar·gu·er** \-gyə-wər\ *n*

ar·gu·fy \'är-gyə-₁fī\ *vb* **-fied; -fy·ing** *vt* (1771) : DISPUTE, DEBATE ~ *vi* : WRANGLE — **ar·gu·fi·er** \-₁fī(-ə)r\ *n*

ar·gu·ment \'är-gyə-mənt\ *n* [ME, fr. MF, fr. L *argumentum,* fr. *arguere*] (14c) **1** *obs* : an outward sign : INDICATION **2 a** : a reason given in proof or rebuttal **b** : discourse intended to persuade **3 a** : the act or process of arguing : ARGUMENTATION **b** : a coherent series of statements leading from a premise to a conclusion **c** : QUARREL, DISAGREEMENT **4** : an abstract or summary esp. of a literary work ⟨a later editor added an ~ to the poem⟩ **5** : the subject matter esp. of a literary work **6 a** : one of the independent variables upon whose value that of a function depends **b** : a substantive (as the direct object of a transitive verb) that is required by a predicate in grammar **c** : the angle assigned to a complex number when it is plotted in a complex plane using polar coordinates — called also *amplitude;* compare ABSOLUTE VALUE 2

ar·gu·men·ta·tion \₁är-gyə-mən-'tā-shən, -₁men-\ *n* (15c) **1** : the act or process of forming reasons and of drawing conclusions and applying them to a case in discussion **2** : DEBATE, DISCUSSION

ar·gu·men·ta·tive \₁är-gyə-'men-tə-tiv\ *adj* (15c) **1** : characterized by argument : CONTROVERSIAL **2** : given to argument : DISPUTATIOUS — **ar·gu·men·ta·tive·ly** *adv*

ar·gu·men·tum \₁är-gyə-'men-təm\ *n, pl* **-men·ta** \-'men-tə\ [L] (1690) : ARGUMENT 3b

Ar·gus \'är-gəs\ *n* [L, fr. Gk *Argos*] **1** : a hundred-eyed monster of Greek mythology **2** : a watchful guardian

Ar·gus–eyed \'är-gəs-₁īd\ *adj* (1603) : vigilantly observant

ar·gy–bar·gy \₁är-jē-'bär-jē, ₁är-gē-'bär-gē\ *n* [redupl. of Sc & E dial. *argy,* alter. of *argue*] (1887) *chiefly Brit* : a lively discussion : ARGUMENT, DISPUTE

ar·gyle *also* **ar·gyll** \'är-₁gī(ə)l, är-'\ *n, often cap* [*Argyle, Argyll,* branch of the Scottish clan of Campbell, fr. whose tartan the design was adapted] (1899) **:** a geometric knitting pattern of varicolored diamonds in solid and outline shapes on a single background color; *also* : a sock knit in this pattern

ar·hat \'är-(₁)hət\ *n* [Skt, fr. prp. of *arhati* he deserves; akin to Gk *alphein* to gain] (1870) : a Buddhist who has reached the stage of enlightenment — **ar·hat·ship** \-₁ship\ *n*

aria \'är-ē-ə\ *n* [It, lit., atmospheric air, modif. of L *aer*] (ca. 1724) **1** : AIR, MELODY, TUNE; *specif* : an accompanied elaborate melody sung (as in an opera) by a single voice **2** : a striking solo performance (as in a movie)

Ar·i·ad·ne \₁ar-ē-'ad-nē\ *n* [L, fr. Gk *Ariadnē*] : a daughter of Minos who helps Theseus escape from the labyrinth

¹Ar·i·an \'ar-ē-ən, 'er-\ *adj* (14c) : of or relating to Arius or his doctrines esp. that the Son is not of the same substance as the Father but

was created as an agent for creating the world — **Ar·i·an·ism** \-ə-₁ni-zəm\ *n*

²Arian *n* (14c) : a supporter of Arian doctrines

³Ar·i·an \'er-ē-ən, 'ar-\ *n* (1917) : ARIES 2b

-ar·i·an *n suffix* [L *-arius -ary*] **1** : believer ⟨necessit*arian*⟩ : advocate ⟨latitudin*arian*⟩ **2** : producer ⟨disciplin*arian*⟩

ari·bo·fla·vin·osis \₁ā-₁rī-bə-₁flā-və-'nō-səs\ *n* [NL] (1939) : a deficiency disease due to inadequate intake of riboflavin and characterized by sores on the mouth

ar·id \'ar-əd\ *adj* [F or L; F *aride,* fr. L *aridus,* fr. *arēre* to be dry; akin to Skt *āsa* ash, OE *asce*] (1652) **1** : excessively dry; *specif* : having insufficient rainfall to support agriculture **2** : lacking in interest and life : JEUNE — **arid·i·ty** \ə-'ri-də-tē, a-\ *n* — **ar·id·ness** \'ar-əd-nəs\ *n*

Ar·i·el \'ar-ē-əl, 'er-\ *n* : a prankish spirit in Shakespeare's *The Tempest*

Ar·i·es \'er-₁ēz, 'ar-, -ē-₁ēz\ *n* [L (gen. *Arietis*), lit., ram; perh. akin to Gk *eriphos* kid, OIr *heirp* she-goat] **1** : a constellation between Pisces and Taurus pictured as a ram **2 a** : the first sign of the zodiac in astrology — see ZODIAC table **b** : one born under the sign of Aries

ari·et·ta \₁är-ē-'e-tə, ₁ar-\ *n* [It, dim. of *aria*] (ca. 1724) : a short aria

aright \ə-'rīt\ *adv* [ME, fr. OE *ariht,* fr. ¹*a-* + *riht* right] (bef. 12c) : RIGHT, CORRECTLY ⟨if I remember ~⟩

Ar·i·ka·ra \ə-'ri-kə-rə\ *n, pl* **Arikara** (1811) **1** : a member of an American Indian people of the Missouri River Valley in No. Dakota **2** : the language of the Arikara

ar·il \'ar-əl\ *n* [prob. fr. NL *arillus,* fr. ML, raisin, grape seed] (1794) : an exterior covering or appendage of some seeds (as of the yew) that develops after fertilization as an outgrowth from the ovule stalk — **ar·il·late** \'ar-ə-₁lāt\ *adj*

ari·o·so \₁är-ē-'ō-(₁)sō, -(₁)zō\ *n, pl* **-sos** *also* **-si** \-(₁)sē, -(₁)zē\ [It, fr. *aria*] (ca. 1724) : a musical passage or composition having a mixture of free recitative and metrical song

arise \ə-'rīz\ *vi* **arose** \-'rōz\; **aris·en** \-'ri-zⁿn\; **aris·ing** \-'rī-ziŋ\ [ME, fr. OE *ārīsan,* fr. *ā-,* perfective prefix + *rīsan* to rise — more at ABIDE] (bef. 12c) **1** : to get up : RISE **2** : to originate from a source **b** : to come into being or to attention **3** : ASCEND *syn* see SPRING

aris·ta \ə-'ris-tə\ *n, pl* **-tae** \-(₁)tē, -₁tī\ *or* **-tas** [NL, fr. L, beard of grain] (1691) : a bristlelike structure or appendage — **aris·tate** \-₁tāt\ *adj*

aris·to \ə-'ris-(₁)tō\ *n, pl* **-tos** [by shortening] (1864) : ARISTOCRAT

ar·is·toc·ra·cy \₁ar-ə-'stä-krə-sē\ *n, pl* **-cies** [MF & LL; MF *aristocratie,* fr. LL *aristocratia,* fr. Gk *aristokratia,* fr. *aristos* best + *-kratia* -cracy] (1561) **1** : government by the best individuals or by a small privileged class **2 a** : a government in which power is vested in a minority consisting of those believed to be best qualified **b** : a state with such a government **3** : a governing body or upper class usu. made up of an hereditary nobility **4** : the aggregate of those believed to be superior

aris·to·crat \ə-'ris-tə-₁krat, a-; 'ar-ə-stə-\ *n* (1789) **1** : a member of an aristocracy; *esp* : NOBLE **2 a** : one who has the bearing and viewpoint typical of the aristocracy **b** : one who favors aristocracy **3** : one believed to be superior of its kind ⟨the ~ of Southern resorts —*Southern Living*⟩

aris·to·crat·ic \ə-₁ris-tə-'kra-tik, (₁)a-₁ris-tə-, ₁ar-ə-stə-\ *adj* [MF *aristocratique,* fr. ML *aristocraticus,* fr. Gk *aristokratikos,* fr. *aristokratia*] (1602) **1** : belonging to, having the qualities of, or favoring aristocracy **2 a** : socially exclusive ⟨an ~ neighborhood⟩ **b** : SNOBBISH — **aris·to·crat·i·cal·ly** \-ti-k(ə-)lē\ *adv*

Ar·is·to·te·lian *also* **Ar·is·to·te·lean** \₁ar-ə-stə-'tēl-yən\ *adj* [L *Aristoteles* Aristotle, fr. Gk *Aristotelēs*] (1607) : of or relating to the Greek philosopher Aristotle or his philosophy — **Aristotelian** *n* — **Ar·is·to·te·lian·ism** \-yə-₁ni-zəm\ *n*

arith·me·tic \ə-'rith-mə-₁tik\ *n* [ME *arsmetrik,* fr. OF *arismetique,* fr. L *arithmetica,* fr. Gk *arithmētikē,* fr. fem. of *arithmētikos* arithmetical, fr. *arithmein* to count, fr. *arithmos* number; akin to OE *rīm* number, and perh. to Gk *arariskein* to fit] (15c) **1 a** : a branch of mathematics that deals esp. with the nonnegative real numbers including sometimes the transfinite cardinals and with the application of the operations of addition, subtraction, multiplication, and division to them **b** : a treatise on arithmetic **2** : COMPUTATION, CALCULATION — **ar·ith·met·ic** \₁ar-ith-'me-tik\ *or* **ar·ith·met·i·cal** \-ti-kəl\ *adj* — **ar·ith·met·i·cal·ly** \-ti-k(ə-)lē\ *adv* — **arith·me·ti·cian** \ə-₁rith-mə-'ti-shən\ *n*

arithmetic mean *n* (1767) : a value that is computed by dividing the sum of a set of terms by the number of terms

arithmetic progression *n* (1594) : a progression (as 3, 5, 7, 9) in which the difference between any term and its predecessor is constant

-ar·i·um *n suffix, pl* **-ar·i·ums** *or* **-ar·ia** [L, fr. neut. of *-arius -ary*] : thing or place relating to or connected with ⟨planet*arium*⟩

ark \'ärk\ *n* [ME, fr. OE *arc,* fr. L *arca* chest; akin to L *arcēre* to hold off, defend, Gk *arkein,* Hitt *hark-* to have, hold] (bef. 12c) **1 a** : a boat or ship held to resemble that in which Noah and his family were preserved from the Flood **b** : something that affords protection and safety **2 a** : the sacred chest representing to the Hebrews the presence of God among them **b** : a repository traditionally in or against the wall of a synagogue for the scrolls of the Torah

ar·kose \'är-₁kōs, -₁kōz\ *n* [F] (1839) : a sandstone characterized by feldspar fragments that is derived from granite or gneiss which has disintegrated rapidly — **ar·ko·sic** \(₁)är-'kō-sik, -zik\ *adj*

¹arm \'ärm\ *n* [ME, fr. OE *earm;* akin to L *armus* shoulder, Skt *īrma* arm] (bef. 12c) **1** : a human upper limb; *esp* : the part between the shoulder and the wrist **2** : something like or corresponding to an arm: as **a** : the forelimb of a vertebrate **b** : a limb of an invertebrate animal **c** : a branch or lateral shoot of a plant **d** : a slender part of a structure, machine, or an instrument projecting from a main part, axis, or fulcrum ⟨the ~ of a chair⟩ **e** : the end of a ship's yard; *also* : the part of an anchor from the crown to the fluke — see ANCHOR illustration **f** : any of the usu. two parts of a chromosome lateral to the centromere **3** : an inlet of water (as from the sea) **4** : a narrow extension of a larger area, mass, or group **5** : POWER, MIGHT ⟨the long ~ of the law⟩ **6** : a support (as on a chair) for the elbow and forearm **7** : SLEEVE **8** : the ability to throw or pitch a baseball well; *also* : a player having such ability **9** : a functional division of a group, organization, institution, or activity ⟨the logistical ~ of the air force⟩ — **arm·less** \'ärm-ləs\ *adj* — **arm·like** \-₁līk\ *adj* — **arm in arm** : with arms linked together ⟨walked down the street *arm in arm*⟩

argyle

²arm *vb* [ME *armen*, fr. OF *armer*, fr. L *armare*, fr. *arma* weapons, tools; akin to L *ars* skill, Gk *harmos* joint, *arariskein* to fit] *vt* (12c) **1** : to furnish or equip with weapons **2** : to furnish with something that strengthens or protects **3** : to fortify morally **4** : to equip or ready for action or operation ⟨~ a bomb⟩ ~ *vi* : to prepare oneself for struggle or resistance

³arm *n, often attrib* [ME *armes* (pl.) weapons, fr. OF, fr. L *arma*] (13c) **1 a** : a means (as a weapon) of offense or defense; *esp* : FIREARM **b** : a combat branch (as of an army) **c** : an organized branch of national defense (as the navy) **2** *pl* **a** : the hereditary heraldic devices of a family **b** : heraldic devices adopted by a government **3** *pl* **a** : active hostilities : WARFARE **b** : military service — **up in arms** : aroused and ready to undertake hostilities

ar·ma·da \är-ˈmä-də, -ˈmā- *also* -ˈma-\ *n* [Sp, fr. ML *armata* army, fleet, fr. L, fem. of *armatus*, pp. of *armare* to arm, fr. *arma*] (1533) **1** : a fleet of warships **2** : a large force or group usu. of moving things ⟨an ~ of fishing boats⟩

ar·ma·dil·lo \ˌär-mə-ˈdi-(ˌ)lō\ *n, pl* **-los** [Sp, fr. dim. of *armado* armed one, fr. L *armatus*] (1577) : any of a family (Dasypodidae) of burrowing edentate mammals found from the southern U.S. to Argentina and having the body and head encased in an armor of small bony plates

Ar·ma·ged·don \ˌär-mə-ˈge-dᵊn\ *n* [Gk *Armageddōn, Harmagedōn*, scene of the battle foretold in Rev 16:14–16] (1534) **1 a** : the site or time of a final and conclusive battle between the forces of good and evil **b** : the battle taking place at Armageddon **2** : a usu. vast decisive conflict or confrontation

Ar·ma·gnac \ˈär-mən-ˌyak\ *n* [F, fr. *Armagnac*, region in southwest France] (1850) : a brandy produced in the Gers department of France

ar·ma·ment \ˈär-mə-mənt *also* ˈärm-mənt\ *n* [F *armement*, fr. L *armamenta* (pl.) utensils, military or naval equipment, fr. *armare*] (1699) **1** : a military or naval force **2 a** : the aggregate of a nation's military strength **b** : WEAPONS, ARMS **3** : the process of preparing for war

ar·ma·men·tar·i·um \ˌär-mə-ˌmen-ˈter-ē-əm, -mən-\ *n, pl* **-tar·ia** \-ē-ə\ [L, armory, fr. *armamenta*] (ca. 1860) **1** : the equipment and methods used esp. in medicine **2** : matter available or utilized for an undertaking or field of activity ⟨a whole ~ of devices to create an illusion of real life —Kenneth Rexroth⟩

arm and a leg *n* (1967) : an exorbitant price

ar·ma·ture \ˈär-mə-ˌchu̇r, -chər, -ˌtyu̇r, -ˌtu̇r\ *n* [L *armatura* armor, equipment, fr. *armatus*] (15c) **1** : an organ or structure (as teeth or thorns) for offense or defense **2 a** : a piece of soft iron or steel that connects the poles of a magnet or of adjacent magnets **b** : a usu. rotating part of an electric machine (as a generator or motor) which consists essentially of coils of wire around a metal core and in which electric current is induced or in which the input current interacts with a magnetic field to produce torque **c** : the movable part of an electromagnetic device (as a loudspeaker) **d** : a framework used by a sculptor to support a figure being modeled in a plastic material **e** : FRAMEWORK 1b ⟨the ~ of the book derives from fourteenth century England —Stanley Kauffmann⟩

arm·band \ˈärm-ˌband\ *n* (1797) : a band usu. worn around the upper part of a sleeve for identification or in mourning

¹arm·chair \ˈärm-ˌcher, -ˌchar\ *n* (1633) : a chair with armrests

²armchair *adj* (1886) **1** : remote from direct dealing with problems : theoretical rather than practical ⟨~ strategists⟩ **2** : sharing vicariously in another's experiences ⟨an ~ traveler⟩

¹armed \ˈärmd\ *adj* (13c) **1 a** : furnished with weapons **b** : furnished with something that provides security, strength, or efficacy **2** : marked by the maintenance of armed forces in readiness

²armed *adj* (1606) : having an arm or arms esp. of a specified kind or number — usu. used in combination ⟨long-*armed*⟩ ⟨two-*armed*⟩

armed forces *n pl* (1943) : the combined military, naval, and air forces of a nation — called also *armed services*

Ar·me·nian \är-ˈmē-nē-ən, -nyən\ *n* (1537) **1** : a member of a people dwelling chiefly in Armenia and neighboring areas (as Turkey or Azerbaijan) **2** : the Indo-European language of the Armenians — see INDO-EUROPEAN LANGUAGES table **3** : a member of the Armenian church established by St. Gregory the Illuminator that adheres to the decisions of the first three ecumenical councils — **Armenian** *adj*

arm·ful \ˈärm-ˌfu̇l\ *n, pl* **arm·fuls** \-ˌfu̇lz\ *or* **arms·ful** \ˈärmz-ˌfu̇l\ (1579) : as much as the arm or arms can hold

arm·hole \ˈärm-ˌhōl\ *n* (ca. 1775) : an opening for the arm in a garment

ar·mi·ger \ˈär-mi-jər\ *n* [ML, fr. L, armor-bearer, fr. *armiger* bearing arms, fr. *arma* arms + *gerere* to carry] (1762) **1** : SQUIRE **2** : one entitled to bear heraldic arms — **ar·mig·er·al** \är-ˈmi-jə-rəl\ *adj*

ar·mig·er·ous \är-ˈmi-jər-əs\ *adj* (1731) : bearing heraldic arms

ar·mil·la·ry sphere \ˈär-mə-ˌler-ē-, är-ˈmi-lə-rē-\ *n* [F *sphère armillaire*, fr. ML *armilla*, fr. L, bracelet, iron ring, fr. *armus* shoulder — more at ARM] (1664) : an old astronomical instrument composed of rings showing the positions of important circles of the celestial sphere

Ar·min·i·an \är-ˈmi-nē-ən\ *adj* (1618) : of or relating to Arminius or his doctrines opposing the absolute predestination of strict Calvinism and maintaining the possibility of salvation for all — **Arminian** *n* — **Ar·min·i·an·ism** \-nē-ə-ˌni-zəm\ *n*

ar·mi·stice \ˈär-mə-stəs\ *n* [F or NL; F, fr. NL *armistitium*, fr. L *arma* + *-stitium* (as in *solstitium* solstice)] (ca. 1707) : temporary suspension of hostilities by agreement between the opponents : TRUCE

Armistice Day *n* [fr. the armistice terminating World War I on November 11, 1918] (1919) : VETERANS DAY — used before the official adoption of *Veterans Day* in 1954

arm·let \ˈärm-lət\ *n* (1535) **1** : a band (as of cloth or metal) worn around the upper arm **2** : a small arm (as of the sea)

arm·load \ˈärm-ˌlōd\ *n* (1906) : ARMFUL

arm·lock \-ˌläk\ *n* (1905) : HAMMERLOCK

ar·moire \ärm-ˈwär, *Southern also* ˈär-mər\ *n* [MF, fr. OF *armaire*, fr. L *armarium*, fr. *arma*] (1571) : a usu. tall cupboard or wardrobe

ar·mor \ˈär-mər\ *n* [ME *armure*, fr. OF, fr. L *armatura* — more at ARMATURE] (13c) **1** : defensive covering for the body; *esp* : covering (as of metal) used in combat **2** : a quality or circumstance that affords protection ⟨the ~ of prosperity⟩ **3** : a protective outer layer (as of a ship, a plant or animal, or a cable) **4** : armored forces and vehicles (as tanks) — **armor** *vt* — **ar·mored** \-mərd\ *adj* — **ar·mor·less** \-mər-ləs\ *adj*

armored scale *n* (ca. 1903) : any of a family (Diaspididae) of scale insects having a firm covering of wax best developed in the female

ar·mor·er \ˈär-mər-ər\ *n* (14c) **1** : one that makes armor or arms **2** : one that repairs, assembles, and tests firearms

ar·mo·ri·al \är-ˈmȯr-ē-əl, -ˈmȯr-\ *adj* [*armory* (heraldry)] (1576) : of, relating to, or bearing heraldic arms — **ar·mo·ri·al·ly** \-ē-ə-lē\ *adv*

Ar·mor·i·can \är-ˈmȯr-i-kən, -ˈmär-\ *or* **Ar·mor·ic** \-ik\ *n* (ca. 1645) : a native or inhabitant of Armorica; *esp* : BRETON — **Armorican** *or* **Armoric** *adj*

ar·mory \ˈärm-rē, ˈär-mə-\ *n, pl* **ar·mor·ies** (14c) **1 a** : a supply of arms for defense or attack **b** : a collection of available resources **2** : a place where arms and military equipment are stored; *esp* : one used for training reserve military personnel **3** : a place where arms are manufactured

ar·mour, ar·moury *chiefly Brit var of* ARMOR, ARMORY

arm·pit \ˈärm-ˌpit\ *n* (14c) **1** : the hollow beneath the junction of the arm and shoulder **2** : the least desirable place : PIT ⟨77th Street Station . . . was the ~ of detective duty —Joseph Wambaugh⟩

arm·rest \-ˌrest\ *n* (ca. 1889) : a support for the arm

arm's length *n* (ca. 1909) **1** : a distance discouraging personal contact or familiarity ⟨kept former friends at *arm's length* now⟩ **2** : the condition or fact that the parties to a transaction are independent and on an equal footing — **arm's–length** *adj*

arm–twist·ing \-ˌtwis-tiŋ\ *n* (1948) : the use of direct personal pressure in order to achieve a desired end ⟨for all the ~, the . . . vote on the measure was unexpectedly tight —*Newsweek*⟩ — **arm–twist** \-ˌtwist\ *vb*

arm wrestling *n* (1973) : a form of wrestling in which two opponents sit face to face gripping usu. their right hands, set corresponding elbows firmly on a surface (as a tabletop), and attempt to force each other's arm down — called also *Indian wrestling*

ar·my \ˈär-mē\ *n, pl* **armies** [ME *armee*, fr. MF, fr. ML *armata* — more at ARMADA] (14c) **1 a** : a large organized body of armed personnel trained for war esp. on land **b** : a unit capable of independent action and consisting usu. of a headquarters, two or more corps, and auxiliary troops **c** *often cap* : the complete military organization of a nation for land warfare **2** : a great multitude ⟨an ~ of bicycles — Norm Fruchter⟩ **3** : a body of persons organized to advance a cause

army ant *n* (1874) : any of a subfamily (Dorylinae) of aggressive nomadic tropical ants that prey on insects and spiders

ar·my·worm \ˈär-mē-ˌwərm\ *n* (1816) : any of numerous moths whose larvae travel in multitudes from field to field destroying grass, grain, and other crops; *esp* : the common armyworm (*Pseudaletia unipuncta*) of the northern U.S.

ar·ni·ca \ˈär-ni-kə\ *n* [NL] (ca. 1753) : any of a genus (*Arnica*) of composite herbs including some with bright yellow ray flowers

ar·oid \ˈar-ˌȯid, ˈer-\ *adj* [NL *Arum*] (ca. 1890) : of or relating to the arum family — **aroid** *n*

aroint \ə-ˈrȯint\ *vb imper* [origin unknown] (1605) *archaic* : BEGONE ⟨~ thee, witch —Shak.⟩

aro·ma \ə-ˈrō-mə\ *n* [ME *aromat* spice, fr. OF, fr. L *aromat-, aroma*, fr. Gk *arōmat-, arōma*] (1814) **1 a** : a distinctive pervasive and usu. pleasant or savory smell; *broadly* : ODOR **b** : the odor of a wine imparted by the grapes from which it is made **2** : a distinctive quality or atmosphere : FLAVOR ⟨the ~ of enjoyment —Stella D. Gibbons⟩ *syn* see SMELL

aro·ma·ther·a·py \ə-ˌrō-mə-ˈther-ə-pē\ *n* [F *aromathérapie*, fr. L *aroma* + F *thérapie* therapy] (1969) : massage of the body and esp. of the face with a preparation of fragrant essential oils extracted from herbs, flowers, and fruits — **aro·ma·ther·a·pist** \-pist\ *n*

¹ar·o·mat·ic \ˌar-ə-ˈma-tik\ *adj* (14c) **1** : of, relating to, or having aroma: **a** : FRAGRANT **b** : having a strong smell **c** : having a distinctive quality **2** *of an organic compound* : characterized by increased chemical stability resulting from the delocalization of electrons in a ring system (as benzene) containing usu. multiple conjugated double bonds — compare ALICYCLIC, ALIPHATIC *syn* see ODOROUS — **ar·o·mat·i·cal·ly** \-ti-k(ə-)lē\ *adv* — **aro·ma·tic·i·ty** \ˌar-ə-mə-ˈti-sə-tē, ə-ˌrō-mə-\ *n*

²aromatic *n* (15c) **1** : an aromatic plant or plant part; *esp* : an aromatic herb or spice **2** : an aromatic organic compound

aro·ma·tize \ə-ˈrō-mə-ˌtīz\ *vt* **-tized; -tiz·ing** (15c) **1** : to make aromatic : FLAVOR **2** : to convert into one or more aromatic compounds — **aro·ma·ti·za·tion** \-ˌrō-mə-tə-ˈzā-shən\ *n*

arose *past of* ARISE

¹around \ə-ˈrau̇nd\ *adv* [ME, fr. ¹*a-* + *²round*] (14c) **1 a** : in a circle or in circumference ⟨the wheel goes ~⟩ ⟨a tree five feet ~⟩ **b** : in, along, or through a circuit ⟨the road goes ~ by the lake⟩ **2 a** : on all or various sides : in every or any direction ⟨papers lying ~⟩ ⟨nothing for miles ~⟩ **b** : in close from all sides so as to surround ⟨people crowded ~⟩ **c** : in or near one's present place or situation ⟨wait ~ awhile⟩ **3 a** : here and there : from one place to another ⟨travels ~ on business⟩ **b** : to a particular place ⟨come ~ for dinner⟩ **4 a** : in rotation or succession ⟨another winter comes ~⟩ **b** : from beginning to end : THROUGH ⟨mild the year ~⟩ **c** : in order ⟨the other way ~⟩

armor 1: *1* helmet, *2* gorget, *3* shoulder piece, *4* pallette, *5* breastplate, *6* brassard, *7* elbow piece, *8* skirt of tasses, *9* tuille, *10* gauntlet, *11* cuisse, *12* knee piece, *13* jambeau, *14* solleret

---

\ə\ abut \ᵊ\ kitten, F table \ər\ further \a\ ash \ā\ ace \ä\ mop, mar \au̇\ out \ch\ chin \e\ bet \ē\ easy \g\ go \i\ hit \ī\ ice \j\ job \ŋ\ sing \ō\ go \ȯ\ law \ȯi\ boy \th\ thin \ṯh\ the \ü\ loot \u̇\ foot \y\ yet \zh\ vision \ā, k̟, ⁿ, œ, œ̄, ue, ūe, ʸ\ *see* Guide to Pronunciation

5 : in or to an opposite direction or position ⟨turn ∼⟩ **6** : with some approach to exactness : APPROXIMATELY ⟨cost ∼ $5⟩
²**around** *prep* (14c) **1 a** : on all sides of **b** : so as to encircle or enclose ⟨seated ∼ the table⟩ **c** : so as to avoid or get past : on or to another side of ⟨find a way ∼ their objections⟩ ⟨went ∼ the lake⟩ ⟨∼ the corner⟩ **d** : NEAR ⟨lives ∼ Chicago⟩ ⟨∼ the turn of the century⟩ **2** : in all directions outward from ⟨look ∼ you⟩ **3** : here and there in or throughout ⟨barnstorming ∼ the country⟩ **4** : so as to have a center or basis in ⟨a society organized ∼ kinship ties⟩
³**around** *adj* (1849) **1** : ABOUT 1 ⟨has been up and ∼ for two days⟩ **2** : being in existence, evidence, or circulation ⟨the most intelligent of the artists ∼ today —R. M. Coates⟩ — **been around** : gone through many varied experiences : become worldly-wise
around–the–clock *adj* (1943) : being in effect, continuing, or lasting 24 hours a day : CONSTANT
arouse \ə-'rau̇z\ *vb* **aroused; arous·ing** [*a-* (as in *arise*) + *rouse*] *vt* (1593) **1** : to awaken from sleep **2** : to rouse or stimulate to action or to physiological readiness for activity : EXCITE ⟨the book *aroused* debate⟩ ∼ *vi* : to awaken from sleep : STIR — **arous·al** \ə-'rau̇-zəl\ *n*
ar·peg·gi·ate \är-'pe-jē-ˌāt\ *vt* **-at·ed; -at·ing** (1953) : to play (as a chord or passage) in arpeggio
ar·peg·gio \är-'pe-jē-ˌō, -'pe-jō\ *n, pl* **-gios** [It, fr. *arpeggiare* to play on the harp, fr. *arpa* harp, of Gmc origin; akin to OHG *harpha* harp] (ca. 1724) **1** : production of the tones of a chord in succession and not simultaneously **2** : a chord played in arpeggio
ar·pent \är-'päⁿ\ *n, pl* **ar·pents** \-'päⁿ(z)\ [MF] (1580) **1** : any of various old French units of land area; *esp* : one used in French sections of Canada and the U.S. equal to about 0.85 acre (0.34 hectare) **2** : a unit of length equal to one side of a square arpent
ar·que·bus \'är-kwi-(ˌ)bəs, -kə-bəs\ *var of* HARQUEBUS
ar·rack \'ar-ək, ə-'rak\ *n* [Ar *'araq* sweet juice, liquor] (1521) : an Asian alcoholic beverage like rum that is distilled from a fermented mash of malted rice with toddy or molasses
ar·raign \ə-'rān\ *vt* [ME *arreinen*, fr. MF *araisner*, fr. OF, fr. *a-* (fr. L *ad-*) + *raisnier* to speak, fr. (assumed) VL *rationare*, fr. L *ration-, ratio* reason — more at REASON] (14c) **1** : to call (a defendant) before a court to answer to an indictment : CHARGE **2** : to accuse of wrong, inadequacy, or imperfection — **ar·raign·ment** \-mənt\ *n*
ar·range \ə-'rānj\ *vb* **-ranged; -rang·ing** [ME *arangen*, fr. MF *arangier*, fr. OF, fr. *a-* + *rengier* to set in a row, fr. *reng* row — more at RANK] *vt* (1789) **1** : to make preparations for : PLAN ⟨*arranged* a reception for the visitor⟩ **2** : to put into a proper order or into a correct or suitable sequence, relationship, or adjustment ⟨∼ flowers in a vase⟩ ⟨∼ cards alphabetically⟩ **3 a** : to adapt (a musical composition) by scoring for voices or instruments other than those for which orig. written **b** : ORCHESTRATE **4** : to bring about an agreement or understanding concerning : SETTLE ⟨∼ an exchange of war prisoners⟩ ∼ *vi* **1** : to bring about an agreement or understanding ⟨*arranged* to have a table at the restaurant⟩ **2** : to make preparations : PLAN ⟨*arranged* for a vacation with his family⟩ *syn* see ORDER — **ar·rang·er** \ə-'rān-jər\ *n*
ar·range·ment \ə-'rānj-mənt\ *n* (1690) **1 a** : the state of being arranged : ORDER ⟨everything in neat ∼⟩ **b** : the act of arranging ⟨the ∼ of the details was quickly accomplished⟩ **2** : something arranged: as **a** : a preliminary measure : PREPARATION ⟨travel ∼s⟩ **b** : an adaptation of a musical composition by rescoring **c** : an informal agreement or settlement esp. on personal, social, or political matters ⟨∼s under the new regime⟩ **3** : something made by arranging parts or things together ⟨a floral ∼⟩
ar·rant \'ar-ənt\ *adj* [alter. of *errant*] (1553) : being notoriously without moderation : EXTREME ⟨we are ∼ knaves, all; believe none of us — Shak.⟩ — **ar·rant·ly** *adv*
ar·ras \'ar-əs\ *n, pl* **arras** [ME, fr. *Arras*, France] (15c) **1** : a tapestry of Flemish origin used esp. for wall hangings and curtains **2** : a wall hanging or screen of tapestry
¹**ar·ray** \ə-'rā\ *vt* [ME, fr. OF *arayer*, fr. (assumed) VL *arredare*, fr. L *ad-* + a base of Gmc origin; akin to Goth *garaiths* arranged — more at READY] (14c) **1** : to dress or decorate esp. in splendid or impressive attire : ADORN **2 a** : to set or place in order : DRAW UP, MARSHAL **b** : to set or set forth in order (as a jury) for the trial of a cause — **ar·ray·er** *n*
²**array** *n* (14c) **1 a** : a regular and imposing grouping or arrangement : ORDER ⟨lined up . . . in soldierly ∼ —Donald Barthelme⟩ **b** : an orderly listing of jurors impaneled **2** : CLOTHING, ATTIRE **b** : rich or beautiful apparel : FINERY **3** : a body of soldiers : MILITIA ⟨the baron and his feudal ∼⟩ **4** : an imposing group : large number ⟨faced a whole ∼ of problems⟩ **5 a** (1) : a number of mathematical elements arranged in rows and columns (2) : a data structure in which similar elements of data are arranged in a table **b** : a series of statistical data arranged in classes in order of magnitude **6** : a group of elements forming a complete unit ⟨an antenna ∼⟩
ar·rear \ə-'rir\ *n* [ME *arrere* behind, backward, fr. MF, fr. (assumed) VL *ad retro* backward, fr. L *ad* to + *retro* backward, behind — more at AT, RETRO-] (1620) **1** : the state of being behind in the discharge of obligations — usu. used in pl. ⟨in ∼s with the rent⟩ **2 a** : an unfinished duty — usu. used in pl. ⟨∼s of work that have piled up⟩ **b** : an unpaid and overdue debt — usu. used in pl. ⟨paying off the ∼s of the past several months⟩
ar·rear·age \-ij\ *n* (14c) **1** : the condition of being in arrears **2** : something that is in arrears; *esp* : something unpaid and overdue
¹**ar·rest** \ə-'rest\ *vt* [ME *aresten*, fr. MF *arester* to rest, arrest, fr. (assumed) VL *arrestare*, fr. L *ad-* + *restare* to remain — more at REST] (14c) **1 a** : to bring to a stop ⟨sickness ∼ed his activities⟩ **b** : CHECK, SLOW **c** : to make inactive ⟨an ∼ed tumor⟩ **2** : SEIZE, CAPTURE; *specif* : to take or keep in custody by authority of law **3** : to catch suddenly and engagingly — **ar·rest·er** *or* **ar·res·tor** \-'res-tər\ *n* — **ar·rest·ment** \-'res(t)-mənt\ *n*
²**arrest** *n* (14c) **1 a** : the act of stopping **b** : the condition of being stopped or inactive **2** : the taking or detaining in custody by authority of law — **under arrest** : in legal custody
ar·res·tant \ə-'res-tənt\ *n* (1962) : a substance that stimulates an insect to stop locomotion
ar·rest·ee \ə-ˌres-'tē\ *n* (1944) : one that is under arrest

ar·rest·ing \ə-'res-tiŋ\ *adj* (1792) : catching the attention : STRIKING, IMPRESSIVE — **ar·rest·ing·ly** \-tiŋ-lē\ *adv*
ar·rhyth·mia \ā-'rith-mē-ə\ *n* [NL, fr. Gk, lack of rhythm, fr. *arrhythmos* unrhythmical, fr. *a-* + *rhythmos* rhythm] (ca. 1860) : an alteration in rhythm of the heartbeat either in time or force
ar·rhyth·mic \-mik\ *adj* [Gk *arrhythmos*] (1853) : lacking rhythm or regularity ⟨∼ locomotor activity⟩
ar·ri·ère–ban \ˌar-ē-ˌer-'bän, ¦ar-¦ē-\ *n* [F] (1523) : a proclamation of a king (as of France) calling his vassals to arms; *also* : the body of vassals summoned
ar·ri·ère–pen·sée \-ˌpäⁿ-'sā\ *n* [F, fr. *arrière* in back + *pensée* thought] (1824) : mental reservation
ar·ris \'ar-əs\ *n, pl* **arris** *or* **ar·ris·es** [prob. modif. of MF *areste*, lit., fishbone, fr. LL *arista* — more at ARÊTE] (1677) : the sharp edge or salient angle formed by the meeting of two surfaces esp. in moldings
ar·riv·al \ə-'rī-vəl\ *n* (14c) **1** : the act of arriving **2** : the attainment of an end or state **3** : one that has recently reached a destination
ar·rive \ə-'rīv\ *vi* **ar·rived; ar·riv·ing** [ME *ariven*, fr. (assumed) VL *arripare* to come to shore, fr. L *ad-* + *ripa* shore — more at RIVE] (13c) **1 a** : to reach a destination **b** : to make an appearance ⟨the guests have *arrived*⟩ **2 a** *archaic* : HAPPEN **b** : to be near in time : COME ⟨the moment has *arrived*⟩ **3** : to achieve success — **ar·riv·er** *n* — **arrive at** : to reach by effort or thought ⟨*arrived at* a decision⟩
ar·ri·vé \ˌar-i-'vā\ *n* [F, fr. pp. of *arriver* to arrive, fr. OF *ariver*] (1925) : one who has risen rapidly to success, power, or fame
ar·ri·viste \-'vēst\ *n* [F, fr. *arriver*] (1901) : one that is a new and uncertain arrival (as in social position or artistic endeavor)
ar·ro·ba \ə-'rō-bə\ *n* [Sp & Pg, fr. Ar *ar-rub'*, lit., the quarter] (1555) **1** : an old Spanish unit of weight equal to about 25 pounds **2** : an old Portuguese unit of weight equal to about 32 pounds
ar·ro·gance \'ar-ə-gən(t)s\ *n* (14c) : a feeling or an impression of superiority manifested in an overbearing manner or presumptuous claims
ar·ro·gant \-gənt\ *adj* [ME, fr. L *arrogant-, arrogans*, prp. of *arrogare*] (14c) **1** : exaggerating or disposed to exaggerate one's own worth or importance in an overbearing manner ⟨an ∼ official⟩ **2** : proceeding from or characterized by arrogance ⟨∼ manners⟩ *syn* see PROUD — **ar·ro·gant·ly** *adv*
ar·ro·gate \-ˌgāt\ *vt* **-gat·ed; -gat·ing** [L *arrogatus*, pp. of *arrogare*, fr. *ad-* + *rogare* to ask — more at RIGHT] (1537) **1 a** : to claim or seize without justification **b** : to make undue claims to having : ASSUME **2** : to claim on behalf of another : ASCRIBE — **ar·ro·ga·tion** \ˌar-ə-'gā-shən\ *n*
ar·ron·disse·ment \ə-'rän-də-smənt, ˌar-ˌōⁿ-(ˌ)dē-'smäⁿ\ *n* [F] (1807) **1** : an administrative district of some large French cities **2** : the largest division of a French department
¹**ar·row** \'ar-(ˌ)ō\ *n* [ME *arwe*, fr. OE; akin to Goth *arhwazna* arrow, L *arcus* bow, arch, arc] (bef. 12c) **1** : a missile weapon shot from a bow and usu. having a slender shaft, a pointed head, and feathers at the butt **2** : something shaped like an arrow; *esp* : a mark (as on a map or signboard) to indicate direction
²**arrow** *vi* (1827) : to move fast and straight like an arrow in flight : DART
ar·row·head \'ar-ō-ˌhed, 'ar-ə-\ *n* (14c) **1** : a wedge-shaped piercing tip usu. fixed to an arrow **2** : something resembling an arrowhead **3** : any of a genus (*Sagittaria*) of marsh or aquatic plants of the water-plantain family with leaves shaped like arrowheads

arrowhead 1

ar·row·root \-ˌrüt, -ˌru̇t\ *n* (1696) **1** : any of a genus (*Maranta* of the family Marantaceae, the arrowroot family) of tropical American plants with tuberous roots; *esp* : one (*M. arundinacea*) whose roots yield an easily digested edible starch **b** : any of several plants (as coontie) that yield starch **2** : starch yielded by an arrowroot
ar·row·wood \-ˌwu̇d\ *n* (1709) : any of several common viburnums (esp. *Viburnum dentatum*) of the eastern U.S.
ar·row·worm \-ˌwərm\ *n* (ca. 1889) : any of a phylum (Chaetognatha) of small planktonic wormlike marine organisms having curved bristles on either side of the head for seizing prey
ar·rowy \'ar-ə-wē\ *adj* (1637) **1** : resembling or suggesting an arrow; *esp* : swiftly moving **2** : consisting of arrows
ar·royo \ə-'ròi-(ˌ)ō, -ə\ *n, pl* **-royos** [Sp] (1843) **1** : a watercourse (as a creek) in an arid region **2** : a water-carved gully or channel
ar·roz con po·llo \ä-¦ròth-(ˌ)kòn-'pōl-(ˌ)yō, -¦pō-(ˌ)yō\ *n* [Sp, lit., rice with chicken] (1938) : chicken cooked with rice and usu. flavored with saffron
arse *var of* ASS
ar·se·nal \'ärs-nəl, 'är-s³n-əl\ *n* [It *arsenale*, ultim. fr. Ar *dār ṣinā'ah* house of manufacture] (1555) **1 a** : an establishment for the manufacture or storage of arms and military equipment **b** : a collection of weapons : STORE, REPERTORY ⟨the team's ∼ of veteran players⟩
ar·se·nate \'ärs-nət, 'är-s³n-ət, -s³n-ˌāt\ *n* (1800) : a salt or ester of an arsenic acid
¹**ar·se·nic** \'ärs-nik, -s³n-ik\ *n* [ME, yellow orpiment, fr. MF & L; MF, fr. L *arsenicum*, fr. Gk *arsenikon, arrhenikon*, fr. Syr *zarnīg*, of Iranian origin; akin to Av *zaranya* gold, Skt *hari* yellowish — more at YELLOW] (14c) **1** : a trivalent and pentavalent solid poisonous element that is commonly metallic steel-gray, crystalline, and brittle — see ELEMENT table **2** : a poisonous trioxide As_2O_3 or As_4O_6 of arsenic used esp. as an insecticide or weed killer — called also *arsenic trioxide*
²**ar·sen·ic** \är-'se-nik\ *adj* (1801) : of, relating to, or containing arsenic esp. with a valence of five
ar·sen·i·cal \är-'se-ni-kəl\ *adj* (1605) : of, relating to, containing, or caused by arsenic ⟨∼ poisoning⟩ — **arsenical** *n*
ar·se·nide \'är-s³n-ˌīd\ *n* (ca. 1859) : a binary compound of arsenic with a more positive element
ar·se·ni·ous \är-'sē-nē-əs\ *adj* (1818) : of, relating to, or containing arsenic esp. when trivalent
ar·se·nite \'är-s³n-ˌīt\ *n* (1800) : a salt or ester of an arsenious acid

ar·se·no·py·rite \ˌär-s⁽ᵊ⁾n-ō-ˈpī-ˌrīt\ *n* (1881) : a mineral consisting of a combined sulfide and arsenide of iron occurring in prismatic orthorhombic crystals or in masses or grains

ar·sine \är-ˈsēn, ˈär-ˌ\ *n* [ISV, fr. *arsenic*] (1876) : a colorless flammable extremely poisonous gas AsH₃ with an odor like garlic; *also* : a derivative of arsine

ar·sis \ˈär-səs\ *n, pl* **ar·ses** \-ˌsēz\ [LL & Gk; LL, raising of the voice, accented part of foot, fr. Gk, upbeat, less important part of foot, lit., act of lifting, fr. *aeirein, airein* to lift] (14c) **1 a** : the lighter or shorter part of a poetic foot esp. in quantitative verse **b** : the accented or longer part of a poetic foot esp. in accentual verse **2** : the unaccented part of a musical measure — compare THESIS

ar·son \ˈär-s⁽ᵊ⁾n\ *n* [AF *arsoun*, alter. of OF *arsin* act of burning, fr. *ars*, pp. of *ardre* to burn, fr. L *ardēre* — more at ARDOR] (ca. 1680) : the willful or malicious burning of property (as a building) esp. with criminal or fraudulent intent — **ar·son·ist** \-ist\ *n* — **ar·son·ous** \-əs\ *adj*

ars·phen·a·mine \ärs-ˈfe-nə-ˌmēn, -mən\ *n* [ISV *arsenic* + *phenamine*] (1917) : a light-yellow toxic hygroscopic powder C₁₂Cl₂H₁₄As₂N₂O₂·2H₂O formerly used in the treatment esp. of syphilis and yaws

¹art \ˈärt, ərt\ [ME, fr. OE *eart*; akin to ON *est, ert* (thou) art, OE *is* is] *archaic pres 2d sing of* BE

²art \ˈärt\ *n* [ME, fr. OF, fr. L *art-, ars* — more at ARM] (13c) **1** : skill acquired by experience, study, or observation ⟨the ~ of making friends⟩ **2 a** : a branch of learning: (1) : one of the humanities (2) *pl* : LIBERAL ARTS **b** *archaic* : LEARNING, SCHOLARSHIP **3** : an occupation requiring knowledge or skill ⟨the ~ of organ building⟩ **4 a** : the conscious use of skill and creative imagination esp. in the production of aesthetic objects; *also* : works so produced **b** (1) : FINE ARTS (2) : one of the fine arts (3) : a graphic art **5 a** *archaic* : a skillful plan **b** : the quality or state of being artful **6** : decorative or illustrative elements in printed matter

syn ART, SKILL, CUNNING, ARTIFICE, CRAFT mean the faculty of executing well what one has devised. ART implies a personal, unanalyzable creative power ⟨the *art* of choosing the right word⟩. SKILL stresses technical knowledge and proficiency ⟨the *skill* of a glassblower⟩. CUNNING suggests ingenuity and subtlety in devising, inventing, or executing ⟨a mystery plotted with great *cunning*⟩. ARTIFICE suggests technical skill esp. in imitating things in nature ⟨believed realism in film could be achieved only by *artifice*⟩. CRAFT may imply expertness in workmanship ⟨the *craft* of a master goldsmith⟩.

-art — see -ARD

art de·co \ˌärt-ˈde-ˌkō; ˌär(t)-dā-ˈkō, ˈär(t)-ˈdā-(ˌ)-\ *n, often cap A&D* [F *Art Déco*, fr. *Exposition Internationale des Arts Décoratifs et Industriels Modernes*, an exposition of modern decorative and industrial arts held in Paris, France, in 1925] (1966) : a popular design style of the 1920s and 1930s characterized esp. by bold outlines, geometric and zigzag forms, and the use of new materials (as plastic)

ar·te·fact *chiefly Brit var of* ARTIFACT

ar·tel \är-ˈtel; -telᵊ\ *n* [Russ *artel'*] (1884) : a workers' or craftsmen's cooperative in Russia and later the U.S.S.R

Ar·te·mis \ˈär-tə-məs\ *n* [Gk] : a Greek moon goddess often portrayed as a virgin huntress — compare DIANA

ar·te·mi·sia \ˌär-tə-ˈmi-zh(ē-)ə, -zē-ə\ *n* [NL, fr. L, artemisia, fr. Gk, wormwood] (14c) : any of a genus (*Artemisia*) of aromatic composite herbs and shrubs (as sagebrush) — compare WORMWOOD 1

arteri- *or* **arterio-** *comb form* [Gk *artēri-, artērio-*, fr. *artēria* artery] **1** : artery ⟨*arteriogram*⟩ **2** : arterial and ⟨*arteriovenous*⟩

¹ar·te·ri·al \är-ˈtir-ē-əl\ *adj* (15c) **1 a** : of or relating to an artery **b** : relating to or being the bright red blood present in most arteries that has been oxygenated in lungs or gills **2** : of, relating to, or constituting through traffic ⟨an ~ highway⟩ — **ar·te·ri·al·ly** \-ē-ə-lē\ *adv*

²arterial *n* (1932) : a through street or highway

ar·te·rio·gram \är-ˈtir-ē-ə-ˌgram\ *n* [ISV] (1929) : a roentgenogram of an artery made by arteriography

ar·te·ri·og·ra·phy \är-ˌtir-ē-ˈä-grə-fē\ *n, pl* **-phies** [ISV] (1929) : the roentgenographic visualization of an artery after injection of a radio-opaque substance — **ar·te·rio·graph·ic** \-ē-ə-ˈgra-fik\ *adj*

ar·te·ri·ole \är-ˈtir-ē-ˌōl\ *n* [F or NL; F *artériole*, prob. fr. NL *arteriola*, dim. of L *arteria*] (ca. 1847) : any of the small terminal twigs of an artery that ends in capillaries — **ar·te·ri·o·lar** \-ˌtir-ē-ˈō-ˌlär, -lər\ *adj*

ar·te·rio·scle·ro·sis \är-ˌtir-ē-ō-sklə-ˈrō-səs\ *n* [NL] (1881) : a chronic disease characterized by abnormal thickening and hardening of the arterial walls with resulting loss of elasticity — **ar·te·rio·scle·rot·ic** \-ˈrä-tik\ *adj or n*

ar·te·rio·ve·nous \-ˈvē-nəs\ *adj* [ISV] (ca. 1880) : of, relating to, or connecting the arteries and veins ⟨an ~ fistula⟩

ar·ter·i·tis \ˌär-tə-ˈrī-təs\ *n* [NL] (1836) : arterial inflammation

ar·tery \ˈär-tə-rē, ˈär-trē\ *n, pl* **-ter·ies** [ME *arterie*, fr. L *arteria*, fr. Gk *artēria*; akin to Gk *aortē* aorta] (14c) **1** : any of the tubular branching muscular- and elastic-walled vessels that carry blood from the heart through the body **2** : a channel (as a river or highway) of transportation or communication; *esp* : the main channel in a branching system

ar·te·sian well \är-ˈtē-zhən-\ *n* [F *artésien*, lit., of Artois, fr. OF, fr. *Arteis* Artois, France] (1842) **1** : a well in which water is under pressure; *esp* : one in which the water flows to the surface naturally **2** : a deep well

art film *n* (1926) : a motion picture produced as an artistic effort

art form *n* (1868) **1** : a recognized form (as a symphony) or medium (as sculpture) of artistic expression **2** : an unconventional form or medium in which impulses regarded as artistic may be expressed ⟨describe pinball as a great American *art form*—Tom Buckley⟩

art·ful \ˈärt-fəl\ *adj* (1615) **1** : performed with or showing art or skill ⟨an ~ performance on the violin⟩ **2 a** : using or characterized by art and skill : DEXTEROUS ⟨an ~ prose stylist⟩ **b** : adroit in attaining an end often by insinuating or indirect means : WILY ⟨an ~ cross-examiner⟩ **3** : ARTIFICIAL ⟨trim walks and ~ bowers —William Wordsworth⟩ *syn* see SLY — **art·ful·ly** \-fə-lē\ *adv* — **art·ful·ness** *n*

art glass *n* (1926) : articles of glass designed primarily for decorative purposes; *esp* : novelty glassware

art historical *adj* (1933) : of or relating to the history of art — **art historically** *adv*

art house *n* (1951) : ART THEATER

arthr- *or* **arthro-** *comb form* [L, fr. Gk, fr. *arthron*; akin to Gk *arariskein* to fit — more at ARM] : joint ⟨*arthro*pathy⟩

ar·thral·gia \är-ˈthral-j(ē-)ə\ *n* [NL] (ca. 1848) : neuralgic pain in one or more joints — **ar·thral·gic** \-jik\ *adj*

ar·thrit·ic \är-ˈthri-tik\ *adj* (14c) **1** : of, relating to, or affected with arthritis **2** : being or showing effects associated with aging ⟨~ anxiety⟩ — **arthritic** *n* — **ar·thrit·i·cal·ly** \-ti-k(ə-)lē\ *adv*

ar·thri·tis \är-ˈthrī-təs\ *n, pl* **-thri·i·des** \-ˈthri-tə-ˌdēz\ [L, fr. Gk, fr. *arthron*] (1543) : inflammation of joints due to infectious, metabolic, or constitutional causes; *also* : a specific arthritic condition

ar·throd·e·sis \är-ˈthrä-də-səs\ *n, pl* **-e·ses** \-ˌsēz\ [NL, fr. *arthr-* + Gk *desis* binding, fr. *dein* to bind] (ca. 1901) : the surgical immobilization of a joint so that the bones grow solidly together

ar·throp·a·thy \är-ˈthrä-pə-thē\ *n, pl* **-thies** (ca. 1860) : a disease of a joint

ar·thro·pod \ˈär-thrə-ˌpäd\ *n* [NL *Arthropoda*, fr. *arthr-* + Gk *pod-, pous* foot — more at FOOT] (1877) : any of a phylum (Arthropoda) of invertebrate animals (as insects, arachnids, and crustaceans) that have a segmented body and jointed appendages, a usu. chitinous exoskeleton molted at intervals, and a dorsal anterior brain connected to a ventral chain of ganglia — **arthropod** *adj* — **ar·throp·o·dan** \är-ˈthrä-pə-dən\ *adj*

ar·thros·co·py \är-ˈthräs-kə-pē\ *n* (ca. 1935) : visual examination of the interior of a joint (as the knee) with a special surgical instrument; *also* : joint surgery using an arthroscope — **ar·thro·scope** \ˈär-thrə-ˌskōp\ *n* — **ar·thro·scop·ic** \ˌär-thrə-ˈskä-pik\ *adj*

ar·thro·sis \är-ˈthrō-səs\ *n, pl* **-thro·ses** \-ˌsēz\ [NL, fr. Gk *arthrōsis* jointing, articulation, fr. *arthroun* to articulate, fr. *arthron*] (1634) **1** : an articulation between bones **2** : a degenerative disease of a joint

ar·thro·spore \ˈär-thrə-ˌspȯr, -ˌspȯr\ *n* (1895) : OIDIUM 1b

Ar·thur \ˈär-thər\ *n* : a legendary king of the Britons whose story is based on traditions of a 6th century military leader

Ar·thu·ri·an \är-ˈthu̇r-ē-ən, -ˈthyu̇r-\ *adj* (1612) : of or relating to King Arthur and his court

ar·ti·choke \ˈär-tə-ˌchōk\ *n* [It dial. *articiocco*, ultim. fr. Ar *al-khurshūf* the artichoke] (1530) **1 a** : a tall composite herb (*Cynara scolymus*) like a thistle with coarse pinnately incised leaves; *also* : its edible immature flower head which is cooked as a vegetable **2** : JERUSALEM ARTICHOKE

¹ar·ti·cle \ˈär-ti-kəl\ *n* [ME, fr. OF, fr. L *articulus* joint, division, dim. of *artus* joint, limb; akin to Gk *arariskein* to fit — more at ARM] (13c) **1 a** : a distinct often numbered section of a writing **b** : a separate clause **c** : a stipulation in a document (as a contract or a creed) **d** : a nonfictional prose composition usu. forming an independent part of a publication (as a magazine) **2** : an item of business : MATTER **3** : any of a small set of words or affixes (as *a, an,* and *the*) used with nouns to limit or give definiteness to the application **4** : a member of a class of things; *esp* : an item of goods ⟨~s of value⟩ **5** : a thing of a particular and distinctive kind ⟨the genuine ~⟩

²article *vt* **ar·ti·cled; ar·ti·cling** \-k(ə-)liŋ\ (1820) : to bind by articles (as of apprenticeship)

article of faith (15c) : a basic belief

ar·tic·u·la·ble \är-ˈti-kyə-lə-bəl\ *adj* (1833) : capable of being articulated

ar·tic·u·la·cy \är-ˈti-kyə-lə-sē\ *n* (1918) *chiefly Brit* : the quality or state of being articulate

ar·tic·u·lar \är-ˈti-kyə-lər\ *adj* [ME *articuler*, fr. L *articularis*, fr. *articulus*] (15c) : of or relating to a joint ⟨~ cartilage⟩

¹ar·tic·u·late \är-ˈti-kyə-lət\ *adj* [L *articulatus* jointed, pp. of *articulare*, fr. *articulus*] (1586) **1 a** : divided into syllables or words meaningfully arranged : INTELLIGIBLE **b** : able to speak **c** : expressing oneself readily, clearly, or effectively; *also* : expressed in this manner **2 a** : consisting of segments united by joints : JOINTED ⟨~ animals⟩ **b** : distinctly marked off — **ar·tic·u·late·ly** *adv* — **ar·tic·u·late·ness** *n*

²ar·tic·u·late \-ˌlāt\ *vb* **-lat·ed; -lat·ing** *vt* (1594) **1 a** : to utter distinctly ⟨*articulating* each note in the musical phrase⟩ **b** : to give clear and effective utterance to : put into words ⟨~ one's grievances⟩ **c** : to give definition to (as a shape or object) ⟨shades of gray were chosen to ~ different spaces —Carol Vogel⟩ **2 a** : to unite by means of a joint : JOINT **b** : to form or fit into a systematic whole ⟨*articulating* a program for all school grades⟩ ~ *vi* **1** : to utter articulate sounds **2** : to become united or connected by or as if by a joint — **ar·tic·u·la·tive** \-lə-tiv, -ˌlā-\ *adj* — **ar·tic·u·la·tor** \-ˌlā-tər\ *n*

ar·tic·u·lat·ed \-lā-təd\ *adj* (1899) *of a vehicle* : having a hinge or pivot connection esp. to allow negotiation of sharp turns ⟨~ lorry⟩ ⟨~ bus⟩

ar·tic·u·la·tion \(ˌ)är-ˌti-kyə-ˈlā-shən\ *n* (15c) **1 a** : a joint or juncture between bones or cartilages in the skeleton of a vertebrate **b** : a movable joint between rigid parts of an animal **2 a** : the action or manner of jointing or interrelating **b** : the state of being jointed or interrelated **3 a** : the act of giving utterance or expression **b** : the act or manner of articulating sounds **c** : an articulated utterance or sound; *specif* : CONSONANT **4** : OCCLUSION 1b

ar·tic·u·la·to·ry \är-ˈti-kyə-lə-ˌtōr-ē, -ˌtȯr-\ *adj* (1818) : of or relating to articulation

ar·ti·fact \ˈär-ti-ˌfakt\ *n* [L *arte* by skill (abl. of *art-, ars* skill) + *factum*, neut. of *factus*, pp. of *facere* to do — more at ARM, DO] (1821) **1 a** : something created by humans usu. for a practical purpose; *esp* : an object remaining from a particular period ⟨caves containing prehistoric ~s⟩ **b** : something characteristic of or resulting from a human institution or activity ⟨self-consciousness ... turns out to be an ~ of our education system —*Times Lit. Supp.*⟩ **2** : a product of artificial character (as in a scientific test) due usu. to extraneous (as human) agency — **ar·ti·fac·tu·al** \ˌär-ti-ˈfak-chə(-wə)l, -ˈfak-shwəl\ *adj*

ar·ti·fice \ˈär-tə-fəs\ *n* [MF, fr. L *artificium*, fr. *artific-, artifex* artificer, fr. L *art-, ars* + *facere*] (ca. 1604) **1 a** : clever or artful skill : INGENUITY ⟨believing that characters had to be created from within rather than with ~ —Garson Kanin⟩ **b** : an ingenious device or expedient **2 a** : an artful stratagem : TRICK **b** : false or insincere behavior ⟨social ~⟩ *syn* see TRICK, ART

\ə\ abut \ᵊ\ kitten, F table \ər\ further \a\ ash \ā\ ace \ä\ mop, mar \au̇\ out \ch\ chin \e\ bet \ē\ easy \g\ go \i\ hit \ī\ ice \j\ job \ŋ\ sing \ō\ go \ȯ\ law \ȯi\ boy \th\ thin \t͟h\ the \ü\ loot \u̇\ foot \y\ yet \zh\ vision \à, k̲, ⁿ, œ, œ̄, ʉ, ᵫ, ᵊ\ see Guide to Pronunciation

ar·ti·fi·cer \är-'ti-fə-sər, 'är-tə-fə-sər\ *n* (14c) **1** : a skilled or artistic worker or craftsman **2** : one that makes or contrives : DEVISER ⟨had been the ~ of his own fortunes —*Times Lit. Supp.*⟩

ar·ti·fi·cial \,är-tə-'fi-shᵊl\ *adj* (14c) **1** : humanly contrived often on a natural model : MAN-MADE ⟨an ~ limb⟩ ⟨~ diamonds⟩ **2 a** : having existence in legal, economic, or political theory **b** : caused or produced by a human and esp. social or political agency ⟨an ~ price advantage⟩ ⟨~ barriers of discrimination —R. C. Weaver⟩ **3** *obs* : ARTFUL, CUNNING **4 a** : lacking in natural or spontaneous quality ⟨an ~ smile⟩ ⟨an ~ excitement⟩ **c** : IMITATION, SHAM ⟨~ flavor⟩ **5** : based on differential morphological characters not necessarily indicative of natural relationships ⟨an ~ key for plant identification⟩ — **ar·ti·fi·ci·al·i·ty** \,är-tə-,fi-shē-'a-lə-tē\ *n* — **ar·ti·fi·cial·ly** \-'fi-shᵊl-ē\ *adv* — **ar·ti·fi·cial·ness** \-'fi-shəl-nəs\ *n*

artificial horizon *n* (1920) : a gyroscopic flight instrument designed to indicate aircraft attitude with respect to the true horizon

artificial insemination *n* (1897) : introduction of semen into the uterus or oviduct by other than natural means

artificial intelligence *n* (1956) **1** : the capability of a machine to imitate intelligent human behavior **2** : a branch of computer science dealing with the simulation of intelligent behavior in computers

artificial respiration *n* (1852) : the rhythmic forcing of air into and out of the lungs of a person whose breathing has stopped

ar·til·ler·ist \är-'ti-lə-rist\ *n* (1781) : GUNNER, ARTILLERYMAN

ar·til·lery \är-'ti-lər-ē, -'til-rē\ *n, pl* **-ler·ies** [ME *artillerie*, fr. MF, fr. *artillier* to equip, arm, alter. of OF *attilier*, fr. (assumed) VL *apticulare*, fr. L *aptare* to don, prepare, fit — more at ADAPT] (15c) **1** : weapons (as bows, slings, and catapults) for discharging missiles **2 a** : large bore crew-served mounted firearms (as guns, howitzers, and rockets) : ORDNANCE **b** : a branch of an army armed with artillery **3** : means of impressing, arguing, or persuading

ar·til·lery·man \-mən\ *n* (1635) : a soldier in the artillery

ar·tio·dac·tyl \,är-tē-ō-'dak-tᵊl\ *n* [NL *Artiodactyla*, fr. Gk *artios* fitting, even-numbered + *daktylos* finger, toe; akin to Gk *arariskein* to fit — more at ARM] (ca. 1879) : any of an order (Artiodactyla) of ungulates (as the camel or pig) with an even number of functional toes on each foot — **artiodactyl** *adj*

ar·ti·san \'är-tə-zən, -sən, *chiefly Brit* ,är-tə-'zan\ *n* [MF, ultim. fr. OIt *artigiano*, fr. *arte* art, fr. L *art-, ars*] (1538) : CRAFTSMAN — **ar·ti·san·al** \-zə-nᵊl, -sə-, -'za-\ *adj* — **ar·ti·san·ship** \-,ship\ *n*

art·ist \'är-tist\ *n* (ca. 1507) **1 a** *obs* : one skilled or versed in learned arts **b** *archaic* : PHYSICIAN **c** *archaic* : ARTISAN **2 a** : one who professes and practices an imaginative art **b** : a person skilled in one of the fine arts **3** : a skilled performer; *esp* : ARTISTE **4** : one who is adept at something ⟨con ~⟩ ⟨strikeout ~⟩

ar·tiste \är-'tēst\ *n* [F] (1823) : a skilled adept public performer; *specif* : a musical or theatrical entertainer

ar·tis·tic \är-'tis-tik\ *adj* (ca. 1753) **1** : of, relating to, or characteristic of art or artists ⟨~ subjects⟩ ⟨an ~ success⟩ **2** : showing imaginative skill in arrangement or execution ⟨~ photography⟩ — **ar·tis·ti·cal·ly** \-ti-k(ə-)lē\ *adv*

art·ist·ry \'är-tə-strē\ *n* (1868) **1** : artistic quality of effect or workmanship ⟨the ~ of his novel⟩ **2** : artistic ability ⟨the ~ of the violinist⟩ ⟨a lawyer's ~ in persuading juries⟩

art·less \'ärt-ləs\ *adj* (1589) **1** : lacking art, knowledge, or skill : UNCULTURED **2 a** : made without skill : CRUDE **b** : free from artificiality : NATURAL ⟨~ grace⟩ **3** : free from guile or craft : sincerely simple — *syn* see NATURAL — **art·less·ly** *adv* — **art·less·ness** *n*

art mo·derne \,är(t)-mō-'dern\ *n, often cap A&M* [F — more at ART DECO] (1931) : ART DECO

art nou·veau \,är(t)-nü-'vō\ *n, often cap A&N* [F, lit., new art] (1908) : a design style of late 19th century origin characterized esp. by sinuous lines and foliate forms

Arts and Crafts *n* (1888) : a movement in European and American design during the late 19th and early 20th centuries promoting handcraftsmanship over industrial mass production

art song *n* (1890) : a usu. through-composed lyric song with melody and accompaniment

art·sy \'ärt-sē\ *adj* (1902) : ARTY

artsy–craftsy \,ärt-sē-'kraf(t)-sē\ *also* **arty–crafty** \,är-tē-'kraf-tē\ *adj* [fr. the phrase *arts and crafts*] (1902) : ARTY

art theater *n* (1923) : a theater that specializes in the presentation of art films

art·work \'ärt-,wərk\ *n* (1877) **1 a** : an artistic production ⟨an 8-foot metal ~⟩ **b** : artistic work ⟨~ being sold on the sidewalk⟩ **2 a** : ART 6 **b** : material (as a drawing or photograph) prepared for reproduction in printed matter

arty \'är-tē\ *adj* **art·i·er; -est** (1901) : showily or pretentiously artistic ⟨~ lighting and photography⟩ — **art·i·ly** \'är-tᵊl-ē\ *adv* — **art·i·ness** \'är-tē-nəs\ *n*

aru·gu·la \ə-'rü-gə-lə, -gyə-\ *n* [prob. fr. It dial.; akin to It dial. (Lombardy) *arigola* arugula, It *ruca* — more at ROCKET] (1967) : a yellowish-flowered European herb (*Eruca vesicaria*) of the mustard family cultivated for its foliage which is used esp. in salads — called also *garden rocket, rocket, rugola*

ar·um \'ar-əm, 'er-\ *n* [NL, fr. L *arum*, fr. Gk *aron*] (14c) : any of a genus (*Arum* of the family Araceae, the arum family) of Old World plants having usu. arrow-shaped leaves and a showy spathe partially enclosing a spadix; *broadly* : a plant of the arum family

¹-ary *US usu* ,er-ē *when an unstressed syllable precedes*, ə-rē *or* rē *when a stressed syllable precedes; Brit usu* ə-rē *or* rē *in all cases*\ *n suffix* [ME *-arie*, fr. OF & L; OF *-aire, -arie*, fr. L *-aria, -aria, -arium*, fr. *-arius*, adj. suffix] **1** : thing belonging to or connected with; *esp* : place of ⟨ovary⟩ **2** : person belonging to, connected with, or engaged in ⟨functionary⟩

²-ary *adj suffix* [ME *-arie*, fr. MF & L; MF *-aire*, fr. L *-arius*] : of, relating to, or connected with ⟨budgetary⟩

¹Ary·an \'ar-ē-ən, 'er-; 'är-yən\ *adj* [Skt *ārya* noble, belonging to the people speaking an Indo-European dialect who migrated into northern India] (1839) **1** : INDO-EUROPEAN **2 a** : of or relating to a hypothetical ethnic type illustrated by or descended from early speakers of Indo-European languages **b** : NORDIC **c** — used in Nazism to designate a supposed master race of non-Jewish Caucasians having esp. Nordic features **3** : of or relating to Indo-Iranian or its speakers

²Aryan *n* (1851) **1** : INDO-EUROPEAN **2 a** : NORDIC **b** : GENTILE

ar·yl \'ar-əl\ *adj* [ISV aromatic + *-yl*] (1906) : having or being a univalent organic group (as phenyl) derived from an aromatic hydrocarbon by the removal of one hydrogen atom — often used in combination

ar·y·te·noid \,ar-ə-'tē-,nȯid, ə-'ri-tᵊn-,ȯid\ *adj* [NL *arytaenoides*, fr. Gk *arytainoeidēs*, lit., ladle-shaped, fr. *arytaina* ladle] (ca. 1751) **1** : relating to or being either of two small laryngeal cartilages to which the vocal cords are attached **2** : relating to or being either of a pair of small muscles or an unpaired muscle of the larynx — **arytenoid** *n*

¹as \əz, (,)az\ *adv* [ME, fr. OE *eallswā* likewise, just as — more at ALSO] (bef. 12c) **1** : to the same degree or amount ⟨~ deaf as a post⟩ ⟨twice ~ long⟩ **2** : for instance ⟨various trees, ~ oak or pine⟩ **3** : when considered in a specified form or relation — usu. used before a preposition or a participle ⟨my opinion ~ distinguished from his⟩

²as *conj* (12c) **1** : AS IF ⟨looks ~ he had seen a ghost —S. T. Coleridge⟩ **2** : in or to the same degree in which ⟨deaf ~ a post⟩ — usu. used as a correlative after an adjective or adverb modified by adverbial *as* or *so* ⟨as cool ~ a cucumber⟩ **3** : in the way or manner that ⟨do ~ I do⟩ **4** : in accordance with what or the way in which ⟨quite good ~ boys go⟩ **5** : WHILE, WHEN ⟨spilled the milk ~ she got up⟩ **6** : regardless of the degree to which : THOUGH ⟨improbable ~ it seems, it's true⟩ **7** : for the reason that : BECAUSE, SINCE ⟨stayed home ~ she had no car⟩ **8** : that the result is ⟨so clearly guilty ~ to leave no doubt⟩ *usage* see LIKE — **as is** : in the presently existing condition without modification ⟨bought the clock at an auction *as is*⟩ — **as it were** : as if it were so : in a manner of speaking

³as *pron* (12c) **1** : THAT, WHO, WHICH — used after *same* or *such* ⟨in the same building ~ my brother⟩ ⟨tears such ~ angels weep —John Milton⟩ and chiefly dial. after a substantive not modified by *same* or *such* ⟨that kind of fruit ~ maids call medlars —Shak.⟩ **2** : a fact that ⟨is a foreigner, ~ is evident from his accent⟩

⁴as *prep* (13c) **1 a** : LIKE 2 ⟨all rose ~ one man⟩ **b** : LIKE 1a ⟨his face was ~ a mask —Max Beerbohm⟩ **2** : in the capacity, character, condition, or role of ⟨speaking ~ an editor⟩

⁵as \'as\ *n, pl* **as·ses** \'a-,sēz, 'a-səz\ [L] (1540) **1 a** : a bronze coin of the ancient Roman republic **b** : a unit of value equivalent to an as coin **2** : LIBRA 2a

as- — see AD-

asa·fet·i·da *or* **asa·foe·ti·da** \,a-sə-'fe-tə-də, -'fē-; *Southern also* -'fi-tə-dē\ *n* [ME *asafetida*, fr. ML *asafoetida*, fr. Per *azā* mastic + L *foetida*, fem. of *foetidus* fetid] (14c) : the fetid gum resin of various oriental plants (genus *Ferula*) of the carrot family formerly used in medicine as an antispasmodic and in folk medicine as a general prophylactic against disease

asa·na \'ä-sə-nə\ *n* [Skt *āsana* manner of sitting, fr. *āste* he sits; akin to Gk *hēsthai* to sit, Hitt *es-*] (ca. 1934) : any of various yogic postures

Asan·te \ə-'san-tē, -'sän-\ *n, pl* **Asante** (1721) : ASHANTI

as·bes·tos \as-'bes-təs, az-\ *n* [ME *albestron* mineral supposed to be inextinguishable when set on fire, prob. fr. MF, fr. ML *asbeston*, alter. of L *asbestos*, fr. Gk, unslaked lime, fr. *asbestos* inextinguishable, fr. *a-* + *sbennynai* to quench] (1607) : any of several minerals (as chrysotile) that readily separate into long flexible fibers, that have been implicated as causes of certain cancers, and that have been used esp. formerly as fireproof insulating materials

as·bes·to·sis \,as-,bes-'tō-səs, ,az-\ *n, pl* **-to·ses** \-,sēz\ (1927) : a pneumoconiosis due to asbestos particles

asc- *or* **asco-** *comb form* [NL, fr. *ascus*] : ascus ⟨*asco*carp⟩

as·ca·ri·a·sis \,as-kə-'rī-ə-səs\ *n, pl* **-a·ses** \-,sēz\ [NL] (ca. 1888) : infestation with or disease caused by ascarids

as·ca·rid \'as-kə-rəd\ *n* [ultim. fr. LL *ascarid-, ascaris* intestinal worm, fr. Gk *askarid-, askaris*, prob. by back-formation fr. *askarizein* to jump, throb, alter. of *skarizein*, fr. *skairein* to gambol] (ca. 1890) : any of a family (Ascaridae) of nematode worms that includes the common roundworm (*Ascaris lumbricoides*) parasitic in the human intestine

as·ca·ris \'as-kə-rəs\ *n, pl* **as·car·i·des** \a-'skar-ə-,dēz\ (14c) : ASCARID

as·cend \ə-'send\ *vb* [ME, fr. L *ascendere*, fr. *ad-* + *scandere* to climb — more at SCAN] *vi* (14c) **1 a** : to move upward **b** : to slope upward **2 a** : to rise from a lower level or degree **b** : to go back in time or in order of genealogical succession ~ *vt* **1** : to go or move up ⟨~ a staircase⟩ **2** : to succeed to : OCCUPY ⟨~ the throne⟩ — **as·cend·able** *or* **as·cend·ible** \-'sen-də-bəl\ *adj*

as·cen·dance *also* **as·cen·dence** \ə-'sen-dən(t)s\ *n* (1742) : ASCENDANCY

as·cen·dan·cy *also* **as·cen·den·cy** \ə-'sen-dən(t)-sē\ *n* (1712) : governing or controlling influence : DOMINATION

¹as·cen·dant *also* **as·cen·dent** \ə-'sen-dənt\ *n* [ME *ascendent*, fr. ML *ascendent-, ascendens*, fr. L, prp. of *ascendere*] (14c) **1** : the point of the ecliptic or degree of the zodiac that rises above the eastern horizon at any moment **2** : a state or position of dominant power or importance **3** : a lineal or collateral relative in the ascending line

²ascendant *also* **ascendent** *adj* (1591) **1 a** : moving upward : RISING **b** : directed upward ⟨an ~ stem⟩ **2 a** : SUPERIOR **b** : DOMINANT — **as·cen·dant·ly** *adv*

as·cend·er \ə-'sen-dər\ *n* (ca. 1867) : the part of a lowercase letter (as b) that rises above the main body of the letter; *also* : a letter that has such a part

as·cend·ing \ə-'sen-diŋ\ *adj* (1599) **1 a** : mounting or sloping upward **b** : rising or increasing to higher levels, values, or degrees ⟨~ powers of *x*⟩ **2** : rising upward usu. from a more or less prostrate base or point of attachment

as·cen·sion \ə-'sen(t)-shən\ *n* [ME, fr. L *ascension-, ascensio*, fr. *ascendere*] (14c) : the act or process of ascending

as·cen·sion·al \ə-'sench-nəl, ə-'sen(t)-shə-nᵊl\ *adj* (1594) : of or relating to ascension or ascent

Ascension Day n (14c) : the Thursday 40 days after Easter observed in commemoration of Christ's ascension into Heaven

as·cen·sive \ə-'sen(t)-siv\ adj (1646) : rising or tending to rise

as·cent \ə-'sent, a-\ n [irreg. fr. ascend] (ca. 1596) **1 a** : the act of rising or mounting upward : CLIMB **b** : an upward slope or rising grade : ACCLIVITY **c** : the degree of elevation : INCLINATION, GRADIENT **2** : an advance in social status or reputation : PROGRESS **3** : a going back in time or upward in order of genealogical succession

as·cer·tain \ˌa-sər-'tān\ vt [ME acertainen, fr. MF acertainer, fr. a- (fr. L ad-) + certain] (15c) **1** archaic : to make certain, exact, or precise **2** : to find out or learn with certainty **syn** see DISCOVER — **as·cer·tain·able** \-'tā-nə-bəl\ adj — **as·cer·tain·ment** \-'tān-mənt\ n

as·ce·sis \ə-'sē-səs\ n, pl **-ce·ses** \-'sē-(ˌ)sēz\ [LL or Gk; LL, fr. Gk askēsis, lit., exercise, fr. askein] (1873) : SELF-DISCIPLINE, ASCETICISM

as·cet·ic \ə-'se-tik, a-\ also **as·cet·i·cal** \-ti-kəl\ adj [Gk askētikos, lit., laborious, fr. askētēs one that exercises, hermit, fr. askein to work, exercise] (1646) **1** : practicing strict self-denial as a measure of personal and esp. spiritual discipline **2** : austere in appearance, manner, or attitude syn see SEVERE — **ascetic** n — **as·cet·i·cal·ly** \-ti-k(ə-)lē\ adv — **as·cet·i·cism** \-'se-tə-ˌsi-zəm\ n

as·cid·i·an \ə-'si-dē-ən\ n [NL Ascidia, group comprising tunicates, fr. Ascidium, genus name, fr. Gk askidion, dim. of askos wineskin, bladder] (1856) : any of a class (Ascidiacea) of solitary or colonial sessile tunicates that have an oral and an atrial siphon — called also sea squirt

ASCII \'as-(ˌ)kē\ n [American Standard Code for Information Interchange] (1963) : a code for representing alphanumeric information

as·ci·tes \ə-'sī-tēz\ n, pl **ascites** [ME aschytes, fr. LL ascites, fr. Gk askītēs, fr. askos] (14c) : accumulation of serous fluid in the spaces between tissues and organs in the cavity of the abdomen — **as·cit·ic** \-'si-tik\ adj

as·cle·pi·ad \ə-'sklē-pē-əd, a-, -ˌad\ n [ultim. fr. Gk asklēpiad-, asklēpias swallowwort, fr. Asklēpios, Greek god of medicine] (1859) : MILKWEED

as·co·carp \'as-kə-ˌkärp\ n (ca. 1887) : the mature fruiting body of an ascomycetous fungus; broadly : such a body with its enclosed asci, spores, and paraphyses — **as·co·car·pic** \ˌas-kə-'kär-pik\ adj

as·co·go·ni·um \ˌas-kə-'gō-nē-əm\ n, pl **-nia** \-nē-ə\ [NL] (1875) : the female sex organ in ascomycetous fungi

as·co·my·cete \ˌas-kō-'mī-ˌsēt, -ˌmī-'sēt\ n [ultim. fr. Gk askos + mykēt-, mykēs fungus; akin to Gk myxa mucus — more at MUCUS] (1875) : any of a class (Ascomycetes) or subdivision (Ascomycotina) of higher fungi (as yeasts or molds) with septate hyphae and spores formed in asci — **as·co·my·ce·tous** \-ˌmī-'sē-təs\ adj

ascor·bate \ə-'skor-ˌbāt, -bət\ n (1941) : a salt of ascorbic acid

ascor·bic acid \ə-'skor-bik-\ n [ISV a- + NL scorbutus scurvy — more at SCORBUTIC] (1933) : VITAMIN C

as·co·spore \'as-kə-ˌspor, -ˌspor\ n (1875) : any of the spores contained in an ascus — **as·co·spor·ic** \ˌas-kə-'spor-ik, -'spor-\ adj

as·cot \'as-kət, -ˌkät\ n [Ascot Heath, racetrack near Ascot, England] (1898) : a broad neck scarf that is looped under the chin

as·cribe \ə-'skrīb\ vt **as·cribed; as·crib·ing** [ME, fr. L ascribere, fr. ad- + scribere to write — more at SCRIBE] (15c) : to refer to a supposed cause, source, or author — **as·crib·able** \-'skrī-bə-bəl\ adj

syn ASCRIBE, ATTRIBUTE, ASSIGN, IMPUTE, CREDIT mean to lay something to the account of a person or thing. ASCRIBE suggests an inferring or conjecturing of cause, quality, authorship ⟨forged paintings formerly ascribed to masters⟩. ATTRIBUTE suggests less tentativeness than ASCRIBE, less definiteness than ASSIGN ⟨attributed to Rembrandt but possibly done by an associate⟩. ASSIGN implies ascribing with certainty or after deliberation ⟨assigned the bones to the Cretaceous Period⟩. IMPUTE suggests ascribing something that brings discredit by way of accusation or blame ⟨tried to impute sinister motives to my actions⟩. CREDIT implies ascribing a thing or esp. an action to a person or other thing as its agent, source, or explanation ⟨credited his teammates for his success⟩.

ascribed adj (1972) : acquired or assigned arbitrarily (as at birth) ⟨~ social status⟩

as·crip·tion \ə-'skrip-shən\ n [LL ascription-, ascriptio, fr. L, written addition, fr. ascribere] (1600) **1** : the act of ascribing : ATTRIBUTION **2** : arbitrary placement (as at birth) in a particular social status

as·crip·tive \ə-'skrip-tiv\ adj (1650) : relating to, marked by, or involving ascription

as·cus \'as-kəs\ n, pl **as·ci** \'as-ˌkī, -ˌkē, 'a-ˌsī\ [NL, fr. Gk askos wineskin, bladder] (1830) : the membranous oval or tubular spore case of an ascomycete

as·dic \'az-(ˌ)dik\ n [fr. asdics underwater echo ranging, prob. fr. Anti= Submarine Division (British Admiralty department 1916–18) + -ics] (1939) chiefly Brit : SONAR

-ase n suffix [F, fr. diastase] : enzyme ⟨protease⟩

asep·sis \(ˌ)ā-'sep-səs, ə-\ n [NL] (1892) **1** : the condition of being aseptic **2** : the methods of making or keeping aseptic

asep·tic \(ˌ)ā-'sep-tik, ə-\ adj [ISV] (ca. 1859) **1 a** : preventing infection ⟨~ techniques⟩ **b** : free or freed from pathogenic microorganisms ⟨an ~ operating room⟩ **2** : lacking vitality, emotion, or warmth ⟨~ essays⟩ — **asep·ti·cal·ly** \-ti-k(ə-)lē\ adv

asex·u·al \(ˌ)ā-'sek-sh(ə-)wəl, -'sek-shəl\ adj (1830) **1** : lacking sex or functional sex organs ⟨~ plants⟩ **2** : involving or reproducing by reproductive processes (as cell division, spore formation, fission, or budding) that do not involve the union of individuals or germ cells ⟨~ reproduction⟩ ⟨an ~ generation⟩ **b** : produced by asexual reproduction ⟨~ spores⟩ **3** : devoid of sexuality ⟨an ~ relationship⟩ — **asex·u·al·i·ty** \ˌā-ˌsek-shə-'wa-lə-tē\ n — **asex·u·al·ly** \(ˌ)ā-'sek-sh(ə-)wə-lē, -ˌsek-shə-)lē\ adv

¹as far as conj (14c) : to the extent or degree that ⟨is safe, as far as we know⟩ — often used in expressions like "as far as (something) goes" and "as far as (something) is concerned" to mean "with regard to (something)" ⟨we felt pretty safe as far as the fire was concerned —Mark Twain⟩ or in expressions like "as far as (someone) is concerned" to mean "in (someone's) opinion" ⟨as far as I'm concerned, it's a mistake⟩

²as far as prep (1523) : with regard to : CONCERNING ⟨neatly groomed and, as far as clothes, casual looking —N.Y. Times⟩ ⟨as far as being mentioned in the Ten Commandments, I think it is —Billy Graham⟩ — chiefly in oral use

as for prep (1533) : with regard to : CONCERNING ⟨as for the others, they'll arrive later⟩

As·gard \'as-ˌgärd, 'az-\ n [ON āsgarthr] : the home of the Norse gods

¹ash \'ash\ n [ME asshe, fr. OE æsc; akin to OHG ask ash, L ornus mountain ash] (bef. 12c) **1** : any of a genus (Fraxinus) of trees of the olive family with pinnate leaves, thin furrowed bark, and gray branchlets **2** : the tough elastic wood of an ash **3** [OE æsc, name of the corresponding runic letter] : the ligature æ used in Old English and some phonetic alphabets to represent a low front vowel \a\

²ash n, often attrib [ME asshe, fr. OE asce — more at ARID] (bef. 12c) **1** : something that symbolizes grief, repentance, or humiliation **2 a** : the solid residue left when combustible material is thoroughly burned or is oxidized by chemical means **b** : fine particles of mineral matter from a volcanic vent **3** pl : the remains of the dead human body after cremation or disintegration **4** pl : deathly pallor ⟨the lip of ~es and the cheek of flame —Lord Byron⟩ **5** pl : RUINS — **ash·less** \-ləs\ adj

³ash vt (1894) : to convert into ash

ashamed \ə-'shāmd\ adj [ME, fr. OE āscamod, pp. of āscamian to shame, fr. ā- (perfective prefix) + scamian to shame — more at ABIDE, SHAME] (bef. 12c) **1 a** : feeling shame, guilt, or disgrace **b** : feeling inferior or unworthy **2** : restrained by anticipation of shame ⟨was ~ to beg⟩ — **asham·ed·ly** \-'shā-məd-lē\ adv

Ashan·ti \ə-'shan-tē, -'shän-\ n, pl **Ashanti** or **Ashantis** [Twi àsàntè] (1721) **1** : a member of a people of southern Ghana **2** : the dialect of Akan spoken by the Ashanti people

ash–blond or **ash–blonde** \'ash-'bländ\ adj (1903) : pale or grayish blond ⟨~ hair⟩

Ash·can \'ash-ˌkan\ adj (1939) : of or relating to a group of 20th century American painters who depicted city life realistically ⟨~ school⟩

ash can n (1899) **1** : a metal receptacle for refuse **2** slang : DEPTH CHARGE

¹ash·en \'a-shən\ adj (bef. 12c) : of, relating to, or made from ash wood

²ashen adj (14c) : resembling ashes (as in color); esp : deathly pale ⟨a face ~ and haggard⟩

Ash·er \'a-shər\ n [Heb Āshēr] : a son of Jacob and the traditional eponymous ancestor of one of the tribes of Israel

ash·fall \'ash-ˌfol\ n (1923) : a deposit of volcanic ash

Ash·ke·nazi \ˌäsh-kə-'nä-zē, ˌash-kə-'na-\ n, pl **-naz·im** \-'nä-zəm, -'na-\ [LHeb Ashkĕnāzī, fr. Ashkĕnāz, medieval rabbinical name for Germany] (1839) : a member of one of the two great divisions of Jews comprising the eastern European Yiddish-speaking Jews — compare SEPHARDI — **Ash·ke·naz·ic** \-'nä-zik, -'na-\ adj

ash·lar \'ash-lər\ n [ME asheler, fr. MF aisselier traverse beam, fr. OF, fr. ais board, fr. L axis, alter. of assis] (14c) **1** : hewn or squared stone; also : masonry of such stone **2** : a thin squared and dressed stone for facing a wall of rubble or brick

ashore \ə-'shor, -'shor\ adv (1582) : on or to the shore

as how conj (1771) : THAT ⟨allowed as how she was glad to be here⟩

ash·ram \'äsh-rəm, -ˌräm; 'ash-ˌram\ n [Skt āśrama, fr. śrama religious exercise] (1917) **1** : a secluded dwelling of a Hindu sage; also : the group of disciples instructed there **2** : a religious retreat

Ash·to·reth \'ash-tə-ˌreth\ n [Heb 'Ashtōreth] : ASTARTE

ash·tray \'ash-ˌtrā\ n (1887) : a receptacle for tobacco ashes and for cigar and cigarette butts

Ashur \'ä-ˌshùr\ n [Akkadian Ashūr] : the chief deity of the Assyrians

Ash Wednesday n (14c) : the first day of Lent — see EASTER table

ashy \a-shē\ adj **ash·i·er; -est** (14c) **1** : of or relating to ashes **2** : ASHEN

Asi·a·go \ˌä-zhē-'ä-(ˌ)gō, ˌä-sē, -shē-\ n [Asiago, town in Italy] (1938) : a pungent hard yellow cheese of Italian origin suitable for grating

¹Asian \'ā-zhən also -shən\ adj (1550) : of, relating to, or characteristic of the continent of Asia or its people

²Asian n (ca. 1890) : a native or inhabitant of Asia

Asian–Amer·i·can \-ə-'mər-ə-kən\ n (1974) : an American of Asian descent — **Asian–American** adj

Asian elephant n (1981) : ELEPHANT 1b

Asian influenza n (1957) : influenza caused by a mutant strain of the influenza virus isolated during the 1957 epidemic in Asia — called also Asian flu

Asi·at·ic \ˌā-zhē-'a-tik, -zē-\ adj (1602) : ASIAN — sometimes taken to be offensive — **Asiatic** n

Asiatic cholera n (1831) : cholera of Asian origin that is caused by virulent strains of the cholera vibrio (Vibrio cholerae)

Asiatic elephant n (1930) : ELEPHANT 1b

¹aside \ə-'sīd\ adv (14c) **1** : to or toward the side ⟨stepped ~⟩ **2** : away from others or into privacy ⟨pulled him ~⟩ **3** : out of the way esp. for future use : AWAY ⟨putting ~ savings⟩ **4** : away from one's thought or consideration ⟨jesting ~⟩

²aside prep (1592) obs : BEYOND, PAST

³aside n (ca. 1751) **1** : an utterance meant to be inaudible to someone; esp : an actor's speech heard by the audience but supposedly not by other characters **2** : a straying from the theme : DIGRESSION

aside from prep (1818) **1** : in addition to : BESIDES **2** : EXCEPT FOR

as if conj (13c) **1** : as it would be if ⟨it was as if he had lost his last friend⟩ **2** : as one would do if ⟨he ran as if ghosts were chasing him⟩ **3** : THAT ⟨it seemed as if the day would never end⟩

as·i·nine \'a-sᵊn-ˌīn\ adj [L asininus, fr. asinus ass] (15c) **1** : marked by inexcusable failure to exercise intelligence or sound judgment ⟨an ~ excuse⟩ **2** : of, relating to, or resembling an ass syn see SIMPLE — **as·i·nine·ly** adv — **as·i·nin·i·ty** \ˌa-sə-'ni-nə-tē\ n

ask \'ask, 'ask; dial 'aks\ vb **asked** \'as(k)t, 'äs(k)t, 'ask; dial 'akst\; **ask·ing** [ME, fr. OE āscian; akin to OHG eiscōn to ask, Lith eiškoti to seek, Skt icchati he seeks] vt (bef. 12c) **1 a** : to call on for an answer **b** : to put a question about : SPEAK, UTTER ⟨~ a question⟩ **2 a** : to make a request of ⟨she ~ed her teacher for help⟩ **b** : to make a request for ⟨she ~ed help from her teacher⟩ **3** : to call for : REQUIRE **4** : to set as a price ⟨~ed $3000 for the car⟩ **5** : INVITE ~ vi **1** : to

---

\ə\ abut \ᵊ\ kitten, F table \ər\ further \a\ ash \ā\ ace \ä\ mop, mar
\aù\ out \ch\ chin \e\ bet \ē\ easy \g\ go \i\ hit \ī\ ice \j\ job
\ŋ\ sing \ō\ go \o\ law \oi\ boy \th\ thin \t͟h\ the \ü\ loot \ù\ foot
\y\ yet \zh\ vision \á, k̲, ⁿ, œ, œ̄, ᵫ, ᵫ̄, ᵻ\ see Guide to Pronunciation

seek information **2** : to make a request ⟨∼ed for food⟩ **3** : LOOK — often used in the phrase *ask for trouble* — **ask·er** *n*

syn ASK, QUESTION, INTERROGATE, QUERY, INQUIRE mean to address a person in order to gain information. ASK implies no more than the putting of a question ⟨*ask* for directions⟩. QUESTION usu. suggests the asking of series of questions ⟨*questioned* them about every detail of the trip⟩. INTERROGATE suggests formal or official systematic questioning ⟨the prosecutor *interrogated* the witness all day⟩. QUERY implies a desire for authoritative information or confirmation ⟨*queried* a librarian about the book⟩. INQUIRE implies a searching for facts or for truth often specifically by asking questions ⟨began to *inquire* of friends and teachers what career she should pursue⟩.

syn ASK, REQUEST, SOLICIT mean to seek to obtain by making one's wants known. ASK implies no more than the statement of the desire ⟨*ask* a favor of a friend⟩. REQUEST implies greater formality and courtesy ⟨*requests* the pleasure of your company⟩. SOLICIT suggests a calling attention to one's wants or desires by public announcement or advertisement ⟨a letter *soliciting* information⟩.

askance \ə-'skan(t)s\ *also* **askant** \-'skant\ *adv* [origin unknown] (ca. 1530) **1** : with a side-glance : OBLIQUELY **2** : with disapproval or distrust : SCORNFULLY

as·ke·sis \ə-'skē-səs\ *var of* ASCESIS

askew \ə-'skyü\ *adv or adj* [prob. fr. ¹*a*- + *skew*] (1573) : out of line : AWRY ⟨the picture hung ∼⟩ — **askew·ness** *n*

asking price *n* (1755) : the price at which something is offered for sale

¹**aslant** \ə-'slant\ *adv or adj* (14c) : in a slanting direction : OBLIQUELY

²**aslant** *prep* (1602) : over or across in a slanting direction

¹**asleep** \ə-'slēp\ *adj* [ME *aslepe*, fr. OE *on slæpe*] (13c) **1** : being in a state of sleep **2** : DEAD **3** : lacking sensation : NUMB **4 a** : INACTIVE, DORMANT **b** : not alert : INDIFFERENT

²**asleep** *adv* (13c) **1** : into a state of sleep **2** : into the sleep of death **3** : into a state of inactivity, sluggishness, or indifference

as long as *conj* (15c) **1** : provided that ⟨can do as they like *as long as* they have a B average⟩ **2** : INASMUCH AS, SINCE ⟨*as long as* you're going, I'll go too⟩

aslope \ə-'slōp\ *adj or adv* (14c) : being in a sloping or slanting position or direction

aso·cial \(ˌ)ā-'sō-shəl\ *adj* (1883) : not social: as **a** : rejecting or lacking the capacity for social interaction **b** : ANTISOCIAL

as of *prep* (1900) : ON, AT, FROM — used to indicate a time or date at which something begins or ends ⟨takes effect *as of* July 1⟩

¹**asp** \'asp\ *n* [ME, fr. OE *æspe*] (bef. 12c) : ASPEN

²**asp** *n* [ME *aspis*, fr. L, fr. Gk] (14c) : a small venomous snake of Egypt usu. held to be a cobra (*Naja haje*)

as·par·a·gine \ə-'spar-ə-ˌjēn\ *n* [F, fr. L *asparagus*] (1813) : a nonessential amino acid $C_4H_8N_2O_3$ that is an amide of aspartic acid

as·par·a·gus \ə-'spar-ə-gəs\ *n, pl* **-gus** [NL, genus name, fr. L, asparagus plant, fr. Gk *asparagos;* perh. akin to Gk *spargan* to swell] (1548) : any of a genus (*Asparagus*) of Old World perennial plants of the lily family having much-branched stems, minute scalelike leaves, and narrow usu. filiform branchlets that function as leaves; *esp* : one (*A. officinalis*) widely cultivated for its edible young shoots

asparagus

as·par·tame \'as-pər-ˌtām, ə-'spär-ˌtām\ *n* [*aspartic* acid + *phenylalanine* + *methyl* + *ester*] (1972) : a crystalline compound $C_{14}H_{18}N_2O_5$ that is a diamide synthesized from phenylalanine and aspartic acid and that is used as a low-calorie sweetener

as·par·tate \ə-'spär-ˌtāt\ *n* (1863) : a salt or ester of aspartic acid

as·par·tic acid \ə-'spär-tik-\ *n* [ISV, irreg. fr. L *asparagus*] (1863) : a crystalline amino acid $C_4H_7NO_4$ found esp. in plants

as·pect \'as-ˌpekt\ *n* [ME *aspectus*, fr. *aspicere* to look at, fr. *ad-* + *specere* to look — more at SPY] (14c) **1 a** : the position of planets or stars with respect to one another held by astrologers to influence human affairs; *also* : the apparent position (as conjunction) of a body in the solar system with respect to the sun **b** : a position facing a particular direction : EXPOSURE ⟨the house has a southern ∼⟩ **c** : the manner of presentation of a plane to a fluid through which it is moving or to a current **2 a** (1) : appearance to the eye or mind (2) : a particular appearance of countenance : MIEN **b** : a particular status or phase in which something appears or may be regarded ⟨studied every ∼ of the question⟩ **3** *archaic* : an act of looking : GAZE **4 a** : the nature of the action of a verb as to its beginning, duration, completion, or repetition and without reference to its position in time **b** : a set of inflected verb forms that indicate aspect — **as·pec·tu·al** \a-'spek-chə-(-wə)l\ *adj*

aspect ratio *n* (1907) : a ratio of one dimension to another: as **a** : the ratio of span to mean chord of an airfoil **b** : the ratio of the width of a television or motion-picture image to its height

as·pen \'as-pən\ *n* [ME, fr. an aspen, fr. *asp* aspen, fr. OE *æspe;* akin to OHG *aspa* aspen, Russ *osina*] (1596) : any of several poplars (esp. *Populus tremula* of Europe and *P. tremuloides* and *P. grandidentata* of No. America) with leaves that flutter in the lightest wind because of their flattened petioles

as per \'az-,pər\ *prep* (1859) : in accordance with : ACCORDING TO — **as per usual** : as usual

as·per·ges \a-'spər-(ˌ)jēz\ *n* [L, thou wilt sprinkle, fr. *aspergere*] (ca. 1587) : a ceremony of sprinkling altar and people with holy water

as·per·gil·lo·sis \ˌas-pər-(ˌ)ji-'lō-səs\ *n, pl* **-lo·ses** \-ˌsēz\ (1898) : infection with or disease caused (as in poultry) by molds (genus *Aspergillus*)

as·per·gil·lum \ˌas-pər-'ji-ləm\ *n, pl* **-la** \-lə\ *or* **-lums** [NL, fr. L *aspergere*] (1649) : a brush or small perforated container with a handle that is used for sprinkling holy water in a liturgical service

as·per·gil·lus \-'ji-ləs\ *n, pl* **-gil·li** \-'ji-ˌlī\ [NL, genus name, fr. *aspergillum*] (ca. 1847) : any of a genus (*Aspergillus*) of ascomycetous fungi with branched radiate sporophores including many common molds

as·per·i·ty \a-'sper-ə-tē, ə-\ *n, pl* **-ties** [ME *asprete*, fr. OF *aspreté*, *aspre* rough, fr. L *asper*, fr. (assumed) OL *absperos*, fr. *ab-* ab- + *-speros;* akin to Skt *apsphura* repelling, L *spernere* to spurn — more at SPURN] (13c) **1** : RIGOR, SEVERITY **2 a** : roughness of surface : UNEVENNESS;

also : a tiny projection from a surface **b** : roughness of sound **3** : roughness of manner or of temper : HARSHNESS

as·perse \ə-'spərs, a-\ *vt* **as·persed; as·pers·ing** [L *aspersus,* pp. of *aspergere,* fr. *ad-* + *spargere* to scatter — more at SPARK] (15c) **1** : SPRINKLE; *esp* : to sprinkle with holy water **2** : to attack with evil reports or false or injurious charges **syn** see MALIGN

as·per·sion \ə-'spər-zhən, -shən\ *n* (ca. 1587) **1 a** : a sprinkling with water esp. in religious ceremonies **b** : the act of calumniating **b** : a calumnious expression ⟨cast ∼s on her integrity⟩

¹**as·phalt** \'as-ˌfȯlt *also* 'ash-, *esp Brit* -ˌfalt\ *also* **as·phal·tum** \as-'fȯl-təm, *esp Brit* -'fal-\ *n* [ME *aspalt,* fr. LL *aspaltus,* fr. Gk *asphaltos*] (14c) **1** : a dark bituminous substance that is found in natural beds and is also obtained as a residue in petroleum refining and that consists chiefly of hydrocarbons **2** : an asphaltic composition used for pavements and as a waterproof cement — **as·phal·tic** \as-'fȯl-tik, *esp Brit* -'fal-\ *adj*

²**asphalt** *vt* (ca. 1859) : to cover with asphalt : PAVE 1

as·phalt·ite \'as-ˌfȯl-ˌtīt, *esp Brit* -ˌfal-\ *n* (ca. 1899) : a native asphalt occurring in vein deposits below the surface of the ground

asphalt jungle *n* (1920) : a big city or a specified part of a big city

as·pher·ic \(ˌ)ā-'sfir-ik, -'sfer-\ *or* **as·pher·i·cal** \-i-kəl\ *adj* (ca. 1922) : departing slightly from the spherical form esp. in order to correct for spherical aberration ⟨an ∼ lens⟩

as·pho·del \'as-fə-ˌdel\ *n* [L *asphodelus,* fr. Gk *asphodelos*] (1597) : any of various Old World usu. perennial herbs (esp. genera *Asphodelus* and *Asphodeline*) of the lily family with flowers in usu. long erect racemes

as·phyx·ia \as-'fik-sē-ə, əs-\ *n* [NL, fr. Gk, stopping of the pulse, fr. *a-* + *sphyzein* to throb] (1778) : a lack of oxygen or excess of carbon dioxide in the body that is usu. caused by interruption of breathing and that causes unconsciousness

as·phyx·i·ate \-sē-ˌāt\ *vb* **-at·ed; -at·ing** *vt* (1836) : to cause asphyxia in; *also* : to kill or make unconscious by inadequate oxygen, presence of noxious agents, or other obstruction to normal breathing ∼ *vi* : to become asphyxiated — **as·phyx·i·a·tion** \-ˌfik-sē-'ā-shən\ *n*

¹**as·pic** \'as-pik\ *n* [MF, alter. of *aspe,* fr. L *aspis*] (1530) *obs* : ²ASP

²**aspic** *n* [F, lit., asp] (1789) : a clear savory jelly (as of fish or meat stock) used as a garnish or to make a meat, fish, or vegetable mold

as·pi·dis·tra \ˌas-pə-'dis-trə\ *n* [NL, irreg. fr. Gk *aspid-, aspis* shield] (1822) : an Asian plant (*Aspidistra elatior*) of the lily family that has large basal leaves and is often grown as a foliage plant

¹**as·pi·rant** \'as-p(ə-)rənt, ə-'spi-rənt\ *n* (1738) : one who aspires ⟨presidential ∼s⟩

²**aspirant** *adj* (1814) : seeking to attain a desired position or status

¹**as·pi·rate** \'as-p(ə-)rət\ *n* (1617) **1** : an independent sound \h\ or a character (as the letter *h*) representing it **2** : a consonant having aspiration as its final component ⟨in English the \p\ of *pit* is an ∼⟩ **3** : material removed by aspiration

²**as·pi·rate** \'as-pə-ˌrāt\ *vt* **-rat·ed; -rat·ing** [L *aspiratus,* pp. of *aspirare*] (ca. 1700) **1** : to pronounce (a vowel or a consonant) with aspiration (sense 1a) **2 a** : to draw by suction **b** : to remove (as blood) by aspiration **c** : to take into the lungs by aspiration

as·pi·ra·tion \ˌas-pə-'rā-shən\ *n* (14c) **1 a** : audible breath that accompanies or comprises a speech sound **b** : the pronunciation or addition of an aspiration; *also* : the symbol of an aspiration **2 a** : a drawing of something in, out, up, or through by or as if by suction: as **a** : the act of breathing and esp. of breathing in **b** : the withdrawal of fluid or tissue from the body **c** : the taking of foreign matter into the lungs with the respiratory current **3 a** : a strong desire to achieve something high or great **b** : an object of such desire **syn** see AMBITION — **as·pi·ra·tion·al** \-'rā-sh(ə-)nəl\ *adj*

as·pi·ra·tor \'as-pə-ˌrā-tər\ *n* (1804) : an apparatus for producing suction or moving or collecting materials by suction; *esp* : a hollow tubular instrument connected with a partial vacuum and used to remove fluid or tissue or foreign bodies from the body

as·pire \ə-'spīr\ *vi* **as·pired; as·pir·ing** [ME, fr. MF or L; MF *aspirer,* fr. L *aspirare,* lit., to breathe upon, fr. *ad-* + *spirare* to breathe] (14c) **1** : to seek to attain or accomplish a particular goal ⟨*aspired* to a career in medicine⟩ **2** : ASCEND, SOAR — **as·pir·er** *n*

as·pi·rin \'as-p(ə-)rən\ *n, pl* **aspirin** *or* **aspirins** [ISV, fr. *acetyl* + *spiraeic* acid (former name of salicylic acid), fr. NL *Spiraea,* genus of shrubs — more at SPIREA] (1899) **1** : a white crystalline derivative $C_9H_8O_4$ of salicylic acid used for relief of pain and fever **2** : a tablet of aspirin

as regards *also* **as respects** *prep* (1840) : in regard to : with respect to

¹**ass** \'as\ *n* [ME, fr. OE *assa,* prob. fr. OIr *asan,* fr. L *asinus*] (bef. 12c) **1** : any of several hardy gregarious African or Asian perissodactyl mammals (genus *Equus*) smaller than the horse and having long ears; *esp* : an African mammal (*E. asinus*) that is the ancestor of the donkey **2** : a stupid, obstinate, or perverse person — often compounded with a preceding adjective ⟨don't be a smart-*ass*⟩; often considered vulgar

²**ass** \'as\ *or* **arse** \'as, 'ärs\ *n* [ME *ars, ers,* fr. OE *ærs, ears;* akin to OHG & ON *ars* buttocks, Gk *orrhos* buttocks, *oura* tail] (bef. 12c) **1 a** : BUTTOCKS — often used in emphatic reference to a specific person ⟨get your ∼ over here⟩ ⟨saved my ∼⟩; often considered vulgar **b** : ANUS — often considered vulgar **2** : SEXUAL INTERCOURSE — usu. considered vulgar

³**ass** *adv* [²*ass*] (1955) — used as a postpositive intensive esp. with words of derogatory implication ⟨fancy-*ass*⟩; often considered vulgar

as·sai \ä-'sī\ *adv* [It, fr. (assumed) VL *ad satis* enough — more at ASSET] (ca. 1724) : VERY — used with tempo direction in music ⟨allegro ∼⟩

as·sail \ə-'sā(ə)l\ *vt* [ME, fr. OF *asaillir,* fr. (assumed) VL *assalire,* alter. of L *assilire* to leap upon, fr. *ad-* + *salire* to leap — more at SALLY] (13c) : to attack violently with blows or words **syn** see ATTACK — **as·sail·able** \-'sā-lə-bəl\ *adj* — **as·sail·ant** \-'sā-lənt\ *n*

As·sam·ese \ˌa-sə-'mēz, -'mēs\ *n, pl* **Assamese** (1826) **1** : a native or inhabitant of Assam, India **2** : the Indo-Aryan language of Assam — **Assamese** *adj*

as·sas·sin \ə-'sa-sᵊn\ *n* [ML *assassinus,* fr. Ar *hashshāshīn,* pl. of *hashshāsh* one who smokes or chews hashish, fr. *hashish* hashish] (ca. 1520) **1** *cap* : one of a secret order of Muslims that at the time of the Crusades terrorized Christians and other enemies by secret murder committed under the influence of hashish **2** : a person who commits murder; *esp* : one who murders a politically important person either for hire or from fanatical motives

as·sas·si·nate \ə-'sa-s³n-ˌāt\ *vt* **-nat·ed; -nat·ing** (1607) **1** : to injure or destroy unexpectedly and treacherously **2** : to murder by sudden or secret attack usu. for impersonal reasons *syn* see KILL — **as·sas·si·na·tion** \-ˌsa-s³n-'ā-shən\ *n* — **as·sas·si·na·tor** \-'sa-s³n-ˌā-tər\ *n*

assassin bug *n* (1895) : any of a family (Reduviidae) of bugs that are usu. predatory on insects though some (as a conenose) suck the blood of mammals — called also *reduviid*

¹as·sault \ə-'sȯlt\ *n* [ME *assaut*, fr. OF, fr. (assumed) VL *assaltus*, fr. *assalire*] (14c) **1 a** : a violent physical or verbal attack **b** : a military attack usu. involving direct combat with enemy forces **c** : a concerted effort (as to reach a goal or defeat an adversary) **2 a** : a threat or attempt to inflict offensive physical contact or bodily harm on a person (as by lifting a fist in a threatening manner) that puts the person in immediate danger of or in apprehension of such harm or contact — compare BATTERY 1b ⟩ : RAPE

²assault *vt* (15c) **1** : to make an assault on **2** : RAPE ~ *vi* : to make an assault *syn* see ATTACK — **as·saul·tive** \-'sȯl-tiv\ *adj* — **as·saul·tive·ly** *adv* — **as·saul·tive·ness** *n*

assault boat *n* (1941) : a small portable boat used in an amphibious military attack or in land warfare for crossing rivers or lakes

assault rifle *n* (1975) : any of various automatic or semiautomatic rifles designed for military use with large capacity magazines

¹as·say \'a-ˌsā, a-'sā\ *n* [ME, fr. OF *essai, assai* test, effort — more at ESSAY] (14c) **1** *archaic* : TRIAL, ATTEMPT **2** : examination and determination as to characteristics (as weight, measure, or quality) **3** : analysis (as of an ore or drug) to determine the presence, absence, or quantity of one or more components **4** : a substance to be assayed; *also* : the tabulated result of assaying

²as·say \a-'sā, 'a-ˌsā\ *vt* (14c) **1** : TRY, ATTEMPT **2 a** : to analyze (as an ore) for one or more specific components **b** : to judge the worth of : ESTIMATE ~ *vi* : to prove up in an assay — **as·say·er** *n*

assed \'ast\ *adj* (1932) : ³ASS — used in combination ⟨smart-*assed*⟩; often considered vulgar

as·se·gai or **as·sa·gai** \'a-si-ˌgī\ *n* [ultim. fr. Ar *az-zaghāya* the assegai, fr. *al-* the + *zaghāya* assegai] (1600) : a slender hardwood spear or light javelin usu. tipped with iron and used in southern Africa

as·sem·blage \ə-'sem-blij, *for 3 also* ˌa-ˌsäm-'bläzh\ *n* (1690) **1** : a collection of persons or things : GATHERING **2** : the act of assembling : the state of being assembled **3 a** : an artistic composition made from scraps, junk, and odds and ends (as of paper, cloth, wood, stone, or metal) **b** : the art of making assemblages

as·sem·blag·ist \-bli-jist, -'blä-zhist\ *n* (1965) : an artist who specializes in assemblages

as·sem·ble \ə-'sem-bəl\ *vb* **as·sem·bled; as·sem·bling** \-b(ə-)liŋ\ [ME, fr. OF *assembler*, fr. (assumed) VL *assimulare*, fr. L *ad-* + *simul* together — more at SAME] *vt* (13c) **1** : to bring together (as in a particular place or for a particular purpose) **2** : to fit together the parts of ~ *vi* : to meet together : CONVENE *syn* see GATHER

as·sem·bler \-b(ə-)lər\ *n* (1635) **1** : one that assembles **2 a** : a computer program that automatically converts instructions written in assembly language into machine language **b** : ASSEMBLY LANGUAGE

as·sem·bly \ə-'sem-blē\ *n, pl* **-blies** [ME *assemblee*, fr. MF, fr. OF, fr. *assembler*] (14c) **1** : a company of persons gathered for deliberation and legislation, worship, or entertainment **2** *cap* : a legislative body; *specif* : the lower house of a legislature **3** : ASSEMBLAGE 1, 2 **4** : a signal for troops to assemble or fall in **5 a** : the fitting together of manufactured parts into a complete machine, structure, or unit of a machine **b** : a collection of parts so assembled **6** : the translation of assembly language to machine language by an assembler

assembly language *n* (ca. 1964) : a programming language that consists of instructions that are mnemonic codes for corresponding machine language instructions

assembly line *n* (1914) **1** : an arrangement of machines, equipment, and workers in which work passes from operation to operation in direct line until the product is assembled **2** : a process for turning out a finished product in a mechanically efficient manner ⟨academic *assembly lines*⟩

as·sem·bly·man \ə-'sem-blē-mən\ *n* (1647) : a member of an assembly

Assembly of God (1952) : a congregation belonging to a Pentecostal body founded in the U.S. in 1914

as·sem·bly·wom·an \-ˌwu̇-mən\ *n* (1969) : a woman who is a member of an assembly

¹as·sent \ə-'sent, a-\ *vi* [ME, fr. OF *assenter*, fr. L *assentari*, fr. *assentire*, fr. *ad-* + *sentire* to feel — more at SENSE] (14c) : to agree to something esp. after thoughtful consideration : CONCUR — **as·sen·tor** or **as·sent·er** \-'sen-tər\ *n*

syn ASSENT, CONSENT, ACCEDE, ACQUIESCE, AGREE, SUBSCRIBE mean to concur with what has been proposed. ASSENT implies an act involving the understanding or judgment and applies to propositions or opinions ⟨voters *assented* to the proposal⟩. CONSENT involves the will or feelings and indicates compliance with what is requested or desired ⟨*consented* to their daughter's going⟩. ACCEDE implies a yielding, often under pressure, of assent or consent ⟨officials *acceded* to the prisoners' demands⟩. ACQUIESCE implies tacit acceptance or forbearance of opposition ⟨*acquiesced* to his boss's wishes⟩. AGREE sometimes implies previous difference of opinion or attempts at persuasion ⟨finally *agreed* to come along⟩. SUBSCRIBE implies not only consent or assent but hearty approval and active support ⟨*subscribes* wholeheartedly to the idea⟩.

²assent *n* (14c) : an act of assenting : ACQUIESCENCE, AGREEMENT

as·sen·ta·tion \ˌa-s³n-'tā-shən, ˌa-ˌsen-\ *n* (15c) : ready assent esp. when insincere or obsequious

as·sert \ə-'sərt, a-\ *vt* [L *assertus*, pp. of *asserere*, fr. *ad-* + *serere* to join — more at SERIES] (ca. 1604) **1** : to state or declare positively and often forcefully or aggressively **2 a** : to demonstrate the existence of ⟨~ his manhood —James Joyce⟩ **b** : POSIT, POSTULATE — **assert oneself** : to compel recognition esp. of one's rights

syn ASSERT, DECLARE, AFFIRM, PROTEST, AVOW mean to state positively usu. in anticipation of denial or objection. ASSERT implies stating confidently without need for proof or regard for evidence ⟨*asserted* that modern music is just noise⟩. DECLARE stresses open or public statement ⟨*declared* her support for the candidate⟩. AFFIRM implies conviction based on evidence, experience, or faith ⟨*affirmed* the existence of an afterlife⟩. PROTEST emphasizes affirming in the face of denial or doubt ⟨*protested* that he really had been misquoted⟩. AVOW stresses

frank declaration and acknowledgment of personal responsibility for what is declared ⟨*avowed* that all investors would be repaid in full⟩. *syn* see in addition MAINTAIN

as·sert·ed·ly \ə-'sər-təd-lē, a-\ *adv* (1937) : by positive and usu. unsubstantiated assertion : ALLEGEDLY

as·ser·tion \ə-'sər-shən, a-\ *n* (15c) : the act of asserting; *also* : DECLARATION, AFFIRMATION

as·ser·tive \ə-'sər-tiv, a-\ *adj* (ca. 1619) **1** : disposed to or characterized by bold or confident assertion **2** : having a strong or distinctive flavor or aroma ⟨~ wines⟩ *syn* see AGGRESSIVE — **as·ser·tive·ly** *adv* — **as·ser·tive·ness** *n*

assertiveness training *n* (1975) : a method of training individuals to act in a bold self-confident manner

asses *pl of* AS *or of* ASS

as·sess \ə-'ses, a-\ *vt* [ME, prob. fr. ML *assessus*, pp. of *assidēre*, fr. L, to sit beside, assist in the office of a judge — more at ASSIZE] (15c) **1** : to determine the rate or amount of (as a tax) **2 a** : to impose (as a tax) according to an established rate **b** : to subject to a tax, charge, or levy **3** : to make an official valuation of (property) for the purposes of taxation **4** : to determine the importance, size, or value of **5** : to charge (a player or team) with a foul or penalty *syn* see ESTIMATE — **as·sess·able** \-'se-sə-bəl\ *adj*

as·sess·ment \ə-'ses-mənt, a-\ *n* (1534) **1** : the action or an instance of assessing : APPRAISAL **2** : the amount assessed

as·ses·sor \ə-'se-sər\ *n* (14c) **1** : an official who assists a judge or magistrate **2** : one that assesses; *esp* : an official who assesses property for taxation

as·set \'a-ˌset *also* -sət\ *n* [back-formation fr. *assets*, sing., sufficient property to pay debts and legacies, fr. AF *asetz*, fr. OF *assez* enough, fr. (assumed) VL *ad satis*, fr. L *ad* to + *satis* enough — more at AT, SAD] (1531) **1** *pl* **a** : the property of a deceased person subject by law to the payment of his or her debts and legacies **b** : the entire property of a person, association, corporation, or estate applicable or subject to the payment of debts **2** : ADVANTAGE, RESOURCE ⟨his wit is his chief ~⟩ **3 a** : an item of value owned **b** *pl* : the items on a balance sheet showing the book value of property owned

as·sev·er·ate \ə-'se-və-ˌrāt\ *vt* **-at·ed; -at·ing** [L *asseveratus*, pp. of *asseverare*, fr. *ad-* + *severus* severe] (1791) : to affirm or aver positively or earnestly — **as·sev·er·a·tion** \-ˌse-və-'rā-shən\ *n* — **as·sev·er·a·tive** \-'se-və-ˌrā-tiv\ *adj*

ass·hole \'as-ˌ(h)ōl\ *n* (14c) **1** : ANUS — usu. considered vulgar **2 a** : a stupid, incompetent, or detestable person — usu. considered vulgar **b** : a despicable place — usu. used in the phrase *asshole of the universe*; usu. considered vulgar

as·si·du·ity \ˌa-sə-'dü-ə-tē, -'dyü-\ *n, pl* **-ities** (1596) **1** : the quality or state of being assiduous : DILIGENCE **2** : persistent personal attention — usu. used in pl.

as·sid·u·ous \ə-'sij-wəs, -'si-jə-\ *adj* [L *assiduus*, fr. *assidēre*] (1660) : marked by careful unremitting attention or persistent application ⟨an ~ book collector⟩ ⟨tended her garden with ~ attention⟩ *syn* see BUSY — **as·sid·u·ous·ly** *adv* — **as·sid·u·ous·ness** *n*

¹as·sign \ə-'sīn\ *vt* [ME, fr. OF *assigner*, fr. L *assignare*, fr. *ad-* + *signare* to mark, fr. *signum* mark, sign] (13c) **1** : to transfer (property) to another esp. in trust or for the benefit of creditors **2 a** : to appoint to a post or duty ⟨~ed them to light duty⟩ ⟨~ed me two clerks⟩ **b** : to appoint as a duty or task ⟨~s 20 pages for homework⟩ **3** : to fix or specify in correspondence or relationship ⟨~ counsel to the defendant⟩ ⟨~ a value to the variable⟩ **4 a** : to ascribe as a motive, reason, or cause esp. after deliberation **b** : to consider to belong to (a specified period of time) *syn* see ASCRIBE — **as·sign·abil·i·ty** \-ˌsī-nə-'bi-lə-tē\ *n* — **as·sign·able** \-'sī-nə-bəl\ *adj* — **as·sign·er** \ə-'sī-nər\ *or* **as·sign·or** \ə-ˌsī-'nȯr, ˌa-ˌsī-, ə-ˌsī-\ *n*

²assign *n* (15c) : ASSIGNEE 3 ⟨heirs and ~s⟩

as·si·gnat \ˌa-(ˌ)sēn-'yä, 'a-sig-ˌnat\ *n* [F, fr. L *assignatus*, pp. of *assignare*] (1790) : a bill issued as currency by the French Revolutionary government (1789–96) on the security of expropriated lands

as·sig·na·tion \ˌa-sig-'nā-shən\ *n* (15c) **1** : the act of assigning or the assignment made **2** : an appointment of time and place for a meeting; *esp* : TRYST ⟨returned from an ~ with his mistress —W. B. Yeats⟩

assigned risk *n* (1946) : a poor risk (as an accident-prone motorist) that insurance companies would normally reject but are forced to insure by state law

as·sign·ee \ˌa-sə-'nē, ˌa-ˌsī-, ə-ˌsī-\ *n* (14c) **1** : a person to whom an assignment is made **2** : a person appointed to act for another **3** : a person to whom a right or property is legally transferred

as·sign·ment \ə-'sīn-mənt\ *n* (14c) **1** : the act of assigning **2 a** : a position, post, or office to which one is assigned **b** : a specified task or amount of work assigned or undertaken as if assigned by authority **3** : the transfer of property; *esp* : the transfer of property to be held in trust or to be used for the benefit of creditors *syn* see TASK

as·sim·i·la·ble \ə-'si-mə-lə-bəl\ *adj* (1667) : capable of being assimilated — **as·sim·i·la·bil·i·ty** \-ˌsi-mə-lə-'bi-lə-tē\ *n*

¹as·sim·i·late \ə-'si-mə-ˌlāt\ *vb* **-lat·ed; -lat·ing** [ME, fr. ML *assimilatus*, pp. of *assimilare*, fr. L *assimulare* to make similar, fr. *ad-* + *simulare* to make similar, simulate] *vt* (15c) **1 a** : to take in and appropriate as nourishment : absorb into the system **b** : to take into the mind and thoroughly comprehend **2 a** : to make similar **b** : to alter by assimilation **c** : to absorb into the culture or mores of a population or group **3** : COMPARE, LIKEN ~ *vi* : to become assimilated — **as·sim·i·la·tor** \-ˌlā-tər\ *n*

usage When *assimilate* is followed by a preposition, transitive senses 2a and 2c commonly take *to* and *into* and less frequently with; 2b regularly takes *to*; sense 3 most often takes *to* and sometimes *with*. The most frequent prepositions used with the intransitive sense are *to* and *into*.

²as·sim·i·late \-lət, -ˌlāt\ *n* (1935) : something that is assimilated

as·sim·i·la·tion \ə-ˌsi-mə-'lā-shən\ *n* (15c) **1 a** : an act, process, or

\ə\ abut \ᵊ\ kitten, F table \ər\ further \a\ ash \ā\ ace \ä\ mop, mar \au̇\ out \ch\ chin \e\ bet \ē\ easy \g\ go \i\ hit \ī\ ice \j\ job \ŋ\ sing \ō\ go \ȯ\ law \ȯi\ boy \th\ thin \t̶h̶\ the \ü\ loot \u̇\ foot \y\ yet \zh\ vision \ā, k̲, ⁿ, œ, œ̄, ᵫ, ᵫ̄, ᵞ\ *see* Guide to Pronunciation instance of assimilating **b** : the state of being assimilated **2** : the incorporation or conversion of nutrients into protoplasm that in animals follows digestion and absorption and in higher plants involves both photosynthesis and root absorption **3** : change of a sound in speech so that it becomes identical with or similar to a neighboring sound ⟨the usual ~ of \z\ to \sh\ in the phrase *his shoe*⟩ **4** : the process of receiving new facts or of responding to new situations in conformity with what is already available to consciousness

as·sim·i·la·tion·ist \-sh(ə-)nist\ *n* (1899) : a person who advocates a policy of assimilating differing racial or cultural groups — **as·sim·i·la·tion·ism** \-shə-,ni-zəm\ *n* — **as·sim·i·la·tion·ist** *adj*

as·sim·i·la·tive \ə-'si-mə-,lā-tiv, -lə-tiv\ *adj* (14c) : of, relating to, or causing assimilation

as·sim·i·la·to·ry \ə-'si-mə-lə-,tōr-ē, -,tȯr-\ *adj* (ca. 1847) : ASSIMILATIVE

As·sin·i·boin or **As·sin·i·boine** \ə-'si-nə-,bȯin\ *n, pl* **-boin** or **-boins** or **boine** or **-boines** [Ojibwa dial. *assini*ⁿ*pwan*, lit., stone Sioux] (1804) : a member of an American Indian people orig. of the area between the upper Missouri and middle Saskatchewan rivers

¹**as·sist** \ə-'sist\ *vb* [MF or L; MF *assister* to help, stand by, fr. L *assistere*, fr. *ad-* + *sistere* to cause to stand; akin to L *stare* to stand — more at STAND] *vt* (15c) : to give usu. supplementary support or aid to ~ *vi* **1** : to give support or aid ⟨~ed at the stove⟩ ⟨another surgeon ~ed on the operation⟩ **2** : to be present as a spectator ⟨the ideal figures ~*ing* at Italian holy scenes —Mary McCarthy⟩

²**assist** *n* (1597) **1** : an act of assistance : AID **2** : the action (as a throw or pass) of a player who enables a teammate to make a putout or score a goal; *also* : official credit given for such an action **3** : a mechanical device that provides assistance

as·sis·tance \ə-'sis-tən(t)s\ *n* (14c) : the act of assisting or the help supplied : AID ⟨financial and technical ~⟩

as·sis·tant \-tənt\ *n* (15c) : a person who assists : HELPER; *also* : a person holding an assistantship — **assistant** *adj*

assistant professor *n* (1851) : a member of a college or university faculty who ranks above an instructor and below an associate professor — **assistant professorship** *n*

as·sis·tant·ship \ə-'sis-tən(t)-,ship\ *n* (1948) : a paid appointment awarded annually to a qualified graduate student that requires part-time teaching, research, or residence hall duties

as·size \ə-'sīz\ *n* [ME *assise*, fr. OF, session, settlement, fr. *asseoir* to seat, fr. (assumed) VL *assedēre*, fr. L *assidēre* to sit beside, assist in the office of a judge, fr. *ad-* + *sedēre* to sit — more at SIT] (14c) **1 a** : a judicial inquest **b** : an action to be decided by such an inquest, the writ for instituting it, or the verdict or finding rendered by the jury **2 a** : the former periodical sessions of the superior courts in English counties for trial of civil and criminal cases — usu. used in pl. **b** : the time or place of holding such a court, the court itself, or a session of it — usu. used in pl.

¹**as·so·ci·ate** \ə-'sō-shē-,āt, -sē-\ *vb* **-at·ed; -at·ing** [ME *associat* associated, fr. L *associatus*, pp. of *associare* to unite, fr. *ad-* + *sociare* to join, fr. *socius* companion — more at SOCIAL] *vt* (14c) **1** : to join as a partner, friend, or companion **2** *obs* : to keep company with : ATTEND **3** : to join or connect together : COMBINE **4** : to bring together or into relationship in any of various intangible ways (as in memory or imagination) ~ *vi* **1** : to come or be together as partners, friends, or companions **2** : to combine or join with other parts : UNITE *syn* see JOIN

²**as·so·ci·ate** \ə-'sō-shē-ət, -sē-, -,āt, -shət\ *adj* (14c) **1** : closely connected (as in function or office) with another **2** : closely related esp. in the mind **3** : having secondary or subordinate status ⟨~ membership in a society⟩

³**as·so·ci·ate** *same as ²*\ *n* (1533) **1** : one associated with another: as **a** : PARTNER, COLLEAGUE **b** : COMPANION, COMRADE **2 a** : an entry-level member (as of a learned society, professional organization, or profession) **b** : EMPLOYEE, WORKER **3** : a degree conferred esp. by a junior college ⟨~ in arts⟩ — **as·so·ci·ate·ship** \-,ship\ *n*

associate professor *n* (1822) : a member of a college or university faculty who ranks above an assistant professor and below a professor — **associate professorship** *n*

as·so·ci·a·tion \ə-,sō-sē-'ā-shən, -shē-\ *n* (1535) **1 a** : the act of associating **b** : the state of being associated : COMBINATION, RELATIONSHIP **2** : an organization of persons having a common interest : SOCIETY **3** : something linked in memory or imagination with a thing or person **4** : the process of forming mental connections or bonds between sensations, ideas, or memories **5** : the aggregation of chemical species to form (as with hydrogen bonds) loosely bound complexes **6** : a major unit in ecological community organization characterized by essential uniformity and usu. by two or more dominant species — **as·so·ci·a·tion·al** \-sh(ə-)nᵊl\ *adj*

association area *n* (ca. 1909) : an area of the cerebral cortex that functions in linking and coordinating the sensory and motor areas

association football *n* (1873) : SOCCER

as·so·ci·a·tion·ism \ə-,sō-sē-'ā-shə-,ni-zəm, -,sō-shē-\ *n* (1875) : a reductionist school of psychology that holds that the content of consciousness can be explained by the association and reassociation of irreducible stimulus and perceptual elements — **as·so·ci·a·tion·ist** \-'ā-sh(ə-)nist\ *n* — **as·so·ci·a·tion·is·tic** \-,ā-shə-'nis-tik\ *adj*

as·so·cia·tive \ə-'sō-shē-ā-tiv, -sē-, -shə-tiv\ *adj* (1812) **1** : of or relating to association esp. of ideas or images **2** : dependent on or acquired by association or learning **3** : of, having, or being the property of producing the same result no matter which pair of elements next to each other in a mathematical expression is used to perform a given operation first if the elements in the expression are listed in a fixed order ⟨addition is ~ since $(a + b) + c = a + (b + c)$⟩ — **as·so·cia·tive·ly** *adv* — **as·so·cia·tiv·i·ty** \-,sō-shē-ə-'ti-və-tē, -sē-, -shə-'ti-\ *n*

associative learning *n* (1957) : a learning process in which discrete ideas and percepts become linked to one another

associative neuron *n* (1935) : a neuron that conveys impulses from one neuron to another

as·soil \a-'sȯi(ə)l\ *vt* [ME, fr. OF *assoldre*, fr. L *absolvere* to absolve] (13c) **1** *archaic* : ABSOLVE, PARDON **2** *archaic* : ACQUIT, CLEAR **3** *archaic* : EXPIATE — **as·soil·ment** \-mənt\ *n, archaic*

as·so·nance \'a-sə-nən(t)s\ *n* [F, fr. L *assonare* to answer with the same sound, fr. *ad-* + *sonare* to sound, fr. *sonus* sound — more at SOUND] (1727) **1** : resemblance of sound in words or syllables **2 a** : relatively close juxtaposition of similar sounds esp. of vowels **b** : repeti-

tion of vowels without repetition of consonants (as in *stony* and *holy*) used as an alternative to rhyme in verse — **as·so·nant** \-nənt\ *adj or n* — **as·so·nant·al** \,a-sə-'nan-tᵊl\ *adj*

as soon as *conj* (14c) : immediately at or shortly after the time that

as·sort \ə-'sȯrt\ *vb* [MF *assortir*, fr. *a-* (fr. L *ad-*) + *sorte* sort] *vt* (15c) **1** : to distribute into groups of a like kind : CLASSIFY **2** : to supply with an assortment (as of goods) ~ *vi* **1** : to agree in kind : HARMONIZE **2** : to keep company : ASSOCIATE — **as·sort·er** *n*

as·sor·ta·tive \ə-'sȯr-tə-tiv\ *adj* (1897) : being nonrandom mating based on like or unlike characteristics — **as·sor·ta·tive·ly** \-lē\ *adv*

as·sort·ed \-'sȯr-təd\ *adj* (ca. 1797) **1** : suited esp. by nature or character ⟨an ill-*assorted* pair⟩ **2** : consisting of various kinds ⟨~ chocolates⟩

as·sort·ment \-'sȯrt-mənt\ *n* (1611) **1 a** : the act of assorting **b** : the state of being assorted **2** : a collection of assorted things or persons

as·suage \ə-'swāj *also* ə-'swäzh *or* -'swäzh\ *vt* **as·suaged; as·suag·ing** [ME *aswagen*, fr. OF *assouagier*, fr. (assumed) VL *assuaviare*, fr. L *ad-* + *suavis* sweet — more at SWEET] (14c) **1** : to lessen the intensity of (something that pains or distresses) : EASE **2** : PACIFY, QUIET **3** : to put an end to by satisfying : APPEASE, QUENCH *syn* see RELIEVE — **as·suage·ment** \-mənt\ *n*

as·sua·sive \ə-'swā-siv, -ziv\ *adj* (1708) : SOOTHING, CALMING

as·sume \ə-'süm\ *vt* **as·sumed; as·sum·ing** [ME, fr. L *assumere*, fr. *ad-* + *sumere* to take — more at CONSUME] (15c) **1 a** : to take up or in : RECEIVE **b** : to take into partnership, employment, or use **2 a** : to take to or upon oneself : UNDERTAKE **b** : TURN ON, DON **3** : to take control of **4** : to pretend to have or be : FEIGN ⟨*assumed* an air of confidence in spite of her dismay⟩ **5** : to take as granted or true : SUPPOSE **6** : to take over (the debts of another) as one's own — **as·sum·abil·i·ty** \-,sü-mə-'bi-lə-tē\ *n* — **as·sum·able** \-'sü-mə-bəl\ *adj* — **as·sum·ably** \-blē\ *adv*

syn ASSUME, AFFECT, PRETEND, SIMULATE, FEIGN, COUNTERFEIT, SHAM mean to put on a false or deceptive appearance. ASSUME often implies a justifiable motive rather than an intent to deceive ⟨*assumed* an air of cheerfulness around the patients⟩. AFFECT implies making a false show of possessing, using, or feeling ⟨*affected* an interest in art⟩. PRETEND implies an overt and sustained false appearance ⟨*pretended* that nothing had happened⟩. SIMULATE suggests a close imitation of the appearance of something ⟨cosmetics that *simulate* a suntan⟩. FEIGN implies more artful invention than PRETEND, less specific mimicry than SIMULATE ⟨*feigned* sickness⟩. COUNTERFEIT implies achieving the highest degree of verisimilitude of any of these words ⟨an actor *counterfeiting* drunkenness⟩. SHAM implies an obvious falseness that fools only the gullible ⟨*shammed* a most unconvincing limp⟩.

as·sum·ing *adj* (1695) : PRETENTIOUS, PRESUMPTUOUS

as·sump·sit \ə-'səm(p)-sət\ *n* [NL, he undertook, fr. L *assumere* to undertake] (1590) **1** : an express or implied promise or contract not under seal on which an action may be brought **2 a** : a former common-law action brought to recover damages alleged from the breach of an assumpsit **b** : an action to recover damages for breach of a contract

as·sump·tion \ə-'səm(p)-shən\ *n* [ME, fr. LL *assumption-, assumptio* taking up, fr. L *assumere*] (13c) **1 a** : the taking up of a person into heaven **b** *cap* : August 15 observed in commemoration of the Assumption of the Virgin Mary **2** : a taking to or upon oneself ⟨the ~ of a new position⟩ **3** : the act of laying claim to or taking possession of something ⟨the ~ of power⟩ **4** : ARROGANCE, PRETENSION **5 a** : an assuming that something is true **b** : a fact or statement (as a proposition, axiom, postulate, or notion) taken for granted **6** : the taking over of another's debts

as·sump·tive \ə-'səm(p)-tiv\ *adj* (1611) : of, relating to, or based on assumption

as·sur·ance \ə-'shur-ən(t)s\ *n* (14c) **1** : the act or action of assuring: as **a** : PLEDGE, GUARANTEE **b** : the act of conveying real property; *also* : the instrument by which it is conveyed **c** *chiefly Brit* : INSURANCE **2** : the state of being assured: as **a** : SECURITY **b** : a being certain in the mind ⟨the puritan's ~ of salvation⟩ **c** : confidence of mind or manner : easy freedom from self-doubt or uncertainty; *also* : excessive self-confidence : BRASHNESS, PRESUMPTION **3** : something that inspires or tends to inspire confidence ⟨gave repeated ~s of goodwill⟩ *syn* see CONFIDENCE

as·sure \ə-'shur\ *vt* **as·sured; as·sur·ing** [ME, fr. MF *assurer*, fr. ML *assecurare*, fr. L *ad-* + *securus* secure] (14c) **1** : to make safe (as from risks or against overthrow) : INSURE **2** : to give confidence to ⟨and hereby we know that we are of the truth, and shall ~ our hearts —1 Jn 3:19 (AV)⟩ **3** : to make sure or certain : CONVINCE ⟨glancing back to ~ himself no one was following⟩ **4** : to inform positively ⟨I ~ you that we will do better next time⟩ **5** : to make certain the coming or attainment of : GUARANTEE ⟨worked hard to ~ accuracy⟩ *syn* see ENSURE

¹**as·sured** \ə-'shurd\ *adj* (15c) **1** : characterized by certainty or security : GUARANTEED ⟨an ~ market⟩ **2 a** : SELF-ASSURED **b** : SELF-SATISFIED **3** : satisfied as to the certainty or truth of a matter ⟨rest ~ we got what we came for⟩ — **as·sured·ness** \-'shur-əd-nəs, -'shurd-\ *n*

²**assured** *n, pl* **assured** *or* **assureds** (1755) : INSURED

as·sured·ly \ə-'shur-əd-lē\ *adv* (14c) **1** : without a doubt : CERTAINLY **2** : in an assured manner : CONFIDENTLY

as·sur·er \ə-'shur-ər\ *or* **as·sur·or** \ə-'shur-ər, ə-,shur-'ȯr\ *n* (1607) : one that assures : INSURER

as·sur·gent \ə-'sər-jənt\ *adj* [L *assurgent-, assurgens*, prp. of *assurgere* to rise, fr. *ad-* + *surgere* to rise — more at SURGE] (1578) : moving upward : RISING; *esp* : ASCENDANT 1b

As·syr·i·an \ə-'sir-ē-ən\ *n* (15c) **1** : a native or inhabitant of ancient Assyria **2** : the dialect of Akkadian spoken by the Assyrians — **Assyrian** *adj*

As·syr·i·ol·o·gy \ə-,sir-ē-'ä-lə-jē\ *n* (1828) : the science or study of the history, language, and antiquities of ancient Assyria and Babylonia — **As·syr·i·o·log·i·cal** \-,sir-ē-ə-'lä-ji-kəl\ *adj* — **As·syr·i·ol·o·gist** \-'ä-lə-jist\ *n*

-ast *n suffix* [ME, fr. L *-astes*, fr. Gk *-astēs*, fr. verbs in *-azein*] : one connected with ⟨ecdysi*ast*⟩

astar·board \ə-'stär-bərd\ *adv* (ca. 1630) : toward or on the starboard side of a ship ⟨put the helm hard ~⟩

As·tar·te \ə-'stär-tē\ n [L, fr. Gk *Astartē*] : the Phoenician goddess of fertility and of sexual love

as·ta·tine \'as-tə-‚tēn\ n [Gk *astatos* unsteady, fr. *a-* + *statos* standing, fr. *histanai* to cause to stand — more at STAND] (1947) : a radioactive halogen element discovered by bombarding bismuth with alpha particles and also formed by radioactive decay — see ELEMENT table

as·ter \'as-tər\ n (1664) **1** [NL, fr. L, aster, fr. Gk *aster-, astēr* star, aster — more at STAR] **a** : any of various chiefly fall-blooming leafy-stemmed composite herbs (*Aster* and closely related genera) with often showy heads containing disk flowers or both disk and ray flowers **b** : CHINA ASTER **2** [NL, fr. Gk *aster-, astēr*] : a system of microtubules arranged radially about a centriole at either end of the mitotic or meiotic spindle

-aster n suffix [ME, fr. L, suffix denoting partial resemblance] : one that is inferior or not genuine ⟨critic*aster*⟩

as·te·ria \a-'stir-ē-ə\ n [L, a precious stone, fr. Gk, fem. of *asterios* starry, fr. *aster-, astēr*] : a gemstone cut to show asterism

as·te·ri·at·ed \-ē-‚ā-təd\ adj [Gk *asterios*] (1816) : exhibiting asterism ⟨~ sapphire⟩

¹as·ter·isk \'as-tə-‚risk, esp in plural also ÷-‚rik\ n [ME, astarisc, fr. LL asteriscus, fr. Gk *asteriskos*, lit., little star, dim. of *aster-, astēr*] (14c) : the character * used in printing or writing as a reference mark, as an indication of the omission of letters or words, to denote a hypothetical or unattested linguistic form, or for various arbitrary meanings — **as·ter·isk·less** \-ləs\ adj

²asterisk vt (ca. 1733) : to mark with an asterisk : STAR

as·ter·ism \'as-tə-‚ri-zəm\ n [Gk *asterismos*, fr. *asterizein* to arrange in constellations, fr. *aster-, astēr*] (1598) **1 a** : CONSTELLATION **b** : a small group of stars **2** : a star-shaped figure exhibited by some crystals by reflected light (as in a star sapphire) or by transmitted light (as in some mica)

astern \ə-'stərn\ adv or adj (1627) **1** : behind a ship **2** : at or toward the stern of a ship **3** : BACKWARD **: STERNFOREMOST, BACKWARD**

¹as·ter·oid \'as-tə-‚ròid\ n [Gk *asteroeidēs* starlike, fr. *aster-, astēr*] (1802) **1** : any of the small celestial bodies found esp. between the orbits of Mars and Jupiter **2** : STARFISH — **as·ter·oi·dal** \‚as-tə-'ròi-d²l\ adj

²asteroid adj (1854) **1** : resembling a star ⟨~ bodies in sporotrichosis⟩ **2** : of or resembling a starfish

asteroid belt n (1952) : the region of interplanetary space between the orbits of Mars and Jupiter in which most asteroids are found

aster yellows n pl (1922) : a widespread disease that affects more than 40 families of plants, is characterized esp. by yellowing and dwarfing, and is caused by a mycoplasma transmitted by leafhoppers

as·the·nia \as-'thē-nē-ə\ n [NL, fr. Gk *asthenes* weak, fr. *a-* + *sthenos* strength] (1802) : lack or loss of strength : DEBILITY

as·then·ic \as-'the-nik\ adj (1789) **1** : of, relating to, or exhibiting asthenia : WEAK **2** : ECTOMORPHIC 2

as·theno·sphere \as-'the-nə-‚sfir\ n [Gk *asthenes* weak + E -o- + sphere] (1914) : a hypothetical zone of a celestial body (as the earth) which lies beneath the lithosphere and within which the material is believed to yield readily to persistent stresses — **as·theno·spher·ic** \-‚the-nə-'sfir-ik, -'sfer-\ adj

asth·ma \'az-mə, Brit 'as-\ n [ME asma, fr. ML, modif. of Gk asthma] (14c) : a condition often of allergic origin that is marked by continuous or paroxysmal labored breathing accompanied by wheezing, by a sense of constriction in the chest, and often by attacks of coughing or gasping — **asth·mat·ic** \az-'ma-tik, Brit as-\ adj or n — **asth·mat·i·cal·ly** \-ti-k(ə-)lē\ adv

as though conj (13c) : AS IF

as·tig·mat·ic \‚as-tig-'ma-tik\ adj [a- + Gk *stigmat-, stigma* stigma] (1849) **1** : affected with, relating to, or correcting astigmatism **2** : showing incapacity for observation or discrimination ⟨an ~ fanaticism, a disregard for the facts —*N.Y. Herald Tribune*⟩ — **astigmatic** n

astig·ma·tism \ə-'stig-mə-‚ti-zəm\ n (1849) **1** : a defect of an optical system (as a lens) causing rays from a point to fail to meet in a focal point resulting in a blurred and imperfect image **2** : a defect of vision due to astigmatism of the refractive system of the eye and esp. to corneal irregularity **3** : distorted understanding suggestive of the blurred vision of an astigmatic person

astil·be \ə-'stil-(‚)bē\ n [NL, fr. ²a- + Gk *stilbē*, fem. of *stilbos* sparkling] : any of a genus (*Astilbe*) of chiefly Asian perennials of the saxifrage family having simple or usu. compound leaves and widely cultivated for their panicles of white or red flowers

astir \ə-'stər\ adj (1823) **1** : exhibiting activity **2** : being out of bed : UP

As·ti Spu·man·te \‚äs-tē-spü-'män-(‚)tē, ‚as-tē-, -spü-'man-\ n [It, fr. Asti, Italy + It spumante effervescent, lit., foaming] (1908) : a sweet sparkling white wine made in and around the village of Asti in Piedmont

as to prep (14c) **1** : AS FOR, ABOUT ⟨at a loss *as to* how to explain the error⟩ **2** : ACCORDING TO, BY ⟨graded *as to* size and color⟩

as·ton·ied \ə-'stä-nēd\ adj [ME, fr. pp. of astonien] (14c) **1** archaic : deprived briefly of the power to act : DAZED **2** archaic : filled with consternation or dismay

as·ton·ish \ə-'stä-nish\ vt [prob. fr. earlier astony (fr. ME astonen, astonien, fr. OF estoner, fr. — assumed — VL extonare, fr. L ex- + tonare to thunder) + -ish (as in abolish) — more at THUNDER] (1535) **1** obs : to strike with sudden fear **2** : to strike with sudden and usu. great wonder or surprise **syn** see SURPRISE

as·ton·ish·ing \-ni-shiŋ\ adj (1543) : causing astonishment : SURPRISING — **as·ton·ish·ing·ly** \-shiŋ-lē\ adv

as·ton·ish·ment \-'stä-nish-mənt\ n (ca. 1586) **1 a** : the state of being astonished **b** : CONSTERNATION **: AMAZEMENT 2** : a cause of amazement or wonder

¹as·tound \ə-'staùnd\ adj [ME astoned, fr. pp. of astonen] (14c) archaic : overwhelmed with astonishment or amazement : ASTOUNDED

²astound vt (1634) : to fill with bewilderment or wonder **syn** see SURPRISE

as·tound·ing \-'staùn-diŋ\ adj (1586) : causing astonishment or amazement — **as·tound·ing·ly** \-diŋ-lē\ adv

astr- or **astro-** comb form [ME astro-, fr. OF, fr. L astr-, astro-, fr. Gk, fr. astron — more at STAR] : star : heavens : outer space : astronomical ⟨astrophysics⟩

¹astrad·dle \ə-'stra-d²l\ adv (1703) : on or above and extending onto both sides : ASTRIDE

²astraddle prep (1935) : with one leg on each side of : ASTRIDE

as·tra·gal \'as-tri-gəl\ n [L astragalus, fr. Gk *astragalos* anklebone, molding; akin to Gk *astakos* lobster, *osteon* bone — more at OSSEOUS] (1563) **1** : a narrow half-round molding **2** : a projecting strip on the edge of a folding door

as·tra·khan \'as-trə-kən, -‚kan\ n, often cap [Astrakhan, Russia] (1766) **1** : karakul of Russian origin **2** : a cloth with a usu. wool, curled, and looped pile resembling karakul

as·tral \'as-trəl\ adj [LL astralis, fr. L astrum star, fr. Gk astron] (1605) **1** : of, relating to, or coming from the stars ⟨~ influences⟩ ⟨unusual ~ occurrences⟩ **2** : of or relating to a mitotic or meiotic aster **3** : of or consisting of a supersensible substance held in theosophy to be next above the tangible world in refinement **4 a** : VISIONARY **b** : elevated in station or position : EXALTED — **as·tral·ly** \-trə-lē\ adv

astray \ə-'strā\ adv or adj [ME, fr. MF estraié wandering, fr. estraier to stray — more at STRAY] (14c) **1** : off the right path or route : STRAYING **2** : in error : away from what is proper or desirable

¹astride \ə-'strīd\ adv (1664) **1** : with one leg on each side : astride a horse ⟨she rode ~, not sidesaddle⟩ **2** : with the legs stretched wide apart ⟨standing ~⟩

²astride prep (1713) **1** : on or above and with one leg on each side of **2** : placed or lying on both sides of **3** : extending over or across : SPANNING, BRIDGING

as·trin·gen·cy \ə-'strin-jən(t)-sē\ n (1601) : the quality or state of being astringent

¹as·trin·gent \-jənt\ adj [prob. fr. MF, fr. L astringent-, astringens, prp. of astringere to bind fast, fr. ad- + stringere to bind tight — more at STRAIN] (1541) **1** : able to draw together the soft organic tissues : STYPTIC, PUCKERY ⟨~ lotions⟩ ⟨an ~ fruit⟩ **2** : suggestive of an astringent effect upon tissue : rigidly severe : AUSTERE ⟨dry ~ comments⟩; also : PUNGENT, CAUSTIC — **as·trin·gent·ly** adv

²astringent n (1626) : an astringent agent or substance

as·tro·bi·ol·o·gy \‚as-trō-(‚)bī-'ä-lə-jē\ n (1955) : EXOBIOLOGY — **as·tro·bi·ol·o·gist** \-(‚)bī-'ä-lə-jist\ n

as·tro·cyte \'as-trə-‚sīt\ n [ISV] (1898) : a star-shaped cell (as of the neuroglia) — **as·tro·cyt·ic** \‚as-trə-'si-tik\ adj

as·tro·cy·to·ma \‚as-trə-sī-'tō-mə\ n, pl **-mas** or **-ma·ta** \-mə-tə\ [NL] (ca. 1923) : a nerve-tissue tumor composed of astrocytes

as·tro·dome \'as-trə-‚dōm\ n [ISV] (1941) : a transparent dome in the upper surface of an airplane from within which the navigator makes celestial observations

as·tro·labe \'as-trə-‚lāb also -‚lab\ n [ME, fr. MF & ML; MF, fr. ML astrolabium, fr. LGk astrolabion, fr. Gk astrolabos, fr. astr- + lambanein to take — more at LATCH] (14c) : a compact instrument used to observe and calculate the position of celestial bodies before the invention of the sextant

as·trol·o·ger \ə-'strä-lə-jər\ n (14c) : one who practices astrology

as·trol·o·gy \ə-'strä-lə-jē\ n [ME astrologie, fr. MF, fr. L astrologia, fr. Gk, fr. astr- + -logia -logy] (14c) **1** archaic : ASTRONOMY **2** : the divination of the supposed influences of the stars and planets on human affairs and terrestrial events by their positions and aspects — **as·tro·log·i·cal** \‚as-trə-'lä-ji-kəl\ adj — **as·tro·log·i·cal·ly** \-k(ə-)lē\ adv

as·trom·e·try \ə-'strä-mə-trē\ n (ca. 1859) : a branch of astronomy that deals with measurements (as of positions and movements) of celestial bodies — **as·tro·met·ric** \‚as-trə-'me-trik\ adj

as·tro·naut \'as-trə-‚nòt, -‚nät\ n [astr- + -naut (as in aeronaut)] (1929) : a person who travels beyond the earth's atmosphere; also : a trainee for spaceflight

as·tro·nau·tics \‚as-trə-'nò-tiks, -'nä-\ n pl but sing or pl in constr (1928) : the science of the construction and operation of vehicles for travel in space beyond the earth's atmosphere — **as·tro·nau·tic** \-tik\ or **as·tro·nau·ti·cal** \-ti-kəl\ adj — **as·tro·nau·ti·cal·ly** \-ti-k(ə-)lē\ adv

as·tron·o·mer \ə-'strä-nə-mər\ n (14c) : one who is skilled in astronomy or who makes observations of celestial phenomena

as·tro·nom·i·cal \‚as-trə-'nä-mi-kəl\ also **as·tro·nom·ic** \-mik\ adj (1556) **1** : of or relating to astronomy **2** : enormously or inconceivably large or great ⟨~ numbers⟩ — **as·tro·nom·i·cal·ly** \-mi-k(ə-)lē\ adv

astronomical unit n (1903) : a unit of length used in astronomy equal to the mean distance of the earth from the sun or about 93 million miles (150 million kilometers)

as·tron·o·my \ə-'strä-nə-mē\ n, pl **-mies** [ME astronomie, fr. OF, fr. L astronomia, fr. Gk, fr. astr- + -nomia -nomy] (13c) : the study of objects and matter outside the earth's atmosphere and of their physical and chemical properties

as·tro·pho·tog·ra·phy \‚as-(‚)trō-fə-'tä-grə-fē\ n [ISV] (ca. 1858) : photography as used in astronomical investigations — **as·tro·pho·to·graph** \-'fō-tə-‚graf\ n — **as·tro·pho·tog·ra·pher** \-fə-'tä-grə-fər\ n

as·tro·phys·ics \‚as-trə-'fi-ziks\ n pl but sing or pl in constr [ISV] (1890) : a branch of astronomy dealing esp. with the behavior, physical properties, and dynamic processes of celestial objects and phenomena — **as·tro·phys·i·cal** \-zi-kəl\ adj — **as·tro·phys·i·cal·ly** \-zi-k(ə-)lē\ adv — **as·tro·phys·i·cist** \-'fi-zə-sist, -'fiz-ə-\ n

as·tute \ə-'stüt, a-, -'styüt\ adj [L astutus, fr. astus craft] (ca. 1611) : having or showing shrewdness and perspicacity ⟨an ~ observer⟩ ⟨~ remarks⟩; also : CRAFTY, WILY **syn** see SHREWD — **as·tute·ly** adv — **as·tute·ness** n

As·ty·a·nax \ə-'stī-ə-‚naks\ n [Gk] : a son of Hector and Andromache hurled by the Greeks from the walls of Troy

asun·der \ə-'sən-dər\ adv or adj (14c) **1** : into parts ⟨torn ~⟩ **2** : apart from each other in position ⟨wide ~⟩

aswarm \ə-'swòrm\ adj (ca. 1869) : filled to overflowing : SWARMING ⟨streets ~ with people⟩

\ə\ abut \ᵊ\ kitten, F table \ər\ further \a\ ash \ā\ ace \ä\ mop, mar \aù\ out \ch\ chin \e\ bet \ē\ easy \g\ go \i\ hit \ī\ ice \j\ job \ŋ\ sing \ō\ go \ò\ law \òi\ boy \th\ thin \t͟h\ the \ü\ loot \ù\ foot \y\ yet \zh\ vision \ä, k̲, ⁿ, œ, œ̄, ᵫ, ᵫ̄, ᵼ\ see Guide to Pronunciation

¹as well as *conj* (15c) : and in addition : AND ⟨brave *as well as* loyal⟩
²as well as *prep* (1589) : in addition to : BESIDES ⟨the coach, *as well as* the team, is ready⟩
aswirl \ə-'swər(-ə)l\ *adj* (1877) : being in a swirl : SWIRLING
aswoon \ə-'swün\ *adj* (14c) : being in a swoon : DAZED
asy·lum \ə-'sī-ləm\ *n* [ME, fr. L, fr. Gk *asylon*, neut. of *asylos* inviolable, fr. *a-* + *sylon* right of seizure] (15c) **1** : an inviolable place of refuge and protection giving shelter to criminals and debtors : SANCTUARY **2** : a place of retreat and security : SHELTER **3 a** : the protection or inviolability afforded by an asylum : REFUGE **b** : protection from arrest and extradition given esp. to political refugees by a nation or by an embassy or other agency enjoying diplomatic immunity **4** : an institution for the care of the destitute or sick and esp. the insane
asym·met·ri·cal \ˌā-sə-'me-tri-kəl\ *or* **asym·met·ric** \-trik\ *adj* [Gk *asymmetria* lack of proportion, fr. *asymmetros* ill-proportioned, fr. *a-* + *symmetros* symmetrical] (1690) **1** : not symmetrical **2** *usu asymmetric, of a carbon atom* : bonded to four different atoms or groups — **asym·met·ri·cal·ly** \-tri-k(ə-)lē\ *adv* — **asym·me·try** \(ˌ)ā-'si-mə-trē\ *n*
asymp·tom·at·ic \ˌā-ˌsim(p)-tə-'ma-tik\ *adj* (1927) : presenting no symptoms of disease — **asymp·tom·at·i·cal·ly** \-ti-k(ə-)lē\ *adv*
as·ymp·tote \'a-səm(p)-ˌtōt\ *n* [prob. fr. (assumed) NL *asymptotus*, fr. Gk *asymptōtos* not meeting, fr. *a-* + *sympiptein* to meet — more at SYMPTOM] (1656) : a straight line associated with a curve such that as a point moves along an infinite branch of the curve the distance from the point to the line approaches zero and the slope of the curve at the point approaches the slope of the line — **as·ymp·tot·ic** \ˌa-səm(p)-'tä-tik\ *adj* — **as·ymp·tot·i·cal·ly** \-ti-k(ə-)lē\ *adv*
asyn·ap·sis \ˌā-sə-'nap-səs\ *n*, *pl* **-ap·ses** \-ˌsēz\ [NL ²*a-* + *synapsis*] (1930) : failure of pairing of homologous chromosomes in meiosis
asyn·chro·nous \(ˌ)ā-'siŋ-krə-nəs, -'sin-\ *adj* (1748) **1** : not synchronous **2** : of, used in, or being digital communication (as between computers) in which there is no timing requirement for transmission and in which the start of each character is individually signaled by the transmitting device — **asyn·chro·nous·ly** *adv*
asyn·chro·ny \-krə-nē\ *or* **asyn·chro·nism** \-krə-ˌni-zəm\ *n* (1875) : the quality or state of being asynchronous : absence or lack of concurrence in time
as·yn·det·ic \ˌa-sᵉn-'de-tik\ *adj* (ca. 1864) : marked by asyndeton — **as·yn·det·i·cal·ly** \-ti-k(ə-)lē\ *adv*
asyn·de·ton \ə-'sin-də-ˌtän, (ˌ)ā-'sin-\ *n*, *pl* **-tons** *or* **-ta** \-də-tə\ [LL, fr. Gk, fr. neut. of *asyndetos* unconnected, fr. *a-* + *syndetos* bound together, fr. *syndein* to bind together, fr. *syn-* + *dein* to bind — more at DIADEM] (1555) : omission of the conjunctions that ordinarily join coordinate words or clauses (as in "I came, I saw, I conquered")
¹at \ət, 'at\ *prep* [ME, fr. OE *æt*; akin to OHG *az* at, L *ad*] (bef. 12c) **1** — used as a function word to indicate presence or occurrence in, on, or near ⟨staying ~ a hotel⟩ ⟨~ a party⟩ ⟨sick ~ heart⟩ **2** — used as a function word to indicate the goal of an indicated or implied action or motion ⟨aim ~ the target⟩ ⟨creditors are ~ him again⟩ **3** — used as a function word to indicate that with which one is occupied or employed ⟨~ work⟩ ⟨~ the controls⟩ ⟨good ~ chess⟩ **4** — used as a function word to indicate situation in an active or passive state or condition ⟨~ liberty⟩ ⟨~ rest⟩ **5** — used as a function word to indicate the means, cause, or manner ⟨sold ~ auction⟩ ⟨laughed ~ my joke⟩ ⟨act ~ your own discretion⟩ **6 a** — used as a function word to indicate the rate, degree, or position in a scale or series ⟨the temperature ~ 90⟩ ⟨~ first⟩ **b** — used as a function word to indicate age or position in time ⟨will retire ~ 65⟩
²at \'ät\ *n*, *pl* **at** [Lao] (1955) — see *kip* at MONEY table
at- — see AD-
At·a·brine \'a-tə-brən, -ˌbrēn\ *trademark* — used for quinacrine
atac·tic \(ˌ)ā-'tak-tik\ *adj* [ISV ²*a-* + *-tactic*] (1957) : of, relating to, or being a polymer exhibiting no stereochemical regularity of structure ⟨~ polypropylene⟩ — compare ISOTACTIC
At·a·lan·ta \ˌa-tᵊl-'an-tə\ *n* [L, fr. Gk *Atalantē*] : a fleet-footed huntress in Greek mythology who challenges her suitors to a race and is defeated by Hippomenes when she stops to pick up three golden apples he has dropped
at all *adv* (14c) : in any way or respect : to the least extent or degree : under any circumstances ⟨doesn't smoke *at all*⟩
at·a·man \ˌa-tə-'man\ *n* [Russ] (1835) : HETMAN
at·a·mas·co lily \ˌa-tə-'mas-(ˌ)kō-\ *n* [Virginia Algonquian *attamusco*] (1743) : any of a genus (*Zephyranthes*) of American bulbous herbs of the amaryllis family with pink, white, or yellowish flowers; *esp* : one (*Z. atamasco*) of the southeastern U.S. with white flowers usu. tinged with purple
at·a·rac·tic \ˌa-tə-'rak-tik\ *or* **at·a·rax·ic** \-'rak-sik\ *n* [ataractic fr. Gk *ataraktos* calm, fr. *a-* + *tarassein* to disturb; ataraxic fr. Gk *ataraxia* calmness, fr. *a-* + *tarassein*] (1955) : TRANQUILIZER — **2** — **ataractic** *or* **ataraxic** *adj*
at·a·vism \'a-tə-ˌvi-zəm\ *n* [F *atavisme*, fr. L *atavus* ancestor, fr. *at-* (prob. akin to *atta* daddy) + *avus* grandfather — more at UNCLE] (1833) **1 a** : recurrence in an organism of a trait or character typical of an ancestral form and usu. due to genetic recombination **b** : recurrence of or reversion to a past style, manner, outlook, or approach ⟨architectural ~⟩ **2** : one that manifests atavism : THROWBACK — **at·a·vis·tic** \ˌa-tə-'vis-tik\ *adj* — **at·a·vis·ti·cal·ly** \-ti-k(ə-)lē\ *adv*
atax·ia \ə-'tak-sē-ə, (ˌ)ā-\ *n* [Gk, fr. *a-* + *tassein* to put in order] (1670) : an inability to coordinate voluntary muscular movements that is symptomatic of some nervous disorders — **atax·ic** \-sik\ *adj*
at bat *n* (1884) : an official time at bat charged to a baseball batter except when he walks, sacrifices, is hit by a pitched ball, or is interfered with by the catcher ⟨three hits in five *at bats*⟩
ate *past of* EAT
Ate \'ä-tē, 'ā-(ˌ)tē; 'ä-ˌtā\ *n* [Gk *Atē*] : a Greek goddess personifying foolhardy and ruinous impulse
¹-ate *n suffix* [ME -*at*, fr. OF, fr. L -*atus*, -*atum*, masc. & neut. of -*atus*, pp. ending] **1** : one acted upon (in a specified way) ⟨distill*ate*⟩ **2** [NL -*atum*, fr. L] : chemical compound or complex anion derived from a (specified) compound or element ⟨phenol*ate*⟩; *esp* : salt or ester of an acid with a name ending in -*ic* and not beginning with *hydro-* ⟨borate⟩
²-ate *n suffix* [ME -*at*, fr. OF, fr. L -*atus*, fr. -*a-*, stem vowel of 1st conj. + -*tus*, suffix of verbal nouns] **1** : office : function : rank : group of persons holding a (specified) office or rank or having a (specified) function ⟨vicar*ate*⟩ **2** : state : dominion : jurisdiction ⟨emir*ate*⟩ ⟨khan*ate*⟩
³-ate *adj suffix* [ME -*at*, L -*atus*, fr. pp. ending of 1st conj. verbs, fr. -*a-*, stem vowel of 1st conj. + -*tus*, pp. suffix — more at -ED] : marked by having ⟨cran*iate*⟩
⁴-ate *vb suffix* [ME -*aten*, fr. L -*atus*, pp. ending] : act on (in a specified way) ⟨insul*ate*⟩ : cause to be modified or affected by ⟨camphor*ate*⟩ : cause to become ⟨activ*ate*⟩ : furnish with ⟨capacit*ate*⟩
-ated *adj suffix* : ³-ATE ⟨pile*ated*⟩
at·el·ec·ta·sis \ˌa-tᵊl-'ek-tə-səs\ *n*, *pl* **-ta·ses** \-ˌsēz\ [NL, fr. Gk *atelēs* incomplete, defective (fr. *a-* ²*a-* + *telos* end) + *ektasis* extension, fr. *ekteinein* to stretch out, fr. *ex-* + *teinein* to stretch — more at TELOS, THIN] (1859) : collapse of the expanded lung; *also* : defective expansion of the pulmonary alveoli at birth
ate·lier \ˌa-tᵊl-'yā\ *n* [F, fr. MF *astelier* woodpile, fr. *astele* splinter, fr. LL *astella*, dim. of L *astula*] (1699) **1** : an artist's or designer's studio or workroom **2** : WORKSHOP
ate·moya \ˌä-tə-'mȯi-ə, ˌa-\ *n* [*ates* sweetsop (fr. Tag) + cheri*moya*] (1914) : a white-pulped tropical fruit of a tree that is a hybrid of the sweetsop and the cherimoya
a tem·po \ä-'tem-(ˌ)pō\ *adv or adj* [It] (ca. 1740) : in time — used as a direction in music to return to the original tempo
atem·po·ral \(ˌ)ā-'tem-p(ə-)rəl\ *adj* (1870) : independent of or unaffected by time : TIMELESS
Ate·ri·an \ə-'tir-ē-ən\ *adj* [F *atérien*, fr. Bir el-*Ater* (Constantine), Algeria] (1928) : of or relating to a Paleolithic culture of northern Africa characterized by Mousterian features, tanged arrow points, and leafshaped spearheads
Ath·a·bas·can \ˌa-thə-'bas-kən\ *or* **Ath·a·pas·kan** \-'pas-\ *also* **Ath·a·bas·kan** \-'bas-\ *or* **Ath·a·pas·can** \-'pas-\ *n* [*Athabasca*, a Cree band, fr. Cree dial. *aδapaskaˑw*, name for the area east of Lake Athabasca, lit., (where) there are reeds one after another] (1846) **1** : a family of American Indian languages spoken primarily in western Canada, Alaska, and the U.S. Southwest **2** : a member of a people speaking an Athabascan language
Ath·a·na·sian \ˌa-thə-'nā-zhən, -shən\ *adj* (1586) : of or relating to Athanasius or his advocacy of the homoousian doctrine against Arianism
Athanasian Creed *n* (1586) : a Christian creed originating in Europe about A.D. 400 and relating esp. to the Trinity and Incarnation
athe·ism \'ā-thē-ˌi-zəm\ *n* [MF *athéisme*, fr. *athée* atheist, fr. Gk *atheos* godless, fr. *a-* + *theos* god] (1546) **1** *archaic* : UNGODLINESS, WICKEDNESS **2 a** : a disbelief in the existence of deity **b** : the doctrine that there is no deity
athe·ist \'ā-thē-ist\ *n* (1571) : one who denies the existence of God — **athe·is·tic** \ˌā-thē-'is-tik\ *or* **athe·is·ti·cal** \ˌā-thē-'is-ti-kəl\ *adj* — **athe·is·ti·cal·ly** \-ti-k(ə-)lē\ *adv*
ath·e·ling \'a-thə-liŋ, -thə-\ *n* [ME, fr. OE *ætheling*, fr. *æthelu* nobility, akin to OHG *adal* nobility] (bef. 12c) : an Anglo-Saxon prince or nobleman; *esp* : the heir apparent or a prince of the royal family
Athe·na \ə-'thē-nə\ *or* **Athe·ne** \-nē\ *n* [L *Athena*, fr. Gk *Athēnē*] : the Greek goddess of wisdom — compare MINERVA
ath·e·nae·um *or* **ath·e·ne·um** \ˌa-thə-'nē-əm\ *n* [L *Athenaeum*, a school in ancient Rome for the study of arts, fr. Gk *Athēnaion*, a temple of Athena, fr. *Athēnē*] (1799) **1** : a building or room in which books, periodicals, and newspapers are kept for use **2** : a literary or scientific association
athe·o·ret·i·cal \ˌā-ˌthē-ə-'re-ti-kəl, -ˌthi(-ə)r-'e-\ *adj* (1969) : not based on or concerned with theory
athero- *comb form* [Gk *athēra*] : atheroma ⟨*athero*genic⟩
ath·ero·gen·e·sis \ˌa-thə-rō-'je-nə-səs\ *n* (1953) : the process of developing atheroma
ath·ero·gen·ic \-'je-nik\ *adj* (1954) : relating to or producing degenerative changes in arterial walls ⟨~ diet⟩
ath·er·o·ma \ˌa-thə-'rō-mə\ *n* [NL *atheromat-, atheroma*, fr. L, a tumor containing matter resembling gruel, fr. Gk *athērōma*, fr. *athēra* gruel] (1875) **1** : fatty degeneration of the inner coat of the arteries **2** : an abnormal fatty deposit in an artery — **ath·er·o·ma·tous** \-'rō-mə-təs\ *adj*
ath·ero·scle·ro·sis \ˌa-thə-ˌrō-sklə-'rō-səs\ *n* [NL] (1910) : an arteriosclerosis characterized by atheromatous deposits and fibrosis of the inner layer of the arteries — **ath·ero·scle·rot·ic** \-sklə-'rä-tik\ *adj*
athirst \ə-'thərst\ *adj* [ME, fr. OE *ofthyrst*, pp. of *ofthyrstan* to suffer from thirst, fr. *of-* off, from + *thyrstan* to thirst — more at OF] (bef. 12c) **1** *archaic* : THIRSTY **2** : having a strong eager desire ⟨I that for ever feel ~ for glory —John Keats⟩ *syn* see EAGER
ath·lete \'ath-ˌlēt, ÷'a-thə-ˌlēt\ *n* [ME, fr. L *athleta*, fr. Gk *athlētēs*, fr. *athlein* to contend for a prize, fr. *athlon* prize, contest] (15c) : a person who is trained or skilled in exercises, sports, or games requiring physical strength, agility, or stamina
athlete's foot *n* (1928) : ringworm of the feet
ath·let·ic \ath-'le-tik, ÷ˌa-thə-'le-\ *adj* (1636) **1** : of or relating to athletes or athletics **2** : characteristic of an athlete; *esp* : VIGOROUS, ACTIVE **3** : MESOMORPHIC **4** : used by athletes — **ath·let·i·cal·ly** \-ti-k(ə-)lē\ *adv* — **ath·let·i·cism** \-'le-tə-ˌsi-zəm\ *n*
ath·let·ics \ath-'le-tiks, ÷ˌa-thə-'le-\ *n pl but sing or pl in constr* (1727) **1** : exercises, sports, or games engaged in by athletes **2** : the practice or principles of athletic activities
athletic supporter *n* (1927) : a supporter for the genitals worn by men participating in sports or strenuous activities
at–home \ət-'hōm\ *adj* (1951) **1** : intended or suitable for one's home ⟨an ~ dress⟩ **2** : being or occurring at one's home ⟨~ entertainment⟩
at home *n* (1745) : a reception given at one's home
-athon *n comb form* [mar*athon*] : event or activity lasting a long time ⟨talk*athon*⟩
ath·ro·cyte \'a-thrə-ˌsīt\ *n* [Gk *athroos* together, collected + ISV -*cyte*] (1938) : a cell that has the ability to store up substances of an excretory nature

¹**athwart** \ə-'thwȯrt, *naut often* -'thȯrt\ *prep* (15c) **1** : ACROSS **2** : in opposition to ⟨a procedure directly ~ the New England prejudices — R. G. Cole⟩

²**athwart** *adv* (ca. 1500) **1** : across esp. in an oblique direction **2** : in opposition to the right or expected course ⟨and quite ~ goes all decorum —Shak.⟩

athwart·ship \-,ship\ *adj* (1879) : being across the ship from side to side ⟨~ and longitudinal framing⟩

athwart·ships \-,ships\ *adv* (1718) : across the ship from side to side

atilt \ə-'tilt\ *adv or adj* (1562) **1** : in a tilted position **2** : with lance in hand ⟨run ~ at death —Shak.⟩

atin·gle \ə-'tiŋ-gəl\ *adj* (1855) : tingling esp. with excitement

-ation *n suffix* [ME -*acioun*, fr. OF -*ation*, fr. L -*ation*-, -*atio*, fr. -*a*-, stem vowel of 1st conj. + -*tion*-, -*tio*, n. suffix] : action or process ⟨flirt*ation*⟩ : something connected with an action or process ⟨discolor*ation*⟩

-ative *adj suffix* [ME, fr. MF -*atif*, fr. L -*ativus*, fr. -*atus* -ate + -*ivus* -ive] : of, relating to, or connected with ⟨authorit*ative*⟩ : tending to ⟨talk*ative*⟩

At·ka mackerel \'at-kə-, 'ät-\ *n* [*Atka* Island, Alaska] (1893) : a greenling (*Pleurogrammus monopterygius*) of Alaska and adjacent regions valued as a food fish

¹**At·lan·te·an** \,at-,lan-'tē-ən, ət-'lan-tē-\ *adj* (1667) : of, relating to, or resembling Atlas : STRONG

²**Atlantean** *adj* (ca. 1828) : of or relating to Atlantis

At·lan·tic \ət-'lan-tik, at-\ *adj* (1601) **1 a** : of, relating to, or found in, on, or near the Atlantic Ocean **b** : of, relating to, or found on or near the east coast of the U.S. **2** : of relating to the nations that border the Atlantic Ocean ⟨the ~ community⟩

Atlantic croaker *n* (ca. 1949) : a small fish (*Micropogonias undulatus*) of the Gulf coast and the Atlantic coast — called also *hardhead*

At·lan·ti·cism \-'lan-tə-,si-zəm\ *n* (1950) : a policy of military cooperation between European powers and the U.S. — **At·lan·ti·cist** \-sist\ *n*

Atlantic salmon *n* (1902) : SALMON 1a

Atlantic time *n* (ca. 1909) : the time of the fourth time zone west of Greenwich that includes the Canadian Maritime Provinces, Puerto Rico, and the Virgin Islands

At·lan·tis \ət-'lan-təs, at-\ *n* [L, fr. Gk, fr. *Atlas*] : a fabled island in the Atlantic that according to legend sank beneath the sea

at·las \'at-ləs\ *n* [L *Atlant*-, *Atlas*, fr. Gk] **1** *cap* : a Titan who for his part in the Titans' revolt against the gods is forced by Zeus to support the heavens on his shoulders **2** *cap* : one who bears a heavy burden **3 a** : a bound collection of maps often including illustrations, informative tables, or textual matter **b** : a bound collection of tables, charts, or plates **4** : the first vertebra of the neck **5** *pl usu* **at·lan·tes** \ət-'lan-(,)tēz, at-\ : a male figure used like a caryatid as a supporting column or pilaster — called also *telamon*

at·latl \'ät-,lät-³l\ *n* [Nahuatl *ahtlatl*] (1871) : a device for throwing a spear or dart that consists of a rod or board with a projection (as a hook or thong) at the rear end to hold the weapon in place until released

At·li \'ät-lē\ *n* [ON] : a king of the Huns figuring in Germanic legend and corresponding to the historical Attila

at·man \'ät-mən, -,män\ *n, often cap* [Skt *ātman*, lit., breath, soul; akin to OE *æthm* breath] (1785) **1** *Hinduism* : the innermost essence of each individual **2** *Hinduism* : the supreme universal self : BRAHMA 2

at·mom·e·ter \at-'mä-mə-tər\ *n* [Gk *atmos* + E -*meter*] (1815) : an instrument for measuring the evaporating capacity of the air

at·mo·sphere \'at-mə-,sfir\ *n* [NL *atmosphaera*, fr. Gk *atmos* vapor + L *sphaera* sphere] (1677) **1 a** : the gaseous envelope of a celestial body (as a planet) **b** : the whole mass of air surrounding the earth **2** : the air of a locality **3** : a surrounding influence or environment ⟨an ~ of hostility⟩ **4** : a unit of pressure equal to the pressure of the air at sea level or approximately 14.7 pounds per square inch (101,325 pascals) **5** : the overall aesthetic effect of a work of art **b** : a dominant aesthetic or emotional effect or appeal — **at·mo·sphered** \-,sfird\ *adj*

at·mo·spher·ic \,at-mə-'sfir-ik, -'sfer-\ *adj* (1783) **1 a** : of, relating to, or occurring in the atmosphere **b** : resembling the atmosphere : AIRY **2** : having, marked by, or contributing aesthetic or emotional atmosphere — **at·mo·spher·i·cal·ly** \-i-k(ə-)lē\ *adv*

at·mo·spher·ics \-iks\ *n pl* (1915) **1** : audible disturbances produced in radio receiving apparatus by atmospheric electrical phenomena (as lightning); *also* : the electrical phenomena causing these disturbances **2** : actions (as official statements) intended to create or suggest a particular atmosphere or mood in politics and esp. international relations; *also* : the mood so created or suggested **3** : realistic detail added (as to a literary work) to create a mood

atoll \'a-,tȯl, -,täl, -,tōl, 'ā-\ *n* [Divehi (Indo-Aryan language of the Maldive Islands) *atolu*] (1625) : a coral island consisting of a reef surrounding a lagoon

at·om \'a-təm\ *n* [ME, fr. L *atomus*, fr. Gk *atomos*, fr. *atomos* indivisible, fr. *a*- + *temnein* to cut] (15c) **1** : one of the minute indivisible particles of which according to ancient materialism the universe is composed **2** : a tiny particle : BIT **3** : the smallest particle of an element that can exist either alone or in combination **4** : the atom considered as a source of vast potential energy

atoll

atom·ic \ə-'tä-mik\ *adj* (1678) **1 a** : of, relating to, or concerned with atoms ⟨~ physics⟩ **b** : NUCLEAR 2 ⟨~ energy⟩ **2 a** : marked by acceptance of the theory of atomism **b** : ATOMISTIC 2 **3** : MINUTE **4** *of a chemical element* : existing in the state of separate atoms — **atom·i·cal·ly** \-mi-k(ə-)lē\ *adv*

atomic bomb *n* (1914) **1** : a bomb whose violent explosive power is due to the sudden release of energy resulting from the splitting of nuclei of a heavy chemical element (as plutonium or uranium) by neutrons in a very rapid chain reaction — called also *atom bomb* **2** : a nuclear weapon (as a hydrogen bomb)

atomic clock *n* (1938) : a precision clock that depends for its operation on an electrical oscillator regulated by the natural vibration frequencies of an atomic system (as a beam of cesium atoms)

atomic mass *n* (1898) : the mass of an atom usu. expressed in atomic mass units; *also* : ATOMIC WEIGHT

atomic mass unit *n* (ca. 1942) : a unit of mass for expressing masses of atoms, molecules, or nuclear particles equal to $1/12$ the mass of a single atom of the most abundant carbon isotope ^{12}C — called also *dalton*

atomic number *n* (1821) : an experimentally determined number characteristic of a chemical element that represents the number of protons in the nucleus which in a neutral atom equals the number of electrons outside the nucleus and that determines the place of the element in the periodic table — see ELEMENT table

atomic reactor *or* **atomic pile** *n* (1945) : REACTOR 3b

atomic theory *n* (ca. 1847) **1** : a theory of the nature of matter: all material substances are composed of minute particles or atoms of a comparatively small number of kinds and all the atoms of the same kind are uniform in size, weight, and other properties **2** : any of several theories of the structure of the atom; *esp* : one based on experimentation and theoretical considerations holding that the atom is composed essentially of a small positively charged comparatively heavy nucleus surrounded by a comparatively large arrangement of electrons

atomic weight *n* (1820) : the mass of one atom of an element; *specif* : the average mass of an atom of an element as it occurs in nature that is expressed in atomic mass units — see ELEMENT table

at·om·ise, at·om·is·er *Brit var of* ATOMIZE, ATOMIZER

at·om·ism \'a-tə-,mi-zəm\ *n* (1678) **1** : a doctrine that the physical or physical and mental universe is composed of simple indivisible minute particles **2** : INDIVIDUALISM 1 — **at·om·ist** \-mist\ *n*

at·om·is·tic \,a-tə-'mis-tik\ *adj* (1809) **1** : of or relating to atoms or atomism **2** : composed of many simple elements; *also* : characterized by or resulting from division into unconnected or antagonistic fragments ⟨an ~ society⟩ — **at·om·is·ti·cal·ly** \-ti-k(ə-)lē\ *adv*

at·om·ize \'a-tə-,mīz\ *vt* -ized; -iz·ing (1845) **1** : to treat as made up of many discrete units **2** : to reduce to minute particles or to a fine spray **3** : DIVIDE, FRAGMENT **4** : to subject to attack by nuclear weapons — **at·om·iza·tion** \,a-tə-mə-'zā-shən\ *n*

at·om·iz·er \'a-tə-,mī-zər\ *n* (1865) : an instrument for atomizing usu. a perfume, disinfectant, or medicament

atom smasher *n* (1937) : ACCELERATOR d

at·o·my \'a-tə-mē\ *n, pl* -mies [irreg. fr. L *atomi*, pl. of *atomus* atom] (1591) : a tiny particle : ATOM, MITE

aton·al \(,)ā-'tō-n³l, ,a-\ *adj* [²*a*- + *tonal*] (1922) : marked by avoidance of traditional musical tonality; *esp* : organized without reference to key or tonal center and using the tones of the chromatic scale impartially — **aton·al·ism** \-n³l-,i-zəm\ *n* — **aton·al·ist** \-ist\ *n* — **aton·al·i·ty** \,ā-tō-'na-lə-tē, ,a-\ *n* — **aton·al·ly** \(,)ā-'tō-n³l-ē, (,)a-\ *adv*

atone \ə-'tōn\ *vb* **atoned**; **aton·ing** [ME, to become reconciled, fr. *at on* in harmony, fr. *at* + *one*] *vt* (1593) **1** *obs* : RECONCILE **2** : to supply satisfaction for : EXPIATE ~ *vi* : to make amends

atone·ment \ə-'tōn-mənt\ *n* (1513) **1** *obs* : RECONCILIATION **2** : the reconciliation of God and man through the sacrificial death of Jesus Christ **3** : reparation for an offense or injury : SATISFACTION **4** *Christian Science* : the exemplifying of man's oneness with God

aton·ic \(,)ā-'tä-nik, (,)a-\ *adj* (1792) **1** : characterized by atony **2** : uttered without accent or stress

at·o·ny \'a-t³n-ē\ *n* [LL *atonia*, fr. Gk, fr. *atonos* without tone, fr. *a*- + *tonos* tone] (1693) : lack of physiological tone esp. of a contractile organ

¹**atop** \ə-'täp\ *prep* (1655) : on top of

²**atop** *adv or adj* (1658) : on, to, or at the top

at·o·py \'a-tə-pē\ *n* [Gk *atopia* uncommonness, fr. *atopos* out of the way, uncommon, fr. *a*- + *topos* place] (1923) : a prob. hereditary allergy characterized by symptoms (as asthma, hay fever, or hives) produced upon exposure to the exciting antigen without inoculation — **atop·ic** \(,)ā-'tä-pik, -'tō-\ *adj*

-ator *n suffix* [ME -*atour*, fr. OF & L; OF, fr. L -*ator*, fr. -*a*-, stem vowel of 1st conj. + -*tor*, agent suffix] : one that does ⟨totaliz*ator*⟩

ATP \,ā-,tē-'pē\ *n* [*adenosine triphosphate*] (1939) : a phosphorylated nucleoside $C_{10}H_{16}N_5O_{13}P_3$ of adenine that supplies energy for many biochemical cellular processes by undergoing enzymatic hydrolysis esp. to ADP — called also *adenosine triphosphate*

ATPase \,ā-,tē-'pē-,ās, -,āz\ *n* (1946) : an enzyme that hydrolyzes ATP; *esp* : one that hydrolyzes ATP to ADP and inorganic phosphate

at·ra·bil·ious \,a-trə-'bil-yəs\ *adj* [L *atra bilis* black bile] (1651) **1** : given to or marked by melancholy : GLOOMY **2** : ILL-NATURED, PEEVISH — **at·ra·bil·ious·ness** *n*

at·ra·zine \'a-trə-,zēn\ *n* [perh. fr. *amino* + *triazine*] (1962) : a photosynthesis-inhibiting persistent herbicide $C_8H_{14}ClN_5$ used esp. to kill annual weeds and quack grass

atrem·ble \ə-'trem-bəl\ *adj* (1862) : shaking involuntarily : TREMBLING ⟨he was white as death and all ~ —Robert Coover⟩

atre·sia \ə-'trē-zhə\ *n* [NL, fr. ²*a*- + Gk *trēsis* perforation, fr. *tetrainein* to pierce — more at THROW] (ca. 1807) **1** : absence or closure of a natural passage of the body **2** : absence or disappearance of an anatomical part (as an ovarian follicle) by degeneration

Atreus \'ā-,trüs, -trē-əs\ *n* [Gk] : a king of Mycenae and father of Agamemnon and Menelaus

atrial natriuretic factor *n* (1984) : a peptide hormone secreted by the cardiac atria that stimulates natriuresis and diuresis and helps regulate blood pressure

atrio·ven·tric·u·lar \,ā-trē-ō-ven-'tri-kyə-lər, -vən-\ *adj* [NL *atrium* + E *ventricular*] (ca. 1860) : of, relating to, or located between an atrium and ventricle of the heart

atrioventricular node *n* (ca. 1934) : a small mass of tissue in the right atrioventricular region of higher vertebrates through which impulses from the sinoatrial node are passed to the ventricles

---

\ə\ abut \ᵊ\ kitten, F table \ər\ further \a\ ash \ā\ ace \ä\ mop, mar \aù\ out \ch\ chin \e\ bet \ē\ easy \g\ go \i\ hit \ī\ ice \j\ job \ŋ\ sing \ō\ go \ȯ\ law \ȯi\ boy \th\ thin \th\ the \ü\ loot \ù\ foot \y\ yet \zh\ vision \à, ḵ, ⁿ, œ, œ̄, ᵫ, ᵭ, ʸ\ *see* Guide to Pronunciation

atrip \ə-'trip\ *adj* (1796) *of an anchor* : AWEIGH

atri·um \'ā-trē-əm\ *n, pl* **atria** \-trē-ə\ *also* **atri·ums** [L] (1577)   1 : the central room of a Roman house   2 *pl usu* **atriums** : a rectangularly shaped open patio around which a house is built; *also* : a many-storied court in a building (as a hotel) usu. with a skylight   3 [NL, fr. L] : an anatomical cavity or passage; *esp* : the chamber or either of the chambers of the heart that receives blood from the veins and forces it into the ventricle or ventricles — see HEART illustration — **atri·al** \-trē-əl\ *adj*

atro·cious \ə-'trō-shəs\ *adj* [L *atroc-, atrox* gloomy, atrocious, fr. *atr-, ater* black + *-oc-, -ox* (akin to Gk *ōps* eye) — more at EYE] (1669)   1 : extremely wicked, brutal, or cruel : BARBARIC   2 : APPALLING, HORRIFYING (the ~ weapons of modern war)   3 **a** : utterly revolting : ABOMINABLE (~ working conditions)   **b** : of very poor quality (~ handwriting) — **atro·cious·ly** *adv* — **atro·cious·ness** *n*

atroc·i·ty \ə-'trä-sə-tē\ *n, pl* **-ties** (1534)   1 : the quality or state of being atrocious   2 : an atrocious act, object, or situation (the . . . sufferings and *atrocities* of trench warfare —Aldous Huxley)

at·ro·phy \'a-trə-fē\ *n, pl* **-phies** [LL *atrophia*, fr. Gk, fr. *atrophos* ill fed, fr. *a-* + *trephein* to nourish] (1601)   1 : decrease in size or wasting away of a body part or tissue; *also* : arrested development or loss of a part or organ incidental to the normal development or life of an animal or plant   2 : a wasting away or progressive decline : DEGENERATION (the ~ of freedom) (was not a solitude of ~, of negation, but of perpetual flowering —Willa Cather) — **atro·phic** \(.)ā-'trō-fik\ *adj* — **atrophy** \'a-trə-fē, -,fī\ *vb*

at·ro·pine \'a-trə-,pēn\ *n* [G *Atropin*, fr. NL *Atropa*, genus name of belladonna, fr. Gk *Atropos*, one of the three Fates] (1836) : a racemic mixture of hyoscyamine obtained from any of various solanaceous plants (as belladonna) and used esp. in the form of its sulfate for its anticholinergic effects (as pupil dilation or inhibition of smooth muscle spasms)

att *var of* ²AT

at·ta·boy \'a-də-,bȯi\ *interj* [prob. alter. of *that's the boy*] (1909) — used to express encouragement, approval, or admiration

at·tach \ə-'tach\ *vb* [ME, fr. MF *attacher*, fr. OF *estachier*, fr. *estache* stake, of Gmc origin; akin to OE *staca* stake] *vt* (14c)   1 : to take by legal authority esp. under a writ (~ed the property)   2 **a** : to bring (oneself) into an association   **b** : to assign temporarily   3 : to bind by personal ties (as of affection or sympathy) (was strongly ~ed to his family)   4 : to make fast (as by tying or gluing) (~ a label to a package)   5 : to associate esp. as a property : ATTRIBUTE (~ed great importance to public opinion polls) ~ *vi* : to become attached : ADHERE *syn* see FASTEN — **at·tach·able** \-'ta-chə-bəl\ *adj*

at·ta·ché \,a-tə-'shā, ,a-,ta-, ,ä-,ta-\ *n* [F, pp. of *attacher*] (1829)   1 : a technical expert on the diplomatic staff of his country at a foreign capital (a military ~)   2 : ATTACHÉ CASE

at·ta·ché case \,a-,tə-'shā-, ,a-tə-; ə-'ta-(,)shā-\ *n* (1904)   1 : a small thin suitcase used esp. for carrying business papers   2 : BRIEFCASE

at·tached \ə-'tacht\ *adj* (1854) : permanently fixed when adult (~ barnacles)

at·tach·ment \ə-'tach-mənt\ *n* (14c)   1 : a seizure by legal process; *also* : the writ or precept commanding such seizure   2 : the state of being personally attached : FIDELITY (~ to a cause)   **b** : affectionate regard (a deep ~ to nature)   3 : a device attached to a machine or implement   4 : the physical connection by which one thing is attached to another   5 : the process of physically attaching

¹**at·tack** \ə-'tak\ *vb* [MF *attaquer*, fr. (assumed) OIt *estaccare* to attach, fr. *stacca* stake, of Gmc origin; akin to OE *staca*] *vt* (1600)   1 : to set upon or work against forcefully   2 : to assail with unfriendly or bitter words   3 : to begin to affect or to act on injuriously   4 : to set to work on   5 : to threaten (a piece in chess) with immediate capture ~ *vi* : to make an attack — **at·tack·er** *n*
syn ATTACK, ASSAIL, ASSAULT, BOMBARD, STORM mean to make an onslaught upon. ATTACK implies taking the initiative in a struggle (plan to *attack* the town at dawn). ASSAIL implies attempting to break down resistance by repeated blows or shots (*assailed* the enemy with artillery fire). ASSAULT suggests a direct attempt to overpower by suddenness and violence of onslaught (commandos *assaulted* the building from all sides). BOMBARD applies to attacking with bombs or shells (*bombarded* the city nightly). STORM implies attempting to break into a defended position (preparing to *storm* the fortress).

²**attack** *n* (1661)   1 : the act of attacking with physical force or unfriendly words : ASSAULT   2 : a belligerent or antagonistic action   3 **a** : a fit of sickness; *esp* : an active episode of a chronic or recurrent disease   **b** : a period of being strongly affected by something (as a desire or mood)   4 **a** : an offensive or scoring action (won the game with an eight-hit ~)   **b** : offensive players or the positions taken up by them   5 : the setting to work on some undertaking (made a new ~ on the problem)   6 : the beginning of destructive action (as by a chemical agent)   7 : the act or manner of beginning a musical tone or phrase

at·tack·man \-,man\ *n* (1940) : a player (as in lacrosse) assigned to an offensive zone or position

at·tain \ə-'tān\ *vb* [ME *atteynen*, fr. OF *ataindre*, fr. (assumed) VL *attangere*, alter. of L *attingere*, fr. *ad-* + *tangere* to touch — more at TANGENT] *vt* (14c)   1 : to reach as an end : GAIN, ACHIEVE (~ a goal)   2 : to come into possession of : OBTAIN (he ~ed preferment over his fellows)   3 : to come to as the end of a progression or course of movement (they ~ed the top of the hill) (~ a ripe old age) ~ *vi* : to come or arrive by motion, growth, or effort — usu. used with *to* — **at·tain·abil·i·ty** \-,tā-nə-'bi-lə-tē\ *n* — **at·tain·able** \-'tā-nə-bəl\ *adj*

at·tain·der \ə-'tān-dər\ *n* [ME *attaynder*, fr. MF *ataindre* to accuse, attain] (15c)   1 : extinction of the civil rights and capacities of a person upon sentence of death or outlawry usu. after a conviction of treason   2 *obs* : DISHONOR

at·tain·ment \ə-'tān-mənt\ *n* (1549)   1 : the act of attaining : the condition of being attained   2 : something attained : ACCOMPLISHMENT (scientific ~s)

¹**at·taint** \ə-'tānt\ *vt* [ME *attaynten*, fr. MF *ataint*, pp. of *ataindre*] (14c)   1 : to affect by attainder   2 **a** : INFECT, CORRUPT   **b** *archaic* : TAINT, SULLY   3 *archaic* : ACCUSE

²**attaint** *n* (1592) *obs* : a stain upon honor or purity : DISGRACE

at·tar \'a-tər, 'a-,tär\ *n* [Per *'aṭir* perfumed, fr. Ar, fr. *'iṭr* perfume] (1798) : a fragrant essential oil (as from rose petals); *also* : FRAGRANCE

¹**at·tempt** \ə-'tem(p)t\ *vt* [ME, fr. MF & L; MF *attempter*, fr. L *attemptare*, fr. *ad-* + *temptare* to touch, try — more at TEMPT] (14c)   1 : to make an effort to do, accomplish, solve, or effect (~ed to swim the swollen river)   2 *archaic* : TEMPT   3 *archaic* : to try to subdue or take by force : ATTACK — **at·tempt·able** \-'tem(p)-tə-bəl\ *adj*
syn ATTEMPT, TRY, ENDEAVOR, ESSAY, STRIVE mean to make an effort to accomplish an end. ATTEMPT stresses the initiation or beginning of an effort (will *attempt* to photograph the rare bird). TRY is often close to ATTEMPT but may stress effort or experiment made in the hope of testing or proving something (*tried* to determine which was the better procedure). ENDEAVOR heightens the implications of exertion and difficulty (*endeavored* to find crash survivors in the mountains). ESSAY implies difficulty but also suggests tentative trying or experimenting (will *essay* a dramatic role for the first time). STRIVE implies great exertion against great difficulty and specifically suggests persistent effort (continues to *strive* for peace).

²**attempt** *n* (1534)   1 **a** : the act or an instance of attempting; *esp* : an unsuccessful effort   **b** : something resulting from or representing an attempt (surrounded by . . . a few ~s at rose bushes —Marian Engel)   2 : ATTACK, ASSAULT (an ~ on the life of the president)

at·tend \ə-'tend\ *vb* [ME, fr. OF *atendre*, fr. L *attendere*, lit., to stretch to, fr. *ad-* + *tendere* to stretch — more at THIN] *vt* (14c)   1 : to pay attention to   2 : to look after : take charge of (campsites . . . ~ed by park rangers —Jackson Rivers)   3 **a** : to go or stay with as a companion, nurse, or servant   **b** : to visit professionally as a physician   4 *archaic* **a** : to wait for   **b** : to be in store for   5 : to be present with : ACCOMPANY   6 : to be present at : go to (~ law school) ~ *vi*   1 : to apply oneself (~ to your work)   2 : to apply the mind or pay attention : HEED   3 **a** : to be ready for service (ministers who ~ upon the king)   **b** *obs* : WAIT, STAY   5 : to direct one's attention : SEE (I'll ~ to that) — **at·tend·er** *n*

at·ten·dance \ə-'ten-dən(t)s\ *n* (14c)   1 : the act or fact of attending (a physician in ~)   2 **a** : the persons or number of persons attending (daily ~ at the fair)   **b** : the number of times a person attends

attendance officer *n* (1884) : one employed by a public-school system to investigate the continued absences of pupils

¹**at·ten·dant** \ə-'ten-dənt\ *n* (15c)   1 : one who attends another to perform a service; *esp* : an employee who waits on customers   2 : something that accompanies : CONCOMITANT   3 : ATTENDEE

²**attendant** *adj* (15c)   1 : accompanying, waiting upon, or following in order to perform service (Cherub and Seraph . . . ~ on their Lord —John Milton)   2 : accompanying or following as a consequence or result (problems ~ upon pollution)

at·tend·ee \ə-,ten-'dē, ,a-\ *n* (1937) : a person who is present on a given occasion or at a given place (~s at a convention)

at·tend·ing \ə-'ten-diŋ\ *adj* (ca. 1923) : serving as a physician on the staff of a teaching hospital (~ surgeon)

at·ten·tion \ə-'ten(t)-shən; *sense 4 often* (ə-)ten(ch)-'hət\ *n* [ME *attencioun*, fr. L *attention-, attentio*, fr. *attendere*] (14c)   1 **a** : the act or state of attending esp. through applying the mind to an object of sense or thought   **b** : a condition of readiness for such attention involving esp. a selective narrowing or focusing of consciousness and receptivity   2 : OBSERVATION, NOTICE; *esp* : consideration with a view to action (a problem requiring prompt ~)   3 **a** : an act of civility or courtesy esp. in courtship   **b** : sympathetic consideration of the needs and wants of others : ATTENTIVENESS   4 : a position assumed by a soldier with heels together, body erect, arms at the sides, and eyes to the front — often used as a command — **at·ten·tion·al** \-'ten(t)-sh(ə-)nəl\ *adj*

attention deficit disorder *n* (1980) : a syndrome of learning and behavioral problems that is not caused by any serious underlying physical or mental disorder and is characterized esp. by difficulty in sustaining attention, by impulsive behavior (as in speaking out of turn), and usu. by excessive activity

attention line *n* (1925) : a line usu. placed above the salutation in a business letter directing the letter to one specified

attention span *n* (1934) : the length of time during which an individual is able to concentrate or remain interested

at·ten·tive \ə-'ten-tiv\ *adj* (14c)   1 : MINDFUL, OBSERVANT (~ to what he is doing)   2 : heedful of the comfort of others : SOLICITOUS   3 : offering attentions in or as if in the role of a suitor — **at·ten·tive·ly** *adv* — **at·ten·tive·ness** *n*

¹**at·ten·u·ate** \ə-'ten-yə-,wāt\ *vb* **-at·ed; -at·ing** [L *attenuatus*, pp. of *attenuare* to make thin, fr. *ad-* + *tenuis* thin — more at THIN] *vt* (15c)   1 : to make thin or slender   2 : to make thin in consistency : RAREFY   3 : to lessen the amount, force, magnitude, or value of : WEAKEN   4 : to reduce the severity, virulence, or vitality of ~ *vi* : to become thin, fine, or less — **at·ten·u·a·tion** \-,ten-yə-'wā-shən\ *n*

²**at·ten·u·ate** \ə-'ten-yə-wət\ *adj* (15c)   1 : attenuated esp. in thickness, density, or force   2 : tapering gradually usu. to a long slender point (~ leaves)

at·ten·u·a·tor \-yə-,wā-tər\ *n* (1924) : a device for attenuating; *esp* : one for reducing the amplitude of an electrical signal without appreciable distortion

at·test \ə-'test\ *vb* [MF *attester*, fr. L *attestari*, fr. *ad-* + *testis* witness — more at TESTAMENT] *vt* (1596)   1 **a** : to affirm to be true or genuine; *specif* : to authenticate by signing as a witness   **b** : to authenticate officially   2 : to establish or verify the usage of   3 : to be proof of : MANIFEST (her record ~s her integrity)   4 : to put on oath ~ *vi* : to bear witness : TESTIFY (~ to a belief)   *syn* see CERTIFY — **at·tes·ta·tion** \,a-,tes-'tā-shən, ,a-tə-'stā-\ *n* — **at·test·er** \ə-'tes-tər\ *n*

at·tic \'a-tik\ *n* [F *attique*, fr. *attique* of Attica, fr. L *Atticus*] (ca. 1696)   1 : a low story or wall above the main order of a facade in the classical styles   2 : a room behind an attic   3 : a room or a space immediately below the roof of a building : GARRET   4 : something resembling an attic (as in being used for storage)

¹**At·tic** \'a-tik\ *adj* [L *Atticus* of Attica, fr. Gk *Attikos*, fr. *Attikē* Attica, Greece] (1599)   1 : of, relating to, or having the characteristics of Athens or its ancient civilization   2 : marked by simplicity, purity, and refinement (an ~ prose style)

²**Attic** *n* (ca. 1771) : a dialect of ancient Greek orig. used in Attica and later the literary language of the Greek-speaking world

at·ti·cism \'a-tə-,si-zəm\ n, often cap (1593)   1 : a witty or well-turned phrase   2 : a characteristic feature of Attic Greek occurring in another language or dialect

¹**at·tire** \ə-'tīr\ vt **at·tired; at·tir·ing** [ME, fr. OF atirier, fr. a- (fr. L ad-) + tire order, rank, of Gmc origin; akin to OE tīr glory, ornament] (14c) : to put garments on : DRESS, ARRAY; esp : to clothe in fancy or rich garments

²**attire** n (14c)   1 : DRESS, CLOTHES; esp : splendid or decorative clothing   2 : the antlers or antlers and scalp of a stag or buck

at·ti·tude \'a-tə-,tüd, -,tyüd\ n [F, It. attitudine, lit., aptitude, fr. LL aptitudin-, aptitudo fitness — more at APTITUDE] (1668)   1 : the arrangement of the parts of a body or figure : POSTURE   2 : a position assumed for a specific purpose ⟨a threatening ~⟩   3 : a ballet position similar to the arabesque in which the raised leg is bent at the knee   4 **a** : a mental position with regard to a fact or state   **b** : a feeling or emotion toward a fact or state   5 : the position of an aircraft or spacecraft determined by the relationship between its axes and a reference datum (as the horizon or a particular star)   6 : an organismic state of readiness to respond in a characteristic way to a stimulus (as an object, concept, or situation)   7 **a** : a negative or hostile state of mind   **b** : a cocky or arrogant manner

at·ti·tu·di·nal \,a-tə-'tüd-ᵊn-əl, -'tyü-\ adj [attitude + -inal (as in aptitudinal, fr. L aptitudin-, aptitudo)] (1831) : relating to, based on, or expressive of personal attitudes or feelings ⟨~ judgment⟩ — **at·ti·tu·di·nal·ly** \-ə-lē\ adv

at·ti·tu·di·nise Brit var of ATTITUDINIZE

at·ti·tu·di·nize \,a-tə-'tüd-ᵊn-,īz, -'tyü-\ vi **-nized; -niz·ing** (1784) : to assume an affected mental attitude : POSE

at·to- \'a-(,)tō\ comb form [ISV, fr. Dan or Norw atten eighteen, fr. ON āttjān; akin to OE eahtatīene eighteen] : one quintillionth (10⁻¹⁸) part of ⟨attogram⟩

at·torn \ə-'tərn\ vi [ME attournen, fr. MF atorner, fr. OF, fr. a- (fr. L ad-) + torner to turn] (15c) : to agree to be tenant to a new owner or landlord of the same property — **at·torn·ment** \-mənt\ n

at·tor·ney \ə-'tər-nē\ n, pl **-neys** [ME attourney, fr. MF atorné, pp. of atorner] (14c) : one who is legally appointed to transact business on another's behalf; specif : a legal agent qualified to act for suitors and defendants in legal proceedings — **at·tor·ney·ship** \-,ship\ n

attorney–at–law n, pl **attorneys–at–law** (1768) : a practitioner in a court of law who is legally qualified to prosecute and defend actions in such court on the retainer of clients

attorney general n, pl **attorneys general** or **attorney generals** (1585) : the chief law officer of a nation or state who represents the government in litigation and serves as its principal legal adviser

at·tract \ə-'trakt\ vb [ME, fr. L attractus, pp. of attrahere, fr. ad- + trahere to pull, draw] vt (15c) : to cause to approach or adhere: as **a** : to pull to or draw toward oneself or itself ⟨a magnet ~s iron⟩   **b** : to draw by appeal to natural or excited interest, emotion, or aesthetic sense : ENTICE ⟨~ attention⟩ ~ vi : to exercise attraction — **at·trac·tor** \-'trak-tər\ n

   syn ATTRACT, ALLURE, CHARM, CAPTIVATE, FASCINATE, ENCHANT mean to draw another by exerting a powerful influence. ATTRACT applies to any degree or kind of ability to exert influence over another ⟨students attracted by the school's locale⟩. ALLURE implies an enticing by what is fair, pleasing, or seductive ⟨an alluring smile⟩. CHARM implies the power of casting a spell over the person or thing affected and so compelling a response ⟨charmed by their hospitality⟩, but it may, like CAPTIVATE, suggest no more than evoking delight or admiration ⟨her performances captivated audiences⟩. FASCINATE suggests a magical influence and tends to stress the ineffectiveness of attempts to resist ⟨a story that continues to fascinate children⟩. ENCHANT is perhaps the strongest of these terms in stressing the appeal of the agent and the degree of delight evoked in the subject ⟨hopelessly enchanted by her beauty⟩.

at·trac·tance \-tən(t)s\ n (1948) : ATTRACTANCY

at·trac·tan·cy \ə-'trak-tən(t)-sē\ n (1948) : the quality or capacity (as of a pheromone) of attracting

at·trac·tant \ə-'trak-tənt\ n (1920) : a substance (as of a pheromone) that attracts insects or other animals

at·trac·tion \ə-'trak-shən\ n (14c)   1 **a** : the act, process, or power of attracting   **b** : personal charm   2 : the action or power of drawing forth a response : an attractive quality   3 : a force acting mutually between particles of matter, tending to draw them together, and resisting their separation   4 : something that attracts or is intended to attract people by appealing to their desires and tastes ⟨coming ~s⟩

   syn ATTRACTION, AFFINITY, SYMPATHY mean the relationship existing between things or persons that are naturally or involuntarily drawn together. ATTRACTION implies the possession by one thing of a quality that pulls another to it ⟨felt an attraction to danger⟩. AFFINITY implies a susceptibility or predisposition on the part of the one drawn ⟨an affinity for mathematics⟩. SYMPATHY implies a reciprocal or natural relation between two things that are both susceptible to the same influence ⟨two minds in sympathy⟩.

at·trac·tive \ə-'trak-tiv\ adj (14c)   1 : having or relating to the power to attract ⟨~ forces between molecules⟩ ⟨an ~ offer⟩   2 : arousing interest or pleasure : CHARMING ⟨an ~ smile⟩ — **at·trac·tive·ly** adv — **at·trac·tive·ness** n

¹**at·tri·bute** \'a-trə-,byüt\ n [ME, fr. L attributus, pp. of attribuere to attribute, fr. ad- + tribuere to bestow — more at TRIBUTE] (14c)   1 : an inherent characteristic; also : an accidental quality   2 : an object closely associated with or belonging to a specific person, thing, or office ⟨a scepter is the ~ of power⟩; esp : such an object used for identification in painting or sculpture   3 : a word ascribing a quality; esp : ADJECTIVE   **syn** see QUALITY

²**at·trib·ute** \ə-'tri-,byüt, -byət\ vt **-ut·ed; -ut·ing** (1530)   1 : to explain by indicating a cause ⟨attributed his success to his coach⟩   2 **a** : to regard as a characteristic of a person or thing   **b** : to reckon as made or originated in an indicated fashion ⟨attributed the invention to a Russian⟩   **c** : CLASSIFY, DESIGNATE   **syn** see ASCRIBE — **at·trib·ut·able** \-byü-tə-bəl, -byə-\ adj

at·tri·bu·tion \,a-trə-'byü-shən\ n (1651)   1 : the act of attributing; esp : the ascribing of a work (as of literature or art) to a particular author or artist   2 : an ascribed quality, character, or right — **at·tri·bu·tion·al** \-sh(ə-)nᵊl\ adj

at·trib·u·tive \ə-'tri-byə-tiv\ adj (1606)   1 : relating to or of the nature of an attribute : ATTRIBUTING   2 : joined directly to a modified noun without a linking verb (as city in city streets) — **attributive** n — **at·trib·u·tive·ly** adv

at·trit·ed \ə-'trī-təd\ adj (1760) : worn by attrition

at·tri·tion \ə-'tri-shən, a-\ n [L attrition-, attritio, fr. atterere to rub against, fr. ad- + terere to rub — more at THROW] (14c)   1 [ME attricioun, fr. ML attrition-, attritio, fr. L] : sorrow for one's sins that arises from a motive other than that of the love of God   2 : the act of rubbing together : FRICTION; also : the act of wearing or grinding down by friction   3 : the act of weakening or exhausting by constant harassment, abuse, or attack   4 : a reduction in numbers usu. as a result of resignation, retirement, or death — **at·tri·tion·al** \-'tri-sh(ə-)nᵊl\ adj

at·tune \ə-'tün, -'tyün\ vt (1596)   1 : to bring into harmony : TUNE   2 : to make aware or responsive ⟨~ businesses to changing trends⟩ — **at·tune·ment** \-mənt\ n

at·wit·ter \ə-'twi-tər\ adj (1833) : nervously concerned : EXCITED ⟨gossips ~ with speculation —Time⟩

atyp·i·cal \(,)ā-'ti-pi-kəl\ adj (1885) : not typical : IRREGULAR, UNUSUAL — **atyp·i·cal·i·ty** \,ā-,ti-pə-'ka-lə-tē\ n — **atyp·i·cal·ly** \(,)ā-'ti-pi-k(ə-)lē\ adv

au·bade \ō-'bäd\ n [F, fr. MF, fr. OProv aubada, fr. alba, auba dawn, fr. (assumed) VL alba, fr. L, fem. of albus white — more at ALB] (ca. 1678)   1 : a song or poem greeting the dawn   2 **a** : a morning love song   **b** : a song or poem of lovers parting at dawn   3 : morning music — compare NOCTURNE

au·berge \ō-'berzh\ n [F, fr. MF, of Gmc origin; akin to OHG heriberga military quarters — more at HARBOR] (1599) : INN 1a

au·ber·gine \'ō-bər-,zhēn\ n [F, fr. Catal albergínia, fr. Ar al-bādhinjān the eggplant] (1794)   1 chiefly Brit : EGGPLANT 1   2 : EGGPLANT 2

¹**au·burn** \'ō-bərn\ adj [ME auborne blond, fr. MF, fr. ML alburnus whitish, fr. L alburnum sapwood] (15c)   1 : of the color auburn   2 : of a reddish brown color

²**auburn** n (1613) : a moderate brown

Au·bus·son \,ō-bə-'sōⁿ\ n [Aubusson, town in France] (1851) : a figured scenic tapestry used for wall hangings and upholstery; also : a rug woven to resemble Aubusson tapestry

au cou·rant \,ō-kú-'rän\ adj [F, lit., in the current] (1762)   1 **a** : fully informed : UP-TO-DATE   **b** : FASHIONABLE, STYLISH   2 : fully familiar : CONVERSANT

¹**auc·tion** \'ōk-shən\ n [L auction-, auctio, fr. augēre to increase — more at EKE] (1595)   1 : a sale of property to the highest bidder   2 : the act or process of bidding in some card games

²**auction** vt **auc·tioned; auc·tion·ing** \-sh(ə-)niŋ\ (ca. 1798) : to sell at auction ⟨~ed off his library⟩

auction bridge n (1908) : a bridge game differing from contract bridge in that tricks made in excess of the contract are scored toward game

auc·tion·eer \,ōk-shə-'nir\ n (ca. 1708) : an agent who sells goods at auction

auc·to·ri·al \ōk-'tōr-ē-əl, -'tȯr-\ adj [L auctor author — more at AUTHOR] (1821) : of or relating to an author

au·da·cious \ȯ-'dā-shəs\ adj [MF audacieux, fr. audace boldness, fr. L audacia, fr. audac-, audax bold, fr. audēre to dare, fr. avidus eager — more at AVID] (1550)   1 **a** : intrepidly daring : ADVENTUROUS ⟨an ~ mountain climber⟩   **b** : recklessly bold : RASH   2 : contemptuous of law, religion, or decorum : INSOLENT   3 : marked by originality and verve — **au·da·cious·ly** adv — **au·da·cious·ness** n

au·dac·i·ty \ȯ-'da-sə-tē\ n, pl **-ties** [ME audacite, fr. L audac-, audax] (15c)   1 : the quality or state of being audacious: as **a** : intrepid boldness   **b** : bold or arrogant disregard of normal restraints   2 : an audacious act — usu. used in pl.   **syn** see TEMERITY

au·di·al \'ȯ-dē-əl\ adj [audio + -al] (1966) : of, relating to, or affecting the sense of hearing : AURAL

¹**au·di·ble** \'ȯ-də-bəl\ adj [LL audibilis, fr. L audire to hear; akin to Gk aisthanesthai to perceive, Skt āvis evidently] (1527) : heard or capable of being heard — **au·di·bil·i·ty** \,ȯ-də-'bi-lə-tē\ n — **au·di·bly** \'ȯ-də-blē\ adv

²**audible** n (1962) : a substitute offensive or defensive play called at the line of scrimmage in football

au·di·ence \'ȯ-dē-ən(t)s, 'ä-\ n [ME, fr. MF, fr. L audientia, fr. audient-, audiens, prp. of audire] (14c)   1 : the act or state of hearing   2 **a** : a formal hearing or interview ⟨an ~ with the pope⟩   **b** : an opportunity of being heard ⟨I would succeed if I were once given ~⟩   3 **a** : a group of listeners or spectators   **b** : a reading, viewing, or listening public   4 : a group of ardent admirers or devotees : FOLLOWING

au·dile \'ȯ-,dīl\ adj [auditory + -ile (as in tactile)] (1897) : AUDITORY

aud·ing \'ȯ-diŋ\ n [L audire + E ¹-ing] (ca. 1949) : the process of hearing, recognizing, and interpreting spoken language

¹**au·dio** \'ȯ-dē-,ō\ adj [audio-] (1916)   1 : of or relating to acoustic, mechanical, or electrical frequencies corresponding to normally audible sound waves which are of frequencies approximately from 15 to 20,000 hertz   2 **a** : of or relating to sound or its reproduction and esp. high-fidelity reproduction   **b** : relating to or used in the transmission or reception of sound — compare VIDEO   **c** : of, relating to, or utilizing recorded sound

²**audio** n (1934)   1 : an audio signal; broadly : SOUND   2 : the section of television or motion-picture equipment that deals with sound   3 : the transmission, reception, or reproduction of sound

audio- comb form [L audire to hear] (1896)   1 : hearing ⟨audiometer⟩   2 : sound ⟨audiophile⟩   3 : auditory and ⟨audiovisual⟩

au·dio–an·i·ma·tron·ic \,ō-dē-ō-,a-nə-mə-'trä-nik\ adj [fr. Audio-Animatronics, a trademark] (1964) : being or consisting of a lifelike electromechanical figure of a person or animal that has synchronized movement and sound

au·dio·cas·sette \,ȯ-dē-(,)ō-kə-'set, -ka-\ n (1971) : an audiotape recording mounted in a cassette

---

\ə\ abut \ᵊ\ kitten, F table \ər\ further \a\ ash \ā\ ace \ä\ mop, mar
\au̇\ out \ch\ chin \e\ bet \ē\ easy \g\ go \i\ hit \ī\ ice \j\ job
\ŋ\ sing \ō\ go \ȯ\ law \ȯi\ boy \th\ thin \t̲h̲\ the \ü\ loot \u̇\ foot
\y\ yet \zh\ vision \ä, k̲, ⁿ, œ, œ̄, ue, ūe, ᵊ\ see Guide to Pronunciation

au·dio·gen·ic \ˌȯ-dē-ō-'je-nik\ adj (1941) : produced by frequencies corresponding to sound waves — used esp. of epileptoid responses

au·dio·gram \'ȯ-dē-ō-ˌgram\ n (1927) : a graphic representation of the relation of vibration frequency and the minimum sound intensity for hearing

au·dio·lin·gual \ˌȯ-dē-ō-'liŋ-gwəl also -gyə-wəl\ adj (1960) : involving a drill routine of listening and speaking in language learning

au·di·ol·o·gy \ˌȯ-dē-'ä-lə-jē\ n (1946) : a branch of science dealing with hearing; specif : therapy of individuals having impaired hearing — **au·di·o·log·i·cal** \-ē-ə-'lä-ji-kəl\ also **au·di·o·log·ic** \-ē-ə-'lä-jik\ adj — **au·di·ol·o·gist** \-ē-'ä-lə-jist\ n

au·di·om·e·ter \ˌȯ-dē-'ä-mə-tər\ n (1879) : an instrument used in measuring the acuity of hearing — **au·di·o·met·ric** \-dē-ō-'me-trik\ adj — **au·di·om·e·try** \-dē-'ä-mə-trē\ n

au·dio·phile \'ȯ-dē-ō-ˌfīl\ n (1951) : a person who is enthusiastic about high-fidelity sound reproduction

au·dio·tape \'ȯ-dē-ō-ˌtāp\ n (1958) : a tape recording of sound

au·dio·vi·su·al \ˌȯ-dē-(ˌ)ō-'vi-zhə-wəl, -zhəl\ adj (1937) **1** : designed to aid in learning or teaching by making use of both hearing and sight **2** : of or relating to both hearing and sight

au·dio·vi·su·als \-zhə-wəlz, -zhəlz\ n pl (1955) : audiovisual teaching materials (as filmstrips accompanied by recordings)

¹au·dit \'ȯ-dət\ n [ME, fr. L auditus act of hearing, fr. audire] (15c) **1 a** : a formal examination of an organization's or individual's accounts or financial situation **b** : the final report of an audit **2** : a methodical examination and review — **au·dit·able** \-di-tə-bəl\ adj

²audit vt (15c) **1** : to perform an audit of or for ⟨∼ the books⟩ ⟨∼ the company⟩ **2** : to attend (a course) without working for or expecting to receive formal credit

¹au·di·tion \ȯ-'di-shən\ n [MF or L; MF, fr. L audition-, auditio, fr. audire] (1599) **1** : the power or sense of hearing **2** : the act of hearing; esp : a critical hearing ⟨an ∼ of new recordings⟩ **3** : a trial performance to appraise an entertainer's merits

²audition vb **au·di·tioned**; **au·di·tion·ing** \-'di-sh(ə-)niŋ\ vt (1934) : to test esp. in an audition ∼ vi : to give a trial performance

au·di·tor \'ȯ-də-tər\ n (14c) **1** : a person authorized to examine and verify accounts **2** : one that hears or listens; esp : one that is a member of an audience **3** : a person who audits a course of study **4** : a person who hears (as a court case) in the capacity of judge

au·di·to·ri·um \ˌȯ-də-'tȯr-ē-əm, -'tȯr-\ n, pl **-ri·ums** or **-ria** \-ē-ə\ [L, lit., lecture room] (ca. 1751) **1** : the part of a public building where an audience sits **2** : a room, hall, or building used for public gatherings

¹au·di·to·ry \'ȯ-də-ˌtȯr-ē, -ˌtȯr-\ n [ME auditorie, fr. L auditorium] (14c) **1** archaic : AUDIENCE **2** archaic : AUDITORIUM

²au·di·to·ry adj [LL auditorius] (1578) : of, relating to, or experienced through hearing — **au·di·to·ri·ly** adv

auditory nerve n (1724) : either of the 8th pair of cranial nerves connecting the inner ear with the brain and transmitting impulses concerned with hearing and balance — see EAR illustration

auditory tube n (1907) : EUSTACHIAN TUBE

audit trail n (1954) : a record of a sequence of events (as actions performed by a computer) from which a history may be reconstructed

Auf·klä·rung \'auf-ˌkler-əŋ, -ˌuŋ\ n [G] (1842) : ENLIGHTENMENT 2

auf Wie·der·seh·en \auf-'vē-dər-ˌzā(-ə)n\ interj [G, lit., till seeing again] (1885) — used to express farewell

Au·ge·an \ȯ-'jē-ən\ adj [L Augeas, king of Elis, fr. Gk Augeias; fr. the legend that his stable, left neglected for 30 years, was finally cleaned by Hercules] (1599) **1** : extremely formidable or difficult and occas. distasteful ⟨an ∼ task⟩

Augean stable n (1635) : a condition or place marked by great accumulation of filth or corruption

au·ger \'ȯ-gər\ n [ME, alter. (resulting from false division of a nauger) of nauger, fr. OE nafogār; akin to OHG nabugēr auger, OE nafu nave, gār spear — more at NAVE, GORE] (bef. 12c) : any of various tools or devices having a helical shaft or member that are used for boring holes (as in wood, earth, or ice) or moving loose material (as snow)

auger: 1, 2 screw, 3 tapering pod

Au·ger effect \(ˌ)ō-'zhā-\ n [Pierre V. Auger b1899 Fr. physicist] (1931) : a process in which an atom that has been ionized through the emission of an electron with energy in the X-ray range undergoes a transition in which a second electron is emitted rather than an X-ray photon — called also Auger process

Auger electron n (1939) : an electron emitted from an atom in the Auger effect

Auger electron spectroscopy n (1970) : an instrumental method for determining the chemical composition of a material's surface by bombardment with an electron beam to produce Auger electrons whose energy spectra are characteristic of their parent atoms — called also Auger spectroscopy

¹aught \'ȯt, 'ät\ pron [ME, fr. OE āwiht, fr. ā ever + wiht creature, thing — more at AYE, WIGHT] (bef. 12c) **1** : ANYTHING **2** : ALL, EVERYTHING ⟨for ∼ I care⟩ ⟨for ∼ we know⟩

²aught adv (13c) archaic : AT ALL

³aught n [alter. (resulting from false division of a naught) of naught] (1872) **1** : ZERO, CIPHER **2** archaic : NONENTITY, NOTHING

au·gite \'ȯ-ˌjīt\ n [L augites, a precious stone, fr. Gk augitēs] (1804) **1** : an aluminous usu. black or dark green pyroxene that is found in igneous rocks **2** : PYROXENE — **au·git·ic** \ȯ-'ji-tik\ adj

¹aug·ment \ȯg-'ment\ vb [ME, fr. MF augmenter, fr. LL augmentare, fr. L augmentum increase, fr. augēre to increase — more at EKE] vt (14c) **1** : to make greater, more numerous, larger, or more intense ⟨the impact of the report was ∼ed by its timing⟩ **2** : to add an augment to **3** : SUPPLEMENT ⟨∼ed her scholarship by working nights⟩ ∼ vi : to become augmented syn see INCREASE — **aug·ment·er** or **aug·men·tor** \-'men-tər\ n

²aug·ment \'ȯg-ˌment\ n (ca. 1771) : a vowel prefixed or a lengthening of the initial vowel to mark past time esp. in Greek and Sanskrit verbs

aug·men·ta·tion \ˌȯg-mən-'tā-shən, -ˌmen-\ n (14c) **1 a** : the act or process of augmenting **b** : the state of being augmented **2** : something that augments : ADDITION

¹aug·men·ta·tive \ȯg-'men-tə-tiv\ adj (15c) **1** : able to augment **2** : indicating large size and sometimes awkwardness or unattractiveness — used of words and affixes; compare DIMINUTIVE

²augmentative n (1804) : an augmentative word or affix

aug·ment·ed \ȯg-'men-təd\ adj (1825) of a musical interval : made one half step greater than major or perfect ⟨an ∼ fifth⟩

augmented matrix n (ca. 1949) : a matrix whose elements are the coefficients of a set of simultaneous linear equations with the constant terms of the equations entered in an added column

au gra·tin \ō-'grä-t²n, ȯ-, -'gra-\ adj [F, lit., with the burnt scrapings from the pan] (1806) : covered with bread crumbs or grated cheese and browned (as under a broiler)

¹au·gur \'ȯ-gər\ n [L; akin to L augēre] (14c) **1** : an official diviner of ancient Rome **2** : one held to foretell events by omens

²augur vt (1601) **1** : to foretell esp. from omens **2** : to give promise of : PRESAGE ⟨higher pay ∼s a better future⟩ ∼ vi : to predict the future esp. from omens

au·gu·ry \'ȯ-gyə-rē, -gə-\ n, pl **-ries** (14c) **1** : divination from auspices or omens; also : an instance of this **2** : OMEN, PORTENT

au·gust \ȯ-'gəst, 'ȯ-(ˌ)gəst\ adj [L augustus; akin to L augur] (1664) : marked by majestic dignity or grandeur — **au·gust·ly** adv — **au·gust·ness** \ȯ-'gəst(t)-nəs, 'ȯ-(ˌ)gəs(t)-\ n

Au·gust \'ȯ-gəst\ n [ME, fr. OE, fr. L Augustus, fr. Augustus Caesar] (bef. 12c) : the 8th month of the Gregorian calendar

Au·gus·tan \ȯ-'gəs-tən, ə-\ adj (1704) **1** : of, relating to, or characteristic of Augustus Caesar or his age **2** : of, relating to, or characteristic of the neoclassical period in England — **Augustan** n

¹Au·gus·tin·i·an \ˌȯ-gə-'sti-nē-ən\ n (1602) **1** : a member of an Augustinian order; specif : a friar of the Hermits of St. Augustine founded in 1256 and devoted to educational, missionary, and parish work **2** : a follower of St. Augustine

²Augustinian adj (1674) **1** : of or relating to St. Augustine or his doctrines **2** : of or relating to any of several orders under a rule ascribed to St. Augustine — **Au·gus·tin·i·an·ism** \-nē-ə-ˌni-zəm\ n

au jus \ō-'zhü(s), -'jüs; ō-zhᵫ\ adj [F, lit., with juice] (ca. 1919) of meat : served in the juice obtained from roasting

auk \'ȯk\ n [Norw or Icel alk, alka, fr. ON ālka] (1674) : any of several black-and-white short-necked diving seabirds (family Alcidae) that breed in colder parts of the northern hemisphere

auk·let \'ȯk-lət\ n (1886) : any of several small auks of the No. Pacific coasts

auld \'ȯl(d), 'äl(d)\ adj (14c) chiefly Scot : OLD

auld lang syne \ˌȯl(d)-ˌ(ˌ)laŋ-'zīn, -ˌȯl(d)-\ n [Sc, lit., old long ago] (1692) : the good old times

au na·tu·rel \ˌō-ˌna-tə-'rel, -ˌna-chə-\ adj [F] (1817) **1** : cooked or served plainly **2 a** : being in natural style or condition **b** : NUDE

aunt \'ant, 'änt\ n [ME, fr. OF ante, fr. L amita; akin to OHG amma mother, nurse, Gk amma nurse] (14c) **1** : a sister of one's father or mother **2** : the wife of one's uncle — **aunt·hood** \-ˌhůd\ n — **aunt·like** \-ˌlīk\ adj — **aunt·ly** adv

Aunt Sal·ly \-'sa-lē\ n, pl **Aunt Sallies** [Aunt Sally, name given to an effigy of a woman smoking a pipe set up as an amusement attraction at English fairs for patrons to throw missiles at] (1898) Brit **1** : an object of criticism or contention; esp : one that is set up to invite criticism or be easily refuted

au pair \'ō-ˌpar, -ˌper\ n, pl **au pairs** \-ˌparz, -ˌperz\ [F, on even terms] (1960) : a usu. young foreign person who does domestic work for a family in return for room and board and the opportunity to learn the family's language

au poivre \ō-'pwäv(r²)\ adj [F, with pepper] (1971) : prepared or served with a generous amount of usu. coarsely ground black pepper ⟨steak au poivre⟩

au·ra \'ȯr-ə\ n [ME, fr. L, puff of air, breeze, fr. Gk; prob. akin to Gk aēr air] (1732) **1 a** : a subtle sensory stimulus (as an aroma) **b** : a distinctive atmosphere surrounding a given source ⟨the place had an ∼ of mystery⟩ **2** : a luminous radiation : NIMBUS **3** : a subjective sensation (as of lights) experienced before an attack of some disorders (as epilepsy or a migraine) **4** : an energy field that is held to emanate from a living being

au·ral \'ȯr-əl\ adj [L auris ear — more at EAR] (1847) : of or relating to the ear or to the sense of hearing — **au·ral·ly** \-ə-lē\ adv

aurar pl of EYRIR

au·re·ate \'ȯr-ē-ət\ adj [ME aureat, fr. ML aureatus decorated with gold, fr. L aureus] (15c) **1** : of a golden color or brilliance **2** : marked by grandiloquent and rhetorical style

au·re·ole \'ȯr-ē-ˌōl\ or **au·re·o·la** \ȯ-'rē-ə-lə, ə-\ n [ME aureole heavenly crown worn by saints, fr. ML aureola, fr. L, fem. of aureolus golden, dim. of aureus] (13c) **1 a** : a radiant light around the head or body of a representation of a sacred personage **b** : something resembling an aureole ⟨an ∼ of hair⟩ **2** : RADIANCE, AURA ⟨an ∼ of youth and health⟩ **3** : the luminous area surrounding the sun or other bright light when seen through thin cloud or mist : CORONA **4** : a ring-shaped zone around an igneous intrusion — **aureole** vt

Au·reo·my·cin \ˌȯr-ē-ō-'mī-s²n\ trademark — used for a preparation of the hydrochloride of chlortetracycline

au·re·us \'ȯr-ē-əs\ n, pl **-rei** \-ē-ˌī\ [L, lit., golden, fr. aurum gold; akin to OPruss ausis gold] (1609) : a gold coin of ancient Rome varying in weight from ¹⁄₃₀ to ¹⁄₇₀ libra

au re·voir \ˌȯr-ə-'vwär, ˌȯr-, F ȯr(-ə)-vwár\ n [F, lit., till seeing again] (1694) : GOOD-BYE — often used interjectionally

au·ric \'ȯr-ik\ adj [L aurum] (ca. 1828) : of, relating to, or derived from gold

au·ri·cle \'ȯr-i-kəl\ n [L auricula, fr. dim. of auris ear — more at EAR] (15c) **1 a** : an atrium of a heart **b** : PINNA 2b **c** : an anterior ear-shaped pouch in each atrium of the human heart **2** : an angular or ear-shaped lobe, process, or appendage

au·ric·u·la \ȯ-'ri-kyə-lə\ n [NL, fr. L, external ear] (1655) : a yellow-flowered Alpine primrose (Primula auricula)

au·ric·u·lar \ȯ-'ri-kyə-lər\ adj (15c) **1** : told privately ⟨an ∼ confession⟩ **2** : understood or recognized by the sense of hearing **3** : of, relating to, or using the ear or the sense of hearing **4** : of or relating to an auricle

au·ric·u·late \ȯ-'ri-kyə-lət\ adj (1713) : having auricles

au·rif·er·ous \ȯ-'ri-f(ə-)rəs\ adj [L aurifer, fr. aurum + -fer -ferous] (1727) : containing gold
Au·ri·ga \ȯ-'rī-gə\ n [L, lit., charioteer] : a constellation between Perseus and Gemini
Au·ri·gna·cian \ˌȯr-ēn-'yā-shən\ adj [F aurignacien, fr. Aurignac, France] (1909) : of or relating to an Upper Paleolithic culture marked by finely made artifacts of stone and bone, paintings, and engravings
au·rochs \'aür-ˌäks, 'ȯr-\ n, pl **aurochs** [G, fr. OHG ūrohso, fr. ūro aurochs + ohso ox; akin to OE ūr aurochs — more at OX] (1766) **1** : an extinct large long-horned wild ox (Bos primigenius) of Europe that is the ancestor of domestic cattle **2** : WISENT
au·ro·ra \ə-'rōr-ə, ȯ-, -'rȯr-\ n, pl **auroras** or **au·ro·rae** \-(ˌ)ē\ [L — more at EAST] (14c) **1** : DAWN **2** cap : the Roman goddess of dawn — compare EOS **3** : a luminous phenomenon that consists of streamers or arches of light appearing in the upper atmosphere of a planet's magnetic polar regions and is caused by the emission of light from atoms excited by electrons accelerated along the planet's magnetic field lines — **au·ro·ral** \-əl\ adj — **au·ro·re·an** \-ē-ən\ adj
aurora aus·tra·lis \-ȯ-'strā-ləs, ä-'strä-\ n [NL, lit., southern dawn] (1741) : an aurora that occurs in earth's southern hemisphere — called also southern lights
aurora bo·re·al·is \-ˌbōr-ē-'a-ləs, -ˌbȯr-\ n [NL, lit., northern dawn] (1717) : an aurora that occurs in earth's northern hemisphere — called also northern lights
aus·cul·tate \'ȯ-skəl-ˌtāt\ vt **-tat·ed; -tat·ing** [back-formation fr. auscultation] (ca. 1860) : to examine by auscultation — **aus·cul·ta·to·ry** \ȯ-'skəl-tə-ˌtōr-ē, -ˌtȯr-\ adj
aus·cul·ta·tion \ˌȯ-skəl-'tā-shən\ n [L auscultation-, auscultatio act of listening, fr. auscultare to listen; akin to L auris ear — more at EAR] (ca. 1828) : the act of listening to sounds arising within organs (as the lungs) as an aid to diagnosis and treatment
aus·land·er \'aüs-ˌlen-dər, -ˌlan-\ n [G Ausländer] (1936) : OUTSIDER, FOREIGNER
aus·pice \'ȯs-pəs\ n, pl **aus·pic·es** \-pə-səz, -ˌsēz\ [L auspicium, fr. auspic-, auspex diviner by birds, fr. avis bird + specere to look, look at — more at AVIARY, SPY] (1533) **1** : observation by an augur esp. of the flight and feeding of birds to discover omens **2** pl : kindly patronage and guidance **3** : a prophetic sign; esp : a favorable sign
aus·pi·cious \ȯ-'spi-shəs\ adj (1593) **1** : affording a favorable auspice : PROPITIOUS ⟨an ~ beginning⟩ **2** : attended by good auspices : PROSPEROUS ⟨an ~ year⟩ syn see FAVORABLE — **aus·pi·cious·ly** adv — **aus·pi·cious·ness** n
Aus·sie \'ȯ-sē, 'ä-sē, Brit & Austral usu 'ȯ-zē\ n [Australian + -ie] (1917) : a native or inhabitant of Australia
aus·ten·ite \'ȯs-tə-ˌnīt, 'äs-\ n [F, fr. Sir W. C. Roberts-Austen †1902 Eng. metallurgist] (1902) : a solid solution in iron of carbon and sometimes other solutes that occurs as a constituent of steel under certain conditions — **aus·ten·it·ic** \ˌȯs-tə-'ni-tik, ˌäs-\ adj
aus·tere \ȯ-'stir also -'ster\ adj [ME, fr. MF, fr. L austerus, fr. Gk austēros harsh, severe; akin to Gk hauos dry — more at SERE] (14c) **1 a** : stern and cold in appearance or manner **b** : SOMBER, GRAVE ⟨an ~ critic⟩ **2** : morally strict : ASCETIC **3** : markedly simple or unadorned ⟨an ~ office⟩ ⟨an ~ style of writing⟩ **4** : giving little or no scope for pleasure ⟨~ diets⟩ **5** of a wine : having the flavor of acid or tannin predominant over fruit flavors usu. indicating a capacity for aging syn see SEVERE — **aus·tere·ly** adv — **aus·tere·ness** n
aus·ter·i·ty \ȯ-'ster-ə-tē also -'stir-\ n, pl **-ties** (14c) **1** : the quality or state of being austere **2 a** : an austere act, manner, or attitude **b** : an ascetic practice **3** : enforced or extreme economy
¹Austr- or **Austro-** comb form [L, fr. Austr-, Auster south wind] : south : southern ⟨Austroasiatic⟩
²Austr- or **Austro-** comb form [prob. fr. NL, fr. Austria] : Austrian and ⟨Austro-Hungarian⟩
¹aus·tral \'ȯs-trəl, 'äs-\ adj [ME, fr. L australis, fr. Austr-, Auster] (14c) **1** : of or relating to the Southern hemisphere **2** cap : AUSTRALIAN
²aus·tral \aü-'sträl\ n, pl **aus·tral·es** \-'strä-lās\ also **australs** [Sp] (1985) : the basic monetary unit of Argentina 1985–91
Aus·tra·lia Day \ȯ-'strāl-yə-, ä-, ə-\ n (1911) : a national holiday in Australia commemorating the landing of the British at Sydney Cove in 1788 and observed on the Monday of or next following Jan. 26
¹Aus·tra·lian \ȯ-'strāl-yən, ä-, ə-\ adj (1814) **1** : of, relating to, or characteristic of the continent or commonwealth of Australia, its inhabitants, or the languages spoken there **2** : of, relating to, or being a biogeographic region that comprises Australia, the islands north of it from Celebes eastward, Tasmania, New Zealand, and Polynesia
²Australian n (1814) **1** : a native or inhabitant of the Australian commonwealth **2** : a group of about 200 languages spoken by the aboriginal inhabitants of Australia
Australian ballot n (1888) : an official ballot printed at public expense on which the names of all the candidates and proposals appear and which is distributed only at the polling place and marked in secret
Australian cattle dog n (1926) : any of a breed of medium-sized dogs that were developed in Australia to herd cattle and that have upright ears and a red or blue mottled coat
Aus·tra·lian·ism \ˌȯ-'strāl-yə-ˌni-zəm, ˌä-, ə-\ n (1883) : a characteristic feature of Australian English
Australian pine n (1919) : any of several casuarinas (esp. Casuarina equisetifolia) now widely grown as ornamentals in warm regions
Australian Rules football n (1904) : a game resembling rugby that is played between two teams of 18 players on a field 180–190 yards long that has four goalposts at each end

Australian cattle dog

Australian shepherd n (1964) : any of a breed of bobtailed medium-sized dogs developed in America and often used in herding
Australian terrier n (1903) : any of a breed of small rather short-legged wirehaired terriers of Australian origin usu. having a tan and blue or sandy coat

Aus·tra·loid \'ȯs-trə-ˌlȯid, 'äs-\ adj [Australia + E -oid] (1901) in some classifications : of or relating to a racial group including the Australian aborigines and other peoples of southern Asia and Pacific islands — **Australoid** n
aus·tra·lo·pith·e·cine \ȯ-ˌstrā-lō-'pi-thə-ˌsīn, ä-; ˌȯs-trə-, ˌäs-\ n [ultim. fr. L australis + Gk pithēkos ape] (1943) : any of a genus (Australopithecus) of extinct southern and eastern African hominids that include gracile and robust forms with near-human dentition and a relatively small brain — **australopithecine** adj
Austrian pine n (1858) : a tall European pine (Pinus nigra) widely cultivated for ornament and having needles in clusters of two
Aus·tro·asi·at·ic \ˌȯs-(ˌ)trō-ˌā-zhē-'a-tik, -zē-'a-, 'äs- also -ˌā-shē-\ adj (1922) : of, relating to, or constituting a family of languages of south and southeast Asia that includes Mon-Khmer and Munda as subfamilies
Aus·tro·ne·sian \ˌȯs-trə-'nē-zhən, ˌäs-, -shən\ adj [Austronesia, islands of the southern Pacific] (1925) : of, relating to, or constituting a family of languages spoken in the area extending from Madagascar eastward through the Malay Peninsula and Archipelago to Hawaii and Easter Island and including practically all the native languages of the Pacific islands with the exception of the Australian and Papuan languages
aut- or **auto-** comb form [Gk, fr. autos same, -self, self] **1** : self : same one ⟨autism⟩ ⟨autobiography⟩ **2** : automatic : self-acting ⟨autopilot⟩
au·ta·coid \'ȯ-tə-ˌkȯid\ n [aut- + Gk akos remedy; prob. akin to OIr icc cure] (1914) : a physiologically active substance (as serotonin, bradykinin, or angiotensin) produced by and acting within the body
au·tar·chic \ȯ-'tär-kik\ adj (1883) : AUTARKIC — **au·tar·chi·cal** \-ki-kəl\ adj
¹au·tar·chy \'ȯ-ˌtär-kē\ n [by alter.] (1617) : AUTARKY
²autarchy n, pl **-chies** [Gk autarchia, fr. aut- + -archia -archy] (1665) **1** : absolute sovereignty **2** : AUTOCRACY
au·tar·kic \ȯ-'tär-kik\ adj (1936) : of, relating to, or marked by autarky — **au·tar·ki·cal** \-ki-kəl\ adj
au·tar·ky \'ȯ-ˌtär-kē\ n [G Autarkie, fr. Gk autarkeia, fr. autarkēs self-sufficient, fr. aut- + arkein to defend, suffice — more at ARK] (1657) **1** : SELF-SUFFICIENCY, INDEPENDENCE; specif : national economic self-sufficiency and independence **2** : a policy of establishing a self-sufficient and independent national economy
aut·ecol·o·gy \ˌȯ-ti-'kä-lə-jē, ˌȯt-ē-\ n [ISV] (1910) : ecology dealing with individual organisms or individual species of organisms — **aut·eco·log·i·cal** \ˌȯt-ˌē-kə-'lä-ji-kəl, -ˌe-kə-\ adj
au·teur \ō-'tər\ n [F, originator, author, fr. OF auctor, fr. L auctor — more at AUTHOR] (1967) : a film director whose practice accords with the auteur theory — **au·teur·ist** \-ist\ adj or n
au·teur theory \ō-'tər-\ n (1962) : a view of filmmaking in which the director is considered the primary creative force in a motion picture
au·then·tic \ə-'then-tik, ȯ-\ adj [ME autentik, fr. MF autentique, fr. LL authenticus, fr. Gk authentikos, fr. authentēs perpetrator, master, fr. aut- + -hentēs (akin to Gk anyein to accomplish, Skt sanoti he gains)] (14c) **1** obs : AUTHORITATIVE **2 a** : worthy of acceptance or belief as conforming to or based on fact ⟨paints an ~ picture of our society⟩ **b** : conforming to an original so as to reproduce essential features ⟨an ~ reproduction of a colonial farmhouse⟩ **c** : made or done the same way as an original ⟨~ Mexican fare⟩ **3** : not false or imitation : REAL, ACTUAL ⟨based on ~ documents⟩ ⟨an ~ cockney accent⟩ **4 a** of a church mode : ranging upward from the keynote — compare PLAGAL 1 **b** of a cadence : progressing from the dominant chord to the tonic — compare PLAGAL 2 **5** : true to one's own personality, spirit, or character — **au·then·ti·cal·ly** \-ti-k(ə-)lē\ adv — **au·then·tic·i·ty** \ˌȯ-ˌthen-'ti-sə-tē, -thən-\ n
syn AUTHENTIC, GENUINE, BONA FIDE mean being actually and exactly what is claimed. AUTHENTIC implies being fully trustworthy as according with fact ⟨an authentic account of the perilous journey⟩; it can also stress painstaking or faithful imitation of an original ⟨an authentic reproduction⟩ ⟨authentic Vietnamese cuisine⟩. GENUINE implies actual character not counterfeited, imitated, or adulterated ⟨genuine piety⟩ ⟨genuine maple syrup⟩; it also connotes definite origin from a source ⟨a genuine Mark Twain autograph⟩. BONA FIDE implies good faith and sincerity of intention ⟨a bona fide offer for the stock⟩.
au·then·ti·cate \ə-'then-ti-ˌkāt, ȯ-\ vt **-cat·ed; -cat·ing** (1653) : to prove or serve to prove the authenticity of syn see CONFIRM — **au·then·ti·ca·tion** \-ˌthen-ti-'kā-shən\ n — **au·then·ti·ca·tor** \-'then-ti-ˌkā-tər\ n
¹au·thor \'ȯ-thər\ n [ME auctour, fr. ONF, fr. L auctor promoter, originator, author, fr. augēre to increase — more at EKE] (14c) **1 a** : one that originates or creates : SOURCE ⟨software ~s⟩ ⟨the ~ of this crime⟩ **b** cap : GOD **1 2** : the writer of a literary work (as a book) — **au·tho·ri·al** \ȯ-'thōr-ē-əl, -'thȯr-\ adj
²author vt (1596) : to be the author of
au·thor·ess \'ȯ-th(ə-)rəs\ n (15c) : a woman author
au·tho·rise Brit var of AUTHORIZE
au·thor·i·tar·i·an \ə-ˌthär-ə-'ter-ē-ən, ȯ-, -ˌthȯr-\ adj (1879) **1** : of, relating to, or favoring blind submission to authority ⟨had ~ parents⟩ **2** : of, relating to, or favoring a concentration of power in a leader or an elite not constitutionally responsible to the people — **authoritarian** n — **au·thor·i·tar·i·an·ism** \-ē-ə-ˌni-zəm\ n
au·thor·i·ta·tive \ə-'thär-ə-ˌtā-tiv, ȯ-, -'thȯr-\ adj (1605) **1 a** : having or proceeding from authority : OFFICIAL ⟨~ church doctrine⟩ **b** : showing evident authority : DEFINITIVE ⟨a most ~ literary critique⟩ **2** : DICTATORIAL 2 — **au·thor·i·ta·tive·ly** adv — **au·thor·i·ta·tive·ness** n
au·thor·i·ty \ə-'thär-ə-tē, ȯ-, -'thȯr-\ n, pl **-ties** [ME auctorite, fr. OF auctorité, fr. L auctoritat-, auctoritas opinion, decision, power, fr. auctor] (13c) **1 a** (1) : a citation (as from a book or file) used in defense or support (2) : the source from which the citation is drawn **b** (1) : a conclusive statement or set of statements (as an official decision of a court) (2) : a decision taken as a precedent (3) : TESTIMONY **c** : an

\ə\ abut \ᵊ\ kitten, F table \ər\ further \a\ ash \ā\ ace \ä\ mop, mar \aü\ out \ch\ chin \e\ bet \ē\ easy \g\ go \i\ hit \ī\ ice \j\ job \ŋ\ sing \ō\ go \ȯ\ law \ȯi\ boy \th\ thin \t͟h\ the \ü\ loot \u̇\ foot \y\ yet \zh\ vision \à, k̇, ⁿ, œ, œ̄, ᵫ, ᵫ̄, ᵊ\ see Guide to Pronunciation individual cited or appealed to as an expert   **2 a :** power to influence or command thought, opinion, or behavior   **b :** freedom granted by one in authority : RIGHT   **3 a :** persons in command; *specif :* GOVERNMENT   **b :** a governmental agency or corporation to administer a revenue-producing public enterprise ⟨the transit ∼⟩   **4 a :** GROUNDS, WARRANT ⟨had excellent ∼ for believing the claim⟩   **b :** convincing force ⟨lent ∼ to the performance⟩   *syn* see INFLUENCE, POWER

au·tho·ri·za·tion \ˌȯ-th(ə-)rə-ˈzā-shən\ *n* (15c)   **1 :** the act of authorizing   **2 :** an instrument that authorizes : SANCTION

au·tho·rize \ˈȯ-thə-ˌrīz\ *vt* **-rized; -riz·ing** (14c)   **1 :** to establish by or as if by authority : SANCTION ⟨a custom *authorized* by time⟩   **2 :** to invest esp. with legal authority : EMPOWER ⟨*authorized* to act for her husband⟩   **3** *archaic :* JUSTIFY 1a — **au·tho·riz·er** *n*

Authorized Version *n* (1824) : a revision of the English Bishops' Bible carried out under James I, published in 1611, and widely used by Protestants — called also *King James Version*

au·thor·ship \ˈȯ-thər-ˌship\ *n* (1710)   **1 :** the profession of writing   **2 :** the source (as the author) of a piece of writing, music, or art   **3 :** the state or act of writing, creating, or causing

au·tism \ˈȯ-ˌti-zəm\ *n* (1912)   **1 :** absorption in self-centered subjective mental activity (as daydreams, fantasies, delusions, and hallucinations) usu. accompanied by marked withdrawal from reality   **2 :** a mental disorder originating in infancy that is characterized by self-absorption, inability to interact socially, repetitive behavior, and language dysfunction (as echolalia) — **au·tis·tic** \ȯ-ˈtis-tik\ *adj or n* — **au·tis·ti·cal·ly** \-ti-k(ə-)lē\ *adv*

au·to \ˈȯ-(ˌ)tō, ˈä-\ *n, pl* **autos** (1899) : AUTOMOBILE

auto- — see AUT-

au·to·an·ti·body \ˌȯ-(ˌ)tō-ˈan-ti-ˌbä-dē\ *n* (ca. 1910) : an antibody active against a tissue constituent of the individual producing it

au·to·bahn \ˈȯ-tō-ˌbän, ˈaů-\ *n* [G, fr. *Auto* + *Bahn* road] (1937) : a German, Swiss, or Austrian expressway

au·to·bi·og·ra·phy \ˌȯ-tō-bī-ˈä-grə-fē, -bē-\ *n* (1771) : the biography of a person narrated by himself — **au·to·bi·og·ra·pher** \-fər\ *n* — **au·to·bio·graph·i·cal** \-ˌbī-ə-ˈgra-fi-kəl\ *also* **au·to·bio·graph·ic** \-fik\ *adj* — **au·to·bio·graph·i·cal·ly** \-fi-k(ə-)lē\ *adv*

au·to·bus \ˈȯ-tō-ˌbəs\ *n* [*auto* + *bus*] (1899) : OMNIBUS 1

au·to·ca·tal·y·sis \ˌȯ-tō-kə-ˈta-lə-səs\ *n, pl* **-y·ses** \-ˌsēz\ [NL] (1891) : catalysis of a reaction by one of its products — **au·to·cat·a·lyt·ic** \-ˌka-tə-ˈli-tik\ *adj* — **au·to·cat·a·lyt·i·cal·ly** \-ti-k(ə-)lē\ *adv*

au·to·ceph·a·lous \ˌȯ-tō-ˈse-f(ə-)ləs\ *adj* [LGk *autokephalos*, fr. Gk *aut-* + *kephalē* head — more at CEPHALIC] (1863) : being independent of external and esp. patriarchal authority — used esp. of Eastern national churches — **au·to·ceph·a·ly** \-fə-lē\ *n*

au·toch·thon \ȯ-ˈtäk-thən\ *n, pl* **-thons** *or* **-tho·nes** \-thə-ˌnēz\ [Gk *autochthōn*, fr. *aut-* + *chthōn* earth — more at HUMBLE] (1590) : one (as a person, plant, or animal) that is autochthonous

au·toch·tho·nous \ȯ-ˈtäk-thə-nəs\ *adj* (1805)   **1 :** INDIGENOUS, NATIVE ⟨an ∼ people⟩   **2 :** formed or originating in the place where found ⟨∼ rock⟩ ⟨an ∼ infection⟩ — **au·toch·tho·nous·ly** *adv*

¹au·to·clave \ˈȯ-tō-ˌklāv\ *n* [F, fr. *aut-* + L *clavis* key — more at CLAVICLE] (1876) : an apparatus in which special conditions (as high or low pressure or temperature) can be established for a variety of applications; *esp :* an apparatus (as for sterilizing) using superheated steam under high pressure

²autoclave *vt* **-claved; -clav·ing** (1911) : to treat in an autoclave

au·to·cor·re·la·tion \ˌȯ-tō-ˌkȯr-ə-ˈlā-shən, -ˌkär-\ *n* (1950) : the correlation between paired values of a function of a mathematical or statistical variable taken at usu. constant intervals that indicates the degree of periodicity of the function

au·toc·ra·cy \ȯ-ˈtä-krə-sē\ *n, pl* **-cies** (1655)   **1 :** the authority or rule of an autocrat   **2 :** government in which one person possesses unlimited power   **3 :** a community or state governed by autocracy

au·to·crat \ˈȯ-tə-ˌkrat\ *n* [F *autocrate*, fr. Gk *autokratēs* ruling by oneself, absolute, fr. *aut-* + *-kratēs* ruling — more at -CRAT] (1803)   **1 :** a person (as a monarch) ruling with unlimited authority   **2 :** one who has undisputed influence or power

au·to·crat·ic \ˌȯ-tə-ˈkra-tik\ *also* **au·to·crat·i·cal** \-ti-kəl\ *adj* (1823)   **1 :** of, relating to, or being an autocracy : ABSOLUTE ⟨an ∼ government⟩   **2 :** characteristic of or resembling an autocrat : DESPOTIC ⟨an ∼ ruler⟩ — **au·to·crat·i·cal·ly** \-ti-k(ə-)lē\ *adv*

au·to·cross \ˈȯ-tō-ˌkrȯs, ˈä-tō-\ *n* [*auto* + *motocross*] (1963) : an automobile gymkhana

au·to·da·fé \ˌaů-tō-də-ˈfā, ˌȯ-tō-\ *n, pl* **au·tos·da·fé** \-tōz-də-\ [Pg *auto da fé*, lit., act of the faith] (1723) : the ceremony accompanying the pronouncement of judgment by the Inquisition and followed by the execution of sentence by the secular authorities; *broadly :* the burning of a heretic

au·to·di·dact \ˌȯ-tō-ˈdī-ˌdakt, -ˌdī-ˈ, -də-ˈ\ *n* [Gk *autodidaktos* self-taught, fr. *aut-* + *didaktos* taught, fr. *didaskein* to teach] (1748) : a self-taught person — **au·to·di·dac·tic** \-ˈdak-tik, -də-\ *adj*

au·toe·cious \ȯ-ˈtē-shəs\ *adj* [*aut-* + Gk *oikia* house — more at VICINITY] (ca. 1882) : passing through all life stages on the same host ⟨∼ rusts⟩ — **au·toe·cious·ly** *adv* — **au·toe·cism** \-ˈtē-ˌsi-zəm\ *n*

au·to·er·o·tism \ˌȯ-tō-ˈer-ə-ˌti-zəm\ *or* **au·to·erot·i·cism** \-i-ˈrä-tə-ˌsi-zəm\ *n* (1898)   **1 :** sexual feeling arising without known external stimulation   **2 :** sexual gratification obtained solely through stimulation by oneself of one's own body — **au·to·erot·ic** \-i-ˈrä-tik\ *adj*

au·tog·a·my \ȯ-ˈtä-gə-mē\ *n* [ISV] (1877) : SELF-FERTILIZATION: as   **a :** pollination of a flower by its own pollen   **b :** conjugation of two sister cells or sister nuclei of protozoans or fungi — **au·tog·a·mous** \-məs\ *adj*

au·tog·e·nous \ȯ-ˈtä-jə-nəs\ *also* **au·to·gen·ic** \ˌȯ-tō-ˈje-nik\ *adj* [Gk *autogenēs*, fr. *aut-* + *-genēs* born, produced — more at -GEN] (1846)   **1 :** produced independently of external influence or aid : ENDOGENOUS   **2 :** originating or derived from sources within the same individual ⟨an ∼ graft⟩ ⟨∼ vaccine⟩   **3 :** not requiring a meal of blood to produce eggs ⟨∼ mosquitoes⟩ — **au·tog·e·nous·ly** *adv* — **au·tog·e·ny** \ȯ-ˈtä-jə-nē\ *n*

au·to·gi·ro *or* **au·to·gy·ro** \ˌȯ-tō-ˈjīr-(ˌ)ō\ *n, pl* **-ros** [fr. *Autogiro*, a trademark] (1923) : a rotary-wing aircraft that employs a propeller for forward motion and a freely rotating rotor for lift

au·to·graft \ˈȯ-tō-ˌgraft\ *n* (ca. 1913) : a tissue or organ that is transplanted from one part to another of the same body — **autograft** *vt*

¹au·to·graph \ˈȯ-tə-ˌgraf\ *n* [LL *autographum*, fr. L, neut. of *autographus* written with one's own hand, fr. Gk *autographos*, fr. *aut-* + *-graphos* written — more at -GRAPH] (ca. 1644) : something written or made with one's own hand: **a :** an original manuscript or work of art   **b :** a person's handwritten signature — **au·tog·ra·phy** \ȯ-ˈtä-grə-fē\ *n*

autogiro

²autograph *vt* (1818)   **1 :** to write with one's own hand   **2 :** to write one's signature in or on

³autograph *adj* (1832) : being in the writer's own handwriting : not copied or duplicated ⟨an ∼ letter⟩

au·to·graph·ic \ˌȯ-tə-ˈgra-fik\ *adj* (1810)   **1 :** of, relating to, or constituting an autograph   **2 a** *of an instrument :* SELF-RECORDING   **b** *of a record :* recorded by a self-recording instrument — **au·to·graph·i·cal·ly** \-fi-k(ə-)lē\ *adv*

Au·to·harp \ˈȯ-tō-ˌhärp\ *trademark* — used for a zither with button-controlled dampers for selected strings

au·to·hyp·no·sis \ˌȯ-tō-hip-ˈnō-səs\ *n* [NL] (1903) : self-induced and usu. automatic hypnosis — **au·to·hyp·not·ic** \-ˈnä-tik\ *adj*

au·to·im·mune \-im-ˈyün\ *adj* (1952) : of, relating to, or caused by autoantibodies or lymphocytes that attack molecules, cells, or tissues of the organism producing them ⟨∼ diseases⟩ — **au·to·im·mu·ni·ty** \-ˈyü-nə-tē\ *n* — **au·to·im·mu·ni·za·tion** \-ˌim-yə-nə-ˈzā-shən *also* -im-ˌyü-\ *n*

au·to·in·fec·tion \-in-ˈfek-shən\ *n* [ISV] (1903) : reinfection with larvae produced by parasitic worms already in the body

au·to·in·tox·i·ca·tion \-in-ˌtäk-sə-ˈkā-shən\ *n* [ISV] (1887) : a state of being poisoned by toxic substances produced within the body

au·to·load·ing \ˌȯ-tō-ˈlō-diŋ\ *adj* (1923) : SEMIAUTOMATIC

au·tol·o·gous \ȯ-ˈtä-lə-gəs\ *adj* [*aut-* + *-ologous* (as in *homologous*)] (ca. 1921) : derived from the same individual ⟨∼ blood transfusion⟩

au·tol·y·sate \ȯ-ˈtä-lə-ˌsāt, -ˌzāt\ *also* **au·tol·y·zate** \-ˌzāt\ *n* (1910) : a product of autolysis

au·tol·yse *Brit var of* AUTOLYZE

au·tol·y·sis \-lə-səs\ *n* [NL] (1902) : breakdown of all or part of a cell or tissue by self-produced enzymes — **au·to·lyt·ic** \ˌȯ-tᵊl-ˈi-tik\ *adj*

au·to·lyze \ˈȯ-tō-ˌlīz\ *vb* **-lyzed; -lyz·ing** [back-formation fr. *autolysis*] *vi* (1910) : to undergo autolysis ∼ *vt* : to subject to autolysis

au·to·mak·er \ˈȯ-tō-ˌmā-kər, ˈä-tō-\ *n* (ca. 1905) : a manufacturer of automobiles

au·to·man \ˈȯ-tō-ˌman, ˈä-tō-\ *n* (1952) : AUTOMAKER

Au·to·mat \ˈȯ-tə-ˌmat\ *service mark* — used for a cafeteria in which food is obtained esp. from vending machines

au·to·mate \ˈȯ-tə-ˌmāt\ *vb* **-mat·ed; -mat·ing** [back-formation fr. *automation*] *vt* (1952)   **1 :** to operate by automation   **2 :** to convert to largely automatic operation : AUTOMATIZE ∼ *vi* : to undergo automation — **au·to·mat·able** \-ˌmā-tə-bəl\ *adj*

automated teller machine *n* (1981) : a computerized electronic machine that performs basic banking functions (as handling check deposits or issuing cash withdrawals) — called also *automatic teller, automatic teller machine*

¹au·to·mat·ic \ˌȯ-tə-ˈma-tik\ *adj* [Gk *automatos* self-acting, fr. *aut-* + *-matos* (akin to L *ment-, mens* mind) — more at MIND] (1748)   **1 a :** largely or wholly involuntary; *esp :* REFLEX 5 ⟨∼ blinking of the eyelids⟩   **b :** acting or done spontaneously or unconsciously   **c :** done or produced as if by machine : MECHANICAL ⟨the answers were ∼⟩   **2 :** having a self-acting or self-regulating mechanism   **3** *of a firearm :* using either gas pressure or force of recoil and mechanical spring action for repeatedly ejecting the empty cartridge shell, introducing a new cartridge, and firing it   *syn* see SPONTANEOUS — **au·to·mat·i·cal·ly** \-ti-k(ə-)lē\ *adv* — **au·to·ma·tic·i·ty** \-mə-ˈti-sə-tē, -ma-\ *n*

²automatic *n* (1902)   **1 :** a machine or apparatus that operates automatically: as   **a :** an automatic firearm   **b :** an automatic gear-shifting mechanism   **2 :** a semiautomatic firearm   **3 :** AUDIBLE

automatic pilot *n* (1916)   **1 :** AUTOPILOT 1   **2 :** a state or condition in which activity or behavior is regulated automatically in a predetermined or instinctive manner ⟨would go on *automatic pilot* and repeat all his standard denunciations —G. J. Church⟩

automatic writing *n* (1883) : writing produced without conscious intention as if of telepathic or spiritualistic origin

au·to·ma·tion \ˌȯ-tə-ˈmā-shən\ *n* [¹*automatic*] (ca. 1948)   **1 :** the technique of making an apparatus, a process, or a system operate automatically   **2 :** the state of being operated automatically   **3 :** automatically controlled operation of an apparatus, process, or system by mechanical or electronic devices that take the place of human organs of observation, effort, and decision

au·tom·a·tism \ȯ-ˈtä-mə-ˌti-zəm\ *n* [F *automatisme*, fr. *automate* automaton, fr. L *automaton*] (1838)   **1 a :** the quality or state of being automatic   **b :** an automatic action   **2 :** the power or fact of moving or functioning without conscious control either independently of external stimuli (as in the beating of the heart) or under the influence of external stimuli (as in pupil dilation)   **3 :** a theory that views the body as a machine and consciousness as a noncontrolling adjunct of the body   **4 :** suspension of the conscious mind to release subconscious images ⟨∼ the surrealist trend toward spontaneity and intuition —*Elle*⟩ — **au·tom·a·tist** \-ˈtä-mə-tist\ *n or adj*

au·tom·a·tize \ȯ-ˈtä-mə-ˌtīz\ *vt* **-tized; -tiz·ing** (1952) : to make automatic — **au·tom·a·ti·za·tion** \ȯ-ˌtä-mə-tə-ˈzā-shən, -ˌtī-ˈzä-\ *n*

au·tom·a·ton \ȯ-ˈtä-mə-tən, -mə-ˌtän\ *n, pl* **-atons** *or* **-a·ta** \-mə-tə, -mə-ˌtä\ [L, fr. Gk, neut. of *automatos*] (1645)   **1 :** a mechanism that is relatively self-operating; *esp :* ROBOT   **2 :** a machine or control mechanism designed to follow automatically a predetermined sequence of operations or respond to encoded instructions   **3 :** an individual who acts in a mechanical fashion

¹au·to·mo·bile \ˈȯ-tō-mō-ˌbē(ə)l, ˌȯ-tə-ˈmō-ˌbēl, -bēl\ *adj* [F, fr. *aut-* + *mobile*] (1883) : AUTOMOTIVE

²automobile *n* (ca. 1889) : a usu. four-wheeled automotive vehicle designed for passenger transportation — **automobile** *vi* — **au·to·mo·bil·ist** \-ˈbē-list, -ˌbē-\ *n*

au·to·mo·bil·i·ty \‚ȯ-tō-mə-'bi-lə-tē, -mō-\ *n* (1903) : the use of automobiles as the major means of transportation

au·to·mor·phism \‚ȯ-tə-'mȯr‚fi-zəm\ *n* [*aut-* + iso*morphism*] (1903) : an isomorphism of a set (as a group) with itself

au·to·mo·tive \‚ȯ-tə-'mō-tiv\ *adj* (1898) **1** : of, relating to, or concerned with self-propelled vehicles or machines **2** : SELF-PROPELLED

au·to·nom·ic \‚ȯ-tə-'nä-mik\ *adj* (1898) **1** : acting or occurring involuntarily ⟨~ reflexes⟩ **2** : relating to, affecting, or controlled by the autonomic nervous system or its effects or activity ⟨~ drugs⟩ — **au·to·nom·i·cal·ly** \-mi-k(ə-)lē\ *adv*

autonomic nervous system *n* (1898) : a part of the vertebrate nervous system that innervates smooth and cardiac muscle and glandular tissues and governs involuntary actions (as secretion and peristalsis) and that consists of the sympathetic nervous system and the parasympathetic nervous system

au·ton·o·mist \ȯ-'tä-nə-mist\ *n* (1865) : one who advocates autonomy

au·ton·o·mous \ȯ-'tä-nə-məs\ *adj* [Gk *autonomos* independent, fr. *aut-* + *nomos* law — more at NIMBLE] (1800) **1** : of, relating to, or marked by autonomy **2 a** : having the right or power of self-government **b** : undertaken or carried on without outside control : SELF-CONTAINED ⟨an ~ school system⟩ **3 a** : existing or capable of existing independently ⟨an ~ zooid⟩ **b** : responding, reacting, or developing independently of the whole ⟨an ~ growth⟩ **4** : controlled by the autonomic nervous system *syn* see FREE — **au·ton·o·mous·ly** *adv*

au·ton·o·my \-mē\ *n, pl* **-mies** (ca. 1623) **1** : the quality or state of being self-governing ; *esp* : the right of self-government **2** : self-directing freedom and esp. moral independence **3** : a self-governing state

au·to·pi·lot \'ȯ-tō-‚pī-lət\ *n* (1935) **1** : a device for automatically steering ships, aircraft, and spacecraft **2** : AUTOMATIC PILOT 2

au·to·poly·ploid \‚ȯ-tō-'pä-li-‚plȯid\ *n* (1930) : an individual or strain whose chromosome complement consists of more than two complete copies of the genome of a single ancestral species — **autopolyploid** *adj* — **au·to·poly·ploi·dy** \-‚plȯi-dē\ *n*

au·top·sy \'ȯ-‚täp-sē, 'ȯ-təp-\ *n, pl* **-sies** [Gk *autopsia* act of seeing with one's own eyes, fr. *aut-* + *opsis* sight, appearance — more at OPTIC] (1678) **1** : an examination of a body after death to determine the cause of death or the character and extent of changes produced by disease **2** : a critical examination, evaluation, or assessment of someone or something past — **autopsy** *vt*

au·to·ra·dio·gram \‚ȯ-tō-'rā-dē-ə-‚gram\ *n* (1949) : AUTORADIOGRAPH

au·to·ra·dio·graph \‚ȯ-tō-'rā-dē-ə-‚graf\ *n* [ISV] (1903) : an image produced on a photographic film or plate by the radiations from a radioactive substance in an object which is in close contact with the emulsion — **au·to·ra·dio·graph·ic** \-‚rā-dē-ə-'gra-fik\ *adj* — **au·to·ra·di·og·ra·phy** \-‚rā-dē-'ä-grə-fē\ *n*

au·to·ro·ta·tion \-rō-'tā-shən\ *n* (1918) : the turning of the rotor of an autogiro or a helicopter with the resulting lift caused solely by the aerodynamic forces induced by motion of the rotor along its flight path — **au·to·ro·tate** \-'rō-‚tāt\ *vi*

au·to·route \'ȯ-tō-‚rüt, -‚raüt\ *n* [F, fr. *auto*mobile + *route*] (1951) : an expressway esp. in France

autos-da-fé *pl of* AUTO-DA-FÉ

au·to·sex·ing \'ȯ-tō-‚sek-siŋ\ *n* (1936) : exhibiting different characters in the two sexes at birth or hatching

au·to·some \'ȯ-tə-‚sōm\ *n* (ca. 1906) : a chromosome other than a sex chromosome — **au·to·so·mal** \‚ȯ-tə-'sō-məl\ *adj* — **au·to·so·mal·ly** \-məl-lē\ *adv*

au·to·stra·da \‚au̇-tō-'strä-də, ‚ȯ-tō-\ *n, pl* **-stradas** *or* **-stra·de** \-'strä-(‚)dā\ [It, fr. *auto*mobile + *strada* street, fr. LL *strata* paved road — more at STREET] (1927) : an expressway esp. in Italy

au·to·sug·ges·tion \‚ȯ-tō-sə(g)-'jes-chən, -'jesh-\ *n* [ISV] (1890) : an influencing of one's own attitudes, behavior, or physical condition by mental processes other than conscious thought : SELF-HYPNOSIS — **au·to·sug·gest** \-sə(g)-'jest\ *vt*

au·to·te·lic \‚ȯ-tō-'te-lik, -'tē-\ *adj* [Gk *autotelēs*, fr. *aut-* + *telos* end — more at TELOS] (ca. 1901) : having a purpose in and not apart from itself

au·to·tet·ra·ploid \‚ȯ-tō-'te-trə-‚plȯid\ *n* (1930) : an individual or strain whose chromosome complement consists of four copies of a single genome due to doubling of an ancestral chromosome complement — **autotetraploid** *adj* — **au·to·tet·ra·ploi·dy** \-‚plȯi-dē\ *n*

au·tot·o·my \ȯ-'tä-tə-mē\ *n* [ISV] (1897) : reflex separation of a part (as an appendage) from the body : division of the body into two or more pieces — **au·to·to·mous** \-məs\ *adj* — **au·tot·o·mize** \-‚mīz\ *vb*

au·to·trans·form·er \‚ȯ-tō-tran(t)s-'fȯr-mər\ *n* (1895) : a transformer in which the primary and secondary coils have part or all of their turns in common

au·to·trans·fu·sion \‚ȯ-tō-tran(t)s-'fyü-zhən\ *n* (ca. 1923) : return of autologous blood to the patient's own circulatory system

au·to·troph \'ȯ-tə-‚trȯf, -‚träf\ *n* [G, fr. *autotroph*, adj.] (1938) : an autotrophic organism

au·to·tro·phic \‚ȯ-tə-'trō-fik\ *adj* [prob. fr. G *autotroph*, fr. Gk *autotrophos* supplying one's own food, fr. *aut-* + *trephein* to nourish] (ca. 1900) **1** : needing only carbon dioxide or carbonates as a source of carbon and a simple inorganic nitrogen compound for metabolic synthesis **2** : not requiring a specified exogenous factor for normal metabolism — **au·to·tro·phi·cal·ly** \-fi-k(ə-)lē\ *adv* — **au·tot·ro·phy** \ȯ-'tä-trə-fē\ *n*

au·to·wor·ker \'ȯ-tō-‚wər-kər, 'ä-\ *n* (1941) : a person employed in the automobile manufacturing industry

au·tox·i·da·tion \ȯ-‚täk-sə-'dā-shən\ *n* (1883) : oxidation by direct combination with oxygen (as in air) at ordinary temperatures

au·tumn \'ȯ-təm\ *n* [ME *autumpne*, fr. L *autumnus*] (14c) **1** : the season between summer and winter comprising in the northern hemisphere usu. the months of September, October, and November or as reckoned astronomically extending from the September equinox to the December solstice — called also *fall* **2** : a period of maturity or incipient decline ⟨in the ~ of life⟩ — **au·tum·nal** \ȯ-'təm-nəl\ *adj* — **au·tum·nal·ly** \-nə-lē\ *adv*

autumn crocus *n* (1885) : an autumn-blooming colchicum (*Colchicum autumnale*)

au·tun·ite \ȯ-'tə-‚nīt, 'ȯ-t³n-\ *n* [*Autun*, town in France] (ca. 1852) : a radioactive lemon-yellow mineral occurring in tabular crystals with basal cleavage and in scales like mica

aux·e·sis \ȯg-'zē-səs, ȯk-'sē-\ *n* [NL, fr. Gk *auxēsis* increase, growth, fr. *auxein* to increase — more at EKE] (ca. 1848) : GROWTH; *specif* : increase of cell size without cell division — **aux·et·ic** \-'ze-tik, -'se-\ *adj or n*

¹aux·il·ia·ry \ȯg-'zil-yə-rē, -'zil-rē, -'zi-lə-\ *adj* [L *auxiliaris*, fr. *auxilium* help; akin to L *augēre* to increase — more at EKE] (15c) **1 a** : offering or providing help **b** : functioning in a subsidiary capacity ⟨an ~ branch of the state university⟩ **2** *of a verb* : accompanying another verb and typically expressing person, number, mood, or tense **3 a** : SUPPLEMENTARY **b** : constituting a reserve ⟨an ~ power plant⟩ **4** : equipped with sails and a supplementary inboard engine

²auxiliary *n, pl* **-ries** (1601) **1 a** : an auxiliary person, group, or device; *specif* : a member of a foreign force serving a nation at war **b** : a Roman Catholic titular bishop assisting a diocesan bishop and not having the right of succession — called also *auxiliary bishop* **2** : an auxiliary boat or ship **3** : an auxiliary verb

aux·in \'ȯk-sən\ *n* [ISV, fr. Gk *auxein*] (1934) **1** : any of various usu. acidic organic substances that promote cell elongation in plant shoots and usu. regulate other growth processes (as root initiation): as **a** : INDOLEACETIC ACID **b** : any of various synthetic substances (as 2,4-D) resembling indoleacetic acid in activity and used esp. in research and agriculture **2** : PLANT HORMONE — **aux·in·ic** \ȯk-'si-nik\ *adj*

auxo·troph \'ȯk-sə-‚trȯf, -‚träf\ *n* (1950) : an auxotrophic strain or individual

auxo·tro·phic \‚ȯk-sə-'trō-fik\ *adj* [Gk *auxein* to increase + *-o-* + E *-trophic*] (1944) : requiring a specific growth substance beyond the minimum required for normal metabolism and reproduction by the parental or wild-type strain ⟨~ mutants of bacteria⟩ — **aux·ot·ro·phy** \ȯk-'sä-trə-fē\ *n*

¹avail \ə-'vāl\ *vb* [ME, prob. fr. *a-* (as in *abaten* to abate) + *vailen* to avail, fr. OF *valoir* to be of worth, fr. L *valēre* — more at WIELD] *vi* (14c) : to be of use or advantage : SERVE ⟨our best efforts did not ~⟩ ~ *vt* **1** : to be of use or advantage to : PROFIT **2** : to result in : bring about ⟨his efforts ~ed him nothing⟩ — **avail oneself of** *also* **avail of** : to make use of : take advantage of

²avail *n* (15c) **1** : advantage toward attainment of a goal or purpose : USE ⟨effort was of little ~⟩ **2** *pl* : profits or proceeds esp. from a business or from the sale of property

avail·abil·i·ty \ə-‚vā-lə-'bi-lə-tē\ *n, pl* **-ties** (1803) **1** : the quality or state of being available **2** : an available person or thing

avail·able \ə-'vā-lə-bəl\ *adj* (15c) **1** *archaic* : having a beneficial effect **2** : VALID — used of a legal plea or charge **3** : present or ready for immediate use **4** : ACCESSIBLE, OBTAINABLE ⟨articles ~ in any drugstore⟩ **5** : qualified or willing to do something or to assume a responsibility ⟨~ candidates⟩ **6** : present in such chemical or physical form as to be usable (as by a plant) ⟨~ nitrogen⟩ ⟨~ water⟩ — **avail·able·ness** *n* — **avail·ably** \-blē\ *adv*

¹av·a·lanche \'a-və-‚lanch\ *n* [F, fr. F dial. *lavantse, avalantse*] (1771) **1** : a large mass of snow, ice, earth, rock, or other material in swift motion down a mountainside or over a precipice **2** : a sudden great or overwhelming rush or accumulation of something ⟨office workers tied down with an ~ of paperwork⟩ **3** : a cumulative process in which photons or accelerated charge carriers produce additional photons or charge carriers through collisions (as with gas molecules)

²avalanche *vb* **-lanched; -lanch·ing** *vi* (1872) : to descend in an avalanche ~ *vt* : OVERWHELM, FLOOD

Av·a·lon \'a-və-‚län\ *n* : a paradise to which Arthur is carried after his death

avant \'ä-‚vänt, 'a-, -‚vȯnt(t), -‚vōⁿ\ *adj* [F *avant-* fore-, front, fr. *avant* before, fr. L *abante*] (1965) : culturally or stylistically advanced : AVANT-GARDE ⟨~ jazz⟩

¹avant-garde \‚ä-‚vänt(t)-'gärd, ‚a-, ‚ä-; ə-'vänt-; ‚a-‚vōⁿ-, ‚a-‚vȯnt(t)-'\ *n* [F, vanguard] (1910) : an intelligentsia that develops new or experimental concepts esp. in the arts — **avant–gard·ism** \-'gär-‚di-zəm\ *n* — **avant–gard·ist** \-'gär-dist\ *n*

²avant-garde *adj* (1925) : of or relating to an avant-garde ⟨~ writers⟩

av·a·rice \'a-və-rəs, 'av-rəs\ *n* [ME, fr. OF, fr. L *avaritia*, fr. *avarus* avaricious, fr. *avēre* to crave — more at AVID] (14c) : excessive or insatiable desire for wealth or gain : GREEDINESS, CUPIDITY

av·a·ri·cious \‚a-və-'ri-shəs\ *adj* (15c) : greedy of gain : excessively acquisitive esp. in seeking to hoard riches *syn* see COVETOUS — **av·a·ri·cious·ly** *adv* — **av·a·ri·cious·ness** *n*

avas·cu·lar \(‚)ā-'vas-kyə-lər\ *adj* (ca. 1900) : having few or no blood vessels ⟨~ tissue⟩ — **avas·cu·lar·i·ty** \‚ā-‚vas-kyə-'lar-ə-tē\ *n*

avast \ə-'vast\ *vb imper* [perh. fr. D *houd vast* hold fast] (1681) — a nautical command to stop or cease

av·a·tar \'a-və-‚tär, ‚a-və-'\ *n* [Skt *avatāra* descent, fr. *avatarati* he descends, fr. *ava-* away + *tarati* he crosses over — more at UKASE, THROUGH] (1784) **1** : the incarnation of a Hindu deity (as Vishnu) **2 a** : an incarnation in human form **b** : an embodiment (as of a concept or philosophy) often in a person **3** : a variant phase or version of a continuing basic entity

avaunt \ə-'vȯnt, -'vänt\ *adv* [ME, fr. MF *avant*, fr. L *abante* forward, before, fr. *ab* from + *ante* before — more at OF, ANTE-] (15c) : AWAY, HENCE

ave \'ä-(‚)vā\ *n* [ME, fr. L, hail] (13c) **1** : an expression of greeting or of leave-taking : HAIL, FAREWELL **2** *often cap* : AVE MARIA

avel·lan \ə-'ve-lən\ *or* **avel·lane** \ə-'ve-‚lān, 'a-və-‚län\ *adj* [L *abellana, avellana* filbert, fr. fem. of *Abellanus* of Abella, fr. *Abella*, ancient town in Italy] (1611) *of a heraldic cross* : having the four arms shaped like conventionalized filberts — see CROSS illustration

Ave Ma·ria \‚ä-(‚)vä-mə-'rē-ə\ *n* [ME, fr. ML, hail, Mary] (13c) : HAIL MARY

avenge \ə-'venj\ *vt* **avenged; aveng·ing** [ME *avengen*, prob. fr. *a-* (as

\ə\ abut \ᵊ\ kitten, F table \ər\ further \a\ ash \ā\ ace \ä\ mop, mar \au̇\ out \ch\ chin \e\ bet \ē\ easy \g\ go \i\ hit \ī\ ice \j\ job \ŋ\ sing \ō\ go \o\ law \oi\ boy \th\ thin \t̷h\ the \ü\ loot \u̇\ foot \y\ yet \zh\ vision \å, ᵏ, ⁿ, œ, œ̄, ᵫ, ūe, ᵞ\ *see* Guide to Pronunciation in *abaten* to abate) + *vengen* to avenge, fr. OF *vengier* — more at VEN-GEANCE] (14c) **1 :** to take vengeance for or on behalf of **2 :** to exact satisfaction for (a wrong) by punishing the wrongdoer — **aveng·er** *n*

av·ens \'a-vənz\ *n, pl* **avens** [ME *avence*, fr. OF] (13c) **:** any of a genus (*Geum*) of perennial herbs of the rose family with white, purple, or yellow flowers

av·en·tail \'a-vən-ˌtāl\ *n* [ME, modif. of OF *ventaille*] (14c) **:** VENTAIL

aven·tu·rine \ə-'ven-chə-ˌrēn, -rən\ *n* [F, fr. *aventure* chance — more at ADVENTURE] (1811) **1 :** glass containing opaque sparkling particles of foreign material usu. copper or chromic oxide **2 :** a translucent quartz spangled throughout with scales of mica or other mineral

av·e·nue \'a-və-ˌnü, -ˌnyü\ *n* [MF, fr. fem. of *avenu*, pp. of *avenir* to come to, fr. L *advenire* — more at ADVENTURE] (1600) **1 :** a way of access **:** ROUTE **2 :** a channel for pursuing a desired object ⟨∼s of com-munication⟩ **3 a** *chiefly Brit* **:** the principal walk or driveway to a house situated off a main road **b :** a broad passageway bordered by trees **4 :** an often broad street or road

aver \ə-'vər\ *vt* **averred; aver·ring** [ME *averren*, fr. MF *averer*, fr. ML *adverare* to confirm as authentic, fr. L *ad-* + *verus* true — more at VERY] (15c) **1 a :** to verify or prove to be true in pleading a cause **b :** to allege or assert in pleading **2 :** to declare positively

¹av·er·age \'a-v(ə-)rij\ *n* [fr. earlier *average* proportionally distributed charge for damage at sea, modif. of MF *avarie* damage to ship or cargo, fr. Olt *avaria*, fr. Ar '*awāriyah* damaged merchandise] (1735) **1 a :** a single value (as a mean, mode, or median) that summarizes or repre-sents the general significance of a set of unequal values **b :** MEAN 1b **2 a :** an estimation of or approximation to an arithmetic mean **b :** a level (as of intelligence) typical of a group, class, or series ⟨above the ∼⟩ **3 :** a ratio expressing the average performance esp. of an athletic team or an athlete computed according to the number of opportunities for successful performance — **on average** *or* **on the average :** tak-ing the typical example of the group under consideration ⟨prices have increased *on average* by five percent⟩

syn AVERAGE, MEAN, MEDIAN, NORM mean something that represents a middle point. AVERAGE is exactly or approximately the quotient ob-tained by dividing the sum total of a set of figures by the number of figures ⟨scored an *average* of 85 on tests⟩. MEAN may be the simple average or it may represent value midway between two extremes ⟨a high of 70° and a low of 50° give a *mean* of 60°⟩. MEDIAN applies to the value that represents the point at which there are as many instances above as there are below ⟨*average* of a group of persons earning 3, 4, 5, 8, and 10 dollars a day is 6 dollars, whereas the *median* is 5 dollars⟩. NORM means the computed or estimated average of performance of a significantly large group, class, or grade ⟨scores about the *norm* for 5th grade arithmetic⟩.

²average *adj* (1770) **1 :** equaling an arithmetic mean **2 a :** being about midway between extremes ⟨a man of ∼ height⟩ **b :** not out of the ordinary **:** COMMON ⟨the ∼ person⟩ — **av·er·age·ly** *adv* — **av·er·age·ness** *n*

³average *vb* **av·er·aged; av·er·ag·ing** *vi* (1769) **1 a :** to be or come to an average ⟨the gain *averaged* out to 20 percent⟩ **b :** to have a me-dial value of ⟨a color *averaging* a pale purple⟩ **2 :** to buy on a falling market or sell on a rising market additional shares or commodities so as to obtain a more favorable average price — usu. used with *down* or *up* ∼ *vt* **1 :** to do, get, or have on the average or as an average sum or quantity ⟨∼s 12 hours of work a day⟩ **2 :** to find the arithmetic mean of ⟨a series of unequal quantities⟩ **3 a :** to bring toward the average **b :** to divide among a number proportionately

aver·ment \ə-'vər-mənt\ *n* (15c) **1 :** the act of averring **2 :** some-thing that is averred **:** AFFIRMATION

averse \ə-'vərs\ *adj* [L *aversus*, pp. of *avertere*] (1597) **:** having an ac-tive feeling of repugnance or distaste ⟨∼ to strenuous exercise⟩ *syn* see DISINCLINED — **averse·ly** *adv* — **averse·ness** *n*

aver·sion \ə-'vər-zhən, -shən\ *n* (1596) **1** *obs* **:** the act of turning away **2 a :** a feeling of repugnance toward something with a desire to avoid or turn from it ⟨regards drunkenness with ∼⟩ **b :** a settled dislike **:** ANTIPATHY ⟨expressed an ∼ to parties⟩ **c :** a tendency to extinguish a behavior or to avoid a thing or situation and esp. a usu. pleasurable one because it is or has been associated with a noxious stimulus **3 :** one that is the object of aversion

aversion therapy *n* (1946) **:** therapy intended to change habits or antisocial behavior by inducing dislike for them through association with a noxious stimulus

aver·sive \ə-'vər-siv, -ziv\ *adj* (1923) **:** tending to avoid or causing avoidance of a noxious or punishing stimulus ⟨behavior modification by ∼ stimulation⟩ — **aver·sive·ly** *adv* — **aver·sive·ness** *n*

avert \ə-'vərt\ *vt* [ME, fr. MF *avertir*, fr. L *avertere*, fr. *ab-* + *vertere* to turn — more at WORTH] (15c) **1 :** to turn away or aside (as the eyes) in avoidance **2 :** to see coming and ward off **:** AVOID

Aves·ta \ə-'ves-tə\ *n* [MPer *Avastāk*, lit., original text] (1856) **:** the book of the sacred writings of Zoroastrianism

Aves·tan \-tən\ *n* (1856) **:** an ancient Iranian language in which the sacred books of Zoroastrianism were written — see INDO-EUROPEAN LANGUAGES table — **Avestan** *adj*

av·gas \'av-ˌgas\ *n* [*aviation gasoline*] (1943) **:** gasoline for airplanes

av·go·lem·o·no \ˌäv-gō-'le-mə-(ˌ)nō\ *n* [NGk *augolemono*, fr. *augo* egg + *lemoni* lemon] (1961) **:** a soup or sauce made of chicken stock, rice, egg yolks, and lemon sauce

avi·an \'ā-vē-ən\ *adj* [L *avis*] (1870) **:** of, relating to, or derived from birds

avi·ary \'ā-vē-ˌer-ē\ *n, pl* **-ar·ies** [L *aviarium*, fr. *avis* bird; akin to Gk *aetos* eagle] (1577) **:** a place for keeping birds confined

avi·ate \'ā-vē-ˌāt, 'a-\ *vi* **-at·ed; -at·ing** [back-formation fr. *aviation*] (1887) **:** to navigate the air (as in an airplane)

avi·a·tion \ˌā-vē-'ā-shən, ˌa-\ *n, often attrib* [F, fr. L *avis*] (1866) **1 :** the operation of heavier-than-air aircraft **2 :** military airplanes **3 :** airplane manufacture, development, and design

avi·a·tor \'ā-vē-ˌā-tər, 'a-\ *n* (1887) **:** the operator or pilot of an aircraft and esp. an airplane

aviator glasses *n pl* (1968) **:** eyeglasses having a lightweight metal frame and relatively large usu. tinted lenses

avi·a·trix \ˌā-vē-'ā-triks, ˌa-\ *n, pl* **-trix·es** \-trik-səz\ *or* **-tri·ces** \-trə-ˌsēz\ (1910) **:** a woman aviator

avi·cul·ture \'ā-və-ˌkəl-chər, 'a-\ *n* [L *avis* + E *culture*] (ca. 1879) **:** the raising and care of birds and esp. of wild birds in captivity — **avi·cul·tur·ist** \ˌā-və-'kəl-ch(ə-)rist, ˌa-\ *n*

av·id \'a-vəd\ *adj* [F or L; F *avide*, fr. L *avidus*, fr. *avēre* to desire, crave; akin to W *ewyllys* desire, OIr *con-oí* he protects] (1769) **1 :** desirous to the point of greed **:** urgently eager **:** GREEDY ⟨∼ for publicity⟩ **2 :** characterized by enthusiasm and vigorous pursuit ⟨∼ readers⟩ *syn* see EAGER — **av·id·ly** *adv* — **av·id·ness** *n*

avi·din \'a-və-dən\ *n* [fr. its avidity for biotin] (1941) **:** a protein found in egg white that inactivates biotin by combining with it

avid·ity \ə-'vi-də-tē, a-\ *n, pl* **-ities** (15c) **1 :** the quality or state of being avid **: a :** keen eagerness **: b :** consuming greed **2 :** AFFINITY 2b(2)

avi·fau·na \ˌā-və-'fó-nə, ˌa-, -'fä-nə\ *n* [NL, fr. L *avis* + NL *fauna*] (1874) **:** the birds or the kinds of birds of a region, period, or environ-ment — **avi·fau·nal** \-'fó-n³l, -'fä-\ *adj*

avi·on·ics \ˌā-vē-'ä-niks, ˌa-\ *n pl* [*aviation electronics*] (1949) **:** elec-tronics designed for use in aerospace vehicles — **avi·on·ic** \-nik\ *adj*

avir·u·lent \(ˌ)ā-'vir-(y)ə-lənt\ *adj* [ISV] (ca. 1900) **:** not virulent — compare NONPATHOGENIC

avi·ta·min·o·sis \ˌā-ˌvī-tə-mə-'nō-səs\ *n, pl* **-o·ses** \-ˌsēz\ [NL] (1919) **:** disease (as pellagra) resulting from a deficiency of one or more vita-mins — **avi·ta·min·ot·ic** \-mə-'nä-tik\ *adj*

A–V node \ˌā-'vē-, ˌä-,\ *n* (1949) **:** ATRIOVENTRICULAR NODE

avo \'ā-(ˌ)vü\ *n, pl* **avos** [Pg, fr. *avo* fractional part, fr. *-avo* ordinal suffix (as in *oitavo* eighth, fr. L *octavus*) — more at OCTAVE] (ca. 1909) — see *pataca* at MONEY table

av·o·ca·do \ˌä-və-'kä-(ˌ)dō, ˌa-\ *n, pl* **-dos** *also* **-does** [modif. of Sp *aguacate*, fr. Nahuatl *āhuacatl* avocado, testicle] (1697) **1 :** a pulpy green to purple nutty-flavored edible fruit of any of various tropical American trees (genus *Persea* esp. *P. americana*) of the laurel family; *also* **:** a tree bearing avocados **2 :** a light yellowish green

avocado pear *n* (1830) *chiefly Brit* **:** AVOCADO 1

av·o·ca·tion \ˌa-və-'kā-shən\ *n* [L *avocation-, avocatio*, fr. *avocare* to call away, fr. *ab-* + *vocare* to call, fr. *voc-, vox* voice — more at VOICE] (ca. 1617) **1** *archaic* **:** DIVERSION, DISTRACTION **2 :** customary employment **:** VOCATION **3 :** a subordinate occupation pursued in addition to one's vocation esp. for enjoyment **:** HOBBY

av·o·ca·tion·al \ˌa-və-'kā-sh(ə-)nəl\ *adj* (1921) **1 :** of or relating to an avocation ⟨an ∼ interest in sports⟩ **2 :** being such by avocation ⟨an ∼ musician⟩ — **av·o·ca·tion·al·ly** \-sh(ə-)nə-lē\ *adv*

av·o·cet \'a-və-ˌset\ *n* [F & It; F *avocette*, fr. It *avocetta*] (1766) **:** any of a genus (*Recurvirostra*) of rather large long-legged shorebirds with webbed feet and slender upward-curving bill

Avo·ga·dro's number \ˌa-və-'gä-(ˌ)drōz-, ˌä-və-, -'gä-\ *n* [Count Amedeo *Avogadro*] (1924) **:** the number 6.023×10^{23} indicating the number of atoms or molecules in a mole of any substance — called also *Avogadro number*

avoid \ə-'vóid\ *vt* [ME, fr. MF *esvuidier*, fr. *es-* (fr. L *ex-*) + *vuidier* to empty — more at VOID] (14c) **1 :** to make legally void **:** ANNUL ⟨∼ a plea⟩ **2** *obs* **:** VOID, EXPEL **3 a :** to keep away from **:** SHUN **b :** to prevent the occurrence or effectiveness of **c :** to refrain from **4** *ar-chaic* **:** to depart or withdraw from **:** LEAVE *syn* see ESCAPE — **avoid·able** \-'vói-də-bəl\ *adj* — **avoid·ably** \-blē\ *adv* — **avoid·er** *n*

avoid·ance \ə-'vói-dᵊn(t)s\ *n* (14c) **1** *obs* **a :** an action of emptying, vacating, or clearing away **b :** OUTLET **2 :** ANNULMENT 1 **3 :** an act or practice of avoiding or withdrawing from something

¹av·oir·du·pois \ˌa-vər-də-'póiz, 'a-vər-də-,\ *n* [ME *avoir de pois* goods sold by weight, fr. OF, lit., goods of weight] (15c) **1 :** AVOIRDUPOIS WEIGHT **2 :** WEIGHT, HEAVINESS; *esp* **:** personal weight

²avoirdupois *adj* (1755) **:** expressed in avoirdupois weight ⟨one ounce ∼⟩

avoirdupois weight *n* (1619) **:** the series of units of weight based on the pound of 16 ounces and the ounce of 16 drams — see WEIGHT table

avouch \ə-'vauch\ *vt* [ME, to cite as authority, fr. MF *avochier* to sum-mon, fr. L *advocare* — more at ADVOCATE] (15c) **1 :** to declare as a matter of fact or as a thing that can be proved **:** AFFIRM **2 :** to vouch for **:** CORROBORATE **3 a :** to acknowledge (as an act) as one's own **b :** CONFESS, AVOW

avouch·ment \-mənt\ *n* (1574) **:** an act of avouching **:** AVOWAL

avow \ə-'vau\ *vt* [ME, fr. MF *avouer*, fr. L *advocare*] (14c) **1 :** to de-clare assuredly **2 :** to declare openly, bluntly, and without shame ⟨ever ready to ∼ his reactionary outlook⟩ *syn* see ACKNOWLEDGE, ASSERT — **avow·er** \-'vau̇(-ə)r\ *n*

avow·al \ə-'vau̇(-ə)l\ *n* (ca. 1732) **:** an open declaration or acknowledg-ment

avow·ed·ly \ə-'vau̇-əd-lē\ *adv* (1656) **1 :** with open acknowledgment **:** FRANKLY ⟨an ∼ hostile review⟩ **2 :** by unsupported assertion or profession alone **:** ALLEGEDLY ⟨politicians remain skeptical of . . . ∼ democratic intentions —Jerry Kirshenbaum⟩

avulse \ə-'vəls\ *vt* **avulsed; avuls·ing** [L *avulsus*, pp. of *avellere* to tear off, fr. *ab-* + *vellere* to pluck — more at VULNERABLE] (ca. 1765) **:** to separate by avulsion

avul·sion \ə-'vəl-shən\ *n* (1622) **:** a forcible separation or detachment: as **a :** a tearing away of a body part accidentally or surgically **b :** a sudden cutting off of land by flood, currents, or change in course of a body of water; *esp* **:** one separating land from one person's property and joining it to another's

avun·cu·lar \ə-'vən-kyə-lər\ *adj* [L *avunculus* maternal uncle — more at UNCLE] (1831) **1 :** of or relating to an uncle **2 :** suggestive of an uncle esp. in kindliness or geniality ⟨∼ indulgence⟩ — **avun·cu·lar·i·ty** \ə-ˌvən-kyə-'la-rə-tē\ *n* — **avun·cu·lar·ly** \ə-'vən-kyə-lər-lē\ *adv*

aw \'ò\ *interj* (1852) — used to express mild disappointment, gentle entreaty, or real or mock sympathy or sentiment

await \ə-'wāt\ *vb* [ME, fr. ONF *awaitier*, fr. *a-* (fr. L *ad-*) + *waitier* to watch — more at WAIT] (13c) **1** *obs* **a :** to lie in wait for **2 a :** to wait for **b :** to remain in abeyance until ⟨a treaty ∼ing ratification⟩ **3 :** to be in store for ⟨wonders what ∼s him next⟩ ∼ *vi* **1** *obs* **:** ATTEND **2 :** to stay or be in waiting **:** WAIT **3 :** to be in store

¹awake \ə-'wāk\ *vb* **awoke** \-'wōk\ *also* **awaked** \-'wākt\; **awo·ken** \-'wō-kən\ *or* **awaked** *also* **awoke; awak·ing** [ME *awaken* (fr. OE *awacan, onwacan,* fr. *¹a-, on* + *wacan* to awake) & *awakien,* fr. OE *awacian, onwacian,* fr. *¹a-* + *wacian* to be awake — more at WAKE] *vi* (bef. 12c) **1 :** to cease sleeping **2 :** to become aroused or active again **3 :** to be-

come conscious or aware of something ⟨*awoke* to the possibilities⟩ ~
vt **1** : to arouse from sleep or a sleeplike state ⟨*awoken* by the storm⟩
2 : to make active : stir up ⟨*awoke* old memories⟩
²**awake** *adj* (13c) : fully conscious, alert, and aware : not asleep *syn*
see AWARE

awak·en \ə-'wā-kən\ *vb* **awak·ened; awak·en·ing** \-'wāk-niŋ, -'wā-
kə-\ [ME, fr. OE *awæcnian*, fr. *a-* + *wæcnian* to waken] (bef. 12c)
: AWAKE — **awak·en·er** \-'wāk-nər, -'wā-kə-\ *n*

¹**award** \ə-'wȯrd\ *vt* [ME, to decide, fr. ONF *eswarder*, fr. *es-* (fr. L *ex-*)
+ *warder* to guard, of Gmc origin; akin to OHG *wartēn* to watch —
more at WARD] (14c) **1** : to give by judicial decree or after careful
consideration **2** : to confer or bestow as being deserved or merited or
needed ⟨~ scholarships to disadvantaged students⟩ *syn* see GRANT —
award·able \-'wȯr-də-bəl\ *adj* — **award·ee** \-,wȯr-'dē\ *n* — **award·
er** \-'wȯr-dər\ *n*
²**award** *n* (14c) **1** **a** : a judgment or final decision; *esp* : the decision
of arbitrators in a case submitted to them **b** : the document containing the decision of arbitrators **2** : something that is conferred or bestowed esp. on the basis of merit or need

aware \ə-'war\ *adj* [ME *iwar*, fr. OE *gewær*, fr. *ge-* (associative
prefix) + *wær* wary — more at CO-, WARY] (bef. 12c) **1** *archaic*
: WATCHFUL, WARY **2** : having or showing realization, perception, or
knowledge — **aware·ness** *n*
syn AWARE, COGNIZANT, CONSCIOUS, SENSIBLE, ALIVE, AWAKE mean having knowledge of something. AWARE implies vigilance in observing or
alertness in drawing inferences from what one experiences ⟨*aware* of
changes in climate⟩. COGNIZANT implies having special or certain
knowledge as from firsthand sources ⟨not fully *cognizant* of the facts⟩.
CONSCIOUS implies that one is focusing one's attention on something or
is even preoccupied by it ⟨*conscious* that my heart was pounding⟩.
SENSIBLE implies direct or intuitive perceiving esp. of intangibles or of
emotional states or qualities ⟨*sensible* of a teacher's influence⟩. ALIVE
adds to SENSIBLE the implication of acute sensitivity to something
⟨*alive* to the thrill of danger⟩. AWAKE implies that one has become alive
to something and is on the alert ⟨a country always *awake* to the threat
of invasion⟩.

awash \ə-'wȯsh, -'wäsh\ *adj* (1833) **1** **a** : alternately covered and
exposed by waves or tide **b** : washing about : AFLOAT **c** : covered
with water **2** : FLOODED **2** : filled, covered, or completely overrun as if
by a flood ⟨a movie ~ in sentimentality⟩

¹**away** \ə-'wā\ *adv* (bef. 12c) **1** : on the way : ALONG ⟨get ~ early⟩ **2**
: from this or that place : HENCE, THENCE ⟨go ~⟩ **3** **a** : in a secure
place or manner ⟨locked ~⟩ **b** : in another direction ⟨look ~⟩ **4**
: out of existence : to an end ⟨echoes dying ~⟩ **5** : from one's possession ⟨gave ~ a fortune⟩ **6** : steadily onward : UNINTERRUPTEDLY
⟨clocks ticking ~⟩ **7** : by a long distance or interval : FAR ⟨~ back in
1910⟩
²**away** *adj* (14c) **1** : absent from a place : GONE ⟨~ for the weekend⟩
2 : distant in space or time ⟨a lake 10 miles ~⟩ ⟨the season is two
months ~⟩ **3** : played on an opponent's grounds ⟨home and ~
games⟩ **4** *baseball* : OUT ⟨two ~ in the ninth⟩ — **away·ness** *n*

¹**awe** \'ȯ\ *n* [ME, fr. ON *agi*; akin to OE *ege* awe, Gk *achos* pain] (13c)
1 : an emotion variously combining dread, veneration, and wonder
that is inspired by authority or by the sacred or sublime ⟨stood in ~ of
the king⟩ ⟨regard nature's wonders with ~⟩ **2** *archaic* **a** : DREAD,
TERROR **b** : the power to inspire dread
²**awe** *vt* **awed; aw·ing** (13c) : to inspire with awe

aweary \ə-'wir-ē\ *adj* (1537) *archaic* : being weary

aweath·er \ə-'we-thər\ *adv* (1599) : on or toward the weather or windward side — compare ALEE

awed \'ȯd\ *adj* (1592) : showing awe ⟨~ respect⟩

aweigh \ə-'wā\ *adj* (1670) : raised just clear of the bottom — used of
an anchor

awe·less *or* **aw·less** \'ȯ-ləs\ *adj* (14c) **1** : feeling no awe **2** *obs* : inspiring no awe

awe·some \'ȯ-səm\ *adj* (1598) **1** : expressive of awe ⟨~ tribute⟩ **2** **a**
: inspiring awe ⟨an ~ task⟩ **b** : TERRIFIC 2, 3; *esp* : EXTRAORDINARY
— **awe·some·ly** *adv* — **awe·some·ness** *n*

awe·struck \-,strək\ *also* **awe·strick·en** \-,stri-kən\ *adj* (1634) : filled
with awe

¹**aw·ful** \'ȯ-fəl\ *adj* (13c) **1** : inspiring awe **2** : filled with awe: as **a**
obs : AFRAID, TERRIFIED **b** : deeply respectful or reverential **3** : extremely disagreeable or objectionable **4** : exceedingly great — used as
an intensive ⟨an ~ lot of money⟩ — **aw·ful·ly** \'ȯ-fə-lē, *esp as adv of
adj senses 3 & 4* -flē\ *adv* — **aw·ful·ness** \-fəl-nəs\ *n*
usage Many grammarians take issue with the senses of *awful* and
awfully that do not convey the etymological connection with *awe*.
However, senses 3 and 4 of the adjective were used in speech and
casual writing by the late 18th century ⟨it is an *awful* while since you
have heard from me —John Keats (letter)⟩ ⟨there was an *awful* crowd
—Sir Walter Scott (letter)⟩ ⟨this is an *awful* thing to say to oil painters
—William Blake⟩. Adverbial use of *awful* as an intensifier began to
appear in print in the early 19th century, as did the senses of *awfully*
corresponding to senses 3 and 4 of the adjective. Both adverbs remain
in widespread use ⟨a sad state of affairs and *awful* tough on art —H.
L. Mencken⟩ ⟨the *awfully* rich young American —Henry James⟩ ⟨de-
cided to play it so *awfully* safe —A. M. Schlesinger *b*1917⟩.
²**awful** *adv* (1818) : VERY, EXTREMELY ⟨~ cold⟩

awhile \ə-'hwī(ə)l, ə-'wī(ə)l\ *adv* (bef. 12c) : for a while
usage Although considered a solecism by many commentators,
awhile, like several other adverbs of time and place, is often used as
the object of a preposition ⟨for *awhile* there is a silence —Lord Dun-
sany⟩.

awhirl \ə-'hwər(-ə)l, -'wər(-ə)l\ *adj* (1883) : being in a whirl

awk·ward \'ȯ-kwərd\ *adj* [ME *awkeward* in the wrong direction, fr.
awke turned the wrong way, fr. ON *ǫfugr*; akin to OHG *abuh* turned
the wrong way] (1530) **1** *obs* : PERVERSE **2** *archaic* : UNFAVORABLE,
ADVERSE **3** **a** : lacking dexterity or skill (as in the use of hands) ⟨~
with a needle and thread⟩ **b** : showing the result of a lack of expertness ⟨~ pictures⟩ **4** **a** : lacking ease or grace (as of movement or
expression) **b** : lacking the right proportions, size, or harmony of
parts : UNGAINLY **5** **a** : lacking social grace and assurance **b** : causing embarrassment ⟨an ~ moment⟩ **6** : not easy to handle or deal

with : requiring great skill, ingenuity, or care ⟨an ~ load⟩ ⟨an ~ diplomatic situation⟩ — **awk·ward·ly** *adv* — **awk·ward·ness** *n*
syn AWKWARD, CLUMSY, MALADROIT, INEPT, GAUCHE mean not marked
by ease (as of performance, movement, or social conduct). AWKWARD
is widely applicable and may suggest unhandiness, inconvenience,
lack of muscular control, embarrassment, or lack of tact ⟨periods of
awkward silence⟩. CLUMSY implies stiffness and heaviness and so may
connote inflexibility, unwieldiness, or lack of ordinary skill ⟨a *clumsy*
mechanic⟩. MALADROIT suggests a tendency to create awkward situations ⟨a *maladroit* politician⟩. INEPT often implies complete failure or
inadequacy ⟨a hopelessly *inept* defense attorney⟩. GAUCHE implies the
effects of shyness, inexperience, or ill breeding ⟨felt *gauche* and unsophisticated at formal parties⟩.

awl \'ȯl\ *n* [ME *al*, fr. ON *alr*; akin to OHG *āla* awl, Skt *ārā*] (bef. 12c)
: a pointed tool for marking surfaces or piercing small holes (as in
leather or wood)

awn \'ȯn\ *n* [ME, fr. OE *agen*, fr. ON *ǫgn*; akin to OHG *agana* awn,
OE *ecg* edge — more at EDGE] (12c) : one of the slender bristles that
terminate the glumes of the spikelet in some cereal and other grasses —
awned \'ȯnd\ *adj* — **awn·less** \'ȯn-ləs\ *adj*

aw·ning \'ȯ-niŋ, 'ä-niŋ\ *n* [origin unknown] (1624) : a rooflike cover
extending over or in front of a place (as over the deck or in front of a
door or window) as a shelter — **aw·ninged** \-niŋd\ *adj*

awoke *past and past part of* AWAKE

awoken *past part of* AWAKE

¹**AWOL** \'ā-,wȯl, ,ā-,də-bəl-yü-,ō-'el\ *adj or adv, sometimes not cap*
[absent without leave] (1919) **1** : ABSENT WITHOUT LEAVE; *broadly* : absent
often without notice or permission ⟨the place looked as if its caretaker
had been ~ for some time —Daniel Ford⟩
²**AWOL** *n, sometimes not cap* (1919) : a person who is AWOL

awry \ə-'rī\ *adv or adj* (14c) **1** : in a turned or twisted position or
direction : ASKEW **2** : off the correct or expected course : AMISS

aw–shucks \'ȯ-,shəks\ *adj* (1951) : being or marked by an unsophisticated, self-conscious, or self-effacing manner

¹**ax** *or* **axe** \'aks\ *n* [ME, fr. OE *æcs*; akin to OHG *ackus* ax, L *ascia*, Gk
axinē] (bef. 12c) **1** : a cutting tool that consists of a heavy edged head
fixed to a handle with the edge parallel to the handle and that is used
esp. for felling trees and chopping and splitting wood **2** : a hammer
with a sharp edge for dressing or spalling stone **3** : abrupt removal
(as from employment or from a budget) — sometimes used in the
phrase *get the ax* **4** : a musical instrument (as a guitar or a saxophone)
— **ax to grind** : an ulterior often selfish purpose to further
²**ax** *or* **axe** *vt* **axed; ax·ing** (1679) **1** **a** : to shape, dress, or trim with
an ax **b** : to chop, split, or sever with an ax **2** : to remove abruptly
(as from employment or from a budget)

ax·el \'ak-səl, 'äk-\ *n, often cap* [*Axel* Paulsen †1938 Norw. figure
skater] (1930) : a jump in figure skating from the outer forward edge
of one skate with 1½ turns taken in the air and a return to the outer
backward edge of the other skate

axe·nic \(,)ā-'ze-nik, -'zē-\ *adj* [²*a-* + Gk *xenos* strange] (1942) : free
from other living organisms — **axe·ni·cal·ly** \-ni-k(ə-)lē\ *adv*

ax·i·al \'ak-sē-əl\ *adj* (ca. 1847) **1** : of, relating to, or having the characteristics of an axis **2** **a** : situated around, in the direction of, on, or
along an axis **b** : extending in a direction essentially perpendicular to
the plane of a cyclic structure (as of cyclohexane) ⟨~ hydrogens⟩ —
compare EQUATORIAL — **ax·i·al·i·ty** \,ak-sē-'a-lə-tē\ *n* — **ax·i·al·ly**
\'ak-sē-ə-lē\ *adv*

axial skeleton *n* (1872) : the skeleton of the trunk and head

ax·il \'ak-səl, -,sil\ *n* [NL *axilla*, fr. L] (1794) : the angle between a
branch or leaf and the axis from which it arises

ax·il·la \ag-'zi-lə, ak-'si-\ *n, pl* **-lae** \-(,)lē, -,lī\ *or* **-las** [L, dim. of *ala*
wing, upper arm, armpit, axil — more at AISLE] (1616) : the cavity
beneath the junction of a forelimb and the body; *esp* : ARMPIT

ax·il·lar \ag-'zi-lər, ak-'si-, 'ag-zə-, 'ak-sə-, -,lär\ *n* (1541) : an axillary
part (as a feather)

¹**ax·il·lary** \'ak-sə-,ler-ē\ *adj* (1615) **1** : of, relating to, or located near
the axilla **2** : situated in or growing from an axil ⟨~ buds⟩
²**axillary** *n, pl* **-lar·ies** (ca. 1889) : one of the feathers arising from the
axilla and closing the space between the flight feathers and body of a
flying bird

ax·i·ol·o·gy \,ak-sē-'ä-lə-jē\ *n* [Gk *axios* + ISV *-logy*] (1908) : the
study of the nature, types, and criteria of values and of value judgments esp. in ethics — **ax·i·o·log·i·cal** \,ak-sē-ə-,lä-ji-kəl\ *adj* — **ax·i·
o·log·i·cal·ly** \-ji-k(ə-)lē\ *adv*

ax·i·om \'ak-sē-əm\ *n* [L *axioma*, fr. Gk *axiōma*, lit., something worthy, fr. *axioun* to think worthy, fr. *axios* worth, worthy; akin to Gk
agein to weigh, drive — more at AGENT] (15c) **1** : a maxim widely
accepted on its intrinsic merit **2** : a statement accepted as true as the
basis for argument or inference : POSTULATE 1 **3** : an established rule
or principle or a self-evident truth

ax·i·om·at·ic \,ak-sē-ə-'ma-tik\ *adj* [MGk *axiōmatikos*, fr. Gk, honorable, fr. *axiōmat-, axiōma*] (1797) **1** : taken for granted : SELF-
EVIDENT **2** : based on or involving an axiom or system of axioms ⟨~
set theory⟩ — **ax·i·om·at·i·cal·ly** \-ti-k(ə-)lē\ *adv*

ax·i·om·a·tisa·tion *chiefly Brit var of* AXIOMATIZATION

ax·i·omat·iza·tion \,ak-sē-ə-,ma-tə-'zā-shən, -sē-,ä-mə-tə-\ *n* (1931)
: the act or process of reducing to a system of axioms — **ax·i·om·a·
tize** \-sē-'ä-mə-,tīz\ *vt*

axiom of choice (1942) : an axiom in set theory that is equivalent to
Zorn's lemma: for every collection of nonempty sets there is a function
which chooses an element from each set

ax·ion \'ak-sē-,än\ *n* [*axial* + ²*-on*] (1978) : a hypothetical subatomic
particle of low mass and energy that is postulated to exist because of
certain properties of the strong force

ax·is \'ak-səs\ *n, pl* **ax·es** \-,sēz\ [L, axis, axle; akin to OE *eax* axis,
axle, Gk *axōn*, Lith *ašis*, Skt *akṣa*] (14c) **1** **a** : a straight line about
which a body or a geometric figure rotates or may be supposed to ro-

\ə\ abut \'ə, ,ə\ kitten, F table \ər\ further \a\ ash \ā\ ace \ä\ mop, mar
\au̇\ out \ch\ chin \e\ bet \ē\ easy \g\ go \i\ hit \ī\ ice \j\ job
\ŋ\ sing \ō\ go \o̊\ law \o̊i\ boy \th\ thin \t͟h\ the \ü\ loot \u̇\ foot
\y\ yet \zh\ vision \á, k̲, ⁿ, œ, œ̄, ʉ, ᵫ, ᵞ\ see Guide to Pronunciation

tate   **b** : a straight line with respect to which a body or figure is symmetrical — called also *axis of symmetry*   **c** : a straight line that bisects at right angles a system of parallel chords of a curve and divides the curve into two symmetrical parts   **d** : one of the reference lines of a coordinate system   **2 a** : the second vertebra of the neck on which the head and first vertebra turn as on a pivot   **b** : any of various central, fundamental, or axial parts   **3** : a plant stem   **4** : one of several imaginary lines assumed in describing the positions of the planes by which a crystal is bounded and the positions of atoms in the structure of the crystal   **5** : a main line of direction, motion, growth, or extension   **6 a** : an implied line in painting or sculpture through a composition to which elements in the composition are referred   **b** : a line actually drawn and used as the basis of measurements in an architectural or other working drawing   **7** : any of three fixed lines of reference in an aircraft that run in the longitudinal, lateral, and vertical directions, are mutually perpendicular, and usu. pass through the aircraft's center of gravity   **8** : PARTNERSHIP, ALLIANCE

Axis *adj* (1938) : of or relating to the three powers Germany, Italy, and Japan engaged against the Allied nations in World War II

ax·i·sym·met·ric \,ak-si-sə-'me-trik\ *also* **axi·sym·met·ri·cal** \-tri-kəl\ *adj* [*axis* + *symmetric*] (1893) : symmetric in respect to an axis — **axi·sym·me·try** \-'si-mə-trē\ *n*

ax·le \'ak-səl\ *n* [ME *axel-* (as in *axeltre*)] (14c)   **1 a** : a pin or shaft on or with which a wheel or pair of wheels revolves   **b** (1) : a fixed bar or beam with bearings at its ends on which wheels (as of a cart) revolve   (2) : the spindle of such a beam   **2** *archaic* : AXIS

axle·tree \-(,)trē\ *n* [ME *axeltre*, fr. ON *ǫxultrē*, fr. *ǫxull* axle + *trē* tree] (14c) : AXLE 1b(1)

ax·man \'ak-smən\ *n* (1671) : one who wields an ax

Ax·min·ster \'ak-,smin(t)-stər\ *n* [*Axminster*, town in England] (1818) : a machine-woven carpet with pile tufts inserted mechanically in a variety of textures and patterns

ax·o·lotl \'ak-sə-,lä-t²l\ *n* [Nahuatl *āxōlōtl*] (ca. 1768) : any of several salamanders (genus *Ambystoma* esp. *A. mexicanum* and *A. tigrinum*) of mountain lakes of Mexico and the western U.S. that ordinarily live and breed without metamorphosing

ax·on \'ak-,sän\ *also* **ax·one** \-,sōn\ *n* [NL *axon*, fr. Gk *axōn*] (ca. 1899) : a usu. long and single nerve-cell process that usu. conducts impulses away from the cell body — see NEURON illustration — **ax·o·nal** \'ak-sə-n²l; ak-'sä-, -'sō-\ *adj*

ax·o·neme \'ak-sə-,nēm\ *n* [Gk *axōn* axis + *nēma* thread, fr. *nēn* to spin — more at NEEDLE] (1901) : the fibrillar bundle of a flagellum or cilium that usu. consists of nine pairs of microtubules arranged in a ring around a single central pair — **ax·o·ne·mal** \,ak-sə-'nē-məl\ *adj*

ax·o·no·met·ric \,ak-sə-nō-'me-trik\ *adj* [Gk *axōn* axis + E *-metric*] (1908) : being or prepared by the projection of objects on the drawing surface so that they appear inclined with three sides showing and with horizontal and vertical distances drawn to scale but diagonal and curved lines distorted ⟨an ~ drawing⟩

axo·plasm \'ak-sə-,pla-zəm\ *n* [*axon* + *-plasm*] (1900) : the protoplasm of an axon — **axo·plas·mic** \,ak-sə-'plaz-mik\ *adj*

ay \'ī\ *interj* [MF *aymi* ay me] (14c) — usu. used with following *me* to express sorrow or regret

ayah \'ī-ə; 'ä-yə, -(,)yä\ *n* [Hindi *āyā*, fr. Pg *aia*, fr. L *avia* grandmother] (1779) : a nurse or maid native to India

aya·hua·sca \,ī-yə-'hwäs-kə, -'wäs-\ *n* [AmerSp] (1949) : an hallucinogenic beverage prepared from the bark of a So. American vine (*Banisteriopsis caapi* of the family Malpighiaceae)

aya·tol·lah \,ī-ə-'tō-lə, -'tä-, -'tə-, 'ī-ə-\ *n* [Per, lit., sign of God, fr. Ar *āya* sign, miracle + *allāh* God] (1953) : a religious leader among Shiite Muslims — used as a title of respect esp. for one who is not an imam

¹aye *also* **ay** \'ā\ *adv* [ME, fr. ON *ei*; akin to OE *ā* always, L *aevum* age, lifetime, Gk *aiōn* age] (13c) : ALWAYS, CONTINUALLY, EVER ⟨love that will ~ endure —W. S. Gilbert⟩

²aye *also* **ay** \'ī\ *adv* [perh. fr. ME *ye, yie* — more at YEA] (1576) : YES ⟨~, ~, sir⟩

³aye *also* **ay** \'ī\ *n, pl* **ayes** (1589) : an affirmative vote or voter ⟨the ~s have it⟩

aye-aye \'ī-,ī\ *n* [F, fr. Malagasy *aiay*] (ca. 1781) : a small primitive nocturnal forest-dwelling primate (*Daubentonia madagascariensis*) of northern Madagascar that has a round head, large eyes and ears, and long thin fingers

ayin \'ī-ən\ *n* [Heb *'ayin*, lit., eye] (1823) : the 16th letter of the Hebrew alphabet — see ALPHABET table

Ay·ma·ra \,ī-mə-'rä\ *n, pl* **Aymara** *or* **Aymaras** [Sp *aymará*] (1860)   **1** : a member of an Indian people of Bolivia and Peru   **2** : the language of the Aymara people

Ayr·shire \'ar-,shir, 'er-, -shər; 'ash-,ir\ *n* [*Ayrshire*, Scotland] (1856) : any of a breed of hardy dairy cattle originated in Ayr and usu. marked with blotches of red or brown with white

az- *or* **azo-** *comb form* [ISV, fr. F *azote* nitrogen, fr. *a-* ²a- + *-zote*, prob. fr. Gk *zōtikos* maintaining life, fr. *zōē* life — more at QUICK] : containing nitrogen esp. as the bivalent group N=N ⟨azine⟩

aza- *or* **az-** *comb form* [ISV *az-* + *-a-*] : containing nitrogen in place of carbon and usu. the bivalent group NH for the group CH₂ or a single trivalent nitrogen atom for the group CH ⟨azathioprine⟩

aza·lea \ə-'zāl-yə\ *n* [NL, genus name, fr. Gk, fem. of *azaleos* dry, fr. *azein* to parch, dry; akin to Hitt *ḫat-* to dry up and prob. to L *ador* emmer] (1767) : any of a subgenus (*Azalea*) of rhododendrons with funnel-shaped corollas and usu. deciduous leaves including many species and hybrid forms cultivated as ornamentals

aza·thi·o·prine \,a-zə-'thī-ə-,prēn\ *n* [*aza-* + *thi-* + *purine*] (1962) : a purine antimetabolite C₉H₇N₇O₂S used esp. as an immunosuppressant

Aza·zel \ə-'zā-zəl, 'a-zə-,zel\ *n* [Heb *'ǎzāzēl*] : an evil spirit of the wilderness to which a scapegoat was sent by the ancient Hebrews in a ritual of atonement

azeo·trope \'ā-zē-ə-,trōp\ *n* [²a- + zeo- (fr. Gk *zein* to boil) + *-trope* something changed, fr. Gk *tropos* turn — more at YEAST, TROPE] (1938) : a liquid mixture that is characterized by a constant minimum or maximum boiling point which is lower or higher than that of any of the components

azide \'ā-,zīd, 'a-\ *n* (ca. 1904) : a compound containing the group N₃ combined with an element or radical

az·i·do \'a-zə-(,)dō\ *adj* [ISV *azide* + *-o-*] (ca. 1926) : relating to or containing the univalent group N₃— often used in combination

az·i·do·thy·mi·dine \ə-,zī-dō-'thī-mə-,dēn\ *n* (1974) : an antiviral drug C₁₀H₁₃N₅O₄ that inhibits replication of some retroviruses (as HIV) and is used to treat AIDS — called also *AZT, zidovudine*

az·i·muth \'az-məth, 'a-zə-\ *n* [ME, fr. (assumed) ML, fr. Ar *as-sumūt* the azimuth, pl. of *as-samt* the way] (14c)   **1** : an arc of the horizon measured between a fixed point (as true north) and the vertical circle passing through the center of an object esp. in astronomy and navigation clockwise from the north point through 360 degrees   **2** : horizontal direction expressed as the angular distance between the direction of a fixed point (as the observer's heading) and the direction of the object — **az·i·muth·al** \,a-zə-'mə-thəl\ *adj* — **az·i·muth·al·ly** \-'mə-thə-lē\ *adv*

azimuthal equidistant projection *n* (1942) : a map projection of the surface of the earth so centered at any given point that a straight line radiating from the center to any other point represents the shortest distance and can be measured to scale

azimuthal equidistant projection, centered on Washington, D.C.: *1* London, *2* Algiers, *3* Moscow, *4* Rio de Janeiro, *5* Tokyo, *6* Auckland

azine \'ā-,zēn, 'a-\ *n* (1887) : a compound of the general formula RCH=NH=CHR or R₂C=NN=CR₂ formed by the action of hydrazine on aldehydes or ketones

azo \'ā-(,)zō, 'a-\ *adj* [*az-*] (ca. 1879) : relating to or containing the bivalent group N=N united at both ends to carbon

azo dye *n* (1884) : any of numerous dyes containing azo groups

azo·ic \(,)ā-'zō-ik\ *adj* [²a- + Gk *zōē* life — more at QUICK] (ca. 1847) : having no life; *esp* : of or relating to the part of geologic time that antedates life — compare ARCHEOZOIC

azole \'ā-,zōl, 'a-\ *n* (ca. 1899) : any of numerous compounds characterized by a 5-membered ring containing at least one nitrogen atom

azon·al \(,)ā-'zō-n²l\ *adj* (1938) : of, relating to, or being a soil or a major group of soils lacking well-developed horizons often because of immaturity — compare INTRAZONAL, ZONAL

azo·o·sper·mia \(,)ā-,zō-ə-'spər-mē-ə\ *n* [NL, fr. Gk *azoos* lifeless (fr. *a-* ²a- + *zōē* life) + *sperma* semen, seed — more at SPERM] (ca. 1881) : absence of spermatozoa from the seminal fluid

azo·te·mia \,a-zō-'tē-mē-ə\ *n* [ISV *azote* nitrogen + NL *-emia* — more at AZ-] (ca. 1900) : an excess of nitrogenous bodies in the blood as a result of kidney insufficiency — compare UREMIA — **azo·te·mic** \-mik\ *adj*

az·oth \'a-,zoth\ *n* [Ar *az-zā'ūq* the mercury] (15c)   **1** : mercury regarded by alchemists as the first principle of metals   **2** : the universal remedy of Paracelsus

azo·to·bac·ter \ā-'zō-tə-,bak-tər\ *n* [NL, genus name, fr. ISV *azote* + NL *bacterium*] (1910) : any of a genus (*Azotobacter*) of large rod= shaped or spherical bacteria occurring in soil and sewage and fixing atmospheric nitrogen

azo·tu·ria \,ā-zō-'tùr-ē-ə, -'tyùr-\ *n* [ISV *azote* + NL *-uria*] (ca. 1838) : an abnormal condition of horses characterized by an excess of urea or other nitrogenous substances in the urine and muscle damage esp. to the hindquarters

AZT \,ā-(,)zē-'tē\ *n* (1985) : AZIDOTHYMIDINE

Az·tec \'az-,tek\ *n* [Sp *azteca*, fr. Nahuatl *aztēcah*, pl. of *aztēcatl*] (1787)   **1 a** : a member of a Nahuatl-speaking people that founded the Mexican empire conquered by Cortes in 1519   **b** : a member of any people under Aztec influence   **2** : NAHUATL — **Az·tec·an** \'az-,te-kən, ,az-'te-\ *adj*

azure \'a-zhər\ *n* [ME *asur*, fr. OF *azur*, prob. fr. OSp, modif. of Ar *lāzaward*, fr. Per *lāzhuward*] (14c)   **1** *archaic* : LAPIS LAZULI   **2 a** : the blue color of the clear sky   **b** : the heraldic color blue   **3** : the unclouded sky — **azure** *adj*

azur·ite \'a-zhə-,rīt\ *n* [F, fr. *azur* azure] (ca. 1868)   **1** : a mineral that consists of blue basic carbonate of copper and is a copper ore   **2** : a semiprecious stone derived from azurite

¹azy·gos \ā-'zī-gəs\ *n* [NL, fr. Gk, unyoked, fr. *a-* + *zygon* yoke — more at YOKE] (1646) : an azygos anatomical part

²azy·gos *also* **azy·gous** \(,)ā-'zī-gəs\ *adj* (1681) : not being one of a pair : SINGLE ⟨an ~ vein⟩

B

b \'bē\ *n, pl* **b's** *or* **bs** \'bēz\ *often cap, often attrib* (bef. 12c) **1 a** : the 2d letter of the English alphabet **b** : a graphic representation of this letter **c** : a speech counterpart of orthographic *b* **2** : the 7th tone of a C-major scale **3** : a graphic device for reproducing the letter *b* **4** : one designated *b* esp. as the 2d in order or class **5 a** : a grade rating a student's work as good but short of excellent **b** : one graded or rated with a B **6** : something shaped like the letter B

baa \'ba, 'bä\ *vi* **baaed; baa·ing** [imit.] (ca. 1586) : to make the bleat of a sheep — **baa** *n*

baal \'bä(-ə)l\ *n, pl* **baals** *or* **baa·lim** \'bä-(ə-)ləm, 'bä-ə-,lim\ *often cap* [Heb *ba'al* lord] (14c) : any of numerous Canaanite and Phoenician local deities — **baal·ism** \'bä-(ə-),li-zəm\ *n, often cap*

baas \'bäs\ *n* [Afrik, fr. D] (1785) *SoAfr* : BOSS, MASTER — used esp. by nonwhites when speaking to or about Europeans in positions of authority

ba·ba \'bä-(,)bä, -bə\ *n* [F, fr. Pol, lit., old woman] (1827) : a rich cake soaked in a rum and sugar syrup

ba·bas·su \,bä-bə-'sü\ *n* [Pg *babaçu*, fr. (assumed) Tupi *iwaβasu*, fr. Tupi *iwa* fruit + *βasu* large] (1917) : a tall pinnate-leaved palm (*Orbignya barbosiana*) of Brazil with hard-shelled nuts yielding a valuable oil

bab·bitt \'ba-bət\ *n* [Isaac *Babbitt* †1862 Am. inventor] (1900) : an alloy used for lining bearings; *esp* : one containing tin, copper, and antimony — called also *babbitt metal* — **bab·bit·ed** \-bə-təd\ *adj*

Bab·bitt \'ba-bət\ *n* [George F. *Babbitt*, character in the novel *Babbitt* (1922) by Sinclair Lewis] (1923) : a business or professional man who conforms unthinkingly to prevailing middle-class standards — **Bab·bitt·ry** \-bə-trē\ *n* — **Bab·bitty** \-tē\ *adj*

bab·ble \'ba-bəl\ *vb* **bab·bled; bab·bling** \-b(ə-)liŋ\ [ME *babelen*, prob. of imit. origin] *vi* (13c) **1 a** : to talk enthusiastically or excessively **b** : to utter meaningless or unintelligible sounds **2** : to make sounds as though babbling ~ *vt* **1** : to utter in an incoherently or meaninglessly repetitious manner **2** : to reveal by talk that is too free — **babble** *n* — **bab·ble·ment** \-bəl-mənt\ *n* — **bab·bler** \-b(ə-)lər\ *n*

babe \'bäb\ *n* [ME, prob. of imit. origin] (14c) **1 a** : INFANT, BABY **b** *slang* : GIRL, WOMAN **2** : a naive inexperienced person — used esp. in the phrase *babe in the woods*

Ba·bel \'bä-bəl, 'ba-\ *n* [Heb *Bābhel*, fr. Akkadian *bāb-ilu* gate of god] **1** : a city in Shinar where the building of a tower is held in Genesis to have been halted by the confusion of tongues **2** *often not cap* **a** : a confusion of sounds or voices **b** : a scene of noise or confusion

ba·be·sia \bə-'bē-zh(ē-)ə\ *n* [NL, fr. Victor *Babeş* †1926 Rom. bacteriologist] (1911) : any of a genus (*Babesia*) of sporozoans parasitic in mammalian red blood cells (as in Texas fever) and transmitted by the bite of a tick — called also *piroplasm*

bab·e·si·o·sis \,ba-bə-'zī-ə-səs\ *n* [NL] (1911) : an infection with or disease caused by babesias

Ba·bin·ski reflex \bə-'bin-skē-\ *n* [J.F.F. *Babinski* †1932 Fr. neurologist] (1900) : a reflex movement in which when the sole is tickled the big toe turns upward instead of downward and which is normal in infancy but indicates damage to the central nervous system (as in the pyramidal tracts) later in life — called also *Babinski sign*, *Ba·bin·ski's reflex* \-skēz-\

bab·i·ru·sa \,ba-bə-'rü-sə, ,bä-\ *n* [Malay, fr. *babi* pig + *rusa* deer] (1673) : a large wild swine (*Babyrousa babyrussa*) of Indonesia

ba·boon \ba-'bün, *chiefly Brit* bə-\ *n* [ME *babewin*, fr. MF *babouin*, fr. *baboue* grimace] (15c) : any of a genus (*Papio*) of large gregarious primates of Africa and southwestern Asia having a long square naked muzzle; *also* : any of several closely related primates

ba·bu *also* **ba·boo** \'bä-(,)bü\ *n, often attrib* [Hindi *bābū*, lit., father] (1776) **1** : a Hindu gentleman — a form of address corresponding to *Mr.* **2 a** : an Indian clerk who writes English **b** : an Indian having some education in English — often used disparagingly

ba·bul \bə-'bül\ *n* [Per *babūl*] (1780) : an acacia tree (*Acacia nilotica* syn. *A. arabica*) widespread in India and northern Africa that yields gum arabic and tannins as well as fodder and timber

ba·bush·ka \bə-'büsh-kə, -'bùsh-\ *n* [Russ, grandmother, dim. of *baba* old woman] (1938) **1 a** : a usu. triangularly folded kerchief for the head **b** : a head covering resembling a babushka **2** : an elderly Russian woman

¹ba·by \'bä-bē\ *n, pl* **babies** [ME, fr. *babe*] (14c) **1 a** (1): an extremely young child; *esp* : INFANT (2): an extremely young animal **b** : the youngest of a group **2 a** : one that is like a baby (as in behavior) **b** : something that is one's special responsibility, achievement, or interest **3** *slang* **a** : GIRL, WOMAN — often used in address **b** : BOY, MAN — often used in address **4** : PERSON, THING (is one tough ~) — **ba·by·hood** \-bē-,hüd\ *n* — **ba·by·ish** \-ish\ *adj*

²baby *adj* (1591) **1** : of, relating to, or being a baby **2** : much smaller than the usual (~ carrots) (a ~ flattop) (take two ~ steps)

³baby *vt* **ba·bied; ba·by·ing** (1742) **1** : to tend to indulge with often excessive or inappropriate care and solicitude (~ing their only child) **2** : to operate or treat with care (~ a new motor) (~ing a sore knee) *syn* see INDULGE

baby blue *n* (1889) : a pale blue

baby blue–eyes \-'blü-,īz\ *n pl but sing or pl in constr* (1887) : a delicate blue-flowered California herb (*Nemophila menziesii*) of the waterleaf family

baby boom *n* (1941) : a marked rise in birthrate (as in the U.S. immediately following the end of World War II) — **baby boomer** *n*

baby bust *n* (1971) : a marked decline in birthrate — **baby buster** *n*

baby carriage *n* (1866) : a small four-wheeled carriage often with a folding top for pushing a baby around in — called also *baby buggy*

baby grand *n* (ca. 1903) : a small grand piano

Bab·y·lon \'ba-bə-,län, -lən\ *n* [*Babylon*, ancient city of Babylonia] (14c) : a city devoted to materialism and sensual pleasure

¹Bab·y·lo·nian \,ba-bə-'lō-nyən, -nē-ən\ *n* (1564) **1** : a native or inhabitant of ancient Babylonia or Babylon **2** : the form of the Akkadian language used in ancient Babylonia

²Babylonian *adj* (1596) **1** : of, relating to, or characteristic of Babylonia or Babylon, the Babylonians, or Babylonian **2** : marked by luxury, extravagance, or the pursuit of sensual pleasure (the ~ halls of the big hotel —G. K. Chesterton) (the ~ delights of the city)

baby's breath *n* (ca. 1890) : GYPSOPHILA; *esp* : a perennial herb (*Gypsophila paniculata*) or an annual herb (*G. elegans*) commonly used in floral arrangements

ba·by-sit \'bä-bē-,sit\ *vb* **-sat** \-,sat\; **-sit·ting** [back-formation fr. *baby-sitter*] *vi* (1947) : to care for children usu. during a short absence of the parents; *broadly* : to give care (~ for a neighbor's pets) ~ *vt* : to baby-sit for; *broadly* : MIND, TEND (~ house plants) (police *baby-sitting* a witness) — **ba·by-sit·ter** *n*

baby talk *n* (1836) **1 a** : the syntactically imperfect speech or phonetically modified forms used by small children learning to talk **b** : the consciously imperfect or altered speech used by adults in speaking to small children **2** : oversimplified speech or writing

baby tooth *n* (1939) : MILK TOOTH

bac·ca·lau·re·ate \,ba-kə-'lòr-ē-ət, -'lär-\ *n* [ML *baccalaureatus*, fr. *baccalaureus* bachelor, alter. of *baccalarius*] (ca. 1649) **1** : the degree of bachelor conferred by universities and colleges **2 a** : a sermon to a graduating class **b** : the service at which this sermon is delivered

bac·ca·rat \,bä-kə-'rä, ,ba-\ *n* [F *baccara*] (1865) : a card game resembling chemin de fer in which three hands are dealt and players may bet either or both hands against the dealer's; *also* : a two-handed version in which players may bet on or against the dealer

Bac·chae \'ba-,kē, -,kī\ *n pl* [L, fr. Gk *Bakchai*, fr. *Bakchos* Bacchus] (ca. 1909) **1** : the female attendants or priestesses of Bacchus : the women participating in the Bacchanalia

¹bac·cha·nal \'ba-kə-nᵊl, 'bä-; ,ba-kə-'nal, ,bä-kə-'näl\ *n* [L, shrine of Bacchus, prob. back-formation fr. *Bacchanalia*] (1550) **1** : ORGY 2, 3 **2 a** : a devotee of Bacchus; *esp* : one who celebrates the Bacchanalia **b** : REVELER

²bac·cha·nal \'ba-kə-nᵊl\ *adj* (1550) : of, relating to, or suggestive of the Bacchanalia : BACCHANALIAN

bac·cha·na·lia \,ba-kə-'näl-yə, ,bä-kə-\ *n, pl bacchanalia* [L, fr. *Bacchus*] (1591) **1** *pl, cap* : a Roman festival of Bacchus celebrated with dancing, song, and revelry **2** : ORGY 2, 3 — **bac·cha·na·lian** \-'näl-yən\ *adj or n*

bac·chant \bə-'kant, -'känt; 'ba-kənt, 'bä-\ *n, pl* **bacchants** *or* **bacchantes** \bə-'kan-tēz, -'käntz, -'kän-tēz, -'kän-,tēz\ [L *bacchant-, bacchans*, fr. prp. of *bacchari* to take part in the orgies of Bacchus] (1699) : BACCHANAL — **bacchant** *adj*

bac·chante \bə-'kant, -'känt; -'kan-tē, -'kän-\ *n* [F, fr. L *bacchant-, bacchans*] (1579) : a priestess or female follower of Bacchus : MAENAD

bac·chic \'ba-kik, 'bä-\ *adj, often cap* (1669) : of, relating to, or suggestive of Bacchus or the Bacchanalia : BACCHANALIAN

Bac·chus \'ba-kəs, 'bä-\ *n* [L, fr. Gk *Bakchos*] : the Greek god of wine — called also *Dionysus*

¹bach \'bach\ *n* (1855) : BACHELOR 3a

²bach *vi* (1870) : to live as a bachelor — often used with *it*

³bach *n* [²*bach*] (1925) *New Zeal* : a small house or weekend cottage

¹bach·e·lor \'bach-lər, 'ba-chə-\ *n* [ME *becheler*, fr. OF] (14c) **1 a** : a young knight who follows the banner of another **2** : a person who has received what is usu. the lowest degree conferred by a four-year college, university, or professional school (~ of arts) **3 a** : an unmarried man **b** : a male animal (as a fur seal) without a mate during breeding time — **bach·e·lor·dom** \-dəm\ *n* — **bach·e·lor·hood** \-,hüd\ *n*

²bachelor *adj* (1857) **1** : suitable for or occupied by a single person (a ~ apartment) **2** : UNMARRIED (~ women) (~ parents)

bach·e·lor·ette \,bach-lə-'ret, ,ba-chə-\ *n* (1938) : a bachelor woman

bachelor's button *n* (1847) : a European composite (*Centaurea cyanus*) having flower heads with blue, pink, or white rays that is often cultivated in No. America — called also *cornflower*

ba·cil·la·ry \'ba-sə-,ler-ē, bə-'si-lə-rē\ *or* **ba·cil·lar** \bə-'si-lər, 'ba-sə-lər\ *adj* [ML & NL *bacillus*] (1865) **1** : shaped like a rod; *also* : consisting of small rods **2** : of, relating to, or caused by bacilli

ba·cil·lus \bə-'si-ləs\ *n, pl* **-li** \-,lī *also* -lē\ [NL, fr. ML, small staff, rod, dim. of L *baculus* staff, alter. of *baculum*] (ca. 1879) **1** : any of a genus (*Bacillus*) of aerobic rod-shaped gram-positive bacteria producing endospores that do not thicken the rod and including many saprophytes and some parasites (as *B. anthracis* of anthrax); *broadly* : a straight rod-shaped bacterium **2** : BACTERIUM; *esp* : a disease-producing bacterium

bac·i·tra·cin \,ba-sə-'trā-sᵊn\ *n* [NL *Bacillus subtilis* (species of bacillus producing the toxin) + Margaret *Tracy b* ab 1936 Am. child in whose tissues it was found] (1945) : a toxic polypeptide antibiotic isolated from a bacillus (*Bacillus subtilis*) and usu. used topically esp. against gram-positive bacteria

¹back \'bak\ *n* [ME, fr. OE *bæc*; akin to OHG *bah* back] (bef. 12c) **1 a** (1): the rear part of the human body esp. from the neck to the end of the spine (2): the body considered as the wearer of clothes (3): capacity for labor, effort, or endurance (4): the back considered as the seat of one's awareness of duty or failings (get off my ~) **b** : the part of a lower animal (as a quadruped) corresponding to the human back **c** : SPINAL COLUMN **d** : BACKBONE 4 **2 a** : the side or surface opposite the front or face : the rear part; *also* : the farther or reverse side **b** : something at or on the back for support (~ of a chair) **c** : a place away from the front (sat in ~) **3** : a position in some games (as football or soccer) behind the front line of players; *also* : a player in this position — **backed** \'bakt\ *adj* — **back·less** \'bak-ləs\ *adj* — **back of one's hand** *or* **back of the hand** : a show of contempt — **back of one's mind** : the remote part of one's mind where thoughts and memories are stored to be drawn on — **behind one's back** : without one's knowledge : in secret — **in back of** : BEHIND

babushka 1a

---

[2]**back** *adv* (14c) **1 a** : to, toward, or at the rear **b** : in or into the past : backward in time; *also* : AGO **c** : to or at an angle off the vertical **d** (1) : under restraint (2) : in a delayed or retarded condition **2 a** : to, toward, or in a place from which a person or thing came **b** : to or toward a former state **c** : in return or reply

[3]**back** *adj* (15c) **1 a** : being at or in the back ⟨∼ door⟩ **b** : distant from a central or main area ⟨∼ roads⟩ **c** : articulated at or toward the back of the oral passage ⟨∼ vowels⟩ **2** : having returned or been returned **3** : being in arrears : OVERDUE **4** : moving or operating backward : REVERSE **5** : not current ⟨∼ numbers of a magazine⟩ **6** : constituting the final 9 holes of an 18-hole golf course

[4]**back** *vt* (1548) **1 a** : to support by material or moral assistance — usu. used with *up* **b** : SUBSTANTIATE **c** : to assume financial responsibility for **d** : to provide musical accompaniment for — often used with *up* **2 a** : to cause to go back or in reverse **b** : to articulate (a sound) with the tongue farther back **3 a** : to furnish with a back **b** : to be at the back of ∼ *vi* **1** : to move backward — often used with *up* **2** *of the wind* : to shift counterclockwise — compare VEER **3** : to have the back in the direction of something *syn* see SUPPORT, RECEDE — **back·er** \'ba-kər\ *n* — **back and fill** **1** : to manage the sails of a ship so as to keep it clear of obstructions as its floats down with the current of a river or channel **2** : to take opposite positions alternately : SHILLY-SHALLY — **back into** : to get into inadvertently ⟨*backed into* the antiques business⟩

back·ache \'bak-,āk\ *n* (1601) : a pain in the lower back

back–and–forth *n* (1941) : DISCUSSION 1, GIVE-AND-TAKE ; *also* : EXCHANGE 1

back and forth *adv* (1613) : backward and forward; *also* : between two places or persons

back away *vi* (1919) : to move away (as from a stand on an issue)

back bacon *n* (1947) *chiefly Brit* : CANADIAN BACON

back·beat \'bak-,bēt\ *n* (1928) : a steady pronounced rhythm stressing the second and fourth beats of a four-beat measure

back·bench *n* (1874) : a bench in a British legislature (as the House of Commons) occupied by rank-and-file members — compare FRONT BENCH — **back·bench·er** \'-'ben-chər\ *n*

back·bite \'-,bīt\ *vb* **-bit; -bit·ten; -bit·ing** *vt* (12c) : to say mean or spiteful things about ∼ *vi* : to backbite a person — **back·bit·er** *n*

backbiting \'bak-,bī-tiŋ\ *n* (12c) : malicious comment about one not present

back·block \-,bläk\ *n* (1870) *Austral & New Zeal* : BOONDOCKS 2 — usu. used in pl.

back·board \-,bōrd, -,bȯrd\ *n* (1761) : a board placed at or serving as the back of something; *esp* : a rounded or rectangular board behind the basket on a basketball court which serves to keep missed shots from going out-of-bounds and from which the ball can be made to rebound into the basket

back·bone \-'bōn, -,bōn\ *n* (14c) **1** : SPINAL COLUMN, SPINE **2** : something that resembles a backbone: as **a** : a chief mountain ridge, range, or system **b** : the foundation or most substantial or sturdiest part of something **c** : the longest chain of atoms or groups of atoms in a usu. long molecule (as a polymer or protein) **3** : firm and resolute character **4** : SPINE 1c

back·break·ing \-,brā-kiŋ\ *adj* (1870) : extremely tiring or demanding : OPPRESSIVE ⟨∼ labor⟩ ⟨∼ rents⟩ — **back·break·er** \-kər\ *n*

back burner *n* (1963) : the condition of being out of active consideration or development — usu. used in the phrase *on the back burner*

back channel *n* (1975) : a secret, unofficial, or irregular means of communication — **back–channel** *adj*

back·chat \'bak-,chat\ *n* (1901) **1** : BACK TALK **2** : gossipy or bantering conversation

back–check \-,chek\ *vi* (1937) : to skate back toward one's own goal while closely defending against the offensive rushes of an opposing player in ice hockey — **back–check·er** \-,che-kər\ *n*

back·cloth \-,klȯth\ *n* (1886) *chiefly Brit* : BACKDROP

back·coun·try \-,kən-trē\ *n, often attrib* (1746) : a remote undeveloped rural area

back·court \-'kōrt, -'kȯrt\ *n* (1890) **1** : the area near or nearest the back boundary lines or back wall of the playing area in a net or court game **2** : a basketball team's defensive half of the court; *also* : the part of the offensive half of the court farthest from the goal **3** : the basketball players who play the backcourt

back·court·man \-mən\ *n* (1954) : a guard on a basketball team

[1]**back·cross** \'bak-,krȯs\ *vt* (1904) : to cross (a first-generation hybrid) with one of the parental types

[2]**backcross** *n* (1918) : a mating that involves backcrossing; *also* : an individual produced by backcrossing

back·date \'bak-,dāt\ *vt* (1944) : to put a date earlier than the actual one on ⟨∼ a memo⟩; *also* : to make retroactive ⟨∼ pension rights⟩

back dive *n* (ca. 1934) : a dive from a position facing the diving board

back·door \'bak-'dȯr, -'dȯr\ *adj* (1805) : INDIRECT, DEVIOUS

back down *vi* (1849) : to withdraw from a commitment or position

back·drop \'bak-,dräp\ *n* (1913) **1** : a painted cloth hung across the rear of a stage **2** : BACKGROUND — **backdrop** *vt*

back·field \-,fēld\ *n* (1920) : the football players whose positions are behind the line of scrimmage; *also* : the positions themselves

back·fill \-,fil\ *vt* (1908) : to refill (as an excavation) usu. with excavated material ∼ *vi* : to backfill an excavation — **backfill** *n*

[1]**back·fire** \-,fīr\ *n* (1839) **1** : a fire started to check an advancing fire by clearing an area **2** : a loud noise caused by the improperly timed explosion of fuel mixture in the cylinder of an internal combustion engine

[2]**backfire** *vi* (1886) **1** : to make or undergo a backfire **2** : to have the reverse of the desired or expected effect

back·fit \'bak-,fit\ *vt* (1967) : RETROFIT — **backfit** *n*

back·flow \-,flō\ *n* (1884) : a flowing back or returning toward a source

back–formation *n* (1889) **1** : a word formed by subtraction of a real or supposed affix from an already existing longer word (as *burgle* from *burglar*) **2** : the formation of back-formations

back·gam·mon \'bak-,ga-mən, bak-'\ *n* [perh. fr. [3]*back* + ME *gamen*, *game* game] (ca. 1645) : a board game played with dice and counters in which players try to be the first to gather their pieces into one corner and then systematically remove them from the board

[1]**back·ground** \'bak-,graůnd\ *n, often attrib* (1672) **1 a** : the scenery or ground behind something **b** : the part of a painting representing what lies behind objects in the foreground **2** : an inconspicuous position **3 a** : the conditions that form the setting within which something is experienced **b** (1) : the circumstances or events antecedent to a phenomenon or development (2) : information essential to understanding of a problem or situation **c** : the total of a person's experience, knowledge, and education **4 a** : intrusive sound or radiation that interferes with received or recorded electronic signals **b** : a more or less steady level of noise above which the effect (as radioactivity) being measured by an apparatus (as a Geiger counter) is detected; *esp* : a somewhat steady level of radiation in the natural environment (as from cosmic rays)

syn BACKGROUND, SETTING, ENVIRONMENT, MILIEU, MISE-EN-SCÈNE mean the place, time, and circumstances in which something occurs. BACKGROUND often refers to the circumstances or events that precede a phenomenon or development ⟨the shocking decision was part of the *background* of the riots⟩. SETTING suggests looking at real-life situations in literary or dramatic terms ⟨a militant reformer who was born into an unlikely social *setting*⟩. ENVIRONMENT applies to all the external factors that have a formative influence on one's physical, mental, or moral development ⟨the kind of *environment* that produces juvenile delinquents⟩. MILIEU applies esp. to the physical and social surroundings of a person or group of persons ⟨an intellectual *milieu* conducive to artistic experimentation⟩. MISE-EN-SCÈNE strongly suggests the use of properties to achieve a particular atmosphere or theatrical effect ⟨a gothic thriller with a carefully crafted *mise-en-scène*⟩.

[2]**background** *vt* (1768) : to provide with background

back·ground·er \'bak-,graůn-dər\ *n* (1960) : an off-the-record briefing for reporters

background music *n* (1928) : music to accompany the dialogue or action of a motion picture or radio or television drama

background radiation *n* (1969) : the microwave radiation pervading the universe that has the spectral energy distribution of a blackbody having a temperature of 2.7 K and that is the principle evidence supporting the big bang theory — called also *cosmic background radiation*

[1]**back·hand** \'bak-,hand\ *n* (1657) **1 a** : a stroke (as in tennis) made with the back of the hand turned in the direction of movement; *also* : the side on which such strokes are made **b** : a catch (as in baseball) made to the side of the body opposite the hand being used **2** : handwriting whose strokes slant downward from left to right

[2]**backhand** *adj* (1695) : made with a backhand ⟨a ∼ tennis stroke⟩

[3]**backhand** *or* **back·hand·ed** \-'han-dəd\ *adv* (1889) : with a backhand

[4]**backhand** *vt* (ca. 1935) : to do, hit, or catch backhand

back·hand·ed \'bak-'han-dəd\ *adj* (1800) **1** : INDIRECT, DEVIOUS; *esp* : SARCASTIC ⟨a ∼ compliment⟩ **2** : using or made with a backhand — **back·hand·ed·ly** *adv*

backhand 1a

back·hand·er \-dər\ *n* (1960) *Brit* : BRIBE

back·hoe \-,hō\ *n* (1928) : an excavating machine having a bucket that is attached to a rigid bar hinged to a boom and that is drawn toward the machine in operation

back·house \-,haůs\ *n* (ca. 1847) : PRIVY 1a

back·ing \'ba-kiŋ\ *n* (1793) **1** : something forming a back **2 a** : SUPPORT, AID **b** : endorsement esp. of a warrant by a magistrate

back judge *n* (ca. 1966) : a football official whose duties include keeping the game's official time and identifying eligible pass receivers

back·land \'bak-,land\ *n* (1681) : BACKCOUNTRY, HINTERLAND — usu. used in pl.

back·lash \'bak-,lash\ *n* (1815) **1 a** : a sudden violent backward movement or reaction **b** : the play between adjacent movable parts (as in a series of gears); *also* : the jar caused by this when the parts are put into action **2** : a snarl in that part of a fishing line wound on the reel **3** : a strong adverse reaction (as to a recent political or social development) — **back·lash·er** *n*

back·light \-,līt\ *n* (ca. 1846) : illumination from behind; *also* : the source of such illumination — **backlight** *vt*

back·list \'bak-,list\ *n* (1964) : a list of books kept in print as distinguished from books newly published

[1]**back·log** \-,lȯg, -,läg\ *n* (1684) **1** : a large log at the back of a hearth fire **2** : an accumulation of tasks unperformed or materials not processed

[2]**backlog** *vb* (1963) : ACCUMULATE

back matter *n* (1947) : matter following the main text of a book

back mutation *n* (1939) : mutation of a previously mutated gene to its former condition

back of *prep* (1694) : BEHIND

back of beyond *n* (1816) : a remote place

back off *vi* (1938) : BACK DOWN

back–office \'bak-'ä-fəs, -'ȯ-fəs\ *adj* (1953) : of or relating to the inner workings of a business or institution : INTERNAL ⟨∼ operations⟩

back out *vi* (1807) : to withdraw esp. from a commitment or contest

[1]**back·pack** \'bak-,pak\ *n* (1914) **1 a** : a load carried on the back **b** : a camping pack (as of canvas or nylon) supported by a usu. aluminum frame and carried on the back **2** : a piece of equipment designed for use while being carried on the back

[2]**backpack** *vt* (1927) : to carry (food or equipment) on the back esp. in hiking ∼ *vi* : to hike with a backpack — **back·pack·er** *n*

back·ped·al \'bak-,pe-d²l\ *vi* (1901) : to retreat or move backward

back·rest \-,rest\ *n* (1859) : a rest for the back

back·room \'bak-'rüm, -'rům\ *adj* (1940) : made or operating in an inconspicuous way : BEHIND-THE-SCENES ⟨∼ deals⟩ ⟨a ∼ politician⟩

back room *n* (1592) **1** : a room situated in the rear **2** : the meeting place of a directing group that exercises its authority in an inconspicuous and indirect way

back·saw \'bak-,sȯ\ *n* (ca. 1877) : a saw with a metal rib along its back

back·scat·ter \-,ska-tər\ *or* **back·scat·ter·ing** \-tə-riŋ\ *n* (1940) : the scattering of radiation or particles in a direction opposite to that of the incident radiation due to reflection from particles of the medium traversed; *also* : the radiation or particles so reversed in direction — **backscatter** *vt*

back-scratch-ing \'bak-ˌskra-chiŋ\ *n* (1924) : the reciprocal exchange of favors, services, assistance, or praise

back-seat \-'sēt\ *n* (1829) **1** : a seat in the back (as of an automobile) **2** : an inferior position ⟨won't take a ~ to anyone⟩

back-set \'bak-ˌset\ *n* (1721) : SETBACK

back-side \-ˌsīd\ *n* (ca. 1500) : BUTTOCKS — often used in pl.

back-slap \-ˌslap\ *vt* (1926) : to display excessive or effusive goodwill for ~ *vi* : to display excessive cordiality or goodwill — **backslap** *n* — **back-slap-per** *n*

back-slide \-ˌslīd\ *vi* **-slid** \-ˌslid\; **-slid** *or* **-slid-den** \-ˌsli-dᵊn\; **-slid-ing** \-ˌslī-diŋ\ (1581) **1** : to lapse morally or in the practice of religion **2** : to revert to a worse condition : RETROGRESS — **back-slid-er** \-ˌslī-dər\ *n*

back-space \-ˌspās\ *vi* (1911) : to move back one space in a text with each depression of a key — **backspace** *n*

back-spin \-ˌspin\ *n* (ca. 1909) : a backward rotary motion of a ball

back-splash \'bak-ˌsplash\ *n* (1947) : a vertical surface (as of tiles) designed to protect the wall behind a stove or countertop

back-stab-bing \-ˌsta-biŋ\ *n* (1946) : betrayal (as by a verbal attack against one not present) esp. by a false friend — **back-stab** \-ˌstab\ *vb* — **back-stab-ber** \-ˌsta-bər\ *n*

¹back-stage \'bak-ˌstāj\ *adj* (1916) **1** : of, relating to, or occurring in the area behind the proscenium and esp. in the dressing rooms **2** : of or relating to the private lives of theater people **3** : of or relating to the inner working or operation (as of an organization)

²back-stage \'bak-ˌstāj\ *adv* (1923) **1** : in or to a backstage area **2** : in private : SECRETLY

back-stairs \-ˌstarz, -ˌsterz\ *adj* (1663) **1** : SECRET, FURTIVE ⟨~ political deals⟩ **2** : SORDID, SCANDALOUS ⟨~ gossip⟩

back-stay \-ˌstā\ *n* (1626) **1** : a stay extending from the mastheads to the side of a ship and slanting aft **2** : a strengthening or supporting device at the back (as of a carriage or a shoe)

back-stitch \-ˌstich\ *n* (1611) : a stitch sewn one stitch length backward on the front side and two stitch lengths forward on the reverse side to form a solid line of stitching on both sides — **backstitch** *vb*

¹back-stop \-ˌstäp\ *n* (1851) **1** : something at the back serving as a stop: as **a** : a screen or fence for keeping a ball from leaving the field of play **b** : a stop (as a pawl) that prevents a backward movement (as of a wheel) **2** : a player (as the catcher) positioned behind the batter

²backstop *vt* (1941) **1** : SUPPORT, BOLSTER **2** : to serve as a backstop to

back-street \'bak-ˌstrēt\ *n* (15c) : a street away from the main thoroughfares

back-stretch \'bak-ˌstrech\ *n* (1839) : the side opposite the homestretch on a racecourse

back-stroke \-ˌstrōk\ *n* (1879) : a swimming stroke executed on the back and usu. consisting of alternating circular arm pulls and a flutter kick

back-swept \-ˌswept\ *adj* (ca. 1918) : swept or slanting backward

back swimmer *n* (1862) : an aquatic bug (family Notonectidae) that swims on its back

back-swing \'bak-ˌswiŋ\ *n* (1899) : the movement of a club, racket, bat, or arm backward to a position from which the forward or downward swing is made

back-sword \-ˌsōrd, -ˌsȯrd\ *n* (1609) : a single-edged sword

back talk *n* (1858) : impudent, insolent, or argumentative replies

back-to-back *adj or adv* (15c) **1** : facing in opposite directions and often touching **2** : coming one after the other : CONSECUTIVE

back-track \'bak-ˌtrak\ *vi* (1904) **1 a** : to retrace one's course **b** : to go back to an earlier point in a sequence **2** : to reverse a position

back-up \-ˌəp\ *n, often attrib* (1951) **1 a** : one that serves as a substitute or support ⟨a ~ plan⟩ **b** : musical accompaniment **2** : an accumulation caused by a stoppage in the flow ⟨traffic ~⟩ **3** : the act or an instance of backing up a computer's hard disk

back up *vi* (1837) : to accumulate in a congested state ⟨traffic *backed up* for miles⟩ ~ *vt* **1** : to move into a position behind (a teammate) in order to assist on a play **2** : HOLD BACK 1 **3** : to make copies of the computer files on (a hard disk) to protect against loss of data

¹back-ward \'bak-wərd\ *or* **back-wards** \-wərdz\ *adv* (14c) **1 a** : toward the back **b** : with the back foremost **2 a** : in a reverse or contrary direction or way **b** : toward the past **c** : toward a worse state — **bend over backward** *or* **lean over backward** : to make extreme efforts (as at concession)

²backward *adj* (14c) **1 a** : directed or turned backward **b** : done or executed backward **2** : DIFFIDENT, SHY **3** : retarded in development — **back-ward-ly** *adv* — **back-ward-ness** *n*

³backward *n* (1610) : the part behind or past

back-wash \'bak-ˌwȯsh, -ˌwäsh\ *n* (1876) **1** : a backward flow or movement (as of water or air) produced esp. by a propelling force; *also* : the fluid that is moving backward **2** : CONSEQUENCE, AFTERMATH

back-wa-ter \-ˌwȯ-tər, -ˌwä-\ *n* (1629) **1 a** : water backed up in its course by an obstruction, an opposing current, or the tide **b** : a body of water (as an inlet or tributary) that is out of the main current of a larger body **2** : an isolated or backward place or condition

back-woods \-'wu̇dz\ *n pl but sing or pl in constr, often attrib* (1709) **1** : wooded or partly cleared areas far from cities **2** : a remote or culturally backward area — **back-woodsy** \-'wu̇d-zē\ *adj*

back-woods-man \ˌbak-'wu̇dz-mən, 'bak-ˌ\ *n* (1774) : one who lives in the backwoods

back-wrap \-ˌrap\ *n* (1951) : a wraparound garment (as a skirt) that fastens in the back

back-yard \-'yärd\ *n* (1659) **1** : an area at the rear of a house **2** : an area that is one's special domain

ba-con \'bā-kən\ *n* [ME, fr. MF, of Gmc origin; akin to OHG *bahho* side of bacon, *bah* back] (14c) : a side of a pig cured and smoked

Ba-co-ni-an \bā-'kō-nē-ən\ *adj* (1812) **1** : of, relating to, or characteristic of Francis Bacon or his doctrines **2** : of or relating to those who believe that Francis Bacon wrote the works usu. attributed to Shakespeare — **Baconian** *n*

bac-ter-emia \ˌbak-tə-'rē-mē-ə\ *n* [NL, alter. of *bacteriemia*, fr. *bacteri-* + *-emia*] (ca. 1890) : the usu. transient presence of bacteria in the blood — **bac-ter-emic** \-'mik\ *adj*

bacteri- *or* **bacterio-** *comb form* [NL *bacterium*] : bacteria ⟨*bacteriolysis*⟩

bac-te-ria \bak-'tir-ē-ə\ *n, pl* **-ri-as** [pl. of *bacterium*] (1884) : a group (as a genus, species, or strain) of bacteria — used chiefly in nontechnical writing and in news broadcasts

usage Bacteria is regularly a plural in scientific and pedagogical use; in speech and in journalism it is also used as a singular ⟨caused by a ~ borne by certain tiny ticks —*Wall St. Jour.*⟩ ⟨more resistant to chlorine and elevated water temperatures than other ~s —Allan Bruckheim, M.D., *Chicago Tribune*⟩. This journalistic use is found in British as well as American sources.

bac-te-ri-al \bak-'tir-ē-əl\ *adj* (1871) : of, relating to, or caused by bacteria ⟨~ infection⟩ — **bac-te-ri-al-ly** \-ə-lē\ *adv*

bac-te-ri-cid-al \bak-ˌtir-ə-'sī-dᵊl\ *adj* (1878) : destroying bacteria — **bac-te-ri-cid-al-ly** \-dᵊl-ē\ *adv* — **bac-te-ri-cide** \-'tir-ə-ˌsīd\ *n*

bac-ter-in \'bak-tə-rən\ *n* (ca. 1912) : a suspension of killed or attenuated bacteria for use as a vaccine

bac-te-rio-chlo-ro-phyll \bak-ˌtir-ē-ō-'klȯr-ə-ˌfil, -'klȯr-, -fəl\ *n* (1938) : a pyrrole derivative in photosynthetic bacteria related to the chlorophyll of higher plants

bac-te-rio-cin \bak-'tir-ē-ə-sən\ *n* [ISV *bacteri-* + *-cin* (as in *colicin*)] (1954) : an antibiotic (as a colicin) produced by bacteria

bac-te-ri-ol-o-gy \(ˌ)bak-ˌtir-ē-'ä-lə-jē\ *n* [ISV] (1884) **1** : a science that deals with bacteria and their relations to medicine, industry, and agriculture **2** : bacterial life and phenomena — **bac-te-ri-o-log-ic** \bak-ˌtir-ē-ə-'lä-jik\ *or* **bac-te-ri-o-log-i-cal** \-'lä-ji-kəl\ *adj* — **bac-te-ri-o-log-i-cal-ly** \-ji-k(ə-)lē\ *adv* — **bac-te-ri-ol-o-gist** \(ˌ)bak-ˌtir-ē-'ä-lə-jist\ *n*

bac-te-ri-ol-y-sis \(ˌ)bak-ˌtir-ē-'ä-lə-səs\ *n* [NL] (1900) : destruction or lysis of bacterial cells — **bac-te-ri-o-lyt-ic** \bak-ˌtir-ē-ō-'li-tik\ *adj*

bac-te-rio-phage \bak-'tir-ē-ə-ˌfāj *also* -ˌfäzh\ *n* [ISV] (1921) : a virus that infects bacteria — **bac-te-ri-oph-a-gy** \(ˌ)bak-ˌtir-ē-'ä-fə-jē\ *n*

bac-te-rio-rho-dop-sin \bak-ˌtir-ē-ə-rō-'däp-sin\ *n* (1974) : a purple-pigmented protein found in the outer membrane of a bacterium (*Halobacterium halobium*) that converts light energy into chemical energy in the synthesis of ATP

bac-te-rio-sta-sis \bak-ˌtir-ē-ō-'stā-səs\ *n* [NL] (1920) : inhibition of the growth of bacteria without destruction

bac-te-rio-stat \-'tir-ē-ō-ˌstat\ *n* (1920) : an agent that causes bacteriostasis — **bac-te-rio-stat-ic** \-ˌtir-ē-ō-'sta-tik\ *adj*

bac-te-ri-um \bak-'tir-ē-əm\ *n, pl* **-ria** \-ē-ə\ [NL, fr. Gk *baktērion* staff] (ca. 1849) : any of a group (as Kingdom Procaryotae or Kingdom Monera) of prokaryotic unicellular round, spiral, or rod-shaped single-celled microorganisms that are often aggregated into colonies or motile by means of flagella, that live in soil, water, organic matter, or the bodies of plants and animals, and that are autotrophic, saprophytic, or parasitic in nutrition and important because of their biochemical effects and pathogenicity

bac-te-ri-uria \bak-ˌtir-ē-'yu̇r-ē-ə\ *n* [NL] (1900) : the presence of bacteria in the urine

bac-te-rize \'bak-tə-ˌrīz\ *vt* **-rized; -riz-ing** (1914) : to subject to bacterial action — **bac-te-ri-za-tion** \ˌbak-tə-rə-'zā-shən\ *n*

bac-te-roid \'bak-tə-ˌrȯid\ *n* (1878) : an irregularly shaped bacterium (as a rhizobium) found esp. in root nodules of legumes

Bac-tri-an camel \'bak-trē-ən-\ *n* (1609) : CAMEL 1b

¹bad \'bad\ *adj* **worse** \'wərs\; **worst** \'wərst\ [ME] (14c) **1 a** : failing to reach an acceptable standard : POOR **b** : UNFAVORABLE ⟨make a ~ impression⟩ **c** : not fresh : SPOILED ⟨~ fish⟩ **d** : not sound : DILAPIDATED ⟨the house was in ~ condition⟩ **2 a** : morally objectionable **b** : MISCHIEVOUS, DISOBEDIENT **3** : inadequate or unsuited to a purpose ⟨a ~ plan⟩ ⟨~ lighting⟩ **4** : DISAGREEABLE, UNPLEASANT ⟨~ news⟩ **5 a** : INJURIOUS, HARMFUL **b** : SERIOUS, SEVERE ⟨in ~ trouble⟩ ⟨a ~ cough⟩ **6** : INCORRECT, FAULTY ⟨~ grammar⟩ **7** : suffering pain or distress ⟨felt generally ~⟩ **b** : UNHEALTHY, DISEASED ⟨~ teeth⟩ **8** : SORROWFUL, SORRY **9** : INVALID, VOID ⟨a ~ check⟩ **10 bad-der; bad-dest** *slang* **a** : GOOD, GREAT **b** : TOUGH, MEAN — **bad-ness** *n*

²bad *n* (15c) **1** : something that is bad **2** : an evil or unhappy state

³bad *adv* (1681) : BADLY

¹bad-ass \-ˌas\ *adj* (1956) : ready to cause or get into trouble : MEAN — often considered vulgar

²badass *n* (1984) : a person who is badass — often considered vulgar

bad blood *n* (1825) : ill feeling : BITTERNESS

bad-die *or* **bad-dy** \'ba-dē\ *n, pl* **baddies** (1937) : one that is bad; *esp* : an opponent of the hero (as in fiction or motion pictures)

bade *past and past part of* BID

badge \'baj\ *n* [ME *bage, bagge*] (14c) **1** : a device or token esp. of membership in a society or group **2** : a characteristic mark **3** : an emblem awarded for a particular accomplishment — **badge** *vt*

¹bad-ger \'ba-jər\ *n* [prob. fr. *badge*; fr. the white mark on its forehead] (1523) **1 a** : any of various burrowing mammals (esp. *Taxidea taxus* and *Meles meles*) that are related to the weasels and are widely distributed in the northern hemisphere **b** : the pelt or fur of a badger **2** *cap* : a native or resident of Wisconsin — used as a nickname

²badger *vt* [fr. the sport of baiting badgers] (1794) : to harass or annoy persistently **syn** see BAIT

ba-di-nage \ˌba-dᵊn-'äzh\ *n* [F] (ca. 1658) : playful repartee : BANTER

bad-land \'bad-ˌland\ *n* (1851) : a region marked by intricate erosional sculpturing, scanty vegetation, and fantastically formed hills — usu. used in pl.

bad-ly \'bad-lē\ *adv* (14c) **1** : in a bad manner ⟨played ~⟩ **2** : to a great or intense degree ⟨want something ~⟩

bad-min-ton \'bad-ˌmin-tᵊn\ *n* [*Badminton*, residence of the Duke of Beaufort, England] (1874) : a court game played with light long-handled rackets and a shuttlecock volleyed over a net

bad-mouth \'bad-ˌmau̇th, -ˌmau̇th\ *vt* (1942) : to criticize severely

bad news *n pl but sing in constr* (1930) : one that is troublesome, unwelcome, or dangerous ⟨stay away from him, he's *bad news*⟩

\ə\ abut \ᵊ\ kitten, F table \ər\ further \a\ ash \ā\ ace \ä\ mop, mar \au̇\ out \ch\ chin \e\ bet \ē\ easy \g\ go \i\ hit \ī\ ice \j\ job \ŋ\ sing \ō\ go \ȯ\ law \ȯi\ boy \th\ thin \t̲h̲\ the \ü\ loot \u̇\ foot \y\ yet \zh\ vision \à, k̲, ⁿ, œ, œ̄, ue, ūe, ʸ\ *see* Guide to Pronunciation

Bae·de·ker \'bā-di-kər, 'be-\ n [Karl Baedeker †1859 Ger. publisher of guidebooks] (1924) : GUIDEBOOK

¹**baf·fle** \'ba-fəl\ vt **baf·fled; baf·fling** \-f(ə-)liŋ\ [prob. alter. of ME (Sc) bawchillen to denounce, discredit publicly] (ca. 1590) **1** : to defeat or check (as a person) by confusing or puzzling : DISCONCERT **2** : to check or break the force or flow of by or as if by a baffle *syn* see FRUSTRATE — **baf·fle·ment** \-fəl-mənt\ n — **baf·fler** \-f(ə-)lər\ n — **baf·fling·ly** \'ba-fliŋ-lē\ adv

²**baffle** n (ca. 1900) : a device (as a plate, wall, or screen) to deflect, check, or regulate flow (as of a fluid, light, or sound) — **baf·fled** \'ba-fəld\ adj

¹**bag** \'bag also 'bàg\ n [ME bagge, fr. ON baggi] (13c) **1** : a usu. flexible container that may be closed for holding, storing, or carrying something: as **a** : PURSE; *esp* : HANDBAG **b** : a bag for game **c** : SUITCASE **2** : something resembling a bag: as **a** : a pouched or pendulous bodily part or organ; *esp* : UDDER **b** : a puffed-out sag or bulge in cloth **c** : a square white stuffed canvas bag to mark a base in baseball **3** : the amount contained in a bag **4 a** : a quantity of game taken; *also* : the maximum legal quantity of game **b** : an assortment or collection esp. of nonmaterial things (a ~ of tricks) **5** : an unattractive woman **6** : something one likes or does regularly or well; *also* : one's characteristic way of doing things — **in the bag** : SURE, CERTAIN (her nomination was *in the bag*)

²**bag** vb **bagged; bag·ging** vi (15c) **1** : to swell out : BULGE **2** : to hang loosely ~ vt **1** : to cause to swell **2** : to put into a bag **3 a** : to take (animals) as game **b** : to get possession of esp. by strategy or stealth **c** : CAPTURE, SEIZE **d** : to shoot down : DESTROY *syn* see CATCH — **bag·ger** n

ba·gasse \bə-'gas\ n [F] (ca. 1826) : plant residue (as of sugarcane or grapes) left after a product (as juice) has been extracted

bag·a·telle \,ba-gə-'tel\ n [F, fr. It bagatella] (1633) **1** : TRIFLE 1 **2** : any of various games involving the rolling of balls into scoring areas **3** : a short literary or musical piece in light style

ba·gel \'bā-gəl\ n [Yiddish beygl, fr. (assumed) MHG böugel ring, fr. MHG bouc ring, fr. OHG; akin to OE bēag ring, būgan to bend — more at BOW] (1932) : a hard glazed doughnut-shaped roll

bag·ful \'bag-,fủl\ n (15c) **1** : as much or as many as a bag will hold **2** : a large number or amount (had a ~ of tricks)

¹**bag·gage** \'ba-gij\ n [ME bagage, fr. MF, fr. bague bundle] (15c) **1** : suitcases, trunks, and personal belongings of travelers : LUGGAGE **2** : transportable equipment esp. of a military force **3** : things (as objects, circumstances, or beliefs) that get in the way : IMPEDIMENTA

²**baggage** n [prob. modif. of MF bagasse, fr. OProv bagassa] (1594) **1** : a contemptible woman; *esp* : PROSTITUTE **2** : a young woman

bag·ging \'ba-giŋ\ n (1732) : material (as cloth) for bags

bag·gy \'ba-gē\ adj **bag·gi·er; -est** (1831) : loose, puffed out, or hanging like a bag (~ trousers) — **bag·gi·ly** \'ba-gə-lē\ adv — **bag·gi·ness** \'ba-gē-nəs\ n

bag·house \'bag-,hàus\ n (1914) : a device or facility in which particulates are removed from a stream of exhaust gases (as from a blast furnace) as the stream passes through a large cloth bag; *also* : the bag used to filter the gas stream

bag lady n (1979) : a homeless woman who roams the streets of a large city carrying her possessions in shopping bags

bag·man \'bag-mən\ n (1765) **1** chiefly Brit : TRAVELING SALESMAN **2** : a person who on behalf of another collects or distributes illicitly gained money

ba·gnio \'ban-(,)yō\ n, pl **bagnios** [It bagno, lit., public baths (fr. the Turks' use of Roman baths at Constantinople as prisons), fr. L balneum, fr. Gk balaneion] (1599) **1** obs : PRISON **2** : BORDELLO

bag of waters (ca. 1881) : the double-walled fluid-filled sac that encloses and protects the fetus in the womb and that breaks releasing its fluid during the birth process

bag·pipe \'bag-,pīp\ n (14c) : a wind instrument consisting of a reed melody pipe and from one to five drones with air supplied continuously either by a bag with valve-stopped mouth tube or by bellows — often used in pl. — **bag·pip·er** \-,pī-pər\ n

ba·guette \ba-'get\ n [F, lit., rod] (1926) **1** : a gem having the shape of a narrow rectangle; *also* : the shape itself **2** : a long thin loaf of French bread

bag·wig \'bag-,wig\ n (1717) : an 18th century wig with the back hair enclosed in a small silk bag

bag·worm \-,wərm\ n (1862) : any of a family (Psychidae) of moths with wingless females and plant-feeding larvae that live in a silk case covered with plant debris; *esp* : one (Thyridopteryx ephemeraeformis) often destructive to deciduous and evergreen trees of the eastern U.S.

bah \'bä, 'ba\ interj (1600) — used to express disdain or contempt

Ba·ha'i \bä-'hä-ē, -'hī\ n, pl **Baha'is** [Per bahā'ī, lit., of glory, fr. bahā glory] (1889) : an adherent of a religious movement originating in Iran in the 19th century and emphasizing the spiritual unity of mankind — **Baha'i** adj — **Ba·ha·ism** \-'hä-,i-zəm, -'hī-,i-\ n — **Ba·ha·ist** \-'hä-(,)ist\ n

Ba·ha·sa In·do·ne·sia \bə-,hä-sə-,in-də-'nē-zhə, -shə\ n [Indonesian bahasa indonésia, lit., Indonesian language] (1952) : INDONESIAN 2b

Ba·hia grass \bə-'hē-ə-\ n [Bahia, state in Brazil] (ca. 1927) : a perennial tropical American grass (Paspalum notatum) used in the southern U.S. as a lawn grass

baht \'bät\ n, pl **baht** also **bahts** [Thai bàad] (1828) — see MONEY table

¹**bail** \'bā(ə)l\ n [ME baille, fr. MF, bucket, fr. ML bajula water vessel, fr. fem. of L bajulus] (14c) : a container used to remove water from a boat

²**bail** vt (1613) **1** : to clear (water) from a boat by dipping and throwing over the side — usu. used with out **2** : to clear water from by dipping and throwing — usu. used with out — **bail·er** n

³**bail** n [ME, custody, bail, fr. MF, custody, fr. baillier to have in charge, deliver, fr. ML bajulare to control, fr. L, to carry a load, fr. bajulus porter] (15c) **1** : the temporary release of a prisoner in exchange for security given for the due appearance of the prisoner **2** : security given for the release of a prisoner on bail **3** : one who provides bail

⁴**bail** vt (1548) **1** : to release under bail **2** : to procure the release of by giving bail — often used with out **3** : to help from a predicament — used with out (~ing out impoverished countries) — **bail·able** adj

⁵**bail** n [ME beil, baile, prob. of Scand origin; akin to Sw bygel bow,

hoop; akin to OE būgan to bend — more at BOW] (15c) **1 a** : a supporting half hoop **b** : a hinged bar for holding paper against the platen of a typewriter **2** : a usu. arched handle (as of a kettle or pail)

⁶**bail** vt [AF baillier, fr. F] (1768) : to deliver (personal property) in trust to another for a special purpose and for a limited period

⁷**bail** n [perh. fr. ⁵bail] (1844) chiefly Brit : a device for confining or separating animals

bail·ee \bā-'lē\ n (1528) : the person to whom personal property is bailed

bai·ley \'bā-lē\ n, pl **baileys** [ME bailli, palisade, bailey, fr. OF baille, balie] (13c) **1** : the outer wall of a castle or any of several walls surrounding the keep **2** : a courtyard within the external wall or between two outer walls of a castle

bai·lie \'bā-lē\ n [ME] (13c) **1** chiefly dial : BAILIFF **2** : a Scottish municipal magistrate corresponding to an English alderman

bai·liff \'bā-ləf\ n [ME baillif, bailie, fr. OF baillif, fr. bail custody, jurisdiction — more at BAIL] (14c) **1 a** : an official employed by a British sheriff to serve writs and make arrests and executions **b** : a minor officer of some U.S. courts usu. serving as a messenger or usher **2** chiefly Brit : one who manages an estate or farm — **bai·liff·ship** \-,ship\ n

bai·li·wick \'bā-li-,wik\ n [ME bailliwik, fr. baillif + wik dwelling place, village, fr. OE wīc, fr. L vicus village — more at VICINITY] (15c) **1** : the office or jurisdiction of a bailiff **2** : a special domain

bail·ment \'bā(ə)l-mənt\ n (1554) : the act of bailing a person or personal property

bail·or \bā-'lór, 'bā-lər\ or **bail·er** \'bā-lər\ n (1602) : a person who delivers personal property to another in trust

bail·out \'bā-,laùt\ n (1951) : a rescue (as of a corporation) from financial distress

bail out vi (1930) **1** : to parachute from an aircraft **2** : to abandon a harmful or difficult situation; *also* : LEAVE, DEPART

bails·man \'bā(ə)lz-mən\ n (1622) : one who gives bail for another

bairn \'barn, 'bern\ n [ME bern, barn, fr. OE bearn & ON barn; akin to OHG barn child] (bef. 12c) chiefly Scot : CHILD

¹**bait** \'bāt\ vb [ME, fr. ON beita; akin to OE bǣtan to bait, bītan to bite] vt (13c) **1 a** : to persecute or exasperate with unjust, malicious, or persistent attacks **b** : TEASE **2** : to harass (as a chained animal) with dogs usu. for sport **b** : to attack by biting and tearing **3 a** : to furnish with bait **b** : ENTICE, LURE **4** : to give food and drink to (an animal) esp. on the road ~ vi, archaic : to stop for food and rest when traveling — **bait·er** n

syn BAIT, BADGER, HECKLE, HECTOR, CHIVY, HOUND mean to harass by efforts to break down. BAIT implies wanton cruelty or delight in persecuting a helpless victim (baited the chained dog). BADGER implies pestering so as to drive a person to confusion or frenzy (badgered her father for a car). HECKLE implies persistent annoying or belligerent interruptions of a speaker (drunks heckled the stand-up comic). HECTOR carries an implication of bullying and domineering (football players hectored by their coach). CHIVY suggests persecution by teasing or nagging (chivied the new student mercilessly). HOUND implies unrelenting pursuit and harassing (hounded by creditors).

²**bait** n [ME, fr. ON beit pasturage & beita food; akin to OE bītan to bite] (14c) **1 a** : something used in luring esp. to a hook or trap **b** : a poisonous material placed where it will be eaten by usu. wild animals considered undesirable or deleterious **2** : LURE, TEMPTATION

bait and switch n (1967) : a sales tactic in which a customer is attracted by the advertisement of a low-priced item but is then encouraged to buy a higher-priced one

bai·za \'bī-(,)zä\ n, pl **baiza** or **baizas** [Ar, fr. Hindi paisā] (1970) — see rial at MONEY table

baize \'bāz\ n [MF baies, pl. of baie baize, fr. fem. of bai bay-colored] (1578) : a coarse woolen or cotton fabric napped to imitate felt

¹**bake** \'bāk\ vb **baked; bak·ing** [ME, fr. OE bacan; akin to OHG bahhan to bake, Gk phōgein to roast] vt (bef. 12c) **1** : to cook (as food) by dry heat esp. in an oven **2** : to dry or harden by subjecting to heat ~ vi **1** : to prepare food by baking it **2** : to become baked **3** : to become extremely hot — **bak·er** n

²**bake** n (1565) **1** : the act or process of baking **2** : a social gathering at which a baked food is served **3** : baked food (a ~ sale)

Ba·ke·lite \'bā-kə-,līt, -,klīt\ trademark — used for any of various synthetic resins and plastics

baker's dozen n (1596) : THIRTEEN

baker's yeast n (1854) : a yeast (as Saccharomyces cerevisiae) used or suitable for use as leaven

bak·ery \'bā-k(ə-)rē\ n, pl **-er·ies** (ca. 1820) : a place for baking or selling baked goods

bake·shop \'bāk-,shäp\ n (1789) : BAKERY

baking powder n (1850) : a powder used as a leavening agent in making baked goods (as quick breads) that consists of a carbonate, an acid substance, and starch or flour

baking soda n (1881) : SODIUM BICARBONATE

bak·la·va \,bä-klə-'vä\ n [Turk] (1653) : a dessert made of thin pastry, nuts, and honey

bak·sheesh \'bak-,shēsh, bak-'\ n [Per bakhshīsh, fr. bakhshīdan to give; akin to Gk phagein to eat, Skt bhajati he allots] (1775) : payment (as a tip or bribe) to expedite service

BAL \,bē-(,)ā-'el\ n [British Anti-Lewisite] (1942) : DIMERCAPROL

Ba·laam \'bā-ləm\ n [Gk, fr. Heb Bil'ām] : an Old Testament prophet who is reproached by the ass he is riding and rebuked by God's angel while on the way to meet with an enemy of Israel

bal·a·cla·va \,ba-lə-'klä-və, -'kla-\ n [Balaclava, Crimea, where a battle of the Crimean War was fought] (1881) : a knit cap for the head and neck — called also balaclava helmet

bal·a·lai·ka \,ba-lə-'lī-kə\ n [Russ] (1788) : a usu. 3-stringed instrument of Russian origin with a triangular body played by plucking or strumming

¹**bal·ance** \'ba-lən(t)s\ n [ME, fr. OF, fr. (as-

balalaika

sumed) VL *bilancia*, fr. LL *bilanc-, bilanx* having two scalepans, fr. L *bi-* + *lanc-, lanx* plate] (13c) **1 :** an instrument for weighing: as **a :** a beam that is supported freely in the center and has two pans of equal weight suspended from its ends **b :** a device that uses the elasticity of a spiral spring for measuring weight or force **c** *cap* **:** LIBRA **2 :** a means of judging or deciding **3 :** a counterbalancing weight, force, or influence **4 :** an oscillating wheel operating with a hairspring to regulate the movement of a timepiece **5 a :** stability produced by even distribution of weight on each side of the vertical axis **b :** equipoise between contrasting, opposing, or interacting elements **c :** equality between the totals of the two sides of an account **6 a :** an aesthetically pleasing integration of elements **b :** the juxtaposition in writing of syntactically parallel constructions containing similar or contrasting ideas **7 a :** physical equilibrium **b :** the ability to retain one's balance **8 a :** weight or force of one side in excess of another **b :** something left over **:** REMAINDER **c :** an amount in excess esp. on the credit side of an account **9 :** mental and emotional steadiness — **bal·anced** \-lən(t)st\ *adj* — **in the balance** *or* **in balance :** with the fate or outcome about to be determined — **on balance :** with all things considered

²**balance** *vb* **bal·anced; bal·anc·ing** *vt* (1588) **1 a** (1) **:** to compute the difference between the debits and credits of (an account) (2) **:** to pay the amount due on **:** SETTLE **b** (1) **:** to arrange so that one set of elements exactly equals another 〈~ a mathematical equation〉 (2) **:** to complete (a chemical equation) so that the same number of atoms and electric charges of each kind appears on each side **2 a :** COUNTERBALANCE, OFFSET **b :** to equal or equalize in weight, number, or proportion **3 :** to weigh in or as if in a balance **4 a :** to bring to a state or position of equipoise **b :** to poise in or as if in balance **c :** to bring into harmony or proportion ~ *vi* **1 :** to become balanced or established in balance **2 :** to be an equal counterpoise **3 :** WAVER **1** 〈~s and temporizes on matters that demand action〉

balance beam *n* (ca. 1949) **1 :** a narrow wooden beam supported in a horizontal position approximately four feet above the floor and used for balancing feats in gymnastics **2 :** an event in gymnastics competition in which the balance beam is used

balance of payments (1844) **:** a summary of the international transactions of a country or region over a period of time including commodity and service transactions, capital transactions, and gold movements

balance of power (1701) **:** an equilibrium of power sufficient to discourage or prevent one nation or party from imposing its will on or interfering with the interests of another

balance of trade (1668) **:** the difference in value over a period of time between a country's imports and exports

bal·anc·er \'ba-lən(t)-sər\ *n* (15c) **:** one that balances; *specif* **:** HALTERE

balance sheet *n* (ca. 1771) **:** a statement of financial condition at a given date

balance wheel *n* (1669) **1 :** a wheel that regulates or stabilizes the motion of a mechanism **2 :** a balancing or stabilizing force

balancing act *n* (1954) **:** an attempt to cope with several often conflicting factors or situations at the same time

Ba·lante \bə-'länt\ *n, pl* **Balante** *or* **Balantes** [F, fr. Balante *Bulanda*] (ca. 1895) **1 :** a member of a people of Senegal and Guinea-Bissau **2 :** the language of the Balante people

bal·as \'ba-ləs\ *n* [ME, fr. MF *balais*, fr. Ar *balakhsh*, fr. *Balakhshān*, ancient region of Afghanistan] (15c) **:** a ruby spinel of a pale rose-red or orange

ba·la·ta \bə-'lä-tə\ *n* [Sp, fr. Carib] (1860) **:** a substance like gutta-percha that is the dried juice of tropical American trees (esp. *Manilkara bidentata*) of the sapodilla family and is used esp. in belting and golf balls; *also* **:** a tree yielding it

bal·boa \bal-'bō-ə\ *n* [Sp, fr. Vasco Núñez de *Balboa*] (ca. 1909) — see MONEY table

bal·brig·gan \bal-'bri-gən\ *n* [*Balbriggan*, town in Ireland] (1885) **:** a knitted cotton fabric used esp. for underwear or hosiery

bal·co·ny \'bal-kə-nē\ *n, pl* **-nies** [It *balcone*, fr. OIt, large window, of Gmc origin; akin to OHG *balko* beam — more at BALK] (1618) **1 :** a platform that projects from the wall of a building and is enclosed by a parapet or railing **2 :** an interior projecting gallery in a public building (as a theater) — **bal·co·nied** \-nēd\ *adj*

¹**bald** \'bold\ *adj* [ME *balled*; prob. akin to Dan *bældet* bald, L *fulica* coot, Gk *phalios* having a white spot] (14c) **1 a :** lacking a natural or usual covering (as of hair, vegetation, or nap) **b :** having little or no tread 〈~ tires〉 **2 :** UNADORNED **3 :** UNDISGUISED, PALPABLE **4 :** marked with white *syn* see BARE — **bald·ish** \'bol-dish\ *adj* — **bald·ly** \'bol(d)-lē\ *adv* — **bald·ness** \'bol(d)-nəs\ *n*

²**bald** *vt* (1602) **:** to make bald ~ *vi* **:** to become bald

bal·da·chin \'bol-də-kən, 'bal-\ *or* **bal·da·chi·no** \,bal-də-'kē-(,)nō, ,bäl-\ *n, pl* **baldachins** *or* **baldachinos** [It *baldacchino*, fr. *Baldacco* Baghdad, Iraq] (1537) **1 :** a cloth canopy fixed or carried over an important person or a sacred object **2 :** a rich embroidered fabric of silk and gold **3 :** an ornamental structure resembling a canopy used esp. over an altar

bald cypress *n* (1709) **1 :** either of two large swamp trees (*Taxodium distichum* and *T. ascendens* of the family Taxodiaceae, the bald cypress family) of the southern U.S. that are related to the sequoias **2 :** the hard red wood of bald cypress that is much used for shingles

bald eagle *n* (1688) **:** an eagle (*Haliaeetus leucocephalus*) of No. America that is brown when young with white only on the undersides of the wings but in full adult plumage has white head and neck feathers and a white tail

Bal·der \'bol-dər\ *n* [ON *Baldr*] **:** the son of Odin and Frigga and Norse god of light and peace slain through the trickery of Loki by a mistletoe sprig

bal·der·dash \'bol-dər-,dash\ *n* [origin unknown] (1674) **:** NONSENSE

bald–faced \'bol(d)-'fast\ *adj* (1943) **:** BAREFACED

bald·head \'bold-,hed\ *n* (1535) **:** a bald-headed person

balding (1938) **:** getting bald (bespectacled and ~)

bald·pate \'bol(d)-,pāt\ *n* (1592) **1 :** BALDHEAD **2 :** a No. American wigeon (*Anas americana*) with a large white patch on each wing and in the male a white crown

bal·dric \'bol-drik\ *n* [ME *baudry, baudrik*, fr. MF *baudré*, fr. OF *baldrei*] (14c) **:** an often ornamented belt worn over one shoulder to support a sword or bugle

¹**bale** \'bā(ə)l\ *n* [ME, fr. OE *bealu*; akin to OHG *balo* evil, OCS *bolĭ* sick person] (bef. 12c) **1 :** great evil **2 :** WOE, SORROW

²**bale** *n* [ME, fr. MF, of Gmc origin; akin to OHG *balla* ball] (14c) **:** a large bundle of goods; *specif* **:** a large closely pressed package of merchandise bound and usu. wrapped 〈a ~ of paper〉 〈a ~ of hay〉

³**bale** *vt* **baled; bal·ing** (1760) **:** to make up into a bale — **bal·er** *n*

ba·leen \bə-'lēn, 'ba-,lēn\ *n* [ME *baleine* whale, baleen, fr. L *balaena* whale; akin to Gk *phallaina* whale] (14c) **:** a horny substance found in two rows of plates from 2 to 12 feet long attached along the upper jaws of baleen whales

baleen whale *n* (1874) **:** any of a suborder (Mysticeti) of usu. large whales lacking teeth but having baleen which is used to filter chiefly small marine crustaceans (as krill) out of large quantities of seawater

bale·fire \'bā(ə)l-,fir\ *n* [ME, fr. OE *bǣlfȳr* funeral fire, fr. *bǣl* pyre + *fȳr* fire] (bef. 12c) **:** an outdoor fire often used as a signal fire

bale·ful \-fəl\ *adj* (bef. 12c) **1 :** deadly or pernicious in influence **2 :** foreboding evil **:** OMINOUS *syn* see SINISTER — **bale·ful·ly** \-fə-lē\ *adv* — **bale·ful·ness** \-fəl-nəs\ *n*

Ba·li·nese \,bä-li-'nēz, ,ba-, -'nēs\ *n* [D *Balinees*, fr. *Bali* island of Indonesia] (1967) **:** any of a breed of slender long-haired cats that originated as a spontaneous mutation of the Siamese

¹**balk** \'bok\ *n* [ME *balke*, fr. OE *balca*; akin to OHG *balko* beam, L *fulcire* to prop, Gk *phalanx* log, phalanx] (bef. 12c) **1 :** a ridge of land left unplowed as a dividing line or through carelessness **2 :** BEAM, RAFTER **3 :** HINDRANCE, CHECK **4 a :** the space behind the balkline on a billiard table **b :** any of the outside divisions made by the balklines **5 :** failure of a player to complete a motion; *esp* **:** an illegal motion of the pitcher in baseball while in position

²**balk** *vt* (15c) **1** *archaic* **:** to pass over or by **2 :** to check or stop by or as if by an obstacle **:** BLOCK ~ *vi* **1 :** to stop short and refuse to proceed **2 :** to refuse abruptly — used with *at* **3 :** to commit a balk in sports *syn* see FRUSTRATE — **balk·er** *n*

bal·kan·ize \'bol-kə-,nīz\ *vt* **-ized; -iz·ing** *often cap* [*Balkan* Peninsula] (1919) **:** to break up (as a region or group) into smaller and often hostile units — **bal·kan·i·za·tion** \,bol-kə-nə-'zā-shən\ *n, often cap*

balk·line \'bok-,klīn\ *n* (1839) **1 :** a line across a billiard table near one end behind which the cue balls are placed in making opening shots **2 a :** one of four lines parallel to the cushions of a billiard table dividing it into nine compartments **b :** a billiards game that sets restrictions in scoring caroms according to these lines

balky \'bo-kē\ *adj* **balk·i·er; -est** (1847) **:** refusing or likely to refuse to proceed, act, or function as directed or expected 〈a ~ mule〉 *syn* see CONTRARY — **balk·i·ness** *n*

¹**ball** \'bol\ *n, often attrib* [ME *bal*, fr. ON *bollr*; akin to OE *bealluc* testis, OHG *balla* ball, OE *blāwan* to blow] (13c) **1 :** a round or roundish body or mass: as **a :** a spherical or ovoid body used in a game or sport **b :** EARTH, GLOBE **c :** a spherical or conical projectile; *also* **:** projectiles used in firearms **d :** a roundish protuberant anatomic structure; *esp* **:** the rounded eminence at the base of the thumb or big toe **2 a :** TESTIS — often considered vulgar **b** *pl* (1) **:** NONSENSE — often used interjectionally; often considered vulgar (2) **:** NERVE **3** — often considered vulgar **3 :** a game in which a ball is thrown, kicked, or struck; *also* **:** quality of play in such a game **4 a :** a pitch not swung at by the batter that fails to pass through the strike zone **b :** a hit or thrown ball in various games 〈foul ~〉 — **on the ball 1 :** COMPETENT, KNOWLEDGEABLE, ALERT 〈the other introductory essay . . . is much more *on the ball* —Times Lit. Supp.〉 〈keep *on the ball*〉 **2 :** of ability or competence 〈if the teacher has something *on the ball*, the pupils won't squirm much —New Yorker〉

²**ball** *vt* (1658) **1 :** to form or gather into a ball 〈~ed the paper into a wad〉 **2 :** to have sexual intercourse with — usu. considered vulgar ~ *vi* **1 :** to form or gather into a ball **2 :** to engage in sexual intercourse — usu. considered vulgar

³**ball** *n* [F *bal*, fr. *baller* to dance, fr. LL *ballare*, fr. Gk *ballizein*] (ca. 1639) **1 :** a large formal gathering for social dancing **2 :** a very pleasant experience **:** a good time

bal·lad \'ba-ləd\ *n* [ME *balade* ballade, song, fr. MF, fr. OProv *balada* dance, song sung while dancing, fr. *balar* to dance, fr. LL *ballare*] (14c) **1 :** a narrative composition in rhythmic verse suitable for singing **b :** an art song accompanying a traditional ballad **2 :** a simple song **:** AIR **3 :** a popular song; *esp* **:** a slow romantic or sentimental song — **bal·lad·ic** \bə-'la-dik, ba-\ *adj*

bal·lade \bə-'läd, ba-\ *n* [ME *balade*, fr. MF, ballad, ballade] (14c) **1 :** a fixed verse form consisting usu. of three stanzas with recurrent rhymes, an envoi, and an identical refrain for each part **2 :** a musical composition usu. for piano suggesting the epic ballad

bal·lad·eer \,ba-lə-'dir\ *n* (1830) **:** a singer of ballads

bal·lad·ist \'ba-lə-dist\ *n* (1858) **:** one who writes or sings ballads

bal·lad·ry \'ba-lə-drē\ *n* (1596) **1 :** the composing or performing of ballads **2 :** BALLADS

ballad stanza *n* (ca. 1934) **:** a stanza consisting of four lines with the first and third lines unrhymed iambic tetrameters and the second and fourth lines rhymed iambic trimeters

ball–and–socket joint *n* (1809) **1 :** a joint in which a ball moves within a socket so as to allow rotary motion in every direction within certain limits **2 :** an articulation (as the hip joint) in which the rounded head of one bone fits into a cuplike cavity of the other and admits movement in any direction

ball-and-socket joint 1

¹**bal·last** \'ba-ləst\ *n* [prob. fr. LG, of Scand origin; akin to Dan & Sw *barlast* ballast; perh. akin to OE *bær* bare & to OE *hlæst* load, *hladan* to load — more at LADE] (1530) **1 :** a heavy substance used to improve the stability and control the draft of a ship or the ascent of a balloon **2**

\ə\ abut \ᵊ\ kitten, F table \ər\ further \a\ ash \ā\ ace \ä\ mop, mar \au̇\ out \ch\ chin \e\ bet \ē\ easy \g\ go \i\ hit \ī\ ice \j\ job \ŋ\ sing \ō\ go \o\̇ law \oi̇\ boy \th\ thin \t̲h̲\ the \ü\ loot \u̇\ foot \y\ yet \zh\ vision \à, k̲, ⁿ, œ, œ̄, ɶ, ǖ, ᵊ\ *see* Guide to Pronunciation

: something that gives stability (as in character or conduct) **3** : gravel or broken stone laid in a railroad bed or used in making concrete **4** : a device used to provide the starting voltage or to stabilize the current in a circuit (as of a fluorescent lamp) — **in ballast** *of a ship* : having only ballast for a load
²**ballast** *vt* (1538) **1** : to steady or equip with or as if with ballast **2** : to fill in (as a railroad bed) with ballast
ball bearing *n* (1883) : a bearing in which the journal turns upon loose hardened steel balls that roll easily in a race; *also* : one of the balls in such a bearing
ball boy *n* (1903) : a male tennis court attendant who retrieves balls for the players
ball·car·ri·er \'bȯl-ˌkar-ē-ər\ *n* (1935) : the football player carrying the ball on an offensive play
ball cock *n* (1790) : an automatic valve whose opening and closing are controlled by a spherical float at the end of a lever
ball control *n* (1928) : an offensive strategy (as in football) in which a team tries to maintain possession of the ball for extended periods of time
bal·le·ri·na \ˌba-lə-'rē-nə\ *n* [It, fr. *ballare* to dance, fr. LL] (1815) : a woman who is a ballet dancer : DANSEUSE
bal·let \'ba-ˌlā, ba-'\ *n* [F, fr. It *balletto*, dim. of *ballo* dance, fr. *ballare*] (1634) **1 a** : a theatrical art form using dancing, music, and scenery to convey a story, theme, or atmosphere **b** : dancing in which conventional poses and steps are combined with light flowing figures (as leaps and turns) **2** : music for a ballet **3** : a group that performs ballets — **bal·let·ic** \ba-'le-tik\ *adj*
bal·let·o·mane \ba-'le-tə-ˌmān\ *n* [*ballet* + -o- + -*mane* (fr. *mania*)] (1930) : a devotee of ballet — **bal·let·o·ma·nia** \-ˌle-tə-'mā-nē-ə, -nyə\ *n*
ball–flow·er \'bȯl-ˌflau̇(-ə)r\ *n* (1845) : an architectural ornament consisting of a ball in the flower-shaped hollow of a circular mold
ball game *n* (1848) **1** : a game played with a ball **2 a** : a set of circumstances : SITUATION ⟨a whole new *ball game*⟩ **b** : CONTEST 1
ball girl *n* (1926) : a female tennis court attendant who retrieves balls for the players
ball handler *n* (1948) : a player who controls the ball in any of various games; *esp* : a player who is skilled at handling the ball (as in basketball) — **ball–han·dling** *n*
bal·lis·ta \bə-'lis-tə\ *n, pl* **-tae** \-ˌtē\ [L, fr. (assumed) Gk *ballistēs*, fr. *ballein* to throw — more at DEVIL] (14c) : an ancient military engine often in the form of a crossbow for hurling large missiles
bal·lis·tic \bə-'lis-tik\ *adj* [L *ballista*] (ca. 1775) **1** : of or relating to ballistics or to a body in motion according to the laws of ballistics **2** : suddenly and extremely upset or angry : WILD — usu. used with *go* — **bal·lis·ti·cal·ly** \-ti-k(ə-)lē\ *adv*
ballistic missile *n* (1954) : a missile guided in the ascent of a high-arch trajectory and freely falling in the descent
bal·lis·tics \bə-'lis-tiks\ *n pl but sing or pl in constr* (ca. 1753) **1 a** : the science of the motion of projectiles in flight **b** : the flight characteristics of a projectile **2 a** : the study of the processes within a firearm as it is fired **b** : the firing characteristics of a firearm or cartridge
ball joint *n* (ca. 1884) : BALL-AND-SOCKET JOINT 1
ball lightning *n* (1857) : a rare form of lightning consisting of luminous balls that may move along solid objects or float in the air
ball mill *n* (1903) : a pulverizing machine consisting of a rotating drum which contains pebbles or metal balls as the grinding implements
ball of fire *n* (ca. 1900) : a person of unusual energy, vitality, or drive
ball of wax *n* (ca. 1953) : AFFAIR, CONCERN ⟨the whole *ball of wax*⟩
bal·lon \ba-'lōⁿ\ *n* [F, lit., balloon] (1830) : lightness of movement that exaggerates the duration of a ballet dancer's jump
bal·lo·net \ˌba-lə-'nā\ *n* [F *ballonnet*, dim. of *ballon*] (1902) : a compartment of variable volume within the interior of a balloon or airship used to control ascent and descent
¹**bal·loon** \bə-'lün\ *n* [F *ballon* large football, balloon, fr. It dial. *ballone* large football, aug. of *balla* ball, of Gmc origin] (1783) **1** : a nonporous bag of tough light material filled with heated air or a gas lighter than air so as to rise and float in the atmosphere **2** : an inflatable bag (as of rubber) usu. used as a toy or for decoration **3** : the outline enclosing words spoken or thought by a figure esp. in a cartoon
²**balloon** *adj* (ca. 1786) **1** : relating to, resembling, or suggesting a balloon ⟨a ∼ sleeve⟩ **2** : being or having a final installment that is much larger than preceding ones in a term or installment note
³**balloon** *vi* (1841) **1** : to swell or puff out : EXPAND ⟨∼ed to 200 pounds⟩ **2** : to ascend or travel in a balloon **3** : to increase rapidly ∼ *vt* : INFLATE, INCREASE
balloon angioplasty *n* (1980) : dilatation of an atherosclerotically obstructed artery by the passage of a balloon catheter through the vessel to the area of disease where inflation of the catheter compresses the plaque against the vessel wall
balloon catheter *n* (1961) : a catheter with an inflatable tip that is used esp. to measure blood pressure in a blood vessel or to expand a partly closed or obstructed bodily passage or tube (as a coronary artery)
bal·loon·ing \bə-'lü-niŋ\ *n* (1784) : the act or sport of riding in a balloon
bal·loon·ist \-nist\ *n* (1784) : a person who rides in a balloon
balloon tire *n* (1923) : a low-pressure pneumatic tire with a flexible carcass and large cross section designed to provide cushioning
balloon vine *n* (1836) : a tropical American vine (*Cardiospermum halicacabum*) of the soapberry family bearing large ornamental pods
¹**bal·lot** \'ba-lət\ *n* [It *ballotta*, fr. It dial., dim. of *balla* ball] (1549) **1 a** : a small ball used in secret voting **b** : a sheet of paper used to cast a secret vote **2 a** : the action or system of secret voting **b** : the right to vote **c** : VOTE 1a **3** : the number of votes cast **4** : the drawing of lots
²**ballot** *vi* (1580) : to vote or decide by ballot — **bal·lot·er** *n*
ballot box *n* (ca. 1680) **1** : a box for receiving ballots **2** : BALLOT 2a
¹**ball·park** \'bȯl-ˌpärk\ *n* (1899) **1** : a park in which ball games (as baseball) are played **2** : a range (as of prices or views) within which comparison or compromise is possible — **in the ballpark** : approximately correct
²**ballpark** *adj* [fr. the expression *in the ballpark*] (1967) : approximately correct ⟨a ∼ figure⟩

ball·play·er \'bȯl-ˌplā-ər\ *n* (1619) : a person who plays ball; *esp* : a baseball player
ball-point \-ˌpȯint\ *n* (1953) : a pen having as the writing point a small rotating metal ball that inks itself by contact with an inner magazine
ball-room \'bȯl-ˌrüm, -ˌru̇m\ *n* (1736) : a large room used for dances
balls–up \'bȯl-ˌzəp\ *n* (1939) *Brit* : FOUL-UP
ball·sy \'bȯl-zē\ *adj* **ball·si·er; -est** \['ball] (1959) : aggressively tough : GUTSY — sometimes considered vulgar
ball up *vt* (1885) : to make a mess of : CONFUSE, MUDDLE ∼ *vi* : to become badly muddled or confused
ball valve *n* (1839) : a valve in which a ball regulates the aperture by its rise and fall due to fluid pressure, a spring, or its own weight
bally \'ba-lē\ *adj or adv* [euphemism for *bloody*, adj., adv.] (1885) *Brit* — used as an intensive
bal·ly·hoo \'ba-lē-ˌhü\ *n, pl* **-hoos** [origin unknown] (1901) **1** : a noisy attention-getting demonstration or talk **2** : flamboyant, exaggerated, or sensational advertising or propaganda — **ballyhoo** *vt*
bal·ly·rag \-ˌrag\ *var of* BULLYRAG
balm \'bä(l)m, *NewEng also* 'bä-\ *n* [ME *basme, baume*, fr. OF, fr. L *balsamum* balsam] (13c) **1** : a balsamic resin; *esp* : one from small tropical evergreen trees (genus *Commiphora* of the family Burseraceae) **2** : an aromatic preparation (as a healing ointment) **3** : any of several aromatic plants of the mint family; *esp* : LEMON BALM **4** : a spicy aromatic odor **5** : a soothing restorative agency
bal·ma·caan \ˌbal-mə-'kan, -'kän\ *n* [*Balmacaan*, estate near Inverness, Scotland] (1919) : a loose single-breasted overcoat usu. having raglan sleeves and a short turnover collar
balm of Gil·e·ad \-'gi-lē-əd\ [*Gilead*, region of ancient Palestine known for its balm] (1703) **1** : a small evergreen African and Asian tree (*Commiphora meccanensis* of the family Burseraceae) with aromatic leaves; *also* : a fragrant oleoresin from this tree **2** : any aromatic agent that soothes, relieves, or heals **3** : either of two poplars: **a** : a hybrid northern tree (*Populus gileadensis*) with broadly cordate leaves that are pubescent esp. on the underside **b** : BALSAM POPLAR
bal·mor·al \bal-'mȯr-əl, -'mär-\ *n* [*Balmoral* Castle, Scotland] (1859) **1** : a laced boot or shoe **2** *often cap* : a round flat cap with a top projecting all around
balmy \'bä-mē, 'bäl-mē, *NewEng also* 'bä-mē\ *adj* **balm·i·er; -est** (15c) **1 a** : having the qualities of balm : SOOTHING **b** : MILD **2** : CRAZY, FOOLISH — **balm·i·ly** \-mə-lē\ *adv* — **balm·i·ness** \-mē-nəs\ *n*
bal·ne·ol·o·gy \ˌbal-nē-'ä-lə-jē\ *n* [ISV, fr. L *balneum* bath — more at BAGNIO] (ca. 1879) : the science of the therapeutic use of baths
¹**ba·lo·ney** \bə-'lō-nē\ *var of* BOLOGNA
²**baloney** *n* [*bologna*] (1923) : pretentious nonsense : BUNKUM — often used as a generalized expression of disagreement
bal·sa \'bȯl-sə\ *n* [Sp] (ca. 1600) **1** : a small raft or boat; *specif* : one made of tightly bundled reeds and used on Lake Titicaca **2** : a tropical American tree (*Ochroma pyramidale* syn. *O. lagopus*) of the silk-cotton family with extremely light strong wood used esp. for floats; *also* : its wood
bal·sam \'bȯl-səm\ *n* [L *balsamum*, fr. Gk *balsamon*, prob. of Sem origin; akin to Heb *bāshām* balsam] (bef. 12c) **1 a** : an aromatic and usu. oily and resinous substance flowing from various plants; *esp* : any of several resinous substances containing benzoic or cinnamic acid and used esp. in medicine **b** : a preparation containing resinous substances and having a balsamic odor **2 a** : a balsam-yielding tree; *esp* : BALSAM FIR **b** : IMPATIENS; *esp* : a common garden ornamental (*Impatiens balsamina*) **3** : BALM 5 — **bal·sam·ic** \bȯl-'sa-mik\ *adj*
balsam fir *n* (1805) : a resinous American fir (*Abies balsamea*) that is widely used for pulpwood and as a Christmas tree and is the source of Canada balsam
balsamic vinegar *n* [trans. of It *aceto balsamico*, lit., curative vinegar] (1982) : an aged Italian vinegar made from the must of white grapes
balsam poplar *n* (1819) : a No. American poplar (*Populus balsamifera*) that is often cultivated as a shade tree and has buds thickly coated with an aromatic resin — called also *balm of Gilead, tacamahac*
Bal·ti \'bȯl-tē, 'bȯl-\ *n* (1901) : a Tibeto-Burman language of northern Kashmir
Bal·tic \'bȯl-tik\ *adj* [ML (*mare*) *balticum* Baltic Sea] (ca. 1590) **1** : of or relating to the Baltic Sea or to the states of Lithuania, Latvia, and Estonia **2** : of or relating to a branch of the Indo-European language family containing Latvian, Lithuanian, and Old Prussian — see INDO-EUROPEAN LANGUAGES table
Bal·ti·more oriole \'bȯl-tə-ˌmȯr-, -ˌmȯr-, -mər-\ *n* [George Calvert, Lord *Baltimore*] (1808) : a northern oriole (*Icterus galbula galbula*) of the eastern and central U.S. and southern Canada in which the male has a solid black head and the female usu. has an olive brown back and orange yellow underside
Bal·to–Slav·ic \ˌbȯl-(ˌ)tō-'slä-vik, -'sla-\ *n* (1896) : a subgroup of Indo-European languages consisting of the Baltic and the Slavic branches — see INDO-EUROPEAN LANGUAGES table
Ba·lu·chi \bə-'lü-chē\ *n, pl* **Baluchis** *also* **Baluchi** [Per *Balūchī* of the Baluchis, fr. *Balūch, Baloch* Baluchi] (1616) **1** : a member of an Indo-Iranian people of Baluchistan **2** : the Iranian language of the Baluchi people
bal·us·ter \'ba-lə-stər\ *n* [F *balustre*, fr. It *balaustro*, fr. *balaustra* wild pomegranate flower, fr. L *balaustium*, fr. Gk *balaustion*; fr. its shape] (1602) **1** : an object or vertical member (as the leg of a table, a round in a chair back, or the stem of a glass) having a vaselike or turned outline **2** : an upright often vase-shaped support for a rail
bal·us·trade \'ba-lə-ˌsträd\ *n* [F, fr. It *balaustrata*, fr. *balaustro*] (1644) **1** : a row of balusters topped by a rail **2** : a low parapet or barrier — **bal·us·trad·ed** \-ˌsträ-dəd\ *adj*
bam *n* [imit.] (1930) : a dull resounding noise (as of a hard blow or impact) — often used interjectionally
Bam·ba·ra \bam-'bär-ə\ *n, pl* **Bambara** *or* **Bambaras** (1883) **1** : a member of an African people of the upper Niger **2** : a Mande language of the Bambara people
bam·bi·no \bam-'bē-(ˌ)nō, bäm-\ *n, pl* **-nos** *or* **-ni** \-(ˌ)nē\ [It, dim. of *bambo* child] (1722) **1** *pl usu* **bambini** : a representation of the infant Christ **2** : CHILD, BABY
bam·boo \(ˌ)bam-'bü, bäm-\ *n, pl* **bamboos** *often attrib* [Malay *bambu*] (1586) : any of various chiefly tropical woody or arborescent grasses (as of the genera *Bambusa, Arundinaria*, and *Dendrocalamus*)

including some with hollow stems used for building, furniture, or utensils and young shoots used for food

bamboo curtain *n, often cap B&C* (1949) : a political, military, and ideological barrier isolating an area of the Orient

bam·boo·zle \bam-'bü-zəl\ *vt* **-boo·zled; -boo·zling** \-'büz-liŋ, -'bü-zə-\ [origin unknown] (1703) : to deceive by underhanded methods : DUPE, HOODWINK — **bam·boo·zle·ment** \-'bü-zəl-mənt\ *n*

¹ban \'ban\ *vb* **banned; ban·ning** [ME *bannen* to summon, curse, fr. OE *bannan* to summon; akin to OHG *bannan* to command, L *fari* to speak, Gk *phanai* to say, *phōnē* sound, voice] *vt* (12c) **1** *archaic* : CURSE **2** : to prohibit esp. by legal means ⟨∼ discrimination⟩; *also* : to prohibit the use, performance, or distribution of ⟨∼ a book⟩ ⟨∼ a pesticide⟩ ∼ *vi* : to utter curses or maledictions

²ban *n* [ME, partly fr. *bannen* & partly fr. OF *ban*, of Gmc origin; akin to OHG *bannan* to command] (14c) **1** : the summoning in feudal times of the king's vassals for military service **2** : ANATHEMA, EXCOMMUNICATION **3** : MALEDICTION, CURSE **4** : legal or formal prohibition **5** : censure or condemnation esp. through social pressure

³ban \'bän\ *n, pl* **ba·ni** \'bä-(,)nē\ [Rom] (1880) — see *leu* at MONEY table

Ba·nach space \'bä-,näk-, -nək-\ *n* [Stefan *Banach* †1945 Pol. mathematician] (1949) : a normed vector space for which the field of multipliers comprises the real or complex numbers and in which every Cauchy sequence converges to a point in the space

ba·nal \bə-'nal, ba-, -'nál; bā-'nal; 'bā-n³l\ *adj* [F, fr. MF, of compulsory feudal service, possessed in common, commonplace, fr. *ban*] (1840) : lacking originality, freshness, or novelty : TRITE *syn* see INSIPID — **ba·nal·i·ty** \bə-'na-lə-tē *also* bā- *or* ba-\ *n* — **ba·nal·ize** \bə-'na-,līz, ba-; -'nä-; bä-'na-; 'bā-n³l-,īz\ *vt* — **ba·nal·ly** \bə-'nal-lē, ba-, -'nál-; bä-'nal-; 'bā-n³l-(l)ē\ *adv*

ba·nana \bə-'na-nə, *esp Brit* -'nä-\ *n, often attrib* [Sp or Pg; Sp, fr. Pg, of African origin; akin to Wolof *banäna* banana] (1597) **1** : an elongated usu. tapering tropical fruit with soft pulpy flesh enclosed in a soft usu. yellow rind **2** : any of several widely cultivated perennial herbs (genus *Musa* of the family Musaceae, the banana family) bearing bananas in compact pendent bunches

banana oil *n* (1926) : a colorless liquid acetate $C_7H_{14}O_2$ of amyl alcohol that has a pleasant fruity odor and is used as a solvent and in the manufacture of artificial fruit essences

banana republic *n* (1935) : a small dependent country usu. of the tropics; *esp* : one run despotically

ba·nan·as \bə-'na-nəz, *esp Brit* -'nä-\ *adj* (1968) : CRAZY ⟨go ∼⟩ ⟨drives me ∼⟩

banana seat *n* (1965) : an elongated bicycle saddle

bananas Fos·ter \-'fòs-tər, -'fäs-\ *n* [Richard *Foster*, friend of New Orleans restaurateur Owen E. Brennan, at whose restaurant the dish was first made] (1976) : a dessert of bananas flamed (as with rum) and served with ice cream

banana split *n* (1920) : ice cream served on a banana sliced in half lengthwise and usu. garnished with flavored syrups, fruits, nuts, and whipped cream

ba·nau·sic \bə-'nò-sik, -zik\ *adj* [Gk *banausikos* of an artisan, nonintellectual, vulgar, fr. *banausos* artisan] (1845) : relating to or concerned with earning a living — used pejoratively ⟨contempt for the ∼ occupations —T. S. Eliot⟩; *also* : UTILITARIAN, PRACTICAL ⟨such mundane and ∼ considerations as comfort and durability —G. B. Boyer⟩

¹band \'band\ *n* [in senses 1 & 2, fr. ME *band, bond* something that constricts, fr. ON *band*; akin to OE *bindan* to bind; in other senses, fr. ME *bande* strip, fr. MF, fr. (assumed) VL *binda*, of Gmc origin; akin to OHG *binta* fillet; akin to OE *bindan* to bind, *bend* fetter] (12c) **1** : something that confines or constricts while allowing a degree of movement **2** : something that binds or restrains legally, morally, or spiritually **3** : a strip serving to join or hold things together: as **a** : BELT 2 **b** : a cord or strip across the back of a book to which the sections are sewn **4** : a thin flat encircling strip esp. for binding: as **a** : a close-fitting strip that confines material at the waist, neck, or cuff of clothing **b** : a strip of cloth used to protect a newborn baby's navel — called also *bellyband* **c** : a ring of elastic **5 a** : a strip (as of living tissue or rock) or a stripe (as on an animal) differentiable (as by color, texture, or structure) from the adjacent material or area **b** : a more or less well-defined range of wavelengths, frequencies, or energies : RANGE 7a **6** : a narrow strip serving chiefly as decoration: as **a** : a narrow strip of material applied as trimming to an article of dress **b** *pl* : a pair of strips hanging at the front of the neck as part of a clerical, legal, or academic dress **c** : a ring without raised portions **7** : TRACK 1e(2)

²band *vt* (15c) **1** : to affix a band to or tie up with a band **2** : to finish or decorate with a band **3** : to gather together : UNITE ⟨∼ed themselves together for protection⟩ ∼ *vi* : to unite for a common purpose — often used with *together* ⟨∼ed together in hopes of attacking the blight that is common to them all —J. B. Conant⟩ — **band·er** *n*

³band *n* [MF *bande* troop, fr. OProv *banda*, of Gmc origin; akin to Goth *bandwo* sign, standard — more at BANNER] (15c) : a group of persons, animals, or things; *esp* : a group of musicians organized for ensemble playing and using chiefly woodwinds, brass, and percussion instruments — compare ORCHESTRA

¹ban·dage \'ban-dij\ *n* [MF, fr. *bande*] (1599) **1** : a strip of fabric used esp. to dress and bind up wounds **2** : a flexible strip or band used to cover, strengthen, or compress something

²bandage *vt* **ban·daged; ban·dag·ing** (1774) : to bind, dress, or cover with a bandage

Band–Aid \'ban-'dād\ *trademark* — used for a small adhesive strip with a gauze pad for covering minor wounds

banana 2

ban·dan·na *or* **ban·dana** \ban-'da-nə\ *n* [Hindi *bādhnū* tie-dyeing, cloth so dyed, fr. *bādhnā* to tie, fr. Skt *badhnāti* he ties; akin to OE *bindan*] (1741) : a large often colorfully patterned handkerchief

¹band·box \'ban(d)-,bäks\ *n* (1631) **1** : a usu. cylindrical box of paperboard or thin wood for holding light articles of attire **2** : a structure (as a baseball park) having relatively small interior dimensions

²bandbox *adj* (1844) : exquisitely neat, clean, or ordered as if just taken from a bandbox ⟨a ∼ perfection of appearance⟩ — **bandbox** *adv*

ban·deau \ban-'dō\ *n, pl* **ban·deaux** \-'dōz\ [F, dim. of *bande*] (1706) **1** : a fillet or band esp. for the hair **2** : BRASSIERE; *also* : a band-shaped covering for the breasts

band·ed \'ban-dəd\ *adj* (1787) : having or marked with bands

ban·de·ril·la \,ban-də-'rē(l)-yə\ *n* [Sp, dim. of *bandera* banner] (1797) : a decorated barbed dart that the banderillero thrusts into the neck or shoulders of the bull in a bullfight

ban·de·ril·le·ro \,ban-də-(,)rē(l)-'yer-(,)ō\ *n, pl* **-ros** [Sp, fr. *banderilla*] (1797) : one who thrusts in the banderillas in a bullfight

ban·de·role *or* **ban·de·rol** \'ban-də-,rōl\ *n* [F *banderole*, fr. It *banderuola*, dim. of *bandiera* banner, of Gmc origin; akin to Goth *bandwo* sign] (1562) **1** : a long narrow forked flag or streamer **2** : a long scroll bearing an inscription or a device

ban·di·coot \'ban-di-,küt\ *n* [Telugu *pandikokku*] (1813) **1** : any of several very large rats (genera *Bandicota* and *Nesokia*) of southern Asia destructive to crops **2** : any of a family (Peramelidae) of small insectivorous and herbivorous marsupial mammals of Australia, Tasmania, and New Guinea

ban·dit \'ban-dət\ *n* [It *bandito*, fr. pp. of *bandire* to banish, of Gmc origin; akin to OHG *bannan* to command — more at BAN] (1591) **1** *pl also* **ban·dit·ti** \ban-'di-tē\ : an outlaw who lives by plunder; *esp* : a member of a band of marauders **2** : ROBBER **3** : an enemy plane — **ban·dit·ry** \'ban-də-trē\ *n*

band·lead·er \'band-,lē-dər\ *n* (1894) : the conductor of a band (as a dance band)

band·mas·ter \'ban(d)-,mas-tər\ *n* (1858) : BANDLEADER; *esp* : a conductor of a military or concert band

ban·dog \'ban-,dòg\ *n* [ME *bandogge*, fr. *band* + *dogge* dog] (14c) : a dog kept tied to serve as a watchdog or because of its ferocity

ban·do·lier *or* **ban·do·leer** \,ban-də-'lir\ *n* [MF *bandouliere*, ultim. fr. OSp *bando* band, of Gmc origin; akin to Goth *bandwo*] (ca. 1577) : a belt worn over the shoulder and across the breast often for the suspending or supporting of some article (as cartridges) or as a part of an official or ceremonial dress

ban·dore \'ban-,dōr, -,dȯr\ *or* **ban·do·ra** \ban-'dōr-ə, -'dȯr-\ *n* [Sp *bandurria* or Pg *bandurra*, fr. LL *pandura* 3-stringed lute, fr. Gk *pandoura*] (1566) : a bass stringed instrument resembling a guitar

band–pass filter \'ban(d)-,pas-\ *n* (1926) : a filter that transmits only frequencies within a selected band

band saw *n* (ca. 1864) : a saw in the form of an endless steel belt running over pulleys; *also* : a power sawing machine using this device

band shell *n* (1926) : a bandstand having at the rear a sounding board shaped like a huge concave seashell

bands·man \'ban(d)z-mən\ *n* (ca. 1842) : a member of a musical band

band·stand \'ban(d)-,stand\ *n* (1859) **1** : a usu. roofed platform on which a band or orchestra performs outdoors **2** : a platform in a ballroom or nightclub on which musicians perform

band·wag·on \'band-,wa-gən\ *n* (1855) **1** : a usu. ornate and high wagon for a band of musicians esp. in a circus parade **2** : a popular party, faction, or cause that attracts growing support — often used in such phrases as *climb on the bandwagon* **3** : a current or fashionable trend

band·width \'band-,width\ *n* (ca. 1937) **1** : a range within a band of wavelengths, frequencies, or energies; *esp* : a range of radio frequencies which is occupied by a modulated carrier wave, which is assigned to a service, or over which a device can operate **2** : the data transfer rate of an electronic communications system

¹ban·dy \'ban-dē\ *vb* **ban·died; ban·dy·ing** [prob. fr. MF *bander* to be tight, to bandy, fr. *bande* strip — more at BAND] *vt* (1577) **1** : to bat (as a tennis ball) to and fro **2 a** : to toss from side to side or pass about from one to another often in a careless or inappropriate manner **b** : EXCHANGE; *esp* : to exchange (words) argumentatively **c** : to discuss lightly or banteringly **d** : to use in a glib or offhand manner — often used with *about* ⟨∼ these statistics about with considerable bravado —Richard Pollak⟩ **3** *archaic* : to band together ∼ *vi* **1** *obs* : CONTEND **2** *archaic* : UNITE

²bandy *n* [perh. fr. MF *bandé*, pp. of *bander*] (1693) : a game similar to hockey and believed to be its prototype

³bandy *adj* [prob. fr. *bandy* (hockey stick)] (1687) **1** *of legs* : BOWED **2** : BOWLEGGED — **ban·dy·legged** \-ban-dē-,legd; ,ban-dē-'le-gəd, -'lā-\ *adj*

¹bane \'bān\ *n* [ME, fr. OE *bana*; akin to OHG *bano* death] (bef. 12c) **1 a** *obs* : KILLER, SLAYER **b** : POISON **c** : DEATH, DESTRUCTION ⟨stop the way of those that seek my ∼ —Philip Sidney⟩ **d** : WOE **2** : a source of harm or ruin : CURSE ⟨national frontiers have been more of a ∼ than a boon for mankind —D. C. Thomson⟩

²bane *vt* **baned; ban·ing** (1578) *obs* : to kill esp. with poison

³bane *n* [ME (northern dial.) *ban*, fr. OE *bān*] (bef. 12c) *chiefly Scot* : BONE

bane·ber·ry \'bān-,ber-ē\ *n* (1755) : any of several perennial herbs (genus *Actaea*) of the buttercup family having acrid poisonous berries; *also* : one of the berries

bane·ful \'bān-fəl\ *adj* (1579) **1** : productive of destruction or woe : seriously harmful ⟨a ∼ influence⟩ **2** *archaic* : POISONOUS *syn* see PERNICIOUS — **bane·ful·ly** \-fə-lē\ *adv*

¹bang \'baŋ\ *vb* [prob. of Scand origin; akin to Icel *banga* to hammer] *vt* (ca. 1550) **1** : to strike sharply : BUMP **2** : to knock, beat, or thrust vigorously often with a sharp noise **3** : to have sexual intercourse with — often considered vulgar ∼ *vi* **1** : to strike with a sharp noise or

\ə\ abut \³\ kitten, F table \ər\ further \a\ ash \ā\ ace \ä\ mop, mar \aù\ out \ch\ chin \e\ bet \ē\ easy \g\ go \i\ hit \ī\ ice \j\ job \ŋ\ sing \ō\ go \ò\ law \òi\ boy \th\ thin \t͟h\ the \ü\ loot \ù\ foot \y\ yet \zh\ vision \à, k̲, ⁿ, œ, œ̄, ᵫ, ᵫ̄, ᵜ\ *see* Guide to Pronunciation thump 2 : to produce a sharp often metallic explosive or percussive noise or series of such noises

²**bang** n (ca. 1550) 1 : a resounding blow 2 : a sudden loud noise — often used interjectionally 3 a : a sudden striking effect b : a quick burst of energy ⟨start off with a ∼⟩ c : THRILL ⟨I get a ∼ out of all this —W. H. Whyte⟩ — **bang for the buck** also **bang for one's buck** : value received from outlay or effort ⟨investment is yielding less bang for the buck —Fortune⟩

³**bang** adv (1828) : RIGHT, DIRECTLY ⟨ran ∼ up against more trouble⟩

⁴**bang** n [prob. short for bangtail (short tail)] (1878) : a fringe of banged hair — usu. used in pl.

⁵**bang** vt (1878) : to cut (as front hair) short and squarely across

ban·ga·lore torpedo \ˈbaŋ-gə-ˌlōr-, -ˌlȯr-\ n [Bangalore, India] (1913) : a metal tube that contains explosives and a firing mechanism and is used to cut barbed wire and detonate buried mines

bang away vi (ca. 1889) 1 : to work with determined effort ⟨students banging away at their homework⟩ 2 : to attack persistently ⟨police are going to keep banging away at you —Erle Stanley Gardner⟩

bang·er \ˈbaŋ-ər\ n (ca. 1919) 1 Brit : SAUSAGE 2 Brit : FIRECRACKER 3 Brit : JALOPY

bang·kok \ˈbaŋ-ˌkäk, baŋ-ˈ\ n [earlier bangkok, a fine straw, fr. Bangkok, Thailand] (1916) : a hat woven of fine palm fiber in the Philippines

ban·gle \ˈbaŋ-gəl\ n [Hindi banglī] (1787) 1 : a stiff usu. ornamental bracelet or anklet slipped or clasped on 2 : an ornamental disk that hangs loosely (as on a bracelet)

bang on adj (1936) chiefly Brit : exactly correct or appropriate

Bang's disease \ˈbaŋz-\ n [Bernhard L. F. Bang †1932 Dan. veterinarian] (ca. 1929) : BRUCELLOSIS; specif : contagious abortion of cattle caused by a brucella (Brucella abortus)

bang·tail \ˈbaŋ-ˌtāl\ n [bangtail (short tail)] (1921) : RACEHORSE

bang–up \ˈbaŋ-ˌəp\ adj [³bang] (1810) : FIRST-RATE, EXCELLENT ⟨a ∼ job⟩

bang up vt [¹bang] (1920) : to cause extensive damage to

bani pl of ³BAN

ban·ish \ˈba-nish\ vt [ME, fr. MF baniss-, stem of banir, of Gmc origin; akin to OHG bannan to command — more at BAN] (14c) 1 : to require by authority to leave a country 2 : to drive out or remove from a home or place of usual resort or continuance 3 : to clear away : DISPEL ⟨his discovery of ∼es anxiety —Stringfellow Barr⟩ — **ban·ish·er** n — **ban·ish·ment** \-nish-mənt\ n

syn BANISH, EXILE, DEPORT, TRANSPORT mean to remove by authority from a state or country. BANISH implies compulsory removal from a country not necessarily one's own ⟨banished for seditious activities⟩. EXILE may imply compulsory removal or an enforced or voluntary absence from one's own country ⟨a writer who exiled himself for political reasons⟩. DEPORT implies sending out of the country an alien who has illegally entered or whose presence is judged inimical to the public welfare ⟨illegal aliens will be deported⟩. TRANSPORT implies sending a convicted criminal to an overseas penal colony ⟨a convict who was transported to Australia⟩.

ban·is·ter \ˈba-nəs-tər\ n [alter. of baluster] (1667) 1 : BALUSTER 2 2 a : a handrail with its supporting posts b : HANDRAIL — **ban·is·tered** \-tərd\ adj

ban·jax \ˈban-ˌjaks\ vt [origin unknown] (1939) chiefly Irish : DAMAGE, RUIN; also : SMASH

ban·jo \ˈban-(ˌ)jō\ n, pl **banjos** also **banjoes** [prob. of African origin; akin to Kimbundu mbanza, a similar instrument] (1739) : a musical instrument with a drumlike body, a fretted neck, and usu. four or five strings which may be plucked or strummed — **ban·jo·ist** \-jō-ist\ n

banjo

banjo clock n (1903) : a pendulum clock whose shape suggests a banjo

¹**bank** \ˈbaŋk\ n [ME, prob. of Scand origin; akin to ON bakki bank; akin to OE benc bench — more at BENCH] (13c) 1 : a mound, pile, or ridge raised above the surrounding level: as a : a piled-up mass of cloud or fog b : an undersea elevation rising esp. from the continental shelf 2 : the rising ground bordering a lake, river, or sea or forming the edge of a cut or hollow 3 a : a steep slope (as of a hill) b : the lateral inward tilt of a surface along a curve or of a vehicle (as an airplane) when taking a curve 4 : a protective or cushioning rim or piece

²**bank** vt (1590) 1 a : to raise a bank about b : to cover (as a fire) with fresh fuel and adjust the draft of air so as to keep in an inactive state c : to build (a curve) with the roadbed or track inclined laterally upward from the inside edge 2 : to heap or pile in a bank 3 : to drive (a ball in billiards) into a cushion 4 : to form or group in a tier ∼ vi 1 : to rise in or form a bank — often used with up ⟨clouds would ∼ up about midday, and showers fall —William Beebe⟩ 2 a : to incline an airplane laterally b (1) : to incline laterally (2) : to follow a curve or incline ⟨skiers ∼ing around the turn⟩

³**bank** n [ME, fr. MF or OIt; MF banque, fr. OIt banca, lit., bench, of Gmc origin; akin to OE benc] (15c) 1 a : an establishment for the custody, loan, exchange, or issue of money, for the extension of credit, and for facilitating the transmission of funds b obs : the table, counter, or place of business of a money changer 2 : a person conducting a gambling house or game; specif : DEALER 3 : a supply of something held in reserve: as a : the fund of supplies (as money, chips, or pieces) held by the banker or dealer for use in a game b : a fund of pieces belonging to a game (as dominoes) from which the players draw 4 : a place where something is held available ⟨memory ∼⟩; esp : a depot for the collection and storage of a biological product of human origin for medical use ⟨blood ∼⟩

⁴**bank** vi (ca. 1751) 1 : to manage a bank 2 : to deposit money or have an account in a bank ∼ vt : to deposit in a bank — **bank on** : to depend or rely on

⁵**bank** n [ME banc bench, fr. OF, of Gmc origin; akin to OE benc] (1614) 1 : a group or series of objects arranged together in a row or a

tier: as a : a set of elevators b : a row or tier of telephones 2 : one of the horizontal and usu. secondary or lower divisions of a headline

bank·able \ˈbaŋk-ə-bəl\ adj (1818) 1 : acceptable to or at a bank 2 : sure to bring in a profit ⟨Hollywood's most ∼ star —Sidney Sheldon⟩ — **bank·abil·i·ty** \ˌbaŋ-kə-ˈbi-lə-tē\ n

bank·book \ˈbaŋk-ˌbuk\ n (1714) : the depositor's book in which a bank records deposits and withdrawals — called also passbook

bank·card \-ˌkärd\ n (1970) : a credit card issued by a bank

bank discount n (1841) : the interest discounted in advance on a note and computed on the face value of the note

¹**bank·er** \ˈbaŋ-kər\ n (1534) 1 : one that engages in the business of banking 2 : the player who keeps the bank in various games — **bank·er·ly** \-lē\ adj

²**banker** n (1666) : a man or boat employed in the cod fishery on the Newfoundland banks

³**banker** n (1677) : a sculptor's or mason's workbench

banker's acceptance n (ca. 1924) : a short-term credit instrument issued by an importer's bank that guarantees payment of an exporter's invoice

bank holiday n (1871) 1 Brit : LEGAL HOLIDAY 2 : a period when banks in general are closed often by government fiat

bank·ing n (1735) : the business of a bank or a banker

bank money n (1904) : a medium of exchange consisting chiefly of checks and drafts

bank·note \ˈbaŋk-ˌnōt\ n (1695) : a promissory note issued by a bank payable to bearer on demand without interest and acceptable as money

¹**bank·roll** \ˈbaŋ-ˌkrōl\ n (1887) : supply of money : FUNDS

²**bankroll** vt (1928) : to supply the capital for or pay the cost of (a business or project) — **bank·roll·er** n

¹**bank·rupt** \ˈbaŋ-(ˌ)krəpt\ n [modif. of MF & OIt; MF banqueroute bankruptcy, fr. OIt bancarotta, fr. banca bank + rotta broken, fr. L rupta, fem. of ruptus, pp. of rumpere to break — more at BANK, REAVE] (1533) 1 a : a person who has done any of the acts that by law entitle his creditors to have his estate administered for their benefit b : a person judicially declared subject to having his estate administered under the bankrupt laws for the benefit of his creditors c : a person who becomes insolvent 2 : one who is destitute of a particular thing ⟨a moral ∼⟩

²**bankrupt** adj (1570) 1 a : reduced to a state of financial ruin : IMPOVERISHED; specif : legally declared a bankrupt ⟨the company went ∼⟩ b : of or relating to bankrupts or bankruptcy ⟨∼ laws⟩ 2 a : BROKEN, RUINED ⟨a ∼ professional career⟩ b : exhausted of valuable qualities : STERILE ⟨a ∼ old culture⟩ c : DESTITUTE — used with of or in ⟨∼ of all merciful feelings⟩

³**bankrupt** vt (1588) 1 : to reduce to bankruptcy 2 : IMPOVERISH ⟨defections had ∼ed the party of its brainpower⟩ syn see DEPLETE

bank·rupt·cy \ˈbaŋ-(ˌ)krəp(t)-sē\ n, pl **-cies** (1700) 1 : the quality or state of being bankrupt 2 : utter failure or impoverishment

bank shot n (1897) 1 : a shot in billiards and pool in which a player banks the cue ball or the object ball 2 : a shot in basketball played to rebound from the backboard into the basket

bank·sia \ˈban(k)-sē-ə\ n [NL, genus name, fr. Sir Joseph Banks] (1788) : any of a genus (Banksia) of Australian evergreen trees or shrubs of the protea family with alternate leathery leaves and flowers in dense cylindrical heads

bank·side \ˈbaŋk-ˌsīd\ n (15c) : the slope of a bank esp. of a stream

¹**ban·ner** \ˈba-nər\ n [ME banere, fr. OF, of Gmc origin; akin to Goth bandwo sign; prob. akin to Gk phainein to show — more at FANCY] (13c) 1 a : a piece of cloth attached by one edge to a staff and used by a leader (as a monarch or feudal lord) as his standard b : ²FLAG 1 c : an ensign displaying a distinctive or symbolic device or legend; esp : one presented as an award of honor or distinction 2 : a headline in large type running across a newspaper page 3 : a strip of cloth on which a sign is painted ⟨welcome ∼s stretched across the street⟩ 4 : a name, slogan, or goal associated with a particular group or ideology ⟨the new ∼ is "community control" —F. M. Hechinger⟩ — often used with under ⟨every new administration arrives . . . under the ∼ of change —John Cogley⟩

²**banner** adj (1840) 1 : prominent in support of a political party ⟨a ∼ Democratic county⟩ 2 : distinguished from all others esp. in excellence ⟨a ∼ year for business⟩

³**banner** vt (1889) 1 : to furnish with a banner 2 : to print (as a news story) under a banner usu. on the front page

¹**ban·ner·et** \ˈba-nə-rət, ˌba-nə-ˈret\ n, often cap [ME baneret, fr. OF, fr. banere] (14c) : a knight leading his vassals into the field under his own banner

²**banneret** also **ban·ner·ette** n (14c) : a small banner

ban·ne·rol \ˈba-nə-ˌrōl\ n (1548) : BANDEROLE

bannister var of BANISTER

ban·nock \ˈba-nək\ n [ME bannok, fr. OE bannuc] (bef. 12c) 1 : a usu. unleavened flat bread or biscuit made with oatmeal or barley meal 2 chiefly NewEng : CORN BREAD; esp : a thin cake baked on a griddle

banns \ˈbanz\ n pl [pl. of bann, fr. ME bane, ban proclamation, ban] (14c) : public announcement esp. in church of a proposed marriage

¹**ban·quet** \ˈbaŋ-kwət, ˈban- also -ˌkwet\ n [MF, fr. OIt banchetto, fr. dim. of banca bench, bank] (15c) 1 : a sumptuous feast; esp : an elaborate and often ceremonious meal for numerous people often in honor of a person ⟨a state ∼⟩ 2 : a meal held in recognition of some occasion or achievement ⟨an awards ∼⟩

²**banquet** vi (ca. 1500) : to partake of a banquet ∼ vt : to treat with a banquet : FEAST — **ban·quet·er** n

banquet room n (1837) : a large room (as in a restaurant or hotel) suitable for banquets

ban·quette \baŋ-ˈket, ban-, 1b is also ˈbaŋ-kət\ n [F, fr. MF, fr. OProv banqueta, dim. of banc bench, of Gmc origin; akin to OE benc bench] (1629) 1 a : a raised way along the inside of a parapet or trench for gunners or guns b Southern : SIDEWALK 2 a : a long upholstered bench b : a sofa having one roll-over arm c : a built-in upholstered bench along a wall

Ban·quo \ˈbaŋ-(ˌ)kwō, ˈban-\ n : a murdered Scottish thane in Shakespeare's Macbeth whose ghost appears to Macbeth

ban·shee \ˈban-(ˌ)shē, ban-ˈ\ n [Ir bean sidhe & ScGael bean sith, lit., woman of fairyland] (1771) : a female spirit in Gaelic folklore whose appearance or wailing warns a family that one of them will soon die

¹**ban·tam** \'ban-təm\ *n* [*Bantam,* former residency in Java] (1749) **1** : any of numerous small domestic fowls that are often miniatures of members of the standard breeds **2** : a person of diminutive stature and often combative disposition

²**bantam** *adj* (1782) **1** : SMALL, DIMINUTIVE **2** : pertly combative

ban·tam·weight \-,wāt\ *n* (1884) : a boxer in a weight division having a maximum limit of 118 pounds for professionals and 119 pounds for amateurs — compare FEATHERWEIGHT, FLYWEIGHT

ban·teng \'bän-,teŋ\ *n* [Malay of Indonesia, fr. Jav *banṭéng*] (1817) : a wild ox (*Bos javanicus* syn. *B. banteng*) of southeastern Asia sometimes domesticated for use as a draft animal or for its meat

¹**ban·ter** \'ban-tər\ *vb* [origin unknown] *vt* (1676) **1** : to speak to or address in a witty and teasing manner **2** *archaic* : DELUDE **3** *chiefly Southern & Midland* : CHALLENGE ~ *vi* : to speak or act playfully or wittily — **ban·ter·er** \-tər-ər\ *n* — **ban·ter·ing·ly** \'ban-tə-riŋ-lē\ *adv*

²**banter** (1690) : good-natured and usu. witty and animated joking

bant·ling \'bant-liŋ\ *n* [perh. modif. of G *Bänkling* bastard, fr. *Bank* bench, fr. OHG — more at BENCH] (1593) : a very young child

Ban·tu \'ban-(,)tü, 'bän-\ *n, pl* **Bantu** *or* **Bantus** (1862) **1** : a family of Niger-Congo languages spoken in central and southern Africa **2** : a member of any of a group of African peoples who speak Bantu languages

Ban·tu·stan \,ban-tù-'stan, ,bän-tú-'stän\ *n* [*Bantu* + *-stan* land (as in *Hindustan*)] (1949) : any of several all-black enclaves in the Republic of So. Africa that have a limited degree of self-government

ban·yan \'ban-yən\ *n* [earlier *banyan* Gujarati trader, fr. Pg *banean,* prob. fr. Tamil *vāṇiyan* trader, fr. Skt *vaṇija;* fr. a tree of the species in Iran under which such traders conducted business] (1634) : an East Indian fig tree (*Ficus benghalensis*) of the mulberry family with branches that send out shoots which grow down to the soil and root to form secondary trunks

ban·zai \(,)bän-'zī, ,bän-,\ *n* [Jp] (1893) : a Japanese cheer or war cry

banzai attack *n* (1944) : a mass attack by Japanese soldiers in World War II; *also* : an all-out usu. desperate attack

banzai charge *n* (1944) **1** : BANZAI ATTACK **2** : a determined often reckless act

bao·bab \'baù-,bab, 'bä-ə-\ *n* [NL *bahobab*] (1640) : a broad-trunked Old World tropical tree (*Adansonia digitata*) of the silk-cotton family with an edible acid fruit resembling a gourd and bark used in making paper, cloth, and rope

bap \'bap\ *n* [origin unknown] (ca. 1575) *Brit* : a small bun or roll

bap·ti·sia \bap-'ti-zh(ē-)ə\ *n* [NL, genus name, fr. Gk *baptisis* a dipping, fr. *baptein*] (ca. 1868) : any of a genus (*Baptisia*) of No. American leguminous plants having showy papilionaceous flowers similar in form to those of the pea plant

bap·tism \'bap-,ti-zəm, *esp Southern* 'bab-\ *n* [ME *baptisme*] (14c) **1 a** : a Christian sacrament marked by ritual use of water and admitting the recipient to the Christian community **b** : a non-Christian rite using water for ritual purification **c** *Christian Science* : purification by or submergence in Spirit **2** : an act, experience, or ordeal by which one is purified, sanctified, initiated, or named — **bap·tis·mal** \bap-'tiz-məl, *esp Southern* bab-\ *adj* — **bap·tis·mal·ly** \-mə-lē\ *adv*

baptismal name *n* (1869) : a name given at christening or confirmation

baptism of fire (1857) **1** : an introductory or initial experience that is a severe ordeal; *specif* : a soldier's first exposure to enemy fire **2** : a spiritual baptism by a gift of the Holy Spirit — often used in allusion to Acts 2:3–4; Mt 3:11 (RSV)

bap·tist \'bap-tist, *esp Southern* 'bab-\ *n* (13c) **1** : one that baptizes **2** *cap* : a member or adherent of an evangelical Protestant denomination marked by congregational polity and baptism by immersion of believers only — **Baptist** *adj*

bap·tis·tery *or* **bap·tis·try** \'bap-tə-strē, *esp Southern* 'bab-\ *n, pl* **-ter·ies** *or* **-tries** (14c) : a part of a church or formerly a separate building used for baptism

bap·tize *also* **bap·tise** \bap-'tīz, 'bap-,, *esp Southern* bab- *or* 'bab-\ *vb* **bap·tized** *also* **bap·tised; bap·tiz·ing** *also* **bap·tis·ing** [ME, fr. OF *baptiser,* fr. LL *baptizare,* fr. Gk *baptizein* to dip, baptize, fr. *baptein* to dip, dye; akin to ON *kvefja* to quench] *vt* (13c) **1** : to administer baptism to **2 a** : to purify or cleanse spiritually esp. by a purging experience or ordeal **b** : INITIATE **3** : to give a name to (as at baptism) : CHRISTEN ~ *vi* : to administer baptism — **bap·tiz·er** *n*

¹**bar** \'bär\ *n, often attrib* [ME *barre,* fr. MF] (12c) **1 a** : a straight piece (as of wood or metal) that is longer than it is wide and has any of various uses (as for a lever, support, barrier, or fastening) **b** : a solid piece or block of material that is usu. considerably longer than it is wide ⟨a ~ of gold⟩ ⟨candy ~⟩ **c** : a usu. rigid piece (as of wood or metal) longer than it is wide that is used as a handle or support; *esp* : a handrail used by ballet dancers to maintain balance while exercising **2** : something that obstructs or prevents passage, progress, or action: as **a** : the destruction of an action or claim in law; *also* : a plea or objection that effects such destruction **b** : an intangible or nonphysical impediment **c** : a submerged or partly submerged bank (as of sand) along a shore or in a river often obstructing navigation **3 a** (1) : the railing in a courtroom that encloses the place about the judge where prisoners are stationed or where the business of the court is transacted in civil cases (2) : COURT, TRIBUNAL (3) : a particular system of courts (4) : an authority or tribunal that hands down judgment **b** (1) : the barrier in the English Inns of Court that formerly separated the seats of the benchers or readers from the body of the hall occupied by the students (2) : the whole body of barristers or lawyers qualified to practice in the courts of any jurisdiction (3) : the profession of barrister or lawyer **4** : a straight stripe, band, or line much longer than it is wide: as **a** : one of two or more horizontal stripes on a heraldic shield **b** : a metal or embroidered strip worn on a usu. military uniform esp. to indicate rank (as of a company officer) or service **5 a** : a counter at which food or esp. alcoholic beverages are served **b** : BARROOM **c** : SHOP **2b 6 a** : a vertical line across the musical staff before the initial measure accent **b** : MEASURE **7** : a lace and embroidery joining covered with buttonhole stitch for connecting various parts of the pattern in needlepoint lace and cutwork — **behind bars** : in jail

²**bar** *vt* **barred; bar·ring** (13c) **1 a** : to fasten with a bar **b** : to place bars across to prevent ingress or egress **2** : to mark with bars : STRIPE **3 a** : to confine or shut in by or as if by bars **b** : to set aside

: RULE OUT **c** : to keep out : EXCLUDE **4 a** : to interpose legal objection to or to the claim of **b** : PREVENT, FORBID

³**bar** *prep* (1714) : EXCEPT

⁴**bar** *n* [G, fr. Gk *baros*] (1910) : a unit of pressure equal to one million dynes per square centimeter

bar- *or* **baro-** *comb form* [Gk *baros;* akin to Gk *barys* heavy — more at GRIEVE] : weight : pressure ⟨*barometer*⟩

Ba·rab·bas \bə-'ra-bəs\ *n* [Gk, fr. Aram *Bar-abba*] : a Jewish prisoner according to Matthew, Mark, and John released in preference to Christ at the demand of the multitude

bar·a·thea \,bar-ə-'thē-ə\ *n* [fr. *Barathea,* a trademark] (1862) : a fabric that has a broken rib weave and a pebbly texture and that is made of silk, worsted, or synthetic fiber or a combination of these

¹**barb** \'bärb\ *n* [ME *barbe* barb, beard, fr. MF, fr. L *barba* — more at BEARD] (14c) **1** : a medieval cloth headdress passing over or under the chin and covering the neck **2 a** : a sharp projection extending backward (as from the point of an arrow or fishhook) and preventing easy extraction; *also* : a sharp projection with its point similarly oblique to something else **b** : a biting or pointedly critical remark or comment **3** : ²BARBEL **4** : any of the side branches of the shaft of a feather — see FEATHER illustration **5** : a plant hair or bristle ending in a hook

²**barb** *vt* (1759) : to furnish with a barb

³**barb** *n* [F *barbe,* fr. It *barbero,* fr. *barbero* of Barbary, fr. *Barberia* Barbary, coastal region in Africa] (1636) : any of a northern African breed of horses that are noted for speed and endurance and are related to Arabians

⁴**barb** *n* (1967) *slang* : BARBITURATE

bar·bar·i·an \bär-'ber-ē-ən, -'bar-\ *adj* [L *barbarus*] (14c) **1** : of or relating to a land, culture, or people alien and usu. believed to be inferior to another land, culture, or people **2** : lacking refinement, learning, or artistic or literary culture — **barbarian** *n* — **bar·bar·i·an·ism** \-ē-ə-,ni-zəm\ *n*

bar·bar·ic \bär-'bar-ik\ *adj* (15c) **1 a** : of, relating to, or characteristic of barbarians **b** : possessing or characteristic of a cultural level more complex than primitive savagery but less sophisticated than advanced civilization **2 a** : marked by a lack of restraint : WILD **b** : having a bizarre, primitive, or unsophisticated quality **3** : BARBAROUS 3 — **bar·bar·i·cal·ly** \-i-k(ə-)lē\ *adv*

bar·ba·rism \'bär-bə-,ri-zəm\ *n* (15c) **1 a** : a barbarian or barbarous social or intellectual condition : BACKWARDNESS **b** : the practice or display of barbarian acts, attitudes, or ideas **2** : an idea, act, or expression that in form or use offends against contemporary standards of good taste or acceptability

bar·bar·i·ty \bär-'bar-ə-tē\ *n, pl* **-ties** (ca. 1570) **1** : BARBARISM **2 a** : barbarous cruelty : INHUMANITY **b** : an act or instance of such cruelty

bar·ba·ri·za·tion \,bär-bə-rə-'zā-shən\ *n* (1822) : the act or process of barbarizing : the state of being barbarized

bar·ba·rize \'bär-bə-,rīz\ *vb* **-rized; -riz·ing** *vt* (1648) : to make barbarian or barbarous ~ *vi* : to become barbarous

bar·ba·rous \'bär-b(ə-)rəs\ *adj* [L *barbarus,* fr. Gk *barbaros* foreign, ignorant] (15c) **1 a** : UNCIVILIZED **b** : lacking culture or refinement : PHILISTINE **2** : characterized by the occurrence of barbarisms **3** : mercilessly harsh or cruel *syn* see FIERCE — **bar·ba·rous·ly** *adv* — **bar·ba·rous·ness** *n*

Bar·ba·ry ape \'bär-b(ə-)rē-\ *n* [*Barbary,* Africa] (1848) : a tailless monkey (*Macaca sylvanus*) of northern Africa and Gibraltar

Barbary Coast *n* (1880) : a district or section of a city noted as a center of gambling, prostitution, and riotous nightlife

Barbary sheep *n* (ca. 1898) : AOUDAD

barbe \'bärb\ *n* [ME, fr. MF, lit., beard] (14c) : ¹BARB 1

¹**bar·be·cue** \'bär-bi-,kyü\ *vt* **-cued; -cu·ing** (1690) **1** : to roast or broil on a rack over hot coals or on a revolving spit before or over a source of heat **2** : to cook in a highly seasoned vinegar sauce — **bar·be·cu·er** *n*

²**barbecue** *also* **bar·be·que** *n* [AmerSp *barbacoa* framework for supporting meat over a fire, prob. fr. Taino] (1709) **1** : a large animal (as a steer) roasted whole or split over an open fire or a fire in a pit; *also* : smaller pieces of barbecued meat **2** : a social gathering esp. in the open air at which barbecued food is eaten **3** : an often portable fireplace over which meat and fish are roasted

barbed \'bärbd\ *adj* (1611) **1** : having barbs **2** : characterized by pointed and biting criticism or sarcasm ⟨~ witticisms⟩

barbed wire \'bärb(d)-'wīr, 'bäb(d)-\ *n* (1881) : twisted wires armed with barbs or sharp points — called also *barbwire*

¹**bar·bel** \'bär-bəl\ *n* [ME, fr. MF, fr. (assumed) VL *barbellus,* dim. of L *barbus* barbel, fr. *barba* beard — more at BEARD] (14c) : a European freshwater cyprinid fish (*Barbus barbus*) with four barbels on its upper jaw; *also* : any of various closely related fishes

²**barbel** *n* [obs. F, fr. MF, dim. of *barbe* barb, beard] (1601) : a slender tactile process on the lips of certain fishes (as catfishes)

bar·bell \'bär-,bel\ *n* (1887) : a bar with adjustable weighted disks attached to each end that is used for exercise and in weight lifting

¹**bar·ber** \'bär-bər\ *n* [ME, fr. MF *barbeor,* fr. *barbe* beard — more at BARB] (14c) : one whose business is cutting and dressing hair, shaving and trimming beards, and performing related services

²**barber** *vb* **bar·bered; bar·ber·ing** \-b(ə-)riŋ\ *vt* (1606) : to perform the services of a barber for ~ *vi* : to perform the services of a barber

bar·ber·ry \'bär-,ber-ē\ *n* [ME *barbere,* fr. MF *barbarin,* fr. Ar *barbārīs*] (14c) : any of a genus (*Berberis* of the family Berberidaceae, the barberry family) of shrubs usu. having spines, yellow flowers, and oblong red berries

¹**bar·ber·shop** \'bär-bər-,shäp\ *n* (1579) : a barber's place of business

²**barbershop** *adj* [fr. the old custom of men in barbershops forming quartets for impromptu singing of sentimental songs] (1910) : of a style of unaccompanied group singing of popular songs usu. marked by highly conventionalized close harmony

---

\ə\ abut \'ə\ kitten, F table \ər\ further \a\ ash \ā\ ace \ä\ mop, mar \aù\ out \ch\ chin \e\ bet \ē\ easy \g\ go \i\ hit \ī\ ice \j\ job \ŋ\ sing \ō\ go \ò\ law \òi\ boy \th\ thin \t̲h̲\ the \ü\ loot \ù\ foot \y\ yet \zh\ vision \á, k̲, ⁿ, œ, œ̄, ṳe, ṳē, ᵊ\ see Guide to Pronunciation

bar·bet \'bär-bət\ n [prob. fr. ¹*barb*] (1824) : any of a family (Capitonidae) of nonpasserine tropical birds with a stout bill bearing bristles and usu. swollen at the base

bar·bette \bär-'bet\ n [F, dim. of *barbe* headdress] (1772) **1** : a mound of earth or a protected platform from which guns fire over a parapet **2** : an armored structure protecting a gun turret on a warship

bar·bi·can \'bär-bi-kən\ n [ME, fr. MF *barbacane*, fr. ML *barbacana*] (13c) : an outer defensive work; *esp* : a tower at a gate or bridge

bar·bi·cel \'bär-bə-ˌsel\ n [NL *barbicella*, dim. of L *barba*] (1869) : any of the small hook-bearing processes on a barbule of a feather — see FEATHER illustration

bar·bi·tal \'bär-bə-ˌtȯl\ n [*barbituric* + *-al* (as in *Veronal*, trademark for barbital)] (1919) : a white crystalline addictive hypnotic $C_8H_{12}N_2O_3$ often administered in the form of its soluble sodium salt

bar·bi·tone \'bär-bə-ˌtōn\ n [*barbituric* + *-one*] (1914) *Brit* : BARBITAL

bar·bi·tu·rate \bär-'bi-chə-rət, -ˌrāt; ˌbär-bə-'tyu̇r-ət, -'tu̇r-, -ˌāt\ n (1928) **1** : a salt or ester of barbituric acid **2** : any of various derivatives of barbituric acid used esp. as sedatives, hypnotics, and antispasmodics

bar·bi·tu·ric acid \ˌbär-bə-'t(y)u̇r-ik-\ n [part trans. of G *Barbitursäure*, irreg. fr. the name *Barbara* + ISV *uric* + G *Säure* acid] (1866) : a synthetic crystalline acid $C_4H_4N_2O_3$ derived from pyrimidine

Bar·bi·zon \ˌbär-bə-'zōn, -'zän\ adj [*Barbizon*, France] (1890) : of, relating to, or being a school of mid-nineteenth century French landscape painters whose naturalistic canvases were based on direct observation of nature

bar·bule \'bär-(ˌ)byü(ə)l\ n (1835) : a minute barb; *esp* : one of the processes that fringe the barbs of a feather — see FEATHER illustration

barb·wire \'bärb-ˌwir, 'bäb-\ n (1880) : BARBED WIRE

bar car n (1945) : CLUB CAR

bar·ca·role *or* **bar·ca·rolle** \'bär-kə-ˌrōl\ n [F *barcarolle*, fr. It dial. (Venice) *barcarola*, fr. *barcarolo* gondolier, fr. *barca* bark, fr. LL] (ca. 1779) **1** : a Venetian boat song usu. in ⁶/₈ or ¹²/₈ time characterized by the alternation of a strong and weak beat that suggests a rowing rhythm **2** : music imitating a barcarole

Bar·ce·lo·na chair \ˌbär-sə-'lō-nə-\ n [*Barcelona*, Spain] (1970) : an armless chair with leather-covered cushions on a stainless steel frame

bar·chan \(ˌ)bär-'kän, -'kän\ n [Russ *barkhan*, fr. Kazakh] (1888) : a moving crescent-shaped sand dune

bar chart n (1914) : BAR GRAPH

bar code n (1963) : a code consisting of a group of printed and variously patterned bars and spaces and sometimes numerals that is designed to be scanned and read into computer memory as identification for the object it labels

¹bard \'bärd\ n [ME, fr. ScGael & Ir] (15c) **1 a** : a tribal poet-singer skilled in composing and reciting verses on heroes and their deeds **b** : a composer, singer, or declaimer of epic or heroic verse **2** : POET — **bard·ic** \'bär-dik\ adj

²bard *or* **barde** \'bärd\ n [MF *barde*, fr. OSp *barda*, fr. Ar *barda'ah*] (15c) : a piece of armor or ornament for a horse's neck, breast, or flank

³bard vt (ca. 1521) **1** : to furnish with bards **2** : to dress meat for cooking by covering with strips of fat

bard·ol·a·ter \bär-'dä-lə-tər\ n [*Bard* (of *Avon*), epithet of Shakespeare + *-o-* + *-later*] (1903) : a person who idolizes Shakespeare — **bard·ol·a·try** \-lə-trē\ n

Bar·do·li·no \ˌbär-dᵊl-'ē-(ˌ)nō\ n, pl **-nos** [*Bardolino*, village on Lake Garda, Italy] (1934) : a light red Italian wine

¹bare \'bar, 'ber\ adj **bar·er**; **bar·est** [ME, fr. OE *bær*; akin to OHG *bar* naked, Lith *basas* barefoot] (bef. 12c) **1 a** : lacking a natural, usual, or appropriate covering **b** (1) : lacking clothing (2) *obs* : BAREHEADED **c** : UNARMED **2** : open to view : EXPOSED **3** : unfurnished or scantily supplied **b** : DESTITUTE 〈~ of all safeguards〉 **4 a** : having nothing left over or added 〈the ~ necessities of life〉 **b** : MERE 〈a two hours' away〉 **c** : devoid of amplification or adornment **5** *obs* : WORTHLESS — **bare·ness** n

syn BARE, NAKED, NUDE, BALD, BARREN mean deprived of naturally or conventionally appropriate covering. BARE implies the removal of what is additional, superfluous, ornamental, or dispensable 〈an apartment with *bare* walls〉. NAKED suggests absence of protective or ornamental covering but may imply a state of nature, of destitution, or of defenselessness 〈poor half-*naked* children〉. NUDE applies esp. to the unclothed human figure 〈a *nude* model posing for art students〉. BALD implies actual or seeming absence of natural covering and may suggest a conspicuous bareness 〈a *bald* mountain peak〉. BARREN often suggests aridity or impoverishment or sterility 〈*barren* plains〉.

²bare vt **bared**; **bar·ing** (bef. 12c) : to make or lay bare : UNCOVER

³bare archaic past of BEAR

bare·back \-ˌbak\ *or* **bare·backed** \-'bakt\ adv or adj (1562) : on the bare back of a horse : without a saddle 〈likes riding ~〉〈~ riding〉

bare·boat \-ˌbōt\ n (ca. 1949) : a boat chartered without its crew

bare bones n pl (1915) : the barest essentials, facts, or elements — **bare—bones** adj

bare·faced \'bar-'fāst, 'ber-\ adj (1590) **1** : having the face uncovered: **a** : having no whiskers : BEARDLESS **b** : wearing no mask **2 a** : OPEN, UNCONCEALED **b** : lacking scruples — **bare·faced·ly** \-'fā-səd-lē, -'fāst-lē\ adv — **bare·faced·ness** \-'fā-səd-nəs, -'fāst(ᵊ)-nəs\ n

bare·foot \-ˌfu̇t\ *or* **bare·foot·ed** \-'fu̇-təd\ adv or adj (bef. 12c) : with the feet bare 〈went ~ most of the summer〉〈~ boy, with cheek of tan —J. G. Whittier〉

barefoot doctor n (1971) : an auxiliary medical worker trained to provide basic health care in rural areas of China

bare—hand·ed \'bar-'han-dəd, 'ber-\ adv or adj (15c) **1** : without gloves **2** : without tools or weapons 〈fight an animal ~〉

bare·head·ed \-'he-dəd\ adv or adj (14c) : without a covering for the head 〈went ~ in the hot sun〉〈a ~ boy who had lost his cap〉

bare—knuck·le \-'nə-kəl\ *also* **bare—knuck·led** \-kəld\ adj or adv (1903) **1** : not using boxing gloves 〈champion ~ prizefighter of England —Dennis Craig〉 〈when men fought ~〉 **2** : having a fierce unrelenting character 〈~ politics〉

bare·ly adv (bef. 12c) **1** : in a meager manner : PLAINLY 〈a ~ furnished room〉 **2** : SCARCELY, HARDLY 〈~ enough money for lunch〉

barf \'bärf\ vi [origin unknown] (1957) : VOMIT

bar·fly \'bär-ˌflī\ n (1910) : a person who spends much time in bars

¹bar·gain \'bär-gən\ n, often attrib (14c) **1** : an agreement between parties settling what each gives or receives in a transaction between them or what course of action or policy each pursues in respect to the other **2** : something acquired by or as if by bargaining; *esp* : an advantageous purchase **3** : a transaction, situation, or event regarded in the light of its results — **into the bargain** *also* **in the bargain** : BESIDES 〈tastes good and is good for you, *into the bargain*〉

²bargain vb [ME, fr. MF *bargaignier*, prob. of Gmc origin; akin to OE *borgian* to borrow — more at BURY] vi (14c) **1** : to negotiate over the terms of a purchase, agreement, or contract : HAGGLE **2** : to come to terms : AGREE ~ vt **1** : to bring to a desired level by bargaining 〈~ a price down〉 **2** : to sell or dispose of by bargaining — **bar·gain·er** n — **bargain for** : EXPECT 〈more work than I *bargained for*〉

bar·gain—base·ment \'bär-gən-'bās-mənt\ adj (1948) **1** : of inferior quality or worth **2** : markedly inexpensive 〈~ rates〉

bargain basement n (1899) : a section of a store (as the basement) where merchandise is sold at reduced prices

¹barge \'bärj\ n [ME, fr. MF, fr. OF, fr. LL *barca*] (14c) : any of various boats: as **a** : a roomy usu. flat-bottomed boat used chiefly for the transport of goods on inland waterways and usu. propelled by towing **b** : a large motorboat supplied to the flag officer of a flagship **c** : a roomy pleasure boat; *esp* : a boat of state elegantly furnished and decorated

²barge vb **barged**; **barg·ing** vt (1649) : to carry by barge ~ vi **1** : to move ponderously or clumsily **2** : to thrust oneself heedlessly or unceremoniously 〈*barged* into the meeting〉

barge·board \'bärj-ˌbȯrd, -ˌbȯrd\ n [origin unknown] (1833) : an often ornamented board that conceals roof timbers projecting over gables

barg·ee \bär-'jē\ n (1666) *Brit* : BARGEMAN

bar·gel·lo \bär-'je-(ˌ)lō\ n [the *Bargello*, museum in Florence, Italy; fr. the use of this stitch in the upholstery of 17th cent. chairs at the Bargello] (ca. 1924) : a needlework stitch that produces a zigzag pattern

barge·man \'bärj-mən\ n (14c) : the master or a deckhand of a barge

bar graph n (1924) : a graphic means of quantitative comparison by rectangles with lengths proportional to the measure of the data or things being compared — called also *bar chart*

bar·hop \'bär-ˌhäp\ vi (1947) : to visit and drink at a series of bars in the course of an evening

bar·ite \'bar-ˌīt, 'ber-\ n [Gk *barytēs* weight, fr. *barys*] (1868) : barium sulfate occurring as a mineral

¹bari·tone \'bar-ə-ˌtōn\ n [F *baryton* or It *baritono*, fr. Gk *barytonos* deep sounding, fr. *barys* heavy + *tonos* tone — more at GRIEVE] (1609) **1** : a male singing voice of medium compass between bass and tenor; *also* : a person having this voice **2** : a member of a family of instruments having a range between tenor and bass; *esp* : the baritone saxhorn or baritone saxophone — **bari·ton·al** \ˌbar-ə-'tō-nᵊl\ adj

²baritone adj (1729) : relating to or having the range or part of a baritone

bar·i·um \'bar-ē-əm, 'ber-\ n [NL, fr. *bar-*] (1808) : a silver-white malleable toxic bivalent metallic element of the alkaline-earth group that occurs only in combination — see ELEMENT table

barium sulfate n (1903) : a colorless crystalline insoluble compound $BaSO_4$ that is used as a pigment and extender, as a filler, and as a substance opaque to X rays in medical photography of the alimentary canal

¹bark \'bärk\ vb [ME *berken*, fr. OE *beorcan*; akin to ON *berkja* to bark, Lith *burgéti* to growl] vi (bef. 12c) **1 a** : to make the characteristic short loud cry of a dog **b** : to make a noise resembling a bark **2** : to speak in a curt loud and usu. angry tone : SNAP ~ vt **1** : to utter in a curt loud usu. angry tone **2** : to advertise by persistent outcry 〈~ing their wares〉 — **bark up the wrong tree** : to proceed under a misapprehension; *also* : to misdirect one's efforts

²bark n (bef. 12c) **1 a** : the sound made by a barking dog **b** : a similar sound **2** : a short sharp peremptory tone of speech or utterance — **bark·less** \'bär-kləs\ adj

³bark n [ME, fr. ON *bark-*, *bȯrkr*; akin to MD & MLG *borke* bark] (14c) **1** : the tough exterior covering of a woody root or stem; *specif* : the tissues outside the cambium that include an inner layer esp. of secondary phloem and an outer layer of periderm **2** : CINCHONA 2 — **bark·less** \'bär-kləs\ adj

⁴bark vt (14c) **1 a** : to treat with an infusion of tanbark **2 a** : to strip the bark from **b** : to rub off or abrade the skin of

⁵bark n [ME, fr. MF *barque*, fr. OProv *barca*, fr. LL] (15c) **1 a** : a small sailing ship **b** : a sailing ship of three or more masts with the aftmost mast fore-and-aft rigged and the others square-rigged **2** : a craft propelled by sails or oars

bark beetle n (1862) : any of numerous beetles (family Scolytidae) that bore under the bark of trees both as a larva and an adult

bar·keep \'bär-ˌkēp\ *also* **bar·keep·er** \-ˌkē-pər\ n (1712) : BARTENDER

bar·ken·tine \'bär-kən-ˌtēn\ n [⁵*bark* + *-entine*, alter. of *-antine* (as in *brigantine*)] (1693) : a sailing ship of three or more masts with the foremast square-rigged and the others fore-and-aft rigged

¹bark·er \'bär-kər\ n (14c) : one that barks; *esp* : a person who advertises by hawking at an entrance to a show

²barker n (1611) : one that removes or prepares bark

barking deer n (1880) : MUNTJAC

barky \'bär-kē\ adj **bark·i·er**; **-est** (1590) : covered with or resembling bark

bar·ley \'bär-lē\ n [ME *barly*, fr. OE *bærlic* of barley; akin to OE *bere* barley, L *far* spelt] (bef. 12c) : a cereal grass (genus *Hordeum*, esp. *H. vulgare*) having the flowers in dense spikes with long awns and three spikelets at each joint of the rachis; *also* : its seed used esp. in malt beverages, breakfast foods, and stock feeds

bar·ley—bree \-ˌbrē\ *also* **bar·ley—broo** \-ˌbrü\ n [*barley* + Sc *bree* or *broo* (bree)] (1724) *chiefly Scot* : WHISKY; *also* : MALT LIQUOR

bar·ley·corn \-ˌkȯrn\ n (1500) **1** : a grain of barley **2** : an old unit of length equal to a third of an inch

Barcelona chair

bar·low \'bär-,lō\ *n* [*Barlow*, family of 18th cent. Eng. knife makers] (1884) : a sturdy inexpensive jackknife

barm \'bärm\ *n* [ME *berme*, fr. OE *beorma*; akin to L *fermentum* yeast, *fervēre* to boil, OIr *berbaid* he boils] (bef. 12c) : yeast formed on fermenting malt liquors

bar·maid \'bär-,mād\ *n* (ca. 1658) : a woman who serves liquor at a bar

bar·man \-mən\ *n* (1837) *chiefly Brit* : BARTENDER

Bar·me·cid·al \,bär-mə-'sī-d°l\ *or* **Bar·me·cide** \'bär-mə-,sīd\ *adj* [*Barmecide*, a wealthy Persian, who, in a tale of *The Arabian Nights' Entertainments*, invited a beggar to a feast of imaginary food] (1842) : providing only the illusion of abundance ⟨a ~ feast⟩

¹bar mitz·vah \bär-'mits-və\ *n, often cap B&M* [Heb *bar miṣwāh*, lit., son of the (divine) law] (1816) **1** : a Jewish boy who reaches his 13th birthday and attains the age of religious duty and responsibility **2** : the initiatory ceremony recognizing a boy as a bar mitzvah

²bar mitzvah *vt* **bar mitz·vahed; bar mitz·vah·ing** (1947) : to administer the ceremony of bar mitzvah to

¹barmy \'bär-mē\ *adj* **barm·i·er; -est** (15c) : full of froth or ferment

²barmy *adj* **barm·i·er; -est** [alter. of *balmy*] (1892) *chiefly Brit* : BALMY 2

barn \'bärn\ *n* [ME *bern*, fr. OE *bereærn*, fr. *bere* barley + *ærn* house, store] (bef. 12c) **1 a** : a usu. large building for the storage of farm products or feed and usu. for the housing of farm animals or farm equipment **b** : an unusually large and usu. bare building ⟨a great ~ of a hotel —W. A. White⟩ **2 a** : a large building for the housing of a fleet of vehicles (as trolley cars or trucks) — **barn·like** \-,līk\ *adj* — **barny** \'bär-nē\ *adj*

Bar·na·bas \'bär-nə-bəs\ *n* [Gk, fr. Aram *Barnebhū'āh*] : a companion of the apostle Paul on his first missionary journey

bar·na·cle \'bär-ni-kəl\ *n* [ME *barnakille*, alter. of *bernake*, *bernekke*] (15c) **1** : BARNACLE GOOSE **2** [fr. a popular belief that the goose grew from the crustacean] : any of numerous marine crustaceans (subclass Cirripedia) with feathery appendages for gathering food that are free-swimming as larvae but permanently fixed (as to rocks, boat hulls, or whales) as adults — **bar·na·cled** \-kəld\ *adj*

barnacle goose *n* (1768) : a European goose (*Branta leucopsis*) that breeds in the arctic and is larger than the related brant

barn burner *n* (ca. 1960) : one that arouses much interest or excitement ⟨the game should be a real *barn burner*⟩

barn dance *n* (1831) : an American social dance orig. held in a barn and featuring several dance forms (as square dancing)

barn lot *n* (1724) *chiefly Southern & Midland* : BARNYARD

barn owl *n* (1674) : a widely distributed owl (*Tyto alba*) that has plumage mottled buff brown and gray above and chiefly white below, frequents barns and other buildings, and preys esp. on rodents

barn raising *n* (1856) : a gathering for the purpose of erecting a barn — compare ³BEE

barn·storm \'bärn-,storm\ *vi* (1883) **1** : to tour through rural districts staging usu. theatrical performances **2** : to travel from place to place making brief stops (as in a political campaign or a promotional tour) **3** : to pilot one's airplane in sight-seeing flights with passengers or in exhibition stunts in an unscheduled course esp. in rural districts ~ *vt* : to travel across while barnstorming — **barn·storm·er** *n*

barn swallow *n* (1851) : a swallow (*Hirundo rustica*) that is widespread in the northern hemisphere, has a deeply forked tail, and often nests in or near buildings

¹barn·yard \-,yärd\ *n* (14c) : a usu. fenced area adjoining a barn

²barnyard *adj* (1927) : SMUTTY, EARTHY, SCATOLOGICAL ⟨~ humor⟩

barnyard grass *n* (1843) : a coarse annual panicled grass (*Echinochloa crusgalli*) that has flowers borne on only one side of the raceme and is nearly cosmopolitan as a weed in cultivated ground

baro- — see BAR-

baro·gram \'bar-ə-,gram\ *n* [ISV] (1884) : a barographic tracing

baro·graph \-,graf\ *n* [ISV] (ca. 1864) : a recording barometer — **baro·graph·ic** \,bar-ə-'gra-fik\ *adj*

Ba·ro·lo \bə-'rō-(,)lō, bä-\ *n* [*Barolo*, village in the Piedmont region, Italy] (1875) : a dry red Italian wine

ba·rom·e·ter \bə-'rä-mə-tər\ *n* (ca. 1666) **1** : an instrument for determining the pressure of the atmosphere and hence for assisting in forecasting weather and for determining altitude **2** : one that indicates fluctuations (as in public opinion) **3** : STANDARD 4 ⟨a ~ to measure high school talent —Jeff Fellenzer⟩ — **baro·met·ric** \,bar-ə-'me-trik\ *adj* — **baro·met·ri·cal·ly** \-tri-k(ə-)lē\ *adv* — **ba·rom·e·try** \bə-'rä-mə-trē\ *n*

barometric pressure *n* (1827) : the pressure of the atmosphere usu. expressed in terms of the height of a column of mercury

bar·on \'bar-ən\ *n* [ME, fr. OF, fr. Gmc origin; akin to OHG *baro* freeman] (13c) **1 a** : one of a class of tenants holding his rights and title by military or other honorable service directly from a feudal superior (as a king) **b** : a lord of the realm : NOBLE, PEER **2 a** : a member of the lowest grade of the peerage in Great Britain **b** : a nobleman on the continent of Europe of varying rank **c** : a member of the lowest order of nobility in Japan **3** : a joint of meat consisting of two sirloins or loins and legs not cut apart at the backbone ⟨a ~ of beef⟩ **4** : a man of great power or influence in some field of activity ⟨cattle ~⟩

bar·on·age \-ə-nij\ *n* (13c) : the whole body of barons or peers : NOBILITY 2

bar·on·ess \'bar-ə-nəs, -,nes, US also ,bar-ə-'nes\ *n* (15c) **1** : the wife or widow of a baron **2** : a woman who holds a baronial title in her own right

bar·on·et \'bar-ə-nət, US also ,bar-ə-'net\ *n* (1614) : the holder of a rank of honor below a baron and above a knight

bar·on·et·age \'bar-ə-nə-(,)tij, ,bar-ə-'ne-tij\ *n* (1760) **1** : BARONETCY **2** : the whole body of baronets

bar·on·et·cy \'bar-ə-nət-sē, ,bar-ə-'net-sē\ *n* (1795) : the rank of a baronet

ba·rong \bə-'ron, -'rän\ *n* [of Austronesian origin; akin to Malay *parang* knife] (1898) : a thick-backed thin-edged knife or sword used by the Moros

ba·ro·ni·al \bə-'rō-nē-əl\ *adj* (1767) **1** : of or relating to a baron or the baronage **2** : STATELY, AMPLE ⟨a ~ room⟩

bar·ony \'bar-ə-nē\ *n, pl* **-on·ies** (14c) **1** : the domain, rank, or dignity of a baron **2** : a vast private landholding **3** : a field of activity under the sway of an individual or a special group

¹ba·roque \bə-'rōk, ba-, -'räk, -'rōk\ *adj, often cap* [F, fr. MF *barroque* irregularly shaped (of a pearl), fr. Pg *barroco* irregularly shaped pearl] (1765) **1** : of, relating to, or having the characteristics of a style of artistic expression prevalent esp. in the 17th century that is marked generally by use of complex forms, bold ornamentation, and the juxtaposition of contrasting elements often conveying a sense of drama, movement, and tension **2** : characterized by grotesqueness, extravagance, complexity, or flamboyance **3** : irregularly shaped — used of gems ⟨a ~ pearl⟩ — **ba·roque·ly** *adv*

²baroque *n, often cap* (1877) : the baroque style or the period in which it flourished

baro·re·cep·tor \,bar-ō-ri-'sep-tər\ *also* **baro·cep·tor** \'bar-ō-,sep-tər\ *n* (1948) : a neural receptor (as of the arterial walls) sensitive to changes in pressure

ba·rouche \bə-'rüsh\ *n* [G *Barutsche*, fr. It *biroccio*, ultim. fr. LL *birotus* two-wheeled, fr. L *bi-* + *rota* wheel — more at ROLL] (1801) : a four-wheeled carriage with a driver's seat high in front, two double seats inside facing each other, and a folding top over the back seat

barque \'bärk\, **bar·quen·tine** \'bär-kən-,tēn\ *var of* BARK, BARKENTINE

bar·quette \bär-'ket\ *n* [F, dim. of *barque* bark (ship)] (ca. 1949) : a small boat-shaped pastry shell

¹bar·rack \'bar-ək, -ik\ *n* [F *baraque* hut, fr. Catal *barraca*] (1686) **1** : a building or set of buildings used esp. for lodging soldiers in garrison **2 a** : a structure resembling a shed or barn that provides temporary housing **b** : housing characterized by extreme plainness or dreary uniformity — usu. used in pl. in all senses

²barrack *vt* (1701) : to lodge in barracks

³barrack *vb* [origin unknown] *vt* (1887) *chiefly Brit* : to shout at derisively or sarcastically ~ *vi* **1** *chiefly Brit* : ROOT, CHEER — usu. used with *for* **2** *chiefly Brit* : JEER, SCOFF — **bar·rack·er** *n*

barracks bag *n* (1938) : a fabric bag for carrying personal equipment; *esp* : DUFFEL BAG

bar·ra·coon \,bar-ə-'kün\ *n* [Sp *barracón*, aug. of *barraca* hut, fr. Catal] (1848) : an enclosure or barracks formerly used for temporary confinement of slaves or convicts — often used in pl.

bar·ra·cou·ta \,bar-ə-'kü-tə\ *n* [modif. of AmerSp *barracuda*] (1835) : a large elongate marine fish (*Thyrsites atun* of the family Gempylidae) used for food

bar·ra·cu·da \,bar-ə-'kü-də\ *n, pl* **-da** *or* **-das** [AmerSp] (1678) **1** : any of a genus (*Sphyraena* of the family Sphyraenidae) of elongate predaceous often large fishes of warm seas that include fishes used for food as well as some forms regarded as toxic **2** : one that uses aggressive, selfish, and sometimes unethical methods to obtain a goal esp. in business

¹bar·rage \'bar-ij\ *n* [F, fr. *barrer* to bar, fr. *barre* bar] (1859) : a dam placed in a watercourse to increase the depth of water or to divert it into a channel for navigation or irrigation

²bar·rage \bə-'räzh, -'räj\ *n* [F (*tir de*) *barrage* barrier fire] (1916) **1** : artillery fire laid on a line close to friendly troops to screen and protect them **2** : a vigorous or rapid outpouring or projection of many things at once ⟨a ~ of protests⟩

³bar·rage \bə-'räzh, -'räj\ *vt* **bar·raged; bar·rag·ing** (1918) : to deliver a barrage against

barrage balloon *n* (ca. 1920) : a small captive balloon used to support wires or nets as protection against air attacks

bar·ra·mun·di \,bar-ə-'mən-dē\ *also* **bar·ra·mun·da** \-də\ *n* [prob. fr. an Australian aboriginal language of Queensland] (1864) : any of several Australian fishes (esp. *Lates calcarifer* of the family Centropomidae) used for food

bar·ran·ca \bə-'raŋ-kə\ *or* **bar·ran·co** \-(,)kō\ *n, pl* **-cas** *or* **-cos** [Sp] (ca. 1691) **1** : a deep gully or arroyo with steep sides **2** : a steep bank or bluff

bar·ra·tor *also* **bar·ra·ter** \'bar-ə-tər\ *n* (15c) : one who engages in barratry

bar·ra·try \'bar-ə-trē\ *n, pl* **-tries** [ME *barratrie*, fr. MF *baraterie* deception, fr. *barater* to deceive, exchange] (15c) **1** : the purchase or sale of office or preferment in church or state **2** : an unlawful act or fraudulent breach of duty on the part of a master of a ship or of the mariners to the injury of the owner of the ship or cargo **3** : the persistent incitement of litigation

Barr body \'bär-\ *n* [Murray Llewellyn *Barr* b 1908 Canad. anatomist] (1963) : material of the inactivated X chromosome present in each of the female's somatic cells of most mammals used as a test of genetic femaleness (as in a fetus or an athlete) — called also *sex chromatin*

barre \'bär\ *n* [F, fr. ML *barra*] (1936) : BAR 1c

barred \'bärd\ *adj* (14c) : marked by or divided off by bars; *esp* : having alternate bands of different color ⟨~ feather⟩

barred owl *n* (1811) : a large American owl (*Strix varia*) with brown eyes and bars of dark brown on the breast

¹bar·rel \'bar-əl\ *n* [ME *barel*, fr. MF *baril*] (14c) **1** : a round bulging vessel of greater length than breadth that is usu. made of staves bound with hoops and has flat ends of equal diameter **2 a** : the amount contained in a barrel; *esp* : the amount (as 31 gal. of fermented beverage or 42 gal. of petroleum) fixed for a certain commodity used as a unit of measure **b** : a great quantity **3** : a drum or cylindrical part: as **a** : the discharging tube of a gun **b** : the cylindrical metal box enclosing the mainspring of a timepiece **c** : the part of a fountain pen or of a pencil containing the ink or lead **d** : a cylindrical or tapering housing containing the optical components of a photographic-lens system and the iris diaphragm **e** : TUMBLING BARREL **f** : the fuel outlet from the carburetor on a gasoline engine **g** : the trunk of a quadruped — **bar·reled** \-əld\ *adj* — **on the barrel** : asking for or granting no credit — **over a barrel** : at a disadvantage : in an awkward position

²**barrel** *vb* **-reled** *or* **-relled; -rel·ing** *or* **-rel·ling** *vt* (15c) : to put or pack in a barrel ~ *vi* : to move at a high speed or without hesitation

bar·rel·age \'bär-ə-lij\ *n* (1890) : amount (as of beer) in barrels

barrel cactus *n* (1881) : any of a genus (*Ferocactus*) of nearly globular deeply ribbed spiny cacti of Mexico and the adjacent U.S.

bar·rel—chest·ed \'bar-əl-,ches-təd\ *adj* (1926) : having a large rounded chest

barrel cuff *n* (1926) : an unfolded cuff (as on a shirt) usu. fastened by a button

bar·rel·ful \'bar-əl-,fúl\ *n, pl* **barrelfuls** \-,fúlz\ *or* **bar·rels·ful** \-əlz-,fúl\ (14c) 1 : as much or as many as a barrel will hold 2 : a large number or amount

bar·rel·head \-,hed\ *n* (1840) : the flat end of a barrel — **on the barrelhead** : asking for or granting no credit ⟨paid cash *on the barrelhead*⟩

barrel cactus

bar·rel·house \-,haús\ *n* (1883) 1 : a cheap drinking and usu. dancing establishment 2 : a strident, uninhibited, and forcefully rhythmic style of jazz or blues

barrel organ *n* (1772) : an instrument for producing music by the action of a revolving cylinder studded with pegs on a series of valves that admit air from a bellows to a set of pipes

barrel racing *n* (1972) : a rodeo event for women in which a mounted rider makes a series of sharp turns around three barrels in a cloverleaf pattern — **barrel race** *n* — **barrel racer** *n*

barrel roll *n* (ca. 1920) : an airplane maneuver in which a complete revolution about the longitudinal axis is made

barrel vault *n* (1849) : a semicylindrical vault — **bar·rel—vault·ed** \-,vȯl-təd\ *adj*

¹**bar·ren** \'bar-ən\ *adj* [ME *bareine*, fr. OF *baraine*] (13c) 1 : not reproducing: as a : incapable of producing offspring — used esp. of females or matings b : not yet or not recently pregnant c : habitually failing to fruit 2 : not productive: as a : producing little or no vegetation : DESOLATE ⟨~ deserts⟩ b : producing inferior crops ⟨~ soil⟩ c : unproductive of results or gain : FRUITLESS ⟨a ~ scheme⟩ 3 : DEVOID, LACKING — used with *of* ⟨~ of excitement⟩ 4 : lacking interest, information, or charm 5 : DULL, UNRESPONSIVE **syn** see BARE — **bar·ren·ly** *adv* — **bar·ren·ness** \-ə(n)-nəs\ *n*

²**barren** *n* (1651) 1 *pl* : an extent of usu. level land having an inferior growth of trees or little vegetation 2 : a tract of barren land

bar·rette \bä-'ret, bə-\ *n* [F, dim. of *barre* bar] (1901) : a clip or bar for holding hair in place

¹**bar·ri·cade** \'bar-ə-,kād, ,bar-ə-'\ *vt* **-cad·ed; -cad·ing** (1592) 1 : to block off or stop up with a barricade 2 : to prevent access to by means of a barricade

²**barricade** *n* [F, fr. MF, fr. *barriquer* to barricade, fr. *barrique* barrel] (1642) 1 : an obstruction or rampart thrown up across a way or passage to check the advance of the enemy 2 : BARRIER 3, OBSTACLE 3 *pl* : a field of combat or dispute

bar·ri·ca·do \,bar-ə-'kā-(,)dō\ *n, pl* **-does** [modif. of MF *barricade*] (1590) *archaic* : BARRICADE — **barricado** *vt, archaic*

bar·ri·er \'bar-ē-ər\ *n* [ME *barrere*, fr. MF *barriere*, fr. *barre*] (14c) 1 a : something material that blocks or is intended to block passage ⟨highway ~s⟩ ⟨a ~ contraceptive⟩ b : a natural formation or structure that prevents or hinders movement or action ⟨geographic ~s to species dissemination⟩ ⟨~ beaches⟩ ⟨drugs that cross the placental ~⟩ 2 *pl, often cap* : a medieval war game in which combatants fight on foot with a fence or railing between them 3 : something immaterial that impedes or separates : OBSTACLE ⟨behavioral ~s⟩ ⟨trade ~s⟩ ⟨a ~ to honest communication⟩

barrier island *n* (1943) : a long broad sandy island lying parallel to a shore that is built up by the action of waves, currents, and winds and that protects the shore from the effects of the ocean

barrier reef *n* (1805) : a coral reef roughly parallel to a shore and separated from it by a lagoon

bar·ring \'bär-iŋ\ *prep* (15c) : excluding by exception : EXCEPTING

bar·rio \'bär-ē-,ō, 'bar-\ *n, pl* **-ri·os** [Sp, fr. Ar *barri* of the open country, fr. *barr* outside, open country] (1841) 1 : a ward, quarter, or district of a city or town in Spanish-speaking countries 2 : a Spanish-speaking quarter or neighborhood in a city or town in the U.S. esp. in the Southwest

bar·ris·ter \'bar-ə-stər\ *n* [ME *barrester*, fr. *barre* bar + *-ster* (as in *legister* lawyer)] (15c) : a counsel admitted to plead at the bar and undertake the public trial of causes in an English superior court — compare SOLICITOR

bar·room \'bär-,rüm, -,rúm\ *n* (1797) : a room or establishment whose main feature is a bar for the sale of liquor

¹**bar·row** \'bar-(,)ō\ *n* [ME *bergh*, fr. OE *beorg*; akin to OHG *berg* mountain, Skt *bṛhant* high] (bef. 12c) 1 : MOUNTAIN, MOUND — used only in the names of hills in England 2 : a large mound of earth or stones over the remains of the dead : TUMULUS

²**barrow** *n* [ME *barow*, fr. OE *bearg*; akin to OHG *barug* barrow] (bef. 12c) : a male hog castrated before sexual maturity

³**barrow** *n* [ME *barew*, fr. OE *bearwe*; akin to OE *beran* to carry — more at BEAR] (bef. 12c) 1 a : HANDBARROW b : WHEELBARROW 2 : a cart with a shallow box body, two wheels, and shafts for pushing it

barrow boy *n* (1939) *Brit* : COSTERMONGER

bar sinister *n* (1823) 1 : a heraldic charge held to be a mark of bastardy 2 : the fact or condition of being of illegitimate birth

bar·tend·er \'bär-,ten-dər\ *n* (1836) : one that serves liquor at a bar

¹**bar·ter** \'bär-tər\ *vb* [ME *bartren*, fr. MF *barater* to deceive, exchange] *vi* (15c) : to trade by exchanging one commodity for another ~ *vt* : to trade or exchange by or as if by bartering — **bar·ter·er** \-tər-ər\ *n*

²**barter** *n* (15c) 1 : the act or practice of carrying on trade by bartering 2 : the thing given in exchange in bartering

Bar·tho·lin's gland \'bär-thə-lənz-, 'bär-t'l-ənz-\ *n* [Kaspar *Bartholin* †1738 Dan. physician] (1901) : either of two oval racemose glands lying one to each side of the lower part of the vagina and secreting a lubricating mucus — compare COWPER'S GLAND

bar·ti·zan \'bär-tə-zən, ,bär-tə-'zan\ *n* [alter. of ME *bretasinge*, fr. *bretais* parapet — more at BRATTICE] (1808) : a small structure (as a turret) projecting from a building and serving esp. for lookout or defense

Ba·ruch \bə-'rük, 'bär-,ük\ *n* [LL, fr. Gk *Barouch*, fr. Heb *Bārükh*] : a homiletic book included in the Roman Catholic canon of the Old Testament and in the Protestant Apocrypha — see BIBLE table

bar·ware \'bär-,war, -,wer\ *n* (1941) : glassware or utensils used in preparing and serving alcoholic beverages

bary·on \'bar-ē-,än\ *n* [ISV *bary*- (fr. Gk *barys* heavy) + ²-*on* — more at GRIEVE] (1953) : any of a group of elementary particles (as nucleons) that are subject to the strong force and are held to be a combination of three quarks — **bary·on·ic** \,bar-ē-'ä-nik\ *adj*

bary·te \'bar-,īt, 'ber-\ *or* **ba·ry·tes** \bə-'rī-tēz\ *var of* BARITE

bary·tone \'bar-ə-,tōn\ *var of* BARITONE

bas·al \'bā-səl, -zəl\ *adj* (1645) 1 a : relating to, situated at, or forming the base b : arising from the base of a stem ⟨~ leaves⟩ 2 a : of or relating to the foundation, base, or essence : FUNDAMENTAL b : of, relating to, or being essential for maintaining the fundamental vital activities of an organism : MINIMAL c : used for teaching beginners ⟨~ readers⟩ — **ba·sal·ly** *adv*

basal body *n* (1902) : a minute distinctively staining cell organelle found at the base of a flagellum or cilium and identical to a centriole in structure — called also *basal granule, kinetosome*

basal cell *n* (ca. 1903) : one of the innermost cells of the deeper epidermis of the skin

basal ganglion *n* (ca. 1889) : any of four deeply placed masses of gray matter (as the amygdala) in each cerebral hemisphere — called also *basal nucleus*

basal metabolic rate *n* (1922) : the rate at which heat is given off by an organism at complete rest

basal metabolism *n* (1913) : the turnover of energy in a fasting and resting organism using energy solely to maintain vital cellular activity, respiration, and circulation as measured by the basal metabolic rate

ba·salt \bə-'sȯlt, 'bȯ-,\ *n* [L *basaltes*, MS var. of *basanites* touchstone, fr. Gk *basanitēs* (*lithos*), fr. *basanos* touchstone, fr. Egypt *bḥnw*] (1601) : a dark gray to black dense to fine-grained igneous rock that consists of basic plagioclase, augite, and usu. magnetite — **ba·sal·tic** \bə-'sȯl-tik\ *adj*

bas·cule \'bas-(,)kyü(ə)l\ *n* [F, seesaw] (1678) : an apparatus or structure (as a drawbridge) in which one end is counterbalanced by the other on the principle of the seesaw or by weights

¹**base** \'bās\ *n, pl* **bas·es** \'bā-səz\ [ME, fr. MF, fr. L *basis*, fr. Gk, step, base, fr. *bainein* to go — more at COME] (13c) 1 a (1) : the lower part of a wall, pier, or column considered as a separate architectural feature (2) : the lower part of a complete architectural design b : the bottom of something considered as its support : FOUNDATION c (1) : a side or face of a geometrical figure from which an altitude can be constructed; *esp* : one on which the figure stands (2) : the length of a base d : that part of a bodily organ by which it is attached to another more central structure of the organism 2 a : main ingredient ⟨paint having a latex ~⟩ b : a supporting or carrying ingredient (as of a medicine) 3 a : the fundamental part of something : GROUNDWORK, BASIS b : the economic factors on which in Marxist theory all legal, social, and political relations are formed 4 : the lower part of a heraldic field 5 a : the starting point or line for an action or undertaking b : a baseline in surveying c : a center or area of operations: as (1) : the place from which a military force draws supplies (2) : a place where military operations begin (3) : a permanent military installation d (1) : a number (as 5 in 5⁶·⁴⁴ or 5⁷) that is raised to a power; *esp* : the number that when raised to a power equal to the logarithm of a number yields the number itself ⟨the logarithm of 100 to the ~ 10 is 2 since 10² = 100⟩ (2) : a number equal to the number of units in a given digit's place that for a given system of writing numbers is required to give the numeral 1 in the next higher place ⟨the decimal system uses a ~ of 10⟩; *also* : such a system of writing numbers using an indicated base ⟨convert from ~ 10 to ~ 2⟩ (3) : a number that is multiplied by a rate or of which a percentage or fraction is calculated ⟨to find the interest on $90 at 10% multiply the ~ 90 by .10⟩ e : ROOT 6 6 a : the starting place or goal in various games b : any one of the four stations at the corners of a baseball infield c : a point to be considered ⟨his opening remarks touched every ~⟩ 7 a : any of various typically water-soluble and bitter tasting compounds that in solution have a pH greater than 7, are capable of reacting with an acid to form a salt, and are molecules or ions able to take up a proton from an acid or able to give up an unshared pair of electrons to an acid b : any of the five purine or pyrimidine bases of DNA and RNA that include cytosine, guanine, adenine, thymine, and uracil 8 : a price level at which a security previously actively declining in price resists further price decline 9 : the part of a transformational grammar that consists of rules and a lexicon and generates the deep structures of a language — **based** \'bāst\ *adj* — **base·less** \'bā-sləs\ *adj* — **off base** 1 : WRONG, MISTAKEN 2 : UNAWARES

²**base** *vt* **based; bas·ing** (1587) 1 : to make, form, or serve as a base for 2 : to find a base or basis for — usu. used with *on* or *upon*

³**base** *adj* [ME *bas*, fr. MF, fr. ML *bassus* short, low] (14c) 1 *archaic* : of little height 2 *obs* : low in place or position 3 *obs* : BASS 4 *archaic* : BASEBORN 5 a : resembling a villein : SERVILE ⟨a ~ tenant⟩ b : held by villenage ⟨~ tenure⟩ 6 a : being of comparatively low value and having relatively inferior properties (as lack of resistance to corrosion) ⟨a ~ metal such as iron⟩ — compare NOBLE b : containing a larger than usual proportion of base metals ⟨~ silver denarii⟩ 7 a : lacking or indicating the lack of higher qualities of mind or spirit : IGNOBLE b : lacking higher values : DEGRADING ⟨a drab ~ way of life⟩ — **base·ly** *adv* — **base·ness** *n*

base of a column:
1 upper torus, *2* scotia, *3* lower torus, *4* plinth, *5* shaft, *6* fillets

syn BASE, LOW, VILE mean deserving of contempt because of the absence of higher values. BASE stresses the ignoble and may suggest cruelty, treachery, greed, or grossness ⟨*base* motives⟩. LOW may connote crafty cunning, vulgarity, or immorality and regularly implies an outraging of one's sense of decency or propriety ⟨refused to listen to such *low* talk⟩. VILE, the strongest of these words, tends to suggest disgusting depravity or filth ⟨a *vile* remark⟩.

base angle *n* (ca. 1949) : either of the angles of a triangle that have one side in common with the base

base·ball \'bās-ˌbȯl\ *n, often attrib* (ca. 1815) : a game played with a bat and ball between two teams of nine players each on a large field having four bases that mark the course a runner must take to score; *also* : the ball used in this game

base·board \-ˌbōrd, -ˌbȯrd\ *n* (1853) : a board situated at or forming the base of something; *specif* : a molding covering the joint of a wall and the adjoining floor

base·born \-'bȯrn\ *adj* (1591) **1 :** MEAN, IGNOBLE **2 a :** of humble birth **b :** of illegitimate birth

base burner *n* (1874) : a stove in which the fuel is fed from a hopper as the lower layer is consumed

base exchange *n* (ca. 1956) : a post exchange at a naval or air force base

base hit *n* (1874) : a hit in baseball that enables the batter to reach base safely without benefit of an error or fielder's choice

base·line \'bās-ˌlīn\ *n, often attrib* (1750) **1 :** a line serving as a basis; *esp* : one of known measure or position used (as in surveying or navigation) to calculate or locate something **2 a :** either of the lines leading from home plate to first base and third base that are extended into the outfield as foul lines **b :** BASE PATH **3 :** a boundary line at either end of a court (as in tennis or basketball) **4 :** a set of critical observations or data used for comparison or a control **5 :** a starting point ⟨the ∼ of this discussion⟩

base·lin·er \'bās-ˌlī-nər\ *n* (ca. 1929) : a tennis player who stays on or near the baseline and seldom moves to the net

base·ment \'bā-smənt\ *n* [prob. fr. ¹*base*] (1730) **1 :** the part of a building that is wholly or partly below ground level **2 :** the ground floor facade or interior in Renaissance architecture **3 :** the lowest or fundamental part of something; *specif* : the rocks underlying stratified rocks **4** *chiefly NewEng* : a toilet or washroom esp. in a school — **base·ment·less** \-ləs\ *adj*

basement membrane *n* (1847) : a thin membranous layer of connective tissue that separates a layer of epithelial cells from the underlying lamina propia

ba·sen·ji \bə-'sen-jē, -'zen-\ *n* [prob. fr. Lingala *basenji*, pl. of *mosenji* native] (1933) : any of a breed of small curly-tailed dogs of African origin that do not bark

base on balls (ca. 1891) : an advance to first base awarded a baseball player who during his turn at bat takes four pitches that are balls

base pair *n* (1962) : one of the pairs of chemical bases composed of a purine on one strand of DNA joined by hydrogen bonds to a pyrimidine on the other that hold together the two complementary strands much like the rungs of a ladder and include adenine linked to thymine or sometimes to uracil and guanine linked to cytosine

base path *n* (1935) : the area between the bases of a baseball field used by a base runner

base pay *n* (1920) : a rate or amount of pay for a standard work period, job, or position exclusive of additional payments or allowances

base runner *n* (1867) : a baseball player of the team at bat who is on base or is attempting to reach a base — **base·run·ning** *n*

bases *pl of* BASE *or of* BASIS

¹bash \'bash\ *vb* [origin unknown] *vt* (1750) **1 :** to strike violently : HIT; *also* : to injure or damage by striking : SMASH — often used with *in* **2 :** to attack physically or verbally ⟨media ∼*ing*⟩ ⟨celebrity ∼*ing*⟩ ∼ *vi* : CRASH — **bash·er** *n*

²bash *n* (1805) **1 :** a forceful blow **2 :** a festive social gathering : PARTY **3 :** TRY, ATTEMPT ⟨have a ∼ at it⟩

ba·shaw \bə-'shȯ\ *var of* PASHA

bash·ful \'bash-fəl\ *adj* [obs. *bash* (to be abashed)] (1548) **1 :** socially shy or timid : DIFFIDENT, SELF-CONSCIOUS **2 :** resulting from or typical of a bashful nature ⟨a ∼ smile⟩ **syn** see SHY — **bash·ful·ly** \-fə-lē\ *adv* — **bash·ful·ness** \-fəl-nəs\ *n*

¹ba·sic \'bā-sik *also* -zik\ *adj* (1842) **1 :** of, relating to, or forming the base or essence : FUNDAMENTAL **2 :** constituting or serving as the basis or starting point **3 a :** of, relating to, containing, or having the character of a chemical base **b :** having an alkaline reaction **4 :** containing relatively little silica ⟨∼ rocks⟩ **5 :** relating to, made by, used in, or being a process of making steel done in a furnace lined with basic material and under basic slag — **ba·sic·i·ty** \bā-'si-sə-tē\ *n*

²basic *n* (1926) **1 :** something that is basic : FUNDAMENTAL ⟨get back to ∼s⟩ **2 :** BASIC TRAINING

BA·SIC \'bā-sik\ *n* [*B*eginner's *A*ll-purpose *S*ymbolic *I*nstruction *C*ode] (1964) : a simplified language for programming a computer

ba·si·cal·ly \'bā-si-k(ə-)lē *also* -zi-\ *adv* (1903) **1 a :** at a basic level : in fundamental disposition or nature ⟨∼ correct⟩ ⟨∼, they are simple people⟩ **b :** for the most part ⟨they ∼ play zone defense⟩ **2 :** in a basic manner : SIMPLY ⟨live ∼⟩

basic slag *n* (1888) : a slag low in silica and high in base-forming oxides that is used in the basic process of steelmaking and that is subsequently useful as a fertilizer

basic training *n* (1943) : the initial period of training of a military recruit

ba·sid·io·my·cete \bə-ˌsi-dē-ō-'mī-ˌsēt, -ˌmī-'sēt\ *n* [ultim. fr. NL *basidium* + Gk *mykēt-, mykēs* fungus; akin to Gk *myxa* mucus — more at MUCUS] (1899) : any of a large class (Basidiomycetes) or subdivision (Basidiomycotina) of higher fungi having septate hyphae, bearing spores on a basidium, and including rusts, smuts, mushrooms, and puffballs — **ba·sid·io·my·ce·tous** \-dē-ō-ˌmī-'sē-təs\ *adj*

ba·sid·io·spore \bə-'si-dē-ə-ˌspōr, -ˌspȯr\ *n* [NL *basidium* + E -*o*- + *spore*] (1859) : a spore produced by a basidium

ba·sid·i·um \bə-'si-dē-əm\ *n, pl* -**ia** \-dē-ə\ [NL, fr. L *basis*] (1859) : a structure on the fruiting body of a basidiomycete in which karyogamy occurs followed by meiosis to form usu. four basidiospores

ba·si·fy \'bā-sə-ˌfī\ *vt* -**fied**; -**fy·ing** (ca. 1847) : to convert into a base or make alkaline — **ba·si·fi·ca·tion** \ˌbā-sə-fə-'kā-shən\ *n*

ba·sil \'ba-zəl, 'bā-, -səl\ *n* [MF *basile*, fr. L *basilicum*, fr. Gk *basilikon*, fr. neut. of *basilikos*] (15c) **1 :** any of several aromatic herbs (genus *Ocimum*) of the mint family; *esp* : SWEET BASIL **2 :** the dried or fresh leaves of a basil used esp. as a seasoning

bas·i·lar \'ba-z³l-ər, -s³l- *also* 'bā-\ *adj* [MF *basilaire*, irreg. fr. *base* base] (1541) : of, relating to, or situated at the base

basilar membrane *n* (1867) : a membrane extending from the bony shelf of the cochlea to the outer wall and supporting the organ of Corti

Ba·sil·i·an \bə-'zi-lē-ən\ *n* (1780) : a member of the monastic order founded by St. Basil in the 4th century in Cappadocia — **Basilian** *adj*

ba·sil·i·ca \bə-'si-li-kə *also* -'zi-\ *n* [L, fr. Gk *basilikē*, fr. fem. of *basilikos* royal, fr. *basileus* king] (1541) **1 :** an oblong building ending in a semicircular apse used in ancient Rome esp. for a court of justice and place of public assembly **2 :** an early Christian church building consisting of nave and aisles with clerestory and a large high transept from which an apse projects **3 :** a Roman Catholic church given ceremonial privileges — **ba·sil·i·can** \-kən\ *adj*

bas·i·lisk \'ba-sə-ˌlisk, 'ba-zə-\ *n* [ME, fr. L *basiliscus*, fr. Gk *basiliskos*, fr. dim. of *basileus*] (14c) **1 :** a legendary reptile with fatal breath and glance **2 :** any of several crested tropical American lizards (genus *Basiliscus*) related to the iguanas and noted for their ability to run on their hind legs — **basilisk** *adj*

ba·sin \'bā-s³n\ *n* [ME, fr. OF *bacin*, fr. LL *bacchinon*] (13c) **1 a :** an open usu. circular vessel with sloping or curving sides used typically for holding water for washing **b** *chiefly Brit* : a bowl used esp. in cooking **c :** the quantity contained in a basin **2 a :** a dock built in a tidal river or harbor **b :** an enclosed or partly enclosed water area **3 a :** a large or small depression in the surface of the land or in the ocean floor **b :** the entire tract of country drained by a river and its tributaries **c :** a great depression in the surface of the lithosphere occupied by an ocean **4 :** a broad area of the earth beneath which the strata dip usu. from the sides toward the center — **ba·sin·al** \-s³n-əl\ *adj* — **ba·sined** \-s³nd\ *adj* — **ba·sin·ful** \-ˌful\ *n*

bas·i·net \ˌba-sə-'net\ *n* [ME *bacinet*, fr. MF, dim. of OF *bacin*] (14c) : a light often pointed steel helmet

ba·sip·e·tal \bā-'si-pə-t³l, -'zi-\ *adj* [L *basis* + *petere* to go toward — more at FEATHER] (1869) : proceeding from the apex toward the base or from above downward ⟨∼ maturation of an inflorescence⟩ — **ba·sip·e·tal·ly** \-t³l-ē\ *adv*

ba·sis \'bā-səs\ *n, pl* **ba·ses** \-ˌsēz\ [L — more at BASE] (14c) **1 :** the bottom of something considered as its foundation **2 :** the principal component of something **3 a :** something on which something else is established or based **b :** an underlying condition or state of affairs ⟨hired on a trial ∼⟩ ⟨on a first-name ∼⟩ **4 :** the basic principle **5 :** a set of linearly independent vectors in a vector space such that any vector in the vector space can be expressed as a linear combination of them with appropriately chosen coefficients

basis point *n* (1967) : one hundredth of one percent in the yield of an investment

bask \'bask\ *vb* [ME, prob. fr. ON *bathask*, refl. of *batha* to bathe; akin to OE *bæth* bath] *vi* (14c) **1 :** to lie in or expose oneself to a pleasant warmth or atmosphere **2 :** to take pleasure or derive enjoyment ∼ *vt, obs* : to warm by continued exposure to heat

bas·ket \'bas-kit, *Brit also* 'bäs-\ *n* [ME, prob. fr. (assumed) ONF *baskot*; akin to OF *baschoue* wooden vessel; both fr. L *bascauda* kind of basin, of Celt origin; akin to MIr *basc* necklace — more at FASCIA] (14c) **1 a :** a receptacle made of interwoven material (as osiers) **b** : any of various lightweight usu. wood containers **c :** the quantity contained in a basket **2 :** something that resembles a basket esp. in shape or use **3 a :** a net open at the bottom and suspended from a metal ring that constitutes the goal in basketball **b :** a field goal in basketball **4 a :** an aggregate of values (as of selected currencies) the average of which serves as a monetary standard **b :** a selection of financial instruments (as equities, futures, or options) the values of which reflect market fluctuations **5 :** a ring around the lower end of a ski pole that keeps the pole from sinking too deep in snow — **bas·ket·like** \-ˌlīk\ *adj*

bas·ket·ball \-ˌbȯl\ *n, often attrib* (1892) **1 :** a usu. indoor court game between two teams of usu. five players each who score by tossing an inflated ball through a raised goal; *also* : the ball used in this game

basket case *n* (1919) **1 :** a person who has all four limbs amputated **2 :** one that is completely incapacitated, inoperative, or worn out (as from nervous tension)

bas·ket·ful \'bas-kit-ˌful\ *n, pl* **bas·ket·fuls** \-ˌfulz\ *also* **bas·kets·ful** \-kits-ˌful\ (14c) : as much or as many as a basket will hold; *also* : a considerable quantity

basket hilt *n* (ca. 1550) : a hilt with a basket-shaped guard to protect the hand — **bas·ket-hilt·ed** \ˌbas-kit-'hil-təd\ *adj*

Basket Maker *n* (1897) : any of three stages of an ancient culture of the plateau area of southwestern U.S.; *also* : a member of the people who produced the Basket Maker culture

basket-of-gold *n* (1930) : a European perennial herb (*Aurinia saxatilis* syn. *Alyssum saxatile*) widely cultivated for its grayish foliage and yellow flowers

bas·ket·ry \'bas-ki-trē\ *n, pl* -**ries** (1851) **1 :** BASKETWORK **2 :** the art or craft of making baskets or objects woven like baskets

basket star *n* (ca. 1915) : any of various brittle stars (suborder Euryalina) with slender complexly branched interlacing arms

basket weave *n* (1912) : a textile weave resembling the checkered pattern of a plaited basket; *also* : something resembling this weave

bas·ket·work \'bas-kit-ˌwərk\ *n* (1769) : objects produced by basketry

bask·ing shark \'bas-kiŋ-\ *n* (ca. 1769) : a large plankton-feeding shark (*Cetorhinus maximus*) that has an oil-rich liver and sometimes attains a length of 40 feet (12 meters)

bas·ma·ti rice \ˌbäz-'mä-tē *also* ˌbaz-\ *n* [Hindi *bāsmatī* kind of rice, lit., something fragrant] (1845) : a cultivated aromatic long-grain rice of South Asian origin — called also *basmati*

bas mitz·vah \bäs-'mits-və\ *n, often cap B&M* [Heb *bath miṣwāh*, lit., daughter of the (divine) law] (1952) **1 :** a Jewish girl who at about 13 years of age assumes religious responsibilities **2 :** the initiatory ceremony recognizing a girl as a bas mitzvah

---

\ə\ abut \ᵊ\ kitten, F table \ər\ further \a\ ash \ā\ ace \ä\ mop, mar \aú\ out \ch\ chin \e\ bet \ē\ easy \g\ go \i\ hit \ī\ ice \j\ job \ŋ\ sing \ō\ go \ȯ\ law \ȯi\ boy \th\ thin \th\ the \ü\ loot \ú\ foot \y\ yet \zh\ vision \à, ḵ, ⁿ, œ, œ, ᵫ, ūᵉ, ᵜ\ *see* Guide to Pronunciation

ba·so·phil \'bā-sə-ˌfil, -zə-\ or **ba·so·phile** \-ˌfīl\ n (ca. 1890) : a basophilic substance or structure; esp : a leukocyte containing basophilic granules that is similar in function to a mast cell

ba·so·phil·ia \ˌbā-sə-'fi-lē-ə, -zə-\ n [NL] (1905) **1** : tendency to stain with basic dyes **2** : an abnormal condition in which some tissue element has increased basophilia

ba·so·phil·ic \-'fi-lik\ adj [ISV base + -o- + -philic] (ca. 1894) : staining readily with basic stains

Ba·so·tho \bä-'sò-ˌtò, -'sü-ˌtü\ n pl (1895) : a Bantu-speaking people of Lesotho

Basque \'bask\ n [F, fr. MF, fr. L Vasco] (1835) **1** : a member of a people inhabiting the western Pyrenees on the Bay of Biscay **2** : the language of the Basques of unknown relationship **3** not cap : a tight-fitting bodice for women — **Basque** adj

bas–re·lief \ˌbä-ri-'lēf, ˌbä-ri-ˌ\ n [F, fr. bas low + relief raised work] (1667) : sculptural relief in which the projection from the surrounding surface is slight and no part of the modeled form is undercut; also : sculpture executed in bas-relief

¹**bass** \'bas\ n, pl **bass** or **bass·es** [ME base, bærs, fr. OE bærs; akin to OHG bersich perch] (bef. 12c) : any of numerous edible spiny-finned marine or freshwater fishes (esp. families Centrarchidae, Serranidae, and Percichthyidae)

²**bass** \'bās\ adj [ME bas base] (15c) **1** : deep or grave in tone **2 a** : of low pitch **b** : relating to or having the range or part of a bass

³**bass** \'bās\ n (15c) **1 a** : the lowest voice part in a 4-part chorus **b** : the lower half of the whole vocal or instrumental tonal range — compare TREBLE **c** : the lowest adult male singing voice; also : a person having this voice **d** : a member of a family of instruments having the lowest range; esp : DOUBLE BASS **2** : a deep or grave tone : a low-pitched sound

⁴**bass** \'bas\ n [alter. of bast] (1691) **1** : BASSWOOD 1 **2** : a coarse tough fiber from palms

bass clef n (ca. 1771) **1** : a clef placing the F below middle C on the fourth line of the staff **2** : the bass staff

bass drum n (1804) : a large drum having two heads and giving a booming sound of low indefinite pitch — see DRUM illustration

bas·set hound \'ba-sət-\ n [F basset, fr. MF, fr. basset short, fr. bas low — more at BASE] (1883) : any of an old breed of short-legged hunting dogs of French origin having very long ears and crooked front legs — called also bassett

bass fiddle n (1951) : DOUBLE BASS

bass horn n (ca. 1846) : an obsolete wind instrument shaped like a bassoon but with a cup-shaped mouthpiece

bas·si·net \ˌba-sə-'net\ n [prob. modif. of F barcelonnette, dim. of berceau cradle] (1854) **1** : a baby's basketlike bed (as of wickerwork or plastic) often with a hood over one end **2** : a perambulator that resembles a bassinet

bass·ist \'bā-sist\ n (ca. 1909) : a person who plays an acoustic or electric bass

bas·so \'ba-(ˌ)sō, 'bä-\ n, pl **bassos** or **bas·si** \'bä-ˌsē\ [It, fr. ML bassus, fr. bassus short, low] (ca. 1724) **1** : a bass singer; esp : an operatic bass **2** : a low deep voice

bas·soon \bə-'sün, ba-\ n [F basson, fr. It bassone, fr. basso] (1724) : a double-reed woodwind instrument having a long U-shaped conical tube connected to the mouthpiece by a thin metal tube and a usual range two octaves lower than that of the oboe — **bas·soon·ist** \-'sü-nist\ n

bas·so pro·fun·do \ˌba-(ˌ)sō-prə-'fən-(ˌ)dō, ˌbä-, -'fün-\ n, pl **bassi profundos** [It, lit., deep bass] (1860) : a deep heavy bass voice with an exceptionally low range; also : a person having this voice

bas·so–re·lie·vo also **bas·so–ri·lie·vo** \ˌba-(ˌ)sō-ri-'lē-(ˌ)vō, ˌbä-(ˌ)sō-rēl-'yä-(ˌ)vō\ n [It bassorilievo, fr. basso low + rilievo relief] (1644) : BAS-RELIEF

bass viol n (1590) **1** : VIOLA DA GAMBA **2** : DOUBLE BASS

bass·wood \'bas-ˌwud\ n (1670) **1** : any of several New World lindens; esp : LINDEN 1b **2** : the straight-grained white wood of a basswood

bast \'bast\ n [ME, fr. OE bæst; akin to OHG & ON bast bast] (bef. 12c) **1** : PHLOEM **2** : BAST FIBER

¹**bas·tard** \'bas-tərd\ n [ME, fr. OF, prob. of Gmc origin; akin to OFris bost marriage, OE bindan to bind] (14c) **1** : an illegitimate child **2** : something that is spurious, irregular, inferior, or of questionable origin **3 a** : an offensive or disagreeable person — used as a generalized term of abuse **b** : MAN, FELLOW — **bas·tard·ly** adj

²**bastard** adj (14c) **1** : ILLEGITIMATE **2** : of mixed or ill-conceived origin ⟨known for coining ~ words⟩ **3** : of abnormal shape or irregular size **4** : of a kind similar to but inferior to or less typical than some standard ⟨~ measles⟩ **5** : lacking genuineness or authority : FALSE

bas·tard·ise Brit var of BASTARDIZE

bas·tard·ize \'bas-tər-ˌdīz\ vt **-ized; -iz·ing** (1587) **1** : to reduce from a higher to a lower state or condition : DEBASE **2** : to declare or prove to be a bastard **3** : to modify esp. by introducing discordant or disparate elements — **bas·tard·i·za·tion** \ˌbas-tər-də-'zā-shən\ n

bastard wing n (1772) : ALULA

bas·tardy \'bas-tər-dē\ n, pl **-tard·ies** (15c) **1** : the quality or state of being a bastard : ILLEGITIMACY **2** : the begetting of an illegitimate child

¹**baste** \'bāst\ vt **bast·ed; bast·ing** [ME, fr. MF bastir, of Gmc origin; akin to OHG besten to patch, OE bæst bast] (15c) : to sew with long loose stitches in order to hold something in place temporarily — **baster** n

²**baste** vt **bast·ed; bast·ing** [ME baisten] (15c) : to moisten (as meat) at intervals with a liquid (as melted butter, fat, or pan drippings) esp. during cooking — **baster** n

³**baste** vt **bast·ed; bast·ing** [prob. fr. ON beysta; akin to OE bēatan to beat] (1533) **1** : to beat severely or soundly : THRASH **2** : to scold vigorously : BERATE

bast fiber n (ca. 1885) : a strong woody fiber obtained chiefly from the phloem of plants and used esp. in cordage, matting, and fabrics

bas·tille \ba-'stēl\ n [F bastille, fr. the Bastille, fortress in Paris, fr. MF bastille, modif. of OProv bastida fortified town, fr. bastir to build, of Gmc origin; akin to OHG besten to patch] (1741) : PRISON, JAIL

Bastille Day n (1920) : July 14 observed in France as a national holiday in commemoration of the fall of the Bastille in 1789

¹**bas·ti·na·do** \ˌbas-tə-'nā-(ˌ)dō, -'nä-\ or **bas·ti·nade** \ˌbas-tə-'nād, -'näd\ n, pl **-na·does** or **-nades** [Sp bastonada, fr. bastón stick, fr. LL bastum] (1572) **1** : a blow with a stick or cudgel **2 a** : a beating esp. with a stick **b** : a punishment consisting of beating the soles of the feet with a stick **3** : STICK, CUDGEL

²**bastinado** vt **-doed; -do·ing** (1599) : to subject to repeated blows

¹**bast·ing** \'bā-stiŋ\ n (15c) **1** : the action of a sewer who bastes **2 a** : the thread used in basting **b** : the stitching made by basting

²**basting** n (1530) **1** : the action of one that bastes food **2** : the liquid used in basting

³**basting** n (1590) : a severe beating

bas·tion \'bas-chən\ n [MF, fr. OIt bastione, aug. of bastia fortress, derivative fr. dial. form of bastire to build, of Gmc origin; akin to OHG besten to patch] (1562) **1** : a projecting part of a fortification **2** : a fortified area or position **3** : something that is considered a stronghold : BULWARK — **bas·tioned** \-chənd\ adj

Ba·su·to \bə-'sü-(ˌ)tō\ n, pl **Basuto** or **Basutos** (1835) : a member of the Basotho people

¹**bat** \'bat\ n [ME, fr. OE batt] (bef. 12c) **1 a** : a stout solid stick : CLUB **2** : a sharp blow : STROKE **3 a** : a usu. wooden implement used for hitting the ball in various games **b** : a paddle used in various games (as table tennis) **c** : the short whip used by a jockey **4 a** : BATSMAN **b** : a turn at batting — usu. used in the phrase at bat **5** : BATT **6** Brit : rate of speed : GAIT **7** : BINGE — **off one's own bat** chiefly Brit : through one's own efforts — **off the bat** : without delay : IMMEDIATELY

²**bat** vb **bat·ted; bat·ting** vt (15c) **1** : to strike or hit with or as if with a bat **2 a** : to advance (a base runner) by batting **b** : to have a batting average of **3** : to discuss at length : consider in detail ~ vi **1 a** : to strike or hit a ball with a bat **b** : to take one's turn at bat **2** : to wander aimlessly

³**bat** n [alter. of ME bakke, prob. of Scand origin; akin to OSw nattbakka bat] (1580) : any of a widely distributed order (Chiroptera) of nocturnal usu. frugivorous or insectivorous flying mammals that have wings formed from four elongated digits of the forelimb covered by a cutaneous membrane and that have adequate visual capabilities but often rely on echolocation

⁴**bat** vt **bat·ted; bat·ting** [prob. alter. of ²bate] (ca. 1838) : to wink esp. in surprise or emotion ⟨never batted an eye⟩; also : FLUTTER ⟨batted his eyelashes⟩

bat·boy \'bat-ˌbòi\ n (ca. 1925) : a boy employed to look after the equipment (as bats) of a baseball team

¹**batch** \'bach\ n [ME bache; akin to OE bacan to bake] (15c) **1** : the quantity baked at one time : BAKING **2 a** : the quantity of material prepared or required for one operation; specif : a mixture of raw materials ready for fusion into glass **b** : the quantity produced at one operation **c** : a group of jobs (as programs) which are submitted for processing on a computer and whose results are obtained at a later time ⟨~ processing⟩ — compare TIME-SHARING **3** : a quantity (as of persons or things) considered as a group

²**batch** vt (1876) : to bring together or process as a batch — **batch·er** n

³**batch** var of BACH

¹**bate** \'bāt\ vb **bat·ed; bat·ing** [ME, short for abaten to abate] vt (14c) **1** : to reduce the force or intensity of : RESTRAIN ⟨with bated breath⟩ **2** : to take away : DEDUCT **3** archaic : to lower esp. in amount or estimation **4** archaic : BLUNT ~ vi, obs : DIMINISH, DECREASE

²**bate** vi **bat·ed; bat·ing** [ME, fr. MF batre to beat, fr. L battuere] (14c) of a falcon or hawk : to attempt to fly off something (as a gauntlet) in fear

bat–eared fox \'bat-ˌird-\ n (1946) : a large-eared yellowish gray fox (Otocyon megalotis) that inhabits arid unforested areas of eastern and southern Africa

ba·teau \ba-'tō\ n, pl **ba·teaux** \-'tō(z)\ [CanF, fr. F, fr. OF batel, fr. OE bāt boat — more at BOAT] (1711) : any of various small craft; esp : a flat-bottomed boat with raked bow and stern and flaring sides

Bates·ian \'bāt-sē-ən\ adj [Henry Walter Bates †1892 Eng. naturalist] (1896) : characterized by or being mimicry involving resemblance of an innocuous species to another that is protected from predators by repellent qualities (as unpalatability) ⟨~ mimic⟩

bat·fish \'bat-ˌfish\ n (1873) : any of several fishes with winglike processes; esp : any of a family (Ogcocephalidae) of flattened pediculate fishes (as a common West Indian form Ogcocephalus vespertillo)

bat·fowl \-ˌfaul\ vi (15c) : to catch birds at night by blinding them with a light and knocking them down with a stick or netting them

¹**bath** \'bath, 'bàth\ n, pl **baths** \'bathz, 'baths, 'bàthz, 'bàths\ [ME, fr. OE bæth; akin to OHG bad bath, OHG bāen to warm] (bef. 12c) **1 a** : a washing or soaking (as in water or steam) of all or part of the body **2 a** : water used for bathing **b** (1) : a contained liquid for a special purpose **c** (1) : a receptacle holding the liquid **c** (1) : a medium for regulating the temperature of something placed in or on it (2) : a vessel containing this medium **3 a** : BATHROOM **b** : a building containing an apartment or a series of rooms designed for bathing **c** : SPA — usu. used in pl. **d** Brit : SWIMMING POOL — often used in pl. **4 a** : the quality or state of being covered with a liquid **b** : FLOOD 3 **5** : BATHTUB **6** : a financial setback : LOSS ⟨took a ~ in the market⟩

batfish

²**bath** vt (15c) Brit : to give a bath to ~ vi, Brit : to take a bath

³**bath** n [Heb] (14c) : an ancient Hebrew liquid measure corresponding to the ephah of dry measure

bath chair \'bath-, 'bàth-\ n, often cap B [Bath, England] (1823) : a hooded and sometimes glassed wheeled chair used esp. by invalids; broadly : WHEELCHAIR

¹**bathe** \'bāth\ vb **bathed; bath·ing** [ME, fr. OE bathian; akin to OE bæth bath] vt (bef. 12c) **1** : MOISTEN, WET **2** : to wash in a liquid (as water) **3** : to apply water or a liquid medicament to **4** : to flow along the edge of : LAVE **5** : to suffuse with or as if with light ~ vi **1**

: to take a bath   **2** : to go swimming   **3** : to become immersed or absorbed — **bath·er** \'bā-thər\ n
²**bathe** n (1831)   **1** *Brit* : ¹BATH 1   **2** *Brit* : SWIM, DIP
ba·thet·ic \bə-'the-tik\ adj [bathos + -etic (as in pathetic)] (ca. 1864) : characterized by bathos — **ba·thet·i·cal·ly** \-ti-k(ə-)lē\ adv
bath·house \'bath-ˌhau̇s, 'bȧth-\ n (1705)   **1** : a building equipped for bathing   **2** : a building containing dressing rooms for bathers
bathing beauty n (1920) : a woman in a bathing suit who is a contestant in a beauty contest
bathing suit n (1873) : SWIMSUIT
bath mat n (1895) : a usu. washable mat used in a bathroom
bath·o·lith \'ba-thə-ˌlith\ n [Gk bathos depth + ISV -lith] (ca. 1900) : a great mass of intruded igneous rock that for the most part stopped in its rise a considerable distance below the surface — **bath·o·lith·ic** \ˌba-thə-'li-thik\ adj
ba·thos \'bā-ˌthäs\ n [Gk, lit., depth] (1727)   **1 a** : the sudden appearance of the commonplace in otherwise elevated matter or style   **b** : ANTICLIMAX   **2** : exceptional commonplaceness : TRITENESS   **3** : insincere or overdone pathos : SENTIMENTALISM
bath·robe \'bath-ˌrōb, 'bȧth-\ n (1902) : a loose often absorbent robe worn before and after bathing or as a dressing gown
bath·room \-ˌrüm, -ˌru̇m\ n (1780)   **1** : a room containing a bathtub or shower and usu. a sink and toilet   **2** : LAVATORY 2
bath salts n pl (1907) : a usu. colored crystalline compound for perfuming and softening bathwater
bath·tub \-ˌtəb\ n (1869) : a usu. fixed tub for bathing
bathtub gin n (1930) : a homemade spirit concocted from raw alcohol, water, essences, and essential oils
bath·wa·ter \'bath-ˌwȯ-tər, 'bȧth-, -ˌwä-tər\ n (14c) : water for a bath
bathy- comb form [ISV, fr. Gk, fr. bathys deep]   **1** : deep : depth ⟨bathyal⟩   **2** : deep-sea ⟨bathysphere⟩
bathy·al \'ba-thē-əl\ adj (1921) : of or relating to the ocean depths or floor usu. from 600 to 6000 feet (180 to 1800 meters)
ba·thym·e·try \bə-'thi-mə-trē\ n, pl -tries [ISV] (ca. 1859) : the measurement of water depth at various places in a body of water; also : the information derived from such measurements — **bathy·met·ric** \ˌba-thi-'me-trik\ also **bathy·met·ri·cal** \-tri-kəl\ adj — **bathy·met·ri·cal·ly** \-tri-k(ə-)lē\ adv
bathy·pe·lag·ic \ˌba-thi-pə-'la-jik\ adj (ca. 1900) : of, relating to, or living in the ocean depths esp. between 2000 and 12,000 feet (600 and 3600 meters)
bathy·scaphe \'ba-thi-ˌskaf, -ˌskȧf\ or **bathy·scaph** \-ˌskaf\ n [ISV bathy- + Gk skaphē light boat] (1947) : a navigable submersible for deep-sea exploration having a spherical watertight cabin attached to its underside
bathy·sphere \-ˌsfir\ n (1930) : a strongly built steel diving sphere for deep-sea observation
bathy·ther·mo·graph \-'thər-mə-ˌgraf\ n (1938) : an instrument designed to record water temperature as a function of depth
ba·tik \bə-'tēk, 'ba-tik\ n [Jav batik] (1880)   **1** : a fabric printed by an Indonesian method of hand-printing textiles by coating with wax the parts not to be dyed; also : the method itself   **2** : a design executed in batik
bat·ing \'bā-tiŋ\ prep (1647) : with the exception of : EXCEPTING
ba·tiste \bə-'tēst, ba-\ n [F] (1697) : a fine soft sheer fabric of plain weave made of various fibers
bat·man \'bat-mən\ n [F bât packsaddle] (1755) : an orderly of a British military officer
bat mitzvah \bät-'mits-və\ often cap B&M, var of BAS MITZVAH
ba·ton \bə-'tän, ba-, -'tōⁿ also 'ba-tⁿn\ n [F bâton, fr. OF baston, fr. LL bastum stick] (1520)   **1** : CUDGEL, TRUNCHEON; specif : BILLY CLUB   **2** : a staff borne as a symbol of office   **3** : a narrow heraldic bend   **4** : a slender rod with which a leader directs a band or orchestra   **5** : a hollow cylinder carried by each member of a relay team and passed to the succeeding runner   **6** : a hollow metal rod with a weighted bulb at one or both ends that is flourished or twirled by a drum major or drum majorette
bat out vt (1941) : to compose esp. in a casual, careless, or hurried manner
ba·tra·chi·an \bə-'trā-kē-ən\ n [ultim. fr. Gk batrachos frog] (ca. 1828) : AMPHIBIAN 1; esp : FROG, TOAD — **batrachian** adj
bats \'bats\ adj (1919) : BATTY 2
bats·man \'bat-smən\ n (1756) : a batter esp. in cricket
batt \'bat\ n (1871) : BATTING 2; also : an often square piece of batting
bat·tail·ous \'ba-tⁿl-əs\ adj [ME bataillous, fr. MF bataillos, fr. bataille battle] (14c) archaic : ready for battle : WARLIKE
bat·ta·lia \bə-'tāl-yə, -'tal-\ n [It battaglia] (1569)   **1** archaic : order of battle   **2** obs : a large body of men in battle array
bat·tal·ion \bə-'tal-yən\ n [MF bataillon, fr. OIt battaglione, aug. of battaglia company of soldiers, battle, fr. LL battalia combat — more at BATTLE] (1579)   **1** : a considerable body of troops organized to act together : ARMY   **2** : a military unit composed of a headquarters and two or more companies, batteries, or similar units   **3** : a large group
bat·teau var of BATEAU
bat·te·ment \ˌbat-'mäⁿ\ n [F, fr. battre to beat, fr. L battuere] (1830) : a ballet movement in which the foot is extended in any direction usu. followed by a beat against the supporting foot
¹**bat·ten** \'ba-tⁿn\ vb **bat·tened; bat·ten·ing** \'bat-niŋ, 'ba-tⁿn-iŋ\ [prob. ON batna to improve; akin to OE betera better] vi (1591)   **1 a** : to grow fat   **b** : to feed gluttonously   **2** : to grow prosperous esp. at the expense of another — usu. used with on ~ vt : FATTEN
²**batten** n [alter. of ME batent, bataunt finished board, fr. MF batant, fr. prp. of battre] (1658)   **1 a** Brit : a piece of lumber used esp. for flooring   **b** : a thin narrow strip of lumber used esp. to seal or reinforce a joint   **2** : a strip, bar, or support resembling or used similarly to a batten
³**batten** vb **bat·tened; bat·ten·ing** \'bat-niŋ, 'ba-tⁿn-iŋ\ vt (1663)   **1** : to furnish with battens   **2** : to fasten with or as if with battens — often used with down ~ vi : to make one secure by or as if by battens ⟨~ing down for the hurricane⟩
¹**bat·ter** \'ba-tər\ vb [ME bateren, prob. freq. of batter to bat, fr. bat] vt (14c)   **1 a** : to beat with successive blows so as to bruise, shatter, or demolish   **b** : BOMBARD   **2** : to subject to strong, overwhelming, or

repeated attack   **3** : to wear or damage by hard usage or blows ⟨a ~ed old hat⟩ ~ vi : to strike heavily and repeatedly : BEAT   syn see MAIM
²**batter** n [ME bater, prob. fr. bateren] (14c)   **1 a** : a mixture consisting chiefly of flour, egg, and milk or water and being thin enough to pour or drop from a spoon   **b** : a mixture (as of flour and egg) used as a coating for food (as chicken) that is to be fried   **2** : an instance of battering
³**batter** vt (1973) : to coat (food) with batter for frying
⁴**batter** n [origin unknown] (1743) : a receding upward slope of the outer face of a structure
⁵**batter** vt (ca. 1882) : to give a receding upward slope to (as a wall)
⁶**batter** n (1773) : one that bats; esp : the player whose turn it is to bat
battered child syndrome n (1962) : the complex of physical injuries sustained by a grossly abused child
bat·te·rie \ˌba-tə-'rē\ n [F, lit., beating — more at BATTERY] (1712) : a ballet movement consisting of beating together the feet or calves of the legs during a leap
battering ram n (1593)   **1** : a military siege engine consisting of a large wooden beam with a head of iron used in ancient times to beat down the walls of a besieged place   **2** : a heavy metal bar with handles used (as by firefighters) to batter down doors and walls
bat·tery \'ba-tə(-)rē\ n, pl -ter·ies [MF batterie, fr. OF, fr. battre to beat, fr. L battuere] (1531)   **1 a** : the act of battering or beating   **b** : an offensive touching or use of force on a person without the person's consent — compare ASSAULT 2a   **2 a** : a grouping of artillery pieces for tactical purposes   **b** : the guns of a warship   **3** : an artillery unit in the army equivalent to a company   **4 a** : a combination of apparatus for producing a single electrical effect   **b** : a group of two or more cells connected together to furnish electric current; also : a single cell that furnishes electric current ⟨a flashlight ~⟩   **5 a** : a number of similar articles, items, or devices arranged, connected, or used together : SET, SERIES ⟨a ~ of tests⟩   **b** : a usu. impressive or imposing group : ARRAY   **6** : the position of readiness of a gun for firing   **7** : the pitcher and catcher of a baseball team
bat·ting \'ba-tiŋ\ n (1773)   **1 a** : the action of one who bats   **b** : the use of or ability with a bat   **2** : layers or sheets of raw cotton or wool or of synthetic fibrous material used for lining quilts or for stuffing or packaging; also : a blanket of thermal insulation (as fiberglass)
batting average n (1867)   **1** : a ratio (as a rate per thousand) of base hits to official times at bat for a baseball player   **2** : a record of achievement or accomplishment
¹**bat·tle** \'ba-tⁿl\ n, often attrib [ME batel, fr. OF bataille battle, fortifying tower, battalion, fr. LL battalia combat, alter. of battualia fencing exercises, fr. L battuere to beat] (13c)   **1** archaic : BATTALION   **2** : a combat between two persons   **3** : a general encounter between armies, ships of war, or aircraft   **4** : an extended contest, struggle, or controversy
²**battle** vb **bat·tled; bat·tling** \'bat-liŋ, 'ba-tⁿl-iŋ\ vi (14c)   **1** : to engage in battle : FIGHT   **2** : to contend with full strength, vigor, skill, or resources : STRUGGLE ~ vt : **1** : to fight against   **2** : to force (as one's way) by battling — **bat·tler** \-lər, 'ba-tⁿl-ər\ n
³**battle** vt **bat·tled; bat·tling** [ME batailen, fr. MF bataillier to fortify, fr. OF, fr. bataille] (14c) archaic : to fortify with battlements
bat·tle–ax \'ba-tⁿl-ˌaks\ n (14c)   **1** : a broadax formerly used as a weapon of war   **2** : a sharp-tongued domineering usu. older woman
battle cruiser n (1911) : a large heavily armed warship that is lighter, faster, and more maneuverable than a battleship
battle cry n (1814) : WAR CRY
battle fatigue n (1945) : COMBAT FATIGUE — **bat·tle–fa·tigued** adj
bat·tle·field \'ba-tⁿl-ˌfēld\ n (1812)   **1** : a place where a battle is fought   **2** : an area of conflict
bat·tle·front \-ˌfrənt\ n (1914) : the military sector in which actual combat takes place
bat·tle·ground \-ˌgrau̇nd\ n (1815) : BATTLEFIELD
battle line (1814)   **1** : a line along which a battle is fought   **2** : a line defining the positions of opposing groups in a conflict or controversy — usu. used in pl. ⟨battle lines were drawn over economic policies⟩
bat·tle·ment \'ba-tⁿl-mənt\ n [ME batelment, fr. MF bataille] (14c) : a parapet with open spaces that surmounts a wall and is used for defense or decoration — **bat·tle·ment·ed** \-ˌmen-təd\ adj

battlement: 1 crenellations, 2 merlons, 3 machicolations

battle royal n, pl **battles royal** or **battle royals** (1672)   **1 a** : a fight participated in by more than two combatants; esp : one in which the last man in the ring or on his feet is declared the winner   **b** : a violent struggle   **2** : a heated dispute
bat·tle·ship \'ba-tⁿl-ˌship\ n [short for line-of-battle ship] (1794) : a warship of the largest and most heavily armed and armored class
bat·tle·wag·on \-ˌwa-gən\ n (ca. 1927) : BATTLESHIP
bat·tu \ba-'tü, -'tyü\ adj [F, fr. pp. of battre to beat] (1947) of a ballet movement : performed with a striking together of the legs
bat·tue \ba-'tü, -'tyü\ n [F, fr. battre to beat] (1816) : the beating of woods and bushes to flush game; also : a hunt in which this procedure is used
bat·ty \'ba-tē\ adj **bat·ti·er; -est** (1590)   **1** : of, relating to, or resembling a bat   **2** : mentally unstable : CRAZY — **bat·ti·ness** n
bau·ble \'bȯ-bəl, 'bä-\ n [ME babel, fr. MF] (14c)   **1** : TRINKET   **2** : a fool's scepter   **3** : TRIFLE
Bau·cis \'bȯ-səs\ n [L, fr. Gk Baukis] : the wife of Philemon
baud \'bȯd, 'bäd, Brit 'bōd\ n, pl **baud** also **bauds** [baud (telegraphic transmission speed unit), fr. J. M. E. Baudot †1903 Fr. inventor] (1931) : a variable unit of data transmission speed (as one bit per second)
Bau·haus \'bau̇-ˌhau̇s\ adj [G Bauhaus, lit., architecture house, school

\ə\ abut \ᵊ\ kitten, F table \ər\ further \a\ ash \ā\ ace \ä\ mop, mar \au̇\ out \ch\ chin \e\ bet \ē\ easy \g\ go \i\ hit \ī\ ice \j\ job \ŋ\ sing \ō\ go \ȯ\ law \ȯi\ boy \th\ thin \th\ the \ü\ loot \u̇\ foot \y\ yet \zh\ vision \ä, k̲, ⁿ, œ, œ̄, ᵫ, ᵺ, ᵻ\ see Guide to Pronunciation founded by Walter Gropius] (1923) : of, relating to, or influenced by a school of design noted esp. for a program that synthesized technology, craftsmanship, and design aesthetics

baulk chiefly Brit var of BALK

Bau·mé \bō-'mā\ adj [Antoine Baumé] (1877) : being, calibrated in accordance with, or according to either of two arbitrary hydrometer scales for liquids lighter than water or for liquids heavier than water that indicate specific gravity in degrees

baum marten \'baùm-ˌmär-tᵊn\ n [part trans. of G Baummarder, fr. Baum tree + Marder marten] (1909) : the pelt or fur of the European marten (Martes martes)

baux·ite \'bȯk-ˌsīt, 'bäk-\ n [F bauxite, fr. Les Baux, near Arles, France] (1861) : an impure mixture of earthy hydrous aluminum oxides and hydroxides that is the principal source of aluminum — **baux·it·ic** \bȯk-'si-tik, bäk-\ adj

Ba·var·i·an \bə-'ver-ē-ən, -'var-\ n (1638) 1 : a native or inhabitant of Bavaria 2 : the High German dialect of southern Bavaria and Austria — **Bavarian** adj

Bavarian cream n (ca. 1879) : flavored custard or pureed fruit combined with gelatin and whipped cream

baw·bee \'bȯ-(ˌ)bē, bȯ-'\ n [prob. fr. Alexander Orrok, laird of Sillebawbe fl 1538 Scot. master of the mint] (1542) 1 : any of various Scottish coins of small value 2 : an English halfpenny

baw·cock \'bȯ-ˌkäk\ n [F beau coq, fr. beau fine + coq fellow, cock] (1599) archaic : a fine fellow

bawd \'bȯd\ n [ME bawde] (14c) 1 obs : PANDER 2 a : one who keeps a house of prostitution : MADAM b : PROSTITUTE

bawd·ry \'bȯ-drē\ n [ME bawderie, fr. bawde] (15c) 1 obs : UNCHASTITY 2 : suggestive, coarse, or obscene language

¹**bawdy** \'bȯ-dē\ adj **bawd·i·er; -est** [bawd] (1513) 1 : OBSCENE, LEWD 2 : boisterously or humorously indecent — **bawd·i·ly** \'bȯ-dᵊl-ē\ adv — **bawd·i·ness** \'bȯ-dē-nəs\ n

²**bawdy** n [prob. fr. ¹bawdy] (1656) : BAWDRY 2

bawdy house n (1552) : BORDELLO

¹**bawl** \'bȯl\ vb [ME, to bark, prob. fr. Scand origin; akin to Icel baula to low\ vi (1570) 1 : to cry out loudly and unrestrainedly : YELL, BELLOW 2 : to cry loudly : WAIL ~ vt : to cry out at the top of one's voice — **bawl·er** n

²**bawl** n (1792) : a loud prolonged cry : OUTCRY

bawl out vt (1905) : to reprimand loudly or severely

¹**bay** \'bā\ adj [ME, fr. MF bai, fr. L badius; akin to OIr buide yellow] (14c) : reddish brown ⟨a ~ mare⟩

²**bay** n (1535) 1 : a bay-colored animal; specif : a horse with a bay-colored body and black mane, tail, and points — compare CHESTNUT 4, ¹SORREL 1 2 : a reddish brown

³**bay** n [ME, fr. MF baee opening, fr. OF, fr. fem. of baé, pp. of baer to gape, yawn — more at ABEYANCE] (14c) 1 : a principal compartment of the walls, roof, or other part of a building or of the whole building 2 : a main division of a structure 3 : any of various compartments or sections used for a special purpose (as in an airplane, spacecraft, or service station) ⟨bomb ~⟩ ⟨cargo ~⟩ 4 : BAY WINDOW 1 5 : a support or housing for electronic equipment

⁴**bay** vb [ME baien, abaien, fr. OF abaiier, of imit. origin] vi (14c) 1 : to bark with prolonged tones 2 : to cry out : SHOUT ~ vt 1 : to bark at 2 : to bring to bay 3 : to pursue with barking 4 : to utter in deep prolonged tones

⁵**bay** n (14c) 1 : a baying of dogs 2 : the position of one unable to retreat and forced to face danger ⟨brought his quarry to ~⟩ 3 : the position of one checked (police kept the rioters at ~⟩

⁶**bay** n, often attrib [ME baye, fr. MF baie] (14c) 1 : an inlet of the sea or other body of water usu. smaller than a gulf 2 : a small body of water set off from the main body 3 : any of various terrestrial formations resembling a bay of the sea

⁷**bay** n [ME, berry, fr. MF baie, fr. L baca] (15c) 1 a : the European laurel (Laurus nobilis) b : any of several shrubs or trees (as of the genera Magnolia, Pimenta, and Gordonia) resembling the laurel 2 a : a garland or crown esp. of laurel given as a prize for victory or excellence b : HONOR, FAME — usu. used in pl.

ba·ya·dere \ˌbī-ə-'dir, -ˌder\ n [F bayadère professional female dancer in India] (1856) : a fabric with horizontal stripes in strongly contrasted colors

bay·ber·ry \'bā-ˌber-ē\ n (1687) 1 : any of several wax myrtles; esp : a hardy shrub (Myrica pensylvanica) of coastal eastern No. America bearing dense clusters of small berries covered with grayish white wax 2 : the fruit of a bayberry

Bayes·ian \'bā-zē-ən, -zhən\ adj (1961) : being, relating to, or concerned with a theory (as of decision making or statistical inference) involving the application of Bayes' theorem and the use of probabilities based on prior knowledge and accumulated experience ⟨~ probability models⟩

Bayes' theorem \'bāz-\ n [Thomas Bayes †1761 Eng. mathematician] (1939) : a theorem about conditional probabilities: the probability that an event A occurs given that another event B has already occurred is equal to the probability that the event B occurs given that A has already occurred multiplied by the probability of occurrence of event A and divided by the probability of occurrence of event B

bay leaf n (15c) : the dried leaf of the European laurel (Laurus nobilis) used in cooking

bay·man \'bā-mən, -ˌman\ n (1641) : a person and esp. a fisherman who lives or works on or about a bay

¹**bay·o·net** \'bā-ə-nət, -ˌnet, ˌbā-ə-'net\ n [F baïonnette, fr. Bayonne, France] (1704) : a steel blade attached at the muzzle end of a shoulder arm (as a rifle) and used in hand-to-hand combat

²**bayonet** also **-net·ed** also **-net·ted; -net·ing** also **-net·ting** vt (1858) 1 : to stab with a bayonet 2 : to compel or drive by or as if by the bayonet ~ vi : to use a bayonet

bay·ou \'bī-(ˌ)ü, -(ˌ)ō\ n [LaF, fr. Choctaw bayuk] (1763) 1 : a creek, secondary watercourse, or minor river that is tributary to another body of water 2 : any of various usu. marshy or sluggish bodies of water

bay rum n (1840) : a fragrant cosmetic and medicinal liquid distilled from the leaves of a West Indian bay tree (Pimenta racemosa) or usu. prepared from essential oils, alcohol, and water

Bay Stat·er \'bā-ˌstā-tər\ n (1845) : a native or resident of Massachusetts — used as a nickname

bay window n (15c) 1 : a window or series of windows forming a bay in a room and projecting outward from the wall 2 : POTBELLY 1

ba·zaar \bə-'zär\ n [Per bāzār] (1612) 1 : an oriental market consisting of rows of shops or stalls selling miscellaneous goods 2 a : a place for the sale of goods b : DEPARTMENT STORE 3 : a fair for the sale of articles esp. for charitable purposes

ba·zoo·ka \bə-'zü-kə\ n [bazooka (a crude musical instrument made of pipes and a funnel)] (1943) : a light portable antitank weapon consisting of an open-breech smoothbore firing tube that launches an armor-piercing rocket and is fired from the shoulder

BB \'bē-(ˌ)bē\ n (1874) 1 : a shot pellet 0.18 inch in diameter for use in a shotgun cartridge 2 : a shot pellet 0.175 inch in diameter for use in an air gun

BCD \ˌbē-(ˌ)sē-'dē\ n [binary coded decimal] (ca. 1962) : a computer code for representing alphanumeric information

B cell n [bone-marrow-derived cell] (1968) : any of the lymphocytes that have antibody molecules on the surface and comprise the antibody-secreting plasma cells when mature — called also B lymphocyte; compare T CELL

BCG vaccine \ˌbē-(ˌ)sē-'jē-\ n [Bacillus Calmette-Guérin (an attenuated strain of tubercle bacilli), fr. Albert Calmette †1933 and Camille Guérin †1961 Fr. bacteriologists] (1927) : a vaccine prepared from a living attenuated strain of tubercle bacilli and used to vaccinate human beings against tuberculosis — called also BCG

B complex n (1934) : VITAMIN B COMPLEX

BC soil \'bē-'sē-\ n (ca. 1938) : a soil whose profile has only B horizons and C horizons

bdel·li·um \'de-lē-əm\ n [ME, fr. L, fr. Gk bdellion] (14c) : a gum resin similar to myrrh obtained from various trees (genus Commiphora) of the East Indies and Africa

be \'bē\ vb, past 1st & 3d sing was \'wəz, 'wäz\; 2d sing were \'wər\; pl were; past subjunctive were; past part been \'bin, chiefly Brit 'bēn\; pres part be·ing \'bē-(i)ŋ\; pres 1st sing am \əm, 'am\; 2d sing are \'är, ər\; 3d sing is \'iz, əz\; pl are; pres subjunctive be [ME, fr. OE bēon; akin to OHG bim am, L fui I have been, futurus about to be, fieri to become, be done, Gk phynai to be born, be by nature, phyein to produce] vi (bef. 12c) 1 a : to equal in meaning : have the same connotation as : SYMBOLIZE ⟨God is love⟩ ⟨January is the first month⟩ ⟨let x ~ 10⟩ b : to have identity with ⟨the first person I met was my brother⟩ c : to constitute the same class as d : to have a specified qualification or characterization ⟨the leaves are green⟩ e : to belong to the class of ⟨the fish is a trout⟩ — used regularly in senses 1a through 1e as the copula of simple predication 2 a : to have an objective existence : have reality or actuality : LIVE ⟨I think, therefore I am⟩ ⟨once upon a time there was a knight⟩ b : to have, maintain, or occupy a place, situation, or position ⟨the book is on the table⟩ c : to remain unmolested, undisturbed, or uninterrupted — used only in infinitive form ⟨let him ~⟩ d : to take place : OCCUR ⟨the concert was last night⟩ e : to come or go ⟨has already been and gone⟩ ⟨has never been to the circus⟩ f archaic : BELONG, BEFALL ~ verbal auxiliary 1 — used with the past participle of transitive verbs as a passive-voice auxiliary ⟨the money was found⟩ ⟨the house is being built⟩ 2 — used as the auxiliary of the present participle in progressive tenses expressing continuous action ⟨he is reading⟩ ⟨I have been sleeping⟩ 3 — used with the past participle of some intransitive verbs as an auxiliary forming archaic perfect tenses ⟨Christ is risen from the dead —1 Cor 15:20 (DV)⟩ 4 — used with the infinitive with to to express futurity, arrangement in advance, or obligation ⟨I am to interview him today⟩ ⟨she was to become famous⟩

be- prefix [ME, fr. OE bi-, be-; akin to OE bī by, near — more at BY] 1 : on : around : over ⟨bedaub⟩ ⟨besmear⟩ 2 : to a great or greater degree : thoroughly ⟨befuddle⟩ ⟨berate⟩ 3 : excessively : ostentatiously — in intensive verbs formed from simple verbs ⟨bedeck⟩ and in adjectives based on adjectives ending in -ed ⟨beribboned⟩ 4 : about : to : at : upon : against : across ⟨bestride⟩ ⟨bespeak⟩ 5 : make : cause to be : treat as ⟨belittle⟩ ⟨befool⟩ ⟨befriend⟩ 6 : call or dub esp. excessively ⟨bedoctor⟩ 7 : affect, afflict, treat, provide, or cover with esp. excessively ⟨bedevil⟩ ⟨befog⟩

¹**beach** \'bēch\ n [origin unknown] (1535) 1 : shore pebbles : SHINGLE 2 a : a shore of a body of water covered by sand, gravel, or larger rock fragments b : a seashore area

²**beach** vt (1840) 1 : to run or drive ashore 2 : to strand on or as if on a beach

beach ball n (1940) : a large inflated ball for use at the beach

beach·boy \-ˌbȯi\ n (1941) : a male beach attendant (as at a club or hotel)

beach buggy n (1943) : DUNE BUGGY

beach·comb·er \'bēch-ˌkō-mər\ n (1840) 1 : a white man living as a drifter or loafer esp. on the islands of the So. Pacific 2 : a person who searches along a shore (as for salable refuse or for seashells) — **beach·comb** \-ˌkōm\ vb

beach flea n (1843) : any of numerous amphipod crustaceans (family Talitridae) living on ocean beaches and leaping like fleas

beach·front \'bēch-ˌfrənt\ n (1921) : a strip of land that fronts a beach

beach·go·er \-ˌgō-ər\ n (1954) : a person who frequently goes to the beach

beach grass n (1681) : any of several tough strongly rooted grasses that grow on exposed sandy shores; esp : any of a genus (Ammophila) of rhizomatous perennials widely planted to bind sandy slopes

beach·head \'bēch-ˌhed\ n (1940) 1 : an area on a hostile shore occupied to secure further landing of troops and supplies 2 : FOOTHOLD

beach pea n (1802) : a wild pea (Lathyrus japonicus syn. L. maritimus) having tough roots and purple flowers that is found along sandy shores

beach plum n (1784) : a shrubby plum (Prunus maritima) having white flowers and growing along the northeastern coast of No. America; also : its edible usu. dark purple fruit that is used esp. in preserves

beach·side \'bēch-ˌsīd\ adj (1952) : located at a beach

beach·wear \-ˌwar, -ˌwer\ n (1928) : clothing for wear at a beach

beachy \'bē-chē\ adj (1597) : covered with pebbles or shingle

¹**bea·con** \'bē-kən\ n [ME beken, fr. OE bēacen sign; akin to OHG bouhhan sign] (14c) 1 : a signal fire commonly on a hill, tower, or pole 2 a : a lighthouse or other signal for guidance b : a radio transmitter emitting signals for guidance of aircraft 3 : a source of light or inspiration

²**bea·con** vt (1821) : to furnish with a beacon ～ vi : to shine as a beacon

¹**bead** \'bēd\ n [ME bede prayer, prayer bead, fr. OE bed, gebed prayer; akin to OE biddan to entreat, pray — more at BID] (bef. 12c) **1 a** obs : PRAYER — usu. used in pl. **b** pl : a series of prayers and meditations made with a rosary **2** : a small piece of material pierced for threading on a string or wire (as in a rosary) **3** pl **a** : ROSARY **b** : a necklace of beads or pearls **4** : a small ball-shaped body: as **a** : a drop of sweat or blood **b** : a bubble formed in or on a beverage **c** : a small metal knob on a firearm used as a front sight **d** : a blob or a line of weld metal **5** : a projecting rim, band, or molding

²**bead** vt (1577) **1** : to furnish, adorn, or cover with beads or beading **2** : to string together like beads ～ vi : to form into a bead

bead·ing n (1845) **1** : a beaded molding **2** : material or a part or a piece consisting of a bead **3** : an openwork trimming **4** : BEADWORK

bea·dle \'bēd²l\ n [ME bedel messenger, fr. OE bydel; akin to OHG butil bailiff, OE bēodan to command — more at BID] (1581) : a minor parish official whose duties include ushering and preserving order at services and sometimes civil functions

bead·roll \'bēd-ˌrōl\ n [fr. the reading in church of a list of names of persons for whom prayers are to be said] (1529) **1** : a list of names : CATALOG **2** : ROSARY

beads·man \'bēdz-mən\ n (13c) archaic : one who prays for another

bead·work \'bēd-ˌwərk\ n (1751) **1** : ornamental work in beads **2** : joinery beading

beady \'bē-dē\ adj bead·i·er; -est (1826) **1 a** : resembling beads **b** : small, round, and shiny with interest or greed (～ eyes) **2** : marked by bubbles or beads (a ～ liquor) — **bead·i·ly** \'bē-də-lē\ adv

bea·gle \'bē-gəl\ n [ME begle] (15c) : any of a breed of small short-legged smooth-coated often black, white, and tan hounds

beak \'bēk\ n [ME bec, fr. OF, fr. L beccus, of Gaulish origin] (13c) **1 a** : the bill of a bird; esp : a strong short broad bill **b** (1) : the elongated sucking mouth of various insects (as the true bugs) (2) : any of various rigid projecting mouth structures (as of a turtle) **c** : the human nose **2 a** : a pointed structure or formation: **a** : a metal-pointed beam projecting from the bow esp. of an ancient galley for piercing an enemy ship **b** : the spout of a vessel **c** : a continuous slight architectural projection ending in an arris — see MOLDING illustration **d** : a process suggesting the beak of a bird **3** chiefly Brit **a** : MAGISTRATE **b** : HEADMASTER — **beaked** \'bēkt\ adj — **beaky** \'bē-kē\ adj

beaked whale n (1877) : any of a widely distributed family (Ziphiidae) of medium-sized toothed whales that have an elongated snout and a small dorsal fin

bea·ker \'bē-kər\ n [ME biker, fr. ON bikarr, prob. fr. OS bikeri, fr. ML bicarium] (14c) **1** : a large drinking cup that has a wide mouth and is sometimes supported on a standard **2** : a deep widemouthed thin-walled vessel usu. with a lip for pouring that is used esp. in science laboratories

be-all and end-all \'bē-ˌȯ-lən-'(d)en-ˌdȯl\ n (1605) **1** : prime cause : essential element **2** : TOTALITY 1

¹**beam** \'bēm\ n [ME beem, fr. OE bēam tree, beam; akin to OHG boum tree] (bef. 12c) **1 a** : a long piece of heavy often squared timber suitable for use in construction **b** : a wood or metal cylinder in a loom on which the warp is wound **c** : the part of a plow to which handles, standard, and coulter are attached **d** : the bar of a balance from which scales hang **e** : one of the principal horizontal supporting members (as of a building or ship) (a steel ～ supporting a floor); also : BOOM, SPAR (the ～ of a crane) **f** : the extreme width of a ship at the widest part **g** : an oscillating lever on a central axis receiving motion at one end from an engine piston rod and transmitting it at the other **2 a** : a ray or shaft of light **b** : a collection of nearly parallel rays (as X rays) or a stream of particles (as electrons) **c** : a constant directional radio signal transmitted for the guidance of pilots; also : the course indicated by a radio beam **3** : the main stem of a deer's antler **4** : the width of the buttocks — **on the beam 1** : following a guiding beam **2** : proceeding or operating correctly

²**beam** vt (15c) **1** : to emit in beams or as a beam **2** : to support with beams **3** : to aim and transmit (a broadcast) by directional antennas or by satellite **b** : to direct to a particular audience ～ vi **1** : to send out beams of light **2** : to smile with joy

beam-ends \'bēm-'en(d)z\ n pl (1773) : the ends of a ship's beams — **on her beam-ends** : inclined so much on one side that the beams approach a vertical position

beam·ish \'bē-mish\ adj (1870) : beaming and bright with optimism, promise, or achievement — **beam·ish·ly** adv

beam splitter n (1935) : a mirror or prism or a combination of the two that is used to divide a beam of radiation into two or more parts

beamy \'bē-mē\ adj (14c) **1** : emitting beams of light : RADIANT **2** : broad in the beam (a ～ cargo ship)

¹**bean** \'bēn\ n [ME bene, fr. OE bēan; akin to OHG bōna bean] (bef. 12c) **1 a** : BROAD BEAN **b** : the seed of any of various erect or climbing leguminous plants (esp. genera Phaseolus, Dolichos, and Vigna) other than the broad bean **c** : a plant bearing beans **d** : an immature bean pod used as a vegetable **2 a** : a valueless item **b** pl : the least amount (didn't know ～s about it) **3** : any of various seeds or fruits that resemble beans or bean pods; also : a plant producing these **4 a** pl : EXUBERANCE — used in the phrase full of beans **b** pl : NONSENSE, BUNKUM — used in the phrase full of beans **5** : HEAD, BRAIN **6** : a protuberance on the upper mandible of waterfowl — see DUCK illustration

²**bean** vt (1910) : to strike (a person) on the head with an object

bean-bag \'bēn-ˌbag\ n (1871) **1** : a cloth bag partially filled typically with dried beans and used as a toy **2** : any of various pellet-filled bags used as furniture (as a chair) or household articles (as an ashtray base)

bean·ball \-ˌbȯl\ n (ca. 1905) : a pitch thrown at a batter's head

bean counter n (1975) : a person involved in corporate financial decisions and esp. one reluctant to spend money

bean curd n (ca. 1889) : a soft vegetable cheese prepared by treating soybean milk with coagulants (as magnesium chloride or dilute acids) — called also tofu

bean·ery \'bēn-rē, 'bē-nə-\ n, pl -er·ies (1887) : RESTAURANT

bean·ie \'bē-nē\ n (1940) : a small round tight-fitting skullcap worn esp. by schoolboys and college freshmen

beano \'bē-(ˌ)nō\ n, pl beanos [by alter.] (1935) : BINGO

bean-pole \'bēn-ˌpō(ə)l\ n (1798) **1** : a pole up which bean vines may climb **2** : a tall thin person

bean sprouts n pl (1921) : the sprouts of bean seeds esp. of the mung bean used as a vegetable

¹**bear** \'bar, 'ber\ n, pl bears often attrib [ME bere, fr. OE bera; akin to OE brūn brown — more at BROWN] (bef. 12c) **1** or pl **bear** : any of a family (Ursidae of the order Carnivora) of large heavy mammals of America and Eurasia that have long shaggy hair, rudimentary tails, and plantigrade feet and feed largely on fruit and insects as well as on flesh **2** : a surly, uncouth, or shambling person **3** [prob. fr. the proverb about selling the bearskin before catching the bear] : one that sells securities or commodities in expectation of a price decline — compare BULL — **bear·like** \-ˌlīk\ adj

²**bear** vb bore \'bōr, 'bȯr\; borne \'bōrn, 'bȯrn\ also born \'bȯrn\; bear·ing [ME beren to carry, bring forth, fr. OE beran; akin to OHG beran to carry, L ferre, Gk pherein] vt (bef. 12c) **1 a** : to move while holding up and supporting **b** : to be equipped or furnished with **c** : BEHAVE, CONDUCT (～ing himself well) **d** : to have as a feature or characteristic **e** : to give as testimony (～ false witness) **f** : to have as an identification (bore the name of John) **g** : to hold in the mind **h** : DISSEMINATE **i** : LEAD, ESCORT **j** : RENDER, GIVE **2 a** : to give birth to **b** : to produce as yield **c** (1) : to permit growth of (2) : CONTAIN (oil-bearing shale) **3 a** : to support the weight of : SUSTAIN **b** : to put up with esp. without giving way (couldn't ～ the pain) **c** : to call for as suitable or essential (it ～s watching) **d** : to hold above, on top, or aloft **e** : to admit of : ALLOW **f** : ASSUME, ACCEPT **x** : THRUST, PRESS ～ vi **1** : to produce fruit : YIELD **2 a** : to force one's way **b** : to extend in a direction indicated or implied **c** : to be situated : LIE **d** : to become directed **e** : to go or incline in an indicated direction **3** : to support a weight or strain — often used with up **4 a** : to exert influence or force **b** : APPLY, PERTAIN — **bear a hand** : to join in and help out — **bear arms 1** : to carry or possess arms **2** : to serve as a soldier — **bear fruit** : to come to satisfying fruition, production, or development — **bear in mind** : to think of esp. as a warning : REMEMBER — **bear with** : to be indulgent, patient, or forbearing with

syn BEAR, SUFFER, ENDURE, ABIDE, TOLERATE, STAND mean to put up with something trying or painful. BEAR usu. implies the power to sustain without flinching or breaking (forced to bear a tragic loss). SUFFER often suggests acceptance or passivity rather than courage or patience in bearing (suffering many insults). ENDURE implies continuing firm or resolute through trials and difficulties (endured years of rejection). ABIDE suggests acceptance without resistance or protest (cannot abide their rudeness). TOLERATE suggests overcoming or successfully controlling an impulse to resist, avoid, or resent something injurious or distasteful (refused to tolerate such treatment). STAND emphasizes even more strongly the ability to bear without discomposure or flinching (unable to stand teasing).

bear·able \'bar-ə-bəl, 'ber-\ adj (ca. 1550) : capable of being borne — **bear·abil·i·ty** \ˌbar-ə-'bi-lə-tē, ˌber-\ n — **bear·ably** \-blē\ adv

bear-bait·ing \'bar-ˌbā-tiŋ, 'ber-\ n (14c) : the practice of setting dogs on a chained bear

bear·ber·ry \-ˌber-ē\ n (1625) : a trailing evergreen plant (Arctostaphylos uva-ursi) of the heath family with astringent foliage and red berries

¹**beard** \'bird\ n [ME berd, fr. OE beard; akin to OHG bart beard, L barba] (bef. 12c) **1** : the hair that grows on a man's face often excluding the mustache **2** : a hairy or bristly appendage or tuft **3** : FRONT 7a — **beard·ed** \'bir-dəd\ adj — **beard·ed·ness** n — **beard·less** \'bird-ləs\ adj

²**beard** vt (1525) **1** : to confront and oppose with boldness, resolution, and often effrontery : DEFY **2** : to furnish with a beard

bearded collie n (1880) : any of a breed of large working dogs of Scottish origin that have a long rough coat and drooping ears

bearded iris n (1923) : any of numerous wild or cultivated irises with a growth of short hairs on each fall

bearded seal n (1913) : a large arctic seal (Erignathus barbatus) with a tuft of long whiskers on each side of the muzzle

bear down vt : OVERCOME, OVERWHELM ～ vi : to exert full strength and concentrated attention — **bear down on 1** : EMPHASIZE **2** : to weigh heavily on : BURDEN

beard-tongue \'bird-ˌtəŋ\ n (1821) : PENSTEMON

bear·er \'bar-ər, 'ber-\ n (13c) : one that bears: as **a** : PORTER 1 **b** : a plant yielding fruit **c** : PALLBEARER **d** : one holding a check, draft, or other order for payment esp. if marked payable to bearer

bear grass n (1750) : any of several plants (genera Yucca, Nolina, or Xerophyllum) of the lily or agave families chiefly of the southern and western U.S. with foliage resembling coarse blades of grass

bear hug n (1921) : a rough tight embrace

bear·ing n (13c) **1** : the manner in which one bears or comports oneself **2 a** : the act, power, or time of bringing forth offspring or fruit **b** : a product of bearing : CROP **3 a** : an object, surface, or point that supports **b** : a machine part in which another part (as a journal or pin) turns or slides **4** : a figure borne on a heraldic field **5** : PRESSURE, THRUST **6 a** : the situation or horizontal direction of one point with respect to another or to the compass **b** : a determination of position **c** pl : comprehension of one's position, environment, or situation **d** : RELATION, CONNECTION; also : PURPORT **7** : the part of a structural member that rests on its supports

syn BEARING, DEPORTMENT, DEMEANOR, MIEN, MANNER, CARRIAGE mean the outward manifestation of personality or attitude. BEARING is the most general of these words but now usu. implies characteristic posture (a woman of regal bearing). DEPORTMENT suggests actions or behavior as formed by breeding or training (your deportment was atrocious). DEMEANOR suggests one's attitude toward others as expressed in outward behavior (the haughty demeanor of the headwaiter). MIEN is a literary term referring both to bearing and demeanor (a mien of supreme self-satisfaction). MANNER implies characteristic or custom-

---

\ə\ abut \ᵊ\ kitten, F table \ər\ further \a\ ash \ā\ ace \ä\ mop, mar
\au̇\ out \ch\ chin \e\ bet \ē\ easy \g\ go \i\ hit \ī\ ice \j\ job
\ŋ\ sing \ō\ go \ȯ\ law \ȯi\ boy \th\ thin \t͟h\ the \ü\ loot \u̇\ foot
\y\ yet \zh\ vision \á, k̲, ⁿ, œ, œ̄, ue, ue̅, ᵊ\ see Guide to Pronunciation

ary way of moving and gesturing and addressing others ⟨the imperious *manner* of a man used to giving orders⟩. CARRIAGE applies chiefly to habitual posture in standing or walking ⟨the kind of *carriage* learned at boarding school⟩.

bearing rein *n* (1794) : CHECKREIN 1

bear·ish \'bar-ish, 'ber-\ *adj* (1744) **1 a** : resembling a bear in build or in roughness, gruffness, or surliness **2 a** : marked by, tending to cause, or fearful of falling prices (as in a stock market) **b** : PESSIMISTIC — **bear·ish·ly** *adv* — **bear·ish·ness** *n*

bé·ar·naise sauce \'ba-ar-,naz-, -ar-; 'ber-\ *n* [F *béarnaise*, fem. of *béarnais* of Béarn, France] (1877) : a sauce of egg yolks and butter flavored with shallots, wine, vinegar, and seasonings

bear out *vt* (15c) : CONFIRM, SUBSTANTIATE

bear·skin \'bar-,skin, 'ber-\ *n* (1752) : an article made of the skin of a bear; *esp* : a military hat made of the skin of a bear

bear up *vt* (13c) : SUPPORT, ENCOURAGE ~ *vi* : to summon up courage, resolution, or strength ⟨*bearing up* under the strain⟩

beast \'best\ *n* [ME *beste*, fr. OF, fr. L *bestia*] (13c) **1 a** : a four-footed mammal as distinguished from a human being, a lower vertebrate, and an invertebrate **b** : a lower animal as distinguished from a human being **c** : an animal as distinguished from a plant **d** : an animal under human control **2** : a contemptible person **3** : something formidably difficult to control or deal with

beast epic *n* (1889) : a poem with epic conventions in which animals speak and act like human beings

beast fable *n* (1865) : a usu. didactic prose or verse fable in which animals speak and act like human beings

beast·ie \'bē-stē\ *n* (ca. 1773) : BEAST, ANIMAL, CRITTER

beas·tings *var of* BEESTINGS

¹beast·ly \'best-lē\ *adj* **beast·li·er; -est** (13c) **1** : BESTIAL 1 **2** : ABOMINABLE, DISAGREEABLE ⟨~ weather⟩ — **beast·li·ness** *n*

²beastly *adv* (1865) : VERY ⟨a ~ cold day⟩

beast of burden *n* (1740) : an animal employed to carry heavy loads or to perform other heavy work (as pulling a plow)

¹beat \'bēt\ *vb* **beat; beat·en** \'bē-t²n\ *or* **beat; beat·ing** [ME *beten*, fr. OE *bēatan*; akin to OHG *bōzan* to beat] *vt* (bef. 12c) **1** : to strike repeatedly: **a** : to hit repeatedly so as to inflict pain — often used with *up* **b** : to walk on : TREAD **c** : to strike directly against forcefully and repeatedly : dash against or thrash at vigorously **e** : to strike at in order to rouse game; *also* : to range over in or as if in quest of game **f** : to mix by stirring : WHIP — often used with *up* **g** : to strike repeatedly in order to produce music or a signal ⟨~ a drum⟩ **2 a** : to drive or force by blows **b** : to pound into a powder, paste, or pulp **c** : to make by repeated treading or driving over **d** (1) : to dislodge by repeated hitting (2) : to lodge securely by repeated striking **e** : to shape by beating ⟨~ swords into plowshares⟩; *esp* : to flatten thin by blows **f** : to sound or express esp. by drumbeat **3** : to cause to strike or flap repeatedly **4 a** : OVERCOME, DEFEAT; *also* : SURPASS — often used with *out* **b** : to prevail despite ⟨~ the odds⟩ **c** : BEWILDER, BAFFLE **d** (1) : FATIGUE, EXHAUST (2) : to leave dispirited, irresolute, or hopeless ⟨~ CHEAT, SWINDLE **5 a** (1) : to act ahead of usu. so as to forestall (2) : to report a news item in advance of **b** : to come or arrive before **c** : CIRCUMVENT ⟨~ the system⟩ **d** : to outmaneuver (a defender) and get free **e** : to score against (a goalkeeper) **6** : to indicate by beating ⟨~ the tempo⟩ ~ *vi* **1 a** : to become forcefully impelled : DASH **b** : to glare or strike with oppressive intensity **c** : to sustain distracting activity **d** : to beat a drum **2 a** : PULSATE, THROB (2) : TICK **b** : to sound upon being struck **3 a** : to strike repeated blows **b** : to strike the air : FLAP **c** : to strike cover in order to rouse game; *also* : to range or scour for or as if for game **4** : to progress with much difficulty **5** : to sail to windward by a series of tacks — **beat·a·ble** \'bē-tə-bəl\ *adj* — **beat about the bush** *or* **beat around the bush** : to fail or refuse to come to the point in discourse — **beat a retreat** : to leave in haste — **beat it 1** : to hurry away : SCRAM **2** : HURRY, RUSH — **beat one's brains out** : to try intently to resolve something difficult by thinking — **beat the bushes** : to search thoroughly through all possible areas — **beat the drum** : to proclaim as meritorious or significant : publicize vigorously — **beat the rap** : to escape or evade the penalties connected with an accusation or charge — **beat up on** : to attack physically or verbally

²beat *n* (1615) **1 a** : a single stroke or blow esp. in a series; *also* : PULSATION, TICK **b** : a sound produced by or as if by beating **c** : a driving impact or force **2** : one swing of the pendulum or balance of a timepiece **3 a** : a regularly traversed round ⟨the cop on the ~⟩ **b** : a group of news sources that a reporter covers regularly **4 a** : a metrical or rhythmic stress in poetry or music or the rhythmic effect of these stresses **b** : the tempo indicated (as by a conductor) to a musical performer **c** : the pronounced rhythm that is the characteristic driving force in jazz or rock music; *also* : ²ROCK 2 **5 a** : one that excels ⟨I've never seen the ~ of it⟩ **b** : the reporting of a news story ahead of competitors **6** : DEADBEAT **7 a** : an act of beating to windward **b** : one of the reaches so traversed : TACK **8** : each of the pulsations of amplitude produced by the union of sound or radio waves or electric currents having different frequencies **9** : an accented stroke (as of one leg or foot against the other) in dancing — **beat·less** \-ləs\ *adj*

³beat *adj* [ME *beten, bete*, fr. pp. of *beten*] (1832) **1 a** : being in a state of exhaustion : EXHAUSTED **b** : sapped of resolution or morale **2** *often cap* : of, relating to, or being beatniks ⟨~ poets⟩

⁴beat *n, often cap* (1957) : BEATNIK

beat·en \'bē-t²n\ *adj* (13c) **1** : hammered into a desired shape ⟨~ gold⟩ **2** : much trodden and worn smooth; *also* : FAMILIAR ⟨a ~ path⟩ **3** : being in a state of exhaustion : EXHAUSTED

beaten biscuit *n* (1876) : a biscuit whose dough is lightened by beating and folding

beat·er \'bē-tər\ *n* (14c) **1** : one that beats: as **a** : EGGBEATER **b** : a rotary blade attached to an electric mixer **c** : DRUMSTICK 1 **2** : one that strikes bushes or other cover to rouse game

be·atif·ic \,bē-ə-'ti-fik\ *adj* [L *beatificus* making happy, fr. *beatus* happy, fr. pp. of *beare* to bless; perh. akin to L *bonus* good — more at BOUNTY] (1649) **1** : of, possessing, or imparting beatitude **2** : having a blissful appearance ⟨a ~ smile⟩ — **be·atif·i·cal·ly** \-fi-k(ə-)lē\ *adv*

beatific vision *n* (1639) : the direct knowledge of God enjoyed by the blessed in heaven

be·at·i·fy \bē-'a-tə-,fī\ *vt* **-fied; -fy·ing** [MF *beatifier*, fr. LL *beatificare*, fr. L *beatus* + *facere* to make — more at DO] (1535) **1** : to make supremely happy **2** : to declare to have attained the blessedness of heaven and authorize the title "Blessed" and limited public religious honor — **be·at·i·fi·ca·tion** \-,a-tə-fə-'kā-shən\ *n*

beat·ing \'bē-tiŋ\ *n* (13c) **1** : an act of striking with repeated blows so as to injure or damage; *also* : the injury or damage thus inflicted **2** : PULSATION **3** : DEFEAT, SETBACK

beating reed *n* (1879) : a reed in a musical instrument that vibrates against the edges of an air opening (as in a clarinet or organ pipe) to which it is attached — compare FREE REED

be·at·i·tude \bē-'a-tə-,tüd, -,tyüd\ *n* [L *beatitudo*, fr. *beatus*] (15c) **1 a** : a state of utmost bliss **b** — used as a title for a primate esp. of an Eastern church **2** : any of the declarations made in the Sermon on the Mount (Mt 5:3–12) beginning in the AV "Blessed are"

beat·nik \'bēt-nik\ *n* [²*beat* + *-nik*] (1958) : a person who rejects the mores of established society (as by dressing and behaving unconventionally) and indulges in exotic philosophizing and self-expression

beat off *vt* (15c) : REPEL ~ *vi* : MASTURBATE — used of a male; usu. considered vulgar

beat out *vt* (1607) **1** : to make or perform by or as if by beating **2** : to mark or accompany by beating **3** : to turn (a routine ground ball) into a hit in baseball by fast running to first base

Be·atrice \,bā-ä-'trē-(,)chā, 'bē-ə-trəs\ *n* [It] : a Florentine woman idealized in Dante's *Vita Nuova* and *Divina Commedia*

beat-up \'bēt-,əp, -'əp\ *adj* (1946) : DILAPIDATED, SHABBY

beau \'bō\ *n, pl* **beaux** \'bōz\ *or* **beaus** [F, fr. *beau* beautiful, fr. L *bellus* pretty] (1684) **1** : DANDY 1 **2** : BOYFRIEND 2

Beau Brum·mell \'bō-'brə-məl\ *n* [nickname of G. B. *Brummell*] (1920) : DANDY 1

beau·coup \'bō-(,)kü\ *adj* [F] (1918) *slang* : great in quantity or amount : MANY, MUCH ⟨spent ~ dollars⟩

Beau·fort scale \'bō-fərt-\ *n* [Sir Francis *Beaufort*] (1858) : a scale in which the force of the wind is indicated by numbers from 0 to 12

BEAUFORT SCALE

BEAUFORT NUMBER	NAME	WIND SPEED		DESCRIPTION
		MPH	KPH	
0	calm	<1	<1	calm; smoke rises vertically
1	light air	1-3	1-5	direction of wind shown by smoke but not by wind vanes
2	light breeze	4-7	6-11	wind felt on face; leaves rustle; wind vane moves
3	gentle breeze	8-12	12-19	leaves and small twigs in constant motion; wind extends light flag
4	moderate breeze	13-18	20-28	wind raises dust and loose paper; small branches move
5	fresh breeze	19-24	29-38	small-leaved trees begin to sway; crested wavelets form on inland waters
6	strong breeze	25-31	39-49	large branches move; overhead wires whistle; umbrellas difficult to control
7	moderate gale or near gale	32-38	50-61	whole trees sway; walking against wind is difficult
8	fresh gale or gale	39-46	62-74	twigs break off trees; moving cars veer
9	strong gale	47-54	75-88	slight structural damage occurs; shingles may blow away
10	whole gale or storm	55-63	89-102	trees uprooted; considerable structural damage occurs
11	storm or violent storm	64-72	103-117	widespread damage occurs
12	hurricane*	>72	>117	widespread damage occurs

*The U.S. uses 74 statute mph as the speed criterion for a hurricane.

beau geste \bō-'zhest\ *n, pl* **beaux gestes** *or* **beau gestes** \bō-'zhest\ [F, lit., beautiful gesture] (1914) **1** : a graceful or magnanimous gesture **2** : an ingratiating conciliatory gesture

beau ide·al \,bō-ī-'dē(-ə)l, ,bō-,ē-dā-'äl\ *n, pl* **beau ideals** [F *beau idéal* ideal beauty] (1809) : the perfect type or model

Beau·jo·lais \,bō-zhō-'lā, -zhə-\ *n, pl* **Beaujolais** [F, fr. *Beaujolais*, region of eastern France] (1863) : a light fruity red burgundy wine made from the Gamay grape

beau monde \bō-'mänd, -'mōⁿd\ *n, pl* **beau mondes** \-'män(d)z\ *or* **beaux mondes** \bō-mōⁿd\ [F, lit., fine world] (1673) : the world of high society and fashion

¹beaut \'byüt\ *n* (1896) : BEAUTY 4

²beaut *adj* (1918) *Austral & NewZeal* : EXCELLENT 2

beau·te·ous \'byü-tē-əs\ *adj* [ME, fr. *beaute*] (15c) : BEAUTIFUL — **beau·te·ous·ly** *adv* — **beau·te·ous·ness** *n*

beau·ti·cian \byü-'ti-shən\ *n* [*beauty* + *-ician*] (1924) : COSMETOLOGIST

beau·ti·ful \'byü-ti-fəl\ *adj* (15c) **1** : having qualities of beauty : exciting aesthetic pleasure **2** : generally pleasing : EXCELLENT — **beau·ti·ful·ly** \-f(ə-)lē\ *adv* — **beau·ti·ful·ness** \-fəl-nəs\ *n*

syn BEAUTIFUL, LOVELY, HANDSOME, PRETTY, COMELY, FAIR mean exciting sensuous or aesthetic pleasure. BEAUTIFUL applies to whatever excites the keenest of pleasure to the senses and stirs emotion through the senses ⟨*beautiful* mountain scenery⟩. LOVELY is close to BEAUTIFUL but applies to a narrower range of emotional excitation in suggesting the graceful, delicate, or exquisite ⟨a *lovely* melody⟩. HANDSOME suggests aesthetic pleasure due to proportion, symmetry, or elegance ⟨a *handsome* Georgian mansion⟩. PRETTY often applies to superficial or insubstantial attractiveness ⟨a painter of conventionally *pretty* scenes⟩. COMELY is like HANDSOME in suggesting what is cooly approved rather than emotionally responded to ⟨the *comely* grace of a dancer⟩. FAIR suggests beauty because of purity, flawlessness, or freshness ⟨*fair* of face⟩.

beautiful people *n pl, often cap B&P* (1964) : wealthy or famous people whose lifestyle is usu. expensive and well-publicized

beau·ti·fy \'byü-tə-,fī\ *vb* **-fied; -fy·ing** *vt* (1526) : to make beautiful or add beauty to : EMBELLISH ∼ *vi* : to grow beautiful **syn** see ADORN — **beau·ti·fi·ca·tion** \,byü-tə-fə-'kā-shən\ *n* — **beau·ti·fi·er** \'byü-tə-,fī(-ə)r\ *n*

beau·ty \'byü-tē\ *n, pl* **beauties** [ME *beaute*, fr. OF *biauté*, fr. *bel, biau* beautiful, fr. L *bellus* pretty; akin to L *bonus* good — more at BOUNTY] (14c) **1** : the quality or aggregate of qualities in a person or thing that gives pleasure to the senses or pleasurably exalts the mind or spirit : LOVELINESS **2** : a beautiful person or thing; *esp* : a beautiful woman **3** : a particularly graceful, ornamental, or excellent quality **4** : a brilliant, extreme, or egregious example or instance ⟨that mistake was a ∼⟩ **5** : a quantum characteristic that accounts for the existence and lifetime of the upsilon particle; *also* : a particle having this characteristic

beauty bush *n* (1926) : a Chinese shrub (*Kolkwitzia amabilis*) of the honeysuckle family with pinkish flowers and bristly fruit

beauty contest *n* (1899) **1** : an assemblage of girls or women at which judges select the most beautiful **2** : a presidential primary election in which the popular vote does not determine the number of convention delegates a candidate receives

beauty part *n* (1951) : the most desirable or beneficial aspect of something

beauty shop *n* (1901) : an establishment or department where hairdressing, facials, and manicures are done — called also *beauty parlor, beauty salon*

beauty spot *n* (1657) **1** : ¹PATCH 2 **2** : NEVUS

¹**beaux arts** \bō-'zär\ *n pl* [F *beaux-arts*] (1821) : FINE ARTS

²**beaux arts** *adj, often cap B&A* [F *École des Beaux-Arts* School of Fine Arts, in Paris] (1924) : characterized by the use of historic forms, rich decorative detail, and a tendency toward monumental conception in architecture

¹**bea·ver** \'bē-vər\ *n, pl* **beavers** [ME *bever*, fr. OE *beofor*; akin to OHG *bibar* beaver, and prob. to OE *brūn* brown — more at BROWN] (bef. 12c) **1** *or pl* **beaver a** : either of two large semiaquatic herbivorous rodents (*Castor canadensis* of No. America and *C. fiber* of Eurasia) having webbed hind feet and a broad flat scaly tail and constructing dams and partially submerged lodges **b** : the fur or pelt of the beaver **2 a** : a hat made of beaver fur or a fabric imitation **b** : SILK HAT **3** : a heavy fabric of felted wool or of cotton napped on both sides **4** : the pudenda of a woman — usu. considered vulgar

²**beaver** *n* [ME *baviere*, fr. MF] (15c) **1** : a piece of armor protecting the lower part of the face **2** : a helmet visor

³**beaver** *vi* (1946) : to work energetically ⟨∼*ing* away at the problem⟩

bea·ver·board \'bē-vər-,bōrd, -,bȯrd\ *n* [fr. *Beaver Board*, a trademark] (1909) : a fiberboard used for partitions and ceilings

be·bop \'bē-,bäp\ *n* [imit.] (1944) : ³BOP 1 — **be·bop·per** *n*

be·calm \bi-'kä(l)m, *NewEng also* -'kám\ *vt* (1582) **1 a** : to keep motionless by lack of wind **b** : to stop the progress of **2** : to make calm : SOOTHE

be·cause \bi-'kȯz, -'kəz *also* -'kós\ *conj* [ME *because that, because*, fr. *by cause that*] (14c) **1** : for the reason that : SINCE ⟨rested ∼ he was tired⟩ **2** : the fact that : THAT ⟨the reason I haven't been fired is ∼ my boss hasn't got round to it yet —E. B. White⟩

because of *prep* (14c) : by reason of : on account of

bé·cha·mel \,bā-shə-'mel\ *n* [F *sauce béchamelle*, fr. Louis de Béchamel †1703 Fr. courtier] (1796) : a rich white sauce

be·chance \bi-'chan(t)s\ *vb* (1527) *archaic* : BEFALL

bêche–de–mer \,besh-də-'mer, ,bäsh-\ *n* [F, alter. of *biche de mer*, fr. Pg *bicho do mar*, lit., sea worm] (1783) **1** *pl* **bêche–de–mer** *or* **bêches–de–mer** \,besh-də-, ,be-shəz-, ,bäsh-\ **1** : TREPANG **2** *cap B&M* : any of several English-based pidgins spoken on islands of the western Pacific

¹**beck** \'bek\ *n* [ME *bek*, fr. ON *bekkr*; akin to OE *bæc* brook, OHG *bah*, Lith *bėgti* to flee — more at PHOBIA] (14c) *Brit* : CREEK 2

²**beck** *n* [ME, alter. of *bekken*] (14c) *archaic* : BECKON

³**beck** *n* (14c) **1** *chiefly Scot* : BOW, CURTSY **2 a** : a beckoning gesture **b** : SUMMONS, BIDDING — **at one's beck and call** : ready to obey one's command immediately

beck·et \'be-kət\ *n* [origin unknown] (ca. 1769) : a device for holding something in place: as **a** : a grommet or a loop of rope with a knot at one end to catch in an eye at the other **b** : a ring of rope or metal **c** : a loop of rope (as for a handle)

beck·on \'be-kⁿn\ *vb* **beck·oned; beck·on·ing** [ME *beknen*, fr. OE *bīecnan*, fr. *bēacen* sign — more at BEACON] (bef. 12c) **1** : to summon or signal typically with a wave or nod **2** : to appear inviting : ATTRACT ∼ *vt* : to beckon to — **beckon** *n*

be·cloud \bi-'klaúd\ *vt* (1598) **1** : to obscure with or as if with a cloud **2** : to prevent clear perception or realization of : MUDDLE ⟨prejudices that ∼ his judgment⟩

be·come \bi-'kəm\ *vb* **-came** \-'kām\; **-come; -com·ing** [ME, to come to, become, fr. OE *becuman*, fr. *be-* + *cuman* to come] *vi* (bef. 12c) **1 a** : to come into existence **b** : to come to be ⟨∼ sick⟩ **2** : to undergo change or development ∼ *vt* : to suit or be suitable to ⟨seriousness *becoming* the occasion⟩ ⟨her clothes ∼ her⟩ — **become of** : to happen to

be·com·ing \-'kə-miŋ\ *adj* (15c) : SUITABLE, FITTING; *esp* : attractively suitable ⟨∼ modesty⟩ — **be·com·ing·ly** \-miŋ-lē\ *adv*

¹**bed** \'bed\ *n* [ME, fr. OE *bedd*; akin to OHG *betti* bed, L *fodere* to dig] (bef. 12c) **1 a** : a piece of furniture on or in which to lie and sleep **b** (1) : a place of sex relations (2) : marital relationship **c** : a place for sleeping **d** : SLEEP; *also* : a time for sleeping ⟨took a walk before ∼⟩ **e** (1) : a mattress filled with soft material (2) : BEDSTEAD **f** : the equipment and services needed to care for one hospitalized patient or hotel guest **2** : a flat or level surface: as **a** : a plot of ground prepared for plants; *also* : the plants grown in such a plot **b** : the bottom of a body of water; *esp* : an area of sea bottom supporting a heavy growth of a particular organism ⟨an oyster ∼⟩ **3** : a supporting surface or structure : FOUNDATION **4** : LAYER, STRATUM **5 a** : the place or material in which a block or brick is laid **b** : the lower surface of a brick, slate, or tile **6** : a mass or heap resembling a bed ⟨a ∼ of ashes⟩ ⟨served on a ∼ of lettuce⟩ — **in bed** : in the act of sexual intercourse

²**bed** *vb* **bed·ded; bed·ding** *vt* (bef. 12c) **1 a** : to find or make sleeping accommodations **b** : to go to bed **2** : to form a layer **3** : to lie flat or flush ∼ *vt* **1 a** : to furnish with a bed or bedding : settle in sleeping quarters — often used with *down* **b** : to put, take, or send to bed **2** : EMBED **b** : to plant or arrange in beds **c** : BASE, ESTABLISH **3 a** : to lay flat or in a layer **b** : to make a bed in or of **4** : to have sexual intercourse with — often used with *down*

be·dab·ble \bi-'da-bəl\ *vt* (1590) *archaic* : to wet or soil by dabbling

bed–and–breakfast *n* (1910) : an establishment (as an inn) offering lodging and breakfast

be·daub \bi-'dȯb, -'däb\ *vt* (1558) **1** : to daub over : BESMEAR **2** : to ornament with vulgar excess

be·daz·zle \bi-'da-zəl\ *vt* (1596) **1** : to confuse by a strong light : DAZZLE **2** : to impress forcefully : ENCHANT — **be·daz·zle·ment** \-mənt\ *n*

bed board *n* (1946) : a stiff thin wide board inserted usu. between a bedspring and mattress esp. to give support to one's back or to protect a mattress from sagging springs

bed·bug \'bed-,bəg\ *n* (1808) : a wingless bloodsucking bug (*Cimex lectularius*) sometimes infesting houses and esp. beds and feeding on human blood

bed·cham·ber \-,chām-bər\ *n* (14c) : BEDROOM

bed check *n* (1927) : a night inspection to check the presence of persons (as soldiers) required by regulations to be in bed or in quarters

bed·clothes \'bed-,klō(th)z\ *n pl* (14c) : the covering (as sheets and blankets) used on a bed

bed·cov·er \-,kə-vər\ *also* **bed·cov·er·ing** \-,kə-v(ə-)riŋ\ *n* (ca. 1656) **1** : BEDSPREAD **2** : BEDCLOTHES — usu. used in pl.

bed·ded \'be-dəd\ *adj* (1788) : having a bed or beds of a specified kind or number — used in combination ⟨a twin-*bedded* room⟩

bed·der \'be-dər\ *n* (1803) **1** : one that makes up beds **2** : a bedding plant

¹**bed·ding** \'be-diŋ\ *n* [ME, fr. OE, fr. *bedd*] (bef. 12c) **1** : BEDCLOTHES **2** : a bottom layer : FOUNDATION **3** : material to provide a bed for livestock **4** : STRATIFICATION

²**bedding** *adj* [fr. gerund of ²*bed*] (1856) : suitable for planting in large groups in flower beds to produce a mass display ⟨∼ plants⟩

be·deck \bi-'dek\ *vt* (ca. 1566) **1** : to clothe with finery : DECK 2 : DECORATE 2

be·dev·il \bi-'de-vəl\ *vt* (1574) **1** : to possess with or as if with a devil **2** : to cause distress : TROUBLE **3** : to change for the worse : SPOIL **4** : to confuse utterly : BEWILDER — **be·dev·il·ment** \-mənt\ *n*

be·dew \bi-'dü, -'dyü\ *vt* (14c) : to wet with or as if with dew

bed·fast \'bed-,fast\ *adj* (1560) : BEDRIDDEN

bed·fel·low \-,fe-(,)lō\ *n* (15c) **1** : one who shares a bed with another **2** : ASSOCIATE, ALLY ⟨political ∼s⟩

Bed·ford cord \'bed-fərd-\ *n* [perh. fr. New *Bedford*, Massachusetts] (1862) : a clothing fabric with lengthwise ribs that resembles corduroy; *also* : the weave used in making this fabric

be·dight \bi-'dīt\ *vt* **be·dight·ed** *or* **bedight; be·dight·ing** (14c) *archaic* : EQUIP, ARRAY

be·dim \bi-'dim\ *vt* (1583) **1** : to make less bright **2** : to make indistinct : OBSCURE

Bed·i·vere \'be-də-,vir\ *n* : a knight of the Round Table

be·di·zen \bi-'dī-zⁿn, -'di-\ *vt* (1661) : to dress or adorn gaudily — **be·di·zen·ment** \-mənt\ *n*

bed·lam \'bed-ləm\ *n* [*Bedlam*, popular name for the Hospital of St. Mary of Bethlehem, London, an insane asylum, fr. ME *Bedlem* Bethlehem] (1522) **1** *obs* : MADMAN, LUNATIC **2** *often cap* : a lunatic asylum **3** : a place, scene, or state of uproar and confusion — **bedlam** *adj*

bed·lam·ite \'bed-lə-,mīt\ *n* (1589) : MADMAN, LUNATIC — **bedlamite** *adj*

Bed·ling·ton terrier \'bed-liŋ-tən-\ *n* [*Bedlington*, England] (1867) : a swift lightly built terrier of English origin with a long narrow head, arched back, and usu. curly coat — called also *Bedlington*

bed·mate \'bed-,māt\ *n* (1583) : one who shares one's bed; *esp* : a sexual partner

bed molding *n* (1703) : the molding of a cornice below the corona and above the frieze; *also* : a molding below a deep projection

bed of roses (1648) : a place or situation of agreeable ease

bed·ou·in *or* **bed·u·in** \'be-də-wən\ *n, pl* **bedouin** *or* **bedouins** *or* **beduin** *or* **beduins** *often cap* [ME *Bedoyne*, fr. MF *bedoin*, fr. Ar *badawī* desert dweller] (15c) : a nomadic Arab of the Arabian, Syrian, or No. African deserts

bed·pan \'bed-,pan\ *n* (1678) : a shallow vessel used by a bedridden person for urination or defecation

bed·plate \-,plāt\ *n* (1850) : a plate or framing used as a support

bed·post \-,pōst\ *n* (1598) : the usu. turned or carved post of a bed

be·drag·gle \bi-'dra-gəl\ *vt* (1727) : to wet thoroughly

\ə\ abut \ᵊ\ kitten, F table \ər\ further \a\ ash \ā\ ace \ä\ mop, mar
\aú\ out \ch\ chin \e\ bet \ē\ easy \g\ go \i\ hit \ī\ ice \j\ job
\ŋ\ sing \ō\ go \ó\ law \ói\ boy \th\ thin \t̲h̲\ the \ü\ loot \ú\ foot
\y\ yet \zh\ vision \á, k̲, ⁿ, œ, œ̄, ūe, ᵊ\ see Guide to Pronunciation

be·drag·gled \bi-'dra-gəld\ *adj* (1824) **1** : left wet and limp by or as if by rain **2** : soiled and stained by or as if by trailing in mud **3** : DILAPIDATED ⟨~ buildings⟩

bed rest *n* (1944) : confinement of a sick person to bed

bed·rid·den \'bed-ˌri-d°n\ *also* **bed·rid** \-ˌrid\ *adj* [alter. of ME *bedrede, bedreden,* fr. OE *bedreda,* fr. *bedreda* one confined to bed, fr. *bedd* bed + *-rida, -reda,* fr. *rīdan* to ride] (bef. 12c) : confined (as by illness) to bed

¹bed·rock \'räk, -ˌräk\ *n* (1850) **1** : the solid rock underlying unconsolidated surface materials (as soil) **2 a** : lowest point : NADIR **b** : BASIS

²bed·rock *adj* (1896) : solidly fundamental, basic, or reliable ⟨traditional ~ values⟩ ⟨a ~ constituency⟩

bed·roll \-ˌrōl\ *n* (1910) : bedding rolled up for carrying

¹bed·room \-ˌrüm, -ˌrum\ *n* (1616) : a room furnished with a bed and intended primarily for sleeping — **bed·roomed** \-ˌrümd, -ˌrumd\ *adj*

²bed·room *adj* (1915) **1** : dealing with, suggestive of, or inviting sexual relations ⟨a ~ farce⟩ ⟨~ eyes⟩ **2** : inhabited or used by commuters ⟨a ~ community⟩

bed·sheet \'bed-ˌshēt\ *n* (15c) : an oblong piece of usu. cotton or linen cloth used as an article of bedding

¹bed·side \'bed-ˌsīd\ *n* (14c) : the side of a bed : a place beside a bed

²bed·side *adj* (1837) **1** : of, relating to, or conducted at the bedside ⟨a ~ diagnosis⟩ **2** : suitable for reading in bed ⟨a ~ book⟩

bedside manner *n* (1869) : the manner that a physician assumes toward patients

bed·sit·ter \'bed-ˌsi-tər\ *n* [*bed-sitting* room + *-er* (as in *fresher* freshman, *rugger* rugby)] (1927) *Brit* : a one-room apartment serving as both bedroom and sitting room — called also *bedsit, bed-sitting-room*

bed·sore \'bed-ˌsōr, -ˌsȯr\ *n* (1861) : an ulceration of tissue deprived of adequate blood supply by prolonged pressure

bed·spread \-ˌspred\ *n* (1845) : a usu. ornamental cloth cover for a bed

bed·spring \-ˌspriŋ\ *n* (1897) : a spring supporting a mattress

bed·stead \'bed-ˌsted\ *n* [ME *bedstede,* fr. *bed* + *stede* stead, place — more at STEAD] (15c) : the framework of a bed

bed·straw \-ˌstrȯ\ *n* [fr. its use for mattresses] (1527) : any of a genus (*Galium*) of herbs of the madder family having squarish stems, whorled leaves, and small flowers

bed table *n* (1811) **1** : an adjustable table used (as for eating or writing) by a person in bed **2** : a small table beside a bed

bed·time \-ˌtīm\ *n* (13c) : a time for going to bed

bedtime story *n* (1899) : a story read or recounted to someone (as a child) at bedtime

be·du \'be-(ˌ)dü\ *n, pl* **bedu** *often cap* [Ar *badw* Bedouins, lit., desert] (1912) : BEDOUIN

bed warmer *n* (1922) : a covered pan containing hot coals used to warm a bed

bed–wet·ting \-ˌwe-tiŋ\ *n* (1890) : enuresis esp. when occurring in bed during sleep — **bed wetter** *n*

¹bee \'bē\ *n* [ME, fr. OE *bēo;* akin to OHG *bia* bee, OIr *bech,* Lith *bitis*] (bef. 12c) **1** : HONEYBEE; *broadly* : any of numerous insects (superfamily Apoidea) that differ from the related wasps esp. in the heavier hairier body and in having sucking as well as chewing mouthparts, that feed on pollen and nectar, and that store both and often also honey **2** : an eccentric notion — FANCY — **bee·like** \-ˌlīk\ *adj* — **bee in one's bonnet** : ¹BEE 2

²bee *n* (14c) : the letter B

³bee *n* [perh. fr. E dial. *been* help given by neighbors, fr. ME *bene* prayer, boon, fr. E dial. *bēn* prayer — more at BOON] (1769) : a gathering of people for a specific purpose ⟨quilting ~⟩

bee balm *n* (1840) **1** : any of several monardas; *esp* : OSWEGO TEA **2** : LEMON BALM

bee-bee *var of* BB

bee·bread \'bē-ˌbred\ *n* (1657) : bitter yellowish brown pollen stored up in honeycomb cells and used mixed with honey by bees as food

beech \'bēch\ *n, pl* **beech·es** *or* **beech** [ME *beche,* fr. OE *bēce;* akin to OE *bōc* beech, OHG *buohha,* L *fagus,* Gk *phēgos* oak] (bef. 12c) : any of a genus (*Fagus* of the family Fagaceae, the beech family) of hardwood trees with smooth gray bark and small edible nuts; *also* : its wood — **beech·en** \'bē-chən\ *adj*

beech·drops \'bēch-ˌdräps\ *n pl but sing or pl in constr* (1815) : a plant (*Epifagus virginiana*) of the broomrape family parasitic on the roots of beeches

beech·nut \-ˌnət\ *n* (1739) : the nut of the beech

bee–eat·er \'bē-ˌē-tər\ *n* (1668) : any of a family (Meropidae) of brightly colored slender-billed insectivorous chiefly tropical Old World birds

¹beef \'bēf\ *n, pl* **beefs** \'bēfs\ *or* **beeves** \'bēvz\ [ME, fr. OF *buef* ox, beef, fr. L *bov-, bos* head of cattle — more at COW] (14c) **1** : the flesh of an adult domestic bovine (as a steer or cow) used as food **2 a** : an ox, cow, or bull in a full-grown or nearly full-grown state; *esp* : a steer or cow fattened for food ⟨quality Texas *beeves*⟩ ⟨a herd of good ~⟩ **b** : a dressed carcass of a beef animal **3** : muscular flesh : BRAWN **4** *pl* **beefs** : COMPLAINT

²beef *vt* (1860) : to add substance, strength, or power to — usu. used with *up* ⟨money to ~ up its staff of professional economists —John Fischer⟩ ~ *vi* : COMPLAIN

beef·a·lo \'bē-fə-ˌlō\ *n, pl* **-a·los** *or* **-a·loes** [blend of ¹*beef* and *buffalo*] (1973) : any of a breed of beef cattle developed in the U.S. that is genetically ⅜ No. American bison and ⅝ domestic bovine

beef·cake \'bēf-ˌkāk\ *n* (1949) : a usu. photographic display of muscular male physiques; *also* : men of the type featured in such a display — compare CHEESECAKE

beef cattle *n pl* (1758) : cattle developed primarily for the efficient production of meat and marked by capacity for rapid growth, heavy well-fleshed body, and stocky build

beef·eat·er \'bē-ˌfē-tər\ *n, often cap* (1671) : a yeoman of the guard of an English monarch

bee fly *n* (1852) : any of a family (Bombyliidae) of dipteran flies many of which resemble bees

beef·steak \'bēf-ˌstāk\ *n* (1711) : a steak of beef usu. from the hindquarter

beefsteak tomato *n* (1968) : a very large globe-shaped red tomato with dense flesh

beef Stro·ga·noff \-'strȯ-gə-ˌnȯf, -'strō-\ *n* [Count Paul Stroganoff, 19th cent. Russ. diplomat] (1932) : beef sliced thin and cooked in a sour-cream sauce

beef Wel·ling·ton \-'we-liŋ-tən\ *n* [prob. fr. the name *Wellington*] (1965) : a fillet of beef covered with pâté de foie gras and baked in a casing of pastry

beef·wood \'bēf-ˌwùd\ *n* (1805) **1** : the hard heavy reddish wood of any of various chiefly tropical trees (as the Australian pine) **2** : AUSTRALIAN PINE

beefy \'bē-fē\ *adj* **beef·i·er; -est** (1743) **1 a** : heavily and powerfully built **b** : SUBSTANTIAL, STURDY **2** : full of beef

bee·hive \'bē-ˌhīv\ *n* (14c) **1** : HIVE 1 **2** : something resembling a hive for bees: as **a** : a scene of crowded activity **b** : a woman's hairdo that is conical in shape — **beehive** *adj*

beehive oven *n* (ca. 1881) : an arched oven used esp. for baking food and formerly for coking coal

bee·keep·er \-ˌkē-pər\ *n* (1817) : a person who raises bees — **bee·keep·ing** *n*

¹bee·line \-ˌlīn\ *n* [fr. the belief that nectar-laden bees return to their hives in a direct line] (1830) : a straight direct course

²beeline *vi* (1940) : to go quickly in a straight direct course

Beel·ze·bub \bē-'el-zi-ˌbəb, 'bēl-zi-, 'bel-\ *n* [*Beelzebub,* prince of devils, fr. L, fr. Gk *Beelzeboub,* fr. Heb *Ba'al zĕbhūbh,* a Philistine god, lit., lord of flies] (bef. 12c) **1** : DEVIL **2** : a fallen angel in Milton's *Paradise Lost* ranking next to Satan

been *past part of* BE

¹beep \'bēp\ *n* [imit.] (1929) : a short usu. high-pitched sound (as from a horn or an electronic device) that serves as a signal or warning

²beep *vi* (1936) **1** : to sound a horn **2** : to make a beep ~ *vt* : to cause (as a horn) to sound

beep·er \'bē-pər\ *n* (1970) : an electronic device that beeps to make contact with the person carrying it when it receives a special radio signal

beer \'bir\ *n* [ME *ber,* fr. OE *bēor;* akin to OHG *bior* beer] (bef. 12c) **1** : an alcoholic beverage usu. made from malted cereal grain (as barley), flavored with hops, and brewed by slow fermentation **2** : a carbonated nonalcoholic or a fermented slightly alcoholic beverage with flavoring from roots or other plant parts ⟨birch ~⟩ **3** : fermented mash **4** : a drink of beer

beer and skittles *n pl but sing or pl in constr* (1857) : a situation of agreeable ease ⟨won't be all *beer and skittles*⟩

beery \'bir-ē\ *adj* **beer·i·er; -est** (1848) **1** : smelling or tasting of beer ⟨~ tavern⟩ **2** : affected or caused by beer ⟨~ voices⟩

bees·tings \'bē-stiŋz\ *n pl but sing or pl in constr* [ME *bestynge,* fr. OE *bȳsting,* fr. *bēost* beestings; akin to OHG *biost* beestings] (bef. 12c) : the colostrum esp. of a cow

bee–stung \'bē-ˌstəŋ\ *adj* (1933) : having a red puffy appearance as if from being stung by a bee ⟨~ lips⟩

bees·wax \'bēz-ˌwaks\ *n* (1676) : WAX 1

beet \'bēt\ *n* [ME *bete,* fr. OE *bēte,* fr. L *beta*] (bef. 12c) : a biennial garden plant (*Beta vulgaris*) of the goosefoot family that has several cultivars (as Swiss chard and sugar beet) and possesses thick long-stalked edible leaves and swollen root used as a vegetable, as a source of sugar, or for forage; *also* : its root

beet armyworm *n* (1902) : an armyworm (*Spodoptera exigua*) that eats the foliage of beets, alfalfa, and vegetables

¹bee·tle \'bē-t°l\ *n* [ME *betylle,* fr. OE *bitula;* akin to *bītan* to bite] (bef. 12c) **1** : any of an order (Coleoptera) of insects having four wings of which the outer pair are modified into stiff elytra that protect the inner pair when at rest **2** : any of various insects resembling a beetle

²beetle *vi* **bee·tled; bee·tling** \'bē-t°l-iŋ\ (ca. 1919) : to scurry like a beetle ⟨editors *beetled* around the office⟩

³beetle *n* [ME *betel,* fr. OE *bietel;* akin to OE *bēatan* to beat] (bef. 12c) **1** : a heavy wooden hammering or ramming instrument **2** : a wooden pestle or bat for domestic tasks

⁴beetle *adj* [ME *bitel-browed* having overhanging brows, prob. fr. *betylle, bitel* beetle] (14c) : being prominent and overhanging ⟨~ brows⟩

⁵bee·tle *vi* **bee·tled; bee·tling** \'bē-t°l-iŋ\ (1602) : PROJECT, JUT ⟨to scale the *beetling* crags —R. L. Stevenson⟩

beet leafhopper *n* (1919) : a leafhopper (*Circulifer tenellus*) that transmits curly top virus to sugar beets and other garden plants

bee tree *n* (1782) : a hollow tree in which honeybees nest

beet·root \'bēt-ˌrüt\ *n* (1579) *chiefly Brit* : a beet grown for its edible usu. red root; *also* : the root

beeves *pl of* BEEF

bee·yard \'bē-ˌyärd\ *n* (15c) : APIARY

be·fall \bi-'fȯl\ *vb* **-fell** \-'fel\; **-fall·en** \-'fȯ-lən\ *vi* (13c) : to happen esp. as if by fate ~ *vt* : to happen to

be·fit \bi-'fit\ *vt* **be·fit·ted; be·fit·ting** (15c) : to be proper or becoming to

be·fit·ting \-'fi-tiŋ\ *adj* (1564) **1** : SUITABLE, APPROPRIATE **2** : PROPER, DECENT — **be·fit·ting·ly** \-tiŋ-lē\ *adv*

be·fog \bi-'fȯg, -'fäg\ *vt* (1601) **1** : CONFUSE **2** : FOG, OBSCURE

be·fool \bi-'fül\ *vt* (14c) **1** : to make a fool of **2** : DELUDE, DECEIVE

¹be·fore \bi-'fȯr, -'fȯr\ *adv or adj* [ME, adv. & prep., fr. OE *beforan,* fr. *be-* + *foran* before, fr. *fore*] (bef. 12c) **1** : in advance : AHEAD ⟨marching on ~⟩ **2** : at an earlier time : PREVIOUSLY ⟨the night ~⟩ ⟨knew her from ~⟩

²before *prep* (bef. 12c) **1 a (1)** : in front of **(2)** : in the presence of **b** : under the jurisdiction or consideration of ⟨the case ~ the court⟩ **c (1)** : at the disposal of **(2)** : in store for **2** : preceding in time : ear-

¹beef \'bē\
beeves \'bēvz\

beef 2b: A wholesale cuts: *1* shank, *2* round with rump and shank cut off, *3* rump, *4* sirloin, *5* short loin, *6* flank, *7* rib, *8* chuck, *9* plate, *10* brisket, *11* shank; B retail cuts: *a* heel pot roast, *b* round steak, *c* rump roast, *d* sirloin steak, *e* pinbone steak, *f* short ribs, *g* porterhouse, *h* T-bone, *i* club steak, *j* flank steak, *k* rib roast, *l* blade rib roast, *m* plate, *n* brisket, *o* crosscut shank, *p* arm pot roast, *q* boneless neck, *r* blade roast

lier than   **3** : in a higher or more important position than ⟨put quantity ~ quality⟩
³before *conj* (13c)   **1 a** (1) : earlier than the time that ⟨call me ~ you go⟩   (2) : sooner or quicker than ⟨I'll be done ~ you know it⟩   (3) : so that . . . do not ⟨get out of there ~ you get dirty⟩   **b** : until the time that ⟨miles to go ~ I sleep —Robert Frost⟩   **c** (1) : or else . . . not ⟨must be convicted ~ he can be removed from office⟩   (2) : or else ⟨get out of here ~ I call a cop⟩   **2** : rather or sooner than ⟨would starve ~ he'd steal⟩
be·fore·hand \bi-'fōr-,hand, -'fȯr-\ *adv or adj* (13c)   **1 a** : in anticipation   **b** : in advance   **2** : ahead of time : EARLY
be·fore·time \-,tīm\ *adv* (14c) *archaic* : FORMERLY
be·foul \bi-'fau̇(ə)l\ *vt* (bef. 12c) : to make foul with or as if with dirt
be·friend \bi-'frend\ *vt* (1559) : to act as a friend to
be·fud·dle \bi-'fə-d⁰l\ *vt* (ca. 1879)   **1** : to muddle or stupefy with or as if with drink   **2** : CONFUSE, PERPLEX — **be·fud·dle·ment** \-mənt\ *n*
beg \'beg\ *vb* **begged; beg·ging** [ME *beggen*] *vt* (13c)   **1** : to ask for as a charity   **2 a** : to ask earnestly for : ENTREAT   **b** : to require as necessary or appropriate   **3 a** : EVADE, SIDESTEP ⟨*begged* the real problems⟩   **b** : to pass over or ignore by assuming to be established or settled ⟨~ the question⟩   ~ *vi*   **1** : to ask for alms   **2** : to ask earnestly ⟨*begged* for mercy⟩
syn BEG, ENTREAT, BESEECH, IMPLORE, SUPPLICATE, ADJURE, IMPORTUNE mean to ask urgently. BEG suggests earnestness or insistence esp. in asking for a favor ⟨children *begging* to stay up late⟩. ENTREAT implies an effort to persuade or to overcome resistance ⟨*entreated* him to change his mind⟩. BESEECH implies great eagerness or anxiety ⟨I *beseech* you to have mercy⟩. IMPLORE adds to BESEECH a suggestion of greater urgency or anguished appeal ⟨*implored* her not to leave him⟩. SUPPLICATE suggests a posture of humility ⟨with bowed heads they *supplicated* their Lord⟩. ADJURE implies advising as well as pleading and suggests the invoking of something sacred ⟨in God's name I *adjure* you to cease⟩. IMPORTUNE suggests an annoying persistence in trying to break down resistance to a request ⟨*importuning* viewers for contributions⟩.
be·get \bi-'get\ *vt* **-got** \-'gät\ *also* **-gat** \-'gat\; **-got·ten** \-'gä-t⁰n\ *or* **-got; -get·ting** [ME *begeten*, alter. of *beyeten*, fr. OE *bigietan* — more at GET] (13c)   **1** : to procreate as the father : SIRE   **2** : to produce esp. as an effect or outgrowth — **be·get·ter** *n*
¹beg·gar \'be-gər\ *n* [ME *beggere, beggare*, fr. *beggen* to beg + *-ere, -are* ²-er] (13c)   **1** : one that begs; *esp* : a person who lives by asking for gifts   **2** : PAUPER   **3** : FELLOW 4c
²beggar *vt* **beg·gared; beg·gar·ing** \'be-gə-riŋ\ (15c)   **1** : to reduce to beggary   **2** : to exceed the resources or abilities of : DEFY ⟨~s description⟩
beg·gar·ly \'be-gər-lē\ *adj* (1526)   **1** : contemptibly mean, scant, petty, or paltry   **2** : befitting or resembling a beggar; *esp* : marked by extreme poverty — **beg·gar·li·ness** *n*
beg·gar's-lice \'be-gərz-,līs\ *or* **beg·gar-lice** \-gər-,līs\ *n pl but sing or pl in constr* (1837) : any of various plants (as of the genera *Hackelia* and *Cynoglossum*) with prickly or adhesive fruits; *also* : one of these fruits
beg·gar–ticks *also* **beg·gar's-ticks** \-,tiks\ *n pl but sing or pl in constr* (ca. 1818)   **1** : BUR MARIGOLD; *also* : its prickly achenes   **2** : BEGGAR'S-LICE
beg·gar·weed \'be-gər-,wēd\ *n* (ca. 1809) : any of various plants (as a knotgrass, spurrey, or dodder) that grow in waste ground   **2** : any of several tick trefoils (genus *Desmodium*); *esp* : a West Indian forage plant (*D. tortuosum*) cultivated in the southern U.S.
beg·gary \'be-gə-rē\ *n, pl* **-gar·ies** (14c)   **1** : POVERTY, PENURY   **2** : the class of beggars   **3** : the practice of begging
be·gin \bi-'gin\ *vb* **be·gan** \-'gan\; **be·gun** \-'gən\; **be·gin·ning** [ME *beginnen*, fr. OE *beginnan*; akin to OHG *biginnan* to begin, OE *onginnan*] *vi* (bef. 12c)   **1** : to do the first part of an action : go into the first part of a process : START   **2 a** : to come into existence : ARISE   **b** : to have a starting point   **3** : to do or succeed in the least degree ⟨I can't ~ to tell you how pleased I am⟩   ~ *vt*   **1** : to set about the activity of : START   **2 a** : to bring into being : FOUND   **b** : ORIGINATE, INVENT — **to begin with** : as the first thing to be considered
syn BEGIN, COMMENCE, START, INITIATE, INAUGURATE, USHER IN mean to take the first step in a course, process, or operation. BEGIN, START, and COMMENCE are often interchangeable. BEGIN, opposed to *end*, is the most general ⟨*begin* a trip⟩ ⟨*began* dancing⟩. START, opposed to *stop*, applies esp. to first actions, steps, or stages ⟨the work *started* slowly⟩. COMMENCE can be more formal or bookish than BEGIN or START ⟨*commence* firing⟩ ⟨*commenced* a conversation⟩. INITIATE implies taking a first step in a process or series that is to continue ⟨*initiated* diplomatic contacts⟩. INAUGURATE suggests a beginning of some formality or notion of significance ⟨the discovery of penicillin *inaugurated* a new era in medicine⟩. USHER IN is somewhat less weighty than INAUGURATE ⟨*ushered* in a period of economic decline⟩.
be·gin·ner \bi-'gi-nər\ *n* (14c) : one that begins something; *esp* : an inexperienced person
¹be·gin·ning \bi-'gi-niŋ\ *n* (12c)   **1** : the point at which something begins : START   **2** : the first part   **3** : ORIGIN, SOURCE   **4** : a rudimentary stage or early period — usu. used in pl.
²beginning *adj* (1576)   **1** : just starting out ⟨a ~ writer⟩   **2 a** : being first or the first part ⟨the ~ chapters⟩   **b** : INTRODUCTORY ⟨~ chemistry⟩
beginning rhyme *n* (1913)   **1** : rhyme at the beginning of successive lines of verse   **2** : ALLITERATION
be·gird \bi-'gərd\ *vt* **-gird·ed** *or* **-girt** \-'gərt\; **-girt·ing** (bef. 12c)   **1** : GIRD 1a   **2** : SURROUND, ENCOMPASS
be·glam·our *also* **be·glam·or** \bi-'gla-mər\ *vt* (1822) : to impress or deceive with glamour
beg off *vi* (1854) : to ask to be excused from something — **beg–off** \'beg-,ȯf\ *n*
be·gone \bi-'gȯn *also* -'gän\ *vi* [ME, fr. *be gone* (imper.)] (14c) : to go away : DEPART — used esp. in the imperative
be·go·nia \bi-'gōn-yə\ *n* [NL, fr. Michel *Bégon* †1710 Fr. governor of Santo Domingo] (1751) : any of a large genus (*Begonia* of the family Begoniaceae, the begonia family) of tropical herbs and shrubs that have asymmetrical leaves and are widely cultivated as ornamentals

be·gor·ra \bi-'gȯr-ə, -'gär-\ *interj* [euphemism for *by God*] (1839) *Irish* — used as a mild oath
be·grime \bi-'grīm\ *vt* **be·grimed; be·grim·ing** (ca. 1553)   **1** : to make dirty with grime   **2** : SULLY, CORRUPT
be·grudge \bi-'grəj\ *vt* (14c)   **1** : to give or concede reluctantly or with displeasure   **2** : to look upon with disapproval — **be·grudg·ing·ly** \-'grə-jiŋ-lē\ *adv*
be·guile \bi-'gī(ə)l\ *vb* **be·guiled; be·guil·ing** *vt* (13c)   **1** : to lead by deception   **2** : HOODWINK   **3** : to while away esp. by some agreeable occupation; *also* : DIVERT 2   **4** : to engage the interest of by or as if by guile   ~ *vi* : to deceive by wiles   **syn** see DECEIVE — **be·guile·ment** \-'gī(ə)l-mənt\ *n* — **be·guil·er** \-'gī-lər\ *n* — **be·guil·ing·ly** \-'gī-liŋ-lē\ *adv*
be·guine \bi-'gēn\ *n* [AmerF *béguine*, fr. F *béguin* flirtation] (1935) : a vigorous popular dance of the islands of Saint Lucia and Martinique that somewhat resembles the rumba
Be·guine \'bā-,gēn, ,bā-'\ *n* [MF] (15c) : a member of one of various ascetic and philanthropic communities of women not under vows founded chiefly in the Netherlands in the 13th century
be·gum \'bā-gəm, 'bē-\ *n* [Hindi *begam*] (1617) : a Muslim woman of high rank (as in India or Pakistan)
be·half \bi-'haf, -'häf\ *n* [ME, fr. *by* + *half* half, side] (14c) : INTEREST, BENEFIT; *also* : SUPPORT, DEFENSE ⟨argued in his ~⟩ — **on behalf of** *or* **in behalf of** : in the interest of; *also* : as a representative of
usage A body of opinion favors *in* with the "interest, benefit" sense of *behalf* and *on* with the "support, defense" sense. This distinction has been observed by some writers but overall has never had a sound basis in actual usage. In current British use, *on behalf* (*of*) has replaced *in behalf* (*of*); both are still used in American English, but the distinction is frequently not observed.
be·have \bi-'hāv\ *vb* **be·haved; be·hav·ing** [ME *behaven*, fr. *be-* + *haven* to have, hold] *vt* (15c)   **1** : to manage the actions of (oneself) in a particular way   **2** : to conduct (oneself) in a proper manner   ~ *vi*   **1** : to act, function, or react in a particular way   **2** : to conduct oneself properly — **be·hav·er** *n*
syn BEHAVE, CONDUCT, DEPORT, COMPORT, ACQUIT mean to act or to cause oneself to do something in a certain way. BEHAVE may apply to the meeting of a standard of what is proper or decorous ⟨the children *behaved* in church⟩. CONDUCT implies action or behavior that shows the extent of one's power to control or direct oneself ⟨*conducted* herself with unfailing good humor⟩. DEPORT implies behaving so as to show how far one conforms to conventional rules of discipline or propriety ⟨the hero *deported* himself in accord with the code of chivalry⟩. COMPORT suggests conduct measured by what is expected or required of one in a certain class or position ⟨*comported* themselves as gentlemen⟩. ACQUIT applies to action under stress that deserves praise or meets expectations ⟨*acquitted* herself well in her first assignment⟩.
be·hav·ior \bi-'hā-vyər\ *n* [alter. of ME *behavour*, fr. *behaven*] (15c)   **1 a** : the manner of conducting oneself   **b** : anything that an organism does involving action and response to stimulation   **c** : the response of an individual, group, or species to its environment   **2** : the way in which someone behaves; *also* : an instance of such behavior   **3** : the way in which something functions or operates — **be·hav·ior·al** \-vyə-rəl\ *adj* — **be·hav·ior·al·ly** \-rə-lē\ *adv*
behavioral science *n* (1951) : a science (as psychology, sociology, or anthropology) that deals with human action and seeks to generalize about human behavior in society — **behavioral scientist** *n*
be·hav·ior·ism \bi-'hā-vyə-,ri-zəm\ *n* (1913) : a school of psychology that takes the objective evidence of behavior (as measured responses to stimuli) as the only concern of its research and the only basis of its theory without reference to conscious experience — compare INTROSPECTIONISM — **be·hav·ior·ist** \-vyə-rist\ *adj or n* — **be·hav·ior·is·tic** \-,hā-vyə-'ris-tik\ *adj*
behavior therapy *n* (1961) : psychotherapy that emphasizes the application of the principles of learning to substitute desirable responses and behavior patterns for undesirable ones — called also *behavior modification*
be·hav·iour *chiefly Brit var of* BEHAVIOR
be·head \bi-'hed\ *vt* (bef. 12c) : to cut off the head of : DECAPITATE
be·he·moth \bi-'hē-məth, 'bē-ə-məth, -,mäth, -,mȯth\ *n, often attrib* [ME, fr. LL, fr. Heb *běhēmōth*] (14c)   **1** *often cap* : a mighty animal described in Job 40:15–24 as an example of the power of God   **2** : something of monstrous size or power
be·hest \bi-'hest\ *n* [ME, promise, command, fr. OE *behǣs* promise, fr. *behātan* to promise, fr. *be-* + *hātan* to command, promise — more at HIGHT] (12c)   **1** : an authoritative order : COMMAND   **2** : an urgent prompting ⟨called at the ~ of my friends⟩
¹be·hind \bi-'hīnd\ *adv or adj* [ME *behinde*, fr. OE *behindan*, fr. *be-* + *hindan* from behind; akin to OE *hinder* behind — more at HIND] (bef. 12c)   **1 a** : in the place or situation that is being or has been departed from ⟨stay ~⟩   **b** : in, to, or toward the back ⟨look ~⟩ ⟨came from ~⟩   **c** : later in time ⟨can spring be far ~⟩   **2 a** : in a secondary or inferior position   **b** : in arrears ⟨~ in the rent⟩   **c** : SLOW   **3** *archaic* : still to come
²behind *prep* (bef. 12c)   **1 a** : in or to a place or situation in back of or to the rear of ⟨look ~ you⟩ ⟨put ~ bars⟩   **b** — used as a function word to indicate something that screens an observer ⟨the sun went ~ a cloud⟩   **c** : following in order ⟨marched ~ the band⟩   **2** — used as a function word to indicate backwardness, delay, or deficiency ⟨~ the times⟩ ⟨~ schedule⟩ ⟨lagged ~ last year's sales⟩   **3 a** : in the background of ⟨the conditions ~ the strike⟩   **b** : out of the mind or consideration of ⟨put our troubles ~ us⟩   **c** : beyond in depth or time ⟨the story ~ the story⟩ ⟨go back ~ St. Augustine⟩   **4 a** : in support of : on the side of ⟨solidly ~ the candidate⟩   **b** : with the support of ⟨won 1–0 ~ brilliant pitching⟩
³behind *n* [¹*behind*] (ca. 1830) : BUTTOCKS

\ə\ abut \ᵊ\ kitten, F table \ər\ further \a\ ash \ā\ ace \ä\ mop, mar
\au̇\ out \ch\ chin \e\ bet \ē\ easy \g\ go \i\ hit \ī\ ice \j\ job
\ŋ\ sing \ō\ go \ȯ\ law \ȯi\ boy \th\ thin \t͟h\ the \ü\ loot \u̇\ foot
\y\ yet \zh\ vision \á, k̲, ⁿ, œ, œ̄, ᵫ, ᵫ̄, ʸ\ see Guide to Pronunciation

be·hind·hand \bi-'hīnd-,hand\ *adj* (1535) **1** : being in arrears **2 a** : being in an inferior position **b** : being behind schedule

behind–the–scenes *adj* (1711) **1** : being or working out of public view or in secret 〈~ wrangling〉 〈a ~ player〉 **2** : revealing or reporting the hidden workings 〈a ~ account〉 〈a ~ glimpse〉

be·hold \bi-'hōld\ *vb* **-held** \-'held\; **-hold·ing** [ME, to keep, behold, fr. OE *behealdan*, fr. *be-* + *healdan* to hold] *vt* (bef. 12c) **1** : to perceive through sight or apprehension : SEE **2** : to gaze upon : OBSERVE ~ *vi* — used in the imperative esp. to call attention — **be·hold·er** *n*

be·hold·en \bi-'hōl-dən\ *adj* [ME, fr. pp. of *beholden*] (14c) : being under obligation for a favor or gift : INDEBTED 〈I'm ~ to you〉

be·hoof \bi-'hüf\ *n* [ME *behof*, fr. OE *behōf* profit, need; akin to OE *hebban* to raise — more at HEAVE] (bef. 12c) : ADVANTAGE, PROFIT 〈for his own ~〉

be·hoove \bi-'hüv\ *vb* **be·hooved; be·hoov·ing** [ME *behoven*, fr. OE *behōfian*, fr. *behōf*] *vt* (bef. 12c) : to be necessary, proper, or advantageous for 〈it ~s us to go〉 ~ *vi* : to be necessary, fit, or proper

be·hove \bi-'hōv\ *chiefly Brit var of* BEHOOVE

¹beige \'bāzh\ *n* [F] (ca. 1858) **1** : cloth made of natural undyed wool **2 a** : a variable color averaging light grayish yellowish brown **b** : a pale to grayish yellow — **beigy** \'bā-zhē\ *adj*

²beige *adj* (1879) **1** : of the color beige **2** : VANILLA 2, VAPID

bei·gnet \bān-'yā, ,ben-\ *n* [AmerF & F; AmerF, fr. F, fr. MF *bignet*, fr. *buyne* bump, bruise] (1835) **1** : FRITTER **2** : a light square doughnut

¹be·ing \'bē-(i)ŋ\ *n* (14c) **1 a** : the quality or state of having existence **b** (1) : something conceivable as existing (2) : something that actually exists (3) : the totality of existing things **c** : conscious existence : LIFE **2** : the qualities that constitute an existent thing : ESSENCE; *esp* : PERSONALITY **3** : a living thing; *esp* : PERSON

²being *adj* [prp. of *be*] (14c) : PRESENT — used in the phrase *for the time being*

³being *conj* (1528) *chiefly dial* : SINCE, BECAUSE — usu. used with *as, as how,* or *that*

Be·ja \'bā-jə\ *n, pl* **Beja** (1819) **1** : a member of a pastoral people living between the Nile and the Red Sea **2** : the Cushitic language of the Beja people

be·je·sus *also* **be·jee·zus** \bi-'jē-zəs, -'jā-, -zəz\ *interj* [alter. of *by Jesus*] (ca. 1908) — used as a mild oath; used as a noun for emphasis 〈scares the ~ out of me〉

be·jew·eled *or* **be·jew·elled** \bi-'jü-əld, -'jüld *also* -'jù(-ə)ld\ *adj* (1557) : ornamented with or as if with jewels

bel \'bel\ *n* [Alexander Graham *Bell*] (1929) : ten decibels

be·la·bor \bi-'lā-bər\ *vt* (1596) **1 a** : to attack verbally **b** : to beat soundly **2** : to explain or insist on excessively 〈~ the obvious〉

be·la·bour *chiefly Brit var of* BELABOR

be·lat·ed \bi-'lā-təd\ *adj* [pp. of *belate* (to make late)] (1670) **1** : delayed beyond the usual time **2** : existing or appearing past the normal or proper time — **be·lat·ed·ly** *adv* — **be·lat·ed·ness** *n*

be·laud \bi-'lòd\ *vt* (ca. 1849) : to praise unduly : to excess

¹be·lay \bi-'lā\ *vb* [ME *beleggen* to beset, fr. OE *belecgan*, fr. *be-* + *lecgan* to lay] *vt* (1548) **1 a** : to secure (as a rope) by turns around a cleat, pin, or bitt **b** : to make fast **2** : STOP **3 a** : to secure (a person) at the end of a rope **b** : to secure (a rope) to a person or object ~ *vi* **1** : to be made fast **2** : STOP, QUIT — used in the imperative 〈~ there〉 **3** : to make a line fast by turns around a cleat, pin, or bitt

²belay *n* (1908) **1** : the securing of a person or a safety rope to an anchor point (as during mountain climbing); *also* : a method of so securing a person or rope **2** : something (as a projection of rock) to which a person or rope is anchored

bel can·to \bel-'kän-(,)tō, -'kan-\ *n* [It, lit., beautiful singing] (1894) : operatic singing originating in 17th century and 18th century Italy and stressing ease, purity, and evenness of tone production and an agile and precise vocal technique

belch \'belch\ *vb* [ME, fr. OE *bealcan*] *vi* (bef. 12c) **1** : to expel gas suddenly from the stomach through the mouth **2** : to erupt, explode, or detonate violently **3** : to issue forth spasmodically : GUSH ~ *vt* **1** : to eject or emit violently **2** : to expel (gas) from the stomach suddenly : ERUCT — **belch** *n*

bel·dam *or* **bel·dame** \'bel-dəm\ *n* [ME *beldam* grandmother, fr. MF *bel* beautiful + ME *dam*] (1580) : an old woman

be·lea·guer \bi-'lē-gər\ *vt* **-guered; -guer·ing** \-g(ə-)riŋ\ [D *belegeren*, fr. *be-* (akin to OE *be-*) + *leger* camp; akin to OHG *legar* bed — more at LAIR] (1587) **1** : BESIEGE **2** : TROUBLE, HARASS 〈~ed parents〉 — **be·lea·guer·ment** \-mənt\ *n*

bel·em·nite \'bel-əm-,nīt\ *n* [NL *belemnites*, fr. Gk *belemnon* dart; akin to Gk *ballein* to throw — more at DEVIL] (1646) : any of a genus (*Belemnites*) of extinct cephalopods that had bullet-shaped internal shells and were esp. abundant in the Mesozoic era

bel·fry \'bel-frē\ *n, pl* **belfries** [ME *belfrey*, alter. of *berfrey*, fr. MF *berfrei* bell tower, siege tower, of Gmc origin (akin to MHG *bërvrit* siege tower); akin to OHG *bergan* to shelter and to OE *frith* peace, refuge — more at BURY] (15c) **1** : a bell tower; *esp* : one surmounting or attached to another structure **2** : a room or framework for enclosing a bell **3** : HEAD 2a 〈batty in the ~〉

Bel·gae \'bel-,gī, -,jē\ *n pl* [L, pl. of *Belga*] (ca. 1895) : a people occupying parts of northern Gaul and Britain in Caesar's time — **Bel·gic** \-jik\ *adj*

Bel·gian \'bel-jən\ *n* (ca. 1623) **1** : a native or inhabitant of Belgium **2** : any of a breed of heavy muscular usu. roan or chestnut draft horses developed in Belgium — **Belgian** *adj*

Belgian endive *n* (1931) : ENDIVE 2

Belgian hare *n* (1900) : any of a breed of slender chestnut-colored domestic rabbits

Belgian Ma·li·nois \-,ma-lən-'wä\ *n* (1968) : any of a breed of squarely built working dogs closely related to the Belgian sheepdog and having relatively short straight hair with a dense undercoat — called also *Malinois*

Belgian sheepdog *n* (1929) : any of a breed of hardy black dogs developed in Belgium esp. for herding sheep

Belgian Ter·vu·ren \-(,)tər-'vyür-ən, -ter-\ *n* [*Tervuren*, commune in Brabant, Belgium] (1964) : any of a breed of working dogs closely related to the Belgian sheepdog but having abundant long straight fawn-colored hair with black tips

Be·lial \'bē-lē-əl, 'bēl-yəl\ *n* [Gk, fr. Heb *bĕlīya'al* worthlessness] (13c) **1** — a biblical name of the devil or one of the fiends **2** : one of the fallen angels in Milton's *Paradise Lost*

be·lie \bi-'lī\ *vt* **-lied; -ly·ing** (bef. 12c) **1 a** : to give a false impression of **b** : to present an appearance not in agreement with **2 a** : to show (something) to be false or wrong **b** : to run counter to : CONTRADICT **3** : DISGUISE 3 — **be·li·er** \-'lī(-ə)r\ *n*

be·lief \bə-'lēf\ *n* [ME *beleave*, prob. alter. of OE *gelēafa*, fr. ge-, associative prefix + *lēafan*; akin to OE *lyfan*] (12c) **1** : a state or habit of mind in which trust or confidence is placed in some person or thing **2** : something believed; *esp* : a tenet or body of tenets held by a group **3** : conviction of the truth of some statement or the reality of some being or phenomenon esp. when based on examination of evidence

syn BELIEF, FAITH, CREDENCE, CREDIT mean assent to the truth of something offered for acceptance. BELIEF may or may not imply certitude in the believer 〈my *belief* that I had caught all the errors〉. FAITH almost always implies certitude even where there is no evidence or proof 〈an unshakable *faith* in God〉. CREDENCE suggests intellectual assent without implying anything about grounds for assent 〈a theory now given *credence* by scientists〉. CREDIT may imply assent on grounds other than direct proof 〈gave full *credit* to the statement of a reputable witness〉. **syn** see in addition OPINION

be·liev·able \-'lē-və-bəl\ *adj* (14c) : capable of being believed esp. as within the range of known possibility or probability — **be·liev·abil·i·ty** \-,lē-və-'bi-lə-tē\ *n* — **be·liev·ably** \-'lē-və-blē\ *adv*

be·lieve \bə-'lēv\ *vb* **be·lieved; be·liev·ing** [ME *beleven*, fr. OE *belēfan*, fr. *be-* + *lyfan*, *lēfan* to allow, believe; akin to OHG *gilouben* to believe, OE *lēof* dear — more at LOVE] *vi* (bef. 12c) **1 a** : to have a firm religious faith **b** : to accept as true, genuine, or real 〈ideals we ~ in〉 〈~s in ghosts〉 **2** : to have a firm conviction as to the goodness, efficacy, or ability of something 〈~ in exercise〉 **3** : to hold an opinion : THINK 〈I ~ so〉 ~ *vt* **1 a** : to consider to be true or honest 〈~ the reports〉 〈you wouldn't ~ how long it took〉 **b** : to accept the word or evidence of 〈I ~ you〉 〈couldn't ~ my ears〉 **2** : to hold as an opinion : SUPPOSE 〈I ~ it will rain soon〉 — **be·liev·er** *n* — **not believe :** to be astounded at 〈I couldn't *believe* my luck〉

be·like \bi-'līk\ *adv* (ca. 1533) *archaic* : most likely : PROBABLY

be·lit·tle \bi-'li-t'l\ *vt* **-lit·tled; -lit·tling** \-'li-t'l-iŋ, -'lit-liŋ\ (1797) **1** : to speak slightingly of : DISPARAGE 〈~s her efforts〉 **2** : to cause (a person or thing) to seem little or less — **syn** see DECRY — **be·lit·tle·ment** \-'li-t'l-mənt\ *n* — **be·lit·tler** \-'li-t'l-ər, -'lit-lər\ *n*

be·live \bi-'līv\ *adv* [ME *bilive* vigorously, fr. *by* + *live*, dat. of *lif* life] (1594) *Scot* : in due time : BY AND BY

¹bell \'bel\ *n* [ME *belle*, fr. OE; perh. akin to OE *bellan* to roar — more at BELLOW] (bef. 12c) **1 a** : a hollow metallic device that gives off a reverberating sound when struck **b** : DOORBELL **2 a** : the sounding of a bell as a signal **b** : a stroke of a bell (as on shipboard) to indicate the time; *also* : the time so indicated **c** : a half hour period of a watch on shipboard indicated by the strokes of a bell — see SHIP'S BELLS table below **3** : something having the form of a bell: as **a** : the corolla of a flower **b** : the part of the capital of a column between the abacus and neck molding **c** : the flared end of a wind instrument **4 a** : a percussion instrument consisting of metal bars or tubes that when struck give out tones resembling bells — usu. used in pl. **b** : GLOCKENSPIEL

SHIP'S BELLS

NO. OF BELLS	HOUR (A.M. OR P.M.)		
1	12:30	4:30	8:30
2	1:00	5:00	9:00
3	1:30	5:30	9:30
4	2:00	6:00	10:00
5	2:30	6:30	10:30
6	3:00	7:00	11:00
7	3:30	7:30	11:30
8	4:00	8:00	12:00

²bell *vt* (14c) **1** : to provide with a bell **2** : to flare the end of (as a tube) into the shape of a bell ~ *vi* : to take the form of a bell : FLARE — **bell the cat :** to do a daring or risky deed

³bell *vi* [ME, fr. OE *bellan*] (bef. 12c) : to make a resonant bellowing or baying sound 〈the wild buck ~s from ferny brake —Sir Walter Scott〉

⁴bell *n* (1862) : BELLOW, ROAR

bel·la·don·na \,be-lə-'dä-nə\ *n* [It, lit., beautiful lady] (1597) **1** : an Old World poisonous plant (*Atropa belladonna*) of the nightshade family having purple or green bell-shaped flowers, glossy black berries, and root and leaves that yield atropine — called also *deadly nightshade* **2** : a medicinal extract (as atropine) from the belladonna plant

belladonna lily *n* (1734) : AMARYLLIS

bell-bird \'bel-,bərd\ *n* (1802) : any of various birds (as of the genera *Procnias* and *Anthornis*) whose notes suggest the sound of a bell

bell–bot·toms \'bel-'bä-təmz\ *n pl* (1898) : pants with wide flaring bottoms — **bell–bottom** *adj*

bell–boy \'bel-,bòi\ *n* (1861) : BELLHOP

bell buoy *n* (1838) : a buoy with a bell rung by the action of the waves

bell captain *n* (1926) : CAPTAIN 2c

bell curve *n* [fr. the shape] (ca. 1941) : NORMAL CURVE

belle \'bel\ *n* [F, fr. fem. of *beau* beautiful — more at BEAU] (1622) : a popular and attractive girl or woman; *esp* : a girl or woman whose charm and beauty make her a favorite 〈the ~ of the ball〉

Bel·leek \bə-'lēk\ *n* [*Belleek*, town in Northern Ireland] (1869) : a very thin translucent porcelain with a lustrous pearly glaze produced in Ireland — called also *Belleek china, Belleek ware*

belle epoque *or* **belle époque** \'bel-ā-'pòk\ *n, often cap B&E* [F, lit., beautiful age] (1954) : a period of high artistic or cultural development; *esp* : such a period in fin de siècle France

Bel·ler·o·phon \bə-'ler-ə-fən, -,fän\ *n* [L, fr. Gk *Bellerophōn*] : a legendary Greek hero noted for killing the Chimera

belles let·tres \bel-'letr'\ *n pl but sing in constr* [F, lit., fine letters] (1710) : literature that is an end in itself and not merely informative; *specif* : light, entertaining, and often profound literature

bel·le·trist \bel-'le-trist\ n [belles lettres] (1816) : a writer of belles lettres — **bel·le·tris·tic** \,be-lə-'tris-tik\ adj
bell-flow·er \bel-,flaú(-ə)r\ n (1578) : any of a genus (Campanula of the family Campanulaceae, the bellflower family) of widely cultivated herbs having alternate leaves and usu. showy flowers
bell-hop \-,häp\ n [short for bell-hopper] (1910) : a hotel or club employee who escorts guests to rooms, assists them with luggage, and runs errands
bel·li·cose \'be-li-,kōs\ adj [ME, fr. L bellicosus, fr. bellicus of war, fr. bellum war] (15c) : favoring or inclined to start quarrels or wars **syn** see BELLIGERENT — **bel·li·cos·i·ty** \,be-li-'kä-sə-tē\ n
bel·lied \'be-lēd\ adj (15c) : having a belly of a specified kind — used in combination ⟨a big-bellied man⟩
bel·lig·er·ence \bə-'lij-rən(t)s, -'li-jə-\ n (1814) : an aggressive or truculent attitude, atmosphere, or disposition
bel·lig·er·en·cy \-rən(t)-sē\ n (1863) 1 : the state of being at war or in conflict; specif : the status of a legally recognized belligerent state or nation 2 : BELLIGERENCE
bel·lig·er·ent \-rənt\ adj [modif. of L belligerant-, belligerans, prp. of belligerare to wage war, fr. belliger waging war, fr. bellum + gerere to wage] (1577) 1 : waging war; specif : belonging to or recognized as a state at war and protected by and subject to the laws of war 2 : inclined to or exhibiting assertiveness, hostility, or combativeness — **belligerent** n — **bel·lig·er·ent·ly** adv
syn BELLIGERENT, BELLICOSE, PUGNACIOUS, QUARRELSOME, CONTENTIOUS mean having an aggressive or fighting attitude. BELLIGERENT implies being actually at war or engaged in hostilities ⟨belligerent nations⟩. BELLICOSE suggests a disposition to fight ⟨a drunk in a bellicose mood⟩. PUGNACIOUS suggests a disposition that takes pleasure in personal combat ⟨a pugnacious thug⟩. QUARRELSOME stresses an ill-natured readiness to fight without good cause ⟨the heat made us all quarrelsome⟩. CONTENTIOUS implies perverse and irritating fondness for arguing and quarreling ⟨wearied by his contentious disposition⟩.
bell jar n (ca. 1859) : a bell-shaped usu. glass vessel designed to cover objects or to contain gases or a vacuum
bell–ly·ra \'bel-'lī-rə\ or **bell lyre** \-,lir\ n [lyra fr. L, lyre] (ca. 1943) : a glockenspiel mounted in a portable lyre-shaped frame and used esp. in marching bands
bell·man \'bel-mən\ n (14c) 1 : a man (as a town crier) who rings a bell 2 : BELLHOP
bell metal n (1541) : bronze that consists usu. of three to four parts of copper to one of tin and that is used for making bells
Bel·lo·na \bə-'lō-nə\ n [L] : the Roman goddess of war
bel·low \'be-(,)lō\ vb [ME belwen, fr. OE bylgian; akin to OE & OHG bellan to roar] vi (bef. 12c) 1 : to make the loud deep hollow sound characteristic of a bull 2 : to shout in a deep voice ~ vt : BAWL ⟨~s the orders⟩ — **bellow** n

bell jar

bel·lows \'be-(,)lōz, -ləz\ n pl but sing or pl in constr [ME belu, fr. OE belg — more at BELLY] (bef. 12c) 1 : an instrument or machine that by alternate expansion and contraction draws in air through a valve or orifice and expels it through a tube; also : any of various other blowers 2 : LUNGS 3 : the pleated expansible part in a camera; also : a metallic or plastic flexible and expansible vessel
bell pepper n (1707) : SWEET PEPPER
bell–pull \'bel-,púl\ n (1832) : a handle or knob attached to a cord by which one rings a bell; also : the cord itself
bell push n (1884) : a button that is pushed to ring a bell
bells and whistles n pl (1969) : items or features that are useful or decorative but not essential : FRILLS
bell–shaped \'bel-,shāpt\ adj (ca. 1828) 1 : shaped like a bell 2 : relating to or being a normal curve or a normal distribution
Bell's palsy \'belz-\ n [Sir Charles Bell †1842 Scot. anatomist] (ca. 1860) : paralysis of the facial nerve producing distortion on one side of the face
bell tower n (1614) : a tower that supports or shelters a bell
bell-weth·er \'bel-'we-thər, -,we-\ n [ME, leading sheep of a flock, leader, fr. belle bell + wether; fr. the practice of belling the leader of a flock] (13c) : one that takes the lead or initiative : LEADER; also : an indicator of trends
bell·wort \'bel-,wȯrt, -,wȯrt\ n (1784) : any of a small genus (Uvularia) of herbs of the lily family with yellow drooping flowers
¹**bel·ly** \'be-lē\ n, pl **bellies** [ME bely bellows, belly, fr. OE belg bag, skin; akin to OHG balg bag, skin, OE blāwan to blow — more at BLOW] (bef. 12c) 1 a : ABDOMEN 1; also : POTBELLY 1 b : the stomach and its adjuncts c : the undersurface of an animal's body; also : hide from this part d : WOMB, UTERUS 2 : an internal cavity : INTERIOR 3 : appetite for food 4 : a surface or object curved or rounded like a human belly 5 a : the enlarged fleshy body of a muscle b : the part of a sail that swells out when filled with wind 6 : GUT 1a(2)
²**belly** vb bel·lied; bel·ly·ing vt (1606) : to cause to swell or fill out ~ vi 1 : SWELL, FILL 2 a : to slide or crawl on one's belly b : BELLYLAND
¹**bel·ly·ache** \'be-lē-,āk\ n (1552) : pain in the abdomen and esp. in the bowels : COLIC
²**bellyache** vi (1881) : to complain whiningly or peevishly : find fault — **bel·ly·ach·er** n
bel·ly·band \'be-lē-,band\ n (15c) : a band around or across the belly: as a : GIRTH 1 b : BAND 4b
belly button n (ca. 1877) : the human navel
belly dance n (1899) : a usu. solo dance emphasizing movements of the belly — **belly dance** vi — **belly dancer** n
belly flop n (1895) : a dive (as into water or in coasting prone on a sled) in which the front of the body strikes flat against another surface — called also belly flopper — **belly flop** vi
bel·ly·ful \'be-lē-,fúl\ n (1535) : an excessive amount ⟨a ~ of advice⟩
bel·ly–land \-,land\ vi (1943) : to land an airplane on its undersurface without use of landing gear — **belly landing** n
belly laugh n (1921) : a deep hearty laugh
bel·ly–up \-'əp\ adj [fr. the floating position of a dead fish] (1939) : hopelessly ruined or defeated; esp : BANKRUPT ⟨the business went ~⟩

belly up vi (1948) : to move close or next to ⟨bellied up to the bar⟩
be·long \bi-'lȯŋ\ vb [ME belongen, fr. be- + longen to be suitable — more at LONG] vi (14c) 1 a : to be suitable, appropriate, or advantageous ⟨a dictionary ~s in every home⟩ b : to be in a proper situation ⟨a man of his ability ~s in teaching⟩ 2 a : to be the property of a person or thing — used with to b : to be attached or bound by birth, allegiance, or dependency c : to be a member of a club, organization, or set 3 : to be an attribute, part, adjunct, or function of a person or thing ⟨nuts and bolts ~ to a car⟩ 4 : to be properly classified ~ verbal auxiliary, chiefly Southern & southern Midland : OUGHT, MUST
be·long·ing \-'lȯŋ-iŋ\ n (1817) 1 : POSSESSION — usu. used in pl. 2 : close or intimate relationship ⟨a sense of ~⟩ — **be·long·ing·ness** n
Belo·rus·sian \,be-lō-'rə-shən, ,bye-\ n (1943) 1 : a native or inhabitant of Belorussia (Belarus) 2 : the Slavic language of the Belorussians — **Belorussian** adj
be·loved \bi-'ləvd, -'lə-vəd\ adj [ME, fr. pp. of beloven to love, fr. be- + loven to love] (14c) : dearly loved : dear to the heart — **beloved** n
¹**be·low** \bi-'lō\ adv [ME bilooghe, fr. bi by + looghe ³low] (14c) 1 : in or to a lower place 2 a : on earth b : in or to Hades or hell 3 : on or to a lower floor or deck 4 a : in, to, at, or by a lower rank or number b : below zero ⟨20 degrees ~⟩ 5 : lower on the same page or on a following page 6 : under the surface of the water
²**below** prep (1575) 1 a : lower in place, rank, or value than : UNDER b : down river from c : south of 2 : inferior to (as in rank) 3 : not suitable to the rank of c : BENEATH
³**below** n (1697) : something that is below
⁴**below** adj (1916) : written or discussed lower on the same page or on a following page
be·low–decks \bi-,lō-'deks; -'lō-,deks\ adv (1909) : inside or into the superstructure of a boat : down to a lower deck
be·low–ground \-'graúnd; ,graúnd\ adj (1928) : being under the ground
Bel·shaz·zar \bel-'sha-zər\ n [Heb Bēlshaṣṣar] : a son of Nebuchadnezzar and king of Babylon
¹**belt** \'belt\ n [ME, fr. OE; akin to OHG balz belt; both fr. L balteus belt] (bef. 12c) 1 a : a strip of flexible material worn esp. around the waist b : a similar article worn as a corset or for protection or safety or as a symbol of distinction 2 : a continuous band of tough flexible material for transmitting motion and power or conveying materials 3 : an area characterized by some distinctive feature (as of culture, habitation, geology, or life forms); esp : one suited to a particular crop ⟨the corn ~⟩ 4 : BELTWAY — **belt·ed** \'bel-təd\ adj — **belt·less** \'belt-ləs\ adj — **below the belt** : UNFAIR, UNFAIRLY — **under one's belt** : in one's possession : as part of one's experience
²**belt** vt (14c) 1 a : to encircle or fasten with a belt b : to strap on 2 a : to beat with or as if with a belt : THRASH b : STRIKE, HIT 3 : to mark with a band 4 : to sing in a forceful manner or style ⟨~ing out popular songs⟩ ~ vi 1 : to move or act in a speedy, vigorous, or violent manner 2 : to sing loudly — **belt·er** \'bel-tər\ n
³**belt** n (1899) 1 : a jarring blow : WHACK 2 : DRINK ⟨a ~ of gin⟩
Bel·tane \'bel-,tān, -tin\ n [ME (Sc), 1st or 3rd of May, fr. ScGael bealltain] (15c) : the Celtic May Day festival
belted kingfisher n (1811) : a No. American kingfisher (Ceryle alcyon syn. Megaceryle alcyon) that is slate blue above and white below with a slate blue breast band and an additional chestnut-colored band in the female
belt·ing \'bel-tiŋ\ n (1567) 1 : BELTS 2 : material for belts
belt–tight·en·ing \'belt-,tīt-niŋ, -,tī-t²n-iŋ\ n (1937) : a reduction in spending
belt up vi (1949) Brit : SHUT UP
belt·way \'belt-,wā\ n (ca. 1952) : a highway skirting an urban area — often used to refer specif. to the beltway around Washington D.C. esp. as delimiting what is seen as an insular political and social world
be·lu·ga \bə-'lü-gə\ n [Russ, fr. belyi white; akin to Gk phalios having a white spot — more at BALD] (1772) 1 a : a large white sturgeon (Huso huso syn. Acipenser huso) of the Black Sea, Caspian Sea, and their tributaries b : caviar processed from beluga roe 2 [Russ belukha, fr. belyi] : WHITE WHALE
bel·ve·dere \'bel-və-,dir\ n [It, lit., beautiful view] (1593) : a structure (as a cupola or a summerhouse) designed to command a view
be·ma \'bē-mə\ n [LL & LGk; LL, fr. LGk bēma, fr. Gk, step, tribunal, fr. bainein to go — more at COME] (1683) 1 : the usu. raised part of an Eastern church containing the altar 2 : a raised platform in a synagogue from which the Pentateuch and the Prophets are read
Bem·ba \'bem-bə\ n, pl **Bemba** or **Bembas** (1940) 1 : a member of a primarily agricultural Bantu-speaking people of northeastern Zambia 2 : a Bantu language of the Bemba people
be·med·aled or **be·med·alled** \bi-'me-d²ld\ adj (1880) : wearing or decorated with medals
be·mire \bi-'mīr\ vt (ca. 1532) 1 : to soil with mud or dirt 2 : to drag through or sink in mire
be·moan \bi-'mōn\ vt (bef. 12c) 1 : to express deep grief or distress over 2 : to regard with displeasure, disapproval, or regret **syn** see DEPLORE
be·mock \bi-'mäk, -'mȯk\ vt (1607) archaic : MOCK
be·muse \bi-'myüz\ vt (1735) 1 : to make confused : BEWILDER 2 : to occupy the attention of : ABSORB — **be·mus·ed·ly** \-'myü-zəd-lē\ adv — **be·muse·ment** \-'myüz-mənt\ n
¹**ben** \'ben\ adv [ME, fr. OE binnan, fr. be- + innan within, from within, fr. in] (bef. 12c) Scot : WITHIN
²**ben** prep (bef. 12c) Scot : WITHIN
³**ben** n (ca. 1799) Scot : the inner room or parlor of a 2-room cottage
Bence–Jones protein \'ben(t)s-'jōnz-\ n [Henry Bence-Jones †1873 Eng. physician and chemist] (ca. 1923) : an immunoglobulin that is composed only of light chain polypeptides and that is found esp. in the urine of persons affected with multiple myeloma
¹**bench** \'bench\ n [ME, fr. OE benc; akin to OHG bank bench] (bef.

\ə\ abut \ᵊ\ kitten, F table \ər\ further \a\ ash \ā\ ace \ä\ mop, mar \aú\ out \ch\ chin \e\ bet \ē\ easy \g\ go \i\ hit \ī\ ice \j\ job \ŋ\ sing \ō\ go \ȯ\ law \ȯi\ boy \th\ thin \t͟h\ the \ü\ loot \ú\ foot \y\ yet \zh\ vision \a, k̲, ⁿ, œ, œ̄, ue, ūe, ʸ\ see Guide to Pronunciation

12c) **1 a :** a long seat for two or more persons **b :** a thwart in a boat **c** (1) : a seat on which the members of an athletic team await a turn or opportunity to play (2) : the reserve players on a team **2 a** : the seat where a judge sits in court **b :** the place where justice is administered : COURT **c :** the office or dignity of a judge **d :** the persons who sit as judges **3 a :** the office or dignity of an official **b :** a seat for an official **c :** the officials occupying a bench **4 a :** a long worktable; *also* : LABORATORY ⟨~ chemist⟩ ⟨~ test⟩ **b :** a table forming part of a machine **5 :** TERRACE, SHELF: as **a :** a former wave-cut shore of a sea or lake or floodplain of a river **b :** a shelf or ridge formed in working an open excavation on more than one level **6 :** a compartmented platform on which dogs or cats are kept at a show when not being judged
²**bench** *vt* (14c) **1 :** to furnish with benches **2 :** to seat on a bench **b** (1) : to remove from or keep out of a game (2) : to remove from the starting lineup **3 :** to exhibit (dogs or cats) to the public on a bench ~ *vi* : to form a bench by natural processes
bench·er \'ben-chər\ *n* (15c) : one who sits on or presides at a bench
bench·land \'bench-,land\ *n* (1857) : BENCH 5a
bench·mark \'bench-,märk\ *n* (ca. 1842) **1** *usu* **bench mark** : a mark on a permanent object indicating elevation and serving as a reference in topographical surveys and tidal observations **2 a :** a point of reference from which measurements may be made **b :** something that serves as a standard by which others may be measured or judged **c :** a standardized problem or test that serves as a basis for evaluation or comparison (as of computer system performance)
bench press *n* (1973) : a press in weight lifting performed by a lifter lying on a bench — **bench-press** *vt*
bench seat *n* (1975) : a seat in an automotive vehicle that extends the full width of the passenger section
bench·warm·er \'bench-,wȯr-mər\ *n* (1892) : a reserve player on an athletic team
bench warrant *n* (1696) : a warrant issued by a presiding judge or by a court against a person guilty of contempt or indicted for a crime
¹**bend** \'bend\ *vb* **bent** \'bent\; **bend·ing** [ME, fr. OE *bendan*; akin to OE *bend* fetter — more at BAND] *vt* (bef. 12c) **1 :** to constrain or strain to tension by curving ⟨~ a bow⟩ **2 a :** to turn or force from straight or even to curved or angular **b :** to force from a proper shape **c :** to force back to an original straight or even condition **3 :** FASTEN ⟨~ a sail to its yard⟩ **4 a :** to cause to turn from a straight course : DEFLECT **b :** to guide or turn toward : DIRECT **c :** INCLINE, DISPOSE **d :** to adapt to one's purpose : DISTORT ⟨~ the rules⟩ **5 :** to direct strenuously or with interest : APPLY **6 :** to make submissive : SUBDUE ~ *vi* **1 :** to curve out of a straight line or position; *specif* : to incline the body in token of submission **2 :** to apply oneself vigorously ⟨~ing to their work⟩ **3 :** INCLINE, TEND **4 :** to make concessions : COMPROMISE — **bend·a·ble** \'ben-də-bəl\ *adj* — **bend one's ear :** to talk to someone at length
²**bend** *n* (15c) **1 :** the act or process of bending : the state of being bent **2 :** something that is bent: as **a :** a curved part of a stream or road **b :** ¹WALE 2 — usu. used in pl. **3** *pl but sing or pl in constr* : a sometimes fatal disorder that is marked by neuralgic pains and paralysis, distress in breathing, and often collapse and that is caused by the release of gas bubbles (as of nitrogen) in tissue upon too rapid decrease in air pressure during a stay in a compressed atmosphere — usu. used with *the*; called also *caisson disease, decompression sickness;* compare AEROEMBOLISM — **around the bend :** MAD, CRAZY
³**bend** *n* [ME, fr. MF *bende,* fr. Gmc origin; akin to OHG *binta, bant* band — more at BAND] (15c) **1 :** a diagonal band that runs from the dexter chief to the sinister base on a heraldic shield — compare BEND SINISTER **2** [ME, band, fr. OE *bend* fetter — more at BAND] : a knot by which one rope is fastened to another or to some object
ben·day \'ben-'dā\ *adj, often cap* [*Benjamin Day* †1916 Am. printer] (1903) : involving a process for adding shaded or tinted areas made up of dots for reproduction by line engraving — **benday** *vt*
bend·er \'ben-dər\ *n* (15c) **1 :** one that bends **2 :** SPREE
bend sinister *n* (1612) : a diagonal bend that runs from the sinister chief to the dexter base on a heraldic shield
bendy \'ben-dē\ *adj* (1928) : FLEXIBLE, PLIABLE ⟨a ~ mast⟩
¹**be·neath** \bi-'nēth\ *adv* [ME *benethe,* fr. OE *beneothan,* fr. *be-* + *neo-than* below; akin to OE *nithera* nether] (bef. 12c) **1 :** in or to a lower position : BELOW **2 :** directly under : UNDERNEATH
²**beneath** *prep* (bef. 12c) **1 a :** in or to a lower position than : BELOW **b :** directly under **c :** at the foot of **2 :** not suitable to the rank of : unworthy of **3 :** under the control, pressure, or influence of **4 :** concealed by : under the guise of ⟨a warm heart ~ a gruff manner⟩
ben·e·dict \'be-nə-,dikt\ *n* [alter. of *Benedick,* character in Shakespeare's *Much Ado about Nothing*] (1821) : a newly married man who has long been a bachelor
Ben·e·dic·tine \,be-nə-'dik-tən, -,tēn\ *n* (15c) : a monk or a nun of one of the congregations following the rule of St. Benedict and devoted esp. to scholarship and liturgical worship — **Benedictine** *adj*
bene·dic·tion \,be-nə-'dik-shən\ *n* [ME *benediccioun,* fr. LL *benedic-tion-, benedictio,* fr. *benedicere* to bless, fr. L, to speak well of, fr. *bene* well (akin to L *bonus* good) + *dicere* to say — more at BOUNTY, DICTION] (15c) **1 :** the invocation of a blessing; *esp* : the short blessing with which public worship is concluded **2 :** something that promotes goodness or well-being **3** *often cap* : a Roman Catholic or Anglo-Catholic devotion including the exposition of the eucharistic Host in the monstrance and the blessing of the people with it **4 :** an expression of good wishes
bene·dic·to·ry \-'dik-t(ə-)rē\ *adj* (1710) : of or expressing benediction
Ben·e·dict's solution \'be-nə-,dik(t)s-\ *n* [Stanley Rossiter *Benedict* †1936 Am. chemist] (1921) : a blue solution containing a carbonate, citrate, and sulfate which yields a red, yellow, or orange precipitate upon warming with a sugar (as glucose) that is a reducing agent
Ben·e·dic·tus \,be-nə-'dik-təs\ *n* [LL, blessed, fr. pp. of *benedicere;* fr. its first word] (1552) **1 :** a canticle from Lk 1:68 beginning "Blessed be the Lord God of Israel" **2 :** a canticle from Mt 21:9 beginning "Blessed is he that cometh in the name of the Lord"
ben·e·fac·tion \,be-nə-'fak-shən\ *n* [LL *benefaction-, benefactio,* fr. L *bene facere* to do good to, fr. *bene* + *facere* to do — more at DO] (ca. 1662) **1 :** the act of benefiting **2 :** a benefit conferred; *esp* : a charitable donation

ben·e·fac·tor \'be-nə-,fak-tər\ *n* (15c) : one that confers a benefit; *esp* : one that makes a gift or bequest
ben·e·fac·tress \'be-nə-,fak-tris\ *n* (1711) : a woman who is a benefactor
be·nef·ic \bə-'ne-fik\ *adj* [L *beneficus,* fr. *bene* + *facere*] (1641) : BE-NEFICENT
ben·e·fice \'be-nə-fəs\ *n* [ME, fr. MF, fr. ML *beneficium,* fr. L, favor, promotion, fr. *beneficus*] (14c) **1 :** an ecclesiastical office to which the revenue from an endowment is attached **2 :** a feudal estate in lands : FIEF — **benefice** *vt*
be·nef·i·cence \bə-'ne-fə-sən(t)s\ *n* [L *beneficentia,* fr. *beneficus*] (15c) **1 :** the quality or state of being beneficent **2 :** BENEFACTION
be·nef·i·cent \-sənt\ *adj* [back-formation fr. *beneficence*] (1616) **1** : doing or producing good; *esp* : performing acts of kindness and charity **2 :** BENEFICIAL — **be·nef·i·cent·ly** *adv*
ben·e·fi·cial \,be-nə-'fi-shəl\ *adj* [L *beneficium* favor, benefit] (15c) **1** : conferring benefits : conducive to personal or social well-being **2** : receiving or entitling one to receive advantage, use, or benefit ⟨a ~ legacy⟩ — **ben·e·fi·cial·ly** \-'fi-sh(ə-)lē\ *adv* — **ben·e·fi·cial·ness** *n*
ben·e·fi·cia·ry \,be-nə-'fi-shē-,er-ē, -'fi-sh(ə-)rē\ *n, pl* **-ries** (1662) **1** : one that benefits from something **2 a :** the person designated to receive the income of a trust estate **b :** the person named (as in an insurance policy) to receive proceeds or benefits — **beneficiary** *adj*
ben·e·fi·ci·a·tion \,be-nə-,fi-shē-'ā-shən\ *n* (ca. 1881) : the treatment of raw material (as iron ore) to improve physical or chemical properties esp. in preparation for smelting — **ben·e·fi·ci·ate** \-'fi-shē-,āt\ *vt*
¹**ben·e·fit** \'be-nə-,fit\ *n* [ME, fr. AF *benfet,* fr. L *bene factum,* fr. neut. of *bene factus,* pp. of *bene facere*] (14c) **1** *archaic* : an act of kindness : BENEFACTION **2 a :** something that promotes well-being : ADVANTAGE **b :** useful aid : HELP **3 a :** financial help in time of sickness, old age, or unemployment **b :** a payment or service provided for under an annuity, pension plan, or insurance policy **4 :** an entertainment or social event to raise funds for a person or cause
²**benefit** *vb* **-fit·ed** \-,fi-təd\ *also* **-fit·ted; -fit·ing** *also* **-fit·ting** *vt* (15c) : to be useful or profitable to ~ *vi* : to receive benefit — **ben·e·fit·er** \-,fi-tər\ *n*
benefit of clergy (15c) **1 :** clerical exemption from trial in a civil court **2 :** the ministration or sanction of the church
be·nev·o·lence \bə-'nev-lən(t)s, -'nev-ə-\ *n* (14c) **1 :** disposition to do good **2 :** an act of kindness **3 :** a generous gift **3 :** a compulsory levy by certain English kings with no other authority than the claim of prerogative
be·nev·o·lent \-lənt\ *adj* [ME, fr. L *benevolent-, benevolens,* fr. *bene* + *volent-, volens,* prp. of *velle* to wish — more at WILL] (15c) **1 a** : marked by or disposed to doing good ⟨a ~ donor⟩ **b :** organized for the purpose of doing good ⟨a ~ society⟩ **2 :** marked by or suggestive of goodwill ⟨~ smiles⟩ — **be·nev·o·lent·ly** *adv* — **be·nev·o·lent·ness** *n*
Ben·gali \ben-'gȯ-lē, beŋ-\ *n* [Hindi *Baṅgālī,* fr. *Baṅgāl* Bengal] (1848) **1 :** a native or resident of Bengal **2 :** the modern Indo-Aryan language of Bengal — **Bengali** *adj*
ben·ga·line \'beŋ-gə-,lēn\ *n* [F, fr. *Bengal*] (1884) : a fabric with a crosswise rib made from textile fibers (as rayon, nylon, cotton, or wool) often in combination
Ben·gal light \'ben-,gȯl-, ,beŋ-, -,gäl-, -gəl-\ *n* (1818) : a usu. blue light or flare used formerly esp. for signaling and illumination
Bengal tiger *n* (ca. 1864) : a tiger (*Panthera tigris tigris*) occurring esp. in India
be·night·ed \bi-'nī-təd\ *adj* (15c) **1 :** overtaken by darkness or night **2 :** existing in a state of intellectual, moral, or social darkness : UNEN-LIGHTENED — **be·night·ed·ly** *adv* — **be·night·ed·ness** *n*
be·nign \bi-'nīn\ *adj* [ME *benigne,* fr. MF, fr. L *benignus,* fr. *bene* + *gignere* to beget — more at KIN] (14c) **1 :** of a gentle disposition : GRACIOUS ⟨a ~ teacher⟩ **2 a :** showing kindness and gentleness ⟨~ faces⟩ **b :** FAVORABLE, WHOLESOME ⟨a ~ climate⟩ **3 a :** of a mild type or character that does not threaten health or life ⟨a ~ tumor⟩ **b :** having no significant effect : HARMLESS ⟨environmentally ~⟩ — **be·nig·ni·ty** \-'nig-nə-tē\ *n* — **be·nign·ly** \-'nīn-lē\ *adv*
be·nig·nan·cy \bi-'nig-nən(t)-sē\ *n* (1876) : benignant quality
be·nig·nant \-nənt\ *adj* [*benign* + *-ant* (as in *malignant*)] (ca. 1782) **1** : serenely mild and kindly : BENIGN **2 :** FAVORABLE, BENEFICIAL ⟨a ~ power⟩ — **be·nig·nant·ly** *adv*
benign neglect *n* (1970) : an attitude or policy of ignoring an often undesirable situation that one is perceived to be responsible for dealing with
ben·i·son \'be-nə-sən, -zən\ *n* [ME *beneson,* fr. MF *beneiçon,* fr. LL *benediction-, benedictio*] (14c) : BLESSING, BENEDICTION
Ben·ja·min \'ben-jə-mən\ *n* [Heb *Binyāmīn*] : a son of Jacob and the traditional eponymous ancestor of one of the tribes of Israel
ben·ne *also* **bene** \'be-nē\ *n* [of African origin; akin to Malinke *bĕne* sesame] (1769) : SESAME 1
ben·ny \'be-nē\ *n, pl* **bennies** [*Benzedrine* + *-ie*] (1949) *slang* : a tablet of amphetamine taken as a stimulant
ben·o·myl \'be-nə-,mil\ *n* [*benz-* + *-o-* + *methyl*] (1969) : a derivative $C_{14}H_{18}N_4O_3$ of carbamate and benzimidazole used esp. as a systemic agricultural fungicide
¹**bent** \'bent\ *n* [ME, grassy place, bent grass, fr. OE *beonot-;* akin to OHG *binuz* rush] (14c) **1 :** unenclosed grassland **2 a** (1) : a reedy grass (2) : a stalk of stiff coarse grass **b :** BENT GRASS
²**bent** *adj* [ME, fr. pp. of *benden* to bend] (14c) **1 :** changed by bending out of an orig. straight or even condition ⟨~ twigs⟩ **2 :** strongly inclined : DETERMINED ⟨was ~ on going⟩ **3** *slang* **a :** different from the normal or usual **b** *chiefly Brit* : DISHONEST, CORRUPT
³**bent** *n* [irreg. fr. ¹*bend*] (1586) **1 a :** a strong inclination or interest : BIAS **b :** a special inclination or capacity : TALENT **2 :** capacity of endurance **3 :** a transverse framework (as in a bridge) to carry lateral as well as vertical loads *syn* see GIFT
bent grass *n* (1778) : any of a genus (*Agrostis*) of grasses including important chiefly perennial and rhizomatous pasture and lawn grasses with fine velvety or wiry herbage
Ben·tham·ism \'ben(t)-thə-,mi-zəm\ *n* (1829) : the utilitarian philosophy of Jeremy Bentham and his followers — **Ben·tham·ite** \-,mīt\ *n or adj*

ben·thic \'ben(t)-thik\ *adj* [*benthos*] (1902) **1** : of, relating to, or occurring at the bottom of a body of water **2** : of, relating to, or occurring in the depths of the ocean

ben·thon·ic \ben-'thä-nik\ *adj* [irreg. fr. *benthos*] (1897) : BENTHIC

ben·thos \'ben-ˌthäs\ *n* [NL, fr. Gk, depth, deep sea; akin to Gk *bathys* deep] (1891) : organisms that live on or in the bottom of a body of water

ben·ton·ite \'ben-tᵊn-ˌīt\ *n* [Fort *Benton*, Mont.] (1898) : an absorptive and colloidal clay used esp. as a sealing agent or carrier (as of drugs) — **ben·ton·it·ic** \ˌben-tᵊn-'i-tik\ *adj*

ben tro·va·to \ˌben-trō-'vä-(ˌ)tō\ *adj* [It, lit., well found] (1876) : characteristic or appropriate even if not true ⟨the story is *ben trovato*⟩

bent·wood \'bent-ˌwu̇d\ *adj* (1862) : made of wood that is bent rather than cut into shape ⟨∼ furniture⟩ — **bentwood** *n*

be·numb \bi-'nəm\ *vt* [ME *benomen*, fr. *benomen*, pp. of *benimen* to deprive, fr. OE *beniman*, fr. *be-* + *niman* to take — more at NIMBLE] (14c) **1** : to make inactive : DEADEN **2** : to make numb esp. by cold

benz- *or* **benzo-** *comb form* [ISV, fr. *benzoin*] : related to benzene or benzoic acid ⟨*benzophenone*⟩ ⟨*benzyl*⟩

benz·al·de·hyde \ben-'zal-də-ˌhīd\ *n* [ISV] (1866) : a colorless nontoxic aromatic liquid C_6H_5CHO found in essential oils (as in peach kernels) and used in flavoring and perfumery, in pharmaceuticals, and in synthesis of dyes

benz·an·thra·cene \ben-'zan(t)-thrə-ˌsēn\ *n* [ISV] (1938) : a crystalline feebly carcinogenic cyclic hydrocarbon $C_{18}H_{12}$ that is found in small amounts in coal tar

Ben·ze·drine \'ben-zə-ˌdrēn\ *trademark* — used for amphetamine

ben·zene \'ben-ˌzēn, ben-'\ *n* [ISV *benz-* + *-ene*] (ca. 1872) : a colorless volatile flammable toxic liquid aromatic hydrocarbon C_6H_6 used in organic synthesis, as a solvent, and as a motor fuel — called also *benzol* — **ben·ze·noid** \'ben-zə-ˌnȯid\ *adj*

benzene hexa·chlo·ride \-ˌhek-sə-'klōr-ˌīd, -'klȯr-\ *n* (1884) : BHC

benzene ring *n* (1877) : a structural arrangement of atoms held to exist in benzene and other aromatic compounds and marked by six carbon atoms linked in a planar symmetrical hexagon with each carbon attached to hydrogen in benzene itself or to other atoms or groups in substituted benzenes — compare META- 4a, ORTH- 4b, PARA- 2b

ben·zi·dine \'ben-zə-ˌdēn\ *n* [ISV *benz-* + *-idine*] (1878) : a crystalline base $C_{12}H_{12}N_2$ prepared from nitrobenzene and used esp. in making dyes

benz·imid·azole \ˌben-ˌzi-mə-'da-ˌzōl, ˌben-zə-'mi-də-ˌzōl\ *n* [ISV] (ca. 1929) : a crystalline base $C_7H_6N_2$ used esp. to inhibit the growth of various viruses, parasitic worms, or fungi; *also* : one of its derivatives

ben·zine \'ben-ˌzēn, ben-'\ *n* [G *Benzin*, fr. *benz-*] (1835) : any of various volatile flammable petroleum distillates used esp. as solvents or as motor fuels

ben·zo·a·py·rene \ˌben-zō-ˌā-'pīr-ˌēn, -zō-ˌal-fə-\ *n* [*benz-* + *-a-*, denoting attachment of the benzene substituent at carbon atoms 1 and 2 of the pyrene molecule + *pyrene*] (1950) : a yellow crystalline carcinogenic hydrocarbon $C_{20}H_{12}$ found in coal tar — *a* often italicized and placed in parentheses or brackets or between hyphens

ben·zo·ate \'ben-zə-ˌwāt\ *n* (1806) : a salt or ester of benzoic acid

ben·zo·caine \'ben-zə-ˌkān\ *n* [ISV *benz-* + *-caine*] (1922) : a white crystalline ester $C_9H_{11}NO_2$ used as a local anesthetic

ben·zo·di·az·e·pine \ˌben-zō-dī-'a-zə-ˌpēn\ *n* [*benz-* + *di-* + *az-* + *-epine* (fr. *hepta-* + *²-ine*)] (1934) : any of a group of aromatic lipophilic amines (as diazepam and chlordiazepoxide) used esp. as tranquilizers

ben·zo·fu·ran \ˌben-zō-'fyu̇r-ˌan, -fyu̇-'ran\ *n* (1946) : a compound C_8H_6O found in coal tar and polymerized with indene to form thermoplastic resins used esp. in adhesives and printing inks

ben·zo·ic acid \ben-'zō-ik-\ *n* [ISV, fr. *benzoin*] (1791) : a white crystalline acid $C_7H_6O_2$ found naturally (as in benzoin or in cranberries) or made synthetically and used esp. as a preservative of foods, in medicine, and in organic synthesis

ben·zo·in \'ben-zə-wən, -ˌwēn; -ˌzȯin\ *n* [MF *benjoin*, fr. Catal *benjuí*, fr. *lubān jāwī*, lit., frankincense of Java] (1562) **1** : a hard fragrant yellowish balsamic resin from trees (genus *Styrax*) of southeastern Asia used esp. in medication, as a fixative in perfumes, and as incense **2** : a white crystalline hydroxy ketone $C_{14}H_{12}O_2$ made from benzaldehyde

ben·zol \'ben-ˌzȯl, -ˌzōl\ *n* [G, fr. *benz-* + *-ol*] (1838) : BENZENE; *also* : a mixture of benzene and other aromatic hydrocarbons

ben·zo·phe·none \ˌben-zō-fi-'nōn, -'fē-ˌnōn\ *n* [ISV *benz-* + *phen-* + *-one*] (1885) : a colorless crystalline ketone $C_{13}H_{10}O$ used chiefly in perfumery and sunscreens; *also* : a derivative of benzophenone

ben·zo·yl \'ben-zə-ˌwil, -ˌzȯil\ *n* [G, fr. *Benzoësäure* benzoic acid + Gk *hylē* matter, lit., wood] (ca. 1855) : the radical C_6H_5CO of benzoic acid

benzoyl peroxide *n* (1924) : a white crystalline flammable compound $C_{14}H_{10}O_4$ used in bleaching and in medicine esp. in the treatment of acne

ben·zyl \'ben-ˌzēl, -zəl\ *n* [ISV *benz-* + *-yl*] (1869) : a univalent radical $C_6H_5CH_2$ derived from toluene — **ben·zyl·ic** \ben-'zi-lik\ *adj*

Be·o·wulf \'bā-ə-ˌwu̇lf\ *n* : a legendary Geatish warrior and hero of the Old English poem *Beowulf*

be·paint \bi-'pānt\ *vt* (ca. 1555) *archaic* : TINGE

be·queath \bi-'kwēth, -'kwēth\ *vt* [ME *bequethen*, fr. OE *becwethan*, fr. *be-* + *cwethan* to say — more at QUOTH] (bef. 12c) **1** : to give or leave by will — used esp. of personal property **2** : to hand down : TRANSMIT — **be·queath·al** \-'kwē-thəl, -thəl\ *n*

be·quest \bi-'kwest\ *n* [ME, irreg. fr. *bequethen*] (14c) **1** : the act of bequeathing **2** : something bequeathed : LEGACY

be·rate \bi-'rāt\ *vt* (1548) : to scold or condemn vehemently and at length *syn* see SCOLD

Ber·ber \'bər-bər\ *n* [Ar *Barbar*] (1732) **1** : a member of any of various peoples living in northern Africa west of Tripoli **2 a** : a branch of the Afro-Asiatic language family comprising languages spoken by various peoples of northern Africa and the Sahara (as the Tuaregs and the Kabyles) **b** : any one of the Berber languages

ber·ber·ine \'bər-bə-ˌrēn\ *n* [G *Berberin*, fr. NL *berberis*] (ca. 1847) : a bitter crystalline yellow alkaloid $C_{20}H_{19}NO_5$ obtained from the roots of various plants (as barberry) and used as a tonic in medicine

ber·ber·is \'bər-bər-əs\ *n* [NL, the genus including barberry, alter. of ML *barberis* barberry, fr. Ar *barbārīs*] (ca. 1868) : BARBERRY

ber·ceuse \ber-'sœs, -'sᵫz\ *n, pl* **ber·ceuses** \-'sœz; -'sᵫz, -'sü-zəz\ [F] (1876) **1** : LULLABY **2** : a musical composition usu. in ⁶/₈ time that resembles a lullaby

be·reave \bi-'rēv\ *vt* **-reaved** *or* **-reft** \-'reft\; **-reav·ing** [ME *bereven*, fr. OE *berēafian*, fr. *be-* + *rēafian* to rob — more at REAVE] (bef. 12c) **1** : to deprive of something — usu. used with *of* ⟨madam, you have *bereft* me of all words —Shak.⟩ **2** : to take away (a valued or necessary possession) esp. by force

¹be·reaved \bi-'rēvd\ *adj* (1828) : suffering the death of a loved one

²bereaved *n, pl* **bereaved** (1943) : one who is bereaved

be·reave·ment \bi-'rēv-mənt\ *n* (ca. 1731) : the state or fact of being bereaved; *esp* : the loss of a loved one by death

be·reft \-'reft\ *adj* (1586) **1 a** : deprived or robbed of the possession or use of something — usu. used with *of* ⟨both players are instantly ∼ of their poise —A. E. Wier⟩ **b** : lacking something needed, wanted, or expected — used with *of* ⟨the book is . . . completely ∼ of an index —*Times Lit. Supp.*⟩ **2** : BEREAVED ⟨a ∼ mother⟩

be·ret \bə-'rā\ *n* [F *béret*, fr. Gascon *berret*, fr. OProv, cap — more at BIRETTA] (1827) : a visorless usu. woolen cap with a tight headband and a soft full flat top

berg \'bərg\ *n* (1823) : ICEBERG

ber·ga·mot \'bər-gə-ˌmät\ *n* [F *bergamote*, fr. It *bergamotta*, modif. of Turk *bey armudu*, lit., the bey's pear] (1696) **1** : a pear-shaped orange (*Citrus aurantium bergamia*) having a rind which yields an essential oil used in perfumery; *also* : this oil **2** : any of several mints (genus *Monarda*) — compare WILD BERGAMOT

be·rib·boned \bi-'ri-bənd\ *adj* (1863) : adorned with ribbons

beri·beri \ˌber-ē-'ber-ē\ *n* [Sinhalese *bæribæri*] (1703) : a deficiency disease marked by inflammatory or degenerative changes of the nerves, digestive system, and heart and caused by a lack of or inability to assimilate thiamine

Berke·le·ian *or* **Berke·ley·an** \'bär-klē-ən, 'bər-; bär-', bər-'\ *adj* (1842) : of, relating to, or suggestive of Bishop Berkeley or his system of philosophical idealism — **Berkeleian** *n* — **Berke·le·ian·ism** \-ə-ˌni-zəm\ *n*

berke·li·um \'bər-klē-əm\ *n* [NL, fr. *Berkeley*, Calif.] (1950) : a radioactive metallic element produced by bombarding americium 241 with helium ions — see ELEMENT table

Berk·shire \'bərk-ˌshir, -shər\ *n* [*Berkshire*, England] (1831) : any of a breed of medium-sized black swine with white markings

berm \'bərm\ *n* [F *berme*, fr. D *berm* strip of ground along a dike; akin to ME *brimme* brim] (1729) **1** : a narrow shelf, path, or ledge typically at the top or bottom of a slope; *also* : a mound or wall of earth ⟨a landscaped ∼⟩

Ber·mu·da bag \(ˌ)bər-'myü-də-, *esp Southern* -'mü-də-\ *n* [*Bermuda* islands, No. Atlantic] (1979) : a round or oval-shaped handbag with a wooden handle and removable cloth covers

Bermuda grass *n* (1808) : a creeping stoloniferous southern European grass (*Cynodon dactylon*) often used as a lawn and pasture grass

Bermuda rig *n* (1853) : a fore-and-aft rig marked by a triangular sail and a mast with an extreme rake

Ber·mu·das \(ˌ)bər-'myü-dəz, *esp Southern* -'mü-dəz\ *n pl* (1961) : BERMUDA SHORTS

Bermuda shorts *n pl* (1951) : knee-length walking shorts

Ber·nese mountain dog \'bər-ˌnēz-, -ˌnēs-\ *n* [*Bern*, Switzerland] (1935) : any of a breed of large powerful long-coated black dogs of Swiss origin that have tan and white markings and were developed as draft animals

Ber·noul·li's principle \bər-'nü-lēz-, ˌbər-ˌnü-'lēz-\ *n* [Daniel *Bernoulli* †1782 Swiss physicist] (1940) : a principle in hydrodynamics: the pressure in a stream of fluid is reduced as the speed of the flow is increased

Bernoulli trial \bər-'nü-lē-, ˌbər-ˌnü-'lē-\ *n* [Jacques *Bernoulli* †1705 Swiss mathematician] (1951) : one of the repetitions of a statistical experiment having two mutually exclusive outcomes with constant probability of occurrence

ber·ried \'ber-ēd\ *adj* (1794) **1** : having or covered with berries ⟨∼ shrub⟩ **2** : bearing eggs ⟨a ∼ lobster⟩

¹ber·ry \'ber-ē\ *n, pl* **berries** [ME *berye*, fr. OE *berie*; akin to OHG *beri* berry] (bef. 12c) **1 a** : a pulpy and usu. edible fruit (as a strawberry, raspberry, or checkerberry) of small size irrespective of its structure **b** : a simple fruit (as a currant, grape, tomato, or banana) with a pulpy or fleshy pericarp **c** : the dry seed of some plants (as wheat) **2** : an egg of a fish or lobster

²berry *vi* **ber·ried; ber·ry·ing** (ca. 1780) **1** : to bear or produce berries ⟨a ∼*ing* shrub⟩ **2** : to gather or seek berries

ber·ry·like \'ber-ē-ˌlīk\ *adj* (1864) **1** : resembling a berry esp. in size or structure **2** : being small and rounded : COCCOID

ber·seem \(ˌ)bər-'sēm\ *n* [Ar *barsīm*, fr. Copt *bersim*] (ca. 1902) : a succulent clover (*Trifolium alexandrinum*) cultivated as a forage plant and green-manure crop esp. in the alkaline soils of the Nile valley and in the southwestern U.S. — called also *Egyptian clover*

¹ber·serk \bə(r)-'sərk, ˌbər-, -'zərk; 'bər-\ *or* **berserk·er** \-'sər-kər, -'zər-; 'bər-\ *n* [ON *berserkr*, fr. *bjorn* bear + *serkr* shirt] (1818) **1** : an ancient Scandinavian warrior frenzied in battle and held to be invulnerable **2** : one whose actions are recklessly defiant

²berserk *adj* (1851) : FRENZIED, CRAZED — usu. used in the phrase *go berserk* ⟨sinister ravings of an imagination gone ∼ —John Gruen⟩ — **berserk** *adv* — **ber·serk·ly** *adv*

¹berth \'bərth\ *n* [prob. fr. ²*bear* + *-th*] (15c) **1 a** : sufficient distance for maneuvering a ship **b** : safe distance — used esp. with *wide* **2 a** : the place where a ship lies when at anchor or at a wharf **b** : a space for an automotive vehicle at rest ⟨a truck-loading ∼⟩ **3** : a place to sit or sleep esp. on a ship or vehicle : ACCOMMODATION **4 a** : a billet on a ship **b** : JOB, POSITION, PLACE ⟨a starting ∼ on the team⟩

²berth *vt* (1667) **1** : to bring into a berth **2** : to allot a berth to ∼ *vi* : to come into a berth

\ə\ abut \ᵊ\ kitten, F table \ər\ further \a\ ash \ā\ ace \ä\ mop, mar \au̇\ out \ch\ chin \e\ bet \ē\ easy \g\ go \i\ hit \ī\ ice \j\ job \ŋ\ sing \ō\ go \ȯ\ law \ȯi\ boy \th\ thin \t͟h\ the \ü\ loot \u̇\ foot \y\ yet \zh\ vision \ä, k̲, ⁿ, œ, œ̄, ᵫ, ᵫ̄, ᵜ\ *see* Guide to Pronunciation

ber·tha \'bər-thə\ *n* [F *berthe*, fr. *Berthe* (Bertha) †783 queen of the Franks] (1842) : a wide round collar covering the shoulders

Ber·til·lon system \'bər-tᵊl-ˌän-, 'ber-tē-ˌyōⁿ-\ *n* [Alphonse *Bertillon* †1914 Fr. criminologist] (1896) : a system of identification of persons by a description based on anthropometric measurements, photographs, and notation of data (as markings, color, and thumb line impressions)

ber·yl \'ber-əl\ *n* [ME, fr. MF *beril*, fr. L *beryllus*, fr. Gk *bēryllos*, back-formation fr. *bēryllion* beryl, of Indo-Aryan origin; akin to Prakrit *verulia, veluriya* beryl] (13c) : a mineral consisting of a silicate of beryllium and aluminum of great hardness and occurring in green, bluish green, yellow, pink, or white hexagonal prisms

be·ryl·li·um \bə-'ri-lē-əm\ *n* [NL, fr. Gk *bēryllion*] (ca. 1847) : a steel-gray light strong brittle toxic bivalent metallic element used chiefly as a hardening agent in alloys — see ELEMENT table

be·seech \bi-'sēch\ *vb* -seeched *or* -sought \-'sȯt\; -seech·ing [ME *besechen*, fr. *be-* + *sechen* to seek] *vt* (12c) 1 : to beg for urgently or anxiously 2 : to request earnestly : IMPLORE ~ *vi* : to make supplication *syn* see BEG — **be·seech·ing·ly** \-'sē-chiŋ-lē\ *adv*

be·seem \bi-'sēm\ *vi* (13c) *archaic* : to be fitting or becoming ~ *vt, archaic* : to be suitable to : BEFIT

be·set \bi-'set, bē-\ *vt* -set; -set·ting [ME *besetten*, fr. OE *besettan*, fr. *be-* + *settan* to set] (bef. 12c) 1 : to set or stud with or as if with ornaments 2 : TROUBLE, HARASS ⟨inflation ~s the economy⟩ 3 **a** : to set upon : ASSAIL ⟨the settlers were ~ by savages⟩ **b** : to hem in : SURROUND — **be·set·ment** \-mənt\ *n*

be·set·ting *adj* (1795) : constantly present or attacking : OBSESSIVE

be·shrew \bi-'shrü, bē-, *esp Southern* -'srü\ *vt* (14c) *archaic* : CURSE

¹**be·side** \bi-'sīd\ *prep* [ME, adv. & prep., fr. OE *be sidan* at or to the side, fr. *be* at (fr. *bi*) + *sidan*, dat. & acc. of *side* side — more at BY] (13c) 1 **a** : by the side of ⟨walk ~ me⟩ **b** : in comparison with **c** : on a par with 2 : BESIDES 3 : not relevant to ⟨~ the point⟩ — **beside oneself** : in a state of extreme excitement

²**beside** *adv* (14c) 1 : NEARBY 2 *archaic* : BESIDES

¹**be·sides** \bi-'sīdz\ *prep* (14c) 1 : OTHER THAN, EXCEPT 2 : together with

²**besides** *adv* (1564) 1 : as well : ALSO 2 : MOREOVER, FURTHERMORE

³**besides** *prep* (1954) : ELSE

be·siege \bi-'sēj\ *vt* -sieged; -sieg·ing (14c) 1 : to surround with armed forces 2 **a** : to press with requests : IMPORTUNE **b** : to cause worry or distress to : BESET ⟨doubts *besieged* him⟩ — **be·sieg·er** *n*

be·smear \bi-'smir\ *vt* (bef. 12c) : SMEAR

be·smirch \bi-'smərch\ *vt* (1599) : SULLY, SOIL

be·som \'bē-zəm\ *n* [ME *beseme*, fr. OE *besma*; akin to OHG *besmo* broom] (bef. 12c) : BROOM 2; *esp* : one made of twigs

besom pocket *n* [origin unknown] (1966) : a pocket with a welted slit opening

be·sot \bi-'sät\ *vt* **be·sot·ted; be·sot·ting** [*be-* + *sot* (to stultify)] (1581) 1 : INFATUATE 2 2 : to make dull or stupid; *esp* : to muddle with drunkenness

be·spat·ter \bi-'spa-tər\ *vt* (1640) : SPATTER

be·speak \bi-'spēk\ *vt* **-spoke** \-'spōk\; **-spo·ken** \-'spō-kən\; **-speaking** (1536) 1 : to hire, engage, or claim beforehand 2 : to speak to esp. with formality : ADDRESS 3 : REQUEST ⟨~ a favor⟩ 4 **a** : INDICATE, SIGNIFY ⟨her performance ~s considerable practice⟩ **b** : to show beforehand : FORETELL

be·spec·ta·cled \bi-'spek-(ˌ)ti-kəld\ *adj* (1742) : wearing spectacles

be·spoke \bi-'spōk\ *or* **be·spo·ken** \-'spō-kən\ *adj* [pp. of *bespeak*] (1607) 1 **a** : CUSTOM-MADE **b** : dealing in or producing custom-made articles 2 *dial* : ENGAGED

be·sprent \bi-'sprent\ *adj* [ME *bespreynt*, fr. pp. of *besprengen* to besprinkle, fr. OE *besprengan*, fr. *be-* + *sprengan* to scatter; akin to OE *springan* to spring] (14c) *archaic* : sprinkled over

be·sprin·kle \bi-'spriŋ-kəl\ *vt* [ME *besprengeln*, freq. of *besprengen*] (15c) : SPRINKLE

Bes·sel function \'be-səl-\ *n* [Friedrich W. *Bessel* †1846 Prussian astronomer] (1872) : one of a class of transcendental functions expressible as infinite series and occurring in the solution of the differential equation

$$x^2 \frac{d^2y}{dx^2} + x\frac{dy}{dx} = (n^2 - x^2)y$$

Bes·se·mer converter \'be-sə-mər-\ *n* (ca. 1887) : the furnace used in the Bessemer process

Bessemer process *n* [Sir Henry *Bessemer*] (1875) : a process of making steel from pig iron by burning out carbon and other impurities by means of a blast of air forced through the molten metal

¹**best** \'best\ *adj, superlative of* GOOD [ME, fr. OE *betst*; akin to OE *bōt* remedy — more at BETTER] (bef. 12c) 1 : excelling all others ⟨the ~ student⟩ 2 : most productive of good or of advantage, utility, or satisfaction ⟨what is the ~ thing to do⟩ 3 : MOST, LARGEST ⟨it rained for the ~ part of their vacation⟩

²**best** *adv, superlative of* WELL (bef. 12c) 1 : in the best way : to greatest advantage ⟨some things are ~ left unsaid⟩ 2 : MOST ⟨those ~ able will provide needed support⟩

³**best** *n, pl* **best** (bef. 12c) 1 : the best state or part 2 : one that is best ⟨the ~ falls short⟩ 3 : the greatest degree of good or excellence 4 : one's maximum effort ⟨do your ~⟩ 5 : best clothes ⟨Sunday ~⟩ — **at best** : under the most favorable circumstances

⁴**best** *vt* (1863) : to get the better of : OUTDO

⁵**best** *verbal auxiliary* (1941) : had best ⟨you ~ listen⟩

best–ball \'best)-'bȯl\ *adj* (1909) : relating to or being a golf match in which one player competes against the best individual score of two or more players for each hole — compare FOUR-BALL

best boy *n* (1937) : the chief assistant to the gaffer in motion-picture or television production

best–case \'best)-'kās\ *adj* (1977) : being, relating to, or based on a projection of future events that assumes only the best possible circumstances ⟨a ~ scenario⟩

¹**be·stead** *or* **be·sted** \bi-'sted\ *adj* [ME *bested*, fr. *be-* + *sted*, pp. of *steden* to place, fr. *stede* place — more at STEAD] (14c) *archaic* : SITUATED

²**bestead** *vt* **be·stead·ed; be·stead; be·stead·ing** [*be-* + *stead*] (1581) 1 *archaic* : HELP 2 *archaic* : to be useful to : AVAIL

bes·tial \'bes-chəl, 'besh-, 'bēs-, 'bēsh-\ *adj* [ME, fr. MF, fr. L *bestialis*, fr. *bestia* beast] (14c) 1 **a** : of or relating to beasts **b** : resembling a beast 2 **a** : lacking intelligence or reason **b** : marked by base or inhuman instincts or desires : BRUTAL *syn* see BRUTAL — **bes·tial·ize** \-chə-ˌlīz\ *vt* — **bes·tial·ly** \-chə-lē\ *adv*

bes·ti·al·i·ty \ˌbes-chē-'a-lə-tē, ˌbesh-, ˌbēs-, ˌbēsh-\ *n, pl* **-ties** (14c) 1 : the condition or status of a lower animal 2 : display or gratification of bestial traits or impulses 3 : sexual relations between a human being and a lower animal

bes·ti·ary \'bes-chē-ˌer-ē, 'besh-, 'bēs-, 'bēsh-\ *n, pl* **-ar·ies** [ML *bestiarium*, fr. L, neut. of *bestiarius* of beasts, fr. *bestia*] (1840) 1 : a medieval allegorical or moralizing work on the appearance and habits of real or imaginary animals 2 : a collection of descriptions of real or imaginary animals

be·stir \bi-'stər\ *vt* (14c) : to rouse to action : get going

best man *n* (ca. 1782) : the principal groomsman at a wedding

be·stow \bi-'stō\ *vt* [ME, fr. *be-* + *stowe* place — more at STOW] (14c) 1 : to put to use : APPLY ⟨~*ed* his spare time on study⟩ 2 : to put in a particular or appropriate place : STOW 3 : to provide with quarters : PUT UP 4 : to convey as a gift — usu. used with *on* or *upon* *syn* see GIVE — **be·stow·al** \-'stō-əl\ *n*

be·strew \bi-'strü\ *vt* **-strewed; -strewed** *or* **-strewn** \-'strün\; **-strew·ing** (bef. 12c) 1 : STREW 2 : to lie scattered over

be·stride \bi-'strīd\ *vt* **-strode** \-'strōd\; **-strid·den** \-'stri-dᵊn\; **-strid·ing** \-'strī-diŋ\ (bef. 12c) 1 : to ride, sit, or stand astride : STRADDLE 2 : to tower over : DOMINATE ⟨the bloated bureaucracy that ~s us all —Edward Ney⟩ 3 *archaic* : to stride across

best–sell·er \'best)-'se-lər\ *n* (1889) : an article (as a book) whose sales are among the highest of its class — **best–sell·er·dom** \-dəm\ *n* — **best–sell·ing** \-'se-liŋ\ *adj*

¹**bet** \'bet\ *n* [origin unknown] (1592) 1 **a** : something that is laid, staked, or pledged typically between two parties on the outcome of a contest or a contingent issue : WAGER **b** : the act of giving such a pledge 2 : something to wager on 3 : a choice made by consideration of probabilities ⟨your best ~ is the back road⟩

²**bet** *vb* **bet** *also* **bet·ted; bet·ting** *vt* (1597) 1 **a** : to stake on the outcome of an issue or the performance of a contestant **b** : to be able to be sure that — usu. used in the expression *you bet* ⟨you ~ I'll be there⟩ 2 **a** : to maintain with or as if with a bet **b** : to make a bet with **c** : to make a bet on ~ *vi* : to lay a bet

¹**be·ta** \'bā-tə, *chiefly Brit* 'bē-\ *n* [ME *betha*, fr. L *beta*, fr. Gk *bēta*, of Sem origin; akin to Heb *bēth* beth] (14c) 1 : the 2d letter of the Greek alphabet — see ALPHABET table 2 : BETA PARTICLE 3 : a measure of a stock's or a portfolio's volatility that is expressed numerically as deviation from the market's volatility taken as unity

²**beta** *adj* (1899) : second in position in the structure of an organic molecule from a particular group or atom ⟨~ substitution⟩ — often used in combination; symbol β

be·ta–ad·ren·er·gic \-ˌa-drə-'nər-jik\ *adj* (1965) : of, relating to, or being a beta-receptor ⟨~ blocking action⟩

be·ta–block·er \-ˌblä-kər\ *n* (1968) : any of a class of drugs (as propranolol) that slow heart action and increase coronary blood flow by blocking the activity of beta-receptors — **be·ta–block·ing** \-kiŋ\ *adj*

be·ta–car·o·tene \-'kar-ə-ˌtēn\ *n* (1938) : an isomer of carotene found in dark green and dark yellow vegetables and fruits

beta cell *n* (1926) : any of the insulin-secreting pancreatic cells in the islets of Langerhans

beta decay *n* (1934) : a radioactive nuclear transformation governed by the weak force in which a nucleon (as a neutron) changes into the other type of nucleon (as a proton) with the emission of an electron or positron and a neutrino and which results in a change in the atomic number of the nucleus of +1 or −1

be·ta–en·dor·phin \-en-'dȯr-fən\ *n* (1977) : an endorphin of the pituitary gland having a much greater analgesic potency than morphine

beta globulin *n* [ISV] (1945) : any of several globulins of plasma or serum that have at alkaline pH electrophoretic mobilities intermediate between those of the alpha globulins and gamma globulins

be·ta·ine \'bē-tə-ˌēn\ *n* [ISV, fr. L *beta* beet] (1879) : a sweet crystalline quaternary ammonium salt $C_5H_{11}NO_2$ occurring esp. in beet juice; *also* : its hydrate $C_5H_{13}NO_3$ or its hydrochloride $C_5H_{12}NO_2Cl$

be·take \bi-'tāk\ *vt* **-took** \-'tuk\; **-tak·en** \-'tā-kən\; **-tak·ing** (14c) 1 *archaic* : COMMIT 2 : to cause (oneself) to go

be·ta–lac·ta·mase \-'lak-tə-ˌmās, -ˌmāz\ *n* [*lactam*, a cyclic amide (fr. ISV *lact-* + *amide*) + *-ase*] (1965) : PENICILLINASE

be·ta–ox·i·da·tion \'bā-tə-ˌäk-sə-'dā-shən\ *n* (ca. 1935) : stepwise catabolism of fatty acids in which two-carbon fragments are successively removed from the carboxyl end of the chain

beta particle *n* (1904) : a high-speed electron; *specif* : one emitted by a radioactive nucleus in beta decay

beta ray *n* (1902) 1 : BETA PARTICLE 2 : a stream of beta particles — called also *beta radiation*

be·ta–re·cep·tor \'bā-tə-ri-'sep-tər\ *n* (1948) : any of a group of receptors postulated to exist on nerve cell membranes of the sympathetic nervous system to explain the specificity of certain adrenergic agents in affecting only some sympathetic activities (as vasodilation, increase in muscular contraction and beat of the heart, and relaxation of smooth muscle in the bronchi and intestine)

be·ta–thal·as·se·mia \-ˌtha-lə-'sē-mē-ə\ *n* (1962) : thalassemia in which the longer hemoglobin chain is affected and which comprises Cooley's anemia in the homozygous condition and a less severe thalassemia in the heterozygous condition

be·ta·tron \'bā-tə-ˌträn\ *n* [ISV] (1941) : an accelerator in which electrons are propelled by the inductive action of a rapidly varying magnetic field

beta wave *n* (1936) : an electrical rhythm of the brain with a frequency of 13 to 30 cycles per second that is associated with normal conscious waking experience — called also *beta, beta rhythm*

be·tel \'bē-tᵊl\ *n* [Pg *bétele*, fr. Tamil *verrilai*] (1553) : a climbing pepper (*Piper betle*) whose leaves are chewed together with betel nut and mineral lime as a stimulant masticatory esp. by southeastern Asians

Be·tel·geuse \'bē-tᵊl-ˌjüs, 'be-, -ˌjüz\ *n* [F *Bételgeuse*, fr. Ar *bayt al-jawzā'* Gemini, lit., the house of the twins (confused with Orion & Betelgeuse)] : a variable red giant star of the first magnitude near one shoulder of Orion

betel nut *n* [fr. its being chewed with betel leaves] (1681) : the astringent seed of the betel palm

betel palm *n* (1875) : an Asian pinnate-leaved palm (*Areca catechu*) that has an orange-colored drupe with an outer fibrous husk

bête noire \,bet-'nwär, ,bät-\ *n, pl* **bêtes noires** \,bet-'nwär(z), ,bät-\ [F, lit., black beast] (1844) : a person or thing strongly detested or avoided : BUGBEAR

beth \'bāth, 'bāt, 'bās\ *n* [Heb *bēth*, fr. *bayith* house] (ca. 1823) : the 2d letter of the Hebrew alphabet — see ALPHABET table

beth·el \'be-thəl\ *n* [Heb *bēth'ēl* house of God] (ca. 1617) **1 :** a hallowed spot **2 a :** a chapel for Nonconformists **b :** a place of worship for seamen

be·think \bi-'thiŋk\ *vt* -**thought** \-'thot\; -**think·ing** (bef. 12c) **1 a :** REMEMBER, RECALL **b :** to cause (oneself) to be reminded **2 :** to cause (oneself) to consider

be·tide \bi-'tīd\ *vi* (12c) : to happen esp. as if by fate ~ *vt* : to happen to : BEFALL — used chiefly in the phrase *woe betide* ⟨woe ~ our enemies⟩

be·times \bi-'tīmz\ *adv* (13c) **1 :** in good time : EARLY **2** *archaic* : in a short time **3 :** at times : OCCASIONALLY

bê·tise \bā-'tēz\ *n, pl* **bê·tises** \-'tēz\ [F] (1827) **1 :** an act of foolishness or stupidity **2 :** lack of good sense : STUPIDITY

be·to·ken \bi-'tō-kən\ *vt* -**to·kened**; -**to·ken·ing** \-'tōk-niŋ, -'tō-kə-\ (15c) **1 :** to typify beforehand : PRESAGE **2 :** to give evidence of : SHOW

be·tray \bi-'trā\ *vb* [ME, fr. *be-* + *trayen* to betray, fr. OF *traïr*, fr. L *tradere* — more at TRAITOR] *vt* (13c) **1 :** to lead astray; *esp* : SEDUCE **2 :** to deliver to an enemy by treachery **3 :** to fail or desert esp. in time of need **4 a :** to reveal unintentionally **b :** SHOW, INDICATE **c :** to disclose in violation of confidence ~ *vi* : to prove false *syn* see REVEAL — **be·tray·al** \-'trā-(ə)l\ *n* — **be·tray·er** \-'trā-ər\ *n*

be·troth \bi-'trōth, -'trŏth\ *vt* [ME, fr. *be-* + *trouthe* truth, troth] (14c) **1 :** to promise to marry **2 :** to give in marriage

be·troth·al \-'trō-thəl, -'trŏ-, -thəl\ *n* (1844) **1 :** the act of betrothing or fact of being betrothed **2 :** a mutual promise or contract for a future marriage

be·trothed \bi-'trōthd, -'trŏtht\ *n* (1588) : the person to whom one is betrothed

bet·ta \'be-tə\ *n* [NL] (1927) : any of a genus (*Betta*) of small brilliantly colored long-finned freshwater fishes of southeastern Asia; *esp* : SIAMESE FIGHTING FISH

1bet·ter \'be-tər\ *adj, comparative of* GOOD [ME *bettre*, fr. OE *betera*; akin to OE *bōt* remedy, Skt *bhadra* fortunate] (bef. 12c) **1 :** greater than half **2 :** improved in health or mental attitude **3 :** more attractive, favorable, or commendable **4 :** more advantageous or effective **5 :** improved in accuracy or performance

2better *vt* (bef. 12c) **1 :** to make better: as **a :** to make more tolerable or acceptable ⟨trying to ~ the lot of slum dwellers⟩ **b :** to make more complete or perfect ⟨looked forward to ~ing her acquaintance with the new neighbors⟩ **2 :** to surpass in excellence : EXCEL ~ *vi* : to become better *syn* see IMPROVE

3better *adv, comparative of* WELL (12c) **1 a :** in a more excellent manner **b :** to greater advantage : PREFERABLY ⟨some things are ~ left unsaid⟩ **2 a :** to a higher or greater degree ⟨he knows the story ~ than you do⟩ **b :** MORE ⟨it is ~ than nine miles to the next town⟩

4better *n* (12c) **1 :** something better **b :** a superior esp. in merit or rank **2 :** ADVANTAGE, VICTORY ⟨get the ~ of him⟩

5better *verbal auxiliary* (1831) : had better ⟨you ~ hurry⟩

bet·ter·ment \'be-tər-mənt\ *n* (1598) **1 :** a making or becoming better **2 :** an improvement that adds to the value of a property or facility

better–off \,be-tə-'rof\ *adj* (ca. 1859) **1 :** being in comfortable economic circumstances ⟨the ~ people live in the older section of town⟩ **2 :** being in a more advantageous position

betting shop *n* (1852) *Brit* : a shop where bets are taken

bet·tor *or* **bet·ter** \'be-tər\ *n* (1609) : one that bets

1be·tween \bi-'twēn\ *prep* [ME *betwene*, prep. & adv., fr. OE *betwēonum*, fr. *be-* + -*twēonum* (dat. pl.) (akin to Goth *tweihnai* two each); akin to OE *twā* two] (bef. 12c) **1 a :** by the common action of : jointly engaging ⟨shared the work ~ the two of them⟩ ⟨talks ~ the three —*Time*⟩ **b :** in common to : shared by ⟨divided ~ his four grandchildren⟩ **2 a :** in the time, space, or interval that separates ⟨be ~ intermediate relation to **3 a :** from one to another of ⟨air service ~ Miami and Chicago⟩ **b :** serving to connect or unite in a relationship ⟨as difference, likeness, or proportion⟩ ⟨a one-to-one correspondence ~ sets⟩ **c :** setting apart ⟨the line ~ fact and fancy⟩ **4 :** in point of comparison of ⟨not much to choose ~ the two coats⟩ **5 :** in confidence restricted to ⟨a secret ~ you and me⟩

usage There is a persistent but unfounded notion that *between* can be used only of two items and that *among* must be used for more than two. *Between* has been used of more than two since Old English; it is esp. appropriate to denote a one-to-one relationship, regardless of the number of items. It can be used when the number is unspecified ⟨economic cooperation *between* nations⟩, when more than two are enumerated ⟨*between* you and me and the lamppost⟩ ⟨partitioned *between* Austria, Prussia, and Russia —Nathaniel Benchley⟩, and even when only one item is mentioned (but repetition is implied) ⟨pausing *between* every sentence to rap the floor —George Eliot⟩. *Among* is more appropriate where the emphasis is on distribution rather than individual relationships ⟨discontent *among* the peasants⟩. When *among* is automatically chosen for more than two, English idiom may be strained ⟨a worthy book that nevertheless falls *among* many stools — John Simon⟩ ⟨the author alternates *among* mod slang, clichés and quotes from literary giants —A. H. Johnston⟩.

2between *adv* (bef. 12c) : in an intermediate space or interval

be·tween–brain \-,brān\ *n* (ca. 1909) : DIENCEPHALON

be·tween·ness \bi-'twēn-nəs\ *n* (1892) : the quality or state of being between two others in an ordered mathematical set

be·tween–times \bi-'twēn-,tīmz\ *adv* (1907) : at or during intervals

be·tween–whiles \-,hwīlz, -,wīlz\ *adv* (1678) : BETWEENTIMES

be·twixt \bi-'twikst\ *adv or prep* [ME, fr. OE *betwux*, fr. *be-* + -*twux* (akin to Goth *tweihnai*)] (bef. 12c) : BETWEEN

betwixt and between *adv or adj* (1832) : in a midway position : neither one thing nor the other

Beu·lah \'byü-lə\ *n* : an idyllic land near the end of life's journey in Bunyan's *Pilgrim's Progress*

beurre blanc \'bər-'blä^n\ *n* [F, lit., white butter] (1931) : a hot butter sauce (as for fish) flavored with vinegar or lemon juice

beurre ma·nié \-män-'yā\ *n* [F, lit., handled butter] (1939) : flour and butter kneaded together used as a thickener in sauces

beurre noir \-'nwär\ *n* [F, lit., black butter] (1856) : butter heated until brown or black and often flavored with vinegar or lemon juice

1bev·el \'be-vəl\ *adj* (ca. 1600) : OBLIQUE, BEVELED

2bevel *n* [(assumed) MF, fr. OF *baïf* with open mouth, fr. *baer* to yawn — more at ABEYANCE] (1610) **1 :** an instrument consisting of two rules or arms jointed together and opening to any angle for drawing angles or adjusting surfaces to be cut at an angle **2 a :** the angle that one surface or line makes with another when they are not at right angles **b :** the slant of such a surface or line **3 :** the part of printing type extending from face to shoulder

3bevel *vb* -**eled** *or* -**elled**; -**el·ing** *or* -**el·ling** \'bev-liŋ, 'be-və-\ *vt* (1677) : to cut or shape to a bevel ~ *vi* : INCLINE, SLANT

bevel gear *n* (1833) : either of a pair of toothed wheels whose working surfaces are inclined to nonparallel axes

bev·er·age \'bev-rij, 'be-və-\ *n* [ME, fr. MF *bevrage*, fr. *beivre* to drink, fr. L *bibere* — more at POTABLE] (14c) : a drinkable liquid

bevel gears

bevy \'be-vē\ *n, pl* **bev·ies** [ME *bevey*] (15c) **1 :** a large group or collection ⟨a ~ of girls⟩ **2 :** a group of animals and esp. quail together

be·wail \bi-'wā(ə)l\ *vt* (14c) **1 :** to wail over **2 :** to express deep sorrow for usu. by wailing and lamentation ⟨wringing her hands and ~ing her fate⟩ *syn* see DEPLORE

be·ware \bi-'war, -'wer\ *vb* [ME *been war*, fr. *been* to be + *war* careful — more at BE, WARE] *vi* (14c) : to be on one's guard ⟨~ of the dog⟩ ~ *vt* : to take care of ⟨~ your wallet⟩ **2 :** to be wary of ⟨we must . . . ~ the exceedingly tenuous generalization —Matthew Lipman⟩

be·whis·kered \-'hwis-kərd, -'wis-\ *adj* (1820) : wearing whiskers

be·wigged \bi-'wigd\ *adj* (1774) : wearing a wig

be·wil·der \bi-'wil-dər\ *vt* -**wil·dered**; -**wil·der·ing** \-d(ə-)riŋ\ (1684) **1 :** to cause to lose one's bearings **2 :** to perplex or confuse esp. by a complexity, variety, or multitude of objects or considerations *syn* see PUZZLE — **be·wil·dered·ly** *adv* — **be·wil·dered·ness** *n* — **be·wil·der·ing·ly** \-d(ə-)riŋ-lē\ *adv*

be·wil·der·ment \-dər-mənt\ *n* (1820) **1 :** the quality or state of being bewildered **2 :** a bewildering tangle or confusion

be·witch \bi-'wich\ *vt* (13c) **1 :** to influence or affect esp. injuriously by witchcraft **b :** to cast a spell over **2 :** to attract as if by the power of witchcraft : ENCHANT ⟨~ed by her beauty⟩ ~ *vi* : to bewitch someone or something — **be·witch·ery** \-'wi-ch(ə-)rē\ *n* — **be·witch·ing·ly** \-'wi-chiŋ-lē\ *adv*

be·witch·ment \-'wich-mənt\ *n* (1607) **1 a :** the act or power of bewitching **b :** a spell that bewitches **2 :** the state of being bewitched

be·wray \bi-'rā\ *vt* [ME, fr. *be-* + *wreyen* to accuse, fr. OE *wrēgan*; akin to OHG *ruogen* to accuse] (13c) *archaic* : DIVULGE, BETRAY

bey \'bā\ *n* [Turk, gentleman, chief] (1595) **1 a :** a provincial governor in the Ottoman Empire **b :** the former native ruler of Tunis or Tunisia **2 :** — used as a courtesy title in Turkey and Egypt

1be·yond \bē-'änd\ *adv* [ME, prep. & adv., fr. OE *begeondan*, fr. *be-* + *geondan* beyond, fr. *geond* yond — more at YOND] (bef. 12c) **1 :** on or to the farther side : FARTHER **2 :** in addition : BESIDES

2beyond *prep* (bef. 12c) **1 :** on or to the farther side of : at a greater distance than **2 a :** out of the reach or sphere of **b :** in a degree or amount surpassing **c :** out of the comprehension of **3 :** in addition to : BESIDES

3beyond *n* (14c) **1 :** something that lies beyond **2 :** something that lies outside the scope of ordinary experience; *specif* : HEREAFTER

be·zant \'be-z^nt, bə-'zant\ *n* [ME *besant*, fr. OF, fr. ML *Byzantius* Byzantine, fr. *Byzantium*, ancient name of Istanbul] (13c) **1 :** SOLIDUS **1 2 :** a flat disk used in architectural ornament

be·zel \'bē-zəl, 'be-\ *n* [prob. fr. dial. form of F *biseau* bezel, fr. MF] (ca. 1616) **1 :** a rim that holds a transparent covering (as on a watch, clock, or headlight) or that is rotatable and has special markings (as on a watch) **2 :** the oblique side or face of a cut gem; *specif* : the upper faceted portion of a brilliant projecting from the setting — see BRILLIANT illustration **3 :** usu. metal rim of a piece of jewelry in which an ornament (as a gem) is set

be·zique \bə-'zēk\ *n* [F *bésique*] (1861) : a card game similar to pinochle that is played with a pack of 64 cards

be·zoar \'bē-,zōr, -,zŏr\ *n* [MF, fr. ML, fr. Ar dial. *bezuwār*, fr. Ar *bāzahr*, fr. Per *pād-zahr*, fr. *pād* protecting (against) + *zahr* poison] (1577) : any of various calculi found chiefly in the gastrointestinal organs and formerly believed to possess magical properties — called also *bezoar stone*

B–girl *n* [prob. fr. *bar* + *girl*] (1936) : a woman who entertains bar patrons and encourages them to spend freely

BHA \,bē-(,)ā-'chä\ *n* [butylated hydroxyanisole] (1950) : a phenolic antioxidant $C_{11}H_{16}O_2$ used esp. to preserve fats and oils in food

Bha·ga·vad Gi·ta \,bä-gə-,väd-'gē-tə\ *n* [Skt *Bhagavadgītā*, lit., song of the blessed one (Krishna)] (ca. 1785) : a Hindu devotional work in poetic form

bhak·ti \'bək-tē\ *n* [Skt, lit., devotion] (1832) : devotion to a deity constituting a way to salvation in Hinduism

\ə\ abut \ə^\ kitten, F table \ər\ further \a\ ash \ā\ ace \ä\ mop, mar \au\ out \ch\ chin \e\ bet \ē\ easy \g\ go \i\ hit \ī\ ice \j\ job \ŋ\ sing \ō\ go \o\ law \oi\ boy \th\ thin \ṯh\ the \ü\ loot \u\ foot \y\ yet \zh\ vision \á, k̲, ^n, œ, œ̄, œ, œ̄, ^y\ see Guide to Pronunciation

bhang \'baŋ, 'bäŋ\ n [Hindi bhāg] (1563) : HEMP 1a, c; also : the leaves and flowering tops of uncultivated hemp : CANNABIS — compare MARIJUANA, HASHISH

bhar·al \'bər-əl, 'bə-räl\ n [Hindi] (1838) : a goatlike artiodactyl mammal (Pseudois nayaur) of the Himalayas and western China having a bluish-gray coat

BHC \,bē-,äch-'sē\ n [benzene hexachloride] (1947) 1 : any of several stereoisomeric chlorine derivatives $C_6H_6Cl_6$ of cyclohexane in which the chlorine atoms are all attached to different carbon atoms 2 : LINDANE

Bhoj·puri \'bōj-,pùr-ē, 'bäj-, -pə-rē\ n [Hindi bhojpuri, fr. Bhojpur, village in Bihar] (1901) : an Indo-Aryan language spoken in western Bihar and eastern Uttar Pradesh, India

B horizon n (1938) : a subsurface soil layer that is immediately beneath the A horizon from which it obtains organic matter chiefly by illuviation and is usu. distinguished by less weathering

BHT \,bē-,äch-'tē\ n [butylated hydroxytoluene] (1961) : a phenolic antioxidant $C_{15}H_{24}O$ used esp. to preserve fats and oils in food, cosmetics, and pharmaceuticals

bi \'bī\ n or adj (ca. 1965) : BISEXUAL

¹bi- prefix [ME, fr. L — more at TWI-] 1 a : two ⟨bilateral⟩ b : coming or occurring every two ⟨bicentennial⟩ c : into two parts ⟨bisect⟩ 2 a : twice : doubly : on both sides ⟨biconvex⟩ b : coming or occurring two times ⟨biannual⟩ — compare SEMI- 3 : between, involving, or affecting two (specified) symmetrical parts ⟨bilabial⟩ 4 a : containing one (specified) constituent in double the proportion of the other constituent or in double the ordinary proportion ⟨bicarbonate⟩ b : DI-2 ⟨biphenyl⟩

usage Many people are puzzled about bimonthly and biweekly, which are often ambiguous because they are formed from both senses 1b and 2b of bi-. This ambiguity has been in existence for nearly a century and a half and cannot be eliminated by the dictionary. The chief difficulty is that many users of these words assume that others know exactly what they mean, and they do not bother to make their context clear. So if you need bimonthly or biweekly, you should leave some clues in your context to the sense of bi- you mean. And if you need the meaning "twice a," you can substitute semi- for bi-. Biannual and biennial are usu. differentiated.

²bi- or **bio-** comb form [Gk, fr. bios mode of life — more at QUICK] : life : living organisms or tissue ⟨bioluminescence⟩

bi·aly \bē-'ä-lē\ n, pl **bialys** [Yiddish, short for bialystoker, fr. bialystoker of Bialystok, city in Poland] (1965) : a flat breakfast roll that has a depressed center and is usu. covered with onion flakes

bi·an·nu·al \(,)bī-'an-yə(-wə)l\ adj (1877) : occurring twice a year; sometimes : BIENNIAL 1 usage see BI- — **bi·an·nu·al·ly** adv

¹bias \'bī-əs\ n [MF biais] (1530) 1 : a line diagonal to the grain of a fabric; esp : a line at a 45° angle to the selvage often utilized in the cutting of garments for smoother fit 2 a : a peculiarity in the shape of a bowl that causes it to swerve when rolled on the green b : the tendency of a bowl to swerve; also : the impulse causing this tendency c : the swerve of the bowl 3 a : BENT, TENDENCY b : an inclination of temperament or outlook; esp : a personal and sometimes unreasoned judgment : PREJUDICE c : an instance of such prejudice d (1) : deviation of the expected value of a statistical estimate from the quantity it estimates (2) : systematic error introduced into sampling or testing by selecting or encouraging one outcome or answer over others 4 a : a voltage applied to a device (as a transistor control electrode) to establish a reference level for operation b : a high-frequency voltage combined with an audio signal to reduce distortion in tape recording **syn** see PREDILECTION — **on the bias** : ASKEW, OBLIQUELY

²bias adj (1551) : DIAGONAL, SLANTING — used chiefly of fabrics and their cut — **bi·as·ness** n

³bias adv (1575) 1 : DIAGONALLY ⟨cut cloth ∼⟩ 2 obs : AWRY

⁴bias vt **bi·ased** or **bi·assed**; **bi·as·ing** or **bi·as·sing** (ca. 1628) 1 : to give a settled and often prejudiced outlook to ⟨his background ∼es him against foreigners⟩ 2 : to apply a slight negative or positive voltage to (as an electron-tube grid) **syn** see INCLINE

bi·as—belt·ed tire \'bī-əs-,bel-təd-\ n (1968) : a pneumatic tire with a belt (as of steel or fiberglass) around the tire under the tread and on top of the ply cords set diagonally to the center line of the tread

bi·ased adj (1649) 1 : exhibiting or characterized by bias; esp : PREJUDICED 2 : tending to yield one outcome more frequently than others in a statistical experiment ⟨a ∼ coin⟩ 3 : having an expected value different from the quantity or parameter estimated ⟨a ∼ estimate⟩

bi·as—ply tire \'bī-əs-,plī-\ n (1968) : a pneumatic tire having crossed layers of ply-cord set diagonally to the center line of the tread

bias tape n (1926) : a narrow strip of cloth cut on the bias, folded, and used for finishing or decorating clothing

bi·ath·lete \'bī-'ath-,lēt\ n [blend of athlete and biathlon] (1968) : a competitor in a biathlon

bi·ath·lon \bī-'ath-lən, -,län\ n [¹bi- + -athlon (as in decathlon)] (1958) : a composite athletic contest consisting of cross-country skiing and rifle sharpshooting

bi·ax·i·al \(,)bī-'ak-sē-əl\ adj (1854) : having or relating to two axes or optic axes ⟨a ∼ crystal⟩ — **bi·ax·i·al·ly** \-ə-lē\ adv

¹bib \'bib\ vb **bibbed**; **bib·bing** [ME] (14c) : DRINK

²bib n (1580) 1 : a cloth or plastic shield tied under the chin to protect the clothes 2 : the part of an apron or of overalls extending above the waist 3 : a patch of differently colored feathers or fur immediately below the bill or chin of a bird or mammal — **bibbed** \'bibd\ adj — **bib·less** \'bib-ləs\ adj

bib and tucker n (1747) : an outfit of clothing — usu. used in the phrase best bib and tucker

bib·ber \'bi-bər\ n (1536) : a person who regularly drinks alcoholic beverages — **bib·bery** \'bi-bə-rē\ n

Bibb lettuce \'bib-\ n [Major John Bibb, 19th cent. Am. grower] (1961) : lettuce of a variety that has a small head and dark green color

bib·cock \'bib-,käk\ also **bibb cock** n (ca. 1853) : a faucet having a bent-down nozzle

bi·be·lot \'bē-bə-,lō\ n, pl **bibelots** \-,lō(z)\ [F] (1873) : a small household ornament or decorative object : TRINKET

bi·ble \'bī-bəl\ n [ME, fr. OF, fr. ML biblia, fr. Gk, pl. of biblion book, dim. of byblos papyrus, book, fr. Byblos, ancient Phoenician city from which papyrus was exported] (14c) 1 cap a : the sacred scriptures of

Christians comprising the Old Testament and the New Testament b : the sacred scriptures of some other religion (as Judaism) 2 obs : BOOK 3 cap : a copy or an edition of the Bible 4 : a publication that is preeminent esp. in authoritativeness or wide readership ⟨the fisherman's ∼⟩ ⟨the ∼ of the entertainment industry⟩

BOOKS OF THE OLD TESTAMENT

ROMAN CATHOLIC CANON	PROTESTANT CANON	ROMAN CATHOLIC CANON	PROTESTANT CANON
Genesis	Genesis	Wisdom	
Exodus	Exodus	Sirach	
Leviticus	Leviticus	Isaiah	Isaiah
Numbers	Numbers	Jeremiah	Jeremiah
Deuteronomy	Deuteronomy	Lamentations	Lamentations
Joshua	Joshua	Baruch	
Judges	Judges	Ezekiel	Ezekiel
Ruth	Ruth	Daniel	Daniel
1 & 2 Samuel	1 & 2 Samuel	Hosea	Hosea
1 & 2 Kings	1 & 2 Kings	Joel	Joel
1 & 2 Chronicles	1 & 2 Chronicles	Amos	Amos
Ezra	Ezra	Obadiah	Obadiah
Nehemiah	Nehemiah	Jonah	Jonah
Tobit		Micah	Micah
Judith		Nahum	Nahum
Esther	Esther	Habakkuk	Habakkuk
Job	Job	Zephaniah	Zephaniah
Psalms	Psalms	Haggai	Haggai
Proverbs	Proverbs	Zechariah	Zechariah
Ecclesiastes	Ecclesiastes	Malachi	Malachi
Song of Songs	Song of Solomon	1 & 2 Maccabees	

JEWISH SCRIPTURE

Law	1 & 2 Kings	Nahum	Song of Songs
Genesis	Isaiah	Habakkuk	Ruth
Exodus	Jeremiah	Zephaniah	Lamentations
Leviticus	Ezekiel	Haggai	Ecclesiastes
Numbers	Hosea	Zechariah	Esther
Deuteronomy	Joel	Malachi	Daniel
Prophets	Amos	Hagiographa	Ezra
Joshua	Obadiah	Psalms	Nehemiah
Judges	Jonah	Proverbs	1 & 2 Chronicles
1 & 2 Samuel	Micah	Job	

PROTESTANT APOCRYPHA

1 & 2 Esdras	Ecclesiasticus or the Wisdom of Jesus Son of Sirach	Prayer of Azariah and the Song of the Three Holy Children	Bel and the Dragon
Tobit			The Prayer of Manasses
Judith			
Additions to Esther			
Wisdom of Solomon	Baruch	Susanna	1 & 2 Maccabees

BOOKS OF THE NEW TESTAMENT

Matthew	Romans	1 & 2 Thessalonians	James
Mark	1 & 2 Corinthians	1 & 2 Peter
Luke	Galatians	1 & 2 Timothy	1, 2, 3 John
John	Ephesians	Titus	Jude
Acts of the Apostles	Philippians	Philemon	Revelation
	Colossians	Hebrews	or Apocalypse

Bible Belt n (1925) : an area chiefly in the southern U.S. believed to hold uncritical allegiance to the literal accuracy of the Bible; broadly : an area characterized by ardent religious fundamentalism

Bible paper n (1903) : INDIA PAPER 2

Bi·ble—thump·er \'bī-bəl-,thəm-pər\ n (1937) : an overzealous proponent of Christian fundamentalism — **Bi·ble—thump·ing** \-piŋ\ adj

bibli- or **biblio-** comb form [MF, fr. L, fr. Gk, fr. biblion] : book ⟨bibliology⟩

bib·li·cal \'bi-bli-kəl\ adj [ML biblicus, fr. biblia] (ca. 1775) 1 : of, relating to, or being in accord with the Bible 2 : suggestive of the Bible or Bible times — **bib·li·cal·ly** \-k(ə-)lē\ adv

bib·li·cism \'bi-blə-,si-zəm\ n, often cap (1851) : adherence to the letter of the Bible — **bib·li·cist** \-lə-sist\ n, often cap

bib·li·og·ra·pher \,bi-blē-'ä-grə-fər\ n (1775) 1 : an expert in bibliography 2 : a compiler of bibliographies

bib·li·og·ra·phy \,bi-blē-'ä-grə-fē\ n, pl **-phies** [prob. fr. NL bibliographia, fr. Gk, the copying of books, fr. bibli- + -graphia -graphy] (1802) 1 : the history, identification, or description of writings or publications 2 a : a list often with descriptive or critical notes of writings relating to a particular subject, period, or author b : a list of works written by an author or printed by a publishing house 3 : the works or a list of the works referred to in a text or consulted by the author in its production — **bib·lio·graph·ic** \,bi-blē-ə-'gra-fik\ also **bib·lio·graph·i·cal** \-fi-kəl\ adj — **bib·lio·graph·i·cal·ly** \-k(ə-)lē\ adv

bib·li·ol·a·ter \,bi-blē-'ä-lə-tər\ n (1847) 1 : one having excessive reverence for the letter of the Bible 2 : one overly devoted to books — **bib·li·ol·a·trous** \-'ä-lə-trəs\ adj — **bib·li·ol·a·try** \-trē\ n

bib·li·ol·o·gy \,bi-blē-'ä-lə-jē\ n (1806) 1 : the history and science of books as physical objects : BIBLIOGRAPHY 2 often cap : the study of the theological doctrine of the Bible

bib·lio·ma·nia \,bi-blē-ə-'mā-nē-ə, -nyə\ n [F bibliomanie, fr. bibli- + manie mania, fr. LL mania] (1734) : extreme preoccupation with collecting books — **bib·lio·ma·ni·ac** \-nē-,ak\ n or adj — **bib·lio·ma·ni·a·cal** \-lē-ō-mə-'nī-ə-kəl\ adj

bib·li·op·e·gy \,bi-blē-'ä-pə-jē\ n [ultim. fr. Gk bibli- + pēgnynai to fasten together — more at PACT] (ca. 1859) : the art of binding books

— **bib·li·o·pe·gic** \ˌbi-blē-ə-ˈpe-jik, -ˈpē-\ adj — **bib·li·op·e·gist** \ˌbi-blē-ˈä-pə-jist\ n

bib·lio·phile \ˈbi-blē-ə-ˌfīl\ n [F, fr. bibli- + -phile] (1824) : a lover of books esp. for qualities of format; also : a book collector — **bib·lio·phil·ic** \ˌbi-blē-ə-ˈfi-lik\ adj — **bib·lio·phil·ism** \-ˈä-fə-ˌli-zəm\ n — **bib·li·oph·i·ly** \-lē\ n

bib·li·o·pole \ˈbi-blē-ə-ˌpōl\ n [L bibliopola bookseller, fr. Gk bibliopōlēs, fr. bibli- + pōlein to sell] (1775) : a dealer esp. in rare or curious books

bib·li·o·the·ca \ˌbi-blē-ə-ˈthē-kə\ n, pl **-cas** or **-cae** \-ˌsē, -ˌkē\ [L, fr. Gk bibliothēkē, fr. bibli- + thēkē case; akin to Gk tithenai to put, place — more at DO] (ca. 1824) 1 : a collection of books 2 : a list of books — **bib·li·o·the·cal** \-ˈthē-kəl\ adj

bib·lio·ther·a·py \ˌbi-blē-ə-ˈ ther-ə-pē\ n (1919) : the use of reading materials for help in solving personal problems or for psychiatric therapy

bib·li·ot·ics \ˌbi-blē-ˈä-tiks\ n pl but sing in constr [bibli- + ¹-otic + -ics] (1901) : the study of handwriting, documents, and writing materials esp. for determining genuineness or authorship — **bib·li·ot·ic** \-tik\ adj — **bib·li·o·tist** \ˈbi-blē-ə-tist\ n

bib·u·lous \ˈbi-byə-ləs\ adj [L bibulus, fr. bibere to drink — more at POTABLE] (1675) 1 : highly absorbent 2 a : fond of alcoholic beverages b : of, relating to, or marked by the consumption of alcoholic beverages — **bib·u·lous·ly** adv — **bib·u·lous·ness** n

bi·cam·er·al \(ˌ)bī-ˈkam-rəl, -ˈka-mə-\ adj [¹bi- + LL camera chamber — more at CHAMBER] (1856) : having, consisting of, or based on two legislative chambers ⟨a ~ legislature⟩ — **bi·cam·er·al·ism** \-rə-ˌli-zəm\ n

bi·carb \(ˌ)bī-ˈkärb, ˈbī-ˌ\ n (1922) : SODIUM BICARBONATE

bi·car·bon·ate \(ˌ)bī-ˈkär-bə-ˌnāt, -nət\ n [ISV] (1819) : an acid carbonate

bicarbonate of soda (ca. 1887) : SODIUM BICARBONATE

bi·cen·te·na·ry \ˌbī-(ˌ)sen-ˈte-nə-rē, (ˌ)bī-ˈsen-tᵊn-ˌer-ē, ˌbī-(ˌ)sen-ˈtē-nə-rē\ n (1872) : BICENTENNIAL — **bicentenary** adj

bi·cen·ten·ni·al \ˌbī-(ˌ)sen-ˈte-nē-əl\ n (1883) : a 200th anniversary or its celebration — **bicentennial** adj

bi·ceps \ˈbī-ˌseps\ n, pl **biceps** also **bi·ceps·es** [NL bicipit-, biceps, fr. L, two-headed, fr. bi- + capit-, caput head — more at HEAD] (1650) : a muscle having two heads: as a : the large flexor muscle of the front of the upper arm b : the large flexor muscle of the back of the upper leg

biceps bra·chii \-ˈbrā-kē-ˌī, -kē-ˌē\ n [NL, lit., biceps of the arm] (ca. 1860) : BICEPS a

biceps fe·mo·ris \-ˈfe-mə-rəs\ n [NL, lit., biceps of the femur] (ca. 1860) : BICEPS b

bi·chlo·ride of mercury \(ˌ)bī-ˈklōr-ˌīd-, -ˈklȯr-\ [ISV] (1810) : MERCURIC CHLORIDE

bi·chon fri·se \bē-ˌshōⁿ-frē-ˈzā\ n, pl **bi·chons fri·ses** \-ˌshōⁿ-frē-ˈzā(z)\ [modif. of F bichon à poil frisé curly-haired lapdog] (1966) : any of a breed of small sturdy dogs of Mediterranean origin having a thick wavy white coat

bi·chro·mate \ˈbī-ˈkrō-ˌmāt, ˈbī-krō-\ n (1836) : a dichromate esp. of sodium or potassium — **bi·chro·mat·ed** \-ˌmā-təd\ adj

bi·chrome \ˈbī-ˌkrōm\ adj (1924) : two-colored

bi·cip·i·tal \bī-ˈsi-pə-tᵊl\ adj (1646) : of, relating to, or being a biceps

¹bick·er \ˈbi-kər\ n [ME biker] (14c) 1 : petulant quarreling : ALTERCATION 2 : a sound of or as if of bickering

²bicker vi **bick·ered; bick·er·ing** \ˈbi-k(ə-)riŋ\ (15c) 1 : to engage in a petulant or petty quarrel 2 a : to move with a rapidly repeated noise ⟨a ~ing stream⟩ b : QUIVER, FLICKER — **bick·er·er** \-kə-rər\ n

bi·coast·al \(ˌ)bī-ˈkōs-təl\ adj (1972) : of or relating to or living or working on both the East and West coasts of the U.S.

bi·col·ored \ˈbī-ˌkə-lərd\ or **bi·col·or** \-lər\ adj [L bicolor, fr. bi- + color] (ca. 1843) : two-colored — **bicolor** n

bi·com·po·nent \(ˌ)bī-kəm-ˈpō-nənt, -käm-, -ˈkäm-ˌ\ adj (1962) : being a fiber made of two polymers having slightly different physical properties so that the fiber has a permanent crimp and fabrics made from it have inherent bulk and stretchability

bi·con·cave \(ˌ)bī-(ˌ)kän-ˈkāv, -ˈkän-\ adj (1833) : concave on both sides — **bi·con·cav·i·ty** \ˌbī-(ˌ)kän-ˈka-və-tē\ n

bi·con·di·tion·al \ˌbī-kən-ˈdish-nəl, -ˈdi-shə-\ n (1940) : a relation between two propositions that is true only when both propositions are simultaneously true or false

bi·con·vex \ˌbī-(ˌ)kän-ˈveks, (ˌ)bī-ˈkän-ˌ\ adj [ISV] (ca. 1852) : convex on both sides — **bi·con·vex·i·ty** \ˌbī-kən-ˈvek-sə-tē, -(ˌ)kän-\ n

bi·corne \ˈbī-ˌkȯrn\ n [F, fr. L bicornis two-horned, fr. bi- + cornu horn — more at HORN] (1936) : COCKED HAT 2

bi·cul·tur·al \(ˌ)bī-ˈkəl-chər-əl\ adj (1940) : of, relating to, or including two distinct cultures ⟨~ education⟩ — **bi·cul·tur·al·ism** \-ə-ˌli-zəm\ n

¹bi·cus·pid \(ˌ)bī-ˈkəs-pəd\ adj [NL bicuspid-, bicuspis, fr. bi- + L cuspid-, cuspis point] (ca. 1839) : having or ending in two points ⟨~ teeth⟩

²bicuspid n (1852) : a human premolar tooth — see TOOTH illustration

bicuspid valve n (ca. 1903) : a cardiac valve consisting of two triangular flaps which allow only unidirectional blood flow from the left atrium to the ventricle — called also mitral valve

¹bi·cy·cle \ˈbī-si-kəl, -ˌsi- also -ˌsī-\ n [F, fr. bi- + -cycle (as in tricycle)] (1868) : a vehicle with two wheels tandem, a steering handle, a saddle seat, and pedals by which it is propelled; also : a stationary exercise machine that resembles such a vehicle

²bicycle vi **bi·cy·cled; bi·cy·cling** \-k(ə-)liŋ\ (1869) : to ride a bicycle — **bi·cy·cler** \-klər\ n — **bi·cy·clist** \-klist\ n

bi·cy·clic \(ˌ)bī-ˈsī-klik, -ˈsi-\ adj [ISV] (ca. 1909) 1 : consisting of or arranged in two cycles 2 : containing two usu. fused rings in the structure of the molecule

¹bid \ˈbid\ vb **bade** \ˈbad, ˈbād\ or **bid; bid·den** \ˈbi-dᵊn\ or **bid** also **bade; bid·ding** [partly fr. ME bidden, fr. OE biddan; akin to OHG bitten to entreat, and perh. to Skt bādhate he presses; partly fr. ME beden to offer, command, fr. OE bēodan; akin to OHG biotan to offer, Gk pynthanesthai to examine, Skt bodhi enlightenment] vt (bef. 12c) 1 a obs : BESEECH, ENTREAT b : to issue an order to : TELL c : to request to come : INVITE 2 : to give expression to ⟨bade a tearful farewell⟩ 3 a : OFFER — usu. used in the phrase to bid defiance b past and past part bid (1) : to offer (a price) whether for payment or acceptance (2) : to make a bid of or in (a suit at cards) ~ vi : to make a bid syn see COMMAND — **bid·der** n — **bid fair** : to seem likely

²bid n (1788) 1 a : the act of one who bids b : a statement of what one will give or take for something; esp : an offer of a price c : something offered as a bid 2 : an opportunity to bid 3 : INVITATION 4 a : an announcement of what a cardplayer proposes to undertake b : the amount of such a bid c : a biddable bridge hand 5 : an attempt or effort to win, achieve, or attract ⟨a ~ for reelection⟩

bid·da·ble \ˈbi-də-bəl\ adj (ca. 1768) 1 : easily led, taught, or controlled : DOCILE 2 : capable of being bid — **bid·da·bil·i·ty** \ˌbi-də-bᵊ-lə-tē\ n — **bid·da·bly** \ˈbi-də-blē\ adv

¹bid·dy \ˈbi-dē\ n, pl **biddies** [perh. imit.] (1601) : HEN 1a; also : a young chicken

²biddy n, pl **biddies** [dim. of the name Bridget] (ca. 1861) 1 : a hired girl or cleaning woman 2 : WOMAN; esp : an elderly woman — usu. used disparagingly

bide \ˈbīd\ vb **bode** \ˈbōd\ or **bid·ed; bided; bid·ing** [ME, fr. OE bīdan; akin to OHG bītan to wait, L fidere to trust, Gk peithesthai to believe] vt (bef. 12c) 1 archaic : to wait for — used chiefly in the phrase bide one's time 2 archaic : WITHSTAND ⟨two men . . . might ~ the winter storm —W. C. Bryant⟩ 3 chiefly dial : to put up with : TOLERATE ~ vi 1 : to continue in a state or condition 2 : to wait awhile : TARRY 3 : to continue in a place : SOJOURN — **bid·er** n

bi·det \bi-ˈdā\ n [F, small horse, bidet, fr. MF, fr. bider to trot] (1766) : a bathroom fixture used esp. for bathing the external genitals and the posterior parts of the body

bi·di·a·lec·tal·ism \ˌbī-ˌdī-ə-ˈlek-tᵊl-ˌi-zəm\ n (1958) : facility in using two dialects of the same language; also : the teaching of Standard English to pupils who normally use a nonstandard dialect — **bi·di·a·lec·tal** adj

bi·di·rec·tion·al \ˌbī-də-ˈrek-shnəl, -dī-, -shə-nᵊl\ adj (1928) : involving, moving, or taking place in two usu. opposite directions ⟨~ flow⟩ ⟨~ replication of DNA⟩ — **bi·di·rec·tion·al·ly** adv

bi·don·ville \ˌbē-dōⁿ-ˈvē(ə)l\ n [F, fr. bidon metal can or drum + ville city] (1952) : a settlement of jerry-built dwellings on the outskirts of a city (as in France or No. Africa)

bid up vt (1864) : to raise the price of (as property at auction) by a succession of offers

Bie·der·mei·er \ˈbē-dər-ˌmī(-ə)r\ adj [after Gottlieb Biedermeier, satirical name for an uninspired Ger. bourgeois] (1905) : of a style of unostentatious furniture and interior decoration popular esp. with the middle class in early 19th century Germany

bi·en·ni·al \(ˌ)bī-ˈe-nē-əl\ adj (1562) 1 : occurring every two years 2 : continuing or lasting for two years; specif : growing vegetatively during the first year and fruiting and dying during the second usage see BI- — **biennial** n — **bi·en·ni·al·ly** \-ə-lē\ adv

bi·en·ni·um \bī-ˈe-nē-əm\ n, pl **-niums** or **-nia** \-nē-ə\ [L, fr. bi- + annus year — more at ANNUAL] (1899) : a period of two years

bier \ˈbir\ n [ME bere, fr. OE bǣr; akin to OE beran to carry — more at BEAR] (bef. 12c) 1 archaic : a framework for carrying 2 : a stand on which a corpse or coffin is placed; also : a coffin together with its stand

bi·face \ˈbī-ˌfās\ n (1934) : a bifacial stone tool

bi·fa·cial \(ˌ)bī-ˈfā-shəl\ adj (ca. 1847) : having opposite sides or faces worked on to form an edge for cutting or scraping — **bi·fa·cial·ly** adv

biff \ˈbif\ n [prob. imit.] (ca. 1889) : WHACK, BLOW — **biff** vt

bi·fid \ˈbī-ˌfid, -fəd\ adj [L bifidus, fr. bi- + -fidus -fid] (1661) : divided into two equal lobes or parts by a median cleft ⟨a ~ leaf⟩

bi·fi·lar \(ˌ)bī-ˈfī-lər\ adj [ISV bi- + L filum thread — more at FILE] (1846) 1 : involving two threads or wires ⟨~ suspension of a pendulum⟩ 2 : involving a single thread or wire doubled back upon itself ⟨a ~ resistor⟩ — **bi·fi·lar·ly** adv

bi·fla·gel·late \(ˌ)bī-ˈfla-jə-lət, -ˌlāt; -flə-ˈje-lət\ adj (1856) : having two flagella ⟨~ gametes⟩

¹bi·fo·cal \ˈbī-ˌfō-kəl\ adj [ISV] (1888) 1 : having two focal lengths 2 : having one part that corrects for near vision and one for distant vision ⟨a ~ eyeglass lens⟩

²bifocal n (1899) 1 pl : eyeglasses with bifocal lenses 2 : a bifocal glass or lens

bi·func·tion·al \(ˌ)bī-ˈfəŋ(k)-shnəl, -shə-nᵊl\ adj (1936) : having two functions; esp : DIFUNCTIONAL

bi·fur·cate \ˈbī-(ˌ)fər-ˌkāt, bī-ˈfər-\ vb **-cat·ed; -cat·ing** [ML bifurcatus, pp. of bifurcare, fr. L bifurcus two-pronged, fr. bi- + furca fork] vt (1615) : to cause to divide into two branches or parts ~ vi : to divide into two branches or parts — **bi·fur·cate** \(ˌ)bī-ˈfər-kət, -ˌkāt; ˈbī-(ˌ)fər-ˌkāt\ adj

bi·fur·ca·tion \ˌbī-(ˌ)fər-ˈkā-shən\ n (1615) 1 a : the point at which bifurcating occurs b : BRANCH 2 : the act of bifurcating : the state of being bifurcated

¹big \ˈbig\ adj **big·ger; big·gest** [ME, perh. of Scand origin; akin to Norw dial. bugge important man] (14c) 1 a obs : of great strength b : of great force ⟨a ~ storm⟩ 2 a : large or great in dimensions, bulk, or extent ⟨a ~ house⟩; also : large or great in quantity, number, or amount ⟨a ~ fleet⟩ b : operating on a large scale ⟨~ government⟩ c : CAPITAL 3 a : PREGNANT 2; esp : nearly ready to give birth b : full to bursting : SWELLING ⟨~ with rage⟩ c of the voice : full and resonant 4 a : CHIEF, PREEMINENT ⟨the ~ issue of the campaign⟩ b : outstandingly worthy or able ⟨a truly ~ man⟩ c : of great importance or significance ⟨the ~ moment⟩ d : IMPOSING, PRETENTIOUS; also : marked by or given to boasting ⟨~ talk⟩ e : MAGNANIMOUS, GENEROUS ⟨was ~ about it⟩ 5 : POPULAR ⟨soft drinks are very ~ in Mexico —Russ Leadabrand⟩ 6 : full-bodied and flavorful — used of wine — **big·ly** adv — **big·ness** n — **big on** : strongly favoring or liking; also : noted for ⟨she is big on blushing —Arnold Hano⟩

²big adv (1807) 1 : in a loud or declamatory manner; also : in a boasting manner ⟨talk ~⟩ 2 : to a large amount or extent ⟨won ~⟩ ⟨lost ~⟩ b : on a large scale ⟨think ~⟩ ⟨worry ~⟩ 3 : HARD ⟨hits her forehand ~⟩

³big n (1965) : an individual or organization of outstanding importance or power; esp : MAJOR LEAGUE — usu. used in pl. ⟨playing in the ~s⟩

\ə\ abut \ᵊ\ kitten, F table \ər\ further \a\ ash \ā\ ace \ä\ mop, mar \aù\ out \ch\ chin \e\ bet \ē\ easy \g\ go \i\ hit \ī\ ice \j\ job \ŋ\ sing \ō\ go \ȯ\ law \ȯi\ boy \th\ thin \t͟h\ the \ü\ loot \ù\ foot \y\ yet \zh\ vision \á, k̲, ⁿ, œ, œ̄, ᵫ, ᵫ̄, ᵘ\ see Guide to Pronunciation

big·a·mous \'bi-gə-məs\ adj (1864) **1** : guilty of bigamy **2** : involving bigamy — **big·a·mous·ly** adv

big·a·my \'bi-gə-mē\ n [ME bigamie, fr. ML bigamia, fr. L bi- + LL -gamia -gamy] (13c) : the act of entering into a marriage with one person while still legally married to another — **big·a·mist** \-mist\ n

bi·ga·rade \,bē-gä-'räd\ n [F, fr. Prov bigarrado, fr. bigarra to variegate] (1703) **1** : SOUR ORANGE **2** : a brown sauce flavored with the juice and grated rind of oranges

big band n (1926) : a band that is larger than a combo and that usu. features a mixture of ensemble playing and solo improvisation typical of jazz or swing

big bang n (1950) : the cosmic explosion that marked the beginning of the universe according to the big bang theory

big bang theory n (1955) : a theory in astronomy: the universe originated billions of years ago in an explosion from a single point of nearly infinite energy density — compare STEADY STATE THEORY

big beat n, often cap both Bs (1958) : music (as rock) characterized by a heavy persistent beat

Big Ben \-'ben\ n [Sir Benjamin Hall †1867 Eng. Chief Commissioner of Works] (ca. 1895) **1** : a large bell in the clock tower of the Houses of Parliament in London **2** : the tower that houses Big Ben; also : the clock in the tower

big boy n (1926) : BIG GUN — usu. used in pl.

big brother n (1863) **1** : an older brother **2** : a man who befriends a delinquent or friendless boy **3** cap both Bs [Big Brother, personification of the power of the state in 1984 (1949) by George Orwell] **a** : the leader of an authoritarian state or movement **b** : an all-powerful government or organization monitoring and directing people's actions ⟨data banks that tell Big Brother all about us —Herbert Brucker⟩

Big Broth·er·ism \-'brə-thər-,i-zəm\ n (1950) : authoritarian attempts at complete control (as of a person or a nation)

big buck n (1970) : a large sum of money — usu. used in pl.; usu. hyphenated when attributive

big business n (1905) **1** : an economic group consisting of large profit-making corporations esp. with regard to their influence on social or political policy **2** : a very profitable enterprise

big C n, often cap B (1968) : CANCER 2

big daddy n, often cap B&D (1958) : one preeminent esp. by reason of power, size, or seniority : one representing paternalistic authority

big deal n (1949) : something of special importance — sometimes used ironically as an interjection

Big Dipper n : the seven principal stars in the constellation of Ursa Major

bi·gem·i·ny \bī-'je-mə-nē\ n [bigeminal (double, paired), fr. LL bigeminus, fr. bi- + geminus twin] (ca. 1923) : the state of having a pulse characterized by two beats close together with a pause following each pair of beats — **bi·gem·i·nal** \-mə-nᵊl\ adj

bi·ge·ner·ic \,bī-jə-'ner-ik\ adj (1885) : of, relating to, or involving two genera ⟨a ~ hybrid⟩

big·eye \'big-,ī\ n (ca. 1889) : either of two small widely distributed reddish to silvery bony fishes (Priacanthus cruentatus and P. arenatus of the family Priacanthidae) of tropical seas

big·foot \'big-,fût\ n, often cap [fr. the size of the footprints ascribed to it] (1958) : SASQUATCH

big game n (1864) **1** : large animals sought or taken by hunting or fishing for sport **2** : an important objective esp. when involving risk

big·ge·ty or big·gi·ty \'bi-gə-tē\ adj [big + -ety (as in persnickety)] (1880) **1** Southern & Midland : CONCEITED, VAIN **2** Southern & Midland : rudely self-important : IMPUDENT ⟨never acted ~ in court, but she would bow her head only so low —Claude Brown⟩

big·gie \'bi-gē\ n (ca. 1931) : one that is big

¹**big·gin or big·ging** \'bi-gən\ n [ME bigging, fr. biggen to dwell, fr. ON byggja; akin to OE bēon to be] (14c) archaic : BUILDING

²**biggin** n [MF beguin] (1530) archaic : CAP **a** : a child's cap **b** : NIGHTCAP

big·gish \'bi-gish\ adj (ca. 1626) : somewhat big

big gun n (1834) : one having preeminent status or power in a field

big·head \'big-,hed\ n (1805) **1** : any of several diseases of animals marked by swelling about the head **2** : an exaggerated opinion of one's importance — usu. used with the — **big·head·ed** \-'he-dəd\ adj

big·heart·ed \-'här-təd\ adj (1868) : GENEROUS, CHARITABLE — **big·heart·ed·ly** adv — **big·heart·ed·ness** n

big·horn sheep \'big-,hȯrn-\ n (1838) : a usu. grayish brown wild sheep (Ovis canadensis) of mountainous and desert regions of western No. America — called also bighorn

big house n, often cap B&H (1916) slang : PENITENTIARY

bight \'bīt\ n [ME, fr. OE byht bend, bay; akin to OE būgan to bend — more at BOW] (15c) **1** : a bend in a coast forming an open bay; also : a bay formed by such a bend **2** : a slack part or loop in a rope

big league n (1899) **1** : MAJOR LEAGUE **2** : BIG TIME 2 — often used in pl. — **big–league** adj — **big leaguer** n

big lie n, sometimes cap B&L (1946) : a deliberate gross distortion of the truth used esp. as a propaganda tactic

big-mouthed \'big-,mau̇thd, 'big-,maû̇tht, 'big-\ adj (1642) **1** : having a large mouth **2** : LOUDMOUTHED

big name n (1932) : a performer or personage of top rank in popular recognition — **big–name** adj

big·no·nia \big-'nō-nē-ə\ n [NL, genus name, fr. J. P. Bignon †1743 Fr. royal librarian] (1785) : any of a genus (Bignonia) of American and Japanese woody vines of the trumpet-creeper family with compound leaves and tubular flowers

bighorn sheep

big·ot \'bi-gət\ n [MF, hypocrite, bigot] (1661) : a person obstinately or intolerantly devoted to his or her own opinions and prejudices — **big·ot·ed** \-gə-təd\ adj — **big·ot·ed·ly** adv

big·ot·ry \'bi-gə-trē\ n, pl **-ries** (ca. 1674) **1** : the state of mind of a bigot **2** : acts or beliefs characteristic of a bigot

big picture n, often cap B&P (ca. 1960) : the entire perspective on a situation or issue — used with the

big shot \'big-,shät\ n (1929) : a person of consequence or prominence

big stick n (1904) : threat esp. of military or political intervention

big-tick·et \'big-'ti-kət\ adj (1945) : having a high price

big time \-,tīm\ n (1910) **1** : a high-paying vaudeville circuit requiring only two performances a day **2** : the top rank of an activity or enterprise — **big–time** adj — **big·tim·er** \-,tī-mər\ n

big toe n (ca. 1887) : the innermost and largest toe of the foot

big top n (1895) **1** : the main tent of a circus **2** : CIRCUS 2a, b, c

big tree n (1853) : a California evergreen (Sequoiadendron giganteum) of the bald cypress family that sometimes exceeds 270 feet (about 82 meters) in height — called also giant sequoia, sequoia

big wheel n (1942) : BIGWIG, BIG SHOT

big·wig \'big-,wig\ n (1703) : an important person

Bi·ha·ri \bi-'här-ē\ n (1882) **1** : a group of Indo-Aryan languages (as Bhojpuri) spoken in Bihar, India, and adjacent areas **2 a** : a native or inhabitant of Bihar **b** : a Muslim born in Bihar who emigrated after the partition of India in 1947; also : a descendant of such a person

bi·jec·tion \(,)bī-'jek-shən\ n [¹bi- + -jection (as in injection)] (1966) : a mathematical function that is a one-to-one and onto mapping — compare INJECTION, SURJECTION — **bi·jec·tive** \-'jek-tiv\ adj

bi·jou \'bē-,zhü\ n, pl **bijous** or **bi·joux** \-,zhü(z)\ [F, fr. Bret bizou ring, fr. biz finger] (1668) **1** : a small dainty usu. ornamental piece of delicate workmanship : JEWEL **2** : something delicate, elegant, or highly prized — **bijou** adj

bi·jou·te·rie \bi-'zhü-tə-(,)rē\ n [F, fr. bijou] (1815) : a collection of trinkets or ornaments : JEWELS; also : DECORATION

¹**bike** \'bīk\ n [ME] (14c) **1** chiefly Scot : a nest of wild bees, wasps, or hornets **2** chiefly Scot : a crowd or swarm of people

²**bike** n [by shortening & alter.] (1882) **1** : BICYCLE **2** : MOTORCYCLE **3** : MOTORBIKE

³**bike** vi biked; bik·ing (1895) : to ride a bike

bik·er \'bī-kər\ n (1883) **1** : BICYCLIST **2** : MOTORCYCLIST; esp : one who is a member of an organized gang

bike·way \'bīk-,wā\ n (1965) : a thoroughfare for bicycles

bik·ie \'bī-kē\ n [²bike + -ie] (1967) : BIKER 2

bi·ki·ni \bə-'kē-nē\ n [F, fr. Bikini, atoll of the Marshall islands] (1947) **1 a** : a woman's scanty two-piece bathing suit **b** : a man's brief swimsuit **2** : a man's or woman's low-cut briefs — **bi·ki·nied** \-nēd\ adj

¹**bi·la·bi·al** \(,)bī-'lā-bē-əl\ adj [ISV] (1894) of a consonant : produced with both lips

²**bilabial** n (1899) : a bilabial consonant

bi·la·bi·ate \-bē-ət\ adj (1794) : having two lips ⟨a ~ corolla⟩

bi·lat·er·al \(,)bī-'la-t(ə-)rəl\ adj (1775) **1** : having two sides **2** : affecting reciprocally two nations or parties ⟨a ~ treaty⟩ ⟨a ~ trade agreement⟩ **3 a** : of, relating to, or affecting the right and left sides of the body or the right and left members of paired organs ⟨a ~ nephrectomy⟩ **b** : having bilateral symmetry — **bi·lat·er·al·ism** \-t(ə-)rə-,li-zəm\ n — **bi·lat·er·al·ly** adv

bilateral symmetry n (1860) : symmetry in which similar anatomical parts are arranged on opposite sides of a median axis so that only one plane can divide the individual into essentially identical halves

bi·lay·er \'bī-,lā-ər, -,le(-ə)r\ n (1963) : a film or membrane with two molecular layers ⟨a ~ of phospholipid molecules⟩ — **bilayer** adj

bil·ber·ry \'bil-,ber-ē\ n [bil- (prob. of Scand origin; akin to Dan bølle whortleberry) + berry] (1577) : any of several ericaceous shrubs (genus Vaccinium) that resemble blueberries but have flowers which arise solitary or in very small clusters from axillary buds; also : its sweet edible fruit

¹**bil·bo** \'bil-(,)bō\ n, pl **bilboes** [perh. fr. Bilboa, Spain] (1557) : a long bar of iron with sliding shackles used to confine the feet of prisoners esp. on shipboard

²**bilbo or bil·boa** \'bil-(,)bō\ n, pl **bilboes** or **bilboas** [Bilboa, Bilbao, Spain] (1565) : SWORD

bil·dungs·ro·man \'bil-dún(k)s-rō-,män, -dûnz-\ n [G, fr. Bildung education + Roman novel] (1910) : a novel about the moral and psychological growth of the main character

bile \'bī(ə)l\ n [L bilis; akin to W bustl bile] (1547) **1 a** : either of two humors associated in old physiology with irascibility and melancholy **b** : a yellow or greenish viscid alkaline fluid secreted by the liver and passed into the duodenum where it aids esp. in the emulsification and absorption of fats **2** : inclination to anger

bile acid n (ca. 1881) : any of several steroid acids (as cholic acid) of or derived from bile

bile duct n (1774) : a duct by which bile passes from the liver or gallbladder to the duodenum

bile salt n (1881) **1** : a salt of bile acid **2** pl : a dry mixture of the principal salts of the gall of the ox used as a liver stimulant and as a laxative

¹**bi·lev·el** \'bī-,le-vəl\ adj (1960) **1** : having two levels of freight or passenger space **2** : divided vertically into two ground-floor levels

²**bi–level** \'bī-,\ n (1966) : a bi-level house

¹**bilge** \'bilj\ n [prob. modif. of MF boulge, bouge leather bag, curved part — more at BUDGET] (1513) **1** : the bulging part of a cask or barrel **2 a** : the part of the underwater body of a ship between the flat of the bottom and the vertical topsides **b** : the lowest point of a ship's inner hull **3** : stale or worthless remarks or ideas

²**bilge** vi bilged; bilg·ing (1728) : to become damaged in the bilge

bilge keel n (1850) : a projection like a fin extending from the hull near the turn of the bilge on either side to check rolling

bilge·wa·ter \'bilj-,wȯ-tər, -,wä-\ n (1706) : water that collects in the bilge of a ship

bil·har·zia \bil-'här-zē-ə; -'härt-sē-\ n [NL, genus name, fr. Theodor Bilharz †1862 Ger. zoologist] (ca. 1881) **1** : SCHISTOSOMIASIS **2** : SCHISTOSOME — **bil·har·zi·al** \-zē-əl, -sē-\ adj

bil·har·zi·a·sis \,bil-,här-'zī-ə-səs; -,härt-'sī-\ n, pl **-a·ses** \-,sēz\ [NL] (ca. 1900) : SCHISTOSOMIASIS

bil•i•ary \'bi-lē-ˌer-ē\ *adj* [F *biliare,* fr. L *bilis*] (1731) **:** of, relating to, or conveying bile; *also* **:** affecting the bile-conveying structures

bi•lin•ear \(ˌ)bī-'li-nē-ər\ *adj* (1886) **:** linear with respect to each of two mathematical variables; *specif* **:** of or relating to an algebraic form each term of which involves one variable to the first degree from each of two sets of variables

bi•lin•gual \(ˌ)bī-'liŋ-gwəl *also* -gyə-wəl\ *adj* [L *bilinguis,* fr. *bi-* + *lingua* tongue — more at TONGUE] (1845) **1 :** having or expressed in two languages **2 :** using or able to use two languages esp. with equal fluency **3 :** of or relating to bilingual education — **bilingual** *n* — **bi•lin•gual•ly** *adv*

bilingual education *n* (1972) **:** education in an English-language school system in which minority students with little fluency in English are taught in their native language

bi•lin•gual•ism \-gwə-ˌli-zəm\ *n* (1873) **:** the ability to speak two languages **:** the frequent oral use of two languages

bil•ious \'bil-yəs\ *adj* [MF *bilieux,* fr. L *biliosus,* fr. *bilis*] (1541) **1 a :** of or relating to bile **b :** marked by or suffering from liver dysfunction and esp. excessive secretion of bile **c :** appearing as if affected by a bilious disorder **2 :** of or indicative of a peevish ill-natured disposition — **bil•ious•ly** *adv* — **bil•ious•ness** *n*

bil•i•ru•bin \ˌbi-li-'rü-bən, 'bi-li-ˌ\ *n* [L *bilis* + *ruber* red — more at RED] (1871) **:** a reddish yellow water insoluble pigment occurring esp. in bile and blood and causing jaundice if accumulated in excess

bil•i•ver•din \-'vər-dᵊn, -ˌvər-\ *n* [Sw, fr. L *bilis* + obs. F *verd* green] (1845) **:** a green pigment that occurs in bile and is an intermediate in the degradation of hemoglobin heme groups to bilirubin

[1]**bilk** \'bilk\ *vt* [perh. alter. of [2]*balk*] (1651) **1 :** to block the free development of **:** FRUSTRATE ⟨fate ~*s* their hopes⟩ **2 a :** to cheat out of something valuable **:** DEFRAUD **b :** to evade payment of or to ⟨~*s* his creditors⟩ **3 :** to slip away from **:** ELUDE ⟨~*ed* her pursuers⟩ — **bilk•er** *n*

[2]**bilk** *n* (1790) **:** an untrustworthy tricky individual **:** CHEAT

[1]**bill** \'bil\ *n* [ME *bile,* fr. OE; akin to OE *bill*] (bef. 12c) **1 :** the jaws of a bird together with their horny covering **2 :** a mouthpart (as the beak of a turtle) that resembles a bird's bill **3 :** the point of an anchor fluke — see ANCHOR illustration **4 :** the visor of a cap or hood

bill 1: *1* flamingo, *2* falcon, *3* pigeon, *4* thrush, *5* merganser, *6* toucan, *7* finch, *8* spoonbill, *9* pelican

[2]**bill** *vi* (1592) **1 :** to touch and rub bill to bill **2 :** to caress affectionately ⟨~*ing* and cooing⟩

[3]**bill** *n* [ME *bil,* fr. OE *bill* sword; akin to OHG *bill* pickax] (14c) **1 :** a weapon in use up to the 18th century that consists of a long staff ending in a hook-shaped blade **2 :** BILLHOOK

[4]**bill** *n* [ME, fr. ML *billa* seal, alter. of *bulla,* fr. L, bubble, boss] (14c) **1 :** an itemized list or a statement of particulars (as a list of materials or of members of a ship's crew) **2 :** a written document or note **3** *obs* **:** a formal petition **4 a :** an itemized account of the separate cost of goods sold, services performed, or work done **:** INVOICE **b :** an amount expended or owed **c :** a statement of charges for food or drink **:** CHECK **5 a :** a written or printed advertisement posted or otherwise distributed to announce an event of interest to the public; *esp* **:** an announcement of a theatrical entertainment **b :** a programmed presentation (as a motion picture, play, or concert) **6 :** a draft of a law presented to a legislature for enactment; *also* **:** the law itself ⟨the GI ~⟩ **7 :** a declaration in writing stating a wrong a complainant has suffered from a defendant or stating a breach of law by some person ⟨a ~ of complaint⟩ **8 a :** a piece of paper money **b :** an individual or commercial note ⟨~*s* receivable⟩ **c** *slang* **:** one hundred dollars — **fill the bill** *or* **fit the bill :** to be exactly what is needed **:** be suitable

[5]**bill** *vt* (14c) **1 a :** to enter in an accounting system **:** prepare a bill of (charges) **b :** to submit a bill of charges to **c :** to enter (as freight) in a waybill **d :** to issue a bill of lading to or for **2 :** to announce (as a performance) esp. by posters or placards **3 :** ADVERTISE, PROMOTE ⟨the book is ~*ed* as a "report" —P. G. Altbach⟩ — **bill•able** *adj*

bil•la•bong \'bi-lə-ˌbȯŋ, -ˌbäŋ\ *n* [Wiradhuri (Australian aboriginal language of central New South Wales) *bilabaŋ*] (1861) **1** *Austral* **a :** a blind channel leading out from a river **b :** a usu. dry streambed that is filled seasonally **2** *Austral* **:** a backwater forming a stagnant pool

[1]**bill•board** \'bil-ˌbōrd, -ˌbȯrd\ *n* (1851) **:** a flat surface (as of a panel, wall, or fence) on which bills are posted; *specif* **:** a large panel designed to carry outdoor advertising

[2]**billboard** *vt* (1950) **:** to promote by a conspicuous display on or as if on a billboard

bill•bug \'bil-ˌbəg\ *n* [[1]*bill* + *bug*] (1861) **:** any of various weevils (as of the genus *Sphenophorus*) having larvae that eat the roots of cereal and other grasses

billed \'bild\ *adj* **:** having a bill of a specified kind — used in combination ⟨spoon-*billed*⟩

bill•er \'bi-lər\ *n* (1920) **:** one that bills; *esp* **:** one that makes out bills

[1]**bil•let** \'bi-lət\ *n* [ME *bylet,* fr. MF *billette,* dim. of *bulle* document, fr. ML *bulla*] (15c) **1** *archaic* **:** a brief letter **:** NOTE **2 a :** an official order directing that a member of a military force be provided with board and lodging (as in a private home) **b :** quarters assigned by or as if by a billet **3 :** POSITION, JOB ⟨a lucrative ~⟩

[2]**billet** *vt* (1594) **1 :** to assign lodging to (as soldiers) by or as if by a billet **2 :** to serve with a billet ⟨~ a householder⟩

[3]**billet** *n* [ME *bylet,* fr. MF *billete,* dim. of *bille* log, of Celt origin; akin to OIr *bile* landmark tree] (15c) **1 a :** a chunky piece of wood (as for firewood) **b** *obs* **:** CUDGEL **2 a :** a bar of metal **b :** a piece of semifinished iron or steel nearly square in section made by rolling an ingot or bloom **c :** a section of nonferrous metal ingot hot-worked by forging, rolling, or extrusion **d :** a nonferrous casting suitable for rolling or extrusion

bil•let–doux \ˌbi-lē-'dü, ˌbi-(ˌ)lā-\ *n, pl* **bil•lets–doux** \-'dü(z)\ [F *billet doux,* lit., sweet letter] (1673) **:** a love letter

bill•fish \'bil-ˌfish\ *n* (1782) **:** a fish with long slender jaws; *esp* **:** any of a family (Istiophoridae) including marlins, spearfishes, and sailfishes

bill•fold \-ˌfōld\ *n* [short for earlier *billfolder*] (1895) **:** a folding pocketbook for paper money **:** WALLET

bill•hook \-ˌhu̇k\ *n* (1611) **:** a cutting or pruning tool with a hooked blade

bil•liard \'bi(l)-yərd\ *n* (1580) — used as an attributive form of *billiards* ⟨~ ball⟩

bil•liards \-yərdz\ *n pl but sing in constr* [MF *billard* billiard cue, billiards, fr. *bille*] (1580) **:** any of several games played on an oblong table by driving small balls against one another or into pockets with a cue; *specif* **:** a game in which one scores by causing a cue ball to hit in succession two object balls — compare POOL

bil•li–bi *also* **bil•ly–bi** \'bi-lē-ˌbē, ˌbi-lē-'\ *n* [F, alter. of *Billy B.,* perh. fr. William B. Leeds, Jr. †1972 Am. industrialist] (1961) **:** a soup of mussel stock, white wine, and cream served hot or cold

bill•ing \'bi-liŋ\ *n* [[5]*bill*] (1875) **1 :** advertising or public promotion (as of a product or personality); *also* **:** relative prominence of a name in such promotion ⟨got top ~⟩ **2 :** total amount of business or investments (as of an advertising agency) within a given period

bil•lings•gate \'bi-liŋz-ˌgāt, *Brit usu* -git\ *n* [*Billingsgate,* old gate and fish market, London, England] (1652) **:** coarsely abusive language ***syn*** see ABUSE

bil•lion \'bi(l)-yən\ *n* [F, fr. *bi-* + *-illion* (as in *million*)] (1834) **1 —** see NUMBER table **2 :** a very large number — **billion** *adj* — **bil•lionth** \-yən(t)th\ *adj or n*

bil•lion•aire \ˌbi(l)-yə-'nar, -'ner, 'bi(l)-yə-ˌ\ *n* [*billion* + *-aire* (as in *millionaire*)] (1860) **:** one whose wealth is estimated at a billion or more (as of dollars or pounds)

bill of exchange (1534) **:** an unconditional written order from one person to another to pay a specified sum of money to a designated person

bill of fare (1636) **1 :** MENU **2 :** PROGRAM

bill of goods (1920) **1 :** a consignment of merchandise **2 :** something intentionally misrepresented **:** something passed off in a deception or fraud — often used in the phrase *sell a bill of goods*

bill of health (1644) **1 :** a certificate given to the ship's master at the time of leaving port that indicates the state of health of a ship's company and of a port with regard to infectious diseases **2 :** a usu. favorable report following an examination or investigation ⟨gave the criticized textbook a clean *bill of health*⟩

bill of indictment (ca. 1530) **:** an indictment before it is found or ignored by the grand jury

bill of lading (1532) **:** a receipt listing goods shipped that is signed by the agent of the owner of a ship or issued by a common carrier

bill of particulars (ca. 1860) **:** a detailed listing of charges or claims brought in a legal action or of a defendant's response or counterclaim

bill of rights *often cap B&R* (1798) **:** a summary of fundamental rights and privileges guaranteed to a people against violation by the state — used esp. of the first 10 amendments to the U.S. Constitution

bill of sale (1608) **:** a formal instrument for the conveyance or transfer of title to goods and chattels

bil•lon \'bi-lən\ *n* [F, fr. MF, fr. *bille* log — more at BILLET] (ca. 1727) **1 :** gold or silver heavily alloyed with a less valuable metal **2 :** an alloy of silver containing more than 50 percent of copper by weight

[1]**bil•low** \'bi-(ˌ)lō\ *n* [ON *bylgja;* akin to OHG *balg* bag — more at BELLY] (1552) **1 :** WAVE; *esp* **:** a great wave or surge of water **2 :** a rolling mass (as of flame or smoke) that resembles a high wave — **bil•lowy** \'bi-lə-wē\ *adj*

[2]**billow** *vi* (1597) **1 :** to rise or roll in waves or surges **2 :** to bulge or swell out (as through action of the wind) ~ *vt* **:** to cause to billow

[1]**bil•ly** \'bi-lē\ *n, pl* **billies** [Sc *billy-pot* cooking utensil] (1839) *chiefly Austral & NewZeal* **:** a metal or enamelware pail or pot with a lid and wire bail — called also *billycan*

[2]**billy** *n, pl* **billies** [prob. fr. the name *Billy*] (1848) **1 :** BILLY CLUB **2 :** BILLY GOAT

billy club *n* [[2]*billy*] (1949) **:** a heavy usu. wooden club; *specif* **:** a police officer's club

bil•ly•cock \'bi-lē-ˌkäk\ *n* [origin unknown] (1721) *Brit* **:** DERBY 3

billy goat *n* [fr. the name *Billy*] (1861) **:** a male goat

bi•lobed \'bī-'lōbd\ *adj* (1756) **:** divided into two lobes ⟨a ~ nucleus⟩

bi•lo•ca•tion \'bī-lō-ˌkā-shən\ *n* (1858) **:** the state of being or ability to be in two places at the same time

bil•tong \'bil-ˌtȯŋ, -ˌtäŋ\ *n* [Afrik, fr. *bil* rump + *tong* tongue] (1815) *chiefly SoAfr* **:** jerked meat

bi•man•u•al \(ˌ)bī-'man-yə-wəl, -yəl\ *adj* (ca. 1889) **:** done with or requiring the use of both hands — **bi•man•u•al•ly** *adv*

bim•bo \'bim-(ˌ)bō\ *n, pl* **bimbos** [perh. fr. It *bimbo* baby] (1919) *slang* **1 :** MAN, WOMAN — usu. used disparagingly ⟨telling a thickheaded pitcher that the ~ at the plate hasn't hit a curve in three seasons —Jay Stuller⟩ and esp. of an attractive but empty-headed person ⟨we didn't want a blond ~ in that role . . . we wanted her to be smart —Hugh Wilson⟩ **2 :** TRAMP 1c ⟨evidence of how her hubby's been cheating on her with various ~*s* —Dan Greenburg⟩

bi•met•al \'bī-ˌme-tᵊl\ *adj* (1924) **:** BIMETALLIC — **bimetal** *n*

bi•me•tal•lic \ˌbī-mə-'ta-lik\ *adj* (1876) **1 :** relating to, based on, or

using bimetallism **2** : composed of two different metals — often used of devices having a part in which two metals that expand differently are bonded together — **bimetallic** *n*

bi·met·al·lism \(,)bī-'me-t³l-,i-zəm\ *n* [F *bimétallisme*, fr. *bi-* + *métal* metal] (1876) : the use of two metals (as gold and silver) jointly as a monetary standard with both constituting legal tender at a predetermined ratio — **bi·met·al·list** \-t³l-ist\ *n* — **bi·met·al·lis·tic** \,bī-,me-t³l-'is-tik\ *adj*

bi·mil·le·na·ry \(,)bī-'mi-lə-,ner-ē, ,bī-mə-'le-nə-rē\ *or* **bi·mil·len·ni·al** \,bī-mə-'le-nē-əl\ *n* (1850) **1** : a period of 2000 years **2** : a 2000th anniversary — **bimillenary** *adj*

bi·mod·al \(,)bī-'mō-d³l\ *adj* (1903) : having or relating to two modes; *esp* : having or occurring with two statistical modes — **bi·mo·dal·i·ty** \,bī-mo-'da-lə-tē\ *n*

bi·mo·lec·u·lar \,bī-mə-'le-kyə-lər\ *adj* [ISV] (1899) **1** : relating to or formed from two molecules **2** : being two molecules thick ⟨~ lipid layers⟩ — **bi·mo·lec·u·lar·ly** *adv*

¹bi·month·ly \(,)bī-'mən(t)th-lē\ *adj* (1846) **1** : occurring every two months **2** : occurring twice a month : SEMIMONTHLY *usage* see BI-

²bimonthly *adv* (1864) **1** : once every two months **2** : twice a month

³bimonthly *n* (ca. 1890) : a bimonthly publication

bi·mor·phe·mic \,bī-mȯr-'fē-mik\ *adj* (1942) : consisting of two morphemes

¹bin \'bin\ *n* [ME *binn*, fr. OE] (bef. 12c) : a box, frame, crib, or enclosed place used for storage

²bin *vt* **binned; bin·ning** (1841) : to put into a bin

bin- *prefix* [ME, fr. LL, fr. L *bini* two by two; akin to OE *twinn* twofold — more at TWIN] : **¹BI-** ⟨*binaural*⟩

¹bi·na·ry \'bī-nə-rē, -,ner-ē\ *n, pl* **-ries** (15c) : something made of or based on two things or parts: as **a** : BINARY STAR **b** : a binary number system

²binary *adj* [LL *binarius*, fr. L *bini*] (1597) **1** : compounded or consisting of or marked by two things or parts **2 a** : DUPLE — used of measure or rhythm **b** : having two musical subjects or two complementary sections **3 a** : relating to, being, or belonging to a system of numbers having 2 as its base ⟨the ~ digits 0 and 1⟩ **b** : involving a choice or condition of two alternatives (as on-off or yes-no) **4 a** : composed of two chemical elements, an element and a radical that acts as an element, or two such radicals **b** : utilizing two harmless ingredients that upon combining form a lethal substance (as a gas) ⟨~ weapon⟩ **5** : relating two logical or mathematical elements ⟨~ operation⟩

binary fission *n* (1897) : reproduction of a cell by division into two approximately equal parts ⟨the *binary fission* of protozoans⟩

binary star *n* (ca. 1847) : a system of two stars that revolve around each other under their mutual gravitation — called also *binary system*

bi·na·tion·al \(,)bī-'na-sh(ə-)nəl\ *adj* (1888) : of or relating to two nations ⟨a ~ board of directors⟩

bin·au·ral \(,)bī-'nȯr-əl, (,)bi-\ *adj* [ISV] (1861) **1** : of, relating to, or involving two or both ears **2** : of, relating to, or constituting sound reproduction involving the use of two separated microphones and two transmission channels to achieve a stereophonic effect — **bin·au·ral·ly** \-ə-lē\ *adv*

¹bind \'bīnd\ *vb* **bound** \'baund\; **bind·ing** [ME, fr. OE *bindan;* akin to OHG *bintan* to bind, Gk *peisma* cable, Skt *badhnāti* he binds] *vt* (bef. 12c) **1 a** : to make secure by tying **b** : to confine, restrain, or restrict as if with bonds **c** : to put under an obligation ⟨~s himself with an oath⟩ **d** : to constrain with legal authority **2 a** : to wrap around with something so as to enclose or cover **b** : BANDAGE **3** : to fasten round about **4** : to tie together (as stocks of wheat) **5 a** : to cause to stick together **b** : to take up and hold (as by chemical forces) : combine with **6** : CONSTIPATE **7** : to make a firm commitment for ⟨a handshake ~s the deal⟩ **8** : to protect, strengthen, or decorate by a band or binding **9** : to apply the parts of the cover to (a book) **10** : to set at work as an apprentice : INDENTURE **11** : to cause or bring about an emotional attachment **12** : to fasten together ~ *vi* **1** : to form a cohesive mass **b** : to combine or be taken up esp. by chemical action ⟨antibody ~s to a specific antigen⟩ **2** : to hamper free movement or natural action **3** : to become hindered from free operation **4** : to exert a restraining or compelling effect ⟨a promise that ~s⟩

²bind *n* (bef. 12c) **1 a** : something that binds **b** : the act of binding : the state of being bound **c** : a place where binding occurs : TIE **3** : a position or situation in which one is hampered, constrained, or prevented from free movement or action — **in a bind** : in trouble

bind·er \'bīn-dər\ *n* (bef. 12c) **1** : a person or machine that binds something (as books) **2** : something used in binding **b** : a usu. detachable cover (as for holding sheets of paper) **3** : something (as tar or cement) that produces or promotes cohesion in loosely assembled substances **4** : a temporary insurance contract that provides coverage until the policy is issued **5** : something (as money) given in earnest; *also* : the agreement arrived at

bind·ery \'bīn-d(ə-)rē\ *n, pl* **-er·ies** (1810) : a place where books are bound

¹bind·ing \'bīn-diŋ\ *n* (13c) **1** : the action of one that binds **2** : a material or device used to bind: as **a** : the cover and materials that hold a book together **b** : a narrow fabric used to finish raw edges **c** : a set of ski fastenings for holding the boot firm on the ski

²binding *adj* (14c) **1** : that binds **2** : imposing an obligation — **bind·ing·ly** \-diŋ-lē\ *adv* — **bind·ing·ness** *n*

binding energy *n* (1932) : the energy required to break up a molecule, atom, or atomic nucleus completely into its constituent particles

bin·dle stiff \'bin-d³l-,stif\ *n* [*bindle*, perh. alter. of *bundle*] (1901) : HOBO; *esp* : one who carries his clothes or bedding in a bundle

bind off *vt* (ca. 1939) : to cast off in knitting

bind over *vt* (1610) : to put under a bond to do something (as to appear in court)

bind·weed \'bīnd-,wēd\ *n* (1548) : any of various twining plants (esp. genus *Convolvulus* of the morning-glory family) that mat or interlace with plants among which they grow

bine \'bīn\ *n* [alter. of ²*bind*] (1727) : a twining stem or flexible shoot (as of the hop); *also* : a plant (as woodbine) whose shoots are bines

Bi·net–Si·mon scale \bi-,nā-sē-'mōn-\ *n* [Alfred *Binet* †1911 and Théodore *Simon* †1961 Fr. psychologists] (1914) : an intelligence test

consisting orig. of tasks graded from the level of the average 3-year-old to that of the average 12-year-old but later extended in range

¹binge \'binj\ *n* [E dial. *binge* (to drink heavily)] (1854) **1 a** : a drunken revel : SPREE **b** : an unrestrained and often excessive indulgence ⟨a buying ~⟩ **2** : a social gathering : PARTY

²binge *vi* **binged; binge·ing** *or* **bing·ing** (1910) : to go on a binge; *esp* : to go on an eating binge — **bing·er** \'bin-jər\ *n*

bin·go \'biŋ-(,)gō\ *interj* [alter. of *bing* (interj. suggestive of a ringing sound)] (1925) **1** — used to announce an unexpected event or instantaneous result **2** — used to announce a winning position in bingo

²bingo *n, pl* **bingos** (1932) : a game of chance played with cards having numbered squares corresponding to numbered balls drawn at random and won by covering five such squares in a row; *also* : a social gathering at which bingo is played

bin·na·cle \'bi-ni-kəl\ *n* [alter. of ME *bitakle*, fr. OPg or OSp; OPg *bitácola* & OSp *bitácula*, fr. L *habitaculum* dwelling place, fr. *habitare* to inhabit — more at HABITATION] (1762) : a housing for a ship's compass and a lamp

bin·oc·u·lar \bī-'nä-kyə-lər, bə-\ *adj* (1738) : of, relating to, using, or adapted to the use of both eyes ⟨~ vision⟩ — **bin·oc·u·lar·i·ty** \(,)bī-,nä-kyə-'lar-ə-tē, bə-\ *n* — **bin·oc·u·lar·ly** \bī-'nä-kyə-lər-lē, bə-\ *adv*

²bin·oc·u·lar \bə-'nä-kyə-lər, bī-\ *n* (1871) **1** : a binocular optical instrument **2** : a handheld optical instrument composed of two telescopes and a focusing device and usu. having prisms to increase magnifying ability — usu. used in pl.

bi·no·mi·al \bī-'nō-mē-əl\ *n* [NL *binomium*, fr. ML, neut. of *binomius* having two names, alter. of L *binominis*, fr. *bi-* + *nomin-, nomen* name — more at NAME] (1557) **1** : a mathematical expression consisting of two terms connected by a plus sign or minus sign **2** : a biological species name consisting of two terms — **binomial** *adj* — **bi·no·mi·al·ly** \-mē-ə-lē\ *adv*

binomial coefficient *n* (ca. 1889) : a coefficient of a term in the expansion of the binomial $(x + y)^n$ according to the binomial theorem

binomial distribution *n* (1911) : a probability function each of whose values gives the probability that an outcome with constant probability of occurrence in a statistical experiment will occur a given number of times in a succession of repetitions of the experiment

binomial nomenclature *n* (1880) : a system of nomenclature in which each species of animal or plant receives a name of two terms of which the first identifies the genus to which it belongs and the second the species itself

binomial theorem *n* (1755) : a theorem that specifies the expansion of a binomial of the form $(x + y)^n$ as the sum of $n + 1$ terms of which the general term is of the form

$$\frac{n!}{(n-k)!\ k!} x^{(n-k)} y^k$$

where k takes on values from 0 to n

bint \'bint\ *n* [Ar, girl, daughter] (1855) *Brit* : GIRL, WOMAN

bi·nu·cle·ate \(,)bī-'nü-klē-ət *also* -'nyü-\ *also* **bi·nu·cle·at·ed** \-klē-,ā-təd\ *adj* (1881) : having two cellular nuclei ⟨~ hepatocytes⟩

bio \'bī-(,)ō\ *n, pl* **bi·os** (1947) : a biography or biographical sketch

bio- — see BI-

bio·acous·tics \,bī-(,)ō-ə-'kü-stiks\ *n pl but sing in constr* (1957) : a branch of science concerned with the production of sound by and its effects on living systems

bio·ac·tive \,bī-ō-'ak-tiv\ *adj* (1965) : having an effect on a living organism ⟨~ molecules⟩ — **bio·ac·tiv·i·ty** \-ak-'ti-və-tē\ *n*

bio·as·say \,bī-(,)ō-'a-,sā, -a-'sā\ *n* (1912) : determination of the relative strength of a substance (as a drug) by comparing its effect on a test organism with that of a standard preparation — **bio·as·say** \-a-'sā, -'a-,sā\ *vt*

bio·avail·abil·i·ty \-ə-,vā-lə-'bi-lə-tē\ *n* (1971) : the degree and rate at which a substance (as a drug) is absorbed into a living system or is made available at the site of physiological activity — **bio·avail·able** \-'vā-lə-bəl\ *adj*

bio·ce·no·sis *or* **bio·coe·no·sis** \,bī-ō-sə-'nō-səs\ *n, pl* **-no·ses** \-,sēz\ [NL, fr. ²*bi-* + Gk *koinōsis* sharing, fr. *koinos* common] (1883) : an ecological community esp. when forming a self-regulating unit

bio·chem·i·cal \,bī-ō-'ke-mi-kəl\ *adj* [ISV] (1851) **1** : of or relating to biochemistry **2** : characterized by, produced by, or involving chemical reactions in living organisms — **biochemical** *n* — **bio·chem·i·cal·ly** \-k(ə-)lē\ *adv*

biochemical oxygen demand *n* (ca. 1927) : the oxygen used in meeting the metabolic needs of aerobic microorganisms in water rich in organic matter (as water polluted with sewage)

bio·chem·is·try \,bī-ō-'ke-mə-strē\ *n* [ISV] (1881) **1** : chemistry that deals with the chemical compounds and processes occurring in organisms **2** : the chemical characteristics and reactions of a particular living system or biological substance (as chlorophyll) ⟨a change in the patient's ~⟩ — **bio·chem·ist** \-'mist\ *n*

bio·chip \'bī-ō-,chip\ *n* (1981) : a hypothetical computer logic circuit or storage device in which the physical or chemical properties of large biological molecules (as proteins) are used to process information

bio·cid·al \,bī-ə-'sī-d³l\ *adj* (1949) : destructive to life

bio·cide \'bī-ə-,sīd\ *n* (1947) : a substance (as DDT) that is destructive to many different organisms

bio·cli·mat·ic \,bī-ō-klī-'ma-tik\ *adj* (1918) : of or relating to the relations of climate and living matter ⟨~ adaptations⟩

bio·com·pat·i·bil·i·ty \-kəm-,pa-tə-'bi-lə-tē\ *n* (1971) : compatibility with living tissue or a living system by not being toxic or injurious and not causing immunological rejection — **bio·com·pat·i·ble** \-'pa-tə-bəl\ *adj*

bio·con·trol \,bī-ō-kən-'trōl\ *n* (1967) : BIOLOGICAL CONTROL

bio·con·ver·sion \,bī-(,)ō-kən-'vər-zhən, -shən\ *n* (1960) : the conversion of organic materials (as wastes) into an energy source (as methane) by processes (as fermentation) involving living organisms

bio·de·grad·able \-di-'grā-də-bəl\ *adj* (1961) : capable of being broken down esp. into innocuous products by the action of living things (as microorganisms) ⟨~ trash bags⟩ — **bio·de·grad·abil·i·ty** \-,grā-də-'bi-lə-tē\ *n* — **bio·deg·ra·da·tion** \-,de-grə-'dā-shən\ *n* — **bio·de·grade** \-di-'grād\ *vb*

bio·de·te·ri·o·ra·tion \-di-,tir-ē-ə-'rā-shən\ *n* (1953) : the breakdown of materials by microbial action

bio·di·ver·si·ty \-də-'vər-sə-tē, -dī-\ *n* (1986) : biological diversity in an environment as indicated by numbers of different species of plants and animals

bio·dy·nam·ic \-di-'na-mik, -dī-\ *adj* (1939) : of or relating to a system of farming that uses only organic materials for fertilizing and soil conditioning

bio·elec·tric \-i-'lek-trik\ *also* **bio·elec·tri·cal** \-tri-kəl\ *adj* (1918) : of or relating to electric phenomena in animals and plants — **bio·elec·tric·i·ty** \-,lek-'tri-sə-tē, -'tris-tē\ *n*

bio·en·er·get·ics \-,e-nər-'je-tiks\ *n pl but sing in constr* (1912) **1** : the biology of energy transformations and energy exchanges (as in photosynthesis) within and between living things and their environments **2** : a system of physical and psychological therapy that is held to increase well-being by releasing blocked physical and psychic energy — **bio·en·er·get·ic** \-'je-tik\ *adj*

bio·en·gi·neer·ing \-,en-jə-'nir-iŋ\ *n* (ca. 1954) : biological or medical application of engineering principles or engineering equipment; *broadly* : BIOTECHNOLOGY 1 — **bio·en·gi·neer** \-'nir\ *n or vt*

bio·eth·ics \-'e-thiks\ *n pl but sing in constr* (1971) : a discipline dealing with the ethical implications of biological research and applications esp. in medicine — **bio·eth·i·cal** \-'e-thi-kəl\ *adj* — **bio·eth·i·cist** \-'e-thə-sist\ *n*

bio·feed·back \-'fēd-,bak\ *n* (1970) : the technique of making unconscious or involuntary bodily processes (as heartbeats or brain waves) perceptible to the senses (as by the use of an oscilloscope) in order to manipulate them by conscious mental control

bio·foul·ing \-'faù-liŋ\ *n* (1943) : the gradual accumulation of waterborne organisms (as bacteria and protozoa) on the surfaces of engineering structures in water that contributes to corrosion of the structures and to a decrease in the efficiency of moving parts

bio·gas \'bī-ō-,gas\ *n* (1974) : a mixture of methane and carbon dioxide produced by the bacterial decomposition of organic wastes and used as a fuel

bio·gen·e·sis \,bī-ō-'je-nə-səs\ *n* [NL] (1870) **1** : the development of life from preexisting life **2** : a supposed tendency for stages in the evolutionary history of a race to briefly recur during the development and differentiation of an individual of that race **3** : the synthesis of chemical compounds or structures in the living organism — compare BIOSYNTHESIS — **bio·ge·net·ic** \-jə-'ne-tik\ *adj* — **bio·ge·net·i·cal·ly** \-ti-k(ə-)lē\ *adv*

biogenetic law *n* (1882) : a theory of development much disputed in biology: an organism passes through successive stages resembling the series of ancestral types from which it has descended so that the ontogeny of the individual is a recapitulation of the phylogeny of the group

bio·gen·ic \-'je-nik\ *also* **bi·og·e·nous** \bī-'ä-jə-nəs\ *adj* (1913) : produced by living organisms (~ methane formation)

bio·geo·chem·i·cal \-,jē-ō-'ke-mi-kəl\ *adj* (1938) : of or relating to the partitioning and cycling of chemical elements and compounds between the living and nonliving parts of an ecosystem — **bio·geo·chem·is·try** \-mə-strē\ *n*

bio·ge·og·ra·phy \-jē-'ä-grə-fē\ *n* [ISV] (1895) : a science that deals with the geographical distribution of animals and plants — **bio·ge·og·ra·pher** \-grə-fər\ *n* — **bio·geo·graph·ic** \-,jē-ə-'gra-fik\ *or* **bio·geo·graph·i·cal** \-fi-kəl\ *adj*

bi·og·ra·phee \bī-,ä-grə-'fē *also* bē-\ *n* (1841) : a person about whom a biography is written

bi·og·ra·pher \-'ä-grə-fər\ *n* (1715) : a writer of a biography

bio·graph·i·cal \,bī-ə-'gra-fi-kəl\ *also* **bio·graph·ic** \-'fik\ *adj* (1738) **1** : of, relating to, or constituting biography **2** : consisting of biographies (a ~ dictionary) **3** : relating to a list briefly identifying persons (~ notes) — **bio·graph·i·cal·ly** \-fi-k(ə-)lē\ *adv*

bi·og·ra·phy \bī-'ä-grə-fē *also* bē-\ *n, pl* **-phies** [LGk *biographia*, fr. Gk *bi-* + *-graphia* -graphy] (1683) **1** : a usu. written history of a person's life **2** : biographical writings as a whole **3** : an account of the life of something (as an animal, a coin, or a building)

bio·haz·ard \'bī-ō-,ha-zərd\ *n* (1967) : a biological agent or condition that constitutes a hazard to humans or the environment; *also* : a hazard posed by such an agent or condition

bi·o·log·ic \,bī-ə-'lä-jik\ *or* **bi·o·log·i·cal** \-ji-kəl\ *n* (1921) : a biological product used in medicine

biological *also* **biologic** *adj* (1859) **1** : of or relating to biology or to life and living processes **2** : used in or produced by applied biology **3** : related by direct genetic relationship rather than by adoption or marriage (~ parents) — **bi·o·log·i·cal·ly** \-ji-k(ə-)lē\ *adv*

biological clock *n* (1955) : an inherent timing mechanism that is inferred to exist in some living systems (as a cell) in order to explain various cyclical behaviors and physiological processes

biological control *n* (1923) : reduction in numbers or elimination of pest organisms by interference with their ecology (as by the introduction of parasites or diseases)

biological oxygen demand *n* (1945) : BIOCHEMICAL OXYGEN DEMAND

biological warfare *n* (1946) : warfare involving the use of living organisms (as disease germs) or their toxic products as weapons; *also* : warfare involving the use of herbicides

bi·ol·o·gism \bī-'ä-lə-,ji-zəm\ *n* (1924) : preoccupation with biological explanations in the analysis of social situations — **bi·ol·o·gis·tic** \-,ä-lə-'jis-tik\ *adj*

bi·ol·o·gy \bī-'ä-lə-jē\ *n* [G *Biologie*, fr. *bi-* + *-logie* -logy] (1819) **1** : a branch of knowledge that deals with living organisms and vital processes **2 a** : the plant and animal life of a region or environment **b** : the life processes esp. of an organism or group; *broadly* : ECOLOGY — **bi·ol·o·gist** \-jist\ *n*

bio·lu·mi·nes·cence \,bī-ō-,lü-mə-'ne-s°n(t)s\ *n* [ISV] (1916) : the emission of light from living organisms; *also* : the light so produced — **bio·lu·mi·nes·cent** \-s°nt\ *adj*

bio·mass \'bī-ō-,mas\ *n* (1934) **1** : the amount of living matter (as in a unit area or volume of habitat) **2** : plant materials and animal waste used esp. as a source of fuel

bio·ma·te·ri·al \,bī-ō-mə-'tir-ē-əl\ *n* (1966) : material used for or suitable for use in prostheses that come in direct contact with living tissues

bio·math·e·mat·ics \-,ma-thə-'ma-tiks, -math-'ma-\ *n pl but usu sing in constr* (1923) : mathematics of special use in biology and medicine —

bio·math·e·mat·i·cal \-ti-kəl\ *adj* — **bio·math·e·ma·ti·cian** \-,math-mə-'ti-shən, -,ma-thə-\ *n*

bi·ome \'bī-,ōm\ *n* [²*bi-* + *-ome*] (1916) : a major ecological community type (as tropical rain forest, grassland, or desert)

bio·me·chan·ics \'bī-ō-mə-'ka-niks\ *n pl but sing or pl in constr* (ca. 1933) : the mechanics of biological and esp. muscular activity (as in locomotion or exercise); *also* : the scientific study of this — **bio·me·chan·i·cal** \-ni-kəl\ *adj* — **bio·me·chan·i·cal·ly** \-ni-k(ə-)lē\ *adv*

bio·med·i·cal \,bī-ō-'me-di-kəl\ *adj* (1955) **1** : of or relating to biomedicine **2** : of, relating to, or involving biological, medical, and physical science

bio·med·i·cine \-'me-də-sən, *Brit usu* -'med-sən\ *n* (1947) : medicine based on the application of the principles of the natural sciences and esp. biology and biochemistry

bio·me·te·o·rol·o·gy \,bī-ō-,mē-tē-ə-'rä-lə-jē\ *n* (1946) : a science that deals with the relationship between living things and atmospheric phenomena — **bio·me·te·o·ro·log·i·cal** \-rə-'lä-ji-kəl\ *adj*

bi·om·e·try \bī-'ä-mə-trē\ *n* [ISV] (1831) : the statistical analysis of biological observations and phenomena — **bio·met·ric** \,bī-ō-'me-trik\ *or* **bio·met·ri·cal** \-tri-kəl\ *adj* — **bio·me·tri·cian** \-me-'tri-shən\ *n* — **bio·met·rics** \-'me-triks\ *n pl but sing or pl in constr*

bio·mol·e·cule \,bī-ō-'mä-li-,kyü(ə)l\ *n* (1901) : an organic molecule and esp. a macromolecule in living organisms — **bio·mo·lec·u·lar** \-mə-'le-kyə-lər\ *adj*

bio·mor·phic \,bī-ə-'mòr-fik\ *adj* (1895) : resembling or suggesting the forms of living organisms (~ sculptures) (~ images)

bi·on·ic \bī-'ä-nik\ *adj* (1963) **1** : of or relating to bionics **2** : having normal biological capability or performance enhanced by or as if by electronic or electromechanical devices

bi·on·ics \bī-'ä-niks\ *n pl but sing or pl in constr* [²*bi-* + *-onics* (as in *electronics*)] (1960) : a science concerned with the application of data about the functioning of biological systems to the solution of engineering problems

bi·o·nom·ics \,bī-ə-'nä-miks\ *n pl but sing or pl in constr* [*bionomic*, adj., prob. fr. F *bionomique*, fr. *bionomie* ecology, fr. *bi-* + *-nomie* -nomy] (1888) : ECOLOGY — **bi·o·nom·ic** \-mik\ *adj*

bio·phys·ics \,bī-ō-'fi-ziks\ *n pl but sing or pl in constr* (1892) : a branch of science concerned with the application of physical principles and methods to biological problems — **bio·phys·i·cal** \-zi-kəl\ *adj* — **bio·phys·i·cist** \-'fi-zə-sist, -'fiz-sist\ *n*

bio·pic \-,(,)ō-,pik\ *n* [²*bio-* + ¹*pic*] (1951) : a biographical movie

bio·poly·mer \,bī-ō-'pä-lə-mər\ *n* (1961) : a polymeric substance (as a protein or polysaccharide) formed in a biological system

bi·op·sy \'bī-,äp-sē\ *n, pl* **-sies** [ISV ²*bi-* + *-opsy* (as in *autopsy*)] (1895) : the removal and examination of tissue, cells, or fluids from the living body — **biopsy** *vt*

bio·re·ac·tor \,bī-ō-rē-'ak-tər\ *n* (1974) : a device or apparatus in which living organisms and esp. bacteria synthesize useful substances (as interferon) or break down harmful ones (as in sewage)

bio·rhythm \'bī-ō-,ri-thəm\ *n* (1960) : an inherent rhythm that appears to control or initiate various biological processes — **bio·rhyth·mic** \-'rith-mik\ *adj*

bio·safe·ty \,bī-ō-'sāf-tē\ *n* (1977) : safety with respect to the effects of biological research on humans and the environment

bio·sci·ence \-'sī-ən(t)s\ *n* (1941) : BIOLOGY 1; *also* : LIFE SCIENCE — **bio·sci·en·tif·ic** \-,sī-ən-'ti-fik\ *adj* — **bio·sci·en·tist** \-'sī-ən-tist\ *n*

bio·sen·sor \-'sen-,sòr, -'sen(t)-sər\ *n* (1962) : a device that is sensitive to a physical or chemical stimulus (as heat or an ion) and transmits information about it or the life process

-biosis *n comb form, pl* **-bioses** [NL, fr. Gk *biōsis*, fr. *bioun* to live, fr. *bios* life — more at QUICK] : mode of life (para*biosis*)

bio·so·cial \,bī-ō-'sō-shəl\ *adj* (1897) : of, relating to, or concerned with the interaction of the biological aspects and social relationships of living organisms (~ science) — **bio·so·cial·ly** \-'sōsh-lē, -'sō-shə-\ *adv*

bio·sphere \'bī-ə-,sfir\ *n* (1899) **1** : the part of the world in which life can exist **2** : living beings together with their environment — **bio·spher·ic** \,bī-ə-'sfir-ik, -'sfer-\ *adj*

bio·sta·tis·tics \,bī-ō-stə-'tis-tiks\ *n pl but sing in constr* (1950) : statistics applied to the analysis of biological data — **bio·sta·tis·ti·cal** \-ti-kəl\ *adj* — **bio·stat·is·ti·cian** \-,sta-tə-'sti-shən\ *n*

bio·strati·graph·ic \-,stra-tə-'gra-fik\ *adj* (1947) : of or relating to the branch of paleontology dealing with the conditions and order of deposition of sedimentary rocks — **bio·stra·tig·ra·phy** \-strə-'ti-grə-fē\ *n*

bio·syn·the·sis \-'sin(t)-thə-səs\ *n* [NL] (1930) : the production of a chemical compound by a living organism — **bio·syn·thet·ic** \-sin-'the-tik\ *adj* — **bio·syn·thet·i·cal·ly** \-ti-k(ə-)lē\ *adv*

bio·sys·te·mat·ics \-,sis-tə-'ma-tiks\ *n pl but sing or pl in constr* (1945) : experimental taxonomy esp. as based on cytogenetics and genetics — **bio·sys·te·mat·ic** \-tik\ *adj* — **bio·sys·tem·atist** \-'sis-tə-mə-tist, -sis-'te-mə-\ *n*

bi·o·ta \bī-'ō-tə\ *n* [NL, fr. Gk *biotē* life; akin to Gk *bios*] (1901) : the flora and fauna of a region

bio·tech \'bī-ō-,tek\ *n* (1974) : BIOTECHNOLOGY 1

bio·tech·ni·cal \,bī-ō-'tek-ni-kəl\ *adj* (1938) : of or relating to biotechnology

bio·tech·nol·o·gy \,bī-ō-tek-'nä-lə-jē\ *n* (1941) **1** : applied biological science (as bioengineering or recombinant DNA technology) **2** : ERGONOMICS — **bio·tech·no·log·i·cal** \-,tek-nə-'läj-i-kəl\ *adj* — **bio·tech·nol·o·gist** \-'nä-lə-jist\ *n*

bio·te·lem·e·try \-tə-'le-mə-trē\ *n* (1963) : the remote detection and measurement of a human or animal function, activity, or condition — **bio·tel·e·met·ric** \-,te-lə-'me-trik\ *adj*

bi·ot·ic \bī-'ä-tik\ *adj* [Gk *biōtikos*, fr. *bioun*] (1868) : of or relating to life; *esp* : caused or produced by living beings (~ diversity)

-biotic *adj comb form* [prob. fr. NL *-bioticus*, fr. Gk *biōtikos*] : having a (specified) mode of life (endo*biotic*)

\ə\ abut \ᵊ\ kitten, F table \ər\ further \a\ ash \ā\ ace \ä\ mop, mar \aù\ out \ch\ chin \e\ bet \ē\ easy \g\ go \i\ hit \ī\ ice \j\ job \ŋ\ sing \ō\ go \ò\ law \òi\ boy \th\ thin \th\ the \ü\ loot \ù\ foot \y\ yet \zh\ vision \à, k̲, ⁿ, œ, œ̄, ʉ̲e, ᵿ̄, ᵞ\ *see* Guide to Pronunciation

biotic potential *n* (1935) : the inherent capacity of an organism or species to reproduce and survive

bi·o·tin \'bī-ə-tən\ *n* [ISV, fr. Gk *biotos* life, sustenance; akin to Gk *bios*] (1936) : a colorless crystalline growth vitamin $C_{10}H_{16}N_2O_3S$ of the vitamin B complex found esp. in yeast, liver, and egg yolk

bi·o·tite \'bī-ə-ˌtīt\ *n* [G *Biotit*, fr. Jean B. *Biot* †1862 Fr. mathematician] (1862) : a generally black or dark green form of mica that is a constituent of crystalline rocks and consists of a silicate of iron, magnesium, potassium, and aluminum — **bi·o·tit·ic** \ˌbī-ə-'ti-tik\ *adj*

bio·tope \'bī-ə-ˌtōp\ *n* [²*bi-* + Gk *topos* place] (1927) : a region uniform in environmental conditions and in its populations of animals and plants for which it is the habitat

bio·trans·for·ma·tion \ˌbī-ō-ˌtran(t)s-fər-'mā-shən, -ˌfȯr-\ *n* (1955) : the transformation of chemical compounds within a living system

bio·type \-ˌtīp\ *n* [ISV] (1906) : the organisms sharing a specified genotype; *also* : the genotype shared or its distinguishing peculiarity — **bio·typ·ic** \ˌbī-ə-'ti-pik\ *adj*

bi·pa·ren·tal \ˌbī-pə-'ren-t°l\ *adj* (1900) : of, relating to, involving, or derived from two parents — **bi·pa·ren·tal·ly** \-t°l-ē\ *adv*

bi·par·ti·san \(ˌ)bī-'pär-tə-zən, -sən, -ˌzan, *chiefly Brit* ˌbī-ˌpär-tə-'zan\ *adj* (ca. 1909) : of, relating to, or involving members of two parties ⟨a ~ commission⟩ — **bi·par·ti·san·ism** \-zə-ˌni-zəm, -sə-\ *n* — **bi·par·ti·san·ship** \-zən-ˌship, -sən-\ *n*

bi·par·tite \(ˌ)bī-'pär-ˌtīt\ *adj* [L *bipartitus*, pp. of *bipartire* to divide in two, fr. *bi-* + *partire* to divide, fr. *part-, pars* part] (1574) **1 a :** being in two parts **b :** having a correspondent part for each of two parties ⟨a ~ contract⟩ **c :** shared by two ⟨a ~ treaty⟩ **2 :** divided into two parts almost to the base ⟨a ~ leaf⟩ — **bi·par·tite·ly** *adv* — **bi·par·ti·tion** \ˌbī-ˌpär-'ti-shən\ *n*

bi·ped \'bī-ˌped\ *n* [L *biped-, bipes*, fr. *bi-* + *ped-, pes* foot — more at FOOT] (1646) : a two-footed animal — **bi·ped·al** \(ˌ)bī-'pe-d°l\ *adj* — **bi·ped·al·ly** \-ē\ *adv*

bi·ped·al·ism \(ˌ)bī-'pe-d°l-ˌi-zəm\ *n* (1907) : the condition of having two feet or of using only two feet for locomotion

bi·pe·dal·i·ty \ˌbī-pə-'da-lə-tē\ *n* (1847) : BIPEDALISM

bi·phas·ic \(ˌ)bī-'fā-zik\ *adj* (ca. 1909) : having two phases ⟨a ~ immune response⟩

bi·phe·nyl \(ˌ)bī-'fe-n°l, -'fē-\ *n* [ISV] (ca. 1923) : a white crystalline hydrocarbon $C_6H_5 \cdot C_6H_5$ used esp. as a heat-transfer medium

bi·pin·nate \-'pi-ˌnāt\ *adj* (1794) : twice pinnate — **bi·pin·nate·ly** *adv*

bi·plane \'bī-ˌplān\ *n* (1874) : an aircraft with two main supporting surfaces usu. placed one above the other

bi·pod \'bī-ˌpäd\ *n* [*bi-* + *-pod* (as in *tripod*)] (1922) : a two-legged support

bi·po·lar \(ˌ)bī-'pō-lər\ *adj* (1810) **1 :** having or marked by two mutually repellent forces or diametrically opposed natures or views **2 a :** having or involving the use of two poles or polarities **b :** relating to, being, or using a transistor in which both electrons and holes are utilized as charge carriers **3 :** relating to, associated with, or occurring in both polar regions ⟨~ species of birds⟩ **4 :** characterized by the alternation of manic and depressive states ⟨a ~ affective disorder⟩ — **bi·po·lar·i·ty** \ˌbī-pō-'lar-ə-tē\ *n* — **bi·po·lar·iza·tion** \(ˌ)bī-ˌpō-lə-rə-'zā-shən\ *n* — **bi·po·lar·ize** \(ˌ)bī-'pō-lə-ˌrīz\ *vt*

bi·pro·pel·lant \ˌbī-prə-'pe-lənt\ *n* (1947) : a rocket propellant consisting of separate fuel and oxidizer that come together only in a combustion chamber

bi·pyr·a·mid \(ˌ)bī-'pir-ə-mid\ *n* (1897) : a crystal consisting of two identical pyramids base to base — **bi·py·ra·mi·dal** \-pə-'ra-mə-d°l\ *adj*

bi·qua·drat·ic \ˌbī-kwä-'dra-tik\ *adj or n* (1668) : QUARTIC

bi·ra·cial \(ˌ)bī-'rā-shəl\ *adj* (1922) : of, relating to, or involving members of two races — **bi·ra·cial·ism** \-shə-ˌli-zəm\ *n*

bi·ra·di·al \(ˌ)bī-'rā-dē-əl\ *adj* (ca. 1909) : having both bilateral and radial symmetry

bi·ra·mous \(ˌ)bī-'rā-məs\ *adj* (1877) : having two branches

¹birch \'bərch\ *n* [ME, fr. OE *beorc*; akin to OHG *birka* birch, OE *beorht* bright, and prob. to L *fraxinus* ash tree — more at BRIGHT] (bef. 12c) **1 :** any of a genus (*Betula* of the family Betulaceae, the birch family) of monoecious deciduous usu. short-lived trees or shrubs having simple petioled leaves and typically a layered membranous outer bark that peels readily **2 :** the hard pale close-grained wood of a birch **3 :** a birch rod or bundle of twigs for flogging — **birch** *or* **birch·en** \-chən\ *adj*

²birch *vt* (1830) : to beat with or as if with a birch : WHIP

Birch·er \'bər-chər\ *n* (1961) : a member or adherent of the John Birch Society — **Birch·ism** \'bər-ˌchi-zəm\ *n* — **Birch·ist** \-chist\ *or* **Birch·ite** \-ˌchīt\ *n or adj*

¹bird \'bərd\ *n, often attrib* [ME, fr. OE *bridd*] (bef. 12c) **1** *archaic* : the young of a feathered vertebrate **2 :** any of a class (Aves) of warm-blooded vertebrates distinguished by having the body more or less completely covered with feathers and the forelimbs modified as wings **3 :** a game bird **4 :** CLAY PIGEON **5 a :** FELLOW **b :** a peculiar person **c** *chiefly Brit* : GIRL **6 :** SHUTTLECOCK **7** *chiefly Brit* **a :** a hissing or jeering expressive of disapproval **b :** dismissal from employment **8 :** a thin piece of meat rolled up with stuffing and cooked **9 :** something (as an aircraft, rocket, or satellite) resembling a bird esp. by flying or being aloft **10 :** an obscene gesture of contempt made by pointing the middle finger upward while keeping the other fingers down — usu. used with *the*; called also *finger* — **bird·like** \-ˌlīk\ *adj* — **for the birds** : WORTHLESS, RIDICULOUS

²bird *vi* (1918) : to observe or identify wild birds in their natural environment

bird·bath \'bərd-ˌbath, -ˌbäth\ *n* (1895) : a usu. ornamental basin set up for birds to bathe in

bird·brain \-ˌbrān\ *n* (1943) **1 :** a stupid person **2 :** SCATTERBRAIN — **bird·brained** \-ˌbrānd\ *adj*

bird·cage \-ˌkāj\ *n* (15c) : a cage for confining birds

bird·call \-ˌkȯl\ *n* (ca. 1625) **1 :** a device for imitating the cry of a bird **2 :** the note or cry of a bird; *also* : a sound imitative of it

bird colonel *n* [fr. the eagle serving as insignia for this rank] (ca. 1947) *slang* : COLONEL 1a

bird–dog \'bərd-ˌdȯg\ *vi* (1943) : to watch closely ~ *vt* : to seek out : FOLLOW, DETECT

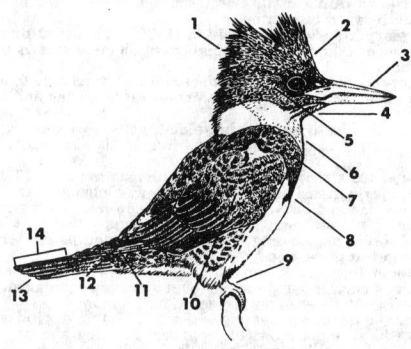

bird 2 (kingfisher): *1* crest, *2* crown, *3* bill, *4* throat, *5* auricular region, *6* breast, *7* scapulars, *8* abdomen, *9* tarsus, *10* upper wing coverts, *11* primaries, *12* secondaries, *13* rectrix, *14* tail

bird dog *n* (ca. 1888) **1 :** a gundog trained to hunt or retrieve birds **2 a :** one (as a canvasser or talent scout) who seeks out something for another **b :** one who steals another's date

bird–dog·ging \-ˌdȯ-giŋ\ *n* (ca. 1941) **1 :** the stealing of another's date (as at a party) **2 :** the action of one that bird-dogs

bird·er \'bər-dər\ *n* (15c) **1 :** a catcher or hunter of birds esp. for market **2 :** a person who birds

bird·house \'bərd-ˌhau̇s\ *n* (1870) : an artificial nesting site for birds; *also* : AVIARY

¹bird·ie \'bər-dē\ *n* (1792) **1 :** a little bird **2 :** a golf score of one stroke less than par on a hole — compare EAGLE

²birdie *vt* **bird·ied; bird·ie·ing** (1948) : to score a birdie on

bird·lime \'bərd-ˌlīm\ *n* (15c) **1 :** a sticky substance usu. made from the bark of a holly (*Ilex aquifolium*) that is smeared on twigs to snare small birds **2 :** something that ensnares — **birdlime** *vt*

bird louse *n* (1826) : BITING LOUSE

bird·man \'bərd-mən, *esp for 1 also* -ˌman\ *n* (1697) **1 :** a person who deals with birds **2 :** a person who flies (as in an aircraft)

bird–of–paradise *n* (ca. 1884) : an ornamental plant (*Strelitzia reginae* of the family Strelitziaceae) having scapes of orange or yellow and purple flowers with three sepals and three very irregular petals

bird of paradise (1638) : any of numerous brilliantly colored plumed oscine birds (family Paradiseidae) of the New Guinea area

bird of passage (1728) **1 :** a migratory bird **2 :** a person who leads a wandering or unsettled life

bird of prey (14c) : a carnivorous bird (as a hawk, falcon, or vulture) that feeds wholly or chiefly on meat taken by hunting or on carrion

bird pepper *n* (1696) : a capsicum (*Capsicum annuum glabriusculum*) having very small oblong extremely pungent red fruits

bird·seed \'bərd-ˌsēd\ *n* (1840) : a mixture of seeds (as of hemp, millet, and sunflowers) used for feeding caged and wild birds

¹bird's–eye \'bərd-ˌzī\ *n* (1597) **1 :** any of numerous plants with small bright-colored flowers; esp : a speedwell (*Veronica chamaedrys*) **2 a :** an allover pattern for textiles consisting of a small diamond with a center dot **b :** a fabric woven with this pattern **3 :** a small spot in wood surrounded with an ellipse of concentric fibers

²bird's–eye *adj* (1665) **1 :** marked with spots resembling birds' eyes **2 :** having or involving a bird's-eye view ⟨~ perspective⟩ ⟨a ~ survey of the topic⟩

bird's–eye view *n* (1762) **1 :** a view from a high angle as if seen by a bird in flight **2 :** an overall or cursory look at something

bird's–foot trefoil \'bərdz-ˌfu̇t-\ *n* (1833) : a European legume (*Lotus corniculatus*) having claw-shaped pods and widely used esp. in the U.S. as a forage and fodder plant or often planted along roadsides

bird's–foot violet *n* (1839) : a common violet (*Viola pedata*) of the eastern U.S. with deeply cleft leaves and pale blue to purple flattened flowers

bird's–nest fern \'bərdz-ˌnest-\ *n* (1858) : a large epiphytic spleenwort (*Asplenium nidus*) of tropical Asia and Polynesia that has large lance-shaped leaves and is often grown as a houseplant

bird's nest soup *n* (1871) : a soup made with the nests of small cave-nesting swifts (genus *Collocalia*) that build them using a glutinous secretion from their salivary glands

bird·song \'bərd-ˌsȯŋ\ *n* (1896) : the song of a bird

bird–watch \'bərd-ˌwäch\ *vi* [back-formation fr. *bird-watcher*] (1948) : BIRD

bird–watch·er \-ˌwä-chər\ *n* (1905) : BIRDER 2

bi·re·frin·gence \ˌbī-ri-'frin-jən(t)s\ *n* [ISV] (1898) : the refraction of light in an anisotropic material (as calcite) in two slightly different directions to form two rays — **bi·re·frin·gent** \-jənt\ *adj*

bi·reme \'bī-ˌrēm\ *n* [L *biremis*, fr. *bi-* + *remus* oar — more at ROW] (1662) : a galley with two banks of oars used esp. by the ancient Greeks and Phoenicians

bi·ret·ta \bə-'re-tə\ *n* [It *berretta*, fr. OProv *berret* cap, fr. ML *birretum*, fr. LL *birrus* cloak with a hood, perh. of Celt origin; akin to MIr *berr* short] (1598) : a square cap with three ridges on top worn by clergymen esp. of the Roman Catholic Church

birk \'birk\ *n* [ME *birch, birk*] (14c) *chiefly Scot* : BIRCH

birk·ie \'bir-kē, 'bər-\ *n* [origin unknown] (1724) **1** *Scot* : a lively smart assertive person **2** *Scot* : FELLOW, BOY

biretta

¹birl \'bər(-ə)l, *Scot also* 'bir(-ə)l\ *vi* [ME fr. OE *byrlian;* prob. akin to OE *beran* to carry — more at BEAR] (ca. 1585) *chiefly Scot* : CAROUSE

²birl *vb* [perh. imit.] *vt* (1790) **1** : SPIN **2** : to cause (a floating log) to rotate by treading ~ *vi* : to progress by whirling — **birl·er** \'bər-lər, 'bir-\ *n*

Bi·ro \'bī-(,)rō\ *trademark* — used for a ballpoint pen

birr \'bər, 'bir\ *n, pl* **birr** [Ar] (ca. 1978) — see MONEY table

birse \'birs, 'bərs\ *n* [(assumed) ME *birst,* fr. OE *byrst* — more at BRISTLE] (bef. 12c) **1** *chiefly Scot* : a bristle or tuft of bristles **2** *chiefly Scot* : ANGER

¹birth \'bərth\ *n, often attrib* [ME, fr. ON *byrth;* akin to OE *beran*] (13c) **1 a** : the emergence of a new individual from the body of its parent **b** : the act or process of bringing forth young from the womb **2** : a state resulting from being born esp. at a particular time or place ⟨a Southerner by ~⟩ **3 a** : LINEAGE, EXTRACTION ⟨marriage between equals in ~⟩ **b** : high or noble birth **4** *archaic* : one that is born **b** : BEGINNING, START ⟨the ~ of an idea⟩

²birth *vt* (1906) **1** *chiefly dial* : to bring forth **2** : to give rise to : ORIGINATE ~ *vi* : to bring forth a child or young

birth canal *n* (1927) : the channel formed by the cervix, vagina, and vulva through which the fetus passes during birth

birth certificate *n* (1900) : a copy of an official record of a person's date and place of birth and parentage

birth control *n* (1914) : control of the number of children born esp. by preventing or lessening the frequency of conception : CONTRACEPTION

birth·day \'bərth-,dā\ *n* (14c) **1 a** : the day of a person's birth **b** : a day of origin **2** : an anniversary of a birth ⟨her 21st ~⟩

birthday suit *n* (1753) : unclothed skin : NAKEDNESS

birth defect *n* (1971) : a physical or biochemical defect that is present at birth and may be inherited or environmentally induced

birth·mark \'bərth-,märk\ *n* (1580) : an unusual mark or blemish on the skin at birth : NEVUS

birth pang *n* (ca. 1887) **1** : one of the regularly recurrent pains that are characteristic of childbirth — usu. used in pl. **2** *pl* : disorder and distress incident esp. to a major social change

birth·place \'bərth-,plās\ *n* (1607) : place of birth or origin

birth·rate \'bərth-,rāt\ *n* (1859) : the ratio between births and individuals in a specified population and time

birth·right \'bərth-,rīt\ *n* (1535) : a right, privilege, or possession to which a person is entitled by birth

birth·root \'bərth-,rüt, -,rut\ *n* (1822) : any of several trilliums with astringent roots used in folk medicine

birth·stone \'bərth-,stōn\ *n* (1907) : a gemstone associated symbolically with the month of one's birth

birth·wort \-,wərt, -,wȯrt\ *n* (1551) : any of several herbs or woody vines (genus *Aristolochia* of the family Aristolochiaceae, the birthwort family) with aromatic roots used in folk medicine to aid childbirth

bis \'bis\ *adv* [L, fr. OL *dvis;* akin to OHG *zwiro* twice, L *duo* two — more at TWO] (1819) **1** : AGAIN — used in music as a direction to repeat **2** : TWICE

Bi·sa·yan \bə-'sī-ən\ *n* [Bisayan *Bisayâ*] (1951) **1** : a member of any of several peoples in the Visayan islands, Philippines **2** : the group of Austronesian languages of the Bisayans

bis·cuit \'bis-kət\ *n, pl* **biscuits** *also* **biscuit** [ME *bisquite,* fr. MF *bescuit,* fr. (pain) *bescuit* twice-cooked bread] (14c) **1 a** : any of various hard or crisp dry baked products: as **(1)** *Brit* : CRACKER 4 **(2)** *Brit* : COOKIE **b** : a small quick bread made from dough that has been rolled out and cut or dropped from a spoon **2** : earthenware or porcelain after the first firing and before glazing **3 a** : a light grayish yellowish brown **b** : a grayish yellow

bi·sect \'bī-,sekt, bī-\ *vb* [*bi-* + inter*sect*] *vt* (ca. 1645) : to divide into two usu. equal parts ~ *vi* : CROSS, INTERSECT — **bi·sec·tion** \'bī-,sek-shən, bī-\ *n* — **bi·sec·tion·al** \-shnəl, -shə-nᵊl\ *adj* — **bi·sec·tion·al·ly** *adv*

bi·sec·tor \'bī-,sek-tər, bī-\ *n* (1864) : one that bisects; *esp* : a straight line that bisects an angle or a line segment

bi·sex·u·al \(,)bī-'sek-sh(ə-)wəl, -shəl\ *adj* (1824) **1 a** : possessing characters of both sexes : HERMAPHRODITIC **b** : sexually oriented toward both sexes **2** : of, relating to, or involving both sexes — **bisexual** *n* — **bi·sex·u·al·i·ty** \,bī-,sek-shə-'wa-lə-tē\ *n* — **bi·sex·u·al·ly** \(,)bī-'sek-sh(ə-)wə-lē, -sh(ə-)lē\ *adv*

bish·op \'bi-shəp\ *n* [ME *bisshop,* fr. OE *bisceop,* fr. LL *episcopus,* fr. Gk *episkopos,* lit., overseer, fr. *epi-* + *skeptesthai* to look — more at SPY] (bef. 12c) **1** : one having spiritual or ecclesiastical supervision: as **a** : an Anglican, Eastern Orthodox, or Roman Catholic clergyman ranking above a priest, having authority to ordain and confirm, and typically governing a diocese **b** : any of various Protestant clerical officials who superintend other clergy **c** : a Mormon high priest presiding over a ward or over all other bishops and over the Aaronic priesthood **2** : either of two pieces of each color in a set of chessmen having the power to move diagonally across any number of adjoining unoccupied squares **3** : mulled port wine flavored with roasted oranges and cloves

bish·op·ric \'bi-shə-(,)prik\ *n* [ME *bisshopriche,* fr. OE *bisceoprice,* fr. *bisceop* + *rice* kingdom — more at RICH] (bef. 12c) **1** : DIOCESE **2** : the office of bishop **3** : the administrative body of a Mormon ward consisting of a bishop and two high priests as counselors

Bishops' Bible *n* (1835) : an officially commissioned English translation of the Bible published in 1568

bis·muth \'biz-məth\ *n* [NL *bismuthum,* modif. of G *Wismut*] (1668) : a heavy brittle grayish white chiefly trivalent metallic element that is chemically like arsenic and antimony and that is used in alloys and pharmaceuticals — see ELEMENT table — **bis·mu·thic** \biz-'mə-thik, -'myü-\ *adj*

bi·son \'bī-sᵊn, -zᵊn\ *n, pl* **bison** [L *bisont-, bison,* of Gmc origin; akin to OHG *wisant* aurochs; akin to OPruss *wissambrs* aurochs] (1611) : any of several large shaggy-maned usu. gregarious recent or extinct bovine mammals (genus *Bison*) having a large head with short horns and heavy forequarters surmounted by a large fleshy hump: as **a** : WISENT **b** : BUFFALO 1c(1) — **bi·son·tine** \-s²n-,tīn, -z²n-\ *adj*

¹bisque \'bisk\ *n* [F] (1647) **1 a** : a thick cream soup made with shellfish or game **b** : a cream soup of pureed vegetables **2** : ice cream containing powdered nuts or macaroons

²bisque *n* [F] (ca. 1656) : odds allowed an inferior player: as **a** : a point taken when desired in a set of tennis **b** : an extra turn in croquet **c** : one or more strokes off a golf score

³bisque *n* [by shortening & alter.] (1664) : BISCUIT 2; *esp* : unglazed china that is not to be glazed but is hard-fired and vitreous

bi·state \'bī-,stāt\ *adj* (1928) : of or relating to two states

bis·ter *or* **bis·tre** \'bis-tər\ *n* [F *bistre*] (ca. 1751) **1** : a yellowish brown to dark brown pigment used in art **2** : a grayish to yellowish brown — **bis·tered** \-tərd\ *adj*

bis·tort \'bis-,tȯrt, bis-\ *n* [MF *bistorte,* fr. (assumed) ML *bistorta,* fr. L *bis* + *torta,* fem. of *tortus,* pp. of *torquēre* to twist — more at TORTURE] (1578) : any of several polygonums; *esp* : a European herb (*Polygonum bistorta*) or a related American plant (*P. bistortoides*) with twisted roots used as astringents

bis·tro \'bēs-(,)trō, 'bis-\ *n, pl* **bistros** [F] (1921) **1** : a small or unpretentious restaurant **2 a** : a small bar or tavern **b** : NIGHTCLUB — **bis·tro·ic** \bēs-'trō-ik, bis-\ *adj*

bi·sul·fate \(,)bī-'səl-,fāt\ *n* (ca. 1846) : an acid sulfate

bi·sul·fide \-,fīd\ *n* [ISV] (1863) : DISULFIDE

bi·sul·fite \-,fīt\ *n* [F, fr. *bi-* + *sulfite*] (ca. 1846) : an acid sulfite

bi–swing \'bī-'swiŋ\ *adj* [¹*bi-* + *swing;* perh. fr. the freedom of movement allowed by this jacket] (1968) : made with a pleat or gusset at the back of the arms ⟨~ jacket⟩

¹bit \'bit\ *n* [ME *bitt,* fr. OE *bite* act of biting; akin to OE *bitan*] (14c) **1 a (1)** : the biting or cutting edge or part of a tool **(2)** : a replaceable part of a compound tool that actually performs the function (as drilling or boring) for which the whole tool is designed **b** *pl* : the jaws of tongs or pincers **2** : something bitten or held with the teeth: **a** : the usu. steel part of a bridle inserted in the mouth of a horse **b** : the rimmed mouth end on the stem of a pipe or cigar holder **3** : something that curbs or restrains **4** : the part of a key that enters the lock and acts on the bolt and tumblers

²bit *vt* **bit·ted; bit·ting** (1583) **1 a** : to put a bit in the mouth of (a horse) **b** : to control as if with a bit **2** : to form a bit on (a key)

³bit *n* [ME, fr. OE *bita;* akin to OE *bitan*] (bef. 12c) **1** : a small quantity of food; *esp* : a small delicacy **2 a** : a small piece or quantity of some material thing **b (1)** : a small coin **(2)** : a unit of value equal to ⅛ of a dollar ⟨four ~s⟩ **3** : something small or unimportant of its kind: as **a** : a brief period : WHILE **b** : an indefinite usu. small degree, extent, or amount ⟨a ~ of a rascal⟩ ⟨every ~ as powerful⟩ **c (1)** : a small part usu. with spoken lines in a theatrical performance **(2)** : a usu. short theatrical routine ⟨a corny comedy ~⟩ **4** : the aggregate of items, situations, or activities appropriate to a given style, genre, or role ⟨rejected the whole ~ about love-marriage-motherhood —Vance Packard⟩ — **a bit** : SOMEWHAT, RATHER ⟨the play was *a bit* dull⟩ — **a bit much** : a little more than one wants to endure — **bit by bit** : by degrees : LITTLE BY LITTLE

⁴bit *n* [*binary digit*] (1948) **1** : a unit of computer information equivalent to the result of a choice between two alternatives (as *yes* or *no, on* or *off*) **2** : the physical representation of a bit by an electrical pulse, a magnetized spot, or a hole whose presence or absence indicates data

bi·tar·trate \(,)bī-'tär-,trāt\ *n* [ISV] (1879) : an acid tartrate

¹bitch \'bich\ *n* [ME *bicche,* fr. OE *bicce*] (bef. 12c) **1** : the female of the dog or some other carnivorous mammals **2 a** : a lewd or immoral woman **b** : a malicious, spiteful, or domineering woman — sometimes used as a generalized term of abuse **3** : something that is highly objectionable or unpleasant **4** : COMPLAINT

²bitch *vt* (1823) **1** : SPOIL, BOTCH ⟨I must have ~ed up my life —Mavis Gallant⟩ **2** : CHEAT, DOUBLECROSS **3** : to complain of or about ~ *vi* : COMPLAIN

bitch·ery \'bi-chə-rē\ *n, pl* **-er·ies** (1936) : malicious, spiteful, or domineering behavior; *also* : an instance of such behavior

bitch goddess *n* (1906) : SUCCESS; *esp* : material or worldly success

bitchy \'bi-chē\ *adj* **bitch·i·er; -est** (1937) : characterized by malicious, spiteful, or arrogant behavior — **bitch·i·ly** \'bi-chə-lē\ *adv* — **bitch·i·ness** \'bi-chē-nəs\ *n*

¹bite \'bīt\ *vb* **bit** \'bit\; **bit·ten** \'bi-t²n\; **bit·ing** \'bī-tiŋ\ [ME, fr. OE *bitan;* akin to OHG *bīzan* to bite, L *findere* to split] *vt* (bef. 12c) **1 a** : to seize esp. with teeth or jaws so as to enter, grip, or wound **b** : to wound, pierce, or sting esp. with a fang or a proboscis **2** : to cut or pierce with or as if with an edged weapon **3** : to cause sharp pain or stinging discomfort to **4** : to take hold of **5** *archaic* : to take in : CHEAT ~ *vi* **1** : to bite or have the habit of biting something **2** *of a weapon or tool* : to cut, pierce, or take hold **3** : to cause irritation or smarting **4** : CORRODE **5** *of fish* : to take a bait **6** : to respond so as to be caught (as by a trick) **6** : to take or maintain a firm hold — **bit·er** \'bī-tər\ *n* — **bite off more than one can chew** : to undertake more than one can perform — **bite the bullet** : to enter with resignation upon a difficult or distressing course of action — **bite the dust** **1** : to fall dead esp. in battle **2** : to suffer humiliation or defeat — **bite the hand that feeds one** : to injure a benefactor maliciously

²bite *n* (15c) **1** : the act or manner of biting **2** : FOOD: as **a** : the amount of food taken at a bite : MORSEL **b** : a small amount of food : SNACK **3** *archaic* **a** : CHEAT, TRICK **b** : SHARPER **4** : a wound made by biting **5** : the hold or grip by which friction is created or purchase is obtained **6** : a surface that creates friction or is brought into contact with another for the purpose of obtaining a hold **7 a** : a keen incisive quality **b** : a sharp penetrating effect **8** : a single exposure of an etcher's plate to the corrosive action of acid **9** : an amount taken usu. in one operation for one purpose : CUT

bite·wing \'bīt-,wiŋ\ *n* (1938) : a dental X-ray film designed to show the crowns of the upper and lower teeth simultaneously

bit·ing \'bī-tiŋ\ *adj* (14c) : having the power to bite ⟨a ~ wind⟩; *esp* : able to grip and impress deeply ⟨the report is ~ in its intolerance of deceit⟩ — **bit·ing·ly** \-tiŋ-lē\ *adv*

\ə\ abut \ᵊ\ kitten, F table \ər\ further \a\ ash \ā\ ace \ä\ mop, mar
\aú\ out \ch\ chin \e\ bet \ē\ easy \g\ go \i\ hit \ī\ ice \j\ job
\ŋ\ sing \ō\ go \ȯ\ law \ȯi\ boy \th\ thin \th\ the \ü\ loot \ù\ foot
\y\ yet \zh\ vision \å, ḵ, ⁿ, œ, œ̄, ᵫ, ᵾ, ᵊ\ *see* Guide to Pronunciation

biting louse *n* (1896) : any of numerous wingless insects (order Mallophaga) that are parasitic esp. on birds — called also *bird louse*
biting midge *n* (1945) : any of a family (Ceratopogonidae) of tiny biting dipteran flies of which some are vectors of filarial worms
bit·stock \'bit-ˌstäk\ *n* (ca. 1887) : BRACE 3
bit·sy \'bit-sē\ *adj* [*itsy-bitsy*] (1905) : TINY
¹**bitt** \'bit\ *n* [perh. fr. ON *biti* beam; akin to OE *bōt* boat] (14c) **1 a** : a post or pair of posts fixed on the deck of a ship for securing lines **2** : BOLLARD 1
²**bitt** *vt* (1769) : to make (a cable) fast about a bitt
¹**bit·ter** \'bi-tər\ *adj* [ME, fr. OE *biter*; akin to OHG *bittar* bitter, OE *bītan*] (bef. 12c) **1 a** : being or inducing the one of the four basic taste sensations that is peculiarly acrid, astringent, or disagreeable and suggestive of an infusion of hops — compare SALT, SOUR, SWEET **b** : distasteful or distressing to the mind : GALLING ⟨a ~ sense of shame⟩ **2** : marked by intensity or severity: **a** : accompanied by severe pain or suffering ⟨a ~ death⟩ **b** : being relentlessly determined : VEHEMENT ⟨a ~ partisan⟩ **c** : exhibiting intense animosity ⟨~ enemies⟩ **d** (1) : harshly reproachful ⟨~ complaints⟩ (2) : marked by cynicism and rancor ⟨~ contempt⟩ **e** : intensely unpleasant esp. in coldness or rawness **3** : expressive of severe pain, grief, or regret ⟨~ tears⟩ — **bit·ter·ish** \-ish\ *adj* — **bit·ter·ly** *adv* — **bit·ter·ness** *n*
²**bitter** *n* (bef. 12c) **1** : bitter quality **2** *a pl* : a usu. alcoholic solution of bitter and often aromatic plant products used esp. in preparing mixed drinks or as a mild tonic **b** *Brit* : a very dry heavily hopped ale
³**bitter** *vt* (12c) : to make bitter ⟨~ed ale⟩
⁴**bitter** *adv* (1749) : to a bitter degree ⟨it's ~ cold⟩
bitter almond *n* (1632) : an almond with a bitter taste that contains amygdalin; *also* : a tree (*Prunus dulcis amara*) producing bitter almonds
bit·ter·brush \'bi-tər-ˌbrəsh\ *n* (1910) : a much-branched silvery shrub (*Purshia tridentata*) of arid western No. America that has 3-toothed leaves and yellow flowers and is valuable for forage
bitter cress *n* (ca. 1890) : any of a genus (*Cardamine*) of cruciferous herbs that produce flat pods and wingless seeds
¹**bitter end** *n* [prob. fr. ²*bitter end*] (1849) : the last extremity however painful or calamitous — **bit·ter·end·er** \ˌbi-tər-'en-dər\ *n*
²**bitter end** *n* [*bitter* (a turn of cable around the bitts)] (ca. 1862) : the inboard end of a ship's anchoring cable
¹**bit·tern** \'bi-tərn\ *n* [ME *bitoure*, fr. MF *butor*, fr. (assumed) VL *butitaurus*, fr. L *buteo* hawk + *taurus* bull] (1515) : any of various small or medium-sized usu. secretive herons (esp. genera *Botaurus* and *Ixobrychus*)
²**bittern** *n* [irreg. fr. ¹*bitter*] (1682) : the bitter water solution of salts that remains after sodium chloride has crystallized out of a brine
bit·ter·root \'bi-tə(r)-ˌrüt, -ˌrüt\ *n* (1838) : a succulent herb (*Lewisia rediviva*) of mountainous slopes of western No. America that has starchy roots and pink or white flowers
¹**bit·ter·sweet** \'bi-tər-ˌswēt\ *n* (14c) **1** : something that is bittersweet; *esp* : pleasure alloyed with pain **2 a** : a sprawling poisonous weedy nightshade (*Solanum dulcamara*) with purple flowers and oval reddish orange berries **b** : a No. American woody climbing plant (*Celastrus scandens*) of the staff-tree family having clusters of small greenish flowers succeeded by yellow capsules that open when ripe and disclose the scarlet aril
²**bittersweet** *adj* (1611) **1** : being at once bitter and sweet; *esp* : pleasant but including or marked by elements of suffering or regret ⟨a ~ ballad⟩ **2** : of or relating to a prepared chocolate containing little sugar — **bit·ter·sweet·ly** *adv* — **bit·ter·sweet·ness** *n*
bit·ter·weed \'bi-tər-ˌwēd\ *n* (1819) : any of several American plants containing a bitter substance: as **a** : HORSEWEED **b** : a sneezeweed (*Helenium amarum* syn. *H. tenuifolium*) **c** : an erect composite herb (*Hymenoxys odorata*) of the southwestern U.S. that has yellow terminal flowerheads and is poisonous to livestock
bit·tock \'bi-tək\ *n* (ca. 1802) *chiefly Scot* : a little bit
¹**bit·ty** \'bi-tē\ *adj* (1892) *chiefly Brit* : made up of or containing bits; *esp* : not cohesive or flowing
²**bitty** *adj* (1905) : SMALL, TINY ⟨a little ~ room⟩
bi·tu·men \bə-'tyü-mən, bī-, -'tü-, *esp Brit also* 'bit-yə-\ *n* [ME *bithumen* mineral pitch, fr. L *bitumin-, bitumen*] (15c) **1** : an asphalt of Asia Minor used in ancient times as a cement and mortar **2** : any of various mixtures of hydrocarbons (as tar) often together with their nonmetallic derivatives that occur naturally or are obtained as residues after heat-refining natural substances (as petroleum); *specif* : such a mixture soluble in carbon disulfide — **bi·tu·mi·ni·za·tion** \bə-ˌtyü-mə-nə-'zā-shən, bī-, -ˌtü-\ *n* — **bi·tu·mi·nize** \-'tyü-mə-ˌnīz, -'tü-\ *vt*
bi·tu·mi·nous \bə-'tyü-mə-nəs, bī-, -'tü-\ *adj* (1620) **1** : containing or impregnated with bitumen **2** : of or relating to bituminous coal
bituminous coal *n* (1827) : a coal that when heated yields considerable volatile bituminous matter — called also *soft coal*
bi·unique \ˌbī-yü-'nēk\ *adj* (1941) : being a correspondence between two sets that is one-to-one in both directions — **bi·unique·ness** *n*
¹**bi·va·lent** \(ˌ)bī-'vā-lənt, 'bī-və-\ *adj* (1869) **1** : DIVALENT **2** : associated in pairs in synapsis
²**bivalent** *n* (ca. 1934) : a pair of synaptic chromosomes
¹**bi·valve** \'bī-ˌvalv\ *adj* (1661) : having a shell composed of two valves
²**bivalve** *n* (1683) : an animal (as a clam) with a 2-valved shell
bi·var·i·ate \(ˌ)bī-'ver-ē-ət, -'var-\ *adj* (1920) : of, relating to, or involving two variables ⟨a ~ frequency distribution⟩
¹**biv·ouac** \'bi-və-ˌwak, 'biv-ˌwak\ *n* [F, fr. LG *biwacht*, fr. *bi* by + *wacht* guard] (ca. 1702) **1** : a usu. temporary encampment under little or no shelter **2 a** : encampment usu. for a night **b** : a temporary shelter or settlement
²**bivouac** *vi* **-ouacked; -ouack·ing** (1809) : to make a bivouac : CAMP
¹**bi·week·ly** \(ˌ)bī-'wē-klē\ *adj* (1832) **1** : occurring twice a week **2** : occurring every two weeks : FORTNIGHTLY *usage* see BI- — **biweekly** *adv*
²**biweekly** *n* (ca. 1890) **1** : a publication issued every two weeks **2** : SEMIWEEKLY
bi·year·ly \(ˌ)bī-'yir-lē\ *adj* (ca. 1909) **1** : BIANNUAL 1 **2** : BIENNIAL 1
biz \'biz\ *n* (1862) : BUSINESS
¹**bi·zarre** \bə-'zär\ *adj* [F, fr. It *bizzarro*] (ca. 1648) : strikingly out of the ordinary: as **a** : odd, extravagant, or eccentric in style or mode **b**

: involving sensational contrasts or incongruities *syn* see FANTASTIC — **bi·zarre·ly** *adv* — **bi·zarre·ness** *n*
²**bizarre** *n* (ca. 1753) : a flower with atypical striped marking
bi·zar·re·rie \bi-ˌzär-ə-'rē\ *n* [F] (1747) **1** : a bizarre quality **2** : something bizarre
bi·zon·al \(ˌ)bī-'zōn-ᵊl\ *adj* (1946) : of or relating to the affairs of a zone governed or administered by two powers acting together — **bi·zone** \'bī-ˌzōn\ *n*
¹**blab** \'blab\ *n* [ME *blabbe*; akin to ME *blaberen*] (14c) **1** *archaic* : one that blabs : TATTLETALE **2** : idle or excessive talk : CHATTER — **blab·by** \'bla-bē\ *adj*
²**blab** *vb* **blabbed; blab·bing** *vi* (15c) **1** : to talk idly or thoughtlessly : PRATTLE **2** : to reveal a secret esp. by indiscreet chatter ~ *vt* : to reveal esp. without reserve or discretion ⟨*blabbed* the whole affair to the press⟩
¹**blab·ber** \'bla-bər\ *vb* **blab·bered; blab·ber·ing** \-b(ə-)riŋ\ [ME *blaberen*] *vi* (14c) : to talk foolishly or excessively ~ *vt* : to say indiscreetly
²**blabber** *n* (ca. 1913) : idle talk : BABBLE
³**blabber** *n* [²*blab*] (1557) : one that blabs
blab·ber·mouth \'bla-bər-ˌmaüth\ *n* (1936) : a person who talks too much; *esp* : TATTLETALE
¹**black** \'blak\ *adj* [ME *blak*, fr. OE *blæc*; akin to OHG *blah* black, and prob. to L *flagrare* to burn, Gk *phlegein*] (bef. 12c) **1 a** : of the color black **b** (1) : very dark in color ⟨his face was ~ with rage⟩ (2) : having a very deep or low register ⟨a bass with a ~ voice⟩ (3) : HEAVY, SERIOUS ⟨the play was a ~ intrigue⟩ **2 a** : having dark skin, hair, and eyes : SWARTHY ⟨the ~ Irish⟩ **b** (1) *often cap* : of or relating to any of various population groups having dark pigmentation of the skin ⟨~ Americans⟩ (2) : of or relating to the Afro-American people or their culture ⟨~ literature⟩ ⟨a ~ college⟩ ⟨~ pride⟩ ⟨~ studies⟩ (3) : typical or representative of the most readily attended parts of black culture ⟨tried to play ~er jazz⟩ **3** : dressed in black **4** : DIRTY, SOILED ⟨hands ~ with grime⟩ **5 a** : characterized by the absence of light ⟨a ~ night⟩ **b** : reflecting or transmitting little or no light ⟨~ water⟩ **c** : served without milk or cream ⟨~ coffee⟩ **6 a** : thoroughly sinister or evil : WICKED ⟨a ~ deed⟩ **b** : indicative of condemnation or discredit ⟨got a ~ mark for being late⟩ **7** : connected with or invoking the supernatural and esp. the devil ⟨~ magic⟩ **8 a** : very sad, gloomy, or calamitous ⟨~ despair⟩ **b** : marked by the occurrence of disaster ⟨~ Friday⟩ **9** : characterized by hostility or angry discontent : SULLEN ⟨~ resentment filled his heart⟩ **10** *chiefly Brit* : subject to boycott by trade-union members as employing or favoring nonunion workers or as operating under conditions considered unfair by the trade union **11 a** *of propaganda* : conducted so as to appear to originate within an enemy country and designed to weaken enemy morale **b** : characterized by or connected with the use of black propaganda ⟨~ radio⟩ **12** : characterized by grim, distorted, or grotesque satire ⟨~ humor⟩ **13** : of or relating to covert intelligence operations ⟨~ government programs⟩ — **black·ish** \'bla-kish\ *adj* — **black·ly** *adv* — **black·ness** *n*
²**black** *n* (bef. 12c) **1** : a black pigment or dye; *esp* : one consisting largely of carbon **2** : the achromatic color of least lightness characteristically perceived to belong to objects that neither reflect nor transmit light **3** : something that is black: as **a** : black clothing ⟨looks good in ~⟩ **b** : a black animal (as a horse) **4 a** : a person belonging to any of various population groups having dark pigmentation of the skin **b** : AFRO-AMERICAN **5** : the pieces of a dark color in a board game for two players (as chess) **6** : total or nearly total absence of light ⟨the ~ of night⟩ **7** : the condition of making a profit — usu. used with *the* ⟨operating in the ~⟩; compare RED
³**black** *vi* (13c) : to become black ~ *vt* **1** : to make black **2** *chiefly Brit* : to declare (as a business or industry) subject to boycott by trade-union members
black alder *n* (1805) : WINTERBERRY 1
black·a·moor \'bla-kə-ˌmür\ *n* [irreg. fr. *black* + *Moor*] (1547) : a dark-skinned person; *esp* : BLACK 4a
black-and-blue \ˌbla-kən-'blü\ *adj* (14c) : darkly discolored from blood effused by bruising
black–and–tan \-kən-'tan\ *adj* (1850) **1** : having a predominantly black color pattern with deep red or rusty tan on the feet, breeching, and cheek patches, above the eyes, and inside the ears **2** : favoring or practicing proportional representation of whites and blacks in politics **3** : frequented by both blacks and whites ⟨a ~ bar⟩
black and tan *n* (1870) **1** : a black-and-tan animal (as a dog) **2** *chiefly Brit* : a drink consisting of a dark beer (as stout or porter) and ale or beer **3** *cap B&T* [fr. the color of his uniform]: a recruit enlisted in England in 1920–21 for service in the Royal Irish Constabulary against the armed movement for Irish independence **4** : a member of a black-and-tan political organization (as in the southern U.S.) — compare LILY-WHITE
black–and–tan coonhound *n* (1948) : any of a breed of strong vigorous coonhounds of American origin with black-and-tan markings
black–and–white \ˌbla-kən-'hwīt, -'wīt\ *adj* (1612) **1** : being in writing or print **2** : partly black and partly white in color **3** : executed in dark pigment on a light background or in light pigment on a dark ground ⟨a ~ drawing⟩ **4** : MONOCHROME 2a ⟨~ film⟩ ⟨~ television⟩ **5 a** : sharply divided into good and evil **b** : evaluating or viewing things as either all good or all bad ⟨~ morality⟩ **c** : sharply defined : CLEAR-CUT ⟨the truth is not always ~⟩
black and white *n* (1599) **1** : WRITING, PRINT **2** : a drawing or print done in black and white or in monochrome **3** : monochrome reproduction of visual images (as by photography or television)
Black Angus *n* (1948) : ANGUS
black–a–vised \'bla-kə-ˌvīst\ *adj* [*black* + F *à vis* as to face] (ca. 1758) : having a dark complexion
¹**black·ball** \'blak-ˌbȯl\ *vt* (1770) **1** : to vote against; *esp* : to exclude from membership by casting a negative vote **2 a** : to exclude socially : OSTRACIZE **b** : BOYCOTT
²**blackball** *n* (ca. 1847) **1** : a small black ball for use as a negative vote in a ballot box **2** : an adverse vote esp. against admitting someone to membership in an organization

black bass n (1815) : any of a genus (*Micropterus*) of freshwater sunfishes native to eastern and central No. America and including the largemouth bass and smallmouth bass

black bean n (1792) 1 : a black kidney bean commonly used in Latin American cuisine 2 : a black soybean commonly used in oriental cuisine

black bear n (1781) : the common American bear (*Ursus americanus*) ranging in color from brown or typical black to white

black beast n (1926) : BÊTE NOIRE

¹**black belt** \'blak-,belt\ n (1870) 1 : an area characterized by rich black soil 2 *often cap both Bs* : an area densely populated by blacks

²**black belt** n (1954) : one who holds the rating of expert in various arts of self-defense (as judo and karate); *also* : the rating itself

black·ber·ry \'blak-,ber-ē\ n (bef. 12c) 1 : the usu. black or dark purple juicy but seedy edible aggregate fruit of various brambles (genus *Rubus*) of the rose family 2 : a plant that bears blackberries

black bile n (1797) : a humor of medieval physiology believed to be secreted by the kidneys or spleen and to cause melancholy

black birch n (1674) : SWEET BIRCH

¹**black·bird** \'blak-,bərd\ n (14c) 1 : any of various birds of which the males are largely or entirely black: as a : a common thrush (*Turdus merula*) of Eurasia and northern Africa having an orange bill and eye rim b : any of several American birds (family Icteridae) 2 : a Pacific islander kidnapped for use as a plantation laborer

²**blackbird** vi (1894) : to engage in the slave trade esp. in the So. Pacific

black·bird·er n (1880) 1 : a person who blackbirds 2 : a ship used in blackbirding

black·board \'blak-,bōrd, -,bórd\ n (1823) : a hard smooth usu. dark surface used esp. in a classroom for writing or drawing on with chalk

black·body \'blak-'bä-dē\ n (1710) : an ideal body or surface that completely absorbs all radiant energy falling upon it with no reflection and that radiates at all frequencies with a spectral energy distribution dependent on its absolute temperature

black book n (1592) : a book containing a blacklist

black box n (ca. 1945) 1 : a usu. complicated electronic device that functions and is packaged as a unit and whose internal mechanism is usu. hidden from or mysterious to the user; *broadly* : anything that has mysterious or unknown internal functions or mechanisms 2 : a crashworthy device in aircraft for recording cockpit conversations and flight data

black·cap \'blak-,kap\ n (1678) 1 : any of several birds with black heads or crowns: as a : a small European warbler (*Sylvia atricapilla*) with a black crown b : CHICKADEE 2 : BLACK RASPBERRY

black–capped \-'kapt\ adj (1781) of a bird : having the top of the head black

black·cock \-,käk\ n (15c) chiefly Brit : BLACK GROUSE; specif : the male black grouse

black cohosh n (1828) : a bugbane (*Cimicifuga racemosa*) of the eastern U.S.

black crappie n (ca. 1827) : a silvery black-mottled sunfish (*Pomoxis nigromaculatus*) of the Mississippi drainage and eastern U.S. having seven or eight protruding spines on the dorsal fins

black–crowned night heron \'blak-,kraùnd-\ n (1844) : a widely distributed night heron (*Nycticorax nycticorax*) having a black crown and back

black damp n (1836) : a carbon dioxide mixture occurring as a mine gas and incapable of supporting life or flame

black death n, often cap B&D [fr. the black patches formed on the skin of its victims] (1780) 1 : PLAGUE 2b 2 : a severe epidemic of plague and esp. bubonic plague that occurred in Asia and Europe in the 14th century

black diamond n (1763) 1 : dense black hematite 2 pl : COAL 3a 3 : ³CARBONADO

black duck n (1637) : any of several ducks that are dark in color; *esp* : a common brown duck (*Anas rubripes*) of eastern No. America

black dwarf n, pl black dwarfs (1945) : a very small star that emits no detectable light

black·en \'bla-kən\ vb black·ened; black·en·ing \'blak-niŋ, 'bla-kə-\ vi (14c) : to become dark or black (the sky ~s) ~ vt 1 : to make black 2 : DEFAME, SULLY — **black·en·er** \'blak-nər, 'bla-kə-\ n

black·ened \-kənd\ adj (1984) : coated with a mixture of cayenne pepper and spices and cooked in a frying pan over extremely high heat (~ redfish)

Black English n (1969) : a nonstandard variety of English spoken by some American blacks — called also *Black English vernacular*

black·en·ing \'blak-niŋ, 'bla-kə-\ n (ca. 1909) : BLACKING

black eye n (1604) 1 : a discoloration of the skin around the eye from bruising 2 : a bad reputation

black–eyed pea \'blak-,īd-\ n (1728) : COWPEA

black–eyed Su·san \-'sü-z²n\ n (1892) : either of two No. American coneflowers (*Rudbeckia hirta* and *R. serotina*) having flower heads with deep yellow to orange rays and dark conical disks

black·face \'blak-,fās\ n (1869) : makeup applied to a performer playing a black person esp. in a minstrel show; *also* : a performer wearing such makeup

black·fish \-,fish\ n (1754) 1 : any of numerous dark-colored fishes: as a : TAUTOG b : a small food fish (*Dallia pectoralis*) of Alaska and Siberia that is noted for its resistance to cold 2 : any of several small toothed whales (genus *Globicephala*) found in warm seas

black–flag \-'flag\ vt (1963) : to signal (a race-car driver) to go immediately to the pits

black flag n (1720) : a pirate's flag usu. bearing a skull and crossbones

black·fly \'blak-,flī\ n, pl -flies or -fly (1608) : any of various small dark-colored insects; *esp* : any of a family (Simuliidae and esp. genus *Simulium*) of bloodsucking dipteran flies whose larvae usu. live in flowing streams

Black·foot \'blak-,fùt\ n, pl Blackfeet or Blackfoot (1794) 1 : a member of an American Indian people of Montana, Alberta, and Saskatchewan 2 : the Algonquian language of the Blackfeet

black–foot·ed albatross \'blak-,fù-təd-\ n (1839) : an albatross (*Diomedea nigripes*) of the Pacific that is chiefly blackish with dusky bill and black feet and legs — called also *gooney*

black–footed ferret n (1846) : a rare weasel (*Mustela nigripes*) of western No. American prairies having a yellowish coat, dark feet and facial mask, and a dark-tipped tail

black gold n (1910) : PETROLEUM

black grouse n (1678) : a large grouse (*Lyrurus tetrix*) of western Asia and Europe of which the male is black with white wing patches and the female is barred and mottled

¹**black·guard** \'bla-gərd, -,gärd; 'blak-,gärd\ n (1535) 1 obs : the kitchen servants of a household 2 a : a rude or unscrupulous person b : a person who uses foul or abusive language — **black·guard·ism** \-gər-,di-zəm, -,gär-\ n — **black·guard·ly** \-gərd-lē, -,gärd-\ adj or adv

²**blackguard** vt (1823) : to talk about or address in abusive terms

black gum n (1709) : a tupelo (*Nyssa sylvatica*) of the eastern U.S. with light and soft but tough wood

black hand n, often cap B&H [Black Hand, a Sicilian and Italian-American secret society of the late 19th and 20th centuries] (1904) : a lawless secret society engaged in criminal activities (as terrorism or extortion) — **black–hand·er** \'blak-,han-dər\ n

black·head \-,hed\ n (ca. 1837) 1 : a small plug of sebum blocking the duct of a sebaceous gland esp. on the face 2 : a destructive disease of turkeys and related birds caused by a protozoan (*Histomonas meleagridis*) that invades the intestinal ceca and liver 3 : a larval clam or mussel attached to the skin or gills of a freshwater fish

black·heart \-,härt\ n (1909) : a plant disease in which the central tissues blacken

black hole n (1968) 1 : a hypothetical celestial object with a gravitational field so strong that light cannot escape from it which is believed to be created in the collapse of a very massive star 2 : something resembling a black hole: as a : something that consumes a resource continually (a financial *black hole*) b : an empty space : VOID

black ice n (1961) : a thin film of ice on paved surfaces (as roads) that is difficult to see

black·ing \'bla-kiŋ\ n (1571) : a substance (as a paste or polish) that is applied to an object to make it black

¹**black·jack** \-,jak\ n (1591) 1 [black + jack (vessel)] : a tankard for beer or ale usu. of tar-coated leather 2 : SPHALERITE 3 : a hand weapon typically consisting of a piece of leather-enclosed metal with a strap or springy shaft for a handle 4 : an often scrubby oak (*Quercus marilandica*) chiefly of the southeastern U.S. — called also *blackjack oak* 5 : a card game the object of which is to be dealt cards having a higher count than those of the dealer up to but not exceeding 21 — called also *twenty-one, vingt-et-un*

²**blackjack** vt (1905) 1 : to strike with a blackjack 2 : to coerce with threats or pressure

black·land \'blak-,land\ n (1803) 1 : a heavy sticky black soil such as that covering large areas in Texas 2 pl : a region of blackland

black·lead \'blak-,led\ n (1583) chiefly Brit : GRAPHITE 1

black·leg \'blak-,leg, -,läg\ n (ca. 1722) 1 : a usu. fatal toxemia esp. of young cattle caused by a soil bacterium (*Clostridium chauvoei*) 2 : a cheating gambler : SWINDLER 3 chiefly Brit : a worker hostile to trade unionism or acting in opposition to union policies : SCAB

black letter n (ca. 1644) : a heavy angular condensed typeface used esp. by the earliest European printers and based on handwriting used chiefly in the 13th to 15th centuries; *also* : this style of handwriting

𝔪𝔫𝔬𝔭𝔮𝔯𝔰𝔱𝔲𝔳

black letter

black light n (1927) 1 : invisible ultraviolet light 2 : a lamp that radiates black light

black–light trap \'blak-,līt-\ n (1961) : a trap for insects that uses a form of black light perceptible to particular insects as an attractant

¹**black·list** \-,list\ n (ca. 1619) : a list of persons who are disapproved of or are to be punished or boycotted

²**blacklist** vt (1718) : to put on a blacklist — **black·list·er** n

black locust n (1787) : a tall tree (*Robinia pseudoacacia*) of eastern No. America with pinnately compound leaves, drooping racemes of fragrant white flowers, and strong stiff wood

black lung n (1837) : pneumoconiosis caused by habitual inhalation of coal dust

black·mail \'blak-,māl\ n [black + ¹mail] (1552) 1 : a tribute anciently exacted on the Scottish border by freebooting chiefs for immunity from pillage 2 a : extortion or coercion by threats esp. of public exposure or criminal prosecution b : the payment that is extorted — **blackmail** vt — **black·mail·er** n

Black Ma·ria \,blak-mə-'rī-ə\ n (1847) : PADDY WAGON

black–mar·ket vi (1943) : to buy or sell goods in the black market ~ vt : to sell in the black market — **black marketeer** or **black mar·keteer** \-,mär-kə-'tir\ n

black market n (1931) : illicit trade in goods or commodities in violation of official regulations; *also* : a place where such trade is carried on

Black Mass n (1893) : a travesty of the Christian mass ascribed to worshipers of Satan

Black Muslim n (1960) : a member of a chiefly black group that professes Islamic religious belief

black nationalist n, often cap B&N (1963) : a member of a group of militant blacks who advocate separatism from the whites and the formation of self-governing black communities — **black nationalism** n, often cap B&N

black·out \'blak-,aùt\ n (1913) 1 a : a turning off of the stage lighting to separate scenes in a play or end a play or skit; *also* : a skit that ends with a blackout b : a period of darkness enforced as a precaution against air raids c : a period of darkness (as in a city) caused by a failure of electrical power 2 : a transient dulling or loss of vision, consciousness, or memory (an alcoholic ~) 3 a : a wiping out : OBLITERATION b : a blotting out by censorship : SUPPRESSION (a news

\ə\ abut \²\ kitten, F table \ər\ further \a\ ash \ā\ ace \ä\ mop, mar
\aù\ out \ch\ chin \e\ bet \ē\ easy \g\ go \i\ hit \ī\ ice \j\ job
\ŋ\ sing \ō\ go \ò\ law \òi\ boy \th\ thin \th\ the \ü\ loot \ù\ foot
\y\ yet \zh\ vision \á, k̲, ⁿ, œ, œ̄, ue, ūe, ᵛ\ see Guide to Pronunciation

~⟩ **4 :** a usu. temporary loss of a radio signal **5 :** the prohibition or restriction of the telecasting of a sports event

black out vi (1921) **1 :** to become enveloped in darkness **2 :** to undergo a temporary loss of vision, consciousness, or memory ~ vt **1 :** to cause to black out ⟨*black out* the stage⟩ **2 :** to make inoperative (as by a power failure) **3 a :** BLOT OUT, ERASE ⟨*blacked out* the event from his mind⟩ **b :** to suppress by censorship ⟨*black out* the news⟩ **4 :** to impose a blackout on

Black Panther n (1965) **:** a member of an organization of militant American blacks

black pepper n (bef. 12c) **:** a spice that consists of the fruit of an East Indian plant (*Piper nigrum*) ground with the black husk still on

black·poll \'blak-ˌpōl\ n (1783) **:** a No. American warbler (*Dendroica striata*) with the male having a black cap when in breeding plumage

black powder n (ca. 1909) **:** an explosive mixture of potassium nitrate or sodium nitrate, charcoal, and sulfur used esp. in fireworks and as a propellant in antique firearms — compare GUNPOWDER

black power n, often cap B&P (1966) **:** the mobilization of the political and economic power of American blacks esp. to compel respect for their rights and improve their condition

black pudding n (1568) chiefly Brit **:** BLOOD SAUSAGE

black racer n (1849) **:** an American blacksnake (*Coluber constrictor constrictor*) common in the eastern U.S.

black raspberry n (ca. 1782) **:** a raspberry (*Rubus occidentalis*) of eastern No. America that has a purplish black fruit and is the source of several cultivated varieties — called also *blackcap*

black rhinoceros n (1850) **:** a rhinoceros (*Diceros bicornis*) of sub-Saharan Africa having a prehensile upper lip that protrudes in the middle — called also *black rhino*

Black Rod n (ca. 1607) **:** the principal usher of the House of Lords

black rot n (1849) **:** a bacterial or fungal rot of plants marked by dark brown discoloration

black sheep n (1792) **:** a discreditable member of a respectable group

Black·shirt \'blak-ˌshərt\ n (1922) **:** a member of a fascist organization having a black shirt as a distinctive part of its uniform; *esp* **:** a member of the Italian Fascist party

black·smith \'blak-ˌsmith\ n [fr. a distinction between black metal (iron) and white metal (tin)] (15c) **:** a smith who forges iron — **black·smith·ing** \-ˌsmi-thiŋ\ n

black smoker n (1980) **:** a vent in a geologically active region of the sea floor from which issues superheated water laden with minerals (as sulfide precipitates)

black·snake \-ˌsnāk\ n (1634) **1 :** any of several snakes that are largely black or very dark in color; *esp* **:** either of two harmless snakes (*Coluber constrictor* and *Elaphe obsoleta*) of the U.S. **2 :** a long tapering braided whip of rawhide or leather

black spot n (ca. 1889) **:** any of several bacterial or fungal diseases of plants characterized by black spots or blotches esp. on the leaves

black·tail \'blak-ˌtāl\ n (1828) **:** BLACK-TAILED DEER

black–tailed deer \ˌblak-ˌtāl(d)-\ n (1806) **:** MULE DEER; *specif* **:** one of a subspecies (*Odocoileus hemionus columbianus*) esp. of British Columbia, Oregon, and Washington

black tea n (1789) **:** tea that is dark in color from complete fermentation of the leaf before firing

black·thorn \'blak-ˌthôrn\ n (14c) **:** a European spiny plum (*Prunus spinosa*) with hard wood and small white flowers

black–tie adj (1933) **:** characterized by or requiring the wearing of semiformal evening clothes consisting of a usu. black tie and tuxedo for men and a formal dress for women ⟨a ~ dinner⟩ — compare WHITE-TIE

black·top \'blak-ˌtäp\ n (1931) **:** a bituminous material used esp. for surfacing roads; *also* **:** a surface paved with blacktop — **blacktop** vt

Blackwall hitch \'blak-ˌwôl-\ n [*Blackwall*, shipyard in London, England] (ca. 1862) **:** a hitch for securing a rope to a hook — see KNOT illustration

black walnut n (1612) **:** a walnut (*Juglans nigra*) of eastern No. America with hard strong heavy dark brown wood and oily edible nuts; *also* **:** its wood or nut

black·wa·ter \'blak-ˌwȯ-tər, -ˌwä-\ n (1800) **:** any of several diseases (as blackwater fever) characterized by dark-colored urine

blackwater fever n (1884) **:** a febrile complication of repeated malarial attacks that is characterized esp. by extensive kidney damage and urine discolored by heme from blood

black widow n (1915) **:** a venomous New World spider (*Latrodectus mactans*) the female of which is black with an hourglass-shaped red mark on the underside of the abdomen

black·wood \'blak-ˌwu̇d\ n (1631) **:** any of several hardwood trees (as the legumes *Acacia melanoxylon* and *Dalbergia latifolia*) or their dark-colored wood

blad·der \'bla-dər\ n [ME, fr. OE *blǣdre*; akin to OHG *blātara* bladder, OE *blāwan* to blow] (bef. 12c) **1 a :** a membranous sac in animals that serves as the receptacle of a liquid or contains gas; *esp* **:** URINARY BLADDER **b :** CYST 2b **2 :** something (as the rubber bag inside a football) resembling a bladder — **blad·der·like** \-ˌlīk\ adj

bladder campion n (1817) **:** an Old World campion (*Silene vulgaris* syn. *S. cucubalus*) with an inflated calyx introduced into temperate No. America

blad·der·nut \'bla-dər-ˌnət\ n (1578) **:** any of a genus (*Staphylea* of the family Staphyleaceae, the bladdernut family) of ornamental shrubs or small trees with panicles of small white flowers followed by inflated capsules; *also* **:** one of the capsules

bladder worm n (1858) **:** a bladderlike larval tapeworm (as a cysticercus)

blad·der·wort \'bla-dər-ˌwərt, -ˌwȯrt\ n (ca. 1815) **:** any of a genus (*Utricularia* of the family Lentibulariaceae, the bladderwort family) of chiefly aquatic plants with leaves usu. having insect-trapping bladders

bladder wrack n (1810) **:** a common rockweed (*Fucus vesiculosus*) used in preparing kelp and as a manure

blade \'blād\ n [ME, fr. OE *blæd*; akin to OHG *blat* leaf, L *folium*, Gk *phyllon*, OE *blōwan* to blossom — more at BLOW] (bef. 12c) **1 a :** LEAF 1a(1); *esp* **:** the leaf of an herb or a grass **b :** the flat expanded part of a leaf as distinguished from the petiole **2 :** something resembling the blade of a leaf: as **a :** the broad flattened part of an oar or paddle **b :** an arm of a screw propeller, electric fan, or steam turbine **c :** the broad flat or concave part of a machine (as a bulldozer or snow-

plow) that comes into contact with the material to be moved **d :** a broad flat body part; *specif* **:** SCAPULA — used chiefly in naming cuts of meat **e :** the flat portion of the tongue immediately behind the tip; *also* **:** this portion together with the tip **3 a :** the cutting part of an implement **b** (1) **:** SWORD (2) **:** SWORDSMAN (3) **:** a dashing lively man **c :** the runner of an ice skate — **blade-like** \-ˌlīk\ adj

blad·ed \'blā-dəd\ adj (1578) **:** having blades — often used in combination ⟨five-*bladed* propeller⟩

blae \'blā\ adj [ME *bla*, *blo*, fr. ON *blār*; akin to OHG *blāo* blue — more at BLUE] (13c) chiefly Scot **:** dark blue or bluish gray

blae·ber·ry \'blā-ˌber-ē, -ˌb(ə-)rē\ n (15c) chiefly Scot **:** WHORTLEBERRY 1

¹blah \'blä\ n [imit.] (1918) **1** also **blah–blah** \-ˌblä\ **:** silly or pretentious chatter or nonsense **2** pl [perh. influenced in meaning by *blasé*] **:** a feeling of boredom, lethargy, or general dissatisfaction

²blah adj (1923) **:** lacking interest **:** MEDIOCRE ⟨a ~ winter day⟩

blain \'blān\ n [ME, fr. OE *blegen*; akin to MLG *bleine* blain, OE *blāwan* to blow] (bef. 12c) **:** an inflammatory swelling or sore

blam·able \'blā-mə-bəl\ adj (14c) **:** deserving blame **:** REPREHENSIBLE — *syn* see BLAMEWORTHY — **blam·ably** \-blē\ adv

¹blame \'blām\ vt **blamed; blam·ing** [ME, fr. OF *blamer*, fr. LL *blasphemare* to blaspheme, fr. Gk *blasphēmein*] (13c) **1 :** to find fault with **:** CENSURE ⟨the right to praise or ~ a literary work⟩ **2 a :** to hold responsible ⟨they ~ me for everything⟩ **b :** to place responsibility for ⟨~s it on me⟩ — **blam·er** n — **to blame :** at fault **:** RESPONSIBLE

usage Use of *blame* in sense 2b with *on* has occas. been disparaged as wrong. Such disparagement is without basis; *blame on* occurs as frequently in carefully edited prose as *blame for*. Both forms are standard.

²blame n (13c) **1 :** an expression of disapproval or reproach **:** CENSURE **2 a :** a state of being blameworthy **:** CULPABILITY **b** archaic **:** FAULT, SIN **3 :** responsibility for something believed to deserve censure ⟨they must share the ~⟩ — **blame·less** \-ləs\ adj — **blame·less·ly** adv — **blame·less·ness** n

blame·ful \'blām-fəl\ adj (14c) **:** BLAMABLE — **blame·ful·ly** \-fə-lē\ adv

blame·wor·thy \-ˌwər-thē\ adj (14c) **:** being at fault **:** deserving blame — **blame·wor·thi·ness** n

syn BLAMEWORTHY, BLAMABLE, GUILTY, CULPABLE mean deserving reproach or punishment. BLAMEWORTHY and BLAMABLE apply to any degree of reprehensibility ⟨conduct adjudged *blameworthy*⟩ ⟨an accident for which no one is *blamable*⟩. GUILTY implies responsibility for or consciousness of crime, sin, or, at the least, grave error or misdoing ⟨*guilty* of a breach of etiquette⟩. CULPABLE is weaker than *guilty* and is likely to connote malfeasance or errors of ignorance, omission, or negligence ⟨*culpable* neglect⟩.

blanc fixe \'blaŋk-ˈfiks\ n [F, lit., fixed white] (1866) **:** barium sulfate prepared as a heavy white powder and used esp. as a filler in paper, rubber, and linoleum or as a pigment

blanch \'blanch\ vb [ME *blaunchen*, fr. MF *blanchir*, fr. OF *blanche*, fem. of *blanc*, adj., white — more at BLANK] vt (15c) **:** to take the color out of: as **a :** to bleach by excluding light ⟨~ celery⟩ **b :** to scald or parboil in water or steam in order to remove the skin from, whiten, or stop enzymatic action (as food for freezing) **c :** to make ashen or pale ⟨fear ~es the cheek⟩ ~ vi **:** to become white or pale — **blanch·er** n

blanc·mange \blə-ˈmänj, -ˈmäⁿzh\ n [ME *blancmanger*, fr. MF *blanc manger*, lit., white food] (14c) **:** a usu. sweetened and flavored dessert made from gelatinous or starchy ingredients and milk

bland \'bland\ adj [L *blandus*] (1661) **1 a :** smooth and soothing in manner or quality ⟨a ~ smile⟩ **b :** exhibiting no personal concern or embarrassment **:** UNPERTURBED ⟨a ~ confession of guilt⟩ **2 a :** not irritating, stimulating, or invigorating **:** SOOTHING **b :** DULL, INSIPID ⟨~ stories with little plot or action⟩ *syn* see SUAVE — **bland·ly** \'blan(d)-lē\ adv — **bland·ness** \'blan(d)-nəs\ n

blan·dish \'blan-dish\ vb [ME, fr. MF *blandiss-*, stem of *blandir*, fr. L *blandiri*, fr. *blandus* mild, flattering] vt (14c) **:** to coax with flattery **:** CAJOLE ⟨~ vi **:** to act or speak in a flattering or coaxing manner — **blan·dish·er** n

blan·dish·ment \-dish-mənt\ n (1591) **:** something that tends to coax or cajole **:** ALLUREMENT — often used in pl.

¹blank \'blaŋk\ adj [ME, fr. MF *blanc* colorless, white, of Gmc origin; akin to OHG *blanch* white; prob. akin to L *flagrare* to burn — more at BLACK] (14c) **1** archaic **:** COLORLESS **2 a :** appearing or causing to appear dazed, confounded, or nonplussed ⟨stared in ~ dismay⟩ **b :** EXPRESSIONLESS ⟨a ~ stare⟩ **3 a :** devoid of covering or content; *esp* **:** free from writing or marks ⟨~ paper⟩ **b :** having spaces to be filled in **c :** lacking interest, variety, or change ⟨~ hours⟩ **4 :** ABSOLUTE, UNQUALIFIED ⟨a ~ refusal⟩ **5 :** UNFINISHED; *esp* **:** having a plain or unbroken surface where an opening is usual ⟨a ~ key⟩ ⟨a ~ arch⟩ *syn* see EMPTY — **blank·ly** adv — **blank·ness** n

²blank n (1554) **1** obs **:** the bull's-eye of a target **2 a :** an empty space (as on a paper) **b :** a paper with spaces for the entry of data ⟨an order ~⟩ **3 a :** a piece of material prepared to be made into something (as a key) by a further operation **b :** a cartridge loaded with propellant and a seal but no projectile **4 a :** an empty or featureless place or space ⟨my mind was a ~⟩ **b :** a vacant or uneventful period ⟨a long ~ in history⟩ **5 :** a dash substituting for an omitted word

³blank vt (ca. 1765) **1 a :** OBSCURE, OBLITERATE ⟨~ off a tunnel⟩ **b :** to stop access to **:** SEAL ⟨~ off a tunnel⟩ **2 :** to keep (an opposing team) from scoring ⟨were ~ed for eight innings⟩ ~ vi **1 :** FADE — usu. used with *out* ⟨the music ~ed out⟩ **2 :** to become confused or abstracted — often used with *out* ⟨his mind ~ed out momentarily⟩

blank check n (1884) **1 :** complete freedom of action or control **:** CARTE BLANCHE **2 :** a signed check with the amount unspecified

¹blan·ket \'blaŋ-kət\ n [ME, fr. OF *blankete*, fr. *blanc*] (14c) **1 a :** a large usu. oblong piece of woven fabric used as a bed covering **b :** a similar piece of fabric used as a body covering (as for an animal) ⟨a horse ~⟩ **2 :** something that resembles a blanket ⟨a ~ of fog⟩ ⟨a ~ of gloom⟩ **3 :** a rubber or plastic sheet on the cylinder in an offset press that transfers the image to the surface being printed — **blan·ket·like** \-ˌlīk\ adj

²blanket vt (1605) **1 :** to cover with or as if with a blanket ⟨new grass ~s the slope⟩ **2 a :** to cover so as to obscure, interrupt, suppress, or extinguish ⟨~ a fire with foam⟩ **b** : to apply or cause to apply to uniformly despite wide separation or diversity among the elements included ⟨freight rates that ~ a region⟩ **c** : to cause to be included ⟨automatically ~ed into the insurance program⟩

³blanket *adj* (1886) **1** : covering all members of a group or class ⟨a ~ wage increase⟩ **2** : effective or applicable in all instances

blan·ket·flow·er \'blaŋ-kət-,flaü(-ə)r\ *n* (1879) : GAILLARDIA

blanket stitch *n* (1880) : a buttonhole stitch with spaces of variable width used on materials too thick to hem — **blanket–stitch** *vt*

blank verse *n* (1588) : unrhymed verse; *specif* : unrhymed iambic pentameter verse

blan·quette \blä⁻'ket\ *n* [F, fr. Prov *blanqueto*, fr. *blanc* white, of Gmc origin; akin to OHG *blanch* white] (1727) : a stew of light meat or seafood in a white sauce ⟨~ of veal⟩ ⟨~ of lobster⟩

¹blare \'blar, 'bler\ *vb* **blared; blar·ing** [ME *bleren;* akin to MD *blēren* to shout] *vi* (15c) : to sound loud and strident ⟨radios *blaring*⟩ ~ *vt* **1** : to sound or utter raucously ⟨sat *blaring* the car horn⟩ **2** : to proclaim flamboyantly ⟨headlines *blared* his defeat⟩

²blare *n* (1809) **1** : a loud strident noise **2** : dazzling often garish brilliance **3** : FLAMBOYANCE

blar·ney \'blär-nē\ *n* [*Blarney stone,* a stone in Blarney Castle, near Cork, Ireland, held to bestow skill in flattery on those who kiss it] (1796) **1** : skillful flattery : BLANDISHMENT **2** : NONSENSE, HUMBUG — **blarney** *vb*

bla·sé \blä⁻'zā\ *also* **bla·se** *adj* [F] (1819) **1** : apathetic to pleasure or excitement as a result of excessive indulgence or enjoyment : WORLD-WEARY **2** : SOPHISTICATED, WORLDLY-WISE **3** : UNCONCERNED *syn* see SOPHISTICATED

blas·pheme \blas-'fēm, 'blas-,\ *vb* **blas·phemed; blas·phem·ing** [ME *blasfemen,* fr. LL *blasphemare* — more at BLAME] *vt* (14c) **1** : to speak of or address with irreverence **2** : REVILE, ABUSE ~ *vi* : to utter blasphemy — **blas·phem·er** \-'fē-mər; 'blas-,fē-mər, -fə-mər\ *n*

blas·phe·mous \'blas-fə-məs\ *adj* (15c) : impiously irreverent : PROFANE — **blas·phe·mous·ly** *adv* — **blas·phe·mous·ness** *n*

blas·phe·my \'blas-fə-mē\ *n, pl* **-mies** (13c) **1 a** : the act of insulting or showing contempt or lack of reverence for God **b** : the act of claiming the attributes of deity **2** : irreverence toward something considered sacred or inviolable

¹blast \'blast\ *n* [ME, fr. OE *blǣst;* akin to OHG *blāst* blast, *blāsan* to blow, OE *blāwan* — more at BLOW] (bef. 12c) **1 a** : a violent gust of wind **b** : the effect or accompaniment (as sleet) of such a gust **2** : the sound produced by an impulsion of air through a wind instrument or whistle **3** : something resembling a gust of wind: as **a** : a stream of air or gas forced through a hole **b** : a vehement outburst **c** : the continuous blowing to which a charge of ore or metal is subjected in a blast furnace **4 a** : a sudden pernicious influence or effect ⟨the ~ of a huge epidemic⟩ **b** : a disease of plants that causes the foliage or flowers to wither **5 a** : an explosion or violent detonation **b** : the violent effect produced in the vicinity of an explosion that consists of a wave of increased atmospheric pressure followed by a wave of decreased atmospheric pressure **6** : SPEED, CAPACITY, OPERATION ⟨go full ~⟩ ⟨in full ~⟩ **7** : an enjoyably exciting experience, occasion, or event; *esp* : PARTY

²blast *vi* (14c) **1** : BLARE ⟨music ~*ing* from the radio⟩ **2** : to make a vigorous attack **3 a** : to use an explosive **b** : SHOOT **4** : to hit a golf ball out of a sand trap with explosive force ~ *vt* **1** : to injure by or as if by the action of wind **b** : BLIGHT **2** : to shatter by or as if by an explosive **b** : to remove, open, or form by or as if by an explosive **c** : SHOOT **3** : to attack vigorously **4** : to cause to blast off ⟨will ~ themselves from the moon's surface⟩ **5** : to hit vigorously and effectively — **blast·er** *n*

blast- *or* **blasto-** *comb form* [G, fr. Gk, fr. *blastos*] : bud : budding : germ ⟨*blastodisc*⟩ ⟨*blastula*⟩

-blast \,blast\ *n comb form* [NL *-blastus,* fr. Gk *blastos* bud, shoot, fr. *blastanein* to bud, sprout] : formative unit esp. of living matter : germ : cell : cell layer ⟨*epiblast*⟩

blast·ed *adj* (1552) **1** : damaged by or as if by an explosive, lightning, wind, or supernatural force ⟨upon this ~ heath —Shak.⟩ ⟨a ~ apple tree⟩ **2** : DAMNED, DETESTABLE ⟨this ~ weather⟩

blas·te·ma \bla-'stē-mə\ *n, pl* **-ma·ta** *or* **-ma·ta** \-mə-tə\ [NL, fr. Gk *blastēma* offshoot, fr. *blastanein*] (ca. 1823) : a mass of living substance capable of growth and differentiation — **blas·te·mal** \-məl\ *or* **blas·te·mat·ic** \,blas-tə-'ma-tik\ *adj*

blast furnace *n* (1706) : a furnace in which combustion is forced by a current of air under pressure; *esp* : one for the reduction of iron ore

-blastic *adj comb form* [ISV, fr. *-blast*] : having (such or so many) buds, germs, cells, or cell layers ⟨*diploblastic*⟩

blast·ie \'blas-tē\ *n* [Sc *blast* to wither, fr. *²blast*] (1787) *Scot* : an ugly little creature

blast·ment \'blas(t)-mənt\ *n* (1602) *archaic* : a blighting influence

blas·to·coel *or* **blas·to·coele** \'blas-tə-,sēl\ *n* [ISV] (1877) : the cavity of a blastula — see BLASTULA illustration — **blas·to·coe·lic** \,blas-tə-'sē-lik\ *adj*

blas·to·cyst \'blas-tə-,sist\ *n* (ca. 1881) : the modified blastula of a placental mammal

blas·to·derm \-,dərm\ *n* [G, fr. *blast-* + *-derm*] (ca. 1843) : a blastodisc after completion of cleavage and formation of the blastocoel

blas·to·der·mic vesicle \'blas-tə-,dər-mik-\ *n* (ca. 1860) : BLASTOCYST

blas·to·disc \'blas-tə-,disk\ *n* (ca. 1881) : the embryo-forming portion of an egg with discoidal cleavage usu. appearing as a small disc on the upper surface of the yolk mass — see EGG illustration

blast·off \'blas-,tȯf\ *n* (1951) : a blasting off (as of a rocket)

blast off *vi* (1951) : TAKE OFF 2d — used esp. of rocket-propelled missiles and vehicles

blas·to·mere \'blas-tə-,mir\ *n* [ISV] (1877) : a cell produced during cleavage of a fertilized egg

blas·to·my·co·sis \,blas-tə-,mī-'kō-səs\ *n* [NL, fr. *Blastomyces,* fungus genus, fr. *blast-* + Gk *mykēs* fungus; akin to Gk *myxa* mucus — more at MUCUS] (ca. 1900) : any of several fungal infections; *esp* : an infec-

tious disease caused by a fungus (*Blastomyces dermtitides*) that affects esp. the lungs and skin

blas·to·pore \'blas-tə-,pȯr, -,pȯr\ *n* (1880) : the opening of the archenteron — **blas·to·por·ic** \-'pȯr-ik, -'pȯr-\ *adj*

blas·to·spore \'blas-tə-,spȯr, -,spȯr\ *n* [*blast-* + *spore*] (ca. 1923) : a fungal spore produced by budding

blas·tu·la \'blas-chə-lə\ *n, pl* **-las** *or* **-lae** \-,lē\ [NL, fr. Gk *blastos*] (1887) : an early metazoan embryo typically having the form of a hollow fluid-filled rounded cavity bounded by a single layer of cells — compare GASTRULA, MORULA — **blas·tu·la·tion** \,blas-chə-'lā-shən\ *n*

section of blastula: *c* blastocoel, *ma* macromere, *mi* micromere, *a* animal pole, *v* vegetal pole

blat \'blat\ *vb* **blat·ted; blat·ting** [perh. alter. of *bleat*] *vi* (1846) **1** : to cry like a calf or sheep : BLEAT **2** : to make a raucous noise **b** : BLAB ~ *vt* : to utter loudly or foolishly : BLURT — **blat** *n*

bla·tan·cy \'blā-t⁹n(t)-sē\ *n, pl* **-cies** (1610) **1** : the quality or state of being blatant **2** : something that is blatant

bla·tant \'blā-t⁹nt\ *adj* [perh. fr. L *blatire* to chatter] (ca. 1656) **1** : noisy esp. in a vulgar or offensive manner : CLAMOROUS **2** : completely obvious, conspicuous, or obtrusive esp. in a crass or offensive manner : BRAZEN *syn* see VOCIFEROUS — **bla·tant·ly** *adv*

blate \'blāt\ *adj* [ME] (1535) *chiefly Scot* : TIMID, SHEEPISH

¹blath·er \'bla-thər\ *vi* **blath·ered; blath·er·ing** [ON *blathra;* akin to MHG *blōdern* to chatter] (1524) : to talk foolishly at length — often used with *on* — **blath·er·er** \-thər-ər\ *n*

²blather *n* (1719) **1** : voluble nonsensical or inconsequential talk or writing **2** : STIR, COMMOTION

blath·er·skite \'bla-thər-,skit\ *n* [*blather* + Sc dial. *skate* a contemptible person] (ca. 1650) **1** : a person who blathers a lot **2** : NONSENSE, BLATHER

blat·ter \'bla-tər\ *vi* [perh. fr. L *blaterare* to chatter] (ca. 1555) *dial* : to talk noisily and fast

blaw \'blȯ\ *vb* **blawed; blawn** \'blȯn\; **blaw·ing** \'blȯ(-)iŋ\ [ME (northern dial.) *blawen,* fr. OE *blāwan*] (bef. 12c) *chiefly Scot* : BLOW

blax·ploi·ta·tion \,blak-(,)splȯi-'tä-shən\ *n* [blend of *blax-* (alter. of *blacks*) and *exploitation*] (1972) : the exploitation of blacks by producers of black-oriented films

¹blaze \'blāz\ *n* [ME *blase,* fr. OE *blǣse* torch] (bef. 12c) **1 a** : an intensely burning fire **b** : intense direct light often accompanied by heat ⟨the ~ of TV lights⟩ **c** : an active burning; *esp* : a sudden bursting forth of flame **2** : something that resembles the blaze of a fire: as **a** : a dazzling display ⟨a ~ of color⟩ **b** : a sudden outburst ⟨a ~ of fury⟩ **c** *pl* : HELL ⟨go to ~s⟩ ⟨as hot as ~s⟩

²blaze *vi* **blazed; blaz·ing** (13c) **1 a** : to burn brightly ⟨the sun *blazed* overhead⟩ **b** : to flare up : FLAME ⟨inflation *blazed* up⟩ **2** : to be conspicuously brilliant or resplendent ⟨fields *blazing* with flowers⟩ **3** : to shoot rapidly and repeatedly — usu. used with *away*

³blaze *vt* **blazed; blaz·ing** [ME *blasen,* fr. MD *blāsen* to blow; akin to OHG *blāst* blast] (1541) : to make public or conspicuous

⁴blaze *n* [G *Blas,* fr. OHG *plas;* akin to OE *blǣse*] (1639) **1 a** : a usu. white stripe down the center of the face of an animal **b** : a white or gray streak in the hair of the head **2** : a trail marker; *esp* : a mark made on a tree by chipping off a piece of the bark

⁵blaze *vt* **blazed; blaz·ing** (1750) **1** : to mark (as a trail) with blazes **2** : to lead in some direction or activity ⟨~ new trails in education⟩

blaz·er \'blā-zər\ *n* (ca. 1635) **1** : one that blazes **2** : a sports jacket often with notched collar and patch pockets

blaz·ing *adj* (1596) : of outstanding power, speed, heat, or intensity ⟨~ eyes⟩ ⟨a ~ fastball⟩ ⟨~ gunfire⟩ — **blaz·ing·ly** *adv*

blazing star *n* (15c) **1** *archaic* : COMET **2** : any of various plants having conspicuous flower clusters or star-shaped flowers: as **a** : any of a genus (*Liatris*) of No. American composite herbs with spikes of rosy purple rayless flowers — called also *button snakeroot* **b** : any of several No. American rough-leaved herbs (genus *Mentzelia* of the family Losaceae)

¹bla·zon \'blā-z⁹n\ *n* [ME *blason,* fr. MF] (14c) **1 a** : armorial bearings : COAT OF ARMS **b** : the proper description or representation of heraldic or armorial bearings **2** : ostentatious display

²blazon *vt* **bla·zoned; bla·zon·ing** \'blāz-niŋ, 'blā-z⁹n-iŋ\ (1534) **1** : to publish widely : PROCLAIM **2 a** : to describe (heraldic or armorial bearings) in technical terms **b** : to represent (armorial bearings) in drawing or engraving **3 a** : DISPLAY **b** : DECK, ADORN ⟨the town was ~ed with flags⟩ — **bla·zon·er** \-z⁹n-ər; -z⁹n-ər\ *n* — **blazoning** *n*

bla·zon·ry \'blā-z⁹n-rē\ *n, pl* **-ries** (1622) **1 a** : BLAZON 1b **b** : BLAZON 1a **2** : a dazzling display

¹bleach \'blēch\ *vb* [ME *blechen,* fr. OE *blǣcean;* akin to OE *blāc* pale; prob. akin to L *flagrare* to burn — more at BLACK] *vt* (bef. 12c) **1** : to remove color or stains from **2** : to make whiter or lighter esp. by physical or chemical removal of color ~ *vi* : to grow white or lose color — **bleach·able** \'blē-chə-bəl\ *adj*

²bleach *n* (1887) **1** : the act or process of bleaching **2** : a preparation used in bleaching **3** : the degree of whiteness obtained by bleaching

bleach·er \'blē-chər\ *n* (1550) **1** : one that bleaches or is used in bleaching **2** : a usu. uncovered stand of tiered planks providing seating for spectators — usu. used in pl. — **bleach·er·ite** \-chə-,rīt\ *n*

bleaching powder *n* (ca. 1846) : a white powder consisting chiefly of calcium hydroxide, calcium chloride, and calcium hypochlorite and used as a bleach, disinfectant, or deodorant

bleak \'blēk\ *adj* [ME *bleke* pale; prob. akin to OE *blāc*] (1574) **1** : exposed and barren and often windswept **2** : COLD, RAW ⟨a ~ November evening⟩ **3 a** : lacking in warmth, life, or kindliness : GRIM **b** : not hopeful or encouraging : DEPRESSING ⟨a ~ outlook⟩ **c** : se-

\ə\ abut \ᵊ\ kitten, F table \ər\ further \a\ ash \ā\ ace \ä\ mop, mar
\aü\ out \ch\ chin \e\ bet \ē\ easy \g\ go \i\ hit \ī\ ice \j\ job
\ŋ\ sing \ō\ go \ȯ\ law \ȯi\ boy \th\ thin \t͟h\ the \ü\ loot \u̇\ foot
\y\ yet \zh\ vision \á, k̲, ⁿ, œ, œ̄, ᴜᴇ, ᴜᴇ̄, ᵞ\ *see* Guide to Pronunciation

verely simple or austere — **bleak·ish** \'blē-kish\ *adj* — **bleak·ly** *adv* — **bleak·ness** *n*

¹blear \'blir\ *vt* [ME *bleren*] (14c) **1** : to make (the eyes) sore or watery **2** : DIM, BLUR

²blear *adj* (14c) **1** : dim with water or tears **2** : obscure to the view or imagination

blear–eyed \-ˌīd\ *adj* (14c) : BLEARY-EYED

bleary \'blir-ē\ *adj* (14c) **1** *of the eyes or vision* : dull or dimmed esp. from fatigue or sleep **2** : poorly outlined or defined : DIM **3** : tired to the point of exhaustion — **blear·i·ly** \'blir-ə-lē\ *adv* — **blear·i·ness** \'blir-ē-nəs\ *n*

bleary–eyed \-ˌīd\ *adj* (ca. 1927) : having the eyes dimmed and watery (as from fatigue, drink, or emotion)

¹bleat \'blēt, *Northern also* 'blat, *Southern usu* 'blāt\ *vb* [ME *bleten*, fr. OE *blǣtan*; akin to L *flēre* to weep, OE *bellan* to roar — more at BELLOW] *vi* (bef. 12c) **1 a** : to utter the natural cry of a sheep or goat or a similar sound **b** : WHIMPER **2 a** : to talk complainingly or with a whine **b** : BLATHER ~ *vt* : to utter in a bleating manner — **bleat·er** *n*

²bleat *n* (ca. 1505) **1** : the cry of a sheep or goat or a similar sound **2** : a feeble outcry, protest, or complaint

bleb \'bleb\ *n* [perh. alter. of *blob*] (1607) **1** : a small blister **2** : BUBBLE; *also* : a small particle — **bleb·by** \'ble-bē\ *adj*

¹bleed \'blēd\ *vb* **bled** \'bled\; **bleed·ing** [ME *bleden*, fr. OE *blēdan*, fr. *blōd* blood] *vi* (bef. 12c) **1 a** : to emit or lose blood **b** : to sacrifice one's blood esp. in battle **2** : to feel anguish, pain, or sympathy ⟨a heart that ~s at a friend's misfortune⟩ **3** : to escape by oozing or flowing (as from a wound) **4** : to give up some constituent (as sap or dye) by exuding or diffusing it **5 a** : to pay out or draw money **b** : to have money extorted **6** : to be printed so as to run off one or more edges of the page after trimming ~ *vt* **1** : to remove or draw blood from **2** : to get or extort money from esp. over a prolonged period **3** : to draw sap from (a tree) **4 a** : to extract or let out some or all of a contained substance from ⟨~ a brake line⟩ **b** : to extract or cause to escape from a container **c** : to diminish gradually — usu. used with *off* ⟨a pilot ~*ing* off airspeed⟩ **5** : to cause (as a printed illustration) to bleed — **bleed white** : to drain of blood or resources

²bleed *n* (ca. 1937) : printed matter (as an illustration) that bleeds; *also* : the part of a bleed trimmed off

bleed·er *n* (1803) **1** : one that bleeds; *esp* : HEMOPHILIAC **2** *Brit* : ROTTER; *also* : BLOKE

bleed·ing \'blē-diŋ, -dən\ *adj or adv* (1858) *chiefly Brit* : BLOODY — used as an intensive

bleeding heart *n* (1691) **1** : a garden plant (*Dicentra spectabilis*) of the fumitory family with racemes of usu. deep pink drooping heart-shaped flowers; *broadly* : any of several plants (genus *Dicentra*) **2** : a person who shows extravagant sympathy esp. for an object of alleged persecution

¹bleep \'blēp\ *n* [imit.] (1953) : a short high-pitched sound (as from electronic equipment)

²bleep *vt* (1968) : BLIP

³bleep *interj* (1970) — used in place of an expletive

¹blem·ish \'ble-mish\ *vt* [ME *blemisshen*, fr. MF *blesmiss-*, stem of *blesmir* to make pale, wound] (14c) : to spoil by a flaw

²blemish *n* (1535) : a noticeable imperfection; *esp* : one that seriously impairs appearance

¹blench \'blench\ *vi* [ME, to deceive, blench, fr. OE *blencan* to deceive; akin to ON *blekkja* to impose on] (13c) : to draw back or turn aside from lack of courage : FLINCH *syn* see RECOIL

²blench *vb* [alter. of *blanch*] (1813) : BLEACH, WHITEN

¹blend \'blend\ *vb* **blend·ed** *also* **blent** \'blent\; **blend·ing** [ME, modif. of ON *blanda*; akin to OE *blandan* to mix, Lith *blandus* impure, cloudy] *vt* (14c) **1** : MIX; *esp* : to combine or associate so that the separate constituents or the line of demarcation cannot be distinguished **2** : to prepare by thoroughly intermingling different varieties or grades ~ *vi* **1 a** : to mingle intimately or unobtrusively **b** : to combine into an integrated whole **2** : to produce a harmonious effect *syn* see MIX

²blend *n* (1883) **1** : something produced by blending: as **a** : a product prepared by blending **b** : a word (as *brunch*) produced by combining other words or parts of words **2** : a group of two or more consecutive consonants that begin a syllable

blende \'blend\ *n* [G, fr. *blenden* to blind, fr. OHG *blenten*; akin to OE *blind*] (ca. 1753) : SPHALERITE

blended whiskey *n* (1940) : whiskey blended from two or more straight whiskeys or from whiskey and neutral spirits

blend·er \'blen-dər\ *n* (ca. 1798) : one that blends; *esp* : an electric appliance for grinding or mixing ⟨a food ~⟩

blending inheritance *n* (1922) : the expression in offspring of phenotypic characters (as pink flower color from red and white parents) intermediate between those of the parents; *also* : inheritance in a now discarded theory in which the genetic material of offspring was held to be a uniform blend of that of the parents

blen·ny \'ble-nē\ *n, pl* **blennies** [L *blennius*, a sea fish, fr. Gk *blennos*] (1774) : any of numerous usu. small and elongated marine fishes (esp. families Blenniidae and Clinidae) including both scaled and scaleless forms

blephar- or **blepharo-** *comb form* [NL, fr. Gk, fr. *blepharon*] **1** : eyelid ⟨*blepharo*spasm⟩ **2** : cilium : flagellum ⟨*blepharo*plast⟩

bleph·a·ro·plast \'ble-fə-rō-ˌplast\ *n* (1897) : a basal body esp. of a flagellated cell

bleph·a·ro·plas·ty \-ˌplas-tē\ *n* (ca. 1881) : plastic surgery on the eyelid esp. to remove fatty or excess tissue

bleph·a·ro·spasm \-ˌspa-zəm\ *n* (1872) : spasmodic winking from involuntary contraction of the orbicular muscle of the eyelids

bles·bok \'bles-ˌbäk\ *n* [Afrik, fr. *bles* blaze + *bok* male antelope] (1824) : a So. African antelope (*Damaliscus dorcas*) having a large white patch down the center of the face

bless \'bles\ *vt* **blessed** \'blest\ *also* **blest** \'blest\; **bless·ing** [ME, fr. OE *blētsian*, fr. *blōd* blood; fr. the use of blood in consecration] (bef. 12c) **1** : to hallow or consecrate by religious rite or word **2** : to hallow with the sign of the cross **3** : to invoke divine care for ⟨~ your heart⟩ **4 a** : PRAISE, GLORIFY ⟨~ his holy name⟩ **b** : to speak well of

: APPROVE **5** : to confer prosperity or happiness upon **6** *archaic* : PROTECT, PRESERVE **7** : ENDOW, FAVOR ⟨~ed with athletic ability⟩

bless·ed \'ble-səd\ *also* **blest** \'blest\ *adj* (bef. 12c) **1 a** : held in reverence : VENERATED ⟨the ~ saints⟩ **b** : honored in worship : HALLOWED ⟨the ~ Trinity⟩ **c** : BEATIFIC ⟨a ~ visitation⟩ **2** : of or enjoying happiness; *specif* : enjoying the bliss of heaven — used as a title for a beatified person **3** : bringing pleasure, contentment, or good fortune **4** — used as an intensive ⟨no one gave us a ~ penny —*Saturday Rev.*⟩ — **bless·ed·ly** *adv* — **bless·ed·ness** *n*

Bless·ed Sacrament \'ble-səd-\ *n* (15c) : the Communion elements; *specif* : the consecrated host

bless·ing *n* (bef. 12c) **1 a** : the act or words of one that blesses **b** : APPROVAL, ENCOURAGEMENT **2** : a thing conducive to happiness or welfare **3** : grace said at a meal

bleth·er \'ble-thər\ *var of* BLATHER

blew *past of* BLOW

¹blight \'blīt\ *n* [origin unknown] (1611) **1 a** : a disease or injury of plants resulting in withering, cessation of growth, and death of parts without rotting **b** : an organism that causes blight **2** : something that frustrates plans or hopes **3** : something that impairs or destroys **4** : a deteriorated condition ⟨urban ~⟩

²blight *vt* (1695) **1** : to affect (as a plant) with blight **2** : to cause to deteriorate ~ *vi* : to suffer from or become affected with blight

blight·er \'blī-tər\ *n* (1822) **1** : one that blights **2** *chiefly Brit* **a** : a disliked or contemptible person **b** : FELLOW, GUY

blimp \'blimp\ *n* [imit.; perh. fr. the sound made by striking the gas bag with the thumb] (1916) **1** : a nonrigid airship **2** *cap* : COLONEL BLIMP

blimp·ish \'blim-pish\ *adj, often cap* : of, relating to, or suggesting a Colonel Blimp — **blimp·ish·ly** *adv* — **blimp·ish·ness** *n*

blin \'blin\ *n, pl* **bli·ni** \'blē-nē, 'bli-; blə-'nē\ *or* **bli·nis** \'blē-nēz, 'bli-; blə-'nēz\ [Russ] (1888) : a thin often buckwheat pancake usu. filled (as with sour cream) and folded

¹blind \'blīnd\ *adj* [ME, fr. OE; akin to OHG *blint* blind, OE *blandan* to mix — more at BLEND] (bef. 12c) **1 a** (1) : SIGHTLESS (2) : having less than ¹/₁₀ of normal vision in the more efficient eye when refractive defects are fully corrected by lenses **b** : of or relating to sightless persons **2 a** : unable or unwilling to discern or judge ⟨~ to a lover's faults⟩ **b** : UNQUESTIONING ⟨~ loyalty⟩ ⟨~ faith⟩ **3 a** : having no regard to rational discrimination, guidance, or restriction ⟨~ choice⟩ **b** : lacking a directing or controlling consciousness ⟨~ chance⟩ **c** : DRUNK **4** : made or done without sight of certain objects or knowledge of certain facts that could serve for guidance ⟨a ~ taste test⟩; *esp* : performed solely by the aid of instruments within an airplane ⟨a ~ landing⟩ **5** : DEFECTIVE: as **a** : lacking a growing point or producing leaves instead of flowers **b** : lacking a complete or legible address ⟨~ mail⟩ **6 a** : difficult to discern, make out, or discover **b** : hidden from sight : COVERED ⟨~ seam⟩ **7** : having but one opening or outlet ⟨~ sockets⟩ **8** : having no opening for light or passage : BLANK ⟨~ wall⟩ — **blind·ly** \'blīn(d)-lē\ *adv* — **blind·ness** \'blīn(d)-nəs\ *n*

²blind *vt* (bef. 12c) **1 a** : to make blind **b** : DAZZLE **2 a** : to withhold light from **b** : HIDE, CONCEAL — **blind·ing·ly** \'blīn-diŋ-lē\ *adv*

³blind *n* (1702) **1** : something to hinder sight or keep out light: as **a** : a window shutter **b** : a roller window shade **c** : VENETIAN BLIND **d** : BLINDER **2 a** : place of concealment; *esp* : a concealing enclosure from which one may shoot game or observe wildlife **3 a** : something put forward for the purpose of misleading : SUBTERFUGE **b** : a person who acts as a decoy or distraction

⁴blind *adv* (ca. 1775) **1** : BLINDLY: as **a** : to the point of insensibility ⟨~ drunk⟩ **b** : without seeing outside an airplane ⟨fly ~⟩ **2** — used as an intensive ⟨was robbed ~⟩

blind alley *n* (1583) : a fruitless or mistaken course or direction

blind date *n* (1925) **1** : a date between two persons who have not previously met **2** : either participant in a blind date

blind·er \'blīn-dər\ *n* (1809) **1** : either of two flaps on a horse's bridle to keep it from seeing objects at its sides **2** *pl* : a limitation or obstruction to sight or discernment

blind·fish \'blīn(d)-ˌfish\ *n* (1843) : any of several small fishes with vestigial functionless eyes found usu. in the waters of caves

¹blind·fold \-ˌfōld\ *vt* [alter. of ME *blindfellen, blindfelden* to strike blind, blindfold, fr. *blind* + *fellen* to fell] (1599) **1** : to cover the eyes of with or as if with a bandage **2** : to hinder from seeing; *esp* : to keep from comprehension — **blindfold** *adj*

²blindfold *n* (1880) **1** : a bandage for covering the eyes **2** : something that obscures mental or physical vision

blind gut *n* (15c) : a digestive cavity open at only one end; *esp* : the cecum of the large intestine

blind-man's buff \'blīn(d)-ˈmanz-\ *n* (1600) : a group game in which a blindfolded player tries to catch and identify another player — called also *blindman's bluff*

blind pig *n* (1887) : BLIND TIGER

blind·side \'blīn(d)-ˌsīd\ *vt* (1968) **1** : to hit unexpectedly from or as if from the blind side **2** : to surprise unpleasantly

blind side *n* (1606) **1** : the side away from which one is looking **2** : the side on which one that is blind in one eye cannot see

blind spot *n* (1872) **1 a** : the nearly circular light-colored area at the back of the retina where the optic nerve enters the eyeball and which is not sensitive to light — called also *optic disk*; see EYE illustration **b** : a portion of a field that cannot be seen or inspected with available equipment **2** : an area in which one fails to exercise judgment or discrimination

blind tiger *n* (1857) : a place that sells intoxicants illegally

blind trust *n* (1969) : an arrangement in which the financial holdings of a person in an influential position (as a government official) are placed in the control of a fiduciary in order to avoid a possible conflict of interest

blind·worm \'blīnd-ˌwərm\ *n* (15c) : SLOWWORM

¹blink \'bliŋk\ *vb* [ME, to open one's eyes] *vi* (14c) **1 a** *obs* : to look glancingly : PEEP **b** : to look with half-shut eyes **c** : to close and open the eyes involuntarily (as when dazzled) **2** : to shine dimly or intermittently **3 a** : to look with too little concern **b** : to look with surprise or dismay ~ *vt* **1 a** : to cause to blink **b** : to remove (as tears) from the eye by blinking **2** : to deny recognition to

²**blink** n (1594) **1** chiefly Scot : GLIMPSE, GLANCE **2** : GLIMMER, SPARKLE **3** : a usu. involuntary shutting and opening of the eye **4** : ICEBLINK — **on the blink** : in or into a disabled or useless condition

¹**blink·er** \'bliŋ-kər\ n (1636) **1** : one that blinks; esp : a light that flashes off and on (as for the directing of traffic or the coded signaling of messages) **2 a** : BLINDER 1 **b** : a cloth hood with shades projecting at the sides of the eye openings used on skittish racehorses — usu. used in pl. **3** pl : BLINDER 2

²**blinker** vt (1865) : to put blinders on

blink·ered \'bliŋ-kərd\ adj (1867) **1** : limited in scope or understanding : NARROW-MINDED **2** : fitted with blinders

blin·tze \'blin(t)-sə\ or **blintz** \'blin(t)s\ n [Yiddish blintse, fr. Slavic origin; akin to Ukrainian mlynets', dim. of mlyn pancake] (1903) : a thin usu. wheat-flour pancake folded to form a casing and then sautéed or baked

¹**blip** \'blip\ n [imit.] (1945) **1** : a trace on an oscilloscope; esp : a spot on a radar screen **2** : a short crisp sound **3** : an interruption of the sound received in a radio or television program or occurring in a recording as a result of blipping **4** : a transient sharp movement up or down (as of a quantity commonly shown on a graph)

²**blip** vt **blipped; blip·ping** (1968) : to remove (recorded sound) from a recording so that there is an interruption of the sound in the reproduction ⟨a censor blipped the swearwords⟩

bliss \'blis\ n [ME blisse, fr. OE bliss; akin to OE blīthe blithe] (bef. 12c) **1** : complete happiness **2** : PARADISE, HEAVEN

blissed—out \'blist-'aút\ adj (1973) : being in a state of bliss : ECSTATIC

bliss·ful \'blis-fəl\ adj (12c) **1** : full of, marked by, or causing bliss **2** : happily benighted ⟨~ ignorance⟩ — **bliss·ful·ly** \-fə-lē\ adv — **bliss·ful·ness** n

¹**blis·ter** \'blis-tər\ n [ME, modif. of OF or MD; OF blostre leprous nodule, fr. MD bluyster blister; akin to OE blǣst blast] (14c) **1** : an elevation of the epidermis containing watery liquid **2** : an enclosed raised spot (as in paint) resembling a blister **3** : an agent that causes blistering **4** : a disease of plants marked by large swollen patches on the leaves **5** : any of various structures that bulge out (as a gunner's compartment on a bomber) — **blis·tery** \-t(ə-)rē\ adj

²**blister** vb **blis·tered; blis·ter·ing** \-t(ə-)riŋ\ vi (15c) : to become affected with a blister — vt **1** : to raise a blister on **2** : LAMBASTE 2

blister beetle n (1816) : a beetle (as the Spanish fly) used medicinally dried and powdered to raise blisters on the skin; broadly : any of a family (Meloidae) of soft-bodied beetles

blister copper n (1861) : metallic copper of a black blistered surface that is the product of converting copper matte and is about 98.5 to 99.5 percent pure

blis·ter·ing adj (1562) : extremely intense or severe — **blistering** adv — **blis·ter·ing·ly** \-t(ə-)riŋ-lē\ adv

blister pack n (1955) : a package holding and displaying merchandise in a clear plastic case sealed to a sheet of cardboard

blister rust n (1916) : any of several diseases of pines that are caused by rust fungi (genus Cronartium) in the aecial stage and that affect the sapwood and inner bark and produce blisters externally

blithe \'blith, 'blith\ adj **blith·er; blith·est** [ME, fr. OE blīthe; akin to OHG blidi joyous] (bef. 12c) **1** : of a happy lighthearted character or disposition **2** : lacking due thought or consideration : CASUAL, HEEDLESS ⟨~ unconcern⟩ **syn** see MERRY — **blithe·ly** adv

blith·er \'bli-thər\ vi or n [by alter.] (1868) : BLATHER

blithe·some \'blith-səm, 'blith-\ adj (1724) : GAY, MERRY — **blithe·some·ly** adv

blitz \'blits\ n (ca. 1939) **1 a** : BLITZKRIEG 1 **b** (1) : an intensive aerial campaign (2) : AIR RAID **2 a** : an intensive nonmilitary campaign : a sudden overwhelming bombardment ⟨an advertising ~⟩ **b** : a rush of the passer by the defensive linebackers in football — **blitz** vb

blitz·krieg \-,krēg\ n [G, fr. Blitz lightning + Krieg war] (1939) **1** : war conducted with great speed and force; specif : a violent surprise offensive by massed air forces and mechanized ground forces in close coordination **2** : BLITZ 2a

bliz·zard \'bli-zərd\ n [origin unknown] (1870) **1** : a long severe snowstorm **2** : an intensely strong cold wind filled with fine snow **3** : an overwhelming run or deluge ⟨the ~ of mail at Christmas⟩ — **bliz·zardy** \'bli-zər-dē\ also **bliz·zard·ly** \-,zərd-lē\ adj

¹**bloat** \'blōt\ adj [alter. of ME blout] (14c) : BLOATED, PUFFY

²**bloat** vt (1677) **1** : to make turgid or swollen **2** : to fill to capacity or overflowing ~ vi : SWELL

³**bloat** n (1860) **1** : one that is bloated **2** : a flatulent digestive disturbance of domestic animals and esp. cattle marked by abdominal bloating

bloat·ed adj (1711) **1** : being much larger than what is warranted ⟨a ~ estimate⟩ **2** : obnoxiously vain

¹**bloat·er** \'blō-tər\ n [obs. bloat (to cure)] (1832) : a large fat herring or mackerel lightly salted and briefly smoked

²**bloater** n [²bloat] (1896) : a small but common cisco (Coregonus hoyi) of the Great Lakes

¹**blob** \'bläb\ n [ME] (15c) **1 a** : a small drop or lump of something viscid or thick **b** : a daub or spot of color **2** : something ill-defined or amorphous

²**blob** vt **blobbed; blob·bing** (15c) : to mark with blobs : SPLOTCH

bloc \'bläk\ n [F, lit., block] (1903) **1 a** : a temporary combination of parties in a legislative assembly **b** : a group of legislators who act together for some common purpose irrespective of party lines **2 a** : a combination of persons, groups, or nations forming a unit with a common interest or purpose **b** : a group of nations united by treaty or agreement for mutual support or joint action

¹**block** \'bläk\ n, often attrib [ME blok, fr. MF bloc, fr. MD blok; akin to OHG bloh block] (14c) **1** : a compact usu. solid piece of substantial material esp. when worked or altered to serve a particular purpose: as **a** : the piece of wood on which the neck of a person condemned to be beheaded is laid for execution **b** : a mold or form on which articles are shaped or displayed **c** : a hollow rectangular building unit usu. of artificial material **d** : a lightweight usu. cubical and solid wooden or plastic building toy that is usu. provided in sets **e** : the casting that contains the cylinders of an internal-combustion engine **2 a** : OBSTACLE **b** : an obstruction of an opponent's play in sports; esp : a halting or impeding of the progress or movement of an opponent in football by

use of the body **c** (1) : interruption of normal physiological function (as of a tissue or organ); esp : HEART BLOCK (2) : local anesthesia (as by injection) produced by interruption of the flow of impulses along a nerve **d** : interruption or cessation esp. of train of thought by competing thoughts or psychological suppression **3** slang : HEAD 1 ⟨threatened to knock his ~ off⟩ **4** : a wooden or metal case enclosing one or more pulleys and having a hook, eye, or strap by which it may be attached **5** : a piece of material (as wood or linoleum) having on its surface a hand-cut design from which impressions are to be printed **6 a** (1) : a usu. rectangular space (as in a city) enclosed by streets and occupied by or intended for buildings (2) : the distance along one of the sides of such a block **b** (1) : a large building divided into separate functional units (2) : a line of row houses (3) : a distinctive part of a building or integrated group of buildings **c** : a short section of railroad track in the block system **7** : a platform from which property is sold at auction **8 a** : a quantity, number, or section of things dealt with as a unit **b** : BLOC 2 — **on the block** : for sale

²**block** vt (1580) **1 a** : to make unsuitable for passage or progress by obstruction **b** archaic : BLOCKADE **c** : to hinder the passage, progress, or accomplishment of by or as if by interposing an obstruction **d** : to shut off from view ⟨forest canopy ~ing the sun⟩ **e** : to interfere usu. legitimately with (as an opponent) in various games or sports **f** : to prevent normal functioning of **g** : to restrict the exchange of (as currency or checks) **2** : to mark or indicate the outline or chief lines of ⟨~ out a design⟩ ⟨~ in a sketched figure⟩ **3** : to shape on, with, or as if with a block ⟨~ a hat⟩ **4** : to secure, support, or provide with a block **5** : to work out or chart the movements of (as stage performers) — often used with out **6** : to make (two or more lines of writing or type) flush at the left or at both left and right ~ vi : to block an opponent in sports **syn** see HINDER — **block·er** n

¹**block·ade** \blä-'kād\ vt **block·ad·ed; block·ad·ing** (1680) **1** : to subject to a blockade **2** : BLOCK, OBSTRUCT — **block·ad·er** n

²**blockade** n (1693) **1** : the isolation by a warring nation of an enemy area (as a harbor) by troops or warships to prevent passage of persons or supplies; broadly : a restrictive measure designed to obstruct the commerce and communications of an unfriendly nation **2** : something that blocks **3** : interruption of normal physiological function (as transmission of nerve impulses) of a tissue or organ

block·ade—run·ner \-'kād-,rə-nər\ n (1863) : a ship or person that runs through a blockade — **block·ade—run·ning** \-,rə-niŋ\ n

block·age \'blä-kij\ n (1874) : an act or instance of obstructing : the state of being blocked ⟨a ~ in a coronary artery⟩

block and tackle n (1838) : pulley blocks with associated rope or cable for hoisting or hauling

block·bust·er \'bläk-,bəs-tər\ n (1942) **1** : a very large high-explosive bomb **2** : one that is notably effective, successful, large, or violent **3** : one who engages in blockbusting

block·bust·ing \-tiŋ\ n (1954) : profiteering by inducing property owners to sell hastily and often at a loss by appeals to fears of depressed values because of threatened minority encroachment and then reselling at inflated prices

block diagram n (1944) : a diagram (as of a system, process, or program) in which labeled figures (as rectangles) and interconnecting lines represent the relationship of parts

blocked \'bläkt\ adj (1945) : exhibiting or affected by a psychological block ⟨a ~ writer⟩

block grant n (1900) : an unrestricted federal grant

block·head \'bläk-,hed\ n (1549) : a stupid person

block·house \-,haús\ n (1512) **1 a** : a structure of heavy timbers formerly used for military defense with sides loopholed and pierced for gunfire and often with a projecting upper story **b** : a small easily defended building for protection from enemy fire **2** : a building usu. of reinforced concrete serving as an observation point for an operation likely to be accompanied by heat, blast, or radiation hazard

blockhouse 1a

block·ish \'blä-kish\ adj (1565) : resembling a block

block letter n (1908) : an often hand-drawn simple capital letter composed of strokes of uniform thickness

block party n (1941) : an outdoor public party put on by the residents of a city block or neighborhood

block plane n (ca. 1884) : a small plane made with the blade set at a lower pitch than other planes and used chiefly on end grains of wood

block system n (1864) : a system by which a railroad track is divided into short sections and trains are run by guidance signals

blocky \'blä-kē\ adj **block·i·er; -est** (ca. 1879) **1** : resembling a block in form : CHUNKY **2** : filled with or made up of blocks or patches

bloke \'blōk\ n [origin unknown] (1851) chiefly Brit : MAN, FELLOW

¹**blond** or **blonde** \'bländ\ adj [MF blond, masc., blonde, fem.] (15c) **1 a** : of a flaxen, golden, light auburn, or pale yellowish brown color ⟨~ hair⟩ **b** : of a pale white or rosy white color ⟨~ skin⟩ **c** : being a blond **2 a** : of a light color **b** : of the color blond **c** : made light-colored by bleaching ⟨a table of ~ walnut⟩ — **blond·ish** \'blän-dish\ adj

²**blond** or **blonde** n (1822) **1** : a person having blond hair and usu. a light complexion and blue or gray eyes **2** : a light yellowish brown to dark grayish yellow

¹**blood** \'bləd\ n, often attrib [ME, fr. OE blōd; akin to OHG bluot blood] (bef. 12c) **1 a** : the fluid that circulates in the heart, arteries, capillaries, and veins of a vertebrate animal carrying nourishment and oxygen to and bringing away waste products from all parts of the body **b** : a comparable fluid of an invertebrate **c** : a fluid resembling blood **2** : the shedding of blood; also : the taking of life **3 a** : LIFEBLOOD;

\ə\ abut \ᵊ\ kitten, F table \ər\ further \a\ ash \ā\ ace \ä\ mop, mar \aú\ out \ch\ chin \e\ bet \ē\ easy \g\ go \i\ hit \ī\ ice \j\ job \ŋ\ sing \ō\ go \ò\ law \òi\ boy \th\ thin \th\ the \ü\ loot \ú\ foot \y\ yet \zh\ vision \à, ḵ, ⁿ, œ, œ̄, ɯ, ūe, ʸ\ see Guide to Pronunciation broadly : LIFE **b** : human stock or lineage; *esp* : royal lineage ⟨a prince of the ∼⟩ **c** : relationship by descent from a common ancestor : KINSHIP **d** : persons related through common descent : KINDRED **e** (1) : honorable or high birth or descent (2) : descent from parents of recognized breed or pedigree **4** **a** : blood regarded as the seat of the emotions : TEMPER **b** *obs* : LUST **c** : a showy foppish man : RAKE **5** : PERSONNEL ⟨a company in need of new ∼⟩ **6** : a black American male — used esp. among blacks

²**blood** *vt* (1633) **1** *archaic* : BLEED **1** **2** : to stain or wet with blood **3** : to expose (a hunting dog) to sight, scent, or taste of the blood of its prey **4** : to give experience to ⟨troops ∼*ed* in battle⟩

blood-and-guts \'bləd-ᵊn-'gəts\ *adj* (1937) : marked by great vigor, violence, or fierceness ⟨∼ competition⟩

blood·bath \'bləd-,bath, -,bàth\ *n* (1867) : a great slaughter

blood–brain barrier \'bləd-'brān-\ *n* (1944) : a barrier created by the modification of brain capillaries (as by reduction in fenestration and formation of tight cell-to-cell contacts) that prevents many substances from leaving the blood and crossing the capillary walls into the brain tissues

blood brother *n* (1890) **1** : a brother by birth **2** : one of two men pledged to mutual loyalty by a ceremonial use of each other's blood — **blood brotherhood** *n*

blood cell *n* (1846) : a cell normally present in blood

blood count *n* (ca. 1900) : the determination of the blood cells in a definite volume of blood; *also* : the number of cells so determined

blood·cur·dling \'bləd-,kərd-liŋ, -,kər-dᵊl-iŋ\ *adj* (1904) : arousing fright or horror ⟨∼ screams⟩

blood doping *n* (1973) : a technique for temporarily improving athletic performance in which oxygen-carrying red blood cells from blood previously withdrawn from an athlete are reinjected just before an event — called also *blood packing*

blood·ed \'bləd-dəd\ *adj* (1595) **1** : having blood of a specified kind — used in combination ⟨cold-*blooded*⟩ **2** : being entirely or largely purebred ⟨a herd of ∼ stock⟩

blood feud *n* (1858) : a feud between different clans or families

blood fluke *n* (1872) : SCHISTOSOME

blood group *n* (1916) : one of the classes (as those designated A, B, AB, or O) into which individuals or their blood can be separated on the basis of the presence or absence of specific antigens in the blood — called also *blood type*

blood·guilt \'bləd-,gilt\ *n* (1593) : guilt resulting from bloodshed — **blood·guilt·i·ness** \-,gil-tē-nəs\ *n* — **blood-guilty** \-tē\ *adj*

blood·hound \'bləd-,haùnd\ *n* (14c) **1** : any of a breed of large powerful hounds of European origin remarkable for acuteness of smell **2** : a person keen in pursuit

blood·less \'bləd-ləs\ *adj* (bef. 12c) **1** : deficient in or free from blood **2** : not accompanied by loss or shedding of blood ⟨a ∼ victory⟩ **3** : lacking in spirit or vitality **4** : lacking in human feeling ⟨∼ statistics⟩ — **blood·less·ly** *adv* — **blood·less·ness** *n*

blood·let·ting \-,le-tiŋ\ *n* (13c) **1** : PHLEBOTOMY **2** : BLOODSHED **3** : elimination of personnel or resources

blood·line \-,līn\ *n* (ca. 1909) : a sequence of direct ancestors esp. in a pedigree; *also* : FAMILY, STRAIN

blood·mo·bile \-mō-,bēl\ *n* (1948) : an automotive vehicle staffed and equipped for collecting blood from donors

blood money *n* (1535) **1** : money obtained at the cost of another's life **2** : money paid by a manslayer or members of his family, clan, or tribe to the next of kin of a person killed by him

blood orange *n* (1855) : a cultivated sweet orange having fruit with usu. red pulp; *also* : its fruit

blood platelet *n* (1898) : one of the minute protoplasmic disks of vertebrate blood that assist in blood clotting

blood poisoning *n* (1863) : SEPTICEMIA

blood pressure *n* (1874) : pressure that is exerted by the blood upon the walls of the blood vessels and esp. arteries and that varies with the muscular efficiency of the heart, the blood volume and viscosity, the age and health of the individual, and the state of the vascular wall

blood·red \'bləd-'red\ *adj* (bef. 12c) : having the color of blood

blood·root \'bləd-,rüt, -,rùt\ *n* (1722) : a plant (*Sanguinaria canadensis*) of the poppy family having a red root and sap and bearing a solitary lobed leaf and white flower in early spring — called also *sanguinaria*

blood sausage *n* (1863) : very dark sausage containing a large proportion of blood — called also *blood pudding*

blood serum *n* (ca. 1909) : blood from which the fibrin and suspended material (as cells) have been removed

blood·shed \'bləd-,shed\ *n* (15c) **1** : the shedding of blood **2** : the taking of life : SLAUGHTER

blood·shot \-,shät\ *adj* (1552) *of an eye* : inflamed to redness

blood sport *n* (1895) : a sport or contest (as hunting or cockfighting) involving bloodshed

blood·stain \-,stān\ *n* (1820) : a discoloration caused by blood

blood·stained \-,stānd\ *adj* (1596) **1** : stained with blood **2** : involved with slaughter ⟨a ∼ chronicle of war⟩

blood·stock \-,stäk\ *n* (1830) : horses of Thoroughbred breeding

blood·stone \-,stōn\ *n* (1551) : a green chalcedony sprinkled with red spots resembling blood — called also *heliotrope*

blood·stream \-,strēm\ *n* (1873) **1** : the flowing blood in a circulatory system **2** : a mainstream of power or vitality ⟨introduce into the economic ∼ a large amount of money —*Harper's*⟩

blood·suck·er \-,sə-kər\ *n* (14c) **1** : an animal that sucks blood; *esp* : LEECH **2** : a person who sponges or preys on another — **blood·suck·ing** \-kiŋ\ *adj*

blood sugar *n* (1918) : the glucose in the blood; *also* : its concentration (as in milligrams per 100 milliliters)

blood test *n* (1912) : a test of the blood; *esp* : a serologic test for the presence of substances indicative of disease (as syphilis) or disease-causing agents (as HIV)

blood·thirsty \'bləd-,thər-stē\ *adj* (1535) : eager for or marked by the shedding of blood, violence, or killing — **blood·thirst·i·ly** \-stə-lē\ *adv* — **blood·thirst·i·ness** \-stē-nəs\ *n*

blood–typ·ing \-,tī-piŋ\ *n* (1926) : the action or process of determining an individual's blood group

blood vessel *n* (1694) : any of the vessels through which blood circulates in the body

blood·worm \'bləd-,wərm\ *n* (1714) **1** : any of various reddish annelid worms (as of genera *Glycera* or *Tubifex*) often used as bait **2** : any of several strongyle worms (genus *Strongylus*) that are parasitic in the large intestine of horses

¹**bloody** \'blə-dē\ *adj* **blood·i·er; -est** (bef. 12c) **1** : containing or made up of blood **b** : of or contained in the blood **2** : smeared or stained with blood **3** : accompanied by or involving bloodshed; *esp* : marked by great slaughter **4** **a** : MURDEROUS **b** : MERCILESS, CRUEL **5** : BLOODRED **6** — used as an intensive; sometimes considered vulgar — **blood·i·ly** \'blə-dᵊl-ē\ *adv* — **blood·i·ness** \'blə-dē-nəs\ *n*

syn BLOODY, SANGUINARY, GORY mean affected by or involving the shedding of blood. BLOODY is applied esp. to something attended by, or someone inclined to, bloodshed ⟨the Civil War was America's most *sanguinary* conflict⟩. GORY suggests a profusion of blood and slaughter ⟨exceptionally *gory*, even for a horror movie⟩.

²**bloody** *vt* **blood·ied; bloody·ing** (1530) : to make bloody or bloodred

³**bloody** *adv* (1676) — used as an intensive; sometimes considered vulgar

Bloody Mary *n, pl* **Bloody Marys** [prob. fr. *Bloody Mary*, appellation of Mary I of England] (1947) : a cocktail consisting essentially of vodka and usu. spiced tomato juice

bloody–mind·ed \,blə-dē-'mīn-dəd\ *adj* (1584) **1** : inclined towards violence or bloodshed **2** *chiefly Brit* : stubbornly contrary or obstructive : CANTANKEROUS — **bloody–mind·ed·ness** *n*

bloody murder *adv* (1925) : in a loud and violent manner ⟨ran off, screaming *bloody murder*⟩; *also* : in vehement protest ⟨screaming *bloody murder* over the pay cut⟩

bloody shirt *n* (1874) : something intended to stir up or revive partisan animosity — usu. used in the phrase *wave the bloody shirt*

¹**bloom** \'blüm\ *n* [ME *blome* lump of metal, fr. OE *blōma*] (bef. 12c) **1** : a mass of wrought iron from the forge or puddling furnace **2** : a bar of iron or steel hammered or rolled from an ingot

²**bloom** *n* [ME *blome*, fr. ON *blōm*; akin to OE *blōwan* to blossom — more at BLOW] (13c) **1** **a** : FLOWER **b** : the flowering state ⟨the roses in ∼⟩ **c** : a period of flowering ⟨the spring ∼⟩ **d** : an excessive growth of plankton **2** **a** : a state or time of beauty, freshness, and vigor **b** : a state or time of high development or achievement ⟨a career in full ∼⟩ **3** : a surface coating or appearance: as **a** : a delicate powdery coating on some fruits and leaves **b** : a rosy appearance of the cheeks; *broadly* : an outward evidence of freshness or healthy vigor **c** : a cloudiness on a film of varnish or lacquer **d** : a grayish discoloration on chocolate **e** : glare caused by an object reflecting too much light into a television camera

³**bloom** *vi* (13c) **1** **a** : to produce or yield flowers **b** : to support abundant plant life ⟨make the desert ∼⟩ **2** **a** (1) : to mature into achievement of one's potential (2) : to flourish in youthful beauty, freshness or excellence **b** : to shine out : GLOW **3** : to appear or occur unexpectedly or in remarkable quantity or degree **4** : to become densely populated with microorganisms and esp. plankton — used of bodies of water ∼ *vt* **1** *obs* : to cause to bloom **2** : to give bloom to

¹**bloom·er** \'blü-mər\ *n* (ca. 1736) **1** : a plant that blooms **2** : a person who reaches full competence or maturity **3** [*blooming*] : a stupid blunder

²**bloo·mer** \'blü-mər\ *n* [Amelia *Bloomer*] (1851) **1** : a costume for women consisting of a skirt over long loose trousers gathered closely about the ankles **2** *pl* **a** : full loose trousers gathered at the knee formerly worn by women for athletics **b** : underpants of similar design worn chiefly by girls and women

bloom·ing \'blü-mən, -miŋ\ *adj or adv* [prob. euphemism for *bloody*] (1882) *chiefly Brit* — used as a generalized intensive ⟨∼ fool⟩

bloomy \'blü-mē\ *adj* (1593) **1** : full of bloom **2** : covered with bloom ⟨∼ plums⟩ **3** : showing freshness or vitality ⟨all the ∼ flush of life is fled —Oliver Goldsmith⟩

bloop \'blüp\ *n* [back-formation fr. *blooper*] (1967) : BLOOPER 1a — **bloop** *vt*

bloop·er \'blü-pər\ *n* [*bloop* (an unpleasant sound)] (1937) **1** **a** : a fly ball hit barely beyond a baseball infield **b** : a high baseball pitch lobbed to the batter **2** : an embarrassing public blunder

¹**blos·som** \'blä-səm\ *n* [ME *blosme*, fr. OE *blōstm*; akin to OE *blōwan*] (bef. 12c) **1** **a** : the flower of a seed plant; *also* : the mass of such flowers on a single plant **b** : the state of bearing flowers **2** : a peak period or stage of development — **blos·somy** \-sə-mē\ *adj*

²**blossom** *vi* (bef. 12c) **1** : BLOOM **2** **a** : to come into one's own : DEVELOP ⟨a ∼*ing* talent⟩ **b** : to become evident : make an appearance

¹**blot** \'blät\ *n* [ME] (14c) **1** **a** : a soiling or disfiguring mark : SPOT **2** : a mark of reproach : moral flaw **3** : a usu. nitrocellulose sheet that contains spots of immobilized macromolecules (as of DNA, RNA, or protein) or their fragments and is used to identify specific components of the spots by applying a molecular probe (as a complementary nucleic acid or a radioactively labeled antibody)

²**blot** *vb* **blot·ted; blot·ting** *vt* (15c) **1** : to spot, stain, or spatter with a discoloring substance **2** *obs* : MAR; *esp* : to stain with infamy **3** **a** : to dry (as writing) with an absorbing agent **b** : to remove with absorbing material ⟨*blotting* up spilled water⟩ ∼ *vi* **1** : to make a blot **2** : to become marked with a blot

³**blot** *n* [origin unknown] (1595) **1** : a lone backgammon man exposed to capture **2** *archaic* : a weak or exposed point

¹**blotch** \'bläch\ *vt* (1604) : to mark or mar with blotches

²**blotch** *n* [perh. blend of ¹*blot* and ³*botch*] (1669) **1** : IMPERFECTION, BLEMISH **2** : a spot or mark (as of color or ink) esp. when large or irregular — **blotch·i·ly** \'blä-chə-lē\ *adv* — **blotchy** \'blä-chē\ *adj*

blot out *vt* (1530) **1** : to make obscure, insignificant, or inconsequential **2** : WIPE OUT, DESTROY

blot·ter \'blä-tər\ *n* (1591) **1** : a piece of blotting paper **2** : a book in which entries (as of transactions or occurrences) are made temporarily pending their transfer to permanent record books ⟨police ∼⟩

blotting paper *n* (15c) : a spongy unsized paper for absorbing ink

blot·to \'blä-(,)tō\ *adj* [prob. irreg. fr. ²*blot*] (1917) : DRUNK 1a

¹**blouse** \'blaùs *also* 'blaùz\ *n, pl* **blous·es** \'blaù-səz, -zəz\ [F] (1828) **1** **a** : a long loose overgarment that resembles a shirt or smock and is worn esp. by workmen, artists, and peasants **b** : the jacket of a uni-

form **2** : a usu. loose-fitting garment esp. for women that covers the body from the neck to the waist — **blousy** \'blau̇-sē, -zē\ *adj*
²**blouse** \'blau̇s, 'blau̇z\ *vb* **bloused; blous·ing** *vi* (1904) : to fall in a fold ⟨coats that ~ above the hip⟩ ~ *vt* : to cause to blouse ⟨trousers are *bloused* over the boots⟩
blou·son \'blau̇-ˌsän, 'blü-ˌzän\ *n* [F, fr. *blouse*] (1904) : a garment (as a dress) having a close waistband with blousing of material over it
¹**blow** \'blō\ *vb* **blew** \'blü\; **blown** \'blōn\; **blow·ing** [ME, fr. OE *blāwan*; akin to OHG *blāen*, L *flare*, Gk *phallos* penis] *vi* (bef. 12c) **1** *of air* : to move with speed or force **2** : to send forth a current of air or other gas **3** : to make a sound by or as if by blowing **b** *of a wind instrument* : SOUND **4 a** : BOAST **b** : to talk windily **5 a** : PANT, GASP ⟨the horse *blew* heavily⟩ **b** *of a cetacean* : to eject moisture-laden air from the lungs through the blowhole **6** : to move or be carried by or as if by wind ⟨just *blew* into town⟩ **7** *of an electric fuse* : to melt when overloaded — often used with *out* **8** *of a tire* : to release the contained air through a spontaneous rupture — usu. used with *out* ~ *vt* **1 a** : to set (gas or vapor) in motion **b** : to act on with a current of gas or vapor **2** : to play or sound on (a wind instrument) **3 a** : to spread by report **b** *past participle* **blowed** \'blōd\ : DAMN ⟨~ the expense⟩ ⟨I'm ~*ed* if I know⟩ **4 a** : to drive with a current of gas or vapor **b** : to clear of contents by forcible passage of a current of air **c** : to project (a gesture or sound made with the mouth) by blowing ⟨*blew* him a kiss⟩ **5 a** : to distend with or as if with gas **b** : to produce or shape by the action of blown or injected air ⟨~*ing* bubbles⟩ ⟨~*ing* glass⟩ **6** *of insects* : to deposit eggs or larvae on or in **7** : to shatter, burst, or destroy by explosion **8 a** : to put out of breath with exertion **b** : to let (as a horse) pause to catch the breath **9 a** : to expend (as money) extravagantly ⟨*blew* $50 on lunch⟩ **b** : to treat with unusual expenditure ⟨I'll ~ you to a steak⟩ **10** : to cause (a fuse) to blow **11** : to rupture by too much pressure ⟨*blew* a gasket⟩ **12** : to foul up hopelessly ⟨*blew* her lines⟩ ⟨*blew* his chance⟩ **13** : to leave hurriedly ⟨*blew* town⟩ **14** : to propel with great force or speed ⟨*blew* a fastball by the batter⟩ — **blow hot and cold** : to be favorable at one moment and adverse the next — **blow off steam** : to release pent-up emotions — **blow one's cool** : to lose one's composure — **blow one's cover** : to reveal one's real identity — **blow one's mind** : to overwhelm one with wonder or bafflement — **blow one's top** or **blow one's stack 1** : to become violently angry **2** : to go crazy — **blow smoke** : to speak idly, misleadingly, or boastfully — **blow the whistle** : to call public or official attention to something (as a wrongdoing) kept secret — usu. used with *on*
²**blow** *n* (1660) **1** : a blowing of wind esp. when strong or violent **2** : BRAG, BOASTING **3** : an act or instance of blowing **4 a** : the time during which air is forced through molten metal to refine it **b** : the quantity of metal refined during that time **5** *slang* : COCAINE
³**blow** *vi* **blew** \'blü\; **blown** \'blōn\; **blow·ing** [ME, fr. OE *blōwan*; akin to OHG *blūoen* to bloom, L *flōrēre* to bloom, *flor-, flos* flower] (bef. 12c) : FLOWER, BLOOM
⁴**blow** *n* (1710) **1** : BLOSSOMS **2** : ²BLOOM 1b ⟨lilacs in full ~⟩
⁵**blow** *n* [ME (northern dial.) *blaw*; prob. akin to OHG *bliuwan* to beat] (15c) **1** : a forcible stroke delivered with a part of the body or with an instrument **2** : a hostile act or state : COMBAT ⟨come to ~s⟩ **3 a** : a forcible or sudden act or effort : ASSAULT **4** : an unfortunate or calamitous happening ⟨failure to land the job came as a ~⟩
blow away *vt* (1776) **1** : to kill by gunfire : shoot dead **2** : to dissipate or remove as if with a current of air ⟨their doubts were *blown away*⟩ **3** : to impress very strongly and usu. favorably **4** : to defeat soundly ⟨*blew* their rivals *away* in the first game⟩
blow-by \'blō-ˌbī\ *n* (1926) : leakage of combustion gases between a piston and the cylinder wall into the crankcase in an automobile
blow–by–blow \'blō-bī-'blō, -bə-\ *adj* (1933) : minutely detailed ⟨a ~ account⟩
blow·down \'blō-ˌdau̇n\ *n* (1895) : an instance of trees being blown down by the wind; *also* : a tree blown down
blow–dried \'blō-ˌdrīd\ *adj* (1976) : having blow-dried hair; *also* : being or appearing well-groomed but superficial or vacuous
blow–dry \-ˌdrī\ *vt* (1966) : to dry and usu. style (hair) with a blow-dryer ~ *vi* : to dry hair with a blow-dryer — **blow–dry** *n*
blow–dryer \-ˌdrī(-ə)r\ *n* (1976) : a handheld hair dryer
blow·er \'blō-(ə)r\ *n* (bef. 12c) **1** : one that blows **2** : a device for producing a current of air or gas **3** : BRAGGART **4** *Brit* : TELEPHONE
blow·fish \'blō-ˌfish\ *n* (ca. 1893) : PUFFER 2a
blow·fly \-ˌflī\ *n* (1821) : any of a family (Calliphoridae) of dipteran flies (as the bluebottle or screwworm) that deposit their eggs esp. on meat or in wounds
blow·gun \-ˌgən\ *n* (1864) : a tube through which a projectile (as a dart) may be impelled by the force of the breath
blow·hard \-ˌhärd\ *n* (1857) : BRAGGART
blow·hole \-ˌhōl\ *n* (1691) **1** : a hole in metal caused by a bubble of gas captured during solidification **2** : a nostril in the top of the head of a cetacean and esp. a whale
blow in *vi* (1895) : to arrive casually or unexpectedly
blow job *n* (1956) : an act of fellatio — usu. considered vulgar
blown \'blōn\ *adj* [ME *blowen*, fr. pp. of *blowen* to blow] (14c) **1 a** : SWOLLEN **b** : affected with bloat **2** : being out of breath
blow off *vt* (1987) **1** : to refuse to take notice of, honor, or deal with : IGNORE ⟨decided to *blow off* two billion viewers — Harry Homburg⟩ **2** : to fail to attend or show up for ⟨*blew off* an official dinner⟩
blow·out \'blō-ˌau̇t\ *n* (1824) **1** : a festive social affair **2** : a bursting of a container (as a tire) by pressure of the contents on a weak spot **3** : an uncontrolled eruption of an oil or gas well **4** : an easy or one-sided victory
blow out *vt* (14c) **1** : to extinguish by a gust **2** : to dissipate (itself) by blowing — used of storms **3** : to defeat easily ~ *vi* **1** : to become extinguished by a gust **2** : to erupt out of control — used of an oil or gas well
blow over *vi* (1617) : to pass away without effect
blow·pipe \'blō-ˌpīp\ *n* (1685) **1** : a small tubular instrument for directing a jet of air or other gas into a flame so as to concentrate and increase the heat **2** : BLOWGUN **3** : a tubular instrument used for revealing or cleaning a bodily cavity by forcing air into it **4** : a long metal tube on the end of which a glassmaker gathers a quantity of molten glass and through which he blows to expand and shape it

blow·sy *also* **blow·zy** \'blau̇-zē\ *adj* [E dial. *blowse, blowze* wench] (ca. 1770) **1** : having a sloppy appearance or aspect : FROWSY **2** : being coarse and ruddy of complexion
blow·torch \'blō-ˌtȯrch\ *n* (1897) : a small burner having a device to intensify combustion by means of a blast of air or oxygen, usu. including a fuel tank pressurized by a hand pump, and used esp. in plumbing
blow–up \'blō-ˌəp\ *n* (1807) : a blowing up: as **a** : EXPLOSION **b** : an outburst of temper **c** : a photographic enlargement
blow up *vt* (1536) **1** : to build up or tout to an unreasonable extent ⟨advertisers *blowing up* their products⟩ **2** : to rend apart, shatter, or destroy by explosion **3** : to fill up with a gas (as air) ⟨*blow up* a balloon⟩ **4** : to make a photographic enlargement of **5** : to bring into existence by blowing of wind ⟨it may *blow up* a storm⟩ ~ *vi* **1 a** : EXPLODE **b** : to be disrupted or destroyed (as by explosion) **c** : to lose self-control; *esp* : to become violently angry **2** : to become or come into being by or as if by blowing of wind **3** : to become filled with a gas (as air) **b** : to become expanded to unreasonable proportions
blowy \'blō-ē\ *adj* (1830) **1** : WINDY ⟨a ~ March day⟩ **2** : readily blown about ⟨~ desert sand⟩
BLT *n* (1952) : a bacon, lettuce, and tomato sandwich
blub \'bləb\ *vi* **blubbed; blub·bing** (1804) *chiefly Brit* : BLUBBER
¹**blub·ber** \'blə-bər\ *vb* **blub·bered; blub·ber·ing** \'blə-b(ə-)riŋ\ [ME *blubren* to make a bubbling sound, fr. *bluber*] *vi* (15c) : to weep noisily ~ *vt* **1** : to swell, distort, or wet with weeping **2** : to utter while weeping
²**blubber** *n* [ME *bluber* bubble, foam, prob. of imit. origin] (15c) **1 a** : the fat of whales and other large marine mammals **b** : excessive fat on the body **2** : the action of blubbering
³**blubber** *adj* (1667) : puffed out : THICK ⟨~ lips⟩
blub·bery \'blə-b(ə-)rē\ *adj* (1791) **1** : having or characterized by blubber **2** : puffed out : THICK
blu·cher \'blü-chər *also* -kər\ *n* [G. L. von *Blücher*] (1831) : a shoe having the tongue and vamp cut in one piece and the quarters lapped over the vamp and laced together for closing
¹**blud·geon** \'blə-jən\ *n* [origin unknown] (ca. 1730) **1** : a short stick that usu. has one thick or loaded end and is used as a weapon **2** : something used to attack or bully ⟨the ~ of satire⟩
²**bludgeon** *vt* (1868) **1** : to hit with heavy impact **2** : to overcome by aggressive argument
blud·ger \'blə-jər\ *n* [prob. contr. of *bludgeoner* pimp, fr. ¹*bludgeon*] (1939) *chiefly Austral & NewZeal* : LOAFER, SHIRKER
¹**blue** \'blü\ *adj* **blu·er; blu·est** [ME, fr. OF *blou*, of Gmc origin; akin to OHG *blāo* blue; akin to L *flavus* yellow] (13c) **1** : of the color blue **2 a** : BLUISH **b** : discolored by or as if by bruising ⟨~ with cold⟩ **c** : bluish gray ⟨~ cat⟩ **3 a** : low in spirits : MELANCHOLY **b** : marked by low spirits : DEPRESSING ⟨a ~ funk⟩ ⟨things looked ~⟩ **4** : wearing blue **5** *of a woman* : LEARNED, INTELLECTUAL **6** : PURITANICAL **7 a** : PROFANE, INDECENT ⟨~ movie⟩ **b** : OFF-COLOR, RISQUÉ ⟨~ jokes⟩ **8** : of, relating to, or used in blues ⟨a ~ song⟩ — **blue·ly** *adv* — **blue·ness** *n* — **blue in the face** : extremely exasperated
²**blue** *n* (13c) **1** : a color whose hue is that of the clear sky or that of the portion of the color spectrum lying between green and violet **2 a** : a pigment or dye that colors blue **b** : BLUING **3 a** : blue clothing or cloth **b** *pl* : a blue costume or uniform **4 a** : a Union soldier in the Civil War **b** : the Union army **5 a** (1) : SKY (2) : the far distance **b** : SEA **6 a** : a blue object **7** : BLUESTOCKING **8** : any of numerous small chiefly blue butterflies (family Lycaenidae) **9** : BLUEFISH **10** : BLUE CHEESE — **out of the blue** : without advance notice : UNEXPECTEDLY ⟨the job offer came *out of the blue*⟩
³**blue** *vb* **blued; blue·ing** or **blu·ing** *vt* (1606) : to make blue ~ *vi* : to turn blue
blue baby *n* (ca. 1899) : an infant with a bluish tint usu. from a congenital heart defect in which mingling of venous and arterial blood occurs
blue·beard \'blü-ˌbird\ *n, often cap* [*Bluebeard*, a fairy-tale character] (1822) : a man who marries and kills one wife after another
blue·bell \-ˌbel\ *n* (1578) **1** : any of various bellflowers; *esp* : HAREBELL **2** : any of various plants bearing blue bell-shaped flowers: as **a** : a European herb (*Endymion nonscriptus* syn. *Scilla nonscripta*) of the lily family having scapose racemes of drooping bell-shaped flowers — called also *wild hyacinth* **b** *pl* : a glabrous erect eastern U.S. herb (*Mertensia virginica*) of the borage family with entire leaves and showy blue flowers pink in the bud — called also *Virginia bluebells*
blue·ber·ry \'blü-ˌber-ē, -b(ə-)rē\ *n* (1709) : the edible blue or blackish berry of any of several plants (genus *Vaccinium*) of the heath family; *also* : a low or tall shrub producing these berries
blue·bird \-ˌbərd\ *n* (1688) : any of several small No. American thrushes (genus *Sialia*) that are blue above and reddish brown or pale blue below
blue blood *n* (1834) **1** \'blü-ˈbləd\ : membership in a noble or socially prominent family **2** \-ˌbləd\ : a member of a noble or socially prominent family — **blue–blood·ed** \-ˈblə-dəd\ *adj*
blue·bon·net \'blü-ˌbä-nət\ *n* (1682) **1 a** : a wide flat round cap of blue wool formerly worn in Scotland **b** : one that wears such a cap; *specif* : SCOT **2** : either of two low-growing annual lupines (*Lupinus subcarnosus* or *L. texensis*) of Texas with silky foliage and blue flowers
blue book *n* (1836) **1** : a register esp. of socially prominent persons **2** : a book of specialized information often published under government auspices **3** : a blue-covered booklet used for writing examinations **4** : a periodically issued price list (as of used cars)
blue·bot·tle \'blü-ˌbä-tᵊl\ *n* (15c) **1** : BACHELOR'S BUTTON **2** : any of several blowflies (genus *Calliphora*) that have the abdomen or the whole body iridescent blue in color and that make a loud buzzing noise in flight
blue catfish *n* (1835) : a large bluish catfish (*Ictalurus furcatus*) of the Mississippi valley that may weigh over 100 pounds (45 kilograms)

\ə\ abut \ᵊ\ kitten, F table \ər\ further \a\ ash \ā\ ace \ä\ mop, mar
\au̇\ out \ch\ chin \e\ bet \ē\ easy \g\ go \i\ hit \ī\ ice \j\ job
\ŋ\ sing \ō\ go \ȯ\ law \ȯi\ boy \th\ thin \th̲\ the \ü\ loot \u̇\ foot
\y\ yet \zh\ vision \à, k̲, ⁿ, œ, œ̄, ᵫ, ᵫ̄, ᷰ\ see Guide to Pronunciation

blue cheese *n* (1925) : cheese having veins of greenish blue mold

blue chip *n* (1929) **1 a :** a stock issue of high investment quality that usu. pertains to a substantial well-established company and enjoys public confidence in its worth and stability **b :** a consistently successful and profitable venture or enterprise **2 a :** an outstandingly worthwhile or valuable property or asset **b :** an athlete rated as excellent or as an excellent prospect — **blue–chip** *adj*

blue–chip·per \'blü-ˌchi-pər\ *n* (1968) : BLUE CHIP 2b

blue–coat \'blü-ˌkōt\ *n* (1593) : a person who wears a blue coat: as **a :** a Union soldier during the Civil War **b :** POLICE OFFICER

blue cohosh *n* (1821) : a perennial herb (*Caulophyllum thalictroides*) of the barberry family that has greenish yellow or purplish flowers and large blue berrylike fruits

blue–col·lar \'blü-ˈkä-lər\ *adj* (1946) : of, relating to, or constituting the class of wage earners whose duties call for the wearing of work clothes or protective clothing — compare WHITE-COLLAR

blue crab *n* (1883) : a large bluish green edible crab (*Callinectes sapidus*) of the Atlantic and Gulf coasts

blue curls *n pl but sing or pl in constr* (1817) : any of several mints (genus *Trichostema*) with irregular blue flowers

blue devils *n pl* (1781) : low spirits : DESPONDENCY

blue–eyed \'blü-ˌīd\ *adj* (1610) **1 :** having blue eyes **2 :** performed by whites ⟨~ soul⟩; *also :* WHITE ⟨a ~ soul singer⟩

blue–eyed grass *n* (1784) : any of several herbs (genus *Sisyrinchium*) of the iris family with grasslike foliage and blue flowers

blue·fin tuna \'blü-ˌfin-\ *n* (1922) : a very large tuna (*Thunnus thynnus*) that is an important food and game fish — called also *bluefin*

blue·fish \-ˌfish\ *n* (ca. 1622) **1 :** an active food and game marine fish (*Pomatomus saltatrix*) that is bluish above with silvery sides **2 :** any of various dark or bluish fishes (as the pollack)

blue flag *n* (1784) : a blue-flowered iris; *esp :* a common iris (*Iris versicolor*) of the eastern U.S. with a root formerly used medicinally

blue flu *n* [fr. the color of a police uniform] (1970) : a sick-out staged by police officers

blue·gill \'blü-ˌgil\ *n* (1881) : a common sunfish (*Lepomis macrochirus*) of the eastern and central U.S. sought for food and sport

blue·grass \-ˌgras\ *n* (1751) **1 :** any of several grasses (genus *Poa*) of which some have bluish green culms; *esp :* KENTUCKY BLUEGRASS **2** [fr. the *Blue Grass Boys*, performing group, fr. *Bluegrass state*, nickname of Kentucky] : country music played on unamplified stringed instruments (as banjo, fiddle, guitar, and mandolin) and characterized by free improvisation and clear, high-pitched harmony

blue–green alga \'blü-ˈgrēn-\ *n* (1899) : any of a group of photosynthetic microorganisms now usu. classified as bacteria (division Cyanobacteria) or sometimes as plants (division Cyanophyta) — called also *blue-green bacterium, cyanobacterium*

blue gum *n* (1799) : any of several Australian trees (genus *Eucalyptus*) that yield valuable timber

blue heron *n* (ca. 1730) : either of two herons with bluish or slaty plumage; *esp :* GREAT BLUE HERON

blue·jack·et \-ˌja-kət\ *n* (1830) : an enlisted man in the navy : SAILOR

blue jay \-ˌjā\ *n* (1709) : a crested bright blue No. American jay (*Cyanocitta cristata*)

blue jeans *n pl* (1901) : pants usu. made of blue denim — **blue–jeaned** \-ˌjēnd\ *adj*

blue law *n* (1781) **1 :** one of numerous extremely rigorous laws designed to regulate morals and conduct in colonial New England **2 :** a statute regulating work, commerce, and amusements on Sundays

blue line *n* (1931) : either of two blue lines that divide an ice-hockey rink into three equal zones and that separate the offensive and defensive zones from the center-ice neutral zone

blue mold *n* (1664) : any of various fungi (genus *Penicillium*) that produce blue or blue-green surface growths

blue moon *n* (1821) : a very long period of time ⟨such people happen along only once in a *blue moon* —*Saturday Rev.*⟩

blue·nose \'blü-ˌnōz\ *n* (1903) : a person who advocates a rigorous moral code

blue note *n* [fr. its frequent use in blues music] (1919) : a variable microtonal lowering of the third, seventh, and occas. fifth degrees of the major scale

blue–pen·cil \'blü-ˈpen(t)-səl\ *vt* (1888) : to edit esp. by shortening or deletion — **blue penciler** *n*

blue pencil *n* (1893) : a writing instrument used for editing; *also :* the act or practice of blue-penciling

blue pe·ter \-ˈpē-tər\ *n* [prob. fr. the name *Peter*] (1823) : a blue signal flag with a white square in the center used to indicate that a merchant vessel is ready to sail

blue pike *n* (1842) : a grayish-blue walleye categorized as either a morph or a subspecies (*Stizostedion vitreum glaucum*)

blue plate *adj* (1926) : being a main course usu. offered at a special price in a restaurant ⟨a *blue plate* luncheon⟩

blue·point \'blü-ˌpȯint\ *n* [*Blue Point*, Long Island] (1789) : a small oyster (*Crassostrea virginica*) typically from the south shore of Long Island

blue point \-ˌpȯint\ *adj* (1944) *of a domestic cat :* having a bluish cream body color with dark gray points — **blue point** *n*

blue·print \-ˌprint\ *n* (1886) **1 :** a photographic print in white on a bright blue ground or blue on a white ground used esp. for copying maps, mechanical drawings, and architects' plans **2 :** something resembling a blueprint; *esp :* a detailed plan or program of action ⟨a ~ for victory⟩ — **blueprint** *vt*

blue racer *n* (1886) : a blue or greenish blue blacksnake (*Coluber constrictor* subsp.) occurring from Michigan and Wisconsin to Texas

blue–ribbon *adj* (1926) : of outstanding quality; *esp :* consisting of individuals selected for quality, reputation, or authority ⟨a ~ committee⟩ ⟨a ~ jury⟩

blue ribbon *n* (1651) **1 :** an honor or award gained for preeminence **2 :** a blue ribbon awarded as an honor (as to the first-place winner in a competition)

blues \'blüz\ *n pl but sing or pl in constr* [*blue devils*] (1741) **1 :** low spirits : MELANCHOLY **2 :** a song often of lamentation characterized by usu. 12-bar phrases, 3-line stanzas in which the words of the second line usu. repeat those of the first, and continual occurrence of blue notes in melody and harmony **3 :** jazz or popular music using harmonic and phrase structures of blues

blue shark *n* (ca. 1672) : a chiefly pelagic shark (*Prionace glauca*) found in all tropical and temperate seas that occas. attacks humans

blue sheep *n* (1911) : BHARAL

blue·shift \'blü-ˈshift\ *n* (1951) : the displacement of the spectrum of an approaching celestial body toward shorter wavelengths — **blueshift·ed** *adj*

blue–sky \'blü-ˈskī\ *adj* (1906) **1 :** having little or no value ⟨~ stock⟩ **2 :** not grounded in the realities of the present : VISIONARY ⟨~ thinking⟩

blue–sky law *n* (1912) : a law providing for the regulation of the sale of securities (as stock)

blues·man \'blüz-mən\ *n* (1966) : a man who plays or sings the blues

blue spruce *n* (1884) : a spruce (*Picea pungens*) of the Rocky Mountains having sharp usu. bluish gray needles and often planted as an ornamental

blue·stem \'blü-ˌstem\ *n* (ca. 1862) **1 :** a tall No. American grass (*Andropogon gerardii* syn. *A. furcatus*) that has smooth bluish leaf sheaths and slender spikes borne in pairs or clusters and is used for hay and forage **2 :** LITTLE BLUESTEM

blue·stock·ing \-ˌstä-kiŋ\ *n* [*Bluestocking* society, 18th cent. literary clubs] (1790) : a woman having intellectual or literary interests

blue·stone \-ˌstōn\ *n* (1709) : a building stone of bluish gray color

blue streak *n* (1830) **1 :** something that moves very fast **2 :** a constant stream of words ⟨talked a *blue streak*⟩

bluesy \'blü-zē\ *adj* **blues·i·er; -est** (1946) : resembling, characteristic of, or suited to the blues

blu·et \'blü-ət\ *n* [prob. fr. ¹*blue*] (ca. 1821) : a No. American plant (*Hedyotis caerulea* syn. *Houstonia caerulea*) of the madder family having tufted stems and bluish or white flowers with yellow centers

blue·tick \-ˌtik\ *n* (1945) : any of a breed of tricolor coonhounds of American origin having the white areas of the coat heavily ticked with black

blue·tongue \'blü-ˌtəŋ\ *n* (1863) : a serious virus disease esp. of sheep characterized by hyperemia, cyanosis, and punctate hemorrhages and by swelling and sloughing of the epithelium esp. about the mouth and tongue

blue vitriol *n* (1728) : a hydrated copper sulfate $CuSO_4 \cdot 5H_2O$

blue water *n* (1582) : the open sea — **blue–wa·ter** \'blü-ˌwȯ-tər, -ˌwä-\ *adj*

blue·weed \'blü-ˌwēd\ *n* (ca. 1837) **1 :** VIPER'S BUGLOSS **2 :** a small weedy sunflower (*Helianthus ciliaris*) of the southwestern U.S. with blue-green or gray-green foliage

blue whale *n* (1851) : a very large baleen whale (*Balaenoptera musculus* syn. *Sibbaldus musculus*) that may reach a weight of 150 tons (135 metric tons) and a length of 100 feet (30 meters) and is generally considered the largest living animal

bluey \'blü-ē\ *n* [fr. the blue blanket commonly used to wrap the bundle] (1877) *Austral :* a swagman's bundle of personal effects; *also :* a bag of clothing carried in travel

¹bluff \'bləf\ *adj* [obs. D *blaf* flat; akin to MLG *blaff* smooth] (1627) **1 a :** having a broad flattened front **b :** rising steeply with a broad flat or rounded front **2 :** good-naturedly frank and outspoken — **bluff·ly** *adv* — **bluff·ness** *n*

syn BLUFF, BLUNT, BRUSQUE, CURT, CRUSTY, GRUFF mean abrupt and unceremonious in speech and manner. BLUFF connotes good-natured outspokenness and unconventionality ⟨a *bluff* manner⟩. BLUNT suggests directness of expression in disregard of others' feelings ⟨a *blunt* appraisal⟩. BRUSQUE applies to a sharpness or ungraciousness ⟨a *brusque* response⟩. CURT implies disconcerting shortness or rude conciseness ⟨a *curt* command⟩. CRUSTY suggests a harsh or surly manner sometimes concealing an inner kindliness ⟨a *crusty* exterior⟩. GRUFF suggests a hoarse or husky speech which may imply bad temper but more often implies embarrassment or shyness ⟨puts on a *gruff* pose⟩.

²bluff *n* (1666) : a high steep bank : CLIFF

³bluff *vb* [prob. fr. D *bluffen* to boast, play a kind of card game] *vt* (1839) **1 a :** to deter or frighten by pretense or a mere show of strength **b :** DECEIVE **c :** FEIGN ⟨the catcher ~ed a throw to first⟩ **2 :** to deceive (an opponent) in cards by a bold bet on an inferior hand ~ *vi :* to bluff someone : act deceptively — **bluff·er** *n*

⁴bluff *n* (1845) **1 a :** an act or instance of bluffing **b :** the practice of bluffing **2 :** one who bluffs

blu·ing *or* **blue·ing** \'blü-iŋ\ *n* (1669) : a preparation used in laundering to counteract yellowing of white fabrics

blu·ish \'blü-ish\ *adj* (14c) : somewhat blue : having a tinge of blue — **blu·ish·ness** *n*

¹blun·der \'blən-dər\ *vb* **blun·dered; blun·der·ing** \-d(ə-)riŋ\ [ME *blundren*] *vi* (14c) **1 :** to move unsteadily or confusedly **2 :** to make a mistake through stupidity, ignorance, or carelessness ~ *vt* **1 :** to utter stupidly, confusedly, or thoughtlessly **2 :** to make a stupid, careless, or thoughtless mistake in — **blun·der·er** \-dər-ər\ *n* — **blun·der·ing·ly** \-d(ə-)riŋ-lē\ *adv*

²blunder *n* (ca. 1706) : a gross error or mistake resulting usu. from stupidity, ignorance, or carelessness *syn* see ERROR

blun·der·buss \'blən-dər-ˌbəs\ *n* [by folk etymology fr. obs. D *donderbus*, fr. D *donder* thunder + obs. D *bus* gun] (1654) **1 :** a muzzle-loading firearm with a short barrel and flaring muzzle to facilitate loading **2 :** a blundering person

blunderbuss 1

¹blunt \'blənt\ *adj* [ME] (13c) **1 a :** slow or deficient in feeling : INSENSITIVE **b :** obtuse in understanding or discernment : DULL **2 :** having an edge or point that is not sharp **3 a :** abrupt in speech or manner **b :** being straight to the point : DIRECT *syn* see DULL, BLUFF — **blunt·ly** *adv* — **blunt·ness** *n*

²blunt *vt* (14c) : to make less sharp or definite ~ *vi :* to become blunt

¹blur \'blər\ *n* [perh. akin to ME *bleren* to blear] (1548) **1 :** a smear or stain that obscures **2 :** something vaguely or indistinctly perceived; *esp :* something moving or occurring too quickly to be clearly perceived

²blur *vb* **blurred; blur·ring** *vt* (1581) **1 :** to obscure or blemish by smearing **2** : SULLY **3** : to make dim, indistinct, or vague in outline or character **4** : to make cloudy or confused ~ *vi* **1** : to make blurs **2** : to become vague or indistinct — **blur·ring·ly** \'blər-iŋ-lē\ *adv*

¹**blurb** \'blərb\ *n* [coined by Gelett Burgess] (1914) : a short publicity notice (as on a book jacket)

²**blurb** *vt* (1915) : to describe or praise in a blurb

blur·ry \'blər-ē\ *adj* **blur·ri·er; -est** (1884) : marked by blurring — **blur·ri·ly** \'blər-ə-lē\ *adv* — **blur·ri·ness** \'blər-ē-nəs\ *n*

blurt \'blərt\ *vt* [prob. imit.] (1573) : to utter abruptly and impulsively — usu. used with *out* — **blurt·er** *n*

¹**blush** \'bləsh\ *n* [ME, prob. fr. *blusshen*] (14c) **1** : outward appearance : VIEW ⟨at first ~⟩ **2** : a reddening of the face esp. from shame, modesty, or confusion **3** : a red or rosy tint — **blush·ful** \-fəl\ *adj*

²**blush** *vi* [ME *blusshen*, fr. OE *blyscan* to redden; akin to OE *blysa* flame, OHG *bluhhen* to burn brightly] (15c) **1** : to become red in the face esp. from shame, modesty, or confusion **2** : to feel shame or embarrassment **3** : to have a rosy or fresh color : BLOOM — **blush·ing·ly** \'blə-shiŋ-lē\ *adv*

blush·er \'blə-shər\ *n* (1665) **1** : one that blushes **2** : a cosmetic applied to the face to give a usu. pink color or to accent the cheekbones

blush wine *n* (1985) : any of various pinkish table wines

¹**blus·ter** \'bləs-tər\ *vb* **blus·tered; blus·ter·ing** \-t(ə-)riŋ\ [ME *blustren*, prob. fr. MLG *blüsteren*] *vi* (15c) **1** : to talk or act with noisy swaggering threats **2** **a** : to blow in stormy noisy gusts **b** : to be windy and boisterous ~ *vt* **1** : to utter with noisy self-assertiveness **2** : to blow or force by blustering — **blus·ter·er** \-tər-ər\ *n* — **blus·ter·ing·ly** \-t(ə-)riŋ-lē\ *adv*

²**bluster** *n* (1583) **1** : a violent boisterous blowing **2** : violent commotion **3** : loudly boastful or threatening speech — **blus·ter·ous** \-t(ə-)rəs\ *adj* — **blus·tery** \-t(ə-)rē\ *adj*

B lymphocyte *n* (1971) : B CELL

B movie *n* (1948) : a cheaply produced motion picture

boa \'bō-ə\ *n* [L, a water snake] (14c) **1** : a large snake (as the boa constrictor, anaconda, or python) that kills by constriction **2** : a long fluffy scarf of fur, feathers, or delicate fabric

boa constrictor *n* (1809) : a tropical American boa (*Constrictor constrictor* syn. *Boa constrictor*) that is light brown barred or mottled with darker brown and reaches a length of 10 feet (3 meters) or more; *broadly* : BOA 1

boar \'bōr, 'bȯr\ *n* [ME *bor*, fr. OE *bār*; akin to OHG & OS *bēr* boar] (bef. 12c) **1** **a** : an uncastrated male swine **b** : the male of any of several mammals (as a guinea pig or raccoon) **2** : WILD BOAR — **boar·ish** \-ish\ *adj*

¹**board** \'bōrd, 'bȯrd\ *n* [ME *bord* piece of sawed lumber, border, ship's side, fr. OE; akin to OHG *bort* ship's side] (bef. 12c) **1** *obs* : BORDER, EDGE **2** : the side of a ship **3** **a** : a piece of sawed lumber of little thickness and length greatly exceeding its width **b** *pl* : STAGE 2a(2) **4** **a** *archaic* : TABLE 3a **b** : a table spread with a meal **c** : daily meals esp. when furnished for pay **d** : a table at which a council or magistrates sit **e** (1) : a group of persons having managerial, supervisory, investigatory, or advisory powers ⟨~ of directors⟩ ⟨~ of examiners⟩ (2) : an examination given by an examining board — often used in pl. ⟨pass the medical ~s⟩ **f** : LEAGUE, ASSOCIATION **g** (1) : the exposed hands of all the players in a stud poker game (2) : an exposed dummy hand in bridge **5** **a** : a flat usu. rectangular piece of material (as wood) designed for a special purpose: as (1) : SPRINGBOARD 1 (2) : SURFBOARD **b** : BACKBOARD; *also* : a rebound in basketball **c** : a surface, frame, or device for posting notices **d** : BLACKBOARD **e** : SWITCHBOARD **6** **a** : PAPERBOARD **b** : the stiff foundation piece for the side of a book cover **7** **a** : securities or commodities exchange **8** *pl* : the low wooden wall enclosing a hockey rink **9** : a sheet of insulating material carrying circuit elements and terminals so that it can be inserted in an electronic apparatus (as a computer) — **board·like** \-ˌlīk\ *adj* — **across the board** : so as to include or affect all classes or categories ⟨cut spending *across the board*⟩; *also* : in all areas or respects ⟨considered an average player *across the board*⟩ — **on board** : ABOARD

²**board** *vt* (15c) **1** *archaic* : to come up against or alongside (a ship) usu. to attack **2** : ACCOST, ADDRESS **3** **a** : to go aboard (as a ship, train, airplane, or bus) **b** : to put aboard ⟨an airliner ~ing passengers⟩ **4** : to cover with boards ⟨~ up a window⟩ **5** : to provide with regular meals and often also lodging usu. for compensation **6** : to check with a board check ~ *vi* : to take one's meals usu. as a paying customer

board check *n* (ca. 1936) : a body check of an opposing player against the rink boards in ice hockey

board·er \'bȯr-dər, 'bȯr-\ *n* (1530) : one that boards; *esp* : one that is provided with regular meals or regular meals and lodging

board foot *n* (1896) : a unit of quantity for lumber equal to the volume of a board 12 × 12 × 1 inches — abbr. *bd ft*

board game *n* (1934) : a game of strategy (as checkers, chess, or backgammon) played by moving pieces on a board

board·ing·house \'bȯr-diŋ-ˌhaús, 'bȯr-\ *n* (1728) : a lodging house at which meals are provided

boarding school *n* (1677) : a school at which meals and lodging are provided

board·man \'bȯrd-ˌman, 'bȯrd-, *esp for 2* -mən\ *n* (ca. 1923) **1** : a member of a board **2** : one who works at a board

board of trade (1780) **1** *cap B&T* : a British governmental department concerned with commerce and industry **2** : a commodities exchange

board·room \'bȯrd-ˌrüm, 'bȯrd-, -ˌrúm\ *n* (1836) : a room that is designated for meetings of a board

board·sail·ing \-ˌsā-liŋ\ *n* (1980) : WINDSURFING — **board·sail·or** \-ˌsā-lər\ *n*

board·walk \-ˌwȯk\ *n* (1872) **1** : a walk constructed of planking **2** : a walk constructed along a beach

boart \'bȯrt, 'bȯrt\ *var of* BORT

¹**boast** \'bōst\ *n* [ME *boost*] (14c) **1** : the act or an instance of boasting **2** : BRAG **2** : a cause for pride — **boast·ful** \'bōst-fəl\ *adj* — **boast·ful·ly** \-fə-lē\ *adv* — **boast·ful·ness** *n*

²**boast** *vi* (14c) **1** : to puff oneself up in speech : speak vaingloriously **2** *archaic* : GLORY, EXULT ~ *vt* **1** : to speak of or assert with excessive pride **2** **a** : to possess and often call attention to (something that is a

source of pride) ⟨~s a new stadium⟩ **b** : HAVE, CONTAIN ⟨a room ~ing no more than a desk and a chair⟩ — **boast·er** *n*

syn BOAST, BRAG, VAUNT, CROW mean to express pride in oneself or one's accomplishments. BOAST often suggests ostentation and exaggeration ⟨*boasts* of every trivial success⟩, but it may imply a claiming with proper and justifiable pride ⟨the town *boasts* one of the best museums in the area⟩. BRAG suggests crudity and artlessness in glorifying oneself ⟨*bragging* of their exploits⟩. VAUNT usu. connotes more pomp and bombast than BOAST and less crudity or naïveté than BRAG ⟨*vaunted* his country's military might⟩. CROW usu. implies exultant boasting or bragging ⟨*crowed* after winning the championship⟩.

³**boast** *vt* [origin unknown] (1823) : to shape (stone) roughly in sculpture and stonecutting as a preliminary to finer work

¹**boat** \'bōt\ *n* [ME *boot*, fr. OE *bāt*; akin to ON *beit* boat] (bef. 12c) **1** **a** : a small vessel for travel on water **b** : SHIP **2** : a boat-shaped container, utensil, or device ⟨a gravy ~⟩ ⟨a laboratory ~⟩ — **boat·ful** \-ˌfúl\ *n* — **boat·like** \-ˌlīk\ *adj* — **in the same boat** : in the same situation or predicament

²**boat** *vt* (1613) : to place in or bring into a boat ~ *vi* : to go by boat

boat·build·er \-ˌbil-dər\ *n* (1679) : one that builds boats — **boat·build·ing** \-ˌbil-diŋ\ *n*

boat·er \'bō-tər\ *n* (1605) **1** : one who travels in a boat **2** : a stiff hat usu. made of braided straw with a brim, hatband, and flat crown

boat hook *n* (ca. 1611) : a pole-handled hook with a point or knob on the back used esp. to pull or push a boat, raft, or log into place

boat·house \-ˌhaús\ *n* (1722) : a building to house and protect boats

boat·load \'bōt-ˌlōd\ *n* (1680) **1** : a load that fills a boat **2** : an indefinitely large number ⟨a ~ of money⟩

boat·man \'bōt-mən\ *n* (14c) : a man who works on, deals in, or operates boats

boat people *n pl* (1977) : refugees fleeing by boat

boat·swain \'bō-sᵊn\ *n* [ME *bootswein*, fr. *boot* boat + *swein* boy, servant — more at SWAIN] (14c) **1** : a petty officer on a merchant ship having charge of hull maintenance and related work **2** : a naval warrant officer in charge of the hull and all related equipment

boat train *n* (1884) : an express train for transporting passengers between a port and a city

boat·yard \'bōt-ˌyärd\ *n* (1847) : a yard where boats are built, repaired, and stored and often sold or rented

¹**bob** \'bäb\ *vb* **bobbed; bob·bing** [ME *boben*] *vt* (13c) **1** : to strike with a quick light blow : RAP **2** : to move up and down in a short quick movement ⟨~ the head⟩ **3** : to polish with a bob : BUFF ~ *vi* **1** **a** : to move up and down briefly or repeatedly ⟨a cork *bobbed* in the water⟩ **b** : to emerge, arise, or appear suddenly or unexpectedly ⟨the question *bobbed* up again⟩ **2** : to nod or curtsy briefly **3** : to try to seize a suspended or floating object with the teeth ⟨~ for apples⟩

²**bob** *n* (1550) **1** **a** : a short quick down-and-up motion **b** *Scot* : any of several folk dances **2** *obs* : a blow or tap esp. with the fist **3** **a** : a modification of the order in change ringing **b** : a method of change ringing using a bob **4** : a small polishing wheel of solid felt or leather with rounded edges

³**bob** *vt* **bobbed; bob·bing** [ME *bobben*, fr. MF *bober*] (14c) **1** *obs* : DECEIVE, CHEAT **2** *obs* : to take by fraud : FILCH

⁴**bob** *n* [ME *bobbe*] (14c) **1** **a** (1) : BUNCH, CLUSTER (2) *Scot* : NOSEGAY **b** : a knob, knot, twist, or curl esp. of ribbons, yarn, or hair **c** : a short haircut on a woman or child **2** : FLOAT 2a **3** : a hanging ball or weight (as on a plumb line) **4** : TRIFLE 1

⁵**bob** *vt* **bobbed; bob·bing** (1675) **1** : to cut shorter : CROP ⟨~ a horse's tail⟩ **2** : to cut (hair) in the style of a bob

⁶**bob** *n, pl* **bob** [perh. fr. the name *Bob*] (1789) *slang Brit* : SHILLING

⁷**bob** *n* (1856) : BOBSLED

¹**bob·ber** \'bä-bər\ *n* (1593) : one that bobs

²**bobber** *n* (1904) : a person who rides or races on a bobsled

bob·bery \'bä-b(ə-)rē\ *n, pl* **-ber·ies** [Hindi *bāp re*, lit., oh father!] (1803) : HUBBUB

bob·bin \'bä-bən\ *n* [origin unknown] (1530) **1** **a** : a cylinder or spindle on which yarn or thread is wound (as in a sewing machine) **b** : any of various small round devices on which threads are wound for working handmade lace **c** : a coil of insulated wire or the reel it is wound on **2** : a cotton cord formerly used by dressmakers for piping

bob·bi·net \ˌbä-bə-ˌnet\ *n* [blend of *bobbin* and *net*] (1814) : a machine-made net of cotton, silk, or nylon usu. with hexagonal mesh

¹**bob·ble** \'bä-bəl\ *vb* **bob·bled; bob·bling** \-b(ə-)liŋ\ [freq. of ¹*bob*] (1812) **1** : ¹BOB **2** : FUMBLE

²**bobble** *n* (1880) **1** : a repeated bobbing movement **2** : a small ball of fabric; *esp* : one in a series used on an edging ⟨curtains with ~s⟩ **3** : ERROR, MISTAKE; *esp* : a mishandling of the ball in baseball or football

bob·by \'bä-bē\ *n, pl* **bobbies** [*Bobby*, nickname for *Robert*, after Sir *Robert* Peel, who organized the London police force] (1844) *Brit* : POLICE OFFICER

bobby pin *n* [perh. fr. ⁴*bob*] (1932) : a flat wire hairpin with prongs that press close together

bobby socks *or* **bobby sox** *n pl* [perh. fr *bobby* pin] (1943) : girls' socks reaching above the ankle

bob·by–sox·er \-ˌsäk-sər\ *n* (1944) : an adolescent girl

bob·cat \'bäb-ˌkat\ *n* [⁴*bob*; fr. the stubby tail] (1888) : a common No. American lynx (*Lynx rufus*) variably reddish in base color with dark markings

bo·beche \bō-'besh, -'bāsh\ *n* [F *bobèche*] (ca. 1897) : a usu. glass collar on a candle socket to catch drippings or on a candlestick or chandelier to hold suspended glass prisms

bob·o·link \'bä-bə-ˌliŋk\ *n* [imit.] (ca. 1801) : an American migratory songbird (*Dolichonyx oryzivorus*) with the breeding male chiefly black

bob·sled \'bäb-ˌsled\ *n* [perh. fr. ⁴*bob*] (1839) **1** : a short sled usu. used as one of a pair joined by a coupling **2** : a large usu. metal sled used in racing and equipped with two pairs of runners in tandem, a

---

\ə\ abut \ᵊ\ kitten, F table \ər\ further \a\ ash \ā\ ace \ä\ mop, mar
\aú\ out \ch\ chin \e\ bet \ē\ easy \g\ go \i\ hit \ī\ ice \j\ job
\ŋ\ sing \ō\ go \ò\ law \òi\ boy \th\ thin \t͟h\ the \ü\ loot \ú\ foot
\y\ yet \zh\ vision \á, k, ⁿ, œ, œ̄, ue, ūe, ᴗ\ *see* Guide to Pronunciation

long seat for two or more people, a steering wheel, and a hand brake — **bobsled** *vi* — **bob·sled·der** *n*

bob·sled·ding \-,sle-diŋ\ *n* (1883) : the act, skill, or sport of riding or racing on a bobsled

bob·stay \'bäb-,stā\ *n* [prob. fr. ²*bob*] (1758) : a stay to hold a ship's bowsprit down

bob·tail \'bäb-,tāl\ *n* [⁴*bob*] (1605) **1 a** : a bobbed tail **b** : a horse, dog, or cat with a bobbed or very short tail; *esp* : OLD ENGLISH SHEEP-DOG **2** : something curtailed — **bobtail** *or* **bob·tailed** \-,tāld\ *adj*

bob veal \'bäb-\ *n* [E dial. *bob* young calf] (1855) : the veal of a very young or unborn calf

bob·white \'bäb-'hwit, -'wit\ *n* [imit.] (1819) : any of a genus (*Colinus*) of quail; *esp* : a popular game bird (*C. virginianus*) of the eastern and central U.S.

bo·cac·cio \bə-'kä-chē-,ō, -chō\ *n* [perh. modif. of Sp *bocacha*, aug. of *boca* mouth] (ca. 1890) : a large rockfish (*Sebastes paucispinis*) of the Pacific coast locally important as a market fish

boc·cie *or* **boc·ci** *or* **boc·ce** \'bä-chē\ *n* [It *bocce*, pl. of *boccia* ball, fr. (assumed) VL *bottia* boss] (1745) : a game of Italian origin similar to lawn bowling played on a long narrow usu. dirt court

bock \'bäk\ *n* [G, short for *Bockbier*, by shortening & alter. fr. *Einbecker Bier*, lit., beer from Einbeck, fr. *Einbeck*, Germany] (1856) : a heavy dark rich beer usu. sold in the early spring

bod \'bäd\ *n* (1933) **1** *Brit* : FELLOW, GUY **2** : BODY

bo·da·cious \bō-'dā-shəs\ *adj* [prob. blend of *bold* and *audacious*] (1845) **1** *Southern & Midland* : OUTRIGHT, UNMISTAKABLE **2** : RE-MARKABLE, NOTEWORTHY ⟨the ~ 1974 comedy —*People*⟩ — **bo·da·cious·ly** *adv*

¹bode \'bōd\ *vt* **bod·ed; bod·ing** [ME, fr. OE *bodian;* akin to OE *bēodan* to proclaim — more at BID] (bef. 12c) **1** *archaic* : to announce beforehand : FORETELL **2** : to indicate by signs : PRESAGE ⟨this controversy . . . will ~ ill for both of us —A. H. Lowe⟩

²bode *past of* BIDE

bo·de·ga \bō-'dā-gə\ *n* [Sp, fr. L *apotheca* storehouse — more at APOTH-ECARY] (1846) **1** : a storehouse for maturing wine **2 a** : WINESHOP **b** (1) : ¹BAR 5a (2) : BARROOM **3** : a store specializing in Hispanic groceries

bode·ment \'bōd-mənt\ *n* (1605) **1** : OMEN, FOREBODING **2** : PREDIC-TION, PROPHECY

bo·dhi·satt·va *or* **bod·dhi·satt·va** \,bō-di-'sət-və, -'sät-\ *n* [Skt *bodhi-sattva* one whose essence is enlightenment, fr. *bodhi* enlightenment + *sattva* being — more at BID] (1828) : a being that compassionately refrains from entering nirvana in order to save others and is worshiped as a deity in Mahayana Buddhism

bodh·ran \'bò-(,)rän, -rən\ *n* [Ir *bodhrán*] (1972) : an Irish goatskin drum

bod·ice \'bä-dəs\ *n* [alter. of *bodies*, pl. of ¹*body*] (ca. 1567) **1** : the upper part of a woman's dress **2** *archaic* : CORSET, STAYS

bodice ripper *n* (1980) : a historical or Gothic romance typically featuring scenes in which the heroine is subjected to sexual violence

bod·ied \'bä-dēd\ *adj* (ca. 1547) : having a body of a specified kind — used in combination ⟨full-*bodied*⟩ ⟨glass-*bodied*⟩

bodi·less \'bä-di-ləs, 'bä-d²l-əs\ *adj* (14c) : having no body

¹bodi·ly \'bä-d²l-ē\ *adj* (14c) **1** : having a body : PHYSICAL **2** : of or relating to the body ⟨~ comfort⟩ ⟨~ organs⟩

²bodily *adv* (14c) **1** : in the flesh **2** : as a whole : ALTOGETHER

bod·ing \'bō-diŋ\ *n* (13c) : FOREBODING

bod·kin \'bäd-kən\ *n* [ME *bodekin*] (14c) **1 a** : DAGGER, STILETTO **b** : a sharp slender instrument for making holes in cloth **c** : an ornamental hairpin shaped like a stiletto **2 a** : a blunt needle with a large eye for drawing tape or ribbon through a loop or hem

¹body \'bä-dē\ *n, pl* **bod·ies** [ME, fr. OE *bodig;* akin to OHG *boteh* corpse] (bef. 12c) **1 a** : the main part of a plant or animal body esp. as distinguished from limbs and head : TRUNK **b** : the main, central, or principal part: as (1) : the nave of a church (2) : the bed or box of a vehicle or one in which the load is placed (3) : the enclosed or partly enclosed part of an automobile **2 a** : the organized physical substance of an animal or plant either living or dead: as (1) : the material part or nature of a human being (2) : the dead organism : CORPSE **b** : a human being : PERSON **3 a** : a mass of matter distinct from other masses ⟨a ~ of water⟩ ⟨a celestial ~⟩ **b** : something that embodies or gives concrete reality to a thing; *also* : a sensible object in physical space **c** : AGGREGATE, QUANTITY ⟨a ~ of evidence⟩ **4 a** : the part of a garment covering the body or trunk **b** : the main part of a literary or journalistic work : TEXT **2b** **c** : the sound box or pipe of a musical instrument **5** : a group of persons or things: as **a** : a fighting unit : FORCE **b** : a group of individuals organized for some purpose ⟨a legislative ~⟩ **6 a** : fullness and richness of flavor (as of wine) **b** : VISCOSITY, CONSISTENCY — used esp. of oils and grease **c** : compactness or firmness of texture **d** : fullness or resonance of a musical tone

²body *vt* **bod·ied; body·ing** (15c) **1** : to give form or shape to : EM-BODY **2** : REPRESENT, SYMBOLIZE — usu. used with *forth*

body bag *n* (1954) : a large zippered usu. rubber bag in which a human corpse is placed esp. for transportation

body blow *n* (1792) **1** : a blow to the body **2** : a damaging or deeply felt blow ⟨an economic *body blow*⟩

body·build·ing \-,bil-diŋ\ *n* (1904) : the developing of the body through exercise and diet; *specif* : the developing of the physique for competitive exhibition — **body·build·er** *n*

body cavity *n* (1875) : a cavity in an animal body; *specif* : COELOM

body·cen·tered \'bä-dē-,sen-tərd\ *adj* (1921) : relating to or being a crystal space lattice in which each cubic unit cell has an atom at its center and at each vertex — compare FACE-CENTERED

body check *n* (1892) : a blocking of an opposing player with the body (as in ice hockey or lacrosse) — **body-check** \'bä-dē-,chek\ *vt*

body clock *n* (1968) : the internal mechanisms that schedule periodic bodily functions and activities — usu. not used technically

body corporate *n* (15c) : CORPORATION

body count *n* (1967) **1** : a count of the bodies of killed enemy soldiers **2** : the number of persons involved in a particular activity

body English *n* (1908) : bodily motions made in a usu. unconscious effort to influence the progress of a propelled object (as a ball)

body·guard \'bä-dē-,gärd\ *n* (ca. 1735) : a usu. armed attendant or group of attendants whose duty is to protect a person

body language *n* (1926) : the gestures, movements, and mannerisms by which a person or animal communicates with others

body louse *n* (1575) : a louse feeding primarily on the body; *esp* : a sucking louse (*Pediculus humanus humanus*) feeding on the body and living in the clothing of humans — called also *cootie*

body mechanics *n pl but sing or pl in constr* (ca. 1970) : systematic exercises designed esp. to develop coordination, endurance, and poise

body politic *n* (15c) **1** : a group of persons politically organized under a single governmental authority **2** *archaic* : CORPORATION **2 3** : a people considered as a collective unit

body shirt *n* (1967) **1** : a close-fitting shirt or blouse **2** : a woman's close-fitting top made with a sewn-in or snapped crotch

body shop *n* (1954) : a shop where automotive bodies are made or repaired

body snatcher *n* (1812) : one that steals corpses from graves

body stocking *n* (1965) : a sheer close-fitting one-piece garment for the torso that often has sleeves and legs

body·suit \'bä-dē-,süt\ *n* (1970) : a close-fitting one-piece garment for the torso

body·surf \'bä-dē-,sərf\ *vi* (1943) : to ride on a wave without a surf-board by planing on the chest and stomach — **body·surf·er** *n*

body wall *n* (1888) : the external surface of the animal body consisting of ectoderm and mesoderm and enclosing the body cavity

body·work \'bä-dē-,wərk\ *n* (1908) **1** : a vehicle body **2** : the act or process of making or repairing vehicle bodies **3** : therapeutic touching or manipulation of the body by using specialized techniques

boehm·ite \'bā-,mīt, 'bə(r)-\ *n* [G *Böhmit*, fr. J. *Böhm* (*Boehm*), 20th cent. Ger. scientist] (ca. 1929) : a mineral consisting of an orthorhombic form of aluminum oxide and hydroxide AlO(OH) found in bauxite

Boer \'bōr, 'bòr, 'bùr\ *n* [D, lit., farmer — more at BOOR] (1834) : a South African of Dutch or Huguenot descent

¹boff \'bäf\ *vt* [fr. *boff* blow, punch, perh. imit.] (1937) : to have sexual intercourse with — sometimes considered vulgar

²boff *or* **bof·fo** \'bä-(,)fō\ *n, pl* **boffs** *or* **boffos** [perh. fr. *box office*] (1946) **1** : a hearty laugh **2** : a gag or line that produces a hearty laugh **3** : something that is conspicuously successful : HIT

bof·fin \'bä-fən\ *n* [origin unknown] (1945) *chiefly Brit* : a scientific expert; *esp* : one involved in technological research

bof·fo \'bä-(,)fō\ *adj* (1949) : extremely successful : SENSATIONAL

bof·fo·la \bä-'fō-lə\ *n* [irreg. fr. *boff*] (1946) : BOFF

Bo·fors gun \'bō-,fòrz-, 'bü-\ *n* [*Bofors*, munition works in Sweden] (1939) : a double-barreled automatic antiaircraft gun

¹bog \'bäg, 'bòg\ *n* [ME (Sc), fr. ScGael & Ir *bog-* (as in *bogluachair* bulrushes), fr. *bog* marshy, lit., soft, fr. MIr *bocc;* prob. akin to OE *būgan* to bend — more at BOW] (14c) : wet spongy ground; *esp* : a poorly drained usu. acid area rich in accumulated plant material, frequently surrounding a body of open water, and having a characteristic flora (as of sedges, heaths, and sphagnum) — **bog·gy** \'bä-gē, 'bò-\ *adj*

²bog *vb* **bogged; bog·ging** *vt* (1599) : to cause to sink into or as if into a bog : IMPEDE, MIRE — usu. used with *down* ~ *vi* : to become impeded or stuck — usu. used with *down*

bog asphodel *n* (1857) : either of two bog herbs (*Narthecium ossi-fragum* of Europe and *N. americanum* of the U.S.) of the lily family

¹bo·gey *also* **bo·gie** *or* **bo·gy** *n, pl* **bogeys** *also* **bogies** [prob. alter. of *bogle*] (1857) **1** \'bù-gē, 'bō-, 'bü-\ : SPECTER, PHANTOM **2** \'bō-gē *also* 'bù- *or* 'bü-\ : a source of fear, perplexity, or harassment **3** \'bō-gē\ **a** *chiefly Brit* : an average golfer's score used as a standard for a particular hole or course **b** : one stroke over par on a hole in golf **4** \'bō-gē\ : a numerical standard of performance set up as a mark to be aimed at in competition **5** \'bō-gē\ : an unidentified aircraft; *esp* : one not positively identified as friendly and so assumed to be hostile

²bo·gey \'bō-gē\ *vt* **bo·geyed; bo·gey·ing** (1948) : to shoot (a hole in golf) in one over par

bo·gey·man *also* **bo·gy·man** \'bù-gē-,man, 'bō-, 'bü-, 'bù-gər-\ *n* (ca. 1890) **1** : a monstrous imaginary figure used in threatening children **2** : a terrifying or dreaded person or thing : BUGBEAR

bog·gle \'bä-gəl\ *vb* **bog·gled; bog·gling** \-g(ə-)liŋ\ [perh. fr. *bogle*] (1598) *vi* **1** : to start with fright or amazement : be overwhelmed ⟨the mind ~s at the research needed⟩ **2** : to hesitate because of doubt, fear, or scruples ~ *vt* **1** : MISHANDLE, BUNGLE **2** : to overwhelm with wonder or bewilderment — **boggle** *n*

bo·gie *also* **bo·gey** \'bō-gē\ *n, pl* **bogies** *also* **bogeys** [origin unknown] (1835) **1** : a low strongly built cart **2 a** *chiefly Brit* : a swiveling railway truck **b** : the driving-wheel assembly consisting of the rear four wheels of a 6-wheel automotive truck **3** : a small supporting or aligning wheel (as on the inside perimeter of a tank tread)

bo·gle \'bō-gəl\ *also* **bog·gle** \'bä-gəl\ *n* [origin unknown] (ca. 1505) *dial Brit* : GOBLIN, SPECTER; *also* : an object of fear or loathing

Bo·go·mil *also* **Bo·go·mile** \,bə-gə-'mē(ə)l\ *n* [MGk *Bogomilos*, fr. *Bogomilos* Bogomil, 10th cent. Bulg. priest, founder of the sect] (1841) : a member of a medieval Bulgarian sect holding that God has two sons, the rebellious Satan and the obedient Jesus

bo·gus \'bō-gəs\ *adj* [*bogus* (a machine for making counterfeit money)] (1825) : not genuine : COUNTERFEIT, SHAM

bo·hea \bō-'hē\ *n, often cap* [Chin (Fujian) *Bú-i*, hills in China where it was grown] (1701) : a black tea

bo·he·mia \bō-'hē-mē-ə\ *n, often cap* [trans. of F *bohème*] (1861) : a community of bohemians : the world of bohemians

Bo·he·mi·an \-mē-ən\ *n* (1603) **1 a** : a native or inhabitant of Bohemia **b** : the group of Czech dialects used in Bohemia **2** *often not cap* **a** : VAGABOND, WANDERER; *esp* : GYPSY **b** : a person (as a writer or an artist) living an unconventional life usu. in a colony with others — **bohemian** *adj, often cap*

Bohemian Brethren *n pl* (ca. 1862) : a Christian body originating in Bohemia in 1467 and forming a parent body of the Moravian Church

bo·he·mi·an·ism \bō-'hē-mē-ə-,ni-zəm\ *n, often cap* (1861) : the unconventional way of life of bohemians

Bohr effect \'bōr-, 'bòr-\ *n* [Christian *Bohr* †1911 Dan. physiologist] (1939) : the decrease in the oxygen affinity of a respiratory pigment (as hemoglobin) in response to decreased blood pH resulting from increased carbon dioxide concentration in the blood

Bohr theory *n* [Niels *Bohr*] (1922) : a theory in early quantum physics: an atom consists of a positively charged nucleus about which revolves one or more electrons of quantized energy

bo·hunk \'bō-,həŋk\ *n* [*Bohemian* + *Hunk* person of central European descent, by shortening & alter. of *Hungarian*] (ca. 1903) : a person of central European descent or birth — usu. used disparagingly

¹boil \'boi(ə)l\ *vb* [ME, fr. OF *boillir*, fr. L *bullire* to bubble, fr. *bulla* bubble] *vi* (13c) **1 a** : to come to the boiling point **b** : to generate bubbles of vapor when heated — used of a liquid **c** : to cook in boiling water **2** : to become agitated like boiling water : SEETHE **3** : to be moved, excited, or stirred up ⟨made his blood ~⟩ **4 a** : to rush headlong **b** : to burst forth : ERUPT ⟨water ~*ing* from a spring⟩ **5** : to undergo the action of a boiling liquid ~ *vt* **1** : to subject to the action of a boiling liquid **2** : to heat to the boiling point **3** : to form or separate (as sugar or salt) by boiling — **boil·able** \'boi-lə-bəl\ *adj*

²boil *n* [ME, alter. of *bile*, fr. OE *bȳl*; akin to OHG *pūlla* bladder] (15c) : a localized swelling and inflammation of the skin resulting from infection in a skin gland, having a hard central core, and forming pus

³boil *n* (15c) **1** : the act or state of boiling **2** : a swirling upheaval (as of water)

boil down *vt* (1845) **1** : to reduce in bulk by boiling **2** : CONDENSE, SUMMARIZE ⟨*boil down* a report⟩ ~ *vi* **1** : to undergo reduction in bulk by boiling **2 a** : to be equivalent in summary : AMOUNT ⟨his speech *boiled down* to a plea for more money⟩ **b** : to reduce ultimately ⟨your choices *boil down* to three⟩

boil·er \'boi-lər\ *n* (ca. 1540) **1** : one that boils **2 a** : a vessel used for boiling **b** : the part of a steam generator in which water is converted into steam and which consists usu. of metal shells and tubes **c** : a tank in which water is heated or hot water is stored

boil·er·mak·er \'boi-lər-,mā-kər\ *n* (1865) **1** : a worker who makes, assembles, or repairs boilers **2** : whiskey with a beer chaser

boil·er·plate \-,plāt\ *n* (1897) **1** : syndicated material supplied esp. to weekly newspapers in matrix or plate form **2 a** : standardized text **b** : formulaic or hackneyed language ⟨bureaucratic ~⟩

boiler room *n* (1903) **1** : a room in which a boiler is located **2** : a room equipped with telephones used for making high-pressure usu. fraudulent sales pitches

boil·er·suit \-,süt\ *n* (1928) : COVERALL

¹boil·ing \'boi-liŋ\ *adj* (14c) **1 a** : heated to the boiling point **b** : TORRID ⟨a ~ sun⟩ **2** : intensely agitated ⟨a ~ sea⟩ ⟨~ with anger⟩

²boiling *adv* (1607) : to an extreme degree : VERY ⟨~ mad⟩ ⟨~ hot⟩

boiling point *n* (1773) **1** : the temperature at which a liquid boils **2 a** : the point at which a person becomes uncontrollably angry **b** : the point of crisis : HEAD 17b ⟨matters had reached the *boiling point*⟩

boil over *vi* (15c) **1** : to overflow while boiling or during boiling **2** : to become so incensed as to lose one's temper

bois d'arc \'bō-,dä(r)k, *dial also* 'bwä-, 'bōr-\ *n*, *pl* **bois d'arcs** *or* **bois d'arc** [AmerF, lit., bow wood] (1805) : OSAGE ORANGE; *also* : its wood

bois·ter·ous \'boi-st(ə-)rəs\ *adj* [ME *boistous* rough] (14c) **1** *obs* **a** : COARSE **b** : DURABLE, STRONG **c** : MASSIVE **2 a** : noisily turbulent **b** : ROWDY **b** : marked by or expressive of exuberance and high spirits **3** : STORMY, TUMULTUOUS *syn* see VOCIFEROUS — **bois·ter·ous·ly** *adv* — **bois·ter·ous·ness** *n*

boîte \'bwät\ *n* [F, lit., box] (1922) : NIGHTCLUB

bok choy \'bäk-'choi\ *n* [Chin (Guangdong) *baahk-choi*, lit., white vegetable] (1938) : a Chinese cabbage (*Brassica chinensis*) forming an open head with long white stalks and green leaves

Bok·mål \'buk-,mōl, 'bōk-\ *n* [Norw, lit., book language] (1931) : a literary form of Norwegian developed by the gradual reform of written Danish — compare NYNORSK

bo·la \'bō-lə\ *or* **bo·las** \-ləs\ *n*, *pl* **bolas** \-ləz\ *also* **bo·las·es** [AmerSp *bolas*, fr. Sp *bola* ball] (1818) : a cord with weights attached to the ends for throwing at and entangling an animal

¹bold \'bōld\ *adj* [ME *beald*; akin to OHG *bald* bold] (bef. 12c) **1 a** : fearless before danger : INTREPID **b** : showing or requiring a fearless daring spirit ⟨a ~ plan⟩ **2** : IMPUDENT, PRESUMPTUOUS **3** *obs* : ASSURED, CONFIDENT **4** : SHEER, STEEP ⟨~ cliffs⟩ **5** : ADVENTUROUS, FREE ⟨a ~ thinker⟩ **6** : standing out prominently **7** : being or set in boldface — **bold·ly** \'bōl(d)-lē\ *adv* — **bold·ness** \'bōl(d)-nəs\ *n*

bola

²bold *n* (ca. 1871) : BOLDFACE

bold·face \'bōl(d)-,fās\ *n* (ca. 1889) : a heavy-faced type; *also* : printing in boldface

bold–faced \'bōl(d)-'fāst\ *adj* (1591) **1** : bold in manner or conduct : IMPUDENT **2** *usu* **bold-faced** : being or set in boldface

bole \'bōl\ *n* [ME, fr. ON *bolr*] (14c) : TRUNK 1a

bo·le·ro \bə-'ler-(,)ō\ *n*, *pl* **-ros** [Sp] (1787) **1** : a Spanish dance characterized by sharp turns, stamping of the feet, and sudden pauses in a position with one arm arched over the head; *also* : music in ¾ time for a bolero **2** : a loose waist-length jacket open at the front

bo·lete \bō-'lēt\ *n* [NL *Boletus*] (1914) : any of a family (Boletaceae) of fleshy stalked pore fungi that usu. grow on the ground in wooded areas; *esp* : BOLETUS

bo·le·tus \bō-'lē-təs\ *n*, *pl* **-tus** *or* **-ti** \-'lē-,tī\ [NL, genus name, fr. L, mushroom] (1601) : any of a genus (*Boletus*) of boletes (as a cèpe) some of which are poisonous and others edible

bo·lide \'bō-,līd, -lid\ *n* [F, fr. L *bolid-*, *bolis*, fr. Gk, fr. *bolē* throw, stroke] (1852) : a large meteor : FIREBALL; *esp* : one that explodes

Bo·li·var \bə-'lē-,vär, 'bä-lə-vər\ *n*, *pl* **-va·res** \,bä-lə-'vär-,ās, ,bō-li-\ *or* **-vars** [AmerSp *bolívar*, fr. Simón *Bolívar*] (ca. 1895) — see MONEY table

bo·li·vi·a·no \bə-,li-vē-'ä-(,)nō\ *n*, *pl* **-nos** [AmerSp] (ca. 1872) — see MONEY table

boll \'bōl\ *n* [ME] (15c) : the pod or capsule of a plant (as cotton)

bol·lard \'bä-lərd, *Brit also* -,lärd\ *n* [perh. fr. *bole*] (ca. 1775) **1** : a post of metal or wood on a wharf around which to fasten mooring lines **2** : BITT 1 **3** *chiefly Brit* : any of a series of short posts set at intervals to delimit an area (as a traffic island) or to exclude vehicles

bol·lix \'bä-liks\ *vt* [alter. of *ballocks*, pl. of *ballock* (testis), fr. ME, fr. OE *bealluc* — more at BALL] (1937) : to throw into disorder; *also* : BUNGLE — usu. used with *up* — **bollix** *n*

boll weevil *n* (1895) : a grayish weevil (*Anthonomus grandis*) that infests the cotton plant and feeds on the squares and bolls

boll·worm \'bōl-,wərm\ *n* (1847) : CORN EARWORM; *also* : any of several other moths or their immature stages that feed on cotton bolls as larvae

bo·lo \'bō-(,)lō\ *n*, *pl* **bolos** [PhilSp] (ca. 1900) : a long heavy single-edged knife of Philippine origin used to cut vegetation and as a weapon

bo·lo·gna \bə-'lō-nē *also* -nyə, -nə\ *n* [short for *Bologna sausage*, fr. *Bologna*, Italy] (1596) : a large smoked sausage of beef, veal, and pork; *also* : a sausage made (as of turkey) to resemble bologna

bo·lom·e·ter \bō-'lä-mə-tər\ *n* [Gk *bolē* stroke, beam of light (fr. *ballein* to throw) + E -*o*- + -*meter* — more at DEVIL] (1881) : a very sensitive thermometer whose electrical resistance varies with temperature and which is used in the detection and measurement of feeble thermal radiation and is esp. adapted to the study of infrared spectra — **bo·lo·met·ric** \,bō-lə-'me-trik\ *adj* — **bo·lo·met·ri·cal·ly** \-tri-k(ə-)lē\ *adv*

bo·lo·ney \bə-'lō-nē\ *var of* BALONEY

bolo tie \'bō-lō-\ *or* **bo·la tie** \-lə-\ *n* [prob. fr. *bola*] (1964) : a cord fastened around the neck with an ornamental clasp and worn as a necktie

Bol·she·vik \'bōl-shə-,vik, 'bōl-, 'bäl-, -,vēk\ *n*, *pl* **Bolsheviks** *also* **Bol·she·vi·ki** \,bōl-shə-'vi-kē, ,bōl-, ,bäl-, -'vē-kē\ [Russ *bol'shevik*, fr. *bol'shii* greater] (1917) **1** : a member of the extremist wing of the Russian Social Democratic party that seized power in Russia by the Revolution of November 1917 **2** : COMMUNIST **3** — **Bolshevik** *adj*

bol·she·vism \'bōl-shə-,vi-zəm, 'bōl-, 'bäl-\ *n*, *often cap* (1917) **1** : the doctrine or program of the Bolsheviks advocating violent overthrow of capitalism **2** : Russian communism

Bol·she·vist \-vist\ *n or adj* (1917) : BOLSHEVIK

bol·she·vize \-,vīz\ *vt* -**vized**; -**viz·ing** (1919) : to make Bolshevist — **Bol·she·vi·za·tion** \,bōl-shə-və-'zā-shən, ,bōl-, ,bäl-\ *n*

bol·shie *or* **bol·shy** \'bōl-shē, 'bōl-, 'bäl-\ *n or adj*, *often cap* [by shortening & alter.] (1918) : BOLSHEVIK

¹bol·ster \'bōl-stər\ *n* [ME, fr. OE; akin to OE *belg* bag — more at BELLY] (bef. 12c) **1** : a long pillow or cushion **2** : a structural part designed to eliminate friction or provide support or bearing

²bolster *vt* **bol·stered; bol·ster·ing** \-st(ə-)riŋ\ (1508) **1** : to support with or as if with a bolster : REINFORCE **2** : to give a boost to ⟨news that ~*ed* his spirits⟩ — **bol·ster·er** \-stər-ər\ *n*

¹bolt \'bōlt\ *n* [ME, fr. OE; akin to OHG *bolz* crossbow bolt, and perh. to Lith *beldéti* to beat] (bef. 12c) **1 a** : a shaft or missile designed to be shot from a crossbow or catapult; *esp* : a short stout usu. blunt-headed arrow **b** : a lightning stroke; *also* : THUNDERBOLT **2 a** : a wood or metal bar or rod used to fasten a door **b** : the part of a lock that is shot or withdrawn by the key **3** : a roll of cloth or wallpaper of specified length **4** : a metal rod or pin for fastening objects together that usu. has a head at one end and a screw thread at the other and is secured by a nut **5 a** : a block of timber to be sawed or cut **b** : a short round section of a log **6** : a metal cylinder that drives the cartridge into the chamber of a firearm, locks the breech, and usu. contains the firing pin and extractor

bolt 4

²bolt *vi* (13c) **1** : to move suddenly or nervously : START **2** : to move rapidly : DASH **3 a** : to dart off or away : FLEE **b** : to break away from control or a set course **4** : to break away from or oppose one's previous affiliation (as with a political party or candidate) **5** : to produce seed prematurely ~ *vt* **1 a** *archaic* : SHOOT, DISCHARGE **b** : FLUSH, START ⟨~ rabbits⟩ **2** : to say impulsively : BLURT **3** : to secure with a bolt **4** : to attach or fasten with bolts **5** : to swallow hastily or without chewing **6** : to break away from or refuse to support (as a political party)

³bolt *adv* (14c) **1** : in an erect or straight-backed position : RIGIDLY ⟨sat ~ upright⟩ **2** *archaic* : DIRECTLY, STRAIGHT

⁴bolt *n* (1550) : the act or an instance of bolting

⁵bolt *vt* [ME *bulten*, fr. OF *buleter*, modif. of MHG *biuteln* to sift, fr. *biutel* bag, fr. OHG *būtil*] (13c) **1** : to sift (as flour) usu. through fine-meshed cloth **2** *archaic* : SIFT 2

bolt–ac·tion \'bōlt-,ak-shən\ *adj* (1896) *of a firearm* : loaded by means of a manually operated bolt

bolt·er \'bōl-tər\ *n* (ca. 1699) : one that bolts: as **a** : a horse given to running away **b** : a voter who bolts from a political party

bolt–hole \'bōlt-,hōl\ *n* (ca. 1851) *chiefly Brit* : a place of escape or refuge

bolt·rope \'bōlt-,rōp\ *n* (ca. 1626) : a strong rope stitched to the edges of a sail to strengthen it

bo·lus \'bō-ləs\ *n* [LL, fr. Gk *bōlos* lump] (1562) : a rounded mass: as **a** : a large pill **b** : a soft mass of chewed food

¹bomb \'bäm\ *n* [F *bombe*, fr. It *bomba*, prob. fr. L *bombus* deep hollow sound, fr. Gk *bombos*, of imit. origin] (1684) **1 a** : an explosive device fused to detonate under specified conditions **b** : ATOMIC BOMB; *also* : nuclear weapons in general — usu. used with *the* **2** : a vessel for compressed gases: as **a** : a pressure vessel for conducting chemical experiments **b** : a container for an aerosol : SPRAY CAN **3** : a rounded mass of lava exploded from a volcano **4** : a lead-lined container for radioactive material **5** : FAILURE, FLOP ⟨the play was a ~⟩ **6** *Brit* : a large sum of money **7** *Brit* : a great success : HIT **8** : a long pass in football

²bomb *vt* (1688) **1** : to attack with or as if with bombs : BOMBARD **2** : to defeat decisively ~ *vi* **1** : to fall flat : FAIL **2** *slang* : to move rapidly ⟨~*ed* down the hill⟩ — **bomb·ing** *n*

¹bom·bard \'bäm-,bärd\ *n* [ME *bombarde*, fr. MF, prob. fr. L *bombus*] (15c) : a late medieval cannon used to hurl large stones

²bom·bard \bäm-'bärd *also* bəm-\ *vt* (1686) **1** : to attack esp. with

\ə\ abut \ᵊ\ kitten, F table \ər\ further \a\ ash \ā\ ace \ä\ mop, mar \au̇\ out \ch\ chin \e\ bet \ē\ easy \g\ go \i\ hit \ī\ ice \j\ job \ŋ\ sing \ō\ go \ȯ\ law \ȯi\ boy \th\ thin \t͟h\ the \ü\ loot \u̇\ foot \y\ yet \zh\ vision \à, k̲, ⁿ, œ, œ̄, ᵫ, u͞e, ū͞e, ᵜ\ see Guide to Pronunciation artillery or bombers **2 :** to assail vigorously or persistently (as with questions) **3 :** to subject to the impact of rapidly moving particles (as electrons) *syn* see ATTACK — **bom·bard·ment** \-mənt\ *n*

bom·bar·dier \ˌbäm-bə-ˈdir, -bər-\ *n* (1560) **1 a** *archaic :* ARTILLERY-MAN **b :** a noncommissioned officer in the British artillery **2 :** a bomber-crew member who releases the bombs

bom·bar·don \ˈbäm-bər-ˌdön, bäm-ˈbär-d²n\ *n* [F, fr. It *bombardone*] (1856) **1 :** a bass tuba **2 :** the bass member of the shawm family

bom·bast \ˈbäm-ˌbast\ *n* [ME *bombast* cotton padding, fr. MF *bombace*, fr. ML *bombac-, bombax* cotton, alter. of L *bombyc-, bombyx* silkworm, silk, fr. Gk *bombyc-, bombyx*] (1589) **:** pretentious inflated speech or writing

bom·bas·tic \bäm-ˈbas-tik\ *adj* (1704) **:** marked by or given to bombast **:** POMPOUS, OVERBLOWN — **bom·bas·ti·cal·ly** \-ti-k(ə-)lē\ *adv*

bom·ba·zine \ˌbäm-bə-ˈzēn\ *n* [MF *bombasin*, fr. ML *bombacinum, bombycinum* silken texture, fr. L, neut. of *bombycinus* of silk, fr. *bombyc-, bombyx*] (1572) **1 :** a twilled fabric with silk warp and worsted filling **2 :** a silk fabric in twill weave dyed black

bombe \ˈbäm, ˈböⁿ(m)b\ *n* [F, lit., bomb] (1892) **:** a frozen dessert usu. containing ice cream and formed in layers in a mold

bom·bé *or* **bom·be** \(ˌ)bäm-ˈbā, (ˌ)böⁿ-\ *adj* [F, fr. *bombe*] (1904) **:** having outward curving lines — usu. used of furniture

bombed \ˈbämd\ *adj* (1959) **:** affected by alcohol or drugs **:** DRUNK, HIGH

bomb·er \ˈbä-mər\ *n* (1915) **1 :** one that bombs; *specif :* an airplane designed for bombing **2 :** BOMBER JACKET

bomber jacket *n* (1952) **:** a zippered usu. leather jacket with front pockets and knitted cuffs and waistband

bom·bi·nate \ˈbäm-bə-ˌnāt\ *vi* **-nat·ed; -nat·ing** [NL *bombinatus*, pp. of *bombinare*, alter. of L *bombilare*, fr. *bombus*] (1880) **:** BUZZ, DRONE — **bom·bi·na·tion** \ˌbäm-bə-ˈnā-shən\ *n*

bomb·proof \ˈbäm-ˈprüf\ *adj* (1702) **:** safe from the force of bombs

bomb·shell \ˈbäm-ˌshel\ *n* (1708) **1 :** BOMB 1a **2 :** one that is stunning, amazing, or devastating ⟨the book was a political ∼⟩

bomb·sight \-ˌsīt\ *n* (1917) **:** a sighting device for aiming bombs

bo·na fide \ˈbō-nə-ˌfīd, ˈbä-; ˌbō-nə-ˈfī-dē, -ˈfī-də\ *adj* [L, lit., in good faith] (1788) **1 :** made in good faith without fraud or deceit ⟨a *bona fide* offer to buy a farm⟩ **2 :** made with earnest intent **:** SINCERE **3 :** neither specious nor counterfeit **:** GENUINE *syn* see AUTHENTIC

bo·na fi·des \ˌbō-nə-ˈfī-ˌdēz, ÷ˈbō-nə-ˌfīdz\ *n* [L, lit., good faith] (1798) **1 :** good faith **:** SINCERITY **2 :** the fact of being genuine — often pl. in constr. **3 :** evidence of one's good faith or genuineness — often pl. in constr. **4 :** evidence of one's qualifications or achievements — often pl. in constr.

bo·nan·za \bə-ˈnan-zə\ *n* [Sp, lit., calm sea, fr. ML *bonacia*, alter. of L *malacia*, fr. Gk *malakia*, lit., softness, fr. *malakos* soft] (1844) **1 :** an exceptionally large and rich mineral deposit (as of an ore, precious metal, or petroleum) **2 a :** something that is very valuable, profitable, or rewarding ⟨a box-office ∼⟩ **b :** an extremely large amount ⟨expected a ∼ of sympathy⟩

Bo·na·part·ism \ˈbō-nə-ˌpär-ˌti-zəm\ *n* (1815) **1 :** support of the French emperors Napoleon I, Napoleon III, or their dynasty **2 :** a political movement associated chiefly with authoritarian rule usu. by a military leader ostensibly supported by a popular mandate — **Bo·na·part·ist** \-ˌpär-tist\ *n or adj*

bon·bon \ˈbän-ˌbän\ *n* [F, redupl. of *bon* good, fr. L *bonus* — more at BOUNTY] (1796) **:** a candy with chocolate or fondant coating and fondant center that sometimes contains fruits and nuts

¹bond \ˈbänd\ *n* [ME *band, bond* — more at BAND] (12c) **1 :** something that binds or restrains **:** FETTER **2 :** a binding agreement **:** COVENANT **3 a :** a band or cord used to tie something **b :** a material or device for binding **c :** an attractive force that holds together the atoms, ions, or groups of atoms in a molecule or crystal **d :** an adhesive, cementing material, or fusible ingredient that combines, unites, or strengthens **4 :** a uniting or binding force or element **:** TIE ⟨the ∼s of friendship⟩ **5 a :** an obligation made binding by a money forfeit; *also* **:** the amount of the money guarantee **b :** one who acts as bail or surety **c :** an interest-bearing certificate of public or private indebtedness **d :** an insurance agreement pledging surety for financial loss caused to another by the act or default of a third person or by some contingency over which the third person may have no control **6 :** the systematic lapping of brick in a wall **7 :** the state of goods made, stored, or transported under the care of bonded agencies until the duties or taxes on them are paid **8 :** a 100-proof straight whiskey aged at least four years under government supervision before being bottled — called also *bonded whiskey* **9 :** BOND PAPER

²bond *vt* (1677) **1 :** to lap (as brick) for solidity of construction **2 a :** to secure payment of duties and taxes on (goods) by giving a bond **b :** to convert into a debt secured by bonds **c :** to provide a bond for or cause to provide such a bond ⟨∼ an employee⟩ **3 a :** to cause to adhere firmly **b :** to embed in a matrix **c :** to hold together in a molecule or crystal by chemical bonds ∼ *vi* **:** to hold together or solidify by or as if by means of a bond or binder **:** COHERE — **bond·able** \ˈbän-də-bəl\ *adj* — **bond·er** *n*

³bond *adj* [ME *bonde*, fr. *bonde* peasant, serf, fr. OE *bonda* householder, fr. ON *bōndi*] (14c) *archaic :* bound in slavery

bond·age \ˈbän-dij\ *n* (14c) **1 :** the tenure or service of a villein, serf, or slave **2 :** a state of being bound usu. by compulsion (as of law or mastery): as **a :** CAPTIVITY, SERFDOM **b :** servitude or subjugation to a controlling person or force ⟨young people in ∼ to drugs⟩

bond·ed \ˈbän-dəd\ *adj* (1945) **:** composed of two or more layers of the same or different fabrics held together by an adhesive ⟨∼ jersey⟩

bond·hold·er \ˈbänd-ˌhōl-dər\ *n* (1823) **:** one that holds a government or corporation bond

bond·ing *n* (1976) **1 :** the formation of a close personal relationship (as between a mother and child) esp. through frequent or constant association **2 :** the attaching of a material (as porcelain) to a tooth surface esp. for cosmetic purposes

bond·maid \ˈbän(d)-ˌmād\ *n* (1526) *archaic :* a female bond servant

bond·man \ˈbän(d)-mən\ *n* (13c) **:** SLAVE, SERF

bond paper *n* (ca. 1877) **:** a durable paper orig. used for documents

bond servant *n* (15c) **:** one bound to service without wages; *also* **:** SLAVE

¹bonds·man \ˈbän(d)z-mən\ *n* (1713) **:** one who assumes the responsibility of a bond **:** SURETY

²bondsman *n* (1735) **:** BONDMAN

bond·stone \ˈbän(d)-ˌstōn\ *n* (ca. 1845) **:** a stone long enough to extend through the full thickness of a wall to bind it together

bond·wom·an \ˈbän(d)-ˌdwů-mən\ *n* (14c) **:** a female slave

¹bone \ˈbōn\ *n, often attrib* [ME *bon*, fr. OE *bān*; akin to OHG & ON *bein* bone, and perh. to OIr *benaid* he hews] (bef. 12c) **1 a :** one of the hard parts of the skeleton of a vertebrate **b :** any of various hard animal substances or structures (as baleen or ivory) akin to or resembling bone **c :** the hard largely calcareous connective tissue of which the adult skeleton of most vertebrates is chiefly composed **2 a :** ESSENCE, CORE ⟨cut costs to the ∼⟩ ⟨a liberal to the ∼⟩ **b :** the most deeply ingrained part **:** HEART — usu. used in pl. ⟨knew in his ∼s that it was wrong⟩ **3 pl a** (1) **:** SKELETON (2) **:** BODY ⟨rested my weary ∼s⟩ (3) **:** CORPSE ⟨inter a person's ∼s⟩ **b :** the basic design or framework (as of a play or novel) **4 :** MATTER, SUBJECT ⟨a ∼ of contention⟩ **5 a** *pl* **:** thin bars of bone, ivory, or wood held in pairs between the fingers and used to produce musical rhythms **b :** a strip of whalebone or steel used to stiffen a corset or dress **c** *pl* **:** DICE **6 :** something that is designed to placate **:** SOP **7 :** a light beige — **boned** \ˈbōnd\ *adj* — **bone·less** \ˈbōn-ləs\ *adj* — **bone to pick :** a matter to argue or complain about

²bone *vb* **boned; bon·ing** *vt* (15c) **1 :** to remove the bones from ⟨∼ a fish⟩ **2 :** to provide (a garment) with stays ∼ *vi* **:** to study hard **:** GRIND ⟨∼ through medical school⟩

³bone *adv* (ca. 1825) **:** EXTREMELY, VERY ⟨∼ tired⟩; *also :* TOTALLY

bone ash *n* (1622) **:** the white porous residue chiefly of tribasic calcium phosphate from bones calcined in air used esp. in making pottery and glass and in cleaning jewelry

bone black *n* (1815) **:** the black residue chiefly of tribasic calcium phosphate and carbon from bones calcined in closed vessels used esp. as a pigment or as a decolorizing adsorbent in sugar manufacturing — called also *bone char*

bone china *n* (ca. 1895) **:** translucent white china made with bone ash or calcium phosphate and characterized by whiteness

bone-dry \ˈbōn-ˈdrī\ *adj* (ca. 1825) **1 :** very dry **2 :** DRY 5

bone·fish \ˈbōn-ˌfish\ *n* (1884) **1 :** a slender silvery small-scaled fish (*Albula vulpes*) that is a notable sport and food fish of warm seas **2 :** LADYFISH 2 — **bone·fish·ing** *n*

¹bone·head \-ˌhed\ *n* (1909) **:** a stupid person **:** NUMSKULL — **bone·head·ed** \-ˈhe-dəd\ *adj* — **bone·head·ed·ness** *n*

²bonehead *adj* (1915) **:** being a college course for students lacking fundamental skills ⟨teaches ∼ English⟩

bone-meal \ˈbōn-ˌmē(ə)l\ *n* (1850) **:** crushed or ground bone used esp. as fertilizer or feed

bon·er \ˈbō-nər\ *n* (ca. 1899) **1 :** one that bones **2 :** HOWLER 2

bone·set \ˈbōn-ˌset\ *n* (1764) **:** any of several composite herbs (genus *Eupatorium*); *esp :* a perennial (*E. perfoliatum*) with opposite perfoliate leaves and white-rayed flower heads used in folk medicine

bone·set·ter \-ˌse-tər\ *n* (15c) **:** a person who sets broken or dislocated bones usu. without being a licensed physician

bone up *vi* (1887) **1 :** to try to master necessary information quickly **:** CRAM ⟨*bone up* for the exam⟩ **2 :** to renew one's skill or refresh one's memory ⟨*boned up* on the speech just before giving it⟩

bone·yard \-ˌyärd\ *n* (1866) **1 :** CEMETERY **2 :** a place where worn-out or damaged objects (as cars) are collected to await disposal

bon·fire \ˈbän-ˌfīr\ *n* [ME *bonefire* a fire of bones, fr. *bon* bone + *fire*] (15c) **:** a large fire built in the open air

¹bong \ˈbäŋ, ˈbóŋ\ *n* [imit.] (1860) **:** the deep resonant sound esp. of a bell — **bong** *vb*

²bong *n* [Thai *bhaung³*] (1971) **:** a simple water pipe consisting of a bottle or vertical tube partially filled with a liquid (as water or liqueur) and a smaller offset tube ending in a bowl

¹bon·go \ˈbäŋ-(ˌ)gō, ˈbóŋ-\ *n, pl* **bongos** *also* **bongoes** [AmerSp *bongó*] (1920) **:** one of a pair of small connected drums of different sizes and pitches played with the hands — **bon·go·ist** \-ˌgō-ist\ *n*

²bongo *n, pl* **bongo** *or* **bongos** [prob. fr. Kele (Bantu language of Gabon)] (1861) **:** an African antelope (*Tragelaphus euryceros* syn. *Boocerus euryceros*) that is chestnut-red with narrow white vertical stripes and is found in forests from Sierra Leone to Kenya

bon·ho·mie \ˌbä-nə-ˈmē, ˌbō-\ *n* [F *bonhomie*, fr. *bonhomme* good-natured man, fr. *bon* good + *homme* man] (1779) **:** good-natured easy friendliness — **bon·ho·mous** \ˈbä-nə-məs\ *adj*

bon·i·face \ˈbä-nə-ˌfäs\ *n* [*Boniface*, innkeeper in *The Beaux' Stratagem* (1707) by George Farquhar] (1803) **:** the proprietor of a hotel, nightclub, or restaurant

bo·ni·to \bə-ˈnē-(ˌ)tō, -ˈnē-tə\ *n, pl* **-tos** *or* **-to** [Sp, fr. *bonito* pretty, dim. of *bueno* good, fr. L *bonus*] (ca. 1565) **:** any of several scombroid fishes (esp. genera *Sarda* and *Euthynnus*) intermediate between the smaller mackerels and the larger tunas

bon·kers \ˈbäŋ-kərz, ˈbóŋ-\ *adj* [perh. fr. *bonk* to hit, bang + *-ers* (as in *crackers*)] (ca. 1948) **:** CRAZY, MAD ⟨if I don't work, I go ∼ —Zoe Caldwell⟩

bon mot \bōⁿ-ˈmō\ *n, pl* **bons mots** \bōⁿ-ˈmō(z)\ *or* **bon mots** \-ˈmō(z)\ [F, lit., good word] (ca. 1730) **:** a clever remark **:** WITTICISM

bonne \ˈbón\ *n* [F, fr. fem. of *bon*] (1771) **:** a French nursemaid or maidservant

¹bon·net \ˈbä-nət\ *n* [ME *bonet*, fr. MF, prob. of Gmc origin; akin to OS *gibund* bundle, OE *bindan* to bind] (14c) **1 a** (1) *chiefly Scot :* a man's or boy's cap (2) **:** a brimless Scotch cap of seamless woolen fabric — compare TAM-O'-SHANTER **2 b :** a cloth or straw hat tied under the chin and worn by women and children **2 a** *Brit :* an automobile hood **b :** a metal covering or cowl (as for a fireplace, valve chamber, or ventilator)

²bonnet *vt* (1858) **:** to provide with or dress in a bonnet

bon·ny *also* **bon·nie** \ˈbä-nē\ *adj* **bon·ni·er; -est** [ME *bonie*, fr. MF *bon* good, fr. L *bonus*] (15c) *chiefly Brit :* ATTRACTIVE, FAIR; *also :* FINE, EXCELLENT — **bon·ni·ly** \ˈbä-nə-lē\ *adv*

bon·ny·clab·ber \ˈbä-nē-ˌkla-bər\ *n* [Ir *bainne clabair*, fr. *bainne* milk + *clabair*, gen. of *clabar* sour thick milk] (1616) *Northern & Midland :* CLABBER

bon·sai \(ˌ)bōn-ˈsī, ˈbōn-, ˈbän-, *also* ˈbän-ˌzī\ *n, pl* **bonsai** [Jp, lit., tray planting] (1900) **:** a potted plant (as a tree) dwarfed and trained to an

artistic shape by special methods of culture; *also* : the art of growing such a plant
bon·spiel \'bän-,spēl\ *n* [perh. fr. D *bond* league + *spel* game] (ca. 1772) : a match or tournament between curling clubs
bon ton \(,)bän-'tän, bän-,\ *n* [F, lit., good tone] (1747) 1 **a** : fashionable manner or style **b** : the fashionable or proper thing **2** : high society
bo·nus \'bō-nəs\ *n* [L, lit., good — more at BOUNTY] (1773) : something in addition to what is expected or strictly due: as **a** : money or an equivalent given in addition to an employee's usual compensation **b** : a premium (as of stock) given by a corporation to a purchaser of its securities, to a promoter, or to an employee **c** : a government payment to war veterans **d** : a sum in excess of salary given an athlete for signing with a team
bon vi·vant \,bän-vē-'vänt, ,bōⁿ-vē-'väⁿ\ *n, pl* **bons vivants** \,bän-vē-'vän(t)s, ,bōⁿ-vē-'väⁿ(z)\ *or* **bon vivants** *same*\ [F, lit., good liver] (ca. 1695) : a person having cultivated, refined, and sociable tastes esp. in respect to food and drink
bon voy·age \,bōⁿ-,vói-'äzh, ,bän-, ,bōⁿ-,vwí-'äzh, ,vwä-'yäzh\ *n* [F, lit., good journey!] (15c) : FAREWELL — often used interjectionally
bony *also* **bon·ey** \'bō-nē\ *adj* **bon·i·er; -est** (14c) **1 a** : consisting of bone **b** : resembling bone **2 a** : full of bones ⟨a ~ piece of fish⟩ **b** : having prominent bones ⟨a rugged ~ face⟩ **3 a** : SKINNY, SCRAWNY **b** : BARREN, LEAN
bony fish *n* (ca. 1890) : any of a major taxon (class Osteichthyes or superclass Teleostomi) comprising fishes (as a sturgeon, salmon, marlin, or ocean sunfish) with a bony rather than a cartilaginous skeleton — called also *teleost;* compare CARTILAGINOUS FISH, JAWLESS FISH
bonze \'bänz\ *n* [MF, fr. Pg *bonzo*, fr. Jp *bonsō*] (1588) : a Buddhist monk
¹boo \'bü\ *interj* [ME *bo*] (15c) — used to express contempt or disapproval or to startle or frighten
²boo *n, pl* **boos** (1575) **1** : a shout of disapproval or contempt **2** : any sound at all — usu. used in negative constructions ⟨never said ~⟩
³boo *vi* (1884) : to deride esp. by uttering boo ~ *vt* : to express disapproval of by booing ⟨the crowd ~ed the referee⟩
⁴boo *n* [origin unknown] (ca. 1959) : MARIJUANA
¹boob \'büb\ *n* [short for ¹*booby*] (1909) **1** : a stupid awkward person **2** : SIMPLETON **2** : BOOR, PHILISTINE — **boob·ish** \'bü-bish\ *adj*
²boob *n* [³*boob*] (1934) *Brit* : MISTAKE, BLUNDER
³boob *vi* [¹*boob*] (1935) *Brit* : GOOF 2
⁴boob *n* [short for ²*booby*] (1945) : BREAST — sometimes considered vulgar
boob·oi·sie \,büb-,wä-'zē\ *n* [blend of ¹*boob* and *bourgeoisie*] (1922) : the general public regarded as consisting of boobs
boo–boo \'bü-(,)bü\ *n, pl* **boo–boos** [prob. baby-talk alter. of *boohoo*, imitation of the sound of weeping] (1953) **1** : a usu. trivial injury (as a bruise or scratch) — used esp. by or of a child **2** : MISTAKE, BLUNDER
boob tube *n* (1966) : TELEVISION — used with *the*
¹boo·by \'bü-bē\ *n, pl* **boobies** [modif. of Sp *bobo*, fr. L *balbus* stammering, prob. of imit. origin] (ca. 1603) **1** : an awkward foolish person : DOPE **2** : any of several tropical seabirds (family Sulidae, esp. genus *Sula*)
²boo·by \'bü-bē, 'bü-\ *n, pl* **boobies** [alter. of *bubby*] (1934) : BREAST — sometimes considered vulgar
booby hatch *n* (1840) **1** : a raised framework with a sliding cover over a small hatch on a ship **2** : an insane asylum
booby prize *n* (1889) **1** : an award for the poorest performance in a game or competition **2** : an acknowledgment of notable inferiority
booby trap *n* (1850) **1** : a trap for the unwary or unsuspecting : PITFALL **2** : a concealed explosive device contrived to go off when some harmless-looking object is touched — **boo·by–trap** *vt*
boo·dle \'bü-d³l\ *n* [D *boedel* estate, lot, fr. MD; akin to ON *būth* booth] (1833) **1** : a collection or lot of persons : CABOODLE **2 a** : bribe money **b** : a large amount esp. of money
boog·er \'bu̇-gər, 'bü-\ *n* [alter. of E dial. *buggard*, *boggart*, fr. ¹*bug* + *-ard*] (1866) **1** : BOGEYMAN **2** : a piece of dried nasal mucus
boo·gey·man \'bu̇-gē-,man, 'bü-\ *also* **boog·er·man** \'bu̇-gər-, 'bü-\ [by alter.] (ca. 1890) : BOGEYMAN
¹boo·gie \'bu̇-gē, 'bü-\ *n* (1929) **1** : BOOGIE-WOOGIE **2** : earthy and strongly rhythmic rock music conducive to dancing; *also* : a period of or occasion for dancing to this music
²boogie *also* **boo·gy** *or* **boo·gey** \'bu̇-gē, 'bü-\ *vi* **boo·gied** *also* **boo·geyed; boo·gy·ing** *also* **boo·gey·ing** (1930) **1** : to dance to rock music; *also* : REVEL, PARTY **2 a** : to move quickly **b** : to get going
boo·gie–woo·gie \,bu̇-gē-'wu̇-gē, ,bü-gē-'wü-gē\ *n* [origin unknown] (1928) : a percussive style of playing blues on the piano characterized by a steady rhythmic ground bass of eighth notes in quadruple time and a series of improvised melodic variations
¹book \'bu̇k\ *n* [ME, fr. OE *bōc;* akin to OHG *buoh* book, Goth *boka* letter] (bef. 12c) **1 a** : a set of written sheets of skin or paper or tablets of wood or ivory **b** : a set of written, printed, or blank sheets bound together into a volume **c** : a long written or printed literary composition **d** : a major division of a treatise or literary work **e** : a record of a business's financial transactions or financial condition — often used in pl. ⟨the ~s show a profit⟩ **2** *cap* : BIBLE 1 **3** : something that yields knowledge or understanding ⟨the great ~ of nature⟩ ⟨her face was an open ~⟩ **4 a** : the total available knowledge and experience that can be brought to bear on a task or problem ⟨tried every trick in the ~⟩ ⟨the ~ on him is that he can't hit a curveball⟩ **b** : the standards or authority relevant in a situation ⟨run by the ~⟩ **5 a** : all the charges that can be made against an accused person ⟨threw the ~ at him⟩ **b** : a position from which one must answer for certain acts : ACCOUNT ⟨bring criminals to ~⟩ **6 a** : LIBRETTO **b** : the script of a play **c** : a book of arrangements for a musician or dance orchestra : musical repertory **7** : a packet of items bound together like a book ⟨a ~ of stamps⟩ ⟨a ~ of matches⟩ **8 a** : BOOKMAKER **b** : the bets registered by a bookmaker; *also* : the business or activity of giving odds and tak-

bonsai

ing bets **9** : the number of tricks a cardplayer or side must win before any trick can have scoring value — **book·ful** \'bu̇k-,fu̇l\ *n* — **in one's book** : in one's own opinion — **in one's good books** : in favor with one — **one for the book** : an act or occurrence worth noting — **on the books** : on the records
²book *adj* (13c) **1** : derived from books and not from practical experience ⟨~ learning⟩ **2** : shown by books of account ⟨~ assets⟩
³book *vt* (1807) **1 a** : to register (as a name) for some future activity or condition (as to engage transportation or reserve lodgings) ⟨~ed to sail on Monday⟩ **b** : to schedule engagements for ⟨~ the band for a week⟩ **c** : to set aside time for **d** : to reserve in advance ⟨~ two seats at the theater⟩ ⟨were all ~ed up⟩ **2 a** : to enter charges against in a police register **b** *chiefly Brit* : to charge (as a soccer player) with an infraction of the rules ~ *vi* **1** : to make a reservation ⟨~ through your travel agent⟩ **2** *chiefly Brit* : to register in a hotel — usu. used with *in* — **book·able** \'bu̇-kə-bəl\ *adj, chiefly Brit* — **book·er** *n*
book·bind·ing \'bu̇k-,bīn-diŋ\ *n* (1771) **1** : the art or trade of binding books **2** : the binding of a book — **book·bind·er** \-,bīn-dər\ *n* — **book·bind·ery** \-d(ə-)rē\ *n*
book·case \-,kās\ *n* (1726) : a piece of furniture consisting of shelves to hold books
book club *n* (1905) : an organization that ships selected books to members usu. on a regular schedule and often at discount prices
book·end \-,end\ *n* (1907) : a support placed at the end of a row of books
book·ie \'bu̇-kē\ *n* [by shortening & alter.] (1885) : BOOKMAKER 2
book·ing \'bu̇-kiŋ\ *n* (1881) **1** : the act of one that books **2** : an engagement or scheduled performance **3** : RESERVATION 1c
booking office *n* (ca. 1837) *chiefly Brit* : a ticket office; *esp* : one in a railroad station
book·ish \'bu̇-kish\ *adj* (1567) **1 a** : of or relating to books **b** : fond of books and reading **2 a** : inclined to rely on book knowledge **b** *of words* : literary and formal as opposed to colloquial and informal **c** : given to literary or scholarly pursuits; *also* : affectedly learned — **book·ish·ly** *adv* — **book·ish·ness** *n*
book·keep·er \'bu̇k-,kē-pər\ *n* (1555) : one who records the accounts or transactions of a business — **book·keep·ing** \-piŋ\ *n*
book·let \'bu̇k-lət\ *n* (1859) : a little book; *esp* : PAMPHLET
book louse *n* (1867) : any of various tiny usu. wingless insects (order Psocoptera) that feed on organic matter; *esp* : an insect (as *Liposcelis divinatorius*) injurious esp. to books
book lung *n* (1879) : a saccular breathing organ in many arachnids containing thin folds of membrane arranged like the leaves of a book
book·mak·er \'bu̇k-,mā-kər\ *n* (1515) **1** : a printer, binder, or designer of books **2** : one who determines odds and receives and pays off bets — **book·mak·ing** \-kiŋ\ *n*
book·man \-mən\ *n* (1583) **1** : one who has a love of books and esp. of reading **2** : one who is involved in the writing, publishing, or selling of books
book·mark \-,märk\ *or* **book·mark·er** \-,mär-kər\ *n* (1838) : a marker for finding a place in a book
book–match \-(,)mach\ *vt* (1942) : to match the grains of (as two sheets of veneer) so that one sheet seems to be the mirrored image of the other
book·mo·bile \'bu̇k-mō-,bēl\ *n* (1926) : a truck that serves as a traveling library
Book of Common Prayer (1549) : the service book of the Anglican Communion
book off *vi* (1971) *Canad* : to notify an employer that one is not reporting for work (as because of sickness)
book·plate \'bu̇k-,plāt\ *n* (1791) : a book owner's identification label that is usu. pasted to the inside front cover of a book
book·sell·er \'bu̇k-,se-lər\ *n* (15c) : one who sells books; *esp* : the proprietor of a bookstore — **book·sell·ing** \-,se-liŋ\ *n*
book·shelf \-,shelf\ *n* (1611) : an open shelf for holding books
book·shop \-,shäp\ *n* (1862) : BOOKSTORE
book·stall \-,stól\ *n* (1800) **1** : a stall where books are sold **2** *chiefly Brit* : NEWSSTAND
book·store \-,stór, -,stȯr\ *n* (ca. 1763) : a place of business where books are the main item offered for sale — called also *bookshop*
book value *n* (1899) : the value of something as shown on bookkeeping records as distinguished from market value: **a** : the value of an asset equal to cost less depreciation **b** : the value of a corporation's capital stock equal to its book value less its liabilities
book·worm \'bu̇k-,wərm\ *n* (1592) : a person unusually devoted to reading and study
Bool·ean \'bü-lē-ən\ *adj* [George Boole †1864 Eng. mathematician] (1851) : of, relating to, or being a logical combinatorial system (as Boolean algebra) that represents symbolically relationships (as those implied by the logical operators AND, OR, and NOT) between entities (as sets, propositions, or on-off computer circuit elements) ⟨~ expression⟩ ⟨~ search strategy for information retrieval⟩
Boolean algebra *n* (1889) : a set that is closed under two commutative binary operations and that can be described by any of various systems of postulates all of which can be deduced from the postulates that an identity element exists for each operation, that each operation is distributive over the other, and that for every element in the set there is another element which when combined with the first under one of the operations yields the identity element of the other operation
¹boom \'büm\ *vb* [imit.] (15c) *vi* **1** : to make a deep hollow sound **2 a** : to increase in importance or esteem **b** : to experience a sudden rapid growth and expansion usu. with an increase in prices ⟨business was ~ing⟩ **c** : to develop rapidly in population and importance ⟨California ~ed when gold was discovered there⟩ ~ *vt* **1** : to cause to resound — often used with *out* ⟨his voice ~s out the lyrics⟩ **2** : to cause a rapid growth or increase of : BOOST
²boom *n* (ca. 1500) **1** : a booming sound or cry **2** : a rapid expansion or increase: as **a** : a general movement in support of a candidate for

\ə\ abut \ᵊ\ kitten, F table \ər\ further \a\ ash \ā\ ace \ä\ mop, mar \au̇\ out \ch\ chin \e\ bet \ē\ easy \g\ go \i\ hit \ī\ ice \j\ job \ŋ\ sing \ō\ go \ȯ\ law \ȯi\ boy \th\ thin \t̷h\ the \ü\ loot \u̇\ foot \y\ yet \zh\ vision \á, k̲, ⁿ, œ, œ̄, ɷ, ɷ̄, ᵜ\ see Guide to Pronunciation office   **b** : rapid settlement and development of a town or district   **c** : a rapid widespread expansion of economic activity

³**boom** *n* [D, tree, beam; akin to OHG *boum* tree — more at BEAM] (1627)   **1 a** : a long spar used to extend the foot of a sail   **2 a** : a chain cable or line of connected floating timbers extended across a river, lake, or harbor (as to obstruct passage or catch floating objects)   **b** : a temporary floating barrier to contain an oil spill   **3 a** : a long beam projecting from the mast of a derrick to support or guide cargo   **b** : a long more or less horizontal supporting arm or brace (as for holding a microphone or for supporting an antenna)   **4** : a spar or outrigger connecting the tail surfaces and the main supporting structure of an aircraft

boom box *n* (1981) : a large portable radio and often tape player with two attached speakers

boom·er *n* (1880)   **1** : one that booms   **2** : one that joins a rush of settlers to a boom area   **3** : a transient worker (as a bridge builder)

boo·mer·ang \'bü-mə-ˌraŋ\ *n* [Dharuk (Australian aboriginal language of the Port Jackson area) *bumariñ*] (1825)   **1** : a bent or angular throwing club typically flat on one side and rounded on the other so that it soars or curves in flight; *esp* : one designed to return near the thrower   **2** : an act or utterance that backfires on its originator — **boomerang** *vi*

boom·let \'büm-lət\ *n* (1880) : a small boom; *specif* : a sudden increase in business activity ⟨a stock market ~⟩

boom·town \'büm-ˌtaùn\ *n* (1896) : a town enjoying a business and population boom

boomy \'bü-mē\ *adj* **boom·i·er; -est** (1888)   **1** : of, relating to, or characterized by an economic boom   **2** : having an excessive accentuation on the tones of lower pitch in reproduced sound

¹**boon** \'bün\ *n* [ME, fr. ON *bōn* petition; akin to OE *bēn* prayer, *bannan* to summon — more at BAN] (12c)   **1** : BENEFIT, FAVOR; *esp* : one that is given in answer to a request   **2** : a timely benefit : BLESSING

²**boon** *adj* [ME *bon*, fr. MF, good — more at BONNY] (14c)   **1** *archaic* : FAVORABLE, CONVIVIAL ⟨a ~ companion⟩

boon·docks \'bün-ˌdäks\ *n pl* [Tag *bundok* mountain] (ca. 1909)   **1** : rough country filled with dense brush   **2** : a rural area : STICKS

boon·dog·gle \'bün-ˌdä-gəl, -ˌdȯ-\ *n* [coined by Robert H. Link †1957 Am. scoutmaster] (1929)   **1** : a braided cord worn by Boy Scouts as a neckerchief slide, hatband, or ornament   **2** : a wasteful or impractical project or activity often involving graft — **boondoggle** *vi* — **boon·dog·gler** \-g(ə-)lər\ *n*

boon·ies \'bü-nēz\ *n pl* (1956) *slang* : BOONDOCKS 2

boor \'bùr\ *n* [D *boer*; akin to OE *būan* to dwell — more at BOWER] (1551)   **1** : PEASANT   **2** : a rude or insensitive person

boor·ish \'bùr-ish\ *adj* (1562) : resembling or befitting a boor (as in crude insensitivity) — **boor·ish·ly** *adv* — **boor·ish·ness** *n*
syn BOORISH, CHURLISH, LOUTISH, CLOWNISH mean uncouth in manners or appearance. BOORISH implies rudeness of manner due to insensitiveness to others' feelings and unwillingness to be agreeable ⟨a drunk's *boorish* behavior⟩. CHURLISH suggests surliness, unresponsiveness, and ungraciousness ⟨*churlish* remarks⟩. LOUTISH implies bodily awkwardness together with stupidity ⟨a *loutish* oaf⟩. CLOWNISH suggests ill-bred awkwardness, ignorance or stupidity, ungainliness, and often a propensity for absurd antics ⟨an adolescent's *clownish* conduct⟩.

¹**boost** \'büst\ *vb* [origin unknown] *vt* (ca. 1815)   **1** : to push or shove up from below   **2** : INCREASE, RAISE ⟨plans to ~ production⟩ ⟨an extra holiday to ~ morale⟩   **3** : to promote the cause or interests of : PLUG ⟨a campaign to ~ the new fashions⟩   **4** : to raise the voltage of or across (an electric circuit)   **5** *slang* : STEAL, SHOPLIFT   ~ *vi*, *slang* : SHOPLIFT   **syn** see LIFT

²**boost** *n* (1825)   **1** : a push upward   **2** : an act that brings help or encouragement : ASSIST   **3** : an increase in amount

boost·er \'bü-stər\ *n* (1890) : one that boosts: as   **a** : an enthusiastic supporter   **b** : an auxiliary device for increasing force, power, pressure, or effectiveness   **c** *slang* : SHOPLIFTER   **d** : a radio-frequency amplifier for a radio or television receiving set   **e** : the first stage of a multistage rocket providing thrust for the launching and the initial part of the flight   **f** : a substance that increases the effectiveness of a medicament; *esp* : BOOSTER SHOT

boost·er·ism \-stə-ˌri-zəm\ *n* (ca. 1913) : the activities and attitudes characteristic of boosters

booster shot *n* (1944) : a supplementary dose of an immunizing agent — called also **booster, booster dose**

¹**boot** \'büt\ *n* [ME, fr. OE *bōt* remedy; akin to OE *betera* better] (bef. 12c)   **1** *archaic* : DELIVERANCE   **2** *chiefly dial* : something to equalize a trade   **3** *obs* : AVAIL — **to boot** : BESIDES

²**boot** *vb* (15c) *archaic* : AVAIL, PROFIT

³**boot** *n* [ME, fr. MF *bote*] (14c)   **1** : a fitted covering (as of leather or rubber) for the foot and usu. reaching above the ankle   **2** : an instrument of torture used to crush the leg and foot   **3** : something that resembles or is likened to a boot; *esp* : an enclosing or protective casing or sheath (as for a rifle or over an electrical or mechanical connection)   **4** : a navy or marine corps recruit undergoing basic training   **5** *Brit* : an automobile trunk   **6 a** : a kick with the foot   **b** : summary dismissal — used with *the*   **c** : momentary pleasure or enjoyment : BANG ⟨got a big ~ out of the joke⟩   **7** : a sheath enclosing the inflorescence

⁴**boot** *vt* (15c)   **1** : to put boots on   **2 a** : KICK   **b** : to eject or discharge summarily — often used with *out* ⟨was ~ed out of office⟩   **3** : to make an error on (a grounder in baseball); *broadly* : BOTCH   **4** : to ride (a horse) in a race ⟨~ed home three winners⟩   **5** [²bootstrap]   **a** : to load (a program) into a computer from a disk   **b** : to start or ready for use esp. by booting a program ⟨~ a microcomputer⟩ — often used with *up*   ~ *vi* : to become loaded into a computer's memory from a disk ⟨the program ~s automatically⟩ — **boot·able** \'bü-tə-bəl\ *adj*

⁵**boot** *n* [¹boot] (1593) *archaic* : BOOTY, PLUNDER

boot·black \'büt-ˌblak\ *n* (1817) : one who shines shoes

boot camp *n* (ca. 1942) : a navy or marine corps camp for basic training

boot·ed \'bü-təd\ *adj* (1552) : wearing boots

boo·tee *or* **boo·tie** \bü-'tē, *of infants' footwear* 'bü-tē\ *n* (1799) : a usu. ankle-length boot, slipper, or sock; *esp* : an infant's knitted or crocheted sock

Bo·ö·tes \bō-'ō-tēz\ *n* [L (gen. *Boötis*), fr. Gk *Boōtēs*, lit., plowman, fr. *bous* head of cattle — more at COW] : a northern constellation containing the bright star Arcturus

booth \'büth, *esp Brit* 'büth\ *n, pl* **booths** \'büthz, 'büths\ [ME *bothe*, of Scand origin; akin to ON *būth* booth; akin to OE *būan* to dwell — more at BOWER] (13c)   **1** : a temporary shelter for livestock or field workers   **2 a** : a stall or stand (as at a fair) for the sale or exhibition of goods   **b** (1) : a small enclosure affording privacy for one person at a time ⟨a telephone ~⟩ ⟨polling ~⟩   (2) : a small enclosure that isolates its occupant esp. from patrons or customers ⟨a ticket ~⟩   (3) : an isolated enclosure used in sound recording or in broadcasting ⟨a radio ~⟩   **c** : a restaurant seating arrangement consisting of a table between two high-back benches

boot·jack \'büt-ˌjak\ *n* (ca. 1841) : a device (as with a V-shaped notch) for pulling off boots

boot·lace \-ˌlās\ *n* (ca. 1887) *Brit* : SHOELACE

¹**boot·leg** \-ˌleg, -ˌläg\ *n* (1634)   **1** : the upper part of a boot   **2** : something bootlegged; *specif* : MOONSHINE   **3** : a football play in which the quarterback fakes a handoff, hides the ball against his hip, and rolls out — compare DRAW 8 — **bootleg** *adj*

²**bootleg** *vt* (1900)   **1 a** : to carry (alcoholic liquor) on one's person illegally   **b** : to manufacture, sell, or transport for sale (alcoholic liquor) illegally   **2 a** : to produce, reproduce, or distribute illicitly or without authorization   **b** : SMUGGLE   ~ *vi*   **1** : to engage in bootlegging   **2** : to run a bootleg play in football — **boot·leg·ger** *n*

bootjack

boot·less \'büt-ləs\ *adj* (1559) : USELESS, UNPROFITABLE — **boot·less·ly** *adv* — **boot·less·ness** *n*

boot·lick \-ˌlik\ *vt* (1845) : to try to gain favor with through a servile or obsequious manner   ~ *vi* : to act obsequiously — **boot·lick·er** *n*

boots \'büts\ *n pl but sing or pl in constr* [fr. pl. of ³*boot*] (ca. 1837) *Brit* : a servant who shines shoes esp. in a hotel

¹**boot·strap** \'büt-ˌstrap\ *n* (1913)   **1** *pl* : unaided efforts — often used in the phrase *by one's own bootstraps*   **2** : a looped strap sewed at the side or the rear top of a boot to help in pulling it on

²**bootstrap** *adj* (1926)   **1** : designed to function independently of outside direction : capable of using one internal function or process to control another ⟨a ~ operation to load a computer⟩   **2** : carried out with minimum resources or advantages : SELF-RELIANT ⟨the city recovered from the flood by the ~ method⟩

³**bootstrap** *vt* (1951) : to promote or develop by initiative and effort with little or no assistance ⟨*bootstrapped* herself to the top⟩

boo·ty \'bü-tē\ *n, pl* **booties** [modif. of MF *butin*, fr. MLG *būte* exchange] (15c)   **1** : plunder taken (as in war); *esp* : plunder taken on land as distinguished from prizes taken at sea   **2** : a rich gain or prize   **syn** see SPOIL

¹**booze** \'büz\ *vi* **boozed; booz·ing** [ME *bousen*, fr. MD *būsen*] (14c) : to drink intoxicating liquor esp. to excess — often used in the phrase *booze it up*

²**booze** *n* (14c)   **1** : intoxicating drink; *esp* : hard liquor — **booz·i·ly** \-zə-lē\ *adv* — **boozy** \-zē\ *adj*

booz·er \'bü-zər\ *n* (ca. 1819)   **1** : a person who boozes : DRUNK   **2** *Brit* : a drinking place : PUB

¹**bop** \'bäp\ *vb* **bopped; bop·ping** [imit.] (1931) : HIT, SOCK

²**bop** *n* (1947) : a blow (as with the fist or a club) that strikes a person

³**bop** *n* [short for *bebop*] (1947)   **1** : jazz characterized by harmonic complexity, convoluted melodic lines, and constant shifting of accent and often played at very rapid tempos   **2** : JIVE 2 — **bop·per** *n*

⁴**bop** *vi* **bopped; bop·ping** (1952)   **1** : to go quickly or unceremoniously : POP ⟨~ into the corner store⟩ — often used with *off*   **2** : to dance or shuffle along to or as if to bop music

bo·peep \(ˌ)bō-'pēp\ *n* [¹*boo* + ³*peep*] (1528) : PEEKABOO

bo·ra \'bȯr-ə, 'bȯr-\ *n* [It, fr. It dial. (Trieste), fr. L *boreas*] (1864) : a violent cold northerly wind of the Adriatic

bo·rac·ic acid \bə-'ras-ik-\ *n* [ML *borac-, borax* borax] (1801) : BORIC ACID

bor·age \'bȯr-ij, 'bär-\ *n* [ME, fr. OF *bourage*] (14c) : a coarse hairy blue-flowered European herb (*Borago officinalis* of the family Boraginaceae, the borage family) used medicinally and in salads

bo·rane \'bȯr-ˌān, 'bȯr-\ *n* [ISV, fr. *boron*] (1916)   **1** : a compound of boron and hydrogen; *specif* : a compound BH_3 known only in the form of its derivatives   **2** : a derivative of borane

bo·rate \-ˌāt\ *n* (1816) : a salt or ester of a boric acid

bo·rat·ed \-ˌā-təd\ *adj* (ca. 1901) : mixed or impregnated with borax or boric acid

¹**bo·rax** \'bȯr-ˌaks, 'bȯr-, -əks\ *n* [ME *boras*, fr. MF, fr. ML *borac-, borax*, fr. Ar *būraq*, fr. Per *būrah*] (14c) : a white crystalline compound that consists of a hydrated sodium borate $Na_2B_4O_7 \cdot 10H_2O$, that occurs as a mineral or is prepared from other minerals, and that is used esp. as a flux, cleansing agent, and water softener, as a preservative, and as a fireproofing agent

²**borax** *n* [origin unknown] (1932) : cheap shoddy merchandise

Bo·ra·zon \'bȯr-ə-ˌzän, 'bȯr-\ *trademark* — used for a boron nitride abrasive

bor·bo·ryg·mus \ˌbȯr-bə-'rig-məs\ *n, pl* **-mi** \-ˌmī\ [NL, fr. Gk *borborygmos*, fr. *borboryzein* to rumble] (ca. 1796) : intestinal rumbling caused by moving gas

Bor·deaux \bȯr-'dō\ *n, pl* **Bor·deaux** \-'dōz\ *often not cap* (ca. 1570)   **1** : white or red wine of the Bordeaux region of France   **2** : CLARET 2

bor·deaux mixture \bȯr-'dō-, 'bȯr-\ *n, often cap B* (1892) : a fungicide made by reaction of copper sulfate, lime, and water

bor·de·laise sauce \ˌbȯr-dᵊl-'āz-\ *n, often cap B* [F *bordelaise*, fem. of *bordelais* of Bordeaux] (1902) : a sauce consisting of stock thickened with roux and flavored typically with red wine and shallots

bor·del·lo \bȯr-'de-(ˌ)lō\ *n, pl* **-los** [It, fr. OF *bordel*, fr. *borde* hut, of Gmc origin; akin to OE *bord* board] (1593) : a building in which prostitutes are available

¹**bor·der** \'bȯr-dər\ *n* [ME *bordure*, fr. MF, fr. OF, fr. *border* to border, fr. *bort* border, of Gmc origin; akin to OE *bord*] (14c)   **1** : an outer part or edge   **2** : an ornamental design at the edge of a fabric or rug   **3**

: a narrow bed of planted ground along the edge of a garden or walk ⟨a ~ of tulips⟩ **4** : BOUNDARY ⟨crossed the ~ into Italy⟩ **5** : a plain or decorative margin around printed matter — **bor·dered** \-dərd\ *adj*

²**border** *vb* **bor·dered; bor·der·ing** \'bȯr-d(ə-)riŋ\ *vt* (14c) **1** : to put a border on **2** : to touch at the edge or boundary : BOUND ⟨~s the city on the south⟩ ~ *vi* **1** : to lie on the border ⟨the U.S. ~s on Canada⟩ **2** : to approach the nature of a specified thing : VERGE ⟨~s on the ridiculous⟩ — **bor·der·er** \-dər-ər\ *n*

Border collie *n* (1941) : any of a breed of medium-sized sheepdogs of British origin noted for their herding abilities

bor·de·reau \,bȯr-də-'rō\ *n, pl* **-reaux** \-'rō(z)\ [F, fr. MF *bordrel*, prob. fr. *bord* border, fr. OF *bort*] (ca. 1858) : a detailed note or memorandum of account; *esp* : one containing an enumeration of documents

bor·der·land \'bȯr-dər-,land\ *n* (1813) **1 a** : territory at or near a border **b** : FRINGE 3a ⟨lives on the ~ of society⟩ **2** : a vague intermediate state or region ⟨the ~ between fantasy and reality⟩

¹**bor·der·line** \-,līn\ *adj* (1907) **1** : being in an intermediate position or state : not fully classifiable as one thing or its opposite; *esp* : not quite up to what is usual, standard, or expected ⟨~ intelligence⟩ **2** : situated at or near a borderline — **borderline** *n*

²**borderline** *adv* (1925) : ALMOST, NEARLY ⟨~ tacky⟩ ⟨~ suicidal⟩

Border terrier *n* (1894) : any of a breed of small terriers of British origin having a harsh dense coat and close undercoat

bor·dure \'bȯr-jər\ *n* [ME] (14c) : a border on a heraldic shield

¹**bore** \'bȯr, 'bȯr\ *vb* **bored; bor·ing** [ME, fr. OE *borian;* akin to OHG *borōn* to bore, L *forare* to bore, *ferire* to strike] *vt* (bef. 12c) **1** : to pierce with a turning or twisting movement of a tool **2** : to make (as a cylindrical hole) by boring or digging away material ⟨*bored* a tunnel⟩ ~ *vi* **1 a** : to make a hole by or as if by boring **b** : to sink a mine shaft or well **2** : to make one's way steadily esp. against resistance ⟨we *bored* through the jostling crowd⟩

²**bore** *n* (14c) **1 a** : a usu. cylindrical hole made by or as if by boring **b** *chiefly Austral & NewZeal* : a borehole drilled esp. to make an artesian well **2 a** : the long usu. cylindrical hollow part of something (as a tube or gun barrel) **b** : the inner surface of a hollow cylindrical object **3** : the size of a bore: as **a** : the interior diameter of a gun barrel; *specif, chiefly Brit* : GAUGE 1a(2) **b** : the diameter of an engine cylinder

³**bore** *past of* BEAR

⁴**bore** *n* [(assumed) ME *bore* wave, fr. ON *bāra*] (1601) : a tidal flood with a high abrupt front

⁵**bore** *n* [origin unknown] (1766) : one that causes boredom: as **a** : a tiresome person **b** : something that is devoid of interest

⁶**bore** *vt* **bored; bor·ing** (1768) : to cause to feel boredom

bo·re·al \'bȯr-ē-əl, 'bȯr-\ *adj* [ME *boriall*, fr. LL *borealis*, fr. L *boreas* north wind, north, fr. Gk, fr. *Boreas*] (15c) **1** : of, relating to, or located in northern regions ⟨~ waters⟩ **2** : of, relating to, or comprising the northern biotic area characterized esp. by dominance of coniferous forests

Bo·re·as \-ē-əs\ *n* [L, fr. Gk] **1** : the Greek god of the north wind **2** : the north wind personified

bore·dom \'bȯr-dəm, 'bȯr-\ *n* (1852) : the state of being weary and restless through lack of interest

bo·reen \bȯr-'ēn, bȯr-\ *n* [Ir *bóthrín*, dim. of *bóthar* road] (1836) *Irish* : a narrow country lane

bore·hole \'bȯr-,hōl, 'bȯr-\ *n* (1708) : a hole bored or drilled in the earth: as **a** : an exploratory well **b** *chiefly Brit* : a small-diameter well drilled esp. to obtain water

bor·er \'bȯr-ər, 'bȯr-\ *n* (14c) **1** : a tool used for boring **2 a** : SHIPWORM **b** : an insect that bores in the woody parts of plants

bore·scope \'bȯr-,skōp, 'bȯr-\ *n* (1941) : an optical device (as a prism or optical fiber) used to inspect an inaccessible space (as an engine cylinder)

boric acid *n* [*boron*] (1869) : a white crystalline acid H_3BO_3 obtained from its salts and used esp. as a weak antiseptic and fire-retardant

bo·ride \'bȯr-,īd, 'bȯr-\ *n* (1863) : a binary compound of boron with a more electropositive element or radical

bor·ing \'bȯr-iŋ, 'bȯr-\ *adj* (1840) : causing boredom : TIRESOME — **bor·ing·ly** \-iŋ-lē\ *adv* — **bor·ing·ness** *n*

born \'bȯrn\ *adj* [ME, fr. OE *boren*, pp. of *beran* to carry — more at BEAR] (bef. 12c) **1 a** : brought forth by or as if by birth **b** : NATIVE — usu. used in combination ⟨American-*born*⟩ **c** : deriving or resulting from — usu. used in combination ⟨poverty-*born* crime⟩ **2 a** : having from birth specified qualities ⟨a ~ leader⟩ **b** : being in specified circumstances from birth ⟨nobly ~⟩ ⟨~ to wealth⟩ **3** : destined from or as if from birth ⟨~ to succeed⟩

born—again *adj* [fr. the verse "Except a man be *born again*, he cannot see the Kingdom of God" ⟨Jn 3:3–AV⟩] (1961) **1** : of, relating to, or being a usu. Christian person who has made a renewed or confirmed commitment of faith esp. after an intense religious experience **2** : having returned to or newly adopted an activity, a conviction, or a persona esp. with a proselytizing zeal ⟨a ~ conservative⟩

¹**borne** \'bȯrn, 'bȯrn\ *past part of* BEAR

²**borne** *adj* [*borne*] (ca. 1559) : transported or transmitted by — used in combination ⟨soil*borne*⟩ ⟨air*borne*⟩

bor·ne·ol \'bȯr-nē-,ȯl, -,ōl\ *n* [ISV, fr. *Borneo*, island of Indonesia] (1876) : a crystalline cyclic alcohol $C_{10}H_{17}OH$ that occurs in two enantiomeric forms, is found in essential oils, and is used esp. in perfumery

born·ite \'bȯr-,nīt\ *n* [G *Bornit*, fr. Ignaz von *Born* †1791 Austrian mineralogist] (ca. 1847) : a brittle metallic-looking mineral that consists of a sulfide of copper and iron and is a valuable copper ore

boro- *comb form* : boron ⟨*boro*silicate⟩

bo·ro·hy·dride \,bȯr-ō-'hī-,drīd, ,bȯr-\ *n* (1940) : the anion BH_4^- of boron and hydrogen that is used esp. as a reducing agent and as a source of hydrogen atoms; *also* : any of various compounds (as of metals) containing the borohydride anion

bo·ron \'bȯr-,än, 'bȯr-\ *n* [*borax* + *-on* (as in *carbon*)] (1812) : a trivalent metalloid element found in nature only in combination and used in metallurgy and in composite structural materials — see ELEMENT table — **bo·ron·ic** \bȯr-'ä-nik, bȯr-\ *adj*

boron carbide *n* (ca. 1909) : a refractory shiny black crystalline compound B_4C that is one of the hardest known materials and is used esp. in abrasives and as a structural reinforcing material

bo·ro·sil·i·cate \,bȯr-ō-'si-lə-,kāt, ,bȯr-, -'si-li-kət\ *n* [ISV] (1817) **1** : a silicate containing boron in the anion and occurring naturally **2** : BOROSILICATE GLASS

borosilicate glass *n* (1933) : a silicate glass that is composed of at least five percent oxide of boron and is used esp. in heat-resistant glassware

bor·ough \'bər-(,)ō, 'bə-(,)rō\ *n* [ME *burgh*, fr. OE *burg* fortified town; akin to OHG *burg* fortified place, and prob. to OE *beorg* hill — more at BARROW] (bef. 12c) **1 a** : a medieval fortified group of houses forming a town with special duties and privileges **b** : a town or urban constituency in Great Britain that sends a member to Parliament **c** : an urban area in Great Britain incorporated for purposes of self-government **2 a** : a municipal corporation proper in some states (as New Jersey and Minnesota) corresponding to the incorporated town or village of the other states **b** : one of the five constituent political divisions of New York City **3** : a civil division of the state of Alaska corresponding to a county in most other states

borough English *n* (14c) : a custom formerly existing in parts of England by which the lands of an intestate descended to the youngest son

borough hall *n* (1939) : the chief administrative building of a borough

bor·row \'bär-(,)ō, 'bȯr-\ *vb* [ME *borwen*, fr. OE *borgian;* akin to OE *beorgan* to preserve — more at BURY] *vt* (bef. 12c) **1 a** : to receive with the implied or expressed intention of returning the same or an equivalent ⟨~ a book⟩ ⟨~*ed* a dollar⟩ **b** : to borrow (money) with the intention of returning the same plus interest **2 a** : to appropriate for one's own use ⟨~ a metaphor⟩ **b** : DERIVE, ADOPT **3** : to take (one) from a digit of the minuend in arithmetical subtraction in order to add as 10 to the digit holding the next lower place **4** : to adopt into one language from another **5** *dial* : LEND ~ *vi* : to borrow something — **bor·row·er** \-ə-wər\ *n* — **borrow trouble** : to do something unnecessarily that may result in adverse reaction or repercussions

bor·rowed time *n* (1898) : an uncertain and usu. uncontrolled postponement of something inevitable — used with *living on*

bor·row·ing \'bär-ə-wiŋ, 'bȯr-\ *n* (ca. 1630) : something borrowed; *esp* : a word or phrase adopted from one language into another

borrow pit *n* (1893) : an excavated area where material has been dug for use as fill at another location

Bors \'bȯrz\ *n* [ME, fr. MF *Bohort*] : a knight of the Round Table and nephew of Lancelot

borscht *or* **borsch** \'bȯrsh(t)\ *n* [Yiddish *borsht* & Ukrainian & Russ *borshch*] (1829) : a soup made primarily of beets and served hot or cold often with sour cream

borscht belt *also* **borsch belt** *n* (1938) : BORSCHT CIRCUIT

borscht circuit *or* **borsch circuit** *n, often cap B&C* [fr. the popularity of borscht on menus of the resorts] (1938) : the theaters and nightclubs associated with the Jewish summer resorts in the Catskills

Bor·stal \'bȯr-st³l\ *n* [*Borstal*, Eng. village where the first such institution was set up] (1907) *Brit* : REFORMATORY

bort \'bȯrt\ *n* [prob. fr. D *boort*] (1622) : imperfectly crystallized diamond or diamond fragments used as an abrasive

bor·zoi \'bȯr-,zȯi\ *n* [Russ *borzoĭ*, fr. *borzoĭ* swift] (1887) : any of a breed of large long-haired dogs of greyhound type developed in Russia esp. for pursuing wolves — called also *Russian wolfhound*

bos·cage *also* **bosk·age** \'bäs-kij\ *n* [ME *boskage*, fr. MF *boscage*, fr. OF, fr. *bois, bosc* forest, of Gmc origin; akin to OHG *busk* forest, bush] (14c) : a growth of trees or shrubs : THICKET

bosh \'bäsh\ *n* [Turk *boş* empty] (1834) : foolish talk or activity : NONSENSE — often used interjectionally

bosk *or* **bosque** \'bäsk\ *n* [prob. back-formation fr. *bosky*] (1814) : a small wooded area

bosky \'bäs-kē\ *adj* [E dial. *bosk* bush, fr. ME *bush, bosk*] (1593) **1** : having abundant trees or shrubs **2** : of or relating to a woods

bos·'n *or* **bo·'s·'n** *or* **bo·sun** *or* **bo'·sun** \'bō-s³n\ *var of* BOATSWAIN

¹**bos·om** \'bu̇-zəm *also* 'bü-\ *n* [ME, fr. OE *bōsm;* akin to OHG *buosam* bosom] (bef. 12c) **1 a** : the human chest and esp. the front part of the chest ⟨hugged the child to his ~⟩ **b** : a woman's breasts regarded esp. as a single feature ⟨a woman with an ample ~⟩; *also* : BREAST **2 a** : the chest conceived of as the seat of the emotions and intimate feelings ⟨a story you will take to your ~⟩ **b** : the security and intimacy of or like that of being hugged to someone's bosom ⟨lived in the ~ of her family⟩ **3** : the part of a garment that covers the chest or the breasts

²**bosom** *adj* (1590) : CLOSE, INTIMATE ⟨~ friends⟩

³**bosom** *vt* (1605) **1** : EMBRACE **2** : to enclose or carry in the bosom

bos·omed \-zəmd\ *adj* (1603) : having a bosom of a specified kind — used in combination ⟨full-*bosomed*⟩

bos·omy \'bu̇-zə-mē *also* 'bü-\ *adj* (1860) **1** : swelling upward or outward ⟨~ hills⟩ **2** : having prominent breasts

bo·son \'bō-,sän, -,zän\ *n* [Satyendranath *Bose* †1974 Indian physicist + E ²-*on*] (1947) : a particle (as a photon or meson) whose spin is zero or an integral number — compare FERMION

bos·quet \'bäs-kət\ *n* [F, fr. It *boschetto*, dim. of *bosco* forest, of Gmc origin; akin to OHG *busk* forest, bush] (ca. 1730) : THICKET

¹**boss** \'bäs, 'bȯs\ *n* [ME *boce*, fr. MF, fr. (assumed) VL *bottia*] (14c) **1 a** : a protuberant part or body ⟨a ~ of granite⟩ ⟨a ~ on an animal's horn⟩ **b** : a raised ornamentation : STUD **c** : an ornamental projecting block used in architecture **2 a** : a soft pad used in ceramics and glassmaking **b** : the hub of a propeller

²**boss** *vt* (15c) **1** : to ornament with bosses : EMBOSS **2** : to treat (as the surface of porcelain) with a boss

³**boss** *n* [D *baas* master] (1679) **1** : a person who exercises control or authority; *specif* : one who directs or supervises workers **2** : a politician who controls votes in a party organization or dictates appointments or legislative measures — **boss·dom** \-dəm\ *n* — **boss·ism** \'bä-,si-zəm, 'bȯ-\ *n*

⁴**boss** \'bȯs\ *adj* (1836) *slang* : EXCELLENT, FIRST-RATE

⁵**boss** \'bȯs\ *vt* (1856) **1** : to act as boss of **2** : to give usu. arbitrary orders to — usu. used with *around*

\ə\ abut \³\ kitten, F table \ər\ further \a\ ash \ā\ ace \ä\ mop, mar
\au̇\ out \ch\ chin \e\ bet \ē\ easy \g\ go \i\ hit \ī\ ice \j\ job
\ŋ\ sing \ō\ go \ȯ\ law \ȯi\ boy \th\ thin \t̲h̲\ the \ü\ loot \u̇\ foot
\y\ yet \zh\ vision \à, k̲, ⁿ, œ, œ̄, ᵫ, ᵫ̄, ᴴ\ see Guide to Pronunciation

⁶boss \'bós, 'bäs\ *n* [E dial., young cow] (1790) : COW, CALF
bos·sa no·va \,bä-sə-'nō-va\ *n* [Pg, lit., new trend] (1962) **1** : popular music of Brazilian origin that is rhythmically related to the samba but with complex harmonies and improvised jazzlike passages **2** : a dance performed to bossa nova music
boss man *n* (1934) : ³BOSS
¹bossy \'bä-sē, 'bó-\ *adj* (1543) **1** : marked by a swelling or roundness **2** : marked by bosses : STUDDED
²bossy \'bó-sē, 'bä-\ *n, pl* **boss·ies** (1843) : COW, CALF
³bossy \'bó-sē, 'bä-\ *adj* **boss·i·er; -est** (1882) : inclined to domineer : DICTATORIAL — **boss·i·ness** *n*
Bos·ton \'bós-tən\ *n* [F, fr. *Boston*, Mass.] (1800) **1** : a variation of whist played with two decks of cards **2** [*Boston*, Mass.] : a dance somewhat like a waltz
Boston cream pie *n* (ca. 1933) : a round cake that is split and filled with a custard or cream filling and usu. frosted with chocolate
Boston fern *n* (ca. 1900) : a luxuriant fern (*Nephrolepis exaltata bostoniensis*) often with drooping much-divided fronds
Boston ivy *n* (ca. 1900) : a woody Asian vine (*Parthenocissus tricuspidata*) of the grape family typically having 3-lobed leaves
Boston rocker *n* (1856) : a wooden rocking chair with a high spindle back, a decorative top panel, and a seat and arms that curve down at the front
Boston terrier *n* (1894) : any of a breed of small smooth-coated terriers originating as a cross of the bulldog and bullterrier and being brindled or black with white markings — called also *Boston bull*
Bos·well \'bäz-,wel, -wəl\ *n* [James *Boswell*] (1858) : a person who records in detail the life of a usu. famous contemporary — **Bos·well·ian** \bäz-'welē-ən\ *adj* — **Bos·well·ize** \'bäz-wə-,līz, -,we-\ *vb*
bot *also* **bott** \'bät\ *n* [ME; akin to D lever*bot* liver fluke] (15c) : the larva of a botfly; *esp* : one infesting the horse
bo·ta \'bō-tə\ *n* [Sp, fr. LL *buttis* cask] (1832) : a leather bottle (as for wine)

Boston rocker

bo·tán·i·ca \bə-'tä-ni-kə\ *n* [AmerSp *botánica*, fr. fem. of Sp *botánico* botanical] (1969) : a shop that deals in herbs and charms used esp. by adherents of Santeria
¹bo·tan·i·cal \bə-'ta-ni-kəl\ *adj* [F *botanique*, fr. Gk *botanikos* of herbs, fr. *botanē* pasture, herb, fr. *boskein* to feed, graze; prob. akin to Lith *guotas* flock] (1658) **1** : of or relating to plants or botany **2** : derived from plants **3** : SPECIES ⟨~ tulips⟩ — **bo·tan·i·cal·ly** \-k(ə-)lē\ *adv*
²botanical *n* (ca. 1926) : a plant part or extract used esp. in skin and hair care products
botanical garden *n* (1785) : a garden often with greenhouses for the culture, study, and exhibition of special plants — called also *bo·tan·ic garden* \bə-'ta-nik-\
bot·an·ise *Brit var of* BOTANIZE
bot·a·nist \'bä-t⁼n-ist, 'bät-nist\ *n* (ca. 1682) : a specialist in botany or in a branch of botany
bot·a·nize \-t⁼n-,īz\ *vb* **-nized; -niz·ing** *vi* (1767) : to collect plants for botanical investigation; *also* : to study plants esp. on a field trip ~ *vt* : to explore for botanical purposes
bot·a·ny \'bä-t⁼n-ē, 'bät-nē\ *n, pl* **-nies** [*botan*ic botanical + ²-*y*] (1696) **1** : a branch of biology dealing with plant life **2 a** : plant life **b** : the properties and life phenomena exhibited by a plant, plant type, or plant group **3** : a botanical treatise or study; *esp* : a particular system of botany
¹botch \'bäch\ *n* [ME *boche*, fr. ONF, fr. (assumed) VL *bottia* boss] (14c) : an inflammatory sore
²botch *vt* [ME *bocchen*] (1530) **1** : to foul up hopelessly — often used with *up* **2** : to put together in a makeshift way — **botch·er** *n*
³botch *n* (1605) **1** : something that is botched : MESS **2** : PATCHWORK, HODGEPODGE — **botchy** \'bä-chē\ *adj*
bot·fly \'bät-,flī\ *n* (1819) : any of various stout dipteran flies (family Oestridae) with larvae parasitic in cavities or tissues of various mammals including humans
¹both \'bōth\ *pron, pl in constr* [ME *bothe*, fr. ON *bāthir*; akin to OHG *beide* both] (12c) : the one as well as the other ⟨~ of us⟩ ⟨we are ~ well⟩ ⟨$1000 fine or 30 days in jail, or ~⟩
²both *conj* (12c) — used as a function word to indicate and stress the inclusion of each of two or more things specified by coordinated words, phrases, or clauses ⟨prized ~ for its beauty and for its utility⟩ ⟨he prayeth well, who loveth well ~ man and bird and beast —S. T. Coleridge⟩
³both *adj* (13c) : being the two : affecting or involving the one and the other ⟨~ feet⟩ ⟨~ his eyes⟩ ⟨~ these armies⟩
¹both·er \'bä-thər\ *vb* **both·ered; both·er·ing** \'bäth-riŋ, 'bä-thə-\ [origin unknown] *vt* (ca. 1745) **1** : to annoy esp. by petty provocation : IRK **2** : to intrude upon : PESTER **3** : to cause to be anxious or concerned — often used interjectionally ~ *vi* **1** : to become concerned **2** : to take pains : take the trouble **syn** see ANNOY
²bother *n* (1834) **1 a** : a state of petty discomfort, annoyance, or worry **b** : something that causes petty annoyance or worry **2** : FUSS
both·er·ation \,bä-thə-'rä-shən\ *n* (1797) **1** : the act of bothering : the state of being bothered **2** : something that bothers — often used interjectionally
both·er·some \'bä-thər-səm\ *adj* (1834) : causing bother : VEXING
bo·thy \'bä-thē, 'bō-\ *n* [Sc, prob. fr. obs. Sc *both* booth] (1771) *chiefly Scot* : HUT
bot·o·née *or* **bot·on·née** \,bä-t⁼n-'ā\ *adj* [MF *botonné*] (15c) *of a heraldic cross* : having a cluster of three balls or knobs at the end of each arm — see CROSS illustration
bo tree \'bō-\ *n* [Sinhalese *bō*, fr. Skt *bodhi* enlightenment; fr. Buddha receiving enlightenment under this tree — more at BID] (1862) : PIPAL
bot·ry·oi·dal \,bä-trē-'ói-d⁼l\ *adj* [Gk *botryoeidēs*, fr. *botrys* bunch of grapes] (1816) : having the form of a bunch of grapes ⟨~ garnets⟩
bo·try·tis \bō-'trī-təs\ *n* [NL, fr. Gk *botrys*] (1900) : any of a genus (*Botrytis*) of imperfect fungi having botryoidal conidia and including several serious plant pathogens
¹bot·tle \'bä-t⁼l\ *n, often attrib* [ME *botel*, fr. MF *bouteille*, fr. ML *butticula*, dim. of LL *buttis* cask] (14c) **1 a** : a rigid or semirigid container typically of glass or plastic having a comparatively narrow neck

or mouth and usu. no handle **b** : a usu. bottle-shaped container made of skin for storing a liquid **2** : the quantity held by a bottle **3 a** : intoxicating drink : the practice of drinking **b** : liquid food (as milk) used in place of mother's milk — **bot·tle·ful** \-,fúl\ *n*
²bottle *vt* **bot·tled; bot·tling** \'bä-t⁼l-iŋ, 'bät-liŋ\ (1600) **1** : to confine as if in a bottle : RESTRAIN — usu. used with *up* ⟨*bottling* up their anger⟩ **2** : to put into a bottle — **bot·tler** \'bä-t⁼l-ər, 'bät-lər\ *n*
bot·tle·brush \'bä-t⁼l-,brəsh\ *n* [fr. the shape of the flowers] (ca. 1841) : any of a genus (*Callistemon*) of Australian trees and shrubs of the myrtle family widely cultivated in warm regions esp. for their spikes of brightly colored flowers
bottle club *n* (1943) : a club serving patrons previously purchased or reserved alcoholic drinks after normal legal closing hours
bottled gas *n* (1930) : gas under pressure in portable cylinders
bot·tle–feed \'bä-t⁼l-,fēd\ *vt* **-fed; -feed·ing** (ca. 1865) : to feed (as an infant) with a bottle
bottle gourd *n* (ca. 1828) : a common cultivated gourd (*Lagenaria siceraria*) with a variably shaped fruit that is sometimes used as a container
bottle green *n* (1804) : a dark green
¹bot·tle·neck \'bä-t⁼l-,nek\ *adj* (1896) : NARROW ⟨~ harbors⟩
²bottleneck *n* (1907) **1 a** : a narrow route **b** : a point of traffic congestion **2 a** : a condition or situation that retards or halts free movement and progress **b** : IMPASSE **3** : a style of guitar playing in which glissando effects are produced by sliding an object (as a knife blade or the neck of a bottle) along the strings
³bottleneck *vt* (1933) : to slow or halt by causing a bottleneck
bot·tle–nosed dolphin \'bä-t⁼l-,nōz-\ *n* (ca. 1909) : a relatively small stout-bodied chiefly gray toothed whale (*Tursiops truncatus*) with a prominent beak and falcate dorsal fin
bottlenose dolphin *n* (1940) : BOTTLE-NOSED DOLPHIN
bot·tling \'bä-t⁼l-iŋ, 'bät-liŋ\ *n* (1954) : a beverage and esp. a wine that is bottled at a particular time
¹bot·tom \'bä-təm\ *n* [ME *botme*, fr. OE *botm;* akin to OHG *bodam* bottom, L *fundus*, Gk *pythmēn*] (bef. 12c) **1 a** : the underside of something **b** : a surface (as the seat of a chair) designed to support something resting on it **c** : the posterior end of the trunk : BUTTOCKS, RUMP **2** : the surface on which a body of water lies **3 a** : the part of a ship's hull lying below the water : BOAT, SHIP **4 a** : the lowest part or place **b** : the remotest or inmost point **c** : the lowest or last place in point of precedence ⟨started work at the ~⟩ **d** : the pants of pajamas — usu. used in pl. **e** : the last half of an inning of baseball : the bass or baritone instruments of a band **5** : BOTTOMLAND — usu. used in pl. **6** : BASIS, SOURCE **7** : capacity (as of a horse) to endure strain **8** : a foundation color applied to textile fibers before dyeing — **bot·tomed** \-təmd\ *adj* — **at bottom** : REALLY, BASICALLY
²bottom *vt* (1544) **1** : to furnish with a bottom **2** : to provide a foundation for **3** : to bring to the bottom **4** : to get to the bottom of : FATHOM ~ *vi* **1** : to become based **2** : to reach the bottom **3** : to reach a low point before rebounding — usu. used with *out* — **bot·tom·er** *n*
³bottom *adj* (1561) **1** : of, relating to, or situated at the bottom ⟨~ rock⟩ **2** : frequenting the bottom ⟨~ fish⟩ **3** : having a quantum characteristic that accounts for the existence and lifetime of upsilon particles and that has a value of zero for most known particles ⟨~ quark⟩
bot·tom·land \'bä-təm-,land\ *n* (1728) : low-lying land along a watercourse
bot·tom·less \-ləs\ *adj* (14c) **1** : having no bottom ⟨a ~ chair⟩ **2 a** : extremely deep **b** : impossible to comprehend : UNFATHOMABLE ⟨a ~ mystery⟩ **c** : BOUNDLESS, UNLIMITED **3 a** [fr. the absence of lower as well as upper garments] : NUDE ⟨~ dancers⟩ **b** : featuring nude entertainers — **bot·tom·less·ly** *adv* — **bot·tom·less·ness** *n*
bottom–line \'bä-təm-,līn\ *adj* (1972) **1** : concerned only with cost or profits **2** : PRAGMATIC, REALISTIC
bottom line *n* (1967) **1 a** : the essential or salient point : CRUX : the primary or most important consideration **2 a** : the line at the bottom of a financial report that shows the net profit or loss **b** : financial considerations (as cost or profit or loss) **c** : the final result : OUTCOME, UPSHOT
bot·tom·most \'bä-tə(m)-,mōst\ *adj* (1861) **1 a** : situated at the very bottom : LOWEST, DEEPEST **b** : LAST ⟨the ~ part of the day —Alfred Kazin⟩ **2** : most basic ⟨the ~ problems facing the world⟩
bottom round *n* (1923) : meat (as beef) sliced from the outer part of a round of beef
bot·u·lin \'bä-chə-lən\ *n* [prob. fr. NL *botulinum*] (ca. 1900) : a neurotoxin formed by botulinum and causing botulism
bot·u·li·num \,bä-chə-'lī-nəm\ *also* **bot·u·li·nus** \-nəs\ *n* [NL, fr. L *botulus* sausage] (1902) : a spore-forming bacterium (*Clostridium botulinum*) that secretes botulin — **bot·u·li·nal** \-'lī-n⁼l\ *adj*
bot·u·lism \'bä-chə-,li-zəm\ *n* (1887) : an acute paralytic disease caused by botulin esp. in food
bou·bou \'bü-,bü\ *n* [F, fr. Malinke *bubu*] (1961) : a long flowing garment worn in parts of Africa
bou·chée \bü-'shā\ *n* [F, lit., mouthful, fr. OF *buchiee*, fr. (assumed) VL *buccata*, fr. L *bucca* cheek, mouth] (1846) : a small patty shell usu. containing a creamed filling
bou·clé *or* **bou·cle** \bü-'klā\ *n* [F *bouclé* curly, fr. pp. of *boucler* to curl, fr. *bocle* buckle, curl] (1895) **1** : an uneven yarn of three plies one of which forms loops at intervals **2** : a fabric of bouclé yarn
bou·doir \'bü-,dwär, 'bú-, ,bü-', ,bú-\ *n* [F, fr. *bouder* to pout] (1781) : a woman's dressing room, bedroom, or private sitting room
bouf·fant \bü-'fänt, 'bü-,\ *adj* [F, fr. MF, fr. prp. of *bouffer* to puff] (1880) : puffed out ⟨~ hairdos⟩ ⟨a ~ veil⟩
bou·gain·vil·lea *also* **bou·gain·vil·laea** \,bü-gən-'vil-yə, ,bō-, ,bü-, -'vē-ə\ *n* [NL, fr. Louis Antoine de *Bougainville*] (1881) : any of a genus (*Bougainvillaea*) of the four-o'clock family of ornamental tropical American woody vines with brilliant purple or red floral bracts
bough \'baú\ *n* [ME, shoulder, bough, fr. OE *bōg;* akin to OHG *buog* shoulder, Gk *pēchys* forearm] (bef. 12c) : a branch of a tree; *esp* : a main branch — **boughed** \'baúd\ *adj*
¹bought \'bót\ *past and past part of* BUY
²bought *adj* [pp. of *buy*] (1599) : STORE 2 ⟨~ clothes⟩

bought·en \'bȯ-t²n\ *adj* [*bought* + *-en* (as in *forgotten*)] (1793) *chiefly dial* : BOUGHT ⟨the only ~ carpet in the region —H. W. Thompson⟩
bou·gie \'bü-ˌzhē, -ˌjē\ *n* [F, fr. *Bougie*, seaport in Algeria] (1755) **1** : a wax candle **2 a** : a tapering cylindrical instrument for introduction into a tubular passage of the body **b** : SUPPOSITORY
bouil·la·baisse \ˌbü-yə-'bās, -'bāz, 'bü-yə-ˌ, -ˌbāz\ *n* [F] (1855) **1** : a highly seasoned fish stew made with at least two kinds of fish **2** : POT-POURRI
bouil·lon \'bü(l)-ˌyän, 'bu(l)-; 'bül-yən; 'bü-ˌyōⁿ\ *n* [F, fr. OF *boillon*, fr. *boillir* to boil] (ca. 1656) : a clear seasoned soup made usu. from lean beef; *broadly* : BROTH
bouillon cube *n* (ca. 1922) : a cube of evaporated meat extract
boul·der \'bōl-dər\ *n* [short for *boulder stone*, fr. ME *bulder ston*, part trans. of a word of Scand origin; akin to Sw dial. *bullersten* large stone in a stream, fr. *buller* noise + *sten* stone] (1617) : a detached and rounded or much-worn mass of rock — **boul·dered** \-dərd\ *adj* — **boul·dery** \-d(ə-)rē\ *adj*
¹**bou·le** \'bü-(ˌ)lē, bü-'lā\ *n* [Gk *boulē*, lit., will, fr. *boulesthai* to wish] (1846) : a legislative council of ancient Greece consisting first of an aristocratic advisory body and later of a representative senate
²**boule** \'bül\ *n* [F, ball — more at BOWL] (1918) : a pear-shaped synthetically formed mass (as of sapphire) with the atomic structure of a single crystal
bou·le·vard \'bu-lə-ˌvärd, 'bü- *also* 'bə-\ *n* [F, modif. of MD *bolwerc* bulwark] (1769) : a broad often landscaped thoroughfare
bou·le·vard·ier \ˌbu-lə-ˌvär-'dyā, ˌbü-, -'dir\ *n* [F, fr. *boulevard*] (1879) : a frequenter of the Parisian boulevards; *broadly* : MAN-ABOUT-TOWN
bou·le·ver·se·ment \bül-ver-sə-mäⁿ\ *n* [F] (1782) **1** : REVERSAL **2** : a violent disturbance : DISORDER
boulle \'bül, 'byü(ə)l\ *n* [André Charles *Boulle* †1732 Fr. cabinet-maker] (1823) : inlaid decoration of tortoiseshell, yellow metal, and white metal in cabinetwork
¹**bounce** \'baun(t)s\ *vb* **bounced; bounc·ing** [ME *bounsen*] *vt* (13c) **1** *obs* : BEAT, BUMP **2** : to cause to rebound ⟨~ a ball⟩ **3 a** : DISMISS, FIRE **b** : to expel precipitately from a place **4** : to issue (a check) drawn on an account with insufficient funds **5** : to present (as an idea) to another person to elicit comments or to gain approval — usu. used with *off* ~ *vi* **1** : to rebound after striking a surface (as the ground) **2** : to recover from a blow or a defeat quickly — usu. used with *back* **3** : to be returned by a bank because of insufficient funds in a checking account ⟨his checks ~⟩ **4 a** : to leap suddenly : BOUND **b** : to walk with springing steps **5** : to hit a baseball so that it hits the ground before it reaches an infielder
²**bounce** *n* (1523) **1 a** : a sudden leap or bound **b** : REBOUND **2** : BLUSTER **3** : VERVE, LIVELINESS
bounc·er \'baun(t)-sər\ *n* (1865) : one that bounces; *esp* : a person employed to restrain or eject disorderly persons
bounc·ing \-siŋ\ *adj* (ca. 1563) **1** : LIVELY, ANIMATED **2** : enjoying good health : ROBUST — **bounc·ing·ly** \-siŋ-lē\ *adv*
bouncing bet \-'bet\ *n, often cap* 2nd *B* [fr. *Bet*, nickname for *Elizabeth*] (ca. 1818) : a European perennial herb (*Saponaria officinalis*) of the pink family that is widely naturalized in the U.S. and has pink or white flowers and leaves which yield a detergent when bruised
bouncy \'baun(t)-sē\ *adj* **bounc·i·er; -est** (1921) **1** : BUOYANT, EXUBERANT **2** : RESILIENT **3** : marked by or producing bounces — **bounc·i·ly** \-sə-lē\ *adv*
¹**bound** \'baund\ *adj* [ME *boun*, fr. ON *būinn*, pp. of *būa* to dwell, prepare; akin to OHG *būan* to dwell — more at BOWER] (13c) **1** *archaic* : READY **2** : intending to go : GOING ⟨~ for home⟩ ⟨college-*bound*⟩
²**bound** *n* [ME, fr. OF *bodne*, fr. ML *bodina*] (13c) **1 a** : a limiting line : BOUNDARY — usu. used in pl. **b** : something that limits or restrains ⟨beyond the ~s of decency⟩ **2** *usu pl* **a** : BORDERLAND **b** : the land within certain bounds **3** : a number greater than or equal to every number in a set (as the range of a function); *also* : a number less than or equal to every number in a set
³**bound** *past and past part of* BIND
⁴**bound** *vt* (14c) **1** : to set limits or bounds to : CONFINE **2** : to form the boundary of : ENCLOSE **3** : to name the boundaries of
⁵**bound** *adj* [ME *bounden*, fr. pp. of *binden* to bind] (14c) **1** : placed under legal or moral restraint or obligation : OBLIGED ⟨duty-*bound*⟩ **2 a** : fastened by or as if by a band : CONFINED ⟨desk-*bound*⟩ **b** : very likely : SURE ⟨~ to rain soon⟩ **3** : made costive : CONSTIPATED **4** *of a book* : secured to the covers by cords, tapes, or glue **5** : DETERMINED, RESOLVED **6** : held in chemical or physical combination **7** : always occurring in combination with another linguistic form ⟨*un-* in *unknown* and *-er* in *speaker* are ~ forms⟩ — compare FREE 11d
⁶**bound** *n* [MF *bond*, fr. *bondir* to leap, fr. (assumed) VL *bombitire* to hum, fr. L *bombus* deep hollow sound — more at BOMB] (ca. 1553) **1** : LEAP, JUMP **2** : the action of rebounding : BOUNCE
⁷**bound** *vi* (1592) **1** : to move by leaping **2** : REBOUND, BOUNCE
bound·ary \'baun-d(ə-)rē\ *n, pl* **-aries** (1626) : something (as a line, point, or plane) that indicates or fixes a limit or extent
boundary layer *n* (1921) : a region of retarded fluid near the surface of a body which moves through a fluid or past which a fluid moves
bound·ed·ness \'baun-dəd-nəs\ *n* (1674) : the quality or state of being bounded
bound·en \'baun-dən\ *adj* [ME] (14c) **1** *archaic* : being under obligation : BEHOLDEN **2** : made obligatory : BINDING ⟨our ~ duty⟩
bound·er \-dər\ *n* (1505) **1** : one that bounds **2** : a man of objectionable social behavior : CAD — **bound·er·ish** \-d(ə-)rish\ *adj*
bound·less \'baun(d)-ləs\ *adj* (1592) : having no boundaries : VAST — **bound·less·ly** *adv* — **bound·less·ness** *n*
bound up *adj* (1611) : closely involved or associated — usu. used with *with*
boun·te·ous \'baun-tē-əs\ *adj* [ME *bountevous*, fr. MF *bontif* kind, fr. OF, fr. *bonté*] (14c) **1** : giving or disposed to give freely **2** : liberally bestowed — **boun·te·ous·ly** *adv* — **boun·te·ous·ness** *n*
boun·tied \'baun-tēd\ *adj* (1788) **1** : having the benefit of a bounty **2** : rewarded or rewardable by a bounty
boun·ti·ful \'baun-ti-fəl\ *adj* (1508) **1** : liberal in bestowing gifts or favors **2** : given or provided abundantly ⟨a ~ harvest⟩ *syn* see LIBERAL — **boun·ti·ful·ly** \-f(ə-)lē\ *adv* — **boun·ti·ful·ness** \-fəl-nəs\ *n*
boun·ty \'baun-tē\ *n, pl* **bounties** [ME *bounte* goodness, fr. OF *bonté*, fr. L *bonitat-, bonitas*, fr. *bonus* good, fr. OL *duenos*; akin to Skt *duva*

reverence, favor] (13c) **1** : something that is given generously **2** : liberality in giving : GENEROSITY **3** : yield esp. of a crop **4** : a reward, premium, or subsidy esp. when offered or given by a government: as **a** : an extra allowance to induce entry into the armed services **b** : a grant to encourage an industry **c** : a payment to encourage the destruction of noxious animals **d** : a payment for the capture of or assistance in the capture of an outlaw
bounty hunter *n* (1930) **1** : one that tracks down and captures outlaws for whom a reward is offered **2** : one that hunts predatory animals for the reward offered
bou·quet \bō-'kā, bü-\ *n* [F, fr. MF, thicket, fr. ONF *bosquet*, fr. OF *bosc* forest — more at BOSCAGE] (ca. 1718) **1 a** : flowers picked and fastened together in a bunch : NOSEGAY **b** : MEDLEY ⟨~ of songs⟩ **2** : COMPLIMENT **3 a** : a distinctive and characteristic fragrance (as of wine) **b** : a subtle aroma or quality (as of an artistic performance)
bou·quet gar·ni \-gär-'nē\ *n, pl* **bou·quets gar·nis** \-'kā(z)-gär-'nē\ [F, lit., garnished bouquet] (ca. 1852) : an herb mixture that is either tied together or enclosed in a porous container and is cooked with a dish but removed before serving
bour·bon \'bür-bən, 'bȯr-, 'bȯr-; *usu* 'bər- *in sense 3*\ *n* [*Bourbon*, seigniory in France] (1600) **1** *cap* : a member of a French family founded in 1272 to which belong the rulers of France from 1589 to 1793 and from 1814 to 1830, of Spain from 1700 to 1808, from 1814 to 1868, from 1875 to 1931, and from 1975, of Naples from 1735 to 1805, and of the Two Sicilies from 1815 to 1860 **2** [*Bourbon* (now Réunion), French island in the Indian Ocean]: a rose (*Rosa borboniana*) of compact upright growth with shining leaves, prickly branches, and clustered flowers **3** [*Bourbon* county, Kentucky] : a whiskey distilled from a mash made up of not less than 51 percent corn plus malt and rye — compare CORN WHISKEY **4** *often cap* : a person who clings obstinately to old social and political ideas; *specif* : an extremely conservative member of the U.S. Democratic party usu. from the South — **bour·bon·ism** \-bə-ˌni-zəm\ *n, often cap*
bourg \'bürg\ *n* [ME, fr. MF, fr. OF *borc*, fr. L *burgus* fortified place, of Gmc origin; akin to OHG *burg* fortified place — more at BOROUGH] (12c) : TOWN, VILLAGE: as **a** : one neighboring a castle **b** : a market town
¹**bour·geois** \'bürzh-ˌwä *also* 'bu̇zh- *or* 'bu̇zh- *or* bürzh-'\ *adj* [MF, fr. OF *borjois*, fr. *borc*] (ca. 1565) **1** : of, relating to, or characteristic of the townsman or of the social middle class **2** : marked by a concern for material interests and respectability and a tendency toward mediocrity **3** : dominated by commercial and industrial interests : CAPITALISTIC — **bour·geois·ifi·ca·tion** \ˌbü(r)zh-ˌwä-zə-fə-'kā-shən\ *n* — **bour·geois·ify** \'bü(r)zh-'wä-zə-ˌfi\ *vb*
²**bourgeois** *n, pl* **bourgeois** \-ˌwä(z), -'wä(z)\ (ca. 1674) **1 a** : BURGHER **b** : a middle-class person **2** : a person with social behavior and political views held to be influenced by private-property interest : CAPITALIST **3** *pl* : BOURGEOISIE
bour·geoise \'bürzh-ˌwäz *also* 'bu̇zh- *or* 'bu̇zh- *or* bürzh-'\ *n* [F, fem. of *bourgeois*] (1794) : a woman of the middle class
bour·geoi·sie \ˌbu̇(r)zh-ˌwä-'zē\ *n* [F, fr. *bourgeois*] (1707) **1** : MIDDLE CLASS **2** : a social order dominated by bourgeois
bour·geon \'bər-jən\ *var of* BURGEON
bour·gui·gnonne \ˌbür-gēn-'yȯn *or* **bour·gui·gnon** \-'yōⁿ\ *adj, often cap* [F, fr. *Bourgogne* Burgundy, region in France] (ca. 1919) : prepared or served in the manner of Burgundy (as with a sauce made with red wine) ⟨beef ~⟩
bourn *or* **bourne** \'bȯrn, 'bȯrn, 'bu̇rn\ *n* [ME *burn, bourne* — more at BURN] (12c) : STREAM, BROOK
bourne *also* **bourn** *n* [MF *bourne*, fr. OF *bodne* — more at BOUND] (1523) **1** : BOUNDARY, LIMIT **2** : GOAL, DESTINATION
bour·rée \bu̇-'rā, 'bü-ˌ\ *n* [F] (1706) **1** : a 17th century French dance usu. in quick duple time; *also* : a musical composition with the rhythm of this dance **2** : PAS DE BOURRÉE
bour·ride \bu̇-'rēd, bə-\ *n* [F, fr. Prov *bourrido*, alter. of *boulido* something boiled, fr. *bouli* to boil, fr. L *bullire* — more at BOIL] (ca. 1919) : a fish stew similar to bouillabaisse that is usu. thickened with egg yolks and strongly flavored with garlic
bourse \'bürs\ *n* [MF, lit., purse, fr. ML *bursa* — more at PURSE] (1597) **1** : EXCHANGE 5a; *specif* : a European stock exchange **2** : a sale of numismatic or philatelic items on tables (as at a convention)
bouse *var of* BOWSE
bou·stro·phe·don \ˌbü-strə-'fē-ˌdän, -d²n\ *n* [Gk *boustrophēdon*, adv., lit., turning like oxen in plowing, fr. *bous* ox, cow + *strephein* to turn — more at COW] (1699) : the writing of alternate lines in opposite directions (as from left to right and from right to left) — **boustrophedon** *adj or adv* — **bou·stro·phe·don·ic** \-fē-'dä-nik\ *adj*
bout \'bau̇t\ *n* [E dial., a trip going and returning in plowing, fr. ME *bought* bend] (1575) : a spell of activity: as **a** : an athletic match (as of boxing) **b** : OUTBREAK, ATTACK ⟨a ~ of lumbago⟩ **c** : SESSION
bou·tique \bü-'tēk\ *n, often attrib* [F, shop, prob. fr. OProv *botica*, ultim. fr. Gk *apothēkē* storehouse — more at APOTHECARY] (1767) **1 a** : a small fashionable specialty shop or business **b** : a small shop within a large department store **2** : a small company that offers highly specialized services ⟨an independent investment ~⟩
bou·ton·niere \ˌbü-t²n-'ir, ˌbü-tən-'yer\ *n* [F *boutonnière* buttonhole, fr. MF, fr. *bouton* button] (ca. 1867) : a flower or bouquet worn in a buttonhole
Bou·vi·er des Flan·dres \ˌbü-vē-ˌā-də-'flän-dərz, -'flänⁿd"\ *n* [F, lit., cowherd of Flanders] (1929) : any of a breed of large powerfully built rough-coated dogs of Belgian origin used esp. for herding and in guard work — called also *Bouvier*
bou·zou·ki \bü-'zü-kē\ *n, pl* **-kis** *also* **-kia** \-kē-ə\ [NGk *mpouzouki*] (1952) : a long-necked stringed instrument of Greek origin that resembles a mandolin
bo·vid \'bō-vid\ *n* [NL *Bovidae*, fr. *Bov-, Bos*, type genus, fr. L *bov-, bos*] (1939) : any of a family (Bovidae) of ruminants that have hollow un-

\ə\ abut \ᵊ\ kitten, F table \ər\ further \a\ ash \ā\ ace \ä\ mop, mar \au̇\ out \ch\ chin \e\ bet \ē\ easy \g\ go \i\ hit \ī\ ice \j\ job \ŋ\ sing \ō\ go \ȯ\ law \ȯi\ boy \th\ thin \t͟h\ the \ü\ loot \u̇\ foot \y\ yet \zh\ vision \ä, k̲, ⁿ, œ, œ̄, ᵫ, ᵫ̄, ᵊ\ *see* Guide to Pronunciation branched permanently attached horns present in both sexes and that include antelopes, oxen, sheep, and goats

¹bo·vine \'bō-,vīn, -,vēn\ *adj* [LL *bovinus*, fr. L *bov-, bos* ox, cow — more at COW] (1817) **1 :** of, relating to, or resembling bovines and esp. the ox or cow **2 :** having qualities (as placidity or dullness) characteristic of oxen or cows — **bo·vine·ly** *adv* — **bo·vin·i·ty** \bō-'vi-nə-tē\ *n*

²bovine *n* (1865) **:** any of a subfamily (Bovinae) of bovids including oxen, bison, buffalo, and their close relatives

¹bow \'bau̇\ *vb* [ME, fr. OE *būgan*; akin to OHG *biogan* to bend, Skt *bhujati* he bends] *vi* (bef. 12c) **1 :** to cease from competition or resistance **:** SUBMIT, YIELD ⟨refusing to ~ to the inevitable —John O'Hara⟩; *also* **:** to suffer defeat ⟨~ed to the champion⟩ **2 :** to bend the head, body, or knee in reverence, submission, or shame **3 :** to incline the head or body in salutation or assent or to acknowledge applause ~ *vt* **1 :** to cause to incline **2 :** to incline (as the head) esp. in respect or submission **3 :** to crush with a heavy burden **4 a :** to express by bowing **b :** to usher in or out with a bow

²bow *n* (ca. 1656) **:** a bending of the head or body in respect, submission, assent, or salutation; *also* **:** a show of respect or submission

³bow \'bō\ *n* [ME *bowe*, fr. OE *boga*; akin to OE *būgan* (bef. 12c) **1 a :** something bent into a simple curve **:** BEND, ARCH **b :** RAINBOW **2 :** a weapon that is made of a strip of flexible material (as wood) with a cord connecting the two ends and holding the strip bent and that is used to propel an arrow **3 :** ARCHER **4 a :** a metal ring or loop forming a handle (as of a key) **b :** a knot formed by doubling a ribbon or string into two or more loops **c :** BOW TIE **d :** a frame for the lenses of eyeglasses; *also* **:** the sidepiece of the frame passing over the ear **5 a :** a wooden rod with horsehairs stretched from end to end used in playing an instrument of the viol or violin family **b :** a stroke of such a bow

⁴bow \'bō\ *vi* (bef. 12c) **1 :** to bend into a curve **2 :** to play a stringed musical instrument with a bow ~ *vt* **1 :** to cause to bend into a curve **2 :** to play (a stringed instrument) with a bow

⁵bow \'bau̇\ *n* [ME *bowe, bowgh*, prob. fr. MD *boech* bow, shoulder; akin to OE *bōg* bough] (15c) **1 :** the forward part of a ship **2 :** ²BOW-MAN

Bow bells \'bō-\ *n pl* (1600) **:** the bells of the Church of St. Mary-le-Bow in London

bowd·ler·ise *Brit var of* BOWDLERIZE

bowd·ler·ize \'bōd-lə-,rīz, 'baud-\ *vt* **-ized; -iz·ing** [Thomas *Bowdler* †1825 Eng. editor] (1836) **1 :** to expurgate (as a book) by omitting or modifying parts considered vulgar **2 :** to modify by abridging, simplifying, or distorting in style or content — **bowd·ler·iza·tion** \,bōd-lə-rə-'zā-shən, ,baud-\ *n* — **bowd·ler·iz·er** *n*

¹bowed \'baud\ *adj* [pp. of ¹*bow*] (14c) **1 :** bent downward and forward ⟨listened with ~ heads⟩ **2 :** having the back and head inclined

²bowed \'bōd\ *adj* [partly fr. ³*bow* + *-ed*; partly fr. pp. of ⁴*bow*] (15c) **:** furnished with or shaped like a bow

bow·el \'bau̇(-ə)l\ *n* [ME, fr. MF *boel*, fr. ML *botellus*, fr. L, dim. of *botulus* sausage] (14c) **1 :** INTESTINE, GUT; *also* **:** one of the divisions of the intestines — usu. used in pl. except in medical use ⟨the large ~⟩ ⟨move your ~s⟩ **2** *archaic* **:** the seat of pity, tenderness, or courage — usu. used in pl. **3** *pl* **:** the interior parts; *esp* **:** the deep or remote parts ⟨~s of the earth⟩ — **bow·el·less** \'bau̇(-ə)l-ləs\ *adj*

¹bow·er \'bau̇(-ə)r\ *n* [ME *bour* dwelling, fr. OE *būr*; akin to OE & OHG *būan* to dwell, OE *bēon* to be — more at BE] (bef. 12c) **1 :** an attractive dwelling or retreat **2 :** a lady's private apartment in a medieval hall or castle **3 :** a shelter (as in a garden) made with tree boughs or vines twined together **:** ARBOR — **bow·ery** \-ē\ *adj*

²bower *vt* (1592) **:** EMBOWER, ENCLOSE

³bower *n* (1652) **:** an anchor carried at the bow of a ship

bow·er·bird \'bau̇(-ə)r-,bərd\ *n* (1845) **:** any of a family (Ptilonorhynchidae) of passerine birds of the Australian region in which the male builds a chamber or passage arched over with twigs and grasses, often adorned with bright-colored objects, and used esp. to attract the female

bow·ery \'bau̇(-ə)r-ē\ *n, pl* **-er·ies** [D *bouwerij*, fr. *bouwer* farmer, fr. *bouwen* to till; akin to OHG *būan* to dwell] (1650) **1 :** a colonial Dutch plantation or farm **2** [*Bowery*, street in New York City] **:** a city district known for cheap bars and derelicts

bow·fin \'bō-,fin\ *n* (1845) **:** a predaceous dull-green iridescent No. American freshwater fish (*Amia calva*) that is the only surviving member of an order (Amiiformes) dating back to the Jurassic

bow·front \-,frənt\ *adj* (1925) **1 :** having an outward curving front ⟨~ furniture⟩ **2 :** having a bow window in front ⟨~ houses⟩

bow·head whale \-,hed-\ *n* (1887) **:** a baleen whale (*Balaena mysticetus*) of arctic and subarctic seas — called also **bowhead**

bow·ie knife \'bü-ē-, 'bō-\ *n* [James *Bowie*] (1836) **:** a stout single-edged hunting knife with part of the back edge curved concavely to a point and sharpened

bow·ing \'bō-iŋ\ *n* (1838) **:** the technique or manner of managing the bow in playing a stringed musical instrument

bow·knot \'bō-,nät\ *n* (1547) **:** a knot with decorative loops

¹bowl \'bōl\ *n* [ME *bolle*, fr. OE *bolla*; akin to OHG *bolla* blister] (bef. 12c) **1 :** a concave usu. hemispherical vessel often used for holding liquids; *esp* **:** a drinking vessel (as for wine) **2 :** the contents of a bowl **3 :** a bowl-shaped or concave part: as **a :** the hollow of a spoon or tobacco pipe **b :** the receptacle of a toilet **4 a :** a natural formation or geographical region shaped like a bowl **b :** a bowl-shaped structure; *esp* **:** an athletic stadium **5 :** a postseason football game between specially invited teams — **bowled** \'bōld\ *adj* — **bowl·ful** \-,fu̇l\ *n*

²bowl *n* [ME *boule*, fr. MF, fr. L *bulla* bubble] (15c) **1 a :** a ball (as of lignum vitae) weighted or shaped to give it a bias when rolled in lawn bowling **b** *pl but sing in constr* **:** LAWN BOWLING **2 :** a delivery of the ball in bowling **3 :** a cylindrical roller or drum (as for a mechanical device)

³bowl *vi* (15c) **1 a :** to participate in a game of bowling **b :** to roll a ball in bowling **c :** to travel smoothly and rapidly (as in a wheeled vehicle) ~ *vt* **1 a :** to roll (a ball) in bowling **b** (1) **:** to complete by bowling ⟨~ a string⟩ (2) **:** to score by bowling ⟨~s 150⟩ **2 :** to strike with a swiftly moving object **3 :** to overwhelm with surprise

bowl·der *var of* BOULDER

bow·leg \'bō-,leg, -,lāg, 'bō-\ *n* (ca. 1864) **:** a leg bowed outward at or below the knee — **bow·legged** \'bō-,le-gəd, -,lā-; -,legd, -,lāgd\ *adj*

¹bowl·er \'bō-lər\ *n* (ca. 1500) **:** a person who bowls; *specif* **:** the player that delivers the ball to the batsman in cricket

²bowl·er \'bō-lər\ *n* [*Bowler*, 19th cent. family of Eng. hatters] (1861) **:** DERBY 3

bow·line \'bō-lən, -,līn\ *n* [ME *bouline*, perh. fr. *bowe* bow + *line*] (13c) **1 :** a rope used to keep the weather edge of a square sail taut forward **2 :** a knot used to form a loop that neither slips nor jams — see KNOT illustration

bowl·ing \'bō-liŋ\ *n* (1535) **:** any of several games in which balls are rolled on a green or down an alley at an object or group of objects

bowl over *vt* (1867) **1 :** to take unawares **2 :** ¹IMPRESS 2

¹bow·man \'bō-mən\ *n* (13c) **:** ARCHER 1

²bow·man \'bau̇-mən\ *n* (1829) **:** a boatman, oarsman, or paddler stationed in the front of a boat

Bow·man's capsule \'bō-mənz-\ *n* [Sir William *Bowman* †1892 Eng. surgeon] (ca. 1860) **:** a thin membranous double-walled capsule surrounding the glomerulus of a vertebrate nephron

bow out *vi* (1942) **:** RETIRE, WITHDRAW

bow saw \'bō-\ *n* (1677) **:** a saw having a narrow blade held under tension by a light bow-shaped frame

bowse \'bau̇z\ *vb* **bowsed; bows·ing** [origin unknown] *vt* (1593) **:** to haul by means of a tackle ~ *vi* **:** to bowse something

bow shock \'bau̇-\ *n* (1950) **:** the shock wave formed by the collision of a stellar wind with another medium (as the magnetosphere of a planet)

bow·sprit \'bau̇-,sprit, 'bō-\ *n* [ME *bouspret*, prob. fr. MLG *bōchsprēt*, fr. *bōch* bow + *sprēt* pole] (13c) **:** a large spar projecting forward from the stem of a ship

bow·string \'bō-,striŋ\ *n* (14c) **:** a waxed or sized cord joining the ends of a shooting bow

bowstring hemp *n* (ca. 1858) **:** any of various Asian and African sansevierias; *also* **:** its soft tough leaf fiber used esp. in cordage

bow tie \'bō-\ *n* (1897) **:** a short necktie tied in a bowknot

bow window \'bō-\ *n* (1753) **:** a usu. curved bay window

bow-wow \'bau̇-,wau̇, bau̇-\ *n* [imit.] (1576) **1 :** the bark of a dog; *also* **:** DOG **2 :** noisy clamor **3 :** arrogant dogmatic manner

bow·yer \'bō-yər\ *n* [ME *bowyere*] (14c) **:** a person who makes shooting bows

¹box \'bäks\ *n, pl* **box** *or* **box·es** [ME, fr. OE, fr. L *buxus*, fr. Gk *pyxos*] (bef. 12c) **:** an evergreen shrub or small tree (genus *Buxus* of the family Buxaceae, the box family) with opposite entire leaves and capsular fruits; *esp* **:** a widely cultivated shrub (*B. sempervirens*) used for hedges, borders, and topiary figures

²box *n* [ME, fr. OE, fr. LL *buxis*, fr. Gk *pyxis*, fr. *pyxos* box tree] (bef. 12c) **1 :** a rigid typically rectangular container with or without a cover ⟨a cigar ~⟩: as **a :** an open cargo container of a vehicle **b :** COFFIN **2 :** the contents of a box esp. as a measure of quantity **3 :** a box or boxlike container and its contents: as **a** *Brit* **:** a gift in a box **b :** an automobile transmission **c :** TELEVISION **d :** a signaling apparatus ⟨alarm ~⟩ **e :** a usu. self-contained piece of electronic equipment **f :** BOOM BOX **4 :** an often small space, compartment, or enclosure: as **a :** an enclosed group of seats for spectators (as in a theater or stadium) **b :** a driver's seat on a carriage or coach **c :** a cell for holding mail **d** *Brit* **:** BOX STALL **e :** PENALTY BOX **5 :** a usu. rectangular space that is frequently outlined or demarcated on a surface: as **a :** any of six spaces on a baseball diamond where the batter, coaches, pitcher, and catcher stand **b :** a space on a page for printed matter or in which to make a mark **6 :** PREDICAMENT, FIX **7 :** a cubical building — **box·ful** \-,fu̇l\ *n* — **box·like** \-,līk\ *adj*

³box *vt* (15c) **1 :** to enclose in or as if in a box **2 :** to hem in (as an opponent) — usu. used with *in, out,* or *up* ⟨~ed out the opposing tackle⟩

⁴box *n* [ME] (14c) **:** a punch or slap esp. on the ear

⁵box *vt* (1519) **1 :** to hit (as the ears) with the hand **2 :** to engage in boxing with ~ *vi* **:** to fight with the fists **:** engage in boxing

⁶box *vt* [prob. fr. Sp *bojar* to circumnavigate, fr. Catal *vogir* to turn, fr. L *volvere* to roll — more at VOLUBLE] (1753) **:** to name the 32 points of (the compass) in their order — used figuratively in the phrase *box the compass* to describe making a complete reversal

box·board \'bäks-,bōrd, -,bȯrd\ *n* (1841) **:** paperboard used for making boxes and cartons

box camera *n* (1902) **:** a box-shaped camera with a simple lens and rotary shutter

¹box·car \'bäks-,kär\ *n* (1856) **:** a roofed freight car usu. with sliding doors in the sides

²boxcar *adj* [fr. the high numbers stenciled on the sides of boxcars] (1944) **:** very large ⟨the judge awarded her a ~ figure⟩

box coat *n* (1822) **1 :** a heavy overcoat formerly worn for driving **2 :** a loose coat usu. fitted at the shoulders

box elder *n* (1787) **:** a No. American maple (*Acer negundo*) with compound leaves

¹box·er \'bäk-sər\ *n* (1742) **1 :** a person who engages in the sport of boxing **2** *pl* **:** SHORT 4b

²boxer *n* (1871) **:** one that makes boxes or packs things in boxes

³boxer *n* [G, fr. E ¹*boxer*] (ca. 1904) **:** a compact medium-sized short-haired usu. fawn or brindled dog of a breed originating in Germany

Box·er \'bäk-sər\ *n* [approx. trans. of Chin (Beijing) *yìhé juàn*, lit., righteous harmonious fist] (1899) **:** a member of a Chinese secret society that in 1900 attempted by violence to drive foreigners out of China and to force Chinese converts to renounce Christianity

boxer shorts *n pl* (1944) **:** SHORT 4b

¹box·ing \'bäk-siŋ\ *n* (1607) **1 :** an act of enclosing in a box **2 :** a boxlike enclosure **:** CASING **3 :** material used for boxes and casings

²boxing *n* (1711) **:** the art of attack and defense with the fists practiced as a sport

Boxing Day *n* (1833) **:** the first weekday after Christmas observed as a legal holiday in parts of the Commonwealth and marked by the giving of Christmas boxes to service workers (as postal workers)

boxing glove *n* (1875) **:** one of a pair of leather mittens heavily padded on the back and worn in boxing

box kite *n* (1897) **:** a tailless kite consisting of two or more open-ended connected boxes

box lunch *n* (1950) **:** a lunch packed in a container (as a box)

box office *n* (1786) **1 a :** an office (as in a theater) where tickets of

admission are sold **b** : income from ticket sales (as for a film) **2** : the ability or power (as of a show) to attract ticket buyers; *also* : something that enhances that ability ⟨any publicity is good *box office*⟩
box pleat *n* (1883) : a pleat made by forming two folded edges one facing right and the other left

box kite

box score *n* [fr. its arrangement in a newspaper box] (1913) : a printed score of a game (as baseball) giving the names and positions of the players and a record of the play arranged in tabular form; *broadly* : total count : SUMMARY
box seat *n* (1849) **1** : ²BOX 4b **2 a** : a seat in a box (as in a theater or grandstand) **b** : a position favorable for viewing something
box social *n* (1928) : a fund-raising affair at which box lunches are auctioned to the highest bidder
box spring *n* (1895) : a bedspring that consists of spiral springs attached to a foundation and enclosed in a cloth-covered frame
box stall *n* (1885) : an individual enclosure within a barn or stable in which an animal may move about freely without a restraining device
box·thorn \'bäks-ˌthȯrn\ *n* (1678) : MATRIMONY VINE
box turtle *n* (ca. 1804) : any of several No. American land turtles (genus *Terrapene*) capable of withdrawing into its shell and closing it by hinged joints in the lower half — called also *box tortoise*
box·wood \'bäks-ˌwud\ *n* (1652) **1** : the very close-grained heavy tough hard wood of the box (*Buxus*); *also* : a wood of similar properties **2** : a plant producing boxwood
boxy \'bäk-sē\ *adj* **box·i·er**; **-est** (ca. 1861) : resembling a box — **box·i·ness** *n*
boy \'bȯi\ *n, often attrib* [ME] (13c) **1** : a male servant — sometimes taken to be offensive **2 a** : a male child from birth to puberty **b** : SON **c** : an immature male : YOUTH **d** : SWEETHEART, BEAU **3 a** : one native to a given place ⟨local ∼⟩ **b** : FELLOW, PERSON ⟨the ∼s at the office⟩ **c** — used interjectionally to express intensity of feeling ⟨∼, what a game⟩ — **boy·hood** \-ˌhud\ *n* — **boy·ish** \-ish\ *adj* — **boy·ish·ly** *adv* — **boy·ish·ness** *n*
bo·yar *also* **bo·yard** \bō-'yär\ *n* [Russ *boyarin*] (1591) : a member of a Russian aristocratic order next in rank below the ruling princes until its abolition by Peter the Great
boy·chick \'bȯi-ˌchik\ *n* [Amer Yiddish *boytshik*, fr. E *boy* + Yiddish *-tshik*, dim. suffix] (ca. 1951) : a young man : BOY
boy·cott \'bȯi-ˌkät\ *vt* [Charles C. *Boycott* †1897 Eng. land agent in Ireland who was ostracized for refusing to reduce rents] (1880) : to engage in a concerted refusal to have dealings with (as a person, store, or organization) usu. to express disapproval or to force acceptance of certain conditions — **boycott** *n* — **boy·cott·er** *n*
boy·friend \'bȯi-ˌfrend\ *n* (1896) **1** : a male friend **2** : a frequent or regular male companion of a girl or woman **3** : a male lover
Boyle's law \'bȯilz-\ *n* [Robert *Boyle*] (ca. 1860) : a statement in physics: the volume of a gas at constant temperature varies inversely with the pressure exerted on it
boyo \'bȯi-(ˌ)ō\ *n, pl* **boy·os** [*boy* + ¹-*o*] (ca. 1870) *Irish* : BOY, LAD
Boy Scout *n* (1909) **1** : a member of any of various national scouting programs (as the Boy Scouts of America) for boys usu. 11 to 17 years of age **2** : a person whose values or actions are characteristic of a Boy Scout
boy·sen·ber·ry \'bȯi-zᵊn-ˌber-ē, -sᵊn-, -zᵊm-\ *n* [Rudolph *Boysen* †1950 Am. horticulturist + E *berry*] (1935) : a large bramble fruit with a raspberry flavor; *also* : the trailing hybrid bramble yielding this fruit and developed by crossing several blackberries and raspberries
boy wonder *n* (1946) : a young man of noteworthy achievements
bo·zo \'bō-(ˌ)zō\ *n, pl* **bozos** [origin unknown] (1920) : a foolish or incompetent person
B picture *n* (ca. 1937) : B MOVIE
bra \'brä\ *n* (1936) : BRASSIERE — **bra·less** *adj*
brab·ble \'bra-bəl\ *vi* **brab·bled; brab·bling** \-b(ə-)liŋ\ [perh. fr. MD *brabbelen*, of imit. origin] (ca. 1530) : SQUABBLE — **brabble** *n*
¹brace \'brās\ *vb* **braced; brac·ing** [ME, fr. MF *bracier* to embrace, fr. *brace*] *vt* (14c) **1** *archaic* : to fasten tightly : BIND **2 a** : to prepare for use by making taut **b** : PREPARE, STEEL ⟨∼ yourself for the shock⟩ **c** : INVIGORATE, FRESHEN **3** : to turn (a sail yard) by means of a brace **4 a** : to furnish or support with a brace ⟨heavily *braced* against the wind⟩ **b** : to make stronger : REINFORCE **5** : to put or plant firmly ⟨∼s his foot in the stirrup⟩ **6** : to waylay esp. with demands or questions ∼ *vi* **1** : to take heart — used with *up* **2** : to get ready (as for an attack)
²brace *n, pl* **brac·es** [ME, clasp, pair, fr. MF, two arms, fr. L *bracchia*, pl. of *bracchium* arm, fr. Gk *brachiōn*, fr. compar. of *brachys* short — more at BRIEF] (14c) **1** : something (as a clasp) that connects or fastens **2** *or pl* **brace** : two of a kind : PAIR ⟨several ∼ of quail⟩ **3** : a crank-shaped instrument for turning a bit **4** : something that transmits, directs, resists, or supports weight or pressure: as **a** : a diagonal piece of structural material that serves to strengthen something (as a framework) **b** : a rope rove through a block at the end of a ship's yard to swing it horizontally **c** *pl* : SUSPENDERS **d** : an appliance for supporting a body part **e** *pl* : dental appliances used to exert pressure to straighten misaligned teeth **5 a** : one of two marks { } used to connect words or items to be considered together **b** : one of these marks connecting two or more musical staffs carrying parts to be performed simultaneously **c** : BRACKET 3a **6** : a position of rigid attention **7** : something that arouses energy or strengthens morale
brace·let \'brās-lət\ *n* [ME, fr. MF, dim. of *bras* arm, fr. L *bracchium*] (15c) **1** : an ornamental band or chain worn around the wrist **2** : something (as handcuffs) resembling a bracelet
¹bra·cer \'brā-sər\ *n* [ME, fr. MF *braciere*, fr. OF, fr. *braz* arm, fr. L *bracchium*] (14c) : an arm or wrist protector esp. for use by an archer
²brac·er \'brā-sər\ *n* (1579) **1** : one that braces, binds, or makes firm **2** : a drink (as of liquor) taken as a stimulant
bra·ce·ro \brä-'ser-(ˌ)ō\ *n, pl* **-ros** [Sp, laborer, fr. *brazo* arm, fr. L *bracchium*] (1920) : a Mexican laborer admitted to the U.S. esp. for seasonal contract labor in agriculture — compare WETBACK
brace root *n* (1892) : PROP ROOT

brachi- *or* **brachio-** *comb form* [L *bracchium, brachium*] **1** : arm ⟨*brachi*al⟩ **2** : brachial and ⟨*brachio*cephalic⟩
bra·chi·al \'brā-kē-əl\ *adj* (1578) : of, relating to, or situated in the arm or an armlike process ⟨the ∼ artery of the upper arm⟩
brachial plexus *n* (ca. 1860) : a network of nerves lying mostly in the armpit and supplying nerves to the chest, shoulder, and arm
bra·chi·ate \'brā-kē-ˌāt\ *vi* **-at·ed; -at·ing** (1932) : to progress by swinging from one hold to another by the arms ⟨a *brachiating* gibbon⟩ — **bra·chi·a·tion** \ˌbrā-kē-'ā-shən\ *n* — **bra·chi·a·tor** \'brā-kē-ˌā-tər\ *n*
bra·chio·ce·phal·ic artery \ˌbrā-kē-(ˌ)ō-sə-ˌfa-lik-\ *n* (ca. 1839) : a short artery that arises from the arch of the aorta and divides into the carotid and subclavian arteries of the right side — called also *innominate artery*
brachiocephalic vein *n* (ca. 1852) : either of two large veins that occur one on each side of the neck, receive blood from the head and neck, and unite to form the superior vena cava — called also *innominate vein*
bra·chio·pod \'brā-kē-ə-ˌpäd\ *n* [ultim. fr. L *bracchium* + Gk *pod-, pous* foot — more at FOOT] (1836) : any of a phylum (Brachiopoda) of marine invertebrates with bivalve shells within which is a pair of arms bearing tentacles by which a current of water is made to bring microscopic food to the mouth — **brachiopod** *adj*
brachy- *comb form* [Gk, fr. *brachys* — more at BRIEF] : short ⟨*brachy*cephalic⟩
brachy·ce·phal·ic \ˌbra-ki-sə-'fa-lik\ *adj* [NL *brachycephalus*, fr. Gk *brachy-* + *kephalē* head — more at CEPHALIC] (ca. 1852) : short-headed or broad-headed with a cephalic index of over 80 — **brachy·ceph·a·ly** \-'se-fə-lē\ *n*
bra·chyp·ter·ous \bra-'kip-tə-rəs\ *adj* [Gk *brachypteros*, fr. *brachy-* + *pteron* wing — more at FEATHER] (ca. 1847) : having rudimentary or abnormally small wings ⟨∼ insects⟩
brac·ing \'brā-siŋ\ *adj* (1750) : giving strength, vigor, or freshness ⟨a ∼ breeze⟩ — **brac·ing·ly** *adv*
bra·ci·o·la \ˌbrä-chē-'ō-lə, -'chō-lə\ *or* **bra·ci·o·le** \-'ō-lä\ *n* [It, lit., slice of meat roasted over coals, fr. *brace* live coals, prob. fr. Gmc origin; akin to Sw *brasa* fire] (ca. 1945) : a thin slice of meat wrapped around a seasoned filling and often cooked in wine
brack·en \'bra-kən\ *n* [ME *braken*, prob. of Scand origin; akin to OSw *brækne* fern] (14c) **1** : a large coarse fern; *esp* : a nearly cosmopolitan brake (*Pteridium aquilinum*) found in most tropical and temperate regions **2** : a growth of brakes
¹brack·et \'bra-kət\ *n* [perh. fr. MF *braguette* codpiece, fr. dim. of *brague* breeches, fr. OProv *braga*, fr. L *braca*, of Celt origin — more at BREECH] (1580) **1** : an overhanging member that projects from a structure (as a wall) and is usu. designed to support a vertical load or to strengthen an angle **2** : a fixture (as for holding a lamp) projecting from a wall or column **3 a** : one of a pair of marks [ ] used in writing and printing to enclose matter or in mathematics and logic as signs of aggregation — called also *square bracket* **b** : one of the pair of marks ⟨ ⟩ used to enclose matter — called also *angle bracket* **c** : PARENTHESIS **3 d** : BRACE 5b **4** : a section of a continuously numbered or graded series (as age ranges or income levels)
²bracket *vt* (ca. 1847) **1 a** : to place within or as if within brackets ⟨editorial comments are ∼*ed*⟩ ⟨news stories ∼*ed* by commercials⟩ **b** : to eliminate from consideration ⟨∼ off politics⟩ **c** : to extend around so as to encompass : INCLUDE ⟨test pressures . . . which ∼ virtually the entire range of passenger-car tire pressures —*Consumer Reports*⟩ **2** : to furnish or fasten with brackets **3** : to put in the same category or group ⟨∼*ed* in a tie for third⟩ **4 a** : to get the range on (a target) by firing over and short ⟨there were mortar rounds ∼*ing* the area —Ed Bradley⟩ **b** : to establish the limits of ⟨∼*ed* the problem neatly⟩ **c** : to take photographs at more than one exposure in order to ensure that the desired exposure is obtained
bracket creep *n* (1975) : movement into a higher tax bracket as a result of income rises intended to offset the effects of inflation
brack·et·ed \-ləd\ *adj of a serif* : joined to the stroke by a curved line
bracket fungus *n* (1899) : a basidiomycete that forms shelflike sporophores
brack·ish \'bra-kish\ *adj* [D *brac* salty; akin to MLG *brac* salty] (1538) **1** : somewhat salty ⟨∼ water⟩ **2 a** : not appealing to the taste ⟨∼ tea⟩ **b** : REPULSIVE — **brack·ish·ness** *n*
brac·o·nid \'bra-kə-(ˌ)nid\ *n* [ultim. fr. Gk *brachys*] (ca. 1893) : any of a large family (Braconidae) of ichneumon flies — **braconid** *adj*
bract \'brakt\ *n* [NL *bractea*, fr. L, thin metal plate] (1770) **1** : a leaf from the axil of which a flower or floral axis arises **2** : a leaf borne on a floral axis; *esp* : one subtending a flower or flower cluster — **brac·te·al** \'brak-tē-əl\ *adj* — **brac·te·ate** \-tē-ət, -ˌāt\ *adj* — **brac·ted** \-təd\ *adj*
brac·te·ole \'brak-tē-ˌōl\ *n* [NL *bracteola*, fr. L, dim. of *bractea*] (ca. 1828) : a small bract esp. on a floral axis
¹brad \'brad\ *n* [ME, fr. ON *broddr* spike; perh. akin to OE *byrst* bristle — more at BRISTLE] (13c) **1** : a thin nail of the same thickness throughout but tapering in width and having a slight projection at the top of one side instead of a head **2** : a slender wire nail with a small barrel-shaped head
²brad *vt* **brad·ded; brad·ding** (1794) : to fasten with brads
brad·awl \'brad-ˌȯl\ *n* (1823) : an awl with chisel edge used to make holes for brads or screws
brady- *comb form* [Gk *bradys*] : slow ⟨*brady*kinin⟩
bra·dy·car·dia \ˌbrā-di-'kär-dē-ə *also* ˌbra-\ *n* [NL] (ca. 1890) : relatively slow heart action — compare TACHYCARDIA
bra·dy·ki·nin \-'kī-nən\ *n* (1949) : a kinin that is formed locally in injured tissue, acts in vasodilation of small arterioles, is considered to play a part in inflammatory processes, and is composed of a chain of nine amino-acid residues

---

\ə\ abut \ᵊ\ kitten, F table \ər\ further \a\ ash \ā\ ace \ä\ mop, mar \aú\ out \ch\ chin \e\ bet \ē\ easy \g\ go \i\ hit \ī\ ice \j\ job \ŋ\ sing \ō\ go \ȯ\ law \ȯi\ boy \th\ thin \t͟h\ the \ü\ loot \ú\ foot \y\ yet \zh\ vision \ä, k̵, ⁿ, œ, œ̄, ᵫ, ᵫ̄, ᴿ\ *see* Guide to Pronunciation

brae \'brā\ *n* [ME *bra*, fr. ON *brā* eyelid; akin to OE *brǣw* eyebrow, and prob. to OE *bregdan* to move quickly — more at BRAID] (13c) *chiefly Scot* : a hillside esp. along a river

¹**brag** \'brag\ *n* [ME] (14c) **1** : a pompous or boastful statement **2** : arrogant talk or manner : COCKINESS **3** : BRAGGART

²**brag** *vb* **bragged; brag·ging** *vi* (14c) : to talk boastfully : engage in self-glorification ~ *vt* : to assert boastfully *syn* see BOAST — **brag·ger** \'bra-gər\ *n* — **brag·gy** \'bra-gē\ *adj*

³**brag** *adj* **brag·ger; brag·gest** (1836) : FIRST-RATE

brag·ga·do·cio \ˌbra-gə-'dō-sē-ˌō, -shē-, -chē-, -(ˌ)shō, -(ˌ)chō\ *n, pl* **-cios** [*Braggadochio*, personification of boasting in *Faerie Queene* by Edmund Spenser] (1594) **1** : BRAGGART **2 a** : empty boasting **b** : arrogant pretension : COCKINESS

brag·gart \'bra-gərt\ *n* (ca. 1577) : a loud arrogant boaster — **brag·gart** *adj*

¹**Brah·ma** \'brä-mə\ *n* [Skt *brahman*] (1690) **1** : the creator god of the Hindu sacred triad — compare SIVA, VISHNU **2** : the ultimate ground of all being in Hinduism

²**Brah·ma** \'brä-mə, 'brä-, 'bra-\ *n* (1938) : BRAHMAN 2

Brah·man *or* **Brah·min** \'brä-mən; 2 is 'brä-, 'brä-, 'bra-\ [ME *Bragman* inhabitant of India, fr. L *Bracmanus*, fr. Gk *Brachman*, fr. Skt *brāhmaṇa* of the Brahman caste, fr. *brahman* Brahman] (15c) **1 a** : a Hindu of the highest caste traditionally assigned to the priesthood **b** : ¹BRAHMA 2 **2** : any of an Indian breed of humped cattle : ZEBU; *esp* : a large vigorous heat-resistant and tick-resistant usu. silvery gray animal developed in the southern U.S. from the zebu **3** *usu* **Brahmin** : a person of high social standing and cultivated intellect and taste ⟨Boston ~s⟩ — **Brah·man·ic** \brä-'ma-nik\ *or* **Brah·man·i·cal** \-ni-kəl\ *adj*

Brah·man·ism \'brä-mə-ˌni-zəm\ *n* (1816) : orthodox Hinduism adhering to the pantheism of the Vedas and to the ancient sacrifices and family ceremonies

¹**braid** \'brād\ *vt* [ME *breyden* to move suddenly, snatch, plait, fr. OE *bregdan;* akin to OHG *brettan* to draw (a sword)] (bef. 12c) **1 a** : to make from braids ⟨~ a rug⟩ **b** : to form (three or more strands) into a braid **2** : to do up (the hair) by interweaving three or more strands **3** : MIX, INTERMINGLE ⟨~ fact with fiction⟩ **4** : to ornament esp. with ribbon or braid — **braid·er** *n*

²**braid** *n* (1530) **1 a** : a length of braided hair **b** : a cord or ribbon having usu. three or more component strands forming a regular diagonal pattern down its length; *esp* : a narrow fabric of intertwined threads used esp. for trimming **2** : high-ranking naval officers

braid·ed *adj* (15c) **1 a** : made by intertwining three or more strands **b** : ornamented with braid **2** : forming an interlacing network of channels ⟨a ~ river⟩

braid·ing \'brā-diŋ\ *n* (15c) : something made of braided material

¹**brail** \'brā(ə)l\ *n* [ME *brayle*, fr. AF *braiel*, fr. OF, strap] (15c) **1** : a rope fastened to the leech of a sail and used for hauling the sail up or in **2** : a dip net with which fish are hauled aboard a boat from a purse seine or trap

²**brail** *vt* (1625) **1** : to take in (a sail) by the brails **2** : to hoist (fish) by means of a brail

braille \'brā(ə)l\ *n, often cap* [Louis *Braille*] (1853) : a system of writing for the blind that uses characters made up of raised dots — **braille** *vt* — **braill·ist** \'brā-list\ *n*

a	b	c	d	e	f	g	h	i	j
1	2	3	4	5	6	7	8	9	0

k	l	m	n	o	p	q	r	s	t

u	v	w	x	y	z	Capital Sign	Numeral Sign

braille alphabet

braille·writ·er \-ˌrī-tər\ *n, often cap* (1942) : a machine for writing braille

¹**brain** \'brān\ *n* [ME, fr. OE *brægen;* akin to MLG *bregen* brain, and perh. to Gk *brechmos* front part of the head] (bef. 12c) **1 a** : the portion of the vertebrate central nervous system that constitutes the organ of thought and neural coordination, includes all the higher nervous centers receiving stimuli from the sense organs and interpreting and correlating them to formulate the motor impulses, is made up of neurons and supporting and nutritive structures, is enclosed within the skull, and is continuous with the spinal cord through the foramen magnum **b** : a nervous center in invertebrates comparable in position and function to the vertebrate brain **2 a** (1) : INTELLECT, MIND ⟨has a clever ~⟩ (2) : intellectual endowment : INTELLIGENCE — often used in pl. ⟨plenty of ~s in that family⟩ **b** (1) : a very intelligent or intellectual person (2) : the chief planner of an organization or enterprise — usu. used in pl. **3** : something that performs the functions of a brain; *esp* : an automatic device (as a computer) for control or computation

²**brain** *vt* (14c) **1** : to kill by smashing the skull **2** : to hit on the head

brain·case \'brān-ˌkās\ *n* (1741) : the cranium enclosing the brain

brain 1a: *1* cerebral hemisphere, *2* corpus callosum, *3* ventricle, *4* fornix, *5* thalamus, *6* pituitary gland, *7* pons, *8* medulla oblongata, *9* spinal cord, *10* cerebellum, *11* midbrain

brain·child \-ˌchīld\ *n* (1631) : a product of one's creative imagination

brain coral *n* (ca. 1711) : a massive reef-building coral (as genus *Maeandra*) having the surface covered by ridges and furrows

brain death *n* (1964) : final cessation of activity in the central nervous system esp. as indicated by a flat electroencephalogram for a predetermined length of time — **brain–dead** *adj*

brain drain *n* (1963) : the departure of educated or professional people from one country, economic sector, or field for another usu. for better pay or living conditions

brained \'brānd\ *adj* (15c) : having a brain of a specified kind — used in combination ⟨feather*brained*⟩

brain hormone *n* (1957) : a hormone that is secreted by neurosecretory cells of the insect brain and that stimulates the prothoracic glands to secrete ecdysone

brain·ish \'brā-nish\ *adj* (ca. 1530) *archaic* : IMPETUOUS, HOTHEADED ⟨and in this ~ apprehension kills the unseen good old man —Shak.⟩

brain·less \'brān-ləs\ *adj* (15c) : devoid of intelligence : STUPID — **brain·less·ly** *adv* — **brain·less·ness** *n*

brain·pan \'brān-ˌpan\ *n* (14c) : BRAINCASE

brain–pick·ing \-ˌpi-kiŋ\ *n* (1954) : the act of gathering information from another's mind — **brain–pick·er** \-kər\ *n*

brain–pow·er \-ˌpau̇(-ə)r\ *n* (1878) **1** : intellectual ability **2** : people with developed intellectual ability

brain·sick \-ˌsik\ *adj* (15c) **1** : mentally disordered **2** : arising from mental disorder ⟨a ~ frenzy⟩ — **brain·sick·ly** *adv*

brain stem *n* (1879) : the part of the brain composed of the mesencephalon, pons, and medulla oblongata and connecting the spinal cord with the forebrain and cerebrum

brain·storm \-ˌstȯrm\ *n* (ca. 1894) **1** : a violent transient fit of insanity **2 a** : a sudden bright idea **b** : a harebrained idea

brain·storm·ing \-ˌstȯr-miŋ\ *n* (ca. 1955) : a group problem-solving technique that involves the spontaneous contribution of ideas from all members of the group — **brain·storm** *vb* — **brain·storm·er** *n*

brains trust *n* (1934) *chiefly Brit* : BRAIN TRUST

brain–teas·er \-ˌtē-zər\ *n* (1923) : something (as a puzzle) that demands mental effort and acuity for its solution

brain trust *n* (1910) : a group of official or unofficial advisers concerned esp. with planning and strategy — **brain trust·er** \-ˌtrəs-tər\ *n*

brain·wash·ing \'brān-ˌwȯ-shiŋ, -ˌwä-\ *n* [trans. of Chin (Beijing) *xǐnǎo*] (1950) **1** : a forcible indoctrination to induce someone to give up basic political, social, or religious beliefs and attitudes and to accept contrasting regimented ideas **2** : persuasion by propaganda or salesmanship — **brain·wash** *vt* — **brainwash** *n* — **brain·wash·er** *n*

brain wave *n* (1890) **1** : BRAINSTORM 2a **2 a** : rhythmic fluctuations of voltage between parts of the brain resulting in the flow of an electric current **b** : a current produced by brain waves

brainy \'brā-nē\ *adj* **brain·i·er; -est** (1874) : having or showing a well-developed intellect : INTELLIGENT — **brain·i·ness** *n*

¹**braise** \'brāz\ *vt* **braised; brais·ing** [F *braisé*, fr. *braise* live coals, fr. OF *breze*, prob. of Gmc origin; akin to Sw *brasa* fire] (1797) : to cook slowly in fat and little moisture in a closed pot

²**braise** *n* (ca. 1885) : an item of braised food

¹**brake** \'brāk\ *archaic past of* BREAK

²**brake** *n* [ME, fern, prob. back-formation fr. *braken* bracken] (14c) : the common bracken fern (*Pteridium aquilinum*)

³**brake** *n* [ME, fr. MLG; akin to OE *brecan* to break] (15c) **1 a** : a toothed instrument or machine for separating out the fiber of flax or hemp by breaking up the woody parts **2** : a machine for bending, flanging, folding, and forming sheet metal

⁴**brake** *n* [ME -*brake*] (1563) : rough or marshy land overgrown usu. with one kind of plant — **braky** \'brā-kē\ *adj*

⁵**brake** *n* [perh. fr. obs. *brake* bridle] (ca. 1782) **1** : a device for arresting or preventing the motion of a mechanism usu. by means of friction **2** : something used to slow down or stop movement or activity ⟨use interest rates as a ~ on spending⟩ — **brake·less** \'brā-kləs\ *adj*

⁶**brake** *vb* **braked; brak·ing** *vt* (1868) : to retard or stop by a brake ~ *vi* **1** : to operate or manage a brake; *esp* : to apply the brake on a vehicle **2** : to become checked by a brake

brake·man \'brāk-mən\ *n* (1833) **1** : a freight or passenger train crew member who inspects the train and assists the conductor **2** : the end man on a bobsled team who operates the brake

bram·ble \'bram-bəl\ *n* [ME *brembel*, fr. OE *brēmel;* akin to OE *brōm* broom] (bef. 12c) : any of a genus (*Rubus*) of usu. prickly shrubs of the rose family including the raspberries and blackberries; *broadly* : a rough prickly shrub or vine — **bram·bly** \-b(ə-)lē\ *adj*

bran \'bran\ *n* [ME, fr. MF] (14c) : the edible broken seed coats of cereal grain separated from the flour or meal by sifting or bolting

¹**branch** \'branch\ *n, often attrib* [ME, fr. MF *branche*, fr. LL *branca* paw] (14c) **1** : a natural subdivision of a plant stem; *esp* : a secondary shoot or stem (as a bough) arising from a main axis (as of a tree) **2** : something that extends from or enters into a main body or source: as **a** (1) : a stream that flows into another usu. larger stream : TRIBUTARY (2) *Southern & Midland* : CREEK **2 b** : a side road or way **c** : a slender projection (as the tine of an antler) **d** : a distinctive part of a mathematical curve **e** : a part of a computer program executed as a result of a program decision **3** : a part of a complex body: as **a** : a division of a family descending from a particular ancestor **b** : an area of knowledge that may be considered apart from related areas ⟨pathology is a ~ of medicine⟩ **c** (1) : a division of an organization (2) : a separate but dependent part of a central organization ⟨the neighborhood ~ of the city library⟩ **d** : a language group less inclusive than a family ⟨the Germanic ~ of the Indo-European language family⟩ — **branched** \'brancht\ *adj* — **branch·less** \'branch-ləs\ *adj* — **branchy** \'bran-chē\ *adj*

²**branch** *vi* (14c) **1** : to put forth branches : RAMIFY **2** : to spring out (as from a main stem) : DIVERGE **3** : to be an outgrowth — used with *from* ⟨poetry that ~ed from religious prose⟩ **4** : to extend activities — usu. used with *out* ⟨the business is ~*ing* out⟩ **5** : to follow one of two or more branches (as in a computer program) ~ *vt* **1** : to ornament with designs of branches **2** : to divide up : SECTION

bran·chi·al \'braŋ-kē-əl\ *adj* [Gk *branchia* gills] (1801) : of, relating to, or supplying the gills or associated structures or their embryonic precursors

bran·chio·pod \'braŋ-kē-ə-ˌpäd\ *n* [ultim. fr. Gk *branchia* gills + *pod-*,

pous foot — more at FOOT] (1836) : any of a group (Branchiopoda) of small usu. freshwater crustaceans (as fairy shrimp or water fleas) with usu. many pairs of setae-bearing appendages — **branchiopod** *adj*
branch·let \'branch-lət\ *n* (ca. 1731) : a small usu. terminal branch
branch·line \-,līn\ *n* (1846) : a secondary line usu. of a railroad
branch water *n* [¹*branch* (creek)] (1835) : plain water ⟨bourbon and *branch water*⟩
¹**brand** \'brand\ *n* [ME, torch, sword, fr. OE; akin to OE *bærnan* to burn] (bef. 12c) **1 a** : a charred piece of wood **b** : FIREBRAND 1 **c** : something (as lightning) that resembles a firebrand **2** : SWORD **3 a** (1) : a mark made by burning with a hot iron to attest manufacture or quality or to designate ownership (2) : a printed mark made for similar purposes : TRADEMARK **b** (1) : a mark put on criminals with a hot iron (2) : a mark of disgrace : STIGMA ⟨the ~ of poverty⟩ **4 a** : a class of goods identified by name as the product of a single firm or manufacturer : MAKE **b** : a characteristic or distinctive kind ⟨a lively ~ of theater⟩ **5** : a tool used to produce a brand
²**brand** *vt* (15c) **1** : to mark with a brand **2** : to mark with disapproval : STIGMATIZE **3** : to impress indelibly ⟨~ the lesson on his mind⟩ — **brand·er** *n*
brand·ed \'bran-dəd\ *adj* (1897) : having a brand name ⟨~ products⟩
¹**bran·dish** \'bran-dish\ *vt* [ME *braundisshen*, fr. MF *brandiss-*, stem of *brandir*, fr. OF, fr. *brand* sword, of Gmc origin; akin to OE *brand*] (14c) **1** : to shake or wave (as a weapon) menacingly **2** : to exhibit in an ostentatious or aggressive manner *syn* see SWING
²**brandish** *n* (1599) : an act or instance of brandishing
brand–name \'bran(d)-'nām\ *adj* (1949) **1** : of or relating to a trade name ⟨~ products⟩ **2** : having a reputation and a loyal following ⟨~ authors⟩
brand name *n* (1922) : TRADE NAME 1b
brand–new \-'nü, -'nyü\ *adj* [¹*brand*] (ca. 1570) : conspicuously new and unused; *also* : recently introduced ⟨a ~ executive officer⟩
¹**bran·dy** \'bran-dē\ *n, pl* **brandies** [short for *brandywine*, fr. D *brandewijn*, fr. MD *brantwijn*, fr. *brant* distilled + *wijn* wine] (1657) : an alcoholic beverage distilled from wine or fermented fruit juice
²**brandy** *vt* **bran·died; bran·dy·ing** (ca. 1848) : to flavor, blend, or preserve with brandy
Bran·gus \'braŋ-gəs\ *trademark* — used for polled solid black beef cattle of a breed developed from a Brahman-Angus cross
bran·ni·gan \'bra-ni-gən\ *n* [prob. fr. the name *Brannigan*] (1927) **1** : a drinking spree **2** : SQUABBLE
brant \'brant\ *n, pl* **brant** *or* **brants** [ME *brand gos*] (14c) : any of several small wild geese (genus *Branta*); *esp* : a small black-necked goose (*Branta bernicla*) about the size of a mallard
¹**brash** \'brash\ *adj* [origin unknown] (1566) **1** : BRITTLE ⟨~ wood⟩ **2 a** : heedless of the consequences : AUDACIOUS ⟨the ~est bush pilot of them all⟩ **b** : done in haste without regard for consequences : RASH ⟨~ acts⟩ **3 a** : full of fresh raw vitality ⟨a ~ frontier town⟩ **b** : uninhibitedly energetic or demonstrative : BUMPTIOUS ⟨a ~ comedian⟩ **4 a** : lacking restraint and discernment : TACTLESS ⟨~ remarks⟩ **b** : aggressively self-assertive : IMPUDENT ⟨~ to the point of arrogance⟩ **5** : piercingly sharp : HARSH ⟨a ~ squeal of brakes⟩ **6** : marked by vivid contrast : BOLD ⟨~ colors⟩ — **brash·ly** *adv* — **brash·ness** *n*
²**brash** *n* [obs. E *brash* to breach a wall] (1787) : a mass of fragments (as of ice)
brass \'bras\ *n* [ME *bras*, fr. OE *bræs*; akin to MLG *bras* metal] (bef. 12c) **1** : an alloy consisting essentially of copper and zinc in variable proportions **2 a** : the brass instruments of an orchestra or band — often used in pl. **b** : a usu. brass memorial tablet **c** : bright metal fittings, utensils, or ornaments **d** : empty cartridge shells **3** : brazen self-assurance : GALL **4** *sing or pl in constr* **a** : high-ranking members of the military **b** : persons in high positions (as in a business or the government) — **brass** *adj*
bras·sard \brə-'särd, 'bra-,\ *n* [F *brassard*, fr. MF *brassal*, fr. OIt *bracciale*, fr. *braccio* arm, fr. L *bracchium* — more at BRACE] (1830) **1** : armor for protecting the arm — see ARMOR illustration **2** : a cloth band worn around the upper arm usu. bearing an identifying mark
brass band *n* (1834) : a band consisting chiefly or solely of brass and percussion instruments
brass·bound \'bras-,baund, -'baund\ *adj* (1687) **1** : having trim made of brass or a metal resembling brass **2 a** (1) : tradition-bound and opinionated (2) : making no concessions : INFLEXIBLE **b** : BRAZEN, PRESUMPTUOUS
brass collar Democrat *n* (1951) : a conservative Democrat esp. in the south who votes the straight Democratic ticket
bras·se·rie \,bras-'rē, ,bra-sə-\ *n* [F, lit., brewery, fr. MF *brasser* to brew, fr. OF *bracier*, fr. (assumed) VL *braciare*, of Celt origin; akin to W *brag* malt] (1864) : an informal usu. French restaurant serving simple hearty food
brass hat *n* [fr. the gold braid worn on the cap] (1893) : a member of the brass
bras·si·ca \'bra-si-kə\ *n* [NL, genus name, fr. L, cabbage] (1832) : any of a large genus (*Brassica*) of Old World temperate zone herbs (as cabbages) of the mustard family with beaked cylindrical pods
bras·siere \brə-'zir *also* ,bra-sē-'er\ *n* [obs. F *brassière* bodice, fr. OF *braciere* arm protector, fr. *bras* arm — more at BRACELET] (1911) : a woman's undergarment to cover and support the breasts
brass instrument *n* (1854) : any of a group of wind instruments (as a French horn, trombone, trumpet, or tuba) that is usu. characterized by a long cylindrical or conical metal tube commonly curved two or more times and ending in a flared bell, that produces tones by the vibrations of the player's lips against a usu. cup-shaped mouthpiece, and that usu. has valves or a slide by which the player may produce all the tones within the instrument's range
brass knuckles *n pl but sing or pl in constr* (1855) : KNUCKLE 4
brass ring *n* (1950) : a rich opportunity : PRIZE
brass tacks *n pl* (1897) : details of immediate practical importance — usu. used in the phrase *get down to brass tacks*
brassy \'bra-sē\ *adj* **brass·i·er; -est** (1576) **1 a** : being shamelessly bold **b** : OBSTREPEROUS **2** : resembling brass esp. in color **3** : resembling the sound of a brass instrument — **brass·i·ly** \'bra-sə-lē\ *adv* — **brass·i·ness** \'bra-sē-nəs\ *n*
brat \'brat\ *n* [perh. fr. E dial. *brat* (coarse garment)] (ca. 1505) **1 a** : CHILD; *specif* : an ill-natured annoying child **b** : an ill-mannered

immature person **2** : the son or daughter of a career military person — **brat·ti·ness** \'bra-tē-nəs\ *n* — **brat·tish** \'bra-tish\ *adj* — **brat·ty** \-tē\ *adj*
brat·tice \'bra-təs, 'bra-tish\ *n* [ME *bretais* parapet, fr. OF *bretesche*, fr. ML *breteschia*] (ca. 1846) : an often temporary partition of planks or cloth used esp. to control mine ventilation — **brattice** *vt*
¹**brat·tle** \'bra-t²l\ *n* [prob. imit.] (ca. 1500) *chiefly Scot* : CLATTER, SCAMPER
²**brattle** *vi* **brat·tled; brat·tling** (1513) *chiefly Scot* : to make a clattering or rattling sound
brat·wurst \'brät-(,)wərst *also* 'brat- *also* -,vù(r)st; *sometimes* -,vùsht\ *n* [G, fr. OHG *brātwurst*, fr. *brāt* meat without waste + *wurst* sausage] (ca. 1888) : fresh pork sausage for frying
braun·schweig·er \'braun-,shwī-gər, -,shvī- *also* 'brän-\ *n* [G *Braunschweiger* (*Wurst*), lit., Brunswick sausage] (1934) : smoked liverwurst
bra·va \'brä-(,)vä, brä-'vä\ *n* [It, fem. of *bravo*] (1803) : BRAVO — used interjectionally in applauding a woman
bra·va·do \brə-'vä-(,)dō\ *n, pl* **-does** *or* **-dos** [MF *bravade* & OSp *bravata*, fr. OIt *bravata*, fr. *bravare* to challenge, show off, fr. *bravo*] (ca. 1580) **1 a** : blustering swaggering conduct **b** : a pretense of bravery **2** : the quality or state of being foolhardy
¹**brave** \'brāv\ *adj* **brav·er; brav·est** [MF, fr. OIt & OSp *bravo* courageous, wild, prob. fr. L *barbarus* barbarous] (15c) **1** : having courage : DAUNTLESS **2** : making a fine show : COLORFUL ⟨~ banners flying in the wind⟩ **3** : EXCELLENT, SPLENDID ⟨the ~ fire I soon had going —J. F. Dobie⟩ — **brave·ly** *adv*
²**brave** *vb* **braved; brav·ing** *vt* (1546) **1** : to face or endure with courage **2** *obs* : to make showy ~ *vi, archaic* : to make a brave show — **brav·er** *n*
³**brave** *n* (1590) **1** *archaic* : BRAVADO **2** : one who is brave; *specif* : an American Indian warrior **3** *archaic* : BULLY, ASSASSIN
brave new world *n* [fr. the dystopian novel *Brave New World* (1932) by Aldous Huxley] (1933) : a future world, situation, or development; *also* : a recent development or recently changed situation
brav·ery \'brāv-rē, 'brā-və-\ *n, pl* **-er·ies** (1548) **1** : the quality or state of being brave : COURAGE **2 a** : fine clothes **b** : showy display
¹**bra·vo** \'brä-(,)vō\ *n, pl* **bravos** *or* **bravoes** [It, fr. *bravo* brave] (1597) **:** VILLAIN, DESPERADO; *esp* : a hired assassin
²**bra·vo** \'brä-(,)vō, brä-'vō\ *n, pl* **bravos** (1761) : a shout of approval — often used interjectionally in applauding a performance
³**bra·vo** *see* ²\ *vt* **bra·voed; bra·vo·ing** (1831) : to applaud by shouts of *bravo*
Bra·vo \'brä-(,)vō\ (1952) — a communications code word for the letter *b*
¹**bra·vu·ra** \brə-'vyùr-ə, brä-, -'vùr-\ *n* [It, lit., bravery, fr. *bravare*] (1757) **1** : a musical passage requiring exceptional agility and technical skill in execution **2** : a florid brilliant style **3** : a show of daring or brilliance
²**bravura** *adj* (1920) **1** : marked by an ostentatious display of skill **2** : ORNATE, SHOWY
braw \'brò, 'brä\ *adj* [modif. of MF *brave*] (ca. 1565) **1** *chiefly Scot* : GOOD, FINE **2** *chiefly Scot* : well dressed
¹**brawl** \'bròl\ *vi* [ME] (14c) **1** : to quarrel or fight noisily : WRANGLE **2** : to make a loud confused noise — **brawl·er** *n*
²**brawl** *n* (15c) **1** : a noisy quarrel or fight **2** : a loud tumultuous noise
brawly \'brò-lē\ *adj* **brawl·i·er; -est** (1940) **1** : inclined to brawl **2** : characterized by brawls or brawling
brawn \'bròn\ *n* [ME, fr. MF *braon* muscle, of Gmc origin; akin to OE *brǣd* flesh] (13c) **1 a** *Brit* : the flesh of a boar **b** : HEADCHEESE **2 a** : full strong muscles **b** : muscular strength
brawny \'brò-nē\ *adj* **brawn·i·er; -est** (1599) **1** : MUSCULAR; *also* : STRONG, POWERFUL **2** : being swollen and hard ⟨a ~ infected foot⟩ — **brawn·i·ly** \-nə-lē\ *adv* — **brawn·i·ness** \-nē-nəs\ *n*
¹**bray** \'brä\ *vb* [ME, fr. MF *braire* to cry, fr. (assumed) VL *bragere*, of Celt origin; akin to OIr *braigid* he breaks wind] *vi* (14c) : to utter the characteristic loud harsh cry of a donkey; *also* : to utter a sound like a donkey's ~ *vt* : to utter or play loudly, harshly, or discordantly — **bray** *n*
²**bray** *vt* [ME, fr. AF *braier*, fr. OF *breier*, of Gmc origin; akin to OHG *brehhan* to break — more at BREAK] (14c) **1** : to crush or grind fine ⟨~ seeds in a mortar⟩ **2** : to spread thin ⟨~ printing ink⟩
bray·er \'brä-ər\ *n* (1688) : a printer's hand inking roller
¹**braze** \'brāz\ *vt* **brazed; braz·ing** [irreg. fr. *brass*] (1602) *archaic* : HARDEN
²**braze** *vt* **brazed; braz·ing** [F *braser*, fr. OF, to burn, fr. *breze* hot coals — more at BRAISE] (1677) : to solder with a nonferrous alloy that melts at a lower temperature than that of the metals being joined — **braz·er** *n*
¹**bra·zen** \'brā-z²n\ *adj* [ME *brasen*, fr. OE *bræsen*, fr. *bræs* brass] (bef. 12c) **1** : made of brass **2 a** : sounding harsh and loud like struck brass **b** : of the color of polished brass **3** : marked by contemptuous boldness — **bra·zen·ly** *adv* — **bra·zen·ness** \'brā-z²n-(n)əs\ *n*
²**brazen** *vt* **bra·zened; bra·zen·ing** \'brāz-niŋ, 'brā-z²n-iŋ\ (ca. 1555) : to face with defiance or impudence — usu. used in the phrase *brazen it out*
bra·zen–faced \'brā-z²n-,fāst\ *adj* (1571) : marked by insolence and bold disrespect ⟨~ assertions⟩
¹**bra·zier** \'brā-zhər\ *n* [ME *brasier*, fr. *bras* brass] (14c) : one that works in brass
²**brazier** *n* [F *brasier*, fr. OF, fire of hot coals, fr. *breze*] (ca. 1690) **1** : a pan for holding burning coals **2** : a utensil in which food is exposed to heat through a wire grill
Bra·zil nut \brə-'zil-\ *n* [*Brazil*, So. America] (1830) : a tall So. American tree (*Bertholletia excelsa* of the family Lecythidaceae) that bears large globular capsules each containing several closely packed roughly triangular oily edible nuts; *also* : its nut

---

\ə\ abut \²\ kitten, F table \ər\ further \a\ ash \ā\ ace \ä\ mop, mar
\aù\ out \ch\ chin \e\ bet \ē\ easy \g\ go \i\ hit \ī\ ice \j\ job
\ŋ\ sing \ō\ go \ò\ law \òi\ boy \th\ thin \th̲\ the \ü\ loot \ù\ foot
\y\ yet \zh\ vision \à, k̲, ⁿ, œ, œ̄, ᵫ, ᵫ̄, ʸ\ see Guide to Pronunciation

bra·zil·wood \brə-'zil-ˌwùd\ n [Sp brasil, fr. brasa live coals (fr. the wood's color), prob. of Gmc origin; akin to Sw brasa fire] (1559) : the heavy wood of any of various tropical leguminous trees (esp. genus Caesalpinia) that is used as red and purple dyewood and in cabinet-work

¹breach \'brēch\ n [ME breche, fr. OE bræc act of breaking; akin to OE brecan to break] (bef. 12c) **1 :** infraction or violation of a law, obligation, tie, or standard **2 a :** a broken, ruptured, or torn condition or area **b :** a gap (as in a wall) made by battering **3 a :** a break in accustomed friendly relations **b :** a temporary gap in continuity : HIATUS **4 :** a leap esp. of a whale out of water

²breach vt (1547) **1 :** to make a breach in **2 :** BREAK, VIOLATE ⟨~ an agreement⟩ ~ vi : to leap out of water ⟨a whale ~ing⟩

breach of promise (1590) : violation of a promise esp. to marry

¹bread \'bred\ n [ME breed, fr. OE brēad; akin to OHG brōt bread, OE brēowan to brew] (bef. 12c) **1 a :** a usu. baked and leavened food made of a mixture whose basic constituent is flour or meal **2 :** FOOD, SUSTENANCE ⟨our daily ~⟩ **3 a :** LIVELIHOOD ⟨earns his ~ as a laborer⟩ **b** slang : MONEY — **bready** \'bre-dē\ adj — **bread upon the waters** : resources risked or charitable deeds performed without expectation of return

²bread vt (1629) : to cover with bread crumbs ⟨a ~ed pork chop⟩

bread–and–butter adj (ca. 1837) **1 a :** being as basic as the earning of one's livelihood ⟨~ issues⟩ **b :** that can be depended on ⟨our ~ repertoire⟩ **2 :** sent or given as thanks for hospitality ⟨a ~ letter⟩

bread and butter n (1732) : a means of sustenance or livelihood

bread and circuses n pl [trans. of L panis et circenses] (1914) : a palliative offered esp. to avert potential discontent

bread·bas·ket \'bred-ˌbas-kət\ n (1753) **1** slang : STOMACH **2 :** a major cereal-producing region

¹bread·board \'bred-ˌbōrd, -ˌbòrd\ n (1857) **1 :** a board on which dough is kneaded or bread cut **2 :** a board on which components are mounted for breadboarding

²breadboard vt (1956) : to make an experimental arrangement of (as an electronic circuit or a mechanical system) to test feasibility

bread·fruit \'bred-ˌfrüt\ n (1697) : a round starchy usu. seedless fruit that resembles bread in color and texture when baked; also : a tall tropical evergreen tree (Artocarpus altilis) of the mulberry family that bears this fruit

bread·line \-ˌlīn\ n (1900) : a line of people waiting to receive free food

bread mold n (1914) : any of various molds found esp. on bread; esp : a rhizopus (Rhizopus nigricans syn. R. stolonifer)

bread·stuff \-ˌstəf\ n (1793) **1 :** a cereal product (as grain or flour) **2** : BREAD

breadth \'bretth, 'bredth, ÷'breth\ n [obs. E brede breadth (fr. ME, fr. OE brǣdu, fr. brād broad) + -th (as in length)] (15c) **1 :** distance from side to side : WIDTH **2 :** something of full width **3 a :** comprehensive quality : SCOPE ⟨~ of his learning⟩ **b :** liberality of views or taste ⟨~ of mind⟩ — **breadth·wise** \-ˌwīz\ adv or adj

bread·win·ner \'bred-ˌwi-nər\ n (1818) **1 :** a means (as a tool or craft) of livelihood **2 :** a member of a family whose wages supply its livelihood — **bread·win·ning** \-ˌwi-niŋ\ n

¹break \'brāk\ vb **broke** \'brōk\; **bro·ken** \'brō-kən\; **break·ing** [ME breken, fr. OE brecan; akin to OHG brehhan to break, L frangere] vt (bef. 12c) **1 a :** to separate into parts with suddenness or violence **b** : FRACTURE ⟨~ an arm⟩ **c :** RUPTURE ⟨~ the skin⟩ **d :** to cut into and turn over the surface of ⟨~ the soil⟩ **e :** to render inoperable ⟨broke his watch⟩ **2 a :** VIOLATE, TRANSGRESS ⟨~ the law⟩ ⟨~ a promise⟩ **b** : to invalidate (a will) by action at law **3 a** archaic : to force entry into **b :** to burst and force a way through ⟨~ the sound barrier⟩ ⟨~ a racial barrier⟩ **c :** to escape by force from ⟨~ jail⟩ **d :** to make or effect by cutting, forcing, or pressing through ⟨~ a trail through the woods⟩ **4 :** to disrupt the order or compactness of ⟨~ ranks⟩ **5 :** to make ineffective as a binding force ⟨~ the spell⟩ **6 a :** to defeat utterly and end as an effective force : DESTROY **b :** to crush the spirit of **c :** to make tractable or submissive: as (1) past part often **broke** : to train (an animal) to adjust to the service or convenience of humans ⟨a halter-broke horse⟩ (2) : INURE, ACCUSTOM **d :** to exhaust in health, strength, or capacity **7 a :** to stop or bring to an end suddenly : HALT ⟨~ a deadlock⟩ **b :** INTERRUPT, SUSPEND ⟨~ the silence with a cry⟩ **c :** to open and bring about suspension of operation ⟨~ an electric circuit⟩ **d :** to destroy unity or completeness of ⟨~ a dining room set by buying a chair⟩ **e :** to change the appearance of uniformity of ⟨a dormer ~s the level roof⟩ **f :** to split the surface of ⟨fish ~ing water⟩ **g :** to cause to discontinue a habit ⟨tried to ~ him of smoking⟩ **8 a :** to make known : TELL ⟨~ the bad news gently⟩ **b :** to bring to attention or prominence initially ⟨radio stations ~ing new musicians⟩ ⟨~ a news story⟩ **9 a :** to ruin financially **b :** to reduce in rank **10 a :** to split into smaller units, parts, or processes : DIVIDE **b** (1) : to give or get the equivalent of (a bill) in smaller denominations (2) : to use as the denomination in paying a bill ⟨didn't want to ~ a $20 bill⟩ — often used with into, up, or down **11 a :** to check the speed, force, or intensity of ⟨the bushes will ~ his fall⟩ ⟨without ~ing her stride⟩ **b** : to cause failure and discontinuance of (a strike) by measures outside bargaining processes **12 :** to cause a sudden significant decrease in the price, value, or volume of ⟨news likely to ~ the market sharply⟩ **13 a** : EXCEED, SURPASS ⟨~ the record⟩ **b :** to score less than (a specified total) ⟨golfer trying to ~ 90⟩ **c :** to win against (an opponent's service) in a racket game **14 :** to open the action of (a breechloader) **15 a :** to find an explanation or solution for : SOLVE ⟨the detective will ~ the case⟩ **b :** to discover the essentials of (a code or cipher system) **16 :** to demonstrate the falsity of ⟨~ an alibi⟩ **17 :** to ruin the prospects of ⟨could make or ~ her career⟩ **18 :** to produce visibly ⟨barely ~s a sweat⟩ ~ vi **1 a :** to escape with sudden forceful effort — often used with out ⟨~ out of jail⟩ **b :** to come into being by or as if by bursting forth ⟨day was ~ing⟩ **c :** to effect a penetration ⟨~ through security lines⟩ **d :** to emerge through the surface of the water **e :** to start abruptly ⟨when the storm broke⟩ **f :** to become known or published ⟨when the news broke⟩ **g :** to make a sudden dash ⟨~ for cover⟩ **h :** to separate after a clinch in boxing **2 a :** to come apart or split into pieces : BURST, SHATTER **b :** to open spontaneously or by pressure from within ⟨his boil finally broke⟩ **c** of a wave : to curl over and fall apart in surf or foam **3 :** to interrupt one's activity or occupation for a brief period ⟨~ for lunch⟩ **4 :** to alter sharply in tone, pitch,

or intensity ⟨a voice ~ing with emotion⟩ **5 :** to become fair : CLEAR ⟨when the weather ~s⟩ **6 :** to make the opening shot of a game of pool **7 :** to end a relationship, connection, or agreement — usu. used with with **8 :** to give way in disorderly retreat **9 a :** to swerve suddenly **b :** to curve, drop, or rise sharply ⟨a pitch that ~s away from the batter⟩ **10 :** to fail in health, strength, vitality, resolve, or control ⟨may ~ under questioning⟩ — often used with down **b :** to become inoperative because of damage, wear, or strain **11 :** to fail to keep a prescribed gait — used of a horse **12 :** to undergo a sudden significant decrease in price, value, or volume ⟨transportation stocks may ~ sharply⟩ **13 :** HAPPEN, DEVELOP ⟨for the team to succeed, everything has to ~ right⟩ **14 :** to win against an opponent's service in a racket game **15 a :** to divide into classes, categories, or types — usu. used with into and often with down ⟨the topic breaks down into three questions⟩ **b :** to fold, bend, lift, or come apart at a seam, groove, or joint **c** of cream : to separate during churning into liquid and fat — **break a leg** — used to wish good luck esp. to a performer — **break bread** : to dine together — **break camp** : to pack up gear and leave a camp or campsite — **break cover** also **break covert** : to start from a covert or lair — **break even** : to achieve a balance; esp : to operate a business or enterprise without either loss or profit — **break ground 1 :** to begin construction — usu. used with for **2** or **break new ground** : to make or show discoveries : PIONEER — **break into 1** : to begin with or as if with a sudden throwing off of restraint ⟨broke into tears⟩ ⟨face breaking into a smile⟩ ⟨the horse breaks into a gallop⟩ **2 :** to make entry or entrance ⟨broke into the house⟩ ⟨break into show business⟩ **3 :** INTERRUPT ⟨break into a TV program with a news flash⟩ — **break one's heart** : to crush emotionally with sorrow — **break one's wrists** : to turn the wrists as part of the swing of a club or bat — **break ranks** also **break rank** : to differ in opinion or action from one's peers — often used with with — **break the back of** : to subdue the main force of ⟨break the back of inflation⟩ — **break the ice 1 :** to make a beginning **2 :** to get through the first difficulties in starting a conversation or discussion — **break wind** : to expel gas from the intestine

²break n (14c) **1 a :** an act or action of breaking **b :** the opening shot in a game of pool or billiards **2 a :** a condition produced by or as if by breaking : GAP ⟨a ~ in the clouds⟩ **b :** a gap in an otherwise continuous electric circuit **3 :** the action or act of breaking in, out, or forth ⟨at ~ of day⟩ ⟨a jail ~⟩ **4 a :** place or situation at which a break occurs; esp : the place at which a word is divided esp. at the end of a line of print or writing **5 :** an interruption in continuity ⟨a ~ in the weather⟩: as **a :** a notable change of subject matter, attitude, or treatment **b** (1) : an abrupt, significant, or noteworthy change or interruption in a continuous process, trend, or surface (2) : a respite from work, school, or duty ⟨coffee ~⟩ ⟨spring ~⟩ (3) : a planned interruption in a radio or television program ⟨a ~ for the commercial⟩ **c :** deviation of a pitched baseball from a straight line **d** mining : FAULT, DISLOCATION **e :** failure of a horse to maintain the prescribed gait **f** : an abrupt change in musical or vocal pitch or quality **g :** the action or an instance of breaking service in a racket game **h :** a usu. solo instrumental passage in jazz, folk, or popular music **6 a :** DASH, RUSH ⟨a base runner making a ~ for home⟩ **b :** FAST BREAK **7 :** a sudden and abrupt decline of prices or values **8 a :** the start of a race **b** : the act of separating after a clinch in boxing **9 a :** a stroke of luck and esp. of good luck ⟨a bad ~⟩ ⟨got the ~s⟩ **b :** a favorable or opportune situation : CHANCE ⟨waiting for a big ~ in show business⟩ **c** : favorable consideration or treatment ⟨a tax ~⟩ ⟨a ~ on the price⟩ **10 a :** a rupture in previously agreeable relations ⟨a ~ between the two countries⟩ **b :** an abrupt split or difference with something previously adhered to or followed ⟨a sharp ~ with tradition⟩ **11 :** BREAKDOWN 1c ⟨suffered a mental ~⟩

break·able \'brā-kə-bəl\ adj (1570) : capable of being broken — **breakable** n

break·age \'brā-kij\ n (1813) **1 a :** the action or an instance of breaking **b :** a quantity broken **2 :** loss due to things broken

¹break·away \'brā-kə-ˌwā\ n (1881) **1 :** one that breaks away **b** : a departure from or rejection of (as a group or tradition) **2 a :** a play (as in hockey) in which an offensive player breaks free of the defenders and rushes toward the goal **b :** a sudden acceleration by one or more bicyclists pulling away from the pack in a race **3 :** an object made to shatter or collapse under pressure or impact

²breakaway adj (1927) **1 :** favoring independence from an affiliation : SECEDING ⟨a ~ faction formed a new party⟩ **2 :** made to break, shatter, or bend easily ⟨~ road signs for highway safety⟩

break away vi (1535) **1 :** to detach oneself esp. from a group : get away **2 :** to depart from former or accustomed ways **3 :** to pull away with a burst of speed

break·bone fever \'brāk-ˌbōn-\ n (ca. 1860) : DENGUE

break dancing n [perh. fr. ²break (solo passage)] (1983) : dancing in which solo dancers perform acrobatics that involve touching various parts of the body (as the back or head) to the ground — **break–dance** \'brāk-ˌdan(t)s\ vb — **break–dancer** \-ˌdan(t)-sər\ n

break·down \'brāk-ˌdaùn\ n (1832) **1 :** the action or result of breaking down: as **a :** a failure to function **b :** failure to progress or have effect : DISINTEGRATION ⟨a ~ of negotiations⟩ **c :** a physical, mental, or nervous collapse **d :** the process of decomposing **e :** division into categories : CLASSIFICATION; also : an account analyzed into categories **2 :** a fast shuffling dance; also : music for such a dance

break down vt (14c) **1 a :** to cause to fall or collapse by breaking or shattering **b :** to make ineffective ⟨break down legal barriers⟩ **2 a** : to divide into parts or categories **b :** to separate (as a chemical compound) into simpler substances : DECOMPOSE **c :** to take apart esp. for storage or shipment and for later reassembling ~ vi **1 a :** to stop functioning because of breakage or wear **b :** to become inoperative or ineffective : FAIL ⟨negotiations broke down⟩ **2** of horses : to tear or strain the tendons of the lower leg **3 a :** to be susceptible to or undergo analysis or subdivision ⟨the statistics break down like this⟩ **b** : to undergo decomposition **syn** see ANALYZE

¹break·er \'brā-kər\ n (12c) **1 a :** one that breaks **b :** a machine or plant for breaking rocks or coal **c** chiefly Brit : one who breaks up ships or cars for salvage **2 :** a wave breaking into foam (as against the shore) **3 :** a strip of fabric under the tread of a tire for extra protection of the carcass

²brea·ker \'brā-kər\ n [by folk etymology fr. Sp *barrica*] (1833) : a small water cask

break·even \'brāk-'ē-vən\ n (1958) : the point at which cost and income are equal and there is neither profit nor loss; *also* : a financial result reflecting neither profit nor loss

break–even \'brāk-'ē-vən\ adj (1931) : having equal cost and income

break·fast \'brek-fəst\ n (15c) 1 : the first meal of the day esp. when taken in the morning 2 : the food prepared for a breakfast ⟨eat your ∼⟩ — **breakfast** vb — **break·fast·er** n

break·front \'brāk-ˌfrənt\ n (1928) : a large cabinet or bookcase whose center section projects beyond the flanking end sections

breakfront

break–in \'brā-ˌkin\ n (1856) 1 : the act or action of breaking in ⟨a rash of ∼s at the new apartment house⟩ 2 : a performance or a series of performances serving as a trial run 3 : an initial period of operation during which working parts begin to function efficiently

break in vi (ca. 1552) 1 : to enter a house or building by force 2 a : IN-TRUDE ⟨*break in* upon his privacy⟩ b : to interrupt a conversation 3 : to start in an activity or enterprise ⟨*breaking in* as a cub reporter⟩ ∼ vt 1 : to accustom to a certain activity or occurrence ⟨*break in* the new clerk⟩ 2 : to overcome the stiffness or newness of

breaking and entering n (1797) : the act of forcing or otherwise gaining unlawful passage into and entering another's building

breaking point n (1908) 1 : the point at which a person gives way under stress 2 : the point at which a situation becomes critical

break·neck \'brāk-ˌnek\ adj (1562) : very fast or dangerous ⟨∼ speed⟩

break off vi (14c) : to stop abruptly ⟨*break off* in the middle of a sentence⟩ ∼ vt : DISCONTINUE ⟨*break off* diplomatic relations⟩

break·out \'brā-ˌkaůt\ n (1820) : a violent or forceful break from a restraining condition or situation; *esp* : a military attack to break from encirclement

break out vi (bef. 12c) 1 : to develop or emerge with suddenness or force ⟨fire *broke out*⟩ ⟨a riot *broke out*⟩ 2 a : to become covered ⟨*break out* in a sweat⟩ b : to become affected with a skin eruption 3 : to make a break from a restraining condition or situation ⟨*broke out* of a slump⟩ ∼ vt 1 a : to make ready for action or use ⟨*break out* the tents and make camp⟩ b : to produce for consumption ⟨*break out* a bottle⟩ 2 : to display flying and unfurled 3 : to separate from a mass of data ⟨*break out* newsstand sales⟩

break·through \'brāk-ˌthrü\ n, often attrib (1918) 1 : an offensive thrust that penetrates and carries beyond a defensive line in warfare 2 : an act or instance of breaking through an obstruction 3 a : a sudden advance esp. in knowledge or technique ⟨a medical ∼⟩ b : a person's first notable success

break through vi (1955) : to make a breakthrough

break·up \'brā-ˌkəp\ n (1794) 1 : an act or instance of breaking up 2 : the breaking, melting, and loosening of ice in the spring

break up vi (15c) 1 a : to cease to exist as a unified whole : DISPERSE ⟨their partnership *broke up*⟩ b : to end a romance 2 : to lose morale, composure, or resolution; *esp* : to become abandoned to laughter ⟨*breaks up* completely, laughing himself into a coughing fit —Gene Williams⟩ ∼ vt 1 : to break into pieces 2 : to bring to an end ⟨*broke up* the fight⟩ 3 : to do away with : DESTROY ⟨*break up* a monopoly⟩ 4 : to disrupt the continuity or flow of ⟨*break up* a dull routine⟩ 5 : DE-COMPOSE ⟨*break up* a chemical⟩ 6 : to cause to laugh heartily ⟨that joke *breaks* me up⟩

breakup value n (1902) : the value esp. of shares of stock of a corporation liquidating its assets

break·wa·ter \'brāk-ˌwȯ-tər, -ˌwä-\ n (ca. 1769) : an offshore structure (as a wall) protecting a harbor or beach from the force of waves

¹bream \'brim, 'brēm\ n, pl **bream** or **breams** [ME *breme*, fr. MF, of Gmc origin; akin to OHG *brahsima* bream, MHG *brehen* to shine] (14c) 1 : a European freshwater cyprinid fish (*Abramis brama*); *broadly* : any of various related fishes 2 a : a porgy or related fish (family *Sparidae*) b : any of various freshwater sunfishes (*Lepomis* and related genera); *esp* : BLUEGILL

²bream \'brēm\ vt [prob. fr. D *brem* furze] (1626) : to clean (a ship's bottom) by heating and scraping

¹breast \'brest\ n [ME *brest*, fr. OE *brēost*; akin to OHG *brust* breast, OIr *brú* belly, Russ *bryukho*] (bef. 12c) 1 : either of the pair of mammary glands extending from the front of the chest in pubescent and adult human females and some other mammals; *also* : either of the analogous but rudimentary organs of the male chest esp. when enlarged 2 a : the fore or ventral part of the body between the neck and the abdomen b : the part of an article of clothing covering the breast 3 : the seat of emotion and thought : BOSOM 4 a : something (as a front, swelling, or curving part) resembling a breast b : FACE 6 — **breast·ed** \'bres-təd\ adj

²breast vt (1599) 1 : to contend with resolutely : CONFRONT ⟨∼*ing* the waves⟩ 2 *chiefly Brit* : CLIMB, ASCEND 3 : to thrust the chest against ⟨the sprinter ∼*ed* the tape⟩

breast–beat·ing \'brest-ˌbē-tiŋ\ n (1940) : noisy demonstrative protestation (as of grief, anger, or self-recrimination)

breast·bone \'brest-ˌbōn\ n (bef. 12c) : STERNUM

breast drill n (1865) : a portable drill with a plate that is pressed by the breast in forcing the drill against the work

breast–feed \'brest-ˌfēd\ vt (1903) : to feed (a baby) from a mother's breast rather than from a bottle

breast·plate \'brest-ˌplāt\ n (14c) 1 : a usu. metal plate worn as defensive armor for the breast — see ARMOR illustration 2 : a vestment worn in ancient times by a Jewish high priest and set with 12 gems bearing the names of the tribes of Israel 3 : a piece against which a worker's breast is pressed in operating a tool (as a breast drill)

breast·stroke \'bres(t)-ˌstrōk\ n (1867) : a swimming stroke executed in a prone position by coordinating a kick in which the legs are brought

forward with the knees together and the feet are turned outward and whipped back with a glide and a backward sweeping movement of the arms — **breast·strok·er** \-ˌstrō-kər\ n

breast·work \'brest-ˌwərk\ n (1642) : a temporary fortification

breath \'breth\ n [ME *breth*, fr. OE *brǣth*; akin to OHG *brādam* breath, and perh. to OE *beorma* yeast — more at BARM] (bef. 12c) 1 a : air filled with a fragrance or odor b : a slight indication : SUGGES-TION ⟨the faintest ∼ of scandal⟩ 2 a : the faculty of breathing ⟨recovering his ∼ after the race⟩ b : an act of breathing ⟨fought to the last ∼⟩ c : opportunity or time to breathe : RESPITE 3 : a slight breeze 4 a : air inhaled and exhaled in breathing ⟨bad ∼⟩ b : something (as moisture on a cold surface) produced by breath or breathing c : IN-HALATION 5 : a spoken sound : UTTERANCE 6 : SPIRIT, ANIMATION — **in one breath** *or* **in the same breath** : almost simultaneously — **out of breath** : breathing very rapidly (as from strenuous exercise)

breath·able \'brē-thə-bəl\ adj (ca. 1731) 1 : suitable for breathing ⟨∼ air⟩ 2 : allowing air to pass through : POROUS ⟨a ∼ synthetic fabric⟩ — **breath·abil·i·ty** \ˌbrē-thə-'bi-lə-tē\ n

Breath·a·ly·zer \'brē-thə-ˌlī-zər\ *trademark* — used for a device that is used to determine the alcohol content of a breath sample

breathe \'brēth\ vb **breathed**; **breath·ing** [ME *brethen*, fr. *breth*] vi (14c) 1 a : to draw air in and expel it from the lungs : RESPIRE; *broadly* : to take in oxygen and give out carbon dioxide through natural processes b : to inhale and exhale freely 2 : LIVE 3 a *obs* : to emit a fragrance or aura b : to become perceptible : be expressed ⟨a personality that ∼s and that distinguishes his work —Bennett Schiff⟩ 4 : to pause and rest before continuing 5 : to blow softly 6 : to feel free of restraint ⟨needs room to ∼⟩ 7 *of wine* : to develop flavor and bouquet by exposure to air 8 a : to permit passage of air or vapor ⟨a fabric that ∼s⟩ b *of an internal-combustion engine* : to use air to support combustion ∼ vt 1 a : to send out by exhaling b : to instill by or as if by breathing ⟨∼ new life into the movement⟩ 2 : to give rest from exertion to 3 : to take in breathing ⟨∼ the scent of pines⟩ 4 : to inhale and exhale ⟨∼ air⟩ 5 a : UTTER, EXPRESS ⟨don't ∼ a word of it to anyone⟩ b : to make manifest : EVINCE ⟨the novel ∼s despair⟩ — **breathe down one's neck** 1 : to threaten esp. in attack or pursuit 2 : to keep one under close or constant surveillance ⟨parents always *breathing down his neck*⟩ — **breathe easily** *or* **breathe freely** : to enjoy relief (as from pressure or danger)

breathed \'bretht\ adj (1555) 1 : having breath esp. of a specified kind — usu. used in combination ⟨sweet-*breathed*⟩ 2 : VOICELESS 2

breath·er \'brē-thər\ n (14c) 1 : one that breathes 2 : a break in activity for rest or relief 3 : a small vent in an otherwise airtight enclosure

breath·ing \'brē-thiŋ\ n (1746) : either of the marks ' and ' used in writing Greek to indicate aspiration or its absence

breathing space n (1650) : some time in which to recover, get organized, or get going — called also *breathing room*, *breathing spell*

breath·less \'breth-ləs\ adj (14c) 1 a : not breathing b : DEAD 2 a : panting or gasping for breath b : leaving one breathless : very rapid or strenuous ⟨go at a ∼ pace⟩ c : holding one's breath from emotion ⟨∼ in anticipation⟩ d : marked by or as if by a holding of one's breath : INTENSE, GRIPPING ⟨∼ tension⟩ 3 : oppressive because of no fresh air or breeze — **breath·less·ly** adv — **breath·less·ness** n

breath·tak·ing \'breth-ˌtā-kiŋ\ adj (1880) 1 : making one out of breath 2 a : EXCITING, THRILLING ⟨a ∼ stock car race⟩ b : very great : ASTONISHING ⟨his ∼ ignorance⟩ — **breath·tak·ing·ly** \-ˌkiŋ-lē\ adv

breathy \'bre-thē\ adj **breath·i·er**; **-est** (1883) : characterized or accompanied by or as if by the audible passage of breath — **breath·i·ly** \-thə-lē\ adv — **breath·i·ness** \-thē-nəs\ n

brec·cia \'bre-ch(ē-)ə\ n [It] (1774) : a rock consisting of sharp fragments embedded in a fine-grained matrix (as sand or clay)

brec·ci·ate \'bre-chē-ˌāt\ vt **-at·ed**; **-at·ing** (1772) 1 : to form (rock) into breccia 2 : to break (rock) into fragments — **brec·ci·a·tion** \ˌbre-chē-'ā-shən\ n

brede \'brēd\ n [var. of *braid*] (1640) *archaic* : EMBROIDERY

bred–in–the–bone \'bre-d^n-thə-ˌbōn\ adj (15c) 1 : DEEP-ROOTED ⟨∼ honesty⟩ 2 : INVETERATE ⟨a ∼ gambler⟩

breech \'brēch\ n [ME, breeches, fr. OE *brēc*, pl. of *brōc* leg covering; akin to OHG *bruoh* breeches, L *brāca* pants] (bef. 12c) 1 pl \'bri-chəz *also* 'brē-\ a : short pants covering the hips and thighs and fitting snugly at the lower edges or just below the knee b : PANTS 2 a : the hind end of the body : BUTTOCKS b : BREECH PRESENTATION; *also* : a fetus that is presented breech first 3 : the part of a firearm at the rear of the barrel

breech·block \'brēch-ˌbläk\ n (1881) : the block in breech-loading firearms that closes the rear of the barrel against the force of the charge and prevents gases from escaping

breech·cloth \'brēch-ˌklȯth, 'brich-\ n (1793) : LOINCLOTH

breech·clout \-ˌklaůt\ n (1757) : LOINCLOTH

breech·es buoy \'brē-chəz- *also* 'bri-\ n (1880) : a canvas seat in the form of breeches hung from a life buoy running on a hawser and used to haul persons from one ship to another or from ship to shore esp. in rescue operations

breech·ing \'brē-chiŋ, 'bri-\ n (ca. 1524) 1 : the part of a harness that passes around the rump of a draft animal 2 : the short coarse wool on the rump and hind legs of a sheep or goat; *also* : the hair on the corresponding part of a dog

breech·load·er \'brēch-'lō-dər\ n (1858) : a firearm that loads at the breech — **breech–load·ing** \-'lō-diŋ\ adj

breech presentation n (1811) : presentation of the fetus in which the breech is the first part to appear at the uterine cervix

¹breed \'brēd\ vb **bred** \'bred\; **breed·ing** [ME *breden*, fr. OE *brēdan*; akin to OE *brōd* brood] vt (bef. 12c) 1 : to produce (offspring) by hatching or gestation 2 a : BEGET 1 b : PRODUCE, ENGENDER ⟨despair often ∼s violence⟩ 3 : to propagate (plants or animals) sexually and usu. under controlled conditions ⟨bred several strains of corn to-

\ə\ abut \ᵊ\ kitten, F table \ər\ further \a\ ash \ā\ ace \ä\ mop, mar \aů\ out \ch\ chin \e\ bet \ē\ easy \g\ go \i\ hit \ī\ ice \j\ job \ŋ\ sing \ō\ go \ȯ\ law \ȯi\ boy \th\ thin \t͟h\ the \ü\ loot \ů\ foot \y\ yet \zh\ vision \à, k̲, ⁿ, œ, œ̄, ᵫ, ᵫ̄, ᵞ\ see Guide to Pronunciation gether to produce a superior variety⟩ **4 a :** BRING UP, NURTURE ⟨born and *bred* in the country⟩ **b :** to inculcate by training ⟨~ good manners into one's children⟩ **5 a :** ⁴MATE **3 b :** to mate with : INSEMINATE **c :** IMPREGNATE 2 **6 :** to produce (a fissionable element) by bombarding a nonfissionable element with neutrons from a radioactive element ~ *vi* **1 a :** to produce offspring by sexual union **b :** COPULATE, MATE **2 :** to propagate animals or plants

²**breed** *n* (1553) **1 a :** a group of animals or plants presumably related by descent from common ancestors and visibly similar in most characters; *esp* : such a group differentiated from the wild type under domestication **2 :** a number of persons of the same stock **3 :** CLASS, KIND ⟨a new ~ of athlete⟩

breed·er \'brē-dər\ *n* (1531) **:** one that breeds: as **a :** an animal or plant kept for propagation **b :** one engaged in the breeding of a specified organism **c :** a nuclear reactor designed to produce more fissionable material than it uses as fuel — called also *breeder reactor*

breed·ing *n* (14c) **1 :** the action or process of bearing or generating **2 :** ANCESTRY **3 a** *archaic* : EDUCATION ⟨she had her ~ at my father's charge.⟩ **b :** training in or observance of the proprieties **4 :** the sexual propagation of plants or animals

breeding ground *n* (1856) **1 :** the place to which animals go to breed **2 :** a place or set of circumstances suitable for or favorable to growth and development ⟨hurricane *breeding grounds*⟩

breeks \'brēks, 'briks\ *n pl* [ME (northern dial.) *breke,* fr. OE *brēc*] (14c) *chiefly Scot* **:** BREECHES

¹**breeze** \'brēz\ *n* [prob. fr. Sp *brisa* northeast wind] (1626) **1 a :** a light gentle wind **b :** a wind of from 4 to 31 miles (6 to 50 kilometers) an hour **2 :** something easily done : CINCH — **breeze·less** \-ləs\ *adj* — **in a breeze :** EASILY

²**breeze** *vi* **breezed; breez·ing** (1907) **1 :** to move swiftly and airily ⟨*breezed* past the protesters⟩ **2 :** to make progress quickly and easily ⟨*breezed* through the exam⟩ ⟨*breezed* to victory⟩

³**breeze** *n* [prob. modif. of F *braise* cinders — more at BRAISE] (1726) **:** residue from the making of coke or charcoal

breeze·way \'brēz-,wā\ *n* (1931) **:** a roofed open passage connecting two buildings (as a house and garage) or halves of a building

breezy \'brē-zē\ *adj* **breez·i·er; -est** (1718) **1 :** swept by breezes **2 a :** briskly informal **b :** AIRY, NONCHALANT — **breez·i·ly** \-zə-lē\ *adv* — **breez·i·ness** \-zē-nəs\ *n*

breg·ma \'breg-mə\ *n, pl* **-ma·ta** \-mə-tə\ [NL *bregmat-, bregma,* fr. LL, front part of the head, fr. Gk; akin to Gk *brechmos* front part of the head — more at BRAIN] (1578) **:** the point of junction of the coronal and sagittal sutures of the skull

brems·strah·lung \'brem(p)-,shträ-lən\ *n* [G, lit., decelerated radiation] (1939) **:** the electromagnetic radiation produced by the sudden retardation of a charged particle in an intense electric field (as of an atomic nucleus); *also* : the process that produces such radiation

brent goose \'brent-\ *n* (1570) *chiefly Brit* **:** BRANT

breth·ren \'breth-rən\ *n pl of* BROTHER (bef. 12c) — used chiefly in formal or solemn address or in referring to the members of a profession, society, or sect

Brethren *n pl* (1822) **:** members of various sects originating chiefly in 18th century German Pietism; *esp* : DUNKERS

Bret·on \'bre-t³n\ *n* [F, fr. ML *Briton-, Brito,* fr. L, Briton] (1653) **1 :** a native or inhabitant of Brittany **2 :** the Celtic language of the Breton people — **Breton** *adj*

breve \'brēv, 'brev\ *n* [L, neut. of *brevis* brief — more at BRIEF] (15c) **1 :** a note equivalent to two whole notes **2 :** a curved mark ˘ used to indicate a short vowel or a short or unstressed syllable

¹**bre·vet** \bri-'vet, *chiefly Brit* 'bre-vit\ *n* [ME, an official message, fr. MF, fr. OF, dim. of *brief* letter — more at BRIEF] (1689) **:** a commission giving a military officer higher nominal rank than that for which pay is received

²**brevet** *vt* **bre·vet·ted** *or* **brev·et·ed; bre·vet·ting** *or* **brev·et·ing** (1824) **:** to confer rank upon by brevet

bre·via·ry \'brē-və-rē, -vyə-, -vē-,er-ē *also* 'bre-\ *n, pl* **-ries** [ME *breviarie,* fr. ML *breviarium,* fr. L, summary, fr. *brevis*] (15c) **1** *often cap* **a :** a book containing the prayers, hymns, psalms, and readings for the canonical hours **b :** DIVINE OFFICE **2** [L *breviarium*] **:** a brief summary : ABRIDGMENT

brev·i·ty \'bre-və-tē\ *n, pl* **-ties** [L *brevitas,* fr. *brevis*] (15c) **:** shortness of duration; *esp* : shortness or conciseness of expression

¹**brew** \'brü\ *vb* [ME, fr. OE *brēowan;* akin to L *fervēre* to boil — more at BARM] *vt* (bef. 12c) **1 :** to prepare (as beer or ale) by steeping, boiling, and fermentation or by infusion and fermentation **2 a :** to bring about : FOMENT ⟨~ trouble⟩ **b :** CONTRIVE, PLOT **3 :** to prepare (as tea) by infusion in hot water ~ *vi* **1 :** to brew beer or ale **2 :** to be in the process of formation ⟨a storm is ~*ing* in the east⟩ — **brew·er** \'brü-ər, 'brů-(ə)r\ *n*

²**brew** *n* (ca. 1510) **1 a :** a brewed beverage (as beer) **b :** a serving of a brewed beverage ⟨quaff a few ~s⟩ **c :** something produced by or as if by brewing **2 :** the process of brewing

brew·age \'brü-ij\ *n* (1542) **:** BREW 1a, 2

brewer's yeast *n* (1871) **:** a yeast used or suitable for use in brewing; *specif* : the dried pulverized cells of such a yeast (*Saccharomyces cerevisiae*) used esp. as a source of B-complex vitamins

brew·ery \'brü-ə-rē, 'brů-(ə)r-ē\ *n, pl* **-er·ies** (1658) **:** a plant where malt liquors are produced

¹**bri·ar** \'brī-(ə)r\ *var of* BRIER

²**briar** *n* (1882) **:** a tobacco pipe made from the root or stem of a brier

bri·ard \brē-'är(d)\ *n* [F, fr. *Brie,* district in France] (ca. 1929) **:** any of an old French breed of large long-coated sheepdogs

¹**bribe** \'brīb\ *n* [ME, something stolen, fr. MF, bread given to a beggar] (15c) **1 :** money or favor given or promised in order to influence the judgment or conduct of a person in a position of trust **2 :** something that serves to induce or influence

²**bribe** *vb* **bribed; brib·ing** *vt* (1528) **:** to induce or influence by or as if by bribery ~ *vi* **:** to practice bribery — **brib·able** \'brī-bə-bəl\ *adj* — **brib·ee** \,brī-'bē\ *n* — **brib·er** *n*

brib·ery \'brī-b(ə-)rē\ *n, pl* **-er·ies** (1549) **:** the act or practice of giving or taking a bribe

bric–a–brac \'bri-kə-,brak\ *n, pl* **bric–a–brac** [F *bric-à-brac*] (1840) **1 :** a miscellaneous collection of small articles commonly of ornamen-

tal or sentimental value : CURIOS **2 :** something suggesting bric-a-brac esp. in extraneous decorative quality

¹**brick** \'brik\ *n, often attrib* [ME *bryke,* fr. MF *brique,* fr. MD *bricke*] (15c) **1** *pl* **bricks** *or* **brick :** a handy-sized unit of building or paving material typically being rectangular and about 2¼ × 3¾ × 8 inches (57 × 95 × 203 millimeters) and of moist clay hardened by heat **2 :** a good-hearted person **3 :** a rectangular compressed mass (as of ice cream) **4 :** a semisoft cheese with numerous small holes, smooth texture, and often mild flavor **5 :** GAFFE, BLUNDER — used esp. in the phrase *drop a brick*

²**brick** *vt* (1592) **:** to close, face, or pave with bricks — usu. used with *up, in,* or *over*

brick·bat \'brik-,bat\ *n* [*brick* + ¹*bat* (lump, fragment)] (ca. 1587) **1 :** a fragment of a hard material (as a brick); *esp* : one used as a missile **2 :** an uncomplimentary remark

brick·field \-,fēld\ *n* (1801) *Brit* **:** BRICKYARD

brick·lay·er \'brik-,lā-ər, -,le(-ə)r\ *n* (15c) **:** a person who lays brick — **brick·lay·ing** \-,lā-iŋ\ *n*

brick·le \'bri-kəl\ *adj* [ME *brekyl*] (13c) *dial* **:** BRITTLE

brick red *n* (1810) **:** a moderate reddish brown

brick·work \'brik-,wərk\ *n* (1580) **:** work of or with bricks and mortar

brick·yard \-,yärd\ *n* (1731) **:** a place where bricks are made

bri·co·lage \,brē-kō-'läzh, ,bri-\ *n* [F, fr. *bricoler* to putter about] (1966) **:** construction or something constructed by using whatever comes to hand

¹**brid·al** \'brī-d³l\ *n* [ME *bridale,* fr. OE *brȳdealu,* fr. *brȳd* + *ealu* ale — more at ALE] (bef. 12c) **:** a marriage festival or ceremony

²**bridal** *adj* (13c) **1 :** of or relating to a bride or a wedding : NUPTIAL **2 :** intended for a newly married couple ⟨a ~ suite⟩

bridal wreath *n* (ca. 1889) **:** a spirea (*Spiraea prunifolia*) widely grown for its umbels of small white flowers borne in spring

bride \'brīd\ *n* [ME, fr. OE *brȳd;* akin to OHG *brūt* bride] (bef. 12c) **:** a woman just married or about to be married

bride·groom \'brīd-,grüm, -,grům\ *n* [ME (Sc) *brydegrome,* by folk etymology fr. ME *bridegome,* fr. OE *brȳdguma,* fr. *brȳd* + *guma* man; akin to OHG *brūtgomo* bridegroom — more at HOMAGE] (14c) **:** a man just married or about to be married

bride–price \-,prīs\ *n* (1876) **:** a payment given by or in behalf of a prospective husband to the bride's family in many cultures

brides·maid \'brīdz-,mād\ *n* (1552) **1 :** a woman attendant of a bride **2 :** one that finishes just behind the winner

bride·well \'brīd-,wel, -,wəl\ *n* [*Bridewell,* London jail] (ca. 1593) **:** PRISON

¹**bridge** \'brij\ *n* [ME *brigge,* fr. OE *brycg;* akin to OHG *brucka* bridge, OCS *brŭvŭno* beam] (bef. 12c) **1 a :** a structure carrying a pathway or roadway over a depression or obstacle **b :** a time, place, or means of connection or transition **2 :** something resembling a bridge in form or function: as **a :** the upper bony part of the nose; *also* : the part of a pair of glasses that rests upon it **b :** a piece raising the strings of a musical instrument — see VIOLIN illustration **c :** the forward part of a ship's superstructure from which the ship is navigated **d :** GANTRY 2b **e :** the hand as a rest for a billiards or pool cue; *also* : a device used as a cue rest **3 a :** a musical passage linking two sections of a composition **b :** a partial denture anchored to adjacent teeth **c :** a connection (as an atom or group of atoms) that joins two different parts of a molecule (as opposite sides of a ring) **4 :** an electrical instrument or network for measuring or comparing resistances, inductances, capacitances, or impedances by comparing the ratio of two opposing voltages to a known ratio — **bridge·less** \-ləs\ *adj*

bridge 1a: *1* simple truss, *2* steel arch, *3* continuous truss, *4* cantilever, *5* suspension

²**bridge** *vt* **bridged; bridg·ing** (bef. 12c) **1 :** to make a bridge over or across ⟨~ the gap⟩; *also* : to join by a bridge **2 :** to provide with a bridge — **bridge·able** \'bri-jə-bəl\ *adj*

³**bridge** *n* [alter. of earlier *biritch,* of unknown origin] (ca. 1897) **:** any of various card games for usu. four players in two partnerships that bid for the right to declare a trump suit, seek to win tricks equal to the final bid, and play with the hand of declarer's partner exposed and played by declarer; *esp* : CONTRACT BRIDGE

bridge·head \-,hed\ *n* (1812) **1 a :** a fortification protecting the end of a bridge nearest an enemy **b :** an area around the end of a bridge **2 :** an advanced position seized in hostile territory

bridge·work \-,wərk\ *n* (1883) **:** dental bridges

¹**bri·dle** \'brī-d³l\ *n* [ME *bridel,* fr. OE *bridel;* akin to OE *bregdan* to move quickly — more at BRAID] (bef. 12c) **1 :** the headgear with which a horse is governed and which carries a bit and reins **2 :** a length of line or cable attached to two parts of something to spread the force of a pull; *esp* : rigging on a kite for attaching line **3 :** CURB, RESTRAINT ⟨set a ~ on his power⟩

²**bridle** *vb* **bri·dled; bri·dling** \'brīd-liŋ, 'brī-d³l-iŋ\ *vt* (bef. 12c) **1 :** to put a bridle on **2 :** to restrain, check, or control with or as if with a bridle ⟨~ your tongue⟩ ~ *vi* **:** to show hostility or resentment (as to

an affront to one's pride or dignity) esp. by drawing back the head and chin *syn* see RESTRAIN

bridle path *n* (1811) : a trail suitable for horseback riding

Brie \'brē\ *n* [F, fr. *Brie*, district in France] (1876) : a soft surface-ripened cheese with a whitish rind and a pale yellow interior

¹**brief** \'brēf\ *adj* [ME *bref, breve*, fr. MF *brief*, fr. L *brevis*; akin to OHG *murg* short, Gk *brachys*] (14c) **1** : short in duration, extent, or length **2 a** : CONCISE **b** : CURT, ABRUPT — **brief·ness** *n*

²**brief** *n* [ME *bref*, fr. MF, fr. ML *brevis*, fr. LL, summary, fr. L *brevis*, adj.] (14c) **1** : an official letter or mandate; *esp* : a papal letter less formal than a bull **2 a** : a concise article **b** : SYNOPSIS, SUMMARY **c** : a concise statement of a client's case made out for the instruction of counsel in a trial at law **3** : an outline of an argument; *esp* : a formal outline esp. in law that sets forth the main contentions with supporting statements or evidence **4** *pl* : short snug pants or underpants — **in brief** : in a few words : BRIEFLY

³**brief** *vt* (15c) **1** : to make an abstract or abridgment of **2 a** : to give final precise instructions to **b** : to coach thoroughly in advance **c** : to give essential information to — **brief·er** *n*

brief·case \'brēf-ˌkās\ *n* (1917) : a flat flexible case for carrying papers or books

brief·ing \'brē-fiŋ\ *n* (1910) : an act or instance of giving precise instructions or essential information

brief·less \'brē-fləs\ *adj* (1824) : having no legal clients

brief·ly \'brē-flē\ *adv* (14c) **1 a** : in a brief way **b** : in brief **2** : for a short time

¹**bri·er** \'brī(-ə)r\ *n* [ME *brere*, fr. OE *brēr*] (bef. 12c) : a plant (as of the genera *Rosa, Rubus,* and *Smilax*) with a woody and thorny or prickly stem; *also* : a mass or tangle of these — **bri·ery** \'brī(-ə)r-ē\ *adj*

²**brier** *n* [F *bruyère* heath, fr. MF *bruiere*, fr. (assumed) VL *brucaria*, fr. LL *brucus* heather, of Celt origin; akin to OIr *froech* heather; akin to Gk *ereikē* heather] (1868) : a heath (*Erica arborea*) of southern Europe whose roots and knotted stems are used for making briar tobacco pipes

¹**brig** \'brig\ *n* [short for *brigantine*] (1712) : a 2-masted square-rigged ship

²**brig** *n* [prob. fr. ¹*brig*] (1852) **1** : a place (as on a ship) for temporary confinement of offenders in the U.S. Navy **2** : GUARDHOUSE, PRISON

¹**bri·gade** \bri-'gād\ *n* [F, fr. It *brigata*, fr. *brigare*] (1637) **1 a** : a large body of troops **b** : a tactical and administrative unit composed of a headquarters, one or more units of infantry or armor, and supporting units **2** : a group of people organized for special activity

²**brigade** *vt* **bri·gad·ed; bri·gad·ing** (1781) : to form or unite into a brigade

brig·a·dier \ˌbri-gə-'dir\ *n* [F, fr. *brigade*] (1678) **1** : an officer in the British army commanding a brigade and ranking immediately below a major general **2** : BRIGADIER GENERAL

brigadier general *n* (1690) : a commissioned officer in the army, air force, or marine corps who ranks above a colonel and whose insignia is one star

Brig·a·doon \ˌbri-gə-'dün\ *n* [fr. *Brigadoon*, village in the musical *Brigadoon* (1947) by A. J. Lerner and F. Loewe] (1968) : a place that is idyllic, unaffected by time, or remote from reality

brig·and \'bri-gənd\ *n* [ME *brigaunt*, fr. MF *brigand*, fr. OIt *brigante*, fr. *brigare* to fight, fr. *briga* strife, of Celt origin; akin to OIr *brig* strength] (14c) : one who lives by plunder usu. as a member of a band : BANDIT — **brig·and·age** \-gən-dij\ *n*

brig·an·dine \'bri-gən-ˌdēn\ *n* [ME, fr. MF, fr. *brigand*] (15c) : medieval body armor of scales or plates

brig·an·tine \'bri-gən-ˌtēn\ *n* [MF *brigantin*, fr. OIt *brigantino*, fr. *brigante*] (1525) : a 2-masted sailing ship that is square-rigged except for a fore-and-aft mainsail

¹**bright** \'brīt\ *adj* [ME, fr. OE *beorht*; akin to OHG *beraht* bright, Skt *bhrājate* it shines] (bef. 12c) **1 a** : radiating or reflecting light : SHINING, SPARKLING ⟨~ lights⟩ ⟨~ eyes⟩ **b** : SUNNY ⟨a ~ day⟩; *also* : radiant with happiness ⟨~ smiling faces⟩ ⟨~ moments⟩ **2** : ILLUSTRIOUS, GLORIOUS ⟨~est star of the opera⟩ **3** : BEAUTIFUL **4** : of high saturation or brilliance ⟨~ colors⟩ **5 a** : LIVELY, CHEERFUL ⟨be ~ and jovial among your guests —Shak.⟩ **b** : INTELLIGENT, CLEVER ⟨a ~ idea⟩ ⟨~ children⟩ **6** : AUSPICIOUS, PROMISING ⟨~ prospects for the future⟩ — **bright** *adv* — **bright·ly** *adv*

syn BRIGHT, BRILLIANT, RADIANT, LUMINOUS, LUSTROUS mean shining or glowing with light. BRIGHT implies emitting or reflecting a high degree of light. BRILLIANT implies intense often sparkling brightness. RADIANT stresses the emission or seeming emission of rays of light. LUMINOUS implies emission of steady, suffused, glowing light by reflection or in surrounding darkness. LUSTROUS stresses an even, rich light from a surface that reflects brightly without sparkling or glittering.

²**bright** *n* (1969) : a bright color — usu. used in pl. ⟨rich earth tones and crisp ~s —Patricia Peterson⟩

bright·en \'brī-t²n\ *vb* **bright·ened; bright·en·ing** \'brīt-niŋ, 'brī-t²n-iŋ\ *vi* (14c) : to become bright or brighter ~ *vt* : to make bright or brighter — **bright·en·er** \'brīt-nər, 'brī-t²n-ər\ *n*

bright·ness *n* (bef. 12c) **1 a** : the quality or state of being bright; *also* : an instance of such a quality or state **b** : LUMINANCE **2** : the attribute of light-source colors by which emitted light is ordered continuously from light to dark in correlation with its intensity — compare HUE 2c, ¹LIGHTNESS 2, SATURATION 4

Bright's disease \'brīts-\ *n* [Richard *Bright* †1858 Eng. physician] (1831) : any of several kidney diseases marked esp. by albumin in the urine

bright·work \'brīt-ˌwərk\ *n* (1841) : polished or plated metalwork

brill \'bril\ *n, pl* **brill** [ME *brell*] (15c) : a European flatfish (*Scophthalmus rhombus* syn. *Bothus rhombus* of the family Bothidae); *broadly* : TURBOT

bril·liance \'bril-yən(t)s\ *n* (1755) : the quality or state of being brilliant

bril·lian·cy \-yən(t)-sē\ *n, pl* **-cies** (1747) **1** : BRILLIANCE **2** : an instance of brilliance

¹**bril·liant** \'bril-yənt\ *adj* [F *brillant*, prp. of *briller* to shine, fr. It *brillare*] (ca. 1681) **1** : very bright : GLITTERING ⟨a ~ light⟩ **2 a** : STRIKING, DISTINCTIVE ⟨a ~ example⟩ **b** : distinguished by unusual mental keenness or alertness *syn* see BRIGHT — **bril·liant·ly** *adv*

²**brilliant** *n* (1690) : a gem (as a diamond) cut in a particular form with numerous facets so as to have special brilliance

bril·lian·tine \'bril-yən-ˌtēn\ *n* (1873) **1** : a light lustrous fabric that is similar to alpaca and is woven usu. with a cotton warp and mohair or worsted filling **2** : a preparation for making hair glossy

¹**brim** \'brim\ *n* [ME *brimme*; akin to MHG *brem* edge] (13c) **1 a** (1) : an upper or outer margin : VERGE (2) *archaic* : the upper surface of a body of water **b** : the edge or rim of a hollow vessel, a natural depression, or a cavity **2** : the projecting rim of a hat — **brim·less** \-ləs\ *adj*

²**brim** *vb* **brimmed; brim·ming** *vt* (1611) : to fill to the brim ~ *vi* **1** : to be or become full often to overflowing **2** : to reach or overflow a brim

brim·ful \'brim-ˈfùl, -ˌfùl\ *adj* (ca. 1530) : full to the brim : ready to overflow

brimmed \'brimd\ *adj* (1606) : having a brim of a specified nature — used in combination ⟨a wide-*brimmed* hat⟩

brim·mer \'bri-mər\ *n* (1663) : a brimming cup or glass

brim·stone \'brim-ˌstōn\ *n* [ME *brinston*, prob. fr. *birnen* to burn + *ston* stone] (12c) : SULFUR

brind·ed \'brin-dəd\ *adj* [ME *brended*] (15c) *archaic* : BRINDLED

brin·dle \'brin-d²l\ *n* [*brindle*, adj.] (1696) **1** : a brindled color **2** : a brindled animal

brin·dled \-d²ld\ *or* **brindle** *adj* [alter. of *brinded*] (1679) : having obscure dark streaks or flecks on a gray or tawny ground

¹**brine** \'brīn\ *n* [ME, fr. OE *brȳne*; akin to MD *brine* brine] (bef. 12c) **1 a** : water saturated or strongly impregnated with common salt **b** : a strong saline solution (as of calcium chloride) **2** : the water of a sea or salt lake

²**brine** *vt* **brined; brin·ing** (1552) : to treat (as by steeping) with brine — **brin·er** *n*

Bri·nell hardness \brə-'nel-\ *n* [Johann A. *Brinell* †1925 Swed. engineer] (1915) : the hardness of a metal or alloy measured by hydraulically pressing a hard ball under a standard load into the specimen

Brinell hardness number *n* (1915) : a number expressing Brinell hardness and denoting the load applied in testing in kilograms divided by the spherical area of indentation produced in the specimen in square millimeters — called also *Brinell number*

brine shrimp *n* (1836) : any of a genus (*Artemia*) of branchiopod crustaceans that can exist in strongly saline environments

bring \'briŋ\ *vb* **brought** \'brot\; **bring·ing** \'briŋ-iŋ\ [ME, fr. OE *bringan*; akin to OHG *bringan* to bring, W *hebrwng* to accompany] *vt* (bef. 12c) **1 a** : to convey, lead, carry, or cause to come along with one toward the place from which the action is being regarded **b** : to cause to be, act, or move in a special way: as (1) : ATTRACT ⟨her screams *brought* the neighbors⟩ (2) : PERSUADE, INDUCE (3) : FORCE, COMPEL (4) : to cause to come into a particular state or condition ⟨~ water to a boil⟩ **c** *dial* : ESCORT, ACCOMPANY **2** : to cause to exist or occur: as **a** : to be the occasion of ⟨winter ~s snow⟩ **b** : to result in **c** : INSTITUTE ⟨~ legal action⟩ **d** : ADDUCE ⟨~ an argument⟩ **3** : PREFER ⟨~ charges⟩ **4** : to procure in exchange : sell for ~ *vi, chiefly Midland* : YIELD, PRODUCE — **bring·er** *n* — **bring forth 1** : BEAR ⟨*brought forth* fruit⟩ **2** : to give birth to : PRODUCE **3** : ADDUCE ⟨*bring forth* persuasive arguments⟩ — **bring forward 1** : to produce to view : INTRODUCE ⟨*brought* new evidence *forward*⟩ **2** : to carry (a total) forward — **bring home** : to make unmistakably clear — **bring to account 1** : to bring to book **2** : REPRIMAND — **bring to bear** : to use with effect ⟨*bring* pressure *to bear*⟩ — **bring to book** : to compel to give an account — **bring to light** : DISCLOSE, REVEAL — **bring to mind** : RECALL — **bring to terms** : to compel to agree, assent, or submit — **bring up the rear** : to come last or behind

bring about *vt* (14c) : to cause to take place : EFFECT

bring around *vt* (1862) **1** : to restore to consciousness : REVIVE **2** : PERSUADE

bring·down \'briŋ-ˌdaùn\ *n* (ca. 1944) : COMEDOWN, LETDOWN

bring down *vt* (14c) **1** : to cause to fall by or as if by shooting **2** : to carry (a total) forward — **bring down the house** : to win the enthusiastic approval of the audience

bring in *vt* (14c) **1** : INCLUDE, INTRODUCE **2** : to produce as profit or return ⟨each sale *brought in* $5⟩ **3** : to enable (a base runner) to reach home plate by hitting the ball **4** : to report to a court ⟨the jury *brought in* a verdict⟩ **5 a** : to cause (as an oil well) to be productive **b** : to win tricks with the cards of (a long suit) in bridge **6** : EARN ⟨*brings in* a good salary⟩

bring off *vt* (1606) **1** : to cause to escape : RESCUE **2** : to carry to a successful conclusion : ACHIEVE, ACCOMPLISH

bring on *vt* (1602) : to cause to appear or occur

bring out *vt* (1605) **1 a** : to make apparent **b** : to effectively develop (as a quality) **2 a** : to present to the public **b** : to introduce formally to society **3** : UTTER

bring to *vt* (1753) **1** : to cause (a boat) to lie to or come to a standstill **2** : to restore to consciousness : REVIVE

bring up *vt* (14c) **1** : to bring (a person) to maturity through nurturing care and education **2** : to cause to stop suddenly **3** : to bring to attention : INTRODUCE **4** : VOMIT ~ *vi* : to stop suddenly

brink \'briŋk\ *n* [ME, of Scand origin; akin to ON *brekka* slope; akin to MD *brink* grassland] (13c) **1** : EDGE; *esp* : the edge at the top of a steep place **2** : a bank esp. of a river **3** : the point of onset : VERGE ⟨on the ~ of war⟩ : the threshold of danger

brink·man·ship \'briŋk-mən-ˌship\ *n* *also* **brinks·man·ship** \'briŋ(k)s-mən-\ *n* (1956) : the art or practice of pushing a dangerous situation or confrontation to the limit of safety esp. to force a desired outcome

brilliant, top and side view: *1* table, *2* bezel, *3* girdle, *4* pavilion, *5* culet

\ə\ abut \ᵊ\ kitten, F table \ər\ further \a\ ash \ā\ ace \ä\ mop, mar \aù\ out \ch\ chin \e\ bet \ē\ easy \g\ go \i\ hit \ī\ ice \j\ job \ŋ\ sing \ō\ go \o\ law \oi\ boy \th\ thin \th\ the \ü\ loot \ù\ foot \y\ yet \zh\ vision \à, k̲, ⁿ, œ, œ̄, ᵫ, ᵬ, ᵞ\ *see* Guide to Pronunciation

briny \'brī-nē\ *adj* **brin·i·er; -est** (1590) : of, relating to, or resembling brine or the sea : SALTY — **brin·i·ness** *n*

brio \'brē-(,)ō\ *n* [It] (1734) : enthusiastic vigor : VIVACITY, VERVE

bri·oche \brē-'ōsh, -'ŏsh\ *n* [F, fr. MF dial., fr. *brier* to knead, of Gmc origin; akin to OHG *brehhan* to break — more at BREAK] (1826) : light slightly sweet bread made with a rich yeast dough

bri·o·lette \,brē-ə-'let\ *n* [F] (1865) : an oval or pear-shaped gemstone cut in triangular facets

bri·quette *or* **bri·quet** \bri-'ket\ *n* [F *briquette*, dim. of *brique* brick] (1883) : a compacted often brick-shaped mass of usu. fine material ⟨a charcoal ~⟩ — **briquette** *vt*

bri·sance \bri-'zän(t)s, -'zäⁿs\ *n* [F, fr. *briser* to break, fr. OF *brisier*, of Celt origin; akin to OIr *brisid* he breaks; perh. akin to L *fricare* to rub — more at FRICTION] (1915) : the shattering or crushing effect of an explosive — **bri·sant** \-'zänt, -'zäⁿ\ *adj*

¹brisk \'brisk\ *adj* [prob. modif. of MF *brusque*] (1560) **1** : keenly alert : LIVELY **2 a** : pleasingly tangy ⟨~ tea⟩ **b** : FRESH, INVIGORATING ⟨~ weather⟩ **3** : sharp in tone or manner **4** : ENERGETIC, QUICK ⟨a ~ pace⟩ — **brisk·ly** *adv* — **brisk·ness** *n*

²brisk *vt* (1628) : to make brisk ~ *vi* : to become brisk — usu. used with *up* ⟨business ~*ed up*⟩

bris·ket \'bris-kət\ *n* [ME *brusket*; akin to OE *brēost* breast] (14c) : the breast or lower chest of a quadruped animal; *also* : a cut of beef from the brisket — see BEEF illustration

bris·ling \'briz-liŋ, 'bris-\ *n* [Norw *brisling*, fr. LG *bretling*, fr. *bret* broad; akin to OE *brād* broad] (ca. 1868) : SPRAT 1a

¹bris·tle \'bris-əl\ *n* [ME *bristil*, fr. *brust* bristle, fr. OE *byrst*; akin to OHG *burst* bristle, and perh. to L *fastigium* top] (14c) : a short stiff coarse hair or filament — **bris·tle-like** \'bris-ə(l)-,lik\ *adj*

²bristle *vb* **bris·tled; bris·tling** \'bris-liŋ, 'bris-ə-\ *vt* (15c) **1** : to furnish with bristles **2** : to make bristly : RUFFLE ~ *vi* **1 a** : to rise and stand stiffly erect ⟨quills *bristling*⟩ **b** : to raise the bristles (as in anger) **2** : to take on an aggressive attitude or appearance (as in response to a slight) **3 a** : to be full of or covered with esp. something suggestive of bristles ⟨roofs *bristled* with chimneys⟩ **b** : to be full of something specified ⟨book ~*s* with detail and irony —W. J. Broad⟩

bris·tle·cone pine \'bris-əl-,kōn-\ *n* (1894) : either of two pines (*Pinus longaeva* and *P. aristata*) of the western U.S. that include the oldest living trees

bris·tle·tail \-,tāl\ *n* (1706) : any of an order (Thysanura) of wingless insects with two or three slender caudal bristles

bris·tly \'bris-lē, 'bris-ə-\ *adj* **bris·tli·er; -est** (ca. 1591) **1 a** : consisting of or resembling bristles **b** : thickly set with bristles **2** : inclined to or exhibiting aggressiveness or anger

bristlecone pine

bris·tol board \'bris-t*ə*l-\ *n* [*Bristol*, England] (1809) : a paperboard with a smooth surface suitable esp. for artwork — called also *bristol*

Bristol fashion *adj* [*Bristol*, England] (1823) : being in good order : SHIPSHAPE

brit *also* **britt** \'brit\ *n* [perh. fr. Corn *brythel* mackerel] (1851) : minute marine animals (as crustaceans and pteropods) on which right whales feed

Brit \'brit\ *n* (1901) : BRITON 2

Bri·tan·nia metal \bri-'tan-yə-, -'ta-nē-ə-\ *n* [*Britannia*, poetic name for Great Britain, fr. L] (1817) : a silver-white alloy largely of tin, antimony, and copper that is similar to pewter

Bri·tan·nic \bri-'ta-nik\ *adj* (1641) : BRITISH

britch·es \'bri-chəz\ *n pl* [alter. of *breeches*] (ca. 1803) : BREECHES, TROUSERS

Brith Mi·lah \'brit-mē-'lä, 'brith-, 'bris-, -'mē-(,)lä\ *n* [LHeb *bĕrith milāh* covenant of circumcision] (ca. 1902) : the Jewish rite of circumcision

Brit·i·cism \'bri-tə-,si-zəm\ *n* [*British* + -*icism* (as in *gallicism*)] (1868) : a characteristic feature of British English

Brit·ish \'bri-tish\ *n* [ME *Bruttische* of Britain, fr. OE *Brettisc*, fr. *Brettas* Britons, of Celt origin; akin to W *Brython* Briton] (13c) **1 a** : the Celtic language of the ancient Britons **b** : BRITISH ENGLISH **2** *pl in constr* : the people of Great Britain or the Commonwealth — **British** *adj* — **Brit·ish·ism** \'bri-ti-,shi-zəm\ *n* — **Brit·ish·ness** *n*

British English *n* (1869) : the native language of most inhabitants of England; *esp* : English characteristic of England and clearly distinguishable from that used elsewhere (as in the U.S. or Australia)

Brit·ish·er \'bri-ti-shər\ *n* (1829) : BRITON 2

British thermal unit *n* (1876) : the quantity of heat required to raise the temperature of one pound of water one degree Fahrenheit at a specified temperature (as 39°F)

Brit·on \'bri-t*ə*n\ *n* [ME *Breton*, fr. MF & L; MF, fr. L *Britton-, Britto*, of Celt origin; akin to W *Brython*] (13c) **1** : a member of one of the peoples inhabiting Britain prior to the Anglo-Saxon invasions **2** : a native or subject of Great Britain; *esp* : ENGLISHMAN

Brit·ta·ny \'bri-t*ə*n-ē\ *n, pl* **Brittanys** *also* **Brittanies** [*Brittany*, region in France] (1967) : any of a breed of medium-sized pointing spaniels of French origin — called also *Brittany spaniel*

¹brit·tle \'bri-t*ə*l\ *adj* **brit·tler** \-t*ə*l-ər, 'bri-t*ə*l-ər\; **brit·tlest** \-ləst, -t*ə*l-əst\ [ME *britil*; akin to OE *brēotan* to break, ON *brjōta*] (14c) **1 a** : easily broken, cracked, or snapped ⟨~ clay⟩ ⟨~ glass⟩ **b** : easily disrupted, overthrown, or damaged : FRAIL ⟨a ~ friendship⟩ **2 a** : PERISHABLE, MORTAL **b** : TRANSITORY, EVANESCENT **3** : easily hurt or offended : SENSITIVE ⟨a ~ personality⟩ **4** : SHARP ⟨~ staccato of snare drums⟩ **5** : lacking warmth, depth, or generosity of spirit : COLD ⟨a ~ selfish person⟩ **6** : affected with or being a form of diabetes characterized by large and unpredictable fluctuations in blood glucose level *syn* see FRAGILE — **brit·tle·ly** \'bri-t*ə*l-(l)ē\ *adv* — **brit·tle·ness** \'bri-t*ə*l-nəs\ *n*

²brittle *n* (1913) : a candy made with caramelized sugar and nuts spread in thin sheets ⟨peanut ~⟩

brittle star *n* (1843) : any of a subclass or class (Ophiuroidea) of echinoderms that have slender flexible arms distinct from the central disk

Brit·ton·ic \bri-'tä-nik\ *adj* [L *Britton-, Britto* Briton] (1923) : BRYTHONIC

Brix \'briks\ *adj* (1897) : of or relating to a Brix scale

Brix scale *n* [Adolf F. *Brix* †1870 Austrian scientist] (1897) : a hydrometer scale for sugar solutions so graduated that its readings at a specified temperature represent percentages by weight of sugar in the solution — called also *Brix*

bro \'brō\ *n, pl* **bros** [by alter.] (1838) **1** : BROTHER 1 **2** : SOUL BROTHER — often used informally as a term of address

¹broach \'brōch\ *n* [ME *broche*, fr. MF, fr. (assumed) VL *brocca*, fr. L, fem. of *broccus* projecting] (13c) **1** : BROOCH **2** : any of various pointed or tapered tools, implements, or parts: as **a** : a spit for roasting meat **b** : a tool for tapping casks **c** : a cutting tool for removing material from metal or plastic to shape an outside surface or a hole

²broach *vt* (15c) **1 a** : to pierce (as a cask) in order to draw the contents; *also* : to open for the first time **b** : to open up or break into (as a mine or stores) **2** : to shape or enlarge (a hole) with a broach **3 a** : to make known for the first time **b** : to open up (a subject) for discussion ~ *vi* : to break the surface from below *syn* see EXPRESS — **broach·er** *n*

³broach *vi* [perh. fr. ²*broach*] (1705) : to veer or yaw dangerously so as to lie broadside to the waves — often used with *to*

¹broad \'brȯd\ *adj* [ME *brood*, fr. OE *brād*; akin to OHG *breit* broad] (bef. 12c) **1 a** : having ample extent from side to side or between limits ⟨~ shoulders⟩ **b** : having a specified extension from side to side ⟨made the path 10 feet ~⟩ **2** : extending far and wide : SPACIOUS ⟨the ~ plains⟩ **3 a** : OPEN, FULL ⟨~ daylight⟩ **b** : PLAIN, OBVIOUS ⟨a ~ hint⟩ **4** : dialectal esp. in pronunciation **5** : marked by lack of restraint, delicacy, or subtlety: **a** *obs* : OUTSPOKEN **b** : COARSE, RISQUÉ ⟨~ humor⟩ **6** *of a vowel* : OPEN — used specif. of *a* pronounced as in *father* **7 a** : LIBERAL, TOLERANT ⟨~ views⟩ **b** : widely applicable or applied : GENERAL **8** : relating to the main or essential points ⟨~ outlines⟩ — **broad·ly** *adv* — **broad·ness** *n*

syn BROAD, WIDE, DEEP mean having horizontal extent. BROAD and WIDE apply to a surface measured or viewed from side to side ⟨a *broad* avenue⟩. WIDE is more common when units of measurement are mentioned ⟨rugs eight feet *wide*⟩ or applied to unfilled space between limits ⟨a *wide* doorway⟩. BROAD is preferred when full horizontal extent is considered ⟨*broad* shoulders⟩. DEEP may indicate horizontal extent away from the observer or from a front or peripheral point ⟨a *deep* cupboard⟩ ⟨*deep* woods⟩.

²broad *adv* (bef. 12c) : in a broad manner : FULLY

³broad *n* (1659) **1** *Brit* : an expansion of a river — often used in pl. **2** *slang* : WOMAN

broad arrow *n* (14c) **1** : an arrow with a flat barbed head **2** *Brit* : a mark shaped like a broad arrow that identifies government property including clothing formerly worn by convicts

broad·ax *or* **broad·axe** \'brȯ-,daks\ *n* (bef. 12c) : a large ax with a broad blade

broad·band \'brȯd-,band\ *adj* (1956) **1** : operating at, responsive to, or comprising a wide band of frequencies ⟨a ~ radio antenna⟩ **2** : of, relating to, or being a communications network in which a frequency range is divided into multiple independent channels for simultaneous transmission of signals (as voice, data, or video)

broad bean *n* (1783) : the large flat edible seed of an Old World upright vetch (*Vicia faba*); *also* : this plant widely grown for its seeds and as fodder

broad–brush \'brȯd-,brəsh\ *adj* (1967) : GENERAL, NONSPECIFIC

¹broad·cast \'brȯd-,kast\ *adj* (1767) **1** : cast or scattered in all directions **2** : made public by means of radio or television **3** : of or relating to radio or television broadcasting

²broadcast *vb* **broadcast** *also* **broad·cast·ed; broad·cast·ing** *vt* (1813) **1** : to scatter or sow (as seed) broadcast **2** : to make widely known **3** : to transmit or make public by means of radio or television ~ *vi* **1** : to transmit a broadcast **2** : to speak or perform on a broadcast program — **broad·cast·er** *n*

³broadcast *adv* (1814) : to or over a broad area

⁴broadcast *n* (1922) **1** : the act of transmitting sound or images by radio or television **2** : a single radio or television program

Broad Church *adj* (1853) : of or relating to a liberal party in the Anglican communion esp. in the later 19th century

broad·cloth \'brȯd-,klŏth\ *n* (15c) **1** : a twilled napped woolen or worsted fabric with smooth lustrous face and dense texture **2** : a fabric usu. of cotton, silk, or rayon made in plain and rib weaves with soft semigloss finish

broad·en \'brȯ-d*ə*n\ *vb* **broad·ened; broad·en·ing** \'brȯd-niŋ, 'brȯ-d*ə*n-iŋ\ *vt* (1726) : to make broad ~ *vi* : to become broad

broad–gauge \'brȯd-'gāj\ *or* **broad–gauged** \-'gājd\ *adj* (1858) **1** : wide in area or scope ⟨a ~ effort⟩ **2** : comprehensive in outlook, range, or capability ⟨a ~ statesman⟩

broad gauge *n* (1844) : a railroad gauge wider than standard gauge

broad jump *n* (1872) : LONG JUMP — **broad jumper** *n*

broad–leaved \-'lēvd\ *or* **broad–leaf** \-'lēf\ *also* **broad–leafed** \-'lēft\ *adj* (1552) **1** : having broad leaves; *specif* : having leaves that are not needles **2** : composed of broad-leaved plants ⟨~ forests⟩

¹broad·loom \-,lüm\ *adj* (1925) : woven on a wide loom; *also* : so woven in solid color

²broadloom *n* (1926) : a broadloom carpet

broad–mind·ed \'brȯd-'mīn-dəd, -,mīn-\ *adj* (1882) **1** : tolerant of varied views **2** : inclined to condone minor departures from conventional behavior — **broad–mind·ed·ly** *adv* — **broad–mind·ed·ness** *n*

broad·scale \-,skā(ə)l\ *adj* (1939) : broad in extent, range, or effect

broad·sheet \-,shēt\ *n* (1705) **1** : BROADSIDE 1 **2** *Brit* : a newspaper with full-size pages as distinguished from a tabloid

¹broad·side \-,sīd\ *n* (1575) **1 a** (1) : a sizable sheet of paper printed on one side (2) : a sheet printed on one or both sides and folded **b** : something (as a ballad) printed on a broadside **2** *archaic* : the side of a ship above the waterline **3 a** : all the guns on one side of a ship; *also* : their simultaneous discharge **b** : a volley of abuse or denunciation **4** : a broad or unbroken surface

²broadside *adj* (1646) : directed or placed broadside ⟨a ~ attack⟩

³broadside *adv* (1870) **1 a** : with the side forward or toward a given point : SIDEWAYS ⟨turned ~⟩ **b** : directly from the side ⟨the car was hit ~⟩ **2** : in one volley **3** : at random

⁴broadside vt (1981) : to hit broadside ⟨the car was *broadsided*⟩

broad–spectrum adj (1952) : effective against a wide range of organisms (as insects or bacteria) ⟨~ antibiotic⟩

broad·sword \'bròd-,sòrd, -,sòrd\ n (bef. 12c) : a large heavy sword with a broad blade for cutting rather than thrusting

broad·tail \-,tāl\ n (1892) **1** : KARAKUL 1 **2** : the fur or skin of a very young or premature karakul lamb having a flat and wavy appearance resembling moiré silk

Broad·way \'bròd-,wā, -'wā\ n [*Broadway*, street in New York City] (1835) : the New York commercial theater and amusement world; specif : playhouses located in the area between the Avenue of the Americas and Ninth Avenue and from W. 41st Street to W. 53d Street — **Broadway** adj — **Broad·way·ite** \-,it\ n

Brob·ding·nag·ian \,bräb-diŋ-'na-gē-ən, -dig-'na-\ adj [*Brobdingnag*, imaginary land of giants in *Gulliver's Travels*, by Jonathan Swift] (1728) : marked by tremendous size — **Brobdingnagian** n

bro·cade \brō-'kād\ n [Sp *brocado*, fr. Catal *brocat*, fr. It *broccato*, fr. *broccare* to spur, brocade, fr. *brocco* small nail, fr. L *broccus* projecting] (1588) **1** : a rich oriental silk fabric with raised patterns in gold and silver **2** : a fabric characterized by raised designs — **brocade** vt — **bro·cad·ed** adj

Bro·ca's area \'brō-kəz-\ n [Paul P. *Broca* †1880 Fr. surgeon] (ca. 1898) : a brain center associated with the motor control of speech and usu. located in the left side of the frontal lobe

broc·a·telle \,brä-kə-'tel\ n [F, fr. It *broccatello*, dim. of *broccato*] (1669) : a stiff decorating fabric with patterns in high relief

broc·co·li \'brä-kə-lē, 'brä-klē\ n [It, pl. of *broccolo* flowering top of a cabbage, dim. of *brocco* small nail, sprout] (1699) **1** chiefly Brit : a large hardy cauliflower **2 a** : either of two garden vegetable plants closely related to the cabbage: (1) : one with a thick central stem and a compact head of dense usu. green florets that is classified with the cauliflower (2) : one (*Brassica oleracea italica*) with slender stems and usu. green or purple florets not arranged in a central head **b** : the stems and immature florets of broccoli used as food

broccoli rabe \-,räb\ n [perh. modif. of It *broccoli di rapa*, lit., flowering tops of the turnip] (1976) : a garden brassica (*Brassica rapa ruvo*) that is related to the turnip and produces edible leafy branching stalks and compact clusters of yellow florets — called also **broccoli raab** \-,räb, -,rab\, *rapini*

bro·chette \brō-'shet\ n [F, fr. OF *brochete*, fr. *broche* pointed tool — more at BROACH] (15c) : SKEWER; also : food broiled on a skewer

bro·chure \brō-'shùr, Brit esp 'brō-,\ n [F, fr. *brocher* to sew, fr. MF, to prick, fr. OF *brochier*, fr. *broche*] (1748) : PAMPHLET, BOOKLET; esp : one containing descriptive or advertising material

brock \'bräk\ n [ME, fr. OE *broc*, of Celt origin; akin to W *broch* badger] (bef. 12c) Brit : BADGER

brock·age \'brä-kij\ n [E dial. *brock* rubbish + E *-age*] (1879) : an imperfectly minted coin

brock·et \'brä-kət\ n [ME *broket*, fr. ONF *broquard*; akin to OF *broche* tine of an antler, pointed tool — more at BROACH] (1837) : any of several small deer (genus *Mazama*) of Central and So. America with unbranched antlers

bro·gan \'brō-gən, -,gan; brō-'gan\ n [Ir *brógán*, dim. of *bróg*] (1835) : a heavy shoe; esp : a coarse work shoe reaching to the ankle

¹brogue \'brōg\ n [Ir *bróg* & ScGael *bròg*, fr. MIr *bróc*, prob. fr. ON *brōk* leg covering; akin to OE *brōc* leg covering — more at BREECH] (1586) **1** : a stout coarse shoe worn formerly in Ireland and the Scottish Highlands **2** : a heavy shoe often with a hobnailed sole : BROGAN **3** : a stout oxford shoe with perforations and usu. a wing tip

²brogue n [Ir *barróg* accent, speech impediment, lit., wrestling hold, tight grip] (1705) : a dialect or regional pronunciation; esp : an Irish accent

broi·der \'bròi-dər\ vt [ME *broideren*, modif. of MF *broder* — more at EMBROIDER] (14c) : EMBROIDER — **broi·dery** \'bròi-d(ə-)rē\ n

¹broil \'bròi(ə)l\ vb [ME, fr. MF *bruler* to burn, modif. of L *ustulare* to singe, fr. *urere* to burn] vt (14c) : to cook by direct exposure to radiant heat : GRILL ~ vi : to be subjected to great or oppressive heat ⟨~ing in the sun⟩

²broil n (1583) : the act or state of broiling

³broil vb [ME, fr. MF *brouiller* to mix, broil, fr. OF *brooilier*, fr. *breu* broth, of Gmc origin; akin to OHG *brod* broth — more at BROTH] vi (15c) : BRAWL ~ vt : EMBROIL

⁴broil n (1525) : a noisy disturbance : TUMULT; esp : BRAWL ⟨a tavern row . . . widens into a general ~ —J. R. Green⟩

broil·er \'bròi-lər\ n (14c) **1** : one that broils **2** : a bird fit for broiling; esp : a young chicken of up to 2½ pounds (1.14 kilograms) dressed weight

¹broke \'brōk\ past of BREAK

²broke adj [ME, alter. of *broken*] (1710) : PENNILESS

bro·ken \'brō-kən\ adj [ME, fr. OE *brocen*, fr. pp. of *brecan* to break] (13c) **1** : violently separated into parts : SHATTERED **2** : damaged or altered by breaking: as **a** : having undergone or been subjected to fracture ⟨a ~ leg⟩ **b** of land surfaces : being irregular, interrupted, or full of obstacles **c** : violated by transgression ⟨a ~ promise⟩ **d** : DISCONTINUOUS, INTERRUPTED **e** : disrupted by change **f** of a flower : having an irregular, streaked, or blotched pattern esp. from virus infection **3** **a** : made weak or infirm **b** : subdued completely : CRUSHED ⟨a ~ spirit⟩ **c** : BANKRUPT **d** : reduced in rank **4 a** : cut off : DISCONNECTED **b** : imperfectly spoken or written ⟨~ English⟩ **5** : not complete or full **6** : disunited by divorce, separation, or desertion of one parent ⟨children from ~ homes⟩ ⟨a ~ family⟩ — **bro·ken·ly** adv — **bro·ken·ness** \-kə(n)-nəs\ n

broken–down adj (1817) : WORN-OUT, DEBILITATED

bro·ken–field \-,fēld\ adj (1923) : characterized by quick changes in direction to avoid widely scattered tacklers ⟨a halfback known for ~ running⟩

bro·ken·heart·ed \-'här-təd\ adj (1526) : overcome by grief or despair

bro·ken·wind·ed \-'win-dəd\ adj (1580) : affected with or as if with heaves

bro·ker \'brō-kər\ n [ME, negotiator, fr. AF *brocour*] (14c) **1** : one who acts as an intermediary: as **a** : an agent who arranges marriages **b** : an agent who negotiates contracts of purchase and sale (as of real estate, commodities, or securities) **2** : POWER BROKER — **broker** vb — **bro·ker·ing** \'brō-k(ə-)riŋ\ n

bro·ker·age \'brō-k(ə-)rij\ n (15c) **1** : the business or establishment of a broker **2** : a broker's fee or commission

bro·kered \-kərd\ adj (1967) : arranged or controlled by power brokers ⟨a ~ political convention⟩

bro·king \-kiŋ\ n (1569) chiefly Brit : the business of a broker : BROKERAGE

brol·ly \'brä-lē\ n, pl **brollies** [by shortening & alter.] (ca. 1874) chiefly Brit : UMBRELLA

brom- or **bromo-** comb form [prob. fr. F *brome*, fr. Gk *brōmos* bad smell] : bromine ⟨*bromide*⟩

bro·mate \'brō-,māt\ n (ca. 1836) : a salt of bromic acid

brome·grass \'brōm-,gras\ n [NL *Bromus*, fr. L *bromos* oats, fr. Gk] (ca. 1791) : any of a large genus (*Bromus*) of tall grasses often having drooping spikelets

bro·me·lain \'brō-mə-lən, -,lān\ also **bro·me·lin** \'brō-mə-lən, brō-'mē-\ n [*bromelain* by alter. of *bromelin*, fr. NL *Bromelia*] (1894) : a protease obtained esp. from the pineapple

bro·me·li·ad \brō-'mē-lē-,ad\ n [NL *Bromelia*, genus of tropical American plants, fr. Olaf *Bromelius* †1705 Swed. botanist] (1866) : any of a family (Bromeliaceae) of chiefly tropical American usu. epiphytic herbaceous plants including the pineapple, Spanish moss, and various ornamentals

bro·mic acid \'brō-mik-\ n (1828) : an unstable strongly oxidizing acid $HBrO_3$ known only in solution or in the form of its salts

bro·mide \'brō-,mīd\ n (1836) **1** : a binary compound of bromine with another element or a radical including some (as potassium bromide) used as sedatives **2 a** : a commonplace or tiresome person : BORE **b** : a commonplace or hackneyed statement or notion

bro·mid·ic \brō-'mi-dik\ adj (1906) : lacking in originality : TRITE

bro·mi·nate \'brō-mə-,nāt\ vt **-nat·ed; -nat·ing** (1873) : to treat or cause to combine with bromine or a compound of bromine — **bro·mi·na·tion** \,brō-mə-'nā-shən\ n

bro·mine \'brō-,mēn\ n [F *brome* bromine + E ²-*ine*] (1827) : a nonmetallic halogen element that is isolated as a deep red corrosive toxic volatile liquid of disagreeable odor — see ELEMENT table

bro·mo \'brō-(,)mō\ n, pl **bromos** [*brom-*] (1923) : a dose of a proprietary effervescent headache remedy and antacid

bro·mo·crip·tine \,brō-mō-'krip-,tēn, -tən\ n [by shortening & alter. fr. *bromoergocryptine*, fr. *brom-* + *ergocryptine*, an ergot derivative, fr. *ergo-* + Gk *kryptos* hidden — more at CRYPT] (1975) : a polypeptide ergot derivative $C_{32}H_{40}BrN_5O_5$ that mimics the activity of dopamine in inhibiting prolactin secretion

bro·mo·ura·cil \,brō-mō-'yùr-ə-,sil, -səl\ n (1960) : a mutagenic uracil derivative $C_4H_3N_2O_2Br$ that is an analogue of thymine and pairs readily with adenine and sometimes with guanine

brom·thy·mol blue \,brōm-'thī-,mòl-\ n (1920) : a dye derived from thymol that is an acid-base indicator — called also **bro·mo·thy·mol blue** \,brō-mō-'thī-,mòl-\

bronc \'bräŋk\ n [short for *bronco*] (1893) : an unbroken or imperfectly broken range horse of western No. America; broadly : MUSTANG

bronch- or **broncho-** comb form [LL, fr. Gk, fr. *bronchos* windpipe] : bronchial tube : bronchial ⟨*bronchitis*⟩

bronchi- or **bronchio-** comb form [NL, fr. *bronchia*, pl., branches of the bronchi, fr. LL, fr. Gk, dim. of *bronchos*] : bronchial tubes ⟨*bronchiectasis*⟩

bron·chi·al \'bräŋ-kē-əl\ adj (1735) : of or relating to the bronchi or their ramifications in the lungs — **bron·chi·al·ly** \-kē-ə-lē\ adv

bronchial asthma n (ca. 1881) : asthma resulting from spasmodic contraction of bronchial muscles

bronchial tube n (1847) : a primary bronchus or any of its branches

bron·chi·ec·ta·sis \,bräŋ-kē-'ek-tə-səs\ n [NL, fr. *bronchi-* + Gk *ektasis* extension — more at ATELECTASIS] (ca. 1860) : a chronic dilatation of bronchi or bronchioles

bron·chi·ole \'bräŋ-kē-,ōl\ n [NL *bronchiolum*, dim. of *bronchia*] (ca. 1860) : a minute thin-walled branch of a bronchus — **bron·chi·o·lar** \,bräŋ-kē-'ō-lər\ adj

bron·chi·tis \brän-'kī-təs, bräŋ-\ n [NL] (1808) : acute or chronic inflammation of the bronchial tubes; also : a disease marked by this — **bron·chit·ic** \-'ki-tik\ adj

bron·cho·di·la·tor \,bräŋ-kō-(,)kō-dī-'lā-tər, -'dī-,\ n (1903) : a drug that relaxes bronchial muscle resulting in expansion of the bronchial air passages — **bronchodilator** adj

bron·cho·gen·ic \,bräŋ-kə-'je-nik\ adj (1927) : of, relating to, or arising in or by way of the air passages of the lungs ⟨~ carcinoma⟩

bron·cho·pneu·mo·nia \,bräŋ-(,)kō-nü-'mō-nyə, -nyü-\ n [NL] (1858) : pneumonia involving many relatively small areas of lung tissue

bron·cho·scope \'bräŋ-kə-,skōp\ n [ISV] (1899) : a tubular illuminated instrument used for inspecting or passing instruments into the bronchi — **bron·cho·scop·ic** \,bräŋ-kə-'skä-pik\ adj — **bron·chos·co·pist** \brän-'käs-kə-pist, bräŋ-\ n — **bron·chos·co·py** \-pē\ n

bron·cho·spasm \'bräŋ-kə-,spa-zəm\ n (ca. 1901) : constriction of the air passages of the lung (as in asthma) by spasmodic contraction of the bronchial muscles — **bron·cho·spas·tic** \,bräŋ-kə-'spas-tik\ adj

bron·chus \'bräŋ-kəs\ n, pl **bron·chi** \'bräŋ-,kī, -,kē\ [NL, fr. Gk *bronchos*] (ca. 1706) : either of the two primary divisions of the trachea that lead respectively into the right and the left lung; broadly : BRONCHIAL TUBE

bron·co also **bron·cho** \'brän-(,)kō\ n, pl **broncos** also **bronchos** [MexSp, fr. Sp, lit., rough, wild] (1850) : BRONC

bron·co·bust·er \-,bəs-tər\ n (1887) : one who breaks wild horses to the saddle

bron·to·sau·rus \,brän-tə-'sòr-əs\ also **bron·to·saur** \'brän-tə-,sòr\ n [NL, fr. Gk *brontē* thunder + *sauros* lizard; akin to Gk *bremein* to roar] (1905) : any of a genus (*Apatosaurus* syn. *Brontosaurus*) of large sauropod dinosaurs of the Jurassic — called also *apatosaurus*

Bronx cheer \'bräŋ(k)s-\ n [*Bronx*, borough of New York City] (1929) : RASPBERRY 2

\ə\ abut \ᵊ\ kitten, F table \ər\ further \a\ ash \ā\ ace \ä\ mop, mar \aù\ out \ch\ chin \e\ bet \ē\ easy \g\ go \i\ hit \ī\ ice \j\ job \ŋ\ sing \ō\ go \ò\ law \òi\ boy \th\ thin \t̲h̲\ the \ü\ loot \ù\ foot \y\ yet \zh\ vision \á, k̲, ⁿ, œ, œ̄, ᵫ, ūe, ᵞ\ see Guide to Pronunciation

¹**bronze** \'bränz\ vt **bronzed; bronz·ing** (1645) : to give the appearance of bronze to ⟨a bronzed sculpture⟩; also : TAN 2 — **bronz·er** n
²**bronze** n, often attrib [F, fr. It bronzo] (1739)   **1 a** : an alloy of copper and tin and sometimes other elements   **b** : any of various copper-base alloys with little or no tin   **2** : a sculpture or artifact of bronze   **3** : a moderate yellowish brown — **bronzy** \'brän-zē\ adj
Bronze Age n (1865) : the period of ancient human culture characterized by the use of bronze that began between 4000 and 3000 B.C. and ended with the advent of the Iron Age
Bronze Star Medal n (1944) : a U.S. military decoration awarded for heroic or meritorious service not involving aerial flights
bronz·ing n (1868) : a bronze coloring or discoloration (as of leaves)
brooch \'brōch also 'brüch\ n [ME broche pointed tool, brooch — more at BROACH] (13c) : an ornament that is held by a pin or clasp and is worn at or near the neck
¹**brood** \'brüd\ n [ME, fr. OE brōd; akin to OE beorma yeast — more at BARM] (bef. 12c)   **1** : the young of an animal or a family of young; esp : the young (as of a bird or insect) hatched or cared for at one time   **2** : a group having a common nature or origin
²**brood** adj (15c) : kept for breeding ⟨a ~ flock⟩
³**brood** vt (15c)   **1 a** : to sit on or incubate (eggs)   **b** : to produce by or as if by incubation : HATCH   **2** of a bird : to cover (young) with the wings   **3** : to think anxiously or gloomily about : PONDER   ~ vi   **1 a** of a bird : to brood eggs or young   **b** : to sit quietly and thoughtfully : MEDITATE   **2** : HOVER, LOOM   **3 a** : to dwell gloomily on a subject : WORRY   **b** : to be in a state of depression — **brood·ing·ly** \'brü-diŋ-lē\ adv
brood·er \'brü-dər\ n (1599)   **1** : one that broods   **2** : a heated structure used for raising young fowl
brood·mare \'brüd-,mar, -,mer\ n (1821) : a mare kept for breeding
broody \'brü-dē\ adj (1523)   **1** : being in a state of readiness to brood eggs that is characterized by cessation of laying and by marked changes in behavior and physiology ⟨a ~ hen⟩   **2** : given or conducive to introspection : CONTEMPLATIVE, MOODY — **brood·i·ness** n
¹**brook** \'bruk\ n [ME, fr. OE brōc; akin to OHG bruoh marshy ground] (bef. 12c) : CREEK 2
²**brook** vt [ME brouken to use, enjoy, fr. OE brūcan; akin to OHG brūhhan to use, L frui to enjoy] (15c) : to stand for : TOLERATE ⟨he would ~ no interference with his plans⟩
brook·ie \'bru-kē\ n (1933) : BROOK TROUT
brook·ite \'brü-,kīt\ n [Henry J. Brooke †1857 Eng. mineralogist] (1825) : titanium dioxide TiO₂ occurring as a mineral in orthorhombic crystals commonly translucent brown or opaque brown to black
brook·let \'brü-klət\ n (1813) : a small brook
Brook·lyn·ese \,brü-klə-'nēz, -'nēs\ n [Brooklyn, borough of New York City] (1939) : the vernacular speech of greater New York City and environs
brook trout n (1836) : the common speckled cold-water char (Salvelinus fontinalis) of No. America
¹**broom** \'brüm, 'brum\ n [ME, fr. OE brōm; akin to OHG brāmo bramble] (bef. 12c)   **1** : any of various leguminous shrubs (esp. genera Cytisus and Genista) with long slender branches, small leaves, and usu. showy yellow flowers; esp : SCOTCH BROOM   **2** : a bundle of firm stiff twigs or fibers bound together on a long handle for sweeping and brushing
²**broom** vt (1838)   **1** : to sweep with or as if with a broom   **2** : to finish (as a concrete surface) by means of a broom
broom·ball \-,bol\ n (1933) : a variation of ice hockey played on ice without skates and with brooms and a soccer ball used instead of sticks and a puck — **broom·ball·er** \-,bo-lər\ n
broom·corn \-,korn\ n (ca. 1782) : any of several tall cultivated sorghums having stiff-branched panicles used in brooms and brushes
broom·rape \-,rāp\ n (1578) : any of a genus (Orobanche of the family Orobanchaceae, the broomrape family) of herbs that have leaves modified to scales and that grow as parasites on the roots of other plants
broom·stick \-,stik\ n (1683) : the long thin handle of a broom
brose \'brōz\ n [perh. alter. of Sc bruis broth, fr. OF broez, nom. sing. of broet, dim. of breu broth — more at BROIL] (1515) : a chiefly Scottish dish made with a boiling liquid and meal
broth \'broth\ n, pl **broths** \'broths, 'brothz\ [ME, fr. OE; akin to OHG brod broth, OE brēowan to brew] (bef. 12c)   **1** : liquid in which meat, fish, cereal grains, or vegetables have been cooked : STOCK   **2** : a fluid culture medium
broth·el \'brä-thəl, 'brò- also -thəl\ n [ME, worthless fellow, prostitute, fr. brothen, pp. of brethen to waste away, go to ruin, fr. OE brēothan to waste away; akin to OE brēotan to break — more at BRITTLE] (ca. 1593) : BORDELLO
broth·er \'brə-thər\ n, pl **brothers** also **breth·ren** \'breth-rən; 'bre-thə-rən, -thərn\ [ME, fr. OE brōthor; akin to OHG bruodor brother, L frater, Gk phratēr member of the same clan] (bef. 12c)   **1** : a male who has the same parents as another or one parent in common with another   **2** : one related to another by common ties or interests   **3** : a fellow member — used as a title for ministers in some evangelical denominations   **4** : one of a type similar to another   **5 a** : KINSMAN   **b** : one who shares with another a common national or racial origin; esp : SOUL BROTHER   **6 a** cap : a member of a congregation of men not in holy orders and usu. in hospital or school work   **b** : a member of a men's religious order who is not preparing for or is not ready for holy orders ⟨a lay ~⟩
broth·er·hood \'brə-thər-,hùd\ n [ME brotherhede, brotherhod, alter. of brotherrede, fr. OE brōthorrǣden, fr. brōthor + rǣden condition — more at KINDRED] (14c)   **1** : the quality or state of being brothers   **2** : FELLOWSHIP, ALLIANCE   **3** : an association (as a labor union) for a particular purpose   **4** : the whole body of persons engaged in a business or profession
broth·er–in–law \'brə-thə-rən-,lò, 'brə-thə-; 'brə-thərn-\ n, pl **broth·ers–in–law** \'brə-thər-zən-\ (14c)   **1** : the brother of one's spouse   **2 a** : the husband of one's sister   **b** : the husband of one's spouse's sister
broth·er·ly \'brə-thər-lē\ adj (bef. 12c)   **1** : of or relating to brothers   **2** : natural or becoming to brothers : AFFECTIONATE ⟨~ love⟩ — **broth·er·li·ness** n — **brotherly** adv
brougham \'brü(-)əm, 'brō(-)əm\ n [Henry Peter Brougham, Baron Brougham and Vaux †1868 Scot. jurist] (1851) : a light closed horse-drawn carriage with the driver outside in front

brought past and past part of BRING
brou·ha·ha \'brü-,hä-,hä, ,brü-,hä-'hä, brü-'hä-,hä\ n [F] (1890) : HUBBUB, UPROAR
¹**brow** \'braù\ n [ME, fr. OE brū; akin to ON brūn eyebrow, Gk ophrys, Skt bhrū] (bef. 12c)   **1 a** : EYEBROW   **b** : FOREHEAD   **2** : the projecting upper part or margin of a steep place   **3** : EXPRESSION, MIEN
²**brow** n [perh. fr. Dan or Sw bro bridge; akin to OE brycg bridge] (1867) : GANGPLANK
brow·beat \'braù-,bēt\ vt **-beat; -beat·en** \-'bē-t²n\ or **-beat; -beat·ing** (1581) : to intimidate or disconcert by a stern manner or arrogant speech : BULLY   syn see INTIMIDATE
browed \'braùd\ adj (15c) : having brows of a specified nature — used in combination ⟨smooth-browed⟩
¹**brown** \'braùn\ adj [ME broun, fr. OE brūn; akin to OHG brūn brown, Gk phrynē toad] (bef. 12c) : of the color brown; esp : of dark or tanned complexion
²**brown** n (13c)   **1** : any of a group of colors between red and yellow in hue, of medium to low lightness, and of moderate to low saturation   **2** : a brown-skinned person — **brown·ish** \'braù-nish\ adj — **browny** \-nē\ adj
³**brown** vi (14c) : to become brown   ~ vt : to make brown
brown alga n (ca. 1899) : any of a division (Phaeophyta) of variable mostly marine algae with chlorophyll masked by brown pigment
brown bagging n (1959)   **1** : the practice of carrying (as to work) one's lunch usu. in a brown paper bag   **2** : the practice of carrying a bottle of liquor into a restaurant or club where setups are available — **brown–bag** \'braùn-,bag\ vb or adj — **brown bagger** n
brown bear n (1805) : any of several bears predominantly brown in color that are sometimes considered a single species (Ursus arctos) including the grizzly bear and that formerly inhabited western No. America from the barrens of Alaska to northern Mexico and much of Europe and Asia but are now much restricted in range
brown Bet·ty \-'be-tē\ n (1864) : a baked pudding of apples, bread crumbs, and spices
brown bread \-,bred\ n (14c)   **1** : bread made of whole wheat flour   **2** : a dark brown steamed bread made usu. of cornmeal, white or whole wheat flours, molasses, soda, and milk or water
brown coal n (ca. 1828) : LIGNITE
brown dwarf n (1978) : a celestial object that is much smaller than a normal star and has insufficient mass for nuclear fusion to begin but that is hot enough to radiate energy esp. at infrared wavelengths
brown earth n (1932) : any of a group of intrazonal soils developed in temperate humid regions under deciduous forests and characterized by a dark brown mull horizon that grades through lighter colored soil into parent material
brown–eyed Su·san \'braù-,nīd-'sü-z²n\ n [brown-eyed + Susan (as in black-eyed Susan)] (1896) : a dark-centered coneflower (Rudbeckia triloba) of eastern No. America often having tripartite lower leaves
brown fat n (1951) : a mammalian heat-producing tissue occurring esp. in human newborns and in hibernators — called also brown adipose tissue
Brown·ian motion \'braù-nē-ən-\ n [Robert Brown †1858 Scot. botanist] (ca. 1889) : a random movement of microscopic particles suspended in liquids or gases resulting from the impact of molecules of the fluid surrounding the particles — called also Brownian movement
brown·ie \'braù-nē\ n [¹brown] (ca. 1500)   **1** : a legendary good-natured elf that performs helpful services at night   **2** cap : a member of a program of the Girl Scouts for girls in the first through third grades in school   **3** : a small square or rectangle of rich usu. chocolate cake often containing nuts
brownie point n, often cap B (ca. 1962) : a credit regarded as earned esp. by currying favor (as with a superior)
Brow·ning automatic rifle \'braù-niŋ-\ n [John M. Browning †1926 Am. designer of firearms] (1920) : a .30 caliber gas-operated air-cooled magazine-fed automatic rifle often provided with a rest for the barrel
Browning machine gun n (1918) : a .30 or .50 caliber recoil-operated air- or water-cooled machine gun fed by a cartridge belt
brown lung n (1969) : BYSSINOSIS
brown·nose \'braù(n)-,nōz\ vt [fr. the implication that servility is equivalent to kissing the hinder parts of the person from whom advancement is sought] (ca. 1939) slang : to ingratiate oneself with : curry favor with — **brownnose** n — **brown·nos·er** n
brown–out \'braù-,naùt\ n [brown + blackout] (1942) : a period of reduced voltage of electricity caused esp. by high demand and resulting in subnormal illumination
brown pelican n (1823) : a pelican (Pelecanus occidentalis) of American coasts that has a brown body and a chiefly white or white with yellow head
brown rat n (1826) : a common domestic rat (Rattus norvegicus) that has been introduced worldwide — called also Norway rat
brown recluse spider n (1964) : a venomous spider (Loxosceles reclusa) of the U.S. that has a violin-shaped mark on the cephalothorax and produces a dangerous cytotoxin
brown rice n (1916) : hulled but unpolished rice that retains most of the bran layers, endosperm, and germ
brown rot n (1894) : a disease of stone fruits caused by fungi (genus Monilinia, esp. M. fructicola)
brown sauce n (1878) : a sauce consisting typically of stock thickened with flour browned in fat
brown·shirt \'braùn-,shərt\ n, often cap (1932) : NAZI; esp : STORM TROOPER
brown·stone \-,stōn\ n (1858)   **1** : a reddish brown sandstone used for building   **2** : a dwelling faced with brownstone
brown study n (1532) : a state of serious absorption or abstraction
brown sugar n (1704) : soft sugar whose crystals are covered by a film of refined dark syrup
Brown Swiss n (1902) : any of a breed of large hardy brown dairy cattle originating in Switzerland
brown–tail moth \'braùn-,tāl-\ n (1782) : a tussock moth (Euproctis chrysorrhoea) introduced in the U.S. and having larvae which feed on foliage and are irritating to the skin
brown trout n (1886) : a speckled European trout (Salmo trutta) widely introduced as a game fish

brow·ridge \'brau̇-ˌrij\ *n* (1898) : a prominence of the frontal bone above the eye caused by the projection of the frontal air sinuses

¹browse \'brau̇z\ *vb* **browsed; brows·ing** *vt* (15c) **1 a** : to consume as browse **b** : GRAZE **2** : to look over casually : SKIM ~ *vi* **1 a** : to feed on or as if on browse **b** : GRAZE **2 a** : to skim through a book reading at random passages that catch the eye **b** : to look over or through an aggregate of things casually esp. in search of something of interest — **brows·er** *n*

²browse *n* [prob. modif. of MF *brouts*, pl. of *brout* sprout, fr. OF *brost*, of Gmc origin; akin to OS *brustian* to sprout, and perh. to OE *brēost* breast] (1523) **1** : tender shoots, twigs, and leaves of trees and shrubs used by animals for food **2** : an act or instance of browsing

bru·cel·la \brü-'se-lə\ *n*, *pl* **-cel·lae** \-'se-(ˌ)lē\ *or* **-cel·las** [NL, fr. Sir David *Bruce*] (1930) : any of a genus (*Brucella*) of nonmotile pleomorphic bacteria that cause disease in humans and domestic animals

bru·cel·lo·sis \ˌbrü-sə-'lō-səs\ *n*, *pl* **-lo·ses** \-ˌsēz\ [NL] (1930) : infection with or disease caused by brucellae

bru·cine \'brü-ˌsēn\ *n* [prob. fr. F, fr. NL *Brucea* (genus name of *Brucea antidysenterica*, a shrub)] (1823) : a poisonous alkaloid $C_{23}H_{26}N_2O_4$ found with strychnine esp. in nux vomica

bru·in \'brü-ən\ *n* [MD, name of the bear in *Reynard the Fox*] (15c) : BEAR 1

¹bruise \'brüz\ *vb* **bruised; bruis·ing** [ME *brusen, brisen*, fr. MF & OE; akin to OE *bruisier* to break, of Celt origin; akin to OIr *bruid* he shatters; OE *brȳsan* to bruise; akin to OIr *bruid*, L *frustum* piece] *vt* (14c) **1 a** *archaic* : DISABLE **b** : BATTER, DENT **2** : to inflict a bruise on : CONTUSE **3** : to break down (as leaves or berries) by pounding : CRUSH **4** : WOUND, INJURE; *esp* : to inflict psychological hurt on ~ *vi* **1** : to inflict a bruise **2** : to undergo bruising

²bruise *n* (1541) **1 a** : an injury involving rupture of small blood vessels and discoloration without a break in the overlying skin : CONTUSION **b** : a similar injury to plant tissue **2** : ABRASION, SCRATCH **3** : an injury esp. to the feelings

bruis·er \'brü-zər\ *n* (1744) : a big husky man

¹bruit *n* [ME, fr. MF, fr. OF, noise] (15c) **1** \'brüt\ *archaic* **a** : NOISE, DIN **b** : REPORT, RUMOR **2** \'brü-ē\ [F, lit., noise] : any of several generally abnormal sounds heard on auscultation

²bruit \'brüt\ *vt* (15c) : to noise abroad : REPORT

bru·mal \'brü-məl\ *adj* [L *brumalis*, fr. *bruma* winter] (1513) *archaic* : indicative of or occurring in the winter

brum·by \'brəm-bē\ *n*, *pl* **brumbies** [origin unknown] (1880) *Austral* : a wild or unbroken horse

brume \'brüm\ *n* [F, mist, winter, fr. OProv *bruma*, fr. L, winter solstice, winter; akin to L *brevis* short — more at BRIEF] (1808) : MIST, FOG — **bru·mous** \'brü-məs\ *adj*

brum·ma·gem \'brə-mi-jəm\ *adj* [alter. of *Birmingham*, England, the source in the 17th cent. of counterfeit groats] (1637) : SPURIOUS; *also* : cheaply showy : TAWDRY — **brummagem** *n*

brunch \'brənch\ *n* [*breakfast* + *lunch*] (1896) : a meal usu. taken late in the morning that combines a late breakfast and an early lunch

¹bru·net *or* **bru·nette** \brü-'net\ *n* (ca. 1539) : a person having brown or black hair and usu. a relatively dark complexion

²brunet *or* **brunette** *adj* [F *brunet*, masc., *brunette*, fem., brownish, fr. OF, fr. *brun* brown, fr. ML *brunus*, of Gmc origin; akin to OHG *brūn* brown] (1752) **1** : being a brunet **2** : of a dark-brown or black color ⟨~ hair⟩

Brun·hild \'brün-ˌhilt\ *n* [G] : a queen in Germanic legend won by Siegfried for Gunther

bru·ni·zem \'brü-nə-ˌzem\ *n* [*bruni-* (fr. ML *brunus* brown) + *-zem* earth (as in *chernozem*)] (1953) : any of a zonal group of deep dark prairie soils developed from loess

Bruns·wick stew \'brənz-(ˌ)wik-\ *n* [*Brunswick* county, Va.] (1856) : a stew made of vegetables and usu. two meats (as chicken and squirrel)

brunt \'brənt\ *n* [ME] (15c) **1** : the principal force, shock, or stress (as of an attack) **2** : the greater part : BURDEN

¹brush \'brəsh\ *n* [ME *brusch*, fr. MF *brusce*] (14c) **1** : BRUSHWOOD **2 a** : scrub vegetation **b** : land covered with scrub vegetation

²brush *n* [ME *brusshe*, fr. MF *broisse*, fr. OF *broce*] (14c) **1** : a device composed of bristles typically set into a handle and used esp. for sweeping, smoothing, scrubbing, or painting **2** : something resembling a brush: as **a** : a bushy tail **b** : a feather tuft worn on a hat **3** : an electrical conductor that makes sliding contact between a stationary and a moving part (as of a generator or a motor) **4 a** : an act of brushing **b** : a quick light touch or momentary contact in passing

³brush *vt* (15c) **1 a** : to apply a brush to **b** : to apply with a brush **2 a** : to remove with passing strokes (as of a brush) **b** : to dispose of in an offhand way : DISMISS ⟨~*ed* him off⟩ **3** : to pass lightly over or across : touch gently against in passing — **brush·er** *n*

⁴brush *n* [*brusche* rush, hostile collision, fr. *bruschen*] (14c) : a brief encounter or skirmish ⟨a ~ with the law⟩

⁵brush *vi* [ME *bruschen* to rush, fr. MF *brosser* to dash through underbrush, fr. *broce*] (1674) **1** : to move lightly or heedlessly ⟨~*ed* past the well-wishers waiting to greet him⟩

brush·abil·i·ty \ˌbrə-shə-'bi-lə-tē\ *n* (1936) : ease of application with a brush ⟨~ of a paint⟩

brush·back \'brəsh-ˌbak\ *n* (1954) : a fastball intentionally thrown near the batter's head or body in baseball — **brush back** *vt*

brush border *n* (1903) : a stria of microvilli on the plasma membrane of an epithelial cell (as in a kidney tubule) that is specialized for absorption

brush cut *n* (1945) : CREW CUT

brush discharge *n* (1849) : a faintly luminous relatively slow electrical discharge having no spark

brushed \'brəsht\ *adj* (1926) **1** : finished with a nap ⟨a ~ fabric⟩ **2** : polished but not shiny ⟨~ aluminum⟩

brush-fire \'brəsh-ˌfīr\ *adj* [*brush fire* (a fire involving brush but not full-sized trees)] (1954) : involving mobilization only on a small and local scale ⟨~ border wars⟩

brush·land \-ˌland\ *n* (1853) : an area covered with brush growth

brush–off \-ˌȯf\ *n* (1941) : a quietly curt or disdainful dismissal

brush up *vt* (ca. 1600) **1** : to improve or polish as if by brushing **2** : to renew one's skill in ⟨*brush up* your Spanish⟩ ~ *vi* : to refresh one's memory : renew one's skill ⟨*brush up* on math⟩ — **brush-up** \'brəsh-ˌəp\ *n*

brush·wood \'brəsh-ˌwu̇d\ *n* (ca. 1613) **1** : wood of small branches esp. when cut or broken **2** : a thicket of shrubs and small trees

brush–work \-ˌwərk\ *n* (1868) : work done with a brush (as in painting); *esp* : the characteristic work of an artist using a brush

¹brushy \'brə-shē\ *adj* **brush·i·er; -est** (1658) : covered with or abounding in brush or brushwood ⟨~ hills⟩ ⟨a ~ habitat⟩

²brushy *adj* **brush·i·er; -est** (1673) : SHAGGY, ROUGH ⟨a ~ moustache⟩

brusque *also* **brusk** \'brəsk\ *adj* [F *brusque*, fr. It *brusco* butcher's-broom (plant with bristly twigs)] (1651) **1** : markedly short and abrupt **2** : blunt in manner or speech often to the point of ungracious harshness *syn* see BLUFF — **brusque·ly** *adv* — **brusqueness** *n*

brus·que·rie \ˌbrəs-kə-'rē\ *n* [F, fr. *brusque*] (1752) : abruptness of manner

Brus·sels carpet \'brə-səlz-\ *n* [*Brussels*, Belgium] (1799) : a carpet made of colored worsted yarns first fixed in a foundation web of strong linen thread and then drawn up in loops to form the pattern

Brussels griffon *n* (1904) : any of a breed of short-faced compact rough- or smooth-coated toy dogs of Belgian origin — called also *griffon*

Brussels lace *n* (1748) **1** : any of various fine needlepoint or bobbin laces with floral designs made orig. in or near Brussels **2** : a machine-made net of hexagonal mesh

brus·sels sprout \'brə-səl-\ *n*, *often cap* B (1796) **1** *pl* : a plant (*Brassica oleracea gemmifera*) of the mustard family that bears small edible green heads on its stem **2** : any of the edible green heads borne on brussels sprouts — usu. used in pl.

brussels sprout 1

brut \'brüt, 'brüēt\ *adj* [F, lit., rough] (1891) *of champagne* : very dry; *specif* : being the driest made by the producer

bru·tal \'brü-tᵊl\ *adj* [ME, fr. MF or ML; MF, fr. ML *brutalis*, fr. L *brutus*] (15c) **1** *archaic* : typical of beasts : ANIMAL **2** : befitting a brute: as **a** : grossly ruthless or unfeeling ⟨a ~ slander⟩ **b** : CRUEL, COLD-BLOODED ⟨a ~ attack⟩ **c** : HARSH, SEVERE ⟨~ weather⟩ **d** : unpleasantly accurate and incisive ⟨the ~ truth⟩ — **bru·tal·ly** \-tᵊl-ē\ *adv*
syn BRUTAL, BRUTISH, BESTIAL, FERAL mean characteristic of an animal in nature, action, or instinct. BRUTAL applies to people, their acts, or their words and suggests a lack of intelligence, feeling, or humanity ⟨a senseless and *brutal* war⟩. BRUTISH stresses likeness to an animal in low intelligence, in base appetites, and in behavior based on instinct ⟨*brutish* stupidity⟩. BESTIAL suggests a degradation unworthy of man and fit only for beasts ⟨*bestial* depravity⟩. FERAL suggests the savagery or ferocity of wild animals ⟨the struggle to survive unleashed their *feral* impulses⟩.

bru·tal·ise *Brit var of* BRUTALIZE

bru·tal·i·ty \brü-'ta-lə-tē\ *n*, *pl* **-ties** (1549) **1** : the quality or state of being brutal **2** : a brutal act or course of action

bru·tal·ize \'brü-tᵊl-ˌīz\ *vt* **-ized; -iz·ing** (ca. 1704) **1** : to make brutal, unfeeling, or inhuman ⟨temperaments *brutalized* by poverty and disease⟩ **2** : to treat brutally ⟨an accord not to ~ prisoners of war⟩ — **bru·tal·iza·tion** \ˌbrü-tᵊl-ə-'zā-shən\ *n*

¹brute \'brüt\ *adj* [ME, fr. MF *brut* rough, fr. L *brutus* brutish, lit., heavy; akin to L *gravis* heavy — more at GRIEVE] (15c) **1** : of or relating to beasts ⟨the ways of the ~ world⟩ **2** : INANIMATE 1a **3** : characteristic of an animal in quality, action, or instinct: as **a** : CRUEL, SAVAGE ⟨~ violence⟩ **b** : not working by reason ⟨~ instinct⟩ **4** : purely physical ⟨~ strength⟩ **5** : unrelievedly harsh ⟨~ facts⟩ ⟨~ necessity⟩

²brute *n* (1611) **1** : BEAST **2** : a brutal person

brut·ish \'brü-tish\ *adj* (1534) **1** : befitting beasts ⟨lived a short and ~ life as a slave⟩ **2 a** : strongly and grossly sensual ⟨~ gluttony⟩ **b** : showing little intelligence or sensibility ⟨a ~ lack of understanding⟩ *syn* see BRUTAL — **brut·ish·ly** *adv* — **brut·ish·ness** *n*

brux·ism \'brək-ˌsi-zəm\ *n* [irreg. fr. Gk *brychein* to gnash the teeth + E *-ism*] (ca. 1940) : the habit of unconsciously gritting or grinding the teeth esp. in situations of stress or during sleep

Bryn·hild \'brin-ˌhild\ *n* [ON *Brynhildr*] : a Valkyrie who is waked from an enchanted sleep by Sigurd and later has him killed when he forgets her

bry·ol·o·gy \brī-'ä-lə-jē\ *n* [Gk *bryon* moss (akin to Gk *bryein* to grow luxuriantly) + ISV *-logy*] (ca. 1859) **1** : moss life or biology **2** : a branch of botany that deals with the bryophytes — **bry·o·log·i·cal** \ˌbrī-ə-'lä-ji-kəl\ *adj* — **bry·ol·o·gist** \brī-'ä-lə-jist\ *n*

bry·o·ny \'brī-ə-nē\ *n*, *pl* **-nies** [ME, fr. L *bryonia*, fr. Gk *bryōnia*; akin to Gk *bryein*] (14c) : any of a genus (*Bryonia*) of tendril-bearing vines of the gourd family with large leaves and red or black fruit

bry·o·phyl·lum \ˌbrī-ə-'fi-ləm\ *n* [NL, fr. Gk *bryon* + *phyllon* leaf — more at BLADE] (ca. 1868) : any of various kalanchoes; *esp* : a succulent kalanchoe (*Kalanchoe pinnata*) often grown as a foliage plant that propagates new plants from its leaves

bry·o·phyte \'brī-ə-ˌfīt\ *n* [ultim. fr. Gk *bryon* + *phyton* plant; akin to Gk *phyein* to bring forth — more at BE] (1878) : any of a division (Bryophyta) of nonflowering plants comprising the mosses, liverworts, and hornworts — **bryo·phyt·ic** \ˌbrī-ə-'fi-tik\ *adj*

bryo·zo·an \ˌbrī-ə-'zō-ən\ *n* [NL *Bryozoa*, fr. Gk *bryon* + NL *-zoa*] (ca. 1864) : any of a phylum (Bryozoa) of aquatic mostly marine invertebrate animals that reproduce by budding and usu. form permanently attached branched or mossy colonies — **bryozoan** *adj*

¹Bry·thon·ic \bri-'thä-nik\ *adj* (1884) : of, relating to, or characteristic of the division of the Celtic languages that includes Welsh, Cornish, and Breton

²Brythonic *n* (1884) : the Brythonic branch of the Celtic languages — see INDO-EUROPEAN LANGUAGES table

\ə\ abut \ᵊ\ kitten, F table \ər\ further \a\ ash \ā\ ace \ä\ mop, mar \au̇\ out \ch\ chin \e\ bet \ē\ easy \g\ go \i\ hit \ī\ ice \j\ job \ŋ\ sing \ō\ go \ȯ\ law \ȯi\ boy \th\ thin \t̷h\ the \ü\ loot \u̇\ foot \y\ yet \zh\ vision \à, k̲, ⁿ, œ, œ̄, ue, ue̅, ʸ\ *see* Guide to Pronunciation

Bt \'bē-'tē\ *n* [NL *Bacillus thuringiensis*, species name, lit., Thuringian bacillus] (1971) : an insecticide composed of a bacterium (*Bacillus thuringiensis*) pathogenic esp. for lepidopteran larvae; *also* : the bacterium itself

bub \'bəb\ *n* [prob. short for *bubby* little boy] (1839) : FELLOW, BUDDY — used in informal address ⟨come on, ~, get moving⟩

¹**bub·ble** \'bə-bəl\ *n, often attrib* [ME *bobel*] (14c) **1** : a small globule typically hollow and light: as **a** : a small body of gas within a liquid **b** : a thin film of liquid inflated with air or gas **c** : a globule in a transparent solid **d** : something (as a plastic or inflatable structure) that is hemispherical or semicylindrical **2** : something that lacks firmness, solidity, or reality **b** : a delusive scheme **3** : a sound like that of bubbling **4** : MAGNETIC BUBBLE

²**bubble** *vb* **bub·bled; bub·bling** \'bə-b(ə-)liŋ\ *vi* (15c) **1 a** : to form or produce bubbles **b** : to rise in or as if in bubbles — usu. used with *up* **2** : to flow with a gurgling sound ⟨a brook *bubbling* over rocks⟩ **3 a** : to become lively or effervescent ⟨*bubbling* with good humor⟩ **b** : to speak in a lively and fluent manner ~ *vt* **1** : to utter (as words) effervescently **2** : to cause to bubble

bubble and squeak *n* (ca. 1785) : a British dish consisting of usu. leftover potatoes, greens (as cabbage), and sometimes meat fried together

bubble chamber *n* (1953) : a chamber of superheated liquid in which the path of an ionizing particle is made visible by a string of vapor bubbles

bub·ble·gum \'bə-bəl-,gəm\ *adj* (1969) : appealing to or characteristic of preteens or adolescents ⟨~ music⟩

bubble gum *n* (1937) **1** : a chewing gum that can be blown into large bubbles **2** *usu* **bub·ble·gum** \'bə-bəl-,gəm\ : rock music characterized by simple repetitive phrasings and intended esp. for young teenagers

bub·ble·head \'bə-bəl-,hed\ *n* (1949) : a foolish or stupid person — **bub·ble·head·ed** \-,he-dəd\ *adj*

bubble memory *n* (1969) : a computer memory that uses magnetic bubbles to store information

bub·bler \'bə-b(ə-)lər\ *n* (1914) **1** : a drinking fountain from which a stream of water bubbles upward **2** : one that bubbles

¹**bub·bly** \'bə-b(ə-)lē\ *adj* **bub·bli·er; -est** (1599) **1** : full of bubbles : EFFERVESCENT ⟨a ~ bottle of pop⟩ **2** : full of or showing good spirits : LIVELY, EFFUSIVE **3** : resembling a bubble ⟨a ~ dome⟩

²**bubbly** *n* (1920) : CHAMPAGNE

bub·by \'bə-bē\ *n, pl* **bubbies** [prob. of imit. origin] (1686) : BREAST 1 — sometimes considered vulgar

bu·bo \'byü-(,)bō, 'bü-\ *n, pl* **buboes** [ML *bubon-, bubo,* fr. Gk *boubōn*] (14c) : an inflammatory swelling of a lymph gland esp. in the groin — **bu·bon·ic** \byü-'bä-nik, bü-\ *adj*

bubonic plague *n* (1885) : plague caused by a bacterium (*Yersinia pestis*) and characterized esp. by the formation of buboes

buc·cal \'bə-kəl\ *adj* [L *bucca* cheek] (ca. 1771) **1** : of, relating to, near, involving, or supplying a cheek ⟨the ~ surface of a tooth⟩ ⟨the ~ branch of the facial nerve⟩ **2** : of, relating to, involving, or lying in the mouth ⟨the ~ cavity⟩ — **buc·cal·ly** *adv*

buc·ca·neer \,bə-kə-'nir\ *n* [F *boucanier*] (ca. 1690) **1** : any of the freebooters preying on Spanish ships and settlements esp. in the West Indies in the 17th century; *broadly* : PIRATE **2** : an unscrupulous adventurer esp. in politics or business — **buccaneer** *vi* — **buc·ca·neer·ish** \-ish\ *adj*

buc·ci·na·tor \'bək-sə-,nā-tər\ *n* [NL, fr. L *bucinator* trumpeter, fr. *bucinare* to sound on the trumpet, fr. *bucina* trumpet, fr. *bov-, bos* cow + *canere* to sing, play — more at COW, CHANT] (1671) : a thin broad muscle forming the wall of the cheek

¹**buck** \'bək\ *n, pl* **bucks** [ME, fr. OE *bucca* stag, he-goat; akin to OHG *boc* he-goat, MIr *bocc*] (bef. 12c) **1** *or pl* **buck** : a male animal; *esp* : a male deer or antelope **2 a** : a male human being : MAN **b** : a dashing fellow : DANDY **3** *or pl* **buck** : ANTELOPE **4 a** : BUCKSKIN; *also* : an article (as a shoe) made of buckskin **b** (1) : DOLLAR 3b (2) : a sum of money esp. to be gained ⟨make a quick ~⟩; *also* : MONEY — usu. used in pl. **5** [short for *sawbuck* sawhorse] **a** : a supporting rack or frame **b** : a short thick leather-covered block for gymnastic vaulting

²**buck** *vt* (1750) **1 a** *archaic* : ¹BUTT **b** : OPPOSE, RESIST ⟨~ing the system⟩ **2** : to throw (as a rider) by bucking **3** : to charge into (as the opponent's line in football) **4 a** : to pass esp. from one person to another **b** : to move or load (as heavy objects) esp. with mechanical equipment ~ *vi* **1** *of a horse or mule* : to spring into the air with the back arched **2** : to charge against something (as an obstruction) **3 a** : to move or react jerkily **b** : to refuse assent : BALK **4** : to strive for advancement sometimes without regard to ethical behavior ⟨~ing for a promotion⟩ — **buck·er** *n*

³**buck** *n* (ca. 1877) : an act or instance of bucking

⁴**buck** *n* [short for earlier *buckhorn knife*] (1865) **1** : an object formerly used in poker to mark the next player to deal; *broadly* : a token used as a mark or reminder **2** : RESPONSIBILITY — used esp. in the phrases *pass the buck* and *the buck stops here*

⁵**buck** *adj* [prob. fr. ¹*buck*] (1918) : of the lowest grade within a military category ⟨~ private⟩

⁶**buck** *adv* [origin unknown] (1928) : STARK ⟨~ naked⟩

buck-and-wing \,bə-kən-'wiŋ\ *n* (1895) : a solo tap dance with sharp foot accents, springs, leg flings, and heel clicks

buck·a·roo *also* **buck·er·oo** \,bə-kə-'rü, 'bə-kə-,\ *n, pl* **-aroos** *also* **-eroos** [by folk etymology fr. Sp *vaquero,* fr. *vaca* cow, fr. L *vacca* — more at VACCINE] (1827) **1** : COWBOY **2** : BRONCOBUSTER

buck·bean \'bək-,bēn\ *n* (1578) **2** : a plant (*Menyanthes trifoliata*) of the family Menyanthaceae) growing in bogs and having racemes of white or purplish flowers

buck·board \-,bōrd, -,bȯrd\ *n* [obs. E *buck* body of a wagon + E *board*] (1839) : a four-wheeled vehicle with a floor made of long springy boards

¹**buck·et** \'bə-kət\ *n* [ME, fr. AF *buket,* fr. OE *būc* pitcher, belly; akin to OHG *būh* belly] (13c) **1** : a typically

buckboard

cylindrical vessel for catching, holding, or carrying liquids or solids **2** : something resembling a bucket: as **a** : the scoop of an excavating machine **b** : one of the receptacles on the rim of a waterwheel **c** : one of the cups of an endless-belt conveyor **d** : one of the vanes of a turbine rotor **3** : BUCKETFUL **4** : BUCKET SEAT **5** : BASKET 3b

²**bucket** *vt* (1649) **1** : to draw or lift in buckets **2** *Brit* **a** : to ride (a horse) hard **b** : to drive hurriedly or roughly **3** : to deal with in a bucket shop ~ *vi* **1** : HUSTLE, HURRY **2** **a** : to move about haphazardly or irresponsibly **b** : to move roughly or jerkily

bucket brigade *n* (1911) : a chain of persons acting to put out a fire by passing buckets of water from hand to hand

buck·et·ful \'bə-kət-,fúl\ *n, pl* **bucketfuls** \-,fúlz\ *or* **buck·ets·ful** \-kəts-,fúl\ (ca. 1563) : as much as a bucket will hold; *broadly* : a large quantity

bucket seat *n* (1908) : a low separate seat for one person (as in an automobile or an airplane)

bucket shop *n* (1875) **1** : a saloon in which liquor was formerly sold from or dispensed in open containers (as buckets or pitchers) **2 a** : a gambling establishment that formerly used market fluctuations (as in securities or commodities) as a basis for gaming **b** : a dishonest brokerage firm; *esp* : one that formerly failed to execute customers' margin orders in expectation of making a profit from market fluctuations adverse to the customers' interests

buck·eye \'bə-,kī\ *n* (1763) **1** : a shrub or tree (genus *Aesculus* of the horse-chestnut family; *also* : its large nutlike seed **2** *cap* : a native or resident of Ohio — used as a nickname

buck fever *n* (1841) : nervous excitement of an inexperienced hunter at the sight of game

¹**buck·le** \'bə-kəl\ *n* [ME *bocle,* fr. MF, boss of a shield, buckle, fr. L *buccula,* dim. of *bucca* cheek] (14c) **1** : a fastening for two loose ends that is attached to one and holds the other by a catch **2** : an ornamental device that suggests a buckle **3** *archaic* : a crisp curl

²**buckle** *vb* **buck·led; buck·ling** \'bə-k(ə-)liŋ\ *vt* (14c) **1** : to fasten with a buckle **2** : to prepare with vigor **3** : to cause to bend, give way, or crumple ~ *vi* **1** : to become fastened with a buckle **2** : to apply oneself with vigor ⟨~s down to the job⟩ **3** : to bend, heave, warp, or kink usu. under the influence of some external agency ⟨wheat *buckling* in the wind⟩ **4** : COLLAPSE ⟨the props *buckled* under the strain⟩ **5** : to give way : YIELD ⟨he *buckled* under pressure⟩

³**buckle** *n* (ca. 1876) **1** : a product of buckling **2** : a coffee cake baked with berries and a crumbly topping ⟨blueberry ~⟩

¹**buck·ler** \'bə-klər\ *n* [ME *bocler,* fr. MF, shield with a boss, fr. *bocle*] (13c) **1 a** : a small round shield held by a handle at arm's length **b** : a shield worn on the left arm **2** : one that shields and protects

²**buckler** *vt* (1590) : to shield or defend with a buckler

buckle up *vi* (1976) : to fasten one's seat belt

buck·min·ster·ful·ler·ene \'bək-(,)min-stər-,fū-lə-'rēn\ *n* [R. *Buckminster Fuller*] (1985) : a spherical fullerene C₆₀ that is an extremely stable form of pure carbon, consists of interconnected pentagons and hexagons suggestive of the geometry of a geodesic dome, and is believed to be a major constituent of soot

bucko \'bə-(,)kō\ *n, pl* **buck·oes** (1883) **1** : a person who is domineering and bullying : SWAGGERER **2** *chiefly Irish* : young fellow : LAD

buck passer *n* (1920) : a person who habitually passes the buck — **buck-pass·ing** \'bək-,pa-siŋ\ *n*

¹**buck·ram** \'bə-krəm\ *n* [ME *bukeram,* fr. OF *boquerant,* fr. OProv *bocaran,* prob. fr. *Bokhara,* city of central Asia] (15c) **1** : a stiff-finished heavily sized fabric of cotton or linen used for interlinings in garments, for stiffening in millinery, and in bookbinding **2** *archaic* : STIFFNESS, RIGIDITY

²**buckram** *adj* (ca. 1589) : suggesting buckram in stiffness

³**buckram** *vt* (1783) **1** : to give strength or stiffness to (as with buckram) **2** *archaic* : to make pretentious

Buck Rogers \'bək-'rä-jərz\ *adj* [*Buck Rogers,* hero of a science-fiction comic strip created by Phil Nowlan] (1941) : marked by futuristic and high-tech qualities : suggestive of science fiction

buck·saw \'bək-,sȯ\ *n* (1856) : a saw set in a usu. H-shaped frame for sawing wood

buck·shee \'bək-(,)shē, ,bək-'\ *n* [Hindi *bakhśiś,* fr. Pers *bakhshīsh* — more at BAKSHEESH] (ca. 1760) **1** *Brit* : something extra obtained free; *esp* : extra rations **2** *Brit* : WINDFALL, GRATUITY

¹**buck·shot** \'bək-,shät\ *n* (1775) : lead shot that is from .24 to .33 inch (about 6.1 to 8.4 millimeters) in diameter

²**buckshot** *adj* (1941) : SCATTERSHOT

buck·skin \-,skin\ *n, often attrib* (14c) **1 a** : the skin of a buck **b** : a soft pliable usu. suede-finished leather **2** *a pl* : buckskin breeches **b** *archaic* : a person dressed in buckskin; *esp* : an early American backwoodsman **3** : a horse of a light yellowish dun color with black mane and tail

buck·skinned \-,skind\ *adj* (1829) : dressed in buckskin

buck·tail \-,tāl\ *n* (1911) : an angler's lure made typically of hairs from the tail of a deer

buck·thorn \-,thȯrn\ *n* (1578) **1** : any of a genus (*Rhamnus* of the family Rhamnaceae, the buckthorn family) of often thorny trees or shrubs some of which yield purgatives or pigments **2** : a tree (*Bumelia lycioides*) of the sapodilla family of the southern U.S.

buck·tooth \-'tüth\ *n* (1753) : a large projecting front tooth — **buck-toothed** \-'tütht\ *adj*

buck up *vb* [²*buck*] *vi* (1844) : to become encouraged ~ *vt* **1** : IMPROVE, SMARTEN **2** : to raise the morale of

buck·wheat \-,hwēt, -,wēt\ *n* [D *boekweit,* fr. MD *boecweit,* fr. *boec-* (akin to OHG *buohha* beech tree) + *weit* wheat — more at BEECH] (1548) **1** : any of a genus (*Fagopyrum* of the family Polygonaceae, the buckwheat family) of herbs with alternate leaves, clusters of apetalous whitish flowers, and triangular seeds; *esp* : either of two plants (*F. esculentum* and *F. tartaricum*) cultivated for their edible seeds **2** : the seed of a buckwheat used as a cereal grain

bucky·ball \'bə-kē-,bȯl\ *n* [R. *Buckminster Fuller* + ⁴-*y*] (1985) : a molecule of buckminsterfullerene

bu·col·ic \byü-'kä-lik\ *adj* [L *bucolicus,* fr. Gk *boukolikos,* fr. *boukolos* cowherd, fr. *bous* head of cattle + *-kolos* (akin to L *colere* to cultivate) — more at COW, WHEEL] (ca. 1609) **1** : of or relating to shepherds or herdsmen : PASTORAL **2** : relating to or typical of rural life — **bu·col·i·cal·ly** \-li-k(ə-)lē\ *adv*

¹**bud** \'bəd\ *n* [ME *budde*] (14c) **1 :** a small lateral or terminal protuberance on the stem of a plant that may develop into a flower, leaf, or shoot **2 :** something not yet mature or at full development: as **a :** an incompletely opened flower **b :** CHILD, YOUTH **c :** an outgrowth of an organism that differentiates into a new individual : GEMMA; *also* : PRIMORDIUM — **in the bud :** in an early stage of development ⟨nipped the rebellion *in the bud*⟩

²**bud** *vb* **bud·ded; bud·ding** *vi* (14c) **1** *of a plant* **a :** to set or put forth buds **b :** to commence growth from buds **2 :** to grow or develop as if from a bud **3 :** to reproduce asexually esp. by the pinching off of a small part of the parent ∼ *vt* **1 :** to produce or develop from buds **2 :** to cause (as a plant) to bud **3 :** to insert a bud from a plant of one kind into an opening in the bark of (a plant of another kind) usu. in order to propagate a desired variety — **bud·der** *n*

Bud·dha \'bü-də, 'bù-\ *n* [Skt, enlightened; akin to Skt *bodhi* enlightenment — more at BID] (1681) **1 :** a person who has attained Buddhahood **2 :** a representation of Gautama Buddha

Bud·dha·hood \-,hùd\ *n* (1837) **:** a state of perfect enlightenment sought in Buddhism

Bud·dhism \'bü-,di-zəm, 'bù-\ *n* (1801) **:** a religion of eastern and central Asia growing out of the teaching of Gautama Buddha that suffering is inherent in life and that one can be liberated from it by mental and moral self-purification — **Bud·dhist** \'bü-dist, 'bù-\ *n or adj* — **Bud·dhis·tic** \bü-'dis-tik, bù-\ *adj*

bud·ding \'bə-diŋ\ *adj* (1581) **:** being in an early stage of development ⟨∼ novelists⟩

bud·dle \'bə-d°l\ *n* [origin unknown] (ca. 1532) **:** an apparatus on which crushed ore is concentrated by washing

bud·dle·ia \'bəd-lē-ə, ,bəd-'lē-\ *n* [NL, genus name, fr. Adam *Buddle* †1715 Eng. botanist] (1791) **:** any of a genus (*Buddleia* of the family Loganiaceae) of shrubs or trees of warm regions with showy terminal clusters of usu. yellow or violet flowers

¹**bud·dy** \'bə-dē\ *n, pl* **buddies** [prob. baby talk alter. of *brother*] (1850) **1 a :** COMPANION, PARTNER **b :** FRIEND 1 **2 :** FELLOW — used esp. in informal address

²**buddy** *vi* **bud·died; bud·dy·ing** (1918) **:** to become friendly — usu. used with *up* or *with*

³**buddy** *adj* (1976) **:** featuring a friendship or partnership between the two main usu. male characters ⟨a ∼ movie⟩

bud·dy–bud·dy \,bə-dē-'bə-dē\ *adj* (1951) **:** familiarly friendly

buddy system *n* (1942) **:** an arrangement in which two individuals are paired (as for mutual safety in a hazardous situation)

¹**budge** \'bəj\ *n* [ME *bugee*, fr. AF *bogee*] (14c) **:** a fur formerly prepared from lambskin dressed with the wool outward

²**budge** *vb* **budged; budg·ing** [MF *bouger*, fr. (assumed) VL *bullicare*, fr. L *bullire* to boil — more at BOIL] *vi* (1590) **1 :** MOVE, SHIFT ⟨the mule wouldn't ∼⟩ **2 :** to give way : YIELD ⟨wouldn't ∼ on the issue⟩ ∼ *vt* **:** to cause to move or change

³**budge** *adj* [origin unknown] (1634) *archaic* **:** POMPOUS, SOLEMN

bud·ger·i·gar \'bə-jə-rē-,gär\ *n* [modif. of Yuwaalaraay (Australian aboriginal language of northern New South Wales) *gijirrigaa*] (1840) **:** a small Australian parrot (*Melopsittacus undulatus*) usu. light green with black and yellow markings in the wild but bred under domestication in many colors

¹**bud·get** \'bə-jət\ *n* [ME *bowgette*, fr. MF *bougette*, dim. of *bouge* leather bag, fr. L *bulga*, of Celt origin; akin to MIr *bolg* bag; akin to OE *belg* bag — more at BELLY] (15c) **1** *chiefly dial* **:** a usu. leather pouch, wallet, or pack; *also* **:** its contents **2 :** STOCK, SUPPLY **3 :** a quantity (as of energy or water) involved in, available for, or assignable to a particular situation; *also* **:** an account of gains and losses of such a quantity **4 a :** a statement of the financial position of an administration for a definite period of time based on estimates of expenditures during the period and proposals for financing them **b :** a plan for the coordination of resources and expenditures **c :** the amount of money that is available for, required for, or assigned to a particular purpose — **bud·get·ary** \'bə-jə,ter-ē\ *adj*

²**budget** *vt* (1618) **1 a :** to put or allow for in a budget **b :** to require to adhere to a budget **2 a :** to allocate funds for in a budget ⟨∼ a new hospital⟩ **b :** to plan or provide for the use of in detail ⟨∼ing manpower⟩ ∼ *vi* **:** to put oneself on a budget ⟨∼ing for a vacation⟩

³**budget** *adj* (1941) **:** suitable for one on a budget : INEXPENSIVE

bud·ge·teer \,bə-jə-'tir\ *also* **bud·get·er** \'bə-jə-tər\ *n* (ca. 1845) **1 :** one who prepares a budget **2 :** one who is restricted to a budget

bud·gie \'bə-jē\ *n* [by shortening and alter.] (1935) **:** BUDGERIGAR

bud scale *n* (ca. 1880) **:** one of the leaves resembling scales that form the sheath of a plant bud

bud·worm \'bəd-,wərm\ *n* (1849) **:** a moth larva that feeds on the buds of plants — compare SPRUCE BUDWORM

¹**buff** \'bəf\ *n* [MF *buffle* wild ox, fr. OIt *bufalo*] (1580) **1 :** a garment (as a uniform) made of buff leather **2 :** the state of being nude ⟨sunbathing in the ∼⟩ **3 a :** a moderate orange yellow **b :** a light to moderate yellow **4 :** a device having a soft absorbent surface (as of cloth) by which polishing material is applied **5** [earlier *buff* an enthusiast about going to fires; perh. fr. the buff overcoats worn by volunteer firefighters in New York City *ab*1820] **:** FAN, ENTHUSIAST

²**buff** *adj* (ca. 1771) **:** of the color buff

³**buff** *vt* (1885) **1 :** POLISH, SHINE ⟨waxed and ∼ed the floor⟩ **2 :** to give a velvety surface to (leather)

¹**buf·fa·lo** \'bə-fə-,lō\ *n, pl* **-lo** *or* **-loes** *also* **-los** *often attrib* [It *bufalo* & Sp *búfalo*, fr. LL *bufalus*, alter. of L *bubalus*, fr. Gk *boubalos* African gazelle] (1562) **1 :** any of several wild bovids: as **a :** WATER BUFFALO **b :** CAPE BUFFALO **c** (1) **:** any of a genus (*Bison*) of bovids; *esp* **:** a large shaggy-maned No. American bovid (*B. bison*) that has short horns and heavy forequarters with a large muscular hump and that was formerly abundant on the central and western plains — compare WISENT (2) **:** the flesh of the buffalo used as food **2 :** any of several suckers (genus *Ictiobus*) found mostly in the Mississippi valley — called also *buffalofish*

²**buffalo** *vt* **-loed; -lo·ing** (ca. 1896) **:** BEWILDER, BAFFLE

buf·fa·lo·ber·ry \-,ber-ē\ *n* (1805) **:** either of two western U.S. shrubs (*Shepherdia argentea* and *S. canadensis*) of the oleaster family with silvery foliage; *also* **:** their edible scarlet berry

buffalo gourd *n* (ca. 1928) **:** a perennial cucurbit (*Cucurbita foetidissima*) of arid lands of the central and southwest U.S. and Mexico with

a large starchy taproot and seeds rich in an oil suitable after processing for use in cooking or as fuel

buffalo grass *n* (1784) **:** a low-growing grass (*Buchloë dactyloides*) of former feeding grounds of the American buffalo; *also* **:** GRAMA

buffalo plaid *n* (1979) **:** a broad checkered plaid pattern usu. of two colors

¹**buff·er** \'bə-fər\ *n, often attrib* [*buff*, v., to react like a soft body when struck] (1835) **1 :** any of various devices or pieces of material for reducing shock or damage due to contact **2 :** a means or device used as a cushion against the shock of fluctuations in business or financial activity **3 :** something that serves as a protective barrier: as **a :** BUFFER STATE **b :** a person who shields another esp. from annoying routine matters **c :** MEDIATOR 1 **4 :** a substance capable in solution of neutralizing both acids and bases and thereby maintaining the original acidity or basicity of the solution; *also* **:** a solution containing such a substance **5 :** a temporary storage unit (as in a computer); *esp* **:** one that accepts information at one rate and delivers it at another — **buffered** \-ford\ *adj*

²**buffer** *vt* **buff·ered; buff·er·ing** \-f(ə-)riŋ\ (1894) **1 :** to lessen the shock of : CUSHION **2 :** to treat (as a solution or its acidity) with a buffer; *also* **:** to prepare (aspirin) with an antacid **3 :** to collect (as data) in a buffer

³**buffer** *n* (1854) **:** one that buffs

buffer state *n* (1883) **:** a usu. neutral state lying between two larger potentially rival powers

buffer zone *n* (1908) **:** a neutral area separating conflicting forces; *broadly* **:** an area designed to separate

¹**buf·fet** \'bə-fət\ *n* [ME, fr. OF, dim. of *buffe* blow] (13c) **1 :** a blow esp. with the hand **2 :** something that strikes with telling force

²**buffet** *vt* (13c) **1 :** to strike sharply esp. with the hand : CUFF **2 :** to strike repeatedly : BATTER ⟨the waves ∼ed the shore⟩ **3 :** to drive, force, move, or attack by or as if by repeated blows ∼ *vi* **:** to make one's way esp. under difficult conditions

³**buf·fet** \(,)bə-'fā, bü-', *Brit* esp 'bü-,\ *n* [F] (1718) **1 :** SIDEBOARD **2 a :** a counter for refreshments **b** *chiefly Brit* **:** a restaurant operated as a public convenience (as in a railway station) **c :** a meal set out as a buffet or table for ready access and informal service

⁴**buf·fet** *same as* ³\ *adj* (1898) **:** served informally (as from a buffet)

buffing wheel *n* (ca. 1889) **:** a wheel covered with polishing material

buff leather *n* (1580) **:** a strong supple oil-tanned leather produced chiefly from cattle hides

buf·fle·head \'bə-fəl-,hed\ *n* [archaic E *buffle* buffalo + E *head*] (1731) **:** a small No. American diving duck (*Bucephala albeola*)

buf·fo \'bü-(,)fō\ *n, pl* **buf·fi** \-(,)fē\ *or* **buffos** [It, fr. *buffone*] (1764) **:** CLOWN, BUFFOON; *specif* **:** a male singer of comic roles in opera

buf·foon \(,)bə-'fün\ *n* [MF *bouffon*, fr. OIt *buffone*] (1585) **1 :** a ludicrous figure : CLOWN **2 :** a gross and usu. ill-educated or stupid person — **buf·foon·ish** \-'fü-nish\ *adj*

buf·foon·ery \-'fü-nə-rē, -'fün-rē\ *n, pl* **-er·ies** (1621) **:** foolish or playful behavior or practice

¹**bug** \'bəg\ *n* [ME *bugge* scarecrow; akin to Norw dial. *bugge* important man] (14c) *obs* **:** BOGEY, BUGBEAR

²**bug** *n* [origin unknown] (1622) **1 a :** an insect or other creeping or crawling invertebrate **b :** any of several insects commonly considered obnoxious: as (1) **:** BEDBUG (2) **:** COCKROACH (3) **:** HEAD LOUSE **c :** any of an order (Hemiptera and esp. its suborder Heteroptera) of insects that have sucking mouthparts, forewings thickened at the base, and incomplete metamorphosis and are often economic pests — called also *true bug* **2 :** an unexpected defect, fault, flaw, or imperfection **3 a :** a germ or microorganism esp. when causing disease **b :** an unspecified or nonspecific sickness usu. presumed due to a bug **4 :** a sudden enthusiasm **5 :** ENTHUSIAST ⟨a camera ∼⟩ **6 :** a prominent person **7 :** a concealed listening device **8** [fr. its designation by an asterisk on race programs] **:** a weight allowance given apprentice jockeys

³**bug** *vt* **bugged; bug·ging** (1949) **1 :** BOTHER, ANNOY ⟨don't ∼ me with petty details⟩ **2 :** to plant a concealed microphone in

⁴**bug** *vb* **bugged; bug·ging** [prob. fr. ²*bug*] *vi* (1877) *of the eyes* **:** PROTRUDE, BULGE — often used with *out* ∼ *vt* **:** to cause to bug ⟨his eyes were *bugged* with horror⟩

bug·a·boo \'bə-gə-,bü\ *n, pl* **-boos** [origin unknown] (1740) **1 :** an imaginary object of fear **2 :** BUGBEAR 2; *also* **:** something that causes fear or distress out of proportion to its importance

bug·bane \'bəg-,bān\ *n* (1804) **:** any of several perennial herbs (genus *Cimicifuga*) of the buttercup family; *esp* **:** BLACK COHOSH

bug·bear \-,bar, -,ber\ *n* (1581) **1 :** an imaginary goblin or specter used to excite fear **2 a :** an object or source of dread **b :** a continuing source of irritation : PROBLEM

bug·eye \-,ī\ *n* (1881) **:** a small boat with a flat bottom, a centerboard, and two raked masts

bug–eyed \-,īd\ *adj* (1922) **:** having the eyes bulging (as with astonishment)

¹**bug·ger** \'bə-gər, 'bu-gər\ *n* [ME *bougre* heretic, fr. MF, fr. ML *Bulgarus*, lit., Bulgarian; fr. the association of Bulgaria with the Bogomils, who were accused of sodomy] (1555) **1 :** SODOMITE **2 :** a worthless person : RASCAL **b :** FELLOW, CHAP **3 :** a small or annoying thing ⟨put down my keys and now I can't find the ∼s⟩

²**bug·ger** \'bə-gər\ *vt* (1598) **1 :** to commit sodomy with — usu. considered vulgar : DAMN

³**bugger** *n* (1955) **:** a person who plants electronic bugs

bugger all *n* (ca. 1937) *slang Brit* **:** NOTHING

bugger off *vi* (1922) *slang Brit* **:** LEAVE, DEPART

bug·gery \'bə-gə-rē\ *n* (1514) **:** SODOMY

¹**bug·gy** \'bə-gē\ *adj* **bug·gi·er; -est** (1714) **:** infested with bugs

²**buggy** *n, pl* **buggies** [origin unknown] (1773) **1 :** a light one-horse carriage made with two wheels in England and with four wheels in the

\ə\ abut \ᵊ\ kitten, F table \ər\ further \a\ ash \ā\ ace \ä\ mop, mar \aù\ out \ch\ chin \e\ bet \ē\ easy \g\ go \i\ hit \ī\ ice \j\ job \ŋ\ sing \ō\ go \ò\ law \òi\ boy \th\ thin \t̲h̲\ the \ü\ loot \ù\ foot \y\ yet \zh\ vision \á, k̲, ⁿ, œ, œ̄, ᵫ, ūᵉ, ᵜ\ see Guide to Pronunciation

U.S. **2** : a small cart or truck for short transportations of heavy materials **3** : BABY CARRIAGE
¹bug·house \'bəg-ˌhau̇s\ *adj* (1895) : mentally deranged : CRAZY
²bughouse *n* (1902) : an insane asylum
¹bu·gle \'byü-gəl\ *n* [ME, fr. OF, fr. LL *bugula*] (13c) : any of a genus (*Ajuga*) of plants of the mint family; *esp* : a European annual (*A. reptans*) that has spikes of blue flowers and is naturalized in the U.S.
²bugle *n* [ME, buffalo, instrument made of buffalo horn, bugle, fr. MF, fr. L *buculus*, dim. of *bos* head of cattle — more at COW] (14c) : a valveless brass instrument that resembles a trumpet and is used esp. for military calls
³bugle *vi* **bu·gled; bu·gling** \-g(ə-)liŋ\ (1884) **1** : to sound a bugle **2** : to utter the characteristic rutting call of the bull elk
⁴bugle *n* [perh. fr. ²*bugle*] (1579) : a small cylindrical bead of glass or plastic used for trimming esp. on women's clothing
bu·gler \'byü-glər\ *n* (1838) : a person who sounds a bugle
bu·gle·weed \'byü-gəl-ˌwēd\ *n* (ca. 1818) **1** : any of a genus (*Lycopus*) of mints; *esp* : one (*L. virginicus*) that is mildly narcotic and astringent **2** : ¹BUGLE
bu·gloss \'byü-ˌgläs, -ˌglös\ *n* [MF *buglosse*, fr. L *buglossa*, irreg. fr. Gk *bouglōssos*, fr. *bous* head of cattle + *glōssa* tongue — more at COW, GLOSS] (14c) : any of several coarse hairy plants (genera *Anchusa, Lycopsis*, and *Echium*) of the borage family — compare VIPER'S BUGLOSS
bug off *vi* [prob. short for *bugger off*] (1971) : LEAVE, DEPART — usu. used as a command
buhl \'bül, 'byü(ə)l\ *var of* BOULLE
buhr·stone \'bər-ˌstōn\ *n* [prob. fr. *burr* + *stone*] (1690) **1** : a siliceous rock used for millstones **2** : a millstone cut from buhrstone
¹build \'bild\ *vb* **built** \'bilt\; **build·ing** [ME *bilden*, fr. OE *byldan*; akin to OE *būan* to dwell — more at BOWER] *vt* (bef. 12c) **1** : to form by ordering and uniting materials by gradual means into a composite whole : CONSTRUCT **2** : to cause to be constructed **3** : to develop according to a systematic plan, by a definite process, or on a particular base **4** : INCREASE, ENLARGE ~ *vi* **1** : to engage in building **2 a** : to progress toward a peak (as of intensity) ⟨~ to a climax⟩ **b** : to develop in extent ⟨a crowd ~ing⟩ — **build a fire under** : to stimulate to vigorous action — **build into** : to make an integral part of ⟨*build* quality *into* the product⟩ — **build on** : to use as a foundation ⟨*building on* past experience⟩
²build *n* (1667) : form or mode of structure : MAKE; *esp* : bodily conformation of a person or lower animal
build·able \'bil-də-bəl\ *adj* (1927) : suitable for building ⟨~ land⟩
build·ed *archaic past of* BUILD
build·er \'bil-dər\ *n* (13c) **1** : one that builds; *esp* : one that contracts to build and supervises building operations **2** : a substance added to or used with detergents to increase their cleansing action
build in *vt* (1933) : to make an integral part of something
build·ing \'bil-diŋ\ *n* (14c) **1** : a usu. roofed and walled structure built for permanent use (as for a dwelling) **2** : the art or business of assembling materials into a structure
building block *n* (1846) : a unit of construction or composition
build-up \'bil-ˌdəp\ *n* (1926) **1** : something produced by building up ⟨fluid ~ in the lungs⟩ **2** : the act or process of building up
build up *vt* (1611) **1** : to develop gradually by increments ⟨*building up* endurance⟩ ⟨*built up* a library⟩ **2** : to promote the health, strength, esteem, or reputation of ~ *vi* **1** : to accumulate or develop appreciably — **build·er-up·per** \'bil-dər-'ə-pər\ *n*
built \'bilt\ *adj* (1621) : formed as to physique or bodily contours ⟨slimly ~⟩; *esp* : well or attractively formed
¹built-in \'bilt-'in\ *adj* (1898) **1** : forming an integral part of a structure; *esp* : constructed as or in a recess in a wall **2** : INHERENT
²built-in \-ˌin\ *n* (1930) : a built-in piece of furniture
built-up \'bilt-'əp\ *adj* (1829) **1** : made of several sections or layers fastened together **2** : covered with buildings
buird·ly \'bu̇r(d)-lē\ *adj* [prob. alter. of *burly*] (1773) *Scot* : STURDY
bulb \'bəlb\ *n* [L *bulbus*, fr. Gk *bolbos* bulbous plant] (ca. 1601) **1 a** : a resting stage of a plant (as the lily, onion, hyacinth, or tulip) that is usu. formed underground and consists of a short stem base bearing one or more buds enclosed in overlapping membranous or fleshy leaves **b** : a fleshy structure (as a tuber or corm) resembling a bulb in appearance **c** : a plant having or developing from a bulb **2** : a bulb-shaped part; *specif* : a glass envelope enclosing the light source of an electric lamp or such an envelope together with the light source it encloses **3** : a rounded or swollen anatomical structure **4** : a camera setting that indicates that the shutter can be opened by pressing on the release and closed by ending the pressure — **bulbed** \'bəlbd\ *adj*

bulb 1a: *1* hyacinth, *2* onion, *3* tulip, *4* lily

bul·bar \'bəl-bər, -ˌbär\ *adj* (1878) : of or relating to a bulb; *specif* : involving the medulla oblongata
bul·bil \'bəl-bəl, -ˌbil\ *n* [F *bulbille*, dim. of *bulbe* bulb, fr. L *bulbus*] (1831) : BULBLET
bulb·let \'bəl-blət\ *n* (1842) : a small or secondary bulb; *esp* : an aerial deciduous bud produced in a leaf axil or replacing the flowers and capable when separated of producing a new plant
bul·bo·ure·thral gland \ˌbəl-(ˌ)bō-yu̇-'rē-thrəl-\ *n* [L *bulbus* bulb + E *urethral*] (ca. 1903) : COWPER'S GLAND
bul·bous \'bəl-bəs\ *adj* (1578) **1** : having a bulb : growing from or bearing bulbs **2** : resembling a bulb esp. in roundness ⟨a ~ nose⟩ — **bul·bous·ly** *adv*
bul·bul \'bu̇l-ˌbu̇l\ *n* [Per, fr. Ar] (1665) **1** : a Persian songbird frequently mentioned in poetry that is prob. a nightingale (*Erithacus megarhynchos*) **2** : any of a group of gregarious passerine birds (family Pycnonotidae) of Asia and Africa
Bul·gar \'bəl-ˌgär, 'bu̇l-\ *n* [ML *Bulgarus*] (1591) : BULGARIAN

Bul·gar·i·an \ˌbəl-'gar-ē-ən, bu̇l-, -'ger-\ *n* (1555) **1** : a native or inhabitant of Bulgaria **2** : the Slavic language of the Bulgarians — **Bulgarian** *adj*
¹bulge \'bəlj *also* 'bu̇lj\ *vb* **bulged; bulg·ing** *vt* (15c) : to cause to bulge ~ *vi* **1** *archaic* : BILGE **2 a** : to jut out : SWELL **b** : to bend outward **c** : to become swollen or protuberant **3** : to be filled to overflowing
²bulge *n* [MF *boulge, bouge* leather bag, curved part — more at BUDGET] (1622) **1** : BILGE 1, 2 **2** : a protuberant or swollen part or place **3** : ADVANTAGE, UPPER HAND **4** : sudden expansion *syn* see PROJECTION — **bulgy** \'bəl-jē *also* 'bu̇l-\ *adj*
bul·gur \'bəl-gər, 'bu̇l-\ *n* [Turk] (1926) : parched cracked wheat
bu·lim·ia \bu̇-'lē-mē-ə, byü-, -'li-\ *n* [NL, fr. Gk *boulimia* great hunger, fr. *bou-*, aug. prefix (fr. *bous* head of cattle) + *limos* hunger — more at COW] (14c) **1** : an abnormal and constant craving for food **2** : a serious eating disorder that occurs chiefly in females, is characterized by compulsive overeating usu. followed by self-induced vomiting or laxative or diuretic abuse, and is often accompanied by guilt and depression — **bu·lim·ic** \-'lē-mik, -'li-\ *adj or n*
¹bulk \'bəlk *also* 'bu̇lk\ *n* [ME, heap, bulk, fr. ON *bulki* cargo] (15c) **1 a** : spatial dimension : MAGNITUDE **b** : material that forms a mass in the intestine; *esp* : FIBER 1d **2 a** : BODY; *esp* : a large or corpulent human body **b** : an organized structure esp. when viewed primarily as a mass of material **c** : a ponderous shapeless mass **3** : the main or greater part — **in bulk 1** : not divided into parts or packaged in separate units **2** : in large quantities
syn BULK, MASS, VOLUME mean the aggregate that forms a body or unit. BULK implies an aggregate that is impressively large, heavy, or numerous ⟨the darkened *bulk* of the skyscrapers⟩. MASS suggests an aggregate made by piling together things of the same kind ⟨a *mass* of boulders⟩. VOLUME applies to an aggregate without shape or outline and capable of flowing or fluctuating ⟨a tremendous *volume* of water⟩.
²bulk *vt* (1540) **1** : to cause to swell or bulge : STUFF **2** : to gather into a mass or aggregate ~ *vi* **1** : SWELL, EXPAND **2** : to appear as a factor : LOOM ⟨a consideration that ~s large in everyone's thinking⟩
³bulk *adj* (1693) **1** : being in bulk ⟨~ cement⟩ **2** : of or relating to materials in bulk
bulk·head \'bəlk-ˌhed, 'bu̇lk-, 'bəl-ˌked\ *n* [*bulk* structure projecting from a building + *head*] (15c) **1** : an upright partition separating compartments **2** : a structure or partition to resist pressure or to shut off water, fire, or gas **3** : a retaining wall along a waterfront **4** : a projecting framework with a sloping door giving access to a cellar stairway or a shaft
bulk up *vi* (1981) : to gain weight esp. by becoming more muscular ~ *vt* : to cause to bulk up
bulky \'bəl-kē *also* 'bu̇l-\ *adj* **bulk·i·er; -est** (15c) **1 a** : having bulk **b** (1) : large of its kind (2) : CORPULENT **2** : having great volume in proportion to weight ⟨a ~ knit sweater⟩ — **bulk·i·ly** \-kə-lē\ *adv* — **bulk·i·ness** \-kē-nəs\ *n*
¹bull \'bu̇l, 'bəl\ *n* [ME *bule*, fr. OE *bula*; akin to ON *boli* bull] (bef. 12c) **1 a** : a male bovine; *esp* : an adult uncastrated male ox **b** : a usu. adult male of various large animals (as elephants, whales, or seals) **2** : one who buys securities or commodities in expectation of a price rise or who acts to effect such a rise — compare BEAR **3** : one that resembles a bull (as in brawny physique) **4** : BULLDOG **5** *slang* : POLICE OFFICER, DETECTIVE **6** *cap* : TAURUS
²bull *adj* (13c) **1 a** : of or relating to a bull **b** : MALE **c** : suggestive of a bull : large of its kind
³bull *vi* (1884) : to advance forcefully ~ *vt* **1** : to act on with violence **2** : FORCE ⟨~ed his way through the crowd⟩
⁴bull *n* [ME *bulle*, fr. ML *bulla*, fr. L, bubble, amulet] (14c) **1** : a solemn papal letter sealed with a bulla or with a red-ink imprint of the device on the bulla **2** : EDICT, DECREE
⁵bull *vt* (1609) *slang* : to fool esp. by fast boastful talk ~ *vi, slang* : to engage in idle and boastful talk
⁶bull *n* [perh. fr. obs. *bull* to mock] (1640) **1** : a grotesque blunder in language **2** *slang* : empty boastful talk **3** *slang* : NONSENSE 2
bul·la \'bu̇-lə\ *n, pl* **bul·lae** \'bu̇-ˌlē, -ˌlī\ (14c) **1** [ML] : the round usu. lead seal attached to a papal bull **2** [NL, fr. L] : a hollow thin-walled rounded bony prominence **3** : a large vesicle or blister
bul·lace \'bu̇-ləs\ *n* [ME *bolace*, fr. MF *beloce*, fr. ML *bolluca*] (14c) : a European plum (*Prunus domestica insititia*) with small ovoid fruit in clusters
bull-bait·ing \'bu̇l-ˌbā-tiŋ, 'bəl-\ *n* (ca. 1580) : the former practice of baiting bulls with dogs
bull-bat \'bu̇l-ˌbat, 'bəl-\ *n* (1838) : NIGHTHAWK 1a
¹bull-dog \'bu̇l-ˌdȯg *also* 'bəl-\ *n* (ca. 1500) **1** : any of a breed of compact muscular short-haired dogs having widely separated forelegs and an undershot lower jaw that were developed in England to fight bulls **2** : a handgun with a thick usu. short barrel **3** : a proctor's attendant at an English university
²bulldog *adj* (1855) : suggestive of a bulldog ⟨~ tenacity⟩
³bulldog *vt* (1907) : to throw (a steer) by seizing the horns and twisting the neck — **bull·dog·ger** *n* — **bull·dog·ging** *n*
bull·doze \'bu̇l-ˌdōz *also* 'bəl-\ *vb* (perh. fr. ²*bull* + alter. of *dose*] *vt* (1876) **1** : to coerce or restrain by threats : BULLY **2** : to move, clear, gouge out, or level off by pushing with or as if with a bulldozer **3** : to force insensitively or ruthlessly ⟨*bulldozed* the program through the legislature⟩ ~ *vi* **1** : to operate a bulldozer **2** : to force one's way like a bulldozer *syn* see INTIMIDATE
bull·doz·er \-ˌdō-zər\ *n* (1876) **1** : one that bulldozes **2** : a tractor-driven machine usu. having a broad blunt horizontal blade for moving earth (as in road building)
bull dyke *n* (ca. 1942) : an aggressively masculine lesbian — often used disparagingly
bul·let \'bu̇-lət *also* 'bə-\ *n, often attrib* [MF *boulette* small ball & *boulet* missile, dims. of *boule* ball — more at BOWL] (1579) **1** : a round or elongated missile (as of lead) to be fired from a firearm; *broadly* : CARTRIDGE 1a **2** : something resembling a bullet (as in curved form) **b** : a large dot placed in printed matter to call attention to a particular passage **3** : a very fast and accurately thrown ball — **bul·let·ed** \-lə-təd\ *adj* — **bul·let-proof** \-ˌprüf\ *adj*
¹bul·le·tin \'bu̇-lə-tⁿn *also* 'bə-\ *n* [F, fr. MF, fr. *bulletin* seal, notice, dim. of *bulle* seal, fr. ML *bulla*] (1765) **1** : a brief public notice issuing usu. from an authoritative source; *specif* : a brief news item intended

for immediate publication or broadcast **2** : PERIODICAL; *esp* : the organ of an institution or association

²**bulletin** *vt* (1838) : to make public by bulletin

bulletin board *n* (1831) **1** : a board for posting notices (as at a school) **2** : a program on a computer system that allows users to read and write public notices and is accessed usu. by modem

bullet train *n* (1966) : a high-speed passenger train esp. of Japan

bull fiddle *n* (1880) : DOUBLE BASS — **bull fiddler** *n*

bull·fight \'bul̇-,fīt *also* 'bəl-\ *n* (1788) : a spectacle in which men ceremonially fight with and in Hispanic tradition kill bulls in an arena for public entertainment — **bull·fight·er** \-,fī-tər\ *n*

bull·fight·ing \-tiŋ\ *n* (ca. 1753) : the action involved in a bullfight

bull·finch \'bul̇-,finch *also* 'bəl-\ *n* (ca. 1570) : a European finch (*Pyrrhula pyrrhula*) having in the male rosy red underparts, blue-gray back, and black cap, chin, tail, and wings; *also* : any of several other finches

bull·frog \-,frȯg, -,fräg\ *n* (1698) : a heavy-bodied deep-voiced frog (*Rana catesbeiana*) of the eastern U.S. and southern Canada that has been introduced elsewhere

bull·head \-,hed\ *n* (15c) : any of various large-headed fishes (as a sculpin); *esp* : any of several common freshwater catfishes (genus *Ameiurus* sometimes included in the genus *Ictalurus*) of the U.S.

bull·head·ed \-'he-dəd\ *adj* (1818) : stupidly stubborn : HEADSTRONG — **bull·head·ed·ly** *adv* — **bull·head·ed·ness** *n*

bull·horn \-,hȯrn\ *n* (1942) : a loudspeaker on a naval ship **2** : a handheld combined microphone and loudspeaker

bul·lion \'bul̇-yən, -,yän\ *n* [ME, fr. AF, mint] (14c) **1 a** : gold or silver considered as so much metal; *specif* : uncoined gold or silver in bars or ingots **b** : metal in the mass ⟨lead ~⟩ **2** : lace, braid, or fringe of gold or silver threads

bull·ish \'bu̇-lish *also* 'bə-\ *adj* (1566) **1** : suggestive of a bull (as in brawniness) **2 a** : marked by, tending to cause, or hopeful of rising prices (as in a stock market) **b** : optimistic about something's or someone's prospects ⟨~ about something ~⟩ — **bull·ish·ly** *adv* — **bull·ish·ness** *n*

bull·mas·tiff \'bul̇-'mas-təf *also* 'bəl-\ *n* (1871) : any of a breed of large powerful dogs developed by crossing bulldogs with mastiffs

Bull Moose *n* [*bull moose*, emblem of the Progressive party of 1912] (1912) : a follower of Theodore Roosevelt in the U.S. presidential campaign of 1912

Bull Moos·er \-'mü-sər\ *n* (1912) : BULL MOOSE

bull neck *n* (1830) : a thick short powerful neck — **bull-necked** \'bul̇-'nekt *also* 'bəl-\ *adj*

bul·lock \'bu̇-lək *also* 'bə-\ *n* (bef. 12c) **1** : a young bull **2** : a castrated bull : STEER — **bull·ocky** \-kē\ *adj*

bul·lous \'bu̇-ləs\ *adj* (1833) : resembling or characterized by bullae : VESICULAR ⟨~ lesions⟩

bull pen *n* (1809) **1** : a large cell where prisoners are detained until brought into court **2 a** : a place on a baseball field where pitchers warm up before they start pitching **b** : the relief pitchers of a baseball team **3** : an open work area not divided into offices

bull·ring \'bul̇-,riŋ\ *n* (1802) : an arena for bullfights

bull session *n* [⁶*bull*] (1920) : an informal discursive group discussion

bull's–eye \'bul̇-,zī *also* 'bəl-\ *n, pl* **bull's–eyes** (1825) **1** : a very hard globular candy **2** : a circular piece of glass with a lump in the middle formed at the end of a glassblower's pipe **3 a** : the center of a target; *also* : something central or crucial **b** : a shot that hits the bull's-eye; *broadly* : something that precisely attains a desired end **4** : a simple lens of short focal distance; *also* : a lantern with such a lens

bull's–eye window *n* (1926) : a circular window; *also* : a window made up of glassblower's bull's-eyes

¹**bull·shit** \'bul̇-,shit *also* 'bəl-\ *n* [¹*bull* & ⁶*bull*] (ca. 1915) : NONSENSE; *esp* : foolish insolent talk — usu. considered vulgar

²**bullshit** *vi* (ca. 1942) **1** : to talk foolishly, boastfully, or idly — usu. considered vulgar **2** : to engage in a discursive discussion — usu. considered vulgar ~ *vt* : to talk nonsense to esp. with the intention of deceiving or misleading — usu. considered vulgar

bull·shot \-,shät\ *n* (1964) : a drink made of vodka and bouillon

bull snake *n* (1784) : any of several large harmless No. American snakes (genus *Pituophis*) that feed chiefly on rodents — called also *gopher snake, pine snake*

bull·ter·ri·er \'bul̇-'ter-ē-ər *also* 'bəl-\ *n* [*bulldog* + *terrier*] (1848) : any of a breed of short-haired terriers originated in England by crossing the bulldog with terriers

bull thistle *n* (1863) : a European thistle (*Cirsium vulgare*) with rather large heads and prickly leaves that is naturalized as a weed in the U.S.

bull tongue *n* (1831) : a wide blade attached to a cultivator or plow to stir the soil, kill weeds, or mark furrows

bull·whip \'bul̇-,(h)wip *also* 'bəl-\ *n* (1852) : a rawhide whip with a very long plaited lash

¹**bul·ly** \'bu̇-lē, 'bə-\ *n, pl* **bullies** [prob. modif. of D *boel* lover, fr. MHG *buole*] (1538) **1** *archaic* **a** : SWEETHEART **b** : a fine chap **2 a** : a blustering browbeating person; *esp* : one habitually cruel to others who are weaker **b** : PIMP **3** : a hired ruffian

²**bully** *adj* (1681) **1** : EXCELLENT, FIRST-RATE — often used in interjectional expressions ⟨~ for you⟩ **2** : resembling or characteristic of a bully

³**bully** *vb* **bul·lied; bul·ly·ing** *vt* (1710) **1** : to treat abusively **2** : to affect by means of force or coercion ~ *vi* : to use browbeating language or behavior : BLUSTER **syn** see INTIMIDATE

⁴**bully** *n* [prob. modif. of F *bœuf* boulli boiled beef] (1753) : pickled or canned usu. corned beef

bul·ly·boy \'bu̇-lē-,bȯi, 'bə-\ *n* (1925) : a swaggering tough

bully pulpit *n* (1976) : a prominent public position (as a political office) that provides an opportunity for expounding one's views; *also* : such an opportunity

bul·ly·rag \-,rag\ *vt* [origin unknown] (ca. 1790) **1** : to intimidate by bullying **2** : to vex by teasing : BADGER

bul·rush *also* **bull·rush** \'bul̇-,rəsh\ *n* [ME *bulrysche*] (15c) : any of several large rushes or sedges growing in wetlands: as **a** : any of a genus of annual or perennial sedges (*Scirpus*, esp. *S. lacustris*) that bear solitary or much-clustered spikelets containing perfect flowers with a perianth of six bristles **b** *Brit* : either of two cattails (*Typha latifolia* and *T. angustifolia*) **c** : PAPYRUS

¹**bul·wark** \'bul̇-(,)wərk, -,wȯrk; 'bəl-(,)wərk; *sense 3 also* 'bə-,läk\ *n* [ME *bulwerke*, fr. MD *bolwerc*, fr. MHG, fr. *bole* plank + *werc* work]

(15c) **1 a** : a solid wall-like structure raised for defense : RAMPART **b** : BREAKWATER, SEAWALL **2** : a strong support or protection **3** : the side of a ship above the upper deck — usu. used in pl.

²**bulwark** *vt* (15c) : to fortify or safeguard with a bulwark

¹**bum** \'bəm\ *n* [ME *bom*] (14c) *chiefly Brit* : BUTTOCKS — sometimes considered vulgar

²**bum** *adj* [perh. fr. ⁴*bum*] (1859) **1 a** : of poor quality or nature : INVALID, INFERIOR ⟨~ advice⟩ ⟨a ~ check⟩ **b** : acutely disagreeable ⟨a ~ trip⟩ **2** : not functioning because of damage or injury : DISABLED ⟨a ~ knee⟩

³**bum** *vb* **bummed; bum·ming** [prob. back-formation fr. ¹*bummer*] *vi* (1863) **1** : LOAF **2** : to spend time unemployed and often wandering — often used with *around* ~ *vt* : to obtain by begging : CADGE

⁴**bum** *n* [prob. short for *bummer*] (1864) **1 a** : one who sponges off others and avoids work **b** : one who performs a function poorly ⟨called the umpire a ~⟩ **c** : one who devotes his time to a recreational activity ⟨a beach ~⟩ ⟨ski ~s⟩ **2** : VAGRANT, TRAMP — **on the bum** : with no settled residence or means of support

⁵**bum** *n* [prob. fr. ³*bum*] (1871) : a drinking spree : BENDER

bum·ber·shoot \'bəm-bər-,shüt\ *n* [*bumber-* (alter. of *umbr-* in *umbrella*) + *-shoot* (alter. of *-chute* in *parachute*)] (ca. 1896) : UMBRELLA

¹**bum·ble** \'bəm-bəl\ *vi* **bum·bled; bum·bling** \-b(ə-)liŋ\ [ME *bomblen* to boom, of imit. origin] (15c) **1** : BUZZ **2** : DRONE, RUMBLE

²**bumble** *vb* **bumbled; bumbling** [perh. alter. of *bungle*] *vi* (1532) **1** : BLUNDER; *specif* : to speak ineptly in a stuttering and faltering manner **2** : to proceed unsteadily : STUMBLE ~ *vt* : BUNGLE — **bum·bler** \-b(ə-)lər\ *n* — **bum·bling·ly** \-b(ə-)liŋ-lē\ *adv*

bum·ble·bee \'bəm-bəl-,bē\ *n* (1530) : any of numerous large robust hairy social bees (genus *Bombus*)

bum·boat \'bəm-,bōt\ *n* [prob. fr. LG *bumboot*, fr. *bum* tree + *boot* boat] (1769) : a boat that brings provisions and commodities for sale to larger ships in port or offshore

bumf *also* **bumph** \'bəm(p)f\ *n* [fr. *bumf* toilet paper, short for *bumfodder*, fr. ¹*bum* + *fodder*] (ca. 1889) *chiefly Brit* : PAPERWORK

bummed \'bəmd\ *adj* [prob. back-formation fr. ²*bummer*] (1971) : DISAPPOINTED, DEPRESSED — usu. used with *out*

¹**bum·mer** \'bə-mər\ *n* [prob. modif. of G *Bummler* loafer, fr. *bummeln* to dangle, loaf] (1855) : one that bums

²**bummer** *n* [²*bum* + ²*-er*] (1967) **1** : an unpleasant experience (as a bad reaction to a hallucinogenic drug) **2** : FAILURE, FLOP

¹**bump** \'bəmp\ *n* [prob. imit. of the sound of a blow] (1592) **1 a** : a relatively abrupt convexity or protuberance on a surface: as **a** : a swelling of tissue **b** : a cranial protuberance **2 a** : a sudden forceful blow, impact, or jolt **b** : DEMOTION **3** : an act of thrusting the hips forward in an erotic manner

²**bump** *vt* (1611) **1** : to strike or knock with force or violence **2** : to collide with **3 a** (1) : to dislodge with a jolt (2) : to subject to a scalar change ⟨rates being ~ed up⟩ **b** : to oust usu. by virtue of seniority or priority ⟨was ~ed from the flight⟩ ~ *vi* **1** : to knock against something with a forceful jolt **2** : to proceed in or as if in a series of bumps **3** : to encounter something that is an obstacle or hindrance ⟨~ed up against a chair⟩ — **bump into** : to encounter esp. by chance

¹**bum·per** \'bəm-pər\ *n* [prob. fr. *bump* to bulge] (1676) **1 a** : a brimming cup or glass **2** : something unusually large

²**bumper** *adj* (1885) **1** : unusually large ⟨a ~ crop⟩ **2** : BANNER 2

³**bump·er** \'bəm-pər\ *n* (1839) **1** : a device for absorbing shock or preventing damage (as in collision); *specif* : a usu. metal bar at either end of an automobile **2** : one that bumps

bumper car *n* (1959) : a small electric car made to be driven around in an enclosure and to be bumped into others (as at an amusement park)

bumper sticker *n* (1967) : a strip of adhesive paper or plastic bearing a printed message and designed to be stuck on a vehicle's bumper

bumper–to–bumper *adj* (1951) : marked by long closed lines of cars

¹**bump·kin** \'bəm(p)-kən\ *n* [perh. fr. Flem *bommekijn* small cask, fr. MD, fr. *bomme* cask] (1570) : an awkward and unsophisticated rustic — **bump·kin·ish** \-kə-nish\ *adj* — **bump·kin·ly** \-kən-lē\ *adj*

²**bumpkin** *or* **bumkin** \'bəm(p)-kən\ *n* [prob. fr. Flem *boomken*, dim. of *boom* tree] (ca. 1632) : a spar projecting from a ship esp. at the stern

bump off *vt* (1910) : to murder casually or cold-bloodedly

bump·tious \'bəm(p)-shəs\ *adj* [¹*bump* + *-tious* (as in *fractious*)] (1803) : presumptuously, obtusely, and often noisily self-assertive : OBTRUSIVE — **bump·tious·ly** *adv* — **bump·tious·ness** *n*

bumpy \'bəm-pē\ *adj* **bump·i·er; -est** (1865) **1** : having or covered with bumps ⟨a ~ road⟩ ⟨~ skin⟩ **2 a** : marked by bumps or jolts ⟨a ~ ride⟩ **b** : marked by or full of difficulties ⟨a ~ relationship⟩ — **bump·i·ly** \-pə-lē\ *adv* — **bump·i·ness** \-pē-nəs\ *n*

bum's rush \'bəmz-\ *n* (1922) : forcible eviction or dismissal

¹**bun** \'bən\ *n* [ME *bunne*] (14c) **1** : a sweet or plain small bread; *esp* : a round roll **2** : a knot of hair shaped like a bun **3** *pl* : BUTTOCKS

²**bun** *n* [perh. fr. ¹*bun*] (1901) : LOAD 4

Bu·na \'byü-nə, 'bü-\ *trademark* — used for any of several rubbers made by polymerization or copolymerization of butadiene

¹**bunch** \'bənch\ *n* [ME *bunche*] (14c) **1** : PROTUBERANCE, SWELLING **2 a** : a number of things of the same kind ⟨a ~ of grapes⟩ **b** : GROUP 2a ⟨a ~ of friends⟩ **c** : a considerable amount : LOT ⟨a ~ of money⟩ — **bunch·i·ly** \'bən-chə-lē\ *adv* — **bunchy** \-chē\ *adj*

²**bunch** *vi* (14c) **1** : SWELL, PROTRUDE **2** : to form a group or cluster — often used with *up* ~ *vt* : to form into a bunch

bunch·ber·ry \'bənch-,ber-ē\ *n* (1845) : a creeping perennial herb (*Cornus canadensis*) of the dogwood family that has whorled leaves and white floral bracts and bears red berries in capitate cymes

bunch·grass \-,gras\ *n* (1839) : any of several grasses (as of the genus *Andropogon*) esp. of the western U.S. that grow in tufts

bun·co *or* **bun·ko** \'bəŋ-(,)kō\ *n, pl* **buncos** *or* **bunkos** [perh. alter. of Sp *banca* bench, banking, bank in gambling, fr. It — more at BANK] (1872) : a swindling game or scheme — **bunco** *vt*

\ə\ abut \ᵊ\ kitten, F table \ər\ further \a\ ash \ā\ ace \ä\ mop, mar
\au̇\ out \ch\ chin \e\ bet \ē\ easy \g\ go \i\ hit \ī\ ice \j\ job
\ŋ\ sing \ō\ go \ȯ\ law \ȯi\ boy \th\ thin \t͟h\ the \ü\ loot \u̇\ foot
\y\ yet \zh\ vision \ä, k̲, ⁿ, œ, œ̄, ue, ūe, ᵊ\ see Guide to Pronunciation

¹**bund** \'bənd\ *n* [Hindi *band*, fr. Per] (1810) **1** : an embankment used esp. in India to control the flow of water **2** : an embanked thoroughfare along a river or the sea esp. in the Far East

²**bund** \'bund, 'bənd, 'bənt\ *n, often cap* [Yiddish *bund* & G *Bund*, fr. MHG *bunt*; akin to OE *byndel*] (1850) : a political association: as **a** : a Jewish socialist organization founded in czarist Russia in 1897 **b** : a pro-Nazi German-American organization of the 1930s — **bund·ist** \'bun-dist, 'bən-\ *n, often cap*

¹**bun·dle** \'bən-dᵊl\ *n* [ME *bundel*, fr. MD; akin to OE *byndel* bundle, *bindan* to bind] (14c) **1 a** : a group of things fastened together for convenient handling **b** : PACKAGE, PARCEL **c** : a considerable number — usu. used in the phrase *do a bunk* **d** : a sizable sum of money **e** : a person embodying a specified quality or characteristic ⟨a ~ of energy⟩ **2 a** : a small band of mostly parallel fibers (as of nerve or muscle) **b** : VASCULAR BUNDLE

²**bundle** *vb* **bun·dled; bun·dling** \'bən(d)-liŋ, 'bən-dᵊl-iŋ\ *vt* (ca. 1628) **1** : to make into a bundle or package : WRAP **2** : to hustle or hurry unceremoniously ⟨*bundled* the children off to school⟩ **3** : to include (a product or service) with a related product for sale at a single price ⟨software is *bundled* with computer hardware⟩ ~ *vi* **1** : HURRY, HUSTLE **2** : to practice bundling — **bun·dler** \-lər, -dᵊl-ər\ *n*

bundle up *vt* (1918) : to dress (someone) warmly ~ *vi* : to dress warmly

bun·dling \'bən(d)-liŋ, 'bən-dᵊl-iŋ\ *n* (1781) : a former custom of an unmarried couple's occupying the same bed without undressing esp. during courtship

¹**bung** \'bəŋ\ *n* [ME, fr. MD *bonne, bonghe*] (15c) **1** : the stopper esp. in the bunghole of a cask; *also* : BUNGHOLE **2** : the cecum or anus esp. of a slaughtered animal

²**bung** *vt* (1589) **1** : to plug with or as if with a bung **2** *Brit* : THROW, TOSS ⟨~ a spanner into the works —P. G. Wodehouse⟩

bun·ga·low \'bəŋ-gə-ˌlō\ *n* [Hindi *baṅglā*, lit., (house) in the Bengal style] (1676) : a usu. one-storied house with a low-pitched roof

bun·gee cord \'bən-jē-\ *n* [origin unknown] (1948) : an elasticized cord used esp. as a fastening or shock-absorbing device — called also *bungee*

bung·hole \'bəŋ-ˌhōl\ *n* (1571) : a hole for emptying or filling a cask

bun·gle \'bəŋ-gəl\ *vb* **bun·gled; bun·gling** \-g(ə-)liŋ\ [perh. of Scand origin; akin to Icel *banga* to hammer] *vi* (1549) : to act or work clumsily and awkwardly ~ *vt* : MISHANDLE, BOTCH — **bungle** *n* — **bun·gler** \-g(ə-)lər\ *n* — **bun·gling·ly** \-g(ə-)liŋ-lē\ *adv*

bun·gle·some \-gəl-səm\ *adj* (ca. 1889) : AWKWARD, CLUMSY

bung up *vt* (1951) : BATTER

bun·ion \'bən-yən\ *n* [prob. alter. of *bunny* swelling] (ca. 1718) : an inflamed swelling of the small sac on the first joint of the big toe

¹**bunk** \'bəŋk\ *n* [prob. short for *bunker*] (1758) **1 a** : BUNK BED **b** : a built-in bed (as on a ship) that is often one of a tier of berths **c** : a sleeping place **2** : a feeding trough for farm animals and esp. cattle

²**bunk** *vi* (1840) : to occupy a bunk or bed : stay the night ⟨~ed with a friend for the night⟩ ~ *vt* : to provide with a bunk or bed

³**bunk** *n* (1900) : BUNKUM, NONSENSE

⁴**bunk** *n* [origin unknown] (ca. 1870) *Brit* : a hurried departure or escape — usu. used in the phrase *do a bunk*

bunk bed *n* (1924) : one of two single beds usu. placed one above the other

¹**bun·ker** \'bəŋ-kər\ *n* [Sc *bonker* chest, box] (1839) **1** : a bin or compartment for storage; *esp* : one on shipboard for the ship's fuel **2 a** : a protective embankment or dugout; *esp* : a fortified chamber mostly below ground often built of reinforced concrete and provided with embrasures **b** : a sand trap or embankment constituting a hazard on a golf course — **bun·kered** \-kərd\ *adj*

²**bunker** *vb* **bun·kered; bun·ker·ing** \-k(ə-)riŋ\ *vi* (1891) : to fill a ship's bunker with coal or oil ~ *vt* **1** : to place or store in a bunker **2** : to hit (a golf ball or shot) into a bunker

bunker mentality *n* (1976) : a state of mind esp. among members of a group that is characterized by chauvinistic defensiveness and self-righteous intolerance of criticism

bunk·house \'bəŋk-ˌhau̇s\ *n* (1876) : a rough simple building providing sleeping quarters

bun·kum *or* **bun·combe** \'bəŋ-kəm\ *n* [*Buncombe* county, N.C.; fr. a remark made by its congressman, who defended an irrelevant speech by claiming that he was speaking to Buncombe] (1845) : insincere or foolish talk : NONSENSE

bun·ny \'bə-nē\ *n, pl* **bunnies** [E dial. *bun* rabbit] (ca. 1690) **1** : RABBIT; *esp* : a young rabbit **2** : a desirable young woman

Bun·ra·ku \bun-'rä-(ˌ)kü\ *n* [Jp] (1920) : Japanese puppet theater featuring large costumed wooden puppets, puppeteers who are onstage, and a chanter who speaks all the lines

Bun·sen burner \'bən(t)-sən-\ *n* [Robert W. *Bunsen*] (ca. 1888) : a gas burner consisting typically of a straight tube with small holes at the bottom where air enters and mixes with the gas to produce an intensely hot blue flame

¹**bunt** \'bənt\ *n* [perh. fr. LG, bundle, fr. MLG; akin to OE *byndel* bundle] (ca. 1582) **1 a** : the middle part of a square sail **b** : the part of a furled sail gathered up in a bunch at the center of the yard **2** : the bagging part of a fishing net

²**bunt** *vb* [alter. of *butt*] *vt* (1584) **1** : to strike or push with or as if with the head : BUTT **2** : to push or tap (a baseball) lightly without swinging the bat ~ *vi* : to bunt a baseball — **bunt·er** *n*

³**bunt** *n* (1767) **1** : an act or instance of bunting **2** : a bunted ball

⁴**bunt** *n* [origin unknown] (ca. 1790) : a destructive covered smut of wheat caused by a fungus (*Tilletia foetida* or *T. caries*)

¹**bun·ting** \'bən-tiŋ\ *n* [ME] (14c) : any of various stout-billed passerine birds (family Emberizidae) included with some of the finches — compare INDIGO BUNTING

²**bunting** *n* [perh. fr. E dial. *bunt* (to sift)] (1711) **1** : a lightweight loosely woven fabric used chiefly for flags and festive decorations **2 a** : FLAGS **b** : decorations esp. in the colors of the national flag

³**bunting** *n* [term of endearment in the nursery rhyme "Bye, baby bunting"] (1922) : an infant's hooded sleeping bag made of napped fabric

bunt·line \'bənt-ˌlīn, -lən\ *n* (1627) : one of the lines attached to the foot of a square sail to haul the sail up to the yard for furling

Bun·yan·esque \ˌbən-yə-'nesk\ *adj* (1888) **1** [John *Bunyan*] : of, relating to, or suggestive of the allegorical writings of John Bunyan **2** [Paul *Bunyan*, legendary giant lumberjack of U.S. & Canada] **a** : of,

relating to, or suggestive of the tales of Paul Bunyan **b** : of fantastically large size

¹**buoy** \'bü-ē, 'bȯi\ *n* [ME *boye*, prob. fr. MD *boeye*; akin to OHG *bouhhan* sign — more at BEACON] (13c) **1** : FLOAT 2; *esp* : a floating object moored to the bottom to mark a channel or something (as a shoal) lying under the water **2** : LIFE BUOY

²**buoy** *vt* (1596) **1** : to mark by or as if by a buoy **2 a** : to keep afloat **b** : SUPPORT, UPLIFT ⟨an economy ~ed by the dramatic postwar growth of industry —*Time*⟩ **3** : to raise the spirits of — usu. used with *up* ⟨hope ~s him up⟩ ~ *vi* : FLOAT — usu. used with *up*

buoy·ance \'bȯi-ən(t)s, 'bü-yən(t)s\ *n* (1821) : BUOYANCY

buoy·an·cy \'bȯi-ən(t)-sē, 'bü-yən(t)-\ *n* (1713) **1 a** : the tendency of a body to float or to rise when submerged in a fluid **b** : the power of a fluid to exert an upward force on a body placed in it; *also* : the upward force exerted **2** : the ability to recover quickly from depression or discouragement : RESILIENCE

buoy·ant \'bȯi-ənt, 'bü-yənt\ *adj* (1578) **1** : having buoyancy: as **a** : capable of floating **b** : CHEERFUL, GAY **c** : capable of recovering : having positive indications ⟨a ~ economy⟩ — **buoy·ant·ly** *adv*

bup·pie \'bə-pē\ *n* [*black* + *yuppie*] (1984) : a college-educated black adult who is employed in a well-paying profession and who lives or works in or near a large city

bur *var of* BURR

Bur·ber·ry \'bər-b(ə-)rē, 'bər-ˌber-ē\ *trademark* — used for various fabrics used esp. for coats for outdoor wear

¹**bur·ble** \'bər-bəl\ *vi* **bur·bled; bur·bling** \-b(ə-)liŋ\ [ME] (14c) **1** : BUBBLE **2** : BABBLE, PRATTLE — **bur·bler** \-b(ə-)lər\ *n*

²**burble** *n* (1898) **1** : PRATTLE **2** : the breaking up of the streamline flow of air about a body (as an airplane wing) — **bur·bly** \-b(ə-)lē\ *adj*

bur·bot \'bər-bət\ *n, pl* **burbot** *also* **burbots** [ME *borbot*, fr. MF *bourbotte*, fr. *bourbeter* to burrow in the mud] (14c) : a Holarctic freshwater fish (*Lota lota*) of the cod family having barbels on the nose and chin

burbs \'bərbz\ *n pl* (1971) : SUBURBS

¹**bur·den** \'bər-dᵊn\ *n* [ME, fr. OE *byrthen*; akin to OE *beran* to carry — more at BEAR] (bef. 12c) **1 a** : something that is carried : LOAD **b** : DUTY, RESPONSIBILITY **2** : something oppressive or worrisome **3 a** : the bearing of a load — usu. used in the phrase *beast of burden* **b** : capacity for carrying cargo ⟨a ship of a hundred tons ~⟩ **4** : the amount of a deleterious parasite, growth, or substance present in a human or animal body ⟨worm ~⟩ ⟨cancer ~⟩

²**burden** *vt* **bur·dened; bur·den·ing** \'bərd-niŋ, 'bər-dᵊn-iŋ\ (1541) : LOAD, OPPRESS ⟨I will not ~ you with a lengthy account⟩

³**burden** *n* [ME *burdoun*, fr. MF *bourdon* a drone bass, of imit. origin] (14c) **1** *archaic* : a bass or accompanying part **2 a** : CHORUS, REFRAIN **b** : a central topic : THEME

burden of proof (1593) : the duty of proving a disputed assertion or charge

bur·den·some \'bər-dᵊn-səm\ *adj* (1578) : imposing or constituting a burden : OPPRESSIVE ⟨~ restrictions⟩ **syn** see ONEROUS

bur·dock \'bər-ˌdäk\ *n* (15c) : any of a genus (*Arctium*) of coarse composite herbs bearing globular flower heads with prickly bracts

bu·reau \'byu̇r-(ˌ)ō\ *n, pl* **bureaus** *also* **bu·reaux** \-(ˌ)ōz\ [F, desk, cloth covering for desks, fr. OF *burel* woolen cloth, fr. (assumed) OF *bure*, fr. LL *burra* shaggy cloth] (1699) **1 a** *Brit* : WRITING DESK; *esp* : one having drawers and a slant top **b** : a low chest of drawers for use in a bedroom **2 a** : a specialized administrative unit; *esp* : a subdivision of an executive department of a government **b** : a branch of a newspaper, newsmagazine, or wire service in an important news center **c** : a usu. commercial agency that serves as an intermediary esp. for exchanging information or coordinating activities ⟨credit ~⟩

bu·reau·cra·cy \byu̇-'rä-krə-sē\ *n, pl* **-cies** [F *bureaucratie*, fr. *bureau* + *-cratie* -cracy] (1818) **1 a** : a body of nonelective government officials **b** : an administrative policy-making group **2** : government characterized by specialization of functions, adherence to fixed rules, and a hierarchy of authority **3** : a system of administration marked by officialism, red tape, and proliferation

bu·reau·crat \'byu̇r-ə-ˌkrat\ *n* (1842) : a member of a bureaucracy

bu·reau·crat·ese \ˌbyu̇r-ə-(ˌ)kra-'tēz, -'tēs\ *n* (1949) : a style of language held to be characteristic of bureaucrats and marked by the prevalence of abstractions, jargon, euphemisms, and circumlocutions

bu·reau·crat·ic \ˌbyu̇r-ə-'kra-tik\ *adj* (1836) : of, relating to, or having the characteristics of a bureaucracy or a bureaucrat ⟨~ government⟩ — **bu·reau·crat·i·cal·ly** \-ti-k(ə-)lē\ *adv*

bu·reau·cra·tise *Brit var of* BUREAUCRATIZE

bu·reau·crat·ism \'byu̇r-ə-(ˌ)kra-ˌti-zəm\ *n* (1880) : a bureaucratic system : BUREAUCRACY

bu·reau·cra·tize \byu̇-'rä-krə-ˌtīz\ *vt* **-tized; -tiz·ing** (1892) : to make bureaucratic — **bu·reau·cra·ti·za·tion** \-ˌrä-krə-tə-'zä-shən\ *n*

bu·rette *or* **bu·ret** \byu̇-'ret\ *n* [MF, cruet, fr. *buire* pitcher, perh. of Gmc origin; akin to OE *būr* storehouse, dwelling — more at BOWER] (1836) : a graduated glass tube with a small aperture and stopcock for delivering measured quantities of liquid or for measuring the liquid or gas received or discharged

burg \'bərg\ *n* [OE — more at BOROUGH] (1753) **1** : an ancient or medieval fortress or walled town **2** [G *Burg*] : CITY, TOWN

bur·gage \'bər-gij\ *n* [ME, property held by burgage tenure, fr. MF *bourgage*, fr. OF, fr. *bourg, borc* town — more at BOURG] (15c) : a tenure by which real property in England and Scotland was held under the king or a lord for a yearly rent or for watching and warding

bur·gee \ˌbər-'jē, 'bər-ˌ\ *n* [perh. fr. F dial. *bourgeais* shipowner] (1750) **1** : a swallow-tailed flag used esp. by ships for signals or identification **2** : the usu. triangular identifying flag of a yacht club

bur·geon \'bər-jən\ *vi* [ME *burjonen*, fr. *burjon* bud, fr. OF, fr. (assumed) VL *burrion-, burrio*, fr. LL *burra* fluff, shaggy cloth] (14c) **1 a** : to send forth new growth (as buds or branches) : SPROUT **b** : BLOOM **2** : to grow and expand rapidly : FLOURISH

bur·ger \'bər-gər\ *n* (1939) **1** : HAMBURGER **2** : a sandwich similar to a hamburger — often used in combination ⟨tofu ~⟩

bur·gess \'bər-jəs\ *n* [ME *burgeis*, fr. OF *borjois*, fr. *borc*] (13c) **1 a** : a citizen of a British borough **b** : a representative of a borough,

buoy 1

corporate town, or university in the British Parliament **2** : a representative in the popular branch of the legislature of colonial Maryland and Virginia

burgh \'bər-(ˌ)ō, 'bə-(ˌ)rō\ *n* [ME — more at BOROUGH] (12c) : BOROUGH; *specif* : an incorporated town in Scotland having local jurisdiction of certain services — **burgh·al** \'bər-gəl\ *adj*

bur·gher \'bər-gər\ *n* (13c) **1** : an inhabitant of a borough or a town **2** : a member of the middle class : a prosperous solid citizen

bur·glar \'bər-glər *also* -gə-lər\ *n* [AF *burgler*, fr. ML *burglator*, prob. alter. of *burgator*, fr. *burgare* to commit burglary] (1541) : one who commits burglary

bur·glar·ize \'bər-glə-ˌrīz *also* 'bər-gə-lə-\ *vb* **-ized; -iz·ing** *vt* (1871) **1** : to break into and steal from **2** : to commit burglary against ~ *vi*

bur·glar·proof \'bər-glər-ˌprüf\ *adj* (1856) : protected against or designed to afford protection against burglary

bur·glary \'bər-glə-rē *also* -gə-lə-rē *also* -gəl-rē\ *n, pl* **-glar·ies** (ca. 1523) : the act of breaking and entering a dwelling at night to commit a felony (as theft); *broadly* : the entering of a building with the intent to commit a crime — **bur·glar·i·ous** \ˌbər-'glär-ē-əs, -'gler-\ *adj* — **bur·glar·i·ous·ly** *adv*

bur·gle \'bər-gəl\ *vt* **bur·gled; bur·gling** \-g(ə-)liŋ\ [back-formation fr. *burglar*] (1870) : BURGLARIZE

bur·go·mas·ter \'bər-gə-ˌmas-tər\ *n* [part modif., part trans. of D *burgemeester*, fr. *burg* town + *meester* master] (1592) : the chief magistrate of a town in some European countries : MAYOR

bur·go·net \'bər-gə-nət, ˌbər-gə-'net\ *n* [modif. of MF *bourguignotte*] (ca. 1587) : a helmet of either of two 16th century styles

bur·goo \'bər-ˌgü, (ˌ)bər-'\ *n, pl* **burgoos** [origin unknown] (1700) **1** : oatmeal gruel **2** : hardtack and molasses cooked together **3 a** : a stew or thick soup of meat and vegetables orig. served at outdoor gatherings **b** : a picnic at which burgoo is served

bur·gun·dy \'bər-gən-dē\ *n, pl* **-dies** [*Burgundy*, region in France] (1668) **1** *often cap* : a red or white unblended wine from Burgundy; *also* : a blended red wine produced elsewhere (as California) **2** : a reddish purple color

buri·al \'ber-ē-əl *also* 'bər-\ *n, often attrib* [ME *beriel, berial*, back-formation fr. *beriels* (taken as a plural), fr. OE *byrgels*; akin to OS *burgisli* tomb, OE *byrgan* to bury — more at BURY] (13c) **1** : GRAVE, TOMB **2** : the act or process of burying

buri·er \'ber-ē-ər *also* 'bər-\ *n* (bef. 12c) : one that buries

bu·rin \'byùr-ən, 'bər-\ *n* [F] (1662) **1** : an engraver's steel cutting tool having the blade ground obliquely to a sharp point **2** : a prehistoric flint tool with a beveled point

burke \'bərk\ *vt* **burked; burk·ing** [fr. *burke* to suffocate, fr. William *Burke* †1829 Irish criminal executed for smothering victims to sell their bodies for dissection] (1840) **1** : to suppress quietly or indirectly ⟨~ an inquiry⟩ **2** : BYPASS, AVOID ⟨~ an issue⟩

Bur·kitt's lymphoma \'bər-kəts-\ *also* **Bur·kitt lymphoma** \-kət-\ *n* [Denis Parsons *Burkitt* †1993 Brit. surgeon] (1963) : a malignant lymphoma that occurs esp. in children of central Africa and is associated with Epstein-Barr virus

burl \'bər(-ə)l\ *n* [ME *burle*, fr. (assumed) MF *bourle* tuft of wool, fr. (assumed) VL *burrula*, dim. of LL *burra* shaggy cloth] (15c) **1 a** : a knot or lump in thread or cloth **2 a** : a hard woody often flattened hemispherical outgrowth on a tree **b** : veneer made from burls

bur·la·de·ro \ˌbùr-lə-'der-(ˌ)ō, ˌbər-\ *n, pl* **-ros** [Sp, fr. *burlar* to make fun of, elude, fr. *burla* joke] (1938) : a wooden shield near the wall in a bullring for bullfighters to take shelter behind if pursued

bur·lap \'bər-ˌlap\ *n* [origin unknown] (ca. 1696) **1** : a coarse heavy plain-woven fabric usu. of jute or hemp used for bagging and wrapping and in furniture and linoleum manufacture **2** : a lightweight material resembling burlap used in interior decoration or for clothing

burled \'bər(-ə)ld\ *adj* (1924) : having a distorted grain due to burls

¹bur·lesque \(ˌ)bər-'lesk\ *n* [*burlesque*, adj., comic, droll, fr. F, fr. It *burlesco*, fr. *burla* joke, fr. Sp] (1667) **1** : a literary or dramatic work that seeks to ridicule by means of grotesque exaggeration or comic imitation **2** : mockery usu. by caricature **3** : theatrical entertainment of a broadly humorous often earthy character consisting of short turns, comic skits, and sometimes striptease acts *syn* see CARICATURE — **burlesque** *adj* — **bur·lesque·ly** *adv*

²burlesque *vb* **bur·lesqued; bur·lesqu·ing** *vt* (1676) : to imitate in a humorous or derisive manner : MOCK ~ *vi* : to employ burlesque — **bur·lesqu·er** *n*

bur·ley \'bər-lē\ *n, often cap* [prob. fr. the name *Burley*] (1881) : a thin-bodied air-cured tobacco grown mainly in Kentucky

bur·ly \'bər-lē\ *adj* **bur·li·er; -est** [ME] (13c) **1** : strongly and heavily built : HUSKY **2** : heartily direct and frank : BLUFF, FORTHRIGHT ⟨an evocative story less ~ than the real thing but entertaining — E. A. Weeks⟩ — **bur·li·ly** \-lə-lē\ *adv* — **bur·li·ness** \-lē-nəs\ *n*

bur marigold *n* (ca. 1818) : any of a genus (*Bidens*) of coarse composite herbs with prickly flattened achenes that adhere to clothing

Bur·mese \ˌbər-'mēz, -'mēs\ *n, pl* **Burmese** (1824) **1** : a native or inhabitant of Burma (Myanmar) **2** : the Tibeto-Burman language of the Burmese people **3** : any of a U.S.-developed breed of slender shorthaired cats having gold eyes and a usu. dark brown coat — **Burmese** *adj*

¹burn \'bərn\ *n* [ME, fr. OE; akin to OHG *brunno* spring of water] (bef. 12c) *Brit* : CREEK 2

²burn \'bərn\ *vb* **burned** \'bərnd, 'bərnt\ *or* **burnt** \'bərnt\; **burn·ing** [ME *birnen, birnan*, v.i., *bærnan*, v.t.; akin to OHG *brinnan* to burn] *vi* (bef. 12c) **1 a** : to consume fuel and give off heat, light, and gases ⟨a small fire ~s on the hearth⟩ **b** : to undergo combustion; *also* : to undergo nuclear fission or nuclear fusion **c** : to contain a fire ⟨a little stove ~*ing* in the corner⟩ **d** : to give off light : SHINE, GLOW ⟨a light ~*ing* in the window⟩ **2 a** : to be hot ⟨the ~*ing* sand⟩ **b** : to produce or undergo discomfort or pain ⟨ears ~*ing* from the cold⟩ **c** : to become emotionally excited or agitated: as (1) : to yearn ardently ⟨~*ing* to tell the story⟩ (2) : to be or become very angry or disgusted ⟨the remark made him ~⟩ **3 a** : to undergo alteration or destruction by the action of fire or heat ⟨the house ~ed down⟩ ⟨the potatoes ~ed to a crisp⟩ **b** : to die in the electric chair **4** : to force or make a way by or as if by burning ⟨her words ~ed into his heart⟩ **5** : to receive sunburn ⟨she ~s easily⟩ ~ *vt* **1 a** : to cause to undergo combustion;

esp : to destroy by fire ⟨~ed the trash⟩ **b** : to use as fuel ⟨this furnace ~s gas⟩ **c** : to use up : CONSUME ⟨~ calories⟩ **2 a** : to transform by exposure to heat or fire ⟨~ clay to bricks⟩ **b** : to produce by burning ⟨~ed a hole in his sleeve⟩ **3 a** : to injure or damage by or as if by exposure to fire, heat, or radiation : SCORCH ⟨~ed his hand⟩ **b** : to execute by burning ⟨~ed heretics at the stake⟩; *also* : ELECTROCUTE **4 a** : IRRITATE, ANNOY — often used with *up* ⟨really ~s me up⟩ **b** : to take advantage of: as (1) : DECEIVE, CHEAT — often used in passive (2) : OUTDO, BEAT ⟨~ed the defense with a touchdown pass⟩ — **burn·able** \'bər-nə-bəl\ *adj* — **burn one's bridges** *also* **burn one's boats** : to cut off all means of retreat — **burn one's ears** : to rebuke strongly — **burn the candle at both ends** : to use one's resources or energies to excess — **burn the midnight oil** : to work or study far into the night

³burn *n* (1594) **1** : an act, process, instance, or result of burning: as **a** : injury or damage resulting from exposure to fire, heat, caustics, electricity, or certain radiations **b** : a burned area ⟨a ~ on the skin⟩ **c** : an abrasion (as of the skin) having the appearance of a burn ⟨rope ~s⟩ **d** : a burning sensation ⟨the ~ of iodine on a cut⟩ **2** : the firing of a spacecraft rocket engine in flight **3** : ANGER; *esp* : increasing fury — used chiefly in the phrase *slow burn*

burned–out \'bərn-'daùt, 'bərnt-'aùt\ *or* **burnt–out** \'bərnt-'aùt\ *adj* (1837) : WORN-OUT; *also* : EXHAUSTED

burn·er \'bər-nər\ *n* (14c) : one that burns; *esp* : the part of a fuel-burning or heat-producing device (as a furnace or stove) where the flame or heat is produced

bur·net \(ˌ)bər-'net, 'bər-nət\ *n* [ME, fr. MF *burnete*, fr. *brun* brown — more at BRUNET] (14c) : any of a genus (*Sanguisorba*) of herbs of the rose family with odd-pinnate stipulate leaves and spikes of apetalous flowers

burn–in \'bərn-ˌnin\ *n* (1966) : the continuous operation of a device (as a computer) as a test for defects or failure prior to putting it to use

burn in *vt* (ca. 1939) : to increase the density of (portions of a photographic print) during enlarging by giving extra exposure

burn·ing \'bər-niŋ\ *adj* (bef. 12c) **1 a** : being on fire **b** : ARDENT, INTENSE ⟨~ enthusiasm⟩ **2 a** : affecting with or as if with heat ⟨a ~ fever⟩ **b** : resembling that produced by a burn ⟨a ~ sensation on the tongue⟩ **3** : of fundamental importance : URGENT ⟨one of the ~ issues of our time⟩ — **burn·ing·ly** \-niŋ-lē\ *adv*

burning bush *n* (1785) : any of several plants associated with fire (as by redness): as **a** : ²WAHOO **b** : SUMMER CYPRESS

burning ghat *n* (1877) : a level space at the head of a ghat for cremation

¹bur·nish \'bər-nish\ *vt* [ME *burnischen*, fr. MF *bruniss-*, stem of *brunir*, lit., to make brown, fr. *brun*] (14c) **1 a** : to make shiny or lustrous esp. by rubbing **b** : POLISH 3 **2** : to rub (a material) with a tool for compacting or smoothing or for turning an edge — **bur·nish·er** *n* — **bur·nish·ing** *adj or n*

²burnish *n* (ca. 1647) : LUSTER, GLOSS

burn off *vi* (ca. 1925) : to be dissipated by the sun's warmth ⟨waiting for the fog to *burn off*⟩ ~ *vt* : to cause to burn off

bur·noose *or* **bur·nous** \(ˌ)bər-'nüs\ *n* [F *burnous*, fr. Ar *burnus*] (1695) : a one-piece hooded cloak worn by Arabs and Berbers — **bur·noosed** \-'nüst\ *adj*

burn·out \'bər-ˌnaùt\ *n* (1940) **1** : the cessation of operation of a jet or rocket engine; *also* : the point at which burnout occurs **2 a** : exhaustion of physical or emotional strength or motivation usu. as a result of prolonged stress or frustration **b** : a person suffering from burnout **3** : a person showing the results of drug abuse

burn out *vt* (1710) **1** : to drive out or destroy the property of by fire **2** : to cause to fail, wear out, or become exhausted esp. from overwork or overuse ~ *vi* : to suffer burnout

burn·sides \'bərn-ˌsīdz\ *n pl* [Ambrose E. *Burnside*] (1875) : SIDE-WHISKERS; *esp* : full muttonchop whiskers

¹burp \'bərp\ *n* [imit.] (ca. 1932) : BELCH

²burp *vi* (ca. 1932) : BELCH ~ *vt* : to help (a baby) expel gas from the stomach esp. by patting or rubbing the back

burp gun *n* (1944) : a small submachine gun

¹burr \'bər\ *n* [ME *burre*; akin to OE *byrst* bristle — more at BRISTLE] (14c) **1** *usu* **bur a** : a rough or prickly envelope of a fruit **b** : a plant that bears burs **2** : something that sticks or clings ⟨a ~ in the throat⟩ **b** : HANGER-ON **3** : an irregular rounded mass; *esp* : a tree burl **4** : a thin ridge or area of roughness produced in cutting or shaping metal **5 a** : a trilled uvular \r\ as used by some speakers of English esp. in northern England and in Scotland **b** : a tongue-point trill that is the usual Scottish \r\ **6 a** : a small rotary cutting tool **b** *usu* **bur** : a bit used on a dental drill **7** : a rough humming sound : WHIR — **burred** \'bərd\ *adj*

²burr *vi* (1798) **1** : to speak with a burr **2** : to make a whirring sound ~ *vt* **1** : to pronounce with a burr **2** : to form into a projecting edge **b** : to remove burrs from — **burr·er** *n*

bur reed *n* (1602) : any of a genus (*Sparganium* of the family Sparganiaceae) of plants with globose fruits resembling burs

bur·ri·to \bə-'rē-(ˌ)tō\ *n, pl* **-tos** [AmerSp, fr. Sp, little donkey, dim. of *burro*] (1934) : a flour tortilla rolled or folded around a filling (as of meat, beans, or cheese) and usu. baked

bur·ro \'bər-(ˌ)ō, 'bùr-; 'bə-(ˌ)rō\ *n, pl* **burros** [Sp, irreg. fr. *borrico*, fr. LL *burricus* small horse] (1800) : DONKEY; *esp* : a small one used as a pack animal

¹bur·row \'bər-(ˌ)ō, 'bə-(ˌ)rō\ *n* [ME *borow*] (13c) : a hole or excavation in the ground made by an animal (as a rabbit) for shelter and habitation

²burrow *vt* (1602) **1** *archaic* : to hide in or as if in a burrow **2 a** : to construct by tunneling **b** : to penetrate by means of a burrow **3** : to make a motion suggestive of burrowing with : NESTLE ⟨~s her hand into mine⟩ ~ *vi* **1** : to conceal oneself in or as if in a burrow **2 a** : to make a burrow **b** : to progress by or as if by digging **3** : to

\ə\ abut \ˈə\ kitten, F table \ər\ further \a\ ash \ā\ ace \ä\ mop, mar \aù\ out \ch\ chin \e\ bet \ē\ easy \g\ go \i\ hit \ī\ ice \j\ job \ŋ\ sing \ō\ go \ò\ law \òi\ boy \th\ thin \t͟h\ the \ü\ loot \ù\ foot \y\ yet \zh\ vision \a, ᵏ, ⁿ, œ, œ̄, ᵫ, ᵫ̄, ᵊ\ see Guide to Pronunciation

make a motion suggestive of burrowing : SNUGGLE, NESTLE ⟨~ed against his back for warmth⟩ — **bur·row·er** n
burrstone var of BUHRSTONE
bur·ry \'bər-ē\ adj **bur·ri·er; -est** (15c) 1 : containing burs 2 : PRICKLY 3 of speech : characterized by a burr
bur·sa \'bər-sə\ n, pl **bur·sas** \-səz\ or **bur·sae** \-,sē, -,sī\ [NL, fr. ML, bag, purse — more at PURSE] (1803) : a bodily pouch or sac: as a : a small serous sac between a tendon and a bone b : BURSA OF FABRICIUS — **bur·sal** \-səl\ adj
bursa of Fa·bri·cius \-fə-'brē-sh(ē-)əs, -'bri-, -s(ē-)əs\ [Johan C. Fabricius †1808 Dan. entomologist] (1945) : a lymphoid organ that opens into the cloaca of birds and functions in B cell production
bur·sar \'bər-sər, -,sär\ n [ML bursarius, fr. bursa] (13c) : an officer (as of a monastery or college) in charge of funds : TREASURER
bur·sa·ry \'bər-sə-rē, 'bərs-rē\ n, pl **-ries** [ML bursaria, fr. bursa] (1695) 1 : the treasury of a college or monastery 2 Brit : a monetary grant to a needy student : SCHOLARSHIP
burse \'bərs\ n [MF bourse, fr. ML bursa] (15c) 1 a : PURSE b : a square cloth case used to carry the corporal in a Communion service 2 obs : EXCHANGE, BOURSE
bur·si·tis \(,)bər-'sī-təs\ n [NL, fr. bursa] (1857) : inflammation of a bursa esp. of the shoulder or elbow
¹**burst** \'bərst\ vb **burst** also **burst·ed; burst·ing** [ME bersten, fr. OE berstan; akin to OHG brestan to burst] vi (bef. 12c) 1 : to break open, apart, or into pieces usu. from impact or from pressure from within 2 a : to give way from an excess of emotion ⟨my heart will ~⟩ b : to give vent suddenly to a repressed emotion ⟨~ into tears⟩ ⟨~ out laughing⟩ 3 a : to emerge or spring suddenly ⟨~ out of the house⟩ b : to move onto the scene⟩ b : LAUNCH, PLUNGE ⟨~ into song⟩ 4 : to be filled to the breaking point ⟨~ing with excitement⟩ ⟨a crate ~ing with fruit⟩ ~ vt 1 : to cause to burst 2 : to force open (as a door) by strong or vigorous action 3 : to produce by or as if by bursting — **burst at the seams** : to be larger, fuller, or more crowded than could reasonably have been anticipated
²**burst** n (1610) 1 a : a sudden outbreak; esp : a vehement outburst (as of emotion) b : EXPLOSION, ERUPTION c : a sudden intense effort ⟨a ~ of speed⟩ d : the duration of fire in one engagement of the mechanism of an automatic firearm 2 : an act of bursting 3 : a result of bursting; esp : a visible puff accompanying the explosion of a shell
burst·er \'bərs-tər\ n (1611) 1 : one that bursts 2 : the celestial source of an outburst of radiation (as X rays)
bur·then \'bər-thən\ var of BURDEN
bur·weed \'bər-,wēd\ n (ca. 1783) : any of various plants (as a cocklebur or burdock) having burry fruit
bury \'ber-ē also 'bər-\ vt **bur·ied; bury·ing** [ME burien, fr. OE byrgan; akin to OHG bergan to shelter, Russ berech' to spare] (bef. 12c) 1 : to dispose of by depositing in or as if in the earth; esp : to inter with funeral ceremonies 2 a : to conceal by or as if by covering with earth b : to cover from view ⟨buried her face in her hands⟩ 3 a : to have done with ⟨~ing their differences⟩ b : to conceal in obscurity ⟨buried the retraction among the classified ads⟩ c : SUBMERGE, ENGROSS — usu. used with in ⟨buried himself in his books⟩ 4 : to put (a playing card) out of play by placing it in or under the dealer's pack 5 : to succeed emphatically or impressively in making (a shot) ⟨~ a jumper⟩ 6 : to defeat overwhelmingly syn see HIDE — **bury the hatchet** : to settle a disagreement : become reconciled
¹**bus** \'bəs\ n, pl **bus·es** or **bus·ses** often attrib [short for omnibus] (ca. 1909) 1 a : a large motor vehicle designed to carry passengers usu. along a fixed route according to a schedule b : AUTOMOBILE 2 : a small hand truck : BUS BAR b : a set of parallel conductors in a computer system that forms a main transmission path 4 : a spacecraft or missile that carries one or more detachable devices (as warheads)
²**bus** vb **bused** or **bussed; bus·ing** or **bus·sing** vi (ca. 1909) 1 : to travel by bus 2 : to work as a busboy ~ vt 1 : to transport by bus 2 a : CLEAR 4d ⟨~ dishes⟩ b : to remove dirty dishes from ⟨~ tables⟩
bus bar n (1893) : a conductor or an assembly of conductors for collecting electric currents and distributing them to outgoing feeders
bus·boy \'bəs-,bȯi\ n [omnibus busboy] (1913) : a waiter's assistant; specif : one who removes dirty dishes and resets tables in a restaurant
bus·by \'bəz-bē\ n, pl **busbies** [prob. fr. the name Busby] (1853) 1 : a military full-dress fur hat with a pendent bag on one side usu. of the color of regimental facings 2 : the bearskin worn by British guardsmen — not used by the guardsmen themselves
¹**bush** \'bush\ n, often attrib [ME; akin to OHG busc forest] (14c) 1 a : SHRUB; esp : a low densely branched shrub b : a close thicket of shrubs suggesting a single plant c : a large uncleared or sparsely settled area (as in Australia) usu. scrub-covered or forested : WILDERNESS — usu. used with the 3 archaic : a bunch of ivy formerly hung outside a tavern to indicate wine for sale b obs : TAVERN c : ADVERTISING ⟨good wine needs no ~ —Shak.⟩ 4 : a bushy tuft or mass ⟨a ~ of hair⟩; esp : ²BRUSH 2a 5 : MINOR LEAGUE — usu. used in pl.
²**bush** vt (15c) : to support, mark, or protect with bushes ~ vi : to extend like a bush : resemble a bush
³**bush** adj (1595) 1 : having a low-growing compact bushy habit — used esp. of cultivated beans ⟨~ snap beans⟩ 2 : serving, occurring in, or used in the bush ⟨~ planes⟩
⁴**bush** n [D bus bushing, box, fr. MD busse box, fr. LL buxis — more at BOX] (1566) chiefly Brit : BUSHING
⁵**bush** adj [short for bush-league] (1970) : falling below acceptable standards : UNPROFESSIONAL ⟨~ behavior⟩
bush baby n (1901) : GALAGO
bush basil n (1597) : a sweet basil of a cultivar with small leaves
bush·buck \'bush-,bək\ n, pl **bushbuck** or **bushbucks** [trans. of Afrik bosbok] (1852) : a small African striped antelope (Tragelaphus scriptus) esp. of sub-Saharan forests that has spirally twisted horns
bush clover n (ca. 1818) : any of several usu. shrubby lespedezas
¹**bushed** \'bushț\ adj (14c) 1 : covered with or as if with a bushy growth 2 chiefly Austral : lost esp. in the bush b : PERPLEXED 1, CONFUSED 3 : TIRED, EXHAUSTED
²**bushed** adj (1907) : having a bushing
¹**bush·el** \'bu-shəl\ n [ME busshel, fr. OF boissel, fr. (assumed) OF boisse one sixth of a bushel, of Celt origin; akin to MIr boss breadth of the hand] (14c) 1 : any of various units of dry capacity — see WEIGHT

table 2 : a container holding a bushel 3 : a large quantity : LOTS ⟨makes ~s of money⟩
²**bushel** vb **bush·eled; bush·el·ing** \-sh(ə-)liŋ\ [prob. fr. G bosseln to do poor work, to patch; akin to OE bēatan to beat] (ca. 1877) : REPAIR, RENOVATE — **bush·el·er** \-sh(ə-)lər\ n
bush·fire \'bush-,fir\ n (1832) Austral : an uncontrolled fire in a bush area
Bu·shi·do \'bu-shi-,dō, 'bü-\ n [Jp bushidō] (1898) : a feudal-military Japanese code of chivalry valuing honor above life
bush·ing \'bu-shiŋ\ n (1839) 1 : a usu. removable cylindrical lining for an opening (as of a mechanical part) used to limit the size of the opening, resist abrasion, or serve as a guide 2 : an electrically insulating lining for a hole to protect a through conductor
bush jacket n [fr. its use in rough country] (ca. 1939) : a long cotton jacket resembling a shirt and having four patch pockets and a belt
bush·land \'bush-,land\ n (1827) : ¹BUSH 2
bush–league adj (1914) : being of an inferior class or group of its kind
bush league n (1909) : MINOR LEAGUE — **bush leaguer** n
bush·man \'bush-mən\ n (1785) 1 cap [modif. of obs. Afrik boschjesman, fr. boschje (dim. of bosch) forest) + Afrik man] a : a member of a group of short-statured peoples of southern Africa who traditionally live by hunting and foraging b : the Khoisan languages spoken by these people 2 a : WOODSMAN b chiefly Austral : a person who lives in the bush
bush·mas·ter \-,mas-tər\ n (1826) : a tropical American pit viper (Lachesis mutus) that is the largest New World venomous snake
bush·pig \-,pig\ n (1840) : a wild usu. reddish to black pig (Potamochoerus porcus) of forests and scrubland of sub-Saharan Africa and Madagascar that has much facial hair, long pointed ears, and a light-colored mane along the top of the neck and back
bush pilot n (1936) : a pilot who flies a small plane into remote areas
bush·rang·er \-,rān-jər\ n (1801) 1 Austral : an outlaw living in the bush 2 : FRONTIERSMAN, WOODSMAN — **bush·rang·ing** \-jiŋ\ n
bush shirt n [fr. its use in rough country] (1909) : a usu. loose-fitting cotton shirt with patch pockets
bush·tit \-,tit\ n (ca. 1889) : a small gray titmouse (Psaltriparus minimus) of western No. America with light underparts that occurs in several geographic forms sometimes placed in separate species
bush·whack \'bush-,hwak, -,wak\ vb [back-formation fr. bushwhacker] vt (1866) : AMBUSH; broadly : to attack suddenly : ASSAULT ~ vi : to clear a path through thick woods esp. by chopping down bushes and low branches — **bush·whack·er** n
bushy \'bu-shē\ adj **bush·i·er; -est** (14c) 1 : full of or overgrown with bushes 2 : resembling a bush; esp : being thick and spreading — **bush·i·ly** \'bu-shə-lē\ adv — **bush·i·ness** \'bu-shē-nəs\ n
busi·ness \'biz-nəs, -nəz, Southern also 'bid-\ n, often attrib (14c) 1 archaic : purposeful activity : BUSYNESS 2 a : ROLE, FUNCTION ⟨how the human mind went about its ~ of learning —H. A. Overstreet⟩ b : an immediate task or objective : MISSION ⟨what is your ~ here⟩ c : a particular field of endeavor ⟨the best in the ~⟩ 3 a : a usu. commercial or mercantile activity engaged in as a means of livelihood : TRADE, LINE ⟨in the restaurant ~⟩ b : a commercial or sometimes an industrial enterprise; also : such enterprises ⟨the ~ district⟩ c : usu. economic dealings : PATRONAGE ⟨took their ~ elsewhere⟩ 4 : AFFAIR, MATTER ⟨the whole ~ got out of hand⟩ ⟨~ as usual⟩ 5 : CREATION, CONCOCTION 6 : movement or action (as lighting a cigarette) by an actor intended esp. to establish atmosphere, reveal character, or explain a situation — called also stage business 7 a : personal concern ⟨none of your ~⟩ b : RIGHT ⟨you have no ~ speaking to me that way⟩ 8 a : serious activity requiring time and effort and usu. the avoidance of distractions ⟨got down to ~⟩ ⟨she means ~⟩ b : maximum effort 9 a : a damaging assault b : REBUKE, TONGUE-LASHING c : DOUBLE CROSS 10 : a bowel movement — used esp. of pets
syn BUSINESS, COMMERCE, TRADE, INDUSTRY, TRAFFIC mean activity concerned with the supplying and distribution of commodities. BUSINESS may be an inclusive term but specifically designates the activities of those engaged in the purchase or sale of commodities or in related financial transactions. COMMERCE and TRADE imply the exchange and transportation of commodities. INDUSTRY applies to the producing of commodities, esp. by manufacturing or processing, usu. on a large scale. TRAFFIC applies to the operation and functioning of public carriers of goods and persons. syn see in addition WORK
business administration n (ca. 1911) : a program of studies in a college or university providing general knowledge of business principles and practices
business card n (1840) : a small card bearing information (as name and address) about a business or business representative
business cycle n (1919) : a cycle of economic activity usu. consisting of recession, recovery, growth, and decline
business end n (1878) : the end with, from, or through which a thing's function is fulfilled ⟨the business end of a revolver⟩
busi·ness·like \'biz-nəs-,līk, -nəz-\ adj (1791) 1 : exhibiting qualities believed to be advantageous in business 2 : SERIOUS, PURPOSEFUL
busi·ness·man \-,man, -mən\ n (1826) : a man who transacts business; esp : a business executive
busi·ness·peo·ple \-,pē-pəl\ n pl (1865) : persons active in business
busi·ness·per·son \-,pər-s²n\ n (1974) : a businessman or businesswoman
business suit n (1870) : a man's suit consisting of matching coat and trousers and sometimes a vest
busi·ness·wom·an \-,wu̇-mən\ n (1844) : a woman who transacts business; esp : a female business executive
bus·ing or **bus·sing** \'bə-siŋ\ n (1923) : the act of transporting by bus; specif : the transporting of children to a school outside their residential area as a means of establishing racial balance in that school
busk·er \'bəs-kər\ n [busk, prob. fr. It buscare to procure, gain, fr. Sp buscar to look for] (1857) chiefly Brit : a person who entertains esp. by playing music on the street — **busk** \'bəsk\ vi
bus·kin \'bəs-kən\ n [prob. modif. of MF brozequin] (1503) 1 a : a laced boot reaching halfway or more to the knee 2 a : COTHURNUS 1 b : TRAGEDY; esp : tragedy resembling that of ancient Greek drama
bus·load \'bəs-,lōd\ n (1938) : a load that fills a bus ⟨~s of tourists⟩
bus·man's holiday \'bəs-mənz-\ n (1893) : a holiday spent in following or observing the practice of one's usual occupation

buss \'bəs\ *n* [perh. alter. of ME *bassen* to kiss] (1570) : KISS — **buss** *vt*
¹bust \'bəst\ *n* [F *buste*, fr. It *busto*, fr. L *bustum* tomb] (1645) **1 :** a sculptured representation of the upper part of the human figure including the head and neck and usu. part of the shoulders and breast **2 :** the upper part of the human torso between neck and waist; *esp* : the breasts of a woman
²bust *vb* **bust·ed** *also* **bust; bust·ing** [alter. of *burst*] *vt* (1806) **1 a :** to break or smash esp. with force; *also* : to make inoperative ⟨~ed my watch⟩ **b :** to bring an end to : BREAK UP ⟨helped ~ trusts —*Newsweek*⟩ — often used with *up* ⟨better not try to ~ up his happy marriage —*Forbes*⟩ **c :** to ruin financially **d :** EXHAUST, WEAR OUT — used in phrases like *bust one's butt* to describe making a strenuous effort **2 :** TAME ⟨bronco ~ing⟩ **3 :** DEMOTE **4** *slang* **a :** ARREST ⟨~ed for carrying guns —Saul Gottlieb⟩ **b :** RAID ⟨~ed the apartment⟩ **5 :** HIT, SLUG ~ *vi* **1 a :** to go broke **2 a :** BURST ⟨laughing fit to ~⟩ **b :** BREAK DOWN **3 a :** to lose at cards by exceeding a limit (as the count of 21 in blackjack) **b :** to fail to complete a straight or flush in poker
³bust *n* (1840) **1 a :** SPREE **b :** a hearty drinking session ⟨a beer ~⟩ **2 a :** a complete failure : FLOP **b :** a business depression **3 :** PUNCH, SOCK **4** *slang* **a :** a police raid **b :** ARREST 2
⁴bust *or* **bust·ed** \'bəs-təd\ *adj* (1837) : BANKRUPT, BROKE ⟨go ~⟩
bus·tard \'bəs-tərd\ *n* [ME, modif. of MF *bistarde*, fr. OIt *bistarda*, fr. L *avis tarda*, lit., slow bird] (15c) : any of a family (Otididae) of large chiefly terrestrial Old World and Australian game birds
bust·er \'bəs-tər\ *n* (1848) **1** *chiefly Austral* : a sudden violent wind often coming from the south ⟨a ~⟩ **2 :** an unusually sturdy child **b** *often cap* : FELLOW — usu. used as a noun of address ⟨hey ~, come here⟩ **3 :** one that breaks, breaks up, or eliminates something ⟨crime ~s⟩: as **a :** PLOW **b** [short for *broncobuster*] : a person who breaks horses **4 :** a bad fall
bus·tier \,büs-tē-'ā, ,bəs-, -'tyä\ *n* [F, fr. *buste*] (1979) : a tight-fitting often strapless top worn as a brassiere or outer garment
¹bus·tle \'bə-səl\ *vi* **bus·tled; bus·tling** \'bəs-liŋ, 'bə-sə-\ [prob. alter. of obs. *buskle* to prepare, freq. of *busk*, fr. ON *búask* to prepare oneself] (1580) **1 :** to move briskly and often ostentatiously **2 :** to be busily astir ⟨~ing~⟩ — **bustling** *adj* — **bus·tling·ly** \-liŋ-lē\ *adv*
²bustle *n* (1634) : noisy, energetic, and often obtrusive activity ⟨the hustle and ~ of the big city⟩
³bustle *n* [origin unknown] (1786) : a pad or framework expanding and supporting the fullness and drapery of the back of a woman's skirt or dress; *also* : the drapery so supported
bust·line \'bəs(t)-,līn\ *n* (1926) **1 :** an arbitrary line encircling the fullest part of the bust **2 :** body circumference at the bust
busty \'bəs-tē\ *adj* **bust·i·er; -est** (1944) : having a large bust
bu·sul·fan \byü-'səl-fən\ *n* [*butane* + *sulfonyl*] (ca. 1954) : an antineoplastic agent C₆H₁₄O₆S₂ used in the treatment of chronic myelogenous leukemia
¹busy \'bi-zē\ *adj* **busi·er; -est** [ME *bisy*, fr. OE *bisig*; akin to MD & MLG *besich* busy] (bef. 12c) **1 a :** engaged in action : OCCUPIED **b :** being in use ⟨found the telephone ~⟩ **2 :** full of activity : BUSTLING ⟨a ~ seaport⟩ **3 :** foolishly or intrusively active : MEDDLING **4 :** full of distracting detail ⟨a ~ design⟩ — **busi·ly** \'bi-zə-lē\ *adv* — **busy·ness** \'bi-zē-nəs\ *n*
  syn BUSY, INDUSTRIOUS, DILIGENT, ASSIDUOUS, SEDULOUS mean actively engaged or occupied. BUSY chiefly stresses activity as opposed to idleness or leisure ⟨too busy to spend time with the children⟩. INDUSTRIOUS implies characteristic or habitual devotion to work ⟨industrious employees⟩. DILIGENT suggests earnest application to some specific object or pursuit ⟨very diligent in her pursuit of a degree⟩. ASSIDUOUS stresses careful and unremitting application ⟨assiduous practice⟩. SEDULOUS implies painstaking and persevering application ⟨a sedulous investigation of the murder⟩.
²busy *vb* **bus·ied; busy·ing** *vt* (bef. 12c) : to make busy : OCCUPY ~ *vi* : BUSTLE ⟨small boats busied to and fro —Quentin Crewe⟩
busy·body \'bi-zē-,bä-dē\ *n* (1526) : an officious or inquisitive person
busy·work \-,wərk\ *n* (1910) : work that usu. appears productive or of intrinsic value but actually only keeps one occupied
¹but \'bət\ *conj* [ME, fr. OE *būtan*, prep. & conj., outside, without, except, except that; akin to OHG *būzan* without, except; akin to OE *be* by, *ūt* out — more at BY, OUT] (bef. 12c) **1 a :** except for the fact ⟨would have protested ~ that he was afraid⟩ **b :** THAT — used after a negative ⟨there is no doubt ~ he won⟩ **c :** without the concomitant that ⟨it never rains ~ it pours⟩ **2 :** if not : UNLESS **3 :** THAN ⟨no sooner started ~ it stopped⟩ — not often in formal use **2 a :** on the contrary : on the other hand : NOTWITHSTANDING — used to connect coordinate elements ⟨he was called ~ he did not answer⟩ ⟨not peace ~ a sword⟩ **b :** YET ⟨poor ~ proud⟩ **c :** with the exception of — used before a word often taken to be the subject of a clause ⟨none ~ the brave deserves the fair —John Dryden⟩ — **but what :** that . . . not — used to indicate possibility or uncertainty ⟨I don't know *but what* I will go⟩
²but *prep* (bef. 12c) **1 a :** with the exception of : BARRING ⟨no one there ~ me⟩ — compare ¹BUT 2c **b :** other than ⟨this letter is nothing ~ an insult⟩ **2** *Scot* : WITHOUT, LACKING **b :** OUTSIDE
³but *adv* (12c) **1 :** ONLY, MERELY ⟨he is ~ a child⟩ **2** *Scot* : OUTSIDE **3 :** to the contrary ⟨who knows ~ that she may succeed⟩ **4** — used as an intensive ⟨get there ~ fast⟩
⁴but *pron* (1556) : that not : who not ⟨nobody ~ has his fault —Shak.⟩
⁵but *n* [Sc *but*, adj. (outer)] (1724) *Scot* : the kitchen or living quarters of a 2-room cottage
bu·ta·di·ene \,byü-tə-'dī-,ēn, -,ēn\ *n* [ISV *butane* + *di-* + *-ene*] (1900) : a flammable gaseous open chain hydrocarbon C₄H₆ used in making synthetic rubbers
bu·tane \'byü-,tān\ *n* [ISV *butyric* + *-ane*] (1875) : either of two isomeric flammable gaseous alkanes C₄H₁₀ obtained usu. from petroleum or natural gas and used as fuels
bu·ta·nol \'byü-t⁰n-,ȯl, -,ōl\ *n* (1894) : either of two flammable four-carbon alcohols C₄H₉OH derived from normal butane
butch \'büch\ *adj* [prob. fr. *Butch*, male nickname] (1941) **1 :** very masculine in appearance or manner **2 :** playing the male role in a homosexual relationship
¹butch·er \'bü-chər\ *n* [ME *bocher*, fr. OF *bouchier*, fr. *bouc* he-goat, prob. of Celt origin; akin to MIr *bocc* he-goat — more at BUCK] (13c) **1 a :** a person who slaughters animals or dresses their flesh **b :** a

dealer in meat **2 :** one that kills ruthlessly or brutally **3 :** one that bungles or botches **4 :** a vendor esp. on trains or in theaters
²butcher *vt* **butch·ered; butch·er·ing** \'büch-riŋ, 'bü-chə-\ (1562) **1 :** to slaughter and dress for market ⟨~ hogs⟩ **2 :** to kill in a barbarous manner **3 :** BOTCH ⟨~ed the play⟩
butch·er–bird \'bü-chər-,bərd\ *n* (1668) : any of various shrikes
butcher block *n* (1967) : a block made with thick strips of usu. laminated hardwood — **butcher–block** *adj*
butch·er·ly \'bü-chər-lē\ *adj* (1513) : resembling a butcher : SAVAGE
butcher paper *n* (1944) : heavy brown or white paper used esp. for wrapping meats
butch·ery \'büch-rē, 'bü-chə-\ *n, pl* **-er·ies** (14c) **1** *chiefly Brit* : SLAUGHTERHOUSE **2 :** the preparation of meat for sale **3 :** cruel and ruthless slaughter of human beings **4 :** BOTCH
bute \'byüt\ *n* (1968) : PHENYLBUTAZONE
bu·tene \'byü-,tēn\ *n* [ISV *butyl* + *-ene*] (1885) : a normal butylene
bu·teo \'byü-tē-,ō\ *n, pl* **-te·os** [NL, genus name, fr. L, a hawk] (1940) : any of a genus (*Buteo*) of hawks with broad rounded wings, relatively short tails, and soaring flight
but for *prep* (12c) : EXCEPT FOR
but·ler \'bət-lər\ *n* [ME *buteler*, fr. OF *bouteillier* bottle bearer, fr. *bouteille* bottle — more at BOTTLE] (13c) **1 :** a manservant having charge of the wines and liquors **2 :** the chief male servant of a household who has charge of other employees, receives guests, directs the serving of meals, and performs various personal services
butler's pantry *n* (1816) : a service room between kitchen and dining room
¹butt \'bət\ *vb* [ME, fr. OF *boter*, of Gmc origin; akin to OHG *bōzan* to beat — more at BEAT] *vi* (13c) : to thrust or push head foremost : strike with the head or horns ~ *vt* : to strike or shove with the head or horns
²butt *n* (1647) : a blow or thrust usu. with the head or horns
³butt *n* [ME, fr. MF *botte*, fr. OProv *bota*, fr. LL *buttis*] (14c) **1 :** a large cask esp. for wine, beer, or water **2 :** any of various units of liquid capacity; *esp* : a measure equal to 108 imperial gallons (491 liters)
⁴butt *n* [ME, partly fr. MF *but* target, end, of Gmc origin; akin to ON *būtr* log, LG *butt* blunt; partly fr. MF *bute* backstop, fr. *but* target] (14c) **1 a :** a backstop (as a mound or bank) for catching missiles shot at a target **b :** TARGET **c** *pl* : RANGE 5c **d :** a blind for shooting birds **2 a** *obs* : LIMIT, BOUND **b** *archaic* : GOAL ⟨here is my journey's end, here is my ~ —Shak.⟩ **3 :** an object of abuse or ridicule : VICTIM ⟨the ~ of all their jokes⟩
⁵butt *n* [ME; prob. akin to ME *buttok* buttock, LG *butt* blunt] (15c) **1 :** BUTTOCKS — often used as a euphemism for *ass* in idiomatic expressions ⟨get your ~ over here⟩ ⟨kick ~⟩ ⟨saved our ~s⟩ **2 :** the large or thicker end part of something : as **a :** a lean upper cut of the pork shoulder **b :** the base of a plant from which the roots spring **c :** the thicker or handle end of a tool or weapon **3 :** an unused remainder **4 :** the part of a hide or skin corresponding to the animal's back and sides
⁶butt *vb* [partly fr. ⁴*butt*, partly fr. ⁵*butt*] *vi* (1785) : ABUT — used with *on* or *against* ~ *vt* **1 :** to place end to end or side to side without overlapping **2 :** to trim or square off (as a log) at the end **3 :** to reduce (as a cigarette) to a butt by stubbing or stamping
butte \'byüt\ *n* [F, knoll, fr. MF *bute*] (1805) : an isolated hill or mountain with steep or precipitous sides usu. having a smaller summit area than a mesa
¹but·ter \'bə-tər\ *n* [ME, fr. OE *butere*, fr. L *butyrum*, fr. Gk *boutyron*, fr. *bous* cow + *tyros* cheese; akin to Av *tūiri-* curds — more at COW] (bef. 12c) **1 :** a solid emulsion of fat globules, air, and water made by churning milk or cream and used as food **2 :** a buttery substance: as **a :** any of various fatty oils remaining nearly solid at ordinary temperatures **b :** a creamy food spread; *esp* : one made of ground roasted nuts ⟨peanut ~⟩ **3 :** FLATTERY — **but·ter·less** \-ləs\ *adj*
²butter *vt* (15c) : to spread with or as if with butter
but·ter–and–eggs \,bə-tər-⁰n-'egz, -'āgz\ *n pl but sing or pl in constr* (1776) : a common Eurasian perennial herb (*Linaria vulgaris*) of the snapdragon family that has showy yellow and orange flowers and is naturalized in much of No. America — called also *toadflax*
but·ter·ball \'bə-tər-,bȯl\ *n* (1813) **1 :** BUFFLEHEAD **2 :** a chubby person
butter bean *n* (ca. 1819) **1 :** LIMA BEAN: as **a** *chiefly Southern & Midland* : a large dried lima bean **b :** SIEVA BEAN **2 :** WAX BEAN **3 :** a green shell bean esp. as opposed to a snap bean
butter clam *n* (1936) : either of two clams (*Saxidomus nuttallii* and *S. giganteus*) of the Pacific coast of No. America
but·ter·cup \'bə-tər-,kəp\ *n* (1777) : any of a genus (*Ranunculus* of the family Ranunculaceae, the buttercup family) of herbs with yellow or white flowers and alternate leaves
but·ter·fat \-,fat\ *n* (1889) : the natural fat of milk and chief constituent of butter consisting essentially of a mixture of glycerides (as those derived from butyric, capric, caproic, and caprylic acids)
but·ter·fin·gered \-,fiŋ-gərd\ *adj* (1615) : apt to let things fall or slip through the fingers : CARELESS — **but·ter·fin·gers** \-gərz\ *n pl but sing or pl in constr*
but·ter·fish \-,fish\ *n* (1674) : any of numerous bony fishes (esp. family Stromateidae) with a slippery coating of mucus
¹but·ter·fly \-,flī\ *n, often attrib* (bef. 12c) **1 :** any of numerous slender-bodied diurnal insects (order Lepidoptera) with broad often brightly colored wings **2 :** something that resembles or suggests a butterfly; *esp* : a person chiefly occupied with the pursuit of pleasure **3 :** a swimming stroke executed in a prone position by moving both arms in a circular motion while kicking both legs up and down **4** *pl* : a feeling of hollowness or queasiness caused esp. by emotional or nervous tension or anxious anticipation

\ə\ abut \ᵊ\ kitten, F table \ər\ further \a\ ash \ā\ ace \ä\ mop, mar \aù\ out \ch\ chin \e\ bet \ē\ easy \g\ go \i\ hit \ī\ ice \j\ job \ŋ\ sing \ō\ go \ȯ\ law \ȯi\ boy \th\ thin \t̲h̲\ the \ü\ loot \ù\ foot \y\ yet \zh\ vision \a, k, ⁿ, œ, œ̄, ᴜᴇ, ᵫ, ᵞ\ see Guide to Pronunciation

²**butterfly** vt **-flied; -fly·ing** (1954) : to split almost entirely and spread apart ⟨a *butterflied* steak⟩ ⟨*butterflied* shrimp⟩

butterfly bush n (1924) : BUDDLEIA

butterfly chair n (1953) : a chair for lounging consisting of a cloth sling supported by a frame of metal tubing or bars

but·ter·fly·er \'bə-tər-,flī(-ə)r\ n (1967) : a swimmer who specializes in the butterfly

butterfly fish n (1740) **1** : any of a family (Chaetodontidae) of small brilliantly colored spiny-finned fishes of tropical seas with a narrow deep body and scaled fins **2** : a small brown freshwater fish (*Pantodon buchholzi* of the family Pantodontidae) of western Africa that has elongate winglike pectoral fins

butterfly chair

butterfly valve n (1846) **1** : a valve consisting of two semicircular clappers hinged to a cross rib that permits fluid flow in only one direction **2** : a damper or valve in a pipe consisting of a disk turning on a diametral axis

butterfly weed n (1816) : an orange-flowered showy milkweed (*Asclepias tuberosa*) of eastern temperate No. America

but·ter·milk \'bə-tər-,milk\ n (15c) **1** : the liquid left after butter has been churned from milk or cream **2** : cultured milk made by the addition of suitable bacteria to sweet milk

but·ter·nut \-,nət\ n (1741) **1** : an eastern No. American tree of the walnut family with sweet egg-shaped nuts and light brown wood — called also *white walnut* **2 a** : a light yellowish brown **b** pl : homespun overalls dyed brown with a butternut extract **c** : a soldier or partisan of the Confederacy during the Civil War

butternut squash n (1945) : a smooth somewhat bottle-shaped buff-colored winter squash with usu. orange flesh

but·ter·scotch \-,skäch\ n (1855) **1** : a candy made from brown sugar, butter, corn syrup, and water; also : the flavor of such candy **2** : a moderate yellowish brown

butter up vt (1819) : to charm or beguile with lavish flattery or praise

but·ter·weed \'bə-tər-,wēd\ n (ca. 1845) : any of several plants having yellow flowers or smooth soft foliage: as **a** : HORSEWEED 1 **b** : a No. American groundsel (*Senecio glabellus*)

but·ter·wort \-,wərt, -,wȯrt\ n (1597) : any of a genus (*Pinguicula*) of herbs of the bladderwort family with fleshy leaves that produce a viscid secretion serving to capture and digest insects

¹**but·tery** \'bə-tə-rē, 'bə-trē\ n, pl **-ter·ies** [ME *boterie*, fr. MF, fr. *botte* cask, butt — more at BUTT] (14c) **1** : a storeroom for liquors **2 a** chiefly dial : PANTRY **b** : a room (as in an English college) stocking provisions for sale to students

²**but·tery** \'bə-tə-rē\ adj (14c) **1 a** : having the qualities of butter **b** : containing or spread with butter **2** : marked by flattery

butt hinge n (1815) : a hinge usu. mortised flush into the edge of a door and its jamb

butt in vi (1900) : to meddle in the affairs of others : INTERFERE

butt·in·sky also **butt·in·ski** \,bə-'din-skē\ n, pl **-skies** [butt in + -sky, -ski (last element in Slavic surnames)] (1902) : a person given to butting in : a troublesome meddler

butt joint n (1823) : a joint made by fastening the parts together end-to-end without overlap and often with reinforcement

but·tock \'bə-tək also -(,)täk\ n [ME *buttok* — more at BUTT] (14c) **1** : the back of a hip that forms one of the fleshy parts on which a person sits **2** pl : the seat of the body **b** : RUMP

¹**but·ton** \'bə-t²n\ n, often attrib [ME *boton*, fr. MF, fr. OF, fr. *boter* to thrust — more at BUTT] (14c) **1 a** : a small knob or disk secured to an article (as of clothing) and used as a fastener by passing it through a buttonhole or loop **b** : a usu. circular metal or plastic badge bearing a stamped design or printed slogan ⟨campaign ~⟩ **2** : something that resembles a button: as **a** : any of various parts or growths of a plant or of an animal: as **(1)** : an immature whole mushroom **(2)** : the terminal segment of a rattlesnake's rattle **b** : a small globule of metal remaining after fusion (as in assaying) **c** : a guard on the tip of a fencing foil **3** : PUSH BUTTON **4** : the point of the chin esp. as a target for a knockout blow — **but·ton·less** \-ləs\ adj — **on the button** : EXACTLY ⟨arrived at noon *on the button*⟩; also : exactly on target : on the nose ⟨the estimate was right *on the button*⟩

²**button** vb **but·toned; but·ton·ing** \'bət-niŋ, 'bə-t²n-iŋ\ vt (14c) **1** : to furnish or decorate with buttons **2 a** : to pass (a button) through a buttonhole or loop **b** : to close or fasten with buttons — often used with *up* ⟨~ up your overcoat⟩ **3 a** : to close (the lips) to prevent speech ⟨~ your lip⟩ **b** : to close or seal tightly — usu. used with *up* ⟨~ up the house for winter⟩ ~ vi : to have buttons for fastening ⟨this dress ~s at the back⟩ — **but·ton·er** \'bət-nər, 'bə-t²n-ər\ n

but·ton·ball \'bə-t²n-,bȯl\ n (1821) : ²PLANE

but·ton·bush \-,bu̇sh\ n (1754) : a No. American shrub (*Cephalanthus occidentalis*) of the madder family with globular flower heads

¹**but·ton-down** \-,da u̇n\ adj (1934) **1 a** of a collar : having the ends fastened to the garment with buttons **b** of a garment : having a button-down collar **2** also **but·toned-down** \-t²n,da u̇n\ : conservatively traditional or conventional; esp : adhering to conventional ideals in dress and behavior ⟨~ businessmen⟩

²**button-down** n (1952) : a shirt with a button-down collar

but·toned-up \'bə-tən-'dəp\ adj (1936) : coldly reserved or standoffish

¹**but·ton·hole** \'bə-t²n-,hōl\ n (1561) **1** : a slit or loop through which a button is passed **2** chiefly Brit : BOUTONNIERE

²**buttonhole** vt (1828) **1** : to furnish with buttonholes **2** : to work with buttonhole stitch — **but·ton·hol·er** \-,hō-lər\ n

³**buttonhole** vt [alter. of *buttonhold*] (1862) : to detain in conversation by or as if by holding on to the outer garments of another

buttonhole stitch n (ca. 1885) : a closely worked loop stitch used to make a firm edge (as on a buttonhole)

but·ton·hook \'bə-t²n-,hu̇k\ n (1870) **1** : a hook for drawing small buttons through buttonholes **2** : an offensive play in football in which the pass receiver runs straight downfield and then abruptly cuts back toward the line of scrimmage — **buttonhook** vi

button man n [perh. fr. *buttons* bellhop] (1966) : a low-ranking member of a criminal underworld organization

button mushroom n (1865) : a small cultivated mushroom (*Agaricus bisporus* syn. *A. brunnescens*)

button quail n (1885) : any of a family (Turnicidae) of small terrestrial Old World birds that resemble quails and have only three toes on a foot with the hind toe being absent

button snakeroot n (1775) **1** : BLAZING STAR 2a **2** : any of several usu. prickly herbs (genus *Eryngium*) of the carrot family

but·ton·wood \'bə-t²n-,wu̇d\ n (1674) : ²PLANE

¹**but·tress** \'bə-trəs\ n [ME *butres*, fr. MF *bouterez*, fr. OF *boterez*, fr. *boter* — more at BUTT] (14c) **1** : a projecting structure of masonry or wood for supporting or giving stability to a wall or building **2** : something that resembles a buttress: as **a** : a projecting part of a mountain or hill **b** : a horny protuberance on a horse's hoof at the heel — see HOOF illustration **c** : the broadened base of a tree trunk or a thickened vertical part of it **3** : something that supports or strengthens ⟨a ~ of the cause of peace⟩ — **but·tressed** \-trəst\ adj

²**buttress** vt (14c) : to furnish or shore up with a buttress; also : SUPPORT, STRENGTHEN ⟨arguments ~ed by solid facts⟩

butt shaft n (1588) : a target arrow without a barb

butt·stock \'bət-,stäk\ n (ca. 1909) : the stock of a firearm in the rear of the breech mechanism

butt weld n (ca. 1864) : a butt joint made by welding — **butt–weld** vt

but·ty \'bə-tē\ n, pl **butties** [origin unknown] (ca. 1790) chiefly Brit : a fellow worker : CHUM, PARTNER

bu·tut \bü-'tüt\ n, pl **bututs** or **butut** [Wolof] (1972) — see *dalasi* at MONEY table

bu·tyl \'byü-t²l\ n [ISV *butyric* + -*yl*] (1869) : any of four isomeric univalent radicals C₄H₉ derived from butanes

butyl alcohol n (ca. 1871) : any of four flammable alcohols C₄H₉OH (as butanol) used in organic synthesis and as solvents

bu·tyl·at·ed \'byü-t²l-,ā-təd\ adj (1942) : combined with the butyl group — **bu·tyl·a·tion** \,byü-t²l-'ā-shən\ n

butylated hy·droxy·an·i·sole \-(,)hī-,dräk-sē-'a-nə-,sōl\ n [*hydroxy* + *anise* + -*ole*] (1950) : BHA

butylated hy·droxy·tol·u·ene \-'täl-yə-,wēn\ n (1961) : BHT

bu·tyl·ene \'byü-t²l-,ēn\ n (1877) : any of three isomeric hydrocarbons C₄H₈ of the ethylene series obtained usu. by cracking petroleum

butyl rubber n (1940) : any of a class of synthetic rubbers that are made by copolymerizing isobutylene with a small amount usu. of isoprene at low temperature

butyr- or **butyro-** comb form [ISV, fr. *butyric*] : butyric ⟨*butyr*aldehyde⟩

bu·tyr·al·de·hyde \,byü-tə-'ral-də-,hīd\ n [ISV] (ca. 1885) : either of two aldehydes C₄H₈O used esp. in making synthetic resins

bu·ty·rate \'byü-tə-,rāt\ n (1873) : a salt or ester of butyric acid

bu·tyr·ic \byü-'tir-ik\ adj [F *butyrique*, fr. L *butyrum* butter — more at BUTTER] (1854) : relating to or producing butyric acid ⟨~ fermentation⟩

butyric acid n (1826) : either of two isomeric fatty acids C₄H₈O₂; esp : an acid of unpleasant odor normally found in perspiration and rancid butter

bu·ty·ro·phe·none \,byü-tə-(,)rō-fə-'nōn\ n [*butyr-* + *phen-* + -*one*] (1970) : any of a class of neuroleptic drugs (as haloperidol) used esp. in the treatment of schizophrenia

bux·om \'bək-səm\ adj [ME *buxsum*, fr. (assumed) OE *bûhsum*; akin to OE *bûgan* to bend — more at BOW] (14c) **1** obs **a** : OBEDIENT, TRACTABLE **b** : offering little resistance : FLEXIBLE, PLIANT ⟨wing silently the ~ air —John Milton⟩ **2** archaic : full of gaiety : BLITHE **3** : vigorously or healthily plump; specif : full-bosomed — **bux·om·ly** adv — **bux·om·ness** n

¹**buy** \'bī\ vb **bought** \'bȯt\; **buy·ing** [ME *byen*, fr. OE *bycgan*; akin to Goth *bugjan* to buy] vt (bef. 12c) **1** : to acquire possession, ownership, or rights to the use or services of by payment esp. of money : PURCHASE **2 a** : to obtain in exchange for something often at a sacrifice ⟨they *bought* peace with their freedom⟩ **b** : REDEEM 6 **3** : BRIBE, HIRE **4** : to be the purchasing equivalent of ⟨the dollar ~s less today than it used to⟩ **5** : ACCEPT, BELIEVE ⟨I don't ~ that hooey⟩ ~ vi : to make a purchase — **buy·er** \'bī(-ə)r\ n — **buy it** or **buy the farm** : to be killed : DIE — **buy time** : to delay an imminent action or decision : STALL

²**buy** n (1879) **1** : something of value at a favorable price; esp : BARGAIN ⟨it's a real ~ at that price⟩ **2** : an act of buying : PURCHASE

buy·back \'bī-,bak\ n (1974) : the act or an instance of buying something back; esp : the repurchase by a corporation of shares of its own common stock on the open market

buyer's market n (1926) : a market in which goods are plentiful, buyers have a wide range of choice, and prices tend to be low — compare SELLER'S MARKET

buy off vt (1629) **1** : to induce to refrain (as from prosecution) by a payment or other consideration **2** : to free (as from military service) by payment

buy·out \'bī-,au̇t\ n (1971) : an act or instance of buying out

buy out vt (1644) **1** : to purchase the share or interest of **2** : to purchase the entire stock-in-trade and the goodwill of (a business)

buy up vt (ca. 1534) **1** : to buy freely or extensively **2** : to buy the entire available supply of

¹**buzz** \'bəz\ vb [ME *bussen*, of imit. origin] vi (14c) **1** : to make a low continuous humming sound like that of a bee **2 a** : MURMUR, WHISPER **b** : to be filled with a confused murmur ⟨the room ~ed with excitement⟩ **3** : to make a signal with a buzzer **4** : to go quickly : HURRY ⟨~ed around town in a sports car⟩; also : SCRAM — usu. used with *off* ~ vt **1** : to utter covertly by or as if by whispering **2** : to cause to buzz **3** : to fly fast and close to ⟨planes ~ the crowd⟩ **4** : to summon or signal with a buzzer **5** dial Eng : to drink to the last drop ⟨get some more port whilst I ~ this bottle —W. M. Thackeray⟩

²**buzz** n (1605) **1** : a persistent vibratory sound **2 a** : RUMOR, GOSSIP **b** : a confused murmur **c** : a flurry of activity **d** : FAD, CRAZE **3 a** : signal conveyed by buzzer; specif : a telephone call **4** : HIGH 4

buz·zard \'bə-zərd\ n [ME *busard*, fr. OF, alter. of *buison*, fr. L *buteon-, buteo* hawk] (14c) **1** chiefly Brit : BUTEO **2** : any of various usu. large birds of prey (as the turkey vulture) **3** : a contemptible or rapacious person

buzz bomb n (1944) : an unguided jet-propelled missile used by the Germans against England in World War II

buzz cut *n* (1983) : CREW CUT
buzz•er \'bə-zər\ *n* (1606) **1** : one that buzzes; *specif* : an electric signaling device that makes a buzzing sound **2** : the sound of a buzzer
buzz saw *n* (1858) : CIRCULAR SAW
buzz•word \'bəz-,wərd\ *n* (1946) **1** : an important-sounding usu. technical word or phrase often of little meaning used chiefly to impress laymen **2** : a voguish word or phrase — called also *buzz phrase*
BVD \,bē-(,)vē-'dē\ *trademark* — used for underwear
B vitamin *n* (1920) : any vitamin of the vitamin B complex
bwa•na \'bwä-nə\ *n* [Swahili, fr. Ar *abūna* our father] (1878) : MASTER, BOSS
¹by \'bī, *before consonants also* bə\ *prep* [ME, prep. & adv., fr. OE, prep., *be, bī*; akin to OHG *bī* by, near, L *ambi-* on both sides, around, Gk *amphi*] (bef. 12c) **1** : in proximity to : NEAR ⟨standing ∼ the window⟩ **2 a** : through or through the medium of : VIA ⟨enter ∼ the door⟩ **b** : in the direction of : TOWARD ⟨north ∼ east⟩ **c** : into the vicinity of and beyond : PAST ⟨went right ∼ him⟩ **3 a** : during the course of ⟨studied ∼ night⟩ **b** : not later than ⟨∼ 2 p.m.⟩ **4 a** : through the agency or instrumentality of ⟨∼ force⟩ **b** : born or begot of **c** : sired or borne by **5** : with the witness or sanction of ⟨swear ∼ all that is holy⟩ **6 a** : in conformity with ⟨acted ∼ the rules⟩ **b** : ACCORDING TO ⟨called her ∼ name⟩ **7 a** : on behalf of ⟨did right ∼ his children⟩ **b** : with respect to ⟨a lawyer ∼ profession⟩ **8 a** : in or to the amount or extent of ⟨win ∼ a nose⟩ **b** *chiefly Scot* : in comparison with : BESIDE **9** — used as a function word to indicate successive units or increments ⟨little ∼ little⟩ ⟨walk two ∼ two⟩ **10** — used as a function word in multiplication, in division, and in measurements ⟨divide *a* ∼ *b*⟩ ⟨multiply 10 ∼ 4⟩ ⟨a room 15 feet ∼ 20 feet⟩ **11** : in the opinion of ⟨okay ∼ me⟩ — **by the by** *or* **by the bye** : INCIDENTALLY 2
²by \'bī\ *adv* (bef. 12c) **1 a** : close at hand : NEAR **b** : at or to another's home ⟨stop ∼⟩ **2** : PAST ⟨saw him go ∼⟩ **3** : ASIDE, AWAY
³by *or* **bye** \'bī\ *adj* (14c) **1** : being off the main route : SIDE **2** : INCIDENTAL
⁴by *or* **bye** \'bī\ *n, pl* **byes** \'bīz\ (1567) : something of secondary importance : a side issue
⁵by *or* **bye** \'bī\ *interj* [short for *goodbye*] (1709) — used to express farewell; often used with following *now*
by–and–by \,bī-ən-'bī\ *n* (1591) : a future time or occasion
by and by *adv* (1526) : before long : SOON
by and large *adv* (1706) : on the whole : in general
by–blow \'bī-,blō\ *n* (1594) **1** : an indirect blow **2** : an illegitimate child
bye \'bī\ *n* [alter. of ²*by*] (1883) : the position of a participant in a tournament who advances to the next round without playing
¹bye–bye *or* **by–by** \'bī-,bī, bī-'bī\ *interj* [baby-talk redupl. of *goodbye*] (ca. 1736) — used to express farewell
²bye–bye *or* **by–by** \'bī-,bī\ *adv* (1917) : out esp. for a walk or ride — used with the verb *go*
³bye–bye *or* **by–by** \'bī-,bī\ *n* (1867) : BED, SLEEP ⟨lie down . . . and go to ∼ —Rudyard Kipling⟩
⁴bye–bye *or* **by–by** \'bī-,bī\ *adv* (1920) : to bed or sleep — used with the verb *go*
by–elec•tion *also* **bye–election** \'bī-ə-,lek-shən\ *n* (1880) : a special election held between regular elections in order to fill a vacancy
by•gone \'bī-,gòn *also* -,gän\ *adj* (15c) : gone by : PAST; *esp* : OUTMODED — **bygone** *n*
by•law *or* **bye•law** \'bī-,lò\ *n* [ME *bilawe*, prob. fr. (assumed) ON *bȳlog*, fr. ON *bȳr* town + *lǫg* law] (14c) **1** : a rule adopted by an organization chiefly for the government of its members and the regulation of its affairs **2** : a local ordinance
¹by•line \'bī-,līn\ *n* (1916) **1** : a secondary line : SIDELINE **2** : a line at the beginning of a news story, magazine article, or book giving the writer's name
²byline *vt* (1938) : to write (an article) under a byline — **by•lin•er** \-,lī-nər\ *n*
by–name \'bī-,nām\ *n* (14c) **1** : a secondary name **2** : NICKNAME
¹by•pass \'bī-,pas\ *n* (1848) **1** : a passage to one side; *esp* : a deflected route usu. around a town **2 a** : a channel carrying a fluid around a part and back to the main stream **b** (1) : SHUNT 1b (2) : SHUNT 1c; *also* : a surgical procedure for the establishment of a shunt ⟨have a coronary ∼⟩
²bypass *vt* (1886) **1 a** : to avoid by means of a bypass **b** : to cause to follow a bypass **2 a** : to neglect or ignore usu. intentionally **b** : CIRCUMVENT
by•past \'bī-,past\ *adj* (15c) : BYGONE
by•path \-,path, -,páth\ *n* (14c) : BYWAY
by•play \-,plā\ *n* (1812) : action engaged in on the side while the main action proceeds (as during a dramatic production)
by–prod•uct \-,prä-(,)dəkt\ *n* (1857) **1** : something produced in a usu. industrial or biological process in addition to the principal product **2** : a secondary and sometimes unexpected or unintended result ⟨unpleasant ∼s of civilization⟩
byre \'bīr\ *n* [ME, fr. OE *bȳre*; akin to OE *būr* dwelling — more at BOWER] (bef. 12c) *chiefly Brit* : a cow barn
by•road \'bī-,rōd\ *n* (1673) : BYWAY
bys•si•no•sis \,bi-sə-'nō-səs\ *n, pl* **-no•ses** \-,sēz\ [NL, fr. L *byssinus* of fine linen, fr. Gk *byssinos*, fr. L *byssos*] (1881) : an occupational respiratory disease associated with inhalation of cotton, flax, or hemp dust and characterized initially by chest tightness, shortness of breath, and cough and eventually by irreversible lung disease
bys•sus \'bi-səs\ *n, pl* **bys•sus•es** *or* **bys•si** \-,sī, -(,)sē\ [ME *bissus*, fr. L *byssus*, fr. Gk *byssos* flax, of Sem origin; akin to Heb *būṣ* linen cloth] (14c) **1** : a fine prob. linen cloth of ancient times **2** [NL, fr. L]: a tuft of long tough filaments by which some bivalve mollusks (as mussels) adhere to a surface
by•stand•er \'bī-,stan-dər\ *n* (ca. 1619) : one present but not taking part in a situation or event : a chance spectator
by•street \-,strēt\ *n* (1672) : a street off a main thoroughfare
byte \'bīt\ *n* [perh. alter. of ²*bite*] (1959) : a group of eight binary digits processed as a unit by a computer and used esp. to represent an alphanumeric character — compare WORD 2c
by•way \'bī-,wā\ *n* (14c) **1** : a little traveled side road **2** : a secondary or little known aspect or field ⟨meandering more and more in the fascinating ∼s of learning —*Times Lit. Supp.*⟩
by•word \-,wərd\ *n* (bef. 12c) **1** : a proverbial saying : PROVERB **2 a** : one that personifies a type **b** : one that is noteworthy or notorious **3** : EPITHET **4** : a frequently used word or phrase
by–your–leave \,bī-yər-'lēv\ *n* (1914) : a request for permission ⟨imposed . . . without so much as a ∼ —J. L. Granatstein⟩
¹Byz•an•tine \'bi-zⁿn-,tēn, 'bi-, -,tīn; bə-'zan-,, bī-'\ *adj* (1794) **1** : of, relating to, or characteristic of the ancient city of Byzantium **2** : of, relating to, or having the characteristics of a style of architecture developed in the Byzantine Empire esp. in the 5th and 6th centuries featuring the dome carried on pendentives over a square and incrustation with marble veneering and with colored mosaics on grounds of gold **3** : of or relating to the churches using a traditional Greek rite and subject to Eastern canon law **4** *often not cap* **a** : of, relating to, or characterized by a devious and usu. surreptitious manner of operation ⟨a ∼ power struggle⟩ **b** : intricately involved : LABYRINTHINE ⟨rules of ∼ complexity⟩
²Byzantine *n* (1836) : a native or inhabitant of Byzantium
By•zan•tin•ist \bi-'zan-ti-nist, bī-\ *n* (1892) : a student of Byzantine culture

\ə\ abut \ᵊ\ kitten, F table \ər\ further \a\ ash \ā\ ace \ä\ mop, mar \aù\ out \ch\ chin \e\ bet \ē\ easy \g\ go \i\ hit \ī\ ice \j\ job \ŋ\ sing \ō\ go \ò\ law \òi\ boy \th\ thin \t͟h\ the \ü\ loot \ù\ foot \y\ yet \zh\ vision \à, k̲, ⁿ, œ, ȫ, ᵫ, ū̇, ʸ\ see Guide to Pronunciation

c \'sē\ *n, pl* **c's** *or* **cs** \'sēz\ *often cap, often attrib* **1 a** : the 3rd letter of the English alphabet **b** : a graphic representation of this letter **c** : a speech counterpart of orthographic *c* **2 a** : one hundred — see NUMBER table **b** *slang* : a sum of $100 **3** : the keynote of a C-major scale **4** : a graphic device for reproducing the letter *c* **5** : one designated *c* esp. as the 3rd in order or class **6 a** : a grade rating a student's work as fair or mediocre in quality **b** : one graded or rated with a C **7** : something shaped like the letter C **8** : a structured programming language designed to produce a compact and efficient translation of a program into machine language

ca' \'kȯ, 'kä\ *Scot var of* CALL

¹cab \'kab, 'käb\ *n* [Heb *qabh*] (1535) : an ancient Hebrew unit of capacity equal to about two quarts (2.2 liters)

²cab \'kab\ *n* [short for *cabriolet*] (1827) **1 a** (1) : CABRIOLET (2) : a similar light closed carriage (as a hansom) **b** : a carriage for hire **2** : TAXICAB **3** [short for *cabin*] **a** : the part of a locomotive that houses the engineer and operating controls **b** : a comparable shelter (as on a truck) housing operating controls

¹ca·bal \kə-'bäl, -'bal\ *n* [F *cabale* cabala, intrigue, cabal, fr. ML *cabbala* cabala, fr. LHeb *qabbālāh*, received (lore)] (1614) : the artifices and intrigues of a group of persons secretly united to bring about an overturn or usurpation esp. in public affairs; *also* : a group engaged in such artifices and intrigues *syn* see PLOT

²cabal *vi* **ca·balled; ca·bal·ling** (1680) : to unite in or form a cabal

ca·ba·la *or* **cab·ba·la** *or* **cab·ba·lah** \kə-'bä-lə, 'ka-bə-lə\ *n, often cap* [ML *cabbala*] (1521) **1** : a medieval and modern system of Jewish theosophy, mysticism, and thaumaturgy marked by belief in creation through emanation and a cipher method of interpreting Scripture **2 a** : a traditional, esoteric, occult, or secret matter **b** : esoteric doctrine or mysterious art — **cab·ba·lism** \'ka-bə-,li-zəm, 'ka-\ *n* — **cab·ba·lis·tic** \,kä-bə-'lis-tik, ,ka-\ *adj*

ca·ba·let·ta \,ka-bə-'le-tə, ,kä-\ *n* [It] (1842) **1** : an operatic song in simple popular style characterized by a uniform rhythm **2** : the lively bravura concluding section of an extended aria or duet

¹ca·ba·list \'ka-bä-list, 'ka-bə-\ *n* (ca. 1533) **1** *often cap* : a student, interpreter, or devotee of the Jewish cabala **2** : one skilled in esoteric doctrine or mysterious art

²cab·al·ist \kə-'ba-list, -'bä-\ *n* (1569) : a member of a cabal

ca·bal·le·ro \,ka-bə-'ler-(,)ō, -bə(l)-'yer-\ *n, pl* **-ros** [Sp, fr. LL *caballarius* hostler — more at CAVALIER] (1749) **1** : KNIGHT, CAVALIER **2** *chiefly Southwest* : HORSEMAN

ca·bana \kə-'ban-yə, -'ba-nə\ *n* [Sp *cabaña*, lit., hut, fr. ML *capanna*] (1890) **1** : a shelter resembling a cabin usu. with an open side facing a beach or swimming pool **2** : a lightweight structure with living facilities

cab·a·ret \,ka-bə-'rä, 'ka-bə-,\ *n* [F, fr. ONF] (1655) **1** *archaic* : a shop selling wines and liquors **2 a** : a restaurant serving liquor and providing entertainment (as by singers or dancers) : NIGHTCLUB **b** : the show provided at a cabaret

¹cab·bage \'ka-bij\ *n, often attrib* [ME *caboche*, fr. ONF, head] (15c) **1** : a leafy garden plant (*Brassica oleracea capitata*) of European origin with a short stem and a dense globular head of usu. green leaves that is used as a vegetable **2** *slang* : PAPER MONEY, BANKNOTES

²cabbage *n* [perh. by folk etymology fr. MF *cabas* cheating, theft] (1663) *Brit* : pieces of cloth left in cutting out garments and traditionally kept by tailors as perquisites

³cabbage *vt* **cab·baged; cab·bag·ing** (1712) : STEAL, FILCH

cabbage butterfly *n* (1816) : any of several largely white butterflies (family Pieridae) whose green larvae are cabbageworms; *esp* : a small cosmopolitan butterfly (*Pieris rapae* syn. *Artogeia rapae*) that is a pest on cabbage — called also *cabbage white*

cabbage looper *n* (ca. 1902) : a noctuid moth (*Trichoplusia ni*) having pale green white-striped larvae that feed on cruciferous plants (as the cabbage)

cabbage palm *n* (ca. 1784) : a palm with terminal buds eaten as a vegetable

cabbage palmetto *n* (1802) : a cabbage palm (*Sabal palmetto*) with fan-shaped leaves that is native to coastal southeastern U.S. and the Bahamas

cabbage butterfly: 1 larva, 2 adult

cabbage rose *n* (1795) : a fragrant garden rose (*Rosa centifolia*) with upright branches and large pink flowers

cab·bage·worm \'ka-bij-,wərm\ *n* (1688) : an insect larva (as of a cabbage butterfly) that feeds on cabbages

cab·bie *or* **cab·by** \'ka-bē\ *n, pl* **cabbies** (1859) : CABDRIVER

cab·driv·er \'kab-,drī-vər\ *n* (1830) : a driver of a cab

ca·ber \'kä-bər, 'kā-\ *n* [ScGael *cabar*] (1505) : POLE; *esp* : a young tree trunk used for tossing as a trial of strength in a Scottish sport

cab·er·net sau·vi·gnon \,ka-bər-'nā-sō-vē-'nyōⁿ\ *n, often cap C&S* [F] (1941) : a dry red wine made from a single widely cultivated variety of black grape — called also *cabernet*

¹cab·in \'ka-bən\ *n* [ME *cabane*, fr. MF, fr. OProv *cabana* hut, fr. ML *capanna*] (14c) **1 a** (1) : a private room on a ship or boat (2) : a compartment below deck on a boat used for living accommodations **b** : the passenger or cargo compartment of a vehicle (as an airplane or automobile) **c** : the crew compartment of an exploratory vehicle (as a spacecraft) **2** : a small one-story dwelling usu. of simple construction **3** *chiefly Brit* : CAB 3

²cabin *vi* (1586) : to live in or as if in a cabin ∼ *vt* : CONFINE

cabin boy *n* (1726) : a boy working as servant on a ship

cabin car *n* (1879) : CABOOSE

cabin class *n* (1929) : a class of accommodations on a passenger ship superior to tourist class and inferior to first class

cabin cruiser *n* (1921) : CRUISER 1b

¹cab·i·net \'kab-nit, 'ka-bə-\ *n* [MF, small room, dim. of ONF *cabine* gambling house] (ca. 1550) **1 a** : a case or cupboard usu. having doors and shelves **b** : a collection of specimens esp. of biological or numismatic interest **c** : CONSOLE 4a **d** : a chamber having tempera-

ture and humidity controls and used esp. for incubating biological samples **2 a** *archaic* : a small room providing seclusion **b** : a small exhibition room in a museum **3 a** *archaic* (1) : the private room serving as council chamber of the chief councillors or ministers of a sovereign (2) : the consultations and actions of these councillors **b** (1) *often cap* : a body of advisers of a head of state (2) : a similar advisory council of a governor of a state or a mayor **c** *Brit* : a meeting of a cabinet

²cabinet *adj* (1631) **1** : of or relating to a governmental cabinet **2** : suitable by reason of size for a small room or by reason of attractiveness or perfection for preservation and display in a cabinet **3 a** : used or adapted for cabinetmaking **b** : done or used by a cabinetmaker

cab·i·net·mak·er \-,mā-kər\ *n* (1681) : a skilled woodworker who makes fine furniture — **cab·i·net·mak·ing** \-,mā-kiŋ\ *n*

cab·i·net·ry \'kab-ni-trē, 'ka-bə-\ *n* (1926) : CABINETWORK; *also* : CABINETS ⟨kitchen ∼⟩

cab·i·net·work \-,wərk\ *n* (1732) : finished woodwork made by a cabinetmaker

cabin fever *n* (1918) : extreme irritability and restlessness from living in isolation or a confined indoor area for a prolonged time

¹ca·ble \'kā-bəl\ *n, often attrib* [ME, fr. ONF, fr. ML *capulum* lasso, fr. L *capere* to take — more at HEAVE] (13c) **1 a** : a strong rope esp. of 10 inches (25 centimeters) or more in circumference **b** : a cable-laid rope **c** : a wire rope or metal chain of great tensile strength **d** : a wire or wire rope by which force is exerted to control or operate a mechanism **2** : CABLE LENGTH **3 a** : an assembly of electrical conductors insulated from each other but laid up together usu. by being twisted around a central core **b** : CABLEGRAM; *also* : a radio message or telegram **4** : something resembling or fashioned like a cable ⟨a fiber-optic ∼⟩ **5** : CABLE TELEVISION

²cable *vb* **ca·bled; ca·bling** \'kā-b(ə-)liŋ\ *vt* (ca. 1500) **1** : to fasten with or as if with a cable **2** : to provide with cables **3** : to telegraph by submarine cable **4** : to make into a cable or into a form resembling a cable ∼ *vi* : to communicate by a submarine cable

cable car *n* (1887) : a vehicle moved by an endless cable: **a** : one suspended from an overhead cable **b** : one that moves along tracks

ca·ble·gram \'kā-bəl-,gram\ *n* (1868) : a message sent by a submarine telegraph cable

ca·ble-laid \'kā-bəl-'lād\ *adj* (1723) : composed of three ropes laid together left-handed with each containing three strands twisted together

cable length *n* (1555) : a maritime unit of length variously reckoned as 100 fathoms, 120 fathoms, or 608 feet

cable television *n* (1965) : a system of television reception in which signals from distant stations are picked up by a master antenna and sent by cable to the individual receivers of paying subscribers — called also *cable TV*

ca·ble·way \'kā-bəl-,wā\ *n* (1899) : a suspended cable used as a track along which carriers can be pulled

cab·man \'kab-mən\ *n* (1834) : CABDRIVER

cab·o·chon \'ka-bə-,shän\ *n* [MF, dim. of ONF *caboche* head] (1578) : a gem or bead cut in convex form and highly polished but not faceted; *also* : this style of cutting — **cabochon** *adv*

ca·boo·dle \kə-'bü-dᵊl\ *n* [prob. fr. *ca-* (intensive prefix) + *boodle*] (ca. 1848) : COLLECTION, LOT ⟨sell the whole ∼⟩

ca·boose \kə-'büs\ *n* [prob. fr. D *kabuis*, fr. MLG *kabūse*] (1769) **1** : a ship's galley **2** : a freight-train car attached usu. to the rear mainly for the use of the train crew **3** : one that follows or brings up the rear

cab·o·tage \'ka-bə-,täzh\ *n* [F, fr. *caboter* to sail along the coast] (1831) **1** : trade or transport in coastal waters or airspace or between two points within a country **2** : the right to engage in cabotage

ca·bret·ta \kə-'bre-tə\ *n* [modif. of Pg and Sp *cabra* goat] (1926) : a light soft leather from skins of hairy sheep

ca·bril·la \kə-'brē-ə, -'brē-yə\ *n* [Sp, dim. of *cabra* goat, fr. L *capra* she-goat, fem. of *caper* he-goat — more at CAPRIOLE] (1859) : any of various sea basses (esp. of the genera *Epinephelus* and *Paralabrax*) of the Mediterranean, the California coast, and the warmer parts of the western Atlantic

cab·ri·ole \'ka-brē-,ōl\ *n* [F, caper] (ca. 1797) **1** : a ballet leap in which one leg is extended in midair and the other struck against it **2** : a curved furniture leg ending in an ornamental foot

cab·ri·o·let \,ka-brē-ə-'lā\ *n* [F, fr. dim. of *cabriole* caper, alter. of MF *capriole*] (1763) **1** : a light 2-wheeled one-horse carriage with a folding leather hood, a large apron, and upward-curving shafts **2** : a convertible coupe

cab·stand \'kab-,stand\ *n* (1848) : a place where cabs await hire

cac- *or* **caco-** *comb form* [NL, fr. Gk *kak-, kako-*, fr. *kakos* bad] : bad ⟨*cacography*⟩

ca' can·ny \kȯ-'ka-nē\ *n* [Sc, vb., to proceed cautiously, fr. *ca'* ('call) + *canny* careful] (1895) *Brit* : SLOWDOWN — **ca' canny** *vi, Brit*

ca·cao \kə-'kau̇, kə-'kā-(,)ō\ *n, pl* **cacaos** [Sp, fr. Nahuatl *cacahuatl* cacao beans] (1555) **1** : the dried partly fermented fatty seeds of a So. American evergreen tree (*Theobroma cacao* of the family Sterculiaceae) that are used in making cocoa, chocolate, and cocoa butter — called also *cacao bean, cocoa bean* **2** : a tree having small yellowish flowers followed by fleshy pods with many seeds that bears cacao

cacao butter *var of* COCOA BUTTER

cac·cia·to·re \,kä-chə-'tȯr-ē, -'tȯr-\ *adj* [It, fr. *cacciatore* hunter] (1942) : cooked with tomatoes and herbs and sometimes wine ⟨chicken ∼⟩

cach·a·lot \'ka-shə-,lät, -,lō\ *n* [F] (1747) : SPERM WHALE

¹cache \'kash\ *n* [F, fr. *cacher* to press, hide, fr. (assumed) VL *coacticare* to press together, fr. L *coactare* to compel, freq. of *cogere* to compel — more at COGENT] (1797) **1 a** : a hiding place esp. for concealing and preserving provisions or implements **b** : a secure place of storage **2** : something hidden or stored in a cache **3** : a computer memory with very short access time used for storage of frequently used instructions or data — called also *cache memory*

²cache *vt* **cached; cach·ing** (1805) : to place, hide, or store in a cache

ca·chec·tic \ka-'kek-tik, ka-\ *adj* [F *cachectique*, fr. L *cachecticus*, fr. Gk *kachektikos*, fr. *kak-* + *echein*] (1634) : affected by cachexia

cache·pot \'kash-,pät, 'kash-,pō, 'ka-shə-\ *n* [F, fr. *cacher* to hide + *pot* pot] (1872) : an ornamental receptacle to hold and usu. to conceal a flowerpot

ca·chet \ka-'shā\ *n* [F, fr. *cacher*] (ca. 1639) **1 a :** a seal used esp. as a mark of official approval **b :** an indication of approval carrying great prestige **2 a :** a characteristic feature or quality conferring prestige **b :** PRESTIGE ⟨being rich . . . doesn't have the ~ it used to — Truman Capote⟩ **3 :** a medicinal preparation for swallowing consisting of a case usu. of rice-flour paste enclosing a medicine **4 a :** a design or inscription on an envelope to commemorate a postal or philatelic event **b :** an advertisement forming part of a postage meter impression **c :** a motto or slogan included in a postal cancellation

ca·chex·ia \ka-'kek-sē-ə, ka-\ *n* [LL *cachexia*, fr. Gk *kachexia* bad condition, fr. *kak-* cac- + *hexis* condition, fr. *echein* to have, be disposed — more at SCHEME] (1541) **:** general physical wasting and malnutrition usu. associated with chronic disease

cach·in·nate \'ka-kə-ˌnāt\ *vi* **-nat·ed; -nat·ing** [L *cachinnatus,* pp. of *cachinnare,* of imit. origin] (1824) **:** to laugh loudly or immoderately — **cach·in·na·tion** \ˌka-kə-'nā-shən\ *n*

ca·chou \ka-'shü, 'ka-,\ *n* [F, fr. Pg *cachu,* fr. Malayalam *kāccu*] (ca. 1879) **:** a pill or pastille used to sweeten the breath

ca·cique \kə-'sēk\ *n* [Sp, fr. Taino, chief] (1555) **1 :** a native Indian chief in areas dominated primarily by a Spanish culture **2 :** a local political boss in Spain and Latin America — **ca·ciqu·ism** \-'sē-ˌki-zəm\ *n*

cack·le \'ka-kəl\ *vi* **cack·led; cack·ling** \-k(ə-)liŋ\ [ME *cakelen,* of imit. origin] (13c) **1 :** to make the sharp broken noise or cry characteristic of a hen esp. after laying **2 :** to laugh esp. in a harsh or sharp manner **3 :** CHATTER — **cackle** *n* — **cack·ler** \-k(ə-)lər\ *n*

caco·de·mon \ˌka-kə-'dē-mən\ *n* [Gk *kakodaimōn,* fr. *kak-* cac- + *daimōn* spirit] (1594) **:** DEMON — **caco·de·mon·ic** \-di-'mä-nik\ *adj*

cacodylic acid \ˌka-kə-'di-lik-\ *n* [G *Kakodyl* the radical As(CH₃)₂, fr. Gk *kakōdēs* foul-smelling, fr. *kak-* + *-ōdēs* (akin to Gk *ozein* to smell) — more at ODOR] (1850) **:** a toxic crystalline compound of arsenic C₂H₇AsO₂ used esp. as an herbicide

caco·ë·thes \ˌka-kə-'wē-(ˌ)thēz\ *n* [L, fr. Gk *kakoēthes* wickedness, fr. neut. of *kakoēthēs* malignant, fr. *kak-* cac- + *ēthos* character — more at SIB] (ca. 1587): an insatiable desire : MANIA

ca·cog·ra·phy \ka-'kä-grə-fē\ *n* (1580) **1 :** bad spelling — compare ORTHOGRAPHY **2 :** bad handwriting — compare CALLIGRAPHY — **caco·graph·i·cal** \ˌka-kə-'gra-fi-kəl\ *adj*

cac·o·mis·tle \'ka-kə-ˌmi-səl, ˌka-kə-'mis(t)-lē\ *n* [MexSp, fr. Nahuatl *tlahcomiztli,* fr. *tlahco* half + *miztli* mountain lion] (1869) **:** RINGTAIL 2

ca·coph·o·nous \ka-'kä-fə-nəs, -'kö- *also* -ka-\ *adj* [Gk *kakophōnos,* fr. *kak-* + *phōnē* voice, sound — more at BAN] (1797) **:** marked by cacophony **:** harsh-sounding — **ca·coph·o·nous·ly** *adv*

ca·coph·o·ny \-nē\ *n, pl* **-nies** (ca. 1656) **:** harsh or discordant sound **:** DISSONANCE 2; *specif* **:** harshness in the sound of words or phrases

cac·tus \'kak-təs\ *n, pl* **cac·ti** \-ˌtī, -(ˌ)tē\ *or* **cac·tus·es** *also* **cactus** [NL, genus name, fr. L, cardoon, fr. Gk *kaktos*] (1767) **:** any of a family (Cactaceae, the cactus family) of plants that have succulent stems and branches with scales or spines instead of leaves and are found esp. in dry areas (as deserts)

ca·cu·mi·nal \ka-'kyü-mə-nᵊl, kə-\ *adj* [ISV, fr. L *cacumin-, cacumen* top, point] (1862) **:** RETROFLEX 2

cad \'kad\ *n* [E dial., unskilled assistant, short for Sc *caddie*] (1833) **1 :** an omnibus conductor **2 :** a man who acts with deliberate disregard for another's feelings or rights

ca·das·tral \kə-'das-trəl\ *adj* (1858) **1 :** of or relating to a cadastre **2 :** showing or recording property boundaries, subdivision lines, buildings, and related details — **ca·das·tral·ly** \-trə-lē\ *adv*

ca·das·tre \kə-'das-tər\ *n* [F, fr. It *catastro,* fr. OIt *catastico,* fr. LGk *katastichon* notebook, fr. Gk *kata* by + *stichos* row, line — more at CATA-, DISTICH] (1804) **:** an official register of the quantity, value, and ownership of real estate used in apportioning taxes

ca·dav·er \kə-'da-vər\ *n* [L, fr. *cadere* to fall] (ca. 1500) **:** a dead body; *esp* **:** one intended for dissection — **ca·dav·er·ic** \-'dav-rik, -'da-və-\ *adj*

ca·dav·er·ine \kə-'da-və-ˌrēn\ *n* (1887) **:** a syrupy colorless poisonous ptomaine C₅H₁₄N₂ formed by decarboxylation of lysine esp. in putrefaction of flesh

ca·dav·er·ous \kə-'dav-rəs, -'da-vər-əs\ *adj* (1627) **1 a :** of or relating to a corpse **b :** suggestive of corpses or tombs **2 a :** PALLID, LIVID **b :** GAUNT, EMACIATED — **ca·dav·er·ous·ly** *adv*

cad·die *or* **cad·dy** \'ka-dē\ *n, pl* **caddies** [F *cadet* military cadet] (ca. 1730) **1** *Scot* **:** one that waits about for odd jobs **2 a :** one who assists a golfer esp. by carrying the clubs **b :** a wheeled device for conveying things not readily carried by hand — **caddie** *or* **caddy** *vi*

¹cad·dis *also* **cad·dice** \'ka-dəs\ *n* [ME *cadas* cotton wool, prob. fr. MF *cadaz,* fr. OProv *cadarz*] (1530) **:** worsted yarn; *specif* **:** a worsted ribbon or binding formerly used for garters and girdles

²caddis (1651) **:** CADDISWORM

caddis fly *n* (1787) **:** any of an order (Trichoptera) of insects with four membranous wings, vestigial mouthparts, slender many-jointed antennae, and aquatic larvae — compare CADDISWORM

cad·dish \'ka-dish\ *adj* (1868) **:** of, relating to, or resembling a cad — **cad·dish·ly** *adv* — **cad·dish·ness** *n*

cad·dis·worm \'ka-dəs-ˌwərm\ *n* [prob. alter. of obs. *codworm;* fr. the case or tube in which it lives] (1622) **:** the larva of a caddis fly that lives in and carries around a silken case covered with bits of debris

Cad·do \'ka-(ˌ)dō\ *n, pl* **Caddo** *or* **Caddos** (1805) **:** a member of a group of American Indian peoples of Louisiana, Arkansas, and eastern Texas

cad·dy \'ka-dē\ *n, pl* **caddies** [Malay *kati* catty] (1792) **1 :** a small box, can, or chest used esp. to keep tea in **2 :** a container or device for storing or holding objects when they are not in use

cade \'kād\ *adj* [E dial. *cade* pet lamb, fr. ME *cad*] (1551) **:** left by its mother and reared by hand : PET ⟨a ~ lamb⟩

-cade *n comb form* [*cavalcade*] **:** procession ⟨motor*cade*⟩

ca·delle \kə-'del\ *n* [F, fr. Prov *cadello,* fr. L *catella,* fem. of *catellus* little dog, dim. of *catulus* young animal] (ca. 1861) **:** a small cosmopolitan black beetle (*Tenebroides mauritanicus*) destructive to stored grain

ca·dence \'kā-dᵊn(t)s\ *n* [ME, fr. OIt *cadenza,* fr. *cadere* to fall, fr. L — more at CHANCE] (14c) **1 a :** a rhythmic sequence or flow of sounds in language **b :** the beat, time, or measure of rhythmical motion or activity **2 a :** a falling inflection of the voice **b :** a concluding and usu. falling strain; *specif* **:** a musical chord sequence moving to a harmonic close or point of rest and giving the sense of harmonic completion **3 :** the modulated and rhythmic recurrence of a sound esp. in nature — **ca·denced** \-dᵊn(t)st\ *adj* — **ca·den·tial** \kā-'den(t)-shəl\ *adj*

ca·den·cy \'kā-dᵊn(t)-sē\ *n, pl* **-cies** (1627) **:** CADENCE

ca·dent \'kā-dᵊnt\ *adj* [L *cadent-, cadens,* prp. of *cadere*] (1605) **1** *archaic* **:** being in the process of falling ⟨with ~ tears fret channels in her cheeks —Shak.⟩ **2 :** having rhythmic cadence

ca·den·za \kə-'den-zə\ *n* [It, cadence, cadenza] (1836) **1 :** a parenthetical flourish in an aria or other solo piece commonly just before a final or other important cadence **2 :** a technically brilliant sometimes improvised solo passage toward the close of a concerto **3 :** an exceptionally brilliant part of an artistic work

cade oil \'kād-\ *n* [*cade* juniper, fr. MF, fr. OProv, fr. ML *catanus*] (1880) **:** JUNIPER TAR

ca·det \kə-'det\ *n, often attrib* [F, fr. Gascon *capdet* chief, fr. LL *capitellum,* dim. of L *capit-, caput* head — more at HEAD] (1610) **1 a :** a younger brother or son **b :** youngest son **c :** a younger branch of a family or a member of it **2 :** one in training for a military or naval commission; *esp* **:** a student in a service academy **3** *slang* **:** PIMP — **ca·det·ship** \-ˌship\ *n*

Ca·dette \kə-'det\ *n* [fr. *cadet*] (1963) **:** a member of a program of the Girl Scouts for girls in the sixth through ninth grades in school

cadge \'kaj\ *vb* **cadged; cadg·ing** [back-formation fr. Sc *cadger* carrier, huckster, fr. ME *cadgear*] (ca. 1812) **:** BEG, SPONGE — **cadg·er** *n*

cad·mi·um \'kad-mē-əm\ *n* [NL, fr. L *cadmia* zinc oxide, fr. Gk *kadmeia,* lit., Theban (earth), fr. fem. of *kadmeios* Theban, fr. *Kadmos;* fr. the occurrence of its ores together with zinc oxide] (1822) **:** a bluish white malleable ductile toxic bivalent metallic element used esp. in protective platings and in bearing metals — see ELEMENT table

cadmium sulfide *n* (ca. 1893) **:** a yellow-brown poisonous salt CdS used esp. in electronic parts, in photoelectric cells, and in medicine

Cad·mus \'kad-məs\ *n* [L, fr. Gk *Kadmos*] **:** the legendary founder of Thebes

cad·re \'ka-ˌdrä, 'kä-, -drē; *esp Brit* 'käd-ə(r), 'kä-, -drə\ *n* [F, fr. It *quadro,* fr. L *quadrum* square — more at QUARREL] (1830) **1 :** FRAME, FRAMEWORK **2 :** a nucleus or core group esp. of trained personnel able to assume control and to train others; *broadly* **:** a group of people having some unifying relationship ⟨a ~ of lawyers⟩ **3 :** a cell of indoctrinated leaders active in promoting the interests of a revolutionary party **4 :** a member of a cadre

ca·du·ceus \kə-'dü-sē-əs, -'dyü-, -shəs\ *n, pl* **-cei** \-sē-ˌī\ [L, modif. of Gk *karykeion,* fr. *karyx, kēryx* herald; akin to Skt *kāru* singer] (1588) **1 :** the symbolic staff of a herald; *specif* **:** a representation of a staff with two entwined snakes and two wings at the top **2 :** an insignia bearing a caduceus and symbolizing a physician

ca·du·ci·ty \kə-'dü-sə-tē, -'dyü-\ *n* [F *caducité,* fr. *caduc* transitory, fr. L *caducus*] (1769) **1 :** SENILITY **2 :** the quality of being transitory or perishable

ca·du·cous \kə-'dü-kəs, -'dyü-\ *adj* [L *caducus* tending to fall, transitory, fr. *cadere* to fall — more at CHANCE] (1808) **:** falling off easily or before the usual time — used esp. of floral organs

cae·cal, cae·cum *var of* CECAL, CECUM

cae·ci·lian \si-'sil-yən, -'sēl-, -'si-lē-ən\ *n* [ultim. fr. L *caecilia* slowworm, fr. *caecus* blind] (ca. 1879) **:** any of an order (Gymnophiona) of chiefly tropical burrowing amphibians resembling worms — **caecilian** *adj*

Caer·phil·ly \kär-'fi-lē\ *n* [*Caerphilly,* urban district in Wales] (ca. 1893) **:** a mild white friable cheese of Welsh origin

Cae·sar \'sē-zər\ *n* [Gaius Julius *Caesar*] (1567) **1 :** any of the Roman emperors succeeding Augustus Caesar — used as a title **2 a** *often not cap* **:** a powerful ruler: (1) **:** EMPEROR (2) **:** AUTOCRAT, DICTATOR **b** [fr. the reference in Mt 22:21]: the civil power **:** a temporal ruler — **Cae·sar·e·an** *or* **Cae·sar·i·an** \si-'zar-ē-ən, -zer-\ *adj*

cae·sar·e·an *also* **cae·sar·i·an** *var of* CESAREAN

Cae·sar·ism \'sē-zə-ˌri-zəm\ *n* (1857) **:** imperial authority or system **:** political absolutism **:** DICTATORSHIP — **Cae·sar·ist** \-zə-rist\ *n*

Caesar salad *n* [*Caesar's,* restaurant in Tijuana, Mexico] (1950) **:** a tossed salad usu. made of romaine, garlic, anchovies, and croutons and dressed with olive oil, coddled egg, lemon juice, and grated cheese

caes·pi·tose \'ses-pə-ˌtōs\ *adj* [NL *caespitosus,* fr. L *caespit-, caespes* turf] (1830) **1 :** growing in clusters or tufts **2 :** forming a dense turf

cae·su·ra \si-'zyúr-ə, -'zhúr-\ *n, pl* **-suras** *or* **-su·rae** \-'zyúr-(ˌ)ē, -'zhúr-\ [LL, fr. L, act of cutting, fr. *caedere* to cut] (1556) **1** *in modern prosody* **:** a usu. rhetorical break in the flow of sound in the middle of a line of verse **2** *Greek & Latin prosody* **:** a break in the flow of sound in a verse caused by the ending of a word within a foot **3 :** BREAK, INTERRUPTION **4 :** a pause marking a rhythmic point of division in a melody — **cae·su·ral** \-'zyúr-əl, -'zhúr-\ *adj*

ca·fé *also* **ca·fe** \ka-'fā, kə-\ *n, often attrib* [F *café* coffee, café, fr. Turk *kahve* — more at COFFEE] (1802) **1 :** a usu. small and informal establishment serving various refreshments (as coffee); *broadly* **:** RESTAURANT **2 :** BARROOM **3 :** CABARET, NIGHTCLUB

ca·fé au lait \(ˌ)ka-ˌfā-ō-'lā\ *n* [F, coffee with milk] (1763) **1 :** coffee with usu. hot milk in about equal parts **2 :** the color of coffee with milk

ca·fé noir \-'nwär\ *n* [F, black coffee] (1841) **:** coffee without milk or cream; *also* **:** DEMITASSE

café society *n* (1937) **:** society of persons who are regular patrons of fashionable cafés

¹caf·e·te·ria \ˌka-fə-'tir-ē-ə\ *n* [AmerSp *cafetería* coffeehouse, fr. *cafetera* coffee maker, fr. F *cafetière,* fr. *café*] (1894) **:** a restaurant in which the customers serve themselves or are served at a counter and take the food to tables to eat

²cafeteria *adj* (1951) **:** providing a selection from which a choice may be made ⟨~ benefit plan⟩ ⟨a ~ curriculum⟩

\ə\ abut \ᵊ\ kitten, F table \ər\ further \a\ ash \ā\ ace \ä\ mop, mar \au̇\ out \ch\ chin \e\ bet \ē\ easy \g\ go \i\ hit \ī\ ice \j\ job \ŋ\ sing \ō\ go \ȯ\ law \ȯi\ boy \th\ thin \t̲h̲\ the \ü\ loot \u̇\ foot \y\ yet \zh\ vision \á, k̲, ⁿ, œ, œ̄, ᵫ, ᵬ, ᶌ\ see Guide to Pronunciation

caf·e·to·ri·um \-'tōr-ē-əm, -'tôr-\ *n* [blend of *cafeteria* and *auditorium*] (1952) : a large room (as in a school building) designed for use both as a cafeteria and an auditorium

caff \'kaf\ *n* (1931) *Brit* : CAFÉ 1

caf·feine \ka-'fēn, 'ka-\ *n* [G *Kaffein*, fr. *Kaffee* coffee, fr. F *café*] (ca. 1823) : a bitter alkaloid $C_8H_{10}N_4O_2$ found esp. in coffee, tea, and kola nuts and used medicinally as a stimulant and diuretic

caf·fe lat·te \'kä-(,)fä-'lä-(,)tā\ *n* [It *caffellatte*, short for *caffè e latte* coffee and milk] (1927) : espresso mixed with hot or steamed milk

caf·tan \'kaf-(,)tan\ *n* [Russ *kaftan*, fr. Turk, fr. Per *qaftān*] (1591) : a usu. cotton or silk ankle-length garment with long sleeves that is common throughout the Levant

¹cage \'kāj\ *n* [ME, fr. OF, fr. L *cavea* cavity, cage, fr. *cavus* hollow — more at CAVE] (13c) **1** : a box or enclosure having some openwork for confining or carrying animals (as birds) **2 a** : a barred cell for confining prisoners **b** : a fenced area for prisoners of war **3** : a framework serving as support ⟨the steel ~ of a skyscraper⟩ **4 a** : an enclosure resembling a cage in form or purpose ⟨a cashier's ~⟩ **b** : an arrangement of atoms or molecules so bonded as to enclose a space in which another atom or ion (as of a metal) can reside **5 a** : a screen placed behind home plate to stop baseballs during batting practice **b** : a goal consisting of posts or a frame with a net attached (as in ice hockey) **6** : a large building containing an area for practicing outdoor sports and often adapted for indoor events — **cage·ful** \-,fùl\ *n*

²cage *vt* **caged; cag·ing** (1577) **1** : to confine or keep in or as if in a cage **2** : to drive (as a puck) into a cage and score a goal

cage·ling \'kāj-liŋ\ *n* (1859) : a caged bird

ca·gey *also* **ca·gy** \'kā-jē\ *adj* **ca·gi·er; -est** [origin unknown] (ca. 1893) **1** : hesitant about committing oneself **2 a** : wary of being trapped or deceived : SHREWD ⟨a ~ consumer⟩ **b** : marked by cleverness ⟨a ~ reply⟩ — **ca·gi·ly** \-jə-lē\ *adv* — **ca·gi·ness** *also* **ca·gey·ness** \-jē-nəs\ *n*

ca·hier \kä-'yā, kī-'ā\ *n* [F, fr. MF *quaer, caier* quire — more at QUIRE] (1789) : a report or memorial concerning policy esp. of a parliamentary body

ca·hoot \kə-'hüt\ *n* [perh. fr. F *cahute* cabin, hut] (1829) : PARTNERSHIP, LEAGUE — usu. used in pl. ⟨they're in ~s⟩

ca·how \kə-'haù\ *n* [imit.] (1615) : a dark-colored petrel (*Pterodroma cahow*) formerly abundant in Bermuda but now nearly extinct

cai·man \'kā-mən; kā-'man, kī-\ *n* [Sp *caimán*, prob. fr. Carib *caymán*] (1577) : any of several Central and So. American crocodilians (genera *Caiman, Melanosuchus,* and *Paleosuchus*) similar to alligators

Cain \'kān\ *n* [Heb *Qayin*] : the brother and murderer of Abel

-caine *n comb form* [G *-kain*, fr. *kokain* cocaine] : synthetic alkaloid anesthetic ⟨*procaine*⟩

ca·ïque \kä-'ēk, 'kīk\ *n* [F, fr. Turk *kayιk*] (1625) **1** : a light skiff used on the Bosporus **2** : a Levantine sailing vessel

caird \'kerd\ *n* [ScGael *ceard* craftsman; akin to Gk *kerdos* profit] (1663) *Scot* : a traveling tinker; *also* : TRAMP, GYPSY

cairn \'karn, 'kern\ *n* [ME (Sc) *carne*, fr. ScGael *carn*; akin to OIr & W *carn* cairn] (15c) : a heap of stones piled up as a memorial or as a landmark — **cairned** \'karnd, 'kernd\ *adj*

cairn·gorm \'karn-,gòrm, 'kern-\ *n* [*Cairngorm*, mountain in Scotland] (1794) : a yellow or smoky-brown crystalline quartz

cairn terrier *n* [fr. its use in hunting among cairns] (1910) : any of a breed of small compactly built hard-coated terriers of Scottish origin

cais·son \'kā-,sän, -s³n, *Brit also* kə-'sün\ *n* [F, fr. MF, fr. OProv, fr. *caissa* chest, fr. L *capsa* — more at CASE] (ca. 1702) **1 a** : a chest to hold ammunition **b** : a usu. 2-wheeled vehicle for artillery ammunition attachable to a horse-drawn limber; *also* : a limber with its attached caisson **2 a** : a watertight chamber used in construction work under water or as a foundation **b** : a hollow floating box or a boat used as a floodgate for a dock or basin **3** : COFFER 3

caisson 1b

caisson disease *n* (1873) : ²BEND 3

cai·tiff \'kā-təf\ *adj* [ME *caitif*, fr. ONF, captive, vile, fr. L *captivus* captive] (14c) : being base, cowardly, or despicable — **caitiff** *n*

caj·e·put \'ka-jə-pət, -,pùt\ *n* [Malay *kayu putih*, fr. *kayu* wood, tree + *putih* white] (1832) : an Australian and southeast Asian tree (*Melaleuca quinquenervia* syn. *M. leucadendron*) of the myrtle family that yields a pungent medicinal oil and has been introduced into Florida

ca·jole \kə-'jōl\ *vt* **ca·joled; ca·jol·ing** [F *cajoler*] (1645) **1** : to persuade with flattery or gentle urging esp. in the face of reluctance : COAX ⟨had to ~ them into going⟩ **2** : to deceive with soothing words or false promises — **ca·jole·ment** \-'jōl-mənt\ *n* — **ca·jol·er** *n* — **ca·jol·ery** \-'jō-lə-rē\ *n*

¹Ca·jun *also* **Ca·jan** \'kā-jən\ *n* [alter. of *Acadian*] (1868) : a Louisianian descended from French-speaking immigrants from Acadia

²Cajun *adj* (1885) **1** : of, relating to, or characteristic of the Cajuns **2** : of, relating to, or prepared in a style of cooking originating among the Cajuns and characterized by the use of hot seasonings (as cayenne pepper)

¹cake \'kāk\ *n* [ME, fr. ON *kaka*; akin to OHG *kuocho* cake] (13c) **1 a** : a breadlike food made from a dough or batter that is usu. fried or baked in small flat shapes and is often unleavened **b** : a sweet baked food made from a dough or thick batter usu. containing flour and sugar and often shortening, eggs, and a raising agent (as baking powder) **c** : a flattened usu. round mass of food that is baked or fried ⟨a fish ~⟩ **2 a** : a block of compacted or congealed matter ⟨a ~ of ice⟩ **b** : a hard or brittle layer or deposit — **cak·ey** \'kā-kē\ *adj*

²cake *vb* **caked; cak·ing** *vt* (1607) **1** : ENCRUST ⟨*caked* with dust⟩ **2** : to fill (a space) with a packed mass ~ *vi* : to form or harden into a mass

cake·walk \'kāk-,wòk\ *n* (1879) **1** : a black American entertainment having a cake as prize for the most accomplished steps and figures in walking **2** : a stage dance developed from walking steps and figures typically involving a high prance with backward tilt **3 a** : a one-sided contest **b** : an easy task — **cakewalk** *vi* — **cake·walk·er** *n*

Cal·a·bar bean \'ka-lə-,bär-\ *n* [*Calabar*, Nigeria] (ca. 1876) : the dark brown highly poisonous seed of a tropical African woody vine (*Physostigma venenosum*) that is used as a source of physostigmine and as an ordeal poison in native witchcraft trials

cal·a·bash \'ka-lə-,bash\ *n* [F & Sp; F *calebasse* gourd, fr. Sp *calabaza*] (1596) **1** : a tropical American tree (*Crescentia cujete*) of the trumpet-creeper family; *also* : its hard globose fruit **2** : GOURD; *esp* : one whose hard shell is used for a utensil **3** : a utensil (as a bottle or dipper) made from the shell of a calabash

cal·a·boose \'ka-lə-,büs\ *n* [Sp *calabozo* dungeon] (1792) : JAIL; *esp* : a local jail

ca·la·di·um \kə-'lā-dē-əm\ *n* [NL, genus name, fr. Malay *kěladi*, an aroid plant] (ca. 1845) : any of a genus (*Caladium*, esp. *C. bicolor*) of tropical American plants of the arum family widely cultivated for their showy variably colored leaves

cal·a·man·der \'ka-lə-,man-dər, ,ka-lə-'\ *n* [prob. fr. D *kalamanderhout* calamander wood] (1804) : the hazel-brown black-striped wood of a southeast Asian tree (genus *Diospyros*, esp. *D. quaesita*) that is used in furniture manufacturing

cal·a·mari \,kä-lə-'mär-ē, 'ka-lə-,mer-ē\ *n* [It, pl. of *calamaro, calamaio*, fr. ML *calamarium* ink pot, fr. L *calamus*; fr. the inky substance the squid secretes] (ca. 1961) : squid used as food

cal·a·mary \'ka-lə-,mer-ē\ *n, pl* **-mar·ies** [ML *calamarium*] (1567) : SQUID

cal·a·mine \'ka-lə-,mīn, -mən\ *n* [ME *calamyn* ore of zinc, fr. ML *calamina*, alter. of L *cadmia* — more at CADMIUM] (15c) : a mixture of zinc oxide with a small amount of ferric oxide used in lotions, liniments, and ointments

cal·a·mint \'ka-lə-,mint\ *n* [ME *calament*, fr. OF, fr. ML *calamentum*, fr. Gk *kalaminthē*] (14c) : any of a genus (*Satureja*, esp. *S. calamintha*) of mints

cal·a·mite \'ka-lə-,mīt\ *n* [NL *Calamites*, genus of fossil plants, fr. L *calamus*] (1837) : a Paleozoic fossil plant (esp. genus *Calamites*) resembling a giant horsetail

ca·lam·i·tous \kə-'la-mə-təs\ *adj* (1547) : being, causing, or accompanied by calamity — **ca·lam·i·tous·ly** *adv*

ca·lam·i·ty \kə-'la-mə-tē\ *n, pl* **-ties** [ME *calamytey*, fr. MF *calamité*, fr. L *calamitat-, calamitas*; perh. akin to L *clades* destruction] (15c) **1** : a state of deep distress or misery caused by major misfortune or loss **2** : an extraordinarily grave event marked by great loss and lasting distress and affliction

cal·a·mon·din \,ka-lə-'män-dən\ *n* [Tag *kalamunding*] (ca. 1928) : a small hybrid citrus tree (*Citrofortunella mitis* syn. *Citrus mitis*); *also* : its tart fruit

cal·a·mus \'ka-lə-məs\ *n, pl* **-mi** \-,mī, -,mē\ [L, reed, reed pen, fr. Gk *kalamos* — more at HAULM] (14c) **1 a** : SWEET FLAG **b** : the aromatic peeled and dried rhizome of the sweet flag that is the source of a carcinogenic essential oil **2** : the hollow basal portion of a feather below the vane : QUILL

ca·lash \kə-'lash\ *n* [F *calèche*, fr. G *Kalesche*, fr. Czech *kolesa* wheels, carriage; akin to Gk *kyklos* wheel — more at WHEEL] (1679) **1 a** : a light small-wheeled 4-passenger carriage with a folding top **b** : CALÈCHE 1b **2** : a large hood worn by women in the 18th century

calc- *or* **calci-** *comb form* [L *calc-, calx* lime — more at CHALK] : calcium : calcium salt ⟨*calcic*⟩ ⟨*calcify*⟩

cal·ca·ne·al \kal-'kā-nē-əl\ *adj* (ca. 1849) : relating to the heel or calcaneus

cal·ca·ne·um \-nē-əm\ *n, pl* **-nea** \-nē-ə\ [L, heel — more at CALK] (ca. 1751) : CALCANEUS

cal·ca·ne·us \-nē-əs\ *n, pl* **-nei** \-nē-,ī\ [LL, heel, alter. of L *calcaneum*] (ca. 1925) : a tarsal bone that in humans is the great bone of the heel

cal·car·e·ous \kal-'kar-ē-əs, -'ker-\ *adj* [L *calcarius* of lime, fr. *calc-, calx*] (1677) **1 a** : resembling calcite or calcium carbonate esp. in hardness **b** : consisting of or containing calcium carbonate; *also* : containing calcium **2** : growing on limestone or in soil impregnated with lime — **cal·car·e·ous·ly** *adv*

calces *pl of* CALX

cal·cic \'kal-sik\ *adj* (1871) : derived from or containing calcium or lime; rich in calcium

cal·ci·cole \'kal-sə-,kōl\ *n* [F, calcicolous, fr. *calc-* + *-cole* -colous] (1882) : a plant normally growing on calcareous soils — **cal·cic·o·lous** \kal-'si-kə-ləs\ *adj*

cal·cif·er·ol \kal-'si-fə-,ròl, -,rōl\ *n* [*calciferous* + *ergosterol*] (1931) : an alcohol $C_{28}H_{43}OH$ usu. prepared by irradiation of ergosterol and used as a dietary supplement in nutrition and medicinally in the control of rickets and related disorders — called also *vitamin* D_2

cal·cif·er·ous \kal-'si-f(ə-)rəs\ *adj* (1799) : producing or containing calcium carbonate

cal·cif·ic \kal-'si-fik\ *adj* [*calcify*] (1861) : involving or caused by calcification ⟨~ lesions⟩

cal·ci·fuge \'kal-sə-,fyüj\ *n* [F, calcifugous, fr. *calc-* + L *fugere* to flee — more at FUGITIVE] (1926) : a plant not normally growing on calcareous soils — **calcifuge** *also* **cal·cif·u·gous** \kal-'si-fyə-gəs\ *adj*

cal·ci·fy \'kal-sə-,fī\ *vb* **-fied; -fy·ing** *vt* (1854) **1** : to make calcareous by deposit of calcium salts **2** : to make inflexible or unchangeable ~ *vi* **1** : to become calcareous **2** : to become inflexible and changeless : HARDEN — **cal·ci·fi·ca·tion** \,kal-sə-fə-'kā-shən\ *n*

cal·ci·mine \'kal-sə-,mīn\ *n* [alter. of *kalsomine*, of unknown origin] (ca. 1859) : a white or tinted wash of glue, whiting or zinc white, and water that is used esp. on plastered surfaces — **calcimine** *vt*

cal·ci·na·tion \,kal-sə-'nā-shən\ *n* (14c) : the act or process of calcining : the state of being calcined

¹cal·cine \kal-'sīn, 'kal-\ *vb* **cal·cined; cal·cin·ing** [ME *calcenen*, fr. ML *calcinare*, fr. LL *calcina* lime, fr. L *calc-, calx*] *vt* (14c) : to heat (as inorganic materials) to a high temperature but without fusing in order to drive off volatile matter or to effect changes (as oxidation or pulverization) ~ *vi* : to undergo calcination

²cal·cine \'kal-,sīn\ *n* (ca. 1909) : a product (as a metal oxide) of calcination or roasting

cal·ci·no·sis \,kal-sə-'nō-səs\ *n, pl* **-no·ses** \-,sēz\ [NL, irreg. (influenced by ISV *calcine*) fr. *calc-* + *-osis*] (ca. 1929) : the abnormal deposition of calcium salts in a part or tissue of the body

cal·cite \'kal-,sīt\ *n* (1849) : a mineral $CaCO_3$ consisting of calcium carbonate crystallized in hexagonal form and including common limestone, chalk, and marble — compare ARAGONITE — **cal·cit·ic** \kal-'si-tik\ *adj*

cal·ci·to·nin \ˌkal-sə-'tō-nən\ *n* [*calci-* + *-tonin* (as in *serotonin*)] (1961) : a polypeptide hormone esp. from the thyroid gland that tends to lower the level of calcium in the blood plasma — called also *thyrocalcitonin*

cal·ci·um \'kal-sē-əm\ *n, often attrib* [NL, fr. L *calc-, calx* lime] (1808) : a silver-white bivalent metallic element of the alkaline-earth group occurring only in combination — see ELEMENT table

calcium carbide *n* (ca. 1888) : a usu. dark gray crystalline compound CaC_2 used esp. for the generation of acetylene and for making calcium cyanamide

calcium carbonate *n* (1873) : a compound $CaCO_3$ found in nature as calcite and aragonite and in plant ashes, bones, and shells and used in making lime and portland cement and as a gastric antacid

calcium channel blocker *n* (1982) : any of a class of drugs that prevent or slow the influx of calcium ions into smooth muscle cells and are used to treat some forms of angina pectoris and some cardiac arrhythmias

calcium chloride *n* (ca. 1885) : a white deliquescent salt $CaCl_2$ used in its anhydrous state as a drying and dehumidifying agent and in a hydrated state for controlling dust and ice on roads

calcium cyanamide *n* (ca. 1893) : a compound $CaCN_2$ used as a fertilizer and a weed killer and as a source of other nitrogen compounds

calcium gluconate *n* (1884) : a white powdery salt $CaC_{12}H_{22}O_{14}$ used esp. to supplement bodily calcium stores

calcium hydroxide *n* (ca. 1889) : a white crystalline strong alkali $Ca(OH)_2$ that is used esp. to make mortar and plaster and to soften water

calcium hypochlorite *n* (ca. 1889) : a white powder $CaCl_2O_2$ used esp. as a bleaching agent and disinfectant

calcium oxalate *n* (1919) : a crystalline salt CaC_2O_4 normally deposited in many plant cells and in animals sometimes excreted in urine or retained in the form of urinary calculi

calcium oxide *n* (ca. 1885) : a caustic solid CaO that is white when pure and that is the chief constituent of lime

calcium phosphate *n* (1869) : any of various phosphates of calcium: as **a** : the phosphate $CaH_4P_2O_8$ used as a fertilizer and in baking powder **b** : the phosphate $CaHPO_4$ used in pharmaceutical preparations and animal feeds **c** : the phosphate $Ca_3P_2O_8$ used as a fertilizer **d** : the naturally occurring phosphate $Ca_5(F,Cl,OH,\frac{1}{2}CO_3)(PO_4)_3$ that contains other elements or radicals and is the chief constituent of phosphate rock, bones, and teeth

calcium silicate *n* (ca. 1888) : any of several silicates of calcium used esp. in construction materials (as portland cement)

calcium sulfate *n* (ca. 1885) : a white salt $CaSO_4$ that occurs esp. as anhydrite, gypsum, and plaster of paris and that in hydrated form is used as a building material and in anhydrous form is used as a drying agent

cal·cu·la·ble \'kal-kyə-lə-bəl\ *adj* (ca. 1734) **1** : subject to or ascertainable by calculation **2** : that may be counted on : DEPENDABLE

cal·cu·late \'kal-kyə-ˌlāt\ *vb* **-lat·ed; -lat·ing** [L *calculatus,* pp. of *calculare,* fr. *calculus* pebble (used in reckoning), perh. irreg. dim. of *calc-, calx* lime — more at CHALK] *vt* (1570) **1 a** : to determine by mathematical processes **b** : to reckon by exercise of practical judgment : ESTIMATE **c** : to solve or probe the meaning of : FIGURE OUT ⟨trying to ~ his expression —Hugh MacLennan⟩ **2** : to design or adapt for a purpose **3 a** : to judge to be true or probable **b** : INTEND ⟨I ~ to do it or perish in the attempt —Mark Twain⟩ ~ *vi* **1 a** : to make a calculation **b** : to forecast consequences **2** : COUNT, RELY

cal·cu·lat·ed \-ˌlā-təd\ *adj* (1722) **1** : APT, LIKELY **2** : worked out by mathematical calculation **b** : engaged in, undertaken, or displayed after reckoning or estimating the statistical probability of success or failure ⟨a ~ risk⟩ **3 a** : planned or contrived to accomplish a purpose **b** : DELIBERATE, INTENDED — **cal·cu·lat·ed·ly** *adv* — **cal·cu·lat·ed·ness** *n*

cal·cu·lat·ing \-ˌlā-tiŋ\ *adj* (1710) **1** : making calculations ⟨~ machine⟩ **2** : marked by prudent analysis or by shrewd consideration of self-interest : SCHEMING — **cal·cu·lat·ing·ly** \-tiŋ-lē\ *adv*

cal·cu·la·tion \ˌkal-kyə-'lā-shən\ *n* (14c) **1 a** : the process or an act of calculating **b** : the result of an act of calculating **2 a** : studied care in analyzing or planning **b** : cold heartless planning to promote self-interest — **cal·cu·la·tion·al** \-'lāsh-nəl, -'lā-shə-n³l\ *adj*

cal·cu·la·tor \'kal-kyə-ˌlā-tər\ *n* (14c) : one that calculates: as **a** : a usu. electronic device for performing mathematical calculations **b** : a person who operates a calculator

cal·cu·lous \'kal-kyə-ləs\ *adj* (1605) : caused by or characterized by a calculus or calculi

cal·cu·lus \-ləs\ *n, pl* **-li** \-ˌlī, -ˌlē\ *also* **-lus·es** [L, stone (used in reckoning)] (1666) **1 a** : a method of computation or calculation in a special notation (as of logic or symbolic logic) **b** : the mathematical methods comprising differential and integral calculus **2** : CALCULATION **3 a** : a concretion usu. of mineral salts around organic material found esp. in hollow organs or ducts : TARTAR 2 **4** : a system or arrangement of intricate or interrelated parts

calculus of variations (1837) : a branch of mathematics concerned with applying the methods of calculus to finding the maxima and minima of a function which depends for its values on another function or a curve

cal·de·ra \kal-'der-ə, kȯl-, -'dir-\ *n* [Sp, lit., cauldron, fr. LL *caldaria* — more at CAULDRON] (1691) : a volcanic crater that has a diameter many times that of the vent and is formed by collapse of the central part of a volcano or by explosions of extraordinary violence

cal·dron *var of* CAULDRON

ca·lèche *or* **ca·leche** \ka-'lesh, -'lash\ *n* [F *calèche* — more at CALASH] (1666) **1 a** : CALASH 1a **b** : a 2-wheeled horse-drawn vehicle with a driver's seat on the splashboard used in Quebec **2** : CALASH 2

cal·e·fac·to·ry \ˌka-lə-'fak-t(ə-)rē\ *n, pl* **-ries** [ML *calefactorium,* fr. L *calefacere* to warm — more at CHAFE] (ca. 1681) : a monastery room warmed and used as a sitting room

¹cal·en·dar \'ka-lən-dər\ *n* [ME *calender,* fr. AF or ML; AF *calender,* fr. ML *kalendarium,* fr. L, moneylender's account book, fr. *kalendae* calends] (13c) **1** : a system for fixing the beginning, length, and divisions of the civil year and arranging days and longer divisions of time (as weeks and months) in a definite order — see MONTH table **2** : a tabular register of days according to a system usu. covering one year and referring the days of each month to the days of the week **3** : an orderly list: as **a** : a list of cases to be tried in court **b** : a list of bills or other items reported out of committee for consideration by a legislative assembly **c** : a list or schedule of planned events or activities giving dates and details **4** *Brit* : a university catalog

²calendar *vt* **-dared; -dar·ing** \-d(ə-)riŋ\ (15c) : to enter in a calendar

calendar year *n* (ca. 1909) **1** : a period of a year beginning and ending with the dates that are conventionally accepted as marking the beginning and end of a numbered year **2** : a period of time equal in length to that of the year in the calendar conventionally in use

¹cal·en·der \'ka-lən-dər\ *vt* **-dered; -der·ing** \-d(ə-)riŋ\ [MF *calandrer,* fr. *calandre* machine for calendering, fr. (assumed) VL *colendra* cylinder, modif. of Gk *kylindros* — more at CYLINDER] (1513) : to press (as cloth, rubber, or paper) between rollers or plates in order to smooth and glaze or to thin into sheets — **cal·en·der·er** \-dər-ər\ *n*

²calender *n* (1688) : a machine for calendering something

³calender *n* [Per *qalandar,* fr. Ar, fr. Per *kalandar* uncouth man] (1621) : a member of a Sufic order of wandering mendicant dervishes

ca·len·dri·cal \kə-'len-dri-kəl, ka-\ *also* **ca·len·dric** \-drik\ *adj* (ca. 1843) : of, relating to, characteristic of, or used in a calendar

ca·lends \'ka-lən(d)z, 'kā-\ *n pl but sing or pl in constr* [ME *kalendes,* fr. L *kalendae, calendae*] (14c) : the first day of the ancient Roman month from which days were counted backward to the ides

ca·len·du·la \kə-'len-jə-lə, -dyü-lə\ *n* [NL, genus name, fr. ML, fr. L *calendae* calends] (1789) : any of a small genus (*Calendula*) of yellow-rayed composite herbs of temperate regions

cal·en·ture \'ka-lən-ˌchu̇r\ *n* [Sp *calentura,* fr. *calentar* to heat, fr. L *calent-, calens,* prp. of *calēre* to be warm — more at LEE] (1593) : a fever formerly supposed to affect sailors in the tropics

¹calf \'kaf, 'kȧf, *dial also* 'kȧf\ *n, pl* **calves** \'kavz, 'kȧvz, 'kȧvz\ *also* **calfs** *often attrib* [ME, fr. OE *cealf;* akin to OHG *kalb* calf] (bef. 12c) **1 a** : the young of the domestic cow; *also* : that of a closely related mammal (as a bison) **b** : the young of various large animals (as the elephant or whale) **2** *pl* **calfs** : the hide of the domestic calf; *esp* : CALFSKIN **3** : an awkward or silly youth — **calf·like** \'kaf-ˌlīk, 'kȧf-, 'kȧf-, *dial also* 'kȧf-\ *adj* — **in calf** : PREGNANT — used of a cow

²calf *n, pl* **calves** \'kavz, 'kȧvz\ [ME, fr. ON *kālfi*] (14c) : the fleshy back part of the leg below the knee

calf-love \-ˌləv\ *n* (1823) : PUPPY LOVE

calf's-foot jelly \'kavz-ˌfu̇t-, 'kȧfs-, 'kȧvz-, 'kȧfs- *also* 'kȧvz-\ *n* (1775) : jelly made from gelatin obtained by boiling calves' feet

calf·skin \'kaf-ˌskin, 'kȧf- *also* 'kȧf-\ *n* (15c) : leather made of the skin of a calf

Cal·gon \'kal-ˌgän\ *trademark* — used for a water softener

Cal·i·ban \'ka-lə-ˌban\ *n* : a savage and deformed slave in Shakespeare's *The Tempest*

cal·i·ber *or* **cal·i·bre** \'ka-lə-bər, *Brit also* kə-'lē-\ *n* [MF *calibre,* fr. OIt *calibro,* fr. Ar *qālib* shoemaker's last] (1567) **1 a** : degree of mental capacity or moral quality **b** : degree of excellence or importance **2 a** : the diameter of a bullet or other projectile **b** : the diameter of a bore of a gun usu. expressed in hundredths or thousandths of an inch and typically written as a decimal fraction ⟨.32 ~⟩ **3** : the diameter of a round body; *esp* : the internal diameter of a hollow cylinder

cal·i·brate \'ka-lə-ˌbrāt\ *vt* **-brat·ed; -brat·ing** (ca. 1864) **1** : to ascertain the caliber of (as a thermometer tube) **2** : to determine, rectify, or mark the graduations of (as a thermometer tube) **3** : to standardize (as a measuring instrument) by determining the deviation from a standard so as to ascertain the proper correction factors **4** : to adjust precisely for a particular function — **cal·i·bra·tor** \-ˌbrā-tər\ *n*

cal·i·bra·tion \ˌka-lə-'brā-shən\ *n* (ca. 1859) **1** : the act or process of calibrating : the state of being calibrated **2** : a set of graduations to indicate values or positions — usu. used in pl. ⟨~s on a gauge⟩

ca·li·che \kə-'lē-chē\ *n* [AmerSp, fr. Sp, flake of lime, fr. *cal* lime, fr. L *calx* — more at CHALK] (ca. 1858) **1** : the nitrate-bearing gravel or rock of the sodium nitrate deposits of Chile and Peru **2** : a crust of calcium carbonate that forms on the stony soil of arid regions

cal·i·co \'ka-li-ˌkō\ *n, pl* **-coes** *or* **-cos** [*Calicut,* India] (1578) **1 a** : cotton cloth imported from India **b** *Brit* : a plain white cotton fabric that is heavier than muslin **c** : any of various cheap cotton fabrics with figured patterns **2** : a blotched or spotted animal; *esp* : one that is predominantly white with red and black patches — **calico** *adj*

calico bass *n* (ca. 1882) : BLACK CRAPPIE

calico bush *n* (1814) : MOUNTAIN LAUREL

Cal·i·for·nia condor \ˌka-lə-'fȯr-nyə-\ *n* [*California,* state of U.S.] (ca. 1889) : a large nearly extinct vulture (*Gymnogyps californianus*) found most recently in the mountains of southern California that is related to the condor of So. America

California laurel *n* (1871) : an evergreen Pacific coast tree (*Umbellularia californica*) of the laurel family with small umbellate flowers

California poppy *n* (1891) : any of a genus (*Eschscholzia*) of herbs of the poppy family; *esp* : one (*E. californica*) widely cultivated for its usu. yellow or orange flowers

California condor

\ə\ abut \ᵊ\ kitten, F table \ər\ further \a\ ash \ā\ ace \ä\ mop, mar
\au̇\ out \ch\ chin \e\ bet \ē\ easy \g\ go \i\ hit \ī\ ice \j\ job
\ŋ\ sing \ō\ go \ȯ\ law \ȯi\ boy \th\ thin \t̲h̲\ the \ü\ loot \u̇\ foot
\y\ yet \zh\ vision \a̱, k̲, ⁿ, œ, œ̄, ᵫ, ᵫ̄, ʸ\ see Guide to Pronunciation

Cal·i·for·nio \,ka-lə-'för-nē-,ō\ n, pl **-nios** [Sp, fr. *California*] (1923) : one of the original Spanish colonists of California or their descendants

cal·i·for·ni·um \,ka-lə-'för-nē-əm\ n [NL, fr. *California*, U.S.] (1950) : a radioactive element discovered by bombarding curium 242 with alpha particles — see ELEMENT table

ca·lig·i·nous \kə-'li-jə-nəs\ adj [MF or L; MF *caligineux*, fr. L *caliginosus*, fr. *caligin-, caligo* darkness] (1548) : MISTY, DARK

¹**cal·i·per** \'ka-lə-pər\ n [alter. of *caliber*] (1588) **1 a** : any of various measuring instruments having two usu. adjustable arms, legs, or jaws used esp. to measure diameter or thickness — usu. used in pl. ⟨a pair of ~s⟩ **b** : a device consisting of two plates lined with a frictional material that press against the sides of a rotating wheel or disc in certain brake systems **2** : thickness esp. of paper, paperboard, or a tree

²**caliper** vt **-pered; -per·ing** \-p(ə-)riη\ (1876) : to measure by or as if by calipers

ca·liph or **ca·lif** \'kā-ləf, 'ka-ləf\ n [ME *caliphe*, fr. MF *calife*, fr. Ar *khalīfah* successor] (14c) : a successor of Muhammad as temporal and spiritual head of Islam — used as a title — **ca·liph·al** \-lə-fəl\ adj

ca·liph·ate \-lə-,fāt, -fət\ n (1614) : the office or dominion of a caliph

cal·is·then·ic \,ka-ləs-'the-nik\ adj (1827) : of or relating to calisthenics

cal·is·then·ics \-niks\ n pl but sing or pl in constr [Gk *kalos* beautiful + *sthenos* strength] (1827) **1** : systematic rhythmic bodily exercises performed usu. without apparatus **2** usu sing in constr : the art or practice of calisthenics

ca·lix \'kā-liks, 'ka-\ n, pl **ca·li·ces** \'kā-lə-,sēz, 'ka-\ [L *calic-, calix* — more at CHALICE] (1698) : CUP

¹**calk** \'kök\, **calk·er** \'kö-kər\ var of CAULK, CAULKER

²**calk** \'kök\ n [prob. alter. of *calkin*, fr. ME *kakun*, fr. MD or ONF; MD *calcoen* horse's hoof, fr. ONF *calcain* heel, fr. L *calcaneum*, fr. *calc-, calx* heel] (1587) : a tapered piece projecting downward on the shoe of a horse to prevent slipping; also : a similar device worn on the sole of a shoe

³**calk** vt (1624) **1** : to furnish with calks **2** : to wound with a calk

¹**call** \'köl\ vb [ME, fr. ON *kalla*; akin to OE *hildecalla* battle herald, OHG *kallōn* to talk loudly, OCS *glasŭ* voice] vi (bef. 12c) **1 a** : to speak in a loud distinct voice so as to be heard at a distance : SHOUT ⟨~ for help⟩ **b** : to make a request or demand ⟨~ for an investigation⟩ **c** of an animal : to utter a characteristic note or cry **d** : to get or try to get into communication by telephone — often used with *up* **e** : to make a demand in card games (as for a particular card or for a show of hands) **f** : to give the calls for a square dance **2** : to make a brief visit ⟨~ed to pay his respects⟩ ⟨~ed on a friend⟩ ~ vt **1 a** (1) : to utter in a loud distinct voice — often used with *out* ⟨~ out a number⟩ (2) : to announce or read loudly or authoritatively ⟨~ the roll⟩ ⟨~ off a row of figures⟩ **b** (1) : to command or request to come or be present ⟨~ed to testify⟩ (2) : to cause to come : BRING ⟨~s to mind an old saying⟩ **c** : to summon to a particular activity, employment, or office ⟨was ~ed to active duty⟩ **d** : to invite or command to meet : CONVOKE ⟨~ a meeting⟩ **e** : to rouse from sleep or summon to get up **f** (1) : to give the order for : bring into action ⟨~ a strike against the company⟩ ⟨a pitchout⟩ (2) : to manage by giving the signals or orders ⟨that catcher ~s a good game⟩ **g** (1) : to make a demand in bridge for (a card or suit) (2) : to require (a player) to show the hand in poker by making an equal bet (3) : to challenge to make good on a statement (4) : to charge with or censure for an offense ⟨deserves to be ~ed on that⟩ **h** : to attract (as game) by imitating the characteristic cry **i** : to halt (as a baseball game) because of unsuitable conditions **j** : to rule on the status of (as a pitched ball or a player's action) ⟨~ balls and strikes⟩ ⟨~ a base runner safe⟩ **k** : to give the calls for (a square dance) — often used with *off* **l** (1) : to demand payment of esp. by formal notice ⟨~ a loan⟩ (2) : to demand presentation of (as a bond or option) for redemption **m** (1) : to get or try to get in communication with by telephone (2) : to generate signals for (a telephone number) in order to reach the party to whom the number is assigned ⟨~ 911⟩ (3) : to make a signal to in order to transmit a message ⟨~ the flagship⟩ **2 a** : to speak of or address by a specified name : give a name to ⟨~ her Kitty⟩ **b** (1) : to regard or characterize as of a certain kind : CONSIDER ⟨can hardly be ~ed generous⟩ (2) : to estimate or consider for purposes of an estimate or for convenience ⟨~ it an even dollar⟩ **c** (1) : to describe correctly in advance of or without knowledge of the event : PREDICT (2) : to name or specify in advance ⟨~ the toss of a coin⟩ **3** : to temporarily transfer control of computer processing to (as a subroutine or procedure) **syn** see SUMMON — **call a spade a spade** : to speak frankly — **call for 1** : to call (as at one's house) to get ⟨I'll *call for* you after dinner⟩ **2** : to require as necessary or appropriate ⟨the job *calls for* typing skills⟩ ⟨the design *calls for* three windows⟩ — **call forth** : ELICIT, EVOKE ⟨these events *call forth* great emotions⟩ — **call in question** or **call into question** : to cast doubt upon — **call it a day** : to stop for the remainder of the day or for the present whatever one has been doing — **call it quits** : to call it a day : QUIT — **call names** : to address or speak of a person or thing contemptuously or offensively — **call on** **1** : to call upon **2** : to elicit a response from (as a student) ⟨the teacher *called on* her first⟩ — **call one's bluff** : to challenge in order to expose an empty pretense or threat — **call the shots** : to be in charge or control : determine the policy or procedure — **call the tune** : to call the shots — **call time** : to ask for or grant a time-out — **call to account** : to hold responsible : REPRIMAND — **call upon 1** : REQUIRE, OBLIGE ⟨may be *called upon* to do several jobs⟩ **2** : to make a demand on : depend on ⟨universities are *called upon* to produce trained professionals⟩

²**call** n (14c) **1 a** : an act of calling with the voice : SHOUT **b** : an imitation of the cry of a bird or other animal made to attract it **c** : an instrument used for calling ⟨a duck ~⟩ **d** : the cry of an animal (as a bird) **2 a** : a request or command to come or assemble **b** : a summons or signal on a drum, bugle, or pipe **c** : admission to the bar as a barrister **d** : an invitation to become the minister of a church or to accept a professional appointment **e** : a divine vocation or strong inner prompting to a particular course of action **f** : a summoning of actors to rehearsal ⟨the ~ is for 11 o'clock⟩ **g** : the attraction or appeal of a particular activity, condition, or place ⟨the ~ of the wild⟩ **h** : an order specifying the number of men to be inducted into the armed

services during a specified period **i** : the selection of a play in football **3 a** : DEMAND, CLAIM **b** : NEED, JUSTIFICATION **c** : a demand for payment of money **d** : an option to buy a specified amount of a security (as stock) or commodity (as wheat) at a fixed price at or within a specified time — compare PUT 2 **e** : an instance of asking for something : REQUEST ⟨many ~s for Christmas stories⟩ **4** : ROLL CALL **5** : a short usu. formal visit **6** : the name or thing called ⟨the ~ was heads⟩ **7** : the act of calling in a card game **8** : the act of calling on the telephone **9** : a direction or a succession of directions for a square dance rhythmically called to the dancers **10** : a decision or ruling made by an official of a sports contest; also : DECISION 1 ⟨a tough ~ to make⟩ **11** : a temporary transfer of control of computer processing to a particular set of instructions (as a subroutine or procedure) — **at call** or **on call** **1 a** : available for use : at the service of ⟨thousands of men *at his call*⟩ **b** : ready to respond to a summons or command ⟨a doctor *on call*⟩ **2** : subject to demand for payment or return without previous notice ⟨money lent *at call*⟩ — **within call** : within hearing or reach of a summons : subject to summons

call·able \'kö-lə-bəl\ adj (1826) : capable of being called; specif : subject to a demand for presentation for payment ⟨~ bond⟩

cal·la lily \'ka-lə-\ n [NL, genus name, modif. of Gk *kallaia* rooster's wattles] (1870) : any of several herbs (genus *Zantedeschia*) of the arum family; esp : a house or greenhouse plant (Z. *aethiopica*) with a white showy spathe and yellow spadix — called also *calla*

cal·la·loo \,ka-lə-'lü, 'ka-lə-,\ n [AmerSp *calalú* plant of the genus *Xanthosoma* whose leaves are used as greens] (1892) : a soup or stew made with greens, onions, and crabmeat

cal·lant \'ka-lənt, 'kä-\ n [D or ONF; D *kalant* customer, fellow, fr. ONF *calland* customer, fr. L *calent-, calens*, prp. of *calēre* to be warm — more at LEE] (ca. 1592) chiefly Scot : BOY, LAD

call·back \'köl-,bak\ n (1926) **1** : a return call **2 a** : RECALL 5 **b** : a recall of an employee to work after a layoff **c** : a second or additional audition for a theatrical part

call–board \-,börd, -,bórd\ n (1886) : BULLETIN BOARD 1

call box n (1885) **1** Brit : a public telephone booth **2** : a telephone usu. located on the side of a road for reporting emergencies (as fires or automobile breakdowns)

call·boy \'köl-,bói\ n (1794) : BELLHOP, PAGE

call down vt (1810) **1** : to cause or entreat to descend ⟨*call down* a blessing⟩ **2** : REPRIMAND ⟨*called me down* for being late⟩

called strike n (1887) : a pitched baseball not struck at by the batter that passes through the strike zone

¹**cal·ler** \'kä-lər\ adj [ME *callour*] (14c) **1** Scot : FRESH **2** Scot : COOL

²**call·er** \'kö-lər\ n (15c) : one that calls

cal·let \'ka-lət\ n [perh. fr. MF *caillette* frivolous person, fr. *Caillette fl* 1500 Fr. court fool] (15c) chiefly Scot : PROSTITUTE

call girl n (ca. 1940) : a prostitute with whom an appointment may be made by telephone

call house n (1929) : a house or apartment where call girls may be procured

cal·lig·ra·pher \kə-'li-grə-fər\ n (1753) **1** : a professional copyist or engrosser **2** : one who writes a beautiful hand **3** : PENMAN ⟨a fair ~⟩

cal·lig·ra·phist \-fist\ n (1816) : CALLIGRAPHER

cal·lig·ra·phy \-fē\ n [F or Gk; F *calligraphie*, fr. Gk *kalligraphia*, fr. *kalli-* beautiful (fr. *kallos* beauty) + *-graphia* -graphy] (1604) **1 a** : artistic, stylized, or elegant handwriting or lettering **b** : the art of producing such writing **2** : PENMANSHIP **3** : an ornamental line in drawing or painting — **cal·li·graph·ic** \,ka-lə-'gra-fik\ adj — **cal·li·graph·i·cal·ly** \-fi-k(ə-)lē\ adv

call–in \'köl-,in\ adj (1967) : allowing listeners to engage in broadcast telephone conversations with the host or a guest ⟨a ~ show⟩

call in vt (1597) **1** : to order to return or to be returned: as **a** : to withdraw from an advanced position ⟨*call in* the outposts⟩ **b** : to withdraw from circulation ⟨*call in* bank notes and issue new ones⟩ **2** : to summon to one's aid or for consultation ⟨*call in* a mediator⟩ **3** : to deliver (a message) by telephone ⟨*call in* an order for pizza⟩ ~ **sick** : to report by telephone that one will be absent because of illness

call·ing \'kö-liη\ n (14c) **1** : a strong inner impulse toward a particular course of action esp. when accompanied by conviction of divine influence **2** : the vocation or profession in which one customarily engages **3** : the characteristic cry of a female cat in heat; also : the period of heat **syn** see WORK

calling card n (1896) **1** : VISITING CARD **2** : a sign or evidence that someone or something is or has been present; broadly : an identifying mark

cal·li·ope \kə-'lī-ə-(,)pē, in sense 2 also 'ka-lē-,ōp\ n [L, fr. Gk *Kalliopē*] **1** cap : the Greek Muse of heroic poetry **2** : a keyboard musical instrument resembling an organ and consisting of a series of whistles sounded by steam or compressed air

cal·li·per chiefly Brit var of CALIPER

cal·li·pyg·ian \,ka-lə-'pi-j(ē-)ən\ or **cal·li·py·gous** \-'pī-gəs\ adj [Gk *kallipygos*, fr. *kalli-* + *pygē* buttocks] (ca. 1800) : having shapely buttocks

Cal·lis·to \kə-'lis-(,)tō\ n [L, fr. Gk *Kallistō*] : a nymph loved by Zeus, changed into a she-bear by Hera, and subsequently changed into the Great Bear constellation

cal·li·thump \'ka-lə-,thəmp\ n [back-formation fr. *callithumpian*, adj., alter. of E dial. *gallithumpian* disturber of order at elections in 18th cent.] (1856) : a noisy boisterous band or parade — **cal·li·thump·ian** \,ka-lə-'thəm-pē-ən\ adj

call letters n pl (1913) : CALL SIGN

call loan n (1852) : a loan payable at the discretion of the borrower or on demand of the lender

call number n (1876) : a combination of characters assigned to a library book to indicate its place on a shelf

call off vt (1633) **1** : to draw away : DIVERT ⟨her attention was *called off* by a new arrival⟩ **2** : CANCEL ⟨*call* the trip *off*⟩

call of nature (1763) : the need to urinate or defecate

cal·los·i·ty \ka-'lä-sə-tē, kə-\ n, pl **-ties** (1578) **1** : the quality or state of being callous: as **a** : marked or abnormal hardness and thickness **b** : lack of feeling or capacity for emotion **2** : CALLUS 1

¹**cal·lous** \'ka-ləs\ adj [MF *calleux*, fr. L *callosus*, fr. *callum, callus* callous skin] (15c) **1 a** : being hardened and thickened **b** : having

calluses 2 **a** : feeling no emotion **b** : feeling no sympathy for others — **cal·lous·ly** adv — **cal·lous·ness** n
²**callous** vt (1834) : to make callous
call out vt (15c) **1** : to summon into action ⟨call out troops⟩ **2** : to challenge to a duel **3** : to order on strike ⟨call out the workers⟩
call·low \'ka-(,)lō\ adj [ME calu bald, fr. OE; akin to OHG kalo bald, OCS golŭ bare] (1580) : lacking adult sophistication : IMMATURE ⟨~ youth⟩ — **cal·low·ness** \'ka-lō-nəs, -lə-nəs\ n
call sign n (1919) : the combination of identifying letters or letters and numbers assigned to an operator, office, activity, or station for use in communication (as in the address of a message sent by radio)
call slip n (1881) : a form filled out by a library patron for a desired book
call to quarters (ca. 1918) : a bugle call usu. shortly before taps that summons soldiers to their quarters
call-up \'kȯ-,ləp\ n (1940) : an order to report for military service
call up vt (1632) **1** : to bring to mind : EVOKE **2** : to summon before an authority **3** : to summon together (as for a united effort) ⟨call up all his forces for the attack⟩ **4** : to summon for active military duty **5** : to bring forward for consideration or action **6** : to retrieve from the memory of a computer esp. for display and user interaction
¹**cal·lus** \'ka-ləs\ n (1563) **1** : a thickening of or a hard thickened area on skin or bark **2** : a mass of exudate and connective tissue that forms around a break in a bone and is converted into bone in healing **3** : soft tissue that forms over a wounded or cut plant surface
²**callus** vi (1864) : to form callus ~ vt : to cause callus to form on
call-waiting n (1986) : a telephone service that signals (as by a click) to the user when an incoming call is received during a call in progress
¹**calm** \'käm, 'kälm, 'kam, 'kȯ(l)m, NewEng also 'kám\ n [ME calme, fr. MF, fr. OIt calma, fr. LL cauma heat, fr. Gk kauma, fr. kaiein to burn] (14c) **1 a** : a period or condition of freedom from storms, high winds, or rough activity of water **b** : complete absence of wind or presence of wind having a speed no greater than one mile (1.6 kilometers) per hour — see BEAUFORT SCALE table **2** : a state of tranquillity
²**calm** vi (14c) : to become calm — usu. used with down ~ vt : to make calm — often used with down
³**calm** adj (14c) **1** : marked by calm : STILL ⟨a ~ sea⟩ **2** : free from agitation, excitement, or disturbance ⟨a ~ manner⟩ — **calm·ly** adv — **calm·ness** n
syn CALM, TRANQUIL, SERENE, PLACID, PEACEFUL mean quiet and free from disturbance. CALM often implies a contrast with a foregoing or nearby state of agitation or violence ⟨the protests ended, and the streets were calm again⟩. TRANQUIL suggests a very deep quietude or composure ⟨the tranquil beauty of a formal garden⟩. SERENE stresses an unclouded and lofty tranquillity ⟨watched the sunset of a serene summer's evening⟩. PLACID suggests an undisturbed appearance and often implies a degree of complacency ⟨remained placid despite the criticism⟩. PEACEFUL implies a state of repose in contrast with or following strife or turmoil ⟨grown peaceful in old age⟩.
calm·ative \'kä-mə-tiv, 'käl-, also 'ka-, 'kȯ(l)-, 'ka-\ n or adj [²calm + -ative (as in sedative)] (1870) : SEDATIVE
cal·mod·u·lin \(,)kal-'mä-jə-lin, -dyü-lin\ n [calcium + modulate + -¹-in] (1979) : a calcium-binding protein that regulates cellular metabolic processes (as the contraction of muscle fibers) by modifying the activity of calcium-sensitive enzymes
ca·ló \kə-'lō\ n [Sp, argot, speech of Span. Gypsies, fr. Romany kalo Gypsy, lit., black, fr. Skt kāla] (ca. 1948) : any of several Spanish argots; esp : an argot used by Chicano youths in cities of the U.S. Southwest
cal·o·mel \'ka-lə-məl, -,mel\ n [prob. fr. (assumed) NL calomelas, fr. Gk kalos beautiful + melas black — more at MELAN-] (1676) : a white tasteless compound Hg₂Cl₂ used esp. as a fungicide and insecticide and occas. in medicine as a purgative — called also mercurous chloride
¹**ca·lo·ric** \kə-'lȯr-ik, -'lär-\ n [F calorique, fr. L calor] (1792) **1** : a supposed form of matter formerly held responsible for the phenomena of heat and combustion **2** archaic : HEAT
²**caloric** adj (ca. 1828) **1** : of or relating to heat **2** : of or relating to calories — **ca·lo·ri·cal·ly** \-i-k(ə-)lē\ adv
cal·o·rie also **cal·o·ry** \'ka-lə-rē, 'kal-rē\ n, pl **-ries** [F calorie, fr. L calor heat, fr. calēre to be warm — more at LEE] (1866) **1 a** : the amount of heat required at a pressure of one atmosphere to raise the temperature of one gram of water one degree Celsius that is equal to about 4.19 joules — called also gram calorie, small calorie; abbr. cal **b** : the amount of heat required to raise the temperature of one kilogram of water one degree Celsius : 1000 gram calories or 3.968 Btu — called also large calorie; abbr. Cal **2 a** : a unit equivalent to the large calorie expressing heat-producing or energy-producing value in food when oxidized in the body **b** : an amount of food having an energy-producing value of one large calorie
cal·o·rif·ic \,ka-lə-'ri-fik\ adj [F or L; F calorifique, fr. L calorificus, fr. calor] (1812) **1** : CALORIC **2** : of or relating to heat production
cal·o·rim·e·ter \,ka-lə-'ri-mə-tər\ n [ISV, fr. L calor] (1794) : any of several apparatuses for measuring quantities of absorbed or evolved heat or for determining specific heats — **cal·o·ri·met·ric** \,ka-lə-rə-'me-trik; kə-,lȯr-ə-, -,lȯr-\ adj — **cal·o·ri·met·ri·cal·ly** \-tri-k(ə-)lē\ adv — **cal·o·rim·e·try** \,ka-lə-'ri-mə-trē\ n
ca·lotte \kə-'lät\ n [F] (1632) : SKULLCAP 1; esp : ZUCCHETTO
cal·o·type \'ka-lə-,tīp\ n [Gk kalos beautiful + -type (as in daguerreotype)] (1845) : a photographic process by which a large number of prints could be produced from a paper negative; also : a positive print so made
cal·pac or **cal·pack** \'kal-,pak, kal-'\ n [Turk kalpak] (1598) : a high-crowned cap worn in Turkey, Iran, and neighboring countries
calque \'kalk\ n [F, lit., copy, fr. calquer to trace, fr. It calcare to trample, trace, fr. L, to trample — more at CAULK] (1937) : LOAN TRANSLATION
cal·trop \'kal-trəp, 'kȯl-\ also **cal·throp** \-,thrəp\ n [ME caltrappe, alter. of calketrappe star thistle, fr. OE calcatrippe, fr. ML calcatrippa] (15c) **1 a** pl but sing or pl in constr : STAR THISTLE 1 **b** : PUNCTURE VINE; also : any of various related herbs (genera Tribulus and Kallstroemia) of the same family (Zygophyllaceae, the caltrop family) **2** : a device with four metal points so arranged that when any three are on the ground the fourth projects upward as a hazard to the hooves of horses or to pneumatic tires

cal·u·met \'kal-yə-,met, -mət\ n [AmerF, fr. F dial., pipe stem, fr. LL calamellus, dim. of L calamus reed — more at CALAMUS] (1673) : a highly ornamented ceremonial pipe of the American Indians

calumet

ca·lum·ni·ate \kə-'ləm-nē-,āt\ vt **-at·ed; -at·ing** (1554) **1** : to utter maliciously false statements, charges, or imputations about **2** : to injure the reputation of by calumny **syn** see MALIGN — **ca·lum·ni·a·tion** \-,ləm-nē-'ā-shən\ n — **ca·lum·ni·a·tor** \-'ləm-nē-,ā-tər\ n
cal·um·ny \'ka-ləm-nē also 'kal-yəm-\ n, pl **-nies** [MF & L; MF calomnie, fr. L calumnia, fr. calvi to deceive; perh. akin to OE hōlian to slander, Gk kēlein to beguile] (15c) **1** : a misrepresentation intended to blacken another's reputation **2** : the act of uttering false charges or misrepresentations maliciously calculated to damage another's reputation — **ca·lum·ni·ous** \kə-'ləm-nē-əs\ adj — **ca·lum·ni·ous·ly** adv
cal·u·tron \'kal-yə-,trän\ n [California University cyclotron] (1945) : an electromagnetic apparatus for separating isotopes according to their masses
cal·va·dos \,kal-və-'dōs, ,käl-\ n, often cap [F, fr. Calvados, department in Normandy, France] (1906) : an applejack made in Calvados
cal·var·i·um \kal-'var-ē-əm, -'ver-\ n, pl **-ia** \-ē-ə\ [NL, fr. L calvaria skull, fr. calvus bald; prob. akin to Skt kulva bald] (14c) : the portion of a skull including the braincase and excluding the lower jaw or lower jaw and facial portion
cal·va·ry \'kal-v(ə-)rē\ n, pl **-ries** [Calvary, the hill near Jerusalem where Jesus was crucified] (1738) **1** : an open-air representation of the crucifixion of Jesus **2** : an experience of usu. intense mental suffering
Calvary cross n (1826) : a Latin cross usu. mounted on three steps — see CROSS illustration
calve \'kav, 'käv\ vb **calved; calv·ing** [ME, fr. OE cealfian, fr. cealf calf] vi (bef. 12c) **1** : to give birth to a calf; also : to produce offspring **2** of an ice mass : to separate or break so that a part becomes detached ~ vt **1** : to produce by birth **2** of an ice mass : to let become detached
calves pl of CALF
Cal·vin cycle \'kal-vən-\ n [Melvin Calvin] (1957) : the cycle of enzyme-catalyzed dark reactions of photosynthesis that occurs in the chloroplasts of plants and in many bacteria and that involves the fixation of carbon dioxide and the formation of a six-carbon sugar
Cal·vin·ism \'kal-və-,ni-zəm\ n [John Calvin] (ca. 1570) : the theological system of Calvin and his followers marked by strong emphasis on the sovereignty of God, the depravity of mankind, and the doctrine of predestination — **Cal·vin·ist** \-və-nist\ n or adj — **Cal·vin·is·tic** \,kal-və-'nis-tik\ adj — **Cal·vin·is·ti·cal·ly** \-ti-k(ə-)lē\ adv
calx \'kalks\ n, pl **calx·es** or **cal·ces** \'kal-,sēz\ [ME cals, fr. L calx lime — more at CHALK] (15c) : the crumbly residue left when a metal or mineral has been subjected to calcination or combustion
¹**ca·lyp·so** \kə-'lip-(,)sō\ n [L, fr. Gk Kalypsō] **1** cap : a sea nymph in Homer's Odyssey who keeps Odysseus seven years on the island of Ogygia **2** pl **calypsos** [NL, genus name, prob. fr. L]: a bulbous bog orchid (Calypso bulbosa) of northern regions bearing a single white or purple flower
²**calypso** n, pl **-sos** or **-soes** [origin unknown] (1934) : a style of music originating in the West Indies, marked by lively duple meter, and having lyrics that are often improvised and usu. satirize local personalities and events; also : a song in this style — **ca·lyp·so·ni·an** \,lip-'sō-nē-ən, ,ka-(,)lip-\ n or adj
ca·lyp·tra \kə-'lip-trə\ n [NL, fr. Gk kalyptra veil, fr. kalyptein to cover — more at HELL] (ca. 1753) : a hoodlike structure in a plant; esp : haploid tissue forming a membranous hood over the capsule in a moss
ca·lyx \'kā-liks also 'ka-\ n, pl **ca·lyx·es** or **ca·ly·ces** \'kā-lə-,sēz also 'ka-\ [L calyc-, calyx, fr. Gk kalyx — more at CHALICE] (1693) **1** : the usu. green outer whorl of a flower consisting of sepals **2** : a cuplike animal structure (as the body wall of a crinoid or a division of the kidney pelvis)
cal·zo·ne \kal-'zōn, -'zō-nē, -'zō-nā; käl-'zō-nā\ n, pl **calzone** or **cal·zones** [It, fr. calzone (sing. of calzoni pants), aug. of calza stocking, fr. ML calcea, fr. L calceus shoe, fr. calc-, calx heel] (ca. 1950) : a baked or fried turnover of pizza dough stuffed with various fillings usu. including cheese
cam \'kam\ n [perh. fr. F came, fr. G Kamm, lit., comb, fr. OHG kamb] (1777) : a rotating or sliding piece in a mechanical linkage used esp. in transforming rotary motion into linear motion or vice versa
ca·ma·ra·de·rie \,käm-'rä-d(ə-)rē, ,kam-, ,kä-mə-, ,ka-, -'ra-\ n [F, fr. camarade comrade] (1840) : a spirit of friendly good-fellowship
cam·a·ril·la \,ka-mə-'ri-lə, -'rē-ə\ n [Sp, lit., small room] (1839) : a group of unofficial often secret and scheming advisers; also : CABAL
cam·as also **cam·ass** \'ka-məs\ n [Chinook Jargon kamass] (1805) : any of a genus (Camassia esp. C. quamash) of plants of the lily family chiefly of the western U.S. with edible bulbs — compare DEATH CAMAS
¹**cam·ber** \'kam-bər\ vb **cam·bered; cam·ber·ing** \-b(ə-)riŋ\ [F cambrer, fr. MF cambre curved, fr. L camur] (1627) : to curve upward in the middle ~ vt **1** : to arch slightly **2** : to impart camber to
²**camber** n (1823) **1** : a slight convexity, arching, or curvature (as of a beam, deck, or road) **2** : the convexity of the curve of an airfoil from the leading edge to the trailing edge **3** : a setting of the wheels of an automotive vehicle closer together at the bottom than at the top
cam·bi·um \'kam-bē-əm\ n, pl **-bi·ums** or **-bia** \-bē-ə\ [NL, ML, exchange, fr. L cambire to exchange — more at CHANGE] (1671) : a thin formative layer between the xylem and phloem of most vascular

\ə\ abut \ᵊ\ kitten, F table \ər\ further \a\ ash \ā\ ace \ä\ mop, mar
\aú\ out \ch\ chin \e\ bet \ē\ easy \g\ go \i\ hit \ī\ ice \j\ job
\ŋ\ sing \ō\ go \ȯ\ law \ȯi\ boy \th\ thin \t͟h\ the \ü\ loot \ú\ foot
\y\ yet \zh\ vision \á, k, ⁿ, œ, œ̄, ᵫ, ᵫ̄, ᵊ\ see Guide to Pronunciation

plants that gives rise to new cells and is responsible for secondary growth — **cam·bi·al** \-bē-əl\ *adj*
Cam·bo·di·an \kam-ˈbō-dē-ən\ *n* (1770)   **1** : a native or inhabitant of Cambodia   **2** : KHMER 2 — **Cambodian** *adj*
Cam·bri·an \ˈkam-brē-ən, ˈkäm-\ *adj* [ML *Cambria* Wales, fr. MW *Cymry* Wales, Welshmen] (ca. 1656)   **1** : WELSH   **2** : of, relating to, or being the earliest geologic period of the Paleozoic era or the corresponding system of rocks marked by fossils of every great animal type except the vertebrates — see GEOLOGIC TIME table — **Cambrian** *n*
cam·bric \ˈkām-brik\ *n* [obs. Flem *Kameryk* Cambrai, city of France] (1530)   **1** : a fine thin white linen fabric   **2** : a cotton fabric that resembles cambric
cambric tea *n* (1888) : a hot drink of water, milk, sugar, and often a small amount of tea
cam·cord·er \ˈkam-ˌkȯr-dər\ *n* [*camera* + *recorder*] (1982) : a small portable combined video camera and videocassette recorder
¹came *past of* COME
²came \ˈkām\ *n* [origin unknown] (1688) : a slender grooved lead rod used to hold together panes of glass esp. in a stained-glass window
cam·el \ˈka-məl\ *n* [ME, fr. OE & ONF, fr. L *camelus*, fr. Gk *kamēlos*, of Sem origin; akin to Heb *gāmāl* camel] (bef. 12c)   **1** : either of two large ruminant mammals (genus *Camelus*) used as draft and saddle animals in desert regions esp. of Africa and Asia: **a** : the one-humped camel (*C. dromedarius*) extant only as a domestic or feral animal — called also *dromedary*   **b** : the two-humped camel (*C. bactrianus* syn. *C. ferus*) of Chinese Turkestan and Mongolia — called also *Bactrian camel*   **2** : a watertight structure used esp. to lift submerged ships   **3** : a light yellowish brown
cam·el·back \ˈkam-əl-ˌbak\ *n* (1860) : the back of a camel
cam·el·eer \ˌka-mə-ˈlir\ *n* (1808) : a camel driver
camel hair *also* **camel's hair** *n* (14c)   **1** : the hair of the camel or a substitute for it (as hair from squirrels' tails)   **2** : cloth made of camel hair or a mixture of camel hair and wool usu. light tan and of soft silky texture
ca·mel·lia \kə-ˈmēl-yə\ *n* [NL *Camellia*, fr. *Camellus* (Georg Josef Kamel †1706 Moravian Jesuit missionary)] (ca. 1753) : any of a genus (*Camellia*) of shrubs or trees of the tea family; *esp* : an ornamental greenhouse shrub (*C. japonica*) with glossy leaves and roselike flowers
ca·mel·o·pard \kə-ˈme-lə-ˌpärd\ *n* [LL *camelopardus*, alter. of L *camelopardalis*, fr. Gk *kamēlopardalis*, fr. *kamēlos* + *pardalis* leopard] (14c)   **1** *archaic* : GIRAFFE   **2** *cap* : CAMELOPARDALIS
Ca·mel·o·par·da·lis \kə-ˌme-lə-ˈpär-dᵊl-əs\ *n* [L (gen. *Camelopardalis*), camelopard] : a northern constellation between Cassiopeia and Ursa Major
Cam·e·lot \ˈka-mə-ˌlät\ *n*   **1** : the site of King Arthur's palace and court   **2** : a time, place, or atmosphere of idyllic happiness
Cam·em·bert \ˈka-məm-ˌber\ *n* [F, fr. *Camembert*, Normandy, France] (1878) : a soft surface-ripened cheese with a thin grayish white rind and a yellow interior
cam·eo \ˈka-mē-ˌō\ *n*, *pl* **-eos** [ME *camew*, fr. MF *camau*, *camaheu*] (15c)   **1   a** : a gem carved in relief; *esp* : a small piece of sculpture on a stone or shell cut in relief in one layer with another contrasting layer serving as background   **b** : a small medallion with a profiled head in relief   **2** : a carving or sculpture made in the manner of a cameo   **3** : a usu. brief literary or filmic piece that brings into delicate or sharp relief the character of a person, place, or event   **4** : a small theatrical role usu. performed by a well-known actor and often limited to a single scene; *broadly* : any brief appearance — **cameo** *adj* — **cameo** *vt*
cam·era \ˈkam-rə, ˈka-mər-ə\ *n* [LL, room — more at CHAMBER] (1712)   **1** : the treasury department of the papal curia   **2** *a* : CAMERA OBSCURA   **b** : a device that consists of a lightproof chamber with an aperture fitted with a lens and a shutter through which the image of an object is projected onto a surface for recording (as on film) or for translation into electrical impulses (as for television broadcast) — **on camera** : before a live television camera
cam·era lu·ci·da \-ˈlü-sə-də\ *n* [NL, lit., light chamber] (1831) : an instrument that by means of a prism or mirrors and often a microscope causes a virtual image of an object to appear as if projected upon a plane surface so that an outline may be traced
cam·era·man \-ˌman, -mən\ *n* (1908) : a person who operates a camera (as for motion pictures or television)
cam·era ob·scu·ra \-əb-ˈskyur-ə\ *n* [NL, lit., dark chamber] (1725) : a darkened enclosure having an aperture usu. provided with a lens through which light from external objects enters to form an image of the objects on the opposite surface
cam·era·per·son \-ˌpər-sᵊn\ *n* (1976) : a cameraman or camerawoman
cam·era·wom·an \-ˌwu̇-mən\ *n* (1971) : a woman who operates a camera
cam·er·len·go \ˌka-mər-ˈleŋ-(ˌ)gō\ *n*, *pl* **-gos** [It *camarlingo*] (1625) : a cardinal who heads the Apostolic Camera
ca·mion \kȧ-ˈmyōⁿ\ *n* [F] (1911) : MOTORTRUCK; *also* : BUS
cam·i·sa·do \ˌka-mə-ˈsä-(ˌ)dō, -ˈsä-\ *n*, *pl* **-does** [prob. fr. obs. Sp *camisada*] (1548) *archaic* : an attack by night
ca·mise \kə-ˈmēz, -ˈmēs\ *n* [Ar *qamīs*, perh. fr. LL *camisia*] (1812) : a light loose long-sleeved shirt, gown, or tunic
cam·i·sole \ˈka-mə-ˌsōl\ *n* [F, fr. Prov *camisolla*, dim. of *camisa* shirt, fr. LL *camisia*] (1795)   **1** : a short negligee jacket for women   **2** : a short sleeveless garment for women
cam·let \ˈkam-lət\ *n* [ME *cameloit*, fr. MF *camelot*, fr. Ar *khamlat* woolen plush] (15c)   **1   a** : a medieval Asian fabric of camel hair or angora wool   **b** : a European fabric of silk and wool   **c** : a fine lustrous woolen   **2** : a garment made of camlet
camomile *var of* CHAMOMILE
ca·mor·ra \kə-ˈmȯr-ə, -ˈmär-\ *n* [It] (1865) : a group of persons united for dishonest or dishonorable ends; *esp* : a secret organization formed about 1820 at Naples, Italy
ca·mor·ris·ta \ˌkä-mō-ˈrē-stə\ *n*, *pl* **-ti** \-(ˌ)stē\ [It, fr. *camorra*] (1897) : a member of a camorra
¹cam·ou·flage \ˈka-mə-ˌfläzh, -ˌfläj\ *n* [F, fr. *camoufler* to disguise] (1917)   **1** : the disguising esp. of military equipment or installations with paint, nets, or foliage; *also* : the disguise so applied   **2   a** : concealment by means of disguise   **b** : behavior or artifice designed to deceive or hide — **cam·ou·flag·ic** \ˌka-mə-ˈflä-zhik, -jik\ *adj*

²camouflage *vb* **-flaged; -flag·ing** *vt* (1917) : to conceal or disguise by camouflage ~ *vi* : to practice camouflage — **cam·ou·flage·able** \ˈka-mə-ˌflä-zhə-bəl, -jə-bəl\ *adj*
³camouflage *adj* (1945) : made in colors or patterns typical of camouflage ⟨a ~ jacket⟩
¹camp \ˈkamp\ *n*, *often attrib* [MF, prob. fr. ONF or OProv, fr. L *campus* plain, field] (1528)   **1   a** : a place usu. away from urban areas where tents or simple buildings (as cabins) are erected for shelter or for temporary residence (as for laborers, prisoners, or vacationers) ⟨migrant labor ~⟩   **b** : a group of tents, cabins, or huts (fishing ~s along the river)   **c** : a settlement newly sprung up in a lumbering or mining region   **d** : a place usu. in the country for recreation or instruction during the summer ⟨goes to ~ every July⟩ ⟨computer ~⟩ ⟨football ~⟩   **2   a** : a body of persons encamped   **b** (1) : a group of persons; *esp* : a group engaged in promoting or defending a theory, doctrine, position, or person (2) : an ideological position   **3** : military service or life
²camp *vi* (1543)   **1** : to make camp or occupy a camp   **2** : to live temporarily in a camp or outdoors — often used with *out*   **3** : to take up one's quarters : LODGE   **4** : to take up one's position : settle down ~ *vt* : to put into a camp; *also* : ACCOMMODATE
³camp *n* [origin unknown] (ca. 1909)   **1** : exaggerated effeminate mannerisms exhibited esp. by homosexuals   **2** : a homosexual displaying camp   **3** : something so outrageously artificial, affected, inappropriate, or out-of-date as to be considered amusing   **4** : something self-consciously exaggerated or theatrical — **camp·i·ly** \ˈkam-pə-lē\ *adv* — **camp·i·ness** \-pē-nəs\ *n* — **campy** \ˈkam-pē\ *adj*
⁴camp *adj* (1909) : of, relating to, being, or displaying camp ⟨~ sendups of the songs of the fifties and sixties—John Elsom⟩
⁵camp *vi* (1925) : to engage in camp : exhibit the qualities of camp ⟨he . . . was ~ing, hands on hips, with a quick eye to notice every man who passed by —R. M. McAlmon⟩
¹cam·paign \(ˌ)kam-ˈpān\ *n* [F *campagne*, prob. fr. It *campagna* level country, campaign, fr. LL *campania* level country, fr. L, the level country around Naples] (ca. 1656)   **1** : a connected series of military operations forming a distinct phase of a war   **2** : a connected series of operations designed to bring about a particular result ⟨election ~⟩
²campaign *vi* (1701) : to go on, engage in, or conduct a campaign — **cam·paign·er** *n*
cam·pa·ni·le \ˌkam-pə-ˈnē-lē, ˌkäm-, -(ˌ)lā, *esp of US structures also* -ˈnē(ə)l\ *n*, *pl* **-ni·les** *or* **-ni·li** \-ˈnē-lē\ [It, fr. *campana* bell, fr. LL] (1640) : a usu. freestanding bell tower
cam·pa·nol·o·gist \ˌkam-pə-ˈnä-lə-jist\ *n* (1857) : one that practices or is skilled in campanology
cam·pa·nol·o·gy \-jē\ *n* [NL *campanologia*, fr. LL *campana* + NL *-o-* + *-logia* -logy] (ca. 1823) : the art of bell ringing
cam·pan·u·la \kam-ˈpan-yə-lə\ *n* [NL, dim. of LL *campana*] (1664) : any of a genus (*Campanula*) of bellflowers
cam·pan·u·late \-lət, -ˌlāt\ *adj* [NL *campanula* bell-shaped part, dim. of LL *campana*] (1668) : shaped like a bell ⟨~ flower⟩
Camp·bell·ite \ˈka-mə-ˌlīt *also* ˈkam-bə-\ *n* [Alexander *Campbell*] (1830) : DISCIPLE 2 — often taken to be offensive
camp·craft \ˈkamp-ˌkraft\ *n* (ca. 1893) : skill and practice in the activities relating to camping
camp·er \ˈkam-pər\ *n* (1856)   **1** : one that camps   **2** : a portable dwelling (as a specially equipped trailer or automotive vehicle) for use during casual travel and camping
cam·pe·si·no \ˌkam-pə-ˈsē-(ˌ)nō\ *n*, *pl* **-nos** [Sp, fr. *campo* field, country, fr. L *campus* field] (1898) : a native of a Latin-American rural area; *esp* : a Latin-American Indian farmer or farm laborer
cam·pes·tral \kam-ˈpes-trəl\ *adj* [L *campestr-*, *campester*, fr. *campus*] (ca. 1750) : of or relating to fields or open country : RURAL
camp·fire \ˈkamp-ˌfir\ *n* (1675) : a fire built outdoors (as at a camp or a picnic)
Camp Fire girl *n* [fr. *Camp Fire Girls*, Inc., former name of Camp Fire, Inc.] (1912) : a girl who is a member of a national organization of young people from ages 5 to 18
camp follower *n* (1810)   **1** : a civilian who follows a military unit to attend or exploit military personnel; *specif* : PROSTITUTE   **2** : a disciple or follower who is not of the main body of members or adherents; *esp* : a politician who joins the party or movement solely for personal gain
camp·ground \ˈkamp-ˌgraund\ *n* (1805) : the area or place (as a field or grove) used for a camp, for camping, or for a camp meeting
cam·phene \ˈkam-ˌfēn\ *n* (ca. 1847) : any of several terpenes related to camphor; *esp* : a colorless crystalline terpene $C_{10}H_{16}$ used in insecticides
cam·phor \ˈkam(p)-fər\ *n* [ME *caumfre*, fr. AF, fr. ML *camphora*, fr. Ar *kāfūr*, fr. Malay *kapur*] (14c) : a tough gummy volatile aromatic crystalline compound $C_{10}H_{16}O$ obtained esp. from the wood and bark of the camphor tree and used as a liniment and mild topical analgesic in medicine, as a plasticizer, and as an insect repellent; *also* : any of several similar compounds (as some terpene alcohols and ketones) — **cam·pho·ra·ceous** \ˌkam(p)-fə-ˈrā-shəs\ *adj*
cam·phor·ate \ˈkam(p)-fə-ˌrāt\ *vt* **-at·ed; -at·ing** (1641) : to impregnate or treat with camphor
camphor tree *n* (1607) : a large Asian evergreen tree (*Cinnamomum camphora*) of the laurel family grown in warm regions
cam·pi·on \ˈkam-pē-ən\ *n* [prob. fr. obs. *campion* (champion)] (1576) : any of various plants (genera *Lychnis* and *Silene*) of the pink family
camp meeting *n* (1803) : a series of evangelistic meetings usu. held outdoors and attended by persons who often camp nearby
cam·po \ˈkam-(ˌ)pō, ˈkäm-\ *n*, *pl* **campos** [AmerSp, fr. Sp, field, fr. L *campus*] (1863) : a grassland plain in So. America with scattered perennial herbs
camp·o·ree \ˌkam-pə-ˈrē\ *n* [*camp* + *jamboree*] (1927) : a gathering of Boy Scouts or Girl Scouts from a given geographic area
camp shirt *n* (1979) : a woman's shirt having a notched collar and often patch pockets
camp·site \ˈkamp-ˌsīt\ *n* (1910) : a place suitable for or used as the site of a camp
cam·pus \ˈkam-pəs\ *n*, *often attrib* [L, plain] (1774)   **1** : the grounds and buildings of a university, college, or school   **2** : a university, college, or school viewed as an academic, social, or spiritual entity   **3**

: grounds that resemble a campus ⟨hospital ~⟩ ⟨landscaped corporate ~⟩

cam·py·lo·bac·ter \,kam-pi-lō-'bak-tər, kam-,pi-lə-\ *n* [NL, fr. Gk *kampylos* bent + NL *bacterium*; akin to Gk *kampē* bend — more at GAMBIT] (1964) : any of a genus (*Campylobacter*) of spirally curved motile gram-negative rod-shaped bacteria of which some are pathogenic in domestic animals and humans

cam·py·lot·ro·pous \,kam-pi-'lä-trə-pəs\ *adj* [Gk *kampylos* + ISV *-tropous* -tropous] (1835) : having the ovule curved

cam·shaft \'kam-,shaft\ *n* (ca. 1877) : a shaft to which a cam is fastened or of which a cam forms an integral part

cam wheel *n* (ca. 1853) : a wheel set or shaped to act as a cam

¹**can** \kən, 'kan\ *vb, past* **could** \kəd, 'kud\; *pres sing & pl* **can** [ME (1st & 3d sing. pres. indic.), fr. OE; akin to OHG *kan* (1st & 3d sing. pres. indic.) know, am able, OE *cnāwan* to know — more at KNOW] *vt* (bef. 12c) **1** *obs* : KNOW, UNDERSTAND **2** *archaic* : to be able to do, make, or accomplish ~ *vi, archaic* : to have knowledge or skill ~ *verbal auxiliary* **1 a** : know how to ⟨she ~ read⟩ **b** : be physically or mentally able to ⟨he ~ lift 200 pounds⟩ **c** — used to indicate possibility ⟨do you think he ~ still be alive⟩ ⟨those things ~ happen⟩; sometimes used interchangeably with *may* **d** : be permitted by conscience or feeling to ⟨~ hardly blame her⟩ **e** : be made possible or probable by circumstances to ⟨he ~ hardly have meant that⟩ **f** : be inherently able or designed to ⟨everything that money ~ buy⟩ **g** : be logically or axiologically able to ⟨2 + 2 ~ also be written 3 + 1⟩ **h** : be enabled by law, agreement, or custom to **2** : have permission to — used interchangeably with *may* ⟨you ~ go if you like⟩

usage *Can* and *may* are most frequently interchangeable in senses denoting possibility; because the possibility of one's doing something may depend on another's acquiescence, they have also become interchangeable in the sense denoting permission. The use of *can* to ask or grant permission has been common since the 19th century and is well established, although some commentators feel *may* is more appropriate in formal contexts. *May* is relatively rare in negative constructions (*mayn't* is not common); *cannot* and *can't* are usual in such contexts.

²**can** \'kan\ *n* [ME *canne*, fr. OE; akin to OHG *channa*] (bef. 12c) : a usu. cylindrical receptacle: **a** : a vessel for holding liquids; *specif* : a drinking vessel **b** : a usu. metal typically cylindrical receptacle usu. with an open top, often with a removable cover, and sometimes with a spout or side handles (as for holding milk or trash) **c** : a container (as of tinplate) in which products (as perishable foods) are hermetically sealed for preservation until use **d** : a jar for packing or preserving fruit or vegetables **2** : JAIL **3 a** : TOILET **b** : BATHROOM **1 4** : BUTTOCKS **5** : DESTROYER 2 **6** *slang* : an ounce of marijuana — **can·ful** \'kan-,ful\ *n* — **in the can** *of a film or videotape* : completed and ready for release

³**can** \'kan\ *vt* **canned; can·ning** (1861) **1 a** : to put in a can : preserve by sealing in airtight cans or jars **b** : to hit (a golf shot) into the cup **c** : to hit (a shot) in basketball **2** : to discharge from employment **3** *slang* : to put a stop or end to — **can·ner** *n*

Ca·naan·ite \'kā-nə-,nīt\ *n* [Gk *Kananitēs*, fr. *Kanaan* Canaan, fr. Heb *Kena'an*] (1535) : a member of a Semitic people inhabiting ancient Palestine and Phoenicia from about 3000 B.C. — **Canaanite** *adj*

Can·a·da balsam \'ka-nə-də-\ *n* [Canada, country in No. America] (1811) : a viscid yellowish to greenish oleoresin exudate of the balsam fir (*Abies balsmea*) that solidifies to a transparent mass and is used as a transparent cement esp. in microscopy

Canada Day *n* (1950) : July 1 observed as a legal holiday in commemoration of the proclamation of dominion status in 1867

Canada goose *n* (1731) : the common wild goose (*Branta canadensis*) of No. America that is chiefly gray and brownish with black head and neck and a white patch running from the sides of the head under the throat

Canada thistle *n* (1799) : a European thistle (*Cirsium arvense*) with pinkish purple or white flowers naturalized as a weed in No. America

Ca·na·di·an \kə-'nā-dē-ən\ *n* (1568) : a native or inhabitant of Canada — **Canadian** *adj*

Canadian bacon *n* (ca. 1934) : bacon cut from the loin that has little fat and is cut into round or oblong slices

Canadian football *n* (1944) : a game resembling American football that is played on a turfed field between two teams of 12 players each

Canadian French *n* (1816) : the language of the French Canadians

Canadian lynx *or* **Canada lynx** *n* (1840) : LYNX c

ca·naille \kə-'nī, -'nā(ə)l\ *n* [F, fr. It *canaglia*, fr. *cane* dog, fr. L *canis* — more at HOUND] (1661) **1** : RABBLE, RIFFRAFF **2** : PROLETARIAN

¹**ca·nal** \kə-'nal\ *n* [ME, fr. L *canalis* pipe, channel, fr. *canna* reed — more at CANE] (15c) **1** : a tubular anatomical passage or channel : DUCT **2** : CHANNEL, WATERCOURSE **3** : an artificial waterway for navigation or for draining or irrigating land **4** : any of various faint narrow lines on the planet Mars seen through telescopes and once thought by some to be canals built by Martians

²**canal** *vt* **-nalled** *or* **-naled; -nal·ling** *or* **-nal·ing** (1819) : to construct a canal through or across

can·a·lic·u·lus \,ka-nə-'li-kyə-ləs\ *n, pl* **-li** \-,lī, -,lē\ [L, dim. of *canalis*] (1854) : a minute canal in a bodily structure — **can·a·lic·u·lar** \-lər\ *adj*

can·a·li·za·tion \,ka-nᵊl-ə-'zā-shən\ *n* (1844) **1** : an act or instance of canalizing **2** : a system of channels

can·a·lize \'ka-nᵊl-,īz\ *vb* **-lized; -liz·ing** *vt* (1860) **1 a** : to provide with a canal or channel **b** : to make into or similar to a canal **2** : to provide with an outlet; *esp* : to direct into preferred channels ~ *vi* **1** : to flow in or into a channel **2** : to establish new channels

can·a·pé \'ka-nə-pē, -,pā\ *n* [F, lit., sofa, fr. ML *canopeum, canapeum* mosquito net — more at CANOPY] (1890) : an appetizer consisting of a piece of bread or toast or a cracker topped with a savory spread (as caviar or cheese) — compare HORS D'OEUVRE

ca·nard \kə-'närd *also* -'när\ *n* [F, lit., duck; in sense 1, fr. MF *vendre des canards à moitié* to cheat, lit., to half-sell ducks] (ca. 1859) **1** : a false or unfounded report or story; *esp* : a fabricated report **2** : an airplane with horizontal stabilizing and control surfaces in front of supporting surfaces; *also* : a small airfoil in front of the wing of an aircraft that increases the aircraft's stability

ca·nary \kə-'ner-ē\ *n, pl* **ca·nar·ies** [MF *canarie*, fr. OSp *canario*, fr. *Islas Canarias* Canary Islands] (1592) **1** : a lively 16th century court dance **2** : a Canary Islands usu. sweet wine similar to Madeira **3** : a small finch (*Serinus canarius*) of the Canary Islands that is usu. greenish to yellow and is kept as a cage bird and singer **4** *slang* : INFORMER 2

canary seed *n* (1597) : seed of a Canary Islands grass (*Phalaris canariensis*) used as food for cage birds

canary yellow *n* (ca. 1865) : a light to a moderate or vivid yellow

ca·nas·ta \kə-'nas-tə\ *n* [Sp, lit., basket] (1948) **1** : a form of rummy using two full decks in which players or partnerships try to meld groups of three or more cards of the same rank and score bonuses for 7-card melds **2** : a meld of seven cards of the same rank in canasta

can·can \'kan-,kan\ *n* [F] (1848) : a woman's dance of French origin characterized by high kicking usu. while holding up the front of a full ruffled skirt

¹**can·cel** \'kan(t)-səl\ *vb* **-celed** *or* **-celled; -cel·ing** *or* **-cel·ling** \-s(ə-)liŋ\ [ME *cancellen*, fr. MF *canceller*, fr. LL *cancellare*, fr. L, to make like a lattice, fr. *cancelli* (pl.), dim. of *cancer* lattice, prob. alter. of *carcer* prison] *vt* (14c) **1 a** : to destroy the force, effectiveness, or validity of : ANNUL ⟨~ a magazine subscription⟩ ⟨a ~ed check⟩ **b** : to bring to nothingness : DESTROY **c** : to match in force or effect : OFFSET — often used with *out* ⟨his irritability ~ed out his natural kindness — Osbert Sitwell⟩ **d** : to call off usu. without expectation of conducting or performing at a later time ⟨~ a football game⟩ **2 a** : to mark or strike out for deletion **b** : OMIT, DELETE **3 a** : to remove (a common divisor) from numerator and denominator **b** : to remove (equivalents) on opposite sides of an equation or account **4** : to deface (a postage or revenue stamp) esp. with a set of ink lines so as to invalidate for reuse ~ *vi* : to neutralize each other's strength or effect : COUNTERBALANCE — **can·cel·able** *or* **can·cel·la·ble** \-s(ə-)lə-bəl\ *adj* — **can·cel·er** *or* **can·cel·ler** \-s(ə-)lər\ *n*

²**cancel** *n* (1806) **1** : CANCELLATION **2 a** : a deleted part or passage **b** (1) : a leaf containing matter to be deleted (2) : a new leaf or slip substituted for matter already printed

can·cel·la·tion *also* **can·cel·a·tion** \,kan(t)-sə-'lā-shən\ *n* (1535) **1** : the act or an instance of canceling **2** : a released accommodation **3** : a mark made to cancel something (as a postage stamp)

can·cel·lous \kan-'se-ləs, 'kan(t)-sə-ləs\ *adj* [NL *cancelli* intersecting osseous plates and bars in cancellous bone, fr. L, lattice] (ca. 1839) *of bone* : having a porous structure

can·cer \'kan(t)-sər\ *n* [ME, fr. L (gen. *Cancri*), lit., crab; akin to Gk *karkinos* crab, cancer] **1** *cap* **a** : a northern zodiacal constellation between Gemini and Leo **b** (1) : the 4th sign of the zodiac in astrology — see ZODIAC table (2) : one born under the sign of Cancer **2** [L, crab, cancer] **a** : a malignant tumor of potentially unlimited growth that expands locally by invasion and systemically by metastasis **b** : an abnormal bodily state marked by such tumors **3** : something evil or malignant that spreads destructively ⟨the ~ of hidden resentment — *Irish Digest*⟩ **4 a** : an enlarged tumorlike plant growth (as that of crown gall) **b** : a plant disease marked by such growths — **can·cer·ous** \'kan(t)s-rəs, 'kan(t)-sə-\ *adj* — **can·cer·ous·ly** *adv*

Can·cer·ian \kan-'ser-ē-ən, -'sir-\ *n* (1911) : CANCER 1b(2)

can·de·la \kan-'dē-lə, -'de-, -'dā-; 'kan-də-lə\ *n* [L, candle] (1949) : the base unit of luminous intensity in the International System of Units that is equal to the luminous intensity in a given direction of a source which emits monochromatic radiation of frequency 540×10^{12} hertz and has a radiant intensity in that direction of $^1/_{683}$ watt per unit solid angle — called also *candle*; abbr. *cd*

can·de·la·bra \,kan-də-'lä-brə *sometimes* -'la-\ *n* [alter. of *candelabrum*, fr. *candela*] (1815) : a branched candlestick or lamp with several lights

can·de·la·brum \-'brəm\ *n, pl* **-bra** \-brə\ *also* **-brums** [L] (1811) : CANDELABRA

can·dent \'kan-dənt\ *adj* [L *candent-, candens,* prp. of *candēre*] (1577) : glowing from or as if from great heat

can·des·cence \kan-'de-sᵊn(t)s\ *n* (ca. 1864) : a candescent state : glowing whiteness

can·des·cent \-sᵊnt\ *adj* [L *candescent-, candescens,* prp. of *candescere,* incho. of *candēre*] (1824) : glowing or dazzling from or as if from great heat

can·did \'kan-dəd\ *adj* [F & L; F *candide,* fr. L *candidus* bright, white, fr. *candēre* to shine, glow; akin to W *can* white, Skt *candati* it shines] (1630) **1** : WHITE ⟨~ flames⟩ **2** : free from bias, prejudice, or malice : FAIR ⟨a ~ observer⟩ **3 a** : marked by honest sincere expression **b** : indicating or suggesting sincere honesty and absence of deception **c** : disposed to criticize severely : BLUNT **4** : relating to photography of subjects acting naturally or spontaneously without being posed : FRANK — **can·did·ly** *adv* — **can·did·ness** *n*

can·di·da \'kan-də-də\ *n* [NL, genus name, fr. L, fem. of *candidus*] (1939) : any of a genus (*Candida*) of parasitic imperfect fungi that resemble yeasts and occur esp. in the mouth, vagina, and intestinal tract and that are usu. benign but can become pathogenic; *esp* : one (*C. albicans*) causing thrush

can·di·da·cy \'kan-də-də-sē, 'ka-nə-\ *n, pl* **-cies** (1864) : the state of being a candidate

can·di·date \'kan-də-,dāt, 'ka-nə-, -dət\ *n* [L *candidatus,* fr. *candidatus* clothed in white, fr. *candidus* white; fr. the white toga worn by candidates for office in ancient Rome] (1600) **1 a** : one that aspires to or is nominated or qualified for an office, membership, or award **b** : one likely or suited to undergo or be chosen for something specified ⟨a ~ for surgery⟩ **2** : a student in the process of meeting final requirements for a degree

can·di·da·ture \'kan-də-də-,chur, 'ka-nə-, -chər\ *n* (1851) *chiefly Brit* : CANDIDACY

candelabra *syn* see FRANK

\ə\ abut \ᵊ\ kitten, F table \ər\ further \a\ ash \ā\ ace \ä\ mop, mar \aủ\ out \ch\ chin \e\ bet \ē\ easy \g\ go \i\ hit \ī\ ice \j\ job \ŋ\ sing \ō\ go \ò\ law \òi\ boy \th\ thin \t͟h\ the \ü\ loot \ủ\ foot \y\ yet \zh\ vision \ȧ, k̲, ⁿ, œ, œ̄, ᵫ, ū̄, ᵉ\ *see* Guide to Pronunciation

candid camera *n* (1929) : a camera used to record subjects in a natural, spontaneous, or unposed manner; *also* : something likened to a camera used in such a manner — **candid–camera** *adj*

can·di·a·sis \kan-də-'dī-ə-səs\ *n, pl* **-a·ses** \-,sēz\ [NL] (1951) : infection with or disease caused by a candida — called also *moniliasis*

can·died \'kan-dēd\ *adj* (ca. 1606) **1** : encrusted or coated with sugar **2** : baked with sugar or syrup until translucent

¹can·dle \'kan-d°l\ *n* [ME *candel*, fr. OE, fr. L *candela*, fr. *candēre*] (bef. 12c) **1** : a usu. molded or dipped mass of wax or tallow containing a wick that may be burned (as to give light, heat, or scent or for celebration or votive purposes) **2** : something resembling a candle in shape or use ⟨a sulfur ~ for fumigating⟩ **3** : required effort, expense, or trouble — usu. used in the phrase *not worth the candle* **4** : CANDELA

²candle *vt* **can·dled; can·dling** \'kan(d)-liŋ, 'kan-d°l-iŋ\ (1879) : to examine by holding between the eye and a light; *esp* : to test (eggs) in this way for staleness, blood clots, fertility, and growth — **can·dler** \'kan(d)-lər, 'kan-d°l-ər\ *n*

can·dle·ber·ry \'kan-d°l-,ber-ē\ *n* (ca. 1730) : a wax myrtle (*Myrica cerifera*); *also* : a bayberry (*Myrica pensylvanica*)

can·dle·fish \-,fish\ *n* (1881) : EULACHON

can·dle·hold·er \-,hōl-dər\ *n* (1932) : CANDLESTICK

can·dle·light \'kan-d°l-,(l)īt\ *n* (bef. 12c) **1 a** : the light of a candle **b** : a soft artificial light **2** : the time for lighting candles : TWILIGHT

can·dle·light·er \-,(l)ī-tər\ *n* (15c) **1** : one who lights the candles for a ceremony **2** : a long-handled implement with a taper and a snuffer that is used for the ceremonial lighting and extinguishing of candles

can·dle·lit \-,(l)it\ *or* **can·dle·light·ed** \-,(l)ī-təd\ *adj* (1917) : illuminated by candlelight ⟨a ~ dinner⟩

Can·dle·mas \'kan-d°l-məs\ *n* [ME *candelmasse*, fr. OE *candelmæsse*, fr. *candel* + *mæsse* mass, feast; fr. the candles blessed and carried in celebration of the feast] (bef. 12c) : February 2 observed as a church festival in commemoration of the presentation of Christ in the temple and the purification of the Virgin Mary

can·dle·nut \-,nət\ *n* (ca. 1836) : the oily seed of a tropical tree (*Aleurites moluccana*) of the spurge family used locally to make candles and commercially as a source of oil; *also* : this tree

can·dle·pin \-,pin\ *n* (1901) **1** : a slender bowling pin tapering toward top and bottom **2** *pl but sing in constr* : a bowling game using candlepins and a smaller ball than that used in tenpins

can·dle·pow·er \-,paù(-ə)r\ *n* (1877) : luminous intensity expressed in candelas; *also* : CANDELA

can·dle·snuff·er \-,snə-fər\ *n* (1552) : an implement for snuffing candles that consists of a small hollow cone attached to a handle

can·dle·stick \-,stik\ *n* (bef. 12c) : a holder with a socket for a candle

can·dle·wick \-,wik\ *n* (bef. 12c) **1** : the wick of a candle **2** : a soft cotton embroidery yarn; *also* : embroidery made with this yarn usu. in tufts

can·dle·wood \-,wùd\ *n* (1712) **1** : any of several trees or shrubs (as ocotillo) chiefly of resinous character **2** : slivers of resinous wood burned for light

can–do \'kan-'dü\ *adj* (1945) : characterized by eager willingness to accept and meet challenges ⟨a ~ attitude⟩

can·dor \'kan-dər, -,dòr\ *n* [F & L; F *candeur*, fr. L *candor*, fr. *candēre* — more at CANDID] (14c) **1 a** : WHITENESS, BRILLIANCE **b** *obs* : unstained purity **2** : freedom from prejudice or malice : FAIRNESS **3** *archaic* : KINDLINESS **4** : unreserved, honest, or sincere expression : FORTHRIGHTNESS ⟨the ~ with which he acknowledged a weakness in his own case —Aldous Huxley⟩

can·dour \'kan-dər\ *chiefly Brit var of* CANDOR

¹can·dy \'kan-dē\ *n, pl* **candies** [ME *sugre candy*, part trans. of MF *sucre candi*, part trans. of OIt *zucchero candi*, fr. *zucchero* sugar + Ar *qandī* candied, fr. *qand* cane sugar] (15c) **1** : crystallized sugar formed by boiling down sugar syrup **2 a** : a confection made with sugar and often flavoring and filling **b** : a piece of such confection — **candy** *adj*

²candy *vb* **can·died; can·dy·ing** *vt* (1533) **1** : to encrust in or coat with sugar; *specif* : to cook (as fruit or fruit peel) in a heavy syrup until glazed **2** : to make attractive : SWEETEN **3** : to crystallize into sugar ~ *vi* : to become coated or encrusted with sugar crystals : become crystallized into sugar

candy floss *n* (1951) **1** *Brit* : COTTON CANDY **2** *usu* **candyfloss** *Brit* : something attractive but insubstantial

candy striper *n* [fr. the striped uniform worn suggesting the stripes on some sticks of candy] (1963) : a teenage volunteer worker at a hospital

can·dy·tuft \'kan-dē-,təft\ *n* [*Candy*, alter. of Candia Crete, Greek island + E *tuft*] (1664) : any of a genus (*Iberis*) of plants of the mustard family cultivated for their white, pink, or purple flowers

¹cane \'kān\ *n* [ME, fr MF, fr. OProv *cana*, fr. L *canna*, fr. Gk *kanna*, of Sem origin; akin to Ar *qanāh* hollow stick, reed] (14c) **1 a** (1) : a hollow or pithy and usu. slender and flexible jointed stem (as of a reed) (2) : any of various slender woody stems; *esp* : an elongated flowering or fruiting stem (as of a rose) usu. arising directly from the ground **b** : any of various tall woody grasses or reeds: as (1) : any of a genus (*Arundinaria*) of coarse grasses (2) : SUGARCANE (3) : SORGHUM **2** : cane dressed for use: as **a** : a cane walking stick; *broadly* : WALKING STICK **b** : a cane or rod for flogging **c** : RATTAN; *esp* : split rattan for wickerwork or basketwork **3** : a tiny glass rod used in decorative glasswork (as in millefiori and paperweights)

²cane *vt* **caned; can·ing** (1667) **1** : to beat with a cane ⟨he sat in a professor's chair and *caned* sophomores for blowing spitballs —H. L. Mencken⟩ **2** : to weave or furnish with cane ⟨~ the seat of a chair⟩

cane·brake \'kān-,brāk\ *n* (1769) : a thicket of cane

can·er \'kā-nər\ *n* (1868) : one that canes chairs

ca·nes·cent \kə-'ne-s°nt, ka-\ *adj* [L *canescent-, canescens,* prp. of *canescere,* incho. of *canēre* to be gray, be white, fr. *canus* white, hoary — more at HARE] (ca. 1828) : growing white, whitish, or hoary; *esp* : having a fine grayish white pubescence ⟨~ leaves⟩

cane sugar *n* (1841) : sugar from sugarcane

cane·ware \'kān-,war, -,wer\ *n* [fr. its color] (1878) : a buff or yellowish stoneware

ca·nic·o·la fever \kə-'ni-kə-lə-\ *n* [NL *canicola,* fr. L *canis* dog + *-cola* inhabitant — more at HOUND, -COLOUS] (1943) : an acute disease in humans and dogs characterized by gastroenteritis and mild jaundice and caused by a spirochete (*Leptospira canicola*)

ca·nic·u·lar \kə-'ni-kyə-lər\ *adj* [ME *caniculer* of the star Sirius, fr. LL *canicularis,* fr. L *Canicula* Sirius, dim. of *canis*] (12c) : of or relating to the dog days

ca·nid \'kā-nəd, 'kā-\ *n* [NL *Canidae,* fr. *Canis,* type genus, fr. L *canis*] (ca. 1889) : any of a family (Canidae) of carnivorous animals that includes the wolves, jackals, foxes, coyote, and the domestic dog

¹ca·nine \'kā-,nīn, Brit also 'ka-\ *n* (15c) **1** [ME, fr. L (*dens*) *caninus* canine tooth] : a conical pointed tooth; *esp* : one situated between the lateral incisor and the first premolar — see TOOTH illustration **2** : CANID; *also* : DOG 1a

²canine *adj* [L *caninus,* fr. *canis* dog — more at HOUND] (1607) **1** : of or resembling that of a dog ⟨~ loyalty⟩ **2** : of or relating to dogs or to the family (Canidae) including the canids

Ca·nis Ma·jor \,kā-nəs-'mā-jər, ,ka-\ *n* [L (gen. *Canis Majoris*), lit., greater dog] : a constellation to the southeast of Orion containing Sirius

Canis Mi·nor \-'mī-nər\ *n* [L (gen. *Canis Minoris*), lit., lesser dog] : a constellation to the east of Orion containing Procyon

can·is·ter *also* **can·nis·ter** \'ka-nə-stər\ *n* [L *canistrum* basket, fr. Gk *kanastron* wicker basket, fr. *kanna* reed — more at CANE] (1711) **1** : an often cylindrical container for holding a usu. specified object or substance ⟨a film ~⟩ **2** : encased shot for close-range artillery fire **3** : a perforated metal box for gas masks with material to adsorb, filter, or detoxify airborne poisons and irritants

¹can·ker \'kaŋ-kər\ *n* [ME, fr. ONF *cancre,* fr. L *cancer* crab, cancer] (13c) **1 a** (1) : an erosive or spreading sore (2) : an area of necrosis in a plant; *also* : a plant disease characterized by cankers **b** : any of various disorders of animals marked by chronic inflammatory changes **2** *archaic* : a caterpillar destructive to plants **3** *chiefly dial* : RUST 1 **4** : a source of corruption or debasement **5** *chiefly dial* : DOG ROSE — **can·ker·ous** \'kaŋ-k(ə-)rəs\ *adj*

²canker *vb* **can·kered; can·ker·ing** \'kaŋ-k(ə-)riŋ\ *vt* (14c) **1** *obs* : to infect with a spreading sore **2** : to corrupt the spirit of ~ *vi* **1** : to become infected with canker **2** : to become corrupted

canker sore *n* (ca. 1909) : a small painful ulcer esp. of the mouth

can·ker·worm \'kaŋ-kər-,wərm\ *n* (1530) : either of two geometrid moths (*Alsophila pometaria* and *Paleacrita vernata*) and esp. their larvae which are serious pests of fruit and shade trees

can·na \'ka-nə\ *n* [NL, genus name, fr. L, reed — more at CANE] (1664) : any of a genus (*Canna* of the family Cannaceae) of tropical herbs with simple stems, large leaves, and a terminal raceme of irregular flowers

can·na·bi·noid \kə-'na-bə-,nòid\ *n* [L *cannabis* + ¹-*in* + ¹-*oid*] (1970) : any of various chemical constituents (as THC or cannabinol) of cannabis or marijuana

can·na·bi·nol \-,nòl, -,nōl\ *n* [L *cannabis* + ¹-*in* + ¹-*ol*] (1896) : a physiologically inactive crystalline cannabinoid $C_{21}H_{26}O_2$

can·na·bis \'ka-nə-bəs\ *n* [L, hemp, fr. Gk *kannabis*; akin to OE *hænep* hemp] (1783) **1** : HEMP 1a **2** : any of the preparations (as marijuana or hashish) or chemicals (as THC) that are derived from the hemp and are psychoactive

canned \'kand\ *adj* (1904) **1 a** : prepared or recorded in advance; *esp* : prepared in standardized form for nonspecific use or wide distribution ⟨~ laughter⟩ ⟨~ music⟩ ⟨~ speeches⟩ **b** : lacking originality or individuality as if mass-produced ⟨~ sales pitch⟩ **2** *slang* : DRUNK 1a

can·nel coal \'ka-n°l-\ *n* [prob. fr. E dial. *cannel* candle, fr. ME *candel*] (1610) : a bituminous coal containing much volatile matter that burns brightly

can·nel·lo·ni \,ka-nə-'lō-nē\ *n pl but sing or pl in constr* [It, pl. of *can-nellone,* aug. of *cannello* segment of cane stalk, fr. *canna*] (1906) : boiled tube-shaped or rolled pasta filled with a meat, fish, cheese, or vegetable mixture and baked in a sauce

can·nery \'ka-nə-rē\ *n, pl* **-ner·ies** (1870) : a factory for the canning of foods

can·ni·bal \'ka-nə-bəl\ *n* [NL *Canibalis* Carib, fr. Sp *Caníbal,* fr. Taino *Caniba,* of Cariban origin; akin to Carib *kari'na* Carib, person] (1553) : one that eats the flesh of its own kind

can·ni·bal·ise *Brit var of* CANNIBALIZE

can·ni·bal·ism \'ka-nə-bə-,li-zəm\ *n* (1796) **1** : the usu. ritualistic eating of human flesh by a human being **2** : the eating of the flesh of an animal by another animal of the same kind **3** : an act of cannibalizing something — **can·ni·bal·is·tic** \,ka-nə-bə-'lis-tik\ *adj*

can·ni·bal·ize \'ka-nə-bə-,līz\ *vb* **-ized; -iz·ing** *vt* (1943) **1 a** : to take salvageable parts from (as a disabled machine) for use in building or repairing another machine **b** : to make use of (a part taken from one thing) in building or repairing something else **2** : to deprive of an essential part or element in creating or sustaining another facility or enterprise ⟨the energy system has begun *cannibalizing* the economic system it is supposed to fuel —Barry Commoner⟩ **3** : to use or draw on material (as another writer or an earlier work) ⟨a volume . . . that not only ~*s* previous publications but is intended itself to be *cannibalized* —R. M. Adams⟩ **4** : to take (sales) away from an existing product by selling or being sold as a similar but new product usu. from the same manufacturer; *also* : to affect (as an existing product) adversely by cannibalizing sales ~ *vi* : to practice cannibalism **2** : to cannibalize one unit for the sake of another of the same kind — **can·ni·bal·i·za·tion** \,ka-nə-bə-lə-'zā-shən\ *n*

can·ni·kin \'ka-ni-kən\ *n* [prob. fr. obs. D *kanneken,* fr. MD *canneken,* dim. of *canne* can; akin to OE *canne* can] (1570) : a small can or drinking vessel

can·no·li \kə-'nō-lē, ,ka-\ *n pl but sing or pl in constr* [It, pl. of *cannolo* small tube, dim. of *canna*] (1943) : a deep-fried tube of pastry filled with sweetened and flavored ricotta cheese

¹can·non \'ka-nən\ *n, pl* **cannons** *or* **cannon** [MF *canon,* fr. It *cannone,* lit., large tube, aug. of *canna* reed, tube, fr. L, cane, reed — more at CANE] (15c) **1** *pl usu* **cannon a** : a large heavy gun usu. mounted on a carriage **b** : a heavy-caliber automatic aircraft gun firing explosive shells **2** *or* **can·on** : the projecting part of a bell by which it is hung : EAR **3** : the part of the leg in which the cannon bone is found

²cannon *vi* (1691) : to discharge cannon ~ *vt* : CANNONADE

¹can·non·ade \,ka-nə-'nād\ *n* (1562) **1** : a heavy fire of artillery **2** : an attack (as with words) likened to artillery fire : BOMBARDMENT

²cannonade *vb* **-ad·ed; -ad·ing** *vt* (ca. 1670) : to attack with or as if with artillery ~ *vi* : to deliver artillery fire

¹**can·non·ball** \'ka-nən-,bȯl\ n (1663) **1 :** a usu. round solid missile made for firing from a cannon **2 :** a jump into water made with the arms holding the knees tight against the chest **3 :** a hard flat tennis service **:** an express train

²**cannonball** vi (1951) **:** to travel with great speed

cannon bone n [F canon, lit., cannon] (1834) **:** a bone in hoofed mammals that extends from the knee or hock to the fetlock

can·non·eer \,ka-nə-'nir\ n (1562) **:** an artillery gunner

cannon fodder n (ca. 1891) **:** soldiers regarded or treated as expendable in battle

can·non·ry \'ka-nən-rē\ n, pl **-ries** (ca. 1840) **:** a battery of cannons or cannon fire

can·not \ka-(,)nät; kə-'nät, ka-'\ (15c) **:** can not — **cannot but** or **cannot help but** also **cannot help :** to be unable to do otherwise than

can·nu·la \'kan-yə-lə\ n, pl **-las** or **-lae** \-,lē, -,lī\ [NL, fr. L, dim. of canna reed — more at CANE] (1684) **:** a small tube for insertion into a body cavity or into a duct or vessel

can·nu·lar \'kan-yə-lər\ adj (1823) **:** TUBULAR

¹**can·ny** \'ka-nē\ adj **can·ni·er; -est** [¹can] (1596) **1 :** CLEVER, SHREWD; also **:** PRUDENT **2** chiefly Scot **a :** CAREFUL, STEADY; also **:** RESTRAINED **b :** QUIET, SNUG ⟨then ∼, in some cozy place, they close the day —Robert Burns⟩ — **can·ni·ly** \'ka-nᵊl-ē\ adv — **can·ni·ness** \'ka-nē-nəs\ n

²**canny** adv (ca. 1796) Scot **:** in a canny manner **:** CAREFULLY

¹**ca·noe** \kə-'nü\ n [F, fr. NL canoa, fr. Sp, fr. Arawakan, of Cariban origin; akin to Carib kana:wa canoe] (1555) **:** a light narrow boat with both ends sharp that is usu. propelled by paddling

²**canoe** vb **ca·noed; ca·noe·ing** vt (1794) **:** to transport in a canoe; also **:** to travel by canoe down (a river) ∼ vi **:** to go or travel in a canoe — **ca·noe·able** \-ə-bəl\ adj — **ca·noe·ist** n

can of worms (1962) **:** PANDORA'S BOX

ca·no·la \kə-'nō-lə\ n [Canada oil—low acid] (1979) **1 :** a rape plant of an improved variety having seeds that are low in erucic acid and are the source of canola oil **2 :** CANOLA OIL

canola oil n (1986) **:** an edible vegetable oil obtained from the seeds of canola that is high in monounsaturated fatty acids

¹**can·on** \'ka-nən\ n [ME, fr. OE, fr. LL, fr. L, ruler, rule, model, standard, fr. Gk kanōn] (bef. 12c) **1 a :** a regulation or dogma decreed by a church council **b :** a provision of canon law **2** [ME, prob. fr. OF, fr. LL, fr. L, model] **:** the most solemn and unvarying part of the Mass including the consecration of the bread and wine **3** [ME, fr. LL, fr. L, standard] **a :** an authoritative list of books accepted as Holy Scripture **b :** the authentic works of a writer **c :** a sanctioned or accepted group or body of related works ⟨the ∼ of great literature⟩ **4 a :** an accepted principle or rule **b :** a criterion or standard of judgment **c :** a body of principles, rules, standards, or norms **5** [LGk kanōn, fr. Gk, model] **:** a contrapuntal musical composition in two or more voice parts in which the melody is imitated exactly and completely by the successive voices though not always at the same pitch syn see LAW

²**canon** n [ME canoun, fr. AF canunie, fr. LL canonicus one living under a rule, fr. L, according to rule, fr. Gk kanonikos, fr. kanōn] (13c) **1 :** a clergyman belonging to the chapter or the staff of a cathedral or collegiate church **2 :** CANON REGULAR

ca·ñon \'kan-yən\ var of CANYON

can·on·ess \'ka-nə-nəs\ n (1682) **1 :** a woman living in community under a religious rule but not under a perpetual vow **2 :** a member of a Roman Catholic congregation of women corresponding to canons regular

ca·non·ic \kə-'nä-nik\ adj (15c) **1 :** CANONICAL **2 :** of or relating to musical canon

ca·non·i·cal \-ni-kəl\ adj (15c) **1 :** of, relating to, or forming a canon **2 :** conforming to a general rule or acceptable procedure **:** ORTHODOX **3 :** of or relating to a clergyman who is a canon **4 :** reduced to the canonical form ⟨a ∼ matrix⟩ — **ca·non·i·cal·ly** \-k(ə-)lē\ adv

canonical form n (1851) **:** the simplest form of something; specif **:** the form of a square matrix that has zero elements everywhere except along the principal diagonal

canonical hour n (15c) **1 :** a time of day canonically appointed for an office of devotion **2 :** one of the daily offices of devotion that compose the Divine Office and include matins with lauds, prime, terce, sext, none, vespers, and compline

ca·non·i·cals \kə-'nä-ni-kəlz\ n pl (1748) **:** the vestments prescribed by canon for an officiating clergyman

can·on·ic·i·ty \,ka-nə-'ni-sə-tē\ n (1797) **:** the quality or state of being canonical

can·on·ist \'ka-nə-nist\ n (1542) **:** a specialist in canon law

can·on·ize \'ka-nə-,nīz\ vt **can·on·ized** \-,nīzd; in "Hamlet" usu kə-'nä-,nīzd\; **can·on·iz·ing** [ME, fr. ML canonizare, fr. LL canon catalog of saints, fr. L, standard] (14c) **1 :** to declare (a deceased person) an officially recognized saint **2 :** to make canonical **3 :** to sanction by ecclesiastical authority **4 :** to attribute authoritative sanction or approval to **5 :** to treat as illustrious, preeminent, or sacred — **can·on·i·za·tion** \,ka-nə-nə-'zā-shən\ n

canon law n (1552) **:** the usu. codified law governing a church

canon lawyer n (ca. 1859) **:** CANONIST

canon regular n, pl **canons regular** (14c) **:** a member of one of several Roman Catholic religious institutes of regular priests living in community under a usu. Augustinian rule

can·on·ry \'ka-nən-rē\ n, pl **-ries** (15c) **:** the office of a canon; also **:** the endowment that financially supports a canon

ca·no·pic jar \kə-'nō-pik-, -'nä-\ n [Canopus, Egypt] (1893) **:** a jar in which the ancient Egyptians preserved the viscera of a deceased person usu. for burial with the mummy

Ca·no·pus \kə-'nō-pəs\ n [L, fr. Gk Kanōpos] **:** a star of the first magnitude in the constellation Carina not visible north of 37° latitude

¹**can·o·py** \'ka-nə-pē\ n, pl **-pies** [ME canope, fr. ML canopeum mosquito net, fr. L conopeum, fr. Gk kōnōpion, fr. kōnōps mosquito] (14c) **1 a :** a

canopic jar

cloth covering suspended over a bed **b :** a cover (as of cloth) fixed or carried above a person of high rank or a sacred object **:** BALDACHIN **c :** a protective covering: as (1) **:** the uppermost spreading branchy layer of a forest (2) **:** AWNING, MARQUEE **2 :** an ornamental rooflike structure **3 a :** the transparent enclosure over an airplane cockpit **b :** the fabric part of a parachute that catches the air

²**canopy** vt **-pied; -py·ing** (1599) **:** to cover with or as if with a canopy

ca·no·rous \kə-'nȯr-əs, -'nȯr-; 'ka-nə-rəs\ adj [L canorus, fr. canor melody, fr. canere to sing — more at CHANT] (1646) **:** pleasant sounding **:** MELODIOUS — **ca·no·rous·ly** adv — **ca·no·rous·ness** n

¹**cant** \'kant\ adj [ME, prob. fr. (assumed) MLG kant] (14c) dial Eng **:** LIVELY, LUSTY

²**cant** vt (ca. 1543) **1 :** to give a cant or oblique edge to **:** BEVEL **2 :** to set at an angle **:** TILT **3** chiefly Brit **:** to throw with a lurch ∼ vi **1 :** to pitch to one side **:** LEAN **2 :** SLOPE

³**cant** n [ME cante edge, prob. fr. MD or ONF; MD, edge, corner, fr. ONF, fr. L canthus, cantus iron tire, perh. of Celt origin; akin to W cant rim; perh. akin to Gk kanthos corner of the eye] (1603) **1** obs **:** CORNER, NICHE **2 :** an external angle (as of a building) **3 :** a log with one or more squared sides **4 a :** an oblique or slanting surface **b :** INCLINATION, SLOPE

⁴**cant** adj (1663) **1 :** having canted corners or sides **2 :** INCLINED 2

⁵**cant** vi [prob. fr. ONF canter to tell, lit., to sing, fr. L cantare — more at CHANT] (1567) **1 :** to talk or beg in a whining or singsong manner **2 :** to speak in cant or jargon **3 :** to talk hypocritically

⁶**cant** n (1640) **1 :** affected singsong or whining speech **2 a :** the private language of the underworld **b** obs **:** the phraseology peculiar to a religious class or sect **c :** JARGON 2 **3 :** a set or stock phrase **4 :** the expression or repetition of conventional or trite opinions or sentiments; esp **:** the insincere use of pious words

can't \'kant, 'kánt, 'känt, esp Southern 'kānt\ (ca. 1652) **:** can not

Can·tab \'kan-,tab\ n [by shortening] (1750) **:** CANTABRIGIAN

can·ta·bi·le \kän-'tä-bi-,lā, -bə-lē\ adv or adj [It, fr. LL cantabilis worthy to be sung, fr. L cantare] (ca. 1724) **:** in a singing manner — often used as a direction in music

Can·ta·brig·i·an \,kan-tə-'bri-j(ē-)ən\ n [ML Cantabrigia Cambridge] (ca. 1540) **1 :** a student or graduate of Cambridge University **2 :** a native or resident of Cambridge, Mass. — **Cantabrigian** adj

can·ta·la \kan-'tä-lə\ n [NL, specific epithet of Agave cantala, perh. fr. Skt kantala babul, fr. kanta thorn] (1911) **:** a hard fiber produced from the leaves of an agave (Agave cantala)

can·ta·loupe also **can·ta·loup** \'kan-tᵊl-,ōp also -,üp\ n [Cantalupo, former papal villa near Rome, Italy] (1739) **1 :** a muskmelon (Cucumis melo reticulatus) having a rind with netted tracery and reddish orange flesh **2 :** any of several muskmelons resembling the cantaloupe; broadly **:** MUSKMELON

can·tan·ker·ous \kan-'taŋ-k(ə-)rəs, kən-\ adj [perh. irreg. fr. obs. contack (contention)] (1772) **:** difficult or irritating to deal with — **can·tan·ker·ous·ly** adv — **can·tan·ker·ous·ness** n

can·ta·ta \kən-'tä-tə\ n [It, fr. L, fem. of cantatus, pp. of cantare] (1724) **:** a composition for one or more voices usu. comprising solos, duets, recitatives, and choruses and sung to an instrumental accompaniment

can·ta·trice \,kän-tə-'trē-(,)chä, ,kä ⁿ-tə-'trēs\ n, pl **-trices** \-'trē-(,)chäz, -'trēs, -trē-səz\ or **-tri·ci** \,kän-tə-'trē-(,)chē\ [It & F, fr. It, fr. LL cantatric-, cantatrix, fem. of L cantator singer, fr. cantare] (1803) **:** a woman who is a singer; esp **:** an opera singer

cant dog n [³cant] (1850) **:** PEAVEY

can·teen \kan-'tēn\ n [F cantine bottle case, sutler's shop, fr. It cantina wine cellar, prob. fr. canto corner, fr. L canthus iron tire — more at CANT] (1737) **1 a :** a portable chest with compartments for carrying bottles or for cooking and eating utensils **b :** a flask for carrying liquids (as on a hike) **c :** MESS KIT **d** Brit **:** a chest for storing flatware **2 a :** a bar at a military post or camp **b :** a general store at a military post **:** EXCHANGE **c :** an establishment that serves as an informal social club (as for soldiers or a community's teenagers) **d :** a small cafeteria or snack bar

¹**cant·er** \'kan-tər\ n (1609) **:** one that uses cant: as **a :** BEGGAR, VAGABOND **b :** a user of professional or religious cant

²**can·ter** \'kan-tər\ vb [short for obs. canterbury, n. (canter), fr. Canterbury, England; fr. the supposed gait of pilgrims riding to Canterbury] vi (1706) **1 :** to move at or as if at a canter **:** LOPE **2 :** to ride a horse at a canter ∼ vt **:** to cause to go at a canter

³**can·ter** n (1755) **1 :** a 3-beat gait resembling but smoother and slower than the gallop **2 :** a ride at a canter

Can·ter·bury bell \'kan-tə(r)-,ber-ē-, -,b(ə-)rē-\ n [Canterbury, England] (1578) **:** any of several bellflowers (as Campanula medium) cultivated for their showy flowers

can·thar·i·din \kan-'thar-ə-dᵊn, -'ther-\ n (1819) **:** a bitter crystalline compound $C_{10}H_{12}O_4$ that is the active blister-producing ingredient of cantharides

can·tha·ris \'kan(t)-thə-rəs\ n, pl **can·thar·i·des** \kan-'thar-ə-,dēz\ [ME & L; ME cantharide, fr. L cantharid-, cantharis, fr. Gk kantharid-, kantharis] (14c) **1 :** SPANISH FLY 1 **2** pl but sing or pl in constr **:** a preparation of dried beetles (as Spanish flies) used in medicine as a counterirritant and formerly as an aphrodisiac

can·tha·xan·thin \,kan(t)-thə-'zan-,thin\ n [ISV cantha- (fr. NL Cantharellus cinnabarinus, mushroom species from which it was obtained) + xanth- + ¹-in] (ca. 1951) **:** a carotenoid $C_{40}H_{52}O_2$ used esp. as a color additive for food

cant hook n [³cant] (ca. 1848) **:** a lumberman's lever that has a pivoting hooked arm and a blunt often toothed metal cap at one end — compare PEAVEY

can·thus \'kan(t)-thəs\ n, pl **can·thi** \'kan-,thī, -,thē\ [LL, fr. Gk kanthos — more at CANT] (1646) **:** either of the angles formed by the meeting of an eye's upper and lower eyelids

---

\ə\ abut \ᵊ\ kitten, F table \ər\ further \a\ ash \ā\ ace \ä\ mop, mar
\aú\ out \ch\ chin \e\ bet \ē\ easy \g\ go \i\ hit \ī\ ice \j\ job
\ŋ\ sing \ō\ go \ȯ\ law \ȯi\ boy \th\ thin \t͟h\ the \ü\ loot \ú\ foot
\y\ yet \zh\ vision \á, k̲, ⁿ, œ, œ, ue, ᵫ, ᵛ\ see Guide to Pronunciation

can·ti·cle \'kan-ti-kəl\ *n* [ME, fr. L *canticulum*, dim. of *canticum* song, fr. *cantus*, pp. of *canere*] (13c) : SONG; *specif* : one of several liturgical songs (as the Magnificat) taken from the Bible

Canticle of Canticles (ca. 1934) : SONG OF SOLOMON

Canticles *n pl but sing in constr* (15c) : SONG OF SOLOMON

can·ti·le·na \,kan-tə-'lā-nə, -'lē-\ *n* [It, fr. L, song, fr. *cantus*] (ca. 1740) : a vocal or instrumental passage of sustained lyricism

¹can·ti·le·ver \'kan-tə-,lē-vər, -,le-\ *n* [perh. fr. ³*cant* + -*i*- + *lever*] (1667) : a projecting beam or member supported at only one end: as   **a** : a bracket-shaped member supporting a balcony or a cornice   **b** : either of the two beams or trusses that project from piers toward each other and that when joined directly or by a suspended connecting member form a span of a cantilever bridge — see BRIDGE illustration

²cantilever *vt* (1902)   **1** : to support by a cantilever ⟨a ~ed shelf⟩   **2** : to build as a cantilever ~ *vi* : to project as a cantilever

can·til·late \'kan-t³l-,āt\ *vt* -**lat·ed; -lat·ing** [L *cantilatus*, pp. of *cantilare* to sing, perh. fr. *cantilena*] (ca. 1828) : to recite with musical tones — **can·til·la·tion** \,kan-t³l-'ā-shən\ *n*

can·ti·na \kan-'tē-nə\ *n* [AmerSp, fr. Sp, canteen, fr. It, wine cellar — more at CANTEEN] (1844)   **1** *Southwest* : a pouch or bag at the pommel of a saddle   **2** *Southwest* : a small barroom : SALOON

cant·ing \'kan-tiŋ\ *adj* [⁵*cant*] (1663) : affectedly pious or righteous

can·tle \'kan-t³l\ *n* [ME *cantel*, fr. ONF, dim. of *can* edge, corner — more at CANT] (14c)   **1** : a segment cut off or out of something : PART, PORTION   **2** : the upward projecting rear part of a saddle

can·to \'kan-(,)tō\ *n, pl* **cantos** [It, fr. L *cantus* song, fr. *canere* to sing — more at CHANT] (1590) : one of the major divisions of a long poem

¹can·ton \'kan-t³n, -,tän\ *n* [MF, fr. L *cantone*, fr. *canto* corner, fr. L *canthus* iron tire — more at CANT] (1522) : a small territorial division of a country: as   **a** : one of the states of the Swiss confederation   **b** : a division of a French arrondissement — **can·ton·al** \'kan-t³n-əl, kan-'tä-n³l\ *adj*

²canton *n* [MF, fr. OProv, fr. *cant* edge, corner, fr. L *canthus*] (1572)   **1** *obs* : DIVISION, SECTION   **2** : the top inner quarter of a flag   **3** : the dexter chief region of a heraldic field

Can·ton·ese \,kan-t³n-'ēz, -'ēs\ *n, pl* **Cantonese** (1857)   **1** : a native or inhabitant of Canton, China   **2** : the dialect of Chinese spoken in and around Canton   **3** : a style of Chinese cooking that is typically based on mild spices — **Cantonese** *adj*

can·ton flannel \'kan-,tän-, -,t³n-\ *n, often cap C* [*Canton*, China] (ca. 1879) : FLANNEL 1c

can·ton·ment \kan-'tōn-mənt, -'tän- *also* -'tün-\ *n* (1756)   **1** : usu. temporary quarters for troops   **2** : a permanent military station in India

Can·ton ware \'kan-,tän-\ *n* (ca. 1902) : ceramic ware exported from China esp. during the 18th and 19th centuries by way of Canton and including blue-and-white and enameled porcelain and various ornamented stonewares

can·tor \'kan-tər\ *n* [L, singer, fr. *canere* to sing] (1538)   **1** : a choir leader : PRECENTOR   **2** : a synagogue official who sings or chants liturgical music and leads the congregation in prayer — **can·to·ri·al** \kan-'tōr-ē-əl, -'tȯr-\ *adj*

can·trip \'kan-trəp\ *n* [prob. alter. of *caltrop*] (1719)   **1** *chiefly Scot* : a witch's trick : SPELL   **2** *chiefly Brit* : HOCUS-POCUS 2

can·tus \'kan-təs\ *n, pl* **can·tus** \'kan-təs, 'kan-,tüs\ (1590)   **1** : CANTUS FIRMUS   **2** : the principal melody or voice

cantus fir·mus \-'fir-məs, -'fər-\ *n* [ML, lit., fixed song] (1847)   **1** : the plainsong or simple Gregorian melody orig. sung in unison and prescribed as to form and use by ecclesiastical tradition   **2** : a melodic theme or subject; *esp* : one for contrapuntal treatment

canty \'kan-tē\ *adj* [¹*cant*] (1720) *dial Brit* : CHEERFUL, SPRIGHTLY

Ca·nuck \kə-'nək *sometimes* -'nük\ *n* [origin unknown] (1835) : a Canadian and esp. a French Canadian

¹can·vas *also* **can·vass** \'kan-vəs\ *n* [ME *canevas*, fr. ONF, fr. (assumed) VL *cannabaceus* hempen, fr. L *cannabis* hemp — more at CANNABIS] (13c)   **1** : a firm closely woven cloth usu. of linen, hemp, or cotton used for clothing and formerly much used for tents and sails   **2** : a set of sails : SAIL   **3** : a piece of canvas used for a particular purpose   **4** : TENT; *also* : a group of tents   **5 a** : a piece of cloth backed or framed as a surface for a painting; *also* : the painting on such a surface   **b** : the background, setting, or scope of an historical or fictional account or narrative   **6** : a coarse cloth so woven as to form regular meshes for working with the needle   **7** : the canvas-covered floor of a boxing or wrestling ring — **can·vas·like** \-vəs-,līk\ *adj*

²canvas *vt* -**vased** *or* -**vassed; -vas·ing** *or* -**vass·ing** (1556) : to cover, line, or furnish with canvas

can·vas·back \'kan-vəs-,bak\ *n* (1782) : a No. American wild duck (*Aythya valisineria*) that has a reddish brown head, black breast, and whitish body and is characterized esp. by the elongate sloping profile of the bill and head

¹can·vass *also* **can·vas** \'kan-vəs\ *vt* (1508)   **1** *obs* : to toss in a canvas sheet in sport or punishment   **2 a** : to examine in detail; *specif* : to examine (votes) officially for authenticity   **b** : DISCUSS, DEBATE   **3** : to go through (a district) or go to (persons) in order to solicit orders or political support or to determine opinions or sentiments ~ *vi* : to seek orders or votes : SOLICIT — **can·vass·er** *also* **can·vas·er** *n*

²canvass *also* **canvas** *n* (ca. 1611) : the act or an instance of canvassing; *esp* : a personal solicitation of votes or survey of public opinion

can·yon \'kan-yən\ *n* [AmerSp *cañón*, prob. alter. of Sp. *callón*, aug. of *calle* street, fr. L *callis* footpath] (1837) : a deep narrow valley with steep sides and often with a stream flowing through it

can·zo·ne \kan-'zō-nē, känt-'sō-(,)nā\ *n, pl* -**nes** \-nēz, -(,)nāz\ *or* -**ni** \-nē\ [It, fr. L *cantion-, cantio* song, fr. *canere* to sing — more at CHANT] (1589)   **1** : a medieval Italian or Provençal lyric poem   **2** : the musical setting of a canzone

can·zo·net \,kan-zə-'net\ *n* [It *canzonetta*, dim. of *canzone*] (1588)   **1** : a light usu. strophic song   **2** : a part-song resembling but less elaborate than a madrigal

caou·tchouc \'kaü-,chúk, -,chük, -,chü\ *n* [F, fr. obs. Sp *cauchuc* (now *caucho*), fr. Quechua *kawchu*] (1775) : ¹RUBBER 2a

¹cap \'kap\ *n, often attrib* [ME *cappe*, fr. OE *cæppe*, fr. LL *cappa* head covering, cloak] (bef. 12c)   **1 a** : a head covering esp. with a visor and no brim   **b** : a distinctive head covering emblematic of a position or office: as   **(1)** : a cardinal's biretta   **(2)** : MORTARBOARD   **2** : a natural

cover or top: as   **a** : an overlying rock layer that is usu. hard to penetrate   **b   (1)** : PILEUS   **(2)** : CALYPTRA   **c** : the top of a bird's head or a patch of distinctively colored feathers in this area   **3 a** : something that serves as a cover or protection esp. for a tip, knob, or end ⟨a bottle ~⟩   **b** : a fitting for closing the end of a tube (as a water pipe or electric conduit)   **c** *Brit* : CERVICAL CAP   **4** : an overlaying or covering structure   **5** : a paper or metal container holding an explosive charge (as for a toy pistol)   **6** : an upper limit (as on expenditures) : CEILING   **7** : the symbol ∩ indicating the intersection of two sets — compare CUP 9   **8** : a cluster of molecules or chemical groups bound to one end or a region of a cell, virus, or molecule — **cap in hand** : in a respectful, humble, or sometimes fearful manner

²cap *vb* **capped; cap·ping** (15c)   **1 a** : to provide or protect with a cap   **b** : to give a cap to as a symbol of honor, rank, or achievement   **2** : to form a cap over : CROWN ⟨the mountains were *capped* with mist — John Buchan⟩   **3 a** : to follow with something more noticeable or more significant : OUTDO   **b** : CLIMAX   **4** : to form a chemical cap on ~ *vi* : to form or produce a chemical cap

ca·pa·bil·i·ty \,kā-pə-'bi-lə-tē\ *n, pl* -**ties** (1587)   **1** : the quality or state of being capable; *also* : ABILITY   **2** : a feature or faculty capable of development : POTENTIALITY   **3** : the facility or potential for an indicated use or deployment ⟨the ~ of a metal to be fused⟩ ⟨nuclear ~⟩

ca·pa·ble \'kā-pə-bəl, *in rapid speech* 'kāp-bəl\ *adj* [MF or LL; MF *capable*, fr. LL *capabilis*, irreg. fr. L *capere* to take — more at HEAVE] (1579)   **1** : SUSCEPTIBLE ⟨a remark ~ of being misunderstood⟩   **2** *obs* : COMPREHENSIVE   **3** : having attributes (as physical or mental power) required for performance or accomplishment ⟨is ~ of intense concentration⟩   **4** : having traits conducive to or features permitting ⟨this woman is ~ of murder by violence —Robert Graves⟩ ⟨an outer coat of light color ~ of reflecting solar heat —*Current Biog.*⟩   **5** : having legal right to own, enjoy, or perform   **6** : having general efficiency and ability — **ca·pa·ble·ness** \'kā-pə-bəl-nəs\ *n* — **ca·pa·bly** \-pə-blē\ *adv*

ca·pa·cious \kə-'pā-shəs\ *adj* [L *capac-, capax* capacious, capable, fr. L *capere*] (1614) : containing or capable of containing a great deal   *syn* see SPACIOUS — **ca·pa·cious·ly** *adv* — **ca·pa·cious·ness** *n*

ca·pac·i·tance \kə-'pa-sə-tən(t)s\ *n* [*capacity*] (1893)   **1 a** : the property of an electric nonconductor that permits the storage of energy as a result of the separation of charge that occurs when opposite surfaces of the nonconductor are maintained at a difference of potential   **b** : the measure of this property that is equal to the ratio of the charge on either surface to the potential difference between the surfaces   **2** : a part of a circuit or network that possesses capacitance — **ca·pac·i·tive** \-'pa-sə-tiv\ *adj* — **ca·pac·i·tive·ly** *adv*

ca·pac·i·tate \kə-'pa-sə-,tāt\ *vt* -**tat·ed; -tat·ing** (1657)   **1** *archaic* : to make capable   **2** : to cause (sperm) to undergo capacitation

ca·pac·i·ta·tion \kə-,pa-sə-'tā-shən\ *n* (1951) : the change undergone by sperm in the female reproductive tract that enables them to penetrate and fertilize an egg

ca·pac·i·tor \kə-'pa-sə-tər\ *n* (1925) : a device giving capacitance and usu. consisting of conducting plates or foils separated by thin layers of dielectric (as air or mica) with the plates on opposite sides of the dielectric layers oppositely charged by a source of voltage and the electrical energy of the charged system stored in the polarized dielectric

¹ca·pac·i·ty \kə-'pa-sə-tē, -'pas-tē\ *n, pl* -**ties** [ME *capacite*, fr. MF *capacité*, fr. L *capacitat-, capacitas*, fr. *capac-, capax*] (15c)   **1** : legal competency or fitness   **2 a** : the potential or suitability for holding, storing, or accommodating   **b** : the maximum amount or number that can be contained or accommodated ⟨a jug with a one-gallon ~⟩ ⟨the auditorium was filled to ~⟩ — see METRIC SYSTEM table, WEIGHT table   **3 a** : an individual's mental or physical ability : APTITUDE, SKILL   **b** : the faculty or potential for treating, experiencing, or appreciating ⟨~ for love⟩   **4** : DUTY, POSITION, ROLE ⟨will be happy to serve in any ~⟩   **5** : the facility or power to produce, perform, or deploy : CAPABILITY ⟨a plan to double the factory's ~⟩; *also* : maximum output ⟨industries running at three-quarter ~⟩   **6 a** : CAPACITANCE   **b** : the quantity of electricity that a battery can deliver under specified conditions

²capacity *adj* (1897) : equaling maximum capacity ⟨a ~ crowd⟩

cap-a-pie *or* **cap-à-pie** \,ka-pə-'pē, -'pā\ *adv* [MF (*de*) *cap a pé* from head to foot] (1523) : from head to foot ⟨armed ~ for battle⟩

¹ca·par·i·son \kə-'par-ə-sən\ *n* [MF *caparaçon*, fr. OSp *caparazón*] (1579)   **1 a** : an ornamental covering for a horse   **b** : decorative trappings and harness   **2** : rich clothing : ADORNMENT

²caparison *vt* (1594)   **1** : to provide with or as if with a rich ornamental covering : ADORN

¹cape \'kāp\ *n, often attrib* [ME *cap*, fr. MF, fr. OProv, fr. L *caput* head — more at HEAD] (14c)   **1** : a point or extension of land jutting out into water as a peninsula or as a projecting point   **2** *often cap* : CAPE COD COTTAGE

²cape *n* [prob. fr. Sp *capa* cloak, fr. LL *cappa* head covering, cloak] (ca. 1578)   **1** : a sleeveless outer garment or part of a garment that fits closely at the neck and hangs loosely over the shoulders   **2** : the short feathers covering the shoulders of a fowl — see DUCK illustration

Cape buffalo \'kāp-\ *n* [*Cape* of Good Hope, Africa] (ca. 1890) : the large reddish brown to black wild buffalo (*Syncerus caffer*) of sub-Saharan Africa — called also *African buffalo*

Cape Cod cottage \(')kāp-'käd-\ *n* [*Cape Cod*, Mass.] (1916) : a compact rectangular dwelling of one or one-and-a-half stories usu. with a central chimney and steep gable roof

Cape gooseberry *n* (1833) : any of several ground-cherries (esp. *Physalis peruviana*) bearing edible acid berries; *also* : its berry

Cape Horn·er \,kāp-'hȯr-nər\ *n* (1840) : a ship that voyages around Cape Horn

cape·let \'kāp-lət\ *n* (1912) : a small cape usu. covering the shoulders

cape·lin \'ka-p(ə-)lən\ *n* [CanF *capelan*, fr. F, codfish, fr. OProv, chaplain, codfish, fr. ML *cappellanus* chaplain — more at CHAPLAIN] (1620) : a small northern sea fish (*Mallotus villosus*) related to the smelts

Ca·pel·la \kə-'pe-lə\ *n* [L, lit., she-goat, fr. *caper* he-goat — more at CAPRIOLE] : a star of the first magnitude in Auriga

¹ca·per \'kā-pər\ *n* [back-formation fr. earlier *capers* (taken as a plural), fr. ME *caperis*, fr. L *capparis*, fr. Gk *kapparis*] (14c)   **1** : any of a genus (*Capparis* of the family Capparidaceae, the caper family) of low prickly shrubs of the Mediterranean region; *esp* : one (*C. spinosa*) cultivated for

its buds **2** : one of the greenish flower buds or young berries of the caper pickled and used as a seasoning or garnish
²**ca·per** *vi* **ca·pered; ca·per·ing** \-p(ə-)riŋ\ [prob. by shortening & alter. fr. *capriole*] (1588) : to leap or prance about in a playful manner
³**ca·per** *n* (1592) **1** : a frolicsome leap **2** : a capricious escapade : PRANK **3** : an illegal or questionable act; *esp* : THEFT
cap·er·cail·lie \ˌka-pər-ˈkā-lē, -ˈkāl-yē\ *or* **cap·er·cail·zie** \-ˈkāl-zē\ *n, pl* **-caillie** *or* **-cailzies** *also* **-caillies** *or* **-cailzie** [ScGael *capalcoille*, lit., horse of the woods] (1536) : the largest Old World grouse (*Tetrao urogallus*)
cape·skin \ˈkāp-ˌskin\ *n* [*Cape* of Good Hope, Africa] (1919) : a light flexible leather made from sheepskins with the natural grain retained and used esp. for gloves and garments
Ca·pe·tian \kə-ˈpē-shən\ *adj* [Hugh *Capet*] (1836) : of or relating to the French royal house that ruled from 987 to 1328 — **Capetian** *n*
cape·work \ˈkāp-ˌwərk\ *n* (1926) : the art of the bullfighter in working a bull with the cape
cap·ful \ˈkap-ˌfu̇l\ *n* (1873) : as much as a cap will hold ⟨a ~ of detergent⟩
capful of wind (1719) : a sudden light breeze
ca·pi·as \ˈkā-pē-əs\ *n* [ME, fr. L, lit., you should seize, fr. *capere* to take — more at HEAVE] (15c) : an arrest warrant
cap·il·lar·i·ty \ˌka-pə-ˈlar-ə-tē\ *n, pl* **-ties** (1830) **1** : the property or state of being capillary **2** : the action by which the surface of a liquid where it is in contact with a solid (as in a capillary tube) is elevated or depressed depending on the relative attraction of the molecules of the liquid for each other and for those of the solid
¹**cap·il·lary** \ˈka-pə-ˌler-ē, *Brit usu* kə-ˈpi-lə-rē\ *adj* [F or L; F *capillaire*, fr. L *capillaris*, fr. *capillus* hair] (14c) **1 a** : resembling a hair **b** : having a very small bore ⟨a ~ tube⟩ **2** : involving, held by, or resulting from surface tension ⟨~ water in the soil⟩ **3** : of or relating to capillaries or capillarity
²**capillary** *n, pl* **-lar·ies** (1667) : a capillary tube; *esp* : any of the smallest blood vessels connecting arterioles with venules and forming networks throughout the body
capillary attraction *n* (1813) : the force of adhesion between a solid and a liquid in capillarity
¹**cap·i·tal** \ˈka-pə-t³l, ˈkap-t³l\ *n* [ME *capitale*, modif. of ONF *capitel*, fr. LL *capitellum* small head, top of column, dim. of L *capit-, caput* head — more at HEAD] (13c) : the uppermost member of a column or pilaster crowning the shaft and taking the weight of the entablature — see COLUMN illustration
²**capital** *adj* [ME, fr. L *capitalis*, fr. *capit-, caput*] (14c) **1** *of a letter* : of or conforming to the series A, B, C, etc. rather than a, b, c, etc. **2 a** : punishable by death ⟨a ~ crime⟩ **b** : involving execution ⟨~ punishment⟩ **c** : most serious ⟨a ~ error⟩ **3 a** : chief in importance or influence ⟨~ ships⟩ **b** : being the ~ importance of criticism in the work of creation itself — T. S. Eliot⟩ **b** : being the seat of government **4** : of or relating to capital; *esp* : relating to or being assets that add to the long-term net worth of a corporation ⟨~ improvements⟩ **5** : EXCELLENT ⟨a ~ book⟩
³**capital** *n* [F or It; F, fr. It *capitale*, fr. *capitale*, adj., chief, principal, fr. L *capitalis*] (ca. 1639) **1 a** (1) : a stock of accumulated goods esp. at a specified time and in contrast to income received during a specified period; *also* : the value of these accumulated goods (2) : accumulated goods devoted to the production of other goods (3) : accumulated possessions calculated to bring in income **b** (1) : net worth (2) : CAPITAL STOCK **c** : persons holding capital **d** : ADVANTAGE, GAIN ⟨make ~ of the situation⟩ **2** [²*capital*] **a** : a capital letter; *esp* : an initial capital letter **b** : a letter belonging to a style of alphabet modeled on the style customarily used in inscriptions **3** [²*capital*] **a** : a city serving as a seat of government **b** : a city preeminent in some special activity ⟨the fashion ~⟩
capital gain *n* (1921) : the increase in value of an asset (as stock or real estate) between the time it is bought and the time it is sold
capital goods *n pl* (1896) : ³CAPITAL 1a(1), 1a(2)
cap·i·tal·ise *Brit var of* CAPITALIZE
cap·i·tal·ism \ˈka-pə-t³l-ˌiz-əm, ˈkap-t³l-, *Brit also* kə-ˈpi-t³l-\ *n* (1877) : an economic system characterized by private or corporate ownership of capital goods, by investments that are determined by private decision, and by prices, production, and the distribution of goods that are determined mainly by competition in a free market
¹**cap·i·tal·ist** \-ist\ *n* (1792) **1** : a person who has capital esp. invested in business; *broadly* : a person of wealth : PLUTOCRAT **2** : a person who favors capitalism
²**capitalist** *or* **cap·i·tal·is·tic** \ˌka-pə-t³l-ˈis-tik, ˌkap-t³l-, *Brit also* kə-ˌpi-t³l-\ *adj* (1845) **1** : owning capital ⟨the ~ class⟩ **2 a** : practicing or advocating capitalism ⟨~ nations⟩ **b** : marked by capitalism ⟨~ period of history⟩ — **cap·i·tal·is·ti·cal·ly** \-ti-k(ə-)lē\ *adv*
cap·i·tal·i·za·tion \ˌka-pə-t³l-ə-ˈzā-shən, ˌkap-t³l-, *Brit also* kə-ˌpi-t³l-\ *n* (1860) **1 a** : the act or process of capitalizing **b** : a sum resulting from a process of capitalizing **c** : the total liabilities of a business including both ownership capital and borrowed capital **d** : the total par value or the stated value of no-par issues of authorized capital stock **2** : the use of a capital letter in writing or printing
cap·i·tal·ize \ˈka-pə-t³l-ˌīz, ˈkap-t³l-, *Brit also* kə-ˈpi-t³l-\ *vb* **-ized; -iz·ing** *vt* (1764) **1** : to write or print with an initial capital or in capitals **2** : to convert into capital ⟨~ the company's reserve fund⟩ **b** : to treat as capital rather than as an expense **3 a** : to compute the present value of (an income extended over a period of time) **b** : to convert (a periodic payment) into an equivalent capital sum ⟨*capitalized* annuities⟩ **4** : to supply capital for ~ *vi* : to gain by turning something to advantage : PROFIT ⟨~ on an opponent's mistake⟩
cap·i·tal·ly \ˈka-pə-t³l-ē, ˈkap-t³l-\ *adv* (1619) **1** : in a manner involving capital punishment **2** : in a capital manner : EXCELLENTLY
capital stock *n* (1709) **1** : the outstanding shares of a joint-stock company considered as an aggregate **2** : CAPITALIZATION 1d **3** : the ownership element of a corporation divided into shares and represented by certificates
cap·i·tate \ˈka-pə-ˌtāt\ *adj* [L *capitatus* headed, fr. *capit-, caput* head] (1661) **1** : forming a head **2** : abruptly enlarged and globose

cap·i·ta·tion \ˌka-pə-ˈtā-shən\ *n* [LL *capitation-, capitatio* poll tax, fr. L *capit-, caput*] (1641) **1** : a direct uniform tax imposed on each head or person : POLL TAX **2** : a uniform per capita payment or fee
cap·i·tol \ˈka-pə-t³l, ˈkap-t³l\ *n* [L *Capitolium*, temple of Jupiter at Rome on the Capitoline hill] (1699) **1 a** : a building in which a state legislative body meets **b** : a group of buildings in which the functions of state government are carried out **2** *cap* : the building in which the U.S. Congress meets at Washington
Capitol Hill *n* [*Capitol Hill*, Washington, site of the U.S. Capitol] (1943) : the legislative branch of the U.S. government
Cap·i·to·line \ˈka-pə-t³l-ˌīn, *Brit usu* kə-ˈpi-tə-ˌlīn\ *adj* [L *capitolinus*, fr. *Capitolium*] (1667) : of or relating to the smallest of the seven hills of ancient Rome, the temple on it, or the gods worshiped there
ca·pit·u·lar \kə-ˈpi-chə-lər\ *adj* [ML *capitularis*, fr. *capitulum*] (ca. 1525) : of or relating to an ecclesiastical chapter
ca·pit·u·lary \-ˌler-ē\ *n, pl* **-lar·ies** [ML *capitulare*, lit., document divided into sections, fr. LL *capitulum* section, chapter — more at CHAPTER] (1650) : a civil or ecclesiastical ordinance; *also* : a collection of ordinances
ca·pit·u·late \kə-ˈpi-chə-ˌlāt\ *vi* **-lat·ed; -lat·ing** [ML *capitulatus*, pp. of *capitulare* to distinguish by heads or chapters, fr. LL *capitulum*] (1537) **1** *archaic* : PARLEY, NEGOTIATE **2 a** : to surrender often after negotiation of terms **b** : to cease resisting : ACQUIESCE **syn** see YIELD
ca·pit·u·la·tion \kə-ˌpi-chə-ˈlā-shən\ *n* (1535) **1** : a set of terms or articles constituting an agreement between governments **2 a** : the act of surrendering or yielding **b** : the terms of surrender
ca·pit·u·lum \kə-ˈpi-chə-ləm\ *n, pl* **-la** \-lə\ [NL, fr. L, small head — more at CHAPTER] (ca. 1755) **1** : a rounded protuberance of an anatomical part (as a bone) **2** : a racemose inflorescence (as of the buttonbush) with the axis shortened and dilated to form a rounded or flattened cluster of sessile flowers — see INFLORESCENCE illustration
Cap·lets \ˈka-pləts\ *trademark* — used for capsule-shaped medicinal tablets
¹**ca·po** \ˈkä-(ˌ)pō\ *n, pl* **capos** [short for *capotasto*, fr. It, lit., head of fingerboard] (1926) : a movable bar attached to the fingerboard of a fretted instrument to uniformly raise the pitch of all the strings
²**ca·po** \ˈkä-(ˌ)pō, ˈka-\ *n, pl* **capos** [It, head, chief, fr. L *caput*] (ca. 1959) : the head of a branch of a crime syndicate
ca·pon \ˈkā-ˌpän, -pən\ *n* [ME, fr. OE *capūn*, prob. fr. ONF *capon*, fr. L *capon-, capo*; akin to Lith *kapoti* to mince, Gk *koptein* to cut] (bef. 12c) : a castrated male chicken
ca·po·na·ta \ˌkä-pə-ˈnä-tə\ *n* [It, fr. It dial. (Sicily) *capunata*, perh. fr. *capuni* capon, fr. L *capon-, capo*] (1951) : a relish of chopped eggplant and assorted vegetables
ca·pote \kə-ˈpōt\ *n* [F, fr. *cape* cloak, fr. LL *cappa*] (1799) : a usu. long and hooded cloak or overcoat
cap·pel·let·ti \ˌka-pə-ˈle-tē\ *n pl but sing or pl in constr* [It, pl. of *cappelletto*, dim. of *cappello* hat, fr. ML *cappellus* cap, dim. of LL *cappa* head covering — more at CAP] (1945) : pasta in the form of little peaked hats filled with a savory mixture
cap·per \ˈka-pər\ *n* (1587) **1** : one that caps: as **a** : a device that fits caps on bottles **b** : FINALE, CLIMAX, CLINCHER **2** : a lure or decoy esp. in an illicit or questionable activity : SHILL
cap·ping \ˈka-piŋ\ *n* (14c) : something that caps
cap·puc·ci·no \ˌka-pə-ˈchē-(ˌ)nō, ˌkä-pu̇-\ *n* [It, lit., Capuchin; fr. the likeness of its color to that of a Capuchin's habit] (1948) : espresso coffee mixed with frothed hot milk or cream and often flavored with cinnamon
cap·ric acid \ˈka-prik-\ *n* [ISV, fr. L *capr-, caper* goat; fr. its odor — more at CAPRIOLE] (1836) : a fatty acid $C_{10}H_{20}O_2$ found in fats and oils and used in flavors and perfumes
ca·pric·cio \kə-ˈprē-ch(ē-ˌ)ō\ *n, pl* **-cios** [It] (1601) **1** : FANCY, WHIMSY **2** : CAPER, PRANK **3** : an instrumental piece in free form usu. lively in tempo and brilliant in style
ca·price \kə-ˈprēs\ *n* [F, fr. It *capriccio* caprice, shudder, perh. fr. *capo* head (fr. L *caput*) + *riccio* hedgehog, fr. L *ericius* — more at HEAD, URCHIN] (1667) **1 a** : a sudden, impulsive, and seemingly unmotivated notion or action **b** : a sudden usu. unpredictable condition, change, or series of changes ⟨the ~s of the weather⟩ **2** : a disposition to do things impulsively **3** : CAPRICCIO 3
syn CAPRICE, WHIM, VAGARY, CROTCHET mean an irrational or unpredictable idea or desire. CAPRICE stresses lack of apparent motivation and suggests willfulness ⟨by sheer *caprice* she quit her job⟩. WHIM implies a fantastic, capricious turn of mind or inclination ⟨an odd antique that was bought on a *whim*⟩. VAGARY stresses the erratic, irresponsible character of the notion or desire ⟨recently he had been prone to strange *vagaries*⟩. CROTCHET implies an eccentric opinion or preference ⟨a serious scientist equally known for his bizarre *crotchets*⟩.
ca·pri·cious \kə-ˈpri-shəs, -ˈprē-\ *adj* (1601) : governed or characterized by caprice : IMPULSIVE, UNPREDICTABLE **syn** see INCONSTANT — **ca·pri·cious·ly** *adv* — **ca·pri·cious·ness** *n*
Cap·ri·corn \ˈka-pri-ˌkȯrn\ *n* [ME *Capricorne*, fr. L *Capricornus* (gen. *Capricorni*), fr. *caper* goat + *cornu* horn — more at HORN] **1** : a southern zodiacal constellation between Sagittarius and Aquarius **2 a** : the 10th sign of the zodiac in astrology — see ZODIAC table **b** : one born under the sign of Capricorn
cap·ri·fi·ca·tion \ˌka-prə-fə-ˈkā-shən\ *n* [L *caprification-, caprificatio*, fr. *caprificare* to pollinate by caprification, fr. *caprificus*] (1601) : artificial pollination of figs that usu. bear only pistillate flowers by hanging male flowering branches of the caprifig in the trees to facilitate pollen transfer by a wasp
cap·ri·fig \ˈka-prə-ˌfig\ *n* [ME *caprifige*, part trans. of L *caprificus*, fr. *capr-, caper* goat + *ficus* fig — more at FIG] (15c) : a wild fig (*Ficus carica sylvestris*) of southern Europe and Asia Minor used for caprification of the edible fig; *also* : its fruit
cap·rine \ˈka-ˌprīn\ *adj* [L *caprinus*, fr. *capr-, caper*] (15c) : of, relating to, or being a goat ⟨~ serum⟩ ⟨the ~ family⟩

\ə\ abut \ᵊ\ kitten, F table \ər\ further \a\ ash \ā\ ace \ä\ mop, mar \au̇\ out \ch\ chin \e\ bet \ē\ easy \g\ go \i\ hit \ī\ ice \j\ job \ŋ\ sing \ō\ go \ȯ\ law \ȯi\ boy \th\ thin \t̲h̲\ the \ü\ loot \u̇\ foot \y\ yet \zh\ vision \ä, k̲, ⁿ, œ, œ̄, ᵫ, ᵫ̄, ᵊ\ *see* Guide to Pronunciation

cap·ri·ole \'ka-prē-,ōl\ *n* [MF or OIt; MF *capriole*, fr. OIt *capriola*, fr. *capriolo* roebuck, fr. L *capreolus* goat, roebuck, fr. *capr-, caper* he-goat; akin to OE *hæfer* goat, Gk *kapros* wild boar] (1594) **1** : a playful leap : CAPER **2** *of a trained horse* : a vertical leap with a backward kick of the hind legs at the height of the leap — **capriole** *vi*

ca·pri pants \kə-'prē-\ *n pl, often cap C* [*Capri*, Italy] (ca. 1956) : close-fitting women's pants that end above the ankle — called also *capris*

cap·rock \'kap-,räk\ *n* (1867) : CAP 2a

ca·pro·ic acid \kə-'prō-ik-\ *n* [ISV, fr. L *capr-, caper*] (ca. 1847) : a liquid fatty acid $C_6H_{12}O_2$ that is found as a glycerol ester in fats and oils or made synthetically and used in pharmaceuticals and flavors

cap·ro·lac·tam \,ka-prō-'lak-,tam\ *n* [*caproic* acid + *lactone* + *amide*] (1944) : a white crystalline cyclic amide $C_6H_{11}NO$ used esp. in making one type of nylon

ca·pryl·ic acid \kə-'pri-lik-\ *n* [ISV *capryl*, a radical contained in it] (1845) : a fatty acid $C_8H_{16}O_2$ of rancid odor occurring in fats and oils and used in perfumes

cap·sa·i·cin \kap-'sā-ə-sən\ *n* [irreg. fr. NL *Capsicum*] (ca. 1890) : a colorless irritant phenolic amide $C_{18}H_{27}NO_3$ that is found in various capsicums and that gives hot peppers their hotness

Cap·si·an \'kap-sē-ən\ *adj* [F *capsien*, fr. L *Capsa* Gafsa, Tunisia] (1915) : of or relating to a Paleolithic culture of northern Africa and southern Europe

cap·si·cum \'kap-si-kəm\ *n* [NL, perh. fr. L *capsa*] (1588) **1** : any of a genus (*Capsicum*) of tropical herbs and shrubs of the nightshade family widely cultivated for their many-seeded usu. fleshy-walled berries — called also *pepper* **2** : the dried ripe fruit of some capsicums (as *C. frutescens*) used as a gastric and intestinal stimulant

cap·sid \'kap-səd\ *n* [F *capside*, fr. L *capsa* case + F *-ide* ²-id] (1960) : the outer protein shell of a virus particle

cap·size \'kap-,sīz, kap-'\ *vb* **cap·sized; cap·siz·ing** [perh. fr. Sp *capuzar* or Catal *cabussar* to thrust (the head) underwater] *vt* (1788) : to cause to overturn 〈~ a canoe〉 ~ *vi* : to become upset or overturned : TURN OVER 〈the canoe *capsized*〉

cap sleeve *n* (1926) : a very short sleeve (as on a dress) that hangs over the edge of the shoulder without extending along the underside of the arm

cap·stan \'kap-stən, -,stan\ *n* [ME, prob. fr. MF *cabestant*] (14c) **1** : a machine for moving or raising heavy weights that consists of a vertical drum which can be rotated and around which cable is turned **2** : a rotating shaft that drives tape at a constant speed in a recorder

cap·stone \'kap-,stōn\ *n* [¹*cap*] (14c) **1** : a coping stone : COPING 2 : the high point : crowning achievement

cap·su·lar \'kap-sə-lər\ *adj* (ca. 1730) **1** : of, relating to, or resembling a capsule **2** : CAPSULATED

cap·su·lat·ed \-,lā-təd\ *adj* (1668) : enclosed in a capsule

¹cap·sule \'kap-səl, -,(,)sül *also* -,syü(ə)l\ *n* [F, fr. L *capsula*, dim. of *capsa* box — more at CASE] (ca. 1693) **1 a** : a membrane or sac enclosing a body part **b** : either of two layers of white matter in the cerebrum **2** : a closed receptacle containing spores or seeds: as **a** : a dry dehiscent usu. many-seeded fruit composed of two or more carpels **b** : the spore case of a moss **3** : a shell usu. of gelatin for packaging something (as a drug or vitamins); *also* : a usu. medicinal or nutritional preparation for oral use consisting of the shell and its contents **4** : an often polysaccharide envelope surrounding a microorganism **5** : an extremely brief condensation : OUTLINE, SURVEY **6 a** : a compact often sealed and detachable container or compartment **b** : a small pressurized compartment or vehicle (as for space flight or emergency escape)

²capsule *vt* **cap·suled; cap·sul·ing** (1859) **1** : to equip with or enclose in a capsule **2** : to condense into or devise in a compact form

³capsule *adj* (1938) **1** : extremely brief **2** : small and very compact

cap·sul·ize \'kap-sə-,līz\ *vt -ized; -iz·ing* (1945) : CAPSULE

¹cap·tain \'kap-tən *also* 'kap-²m\ *n* [ME *capitaine*, fr. MF *capitain*, fr. LL *capitaneus*] *adj. & n.*, chief, fr. L *capit-, caput* head — more at HEAD] (14c) **1 a** (1) : a military leader : the commander of a unit or a body of troops (2) : a subordinate officer commanding under a sovereign or general (3) : a commissioned officer in the army, air force, or marine corps ranking above a first lieutenant and below a major **b** : a naval officer who is master or commander of a ship; *esp* : a commissioned officer in the navy ranking above a commander and below a commodore and in the coast guard ranking above a commander and below a rear admiral **c** : a senior pilot who commands the crew of an airplane **d** : an officer in a police department or fire department in charge of a unit (as a precinct or company) and usu. ranking above a lieutenant and below a chief **2** : one who leads or supervises: as **a** : a leader of a sports team or side **b** : HEADWAITER **c** : a person in charge of hotel bellhops — called also *bell captain* **3** : a person of importance or influence in a field 〈~s of industry〉 — **cap·tain·cy** \'kap-tən-sē\ *n* — **cap·tain·ship** \-,ship\ *n*

²captain *vt* (1598) : to be captain of : LEAD 〈~ed the football team〉

captain's chair *n* (1946) : an armchair with a saddle seat and a low curved back with vertical spindles

captain's mast *n* (1941) : MAST 3

cap·tan \'kap-,tan\ *n* [short for *mercaptan*] (1952) : a fungicide $C_9H_8Cl_3NO_2S$ used on agricultural crops

¹cap·tion \'kap-shən\ *n* [ME *capcioun*, fr. L *caption-, captio* act of taking, fr. *capere* to take — more at HEAVE] (1670) **1** : the part of a legal document that shows where, when, and by what authority it was taken, found, or executed **2 a** : the heading esp. of an article or document : TITLE **b** : the explanatory comment or designation accompanying a pictorial illustration **c** : a motion-picture subtitle — **cap·tion·less** \-ləs\ *adj*

²caption *vt* **cap·tioned; cap·tion·ing** \-sh(ə-)niŋ\ (1901) : to furnish with a caption

cap·tious \'kap-shəs\ *adj* [ME *capcious*, fr. MF or L; MF *captieux*, fr. L *captiosus*, fr. *captio*] (14c) **1** : marked by an often ill-natured inclination to stress faults and raise objections **2** : calculated to confuse, entrap, or entangle in argument *syn* see CRITICAL — **cap·tious·ly** *adv* — **cap·tious·ness** *n*

cap·ti·vate \'kap-tə-,vāt\ *vt* **-vat·ed; -vat·ing** (ca. 1555) **1** *archaic* : SEIZE, CAPTURE **2** : to influence and dominate by some special charm,

art, or trait and with an irresistible appeal *syn* see ATTRACT — **cap·ti·va·tion** \,kap-tə-'vā-shən\ *n* — **cap·ti·va·tor** \'kap-tə-,vā-tər\ *n*

cap·tive \'kap-tiv\ *adj* [ME, fr. L *captivus*, fr. *captus*, pp. of *capere*] (14c) **1 a** : taken and held as or as if a prisoner of war **b** : kept within bounds : CONFINED **2** : held under control of another but having the appearance of independence : *esp* : owned or controlled by another concern and operated for its needs rather than for an open market 〈a ~ mine〉 **3** : being such involuntarily because of a situation that makes free choice or departure difficult 〈the airline passengers were a ~ audience〉 — **captive** *n*

cap·tiv·i·ty \kap-'ti-və-tē\ *n* (14c) **1** : the state of being captive 〈some birds thrive in ~〉 **2** *obs* : a group of captives

cap·to·pril \'kap-tə-,pril\ *n* [*mercaptan* + *-o-* + *proline* + *-il*, alter. of *-yl*] (1978) : an antihypertensive drug $C_9H_{15}NO_3S$ that is an ACE inhibitor

cap·tor \'kap-tər, -,tȯr\ *n* [LL, fr. L *capere*] (ca. 1688) : one that has captured a person or thing

¹cap·ture \'kap-chər, -shər\ *n* [MF, fr. L *captura*, fr. *captus*] (ca. 1542) **1** : an act or instance of capturing: as **a** : an act of catching, winning, or gaining control by force, stratagem, or guile **b** : a move in a board game (as chess or checkers) that gains an opponent's piece **c** : the absorption by an atom, nucleus, or particle of a subatomic particle that often results in subsequent emission of radiation or in fission **d** : the act of recording in a permanent file 〈data ~〉 **2** : one that has been taken (as a prize ship)

²capture *vt* **cap·tured; cap·tur·ing** \'kap-chə-riŋ, 'kap-shriŋ\ (1795) **1 a** : to take captive; *also* : to gain control of esp. by force 〈~ a city〉 **b** : to gain or win esp. through effort 〈*captured* 60% of the vote〉 **2** : to emphasize, represent, or preserve (as a scene, mood, or quality) in a more or less permanent form 〈at any such moment as a photograph might —C. E. Montague〉 **3** : to captivate and hold the interest of **4** : to take according to the rules of a game **5** : to bring about the capture of (a subatomic particle) **6** : to record in a permanent file (as in a computer) *syn* see CATCH

capture the flag *n* (ca. 1925) : a game in which players on each of two teams seek to capture the other team's flag and return it to their side without being captured and imprisoned

ca·puche \kə-'püch, -'püsh\ *n* [MF, fr. It *cappuccio*, fr. *cappa* cloak, fr. LL] (ca. 1600) : HOOD; *esp* : the cowl of a Capuchin friar

ca·pu·chin \'ka-pyə-shən, -pə-, *esp for 3 also* kə-'pyü-, -'pü-\ *n* [MF, fr. OIt *cappuccino*, fr. *cappuccio*; fr. his cowl] (1589) **1** *cap* : a member of the Order of Friars Minor Capuchin forming since 1529 an austere branch of the first order of St. Francis of Assisi engaged in missionary work and preaching **2** : a hooded cloak for women **3** : any of a genus (*Cebus*) of So. American monkeys; *esp* : one (*C. capucinus*) with the hair on its crown resembling a monk's cowl

Cap·u·let \'ka-pyə-lət\ *n* : the family of Juliet in Shakespeare's *Romeo and Juliet*

cap·y·bara \,ka-pi-'bar-ə, -'bär-\ *n* [Pg *capibara*, fr. Tupi] (1774) : a tailless largely aquatic So. American rodent (*Hydrochaerus hydrochaeris*) often exceeding four feet (1.2 meters) in length

car \'kär, *dial also* 'kȯr, 'kyär\ *n* [ME *carre*, fr. AF, fr. L *carra*, pl. of *carrum*, alter. of *carrus*, of Celt origin; akin to OIr & MW *carr* vehicle; akin to L *currere* to run] (14c) **1** : a vehicle moving on wheels: as **a** *archaic* : CARRIAGE, CHARIOT **b** : a vehicle designed to move on rails (as of a railroad) **c** : AUTOMOBILE **2** : the passenger compartment of an elevator **3** : the part of an airship or balloon that carries the passengers and cargo

ca·ra·bao \,kär-ə-'baù, ,kär-\ *n, pl* **-bao** *or* **-baos** [PhilSp, fr. Bisayan of Samar and Leyte *karabáw*] (1900) : WATER BUFFALO

ca·ra·bid \'kar-ə-bəd, kə-'ra-bəd\ *n* [ultim. fr. Gk *karabos* horned beetle] (1880) : GROUND BEETLE

car·a·bi·neer *or* **car·a·bi·nier** \,kar-ə-bə-'nir\ *n* [F *carabinier*, fr. *carabine* carbine] (1672) : a cavalry soldier armed with a carbine

car·a·bi·ner \,kar-ə-'bē-nər\ *n* [G *Karabiner*, short for *Karabinerhaken*, lit., carabineer's hook] (1920) : an oblong metal ring with one spring-hinged side that is used esp. in mountain climbing as a connector and to hold a freely running rope

ca·ra·bi·ne·ro \,kär-ə-bə-'ner-(,)ō, ,kär-\ *n, pl* **-ros** [Sp, fr. *carabina* carbine, fr. F *carabine*] (1845) **1** : a member of a Spanish national police force serving esp. as frontier guards **2** : a customs or coast guard officer in the Philippines

ca·ra·bi·nie·re \,kar-ə-bən-'yer-(,)ā, ,kär-\ *n, pl* **-nie·ri** \-'yer-ē\ [It, fr. F *carabinier*] (1847) : a member of the Italian national police force

car·a·cal \'kar-ə-,kal\ *n* [F, fr. Turk *karakulak*, fr. *kara* black + *kulak* ear] (1760) : a long-legged reddish brown nocturnal cat (*Felis caracal*) of savannas in Africa and parts of Asia that has long pointed ears with a tuft of black hairs at the tip

carabiner

ca·ra·ca·ra \,kar-ə-'kar-ə, -ə-kə-'rä\ *n* [Sp *caracara* & Pg *caracará*, fr. Tupi *caracará*] (1838) : any of various large long-legged mostly So. American hawks classified with the falcons

car·a·cole \'kar-ə-,kōl\ *n* [F, fr. Sp *caracol* snail, spiral stair, caracole] (1614) : a half turn to right or left executed by a mounted horse — **caracole** *vb*

car·a·cul \'kar-ə-kəl\ *n* [alter. of *karakul*] (1894) : the pelt of a karakul lamb after the curl begins to loosen

ca·rafe \kə-'raf, -'räf\ *n* [F, fr. It *caraffa*, fr. Ar *gharrāfah*] (1786) : a bottle with a flaring lip used to hold beverages and esp. wine

car·am·bo·la \,kar-əm-'bō-lə\ *n* [Pg, fr. Marathi *karambal*, fr. Skt *karmaphala*] (1598) **1** : a five-angled green to yellow tropical fruit of star-shaped cross section — called also *starfruit* **2** : a tropical tree (*Averrhoa carambola*) of the wood-sorrel family widely cultivated for carambolas

car·a·mel \'kär-məl, 'kar-ə-məl, -,mel\ *n* [F, fr. Sp *caramelo*, fr. Pg, icicle, caramel, fr. LL *calamellus* small reed — more at SHAWM] (1725) **1** : an amorphous brittle brown and somewhat bitter substance obtained by heating sugar and used as a coloring and flavoring agent **2** : a firm chewy usu. caramel-flavored candy

car·a·mel·ise *Brit var of* CARAMELIZE

car·a·mel·ize \-mə-ˌlīz\ vb **-ized; -iz·ing** vt (1842) : to change (as sugar) into caramel ~ vi : to change to caramel

ca·ran·gid \kə-ˈran-jəd, -ˈraŋ-gəd\ adj [ultim. fr. F carangue shad, horse mackerel, fr. Sp caranga] (1931) : of or relating to a large family (Carangidae of the order Perciformes) of marine spiny-finned bony fishes including important food fishes — **carangid** n

car·a·pace \ˈkar-ə-ˌpās\ n [F, fr. Sp carapacho] (1836) **1 :** a bony or chitinous case or shield covering the back or part of the back of an animal (as a turtle or crab) **2 :** a protective, decorative, or disguising shell ⟨the ~ of reserve he built around himself —M. M. Mintz⟩

¹carat var of KARAT

²car·at \ˈkar-ət\ n [ME, fr. MF, fr. It carato, fr. Ar qīrāṭ bean pod, a small weight, fr. Gk keration carob bean, a small weight, fr. dim. of kerat-, keras horn — more at HORN] (1555) : a unit of weight for precious stones equal to 200 milligrams

¹car·a·van \ˈkar-ə-ˌvan\ n [It caravana, fr. Per kārwān] (1588) **1 a :** a company of travelers on a journey through desert or hostile regions; also : a train of pack animals **b :** a group of vehicles traveling together in a file **2 a :** a covered wagon or motor vehicle equipped as traveling living quarters **b** Brit : TRAILER 3b

²caravan vi **-vanned** or **-vaned; -van·ning** or **-van·ing** (1885) : to travel in a caravan

car·a·van·ner or **car·a·van·er** \-ˌva-nər\ n (1909) **1 :** one that travels in a caravan **2** Brit : one who goes camping with a trailer

car·a·van·sa·ry \ˌkar-ə-ˈvan(t)-sə-rē\ or **car·a·van·se·rai** \-sə-ˌrī\ n, pl **-ries** or **-rais** or **-rai** [Per kārwānsarāi, fr. kārwān caravan + sarāi palace, inn] (1599) **1 :** an inn surrounding a court in eastern countries where caravans rest at night **2 :** HOTEL, INN

car·a·vel \ˈkar-ə-ˌvel, -vəl\ n [MF caravelle, fr. OPg caravela] (1527) : any of several sailing ships; specif : a small 15th and 16th century ship that has broad bows, high narrow poop, and usu. three masts with lateen or both square and lateen sails

car·a·way \ˈkar-ə-ˌwā\ n [ME, prob. fr. ML carvi, fr. Ar karawyā, fr. Gk karon] (13c) **1 :** a biennial usu. white-flowered aromatic herb (Carum carvi) of the carrot family **2 :** the pungent fruit of the caraway used in seasoning and medicine — called also caraway seed

¹carb \ˈkärb\ n (ca. 1942) slang : CARBURETOR

²carb \ˈkärb\ or **carb-bo** \ˈkärb-(ˌ)bō\ n (1965) : CARBOHYDRATE; also : a high-carbohydrate food — usu. used in pl.

carb- or **carbo-** comb form [F, fr. carbone] : carbon : carbonic : carbonyl : carboxyl ⟨carbide⟩ ⟨carbohydrate⟩

car·ba·chol \ˈkär-bə-ˌkōl, -ˌkōl\ n [carbamic acid + choline] (ca. 1940) : a synthetic parasympathomimetic drug $C_6H_{15}ClN_2O_2$ that is used in veterinary medicine and topically in glaucoma

car·ba·mate \ˈkär-bə-ˌmāt, kär-ˈba-ˌmāt\ n (1888) : a salt or ester of carbamic acid; esp : one that is a synthetic organic insecticide

car·bam·ic acid \(ˌ)kär-ˈba-mik-\ n [ISV carbamide + ¹-ic] (1869) : an acid CH_3NO_2 known in the form of salts and esters that is a half amide of carbonic acid

car·bam·ide \ˈkär-bə-ˌmīd, kär-ˈba-məd\ n [ISV carb- + amide] (1865) : UREA

carb·ami·no \ˌkär-bə-ˈmē-(ˌ)nō\ adj (1922) : relating to any carbamic acid derivative formed by reaction of carbon dioxide with an amino acid or a protein (as hemoglobin)

carb·an·ion \ˌkär-ˈba-ˌnī-ən, -ˌnī-ˌän\ n (1933) : an organic ion carrying a negative charge on a carbon atom — compare CARBONIUM ION

car·barn \ˈkär-ˌbärn\ n (1880) : a building that houses the cars of a street railway or the buses of a bus system

car·ba·ryl \ˈkär-bə-ˌril\ n [carbamate + aryl] (1963) : a carbamate insecticide $C_{12}H_{11}NO_2$ effective esp. against numerous crop, forage, and forest pests

car·ba·zole \ˈkär-bə-ˌzōl\ n [ISV carb- + az- + -ole] (1887) : a crystalline slightly basic cyclic compound $C_{12}H_9N$ found in anthracene and used in making dyes

car·bide \ˈkär-ˌbīd\ n [ISV] (ca. 1865) **1 :** a binary compound of carbon with a more electropositive element; esp : CALCIUM CARBIDE **2 :** a very hard material made of carbon and one or more heavy metals

car·bine \ˈkär-ˌbēn, -ˌbīn\ n [F carabine, fr. MF carabin carabineer] (1605) **1 :** a short-barreled lightweight firearm orig. used by cavalry **2 :** a light short-barreled repeating rifle that is used as a supplementary military arm or for hunting in dense brush

car·bi·nol \ˈkär-bə-ˌnōl, -ˌnȯl\ n [ISV, fr. obs. G Karbin methyl, fr. G karb- carb-] (ca. 1885) : METHANOL; also : an alcohol derived from it

car·bo·cy·clic \ˌkär-bō-ˈsī-klik, -ˈsi-\ adj [ISV] (1899) : being or having an organic ring composed of carbon atoms

car·bo·hy·drase \ˌkär-bō-ˈhī-ˌdrās, -bə-, -ˌdrāz\ n [ISV] (1910) : any of a group of enzymes (as amylase) that promote hydrolysis or synthesis of a carbohydrate (as a disaccharide)

car·bo·hy·drate \-ˌdrāt, -drət\ n (ca. 1869) : any of various neutral compounds of carbon, hydrogen, and oxygen (as sugars, starches, and celluloses) most of which are formed by green plants and which constitute a major class of animal foods

car·bol·ic \kär-ˈbä-lik\ n (1884) : PHENOL 1

carbolic acid n [ISV carb- + L oleum oil — more at OIL] (ca. 1859) : PHENOL 1

car bomb n (1973) : an explosive device concealed in an automobile for use as a weapon of terrorism

car·bon \ˈkär-bən\ n, often attrib [F carbone, fr. L carbon-, carbo ember, charcoal] (1789) **1 :** a nonmetallic chiefly tetravalent element found native (as in the diamond and graphite) or as a constituent of coal, petroleum, and asphalt, of limestone and other carbonates, and of organic compounds or obtained artificially in varying degrees of purity esp. as carbon black, lampblack, activated carbon, charcoal, and coke — see ELEMENT table **2 :** a carbon rod used in an arc lamp **3 a :** a sheet of carbon paper **b :** CARBON COPY

car·bo·na·ceous \ˌkär-bə-ˈnā-shəs\ adj (1791) **1 :** rich in carbon **2 :** relating to, containing, or composed of carbon

¹car·bo·na·do \ˌkär-bə-ˈnä-(ˌ)dō, -ˈnä-\ n, pl **-dos** or **-does** [Sp carbonada] (1586) archaic : a piece of meat scored before grilling

²carbonado vt (1599) **1** archaic : to make a carbonado of **2** archaic : CUT, SLASH

³carbonado n, pl **-dos** [Pg, lit., carbonated] (1853) : an impure opaque dark-colored fine-grained aggregate of diamond particles valuable for its superior toughness

car·bo·nara \ˌkär-bə-ˈnär-ə\ n [It dial. (alla) carbonara, lit., in the manner of a charcoal maker] (1963) : a dish of hot pasta into which other ingredients (as eggs, bacon or ham, and grated cheese) have been mixed — often used as a postpositive modifier ⟨spaghetti ~⟩

¹car·bon·ate \ˈkär-bə-ˌnāt, -nət\ n (1794) : a salt or ester of carbonic acid

²car·bon·ate \-ˌnāt\ vt **-at·ed; -at·ing** (1805) **1 :** to convert into a carbonate **2 :** to combine or impregnate with carbon dioxide ⟨carbonated beverages⟩ — **car·bon·ation** \ˌkär-bə-ˈnā-shən\ n

carbon black n (ca. 1889) : any of various colloidal black substances consisting wholly or principally of carbon obtained usu. as soot and used esp. in tires and as pigments

carbon copy n (1895) **1 :** a copy made by carbon paper **2 :** DUPLICATE

carbon cycle n (1912) **1 :** the cycle of carbon in the earth's ecosystems in which carbon dioxide is fixed by photosynthetic organisms to form organic nutrients and is ultimately restored to the inorganic state by respiration and protoplasmic decay **2 :** a cycle of thermonuclear reactions in which four hydrogen atoms synthesize into a helium atom by the catalytic action of carbon with the release of nuclear energy and which is held to be the source of most of the energy radiated by the sun and stars

carbon dating n (1951) : the determination of the age of old material (as an archaeological or paleontological specimen) by means of the content of carbon 14 — **carbon–date** \ˈkär-bən-ˈdāt\ vt

carbon dioxide n (1873) : a heavy colorless gas CO_2 that does not support combustion, dissolves in water to form carbonic acid, is formed esp. in animal respiration and in the decay or combustion of animal and vegetable matter, is absorbed from the air by plants in photosynthesis, and is used in the carbonation of beverages

carbon disulfide n (1869) : a colorless flammable poisonous liquid CS_2 used as a solvent for rubber and as an insect fumigant — called also carbon bisulfide

carbon fiber n (1960) : a very strong lightweight synthetic fiber made esp. by carbonizing acrylic fiber at high temperatures

carbon 14 \see FOURTEEN\ n (1936) : a heavy radioactive isotope of carbon of mass number 14 used esp. in tracer studies and in dating archaeological and geological materials

car·bon·ic \kär-ˈbä-nik\ adj (1791) : of, relating to, or derived from carbon, carbonic acid, or carbon dioxide

carbonic acid n (1791) : a weak dibasic acid H_2CO_3 known only in solution that reacts with bases to form carbonates

carbonic acid gas n (ca. 1880) : CARBON DIOXIDE

carbonic an·hy·drase \-an-ˈhī-ˌdrās, -ˌdrāz\ n [anhydrous + -ase; fr. its promotion of dehydration] (1932) : a zinc-containing enzyme that occurs in living tissues (as red blood cells) and aids carbon-dioxide transport from the tissues and its release from the blood in the lungs by catalyzing the reversible hydration of carbon dioxide to carbonic acid

car·bon·if·er·ous \ˌkär-bə-ˈni-f(ə-)rəs\ adj (1799) **1 :** producing or containing carbon or coal **2** cap : of, relating to, or being the period of the Paleozoic era between the Devonian and the Permian or the corresponding system of rocks that includes coal beds — see GEOLOGIC TIME table — **Carboniferous** n

car·bo·ni·um \kär-ˈbō-nē-əm-\ n [carb- + -onium] (1942) : an organic ion carrying a positive charge on a carbon atom — compare CARBANION

car·bon·iza·tion \ˌkär-bə-nə-ˈzā-shən\ n (1804) : the process of carbonizing; esp : DESTRUCTIVE DISTILLATION

car·bon·ize \ˈkär-bə-ˌnīz\ vb **-ized; -iz·ing** vt (1806) **1 :** to convert into carbon or a carbonic residue **2 :** CARBURIZE 1 ~ vi : to become carbonized > CHAR

car·bon·less \ˈkär-bən-ləs\ adj (1850) **1 :** being without carbon **2 :** being or composed of paper that makes multiple copies without intervening layers of carbon paper ⟨~ forms⟩

carbon monoxide n (1873) : a colorless odorless very toxic gas CO that burns to carbon dioxide with a blue flame and is formed as a product of the incomplete combustion of carbon

car·bon·nade also **car·bo·nade** \ˌkär-bə-ˈnäd\ n [F, lit., dish of grilled meat, fr. It carbonata, fr. carbone charcoal, coal, fr. L carbon-, carbo] (1877) : a beef stew cooked in beer

carbon paper n (1895) : a thin paper faced with a waxy pigmented coating so that when placed between two sheets of paper the pressure of writing or typing on the top sheet causes transfer of pigment to the bottom sheet

carbon steel n (1903) : a strong hard steel that derives its physical properties from the presence of carbon and is used in hand tools and kitchen utensils

carbon tetrachloride n (1866) : a colorless nonflammable toxic liquid CCl_4 that has an odor resembling that of chloroform and is used as a solvent and a refrigerant

carbon 13 \-thir-ˈtēn, -ˈthir-ˌtēn\ n (1939) : an isotope of carbon of mass number 13 that constitutes about $1/90$ of natural carbon and is used as a tracer esp. in spectroscopy utilizing nuclear magnetic resonance

carbon 12 \-ˈtwelv\ n (1946) : an isotope of carbon of mass number 12 that is the most abundant carbon isotope and is used as a standard for measurements of atomic weight

car·bon·yl \ˈkär-bə-ˌnil, -ˌnēl\ n (1869) **1 :** an organic functional group —CO— occurring in aldehydes, ketones, carboxylic acids, esters, and their derivatives **2 :** a coordination complex involving the neutral radical CO ⟨chromium ~⟩ — **car·bon·yl·ic** \ˌkär-bə-ˈni-lik\ adj

car·bon·yl·a·tion \(ˌ)kär-ˌbä-nə-ˈlā-shən\ n (1946) : the synthesis of a carbonyl compound by a reaction involving carbon monoxide

Car·bo·run·dum \ˌkär-bə-ˈrən-dəm\ trademark — used for various abrasives

carboxy- or **carbox-** comb form : carboxyl ⟨carboxypeptidase⟩

\ə\ abut \ᵊ\ kitten, F table \ər\ further \a\ ash \ā\ ace \ä\ mop, mar \aú\ out \ch\ chin \e\ bet \ē\ easy \g\ go \i\ hit \ī\ ice \j\ job \ŋ\ sing \ō\ go \ȯ\ law \ȯi\ boy \th\ thin \t͟h\ the \ü\ loot \ú\ foot \y\ yet \zh\ vision \à, ̇k, ⁿ, œ, œ̄, ᵫ, ūe, ᵜ\ see Guide to Pronunciation

car·box·yl \kär-'bäk-səl\ n [ISV] (1869) : a univalent radical COOH typical of organic acids — called also *carboxyl group* — **car·box·yl·ic** \,kär-(,)bäk-'si-lik\ adj

car·box·yl·ase \kär-'bäk-sə-,lās, -,lāz\ n [ISV] (1911) : an enzyme that catalyzes decarboxylation or carboxylation

¹**car·box·yl·ate** \-,lāt, -lət\ n (1927) : a salt or ester of a carboxylic acid

²**car·box·yl·ate** \-,lāt\ vt **-at·ed; -at·ing** (ca. 1928) : to introduce carboxyl or carbon dioxide into (a compound) with formation of a carboxylic acid — **car·box·yl·a·tion** \(,)kär-,bäk-sə-'lā-shən\ n

carboxylic acid n (1902) : an organic acid (as acetic acid) containing one or more carboxyl groups

car·boxy·meth·yl·cel·lu·lose \kär-,bäk-sē-,me-thəl-'sel-yə-,lōs, -,lōz\ n (1947) : an acid ether derivative of cellulose that in the form of its sodium salt is used as a thickening, emulsifying, and stabilizing agent and as a bulk laxative in medicine

car·boxy·pep·ti·dase \-'pep-tə-,dās, -,dāz\ n (1937) : an enzyme that hydrolyzes peptides and esp. polypeptides by splitting off sequentially the amino acids at the end of the peptide chain which contain free carboxyl groups

car·boy \'kär-,bói\ n [Per *qarāba*, fr. Ar *qarrābah* demijohn] (1753) : a large container for liquids

car·bun·cle \'kär-,bən-kəl\ n [ME, fr. OF, fr. L *carbunculus* small coal, carbuncle, dim. of *carbon-, carbo* charcoal, ember] (13c) **1 a** obs : any of several red precious stones **b** : the garnet cut cabochon **2** : a painful local purulent inflammation of the skin and deeper tissues with multiple openings for the discharge of pus and usu. necrosis and sloughing of dead tissue — **car·bun·cled** \-kəld\ adj — **car·bun·cu·lar** \kär-'bəŋ-kyə-lər\ adj

car·bu·ret·ed \'kär-bə-,rā-təd, -byə-, esp by chemists -,re-təd\ adj [back-formation fr. *carburetor*] (1972) : equipped with a carburetor ⟨a ~ engine⟩

car·bu·re·tion \,kär-bə-'rā-shən, -byə-\ n [*carburet* to combine chemically with carbon, fr. obs. *carburet* carbide] (1896) : the process of mixing (as in a carburetor) the vapor of a flammable hydrocarbon (as gasoline) with air to form an explosive mixture esp. for use in an internal-combustion engine

car·bu·re·tor \'kär-bə-,rā-tər, -byə-\ n (1896) : an apparatus for supplying an internal combustion engine with an explosive mixture of vaporized fuel and air

car·bu·ret·tor also **car·bu·ret·ter** \,kär-byə-'re-tər, 'kär-byə-,\ chiefly Brit var of CARBURETOR

car·bu·rise Brit var of CARBURIZE

car·bu·rize \'kär-bə-,rīz, -byə-\ vt **-rized; -riz·ing** [obs. *carburet* carbide] (ca. 1889) : to combine or impregnate (as metal) with carbon — **car·bu·ri·za·tion** \,kär-bə-rə-'zā-shən, -byə-\ n

car·ca·net \'kär-kə-nət\ n [MF *carcan*] (ca. 1530) archaic : an ornamental necklace, chain, collar, or headband

car·case \'kär-kəs\ Brit var of CARCASS

car·cass \'kär-kəs\ n [ME *carcays*, fr. MF *carcasse*, fr. OF *carcois*] (14c) **1** : a dead body : CORPSE; esp : the dressed body of a meat animal **2** : the living, material, or physical body **3** : the decaying or worthless remains of a structure ⟨the ~ of an abandoned automobile⟩ **4** : the underlying structure or frame of something (as of a piece of furniture)

carcin- or **carcino-** comb form [Gk *karkin-, karkino-*, fr. *karkinos* ulcerous sore, lit., crab — more at CANCER] : tumor : cancer ⟨*carcinogenic*⟩

car·ci·no·em·bry·on·ic antigen \,kär-sⁿ-ō-,em-brē-'ä-nik-\ n (1967) : a glycoprotein present in fetal gut tissues during the first two trimesters of pregnancy and in peripheral blood of patients with some forms of cancer

car·cin·o·gen \kär-'si-nə-jən, 'kär-sⁿ-ə-,jen\ n (1853) : a substance or agent producing or inciting cancer — **car·ci·no·gen·ic** \,kär-sⁿ-ō-'je-nik\ adj — **car·ci·no·ge·nic·i·ty** \-jə-'ni-sə-tē\ n

car·ci·no·gen·e·sis \,kär-sⁿ-ō-'je-nə-sis\ n (ca. 1923) : the production of cancer

car·ci·noid \'kär-sⁿ-,óid\ n (1925) : a benign or malignant tumor arising esp. from the mucosa of the gastrointestinal tract

car·ci·no·ma \,kär-sⁿ-'ō-mə\ n, pl **-mas** or **-ma·ta** \-mə-tə\ [L, fr. Gk *karkinōma* cancer, fr. *karkinos*] (ca. 1751) : a malignant tumor of epithelial origin — **car·ci·no·ma·tous** \-'ō-mə-təs\ adj

car·ci·no·ma·to·sis \-,ō-mə-'tō-səs\ n [NL, fr. L *carcinomat-, carcinoma*] (1903) : a condition in which multiple carcinomas develop simultaneously usu. after dissemination from a primary source

car·ci·no·sar·co·ma \,kär-sⁿ-ō-,(,)sär-'kō-mə\ n, pl **-mas** or **-ma·ta** \-mə-tə\ (ca. 1919) : a malignant tumor combining elements of carcinoma and sarcoma

car coat n (1958) : a three-quarter-length overcoat

¹**card** \'kärd\ vt (14c) : to cleanse, disentangle, and collect together (as fibers) by the use of cards preparatory to spinning — **card·er** n

²**card** n [ME *carde*, fr. MF, fr. LL *cardus* thistle, fr. L *carduus* — more at CHARD] (15c) **1** : an instrument or machine for carding fibers that consists usu. of bent wire teeth set closely in rows in a thick piece of leather fastened to a back **2** : an implement for raising a nap on cloth

³**card** n [ME *carde*, modif. of MF *carte*, prob. fr. OIt *carta*, lit., leaf of paper, fr. L *charta* leaf of papyrus, fr. Gk *chartēs*] (15c) **1** : PLAYING CARD **2** pl but sing or pl in constr **a** : a game played with cards **b** : card playing **3** : something compared to a valuable playing card in one's hand **4** : a usu. clownishly amusing person : WAG **5** : COMPASS CARD **6 a** : a flat stiff usu. small and rectangular piece of material (as paper, paperboard, or plastic) usu. bearing information: as (1) : POST-CARD (2) : VISITING CARD (3) : CREDIT CARD (4) : one bearing a picture (as of a baseball player) on one side and usu. statistical data on the other (5) : one on which computer information is stored (as in the form of punched holes or magnetic encoding) (6) : one bearing electronic circuit components for insertion into a larger electronic device (as a computer) **b** : PROGRAM; esp : a sports program **c** (1) : a wine list (2) : MENU **d** : GREETING CARD ⟨a birthday ~⟩ — **in the cards** also **on the cards** : INEVITABLE

⁴**card** vt (1884) **1** : to place or fasten on or by means of a card **2** : to provide with a card **3** : to list or record on a card **4** : SCORE **5** : to ask for identification (as in a bar)

car·da·mom \'kär-də-məm, -,mäm\ n [L *cardamomum*, fr. Gk *kardamōmon*, blend of *kardamon* peppergrass and *amōmon*, an Indian spice plant] (1553) : the aromatic capsular fruit of an East Indian herb (*Elettaria cardamomum*) of the ginger family with seeds used as a spice or condiment and in medicine; also : this plant

¹**card·board** \'kärd-,bórd, -,bȯrd\ n (1848) : PAPERBOARD

²**cardboard** adj (1893) **1 a** : made of or as if of cardboard **b** : FLAT, TWO-DIMENSIONAL **2** : UNREAL, STEREOTYPED ⟨a play with ~ characters⟩

card–car·ry·ing \'kärd-,kar-ē-iŋ\ adj [fr. the assumption that such a person carries an identification card] (1948) **1** : being a full-fledged member esp. of a Communist party **2** : being strongly identified with a group (as of people with a common interest) ⟨~ members of the ecology movement —Richard Neuhaus⟩

card catalog n (1854) : a catalog (as of books) in which the entries are arranged systematically on cards

card·hold·er \'kärd-,hōl-dər\ n (1909) : one who possesses a card and esp. a credit card

cardi- or **cardio-** comb form [Gk *kardi-, kardio-*, fr. *kardia* — more at HEART] : heart : cardiac : cardiac and ⟨*cardiogram*⟩ ⟨*cardiovascular*⟩

car·dia \'kär-dē-ə\ n, pl **car·di·ae** \-dē-,ē\ or **-dias** [NL, fr. Gk *kardia* heart, upper orifice of the stomach] (1782) : the opening of the esophagus into the stomach; also : the part of the stomach adjoining this opening

-cardia n comb form [NL, fr. Gk *kardia*] : heart action or location (of a specified type) ⟨*tachycardia*⟩

¹**car·di·ac** \'kär-dē-,ak\ adj [L *cardiacus*, fr. Gk *kardiakos*, fr. *kardia*] (1601) **1 a** : of, relating to, situated near, or acting on the heart **b** : of or relating to the cardia of the stomach **2** : of, relating to, or affected with heart disease

²**cardiac** n (ca. 1929) : a person with heart disease

cardiac muscle n (ca. 1881) : the principal muscle tissue of the vertebrate heart made up of striated fibers that appear to be separated from each other under the electron microscope but that function in long-term rhythmic contraction as if in protoplasmic continuity

car·di·gan \'kär-di-gən\ n [James Thomas Brudenell, 7th Earl of *Cardigan* †1868 Eng. soldier] (1868) : a usu. collarless sweater or jacket that opens the full length of the center front

Cardigan Welsh corgi n [*Cardigan*, former county in Wales] (1935) : a Welsh corgi with rounded ears, slightly bowed forelegs, and long tail — called also *Cardigan*; see WELSH CORGI illustration

¹**car·di·nal** \'kärd-nəl, 'kärd-ⁿ-əl\ n [ME, fr. ML *cardinalis*, fr. LL *cardinalis*, adj.] (12c) **1** : a high ecclesiastical official of the Roman Catholic Church who ranks next below the pope and is appointed by him to assist him as a member of the college of cardinals : CARDINAL NUMBER — usu. used in pl. **3** : a woman's short hooded cloak orig. of scarlet cloth **4** [fr. its color, resembling that of the cardinal's robes] : a crested finch (*Cardinalis cardinalis*) of the eastern U.S. and adjacent Canada, the southwestern U.S., and Mexico to Belize which has a black face and heavy red bill in both sexes and is nearly completely red in the male — **car·di·nal·ship** \-,ship\ n

²**cardinal** adj [ME, fr. LL *cardinalis*, fr. L, serving as a hinge, fr. *cardin-, cardo* hinge] (14c) : of basic importance : MAIN, CHIEF, PRIMARY syn see ESSENTIAL — **car·di·nal·ly** adv

car·di·nal·ate \'kärd-nə-lət, 'kärd-ⁿ-ə-,lāt\ n (1645) : the office, rank, or dignity of a cardinal

cardinal flower n (1698) : a No. American lobelia (*Lobelia cardinalis*) that bears a spike of brilliant red flowers

car·di·nal·i·ty \,kärd-ⁿ-'a-lə-tē\ n, pl **-ties** [¹*cardinal* + *-ity*] (1935) : the number of elements in a given mathematical set

cardinal number n (1591) **1** : a number (as 1, 5, 15) that is used in simple counting and that indicates how many elements there are in an assemblage — see NUMBER table **2** : the property that a mathematical set has in common with all sets that can be put in one-to-one correspondence with it

cardinal point n (1755) : one of the four principal compass points north, south, east, and west

cardinal virtue n (14c) **1** : one of the four classically defined natural virtues prudence, justice, temperance, or fortitude **2** : a quality designated as a major virtue

car·dio·gen·ic \,kär-dē-ō-'je-nik\ adj (ca. 1923) : originating in the heart : caused by a cardiac condition ⟨~ shock⟩

car·dio·gram \'kär-dē-ə-,gram\ n [ISV] (1876) : the curve or tracing made by a cardiograph

car·dio·graph \-,graf\ n [ISV] (1870) : an instrument that registers graphically movements of the heart — **car·dio·graph·ic** \,kär-dē-ə-'gra-fik\ adj — **car·di·og·ra·phy** \,kär-dē-'ä-grə-fē\ n

car·di·oid \'kär-dē-,óid\ n (1753) : a heart-shaped curve that is traced by a point on the circumference of a circle rolling completely around an equal fixed circle and has the general equation $\rho = a(1 + \cos\theta)$ in polar coordinates

car·di·ol·o·gy \,kär-dē-'ä-lə-jē\ n [ISV] (1847) : the study of the heart and its action and diseases — **car·dio·log·i·cal** \-dē-ə-'lä-ji-kəl\ adj — **car·di·ol·o·gist** \-dē-'ä-lə-jist\ n

car·dio·my·op·a·thy \'kär-dē-ō-(,)mī-'ä-pə-thē\ n, pl **-thies** (1961) : a typically chronic disorder of heart muscle that may involve hypertrophy and obstructive damage to the heart

car·di·op·a·thy \,kär-dē-'ä-pə-thē\ n, pl **-thies** (1885) : any disease of the heart

car·dio·pul·mo·nary \,kär-dē-ō-'pùl-mə-,ner-ē, -'pəl-\ adj (ca. 1881) : of or relating to the heart and lungs

cardiopulmonary resuscitation n (1972) : a procedure designed to restore normal breathing after cardiac arrest that includes the clearance of air passages to the lungs, mouth-to-mouth method of artificial respiration, and heart massage by the exertion of pressure on the chest

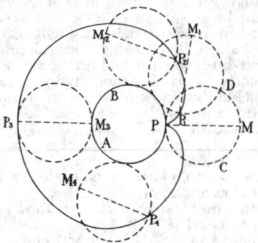

cardioid: *ABP* fixed circle; *PCD* first position of rolling circle; *P* tracing point; *PM* diameter through *P*; P_1, P_2, P_3, P_4 various positions of *P*; P_1M_1, P_2M_2, P_3M_3, P_4M_4 various positions of *PM*

car·dio·re·spi·ra·to·ry \ˌkär-dē-ō-'res-p(ə-)rə-ˌtōr-ē, -ri-'spī-rə-, -ˌtòr-\ *adj* (1892) : of or relating to the heart and the respiratory system

car·dio·tho·rac·ic \-thə-'ra-sik\ *adj* (1962) : relating to or involving the heart and chest

car·dio·ton·ic \-'tä-nik\ *adj* (1927) : tending to increase the tonus of heart muscle — **cardiotonic** *n*

car·dio·vas·cu·lar \-'vas-kyə-lər\ *adj* [ISV] (1879) : of, relating to, or involving the heart and blood vessels

-cardium *n comb form, pl* **-cardia** [NL, fr. Gk *kardia*] : heart ⟨epicardium⟩

car·doon \kär-'dün\ *n* [F *cardon*, fr. LL *cardon-, cardo* thistle, fr. *cardus*, fr. L *carduus* thistle, cardoon] (1611) : a large perennial plant (*Cynara cardunculus*) related to the artichoke and cultivated for its edible root and petioles; *also* : the root and petioles

card·play·er \'kärd-ˌplā-ər\ *n* (1589) : one that plays cards

card·sharp·er \-ˌshär-pər\ *or* **card·sharp** \-ˌshärp\ *n* (1859) : one who habitually cheats at cards

¹care \'ker, 'kar\ *n* [ME, fr. OE *caru*; akin to OHG *kara* lament, L *garrire* to chatter] (bef. 12c) **1** : suffering of mind : GRIEF **2 a** : a disquieted state of mixed uncertainty, apprehension, and responsibility **b** : a cause for such anxiety **3 a** : painstaking or watchful attention **b** : MAINTENANCE ⟨floor-*care* products⟩ **4** : regard coming from desire or esteem **5** : CHARGE, SUPERVISION ⟨under a doctor's ∼⟩ **6** : a person or thing that is an object of attention, anxiety, or solicitude

syn CARE, CONCERN, SOLICITUDE, ANXIETY, WORRY mean a troubled or engrossed state of mind or the thing that causes this. CARE implies oppression of the mind weighed down by responsibility or disquieted by apprehension ⟨a face worn by years of *care*⟩. CONCERN implies a troubled state of mind because of personal interest, relation, or affection ⟨crimes caused *concern* in the neighborhood⟩. SOLICITUDE implies great concern and connotes either thoughtful or hovering attentiveness toward another ⟨acted with typical maternal *solicitude*⟩. ANXIETY stresses anguished uncertainty or fear of misfortune or failure ⟨plagued by *anxiety* and self-doubt⟩. WORRY suggests fretting over matters that may or may not be real cause for anxiety ⟨financial *worries*⟩.

²care *vb* **cared; car·ing** *vi* (bef. 12c) **1 a** : to feel trouble or anxiety **b** : to feel interest or concern ⟨∼ about freedom⟩ **2** : to give care ⟨∼ for the sick⟩ **3 a** : to have a liking, fondness, or taste ⟨don't ∼ for your attitude⟩ **b** : to have an inclination ⟨would you ∼ for some pie⟩ ∼ *vt* **1** : to be concerned about or to the extent of **2** : WISH ⟨if you ∼ to go⟩ — **car·er** *n* — **care less** : not to care — used positively and negatively with the same meaning ⟨I could *care less* what happens⟩ ⟨I couldn't *care less* what happens⟩

¹ca·reen \kə-'rēn\ *n* [fr. *carine* side of a ship, fr. MF, submerged part of a hull, fr. L *carina* hull, half of a nutshell; perh. akin to Gk *karyon* nut] *vt* (ca. 1583) **1** : to put (a ship or boat) on a beach esp. in order to clean, caulk, or repair the hull **2** : to cause to heel over ∼ *vi* **1 a** : to careen a boat **b** : to undergo this process **2** : to heel over **3** : to sway from side to side : LURCH ⟨a ∼*ing* carriage being pulled wildly . . . by a team of runaway horses —J. P. Getty⟩ **4** : CAREER

²careen *vi* (1712) *archaic* : the act or process of careening : the state of being careened

¹ca·reer \kə-'rir\ *n* [MF *carrière*, fr. OProv *carriera* street, fr. ML *carraria* road for vehicles, fr. L *carrus* car] (1580) **1 a** : speed in a course ⟨ran at full ∼⟩ **b** : COURSE, PASSAGE **2** : ENCOUNTER, CHARGE **3** : a field for or pursuit of consecutive progressive achievement esp. in public, professional, or business life ⟨Washington's ∼ as a soldier⟩ **4** : a profession for which one trains and which is undertaken as a permanent calling ⟨a ∼ diplomat⟩

²career *vi* (1647) : to go at top speed esp. in a headlong manner ⟨a car ∼ed off the road⟩

ca·reer·ism \-ˌi-zəm\ *n* (1933) : the policy or practice of advancing one's career often at the cost of one's integrity — **ca·reer·ist** \-ist\ *n*

care·free \'ker-ˌfrē, 'kar-\ *adj* (1795) : free from care: as **a** : having no worries or troubles **b** : IRRESPONSIBLE ⟨is ∼ with his money⟩

care·ful \-fəl\ *adj* **care·ful·ler; care·ful·lest** (bef. 12c) **1** *archaic* **a** : SOLICITOUS, ANXIOUS **b** : filling with care or solicitude **2** : exercising or taking care **3 a** : marked by attentive concern and solicitude **b** : marked by wary caution or prudence ⟨be very ∼ with knives⟩ **c** : marked by painstaking effort to avoid errors or omissions — often used with *of* or an infinitive ⟨∼ of money⟩ ⟨∼ to adjust the machine⟩ — **care·ful·ly** \-f(ə-)lē\ *adv* — **care·ful·ness** \-fəl-nəs\ *n*

syn CAREFUL, METICULOUS, SCRUPULOUS, PUNCTILIOUS mean showing close attention to detail. CAREFUL implies attentiveness and cautiousness in avoiding mistakes ⟨a *careful* worker⟩. METICULOUS may imply either commendable extreme carefulness or a hampering finicky caution over small points ⟨*meticulous* scholarship⟩. SCRUPULOUS applies to what is proper or fitting or ethical ⟨*scrupulous* honesty⟩. PUNCTILIOUS implies minute, even excessive attention to fine points ⟨*punctilious* observance of ritual⟩.

care·giv·er \-ˌgi-vər\ *n* (1975) : a person who provides direct care (as for children or the chronically ill) — **care·giv·ing** \-ˌgi-viŋ\ *n*

care·less \-ləs\ *adj* (bef. 12c) **1 a** : free from care : UNTROUBLED ⟨∼ days⟩ **b** : INDIFFERENT, UNCONCERNED ⟨∼ of the consequences⟩ **2** : not taking care **3** : not showing or receiving care: **a** : NEGLIGENT, SLOVENLY ⟨∼ writing⟩ **b** : UNSTUDIED, SPONTANEOUS ⟨∼ grace⟩ **c** *obs* : UNVALUED, DISREGARDED — **care·less·ly** *adv* — **care·less·ness** *n*

¹ca·ress \kə-'res\ *n* [F *caresse*, fr. It *carezza*, fr. *caro* dear, fr. L *carus* — more at CHARITY] (ca. 1611) **1** : an act or expression of kindness or affection : ENDEARMENT **2 a** : a light stroking, rubbing, or patting **b** : KISS — **ca·res·sive** \-'re-siv\ *adj* — **ca·res·sive·ly** *adv*

²caress *vt* (1658) **1** : to treat with tokens of fondness, affection, or kindness : CHERISH **2 a** : to touch or stroke lightly in a loving or endearing manner **b** : to touch or affect as if with a caress ⟨echoes that ∼ the ear⟩ — **ca·ress·er** *n* — **ca·ress·ing·ly** \kə-'re-siŋ-lē\ *adv*

car·et \'kar-ət\ *n* [L, there is lacking, fr. *carēre* to lack, be without] (1681) : a wedge-shaped mark made on written or printed matter to indicate the place where something is to be inserted

care·tak·er \'ker-ˌtā-kər, 'kar-\ *n* (1858) **1** : one that gives physical or emotional care and support ⟨served as ∼ to the younger children⟩ **2** : one that takes care of the house or land of an owner who may be absent **3** : one temporarily fulfilling the function of office ⟨a ∼ government⟩ — **care·take** \-ˌtāk\ *vb* — **care·tak·ing** *n*

care·worn \-ˌwòrn, -ˌwòrn\ *adj* (1828) : showing the effect of grief or anxiety ⟨a ∼ face⟩

car·fare \'kär-ˌfar, -ˌfer\ *n* (1870) : passenger fare (as on a bus)

car·ful \'kär-ˌfùl\ *n* (1832) : as much or as many as a car will hold

car·go \'kär-(ˌ)gō\ *n, pl* **cargoes** *or* **cargos** [Sp, load, charge, fr. *cargar* to load, fr. LL *carricare* — more at CHARGE] (1657) : the goods or merchandise conveyed in a ship, airplane, or vehicle : FREIGHT

cargo cult *n* (1949) : any of various Melanesian religious groups characterized by the belief that material wealth (as money or manufactured goods) can be obtained through ritual worship

cargo pocket *n* (1974) : a large pocket usu. with a flap and a pleat

car·hop \'kär-ˌhäp\ *n* [*car* + *-hop* (as in *bellhop*)] (1937) : one who serves customers at a drive-in restaurant

Car·ib \'kar-əb\ *n* [NL *Caribes* (pl.), fr. Sp *Caribe*, of Cariban origin — more at CANNIBAL] (1555) **1** : a member of an Indian people of northern So. America and the Lesser Antilles **2** : the language of the Caribs

Ca·ri·ban \'kar-ə-bən, kə-'rē-bən\ *n* (1901) **1** : a member of a group of Indian peoples of So. America and the Lesser Antilles **2** : the language family comprising the languages of the Cariban peoples

Ca·rib·be·an \ˌkar-ə-'bē-ən, kə-'ri-bē-ən\ *adj* [NL *Caribbaeus*, fr. *Caribes*] (1777) : of or relating to the Caribs, the eastern and southern West Indies, or the Caribbean Sea

ca·ri·be \kə-'rē-bē\ *n* [AmerSp, fr. Sp, Carib, cannibal] (1868) : PIRANHA

car·i·bou \'kar-ə-ˌbü\ *n, pl* **-bou** *or* **-bous** [CanF, fr. Micmac *γalipu*] (ca. 1665) : a large gregarious deer (*Rangifer tarandus*) of Holarctic taiga and tundra that usu. has palmate antlers in both sexes — used esp. for one of the New World; called also *reindeer*

caribou

¹car·i·ca·ture \'kar-i-kə-ˌchùr, -ˌchər, -ˌtyùr, -ˌtùr\ *n* [It *caricatura*, lit., act of loading, fr. *caricare* to load, fr. LL *carricare*] (1712) **1** : exaggeration by means of often ludicrous distortion of parts or characteristics **2** : a representation in literature or art that has the qualities of caricature **3** : a distortion so gross as to seem like caricature — **car·i·ca·tur·al** \ˌkar-i-kə-'chùr-əl, -'chər-, -'tyùr-, -'tùr-\ *adj* — **car·i·ca·tur·ist** \'kar-i-kə-ˌchùr-ist, -ˌchər-, -ˌtyùr-, -ˌtùr-\ *n*

syn CARICATURE, BURLESQUE, PARODY, TRAVESTY mean a comic or grotesque imitation. CARICATURE implies ludicrous exaggeration of the characteristic features of a subject ⟨*caricatures* of politicians in cartoons⟩. BURLESQUE implies mockery esp. through giving a serious or lofty subject a frivolous treatment ⟨a nightclub *burlesque* of a trial in court⟩. PARODY applies esp. to treatment of a trivial or ludicrous subject in the exactly imitated style of a well-known author or work ⟨a witty *parody* of a popular novel⟩. TRAVESTY implies that the subject remains unchanged but that the style is extravagant or absurd ⟨this production is a *travesty* of the opera⟩.

²caricature *vt* **-tured; -tur·ing** (ca. 1771) : to make or draw a caricature of : represent in caricature ⟨the portrait *caricatured* its subject⟩

car·ies \'kar-ēz, 'ker-\ *n, pl* **caries** [L, decay; akin to OIr *ara-chrinn* it decays] (1634) : a progressive destruction of bone or tooth; *esp* : tooth decay

car·il·lon \'kar-ə-ˌlän, -lən; 'kar-ē-ˌän, -ˌōn; kə-'ril-yən\ *n* [F, alter. of OF *quarregnon*, modif. of LL *quaternion-, quaternio* set of four — more at QUATERNION] (1775) **1** : a set of fixed chromatically tuned bells sounded by hammers controlled from a keyboard **b** : an electronic instrument imitating a carillon **2** : a composition for the carillon

car·il·lon·neur \ˌkar-ə-lə-'nər, ˌkar-ē-ə-'nər, kə-ˌril-yə-'nər\ *n* [F, fr. *carillon*] (1772) : a carillon player

ca·ri·na \kə-'rī-nə, -'rē-nə\ *n, pl* **-nas** *or* **-nae** \-'rī-ˌnē, -'rē-ˌnī\ [NL, fr. L, hull, keel — more at CAREEN] (ca. 1704) **1** : a keel-shaped anatomical part, ridge, or process **2** *cap* : a constellation in the southern hemisphere lying near the Southern Cross

car·i·nate \'kar-ə-ˌnāt, -nət\ *or* **car·i·nat·ed** \-ˌnā-təd\ *adj* (1781) : having or shaped like a keel or carina

ca·ri·o·ca \ˌkar-ē-'ō-kə\ *n* [Brazilian Pg] (1830) **1** *cap* : a native or resident of Rio de Janeiro **2** : a variation of the samba **b** : the music for this dance

car·io·gen·ic \ˌkar-ē-ə-'je-nik, ˌker-, -'jē-\ *adj* [*caries* + *-o-* + *-genic*] (1930) : producing or promoting the development of tooth decay ⟨∼ foods⟩

car·i·ous \'kar-ē-əs, 'ker-\ *adj* [L *cariosus*, fr. *caries*] (1676) : affected with caries

car·jack·ing \'kär-ˌja-kiŋ\ *n* [*car* + *hijack* + *-ing*] (1991) : the theft of an automobile from its driver by force or intimidation — **car·jack·er** *n*

cark·ing \'kär-kiŋ\ *adj* [ME, fr. *carken*, lit., to load, burden, fr. ONF *carquier*, fr. LL *carricare*] (ca. 1565) : BURDENSOME, ANNOYING

carl *or* **carle** \'kär(-ə)l\ *n* [ME, fr. OE *-carl*, fr. ON *karl* man, carl — more at CHURL] (bef. 12c) **1** : a man of the common people **2** *chiefly dial* : CHURL, BOOR

car·line *or* **car·lin** \'kär-lən\ *n* [ME *kerling*, fr. ON, fr. *karl* man] (14c) *chiefly Scot* : WOMAN; *esp* : an old woman

Car·list \'kär-list\ *n* [Sp *carlista*, fr. Don *Carlos*] (1830) : a supporter of Don Carlos or his successors as having rightful title to the Spanish throne — **Carlist** *adj*

car·load \'kär-ˌlōd, -ˌlōd\ *n* (1854) **1** : a load that fills a car **2** : the minimum number of tons required for shipping at carload rates

---

\ə\ abut \ˀ\ kitten, F table \ər\ further \a\ ash \ā\ ace \ä\ mop, mar
\aù\ out \ch\ chin \e\ bet \ē\ easy \g\ go \i\ hit \ī\ ice \j\ job
\ŋ\ sing \ō\ go \ò\ law \òi\ boy \th\ thin \t͟h\ the \ü\ loot \ù\ foot
\y\ yet \zh\ vision \ä, k̲, ⁿ, œ, œ̄, ᵫ, ᵫ̄, ᵊ\ *see* Guide to Pronunciation

carload rate *n* (1906) : a rate for large shipments lower than that quoted for less-than-carload lots of the same class

Car·lo·vin·gian \ˌkär-lə-'vin-j(ē-)ən\ *adj* [F *carlovingien*, fr. ML *Carlus* Charles + F *-ovingien* (as in *mérovingien* Merovingian)] (1781) : CAROLINGIAN

car·ma·gnole \ˈkär-mən-ˌyōl\ *n* [F] (1793) **1** : a lively song popular at the time of the first French Revolution **2** : a street dance in a meandering course to the tune of the carmagnole

car·mak·er \ˈkär-ˌmā-kər\ *n* (1954) : an automobile manufacturer

Car·mel·ite \ˈkär-mə-ˌlīt\ *n* [ME, fr. ML *carmelita*, fr. *Carmel* Mount Carmel, Palestine] (15c) : a member of the Roman Catholic mendicant Order of Our Lady of Mount Carmel founded in the 12th century — **Carmelite** *adj*

car·mi·na·tive \kär-'mi-nə-tiv, 'kär-mə-ˌnā-\ *adj* [F *carminatif*, fr. L *carminatus*, pp. of *carminare* to card, fr. (assumed) L *carmin-*, *carmen* card, fr. L *carrere* to card; akin to Lith *karšti* to card] (15c) : expelling gas from the alimentary canal so as to relieve colic or griping — **carminative** *n*

car·mine \ˈkär-mən, -ˌmīn\ *n* [F *carmin*, fr. ML *carminium*, irreg. fr. Ar *qirmiz* kermes + L *minium* cinnabar] (1712) **1** : a rich crimson or scarlet lake made from cochineal **2** : a vivid red

car·nage \ˈkär-nij\ *n* [F, fr. ML *carnaticum* tribute consisting of animals or meat, fr. L *carn-, caro*] (ca. 1656) **1** : the flesh of slain animals or men **2** : great and bloody slaughter (as in battle)

car·nal \ˈkär-nᵊl\ *adj* [ME, fr. ONF or LL; ONF, fr. LL *carnalis*, fr. L *carn-, caro* flesh; akin to Gk *keirein* to cut — more at SHEAR] (14c) **1 a** : relating to or given to crude bodily pleasures and appetites **b** : marked by sexuality **2** : BODILY, CORPOREAL **3 a** : TEMPORAL **b** : WORLDLY — **car·nal·i·ty** \kär-'na-lə-tē\ *n* — **car·nal·ly** \ˈkär-nᵊl-ē\ *adv*

syn CARNAL, FLESHLY, SENSUAL, ANIMAL mean having a relation to the body. CARNAL may mean only this but more often connotes derogatorily an action or manifestation of a person's lower nature ⟨a slave to *carnal* desires⟩. FLESHLY is less derogatory than CARNAL ⟨a saint who had experienced *fleshly* temptations⟩. SENSUAL may apply to any gratification of a bodily desire or pleasure but commonly implies sexual appetite with absence of the spiritual or intellectual ⟨fleshpots providing *sensual* delights⟩. ANIMAL stresses the physical as distinguished from the rational nature of a person ⟨led a mindless *animal* existence⟩.

car·nall·ite \ˈkär-nᵊl-ˌīt\ *n* [G *Carnallit*, fr. Rudolf von *Carnall* †1874 Ger. mining engineer] (1876) : a mineral consisting of hydrous potassium-magnesium chloride that is an important source of potassium

car·nas·si·al \kär-'na-sē-əl\ *adj* [F *carnassier* carnivorous, ultim. fr. L *carn-, caro*] (ca. 1852) : of, relating to, or being teeth of a carnivore often larger and longer than adjacent teeth and adapted for cutting rather than tearing — **carnassial** *n*

car·na·tion \kär-'nā-shən\ *n* [MF, fr. OIt *carnagione*, fr. *carne* flesh, fr. L *carn-, caro*] (ca. 1535) **1 a** (1) : the variable color of human flesh (2) : a pale to grayish yellow **b** : a moderate red **2** : a plant of any of numerous often cultivated and usu. double-flowered varieties or subspecies of an Old World pink (*Dianthus caryophyllus*) orig. flesh-colored but now found in many color variations

car·nau·ba \kär-'nȯ-bə, -'naú-; ˌkär-nə-'ü-bə\ *n* [Pg] (1866) : a fan-leaved palm (*Copernicia prunifera* syn. *C. cerifera*) of Brazil that has an edible root and yields a useful leaf fiber and carnauba wax

carnauba wax *n* (1854) : a hard brittle high-melting wax obtained from the leaves of the carnauba palm and used chiefly in polishes

car·ne·lian \kär-'nēl-yən\ *n* [alter. of *cornelian*, fr. ME *corneline*, fr. MF, perh. fr. *cornelle* cornel] (1695) : a hard tough chalcedony that has a reddish color and is used in jewelry

car·ni·tine \ˈkär-nə-ˌtēn\ *n* [ISV, fr. L *carn-, caro*] (ca. 1922) : a quaternary ammonium compound $C_7H_{15}NO_3$ that is present esp. in vertebrate muscle and is involved in the transfer of fatty acids across mitochondrial membranes

car·ni·val \ˈkär-nə-vəl\ *n* [It *carnevale*, alter. of earlier *carnelevare*, lit., removal of meat, fr. *carne* flesh (fr. L *carn-, caro*) + *levare* to remove, fr. L, to raise] (1549) **1** : a season or festival of merrymaking before Lent **2 a** : an instance of merrymaking, feasting, or masquerading **b** : an instance of riotous excess ⟨a ~ of violence⟩ **3 a** : a traveling enterprise offering amusements **b** : an organized program of entertainment or exhibition : FESTIVAL ⟨a winter ~⟩

car·niv·o·ra \kär-'ni-və-rə\ *n pl* [L, neut. pl. of *carnivorus*] (1830) : carnivorous mammals

car·ni·vore \ˈkär-nə-ˌvȯr, -ˌvȯr\ *n* [ultim. fr. L *carnivorus*] (1840) **1** : a carnivorous animal; *esp* : any of an order (Carnivora) of flesh-eating mammals **2** : a carnivorous plant

car·niv·o·rous \kär-'ni-v(ə-)rəs\ *adj* [L *carnivorus*, fr. *carn-, caro* + *-vorus* -vorous] (1592) **1** : subsisting or feeding on animal tissues **2** *of a plant* : subsisting on nutrients obtained from the breakdown of animal protoplasm **3** : of or relating to the carnivores **4** : RAPACIOUS — **car·niv·o·rous·ly** *adv* — **car·niv·o·rous·ness** *n*

car·no·tite \ˈkär-nə-ˌtīt\ *n* [F, fr. M. A. *Carnot* †1920 Fr. inspector general of mines] (1899) : a mineral consisting of a hydrous radioactive vanadate of uranium and potassium that is a source of radium and uranium

car·ny *or* **car·ney** *or* **car·nie** \ˈkär-nē\ *n, pl* **carnies** *or* **carneys** *often attrib* (ca. 1933) **1** : CARNIVAL 3a **2** : a person who works with a carnival

car·ob \ˈkar-əb\ *n* [MF *carobe*, fr. ML *carrubium*, fr. Ar *kharrūbah*] (1548) **1** : a Mediterranean evergreen leguminous tree (*Ceratonia siliqua*) with racemose red flowers **2** : a carob pod or its sweet pulp having a flavor similar to that of chocolate

ca·roche \kə-'rōch, -'rōsh\ *n* [MF *carroche*, fr. OIt *carroccio*, aug. of *carro* car, fr. L *carrus*] (1591) : a luxurious horse-drawn carriage

¹car·ol \ˈkar-əl\ *n* [ME *carole*, fr. MF, fr. ML *choraula* choral song, fr. L, choral accompanist, fr. Gk *choraulēs*, fr. *choros* chorus + *aulein* to play a reed instrument, fr. *aulos*, a reed instrument — more at ALVEOLUS] (14c) **1** : an old round dance with singing **2** : a song of joy or mirth ⟨the ~ of a bird —Lord Byron⟩ **3** : a popular song or ballad of religious joy

²carol *vb* **-oled** *or* **-olled; -ol·ing** *or* **-ol·ling** *vi* (14c) **1** : to sing esp. in a joyful manner **2** : to sing carols; *specif* : to go about outdoors in a group singing Christmas carols ~ *vt* **1** : to praise in or as if in song

2 : to sing esp. in a cheerful manner : WARBLE — **car·ol·er** *or* **car·ol·ler** \-ə-lər\ *n*

Car·o·line \ˈkar-ə-ˌlīn, -lən\ *or* **Car·o·le·an** \ˌkar-ə-'lē-ən\ *adj* [NL *carolinus*, fr. ML *Carolus* Charles] (1652) : of or relating to Charles — used esp. with reference to Charles I and Charles II of England

Car·o·lin·gi·an \ˌkar-ə-'lin-j(ē-)ən\ *adj* [F *carolingien*, fr. ML *Karolingi* Carolingians, fr. *Karol*us Charlemagne + *-ingi* (as in *Merovingi* Merovingians)] (1881) : of or relating to a Frankish dynasty dating from about A.D. 613 and including among its members the rulers of France from 751 to 987, of Germany from 752 to 911, and of Italy from 774 to 961 — **Carolingian** *n*

¹car·om \ˈkar-əm\ *n* [by shortening & alter. fr. obs. *carambole*, fr. Sp *carambola*] (1779) **1 a** : a shot in billiards in which the cue ball strikes each of two object balls **b** : a shot in pool in which an object ball strikes another ball before falling into a pocket — compare COMBINATION SHOT **2** : a rebounding esp. at an angle

²carom *vi* (1860) **1** : to strike and rebound : GLANCE ⟨the car ~ed off a tree⟩ **2** : to make a carom **3** : to proceed by or as if by caroms

car·o·tene \ˈkar-ə-ˌtēn\ *n* [ISV, fr. LL *carota* carrot] (1861) : any of several orange or red crystalline hydrocarbon pigments $C_{40}H_{56}$ that occur in the chromoplasts of plants and in the fatty tissues of plant-eating animals and are convertible to vitamin A

ca·rot·en·oid *also* **ca·rot·in·oid** \kə-'rä-tᵊn-ˌȯid\ *n* (1911) : any of various usu. yellow to red pigments (as carotenes) found widely in plants and animals and characterized chemically by a long aliphatic polyene chain composed of eight isoprene units — **carotenoid** *adj*

ca·rot·id \kə-'rä-təd\ *adj* [F or Gk; F *carotide*, fr. Gk *karōtides* carotid arteries, fr. *karoun* to stupefy; akin to Gk *kara* head — more at CEREBRAL] (1543) : of, relating to, or being the chief artery or pair of arteries that pass up the neck and supply the head — **carotid** *n*

carotid body *n* (1940) : a small body of vascular tissue that adjoins the carotid sinus, functions as a chemoreceptor sensitive to change in the oxygen content of blood, and mediates reflex changes in respiratory activity

carotid sinus *n* (ca. 1923) : a small but richly innervated arterial enlargement that is located near the point in the neck where either carotid artery divides to form its main branches and that functions in the regulation of heart rate and blood pressure

ca·rous·al \kə-'raú-zəl\ *n* (1765) : CAROUSE 2

¹ca·rouse \kə-'raúz\ *n* [MF *carrousse*, fr. *carous*, adv., all out (in *boire carous* to empty the cup), fr. G *gar aus*] (1559) **1** *archaic* : a large draft of liquor : TOAST **2** : a drunken revel

²carouse *vb* **ca·roused; ca·rous·ing** *vi* (1567) **1** : to drink liquor deeply or freely **2** : to take part in a carouse : engage in dissolute behavior ~ *vt, obs* : to drink up : QUAFF — **ca·rous·er** *n*

car·ou·sel \ˌkar-ə-'sel *also* -'zel; 'kar-ə-ˌ\ *n* [F *carrousel*, fr. It *carosello*] (1650) **1** : a tournament or exhibition in which horsemen execute evolutions **2 a** : MERRY-GO-ROUND **b** : a circular conveyer ⟨the luggage ~ at the airport⟩ **c** : a revolving case used for storage or display

¹carp \ˈkärp\ *vi* [ME, of Scand origin; akin to Icel *karpa* to dispute] (14c) : to find fault or complain querulously — **carp·er** *n*

²carp *n* (1904) : COMPLAINT

³carp *n, pl* **carp** *or* **carps** [ME *carpe*, fr. MF, fr. LL *carpa*, prob. of Gmc origin; akin to OHG *karpfo* carp] (15c) **1** : a large variable Asian soft-finned freshwater cyprinid fish (*Cyprinus carpio*) of sluggish waters that is often raised for food and has been widely introduced into U.S. waters; *also* : any of various related fishes **2** : a fish (as the European sea bream) resembling a carp

carp- *or* **carpo-** *comb form* [F & NL, fr. Gk *karp-*, *karpo-*, fr. *karpos* — more at HARVEST] : fruit ⟨*carpogonium*⟩

-carp *comb form* [NL *-carpium*, fr. Gk *-karpion*, fr. *karpos*] : part of a fruit ⟨*mesocarp*⟩ : fruit ⟨*schizocarp*⟩

car·pac·cio \kär-'pä-ch(ē-)ō\ *n* [Vittore *Carpaccio*; fr. the prominent use of red in his painting] (1969) : thinly sliced raw meat or fish served with a sauce — often used as a postpositive modifier ⟨beef ~⟩

¹car·pal \ˈkär-pəl\ *adj* [NL *carpalis*, fr. *carpus*] (1743) : relating to the carpus

²carpal *n* (1855) : a carpal element or bone

carpal tunnel syndrome *n* (1954) : a condition caused by compression of a nerve where it passes through the wrist into the hand and characterized esp. by weakness, pain, and disturbances of sensation in the hand

car park *n* (1926) *chiefly Brit* : PARKING LOT

car·pe di·em \ˈkär-pe-'dē-ˌem, -'dī-, -əm\ *n* [L, lit., pluck the day] (1817) : the enjoyment of the pleasures of the moment without concern for the future

car·pel \ˈkär-pəl\ *n* [NL *carpellum*, fr. Gk *karpos* fruit] (1835) : one of the ovule-bearing structures in an angiosperm that comprises the innermost whorl of a flower — compare PISTIL — **car·pel·lary** \-pə-ˌler-ē\ *adj* — **car·pel·late** \-ˌlāt, -lət\ *adj*

¹car·pen·ter \ˈkär-pən-tər, 'kärp-ᵊm-tər\ *n* [ME, fr. ONF *carpentier*, fr. L *carpentarius* carriage maker, fr. *carpentum* carriage, of Celt origin; akin to OIr *carpat* chariot, *carr* vehicle — more at CAR] (14c) : a worker who builds or repairs wooden structures or their structural parts

²carpenter *vb* **-tered; -ter·ing** \-t(ə-)riŋ\ *vi* (ca. 1815) : to follow the trade of a carpenter ⟨~ed when he was young⟩ ~ *vt* **1** : to make by or as if by carpentry **2** : to put together often in a mechanical manner ⟨~ed many television scripts⟩

carpenter ant *n* (1883) : an ant (esp. genus *Camponotus*) that gnaws galleries esp. in dead or decayed wood

carpenter bee *n* (1838) : any of various solitary bees (genera *Xylocopa* and *Ceratina*) that nest in wood

car·pen·try \-trē\ *n* (14c) **1** : the art or trade of a carpenter; *specif* : the art of shaping and assembling structural woodwork **2** : timber-work constructed by a carpenter **3** : the form or manner of putting together the parts (as of a literary or musical composition)

car·pet \ˈkär-pət\ *n* [ME, fr. MF *carpite*, fr. OIt *carpita*, fr. *carpire* to pluck, modif. of L *carpere* to pluck — more at HARVEST] (15c) **1** : a heavy often tufted fabric used as a floor covering; *also* : a floor covering made of this fabric **2** : a surface resembling or suggesting a carpet — **carpet** *vt* — **on the carpet** : before an authority for censure or reproof

¹car·pet·bag \-ˌbag\ *n* (1830) : a traveler's bag made of carpet and widely used in the U.S. in the 19th century

²carpetbag *or* **car·pet·bag·ging** \-ˌba-giŋ\ *adj* (1870) : of, relating to, or characteristic of carpetbaggers ⟨a ~ government⟩

car·pet·bag·ger \-ˌba-gər\ *n* [fr. their carrying all their belongings in carpetbags] (1868) **1** : a Northerner in the South after the American Civil War usu. seeking private gain under the reconstruction governments **2** : OUTSIDER; *esp* : a nonresident or new resident who meddles in politics — **car·pet·bag·gery** \-ˌba-g(ə-)rē\ *n*

carpetbag steak *n* (1958) : a thick piece of steak in which a pocket is cut and stuffed (as with oysters)

carpet beetle *n* (1889) : any of several small dermestid beetles (genera *Anthrenus* and *Attagenus* whose larvae are destructive esp. to woolen goods

carpet bombing *n* (1944) : the dropping of large numbers of bombs so as to cause uniform devastation over a given area — **carpet bomb** *vb*

car·pet·ing \ˈkär-pə-tiŋ\ *n* (1758) : material for carpets; *also* : CARPETS

car·pet·weed \ˈkär-pət-ˌwēd\ *n* (1784) : a No. American mat-forming weed (*Mollugo verticillata* of the family Aizoaceae, the carpetweed family)

-carpic *adj comb form* [prob. fr. NL *-carpicus*, fr. Gk *karpos* fruit] : -CARPOUS ⟨monocarpic⟩

carp·ing \ˈkär-piŋ\ *adj* (1581) : marked by or inclined to querulous and often perverse criticism *syn* see CRITICAL — **carp·ing·ly** \-piŋ-lē\ *adv*

car·po·go·ni·um \ˌkär-pə-ˈgō-nē-əm\ *n, pl* **-nia** \-nē-ə\ [NL] (1882) : the flask-shaped egg-bearing portion of the female reproductive branch in some thallophytes (as red algae) — **car·po·go·ni·al** \-nē-əl\ *adj*

car·pool \ˈkär-ˌpü(ə)l\ *vi* (1962) : to participate in a car pool — **car-pool·er** *n*

car pool *n* (1942) : an arrangement in which a group of people commute together by car; *also* : the group entering into such an arrangement

car·po·phore \ˈkär-pə-ˌfōr, -ˌfor\ *n* [prob. fr. NL *carpophorum*, fr. *carp-* + *-phorum* -phore] (ca. 1859) **1** : the stalk of a fungal fruiting body; *also* : the entire fruiting body **2** : a slender prolongation of a floral axis from which the carpels are suspended

car·port \ˈkär-ˌpōrt, -ˌport\ *n* (1939) : an open-sided automobile shelter by the side of a building

car·po·spore \ˈkär-pə-ˌspōr, -ˌspor\ *n* (1881) : a diploid spore of a red alga

-carpous *adj comb form* [NL *-carpus*, fr. Gk *-karpos*, fr. *karpos* fruit — more at HARVEST] : having (such) fruit or (so many) fruits ⟨syncarpous⟩ — **-carpy** *n comb form*

car·pus \ˈkär-pəs\ *n, pl* **car·pi** \-ˌpī, -(ˌ)pē\ [NL, fr. Gk *karpos* — more at WHARF] (1679) **1** : WRIST **2** : the bones of the wrist

carr \ˈkär\ *n* [ME *ker*, of Scand origin; akin to ON *kjarr* underbrush] (14c) *chiefly dial* : ¹FEN

car·rack \ˈkar-ək, -ik\ *n* [ME *carrake*, fr. MF *caraque*, fr. OSp *carraca*, fr. *qarāqīr*, pl. of *qurqūr* merchant ship] (14c) : a beamy sailing ship esp. of the 15th and 16th centuries

car·ra·geen *also* **car·ra·gheen** \ˈkar-ə-ˌgēn\ *n* [*Carragheen*, near Waterford, Ireland] (1829) **1** : IRISH MOSS 2 **2** : CARRAGEENAN

car·ra·geen·an *or* **car·ra·geen·in** \ˌkar-ə-ˈgē-nən\ *n* [*carrageen* + ³-*an* or ¹-*in*] (ca. 1889) : a colloid extracted from various red algae and esp. Irish moss and used esp. as a stabilizing or thickening agent

car·re·four \ˌkar-ə-ˈfür\ *n* [MF, fr. LL *quadrifurcum*, neut. of *quadrifurcus* having four forks, fr. L *quadri-* + *furca* fork] (15c) **1** : CROSSROADS **2** : SQUARE, PLAZA ⟨the farmers . . . preferred the open ~ for their transactions —Thomas Hardy⟩

car·rel \ˈkar-əl\ *n* [alter. of ME *caroll*, fr. ML *carola*, perh. fr. *carola* round dance, something circular, fr. LL *choraula* choral song — more at CAROL] (1593) : a table that is often partitioned or enclosed and is used for individual study esp. in a library

car·riage \ˈkar-ij\ *n* [ME *cariage*, fr. ONF, fr. *carier* to transport in a vehicle — more at CARRY] (14c) **1** : the act of carrying **2 a** *archaic* : DEPARTMENT **b** : manner of bearing the body : POSTURE **3** *archaic* : MANAGEMENT **4** *chiefly Brit* : the price or expense of carrying **5** *obs* : BURDEN, LOAD **6 a** : a wheeled vehicle; *esp* : a horse-drawn vehicle designed for private use and comfort **b** *Brit* : a railway passenger coach **7** : a wheeled support carrying a burden **8** *obs* : IMPORT, SENSE 9 **9** : a hanger for a sword **10** : a movable part of a machine for supporting some other movable object or part ⟨a typewriter ~⟩ *syn* see BEARING

carriage trade *n* (ca. 1909) : trade from well-to-do or upper-class people; *also* : well-to-do people

car·riage·way \ˈkar-ij-ˌwā\ *n* (1800) *Brit* : a road used by vehicular traffic : HIGHWAY

car·rick bend \ˈkar-ik-\ *n* [prob. fr. obs. E *carrick* carrack, fr. ME *carrake*, *carryk*] (1819) : a knot used to join the ends of two large ropes — see KNOT illustration

car·ri·er \ˈkar-ē-ər\ *n* (14c) **1** : one that carries : BEARER, MESSENGER **2 a** : an individual or organization engaged in transporting passengers or goods for hire **b** : a transportation line carrying mail between post offices **c** : a postal employee who delivers or collects mail **d** : one that delivers newspapers **e** : an entity (as a hole or an electron) capable of carrying an electric charge **3 a** : a container for carrying **b** : a device or machine that carries : CONVEYER **4** : AIRCRAFT CARRIER **5 a** : a bearer and transmitter of a causative agent of an infectious disease; *esp* : one who carries the causative agent of a disease (as typhoid fever) systemically but is immune to it **b** : an individual (as one heterozygous for a recessive) having a specified gene that is not expressed or only weakly expressed in its phenotype **6 a** : a usu. inactive accessory substance : VEHICLE ⟨a ~ for a drug or an insecticide⟩ **b** : a substance (as a catalyst) by whose agency some element or group is transferred from one compound to another **7 a** : an electromagnetic wave or alternating current whose modulations are used as signals in radio, telephonic, or telegraphic transmission **b** : a telecommunication company **8** : an organization acting as an insurer

carrier pigeon *n* (1647) **1** : a pigeon used to carry messages; *esp* : HOMING PIGEON **2** : any of a breed of large long-bodied show pigeons

car·ri·on \ˈkar-ē-ən\ *n* [ME *caroine*, fr. AF, fr. (assumed) VL *caronia*, irreg. fr. L *carn-*, *caro* flesh — more at CARNAL] (14c) : dead and putrefying flesh; *also* : flesh unfit for food

carrion crow *n* (1528) : a uniformly black crow (*Corvus corone corone*) occurring in much of western Europe

car·ron·ade \ˌkar-ə-ˈnād\ *n* [*Carron*, Scotland] (1779) : a short-barreled gun of the late 18th and 19th centuries that fired large shot at short range and was used esp. on warships

car·rot \ˈkar-ət\ *n* [MF *carotte*, fr. LL *carota*, fr. Gk *karōton*] (1533) **1** : a biennial herb (*Daucus carota* of the family Umbelliferae, the carrot family) with a usu. orange spindle-shaped edible root; *also* : its root **2** : a reward or advantage offered esp. as an inducement

car·rot-and-stick \ˌkar-ət-ᵊn-ˈstik\ *adj* [fr. the traditional alternatives of driving a donkey on by either holding out a carrot or whipping it with a stick] (1951) : characterized by the use of both reward and punishment to induce cooperation ⟨~ foreign policy⟩

car·rot·top \ˈkar-ə(t)-ˌtäp\ *n* (ca. 1902) : REDHEAD 1 — **car·rot·topped** \-ˌtäpt\ *adj*

car·roty \ˈkar-ə-tē\ *adj* (1696) : resembling carrots in color ⟨~ hair⟩

car·rou·sel *var of* CAROUSEL

¹car·ry \ˈkar-ē, ˈker-\ *vb* **car·ried; car·ry·ing** [ME *carien*, fr. ONF *carier* to transport in a vehicle, fr. *car* vehicle, fr. L *carrus* — more at CAR] *vt* (14c) **1** : to move while supporting : TRANSPORT ⟨her legs refused to ~ her further —Ellen Glasgow⟩ **2** : to convey by direct communication ⟨~ tales about a friend⟩ **3** *chiefly dial* : CONDUCT, ESCORT **4** : to influence by mental or emotional appeal : SWAY **5** : to get possession or assent : CAPTURE ⟨carried off the prize⟩ **6** : to transfer from one place (as a column) to another ⟨~ a number in adding⟩ **7** : to contain and direct the course of ⟨the drain *carries* sewage⟩ **8 a** : to wear or have on one's person **b** : to bear upon or within one ⟨is ~*ing* an unborn child⟩ **9 a** : to have or bear esp. as a mark, attribute, or property ⟨~ a scar⟩ **b** : IMPLY, INVOLVE ⟨the crime *carried* a heavy penalty⟩ **10** : to hold or comport (as one's person) in a specified manner **11** : to sustain the weight or burden of ⟨pillars ~ an arch⟩ **12** : to bear as a crop **13** : to sing with reasonable correctness of pitch ⟨~ a tune⟩ **14 a** : to keep in stock for sale **b** : to provide sustenance for ⟨land ~*ing* 10 head of cattle⟩ **c** : to have or maintain on a list or record ⟨~ a person on a payroll⟩ **15** : to be chiefly or solely responsible for the success, effectiveness, or continuation of ⟨a player capable of ~*ing* a team⟩ ⟨her performance *carried* the play⟩ **16** : to prolong in space, time, or degree ⟨~ a principle too far⟩ **17 a** : to gain victory for; *esp* : to secure the adoption or passage of **b** : to win a majority of votes in (as a legislative body or a state) **18** : to present for public consumption ⟨newspapers ~ weather reports⟩ ⟨channel 9 will ~ the game⟩ **19 a** : to bear the charges of holding or having (as stocks or merchandise) from one time to another **b** : to keep on one's books as a debtor ⟨a merchant *carries* a customer⟩ **20** : to hold to and follow after (as a hazard) at a single stroke in golf ⟨~ a bunker⟩ **22** : to pass over (as a hazard) at a single stroke in golf ⟨~ a bunker⟩ **23** : to propel and control (a puck or ball) along a playing surface ~ *vi* **1** : to act as a bearer **2 a** : to reach or penetrate to a distance ⟨voices ~ well⟩ ⟨fly balls don't ~ well in cold air⟩ **b** : to convey itself to a reader or audience **3** : to undergo or admit of carriage in a specified way **4** *of a hunting dog* : to keep and follow the scent **5** : to win adoption ⟨the motion *carried* by a vote of 71–25⟩ — **carry a torch** *or* **carry the torch** **1** : CRUSADE **2** : to be in love esp. without reciprocation : cherish a longing or devotion ⟨still *carrying a torch* for a former lover⟩ — **carry the ball** : to perform or assume the chief role : bear the major portion of work or responsibility — **carry the day** : WIN, PREVAIL

²carry *n, pl* **car·ries** (1858) **1** : carrying power; *esp* : the range of a gun or projectile or of a struck or thrown ball **2 a** : PORTAGE **b** : the act or method of carrying ⟨fireman's ~⟩ **c** : the act of rushing with the ball in football ⟨averaged four yards per ~⟩ **3** : the position assumed by a color-bearer with the flag or guidon held in position for marching **4** : a quantity that is transferred in addition from one number place to the adjacent one of higher place value

car·ry·all \ˈkar-ē-ˌōl, ˈker-\ *n* (1714) **1** [by folk etymology fr. F *carriole*, fr. OProv *carriola*, ultim. fr. L *carrus* car] **a** : a light covered carriage for four or more persons **b** : a passenger automobile used as a small bus **2** [¹*carry* + ³*all*] : a capacious bag or carrying case

carry away *vt* (1570) **1** : to arouse to a high and often excessive degree of emotion or enthusiasm **2** : CARRY OFF 1

car·ry·back \ˈkar-ē-ˌbak, ˈker-\ *n* (1942) : a loss sustained or a portion of a credit not used in a given period that may be deducted from taxable income of a prior period

car·ry·cot \-ˌkät\ *n* (1943) *Brit* : a portable bed for an infant

car·ry·for·ward \ˈkar-ē-ˈfȯr-wərd, ˈker-, -ˌfȯr-, *Southern also* -ˈfär-, -ˌfär-\ *n* (1898) : CARRYOVER

carrying capacity *n* (1921) : the population (as of deer) that an area will support without undergoing deterioration

carrying charge *n* (1914) **1** : expense incident to ownership or use of property **2** : a charge added to the price of merchandise sold on the installment plan

car·ry·ing-on \ˌkar-ē-iŋ-ˈȯn, ˌker-, -ˈän\ *n, pl* **carryings-on** (1663) : foolish, excited, or improper behavior; *also* : an instance of such behavior

carry off *vt* (ca. 1680) **1** : to cause the death of ⟨the plague *carried off* thousands⟩ **2** : to perform or manage successfully : BRING OFF ⟨tried to look suave but couldn't *carry it off*⟩

¹car·ry-on \ˈkar-ē-ˌȯn, ˈker-, -ˌän\ *n* (1890) **1** *Brit* : CARRYING-ON **2** : a piece of luggage suitable for being carried aboard an airplane by a passenger

²carry-on *adj* (1967) : carried or suitable for being carried aboard ⟨~ baggage⟩

carry on *vt* (1644) : to continue doing, pursuing, or operating ⟨*carry on* research⟩ ⟨*carried on* the business⟩ ~ *vi* **1** : to behave or speak in a

\ə\ abut \ᵊ\ kitten, F table \ər\ further \a\ ash \ā\ ace \ä\ mop, mar
\au̇\ out \ch\ chin \e\ bet \ē\ easy \g\ go \i\ hit \ī\ ice \j\ job
\ŋ\ sing \ō\ go \ȯ\ law \ȯi\ boy \th\ thin \t̲h̲\ the \ü\ loot \u̇\ foot
\y\ yet \zh\ vision \a, k, ⁿ, œ, œ̄, ue̅, ᵉ\ *see* Guide to Pronunciation

foolish, excited, or improper manner ⟨embarrassed by the way he *carries on*⟩ **2 :** to continue esp. in spite of hindrance or discouragement

car·ry·out \'kar-ē-,aut, 'ker-\ *n* (1964) **1 :** prepared food packaged to be consumed away from its place of sale **2 :** an establishment selling carryout — **carryout** *adj*

carry out *vt* (1605) **1 :** to put into execution ⟨*carry out* a plan⟩ **2 :** to bring to a successful issue : COMPLETE, ACCOMPLISH ⟨you will be paid when you have *carried out* the assignment⟩ **3 :** to continue to an end or stopping point

car·ry·over \'kar-ē-,ō-vər, 'ker-\ *n* (1894) **1 :** the act or process of carrying over **2 :** something retained or carried over

carry over *vt* (1745) **1 a :** to transfer (an amount) to the next column, page, or book relating to the same account **b :** to hold over (as goods) for another time or season **2 :** to deduct (a loss or an unused credit) from taxable income of a later period ~ *vi* **:** to persist from one stage or sphere of activity to another

carry through *vt* (1605) **:** CARRY OUT ~ *vi* **:** PERSIST, SURVIVE ⟨feelings that *carry through* to the present⟩

car·sick \'kär-,sik\ *adj* (1908) **:** affected with motion sickness esp. in an automobile — **car sickness** *n*

¹cart \'kärt\ *n* [ME, prob. fr. ON *kartr*; akin to OE *cræt* cart] (13c) **1 :** a heavy usu. horse-drawn 2-wheeled vehicle used for farming or transporting freight **2 :** a lightweight 2-wheeled vehicle drawn by a horse, pony, or dog **3 :** a small wheeled vehicle

²cart *vt* (14c) **1 :** to carry or convey in or as if in a cart ⟨buses to ~ the kids to and from school —L. S. Gannett⟩ **2 :** to take or drag away without ceremony or by force — usu. used with *off* ⟨they ~*ed* him off to jail⟩ — **cart·er** *n*

cart·age \'kär-tij\ *n* (15c) **:** the action of or rate charged for carting

carte blanche \'kärt-'blän^sh, -'blänch\ *n, pl* **cartes blanches** \'kärt(s)-\ [F, lit., blank document] (1754) **:** full discretionary power ⟨was given *carte blanche* to furnish the house⟩

carte du jour \,kärt-də-'zhür\ *n, pl* **cartes du jour** \,kärt(s)-\ [F, lit., card of the day] (1936) **:** MENU

car·tel \kär-'tel\ *n* [F, letter of defiance, fr. OIt *cartello*, lit., placard, fr. *carta* leaf of paper — more at CARD] (1692) **1 :** a written agreement between belligerent nations **2 :** a combination of independent commercial or industrial enterprises designed to limit competition or fix prices **3 :** a combination of political groups for common action

car·tel·ise *Brit var of* CARTELIZE

car·tel·ize \'kär-tə-,līz\ *vt* **-ized; -iz·ing** (1915) **:** to bring under the control of a cartel — **car·tel·i·za·tion** \,kär-tə-lə-'zā-shən\ *n*

Car·te·sian \kär-'tē-zhən\ *adj* [NL *cartesianus*, fr. *Cartesius* Descartes] (1656) **:** of or relating to René Descartes or his philosophy — **Cartesian** *n* — **Car·te·sian·ism** \-zhə-,ni-zəm\ *n*

Cartesian coordinate *n* (ca. 1888) **1 :** either of two coordinates that locate a point on a plane and measure its distance from either of two intersecting straight-line axes along a line parallel to the other axis **2 :** any of three coordinates that locate a point in space and measure its distance from any of three intersecting coordinate planes measured parallel to that one of three straight-line axes that is the intersection of the other two planes

Cartesian plane *n* (1960) **:** a plane whose points are labeled with Cartesian coordinates

Cartesian product *n* (1958) **:** a set that is constructed from two given sets and comprises all pairs of elements such that the first element of the pair is from the first set and the second is from the second set

Car·thu·sian \kär-'thü-zhən, -'thyü-\ *n* [ML *Cartusiensis*, fr. *Cartusia* Chartreuse, motherhouse of the Carthusian order, near Grenoble, France] (1526) **:** a member of an ascetic contemplative religious order founded by St. Bruno in 1084 — **Carthusian** *adj*

car·ti·lage \'kär-t^l-ij, 'kärt-lij\ *n* [L *cartilagin-, cartilago*] (15c) **1 :** a usu. translucent somewhat elastic tissue that composes most of the skeleton of vertebrate embryos and except for a small number of structures (as some joints, respiratory passages, and the external ear) is replaced by bone during ossification in the higher vertebrates **2 :** a part or structure composed of cartilage

car·ti·lag·i·nous \,kär-tə-'la-jə-nəs\ *adj* (14c) **:** composed of, relating to, or resembling cartilage

cartilaginous fish *n* (1695) **:** any of a class (Chondrichthyes) of fishes (as a shark, ray, or chimaera) having the skeleton wholly or largely composed of cartilage — compare BONY FISH, JAWLESS FISH

cart·load \'kärt-,lōd, -,löd\ *n* (14c) **:** as much as a cart will hold

car·tog·ra·pher \kär-'tä-grə-fər\ *n* (ca. 1847) **:** one that makes maps

car·tog·ra·phy \-fē\ *n* [F *cartographie*, fr. *carte* card, map + *-graphie* -graphy — more at CARD] (1843) **:** the science or art of making maps — **car·to·graph·ic** \,kär-tə-'gra-fik\ *also* **car·to·graph·i·cal** \-fi-kəl\ *adj* — **car·to·graph·i·cal·ly** \-fi-k(ə-)lē\ *adv*

¹car·ton \'kär-t^n\ *n* [F, fr. It *cartone* pasteboard] (ca. 1859) **:** a box or container usu. made of paperboard and often of corrugated paperboard

²carton *vt* (1921) **:** to pack or enclose in a carton ~ *vi* **:** to shape cartons from paperboard sheets

car·toon \kär-'tün\ *n, often attrib* [It *cartone* pasteboard, fr. *carta*, aug. of *carta* leaf of paper — more at CARD] (1671) **1 :** a preparatory design, drawing, or painting (as for a fresco) **2 a :** a drawing intended as satire, caricature, or humor ⟨a political ~⟩ **b :** COMIC STRIP **3 :** ANIMATED CARTOON **4 :** a ludicrously simplistic, unrealistic, or one= dimensional portrayal or version ⟨the film's villain is an entertaining ~⟩ — **cartoon** *vb* — **car·toon·ing** *n* — **car·toon·ish** \-'tü-nish\ *adj* — **car·toon·ish·ly** *adv* — **car·toon·ist** \-'tü-nist\ *n* — **car·toon·like** \-'tün-,līk\ *adj* — **car·toony** \-'tü-nē\ *adj*

car·top \'kär-,täp\ *adj* (1946) **:** suitable in size and weight for carrying on top of an automobile ⟨a ~ fishing boat⟩ — **car·top·per** \-,tä-pər\ *n*

car·touche *also* **car·touch** \kär-'tüsh\ *n* [F *cartouche*, fr. It *cartoccio*, fr. *carta*] (1611) **1 :** a gun cartridge with a paper case **2 :** an ornate or ornamental frame **3 :** an oval or oblong figure (as on ancient Egyptian monuments) enclosing a sovereign's name

car·tridge \'kär-trij, *dial* 'ka-trij\ *n* [alter. of earlier *cartage*, modif. of MF *cartouche*] (1579) **:** a case or container that holds a substance, device, or material which is difficult, troublesome, or awkward to handle and that usu. can be easily changed: as **a :** a tube (as of metal) containing a complete charge for a firearm and usu. an initiating device (as a primer) **b :** a case containing an explosive charge for blasting **c**

: an often cylindrical container for insertion into a larger mechanism or apparatus **d :** CASSETTE 2 **e :** a small case that contains a phonograph needle and transducer and is attached to a tonearm **f :** a case containing a reel of magnetic tape arranged for insertion into a recorder or player **g :** a removable case containing a magnetic tape or one or more disks and used as a computer storage medium **h :** a case for holding printed circuit chips containing a computer program ⟨a video= game ~⟩

cartridge belt *n* (1874) **1 :** a belt having a series of loops for holding cartridges **2 :** a belt worn around the waist and designed for carrying various attachable equipment (as a cartridge case, canteen, or compass)

car·tu·lary \'kär-chə-,ler-ē\ *n, pl* **-lar·ies** [ML *chartularium*, fr. *chartula* charter — more at CHARTER] (1541) **:** a collection of charters; *esp* **:** a book holding copies of the charters and title deeds of an estate

¹cart·wheel \'kärt-,hwēl, -,wēl\ *n* (1855) **1 :** a large coin (as a silver dollar) **2 :** a lateral handspring with arms and legs extended

²cartwheel *vi* (1917) **:** to move like a turning wheel; *specif* **:** to perform cartwheels — **cart·wheel·er** *n*

car·un·cle \'kar-,əŋ-kəl, kə-'rəŋ-\ *n* [obs. F *caruncule*, fr. L *caruncula* little piece of flesh, dim. of *caro* flesh — more at CARNAL] (1615) **1 :** a naked fleshy outgrowth (as a bird's wattle) **2 :** an outgrowth on a seed adjacent to the micropyle

car·va·crol \'kär-və-,król, -,krōl\ *n* [ISV, fr. NL *carvi* (specific epithet of *Carum carvi* caraway) + L *acr-, acer* sharp — more at CARAWAY, EDGE] (1854) **:** a liquid phenol $C_{10}H_{14}O$ found in essential oils of various mints (as thyme) and used as a fungicide and disinfectant

carve \'kärv\ *vb* **carved; carv·ing** [ME *kerven*, fr. OE *ceorfan*; akin to OHG *kerban* to notch, Gk *graphein* to scratch, write] *vt* (bef. 12c) **1 :** to cut with care or precision ⟨*carved* fretwork⟩ **2 :** to make or get by or as if by cutting — often used with *out* ⟨~ out a career⟩ **3 :** to cut into pieces or slices ⟨*carved* the turkey⟩ ~ *vi* **1 :** to cut up and serve meat **2 :** to work as a sculptor or engraver — **carv·er** *n*

car·vel-built \'kär-vəl-,bilt, -,vel-\ *adj* [prob. fr. D *karveel-*, fr. *karveel* caravel, fr. MF *carvelle*] (1798) **:** built with the planks meeting flush at the seams

carv·en \'kär-vən\ *adj* (14c) **:** wrought or ornamented by carving

carv·ing \'kär-viŋ\ *n* (13c) **1 :** the act or art of one who carves **2 :** a carved object, design, or figure

car wash *n* (1956) **:** an area or structure equipped with facilities for washing automobiles

cary- *or* **caryo-** — see KARY-

cary·at·id \,kar-ē-'a-təd, ,kar-ē-ə-,tid\ *n, pl* **-ids** *or* **-i·des** \,kar-ē-'a-tə-,dēz\ [L *caryatides*, pl., fr. Gk *karyatides* priestesses of Artemis at Caryae, caryatids, fr. *Karyai* Caryae in Laconia] (1563) **:** a draped female figure supporting an entablature

cary·op·sis \,kar-ē-'äp-səs\ *n, pl* **-op·ses** \-,sēz\ *also* **-si·des** \-sə-,dēz\ [NL] (1830) **:** a small one-seeded dry indehiscent fruit (as of Indian corn or wheat) in which the fruit and seed fuse in a single grain

ca·sa \'kä-sə\ *n* [Sp & It, fr. L, cottage] (1844) *chiefly Southwest* **:** DWELLING

ca·sa·ba \kə-'sä-bə\ *n* [*Kasaba* (now Turgutlu, Turkey) (1889) **:** any of several winter melons with yellow rind and sweet flesh

Ca·sa·no·va \,ka-zə-'nō-və, ,ka-sə-\ *n* [Giacomo Girolamo *Casanova*] (1888) **:** LOVER; *esp* **:** a man who is a promiscuous and unscrupulous lover

Cas·bah \'kaz-,bä, 'käz-\ *n* [F, fr. Ar dial. *qasbah*] (1944) **1 :** a No. African castle or fortress **2 :** the native section of a No. African city

cas·ca·bel \'kas-kə-,bel\ *n* [Sp, lit., small bell] (1639) **1 :** a projection behind the breech of a muzzle-loading cannon **2 :** a small hollow perforated spherical bell enclosing a loose pellet

¹cas·cade \(,)kas-'kād\ *n* [F, fr. It *cascata*, fr. *cascare* to fall, fr. (assumed) VL *casicare*, fr. L *casus* fall] (1641) **1 :** a steep usu. small fall of water; *esp* **:** one of a series **2 a :** something arranged or occurring in a series or in a succession of stages so that each stage derives from or acts upon the product of the preceding ⟨blood clotting involves a biochemical ~⟩ **b :** a fall of material (as lace) that hangs in a zigzag line **3 :** something falling or rushing forth in quantity ⟨a ~ of sound⟩ ⟨a ~ of events⟩

²cascade *vb* **cas·cad·ed; cas·cad·ing** *vi* (1702) **:** to fall, pour, or rush in or as if in a cascade ~ *vt* **1 :** to cause to fall like a cascade **2 :** to connect in a cascade arrangement

cas·cara \ka-'skar-ə\ *n* [Sp *cáscara* husk, bark, prob. fr. *cascar* to crack, break, fr. (assumed) VL *quassicare* to shake, fr. L *quassare* — more at QUASH] (1879) **1 :** CASCARA BUCKTHORN **2 :** CASCARA SAGRADA

cascara buckthorn *n* (ca. 1900) **:** a buckthorn (*Rhamnus purshiana*) of the Pacific coast of the U.S. yielding cascara sagrada

cascara sa·gra·da \-sə-'grä-də\ *n* [AmerSp *cáscara sagrada*, lit., sacred bark] (1885) **:** the dried bark of cascara buckthorn used as a laxative

cas·ca·ril·la \,kas-kə-'ri-lə, -'rē-ə\ *n* [Sp, dim. of *cáscara*] (1686) **:** the aromatic bark of a West Indian shrub (*Croton eluteria*) of the spurge family used for making incense and as a tonic; *also* **:** this shrub

¹case \'kās\ *n* [ME *cas*, fr. OF, fr. L *casus* fall, chance, fr. *cadere* to fall — more at CHANCE] (13c) **1 a :** a set of circumstances or conditions ⟨is the statement true in all three ~s⟩ **b** (1) **:** a situation requiring investigation or action (as by the police) (2) **:** the object of investigation or consideration **2 :** CONDITION; *specif* **:** condition of body or mind **3** [ME *cas*, fr. MF, fr. L *casus*, trans. of Gk *ptōsis*, lit., fall] **a :** an inflectional form of a noun, pronoun, or adjective indicating its grammatical relation to other words **b :** such a relation whether indicated by inflection or not **4 :** what actually exists or happens : FACT **5 a :** a suit or action in law or equity **b** (1) **:** the evidence supporting a conclusion or judgment (2) **:** ARGUMENT; *esp* **:** a convincing argument **6 a :** an instance of disease or injury; *also* **:** PATIENT **b :** an instance that directs attention to a situation or exhibits it in action **:** EXAMPLE **c :** a peculiar person **:** CHARACTER **7 :** oneself considered as an object of harassment ⟨get off my ~⟩ *syn* see INSTANCE — **in any case :** without regard to or in spite of other considerations ⟨whatever else is done or is the case ⟨war is inevitable *in any case*⟩ ⟨*in any case* the report will be made public next month⟩ — **in case :** as a

caryatid

precaution ⟨took an umbrella, just *in case*⟩ — **in case of :** in the event of ⟨*in case of* trouble, yell⟩

²**case** *n* [ME *cas*, fr. ONF *casse*, fr. L *capsa* chest, case, prob. fr. *capere* to take — more at HEAVE] (14c) **1 a :** a box or receptacle for holding something **b :** a box together with its contents **c :** SET; *specif :* PAIR **2 a :** an outer covering or housing ⟨a pastry ~⟩ **b :** a tube into which the components of a round of ammunition are loaded **3 :** a divided tray for holding printing type **4 :** the frame of a door or window : CASING

³**case** *vt* **cased; cas·ing** (1575) **1 :** to enclose in or cover with or as if with a case : ENCASE **2 :** to line (as a well) with supporting material (as metal pipe) **3 :** to inspect or study esp. with intent to rob

ca·se·ation \ˌkā-sē-ˈā-shən\ *n* [L *caseus* cheese] (1866) : necrosis with conversion of damaged tissue into a soft cheesy substance — **ca·se·ate** \ˈkā-sē-ˌāt\ *vi*

case·bear·er \ˈkās-ˌbar-ər, -ˌber-\ *n* (ca. 1889) : an insect larva that forms a protective case (as of silk)

case·book \-ˌbùk\ *n* (1762) **1 :** a book containing records of illustrative cases that is used for reference and instruction (as in law or medicine) **2 :** a compilation of primary and secondary documents relating to a central topic together with scholarly comment, exercises, and study aids that is designed to serve as a sourcebook for short papers (as in a writing course) or as a point of departure for a research paper

cased glass \ˈkāst-\ *n* (1849) : glass consisting of two or more fused layers of different colors often decorated by cutting so that the inner layers show through — called also *case glass*

case goods *n pl* (1922) **1 :** furniture (as bureaus or bookcases) that provides interior storage space; *also :* dining-room and bedroom furniture sold as sets **2 :** products often sold by the case

case–hard·en \ˈkās-ˌhär-dᵊn\ *vt* (1677) **1 :** to harden (a ferrous alloy) so that the surface layer is harder than the interior **2 :** to make callous or insensible — **case–hard·ened** *adj*

case history *n* (1894) : a record of history, environment, and relevant details of a case esp. for use in analysis or illustration

ca·sein \ˈkā-ˌsēn, kā-ˈ\ *n* [prob. fr. F *caséine*, fr. L *caseus*] (1841) : a phosphoprotein of milk: as **a :** one that is precipitated from milk by heating with an acid or by the action of lactic acid in souring and is used in making paints and adhesives **b :** one that is produced when milk is curdled by rennet, is the chief constituent of cheese, and is used in making plastics

ca·sein·ate \kā-ˈsē-ˌnāt, ˈkā-si-ˌnāt\ *n* (1904) : a compound of casein with a metal (as calcium or sodium)

case in point (1965) : an illustrative, relevant, or pertinent case

case knife *n* (1704) **1 :** SHEATH KNIFE **2 :** a table knife

case law *n* (1861) : law established by judicial decision in cases

case·load \ˈkās-ˌlōd\ *n* (1938) : the number of cases handled (as by a court or clinic) usu. in a particular period

case·mate \ˈkās-ˌmāt\ *n* [MF, fr. OIt *casamatta*] (1575) : a fortified position or chamber or an armored enclosure on a warship from which guns are fired through embrasures

case·ment \ˈkās-mənt\ *n* [ME, hollow molding, prob. fr. ONF *encassement* frame, fr. *encasser* to enclose, frame, fr. *en-* + *casse*] (15c) : a window sash that opens on hinges at the side; *also :* a window with such a sash

ca·se·ous \ˈkā-sē-əs\ *adj* [L *caseus* cheese] (1661) : marked by caseation; *also :* CHEESY

ca·sern *or* **ca·serne** \kə-ˈzərn\ *n* [F *caserne*] (1696) : a military barracks in a garrison town

case study *n* (1875) **1 :** an intensive analysis of an individual unit (as a person or community) stressing developmental factors in relation to environment **2 :** CASE HISTORY

case system *n* (ca. 1889) : a system of teaching law in which instruction is chiefly on the basis of leading or selected cases as primary authorities instead of from textbooks

case·work \ˈkās-ˌwərk\ *n* (1886) : social work involving direct consideration of the problems, needs, and adjustments of the individual case (as a person or family) — **case·work·er** \-ˌwər-kər\ *n*

¹**cash** \ˈkash\ *n* [modif. of MF or OIt; MF *casse* money box, fr. OIt *cassa*, fr. L *capsa* chest — more at CASE] (1596) **1 :** ready money **2 :** money or its equivalent (as a check) paid for goods or services at the time of purchase or delivery — **cash·less** \-ləs\ *adj*

²**cash** *adj* (1622) : being a method of accounting that includes as income only what has been received in cash and as expenses only those paid in cash

³**cash** *vt* (1811) **1 :** to pay or obtain cash for ⟨~ a check⟩ **2 :** to lead and win a bridge trick with (a card that is the highest remaining card of its suit) — **cash·able** \ˈka-shə-bəl\ *adj*

⁴**cash** *n, pl* **cash** [Pg *caixa*, fr. Tamil *kācu*, a small copper coin, fr. Skt *karṣa*, a weight of gold or silver] (1598) **1 :** any of various coins of small value in China and southern India; *esp :* a Chinese coin with a square hole in the center **2 :** a unit of value equivalent to one cash

¹**cash–and–car·ry** \ˌka-shᵊn-ˈkar-ē, -ˈker-\ *adj* (1917) : sold or provided for cash and usu. without delivery service

²**cash–and–carry** *n* (1921) : the policy of selling on a cash-and-carry basis

cash bar *n* (1968) : a bar (as at a reception) at which drinks are sold — compare OPEN BAR

cash·book \ˈkash-ˌbùk\ *n* (1622) : a book in which record is kept of all cash receipts and disbursements

cash cow *n* (1979) : a consistently profitable business, property, or product whose profits are used to finance a company's investments in other areas

cash crop *n* (1868) : a readily salable crop (as cotton or tobacco) produced or gathered primarily for market

cash discount *n* (1917) : a discount granted in consideration of immediate payment or payment within a prescribed time

cash·ew \ˈka-(ˌ)shü, kə-ˈshü\ *n* [Pg *acaju, cajú*, fr. Tupi *acajú*] (1598) : a tropical American tree (*Anacardium occidentale* of the family Anacardiaceae, the cashew family) grown for a phenolic oil and the edible kernel of its nut and for a gum from its stem; *also :* CASHEW NUT

cashew nut *n* (1796) : the kidney-shaped kernel of the fruit of the cashew that is edible when roasted

cash flow *n* (1954) **1 :** a measure of an organization's liquidity that usu. consists of net income plus noncash charges (as depre-

ciation) against income **2 :** a flow of cash; *esp :* one that provides solvency

¹**ca·shier** \ka-ˈshir, kə-\ *vt* [D *casseren*, fr. MF *casser* to discharge, annul — more at QUASH] (1592) **1 :** to dismiss from service; *esp :* to dismiss dishonorably **2 :** REJECT, DISCARD

²**cash·ier** \(ˌ)ka-ˈshir\ *n* [D or MF; D *kassier*, fr. MF *cassier*, fr. *casse* money box] (1596) : one that has charge of money: as **a :** a high officer in a bank or trust company responsible for moneys received and expended **b :** one who collects and records payments

cashier's check *n* (1867) : a check drawn by a bank on its own funds and signed by the cashier

cash in *vt* (1888) : to obtain cash for ⟨*cashed in* the bonds⟩ ~ *vi* **1 a :** to retire from a gambling game **b :** to settle accounts and withdraw from an involvement (as a business deal) **2 :** to obtain advantage or financial profit — often used with *on* ⟨*cash in* on a best-seller⟩

cash·mere \ˈkazh-ˌmir, ˈkash-\ *n* [*Cashmere* (Kashmir)] (1684) **1 :** fine wool from the undercoat of the cashmere goat; *also :* a yarn of this wool **2 :** a soft twilled fabric made orig. from cashmere

cashmere goat *n* (ca. 1890) : an Indian goat raised esp. for its undercoat of fine soft wool that constitutes the cashmere wool of commerce

cash register *n* (1879) : a business machine that usu. has a money drawer, indicates the amount of each sale, and records the amount of money received and often automatically makes change

cas·ing \ˈkā-siŋ\ *n* (1791) **1 :** something that encases : material for encasing: as **a :** an enclosing frame esp. around a door or window opening **b :** a metal pipe used to case a well **c :** ⁴TIRE 2 **d :** a membranous case for processed meat **2 :** a space formed between two parallel lines of stitching through at least two layers of cloth into which something (as a rod or string) may be inserted

ca·si·no \kə-ˈsē-(ˌ)nō\ *n, pl* **-nos** [It, fr. *casa* house, fr. L, cottage] (1744) **1 :** a building or room used for social amusements; *specif :* one used for gambling **2** *also* **cas·si·no :** a card game in which cards are won by matching or combining cards in a hand with those exposed on the table **3 :** SUMMERHOUSE 2

ca·si·ta \kə-ˈsē-tə\ *n* [Sp, dim. of *casa*] (1923) : a small house

cask \ˈkask\ *n* [ME *caske*, perh. fr. MF *casque* helmet, fr. Sp *casco* potsherd, skull, helmet] (15c) **1 :** a barrel-shaped vessel of staves, headings, and hoops usu. for liquids **2 :** a cask and its contents; *also :* the quantity contained in a cask

cas·ket \ˈkas-kət\ *n* [ME, perh. modif. of MF *cassette*] (15c) **1 :** a small chest or box (as for jewels) **2 :** a usu. fancy coffin — **casket** *vt*

casque \ˈkask\ *n* [MF — more at CASK] (1580) **1 :** a piece of armor for the head : HELMET 1a **2 :** an anatomic structure suggestive of a helmet

Cas·san·dra \kə-ˈsan-drə, -ˈsän-\ *n* [L, fr. Gk *Kassandra*] **1 :** a daughter of Priam endowed with the gift of prophecy but fated never to be believed **2 :** one that predicts misfortune or disaster

cas·sa·va \kə-ˈsä-və\ *n* [Sp *cazabe* cassava bread, fr. Taino *caçábi*] (1555) : any of several plants (genus *Manihot* and esp. *M. esculenta*) of the spurge family grown in the tropics for their fleshy edible rootstocks which yield a nutritious starch; *also :* the rootstock

cas·se·role \ˈka-sə-ˌrōl *also* ˈka-zə-\ *n* [F, saucepan, fr. MF, dim. of *casse* ladle, dripping pan, fr. OProv *cassa*, prob. ultim. fr. Gk *kyathos* ladle] (1708) **1 :** a dish in which food may be baked and served **2 :** food cooked and served in a casserole **3 :** a deep round usu. porcelain dish with a handle used for heating substances in the laboratory

cas·sette *also* **ca·sette** \kə-ˈset, ka-\ *n* [F, fr. MF, dim. of ONF *casse* case] (1793) **1 :** CASKET 1 **2 :** a usu. flat case or container that is used esp. in a device or machine, that holds something which is difficult, troublesome, or awkward to handle, and that can be easily loaded or unloaded: as **a :** a lightproof magazine for holding film or plates for use in a camera **b :** a plastic cartridge containing magnetic tape with the tape on one reel passing to the other

cas·sia \ˈka-shə\ *n* [ME, fr. OE, fr. L, fr. Gk *kassia*, of Sem origin; akin to Heb *qĕṣiʿāh* cassia] (bef. 12c) **1 :** a coarse cinnamon bark (as from *Cinnamomum cassia*) **2 :** any of a genus (*Cassia*) of leguminous herbs, shrubs, and trees of warm regions

cas·si·mere \ˈka-zə-ˌmir, ˈka-sə-\ *n* [obs. *Cassimere* (Kashmir)] (1774) : a closely woven smooth twill usu. wool fabric (as for suits)

Cas·si·ni division \kə-ˈsē-nē-\ *n* [Gian Domenico *Cassini* †1712 Ital. astronomer] (ca. 1909) : the dark region between the two brightest rings of Saturn — called also *Cassini's division*

Cas·si·o·pe·ia \ˌka-sē-ə-ˈpē-ə\ *n* [L, fr. Gk *Kassiopeia*] **1 :** the wife of King Cepheus who gives birth to Andromeda and is later changed into a constellation **2** [L (gen. *Cassiopeiae*), fr. Gk *Kassiopeia*] : a northern constellation between Andromeda and Cepheus

cas·sis \kə-ˈsēs\ *n* [F, lit., black currants, perh. fr. L *cassia*] (1899) : a liqueur made from black currants

cas·sit·er·ite \kə-ˈsi-tə-ˌrīt\ *n* [F *cassitérite*, fr. Gk *kassiteros* tin] (1858) : a brown or black mineral that consists of tin dioxide and is the chief source of metallic tin

cas·sock \ˈka-sək\ *n* [MF *casaque*] (1631) : a close-fitting ankle-length garment worn esp. in Roman Catholic and Anglican churches by the clergy and by laymen assisting in services

cas·sou·let \ˌka-sə-ˈlā\ *n* [F, fr. Prov, lit., earthenware dish, dim. of *cassolo* dish, dim. of *casso* ladle, fr. OProv *cassa*] (ca. 1929) : a casserole of white beans baked with herbs and meat (as pork, lamb, and goose or duck)

cas·so·wary \ˈka-sə-ˌwer-ē\ *n, pl* **-war·ies** [Malay *kĕsuari*, fr. an Austronesian language of the Moluccas] (1611) : any of a genus (*Casuarius*) of large ratite birds chiefly of New Guinea and northern Australia that have a horny casque on the head and are closely related to the emu

¹**cast** \ˈkast\ *vb* **cast; cast·ing** [ME, fr. ON *kasta*; akin to ON *kǫs* heap] *vt* (13c) **1 a :** to cause to move or send forth by throwing ⟨~ a fishing lure⟩ ⟨~ dice⟩ **b :** DI-

cassock

\ə\ abut \ᵊ\ kitten, F table \ər\ further \a\ ash \ā\ ace \ä\ mop, mar
\aù\ out \ch\ chin \e\ bet \ē\ easy \g\ go \i\ hit \ī\ ice \j\ job
\ŋ\ sing \ō\ go \ò\ law \òi\ boy \th\ thin \th\ the \ü\ loot \ù\ foot
\y\ yet \zh\ vision \à, ᵏ, ⁿ, œ, œ̄, ue, ūe, ʸ\ *see* Guide to Pronunciation

RECT ⟨~ a glance⟩ **c** (1) : to put forth ⟨the fire ~s a warm glow⟩ (2) : to place as if by throwing ⟨~ doubt on their reliability⟩ **d** : to deposit (a ballot) formally **e** (1) : to throw off or away ⟨the horse ~ a shoe⟩ (2) : to get rid of : DISCARD ⟨~ off all restraint⟩ (3) : SHED, MOLT (4) : to bring forth; *esp* : to give birth to prematurely **f** : to throw to the ground esp. in wrestling **g** : to build by throwing up earth **2 a** (1) : to perform arithmetical operations on : ADD (2) : to calculate by means of astrology **b** *archaic* : DECIDE, INTEND **3 a** : to dispose or arrange into parts or into a suitable form or order **b** (1) : to assign the parts of (a dramatic production) to actors (2) : to assign (as an actor) to a role or part **4 a** : to give a shape to (a substance) by pouring in liquid or plastic form into a mold and letting harden without pressure ⟨~ steel⟩ **b** : to form by this process **5** : TURN ⟨~ the scale slightly⟩ **6** : to make (a knot or stitch) by looping or catching up **7** : TWIST, WARP ⟨a beam ~ by age⟩ **~ vi 1** : to throw something; *specif* : to throw out a lure with a fishing rod **2** *dial Brit* : VOMIT **3** *dial Eng* : to bear fruit : YIELD **4** : to perform addition **b** *obs* : ESTIMATE, CONJECTURE **5** : WARP **6** : to range over land in search of a trail — used of hunting dogs or trackers **7** : VEER *syn* see DISCARD, THROW — **cast·abil·i·ty** \ˌkas-tə-'bi-lə-tē\ *n* — **cast·able** \'kas-tə-bəl\ *adj* — **cast lots** : to draw lots to determine a matter by chance

²**cast** *n* (14c) **1 a** : an act of casting **b** : something that happens as a result of chance **c** : a throw of dice **d** : a throw of a line (as a fishing line) or net **2 a** : the form in which a thing is constructed **b** (1) : the set of actors in a dramatic production (2) : a set (as in a narrative) of characters or persons **c** : the arrangement of draperies in a painting **3** : the distance to which a thing can be thrown; *specif* : the distance a bow can shoot **4 a** : a turning of the eye in a particular direction; *also* : EXPRESSION ⟨this freakish, elfish ~ came into the child's eye —Nathaniel Hawthorne⟩ **b** : a slight strabismus **5** : something that is thrown or the quantity thrown; *esp, Brit* : the leader of a fishing line **6 a** : something that is formed by casting in a mold or form: as (1) : a reproduction (as of a statue) in metal or plaster : CASTING (2) : a fossil reproduction of the details of a natural object by mineral infiltration **b** : an impression taken from an object with a liquid or plastic substance : MOLD **c** : a rigid dressing of gauze impregnated with plaster of paris for immobilizing a diseased or broken part **7** : FORECAST, CONJECTURE **8 a** : an overspread of a color or modification of the appearance of a substance by a trace of some added hue : SHADE ⟨gray with a greenish ~⟩ **b** : TINGE, SUGGESTION **9 a** : a ride on one's way in a vehicle : LIFT **b** *Scot* : HELP, ASSISTANCE **10 a** : SHAPE, APPEARANCE ⟨the delicate ~ of her features⟩ **b** : characteristic quality ⟨his father's conservative ~ of mind⟩ **11** : something that is shed, ejected, or thrown out or off: as **a** : the excrement of an earthworm **b** : a mass of soft matter formed in cavities of diseased organs and discharged from the body **c** : the skin of an insect **12** : the ranging in search of a trail by a dog, hunting pack, or tracker

cast about *vi* (1575) : to look around : SEEK ⟨cast about for a seat⟩ ~ *vt* : to lay plans concerning : CONTRIVE ⟨cast about how he was to go⟩

cas·ta·net \ˌkas-tə-'net\ *n* [Sp *castañeta*, fr. *castañeta* chestnut, fr. L *castanea* — more at CHESTNUT] (ca. 1647) : a percussion instrument used esp. by dancers that consists of two small shells of hard wood, ivory, or plastic usu. fastened to the thumb and clicked together by the other fingers — usu. used in pl.

cast around *vi* (1946) : CAST ABOUT

cast·away \'kas-tə-ˌwā\ *adj* (1534) **1** : thrown away : REJECTED **2 a** : cast adrift or ashore as a survivor of a shipwreck **b** : thrown out or left without friends or resources — **castaway** *n*

cast down *adj* (14c) : DOWNCAST

caste \'kast *also* 'käst\ *n* [Pg *casta*, lit., race, lineage, fr. fem. of *casto* pure, chaste, fr. L *castus*] (1613) **1** : one of the hereditary social classes in Hinduism that restrict the occupation of their members and their association with the members of other castes **2 a** : a division of society based on differences of wealth, inherited rank or privilege, profession, or occupation **b** : the position conferred by caste standing : PRESTIGE **3** : a system of rigid social stratification characterized by hereditary status, endogamy, and social barriers sanctioned by custom, law, or religion **4** : a specialized form (as the worker of an ant or bee) of a polymorphic social insect that carries out a particular function in the colony — **caste·ism** \'kas-ˌti-zəm\ *n*

cas·tel·lan \'kas-tə-lən\ *n* [ME *castellayn*, fr. ONF *castelain*, fr. L *castellanus* occupant of a castle, fr. *castellanus* of a castle, fr. *castellum* castle] (14c) : a governor or warden of a castle or fort

cas·tel·lat·ed \'kas-tə-ˌlā-təd\ *adj* [ML *castellatus*, pp. of *castellare* to fortify, fr. L *castellum*] (1679) **1** : having battlements like a castle **2** : having or supporting a castle

cast·er \'kas-tər\ *n* (14c) **1** : one that casts; *esp* : a machine that casts type **2** *or* **cas·tor** \-tər\ **a** : a usu. silver table vessel with a perforated top for sprinkling a seasoning (as sugar or spice) **b** : a usu. revolving metal stand bearing condiment containers (as cruets, mustard pot, and often shakers) for table use : a cruet stand **3** : any of a set of wheels or rotating balls mounted in a swivel frame and used for the support and movement of furniture, trucks, and portable equipment **4** : the slight usu. backward tilt of the upper end of the kingbolt of an automobile for giving directional stability to the front wheels

cas·ti·gate \'kas-tə-ˌgāt\ *vt* **-gat·ed; -gat·ing** [L *castigatus*, pp. of *castigare* — more at CHASTEN] (1607) : to subject to severe punishment, reproof, or criticism *syn* see PUNISH — **cas·ti·ga·tion** \ˌkas-tə-'gā-shən\ *n* — **cas·ti·ga·tor** \'kas-tə-ˌgā-tər\ *n*

cas·tile soap \(ˌ)kas-ˌtēl-\ *n, often cap C* [ME *castell sope*, fr. *Castell* Castile] (15c) : a fine hard bland soap made from olive oil and sodium hydroxide; *also* : any of various similar soaps

Cas·til·ian \ka-'stil-yən\ *n* (1796) **1** : a native or inhabitant of Castile; *broadly* : SPANIARD **2 a** : the dialect of Castile **b** : the official and literary language of Spain based on this dialect — **Castilian** *adj*

cast·ing *n* (14c) **1** : something (as excrement) that is cast out or off **2** : the act of one that casts: as **a** : the throwing of a fishing line by means of a rod and reel **b** : the assignment of parts and duties to actors or performers **3** : something cast in a mold

casting director *n* (1922) : a person who supervises the casting of dramatic productions (as films and plays)

casting vote *n* (1678) : a deciding vote cast by a presiding officer to break a tie

cast–iron *adj* (1692) **1** : made of cast iron **2** : resembling cast iron: as **a** : capable of withstanding great strain ⟨a ~ stomach⟩ **b** : not admitting change, adaptation, or exception : RIGID ⟨a ~ will⟩

cast iron *n* (1664) : a commercial alloy of iron, carbon, and silicon that is cast in a mold and is hard, brittle, nonmalleable, and incapable of being hammer-welded but more easily fusible than steel

¹**cas·tle** \'ka-səl\ *n* [ME *castel*, fr. OE, fr. ONF, fr. L *castellum* fortress, castle, dim. of *castrum* fortified place; perh. akin to L *castrare* to castrate] (bef. 12c) **1 a** : a large fortified building or set of buildings **b** : a massive or imposing house **2** : a retreat safe against intrusion or invasion **3** : ³ROOK

²**castle** *vb* **cas·tled; cas·tling** \'ka-s(ə-)liŋ\ *vt* (1587) **1** : to establish in a castle **2** : to move (the chess king) in castling ~ *vi* : to move a chess king two squares toward a rook and in the same move the rook to the square next past the king

cas·tled \'ka-səld\ *adj* (1789) : CASTELLATED

castle in the air *n* (1580) : an impracticable project : DAYDREAM — called also *castle in Spain*

cast–off \'kas-ˌtóf\ *adj* (1746) : thrown away or aside — **cast-off** *n*

cast off *vt* (1602) **1** : LOOSE ⟨cast off a hunting dog⟩ **2** : UNFASTEN ⟨cast off a boat⟩ **3** : to remove (a stitch) from a knitting needle in such a way as to prevent unraveling ~ *vi* **1** : to unfasten or untie a boat or a line **2** : to turn one's partner in a square dance and pass around the outside of the set and back **3** : to finish a knitted fabric by casting off all stitches

cast on *vt* (1840) : to place (stitches) on a knitting needle for beginning or enlarging knitted work

cas·tor \'kas-tər\ *n* [ME, fr. L, fr. Gk *kastōr*, fr. *Kastōr* Castor] (14c) **1** : BEAVER 1a **2** : CASTOREUM **3** : a beaver hat

Cas·tor \'kas-tər\ *n* [L, fr. Gk *Kastōr*] **1** : one of the Dioscuri **2** : the more northern of the two bright stars in Gemini

castor bean *n* (1819) : the very poisonous seed of the castor-oil plant; *also* : CASTOR-OIL PLANT

cas·to·re·um \ka-'stör-ē-əm, -'stör-\ *n* [ME *castorium*, fr. L *castoreum*, fr. *castor*] (14c) : a bitter strong-smelling creamy orange-brown substance that consists of the dried perineal glands of the beaver and their secretion and is used esp. by perfumers — called also *castor*

castor oil *n* [prob. fr. its former use as a substitute for castoreum in medicine] (1746) : a pale viscous fatty oil from castor beans used esp. as a cathartic and as a lubricant and plasticizer

castor–oil plant *n* (1836) : a tropical Old World herb (*Ricinus communis*) widely grown as an ornamental or for its oil-rich castor beans

castor sugar *or* **caster sugar** *n* [*caster*] (1855) *chiefly Brit* : finely granulated white sugar

cast out *vt* (13c) : to drive out : EXPEL

cas·trate \'kas-ˌtrāt\ *vt* **cas·trat·ed; cas·trat·ing** [L *castratus*, pp. of *castrare*; akin to Gk *keazein* to split, Skt *śasati* he slaughters] (1609) **1 a** : to deprive of the testes : GELD **b** : to deprive of the ovaries : SPAY **2** : to render impotent or deprive of vitality esp. by psychological means — **castrate** *n* — **cas·tra·tion** \kas-'trā-shən\ *n* — **cas·tra·tor** \-ˌtrā-tər\ *n* — **cas·tra·to·ry** \'kas-trə-ˌtōr-ē, -ˌtör-\ *adj*

cas·tra·to \ka-'strä-(ˌ)tō, kə-\ *n, pl* **-ti** \-tē\ [It, fr. pp. of *castrare* to castrate, fr. L] (1763) : a singer castrated before puberty to preserve the soprano or contralto range of his voice

Cas·tro·ism \'kas-(ˌ)trō-ˌi-zəm\ *n* (1960) : the political, economic, and social principles and policies of Fidel Castro — **Cas·tro·ite** \-ˌīt\ *n*

¹**ca·su·al** \'kazh-wəl, 'ka-zhə-wəl, 'ka-zhəl\ *adj* [ME, fr. MF & LL; MF *casuel*, fr. LL *casualis*, fr. L *casus* fall, chance — more at CASE] (14c) **1** : subject to, resulting from, or occurring by chance **2 a** : occurring without regularity : OCCASIONAL **b** : employed for irregular periods **3 a** : feeling or showing little concern : NONCHALANT **b** (1) : INFORMAL, NATURAL (2) : designed for informal use *syn* see ACCIDENTAL, RANDOM — **ca·su·al·ly** *adv* — **ca·su·al·ness** *n*

²**casual** *n* (ca. 1852) **1** : a casual or migratory worker **2** : an officer or enlisted man awaiting assignment or transportation to a unit

ca·su·al·ty \'ka-zhəl-tē, 'kazh-wəl-, 'ka-zhə-wəl-\ *n, pl* **-ties** (15c) **1** *archaic* : CHANCE, FORTUNE ⟨losses that befall them by mere ~ —Sir Walter Raleigh⟩ **2** : serious or fatal accident : DISASTER **3 a** : a military person lost through death, wounds, injury, sickness, internment, or capture or through being missing in action **b** : a person or thing injured, lost, or destroyed : VICTIM ⟨the ex-senator was a ~ of the last election⟩

casual water *n* (1899) : a temporary accumulation of water not forming a regular hazard of a golf course

ca·su·a·ri·na \ˌka-zhə-(wə-)'rē-nə\ *n* [NL, genus name, fr. Malay (*pohon*) *kĕsuari*, lit., cassowary tree; fr. the resemblance of its twigs to cassowary feathers] (1806) : any of a genus (*Casuarina* of the family Casuarinaceae) of dicotyledonous chiefly Australian trees which have whorls of scalelike leaves and jointed stems resembling horsetails and some of which yield a heavy hard wood

ca·su·ist \'ka-zhü-ist, 'kazh-wist\ *n* [prob. fr. Sp *casuista*, fr. L *casus* fall, chance — more at CASE] (1609) : one skilled in or given to casuistry — **ca·su·is·tic** \ˌka-zhə-'wis-tik\ *or* **ca·su·is·ti·cal** \-ti-kəl\ *adj*

ca·su·ist·ry \'kazh-wə-strē, 'ka-zhə-\ *n, pl* **-ries** (1725) **1** : a resolving of specific cases of conscience, duty, or conduct through interpretation of ethical principles or religious doctrine **2** : specious argument : RATIONALIZATION

ca·sus bel·li \ˌkä-səs-'be-ˌlē, ˌkä-səs-'be-ˌlī\ *n, pl* **ca·sus belli** \ˌkä-ˌsüs-, ˌkä-ˌsüs-\ [NL, occasion of war] (1849) : an event or action that justifies or allegedly justifies a war or conflict

¹**cat** \'kat\ *n, often attrib* [ME, fr. OE *catt*, prob. fr. LL *cattus*, *catta* cat] (bef. 12c) **1 a** : a carnivorous mammal (*Felis catus*) long domesticated as a pet and for catching rats and mice **b** : any of a family (Felidae) of carnivorous usu. solitary and nocturnal mammals (as the domestic cat, lion, tiger, leopard, jaguar, cougar, wildcat, lynx, and cheetah) **2** : a malicious woman **3** : a strong tackle used to hoist an anchor to the cathead of a ship **4 a** : CATBOAT **b** : CATAMARAN **5** : CAT-O'-NINE-TAILS **6** : CATFISH **7 a** : a player or devotee of jazz **b** : GUY

²**cat** *vb* **cat·ted; cat·ting** *vt* (1769) : to bring (an anchor) up to the cathead ~ *vi* : to search for a sexual mate — often used with *around*

Cat \'kat\ *trademark* — used for a Caterpillar tractor

cata- or **cat-** or **cath-** prefix [Gk kata-, kat-, kath-, fr. kata down, in accordance with, by; akin to OW cant with, Hitt katta] : down ⟨cation⟩ ⟨cathode⟩

ca·tab·o·lism \kə-'ta-bə-,li-zəm\ n [Gk katabolē throwing down, fr. kataballein to throw down, fr. kata- + ballein to throw — more at DEVIL] (1876) : destructive metabolism involving the release of energy and resulting in the breakdown of complex materials within the organism — compare ANABOLISM — **cat·a·bol·ic** \,ka-tə-'bä-lik\ adj — **cat·a·bol·i·cal·ly** \-li-k(ə-)lē\ adv

ca·tab·o·lite \-,līt\ n (ca. 1909) : a product of catabolism

ca·tab·o·lize \-,līz\ vb -lized; -liz·ing vt (ca. 1926) : to subject to catabolism ~ vi : to undergo catabolism

cat·a·chre·sis \,ka-tə-'krē-səs\ n, pl -chre·ses \-,sēz\ [L, fr. Gk katachrēsis misuse, fr. katachrēsthai to use up, misuse, fr. kata- + chrēsthai to use] (1553) 1 : use of the wrong word for the context 2 : use of a forced and esp. paradoxical figure of speech (as blind mouths) — **cat·a·chres·tic** \-'kres-tik\ or **cat·a·chres·ti·cal** \-ti-kəl\ adj — **cat·a·chres·ti·cal·ly** \-ti-k(ə-)lē\ adv

cat·a·clysm \'ka-tə-,kli-zəm\ n [F cataclysme, fr. L cataclysmos, fr. Gk kataklysmos, fr. kataklyzein to inundate, fr. kata- + klyzein to wash — more at CLYSTER] (1637) 1 : FLOOD, DELUGE 2 : CATASTROPHE 3a 3 : a momentous and violent event marked by overwhelming upheaval and demolition; broadly : an event that brings great changes — **cat·a·clys·mal** \,ka-tə-'kliz-məl\ or **cat·a·clys·mic** \-mik\ adj — **cat·a·clys·mi·cal·ly** \-mi-k(ə-)lē\ adv

cat·a·comb \'ka-tə-,kōm\ n [MF catacombe, prob. fr. OIt catacomba, fr. LL catacumbae, pl.] (15c) 1 : a subterranean cemetery of galleries with recesses for tombs — usu. used in pl. 2 : something resembling a catacomb: as a : an underground passageway or group of passageways b : a complex set of interrelated things ⟨the endless ~s of formal education —Kingman Brewster, Jr.⟩

cata·di·op·tric \,ka-tə-dī-'äp-trik\ adj (1723) : belonging to, produced by, or involving both the reflection and the refraction of light

ca·tad·ro·mous \kə-'ta-drə-məs\ adj [prob. fr. NL catadromus, fr. cata- + -dromus -dromous] (1880) : living in fresh water and going to the sea to spawn ⟨~ eels⟩ — compare ANADROMOUS

cat·a·falque \'ka-tə-,fo(l)k, -,falk\ n [It catafalco, fr. (assumed) VL catafalicum scaffold, fr. cata- + L fala siege tower] (1641) 1 : an ornamental structure sometimes used in funerals for the lying in state of the body 2 : a pall-covered coffin-shaped structure used at requiem masses celebrated after burial

Cat·a·lan \'ka-tə-lən, -,lan\ n [Sp catalán] (15c) 1 : a native or inhabitant of Catalonia 2 : the Romance language of Catalonia, Valencia, Andorra, and the Balearic islands — **Catalan** adj

cat·a·lase \'ka-tə-,lās, -,lāz\ n [catalysis] (1901) : a red crystalline enzyme that consists of a protein complex with hematin groups and catalyzes the decomposition of hydrogen peroxide into water and oxygen — **cat·a·lat·ic** \,ka-tə-'la-tik\ adj

cat·a·lec·tic \,ka-tə-'lek-tik\ adj [LL catalecticus, fr. Gk katalēktikos, fr. katalēgein to leave off, fr. kata- + lēgein to stop — more at SLACK] (1589) : lacking a syllable at the end or ending in an incomplete foot — **catalectic** n

cat·a·lep·sy \'ka-tə-,lep-sē\ n, pl -sies [ME catalempsi, fr. ML catalepsia, fr. LL catalepsis, fr. Gk katalēpsis, lit., act of seizing, fr. katalambanein to seize, fr. kata- + lambanein to take — more at LATCH] (14c) : a condition of suspended animation and loss of voluntary motion in which the limbs remain in whatever position they are placed — **cat·a·lep·tic** \,ka-tə-'lep-tik\ adj or n — **cat·a·lep·ti·cal·ly** \-ti-k(ə-)lē\ adv

cat·a·lex·is \,ka-tə-'lek-səs\ n, pl -lex·es \-,sēz\ [NL, fr. Gk katalēxis close, cadence, fr. katalēgein] (1830) : omission or incompleteness usu. in the last foot of a line in metrical verse

¹**cat·a·log** or **cat·a·logue** \'ka-tə-,lóg, -,läg\ n [ME cateloge, fr. MF catalogue, fr. LL catalogus, fr. Gk katalogos, fr. katalegein to list, enumerate, fr. kata- + legein to gather, speak — more at LEGEND] (15c) 1 : LIST, REGISTER 2 a : a complete enumeration of items arranged systematically with descriptive details b : a pamphlet or book that contains such a list c : material in such a list

²**catalog** or **catalogue** vb -loged or -logued; -log·ing or -logu·ing vt (1598) 1 : to make a catalog of 2 a : to enter in a catalog b : to classify (as books or information) descriptively ~ vi 1 : to make or work on a catalog 2 : to become listed in a catalog at a specified price ⟨this stamp ~s at $2⟩ — **cat·a·log·er** or **cat·a·logu·er** n

catalogue rai·son·né \,rā-z⁼n-'ā\ n, pl **cat·a·logues rai·son·nés** \,lōg(z)-,rā-z⁼n-'ā\ [F, lit., reasoned catalog] (1784) : a systematic annotated catalog; esp : a critical bibliography

ca·tal·pa \kə-'tal-pə, -'tól-\ n [Creek katalpa, fr. iká head + talpa wing] (ca. 1730) : any of a genus (Catalpa) of American and Asian trees of the trumpet-creeper family with pale showy flowers in terminal clusters

ca·tal·y·sis \kə-'ta-lə-səs\ n, pl -y·ses \-,sēz\ [Gk katalysis dissolution, fr. katalyein to dissolve, fr. kata- + lyein to dissolve, release — more at LOSE] (1836) 1 : a modification and esp. increase in the rate of a chemical reaction induced by material unchanged chemically at the end of the reaction 2 : a reaction between two or more persons or forces precipitated by a separate agent ⟨a representative list of questions . . . valuable for the ~ of class discussions —B. S. Meyer & D. B. Anderson⟩

cat·a·lyst \'ka-t⁼l-əst\ n (1902) 1 : a substance (as an enzyme) that enables a chemical reaction to proceed at a usu. faster rate or under different conditions (as at a lower temperature) than otherwise possible 2 : an agent that provokes or speeds significant change or action

cat·a·lyt·ic \,ka-tə-'li-tik\ adj (1836) : causing, involving, or relating to catalysis — **cat·a·lyt·i·cal·ly** \-'li-ti-k(ə-)lē\ adv

catalytic converter n (1964) : an automobile exhaust-system component containing a catalyst that causes decomposition of harmful gases into mostly harmless products (as water and carbon dioxide)

catalytic cracker n (1947) : the unit in a petroleum refinery in which cracking is carried out in the presence of a catalyst

cat·a·lyze \'ka-tə-,līz\ vt -lyzed; -lyz·ing (1902) 1 : to bring about the catalysis of (a chemical reaction) 2 : BRING ABOUT, INSPIRE 3 : to alter significantly by catalysis ⟨innovations in basic chemical theory that have catalyzed the field —Newsweek⟩ — **cat·a·lyz·er** n

cat·a·ma·ran \,ka-tə-mə-'ran, 'ka-tə-mə-,ran\ n [Tamil kaṭṭumaram, fr. kaṭṭu to tie + maram tree, wood] (1673) : a vessel (as a sailboat) with twin hulls and usu. a deck or superstructure connecting the hulls

cat·a·me·nia \,ka-tə-'mē-nē-ə\ n pl [NL, fr. Gk katamēnia, fr. neut. pl. of katamēnios monthly, fr. kata by + mēn month — more at CATA-, MOON] (1750) : MENSES — **cat·a·me·ni·al** \-nē-əl\ adj

cat·a·mite \'ka-tə-,mīt\ n [L catamitus, fr. Catamitus Ganymede, fr. Etruscan Catmite, fr. Gk Ganymēdēs] (1593) : a boy kept by a pederast

cat·a·mount \'ka-tə-,maúnt\ n [short for cat-a-mountain] (1664) : any of various wild cats: as a : COUGAR b : LYNX

cat–a–moun·tain \,ka-tə-'maún-t⁼n\ n [ME cat of the mountaine] (15c) : any of various wild cats

cat and mouse n (1887) : behavior like that of a cat with a mouse: as a : the act of toying with or tormenting something before destroying it b : a contrived action involving constant pursuit, near captures, and repeated escapes ⟨played a game of cat and mouse with the police⟩; broadly : an evasive action

ca·taph·o·ra \kə-'ta-fə-rə\ n [cata- + anaphora] (1976) : the use of a grammatical substitute (as a pronoun) that has the same reference as a following word or phrase

cat·a·pho·re·sis \,ka-tə-fə-'rē-səs\ n, pl -re·ses \-,sēz\ [NL] (1889) : ELECTROPHORESIS — **cat·a·pho·ret·ic** \-'re-tik\ adj — **cat·a·pho·ret·i·cal·ly** \-i-k(ə-)lē\ adv

cat·a·phor·ic \,ka-tə-'fór-ik\ adj (1968) : of or relating to cataphora; esp : being a word or phrase (as a pronoun) that takes its reference from a following word or phrase (as her in before her Jane saw nothing but desert) — compare ANAPHORIC

cat·a·plasm \'ka-tə-,pla-zəm\ n [MF cataplasme, fr. L cataplasma, fr. Gk kataplasma, fr. kataplassein to plaster over, fr. kata- + plassein to mold — more at PLASTER] (15c) : POULTICE

cat·a·plexy \'ka-tə-,plek-sē\ n, pl -plex·ies \-,sēz\ [G Kataplexie, fr. Gk kataplēxis, fr. kataplēssein to strike down, terrify, fr. kata- + plēssein to strike — more at PLAINT] (1883) : sudden loss of muscle power following a strong emotional stimulus

¹**cat·a·pult** \'ka-tə-,pəlt, -,púlt\ n [MF or L; MF catapulte, fr. L catapulta, fr. Gk katapaltēs, fr. kata- + pallein to hurl] (1577) 1 : an ancient military device for hurling missiles 2 : a device for launching an airplane at flying speed (as from an aircraft carrier)

²**catapult** vt (1848) : to throw or launch by or as if by a catapult ~ vi : to become catapulted

cat·a·ract \'ka-tə-,rakt\ n [L cataracta waterfall, portcullis, fr. Gk kataraktēs, fr. katarassein to dash down, fr. kata- + arassein to strike, dash] (14c) 1 [ME, fr. MF or ML; MF cataracte, fr. ML cataracta, fr. L, portcullis] : a clouding of the lens of the eye or of its surrounding transparent membrane that obstructs the passage of light 2 a obs : WATERSPOUT b : WATERFALL; esp : a large one over a precipice c : steep rapids in a river d : DOWNPOUR, FLOOD ⟨~s of rain⟩ ⟨~s of information⟩ — **cat·a·rac·tous** \,ka-tə-'rak-təs\ adj

ca·tarrh \kə-'tär\ n [MF or LL; MF catarrhe, fr. LL catarrhus, fr. Gk katarrhous, fr. katarrhein to flow down, fr. kata- + rhein to flow — more at STREAM] (15c) : inflammation of a mucous membrane; esp : one chronically affecting the human nose and air passages — **ca·tarrh·al** \-əl\ adj — **ca·tarrh·al·ly** \-ə-lē\ adv

cat·ar·rhine \'ka-tə-,rīn\ adj [NL Catarrhina, fr. Gk katarrhina, neut. pl. of katarrhin hook-nosed, fr. kata- + rhin-, rhis nose] (1863) : of, relating to, or being any of a division (Catarrhina) of primates comprising the Old World monkeys, higher apes, and hominids that have the nostrils close together and directed downward, 32 teeth, and the tail when present never prehensile — **catarrhine** n

ca·tas·tro·phe \kə-'tas-trə-(,)fē\ n [Gk katastrophē, fr. katastrephein to overturn, fr. kata- + strephein to turn] (1540) 1 : the final event of the dramatic action esp. of a tragedy 2 : a momentous tragic event ranging from extreme misfortune to utter overthrow or ruin 3 a : a violent and sudden change in a feature of the earth b : a violent usu. destructive natural event (as a supernova) 4 : utter failure : FIASCO — **cat·a·stroph·ic** \,ka-tə-'strä-fik\ adj — **cat·a·stroph·i·cal·ly** \-fi-k(ə-)lē\ adv

catastrophe theory n (1976) : mathematical theory and conjecture that uses topology to explain events (as an earthquake or a stock market crash) characterized by major abrupt changes

ca·tas·tro·phism \kə-'tas-trə-,fi-zəm\ n (1869) : a geological doctrine that changes in the earth's crust have in the past been brought about suddenly by physical forces operating in ways that cannot be observed today — compare UNIFORMITARIANISM — **ca·tas·tro·phist** \-fist\ n

cat·a·to·nia \,ka-tə-'tō-nē-ə\ n [NL, fr. G katatonie, fr. kata- cata- + NL -tonia] (ca. 1891) : catatonic schizophrenia

cat·a·ton·ic \-'tä-nik\ adj (1904) 1 : of, relating to, being, resembling, or affected by schizophrenia characterized esp. by a marked psychomotor disturbance that may involve stupor or mutism, negativism, rigidity, purposeless excitement, and inappropriate or bizarre posturing 2 : characterized by a marked lack of movement, activity, or expression — **catatonic** n — **cat·a·ton·i·cal·ly** \-ni-k(ə-)lē\ adv

Ca·taw·ba \kə-'tó-bə\ n (1715) 1 pl **Catawba** or **Catawbas** : a member of an American Indian people of No. Carolina and So. Carolina 2 : the language of the Catawba people 3 : any of various wines produced from a pale red native American grape

cat·bird \'kat-,bərd\ n (1709) : an American songbird (Dumetella carolinensis) that is dark gray in color with a black cap and reddish coverts under the tail and is related to the mockingbird

catbird seat n (1942) : a position of great prominence or advantage

cat·boat \'kat-,bōt\ n (1878) : a sailboat

catboat

\ə\ abut \ᵊ\ kitten, F table \ər\ further \a\ ash \ā\ ace \ä\ mop, mar \aú\ out \ch\ chin \e\ bet \ē\ easy \g\ go \i\ hit \ī\ ice \j\ job \ŋ\ sing \ō\ go \ò\ law \òi\ boy \th\ thin \t͟h\ the \ü\ loot \ú\ foot \y\ yet \zh\ vision \à, k̲, ⁿ, œ, œ̄, ᴜe, ᵫ, ᵊ\ see Guide to Pronunciation having a cat rig and usu. a centerboard and being of light draft and broad beam

cat·bri·er \-ˌbrī(-ə)r\ *n* (1839) : any of a genus (*Smilax*) of dioecious often prickly climbing plants of the lily family

cat burglar *n* (1907) : a burglar who is adept at entering and leaving the burglarized place without attracting notice

cat·call \-ˌkȯl\ *n* (1749) : a loud or raucous cry made esp. to express disapproval (as at a sports event) — **catcall** *vb*

¹catch \ˈkach, ˈkech\ *vb* **caught** \ˈkȯt *also* ˈkät\; **catch·ing** [ME *cacchen*, fr. ONF *cachier* to hunt, fr. (assumed) VL *captiare*, alter. of L *captare* to chase, freq. of *capere* to take — more at HEAVE] *vt* (13c) **1 a :** to capture or seize esp. after pursuit **b :** to take or entangle in or as if in a snare **c :** DECEIVE **d :** to discover unexpectedly **e :** FIND ⟨*caught* in the act⟩ **e :** to check (oneself) suddenly or momentarily **f :** to become suddenly aware of ⟨*caught* me looking at him⟩ **2 a :** to take hold of : SEIZE **b :** to affect suddenly **c :** INTERCEPT **d :** to avail oneself of : TAKE **e :** to obtain through effort : GET **f :** to get entangled ⟨~ a sleeve on a nail⟩ **3 :** to become affected by: as **a :** CONTRACT ⟨~ a cold⟩ **b :** to respond sympathetically to the point of being imbued with ⟨~ the spirit of an occasion⟩ **c :** to be struck by **d :** to be subjected to : RECEIVE ⟨~ hell⟩ **4 a :** to seize and hold firmly **b :** FASTEN **5 :** to take or get usu. momentarily or quickly ⟨~ a glimpse of a friend⟩ ⟨~ a nap⟩ **6 a :** OVERTAKE **b :** to get aboard in time ⟨~ the bus⟩ **7 :** to attract and hold : ARREST, ENGAGE ⟨*catch* my attention⟩ ⟨*caught* her eye⟩ **8 :** to make contact with : STRIKE **9 a :** to grasp by the senses or the mind ⟨you ~ what I mean?⟩ ⟨didn't ~ the name⟩ **b :** to apprehend and fix by artistic means **10 a :** SEE, WATCH ⟨~ a game on TV⟩ **b :** to listen to **11 :** to serve as a catcher in baseball **12 :** to meet with socially ⟨~ you later⟩ ~ *vi* **1 :** to grasp hastily or try to grasp **2 :** to become caught **3 :** to catch fire **4** *of a crop* : to come up and become established **5 :** to play the position of catcher on a baseball team **6 :** KICK OVER — **catch·able** \ˈka-chə-bəl, ˈke-\ *adj* — **catch a crab :** to fail to raise an oar clear of the water on recovery of a stroke — **catch dead :** willing to be publicly exposed — used in negative constructions ⟨wouldn't be *caught dead* in that shirt⟩ — **catch fire 1 :** to become ignited **2 :** to become fired with enthusiasm **3 :** to increase greatly in scope, popularity, interest, or effectiveness ⟨this stock has not *caught fire*—yet —Forbes⟩ — **catch it :** to incur blame, reprimand, or punishment — **catch one's breath :** to rest long enough to restore normal breathing; *broadly* : to rest after a period of intense activity

syn CATCH, CAPTURE, TRAP, SNARE, ENTRAP, ENSNARE, BAG mean to come to possess or control by or as if by seizing. CATCH implies the seizing of something in motion or in flight or in hiding ⟨*caught* the dog as it ran by⟩. CAPTURE suggests taking by overcoming resistance or difficulty ⟨*capture* an enemy stronghold⟩. TRAP, SNARE, ENTRAP, ENSNARE imply seizing by some device that holds the one caught at the mercy of the captor. TRAP and SNARE apply more commonly to physical seizing ⟨*trap* animals⟩ ⟨*snared* butterflies with a net⟩. ENTRAP and ENSNARE more often are figurative ⟨*entrapped* the witness with a trick question⟩ ⟨a sting operation that *ensnared* burglars⟩. BAG implies shooting down a fleeing or distant prey ⟨*bagged* a brace of pheasants⟩.

²catch *n* (15c) **1 :** something caught; *esp* : the total quantity caught at one time ⟨a large ~ of fish⟩ **2 a :** the act, action, or fact of catching **b :** a game in which a ball is thrown and caught **3 :** something that checks or holds immovable ⟨a safety ~⟩ **4 :** one worth catching esp. as a spouse **5 :** a round for three or more unaccompanied usu. male voices often with suggestive or obscene lyrics **6 :** FRAGMENT, SNATCH **7 :** a concealed difficulty or complication ⟨there must be a ~⟩ **8 :** the germination of a field crop to such an extent that replanting is unnecessary

catch·all \ˈka-ˌchȯl, ˈke-\ *n, often attrib* (1838) : something that holds or includes odds and ends or a wide variety of things

catch–as–catch–can *adj* (1764) : using any available means or method : UNPLANNED ⟨a ~ existence begging and running errands —*Time*⟩

catch·er \ˈka-chər, ˈke-\ *n* (15c) : one that catches; *specif* : a baseball player positioned behind home plate

catch·fly \ˈkach-ˌflī, ˈkech-\ *n* (1597) : any of various plants (as of the genera *Lychnis* and *Silene*) of the pink family often with viscid stems

catch·ing *adj* (1590) **1 :** INFECTIOUS, CONTAGIOUS ⟨the flu is ~⟩ ⟨his spirit is ~⟩ **2 :** CATCHY, ALLURING

catch·ment \ˈkach-mənt, ˈkech-\ *n* (1847) **1 :** something that catches water; *also* : the amount of water caught **2 :** the action of catching water

catchment area *n* (1940) : the geographical area served by an institution

catch on *vi* (1883) **1 :** to become aware : LEARN; *also* : UNDERSTAND ⟨didn't *catch on* to what was going on⟩ **2 :** to become popular ⟨this idea has already *caught on*⟩

catch out *vt* (1816) : to detect in error or wrongdoing ⟨delighting to *catch* his literary victims in error —John Clive⟩

catch·pen·ny \ˈkach-ˌpe-nē, ˈkech-\ *adj* (1748) : using sensationalism or cheapness for appeal ⟨a ~ newspaper⟩

catch·phrase \-ˌfrāz\ *n* (ca. 1850) : an expression that has caught on and is used repeatedly

catch·pole *or* **catch·poll** \-ˌpōl\ *n* [ME *cacchepol*, fr. OE *cæcepol*, fr. (assumed) ONF *cachepol*, lit., chicken chaser, fr. ONF *cachier* + *pol* chicken, fr. L *pullus* — more at CATCH, PULLET] (bef. 12c) : a sheriff's deputy; *esp* : one who makes arrests for failure to pay a debt

catch–22 \-ˌtwen-tē-ˈtü\ *n, pl* **catch–22's** *or* **catch–22s** *often cap* [fr. *Catch-22*, paradoxical rule in the novel *Catch-22* (1961) by Joseph Heller] (1961) **1 :** a problematic situation for which the only solution is denied by a circumstance inherent in the problem or by a rule ⟨the show-business ~—no work unless you have an agent, no agent unless you've worked —Mary Murphy⟩; *also* : the circumstance or rule that denies a solution **2 a :** an illogical, unreasonable, or senseless situation **b :** a measure or policy whose effect is the opposite of what was intended **c :** a situation presenting two equally undesirable alternatives **3 :** a hidden difficulty or means of entrapment : CATCH

catch·up \ˈke-chəp, ˈka-; ˈkat-səp\ *var of* KETCHUP

¹catch–up \ˈkach-ˌəp, ˈkech-\ *adj* (1945) : intended to catch up to a theoretical norm or a competitor's accomplishments

²catch–up *n* (1948) : the act or fact of catching up or trying to catch up (as with a norm or competitor) ⟨had to play ~⟩; *also* : an increase intended to achieve catch-up

catch up *vt* (14c) **1 a :** to pick up often abruptly ⟨the thief *caught* the purse *up* and ran⟩ **b :** ENSNARE, ENTANGLE ⟨education has been *caught up* in a stultifying mythology —N. M. Pusey⟩ **c :** ENTHRALL ⟨the ... public was *caught up* in the car's magic —D. A. Jedlicka⟩ **2 :** to provide with the latest information ⟨*catch* me *up* on the news⟩ ~ *vi* **1 :** to travel fast enough to overtake an advance party **b :** to reach a state of parity or of being able to cope ⟨kids left behind in preschool may never *catch up*⟩ **2 :** to bring about arrest for illicit activities ⟨the police *caught up* with the thieves⟩ **3 a :** to complete or compensate for something belatedly ⟨*catch up* on lost sleep⟩ **b :** to acquire belated information ⟨*catch up* on the news⟩

catch·word \ˈkach-ˌwərd, ˈkech-\ *n* (ca. 1736) **1 a :** a word under the right-hand side of the last line on a book page that repeats the first word on the following page **b :** GUIDE WORD **2 :** a word or expression repeated until it becomes representative of a party, school, or point of view

catchy \ˈka-chē, ˈke-chē\ *adj* **catch·i·er; -est** (1831) **1 :** tending to catch the interest or attention ⟨a ~ title⟩ **2 :** FITFUL, IRREGULAR ⟨~ breathing⟩ **3 :** TRICKY ⟨a ~ question⟩

cat·claw \ˈkat-ˌklȯ\ *n* (1898) : a yellow-flowered spiny acacia (*Acacia greggii*) of the southwestern U.S. and Mexico

cat distemper *n* (ca. 1950) : PANLEUKOPENIA

cate \ˈkāt\ *n* [ME, article of purchased food, short for *acate*, fr. ONF *acat* purchase, fr. *acater* to buy, fr. (assumed) VL *accaptare*, fr. L *acceptare* to accept] (15c) *archaic* : a dainty or choice food

cat·e·che·sis \ˌka-tə-ˈkē-səs\ *n, pl* **-che·ses** \-ˌsēz\ [LL, fr. Gk *katēchēsis*, fr. *katēchein* to teach] (1753) : oral instruction of catechumens — **cat·e·chet·i·cal** \-ˈke-ti-kəl\ *adj*

cat·e·chin \ˈka-tə-ˌkin\ *n* [ISV *catechu* + ¹-*in*] (1853) : a crystalline compound $C_{15}H_{14}O_6$ or its derivatives related chemically to the flavones and used in dyeing and tanning

cat·e·chism \ˈka-tə-ˌki-zəm\ *n* (1502) **1 :** oral instruction **2 :** a manual for catechizing; *specif* : a summary of religious doctrine often in the form of questions and answers **3 a :** a set of formal questions put as a test **b :** something resembling a catechism esp. in being a rote response or formulaic statement — **cat·e·chis·mal** \ˌka-tə-ˈkiz-məl\ *adj* — **cat·e·chis·tic** \-ˈkis-tik\ *adj*

cat·e·chist \ˈka-tə-kist\ *n* (ca. 1563) : one that catechizes: as **a :** a teacher of catechumens **b :** a native in a missionary district who does Christian teaching

cat·e·chize \ˈka-tə-ˌkīz\ *vt* **-chized; -chiz·ing** [LL *catechizare*, fr. Gk *katēchizein* to teach, lit., to din into, fr. *kata-* cata- + *ēchein* to resound, fr. *ēchē* sound — more at ECHO] (15c) **1 :** to instruct systematically esp. by questions, answers, and explanations and corrections; *specif* : to give religious instruction in such a manner **2 :** to question systematically or searchingly — **cat·e·chi·za·tion** \ˌka-ti-kə-ˈzā-shən\ *n* — **cat·e·chiz·er** \ˈka-tə-ˌkī-zər\ *n*

cat·e·chol \ˈka-tə-ˌkȯl, -ˌkōl\ *n* (1880) **1 :** CATECHIN **2 :** PYROCATECHOL

cat·e·chol·amine \ˌka-tə-ˈkō-lə-ˌmēn, -ˈkȯ-\ *n* (1954) : any of various amines (as epinephrine, norepinephrine, and dopamine) that function as hormones or neurotransmitters or both

cat·e·chol·amin·er·gic \-ˌkō-lə-mē-ˈnər-jik, -ˌkȯ-, -ˌkȯ-, -mi-\ *adj* (1970) : involving, liberating, or mediated by catecholamine

cat·e·chu \ˈka-tə-ˌchü, -ˌshü\ *n* [prob. modif. of Malay *kachu*, of Dravidian origin; akin to Tamil & Kannada *kācu* catechu] (1683) : any of several dry, earthy, or resinous astringent substances obtained from tropical plants of Asia: as **a :** an extract of the heartwood of an East Indian acacia (*Acacia catechu*) **b :** GAMBIER

cat·e·chu·men \ˌka-tə-ˈkyü-mən\ *n* [ME *cathecumyn*, fr. MF *cathecumine*, fr. LL *catechumenus*, fr. Gk *katēchoumenos*, pres. pass. part. of *katēchein*] (15c) **1 :** a convert to Christianity receiving training in doctrine and discipline before baptism **2 :** one receiving instruction in the basic doctrines of Christianity before admission to communicant membership in a church

cat·e·gor·i·cal \ˌka-tə-ˈgȯr-i-kəl, -ˈgär-\ *also* **cat·e·gor·ic** \-ik\ *adj* [LL *categoricus*, fr. Gk *katēgorikos*, fr. *katēgoria*] (1588) **1 :** ABSOLUTE, UNQUALIFIED ⟨a ~ denial⟩ **2 a :** of, relating to, or constituting a category **b :** involving, according with, or considered with respect to specific categories — **cat·e·gor·i·cal·ly** \-i-k(ə-)lē\ *adv*

categorical imperative *n* (1827) : a moral obligation or command that is unconditionally and universally binding

cat·e·go·rise *Brit var of* CATEGORIZE

cat·e·go·rize \ˈka-ti-gə-ˌrīz\ *vt* **-rized; -riz·ing** (1705) : to put into a category : CLASSIFY — **cat·e·go·ri·za·tion** \ˌka-ti-gə-rə-ˈzā-shən\ *n*

cat·e·go·ry \ˈka-tə-ˌgȯr-ē, -ˌgȯr-\ *n, pl* **-ries** [LL *categoria*, fr. Gk *katēgoria* predication, fr. *katēgorein* to accuse, affirm, predicate, fr. *kata-* + *agora* public assembly, fr. *ageirein* to gather] (1588) **1 :** any of several fundamental and distinct classes to which entities or concepts belong **2 :** a division within a system of classification

ca·te·na \kə-ˈtē-nə\ *n, pl* **-nae** \-(ˌ)nē\ *or* **-nas** [ML, fr. L, chain] (1641) : a connected series of related things

cat·e·nary \ˈka-tə-ˌner-ē, *esp Brit* kə-ˈtē-nə-rē\ *n, pl* **-nar·ies** [NL *catenaria*, fr. L, fem. of *catenarius* of a chain, fr. *catena*] (1788) **1 :** the curve assumed by a cord of uniform density and cross section that is perfectly flexible but not capable of being stretched and that hangs freely from two fixed points **2 :** something in the form of a catenary — **catenary** *adj*

cat·e·nate \ˈka-tə-ˌnāt\ *vt* **-nat·ed; -nat·ing** [L *catenatus*, pp. of *catenare*, fr. *catena*] (ca. 1623) : to connect in a series : LINK — **cat·e·na·tion** \ˌka-tə-ˈnā-shən\ *n*

ca·ter \ˈkā-tər\ *vb* [obs. *cater* buyer of provisions, fr. ME *catour*, short for *acatour*, fr. AF, fr. ONF *acater* to buy — more at CATE] *vi* (1600) **1 :** to provide a supply of food **2 :** to supply what is required or desired ⟨~*ing* to middle-class tastes⟩ ~ *vt* : to provide food and service for ⟨~*ed* the banquet⟩ — **ca·ter·er** \-tər-ər\ *n*

cat·er·an \ˈka-tə-rən\ *n* [ME *ketharan*, prob. fr. ScGael *ceathairneach* freebooter, robber] (14c) : a former military irregular or brigand of the Scottish Highlands

cat·er·cor·ner \'ka-tē-,kȯr-nər, 'ka-tə-, 'ki-tē-\ *also* **cat·er·cor·nered** \-nərd\ *adv or adj* [obs. *cater* four + *corner*] (1838) : in a diagonal or oblique position : on a diagonal or oblique line ⟨the house stood ~ across the square⟩

ca·ter-cous·in \'kā-tər-,kə-z²n\ *n* [perh. fr. obs. *cater* buyer of provisions] (1519) : an intimate friend

cat·er·pil·lar \'ka-tə(r)-,pi-lər\ *n, often attrib* [ME *catyrpel*, fr. ONF *catepelose*, lit., hairy cat] (15c) : the elongated wormlike larva of a butterfly or moth; *also* : any of various similar larvae

Caterpillar *trademark* — used for a tractor made for use on rough or soft ground and moved on two endless metal belts

cat·er·waul \'ka-tər-,wȯl\ *vi* [ME *caterwawen*] (14c) **1** : to make a harsh cry **2** : to quarrel noisily — **caterwaul** *n*

cat·fac·ing \'kat-,fā-siŋ\ *n* (1940) : a disfigurement or malformation of fruit suggesting a cat's face in appearance

cat·fight \-,fīt\ *n* (1919) : an intense fight or argument between two women

cat·fish \-,fish\ *n* (1612) : any of an order (Siluriformes) of chiefly freshwater stout-bodied scaleless bony fishes having long tactile barbels

cat·gut \-,gət\ *n* (1599) : a tough cord made usu. from sheep intestines

cath- — see CATA-

Cath·ar \'ka-,thär\ *n, pl* **Cath·a·ri** \'ka-thə-,rī, -,rē\ *or* **Cathars** [LL *cathari* (pl.), fr. LGk *katharoi*, fr. Gk, pl. of *katharos* pure] (1637) : a member of one of various ascetic and dualistic Christian sects esp. of the later Middle Ages teaching that matter is evil and professing faith in an angelic Christ who did not really undergo human birth or death — **Cath·a·rism** \'ka-thə-,ri-zəm\ *n* — **Cath·a·rist** \-rist\ *or* **Cath·a·ris·tic** \,ka-thə-'ris-tik\ *adj*

ca·thar·sis \kə-'thär-səs\ *n, pl* **ca·thar·ses** \-,sēz\ [NL, fr. Gk *katharsis*, fr. *kathairein* to cleanse, purge, fr. *katharos*] (ca. 1775) **1** : PURGATION **2 a** : purification or purgation of the emotions (as pity and fear) primarily through art **b** : a purification or purgation that brings about spiritual renewal or release from tension **3** : elimination of a complex by bringing it to consciousness and affording it expression

¹ca·thar·tic \kə-'thär-tik\ *adj* [LL or Gk; LL *catharticus*, fr. Gk *kathartikos*, fr. *kathairein*] (1612) : of, relating to, or producing catharsis

²cathartic *n* (1651) : a cathartic medicine : PURGATIVE

cat·head \'kat-,hed\ *n* (1626) : a projecting piece of timber or iron near the bow of a ship to which the anchor is hoisted and secured

ca·thect \kə-'thekt, ka-\ *vt* [back-formation fr. *cathectic*] (1925) : to invest with mental or emotional energy

ca·thec·tic \kə-'thek-tik, ka-\ *adj* [NL *cathexis*] (1927) : of, relating to, or invested with mental or emotional energy

ca·the·dra \kə-'thē-drə\ *n* [L, chair — more at CHAIR] (ca. 1797) : a bishop's official throne

¹ca·the·dral \kə-'thē-drəl\ *adj* (14c) **1** : of, relating to, or containing a cathedra **2** : emanating from a chair of authority **3** : suggestive of a cathedral

²cathedral *n* (1587) **1** : a church that is the official seat of a diocesan bishop **2** : something that resembles or suggests a cathedral

ca·thep·sin \kə-'thep-sən\ *n* [Gk *kathepsein* to digest (fr. *kata*- cata- + *hepsein* to boil) + E ²*-in*] (1929) : any of several intracellular proteases of animal tissue that aid in autolysis

Cath·er·ine wheel \'ka-th(ə-)rin-\ *n* [St. *Catherine* of Alexandria †*ab*307 Christian martyr] (1584) **1** : a wheel with spikes projecting from the rim **2** : PINWHEEL 1 **3** : CARTWHEEL 2

cath·e·ter \'ka-thə-tər, 'kath-tər\ *n* [LL, fr. Gk *kathetēr*, fr. *kathienai* to send down, fr. *kata*- cata- + *hienai* to send — more at JET] (1601) : a tubular medical device for insertion into canals, vessels, passageways, or body cavities usu. to permit injection or withdrawal of fluids or to keep a passage open

cath·e·ter·iza·tion \,ka-thə-tə-rə-'zā-shən, ,kath-tə-rə-\ *n* (ca. 1852) : the use or introduction of a catheter (as in or into the bladder, trachea, or heart) — **cath·e·ter·ize** \'ka-thə-tə-,rīz, 'kath-tə-\ *vt*

ca·thex·is \kə-'thek-səs, ka-\ *n, pl* **ca·thex·es** \-,sēz\ [NL (intended as trans. of G *Besetzung*), fr. Gk *kathexis* holding, fr. *katechein* to hold fast, occupy, fr. *kata*- + *echein* to have, hold — more at SCHEME] (1922) : investment of mental or emotional energy in a person, object, or idea

cath·ode \'ka-,thōd\ *n* [Gk *kathodos* way down, fr. *kata*- + *hodos* way] (1834) **1** : the electrode of an electrochemical cell at which reduction occurs: **a** : the negative terminal of an electrolytic cell **b** : the positive terminal of a galvanic cell **2** : the electron-emitting electrode of an electron tube — compare ANODE — **cath·od·al** \'ka-,thō-d²l\ *adj* — **cath·od·al·ly** *adv* — **ca·thod·ic** \ka-'thä-dik, -'thō-\ *adj* — **ca·thod·i·cal·ly** \-di-k(ə-)lē\ *adv*

cathode ray *n* (1880) **1** *pl* : the high-speed electrons emitted in a stream from the heated cathode of a vacuum tube **2** : a stream of electrons emitted from the cathode of a vacuum tube — usu. used in pl.

cathode—ray tube *n* (1905) : a vacuum tube in which a beam of electrons is projected on a fluorescent screen to produce a luminous spot at a point on the screen determined by the effect on the electron beam of a variable magnetic field within the tube

cathodic protection *n* (1930) : the prevention of electrolytic corrosion of a usu. metallic structure (as a pipeline) by causing it to act as the cathode rather than as the anode of an electrochemical cell

cath·o·lic \'kath-lik, 'ka-thə-\ *adj* [MF & LL; MF *catholique*, fr. LL *catholicus*, fr. Gk *katholikos* universal, general, fr. *katholou* in general, fr. *kata* by + *holos* whole — more at CATA-, SAFE] (14c) **1 a** *often cap* : of, relating to, or forming the church universal **b** *often cap* : of, relating to, or forming the ancient undivided Christian church or a church claiming historical continuity from it **c** *cap* : ROMAN CATHOLIC **2** : COMPREHENSIVE, UNIVERSAL; *esp* : broad in sympathies, tastes, or interests — **ca·thol·i·cal·ly** \kə-'thä-li-k(ə-)lē\ *adv* — **ca·thol·i·cize** \-'thä-lə-,sīz\ *vb*

Cath·o·lic \'kath-lik, 'ka-thə-\ *n* (15c) **1** : a person who belongs to the universal Christian church **2** : a member of a Catholic church; *esp* : ROMAN CATHOLIC

Catholic Apostolic *adj* (1888) : of or relating to a Christian sect founded in 19th century England in anticipation of Christ's second coming

ca·thol·i·cate \kə-'thä-lə-,kāt, -kət\ *n* (1850) : the jurisdiction of a catholicos

Catholic Epistles *n pl* (1582) : the five New Testament letters including James, I and II Peter, I John, and Jude addressed to the early Christian churches at large

Ca·thol·i·cism \kə-'thä-lə-,si-zəm\ *n* (ca. 1617) **1** : ROMAN CATHOLICISM **2** : the faith, practice, or system of Catholic Christianity

cath·o·lic·i·ty \,ka-thə-'li-sə-tē, ,kath-'li-\ *n, pl* **-ties** (1704) **1** *cap* : the character of being in conformity with a Catholic church **2 a** : liberality of sentiments or views ⟨~ of viewpoint —W. V. O'Connor⟩ **b** : UNIVERSALITY **c** : comprehensive range ⟨~ of topics⟩

ca·thol·i·con \kə-'thä-lə-,kän\ *n* [ME, fr. ML, fr. Gk *katholikon*, neut. of *katholikos*] (15c) : CURE-ALL, PANACEA

ca·thol·i·cos \kə-'thȯ-li-kȯs\ *n, pl* **-i·cos·es** \-kȯ-səz\ *or* **-i·coi** \-'thȯ-lə-,kȯi\ *often cap* [LGk *katholikos*, fr. Gk, general] (1878) : a primate of certain Eastern churches and esp. of the Armenian or of the Nestorian church

cat·house \'kat-,haůs\ *n* (1931) : BORDELLO

cat·ion \'kat-,ī-ən, 'ka-(,)tī-ən\ *n* [Gk *kation*, neut. of *kation*, prp. of *katienai* to go down, fr. *kata*- cata- + *ienai* to go — more at ISSUE] (1834) : the ion in an electrolyzed solution that migrates to the cathode; *broadly* : a positively charged ion

cat·ion·ic \,kat-,ī-'ä-nik, ,ka-(,)tī-\ *adj* (ca. 1920) **1** : of, relating to, or being a cation **2** : characterized by an active and esp. surface-active cation ⟨a ~ dye⟩ — **cat·ion·i·cal·ly** \-ni-k(ə-)lē\ *adv*

cat·kin \'kat-kən\ *n* [fr. its resemblance to a cat's tail] (1578) : a spicate inflorescence (as of the willow, birch, or oak) bearing scaly bracts and unisexual usu. apetalous flowers — called also *ament*

cat·like \'kat-,līk\ *adj* (1600) : resembling a cat; *esp* : STEALTHY ⟨with ~ tread, upon our prey we steal —W. S. Gilbert⟩

cat·mint \-,mint\ *n* (13c) : CATNIP

cat·nap \-,nap\ *n* (1823) : a very short light nap — **catnap** *vi*

cat·nap·per *also* **cat·nap·er** \'kat-,na-pər\ *n* [¹*cat* + *-napper* (as in *kidnapper*)] (1942) : one that steals cats usu. to sell them for research

cat·nip \-,nip\ *n* [¹*cat* + obs. *nep* catnip, fr. ME, fr. OE *nepte*, fr. L *nepeta*] (1712) **1** : a strong-scented mint (*Nepeta cataria*) that has whorls of small pale flowers in terminal spikes and contains a substance attractive to cats **2** : something very attractive

cat-o'-nine-tails \,ka-tə-'nīn-,tālz\ *n, pl* **cat-o'-nine-tails** [fr. the resemblance of its scars to the scratches of a cat] (1665) : a whip made of usu. nine knotted lines or cords fastened to a handle

ca·top·tric \kə-'täp-trik\ *adj* [Gk *katoptrikos*, fr. *katoptron* mirror, fr. *katopsesthai* to be going to observe, fr. *kata*- + *opsesthai* to be going to see — more at OPTIC] (ca. 1774) : being or using a mirror to focus light

cat rig *n* (1867) : a rig consisting of a single mast far forward carrying a single large sail extended by a boom — **cat—rigged** \'kat-'rigd\ *adj*

cats and dogs *adv* (1738) : in great quantities : very hard ⟨it was raining *cats and dogs*⟩

CAT scan \'kat-\ *n* [computerized *a*xial *t*omography] (1975) : an image made by computed tomography — **CAT scanning** *n*

CAT scanner *n* (1975) : a medical instrument consisting of integrated X-ray and computing equipment and used for computed tomography

cat's cradle *n* (1768) **1** : a game in which a string looped in a pattern like a cradle on the fingers of one person's hands is transferred to the hands of another so as to form a different figure **2** : something that is intricate, complicated, or elaborate ⟨a *cat's cradle* of red tape⟩

cat's cradle 1

cat scratch disease *n* (1952) : an illness characterized by swelling of the lymph glands, fever, and chills and assumed to be caused by a bacterium transmitted esp. by a cat scratch — called also *cat scratch fever*

cat's-eye \'kat-,sī\ *n, pl* **cat's-eyes** (ca. 1599) **1** : any of various gems (as a chrysoberyl or a chalcedony) exhibiting opalescent reflections from within **2** : a marble with eyelike concentric circles

cat's meow *n* (1926) : a highly admired person or thing

cat's-paw \'kats-,pȯ\ *n, pl* **cat's-paws** (ca. 1769) **1** : a light air that ruffles the surface of the water in irregular patches during a calm **2** [fr. the fable of the monkey that used a cat's paw to draw chestnuts from the fire] : one used by another as a tool : DUPE **3** : a hitch formed with two eyes for attaching a line to a hook — see KNOT illustration

cat·sup *var of* KETCHUP

cat·tail \'kat-,tāl\ *n* (1548) : any of a genus (*Typha* of the family Typhaceae, the cattail family) of tall reedy marsh plants with brown furry fruiting spikes; *esp* : a plant (*Typha latifolia*) with long flat leaves used esp. for making mats and chair seats

cat·tery \'ka-tə-rē\ *n, pl* **-ter·ies** (ca. 1843) : an establishment for the breeding and boarding of cats

cat·tle \'ka-t²l\ *n pl* [ME *catel*, fr. ONF, personal property, fr. ML *capitale*, fr. L, neut. of *capitalis* of the head — more at CAPITAL] (14c) **1** : domesticated quadrupeds held as property or raised for use; *specif* : bovine animals on a farm or ranch **2** : human beings esp. en masse

cattle call *n* (1952) : a mass audition (as of actors)

cattle egret *n* (ca. 1899) : a small Old World white egret (*Bubulcus ibis*) introduced into the New World and having a yellow bill and in the breeding season buff on the crown, breast, and back

cattle grub *n* (1926) : either of two warble flies (genus *Hypoderma*) esp. in the larval stage: **a** : COMMON CATTLE GRUB **b** : a related warble fly (*H. bovis*)

cat·tle·man \-mən, -,man\ *n* (1864) : one who tends or raises cattle

cattle tick *n* (1869) : either of two ixodid ticks (*Boophilus annulatus* and *B. microplus*) that infest cattle and transmit the protozoan which causes Texas fever

cat·tle·ya \'kat-lē-ə; kat-'lā-ə, -'lē-\ *n* [NL, fr. Wm. *Cattley* †1832 Eng. patron of botany] (1828) : any of a genus (*Cattleya*) of tropical American epiphytic orchids with showy hooded flowers

\ə\ abut \ᵊ\ kitten, F table \ər\ further \a\ ash \ā\ ace \ä\ mop, mar \aů\ out \ch\ chin \e\ bet \ē\ easy \g\ go \i\ hit \ī\ ice \j\ job \ŋ\ sing \ō\ go \ȯ\ law \ȯi\ boy \th\ thin \t͟h\ the \ü\ loot \ů\ foot \y\ yet \zh\ vision \à, k̲, ⁿ, œ, œ̄, ɥ, ū̄, ʸ\ see Guide to Pronunciation

¹**cat·ty** \'ka-tē\ *n, pl* **catties** [Malay *katī*] (1598) : any of various units of weight of China and southeast Asia varying around 1⅓ pounds (about 600 grams); *also* : a standard Chinese unit equal to 1.1023 pounds (500 grams)

²**catty** *adj* **cat·ti·er; -est** (1886) **1** : resembling a cat; *esp* : slyly spiteful : MALICIOUS **2** : of or relating to a cat — **cat·ti·ly** \'ka-t⁹l-ē\ *adv* — **cat·ti·ness** \'ka-tē-nəs\ *n*

cat·ty-cor·ner *or* **cat·ty—cor·nered** *var of* CATERCORNER

cat·walk \'kat-,wȯk\ *n* (1885) : a narrow walkway (as along a bridge)

Cau·ca·sian \kȯ-'kā-zhən, kä- *also* -'ka-zhən\ *adj* (1807) **1** : of or relating to the Caucasus or its inhabitants **2 a** : of or relating to the white race of humankind as classified according to physical features **b** : of or relating to the white race as defined by law specif. as composed of persons of European, No. African, or southwest Asian ancestry — **Caucasian** *n* — **Cau·ca·soid** \'kȯ-kə-,sȯid\ *adj or n*

Cau·chy sequence \kō-'shē-, 'kō-shē-\ *n* [Augustin-Louis *Cauchy* †1857 Fr. mathematician] (ca. 1949) : a sequence of elements in a metric space such that for any positive number no matter how small there exists a term in the sequence for which the distance between any two terms beyond this term is less than the arbitrarily small number

¹**cau·cus** \'kȯ-kəs\ *n* [origin unknown] (1763) : a closed meeting of a group of persons belonging to the same political party or faction usu. to select candidates or to decide on policy; *also* : a group of people united to promote an agreed-upon cause

²**caucus** *vi* (1788) : to meet in or hold a caucus

cau·dad \'kȯ-,dad\ *adv* [L *cauda*] (1889) : toward the tail or posterior end

cau·dal \'kȯ-d⁹l\ *adj* [NL *caudalis*, fr. L *cauda* tail] (1661) **1** : of, relating to, or being a tail **2** : situated in or directed toward the hind part of the body — **cau·dal·ly** \-d⁹l-ē\ *adv*

cau·date \'kȯ-,dāt\ *adj* (1600) : having a tail or a taillike appendage

caudate nucleus *n* (ca. 1903) : the most medial of the four basal ganglia in each cerebral hemisphere — called *also caudate*

cau·dex \'kȯ-,deks\ *n, pl* **cau·di·ces** \'kȯ-də-,sēz\ *or* **cau·dex·es** \-,deks-əz\ (ca. 1797) **1** : the stem of a palm or tree fern **2** : the woody base of a perennial plant

cau·dil·lis·mo \,kaù-thē-'yēz-(,)mō, -,thēl-'yēz-\ *n* [Sp, fr. *caudillo*] (1927) : the doctrine or practice of a caudillo

cau·di·llo \kaù-'thē-(,)yō, -'thēl-(,)yō\ *n, pl* **-llos** [Sp, fr. LL *capitellum* small head — more at CADET] (1852) : a Spanish or Latin-American military dictator

cau·dle \'kȯ-d⁹l\ *n* [ME *caudel*, fr. ONF, fr. *caut* warm, fr. L *calidus* — more at CAULDRON] (14c) : a drink (as for invalids) usu. of warm ale or wine mixed with bread or gruel, eggs, sugar, and spices

¹**caught** \'kȯt\ *past and past part of* CATCH

²**caught** *adj* (1858) : PREGNANT — often used in the phrase *get caught*

caul \'kȯl\ *n* [ME *calle*, fr. MF *cale*] (14c) **1** : the large fatty omentum covering the intestines (as of a cow, sheep, or pig) **2** : the inner fetal membrane of higher vertebrates esp. when covering the head at birth

caul·dron \'kȯl-drən\ *n* [ME, alter. of *cauderon*, fr. ONF, dim. of *caudiere*, fr. LL *caldaria*, fr. fem. of L *caldarius* used for hot water, fr. *calidus* warm, fr. *calēre* to be warm — more at LEE] (14c) **1** : a large kettle or boiler **2** : something resembling a boiling cauldron ⟨a ~ of intense emotions⟩

cau·li·flow·er \'kȯ-li-,flaù(-ə)r, 'kä-\ *n, often attrib* [It *cavolfiore*, fr. *cavolo* cabbage (fr. LL *caulus*, fr. L *caulis* stem, cabbage) + *fiore* flower, fr. L *flor-, flos* — more at COLE, BLOW] (1597) : a garden plant (*Brassica oleracea botrytis*) related to the cabbage and grown for its compact edible head of usu. white undeveloped flowers; *also* : its flower cluster used as a vegetable

cauliflower ear *n* (1909) : an ear deformed from injury and excessive growth of reparative tissue

cau·li·flow·er·et \,kȯ-li-,flaù(-ə)-'ret, ,kä-\ *n* (1946) : a bite-size piece of cauliflower

cau·line \'kȯ-,lin\ *adj* [prob. fr. NL *caulinus*, fr. L *caulis*] (1756) : of, relating to, or growing on a stem and esp. on the upper part

¹**caulk** \'kȯk\ *vt* [ME *caulken*, fr. ONF *cauquer* to trample, fr. L *calcare*, fr. *calc-, calx* heel] (15c) : to stop up and make tight against leakage (as a boat or its seams, the cracks in a window frame, or the joints of a pipe) — **caulk·er** *n*

²**caulk** *also* **caulk·ing** \'kȯ-kiŋ\ *n* (1954) : material used to caulk

³**caulk** *var of* ²CALK

caus·al \'kȯ-zəl\ *adj* (ca. 1530) **1** : expressing or indicating cause : CAUSATIVE ⟨a ~ clause introduced by *since*⟩ **2** : of, relating to, or constituting a cause ⟨the ~ agent of a disease⟩ **3** : involving causation or a cause ⟨the relationship . . . was not one of ~ antecedence so much as one of analogous growth —H. O. Taylor⟩ **4** : arising from a cause ⟨a ~ development⟩ — **caus·al·ly** \-zə-lē\ *adv*

cau·sal·gia \kȯ-'zal-j(ē-)ə, -'sal-\ *n* [NL, fr. Gk *kausos* fever (fr. *kaiein* to burn) + NL *-algia*] (1872) : a constant usu. burning pain resulting from injury to a peripheral nerve — **cau·sal·gic** \-jik\ *adj*

cau·sal·i·ty \kȯ-'za-lə-tē\ *n, pl* **-ties** (1603) **1** : a causal quality or agency **2** : the relation between a cause and its effect or between regularly correlated events or phenomena

cau·sa·tion \kȯ-'zā-shən\ *n* (1615) **1 a** : the act or process of causing **b** : the act or agency which produces an effect **2** : CAUSALITY

caus·a·tive \'kȯ-zə-tiv\ *adj* (15c) **1** : effective or operating as a cause or agent ⟨~ bacteria of cholera⟩ **2** : expressing causation; *specif* : being a linguistic form that indicates that the subject causes an act to be performed or a condition to come into being — **causative** *n* — **caus·a·tive·ly** *adv*

¹**cause** \'kȯz\ *n* [ME, fr. OF, fr. L *causa*] (13c) **1 a** : a reason for an action or condition : MOTIVE **b** : something that brings about an effect or a result **c** : a person or thing that is the occasion of an action or state; *esp* : an agent that brings something about **d** : sufficient reason ⟨discharged for ~⟩ **2 a** : a ground of legal action **b** : CASE **3** : a matter or question to be decided **4 a** : a principle or movement militantly defended or supported **b** : a charitable undertaking ⟨for a good ~⟩ — **cause·less** \-ləs\ *adj*

²**cause** *vt* **caused; caus·ing** (14c) **1** : to serve as a cause or occasion of : MAKE **2** : to effect by command, authority, or force — **caus·er** *n*

³**cause** \'kȯz, kəz\ *conj* (15c) : BECAUSE

cause cé·lè·bre *also* **cause ce·le·bre** \,kȯz-sə-'leb, -'le-brə, ,kȯz-, -'lebr⁻\ *n, pl* **causes cé·lè·bres** *also* **causes celebres** *same*\ [F, lit.,

celebrated case] (1763) **1** : a legal case that excites widespread interest **2** : a notorious person, thing, incident, or episode

cau·se·rie \,kōz-'rē, ,kō-zə-\ *n* [F, fr. *causer* to chat, fr. L *causari* to plead, discuss, fr. *causa*] (1827) **1** : an informal conversation : CHAT **2** : a short informal essay

cause·way \'kȯz-,wā\ *n* [ME *cauciwey*, fr. *cauci* + *wey* way] (15c) **1** : a raised way across wet ground or water **2** : HIGHWAY; *esp* : one of ancient Roman construction in Britain — **causeway** *vt*

cau·sey \'kȯ-zē\ *n, pl* **causeys** [ME *cauci*, fr. ONF *caucie*, fr. ML *calciata* paved highway, prob. fr. L *calc-, calx* limestone — more at CHALK] (14c) **1** : CAUSEWAY 1 **2** *obs* : CAUSEWAY 2

¹**caus·tic** \'kȯs-tik\ *adj* [L *causticus*, fr. Gk *kaustikos*, fr. *kaiein* to burn] (14c) **1** : capable of destroying or eating away by chemical action : CORROSIVE **2** : marked by incisive sarcasm **3** : relating to or being the surface or curve of a caustic — **caus·ti·cal·ly** \-ti-k(ə-)lē\ *adv* — **caus·tic·i·ty** \kȯ-'sti-sə-tē\ *n*

syn CAUSTIC, MORDANT, ACRID, SCATHING mean stingingly incisive. CAUSTIC suggests a biting wit ⟨*caustic* comments⟩. MORDANT suggests a wit that is used with deadly effectiveness ⟨*mordant* reviews of the play⟩. ACRID implies bitterness and often malevolence ⟨*acrid* invective⟩. SCATHING implies indignant attacks delivered with fierce severity ⟨a *scathing* satire⟩.

²**caustic** *n* (15c) **1** : a caustic agent: as **a** : a substance that burns or destroys organic tissue by chemical action **b** : SODIUM HYDROXIDE **2** : the envelope of rays emanating from a point and reflected or refracted by a curved surface

caustic potash *n* (1869) : POTASSIUM HYDROXIDE

caustic soda *n* (1876) : SODIUM HYDROXIDE

cau·ter·ize \'kȯ-tə-,rīz\ *vt* **-ized; -iz·ing** (14c) **1** : to sear with a cautery or caustic **2** : to make insensible : DEADEN ⟨must oust the feeling, or ~ it —Robert Craft⟩ — **cau·ter·iza·tion** \,kȯ-tə-rə-'zā-shən\ *n*

cau·tery \'kȯ-tə-rē\ *n, pl* **-ter·ies** [L *cauterium*, fr. Gk *kautērion* branding iron, fr. *kaiein*] (14c) **1** : the act or effect of cauterizing : CAUTERIZATION **2** : an agent (as a hot iron or caustic) used to burn, sear, or destroy tissue

¹**cau·tion** \'kȯ-shən\ *n* [L *caution-, cautio* precaution, fr. *cavēre* to be on one's guard — more at HEAR] (1596) **1** : WARNING, ADMONISHMENT **2** : PRECAUTION **3** : prudent forethought to minimize risk **4** : one that astonishes or commands attention ⟨some shoes you see . . . these days are a ~ —*Esquire*⟩ — **cau·tion·ary** \-shə-,ner-ē\ *adj*

²**caution** *vt* **cau·tioned; cau·tion·ing** \'kȯ-sh(ə-)niŋ\ (1683) : to advise caution to

cau·tious \'kȯ-shəs\ *adj* (ca. 1640) : marked by or given to caution — **cau·tious·ly** *adv* — **cau·tious·ness** *n*

syn CAUTIOUS, CIRCUMSPECT, WARY, CHARY mean prudently watchful and discreet in the face of danger or risk. CAUTIOUS implies the exercise of forethought usu. prompted by fear of danger ⟨a *cautious* driver⟩. CIRCUMSPECT suggests less fear and stresses the surveying of all possible consequences before acting or deciding ⟨*circumspect* in his business dealings⟩. WARY emphasizes suspiciousness and alertness in watching for danger and cunning in escaping it ⟨keeps a *wary* eye on the competition⟩. CHARY implies a cautious reluctance to give, act, or speak freely ⟨*chary* of signing papers without having read them first⟩.

cav·al·cade \,ka-vəl-'kād, 'ka-vəl-,\ *n* [F, ride on horseback, fr. OIt *cavalcata*, fr. *cavalcare* to go on horseback, fr. LL *caballicare*, fr. L *caballus* horse; akin to Gk *kaballeion* horse, MIr *capall* workhorse] (1644) **1 a** : a procession of riders or carriages **b** : a procession of vehicles or ships **2** : a dramatic sequence or procession : SERIES

¹**cav·a·lier** \,ka-və-'lir\ *n* [MF, fr. OIt *cavaliere*, fr. OProv *cavalier*, fr. LL *caballarius* horseman, fr. L *caballus*] (1589) **1** : a gentleman trained in arms and horsemanship **2** : a mounted soldier : KNIGHT **3** *cap* : an adherent of Charles I of England **4** : GALLANT

²**cavalier** *adj* (ca. 1641) **1** : DEBONAIR **2** : marked by or given to offhand and often disdainful dismissal of important matters **3** *a cap* : of or relating to the party of Charles I of England in his struggles with the Puritans and Parliament **b** : ARISTOCRATIC *c cap* : of or relating to the English Cavalier poets of the mid-17th century — **ca·va·lier·ism** \-,i-zəm\ *n* — **cav·a·lier·ly** *adv*

cavalier King Charles spaniel \-'chär(-ə)lz-\ *n* [¹*cavalier* + *King Charles spaniel*, a breed of toy spaniel, fr. *Charles II* of England] (1969) : any of a breed of toy spaniels with a tapered muzzle and a long silky coat

ca·val·la \kə-'va-lə\ *n, pl* **-la** *or* **-las** [Sp *caballa*, a fish, fr. LL, mare, fem. of L *caballus*] (1624) **1** *also* **ca·val·ly** \-'va-lē\ : any of various carangid fishes (esp. genus *Caranx*) **2** : CERO

cav·al·let·ti *also* **cav·a·let·ti** \,ka-və-'le-tē\ *n pl but sing or pl in constr* [It, pl. of *cavalletto* trestle, dim. of *cavallo* horse, fr. L *caballus*] (1950) : a series of timber jumps that are adjustable in height for schooling horses

cav·al·ry \'ka-vəl-rē, ÷'kal-və-rē\ *n, pl* **-ries** [It *cavalleria* cavalry, chivalry, fr. *cavaliere*] (1546) **1 a** : an army component mounted on horseback **b** : an army component moving in motor vehicles or helicopters and assigned to combat missions that require great mobility **2** : HORSEMEN ⟨a thousand ~ in flight⟩

cav·al·ry·man \-rē-mən, -,man\ *n* (1860) : a cavalry soldier

cavalry twill *n* (1942) : TRICOTINE

cav·a·ti·na \,ka-və-'tē-nə, ,kä-\ *n* [It, fr. *cavata* production of sound from an instrument, extraction, fr. *cavare* to dig out, fr. L, to make hollow, fr. *cavus*] (1813) **1** : an operatic solo simpler and briefer than an aria **2** : a songlike instrumental piece or movement

¹**cave** \'kāv\ *n* [ME, fr. OF, fr. L *cava*, fr. *cavus* hollow; akin to Gk *koilos* hollow, and prob. to Gk *kyein* to be pregnant — more at CYME] (13c) **1** : a natural underground chamber or series of chambers open to the surface **2** : a usu. underground chamber for storage ⟨a wine ~⟩; *also* : the articles stored there

²**cave** *vb* **caved; cav·ing** *vt* (15c) : to form a cave in or under : HOLLOW, UNDERMINE ~ *vi* : to explore caves esp. as a sport or hobby — **cav·er** \'kā-vər\ *n*

³**cave** \'kāv\ *vb* **caved; cav·ing** [prob. alter. of *calve*] *vi* (1513) **1** : to fall in or down esp. from being undermined — usu. used with *in* **2** : to cease to resist : SUBMIT — usu. used with *in* ~ *vt* : to cause to fall or collapse — usu. used with *in*

ca·ve·at \'ka-vē-,ät, -,at; 'kä-vē-,ät; 'kā-vē-,at\ *n* [L, let him beware, fr. *cavēre* — more at HEAR] (1533) **1 a** : a warning enjoining one from certain acts or practices **b** : an explanation to prevent misinterpretation **2** : a legal warning to a judicial officer to suspend a proceeding until the opposition has a hearing

caveat emp·tor \-'em(p)-tər, -,tȯr\ *n* [NL, let the buyer beware] (1523) : a principle in commerce: without a warranty the buyer takes the risk

cave dweller *n* (1865) **1** : one (as a prehistoric man) that dwells in a cave **2** : one that lives in a city apartment building

cave–in \'kā-,vin\ *n* (1860) **1** : the action of caving in **2** : a place where earth has caved in

cave·man \'kāv-,man\ *n* (1865) **1** : a cave dweller esp. of the Stone Age **2** : a man who acts in a rough or crude manner

¹cav·ern \'ka-vərn *also* -vrən\ *n* [ME *caverne*, fr. MF, fr. L *caverna*, fr. *cavus*] (14c) : one of large or indefinite extent

²cavern *vt* (ca. 1630) **1** : to place in or as if in a cavern **2** : to form a cavern of : HOLLOW — used with *out*

cav·er·nic·o·lous \,ka-vər-'ni-kə-ləs\ *adj* (ca. 1889) : inhabiting caves

cav·ern·ous \'ka-vər-nəs\ *adj* (15c) **1 a** : having caverns or cavities **b** *of animal tissue* : composed largely of vascular sinuses and capable of dilating with blood to bring about the erection of a body part **2** : constituting or suggesting a cavern — **cav·ern·ous·ly** *adv*

ca·vet·to \kə-'ve-(,)tō, kä-\ *n, pl* **-ti** \-tē\ [It, fr. *cavo* hollow, fr. L *cavus*] (1664) : a concave molding having a curve that approximates a quarter circle — see MOLDING illustration

cav·i·ar *or* **cav·i·are** \'ka-vē-,är *also* 'kä-\ *n* [earlier *cavery, caviarie*, fr. obs. It *caviari*, pl. of *caviaro*, fr. Turk *havyar*] (ca. 1560) **1** : processed salted roe of large fish (as sturgeon) **2** : something considered too delicate or lofty for mass appreciation — usu. used in the phrase *caviar to the general* **3** : something considered the best of its kind ⟨the ~ of porcelain⟩

cav·il \'ka-vəl\ *vb* **-iled** *or* **-illed; -il·ing** *or* **-il·ling** \'ka-və-liŋ, 'kav-liŋ\ [L *cavillari* to jest, cavil, fr. *cavilla* raillery; akin to L *calvi* to deceive — more at CALUMNY] *vi* (1542) : to raise trivial and frivolous objection ~ *vt* : to raise trivial objections to — **cavil** *n* — **cav·il·er** *or* **cav·il·ler** \'ka-və-lər, 'kav-lər\ *n*

cav·ing \'kā-viŋ\ *n* (1932) : the sport of exploring caves : SPELUNKING

cav·i·tary \'ka-və-,ter-ē\ *adj* (1835) : of, relating to, or characterized by bodily cavitation ⟨~ tuberculosis⟩ ⟨~ lesions⟩

cav·i·tate \'ka-və-,tāt\ *vb* **-tat·ed; -tat·ing** *vi* (1909) **1** : to form cavities or bubbles ~ *vt* : to cavitate in

cav·i·ta·tion \,ka-və-'tā-shən\ *n* [*cavity* + *-ation*] (1895) : the process of cavitating: as **a** : the formation of partial vacuums in a liquid by a swiftly moving solid body (as a propeller) or by high-intensity sound waves; *also* : the pitting and wearing away of solid surfaces (as of metal or concrete) as a result of the collapse of these vacuums in surrounding liquid **b** : the formation of cavities in an organ or tissue esp. in disease

cav·i·ty \'ka-və-tē\ *n, pl* **-ties** [MF *cavité*, fr. LL *cavitas*, fr. L *cavus*] (1541) **1** : an unfilled space within a mass; *esp* : a hollowed-out space **2** : an area of decay in a tooth : CARIES

ca·vort \kə-'vȯrt\ *vi* [perh. alter. of *curvet*] (1794) **1** : PRANCE **2** : to engage in extravagant behavior

ca·vy \'kā-vē\ *n, pl* **cavies** [NL *Cavia*, genus name, fr. obs. Pg *çavía* (now *savía*), fr. Tupi *sawiya* rat] (1796) : any of several short-tailed rough-haired So. American rodents (family Caviidae); *esp* : GUINEA PIG

caw \'kȯ\ *vi* [imit.] (1589) : to utter the harsh raucous natural call of the crow or a similar cry — **caw** *n*

cay \'kē, 'kā\ *n* [Sp *cayo* — more at KEY] (1707) : a low island or reef of sand or coral

cay·enne pepper \(,)kī-'en-, (,)kā-; 'kī-, 'kā-,\ *n* [by folk etymology fr. earlier *cayan*, modif. of Tupi *kyinha*] (1756) **1** : a pungent condiment consisting of the ground dried fruits or seeds of hot peppers **2** : HOT PEPPER; *esp* : a cultivated pepper with very long twisted pungent red fruits **3** : the fruit of a cayenne pepper

cay·man *var of* CAIMAN

Ca·yu·ga \kā-'yü-gə, kī-\ *n, pl* **Cayuga** *or* **Cayugas** (1744) **1** : a member of an American Indian people of New York **2** : the Iroquoian language of the Cayuga people

Cay·use \'kī-,yüs, kī-'\ *n, pl* **Cayuse** *or* **Cayuses** (1825) **1** : a member of an American Indian people of Oregon and Washington **2** *pl cayuses, not cap, West* : a native range horse

CB \'sē-'bē\ *n* (1959) : CITIZENS BAND; *also* : the radio transmitting and receiving set used for citizens-band communications

CBer \(,)sē-'bē-ər, -'bir\ *n* (1959) : one that operates a CB radio

CCD \,sē-(,)sē-'dē\ *n* (1973) : CHARGE-COUPLED DEVICE

C–clamp \'sē-,klamp\ *n* (1926) : a C-shaped general-purpose clamp

C clef *n* (1596) : a movable clef indicating middle C by its placement on one of the lines of the staff

CD \,sē-'dē\ *n* (1979) : COMPACT DISC

CD4 \,sē-(,)dē-'fȯr, -'fȯr\ *n* [cluster of differentiation] (1985) : a large glycoprotein that is found on the surface of T4 cells and is the receptor for HIV

cDNA \'sē-,dē-(,)en-'ā, ,sē-\ *n* [complementary] (1973) : a strand of DNA that is complementary to a given messenger RNA and that serves as a template for production of the messenger RNA in the presence of reverse transcriptase

CD–ROM \,sē-,dē-'räm\ *n* [compact disc read-only memory] (1983) : a compact disc containing data that can be read by a computer

ce·a·no·thus \,sē-ə-'nō-thəs\ *n* [NL, fr. Gk *keanōthos*, a thistle] (1785) : any of a genus (*Ceanothus*) of American vines, shrubs, and small trees of the buckthorn family having the calyx disk adherent to the ovary

¹cease \'sēs\ *vb* **ceased; ceas·ing** [ME *cesen*, fr. MF *cesser*, fr. L *cessare* to hold back, be remiss, freq. of *cedere*] *vt* (14c) : to cause to come to an end esp. gradually : no longer continue ~ *vi* **1 a** : to come to an end **b** : to bring an activity or action to an end : DISCONTINUE **2** *obs* : to become extinct : DIE OUT *syn* see STOP

²cease *n* (14c) : CESSATION — usu. used with *without*

cease and desist order *n* (1926) : an order from an administrative agency to refrain from a method of competition or a labor practice found by the agency to be unfair

cease–fire \'sēs-'fīr\ *n* (1859) **1** : a military order to cease firing **2** : a suspension of active hostilities

cease·less \'sēs-ləs\ *adj* (1586) : continuing without cease : CONSTANT — **cease·less·ly** *adv* — **cease·less·ness** *n*

ce·cro·pia moth \si-'krō-pē-ə-\ *n* [NL *cecropia*, fr. L, fem. of *Cecropius* Athenian, fr. Gk *Kekropios*, fr. *Kekrops* Cecrops, legendary king of

Athens] (1885) : a large No. American saturniid moth (*Hyalophora cecropia*) that is brown with red, white, and black markings

ce·cum \'sē-kəm\ *n, pl* **ce·ca** \-kə\ [NL, fr. L *intestinum caecum*, lit., blind intestine] (ca. 1721) : a cavity open at one end (as the blind end of a duct); *esp* : the blind pouch at the beginning of the large intestine into which the ileum opens from one side and which is continuous with the colon — **ce·cal** \-kəl\ *adj* — **ce·cal·ly** \-kə-lē\ *adv*

ce·dar \'sē-dər\ *n* [ME *cedre*, fr. OF, fr. L *cedrus*, fr. Gk *kedros*] (14c) **1 a** : any of a genus (*Cedrus*) of usu. tall coniferous trees (as the cedar of Lebanon or the deodar) of the pine family noted for their fragrant durable wood **b** : any of numerous coniferous trees (as of the genera *Juniperus, Chamaecyparis,* or *Thuja*) that resemble the true cedars esp. in the fragrance and durability of their wood **2** : the wood of a cedar

ce·dar–ap·ple rust \'sē-dər-'a-pəl-\ *n* (1946) : a gall-producing disease esp. of the apple caused by a rust fungus (*Gymnosporangium juniperi-virginianae*) that completes the first part of its life cycle on the common red cedar (*Juniperus virginiana*) and the second on the leaves and fruit of the apple

ce·dar·bird \-,bərd\ *n* (1883) : CEDAR WAXWING

ce·darn \'sē-dərn\ *adj* (1634) *archaic* : made or suggestive of cedar

cedar of Leb·a·non \-'leb-nən, -'le-bə-, -nən\ *n* (14c) : a long-lived cedar (*Cedrus libani*) native to Asia Minor with short fascicled leaves and erect cones

cedar waxwing *n* (ca. 1844) : a brown gregarious American waxwing (*Bombycilla cedrorum*) with a yellow band on the tip of the tail and a pale yellow belly

ce·dar·wood \'sē-dər-,wùd\ *n* (14c) : the wood of a cedar that is esp. repellent to insects

cede \'sēd\ *vt* **ced·ed; ced·ing** [F or L; F *céder*, fr. L *cedere* to go, withdraw, yield] (1754) **1** : to yield or grant typically by treaty **2** : ASSIGN, TRANSFER — **ced·er** *n*

ce·di \'sā-dē\ *n* [Twi *sedi* cowry] (1965) — see MONEY table

ce·dil·la \si-'di-lə\ *n* [Sp, the obs. letter ç (actually a medieval form of the letter z), cedilla, fr. dim. of *ceda, zeda* the letter z, fr. LL *zeta* — more at ZED] (1599) : the diacritical mark . placed under a letter (as ç in French) to indicate an alteration or modification of its usual phonetic value (as in the French word *façade*)

cee \'sē\ *n* (1542) : the letter c

cei·ba \'sā-bə\ *n* [Sp] (1790) **1** : a massive tropical tree (*Ceiba pentandra*) of the silk-cotton family with large pods filled with seeds invested with a silky floss that yields the fiber kapok **2** : KAPOK

ceil \'sē(ə)l\ *vt* [ME *celen*, fr. ML *celare, caelare,* perh. fr. L *caelare* to carve, fr. *caelum* chisel; akin to L *caedere* to cut] (15c) **1** : to furnish (as a wooden ship) with a lining **2** : to furnish with a ceiling

ceil·ing \'sē-liŋ\ *n* [ME *celing,* fr. *celen*] (1535) **1 a** : the overhead inside lining of a room **b** : material used to ceil a wall or roof of a room **2** : something thought of as an overhanging shelter or a lofty canopy ⟨a ~ of stars⟩ **3 a** : the height above the ground from which prominent objects on the ground can be seen and identified **b** : the height above the ground of the base of the lowest layer of clouds when over half of the sky is obscured **4 a** : ABSOLUTE CEILING **b** : SERVICE CEILING **5** : an upper usu. prescribed limit ⟨a ~ on prices, rents, and wages⟩ — **ceil·inged** \-liŋd\ *adj*

ceil·om·e·ter \sē-'lä-mə-tər\ *n* [*ceiling* + *-o-* + *-meter*] (1943) : a photoelectric instrument for determining by triangulation the height of the cloud ceiling above the earth

cein·ture \sa⁽ⁿ⁾-'tyür, -'tür, 'san-chər\ *n* [ME *seynture,* fr. MF *cein-ture,* fr. L *cinctura* — more at CINCTURE] (15c) : a belt or sash for the waist

cel *also* **cell** \'sel\ *n* [short for *celluloid*] (1938) : a transparent sheet of celluloid on which objects are drawn or painted in the making of animated cartoons

cel·a·don \'se-lə-,dän, -lə-d'n\ *n* [F *céladon*] (ca. 1768) **1** : a grayish yellow green **2** : a ceramic glaze originated in China that is greenish in color; *also* : an article with a celadon glaze

cel·an·dine \'se-lən-,dīn, -,dēn\ *n* [ME *celidoine,* fr. MF, fr. L *chelidonia,* fr. fem. of *chelidonius* of the swallow, fr. Gk *chelidonios,* fr. *chelidon-, chelidōn* swallow] (12c) **1** : a yellow-flowered Eurasian biennial herb (*Chelidonium majus*) of the poppy family naturalized in the eastern U.S. **2** : LESSER CELANDINE

-cele *n comb form* [MF, fr. L, fr. Gk *kēlē*; akin to OE *hēala* hernia] : tumor : hernia ⟨varicocele⟩

ce·leb \sə-'leb\ *n* (ca. 1912) : CELEBRITY 2

cel·e·brant \'se-lə-brənt\ *n* (1839) : one who celebrates; *specif* : the priest officiating at the Eucharist

cel·e·brate \'se-lə-,brāt\ *vb* **-brat·ed; -brat·ing** [L *celebratus,* pp. of *celebrare* to frequent, celebrate, fr. *celebr-, celeber* much frequented, famous; perh. akin to L *celer*] *vt* (15c) **1** : to perform (a sacrament or solemn ceremony) publicly and with appropriate rites ⟨~ the mass⟩ **2 a** : to honor (as a holiday) by solemn ceremonies or by refraining from ordinary business **b** : to mark (as an anniversary) by festivities or other deviation from routine **3** : to hold up or play up for public notice ⟨her poetry ~s the glory of nature⟩ ~ *vi* **1** : to observe a holiday, perform a religious ceremony, or take part in a festival **2** : to observe a notable occasion with festivities *syn* see KEEP — **cel·e·bra·tion** \,se-lə-'brā-shən\ *n* — **cel·e·bra·tor** \'se-lə-,brā-tər\ *n* — **cel·e·bra·to·ry** \,se-lə-,tōr-ē, -,tȯr-; ,se-lə-'brā-\ *adj*

cel·e·brat·ed *adj* (ca. 1669) : widely known and often referred to *syn* see FAMOUS — **cel·e·brat·ed·ness** *n*

ce·leb·ri·ty \sə-'le-brə-tē\ *n, pl* **-ties** (14c) **1** : the state of being celebrated **2** : a celebrated person

ce·le·ri·ac \sə-'ler-ē-,ak, -'lir-\ *n* [irreg. fr. *celery*] (1743) : a celery (*Apium graveolens rapaceum*) grown for its knobby edible root — called *also celery root*

ce·ler·i·ty \sə-'ler-ə-tē\ *n* [ME *celerite,* fr. MF, fr. L *celeritat-, celeritas,* fr. *celer* swift — more at HOLD] (15c) : rapidity of motion or action

cel·ery \'se-lə-rē, 'sel-rē\ *n, pl* **-er·ies** [obs. F *celeris,* fr. It dial. *seleri,* pl.

\ə\ abut \ᵊ\ kitten, F table \ər\ further \a\ ash \ā\ ace \ä\ mop, mar \aᴜ\ out \ch\ chin \e\ bet \ē\ easy \g\ go \i\ hit \ī\ ice \j\ job \ŋ\ sing \ō\ go \ȯ\ law \ȯi\ boy \th\ thin \t̲h̲\ the \ü\ loot \ᴜ\ foot \y\ yet \zh\ vision \ȧ, k̲, ⁿ, œ, ᴇ̄, ᵫ, ᵫ̄, ᵊ\ *see* Guide to Pronunciation of *selero,* modif. of LL *selinon,* fr. Gk] (1664) : a European herb (*Apium graveolens*) of the carrot family; *specif* : one of a cultivated variety (*A. graveolens dulce*) with leafstalks eaten raw or cooked

celery cabbage *n* (1930) : CHINESE CABBAGE b

ce·les·ta \sə-'les-tə, chə-\ *or* **ce·leste** \sə-'lest, chə-\ *n* [F *célesta,* alter. of *céleste,* lit., heavenly, fr. L *caelestis*] (1899) : a keyboard instrument with hammers that strike steel plates producing a tone similar to that of a glockenspiel

¹ce·les·tial \sə-'les-chəl, -'lesh-, -'les-tē-əl\ *adj* [ME, fr. MF, fr. L *caelestis* celestial, fr. *caelum* sky] (14c) **1** : of, relating to, or suggesting heaven or divinity **2** : of or relating to the sky or visible heavens 〈the sun, moon, and stars are ~ bodies〉 **3 a** : ETHEREAL, OTHERWORLDLY **b** : OLYMPIAN, SUPREME **4** *cap* [*Celestial* Empire, old name for China] : of or relating to China or the Chinese — **ce·les·tial·ly** \-chə-lē, -tē-ə-lē\ *adv*

²celestial *n* (1573) **1** : a heavenly or mythical being **2** *cap* : CHINESE 1a

celestial equator *n* (1875) : the great circle on the celestial sphere midway between the celestial poles

celestial globe *n* (ca. 1771) : a globe depicting the celestial bodies

celestial hierarchy *n* (1883) : a traditional hierarchy of angels ranked from lowest to highest into the following nine orders: angels, archangels, principalities, powers, virtues, dominions, thrones, cherubim, and seraphim

celestial marriage *n* (1919) : a special order of Mormon marriage solemnized in a Mormon temple and held to be binding for a future life as well as the present one

celestial navigation *n* (1939) : navigation by observation of the positions of celestial bodies

celestial pole *n* (1868) : either of the two points on the celestial sphere around which the diurnal rotation of the stars appears to take place

celestial sphere *n* (1879) : an imaginary sphere of infinite radius against which the celestial bodies appear to be projected and of which the apparent dome of the visible sky forms half

ce·les·tite \'se-ləs-ˌtīt, sə-'les-ˌtīt\ *n* [G *Zölestin,* fr. L *caelestis*] (1854) : a usu. white mineral consisting of the sulfate of strontium

ce·li·ac \'sē-lē-ˌak\ *adj* [L *coeliacus,* fr. Gk *koiliakos,* fr. *koilia* cavity, fr. *koilos* hollow — more at CAVE] (1662) : of or relating to the abdominal cavity

celiac disease *n* (1911) : a chronic nutritional disorder esp. in young children that is characterized by defective digestion and utilization of fats and often by abdominal distention, diarrhea, and fatty stools

cel·i·ba·cy \'se-lə-bə-sē\ *n* (1663) **1** : the state of not being married **2 a** : abstention from sexual intercourse **b** : abstention by vow from marriage

cel·i·bate \'se-lə-bət\ *n* [L *caelibatus,* fr. *caelib-, caelebs* unmarried] (ca. 1847) : a person who lives in celibacy — **celibate** *adj*

cell \'sel\ *n* [ME, fr. OE, religious house and OF *celle* hermit's cell, fr. L *cella* small room; akin to L *celare* to conceal — more at HELL] (12c) **1** : a small religious house dependent on a monastery or convent **2 a** : a one-room dwelling occupied by a solitary person (as a hermit) **b** : a single room (as in a convent or prison) usu. for one person **3** : a small compartment, cavity, or bounded space: as **a** : one of the compartments of a honeycomb **b** : a membranous area bounded by veins in the wing of an insect **4** : a small usu. microscopic mass of protoplasm bounded externally by a semipermeable membrane, usu. including one or more nuclei and various other organelles with their products, capable alone or interacting with other cells of performing all the fundamental functions of life, and forming the smallest structural unit of living matter capable of functioning independently **5 a** (1) : a receptacle (as a cup or jar) containing electrodes and an electrolyte either for generating electricity by chemical action or for use in electrolysis (2) : FUEL CELL **b** : a single unit in a device for converting radiant energy into electrical energy or for varying the intensity of an electrical current in accordance with radiation **6** : a unit in a statistical array (as a spreadsheet) formed by the intersection of a column and a row **7** : the basic and usu. smallest unit of an organization or movement 〈a communist ~〉 **8** : a portion of the atmosphere that behaves as a unit **9** : any of the small sections of a geographic area of a cellular telephone system

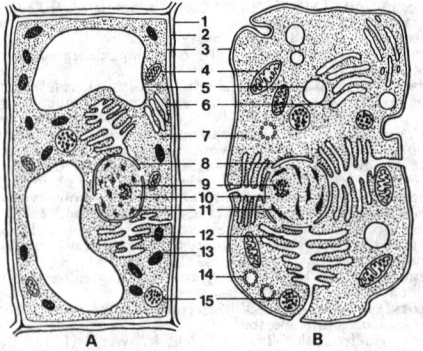

cell 4 (schematic): *A* plant, *B* animal; *1* cell wall, *2* middle lamella, *3* plasma membrane, *4* mitochondrion, *5* vacuole, *6* Golgi apparatus, *7* cytoplasm, *8* nuclear membrane, *9* nucleolus, *10* nucleus, *11* chromatin, *12* endoplasmic reticulum with associated ribosomes, *13* chloroplast, *14* centriole, *15* lysosome

¹cel·lar \'se-lər\ *n* [ME *celer,* fr. AF, fr. L *cellarium* storeroom, fr. *cella*] (13c) **1 a** : BASEMENT; *also* : a covered excavation **b** : the lowest grade or rank; *esp* : the lowest place in the standings (as of an athletic league) **2** : a stock of wines

²cellar *vt* (1677) : to put into a cellar (as for storage)

cel·lar·age \'se-lə-rij\ *n* (1602) : cellar space esp. for storage

cel·lar·er \'se-lər-ər\ *n* [ME *celerer,* fr. OF, fr. LL *cellariarius,* fr. L *cellarium*] (13c) : an official (as in a monastery) in charge of provisions

cel·lar·ette *or* **cel·lar·et** \ˌse-lə-'ret\ *n* (ca. 1807) : a case or sideboard for holding bottles of wine or liquor

cell body *n* (1878) : the nucleus-containing central part of a neuron exclusive of its axons and dendrites — see NEURON illustration

cell cycle *n* (1961) : the complete series of events from one cell division to the next — compare G₁ PHASE, G₂ PHASE, M PHASE, S PHASE

cell division *n* (1882) : the process by which cells multiply involving both nuclear and cytoplasmic division — compare MEIOSIS, MITOSIS

celled \'seld\ *adj* : having (such or so many) cells — used in combination 〈single-*celled* organisms〉

cell-me·di·at·ed \'sel-'mē-dē-ˌā-təd\ *adj* (1967) : relating to or being the part of immunity or the immune response that is mediated primarily by T cells

cell membrane *n* (1870) : PLASMA MEMBRANE

cel·lo \'che-(ˌ)lō\ *n, pl* **cello** *also* **cel·li** \-lē\ [short for *violoncello*] (ca. 1876) : the bass member of the violin family tuned an octave below the viola — **cel·list** \'che-list\ *n*

cel·lo·bi·ose \ˌse-lə-'bī-ˌōs, -ˌōz\ *n* [ISV *cellu*lose + *-o-* + *biose* disaccharide, fr. ¹*bi-* + ²*-ose*] (1902) : a faintly sweet disaccharide $C_{12}H_{22}O_{11}$ obtained by partial hydrolysis of cellulose

cel·loi·din \se-'lȯi-dᵊn\ *n* [*cellu*lose + ¹*-oid* + ¹*-in*] (1883) : a purified pyroxylin used chiefly in microscopy

cel·lo·phane \'se-lə-ˌfān\ *n* [F, fr. *cellu*lose + *-phane* (as in *diaphane* diaphanous), fr. ML *diaphanus*] (1912) : regenerated cellulose in thin transparent sheets used esp. for packaging

cell plate *n* (1882) : a disk formed in the phragmoplast of a dividing plant cell that eventually forms the middle lamella of the wall between the daughter cells

cell sap *n* (ca. 1889) **1** : the liquid contents of a plant cell vacuole **2** : CYTOSOL

cell theory *n* (ca. 1890) : a theory in biology that includes one or both of the statements that the cell is the fundamental structural and functional unit of living matter and that the organism is composed of autonomous cells with all its properties being the sum of those of its cells

cel·lu·lar \'sel-yə-lər\ *adj* [NL *cellularis,* fr. *cellula* living cell, fr. L, dim. of *cella* small room] (ca. 1739) **1** : of, relating to, or consisting of cells **2** : containing cavities : having a porous texture 〈~ rocks〉 **3** : of, relating to, or being a radiotelephone system in which a geographical area (as a city) is divided into small sections each served by a transmitter of limited range so that any available radio channel can be used in different parts of the area simultaneously — **cel·lu·lar·i·ty** \ˌsel-yə-'lar-ə-tē\ *n*

cel·lu·lase \'sel-yə-ˌlās, -ˌlāz\ *n* [ISV] (1903) : an enzyme that hydrolyzes cellulose

cel·lule \'sel-(ˌ)yü(ə)l\ *n* [L *cellula*] (ca. 1693) : a small cell

cel·lu·lite \'sel-yə-ˌlīt, -ˌlēt\ *n* [F, lit., accumulation of subcutaneous fat, cellulitis, fr. *cellule* cell + *-ite* -itis] (1968) : lumpy fat found in the thighs, hips, and buttocks of some women

cel·lu·li·tis \ˌsel-yə-'lī-təs\ *n* [NL, fr. *cellula*] (1861) : diffuse and esp. subcutaneous inflammation of connective tissue

cel·lu·loid \'sel-yə-ˌlȯid\ *n* [fr. *Celluloid,* a trademark] (1871) **1** : a tough flammable thermoplastic composed essentially of cellulose nitrate and camphor **2** : a motion-picture film 〈a work . . . making its third appearance on ~ —John McCarten〉 — **celluloid** *adj*

cel·lu·lo·lyt·ic \ˌsel-yə-lō-'li-tik\ *adj* [*cellu*lose + *-o-* + *-lytic*] (1943) : hydrolyzing or having the capacity to hydrolyze cellulose

cel·lu·lose \'sel-yə-ˌlōs, -ˌlōz\ *n* [F, fr. *cellule* living cell, fr. NL *cellula*] (1848) : a polysaccharide $(C_6H_{10}O_5)_x$ of glucose units that constitutes the chief part of the cell walls of plants, occurs naturally in such fibrous products as cotton and kapok, and is the raw material of many manufactured goods (as paper, rayon, and cellophane)

cellulose acetate *n* (1895) : any of several compounds insoluble in water that are formed esp. by the action of acetic acid, anhydride of acetic acid, and sulfuric acid on cellulose and are used for making textile fibers, packaging sheets, photographic films, and varnishes

cellulose nitrate *n* (1880) : NITROCELLULOSE

cel·lu·los·ic \ˌsel-yə-'lō-sik, -zik\ *adj* (1881) : of, relating to, or made from cellulose — **cellulosic** *n*

cell wall *n* (ca. 1849) : the usu. rigid nonliving permeable wall that surrounds the plasma membrane and encloses and supports the cells of most plants, bacteria, fungi, and algae — see CELL illustration

Cel·si·us \'sel-sē-əs, -shəs\ *adj* [Anders *Celsius*] (ca. 1850) : relating to, conforming to, or having the international thermometric scale on which the interval between the triple point of water and the boiling point of water is divided into 99.99 degrees with 0.01° representing the triple point and 100° the boiling point 〈10° ~〉 — abbr. C; compare CENTIGRADE

celt \'selt\ *n* [LL *celtis* chisel] (1715) : a prehistoric stone or metal implement shaped like a chisel or ax head

Celt \'kelt, 'selt\ *n* [L *Celtae,* pl., fr. Gk *Keltoi*] (1550) **1** : a member of a division of the early Indo-European peoples distributed from the British Isles and Spain to Asia Minor **2** : a modern Gael, Highland Scot, Irishman, Welshman, Cornishman, or Breton

¹Celt·ic \'kel-tik, 'sel-\ *adj* (1590) : of, relating to, or characteristic of the Celts or their languages

²Celtic *n* (1739) : a group of Indo-European languages usu. subdivided into Brythonic and Goidelic and now largely confined to Brittany, Wales, western Ireland, and the Scottish Highlands — see INDO-EUROPEAN LANGUAGES table

Celtic cross *n* (1873) : a cross having essentially the form of a Latin cross with a ring about the intersection of the crossbar and upright shaft — see CROSS illustration

Celt·i·cist \'kel-tə-sist, 'sel-\ *n* (1912) : a specialist in Celtic languages or cultures

cem·ba·lo \'chem-bə-ˌlō\ *n, pl* **-ba·li** \-(ˌ)lē\ *or* **-balos** [It] (ca. 1801) : HARPSICHORD

¹ce·ment \si-'ment *also* 'sē-ment\ *n* [ME *sement,* fr. MF *ciment,* fr. L *caementum* stone chips used in making mortar, fr. *caedere* to cut] (14c) **1 a** : a powder of alumina, silica, lime, iron oxide, and magnesium oxide burned together in a kiln and finely pulverized and used as an ingredient of mortar and concrete; *also* : any mixture used for a similar purpose **b** : CONCRETE 2 : a binding element or agency: as **a** : a substance to make objects adhere to each other **b** : something serving to unite firmly ⟨justice is the ~ that holds a political community together —R. M. Hutchins⟩ 3 : CEMENTUM 4 : a plastic composition made esp. of zinc or silica for filling dental cavities 5 : the fine= grained groundmass or glass of a porphyry

²**cement** *vt* (14c) 1 : to unite or make firm by or as if by cement 2 : to overlay with concrete ~ *vi* : to become cemented — **ce·ment·er** *n*

ce·men·ta·tion \ˌsē-ˌmen-'tā-shən\ *n* (1594) 1 : a process of surrounding a solid with a powder and heating the whole so that the solid is changed by chemical combination with the powder 2 : the act or process of cementing : the state of being cemented

ce·ment·ite \si-'men-ˌtīt\ *n* [¹*cement*] (1888) : a hard brittle iron carbide Fe₃C that occurs in steel, cast iron, and iron-carbon alloys

ce·men·ti·tious \ˌsē-ˌmen-'ti-shəs\ *adj* (ca. 1828) : having the properties of cement

ce·men·tum \si-'men-təm\ *n* [NL, fr. L *caementum*] (1842) : a specialized external bony layer covering the dentin of the part of a tooth normally within the gum — see TOOTH illustration

cem·e·tery \'se-mə-ˌter-ē\ *n, pl* **-ter·ies** [ME *cimitery*, fr. MF *cimitere*, fr. LL *coemeterium*, fr. Gk *koimētērion* sleeping chamber, burial place, fr. *koiman* to put to sleep; akin to Gk *keisthai* to lie, Skt *śete* he lies] (15c) : a burial ground

cen·a·cle \'se-ni-kəl\ *n* [LL *cenaculum* the room where Christ and his disciples had the Last Supper, fr. L, top story, prob. fr. *cena* dinner] (1889) : a retreat house; *esp* : one for Roman Catholic women directed by nuns of the Society of Our Lady of the Cenacle

-cene *adj comb form* [Gk *kainos* new, recent — more at RECENT] : recent — in names of geologic periods ⟨*Eocene*⟩

cen·o·bite \'se-nə-ˌbit, *esp Brit* 'sē-\ *n* [LL *coenobita*, fr. *coenobium* monastery, fr. LGk *koinobion*, ultim. fr. Gk *koin-* coen- + *bios* life — more at QUICK] (ca. 1500) : a member of a religious group living together in a monastic community — **cen·o·bit·ic** \ˌse-nə-'bi-tik, ˌsē-\ *adj*

ce·no·spe·cies \'sē-nə-ˌspē-(ˌ)shēz, 'se-, -(ˌ)sēz\ *n* [*coen-* + *species*] (1922) : a group of related biological taxonomic units capable by reason of closely related genotypes of essentially free gene interchange

ceno·taph \'se-nə-ˌtaf, -ˌtäf\ *n* [F *cénotaphe*, fr. L *cenotaphium*, fr. Gk *kenotaphion*, fr. *kenos* empty + *taphos* tomb] (1603) : a tomb or a monument erected in honor of a person or group of persons whose remains are elsewhere

ce·no·te \si-'nō-tē\ *n* [MexSp, fr. Yucatec *ts'onot*] (1841) : a deep sinkhole in limestone with a pool at the bottom that is found esp. in Yucatán

Ce·no·zo·ic \ˌsē-nə-'zō-ik, ˌse-\ *adj* [Gk *kainos* + E *-zoic*] (1854) : of, relating to, or being an era of geological history that extends from the beginning of the Tertiary period to the present time and is marked by a rapid evolution of mammals and birds and of angiosperms and esp. grasses and by little change in the invertebrates — see GEOLOGIC TIME table — **Cenozoic** *n*

cense \'sen(t)s\ *vt* **censed; cens·ing** [ME, prob. short for *encensen* to incense, fr. MF *encenser*, fr. LL *incensare*, fr. *incensum* incense] (14c) : to perfume esp. with incense

cen·ser \'sen(t)-sər\ *n* (13c) : a vessel for burning incense; *esp* : a covered incense burner swung on chains in a religious ritual

¹**cen·sor** \'sen(t)-sər\ *n* [L, fr. *censēre* to give as one's opinion, assess; perh. akin to Skt *śaṃsati* he praises] (1531) 1 : one of two magistrates of early Rome acting as census takers, assessors, and inspectors of morals and conduct 2 : one who supervises conduct and morals: as **a** : an official who examines materials (as publications or films) for objectionable matter **b** : an official (as in time of war) who reads communications (as letters) and deletes material considered sensitive or harmful 3 : a hypothetical psychic agency that represses unacceptable notions before they reach consciousness — **cen·so·ri·al** \sen-'sōr-ē-əl, -'sȯr-\ *adj*

²**censor** *vt* **cen·sored; cen·sor·ing** \'sen(t)-sə-riŋ, 'sen(t)s-riŋ\ (1882) : to examine in order to suppress or delete anything considered objectionable

cen·so·ri·ous \sen-'sōr-ē-əs, -'sȯr-\ *adj* [L *censorius* of a censor, fr. *censor*] (1536) : marked by or given to censure **syn** see CRITICAL — **cen·so·ri·ous·ly** *adv* — **cen·so·ri·ous·ness** *n*

cen·sor·ship \'sen(t)-sər-ˌship\ *n* (ca. 1591) 1 **a** : the institution, system, or practice of censoring **b** : the actions or practices of censors; *esp* : censorial control exercised repressively 2 : the office, power, or term of a Roman censor 3 : exclusion from consciousness by the psychic censor

cen·sur·able \'sen(t)-sh(ə-)rə-bəl\ *adj* (1634) : deserving or open to censure

¹**cen·sure** \'sen(t)-shər\ *n* [L *censura*, fr. *censēre*] (14c) 1 : a judgment involving condemnation 2 *archaic* : OPINION, JUDGMENT 3 : the act of blaming or condemning sternly 4 : an official reprimand

²**censure** *vt* **cen·sured; cen·sur·ing** \'sen(t)-sh(ə-)riŋ\ (1587) 1 *obs* : ESTIMATE, JUDGE 2 : to find fault with and criticize as blameworthy **syn** see CRITICIZE — **cen·sur·er** \'sen(t)-shər-ər\ *n*

cen·sus \'sen(t)-səs\ *n* [L, fr. *censēre*] (1634) 1 : a count of the population and a property evaluation in early Rome 2 : a usu. complete enumeration of a population; *specif* : a periodic governmental enumeration of population 3 : COUNT, TALLY — **census** *vt*

cent \'sent\ *n* [MF, hundred, fr. L *centum* — more at HUNDRED] (1782) 1 : a monetary unit equal to ¹/₁₀₀ of a basic unit of value — see *birr, dollar, gulden, leone, lilangeni, lira, pound, rand, rupee, shilling* at MONEY table 2 : a coin, token, or note representing one cent 3 : the fen of the People's Republic of China

cen·tal \'sen-t³l\ *n* [L *centum* + E *-al* (as in *quintal*)] (1870) *chiefly Brit* : HUNDREDWEIGHT 1

censer

cen·taur \'sen-ˌtȯr\ *n* [ME, fr. L *Centaurus*, fr. Gk *Kentauros*] (14c) : any of a race of creatures fabled to be half man and half horse and to live in the mountains of Thessaly

cen·tau·rea \sen-'tȯr-ē-ə\ *n* [NL, genus name, fr. ML] (ca. 1829) : any of a large genus (*Centaurea*) of composite herbs (as knapweed) including several cultivated for their showy heads of tubular florets

Cen·tau·rus \-'tȯr-əs\ *n* [L (gen. *Centauri*)] : a southern constellation between the Southern Cross and Hydra

cen·tau·ry \'sen-ˌtȯr-ē\ *n, pl* **-ries** [ME *centaure*, fr. MF *centaurée*, fr. ML *centaurea*, fr. L *centaureum*, fr. Gk *kentaureion*, fr. *Kentauros*] (14c) 1 : any of a genus (*Centaurium*) of low herbs of the gentian family; *esp* : an Old World herb (*C. umbellatum*) formerly used as a tonic 2 : an herb (*Sabatia angularis*) of the eastern U.S. closely related to centaury

¹**cen·ta·vo** \sen-'tä-(ˌ)vō\ *n, pl* **-vos** [Sp, lit., hundredth, fr. *ciento* hundred, fr. L *centum*] (1883) — see *boliviano, colón, cordoba, lempira, peso, quetzal, sol, sucre* at MONEY table

²**cen·ta·vo** \-'tä-(ˌ)vü, -(ˌ)vō\ *n, pl* **-vos** [Pg, fr. Sp] (1920) — see *escudo, metical* at MONEY table

cen·te·nar·i·an \ˌsen-tə-'ner-ē-ən\ *n* (ca. 1841) : one that is 100 years old or older — **centenarian** *adj*

cen·te·na·ry \sen-'te-nə-rē, 'sen-tə-ˌner-ē, *esp Brit* sen-'tē-nə-rē\ *n, pl* **-ries** [LL *centenarium*, fr. L *centenarius* of a hundred, fr. *centeni* one hundred each, fr. *centum* hundred — more at HUNDRED] (1788) : CENTENNIAL — **centenary** *adj*

cen·ten·ni·al \sen-'te-nē-əl\ *n* [L *centum* + E *-ennial* (as in *biennial*)] (1876) : a 100th anniversary or its celebration — **centennial** *adj* — **cen·ten·ni·al·ly** \-ə-lē\ *adv*

¹**cen·ter** \'sen-tər, 'se-nər\ *n* [ME *centre*, fr. MF, fr. L *centrum*, fr. Gk *kentron* sharp point, center of a circle, fr. *kentein* to prick; prob. akin to OHG *hantag* pointed] (14c) 1 **a** : the point around which a circle or sphere is described; *broadly* : a point that is related to a geometrical figure in such a way that for any point on the figure there is another point on the figure such that a straight line joining the two points is bisected by the original point — called also *center of symmetry* **b** : the center of the circle inscribed in a regular polygon 2 **a** : a point, area, person, or thing that is most important or pivotal in relation to an indicated activity, interest, or condition ⟨a railroad ~⟩ ⟨the ~ of the controversy⟩ **b** : a source from which something originates ⟨a propaganda ~⟩ **c** : a group of nerve cells having a common function ⟨respiratory ~⟩ **d** : a region of concentrated population ⟨an urban ~⟩ **e** : a facility providing a place for a particular activity or service ⟨a day= care ~⟩ 3 **a** : the middle part (as of the forehead or a stage) **b** *often cap* (1) : a grouping of political figures holding moderate views esp. between those of conservatives and liberals (2) : the views of such politicians (3) : the adherents of such views 4 **a** : a player occupying a middle position on a team: as (1) : the football player in the middle of a line who passes the ball between his legs to a back to start a down (2) : the usu. tallest player on a basketball team who usu. plays near the basket **b** : CENTER FIELD 5 **a** : either of two tapered rods which support work in a lathe or grinding machine and about or with which the work revolves **b** : a conical recess in the end of work (as a shaft) for receiving such a center — **cen·ter·less** \-ləs\ *adj*

²**center** *vb* **cen·tered; cen·ter·ing** \'sen-t(ə-)riŋ, 'se-nər-iŋ\ *vt* (1610) 1 : to place or fix at or around a center or central area or position ⟨~ the picture on the wall⟩ 2 : to give a central focus or basis ⟨~s her hopes on her son⟩ ⟨the plot was ~ed on espionage⟩ 3 : to adjust (as lenses) so that the axes coincide 4 **a** : to pass (a ball or puck) from either side toward the middle of the playing area **b** : to hand or pass (a football) backward between one's legs to a back to start a down ~ *vi* : to have a specified center : FOCUS

usage The intransitive verb *center* is most commonly used with the prepositions *in, on, at,* and *around. At* appears to be favored in mathematical contexts; the others are found in a broad range of contexts. *Center around,* a standard idiom, has often been objected to as illogical. The logic on which the objections are based is irrelevant, since *center around* is an idiom and idioms have their own logic. *Center on* is currently more common in edited prose, and *revolve around* and similar verbs are available if you want to avoid *center around.*

cen·ter·board \'sen-tər-ˌbōrd, 'se-nər-, -ˌbȯrd\ *n* (1867) : a retractable keel used esp. in sailboats

cen·tered \'sen-tərd, 'se-nərd\ *adj* (ca. 1893) 1 : having a center — often used in combination ⟨a dark-*centered* coneflower⟩ 2 : having a center of curvature — often used in combination ⟨a 3-*centered* arch⟩ 3 : emotionally stable and secure — **cen·tered·ness** \-nəs\ *n*

center field *n* (1857) 1 : the position of the player for defending center field 2 : the part of the baseball outfield between right and left field — **center fielder** *n*

cen·ter·fold \'sen-tər-ˌfōld, 'se-nər-\ *n* (1952) 1 : a foldout that is the center spread of a magazine 2 : a picture (as of a nude) on a centerfold; *also* : a model featured in such a picture

cen·ter·line \-'līn, -ˌlīn\ *n* (1807) : a real or imaginary line that is equidistant from the surface or sides of something

center of curvature (ca. 1856) : the center of the circle whose center lies on the concave side of a curve on the normal to a given point of the curve and whose radius is equal to the radius of curvature at that point

center of gravity (1659) 1 : CENTER OF MASS 2 : the point at which the entire weight of a body may be considered as concentrated so that if supported at this point the body would remain in equilibrium in any position 3 : CENTER 2a

center of mass (1879) : the point in a body or system of bodies at which the whole mass may be considered as concentrated

cen·ter·piece \-ˌpēs\ *n* (1803) 1 : an object occupying a central position; *esp* : an adornment in the center of a table 2 : one that is of central importance or interest in a larger whole

---

\ə\ abut \ᵊ\ kitten, F table \ər\ further \a\ ash \ā\ ace \ä\ mop, mar \aủ\ out \ch\ chin \e\ bet \ē\ easy \g\ go \i\ hit \ī\ ice \j\ job \ŋ\ sing \ō\ go \ȯ\ law \ȯi\ boy \th\ thin \t̷h\ the \ü\ loot \ủ\ foot \y\ yet \zh\ vision \á, k̲, ⁿ, œ, œ̄, ŵ, ǖ, ᵞ\ *see* Guide to Pronunciation

center punch *n* (1879) : a hand punch consisting of a short steel bar with a hardened conical point at one end used for marking the centers of holes to be drilled

center stage *n* (1954)   **1** : the central part of a theatrical stage   **2** : a central or highly prominent position — **center stage** *adj or adv*

cen·tes·i·mal \sen-'te-sə-məl\ *adj* [L *centesimus* hundredth, fr. *centum*] (1809) : marked by or relating to division into hundredths

¹cen·tes·i·mo \chen-'te-zə-,mō\ *n, pl* -**mi** \-(,)mē\ [It] (1851) — see *lira* at MONEY table

²cen·tes·i·mo \sen-'te-sə-,mō\ *n, pl* -**mos** [Sp *centésimo*] (ca. 1883) — see *balboa, peso* at MONEY table

centi- *comb form* [F&L; F, hundredth, fr. L, hundred, fr. *centum* — more at HUNDRED]   **1** : hundred ⟨*centipede*⟩   **2** : hundredth part ⟨*centimeter*⟩

cen·ti·grade \'sen-tə-,grād, 'sän-\ *adj* [F, fr. L *centi*- hundred + F *grade*] (1801) : relating to, conforming to, or having a thermometric scale on which the interval between the freezing point of water and the boiling point of water is divided into 100 degrees with 0° representing the freezing point and 100° the boiling point ⟨10° ∼⟩ — abbr. *C*; compare CELSIUS

cen·ti·gram \-,gram\ *n* (1801) — see METRIC SYSTEM table

cen·ti·li·ter \-,sen-ti-,lē-tər, 'sän-\ *n* (1801) — see METRIC SYSTEM table

cen·til·lion \sen-'til-yən\ *n, often attrib* [L *centum* + E -*illion* (as in *million*)] (ca. 1889) — see NUMBER table

cen·time \'sän-,tēm, 'sen-\ *n* [F, fr. *cent* hundred, fr. L *centum*] (1801) — see *dinar, dirham, franc, gourde* at MONEY table

cen·ti·me·ter \'sen-tə-,mē-tər, 'sän-\ *n* (1801) — see METRIC SYSTEM table

centimeter–gram–second *adj* (1875) : of, relating to, or being a system of units based on the centimeter as the unit of length, the gram as the unit of mass, and the second as the unit of time — abbr. *cgs*

cen·ti·mo \'sen-tə-,mō\ *n, pl* -**mos** [Sp *céntimo*] (1899) — see *bolivar, colon, dobra, guarani, peseta* at MONEY table

cen·ti·mor·gan \'sen-tə-,mór-gən, 'sän-\ *n* (1919) : a genetic unit equivalent to ¹⁄₁₀₀ of a morgan

cen·ti·pede \'sen-tə-,pēd\ *n* [L *centipeda*, fr. *centi*- + *ped*-, *pes* foot — more at FOOT] (1601) : any of a class (Chilopoda) of long flattened many-segmented predaceous arthropods with each segment bearing one pair of legs of which the foremost pair is modified into poison fangs

cent·ner \'sent-nər\ *n* [prob. fr. LG] (1683) : any of various units of weight used esp. in Europe and usu. equal to about 110 pounds (about 50 kilograms)

cen·to \'sen-(,)tō\ *n, pl* **cen·to·nes** \sen-'tō-(,)nēz\ [LL, fr. L, patchwork garment; perh. akin to Skt *kanthā* patched garment] (1605) : a literary work made up of parts from other works

centr- *or* **centri-** *or* **centro-** *comb form* [Gk *kentr*-, *kentro*-, fr. *kentron* center — more at CENTER] : center ⟨*centri*fugal⟩ ⟨*centro*id⟩

centra *pl of* CENTRUM

¹cen·tral \'sen-trəl\ *adj* [L *centralis*, fr. *centrum* center] (1647)   **1** : containing or constituting a center   **2** : of cardinal importance : ESSENTIAL, PRINCIPAL ⟨the ∼ character of the novel⟩   **3   a** : situated at, in, or near the center   **b** : easily accessible from outlying districts ⟨a ∼ location for the new theater⟩   **4   a** : centrally placed and superseding separate scattered units ⟨∼ heating⟩   **b** : controlling or directing local or branch activities ⟨the ∼ committee⟩   **5** : holding to a middle between extremes : MODERATE   **6** : of, relating to, or comprising the brain and spinal cord; *also* : originating within the central nervous system ⟨∼ deafness⟩ — **cen·tral·ly** \-trə-lē\ *adv*

²central *n* (1889)   **1** : a telephone exchange or operator   **2** : a central office or bureau usu. controlling others ⟨weather ∼⟩

central angle *n* (1904) : an angle formed by two radii of a circle

central bank *n* (1922) : a national bank that operates to establish monetary and fiscal policy and to control the money supply and interest rate — **central banker** *n*

central casting *n* (1957) : the department of a movie studio responsible for casting actors — usu. used figuratively ⟨a politician right out of *central casting*⟩

central city *n* (1950) : a city that constitutes the densely populated center of a metropolitan area

cen·tral·ise *Brit var of* CENTRALIZE

cen·tral·ism \'sen-trə-,li-zəm\ *n* (1831) : the concentration of power and control in the central authority of an organization (as a political or educational system) — compare FEDERALISM — **cen·tral·ist** \-list\ *n or adj* — **cen·tral·is·tic** \,sen-trə-'lis-tik\ *adj*

cen·tral·i·ty \sen-'tra-lə-tē\ *n, pl* -**ties** (1647)   **1** : the quality or state of being central   **2** : central situation   **3** : tendency to remain in or at the center

cen·tral·ize \'sen-trə-,līz\ *vb* -**ized; -iz·ing** *vi* (1800) : to form a center : cluster around a center ∼ *vt*   **1** : to bring to a center : CONSOLIDATE ⟨∼ all the data in one file⟩   **2** : to concentrate by placing power and authority in a center or central organization — **cen·tral·i·za·tion** \,sen-trə-lə-'zā-shən\ *n* — **cen·tral·iz·er** \'sen-trə-,lī-zər\ *n*

central limit theorem *n* (1951) : any of several fundamental theorems of probability and statistics that state the conditions under which the distribution of a sum of independent random variables is approximated by the normal distribution; *esp* : one which is much applied in sampling and which states that the distribution of a mean of a sample from a population with finite variance is approximated by the normal distribution as the number in the sample becomes large

central nervous system *n* (ca. 1907) : the part of the nervous system which in vertebrates consists of the brain and spinal cord, to which sensory impulses are transmitted and from which motor impulses pass out, and which coordinates the activity of the entire nervous system — compare AUTONOMIC NERVOUS SYSTEM

central processing unit *n* (1961) : PROCESSOR 2a(2) — abbr. *cpu*

central tendency *n* (ca. 1928) : the degree of clustering of the values of a statistical distribution that is usu. measured by the arithmetic mean, mode, or median

central time *n, often cap C* (1883) : the time of the 6th time zone west of Greenwich that includes the central U.S. — see TIME ZONE illustration

cen·tre *chiefly Brit var of* CENTER

cen·tric \'sen-trik\ *adj* [Gk *kentrikos* of the center, fr. *kentron*] (ca. 1590)   **1** : located in or at a center : CENTRAL ⟨a ∼ point⟩   **2** : concentrated about or directed to a center ⟨a ∼ activity⟩   **3** : of, relating to, or having a centromere   **4** : of, relating to, or resembling an order (Centrales) of radially symmetrical diatoms — **cen·tri·cal·ly** \-tri-k(ə-)lē\ *adv* — **cen·tric·i·ty** \sen-'tri-sə-tē\ *n*

-centric *adj comb form* [ML -*centricus*, fr. L *centrum* center]   **1** : having (such) a center or (such or so many) centers ⟨poly*centric*⟩   **2** : having (something specified) as its center ⟨helio*centric*⟩

¹cen·trif·u·gal \sen-'tri-fyə-gəl, -'tri-fi-, *esp Brit* ,sen-tri-'fyü-gəl\ *adj* [NL *centrifugus*, fr. *centr*- + L *fugere* to flee — more at FUGITIVE] (ca. 1721)   **1** : proceeding or acting in a direction away from a center or axis   **2** : using or acting by centrifugal force ⟨a ∼ pump⟩   **3** : EFFERENT   **4** : tending away from centralization : SEPARATIST ⟨∼ tendencies in modern society⟩ — **cen·trif·u·gal·ly** \-gə-lē\ *adv*

²centrifugal *n* (1866) : a centrifugal machine or a drum in such a machine

centrifugal force *n* (ca. 1721)   **1** : the force that tends to impel a thing or parts of a thing outward from a center of rotation   **2** : the force that an object moving along a circular path exerts on the body constraining the object and that acts outwardly away from the center of rotation ⟨a stone whirled on a string exerts *centrifugal force* on the string⟩

cen·tri·fu·ga·tion \,sen-trə-fyü-'gä-shən, -f(y)ə-\ *n* (1903) : the process of centrifuging

¹cen·tri·fuge \'sen-trə-,fyüj\ *n* [F, fr. *centrifuge* centrifugal, fr. NL *centrifugus*] (1887) : a machine using centrifugal force for separating substances of different densities, for removing moisture, or for simulating gravitational effects

²centrifuge *vt* -**fuged; -fug·ing** (ca. 1895) : to subject to centrifugal action esp. in a centrifuge

cen·tri·ole \'sen-trē-,ōl\ *n* [G *Zentriol*, fr. *Zentrum* center] (ca. 1896) : one of a pair of cellular organelles that occur esp. in animals, are adjacent to the nucleus, function in the formation of the spindle apparatus during cell division, and consist of a cylinder with nine microtubules arranged peripherally in a circle — see CELL illustration

cen·trip·e·tal \sen-'tri-pə-t²l\ *adj* [NL *centripetus*, fr. *centr*- + L *petere* to go to, seek — more at FEATHER] (1709)   **1** : proceeding or acting in a direction toward a center or axis   **2** : AFFERENT   **3** : tending toward centralization : UNIFYING — **cen·trip·e·tal·ly** \-t²l-ē\ *adv*

centripetal force *n* (1709) : the force that is necessary to keep an object moving in a circular path and that is directed inward toward the center of rotation ⟨a string on the end of which a stone is whirled about exerts *centripetal force* on the stone⟩

cen·trist \'sen-trist\ *n* (1872)   **1** *often cap* : a member of a center party   **2** : one who holds moderate views — **cen·trism** \-,tri-zəm\ *n* — **centrist** *adj*

cen·troid \'sen-,tróid\ *n* (1882)   **1** : CENTER OF MASS   **2** : a point whose coordinates are the averages of the corresponding coordinates of a given set of points and which for a given planar or three-dimensional figure (as a triangle or sphere) corresponds to the center of mass of a thin plate of uniform thickness and consistency or a body of uniform consistency having the same boundary

cen·tro·mere \'sen-trə-,mir\ *n* [ISV] (ca. 1925) : the point or region on a chromosome to which the spindle attaches during mitosis and meiosis — **cen·tro·mer·ic** \,sen-trə-'mir-ik, -'mer-\ *adj*

cen·tro·some \'sen-trə-,sōm\ *n* [ISV] (1889)   **1** : CENTRIOLE   **2** : the centriole-containing region of clear cytoplasm adjacent to the cell nucleus

cen·tro·sym·met·ric \,sen-trə-sə-'me-trik\ *adj* (ca. 1909) : symmetric with respect to a central point ⟨∼ molecules⟩ ⟨a ∼ curve⟩

cen·trum \'sen-trəm\ *n, pl* **centrums** *or* **cen·tra** \-trə\ [L — more at CENTER] (1854)   **1** : CENTER   **2** : the body of a vertebra ventral to the neural arch

cen·tum \'ken-təm, -,tùm\ *adj* [L, hundred; fr. the fact that its initial sound (a velar stop) is the representative of an IE palatal stop — more at HUNDRED] (1901) : of, relating to, or constituting an Indo-European language group in which the palatal stops did not in prehistoric times become palatal or alveolar fricatives — compare SATEM

cen·tu·ri·on \sen-'chúr-ē-ən, -'tyùr-, -'tür-\ *n* [ME, fr. MF & L; MF, fr. L *centurion*-, *centurio*, fr. *centuria*] (13c) : an officer commanding a Roman century

cen·tu·ry \'sen(t)-sh(ə-)rē\ *n, pl* -**ries** [L *centuria*, irreg. fr. *centum* hundred] (1533)   **1** : a subdivision of the Roman legion   **2** : a group, sequence, or series of 100 like things   **3** : a period of 100 years esp. of the Christian era or of the preceding period of human history   **4** : a race over a hundred units (as yards or miles)

century plant *n* (1764) : a Mexican agave (*Agave americana*) that takes many years to mature, flowers only once, and then dies

CEO \,sē-(,)ē-'ō\ *n* [chief executive officer] (1975) : the executive with the chief decision-making authority in an organization or business

ceorl \'chä-,órl\ *n* [OE — more at CHURL] (bef. 12c) : a freeman of the lowest rank in Anglo-Saxon England

cèpe *or* **cepe** \'sep\ *n, pl* **cèpes** *or* **cepes** *also* **cèp** \'sep\ *n* [F, fr. Gascon *cep* tree trunk, mushroom, fr. L *cippus* stake, post] (1865) : a wild edible boletus mushroom (esp. *Boletus edulis*)

cephal- *or* **cephalo-** *comb form* [L, fr. Gk *kephal*-, *kephalo*-, fr. *kephalē*] : head ⟨*cephalo*pod⟩

ceph·a·lad \'se-fə-,lad\ *adv* (1887) : toward the head or anterior end of the body

ceph·a·lex·in \,se-fə-'lek-sən\ *n* [*cephalo*sporin + -*ex*- (of unknown origin) + ¹-*in*] (1967) : a semisynthetic cephalosporin $C_{16}H_{17}N_3O_4S$ with a spectrum of antibiotic activity similar to the penicillins

ce·phal·ic \sə-'fa-lik\ *adj* [MF *céphalique*, fr. L *cephalicus*, fr. Gk *kephalikos*, fr. *kephalē* head; akin to OHG *gebal* skull, ON *gafl* gable, Toch A *śpäl* head] (1599)   **1** : of or relating to the head   **2** : directed toward or situated on or in or near the head — **ce·phal·i·cal·ly** \-li-k(ə-)lē\ *adv*

cephalic index *n* (1866) : the ratio multiplied by 100 of the maximum breadth from side to side of the head to its maximum length from front to back in living individuals — compare CRANIAL INDEX

ceph·a·lin \'ke-fə-lən, 'se-\ *n* [ISV] (ca. 1899) : PHOSPHATIDYL-ETHANOLAMINE

ceph·a·li·za·tion \,se-fə-lə-'zā-shən\ *n* (1864) : a tendency in the evolution of organisms to concentrate the sensory and neural organs in an anterior head

ceph·a·lom·e·try \,se-fə-'lä-mə-trē\ n [ISV] (ca. 1889) : the science of measuring the head in living individuals — compare CRANIOMETRY — **ceph·a·lo·met·ric** \-lō-'me-trik\ adj

ceph·a·lo·pod \'se-fə-lə-,päd\ n [ultim. fr. cephal- + Gk pod-, pous foot — more at FOOT] (1826) : any of a class (Cephalopoda) of marine mollusks including the squids, cuttlefishes, and octopuses that move by expelling water from a tubular siphon under the head and that have a group of muscular usu. sucker-bearing arms around the front of the head, highly developed eyes, and usu. a sac containing ink which is ejected for defense or concealment — **cephalopod** adj

ceph·a·lor·i·dine \,se-fə-'lòr-ə-,dēn, -'lär-\ n [prob. fr. cephalosporin + -idine] (1965) : a semisynthetic broad-spectrum antibiotic C₁₉H₁₇N₃O₄S₂ derived from cephalosporin

ceph·a·lo·spo·rin \,se-fə-lə-'spòr-ən, -'spòr-\ n [Cephalosporium, genus of fungi + ¹-in] (1951) : any of several antibiotics produced by an imperfect fungus (genus Cephalosporium)

ceph·a·lo·thin \'se-fə-lə-thən, -,thin\ n [cephalosporin + thi- + ¹-in] (1962) : a semisynthetic broad-spectrum antibiotic derived from cephalosporin and used as the sodium salt C₁₆H₁₅N₂NaO₆S₂

ceph·a·lo·tho·rax \,se-fə-lə-'thòr-,aks, -'thòr-\ n [ISV] (1835) : the united head and thorax of an arachnid or higher crustacean

Ce·phe·id \'se-f(ē-)id, 'sē-\ n [ISV, fr. Cepheus] (ca. 1903) : any of a class of pulsating stars whose very regular light variations are related directly to their intrinsic luminosities and whose apparent luminosities are used to estimate distances in astronomy

Ce·pheus \'sē-,fyüs, 'sē-fē-əs, 'se-\ n [L (gen. Cephei), fr. Gk Kēpheus] : a constellation between Cygnus and the north pole

¹ce·ram·ic \sə-'ra-mik, esp Brit kə-\ adj [Gk keramikos, fr. keramos potter's clay, pottery] (1850) : of or relating to the manufacture of any product (as earthenware, porcelain, or brick) made essentially from a nonmetallic mineral (as clay) by firing at a high temperature; also : of or relating to such a product

²ceramic n (1859) 1 pl but sing in constr : the art or process of making ceramic articles 2 : a product of ceramic manufacture

ce·ra·mist \sə-'ra-mist, 'ser-ə-\ or **ce·ram·i·cist** \sə-'ra-mə-sist\ n (1855) : one who engages in ceramics

ce·ras·tes \sə-'ras-(,)tēz\ n [ME, fr. L, fr. Gk kerastēs, lit., horned, fr. keras horn] (14c) : a venomous viper (Cerastes cornutus) of the Near East having a horny process over each eye — called also horned viper

ce·rate \'sir-,āt\ n [ME, fr. L ceratum wax salve, fr. cera wax — more at CERUMEN] (15c) : an unctuous preparation for external use consisting of wax or resin or spermaceti mixed with oil, lard, and medicinal ingredients

cer·a·top·sian \,ser-ə-'täp-sē-ən\ n [NL Ceratopsia, fr. Ceratops, a genus, fr. Gk kerat-, keras horn + ōps face — more at HORN, EYE] (1909) : any of a suborder (Ceratopsia) of ornithiscian dinosaurs of the Late Cretaceous having horns, a sharp horny beak, and a bony frill projecting backward from the skull — **ceratopsian** adj

Cer·ber·us \'sər-b(ə-)rəs\ n [L, fr. Gk Kerberos] : a 3-headed dog that in Greek mythology guards the entrance to Hades — **Cer·ber·e·an** \,sər-bə-'rē-ən\ adj

-cercal adj comb form [F -cerque, fr. Gk kerkos tail] : -tailed ⟨homocercal⟩

cer·car·ia \(,)sər-'kar-ē-ə, -'ker-\ n, pl **-i·ae** \-ē-,ē\ [NL, fr. Gk kerkos] (ca. 1871) : a usu. tadpole-shaped larval trematode worm that develops in a molluscan host from a redia — **cer·car·i·al** \-ē-əl\ adj

cer·cus \'sər-kəs\ n, pl **cer·ci** \'sər-,sī, -,kī\ [NL, fr. Gk kerkos] (1826) : either of a pair of simple or segmented appendages at the posterior end of various arthropods that usu. act as sensory organs

¹cere \'sir\ vt **cered; cer·ing** [ME, to wax, fr. MF cirer, fr. L cerare, fr. cera] (15c) : to wrap in or as if in a cerecloth

²cere n [ME sere, fr. MF cere, fr. ML cera, fr. L, wax] (15c) : a usu. waxy protuberance or enlarged area at the base of the bill of a bird

¹ce·re·al \'sir-ē-əl\ adj [F or L; F céréale, fr. L cerealis of Ceres, of grain, fr. Ceres] (1818) : relating to grain or to the plants that produce it; also : made of grain

²cereal n (1832) 1 : a plant (as a grass) yielding starchy grain suitable for food; also : its grain 2 : a prepared foodstuff of grain

cereal leaf beetle n (1962) : a small reddish brown black-headed Old World chrysomelid beetle (Oulema melanopus) that feeds on cereal grasses and is a serious threat to U.S. grain crops

cer·e·bel·lum \,ser-ə-'be-ləm\ n, pl **-bellums** or **-bel·la** \-'be-lə\ [ML, fr. L, dim. of cerebrum] (1543) : a large dorsally projecting part of the brain concerned esp. with the coordination of muscles and the maintenance of bodily equilibrium, situated between the brain stem and the back of the cerebrum, and formed in humans of two lateral lobes and a median lobe — see BRAIN illustration — **cer·e·bel·lar** \-'be-lər\ adj

cerebr- or **cerebro-** comb form [cerebrum] 1 : brain : cerebrum ⟨cerebration⟩ 2 : cerebral and ⟨cerebrospinal⟩

ce·re·bral \sə-'rē-brəl, 'ser-ə-\ adj [F cérébral, fr. L cerebrum brain; akin to OHG hirni brain, Gk kara head, keras horn, Skt śiras head — more at HORN] (1816) 1 a : of or relating to the brain or the intellect b : of, relating to, or being the cerebrum 2 a : appealing to intellectual appreciation ⟨~ drama⟩ b : primarily intellectual in nature ⟨a ~ society⟩ — **ce·re·bral·ly** \-brə-lē\ adv

cerebral cortex n (1926) : the surface layer of gray matter of the cerebrum that functions chiefly in coordination of sensory and motor information

cerebral hemisphere n (1816) : either of the two hollow convoluted lateral halves of the cerebrum — see BRAIN illustration

cerebral palsy n (1889) : a disability resulting from damage to the brain before, during, or shortly after birth and outwardly manifested by muscular incoordination and speech disturbances — compare SPASTIC PARALYSIS — **cerebral–palsied** adj

cer·e·brate \'ser-ə-,brāt\ vi **-brat·ed; -brat·ing** [back-formation fr. cerebration, fr. cerebrum] (1915) : to use the mind : THINK — **cer·e·bra·tion** \,ser-ə-'brā-shən\ n

ce·re·bro·side \'ser-ə-brə-,sīd, sə-'rē-\ n [cerebrose galactose] (1883) : any of various lipids found esp. in nerve tissue

ce·re·bro·spi·nal \sə-,rē-brō-'spī-n³l, ,ser-ə-brō-\ adj (1826) : of or relating to the brain and spinal cord or to these together with the cranial and spinal nerves that innervate voluntary muscles

cerebrospinal fluid n (ca. 1889) : a liquid that is comparable to serum, is secreted from the blood into the lateral ventricles of the brain,

and serves chiefly to maintain uniform pressure within the brain and spinal cord

cerebrospinal meningitis n (1889) : inflammation of the meninges of both brain and spinal cord; specif : an infectious epidemic and often fatal meningitis caused by the meningococcus

ce·re·bro·vas·cu·lar \sə-,rē-brō-'vas-kyə-lər, ,ser-ə-brō-\ adj (1935) : of or involving the cerebrum and the blood vessels supplying it

ce·re·brum \sə-'rē-brəm, 'ser-ə-brəm\ n, pl **-brums** or **-bra** \-brə\ [L] (1615) 1 : BRAIN 1a 2 : an enlarged anterior or upper part of the brain; esp : the expanded anterior portion of the brain that in higher mammals overlies the rest of the brain, consists of cerebral hemispheres and connecting structures, and is considered to be the seat of conscious mental processes : TELENCEPHALON

cere·cloth \'sir-,klòth\ n [alter. of earlier cered cloth (waxed cloth)] (1553) : cloth treated with melted wax or gummy matter and formerly used esp. for wrapping a dead body

cere·ment \'ser-ə-mənt, 'sir-ment\ n (1602) : a shroud for the dead; esp : CERECLOTH — usu. used in pl.

¹cer·e·mo·ni·al \,ser-ə-'mō-nē-əl\ adj (14c) : marked by, involved in, or belonging to ceremony : stressing careful attention to form and detail — **cer·e·mo·ni·al·ism** \-ə-,li-zəm\ n — **cer·e·mo·ni·al·ist** \-ə-list\ n — **cer·e·mo·ni·al·ly** \-ē-ə-lē\ adv

syn CEREMONIAL, CEREMONIOUS, FORMAL, CONVENTIONAL mean marked by attention to or adhering strictly to prescribed forms. CEREMONIAL and CEREMONIOUS both imply strict attention to what is prescribed by custom or by ritual, but CEREMONIAL applies to things that are associated with ceremonies ⟨a ceremonial offering⟩, CEREMONIOUS to persons given to ceremony or to acts attended by ceremony ⟨made his ceremonious entrance⟩. FORMAL applies both to things prescribed by and to persons obedient to custom and may suggest stiff, restrained, or old= fashioned behavior ⟨a formal report⟩ ⟨the headmaster's formal manner⟩. CONVENTIONAL implies accord with general custom and usage ⟨conventional courtesy⟩ and may suggest a stodgy lack of originality or independence ⟨conventional fiction⟩.

²ceremonial n (14c) : a ceremonial act, action, or system

cer·e·mo·ni·ous \,ser-ə-'mō-nē-əs\ adj (1553) 1 : devoted to forms and ceremony : PUNCTILIOUS 2 : of, relating to, or constituting a ceremony 3 : according to formal usage or prescribed procedures 4 : marked by ceremony syn see CEREMONIAL — **cer·e·mo·ni·ous·ly** adv — **cer·e·mo·ni·ous·ness** n

cer·e·mo·ny \'ser-ə-,mō-nē\ n, pl **-nies** [ME ceremonie, fr. MF cérémonie, fr. L caerimonia] (14c) 1 : a formal act or series of acts prescribed by ritual, protocol, or convention ⟨the marriage ~⟩ 2 a : a conventional act of politeness or etiquette ⟨the ~ of introduction⟩ b : an action performed only formally with no deep significance c : a routine action performed with elaborate pomp 3 a : prescribed procedures : USAGES ⟨the ~ attending an inauguration⟩ b : observance of an established code of civility or politeness ⟨opened the door without ~ and strode in⟩

Ce·ren·kov radiation \chə-'ren-kòf-, chər-'yen-\ n [P. A. Cherenkov] (1939) : light produced by charged particles (as electrons) traversing a transparent medium at a speed greater than that of light in the same medium — called also Cerenkov light

Ce·res \'sir-(,)ēz\ n [L] : the Roman goddess of agriculture — compare DEMETER

ce·re·us \'sir-ē-əs\ n [NL, genus name, fr. L, wax candle, fr. cera wax — more at CERUMEN] (1730) : any of various cacti (as of the genus Cereus) of the western U.S. and tropical America

ce·ric \'sir-ik, 'ser-\ adj (ca. 1879) : of, relating to, or containing cerium esp. with a valence of four

ce·rise \sə-'rēs, -'rēz\ n [F, lit., cherry, fr. LL ceresia — more at CHERRY] (1844) : a moderate red

ce·ri·um \'sir-ē-əm\ n [NL, fr. Ceres] (1804) : a malleable ductile metallic element that is the most abundant of the rare-earth group — see ELEMENT table

cer·met \'sər-,met\ n [ceramic + metal] (1948) : a composite structural material of a heat-resistant compound (as titanium carbide) and a metal (as nickel) used esp. for turbine blades

cero \'ser-(,)ō\ n, pl **cero** or **ceros** [modif. of Sp sierra saw, cero] (1884) : either of two large food and sport fishes (Scomberomorus regalis and S. cavalla of the warmer parts of the western Atlantic

ce·rous \'sir-əs\ adj (ca. 1872) : of, relating to, or containing cerium esp. with a valence of three

¹cer·tain \'sər-t³n\ adj [ME, fr. OF, fr. (assumed) VL certanus, fr. L certus, fr. pp. of cernere to sift, discern, decide; akin to Gk krinein to separate, decide, judge, OIr criathar sieve] (13c) 1 : FIXED, SETTLED ⟨a ~ percentage of the profit⟩ 2 : of a specific but unspecified character, quantity, or degree ⟨the house has a ~ charm⟩ 3 a : DEPENDABLE, RELIABLE ⟨a ~ remedy for the disease⟩ b : known or proved to be true : INDISPUTABLE ⟨it is ~ that we exist⟩ 4 a : INEVITABLE ⟨the ~ advance of age⟩ b : incapable of failing : DESTINED — used with a following infinitive ⟨she is ~ to do well⟩ 5 : assured in mind or action syn see SURE — **for certain** : as a certainty : ASSUREDLY

²certain pron, pl in constr (15c) : certain ones

cer·tain·ly \-lē\ adv (14c) 1 : in a manner that is certain : with certainty 2 : it is certain that : ASSUREDLY

cer·tain·ty \'sər-t³n-tē\ n, pl **-ties** (14c) 1 : something that is certain 2 : the quality or state of being certain esp. on the basis of evidence syn CERTAINTY, CERTITUDE, CONVICTION mean a state of being free from doubt. CERTAINTY and CERTITUDE are very close; CERTAINTY may stress the existence of objective proof ⟨claims that cannot be confirmed with scientific certainty⟩, while CERTITUDE may emphasize a faith in something not needing or not capable of proof ⟨believes with certitude in an afterlife⟩. CONVICTION applies esp. to belief strongly held by an individual ⟨holds firm convictions on every issue⟩.

cer·tes \'sər-,tēz, 'sərts\ adv [ME, fr. OF, fr. cert certain, fr. L certus] (13c) archaic : in truth : CERTAINLY

\ə\ abut \³\ kitten, F table \ər\ further \a\ ash \ā\ ace \ä\ mop, mar \aů\ out \ch\ chin \e\ bet \ē\ easy \g\ go \i\ hit \ī\ ice \j\ job \ŋ\ sing \ō\ go \ò\ law \òi\ boy \th\ thin \t̲h̲\ the \ü\ loot \ů\ foot \y\ yet \zh\ vision \à, k̲, ⁿ, œ, œ̄, ᵫ, ᵫ̄, ʸ\ see Guide to Pronunciation

¹**cer·tif·i·cate** \(,)sər-'ti-fi-kət\ *n* [ME *certificat*, fr. MF, fr. ML *certificatum*, fr. LL, neut. of *certificatus*, pp. of *certificare* to certify] (15c) **1** : a document containing a certified statement esp. as to the truth of something; *specif* : a document certifying that one has fulfilled the requirements of and may practice in a field **2** : something serving the same end as a certificate **3** : a document evidencing ownership or debt ⟨a ～ of deposit⟩

²**cer·tif·i·cate** \-'ti-fə-,kāt\ *vt* **-cat·ed; -cat·ing** (1883) : to testify to or authorize by a certificate; *esp* : to recognize as having met special qualifications (as of a governmental agency or professional board) within a field — **cer·tif·i·ca·to·ry** \-'ti-fi-kə-,tōr-ē, -,tȯr-\ *adj*

cer·ti·fi·ca·tion \,sər-tə-fə-'kā-shən\ *n* (15c) **1** : the act of certifying : the state of being certified **2** : a certified statement

certification mark *n* (1947) : a mark or device used to identify a product or service that has been certified to conform to a particular set of standards

certified mail *n* (1955) : first class mail for which proof of delivery is secured but no indemnity value is claimed

certified milk *n* (1899) : milk produced in dairies that operate under the rules and regulations of an authorized medical milk commission

certified public accountant *n* (1896) : an accountant who has met the requirements of a state law and has been granted a certificate

cer·ti·fy \'sər-tə-,fī\ *vt* **-fied; -fy·ing** [ME *certifien*, fr. MF *certifier*, fr. LL *certificare*, fr. L *certus* certain — more at CERTAIN] (14c) **1** : to attest authoritatively: as **a** : CONFIRM **b** : to present in formal communication **c** : to attest as being true or as represented or as meeting a standard **d** : to attest officially to the insanity of **2** : to inform with certainty : ASSURE **3** : to guarantee (a personal check) as to signature and amount by so indicating on the face **4** : CERTIFICATE, LICENSE — **cer·ti·fi·able** \-,fī-ə-bəl\ *adj* — **cer·ti·fi·ably** \-blē\ *adv* — **cer·ti·fi·er** \-,fī(-ə)r\ *n*

syn CERTIFY, ATTEST, WITNESS, VOUCH mean to testify to the truth or genuineness of something. CERTIFY usu. applies to a written statement, esp. one carrying a signature or seal ⟨*certified* that the candidate had met all requirements⟩. ATTEST applies to oral or written testimony usu. from experts or witnesses ⟨*attested* to the authenticity of the document⟩. WITNESS applies to the subscribing of one's own name to a document as evidence of its genuineness ⟨*witnessed* the signing of the will⟩. VOUCH applies to one who testifies as a competent authority or a reliable person ⟨willing to *vouch* for her integrity⟩. **syn** see in addition APPROVE

cer·tio·ra·ri \,sər-sh(ē-)ə-'rar-ē, -'rär-ē\ *n* [ME, fr. L, lit., to be informed; fr. the use of the word in the writ] (15c) : a writ of superior court to call up the records of an inferior court or a body acting in a quasi-judicial capacity

cer·ti·tude \'sər-tə-,tüd *also* -,tyüd\ *n* [ME, fr. LL *certitudo*, fr. L *certus*] (15c) **1** : the state of being or feeling certain **2** : certainty of act or event **syn** see CERTAINTY

ce·ru·le·an \sə-'rü-lē-ən\ *adj* [L *caeruleus* dark blue] (1667) : resembling the blue of the sky

ce·ru·lo·plas·min \sə-,rü-lō-'plaz-mən\ *n* [ISV *cerulo-* (fr. L *caeruleus*) + *plasma* + ¹-*in*] (ca. 1952) : a blue copper-binding serum alpha globulin with enzymatic activity

ce·ru·men \sə-'rü-mən\ *n* [NL, irreg. fr. L *cera* wax; akin to Gk *kēros* wax] (1741) : the yellow waxy secretion from the glands of the external ear — called also *earwax* — **ce·ru·mi·nous** \-mə-nəs\ *adj*

ce·ruse \sə-'rüs, 'sir-,üs\ *n* [ME, fr. MF *céruse*, fr. L *cerussa*] (14c) **1** : white lead as a pigment **2** : a cosmetic containing white lead

ce·rus·site \sə-'rə-,sīt\ *n* [G *Zerussit*, fr. L *cerussa*] (1850) : a mineral that consists of lead carbonate occurring in colorless transparent crystals and also in massive form and is a source of white lead

cer·ve·lat \'sər-və-,lat, -,lä\ *n* [obs. F (now *cervelas*)] (1613) : smoked sausage made from a combination of pork and beef

cer·vi·cal \'sər-vi-kəl\ *adj* (1681) : of or relating to a neck or cervix

cervical cap *n* (1923) : a contraceptive device in the form of a thimble-shaped molded cap that fits over the uterine cervix and blocks sperm from entering the uterus

cer·vi·ci·tis \,sər-və-'sī-təs\ *n* [NL] (1889) : inflammation of the uterine cervix

cer·vine \'sər-,vīn\ *adj* [L *cervinus* of a deer, fr. *cervus* stag, deer — more at HART] (ca. 1828) : of, relating to, or resembling deer

cer·vix \'sər-viks\ *n, pl* **cer·vi·ces** \'sər-və-,sēz, (,)sər-'vī-(,)sēz\ *or* **cer·vix·es** [L *cervic-, cervix*] (15c) **1** : NECK; *esp* : the back part of the neck **2** : a constricted portion of an organ or part; *esp* : the narrow outer end of the uterus

ce·sar·e·an *also* **ce·sar·i·an** \si-'zar-ē-ən, -'zer-\ *n* (ca. 1903) : CESAREAN SECTION — **cesarean** *also* **cesarian** *adj*

cesarean section *also* **cesarian section** *n* [fr. the belief that Julius Caesar was born this way] (1615) : surgical incision of the walls of the abdomen and uterus for delivery of offspring

ce·si·um \'sē-zē-əm *also* -zhē-\ *n* [NL, fr. L *caesius* bluish gray] (1861) : a silver-white soft ductile element of the alkali metal group that is the most electropositive element known and that is used esp. in photoelectric cells — see ELEMENT table

cesium 133 *n* (1966) : an isotope of cesium used esp. in atomic clocks and one of whose atomic transitions is used as a scientific time standard

cess \'ses\ *n* [prob. short for *success*] (1830) *chiefly Irish* : LUCK — usu. used in the phrase *bad cess to you*

ces·sa·tion \se-'sā-shən\ *n* [ME *cessacioun*, fr. MF *cessation*, fr. L *cessation-, cessatio* delay, idleness, fr. *cessare* to delay, to be idle — more at CEASE] (14c) : a temporary or final ceasing (as of action) : STOP

ces·sion \'se-shən\ *n* [ME, fr. MF, fr. L *cession-, cessio*, fr. *cedere* to withdraw — more at CEDE] (15c) : a yielding to another : CONCESSION

cess·pit \'ses-,pit\ *n* [*cesspool* + *pit*] (1777) : a pit for the disposal of refuse (as sewage)

cess·pool \-,pü(ə)l\ *n* [by folk etymology fr. ME *suspiral* vent, cesspool, fr. MF *souspirail* ventilator, fr. *souspirer* to sigh, fr. L *suspirare*, lit., to draw a long breath — more at SUSPIRE] (1782) : an underground reservoir for liquid waste (as household sewage)

ces·ta \'ses-tə\ *n* [Sp, lit., basket, fr. L *cista* box, basket] (ca. 1902) : a narrow curved wicker basket used to catch and propel the ball in jai alai

ces·tode \'ses-,tōd\ *n* [NL *Cestoda*, taxonomic group comprising tapeworms, ultim. fr. Gk *kestos* girdle] (ca. 1890) : TAPEWORM — **cestode** *adj*

¹**ces·tus** \'ses-təs\ *n, pl* **ces·ti** \-,tī\ [L, girdle, belt, fr. Gk *kestos*, fr. *kestos* stitched, fr. *kentein* to prick — more at CENTER] (1557) : a woman's belt; *esp* : a symbolic one worn by a bride

²**cestus** *n* [L *cestus, caestus*] (ca. 1720) : a hand covering of leather bands often loaded with lead or iron and used by boxers in ancient Rome

ce·su·ra *var of* CAESURA

ce·ta·cean \si-'tā-shən\ *n* [ultim. fr. L *cetus* whale, fr. Gk *kētos*] (1836) : any of an order (Cetacea) of aquatic mostly marine mammals that include the whales, dolphins, porpoises, and related forms and that have a torpedo-shaped nearly hairless body, paddle-shaped forelimbs but no hind limbs, one or two nares opening externally at the top of the head, and a horizontally flattened tail used for locomotion — **cetacean** *adj* — **ce·ta·ceous** \-shəs\ *adj*

cesta

ce·tane \'sē-,tān\ *n* [fr. *cetyl*, the radical $C_{16}H_{33}$] (1871) : a colorless oily hydrocarbon $C_{16}H_{34}$ found in petroleum

cetane number *n* (1935) : a measure of the ignition value of a diesel fuel that represents the percentage by volume of cetane in a mixture of liquid methylnaphthalene that gives the same ignition lag as the oil being tested — called also *cetane rating*; compare OCTANE NUMBER

ce·te·ris pa·ri·bus \'kā-tər-əs-'par-ə-bəs, 'kē-, 'se-\ *adv* [NL, other things being equal] (1601) : if all other relevant things, factors, or elements remain unaltered

ce·tol·o·gy \sē-'tä-lə-jē\ *n* [L *cetus* whale] (ca. 1828) : a branch of zoology dealing with the cetaceans — **ce·tol·o·gist** \-jist\ *n*

Ce·tus \'sē-təs\ *n* [L (gen. *Ceti*), lit., whale] : an equatorial constellation south of Pisces and Aries

ce·tyl alcohol \'sē-t⁹l-\ *n* [ISV *cet-* (fr. L *cetus* whale) + *-yl*; fr. its occurrence in spermaceti] (1873) : a waxy crystalline alcohol $C_{16}H_{34}O$ obtained by the saponification of spermaceti or the hydrogenation of palmitic acid and used esp. in pharmaceutical and cosmetic preparations and in making detergents

ce·vi·che \sə-'vē-(,)chā, -chē\ *var of* SEVICHE

Cha·blis \sha-'blē, shə-, shä-; 'sha-(,)blē\ *n, pl* **Cha·blis** \-'blēz, -(,)blēz\ [F, fr. *Chablis*, town in France] (1668) **1** : a dry sharp white burgundy wine **2** : a semidry soft white California wine

cha–cha \'chä-(,)chä\ *n* [AmerSp *cha-cha-cha*] (1954) : a fast rhythmic ballroom dance of Latin-American origin with a basic pattern of three steps and a shuffle

chac·ma baboon \'chäk-mə-\ *n* [Khoikhoi] (ca. 1909) : a large dusky baboon (*Papio ursinus*) of southern African savannas — called also *chacma*

cha·conne \shä-'kȯn, sha-, -'kän, -'kən\ *n* [F&Sp; F *chaconne*, fr. Sp *chacona*] (1685) **1** : an old Spanish dance tune of Latin American origin **2** : a musical composition in moderate triple time typically consisting of variations on a repeated succession of chords

chad \'chad\ *n* [origin unknown] (1947) : small pieces of paper or cardboard produced in punching paper tape or data cards; *also* : a piece of chad — **chad·less** \-ləs\ *adj*

Chad·ic \'cha-dik\ *or* **Chad** \'chad\ *n* (ca. 1950) : a subfamily of the Afro-Asiatic language family comprising numerous languages of northern Nigeria, northern Cameroon, and Chad — **Chadic** *adj*

cha·dor \'chə-dor, 'chä-\ *n* [Hindi & Pers; Hindi *caddar*, fr. Pers *chaddar, chādar*] (1614) : a large cloth worn as a combination head covering, veil, and shawl usu. by Muslim women esp. in Iran

chae·ta \'kē-tə\ *n, pl* **chae·tae** \'kē-,tē\ [NL, fr. Gk *chaitē* long flowing hair] (ca. 1866) : BRISTLE, SETA — **chae·tal** \'kē-t⁹l\ *adj*

chae·to·gnath \'kē-,täg-,nath, -nə(g)-\ *n* [NL *Chaetognatha*, class or phylum name, ultim. fr. Gk *chaitē* + *gnathos* jaw — more at -GNATHOUS] (ca. 1889) : ARROWWORM — **chaetognath** *adj*

¹**chafe** \'chāf\ *vb* **chafed; chaf·ing** [ME *chaufen* to warm, fr. MF *chaufer*, fr. (assumed) VL *calfare*, alter. of L *calefacere*, fr. *calēre* to be warm + *facere* to make — more at LEE, DO] *vt* (14c) **1** : IRRITATE, VEX **2** : to warm by rubbing esp. with the hands **3 a** : to rub so as to wear away : ABRADE ⟨the boat *chafed* its sides against the dock⟩ **b** : to make sore by or as if by rubbing ～ *vi* **1** : to feel irritation or discontent : FRET ⟨～s at his restrictive desk job⟩ **2** : to rub and thereby cause wear or irritation

²**chafe** *n* (1551) **1** : a state of vexation : RAGE **2** : injury or wear caused by friction; *also* : FRICTION, RUBBING

cha·fer \'chā-fər\ *n* [ME *cheaffer*, fr. OE *ceafor*; prob. akin to OE *ceafl* jowl — more at JOWL] (bef. 12c) : any of various scarab beetles (as a cockchafer) that feed on leaves and flowers and whose larvae feed on plant roots

¹**chaff** \'chaf\ *n* [ME *chaf*, fr. OE *ceaf*; akin to OHG *cheva* husk] (bef. 12c) **1** : the seed coverings and other debris separated from the seed in threshing grain **2** : something comparatively worthless **3** : the scales borne on the receptacle among the florets in the heads of many composite plants **4** : material (as strips of foil or clusters of fine wires) ejected into the air for reflecting radar waves (as for confusing an enemy's radar detection or for tracking a descending spacecraft) — **chaffy** \'cha-fē\ *adj*

²**chaff** *n* [prob. fr. ¹*chaff*] (1821) : light jesting talk : BANTER

³**chaff** *vt* (1827) : to tease good-naturedly ～ *vi* : JEST, BANTER

¹**chaf·fer** \'cha-fər\ *n* [ME *chaffare*, fr. *chep* trade + *fare* journey — more at CHEAP, FARE] (13c) *archaic* : a haggling about price

²**chaffer** *vb* **chaf·fered; chaf·fer·ing** \'cha-f(ə-)riŋ\ *vi* (14c) **1** : HAGGLE **2** *Brit* : to exchange small talk : CHATTER ～ *vt* **1** : EXCHANGE, BARTER **2** : to bargain for — **chaf·fer·er** \-fər-ər\ *n*

chaf·finch \'cha-(,)finch\ *n* [ME, fr. OE *ceaffinc*, fr. *ceaf* + *finc* finch] (bef. 12c) : a common European finch (*Fringilla coelebs*) of which the male has a pinkish-brown breast

chaf·ing dish \'chā-fiŋ-\ *n* [ME *chafing*, prp. of *chaufen, chafen* to warm] (15c) : a utensil for cooking or keeping food warm esp. at the table

Cha·gas' disease \'shä-gəs-, -gə-səz-\ *n* [Carlos *Chagas* †1934 Braz. physician] (1912) : a tropical American disease that is caused by a trypanosome (*Trypanosoma cruzi*) and is marked by prolonged high fever, edema, and enlargement of the spleen, liver, and lymph nodes

¹cha·grin \shə-'grin\ *n* [F, fr. *chagrin* sad] (ca. 1681) : disquietude or distress of mind caused by humiliation, disappointment, or failure

²chagrin *vt* **cha·grined** \-'grind\; **cha·grin·ing** \-'gri-niŋ\ (1733) : to vex or unsettle by disappointing or humiliating

¹chain \'chān\ *n, often attrib* [ME *cheyne*, fr. MF *chaeine*, fr. L *catena*] (14c) **1 a** : a series of usu. metal links or rings connected to or fitted into one another and used for various purposes (as support, restraint, transmission of mechanical power, or measurement) **b** : a series of links used or worn as an ornament or insignia **c** (1) : a measuring instrument of 100 links used in surveying (2) : a unit of length equal to 66 feet (20 meters) **2** : something that confines, restrains, or secures **3 a** : a series of things linked, connected, or associated together (a ~ of events) **b** : a group of enterprises or institutions of the same kind or function usu. under a single ownership, management, or control (fast-food ~s) **c** : a number of atoms or chemical groups united like links in a chain

²chain *vt* (14c) **1** : to obstruct or protect by a chain **2** : to fasten, bind, or connect with or as if with a chain; *also* : FETTER

chaî·né \shā-'nā\ *n* [F, fr. pp. of *chaîner* to chain] (1897) : a series of short usu. fast turns by which a ballet dancer moves across the stage

chain gang *n* (1834) : a gang of convicts chained together esp. as an outside working party

chain letter *n* (1905) : a letter sent to several persons with a request that each send copies of the letter to an equal number of persons

chain–link fence *n* (ca. 1927) : a fence of heavy steel wire woven to form a diamond-shaped mesh

chain mail *n* (1822) : flexible armor of interlinked metal rings

chain of command (1898) : a series of executive positions in order of authority (a military *chain of command*)

chain pickerel *n* [fr. the markings resembling chains on the sides] (1887) : a large greenish black pickerel (*Esox niger*) with dark markings along the sides that is common in quiet waters of eastern No. America

chain reaction *n* (ca. 1902) **1 a** : a series of events so related to each other that each one initiates the next **b** : a number of events triggered by the same initial event **2** : a self-sustaining chemical or nuclear reaction yielding energy or products that cause further reactions of the same kind — **chain–re·act** \'chān-rē-'akt\ *vi*

chain rule *n* (ca. 1847) : a mathematical rule concerning the differentiation of a function of a function (as *f*[*u*(*x*)]) by which under suitable conditions of continuity and differentiability one function is differentiated with respect to the second function considered as an independent variable and then the second function is differentiated with respect to its independent variable

chain saw *n* (1944) : a portable power saw that has teeth linked together to form an endless chain — **chain–saw** \'chān-,sȯ\ *vt*

chain–smoke \'chān-'smōk\ *vi* (1930) : to smoke esp. cigarettes continually ~ *vt* : to smoke (as cigarettes) almost without interruption — **chain–smok·er** \-,smō-kər\ *n*

chain stitch *n* (1820) **1** : an ornamental stitch like chain links **2** : a machine stitch forming a chain on the underside of the work

chain store *n* (1910) : one of numerous usu. retail stores having the same ownership and selling the same lines of goods

chain·wheel \'chān-,hwēl, -,wēl\ *n* (1845) : SPROCKET 1

¹chair \'cher, 'char\ *n* [ME *chaiere*, fr. OF, fr. L *cathedra*, fr. Gk *kathedra*, fr. *kata-* cata- + *hedra* seat — more at SIT] (13c) **1 a** : a seat typically having four legs and a back for one person **b** : ELECTRIC CHAIR — used with *the* **2 a** : an official seat or a seat of authority, state, or dignity **b** : an office or position of authority or dignity **c** : PROFESSORSHIP (holds a university ~) **d** : CHAIRMAN 1 **3** : a sedan chair **4** : a position of employment usu. of one occupying a chair or desk; *specif* : the position of a player in an orchestra or band **5** : any of various devices that hold up or support

²chair *vt* (1552) **1** : to install in office **2** *chiefly Brit* : to carry on the shoulders in acclaim (we ~ed you through the market place —A. E. Housman) **3** : to preside as chairman of

chair car *n* (1880) **1** : a railroad car having pairs of chairs with individually adjustable backs on each side of the aisle **2** : PARLOR CAR

chair·lift \'cher-,lift, 'char-\ *n* (1940) : a motor-driven conveyor consisting of a series of seats suspended from a cable and used for transporting skiers or sightseers up or down a long slope or mountainside

¹chair·man \-mən\ *n* (1650) **1 a** : the presiding officer of a meeting or an organization or committee **b** : the administrative officer of a department of instruction (as in a college) **2** : a carrier of a sedan chair — **chair·man·ship** \-,ship\ *n*

²chairman *vt* **-maned** *or* **-manned**; **-man·ing** *or* **-man·ning** (1888) : CHAIR 3

chair·per·son \-,pər-s²n\ *n* (1971) : CHAIRMAN 1

chair·wom·an \-,wu̇-mən\ *n* (1685) : a woman who acts as chairman

chaise \'shāz\ *n* [F, chair, chaise, alter. of OF *chaiere*] (1701) **1** : any of various light horse-drawn vehicles: as **a** : a two-wheeled carriage for one or two persons with a folding top **b** : POST CHAISE **2** : CHAISE LONGUE

chaise longue \'shāz-'lȯŋ\ *n, pl* **chaise longues** *also* **chaises longues** \'shāz-'lȯŋ(z)\ [F, lit., long chair] (1800) : a long reclining chair

chaise lounge \'shāz-'lau̇nj, 'chās-\ *n* [by folk etymology fr. F *chaise longue*] (1926) : CHAISE LONGUE

chak·ra \'chä-krə, 'shä-, 'chə-\ *n* [Skt *cakra*, lit., wheel — more at WHEEL] (1888) : any of several points of physical or spiritual energy in the human body according to yoga philosophy

cha·la·za \kə-'lā-zə, -'la-\ *n, pl* **-zae** \-,zē\ *or* **-zas** [NL, fr. Gk, hailstone] (ca. 1704) **1** : either of two spiral bands in the white of a bird's egg that extend from the yolk and attach to opposite ends of the lining membrane — see EGG illustration **2** : the basal part of a plant ovule where the nucellus is fused to the surrounding integument and to which the funiculus is usu. attached — **cha·la·zal** \'lā-zəl, -'la-\ *adj*

Chal·ce·do·ni·an \,kal-sə-'dō-nē-ən\ *adj* (1788) : of or relating to Chalcedon or the ecumenical council held there in A.D. 451 declaring Monophysitism heretical — **Chalcedonian** *n*

chal·ce·do·ny \kal-'se-d²n-ē, chal-; 'kal-sə-,dō-nē, 'chal-, -,dä-\ *n, pl* **-nies** [ME *calcedonie*, a precious stone, fr. LL *chalcedonius*, fr. Gk *Chalkēdōn* Chalcedon] (13c) : a translucent quartz that is commonly pale blue or gray with nearly waxlike luster — **chal·ce·don·ic** \,kal-sə-'dä-nik\ *adj*

chal·cid \'kal-səd\ *n* [ultim. fr. Gk *chalkos* copper, bronze] (1893) : any of a large superfamily (Chalcidoidea) of mostly minute hymenopterous insects parasitic in the larval state on the larvae or pupae of other insects — **chalcid** *adj*

chal·co·cite \'kal-kə-,sīt\ *n* [alter. of *chalcosine*, fr. F, irreg. fr. Gk *chalkos*] (1868) : a black or gray lustrous metallic mineral that consists of a sulfide of copper and is an important copper ore

chal·co·gen \'kal-kə-jən\ *n* [ISV *chalk-* bronze, ore (fr. Gk *chalkos*) + *-gen*; fr. the occurrence of copper and sulfur in many ores] (ca. 1961) : any of the elements oxygen, sulfur, selenium, and tellurium

chal·co·gen·ide \-jə-,nīd\ *n* (1945) : a binary compound of a chalcogen with a more electropositive element or radical

chal·co·py·rite \,kal-kə-'pī-,rīt\ *n* [NL *chalcopyrites*, fr. Gk *chalkos* + L *pyrites*] (1835) : a yellow mineral consisting of copper-iron sulfide and constituting an important ore of copper

Chal·da·ic \kal-'dā-ik, kȯl-, käl-\ *adj or n* (1662) : CHALDEAN

Chal·de·an \kal-'dē-ən, kȯl-, käl-\ *n* [L *Chaldaeus* Chaldean, astrologer, fr. Gk *Chaldaios*, fr. *Chaldaia* Chaldea, region of ancient Babylonia] (1581) **1 a** : a member of an ancient Semitic people that became dominant in Babylonia **b** : the Semitic language of the Chaldeans **2** : a person versed in the occult arts — **Chaldean** *adj*

Chal·dee \'kal-,dē, 'kȯl-, 'käl-\ *n* [ME *Caldey*, prob. fr. MF *chaldée*, fr. L *Chaldaeus*] (14c) **1** : CHALDEAN 1a **2** : the Aramaic vernacular that was the original language of some parts of the Bible

chal·dron \'chȯl-drən, 'chäl-\ *n* [MF *chauderon*, fr. *chaudere* pot, fr. LL *caldaria* — more at CAULDRON] (1615) : any of various old units of measure varying from 32 to 72 imperial bushels

cha·let \sha-'lā, 'sha-(,)lā\ *n* [F] (1782) **1** : a remote herdsman's hut in the Alps **2 a** : a Swiss dwelling with unconcealed structural members and a wide overhang at the front and sides **b** : a cottage or house in chalet style

chal·ice \'cha-ləs\ *n* [ME, fr. AF, fr. L *calic-, calix*; akin to Gk *kalyx* calyx] (14c) **1** : a drinking cup : GOBLET; *esp* : the eucharistic cup **2** : the cup-shaped interior of a flower

¹chalk \'chȯk\ *n* [ME, fr. OE *cealc*, fr. L *calc-, calx* lime; akin to Gk *chalix* pebble] (bef. 12c) **1 a** : a soft white, gray, or buff limestone composed chiefly of the shells of foraminifers **b** : chalk or a material resembling chalk esp. when used in the form of a crayon **2 a** : a mark made with chalk **b** *Brit* : a point scored in a game — **chalky** \'chȯ-kē\ *adj*

chalet 2a

²chalk *vt* (1580) **1** : to write or draw with chalk **2** : to rub or mark with chalk **3 a** : to delineate roughly : SKETCH (~ out a plan of attack) **b** : to set down or add up with or as if with chalk : RECORD — usu. used with *up* (~ up a victory) ~ *vi* : to become chalky

chalk·board \'chȯk-,bȯrd, -,bȯrd\ *n* (1936) : BLACKBOARD

chalk talk \'chȯk-,tȯk\ *n* (1881) : a talk or lecture illustrated at a blackboard

chalk up *vt* (1826) **1** : ASCRIBE, CREDIT **2** : ATTAIN, ACHIEVE (*chalk up* a record score for the season)

chal·lah *also* **chal·la** \'kä-lə, 'hä-\ *n* [Yiddish *khale*, fr. Heb *ḥallāh*] (1927) : egg-rich yeast-leavened bread that is usu. braided or twisted before baking and is traditionally eaten by Jews on the Sabbath and holidays

¹chal·lenge \'cha-lənj\ *vb* **chal·lenged**; **chal·leng·ing** [ME *chalengen* to accuse, fr. OF *chalengier*, fr. L *calumniari* to accuse falsely, fr. *calumnia* calumny] *vt* (13c) **1** : to demand as due or deserved : REQUIRE (an event that ~s explanation) **2** : to order to halt and prove identity (the sentry *challenged* the stranger) **3** : to dispute esp. as being unjust, invalid, or outmoded : IMPUGN (new data that ~s old assumptions) **4** : to question formally the legality or legal qualifications of **5 a** : to confront or defy boldly : DARE **b** : to call out to duel or combat **c** : to invite into competition **6** : to arouse or stimulate esp. by presenting with difficulties **7** : to administer a physiological and esp. an immunologic challenge to (an organism or cell) ~ *vi* **1** : to make or present a challenge **2** : to take legal exception — **chal·leng·er** *n*

²challenge *n* (14c) **1 a** : a summons that is often threatening, provocative, stimulating, or inciting; *specif* : a summons to a duel to answer an affront **b** : an invitation to compete in a sport **2 a** : a calling to account or into question : PROTEST **b** : an exception taken to a juror before he is sworn **c** : a sentry's command to halt and prove identity **d** : a questioning of the right or validity of a vote or voter **3** : a stimulating task or problem (looking for new ~s) **4** : the process of provoking or testing physiological activity by exposure to a specific substance; *esp* : a test of immunity by exposure to an antigen

chal·leng·ing \-lən-jiŋ\ *adj* (1842) **1** : arousing competitive interest, thought, or action (a ~ course of study) **2** : invitingly provocative : FASCINATING (a ~ personality) — **chal·leng·ing·ly** \-jiŋ-lē\ *adv*

chal·lis \'sha-lē\ *n, pl* **chal·lises** \'sha-lēz\ [prob. fr. the name *Challis*] (ca. 1837) : a lightweight soft clothing fabric made of cotton, wool, or synthetic yarns

cha·lone \'kā-,lōn, 'ka-\ *n* [Gk *chalōn*, prp. of *chalan* to slacken] (1914) : an internal secretion that is held to inhibit mitosis in a specific tissue — compare HORMONE

¹cha·ly·be·ate \kə-'lē-bē-ət, -'li-\ *adj* [prob. fr. NL *chalybeatus*, irreg. fr. L *chalybs* steel, fr. Gk *chalyb-, chalyps*, fr. *Chalybes*, ancient people in Asia Minor] (1634) : impregnated with salts of iron; *also* : having a taste due to iron (~ springs)

²chalybeate *n* (1667) : a chalybeate liquid or medicine

cham \'kam\ *var of* KHAN

\ə\ abut \²\ kitten, F table \ər\ further \a\ ash \ā\ ace \ä\ mop, mar \au̇\ out \ch\ chin \e\ bet \ē\ easy \g\ go \i\ hit \ī\ ice \j\ job \ŋ\ sing \ō\ go \ȯ\ law \ȯi\ boy \th\ thin \t͟h\ the \ü\ loot \u̇\ foot \y\ yet \zh\ vision \a, k, ⁿ, œ, œ̄, ᵫ, ᵫ̄, ᵞ\ see Guide to Pronunciation

cham·ae·phyte \'ka-mi-ˌfīt\ n [Gk chamai on the ground + E -phyte — more at HUMBLE] (1913) : a perennial plant that bears its perennnating buds just above the surface of the soil

¹**cham·ber** \'chām-bər\ n [ME chambre, fr. OF, fr. LL camera, fr. L, arched roof, fr. Gk kamara vault] (13c) **1** : ROOM: esp : BEDROOM **2** : a natural or artificial enclosed space or cavity **3 a** : a hall for the meetings of a deliberative, legislative, or judicial body ⟨the senate ∼⟩ **b** : a room where a judge transacts business — usu. used in pl. **c** : the reception room of a person of rank or authority **4 a** : a legislative or judicial body; esp : either of the houses of a bicameral legislature **b** : a voluntary board or council **5 a** : the part of the bore of a gun that holds the charge **b** : a compartment in the cartridge cylinder of a revolver — **cham·bered** \-bərd\ adj

²**chamber** vt **cham·bered; cham·ber·ing** \-b(ə-)riŋ\ (1575) **1** : to place in or as if in a chamber : HOUSE **2** : to serve as a chamber for; esp : to accommodate in the chamber of a firearm

³**chamber** adj (1706) : being, relating to, or performing chamber music

chambered nautilus n (1858) : NAUTILUS 1

cham·ber·lain \'chām-bər-lən\ n [ME, fr. OF chamberlayn, of Gmc origin; akin to OHG chamarling chamberlain, fr. chamara chamber, fr. LL camera] (13c) **1** : an attendant on a sovereign or lord in his bedchamber **2 a** : a chief officer in the household of a king or nobleman **b** : TREASURER **3** : an often honorary papal attendant; specif : a priest having a rank of honor below domestic prelate

cham·ber·maid \-ˌmād\ n (1587) : a maid who makes beds and does general cleaning of bedrooms (as in a hotel)

chamber music n (ca. 1789) : music and esp. instrumental ensemble music intended for performance in a private room or small auditorium and usu. having one performer for each part

chamber of commerce (1797) : an association of businessmen to promote commercial and industrial interests in the community

chamber of horrors (1849) : a place in which macabre or horrible objects are exhibited; also : a collection of such exhibits

chamber orchestra n (ca. 1927) : a small orchestra usu. with one player for each part

chamber pot n (1540) : a bedroom vessel for urination and defecation

cham·bray \'sham-ˌbrā, -brē\ n [irreg. fr. Cambrai, France] (1814) : a lightweight clothing fabric with colored warp and white filling yarns

cha·me·leon \kə-'mēl-yən\ n, often attrib [ME camelion, fr. MF, fr. L chamaeleon, fr. Gk chamaileōn, fr. chamai on the ground + leōn lion — more at HUMBLE] (14c) **1** : any of a family (Chamaeleontidae) of chiefly arboreal Old World lizards with prehensile tail, independently movable eyeballs, and unusual ability to change the color of the skin **2 a** : a person given to often expedient or facile change in ideas or character **b** : one that is subject to quick or frequent change esp. in appearance **3** : AMERICAN CHAMELEON — **cha·me·le·on·ic** \-ˌmē-lē-'ä-nik\ adj — **cha·me·le·on·like** \-ˌlik\ adj

¹**cham·fer** \'cham(p)-fər, 'cham-pər\ vt **cham·fered; cham·fer·ing** \-f(ə-)riŋ, -p(ə-)riŋ\ [back-formation fr. chamfering, alter. of MF chanfreint, fr. pp. of chanfraindre to bevel, fr. chant edge (fr. L canthus iron tire) + fraindre to break, fr. L frangere — more at CANT, BREAK] (ca. 1573) **1** : to cut a furrow in (as a column) : GROOVE **2** : to make a chamfer on : BEVEL

²**chamfer** n (ca. 1847) : a beveled edge

cham·fron \'sham-frən, 'cham-\ n [ME shamfron, fr. MF chanfrein] (15c) : the headpiece of a horse's bard

cham·ois \'sha-mē, sense 1 also sham-'wä\ n, pl **cham·ois** also **chamois** \sense 1 'sha-mē(z) or sham-'wä(z), senses 2 & 3 'sha-mēz\ [MF, fr. LL camox] (1560) **1** : a small goatlike antelope (Rupicapra rupicapra) of mountainous regions from southern Europe to the Caucasus **2** also **cham·my** or **sham·my** \'sha-mē\ : a soft pliant leather prepared from the skin of the chamois or from sheepskin **3** : a cotton fabric made in imitation of chamois leather

¹**cham·o·mile** \'ka-mə-ˌmil, -ˌmēl\ n [ME camemille, fr. ML camomilla, modif. of L chamaemelon, fr. Gk chamaimēlon, fr. chamai + mēlon apple] (13c) **1** : a composite herb (Chamaemelum nobile syn. Anthemis nobilis) of Europe and No. Africa with strong-scented foliage and flower heads that contain a bitter medicinal substance **2** : any of several composite plants (genera Matricaria and Anthemis) related to chamomile; esp : a Eurasian herb (M. recutita syn. M. chamomilla) naturalized in No. America

¹**champ** \'champ, 'chämp, 'chomp\ vb [perh. imit.] vt (14c) **1** : CHOMP **2** : MASH, TRAMPLE ∼ vi **1** : to make biting or gnashing movements **2** : to show impatience of delay or restraint — usu. used in the phrase champing at the bit ⟨he was ∼ing at the bit to begin⟩

²**champ** \'champ\ n (1868) : CHAMPION

cham·pac or **cham·pak** \'cham-ˌpak, 'chəm-ˌ(ˌ)pək\ n [Hindi & Skt; Hindi campak, fr. Skt campaka] (ca. 1770) : an Asian tree (Michelia champaca) of the magnolia family with yellow flowers

cham·pagne \sham-'pān\ n [F, fr. Champagne, France] (1664) **1** : a white sparkling wine made in the old province of Champagne, France; also : a similar wine made elsewhere **2** : a pale orange yellow to light grayish yellowish brown

cham·paign \sham-'pān\ n [ME champaine, fr. MF champagne, fr. LL campania — more at CAMPAIGN] (15c) **1** : an expanse of level open country : PLAIN **2** archaic : BATTLEFIELD — **champaign** adj

cham·pers \'sham-pərz\ n pl but sing in constr [by alter.] (1955) Brit : CHAMPAGNE 1

cham·per·ty \'cham-pər-tē\ n [ME champartie, fr. MF champart field rent, fr. champ field (fr. L campus) + part portion — more at PART] (15c) : a proceeding by which a person not a party in a suit bargains to aid in or carry on its prosecution or defense in consideration of a share of the matter in suit — **cham·per·tous** \-pər-təs\ adj

cham·pi·gnon \(ˌ)sham-pē-'nyōn, (ˌ)shäm-, -'nyōn; sham-'pin-yən, cham-\ n [F, fr. MF, alter. of champigneul, ultim. fr. LL campania] (1670) : an edible fungus; esp : MEADOW MUSHROOM

¹**cham·pi·on** \'cham-pē-ən\ n [ME, fr. OF, fr. ML campion-, campio, of WGmc origin; akin to OE cempa warrior] (13c) **1** : WARRIOR, FIGHTER **2** : a militant advocate or defender ⟨a ∼ of civil rights⟩ **3** : one that does battle for another's rights or honor ⟨God will raise me up a ∼ —

Sir Walter Scott⟩ **4** : a winner of first prize or first place in competition; also : one who shows marked superiority ⟨a ∼ at selling⟩

²**champion** vt (1605) **1** archaic : CHALLENGE, DEFY **2** : to protect or fight for as a champion **3** : to act as militant supporter of : UPHOLD, ADVOCATE ⟨always ∼s the cause of the underdog⟩ **syn** see SUPPORT

cham·pi·on·ship \-ˌship\ n (1825) **1** : designation as champion **2** : the act of championing : DEFENSE ⟨his ∼ of freedom of speech⟩ **3** : a contest held to determine a champion

champ·le·vé \ˌshän-l(ə-)-'vā\ adj [F] (1856) : of, relating to, or being a style of enamel decoration in which the enamel is applied and fired in cells depressed (as by incising) into a metal background — compare CLOISONNÉ— **champlevé** n

¹**chance** \'chan(t)s\ n [ME, fr. OF, fr. (assumed) VL cadentia fall, fr. L cadent-, cadens, prp. of cadere to fall; perh. akin to Skt śad- to fall off] (14c) **1 a** : something that happens unpredictably without discernible human intention or observable cause **b** : the assumed impersonal purposeless determiner of unaccountable happenings : LUCK **c** : the fortuitous or incalculable element in existence : CONTINGENCY **2** : a situation favoring some purpose : OPPORTUNITY ⟨needed a ∼ to relax⟩ **3** : a fielding opportunity in baseball **4 a** : the possibility of a particular outcome in an uncertain situation; also : the degree of likelihood of such an outcome ⟨a small ∼ of success⟩ **b** pl : the more likely indications ⟨∼s are he's already gone⟩ **5 a** : RISK ⟨not taking any ∼s⟩ **b** : a raffle ticket — **chance** adj — **by chance** : in the haphazard course of events ⟨they met by chance⟩

²**chance** vb **chanced; chanc·ing** vi (14c) **1 a** : to take place or come about by chance : HAPPEN **b** : to be found by chance ⟨∼ to have the good or bad luck ⟨we chanced to meet⟩ **2** : to come or light by chance ∼ vt **1** : to leave the outcome of to chance **2** : to accept the hazard of : RISK — **chance one's arm** Brit : to take a risk

chance·ful \'chan(t)s-fəl\ adj (1594) **1** archaic : CASUAL **2** : EVENTFUL

chan·cel \'chan(t)-səl\ n [ME, fr. MF, fr. LL cancellus lattice, fr. L cancelli; fr. the latticework enclosing it — more at CANCEL] (14c) : the part of a church containing the altar and seats for the clergy and choir

chan·cel·lery or **chan·cel·lory** \'chan(t)-s(ə-)lə-rē, -səl-rē\ n, pl **-leries** or **-lor·ies** (14c) **1 a** : the position, court, or department of a chancellor **b** : the building or room where a chancellor has his office **2** : the office of secretary of the court of a person high in authority **3** : the office or staff of an embassy or consulate

chan·cel·lor \'chan(t)-s(ə-)lər\ n [ME chanceler, fr. OF chancelier, fr. LL cancellarius doorkeeper, secretary, fr. cancellus] (14c) **1 a** : the secretary of a nobleman, prince, or king **b** : the lord chancellor of Great Britain **c** Brit : the chief secretary of an embassy **d** : a Roman Catholic priest heading the office in which diocesan business is transacted and recorded **2 a** : the titular head of a British university **b** (1) : a university president (2) : the chief executive officer in some state systems of higher education **3 a** : a lay legal officer or adviser of an Anglican diocese **b** : a judge in a court of chancery or equity in various states of the U.S. **4** : the chief minister of state in some European countries — **chan·cel·lor·ship** \-ˌship\ n

chancellor of the exchequer often cap C&E (1672) : a member of the British cabinet in charge of the public income and expenditure

chance–med·ley \'chan(t)s-'med-lē\ n [AF chance medlée mingled chance] (15c) **1** : accidental homicide not entirely without fault of the killer but without evil intent **2** : haphazard action : CONFUSION

chan·cery \'chan(t)-sə-rē, 'chan(t)s-rē\ n, pl **-cer·ies** [ME chancerie, alter. of chancellerie chancellery, fr. OF, fr. chancelier] (14c) **1 a** cap : a high court of equity in England and Wales with common-law functions and jurisdiction over causes in equity **b** : a court of equity in the American judicial system **c** : the principles and practice of judicial equity **2** : a record office for public archives or those of ecclesiastical, legal, or diplomatic proceedings **3 a** : a chancellor's court or office or the building in which it is located **b** : the office in which the business of a Roman Catholic diocese is transacted and recorded **c** : the office of an embassy : CHANCELLERY 3 — **in chancery** **1** : in litigation in a court of chancery; also : under the superintendence of the lord chancellor ⟨a ward in chancery⟩ **2** : in a hopeless predicament

chan·cre \'shaŋ-kər\ n [F, fr. L cancer] (ca. 1605) : a primary sore or ulcer at the site of entry of a pathogen (as in tularemia); esp : the initial lesion of syphilis — **chan·crous** \-k(ə-)rəs\ adj

chan·croid \'shaŋ-ˌkroid\ n (1861) : a venereal disease caused by a hemophilic bacterium (Hemophilus ducreyi) and characterized by chancres unlike those of syphilis in lacking firm indurated margins — called also soft chancre — **chan·croi·dal** \shaŋ-'kroi-d²l\ adj

chancy \'chan(t)-sē\ adj **chanc·i·er; -est** (1513) **1** Scot : bringing good luck : AUSPICIOUS **2** : uncertain in outcome or prospect : RISKY **3** : occurring by chance : HAPHAZARD — **chanc·i·ness** n

chan·de·lier \ˌshan-də-'lir\ n [F, lit., candlestick, modif. of L candelabrum] (1736) : a branched often ornate lighting fixture suspended from a ceiling — **chan·de·liered** \-'lird\ adj

chan·delle \shan-'del, shän-\ n [F, lit., candle] (1918) : an abrupt climbing turn of an airplane in which the momentum of the plane is used to attain a higher rate of climb — **chandelle** vi

chan·dler \'chan(d)-lər\ n [ME chandeler, fr. MF chandelier, fr. OF, fr. chandelle candle, fr. L candela] (14c) **1** : a maker or seller of tallow or wax candles and usu. soap **2** : a retail dealer in provisions and supplies or equipment of a specified kind ⟨a yacht ∼⟩

chan·dlery \-lə-rē\ n, pl **-dler·ies** (15c) **1** : a place where candles are kept **2** : the business of a chandler **3** : the commodities sold by a chandler

¹**change** \'chānj\ vb **changed; chang·ing** [ME, fr. OF changier, fr. L cambiare to exchange, prob. of Celt origin; akin to OIr camm crooked] vt (13c) **1 a** : to make different in some particular : ALTER ⟨never bothered to ∼ the will⟩ **b** : to make radically different : TRANSFORM ⟨can't ∼ human nature⟩ **c** : to give a different position, course, or direction to **2 a** : to replace with another ⟨let's ∼ the subject⟩ **b** : to make a shift from one to another : SWITCH ⟨always ∼s sides in an argument⟩ **c** : to exchange for an equivalent sum or comparable item **d** : to undergo a modification of ⟨foliage changing color⟩ **e** : to put fresh clothes or covering on ⟨∼ a bed⟩ ∼ vi **1** : to become different ⟨her mood ∼s every hour⟩ **2** of the moon : to pass from one phase to another **3** : to shift one's means of conveyance : TRANSFER ⟨on the bus trip he had to ∼ twice⟩ **4** of the voice : to shift to lower register : BREAK **5** : to undergo transformation, transition, or substitution

chamomile

⟨winter *changed* to spring⟩ **6** : to put on different clothes **7** : EXCHANGE, SWITCH ⟨neither liked his seat so they *changed* with each other⟩ — **chang·er** n — **change hands** : to pass from the possession of one owner to that of another ⟨money *changes hands* many times⟩

syn CHANGE, ALTER, VARY, MODIFY mean to make or become different. CHANGE implies making either an essential difference often amounting to a loss of original identity or a substitution of one thing for another ⟨*changed* the shirt for a larger size⟩. ALTER implies a difference in some particular respect without suggesting loss of identity ⟨slightly *altered* the original design⟩. VARY stresses a breaking away from sameness, duplication, or exact repetition ⟨*vary* your daily routine⟩. MODIFY suggests a difference that limits, restricts, or adapts to a new purpose ⟨*modified* the building for use by the handicapped⟩.

²change n (13c) **1** : the act, process, or result of changing: as **a** : ALTERATION ⟨a ~ in the weather⟩ **b** : TRANSFORMATION ⟨a time of vast social ~⟩ ⟨going through ~s⟩ **c** : SUBSTITUTION ⟨a ~ of scenery⟩ **d** : the passage of the moon from one monthly revolution to another; *also* : the passage of the moon from one phase to another **2** : a fresh set of clothes **3** *Brit* : EXCHANGE 5a **4 a** : money in small denominations received in exchange for an equivalent sum in larger denominations **b** : money returned when a payment exceeds the amount due **c** : coins esp. of low denominations ⟨a pocketful of ~⟩ **d** : a negligible additional amount ⟨only six minutes and ~ left in the game⟩ **5** : an order in which a set of bells is struck in change ringing **6** : CHANGE-UP

change·able \'chān-jə-bəl\ adj (13c) : capable of change: as **a** : able or apt to vary ⟨~ weather⟩ **b** : subject to change : ALTERABLE **c** : FICKLE **d** : IRIDESCENT — **change·abil·i·ty** \,chān-jə-'bi-lə-tē\ n — **change·able·ness** \'chān-jə-bəl-nəs\ n — **change·ably** \-blē\ adv

change·ful \-fəl\ adj (1591) : notably variable : UNCERTAIN — **change·ful·ly** \-fə-lē\ adv — **change·ful·ness** n

change·less \'chānj-ləs\ adj (1580) : marked by the absence of change : CONSTANT — **change·less·ly** adv — **change·less·ness** n

change·ling \'chānj-liŋ\ n (1537) **1** *archaic* : TURNCOAT **2** : a child secretly exchanged for another in infancy **3** *archaic* : IMBECILE — **changeling** adj

change off vi (1873) **1** : to alternate with another at doing an act **2** : to alternate between two different acts or instruments or between an action and a rest period

change of heart (ca. 1828) : a reversal in position or attitude

change of life (1834) : ²CLIMACTERIC 2

change of pace (1912) **1** : CHANGE-UP **2** : an interruption of continuity by a shift to a different activity

change·over \'chānj-jō-vər\ n (1907) **1** : CONVERSION, TRANSITION **2** : a pause in a tennis match during which the players change sides of the court

change ringing n (1872) : the art or practice of ringing a set of tuned bells (as in the bell tower of a church) in continually varying order

change-up \'chān-jəp\ n (1949) : a slow pitch in baseball thrown with the same motion as a fastball in order to deceive the batter

¹chan·nel \'cha-nᵊl\ n [ME *chanel*, fr. MF, fr. L *canalis* channel — more at CANAL] (14c) **1 a** : the bed where a natural stream of water runs **b** : the deeper part of a river, harbor, or strait **c** : a strait or narrow sea between two close landmasses **d** : a means of communication or expression: as **(1)** : a path along which information (as data or music) in the form of an electrical signal passes **(2)** *pl* : a fixed or official course of communication ⟨went through established military ~s with his grievances⟩ **e** : a way, course, or direction of thought or action ⟨new ~s of exploration⟩ **f** : a band of frequencies of sufficient width for a single radio or television communication **g** : CHANNELER **2 a** : a usu. tubular enclosed passage : CONDUIT **b** : a passage created in a selectively permeable membrane by a conformational change in membrane proteins **3** : a long gutter, groove, or furrow **4** : a metal bar of flattened U-shaped section

²channel vt **-neled** or **-nelled; -nel·ing** or **-nel·ling** (15c) **1 a** : to form, cut, or wear a channel in **b** : to make a groove in ⟨~ a chair leg⟩ **2** : to convey or direct into or through a channel ⟨~ his energy into constructive activities⟩ **3** : to serve as a channeler or intermediary for

³channel n [alter. of *chainwale*, fr. ¹*chain* + ¹*wale*] (1769) : one of the flat ledges of heavy plank or metal bolted edgewise to the outside of a ship to increase the spread of the shrouds

channel bass n (1887) : a large coppery drum (*Sciaenops ocellatus*) chiefly of the Atlantic coast of No. America that has a black spot at the base of the tail and is an important game and food fish — called also *red drum*, *redfish*

channel catfish n (1820) : a large black-spotted catfish (*Ictalurus punctatus*) that is an important freshwater food fish of the U.S. and Canada — called also *channel cat*

chan·nel·er \'cha-nᵊl-ər\ n (1987) : a person who conveys thoughts or energy from a source believed to be outside the person's body or conscious mind; *specif* : one who speaks for nonphysical beings or spirits

chan·nel·ize \'cha-nᵊl-,īz\ vt **-ized; -iz·ing** (1609) **1** : CHANNEL 1, 2 **2** : to straighten by means of a channel ⟨~ a stream⟩ — **chan·nel·i·za·tion** \,cha-nᵊl-ə-'zā-shən\ n

channel surfing n (1990) : the act or practice of scanning through television programs usu. by use of a remote control to find something of interest — **channel surf** vi — **channel surfer** n

chan·son \shän-'sōⁿ\ n, pl **chan·sons** \-'sōⁿ(z)\ [F, fr. L *cantion-*, *cantio*, fr. *canere*] (1602) : SONG; *specif* : a music-hall or cabaret song

chanson de geste \-də-'zhest\ n, pl **chansons de geste** *same*\ [F, lit., song of heroic deeds] (1868) : any of several Old French epic poems of the 11th to the 13th centuries

chan·son·nier \shäⁿ-sō-'nyā\ n [F, fr. *chanson*] (1887) : a writer or singer of chansons; *esp* : a cabaret singer

¹chant \'chant\ vb [ME *chaunten*, fr. MF *chanter*, fr. L *cantare*, freq. of *canere* to sing; akin to OE *hana* rooster, OIr *canid* he sings] vi (14c) **1** : to make melodic sounds with the voice; *esp* : to sing a chant **2** : to recite in a monotonous repetitive tone ~ vt **1** : to utter as in chanting **2** : to celebrate or praise in song or chant

²chant n (1671) **1** : SONG **2 a** : PLAINSONG **b** : a rhythmic monotonous utterance or song **c** : a composition for chanting

chant·er \'chan-tər\ n (14c) **1** : one that chants: **a** : CHORISTER **b** : CANTOR **2** : the chief singer in a chantry **3** : the reed pipe of a bagpipe with finger holes on which the melody is played

chan·te·relle \,shan-tə-'rel, ,shän-\ n [F] (1775) : a fragrant edible mushroom (*Cantharellus cibarius*) of rich yellow color

chan·teuse \shan-'tüz, shäⁿ-'tə(r)z\ n, pl **chan·teuses** \-'tüz, -'tü-zəz, -'tə(r)z, -'tə(r)-zəz\ [F, fem. of *chanteur* singer, fr. *chanter*] (1888) : a woman who is a concert or nightclub singer

chan·tey or **chan·ty** \'shan-tē, 'chan-\ n, pl **chanteys** or **chanties** [modif. of F *chanter*] (1856) : a song sung by sailors in rhythm with their work

chan·ti·cleer \,chan-tə-'klir, ,shan-\ n [ME *Chantecleer*, rooster in verse narratives, fr. OF *Chantecler*, rooster in the *Roman de Renart*] (14c) : ROOSTER

Chan·til·ly lace \shan-'ti-lē-\ n [*Chantilly*, France] (1848) : a delicate silk, linen, or synthetic lace having a six-sided mesh ground and a floral or scrolled design — called also *Chantilly*

chan·try \'chan-trē\ n, pl **chantries** [ME *chanterie*, fr. MF, singing, fr. *chanter*] (14c) **1** : an endowment for the chanting of masses commonly for the founder **2** : a chapel endowed by a chantry

Cha·nu·kah \'kä-nə-kə, 'hä-\ var of HANUKKAH

cha·os \'kā-,äs\ n [L, fr. Gk — more at GUM] (15c) **1** *obs* : CHASM, ABYSS **2 a** *often cap* : a state of things in which chance is supreme; *esp* : the confused unorganized state of primordial matter before the creation of distinct forms — compare COSMOS **b** : the inherent unpredictability in the behavior of a natural system (as the atmosphere, boiling water, or the beating heart) **3 a** : a state of utter confusion **b** : a confused mass or mixture ⟨a ~ of television antennas⟩ — **cha·ot·ic** \kā-'ä-tik\ adj — **cha·ot·i·cal·ly** \-ti-k(ə-)lē\ adv

¹chap \'chap\ n (14c) : a crack in or a sore roughening of the skin caused by exposure to wind or cold

²chap vb **chapped; chap·ping** [ME *chappen*; akin to MD *cappen* to cut down] vi (15c) **1** : to open in cracks, slits, or chinks; *also* : to become cracked, roughened, or reddened esp. by the action of wind or cold ⟨hands often ~ in winter⟩ ~ vt : to cause to chap ⟨wind-*chapped* lips⟩

³chap \'chap, 'chäp\ n [origin unknown] (1555) **1 a** : the fleshy covering of a jaw; *also* : JAW — usu. used in pl. ⟨a wolf's ~s⟩ **2** : the forepart of the face — usu. used in pl.

⁴chap n [short for *chapman*] (1716) **1** : FELLOW 4c **2** *Southern & Midland* : BABY, CHILD

chap·a·ra·jos or **chap·a·re·jos** \,sha-pə-'rä-(,)ōs, -'rä-\ n pl [modif. of MexSp *chaparreras*, fr. *chaparro*] (1887) : CHAPS

chap·ar·ral \,sha-pə-'ral, -rel\ n [Sp, fr. *chaparro* dwarf evergreen oak, fr. Basque *txapar*] (1845) **1** : a thicket of dwarf evergreen oaks; *broadly* : a dense impenetrable thicket of shrubs or dwarf trees **2** : an ecological community composed of shrubby plants adapted to dry summers and moist winters that occurs esp. in southern California

chaparral cock n (1853) : ROADRUNNER — called also *chaparral bird*

cha·pa·ti also **cha·pa·ti** \chə-'pä-tē\ n, pl **chapatis** also **chappatis** [Hindi *capātī*] (1810) : a round flat unleavened bread of India that is usu. made of whole wheat flour and cooked on a griddle

chap·book \'chap-,bùk\ n [*chap*man + *book*] (1798) : a small book containing ballads, poems, tales, or tracts

chape \'chāp, 'chap\ n [ME, scabbard, fr. MF, cape, fr. LL *cappa*] (14c) : the metal mounting or trimming of a scabbard or sheath

cha·peau \sha-'pō, shə-\ n, pl **cha·peaus** \-'pōz\ or **cha·peaux** \-'pō(z)\ [MF, fr. OF *chapel* — more at CHAPLET] (1523) : HAT

chap·el \'cha-pəl\ n [ME, fr. OF *chapele*, fr. ML *cappella*, fr. dim. of LL *cappa* cloak; fr. the cloak of St. Martin of Tours preserved as a sacred relic in a chapel built for that purpose] (13c) **1** : a subordinate or private place of worship: as **a** : a place of worship serving a residence or institution **b** : a small house of worship usu. associated with a main church **c** : a room or recess in a church for meditation and prayer or small religious services **2** : a place of worship used by a Christian group other than an established church **3** : a choir of singers belonging to a chapel **4** : a chapel service or assembly at a school or college **5** : an association of the employees in a printing office **6 a** : FUNERAL HOME **b** : a room for funeral services in a funeral home

chapel of ease (1538) : a chapel or dependent church built to accommodate an expanding parish

¹chap·er·on or **chap·er·one** \'sha-pə-,rōn\ n [F *chaperon*, lit., hood, fr. MF, head covering, fr. *chape*] (1720) **1** : a person (as a matron) who for propriety accompanies one or more young unmarried women in public or in mixed company **2** : an older person who accompanies young people at a social gathering to ensure proper behavior; *broadly* : one delegated to ensure proper behavior

²chaperon or **chaperone** vt **-oned; -on·ing** vt (1796) **1** : ESCORT 2 : to act as chaperon to or for ~ vi : to act as a chaperon — **chap·er·on·age** \-,rō-nij\ n

chap·fall·en \'chap-,fò-lən, 'chäp-\ adj (1598) **1** : having the lower jaw hanging loosely **2** : cast down in spirit : DEPRESSED

chap·i·ter \'cha-pə-tər\ n [ME *chapitre*, fr. MF, alter. of OF *chapitle*, fr. L *capitulum*, lit., little head] (15c) : the capital of a column

chap·lain \'cha-plən\ n [ME *chapelain*, fr. OF, fr. ML *cappellanus*, fr. *cappella*] (14c) **1** : a clergyman in charge of a chapel **2** : a clergyman officially attached to a branch of the military, to an institution, or to a family or court **3** : a person chosen to conduct religious exercises (as at a meeting of a club or society) **4** : a clergyman appointed to assist a bishop (as at a liturgical function) — **chap·lain·cy** \-sē\ n

chap·let \'chap-lət\ n [ME *chapelet*, fr. MF, fr. OF, dim. of *chapel* hat, garland, fr. ML *cappellus* head covering, fr. LL *cappa*] (14c) **1** : a wreath to be worn on the head **2 a** : a string of beads **b** : a part of a rosary comprising five decades **3** : a small molding carved with small decorative forms — **chap·let·ed** \-lə-təd\ adj

chap·man \'chap-mən\ n [ME, fr. OE *cēapman*, fr. *cēap* trade + *man* — more at CHEAP] (bef. 12c) **1** *archaic* : MERCHANT, TRADER **2** *Brit* : PEDDLER

chaps \'shaps, 'chaps\ n pl [modif. of MexSp *chaparreras*] (1844) : leather leggings joined by a belt or lacing, often having flared outer

\ə\ abut \ᵊ\ kitten, F table \ər\ further \a\ ash \ā\ ace \ä\ mop, mar \au̇\ out \ch\ chin \e\ bet \ē\ easy \g\ go \i\ hit \ī\ ice \j\ job \ŋ\ sing \ō\ go \ȯ\ law \ȯi\ boy \th\ thin \t̲h̲\ the \ü\ loot \u̇\ foot \y\ yet \zh\ vision \ä, k̲, ⁿ, œ, œ̄, ᵫ, ᵫ̄, ᵊ\ see Guide to Pronunciation flaps, and worn over the trousers (as by western ranch hands)

chap·ter \'chap-tər\ n [ME chapitre, fr. OF, fr. LL capitulum division of a book & ML, meeting place of canons, fr. L, dim. of capit-, caput head — more at HEAD] (13c) **1 a** : a main division of a book **b** : something resembling a chapter in being a significant specified unit ⟨a new ~ in my life⟩ **2 a** : a regular meeting of the canons of a cathedral or collegiate church or of the members of a religious house **b** : the body of canons of a cathedral or collegiate church **3** : a local branch of an organization

chapter and verse n (1628) **1** : the exact reference or source of information or justification for an assertion ⟨clinched their arguments by citing chapter and verse —J. M. Burns⟩ **2** : full precise information or detail ⟨can give chapter and verse on the effects of diverting defense spending —Horace Sutton⟩ — **chapter and verse** adv

¹char \'chär\ n, pl **char** or **chars** [origin unknown] (1662) : any of a genus (Salvelinus) of small-scaled trouts with light-colored spots

²char vb **charred; char·ring** [charcoal] vt (1679) **1** : to convert to charcoal or carbon usu. by heat : BURN **2** : to burn slightly or partly : SCORCH ⟨the fire charred the beams⟩ ~ vi : to become charred

³char n (1879) : a charred substance : CHARCOAL; specif : a combustible residue remaining after the destructive distillation of coal

⁴char vi **charred; char·ring** [charwoman] (1732) : to work as a cleaning woman

⁵char n [by shortening] (1906) Brit : CHARWOMAN

char·a·banc \'shar-ə-baŋ, -ˌbaŋ\ n [F char à bancs, lit., wagon with benches] (1914) Brit : a sight-seeing motor coach

char·a·cin \'kar-ə-sən\ n [ultim. fr. Gk charak-, charax pointed stake, a fish] (1882) : any of a family (Characidae) of usu. small brightly colored tropical freshwater fishes that includes many aquarium fishes — **characin** adj

¹char·ac·ter \'kar-ik-tər\ n [ME caracter, fr. MF caractère, fr. L character mark, distinctive quality, fr. Gk charaktēr, fr. charassein to scratch, engrave; perh. akin to Lith žeyti to scratch] (14c) **1 a** : a conventionalized graphic device placed on an object as an indication of ownership, origin, or relationship **b** : a graphic symbol (as a hieroglyph or alphabet letter) used in writing or printing **c** : a magical or astrological emblem **e** (1) : ALPHABET **e** (1) : WRITING, PRINTING (2) : style of writing or printing (3) : CIPHER **f** : a symbol (as a letter or number) that represents information; also : a representation of such a character that may be accepted by a computer **2 a** : one of the attributes or features that make up and distinguish an individual **b** (1) : a feature used to separate distinguishable things into categories; also : a group or kind so separated ⟨advertising of a very primitive ~⟩ (2) : the detectable expression of the action of a gene or group of genes (3) : the aggregate of distinctive qualities characteristic of a breed, strain, or type ⟨a wine of great ~⟩ **c** : the complex of mental and ethical traits marking and often individualizing a person, group, or nation **d** : main or essential nature esp. as strongly marked and serving to distinguish ⟨excess sewage gradually changed the ~ of the lake⟩ **3** : POSITION, CAPACITY ⟨his ~ as a town official⟩ **4** : REFERENCE 4b **5** : REPUTATION **6** : moral excellence and firmness ⟨a man of sound ~⟩ **7 a** : a person marked by notable or conspicuous traits ⟨quite a ~⟩ **b** : one of the persons of a drama or novel **c** : the personality or part which an actor recreates **d** : characterization esp. in drama or fiction **e** : PERSON, INDIVIDUAL ⟨some ~ just stole her purse⟩ **8** : a short literary sketch of the qualities of a social type **syn** see DISPOSITION, QUALITY, TYPE — **char·ac·ter·less** \-ləs\ adj — **in character** : in accord with a person's usual qualities or traits — **out of character** : not in accord with a person's usual qualities or traits

²character vt (1591) **1** archaic : ENGRAVE, INSCRIBE **2 a** archaic : REPRESENT, PORTRAY **b** : CHARACTERIZE

³character adj (1893) **1** : capable of portraying an unusual or eccentric personality often markedly different from the player ⟨a ~ actor⟩ **2** : requiring the qualities of a character actor ⟨a ~ role⟩

character assassination n (1949) : the slandering of a person usu. with the intention of destroying public confidence in that person

char·ac·ter·ful \'kar-ik-tər-fəl\ adj (1901) **1** : markedly expressive of character ⟨a ~ face⟩ **2** : marked by character ⟨a ~ decision⟩

¹char·ac·ter·is·tic \ˌkar-ik-tə-'ris-tik\ n (1664) **1** : a distinguishing trait, quality, or property **2** : the integral part of a common logarithm **3** : the smallest positive integer n which for an operation in a ring or field yields 0 when any element is used n times with the operation

²characteristic adj (1665) : revealing, distinguishing, or typical of an individual character — **char·ac·ter·is·ti·cal·ly** \-ti-k(ə-)lē\ adv
syn CHARACTERISTIC, INDIVIDUAL, PECULIAR, DISTINCTIVE mean indicating a special quality or identity. CHARACTERISTIC applies to something that distinguishes or identifies a person or thing or class ⟨responded with her characteristic wit⟩. INDIVIDUAL stresses qualities that distinguish one from all other members of the same kind or class ⟨a highly individual writing style⟩. PECULIAR applies to qualities possessed only by a particular individual or class or kind and stresses rarity or uniqueness ⟨an eccentricity that is peculiar to the British⟩. DISTINCTIVE indicates qualities distinguishing and uncommon and often superior or praiseworthy ⟨a distinctive aura of grace and elegance⟩.

characteristic equation n (ca. 1925) : an equation in which the characteristic polynomial of a matrix is set equal to 0

characteristic polynomial n (ca. 1957) : the determinant of a square matrix in which an arbitrary variable (as x) is subtracted from each of the elements along the principal diagonal

characteristic root n (ca. 1957) : EIGENVALUE

characteristic value n (1956) : EIGENVALUE

characteristic vector n (1957) : EIGENVECTOR

char·ac·ter·iza·tion \ˌkar-ik-t(ə-)rə-'zā-shən\ n (1814) : the act of characterizing; esp : the artistic representation (as in fiction or drama) of human character or motives

char·ac·ter·ize \'kar-ik-tə-ˌrīz\ vt **-ized; -iz·ing** (1633) **1** : to describe the character or quality of : DISTINGUISH ⟨an era characterized by greed⟩ **2** : to be a characteristic of : DISTINGUISH

char·ac·ter·olog·i·cal \ˌkar-ik-t(ə-)rə-'lä-ji-kəl\ adj [characterology]

chaps

study of character] (1916) : of, relating to, or based on character or the study of character including its development and its differences in different individuals — **char·ac·ter·olog·i·cal·ly** \-'lä-ji-k(ə-)lē\ adv

character witness n (1952) : a person who gives evidence in a legal action concerning the reputation, conduct, and moral nature of a party

char·ac·tery \'kar-ik-t(ə-)rē, kə-'rak-\ n, pl **-ter·ies** (1598) : a system of written letters or symbols used in the expression of thought

cha·rade \shə-'rād, -'räd\ n [F, fr. Prov charrado chat, fr. charrá to chat, chatter] (1776) **1** : a word represented in riddling verse or by picture, tableau, or dramatic action **2 pl** : a game in which some of the players try to guess a word or phrase from the actions of another player who may not speak **3** : an empty or deceptive act or pretense ⟨his concern was a ~⟩

cha·ras \'chär-əs\ n [Hindi caras] (ca. 1860) : HASHISH

char·broil \'chär-ˌbroi(ə)l\ vt (1968) : to broil on a rack over hot charcoal — **char·broil·er** \-ˌbroi-lər\ n

¹char·coal \'chär-ˌkōl\ n [ME charcole] (14c) **1** : a dark or black porous carbon prepared from vegetable or animal substances (as from wood by charring in a kiln from which air is excluded) **2 a** : a piece or pencil of fine charcoal used in drawing **b** : a charcoal drawing **3** : a dark gray

²charcoal vt (1965) : CHARBROIL

char·cu·te·rie \ˌ(ˌ)shär-ˌkü-tə-'rē\ n [F, lit., pork-butcher's shop, fr. MF chaircuiterie, fr. chaircutier pork butcher, fr. chair cuite cooked meat] (ca. 1858) : a delicatessen specializing in dressed meats and meat dishes; also : the products sold in such a shop

chard \'chärd\ n [modif. of F carde, fr. Prov cardo, fr. L carduus thistle, cardoon] (1664) : SWISS CHARD

char·don·nay \ˌshär-d°n-'ā\ n, often cap [F] (ca. 1941) : a dry white table wine of Chablis type

chare \'char, 'cher\ or chare \'chär\ n [ME char turn, piece of work, fr. OE cierr; akin to OE cierran to turn] (bef. 12c) : CHORE

¹charge \'chärj\ n [ME, fr. OF, fr. chargier] (13c) **1 a** obs : a material load or weight **b** : a figure borne on a heraldic field **2 a** : the quantity that an apparatus is intended to receive and fitted to hold **b** : a store or accumulation of impelling force ⟨the deeply emotional ~ of the drama⟩ **c** : a definite quantity of electricity; esp : an excess or deficiency of electrons in a body ⟨got a ~ out of the game⟩ **3 a** : OBLIGATION, REQUIREMENT **b** : MANAGEMENT, SUPERVISION ⟨has ~ of the home office⟩ **c** : the ecclesiastical jurisdiction (as a parish) committed to a clergyman **d** : a person or thing committed to the care of another **4 a** : INSTRUCTION, COMMAND **b** : instruction in points of law given by a court to a jury **5 a** : EXPENSE, COST ⟨gave the banquet at his own ~⟩ **b** : the price demanded for something ⟨no admission ~⟩ **c** : a debit to an account ⟨the purchase was a ~⟩ **d** : the record of a loan (as of a book from a library) **e** Brit : an interest in property granted as security for a loan **6 a** : a formal assertion of illegality ⟨a ~ of murder⟩ **b** : a statement of complaint or hostile criticism ⟨denied the ~s of nepotism that were leveled against him⟩ **7** : a violent rush forward (as to attack) — **in charge** : having control or custody of something ⟨he is in charge of the training program⟩

²charge vb **charged; charg·ing** [ME, fr. OF chargier, fr. LL carricare, fr. L carrus wheeled vehicle — more at CAR] vt (14c) **1 a** archaic : to lay or put a load on or in : LOAD **b** (1) : to place a charge (as of powder) in (2) : to load or fill to capacity **c** (1) : to restore the active materials in (a storage battery) by the passage of a direct current through in the opposite direction to that of discharge (2) : to give an electric charge to ⟨~ a capacitor⟩ **d** (1) : to assume as a heraldic bearing (2) : to place a heraldic bearing on **e** : to fill or furnish fully ⟨the music is charged with excitement⟩ **2 a** : to impose a task or responsibility on ⟨~ him with the job of finding a new meeting place⟩ **b** : to command, instruct, or exhort with authority ⟨I ~ you not to go⟩ **c** of a judge : to give a charge to (a jury) **3 a** : to make an assertion against esp. by ascribing guilt or blame ⟨~s him with armed robbery⟩ ⟨they were charged as being instigators⟩ **b** : to place the guilt or blame for ⟨~ her failure to negligence⟩ **c** : to assert as an accusation ⟨~s that he distorted the data⟩ **4 a** : to bring (a weapon) into position for attack : LEVEL ⟨~ a lance⟩ **b** : to rush against : ATTACK; also : to rush into (an opponent) usu. illegally in various sports **5 a** (1) : to impose a financial burden on ⟨~ his estate with debts incurred⟩ (2) : to fix or record as financial obligation ⟨~ debts on an estate⟩ **b** (1) : to fix or ask as fee or payment ⟨~s $50 for an office visit⟩ (2) : to ask payment of (a person) ⟨~ a client for expenses⟩ **c** : to record (an item) as an expense, debt, obligation, or liability ⟨charged a new sofa⟩ ~ vi **1** : to rush forward in or as if in assault : ATTACK; also : to charge an opponent in sports **2** : to ask or set a price ⟨do you ~ for this service?⟩ **3** : to charge an item to an account ⟨~ now, pay later⟩ **syn** see COMMAND

charge·able \'chär-jə-bəl\ adj (14c) **1** archaic : financially burdensome : EXPENSIVE **2** : liable to be charged: as **a** : liable to be accused or held responsible **b** : suitable to be charged to a particular account **c** : qualified to be made a charge on the county or parish

charge account n (1903) : a customer's account with a creditor (as a merchant) to which the purchase of goods is charged

charge card n (1950) : CREDIT CARD

charge–coupled device n (1971) : a semiconductor device that is used esp. as an optical sensor and that stores charge and transfers it sequentially to an amplifier and detector — called also CCD

charged \'chärjd\ adj (1934) **1** : possessing or showing strong emotion ⟨attacked the author in a highly ~ review⟩ **2** : capable of arousing strong emotion ⟨a politically ~ subject⟩

char·gé d'af·faires \ˌ(ˌ)shär-ˌzhä-də-'far, -'fer\ n, pl **chargés d'af·faires** \-ˌzhä-də-, -ˌzhäz-də-\ [F, lit., one charged with affairs] (1767) **1** : a subordinate diplomat who substitutes for an absent ambassador or minister **2** : a diplomat inferior in rank to an ambassador or minister who heads a mission when no ambassador or minister is assigned

charge·hand \'chärj-ˌhand\ n (1916) Brit : FOREMAN

charge off vt (ca. 1923) : to treat as a loss or expense — **charge-off** \'chärj-ˌof\ n

charge of quarters n (1918) : an enlisted man designated to handle administrative matters in his unit esp. after duty hours — abbr. CQ

¹char·ger \'chär-jər\ n [ME chargeour; akin to ME chargen to charge] (14c) : a large flat dish or platter

²charg·er n (1539) **1** : one that charges: as **a** : an appliance for holding or inserting a charge of powder or shot in a gun **b** : a cartridge clip **c** : a device for charging storage batteries **2** : a horse for battle or parade

char·i·ness \'char-ē-nəs, 'cher-\ *n* (1571) **1** : the quality or state of being chary : CAUTION **2** : carefully preserved state : INTEGRITY

¹char·i·ot \'char-ē-ət\ *n* [ME, fr. MF, fr. OF, fr. *char* wheeled vehicle, fr. L *carrus* — more at CAR] (14c) **1** : a light four-wheeled pleasure or state carriage **2** : a two-wheeled horse-drawn battle car of ancient times used also in processions and races

²chariot *vi* (1550) : to drive or ride in or as if in a chariot ~ *vt* : to carry in or as if in a chariot

char·i·ot·eer \,char-ē-ə-'tir\ *n* (14c) **1** : one who drives a chariot **2** *cap* : AURIGA

cha·ris·ma \kə-'riz-mə\ *also* **char·ism** \'kar-,i-zəm\ *n*, *pl* **cha·ris·ma·ta** \kə-'riz-mə-tə, ,kər-iz-'mä-tə\ *also* **charisms** [Gk *charisma* favor, gift, fr. *charizesthai* to favor, fr. *charis* grace; akin to Gk *chairein* to rejoice — more at YEARN] (ca. 1641) **1** : an extraordinary power (as of healing) given a Christian by the Holy Spirit for the good of the church **2 a** : a personal magic of leadership arousing special popular loyalty or enthusiasm for a public figure (as a political leader) **b** : a special magnetic charm or appeal ⟨the ~ of a popular actor⟩

¹char·is·mat·ic \,kar-əz-'ma-tik\ *adj* [*charisma*] (ca. 1868) **1** : of, relating to, or constituting charisma **2** : having, exhibiting, or based on charisma ⟨~ sects⟩ ⟨~ leader⟩

²charismatic *n* (1951) : a member of a charismatic religious group or movement

char·i·ta·ble \'char-ə-tə-bəl\ *adj* (14c) **1** : full of love for and goodwill toward others : BENEVOLENT **2 a** : liberal in benefactions to the needy : GENEROUS **b** : of or relating to charity ⟨~ institutions⟩ **3** : merciful or kind in judging others : LENIENT — **char·i·ta·ble·ness** *n* — **char·i·ta·bly** \-blē\ *adv*

char·i·ty \'char-ət-ē\ *n*, *pl* **-ties** [ME *charite*, fr. OF *charité*, fr. LL *caritat-, caritas* Christian love, fr. L, dearness, fr. *carus* dear; akin to OIr *carae* friend, Skt *kāma* love] (13c) **1** : benevolent goodwill toward or love of humanity **2 a** : generosity and helpfulness esp. toward the needy or suffering; *also* : aid given to those in need **b** : an institution engaged in relief of the poor **c** : public provision for the relief of the needy **3 a** : a gift for public benevolent purposes **b** : an institution (as a hospital) founded by such a gift **4** : lenient judgment of others *syn* see MERCY

cha·ri·va·ri \,shi-və-'rē, 'shi-və-,\ *n* [F, perh. fr. LL *caribaria* headache, fr. Gk *karēbaria*, fr. *kara, karē* head + *barys* heavy — more at CEREBRAL, GRIEVE] (ca. 1681) : SHIVAREE

char·la·tan \'shär-lə-tən\ *n* [It *ciarlatano*, alter. of *cerretano*, lit., inhabitant of Cerreto, fr. *Cerreto*, Italy] (1618) **1** : QUACK **2** ⟨~s killing their patients with empirical procedures⟩ **2** : one making usu. showy pretenses to knowledge or ability : FRAUD, FAKER — **char·la·tan·ism** \-tə-,ni-zəm\ *n* — **char·la·tan·ry** \-rē\ *n*

Charles's Wain \'chärlz-'wän, ,chärl-zəz-\ *n* [*Charlemagne*] : BIG DIPPER

Charles·ton \'chärl-stən\ *n* [*Charleston*, S. C.] (1925) : a lively ballroom dance in which the knees are twisted in and out and the heels are swung sharply outward on each step

char·ley horse \'chär-lē-,hórs\ *n* [fr. *Charley*, nickname for *Charles*] (1888) : a muscular pain, cramping, or stiffness esp. of the quadriceps that results from a strain or bruise

char·lie *also* **char·ley** \'chär-lē\ *n*, *often cap* [fr. the name *Charlie*] (ca. 1946) *Brit* : FOOL

Char·lie \'chär-lē\ [fr. the name *Charlie*] (1946) — a communications code word for the letter *c*

char·lock \'chär-,läk, -lək\ *n* [ME *cherlok*, fr. OE *cerlic*] (bef. 12c) : a mustard (*Brassica kaber*) that is a common weed in grainfields — called also *wild mustard*

char·lotte \'shär-lət\ *n* [F] (1796) : a dessert consisting of a filling (as of fruit, whipped cream, or custard) layered with or placed in a mold lined with strips of bread, cake, or biscuits

char·lotte russe \'shär-lət-'rüs\ *n* [F, lit., Russian charlotte] (ca. 1845) : a charlotte made with sponge cake or ladyfingers and a whipped-cream or custard-gelatin filling

¹charm \'chärm\ *n* [ME *charme*, fr. MF, fr. L *carmen* song, fr. *canere* to sing — more at CHANT] (14c) **1 a** : the chanting or reciting of a magic spell : INCANTATION **b** : a practice or expression believed to have magic power **2** : something worn about the person to ward off evil or ensure good fortune : AMULET **3 a** : a trait that fascinates, allures, or delights **b** : a physical grace or attraction — used in pl. **c** : compelling attractiveness ⟨the island possessed great ~⟩ **4** : a small ornament worn on a bracelet or chain **5** : a quantum characteristic of subatomic particles that accounts for the unexpectedly long lifetime of the J/psi particle, explains difficulties in the theory of the weak force, is conserved in interactions involving electromagnetism or the strong force, and has a value of zero for most known particles — **charm·less** \-ləs\ *adj*

²charm *vt* (14c) **1 a** : to affect by or as if by magic : COMPEL **b** : to please, soothe, or delight by compelling attraction ⟨~s customers with his suave manner⟩ **2** : to endow with or as if with supernatural powers by means of charms; *also* : to protect by or as if by spells, charms, or supernatural influences **3** : to control (an animal) typically by charms (as the playing of music) ⟨~ a snake⟩ ~ *vi* **1** : to practice magic and enchantment **2** : to have the effect of a charm : FASCINATE *syn* see ATTRACT — **charm·er** \'chär-mər\ *n*

charmed \'chärmd\ *adj* (1964) : having the quantum characteristic of charm ⟨a ~ antiquark⟩

charmed circle *n* (1898) : a group marked by exclusiveness

char·meuse \(,)shär-'müz, -'müs, -'myüz, -'mə(r)z\ *n* [F, fem. of *charmeur* charmer, fr. *charmer* to charm] (1907) : a fine semilustrous crepe in satin weave

charm·ing \'chär-miŋ\ *adj* (1663) : extremely pleasing or delightful : ENTRANCING — **charm·ing·ly** \-miŋ-lē\ *adv*

char·nel \'chär-n°l\ *n* [ME, fr. MF, fr. ML *carnale*, fr. LL, neut. of *carnalis* of the flesh — more at CARNAL] (14c) : a building or chamber in which bodies or bones are deposited — called also *charnel house* — **charnel** *adj*

Cha·ro·lais \,shar-ə-'lä\ *n* [*Charolais*, district in eastern France] (1893) : any of a breed of large white cattle developed in France and used primarily for beef and crossbreeding

Char·on \'kar-ən, 'ker-, -än\ *n* [L, fr. Gk *Charōn*] : a son of Erebus who in Greek mythology ferries the souls of the dead over the Styx

char·poy \'chär-,pói\ *n*, *pl* **charpoys** [Hindi *cārpāī*] (1845) : a bed used esp. in India consisting of a frame strung with tapes or light rope

charr \'chär\ *var of* ¹CHAR

¹chart \'chärt\ *n* [MF *charte*, fr. L *charta* piece of papyrus, document — more at CARD] (1571) **1** : MAP: as **a** : an outline map exhibiting something (as climatic or magnetic variations) in its geographical aspects **b** : a map for the use of navigators **2 a** : a sheet giving information in tabular form **b** : GRAPH **c** : DIAGRAM **d** : a sheet of paper ruled and graduated for use in a recording instrument **e** : a listing by rank (as of sales) — usu. used in pl. ⟨number one on the ~s —Tim Cahill⟩ **3** : a musical arrangement; *also* : a part in such an arrangement

²chart *vt* (1842) **1** : to lay out a plan for **2** : to make a map or chart of ~ *vi* : to be ranked on a chart ⟨the song ~ed for three months⟩

¹char·ter \'chär-tər\ *n* [ME *chartre*, fr. OF, fr. ML *chartula*, fr. L, dim. of *charta*] (13c) **1** : a written instrument or contract (as a deed) executed in due form **2 a** : a grant or guarantee of rights, franchises, or privileges from the sovereign power of a state or country **b** : a written instrument that creates and defines the franchises of a city, educational institution, or corporation **c** : CONSTITUTION **3** : a written instrument from the authorities of a society creating a lodge or branch **4** : a special privilege, immunity, or exemption **5** : a mercantile lease of a ship or some principal part of it **6** : a charter travel arrangement

²charter *vt* (15c) **1 a** : to establish, enable, or convey by charter **b** *Brit* : CERTIFY ⟨a ~ed mechanical engineer⟩ **2** : to hire, rent, or lease for usu. exclusive and temporary use ⟨~ed a boat for deep-sea fishing⟩ *syn* see HIRE — **char·ter·er** \-tər-ər\ *n*

³charter *adj* (1922) : of, relating to, or being a travel arrangement in which transportation (as a bus or plane) is hired by and for one specific group of people ⟨a ~ flight⟩

chartered accountant *n* (1855) *Brit* : a member of a chartered institute of accountants

charter member *n* (ca. 1909) : an original member of a group (as a society or corporation) — **charter membership** *n*

Char·tism \'chär-,ti-zəm\ *n* [ML *charta* charter, fr. L, document] (1839) : the principles and practices of a body of 19th century English political reformers advocating better social and industrial conditions for the working classes — **Char·tist** \'chär-tist\ *n or adj*

chart·ist \'chär-tist\ *n* (1919) **1** : an analyst of market action whose predictions of market courses are based on study of graphic presentations of past market performance **2** : CARTOGRAPHER

char·treuse \shär-'trüz, -'trüs\ *n* [*Chartreuse*] (1884) : a variable color averaging a brilliant yellow green

Chartreuse *trademark* — used for a usu. green or yellow liqueur

char·tu·lary \'kär-chə-,ler-ē\ *n*, *pl* **-lar·ies** [ML *chartularium*] (1571) : CARTULARY

char·wom·an \'chär-,wu̇-mən\ *n* [*chare* + *woman*] (1596) : a cleaning woman esp. in a large building

chary \'char-ē, 'cher-\ *adj* **chari·er; -est** [ME, sorrowful, dear, fr. OE *cearig* sorrowful, fr. *caru* sorrow — more at CARE] (15c) **1** *archaic* : DEAR, TREASURED **2** : discreetly cautious: as **a** : hesitant and vigilant about dangers and risks **b** : slow to grant, accept, or expend ⟨a person very ~ of compliments⟩ *syn* see CAUTIOUS — **chari·ly** \'char-ə-lē, 'cher-\ *adv*

Cha·ryb·dis \kə-'rib-dəs *also* shə- or chə-\ *n* [L, fr. Gk] : a whirlpool off the coast of Sicily personified in Greek mythology as a female monster — compare SCYLLA

¹chase \'chäs\ *n* (13c) **1 a** : the hunting of wild animals — used with *the* **b** : the act of chasing : PURSUIT **c** : an earnest or frenzied seeking after something desired **2** : something pursued : QUARRY **3** : a tract of unenclosed land used as a game preserve **4** : STEEPLECHASE 1 **5** : a sequence (as in a movie) in which the characters pursue one another

²chase *vb* **chased; chas·ing** [ME, fr. MF *chasser*, fr. (assumed) VL *captiare* — more at CATCH] *vt* (14c) **1 a** : to follow rapidly : PURSUE **b** : HUNT **c** : to follow regularly or persistently with the intention of attracting or alluring **2** *obs* : HARASS **3** : to seek out — often used with *down* ⟨detectives *chasing* down clues⟩ **4** : to cause to depart or flee : DRIVE ⟨~ the dog out of the garden⟩ **5** : to cause the removal of (a baseball pitcher) by a batting rally ~ *vi* **1** : to chase an animal, person, or thing ⟨~ after material possessions⟩ **2** : RUSH, HASTEN ⟨*chased* all over town looking for a place to stay⟩

syn CHASE, PURSUE, FOLLOW, TRAIL mean to go after or on the track of something or someone. CHASE implies going swiftly after and trying to overtake something fleeing or running ⟨a dog *chasing* a cat⟩. PURSUE suggests a continuing effort to overtake, reach, or attain ⟨*pursued* the criminal through narrow streets⟩. FOLLOW puts less emphasis upon speed or intent to overtake ⟨friends *followed* me home in their car⟩. TRAIL may stress a following of tracks or traces rather than a visible object ⟨*trail* a suspect across the country⟩.

³chase *vt* **chased; chas·ing** [ME *chassen*, modif. of MF *enchasser* to set] (15c) **1 a** : to ornament (metal) by indenting with a hammer and tools without a cutting edge **b** : to make by such indentation **c** : to set with gems **2 a** : GROOVE, INDENT **b** : to cut (a thread) with a chaser

⁴chase *n* [F *chas* eye of a needle, fr. LL *capsus* enclosed space, alter. of L *capsa* box — more at CASE] (1611) **1** : GROOVE, FURROW **2** : the bore of a cannon **3 a** : TRENCH **b** : a channel (as in a wall) for something to lie in or pass through

⁵chase *n* [prob. fr. F *châsse* frame, reliquary, fr. MF *chasse*, fr. L *capsa*] (1612) : a rectangular steel or iron frame in which letterpress matter is locked (as for printing)

---

¹chaser \'chā-sər\ n (13c) **1** : one that chases **2** : a mild drink (as beer) taken after hard liquor

²chaser n (1707) **1** : a skilled worker who produces ornamental chasing **2** : a tool for cutting screw threads

Chas·sid or **Chas·sid** \'ha-səd, 'kä-\ n, pl **Cha·si·dim** or **Chas·si·dim** \'ha-sə-dəm, kä-'sē-\ var of HASID

chasm \'ka-zᵊm\ n [L chasma, fr. Gk; akin to L hiare to yawn — more at YAWN] **1** : a deep cleft in the surface of a planet (as the earth) : GORGE **2** : a marked division, separation, or difference ⟨a political ~ between the two countries⟩

¹chas·sé \sha-'sā\ vi **chas·séd; chas·sé·ing** (1803) **1** : to make a chassé **2** : SASHAY

²chassé n [F, fr. pp. of chasser to chase] (1828) : a sliding dance step resembling the galop

chasse·pot \'shas-,pō, 'sha-sə-\ n [F, fr. Antoine A. Chassepot †1905 Fr. inventor] (1869) : a bolt-action rifle firing a paper cartridge

chas·seur \sha-'sər\ n [F, fr. MF chaceor] (1795) **1** : HUNTER, HUNTSMAN **2** : one of a body of light cavalry or infantry trained for rapid maneuvering **3** : a liveried attendant : FOOTMAN

chas·sis \'cha-sē, 'sha-sē also 'cha-səs\ n, pl **chas·sis** \-sēz\ [F châssis, fr. MF chaciz, fr. chasse] (ca. 1864) : the supporting frame of a structure (as an automobile or television); also : the frame and working parts (as of an automobile or electronic device) exclusive of the body or housing

chaste \'chāst\ adj **chast·er; chast·est** [ME, fr. OF, fr. L castus pure] (13c) **1** : innocent of unlawful sexual intercourse **2** : CELIBATE **3** : pure in thought and act : MODEST **4** **a** : severely simple in design or execution : AUSTERE ⟨~ classicism⟩ **b** : CLEAN, SPOTLESS — **chaste·ly** adv — **chaste·ness** \'chās(t)-nəs\ n

syn CHASTE, PURE, MODEST, DECENT mean free from all taint of what is lewd or salacious. CHASTE primarily implies a refraining from acts or even thoughts or desires that are not virginal or not sanctioned by marriage vows ⟨they maintained chaste relations⟩. PURE differs from CHASTE in implying innocence and absence of temptation rather than control of one's impulses and actions ⟨the pure of heart⟩. MODEST and DECENT apply esp. to deportment and dress as outward signs of inward chastity or purity ⟨preferred more modest swimsuits⟩ ⟨decent people didn't go to such movies⟩.

chas·ten \'chā-sᵊn\ vt **chas·tened; chas·ten·ing** \'chās-niŋ, 'chā-sᵊn-iŋ\ [alter. of obs. E chaste to chasten, fr. ME, fr. OF chastier, fr. L castigare, fr. castus + -igare (fr. agere to drive) — more at ACT] (13c) **1** : to correct by punishment or suffering : DISCIPLINE; also : PURIFY **2** **a** : to prune (as a work or style of art) of excess, pretense, or falsity : REFINE **b** : to cause to be more humble or restrained : SUBDUE **syn** see PUNISH — **chas·ten·er** \'chās-nər, 'chā-sᵊn-ər\ n

chas·tise \(,)chas-'tīz\ vt **chas·tised; chas·tis·ing** [ME chastisen, alter. of chasten] (14c) **1** : to inflict punishment on (as by whipping) **2** : to censure severely : CASTIGATE **3** archaic : CHASTEN **2** **syn** see PUNISH — **chas·tise·ment** \(,)chas-'tīz-mənt also 'chas-təz-\ n — **chas·tis·er** \(,)chas-'tī-zər\ n

chas·ti·ty \'chas-tə-tē\ n (13c) **1** : the quality or state of being chaste: as **a** : abstention from unlawful sexual intercourse **b** : abstention from all sexual intercourse **c** : purity in conduct and intention **d** : restraint and simplicity in design or expression **2** : personal integrity

chastity belt n (1931) : a belt device (as of medieval times) designed to prevent sexual intercourse on the part of the woman wearing it

cha·su·ble \'cha-zə-bəl, -zhə-, -sə-\ n [MF, fr. LL casubla hooded garment] (14c) : a sleeveless outer vestment worn by the officiating priest at mass

¹chat \'chat\ vb **chat·ted; chat·ting** [ME chatten, short for chatteren] vi (15c) **1** : CHATTER, PRATTLE **2** : to talk in an informal or familiar manner ~ vt, chiefly Brit : to talk to; esp : to talk lightly, glibly, or flirtatiously with — often used with up

²chat n (1530) **1** : idle small talk : CHATTER **2** : light familiar talk; esp : CONVERSATION **3** [imit.] : any of several songbirds (as of the genera Saxicola, Granatellus, or Icteria)

chasuble: 1 Gothic, 2 fiddle-back

châ·teau \sha-'tō\ n, pl **châteaus** \-'tōz\ or **châ·teaux** \-'tō(z)\ [F, fr. L castellum castle] (1739) **1** : a feudal castle or fortress in France **2** : a large country house : MANSION **3** : a French vineyard estate

cha·teau·bri·and \(,)sha-,tō-brē-'äⁿ\ n, often cap [François René de Chateaubriand] (1877) : a large tenderloin steak usu. grilled or broiled and served with a sauce (as béarnaise)

chat·e·lain \'sha-tᵊl-,ān\ n [MF châtelain, fr. L castellanus occupant of a castle] (15c) : CASTELLAN

chat·e·laine \'sha-tᵊl-,ān\ n [F châtelaine, fem. of châtelain] (1845) **1** **a** : the wife of a castellan : the mistress of a château **b** : the mistress of a household or of a large establishment **2** : a clasp or hook for a watch, purse, or bunch of keys

cha·toy·ance \shə-'tȯi-ən(t)s\ n (1910) : CHATOYANCY

cha·toy·an·cy \-ən(t)-sē\ n (1894) : the quality or state of being chatoyant

¹cha·toy·ant \shə-'tȯi-ənt\ adj [F, fr. prp. of chatoyer to shine like a cat's eyes] (1816) : having a changeable luster or color with an undulating narrow band of white light ⟨a ~ gem⟩

²chatoyant n (ca. 1828) : a chatoyant gem

chat show n (1969) Brit : TALK SHOW

chat·tel \'cha-tᵊl\ n [ME chatel property, fr. MF, fr. ML capitale — more at CATTLE] (14c) **1** : an item of tangible movable or immovable property except real estate, freehold, and things (as buildings) connected with real property **2** : SLAVE, BONDSMAN

¹chat·ter \'cha-tər\ vb [ME chatteren, of imit. origin] vi (13c) **1** : to utter rapid short sounds suggestive of language but inarticulate and indistinct ⟨squirrels ~ed angrily⟩ ⟨a ~ing stream⟩ **2** : to talk idly, incessantly, or fast : JABBER **3** **a** : to click repeatedly or uncontrollably ⟨teeth ~ing with cold⟩ ⟨machine guns ~ing⟩ **b** : to vibrate rapidly

esp. as a consequence of repeated sticking and slipping ⟨~ing brakes⟩ ~ vt : to utter rapidly, idly, or indistinctly — **chat·ter·er** n

²chatter n (13c) **1** : the action or sound of chattering **2** : idle talk : PRATTLE

chat·ter·box \'cha-tər-,bäks\ n (1774) : one who engages in much idle talk

chatter mark n (1888) **1** : a fine undulation formed on the surface of work by a chattering tool **2** : one of a series of short curved cracks on a glaciated rock surface transverse to the glacial striae

chat·ty \'cha-tē\ adj **chat·ti·er; -est** (ca. 1762) **1** : fond of chatting : TALKATIVE ⟨a ~ neighbor⟩ **2** : having the style and manner of light familiar conversation ⟨a ~ letter⟩ — **chat·ti·ly** \'cha-tᵊl-ē\ adv — **chat·ti·ness** \'cha-tē-nəs\ n

¹chauf·feur \'shō-fər, shō-'\ n [F, lit., stoker, fr. chauffer to heat, fr. MF chaufer — more at CHAFE] (1899) **1** : a person employed to drive a motor vehicle **2** : one that transports others by operating a motor vehicle

²chauffeur vb **chauf·feured; chauf·feur·ing** \'shō-f(ə-)riŋ, shō-'fər-iŋ\ vi (1917) : to do the work of a chauffeur ~ vt **1** : to transport in the manner of a chauffeur ⟨~s the children to school⟩ **2** : to operate (as an automobile) as chauffeur

chaul·moo·gra \chȯl-'mü-grə\ n [Beng cālmugrā] (ca. 1815) : any of several East Indian trees (family Flacourtiaceae) that yield an acrid oil used esp. formerly in treating leprosy and skin diseases

chaunt \'chȯnt, 'chänt\, **chaunt·er** var of CHANT, CHANTER

chaus·sure \shō-'sᵫr\ n, pl **chaussures** \same\ [ME chaucer, fr. MF chaussure, fr. chausser to put on footwear, fr. L calceare, fr. calceus shoe — more at CALZONE] (14c) **1** : FOOTGEAR **2** pl : SHOES

chau·tau·qua \shə-'tȯ-kwə\ n, often cap [Chautauqua Lake] (1873) : an institution that flourished in the late 19th and early 20th centuries providing popular education combined with entertainment in the form of lectures, concerts, and plays often presented outdoors or in a tent

chau·vin·ism \'shō-və-,ni-zəm\ n [F chauvinisme, fr. Nicolas Chauvin, character noted for his excessive patriotism and devotion to Napoleon in Théodore and Hippolyte Cogniard's play La Cocarde tricolore (1831)] (1870) **1** : excessive or blind patriotism — compare JINGOISM **2** : undue partiality or attachment to a group or place to which one belongs or has belonged **3** : an attitude of superiority toward members of the opposite sex; also : behavior expressive of such an attitude — **chau·vin·ist** \-və-nist\ n or adj — **chau·vin·is·tic** \,shō-və-'nis-tik\ adj — **chau·vin·is·ti·cal·ly** \-ti-k(ə-)lē\ adv

¹chaw \'chȯ\ vb [by alter.] (1506) : CHEW

²chaw n (1709) : a chew esp. of tobacco

chaw·ba·con \'chȯ-,bā-kən\ n [¹chaw + bacon] (1537) : BUMPKIN, HICK

cha·yo·te \chī-'yō-tē, chē-, -ị\tā\ n [Sp, fr. Nahuatl chayohtli] (1887) : the pear-shaped fruit of a West Indian annual vine (Sechium edule) of the gourd family that is widely eaten as a vegetable; also : the plant — called also mirliton

¹cheap \'chēp\ n [ME chep, fr. OE cēap trade; akin to OHG kouf trade; both fr. L caupo tradesman] (bef. 12c) obs : BARGAIN — **on the cheap** : at minimum expense : CHEAPLY

²cheap adj (1509) **1** **a** : purchasable below the going price or the real value **b** : charging or obtainable at a low price **c** : depreciated in value (as by currency inflation) ⟨~ dollars⟩ **2** : gained with little effort ⟨a ~ victory⟩ **3** **a** : of inferior quality or worth : TAWDRY, SLEAZY **b** : contemptible because of lack of any fine, lofty, or redeeming qualities : STINGY **4** **a** : yielding small satisfaction **b** : paying or able to pay less than going prices **5** of money : obtainable at a low rate of interest — **cheap** adv — **cheap·ish** \'chē-pish\ adj — **cheap·ish·ly** adv — **cheap·ly** \'chē-plē\ adv — **cheap·ness** n

cheap·en \'chē-pən\ vb **cheap·ened; cheap·en·ing** \'chēp-niŋ, 'chē-pə-\ vt (1574) **1** [obs. E cheap to price, bid for] archaic **a** : to ask the price of **b** : to bid or bargain for **2** **a** : to make cheap in price or value **b** : to lower in general esteem **c** : to make tawdry, vulgar, or inferior ~ vi : to become cheap

cheap·ie \'chē-pē\ n (ca. 1898) : one that is cheap; esp : an inexpensively produced motion picture — **cheapie** adj

¹cheap·jack \'chēp-,jak\ n [cheap + the name Jack] (1851) **1** : a haggling huckster **2** : a dealer in cheap merchandise

²cheapjack adj (1865) **1** : being inferior, cheap, or worthless ⟨~ movie companies⟩ **2** : unscrupulously opportunistic ⟨~ speculators⟩

cheapo \'chē-(,)pō\ adj (1972) : CHEAP

cheap shot n (1971) **1** : an act of deliberate roughness against a defenseless opponent esp. in a contact sport **2** : a critical statement that takes unfair advantage of a known weakness of the target

cheap·skate \'chēp-,skāt\ n (1896) : a miserly or stingy person; also : one who tries to avoid paying a fair share of costs or expenses

¹cheat \'chēt\ vt (1590) **1** : to deprive of something valuable by the use of deceit or fraud **2** : to influence or lead by deceit, trick, or artifice **3** : to elude or thwart by or as if by outwitting ⟨~ death⟩ ~ vi **1** **a** : to practice fraud or trickery **b** : to violate rules dishonestly (as at cards or on an examination) **2** : to be sexually unfaithful — usu. used with on — **cheat·er** n

syn CHEAT, COZEN, DEFRAUD, SWINDLE mean to get something by dishonesty or deception. CHEAT suggests using trickery that escapes observation ⟨cheated me out of a dollar⟩. COZEN implies artful persuading or flattering to attain a thing or a purpose ⟨always able to cozen her grandfather out of a few dollars⟩. DEFRAUD stresses depriving one of his or her rights and usu. connotes deliberate perversion of the truth ⟨defrauded of her inheritance by an unscrupulous lawyer⟩. SWINDLE implies large-scale cheating by misrepresentation or abuse of confidence ⟨swindled of their savings by con artists⟩.

²cheat n [earlier cheat forfeited property, fr. ME chet escheat, short for eschete — more at ESCHEAT] (1631) **1** : the act or an instance of fraudulently deceiving : DECEPTION, FRAUD **2** : one that cheats : PRETENDER, DECEIVER **3** : any of several grasses; esp : the common chess (Bromus secalinus) **4** : the obtaining of property from another by an intentional active distortion of the truth

¹check \'chek\ n [ME chek, fr. MF eschec, fr. Ar shāh, fr. Per, lit., king; akin to Gk ktasthai to acquire, Skt kṣatra dominion] (15c) **1** : exposure of a chess king to an attack from which he must be protected or moved to safety **2** **a** : a sudden stoppage of a forward course or progress : ARREST **b** : a checking of an opposing player (as in ice hockey) **3** : a sudden pause or break in a progression **4** archaic

: REPRIMAND, REBUKE **5** : one that arrests, limits, or restrains : RESTRAINT ⟨against all ~s, rebukes, and manners, I must advance — Shak.⟩ **6 a** : a standard for testing and evaluation : CRITERION **b** : EXAMINATION **c** : INSPECTION, INVESTIGATION ⟨a loyalty ~ on government employees⟩ **d** : the act of testing or verifying; *also* : the sample or unit used for testing or verifying **7** : a written order directing a bank to pay money as instructed : DRAFT **8 a** : a ticket or token showing ownership or identity or indicating payment made ⟨a baggage ~⟩ **b** : a counter in various games **c** : a slip indicating the amount due : BILL **9** [ME *chek*, short for *cheker* checker] **a** : a pattern in squares that resembles a checkerboard **b** : a fabric woven or printed with such a design **10** : a mark typically ✓ placed beside an item to show it has been noted, examined, or verified **11** : CRACK, BREAK — **check·less** \'che-kləs\ *adj* — **in check** : under restraint or control
²check *vt* (14c) **1 a** : to put (a chess king) in check **2** *chiefly dial* : REBUKE, REPRIMAND **3 a** : to slow or bring to a stop : BRAKE ⟨hastily ~ed the impulse⟩ **b** : to block the progress of (as a hockey player) **4 a** : to restrain or diminish the action or force of : CONTROL **b** : to slack or ease off and then belay again (as a rope) **5 a** : to compare with a source, original, or authority : VERIFY **b** : to inspect, examine, or look at appraisingly — usu. used with *out* or *over* ⟨~ing out new cars⟩ **c** : to mark with a check as examined, verified, or satisfactory — often used with *off* ⟨~ed off each item⟩ **6 a** : to consign (as luggage) to a common carrier from which one has purchased a passenger ticket ⟨~ed our bags before boarding⟩ **b** : to ship or accept for shipment under such a consignment **7** : to mark into squares : CHECKER **8** : to leave or accept for safekeeping in a checkroom **9** : to make checks or chinks : cause to crack ⟨the sun ~s timber⟩ ~ *vi* **1 a** *of a dog* : to stop in a chase esp. when scent is lost **b** : to halt through caution, uncertainty, or fear : STOP **2 a** : to investigate conditions ⟨~ed on the passengers' safety⟩ **b** : to prove to be consistent or truthful ⟨the description ~s with the photograph⟩ — often used with *out* ⟨the story ~ed out⟩ **3** : to draw a check on a bank **4** : to waive the right to initiate the betting in a round of poker **5** : CRACK, SPLIT *syn* see RESTRAIN — **check into** **1** : to check in at ⟨*check into* a hotel⟩ **2** : INVESTIGATE — **check up on** : INVESTIGATE
check·able *adj* (18?7) **1** : capable of being checked ⟨a ~ story⟩ **2** : held in or being a bank account on which checks can be drawn ⟨~ deposits⟩
check·book \'chek-ˌbŭk\ *n* (ca. 1846) : a book containing blank checks to be drawn on a bank
checkbook journalism *n* (1975) : the practice of paying someone for a news story and esp. for granting an interview
¹check·er \'che-kər\ *n* [ME *cheker*, fr. MF *eschequier*, fr. *eschec*] (14c) **1** *archaic* : CHESSBOARD **2** : a square or spot resembling the markings of a checkerboard **3** [sing. of *checkers*] : a piece in checkers
²checker *vt* **check·ered; check·er·ing** \'che-k(ə-)riŋ\ (15c) **1 a** : to variegate with different colors or shades **b** : to vary with contrasting elements or situations ⟨had a ~ed career⟩ **2** : to mark into squares
³checker *n* (1535) **1** : one that checks ⟨a fact ~⟩ ⟨spelling ~⟩ **2** : an employee who checks out purchases in a self-service store
check·er·ber·ry \'che-kər-ˌber-ē\ *n* [*checker* wild service tree + *berry*] (1776) **1** : the spicy red berrylike fruit of an American wintergreen (*Gaultheria procumbens*) **2** : a plant producing checkerberries
check·er·board \-ˌbȯrd, -ˌbȯrd\ *n* (1775) **1** : a board used in various games (as checkers) with usu. 64 squares in 2 alternating colors **2** : something that has a pattern or arrangement like a checkerboard
check·ers \'che-kərz\ *n pl but sing in constr* (1712) : a checkerboard game for 2 players each with 12 pieces
check–in \'che-ˌkin\ *n* (1927) : an act or instance of checking in
check in *vi* (1918) **1** : to register at a hotel **2** : to report one's presence or arrival ⟨*check in* at a convention⟩ ~ *vt* : to satisfy all requirements in returning ⟨*check in* the equipment after using⟩
checking account *n* (ca. 1909) : a bank account against which the depositor can draw checks
check·list \'chek-ˌlist\ *n* (1853) : a list of things to be checked or done ⟨a pilot's ~ before takeoff⟩; *also* : a comprehensive list ⟨a ~ of bird species⟩
check mark *n* (1917) : CHECK 10 — **check·mark** *vt*
¹check·mate \'chek-ˌmāt\ *vt* [ME *chekmaten*, fr. *chekmate*, interj. used to announce checkmate, fr. MF *eschec mat*, fr. Ar *shāh māt*, fr. Per, lit., the king is left unable to escape] (14c) **1** : to arrest, thwart, or counter completely **2** : to check (a chess opponent's king) so that escape is impossible
²checkmate *n* (15c) **1 a** : the act of checkmating **b** : the situation of a checkmated king **2** : a complete check
check·off \'che-ˌkȯf\ *n* (1911) **1 a** : the deduction of union dues from a worker's paycheck by the employer **b** : designation on an income tax return of a small amount of money to be applied to a special fund (as for financing political campaigns) **2** : AUTOMATIC 2
check off *vt* (1839) **1** : to eliminate from further consideration **2** : to deduct (union dues) from a worker's paycheck ~ *vi* : to change a play at the line of scrimmage in football by calling an automatic
check·out \'che-ˌkaůt\ *n* (1933) **1** : the action or an instance of checking out **2** : the time at which a lodger must vacate a room (as in a hotel) or be charged for retaining it **3** : a counter or area in a store where goods are checked out **4 a** : the action of examining and testing something for performance, suitability, or readiness **b** : the action of familiarizing oneself with the operation of a mechanical thing (as an airplane)
check out *vi* (1921) : to vacate and pay for one's lodging (as at a hotel) ~ *vt* **1** : to satisfy all requirements in taking away ⟨*checked out* a library book⟩ **2** : to itemize and total the cost of and receive payment for (outgoing merchandise) esp. in a self-service store **b** : to have the cost totaled and pay for (purchases) at a checkout
check·point \'chek-ˌpȯint\ *n* (1926) : a point at which a check is performed ⟨vehicles were inspected at various ~s⟩
check·rein \-ˌrān\ *n* (ca. 1809) **1** : a short rein looped over a hook on the saddle of a harness to prevent a horse from lowering its head **2** : a branch rein connecting the driving rein of one horse of a pair with the bit of the other
check·room \-ˌrüm, -ˌrům\ *n* (1900) : a room at which baggage, parcels, or clothing is checked

check·up \'che-ˌkəp\ *n* (1921) : EXAMINATION; *esp* : a general physical examination
check valve *n* (ca. 1877) : a valve that permits flow in one direction only
ched·dar \'che-dər\ *n, often cap* [*Cheddar*, England] (ca. 1661) : a hard white, yellow, or orange smooth-textured cheese with a flavor that ranges from mild to strong as the cheese matures — called also *cheddar cheese*
che·der \'kä-dər, 'ke-\ *var of* HEDER
chee·cha·ko \'chē-'chä-(ˌ)kō, -'chȯ- *also* -'cha-\ *n, pl* **-kos** [Chinook Jargon, fr. *chee* new (fr. Lower Chinook *čxi* right away) + *chako* come, fr. Nootka *čokʷaˑ* come, imper.] (1897) : TENDERFOOT 1 — used chiefly in Alaska
¹cheek \'chēk\ *n* [ME *cheke*, fr. OE *cēace*; akin to MLG *kāke* jawbone] (bef. 12c) **1** : the fleshy side of the face below the eye and above and to the side of the mouth; *broadly* : the lateral aspect of the head **2** : something suggestive of the human cheek in position or form; *esp* : one of two laterally paired parts **3** : insolent boldness and selfassurance **4** : BUTTOCK 1 *syn* see TEMERITY — **cheek·ful** \-ˌfül\ *n*
²cheek *vt* (1840) *chiefly Brit* : to speak rudely or impudently to
cheek·bone \'chēk-ˌbōn\ *n* (ca. 1775) : the prominence below the eye that is formed by the zygomatic bone; *also* : ZYGOMATIC BONE
cheek by jowl *adv* (1577) : SIDE BY SIDE
cheeked \'chēkt\ *adj* (1592) : having cheeks of a specified nature — used in combination ⟨rosy-*cheeked*⟩
cheek tooth *n* (14c) : any of the molar or premolar teeth
cheeky \'chē-kē\ *adj* **cheek·i·er; -est** (1859) : having or showing cheek : IMPUDENT — **cheek·i·ly** \-kə-lē\ *adv* — **cheek·i·ness** \-kē-nəs\ *n*
cheep \'chēp\ *vi* [imit.] (1513) **1** : to utter faint shrill sounds : PEEP **2** : to utter a single word or sound — **cheep** *n*
¹cheer \'chir\ *n* [ME *chere* face, cheer, fr. OF, face, fr. ML *cara*, prob. fr. Gk *kara* head, face — more at CEREBRAL] (13c) **1 a** *obs* : FACE **b** *archaic* : facial expression **2** : state of mind or heart : SPIRIT ⟨be of good ~ —Mt 9:2(AV)⟩ **3** : lightness of mind and feeling : ANIMATION, GAIETY **4** : hospitable entertainment : WELCOME **5** : food and drink for a feast : FARE **6** : something that gladdens ⟨words of ~⟩ **7** : a shout of applause or encouragement
²cheer *vt* (14c) **1 a** : to instill with hope or courage : COMFORT — usu. used with *up* **b** : to make glad or happy — usu. used with *up* **2** : to urge on or encourage esp. by shouts ⟨~ed the team on⟩ **3** : to applaud with shouts ~ *vi* **1** *obs* : to be mentally or emotionally disposed **2** : to grow or be cheerful : REJOICE — usu. used with *up* **3** : to utter a shout of applause or triumph — **cheer·er** *n*
cheer·ful \'chir-fəl\ *adj* (15c) **1 a** : full of good spirits : MERRY **b** : UNGRUDGING ⟨~ obedience⟩ **2** : conducive to cheer : likely to dispel gloom or worry ⟨sunny ~ room⟩ — **cheer·ful·ly** \-f(ə-)lē\ *adv* — **cheer·ful·ness** \-fəl-nəs\ *n*
cheer·io \ˌchir-ē-'ō\ *interj* [*cheery* + -*o*] (1910) *chiefly Brit* — usu. used as a farewell and sometimes as a greeting or toast
cheer·lead·er \'chir-ˌlē-dər\ *n* (1903) : one that calls for and directs organized cheering (as at a football game) — **cheer·lead** \-ˌlēd\ *vt*
cheer·less \-ləs\ *adj* (1579) : lacking qualities that cheer : BLEAK, JOYLESS ⟨a ~ room⟩ — **cheer·less·ly** *adv* — **cheer·less·ness** *n*
cheers \'chirz\ *interj* (1919) — used as a toast
cheery \'chir-ē\ *adj* **cheer·i·er; -est** (15c) **1** : marked by cheerfulness or good spirits **2** : causing or suggesting cheerfulness — **cheer·i·ly** \'chir-ə-lē\ *adv* — **cheer·i·ness** \'chir-ē-nəs\ *n*
¹cheese \'chēz\ *n, often attrib* [ME *chese*, fr. OE *cēse*, fr. L *caseus* cheese] (bef. 12c) **1 a** : a food consisting of the coagulated, compressed, and usu. ripened curd of milk separated from the whey **b** : an often cylindrical cake of this food **2** : something resembling cheese in shape or consistency
²cheese *vt* **cheesed; chees·ing** [origin unknown] (ca. 1811) : to put an end to : STOP — **cheese it** — used in the imperative as a warning of danger ⟨*cheese it*, the cops⟩
³cheese *n* [perh. fr. Urdu *chīz* thing] (1920) *slang* : someone important
cheese·burg·er \'chēz-ˌbər-gər\ *n* [*cheese* + ham*burger*] (ca. 1938) : a hamburger topped with a slice of cheese
cheese·cake \-ˌkāk\ *n* (15c) **1** : a dessert consisting of a creamy filling usu. containing cheese baked in a pastry or pressed-crumb shell **2** : a photographic display of shapely and scantily clothed female figures — compare BEEFCAKE
cheese·cloth \-ˌklȯth\ *n* [fr. its use in the making of cheese] (14c) : a very lightweight unsized cotton gauze
cheese·par·ing \-ˌpar-iŋ, -ˌper-\ *n* (1597) **1** : something worthless or insignificant **2** : miserly economizing — **cheeseparing** *adj*
cheesy \'chē-zē\ *adj* **chees·i·er; -est** (14c) **1 a** : resembling or suggesting cheese esp. in consistency or odor **b** : containing cheese **2** : SHABBY 3c, CHEAP — **chees·i·ness** *n*
chee·tah \'chē-tə\ *n, pl* **cheetahs** *also* **cheetah** [Hindi *cītā* leopard, fr. Skt *citraka*, fr. *citra* bright, variegated; akin to OHG *heitar* bright — more at ·HOOD] (1610) : a long-legged spotted swift-moving African and formerly Asian cat (*Acinonyx jubatus*) about the size of a small leopard that has blunt nonretractile claws and is often trained to run down game
chef \'shef\ *n* [F, head, fr. *chef de cuisine* head of the kitchen] (1826) **1** : a skilled cook who manages the kitchen (as of a restaurant) **2** : COOK — **chef** *vi* — **chef·dom** \-dəm\ *n*
chef d'oeu·vre \shā-dœvr', (ˌ)shā-'da(r)v\ *n, pl* **chefs d'oeuvre** \-dœvr', -'də(r)v(z)\ [F *chef-d'oeuvre*, lit., leading work] (1619) : a masterpiece esp. in art or literature
che·la \'kē-lə\ *n, pl* **che·lae** \-(ˌ)lē\ [NL, fr. Gk *chēlē* claw] (1646) : a pincerlike organ or claw borne by a limb of a crustacean or arachnid
¹che·late \'kē-ˌlāt *also* 'chē-\ *adj* (1826) **1** : resembling or having chela **2** : of, relating to, or being a chelate
²chelate *vb* **che·lat·ed; che·lat·ing** *vt* (1922) : to combine with (a

\ə\ abut \ᵊ\ kitten, F table \ər\ further \a\ ash \ā\ ace \ä\ mop, mar \aů\ out \ch\ chin \e\ bet \ē\ easy \g\ go \i\ hit \ī\ ice \j\ job \ŋ\ sing \ō\ go \ȯ\ law \ȯi\ boy \th\ thin \t͟h\ the \ü\ loot \ů\ foot \y\ yet \zh\ vision \ȧ, k̲, ⁿ, œ, œ̄, ᵫ, ᵫ̄, ᵞ\ *see* Guide to Pronunciation

metal) so as to form a chelate ring ~ vi : to react so as to form a chelate ring — **che·lat·able** \-,lā-tə-bəl\ adj — **che·la·tion** \kē-'lā-shən
also chē-\ n — **che·la·tor** \-,lā-tər\ n
³**chelate** n (1943) : a compound having a ring structure that usu. contains a metal ion held by coordinate bonds
che·lic·era \ki-'li-sə-rə\ n, pl **-er·ae** \-,rē\ [NL, fr. F chélicère, fr. Gk
chēlē + keras horn — more at HORN] (1835) : one of the anterior pair
of appendages of an arachnid often specialized as fangs — **che·lic·er-
al** \-sə-rəl\ adj
che·li·ped \'kē-lə-,ped\ n [Gk chēlē claw + E -i- + -ped] (1869) : one
of the pair of legs that bears the large chelae in decapod crustaceans
Chel·le·an or **Chel·li·an** \'she-lē-ən\ adj [F chelléen, fr. Chelles,
France] (1893) : ABBEVILLIAN
che·lo·ni·an \ki-'lō-nē-ən\ n [Gk chelōnē tortoise] (1828) : TURTLE —
chelonian adj
chem- or **chemo-** also **chemi-** comb form [NL, fr. LGk chēmeia alchemy — more at ALCHEMY] 1 : chemical : chemistry ⟨chemotaxis⟩
2 : chemically ⟨chemisorb⟩
chem·ic \'ke-mik\ adj [NL chimicus alchemist, fr. ML alchimicus, fr.
alchymia alchemy] (1576) 1 archaic : ALCHEMIC 2 : CHEMICAL
¹**chem·i·cal** \'ke-mi-kəl\ adj (1576) 1 : of, relating to, used in, or produced by chemistry 2 a : acting or operated or produced by chemicals b : detectable by chemical means — **chem·i·cal·ly** \-mi-k(ə-)lē\
adv
²**chemical** n (1747) : a substance obtained by a chemical process or
used for producing a chemical effect
chemical engineering n (1888) : engineering dealing with the industrial application of chemistry
chemical warfare n (1917) : tactical warfare using incendiary mixtures, smokes, or irritant, burning, poisonous, or asphyxiating gases
chemical weapon n (1980) : a weapon used in chemical warfare
chemi·lu·mi·nes·cence \,ke-mē-,lü-mə-'ne-sᵊn(t)s, ,kē-\ n [ISV] (1889)
: luminescence (as bioluminescence) due to chemical reaction —
chemi·lu·mi·nes·cent \-'ne-sᵊnt\ adj
che·min de fer \shə-,man-də-'fer\ n, pl **che·mins de fer** \same\ [F,
lit., railroad] (1891) : a card game in which two hands are dealt, any
number of players may bet against the dealer, and the winning hand is
the one that comes closer to but does not exceed a count of nine on two
or three cards
chemi·os·mot·ic \,ke-mē-äz-'mä-tik, ,kē-\ adj (1966) : relating to or
being a hypothesis that seeks to explain the mechanism of ATP formation in oxidative phosphorylation by mitochondria and chloroplasts
without recourse to the formation of high-energy intermediates by
postulating the formation of an energy gradient of hydrogen ions
across the organelle membranes that results in the reversible movement
of hydrogen ions to the outside and is generated by electron transport
or the activity of electron carriers
che·mise \shə-'mēz, sometimes -'mēs\ n [ME, fr. OF, shirt, fr. LL ca-
misia] (13c) 1 : a woman's one-piece undergarment 2 : a loose
straight-hanging dress
chem·i·sette \,she-mi-'zet\ n [F, dim. of chemise] (1807) : a woman's
garment; esp : one (as of lace) to fill the open front of a dress
chem·i·sorb \'ke-mi-,sȯrb, ,kē-, -,zȯrb\ vt [chem- + -sorb (as in adsorb)]
(1935) : to take up and hold usu. irreversibly by chemical forces —
chem·i·sorp·tion \,ke-mi-'sȯrp-shən, ,kē-, -'zȯrp-\ n
chem·ist \'ke-mist\ n [NL chimista, short for ML alchimista] (1562) 1
a obs : ALCHEMIST 2 : one trained in chemistry 2 Brit : PHARMACIST
chem·is·try \'ke-mə-strē\ n, pl **-tries** (1646) 1 : a science that deals
with the composition, structure, and properties of substances and with
the transformations that they undergo 2 a : the composition and
chemical properties of a substance ⟨the ~ of iron⟩ b : chemical processes and phenomena (as of an organism) ⟨blood ~⟩ 3 : a strong
mutual attraction, attachment, or sympathy ⟨they have a special ~⟩
che·mo \'kē-(,)mō\ n (1982) : CHEMOTHERAPY
che·mo·au·to·tro·phic \,kē-mō-,ȯ-tə-'trō-fik also ,ke-\ adj (1945) : being autotrophic and oxidizing an inorganic compound as a source of
energy ⟨~ bacteria⟩ — **che·mo·au·tot·ro·phy** \-ȯ-'tä-trə-fē\ n
che·mo·pro·phy·lax·is \-,prō-fə-'lak-səs also -,prä-fə-\ n (1936) : the
prevention of infectious disease by the use of chemical agents — **che-
mo·pro·phy·lac·tic** \-'lak-tik\ adj
che·mo·re·cep·tion \-ri-'sep-shən\ n [ISV] (1919) : the physiological
reception of chemical stimuli — **che·mo·re·cep·tive** \-'sep-tiv\ adj
che·mo·re·cep·tor \-ri-'sep-tər\ n [ISV] (1906) : a sense organ (as a
taste bud) responding to chemical stimuli
che·mo·sur·gery \,kē-mō-'sərj-rē, -'sər-jə-rē\ n (ca. 1944) : chemical
removal of diseased or unwanted tissue — **che·mo·sur·gi·cal** \-'sər-ji-
kəl\ adj
che·mo·syn·the·sis \-'sin(t)-thə-səs\ n [NL] (1901) : synthesis of organic compounds (as in living cells) by energy derived from chemical
reactions — **che·mo·syn·thet·ic** \-sin-'the-tik\ adj
che·mo·tac·tic \-'tak-tik\ adj (1893) : involving, inducing, or exhibiting chemotaxis — **che·mo·tac·ti·cal·ly** \-ti-k(ə-)lē\ adv
che·mo·tax·is \-'tak-səs\ n [NL] (ca. 1887) : orientation or movement
of an organism or cell in relation to chemical agents
che·mo·tax·on·o·my \-(,)tak-'sä-nə-mē\ n (1963) : the classification of
plants and animals based on similarities and differences in biochemical
composition — **che·mo·tax·o·nom·ic** \-,tak-sə-'nä-mik\ adj — **che-
mo·tax·on·o·mist** \-(,)tak-'sä-nə-mist\ n
che·mo·ther·a·peu·tic \-,ther-ə-'pyü-tik\ adj (1907) : of, relating to,
or used in chemotherapy — **chemotherapeutic** n — **che·mo·ther·a-
peu·ti·cal·ly** \-ti-k(ə-)lē\ adv
che·mo·ther·a·py \-'ther-ə-pē\ n [ISV] (1910) : the use of chemical
agents in the treatment or control of disease or mental illness — **che-
mo·ther·a·pist** \-pist\ n
che·mot·ro·pism \ki-'mä-trə-,pi-zəm, ke-\ n [ISV] (1897) : orientation
of cells or organisms in relation to chemical stimuli
che·nille \shə-'nē(ə)l\ n [F, lit., caterpillar, fr. L canicula, dim. of canis
dog; fr. its hairy appearance — more at HOUND] (ca. 1739) 1 : a wool,
cotton, silk, or rayon yarn with protruding pile; also : a pile-face fabric
with a filling of this yarn 2 : an imitation of chenille yarn or fabric
che·no·pod \'kē-nə-,päd, 'ke-\ n [ultim. fr. Gk chēn goose + podion,
dim. of pod-, pous foot — more at GOOSE, FOOT] (1555) : any plant of
the goosefoot family

cheong·sam \'chȯŋ-,säm\ n [Chin (Guangdong) chèuhng-sāam, lit.,
long gown] (1952) : an oriental dress with a slit skirt and a mandarin
collar
cheque \'chek\ chiefly Brit var of ¹CHECK 7
che·quer \'che-kər\ chiefly Brit var of CHECKER
cher·i·moya \,cher-ə-'mȯi-ə, ,chir-\ n [Sp chirimoya] (1736) : a round,
oblong, or heart-shaped fruit with a pitted rind that is borne by a
widely cultivated tropical American tree (Annona cherimola) of the
custard-apple family; also : this tree
cher·ish \'cher-ish\ vt [ME cherisshen, stem of cherir to
cherish, fr. OF, fr. chier dear, fr. L carus — more at CHARITY] (14c) 1
a : to hold dear : feel or show affection for b : to keep or cultivate
with care and affection : NURTURE 2 : to entertain or harbor in the
mind deeply and resolutely ⟨still ~es that memory⟩ syn see APPRECI-
ATE — **cher·ish·able** \-i-shə-bəl\ adj — **cher·ish·er** \-i-shər\ n
cher·no·zem \,cher-nə-'zyȯm, -'zem\ n [Russ, fr. chërnyĭ black + zemlya earth] (1841) : any of a group of dark-colored zonal soils with a
deep rich humus horizon found in regions (as the grasslands of central
No. America) of temperate to cool climate — **cher·no·zem·ic** \-'zyȯ-
mik, -'ze-\ adj
Cher·o·kee \'cher-ə-(,)kē\ n, pl **Cherokee** or **Cherokees** [prob. fr.
Creek tciloki people of a different speech] (1674) 1 : a member of an
American Indian people orig. of Tennessee and No. Carolina 2 : the
language of the Cherokee people
Cherokee rose n (1823) : a Chinese climbing rose (Rosa laevigata)
with a fragrant white blossom
che·root \shə-'rüt, chə-\ n [Tamil curuṭṭu, lit., roll] (ca. 1679) : a cigar
cut square at both ends
cher·ry \'cher-ē\ n, pl **cherries** [ME chery, fr. ONF cherise (taken as a
plural), fr. LL ceresia, fr. L cerasus cherry tree, fr. Gk kerasos] (14c) 1
a : any of numerous trees and shrubs (genus Prunus) of the rose family
that bear pale yellow to deep red or blackish smooth-skinned drupes
enclosing a smooth seed and that include some cultivated for their
fruits or ornamental flowers — compare SWEET CHERRY b : the fruit of
a cherry c : the wood of a cherry 2 : a variable color averaging a
moderate red 3 a : HYMEN b : VIRGINITY — **cher·ry·like** \-,līk\ adj
cherry bomb n (1953) : a powerful globular red firecracker
cherry picker n (ca. 1944) : a traveling crane equipped for holding a
passenger at the end of the boom
cher·ry·stone \'cher-ē-,stōn\ n (1880) : a small quahog
cherry tomato n (1847) : a small globose red or orange tomato borne
in long dense clusters; also : a plant (Lycopersicon lypersicum cerasi-
forme) bearing cherry tomatoes
chert \'chərt, 'chat\ n [origin unknown] (1679) : a rock resembling
flint and consisting essentially of a large amount of fibrous chalcedony
with smaller amounts of cryptocrystalline quartz and amorphous silica
— **cherty** \'chər-tē, 'cha-\ adj
cher·ub \'cher-əb\ n, pl usu **cher·u·bim** \'cher-ə-,bim, 'ker- also 'cher-
yə-\ [L, fr. Gk cheroub, fr. Heb kĕrūbh] (13c) 1 pl : an order of angels
— see CELESTIAL HIERARCHY 2 pl usu **cherubs** a : a beautiful usu.
winged child in painting and sculpture b : an innocent-looking usu.
chubby and rosy person — **che·ru·bic** \chə-'rü-bik also 'cher-ə-\ adj —
che·ru·bi·cal·ly \-bi-k(ə-)lē\ adv — **cher·ub·like** \'cher-əb-,līk\
adj
cher·vil \'chər-vəl\ n [ME cherville, fr. OE cerfille, fr. L caerefolium,
modif. of (assumed) Gk chairephyllon, fr. chairein to rejoice + phyllon
leaf — more at YEARN, BLADE] (bef. 12c) : an aromatic herb (Anthriscus
cerefolium) of the carrot family with divided leaves that are often used
in soups and salads; also : any of several related plants
Ches·a·peake Bay retriever \'che-sə-,pēk-'bā-\ n (1891) : any of a
breed of large brown sporting dogs developed in Maryland and having
a dense oily water-shedding coat
Chesh·ire cat \'che-shər-\ n [Cheshire, England] (1866) : a broadly
grinning cat in Lewis Carroll's Alice's Adventures in Wonderland
Cheshire cheese n (1597) : a cheese similar to cheddar made chiefly in
Cheshire, England
¹**chess** \'ches\ n [ME ches, fr. MF
esches, acc. pl. of eschec check at
chess — more at CHECK] (14c) : a
game for 2 players each of whom
moves 16 pieces according to fixed
rules across a checkerboard and
tries to checkmate the opponent's
king
²**chess** n [origin unknown] (1736) : a
weedy annual bromegrass (Bromus
secalinus) widely distributed as a
weed esp. in grain; broadly : any of
several weedy bromegrasses
chess·board \'ches-,bȯrd, -bȯrd\ n
(15c) : a checkerboard used in the
game of chess
chess·man \-,man, -mən\ n (15c)
: any of the pieces used in chess
chess pie n [perh. alter. of chest]
(1932) : a pie or tart with a filling
made esp. of eggs, butter, and sugar

chessboard with chess pieces
arranged as at the beginning of a
game

chest \'chest\ n [ME, fr. OE cest, cist
chest, box, fr. L cista basket, hamper] (bef. 12c) 1 a : a
container for storage or shipping; esp : a box with a lid used esp. for
the safekeeping of belongings b : a cupboard used esp. for the storing
of medicines or first-aid supplies 2 : the place where money of a public institution is kept : TREASURY; also : the fund so kept 3 a : THO-
RAX; esp : the human thorax ⟨a pain in the ~⟩ b : BREAST 2a ⟨a hairy
~⟩ — **chest·ful** \-,fùl\ n
chest·ed \'ches-təd\ adj (1662) : having a chest of a specified kind —
used in combination ⟨flat-chested⟩
ches·ter·field \'ches-tər-,fēld\ n [fr. a 19th cent. Earl of Chesterfield]
(1852) 1 : a single-breasted or double-breasted semifitted overcoat
with velvet collar 2 : a davenport usu. with upright armrests
Ches·ter White \'ches-tər-\ n [Chester County, Pa.] (1856) : any of a
breed of large white swine
¹**chest·nut** \'ches(t)-(,)nət\ n [ME chasteine, chesten chestnut tree, fr.
MF chastaigne, fr. L castanea, fr. Gk kastanea] (14c) 1 a : any of a

genus (*Castanea*) of trees or shrubs of the beech family; *esp* : an American tree (*C. dentata*) that was formerly a dominant or codominant member of many deciduous forests of the eastern U.S. but has now been largely eliminated by the chestnut blight and seldom grows beyond the shrub or sapling stage **b** : the edible nut of a chestnut **c** : the wood of a chestnut **2** : a grayish to reddish brown **3** : HORSE CHESTNUT **4** : a chestnut-colored animal; *specif* : a horse having a body color of any shade of pure or reddish brown with mane, tail, and points of the same or a lighter shade — compare 2BAY 1, 1SORREL 1 **5** : a callosity on the inner side of the leg of the horse — see HORSE illustration **6** **a** : an old joke or story **b** : something (as a musical piece or a saying) repeated to the point of staleness

2**chestnut** *adj* (1555) **1** : of the color chestnut **2** : of, relating to, or resembling a chestnut

chestnut blight *n* (ca. 1909) : a destructive disease of the American chestnut marked by cankers of the bark and cambium and caused by an imported fungus (*Endothia parasitica* syn. *Cryphonectria parasitica*)

chestnut oak *n* (1703) : any of several oaks having oblong to lanceolate leaves with crenate or serrate edges: as **a** : CHINQUAPIN OAK **b** : a medium-sized oak (*Quercus prinus*) of eastern No. America with large acorns and leaves that are shiny yellow-green above and paler below

chest of drawers (1649) : a piece of furniture designed to contain a set of drawers (as for holding clothing)

chesty \'ches-tē\ *adj* **chest·i·er; -est** (1899) **1** : proudly or arrogantly self-assertive **2** : marked by a large or well-developed chest

chet·rum \'chē-trəm, 'che-\ *n, pl* **chetrums** *or* **chetrum** [Tibetan] (1973) — see ngultrum at MONEY table

che·val–de–frise \shə-ˌval-də-'frēz\ *n, pl* **che·vaux–de–frise** \shə-ˌvō-\ [F, lit., horse from Friesland] (1668) **1** : a defense consisting of a timber or an iron barrel covered with projecting spikes and often strung with barbed wire **2** : a protecting line (as of spikes) on top of a wall — usu. used in pl.

che·val glass \shə-'val-\ *n* [F *cheval* horse, support] (1828) : a full-length mirror in a frame in which it may be tilted

che·va·lier \ˌshe-və-'lir, *esp for 1b & 2 also* shə-'val-ˌyā\ *n* [ME, fr. MF, fr. LL *caballarius* horseman — more at CAVALIER] (14c) **1** **a** : CAVALIER **2** **b** : a member of any of various orders of knighthood or of merit (as the Legion of Honor) **2** **a** : a member of the lowest rank of French nobility **b** : a cadet of the French nobility **3** : a chivalrous man

che·ve·lure \shəv-lūer\ *n* [F, fr. LL *capillatura*, fr. L *capillatus* having long hair, fr. *capillus* hair] (15c) : a head of hair

chev·i·ot \'she-vē-ət, *esp Brit* 'che-\ *n, often cap* (1815) **1** : any of a breed of hardy hornless relatively small sheep that are a source of quality mutton and have their origin in the Cheviot hills **2** **a** : a fabric of cheviot wool **b** : a heavy rough napped plain or twill fabric of coarse wool or worsted **c** : a sturdy soft-finished plain or twill cotton shirting

chèvre \'shev(r²), 'shev-rə\ *n* [F, lit., goat, fr. OF *chievre*, fr. L *capra* she-goat, fr. *caper* he-goat — more at CAPRIOLE] (1950) : GOAT CHEESE

chev·ron \'shev-rən\ *n* [ME, fr. MF, rafter, chevron, fr. (assumed) VL *caprion-, caprio* rafter; akin to L *caper* goat] (14c) : a figure, pattern, or object having the shape of a V or an inverted V: as **a** *or* **chev·er·on** \'shev-rən, 'she-və-\ : a heraldic charge consisting of two diagonal stripes meeting at an angle usu. with the point up **b** : a sleeve badge that usu. consists of one or more chevron-shaped stripes that indicates the wearer's rank and service (as in the armed forces)

1**chew** \'chü\ *vb* [ME *chewen*, fr. OE *cēowan*; akin to OHG *kiuwan* to chew, Russ *zhevat'*] *vt* (bef. 12c) : to crush, grind, or gnaw (as food) with or as if with the teeth : MASTICATE ~ *vi* : to chew something; *specif* : to chew tobacco — **chew·able** \-ə-bəl\ *adj* — **chew·er** *n* — **chewy** \'chü-ē\ *adj* — **chew the rag** *or* **chew the fat** *slang* : to make friendly familiar conversation : CHAT

2**chew** *n* (13c) **1** : the act of chewing **2** : something for chewing

chewing gum *n* (1850) : a sweetened and flavored insoluble plastic material (as a preparation of chicle) used for chewing

che·wink \chi-'wiŋk\ *n* [imit.] (1793) : TOWHEE 1

chew out *vt* (1943) : REPRIMAND, BAWL OUT

chew over *vt* (1939) : to meditate on : think about reflectively

Chey·enne \shī-'an, -'en\ *n, pl* **Cheyenne** *or* **Cheyennes** [CanF, fr. Dakota *šahíyena*] (1778) **1** : a member of an American Indian people of the western plains of the U.S. **2** : the Algonquian language of the Cheyenne people

chez \'shā\ *prep* [F, fr. L *casae* at home, locative of *casa* cottage] (1740) : at or in the home or business place of

chi \'kī, 'kē\ *n* [Gk *chei, chi*] (15c) : the 22nd letter of the Greek alphabet — see ALPHABET table

Chi·a·ni·na \ˌkē-ə-'nē-nə\ *n, pl* **Chianina** *or* **Chianinas** [It, fr. fem. of *chianino* of the *Chiani* River valley, Italy] (1914) : any of a breed of tall white cattle of Italian origin noted esp. for producing lean meat

Chi·an·ti \kē-'än-tē, -'an-\ *n* [It, fr. the *Chianti* region, Italy] (1833) : a dry usu. red wine from the Tuscany region of Italy; *also* : a similar wine made elsewhere

chiar·oscu·rist \kē-ˌär-ə-'skyùr-ist, kē-ˌar-, -'skùr-\ *n* (ca. 1798) : an artist who specializes in chiaroscuro

chiar·oscu·ro \-'skyùr-(ˌ)ō, -'skùr-\ *n, pl* **-ros** [It, fr. *chiaro* clear, light + *oscuro* obscure, dark] (1686) **1** : pictorial representation in terms of light and shade without regard to color **2** **a** : the arrangement or treatment of light and dark parts in a pictorial work of art **b** : the interplay or contrast of dissimilar qualities (as of mood or character) **3** : a 16th century woodcut technique involving the use of several blocks to print different tones of the same color; *also* : a print made by this technique **4** : the interplay of light and shadow on or as if on a surface **5** : the quality of being veiled or partly in shadow

chi·asm \'kī-ˌa-z²m, 'kē-\ *n* [NL *chiasma*] (1870) : CHIASMA 1

chi·as·ma \kī-'az-mə, kē-\ *n, pl* **-ma·ta** \-mə-tə\ [NL, X-shaped configuration, fr. Gk, crosspiece, fr. *chiazein* to mark with a chi, fr. *chi* (x)] (1839) **1** : an anatomical intersection or decussation — compare OPTIC CHIASMA **2** : a cross-shaped configuration of paired chromatids visible in the diplotene of meiotic prophase and considered the cytological equivalent of genetic crossing-over — **chi·as·mat·ic** \ˌkī-əz-'ma-tik, ˌkē-\ *adj*

chi·as·mus \kī-'az-məs, kē-\ *n* [NL, fr. Gk *chiasmos*, fr. *chiazein* to mark with a chi] (1871) : an inverted relationship between the syntac-

tic elements of parallel phrases (as in Goldsmith's *to stop too fearful, and too faint to go*)

chiaus \'chaùs, 'chaùsh\ *n* [Turk *çavuş*] (1595) : a Turkish messenger or sergeant

Chib·cha \'chib-(ˌ)chä\ *n, pl* **Chibcha** *or* **Chibchas** [Sp] (1814) **1** : a member of an Indian people of central Colombia **2** : the extinct language of the Chibcha people

Chib·chan \-chən\ *adj* (1902) : of, relating to, or constituting a language family of Colombia and Central America

chi·bouk *or* **chi·bouque** \chə-'bük, shə-\ *n* [F *chibouque*, fr. Turk *çubuk*] (1813) : a long-stemmed Turkish tobacco pipe with a clay bowl

1**chic** \'shēk\ *n* [F] (1856) **1** : smart elegance and sophistication esp. of dress or manner : STYLE (wears her clothes with superb ~) **2** : a distinctive mode of dress or manner associated with a fashionable lifestyle, ideology, or pursuit

2**chic** *adj* (1865) **1** : cleverly stylish : SMART (the woman who is ~ adapts fashion to her own personality —Elizabeth L. Post) **2** : currently fashionable (a ~ restaurant) — **chic·ly** *adv* — **chic·ness** *n*

Chi·ca·na \chi-'kä-nə *also* shi-\ *n* [MexSp, fem. of *chicano*] (1967) : an American woman or girl of Mexican descent — **Chicana** *adj*

1**chi·cane** \shi-'kän, chi-\ *vb* **chi·caned; chi·can·ing** [F *chicaner*, fr. MF, to quibble, prevent justice] *vi* (ca. 1672) : to use chicanery (a wretch he had taught to lie and ~ —George Meredith) ~ *vt* : TRICK, CHEAT

2**chicane** *n* (1686) **1** : CHICANERY **2** **a** : an obstacle on a racecourse **b** : a series of tight turns in opposite directions in an otherwise straight stretch of a road-racing course **3** : the absence of trumps in a hand of cards

chi·ca·nery \-'kän-rē, -'kä-nə-\ *n, pl* **-ner·ies** (1609) **1** : deception by artful subterfuge or sophistry : TRICKERY **2** : a piece of sharp practice (as at law) : TRICK

Chi·ca·no \chi-'kä-(ˌ)nō *also* shi-\ *n, pl* **-nos** [MexSp, alter. of Sp *mexicano* Mexican] (1947) : an American of Mexican descent — **Chicano** *adj*

1**chi·chi** \'shē-(ˌ)shē *also* 'chē-(ˌ)chē\ *n* [F] (1908) **1** : frilly or elaborate ornamentation **2** : AFFECTATION, PRECIOSITY **3** : CHIC

2**chichi** *adj* (1926) **1** : elaborately ornamented : SHOWY, FRILLY (a ~ dress) **2** : ARTY, PRECIOUS (~ poetry) **3** : CHIC, FASHIONABLE (a ~ nightclub)

chick \'chik\ *n* [ME *chyke*, alter. of *chiken*] (15c) **1** **a** : a domestic chicken; *esp* : one newly hatched **b** : the young of any bird **2** : CHILD **3** *slang* : a young woman

chick·a·dee \'chi-kə-(ˌ)dē\ *n* [imit.] (1838) : any of several crestless American titmice (genus *Parus*) usu. with the crown of the head sharply demarked and darker than the body

chick·a·ree \'chi-kə-ˌrē\ *n* [imit.] (1829) : RED SQUIRREL; *also* : a related squirrel (*Tamiasciurus douglasii*) of forests from southwestern British Columbia to central California

Chick·a·saw \'chi-kə-ˌsȯ\ *n, pl* **Chickasaw** *or* **Chickasaws** (1674) **1** : a member of an American Indian people of Mississippi and Alabama **2** : a dialect of Choctaw spoken by the Chickasaw

1**chick·en** \'chi-k²n, *sometimes* -k²ŋ\ *n* [ME *chiken*, fr. OE *cicen* young chicken; akin to OE *cocc* cock] (14c) **1** **a** : the common domestic fowl (*Gallus gallus*) esp. when young; *also* : its flesh used as food — compare JUNGLE FOWL **b** : any of various birds or their young **2** **a** : a young woman **3** **a** : COWARD **b** : any of various contests in which the participants risk personal safety in order to see which one will give up first **4** [short for *chickenshit*]: *slang* : petty details **5** : a young male homosexual

2**chicken** *adj* (1941) **1** **a** : SCARED **b** : TIMID, COWARDLY **2** *slang* **a** : insistent on petty details of duty or discipline **b** : PETTY, UNIMPORTANT

3**chicken** *vi* **chick·ened; chick·en·ing** \'chi-k²n-iŋ, 'chik-niŋ\ (1943) : to lose one's nerve — usu. used with *out* (seemed to exhibit courage, manliness, and conviction when others ~ed out —J. R. Seeley)

chicken–and–egg *adj* [fr. the proverbial question "which came first, the chicken or the egg?"] (1959) : of, relating to, or being a cause-and-effect dilemma

chicken colonel *n* [fr. the eagle serving as insignia of the rank] (1947) *slang* : COLONEL 1a

chicken feed *n* (1836) *slang* : a paltry sum (as in profits or wages)

chick·en–fried steak \'chi-k²n-'frīd-\ *n* (1952) : steak coated with batter, fried, and served with gravy

chicken hawk *n* (1827) : a hawk that preys or is believed to prey on chickens

chick·en–heart·ed \'chi-kən-ˌhär-təd\ *adj* (1681) : TIMID, COWARDLY

chick·en–liv·ered \-ˌli-vərd\ *adj* (1872) : FAINTHEARTED, COWARDLY

chicken pox *n* (ca. 1738) : an acute contagious disease esp. of children marked by low-grade fever and formation of vesicles and caused by a herpesvirus — compare HERPES ZOSTER

1**chick·en–shit** \'chi-k²n-ˌshit\ *n* (1947) **1** : the petty details of a duty or discipline — usu. considered vulgar **2** : COWARD, CHICKEN — usu. considered vulgar

2**chickenshit** *adj* (1951) **1** : PETTY, INSIGNIFICANT — usu. considered vulgar **2** : lacking courage, manliness, or effectiveness — usu. considered vulgar

chicken snake *n* (1709) : RAT SNAKE

chicken wire *n* [fr. its use for making enclosures for chickens] (ca. 1904) : a light galvanized wire netting of hexagonal mesh

chick·pea \'chik-ˌpē\ *n* [alter. of *chich pea*, fr. ME *chiche*, fr. MF, fr. L *cicer*] (ca. 1722) : an Asian leguminous herb (*Cicer arietinum*) cultivated for its short pods with one or two seeds; *also* : its seed

chick·weed \-ˌwēd\ *n* (14c) : any of various low-growing small-leaved weedy plants of the pink family (esp. genera *Cerastium* and *Stellaria*); *esp* : a cosmopolitan weed (*Stellaria media*) naturalized in the U.S. from Eurasia

---

\ə\ abut \²\ kitten, F table \ər\ further \a\ ash \ā\ ace \ä\ mop, mar \aù\ out \ch\ chin \e\ bet \ē\ easy \g\ go \i\ hit \ī\ ice \j\ job \ŋ\ sing \ō\ go \ȯ\ law \ȯi\ boy \th\ thin \t̲h̲\ the \ü\ loot \ù\ foot \y\ yet \zh\ vision \a, k̲, ⁿ, œ, œ̄, ᵫ, ᵫ̄, ᵊ\ *see* Guide to Pronunciation

chi·cle \'chi-kəl, 'chi-klē\ n [AmerSp, fr. Nahautl *tzictli*] (ca. 1889) : a gum from the latex of the sapodilla used as the chief ingredient of chewing gum

chic·o·ry also **chick·o·ry** \'chi-k(ə-)rē\ n, pl **-ries** [ME *cicoree*, fr. MF *cichorée, chicorée*, fr. L *cichoreum*, fr. Gk *kichoreia*] (15c) 1 : a thick=rooted usu. blue-flowered European perennial composite herb (*Cichorium intybus*) widely grown for its roots and as a salad plant — compare ENDIVE 2, RADICCHIO 2 : the dried ground roasted root of chicory used to flavor or adulterate coffee

chide \'chīd\ vb **chid** \'chid\ or **chid·ed** \'chī-dəd\; **chid** or **chid·den** \'chi-dᵊn\ or **chided**; **chid·ing** \'chī-diŋ\ [ME, fr. OE *cidan* to quarrel, chide, fr. *cid* strife] vi (bef. 12c) : to speak out in angry or displeased rebuke ~ vt : to voice disapproval to : reproach in a usu. mild and constructive manner : SCOLD **syn** see REPROVE

¹**chief** \'chēf\ adj (14c) 1 : accorded highest rank or office (~ librarian) 2 : of greatest importance or influence (the ~ reasons)

²**chief** (14c) adv archaic : CHIEFLY

³**chief** n [ME, fr. MF, head, chief, fr. L *caput* head — more at HEAD] (15c) 1 : the upper part of a heraldic field 2 : the head of a body of persons or an organization : LEADER (~ of police) 3 : the principal or most valuable part — **chief·dom** \-dəm\ n — **chief·ship** \-,ship\ n — **in chief** : in the chief position or place — often used in titles (commander *in chief*)

chief executive n (1833) : a principal executive officer: as a : the president of a republic b : the governor of a state

chief justice n (1534) : the presiding or principal judge of a court of justice

¹**chief·ly** \'chē-flē\ adv (14c) 1 : most importantly : PRINCIPALLY, ESPECIALLY 2 : for the most part : MOSTLY, MAINLY

²**chiefly** adj (1870) : of or relating to a chief (~ duties)

chief master sergeant n (1959) : a noncommissioned officer in the air force ranking above a senior master sergeant

chief master sergeant of the air force (ca. 1961) : the ranking noncommissioned officer in the air force serving as adviser to the chief of staff

chief of naval operations (1915) : the commanding officer of the navy and a member of the Joint Chiefs of Staff

chief of staff (ca. 1881) 1 : the ranking officer of a staff in the armed forces serving as principal adviser to a commander 2 : the commanding officer of the army or air force and a member of the Joint Chiefs of Staff

chief of state (1950) : the formal head of a national state as distinguished from the head of the government

chief petty officer n (ca. 1887) : an enlisted man in the navy or coast guard ranking above a petty officer first class and below a senior chief petty officer

chief·tain \'chēf-tən\ n [ME *chieftaine*, fr. MF *chevetain*, fr. LL *capitaneus* chief — more at CAPTAIN] (14c) : a chief esp. of a band, tribe, or clan — **chief·tain·ship** \-,ship\ n

chief·tain·cy \-sē\ n, pl **-cies** (1788) 1 : the rank, dignity, office, or rule of a chieftain 2 : a region or a people ruled by a chief : CHIEFDOM

chief warrant officer n (1956) : a warrant officer of senior rank in the armed forces; also : a commissioned officer in the navy or coast guard ranking below an ensign

chiel \'chē(ə)l\ or **chield** \'chē(ə)ld\ n [ME (Sc) *cheld*, alter. of ME *child* child] (1728) chiefly Scot : FELLOW, LAD

chiff·chaff \'chif-,chaf\ n [imit.] (1780) : a small grayish European warbler (*Phylloscopus collybita*)

¹**chif·fon** \shi-'fän, 'shi-\ n [F, lit., rag, fr. *chiffe* old rag, alter. of MF *chipe*, fr. ME *chip* chip] (1765) 1 : an ornamental addition (as a knot of ribbons) to a woman's dress 2 : a sheer fabric esp. of silk

²**chiffon** adj (1903) : resembling chiffon in sheerness or softness 2 : having a light delicate texture achieved usu. by adding whipped egg whites or whipped gelatin (lemon ~ pie)

chif·fo·nade \,shi-fə-'näd, -'näd\ n [F *chiffonnade*, fr. *chiffonner* to crumple, fr. *chiffon*] (1877) : shredded or finely cut vegetables used esp. as a garnish

chif·fo·nier \,shi-fə-'nir\ n [F *chiffonnier*, fr. *chiffon*] (1765) : a high narrow chest of drawers

chif·fo·robe \'shi-fə-,rōb\ n [*chiffonier* + *wardrobe*] (1908) : a combination of wardrobe and chest of drawers

chig·ger \'chi-gər, 'ji-\ n (1756) 1 : CHIGOE 1 2 [alter. of ²*jigger*] : a 6-legged mite larva (family Trombiculidae) that sucks the blood of vertebrates and causes intense irritation

chi·gnon \'shēn-,yän also -,yòn\ n [F, fr. MF *chaignon* chain, collar, nape] (1783) : a knot of hair that is worn at the back of the head and esp. at the nape of the neck

chi·goe \'chi-(,)gō, 'chē-\ n [Carib *chico*] (1691) 1 : a tropical flea (*Tunga penetrans*) of which the fertile female causes great discomfort by burrowing under the skin 2 : CHIGGER 2

Chi·hua·hua \chə-'wä-(,)wä, shə-, -wə\ n [MexSp, fr. *Chihuahua*, Mexico] (1858) : any of a breed of very small roundheaded dogs that occur in short-coated and long-coated varieties

chifforobe

chil·blain \'chil-,blān\ n [¹*chill*] (1547) : an inflammatory swelling or sore caused by exposure (as of the feet or hands) to cold

child \'chī(ə)ld\ n, pl **chil·dren** \'chil-drən, -dərn\ often attrib [ME, fr. OE *cild*; akin to Goth *kilthei* womb, and perh. to Skt *jathara* belly] (bef. 12c) 1 a : an unborn or recently born person b : *dial* : a female infant 2 a : a young person esp. between infancy and youth b : a childlike or childish person c : a person not yet of age 3 usu **childe** \'chī(ə)ld\ archaic : a youth of noble birth 4 a : a son or daughter of human parents b : DESCENDANT 5 : one strongly influenced by another or by a place or state of affairs 6 : PRODUCT, RESULT (barbed wire . . . is truly a ~ of the plains —W. P. Webb) — **child·less** \'chī(ə)ld-ləs\ adj — **child·less·ness** n — **with child** : PREGNANT

child-bear·ing \'chī(ə)ld-,bar-iŋ, -,ber-\ adj (14c) : of or relating to the process of conceiving, being pregnant with, and giving birth to children (women of ~ age) — **childbearing** n

child·bed \-,bed\ n (13c) : the condition of a woman in childbirth

childbed fever n (1928) : PUERPERAL FEVER

child·birth \'chīl(d)-,bərth\ n (15c) : PARTURITION

child·hood \'chīld-,hůd\ n (bef. 12c) 1 : the state or period of being a child 2 : the early period in the development of something

child·ish \'chīl-dish\ adj (bef. 12c) 1 : of, relating to, or befitting a child or childhood 2 a : marked by or suggestive of immaturity and lack of poise (a ~ spiteful remark) b : lacking complexity : SIMPLE (it's a ~ device, but it works) c : deteriorated with age esp. in mind : SENILE — **child·ish·ly** adv — **child·ish·ness** n

child·like \'chīl(d)l(d)-,līk\ adj (1586) : of, relating to, or resembling a child or childhood; esp : marked by innocence, trust, and ingenuousness — **child·like·ness** n

child·ly \'chī(ə)l(d)-lē\ adj (bef. 12c) : CHILDLIKE

child·proof \'chīl(d)-,prüf\ adj (1956) : designed to prevent tampering or opening by children (~ pill bottles)

child's play n (14c) 1 : an extremely simple task or act 2 : something that is insignificant (his injury was *child's play* compared with the damage he inflicted)

Chile saltpeter \'chi-lē-, 'chē-(,)lä-\ n [*Chile*, So. America] (ca. 1909) : sodium nitrate esp. occurring naturally (as in caliche)

chili or **chile** or **chil·li** \'chi-lē\ n, pl **chil·ies** or **chil·es** or **chil·lies** [Sp *chile*, fr. Nahuatl *chīlli*] (1604) 1 a : HOT PEPPER b usu *chilli*, chiefly *Brit* : a pepper whether hot or sweet 2 a : a thick sauce of meat and chilies b : CHILI CON CARNE

chil·i·ad \'ki-lē-,ad, -əd\ n [LL *chiliad-, chilias*, fr. Gk, fr. *chilioi* thousand] (1598) 1 : a group of 1000 2 : MILLENNIUM 2a

chil·i·asm \'ki-lē-,a-zᵊm\ n [NL *chiliasmus*, fr. LL *chiliastes* one that believes in chiliasm, fr. Gk, fr. *chilias*] (1610) : MILLENARIANISM — **chil·i·ast** \-lē-,ast, -lē-əst\ n — **chil·i·as·tic** \,ki-lē-'as-tik\ adj

chili con car·ne \,chi-lē-,kän-'kär-nē, -kən-\ n [AmerSp *chile con carne* chili with meat] (1857) : a spiced stew of ground beef and minced chilies or chili powder usu. with beans

chili dog n (1969) : a hot dog topped with chili

chili powder n (1938) : a condiment made with chilies ground to a powder

chili sauce n (1880) : a spiced tomato sauce usu. made with red and green peppers

¹**chill** \'chil\ n [ME *chile* chill, frost, fr. OE *ciele*; akin to OE *ceald* cold] (bef. 12c) 1 a : a sensation of cold accompanied by shivering b : a disagreeable sensation of coldness 2 : a moderate but disagreeable degree of cold 3 : a check to enthusiasm or warmth of feeling (felt the ~ of his opponent's stare)

²**chill** adj (14c) 1 a : moderately cold b : COLD, RAW 2 : affected by cold (~ travelers) 3 : DISTANT, FORMAL (a ~ reception) 4 : DEPRESSING, DISPIRITING (~ penury —Thomas Gray) — **chill·ness** n

³**chill** vi (14c) 1 a : to become cold b : to shiver or quake with or as if with cold 2 : to become taken with a chill ~ vt 1 a : to make cold or chilly b : to make cool esp. without freezing 2 : to affect as if with cold : DISPIRIT, DISCOURAGE (were ~ed by the drab austerity — William Attwood) — **chill·ing·ly** \'chi-liŋ-lē\ adv

chill·er \'chi-lər\ n (1798) 1 : one that chills 2 : an eerie or frightening story of murder, violence, or the supernatural

chill factor n (1965) : WINDCHILL

chill out vi (1983) slang : to calm down : go easy : RELAX — often used in the imperative

chil·lum \'chi-ləm\ n [Hindi *cilam*, fr. Per *chilam*] (1781) 1 : the part of a water pipe that contains the substance (as tobacco or hashish) which is smoked; also : a quantity of a substance thus smoked 2 : a funnel-shaped clay pipe for smoking

chilly \'chi-lē\ adj **chill·i·er; -est** (1570) 1 : noticeably cold : CHILLING 2 : unpleasantly affected by cold 3 : lacking warmth of feeling 4 : tending to arouse fear or apprehension (~ suspicions) — **chill·i·ly** \'chi-lə-lē\ adv — **chill·i·ness** \'chi-lē-nəs\ n

¹**chi·mae·ra** \kī-'mir-ə, kə-\ var of CHIMERA

²**chimaera** n [NL, genus name, fr. L, chimera] (1804) : any of a family (Chimaeridae) of marine cartilaginous fishes with a tapering or thread-like tail and usu. a long snout

chi·mae·ric, chi·mae·rism *Brit var of* CHIMERIC, CHIMERISM

¹**chime** \'chīm\ n [ME *chimbe*, fr. OE *cimb-*; akin to MD *kimme* edge of a cask] (14c) : the edge or rim of a cask or drum

²**chime** vb **chimed; chim·ing** vi (14c) 1 a : to make a musical and esp. a harmonious sound b : to make the sounds of a chime 2 : to be or act in accord (the music and the mood *chimed* well together) ~ vt 1 : to cause to sound musically by striking 2 : to produce by chiming 3 : to call or indicate by chiming (the clock *chimed* midnight) 4 : to utter repetitively : DIN 2 — **chim·er** n

³**chime** n [ME, cymbal, fr. MF *chimbe*, fr. OF, fr. L *cymbalum* cymbal] (15c) 1 : an apparatus for chiming a bell or set of bells 2 a : a musically tuned set of bells b : one of a set of objects giving a bell-like sound when struck 3 a : the sound of a set of bells — usu. used in pl. b : a musical sound suggesting that of bells 4 : ACCORD, HARMONY (such happy ~ of fact and theory —Henry Maudsley)

chime in vi (1681) 1 : to combine harmoniously (the artist's illustrations *chime in* perfectly with the text —*Book Production*) 2 : to break into a conversation or discussion esp. to express an opinion ~ vt : to remark while chiming in

chi·me·ra \kī-'mir-ə, kə-\ n [L *chimaera*, fr. Gk *chimaira* she-goat, chimera; akin to ON *gymbr* yearling ewe, Gk *cheimōn* winter — more at HIBERNATE] 1 a cap : a fire-breathing she-monster in Greek mythology having a lion's head, a goat's body, and a serpent's tail b : an imaginary monster compounded of incongruous parts 2 : an illusion or fabrication of the mind; esp : an unrealizable dream (a fancy, a ~ in my brain, troubles me in my prayer —John Donne) 3 : an individual, organ, or part consisting of tissues of diverse genetic constitution

chi·mere \shə-'mir, chə-\ n [ME *chimmer, chemeyr*] (14c) : a loose sleeveless robe worn by Anglican bishops over the rochet

chi·me·ric \kī-'mir-ik, kə-, -'mer-\ adj (1973) : relating to, derived from, or being a genetic chimera or its genetic material (a ~ cat) (~ genes)

chi·me·ri·cal \kī-'mer-i-kəl, kə-, -'mir-\ adj [*chimera*] (1638) 1 : existing only as the product of unchecked imagination : fantastically visionary or improbable 2 : given to fantastic schemes **syn** see IMAGINARY — **chi·me·ri·cal·ly** \-i-k(ə-)lē\ adv

chi·me·rism \kī-'mir-ˌi-zəm, kə-; 'kī-mə-ˌri-\ *n* (1961) : the state of being a genetic chimera

chi·mi·chan·ga \ˌchi-mē-'chän-gə\ *n* [MexSp, trinket] (1982) : a tortilla wrapped around a filling (as of meat) and deep-fried

chim·ney \'chim-nē\ *n, pl* **chimneys** [ME, fr. MF cheminée, fr. LL caminata, fr. L caminus furnace, fireplace, fr. Gk kaminos; perh. akin to Gk kamara vault] (14c) **1** *dial* : FIREPLACE, HEARTH **2** : a vertical structure incorporated into a building and enclosing a flue or flues that carry off smoke; *esp* : the part of such a structure extending above a roof **3** : SMOKESTACK **4** : a tube usu. of glass placed around a flame (as of a lamp) **5** : something resembling a chimney: as **a** : a narrow cleft in rock **b** : a tall column of rock on the ocean floor that is formed by the precipitation of minerals from superheated water issuing from a vent in the earth's crust and rising through the column of rock — **chim·ney·like** \-ˌlīk\ *adj*

chim·ney·piece \'chim-nē-ˌpēs\ *n* (1680) : an ornamental construction over and around a fireplace that includes the mantel

chimney pot *n* (ca. 1806) : a usu. earthenware pipe placed at the top of a chimney

chimney sweep *n* (1727) : a person whose occupation is cleaning soot from chimney flues — called also *chimney sweeper*

chimney swift *n* (1849) : a small sooty-gray swift (Chaetura pelagica) with long narrow wings that often builds its nest inside an unused chimney — called also *chimney swallow*

chimp \'chimp *sometimes* 'shimp\ *n* (1877) : CHIMPANZEE

chim·pan·zee \ˌ(ˌ)chim-ˌpan-'zē, -pən-'zē, -'pan-zē *sometimes* (ˌ)shim-\ *n* [Kongo dial. chimpenzi] (1738) : an anthropoid ape (Pan troglodytes) of equatorial Africa that is smaller and more arboreal than the gorilla — compare PYGMY CHIMPANZEE

¹chin \'chin\ *n* [ME, fr. OE cinn; akin to OHG kinni chin, L gena cheek, Gk genys jaw, cheek] (bef. 12c) **1** : the lower portion of the face lying below the lower lip and including the prominence of the lower jaw **2** : the surface beneath or between the branches of the lower jaw — **chin·less** \-ləs\ *adj*

²chin *vb* **chinned; chin·ning** *vt* (1869) **1** : to bring to or hold with the chin ⟨~ a violin⟩ **2** : to raise (oneself) while hanging by the hands until the chin is level with the support ~ *vi, slang* : to talk idly

chi·na \'chī-nə\ *n* [Per chīnī Chinese porcelain] (1579) **1** : PORCELAIN; *also* : vitreous porcelain wares (as dishes, vases, or ornaments) for domestic use **2** : earthenware or porcelain tableware

China aster *n* (1794) : a common annual garden aster (Callistephus chinensis) native to northern China that occurs in many showy forms

chi·na·ber·ry \'chī-nə-ˌber-ē, Southern also 'chä-nē-ˌber-ē\ *n* (1890) : a small Asian tree (Melia azedarach) of the mahogany family naturalized in the southern U.S. where it is widely used for shade or ornament

china clay *n* (1840) : KAOLIN

china closet *n* (1771) : a cabinet or cupboard for the storage or display of household china

Chi·na·man \'chī-nə-mən\ *n* (1849) : a native of China : CHINESE — often taken to be offensive

China rose *n* (ca. 1731) : any of numerous garden roses derived from a shrubby Chinese rose (Rosa chinensis)

China Syndrome *n* [fr. the notion that the molten reactor contents could theoretically sink through the earth to reach China] (1970) : MELTDOWN 1

Chi·na·town \'chī-nə-ˌtaún\ *n* (1857) : the Chinese quarter of a city

China tree *n* (1819) : CHINABERRY

chi·na·ware \'chī-nə-ˌwar, -ˌwer\ *n* (1634) : tableware made of china

chin·bone \'chin-ˌbōn\ *n* (bef. 12c) : MANDIBLE; *esp* : the median anterior part of the human mandible

chinch \'chinch\ *n* [Sp chinche, fr. L cimic-, cimex] (1616) : BEDBUG

chinch bug *n* (1785) : a small black-and-white bug (Blissus leucopterus) very destructive to cereal grasses

chin·che·rin·chee \ˌchin-chə-ri(n)-'chē, ˌchiŋ-kə-\ *n, pl* **chincherin·chee** *or* **chincherinchees** [Afrik tjienkerientjee] (1904) : a southern African perennial bulbous herb (Ornithogalum thyrsoides) of the lily family with spikes of white to golden-yellow blossoms

chin·chil·la \chin-'chil-ə\ *n* [Sp] (1604) **1** : either of two small So. American rodents (Chinchilla laniger and C. brevicaudata) of the high Andes that are the size of large squirrels, have very soft pearly gray fur, and are extensively bred in captivity; *also* : the fur of a chinchilla **2** : a heavy twilled woolen coating

¹chine \'chīn\ *n* [ME, fr. MF eschine, of Gmc origin; akin to OHG scina shinbone, needle — more at SHIN] (14c) **1** : BACKBONE, SPINE; *also* : a cut of meat including all or part of the backbone **2** : the intersection of the bottom and the sides of a flat or V-bottomed boat

²chine *vt* **chined; chin·ing** (ca. 1611) : to cut through the backbone of (as in butchering)

chinchilla

Chi·nese \chī-'nēz, -'nēs\ *n, pl* **Chinese** (1606) **1 a** : a native or inhabitant of China **b** : a person of Chinese descent **2** : a group of related languages used by the people of China that are often mutually unintelligible in their spoken form but share a single system of writing and that constitute a branch of the Sino-Tibetan language family; *esp* : MANDARIN — **Chinese** *adj*

Chinese boxes *n pl* (1829) **1** : a set of boxes graduated in size so that each fits into the next larger one **2** : something that resembles a set of Chinese boxes esp. in complexity

Chinese cabbage *n* (1842) : either of two Asian brassicas now grown in the U.S. and widely used as greens: **a** : BOK CHOY **b** : one (Brassica rapa pekinensis) that forms elongate more or less solid cylindrical heads and has pale green or cream-colored leaves

Chinese checkers *n pl but sing or pl in constr* (1938) : a game in which each player seeks to be the first to transfer a set of marbles from a home point to the opposite point of a pitted 6-pointed star by single moves or jumps

Chinese chestnut *n* (ca. 1909) : an Asian chestnut (Castanea mollissima) that is resistant to chestnut blight

Chinese copy *n* (1920) : an exact imitation or duplicate that includes defects as well as desired qualities

Chinese crested *n* (1976) : any of a breed of hairless or coated dogs with a plumed tail and a crest of hair on the head

Chinese gooseberry *n* (1925) : a subtropical vine (Actinidia chinensis) of the family Actinidiaceae) that bears kiwifruit; *also* : KIWIFRUIT

Chinese lantern *n* (1825) : a collapsible translucent covering for a light

Chinese parsley *n* (ca. 1953) : CILANTRO

Chinese puzzle *n* (ca. 1815) **1** : an intricate or ingenious puzzle **2** : something intricate and obscure

Chinese restaurant syndrome *n* (1968) : a group of symptoms (as numbness of the neck, arms, and back with headache, dizziness, and palpitations) that is held to affect susceptible persons eating food and esp. Chinese food heavily seasoned with monosodium glutamate

chinese shar–pei *n* (1975) : SHAR-PEI

Chinese wall *n* [Chinese Wall, a defensive wall built in the 3d cent. B.C. between China and Mongolia] (1900) : a strong barrier; *esp* : a serious obstacle to understanding

Chinese white *n* (ca. 1884) : ZINC WHITE

Ching *or* **Ch'ing** \'chiŋ\ *n* [Chin (Beijing) Qīng] (1795) : a Manchu dynasty in China dated 1644–1912 and the last imperial dynasty

¹chink \'chiŋk\ *n* [prob. alter. of ME chine crack, fissure] (1535) **1** : a small cleft, slit, or fissure ⟨a ~ in the curtain⟩ **2** : a weak spot that may leave one vulnerable **3** : a narrow beam of light shining through a chink

²chink *vt* (1748) : to fill the chinks of (as by caulking) ⟨~ a log cabin⟩

³chink *n* [imit.] (1573) **1** *archaic* : COIN, MONEY **2** : a short sharp sound

⁴chink *vi* (1589) : to make a slight sharp metallic sound ~ *vt* : to cause to make a chink

Chink \'chiŋk\ *n or adj* [perh. alter. of Chinese] (1887) : CHINESE — usu. taken to be offensive

chi·no \'chē-(ˌ)nō, 'shē-\ *n, pl* **chinos** [origin unknown] (1943) **1** : a usu. khaki cotton or synthetic-fiber twill of the type used for military uniforms **2** *pl* : an article of clothing made of chino

chi·noi·se·rie \shēn-ˌwäz-rē, -'wä-zə-; ˌshēn-ˌwäz-'rē, -wä-zə-\ *n* [F, fr. chinois Chinese, fr. Chine China] (1883) : a style in art (as in decoration) reflecting Chinese qualities or motifs; *also* : an object or decoration in this style

Chi·nook \shə-'núk, chə-, -'núk\ *n, pl* **Chinook** *or* **Chinooks** [Lower Chehalis (Salishan language of western Washington) činúk, name of a Chinook village] (1805) **1** : a member of an American Indian people of the north shore of the Columbia River at its mouth **2** : a Chinookan language of the Chinook and other nearby peoples **3** *often not cap* : a warm moist southwest wind of the coast from Oregon northward **b** : a warm dry wind that descends the eastern slopes of the Rocky Mountains **4** *not cap* : CHINOOK SALMON

Chi·nook·an \-'nú-kən, -'nú-\ *n* (ca. 1890) : an American Indian language family of Washington and Oregon — **Chinookan** *adj*

Chinook jargon *n, often cap J* (1840) : a pidgin language based on Chinook and other Indian languages, French, and English and formerly used as a lingua franca in the northwestern U.S. and on the Pacific coast of Canada and Alaska

chinook salmon *n* (1851) : a large commercially important Pacific salmon (Oncorhynchus tshawytscha) with red flesh that occurs in the northern Pacific Ocean — called also *king salmon*

chin·qua·pin *or* **chin·ka·pin** \'chiŋ-ki-ˌpin\ *n* [prob. modif. of Virginia Algonquian chechinquamin chinquapin nut] (1612) **1** : the edible nut of a chinquapin **2** : any of several trees (genera Castanea and Castanopsis); *esp* : a dwarf chestnut (Castanea pumila) of the U.S.

chinquapin oak *n* (1785) : either of two chestnut oaks (Quercus muhlenbergii and Q. prinoides) of the eastern U.S.

chintz \'chin(t)s\ *n* [earlier chints, pl. of chint, fr. Hindi chīṭ] (1614) **1** : a printed calico from India **2** : a usu. glazed printed cotton fabric

chintzy \'chin(t)-sē\ *adj* **chintz·i·er; -est** (1851) **1** : decorated with or as if with chintz **2 a** : GAUDY, CHEAP ⟨~ toys⟩ **b** : STINGY

chin–up \'chin-(ˌ)nəp\ *n* (1954) : the act or an instance of chinning oneself performed esp. as a conditioning exercise

chin–wag \'chin-ˌwag\ *n* (1879) *slang* : CONVERSATION, CHAT

chi·o·no·doxa \ˌkī-ə-nō-'däk-sə, kī-ˌä-nə-\ *n* [NL, genus name, fr. Gk chion-, chiōn snow (akin to Gk cheimōn winter) + doxa glory — more at HIBERNATE, DOXOLOGY] (1879) : GLORY-OF-THE-SNOW

¹chip \'chip\ *n* [ME; akin to OE -cippian] (14c) **1 a** : a small usu. thin and flat piece (as of wood or stone) cut, struck, or flaked off **b** (1) : a small thin slice of food; *esp* : POTATO CHIP (2) : FRENCH FRY **2** : something small, worthless, or trivial **3 a** : one of the counters used as a token for money in poker and other games **b** *pl* : MONEY — used esp. in the phrase *in the chips* **c** : something valuable that can be used for advantage in negotiation or trade ⟨a bargaining ~⟩ **4** : a piece of dried dung — usu. used in combination ⟨cow ~⟩ **5** : a flaw left after a chip is removed **6 a** : INTEGRATED CIRCUIT **b** : a small wafer of semiconductor material that forms the base for an integrated circuit **7** : CHIP SHOT — **chip off the old block** : a child that resembles his or her parent — **chip on one's shoulder** : a challenging or belligerent attitude

²chip *vb* **chipped; chip·ping** [ME chippen, fr. OE -cippian (as in forcippian to cut off); akin to OE cipp beam, OHG chipfa stave] *vt* (15c) **1 a** : to cut or hew with an edged tool **b** (1) : to cut or break (a small piece) from something (2) : to cut or break a fragment from (3) : to cut into chips ⟨~ a tree stump⟩ **2** : CHAFF, BANTER **3** : to hit (a return in tennis) with backspin ~ *vi* **1** : to break off in small pieces **2** : to play a chip shot

chip·board \'chip-ˌbörd, -ˌbòrd\ *n* (1919) : a paperboard usu. made entirely from wastepaper

chip in *vi* (1861) **1** : CONTRIBUTE ⟨everyone chipped in for the gift⟩ **2** *chiefly Brit* : CHIME IN 2 ~ *vt* : CONTRIBUTE

\ə\ abut \ᵊ\ kitten, F table \ər\ further \a\ ash \ā\ ace \ä\ mop, mar \aú\ out \ch\ chin \e\ bet \ē\ easy \g\ go \i\ hit \ī\ ice \j\ job \ŋ\ sing \ō\ go \ò\ law \òi\ boy \th\ thin \t͟h\ the \ü\ loot \ù\ foot \y\ yet \zh\ vision \à, ḵ, ⁿ, œ, œ̄, ue, ū̄, ᵞ\ *see* Guide to Pronunciation

chip·munk \'chip-,məŋk\ *n* [alter. of earlier *chitmunk*, prob. fr. Ojibwa *ačitamo*[n]? red squirrel] (1832) : any of a genus (*Tamias*) of small striped No. American and Asian rodents of the squirrel family

chipped beef \'chip(t)-\ *n* (1859) : smoked dried beef sliced thin

Chip·pen·dale \'chi-pən-,dāl\ *adj* [Thomas *Chippendale*] (1876) : of or relating to an 18th century English furniture style characterized by graceful outline and often ornate rococo ornamentation

¹**chip·per** \'chi-pər\ *n* (1513) : one that chips

²**chipper** *adj* [perh. alter. of E dial. *kipper* (lively)] (1838) : SPRIGHTLY

Chip·pe·wa \'chi-pə-,wȯ, -,wä, -,wä, -wə\ *n, pl* **Chippewa** or **Chippewas** (1671) : OJIBWA

chip·ping sparrow \'chi-piŋ-\ *n* [*chip* to cheep] (1791) : a small gray-breasted No. American sparrow (*Spizella passerina*) with a black line through the eye, a white line above it, and in breeding plumage a reddish patch on the top of the head

chip·py \'chi-pē\ *adj* **chip·pi·er; -est** [*chip* on one's shoulder] (1898) : aggressively belligerent ⟨a ~ hockey player⟩; *also* : marked by much fighting ⟨a ~ game⟩

chip shot *n* (1909) : a short usu. low approach shot in golf that lofts the ball to the green and allows it to roll

chir- *or* **chiro-** *comb form* [L, fr. Gk *cheir-, cheiro-*, fr. *cheir;* akin to Hitt *keššar* hand] : hand ⟨*chiropractic*⟩

chi·ral \'kī-rəl\ *adj* [*chir-* + ¹-*al*] (1894) : of or relating to a molecule that is not superimposable on its mirror image — **chi·ral·i·ty** \kī-'ra-lə-tē, kə-\ *n*

chiral center *n* (1970) : an atom esp. in an organic molecule that has four different atoms or groups attached to it

Chi-Rho \'kī-'rō, 'kē-\ *n, pl* **Chi-Rhos** [*chi* + *rho*] (1868) : a Christian monogram and symbol formed from the first two letters X and P of the Greek word for *Christ* — called also *Christogram*

Chir·i·ca·hua \,chir-ə-'kä-wə\ *n, pl* **Chiricahua** or **Chiricahuas** (1885) : a member of an Apache people of Arizona

chir·i·moya *var of* CHERIMOYA

chirk \'chərk\ *vb* [ME *charken, chirken* to creak, chirp, fr. OE *cearcian* to creak; akin to OE *cracian* to crack] (1843) : CHEER ⟨play with her and ~ her up a little —Harriet B. Stowe⟩

chi·rog·ra·phy \kī-'rä-grə-fē\ *n* (1654) **1** : HANDWRITING, PENMANSHIP **2** : CALLIGRAPHY 1 — **chi·rog·ra·pher** \-fər\ *n* — **chi·ro·graph·ic** \,kī-rə-'gra-fik\ *or* **chi·ro·graph·i·cal** \-fi-kəl\ *adj*

chi·ro·man·cy \'kī-rə-,man(t)-sē\ *n* [prob. fr. MF *chiromancie*, fr. ML *chiromantia*, fr. Gk *cheir-* chir- + *-manteia* -mancy] (ca. 1528) : PALMISTRY — **chi·ro·man·cer** \-,man(t)-sər\ *n*

chi·ron·o·mid \kī-'rä-nə-məd\ *n* [ultim. fr. Gk *cheironomos* one who gestures with his hands] (1915) : any of a family (Chironomidae) of midges that lack piercing mouthparts — **chironomid** *adj*

chi·rop·o·dy \kə-'rä-pə-dē, shə- *also* ki-\ *n* [*chir-* + *pod-;* fr. its original concern with both hands and feet] (1886) : PODIATRY — **chi·rop·o·dist** \-dist\ *n*

chi·ro·prac·tic \'kī-rə-,prak-tik, ,kī-rə-'\ *n* [*chir-* + Gk *praktikos* practical, operative — more at PRACTICAL] (1898) : a system of therapy which holds that disease results from a lack of normal nerve function and which employs manipulation and specific adjustment of body structures (as the spine) — **chi·ro·prac·tor** \-tər\ *n*

chi·rop·ter·an \kī-'räp-tə-rən\ *n* [ultim. fr. Gk *cheir* hand + *pteron* wing — more at FEATHER] (1835) : ³BAT

chirp \'chərp\ *n* [imit.] (ca. 1755) : the characteristic short sharp sound esp. of a small bird or insect — **chirp** *vi*

chirpy \'chər-pē\ *adj* **chirp·i·er; -est** (1837) **1** : cheerfully lively ⟨a ~ manner⟩ **2 a** : making chirps **b** : suggestive of chirping ⟨a ~ voice⟩ — **chirp·i·ly** \-pə-lē\ *adv*

chirr \'chər\ *n* [imit.] (ca. 1600) : the short vibrant or trilled sound characteristic of an insect (as a grasshopper or cicada) — **chirr** *vi*

chir·rup \'chər-əp, 'chir-\ *n* [imit.] (1788) : CHIRP — **chirrup** *vi*

chir·rupy \'chər-ə-pē, 'chir-\ *adj* (1874) : CHIRPY

chir·rur·geon \'kī-'rər-jən\ *n* [ME *cirurgian*, fr. OF *cirurgien*, fr. *cirurgie* surgery] (13c) *archaic* : SURGEON

¹**chis·el** \'chi-z³l\ *n* [ME, fr. ONF, fr. (assumed) VL *cisellum*, alter. of *caesellum*, fr. L *caesus*, pp. of *caedere* to cut] (14c) : a metal tool with a sharpened edge at one end used to chip, carve, or cut into a solid material (as wood, stone, or metal)

²**chisel** *vb* **-eled** *or* **-elled; -el·ing** *or* **-el·ling** \'chi-z³l-iŋ, 'chiz-liŋ\ *vt* (1509) **1** : to cut or work with or as if with a chisel **2** : to employ shrewd or unfair practices on in order to obtain one's end; *also* : to obtain by such practices ⟨~ a job⟩ ~ *vi* **1** : to work with or as if with a chisel **2 a** : to employ shrewd or unfair practices **b** : to thrust oneself : INTRUDE ⟨~ in on a racket⟩ — **chis·el·er** *or* **chis·el·ler** \'chi-z³l-ər, 'chiz-lər\ *n*

chis·eled *or* **chis·elled** \'chi-z³ld\ *adj* (1821) : formed or crafted as if with a chisel ⟨~ good looks⟩ ⟨a ~ essay⟩

chi-square \'kī-,skwar, -'skwer\ *n, often attrib* (ca. 1934) : a statistic that is a sum of terms each of which is a quotient obtained by dividing the square of the difference between the observed and theoretical values of a quantity by the theoretical value

chi-square distribution *n* (ca. 1956) : a probability density function that gives the distribution of the sum of the squares of a number of independent random variables each with a normal distribution with zero mean and unit variance, that has the property that the sum of two or more random variables with such a distribution also has one, and that is widely used in testing statistical hypotheses esp. about the theoretical and observed values of a quantity and about population variances and standard deviations

¹**chit** \'chit\ *n* [ME *chitte* kitten, cub] (ca. 1624) **1** : CHILD **2** : a pert young woman

²**chit** *n* [Hindi *ciṭṭhī*] (1757) **1** : a short letter or note; *esp* : a signed voucher of a small debt (as for food) **2** : a small slip of paper with writing on it

chit·chat \'chit-,chat\ *n* [redupl. of *chat*] (1710) : SMALL TALK, GOSSIP — **chitchat** *vi*

chi·tin \'kī-t³n\ *n* [F *chitine*, fr. Gk *chitōn*] (ca. 1839) : a horny polysaccharide that forms part of the hard outer integument esp. of insects, arachnids, and crustaceans — **chi·tin·ous** \'kī-t³n-əs, 'kīt-nəs\ *adj*

chi·ton \'kī-t³n, 'kī-,tän\ *n* [NL, genus name, fr. Gk *chitōn* tunic, of Sem origin; akin to Heb *kuttōneth* tunic] (1816) **1** : any of a class (Polyplacophora) of elongated bilaterally symmetrical marine mollusks with

a dorsal shell of calcareous plates **2** [Gk *chitōn*] : the basic garment of ancient Greece worn usu. knee-length by men and full-length by women

chit·ter \'chi-tər\ *vi* [ME *chiteren*, prob. fr. imit. origin] (13c) : TWITTER, CHIRP; *also* : CHATTER

chit·ter·lings *or* **chit·lins** \'chit-lənz\ *n pl* [ME *chiterling*] (13c) : the intestines of hogs esp. when prepared as food

chi·val·ric \shə-'val-rik\ *adj* (1797) : relating to chivalry : CHIVALROUS

chiv·al·rous \'shi-vəl-rəs\ *adj* (14c) **1** : VALIANT **2** : of, relating to, or characteristic of chivalry and knight-errantry **3 a** : marked by honor, generosity, and courtesy **b** : marked by gracious courtesy and high-minded consideration esp. to women *syn* see CIVIL — **chiv·al·rous·ly** *adv* — **chiv·al·rous·ness** *n*

chiv·al·ry \'shi-vəl-rē\ *n, pl* **-ries** [ME *chivalrie*, fr. MF *chevalerie*, fr. *chevalier* knight — more at CHEVALIER] (14c) **1** : mounted men-at-arms **2** *archaic* **a** : martial valor **b** : knightly skill **3** : gallant or distinguished gentlemen **4** : the system, spirit, or customs of medieval knighthood **5** : the qualities of the ideal knight : chivalrous conduct

chive \'chiv\ *n* [ME, fr. ONF, fr. L *cepa* onion] (14c) : a perennial plant (*Allium schoenoprasum*) related to the onion and having slender leaves used as a seasoning — usu. used in pl.

chivy *or* **chiv·vy** \'chi-vē\ *vt* **chiv·ied** *or* **chiv·vied; chivy·ing** *or* **chiv·vy·ing** [*chivy*, n. (chase, hunt), prob. fr. E dial. *Chevy Chase* chase, confusion, fr. the name of a ballad describing the battle of Otterburn (1388)] (1918) **1** : to tease or annoy with persistent petty attacks **2** : to move or obtain by small maneuvers *syn* see BAIT

chla·myd·ia \klə-'mi-dē-ə\ *n, pl* **-i·ae** \-dē-,ē\ [NL, fr. Gk *chlamyd-, chlamys*] (1966) **1** : any of a genus (*Chlamydia*, family Chlamydiaceae) of spherical gram-negative intracellular bacteria; *esp* : one (*C. trachomatis*) that causes or is associated with various diseases of the eye and urogenital tract including trachoma, lymphogranuloma venereum, cervicitis, and some forms of urethritis **2** : a disease or infection caused by chlamydiae — **chla·myd·i·al** \-dē-əl\ *adj*

chla·my·do·spore \klə-'mi-də-,spȯr, -,spȯr\ *n* [L *chlamyd-, chlamys* + ISV *spore*] (1884) : a thick-walled usu. resting fungal spore

chla·mys \'kla-məs, 'klā-\ *n, pl* **chla·mys·es** *or* **chla·my·des** \-mə-,dēz\ [L *chlamyd-, chlamys*, fr. Gk] (1699) : a short oblong mantle worn by young men of ancient Greece

Chloe \'klō-ē\ *n* [L, fr. Gk *Chloē*] : a lover of Daphnis in a Greek pastoral romance

chlor- *or* **chloro-** *comb form* [NL, fr. Gk, fr. *chlōros* greenish yellow — more at YELLOW] **1** : green ⟨*chlorine*⟩ ⟨*chlorosis*⟩ **2** : chlorine : containing chlorine ⟨*chloroprene*⟩

chlor·ac·ne \klō-'rak-nē, klȯ-\ *n* (ca. 1928) : a skin eruption resembling acne and resulting from exposure to chlorine or its compounds

chlo·ral \'klȯr-əl, 'klȯr-\ *n* [F, fr. *chlor-* + *alcool* alcohol] (1838) **1** : a pungent colorless oily aldehyde CCl_3CHO used in making DDT and chloral hydrate **2** : CHLORAL HYDRATE

chloral hydrate *n* (1874) : a bitter white crystalline drug $C_2H_3Cl_3O_2$ used as a hypnotic and sedative or in knockout drops

chlo·ral·ose \'klȯr-ə-,lōs, 'klȯr-, -,lōz\ *n* (1893) : a bitter crystalline compound $C_8H_{11}Cl_3O_6$ used esp. to anesthetize animals — **chlo·ral·osed** \-,lōst, -,lōzd\ *adj*

chlo·ra·mine \'klȯr-ə-,mēn, 'klȯr-\ *n* [ISV] (1893) : any of various compounds containing nitrogen and chlorine

chlor·am·phen·i·col \,klȯr-,am-'fe-ni-,kȯl, ,klȯr-, -,kȯl\ *n* [*chlor-* + *amide* + *phen-* + *nitr-* + *glycol*] (1949) : a broad-spectrum antibiotic $C_{11}H_{12}Cl_2N_2O_5$ isolated from cultures of a soil actinomycete (*Streptomyces venezuelae*) or prepared synthetically

chlo·rate \'klȯr-,āt, 'klȯr-\ *n* (1823) : a salt containing the anion ClO_3^- ⟨~ of potassium⟩

chlor·dane \'klȯr-,dān\ *n* [*chlor-* + *indane* (C_9H_{10})] (1947) : a highly chlorinated viscous volatile liquid insecticide $C_{10}H_6Cl_8$

chlor·di·az·epox·ide \,klȯr-dī-,a-zə-'päk-,sīd, ,klȯr-\ *n* [*chlor-* + *di-* + *az-* + *epoxide*] (1961) : a benzodiazepine $C_{16}H_{14}ClN_3O$ related to diazepam and used in the form of its hydrochloride esp. as a tranquilizer and in the treatment of alcoholism

chlo·rel·la \klə-'re-lə\ *n* [NL, genus name, fr. Gk *chlōros*] (1904) : any of a genus (*Chlorella*) of unicellular green algae

chlor·en·chy·ma \klȯr-'eŋ-kə-mə, klȯr-\ *n* (1894) : chlorophyll-containing parenchyma of plants

chlo·ride \'klȯr-,īd, 'klȯr-\ *n* [G *Chlorid*, fr. *chlor-* + *-id* -ide] (1812) **1** : a compound of chlorine with another element or group; *esp* : a salt or ester of hydrochloric acid **2** : a univalent anion consisting of one atom of chlorine

chloride of lime (1826) : BLEACHING POWDER

chlo·ri·nate \'klȯr-ə-,nāt, 'klȯr-\ *vt* **-nat·ed; -nat·ing** (1856) : to treat or combine with chlorine or a chlorine compound — **chlo·ri·na·tion** \,klȯr-ə-'nā-shən, ,klȯr-\ *n* — **chlo·ri·na·tor** \'klȯr-ə-,nā-tər, 'klȯr-\ *n*

chlorinated lime (1876) : BLEACHING POWDER

chlo·rine \'klȯr-,ēn, 'klȯr-, -ən\ *n* (1810) : a halogen element that is isolated as a heavy greenish yellow gas of pungent odor and is used esp. as a bleach, oxidizing agent, and disinfectant in water purification — see ELEMENT table

chlo·rin·i·ty \klō-'ri-nə-tē, klȯ-\ *n* (ca. 1931) : a measure of the concentration of halides in one kilogram of seawater

¹**chlo·rite** \'klȯr-,īt, 'klȯr-\ *n* [G *Chlorit*, fr. L *chloritis*, a green stone, fr. Gk *chlōritis*, fr. *chlōros*] (1794) : any of a group of monoclinic usu. green minerals associated with and resembling the micas — **chlo·rit·ic** \klō-'ri-tik, klȯ-\ *adj*

²**chlorite** *n* [prob. fr. F, fr. *chlor-*] (1853) : a salt containing the anion ClO_2^- ⟨~ of sodium⟩

chloro- — see CHLOR-

chlo·ro·ben·zene \,klȯr-ō-'ben-,zēn, ,klȯr-, -'ben-\ *n* [ISV] (ca. 1889) : a colorless flammable volatile toxic liquid C_6H_5Cl used in organic synthesis (as of DDT) and as a solvent

chlo·ro·fluo·ro·car·bon \,klȯr-ō-,flȯr-ō-'kär-bən, ,klȯr-, -,flȯr-, -,flȯr-\ *n* (1949) : any of several simple gaseous compounds that contain carbon, chlorine, fluorine, and sometimes hydrogen, that are used as refrigerants, cleaning solvents, and aerosol propellants and in the manufacture of plastic foams, and that are suspected to be a major cause of stratospheric ozone depletion — abbr. *CFC*

chlo·ro·fluo·ro·meth·ane \-'me-,thān, *Brit usu* -'mē-\ *n* (1965) : a chlorofluorocarbon derived from methane

¹chlo·ro·form \'klōr-ə-ˌfȯrm, 'klȯr-\ n [F *chloroforme*, fr. *chlor-* + *formyle* formyl; fr. its having been regarded as a trichloride of this group] (1838) : a colorless volatile heavy toxic liquid CHCl₃ with an ether odor used esp. as a solvent or as a veterinary anesthetic
²chloroform vt (1848) : to treat with or as if with chloroform esp. so as to produce anesthesia, insensibility, or death
chlo·ro·gen·ic acid \ˌklōr-ə-'je-nik-, ˌklȯr-\ n (ca. 1889) : a crystalline acid C₁₆H₁₈O₉ occurring in various plant parts (as coffee beans)
chlo·ro·hy·drin \ˌklōr-ō-'hī-drən, ˌklȯr-\ n [ISV *chlor-* + *hydr-* + '-*in*] (ca. 1890) : any of various organic compounds derived from diols or polyhydroxy alcohols by substitution of chlorine for part of the hydroxyl groups
Chlo·ro·my·ce·tin \ˌklōr-ō-mī-'sē-t²n, ˌklȯr-\ *trademark* — used for chloramphenicol
chlo·ro·phyll \'klōr-ə-ˌfil, 'klȯr-, -fəl\ n [F *chlorophylle*, fr. *chlor-* + Gk *phyllon* leaf — more at BLADE] (1819) **1** : the green photosynthetic pigment found chiefly in the chloroplasts of plants and occurring esp. as a blue-black ester C₅₅H₇₂MgN₄O₅ or a dark green ester C₅₅H₇₀MgN₄O₆ — called also respectively *chlorophyll a*, *chlorophyll b* **2** : a waxy green chlorophyll-containing substance extracted from green plants and used as a coloring agent or deodorant — **chlo·ro·phyl·lous** \ˌklōr-ə-'fi-ləs, ˌklȯr-\ adj
chlo·ro·pic·rin \ˌklōr-ə-'pi-krən, ˌklȯr-\ n [G *Chlorpikrin*, fr. *chlor-* + Gk *pikros* sharp — more at PAINT] (ca. 1889) : a colorless liquid CCl₃NO₂ that causes tears and vomiting and is used esp. as a soil fumigant
chlo·ro·plast \'klōr-ə-ˌplast, 'klȯr-\ n [ISV] (1887) : a plastid that contains chlorophyll and is the site of photosynthesis — see CELL illustration — **chlo·ro·plas·tic** \ˌklōr-ə-'plas-tik, ˌklȯr-\ adj
chlo·ro·prene \-ˌprēn\ n [*chlor-* + *isoprene*] (1931) : a colorless liquid C₄H₅Cl used esp. in making neoprene by polymerization
chlo·ro·quine \'klōr-ə-ˌkwēn, 'klȯr-\ n [*chlor-* + *quinoline*] (1946) : an antimalarial drug C₁₈H₂₆ClN₃ administered as the bitter crystalline diphosphate
chlo·ro·sis \klə-'rō-səs\ n (1678) **1** : an iron-deficiency anemia esp. of adolescent girls that may impart a greenish tint to the skin — called also *greensickness* **2** : a diseased condition in green plants marked by yellowing or blanching — **chlo·rot·ic** \-'rä-tik\ adj
chlo·ro·thi·a·zide \ˌklōr-ə-'thī-ə-ˌzid, ˌklȯr-, -zəd\ n (1957) : a thiazide diuretic C₇H₆ClN₃O₄S₂ used esp. to treat edema and to increase the effectiveness of antihypertensive drugs
chlor·prom·a·zine \klōr-'prä-mə-ˌzēn, klȯr-\ n [*chlor-* + *propyl* + *methyl* + *azine*] (1952) : a phenothiazine C₁₇H₁₉ClN₂S used as a tranquilizer esp. in the form of its hydrochloride to suppress the more flagrant symptoms of psychotic disorders (as in schizophrenia)
chlor·prop·amide \-'prä-pə-ˌmīd, -'prō-\ n [*chlor-* + *propane* + *amide*] (1960) : a sulfonylurea drug C₁₀H₁₃ClN₂O₃S used orally to reduce blood sugar in the treatment of mild diabetes
chlor·tet·ra·cy·cline \ˌklōr-ˌte-trə-'sī-ˌklēn, klȯr-\ n (1953) : a yellow crystalline broad-spectrum antibiotic C₂₂H₂₃ClN₂O₈ that is produced by a soil actinomycete (*Streptomyces aureofaciens*) and is sometimes used in animal feeds to stimulate growth
cho·ano·cyte \kō-'a-nə-ˌsīt\ n [ISV *choan-* funnel-shaped (fr. Gk *choanē* funnel) + *-cyte*] (1888) : COLLAR CELL
¹chock \'chäk\ n [origin unknown] (1769) **1** : a wedge or block for steadying a body (as a cask) and holding it motionless, for filling in an unwanted space, or for blocking the movement of a wheel **2** : a heavy metal casting (as on the bow or stern of a ship) with two short horn-shaped arms curving inward between which ropes or hawsers may pass for mooring or towing
²chock adv (1834) : as close or as completely as possible
³chock vt (1854) : to stop or make fast with or as if with chocks
¹chock-a-block \'chä-kə-ˌbläk\ adv (1850) : CHOCK ⟨~ full⟩
²chockablock adj (ca. 1890) **1** : brought close together **2** : very full
chock–full or **chock·ful** \'chək-'fu̇l, 'chäk-, -ˌfu̇l\ adj [ME *chokkefull*, prob. fr. *choken* to choke + *full*] (15c) : full to the limit
choc·o·hol·ic \ˌchä-kə-'hȯ-lik, ˌchó-, -'hä-\ n [*chocolate* + *-oholic* (as in *alcoholic*)] (1968) : a person who craves or compulsively consumes chocolate
choc·o·late \'chä-k(ə-)lət, 'chȯ-\ n [Sp, fr. Nahuatl *chocolātl*] (1604) **1** : a beverage made by mixing chocolate with water or milk **2** : a food prepared from ground roasted cacao beans **3** : a small candy with a center (as a fondant) and a chocolate coating **4** : a brownish gray — **chocolate** adj
chocolate–box adj [fr. the pictures formerly commonly seen on boxes of chocolates] (1901) : superficially pretty or sentimental
choc·o·la·tier \ˌchä-k(ə-)lə-'tir, ˌchó-\ n [F, fr. *chocolat* chocolate] (1888) : a maker or seller of chocolate candy
choc·o·laty or **choc·o·lat·ey** \'chä-k(ə-)lə-tē, 'chó-\ adj (1926) : made of or like chocolate; *also* : having a rich chocolate flavor
Choc·taw \'chäk-(ˌ)tȯ\ n, pl **Choctaw** or **Choctaws** [Choctaw *čahta*] (1722) **1** : a member of an American Indian people of Mississippi, Alabama, and Louisiana **2** : the language of the Choctaw and Chickasaw people
¹choice \'chȯis\ n [ME *chois*, fr. OF, fr. *choisir* to choose, of Gmc origin; akin to OHG *kiosan* to choose — more at CHOOSE] (13c) **1** : the act of choosing : SELECTION **2** : power of choosing : OPTION **3 a** : the best part : CREAM **b** : a person or thing chosen **4** : a sufficient number and variety to choose among **5** : care in selecting **6** : a grade of meat between prime and good — **of choice** : to be preferred
syn CHOICE, OPTION, ALTERNATIVE, PREFERENCE, SELECTION, ELECTION mean the act or opportunity of choosing or the thing chosen. CHOICE suggests the opportunity or privilege of choosing freely ⟨freedom of *choice*⟩. OPTION implies a power to choose that is specifically granted or guaranteed ⟨the *option* of paying now or later⟩. ALTERNATIVE implies a necessity to choose one and reject another possibility ⟨equally attractive *alternatives*⟩. PREFERENCE suggests the guidance of choice by one's judgment or predilections ⟨a *preference* for cool weather⟩. SELECTION implies a wide range of choice ⟨a varied *selection* of furniture⟩. ELECTION implies an end or purpose which requires exercise of judgment ⟨doing a tax return forces certain *elections* on you⟩.
²choice adj **choic·er**; **choic·est** (14c) **1** : worthy of being chosen **2** : selected with care **3 a** : of high quality **b** : of a grade between prime and good ⟨~ meat⟩ — **choice·ly** adv — **choice·ness** n

syn CHOICE, EXQUISITE, ELEGANT, RARE, DELICATE, DAINTY mean having qualities that appeal to a cultivated taste. CHOICE stresses preeminence in quality or kind ⟨*choice* fabric⟩. EXQUISITE implies a perfection in workmanship or design that appeals only to very sensitive taste ⟨an *exquisite* gold bracelet⟩. ELEGANT applies to what is rich and luxurious but restrained by good taste ⟨a sumptuous but *elegant* dining room⟩. RARE suggests an uncommon excellence ⟨*rare* beauty⟩. DELICATE implies exquisiteness, subtlety, and fragility ⟨*delicate* craftsmanship⟩. DAINTY sometimes carries an additional suggestion of smallness and of appeal to the eye or palate ⟨*dainty* sandwiches⟩.
¹choir \'kwi(-ə)r\ n [ME *quer*, fr. MF *cuer*, fr. ML *chorus*, fr. L, chorus — more at CHORUS] (14c) **1** : an organized company of singers (as in a church service) **2** : a group of instruments of the same class ⟨a brass ~⟩ **3** : an organized group of persons or things **4** : a division of angels **5** : the part of a church occupied by the singers or by the clergy; *also* : the part of a church where the services are performed **6** : a group organized for ensemble speaking
²choir vi (1596) : to sing or sound in chorus or concert
choir·boy \'kwī(-ə)r-ˌbȯi\ n (1837) : a boy member of a choir
choir loft n (1929) : a gallery occupied by a church choir
choir·mas·ter \-ˌmas-tər\ n (1860) : the director of a choir (as in a church)
¹choke \'chōk\ vb **choked**; **chok·ing** [ME, alter. of *achoken*, fr. OE *āceōcian*, fr. ā-, perfective prefix + *cēoce, cēace* jaw, cheek — more at ABIDE, CHEEK] vt (14c) **1** : to check normal breathing of by compressing or obstructing the trachea or by poisoning or adulterating available air **2 a** : to check the growth, development, or activity of ⟨the flowers were *choked* by the weeds⟩ **b** : to obstruct by filling up or clogging ⟨leaves *choked* the drain⟩ **c** : to fill completely : JAM ⟨roads *choked* with traffic⟩ **3** : to enrich the fuel mixture of (a motor) by partially shutting off the air intake of the carburetor **4** : to grip (as a baseball bat) some distance from the end of the handle ~ vi **1** : to become choked in breathing **2 a** : to become obstructed or checked **b** : to become or feel constricted in the throat (as from strong emotion) — usu. used with *up* ⟨*choked* up and couldn't finish the speech⟩ **3** : to shorten one's grip esp. on the handle of a bat — usu. used with *up* **4** : to lose one's composure and fail to perform effectively in a critical situation
²choke n (1736) **1** : the filamentous inedible center of an artichoke head; *broadly* : an artichoke head **2** : something that obstructs passage or flow: as **a** : a valve for choking a gasoline engine **b** : a constriction in an outlet (as of an oil well) that restricts flow **c** : REACTOR **2 d** : a constriction (as a narrowing of the barrel or an attachment) at the muzzle of a shotgun that serves to limit the spread of shot **3** : the act of choking
choke·ber·ry \-ˌber-ē\ n (1778) : a small berrylike astringent fruit; *also* : any of a genus (*Aronia*) of shrubs of the rose family bearing chokeberries
choke chain n (1955) : a collar that may be tightened as a noose and that is used esp. in training and controlling powerful or stubborn dogs — called also *choke collar*
choke·cher·ry \'chōk-ˌcher-ē\ n (1784) : an American wild cherry (*Prunus virginiana*) with bitter or astringent red to black edible fruit; *also* : this fruit
choke coil n (ca. 1896) : REACTOR 2
choke off vt (1818) : to bring to a stop or to an end as if by choking
choke point n (1944) : a strategic narrow route providing passage through or to another region
chok·er \'chō-kər\ n (ca. 1552) **1** : one that chokes **2** : something (as a collar or necklace) worn closely about the throat or neck
chok·ing \'chō-kiŋ\ adj (1562) **1** : producing the feeling of strangulation ⟨a ~ cloud of smog⟩ **2** : indistinct in utterance — used esp. of a person's voice ⟨a low ~ laugh⟩ — **chok·ing·ly** \-kiŋ-lē\ adv
choky \'chō-kē\ adj (1579) : tending to cause choking or to become choked
chol- or **chole-** or **cholo-** comb form [Gk *chol-, cholē-, cholo-*, fr. *cholē, cholos* — more at GALL] : bile : gall ⟨*cholate*⟩
chol·an·gi·og·ra·phy \kə-ˌlan-jē-'ä-grə-fē, (ˌ)kō-\ n (1936) : radiographic visualization of the bile ducts after injection of a radiopaque substance — **chol·an·gio·graph·ic** \-jē-ə-'gra-fik\ adj — **chol·an·gio·gram** \-'lan-jē-ə-ˌgram\ n
cho·late \'kō-ˌlāt\ n (ca. 1846) : a salt or ester of cholic acid
cho·le·cal·cif·er·ol \ˌkō-lə-(ˌ)kal-'si-fə-ˌrȯl, -ˌrōl\ n [ISV] (1955) : a sterol C₂₇H₄₃OH that is a natural form of vitamin D found esp. in fish, egg yolks, and fish-liver oils and is formed in the skin on exposure to sunlight or ultraviolet rays — called also *vitamin D₃*
cho·le·cys·tec·to·my \-(ˌ)sis-'tek-tə-mē\ n, pl **-mies** [NL *cholecystis* gallbladder (fr. *chol-* + Gk *kystis* bladder) + ISV *-ectomy* — more at CYST] (1885) : surgical excision of the gallbladder — **cho·le·cys·tec·to·mized** \-ˌmīzd\ adj
cho·le·cys·ti·tis \-(ˌ)sis-'tī-təs\ n [NL, fr. *cholecystis*] (1866) : inflammation of the gallbladder
cho·le·cys·to·ki·nin \-ˌsis-tə-'kī-nən\ n [NL *cholecystis* + E *-o-* + *kinin*] (ca. 1929) : a hormone secreted esp. by the duodenal mucosa that regulates the emptying of the gallbladder and secretion of enzymes by the pancreas and that has been found in the brain — called also *cholecystokinin-pancreozymin, pancreozymin*
cho·le·li·thi·a·sis \ˌkō-lə-li-'thī-ə-səs\ n [NL] (ca. 1860) : production of gallstones; *also* : the resulting abnormal condition
cho·ler \'kä-lər, 'kō-\ n [ME *coler*, fr. MF *colere*, fr. L *cholera* cholera, fr. Gk] (14c) **1 a** *archaic* : YELLOW BILE **b** *obs* : BILE 1a **2** *obs* : the quality or state of being bilious **3** : ready disposition to irritation : IRASCIBILITY; *also* : ANGER
chol·era \'kä-lə-rə\ n [L] (1601) : any of several diseases of humans and domestic animals usu. marked by severe gastrointestinal symptoms; *esp* : an acute diarrheal disease caused by an enterotoxin produced by a comma-shaped gram-negative bacillus (*Vibrio cholerae* syn.

\ə\ abut \ᵊ\ kitten, F table \ər\ further \a\ ash \ā\ ace \ä\ mop, mar \au̇\ out \ch\ chin \e\ bet \ē\ easy \g\ go \i\ hit \ī\ ice \j\ job \ŋ\ sing \ō\ go \ȯ\ law \ȯi\ boy \th\ thin \t̲h̲\ the \ü\ loot \u̇\ foot \y\ yet \zh\ vision \à, ḵ, ⁿ, œ, œ̄, ᵫ, ᵫ̄, ᵞ\ *see* Guide to Pronunciation

V. comma) when it is present in large numbers in the proximal part of the human small intestine

chol·era mor·bus \-'mȯr-bəs, *dial* -'mä(r)-; *dial* 'kä-lē-\ *n* [NL, lit., the disease cholera] (1673) : gastrointestinal illness characterized by griping, diarrhea, and sometimes vomiting — not used technically

cho·ler·ic \'kä-lə-rik, kə-'ler-ik\ *adj* (1583) **1** : easily moved to often unreasonable or excessive anger : hot-tempered **2** : ANGRY, IRATE — **cho·ler·i·cal·ly** \-ri-k(ə-)lē, -i-k(ə-)lē\ *adv*

cho·le·sta·sis \ˌkō-lə-'stā-səs\ *n, pl* **-sta·ses** \-ˌsēz\ [NL] (ca. 1935) : a checking or failure of bile flow — **cho·le·stat·ic** \-'sta-tik\ *adj*

cho·le·ster·ic \kō-'les-tə-rik, kə-'les-tə-rik\ *adj* [*cholesteric* relating to cholesterol, fr. F *cholesterique*] (1942) : of, relating to, or being the phase of a liquid crystal characterized by arrangement of molecules in layers with the long molecular axes parallel to one another in the plane of each layer and incrementally displaced in successive layers to give helical stacking — compare NEMATIC, SMECTIC

cho·les·ter·ol \kə-'les-tə-ˌrȯl, -ˌrȯl\ *n* [ISV, fr. *chol-* + Gk *stereos* solid] (1894) : a steroid alcohol $C_{27}H_{45}OH$ that is present in animal cells and body fluids, regulates membrane fluidity, and functions as a precursor molecule in various metabolic pathways and as a constituent of LDL may cause arteriosclerosis

cho·le·styr·amine \(ˌ)kō-ˌles-tə-'ra-ˌmēn, kə-; ˌkō-lə-'stir-ə-ˌmēn\ *n* [*chol-* + *styrene* + *amine*] (ca. 1962) : a strongly basic synthetic resin that forms insoluble complexes with bile acids and has been used to lower cholesterol levels in hypercholesterolemic patients

cho·lic acid \'kō-lik-\ *n* [Gk *cholikos* bilious, fr. *cholē*] (1846) : a crystalline bile acid $C_{24}H_{40}O_5$

cho·line \'kō-ˌlēn\ *n* [ISV] (ca. 1871) : a base $C_5H_{15}NO_2$ that occurs as a component of phospholipids esp. in animals, is a precursor of acetylcholine, and is essential to liver function

cho·lin·er·gic \ˌkō-lə-'nər-jik\ *adj* [ISV] (1934) **1** : liberating, activated by, or involving acetylcholine 〈~ nerve fiber〉 〈~ functions〉 **2** : resembling acetylcholine esp. in physiologic action 〈a ~ drug〉 — **cho·lin·er·gi·cal·ly** \-ji-k(ə-)lē\ *adv*

cho·lin·es·ter·ase \ˌkō-lə-'nes-tə-ˌrās, -ˌrāz\ *n* (1932) **1** : ACETYLCHOLINESTERASE **2** : an enzyme that hydrolyzes choline esters and that is found esp. in blood plasma — called also *pseudocholinesterase*

chol·la \'chȯi-yə\ *n* [MexSp, fr. Sp, head] (1846) : any of numerous shrubby opuntias chiefly of the southwestern U.S. and Mexico that have needlelike spines partly enclosed in a papery sheath and cylindrical joints

chomp \'chämp, 'chȯmp\ *vb* [alter. of *champ*] *vi* (ca. 1847) : to chew or bite on something 〈~ *vt* : to chew or bite on

chon \'chän\ *n, pl* **chon** [Korean *chŏn*] — see *won* at MONEY table

chon·drio·some \'kän-drē-ə-ˌsōm\ *n* [Gk *chondrion*, dim. of *chondros* grain + ISV *-some*] (1910) : MITOCHONDRION

chon·drite \'kän-ˌdrīt\ *n* [ISV, fr. Gk *chondros* grain] (1883) : a meteoric stone characterized by the presence of chondrules — **chon·drit·ic** \kän-'dri-tik\ *adj*

chon·dro·cra·ni·um \ˌkän-drō-'krā-nē-əm\ *n* [Gk *chondros* grain, cartilage] (1875) : the cartilaginous parts of an embryonic cranium; *also* : the part of the adult skull derived therefrom

chon·droi·tin \kän-'drȯi-t³n, -'drō-ə-t³n\ *n* [ISV *chondroitic* acid, an acid found in cartilage + *-in*] (1895) : a mucopolysaccharide occurring in sulfated form in various animal tissues (as cartilage)

chon·drule \'kän-(ˌ)drül\ *n* [Gk *chondros* grain] (ca. 1889) : a rounded granule of cosmic origin often found embedded in meteoric stones and sometimes free in marine sediments

chook \'chük\ *n* [imit.] (1880) *Austral & NewZeal* : CHICKEN 1

choose \'chüz\ *vb* **chose** \'chōz\; **cho·sen** \'chō-z³n\; **choos·ing** \'chü-ziŋ\ [ME *chosen*, fr. OE *cēosan*; akin to OHG *kiosan* to choose, L *gustare* to taste] *vt* (bef. 12c) **1 a** : to select freely and after consideration 〈~ a career〉 **b** : to decide on esp. by vote : ELECT 〈*chose* her as captain〉 **2 a** : to have a preference for 〈~ one car over another〉 **b** : DECIDE 〈*chose* to go by train〉 ~ *vi* **1** : to make a selection **2** : to take an alternative — used after *cannot* and usu. followed by *but* 〈when earth is so kind, men cannot ~ but be happy —J. A. Froude〉 — **choos·er** \'chü-zər\ *n*

choose up *vt* (1910) : to form (sides) esp. for a game by having opposing captains choose their players ~ *vi* : to form sides for a game 〈let's *choose up* and play ball〉

choosy *or* **choos·ey** \'chü-zē\ *adj* **choos·i·er; -est** (1862) : fastidiously selective : PARTICULAR

¹chop \'chäp\ *vb* **chopped; chop·ping** [ME *chappen, choppen* — more at CHAP] *vt* (14c) **1 a** : to cut into or sever usu. by repeated blows of a sharp instrument **b** : to cut into pieces — often used with *up* **c** : to weed and thin out (young cotton) **d** : to cut as if by chopping 〈~ prices〉 〈a bridge ~s the lake in two〉 **2** : to strike (as a ball) with a short quick downward stroke **3** : to subject to the action of a chopper 〈~ a beam of light〉 ~ *vi* **1** : to make a quick stroke or repeated strokes with or as if with a sharp instrument (as an ax) **2** *archaic* : to move or act suddenly or violently

²chop *n* (14c) **1 a** : a forceful usu. slanting blow with or as if with an ax or cleaver **b** : a sharp downward blow or stroke **2** : a small cut of meat often including part of a rib — see LAMB illustration **3** : a mark made by or as if by chopping **4** : material that has been chopped up **5 a** : a short abrupt motion (as of a wave) **b** : a stretch of choppy sea **6** : CHOPPER 6 **7** *chiefly Brit* : AX 3

³chop *vi* **chopped; chop·ping** [ME *chappen, choppen* to barter, fr. OE *cēapian*] (1540) **1** : to change direction **2** : to veer with or as if with wind — **chop logic** : to argue with sophistical reasoning and minute distinctions

⁴chop *n* [Hindi *chāp* stamp] (1614) **1 a** : a seal or official stamp or its impression **b** : a license validated by a seal **2 a** : a mark on goods or coins to indicate nature or quality **b** : a kind, brand, or lot of goods bearing the same chop 〈: QUALITY, GRADE 〈of the first ~〉

chop-chop \ˌchäp-'chäp, 'chäp-\ *adv* [Chin Pidgin E, redupl. of *chop* fast] (1834) : without delay : QUICKLY

chop·fall·en \'chäp-ˌfȯ-lən\ *var of* CHAPFALLEN

chop·house \'chäp-ˌhau̇s\ *n* (ca. 1690) : RESTAURANT

cho·pine \shä-'pēn, chä-\ *n* [MF *chapin*, fr. OSp] (1577) : a woman's shoe of the 16th and 17th centuries with a very high sole designed to increase stature and protect the feet from mud and dirt

chop·log·ic \'chäp-ˌlä-jik\ *n* [obs. *chop* to exchange, trade, fr. ME *choppen* to barter] (1533) : involved and often specious argumentation — **choplogic** *adj*

chop mark *n* (1949) : an indentation made on a coin to attest weight, silver content, or legality — **chop-marked** \'chäp-ˌmärkt\ *adj*

chopped liver *n* (1980) *slang* : one that is insignificant or not worth considering

¹chop·per \'chä-pər\ *n* (1552) **1** : one that chops **2** *pl, slang* : TEETH **3** : a device that interrupts an electric current or a beam of radiation (as light) at short regular intervals **4** : MACHINE GUN **5** : HELICOPTER **6** : a high-bouncing batted baseball **7** : a customized motorcycle

²chopper *vb* (1955) : HELICOPTER

chop·pi·ness \'chä-pē-nəs\ *n* (1881) : the quality or state of being choppy

chopping block *n* (1703) : a wooden block on which material (as meat, wood, or vegetables) is cut, split, or diced

¹chop·py \'chä-pē\ *adj* **chop·pi·er; -est** [²*chop*] (1605) **1** : being roughened : CHAPPED **2** : rough with small waves **3 a** : interrupted by ups and downs 〈~ country〉 **b** : JERKY 〈short ~ strides〉 **c** : DISCONNECTED 〈~ writing〉 — **chop·pi·ly** \'chä-pə-lē\ *adv*

²choppy *adj* **chop·pi·er; -est** [³*chop*] (1865) : CHANGEABLE, VARIABLE 〈a ~ wind〉

chops \'chäps\ *n pl* [alter. of ³*chap*] (1589) **1** : JAW **2 a** : MOUTH **b** : the fleshy covering of the jaws 〈a dog licking its ~〉 **3** *slang* : EMBOUCHURE; *broadly* : the technical facility of a musical performer

chop shop *n* (1977) : a place where stolen automobiles are stripped of salable parts

chop·stick \'chäp-ˌstik\ *n* [Chin Pidgin E *chop* fast + E *stick*] (1699) : one of a pair of slender sticks held between thumb and fingers and used chiefly in oriental countries to lift food to the mouth

chop su·ey \ˌchäp-'sü-ē\ *n, pl* **chop sueys** [Chin (Guangdong) *jaahp-seui* odds and ends, fr. *jaahp* miscellaneous + *seui* bits] (1888) : a dish prepared chiefly from bean sprouts, bamboo shoots, water chestnuts, onions, mushrooms, and meat or fish and served with rice and soy sauce

cho·ra·gus \kə-'rä-gəs\ *or* **cho·re·gus** \-'rē-, -'rā-\ *n* [L & Gk; L *choragus*, fr. Gk *choragos, chorēgos*, fr. *choros* chorus + *agein* to lead — more at AGENT] (1625) **1** : the leader of a chorus or choir; *broadly* : the leader of any group or movement **2** : a leader of a dramatic chorus in ancient Greece — **cho·rag·ic** \-'ra-jik\ *adj*

cho·ral \'kȯr-əl, 'kȯr-\ *adj* [F or ML; F *choral*, fr. ML *choralis*, fr. L *chorus*] (1587) **1** : of or relating to a chorus or choir 〈a ~ group〉 **2** : sung or designed for singing by a choir 〈a ~ arrangement〉 — **cho·ral·ly** \-ə-lē\ *adv*

cho·rale \kə-'ral, -'räl\ *n* [G *Choral*, short for *Choralgesang* choral song] (1841) **1** : a hymn or psalm sung to a traditional or composed melody in church; *also* : a harmonization of a chorale melody 〈a Bach ~〉 **2** : CHORUS, CHOIR

chorale prelude *n* (ca. 1924) : a composition usu. for organ based on a chorale

¹chord \'kȯrd\ *n* [alter. of ME *cord*, short for *accord*] (1608) : three or more musical tones sounded simultaneously

²chord *vi* **1** : ACCORD **2** : to play chords esp. on a stringed instrument ~ *vt* **1** : to make chords on **2** : HARMONIZE

³chord *n* [alter. of ¹*cord*] (1543) **1** : CORD 3a **2** : a straight line segment joining and included between two points on a circle; *broadly* : a straight line joining two points on a curve **3** : an individual emotion or disposition 〈struck a responsive ~〉 **4** : either of the two outside members of a truss connected and braced by the web members **5** : the straight line distance joining the leading and trailing edges of an airfoil

chord·al \'kȯr-d³l\ *adj* (1848) **1** : of, relating to, or suggesting a chord **2** : relating to music characterized more by harmony than by counterpoint

chor·da·meso·derm \ˌkȯr-də-'me-zə-ˌdərm *also* -'me-sə-\ *n* [NL *chorda* cord + E *mesoderm*] (1939) : the portion of the embryonic mesoderm that forms notochord and related structures and induces the formation of neural structures — **chor·da·meso·der·mal** \-ˌme-zə-'dər-məl, -ˌme-sə-\ *adj*

chor·date \'kȯr-ˌdāt, -dət\ *n* [ultim. fr. L *chorda* cord] (1897) : any of a phylum (Chordata) of animals having at least at some stage of development a notochord, dorsally situated central nervous system, and gill clefts and including the vertebrates, lancelets, and tunicates — **chordate** *adj*

chore \'chȯr, 'chȯr\ *n* [alter. of *chare*] (1746) **1** *pl* : the regular or daily light work of a household or farm **2** : a routine task or job **3** : a difficult or disagreeable task **syn** see TASK

cho·rea \kə-'rē-ə\ *n* [NL, fr. L, dance, fr. Gk *choreia*, fr. *choros* chorus] (1804) : a nervous disorder (as of humans or dogs) marked by spasmodic movements of limbs and facial muscles and by incoordination — **cho·re·ic** \-'rē-ik\ *adj*

cho·re·i·form \kə-'rē-ə-ˌform\ *adj* [ISV] (ca. 1899) : resembling chorea 〈~ convulsions〉

cho·reo·graph \'kȯr-ē-ə-ˌgraf, 'kȯr-\ *vt* (1943) **1** : to compose the choreography of **2** : to arrange or direct the movements, progress, or details of ~ *vi* : to engage in choreography — **cho·re·og·ra·pher** \ˌkȯr-ē-'ä-grə-fər, ˌkȯr-\ *n*

cho·re·og·ra·phy \ˌkȯr-ē-'ä-grə-fē, ˌkȯr-\ *n, pl* **-phies** [F *chorégraphie*, fr. Gk *choreia* + F *-graphie* -graphy] (ca. 1789) **1** : the art of symbolically representing dancing **2** : the composition and arrangement of dances esp. for ballet **3** : something resembling choreography 〈a snail-paced ~ of delicate high diplomacy —Wolfgang Saxon〉 — **cho·reo·graph·ic** \ˌkȯr-ē-ə-'gra-fik, ˌkȯr-\ *adj* — **cho·reo·graph·i·cal·ly** \-fi-k(ə-)lē\ *adv*

cho·ric \'kȯr-ik, 'kȯr-, 'kär-\ *adj* (1830) : of, relating to, or being in the style of a chorus and esp. a Greek chorus

cho·rine \'kȯr-ˌēn, 'kȯr-\ *n* [chorus + -ine, fem. n. suffix (as in Pauline)] (1922) : CHORUS GIRL

cho·rio·al·lan·to·is \ˌkȯr-ē-(ˌ)ō-ə-'lan-tə-wəs, ˌkȯr-\ *n* [NL, fr. Gk *chorion* + NL *allantois*] (1933) : a vascular fetal membrane composed of the fused chorion and adjacent wall of the allantois that in the hen's egg is used as a living culture medium for viruses and for tissues — called also *chorioallantoic membrane* — **cho·rio·al·lan·to·ic** \-,a-lən-'tō-ik\ *adj*

cho·rio·car·ci·no·ma \-,kär-sᵊn-'ō-mə\ *n* [NL, fr. *chorion* + *carcinoma*] (1901) : a malignant tumor developing in the uterus from the trophoblast and rarely in the testes from a neoplasm

cho·ri·on \'kōr-ē-,än, 'kòr-\ *n* [NL, fr. Gk] (1545) : the highly vascular outer embryonic membrane of reptiles, birds, and mammals that in placental mammals is associated with the allantois in the formation of the placenta

cho·ri·on·ic \,kōr-ē-'ä-nik, ,kòr-\ *adj* (1892) **1** : of, relating to, or being part of the chorion 〈~ villi〉 **2** : secreted or produced by chorionic or related tissue (as in the placenta or a choriocarcinoma) 〈human ~ gonadotropin〉

cho·ris·ter \'kòr-ə-stər, 'kòr-, 'kär-\ *n* [ME *querister*, fr. AF *cueristre*, fr. ML *chorista*, fr. L *chorus*] (14c) **1** : a singer in a choir; *specif* : CHOIRBOY **2** : the leader of a church choir

cho·ri·zo \cha-'rē-(,)zō, -(,)sō\ *n, pl* **-zos** [Sp] (1846) : a pork sausage highly seasoned esp. with chili powder and garlic

C horizon *n* (1935) : the soil layer lying beneath the B horizon and consisting essentially of more or less weathered parent rock

cho·rog·ra·phy \ka-'rä-gra-fē\ *n* [L *chorographia*, fr. Gk *chōrographia*, fr. *chōros* place + *-graphia* -graphy] (1559) **1** : the art of describing or mapping a region or district **2** : a description or map of a region; *also* : the physical conformation and features of such a region — **cho·rog·ra·pher** \-gra-fər\ *n* — **cho·ro·graph·ic** \,kòr-ə-'graf-ik, ,kär-\ *adj*

cho·roid \'kōr-,òid, 'kòr-\ *also* **cho·ri·oid** \'kōr-ē-,òid, 'kòr-\ *n* [NL *choroides* resembling the chorion, fr. Gk *chorioeidēs*, fr. *chorion* chorion] (1683) : a vascular membrane containing large branched pigmented cells that lies between the retina and the sclera of the vertebrate eye — called also *choroid coat*; see EYE illustration — **choroid** *or* **cho·roi·dal** \kə-'ròi-dᵊl\ *adj*

chor·tle \'chòrt-ᵊl\ *vb* **chor·tled; chor·tling** \'chòrt-liŋ, 'chòrt-ᵊl-iŋ\ [prob. blend of *chuckle* and *snort*] *vi* (1872) **1** : to sing or chant exultantly 〈he chortled in his joy —Lewis Carroll〉 **2** : to laugh or chuckle esp. in satisfaction or exultation ~ *vt* : to say or sing with a chortling intonation — **chortle** *n* — **chor·tler** \'chòrt-lər, 'chòrt-ᵊl-ər\ *n*

¹cho·rus \'kōr-əs, 'kòr-\ *n* [L, ring dance, chorus, fr. Gk *choros*] (1586) **1 a** : a company of singers and dancers in Athenian drama participating in or commenting on the action; *also* : a similar company in later plays **b** : a character in Elizabethan drama who speaks the prologue and epilogue and comments on the action **c** : an organized company of singers who sing in concert : CHOIR; *esp* : a body of singers who sing the choral parts of a work (as in opera) **d** : a group of dancers and singers supporting the featured players in a musical comedy or revue **2 a** : a part of a song or hymn recurring at intervals **b** : the part of a drama sung or spoken by the chorus **c** : a composition to be sung by a number of voices in concert **d** : the main part of a popular song; *also* : a jazz variation on a melodic theme **3 a** : something performed, sung, or uttered simultaneously or unanimously by a number of persons or animals 〈a ~ of boos〉〈that eternal ~ of: "Are we there yet?" from the back seat —Sheila More〉 **b** : sounds so uttered 〈visitors are taken to the woods by car to hear the mournful ~es of howling wolves —Bob Gaines〉 — **in chorus** : in unison

²chorus *vt* (1826) : to sing or utter in chorus

chorus boy *n* (1943) : a young man who sings or dances in the chorus of a theatrical production (as a musical or revue)

chorus girl *n* (1894) : a young woman who sings or dances in the chorus of a theatrical production (as a musical or revue)

¹chose *past of* CHOOSE

²chose \'shōz\ *n* [F, fr. L *causa* cause, reason] (1670) : a piece of personal property : THING

¹cho·sen \'chō-zᵊn\ *n, pl* **chosen** (13c) : one who is the object of choice or of divine favor : an elect person

²chosen *adj* [ME, fr. pp. of *chosen* to choose] (14c) **1** : ELECT **2** : selected or marked for favor or special privilege 〈a ~ few〉

Chou \'jō\ *n* [Chin (Beijing) *Zhōu*] (1771) : a Chinese dynasty traditionally dated 1122 to about 256 B.C. and marked by the development of the philosophical schools of Confucius, Mencius, Lao-tzu, and Mo Ti

chough \'chəf\ *n* [ME] (13c) : either of two Old World birds (*Pyrrhocorax pyrrhocorax* and *P. graculus*) that are related to the crows and have red legs and glossy blue-black plumage

¹chouse \'chaùs\ *vt* **choused; chous·ing** [perh. fr. Turk *çavuş* doorkeeper, messenger] (1708) : CHEAT, TRICK

²chouse *or* **choused; chous·ing** [origin unknown] (1904) *West* : to drive or herd roughly

¹chow \'chaù\ *n* [short for *chowchow*] (1856) : FOOD, VICTUALS

²chow *vi* (1917) : EAT — often used with *down*

³chow *n* [by shortening] (1889) : CHOW CHOW

chow-chow \'chaù-,chaù\ *n* [Chin Pidgin E *chowchow* food] (1850) **1** : a Chinese preserve of ginger, fruits, and peels in heavy syrup **2** : a relish of chopped mixed pickles in mustard sauce

chow chow \'chaù-,chaù\ *n, often cap both Cs* [perh. fr. *chow-chow* Chinese person, fr. Chin Pidgin E *chowchow* food] (1886) : any of a breed of heavy-coated blocky dogs of Chinese origin having a broad head and muzzle, a distinctive blue-black tongue and black-lined mouth, and either a long dense coat with a full ruff or a short smooth coat — called also *chow*

chow chow

¹chow·der \'chaù-dər\ *vt* (1732) : to make chowder of

²chowder *n* [F *chaudière* kettle, contents of a kettle, fr. LL *caldaria* — more at CAULDRON] (1751) : a soup or stew of seafood (as clams or fish) usu. made with milk or tomatoes, salt pork, onions, and other vegetables (as potatoes); *also* : a soup resembling chowder 〈corn ~〉

chow·der·head \-,hed\ *n* [alter. of dial. *jolterhead* blockhead] (1833) : DOLT, BLOCKHEAD — **chow·der·head·ed** \'chaù-dər-,he-dəd\ *adj*

chow·hound \'chaù-,haùnd\ *n* (1942) : one fond of eating

chow line *n* (1919) : a line of people waiting to be served food

chow mein \'chaù-'mān\ *n* [Chin (Guangdong) *cháau-mihn* fried noodles] (1903) : a seasoned stew of shredded or diced meat, mushrooms, and vegetables that is usu. served with fried noodles

chres·tom·a·thy \kre-'stä-mə-thē\ *n, pl* **-thies** [NL *chrestomathia*, fr. Gk *chrēstomatheia*, fr. *chrēstos* useful + *manthanein* to learn — more at MATHEMATICAL] (1832) **1** : a selection of passages compiled as an aid to learning a language **2** : a volume of selected passages or stories of an author

chrism \'kri-zəm\ *n* [ME *crisme*, fr. OE *crisma*, fr. LL *chrisma*, fr. Gk, ointment, fr. *chriein* to anoint] (bef. 12c) : consecrated oil used in Greek and Latin churches esp. in baptism, chrismation, confirmation, and ordination

chris·ma·tion \kriz-'mä-shən\ *n* [ML *chrismation-, chrismatio* anointment with chrism, fr. LL *chrismare* to anoint with chrism, fr. *chrisma*] (1642) : a confirmatory sacrament of the Eastern Orthodox Church in which a baptized member is anointed with chrism

chris·mon \'kriz-,män\ *n, pl* **chris·ma** \-mə\ *or* **chrismons** [ML, fr. L *Christus* Christ + LL *monogramma* monogram] (1872) : CHI-RHO

chris·om \'kri-zəm\ *n* [ME *crisom*, short for *crisom cloth*, fr. *crisom* chrism + *cloth*] (13c) : a white cloth or robe put on a person at baptism as a symbol of innocence

chrisom child *n* (1593) : a child that dies in its first month

Christ \'krīst\ *n* [ME *Crist*, fr. OE, fr. L *Christus*, fr. Gk *Christos*, lit., anointed, fr. *chriein*] (bef. 12c) **1** : MESSIAH **2** : JESUS **3** : an ideal type of humanity **4** *Christian Science* : the ideal truth that comes as a divine manifestation of God to destroy incarnate error — **Christ-like** \-,līk\ *adj* — **Christ·ly** \-lē\ *adj*

chris·ten \'kri-sᵊn\ *vt* **chris·tened; chris·ten·ing** \'kris-niŋ, 'kri-sᵊn-iŋ\ [ME *cristnen*, fr. OE *cristnian*, fr. *cristen* Christian, fr. L *christianus*] (bef. 12c) **1 a** : BAPTIZE **b** : to name at baptism **2** : to name or dedicate (as a ship) by a ceremony suggestive of baptism **3** : NAME **4** : to use for the first time

Chris·ten·dom \'kri-sᵊn-dəm\ *n* [ME *cristendom*, fr. OE *cristendōm*, fr. *cristen*] (bef. 12c) **1** : CHRISTIANITY 1 **2** : the part of the world in which Christianity prevails

chris·ten·ing *n* (14c) : the ceremony of baptizing and naming a child

¹Chris·tian \'kris-chən, 'krish-\ *n* [L *christianus*, adj. & n., fr. Gk *Christianos*, fr. *Christos*] (1526) **1 a** : one who professes belief in the teachings of Jesus Christ **b** (1) : DISCIPLE 2 (2) : a member of one of the Churches of Christ separating from the Disciples of Christ in 1906 (3) : a member of the Christian denomination having part in the union of the United Church of Christ concluded in 1961 **2** : the hero in Bunyan's *Pilgrim's Progress*

²Christian *adj* (1553) **1 a** : of or relating to Christianity 〈~ scriptures〉 **b** : based on or conforming with Christianity 〈~ ethics〉 **2 a** : of or relating to a Christian 〈~ responsibilities〉 **b** : professing Christianity 〈a ~ affirmation〉 **3** : commendably decent or generous 〈has a very ~ concern for others〉 — **Chris·tian·ly** *adj or adv*

Christian Brother *n* (1883) : a member of the Roman Catholic institute of Brothers of the Christian Schools founded by St. John Baptist de la Salle in France in 1684 and dedicated to education

Christian era *n* (1657) : the period dating from the birth of Christ

chris·ti·ania \,kris-chē-'ä-nē-ə, ,krish-, -'chä-nə-, -'ä-nē-ə\ *n* [*Christiania*, former name of Oslo, Norway] (1905) : CHRISTIE

Chris·tian·i·ty \,kris-chē-'a-nə-tē, ,krish-, -'cha-nə-, ,kris-tē-'a-\ *n* (14c) **1** : the religion derived from Jesus Christ, based on the Bible as sacred scripture, and professed by Eastern, Roman Catholic, and Protestant bodies **2** : conformity to the Christian religion **3** : CHRISTENDOM 2

Chris·tian·ize \'kris-chə-,nīz, 'krish-\ *vt* **-ized; -iz·ing** (1593) : to make Christian — **Chris·tian·i·za·tion** \,kris-chə-nə-'zä-shən, ,krish-\ *n* — **Chris·tian·iz·er** \'kris-chə-,nī-zər, 'krish-\ *n*

Christian name *n* (1549) : GIVEN NAME

Christian Science *n* (ca. 1867) : a religion founded by Mary Baker Eddy in 1866 that was organized under the official name of the Church of Christ, Scientist, that derives its teachings from the Scriptures as understood by its adherents, and that includes a practice of spiritual healing based on the teaching that cause and effect are mental and that sin, sickness, and death will be destroyed by a full understanding of the divine principle of Jesus's teaching and healing — **Christian Scientist** *n*

chris·tie *or* **chris·ty** \'kris-tē\ *n, pl* **christies** [by shortening & alter. fr. *christiania*] (1925) : a skiing turn used for altering the direction of hill descent or for stopping and executed usu. at high speed by shifting the body weight forward and skidding into a turn with parallel skis

Christ·mas \'kris-məs\ *n, often attrib* [ME *Christemasse*, fr. OE *Cristes mæsse*, lit., Christ's mass] (bef. 12c) **1** : a Christian feast on December 25 or among some Eastern Orthodox on January 7 that commemorates the birth of Christ and is usu. observed as a legal holiday **2** : CHRISTMASTIDE — **Christ·mas·sy** *or* **Christ·masy** \-mə-sē\ *adj*

Christmas cactus *n* [fr. its annual blooming around Christmastime] (ca. 1900) : a branching Brazilian cactus (*Schlumbergera truncata* syn. *Zygocactus truncatus*) with flat stems, joints with margins having one to several blunt teeth, and showy usu. red, pink, white, or violet zygomorphic flowers — called also *crab cactus*

Christmas card *n* (1878) : a greeting card sent at Christmas

Christmas club *n* (ca. 1925) : a savings account in which regular deposits are made throughout the year to provide money for Christmas shopping

Christmas fern *n* (1878) : a No. American evergreen fern (*Polystichum acrostichoides*)

Christmas rose *n* (1688) : a European evergreen herb (*Helleborus niger*) of the buttercup family that has usu. white flowers produced in winter

\ə\ abut \ᵊ\ kitten, F table \ər\ further \a\ ash \ā\ ace \ä\ mop, mar \aù\ out \ch\ chin \e\ bet \ē\ easy \g\ go \i\ hit \ī\ ice \j\ job \ŋ\ sing \ō\ go \ò\ law \òi\ boy \th\ thin \th\ the \ü\ loot \ù\ foot \y\ yet \zh\ vision \ä, k̲, ⁿ, œ, œ̄, ᵫ, ᵬᴇ, ᵞ\ *see* Guide to Pronunciation

Christ·mas·tide \'kris-məs-ˌtīd\ n (1626) : the festival season from Christmas Eve till after New Year's Day or esp. in England till Epiphany

Christ·mas·time \-ˌtīm\ n (1837) : the Christmas season

Christmas tree n (1835) **1** : a usu. evergreen tree decorated at Christmas **2** : an oil-well control device consisting of an assembly of fittings placed at the top of the well

Chris·to·cen·tric \ˌkris-tə-'sen-trik, ˌkris-\ adj [Gk Christos Christ + E -centric] (1873) : centering theologically on Christ

Chris·to·gram \'kris-tə-ˌgram, 'kris-\ n [Gk Christos + E -gram] (1900) : a graphic symbol of Christ; esp : CHI-RHO

Chris·tol·o·gy \kris-'tä-lə-jē, krīs-\ n, pl -gies [Gk Christos + E -logy] (1673) : theological interpretation of the person and work of Christ — **Chris·to·log·i·cal** \ˌkris-tə-'lä-ji-kəl, 'krīs-\ adj

Christ's–thorn \'krī(ts)-'thȯrn\ n (1562) : any of several prickly or thorny shrubs (as the shrub Paliurus spina-christi or the jujube Ziziphus jujuba)

chrom- or **chromo-** comb form [ISV, fr. Gk chrōma color] **1** : chromium ⟨chromize⟩ **2 a** : color : colored ⟨chromolithograph⟩ **b** : pigment ⟨chromogen⟩

chro·ma \'krō-mə\ n [Gk chrōma] (ca. 1889) **1** : SATURATION 4a **2** : a quality of color combining hue and saturation

chro·maf·fin \'krō-mə-fən\ adj [ISV chrom- + L affinis bordering on, related — more at AFFINITY] (1903) : staining deeply with chromium salts ⟨~ cells of the adrenal medulla⟩

chromat- or **chromato-** comb form [Gk chrōmat-, chrōma] **1** : color ⟨chromatid⟩ **2** : chromatin ⟨chromatolysis⟩

chro·mate \'krō-ˌmāt\ n [F, fr. Gk chrōma] (1819) : a salt of chromic acid

¹chro·mat·ic \krō-'ma-tik\ n (1708) : ACCIDENTAL 2

²chromatic adj [Gk chrōmatikos, fr. chrōmat-, chrōma skin, color, modified tone; akin to Gk chrōs color] (ca. 1798) **1 a** : of or relating to color or color phenomena or sensations **b** : highly colored **2** : of or relating to chroma **3 a** : of, relating to, or giving all the tones of the chromatic scale **b** : characterized by frequent use of accidentals — **chro·mat·i·cal·ly** \-ti-k(ə-)lē\ adv — **chro·mat·i·cism** \-'ma-tə-ˌsi-zəm\ n

chromatic aberration n (1831) : aberration caused by the differences in refraction of the colored rays of the spectrum

chro·ma·tic·i·ty \ˌkrō-mə-'ti-sə-tē\ n (1922) : the quality of color characterized by its dominant or complementary wavelength and purity taken together

chro·mat·ics \krō-'ma-tiks\ n pl but sing in constr (ca. 1790) : the branch of colorimetry that deals with hue and saturation

chromatic scale n (ca. 1789) : a musical scale consisting entirely of half steps

chro·ma·tid \'krō-mə-təd\ n (1900) : one of the usu. paired and parallel strands of a duplicated chromosome joined by a single centromere

chro·ma·tin \'krō-mə-tən\ n (1882) : a complex of nucleic acid and basic proteins (as histone) in eukaryotic cells that is usu. dispersed in the interphase nucleus and condensed into chromosomes in mitosis and meiosis — compare EUCHROMATIN, HETEROCHROMATIN; see CELL illustration — **chro·ma·tin·ic** \ˌkrō-mə-'ti-nik\ adj

chro·mato·gram \krō-'ma-tə-ˌgram, krə-\ n (1922) **1** : the pattern formed on the adsorbent medium by the layers of components separated by chromatography **2** : a time-based graphic record (as of concentration of eluted materials) of a chromatographic separation

chro·mato·graph \krō-'ma-tə-ˌgraf, krə-\ n (1946) : an instrument for performing chromatographic separations and producing chromatograms — **chromatograph** vb — **chro·ma·tog·ra·pher** \ˌkrō-mə-'tä-grə-fər\ n

chro·ma·tog·ra·phy \ˌkrō-mə-'tä-grə-fē\ n (1937) : a process in which a chemical mixture carried by a liquid or gas is separated into components as a result of differential distribution of the solutes as they flow around or over a stationary liquid or solid phase — **chro·mato·graph·ic** \ˌkrō-mə-tə-'gra-fik, krə-\ adj — **chro·mato·graph·i·cal·ly** \-fi-k(ə-)lē\ adv

chro·ma·tol·y·sis \ˌkrō-mə-'tä-lə-səs\ n [NL] (1901) : the dissolution and breaking up of chromophil material (as chromatin) of a cell and esp. a nerve cell — **chro·mato·lyt·ic** \krō-ˌma-tə-'li-tik, krə-\ adj

chro·mato·phore \krō-'ma-tə-ˌfōr, krə-, -ˌfȯr\ n [ISV] (ca. 1859) **1** : a pigment-bearing cell; esp : one of the cells of an animal integument capable of causing integumentary color changes by expanding or contracting **2** : the organelle of photosynthesis in blue-green algae and photosynthetic bacteria; broadly : CHROMOPLAST, CHLOROPLAST

¹chrome \'krōm\ n [F, fr. Gk chrōma] (1800) **1 a** : CHROMIUM **b** : a chromium pigment **2** : something plated with an alloy of chromium

²chrome vt chromed; chrom·ing (1876) **1** : to treat with a compound of chromium (as in dyeing) **2** : CHROMIZE

-chrome \ˌkrōm\ n comb form or adj comb form [ML -chromat-, -chroma colored thing, fr. Gk chrōmat-, chrōma] **1** : colored thing ⟨heliochrome⟩ **2** : coloring matter ⟨urochrome⟩

chrome green n (ca. 1859) : any of various brilliant green pigments containing or consisting of chromium compounds

chrome yellow n (1819) : a yellow pigment consisting essentially of neutral lead chromate $PbCrO_4$

chro·mic \'krō-mik\ adj (ca. 1828) : of, relating to, or derived from chromium esp. with a valence of three

chromic acid n (1800) : an acid H_2CrO_4 analogous to sulfuric acid but known only in solution and esp. in the form of its salts

chro·mi·nance \'krō-mə-nən(t)s\ n [chrom- + luminance] (1952) : the difference between a color and a chosen reference color of the same luminous intensity in color television

chro·mite \'krō-ˌmīt\ n [G Chromit, fr. chrom-] (1840) **1** : a mineral that consists of an oxide of iron and chromium **2** : an oxide of bivalent chromium

chro·mi·um \'krō-mē-əm\ n [NL, fr. F chrome] (1807) : a blue-white metallic element found naturally only in combination and used esp. in alloys and in electroplating — see ELEMENT table

chro·mize \'krō-ˌmīz\ vt chro·mized; chro·miz·ing (1939) : to treat (metal) with chromium in order to form a protective surface alloy

chro·mo \'krō-(ˌ)mō\ n, pl chromos (1869) : CHROMOLITHOGRAPH

chro·mo·cen·ter \'krō-mə-ˌsen-tər\ n (1926) : a densely staining aggregation of heterochromatic regions in the nucleus of some cells

chro·mo·dy·nam·ics \ˌkrō-mə-dī-'na-miks\ n pl but sing in constr (1976) : QUANTUM CHROMODYNAMICS

chro·mo·gen \'krō-mə-jən\ n [ISV] (1858) **1** : a precursor of a biochemical pigment **2** : a pigment-producing microorganism

chro·mo·gen·ic \ˌkrō-mə-'je-nik\ adj (1884) **1** : of or relating to a chromogen **2** : being a process of photographic film development in which silver halides activate precursors of chemical dyes that form the final image while the silver is removed; also : being a film developed by this process

chro·mo·litho·graph \ˌkrō-mə-'li-thə-ˌgraf\ n (1860) : a picture printed in colors from a series of lithographic stones or plates — **chro·molithograph** vt — **chro·mo·litho·graph·ic** \-ˌli-thə-'gra-fik\ adj — **chro·mo·li·thog·ra·pher** \-li-'thä-grə-fər\ n — **chro·mo·li·thog·ra·phy** \-grə-fē\ n

chro·mo·mere \'krō-mə-ˌmir\ n [ISV] (1896) : one of the small bead-shaped and heavily staining masses of coiled chromatin that are linearly arranged along the chromosome — **chro·mo·mer·ic** \ˌkrō-mə-'mer-ik, -'mir-\ adj

chro·mo·ne·ma \ˌkrō-mə-'nē-mə\ n, pl -ne·ma·ta \-'nē-mə-tə\ [NL, fr. chrom- + Gk nēmat-, nēma thread — more at NEMAT-] (ca. 1925) : the coiled filamentous core of a chromatid — **chro·mo·ne·mat·ic** \-ni-'ma-tik\ adj

chro·mo·phil \'krō-mə-ˌfil\ adj [ISV] (1899) : staining readily with dyes

chro·mo·phobe \-ˌfōb\ adj (ca. 1909) : resisting staining with dyes

chro·mo·phore \'krō-mə-ˌfōr, -ˌfȯr\ n [ISV] (1879) : a chemical group (as an azo group) that absorbs light at a specific frequency and so imparts color to a molecule; also : a colored chemical compound — **chro·mo·phor·ic** \ˌkrō-mə-'fōr-ik, -'fär-\ adj

chro·mo·plast \'krō-mə-ˌplast\ n [ISV] (1900) : a colored plastid usu. containing red or yellow pigment (as carotene)

chro·mo·pro·tein \ˌkrō-mə-'prō-ˌtēn, -'prō-tē-ən\ n (1924) : any of various proteins (as hemoglobins, carotenoids, or flavoproteins) having a pigment as a prosthetic group

chro·mo·some \'krō-mə-ˌsōm, -ˌzōm\ n [ISV] (1889) : one of the linear or sometimes circular DNA-containing bodies of viruses, prokaryotic organisms, and the cell nucleus of eukaryotic organisms that contain most or all of the genes of the individual — compare CHROMATIN — **chro·mo·som·al** \ˌkrō-mə-'sō-məl, -'zō-\ adj — **chro·mo·som·al·ly** \-mə-lē\ adv

chromosome number n (1910) : the usu. constant number of chromosomes characteristic of a particular kind of animal or plant

chro·mo·sphere \'krō-mə-ˌsfir\ n (1868) : the region of the atmosphere of a star (as the sun) between the star's photosphere and its corona — **chro·mo·spher·ic** \ˌkrō-mə-'sfir-ik, -'sfer-\ adj

chro·mous \'krō-məs\ adj (1840) : of, relating to, or derived from chromium esp. with a valence of two

chron- or **chrono-** comb form [Gk, fr. chronos] : time ⟨chronogram⟩

chron·ax·ie also **chron·axy** \'krō-ˌnak-sē, 'krä-\ n [F chronaxie, fr. chron- + Gk axia value, fr. axios worthy — more at AXIOM] (1917) : the minimum time required for excitation of a structure (as a nerve cell) by a constant electric current of twice the threshold voltage

chron·ic \'krä-nik\ adj [F chronique, fr. Gk chronikos of time, fr. chronos] (1601) **1 a** : marked by long duration or frequent recurrence : not acute ⟨~ indigestion⟩ ⟨~ experiments⟩ **b** : suffering from a chronic disease ⟨the special needs of ~ patients⟩ **2 a** : always present or encountered; esp : constantly vexing, weakening, or troubling ⟨~ petty warfare⟩ **b** : being such habitually ⟨a ~ grumbler⟩ syn see INVETERATE — **chronic** n — **chron·i·cal·ly** \-ni-k(ə-)lē\ adv — **chro·nic·i·ty** \krä-'ni-sə-tē, krō-\ n

¹chron·i·cle \'krä-ni-kəl\ n [ME cronicle, fr. AF, alter. of OF chronique, fr. L chronica, fr. Gk chronika, fr. neut. pl. of chronikos] (14c) **1** : a usu. continuous historical account of events arranged in order of time without analysis or interpretation **2** : NARRATIVE

²chronicle vt -cled; -cling \-k(ə-)liŋ\ (15c) **1** : to record in or as if in a chronicle **2** : LIST, DESCRIBE — **chron·i·cler** \-k(ə-)lər\ n

chronicle play n (1902) : a play with a theme from history consisting usu. of rather loosely connected episodes chronologically arranged

Chron·i·cles \'krä-ni-kəlz\ n pl but sing in constr : either of two historical books of canonical Jewish and Christian Scripture — called also Paralipomenon; see BIBLE table

chro·no·bi·ol·o·gy \ˌkrä-nō-bī-'ä-lə-jē, ˌkrō-\ n (1972) : the study of biological rhythms — **chro·no·bi·o·log·ic** \-bī-ə-'lä-jik\ or **chro·no·bi·o·log·i·cal** \-ji-kəl\ adj — **chro·no·bi·ol·o·gist** \-bī-'ä-lə-jist\ n

chro·no·gram \'krä-nə-ˌgram, 'krō-\ n (1621) : an inscription, sentence, or phrase in which certain letters express a date or epoch

chro·no·graph \'krä-nə-ˌgraf, 'krō-\ n (1868) : an instrument for measuring and recording time intervals: as **a** : an instrument having a revolving drum on which a stylus makes marks **b** : STOPWATCH; also : a watch incorporating the functions of a stopwatch **c** : an instrument for measuring the time of flight of projectiles — **chro·no·graph·ic** \ˌkrä-nə-'gra-fik, ˌkrō-\ adj — **chro·nog·ra·phy** \krə-'nä-grə-fē\ n

chro·no·log·i·cal \ˌkrä-nə-'lä-ji-kəl, ˌkrō-\ also **chro·no·log·ic** \-jik\ adj (1614) : of, relating to, or arranged in or according to the order of time ⟨~ tables of American history⟩; also : reckoned in units of time ⟨~ age⟩ — **chro·no·log·i·cal·ly** \-ji-k(ə-)lē\ adv

chro·nol·o·gist \krə-'nä-lə-jist\ n (1611) : an expert in chronology

chro·nol·o·gy \-jē\ n, pl -gies [NL chronologia, fr. chron- + -logia -logy] (1593) **1** : the science that deals with measuring time by regular divisions and that assigns to events their proper dates **2** : a chronological table, list, or account **3** : an arrangement (as of events) in order of occurrence ⟨reconstruct the ~ of the trip⟩

chro·nom·e·ter \krə-'nä-mə-tər\ n (ca. 1735) : TIMEPIECE; esp : one designed to keep time with great accuracy

chro·no·met·ric \ˌkrä-nə-'me-trik, ˌkrō-\ also **chro·no·met·ri·cal** \-tri-kəl\ adj (1830) : of or relating to a chronometer or chronometry — **chro·no·met·ri·cal·ly** \-tri-k(ə-)lē\ adv

chro·nom·e·try \krə-'nä-mə-trē\ n (1833) : the measuring of time

chro·no·ther·a·py \ˌkrä-nō-'ther-ə-pē, ˌkrō-\ n (1973) : treatment of a sleep disorder (as insomnia) by changing sleeping and waking times in an attempt to reset the patient's biological clock

chrys- or **chryso-** comb form [Gk, fr. chrysos] : gold : yellow ⟨chrysarobin⟩

chrys·a·lid \'kri-sə-ləd\ *n* (1777) : CHRYSALIS — **chrysalid** *adj*
chrys·a·lis \'kri-sə-ləs\ *n, pl* **chry·sal·i·des** \kri-'sa-lə-ˌdēz\ *or* **chrys·a·lis·es** [L *chrysallid-, chrysallis* gold-colored pupa of butterflies, fr. Gk, fr. *chrysos* gold, of Sem origin; akin to Heb *ḥārūṣ* gold] (1601) 1 : a pupa of a butterfly; *broadly* : an insect pupa 2 : a protecting covering : a sheltered state or stage of being or growth ⟨a budding writer could not emerge from his ~ too soon —William Du Bois⟩
chry·san·the·mum \kri-'san(t)-thə-məm *also* -'zan(t)-\ *n* [L, fr. Gk *chrysanthemon*, fr. *chrys-* + *anthemon* flower; akin to Gk *anthos* flower] (1551) 1 : any of various composite plants (genus *Chrysanthemum*) including weeds, ornamentals grown for their brightly colored often double flower heads, and others important as sources of medicinals and insecticides 2 : a flower head of an ornamental chrysanthemum
chrys·a·ro·bin \ˌkris-ə-'rō-bən\ *n* [*chrys-* + araroba, powder found in the wood of a Brazilian tree (*Andira araroba*) + ¹-*in*] (1887) : a powder derived from the wood of a tropical tree used to treat skin diseases
Chry·se·is \krī-'sē-əs\ *n* [L, fr. Gk *Chrysēis*] : a daughter of a priest of Apollo in the *Iliad* narrative taken at Troy by Agamemnon but later restored to her father
chrys·o·ber·yl \'kri-sə-ˌber-əl\ *n* [L *chrysoberyllus*, fr. Gk *chrysobēryllos*, fr. *chrys-* + *bēryllos* beryl] (1661) 1 *obs* : a yellowish beryl 2 : a usu. yellow or pale green mineral consisting of beryllium aluminum oxide with a little iron and sometimes used as a gem
chrys·o·lite \'kri-sə-ˌlīt\ *n* [ME *crisolite*, fr. MF, fr. L *chrysolithos*, fr. Gk, fr. *chrys-* + *-lithos* -lite] (13c) : OLIVINE
chrys·o·me·lid \ˌkri-sə-'me-ləd, -'mē-\ *n* [ultim. fr. Gk *chrysomēlolonthē* golden cockchafer] (ca. 1904) : any of a large family (Chrysomelidae) of small, usu. oval and smooth, shining, and brightly colored beetles (as the Colorado potato beetle) — **chrysomelid** *adj*
chrys·o·phyte \'kri-sə-ˌfīt\ *n* [ultim. fr. Gk *chrysos* + *phyton* plant — more at PHYT-] (1959) : GOLDEN-BROWN ALGA
chrys·o·prase \'kri-sə-ˌprāz\ *n* [alter. of ME *crisopace*, fr. OF, fr. L *chrysoprasus*, fr. Gk *chrysoprasos*, fr. *chrys-* + *prason* leek; akin to L *porrum* leek] (1646) : an apple-green chalcedony valued as a gem
chrys·o·tile \-ˌtīl\ *n* [G *Chrysotil*, fr. *chrys-* + *-til* fiber, fr. Gk *tillein* to pluck] (1850) : a mineral consisting of a fibrous silky serpentine and constituting a kind of asbestos
chthon·ic \'thä-nik\ *also* **chtho·ni·an** \'thō-nē-ən\ *adj* [Gk *chthon-, chthōn* earth — more at HUMBLE] (1882) : of or relating to the underworld : INFERNAL ⟨~ deities⟩
chub \'chəb\ *n, pl* **chub** *or* **chubs** [ME *chubbe*] (15c) 1 : any of numerous freshwater cyprinid fishes (as of the genera *Gila* and *Nocomis*) 2 : any of several marine or freshwater fishes that are not cyprinids
chub·bi·ly \'chə-bə-lē\ *adv* (1909) : in the manner of one that is chubby
chub·by \'chə-bē\ *adj* **chub·bi·er; -est** [*chub*] (1722) : PLUMP ⟨a ~ boy⟩ — **chub·bi·ness** \'chə-bē-nəs\ *n*
¹**chuck** \'chək\ *vb* [ME *chukken*, of imit. origin] (14c) : CLUCK
²**chuck** *n* [perh. fr. *chuck* chicken] (1595) — used as an endearment
³**chuck** *vt* [origin unknown] (1583) 1 : PAT, TAP 2 a : TOSS b : DISCARD ⟨~*ed* his old shirt⟩ c : DISMISS, OUST — used esp. with *out* ⟨was ~*ed* out of office⟩ 3 : to have done with ⟨~*ed* his job⟩ ⟨~ it all and retire⟩
⁴**chuck** *n* (1611) 1 : a pat or nudge under the chin 2 : an abrupt movement or toss
⁵**chuck** *n* [E dial. *chuck* lump] (1723) 1 : a cut of beef that includes most of the neck, the parts about the shoulder blade, and those about the first three ribs — see BEEF illustration 2 *chiefly West* : FOOD 3 : an attachment for holding a workpiece or tool in a machine (as a drill or lathe)
chuck·hole \'chək-ˌhōl\ *n* [perh. fr. ³*chuck* + *hole*] (1836) : a hole or rut in a road : POTHOLE
chuck·le \'chə-kᵊl\ *vi* **chuck·led; chuck·ling** [prob. freq. of ¹*chuck*] (1803) 1 : to laugh inwardly or quietly 2 : to make a continuous gentle sound resembling suppressed mirth ⟨the clear bright water chuckled over gravel —B. A. Williams⟩ — **chuckle** *n* — **chuck·le·some** \-səm\ *adj* — **chuck·ling·ly** \-iŋ-lē\ *adv*
chuck·le·head \'chə-kᵊl-ˌhed\ *n* [*chuckle* lumpish + *head*] (1748) : BLOCKHEAD — **chuck·le·head·ed** \-ˌhe-dəd\ *adj*
chuck wagon *n* [⁵*chuck*] (1890) : a wagon carrying supplies and provisions for cooking (as on a ranch)
chuck·wal·la \'chək-ˌwä-lə\ *or* **chuck·a·wal·la** \'chə-kə-ˌwä-lə\ *n* [AmerSp *chacahuala*, fr. Cahuilla (Uto-Aztecan language of southeast California) *čáxwal*] (1893) : a large herbivorous lizard (*Sauromalus obesus* of the family Iguanidae) of desert regions of the southwestern U.S.
chuck–will's–wid·ow \ˌchək-ˌwilz-'wi-(ˌ)dō\ *n* [imit.] (1791) : a nightjar (*Caprimulgus carolinensis*) of the southern U.S.

chuckwalla

¹**chuff** \'chəf\ *n* [ME *chuffe*] (15c) : BOOR, CHURL
²**chuff** *vi* [imit.] (1914) : to produce noisy exhaust or exhalations : proceed or operate with chuffs ⟨the ~*ing* and snorting of switch engines —Paul Gallico⟩
³**chuff** *n* (1915) : the sound of noisy exhaust or exhalations
chuffed \'chəft\ *adj* [E dial. *chuff* pleased, puffed with fat] (1957) *Brit* : PROUD, SATISFIED
chuf·fy \'chə-fē\ *adj* **chuf·fi·er; -est** [E dial. *chuff* puffed with fat] (1611) : FAT, CHUBBY
¹**chug** \'chəg\ *n* [imit.] (1866) : a dull explosive sound made by or as if by a laboring engine
²**chug** *vi* **chugged; chug·ging** (1896) : to move or go with or as if with chugs ⟨a locomotive *chugging* along⟩ — **chug·ger** *n*
³**chug** *vt* **chugged; chug·ging** (ca. 1968) : CHUGALUG
chug·a·lug \'chə-gə-ˌləg\ *vb* **-lugged; -lug·ging** [imit.] *vt* (1956) : to drink a container of (as beer) without pause; *also* : GUZZLE ~ *vi* : to drink a container (as of beer) without pause
chu·kar \'chə-kər *also* chə-'kär\ *n* [Hindi *cakor*] (1814) : a grayish brown Eurasian partridge (*Alectoris chukar*) introduced as a game bird

into arid mountainous regions of the western U.S. — called also *chukar partridge*
chuk·ka \'chə-kə\ *n* [*chukka*, alter. of *chukker*; fr. a similar polo player's boot] (1948) : a usu. ankle-length leather boot with two or three pairs of eyelets or a buckle and strap
chuk·ker \'chə-kər\ *also* **chuk·ka** \'chə-kə\ *n* [Hindi *cakkar* circular course, fr. Skt *cakra* wheel, circle — more at WHEEL] (1898) : a playing period of a polo game
¹**chum** \'chəm\ *n* [perh. by shortening & alter. fr. *chamber fellow* roommate] (1684) : a close friend : PAL — **chum·ship** \-ˌship\ *n*
²**chum** *vi* **chummed; chum·ming** (1730) 1 : to room together 2 a : to be a close friend b : to show affable friendliness
³**chum** *n* [origin unknown] (1857) : animal or vegetable matter (as chopped fish or corn) thrown overboard to attract fish
⁴**chum** *vb* **chummed; chum·ming** *vt* (1857) : to attract with chum ~ *vi* : to throw chum overboard to attract fish
⁵**chum** *n* [Chinook Jargon *com* spotted, striped, fr. Lower Chinook *čóm* variegated] (1902) : CHUM SALMON
Chu·mash \'chü-ˌmash\ *n* (1891) : a member of an American Indian people of southwestern California
chum·my \'chə-mē\ *adj* **chum·mi·er; -est** (1884) : INTIMATE, SOCIABLE — **chum·mi·ly** \'chə-mə-lē\ *adv* — **chum·mi·ness** \'chə-mē-nəs\ *n*
chump \'chəmp\ *n* [perh. blend of *chunk* and *lump*] (1883) : FOOL, DUPE
chump change *n* (ca. 1968) : a relatively small or insignificant amount of money
chum salmon *n* [⁵*chum*] (1907) : a salmon (*Oncorhynchus keta*) of the northern Pacific — called also *chum*
¹**chunk** \'chəŋk\ *n* [perh. alter. of *chuck* short piece of wood] (1691) 1 : a short thick piece or lump (as of wood or coal) 2 : a large noteworthy quantity ⟨bet a sizable ~ of money on the race⟩ 3 : a strong thickset horse usu. smaller than a draft horse
²**chunk** *vi* [imit.] (1890) : to make a dull plunging or explosive sound ⟨the rhythmic ~*ing* of thrown quoits —John Updike⟩
chunky \'chəŋ-kē\ *adj* **chunk·i·er; -est** (1751) 1 : short and thick or broad; *esp* : STOCKY 2 : filled with chunks ⟨~ peanut butter⟩ — **chunk·i·ly** \-kə-lē\ *adv*
chun·ter \'chən-tər\ *vi* [prob. of imit. origin] (1599) *Brit* : to talk in a low inarticulate way : MUTTER
¹**church** \'chərch\ *n* [ME *chirche*, fr. OE *cirice*, ultim. fr. LGk *kyriakon*, fr. Gk, neut. of *kyriakos* of the lord, fr. *kyrios* lord, master; akin to Skt *śūra* hero, warrior] (bef. 12c) 1 : a building for public and esp. Christian worship 2 : the clergy or officialdom of a religious body 3 : a body or organization of religious believers: as a : the whole body of Christians b : DENOMINATION c : CONGREGATION 4 : a public divine worship ⟨goes to ~ every Sunday⟩ 5 : the clerical profession ⟨considered the ~ as a possible career⟩
²**church** *adj* (bef. 12c) 1 : of or relating to a church ⟨~ government⟩ 2 *chiefly Brit* : of or relating to the established church
³**church** *vt* (14c) : to bring to church to receive one of its rites
churched \'chərcht\ *adj* (14c) : affiliated with a church
church father *n* (1856) : FATHER 4
church·go·er \'chərch-ˌgō(-ə)r\ *n* (1687) : one who habitually attends church — **church·go·ing** \-ˌgō-iŋ, -ˌgó(-)iŋ\ *adj or n*
church·i·an·i·ty \ˌchər-chē-'a-nə-tē\ *n* [*church* + -*ianity* (as in *Christianity*)] (1837) : the usu. excessive or sectarian attachment to the practices and interests of a particular church
church·ing *n* (15c) : the administration or reception of a rite of the church; *specif* : a ceremony in some churches by which women after childbirth are received in the church with prayers, blessings, and thanksgiving
church key *n* (ca. 1953) : an implement with a triangular pointed head at one end for piercing the tops of cans and often with a rounded head at the other end for opening bottles
church·less \'chərch-ləs\ *adj* (1641) : not affiliated with a church
church·ly \'chərch-lē\ *adj* (bef. 12c) 1 : of or relating to a church 2 : suitable to or suggestive of a church 3 : adhering to a church 4 : CHURCHY 1 — **church·li·ness** *n*
church·man \'chərch-mən\ *n* (14c) 1 : CLERGYMAN 2 : a member of a church
church·man·ship \-mən-ˌship\ *n* (ca. 1680) : the attitude, belief, or practice of a churchman
church mode *n* (ca. 1864) : one of eight scales prevalent in medieval music each utilizing a different pattern of intervals and beginning on a different tone
Church of England (1534) : the established episcopal church of England
church register *n* (1846) : a parish register of baptisms, marriages, and deaths
church school *n* (1862) 1 : a school providing a general education but supported by a particular church in contrast to a public school or a nondenominational private school 2 : an organization of officers, teachers, and pupils for purposes of moral and religious education under the supervision of a local church
Church Slavonic *n* (1850) : any of several Slavic literary and liturgical languages that continue Old Church Slavonic but vary regionally under influence of vernacular languages
church·war·den \'chərch-ˌwör-dᵊn\ *n* (15c) 1 : one of two lay parish officers in Anglican churches with responsibility esp. for parish property and alms 2 : a long-stemmed clay pipe
church·wom·an \-ˌwu-mən\ *n* (1722) : a woman who is a member of a church
churchy \'chər-chē\ *adj* (1843) 1 : marked by strict conformity or zealous adherence to the forms or beliefs of a church 2 : of or suggestive of a church or church services
church·yard \'chərch-ˌyärd\ *n* (12c) : a yard that belongs to a church and is often used as a burial ground
churl \'chər(-ə)l\ *n* [ME, fr. OE *ceorl* man, ceorl; akin to ON *karl* man,

---

\ə\ abut \ᵊ\ kitten, F table \ər\ further \a\ ash \ā\ ace \ä\ mop, mar \aú\ out \ch\ chin \e\ bet \ē\ easy \g\ go \i\ hit \ī\ ice \j\ job \ŋ\ sing \ō\ go \ò\ law \òi\ boy \th\ thin \th\ the \ü\ loot \ú\ foot \y\ yet \zh\ vision \á, k̩, ⁿ, œ, œ̄, ᵾ, ᵫ, ᵊ\ *see* Guide to Pronunciation husband] (bef. 12c) **1** : CEORL **2** : a medieval peasant **3** : RUSTIC, COUNTRYMAN **4 a** : a rude ill-bred person **b** : a stingy morose person

churl·ish \'chər-lish\ adj (bef. 12c) **1** : of, resembling, or characteristic of a churl : VULGAR **2** : marked by a lack of civility or graciousness : SURLY **3** : difficult to work with or deal with : INTRACTABLE ⟨∼ soil⟩ **syn** see BOORISH — **churl·ish·ly** adv — **churl·ish·ness** n

¹churn \'chərn\ n [ME chyrne, fr. OE cyrin; akin to ON kjarni churn] (bef. 12c) : a vessel for making butter in which milk or cream is agitated in order to separate the oily globules from the watery medium

²churn vt (15c) **1** : to agitate (milk or cream) in a churn in order to make butter **2 a** : to stir or agitate violently ⟨an old stern-wheeler ∼ing the muddy river⟩ **b** : to make (as foam) by so doing **3** : to make (the account of a client) excessively active by frequent purchases and sales primarily in order to generate commissions ∼ vi **1** : to work a churn **2 a** : to produce or be in violent motion **b** : to proceed by means of rotating members (as wheels)

churn out vt (1912) : to produce mechanically or copiously : GRIND OUT ⟨the usual pap which has been churned out about this superstar — W. S. Murphy⟩

churr \'chər\ vi [imit.] (1555) : to make a vibrant or whirring noise like that made by some insects (as the cockchafer) or some birds (as the partridge) — **churr** n

chur·ri·gue·resque \,chür-i-gə-'resk\ adj, often cap [Sp churrigueresco, fr. José Churriguera †1725 Span. architect] (1845) : of or relating to a Spanish baroque architectural style characterized by elaborate surface decoration or its Latin-American adaptation

¹chute \'shüt\ n [F, fr. OF, fr. cheoir to fall, fr. L cadere — more at CHANCE] (1805) **1 a** : FALL 6b **b** : a quick descent (as in a river) : RAPID **2** : an inclined plane, sloping channel, or passage down or through which things may pass : SLIDE **3** : PARACHUTE

²chute vb **chut·ed; chut·ing** vt (1884) : to convey by a chute ∼ vi **1** : to go in or as if in a chute **2** : to utilize a chute (as by passing ore down it)

chut·ist \'shü-tist\ n (1920) : PARACHUTIST

chut·ney \'chət-nē\ n, pl **chutneys** [Hindi caṭnī] (1813) : a thick sauce of Indian origin that contains fruits, vinegar, sugar, and spices and is used as a condiment

chutz·pah also **chutz·pa** \'hut-spə, 'kut-, -(,)spä\ n [Yiddish khutspe, fr. LHeb ḥuṣpāh] (1892) : supreme self-confidence : NERVE, GALL **syn** see TEMERITY

chyle \'kī(ə)l\ n [LL chylus, fr. Gk chylos juice, chyle; akin to Gk chein to pour — more at FOUND] (1541) : lymph that is milky from emulsified fats, characteristically present in the lacteals, and most apparent during intestinal absorption of fats — **chy·lous** \'kī-ləs\ adj

chy·lo·mi·cron \,kī-lō-'mī-,krän\ n [Gk chylos + mikron, neut. of mikros small — more at MICRO-] (1921) : a microscopic lipid particle common in the blood during fat digestion and assimilation

chyme \'kīm\ n [NL chymus, fr. LL, chyle, fr. Gk chymos juice; akin to Gk chein] (1607) : the semifluid mass of partly digested food expelled by the stomach into the duodenum

chy·mo·tryp·sin \,kī-mō-'trip-sən\ n [chyme + -o- + trypsin] (1933) : a protease that hydrolyzes peptide bonds and is formed in the intestine from chymotrypsinogen — **chy·mo·tryp·tic** \-tik\ adj

chy·mo·tryp·sin·o·gen \-,trip-'si-nə-jən\ n (1933) : a zymogen that is secreted by the pancreas and is converted by trypsin to chymotrypsin

ciao \'chaü\ interj [It, fr. It dial., lit., (I am your) slave, fr. ML sclavus — more at SLAVE] (1929) — used conventionally as an utterance at meeting or parting

ci·bo·ri·um \sə-'bōr-ē-əm, -'bȯr-\ n, pl **-ria** \-ē-ə\ [ML, fr. L, cup, fr. Gk kibōrion] (1651) **1** : a goblet-shaped vessel for holding eucharistic bread **2** : BALDACHIN; specif : a freestanding vaulted canopy supported by four columns over a high altar

ci·ca·da \sə-'kā-də, -'kä-; sī-'kā-\ n, pl **-das** also **-dae** \-'kā-(,)dē, -'kä-\ [NL, genus name, fr. L, cicada] (14c) : any of a family (Cicadidae) of homopterous insects which have a stout body, wide blunt head, and large transparent wings and the males of which produce a loud buzzing noise usu. by stridulation

ci·ca·la \sə-'kä-lə\ n [It, fr. ML, alter. of L cicada] (1820) : CICADA

cic·a·tri·cial \,si-kə-'tri-shəl\ adj (1881) : of or relating to a cicatrix

cic·a·trix \'si-kə-,triks, sə-'kā-triks\ n, pl **ci·ca·tri·ces** \,si-kə-'trī-(,)sēz, sə-'kā-trə-,sēz\ [L cicatric-, cicatrix] (1641) **1** : a scar resulting from formation and contraction of fibrous tissue in a wound **2** : a mark resembling a scar esp. when caused by the previous attachment of an organ or part (as a leaf)

cic·a·tri·za·tion \,si-kə-trə-'zā-shən\ n (15c) : scar formation at the site of a healing wound — **cic·a·trize** \'si-kə-,trīz\ vt

cic·e·ro·ne \,si-sə-'rō-nē, ,che-chə-\ n, pl **-ni** \-(,)nē\ [It, fr. Cicerone Cicero] (1726) : a guide who conducts sightseers

cich·lid \'si-kləd\ n [ultim. fr. Gk kichlē thrush, a kind of wrasse; perh. akin to Gk chelidōn swallow] (1884) : any of a family (Cichlidae) of mostly tropical spiny-finned usu. freshwater fishes including several kept in tropical aquariums — **cichlid** adj

ci·cis·beo \,chē-chəz-'bā-ō, -'bē-\ n, pl **-bei** \-'bā-,ē\ [It] (1718) : LOVER, GALLANT — **ci·cis·be·ism** \-'bā-,i-zəm\ n

-cidal adj comb form [LL -cidalis, fr. L -cida] : killing : having power to kill ⟨insecticidal⟩

-cide n comb form [MF, fr. L -cida, fr. caedere to cut, kill] **1** : killer ⟨insecticide⟩ **2** [MF, fr. L -cidium, fr. caedere] : killing ⟨suicide⟩

ci·der \'sī-dər\ n [ME sidre, fr. MF, fr. LL sicera strong drink, fr. Gk sikera, fr. Heb shēkhār] (13c) **1** : fermented apple juice often made sparkling by carbonation or fermentation in a sealed container **2** : the expressed juice of fruit (as apples) used as a beverage or for making other products (as applejack)

cider vinegar n (1851) : vinegar made from fermented cider

ci—de·vant \,sē-də-'vän\ adj [F, lit., formerly] (1790) : FORMER

ci·gar \si-'gär\ n [Sp cigarro] (1730) : a small roll of tobacco leaf for smoking

cig·a·rette also **cig·a·ret** \,si-gə-'ret, 'si-gə-,\ n [F cigarette, dim. of cigare cigar, fr. Sp cigarro] (1835) : a slender roll of cut tobacco enclosed in paper and meant to be smoked; also : a similar roll of another substance (as marijuana)

cig·a·ril·lo \,si-gə-'ri-(,)lō, -'rē-(,)yō\ n, pl **-los** [Sp cigarrillo cigarette, dim. of cigarro cigar] (1832) **1** : a very small cigar **2** : a cigarette wrapped in tobacco rather than paper

ci·gua·tera \,sē-gwə-'ter-ə, ,si-\ n [AmerSp, fr. ciguato person ill with ciguatera, perh. fr. cigua sea snail] (1862) : poisoning caused by the ingestion of various normally edible tropical fish in whose flesh a toxic substance has accumulated

ci·lan·tro \si-'län-(,)trō, -'lan-\ n [Sp, coriander, fr. ML celiandrum, alter. of L coriandrum — more at CORIANDER] (1903) : leaves of coriander used as a flavoring or garnish; also : CORIANDER 1

cil·i·ary \'si-lē-,er-ē\ adj (1691) **1** : of or relating to cilia **2** : of, relating to, or being the annular suspension of the lens of the eye

cil·i·ate \'si-lē-ət, -lē-,āt\ n (1916) : any of a phylum or subphylum (Ciliophora) of ciliated protozoans (as paramecia)

cil·i·at·ed \'si-lē-,ā-təd\ or **cil·i·ate** \-lē-ət, -lē-,āt\ adj (1753) : possessing cilia ⟨ciliated epithelial cells⟩ ⟨leaves with ciliate petioles⟩ — **cil·i·a·tion** \,si-lē-'ā-shən\ n

cil·i·um \'si-lē-əm\ n, pl **cil·ia** \-lē-ə\ [NL, fr. L, eyelid; akin to L celare to conceal — more at HELL] (1794) **1** : a minute short hairlike process often forming part of a fringe; esp : one on a cell that is capable of lashing movement and serves esp. in free unicellular organisms to produce locomotion or in higher forms a current of fluid **2** : EYELASH

ci·met·i·dine \sī-'me-tə-,dēn\ n [ci- (alter. of cyan-) + methyl + -idine] (1975) : a histamine analogue $C_{10}H_{16}N_6S$ used esp. in the treatment of duodenal ulcers

¹Cim·me·ri·an \sə-'mir-ē-ən\ adj (1580) : very dark or gloomy ⟨under ebon shades . . . in dark ∼ desert ever dwell —John Milton⟩

²Cimmerian n [L Cimmerii, a mythical people, fr. Gk Kimmerioi] (1584) : any of a mythical people described by Homer as dwelling in a remote realm of mist and gloom

¹cinch \'sinch\ n [Sp cincha, fr. L cingula girdle, girth, fr. cingere] (1859) **1** : a girth for a pack or saddle **2** : a tight grip **3 a** : a thing done with ease **b** : a certainty to happen

²cinch vt (1866) **1** : to put a cinch on **2** : to make certain : ASSURE ∼ vi : to tighten the cinch — often used with up

cin·cho·na \sin-'kō-nə, sin-'chō-\ n [NL, genus name, fr. the countess of Chinchón †1641 wife of the Peruvian viceroy] (1786) **1** : any of a genus (Cinchona) of So. American trees and shrubs of the madder family **2** : the dried bark of a cinchona (as C. ledgeriana) containing alkaloids (as quinine) and formerly used as a specific in malaria

cin·cho·nine \'sin-kə-,nēn, 'sin-chə-\ n (1825) : a bitter white crystalline alkaloid $C_{19}H_{22}N_2O$ found esp. in cinchona bark and used like quinine

cin·cho·nism \'sin-kə-,ni-zəm, 'sin-chə-\ n (1857) : a disorder due to excessive or prolonged use of cinchona or its alkaloids and marked by temporary deafness, ringing in the ears, headache, dizziness, and rash

cinc·ture \'sin(k)-chər\ n [L cinctura girdle, fr. cinctus, pp. of cingere to gird; prob. akin to Skt kāñcī girdle] (1600) **1** : the act of encircling **2 a** : an encircling area **b** : GIRDLE, BELT; esp : a cord or sash of cloth worn around an ecclesiastical vestment (as an alb) or the habit of a religious

cin·der \'sin-dər\ n [ME sinder, fr. OE; akin to OHG sintar dross, slag, Serbo-Croatian sedra calcium carbonate] (bef. 12c) **1** : the slag from a metal furnace : DROSS **2 a** pl : ASHES **b** : a fragment of ash **3 a** : a partly burned combustible in which fire is extinct **b** : a hot coal without flame **c** : a partly burned coal capable of further burning without flame **4** : a fragment of lava from an erupting volcano — **cin·dery** \-d(ə-)rē\ adj

cinder block n (1926) : a hollow rectangular building block made of cement and coal cinders

cinder cone n (1849) : a conical hill formed by the accumulation of volcanic debris around a vent

Cin·der·el·la \,sin-də-'re-lə\ n [after Cinderella, fairy-tale heroine who is used as a drudge by her stepmother but ends up married to a prince] (1840) : one resembling the fairy-tale Cinderella: as **a** : one suffering undeserved neglect **b** : one suddenly lifted from obscurity to honor or significance

cine \'si-nē\ n [prob. fr. F ciné, short for cinéma cinema] (1920) : MOTION PICTURE

cine·ast \'si-nē-,ast, -nē-əst\ or **cine·aste** \-,ast\ or **ciné·aste** \-,ast\ n [F cinéaste, fr. ciné + -aste (as in enthousiaste enthusiast)] (1926) : a devotee of motion pictures; also : MOVIEMAKER

cin·e·ma \'si-nə-mə, Brit also -,mä\ n [short for cinematograph] (1909) **1 a** : MOTION PICTURE — usu. used attributively **b** : a motion-picture theater **2 a** : MOVIES; esp : the film industry **b** : the art or technique of making motion pictures

cin·e·ma·go·er \-,gō(-ə)r\ n (1920) : MOVIEGOER

cin·e·ma·theque \,si-nə-mə-'tek\ n [F cinémathèque film library, fr. cinéma + -thèque (as in bibliothèque library)] (1966) : a small movie house specializing in avant-garde films

cin·e·mat·ic \,si-nə-'ma-tik\ adj (1916) **1** : of, relating to, suggestive of, or suitable for motion pictures or the filming of motion pictures ⟨∼ principles and techniques⟩ **2** : filmed and presented as a motion picture ⟨∼ fantasies⟩ — **cin·e·mat·i·cal·ly** \-'ma-ti-k(ə-)lē\ adv

cin·e·ma·tize \'si-nə-mə-,tīz\ vt **-tized; -tiz·ing** (1916) : to make a motion picture of (as a novel) : adapt for motion pictures

cin·e·mat·o·graph \,si-nə-'ma-tə-,graf\ n [F cinématographe, fr. kinēmat-, kinēma movement (fr. kinein to move) + F -o- + -graphe -graph — more at KINESIS] (1896) chiefly Brit : a motion-picture camera, projector, theater, or show

cin·e·ma·tog·ra·pher \,si-nə-mə-'tä-grə-fər\ n (1897) **1** : a motion-picture cameraman **2** : a motion-picture projectionist

cin·e·ma·tog·ra·phy \,si-nə-mə-'tä-grə-fē\ n (1897) : the art or science of motion-picture photography — **cin·e·mat·o·graph·ic** \-,ma-tə-'gra-fik\ adj — **cin·e·mat·o·graph·i·cal·ly** \-fi-k(ə-)lē\ adv

ci·ne·ma ve·ri·té \,si-nə-mə-,ver-i-'tā; si-nä-'mä-ve-rē-'tä\ n [F cinéma-vérité, lit., cinema-truth, trans. of Russ kinopravda] (1963) : the art or technique of filming a motion picture so as to convey candid realism

cin·e·ole \'si-nē-,ōl\ n [ISV, by transposition fr. NL oleum cinae wormseed oil] (1885) : a liquid $C_{10}H_{18}O$ with a camphor odor contained in many essential oils (as of eucalyptus) and used esp. as an expectorant and flavoring agent — called also eucalyptol

cin·er·ar·ia \,si-nə-'rer-ē-ə, -'rar-\ n [NL, fr. L, fem. of cinerarius of ashes, fr. ciner-, cinis ashes — more at INCINERATE] (1597) : any of several garden or potted plants derived from a perennial composite herb (*Senecio cruentus*) of the Canary Islands and having heart-shaped leaves and clusters of bright flower heads

cin·er·ar·i·um \-ē-əm\ *n, pl* **-ia** \-ē-ə\ [L, fr. *ciner-, cinis*] (1880) : a place to receive the ashes of the cremated dead — **cin·er·ary** \'si-nə-ˌrer-ē\ *adj*

ci·ne·re·ous \sə-'nir-ē-əs\ *adj* [L *cinereus*, fr. *ciner-, cinis*] (1661) **1** : gray tinged with black **2** : resembling or consisting of ashes

cin·er·in \'si-nə-rən\ *n* [L *ciner-, cinis*] (1948) : either of two oily liquid esters $C_{20}H_{28}O_3$ and $C_{21}H_{28}O_5$ occurring esp. in the flowers of pyrethrum and possessing insecticidal properties

cin·gu·lum \'siŋ-gyə-ləm\ *n, pl* **-la** \-lə\ [NL, fr. L, girdle, fr. *cingere* to gird — more at CINCTURE] (1845) : an anatomical band or encircling ridge — **cin·gu·late** \-lət\ *adj*

cin·na·bar \'si-nə-ˌbär\ *n* [ME *cynabare*, fr. MF & L; MF *cenobre*, fr. L *cinnabaris*, fr. Gk *kinnabari*, of non-IE origin; akin to Ar *zinjafr* cinnabar] (14c) **1** : artificial red mercuric sulfide used esp. as a pigment **2** : native red mercuric sulfide HgS that is the only important ore of mercury — **cin·na·bar·ine** \-bə-ˌrin, -ˌbär-in\ *adj*

cinnabar moth *n* (ca. 1893) : a European moth (*Tyria jacobeae*) that has been introduced into the western U.S. in attempts to control the tansy ragwort on which its larvae feed — called also *cinnabar*

cin·nam·ic acid \sə-'na-mik-\ *n* [F *cinnamique* of cinnamon, fr. *cinname* cinnamon, fr. L *cinnamomum*] (ca. 1864) : a white crystalline odorless acid $C_9H_8O_2$ found esp. in cinnamon oil and storax

cin·na·mon \'si-nə-mən\ *n, often attrib* [ME *cynamone*, fr. L *cinnamomum, cinnamon*, fr. Gk *kinnamōmon, kinnamon*, of non-IE origin; akin to Heb *qinnāmōn* cinnamon] (14c) **1 a** : any of several Asian trees (genus *Cinnamomum*) of the laurel family **b** : an aromatic spice prepared from the dried inner bark of a cinnamon (esp. *C. zeylanicum*); *also* : the bark **2** : a light yellowish brown

cinnamon fern *n* (1818) : a large fern (*Osmunda cinnamomea*) with cinnamon-colored spore-bearing fronds shorter than and separate from the green foliage fronds

cinnamon stone *n* (1805) : ESSONITE

cin·quain \'siŋ-ˌkān, siŋ-\ *n* [F, fr. *cinq* five, fr. L *quinque* — more at FIVE] (1882) : a 5-line stanza

cin·que·cen·tist \ˌchin-kwi-'chen-tist\ *n* (1871) : an Italian of the cinquecento; *esp* : a poet or artist of this period

cin·que·cen·to \ˌchiŋ-kwi-'chen-(ˌ)tō\ *n* [It, lit., five hundred, fr. *cinque* five (fr. L *quinque*) + *cento* hundred, fr. L *centum* — more at HUNDRED] (1760) : the 16th century esp. in Italian art and literature

cinque·foil \'siŋk-ˌfȯil, 'saŋk-\ *n* [ME *sink foil*, fr. MF *cincfoille*, fr. L *quinquefolium*, fr. *quinque* five + *folium* leaf — more at BLADE] (14c) **1** : any of a genus (*Potentilla*) of herbs and shrubs of the rose family with 5-lobed leaves and 5-petaled flowers — called also *potentilla* **2** : a design enclosed by five joined foils

ciop·pi·no \chə-'pē-(ˌ)nō\ *n* [perh. fr. It dial.] (1936) : a dish of fish and shellfish cooked usu. with tomatoes, wine, spices, and herbs

cinquefoil 2

¹ci·pher \'sī-fər\ *n, often attrib* [ME, fr. MF *cifre*, fr. ML *cifra*, fr. Ar *ṣifr* empty, cipher, zero] (14c) **1 a** : ZERO 1a **b** : one that has no weight, worth, or influence : NONENTITY **2 a** : a method of transforming a text in order to conceal its meaning — compare CODE 3b **b** : a message in code **3** : ARABIC NUMERAL **4** : a combination of symbolic letters; *esp* : the interwoven initials of a name

²cipher *vb* **ci·phered; ci·pher·ing** \-f(ə-)riŋ\ *vi* (ca. 1530) : to use figures in a mathematical process ~ *vt* **1** : ENCIPHER **2** : to compute arithmetically

ci·pher·text \'sī-fər-ˌtekst\ *n* (1939) : the enciphered form of a text or of its elements — compare PLAINTEXT

cir·ca \'sər-kə\ *prep* [L, fr. *circum* around — more at CIRCUM-] (1861) : at, in, or of approximately — used esp. with dates ⟨born ~ 1600⟩

cir·ca·di·an \sər-'kā-dē-ən\ *adj* [L *circa* about + *dies* day + E ²-an — more at DEITY] (1959) : being, having, characterized by, or occurring in approximately 24-hour periods or cycles (as of biological activity or function) ⟨~ rhythms in activity⟩

Cir·cas·sian \(ˌ)sər-'ka-sh(ē-)ən\ *n* [*Circassia*, region of the Caucasus] (1555) **1** : a member of a group of peoples of the northwestern Caucasus **2** : the language of the Circassian peoples — **Circassian** *adj*

Circassian walnut *n* (1914) : the light brown irregularly black-veined wood of the English walnut much used for veneer and cabinetwork

Cir·ce \'sər-(ˌ)sē\ *n* [L, fr. Gk *Kirkē*] : a sorceress who changes Odysseus' men into swine but is forced by Odysseus to change them back

cir·ci·nate \'sər-sⁿ-ˌāt\ *adj* [L *circinatus*, pp. of *circinare* to round, fr. *circinus* pair of compasses, fr. *circus*] (1830) : ROUNDED, COILED; *esp* : rolled in the form of a flat coil with the apex as a center ⟨~ fern fronds unfolding⟩ — **cir·ci·nate·ly** *adv*

¹cir·cle \'sər-kəl\ *n, often attrib* [ME *cercle*, fr. OF, fr. L *circulus*, dim. of *circus* circle, circus, fr. or akin to Gk *krikos, kirkos* ring; akin to OE *hring* ring — more at RING] (14c) **1 a** : RING, HALO **b** : a closed plane curve every point of which is equidistant from a fixed point within the curve **c** : the plane surface bounded by such a curve **2** : the orbit of a celestial body **3** : something in the form of a circle or section of a circle: as **a** : DIADEM **b** : an instrument of astronomical observation the graduated limb of which consists of an entire circle **c** : a balcony or tier of seats in a theater **d** : a circle formed on the surface of a sphere by the intersection of a plane that passes through it ⟨~ of latitude⟩ **e** : ROTARY 2 **4** : an area of action or influence : REALM **5 a** : CYCLE, ROUND ⟨the wheel has come full ~⟩ **b** : fallacious reasoning in which something to be demonstrated is covertly assumed **6** : a group of persons sharing a common interest or revolving about a common center ⟨the sewing ~ of her church⟩ ⟨family ~⟩ ⟨the

circle 1b: *AB* diameter; *C* center; *CD, CA, CB* radii; *EKF* arc on chord *EF; EFKL* (area) segment on chord *EF; ACD* (area) sector; *GH* secant; *TPM* tangent at point *P; EKFBPDA* circumference

gossip of court ~s⟩ **7** : a territorial or administrative division or district **8** : a curving side street

²circle *vb* **cir·cled; cir·cling** \-k(ə-)liŋ\ *vt* (14c) **1** : to enclose in or as if in a circle **2** : to move or revolve around ~ *vi* **1 a** : to move in or as if in a circle **b** : CIRCULATE **2** : to describe or extend in a circle — **cir·cler** \-k(ə-)lər\ *n*

circle graph *n* (1928) : PIE CHART

cir·clet \'sər-klət\ *n* (15c) : a little circle; *esp* : a circular ornament

¹cir·cuit \'sər-kət\ *n, often attrib* [ME, fr. MF *circuite*, fr. L *circuitus*, fr. *circumire, circuire* to go around, fr. *circum-* + *ire* to go — more at ISSUE] (14c) **1 a** : a usu. circular line encompassing an area **b** : the space enclosed within such a line **2 a** : a course around a periphery **b** : a circuitous or indirect route **3 a** : a regular tour (as by a traveling judge or preacher) around an assigned district or territory **b** : the route traveled **c** : a group of church congregations ministered to by one pastor **4 a** : the complete path of an electric current including usu. the source of electric energy **b** : an assemblage of electronic elements : HOOKUP **c** : a two-way communication path between points (as in a computer) **5 a** : an association of similar groups : LEAGUE **b** : a number or series of public outlets (as theaters, radio shows, or arenas) offering the same kind of presentation **c** : a number of similar social gatherings (cocktail ~) — **cir·cuit·al** \-kə-tᵊl\ *adj*

²circuit *vt* (15c) : to make a circuit about ~ *vi* : to make a circuit

circuit board *n* (1948) : BOARD 9

circuit breaker *n* (1872) : a switch that automatically interrupts an electric circuit under an infrequent abnormal condition

circuit court *n* (1708) : a court that sits at two or more places within one judicial district

circuit judge *n* (1801) : a judge who holds a circuit court

cir·cu·i·tous \(ˌ)sər-'kyü-ə-təs\ *adj* [perh. fr. ML *circuitosus*, fr. L *circuitus*] (1664) **1** : having a circular or winding course ⟨a ~ route⟩ **2** : not being forthright or direct in language or action — **cir·cu·i·tous·ly** *adv* — **cir·cu·i·tous·ness** *n*

circuit rider *n* (1837) : a clergyman assigned to a circuit esp. in a rural area

cir·cuit·ry \'sər-kə-trē\ *n, pl* **-ries** (1946) **1** : the detailed plan or arrangement of an electric circuit **2** : the components of an electric circuit

cir·cu·ity \(ˌ)sər-'kyü-ə-tē\ *n, pl* **-ities** [*circuitous*] (ca. 1626) : lack of straightforwardness : INDIRECTION

¹cir·cu·lar \'sər-kyə-lər\ *adj* [ME *circuler*, fr. MF, fr. L *circularis*, fr. L *circulus* circle] (15c) **1 a** : having the form of a circle : ROUND **b** : moving in or describing a circle or spiral **2 a** : of or relating to a circle or its mathematical properties ⟨a ~ arc⟩ **b** : having a circular base or bases ⟨a ~ cylinder⟩ **3** : CIRCUITOUS, INDIRECT **4** : marked by or moving in a cycle **5** : being or involving reasoning that uses in the argument or proof a conclusion to be proved or one of its unproved consequences **6** : intended for circulation — **cir·cu·lar·i·ty** \ˌsər-kyə-'lar-ə-tē\ *n* — **cir·cu·lar·ly** \'sər-kyə-lər-lē\ *adv* — **cir·cu·lar·ness** *n*

²circular *n* (1789) : a paper (as a leaflet) intended for wide distribution

circular dichroism *n* (ca. 1961) **1** : the property (as of an optically active medium) of unequal absorption of right and left plane-polarized light so that the emergent light is elliptically polarized **2** : a spectroscopic technique that makes use of circular dichroism

circular file *n* (1967) : WASTEBASKET

circular function *n* (1884) : TRIGONOMETRIC FUNCTION

cir·cu·lar·ise *Brit var of* CIRCULARIZE

cir·cu·lar·ize \'sər-kyə-lə-ˌrīz\ *vt* **-ized; -iz·ing** (1848) **1 a** : to send circulars to **b** : to poll by questionnaire **2** : PUBLICIZE — **cir·cu·lar·i·za·tion** \ˌsər-kyə-lə-rə-'zā-shən\ *n*

circular saw *n* (1817) : a power saw with a circular cutting blade; *also* : the blade itself

cir·cu·late \'sər-kyə-ˌlāt\ *vb* **-lat·ed; -lat·ing** [L *circulatus*, pp. of *circulare, fr. circulus*] *vi* (ca. 1650) **1** : to move in a circle, circuit, or orbit; *esp* : to follow a course that returns to the starting point ⟨blood ~s through the body⟩ **2** : to pass from person to person or place to place: as **a** : to flow without obstruction **b** : to become well-known or widespread ⟨rumors *circulated* through the town⟩ **c** : to go from group to group at a social gathering **d** : to come into the hands of readers; *specif* : to become sold or distributed ~ *vt* **1** : to cause to circulate — **cir·cu·lat·able** \-ˌlā-tə-bəl\ *adj* — **cir·cu·la·tive** \-ˌlā-tiv\ *adj* — **cir·cu·la·tor** \-ˌlā-tər\ *n*

circulating decimal *n* (1768) : REPEATING DECIMAL

cir·cu·la·tion \ˌsər-kyə-'lā-shən\ *n* (1654) **1** : orderly movement through a circuit; *esp* : the movement of blood through the vessels of the body induced by the pumping action of the heart **2** : FLOW **3 a** : passage or transmission from person to person or place to place; *esp* : the interchange of currency ⟨coins in ~⟩ **b** : the extent of dissemination: as (1) : the average number of copies of a publication sold over a given period (2) : the total number of items borrowed from a library

cir·cu·la·to·ry \'sər-kyə-lə-ˌtōr-ē, -ˌtȯr-\ *adj* (1605) : of or relating to circulation or the circulatory system ⟨~ failure⟩

circulatory system *n* (1862) : the system of blood, blood vessels, lymphatics, and heart concerned with the circulation of the blood and lymph

circum- *prefix* [OF or L; OF, fr. L, fr. *circum*, fr. *circus* circle — more at CIRCLE] : around : about ⟨*circumpolar*⟩

cir·cum·am·bi·ent \ˌsər-kᵊm-'am-bē-ənt\ *adj* [LL *circumambient-, circumambiens*, prp. of *circumambire* to surround in a circle, fr. L *circum-* + *ambire* to go around — more at AMBIENT] (1633) : being on all sides : ENCOMPASSING — **cir·cum·am·bi·ent·ly** *adv*

cir·cum·am·bu·late \-'am-byə-ˌlāt\ *vt* **-lat·ed; -lat·ing** [LL *circumambulatus*, pp. of *circumambulare*, fr. L *circum-* + *ambulare* to walk] (ca. 1656) : to circle on foot esp. ritualistically — **cir·cum·am·bu·la·tion** \-ˌam-byə-'lā-shən\ *n*

\ə\ abut \ᵊ\ kitten, F table \ər\ further \a\ ash \ā\ ace \ä\ mop, mar \au̇\ out \ch\ chin \e\ bet \ē\ easy \g\ go \i\ hit \ī\ ice \j\ job \ŋ\ sing \ō\ go \ȯ\ law \ȯi\ boy \th\ thin \t͟h\ the \ü\ loot \u̇\ foot \y\ yet \zh\ vision \à, k̲, ⁿ, œ, œ̄, ᵫ, ᵫ̄, ᵉ\ *see* Guide to Pronunciation

cir·cum·cen·ter \'sər-k⁹m-ˌsen-tər\ n (ca. 1889) : the point at which the perpendicular bisectors of the sides of a triangle intersect and which is equidistant from the three vertices

cir·cum·cir·cle \-ˌsər-kəl\ n (1885) : a circle which passes through all the vertices of a polygon (as a triangle)

cir·cum·cise \'sər-k⁹m-ˌsīz\ vt -cised; -cis·ing [ME, fr. L circumcisus, pp. of circumcidere, fr. circum- + caedere to cut] (13c) : to cut off the prepuce of (a male) or the clitoris of (a female) — **cir·cum·cis·er** n

cir·cum·ci·sion \ˌsər-k⁹m-'si-zhən, 'sər-k⁹m-ˌ\ n (12c) **1 a** : the act of circumcising; esp : a Jewish rite performed on male infants as a sign of inclusion in the Jewish religious community **b** : the condition of being circumcised **2** cap : January 1 observed as a church festival in commemoration of the circumcision of Jesus

cir·cum·fer·ence \sə(r)-'kəm(p)-fərn(t)s, -f(ə-)rən(t)s\ n [ME, fr. MF, fr. L circumferentia, fr. circumferre to carry around, fr. circum- + ferre to carry — more at BEAR] (14c) **1** : the perimeter of a circle **2** : the external boundary or surface of a figure or object : PERIPHERY — **cir·cum·fer·en·tial** \-ˌkəm(p)-fə-'ren(t)-shəl\ adj

¹cir·cum·flex \'sər-k⁹m-ˌfleks\ adj [L circumflexus, pp. of circumflectere to bend around, mark with a circumflex, fr. circum- + flectere to bend] (ca. 1577) **1** : characterized by the pitch, quantity, or quality indicated by a circumflex **2** : marked with a circumflex

²circumflex n (1609) : a mark ˆ, ˜, or ˉ orig. used in Greek over long vowels to indicate a rising-falling tone and in other languages to mark length, contraction, or a particular vowel quality

cir·cum·flu·ent \(ˌ)sər-'kəm-flü-ənt\ adj [fr. L circumfluent-, circumfluens, prp. of circumfluere to flow around, fr. circum- + fluere to flow — more at FLUID] (1577) : flowing round or surrounding in the manner of a fluid — **cir·cum·flu·ous** \(ˌ)sər-'kəm-flü-əs\ adj

cir·cum·fuse \ˌsər-k⁹m-'fyüz\ vt -fused; -fus·ing [L circumfusus, pp. of circumfundere to pour around, fr. circum- + fundere to pour — more at FOUND] (1605) : SURROUND, ENVELOP — **cir·cum·fu·sion** \-'fyü-zhən\ n

cir·cum·ja·cent \ˌsər-k⁹m-'jā-s⁹nt\ adj [L circumjacent-, circumjacens, prp. of circumjacēre to lie around, fr. circum- + jacēre to lie — more at ADJACENT] (15c) : lying adjacent on all sides : SURROUNDING

cir·cum·lo·cu·tion \ˌsər-k⁹m-lō-'kyü-shən\ n [L circumlocution-, circumlocutio, fr. circum- + locutio speech, fr. loqui to speak] (15c) **1** : the use of an unnecessarily large number of words to express an idea **2** : evasion in speech — **cir·cum·loc·u·to·ry** \-'lä-kyə-ˌtōr-ē, -ˌtòr-\ adj

cir·cum·lu·nar \ˌsər-kəm-'lü-nər\ adj (ca. 1909) : revolving about or surrounding the moon

cir·cum·nav·i·gate \-'na-və-ˌgāt\ vt [L circumnavigatus, pp. of circumnavigare to sail around, fr. circum- + navigare to navigate] (1634) : to go completely around (as the earth) esp. by water; also : to go around instead of through : BYPASS ⟨∼ a congested area⟩ — **cir·cum·nav·i·ga·tion** \-ˌna-və-'gā-shən\ n — **cir·cum·nav·i·ga·tor** \-'na-və-ˌgā-tər\ n

cir·cum·po·lar \ˌsər-k⁹m-'pō-lər\ adj (1686) **1** : continually visible above the horizon ⟨a ∼ star⟩ **2** : surrounding or found in the vicinity of a terrestrial pole

cir·cum·scis·sile \-'si-səl, -ˌsīl\ adj [L circumscissus, pp. of circumscindere to tear around, fr. circum- + scindere to cut, split — more at SHED] (1835) : dehiscing by fissure around the capsule of the fruit

cir·cum·scribe \'sər-k⁹m-ˌskrīb\ vt [L circumscribere, fr. circum- + scribere to write, draw — more at SCRIBE] (1835) **1 a** : to constrict the range or activity of definitely and clearly **b** : to define or mark off carefully **2 a** : to draw a line around **b** : to surround by or as if by a boundary **3** : to construct or be constructed around a (geometrical figure) so as to touch as many points as possible **syn** see LIMIT

cir·cum·scrip·tion \ˌsər-k⁹m-'skrip-shən\ n [L circumscription-, circumscriptio, fr. circumscribere] (1531) **1** : the act of circumscribing : the state of being circumscribed: as **a** : DEFINITION, DELIMITATION **b** : LIMITATION **2** : something that circumscribes: as **a** : LIMIT, BOUNDARY **b** : RESTRICTION **3** : a circumscribed area or district

cir·cum·spect \'sər-k⁹m-ˌspekt\ adj [ME, fr. MF or L; MF circonspect, fr. L circumspectus, fr. pp. of circumspicere to look around, be cautious, fr. circum- + specere to look — more at SPY] (15c) : careful to consider all circumstances and possible consequences : PRUDENT **syn** see CAUTIOUS — **cir·cum·spec·tion** \ˌsər-k⁹m-'spek-shən\ n — **cir·cum·spect·ly** \'sər-k⁹m-ˌspek(t)-lē\ adv

cir·cum·stance \'sər-k⁹m-ˌstan(t)s, -stən(t)s\ n [ME, fr. OF, fr. L circumstantia, fr. circumstant-, circumstans, prp. of circumstare to stand around, fr. circum- + stare to stand — more at STAND] (13c) **1 a** : a condition, fact, or event accompanying, conditioning, or determining another : an essential or inevitable concomitant ⟨the weather is a ∼ to be taken into consideration⟩ **b** : a subordinate or accessory fact or detail ⟨cost is a minor ∼ in this case⟩ **c** : a piece of evidence that indicates the probability or improbability of an event (as a crime) ⟨the ∼ of the missing weapon told against him⟩ ⟨the ∼s suggest murder⟩ **2 a** : the sum of essential and environmental factors (as of an event or situation) ⟨constant and rapid change in economic ∼ —G. M. Trevelyan⟩ **b** : state of affairs : EVENTUALITY ⟨open rebellion was a rare ∼⟩ — often used in pl. ⟨a victim of ∼s⟩ **c** pl : situation with regard to wealth ⟨he was in easy ∼s⟩ **3** : attendant formalities and ceremonial ⟨pride, pomp, and ∼ of glorious war —Shak.⟩ **4** : an event that constitutes a detail (as of a narrative or course of events) ⟨considering each ∼ in turn⟩ **syn** see OCCURRENCE

cir·cum·stanced \-ˌstan(t)st, -stən(t)st\ adj (ca. 1611) : placed in particular circumstances esp. in regard to property or income

cir·cum·stan·tial \ˌsər-k⁹m-'stan(t)-shəl\ adj (1600) **1** : belonging to, consisting in, or dependent on circumstances **2** : pertinent but not essential : INCIDENTAL **3** : marked by careful attention to detail : abounding in factual details ⟨a ∼ account of the fight⟩ **4** : CEREMONIAL — **cir·cum·stan·ti·al·i·ty** \-ˌstan(t)-shē-'a-lə-tē\ n — **cir·cum·stan·tial·ly** \-'stan(t)-sh(ə-)lē\ adv

syn CIRCUMSTANTIAL, MINUTE, PARTICULAR, DETAILED mean dealing with a matter fully and usu. point by point. CIRCUMSTANTIAL implies fullness of detail that fixes something described in time and space ⟨a circumstantial account of our visit⟩. MINUTE implies close and searching attention to the smallest details ⟨a minute examination of a fossil⟩. PARTICULAR implies a precise attention to every detail ⟨a particular description of the scene of the crime⟩. DETAILED stresses abundance or completeness of detail ⟨a detailed analysis of the event⟩.

circumstantial evidence n (1736) : evidence that tends to prove a fact by proving other events or circumstances which afford a basis for a reasonable inference of the occurrence of the fact at issue

cir·cum·stan·ti·ate \ˌsər-k⁹m-'stan(t)-shē-ˌāt\ vt -at·ed; -at·ing (ca. 1652) : to supply with circumstantial evidence or support

cir·cum·stel·lar \ˌsər-k⁹m-'ste-lər\ adj (1951) : surrounding or occurring in the vicinity of a star

¹cir·cum·val·late \-'va-ˌlāt\ vt -lat·ed; -lat·ing [L circumvallatus, pp. of circumvallare to surround with siege works, fr. circum- + vallum rampart — more at WALL] (ca. 1798) : to surround by or as if by a rampart — **cir·cum·val·la·tion** \-ˌva-'lā-shən\ n

²cir·cum·val·late \-'va-ˌlāt, -'va-lət\ adj (ca. 1852) : being any of approximately 12 large papillae near the back of the tongue each of which is surrounded with a marginal sulcus and supplied with taste buds responsive esp. to bitter flavors

cir·cum·vent \ˌsər-k⁹m-'vent\ vt [L circumventus, pp. of circumvenire, fr. circum- + venire to come — more at COME] (1539) **1 a** : to hem in **b** : to make a circuit around **2** : to manage to get around esp. by ingenuity or stratagem ⟨the setup ∼ed the red tape —Lynne McTaggart⟩ — **cir·cum·ven·tion** \-'ven(t)-shən\ n

cir·cum·vo·lu·tion \ˌsər-ˌkəm-və-'lü-shən, ˌsər-k⁹m-vō-\ n [ME circumvolucioun, fr. ML circumvolution-, circumvolutio, fr. L circumvolvere to revolve, fr. circum- + volvere to roll — more at VOLUBLE] (15c) : an act or instance of turning around an axis

cir·cus \'sər-kəs\ n, often attrib [L, circle, circus — more at CIRCLE] (14c) **1 a** : a large arena enclosed by tiers of seats on three or all four sides and used esp. for sports or spectacles (as athletic contests, exhibitions of horsemanship, or in ancient times chariot racing) **b** : a public spectacle **2 a** : an arena often covered by a tent and used for variety shows usu. including feats of physical skill, wild animal acts, and performances by clowns **b** : a circus performance **c** : the physical plant, livestock, and personnel of such a circus **d** : something suggestive of a circus (as in frenzied activity, sensationalism, theatricality, or razzle-dazzle) **3 a** obs : CIRCLE, RING **b** Brit : a usu. circular area at an intersection of streets — **cir·cusy** \-kə-sē\ adj

circus catch n (1893) : a catch (as in baseball or football) requiring an extraordinary or spectacular effort

ci·ré also **ci·re** \sə-'rā, sē-\ n [F, fr. pp. of cirer to wax, fr. cire wax, fr. L cera — more at CERUMEN] (1921) **1** : a highly glazed finish for fabrics usu. achieved by applying wax to the fabric **2** : a fabric or garment with a ciré finish

cirque \'sərk\ n [F, fr. L circus] (1601) **1** archaic : CIRCUS **2** : CIRCLET, CIRCLET **3** : a deep steep-walled basin on a mountain usu. forming the blunt end of a valley

cir·rho·sis \sə-'rō-səs\ n, pl **-rho·ses** \-ˌsēz\ [NL, fr. Gk kirrhos orange-colored; akin to OE hār gray — more at HOAR] (ca. 1847) : widespread disruption of normal liver structure by fibrosis and the formation of regenerative nodules that is caused by any of various chronic progressive conditions affecting the liver (as long term alcohol abuse or hepatitis) — **cir·rhot·ic** \-'rä-tik\ adj or n

cirque 3

cirro- comb form [NL cirrus] : cirrus ⟨cirrostratus⟩

cir·ro·cu·mu·lus \ˌsir-ō-'kyü-myə-ləs\ n [NL] (ca. 1803) : a cloud form of small white rounded masses at a high altitude usu. in regular groupings forming a mackerel sky — see CLOUD illustration

cir·ro·stra·tus \ˌsir-ō-'strā-təs, -'stra-\ n [NL] (ca. 1803) : a fairly uniform layer of high stratus darker than cirrus — see CLOUD illustration

cir·rus \'sir-əs\ n, pl **cir·ri** \'sir-ˌī\ [NL, fr. L, curl] (1708) **1** : TENDRIL **2** : a slender usu. flexible animal appendage: as **a** : an arm of a barnacle **b** : a filament of a crinoid **c** : a fused group of cilia functioning like a limb on some protozoans **d** : the male copulatory organ of various invertebrate animals **3** : a wispy white cloud usu. of minute ice crystals formed at altitudes of 20,000 to 40,000 feet (6,000 to 12,000 meters) — see CLOUD illustration

cis \'sis\ adj [L, lit., on this side] (1888) : characterized by having certain atoms or groups of atoms on the same side of the longitudinal axis of a double bond or of the plane of a ring in a molecule

cis- prefix [L, fr. cis — more at HE] **1** : on this side ⟨cislunar⟩ **2** usu ital : cis ⟨cis-dichloroethylene⟩ — compare TRANS- 2b

cis·al·pine \(ˌ)sis-'al-ˌpīn\ adj (1542) : situated on the south side of the Alps ⟨Cisalpine Gaul⟩ — compare TRANSALPINE

cis·co \'sis-(ˌ)kō\ n, pl **ciscoes** [short for CanF ciscoette] (1848) : any of various whitefishes (genus Coregonus); esp : LAKE HERRING

cis·lu·nar \(ˌ)sis-'lü-nər\ adj (ca. 1877) : lying between the earth and the moon or the moon's orbit ⟨∼ space⟩

cis·plat·in \(ˌ)sis-'pla-t⁹n\ n [cis- + platinum] (1977) : a platinum-containing antineoplastic drug $Cl_2H_6N_2Pt$ used esp. in the treatment of testicular and ovarian tumors and advanced bladder cancer

cis–plat·i·num \-'plat-nəm, -'pla-t⁹n-əm\ n (1977) : CISPLATIN

cissy Brit var of SISSY

cist \'sist, 'kist\ n [W, chest, fr. L cista] (1804) : a neolithic or Bronze Age burial chamber typically lined with stone

Cis·ter·cian \sis-'tər-shən\ n [ML Cistercium Cîteaux] (1611) : a member of a monastic order founded by St. Robert of Molesme in 1098 at Cîteaux, France, under Benedictine rule — **Cistercian** adj

cis·tern \'sis-tərn\ n [ME, fr. OF cisterne, fr. L cisterna, fr. cista box, chest — more at CHEST] (13c) **1** : an artificial reservoir (as an underground tank) for storing liquids and esp. water (as rainwater) **2** : a large usu. silver vessel formerly used (as in cooling wine) at the dining table **3** : a fluid-containing sac or cavity in an organism

cis·ter·na \sis-'tər-nə\ n, pl **-nae** \-ˌnē\ [NL, fr. L, reservoir] (ca. 1860) : CISTERN 3: as **a** : one of the large spaces under the arachnoid membrane **b** : one of the interconnected flattened vesicles comprising the part of the endoplasmic reticulum that is studded with ribosomes — **cis·ter·nal** \-nᵊl\ adj

cis·tron \'sis-ˌträn\ n [cis- + trans- + ²-on] (1957) : a segment of DNA that is equivalent to a gene and that specifies a single functional unit (as a protein or enzyme) — **cis·tron·ic** \sis-'trä-nik\ adj

cit·a·del \'si-tə-d²l, -ˌdel\ n [MF citadelle, fr. OIt cittadella, dim. of cittade city, fr. ML civitat-, civitas — more at CITY] (1562) **1 :** a fortress that commands a city **2 :** STRONGHOLD

ci·ta·tion \si-'tā-shən\ n (13c) **1 :** an official summons to appear (as before a court) **2 a :** an act of quoting; esp **:** the citing of a previously settled case at law **b :** EXCERPT, QUOTE **3 :** MENTION: as **a :** a formal statement of the achievements of a person receiving an academic honor **b :** specific reference in a military dispatch to meritorious performance of duty syn see ENCOMIUM — **ci·ta·tion·al** \-shnəl, -shə-n²l\ adj

cite \'sīt\ vt **cit·ed; cit·ing** [MF citer to cite, summon, fr. L citare to put in motion, rouse, summon, fr. freq. of ciēre to stir, move — more at -KINESIS] (15c) **1 :** to call upon officially or authoritatively to appear (as before a court) **2 :** to quote by way of example, authority, or proof **3 a :** to refer to; esp **:** to mention formally in commendation or praise **b :** to name in a citation **4 :** to bring forward or call to another's attention esp. as an example, proof, or precedent syn see SUMMON — **cit·able** \'si-tə-bəl\ adj

citl·a·ra \'si-thə-rə, 'ki-\ var of KITHARA

cith·er \'si-thər, -thər\ n [F cithare, fr. L cithara kithara, fr. Gk kithara] (1606) **:** CITTERN

cit·ied \'si-tēd\ adj (1612) **:** occupied by cities

cit·i·fied \'si-ti-ˌfīd\ adj (1828) **:** of, relating to, or characteristic of a sophisticated urban style of living — often used disparagingly

cit·i·fy \-ˌfī\ vt **-fied; -fy·ing** (1828) **:** URBANIZE — **cit·i·fi·ca·tion** \ˌsi-tə-fi-'kā-shən\ n

cit·i·zen \'si-tə-zən also -sən\ n [ME citizein, fr. AF citezein, alter. of OF citeien, fr. cité city] (14c) **1 :** an inhabitant of a city or town; esp **:** one entitled to the rights and privileges of a freeman **2 a :** a member of a state **b :** a native or naturalized person who owes allegiance to a government and is entitled to protection from it **3 :** a civilian as distinguished from a specialized servant of the state — **cit·i·zen·ly** \-zən-lē also -sən-\ adj

syn CITIZEN, SUBJECT, NATIONAL mean a person owing allegiance to and entitled to the protection of a sovereign state. CITIZEN is preferred for one owing allegiance to a state in which sovereign power is retained by the people and sharing in the political rights of those people ⟨the rights of a free citizen⟩. SUBJECT implies allegiance to a personal sovereign such as a monarch ⟨the king's subjects⟩. NATIONAL designates one who may claim the protection of a state and applies esp. to one living or traveling outside that state ⟨American nationals working in the Middle East⟩.

cit·i·zen·ess \-zə-nəs also -sə-\ n (1796) **:** a female citizen

cit·i·zen·ry \-zən-rē also -sən-\ n, pl **-ries** (1819) **:** a whole body of citizens

citizen's arrest n (1941) **:** an arrest made not by a law officer but by a citizen who derives authority from the fact of being a citizen

citizens band n (1948) **:** a range of radio-wave frequencies that in the U.S. is allocated officially for private radio communications

cit·i·zen·ship \'si-tə-zən-ˌship\ n (1611) **1 :** the status of being a citizen **2 a :** membership in a community (as a college) **b :** the quality of an individual's response to membership in a community

citr- or citri- or citro- comb form [NL, fr. Citrus, genus name] **1 :** citrus ⟨citriculture⟩ **2 :** citric acid ⟨citrate⟩

cit·ral \'si-ˌtral\ n [ISV] (1891) **:** an unsaturated liquid isomeric aldehyde $C_{10}H_{16}O$ of many essential oils that has a strong lemon odor and is used esp. in perfumery and as a flavoring

cit·rate \'si-ˌtrāt\ n [ISV] (1794) **:** a salt or ester of citric acid

cit·ric acid \'si-trik-\ n [ISV] (1813) **:** a tricarboxylic acid $C_6H_8O_7$ occurring in cellular metabolism, obtained esp. from lemon and lime juices or by fermentation of sugars, and used as a flavoring

citric acid cycle n (1942): KREBS CYCLE

cit·ri·cul·ture \'si-trə-ˌkəl-chər\ n (1916) **:** the cultivation of citrus fruits — **cit·ri·cul·tur·ist** \ˌsi-trə-'kəl-ch(ə-)rist\ n

¹cit·rine \'si-ˌtrēn\ adj [ME, fr. MF citrin, fr. ML citrinus, fr. L citrus citron tree] (14c) **:** resembling a citron or lemon esp. in color

²ci·trine \si-'trēn\ n (1748) **:** a semiprecious yellow stone resembling topaz formed by heating a black quartz in order to change its color

ci·tri·nin \si-'trī-nən\ n [NL citrinum, specific epithet of Penicillium citrinum] (1931) **:** a toxic antibiotic $C_{13}H_{14}O_5$ that is produced esp. by a penicillium (Penicillium citrinum) and an aspergillus (Aspergillus niveus) and is effective against some gram-positive bacteria

cit·ron \'si-trən\ n [ME, fr. MF, modif. of L citrus] (15c) **1 a :** a citrus fruit resembling a lemon but larger with little pulp and a very thick rind **b :** a small shrubby tree (Citrus medica) that produces citrons and is cultivated in tropical regions **c :** the preserved rind of the citron used esp. in cakes and puddings **2 :** a small hard-fleshed watermelon used esp. in pickles and preserves

cit·ro·nel·la \ˌsi-trə-'ne-lə\ n [NL, fr. F citronnelle lemon balm, fr. citron] (ca. 1858) **:** a fragrant grass (Cymbopogon nardus) of southern Asia that yields an oil used in perfumery and as an insect repellent; also **:** its oil

cit·ro·nel·lal \-'ne-ˌlal\ n [ISV, fr. NL citronella] (1893) **:** a lemon–odored aldehyde $C_{10}H_{18}O$ that is derived esp. from citronella oil and is used in perfumery and as an insect repellent

cit·ro·nel·lol \-'ne-ˌlȯl, -ˌlōl\ n [ISV, fr. NL citronella] (1872) **:** an unsaturated liquid alcohol $C_{10}H_{20}O$ with a roselike odor that is found in two optically active forms in many essential oils (as rose oil) and is used in perfumery and soaps

ci·trov·o·rum factor \sə-'trä-və-rəm-\ n [NL citrovorum, specific epithet of Leuconostoc citrovorum, bacterium that requires this form of folic acid] (1948) **:** a metabolically active form of folic acid that has been used in cancer therapy to protect normal cells against methotrexate

cit·rul·line \'si-trə-ˌlēn\ n [ISV, fr. NL Citrullus, genus name of the watermelon] (1930) **:** a crystalline amino acid $C_6H_{13}N_3O_3$ formed esp. as an intermediate in the conversion of ornithine to arginine in the living system

cit·rus \'si-trəs\ n, pl **citrus** or **cit·rus·es** often attrib [NL, genus name, fr. L] (1825) **:** any of a group of often thorny trees and shrubs (Citrus and related genera) of the rue family grown in warm regions for their edible fruit (as the orange or lemon) with firm usu. thick rind and pulpy flesh; also **:** the fruit — **cit·rusy** \'si-trə-sē\ adj

citrus canker n (1916) **:** a destructive disease of citrus caused by a bacterium (Xanthomonas campestris citri) that produces lesions on the leaves, twigs, and fruits

citrus red mite n (1935) **:** a relatively large mite (Panonychus citri) that is a destructive pest on the foliage of citrus

cit·tern \'si-tərn\ also **cith·ern** \'si-thərn, -thərn\ or **cith·ren** \'si-thrən\ n [blend of cither and gittern] (1566) **:** a Renaissance stringed instrument like a guitar with a flat pear-shaped body

city \'si-tē\ n, pl **cit·ies** often attrib [ME citie large or small town, fr. OF cité, fr. ML civitat-, civitas, fr. L, citizenship, state, city of Rome, fr. civis citizen — more at CITY] (13c) **1 a :** an inhabited place of greater size, population, or importance than a town or village **b :** an incorporated British town usu. of major size or importance having the status of an episcopal see **c** cap **(1) :** the financial district of London **(2) :** the influential financial interests of the British economy **d :** a usu. large or important municipality in the U.S. governed under a charter granted by the state **e :** an incorporated municipal unit of the highest class in Canada **2 :** CITY-STATE **3 :** the people of a city **4** slang — used with a preceding adjective or noun naming an abundant or quintessential feature or quality ⟨the movie was shoot-out ∼⟩

city clerk n (1919) **:** a public officer charged with recording the official proceedings and vital statistics of a city

city council n (1789) **:** the legislative body of a city

city editor n (1834) **:** a newspaper editor usu. in charge of local news and staff assignments

city father n (1845) **:** a member (as an alderman or councilman) of the governing body of a city

city hall n (1675) **1 :** the chief administrative building of a city **2 a :** a municipal government **b :** city officialdom or bureaucracy ⟨you can't fight city hall⟩

city manager n (1913) **:** an official employed by an elected council to direct the administration of a city government

city planning n (1912) **:** the drawing up of an organized arrangement (as of streets, parks, and business and residential areas) of a city — **city planner** n

city room n (1919) **:** the department where local news is handled in a newspaper editorial office

city·scape \'si-tē-ˌskāp\ n (1856) **1 :** a city viewed as a scene **2 :** an artistic representation of a city

city slicker n (1924) **:** SLICKER 2b

city–state \'si-tē-ˌstāt also -'stāt\ n (1893) **:** an autonomous state consisting of a city and surrounding territory

city-wide \'si-tē-ˌwid\ adj (1961) **:** including all parts of a city

civ·et \'si-vət\ n [MF civette, fr. OIt zibetto, fr. Ar zabād civet perfume] (1532) **1 :** any of various Old World carnivorous mammals (family Viverridae) with long bodies, short legs, and a usu. long tail **2 :** a thick yellowish musky-odored substance found in a pouch near the sexual organs of the civet (esp. genera Civettictis, Viverra, and Viverricula) and used in perfume

civet

civet cat n (1607) **1 :** CIVET **2 :** RINGTAIL 2 **3 :** any of the small spotted skunks (genus Spilogale) of western No. America

civ·ic \'si-vik\ adj [L civicus, fr. civis citizen] (ca. 1656) **:** of or relating to a citizen, a city, citizenship, or civil affairs — **civ·i·cal·ly** \'si-vi-k(ə-)lē\ adv

civ·ic–mind·ed \ˌsi-vik-'mīn-dəd\ adj (1947) **:** disposed to look after civic needs and interests — **civ·ic–mind·ed·ness** n

civ·ics \'si-viks\ n pl but sing or pl in constr (1886) **:** a social science dealing with the rights and duties of citizens

civ·il \'si-vəl\ adj [ME, fr. MF, fr. L civilis, fr. civis] (14c) **1 a :** of or relating to citizens **b :** of or relating to the state or its citizenry **2 a :** CIVILIZED ⟨∼ society⟩ **b :** adequate in courtesy and politeness **:** MANNERLY **3 a :** of, relating to, or based on civil law **b :** relating to private rights and to remedies sought by action or suit distinct from criminal proceedings **c :** established by law **4 :** of, relating to, or involving the general public, their activities, needs, or ways, or civil affairs as distinguished from special (as military or religious) affairs **5** of time **:** based on the mean sun and legally recognized for use in ordinary affairs

syn CIVIL, POLITE, COURTEOUS, GALLANT, CHIVALROUS mean observant of the forms required by good breeding. CIVIL often suggests little more than the avoidance of overt rudeness ⟨owed the questioner a civil reply⟩. POLITE commonly implies polish of speech and manners and sometimes suggests an absence of cordiality ⟨if you can't be pleasant, at least be polite⟩. COURTEOUS implies more actively considerate or dignified politeness ⟨clerks who were unfailingly courteous to customers⟩. GALLANT and CHIVALROUS imply courteous attentiveness esp. to women. GALLANT suggests spirited and dashing behavior and ornate expressions of courtesy ⟨a gallant suitor of the old school⟩. CHIVALROUS suggests high-minded and self-sacrificing behavior ⟨a chivalrous display of duty⟩.

civil death n (1767) **:** the status of a living person equivalent in its legal consequences to natural death; specif **:** deprivation of civil rights

civil defense n (1939) **:** the system of protective measures and emergency relief activities conducted by civilians in case of hostile attack, sabotage, or natural disaster

civil disobedience n (1866) **:** refusal to obey governmental demands or commands esp. as a nonviolent and usu. collective means of forcing concessions from the government

civil engineer n (ca. 1792) **:** an engineer whose training or occupation is in the design and construction esp. of public works (as roads or harbors) — **civil engineering** n

---

\ə\ abut \'ə\ kitten, F table \ər\ further \a\ ash \ā\ ace \ä\ mop, mar \aú\ out \ch\ chin \e\ bet \ē\ easy \g\ go \i\ hit \ī\ ice \j\ job \ŋ\ sing \ō\ go \ȯ\ law \ȯi\ boy \th\ thin \t͟h\ the \ü\ loot \ú\ foot \y\ yet \zh\ vision \à, ḵ, ⁿ, œ, œ̄, ᵫ, ᵫ̄, ʸ\ see Guide to Pronunciation

ci·vil·ian \sə-'vil-yən *also* -'vil-yən\ *n* (14c) **1** : a specialist in Roman or modern civil law **2 a** : one not on active duty in a military, police, or fire-fighting force **b** : OUTSIDER 1 — **civilian** *adj*

ci·vil·ian·ize \-yə-,nīz\ *vt* **-ized; -iz·ing** (1870) : to convert from military to civilian status or control — **ci·vil·ian·i·za·tion** \-,vil-yə-nə-'zā-shən\ *n*

civ·i·li·sa·tion, civ·i·lise *chiefly Brit var of* CIVILIZATION, CIVILIZE

ci·vil·i·ty \sə-'vil-ə-tē\ *n, pl* **-ties** (1533) **1** *archaic* : training in the humanities **2 a** : COURTESY, POLITENESS **b** : a polite act or expression

civ·i·li·za·tion \,si-və-lə-'zā-shən\ *n* (1772) **1 a** : a relatively high level of cultural and technological development; *specif* : the stage of cultural development at which writing and the keeping of written records is attained **b** : the culture characteristic of a particular time or place **2** : the process of becoming civilized **3 a** : refinement of thought, manners, or taste **b** : a situation of urban comfort — **civ·i·li·za·tion·al** \-shnəl, -shə-nᵊl\ *adj*

civ·i·lize \'si-və-,līz\ *vt* **-lized; -liz·ing** (1601) **1** : to cause to develop out of a primitive state; *esp* : to bring to a technically advanced and rationally ordered stage of cultural development **2 a** : EDUCATE, REFINE **b** : SOCIALIZE 1 ∼ *vi* : to acquire the customs and amenities of a civil community — **civ·i·liz·er** *n*

civilized *adj* (1611) : characteristic of a state of civilization 〈∼ society〉; *esp* : characterized by taste, refinement, or restraint 〈a ∼ way to spend the evening〉

civil law *n, often cap C&L* (14c) **1** : Roman law esp. as set forth in the Justinian code **2** : the body of private law developed from Roman law and used in Louisiana and in many countries outside the English-speaking world **3** : the law established by a nation or state for its own jurisdiction **4** : the law of civil or private rights

civil liberty *n* (1644) : freedom from arbitrary governmental interference (as with the right of free speech) specif. by denial of governmental power and in the U.S. esp. as guaranteed by the Bill of Rights — usu. used in pl. — **civil libertarian** *n or adj*

civ·il·ly \'si-və(l)-lē\ *adv* (15c) **1** : in terms of civil rights, law, or matters 〈∼ dead〉 **2** : in a civil manner : POLITELY

civil marriage *n* (ca. 1889) : a marriage performed by a magistrate

civil rights *n pl* (1721) : the nonpolitical rights of a citizen; *esp* : the rights of personal liberty guaranteed to U.S. citizens by the 13th and 14th amendments to the Constitution and by acts of Congress

civil servant *n* (1800) **1** : a member of a civil service **2** : a member of the administrative staff of an international agency (as the United Nations)

civil service *n* (ca. 1785) : the administrative service of a government or international agency exclusive of the armed forces; *esp* : one in which appointments are determined by competitive examination

civil war *n* (15c) : a war between opposing groups of citizens of the same country

Civ·i·tan \'si-və-,tan\ *n* [*Civitan (Club)*] (1926) : a member of a major national and international service club

civ·vy *also* **civ·ie** \'si-vē\ *n, pl* **civvies** *also* **civies** (ca. 1889) **1** *pl* : civilian clothes as distinguished from a particular uniform (as of the military) **2** : CIVILIAN

civvy street *n, often cap C&S* (1943) *Brit* : civilian life

¹clab·ber \'kla-bər\ *n* [short for *bonnyclabber*] (1634) *chiefly dial* : sour milk that has thickened or curdled

²clabber *vi* (ca. 1879) *chiefly dial* : CURDLE

clach·an \'kla-kən\ *n* [ME, fr. ScGael] (15c) *Scot & Irish* : HAMLET

¹clack \'klak\ *vb* [ME, of imit. origin] *vi* (13c) **1** : CHATTER, PRATTLE **2** : to make an abrupt striking sound or series of sounds **3** *of fowl* : CACKLE, CLUCK ∼ *vt* **1** : to cause to make a clatter **2** : to produce with a chattering sound; *specif* : BLAB — **clack·er** *n*

²clack *n* (15c) **1 a** : rapid continuous talk : CHATTER **b** : TONGUE **2** *archaic* : an object (as a valve) that produces clapping or rattling noises usu. in regular rapid sequence **3** : a sound of clacking 〈the ∼ of a typewriter〉

Clac·to·ni·an \klak-'tō-nē-ən\ *adj* [*Clacton-on-Sea, England*] (1932) : of or relating to a Lower Paleolithic culture usu. characterized by stone flakes with a half cone at the point of striking

¹clad \'klad\ *past and past part of* CLOTHE

²clad *adj* [ME, pp. of *clothen* to clothe] (14c) **1** : being covered or clothed 〈ivy-*clad* buildings〉 **2** *of a coin* : consisting of outer layers of one metal bonded to a core of a different metal

³clad *vt* **clad; clad·ding** (1939) **1** : SHEATHE, FACE; *specif* : to cover (a metal) with another metal by bonding

⁴clad *n* (1941) **1 a** : a composite material formed by cladding **b** : a clad coin **2** : CLADDING; *specif* : the outer layer of a clad coin

clad- *or* **clado-** *comb form* [NL, fr. Gk *klad-, klado-,* fr. *klados* branch, shoot of a tree; akin to OE *holt* woods — more at HOLT] : slip : sprout 〈*cladophyll*〉

clad·ding \'kla-diŋ\ *n* (1936) : something that covers or overlays; *specif* : metal coating bonded to a metal core

clade \'klād\ *n* [Gk *klados*] (1911) : a group of biological taxa (as species) that includes all descendants of one common ancestor

cla·dis·tics \klə-'dis-tiks, kla-\ *n pl but sing in constr* (1965) : a system of biological taxonomy that defines taxa uniquely by shared characteristics not found in ancestral groups and uses inferred evolutionary relationships to arrange taxa in a branching hierarchy such that all members of a given taxon have the same ancestors — **cla·dist** \'kla-dist\ *n* — **cla·dis·tic** \-'dis-tik\ *adj* — **cla·dis·ti·cal·ly** \-ti-k(ə-)lē\ *adv*

cla·doc·er·an \klə-'dä-sə-rən\ *n* [NL *Cladocera,* fr. *clad-* + Gk *keras* horn — more at HORN] (1909) : any of an order (Cladocera) of minute chiefly freshwater branchiopod crustaceans that includes the water fleas

clad·ode \'kla-,dōd\ *n* [NL *cladodium,* fr. Gk *klados*] (1870) : CLADO-PHYLL — **cla·do·di·al** \'klə-'dō-dē-əl\ *adj*

clad·o·gen·e·sis \,kla-də-'je-nə-səs\ *n* (1953) : evolutionary change characterized by treelike branching of taxa — compare ANAGENESIS — **clad·o·ge·net·ic** \,kla-dō-jə-'ne-tik\ *adj* — **clad·o·ge·net·i·cal·ly** \-ti-k(ə-)lē\ *adv*

clad·o·gram \'kla-də-,gram\ *n* (1966) : a branching diagrammatic tree used in cladistic classification to illustrate phylogenetic relationships

clad·o·phyll \'kla-də-,fil\ *n* (1879) : a flattened photosynthetic branch assuming the form of and closely resembling an ordinary foliage leaf

¹claim \'klām\ *vt* [ME, fr. MF *clamer,* fr. L *clamare* to cry out, shout; akin to L *calare* to call — more at LOW] (14c) **1 a** : to ask for esp. as a right 〈∼ed the inheritance〉 **b** : to call for : REQUIRE 〈this matter ∼s our attention〉 **c** : TAKE 16b 〈the accident ∼ed her life〉 **2** : to take as the rightful owner 〈went to ∼ their bags at the station〉 **3 a** : to assert in the face of possible contradiction : MAINTAIN 〈∼ed that he'd been cheated〉 **b** : to claim to have 〈organization... which ∼s 11,000... members —*Rolling Stone*〉 **c** : to assert to be rightfully one's own 〈∼ed responsibility for the attack〉 *syn* see DEMAND — **claim·able** \'klā-mə-bəl\ *adj*

²claim *n* (14c) **1** : a demand for something due or believed to be due 〈insurance ∼〉 **2 a** : a right to something; *specif* : a title to a debt, privilege, or other thing in the possession of another **b** : an assertion open to challenge 〈a ∼ of authenticity〉 **3** : something that is claimed; *esp* : a tract of land staked out

claim·ant \'klā-mənt\ *n* (15c) : one that asserts a right or title 〈a ∼ to an estate〉

claim·er \'klā-mər\ *n* (15c) **1** : one that claims **2** : a horse running in a claiming race

claiming race *n* (1935) : a horse race in which each entry is offered for sale for a specified price that must be deposited before the race

clair·au·di·ence \klar-'ȯ-dē-ən(t)s, kler-, -'ä-\ *n* [*clair-* (as in *clairvoyance*) + *audience* (act of hearing)] (1864) : the power or faculty of hearing something not present to the ear but regarded as having objective reality — **clair·au·di·ent** \-ənt\ *adj* — **clair·au·di·ent·ly** *adv*

clair·voy·ance \klar-'vȯi-ən(t)s, kler-\ *n* (1840) **1** : the power or faculty of discerning objects not present to the senses **2** : ability to perceive matters beyond the range of ordinary perception : PENETRATION

¹clair·voy·ant \-ənt\ *adj* [F, fr. *clair* clear (fr. L *clarus*) + *voyant,* prp. of *voir* to see, fr. L *vidēre* — more at WIT] (1671) **1** : unusually perceptive : DISCERNING **2** : of or relating to clairvoyance — **clair·voy·ant·ly** *adv*

²clairvoyant *n* (1851) : one having the power of clairvoyance

¹clam \'klam\ *n* [ME, fr. OE *clamm* bond, fetter; akin to OHG *klamma* constriction, L *glomus* ball] (bef. 12c) : CLAMP, CLASP

²clam *n, often attrib* [¹*clam;* fr. the clamping action of the shells] (ca. 1520) **1 a** : any of numerous edible marine bivalve mollusks living in sand or mud **b** : a freshwater mussel **2** : a stolid or closemouthed person **3** : CLAMSHELL **4** : DOLLAR 3

³clam *vi* **clammed; clam·ming** (1636) : to gather clams esp. by digging — **clam·mer** \'kla-mər\ *n*

clam 1a: *a* incurrent orifice, *b* siphon, *c* excurrent orifice, *d* mantle, *e* shell, *f* foot

cla·mant \'klā-mənt, 'kla-\ *adj* [L *clamant-, clamans,* prp. of *clamare* to cry out] (1639) **1** : CLAMOROUS, BLATANT **2** : demanding attention : URGENT — **cla·mant·ly** *adv*

clam·bake \'klam-,bāk\ *n* (1835) **1 a** : an outdoor party; *esp* : a seashore outing where food is usu. cooked on heated rocks covered by seaweed **b** : the food served at a clambake **2** : a gathering characterized by noisy sociability; *esp* : a political rally

clam·ber \'klam-bər, 'kla-mər\ *vi* **clam·bered; clam·ber·ing** \-b(ə-)riŋ, 'klam-riŋ, 'kla-mər-iŋ\ [ME *clambren;* akin to OE *climban* to climb] (14c) : to climb awkwardly (as by scrambling) 〈∼ed over the rocks〉 — **clam·ber·er** \-bər-ər, -mər-ər\ *n*

clam·my \'kla-mē\ *adj* **clam·mi·er; -est** [ME, prob. fr. *clammen* to smear, stick, fr. OE *clǣman;* akin to OE *clǣg* clay] (14c) **1** : being damp, soft, sticky, and usu. cool 〈a ∼ and intensely cold mist —Charles Dickens〉 **2** : lacking normal human warmth 〈the ∼ atmosphere of an institution〉 — **clam·mi·ly** \'kla-mə-lē\ *adv* — **clam·mi·ness** \'kla-mē-nəs\ *n*

¹clam·or \'kla-mər\ *n* [ME, fr. MF *clamour,* fr. L *clamor,* fr. *clamare* to cry out — more at CLAIM] (14c) **1 a** : noisy shouting **b** : a loud continuous noise **2** : insistent public expression (as of support or protest) 〈a ∼ against increased taxes〉

²clamor *vb* **clam·ored; clam·or·ing** \'klam-riŋ, 'kla-mər-iŋ\ *vi* (14c) **1** : to make a din **2** : to become loudly insistent 〈∼ed for his impeachment〉 ∼ *vt* **1** : to utter or proclaim insistently and noisily **2** : to influence by means of clamor

³clamor *vt* [origin unknown] (1611) *obs* : SILENCE

clam·or·ous \'klam-rəs, 'kla-mər-əs\ *adj* (15c) **1** : marked by confused din or outcry : TUMULTUOUS 〈the busy ∼ market〉 **2** : noisily insistent *syn* see VOCIFEROUS — **clam·or·ous·ly** *adv* — **clam·or·ous·ness** *n*

clam·our \'kla-mər\ *chiefly Brit var of* CLAMOR

¹clamp \'klamp\ *n* [ME, prob. fr. (assumed) MD *klampe;* akin to OE *clamm* bond, fetter — more at CLAM] (14c) **1** : a device designed to bind or constrict or to press two or more parts together so as to hold them firmly **2** : any of various instruments or appliances having parts brought together for holding or compressing something

²clamp *vt* (ca. 1696) **1** : to fasten with or as if with a clamp **2 a** : to place by decree : IMPOSE — often used with *on* 〈∼ed on a curfew after the riots〉 **b** : to hold tightly

clamp·down \'klamp-,daún\ *n* (1940) : the act or action of making regulations and restrictions more stringent 〈a ∼ on charge accounts, bank loans, and other inflationary influences —*Time*〉

clamp down *vi* (1940) : to impose restrictions : CRACK DOWN 〈the police are *clamping down* on speeders〉

clams casino *n pl but sing or pl in constr, often cap 2d C* (1952) : clams on the half shell usu. topped with green pepper and baked or broiled

clam·shell \'klam-,shel\ *n* (ca. 1520) **1** : the shell of a clam **2 a** : a bucket or grapple (as on a dredge) having two hinged jaws **b** : an excavating machine having a clamshell **c** : either of a pair of doors (as in an airplane tail) that open out and away from each other

clam up *vi* (1916) : to become silent

clam worm *n* (1885) : any of several large burrowing polychaete worms (as a nereid) often used as bait

clan \'klan\ *n* [ME, fr. ScGael *clann* offspring, clan, fr. OIr *cland* plant, offspring, fr. L *planta* plant] (15c) **1 a** : a Celtic group esp. in the Scottish Highlands comprising a number of households whose heads claim descent from a common ancestor **b** : a group of people tracing descent from a common ancestor **2** : a group united by a common interest or common characteristics

clan·des·tine \klan-'des-tən *also* -ˌtin *or* -ˌtēn *or* 'klan-dəs-\ *adj* [MF or L; MF *clandestin*, fr. L *clandestinus*, fr. *clam* secretly; akin to L *celare* to hide — more at HELL] (1566) : marked by, held in, or conducted with secrecy : SURREPTITIOUS *syn* see SECRET — **clan·des·tine·ly** *adv* — **clan·des·tine·ness** *n* — **clan·des·tin·i·ty** \ˌklan-də-'sti-nə-tē, -des-'ti-\ *n*

¹clang \'klaŋ\ *vb* [L *clangere*; akin to Gk *klazein* to scream, bark, OE *hliehhan* to laugh] *vi* (1576) **1 a** : to make a loud metallic ringing sound ⟨anvils ~*ed*⟩ **b** : to go with a clang **2** : to utter the characteristic harsh cry of a bird ~ *vt* : to cause to clang ⟨~ a bell⟩

²clang *n* (1596) **1** : a loud ringing metallic sound ⟨the ~ of a fire alarm⟩ **2** : a harsh cry of a bird (as a crane or goose)

clang·er \'klaŋ-ər\ *n* (1948) *Brit* : a conspicuous blunder — often used in the phrase *drop a clanger*

¹clan·gor \'klaŋ-ər *also* -gər\ *n* [L *clangor*, fr. *clangere*] (1593) : a resounding clang or medley of clangs ⟨the ~ of hammers⟩ — **clan·gor·ous** \-(g)ə-rəs\ *adj* — **clan·gor·ous·ly** *adv*

²clangor *vi* (1837) : to make a clangor

clan·gour \'klaŋ-ər, -gər\ *chiefly Brit var of* CLANGOR

¹clank \'klaŋk\ *vb* [prob. imit.] *vi* (1656) **1** : to make a clank or series of clanks ⟨the radiator hissed and ~*ed*⟩ **2** : to go with or as if with a clank ⟨~*ing* through the streets⟩ ~ *vt* : to cause to clank — **clank·ing·ly** \'klaŋ-kiŋ-lē\ *adv*

²clank *n* (1656) : a sharp brief metallic ringing sound

clan·nish \'kla-nish\ *adj* (1776) **1** : of or relating to a clan **2** : tending to associate only with a select group of similar background or status — **clan·nish·ly** *adv* — **clan·nish·ness** *n*

clans·man \'klanz-mən\ *n* (1810) : a member of a clan

¹clap \'klap\ *vb* **clapped** *also* **clapt**; **clap·ping** [ME *clappen*, fr. OE *clæppan* to throb; akin to OHG *klaphōn* to beat] *vt* (14c) **1** : to strike (as two flat hard surfaces) together so as to produce a sharp percussive noise **2** : to strike (the hands) together repeatedly usu. in applause **b** : APPLAUD **3** : to strike with the flat of the hand in a friendly way ⟨*clapped* his friend on the shoulder⟩ **4** : to place, put, or set esp. energetically ⟨~ him into jail⟩ ⟨since I first *clapped* eyes on it⟩ **5** : to improvise hastily ~ *vi* **1** : to produce a percussive sound; *esp* : SLAM **2** : to go abruptly or briskly **3** : APPLAUD

²clap *n* (13c) **1** : a device that makes a clapping noise **2** *obs* : a sudden stroke of fortune and esp. ill fortune **3** : a loud percussive noise; *specif* : a sudden crash of thunder **4 a** : a sudden blow **b** : a friendly slap **5** : the sound of clapping hands; *esp* : APPLAUSE

³clap *n* [MF *clapoir* bubo] (1587) : GONORRHEA — often used with *the*

clap·board \'kla-bərd; 'kla(p)-ˌbōrd, -ˌbôrd\ *n* [part trans. of D *klaphout* stave wood] (ca. 1520) **1** *archaic* : a size of board for making staves and wainscoting **2** : a narrow board usu. thicker at one edge than the other used for siding **3** \'klap-ˌbōrd, -ˌbôrd\ : a pair of hinged boards one of which has a slate with data identifying a piece of film and which are banged together in front of a motion-picture camera at the start of a take to facilitate editing — called also *clapper board* — **clapboard** *vt*

clapped-out \ˌklapt-'aut\ *adj* (1946) *Brit* : WORN-OUT; *also* : TIRED

clap·per \'kla-pər\ *n* (14c) : one that claps: as **a** : the tongue of a bell **b** : a mechanical device that makes noise esp. by the banging of one part against another **c** : a person who applauds

clap·per·claw \'kla-pər-ˌklô\ *vt* [perh. fr. *clapper* + *claw* (v.)] (1590) **1** *dial Eng* : to claw with the nails **2** *dial Eng* : SCOLD, REVILE

¹clap·trap \'klap-ˌtrap\ *n* [²*clap*; fr. its attempt to win applause] (1799) : pretentious nonsense : TRASH

²claptrap *adj* (1815) : characterized by or suggestive of claptrap; *esp* : of a cheap showy nature ⟨~ sentiment⟩

claque \'klak\ *n* [F, fr. *claquer* to clap, of imit. origin] (1864) **1** : a group hired to applaud at a performance **2** : a group of sycophants

cla·queur \kla-'kər\ *n* [F, fr. *claquer* to clap] (1837) : a member of a claque

clar·et \'klar-ət\ *n* [ME, fr. MF (*vin*) *claret* clear wine, fr. *claret* clear, fr. *cler* clear] (1707) **1** : a red Bordeaux wine; *also* : a similar wine produced elsewhere **2** : a dark purplish red — **claret** *adj*

clar·i·fy \'klar-ə-ˌfī\ *vb* **-fied**; **-fy·ing** [ME *clarifien*, fr. MF *clarifier*, fr. LL *clarificare*, fr. L *clarus* clear — more at CLEAR] *vt* (14c) **1** : to make (as a liquid) clear or pure usu. by freeing from suspended matter **2** : to free of confusion **3** : to make understandable ~ *vi* : to become clear — **clar·i·fi·ca·tion** \ˌklar-ə-fə-'kā-shən\ *n* — **clar·i·fi·er** \'klar-ə-ˌfī(-ə)r\ *n*

clar·i·net \ˌklar-ə-'net, 'klar-ə-nət\ *n* [F *clarinette*, prob. ultim. fr. ML *clarion-*, *clario*] (1796) : a single-reed woodwind instrument having a cylindrical tube with a moderately flared bell and a usual range from D below middle C upward for 3½ octaves — **clar·i·net·ist** *or* **clar·i·net·tist** \ˌklar-ə-'ne-tist\ *n*

¹clar·i·on \'klar-ē-ən\ *n* [ME, fr. MF & ML; MF *clairon*, fr. ML *clarion-*, *clario*, fr. L *clarus*] (14c) **1** : a medieval trumpet with clear shrill tones **2** : the sound of or as if of a clarion

²clarion *adj* (1841) : brilliantly clear ⟨her ~ top notes⟩; *also* : loud and clear ⟨a ~ call to action⟩

clar·i·ty \'klar-ə-tē\ *n* [ME *clarite*, fr. L *claritat-*, *claritas*, fr. *clarus*] (1616) : the quality or state of being clear : LUCIDITY

clark·ia \'klär-kē-ə\ *n* [NL, fr. William *Clark*] (1827) : any of a genus (*Clarkia*) of showy annual herbs of the evening-primrose family that are native to the Pacific slope of No. America and southwestern So. America

cla·ro \'klär-(ˌ)ō\ *n*, *pl* **claros** [Sp, fr. *claro* light, fr. L *clarus*] (1891) : a light-colored usu. mild cigar

clary \'klar-ē, 'kler-\ *n*, *pl* **clar·ies** [ME *clarie*, fr. MF *sclaree*, fr. ML *sclareia*] (14c) : an aromatic mint (*Salvia sclarea*) of southern Europe that is widely cultivated esp. as an ornamental

¹clash \'klash\ *vb* [imit.] *vi* (ca. 1500) **1** : to make a clash ⟨cymbals ~*ed*⟩ **2** : to come into conflict ⟨where ignorant armies ~ by night — Matthew Arnold⟩; *also* : to be incompatible ⟨the colors ~*ed*⟩ ~ *vt* : to cause to clash — **clash·er** *n*

²clash *n* (1513) **1** : a noisy usu. metallic sound of collision **2** : a hostile encounter : SKIRMISH **b** : a sharp conflict ⟨a ~ of opinions⟩

¹clasp \'klasp\ *n* [ME *claspe*] (14c) **1 a** : a device (as a hook) for holding objects or parts together **b** : a device (as a bar) attached to a military medal to indicate an additional award of the medal or the action or service for which it was awarded **2** : a holding or enveloping with or as if with the hands or arms

²clasp *vt* (14c) **1** : to fasten with or as if with a clasp ⟨a robe ~*ed* with a brooch⟩ **2** : to enclose and hold with the arms; *specif* : EMBRACE **3** : to seize with or as if with the hand : GRASP

clasp·er \'klas-pər\ *n* (ca. 1847) : a male copulatory structure: as **a** : one of a pair of external anal processes of an insect that are used to grasp a female **b** : one of a pair of organs that are extensions of the pelvic fins of cartilaginous fishes

clasp knife *n* (ca. 1755) : POCKETKNIFE; *esp* : a large one-bladed folding knife having a catch to hold the blade open

¹class \'klas\ *n*, *often attrib* [F *classe*, fr. L *classis* group called to military service, fleet, class; perh. akin to L *calare* to call — more at LOW] (1602) **1 a** : a body of students meeting regularly to study the same subject **b** : the period during which such a body meets **c** : a course of instruction **d** : a body of students or alumni whose year of graduation is the same **2 a** : a group sharing the same economic or social status ⟨the working ~⟩ **b** : social rank; *esp* : high social rank **c** : high quality : ELEGANCE **3** : a group, set, or kind sharing common attributes: as **a** : a major category in biological taxonomy ranking above the order and below the phylum or division **b** : a collection of adjacent and discrete or continuous values of a random variable **4** : a division or rating based on grade or quality **5** : the best of its kind ⟨the ~ of the league⟩

²class *vt* (1705) : CLASSIFY

class act *n* (1976) : an example of outstanding quality or prestige

class action *n* (1952) : a legal action undertaken by one or more plaintiffs on behalf of themselves and all other persons having an identical interest in the alleged wrong

class–conscious *adj* (1903) **1** : actively aware of one's common status with others in a particular economic or social level of society **2** : believing in class struggle — **class consciousness** *n*

¹clas·sic \'kla-sik\ *adj* [F or L; F *classique*, fr. L *classicus* of the highest class of Roman citizens, of the first rank, fr. *classis*] (ca. 1604) **1 a** : serving as a standard of excellence : of recognized value **b** : TRADITIONAL, ENDURING **c** : characterized by simple tailored lines in fashion year after year ⟨a ~ suit⟩ **2** : of or relating to the ancient Greeks and Romans or their culture : CLASSICAL **3 a** : historically memorable **b** : noted because of special literary or historical associations ⟨Paris is the ~ refuge of expatriates⟩ **c** : AUTHENTIC, AUTHORITATIVE **b** : TYPICAL ⟨a ~ example of chicanery⟩ **5** *cap* : of or relating to the period of highest development of Mesoamerican and esp. Mayan culture about A.D. 300–900

²classic *n* (1711) **1** : a literary work of ancient Greece or Rome **2 a** : a work of enduring excellence; *also* : its author **b** : an authoritative source **3** : a typical or perfect example **4** : a traditional event ⟨a football ~⟩

clas·si·cal \'kla-si-kəl\ *adj* [L *classicus*] (1599) **1** : STANDARD, CLASSIC **2 a** : of or relating to the ancient Greek and Roman world and esp. to its literature, art, architecture, or ideals **b** : versed in the classics **3 a** : of or relating to music of the late 18th and early 19th centuries characterized by an emphasis on balance, clarity, and moderation **b** : of, relating to, or being music in the educated European tradition that includes such forms as art song, chamber music, opera, and symphony as distinguished from folk or popular music or jazz **4 a** : AUTHORITATIVE, TRADITIONAL **b** (1) : of or relating to a form or system considered of first significance in earlier times ⟨~ Mendelian genetics⟩ (2) : not involving relativity, wave mechanics, or quantum theory ⟨~ physics⟩ **c** : conforming to a pattern of usage sanctioned by a body of literature rather than by everyday speech **5** : concerned with or giving instruction in the humanities, the fine arts, and the broad aspects of science ⟨a ~ curriculum⟩

classical conditioning *n* (1949) : conditioning in which the conditioned stimulus (as the sound of a bell) is paired with and precedes the unconditioned stimulus (as the sight of food) until the conditioned stimulus alone is sufficient to elicit the response (as salivation in a dog) — compare OPERANT CONDITIONING

clas·si·cal·i·ty \ˌkla-sə-'ka-lə-tē\ *n* (1819) **1** : the quality or state of being classic **2** : classical scholarship

clas·si·cal·ly \'kla-si-k(ə-)lē\ *adv* (1772) **1** : in a classic or classical manner ⟨~ exact forms of the dance⟩ ⟨~ trained⟩ **2 a** : in classic or traditional circumstances : TYPICALLY ⟨~, the whole fish is stuffed⟩ **b** : as a classic example ⟨~ bad writing⟩

clas·si·cism \'kla-sə-ˌsi-zəm\ *n* (1830) **1 a** : the principles or style embodied in the literature, art, or architecture of ancient Greece and Rome **b** : classical scholarship **c** : a classical idiom or expression **2** : adherence to traditional standards (as of simplicity, restraint, and proportion) that are universally and enduringly valid

clas·si·cist \-sist\ *n* (1830) **1** : an advocate or follower of classicism **2** : a classical scholar — **clas·si·cis·tic** \ˌkla-sə-'sis-tik\ *adj*

clas·si·cize \'kla-sə-ˌsīz\ *vb* **-cized**; **-ciz·ing** *vt* (1854) : to make classic or classical ~ *vi* : to follow classic style

clas·si·co \'kla-si-(ˌ)kō\ *adj* [It, fr. L *classicus*] (1968) : produced in a delimited area of Italy known for its standards of quality ⟨Chianti ~⟩

clas·si·fi·ca·tion \ˌkla-sə-fə-'kā-shən\ *n* (1790) **1** : the act or process of classifying **2** : systematic arrangement in groups or categories according to established criteria; *specif* : TAXONOMY **b** : CLASS, CATEGORY — **clas·si·fi·ca·to·ry** \'kla-sə-fi-kə-ˌtōr-ē, kla-'si-fə-, -ˌtôr-; 'kla-sə-fə-ˌkā-tə-rē\ *adj*

clas·si·fied \'kla-sə-ˌfīd\ *adj* (1889) **1** : divided into classes or placed in a class ⟨~ ads⟩ **2** : withheld from general circulation for reasons of national security ⟨~ information⟩

clas·si·fi·er \'kla-sə-ˌfī(-ə)r\ *n* (1819) **1** : one that classifies; *specif* : a machine for sorting out the constituents of a substance (as ore) **2** : a word or morpheme used with numerals or with nouns designating countable or measurable objects

---

\ə\ abut \ᵊ\ kitten, F table \ər\ further \a\ ash \ā\ ace \ä\ mop, mar \au̇\ out \ch\ chin \e\ bet \ē\ easy \g\ go \i\ hit \ī\ ice \j\ job \ŋ\ sing \ō\ go \ȯ\ law \ȯi\ boy \th\ thin \t͟h\ the \ü\ loot \u̇\ foot \y\ yet \zh\ vision \ä, k̟, ⁿ, œ, œ̄, ᴜᴇ, ᵫ, ᵊ\ *see* Guide to Pronunciation

clas·si·fy \'kla-sə-ˌfī\ vt **-fied; -fy·ing** (1799) **1** : to arrange in classes 〈~ing books according to subject matter〉 **2** : to assign (as a document) to a category — **clas·si·fi·able** \ˌkla-sə-'fī-ə-bəl\ adj

class interval n (1929) : CLASS 3b; also : its numerical width

clas·sis \'kla-sis\ n, pl **clas·ses** \'kla-ˌsēz\ [NL, fr. L, class] (1593) **1** : a governing body in some Reformed churches (as in the former Reformed Church in the U.S.) corresponding to a presbytery **2** : the district governed by a classis

class·ism \'kla-ˌsi-zəm\ n (1842) : prejudice or discrimination based on class — **class·ist** \'kla-sist\ adj

class·less \'klas-ləs\ adj (1878) **1** : belonging to no particular social class **2** : free from distinctions of social class 〈a ~ society〉 — **class·less·ness** n

class·mate \-ˌmāt\ n (1713) : a member of the same class in a school or college

class·room \-ˌrüm, -ˌrùm\ n (1870) : a place where classes meet

classy \'kla-sē\ adj **class·i·er; -est** (1891) : ELEGANT, STYLISH 〈a ~ clientele〉; also : notably superior 〈a ~ outfielder〉 — **class·i·ness** n

clast \'klast\ n [Gk klastos broken, fr. klan to break; perh. akin to L clades disaster] (1952) : a fragment of rock

clas·tic \'klas-tik\ adj [ISV] (1877) : made up of fragments of preexisting rocks 〈a ~ sediment〉 — **clastic** n

clath·rate \'kla-ˌthrāt\ adj [L clathratus, furnished with a lattice, fr. clathri (pl.) lattice, fr. Gk klēithron bar, fr. kleiein to close — more at CLAVICLE] (1906) : relating to or being a compound formed by the inclusion of molecules of one kind in cavities of the crystal lattice of another — **clathrate** n

¹clat·ter \'kla-tər\ vb [ME clatren, fr. (assumed) OE clatrian; of imit. origin] vi (13c) **1** : to make a rattling sound 〈the dishes ~ed on the shelf〉 **2** : to talk noisily or rapidly **3** : to move or go with a clatter 〈~ed down the stairs〉 ~ vt : to cause to clatter — **clat·ter·er** \-tər-ər\ n — **clat·ter·ing·ly** \'kla-tə-riŋ-lē\ adv

²clatter n (14c) **1** : a rattling sound (as of hard bodies striking together) 〈the ~ of pots and pans〉 **2** : COMMOTION 〈the midday ~ of the business district〉 **3** : noisy chatter — **clat·tery** \'kla-tə-rē\ adj

clau·di·ca·tion \ˌklȯ-də-'kā-shən\ n [L claudication-, claudicatio, fr. claudicare to limp, fr. claudus lame] (15c) : the quality or state of being lame : LIMPING

claus·al \'klȯ-zəl\ adj (1904) : relating to or of the nature of a clause

clause \'klȯz\ n [ME, fr. OF, fr. ML clausa close of a rhetorical period, fr. L, fem. of clausus, pp. of claudere to close — more at CLOSE] (13c) **1** : a group of words containing a subject and predicate and functioning as a member of a complex or compound sentence **2** : a separate section of a discourse or writing; specif : a distinct article in a formal document

claus·tral \'klȯs-trəl\ adj [ME, fr. ML claustralis, fr. claustrum cloister, fr. L, bar, bolt, confining space, fr. claudere] (15c) : CLOISTRAL

claus·tro·pho·bia \ˌklȯs-trə-'fō-bē-ə\ n [NL, fr. L claustrum + NL -phobia] (1879) : abnormal dread of being in closed or narrow spaces — **claus·tro·phobe** \'klȯs-trə-ˌfōb\ n

claus·tro·pho·bic \ˌklȯs-trə-'fō-bik\ adj (ca. 1889) **1** : affected with or inclined to claustrophobia **2** : inducing or suggesting claustrophobia — **claus·tro·pho·bi·cal·ly** \-bi-k(ə-)lē\ adv

claus·trum \'klȯs-trəm, 'klaùs-\ n, pl **claus·tra** \-trə\ [NL, fr. L, bar] (1848) : the one of the four basal ganglia in each cerebral hemisphere that consists of a thin lamina of gray matter separated from the lenticular nucleus by a layer of white matter

cla·vate \'klā-ˌvāt\ adj [NL clavatus, fr. L clava club, fr. clavus nail, knot in wood] (1813) : gradually thickening near the distal end : shaped like a club

¹clave past of CLEAVE

²clave \'klā-(ˌ)vā, 'klä\ n [AmerSp, fr. Sp, keystone, clef, fr. L clavis] (1928) : one of a pair of cylindrical hardwood sticks that are used as a percussion instrument

cla·ver \'klā-vər\ vi [prob. of Celt origin; akin to ScGael clabaire babbler] (ca. 1605) chiefly Scot : PRATE, GOSSIP — **claver** n, chiefly Scot

clav·i·chord \'kla-və-ˌkȯrd\ n [ML clavichordium, fr. L clavis key + chorda string — more at CORD] (15c) : an early keyboard instrument having strings struck by tangents attached directly to the key ends — **clav·i·chord·ist** \-ˌkȯr-dist\ n

clav·i·cle \'kla-vi-kəl\ n [F clavicule, fr. NL clavicula, fr. L, dim. of L clavis; akin to Gk kleid-, kleis key, kleiein to close] (1615) : a bone of the vertebrate pectoral girdle typically serving to link the scapula and sternum — called also collarbone — **cla·vic·u·lar** \kla-'vi-kyə-lər, klə-\ adj

cla·vier \klə-'vir; 'klā-vē-ər, 'kla-\ n [F, fr. OF, key bearer, fr. L clavis] (1708) **1** : the keyboard of a musical instrument **2** [G Klavier, fr. F clavier] : an early keyboard instrument — **cla·vier·ist** \klə-'vir-ist; 'klā-vē-ə-rist, 'kla-\ n — **cla·vier·is·tic** \klə-ˌvi-'ris-tik; ˌklā-vē-ə-'ris-tik, ˌkla-\ adj

¹claw \'klȯ\ n, often attrib [ME clawe, fr. OE clawu hoof, claw; akin to ON klō toe, and prob. to OE cliewen ball — more at CLEW] (bef. 12c) **1** : a sharp usu. slender and curved nail on the toe of an animal **2** : any of various sharp curved processes esp. at the end of a limb (as of an insect); also : a limb ending in such a process **3** : one of the pincerlike organs terminating some limbs of various arthropods (as a lobster or scorpion) **4** : something that resembles a claw; specif : the forked end of a tool (as a hammer) — **clawed** \'klȯd\ adj — **claw·like** \-ˌlīk\ adj

²claw vt (bef. 12c) : to rake, seize, dig, or progress with or as if with claws ~ vi : to scrape, scratch, dig, or pull with or as if with claws

claw back vt (1953) chiefly Brit : to get back (as money) by strenuous or forceful means (as taxation) — **claw–back** \'klȯ-ˌbak\ n

claw·ham·mer \'klȯ-ˌha-mər\ adj (1964) : of or relating to a style of banjo playing using the thumb and one or more fingers picking or strumming in a downward direction

claw hammer n (ca. 1769) **1** : a hammer with one end of the head forked for pulling out nails **2** : TAILCOAT

¹clay \'klā\ n, often attrib [ME, fr. OE clǣg; akin to OHG klīwa bran, L gluten glue, MGk glia] (bef. 12c) **1 a** : an earthy material that is plastic when moist but hard when fired, that is composed mainly of fine particles of hydrous aluminum silicates and other minerals, and that is used for brick, tile, and pottery; specif : soil composed chiefly of this material having particles less than a specified size **b** : EARTH, MUD

2 a : a substance that resembles clay in plasticity and is used for modeling **b** : the human body as distinguished from the spirit **c** : fundamental nature or character 〈the common ~〉 **3** : CLAY COURT

clay·ey \'klā-ē\ adj — **clay·ish** \'klā-ish\ adj — **clay·like** \-ˌlīk\ adj

clay·bank \'klā-ˌbaŋk\ n (1851) : a horse of yellowish color

clay court n (1885) : a tennis court with a clay surface or a synthetic surface that resembles clay

clay loam n (ca. 1889) : a loam containing from 20 to 30 percent clay

clay mineral n (1947) : any of a group of hydrous silicates of aluminum and sometimes other metals formed chiefly in weathering processes and occurring esp. in clay and shale

clay·more \'klā-ˌmȯr, -ˌmòr\ n [ScGael claidheamh mór, lit., great sword] (1772) : a large 2-edged sword formerly used by Scottish Highlanders; also : their basket-hilted broadsword

claymore mine n [perh. fr. claymore] (1961) : a usu. electrically fired land mine that contains steel fragments which are discharged in a predetermined direction

clay·pan \-ˌpan\ n (1837) **1** : hardpan consisting mainly of clay **2** Austral : a shallow depression in which water collects after rain

clay pigeon n (1888) : a saucer-shaped target usu. made of baked clay or limestone and pitch and thrown from a trap in skeet and trapshooting

clay·ware \'klā-ˌwar, -ˌwer\ n (1896) : articles made of fired clay

¹clean \'klēn\ adj [ME clene, fr. OE clǣne; akin to OHG kleini delicate, dainty] (bef. 12c) **1 a** : free from dirt or pollution 〈changed to ~ clothes〉 〈~ solar energy〉 **b** : free from contamination or disease **c** : free or relatively free from radioactivity 〈a ~ atomic explosion〉 **2 a** : UNADULTERATED, PURE 〈the ~ thrill of one's first flight〉 **b** of a precious stone : having no interior flaws visible **c** : free from growth that hinders tillage **3 a** : free from moral corruption or sinister connections of any kind 〈a candidate with a ~ record〉 **b** : free from offensive treatment of sexual subjects and from the use of obscenity 〈a ~ joke〉 **c** : observing the rules : FAIR 〈a ~ fight〉 **4** : ceremonially or spiritually pure 〈and all who are ~ may eat flesh —Lev 7:19 (RSV)〉 **5 a** : THOROUGH, COMPLETE 〈a ~ break with the past〉 **b** : deftly executed : SKILLFUL 〈a ~ ballet technique〉 **c** : hit beyond the reach of an opponent 〈a ~ single to center〉 **6 a** : relatively free from error or blemish : CLEAR; specif : LEGIBLE 〈~ copy〉 **b** : UNENCUMBERED 〈~ bill of sale〉 **7 a** : characterized by clarity and precision : TRIM 〈a ~ prose style〉 〈architecture with ~ almost austere lines〉 **b** : EVEN, SMOOTH 〈a ~ edge〉 〈a sharp blow causing a ~ break〉 **c** : free from impedances to smooth flow (as of water or air) 〈a ~ airplane〉 〈a ship with a ~ bottom〉 **8 a** : EMPTY 〈the ship returned with a ~ hold〉 **b** : free from drug addiction **c** slang : having no contraband (as weapons or drugs) in one's possession **9** : habitually neat — **clean·ness** \'klēn-nəs\ n

²clean adv (bef. 12c) **1 a** : so as to clean 〈a new broom sweeps ~〉 **b** : in a clean manner 〈play the game ~〉 **2** : all the way : COMPLETELY 〈the bullet went ~ through his arm〉

³clean vt (15c) **1 a** : to make clean: as (1) : to rid of dirt, impurities, or extraneous matter (2) : to rid of corruption 〈vowing to ~ up city hall〉 **b** : REMOVE, ERADICATE — usu. used with up or off 〈~ up that mess〉 **2 a** : STRIP, EMPTY 〈a tree ~ed of fruit〉 **b** : to remove the entrails from 〈~ fish〉 **c** : to deprive of money or possessions — often used with out 〈they ~ed him out completely〉 ~ vi **1** : to undergo or perform a process of cleaning 〈~ up before dinner〉 — **clean·abil·i·ty** \ˌklē-nə-'bi-lə-tē\ n — **clean·able** \'klē-nə-bəl\ adj — **clean house 1** : to clean a house and its furniture **2** : to make sweeping reforms or changes (as of personnel) — **clean one's clock** : to beat one badly in a fight or competition — **clean up one's act** : to behave in a more acceptable manner

⁴clean n (ca. 1889) : an act of cleaning dirt esp. from the surface of something

clean and jerk n (1939) : a lift in weight lifting in which the weight is raised to shoulder height, held momentarily, and then quickly thrust overhead usu. with a lunge or a spring from the legs — compare PRESS, SNATCH

clean–cut \'klēn-'kət\ adj (1843) **1** : cut so that the surface or edge is smooth and even **2** : sharply defined **3** : of wholesome appearance

clean·er \'klē-nər\ n (ca. 1792) **1 a** : one whose work is cleaning **b** : DRY CLEANER **2** : a preparation for cleaning **3** : an implement or machine for cleaning

clean–hand·ed \'klēn-'han-dəd\ adj (1728) : innocent of wrongdoing

clean–limbed \'klēn-'limd\ adj (15c) : well proportioned : TRIM 〈~ youths〉

¹clean·ly \'klēn-lē\ adv (13c) : in a clean manner

²clean·ly \'klen-lē\ adj **clean·li·er; -est** (ca. 1500) **1** : careful to keep clean : FASTIDIOUS **2** : habitually kept clean — **clean·li·ness** n

clean room \'klēn-ˌrüm, -ˌrùm\ n (1963) : a room for the manufacture or assembly of objects (as precision parts) that is maintained in a high level of cleanliness by special means

cleanse \'klenz\ vb **cleansed; cleans·ing** [ME clensen, fr. OE clǣnsian to purify, fr. clǣne clean] (bef. 12c) : CLEAN; esp : to rid of impurities by or as if by washing

cleans·er \'klen-zər\ n (bef. 12c) **1** : one that cleanses **2** : a preparation (as a scouring powder or a skin cream) used for cleaning

¹clean-up \'klē-ˌnəp\ n (1872) **1** : an act or instance of cleaning **2** : an exceptionally large profit : KILLING

²cleanup adj (1937) : being in the fourth position in the batting order of a baseball team 〈a ~ hitter〉 — **cleanup** adv

clean up n (1920) : to make a spectacular profit in a business enterprise or a killing in speculation or gambling

¹clear \'klir\ adj [ME clere, fr. OF cler, fr. L clarus clear, bright; akin to L calare to call — more at LOW] (13c) **1 a** : BRIGHT, LUMINOUS **b** : CLOUDLESS; specif : less than one-tenth covered 〈a ~ sky〉 **c** : free from mist, haze, or dust 〈a ~ day〉 **d** : UNTROUBLED, SERENE 〈a ~ gaze〉 **2** : CLEAN, PURE: as **a** : free from blemishes **b** : easily seen through : TRANSPARENT **c** : free from abnormal sounds on auscultation **3 a** : easily heard **b** : easily visible : PLAIN **c** : free from obscurity or ambiguity : easily understood : UNMISTAKABLE **4 a** : capable of sharp discernment : KEEN **b** : free from doubt : SURE **5** : free from guile or guilt : INNOCENT **6** : unhampered by restriction or limitation: as **a** : unencumbered by debts or charges **b** : NET 〈a ~ profit〉 **c** : UNQUALIFIED, ABSOLUTE **d** : free from obstruction **e** : emptied of

contents or cargo **f** : free from entanglement **g** : BARE, DENUDED — **clear·ness** *n*
syn CLEAR, TRANSPARENT, TRANSLUCENT, LIMPID mean capable of being seen through. CLEAR implies absence of cloudiness, haziness, or muddiness ⟨*clear* water⟩. TRANSPARENT implies being so clear that objects can be seen distinctly ⟨a *transparent* sheet of film⟩. TRANSLUCENT implies the passage of light but not a clear view of what lies beyond ⟨*translucent* frosted glass⟩. LIMPID suggests the soft clearness of pure water ⟨her eyes were *limpid* pools of blue⟩.
syn CLEAR, PERSPICUOUS, LUCID mean quickly and easily understood. CLEAR implies freedom from obscurity, ambiguity, or undue complexity ⟨*clear* instructions⟩. PERSPICUOUS applies to a style that is simple and elegant as well as clear ⟨a *perspicuous* style⟩. LUCID suggests a clear logical coherence and evident order of arrangement ⟨a *lucid* explanation⟩. *syn* see in addition EVIDENT
²**clear** *adv* (14c)   **1** : in a clear manner ⟨to cry loud and ∼⟩   **2** : all the way ⟨drove ∼ across the state⟩
³**clear** *vt* (14c)   **1 a** : to make clear or translucent   **b** : to free from pollution or cloudiness   **2** : to free from accusation or blame : EXONERATE, VINDICATE ⟨the opportunity to ∼ himself⟩   **3 a** : to give insight to : ENLIGHTEN   **b** : to make intelligible : EXPLAIN ⟨∼ up the mystery⟩   **4 a** : to free from what obstructs or is unneeded: as (1) : OPEN 1b ⟨∼ a path⟩ (2) : to remove unwanted growth or items from ⟨∼ the land of timber⟩ (3) : to rid or make a rasping noise as if ridding (the throat) of phlegm (4) : to erase stored or displayed data from (as a computer or calculator)   **b** : to empty of occupants ⟨∼ the room⟩   **c** : DISENTANGLE ⟨∼ a fishing line⟩   **d** : to remove from an area or place ⟨∼ the dishes from the table⟩ : TRANSMIT, DISPATCH   **5 a** : to submit for approval ⟨∼ it with me first⟩   **b** : AUTHORIZE, APPROVE ⟨∼ed the article for publication⟩: as (1) : to certify as trustworthy ⟨∼ a person for classified information⟩ (2) : to permit (an aircraft) to proceed usu. with a specified action   **6 a** : to free from obligation or encumbrance   **b** : SETTLE, DISCHARGE ⟨∼ an account⟩ (1) : to free (a ship or shipment) by payment of duties or harbor fees (2) : to pass through (customs)   **d** : to gain without deduction : NET ⟨∼ a profit⟩   **e** : to put through a clearinghouse   **7 a** : to go over, under, or by without touching   **b** : PASS ⟨the bill ∼ed the legislature⟩ ∼ *vi*   **1 a** : to become clear ⟨it ∼ed up quickly after the rain⟩   **b** : to go away : VANISH ⟨the symptoms ∼ed gradually⟩   **c** : SELL   **2 a** : to obtain permission to discharge cargo   **b** : to conform to regulations or pay requisite fees prior to leaving port   **3** : to pass through a clearinghouse   **4** : to go to an authority (as for approval) before becoming effective — **clear·able** \ˈklir-ə-bəl\ *adj* — **clear·er** \ˈklir-ər\ *n* — **clear the air** *also* **clear the atmosphere** : to remove elements of hostility, tension, confusion, or uncertainty ⟨had a long meeting to *clear the air*⟩ — **clear the decks** : to make sweeping preparations for action
⁴**clear** *n* (1674)   **1** : a clear space or part   **2** : a high arcing shot over an opponent's head in badminton — **in the clear**   **1** : in inside measurement   **2** : free from guilt or suspicion   **3** : in plaintext : not in code or cipher ⟨a message sent *in the clear*⟩
clear–air turbulence *n* (1955) : sudden severe turbulence occurring in cloudless regions that causes violent jarring or buffeting of aircraft
clear·ance \ˈklir-ən(t)s\ *n* (1540)   **1** : an act or process of clearing: as **a** : the removal of buildings from an area (as a city slum)   **b** : the act of clearing a ship at the customhouse; *also* : the papers showing that a ship has cleared   **c** : the offsetting of checks and other claims among banks through a clearinghouse   **d** : certification as clear of objection : AUTHORIZATION ⟨security ∼⟩   **e** : a sale to clear out stock   **f** : authorization for an aircraft to proceed esp. with a specified action ⟨∼ to land⟩   **2** : the distance by which one object clears another or the clear space between them   **3** : the volume of blood or plasma that could be freed of a specified constituent in a specified time (usu. one minute) by its excretion into the urine through the kidneys — called also *renal clearance*
¹**clear–cut** \ˈklir-ˈkət\ *adj* (1855)   **1** : sharply outlined : DISTINCT   **2** : free from ambiguity or uncertainty : UNAMBIGUOUS
²**clear–cut** \-ˌkət\ *n* (ca. 1958) : an area of forest which has been clear-cut; *also* : CLEAR-CUTTING
clear–cut·ting \-ˌkə-tiŋ\ *n* (1922) : removal of all the trees in a stand of timber — **clear–cut** *vb*
clear–eyed \ˈklir-ˌīd\ *adj* (1530) : CLEAR-SIGHTED
clear–head·ed \-ˌhe-dəd\ *adj* (1709)   **1** : having a clear understanding : PERCEPTIVE   **2** : able to think clearly — **clear·head·ed·ly** *adv* — **clear·head·ed·ness** *n*
clear·ing \ˈklir-iŋ\ *n* (14c)   **1** : the act or process of making or becoming clear   **2** : a tract of land cleared of wood and brush   **3 a** : a method of exchanging and offsetting commercial papers or accounts with cash settlement only of the balances due after the clearing   **b** *pl* : the gross amount of balances so adjusted
clear·ing·house \-ˌhaús\ *n* (1832)   **1** : an establishment maintained by banks for settling mutual claims and accounts   **2** : a central agency for the collection, classification, and distribution esp. of information; *broadly* : an informal channel for distributing information or assistance
clear·ly \ˈklir-lē\ *adv* (14c)   **1** : in a clear manner ⟨speaking ∼⟩   **2** : it is clear ⟨∼, a new approach is needed⟩ *usage* see HOPEFULLY
clear out *vi* (1792)   **1** : to drive out or away usu. forcibly ∼ *vt* : to take out : REMOVE
clear–sight·ed \ˈklir-ˌsī-təd\ *adj* (1586)   **1** : having clear vision   **2** : DISCERNING — **clear–sight·ed·ly** *adv* — **clear–sight·ed·ness** *n*
clear–sto·ry *var of* CLERESTORY
clear·wing \-ˌwiŋ\ *n* (1868) : a moth (as of the families Aegeriidae or Sphingidae) having the wings largely transparent and devoid of scales
¹**cleat** \ˈklēt\ *n* [ME *clete* wedge, fr. (assumed) OE *clēat;* akin to MHG *klōz* lump — more at CLOUT] (14c)   **1 a** : a wedge-shaped piece fastened to or projecting from something and serving as a support or check   **b** : a wooden or metal fitting usu. with two projecting horns around which a rope may be made fast   **2 a** : a strip fastened across something to give strength or hold in position   **b** (1) : a projecting piece (as on the bottom of a shoe) that furnishes a grip (2) *pl* : shoes equipped with cleats
²**cleat** *vt* (1794)   **1** : to secure to or by a cleat   **2** : to provide with a cleat
cleav·able \ˈklē-və-bəl\ *adj* (ca. 1864) : capable of being split
cleav·age \ˈklē-vij\ *n* (1816)   **1 a** : the quality of a crystallized sub-

stance or rock of splitting along definite planes; *also* : the occurrence of such splitting   **b** : a fragment (as of a diamond) obtained by splitting   **2** : the action of cleaving : the state of being cleft   **3** : the series of synchronized mitotic cell divisions of the fertilized egg that results in the formation of the blastomeres and changes the single-celled zygote into a multicellular embryo; *also* : one of these cell divisions   **4** : the splitting of a molecule into simpler molecules   **5** : the depression between a woman's breasts esp. when made visible by the wearing of a low-cut dress
¹**cleave** \ˈklēv\ *vi* **cleaved** \ˈklēvd\ *or* **clove** \ˈklōv\ *also* **clave** \ˈklāv\; **cleaved; cleav·ing** [ME *clevien,* fr. OE *clifian;* akin to OHG *kleben* to stick] (bef. 12c) : to adhere firmly and closely or loyally and unwaveringly   *syn* see STICK
²**cleave** *vb* **cleaved** \ˈklēvd\ *also* **cleft** \ˈkleft\ *or* **clove** \ˈklōv\; **cleaved** *also* **cleft** *or* **clo·ven** \ˈklō-vən\; **cleav·ing** [ME *cleven,* fr. OE *clēofan;* akin to ON *kljūfa* to split, L *glubere* to peel, Gk *glyphein* to carve] *vt* (bef. 12c)   **1** : to divide by or as if by a cutting blow : SPLIT   **2** : to separate into distinct parts or esp. into groups having divergent views   **3** : to subject to chemical cleavage ⟨a protein *cleaved* by an enzyme⟩ ∼ *vi*   **1** : to split esp. along the grain   **2** : to penetrate or pass through something by or as if by cutting   *syn* see TEAR
cleav·er \ˈklē-vər\ *n* (15c)   **1** : one that cleaves; *esp* : a butcher's implement for cutting animal carcasses into joints or pieces   **2** : a prehistoric stone tool having a sharp edge at one end
cleav·ers \ˈklē-vərz\ *n pl but sing or pl in constr* [ME *clivre,* alter. of OE *clife* burdock, cleavers; akin to OE *clifian*] (14c) : an annual bedstraw (*Galium aparine*) that has numerous stalked white flowers, stems covered with curved prickles, and whorls of bristle-tipped leaves; *also* : any of several related plants
cleek \ˈklēk\ *n* [ME (northern) *cleke,* fr. *cleken* to clutch] (15c) *chiefly Scot* : a large hook (as for a pot over a fire)
clef \ˈklef\ *n* [F, lit., key, fr. L *clavis* — more at CLAVICLE] (ca. 1577) : a sign placed at the beginning of a musical staff to determine the pitch of the notes
¹**cleft** \ˈkleft\ *n* [ME *clift,* fr. OE *geclyft;* akin to OE *clēofan* to cleave] (14c)   **1** : a space or opening made by or as if by splitting : FISSURE   **2** : a usu. V-shaped indented formation : a hollow between ridges or protuberances ⟨the anal ∼ of the human body⟩
²**cleft** *adj* [ME, fr. pp. of *cleven*] (14c) : partially split or divided; *specif* : divided about halfway to the midrib ⟨a ∼ leaf⟩
cleft lip *n* (ca. 1946) : HARELIP
cleft palate *n* (1847) : congenital fissure of the roof of the mouth
clei·do·ic \klī-ˈdō-ik\ *adj* [Gk *kleidoun* to fasten, lock in, fr. *kleid-, kleis* key — more at CLAVICLE] (1931) *of an egg* : enclosed in a relatively impervious shell which reduces free exchange with the environment
cleis·tog·a·mous \klī-ˈstä-gə-məs\ *also* **cleis·to·gam·ic** \ˌklī-stə-ˈga-mik\ *adj* [Gk *kleistos* closed (fr. *kleiein* to close) + ISV *-gamous* — more at CLAVICLE] (1874) : characterized by or being small inconspicuous closed self-pollinating flowers additional to and often more fruitful than showier ones on the same plant ⟨violets are ∼⟩ — **cleis·tog·a·mous·ly** \klī-ˈstä-gə-məs-lē\ *adv* — **cleis·tog·a·my** \-ˈstä-gə-mē\ *n*
cle·ma·tis \ˈkle-mə-təs; kli-ˈma-təs, -ˈmä-, -ˈmä-\ *n* [NL, genus name, fr. L, fr. Gk *klēmatis* brushwood, clematis, fr. *klēmat-, klēma* twig, fr. *klan* to break — more at CLAST] (1578) : any of a genus (*Clematis*) of vines or herbs of the buttercup family having three leaflets on each leaf and usu. white, red, pink, or purple flowers
clem·en·cy \ˈkle-mən(t)-sē\ *n, pl* **-cies** (15c)   **1 a** : disposition to be merciful and esp. to moderate the severity of punishment due   **b** : an act or instance of leniency   **2** : pleasant mildness of weather   *syn* see MERCY
clem·ent \ˈkle-mənt\ *adj* [ME, fr. L *clement-, clemens*] (15c)   **1** : inclined to be merciful : LENIENT ⟨a ∼ judge⟩   **2** : MILD ⟨∼ weather for November⟩ — **clem·ent·ly** *adv*
clench \ˈklench\ *vt* [ME *clenccan;* akin to OE *clingan* to cling] (13c)   **1** : CLINCH 2   **2** : to hold fast : CLUTCH ⟨∼ed the arms of the chair⟩   **3** : to set or close tightly ⟨∼ one's teeth⟩ ⟨∼ one's fists⟩ — **clench** *n*
clepe \ˈklep\ *vt* **cleped** \ˈklept\; **yclept** \i-ˈklept\ *also* **cleped** *or* **ycleped** \i-ˈklept\; **clep·ing** \ˈklep-iŋ\ [ME, fr. OE *clipian* to speak, call; akin to OFris *kleppa* to ring] (bef. 12c) *archaic* : NAME, CALL
clep·sy·dra \ˈklep-sə-drə\ *n, pl* **-dras** *or* **-drae** \-ˌdrē, -ˌdrī\ [L, fr. Gk *klepsydra,* fr. *kleptein* to steal + *hydōr* water — more at KLEPT-, WATER] (1646) : WATER CLOCK
clere·sto·ry \ˈklir-ˌstōr-ē, -ˌstȯr-, -st(ə-)rē\ *n* [ME, fr. *clere* clear + *story*] (15c)   **1** : an outside wall of a room or building that rises above an adjoining roof and contains windows   **2** : GALLERY
cler·gy \ˈklər-jē\ *n, pl* **clergies** [ME *clergie,* fr. OF, fr. *clerc* clergyman] (13c)   **1** : a group ordained to perform pastoral or sacerdotal functions in a Christian church   **2** : the official or sacerdotal class of a non-Christian religion
cler·gy·man \-mən\ *n* (1577) : a member of the clergy
cler·gy·wom·an \-ˌwú-mən\ *n* (1673) : a woman who is a member of the clergy
cler·ic \ˈkler-ik\ *n* [LL *clericus*] (1621) : a member of the clergy

clef: *1* treble clef, *2* bass clef

clerestory *1*

\ə\ abut \ᵊ\ kitten, F table \ər\ further \a\ ash \ā\ ace \ä\ mop, mar \aú\ out \ch\ chin \e\ bet \ē\ easy \g\ go \i\ hit \ī\ ice \j\ job \ŋ\ sing \ō\ go \ò\ law \òi\ boy \th\ thin \t̲h̲\ the \ü\ loot \ú\ foot \y\ yet \zh\ vision \à, k̫, ⁿ, œ, œ̄, ᵫ, ᵫ̄, ʸ\ see Guide to Pronunciation

¹cler·i·cal \'kler-i-kəl\ adj (1592)   1 : of, relating to, or characteristic of the clergy   2 : of or relating to a clerk — cler·i·cal·ly \-i-k(ə-)lē\ adv

²clerical n (1605)   1 : a member of the clergy   2 : CLERICALIST   3 : CLERK   4 pl : clerical garments

clerical collar n (1948) : a narrow stiffly upright white collar worn buttoned at the back of the neck by members of the clergy

cler·i·cal·ism \'kler-i-kə-ˌli-zəm\ n (1864) : a policy of maintaining or increasing the power of a religious hierarchy

cler·i·cal·ist \-list\ n (1881) : one that favors maintained or increased ecclesiastical power and influence

cler·i·hew \'kler-i-ˌhyü\ n [Edmund Clerihew Bentley †1956 Eng. writer] (1928) : a light verse quatrain rhyming aabb and usu. dealing with a person named in the initial rhyme

cler·i·sy \'kler-ə-sē\ n [G Klerisei clergy, fr. ML clericia, fr. LL clericus cleric] (1818) : INTELLIGENTSIA

¹clerk \'klərk, Brit usu 'klärk\ n [ME, fr. OF clerc & OE cleric, clerc, both fr. LL clericus, fr. LGk klērikos, fr. Gk klēros lot, inheritance (in allusion to Deut 18:2), stick of wood; akin to Gk klan to break — more at CLAST] (bef. 12c)   1 : CLERIC   2 archaic : SCHOLAR   3   a : an official responsible (as to a government agency) for correspondence, records, and accounts and vested with specified powers or authority (as to issue writs or other processes as ordered by a court) ⟨city ~⟩   b : one employed to keep records or accounts or to perform general office work   c : one who works at a sales or service counter — clerk·ship \-ˌship\ n

²clerk vi (1551) : to act or work as a clerk

clerk·ly \'klər-klē, Brit usu 'klär-\ adj (15c)   1 : of, relating to, or characteristic of a clerk   2 archaic : SCHOLARLY — clerkly adv

Cleve·land bay \'klēv-lənd-\ n [Cleveland, district in Yorkshire, England] (1796) : a large strong horse of a breed of English origin that is uniformly bay with black legs, mane, and tail

clev·er \'kle-vər\ adj [ME cliver, perh. of Scand origin; akin to Dan dial. kløver alert, skillful] (ca. 1595)   1   a : skillful or adroit in using the hands or body : NIMBLE   b : mentally quick and resourceful but often lacking in depth and soundness   2 : marked by wit or ingenuity   3 dial   a : GOOD   b : easy to use or handle — clev·er·ish \-v(ə-)rish\ adj — clev·er·ly \-vər-lē\ adv — clev·er·ness \-vər-nəs\ n

syn CLEVER, ADROIT, CUNNING, INGENIOUS mean having or showing practical wit or skill in contriving. CLEVER stresses physical or mental quickness, deftness, or great aptitude ⟨a person clever with horses⟩. ADROIT often implies a skillful use of expedients to achieve one's purpose in spite of difficulties ⟨an adroit negotiator⟩. CUNNING implies great skill in constructing or creating ⟨a filmmaker cunning in his use of special effects⟩. INGENIOUS suggests the power of inventing or discovering a new way of accomplishing something ⟨an ingenious software engineer⟩. syn see in addition INTELLIGENT

clev·is \'kle-vəs\ n [earlier clevi, perh. of Scand origin; akin to ON kljufa to split — more at CLEAVE] (1592) : SHACKLE 3

¹clew \'klü\ n [ME clewe, fr. OE cliewen; akin to OHG kliuwa ball, Skt glau lump] (bef. 12c)   1 : a ball of thread, yarn, or cord : CLUE 3   a : a lower corner or only the after corner of a sail   b : a metal loop attached to the lower corner of a sail   c pl : a combination of lines by which a hammock is suspended

²clew vt (15c)   1 : to roll into a ball : CLUE 3   2 : to haul (a sail) up or down by ropes through the clews

cli·ché also cli·che \klē-'shā, 'klē-ˌ, kli-\ n [F, lit., printer's stereotype, fr. pp. of clicher to stereotype, of imit. origin] (1892)   1 : a trite phrase or expression; also : the idea expressed by it   2 : a hackneyed theme, characterization, or situation   3 : something (as a mere item) that has become overly familiar or commonplace — cliché adj

cli·chéd \-'shād\ adj (1928)   1 : marked by or abounding in clichés   2 : HACKNEYED

¹click \'klik\ vb [prob. imit.] vt (1581)   1 : to strike, move, or produce with a click ⟨~ed his heels together⟩   ~ vi   1 : to make a click   2   a : to fit or agree exactly   b : to fit together : hit it off ⟨they did not ~ as friends⟩   c : to function smoothly ⟨a movie that ~s⟩   3 : SUCCEED ⟨a movie that ~s⟩

²click n (1611)   1   a : a slight sharp noise : b speech sound in some languages made by enclosing air between two stop articulations of the tongue, enlarging the enclosure to rarefy the air, and suddenly opening the enclosure   2 : DETENT

click beetle n (ca. 1864) : any of a family (Elateridae) of beetles able to right themselves with a click when inverted by flexing the articulation between the prothorax and mesothorax

click stop n (1950) : a turnable control device (as for a camera diaphragm opening) that engages with a definite click at specific settings

cli·ent \'klī-ənt\ n [ME, fr. MF & L; MF client, fr. L client-, cliens, perh. akin to L clinare to lean — more at LEAN] (14c)   1 : one that is under the protection of another : DEPENDENT   2   a : a person who engages the professional advice or services of another ⟨a lawyer's ~s⟩   b : CUSTOMER ⟨hotel ~s⟩   c : a person served by or utilizing the services of a social agency ⟨a welfare ~⟩   3 : CLIENT STATE — cli·ent·age \-ən-tij\ n — cli·en·tal \klī-'en-tᵊl, 'klī-ən-\ adj — cli·ent·less \'klī-ənt-ləs\ adj

cli·en·tele \ˌklī-ən-'tel, ˌklē-ən- also ˌklē-ˌän-\ n [F clientèle, fr. L clientela, fr. client-, cliens] (ca. 1587) : a body of clients ⟨a shop that caters to an exclusive ~⟩

client state n (1918) : a country that is economically, politically, or militarily dependent on another country

¹cliff \'klif\ n [ME clif, fr. OE; akin to OHG klep] (bef. 12c) : a very steep, vertical, or overhanging face of rock, earth, or ice : PRECIPICE — cliffy \'kli-fē\ adj

cliff dweller n (1881)   1 often cap C&D   a : a member of a prehistoric American Indian people of the southwestern U.S. who built their homes on rock ledges or in the natural recesses of canyon walls and cliffs   b : a member of any cliff-dwelling people   2 : a resident of a large usu. metropolitan apartment building — cliff dwelling n

cliff–hang \'klif-ˌhaŋ\ vi [back-formation fr. cliff-hanger] (1946) : to await the outcome of a suspenseful situation

cliff–hang·er \-ˌhaŋ-ər\ n (ca. 1937)   1 : an adventure serial or melodrama; esp : one presented in installments each ending in suspense   2 : a contest whose outcome is in doubt up to the very end; broadly : a suspenseful situation — cliff–hang·ing \-iŋ\ adj

cliff swallow n (1825) : a colonial swallow (Petrochelidon pyrrhonota) of the New World with a pale buff rump and dark throat patch that builds mud nests like jugs esp. under eaves and on cliffs

¹cli·mac·ter·ic \klī-'mak-t(ə-)rik; ˌklī-ˌmak-'ter-ik, -'tir-\ adj [L climactericus, fr. Gk klimaktērikos, fr. klimaktēr critical point, lit., rung of a ladder, fr. klimak-, klimax ladder] (1582)   1 : constituting or relating to a climacteric   2 : CRITICAL, CRUCIAL

²climacteric n (ca. 1630)   1   a : a major turning point or critical stage   2 : MENOPAUSE; also : a corresponding period in the male usu. occurring with less well-defined physiological and psychological changes   3 : the marked and sudden rise in the respiratory rate of fruit just prior to full ripening

cli·mac·tic \klī-'mak-tik, klə-\ adj (1872) : of, relating to, or constituting a climax — cli·mac·ti·cal·ly \-ti-k(ə-)lē\ adv

cli·mate \'klī-mət\ n [ME climat, fr. MF, fr. LL climat-, clima, fr. Gk klimat-, klima inclination, latitude, climate, fr. klinein to lean — more at LEAN] (14c)   1 : a region of the earth having specified climatic conditions   2   a : the average course or condition of the weather at a place usu. over a period of years as exhibited by temperature, wind velocity, and precipitation   b : the prevailing set of conditions (as of temperature and humidity) indoors ⟨a climate-controlled office⟩   3 : the prevailing influence or environmental conditions characterizing a group or period : ATMOSPHERE ⟨a ~ of fear⟩

cli·mat·ic \klī-'ma-tik, klə-\ adj (ca. 1828)   1 : of or relating to climate   2 : resulting from or influenced by the climate rather than the soil ⟨forests that had reverted to the ~ type⟩ — compare EDAPHIC 2 — cli·mat·i·cal·ly \-ti-k(ə-)lē\ adv

climatic climax n (ca. 1928) : the one of the ecological climaxes possible in a particular climatic area whose stability is directly due to the influence of climate — compare EDAPHIC CLIMAX

cli·ma·tol·o·gy \ˌklī-mə-'tä-lə-jē\ n (1843) : the science that deals with climates and their phenomena — cli·ma·to·log·i·cal \ˌklī-mə-tə-'lä-ji-kəl\ adj — cli·ma·to·log·i·cal·ly \-k(ə-)lē\ adv — cli·ma·tol·o·gist \-mə-'tä-lə-jist\ n

¹cli·max \'klī-ˌmaks\ n [L, fr. Gk klimax ladder, fr. klinein to lean] (ca. 1550)   1   a : a figure of speech in which a series of phrases or sentences is arranged in ascending order of rhetorical forcefulness   2   a : the highest point : CULMINATION   b : the point of highest dramatic tension or a major turning point in the action (as of a play)   c : ORGASM   d : MENOPAUSE   3 : a relatively stable ecological stage or community esp. of plants that is achieved through successful adjustment to an environment; esp : the final stage in ecological succession   syn see SUMMIT — cli·max·less adj

²climax vt (1835) : to bring to a climax ⟨~ed his boxing career with a knockout⟩   ~ vi : to come to a climax ⟨a riot ~ing in the destruction of several houses⟩

¹climb \'klīm\ vb [ME, fr. OE climban; prob. akin to OE clifian to adhere — more at CLEAVE] vi (bef. 12c)   1   a : to go upward with gradual or continuous progress : RISE, ASCEND   b : to increase gradually   c : to slope upward   2   a : to go upward or raise oneself esp. by grasping or clutching with the hands ⟨~ed upon her father's knee⟩   b of a plant : to ascend in growth (as by twining)   3 : to go about or down usu. by grasping or holding with the hands ⟨~ down the ladder⟩   4 : to get into or out of clothing usu. with some haste or effort ⟨the firemen ~ed into their clothes⟩   ~ vt   1 : to go upward on or along, to the top of, or over ⟨~ a hill⟩   2 : to draw or pull oneself up, over, or to the top of by using hands and feet ⟨children ~ing the tree⟩   3 : to grow up or over — climb·able \'klī-mə-bəl\ adj

²climb n (ca. 1587)   1 : a place where climbing is necessary to progress   2 : the act or an instance of climbing : RISE, ASCENT

climb·er \'klī-mər\ n (15c)   1   a : one that climbs or helps in climbing   b : a vine or twining plant (as a rose or sweet pea) that readily grows up a support or over other plants   2 : one who attempts to gain a superior social or business position

climbing iron n (1857) : a steel framework with spikes attached that may be affixed to one's boots for climbing (as a pole or tree)

clime \'klīm\ n [LL clima] (14c) : CLIMATE ⟨traveled to warmer ~s⟩

-clinal adj comb form [ISV, fr. Gk klinein to lean — more at LEAN] : sloping ⟨isoclinal⟩

¹clinch \'klinch\ vb [prob. alter. of clench] vt (1542)   1 : CLENCH 3   a : to turn over or flatten the protruding pointed end of (a driven nail); also : to treat (as a screw, bolt, or rivet) in a similar way   b : to fasten in this way   3   a : to make final or irrefutable : SETTLE ⟨that ~ed the argument⟩   b : to secure conclusively : WIN   ~ vi   1 : to hold an opponent (as in boxing) at close quarters with one or both arms   2 : to hold fast or firmly — clinch·ing·ly \'klin-chiŋ-lē\ adv

²clinch n (1659)   1 : a fastening by means of a clinched nail, rivet, or bolt; also : the clinched part of a nail, rivet, or bolt   2 archaic : PUN   3 : an act or instance of clinching in boxing   4 : EMBRACE

clinch·er \'klin-chər\ n (1737) : one that clinches: as   a : a decisive fact, argument, act, or remark ⟨the expense was the ~ that persuaded us to give up the enterprise⟩   b : a tire with flanged beads fitting into the wheel rim

cline \'klīn\ n [Gk klinein] (1938) : a gradient of morphological or physiological change in a group of related organisms usu. along a line of environmental or geographic transition — clin·al \'klī-nᵊl\ adj — clin·al·ly \-nᵊl-ē\ adv

-cline n comb form [back-formation fr. -clinal] : slope ⟨monocline⟩

¹cling \'kliŋ\ vi clung \'kləŋ\; cling·ing \'kliŋ\ [ME, fr. OE clingan; akin to OHG klunga tangled ball of thread] (bef. 12c)   1   a : to hold together   b : to adhere as if glued firmly   c : to hold or hold on tightly or tenaciously   2   a : to have a strong emotional attachment or dependence   b : to remain or linger as if resisting complete dissipation or dispersal ⟨the odor clung to the room for hours⟩   syn see STICK — cling·er \'kliŋ-ər\ n — clingy \'kliŋ-ē\ adj

²cling n (ca. 1625) : an act or instance of clinging : ADHERENCE

cling·stone \'kliŋ-ˌstōn\ n (1705) : any of various stone fruits (as some peaches or plums) with flesh that adheres strongly to the pit

clin·ic \'kli-nik\ n [F clinique, fr. Gk klinikē medical practice at the sickbed, fr. fem. of klinikos of a bed, fr. klinē bed, fr. klinein to lean, recline — more at LEAN] (ca. 1843)   1 : a class of medical instruction in which patients are examined and discussed   2 : a group meeting devoted to the analysis and solution of concrete problems or to the acquiring of specific skills or knowledge ⟨writing ~s⟩ ⟨golf ~s⟩   3

: a facility (as of a hospital) for diagnosis and treatment of outpatients **b** : a group practice in which several physicians work cooperatively

-clinic *adj comb form* [ISV, fr. Gk *klinein*] **1** : inclining : dipping **2** : having (so many) oblique intersections of the axes ⟨mono*clinic*⟩ ⟨tri*clinic*⟩

clin·i·cal \'kli-ni-kəl\ *adj* (ca. 1780) **1** : of, relating to, or conducted in or as if in a clinic: as   **a** : involving direct observation of the patient   **b** : diagnosable by or based on clinical observation   **2** : analytical or coolly dispassionate ⟨a ~ attitude⟩ — **clin·i·cal·ly** \-k(ə-)lē\ *adv*

clinical thermometer *n* (1878) : a thermometer for measuring body temperature that has a constriction in the tube where the column of liquid breaks when the temperature drops from its maximum and that continues to indicate the maximum temperature by the part of the column above the constriction until reset by shaking

cli·ni·cian \kli-'ni-shən\ *n* (1875) **1** : a person qualified in the clinical practice of medicine, psychiatry, or psychology as distinguished from one specializing in laboratory or research techniques or in theory **2** : a person who conducts a clinic

clin·i·co·path·o·log·ic \,kli-ni-(,)kō-,pa-thə-'lä-jik\ *or* **clin·i·co·path·o·log·i·cal** \-'lä-ji-kəl\ *adj* [*clinical*] (1898) : relating to or concerned both with the signs and symptoms directly observable by the physician and with the results of laboratory examination — **clin·i·co·path·o·log·i·cal·ly** \-ji-k(ə-)lē\ *adv*

¹clink \'kliŋk\ *vb* [ME, of imit. origin] *vi* (14c) : to give out a slight sharp short metallic sound ~ *vt* : to cause to clink

²clink *n* (15c) : a clinking sound

³clink *n* [prob. fr. *Clink*, a prison in Southwark, London, England] (1515) **1** *slang* : a prison cell **2** *slang* : JAIL, PRISON

¹clin·ker \'kliŋ-kər\ *n* [alter. of earlier *klincard* a hard yellowish Dutch brick] (1641) **1** : a brick that has been burned too much in the kiln **2** : stony matter fused together : SLAG

²clink·er \'kliŋ-kər\ *n* [¹*clink*] (1733) **1** *Brit* : something first-rate **2 a** : a wrong note **b** : a serious mistake or error : BONER **c** : an utter failure : FLOP **d** : something of poor quality

clink·er–built \-,bilt\ *adj* [*clinker*, n., clinch] (1769) : having the external planks or plates overlapping like the clapboards on a house ⟨a ~ boat⟩

clink·ety–clank \'kliŋ-kə-tē-'klaŋk\ *n* [imit.] (1901) : a repeated usu. rhythmic clanking sound ⟨the ~ of a loose tire chain⟩

cli·nom·e·ter \kli-'nä-mə-tər\ *n* [Gk *klinein* to lean] (1811) : any of various instruments for measuring angles of elevation or inclination

-clinous *adj comb form* [prob. fr. NL *-clinus*, fr. Gk *klinē* bed — more at CLINIC] : having the androecium and gynoecium in a (single or different) flower or (two separate) flowers ⟨di*clinous*⟩

¹clin·quant \'kliŋ-kənt, klaⁿ-'käⁿ\ *adj* [MF, fr. prp. of *clinquer* to glitter, lit., to clink, of imit. origin] (1591) : glittering with gold or tinsel

²clinquant *n* [F, fr. *clinquant*, adj.] (1682) : TINSEL

clin·to·nia \klin-'tō-nē-ə\ *n* [NL, genus name, fr. DeWitt *Clinton*] (1843) : any of a genus (*Clintonia*) of herbs of the lily family with yellow or white flowers

Clio \'kli-(,)ō, 'klē-\ *n* [L, fr. Gk *Kleiō*] **1** : the Greek Muse of history **2** *pl* **Cli·os** : a statuette awarded annually by a professional organization for notable achievement in radio and television commercials

clio·met·rics \,kli-ə-'me-triks\ *n pl but sing in constr* [*Clio* + *-metrics* (as in *econometrics*)] (1966) : the application of methods developed in other fields (as economics, statistics, and data processing) to the study of history — **clio·met·ric** \-trik\ *adj* — **clio·met·ri·cian** \-me-'tri-shən\ *n*

¹clip \'klip\ *vt* **clipped; clip·ping** [ME *clippen*, fr. OE *clyppan*; akin to OHG *kläftra* fathom, Lith *globti* to embrace] (bef. 12c) **1** : ENCOMPASS **2 a** : to hold in a tight grip : CLUTCH **b** : to clasp or fasten with a clip

²clip *n* (15c) **1** : any of various devices that grip, clasp, or hook **2** : a device to hold cartridges for charging the magazines of some rifles; *also* : a magazine from which ammunition is fed into the chamber of a firearm **3** : a piece of jewelry held in position by a clip

³clip *vb* **clipped; clip·ping** [ME *clippen*, fr. ON *klippa*] *vt* (13c) **1 a** : to cut or cut off with or as if with shears ⟨~ a dog's hair⟩ ⟨~ an hour off traveling time⟩ **b** : to cut off the distal or outer part of **c** (1) : ³EXCISE ·(2) : to cut items out of (as a newspaper) **2 a** : CURTAIL, DIMINISH **b** : to abbreviate in speech or writing **3** : HIT, PUNCH **4** : to illegally block (an opposing player) in football **5** : to make money from unfairly or dishonestly esp. by overcharging ⟨the nightclub *clipped* the tourist for $200⟩ ~ *vi* **1** : to clip something **2** : to travel or pass rapidly **3** : to clip an opposing player in football

⁴clip *n* (15c) **1 a** *pl*, *Scot* : SHEARS **b** : a 2-bladed instrument for cutting esp. the nails **2** : something that is clipped: as   **a** : the product of a single shearing (as of sheep) **b** : a crop of wool of a sheep, a flock, or a region   **c** : a section of filmed or videotaped material **d** : a clipping esp. from a newspaper **3** : an act of clipping **4** : a sharp blow **5** : RATE 4a ⟨continues at a brisk ~⟩ **6** : a single instance or occasion : TIME ⟨he charged $10 a ~⟩ — often used in the phrase *at a clip* ⟨trained 1000 workers at a ~⟩

clip·board \'klip-,bȯrd, -,bȯrd\ *n* (1896) : a small writing board with a clip at the top for holding papers

clip–clop \'klip-,kläp\ *n* [imit.] (1884) : the sound made by or as if by a horse walking on a hard surface — **clip–clop** *vi*

clip joint *n* (1933) **1** *slang* : a place of public entertainment (as a nightclub) that makes a practice of defrauding patrons (as by overcharging) **2** *slang* : a business that makes a practice of overcharging

clip–on \'klip-,pȯn, -,pän\ *adj* (1909) : of or relating to something that attaches with a clip ⟨a ~ tie⟩ ⟨~ earrings⟩ — **clip–on** *n*

clip·per \'kli-pər\ *n* (14c) **1** : one that clips something **2** : an implement for clipping esp. hair, fingernails, or toenails — usu. used in pl. **3 a** : one that moves swiftly **b** : a fast sailing ship; *esp* : one with long slender lines, an overhanging bow, tall masts, and a large sail area

clip·ping \'kli-piŋ\ *n* (15c) : something that is clipped off or out of something; *esp* : an item clipped from a publication

clip·sheet \'klip-,shēt\ *n* (1926) : a sheet of newspaper material issued by an organization for clipping and reprinting

clique \'klēk, 'klik\ *n* [F] (1711) : a narrow exclusive circle or group of persons; *esp* : one held together by common interests, views, or purposes — **cliqu·ey** *also* **cliquy** \'klē-kē, 'kli-\ *adj* — **cliqu·ish** \'kli-kish\ *adj* — **cliqu·ish·ly** *adv* — **cliqu·ish·ness** *n*

cli·tel·lum \kli-'te-ləm\ *n*, *pl* **-la** \-lə\ [NL, modif. of L *clitellae* pack-saddle] (1839) : a thickened glandular section of the body wall of some annelids that secretes a viscid sac in which the eggs are deposited

clit·ic \'kli-tik\ *n* [*enclitic* or *proclitic*] (1946) : a word that is treated in pronunciation as forming a part of a neighboring word and that is often unaccented or contracted

clit·o·ri·dec·to·my \,kli-tə-ri-'dek-tə-mē\ *also* **clit·o·rec·to·my** \,kli-tə-'rek-tə-mē\ *n*, *pl* **-mies** : excision of all or part of the clitoris

clit·o·ris \'kli-tə-rəs, kli-'tȯr-əs\ *n*, *pl* **clit·o·ri·des** \kli-'tȯr-ə-,dēz\ [NL, fr. Gk *kleitoris*] (1615) : a small erectile organ at the anterior or ventral part of the vulva homologous to the penis — **clit·o·ral** \'kli-tə-rəl\ *or* **clit·or·ic** \kli-'tȯr-ik, -'tär-\ *adj*

clo·a·ca \klō-'ā-kə\ *n*, *pl* **-a·cae** \-,kē, -,sē\ [L; akin to Gk *klyzein* to wash — more at CLYSTER] (1599) **1** : ³SEWER **2** [NL, fr. L] : the common chamber into which the intestinal, urinary, and generative canals discharge in birds, reptiles, amphibians, and many fishes; *also* : a comparable chamber of an invertebrate — **clo·a·cal** \-'ā-kəl\ *adj*

¹cloak \'klōk\ *n* [ME *cloke*, fr. ONF *cloque* bell, cloak, fr. ML *clocca* bell; fr. its shape] (13c) **1** : a loose outer garment **2** : something that conceals : PRETENSE, DISGUISE

²cloak *vt* (1509) : to cover or hide with or as if with a cloak   *syn* see DISGUISE

cloak–and–dagger *adj* (1860) : dealing in or suggestive of melodramatic intrigue and action usu. involving secret agents and espionage — **cloak–and–dagger** *n*

cloak·room \'klōk-,rüm, -,rüm\ *n* (ca. 1852) **1 a** : a room in which outdoor clothing may be placed during one's stay **b** : a room or cubicle where garments, parcels, and luggage may be checked for temporary safekeeping **2** : an anteroom of a legislative chamber where members may relax and confer with colleagues **3** *Brit* : LAVATORY 2

¹clob·ber \'klä-bər\ *n* [origin unknown] (1879) *slang Brit* : CLOTHES 1

²clobber *vt* **clob·bered; clob·ber·ing** \-b(ə-)riŋ\ [origin unknown] (ca. 1943) **1** : to pound mercilessly; *also* : to hit with force : SMASH **2** : to defeat overwhelmingly

clo·chard \klō-'shär\ *n* [F, fr. *clocher* to limp, fr. (assumed) VL *cloppicare*, fr. LL *cloppus* lame] (1937) : TRAMP, VAGRANT

cloche \'klōsh\ *n* [F, lit., bell, fr. ML *clocca*] (1882) **1** : a transparent plant cover used outdoors esp. for protection against cold **2** : a woman's small close-fitting hat usu. with deep rounded crown and very narrow brim

¹clock \'kläk\ *n*, *often attrib* [ME *clok*, fr. MD *clocke* bell, clock, fr. ONF or ML; ONF *cloque* bell, fr. ML *clocca*, of Celt origin; akin to MIr *clocc* bell] (14c) **1** : a device other than a watch for indicating or measuring time commonly by means of hands moving on a dial; *broadly* : any periodic system by which time is measured **2** : a registering device usu. with a dial; *specif* : ODOMETER **3** : TIME CLOCK **4** : a synchronizing device (as in a computer) that produces pulses at regular intervals **5** : BIOLOGICAL CLOCK — **around the clock** *also* **round the clock** **1** : continuously for 24 hours : day and night without cessation **2** : without relaxation and heedless of time — **kill the clock** *or* **run out the clock** : to use up as much as possible of the playing time remaining in a game (as football) while retaining possession of the ball or puck esp. to protect a lead

²clock *vt* (1883) **1** : to time with a stopwatch or by an electric timing device **2** : to register on a mechanical recording device ⟨wind velocities were ~ed at 80 miles per hour⟩ **3** : to hit hard **4** *chiefly Brit* : ATTAIN, REALIZE — usu. used with *up* ⟨just ~ed up a million . . . paperback sales —*Punch*⟩ ~ *vi* : to register on a time sheet or time clock : PUNCH — used with *in, out, on, off* ⟨he ~ed in late⟩ — **clock·er** *n*

³clock *n* [perh. fr. ¹*clock*] (1530) : an ornamental figure on the ankle or side of a stocking or sock

clock·like \'kläk-,līk\ *adj* (ca. 1770) : unusually regular, undeviating, and precise ⟨does his job with ~ efficiency⟩

clock radio *n* (1949) : a combination clock and radio device in which the clock can be set to turn on the radio at a designated time

clock–watch·er \-,wä-chər\ *n* (1911) : a person (as a worker or student) who keeps close watch on the passage of time — **clock–watch·ing** \-chiŋ\ *n*

clock·wise \'kläk-,wīz\ *adv* (1888) : in the direction which the hands of a clock rotate as viewed from in front or as if standing on a clock face — **clockwise** *adj*

clock·work \-,wərk\ *n* (1628) **1** : the inner workings of something **2** : the machinery (as springs and a train of gears) that run a clock; *also* : a similar mechanism running a mechanical device (as a toy) **3** : the precision, regularity, or absence of variation associated with a clock or clockwork ⟨a ~ operation⟩ ⟨the planning went like ~⟩

clod \'kläd\ *n* [ME *clodde*, fr. OE *clod-* (in *clodhamer* fieldfare)] (15c) **1 a** : a lump or mass esp. of earth or clay **b** : SOIL, EARTH **2** : OAF, DOLT — **clod·dish** \'klä-dish\ *adj* — **clod·dish·ness** *n* — **clod·dy** \'klä-dē\ *adj*

clod·hop·per \'kläd-,hä-pər\ *n* (1721) **1** : a clumsy and uncouth rustic **2** : a large heavy work shoe or boot

clod·hop·ping \-,hä-piŋ\ *adj* (1843) : BOORISH, RUDE

clod·poll *or* **clod·pole** \'kläd-,pōl\ *n* (1601) : BLOCKHEAD

clo·fi·brate \klō-'fi-,brāt, -'fi-\ *n* [perh. fr. *chlor-* + *fibr-* + ¹*-ate*] (1964) : a compound $C_{12}H_{15}ClO_3$ used esp. to lower abnormally high concentrations of fats and cholesterol in the blood

¹clog \'kläg, 'klȯg\ *n* [ME *clogge* short thick piece of wood] (14c) **1 a** : a weight attached esp. to an animal to hinder motion **b** : something that shackles or impedes : ENCUMBRANCE 1 **2** : a shoe, sandal, or overshoe having a thick typically wooden sole

²clog *vb* **clogged; clog·ging** *vt* (1526) **1 a** : to impede with a clog : HINDER **b** : to halt or retard the progress, operation, or growth of : ENCUMBER ⟨restraints that have been *clogging* the market —T. W. Arnold⟩ **2** : to fill beyond capacity : OVERLOAD ⟨cars *clogged* the main street⟩ ⟨a speech *clogged* with clichés⟩ ~ *vi* **1** : to become filled with

\ə\ abut \ᵊ\ kitten, F table \ər\ further \a\ ash \ā\ ace \ä\ mop, mar \au̇\ out \ch\ chin \e\ bet \ē\ easy \g\ go \i\ hit \ī\ ice \j\ job \ŋ\ sing \ō\ go \ȯ\ law \ȯi\ boy \th\ thin \t͟h\ the \ü\ loot \u̇\ foot \y\ yet \zh\ vision \à, ᵏ, ⁿ, œ, œ̄, ᵫ, ᵬ, ᐟ\ *see* Guide to Pronunciation extraneous matter **2 :** to unite in a mass : CLOT **3 :** to dance a clog dance *syn* see HAMPER — **clog·ger** \'klä-gər, 'klò-\ *n*

clog dance *n* (1869) : a dance in which the performer wears clogs and beats out a clattering rhythm on the floor — **clog dancer** *n* — **clog dancing** *n*

cloi·son·né *also* **cloi·son·ne** \ˌklȯi-zə-'nā, ˌklwä-\ *adj* [F, fr. pp. of *cloisonner* to partition] (1863) : of, relating to, or being a style of enamel decoration in which the enamel is applied and fired in raised cells (as of soldered wires) on a usu. metal background — compare CHAMPLEVÉ — **cloisonné** *n*

¹clois·ter \'klȯi-stər\ *n* [ME *cloistre*, fr. OF, fr. ML *claustrum*, fr. L, bar, bolt, fr. *claudere* to close — more at CLOSE] (13c) **1 a :** a monastic establishment **b :** an area within a monastery or convent to which the religious are normally restricted **c :** monastic life **d :** a place or state of seclusion **2 :** a covered passage on the side of a court usu. having one side walled and the other an open arcade or colonnade

cloister 2

²cloister *vt* **clois·tered; clois·ter·ing** \-st(ə-)riŋ\ (1581) **1 :** to seclude from the world in or as if in a cloister ⟨a scientist who ~s herself in a laboratory⟩ **2 :** to surround with a cloister ⟨~ed gardens⟩

clois·tered \'klȯi-stərd\ *adj* (1581) **1 :** being or living in or as if in a cloister **2 :** providing shelter from contact with the outside world ⟨the ~ atmosphere of a small college⟩

clois·tral \'klȯi-strəl\ *adj* (1605) : of, relating to, or suggestive of a cloister

clois·tress \'klȯi-strəs\ *n* (1601) *obs* : NUN

clo·mi·phene \'klō-mə-ˌfēn\ *n* [*chlor-* + *amine* + *-phene* (fr. *phenyl*)] (1963) : a synthetic drug $C_{26}H_{28}ClNO$ used in the form of its citrate to induce ovulation

clomp \'klämp, 'klȯmp, 'kləmp\ *vi* [by alter.] (1829) : CLUMP 1

¹clone \'klōn\ *n* [Gk *klōn* twig, slip; akin to Gk *klan* to break — more at CLAST] (1903) **1 a :** the aggregate of the asexually produced progeny of an individual; *also* : a group of replicas of all or part of a macromolecule (as DNA or an antibody) **b :** an individual grown from a single somatic cell of its parent and genetically identical to it **2 :** one that appears to be a copy of an original form ⟨a ~ of a personal computer⟩ — **clon·al** \'klō-n²l\ *adj* — **clon·al·ly** \-n²l-ē\ *adv*

²clone *vb* **cloned; clon·ing** *vt* (ca. 1948) **1 :** to propagate a clone from **2 :** to make a copy of ~ *vi* : to produce a clone

clo·ni·dine \'klä-nə-ˌdēn, 'klō-, -ˌdin\ *n* [*chlor-* + *aniline* + *imide* + *²-ine*] (1970) : an antihypertensive drug $C_9H_9Cl_2N_3$ used to treat essential hypertension, to prevent migraine headache, and to diminish withdrawal symptoms

clonk \'kläŋk, 'klòŋk\ *vb* [imit.] *vi* (1930) : to make a dull hollow thumping sound ~ *vt* : to cause to clonk — **clonk** *n*

clo·nus \'klō-nəs\ *n* [NL, fr. Gk *klonos* agitation — more at HOLD] (1817) : a rapid succession of alternating contractions and partial relaxations of a muscle occurring in some nervous diseases — **clon·ic** \'klä-nik\ *adj* — **clo·nic·i·ty** \klō-'ni-sə-tē, klä-\ *n*

cloot \'klüt\ *n* [prob. of Scand origin; akin to ON *klō* claw — more at CLAW] (1725) **1** *Scot* : a cloven hoof **2** *pl, cap, Scot* : CLOOTIE

Cloot·ie \'klü-tē\ *n* [dim. of *cloot*] *chiefly Scot* — used as a name of the devil

clop \'kläp\ *n* [imit.] (1899) : a sound made by or as if by a hoof or wooden shoe against the pavement — **clop** *vi*

clop-clop \'kläp-ˌkläp\ *n* (1901) : a sound of rhythmically repeated clops — **clop-clop** *vi*

clo·que *also* **clo·qué** \klō-'kā, 'klō-\ *n* [F *cloqué*, fr. pp. of *cloquer* to become blistered, fr. F dial. (Picard) *cloque* bell, bubble, fr. ML *clocca* bell — more at CLOCK] (1936) **1 :** a fabric with an embossed design **2 :** a fabric esp. of piqué with small woven figures

¹close \'klōz\ *vb* **closed; clos·ing** [ME, fr. OF *clos-*, stem of *clore*, fr. L *claudere* to shut, close; perh. akin to Gk *kleiein* to close — more at CLAVICLE] *vt* (13c) **1 a :** to move so as to bar passage through something ⟨~ the gate⟩ **b :** to block against entry or passage ⟨~ a street⟩ **c :** to deny access to ⟨the city *closed* the beach⟩ **d :** SCREEN, EXCLUDE ⟨~ a view⟩ **e :** to suspend or stop the operations of ⟨~ school⟩ — often used with *down* **2** *archaic* : ENCLOSE, CONTAIN **3 a :** to bring to an end or period ⟨~ an account⟩ **b :** to conclude discussion or negotiation about ⟨the question is *closed*⟩; *also* : to consummate by performing something previously agreed ⟨~ a transfer of real estate title⟩ **c :** to terminate access to ⟨a computer file⟩ **4 a :** to bring or bind together the parts or edges of ⟨a *closed* book⟩ **b :** to fill up (as an opening) **c :** to make complete by circling or enveloping or by making continuous ⟨~ a circuit⟩ **d :** to reduce to nil ⟨*closed* the distance to the lead racer⟩ ~ *vi* **1 a :** to contract, fold, swing, or slide so as to leave no opening ⟨the door *closed* quietly⟩ **b :** to cease operation ⟨the factory *closed* down⟩ ⟨the stores ~ at 9 p.m.⟩ **2 a :** to draw near ⟨the ship was *closing* with the island⟩ **b :** to engage in a struggle at close quarters : GRAPPLE ⟨~ with the enemy⟩ **3 a :** to come together : MEET **b :** to draw the free foot up to the supporting foot in dancing **4 :** to enter into or complete an agreement **5 :** to come to an end or period **6 :** to reduce a gap ⟨*closed* to within two points⟩ — **clos·able** *or* **close·able** \'klō-zə-bəl\ *adj* — **clos·er** *n* — **close one's doors 1** : to refuse admission ⟨the nation *closed* its doors to immigrants⟩ **2 :** to go out of business — **close one's eyes to** : to ignore deliberately — **close ranks** : to unite in a concerted stand esp. to meet a challenge — **close the door** : to be uncompromisingly obstructive ⟨*closed the door* to further negotiation⟩

syn CLOSE, END, CONCLUDE, FINISH, COMPLETE, TERMINATE mean to bring or come to a stopping point or limit. CLOSE usu. implies that something has been in some way open as well as unfinished ⟨*close* a debate⟩. END conveys a strong sense of finality ⟨*ended* his life⟩. CONCLUDE may imply a formal closing (as of a meeting) ⟨the service *concluded* with a blessing⟩. FINISH may stress completion of a final step in a process ⟨after it is painted, the house will be *finished*⟩. COMPLETE implies the removal of all deficiencies or a successful finishing of what has

been undertaken ⟨the resolving of this last issue *completes* the agreement⟩. TERMINATE implies the setting of a limit in time or space ⟨your employment *terminates* after three months⟩.

²close \'klōz\ *n* (14c) **1 a :** a coming or bringing to a conclusion ⟨at the ~ of the party⟩ **b :** a conclusion or end in time or existence : CESSATION ⟨the decade drew to a ~⟩ **c :** the concluding passage (as of a speech or play) **2 :** the conclusion of a musical strain or period : CADENCE **3** *archaic* : a hostile encounter **4 :** the movement of the free foot in dancing toward or into contact with the supporting foot

³close \'klōs, *U.S. also* 'klōz\ *n* [ME *clos*, lit., enclosure, fr. OF *clos*, fr. L *clausum*, fr. neut. of *clausus*, pp.] (13c) **1 a :** an enclosed area **b** *chiefly Brit* : the precinct of a cathedral **2** *chiefly Brit* **a :** a narrow passage leading from a street to a court and the houses within or to the common stairway of tenements **b :** a road closed at one end

⁴close \'klōs\ *adj* **clos·er; clos·est** [ME *clos*, fr. MF, fr. L *clausus*, pp. of *claudere*] (14c) **1 :** having no openings : CLOSED **2 a :** confined or carefully guarded ⟨~ arrest⟩ **b** (1) *of a vowel* : HIGH 13 (2) : formed with the tongue in a higher position than for the other vowel of a pair **3 :** restricted to a privileged class **4 a :** SECLUDED, SECRET **b :** SECRETIVE ⟨she could tell us something if she would . . . but she was as ~ as wax —A. Conan Doyle⟩ **5 :** STRICT, RIGOROUS ⟨keep ~ watch⟩ **6 :** hot and stuffy **7 :** not generous in giving or spending : TIGHT **8 :** having little space between items or units ⟨a ~ weave⟩ **9 a :** fitting tightly or exactly **b :** very short or near to the surface ⟨a ~ haircut⟩ **10 :** being near in time, space, effect, or degree **11 :** INTIMATE, FAMILIAR **12 a :** ACCURATE, PRECISE ⟨a ~ study⟩ **b :** marked by fidelity to an original ⟨a ~ copy of an old master⟩ **c :** TERSE, COMPACT **13 :** decided or won by a narrow margin ⟨a ~ baseball game⟩ **14 :** difficult to obtain ⟨money is ~⟩ **15** *of punctuation* : characterized by liberal use esp. of commas *syn* see STINGY — **close·ly** *adv* — **close·ness** *n* — **close to home** : within one's personal interests so that one is strongly affected ⟨the speaker's remarks hit *close to home*⟩ — **close to the vest** : in a reserved or cautious manner

⁵close \'klōs\ *adv* (15c) : in a close position or manner

close call \'klōs-\ *n* (1881) : a narrow escape

close corporation \'klōs-\ *n* (ca. 1902) : a corporation whose stock is not publicly traded but held by a few persons (as those in management)

close-cropped \'klōs-ˌkräpt\ *adj* (ca. 1893) **1 :** clipped short **2 :** having the hair clipped short

closed \'klōzd\ *adj* (13c) **1 a :** not open **b :** ENCLOSED **c :** composed entirely of closed tubes or vessels ⟨a ~ circulatory system⟩ **2 a :** forming a self-contained unit allowing no additions ⟨~ association⟩ **b** (1) : traced by a moving point that returns to an arbitrary starting point ⟨~ curve⟩; *also* : so formed that every plane section is a closed curve ⟨~ surface⟩ (2) : characterized by mathematical elements that when subjected to an operation produce only elements of the same set ⟨the set of whole numbers is ~ under addition and multiplication⟩ (3) : containing all the limit points of every possible subset ⟨a ~ interval contains its endpoints⟩ **c :** characterized by continuous return and reuse of the working substance ⟨a ~ cooling system⟩ **d** *of a racecourse* : having the same starting and finishing point **3 a :** confined to a few ⟨~ membership⟩ **b :** excluding participation of outsiders or witnesses : conducted in strict secrecy **c :** rigidly excluding outside influence ⟨a ~ mind⟩ **4 :** ending in a consonant ⟨~ syllable⟩

closed book *n* (1913) : something beyond comprehension : ENIGMA

closed–cap·tioned \'klōz(d)-'kap-shənd\ *adj* (1980) *of a television program* : broadcast with captions that appear only on the screen of a receiver equipped with a decoder

closed–cir·cuit \-'sər-kət\ *adj* (1949) : used in, shown on, or being a television installation in which the signal is transmitted by wire to a limited number of receivers

closed corporation *n* (1924) : CLOSE CORPORATION

closed couplet *n* (1910) : a rhymed couplet in which the sense is complete

closed–door \'klōz(d)-'dòr, -'dòr\ *adj* (1950) : barring public and press ⟨a ~ session of the investigating committee⟩

closed–end \'klōz(d)-'end\ *adj* (ca. 1938) : having a fixed capitalization of shares that are traded on the market at prices determined by the operation of the law of supply and demand ⟨a ~ investment company⟩ — compare OPEN-END

closed loop *n* (1951) : an automatic control system for an operation or process in which feedback in a closed path or group of paths acts to maintain output at a desired level

closed–down \'klōz-ˌdaún\ *n* (1889) : an instance of suspending or stopping operations

closed shop *n* (1904) : an establishment in which the employer by agreement hires only union members in good standing

closed stance *n* (ca. 1934) : a stance (as in golf) in which the forward foot is closer to the line of play than the back foot — compare OPEN STANCE

close-fist·ed \'klōs-ˌfis-təd\ *adj* (1608) : STINGY, TIGHTFISTED

close-grained \-'grānd\ *adj* (1754) : having a compacted smooth texture; *esp* : having narrow annual rings or small wood elements

close-hauled \-'hòld\ *adj* (1769) : having the sails set for sailing as nearly against the wind as the vessel will go

close–in \'klōs-'in\ *adj* (1945) : near a center of activity and esp. a city ⟨~ suburbs⟩

close in \'klōz-\ *vt* (14c) **1 :** to encircle closely and isolate **2 :** to enshroud to such an extent as to preclude entrance or exit ⟨the airport was *closed in* by the storm⟩ ~ *vi* **1 :** to gather in close all around with an oppressing or isolating effect ⟨despair *closed in* on her⟩ **2 :** to approach to close quarters esp. for an attack, raid, or arrest ⟨the police *closed in*⟩ **3 :** to grow dark ⟨the short November day was already *closing in* —Ellen Glasgow⟩

close–knit \'klōs-'nit\ *adj* (1926) : bound together by intimate social or cultural ties or by close economic or political ties ⟨~ families⟩

closely held *adj* (1946) : having most stock shares and voting rights in the hands of a few ⟨a *closely held* business⟩

close-mouthed \'klōs-'maúthd, -'maútht\ *adj* (1881) : cautious in speaking : UNCOMMUNICATIVE; *also* : SECRETIVE

close order *n* (ca. 1797) : an arrangement of troops in a typical marching formation

close-out \'klō-,zaut\ *n* (1925) **1** : a clearing out by a sale usu. at reduced prices of the whole remaining stock (as of a business) **2** : an article offered or bought at a closeout

close out \'klōz-\ *vt* (14c) **1 a** : EXCLUDE **b** : PRECLUDE ⟨*close out* his chances⟩ **2 a** : to dispose of a whole stock of by sale **b** : to dispose of (a business) **c** : SELL ⟨*closed out* his share of the business⟩ **d** : to put (an account) in order for disposal or transfer **3 a** : to bring to an often rapid or abrupt conclusion **b** : to discontinue operation of ∼ *vi* **1** : to sell out a business **2** : to buy or sell securities or commodities in order to terminate an account

close quarters \'klōs-\ *n pl* (1809) : immediate contact or close range ⟨fought at *close quarters*⟩

close shave \'klōs-, 'klōsh-\ *n* (1834) : a narrow escape

close-stool \'klōs-,stül\ *n* (15c) : a stool holding a chamber pot

¹**clos-et** \'klä-zət, 'klo-\ *n* [ME, fr. MF, dim. of *clos* enclosure — more at CLOSE] (14c) **1 a** : an apartment or small room for privacy **b** : a monarch's or official's private chamber **2** : a cabinet or recess for esp. china, household utensils, or clothing **3** : a place of retreat or privacy **4** : WATER CLOSET **5** : a state or condition of secrecy, privacy, or obscurity ⟨came out of the ∼⟩ — **clos-et-ful** \-,fül\ *n*

²**closet** *vt* (1595) **1** : to shut up in or as if in a closet **2** : to take into a closet for a secret interview

³**closet** *adj* (ca. 1615) **1** : closely private **2** : working in or suited to the closet as the place of seclusion or study : THEORETICAL **3** : being so in private ⟨a ∼ racist⟩

closet drama *n* (1922) : drama suited primarily for reading rather than production

closet queen *n* (1967) : one who secretly engages in homosexual activities while leading an ostensibly heterosexual life — often used disparagingly

¹**close-up** \'klō-,səp\ *n* (1913) **1** : a photograph or movie shot taken at close range **2** : an intimate view or examination of something

²**close-up** \'klō-'səp\ *adv or adj* (1926) : at close range

clos-ing \'klō-ziŋ\ *n* (1596) **1** : a concluding part (as of a speech) **2** : a closable gap (as in an article of clothing) **3** : a meeting of parties to a real-estate deal for formally transferring title

clos-trid-i-um \klä-'stri-dē-əm\ *n, pl* **-ia** \-dē-ə\ [NL, genus name, fr. Gk *klōstēr* spindle, fr. *klōthein* to spin] (1884) : any of a genus (*Clostridium*) of spore-forming mostly anaerobic soil or intestinal bacteria — compare BOTULINUM — **clos-trid-i-al** \-dē-əl\ *adj*

clo-sure \'klō-zhər\ *n* [ME, fr. MF, fr. L *clausura*, fr. *clausus*, pp. of *claudere* to close — more at CLOSE] (14c) **1** *archaic* : means of enclosing : ENCLOSURE **2** : an act of closing : the condition of being closed ⟨∼ of the eyelids⟩ **3** : something that closes (pocket with zipper ∼) **4** [trans. of F *clôture*] : CLOTURE **5** : the property that a number system or a set has when it is mathematically closed under an operation **6** : a set that contains a given set together with all the limit points of the given set

¹**clot** \'klät\ *n* [ME, fr. OE *clott*; akin to MHG *klōz* lump, ball — more at CLOUT] (bef. 12c) **1** : a portion of a substance cleaving together in a thick nondescript mass (as of clay or gum) **2 a** : a roundish viscous lump formed by coagulation of a portion of liquid or by melting **b** : a coagulated mass produced by clotting of blood **3** *Brit* : BLOCKHEAD **4** : CLUSTER, GROUP ⟨a ∼ of spectators⟩

²**clot** *vb* **clot-ted; clot-ting** *vi* (15c) **1** : to become a clot : form clots **2** : to undergo a sequence of complex chemical and physical reactions that results in conversion of fluid blood into a coagulated mass : COAGULATE ∼ *vt* **1** : to cause to form into or as if into a clot **2** : to fill with clots

cloth \'klȯth\ *n, pl* **cloths** \'klȯthz, 'klȯths\ *often attrib* [ME, fr. OE *clāth* cloth, garment; akin to MHG *kleit* garment] (bef. 12c) **1 a** : a pliable material made usu. by weaving, felting, or knitting natural or synthetic fibers and filaments **b** : a similar material (as of glass) **2 a** : a piece of cloth adapted for a particular purpose; *esp* : TABLECLOTH **3 a** : a distinctive dress of a profession or calling **b** : the dress of the clergy; *specif* : CLERGY

cloth-bound \-,baund\ *adj* (1860) *of a book* : bound in stiff boards covered with cloth

clothe \'klōth\ *vt* **clothed** *or* **clad** \'klad\; **cloth-ing** [ME, fr. OE *clāthian*, fr. *clāth*] (bef. 12c) **1 a** : to cover with or as if with cloth or clothing : DRESS **b** : to provide with clothes **2** : to express or enhance by suitably significant language : COUCH ⟨treaties *clothed* in stately phraseology⟩ **3** : to endow esp. with power or a quality

clothes \'klōz *also* 'klōthz\ *n pl, often attrib* [ME, fr. OE *clāthas*, pl. of *clāth*] (bef. 12c) **1** : CLOTHING **2** : BEDCLOTHES **3** : all the cloth articles of personal and household use that can be washed

clothes-horse \-,hȯrs\ *n* (1775) **1** : a frame on which to hang clothes **2** : a conspicuously dressy person

¹**clothes-line** \-,līn\ *n* (1830) : a line (as of cord) on which clothes may be hung to dry

²**clothesline** *vt* (1964) : to knock down (a football player) by catching by the neck with an outstretched arm

clothes moth *n* (1753) : any of several small yellowish or buff-colored moths (esp. *Tinea pellionella* and *Tineola bisselliella* of the family Tineidae) whose larvae eat wool, fur, or feathers

clothes-peg \'klōz-,peg *also* 'klōthz-\ *n* (1825) *Brit* : CLOTHESPIN

clothes-pin \-,pin\ *n* (1846) : a forked piece of wood or plastic or a small spring clamp used for fastening clothes on a clothesline

clothes-press \-,pres\ *n* (1713) : a receptacle for clothes

cloth-ier \'klōth-yər, 'klō-thē-ər\ *n* [ME, alter. of *clother*, fr. *cloth*] (14c) : one who makes or sells clothing

cloth-ing \'klō-thiŋ\ *n* (13c) : garments in general; *also* : COVERING

cloth yard *n* (15c) : a yard esp. for measuring cloth; *specif* : a unit of 37 inches equal to the Scottish ell and used also as a length for arrows

clotted cream *n* (1878) : a thick cream made chiefly in England by slowly heating whole milk on which the cream has been allowed to rise and then skimming the cooled cream from the top — called also *Devonshire cream*

clo-ture \'klō-chər\ *n* [F *clôture*, lit., closure, alter. of MF *closure*] (1871) : the closing or limitation of debate in a legislative body esp. by calling for a vote — **cloture** *vt*

¹**cloud** \'klaud\ *n, often attrib* [ME, rock, cloud, fr. OE *clūd*; perh. akin to Gk *gloutos* buttock] (14c) **1** : a visible mass of particles of condensed vapor (as water or ice) suspended in the atmosphere of a planet (as the earth) or moon **2** : something resembling or suggesting a cloud: as **a** : a light filmy, puffy, or billowy mass seeming to float in the air ⟨a ∼ of blond hair⟩ ⟨a ship under a ∼ of sail⟩ **b** (1) : a usu. visible mass of minute particles suspended in the air or a gas (2) : an aggregation of usu. obscuring matter esp. in interstellar space (3) : an aggregate of charged particles (as electrons) **c** : a great crowd or multitude : SWARM ⟨∼s of mosquitoes⟩ **3** : something that has a dark, lowering, or threatening aspect ⟨∼s of war⟩ ⟨a ∼ of suspicion⟩ **4** : something that obscures or blemishes ⟨a ∼ of ambiguity⟩ **5** : a dark or opaque vein or spot (as in marble or a precious stone)

²**cloud** *vi* (1562) **1** : to grow cloudy — usu. used with *over* or *up* ⟨∼ed over before the storm⟩ **2 a** *of facial features* : to become troubled, apprehensive, or distressed in appearance **b** : to become blurry, dubious, or ominous — often used with *over* **3** : to billow up in the form of a cloud ∼ *vt* **1 a** : to envelop or hide with or as if with a cloud ⟨smog ∼ed our view⟩ **b** : to make opaque esp. by condensation of moisture **c** : to make murky esp. with smoke or mist **2** : to make unclear or confused ⟨∼ the issue⟩ **3** : TAINT, SULLY ⟨a ∼ed reputation⟩ **4** : to cast gloom over

cloud-ber-ry \'klaud-,ber-ē\ *n* (1597) : a creeping herbaceous raspberry (*Rubus chamaemorus*) of north temperate regions; *also* : its pale amber-colored edible fruit

cloud-burst \-,bərst\ *n* (1869) **1** : a sudden copious rainfall **2** : DELUGE 2

cloud chamber *n* (1897) : a vessel containing air saturated with water vapor whose sudden expansion reveals the passage of an ionizing particle by a trail of visible droplets

cloud–cuck-oo–land \,klaud-'kü-(,)kü-,land, -'kü-\ *n* [trans. of Gk *nephelokokkygia*] (1899) : a realm of fantasy or of whimsical or foolish behavior

cloud-ed leopard \'klau-dəd-\ *n* (1910) : a medium-sized cat (*Neofelis nebulosa*) that occurs from Nepal to southeast China and Indonesia and is grayish to yellowish with darker irregular rings, ovals, and rosettes

cloud forest *n* (1922) : a wet tropical mountain forest at an altitude usu. between 3000 and 8000 ft. (1000 and 2500 meters) that is characterized by a profusion of epiphytes and the presence of clouds even in the dry season

cloud-land \'klaud-,land\ *n* (1817) **1** : the region of the clouds **2** : the realm of visionary speculation or poetic imagination

cloud-less \-ləs\ *adj* (14c) : free from clouds : CLEAR — **cloud-less-ly** *adv* — **cloud-less-ness** *n*

cloud-let \'klaud-lət\ *n* (1788) : a small cloud

cloud nine *n* (1959) : a feeling of well-being or elation — usu. used with *on*

cloud-scape \'klaud-,skāp\ *n* (1880) : a view or pictorial representation of a cloud formation

cloud street *n* (1943) : a row of cumulus clouds

cloudy \'klau-dē\ *adj* **cloud-i-er; -est** (14c) **1** : of, relating to, or resembling cloud **2** : darkened by gloom or anxiety **3 a** : overcast with clouds **b** : having a cloudy sky **4** : obscure in meaning ⟨∼ issues⟩; *also* : uncertain as to fact or outcome ⟨a ∼ future⟩ **5** : dimmed or dulled as if by clouds ⟨a ∼ mirror⟩ **6** : uneven in color or texture **7** : having visible material in suspension : MURKY — **cloud-i-ly** \'klau-də-lē\ *adv* — **cloud-i-ness** \'klau-dē-nəs\ *n*

¹**clout** \'klaut\ *n* [ME, fr. OE *clūt*; akin to MHG *klōz* lump, Russ *gluda*] (bef. 12c) **1** *dial chiefly Brit* : a piece of cloth or leather : RAG **2** : a blow esp. with the hand; *also* : a hard hit in baseball **3** : a white cloth on a stake or frame used as a target in archery **4** : PULL, INFLUENCE ⟨political ∼⟩

²**clout** *vt* (14c) : to cover or patch with a clout **2** : to hit forcefully

¹**clove** \'klōv\ *n* [ME, fr. OE *clufu*; akin to OE *clēofan* to cleave] (bef. 12c) : one of the small bulbs (as in garlic) developed in the axils of the scales of a large bulb

²**clove** *past of* CLEAVE

³**clove** \'klōv\ *n* [alter. of ME *clowe*, fr. OF *clou* (*de girofle*), lit., nail of clove, fr. L *clavus* nail] (13c) : the dried flower bud of a tropical tree (*Syzygium aromaticum* syn. *Eugenia aromatica*) of the myrtle family that is used as a spice and is the source of an oil; *also* : this tree

clove hitch \'klōv-\ *n* [ME *cloven*, clove divided, fr. pp. of *clevien* to cleave] (ca. 1769) : a knot securing a rope temporarily to an object (as a post or spar) and consisting of a turn around the object, over the standing part, around the object again, and under the last turn — see KNOT illustration

clo-ven \'klō-vən\ *past part of* CLEAVE

cloven foot *n* (13c) : CLOVEN HOOF — **clo-ven–foot-ed** \'klō-vən-,fu-təd\ *adj*

cloven hoof *n* (1870) **1** : a foot (as of a sheep) divided into two parts at its distal extremity **2** [fr. the traditional representation of Satan as cloven-hoofed] : the sign of devilish character — **clo-ven–hoofed** \'klō-vən-,huft, -,hüft, -,huvd, -,hüvd\ *adj*

clove pink *n* (ca. 1855) : CARNATION 2

clo-ver \'klō-vər\ *n* [ME, fr. OE *clāfre*; akin to OHG *klēo* clover] (bef. 12c) **1** : any of a genus (*Trifolium*) of low leguminous herbs having trifoliolate leaves and flowers in dense heads and including many that are valuable for forage and attractive to bees **2** : any of various leguminous plants (as of the genera *Melilotus*, *Lespedeza*, or *Medicago*)

cloud 1: *1* cirrus, *2* cirrostratus, *3* cirrocumulus, *4* altostratus, *5* altocumulus, *6* stratocumulus, *7* nimbostratus, *8* cumulus, *9* cumulonimbus, *10* stratus

\ə\ abut \ᵊ\ kitten, F table \ər\ further \a\ ash \ā\ ace \ä\ mop, mar \au̇\ out \ch\ chin \e\ bet \ē\ easy \g\ go \i\ hit \ī\ ice \j\ job \ŋ\ sing \ō\ go \ȯ\ law \ȯi\ boy \th\ thin \t̲h̲\ the \ü\ loot \u̇\ foot \y\ yet \zh\ vision \ȧ, k̲, ⁿ, œ, œ̄, ᵫ, ᵫ̄, ᵊ\ *see* Guide to Pronunciation other than the clovers (genus *Trifolium*) — **in clover** *or* **in the clover** : in prosperity or in pleasant circumstances

¹clo·ver·leaf \-,lēf\ *adj* (1917) : resembling a clover leaf in shape

²cloverleaf *n, pl* **-leafs** \-,lēfs\ *or* **-leaves** \-,lēvz\ (1931) : an interchange between two major highways that allows traffic to change from one to the other without requiring any left turns or crossings and that from above resembles a four-leaf clover

cloverleaf

Clo·vis \'klō-vəs\ *adj* [*Clovis*, New Mexico] (1956) : of or relating to a widely distributed prehistoric culture of No. America characterized by leaf-shaped flint projectile points having fluted sides

¹clown \'klaün\ *n* [prob. of LG origin; akin to Fris *klönne* clumsy fellow, OE *clyne* lump of metal] (1563) **1** : FARMER, COUNTRYMAN **2** : a rude ill-bred person : BOOR **3 a** : a fool, jester, or comedian in an entertainment (as in a play); *specif* : a grotesquely dressed comedy performer in a circus **b** : a person who habitually plays the buffoon **c** : JOKER 1b

²clown *vi* (1599) : to act as or like a clown

clown·ery \'klaü-nə-rē\ *n, pl* **-er·ies** (1589) : clownish behavior or an instance of clownishness : BUFFOONERY

clown·ish \'klaü-nish\ *adj* (ca. 1570) : resembling or befitting a clown (as in ignorance and lack of sophistication) *syn* see BOORISH — **clown·ish·ly** *adv* — **clown·ish·ness** *n*

clox·a·cil·lin \,kläk-sə-'si-lən\ *n* [*chlor-* + *oxacillin*] (1963) : a semisynthetic oral penicillin $C_{19}H_{17}ClN_3NaO_5S$ effective esp. against staphylococci which secrete penicillinase

cloy \'klói\ *vb* [alter. of ME *acloien* to lame, fr. MF *encloer* to drive in a nail, fr. ML *inclavare*, fr. L *in* + *clavus* nail] *vt* (1528) : to surfeit with an excess usu. of something orig. pleasing ~ *vi* : to cause surfeit *syn* see SATIATE

cloy·ing \'klói-iŋ, 'klóiŋ\ *adj* (1594) : disgusting or distasteful by reason of excess (~ sweetness); *also* : excessively sweet or sentimental (a ~ romantic comedy) — **cloy·ing·ly** *adv*

cloze \'klōz\ *adj* [by shortening & alter. fr. *closure*] (1953) : of, relating to, or being a test of reading comprehension that involves having the person being tested supply words which have been systematically deleted from a text

¹club \'kləb\ *n, often attrib* [ME *clubbe*, fr. ON *klubba*; akin to OHG *kolbo* club] (13c) **1 a** : a heavy usu. tapering staff esp. of wood wielded as a weapon **b** : a stick or bat used to hit a ball in any of various games **c** : something resembling a club **2 a** : a playing card marked with a stylized figure of a black clover **b** *pl but sing or pl in constr* : the suit comprising cards marked with clubs **3 a** : an association of persons for some common object usu. jointly supported and meeting periodically; *also* : a group identified by some common characteristic (nations in the nuclear ~) **b** : the meeting place of a club **c** : an association of persons participating in a plan by which they agree to make regular payments or purchases in order to secure some advantage **d** : NIGHTCLUB **e** : an athletic association or team — **club·bish** \'klə-bish\ *adj*

²club *vb* **clubbed; club·bing** *vt* (1593) **1 a** : to beat or strike with or as if with a club **b** : to gather into a club-shaped mass (*clubbed* her hair) **2 a** : to unite or combine for a common cause **b** : to contribute to a common fund ~ *vi* **1** : to form a club : COMBINE **2** : to pay a share of a common expense

club·ba·ble *also* **club·able** \'klə-bə-bəl\ *adj* (1783) : SOCIABLE

clubbed \'kləbd\ *adj* (14c) : shaped like a club (~ antennae)

club·ber \'klə-bər\ *n* (1633) : a member of a club

club·by \'klə-bē\ *adj* **club·bi·er; -est** (1859) : characteristic of a club or club members: as **a** : displaying friendliness esp. to other members of the same social group : SOCIABLE **b** : open only to qualified or approved persons : SELECT, ELITE — **club·bi·ness** *n*

club car *n* (1886) : a railroad passenger car with facilities for serving refreshments and drinks — called also *bar car, lounge car*

club chair *n* (1919) : a deep low thickly upholstered easy chair often with rather low back and heavy sides and arms

club cheese *n* (1916) : a process cheese made by grinding cheddar and other cheeses usu. with added condiments and seasoning

club·foot \'kləb-,füt\ *n* (1538) : a misshapen foot twisted out of position from birth; *also* : this deformity — **club·foot·ed** \-,fü-təd\ *adj*

club fungus *n* (1899) : any of a family (Clavariaceae) of basidiomycetes with a simple or branched often club-shaped sporophore

club·house \'kləb-,haüs\ *n* (1818) **1** : a house occupied by a club or used for club activities **2** : locker rooms used by an athletic team

club·man \'kləb-mən, -,man\ *n* (1851) : a usu. wealthy man given to club life

club moss *n* (1597) : any of an order (Lycopodiales) of primitive vascular plants (as ground pine) often with the sporangia borne in club-shaped strobili

club·root \'kləb-,rüt, -,rüt\ *n* (1846) : a disease of cruciferous plants and esp. of cabbage caused by a slime mold (*Plasmodiophora brassicae*) producing swellings or distortions of the root

club sandwich *n* (1903) : a sandwich of three slices of bread with two layers of meat (as turkey) and lettuce, tomato, and mayonnaise

club soda *n* (1942) : SODA WATER 2

club steak *n* (1915) : a small steak cut from the end of the short loin — see BEEF illustration

¹cluck \'klək\ *vb* [imit.] *vi* (15c) **1** : to make a cluck **2** : to make a clicking sound with the tongue **3** : to express interest or concern (critics ~*ed* over the new developments) ~ *vt* **1** : to call with a cluck **2** : to express with interest or concern

²cluck *n* (1703) **1** : the characteristic sound made by a hen esp. in calling her chicks **2** : a stupid or naive person

¹clue \'klü\ *n* [alter. of *clew*] (1596) : something that guides through an intricate procedure or maze of difficulties; *specif* : a piece of evidence that leads one toward the solution of a problem

²clue *vt* **clued; clue·ing** *or* **clu·ing** (1663) **1** : to provide with a clue **2** : to give reliable information to (~ me in on how it happened)

clue·less \'klü-ləs\ *adj* (1862) **1** : providing no clue **2** : completely or hopelessly bewildered, unaware, ignorant, or foolish

clum·ber spaniel \'kləm-bər-\ *n, often cap C* [*Clumber*, estate in Nottinghamshire, England] (1883) : any of a breed of large massive heavyset spaniels with a dense silky largely white coat

¹clump \'kləmp\ *n* [prob. fr. LG *klump*] (ca. 1586) **1** : a group of things clustered together (a ~ of bushes) **2** : a compact mass **3** : a heavy tramping sound — **clumpy** \'kləm-pē\ *adj*

²clump *vi* (1665) **1** : to walk or move clumsily and noisily **2** : to form clumps ~ *vt* : to arrange in or cause to form clumps (the serum ~*s* the bacteria)

clum·sy \'kləm-zē\ *adj* **clum·si·er; -est** [prob. fr. obs. E *clumse* benumbed with cold] (ca. 1598) **1 a** : lacking dexterity, nimbleness, or grace (~ fingers) **b** : lacking tact or subtlety (a ~ joke) **2** : awkward or inefficient in use or construction : UNWIELDY *syn* see AWKWARD — **clum·si·ly** \-zə-lē\ *adv* — **clum·si·ness** \-zē-nəs\ *n*

clung *past and past part of* CLING

¹clunk \'kləŋk\ *vb* [imit.] *vi* (ca. 1796) **1** : to make a clunk **2** : to hit something with a clunk ~ *vt* : to strike or hit with a clunk

²clunk *n* (1823) **1** : a blow or the sound of a blow : THUMP **2** : a dull or stupid person

clunk·er \'kləŋ-kər\ *n* (1943) **1** : an old or badly working piece of machinery; *esp* : a dilapidated automobile **2** : someone or something notably unsuccessful

clunky \'kləŋ-kē\ *adj* **clunk·i·er; -est** (1968) : clumsy in style, form, or execution (a ~ thriller) (~ earrings)

clu·pe·id \'klü-pē-əd\ *n* [deriv. of L *clupea*, a small river fish] (1880) : any of a large family (Clupeidae) of soft-finned bony fishes (as herrings) that have a laterally compressed body and a forked tail and usu. occur in schools — **clupeid** *adj*

¹clus·ter \'kləs-tər\ *n* [ME, fr. OE *clyster*; akin to OE *clott* clot] (bef. 12c) : a number of similar individuals that occur together: as **a** : two or more consecutive consonants or vowels in a segment of speech **b** : a group of buildings and esp. houses built close together on a sizable tract in order to preserve open spaces larger than the individual yard for common recreation **c** : an aggregation of stars or galaxies that appear close together in the sky and are gravitationally associated — **clus·tery** \-t(ə-)rē\ *adj*

²cluster *vb* **clus·tered; clus·ter·ing** \-t(ə-)riŋ\ *vt* (14c) **1** : to collect into a cluster (~ the tents together) **2** : to furnish with clusters ~ *vi* : to grow, assemble, or occur in a cluster

cluster analysis *n* (1948) : a statistical classification technique for discovering whether the individuals of a population fall into different groups by making quantitative comparisons of multiple characteristics

cluster bomb *n* (1967) : an aircraft-dropped canister of small fragmentation bombs

cluster headache *n* (1953) : a headache that is characterized by severe pain in the eye or temple and tends to recur in a series of attacks

¹clutch \'kləch\ *vb* [ME *clucchen*, fr. OE *clyccan*] *vt* (bef. 12c) **1** : to grasp or hold with or as if with the hand or claws usu. strongly, tightly, or suddenly **2** *obs* : CLENCH ~ *vi* **1** : to seek to grasp and hold **2** : to operate an automobile clutch *syn* see TAKE

²clutch *n* (13c) **1 a** : the claws or a hand in the act of grasping or seizing firmly **b** : an often cruel or unrelenting control, power, or possession (the fell ~ of circumstance —W. E. Henley) **c** : the act of grasping, holding, or restraining **2 a** : a coupling used to connect and disconnect a driving and a driven part of a mechanism **b** : a lever (as a pedal) operating such a clutch **3** : a tight or critical situation : PINCH (come through in the ~) **4** : CLUTCH BAG

³clutch *adj* (1944) **1** : made or done in a crucial situation (a ~ hit) **2** : successful in a crucial situation (a ~ pitcher)

⁴clutch *n* [alter. of dial. E *cletch* hatching, brood] (1721) **1** : a nest of eggs or a brood of chicks **2** : GROUP, BUNCH

clutch bag *n* (1949) : a woman's small usu. strapless handbag

¹clut·ter \'klə-tər\ *vb* [ME *clotteren* to clot, fr. *clot*] *vi* (1556) *chiefly dial* : to run in disorder ~ *vt* : to fill or cover with scattered or disordered things that impede movement or reduce effectiveness — often used with *up*

²clutter *n* (1649) **1 a** : a crowded or confused mass or collection **b** : things that clutter a place **2** : interfering radar echoes caused by reflection from objects (as on the ground) other than the target **3** *chiefly dial* : DISTURBANCE, HUBBUB

Clyde \'klīd\ *n* (1894) : CLYDESDALE

Clydes·dale \'klīdz-,dāl\ *n* (1786) : a heavy draft horse with feathering on the legs of a breed orig. from Clydesdale, Scotland

clyp·e·us \'kli-pē-əs\ *n, pl* **clyp·ei** \-pē-,ī, -pē-,ē\ [NL, fr. L, round shield] (1834) : a plate on the anterior median aspect of an insect's head

clys·ter \'klis-tər\ *n* [ME, fr. MF or L; MF *clistere*, fr. L *clyster*, fr. Gk *klystēr*, fr. *klyzein* to wash out; akin to W *clir* pure, OE *hlūtor* clean] (14c) : ENEMA

Cly·tem·nes·tra \,klī-təm-'nes-trə\ *n* [L, fr. Gk *Klytaimnēstra*] : the wife and murderess of Agamemnon

cni·dar·i·an \nī-'dar-ē-ən, -'der-\ *n* [ultim. fr. NL *cnida* nematocyst, fr. Gk *knidē* nettle] (ca. 1909) : COELENTERATE — **cnidarian** *adj*

co- *prefix* [ME, fr. L, fr. *com-*; akin to OE *ge-*, perfective and collective prefix, OIr *com-* with] **1** : with; together : joint : jointly (*coexist*) (*coheir*) **2** : in or to the same degree (*coextensive*) **3 a** : one that is associated in an action with another : fellow : partner (*coauthor*) (*coworker*) **b** : having a usu. lesser share in duty or responsibility : alternate : deputy (*copilot*) **4** : of, relating to, or constituting the complement of an angle (*cosine*) (*codeclination*)

co·act	co·chair	co·cre·ator
co·ac·tive	co·chair·man	co·cul·ti·vate
co·ac·tor	co·chair·per·son	co·cul·ti·va·tion
co·ad·min·is·tra·tion	co·chair·wom·an	co·cul·ture
co·an·chor	co·cham·pi·on	co·cu·ra·tor
co·au·thor	co·com·pos·er	co·de·fen·dant
co·au·thor·ship	co·con·spir·a·tor	co·de·sign
co·cap·tain	co·coun·sel	co·de·vel·op
co·cat·a·lyst	co·cre·ate	co·de·vel·op·er

co·di·rect
co·di·rec·tion
co·di·rec·tor
co·dis·cov·er
co·dis·cov·er·er
co·drive
co·driv·er
co·ed·it
co·ed·i·tor
co·eter·nal
co·ex·ec·u·tor
co·fa·vor·ite
co·fea·ture
co·fi·nance
co·found
co·found·er
co·head
co·heir
co·heir·ess
co·hold·er
co·host
co·host·ess
co·in·vent
co·in·ven·tor
co·in·ves·ti·ga·tor
co·in·ves·tor

co·join
co·lead
co·lead·er
co·man·age
co·man·age·ment
co·man·ag·er
co·mem·ber
co·nom·i·nee
co·oc·cur
co·oc·cur·rence
co·oc·cur·rent
co·of·fi·cial
co·or·ga·niz·er
co·own
co·own·er
co·own·er·ship
co·part·ner
co·part·ner·ship
co·pre·sent
co·pres·i·dent
co·prince
co·prin·ci·pal
co·pris·on·er
co·pro·cess·ing
co·pro·duce
co·pro·duc·er

co·pro·duc·tion
co·pro·mot·er
co·pro·pri·etor
co·pros·per·i·ty
co·pub·lish
co·pub·lish·er
co·re·cip·i·ent
co·re·search·er
co·res·i·dent
co·res·i·dent·tial
co·rul·er
co·script
co·spon·sor
co·spon·sor·ship
co·star
co·sur·fac·tant
co·ten·ant
co·trans·duce
co·trans·duc·tion
co·trans·fer
co·trans·port
co·trust·ee
co·win·ner
co·work·er
co·write

co·ac·er·vate \kō-'a-sər-ˌvāt\ n [L coacervatus, pp. of coacervare to heap up, fr. co- + acervus heap] (1929) : an aggregate of colloidal droplets held together by electrostatic attractive forces — **co·acer·vate** \ˌkō-ə-'sər-vət\ adj — **co·ac·er·va·tion** \(ˌ)kō-ˌa-sər-'vā-shən\ n

¹coach \'kōch\ n, often attrib [ME coche, fr. MF, fr. G Kutsche, fr. Hung kocsi (szekér), lit., wagon from Kocs, Hungary] (1556) **1 a :** a large usu. closed four-wheeled horse-drawn carriage having doors in the sides and an elevated seat in front for the driver **b :** a railroad passenger car intended primarily for day travel **c :** BUS la **d :** TRAILER 3b **e :** a two-door enclosed automobile **f :** a class of passenger air transportation at a lower fare than first class **2** [fr. the concept that the tutor conveys the student through his examinations] **a :** a private tutor **b :** one who instructs or trains a performer or a team of performers; specif : one who instructs players in the fundamentals of a competitive sport and directs team strategy ⟨football ~⟩

²coach vi (1630) **1 :** to go in a coach **2 :** to instruct, direct, or prompt as a coach ~ vt **1 :** to train intensively (as by instruction and demonstration) ⟨~ pupils⟩ **2 :** to act as coach of ⟨~ tennis⟩ ⟨~ a team⟩ — **coach·able** \'kō-chə-bəl\ adj — **coach·er** n

coach dog n (1840) : DALMATIAN

coach·man \'kōch-mən\ n (1579) : a man who drives a coach or carriage

coach·work \-ˌwərk\ n (1906) : an automobile body : BODYWORK

co·ac·tion \-'ak-shən\ n (1625) **1 :** joint action **2 :** the interaction between individuals or kinds (as species) in an ecological community

co·adapt·ed \ˌkō-ə-'dap-təd\ adj (1836) : mutually adapted esp. by natural selection ⟨~ gene complexes⟩ — **co·ad·ap·ta·tion** \ˌkō-ˌa-ˌdap-'tā-shən, -dəp-'\ n

co·ad·ju·tor \ˌkō-ə-'jü-tər, kō-'a-jə-tər\ n [ME coadjutour, fr. MF coadjuteur, fr. LL coadjutor, fr. L co- + adjutor helper, fr. adjuvare to help — more at AID] (15c) **1 :** one who works together with another : AS-SISTANT **2 :** a bishop assisting a diocesan bishop and often having the right of succession — **coadjutor** adj

co·ad·ju·trix \ˌkō-ə-'jü-triks, kō-'a-jə-(ˌ)triks\ n, pl **co·ad·ju·tri·ces** \ˌkō-ə-'jü-trə-ˌsēz, (ˌ)kō-ˌa-jə-'trī-(ˌ)sēz\ [NL, fem. of coadjutor] (1646) : a female coadjutor

co·ag·u·lant \kō-'a-gyə-lənt\ n (1770) : something that produces coagulation

co·ag·u·lase \kō-'a-gyə-ˌlās, -ˌlāz\ n (1914) : any of several enzymes that cause coagulation (as of blood)

¹co·ag·u·late \kō-'a-gyə-lət\ adj (14c) archaic : being clotted or congealed

²co·ag·u·late \kō-'a-gyə-ˌlāt\ vb **-lat·ed; -lat·ing** [L coagulatus, pp. of coagulare to curdle, fr. coagulum curdling agent, fr. cogere to drive together — more at COGENT] vt (15c) **1 :** to cause to become viscous or thickened into a coherent mass : CURDLE, CLOT **2 :** to gather together or form into a mass or group ~ vi **:** to become coagulated — **co·ag·u·la·bil·i·ty** \kō-ˌa-gyə-lə-'bi-lə-tē\ n — **co·ag·u·la·ble** \-'a-gyə-lə-bəl\ adj — **co·ag·u·la·tor** \-ˌlā-tər\ n

co·ag·u·lum \kō-'a-gyə-ləm\ n, pl **-u·la** \-lə\ or **-ulums** [L] (1658) : a coagulated mass or substance : CLOT

¹coal \'kōl\ n, often attrib [ME col, fr. OE; akin to OHG & ON kol burning ember, MIr gúal coal] (bef. 12c) **1 :** a piece of glowing carbon or charred wood : EMBER **2 :** CHARCOAL 1 **3 a :** a black or brownish black solid combustible substance formed by the partial decomposition of vegetable matter without free access of air and under the influence of moisture and often increased pressure and temperature that is widely used as a natural fuel **b** pl, Brit : pieces or a quantity of the fuel broken up for burning

²coal vt (1602) **1 :** to burn to charcoal : CHAR **2 :** to supply with coal ~ vi : to take in coal

co·a·lesce \ˌkō-ə-'les\ vb **co·a·lesced; co·a·lesc·ing** [L coalescere, fr. co- + alescere to grow — more at OLD] vi (1656) **1 :** to grow together **2 a :** to unite into a whole : FUSE ⟨separate townships have coalesced into a single, sprawling colony —Donald Gould⟩ **b :** to unite for a common end : join forces ⟨people with different points of view ~ into opposing factions —I. L. Horowitz⟩ **3 :** to arise from the combination of distinct elements ⟨an organized and a popular resistance immediately coalesced —C. C. Menges⟩ ~ vt : to cause to unite ⟨sometimes a book ~s a public into a mass market —Walter Meade⟩ **syn** see MIX — **co·a·les·cence** \-'le-sᵊn(t)s\ n — **co·a·les·cent** \-sᵊnt\ adj

coal·field \'kōl-ˌfēld\ n (1813) : a region rich in coal deposits

coal·fish \-ˌfish\ n (1603) : any of several blackish or dark-backed fishes (as a pollack, cobia, or sablefish)

coal gas n (1809) : gas made from coal: as **a :** the mixture of gases thrown off by burning coal **b :** gas made by carbonizing bituminous coal in retorts and used for heating and lighting

coal·hole \'kōl-ˌhōl\ n (ca. 1662) **1** Brit : a compartment for storing coal **2 :** a hole for coal (as an opening in a sidewalk leading to a coal bin)

coal·i·fi·ca·tion \ˌkō-lə-fə-'kā-shən\ n (1911) : a process in which vegetable matter becomes converted into coal of increasingly higher rank with anthracite as the final product — **coal·i·fy** \'kō-lə-ˌfī\ vt

co·a·li·tion \ˌkō-ə-'li-shən\ n [F, fr. L coalescere] (1612) **1 a :** the act of coalescing : UNION **b :** a body formed by the coalescing of orig. distinct elements : COMBINATION **2 :** a temporary alliance of distinct parties, persons, or states for joint action — **co·a·li·tion·ist** \-'li-sh(ə-)nist\ n

coal measures n pl (1832) : beds of coal with the associated rocks

coal oil n (1858) **1 :** petroleum or a refined oil prepared from it **2 :** KEROSENE

coal seam n (1849) : a bed of coal usu. thick enough to be profitably mined

coal tar n (1785) : tar obtained by distillation of bituminous coal and used esp. in making dyes and drugs

coam·ing \'kō-miŋ\ n [prob. irreg. fr. comb] (1611) : a raised frame (as around a hatchway in the deck of a ship) to keep out water

co·apt \kō-'apt\ vt [LL coaptare, fr. L co- + aptus fastened, fit — more at APT] (1570) : to fit together and make fast — **co·ap·ta·tion** \(ˌ)kō-ˌap-'tā-shən\ n

co·arc·ta·tion \(ˌ)kō-ˌärk-'tā-shən\ n (1545) : a stricture or narrowing esp. of a canal or vessel (as the aorta)

coarse \'kōrs, 'kȯrs\ adj **coars·er; coars·est** [ME cors, perh. fr. course, n.] (14c) **1 :** of ordinary or inferior quality or value : COMMON **2 a** (1) **:** composed of relatively large parts or particles ⟨~ sand⟩ (2) **:** loose or rough in texture ⟨~ cloth⟩ **b :** adjusted or designed for heavy, fast, or less delicate work ⟨a ~ saw with large teeth⟩ **c :** not precise or detailed with respect to adjustment or discrimination **3 :** crude or unrefined in taste, manners, or language **4 :** harsh, raucous, or rough in tone **5** chiefly Brit : of or relating to coarse fish ⟨~ fishing⟩ — **coarse·ly** adv — **coarse·ness** n
syn COARSE, VULGAR, GROSS, OBSCENE, RIBALD mean offensive to good taste or morals. COARSE implies roughness, crudeness, or crudeness of spirit, behavior, or language ⟨found the coarse humor of coworkers offensive⟩. VULGAR often implies boorishness or ill-breeding ⟨a loud vulgar belch⟩. GROSS implies extreme coarseness and insensitiveness ⟨gross eating habits⟩. OBSCENE applies to anything strongly repulsive to the sense of decency and propriety esp. in sexual matters ⟨obscene language not allowed on the air⟩. RIBALD applies to what is amusingly or picturesquely vulgar or irreverent or mildly indecent ⟨entertained the campers with ribald folk songs⟩.

coarse fish n (1886) **1** chiefly Brit : a freshwater fish other than a salmonid **2 :** ROUGH FISH

coarse–grained \'kȯrs-ˌgrānd, 'kȯrs-\ adj (ca. 1774) **1 :** having a coarse grain **2 :** CRUDE

coars·en \'kȯr-sᵊn, 'kȯr-\ vb **coars·ened; coars·en·ing** vt (1805) : to make coarse ~ vi : to become coarse

¹coast \'kōst\ n [ME cost, fr. MF coste, fr. L costa rib, side; akin to OCS kostĭ bone] (14c) **1 :** the land near a shore : SEASHORE **2** obs : BORDER, FRONTIER **3 a :** a hill or slope suited to coasting **b :** a slide down a slope (as on a sled) **4** often cap : the Pacific coast of the U.S. **5 :** the immediate area of view — used in the phrase the coast is clear — **coast·al** \'kōs-tᵊl\ adj — **coast·wise** \'kōst-ˌwīz\ adv or adj — **from coast to coast :** across an entire nation or continent

²coast vt (14c) **1** obs : to move along or past the side of : SKIRT **2 :** to sail along the shore of ~ vi **1 a** archaic : to travel on land along a coast or along or past the side of something **b :** to sail along the shore **2 a :** to slide, run, or glide downhill by the force of gravity **b :** to move along without or as if without further application of propulsive power (as by momentum or gravity) **c :** to proceed easily without special application of effort or concern ⟨~ed through school⟩

coast·er \'kōs-tər\ n (1574) **1 :** one that coasts: as **a :** a person engaged in coastal traffic or commerce **b :** a ship sailing along a coast or engaged in trade between ports of the same country **2 :** a resident of a seacoast **3 a :** a tray or decanter stand usu. of silver and sometimes on wheels **b :** a shallow container or a plate or mat to protect a surface **4 a :** a small vehicle (as a sled or wagon) used in coasting **b :** ROLLER COASTER

coaster brake n (1899) : a brake in the hub of the rear wheel of a bicycle operated by reverse pressure on the pedals

coaster wagon n (1911) : a child's toy wagon often used for coasting

coast guard n (1833) **1 :** a military or naval force employed in guarding a coast or responsible for the safety, order, and operation of maritime traffic in neighboring waters **2** usu **coast-guard** chiefly Brit : COASTGUARDSMAN

coast-guards·man \'kōs(t)-ˌgärdz-mən\ or **coast-guard-man** \-ˌgärd-mən\ n (ca. 1891) : a member of a coast guard

coast·land \-ˌland\ n (1852) : land bordering the sea

coast·line \-ˌlīn\ n (ca. 1859) **1 :** a line that forms the boundary between the land and the ocean or a lake **2 :** the outline of a coast

coast redwood n (ca. 1897) : REDWOOD 3a

coast–to–coast \'kōs-tə-'kōst\ adj (1911) : extending or airing across an entire nation or continent

coast·ward \'kōs-twərd\ or **coast·wards** \-twərdz\ adv (1853) : toward the coast — **coastward** adj

¹coat \'kōt\ n, often attrib [ME cote, fr. MF, of Gmc origin; akin to OHG kozza coarse wool mantle] (14c) **1 a :** an outer garment worn on the upper body and varying in length and style according to fashion and use **b :** something resembling a coat **2 :** the external growth on an animal **3 :** a layer of one substance covering another ⟨a ~ of paint⟩ — **coat·ed** \'kō-təd\ adj — **coat·less** adj

²coat vt (14c) **1 :** to cover with a coat **2 :** to cover or spread with a finishing, protecting, or enclosing layer — **coat·er** n

---

\ə\ abut \ᵊ\ kitten, F table \ər\ further \a\ ash \ā\ ace \ä\ mop, mar \au̇\ out \ch\ chin \e\ bet \ē\ easy \g\ go \i\ hit \ī\ ice \j\ job \ŋ\ sing \ō\ go \ȯ\ law \ȯi\ boy \th\ thin \t͟h\ the \ü\ loot \u̇\ foot \y\ yet \zh\ vision \á, k̲, ⁿ, œ, œ̄, ᴜₑ, ᵫ, ᵊ\ see Guide to Pronunciation

coat·dress \'kōt-,dres\ n (1854) : a dress styled like a coat usu. with a front buttoning from neckline to hemline

coat hanger n (1895) : a device which is shaped like the outline of a person's shoulders and over which garments may be hung

co·a·ti \kə-'wä-tē, kwä-'tē\ n [Pg coati, fr. Tupi] (1676) : either of two tropical American mammals (Nasua nasua and N. nelsoni) related to the raccoon but with a longer body and tail and a long flexible snout

co·a·ti·mun·di \kə-,wä-ti-'mən-dē, ,kwä-, -'mún-\ n [Tupi] (1676) : CO-ATI

coat·ing \'kō-tiŋ\ n (1768) **1** : cloth for coats **2** : COAT, COVERING

coat of arms [ME cote of armes, trans. of MF cote d'armes] (14c) **1** : a tabard or surcoat embroidered with armorial bearings **2 a** : the particular heraldic bearings (as of a person) usu. depicted on an escutcheon often with accompanying adjuncts (as a crest, motto, and supporters) **b** : a similar symbolic emblem

coat of mail (15c) : a garment of metal scales or chain mail worn as armor

coat·rack \'kōt-,rak\ n (1915) : a stand or rack fitted with pegs, hooks, or hangers and used for the temporary storage of garments

coat·room \-,rüm, -,rúm\ n (1870) : CLOAKROOM

coat·tail \'kōt-,tāl\ n (ca. 1600) **1** : the rear flap of a man's coat **2** pl : the skirts of a dress coat, cutaway, or frock coat **3** pl : the influence or pulling power of a popular movement or candidate ⟨congressmen riding into office on the president's ∼s⟩

¹coax \'kōks\ vt [earlier cokes, fr. cokes simpleton] (1589) **1** obs : FON-DLE, PET **2** : to influence or gently urge by caressing or flattering : WHEEDLE **3** : to draw, gain, or persuade by means of gentle urging or flattery **4** : to manipulate with great perseverance and usu. with considerable effort toward a desired state or activity ⟨∼ a fire to burn⟩

²co·ax \'kō-,aks\ n (1949) : COAXIAL CABLE

co·ax·i·al \(,)kō-'ak-sē-əl\ adj (1881) **1** : having coincident axes **2** : mounted on concentric shafts — **co·ax·i·al·ly** \-sē-ə-lē\ adv

coaxial cable n (1936) : a transmission line that consists of a tube of electrically conducting material surrounding a central conductor held in place by insulators and that is used to transmit telegraph, telephone, and television signals of high frequency — called also coax cable

cob \'käb\ n [ME cobbe cobbler] (15c) **1** : a male swan **2** pl : a rounded mass, lump, or heap **3** : a crudely struck old Spanish coin of irregular shape **4** : CORNCOB 1 **5** : a stocky short-legged riding horse — **cob·by** \'kä-bē\ adj

co·bal·a·min \kō-'ba-lə-mən\ n [cobalt + vitamin] (1956) : VITAMIN B₁₂

co·balt \'kō-,bȯlt\ n [G Kobalt, alter. of Kobold, lit., goblin, fr. MHG kobolt; fr. its occurrence in silver ore, believed to be due to goblins] (1683) **1** : a tough lustrous silver-white magnetic metallic element that is related to and occurs with iron and nickel and is used esp. in alloys — see ELEMENT table **2** : COBALT BLUE 2

cobalt blue n (1835) **1** : a greenish blue pigment consisting essentially of cobalt oxide and alumina **2** : a strong greenish blue

cobalt chloride n (1885) : a chloride of cobalt; esp : the dichloride CoCl₂ that is blue when dehydrated, turns red in the presence of moisture, and is used to indicate humidity

co·bal·tic \kō-'bȯl-tik\ adj (1782) : of, relating to, or containing cobalt esp. with a valence of three

co·balt·ite \kō-'bȯl-,tīt, kō-\ or **co·balt·ine** \-,tēn\ n [cobaltite, alter. of cobaltine, fr. F, fr. cobalt] (1868) : a mineral consisting of a grayish to silver-white cobalt sulfur arsenide used in making smalt

co·bal·tous \kō-'bȯl-təs\ adj (1863) : of, relating to, or containing cobalt esp. with a valence of two

cobalt 60 n (1946) : a heavy radioactive isotope of cobalt of the mass number 60 produced in nuclear reactors and used as a source of gamma rays (as for radiotherapy)

cob·ber \'kȯ-bər\ n [origin unknown] (1893) Austral & NewZeal : BUDDY

¹cob·ble \'kä-bəl\ vt **cob·bled; cob·bling** \-b(ə-)liŋ\ [ME coblen, perh. back-formation fr. cobelere cobbler] (15c) **1** chiefly Brit : to mend or patch coarsely **2** : REPAIR, MAKE ⟨∼ shoes⟩ **3** : to make or put together roughly or hastily — often used with together or up

²cobble n (1600) **1** : COBBLESTONE **2** pl, chiefly Brit : lump coal about the size of small cobblestones

cobbled adj (1853) : paved with cobblestones

cob·bler \'kä-blər\ n [ME cobelere] (13c) **1** : a mender or maker of shoes and often of other leather goods **2** archaic : a clumsy workman **3** : a tall iced drink consisting usu. of wine, rum, or whiskey and sugar garnished with mint or a slice of lemon or orange **4** : a deep-dish fruit dessert with a thick top crust

cob·ble·stone \'kä-bəl-,stōn\ n [ME, fr. cobble- (prob. fr. cob) + stone] (15c) : a naturally rounded stone larger than a pebble and smaller than a boulder; esp : such a stone used in paving a street or in construction — **cob·ble·stoned** \-,stōnd\ adj

cob·by \'kä-bē\ adj **cob·bi·er; -est** (1883) : STOCKY ⟨a ∼ horse⟩

co·bel·lig·er·ent \,kō-bə-'lij-rənt, -'li-jə-\ n (1813) : a country fighting with another power against a common enemy — **cobelligerent** adj

co·bia \'kō-bē-ə\ n [origin unknown] (ca. 1873) : a large bony fish (Rachycentron canadum of the family Rachycentridae) of warm seas that is a food and sport fish

co·ble \'kō-bəl\ n [ME] (14c) : a flat-bottomed boat propelled chiefly by oars and used in Scotland and northern England esp. for fishing

cob·nut \'käb-,nət\ n (1580) : the fruit of a European hazel (Corylus avellana grandis); also : the plant bearing this fruit

CO·BOL or **Co·bol** \'kō-,bȯl\ n [common business oriented language] (1960) : a computer programming language designed for business applications

co·bra \'kō-brə\ n [Pg cobra (de capello), lit., hooded snake, fr. L colubra snake] (1802) : any of several venomous Asian and African elapid snakes (genera Naja and Ophiophagus) that when excited expand the skin of the neck into a hood by movement of the anterior ribs; also : any of several related African snakes

cob·web \'käb-,web\ n [ME coppeweb, fr. coppe spider (fr. OE ātorcoppe) + web; akin to MD coppe spider] (14c) **1 a** : the network spread by a spider : SPIDERWEB **b** : tangles of the silken threads of a cobweb usu. covered with accumulated dirt and dust **2** : something that entangles, obscures, or confuses ⟨a ∼ of law and politics⟩ — **cob·webbed** \-,webd\ adj — **cob·web·by** \-,we-bē\ adj

co·ca \'kō-kə\ n [Sp, fr. Quechua kuka] (1577) **1** : any of several So.

American shrubs (genus Erythroxylon, family Erythroxylaceae); esp : one (E. coca) that is the primary source of cocaine **2** : dried leaves of a coca (esp. Erythroxylon coca) containing alkaloids including cocaine

co·caine \kō-'kān, 'kō-,\ n (1874) : a bitter crystalline alkaloid C₁₇H₂₁NO₄ obtained from coca leaves that is used medically as a topical anesthetic and illicitly for its euphoric effects and that may result in a compulsive psychological need

co·cain·ize \kō-'kā-,nīz\ vt **-ized; -iz·ing** (1887) : to treat or anesthetize with cocaine — **co·cain·i·za·tion** \-,kā-nə-'zā-shən\ n

co·car·box·yl·ase \,kō-kär-'bäk-sə-,lās, -,lāz\ n (1932) : a coenzyme C₁₂H₁₉ClN₄O₇P₂S·H₂O that is a pyrophosphate of thiamine and is important in metabolic reactions (as decarboxylation in the Krebs cycle)

co·car·cin·o·gen \,kō-kär-'si-nə-jən, kō-'kär-sⁿn-ə-jen\ n (1938) : an agent that aggravates the carcinogenic effects of another substance — **co·car·cin·o·gen·ic** \,kō-,kär-sⁿn-ō-'je-nik\ adj

coc·cid \'käk-səd\ n [NL Coccus, genus of scales, fr. Gk kokkos grain, kermes] (ca. 1889) : SCALE INSECT

coc·cid·i·oi·do·my·co·sis \(,)käk-,si-dē-,ȯi-dō-(,)mī-'kō-səs\ n [NL, fr. Coccidioides, genus of fungi (fr. coccidium) + mycosis] (1937) : a disease esp. of humans and domestic animals caused by a fungus (Coccidioides immitis) and marked esp. by fever and pulmonary symptoms

coc·cid·i·o·sis \(,)käk-,si-dē-'ō-səs\ n, pl **-o·ses** \-,sēz\ [NL] (1892) : infestation with or disease caused by coccidia

coc·cid·i·um \käk-'si-dē-əm\ n, pl **-ia** \-dē-ə\ [NL, dim. of coccus] (ca. 1879) : any of an order (Coccidia) of protozoans usu. parasitic in the digestive epithelium of vertebrates

coc·coid \'kä-,kȯid\ adj (1893) : of, relating to, or resembling a coccus : GLOBULAR 1a(1) — **coccoid** n

coc·cus \'kä-kəs\ n, pl **coc·ci** \'kä-,kī, -,kē; 'käk-,sī, -,sē\ [NL, fr. Gk kokkos] (1888) : a spherical bacterium — **coc·cal** \'kä-kəl\ adj

-coccus n comb form, pl **-cocci** [NL] : berry-shaped microorganism ⟨micrococcus⟩

coc·cy·geal \käk-'si-j(ē-)əl\ adj [ML coccygeus of the coccyx, fr. Gk kokkyk-, kokkyx] (1836) : of or relating to the coccyx

coc·cyx \'käk-siks\ n, pl **coc·cy·ges** \'käk-sə-,jēz\ also **coc·cyx·es** \'käk-sik-səz\ [NL, fr. Gk kokkyx cuckoo, coccyx; fr. its resemblance to a cuckoo's beak] (1615) : a small bone that articulates with the sacrum and that usu. consists of four fused vertebrae which form the terminus of the spinal column in humans and tailless apes

Co·chin \'kō-chin\ n [Cochin China, part of French Indochina] (1853) : any of an Asian breed of large domestic fowl with thick plumage, small wings and tail, and densely feathered legs and feet — called also Cochin China

co·chi·neal \'kä-chə-,nēl, 'kō-\ n [MF & Sp; MF cochenille, fr. OSp cochinilla cochineal insect] (1582) **1** : a red dye consisting of the dried bodies of female cochineal insects **2** : COCHINEAL INSECT

cochineal insect n (1801) : a small red cactus-feeding scale insect (Dactylopius coccus) the females of which are the source of cochineal

co·chlea \'kō-klē-ə, 'kä-klē-\ n, pl **co·chle·as** or **co·chle·ae** \-klē-,ē, -,ī\ [NL, fr. L, snail, snail shell, fr. Gk kochlias, fr. kochlos snail; prob. akin to Gk konchē mussel] (1688) : a division of the bony labyrinth of the inner ear of higher vertebrates that is usu. coiled like a snail shell and is the seat of the hearing organ — see EAR illustration — **co·chle·ar** \'kō-klē-ər, 'kä-\ adj

¹cock \'käk\ n [ME cok, fr. OE cocc, of imit. origin] (bef. 12c) **1 a** : the adult male of the domestic fowl (Gallus gallus) **b** : the male of birds other than the domestic fowl **c** : WOODCOCK **d** archaic : the crowing of a cock; also : COCKCROW **e** : WEATHERCOCK **2 a** : a device (as a faucet or valve) for regulating the flow of a liquid **3 a** : a chief person : LEADER **b** : a person of spirit and often of a certain swagger or arrogance **4 a** : the hammer in the lock of a firearm **b** : the cocked position of the hammer **5** : PENIS — usu. considered vulgar — **cock of the walk** : one that dominates a group or situation esp. overbearingly

²cock vi (1575) **1** : STRUT, SWAGGER **2** : to turn, tip, or stick up **3** : to position the hammer of a firearm for firing ∼ vt **1 a** : to draw the hammer of (a firearm) back and set for firing; also : to set (the trigger) for firing **b** : to draw or bend back in preparation for throwing or hitting **c** : to set a mechanism (as a camera shutter) for tripping **2 a** : to set erect **b** : to turn, tip, or tilt usu. to one side **3** : to turn up (as a hat brim) — **cock a snook** also **cock snooks** : to thumb the nose

³cock n (1717) : TILT, SLANT ⟨∼ of the head⟩

⁴cock n [ME cok, of Scand origin] (14c) : a small pile (as of hay)

⁵cock vt (14c) : to put (as hay) into cocks

cock·ade \kä-'kād\ n [modif. of F cocarde, fr. fem. of cocard vain, fr. coq cock, fr. OF coc, of imit. origin] (1709) : an ornament (as a rosette) usu. worn on a hat as a badge — **cock·ad·ed** \-'kā-dəd\ adj

cock–a–hoop \,kä-kə-'hüp, -'hup\ adj [fr. the phrase to set cock a hoop to be festive] (1663) **1** : triumphantly boastful : EXULTING **2** : AWRY

Cock·aigne \kä-'kān\ n [ME cokaygne, fr. MF (pais de) cocaigne land of plenty] (13c) : an imaginary land of great luxury and ease

cock–a–leek·ie \,kä-ki-'lē-kē\ n [alter. of cockie (dim. of ¹cock) + leekie, dim. of leek] (1737) : a soup made of chicken and leeks

cock·a·lo·rum \,kä-kə-'lōr-əm, -'lȯr-\ n, pl **-rums** [prob. modif. of obs. Flem kockeloeren to crow, of imit. origin] (ca. 1715) **1** : a boastful and self-important person **2** : LEAPFROG **3** : boastful talk

cock·a·ma·my or **cock·a·mie·mie** \,kä-kə-'mā-mē\ adj [perh. alter. of decalcomania] (1960) : RIDICULOUS, INCREDIBLE ⟨of all the ∼ excuses I ever heard —Leo Rosten⟩

cock–and–bull story \,kä-kən-'bùl-\ n (1795) : an incredible story told as true

cock·a·poo \'kä-kə-,pü\ n [alter. of cocker (spaniel) + poodle] (1970) : a dog that is a cross between a cocker spaniel and a poodle

cock·a·tiel \,kä-kə-,tē(ə)l\ n [D kaketielje, fr. Pg cacatilha, fr. cacatua cockatoo] (1877) : a crested small gray Australian parrot (Nymphicus hollandicus) with a yellow head

cock·a·too \'kä-kə-,tü\ n, pl **-toos** [D kaketoe, fr. Malay kakatua] (1634) : any of various large noisy chiefly Australasian crested parrots (family Cacatuidae and esp. genus Cacatua)

cock·a·trice \'kä-kə-trəs, -,tris\ n [ME cocatrice, fr. MF cocatris ichneumon, cockatrice, fr. ML cocatric-, cocatrix ichneumon] (14c) : a legendary serpent that is hatched by a reptile from a cock's egg and that has a deadly glance

cock-boat \'käk-ˌbōt\ *n* (15c) : a small boat; *esp* : one used as a tender to a larger boat

cock-cha-fer \'käk-ˌchä-fər\ *n* [¹*cock* + *chafer*] (1712) : a large European beetle (*Melolontha melolontha*) destructive to vegetation as an adult and to roots as a larva; *also* : any of various related beetles

cock-crow \'käk-ˌkrō\ *n* (13c) : DAWN

cocked hat \'käkt-\ *n* (1673) **1 a** : a hat with brim turned up to give a 3-cornered appearance **2 a** : a hat with brim turned up on two sides and worn either front to back or sideways

¹cock-er \'kä-kər\ *vt* [ME *cokeren*] (15c) : INDULGE, PAMPER

²cocker *n* (1689) : a keeper or handler of fighting cocks

³cocker *n* (ca. 1811) : COCKER SPANIEL

cock-er-el \'kä-k(ə-)rəl\ *n* [ME *cokerelle*, fr. MF dial. *kokerel*, dim. of OF *coc*] (15c) : a young male of the domestic fowl (*Gallus gallus*)

cock-er spaniel \'kä-kər-\ *n* [*cocking* woodcock hunting] (1840) **1** : ENGLISH COCKER SPANIEL **2** : any of a breed of spaniels developed in the U.S. from the English cocker spaniel that are smaller in size and have a shorter muzzle and longer thicker coat

cock-eye \'käk-ˈī, -ˌī\ *n* (ca. 1825) : a squinting eye

cock-eyed \'käk-ˌīd\ *adj* (1821) **1** : having a cockeye **2 a** : ASKEW, AWRY **b** : slightly crazy : TOPSY-TURVY ⟨a ~ scheme⟩ **c** : DRUNK 1a — **cock-eyed-ly** \-ˌī(-ə)d-lē\ *adv* — **cock-eyed-ness** \-ˌīd-nəs\ *n*

cock-fight \'käk-ˌfīt\ *n* (ca. 1566) : a contest in which gamecocks usu. fitted with metal spurs are pitted against each other — **cock-fight-ing** \-ˌfī-tiŋ\ *adj or n*

cock-horse \'käk-ˌhȯrs\ *n* [perh. fr. *cock*, adj., (male) + *horse*] (ca. 1541) : ROCKING HORSE

¹cock-le \'kä-kəl\ *n* [ME, fr. OE *coccel*] (bef. 12c) : any of several weedy plants of the pink family; *esp* : CORN COCKLE

²cockle *n* [ME *cokille*, fr. MF *coquille* shell, modif. of L *conchylia*, pl. of *conchylium*, fr. Gk *konchylion*, fr. *konchē* conch] (14c) **1** : any of various chiefly marine bivalve mollusks (family Cardiidae) having a shell with convex radially ribbed valves; *esp* : a common edible European bivalve (*Cerastoderma edule* syn. *Cardium edule*) **2** : COCKLESHELL

³cockle *n* [ME *kokell*, ultim. fr. MF *coquillé* wavy or rounded like a shell, fr. *coquille*] (15c) : PUCKER, WRINKLE — **cockle** *vb*

cock-le-bur \'kä-kəl-ˌbər, -kə-\ *n* (1804) : any of a genus (*Xanthium*) of prickly-fruited composite plants; *also* : one of its stiff-spined fruits

cock-le-shell \'kä-kəl-ˌshel\ *n* (15c) **1 a** : the shell or one of the shell valves of a cockle **b** : a shell (as a scallop shell) suggesting a cockleshell **2 a** : a light flimsy boat

cockles of the heart [perh. fr. ²*cockle*] (1671) : the core of one's being — usu. used in the phrase *warm the cockles of the heart*

cockleshell 1a

cock-loft \'käk-ˌlȯft\ *n* [prob. fr. ¹*cock*] (1589) : a small garret

cock-ney \'käk-nē\ *n, pl* **cockneys** [ME *cokeney*, lit., cocks' egg, fr. *coken* (gen. pl. of *cok* cock) + *ey* egg, fr. OE *ǣg*] (14c) **1** *obs* **a** : a spoiled child **b** : a squeamish woman **2** *often cap* **a** : a native of London and esp. of the East End of London **b** : the dialect of London or of the East End of London — **cockney** *adj* — **cock-ney-fy** \'käk-ni-ˌfī\ *vt* — **cock-ney-ish** \-nē-ish\ *adj* — **cock-ney-ism** \-ˌi-zəm\ *n*

cock-pit \'käk-ˌpit\ *n* (1587) **1 a** : a pit or enclosure for cockfights **b** : a place noted for esp. bloody, violent, or long-continued conflict **2** *obs* : the pit of a theater **3** : a compartment in a sailing warship used as quarters for junior officers and for treatment of the wounded in an engagement **4** : a space or compartment in a usu. small vehicle (as a boat, airplane, or automobile) from which it is steered, piloted, or driven — see AIRPLANE illustration

cock-roach \'käk-ˌrōch\ *n* [by folk etymology fr. Sp *cucaracha* cockroach, fr. *cuca* caterpillar] (1623) : any of an order or suborder (Blattodea syn. Blattaria) of chiefly nocturnal insects including some that are domestic pests

cocks-comb \'käks-ˌkōm\ *n* (1542) **1** : COXCOMB **2** : a garden plant (*Celosia cristata*) of the amaranth family grown for its flowers

cocks-foot \-ˌfût\ *n* (1697) : ORCHARD GRASS

cock-shut \'käk-ˌshət\ *n* [fr. the time poultry are shut in to rest] (1598) *dial Eng* : evening twilight

cock-shy \-ˌshī\ *n, pl* **cockshies** [¹*cock* + *shy*, n.] (1836) **1 a** : a throw at an object set up as a mark **b** : a mark or target so set up **2** : an object or person taken as a butt (as of criticism)

cock-suck-er \-ˌsə-kər\ *n* (ca. 1891) : one who performs fellatio — usu. considered obscene; often used as a generalized term of abuse

cock-sure \'käk-ˈshùr\ *adj* [prob. fr. ¹*cock* + *sure*] (1672) **1** : feeling perfect assurance sometimes on inadequate grounds **2** : marked by overconfidence or presumptuousness : COCKY *syn* see SURE — **cock-sure-ly** *adv* — **cock-sure-ness** *n*

¹cock-tail \'käk-ˌtāl\ *n* [prob. fr. ¹*cock* + *tail*] (1806) **1 a** : an iced drink of wine or distilled liquor mixed with flavoring ingredients **b** : something resembling or suggesting such a drink **c** : a solution of agents taken or used together esp. for medical treatment or diagnosis **2** : an appetizer served as a first course at a meal

²cocktail *adj* (1865) **1** : of, relating to, or set aside for cocktails ⟨a ~ hour⟩ **2** : designed for semiformal wear ⟨~ dress⟩

³cocktail *n* [¹*cock* + *tail*] (1808) : a horse with its tail docked

cocktail glass *n* (1907) : a bell-shaped drinking glass usu. having a foot and stem and holding about three ounces (90 milliliters)

cocktail lounge *n* (1939) : a public room (as in a hotel, club, or restaurant) where cocktails and other drinks are served

cocktail party *n* (1928) : an informal or semiformal party or gathering at which cocktails are served

cocktail table *n* (1946) : COFFEE TABLE

cock-up \'kä-ˌkəp\ *n* (ca. 1948) *Brit* : MESS 3b

cocky \'kä-kē\ *adj* **cock-i-er; -est** (1768) **1** : boldly or brashly self-confident **2** : JAUNTY — **cock-i-ly** \'kä-kə-lē\ *adv* — **cock-i-ness** \'kä-kē-nəs\ *n*

co-co \'kō-(ˌ)kō\ *n, pl* **cocos** [Sp *coco* & Pg *côco* bogeyman, grimace, coconut] (1555) : the coconut palm; *also* : its fruit

co-coa \'kō-(ˌ)kō\ *n* [modif. of Sp *cacao*] (1788) **1 a** : powdered ground roasted cacao beans from which a portion of the fat has been removed **b** : a beverage prepared by heating cocoa with water or milk **2** : CACAO 2 **3** : a medium brown color

cocoa bean *n* (1855) : CACAO 1

cocoa butter *n* (1872) : a pale vegetable fat with a low melting point obtained from cacao beans

co-co-nut \'kō-kə-(ˌ)nət\ *n* (1613) **1** : the drupaceous fruit of the coconut palm whose outer fibrous husk yields coir and whose nut contains thick edible meat and coconut milk **2** : the edible meat of the coconut

coconut crab *n* (ca. 1889) : a large edible coconut-eating burrowing land crab (*Birgus latro*) widely distributed about islands of the tropical Indian and Pacific Oceans

coconut oil *n* (1838) : a fatty oil or semisolid fat extracted from fresh coconuts and used esp. in making soaps and food products

coconut palm *n* (1852) : a tall pinnate-leaved coconut-bearing palm (*Cocos nucifera*) that grows along tropical coasts

¹co-coon \kə-ˈkün\ *n* [F *cocon*, fr. Prov *coucoun*, fr. *coco* shell, prob. fr. L *coccum* kermes (thought to be a gall or berry), fr. Gk *kokkos* berry, kermes] (1699) **1 a** : an envelope often largely of silk which an insect larva forms about itself and in which it passes the pupa stage **b** : any of various other protective coverings produced by animals **2 a** : a covering suggesting a cocoon **b** : a protective covering placed or sprayed over military or naval equipment in storage

²cocoon *vt* (1881) : to wrap or envelop in or as if in a cocoon

co-coon-ing \-ˈkü-niŋ\ *n* (1987) : the practice of spending leisure time at home in preference to going out

co-cotte \kō-ˈkȯt\ *n, pl* **cocottes** \-ˈkȯt(s)\ [F] (1867) **1** : PROSTITUTE **2** : a shallow individual baking dish usu. with one or two handles

co-co-yam \'kō-(ˌ)kō-yam\ *n* [prob. *coco* + *yam*] (1922) **1** : TARO **2** : YAUTIA

co-cur-ric-u-lar \ˌkō-kə-ˈri-kyə-lər\ *adj* (1949) : being outside of but usu. complementing the regular curriculum

cod \'käd\ *n, pl* **cod** *also* **cods** [ME] (14c) **1** : any of various bottom-dwelling fishes (family Gadidae, the cod family) that usu. occur in cold marine waters and often have barbels and three dorsal fins: as **a** : one (*Gadus morhua*) of the No. Atlantic that is an important food fish **b** : one (*Gadus macrocephalus*) of the Pacific Ocean **2** : any of various bony fishes resembling the true cods

co-da \'kō-də\ *n* [It, lit., tail, fr. L *cauda*] (ca. 1753) **1 a** : a concluding musical section that is formally distinct from the main structure **b** : a concluding part of a literary or dramatic work **2** : something that serves to round out, conclude, or summarize yet has its own interest

cod-dle \'kä-dᵊl\ *vt* **cod-dled; cod-dling** \'käd-liŋ, 'kä-dᵊl-iŋ\ [perh. fr. *caudle*] (1598) **1** : to cook (as eggs) in liquid slowly and gently just below the boiling point **2** : to treat with extreme care : PAMPER — **cod-dler** \'kä-dᵊl-ər\ *n*

¹code \'kōd\ *n* [ME, fr. MF, fr. L *caudex, codex* trunk of a tree, document formed orig. from wooden tablets] (14c) **1** : a systematic statement of a body of law; *esp* : one given statutory force **2** : a system of principles or rules ⟨moral ~⟩ **3 a** : a system of signals or symbols for communication **b** : a system of symbols (as letters or numbers) used to represent assigned and often secret meanings **4** : GENETIC CODE **5** : a set of instructions for a computer — **code-less** \-ləs\ *adj*

²code *vb* **cod-ed; cod-ing** *vt* (1815) : to put in or into the form or symbols of a code ~ *vi* : to specify the genetic code ⟨a gene that ~s for a protein⟩ — **cod-able** \'kō-də-bəl\ *adj* — **cod-er** *n*

code-book *n* (1884) : a book containing an alphabetical list of words or expressions with their code equivalents

co-deine \'kō-ˌdēn\ *n* [F *codéine*, fr. Gk *kōdeia* poppyhead] (1881) : a morphine derivative $C_{18}H_{21}NO_3 \cdot H_2O$ that is found in opium, is weaker in action than morphine, and is used esp. in cough remedies

code name *n* (1919) : a designation having a secret meaning — **code-name** \'kōd-ˌnām\ *vt*

co-de-pen-dence \ˌkō-di-ˈpen-dən(t)s\ *n* (1989) : CODEPENDENCY

co-de-pen-den-cy \-dən(t)-sē\ *n* (1987) : a psychological condition or a relationship in which a person is controlled or manipulated by another who is affected with a pathological condition (as an addiction to alcohol or heroin) — **co-de-pen-dent** \-dənt\ *n or adj*

co-de-ter-mi-na-tion \ˌkō-di-ˌtər-mə-ˈnā-shən\ *n* (1949) : the participation of labor with management in determining business policy

code word *n* (1884) **1** : CODE NAME **2** : EUPHEMISM

co-dex \'kō-ˌdeks\ *n, pl* **co-di-ces** \'kō-də-ˌsēz, 'kä-\ [L] (1670) : a manuscript book esp. of Scripture, classics, or ancient annals

cod-fish \'käd-ˌfish\ *n* (14c) : COD; *also* : its flesh used as food

cod-ger \'kä-jər\ *n* [prob. alter. of *cadger*] (1756) : an often mildly eccentric and usu. elderly fellow ⟨old ~⟩

cod-i-cil \'kä-də-səl, -ˌsil\ *n* [MF *codicille*, fr. L *codicillus*, dim. of *codic-, codex*] (15c) **1** : a legal instrument made to modify an earlier will **2** : APPENDIX, SUPPLEMENT — **cod-i-cil-la-ry** \ˌkä-də-ˈsi-lə-rē\ *adj*

co-di-col-o-gy \ˌkō-də-ˈkä-lə-jē, ˌkä-\ *n* [L *codic-, codex* + -o- + E *-logy*] (1953) : the study of manuscripts as cultural artifacts for historical purposes — **co-di-co-log-i-cal** \-kə-ˈlä-ji-kəl\ *adj*

cod-i-fy \'kä-də-ˌfī, 'kō-\ *vt* **-fied; -fy-ing** (ca. 1800) **1** : to reduce to a code **2** : SYSTEMATIZE **b** : CLASSIFY — **cod-i-fi-abil-i-ty** \ˌkä-də-ˌfī-ə-ˈbi-lə-tē, ˌkō-\ *n* — **cod-i-fi-ca-tion** \-fə-ˈkä-shən\ *n*

¹cod-ling \'käd-liŋ\ *n* (13c) : a young cod **2** : any of several hakes (esp. genus *Urophycis*)

²cod-ling \'käd-liŋ\ *or* **cod-lin** \-lən\ *n* [alter. of ME *querdlyng*] (15c) : a small immature apple; *also* : any of several elongated greenish English cooking apples

codling moth *n* (1747) : a small tortricid moth (*Cydia pomonella*) having larvae that live in apples, pears, quinces, and English walnuts

cod—liver oil *n* (1783) : an oil obtained from the liver of the cod and closely related fishes and used as a source of vitamins A and D

co-dom-i-nant \ˌkō-ˈdä-mə-nənt, -ˈdäm-nənt\ *adj* (ca. 1900) **1 a** : forming part of the main canopy of a forest ⟨~ trees⟩ **b** : sharing in the controlling influence of a biotic community **2** : being fully expressed in the heterozygous condition ⟨~ alleles⟩ — **codominant** *n*

co-don \'kō-ˌdän\ *n* [¹*code* + ²*-on*] (1963) : a specific sequence of three consecutive nucleotides that is part of the genetic code and that speci-

\ə\ abut \ᵊ\ kitten, F table \ər\ further \a\ ash \ā\ ace \ä\ mop, mar \au̇\ out \ch\ chin \e\ bet \ē\ easy \g\ go \i\ hit \ī\ ice \j\ job \ŋ\ sing \ō\ go \ȯ\ law \ȯi\ boy \th\ thin \th̸\ the \ü\ loot \u̇\ foot \y\ yet \zh\ vision \ä, k̟, ⁿ, œ, œ̄, ue̷, ūe̷, ᵞ\ see Guide to Pronunciation fies a particular amino acid in a protein or starts or stops protein synthesis

cod·piece \'käd-ˌpēs\ n [ME codpese, fr. cod bag, scrotum (fr. OE codd) + pese piece] (15c) : a flap or bag concealing an opening in the front of men's breeches esp. in the 15th and 16th centuries

cods·wal·lop \'kädz-ˌwä-ləp, 'kädz-\ n [origin unknown] (1963) Brit : NONSENSE

¹co·ed \'kō-(ˌ)ed\ adj (1889)   **1** : of or relating to a coed   **2** : of or relating to coeducation   **3** : open to or used by both men and women

²coed n [short for coeducational student] (ca. 1893) : a student and esp. a female student in a coeducational institution

co—edi·tion \ˌkō-ə-'di-shən\ n (1964) : an edition of a book published simultaneously by more than one publisher usu. in different countries and in different languages

co·ed·u·ca·tion \(ˌ)kō-ˌe-jə-'kā-shən\ n (1852) : the education of students of both sexes at the same institution — **co·ed·u·ca·tion·al** \-shnəl, -shə-nᵊl\ adj — **co·ed·u·ca·tion·al·ly** adv

co·ef·fi·cient \ˌkō-ə-'fi-shənt\ n [NL coefficient-, coefficiens, fr. L co- + efficient-, efficiens efficient] (ca. 1715)   **1** : any of the factors of a product considered in relation to a specific factor; esp : a constant factor of a term as distinguished from a variable   **2 a** : a number that serves as a measure of some property or characteristic (as of a substance, device, or process) ⟨~ of expansion of a metal⟩   **b** : MEASURE

coefficient of correlation (1896) : CORRELATION COEFFICIENT

coefficient of viscosity (1866) : VISCOSITY 3

coe·la·canth \'sē-lə-ˌkan(t)th\ n [ultim. fr. Gk koilos hollow + akantha spine — more at CAVE] (1857) : any of an order (Coelacanthiformes) of lobe-finned fishes known chiefly from Paleozoic and Mesozoic fossils

coelacanth

-coele or **-coel** n comb form [prob. fr. NL -coela, fr. neut. pl. of -coelus hollow, concave, fr. Gk -koilos, fr. koilos] : cavity : chamber : ventricle ⟨blastocoel⟩ ⟨enterocoele⟩

coe·len·ter·ate \si-'len-tə-ˌrāt, -rət\ n [ultim. fr. Gk koilos + enteron intestine — more at INTER-] (1872) : any of a phylum (Cnidaria syn. Coelenterata) of radially symmetrical invertebrate animals including the corals, sea anemones, jellyfishes, and hydroids — called also cnidarian — **coelenterate** adj

coe·len·ter·on \-'rän, -rən\ n, pl **-tera** \-rə\ [NL, fr. Gk koilos + enteron] (1893) : the internal cavity of a coelenterate

coe·li·ac \'sē-lē-ˌak\ var of CELIAC

coe·lom \'sē-ləm\ n, pl **coeloms** or **coe·lo·ma·ta** \si-'lō-mə-tə\ [G, fr. Gk koilōma cavity, fr. koilos] (1878) : the usu. epithelium-lined space between the body wall and the digestive tract of metazoans above the lower worms — **coe·lo·mate** \'sē-lə-ˌmāt\ adj or n — **coe·lo·mic** \si-'lä-mik, -'lō-\ adj

coen- or **coeno-** comb form [NL, fr. Gk koin-, koino-, fr. koinos] : common : general ⟨coenocyte⟩

coe·no·bite \'sē-nə-ˌbit\ var of CENOBITE

coe·no·cyte \'sē-nə-ˌsīt\ n [ISV] (1897)   **1 a** : a multinucleate mass of protoplasm resulting from repeated nuclear division unaccompanied by cell fission   **b** : an organism consisting of such a structure   **2** : SYNCYTIUM 1 — **coe·no·cyt·ic** \ˌsē-nə-'si-tik\ adj

coe·nu·rus \si-'nür-əs, -'nyür-\ n, pl **-nu·ri** \-ˌi\ [NL, fr. coen- + Gk oura tail] (1876) : a complex tapeworm larva consisting of a sac from the inner wall of which numerous scolices develop

co·en·zyme \(ˌ)kō-'en-ˌzīm\ n (1908) : a thermostable nonprotein compound that forms the active portion of an enzyme system after combination with an apoenzyme — **co·en·zy·mat·ic** \(ˌ)kō-ˌen-zə-'ma-tik, -(ˌ)zī-\ adj — **co·en·zy·mat·i·cal·ly** \-ti-k(ə-)lē\ adv

coenzyme A n (1949) : a coenzyme $C_{21}H_{36}N_7O_{16}P_3S$ that occurs in all living cells and is essential to the metabolism of carbohydrates, fats, and some amino acids — compare ACETYL COENZYME A

coenzyme Q n (1958) : UBIQUINONE

co·equal \(ˌ)kō-'ē-kwəl\ adj (14c) : equal with one another — **coequal** n — **co·equal·i·ty** \ˌkō-ē-'kwä-lə-tē\ n — **co·equal·ly** \(ˌ)kō-'ē-kwə-lē\ adv

co·erce \kō-'ərs\ vt **co·erced; co·erc·ing** [L coercēre, fr. co- + arcēre to shut up, enclose — more at ARK] (15c)   **1** : to restrain or dominate by force ⟨religion in the past has tried to ~ the irreligious —W. R. Inge⟩   **2** : to compel to an act or choice   **3** : to bring about by force or threat ⟨~ the compliance of the rest of the community —Scott Buchanan⟩   **syn** see FORCE — **co·erc·ible** \-'ər-sə-bəl\ adj

co·er·cion \-'ər-zhən, -shən\ n (15c) : the act, process, or power of coercing

co·er·cive \-'ər-siv\ adj (ca. 1600) : serving or intended to coerce — **co·er·cive·ly** adv — **co·er·cive·ness** n

coercive force n (1827) : the opposing magnetic intensity that must be applied to a magnetized material to remove the residual magnetism

co·er·civ·i·ty \ˌkō-ˌər-'si-və-tē\ n (1898) : the property of a material determined by the value of the coercive force when the material has been magnetized to saturation

co·e·ta·ne·ous \ˌkō-ə-'tā-nē-əs\ adj [L coaetaneus, fr. co- + aetas age — more at AGE] (1608) : COEVAL

co·e·val \kō-'ē-vəl\ adj [L coaevus, fr. co- + aevum age, lifetime — more at AYE] (ca. 1662) : of the same or equal age, antiquity, or duration   **syn** see CONTEMPORARY — **coeval** n — **co·e·val·i·ty** \ˌkō-(ˌ)ē-'va-lə-tē\ n

co·evo·lu·tion \ˌkō-ˌe-və-'lü-shən also -ˌē-və-\ n (1965) : evolution involving successive changes in two or more ecologically interdependent species (as of a plant and its pollinators) that affect their interactions — **co·evo·lu·tion·ary** \-shə-ˌner-ē\ adj — **co·evolve** \ˌkō-i-'välv, -'vōlv\ vi

co·ex·ist \ˌkō-ig-'zist\ vi (1667)   **1** : to exist together or at the same time   **2** : to live in peace with each other esp. as a matter of policy — **co·ex·is·tence** \-'zis-tən(t)s\ n — **co·ex·is·tent** \-tənt\ adj

co·ex·ten·sive \ˌkō-ik-'sten(t)-siv\ adj (1771) : having the same spatial or temporal scope or boundaries — **co·ex·ten·sive·ly** adv

co·fac·tor \'kō-ˌfak-tər\ n (ca. 1909)   **1** : the signed minor of an element of a square matrix or of a determinant with the sign positive if the sum of the column number and row number of the element is even and

with the sign negative if it is odd   **2** : a substance that acts with another substance to bring about certain effects; esp : COENZYME

cof·fee \'kȯ-fē, 'kä-\ n, often attrib [It & Turk; It caffè, fr. Turk kahve, fr. Ar qahwa] (1598)   **1 a** : a beverage made by percolation, infusion, or decoction from the roasted and ground seeds of a coffee plant   **b** : any of several Old World tropical plants (genus Coffea and esp. C. arabica and C. canephora) of the madder family that are widely cultivated in warm regions for their seeds from which coffee is prepared   **c** : coffee seeds esp. roasted and often ground — compare ARABICA, ROBUSTA   **d** : a dehydrated product made from brewed coffee ⟨instant ~⟩; also : a beverage made from this   **2** : a cup of coffee ⟨two ~s⟩   **3** : COFFEE HOUR

coffee break n (1951) : a short period for rest and refreshments

coffee cake n (1879) : a sweet rich bread often with added fruit, nuts, and spices that is sometimes glazed after baking

coffee hour n (1952)   **1** : a usu. fixed occasion of informal meeting and chatting at which refreshments are served   **2** : COFFEE BREAK

cof·fee·house \-ˌhau̇s\ n (1612) : an establishment that sells coffee and usu. other refreshments and that commonly serves as an informal club for its regular customers

coffee klatch also **cof·fee—klatsch** \-ˌklach, -ˌkläch, -ˌklȯch\ n [part trans. of G Kaffeeklatsch] (1895) : KAFFEEKLATSCH

cof·fee·mak·er \-ˌmā-kər\ n (1930) : a utensil or appliance in which coffee is brewed

coffee mill n (1691) : a mill for grinding coffee beans

cof·fee·pot \-ˌpät\ n (1704) : a pot for brewing and serving coffee

coffee ring n (1924) : coffee cake in the shape of a ring

coffee roll n (1945) : a sweet roll

coffee room n (1712) : a room where refreshments are served

coffee royal n (1921) : a drink of black coffee and a liquor

coffee shop n (1836) : a small restaurant

coffee—table adj (1962) : of, relating to, or being an article (as a book or magazine) intended for display ⟨as on a coffee table⟩

coffee table n (1877) : a low table customarily placed in front of a sofa — called also cocktail table

coffee tree n (1741)   **1** : a tree (as arabica) that produces coffee   **2** : KENTUCKY COFFEE TREE

¹cof·fer \'kȯ-fər, 'kä-\ n [ME coffre, fr. OF, fr. L cophinus basket, fr. Gk kophinos] (13c)   **1** : CHEST, BOX; esp : STRONGBOX   **2** : TREASURY — usu. used in pl.   **3** : a recessed panel in a vault, ceiling, or soffit

²coffer vt (14c)   **1** : to store or hoard up in a coffer   **2** : to form (as a ceiling) with recessed panels

cof·fer·dam \-ˌdam\ n (1736)   **1** : a watertight enclosure from which water is pumped to expose the bottom of a body of water and permit construction (as of a pier)   **2** : a watertight structure for making repairs below the waterline of a ship

¹cof·fin \'kȯ-fən\ n [ME, basket, receptacle, fr. MF cofin, fr. L cophinus] (1525) : a box or chest for burying a corpse

²coffin vt (1564) : to enclose in or as if in a coffin

coffin bone n (ca. 1720) : the principal bone enclosed within the hoof of a horse — called also pedal bone

coffin corner n (1940) : one of the corners formed by a goal line and a sideline on a football field into which a punt is often aimed so that it may go out of bounds close to the defender's goal line

coffin nail n (1888) slang : CIGARETTE

cof·fle \'kȯ-fəl, 'kä-\ n [Ar qāfila caravan] (1799) : a train of slaves or animals fastened together

co·func·tion \'kō-ˌfəŋ(k)-shən\ n (1909) : a trigonometric function whose value for the complement of an angle is equal to the value of a given trigonometric function of the angle itself ⟨the sine is the ~ of the cosine⟩

¹cog \'käg\ n [ME cogge, of Scand origin; akin to Norw kug cog] (13c)   **1** : a tooth on the rim of a wheel or gear   **2** : a subordinate but vital person or part — **cogged** \'kägd\ adj

²cog vb **cogged; cog·ging** [obs. cog a trick] vi (1532)   **1** obs : to cheat in throwing dice   **2** obs : DECEIVE   **3** obs : to use venal flattery ~ vt   **1** : to direct the fall of (dice) fraudulently   **2** obs : WHEEDLE

³cog vt **cogged; cog·ging** [prob. alter. of cock to cog] (1823) : to connect (as timbers or stones) by means of mortises and tenons

⁴cog n (ca. 1858) : a tenon on a beam or timber

co·gen·cy \'kō-jən(t)-sē\ n (1667) : the quality or state of being cogent

co·gen·er·a·tion \ˌkō-je-nə-'rā-shən\ n (1978) : the production of electricity using waste heat (as in steam) from an industrial process or the use of steam from electric power generation as a source of heat — **co·gen·er·a·tor** \'je-nə-ˌrā-tər\ n

co·gent \'kō-jənt\ adj [L cogent-, cogens, prp. of cogere to drive together, collect, fr. co- + agere to drive — more at AGENT] (1659)   **1** : having power to compel or constrain ⟨~ forces⟩   **2 a** : appealing forcibly to the mind or reason : CONVINCING ⟨~ evidence⟩   **b** : PERTINENT, RELEVANT ⟨a ~ analysis of a problem⟩   **syn** see VALID — **co·gent·ly** adv

cog·i·ta·ble \'kä-jə-tə-bəl\ adj (15c) : CONCEIVABLE, THINKABLE

cog·i·tate \'kä-jə-ˌtāt\ vb **-tat·ed; -tat·ing** [L cogitatus, pp. of cogitare to think, think about, fr. co- + agitare to drive, agitate] vt (ca. 1587) : to ponder or meditate on usu. intently ~ vi : to meditate deeply or intently   **syn** see THINK

cog·i·ta·tion \ˌkä-jə-'tā-shən\ n (13c)   **1 a** : the act of cogitating : MEDITATION   **b** : the capacity to think or reflect   **2** : a single thought

cog·i·ta·tive \'kä-jə-ˌtā-tiv\ adj (15c)   **1** : of or relating to cogitation   **2** : capable of or given to cogitation

cog·i·to \'kä-gi-ˌtō, 'kō-, 'kä-ji-\ n [NL cogito, ergo sum, lit., I think, therefore I am, principle stated by René Descartes] (1838)   **1** : the philosophic principle that one's existence is demonstrated by the fact that one thinks   **2** : the intellectual processes of the self or ego

co·gnac \'kȯn-ˌyak also 'kȯn- or 'kän-\ n [F, fr. Cognac, France] (1755) : a brandy from the departments of Charente and Charente-Maritime distilled from white wine

¹cog·nate \'käg-ˌnāt\ adj [L cognatus, fr. co- + gnatus, natus, pp. of nasci to be born; akin to L gignere to beget — more at KIN] (ca. 1645)   **1** : of the same or similar nature : generically alike   **2** : related by blood; also : related on the mother's side   **3 a** : related by descent from the same ancestral language   **b** of a word or morpheme : related by derivation, borrowing, or descent   **c** of a substantive : related to a verb usu. by derivation and serving as its object to reinforce the meaning — **cog·nate·ly** adv

²**cognate** n (1754) : one that is cognate with another

cog·na·tion \käg-'nā-shən\ n (14c) : cognate relationship

cog·ni·tion \käg-'ni-shən\ n [ME cognicioun, fr. L cognition-, cognitio, fr. cognoscere to become acquainted with, know, fr. co- + gnoscere to come to know — more at KNOW⟩ (15c) : the act or process of knowing including both awareness and judgment; also : a product of this act — **cog·ni·tion·al** \-'nish-nəl, -'ni-shə-n²l\ adj

cog·ni·tive \'käg-nə-tiv\ adj (1586) 1 : of, relating to, or involving cognition ⟨the ~ elements of perception —C. H. Hamburg⟩ 2 : based on or capable of being reduced to empirical factual knowledge — **cog·ni·tive·ly** adv

cognitive dissonance n (1957) : psychological conflict resulting from incongruous beliefs and attitudes held simultaneously

cognitive science n (1976) : an interdisciplinary science that draws on many fields (as psychology, artificial intelligence, linguistics, and philosophy) in developing theories about human perception, thinking, and learning

cog·ni·za·ble \'käg-nə-zə-bəl, käg-'nī-\ adj (1678) 1 : capable of being known 2 : capable of being judicially heard and determined — **cog·ni·za·bly** \-blē\ adv

cog·ni·zance \'käg-nə-zən(t)s\ n [ME conisaunce, fr. MF conoissance, fr. conoistre to know, fr. L cognoscere⟩ (14c) 1 : a distinguishing mark or emblem (as a heraldic bearing) 2 a : KNOWLEDGE, AWARENESS ⟨had no ~ of the situation⟩ b : NOTICE, ACKNOWLEDGMENT ⟨take ~ of their achievement⟩ 3 : JURISDICTION, RESPONSIBILITY

cog·ni·zant \-zənt\ adj (1820) : knowledgeable of something esp. through personal experience; MINDFUL syn see AWARE

cog·nize \käg-'nīz, 'käg-,\ vt cog·nized; cog·niz·ing [back-formation fr. cognizance⟩ (ca. 1837) : KNOW, UNDERSTAND — **cog·niz·er** n

cog·no·men \käg-'nō-mən, 'käg-nə-\ n, pl **cognomens** or **cog·no·mi·na** \käg-'nä-mə-nə, -'nō-\ [L, irreg. fr. co- + nomen name — more at NAME⟩ (1809) 1 : SURNAME; esp : the third of usu. three names borne by a male citizen of ancient Rome 2 : NAME; esp : a distinguishing nickname or epithet — **cog·nom·i·nal** \käg-'nä-mə-n²l\ adj

co·gno·scen·te \,kän-yə-'shen-tē, ,käg-nə-, -'sen-\ n, pl **-scen·ti** \-tē\ [obs. It (now conoscente), fr. cognoscente, adj., wise, fr. L cognoscent-, cognoscens, prp. of cognoscere⟩ (1776) : a person who is esp. knowledgeable in a subject : CONNOISSEUR

cog·nos·ci·ble \käg-'nä-sə-bəl\ adj [LL cognoscibilis, fr. L cognoscere⟩ (ca. 1644) : COGNIZABLE, KNOWABLE

co·gon \kō-'gōn\ n [Sp cogón, fr. Tag & Bisayan kugon⟩ (1898) : any of several coarse tall grasses (genus Imperata) used esp. in the Philippines for thatching

cog railway n (1896) : a steep mountain railroad that has a rail with cogs engaged by a cogwheel on the locomotive to ensure traction

cog·wheel \'käg-,hwēl, -,wēl\ n (14c) : a wheel with cogs : GEAR 6a(2)

co·hab·it \(,)kō-'ha-bət\ vi [LL cohabitare, fr. L co- + habitare to inhabit, fr. freq. of habēre to have — more at GIVE⟩ (ca. 1530) 1 : to live together as or as if a married couple 2 a : to live together or in company ⟨buffaloes ~ing with crossbred cows —Biol. Abstracts⟩ b : to exist together ⟨two strains in his philosophy . . . ~ in each of his major works —Justus Buchler⟩ — **co·hab·i·tant** \-bə-tənt\ n — **co·hab·i·ta·tion** \(,)kō-,ha-bə-'tā-shən\ n

co·here \kō-'hir\ vb **co·hered; co·her·ing** [L cohaerēre, fr. co- + haerēre to stick⟩ vi (1598) 1 a : to hold together firmly as parts of the same mass; broadly : STICK, ADHERE b : to display cohesion of plant parts 2 : to hold together as a mass of parts that cohere 3 a : to become united in principles, relationships, or interests b : to be logically or aesthetically consistent ~ vt : to cause (parts or components) to cohere syn see STICK

co·her·ence \kō-'hir-ən(t)s, -'her-\ n (1580) 1 : the quality or state of cohering: as a : systematic or logical connection or consistency b : integration of diverse elements, relationships, or values 2 : the property of being coherent

co·her·en·cy \-ən(t)-sē, -'her-\ n, pl **-cies** (1630) : COHERENCE

co·her·ent \-ənt\ adj [MF or L; MF cohérent, fr. L cohaerent-, cohaerens, prp. of cohaerēre⟩ (ca. 1555) 1 a : logically or aesthetically ordered or integrated : CONSISTENT ⟨~ style⟩ ⟨a ~ argument⟩ b : having clarity or intelligibility : UNDERSTANDABLE ⟨a ~ person⟩ ⟨a ~ passage⟩ 2 : having the quality of cohering; esp : COHESIVE, COORDINATED ⟨a ~ plan for action⟩ 3 a : relating to or composed of waves having a constant difference in phase ⟨~ light⟩ b : producing coherent light ⟨a ~ source⟩ — **co·her·ent·ly** adv

co·her·er \kō-'hir-ər\ n (1894) : a radio detector in which an imperfectly conducting contact between pieces of conductive material loosely resting against each other is materially improved in conductance by the passage of high-frequency current

co·he·sion \kō-'hē-zhən\ n [L cohaesus, pp. of cohaerēre⟩ (1660) 1 : the act or state of sticking together tightly; esp : UNITY ⟨the lack of ~ in the Party —Times Lit. Supp.⟩ 2 : union between similar plant parts or organs 3 : molecular attraction by which the particles of a body are united throughout the mass — **co·he·sion·less** \-ləs\ adj

co·he·sive \kō-'hē-siv, -ziv\ adj (ca. 1731) : exhibiting or producing cohesion or coherence ⟨a ~ social unit⟩ ⟨~ soils⟩ — **co·he·sive·ly** adv — **co·he·sive·ness** n

co·ho \'kō-(,)hō\ n, pl **cohos** or **coho** [Halkomelem (Salishan language of southwest British Columbia) k̓wôx̌wəθ⟩ (1869) : a rather small Pacific salmon (Oncorhynchus kisutch) that has light-colored flesh and is native to both coasts of the No. Pacific and is stocked in the Great Lakes

co·ho·mol·o·gy \(,)kō-hō-'mä-lə-jē\ n (ca. 1959) : a part of the theory of topology in which groups are used to study the properties of topological spaces and which is related in a complementary way to homology theory — called also cohomology theory — **co·ho·mo·log·i·cal** \-,hō-mə-'lä-ji-kəl, -,hä-\ adj

co·hort \'kō-,hört\ n [MF & L; MF cohorte, fr. L cohort-, cohors — more at COURT⟩ (15c) 1 a : one of 10 divisions of an ancient Roman legion b : a group of warriors or soldiers c : BAND, GROUP d : a group of individuals having a statistical factor (as age or class membership) in common in a demographic study ⟨a ~ of premedical students⟩ 2 : COMPANION, COLLEAGUE ⟨a few of their . . . ~s decided to form a company —Burt Hochberg⟩

co·hosh \'kō-,häsh\ n [Eastern Abenaki kk"àhas⟩ (1789) : any of several American medicinal or poisonous plants: as a : BLACK COHOSH b : BLUE COHOSH c : BANEBERRY

¹**coif** \'kȯif, in sense 2 also 'kwäf\ n [ME coife, fr. MF, fr. LL cofea⟩ (14c) 1 : a close-fitting cap: as a : a hoodlike cap worn under a veil by nuns b : a protective usu. metal skullcap formerly worn under a hood of mail c : a white cap formerly worn by English lawyers and esp. by serjeants-at-law; also : the order or rank of a serjeant-at-law 2 : COIFFURE

²**coif** \'kȯif, 'kwäf\ vt **coiffed** or **coifed; coif·fing** or **coif·ing** (15c) 1 : to cover or dress with or as if with a coif 2 : to arrange (hair) by brushing, combing, or curling

coif·feur \kwä-'fər\ n [F, fr. coiffer⟩ (1847) : a man who is a hairdresser

coif·feuse \kwä-'fə(r)z, -'fyüz, -'füz\ n [F, fem. of coiffeur⟩ (1870) : a woman who is a hairdresser

coif·fure \kwä-'fyür\ n [F, fr. coiffer to cover with a coif, arrange (hair), fr. coife⟩ (ca. 1631) : a style or manner of arranging the hair

coif·fured \-'fyürd\ adj (1907) 1 : being dressed ⟨beautifully ~ hair⟩ 2 : having the hair brushed, combed, and curled ⟨stylishly ~ women⟩

coign of van·tage \,kȯi-nə-'van-tij\ [coign, earlier spelling of ¹coin (corner)⟩ (1605) : an advantageous position

¹**coil** \'kȯi(ə)l\ n [origin unknown⟩ (1567) 1 : TURMOIL 2 : TROUBLE; also : everyday cares and worries ⟨when we have shuffled off this mortal ~ —Shak.⟩

²**coil** vb [F coillir, cuillir to gather — more at CULL⟩ vt (1611) 1 : to wind into rings or spirals 2 : to roll or twist into a shape resembling a coil ~ vi 1 : to move in a circular or spiral course 2 : to form or lie in a coil — **coil·abil·i·ty** \,kȯi-lə-'bi-lə-tē\ n

³**coil** n (1627) 1 a (1) : a series of loops (2) : SPIRAL b : a single loop of such a coil 2 a : a number of turns of wire wound around a core (as of iron) to create a magnetic field for an electromagnet or an induction coil b : INDUCTION COIL 3 : a series of connected pipes in rows, layers, or windings 4 : a roll of postage stamps; also : a stamp from such a roll

¹**coin** \'kȯin\ n [ME, fr. MF, wedge, corner, fr. L cuneus wedge⟩ (14c) 1 archaic a : CORNER, CORNERSTONE, QUOIN b : WEDGE 2 a : a usu. flat piece of metal issued by governmental authority as money b : metal money c : something resembling a coin esp. in shape 3 : something used as if it were money (as in verbal or intellectual exchange) ⟨perhaps wisecracks . . . are respectable literary ~ in the U.S. —Times Lit. Supp.⟩ ⟨would repay him with the full ~ of his mind —Ian Fleming⟩ 4 : something having two different and usu. opposing sides — usu. used in the phrase the other side of the coin 5 : MONEY ⟨I'm in it for the ~ —Sinclair Lewis⟩

²**coin** vt (14c) 1 a : to make (a coin) esp. by stamping : MINT b : to convert (metal) into coins 2 : CREATE, INVENT ⟨~ a phrase⟩ — **coin·er** \'kȯi-nər\ n — **coin money** : to get rich quickly

³**coin** adj (ca. 1566) 1 : of or relating to coins : operated by coins

coin·age \'kȯi-nij\ n (14c) 1 : the act or process of coining 2 a : COINS b : something (as a word) made up or invented

co·in·cide \,kō-ən-'sīd, 'kō-ən-,\ vi **-cid·ed; -cid·ing** [ML coincidere, fr. L co- + incidere to fall on, fr. in- + cadere to fall — more at CHANCE⟩ (1719) 1 a : to occupy the same place in space or time b : to occupy exactly corresponding or equivalent positions on a scale or in a series 2 : to correspond in nature, character, or function 3 : to be in accord or agreement : CONCUR syn see AGREE

co·in·ci·dence \kō-'in(t)-sə-dən(t)s, -sə-,den(t)s\ n (1605) 1 : the act or condition of coinciding : CORRESPONDENCE 2 : the occurrence of events that happen at the same time by accident but seem to have some connection; also : any of these occurrences

co·in·ci·dent \-sə-dənt, -,dent\ adj [F coincident, fr. ML coincident-, coincidens, prp. of coincidere⟩ (ca. 1587) 1 : of similar nature : HARMONIOUS ⟨a theory ~ with the facts⟩ 2 : occupying the same space or time ⟨~ events⟩ syn see CONTEMPORARY — **co·in·ci·dent·ly** \-sə-dənt-lē, -,dent-;⟩ (,)kō-,in(t)-sə-'dent-lē⟩ adv

co·in·ci·den·tal \(,)kō-,in(t)-sə-'den-t²l\ adj (ca. 1800) 1 : resulting from a coincidence 2 : occurring or existing at the same time — **co·in·ci·den·tal·ly** \-'dent-lē, -'den-t²l-ē\ adv

coin-op \'kȯin-,näp\ n (1961) : a self-service laundry where the machines are operated by coins

co·in·sur·ance \,kō-ən-'shür-ən(t)s also -'in-,\ n (ca. 1889) 1 : joint assumption of risk (as by two underwriters) with another 2 : insurance (as fire insurance) in which the insured is obligated to maintain coverage on a risk at a stipulated percentage of its total value or in the event of loss suffer a penalty in proportion to the deficiency

co·in·sure \,kō-ən-'shür\ vt (ca. 1899) : to insure jointly — **co·in·sur·er** n

coir \'kȯi(-ə)r\ n [Tamil kayiṟu rope⟩ (1582) : a stiff coarse fiber from the outer husk of a coconut

cois·trel \'kȯi-strəl\ n [MF coustiller soldier carrying a short sword, fr. coustille short sword, fr. L cultellus knife — more at CUTLASS⟩ (1581) archaic : a mean fellow : VARLET

co·i·tion \kō-'i-shən\ n [LL, fr. L coition-, coitio a coming together, fr. coire to come together, fr. co- + ire to go — more at ISSUE⟩ (1615) : COITUS — **co·i·tion·al** \-'ish-nəl, -'i-shə-n²l\ adj

co·i·tus \'kō-ə-təs, kō-'ē-, 'kȯi-təs\ n [L, fr. coire⟩ (1855) : physical union of male and female genitalia accompanied by rhythmic movements usu. leading to the ejaculation of semen from the penis into the female reproductive tract; also : INTERCOURSE 3 — compare ORGASM — **co·i·tal** \-t²l\ adj — **co·i·tal·ly** \-t²l-ē\ adv

coitus in·ter·rup·tus \-,in-tə-'rəp-təs\ n [NL, interrupted coitus⟩ (1900) : coitus in which the penis is withdrawn prior to ejaculation to prevent the deposit of sperm into the vagina

¹**coke** \'kōk\ n [perh. fr. dial. coke, colk core, fr. ME; akin to Sw kälk pith⟩ (1669) : the residue of coal left after destructive distillation and

\ə\ abut \²\ kitten, F table \ər\ further \a\ ash \ā\ ace \ä\ mop, mar \aü\ out \ch\ chin \e\ bet \ē\ easy \g\ go \i\ hit \ī\ ice \j\ job \ŋ\ sing \ō\ go \ȯ\ law \ȯi\ boy \th\ thin \th\ the \ü\ loot \ü\ foot \y\ yet \zh\ vision \ə, k̲, ⁿ, œ, œ̄, ue, ūe, ᵊ\ see Guide to Pronunciation used as fuel; *also* : a similar residue left by other materials (as petroleum) distilled to dryness

²**coke** *vb* **coked; cok·ing** *vt* (1763) : to change into coke ∼ *vi* : to become coke or like coke

³**coke** *n* [by shortening & alter.] (ca. 1903) : COCAINE

Coke \'kōk\ *trademark* — used for a cola drink

coke·head \'kō-ked, 'kōk-,hed\ *n* (ca. 1927) : a person who uses cocaine compulsively

col \'käl\ *n* [F, fr. MF, neck, fr. L *collum*] (1853) : SADDLE 3

¹**col-** — see COM-

²**col-** *or* **coli-** *or* **colo-** *comb form* [NL, fr. L *colon*]   **1** : colon ⟨*colitis*⟩ ⟨*colostomy*⟩   **2** [NL *Escherichia coli*, species of colon bacillus]: colon bacillus ⟨*coliform*⟩

¹**cola** *pl of* COLON

²**co·la** \'kō-lə\ *n* [fr. *Coca-Cola*, a trademark] (1920) : a carbonated soft drink colored usu. with caramel and flavored usu. with extracts from kola nuts

col·an·der \'kəl-ən-dər, 'kal-\ *n* [ME *colyndore*, prob. modif. of OProv *colador*, fr. ML *colatorium*, fr. L *colare* to sieve, fr. *colum* sieve] (14c) : a perforated utensil for washing or draining food

co·lat·i·tude \(,)kō-'la-tə-,tüd, -,tyüd\ *n* (1790) : the complement of the latitude

Col·by \'kōl-bē\ *n* [prob. fr. the name *Colby*] (1942) : a moist mild cheese similar to cheddar

col·can·non \käl-'ka-nən\ *n* [Ir *cál ceannan*, lit., white-headed cabbage] (ca. 1785) : potatoes and cabbage boiled and mashed together with butter and seasoning

col·chi·cine \'käl-chə-,sēn, 'käl-kə-\ *n* (ca. 1847) : a poisonous alkaloid $C_{22}H_{25}NO_6$ that inhibits mitosis, is extracted from the corms or seeds of the autumn crocus (*Colchicum autumnale*), and is used esp. in the treatment of gout and to produce polyploidy in plants

col·chi·cum \'käl-chi-kəm, 'käl-ki-\ *n* [NL, genus name, fr. L, a kind of plant with a poisonous root, fr. Gk *kolchikon*, lit., product of Colchis] (1597)   **1** : any of a genus (*Colchicum*) of Old World corm-producing herbs of the lily family with flowers that resemble crocuses   **2** : the dried corm or dried seeds of autumn crocus containing colchicine, possessing emetic, diuretic, and cathartic action, and used to treat gout

¹**cold** \'kōld\ *adj* [ME, fr. OE *ceald, cald*; akin to OHG *kalt* cold, L *gelu* frost, *gelare* to freeze] (bef. 12c)   **1 a** : having or being a temperature that is uncomfortably low for humans ⟨it is ∼ outside today⟩   **b** : having a relatively low temperature or one lower than normal or expected ⟨the bath water has gotten ∼⟩   **c** : not heated: as   **(1)** *of food* : served without heating esp. after initial cooking or processing ⟨∼ cereal⟩ ⟨∼ roast beef⟩   **(2)** : served chilled or with ice ⟨a ∼ drink⟩   **3** : involving processing without the use of heat ⟨∼ working of steel⟩   **2 a** : marked by a lack of the warmth of normal human emotion, friendliness, or compassion ⟨got a ∼ reception⟩; *also* : not moved to enthusiasm ⟨the movie leaves me ∼⟩   **b** : not colored or affected by personal feeling or bias : DETACHED, INDIFFERENT ⟨∼ chronicles recorded by an outsider —Andrew Sarris⟩; *also* : IMPERSONAL, OBJECTIVE ⟨∼ facts⟩ ⟨∼ reality⟩   **c** : marked by sure familiarity : PAT ⟨had her lines ∼ weeks before opening night⟩   **3** : conveying the impression of being cold: as   **a** : DEPRESSING, GLOOMY ⟨∼ gray skies⟩   **b** : COOL 6a   **4 a** : marked by the loss of normal body heat ⟨∼ hands⟩; *esp* : DEAD   **b** : giving the appearance of being dead : UNCONSCIOUS ⟨passed out ∼⟩   **5 a** : having lost freshness or vividness : STALE ⟨dogs trying to pick up a ∼ scent⟩   **b** : far off the mark : not close to finding or solving — used esp. in children's games   **c** : marked by poor or unlucky performance ⟨the team's shooting turned ∼ in the second half⟩   **d** : not prepared or suitably warmed up — **cold·ish** \'kōl-dish\ *adj* — **cold·ly** \'kōl(d)-lē\ *adv* — **cold·ness** \'kōl(d)-nəs\ *n* — **in cold blood** : with premeditation : DELIBERATELY

²**cold** *n* (13c)   **1** : bodily sensation produced by loss or lack of heat   **2** : a condition of low temperature; *esp* : cold weather   **3** : a bodily disorder popularly associated with chilling; *specif* : COMMON COLD — **out in the cold** : deprived of benefits given others ⟨the plan benefits management but leaves labor *out in the cold*⟩

³**cold** *adv* (1889)   **1** : with utter finality : ABSOLUTELY, COMPLETELY ⟨turned down ∼⟩; *also* : ABRUPTLY ⟨stopped them ∼⟩   **2 a** : without introduction or advance notice   **b** : without preparation or warm-up

cold–blood·ed \'kōl(d)-'blə-dəd\ *adj* (1595)   **1 a** : done or acting without consideration, compunction, or clemency ⟨∼ murder⟩   **b** : MATTER-OF-FACT, EMOTIONLESS ⟨a ∼ assessment⟩   **2** : having cold blood; *specif* : having a body temperature not internally regulated but approximating that of the environment   **3** *or* **cold-blood** \-'bləd\ : of mixed or inferior breeding   **4** : noticeably sensitive to cold — **cold–blood·ed·ly** *adv* — **cold–blood·ed·ness** *n*

cold call *n* (1966) : a telephone call soliciting business made directly to a potential customer without prior contact or without a lead — **cold–call** *vb*

cold cash *n* (1925) : money in hand

cold chisel *n* (1699) : a chisel made of tool steel of a strength, shape, and temper suitable for chipping or cutting cold metal

cold–cock \'kōl(d)-'käk, ,kōl(d)-'\ *vt* [perh. ²*cock*] (ca. 1927) : to knock unconscious

cold comfort *n* (14c) : quite limited sympathy, consolation, or encouragement

cold cream *n* (1709) : a soothing and cleansing cosmetic

cold cuts *n pl* (1945) : sliced assorted cold cooked meats

cold duck *n* [trans. of G *Kalte Ente*] (1969) : a beverage that consists of a blend of sparkling burgundy and champagne

cold–eyed \'kōl-'dīd, -,did\ *adj* (1950) : cold in manner or appearance; *esp* : coolly dispassionate ⟨∼ analysis⟩

cold feet *n pl* (1893) : apprehension or doubt strong enough to prevent a planned course of action

cold fish *n* (1924) : a cold aloof person

cold frame *n* (1851) : a usu. glass- or plastic-covered frame without artificial heat used to protect plants and seedlings outdoors

cold frame

cold front *n* (1921) : an advancing edge of a cold air mass

cold-heart·ed \'kōld-'här-təd\ *adj* (1606) : marked by lack of sympathy, interest, or sensitivity — **cold-heart·ed·ly** *adv* — **cold-heart·ed·ness** *n*

cold shoulder *n* (1816) : intentionally cold or unsympathetic treatment — **cold–shoulder** *vt*

cold sore *n* (ca. 1889) : a group of blisters appearing about or within the mouth and caused by a herpes simplex virus

cold storage *n* (1877)   **1** : storage (as of food) in a cold place for preservation   **2** : a condition of being held or continued without being acted on : ABEYANCE

cold store *n* (1895) : a building for cold storage

cold sweat *n* (1706) : concurrent perspiration and chill usu. associated with fear, pain, or shock

¹**cold turkey** *n* (1921)   **1** : abrupt complete cessation of the use of an addictive drug; *also* : the symptoms experienced by a person undergoing withdrawal from a drug   **2** : unrelieved blunt language or procedure   **3** : a cold aloof person — **cold turkey** *vt*

²**cold turkey** *adv* (1941) : without a period of gradual adjustment, adaptation, or withdrawal : all at once ⟨quit smoking *cold turkey*⟩

cold type *n* (1949) : composition or typesetting (as photocomposition) done without the casting of metal; *specif* : such composition produced directly on paper by a typewriter mechanism

cold war *n* (1945)   **1** : a conflict over ideological differences carried on by methods short of sustained overt military action and usu. without breaking off diplomatic relations; *specif, often cap C&W* : the ideological conflict between the U.S. and the U.S.S.R. — compare HOT WAR   **2** : a condition of rivalry, mistrust, and often open hostility short of violence esp. between power groups (as labor and management)

cold warrior *n* (1949) : one that supports or is engaged in a cold war

cold–water *adj* (1942) : having only running water without heat or utility services provided ⟨a ∼ flat⟩

cold water *n* (1808) : depreciation of something as being ill-advised, unwarranted, or worthless ⟨threw *cold water* on our hopes⟩

cold wave *n* (1876)   **1** : an unusually large and rapid drop in temperature over a short period of time (as 24 hours)   **2** : a permanent wave set by a chemical preparation without the use of heat

cole \'kōl\ *n* [ME, fr. OE *cāl*, fr. L *caulis* stem, cabbage; akin to Gk *kaulos* stem, Latvian *kauls*] (bef. 12c) : any of several brassicas; *esp* : any of various crop plants (as broccoli, kale, brussels sprouts, cabbage, cauliflower, and kohlrabi) derived from the same wild ancestor (*Brassica oleracea*)

cole·man·ite \'kōl-mə-,nīt\ *n* [William T. *Coleman* †1893 Am. businessman and mine owner] (1884) : a mineral consisting of a hydrous calcium borate occurring in brilliant colorless or white massive monoclinic crystals

co·le·op·tera \,kō-lē-'äp-tə-rə\ *n pl* [NL, ultim. fr. Gk *koleon* sheath + *pteron* wing — more at FEATHER] (1873) : insects that are beetles — **co·le·op·ter·ist** \-tə-rist\ *n* — **co·le·op·ter·ous** \-tə-rəs\ *adj*

co·le·op·ter·an \-tə-rən\ *n* (ca. 1847) : ¹BEETLE 1 — **coleopteran** *adj*

co·le·op·tile \-'äp-t⁸l\ *n* [NL *coleoptilum*, fr. Gk *koleon* + *ptilon* down; akin to Gk *pteron*] (ca. 1866) : the first leaf of a monocotyledon forming a protective sheath about the plumule

co·le·o·rhi·za \,kō-lē-ə-'rī-zə\ *n, pl* **-zae** \-(,)zē\ [NL, fr. Gk *koleon* + NL *-rhiza*] (ca. 1866) : the sheath investing the hypocotyl in some monocotyledonous plants through which the roots burst

cole·slaw \'kōl-,slȯ\ *n* [D *koolsla*, fr. *kool* cabbage + *sla* salad] (1794) : a salad made of raw sliced or chopped cabbage

co·le·us \'kō-lē-əs\ *n* [NL, genus name, fr. Gk *koleos, koleon* sheath] (1885) : any of a large genus (*Coleus*) of herbs of the mint family

cole·wort \'kōl-,wərt, -,wȯrt\ *n* (14c) : COLE; *esp* : one (as kale) that forms no head

coli- — see COL-

¹**col·ic** \'kä-lik\ *n* [ME, fr. MF *colique*, fr. LL *colicus* colicky, fr. Gk *kōlikos*, fr. *kōlon*, alter. of *kolon* colon] (15c) : a paroxysm of acute abdominal pain localized in a hollow organ and often caused by spasm, obstruction, or twisting

²**colic** *adj* (15c) : of or relating to colic : COLICKY ⟨∼ crying⟩

³**col·ic** \'kō-lik, 'kä-\ *adj* (1615) : of or relating to the colon ⟨∼ lymph nodes⟩

co·li·cin \'kō-lə-sən\ *also* **co·li·cine** \-,sēn\ *n* [F *colicine*, fr. *col-* + *-cine* (as in *streptomycine* streptomycin)] (1946) : any of various antibacterial substances that are produced by strains of intestinal bacteria (as of *Escherichia coli*) having a specific plasmid and that often act to inhibit macromolecular synthesis in related strains

col·icky \'kä-li-kē\ *adj* (1742)   **1** : relating to or associated with colic ⟨∼ pain⟩   **2** : suffering from colic ⟨∼ babies⟩

col·ic·root \'kä-lik-,rüt, -,rút\ *n* (1833) : any of several plants having roots used in folk medicine to treat colic; *esp* : either of two bitter herbs (*Aletris farinosa* and *A. aurea*) of the lily family

co·li·form \'kō-lə-,fȯrm, 'kä-\ *adj* (1906) : relating to, resembling, or being the colon bacillus — **coliform** *n*

co·lin·ear \(,)kō-'li-nē-ər\ *adj* (1927)   **1** : COLLINEAR   **2** : having corresponding parts arranged in the same linear order ⟨a gene and the protein it determines are ∼⟩ — **co·lin·ear·i·ty** \(,)kō-,li-nē-'ar-ə-tē\ *n*

co·li·phage \'kō-lə-,fāj, -,fäzh\ *n* (1940) : any bacteriophage active against the colon bacillus

col·i·se·um \,kä-lə-'sē-əm\ *n* [ML *Colosseum, Colisseum*] (ca. 1715)   **1** *cap* : COLOSSEUM 1   **2** : a large sports stadium or building designed like the Colosseum for public entertainments

co·lis·tin \kə-'lis-tən, kō-\ *n* [NL *colistinus*, specific epithet of the bacterium producing it] (1951) : a polymyxin produced by a bacterium (*Bacillus polymyxa* var. *colistinus*) from Japanese soil

co·li·tis \kō-'lī-təs, kə-\ *n* (ca. 1860) : inflammation of the colon

coll- *or* **collo-** *comb form* [NL, fr. Gk *koll-, kollo-*, fr. *kolla* — more at PROTOCOL]   **1** : glue ⟨*collenchyma*⟩   **2** : colloid ⟨*collotype*⟩

col·lab·o·rate \kə-'la-bə-,rāt\ *vi* **-rat·ed; -rat·ing** [LL *collaboratus*, pp. of *collaborare* to labor together, fr. L *com-* + *laborare* to labor] (1871)   **1** : to work jointly with others or together esp. in an intellectual endeavor   **2** : to cooperate with or willingly assist an enemy of one's country and esp. an occupying force   **3** : to cooperate with an agency or instrumentality with which one is not immediately connected — **col·lab·o·ra·tion** \-,la-bə-'rā-shən\ *n* — **col·lab·o·ra·tive** \-'la-bə-,rā-tiv, -b(ǝ)rǝ-\ *adj or n* — **col·lab·o·ra·tive·ly** \-lē\ *adv* — **col·lab·o·ra·tor** \-'la-bǝ-‚rā-tǝr\ *n*

col·lab·o·ra·tion·ism \kǝ-‚la-bǝ-'rā-shǝ-‚ni-zǝm\ *n* (1923) : the advocacy or practice of collaboration with an enemy — **col·lab·o·ra·tion·ist** \-sh(ǝ-)nist\ *adj or n*

col·lage \kǝ-'läzh, kò-, kō-\ *n* [F, lit., gluing, fr. *coller* to glue, fr. *colle* glue, fr. (assumed) VL *colla*, fr. Gk *kolla*] (1919) **1** : an artistic composition made of various materials (as paper, cloth, or wood) glued on a surface **2** : the art of making collages **3** : an assembly of diverse fragments ⟨a ~ of ideas⟩ **4** : a work (as a film) having disparate scenes in rapid succession without transitions — **collage** *vt* — **col·lag·ist** \-'lä-zhist\ *n*

col·la·gen \'kä-lǝ-jǝn\ *n* [Gk *kolla* + ISV *-gen*] (ca. 1865) : an insoluble fibrous protein that occurs in vertebrates as the chief constituent of connective tissue fibrils and in bones and yields gelatin and glue on prolonged heating with water — **col·lag·e·nous** \kǝ-'la-jǝ-nǝs\ *adj*

col·la·ge·nase \'kä-lǝ-jǝ-‚nās, 'kä-lǝ-jǝ-, -‚nāz\ *n* (1926) : any of a group of proteolytic enzymes that decompose collagen and gelatin

¹**col·lapse** \kǝ-'laps\ *vb* **col·lapsed; col·laps·ing** [L *collapsus*, pp. of *collabi*, fr. *com-* + *labi* to fall, slide — more at SLEEP] *vi* (1732) **1** : to fall or shrink together abruptly and completely : fall into a jumbled or flattened mass through the force of external pressure ⟨a blood vessel that *collapsed*⟩ **2** : to break down completely : DISINTEGRATE ⟨his case had *collapsed* in a mass of legal wreckage —Erle Stanley Gardner⟩ **3** : to cave or fall in or give way **4** : to suddenly lose force, significance, effectiveness, or worth **5** : to break down in vital energy, stamina, or self-control through exhaustion or disease; *esp* : to fall helpless or unconscious **6** : to fold down into a more compact shape ⟨a chair that ~s⟩ ~ *vt* : to cause to collapse — **col·laps·ibil·i·ty** \-‚lap-sǝ-'bi-lǝ-tē\ *n* — **col·laps·ible** \-'lap-sǝ-bǝl\ *adj*

²**collapse** *n* (1801) **1 a** : a breakdown in vital energy, strength, or stamina **b** : a state of extreme prostration and physical depression (as from circulatory failure or great loss of body fluids) **c** : an airless state of all or part of a lung originating spontaneously or induced surgically **2** : the act or action of collapsing ⟨the cutting of many tent ropes, the ~ of the canvas —Rudyard Kipling⟩ **3** : a sudden failure : BREAKDOWN, RUIN **4** : a sudden loss of force, value, or effect ⟨the ~ of respect for ancient law and custom —L. S. B. Leakey⟩

¹**col·lar** \'kä-lǝr\ *n* [ME *coler*, fr. OF, fr. L *collare*, fr. *collum* neck; akin to OE *heals* neck, and prob. to OE *hwēol* wheel — more at WHEEL] (14c) **1** : a band, strip, or chain worn around the neck: as **a** : a band that serves to finish or decorate the neckline of a garment **b** : a short necklace **c** : a band placed about the neck of an animal **d** : a part of the harness of draft animals fitted over the shoulders and taking strain when a load is drawn **e** : an indication of control : a token of subservience **f** : a protective or supportive device (as a brace or cast) worn around the neck **g** : CLERICAL COLLAR **2** : something resembling a collar in shape or use (as a ring or round flange to restrain motion or hold something in place) **3** : any of various animal structures or markings similar to a collar **4** : an act of collaring : ARREST, CAPTURE — **col·lared** \-lǝrd\ *adj* — **col·lar·less** \-lǝr-lǝs\ *adj*

²**collar** *vt* (1613) **1 a** : to seize by the collar or neck **b** : ARREST, GRAB **c** : to get control of : PREEMPT ⟨we can ~ nearly the whole of this market —Roald Dahl⟩ **d** : to stop and detain in unwilling conversation **2** : to put a collar on

col·lar·bone \'kä-lǝr-‚bōn\ *n* (15c) : CLAVICLE

collar cell *n* (ca. 1889) : a flagellated endodermal cell that lines the cavity of a sponge and has a contractile protoplasmic cup surrounding the flagellum — called also *choanocyte*

col·lard \'kä-lǝrd\ *n* [alter. of *colewort*] (1755) : a stalked smooth-leaved kale — usu. used in pl.

col·late \kǝ-'lāt, kä-, kō-; 'kä-‚ 'kō-\ *vt* **col·lat·ed; col·lat·ing** [back-formation fr. *collation*] (1612) **1 a** : to compare critically **b** : to collect, compare carefully in order to verify, and often to integrate or arrange in order **2** [L *collatus*, pp.]: to institute (a cleric) to a benefice **3 a** : to verify the order of (printed sheets) **b** : to assemble in proper order; *esp* : to assemble (as printed sheets) in order for binding — **syn** see COMPARE — **col·la·tor** \'lā-tǝr, -‚lä-\ *n*

¹**col·lat·er·al** \kǝ-'la-t(ǝ-)rǝl\ *adj* [ME, prob. fr. MF, fr. ML *collateralis*, fr. L *com-* + *lateralis* lateral] (14c) **1 a** : accompanying as secondary or subordinate : CONCOMITANT ⟨digress into ~ matters⟩ **b** : INDIRECT **c** : serving to support or reinforce : ANCILLARY **2** : belonging to the same ancestral stock but not in a direct line of descent — compare LINEAL 3a **3** : parallel, coordinate, or corresponding in position, order, time, or significance ⟨~ states like Athens and Sparta⟩ **4 a** : of, relating to, or being collateral used as security (as for payment of a debt or performance of a contract) **b** : secured by collateral — **col·lat·er·al·i·ty** \-‚la-tǝ-'ra-lǝ-tē\ *n* — **col·lat·er·al·ly** \-'la-t(ǝ-)rǝ-lē\ *adv*

²**collateral** *n* (1691) **1** : a collateral relative **2** : property (as securities) pledged by a borrower to protect the interests of the lender **3** : a branch of a bodily part (as a vein)

col·lat·er·al·ize \kǝ-'la-t(ǝ-)rǝ-‚līz\ *vt* **-ized; -iz·ing** (1941) **1** : to make (a loan) secure with collateral **2** : to use (as securities) for collateral

col·la·tion \kǝ-'lā-shǝn, kä-, kō-\ *n* (14c) **1** [ME, fr. ML *collation-, collatio*, fr. LL, conference, fr. L, bringing together, comparison, fr. *conferre* (pp. *collatus*) to bring together — more at CONFER, TOLERATE] **a** : a light meal allowed on fast days in place of lunch or supper **b** : a light meal **2** [ME, fr. L *collation-, collatio*]: the act, process, or result of collating

col·league \'kä-(‚)lēg\ *n* [MF *collegue*, fr. L *collega*, fr. *com-* + *legare* to depute — more at LEGATE] (ca. 1533) : an associate in a profession or in a civil or ecclesiastical office — **col·league·ship** \-‚ship\ *n*

¹**col·lect** \'kä-likt *also* -‚lekt\ *n* [ME *collecte*, fr. OF, fr. ML *collecta* (short for *oratio ad collectam* prayer upon assembly), fr. LL, assembly, fr. L, assemblage, fr. fem. of *collectus*] (13c) **1** : a short prayer comprising an invocation, petition, and conclusion; *specif, often cap* : one preceding the eucharistic Epistle and varying with the day **2** : COLLECTION

²**col·lect** \kǝ-'lekt\ *vb* [L *collectus*, pp. of *colligere* to collect, fr. *com-* + *legere* to gather — more at LEGEND] *vt* (1563) **1 a** : to bring together into one body or place **b** : to gather or exact from a number of persons or sources ⟨~ taxes⟩ **2** : INFER, DEDUCE **3** : to gain or regain control of ⟨~ his thoughts⟩ **4** : to claim as due and receive payment

for **5** : to get and bring with one; *specif* : PICK UP ⟨went to ~ her at the train station⟩ ~ *vi* **1** : to come together in a band, group, or mass : GATHER **2 a** : to collect objects **b** : to receive payment ⟨~ing on the insurance⟩ **syn** see GATHER

³**col·lect** \kǝ-'lekt\ *adv or adj* (1893) : to be paid for by the receiver

col·lec·ta·nea \‚kä-‚lek-'tā-nē-ǝ\ *n pl* [L, neut. pl. of *collectaneus* collected, fr. *collectus*, pp.] (1791) : collected writings; *also* : literary items forming a collection

col·lect·ed \kǝ-'lek-tǝd\ *adj* (1610) **1** : possessed of calmness and composure often through concentrated effort **2** : gathered together ⟨the ~ works of Scott⟩ **3** *of a horse's gait* : performed slowly and restrainedly with the animal's center of gravity toward the hindquarters — compare EXTENDED **syn** see COOL — **col·lect·ed·ly** *adv* — **col·lect·ed·ness** *n*

¹**col·lect·ible** *or* **col·lect·able** \kǝ-'lek-tǝ-bǝl\ *adj* (1660) **1** : suitable for being collected **2** : due for present payment : PAYABLE

²**collectible** *or* **collectable** *n* (1953) : an object that is collected by fanciers; *esp* : one other than such traditionally collectible items as art, stamps, coins, and antiques

col·lec·tion \kǝ-'lek-shǝn\ *n* (14c) **1** : the act or process of collecting **2 a** : something collected; *esp* : an accumulation of objects gathered for study, comparison, or exhibition or as a hobby **b** : GROUP, AGGREGATE **c** : a set of apparel designed for sale usu. in a particular season

¹**col·lec·tive** \kǝ-'lek-tiv\ *adj* (15c) **1** : denoting a number of persons or things considered as one group or whole ⟨*flock* is a ~ word⟩ **2 a** : formed by collecting : AGGREGATED **b** *of a fruit* : MULTIPLE **3 a** : of, relating to, or being a group of individuals **b** : involving all members of a group as distinct from its individuals **4** : marked by similarity among or with the members of a group **5** : collectivized or characterized by collectivism **6** : shared or assumed by all members of the group ⟨~ responsibility⟩ — **col·lec·tive·ly** *adv*

²**collective** *n* (1655) **1** : a collective body : GROUP **2** : a cooperative unit or organization; *specif* : COLLECTIVE FARM

collective bargaining *n* (1891) : negotiation between an employer and a labor union usu. on wages, hours, and working conditions

collective farm *n* (1925) : a farm esp. in a communist country formed from many small holdings collected into a single unit for joint operation under governmental supervision

collective mark *n* (1938) : a trademark or a service mark of a group (as a cooperative association)

collective security *n* (1934) : the maintenance by common action of the security of all members of an association of nations

collective unconscious *n* (1917) : the genetically determined part of the unconscious that esp. in the psychoanalytic theory of C. G. Jung occurs in all the members of a people or race

col·lec·tiv·ise *chiefly Brit var of* COLLECTIVIZE

col·lec·tiv·ism \kǝ-'lek-ti-‚vi-zǝm\ *n* (1857) : a political or economic theory advocating collective control esp. over production and distribution; *also* : a system marked by such control — **col·lec·tiv·ist** \-vist\ *adj or n* — **col·lec·tiv·is·tic** \-‚lek-ti-'vis-tik\ *adj* — **col·lec·tiv·is·ti·cal·ly** \-ti-k(ǝ-)lē\ *adv*

col·lec·tiv·i·ty \kǝ-‚lek-'ti-vǝ-tē, ‚kä-\ *n, pl* **-ties** (1862) **1** : the quality or state of being collective **2** : a collective whole; *esp* : the people as a body

col·lec·tiv·ize \kǝ-'lek-ti-‚vīz\ *vt* **-ized; -iz·ing** (1893) : to organize by collectivism — **col·lec·tiv·i·za·tion** \kǝ-‚lek-ti-vǝ-'zā-shǝn\ *n*

col·lec·tor \kǝ-'lek-tǝr\ *n* (14c) : one that collects: as **a** : an official who collects funds or moneys **b** : a person who makes a collection ⟨stamp ~⟩ **c** : an object or device that collects ⟨the statuette was a dust ~⟩ **d** : SOLAR COLLECTOR — **col·lec·tor·ship** \-‚ship\ *n*

collector's item *n* (1932) : an item whose rarity or excellence makes it esp. worth collecting; *broadly* : COLLECTIBLE

col·leen \kä-'lēn, 'kä-‚\ *n* [Ir *cailín*] (1828) : an Irish girl

col·lege \'kä-lij\ *n, often attrib* [ME, fr. MF, fr. L *collegium* society, fr. *collega* colleague — more at COLLEAGUE] (14c) **1** : a body of clergy living together and supported by a foundation **2** : a building used for an educational or religious purpose **3 a** : a self-governing constituent body of a university offering living quarters and instruction but not granting degrees ⟨Balliol and Magdalen *Colleges* at Oxford⟩ **b** : a preparatory or high school **c** : an independent institution of higher learning offering a course of general studies leading to a bachelor's degree **d** : a part of a university offering a specialized group of courses **e** : an institution offering instruction usu. in a professional, vocational, or technical field ⟨business ~⟩ **4** : COMPANY, GROUP; *specif* : an organized body of persons engaged in a common pursuit or having common interests or duties **5 a** : a group of persons considered by law to be a unit **b** : a body of electors — compare ELECTORAL COLLEGE **6** : the faculty, students, or administration of a college

College Board *service mark* — used for administration of tests of aptitude and achievement considered by some colleges in determining admission and placement of students

college try *n* [fr. the phrase "give it the old *college try*"] (1947) : a zealous all-out effort

col·le·gial \kǝ-'lē-j(ē-)ǝl, *esp for 2a also* -'lē-gē-ǝl\ *adj* (14c) **1** : COLLEGIATE 2 **2 a** : marked by power or authority vested equally in each of a number of colleagues **b** : characterized by equal sharing of authority esp. by Roman Catholic bishops **3** : marked by camaraderie among colleagues — **col·le·gial·ly** *adv*

col·le·gi·al·i·ty \-‚lē-jē-'a-lǝ-tē, -‚lē-gē-\ *n* (1887) : the relationship of colleagues; *specif* : the participation of bishops in the government of the Roman Catholic Church in collaboration with the pope

col·le·gian \kǝ-'lē-j(ē-)ǝn\ *n* (15c) : a student or recent graduate of a college

col·le·giate \kǝ-'lē-jǝt, -jē-ǝt\ *adj* [ML *collegiatus*, fr. L *collegium*] (15c) **1** : of or relating to a collegiate church **2** : of, relating to, or comprising a college **3** : COLLEGIAL 2 **4** : designed for or characteristic of college students — **col·le·giate·ly** *adv*

\ǝ\ abut \ᵊ\ kitten, F table \ǝr\ further \a\ ash \ā\ ace \ä\ mop, mar \au̇\ out \ch\ chin \e\ bet \ē\ easy \g\ go \i\ hit \ī\ ice \j\ job \ŋ\ sing \ō\ go \ò\ law \òi\ boy \th\ thin \th̲\ the \ü\ loot \u̇\ foot \y\ yet \zh\ vision \a, k̲, ⁿ, œ, œ̄, ᵫ, ᵫ̄, ᵞ\ *see* Guide to Pronunciation

col·le·giate church *n* (15c) **1** : a church other than a cathedral that has a chapter of canons **2** : a church or corporate group of churches under the joint pastorate of two or more ministers

col·le·gi·um \kə-'le-gē-əm, -'lā-\ *n, pl* **-gia** \-gē-ə\ *or* **-giums** [modif. of Russ *kollegiya*, fr. L *collegium*] (1917) : a group in which each member has approximately equal power and authority

col·lem·bo·lan \kə-'lem-bə-lən\ *n* [ultim. fr. *coll-* + Gk *embolos* wedge, stopper — more at EMBOLUS] (1873) : SPRINGTAIL — **collembolan** *or* **col·lem·bo·lous** \-ləs\ *adj*

col·len·chy·ma \kə-'len-kə-mə, kä-\ *n* [NL] (1857) : a plant tissue that consists of living usu. elongated cells with unevenly thickened walls and acts as support esp. in areas of primary growth — compare SCLERENCHYMA — **col·len·chy·ma·tous** \,kä-lən-'ki-mə-təs, -'kī-\ *adj*

col·let \'kä-lət\ *n* [MF, dim. of *col* collar, fr. L *collum* neck — more at COLLAR] (1528) : a metal band, collar, ferrule, or flange: as **a** : a casing or socket for holding a tool (as a drill bit) **b** : a circle or flange in which a gem is set

col·le·te·ri·al gland \,kä-lə-'tir-ē-əl-, -'ter-\ *n* [NL *colleterium* colleterial gland, irreg. fr. Gk *kollan* to glue — more at PROTOCOL] (1870) : a gland in female insects that secretes a cement by which the eggs are glued together or attached to an external object

col·lide \kə-'līd\ *vi* **col·lid·ed; col·lid·ing** [L *collidere*, fr. *com-* + *laedere* to injure by striking] (1700) **1** : to come together with solid or direct impact **2** : CLASH

col·lid·er \kə-'lī-dər\ *n* (1980) : a particle accelerator in which two beams of particles moving in opposite directions are made to collide

col·lie \'kä-lē\ *n* [prob. fr. E dial. *colly* black] (ca. 1651) : any of a breed of large dogs developed in Scotland that occur in rough-coated and smooth-coated varieties

col·lier \'käl-yər\ *n* [ME *colier*, fr. *col* coal] (13c) **1** : one that produces charcoal **2** : a coal miner **3** : a ship for transporting coal

col·liery \'käl-yə-rē\ *n, pl* **-lier·ies** (1635) : a coal mine and its connected buildings

col·lie-shang·ie \'kä-lē-,shaŋ-ē, 'kə-\ *n* [perh. fr. *collie* + *shang* kind of meal] (1737) *Scot* : SQUABBLE, BRAWL

col·li·gate \'kä-lə-gāt\ *vb* **-gat·ed; -gat·ing** [L *colligatus*, pp. of *colligare*, fr. *com-* + *ligare* to tie — more at LIGATURE] *vt* (1545) **1** : to bind, unite, or group together **2** : to subsume (isolated facts) under a general concept ~ *vi* : to be or become a member of a group or unit — **col·li·ga·tion** \,kä-lə-'gā-shən\ *n*

col·li·ga·tive \'kä-lə-,gā-tiv, kə-'li-gə-\ *adj* (1901) : depending on the number of particles (as molecules) and not on the nature of the particles ⟨pressure is a ~ property⟩

col·li·mate \'kä-lə-,māt\ *vt* **-mat·ed; -mat·ing** [L *collimatus*, pp. of *collimare*, MS var. of *collineare* to make straight, fr. *com-* + *linea* line] (1878) : to make (as light rays) parallel — **col·li·ma·tion** \,kä-lə-'mā-shən\ *n*

col·li·ma·tor \'kä-lə-,mā-tər\ *n* (1865) **1** : a device for producing a beam of parallel rays (as of light) or for forming an infinitely distant virtual image that can be viewed without parallax **2** : a device for obtaining a beam (as of particles) of limited cross section

col·lin·ear \kä-'li-nē-ər, kä-\ *adj* [ISV] (1863) **1** : lying on or passing through the same straight line **2** : having axes lying end to end in a straight line ⟨~ antenna elements⟩ — **col·lin·ear·i·ty** \-,li-nē-'ar-ə-tē\ *n*

col·lins \'kä-lənz\ *n* [prob. fr. the name *Collins*] (ca. 1887) : a tall iced drink of soda water, sugar, lemon or lime juice, and liquor (as gin)

col·li·sion \kə-'li-zhən\ *n* [ME, fr. L *collision-, collisio*, fr. *collidere*] (15c) **1** : an act or instance of colliding : CLASH **2** : an encounter between particles (as atoms or molecules) resulting in exchange or transformation of energy — **col·li·sion·al** \-'lizh-nəl, -'li-zhə-nᵊl\ *adj* — **col·li·sion·al·ly** *adv*

collision course *n* (1944) : a course (as of moving bodies or antithetical philosophies) that will result in collision or conflict if continued unaltered

collo- — see COLL-

col·lo·cate \'kä-lə-,kāt\ *vb* **-cat·ed; -cat·ing** [L *collocatus*, pp. of *collocare*, fr. *com-* + *locare* to place, fr. *locus* place — more at STALL] *vt* (1513) : to set or arrange in a place or position; *esp* : to set side by side ~ *vi* : to occur in conjunction with something

col·lo·ca·tion \,kä-lə-'kā-shən\ *n* (1605) : the act or result of placing or arranging together; *specif* : a noticeable arrangement or conjoining of linguistic elements (as words) — **col·lo·ca·tion·al** \-shnəl, -shə-nᵊl\ *adj*

col·lo·di·on \kə-'lō-dē-ən\ *n* [modif. of NL *collodium*, fr. Gk *kollōdēs* glutinous, fr. *kolla* glue — more at PROTOCOL] (1851) : a viscous solution of pyroxylin used esp. as a coating for wounds or for photographic films

col·logue \kä-'lōg\ *vi* **col·logued; col·logu·ing** [origin unknown] (1646) **1** *dial* : INTRIGUE, CONSPIRE **2** : to talk privately : CONFER

col·loid \'kä-,lȯid\ *n* [ISV *coll-* + *-oid*] (ca. 1852) **1** : a gelatinous or mucinous substance found in tissues in disease (as in the thyroid) or normally **2 a** : a substance that consists of particles dispersed throughout another substance which are too small for resolution with an ordinary light microscope but are incapable of passing through a semipermeable membrane **b** : a mixture consisting of a colloid together with the medium in which it is dispersed ⟨smoke is a ~⟩ — **col·loi·dal** \kə-'lȯi-dᵊl, kä-\ *adj* — **col·loi·dal·ly** *adv*

col·lop \'kä-ləp\ *n* [ME] (14c) **1** : a small piece or slice esp. of meat **2** : a fold of fat flesh

col·lo·qui·al \kə-'lō-kwē-əl\ *adj* (1751) **1** : of or relating to conversation : CONVERSATIONAL **2 a** : used in or characteristic of familiar and informal conversation; *also* : unacceptably informal **b** : using conversational style — **colloquial** *n* — **col·lo·qui·al·i·ty** \-,lō-kwē-'a-lə-tē\ *n* — **col·lo·qui·al·ly** \-'lō-kwē-ə-lē\ *adv*

col·lo·qui·al·ism \-'lō-kwē-ə-,li-zəm\ *n* (1810) **1 a** : a colloquial expression **b** : a local or regional dialect expression **2** : colloquial style

col·lo·quist \'kä-lə-kwist\ *n* (1792) : SPEAKER

col·lo·qui·um \kə-'lō-kwē-əm\ *n, pl* **-qui·ums** *or* **-quia** \-kwē-ə\ [L, colloquy] (1844) : a usu. academic meeting at which specialists deliver addresses on a topic or on related topics and then answer questions relating to them

col·lo·quy \'kä-lə-kwē\ *n, pl* **-quies** [L *colloquium*, fr. *colloqui* to converse, fr. *com-* + *loqui* to speak] (15c) **1** : CONVERSATION, DIALOGUE **2** : a high-level serious discussion : CONFERENCE

col·lo·type \'kä-lə-,tīp\ *n* [ISV] (1883) **1** : a photomechanical process for making prints directly from a hardened film of gelatin or other colloid that has ink-receptive and ink-repellent parts **2** : a print made by collotype

col·lude \kə-'lüd\ *vi* **col·lud·ed; col·lud·ing** [L *colludere*, fr. *com-* + *ludere* to play, fr. *ludus* game — more at LUDICROUS] (1535) : CONSPIRE, PLOT

col·lu·sion \kə-'lü-zhən\ *n* [ME, fr. MF, fr. L *collusion-, collusio*, fr. *colludere*] (14c) : secret agreement or cooperation esp. for an illegal or deceitful purpose — **col·lu·sive** \-'lü-siv, -ziv\ *adj* — **col·lu·sive·ly** *adv*

col·lu·vi·um \kə-'lü-vē-əm\ *n, pl* **-via** \-vē-ə\ *or* **-vi·ums** [NL, fr. ML, offscourings, alter. of L *colluvies*, fr. *colluere* to wash, fr. *com-* + *lavere* to wash — more at LYE] (ca. 1936) : rock detritus and soil accumulated at the foot of a slope — **col·lu·vi·al** \-vē-əl\ *adj*

col·ly \'kä-lē\ *vt* **col·lied; col·ly·ing** [alter. of ME *colwen*, fr. (assumed) OE *colgian*, fr. OE *col* coal] (1590) *dial chiefly Brit* : to blacken with or as if with soot

col·lyr·i·um \kə-'lir-ē-əm\ *n, pl* **-ia** \-ē-ə\ *or* **-i·ums** [ME *collirium*, fr. L *collyrium*, fr. Gk *kollyrion* pessary, eye salve, fr. dim. of *kollyra* roll of bread] (14c) : EYEWASH 1

col·ly·wob·bles \'kä-lē-,wä-bəlz\ *n pl but sing or pl in constr* [perh. by folk etymology fr. NL *cholera morbus*, lit., the disease cholera] (ca. 1823) : BELLYACHE

colo- — see COL-

col·o·bus monkey \'kä-lə-bəs-\ *n* [NL *colobus*, fr. Gk *kolobos* docked, mutilated, fr. *kolos* docked; prob. akin to Gk *klan* to break — more at CLAST] (1889) : any of various long-tailed African monkeys (genus *Colobus* and related genera) — called also *colobus*

co·lo·cate \(,)kō-'lō-,kāt, ,kō-'kāt\ *vt* (1965) : to locate together; *esp* : to place two or more units close together so as to share common facilities

col·o·cynth \'kä-lə-,sin(t)th\ *n* [L *colocynthis*, fr. Gk *kolokynthis*] (1543) : a Mediterranean and African herbaceous vine (*Citrullus colocynthis*) related to the watermelon; *also* : its spongy fruit from which a powerful cathartic is prepared

co·log·a·rithm \(,)kō-'lȯ-gə-,ri-thəm, -'lä-\ *n* (1881) : the logarithm of the reciprocal of a number

co·logne \kə-'lōn\ *n* [*Cologne*, Germany] (1814) **1** : a perfumed liquid composed of alcohol and fragrant oils **2** : a cream or paste of cologne sometimes formed into a semisolid stick — **co·logned** \-'lōnd\ *adj*

¹**co·lon** \'kō-lən\ *n, pl* **colons** *or* **co·la** \-lə\ [ME, fr. L, fr. Gk *kolon*] (14c) : the part of the large intestine that extends from the cecum to the rectum — **co·lon·ic** \kō-'lä-nik, kə-\ *adj*

²**colon** *n, pl* **colons** *or* **co·la** \-lə\ [L, part of a poem, fr. Gk *kōlon* limb, part of a strophe] (ca. 1550) **1** *pl* **cola** : a rhythmical unit of an utterance; *specif, in Greek or Latin verse* : a system or series of from two to not more than six feet having a principal accent and forming part of a line **2** *pl* **colons** : a punctuation mark : used chiefly to direct attention to matter (as a list, explanation, or quotation) that follows **b** : the sign : used between the parts of a numerical expression of time in hours and minutes (as in 1:15) or in hours, minutes, and seconds (as in 8:25:30), in a bibliographical reference (as in *Nation* 130:20), in a ratio where it is usu. read as "to" (as in 4:1 read "four to one"), or in a proportion where it is usu. read as "is to" or when doubled as "as" (as in 2:1::8:4 read "two is to one as eight is to four")

³**co·lon** \kō-'lōⁿ, kə-'lōn\ *n* [F, fr. L *colonus*] (1888) : a colonial farmer or plantation owner

co·lón *also* **co·lone** \kə-'lōn\ *n, pl* **co·lo·nes** \-'lō-,nās\ [Sp *colón*, fr. Cristóbal *Colón* Christopher Columbus] (1916) — see MONEY table

colon bacillus *n* (ca. 1909) : any of various bacilli (esp. genera *Escherichia* and *Aerobacter*) that are normally commensal in vertebrate intestines; *esp* : one (*E. coli*) used extensively in genetic research

col·o·nel \'kər-nᵊl\ *n* [alter. of *coronel*, fr. MF, modif. of OIt *colonnello* column of soldiers, colonel, dim. of *colonna* column, fr. L *columna*] (1548) **1 a** : a commissioned officer in the army, air force, or marine corps ranking above a lieutenant colonel and below a brigadier general **b** : LIEUTENANT COLONEL **2** : a minor titular official of a state esp. in southern or midland U.S. — used as an honorific title — **col·o·nel·cy** \-nᵊl-sē\ *n*

Colonel Blimp \-'blimp\ *n* [*Colonel Blimp*, cartoon character created by David Low] (1937) : a pompous person with out-of-date or ultraconservative views; *broadly* : REACTIONARY — **Colonel Blimp·ism** \-'blim-,pi-zəm\ *n*

¹**co·lo·nial** \kə-'lō-nē-əl, -nyəl\ *adj* (1776) **1** : of, relating to, or characteristic of a colony **2** *often cap* : of or relating to the original 13 colonies forming the United States: as **a** : made or prevailing in America during the colonial period ⟨~ architecture⟩ **b** : adapted from or reminiscent of an American colonial mode of design ⟨~ furniture⟩ **3** : forming or existing in a colony ⟨~ organisms⟩ **4** : possessing or composed of colonies ⟨a ~ empire⟩ — **co·lo·nial·ize** \-nē-ə-,līz, -nyə-,līz\ *vt* — **co·lo·nial·ly** *adv* — **co·lo·nial·ness** *n*

²**colonial** *n* (1798) **1** : a member or inhabitant of a colony **2 a** : a product made for use in a colony **b** : a product (as a house) exhibiting colonial style

co·lo·nial·ism \kə-'lō-nē-ə-,li-zəm, -nyə-,li-\ *n* (1853) **1** : the quality or state of being colonial **2** : something characteristic of a colony **3 a** : control by one power over a dependent area or people **b** : a policy advocating or based on such control — **co·lo·nial·ist** \-list\ *n or adj* — **co·lo·nial·is·tic** \-,lō-nē-ə-'lis-tik, -nyə-'lis-\ *adj*

¹**co·lon·ic** \kō-'lä-nik, kə-\ *adj* (ca. 1885) : of or relating to the colon of the intestine

²**colonic** *n* (1939) : irrigation of the colon : ENEMA

col·o·ni·sa·tion, col·o·nise *Brit var of* COLONIZATION, COLONIZE

col·o·nist \'kä-lə-nist\ *n* (1701) **1** : a member or inhabitant of a colony **2** : one that colonizes or settles in a new country

col·o·ni·za·tion \,kä-lə-nə-'zā-shən\ *n* (1770) : an act or instance of colonizing — **col·o·ni·za·tion·ist** \-sh(ə-)nist\ *n*

col·o·nize \'kä-lə-,nīz\ *vb* **-nized; -niz·ing** *vt* (1622) **1 a** : to establish a colony in or on or of **b** : to establish in a colony **2** : to send illegal or irregularly qualified voters into ⟨*colonizing* doubtful districts⟩

3 : to infiltrate with usu. subversive militants for propaganda and strategy reasons ⟨~ industries⟩ ~ *vi* : to make or establish a colony : SETTLE — **col·o·niz·er** *n*

col·on·nade \ˌkä-lə-ˈnäd\ *n* [F, fr. It *colonnato*, fr. *colonna* column] (1718) : a series of columns set at regular intervals and usu. supporting the base of a roof structure — **col·on·nad·ed** \-ˈnä-dəd\ *adj*

co·lo·nus \kə-ˈlō-nəs\ *n, pl* **-ni** \-ˌnī, -ˌnē\ [L, lit., farmer] (1888) : a free-born serf in the later Roman Empire who could sometimes own property but who was bound to the land and obliged to pay a rent usu. in produce

col·o·ny \ˈkä-lə-nē\ *n, pl* **-nies** [ME *colonie*, fr. MF & L; MF, fr. L *colonia*, fr. *colonus* farmer, colonist, fr. *colere* to cultivate — more at WHEEL] (14c) **1 a** : a body of people living in a new territory but retaining ties with the parent state **b** : the territory inhabited by such a body **2** : a distinguishable localized population within a species ⟨~ of termites⟩ **3 a** : a circumscribed mass of microorganisms usu. growing in or on a solid medium **b** : the aggregation of zooids of a compound animal **4 a** : a group of individuals or things with common characteristics or interests situated in close association ⟨an artist ~⟩ **b** : the section occupied by such a group **5** : a group of persons institutionalized away from others ⟨a leper ~⟩ ⟨a penal ~⟩; *also* : the land or buildings occupied by such a group

colony–stimulating factor *n* (1969) : any of several glycoproteins that promote the differentiation of stem cells esp. into blood granulocytes and macrophages and that stimulate their proliferation into colonies in culture

col·o·phon \ˈkä-lə-fən, -ˌfän\ *n* [L, fr. Gk *kolophōn* summit, finishing touch; perh. akin to L *culmen* top — more at HILL] (1774) **1** : an inscription placed at the end of a book or manuscript usu. with facts relative to its production **2** : an identifying device used by a printer or a publisher

co·lo·pho·ny \kə-ˈlä-fə-nē, ˈkä-lə-ˌfō-\ *n, pl* **-nies** [ME *colophonie*, ultim. fr. Gk *Kolophōn* Colophon, an Ionian city] (14c) : ROSIN

¹col·or \ˈkə-lər\ *n, often attrib* [ME *colour*, fr. OF, fr. L *color*; akin to L *celare* to conceal — more at HELL] (13c) **1 a** : a phenomenon of light (as red, brown, pink, or gray) or visual perception that enables one to differentiate otherwise identical objects **b** : the aspect of objects and light sources that may be described in terms of hue, lightness, and saturation for objects and hue, brightness, and saturation for light sources **c** : a hue as contrasted with black, white, or gray **2 a** : an outward often deceptive show : APPEARANCE ⟨his story has the ~ of truth⟩ **b** : a legal claim to or appearance of a right, authority, or office **c** : a pretense offered as justification : PRETEXT ⟨she could have drawn from the Versailles treaty the ~ of legality for any action she chose — *Yale Rev.*⟩ **d** : an appearance of authenticity : PLAUSIBILITY ⟨lending ~ to this notion⟩ **3** : complexion tint: **a** : the tint characteristic of good health **b** : BLUSH **4** : vividness or variety of effects of language **b** : LOCAL COLOR **5 a** : an identifying badge, pennant, or flag — usu. used in pl. ⟨a ship sailing under Swedish ~s⟩ **b** : colored clothing distinguishing one as a member of a particular group or representative of a particular person or thing — usu. used in pl. ⟨a jockey wearing the ~s of the stable⟩ **6 a** *pl* : position as to a question or course of action : STAND ⟨the USSR changed neither its ~s nor its stripes during all of this —Norman Mailer⟩ **b** : CHARACTER, NATURE — usu. used in pl. ⟨showed himself in his true ~s⟩ **7 a** : the use or combination of colors **b** : two or more hues employed in a medium of presentation ⟨movies in ~⟩ ⟨~ television⟩ **8** *pl* **a** : a naval or nautical salute to a flag being hoisted or lowered **b** : ARMED FORCES **9** : VITALITY, INTEREST ⟨the play had a good deal of ~ to it⟩ **10** : something used to give color : PIGMENT **11** : tonal quality in music ⟨the ~ and richness of the cello⟩ **12** : skin pigmentation esp. other than white characteristic of race ⟨a person of ~⟩ **13** : a small particle of gold in a gold miner's pan after washing **14** : analysis of game action or strategy, statistics and background information on participants, and often anecdotes provided by a sportscaster to give variety and interest to the broadcast of a game or contest **15** : a hypothetical property of quarks that differentiates each type into three forms having a distinct role in binding quarks together — **col·or·ism** \-lə-ˌri-zəm\ *n*

²color *vt* (14c) **1 a** : to give color to **b** : to change the color of (as by dyeing, staining, or painting) **2** : to change as if by dyeing or painting: as **a** : MISREPRESENT, DISTORT **b** : GLOSS, EXCUSE ⟨~ a lie⟩ **c** : INFLUENCE ⟨the lives of most of us have been ~ed by politics —Christine Weston⟩ **3** : CHARACTERIZE, LABEL ⟨call it progress; ~ it inevitable with shades of job security —C. E. Price⟩ ~ *vi* : to take on color; *specif* : BLUSH — **col·or·er** \ˈkə-lər-ər\ *n*

col·or·able \ˈkə-lə-rə-bəl, ˈkəl-rə-\ *adj* (14c) **1** : seemingly valid or genuine **2** : intended to deceive : COUNTERFEIT — **col·or·ably** \-blē\ *adv*

Col·o·ra·do blue spruce \ˌkä-lə-ˈra-dō-, -ˈrä-\ *n* [Colorado, state of the U.S.] (1897) : BLUE SPRUCE

Colorado potato beetle *n* (1868) : a black-and-yellow striped beetle (*Leptinotarsa decemlineata*) that feeds on the leaves of the potato — called also *potato beetle, potato bug*

col·or·ant \ˈkə-lə-rənt\ *n* (1884) : a substance used for coloring a material : DYE, PIGMENT

col·or·a·tion \ˌkə-lə-ˈrā-shən\ *n* (1617) **1 a** : the state of being colored ⟨the dark ~ of his skin⟩ **b** : use or choice of colors (as by an artist) **c** : arrangement of colors ⟨the ~ of a butterfly's wing⟩ **2 a** : characteristic quality ⟨the newspapers . . . took on the former ~ of the magazine —L. B. Seltzer⟩ **b** : aspect suggesting an attitude : PERSUASION ⟨the chameleon talent for taking on the intellectual ~ of whatever idea he happened to fasten onto —Budd Schulberg⟩ **3** : subtle variation of intensity or quality of tone ⟨a wide range of ~ from the orchestra⟩

col·or·a·tu·ra \ˌkə-lə-rə-ˈtür-ə, -ˈtyùr-\ *n* [obs. It, lit., coloring, fr. LL, fr. L *coloratus*, pp. of *colorare* to color, fr. *color*] (1740) **1** : elaborate embellishment in vocal music; *broadly* : music with ornate figuration **2** : a soprano with a light agile voice specializing in coloratura

color bar *n* (1913) : a barrier preventing colored persons from participating with whites in various activities — called also *color line*

Colorado potato beetle

col·or–bear·er \ˈkə-lər-ˌbar-ər, -ˌber-\ *n* (ca. 1891) : one that carries a color or standard esp. in a military parade or drill

col·or–blind \-ˌblīnd\ *adj* (1854) **1** : affected with partial or total inability to distinguish one or more chromatic colors **2** : INSENSITIVE, OBLIVIOUS **3** : not recognizing differences of race ⟨tried to get the welfare establishment . . . to abandon its ~ policy —D. P. Moynihan⟩; *esp* : free from racial prejudice ⟨a white man with an invisible black skin in a ~ community —James Farmer⟩ — **color blindness** *n*

col·or–bred \-ˌbred\ *adj* (1948) : selectively bred for the development of particular colors ⟨pure ~ dogs⟩

co·lo·rec·tal \ˌkō-lō-ˈrek-tᵊl\ *adj* (1962) : relating to or affecting the colon and rectum ⟨~ cancer⟩

¹col·ored \ˈkə-lərd\ *adj* (14c) **1** : having color **2 a** : COLORFUL **b** : marked by exaggeration or bias **3 a** : of a race other than the white; *esp* : BLACK 2b — sometimes taken to be offensive **b** : of mixed race — sometimes taken to be offensive **4** : of or relating to colored persons — sometimes taken to be offensive

²colored *n, pl* **colored** *or* **coloreds** *often cap* (1916) : a colored person — sometimes taken to be offensive

col·or·fast \ˈkə-lər-ˌfast\ *adj* (1926) : having color that retains its original hue without fading or running — **col·or·fast·ness** \-ˌfas(t)-nəs\ *n*

col·or–field \-ˌfē(ə)ld\ *n, often attrib* (1964) : abstract painting in which color is emphasized and form and surface are correspondingly de-emphasized

color filter *n* (1900) : FILTER 3b

col·or·ful \ˈkə-lər-fəl\ *adj* (1889) **1** : having striking colors **2** : full of variety or interest — **col·or·ful·ly** \-f(ə-)lē\ *adv* — **col·or·ful·ness** \-fəl-nəs\ *n*

color guard *n* (ca. 1823) : an honor guard for the colors of an organization

col·or·if·ic \ˌkə-lə-ˈri-fik\ *adj* (1676) : capable of communicating color

col·or·im·e·ter \ˌkə-lə-ˈri-mə-tər\ *n* [ISV] (ca. 1872) : an instrument or device for determining and specifying colors; *specif* : one used for chemical analysis by comparison of a liquid's color with standard colors — **col·or·i·met·ric** \ˌkə-lə-rə-ˈme-trik\ *adj* — **col·or·i·met·ri·cal·ly** \-tri-k(ə-)lē\ *adv* — **col·or·im·e·try** \ˌkə-lə-ˈri-mə-trē\ *n*

col·or·ing \ˈkə-lə-riŋ\ *n* (14c) **1 a** : the act of applying colors **b** : something that produces color or color effects **c** (1) : the effect produced by applying or combining colors (2) : natural color (3) : COMPLEXION, COLORATION **d** : change of appearance (as by adding color) **2** : INFLUENCE, BIAS **3** : COLOR 4 **4** : TIMBRE, QUALITY

col·or·ist \ˈkə-lə-rist\ *n* (1686) : one that colors or deals with color — **col·or·is·tic** \ˌkə-lə-ˈris-tik\ *adj* — **col·or·is·ti·cal·ly** \-ti-k(ə-)lē\ *adv*

col·or·ize \ˈkə-lə-ˌrīz\ *vt* **-ized**; **-iz·ing** (1979) : to add color to (a black-and-white film) by means of a computer — **col·or·i·za·tion** \ˌkə-lə-rə-ˈzā-shən\ *n*

col·or·less \ˈkə-lər-ləs\ *adj* (14c) **1** : lacking color: as **a** : PALLID, BLANCHED **b** : DULL, UNINTERESTING — **col·or·less·ly** *adv* — **col·or·less·ness** *n*

col·or·man \-ˌman\ *n* (1973) : a sportscaster who provides color

color phase *n* (1927) **1** : a seasonally variant pelage color **2 a** : a genetic variant manifested by the occurrence of a skin or pelage color unlike the wild type of the animal group in which it appears **b** : an individual marked by such a variant

col·or·point shorthair \ˈkə-lər-ˌpòint-\ *n* (1974) : any of a breed of domestic cats of Siamese type and coat pattern but occurring in different colors — called also *colorpoint*

color temperature *n* (1916) : the temperature at which a blackbody emits radiant energy competent to evoke a color the same as that evoked by radiant energy from a given source (as a lamp)

color wheel *n* (ca. 1893) : a circular diagram of the spectrum used to show the relationships between the colors

co·los·sal \kə-ˈlä-səl\ *adj* (1712) **1** : of, relating to, or resembling a colossus **2** : of a bulk, extent, power, or effect approaching or suggesting the stupendous or incredible **3** : of an exceptional or astonishing degree *syn* see ENORMOUS — **co·los·sal·ly** \-sə-lē\ *adv*

co·los·se·um \ˌkä-lə-ˈsē-əm\ *n* [ML, fr. L, neut. of *colosseus* colossal, fr. *colossus*] (ca. 1715) **1** *cap* : an amphitheater built in Rome in the first century A.D. **2** : COLISEUM 2

Co·los·sians \kə-ˈlä-shənz *also* -shē-ənz, -sē-\ *n pl but sing in constr* : a letter written by St. Paul to the Christians of Colossae and included as a book in the New Testament — see BIBLE table

co·los·sus \kə-ˈlä-səs\ *n, pl* **co·los·si** \-ˈlä-ˌsī\ [L, fr. Gk *kolossos*] (14c) **1** : a statue of gigantic size and proportions **2** : one that resembles a colossus in size or scope

co·los·to·my \kə-ˈläs-tə-mē\ *n, pl* **-mies** [ISV ²*col-* + *-stomy*] (1888) : surgical formation of an artificial anus

co·los·trum \kə-ˈläs-trəm\ *n* [L, beestings] (1577) : milk secreted for a few days after parturition and characterized by high protein and antibody content — **co·los·tral** \-trəl\ *adj*

col·our \ˈkə-lər\ *chiefly Brit var of* COLOR

-col·ous *adj comb form* [L *-cola* inhabitant; akin to L *colere* to inhabit — more at WHEEL] : living or growing in or on ⟨arenicolous⟩

col·por·tage \ˈkäl-ˌpōr-tij, -ˌpòr-; ˌkäl-pōr-ˈtäzh, -pòr-\ *n* (ca. 1846) : a colporteur's work

col·por·teur \ˈkäl-ˌpōr-tər, -ˌpòr-; ˌkäl-pōr-ˈtər, -pòr-\ *n* [F, alter. of MF *comporteur*, fr. *comporter* to bear, peddle] (1796) : a peddler of religious books

colt \ˈkōlt\ *n* [ME, fr. OE; akin to Sw dial. *kult* half-grown pig] (bef. 12c) **1 a** : FOAL **b** : a young male horse that is either sexually immature or has not attained an arbitrarily designated age **2** : a young untried person

colt·ish \ˈkōl-tish\ *adj* (14c) **1 a** : not subjected to discipline **b** : FRISKY, PLAYFUL **2** : of, relating to, or resembling a colt — **colt·ish·ly** *adv* — **colt·ish·ness** *n*

colts·foot \ˈkōlts-ˌfut\ *n, pl* **coltsfoots** (14c) : any of various plants with large rounded leaves resembling the foot of a colt; *esp* : a peren-

\ə\ abut \ᵊ\ kitten, F table \ər\ further \a\ ash \ā\ ace \ä\ mop, mar \aù\ out \ch\ chin \e\ bet \ē\ easy \g\ go \i\ hit \ī\ ice \j\ job \ŋ\ sing \ō\ go \ò\ law \òi\ boy \th\ thin \t͟h\ the \ü\ loot \ù\ foot \y\ yet \zh\ vision \à, ḳ, ⁿ, œ, œ̄, ᵫ, ᵫ̄, ᵞ\ see Guide to Pronunciation nial composite herb (*Tussilago farfara*) with yellow flower heads appearing before the leaves

col·u·brid \'käl-yə-brəd, 'kä-lə-\ *n* [ultim. fr. L *colubra* snake] (1887) : any of a large cosmopolitan family (Colubridae) of chiefly nonvenomous snakes — **colubrid** *adj*

col·u·brine \-‚brīn\ *adj* (ca. 1528) **1** : of, relating to, or resembling a snake **2** : of or relating to colubrids : COLUBRID

co·lu·go \kə-'lü-(‚)gō\ *n, pl* **-gos** [perh. fr. a language of the Philippines] (ca. 1890) : FLYING LEMUR

col·um·bar·i·um \‚kä-ləm-'bar-ē-əm, -'ber-\ *n, pl* **-ia** \-ē-ə\ [L, lit., dovecote, fr. *columba* dove] (1846) **1** : a structure of vaults lined with recesses for cinerary urns **2** : a recess in a columbarium

Co·lum·bia \kə-'ləm-bē-ə\ *n* [NL, fr. Christopher *Columbus*] (1775) : the United States

Co·lum·bi·an \-bē-ən\ *adj* (1757) : of or relating to the United States or to Christopher Columbus

col·um·bine \'kä-ləm-‚bīn\ *n* [ME, fr. ML *columbina*, fr. L, fem. of *columbinus* like a dove, fr. *columba* dove; akin to OHG *holuntar* elder tree, Gk *kolymbos* a small grebe, *kelainos* black] (14c) : any of a genus (*Aquilegia*) of plants of the buttercup family with irregular showy spurred flowers: as **a** : a red-flowered plant (*A. canadensis*) of eastern No. America **b** : a blue-flowered plant (*A. caerulea*) of the Rocky Mountains

Col·um·bine \-‚bīn, -‚bēn\ *n* [It *Colombina*] : the saucy sweetheart of Harlequin in comedy and pantomime

co·lum·bite \kə-'ləm-‚bīt, 'kä-ləm-\ *n* [NL *columbium*] (1805) : a black mineral consisting mostly of iron and niobium

co·lum·bi·um \kə-'ləm-bē-əm\ *n* [NL, fr. *Columbia*] (1801) : NIOBIUM

Co·lum·bus Day \kə-'ləm-bəs-\ *n* (1893) **1** : October 12 formerly observed as a legal holiday in many states of the U.S. in commemoration of the landing of Columbus in the Bahamas in 1492 **2** : the second Monday in October observed as a legal holiday in many states of the U.S.

col·u·mel·la \‚käl-yə-'me-lə\ *n, pl* **-mel·lae** \-'me-(‚)lē, -‚lī\ [NL, fr. L, dim. of *columna*] (ca. 1755) **1** : the central column or axis of a spiral univalve shell **2** : the axis of the capsule in mosses and in some liverworts **3** : the bony or partly cartilaginous rod connecting the tympanic membrane with the internal ear in birds and in many reptiles and amphibians **b** : the bony central axis of the cochlea **4** : the central sterile portion of the sporangium in various fungi (*Mucor* and related genera) — **col·u·mel·lar** \-'me-lər\ *adj*

col·umn \'kä-ləm *also* 'käl-yəm\ *n* [ME *columne*, fr. MF *colomne*, fr. L *columna*, fr. *columen* top; akin to L *collis* hill — more at HILL] (15c) **1 a** : a vertical arrangement of items printed or written on a page **b** : one of two or more vertical sections of a printed page separated by a rule or blank space **c** : an accumulation arranged vertically : STACK **d** : one in a usu. regular series of newspaper or magazine articles ⟨gossip ~⟩ **2** : a supporting pillar; *esp* : one consisting of a usu. round shaft, a capital, and a base **3 a** : something resembling a column in form, position, or function ⟨a ~ of water⟩ **b** : a tube or cylinder in which a chromatographic separation takes place **4** : a long row (as of soldiers) **5** : one of the vertical lines of elements of a determinant or matrix — **col·umned** \-ləmd, -yəmd\ *adj*

co·lum·nar \kə-'ləm-nər\ *adj* (1728) **1** : of, relating to, resembling, or characterized by columns **2** : of, relating to, being, or composed of tall narrow somewhat cylindrical or prismatic epithelial cells

col·um·ni·a·tion \kə-‚ləm-nē-'ā-shən\ *n* [prob. fr. *intercolumniation*] (1664) : the employment or the arrangement of columns in a structure

col·um·nist \'kä-ləm-nist, -lə-mist *also* 'käl-yəm-nist, -yə-mist\ *n* (1920) : one who writes a newspaper or magazine column — **col·um·nis·tic** \‚kä-ləm-'nis-tik *also* ‚käl-yəm-\ *adj*

col·za \'käl-zə, 'kōl-\ *n* [F, fr. D *koolzaad*, fr. MD *coolsaet*, fr. *coole* cabbage + *saet* seed] (1712) **1** : any of several coles; *esp* : one (as rape) producing seed used as a source of oil **2** : RAPESEED

com- *or* **col-** *or* **con-** *prefix* [ME, fr. OF, fr. L, with, together, thoroughly — more at CO-] : with : together : jointly — usu. *com-* before *b*, *p*, or *m* ⟨commingle⟩, *col-* before *l* ⟨collinear⟩, and *con-* before other sounds ⟨concentrate⟩

¹co·ma \'kō-mə\ *n* [NL, fr. Gk *kōma* deep sleep] (1646) **1** : a state of profound unconsciousness caused by disease, injury, or poison **2** : a state of mental or physical sluggishness : TORPOR

²coma *n, pl* **co·mae** \-‚mē, -‚mī\ [L, hair, fr. Gk *komē*] (1669) **1** : a tufted bunch (as of branches, bracts, or seed hairs) **2** : the head of a comet usu. containing a nucleus **3** : an optical aberration in which the image of a point source is a comet-shaped blur — **co·mat·ic** \kō-'ma-tik\ *adj*

Co·ma Ber·e·ni·ces \'kō-mə-‚ber-ə-'nī-(‚)sēz\ *n* [L (gen. *Comae Berenices*), lit., Berenice's hair] : a constellation north of Virgo and between Boötes and Leo

co·mak·er \(‚)kō-'mā-kər\ *n* (ca. 1934) : one that participates in an agreement; *specif* : one who stands to meet a financial obligation in the event of the maker's default

Co·man·che \kə-'man-chē\ *n, pl* **Comanche** *or* **Comanches** [AmerSp, fr. Southern Paiute *kɨmmancɨ⁼i* Shoshones, strangers] (1806) **1** : a member of an American Indian people ranging from Wyoming and Nebraska south into New Mexico and northwestern Texas **2** : the Uto-Aztecan language of the Comanche people

co·mate \(‚)kō-'māt, 'kō-‚\ *n* (1576) : COMPANION

co·ma·tose \'kō-mə-‚tōs, 'kä-\ *adj* [F *comateux*, fr. Gk *kōmat-, kōma*] (1755) **1** : of, resembling, or affected with coma **2** : characterized by lethargic inertness : TORPID ⟨a ~ economy⟩

¹comb \'kōm\ *n* [ME, fr. OE *camb*; akin to OHG *kamb* comb, Gk *gomphos* tooth] (bef. 12c) **1 a** : a toothed instrument used esp. for adjusting, cleaning, or confining hair **b** : a structure resembling such a comb; *esp* : any of several toothed devices used in handling or ordering textile fibers **c** : CURRYCOMB **2 a** : a fleshy crest on the head of the domestic fowl and other gallinaceous birds **b** : something (as the

ridge of a roof) resembling the comb of a cock **3** : HONEYCOMB — **combed** \'kōmd\ *adj* — **comb·like** \'kōm-‚līk\ *adj*

²comb *vt* (14c) **1** : to draw a comb through for the purpose of arranging or cleaning **2** : to pass across with a scraping or raking action **3 a** : to eliminate (as with a comb) by a thorough going-over **b** : to search or examine systematically **4** : to use in a combing action ~ *vi* **1** *of a wave or its crest* : to roll over or break into foam **2** : to make a thorough search ⟨~ through the classified ads⟩

¹com·bat \käm-‚bat\ *n* (1546) **1** : a fight or contest between individuals or groups **2** : CONFLICT, CONTROVERSY **3** : active fighting in a war : ACTION ⟨casualties suffered in ~⟩

²com·bat \kəm-'bat, 'käm-‚\ *vb* **-bat·ed** *or* **-bat·ted; -bat·ing** *or* **-bat·ting** [MF *combattre*, fr. (assumed) VL *combattere*, fr. L *com-* + *battuere* to beat] *vi* (1564) : to engage in combat : FIGHT ~ *vt* **1** : to fight with : BATTLE **2** : to struggle against; *esp* : to strive to reduce or eliminate ⟨~ pollution⟩ *syn* see OPPOSE

³com·bat \'käm-‚bat\ *adj* (1825) **1** : relating to combat ⟨~ missions⟩ **2** : designed or destined for combat ⟨~ boots⟩ ⟨~ troops⟩

com·bat·ant \kəm-'ba-tᵊnt *also* ‚käm-bə-tənt\ *n* (15c) : one that is engaged in or ready to engage in combat — **combatant** *adj*

combat fatigue *n* (1943) : a traumatic psychoneurotic reaction or an acute psychotic reaction occurring under conditions (as wartime combat) that cause intense stress — called also *battle fatigue*

com·bat·ive \kəm-'ba-tiv\ *adj* (ca. 1834) : marked by eagerness to fight or contend — **com·bat·ive·ly** *adv* — **com·bat·ive·ness** *n*

combe \'küm, 'kōm\ *n* [ME *coumbe, cumbe*, fr. OE *cumb*, of Celt origin; akin to W *cwm* valley] (bef. 12c) **1** *Brit* : a deep narrow valley **2** *Brit* : a valley or basin on the flank of a hill

comb·er \'kō-mər\ *n* (ca. 1682) **1** : one that combs **2** : a long curling wave of the sea

com·bi·na·tion \‚käm-bə-'nā-shən\ *n, often attrib* (14c) **1 a** : a result or product of combining; *esp* : an alliance of individuals, corporations, or states united to achieve a social, political, or economic end **b** : two or more persons working as a team **2** : an ordered sequence: as **a** : a sequence of letters or numbers chosen in setting a lock; *also* : the mechanism operating or moved by the sequence **b** : a rapid sequence of punches in boxing **c** : any subset of a set considered without regard to order within the subset **3** : any of various one-piece undergarments for the upper and lower parts of the body — usu. used in pl. **4** : an instrument designed to perform two or more tasks **5 a** : the act or process of combining; *esp* : that of uniting to form a chemical compound **b** : the quality or state of being combined — **com·bi·na·tion·al** \-shnəl, -shə-nᵊl\ *adj*

combination shot *n* (ca. 1909) : a shot in pool in which a ball is pocketed by an object ball

com·bi·na·tive \'käm-bə-‚nā-tiv, kəm-'bī-nə-\ *adj* (1855) **1** : tending or able to combine **2** : resulting from combination

com·bi·na·to·ri·al \‚käm-bə-nə-'tōr-ē-əl, kəm-‚bī-nə-, -(‚)bi-, -'tòr-\ *adj* (1818) **1** : of, relating to, or involving combinations **2** : of or relating to the arrangement of, operation on, and selection of discrete mathematical elements belonging to finite sets or making up geometric configurations — **com·bi·na·to·ri·al·ly** \-ē-ə-lē\ *adv*

com·bi·na·tor·ics \-'tòr-iks, -'tär-\ *n pl but sing in constr* (1951) : combinatorial mathematics

com·bi·na·to·ry \kəm-'bī-nə-‚tōr-ē, -‚tòr-\ *adj* (1647) : COMBINATIVE

¹com·bine \kəm-'bīn\ *vb* **com·bined; com·bin·ing** [ME, fr. MF *combiner*, fr. LL *combinare*, fr. L *com-* + *bini* two by two — more at BIN-] *vt* (15c) **1 a** : to bring into such close relationship as to obscure individual characters : MERGE **b** : to cause to unite into a chemical compound **c** : to unite into a single number or expression ⟨~ fractions and simplify⟩ **2** : INTERMIX, BLEND **3** : to possess in combination ~ *vi* **1 a** : to become one **b** : to unite to form a chemical compound **2** : to act together *syn* see JOIN — **com·bin·able** \-'bī-nə-bəl\ *adj* — **com·bin·er** *n*

²com·bine \'käm-‚bīn\ *n* (1886) **1** : a combination esp. of business or political interests **2** : a harvesting machine that heads, threshes, and cleans grain while moving over a field

³com·bine \'käm-‚bīn\ *vb* **com·bined; com·bin·ing** *vt* (1926) : to harvest with a combine ~ *vi* : to combine a crop

comb·ing \'kō-miŋ\ *var of* COAMING

comb·ings \'kō-miŋz\ *n pl* (1656) : loose hair removed by a comb

combing wool *n* (1757) : long-staple strong-fibered wool found suitable for combing and used esp. in the manufacture of worsteds

combining form *n* (1884) : a linguistic form that occurs only in compounds or derivatives and can be distinguished descriptively from an affix by its ability to occur as one immediate constituent of a form whose only other immediate constituent is an affix (as *cephal-* in *cephalic*) or by its being an allomorph of a morpheme having another allomorph that may occur alone or can be distinguished historically from an affix by the fact that it is borrowed from another language in which it is descriptively a word or a combining form

comb jelly *n* (ca. 1889) : CTENOPHORE

com·bo \'käm-(‚)bō\ *n, pl* **combos** [*combination* + *¹-o*] (1924) **1** : a usu. small jazz or dance band **2** : COMBINATION

com·bust \kəm-'bəst\ *vb* [L *combustus*, pp. of *comburere* to burn up, irreg. fr. *com-* + *urere* to burn — more at EMBER] (15c) : BURN

com·bus·ti·ble \kəm-'bəs-tə-bəl\ *adj* (1529) **1** : capable of combustion **2** : easily excited — **com·bus·ti·bil·i·ty** \-‚bəs-tə-'bi-lə-tē\ *n* — **combustible** *n* — **com·bus·ti·bly** \-'bəs-tə-blē\ *adv*

com·bus·tion \kəm-'bəs-chən\ *n* (15c) **1** : an act or instance of burning **2** : a usu. rapid chemical process (as oxidation) that produces heat and usu. light; *also* : a slower oxidation (as in the body) **3** : violent agitation : TUMULT — **com·bus·tive** \-'bəs-tiv\ *adj*

com·bus·tor \-'bəs-tər\ *n* (1945) : a chamber (as in a gas turbine or a jet engine) in which combustion occurs — called also *combustion chamber*

¹come \'kəm\ *vb* **came** \'kām\; **come; com·ing** \'kə-miŋ\ [ME, fr. OE *cuman*; akin to OHG *queman* to come, L *venire*, Gk *bainein* to walk, go] *vi* (bef. 12c) **1 a** : to move toward something : APPROACH ⟨~ here⟩ **b** : to move or journey to a vicinity with a specified purpose ⟨~ see us⟩ ⟨~ and see what's going on⟩ **c** (1) : to reach a particular station in a series ⟨now we ~ to the section on health⟩ (2) : to arrive in due course ⟨the time has ~⟩ **d** (1) : to approach in kind or quality ⟨this ~s near perfection⟩ (2) : to reach a condition or conclusion

[diagram of a classical column labeled: CORNICE, FRIEZE, ARCHITRAVE, CAPITAL, SHAFT, BASE, PEDESTAL, with side labels ENTABLATURE and COLUMN]

column 2

⟨*came* to regard him as a friend⟩ ⟨~ to think of it, you may be right⟩ **e** (1) : to advance toward accomplishment ⟨learning new ways doesn't ~ easy⟩ ⟨the job is *coming* nicely⟩ (2) : to advance in a particular manner ⟨~ running when I call⟩ (3) : to advance, rise, or improve in rank or condition ⟨has ~ a long way⟩ **f** : to get along : FARE — often used with *along* **g** : EXTEND ⟨her dress *came* to her ankles⟩ **2 a** (1) : to arrive at a particular place, end, result, or conclusion ⟨*came* to his senses⟩ ⟨~ untied⟩ (2) : AMOUNT ⟨the taxes on it ~ to more than it's worth⟩ **b** (1) : to appear to the mind ⟨the answer *came* to them⟩ (2) : to appear on a scene : make an appearance ⟨children ~ equipped to learn any language⟩ **c** (1) : HAPPEN, OCCUR ⟨no harm will ~ to you⟩ (2) : to come to pass : take place — used in the subjunctive with inverted subject and verb to express the particular time or occasion ⟨~ spring the days will be longer⟩ **d** : ORIGINATE, ARISE ⟨wine ~s from grapes⟩ ⟨~ of sturdy stock⟩ **e** : to enter or assume a condition ⟨artillery *came* into action⟩ **f** : to fall within a field of view or a range of application ⟨this ~s within the terms of the treaty⟩ **g** : to issue forth ⟨a sob *came* from her throat⟩ **h** : to take form ⟨churn till the butter ~s⟩ **i** : to be available ⟨this model ~s in several sizes⟩ ⟨as good as they ~⟩ **j** : to experience orgasm — often considered vulgar **3** : to fall to a person in a division or inheritance of property **4** *obs* : to become moved favorably : RELENT ⟨to turn out to be ⟨good clothes ~ high⟩ **6** : BECOME ⟨a dream that *came* true⟩ ~ *vt* **1** : to approach or be near ⟨an age⟩ ⟨a child *coming* eight years old⟩ **2** : to take on the aspect of ⟨~ the stern parent⟩ — **come a cropper** : to fail completely — **come clean** : to tell the whole story : CONFESS — **come into** : to acquire as a possession or achievement ⟨*come into* a fortune⟩ — **come into one's own** : to achieve one's potential; *also* : to gain recognition — **come of age** : to reach maturity — **come off it** : to cease foolish or pretentious talk or behavior — **come over** : to seize suddenly and strangely ⟨what's *come over* you⟩ — **come to** : to be a question of ⟨when it *comes* to pitching horseshoes, he's the champ⟩ — **come to grips with** : to meet or deal with firmly, frankly, or straightforwardly ⟨*come to grips with* the unemployment problem⟩ — **come to oneself** : to get hold of oneself : regain self-control — **come to pass** : HAPPEN — **come to terms 1** : to reach an agreement — often used with *with* **2** : to become adjusted esp. emotionally or intellectually — usu. used with ⟨*come to terms* with modern life⟩

²**come** *n* (1923) **1** : SEMEN — often considered vulgar **2** : ORGASM — often considered vulgar

come about *vi* (14c) **1** : HAPPEN **2** : to change direction ⟨the wind has *come about* into the north⟩ **3** : to shift to a new tack

come across *vi* (1910) **1** : to give over or furnish something demanded; *esp* : to pay over money **2** : to produce an impression ⟨*comes across* as a good speaker⟩ **3** : COME THROUGH 2

come along *vi* (1694) **1** : to accompany someone who leads the way ⟨asked me to *come along* on the trip⟩ **2** : to make progress ⟨work is *coming along* well⟩ **3** : to make an appearance ⟨won't just marry the first man that *comes along*⟩

come around *vi* (1934) **1** : COME ROUND **2** : MENSTRUATE

come-back \'kəm-ˌbak\ *n* (1889) **1 a** : a sharp or witty reply : RETORT **b** : a cause for complaint **2** : a return to a former position or condition (as of success or prosperity) : RECOVERY, REVIVAL ⟨staging his ultimate ~ from self-imposed exile —Howard Mandel⟩

come back *vi* (1850) **1** : to return to life or vitality **2** : to return to memory ⟨it's all *coming back* to me now⟩ **3** : REPLY, RETORT **4** : to regain a former favorable condition or position

come by *vi* (1863) : to make a visit ~ *vt* : to get possession of : ACQUIRE ⟨a good job is hard to *come by*⟩

co·me·di·an \kə-'mē-dē-ən\ *n* (1581) **1** *archaic* **a** : a writer of comedies **b** : an actor who plays comic roles **2** : a comical individual; *specif* : a professional entertainer who uses any of various physical or verbal means to be amusing

co·me·dic \-'mē-dik\ *adj* (1639) **1** : of or relating to comedy **2** : COMICAL **2** — **co·me·dic·al·ly** \-di-k(ə-)lē\ *adv*

co·me·di·enne \-ˌmē-dē-'en\ *n* [F *comédienne*, fem. of *comédien* comedian, fr. *comédie*] (ca. 1859) : a woman who is a comedian

come-do \'kä-mə-ˌdō\ *n, pl* **come-do-nes** \ˌkä-mə-'dō-(ˌ)nēz\ [NL, fr. L, glutton, fr. *comedere* to eat — more at COMESTIBLE] (1866) : BLACKHEAD

come-down \'kəm-ˌdaún\ *n* (1840) : a descent in rank or dignity

come down *vi* (1711) **1 a** : to pass by tradition ⟨a story that has *come down* from medieval times⟩ **b** : to pass from a usu. high source ⟨word *came down* that the strike was over⟩ **2 a** : to reduce itself : AMOUNT ⟨it *comes down* to this⟩ **b** : to deal with a subject directly ⟨when you *come down* to it, we all depend on others⟩ **3** : to lose or fall in estate or condition ⟨has *come down* in the world⟩ **4** : to place oneself in opposition ⟨*came down* hard on gambling⟩ **5** : to become ill ⟨*came down* with measles⟩ **6** : COME OUT 2

com·e·dy \'kä-mə-dē\ *n, pl* **-dies** [ME, fr. MF *comedie*, fr. L *comoedia*, fr. Gk *kōmōidia*, fr. *kōmos* revel + *aeidein* to sing — more at ODE] (14c) **1 a** : a medieval narrative that ends happily ⟨Dante's *Divine Comedy*⟩ **b** : a literary work written in a comic style or treating a comic theme **2 a** : a drama of light and amusing character and typically with a happy ending **b** : the genre of dramatic literature dealing with the comic or with the serious in a light or satirical manner — compare TRAGEDY **3** : a ludicrous or farcical event or series of events **4 a** : the comic element ⟨the ~ of many life situations⟩ **b** : humorous entertainment ⟨nightclub ~⟩

comedy drama *n* (1885) : serious drama that is interspersed with comedy

comedy of manners (1822) : comedy that satirically portrays the manners and fashions of a particular class or set

come-hith·er \(ˌ)kəm-'hi-thər, (ˌ)kə-'mi-\ *adj* (1925) : sexually provocative ⟨that ~ look in your eyes⟩

come in *vi* (14c) **1 a** : to arrive on a scene ⟨new models *coming in*⟩ **b** : to become available ⟨data began *coming in*⟩ **2** : to place among those finishing ⟨*came in* last⟩ **3 a** : to function in an indicated manner ⟨*come in* handy⟩ **b** *of a telecommunications signal* : to be received ⟨*came in* loud and clear⟩ **4** : to assume a role or function ⟨that's where you *come in*⟩ **5** : to attain maturity, fruitfulness, or production — **come in for** : to become subject to ⟨*coming in for* increasing criticism⟩

come·ly \'kəm-lē *also* 'kōm- *or* 'käm-\ *adj* **come·li·er; -est** [ME *comly*,

alter. of OE *cȳmlic* glorious, fr. *cȳme* lively, fine; akin to OHG *kūmig* weak] (13c) **1** : pleasurably conforming to notions of good appearance, suitability, or proportion **2** : having a pleasing appearance : not homely or plain **syn** see BEAUTIFUL — **come·li·ness** *n*

come off *vi* (1596) **1 a** : to acquit oneself : FARE ⟨*came off* well in the contest⟩ **b** : APPEAR, SEEM **2** : SUCCEED ⟨a television series that never *came off* —*TV Guide*⟩ **3** : HAPPEN, OCCUR ~ *vt* : to have recently completed or recovered from ⟨*coming off* a good year⟩ ⟨*coming off* an injury⟩

come-on \'kə-ˌmón, -ˌmän\ *n* (1902) **1** : something (as an advertising promotion) intended to entice or allure **2** : a usu. sexual advance

come on *vi* (15c) **1 a** : to advance by degrees ⟨darkness *came on*⟩ **b** : to begin by degrees ⟨rain *came on* toward noon⟩ **2 a** : PLEASE — used in cajoling or pleading **b** — used interjectionally to express astonishment, incredulity, or recognition of a put-on **3** : to project an indicated personal image ⟨*comes on* as a conservative⟩ **4** : to show sexual interest in someone; *also* : to make sexual advances ⟨tried to *come on* to her⟩

come out *vi* (13c) **1 a** : to come into public view : make a public appearance ⟨a new magazine has *come out*⟩ **b** : to become evident ⟨his pride *came out* in his refusal to accept help⟩ **2** : to declare oneself esp. in public utterance ⟨*came out* in favor of the proposal⟩ **3** : to turn out in an outcome : end up ⟨everything *came out* all right⟩ **4** : to make a debut **5** : to openly declare one's homosexuality — **com·ing-out** \ˌkə-miŋ-'aút\ *adj* — **come out with 1** : to give expression to ⟨*came out with* a new proposal⟩ **2** : PUBLISH

come-out·er \(ˌ)kə-'maú-tər\ *n* (1840) **1** : a person who withdraws from something established (as a religious body) **2** : a person who advocates political reform

come over *vi* (1576) **1 a** : to change from one side (as of a controversy) to the other **b** : to visit casually : DROP IN ⟨*come over* whenever you like⟩ **2** *Brit* : BECOME

com·er \'kə-mər\ *n* (14c) **1** : one that comes or arrives ⟨all ~s⟩ **2** : one making rapid progress or showing promise

come round *vi* (1818) **1** : to change direction **2** : to return to a former condition; *esp* : COME TO 1 **3** : to accede to a particular opinion or course of action ⟨knew you'd *come round* to our side eventually⟩

¹**co·mes·ti·ble** \kə-'mes-tə-bəl\ *adj* [MF, fr. ML *comestibilis*, fr. L *comestus*, pp. of *comedere* to eat, fr. *com-* + *edere* to eat — more at EAT] (15c) : EDIBLE

²**comestible** *n* (1837) : FOOD — usu. used in pl.

com·et \'kä-mət\ *n* [ME *comete*, fr. OE *cometa*, fr. L, fr. Gk *komētēs*, lit., long-haired, fr. *koman* to wear long hair, fr. *komē* hair] (bef. 12c) : a celestial body that consists of a fuzzy head usu. surrounding a bright nucleus, that has a usu. highly eccentric orbit, and that often when in the part of its orbit near the sun develops a long tail which points away from the sun — **com·e·tary** \-mə-ˌter-ē\ *adj* — **co·met·ic** \kə-'me-tik, kä-\ *adj*

come through *vi* (1914) **1** : to do what is needed or expected ⟨*came through* in the clutch⟩ **2** : to become communicated

come to *vi* (ca. 1572) **1** : to recover consciousness **2 a** : to bring a ship's head nearer the wind : LUFF **b** : to come to anchor or to a stop

come up *vi* (14c) **1** : RISE 6 **2** : to come near : make an approach ⟨*came up* and introduced himself⟩ **3** : to rise in rank or status ⟨an officer who *came up* from the ranks⟩ **4 a** : to come to attention or consideration ⟨the question never *came up*⟩ **b** : to occur in the course of time ⟨any problem that may *come up*⟩ **5** : to turn out to be ⟨the coin *came up* tails⟩ — **come up with** : to produce esp. in dealing with a problem or challenge ⟨*came up with* a solution⟩

come-up·pance \(ˌ)kə-'mə-pən(t)s\ *n* [*come up* + *-ance*] (1859) : a deserved rebuke or penalty : DESERTS

com·fit \'kəm(p)-fət, 'käm(p)-\ *n* [ME *confit*, fr. MF, fr. pp. of *confire* to prepare, fr. L *conficere*, fr. *com-* + *facere* to make — more at DO] (14c) : a candy consisting of a piece of fruit, a root (as licorice), a nut, or a seed coated and preserved with sugar

¹**com·fort** \'kəm(p)-fərt\ *vt* [ME, fr. OF *conforter*, fr. LL *confortare* to strengthen greatly, fr. L *com-* + *fortis* strong] (13c) **1** : to give strength and hope to : CHEER **2** : to ease the grief or trouble of : CONSOLE — **com·fort·ing·ly** \-fər-tiŋ-lē\ *adv*

²**comfort** *n* (13c) **1** : strengthening aid: **a** : ASSISTANCE, SUPPORT ⟨accused of giving aid and *comfort* to the enemy⟩ **b** : consolation in time of trouble or worry : SOLACE **2 a** : a feeling of relief or encouragement **b** : contented well-being **3** : a satisfying or enjoyable experience **4** : one that gives or brings comfort ⟨all the ~s of home⟩ — **com·fort·less** \-ləs\ *adj*

com·fort·able \'kəm(p)(f)-tə(r)-bəl, 'kəm(p)-fə(r)-tə-bəl, 'kəm-fə(r)-bəl\ *adj* (1769) **1 a** : affording or enjoying contentment and security ⟨a ~ income⟩ **b** : affording or enjoying physical comfort ⟨a ~ chair⟩ ⟨was too ~ to move⟩ **2** : free from vexation or doubt ⟨~ assumptions⟩ **b** : free from stress or tension ⟨a ~ routine⟩ — **com·fort·able·ness** *n* — **com·fort·ably** \-blē\ *adv*

syn COMFORTABLE, COZY, SNUG, EASY, RESTFUL mean enjoying or providing a position of contentment and security. COMFORTABLE applies to anything that encourages serenity, well-being, or complacency as well as physical ease ⟨comfortable in our new surroundings⟩. COZY suggests warmth, shelter, assured ease, and friendliness ⟨a cozy neighborhood coffee shop⟩. SNUG suggests having just enough space for comfort and safety but no more ⟨a snug little cottage⟩. EASY implies relief from or absence of anything likely to cause physical or mental discomfort or constraint ⟨living in easy circumstances⟩. RESTFUL applies to whatever induces or contributes to rest or relaxation ⟨a quiet restful vacation⟩.

com·fort·er \'kəm(p)-fə(r)-tər\ *n* (14c) **1 a** *cap* : HOLY SPIRIT **b** : one that gives comfort **2 a** : a long narrow usu. knitted neck scarf **b** : a thick bed covering made of two layers of cloth containing a filling (as down)

comfort station *n* (ca. 1913) : REST ROOM

\ə\ abut \ᵊ\ kitten, F table \ər\ further \a\ ash \ā\ ace \ä\ mop, mar \aú\ out \ch\ chin \e\ bet \ē\ easy \g\ go \i\ hit \ī\ ice \j\ job \ŋ\ sing \ō\ go \ó\ law \ói\ boy \th\ thin \th\ the \ü\ loot \ú\ foot \y\ yet \zh\ vision \á, k̟, ⁿ, œ, œ̄, ю̆, ю̄, ᵞ\ *see* Guide to Pronunciation

com·frey \'kəm(p)-frē\ *n, pl* **comfreys** [ME *cumfirie,* fr. OF, fr. L *conferva* a water plant, fr. *confervēre* to grow together (of bones), fr. *com-* + *fervēre* to boil — more at BARM] (13c) : any of a genus (*Symphytum*) of perennial herbs of the borage family with coarse hairy entire leaves and flowers in one-sided racemes

com·fy \'kəm(p)-fē\ *adj* [by shortening & alter.] (1829) : COMFORTABLE

¹**com·ic** \'kä-mik\ *adj* [L *comicus,* fr. Gk *kōmikos,* fr. *kōmos* revel] (1576) **1** : of, relating to, or marked by comedy **2** : causing laughter or amusement : FUNNY **3** : of or relating to comic strips **syn** see LAUGHABLE

²**comic** *n* (1581) **1** : COMEDIAN **2** : the comic element **3 a** : COMIC STRIP **b** : COMIC BOOK **c** *pl* : the part of a newspaper devoted to comic strips

com·i·cal \'kä-mi-kəl\ *adj* (15c) **1** *obs* : of or relating to comedy **2** : causing laughter esp. because of a startlingly or unexpectedly humorous impact **syn** see LAUGHABLE — **com·i·cal·i·ty** \ˌkä-mi-'ka-lə-tē\ *n* — **com·i·cal·ly** \'kä-mi-k(ə-)lē\ *adv*

comic book *n* (1941) : a magazine containing sequences of comic strips

comic–opera *adj* (1906) : not to be taken seriously ⟨a ∼ regime⟩

comic opera *n* (1762) : opera of a humorous character with a happy ending and usu. some spoken dialogue

comic relief *n* (1875) : a relief from the emotional tension of a drama that is provided by the interposition of a comic episode or element

comic strip *n* (1920) : a group of cartoons in narrative sequence

¹**com·ing** \'kə-miŋ\ *n* (13c) : an act or instance of arriving

²**coming** *adj* (15c) **1** : immediately due in sequence or development ⟨in the ∼ year⟩ **2** : gaining importance

co·min·gle \kə-'miŋ-gəl\ *vt* (1602) : COMMINGLE

coming–of–age *n* (1916) : the attainment of prominence, respectability, recognition, or maturity

Com·in·tern \'kä-mən-ˌtərn\ *n* [Russ *Komintern,* fr. *Kommunisticheskii Internatsional* Communist International] (1923) : the Communist International established in 1919 and dissolved in 1943

co·mi·tia \kə-'mi-sh(ē-)ə\ *n, pl* **comitia** [L, pl. of *comitium,* fr. *com-* + *-it-* (akin to *ire* to go) — more at ISSUE] (1600) : any of several public assemblies of the people in ancient Rome for legislative, judicial, and electoral purposes — **co·mi·tial** \-'mi-shəl\ *adj*

co·mi·ty \'kä-mə-tē, 'kō-\ *n, pl* **-ties** [L *comitat-, comitas,* fr. *comis* courteous, prob. fr. OF *cosmis,* fr. *com-* + *-smis* (akin to Skt *smayate* he smiles) — more at SMILE] (1543) **1 a** : friendly social atmosphere : social harmony ⟨group activities promoting ∼⟩ **b** : a loose widespread community based on common social institutions ⟨the ∼ of civilization⟩ **c** : COMITY OF NATIONS **d** : the informal and voluntary recognition by courts of one jurisdiction of the laws and judicial decisions of another **2** : avoidance of proselytizing members of another religious denomination

comity of nations (1862) **1** : the courtesy and friendship of nations marked esp. by mutual recognition of executive, legislative, and judicial acts **2** : the group of nations practicing international comity

com·ma \'kä-mə\ *n* [LL, fr. L, part of a sentence, fr. Gk *komma* segment, clause, fr. *koptein* to cut — more at CAPON] (1554) **1** : a punctuation mark, used esp. as a mark of separation within the sentence **2** : PAUSE, INTERVAL **3** : any of several nymphalid butterflies (genus *Polygonia*) with a silvery comma-shaped mark on the underside of the hind wings

comma fault *n* (ca. 1934) : COMMA SPLICE

¹**com·mand** \kə-'mand\ *vb* [ME *comanden,* fr. MF *comander,* fr. (assumed) VL *commandare,* alter. of L *commendare* to commit to one's charge — more at COMMEND] *vt* (14c) **1** : to direct authoritatively : ORDER **2** : to exercise a dominating influence over : have command of: as **a** : to have at one's immediate disposal **b** : to demand or receive as one's due ⟨∼s a high fee⟩ **c** : to overlook or dominate from or as if from a strategic position **d** : to have military command of as senior officer **3** *obs* : to order or request to be given ∼ *vi* **1** : to have or exercise direct authority : GOVERN **2** : to give orders **3** : to be commander **4** : to dominate as if from an elevated place — **com·mand·able** \-'man-də-bəl\ *adj*

syn COMMAND, ORDER, BID, ENJOIN, DIRECT, INSTRUCT, CHARGE mean to issue orders. COMMAND and ORDER imply authority and usu. some degree of formality and impersonality. COMMAND stresses official exercise of authority ⟨a general *commanding* troops⟩. ORDER may suggest peremptory or arbitrary exercise ⟨*ordered* his employees about like slaves⟩. BID suggests giving orders peremptorily ⟨as to children or servants⟩ ⟨she *bade* him be seated⟩. ENJOIN implies giving an order or direction authoritatively and urgently and often with admonition or solicitude ⟨a sign *enjoining* patrons to be quiet⟩. DIRECT and INSTRUCT both connote expectation of obedience and usu. concern specific points of procedure or method, INSTRUCT sometimes implying greater explicitness or formality ⟨*directed* her assistant to hold all calls⟩ ⟨the judge *instructed* the jury to ignore the remark⟩. CHARGE adds to ENJOIN an implication of imposing as a duty or responsibility ⟨*charged* by the President with a secret mission⟩.

²**command** *n* (15c) **1 a** : an order given **b** : a signal that actuates a device ⟨as a control mechanism in a spacecraft or one step in a computer⟩; *also* : the activation of a device by means of such a signal **2 a** : the ability to control : MASTERY **b** : the authority or right to command ⟨the officer in ∼⟩ **c** (1) : the power to dominate (2) : scope of vision **d** : facility in use ⟨a good ∼ of French⟩ **3** : the act of commanding **4** : the personnel, area, or organization under a commander; *specif* : a unit of the U.S. Air Force higher than an air force **5** : a position of highest usu. military authority **syn** see POWER

³**command** *adj* (1826) : done on command or request ⟨a ∼ performance⟩

com·man·dant \'kä-mən-ˌdänt, -ˌdant\ *n* (1687) : COMMANDING OFFICER

command car *n* (1941) : an open armored car designed esp. for military reconnaissance and capable of traveling over rough terrain

com·man·deer \ˌkä-mən-'dir\ *vt* [Afrik *kommandeer,* fr. F *commander* to command, fr. OF *comander*] (1881) **1 a** : to compel to perform military service **b** : to seize for military purposes **2** : to take arbitrary or forcible possession of

com·mand·er \kə-'man-dər\ *n* (14c) **1** : one in an official position of command or control: as **a** : COMMANDING OFFICER **b** : the presiding

officer of a society or organization **2** : a commissioned officer in the navy or coast guard ranking above a lieutenant commander and below a captain — **com·mand·er·ship** \-ˌship\ *n*

commander in chief (1654) : one who holds the supreme command of an armed force

com·mand·ery \kə-'man-d(ə-)rē\ *n, pl* **-er·ies** (15c) **1** : a district under the control of a commander of an order of knights **2** : an assembly or lodge in a secret order

com·mand·ing \kə-'man-diŋ\ *adj* (1591) **1** : drawing attention or priority ⟨a ∼ presence⟩ **2** : difficult to overcome ⟨a ∼ lead⟩ — **command·ing·ly** \-diŋ-lē\ *adv*

commanding officer *n* (1720) : an officer in command; *esp* : an officer in the armed forces in command of an organization or installation

com·mand·ment \kə-'man(d)-mənt\ *n* (13c) **1** : the act or power of commanding **2** : something that is commanded; *esp* : one of the biblical Ten Commandments

command module *n* (1962) : a space vehicle module designed to carry the crew, the chief communication equipment, and the equipment for reentry

com·man·do \kə-'man-(ˌ)dō\ *n, pl* **-dos** *or* **-does** [Afrik *kommando,* fr. D *commando* command, fr. Sp *comando,* fr. *comandar* to command, fr. LL *commandare*] (1884) **1** *SoAfr* **a** : a military unit or command of the Boers **b** : a raiding expedition **2 a** : a military unit trained and organized as shock troops esp. for hit-and-run raids into enemy territory **b** : a member of such a unit

command post *n* (ca. 1918) : a post at which the commander of a unit in the field receives orders and exercises command

command sergeant major *n* (1967) : a noncommissioned officer in the army ranking above a first sergeant

comma splice *n* (1924) : the careless or unjustified use of a comma between coordinate main clauses not connected by a conjunction (as in "nobody goes there anymore, it's boring")

com·me·dia dell'ar·te \kə-ˌmā-dē-ə-(ˌ)del-'är-tē, kə-ˌme-\ [It, lit., comedy of art] (1877) : Italian comedy of the 16th to 18th centuries improvised from standardized situations and stock characters

comme il faut \ˌkə-mē(l)-'fō\ *adj* [F, lit., as it should be] (1756) : conforming to accepted standards : PROPER

com·mem·o·rate \kə-'me-mə-ˌrāt\ *vt* **-rat·ed; -rat·ing** [L *commemoratus,* pp. of *commemorare,* fr. *com-* + *memorare* to remind of, fr. *memor* mindful — more at MEMORY] (1599) **1** : to call to remembrance **2** : to mark by some ceremony or observation : OBSERVE **3** : to serve as a memorial of ⟨a plaque that ∼s the battle⟩ **syn** see KEEP — **com·mem·o·ra·tor** \-ˌrā-tər\ *n*

com·mem·o·ra·tion \kə-ˌme-mə-'rā-shən\ *n* (14c) **1** : the act of commemorating **2** : something that commemorates

com·mem·o·ra·tive \kə-'mem-rə-tiv, -'me-mə-; -'me-mə-ˌrā-tiv\ *adj* (1612) **1** : intended as a commemoration; *esp* : issued in limited quantities for a relatively short period in commemoration of a person, place, or event ⟨a ∼ stamp⟩ — **commemorative** *n* — **com·mem·o·ra·tive·ly** *adv*

com·mence \kə-'men(t)s\ *vb* **com·menced; com·menc·ing** [ME *comencen,* fr. MF *comencer,* fr. (assumed) VL *cominitiare,* fr. L *com-* + LL *initiare* to begin, fr. L, to initiate] *vt* (14c) : to enter upon : BEGIN ⟨∼ proceedings⟩ ∼ *vi* **1** : to have or make a beginning : START **2** *chiefly Brit* : to begin to be or to act as **3** *chiefly Brit* : to take a degree at a university **syn** see BEGIN — **com·menc·er** *n*

com·mence·ment \kəm-'men(t)s-mənt\ *n* (13c) **1** : an act, instance, or time of commencing **2 a** : the ceremonies or the day for conferring degrees or diplomas **b** : the period of activities at this time

com·mend \kə-'mend\ *vb* [ME, fr. L *commendare,* fr. *com-* + *mandare* to entrust — more at MANDATE] *vt* (14c) **1** : to entrust for care or preservation **2** : to recommend as worthy of confidence or notice **3** : to mention with approbation : PRAISE ∼ *vi* : to commend or serve as a commendation of something — **com·mend·able** \-'men-də-bəl\ *adj* — **com·mend·ably** \-blē\ *adv* — **com·mend·er** *n*

com·men·da·tion \ˌkä-mən-'dā-shən, -men-\ *n* (14c) **1 a** : an act of commending **b** : something (as a formal citation) that commends **2** *archaic* : COMPLIMENT

com·men·da·to·ry \kə-'men-də-ˌtōr-ē, -ˌtòr-\ *adj* (1555) : serving to commend

com·men·sal \kə-'men(t)-səl\ *adj* [ME, fr. ML *commensalis,* fr. L *com-* + LL *mensalis* of the table, fr. L *mensa* table] (1877) : of, relating to, or living in a state of commensalism — **commensal** *n* — **com·men·sal·ly** \-sə-lē\ *adv*

com·men·sal·ism \-sə-ˌli-zəm\ *n* (1870) : a relation between two kinds of organisms in which one obtains food or other benefits from the other without damaging or benefiting it

com·men·su·ra·ble \kə-'men(t)s-rə-bəl, -'men(t)sh-; -'men(t)-sə-, -shə-\ *adj* (1557) **1** : having a common measure; *specif* : divisible by a common unit an integral number of times **2** : COMMENSURATE **2** — **com·men·su·ra·bil·i·ty** \-ˌmen(t)s-rə-'bi-lə-tē, -ˌmen(t)sh-; -ˌmen(t)-sə-, -shə-\ *n* — **com·men·su·ra·bly** \-'men(t)s-rə-blē, -'men(t)sh-; -'men(t)-sə-, -shə-\ *adv*

com·men·su·rate \kə-'men(t)s-rət, -'men(t)sh-; -'men(t)-sə-, -shə-\ *adj* [LL *commensuratus,* fr. L *com-* + LL *mensuratus,* pp. of *mensurare* to measure, fr. L *mensura* measure — more at MEASURE] (1641) **1** : equal in measure or extent : COEXTENSIVE ⟨lived a life ∼ with the early years of the republic⟩ **2** : corresponding in size, extent, amount, or degree : PROPORTIONATE ⟨was given a job ∼ with her abilities⟩ **3** : COMMENSURABLE **1** — **com·men·su·rate·ly** *adv* — **com·men·su·ra·tion** \-ˌmen(t)s-ə-'rā-shən, -shə-\ *n*

¹**com·ment** \'kä-ˌment\ *n* [ME, fr. LL *commentum,* fr. L, invention, fr. neut. of *commentus,* pp. of *comminisci* to invent, fr. *com-* + *-minisci* (akin to *ment-, mens* mind) — more at MIND] (14c) **1** : COMMENTARY **2** : a note explaining, illustrating, or criticizing the meaning of a writing **3 a** : an observation or remark expressing an opinion or attitude **b** : a judgment expressed indirectly

²**comment** *vt* (15c) : to make a comment on ⟨the discovery . . . is hardly ∼ed by the press —*Nation*⟩ ∼ *vi* : to explain or interpret something by comment ⟨∼ing on recent developments⟩

com·men·tary \'kä-mən-ˌter-ē\ *n, pl* **-tar·ies** (15c) **1 a** : an explanatory treatise — usu. used in pl. **b** : a record of events usu. written by a participant — usu. used in pl. **2 a** : a systematic series of explanations or interpretations (as of a writing) **b** : COMMENT **2 3 a** : something that serves for illustration or explanation ⟨the dark, airless apartments and sunless factories... are a sad ~ upon our civilization —H. A. Overstreet⟩ **b** : an expression of opinion

com·men·tate \'kä-mən-ˌtāt\ *vb* **-tat·ed; -tat·ing** [back-formation fr. *commentator*] *vt* (1794) : to give a commentary on ~ *vi* : to comment in a usu. expository or interpretive manner; *also* : to act as a commentator

com·men·ta·tor \-ˌtā-tər\ *n* (14c) : one who gives a commentary; *esp* : one who reports and discusses news on radio or television

¹**com·merce** \'kä-(ˌ)mərs\ *n* [MF, fr. L *commercium*, fr. *com-* + *merc-, merx* merchandise] (1537) **1** : social intercourse : interchange of ideas, opinions, or sentiments **2** : the exchange or buying and selling of commodities on a large scale involving transportation from place to place **3** : SEXUAL INTERCOURSE *syn* see BUSINESS

²**com·merce** \'kä-(ˌ)mərs, kə-'mərs\ *vi* **com·merced; com·merc·ing** (1596) *archaic* : COMMUNE

¹**com·mer·cial** \kə-'mər-shəl\ *adj* (1598) **1 a** (1) : occupied with or engaged in commerce or work intended for commerce ⟨a ~ artist⟩ (2) : of or relating to commerce ⟨~ regulations⟩ (3) : characteristic of commerce ⟨~ weights⟩ (4) : suitable, adequate, or prepared for commerce ⟨found oil in ~ quantities⟩ **b** (1) : being of an average or inferior quality ⟨~ oxalic acid⟩ ⟨show-quality versus ~ cattle⟩ (2) : producing artistic work of low standards for quick market success **2 a** : viewed with regard to profit ⟨a ~ success⟩ **b** : designed for a large market **3** : emphasizing skills and subjects useful in business **4** : supported by advertisers ⟨~ TV⟩ — **com·mer·ci·al·i·ty** \kə-ˌmər-shē-'a-lə-tē\ *n* — **com·mer·cial·ly** \-'mər-sh(ə-)lē\ *adv*

²**commercial** *n* (1935) : an advertisement broadcast on radio or television

commercial bank *n* (1910) : a bank organized chiefly to handle the everyday financial transactions of businesses (as through demand deposit accounts and short-term commercial loans)

com·mer·cial·ise *Brit var of* COMMERCIALIZE

com·mer·cial·ism \kə-'mər-shə-ˌli-zəm\ *n* (1849) **1** : commercial spirit, institutions, or methods **2** : excessive emphasis on profit — **com·mer·cial·ist** \-'mər-sh(ə-)list\ *n* — **com·mer·cial·is·tic** \-ˌmər-shə-'lis-tik\ *adj*

com·mer·cial·ize \kə-'mər-shə-ˌlīz\ *vt* **-ized; -iz·ing** (1830) **1 a** : to manage on a business basis for profit **b** : to develop commerce in **2** : to exploit for profit ⟨~ Christmas⟩ **3** : to debase in quality for more profit — **com·mer·cial·i·za·tion** \-ˌmər-sh(ə-)lə-'zā-shən\ *n*

commercial paper *n* (1836) : short-term unsecured discounted paper usu. sold by one company to another for immediate cash needs

commercial traveler *n* (1807) : TRAVELING SALESMAN

com·mie \'kä-mē\ *n, often cap* [by shortening & alter.] (1940) : COMMUNIST

com·mi·na·tion \ˌkä-mə-'nā-shən\ *n* [ME, fr. MF or L; MF, fr. L *commination, comminatio*, fr. *comminari* to threaten, fr. *com-* + *minari* to threaten — more at MOUNT] (15c) : DENUNCIATION — **com·mi·na·to·ry** \'kä-mə-nə-ˌtōr-ē, -ˌtor-; kə-'mi-nə-, -'mī-\ *adj*

com·min·gle \kə-'miŋ-gəl, kä-\ *vt* (ca. 1626) **1** : to blend thoroughly into a harmonious whole **2** : to combine (funds or properties) into a common fund or stock ~ *vi* : to become commingled *syn* see MIX

com·mi·nute \'kä-mə-ˌnüt, -ˌnyüt\ *vt* **-nut·ed; -nut·ing** [L *comminutus,* pp. of *comminuere*, fr. *com-* + *minuere* to lessen — more at MINOR] (1626) : to reduce to minute particles : PULVERIZE — **com·mi·nu·tion** \ˌkä-mə-'nü-shən, -'nyü-\ *n*

com·mis·er·ate \kə-'mi-zə-ˌrāt\ *vb* **-at·ed; -at·ing** [L *commiseratus,* pp. of *commiserari*, fr. *com-* + *miserari* to pity, fr. *miser* wretched] *vt* (1599) : to feel or express sympathy : CONDOLE ⟨~s with them on their loss⟩ ~ *vi* : to feel or express sorrow or compassion for — **com·mis·er·at·ing·ly** *adv* — **com·mis·er·a·tion** \-ˌmi-zə-'rā-shən\ *n* — **com·mis·er·a·tive** \-'mi-zə-ˌrā-tiv\ *adj*

com·mis·sar \'kä-mə-ˌsär\ *n* [Russ *komissar*, fr. G *Kommissar*, fr. ML *commissarius*] (1918) **1 a** : a Communist party official assigned to a military unit to teach party principles and policies and to ensure party loyalty **b** : one that attempts to control public opinion or its expression **2** : the head of a government department in the U.S.S.R. until 1946 — **com·mis·sar·i·al** \ˌkä-mə-'sär-ē-əl, -'ser-\ *adj*

com·mis·sar·i·at \ˌkä-mə-'ser-ē-ət, -'sar-, *esp for 3* -'sär-\ *n* [NL *commissariatus*, fr. ML *commissarius*] (1779) **1** : a system for supplying an army with food **2** : food supplies **3** [Russ *komissariat*, fr. G *Kommissariat*, fr. NL *commissariatus*] : a government department in the U.S.S.R. until 1946 **4** : a board of commissioners

com·mis·sary \'kä-mə-ˌser-ē\ *n, pl* **-sar·ies** [ME *commissarie*, fr. ML *commissarius*, fr. L *commissus*, pp. of *committere*] (14c) **1** : one delegated by a superior to execute a duty or an office **2 a** : a store for equipment and provisions; *esp* : a supermarket for military personnel **b** : food supplies **c** : a lunchroom esp. in a motion-picture studio

¹**com·mis·sion** \kə-'mi-shən\ *n* [ME, fr. MF, fr. L *commission-, commissio* act of bringing together, fr. *committere*] (14c) **1 a** : a formal written warrant granting the power to perform various acts or duties **b** : a certificate conferring military rank and authority; *also* : the rank and authority so conferred **2** : an authorization or command to act in a prescribed manner or to perform prescribed acts : CHARGE **3 a** : authority to act for, in behalf of, or in place of another **b** : a task or matter entrusted to one as an agent for another **4 a** : a group of persons directed to perform some duty **b** : a government agency having administrative, legislative, or judicial powers **c** : a city council having legislative and executive functions **5** : an act of committing something **6** : a fee paid to an agent or employee for transacting a piece of business or performing a service; *esp* : a percentage of the money received from a total paid to the agent responsible for the business **7** : an act of entrusting or giving authority — **in commission** or **into commission 1** : under the authority of commissioners **2** *of a ship* : ready for active service **3** : in use or in condition for use — **on commission** : with commission serving as partial or full pay for work done — **out of commission 1** : out of active service or use **2** : out of working order

²**commission** *vt* **-mis·sioned; -mis·sion·ing** \-'mi-sh(ə-)niŋ\ (ca. 1661) **1** : to furnish with a commission: as **a** : to confer a formal commission on ⟨was ~ed lieutenant⟩ **b** : to appoint or assign to a task or function ⟨was ~ed to do the biography⟩ **2** : to order to be made ⟨~ed a portrait⟩ **3** : to put (a ship) in commission

com·mis·sion·aire \kə-ˌmi-shə-'nar, -'ner\ *n* [F *commissionnaire*, fr. *commission*] (1641) *chiefly Brit* : a uniformed attendant

commissioned officer *n* (15c) : an officer of the armed forces holding by a commission a rank of second lieutenant or ensign or above

com·mis·sion·er \kə-'mi-sh(ə-)nər\ *n* (15c) : a person with a commission: as **a** : a member of a commission **b** : the representative of the governmental authority in a district, province, or other unit often having both judicial and administrative powers **c** : the officer in charge of a department or bureau of the public service **d** : the administrative head of a professional sport — **com·mis·sion·er·ship** \-ˌship\ *n*

commission merchant *n* (1796) : BROKER 1b

commission plan *n* (1919) : a method of municipal government under which a small elective commission exercises both executive and legislative powers and each commissioner directly administers one or more municipal departments

com·mis·sure \'kä-mə-ˌshur\ *n* [ME, fr. MF or L; MF, fr. L *commissura* a joining, fr. *commissus*, pp.] (15c) **1** : a point or line of union or junction esp. between two anatomical parts (as adjacent heart valves) **2** : a connecting band of nerve tissue in the brain or spinal cord — **com·mis·sur·al** \ˌkä-mə-'shur-əl\ *adj*

com·mit \kə-'mit\ *vb* **com·mit·ted; com·mit·ting** [ME *committen*, fr. L *committere* to connect, entrust, fr. *com-* + *mittere* to send] *vt* (14c) **1 a** : to put into charge or trust : ENTRUST **b** : to place in a prison or mental institution **c** : to consign or record for preservation ⟨~ it to memory⟩ **d** : to put into a place for disposal or safekeeping **e** : to refer (as a legislative bill) to a committee for consideration and report **2** : to carry into action deliberately : PERPETRATE ⟨~ a crime⟩ **3 a** : OBLIGATE, BIND **b** : to pledge or assign to some particular course or use ⟨~ all troops to the attack⟩ **c** : to reveal the views of ⟨refused to ~ himself on the issue⟩ ~ *vi* **1** *obs* : to perpetrate an offense **2** : to obligate or pledge oneself — **com·mit·ta·ble** \-'mi-tə-bəl\ *adj*

syn COMMIT, ENTRUST, CONFIDE, CONSIGN, RELEGATE mean to assign to a person or place for a definite purpose. COMMIT may express the general idea of delivering into another's charge or the special sense of transferring to a superior power or to a special place of custody ⟨*committed* the felon to prison⟩. ENTRUST implies committing with trust and confidence ⟨the president is *entrusted* with broad powers⟩. CONFIDE implies entrusting with great assurance or reliance ⟨*confided* complete control of my affairs to my attorney⟩. CONSIGN suggests removing from one's control with formality or finality ⟨*consigned* the damaging notes to the fire⟩. RELEGATE implies a consigning to a particular class or sphere often with a suggestion of getting rid of ⟨*relegated* to an obscure position in the company⟩.

com·mit·ment \kə-'mit-mənt\ *n* (1621) **1 a** : an act of committing to a charge or trust: as (1) : a consignment to a penal or mental institution (2) : an act of referring a matter to a legislative committee **b** : MITTIMUS **2 a** : an agreement or pledge to do something in the future; *esp* : an engagement to assume a financial obligation at a future date **b** : something pledged **c** : the state or an instance of being obligated or emotionally impelled ⟨a ~ to a cause⟩

com·mit·tal \kə-'mi-t⁰l\ *n* (1818) : COMMITMENT, CONSIGNMENT

com·mit·tee \kə-'mi-tē, *sense 1 also* ˌkä-mi-'tē\ *n* (15c) **1** *archaic* : a person to whom a charge or trust is committed **2 a** : a body of persons delegated to consider, investigate, take action on, or report on some matter; *esp* : a group of fellow legislators chosen by a legislative body to give consideration to legislative matters **b** : a self-constituted organization for the promotion of a common object

com·mit·tee·man \kə-'mi-tē-mən, -ˌman\ *n* (1654) **1** : a member of a committee **2** : a party leader of a ward or precinct

committee of the whole (1775) : the whole membership of a legislative house sitting as a committee and operating under informal rules

com·mit·tee·wom·an \-ˌwu̇-mən\ *n* (1853) **1** : a woman who is a member of a committee **2** : a woman who is a party leader of a ward or precinct

com·mix \kə-'miks, kä-\ *vb* [back-formation fr. ME *comixt* blended, fr. L *commixtus*, pp. of *commiscēre* to mix together, fr. *com-* + *miscēre* to mix — more at MIX] *vt* (15c) : MINGLE, BLEND ~ *vi* : to become mingled or blended

com·mix·ture \-chər\ *n* [L *commixtura*, fr. *commixtus*] (1592) **1** : the act or process of mixing : the state of being mixed **2** : COMPOUND, MIXTURE

com·mode \kə-'mōd\ *n* [F, fr. *commode*, adj., suitable, convenient, fr. L *commodus*, fr. *com-* + *modus* measure — more at METE] (1688) **1** : a woman's ornate cap popular in the late 17th and early 18th centuries **2 a** : a low chest of drawers **b** : a movable washstand with a cupboard underneath **c** : a boxlike structure holding a chamber pot under an open seat; *also* : CHAMBER POT 2 : TOILET 3b

com·mod·i·fy \kə-'mä-də-ˌfī\ *vt* **-fied; -fy·ing** (1982) : to turn (as an intrinsic value or a work of art) into a commodity — **com·mod·i·fi·ca·tion** \-ˌmä-də-fə-'kā-shən\ *n*

com·mo·di·ous \kə-'mō-dē-əs\ *adj* [ME, useful, fr. MF *commodieux*, fr. ML *commodiosus*, irreg. fr. L *commodum* convenience, fr. neut. of *commodus*] (15c) **1** : comfortably or conveniently spacious : ROOMY ⟨a ~ closet⟩ **2** *archaic* : HANDY, SERVICEABLE *syn* see SPACIOUS — **com·mo·di·ous·ly** *adv* — **com·mo·di·ous·ness** *n*

com·mod·i·ty \kə-'mä-də-tē\ *n, pl* **-ties** [ME *commoditee*, fr. MF *commodité*, fr. L *commoditat-, commoditas*, fr. *commodus*] (15c) **1** : an economic good: as **a** : a product of agriculture or mining **b** : an article of commerce esp. when delivered for shipment ⟨*commodities* futures⟩ **c** : a mass-produced unspecialized product ⟨~ chemicals⟩

commode 1

\ə\ abut \ᵊ\ kitten, F table \ər\ further \a\ ash \ā\ ace \ä\ mop, mar \au̇\ out \ch\ chin \e\ bet \ē\ easy \g\ go \i\ hit \ī\ ice \j\ job \ŋ\ sing \ō\ go \ȯ\ law \ȯi\ boy \th\ thin \t͟h\ the \ü\ loot \u̇\ foot \y\ yet \zh\ vision \ä, ḵ, ⁿ, œ, œ̄, ᵫ, ᵬ, ᵌ\ *see* Guide to Pronunciation

⟨~ memory chips⟩ **2 a :** something useful or valued ⟨that valuable ~ patience⟩ **b :** CONVENIENCE, ADVANTAGE **3** obs : QUANTITY, LOT

com·mo·dore \'kä-mə-ˌdȯr, -ˌdȯr\ n [prob. modif. of D commandeur commander, fr. F, fr. OF comandeor, fr. comander to command] (1695) **1 a :** a captain in the navy in command of a squadron **b :** a commissioned officer in the navy formerly ranking above captain and below rear admiral and having an insignia of one star **2 :** the ranking officer commanding a body of merchant ships **3 :** the chief officer of a yacht club or boating association

¹**com·mon** \'kä-mən\ adj [ME commun, fr. OF, fr. L communis — more at MEAN] (13c) **1 a :** of or relating to a community at large : PUBLIC ⟨work for the ~ good⟩ **b :** known to the community ⟨~ nuisances⟩ **2 a :** belonging to or shared by two or more individuals or things or by all members of a group ⟨a ~ friend⟩ ⟨buried in a ~ grave⟩ **b :** belonging equally to two or more mathematical entities ⟨triangles with a ~ base⟩ **c :** having two or more branches ⟨~ carotid artery⟩ **3 a :** occurring or appearing frequently : FAMILIAR ⟨a ~ sight⟩ **b :** of the best known kind **c :** VERNACULAR 2 ⟨~ names⟩ **4 a :** WIDESPREAD, GENERAL ⟨~ knowledge⟩ **b :** characterized by a lack of privilege or special status ⟨~ people⟩ **c :** just satisfying accustomed criteria : ELEMENTARY ⟨~ decency⟩ **5 a :** falling below ordinary standards : SECOND-RATE **b :** lacking refinement : COARSE **6 :** denoting nominal relations by a single linguistic form that in a more highly inflected language might be denoted by two or more different forms ⟨~ gender⟩ ⟨~ case⟩ **7 :** of, relating to, or being common stock — **com·mon·ly** adv — **com·mon·ness** \-mən-nəs\ n

syn COMMON, ORDINARY, PLAIN, FAMILIAR, POPULAR, VULGAR mean generally met with and not in any way special, strange, or unusual. COMMON implies usual everyday quality or frequency of occurrence ⟨a common error⟩ ⟨lacked common honesty⟩ and may additionally suggest inferiority or coarseness ⟨common manners⟩. ORDINARY stresses conformance in quality or kind with the regular order of things ⟨an ordinary pleasant summer day⟩ ⟨a very ordinary sort of man⟩. PLAIN is likely to suggest homely simplicity ⟨plain hard-working people⟩. FAMILIAR stresses the fact of being generally known and easily recognized ⟨a familiar melody⟩. POPULAR applies to what is accepted by or prevalent among people in general sometimes in contrast to upper classes or special groups ⟨a writer of popular romances⟩. VULGAR, otherwise similar to POPULAR, is likely to carry derogatory connotations (as of inferiority or coarseness) ⟨souvenirs designed to appeal to the vulgar taste⟩.

²**common** n (14c) **1** pl : the common people **2** pl but sing in constr : a dining hall **3** pl but sing or pl in constr, often cap **a :** the political group or estate comprising the commoners **b :** the parliamentary representatives of the commoners **c :** HOUSE OF COMMONS **4 :** the legal right of taking a profit in another's land in common with the owner or others **5 a :** a piece of land subject to common use: as **a :** undivided land used esp. for pasture **b :** a public open area in a municipality **6 a :** a religious service suitable for any of various festivals **b :** ORDINARY 2 **7 :** COMMON STOCK — **in common :** shared together

com·mon·age \'kä-mə-nij\ n (1649) **1 :** community land **2 :** COMMONALTY 1a(2)

com·mon·al·i·ty \ˌkä-mə-'na-lə-tē\ n, pl **-ties** [ME communalite commonwealth, alter. of communalite] (1582) **1 :** the common people **2 a :** possession of common features or attributes : COMMONNESS **b :** a common feature or attribute

com·mon·al·ty \'kä-mə-nⁿl-tē\ n, pl **-ties** [ME communalte, fr. MF comunalté, fr. comunal communal] (14c) **1 a** (1) : the common people (2) : the political estate formed by the common people **b :** a usage or practice common to members of a group **2 :** a general group or body

common carrier n (15c) : a business or agency that is available to the public for transportation of persons, goods, or messages

common cattle grub n (1947) : a cattle grub (Hypoderma lineatum) which is found throughout the U.S. and whose larva is particularly destructive to cattle

common cold n (1786) : an acute virus disease of the upper respiratory tract marked by inflammation of the mucous membranes of the nose, throat, eyes, and eustachian tubes and by a watery then purulent discharge

common denominator n (1594) **1 :** a common multiple of the denominators of a number of fractions **2 :** a common trait or theme

common difference n (ca. 1891) : the difference between two consecutive terms of an arithmetic progression

common divisor n (ca. 1847) : a number or expression that divides two or more numbers or expressions without remainder — called also common factor

com·mon·er \'kä-mə-nər\ n (14c) **1 a :** one of the common people **b :** one who is not of noble rank **2 a :** a student (as at Oxford) who pays for his own board

Common Era n (ca. 1889) : CHRISTIAN ERA

common fraction n (ca. 1897) : a fraction in which the numerator and denominator are both integers and are separated by a horizontal or slanted line — compare DECIMAL FRACTION

common ground n (1874) : a basis of mutual interest or agreement

common-law adj (1848) **1 :** of, relating to, or based on the common law **2 :** relating to or based on a common-law marriage

common law n (14c) : the body of law developed in England primarily from judicial decisions based on custom and precedent, unwritten in statute or code, and constituting the basis of the English legal system and of the system in all of the U.S. except Louisiana

common-law marriage n (1900) **1 :** a marriage recognized in some jurisdictions and based on the parties' agreement to consider themselves married and sometimes also on their cohabitation **2 :** the cohabitation of a couple even when it does not constitute a legal marriage

common logarithm n (ca. 1903) : a logarithm whose base is 10

common market n (1952) : an economic association (as of nations) formed to remove trade barriers among its members

common measure n (1922) : a meter consisting chiefly of iambic lines of 7 accents each arranged in rhymed pairs usu. printed in 4-line stanzas — called also common meter

common multiple n (ca. 1890) : a multiple of each of two or more numbers or expressions ⟨90 is a common multiple of 6 and 10⟩

common noun n (ca. 1864) : a noun that may occur with limiting modifiers (as a or an, some, every, and my) and that designates any one of a class of beings or things

common or garden adj (1892) chiefly Brit : ORDINARY

¹**com·mon·place** \'kä-mən-ˌplās\ n [trans. of L locus communis widely applicable argument, trans. of Gk koinos topos] (1561) **1** archaic : a striking passage entered in a commonplace book **2 a :** an obvious or trite comment : TRUISM **b :** something commonly found

²**commonplace** adj (1609) **1 :** commonly found : ORDINARY, UNREMARKABLE — **com·mon·place·ness** n

commonplace book n (1578) : a book of memorabilia

common pleas n pl (1531) **1** sing in constr : COURT OF COMMON PLEAS **2 a :** actions over which the English crown did not exercise exclusive jurisdiction **b :** civil actions between English subjects

common ratio n (1875) : the ratio of each term of a geometric progression to the term preceding it

common room n (1683) **1 :** a lounge available to all members of a residential community **2 :** a room in a college for faculty use

common salt n (1676) : SALT 1a

common school n (ca. 1657) : a free public school

common sense n (1535) **1 :** the unreflective opinions of ordinary people **2 :** sound and prudent but often unsophisticated judgment **syn** see SENSE — **com·mon-sense** \'kä-mən-'sen(t)s\ adj — **com·mon-sen·si·ble** \-'sen(t)-sə-bəl\ adj — **com·mon-sen·si·cal** \-'sen(t)-si-kəl\ adj — **com·mon-sen·si·cal·ly** \-si-k(ə-)lē\ adv

common situs picketing n (1965) : the picketing of an entire construction site by a trade union having a grievance with only a single subcontractor working there

common stock n (1888) : capital stock other than preferred stock

common time n (1674) : a musical meter marked by four beats per measure with the quarter note receiving a single beat

common touch n (1944) : the gift of appealing to or arousing the sympathetic interest of the common people

com·mon·weal \'kä-mən-ˌwēl\ n (14c) **1** archaic : COMMONWEALTH **2 :** the general welfare

com·mon·wealth \-ˌwelth also -ˌweltth\ n (15c) **1** archaic : COMMONWEAL 2 **2 :** a nation, state, or other political unit: as **a :** one founded on law and united by compact or tacit agreement of the people for the common good **b :** one in which supreme authority is vested in the people **c :** REPUBLIC **3** cap **a :** the English state from the death of Charles I in 1649 to the Restoration in 1660 **b :** PROTECTORATE 1b **4 :** a state of the U.S. — used officially of Kentucky, Massachusetts, Pennsylvania, and Virginia **5** cap **:** a federal union of constituent states — used officially of Australia **6** often cap : an association of self-governing autonomous states more or less loosely associated in a common allegiance (as to the British crown) **7** often cap : a political unit having local autonomy but voluntarily united with the U.S. — used officially of Puerto Rico and of the Northern Mariana Islands

Commonwealth Day n (1959) : May 24 observed in parts of the Commonwealth of Nations as the anniversary of Queen Victoria's birthday

common year n (ca. 1909) : a calendar year containing no intercalary period

com·mo·tion \kə-'mō-shən\ n [ME, fr. MF, fr. L commotion-, commotio, fr. commovēre] (15c) **1 :** a condition of civil unrest or insurrection **2 :** steady or recurrent motion **3 :** mental excitement or confusion **4 a :** an agitated disturbance : TO-DO **b :** noisy confusion : AGITATION

com·move \kə-'müv, kä-\ vt **com·moved; com·mov·ing** [ME commoeven, fr. MF commuev-, pres. stem of commovoir, fr. L commovēre, fr. com- + movēre to move] (14c) **1 :** to move violently : AGITATE **2 :** to rouse intense feeling in : excite to passion

com·mu·nal \kə-'myü-nⁿl, 'käm-yə-nⁿl\ adj [F, fr. LL communalis, fr. L communis] (1811) **1 :** of or relating to one or more communes **2 :** of or relating to a community **3 a :** characterized by collective ownership and use of property **b :** participated in, shared, or used in common by members of a group or community **4 :** of, relating to, or based on racial or cultural groups — **com·mu·nal·ize** \kə-'myü-nⁿl-ˌīz, 'käm-yə-\ vt — **com·mu·nal·ly** adv

com·mu·nal·ism \-nⁿl-ˌi-zəm\ n (1871) **1 :** social organization on a communal basis **2 :** loyalty to a sociopolitical grouping based on religious or ethnic affiliation — **com·mu·nal·ist** \-nⁿl-ist\ n or adj

com·mu·nal·i·ty \ˌkäm-yü-'na-lə-tē\ n, pl **-ties** (1901) **1 :** communal state or character **2 :** a feeling of group solidarity

com·mu·nard \ˌkäm-yü-'när(d)\ n [F] (1874) **1** cap : one who supported or participated in the Commune of Paris in 1871 **2 :** a person who lives in a commune

¹**com·mune** \kə-'myün\ vb **com·muned; com·mun·ing** [ME, to converse, administer Communion, fr. MF comunier to converse, administer or receive Communion, fr. LL communicare, fr. L] vt (15c) obs : TALK OVER, DISCUSS ⟨have more to ~ —Shak.⟩ ~ vi **1 :** to receive Communion **2 :** to communicate intimately ⟨~ with nature⟩

²**com·mune** \'käm-ˌyün; kə-'myün, kä-\ n [F, alter. of MF comugne, fr. ML communia, fr. L neut. pl. of communis] (1673) **1 :** the smallest administrative district of many countries esp. in Europe **2 :** COMMONALTY 1a **3 a :** a medieval usu. municipal corporation **b** (1) : MIR (2) : an often rural community organized on a communal basis

com·mu·ni·ca·ble \kə-'myü-ni-kə-bəl\ adj (1534) **1 :** capable of being communicated : TRANSMITTABLE ⟨~ disease⟩ **2 :** COMMUNICATIVE — **com·mu·ni·ca·bil·i·ty** \-ˌmyü-ni-kə-'bi-lə-tē\ n — **com·mu·ni·ca·ble·ness** \-'myü-ni-kə-bəl-nəs\ n — **com·mu·ni·ca·bly** \-blē\ adv

com·mu·ni·cant \-'myü-ni-kənt\ n (1552) **1 :** a church member entitled to receive Communion; broadly : a member of a fellowship **2 :** one that communicates; specif : INFORMANT — **communicant** adj

com·mu·ni·cate \kə-'myü-nə-ˌkāt\ vb **-cat·ed; -cat·ing** [L communicatus, pp. of communicare to impart, participate, fr. communis common — more at MEAN] vt (1526) **1** archaic : SHARE **2 a :** to convey knowledge of or information about : make known ⟨~ a story⟩ **b :** to reveal by clear signs ⟨his fear communicated itself to his friends⟩ **3 :** to cause to pass from one to another ⟨some diseases are easily communicated⟩ — vi **1 :** to receive Communion **2 :** to transmit information, thought, or feeling so that it is satisfactorily received or understood **3 :** to open into each other : CONNECT ⟨the rooms ~⟩ — **com-**

mu·ni·ca·tee \-ˌmyü-ni-kə-'tē\ n — com·mu·ni·ca·tor \-'myü-nə-ˌkā-tər\ n

com·mu·ni·ca·tion \kə-ˌmyü-nə-'kā-shən\ n (14c) 1 : an act or instance of transmitting 2 a : information communicated b : a verbal or written message 3 a : a process by which information is exchanged between individuals through a common system of symbols, signs, or behavior ⟨the function of pheromones in insect ~⟩; also : exchange of information b : personal rapport ⟨a lack of ~ between old and young persons⟩ 4 pl a : a system (as of telephones) for communicating b : a system of routes for moving troops, and vehicles c : personnel engaged in communicating 5 pl but sing or pl in constr a : a technique for expressing ideas effectively (as in speech) b : the technology of the transmission of information (as by print or telecommunication) — com·mu·ni·ca·tion·al \-shnəl, -shə-nᵊl\ adj

com·mu·ni·ca·tive \kə-'myü-nə-ˌkā-tiv, -ni-kə-tiv\ adj (14c) 1 : tending to communicate : TALKATIVE 2 : of or relating to communication — com·mu·ni·ca·tive·ly adv — com·mu·ni·ca·tive·ness n

com·mu·ni·ca·to·ry \kə-'myü-ni-kə-ˌtōr-ē, -ˌtor-\ adj (1646) 1 : designed to communicate information ⟨~ letters⟩ 2 : COMMUNICATIVE 2

com·mu·nion \kə-'myü-nyən\ n [ME, fr. L communion-, communio mutual participation, fr. communis] (14c) 1 : an act or instance of sharing 2 a cap : a Christian sacrament in which consecrated bread and wine are consumed as memorials of Christ's death or as symbols for the realization of a spiritual union between Christ and communicant or as the body and blood of Christ b : the act of receiving Communion c cap : the part of a Communion service in which the sacrament is received 3 : intimate fellowship or rapport : COMMUNICATION 4 : a body of Christians having a common faith and discipline ⟨the Anglican ~⟩

com·mu·ni·qué \kə-'myü-nə-ˌkā, -ˌmyü-nə-'\ n [F, fr. pp. of communiquer to communicate, fr. L communicare] (1852) : BULLETIN 1

com·mu·nise Brit var of COMMUNIZE

com·mu·nism \'käm-yə-ˌni-zəm\ n [F communisme, fr. commun common] (1840) 1 a : a theory advocating elimination of private property b : a system in which goods are owned in common and are available to all as needed 2 cap a : a doctrine based on revolutionary Marxian socialism and Marxism-Leninism that was the official ideology of the U.S.S.R. b : a totalitarian system of government in which a single authoritarian party controls state-owned means of production c : a final stage of society in Marxist theory in which the state has withered away and economic goods are distributed equitably d : communist systems collectively

com·mu·nist \'käm-yə-nist\ n (1840) 1 : an adherent or advocate of communism 2 cap : COMMUNARD 3 a cap : a member of a Communist party or movement b often cap : an adherent or advocate of a Communist government, party, or movement 4 often cap : one held to engage in left-wing, subversive, or revolutionary activities — communist adj, often cap — com·mu·nis·tic \ˌkäm-yə-'nis-tik\ adj, often cap — com·mu·nis·ti·cal·ly \-ti-k(ə-)lē\ adv

com·mu·ni·tar·i·an \kə-ˌmyü-nə-'ter-ē-ən\ adj (ca. 1909) : of or relating to social organization in small cooperative partially collectivist communities — communitarian n — com·mu·ni·tar·i·an·ism \-ē-ə-ˌni-zəm\ n

com·mu·ni·ty \kə-'myü-nə-tē\ n, pl -ties often attrib [ME comunete, fr. MF comuneté, fr. L communitat-, communitas, fr. communis] (14c) 1 : a unified body of individuals: as a : STATE, COMMONWEALTH b : the people with common interests living in a particular area; broadly : the area itself ⟨the problems of a large ~⟩ c : an interacting population of various kinds of individuals (as species) in a common location d : a group of people with a common characteristic or interest living together within a larger society ⟨a ~ of retired persons⟩ e : a group linked by a common policy f : a body of persons or nations having a common history or common social, economic, and political interests ⟨the international ~⟩ g : a body of persons of common and esp. professional interests scattered through a larger society ⟨the academic ~⟩ 2 : society at large 3 a : joint ownership or participation ⟨~ of goods⟩ b : common character : LIKENESS ⟨~ of interests⟩ c : social activity : FELLOWSHIP b : a social state or condition

community antenna television n (1953) : CABLE TELEVISION

community center n (1915) : a building or group of buildings for a community's educational and recreational activities

community chest n (1919) : a general fund accumulated from individual subscriptions to defray demands on a community for charity and social welfare

community college n (1948) : a 2-year government-supported college that offers an associate degree

community property n (ca. 1925) : property held jointly by husband and wife

com·mu·nize \'käm-yə-ˌnīz\ vt -nized; -niz·ing [back-formation fr. communization] (1888) 1 a : to make common b : to make into state-owned property 2 : to subject to Communist principles of organization — com·mu·ni·za·tion \ˌkäm-yə-nə-'zā-shən\ n

com·mu·tate \'käm-yə-ˌtāt\ vt -tat·ed; -tat·ing [back-formation fr. commutation] (1893) : to reverse every other half cycle of (an alternating current) so as to form a unidirectional current

com·mu·ta·tion \ˌkäm-yə-'tā-shən\ n [ME, fr. MF, fr. L commutation-, commutatio, fr. commutare] (15c) 1 : EXCHANGE, TRADE 2 : REPLACEMENT; specif : a substitution of one form of payment or charge for another 3 : a change of a legal penalty or punishment to a lesser one 4 : an act or process of commuting 5 : the action of commutating

commutation ticket n (1848) : a transportation ticket sold for a fixed number of trips over the same route during a limited period

com·mu·ta·tive \'käm-yə-ˌtā-tiv, kə-'myü-tə-tiv, 'käm-yə-tə-tiv\ adj (1612) 1 : of, relating to, or showing commutation 2 : of, relating to, having, or being the property that a given mathematical operation and set have when the result obtained using any two elements of the set with the operation does not differ with the order in which the elements are used ⟨a ~ group⟩ ⟨addition of the positive integers is ~⟩

com·mu·ta·tiv·i·ty \kə-ˌmyü-tə-'ti-və-tē, ˌkäm-yə-tə-\ n (1929) : the property of being commutative ⟨the ~ of a mathematical operation⟩

com·mu·ta·tor \'käm-yə-ˌtā-tər\ n (1880) 1 : a series of bars or segments so connected to armature coils of a generator or motor that rotation of the armature will in conjunction with fixed brushes result in unidirectional current output in the case of a generator and in the re-

versal of the current into the coils in the case of a motor 2 : an element of a mathematical group that when used to multiply the product of two given elements either on the right side or on the left side but not necessarily on both sides yields the product of the two given elements in reverse order

¹com·mute \kə-'myüt\ vb com·mut·ed; com·mut·ing [L commutare to change, exchange, fr. com- + mutare to change — more at MUTABLE] vt (15c) 1 a : CHANGE, ALTER b : to give in exchange for another : EXCHANGE 2 : to convert (as a payment) into another form 3 : to exchange (a penalty) for another less severe 4 : COMMUTATE ~ vi 1 : MAKE UP, COMPENSATE 2 : to pay in gross 3 : to travel back and forth regularly (as between a suburb and a city) 4 : to yield the same mathematical result regardless of order — used of two elements undergoing an operation or of two operations on elements — com·mut·able \-'myüt-ə-bəl\ adj

²commute n (1954) 1 : an act or an instance of commuting 2 : the distance covered in commuting

com·mut·er \kə-'myü-tər\ n (ca. 1859) 1 : a person who commutes (as between a suburb and a city) 2 : a small airline that carries passengers relatively short distances on a regular schedule

co·mo·no·mer \(ˌ)kō-'mä-nə-mər, -'mō-\ n [co- + monomer] (1945) : one of the constituents of a copolymer

¹comp \'kämp\ n [short for complimentary] (1887) : a complimentary ticket; broadly : something provided free of charge

²comp \'komp, 'kämp\ vi [short for accompany] (1949) : to punctuate and support a jazz solo with irregularly spaced chords

¹com·pact \kəm-'pakt, käm-', 'käm-\ adj [ME, firmly put together, fr. L compactus, fr. pp. of compingere to put together, fr. com- + pangere to fasten — more at PACT] (14c) 1 : predominantly formed or filled : COMPOSED, MADE 2 a : having a dense structure or parts or units closely packed or joined ⟨a ~ woolen⟩ ⟨~ bone⟩ b : not diffuse or verbose ⟨a ~ statement⟩ c : occupying a small volume by reason of efficient use of space ⟨a ~ camera⟩ ⟨a ~ formation of troops⟩ d : short-bodied, solid, and without excess flesh 3 : being a topological space in which a subset is equivalent to a metric space with the property that for any collection of open sets which contains it there is a subset of the collection with a finite number of elements which also contains it — com·pact·ly \-'pakt(t)-lē, -ˌpakt(t)-\ adv — com·pact·ness \-'pakt(t)-nəs, -ˌpakt(t)-\ n

²compact vt (15c) 1 : to make up by connecting or combining : COMPOSE 2 a : to knit or draw together : COMBINE b : to press together : COMPRESS ~ vi : to become compacted — com·pact·ible \-'pak-tə-bəl, -ˌpak-\ adj — com·pac·tor also com·pact·er \-'pak-tər, -ˌpak-\ n

³com·pact \'käm-ˌpakt\ n (1601) : something that is compact or compacted: a : a small cosmetic case (as for compressed powder) b : an automobile smaller than an intermediate but larger than a subcompact

⁴com·pact \'käm-ˌpakt\ n [L compactum, fr. neut. of compactus, pp. of compacisci to make an agreement, fr. com- + pacisci to contract — more at PACT] (1591) : an agreement or covenant between two or more parties

compact disc \'käm-ˌpakt-\ n (1979) : a small plastic optical disc usu. containing recorded music or computer data

com·pac·tion \kəm-'pak-shən, käm-\ n (14c) : the act or process of compacting : the state of being compacted

¹com·pan·ion \kəm-'pan-yən\ n [ME compainoun, fr. OF compagnon, fr. LL companion-, companio, fr. L com- + panis bread, food — more at FOOD] (13c) 1 : one that accompanies another : COMRADE, ASSOCIATE; also : one that keeps company with another 2 obs : RASCAL 3 a : one that is closely connected with something similar b : one employed to live with and accompany another

²companion vt (1622) : ACCOMPANY ~ vi : to keep company

³companion n [by folk etymology fr. D kampanje poop deck] (1762) 1 : a hood covering at the top of a companionway 2 : COMPANIONWAY

com·pan·ion·able \kəm-'pan-yə-nə-bəl\ adj (14c) : marked by, conducive to, or suggestive of companionship : SOCIABLE — com·pan·ion·abil·i·ty \-ˌpan-yə-nə-'bi-lə-tē\ n — com·pan·ion·able·ness n — com·pan·ion·ably \-'pan-yə-nə-blē\ adv

com·pan·ion·ate \kəm-'pan-yə-nət\ adj (1926) : relating to or having the manner of companions; specif : harmoniously or suitably accompanying

companion cell n (1887) : a living nucleated cell that is closely associated in origin, position, and probably function with a cell making up part of a sieve tube of a vascular plant

companion piece n (1844) : a work (as of literature) that is associated with and complements another

com·pan·ion·ship \kəm-'pan-yən-ˌship\ n (1548) : the fellowship existing among companions : COMPANY

com·pan·ion·way \-yən-ˌwā\ n [³companion] (1840) : a ship's stairway from one deck to another

¹com·pa·ny \'kəmp-nē, 'kəm-pə-\ n, pl -nies often attrib [ME companie, fr. OF compaignie, fr. compain companion, fr. LL companio] (13c) 1 a : association with another : FELLOWSHIP ⟨enjoy a person's ~⟩ b : COMPANIONS, ASSOCIATES ⟨know a person by the ~ she keeps⟩ c : VISITORS, GUESTS ⟨having ~ for dinner⟩ 2 a : a group of persons or things ⟨a ~ of horsemen⟩ b : a body of soldiers; esp : a unit (as of infantry) consisting usu. of a headquarters and two or more platoons c : an organization of performing artists d : the officers and crew of a ship e : a fire-fighting unit 3 a : a chartered commercial organization or medieval trade guild b : an association of persons for carrying on a commercial or industrial enterprise c : those members of a partnership firm whose names do not appear in the firm name ⟨John Doe and Company⟩

²company vb -nied; -ny·ing vt (14c) : ACCOMPANY ⟨may . . . fair winds ~ your safe return —John Masefield⟩ ~ vi : ASSOCIATE

company man n (ca. 1921) : a worker who acquiesces in company policy without complaint

company officer n (1844) : a commissioned officer in the army, air force, or marine corps of the rank of captain, first lieutenant, or second

---

\ə\ abut \ᵊ\ kitten, F table \ər\ further \a\ ash \ā\ ace \ä\ mop, mar
\aů\ out \ch\ chin \e\ bet \ē\ easy \g\ go \i\ hit \ī\ ice \j\ job
\ŋ\ sing \ō\ go \ò\ law \òi\ boy \th\ thin \t̲h̲\ the \ü\ loot \ů\ foot
\y\ yet \zh\ vision \à, k̲, ⁿ, œ, œ̄, ɵ, ɵ̄, ʸ\ see Guide to Pronunciation

lieutenant — called also *company grade officer;* compare FIELD OFFICER, GENERAL OFFICER

company town *n* (1927) : a community that is dependent on one firm for all or most of the necessary services or functions of town life (as employment, housing, and stores)

company union *n* (1917) : an unaffiliated labor union of the employees of a single firm; *esp* : one dominated by the employer

com·pa·ra·bil·i·ty \ˌkäm-p(ə-)rə-'bi-lə-tē, ÷kəm-ˌpar-ə-\ *n* (1843) : the quality or state of being comparable

com·pa·ra·ble \'käm-p(ə-)rə-bəl, ÷kəm-'par-ə-bəl\ *adj* (15c) 1 : capable of or suitable for comparison 2 : SIMILAR, LIKE ⟨fabrics of ∼ quality⟩ — **com·pa·ra·ble·ness** *n* — **com·pa·ra·bly** \-blē\ *adv*

comparable worth *n* (1983) : the concept that women and men should receive equal pay for jobs calling for comparable skill and responsibility

com·par·a·tist \kəm-'par-ə-tist\ *n* [*comparative* + *-ist*] (1933) : one that uses a comparative method (as in the study of literature)

¹com·par·a·tive \kəm-'par-ə-tiv\ *adj* (15c) 1 : of, relating to, or constituting the degree of comparison in a language that denotes increase in the quality, quantity, or relation expressed by an adjective or adverb 2 : considered as if in comparison to something else as a standard not quite attained : RELATIVE ⟨a ∼ stranger⟩ 3 : characterized by systematic comparison esp. of likenesses and dissimilarities ⟨∼ anatomy⟩ — **com·par·a·tive·ly** *adv* — **com·par·a·tive·ness** *n*

²comparative *n* (15c) 1 a : one that compares with another esp. on equal footing : RIVAL b : one that makes witty or mocking comparisons 2 : the comparative degree or form in a language

com·par·a·tiv·ist \kəm-'par-ə-ti-vist\ *n* (1887) : COMPARATIST

com·par·a·tor \kəm-'par-ə-tər\ *n* (1883) : a device for comparing something with a similar thing or with a standard measure

¹com·pare \kəm-'par, -'per\ *vb* **com·pared; com·par·ing** [ME, fr. MF *comparer*, fr. L *comparare* to couple, compare, fr. *compar* like, fr. *com-* + *par* equal] *vt* (14c) 1 : to represent as similar : LIKEN ⟨shall I ∼ thee to a summer's day? —Shak.⟩ 2 a : to examine the character or qualities of esp. in order to discover resemblances or differences ⟨∼ your responses with the answers⟩ b : to view in relation to ⟨tall compared to me⟩ 3 : to inflect or modify (an adjective or adverb) according to the degrees of comparison ∼ *vi* 1 : to bear being compared 2 : to make comparisons 3 : to be equal or alike ⟨nothing ∼s to you⟩ *syn* COMPARE, CONTRAST, COLLATE mean to set side by side in order to show differences and likenesses. COMPARE implies an aim of showing relative values or excellences by bringing out characteristic qualities whether similar or divergent ⟨*compared* the convention facilities of the two cities⟩. CONTRAST implies an emphasis on differences ⟨*contrasted* the computerized system with the old filing cards⟩. COLLATE implies minute and critical inspection in order to note points of agreement or divergence ⟨data from districts around the country will be *collated*⟩.

²compare *n* (1589) : the possibility of comparing ⟨beauty beyond ∼⟩; *also* : something with which to be compared ⟨a city without ∼⟩

com·par·i·son \kəm-'par-ə-sən\ *n* [ME, fr. MF *comparaison*, fr. L *comparation-, comparatio*, fr. *comparare*] (14c) 1 : the act or process of comparing: as a : the representing of one thing or person as similar to or like another b : an examination of two or more items to establish similarities and dissimilarities 2 : identity of features : SIMILARITY ⟨several points of ∼ between the two⟩ 3 : the modification of an adjective or adverb to denote different levels of quality, quantity, or relation

comparison shop *vi* (1970) : to compare prices (as of competing brands) in order to find the best value

¹com·part·ment \kəm-'pärt-mənt\ *n* [MF *compartiment*, fr. It *compartimento*, fr. *compartire* to mark out in parts, fr. LL *compartiri* to share out, fr. L *com-* + *partiri* to share, fr. *part-, pars* part, share] (ca. 1578) 1 : a separate division or section 2 : one of the parts into which an enclosed space is divided — **com·part·men·tal** \kəm-ˌpärt-'men-t²l, ˌkäm-\ *adj*

²com·part·ment \-ˌment, -mənt\ *vt* (1918) : COMPARTMENTALIZE

com·part·men·tal·ise *Brit var of* COMPARTMENTALIZE

com·part·men·tal·ize \kəm-ˌpärt-'men-t²l-ˌīz, ˌkäm-\ *vt* **-ized; -iz·ing** (1925) : to separate into isolated compartments or categories — **com·part·men·tal·i·za·tion** \-ˌmen-t²l-ə-'zā-shən\ *n*

com·part·men·ta·tion \kəm-ˌpärt-mən-'tā-shən, -ˌmen-\ *n* (1926) : division into separate sections or units

¹com·pass \'kəm-pəs *also* 'käm-\ *vt* [ME, fr. OF *compasser* to measure, fr. (assumed) VL *compassare* to pace off, fr. L *com-* + *passus* pace] (14c) 1 : to devise or contrive often with craft or skill 2 : ENCOMPASS 3 a : BRING ABOUT, ACHIEVE b : to get into one's possession or power : OBTAIN 4 : COMPREHEND — **com·pass·able** \-pə-sə-bəl\ *adj*

²compass *n* (14c) 1 a : BOUNDARY, CIRCUMFERENCE ⟨within the ∼ of the city walls⟩ b : a circumscribed space ⟨within the narrow ∼ of 21 pages —V. L. Parrington⟩ c : RANGE, SCOPE ⟨the ∼ of a voice⟩ 2 : a curved or roundabout course ⟨a ∼ of seven days' journey —2 Kings 3:9 (AV)⟩ 3 a : a device for determining directions by means of a magnetic needle or group of needles turning freely on a pivot and pointing to the magnetic north b : any of various nonmagnetic devices that indicate direction c : an instrument for describing circles or transferring measurements that consists of two pointed branches joined at the top by a pivot — usu. used in pl.; called also *pair of compasses* 4 : DIRECTION 6c *syn* see RANGE

³compass *adj* (1523) : forming a curve : CURVED ⟨a ∼ timber⟩

compass 3a

compass card *n* (ca. 1859) : the circular card attached to the needles of a mariner's compass on which are marked the 32 points of the compass and the 360° of the circle

com·pas·sion \kəm-'pa-shən\ *n* [ME, fr. MF or LL; MF, fr. LL *compassion-, compassio*, fr. *compati* to sympathize, fr. L *com-* + *pati* to bear, suffer — more at PATIENT] (14c) : sympathetic consciousness of others' distress together with a desire to alleviate it *syn* see PITY — **com·pas·sion·less** \-ləs\ *adj*

¹com·pas·sion·ate \kəm-'pa-sh(ə-)nət\ *adj* (1587) 1 : having or showing compassion : SYMPATHETIC 2 : granted because of unusual

distressing circumstances affecting an individual — used of some military privileges (as leave) — **com·pas·sion·ate·ly** *adv* — **com·pas·sion·ate·ness** *n*

²com·pas·sion·ate \-'pa-shə-ˌnāt\ *vt* **-at·ed; -at·ing** (1592) : PITY

compass plant *n* (1848) : a coarse yellow-flowered composite plant (*Silphium laciniatum*) with large pinnatifid leaves that occurs in prairies and along roadsides and railroad tracks of the central U.S.

compass rose *n* (ca. 1891) : a circle graduated to degrees or quarters and printed on a chart to show direction

com·pat·i·ble \kəm-'pa-tə-bəl\ *adj* [ME, fr. MF, fr. ML *compatibilis*, lit., sympathetic, fr. LL *compati*] (15c) 1 : capable of existing together in harmony ⟨∼ theories⟩ 2 : capable of cross-fertilizing freely or uniting vegetatively 3 : capable of forming a homogeneous mixture that neither separates nor is altered by chemical interaction 4 : capable of being used in transfusion or grafting without immunological reaction (as agglutination or tissue rejection) 5 : designed to work with another device or system without modification; *esp* : being a computer designed to operate in the same manner and use the same software as another computer — **com·pat·i·bil·i·ty** \-ˌpa-tə-'bi-lə-tē\ *n* — **compatible** *n* — **com·pat·i·ble·ness** \-'pa-tə-bəl-nəs\ *n* — **com·pat·i·bly** \-blē\ *adv*

com·pa·tri·ot \kəm-'pā-trē-ət, käm-, -trē-ˌät, *chiefly Brit* -'pa-\ *n* [F *compatriote*, fr. LL *compatriota*, fr. L *com-* + LL *patriota* fellow countryman — more at PATRIOT] (1611) 1 : a person born, residing, or holding citizenship in the same country as another 2 : COMPEER, COLLEAGUE — **com·pa·tri·ot·ic** \kəm-ˌpā-trē-'ä-tik, ˌkäm-, *chiefly Brit* -ˌpa-\ *adj*

¹com·peer \'käm-ˌpir, käm-'; kəm-\ *n* [ME, fr. OF *compere*, lit., godfather, fr. ML *compater*, fr. L *com-* + *pater* father — more at FATHER] (13c) : COMPANION

²compeer *n* [ME *compere*, fr. OF, fr. L *compar*, fr. *compar*, adj., like — more at COMPARE] (15c) : EQUAL, PEER — **compeer** *vt, obs*

com·pel \kəm-'pel\ *vt* **com·pelled; com·pel·ling** [ME *compellen*, fr. MF *compellir*, fr. L *compellere*, fr. *com-* + *pellere* to drive — more at FELT] (14c) 1 : to drive or urge forcefully or irresistibly 2 : to cause to do or occur by overwhelming pressure 3 *archaic* : to drive together *syn* see FORCE — **com·pel·la·ble** \-'pe-lə-bəl\ *adj*

com·pel·la·tion \ˌkäm-pə-'lā-shən, -ˌpe-\ *n* [L *compellation-, compellatio*, fr. *compellare* to address, fr. *com-* + *-pellare* (as in *appellare* to accost, appeal to)] (1603) 1 : an act or action of addressing someone 2 : APPELLATION 1

com·pel·ling \kəm-'pe-liŋ\ *adj* (1606) : that compels: as a : FORCEFUL ⟨a ∼ personality⟩ b : demanding attention ⟨for ∼ reasons⟩ c : CONVINCING ⟨no ∼ evidence⟩ — **com·pel·ling·ly** *adv*

com·pend \'käm-ˌpend\ *n* [ML *compendium*] (1596) : COMPENDIUM

com·pen·di·ous \kəm-'pen-dē-əs\ *adj* (14c) : marked by brief expression of a comprehensive matter : concise and comprehensive; *also* : COMPREHENSIVE *syn* see CONCISE — **com·pen·di·ous·ly** *adv* — **com·pen·di·ous·ness** *n*

com·pen·di·um \kəm-'pen-dē-əm\ *n, pl* **-di·ums** *or* **-dia** \-dē-ə\ [ML, fr. L, saving, shortcut, fr. *compendere* to weigh together, fr. *com-* + *pendere* to weigh — more at PENDANT] (1589) 1 : a brief summary of a larger work or of a field of knowledge : ABSTRACT 2 a : a list of a number of items b : COLLECTION, COMPILATION

com·pen·sa·ble \kəm-'pen(t)-sə-bəl\ *adj* (1661) : that is to be or can be compensated ⟨a ∼ job-related injury⟩ — **com·pen·sa·bil·i·ty** \kəm-ˌpen(t)-sə-'bi-lə-tē, ˌkäm-\ *n*

com·pen·sate \'käm-pən-ˌsāt, -ˌpen-\ *vb* **-sat·ed; -sat·ing** [L *compensatus*, pp. of *compensare*, freq. of *compendere*] *vt* (1646) 1 : to be equivalent to : COUNTERBALANCE 2 : to make an appropriate and usu. counterbalancing payment to 3 a : to provide with means of counteracting variation b : to neutralize the effect of (variations) ∼ *vi* 1 : to supply an equivalent — used with *for* 2 : to offset an error, defect, or undesired effect 3 : to undergo or engage in psychological or physiological compensation *syn* see PAY — **com·pen·sa·tive** \'käm-pən-ˌsā-tiv, -ˌpen-; kəm-'pen(t)-sə-\ *adj* — **com·pen·sa·tor** \'käm-pən-ˌsā-tər, -ˌpen-\ *n* — **com·pen·sa·to·ry** \kəm-'pen(t)-sə-ˌtōr-ē, -ˌtōr-\ *adj*

com·pen·sa·tion \ˌkäm-pən-'sā-shən, -ˌpen-\ *n* (14c) 1 a : the act of compensating : the state of being compensated b : correction of an organic defect or loss by hypertrophy or by increased functioning of another organ or unimpaired parts of the same organ c : a psychological mechanism by which feelings of inferiority, frustration, or failure in one field are counterbalanced by achievement in another 2 a (1) : something that constitutes an equivalent or recompense ⟨age has its ∼s⟩ (2) : payment to unemployed or injured workers or their dependents b : PAYMENT, REMUNERATION — **com·pen·sa·tion·al** \-shnəl, -shə-n²l\ *adj*

compensatory education *n* (1965) : educational programs intended to make up for experiences (as cultural) lacked by disadvantaged children

¹com·pere *or* **com·père** \'käm-ˌper\ *n* [F *compère*, lit., godfather — more at COMPEER] (1914) *chiefly Brit* : the master of ceremonies of an entertainment (as a television program)

²compere *or* **compère** *vb* **com·pered** *or* **com·pèred; com·per·ing** *or* **com·pèr·ing** *vt* (1933) *chiefly Brit* : to act as compere for ∼ *vi, chiefly Brit* : to act as a compere

com·pete \kəm-'pēt\ *vi* **com·pet·ed; com·pet·ing** [LL *competere* to seek together, fr. L, to come together, agree, be suitable, fr. *com-* + *petere* to go to, seek — more at FEATHER] (1620) : to strive consciously or unconsciously for an objective (as position, profit, or a prize) : be in a state of rivalry

com·pe·tence \'käm-pə-tən(t)s\ *n* (1632) 1 : a sufficiency of means for the necessities and conveniences of life ⟨provided his family with a comfortable ∼ —Rex Ingamells⟩ 2 : the quality or state of being competent: as a : the properties of an enzyme field that enable it to respond in a characteristic manner to an organizer b : readiness of bacteria to undergo genetic transformation 3 : the knowledge that enables a person to speak and understand a language — compare PERFORMANCE

com·pe·ten·cy \-pə-tən(t)-sē\ *n, pl* **-cies** (1596) : COMPETENCE

com·pe·tent \'käm-pə-tənt\ *adj* [ME, suitable, fr. MF & L; MF, fr. L *competent-, competens*, fr. prp. of *competere*] (15c) 1 : proper or rightly pertinent 2 : having requisite or adequate ability or qualities

: FIT ⟨a ~ teacher⟩ ⟨a ~ piece of work⟩ **3** : legally qualified or adequate ⟨a ~ witness⟩ **4** : having the capacity to function or develop in a particular way; *specif* : having the capacity to respond (as by producing an antibody) to an antigenic determinant ⟨immunologically ~ cells⟩ *syn* see SUFFICIENT — **com·pe·tent·ly** *adv*

com·pe·ti·tion \ˌkäm-pə-'ti-shən\ *n* [LL *competition-*, *competitio*, fr. L *competere*] (1605) **1** : the act or process of competing : RIVALRY: as **a** : the effort of two or more parties acting independently to secure the business of a third party by offering the most favorable terms **b** : active demand by two or more organisms or kinds of organisms for some environmental resource in short supply **2** : a contest between rivals; *also* : one's competitors ⟨faced tough ~⟩

com·pet·i·tive \kəm-'pe-tə-tiv\ *adj* (1829) **1** : relating to, characterized by, or based on competition ⟨~ sports⟩ **2** : inclined, desiring, or suited to compete ⟨a ~ personality⟩ ⟨salary benefits must be ~ —M. S. Eisenhower⟩ **3** : depending for effectiveness on the relative concentration of two or more substances ⟨~ inhibition of an enzyme⟩ — **com·pet·i·tive·ly** *adv* — **com·pet·i·tive·ness** *n*

com·pet·i·tor \kəm-'pe-tə-tər\ *n* (1534) : one that competes: as **a** : RIVAL **b** : one selling or buying goods or services in the same market as another **c** : an organism that lives in competition with another

com·pi·la·tion \ˌkäm-pə-'lā-shən *also* -ˌpī-\ *n* (15c) **1** : the act or process of compiling **2** : something compiled

com·pile \kəm-'pī(ə)l\ *vt* **com·piled; com·pil·ing** [ME, fr. MF *compiler*, fr. L *compilare* to plunder] (14c) **1** : to compose out of materials from other documents **2** : to collect and edit into a volume **3** : to run (as a program) through a compiler **4** : to build up gradually ⟨*compiled* a record of four wins and two losses⟩

com·pil·er \kəm-'pī-lər\ *n* (14c) **1** : one that compiles **2** : a computer program that translates an entire set of instructions written in a higher-level symbolic language (as Pascal) into machine language before the instructions can be executed

com·pla·cence \kəm-'plā-s²n(t)s\ *n* (15c) **1** : calm or secure satisfaction with oneself or one's lot : SELF-SATISFACTION **2** *obs* : COMPLAISANCE **3** : UNCONCERN

com·pla·cen·cy \-s²n(t)-sē\ *n, pl* **-cies** (1650) **1** : COMPLACENCE; *esp* : self-satisfaction accompanied by unawareness of actual dangers or deficiencies **2** : an instance of complacency

com·pla·cent \kəm-'plā-s²nt\ *adj* [L *complacent-, complacens*, prp. of *complacēre* to please greatly, fr. *com-* + *placēre* to please — more at PLEASE] (1767) **1** : SELF-SATISFIED ⟨a ~ smile⟩ **2** : COMPLAISANT 1 **3** : UNCONCERNED — **com·pla·cent·ly** *adv*

com·plain \kəm-'plān\ *vi* [ME *compleynen*, fr. MF *complaindre*, fr. (assumed) VL *complangere*, fr. L *com-* + *plangere* to lament — more at PLAINT] (14c) **1** : to express grief, pain, or discontent **2** : to make a formal accusation or charge — **com·plain·er** *n* — **com·plain·ing·ly** \-'plā-niŋ-lē\ *adv*

com·plain·ant \kəm-'plā-nənt\ *n* (15c) : the party who makes the complaint in a legal action or proceeding

com·plaint \kəm-'plānt\ *n* [ME *compleynte*, fr. MF *complainte*, fr. OF, fr. *complaindre*] (14c) **1** : expression of grief, pain, or dissatisfaction **2** **a** : something that is the cause or subject of protest or outcry **b** : a bodily ailment or disease **3** : a formal allegation against a party

com·plai·sance \kəm-'plā-s²n(t)s, -z²n(t)s; ˌkäm-plā-'zan(t)s, -plə-, -'zän(t)s\ *n* (1651) : disposition to please or comply : AFFABILITY

com·plai·sant \-s²nt, -z²nt, -'zant, -'zänt\ *adj* [F, fr. MF, fr. prp. of *complaire* to gratify, acquiesce, fr. L *complacēre*] (1647) **1** : marked by an inclination to please or oblige **2** : tending to consent to others' wishes *syn* see AMIABLE — **com·plai·sant·ly** *adv*

com·pleat \kəm-'plēt\ *adj* [archaic variant of *complete* in *The Compleat Angler* (1653) by Izaak Walton] (1526) : COMPLETE 3

com·plect·ed \kəm-'plek-təd\ *adj* [irreg. fr. *complexion*] (1806) : having a specified facial complexion ⟨a tall, thin man, fairly dark ~ —E. J. Kahn⟩

usage Not an error, nor a dialectal term, nor nonstandard—all of which it has been labeled—*complected* still manages to raise hackles. It is an Americanism, apparently nonexistent in British English. Its currency in American English is attested as early as 1806 (by Meriwether Lewis) and it appears in the works of such notable American writers as Mark Twain, O. Henry, James Whitcomb Riley, and William Faulkner. *Complexioned*, recommended by handbooks, has less use than *complected*. Literary use, old and new, slightly favors *complected*.

¹**com·ple·ment** \'käm-plə-mənt\ *n* [ME, fr. L *complementum*, fr. *complēre* to fill up, complete, fr. *com-* + *plēre* to fill — more at FULL] (14c) **1** **a** : something that fills up, completes, or makes perfect **b** : the quantity or number required to make a thing complete ⟨the usual ~ of eyes and ears —Francis Parkman⟩; *esp* : the whole force or personnel of a ship **c** : one of two mutually completing parts : COUNTERPART **2** **a** : the angle or arc that when added to a given angle or arc equals a right angle in measure **b** : the set of all elements that do not belong to a given set and are contained in a particular mathematical set containing the given set **c** : a number that when added to another number of the same sign yields zero if the significant digit farthest to the left is discarded — used esp. in assembly language programming **3** : the musical interval required with a given interval to complete the octave **4** : an added word or expression by which a predication is made complete (as *president* in "they elected him president" and *beautiful* in "he thought her beautiful") **5** : the thermolabile group of proteins in normal blood serum and plasma that in combination with antibodies causes the destruction esp. of particulate antigens (as bacteria and foreign blood corpuscles)

complement 2a: *ACB* right angle, *ACD* complement of *DCB* (and vice versa), *AD* complement of *DB* (and vice versa)

²**com·ple·ment** \-ˌment\ *vi* (1602) *obs* : to exchange formal courtesies ~ *vt* **1** : to be complementary to **2** *obs* : COMPLIMENT

com·ple·men·tal \ˌkäm-plə-'men-t²l\ *adj* (1597) **1** : relating to or being a complement **2** *obs* : CEREMONIOUS, COMPLIMENTARY

com·ple·men·tar·i·ty \ˌkäm-plə-(ˌ)men-'tar-ə-tē, -mən-\ *n* (1911) : the quality or state of being complementary

com·ple·men·ta·ry \ˌkäm-plə-'men-t(ə-)rē\ *adj* (1829) **1** : relating to or constituting one of a pair of contrasting colors that produce a neutral color when combined in suitable proportions **2** : serving to fill out or complete **3** : mutually supplying each other's lack **4** : being complements of each other ⟨~ acute angles⟩ **5** : characterized by the capacity for precise pairing of purine and pyrimidine bases between strands of DNA and sometimes RNA such that the structure of one strand determines the other — **com·ple·men·ta·ri·ly** \-'men-t(ə-)rə-lē, -(ˌ)men-'ter-ə-lē\ *adv* — **com·ple·men·ta·ri·ness** \-'men-t(ə-)rē-nəs\ *n* — **complementary** *n*

com·ple·men·ta·tion \ˌkäm-plə-(ˌ)men-'tā-shən, -mən-\ *n* (1942) **1** : the operation of determining the complement of a mathematical set **2** : production of normal phenotype in an individual heterozygous for two closely related mutations with one on each homologous chromosome and at a slightly different position

complement fixation *n* (1906) : the process of binding serum complement to the product formed by the union of an antibody and the antigen for which it is specific that occurs when complement is added to a suitable mixture of such an antibody and antigen

complement–fixation test *n* (1911) : a diagnostic test for the presence of a particular antibody in the serum of a patient that involves inactivation of the complement in the serum, addition of measured amounts of the antigen for which the antibody is specific and of foreign complement, and detection of the presence or absence of complement fixation by the addition of a suitable indicator system — compare WASSERMANN TEST

com·ple·men·ti·zer \'käm-plə-mən-ˌtī-zər, -(ˌ)men-\ *n* (1965) : a function word or morpheme that combines with a clause or verbal phrase to form a subordinate clause

¹**com·plete** \kəm-'plēt\ *adj* **com·plet·er; -est** [ME *complet*, fr. MF, fr. L *completus*, fr. pp. of *complēre*] (14c) **1** **a** : having all necessary parts, elements, or steps ⟨~ diet⟩ **b** : having all four sets of floral organs **c** *of a subject or predicate* : including modifiers, complements, or objects **2** : brought to an end : CONCLUDED ⟨a ~ period of time⟩ **3** : highly proficient ⟨a ~ artist⟩ **4** **a** : fully carried out : THOROUGH ⟨a ~ renovation⟩ **b** : TOTAL, ABSOLUTE ⟨~ silence⟩ **5** *of insect metamorphosis* : characterized by the occurrence of a pupal stage between the motile immature stages and the adult — compare INCOMPLETE 1b **6** *of a metric space* : having the property that every Cauchy sequence of elements converges to a limit in the space ⟨~ space⟩ — **com·plete·ly** *adv* — **com·plete·ness** *n* — **com·ple·tive** \-'plē-tiv\ *adj* — **complete with** : made complete by the inclusion of ⟨a birthday cake complete with candles⟩

²**complete** *vt* **com·plet·ed; com·plet·ing** (15c) **1** : to bring to an end and esp. into a perfected state ⟨~ a painting⟩ **2** **a** : to make whole or perfect ⟨its song ~s the charm of this bird⟩ **b** : to mark the end of ⟨a rousing chorus ~s the show⟩ **c** : EXECUTE, FULFILL ⟨~ a contract⟩ **3** : to carry out ⟨a forward pass⟩ successfully *syn* see CLOSE

complete fertilizer *n* (1900) : a fertilizer that contains the three chief plant nutrients nitrogen, phosphoric acid, and potash

com·ple·tion \kəm-'plē-shən\ *n* (1657) **1** : the act or process of completing **2** : the quality or state of being complete **3** : a completed forward pass in football

¹**com·plex** \'käm-ˌpleks\ *n* [LL *complexus* totality, fr. L, embrace, fr. *complecti*] (1643) **1** : a whole made up of complicated or interrelated parts ⟨a ~ of university buildings⟩ ⟨a ~ of welfare programs⟩ ⟨the military-industrial ~⟩ **2** **a** : a group of culture traits relating to a single activity (as hunting), process (as use of flint), or culture unit **b** (1) : a group of repressed desires and memories that exerts a dominating influence upon the personality (2) : an exaggerated reaction to a subject or situation **c** : a group of obviously related units of which the degree and nature of the relationship is imperfectly known **3** : a chemical association of two or more species (as ions or molecules) joined esp. by weak electrostatic bonds rather than covalent bonds

²**com·plex** \käm-'pleks, kəm-', 'käm-ˌ\ *adj* [L *complexus*, pp. of *complecti* to embrace, comprise (a multitude of objects), fr. *com-* + *plectere* to braid — more at PLY] (ca. 1652) **1** **a** : composed of two or more parts : COMPOSITE **b** (1) *of a word* : having a bound form as one or more of its immediate constituents ⟨*unmanly* is a ~ word⟩ (2) *of a sentence* : consisting of a main clause and one or more subordinate clauses **2** : hard to separate, analyze, or solve **3** : of, concerned with, being, or containing complex numbers ⟨a ~ root⟩ ⟨~ analysis⟩ — **com·plex·ly** *adv* — **com·plex·ness** *n*

syn COMPLEX, COMPLICATED, INTRICATE, INVOLVED, KNOTTY mean having confusingly interrelated parts. COMPLEX suggests the unavoidable result of a necessary combining and does not imply a fault or failure ⟨a complex recipe⟩. COMPLICATED applies to what offers great difficulty in understanding, solving, or explaining ⟨complicated legal procedures⟩. INTRICATE suggests such interlacing of parts as to make it nearly impossible to follow or grasp them separately ⟨an intricate web of deceit⟩. INVOLVED implies extreme complication and often disorder ⟨a rambling, involved explanation⟩. KNOTTY suggests complication and entanglement that make solution or understanding improbable ⟨knotty ethical questions⟩.

³**com·plex** *same as* ²\ *vt* (1658) **1** : to make complex or into a complex **2** : CHELATE — **com·plex·a·tion** \ˌkäm-ˌplek-'sā-shən, kəm-\ *n*

complex fraction *n* (1827) : a fraction with a fraction or mixed number in the numerator or denominator or both — compare SIMPLE FRACTION

com·plex·i·fy \käm-'plek-sə-ˌfī, kəm-\ *vb* **-fied; -fy·ing** *vt* (1830) : to make complex ~ *vi* : to become complex

com·plex·ion \kəm-'plek-shən\ *n* [ME, fr. MF, fr. ML *complexion-, complexio*, fr. L, combination, fr. *complecti*] (14c) **1** : the combination of the hot, cold, moist, and dry qualities held in medieval physiology to determine the quality of a body **2** **a** : an individual complex of ways of thinking or feeling **b** : a complex of attitudes and inclinations **3** : the hue or appearance of the skin and esp. of the face ⟨a dark ~⟩ **4**

\ə\ abut \²\ kitten, F table \ər\ further \a\ ash \ā\ ace \ä\ mop, mar \aú\ out \ch\ chin \e\ bet \ē\ easy \g\ go \i\ hit \ī\ ice \j\ job \ŋ\ sing \ō\ go \ó\ law \ói\ boy \th\ thin \t͟h\ the \ü\ loot \ú\ foot \y\ yet \zh\ vision \ä, k̟, ⁿ, œ, œ̄, ue, ūe, ᵊ\ *see* Guide to Pronunciation

: overall aspect or character ⟨by changing the ~ of the legislative branch —Trevor Armbrister⟩ — **com·plex·ion·al** \-shnəl, -shə-n⁷l\ adj — **com·plex·ioned** \-shənd\ adj

com·plex·i·ty \kəm-'plek-sə-tē, käm-\ n, pl **-ties** (1685) **1** : the quality or state of being complex **2** : something complex

complex number n (1860) : a number of the form $a + b\sqrt{-1}$ where a and b are real numbers

complex plane n (ca. 1909) : a plane whose points are identified by means of complex numbers; esp : ARGAND DIAGRAM

com·pli·ance \kəm-'plī-ən(t)s\ n (1647) **1 a** : the act or process of complying to a desire, demand, or proposal or to coercion **b** : conformity in fulfilling official requirements **2** : a disposition to yield to others **3** : the ability of an object to yield elastically when a force is applied : FLEXIBILITY

com·pli·an·cy \-ən(t)-sē\ n (1643) : COMPLIANCE

com·pli·ant \-ənt\ adj (1642) : ready or disposed to comply : SUBMISSIVE — **com·pli·ant·ly** adv

com·pli·ca·cy \'käm-pli-kə-sē\ n, pl **-cies** [²complicate] (ca. 1828) **1** : the quality or state of being complicated **2** : something that is complicated

¹com·pli·cate \'käm-plə-ˌkāt\ vt **-cat·ed; -cat·ing** (1621) **1** : to combine esp. in an involved or inextricable manner **2** : to make complex or difficult **3** : INVOLVE; esp : to cause to be more complex or severe ⟨a virus disease complicated by bacterial infection⟩

²com·pli·cate \-pli-kət\ adj [L complicatus, pp. of complicare to fold together, fr. com- + plicare to fold — more at PLY] (1638) **1** : COMPLEX, INTRICATE **2** : CONDUPLICATE

com·pli·cat·ed \'käm-plə-ˌkā-təd\ adj (1656) **1** : consisting of parts intricately combined **2** : difficult to analyze, understand, or explain **syn** see COMPLEX — **com·pli·cat·ed·ly** adv — **com·pli·cat·ed·ness** n

com·pli·ca·tion \ˌkäm-plə-'kā-shən\ n (15c) **1 a** : COMPLEXITY, INTRICACY; esp : a situation or a detail of character complicating the main thread of a plot **b** : a making difficult, involved, or intricate **c** : a complex or intricate feature or element **d** : a difficult factor or issue often appearing unexpectedly and changing existing plans, methods, or attitudes **2** : a secondary disease or condition developing in the course of a primary disease or condition

com·plice \'käm-pləs, 'käm-\ n [ME, fr. MF, fr. LL complic-, complex, fr. L, closely connected, fr. complicare] (15c) archaic : ASSOCIATE

com·plic·it \kəm-'pli-sət\ adj (1973) : having complicity

com·plic·it·ous \-'pli-sə-təs\ adj (1860) : COMPLICIT

com·plic·i·ty \kəm-'pli-s(ə-)tē\ n, pl **-ties** (ca. 1656) **1** : association or participation in or as if in a wrongful act **2** : an instance of complicity

com·pli·er \-'plī(-ə)r\ n (1660) : one that complies

¹com·pli·ment \'käm-plə-mənt\ n [F, fr. It complimento, fr. Sp cumplimiento, fr. cumplir to be courteous — more at COMPLY] (1654) **1 a** : an expression of esteem, respect, affection, or admiration; esp : an admiring remark **b** : formal and respectful recognition : HONOR **2** pl : best wishes : REGARDS ⟨accept my ~s⟩ ⟨~s of the season⟩

²com·pli·ment \-ˌment\ vt (1735) **1** : to pay a compliment to **2** : to present with a token of esteem

com·pli·men·ta·ry \ˌkäm-plə-'men-t(ə-)rē\ adj (1716) **1 a** : expressing or containing a compliment **b** : FAVORABLE ⟨the novel received ~ reviews⟩ **2** : given free as a courtesy or favor ⟨~ tickets⟩ — **com·pli·men·ta·ri·ly** \-'men-t(ə-)rə-lē, -ˌ(ˌ)men-'ter-ə-lē\ adv

complimentary close n (1919) : the words (as sincerely yours) that conventionally come immediately before the signature of a letter and express the sender's regard for the receiver — called also complimentary closing

com·pline \'käm-plən, -ˌplīn\ n, often cap [ME compline, complie, fr. OF complie, modif. of LL completa, fr. L, fem. of completus complete] (13c) : the seventh and last of the canonical hours

¹com·plot \'käm-ˌplät\ n [MF complot crowd, plot] (1577) archaic : PLOT, CONSPIRACY

²com·plot \kəm-'plät, käm-\ vb (1579) archaic : PLOT

com·ply \kəm-'plī\ vi **com·plied; com·ply·ing** [It complire, fr. Sp cumplir to complete, perform what is due, be courteous, modif. of L complēre to complete] (1602) **1** obs : to be ceremoniously courteous **2** : to conform or adapt one's actions to another's wishes, to a rule, or to necessity

com·po \'käm-(ˌ)pō\ n, pl **compos** [short for composition] (1823) : any of various composition materials

¹com·po·nent \kəm-'pō-nənt, 'käm-, käm-\ n [L component-, componens, prp. of componere to put together — more at COMPOUND] (1645) **1** : a constituent part : INGREDIENT **2 a** : any one of the vector terms added to form a vector sum or resultant **b** : a coordinate of a vector; also : either member of an ordered pair of numbers **syn** see ELEMENT — **com·po·nen·tial** \ˌkäm-pə-'nen(t)-shəl\ adj

²component adj (1664) : serving or helping to constitute : CONSTITUENT

¹com·port \kəm-'pōrt, -'pȯrt\ vb [MF comporter to bear, conduct, fr. L comportare to bring together, fr. com- + portare to carry — more at FARE] vi (1589) : to be fitting : ACCORD ⟨actions that ~ with policy⟩ ~ vt : BEHAVE; esp : to behave in a manner conformable to what is right, proper, or expected ⟨~ed himself well in the crisis⟩ **syn** see BEHAVE — **com·port·ment** \-mənt\ n

²com·port \'käm-ˌpōrt, -ˌpȯrt\ n (1771) : COMPOTE 2

com·pose \kəm-'pōz\ vb **com·posed; com·pos·ing** [ME, fr. MF composer, fr. L componere (perf. indic. composui) — more at COMPOUND] vt (15c) **1 a** : to form by putting together : FASHION ⟨a committee composed of three representatives —Current Biog.⟩ **b** : to form the substance of : CONSTITUTE ⟨composed of many ingredients⟩ **c** : to produce (as columns or pages of type) by composition **2 a** : to create by mental or artistic labor : PRODUCE ⟨~ a sonnet⟩ **b** (1) : to formulate and write (a piece of music) (2) : to compose music for **3** : to deal with or act on so as to reduce to a minimum ⟨~ their differences⟩ **4** : to arrange in proper or orderly form **5** : to free from agitation : CALM, SETTLE ⟨composed himself⟩ ~ vi : to practice composition

com·posed \-'pōzd\ adj (1607) : free from agitation : CALM; esp : SELF-POSSESSED **syn** see COOL — **com·pos·ed·ly** \-'pō-zəd-lē\ adv — **com·pos·ed·ness** n

com·pos·er \kəm-'pō-zər\ n (1597) : one that composes; esp : a person who writes music

composing room n (1737) : the department in a printing office where typesetting and related operations are performed

composing stick n (1679) : a tray with an adjustable slide that a compositor holds in one hand and sets type into with the other

composing stick

¹com·pos·ite \käm-'pä-zət, kəm-', esp Brit 'käm-pə-zit\ adj [L compositus, pp. of componere] (1563) **1** : made up of distinct parts **a** cap : relating to or being a modification of the Corinthian order combining angular Ionic volutes with the acanthus-circled bell of the Corinthian **b** : of or relating to a very large family (Compositae) of dicotyledonous herbs, shrubs, and trees often considered to be the most highly evolved plants and characterized by florets arranged in dense heads that resemble single flowers **c** : factorable into two or more prime factors other than 1 and itself ⟨8 is a positive ~ integer⟩ **2** : combining the typical or essential characteristics of individuals making up a group ⟨the ~ man called the Poet —Richard Poirier⟩ **3** of a statistical hypothesis : specifying a range of values for one or more statistical parameters — compare SIMPLE 10 — **com·pos·ite·ly** adv

²composite n (1656) **1** : something composite : COMPOUND **2** : a composite plant **3** : COMPOSITE FUNCTION **4** : a solid material which is composed of two or more substances having different physical characteristics and in which each substance retains its identity while contributing desirable properties to the whole; esp : a structural material made of plastic within which a fibrous material (as silicon carbide) is embedded

³composite vt **-it·ed; -it·ing** (1923) : to make composite or into something composite ⟨composited four soil samples⟩

composite function n (1965) : a function whose values are found from two given functions by applying one function to an independent variable and then applying the second function to the result and whose domain consists of those values of the independent variable for which the result yielded by the first function lies in the domain of the second

com·po·si·tion \ˌkäm-pə-'zi-shən\ n [ME composicioun, fr. MF composition, fr. L composition-, compositio, fr. componere] (14c) **1 a** : the act or process of composing; specif : arrangement into specific proportion or relation and esp. into artistic form **b** (1) : the arrangement of type for printing (2) : the production of type or typographic characters (as in photocomposition) arranged for printing **2 a** : the manner in which something is composed **b** : general makeup ⟨the changing ethnic ~ of the city —Leonard Buder⟩ **c** : the qualitative and quantitative makeup of a chemical compound **3** : mutual settlement or agreement **4** : a product of mixing or combining various elements or ingredients **5** : an intellectual creation: as **a** : a piece of writing; esp : a school exercise in the form of a brief essay **b** : a written piece of music esp. of considerable size and complexity **6** : the quality or state of being compound **7** : the operation of forming a composite function; also : COMPOSITE FUNCTION — **com·po·si·tion·al** \-'zish-nəl, -'zi-shə-n⁷l\ adj — **com·po·si·tion·al·ly** adv

com·pos·i·tor \kəm-'pä-zə-tər\ n (1569) : one who sets type

com·pos men·tis \ˌkäm-pəs-'men-təs\ adj [L, lit., having mastery of one's mind] (1616) : of sound mind, memory, and understanding

¹com·post \'käm-ˌpōst, esp Brit -ˌpäst\ n [MF, fr. ML compostum, fr. L, neut. of compositus, compostus, pp. of componere] (1587) **1** : a mixture that consists largely of decayed organic matter and is used for fertilizing and conditioning land **2** : MIXTURE, COMPOUND

²compost vt (1829) : to convert (as plant debris) to compost

com·po·sure \kəm-'pō-zhər\ n (1647) : a calmness or repose esp. of mind, bearing, or appearance : SELF-POSSESSION **syn** see EQUANIMITY

com·pote \'käm-ˌpōt\ n [F, fr. OF composte, fr. L composta, fem. of compostus, pp.] (1693) **1** : a dessert of fruit cooked in syrup **2** : a bowl of glass, porcelain, or metal usu. with a base and stem from which compotes, fruits, nuts, or sweets are served

¹com·pound \käm-'paúnd, kəm-', 'käm-ˌ\ vb [ME compounen, fr. MF compondre, fr. L componere, fr. com- + ponere to put — more at POSITION] vt (14c) **1** : to put together so as to form a whole : COMBINE ⟨~ ingredients⟩ **2** : to form by combining parts ⟨~ a medicine⟩ **3 a** : to settle amicably : adjust by agreement **b** : to agree for a consideration not to prosecute (an offense) ⟨~ a felony⟩ **4 a** : to pay (interest) on both the accrued interest and the principal **b** : to add to : AUGMENT ⟨we ~ed our error in later policy —Robert Lekachman⟩ ~ vi **1** : to become joined in a compound **2** : to come to terms of agreement — **com·pound·able** \-'paún-də-bəl, -ˌpaún-\ adj — **com·pound·er** n

²com·pound \'käm-ˌpaúnd, käm-, kəm-\ adj [ME compouned, pp. of compounen] (14c) **1** : composed of or resulting from union of separate elements, ingredients, or parts: as **a** : composed of united similar elements esp. of a kind usu. independent ⟨a ~ plant ovary⟩ **b** : having the blade divided to the midrib and forming two or more leaflets on a common axis ⟨a ~ leaf⟩ **2** : involving or used in a combination **3 a** of a word : constituting a compound **b** of a sentence : having two or more main clauses

³com·pound \'käm-ˌpaúnd\ n (1530) **1 a** : a word consisting of components that are words (as rowboat, high school, devil-may-care) **b** : a word (as anthropology, kilocycle, builder) consisting of any of various combinations of words, combining forms, or affixes **2** : something formed by a union of elements or parts; esp : a distinct substance formed by chemical union of two or more ingredients in definite proportion by weight

⁴com·pound \'käm-ˌpaúnd\ n [by folk etymology fr. Malay kampung group of buildings, village] (1679) : a fenced or walled-in area containing a group of buildings and esp. residences

compound–complex adj (1923) of a sentence : having two or more main clauses and two or more subordinate clauses

compound eye n (1836) : an eye (as of an insect) made up of many separate visual units

compound fracture n (1543) : a bone fracture resulting in an open wound through which bone fragments usu. protrude

compound interest n (1660) : interest computed on the sum of an original principal and accrued interest

compound microscope n (ca. 1859) : a microscope consisting of an objective and an eyepiece mounted in a drawtube

compound number n (15c) : a number (as 2 ft. 5 in.) involving different denominations or more than one unit

com·pra·dor or **com·pra·dore** \ˌkäm-prə-ˈdȯr, -ˈdȯr\ n [Pg comprador, lit., buyer] (1840) **1** : a Chinese agent engaged by a foreign establishment in China to have charge of its Chinese employees and to act as an intermediary in business affairs **2** : INTERMEDIARY

com·pre·hend \ˌkäm-pri-ˈhend\ vt [ME, fr. L comprehendere, fr. com- + prehendere to grasp — more at GET] (14c) **1** : to grasp the nature, significance, or meaning of **2** : to contain or hold within a total scope, significance, or amount ⟨philosophy's scope ∼s the truth of everything which man may understand —H. O. Taylor⟩ **3** : to include by construction or implication ⟨does not prudence ∼ all the virtues? —Thomas B. Silver⟩ syn see UNDERSTAND, INCLUDE — **com·pre·hend·ible** \-ˈhen-də-bəl\ adj

com·pre·hen·si·ble \-ˈhen(t)-sə-bəl\ adj (1598) : capable of being comprehended : INTELLIGIBLE — **com·pre·hen·si·bil·i·ty** \-ˌhen(t)-sə-ˈbi-lə-tē\ n — **com·pre·hen·si·ble·ness** \-ˈhen(t)-sə-bəl-nəs\ n — **com·pre·hen·si·bly** \-blē\ adv

com·pre·hen·sion \ˌkäm-pri-ˈhen(t)-shən\ n [MF & L; MF, fr. L comprehension-, comprehensio, fr. comprehendere to understand, comprise] (15c) **1 a** : the act or action of grasping with the intellect : UNDERSTANDING **b** : knowledge gained by comprehending **c** : the capacity for understanding fully **2 a** : the act or process of comprising **b** : the faculty or capability of including : COMPREHENSIVENESS **3** : CONNOTATION 3

com·pre·hen·sive \-ˈhen(t)-siv\ adj (1614) **1** : covering completely or broadly : INCLUSIVE ⟨∼ examinations⟩ ⟨∼ insurance⟩ **2** : having or exhibiting wide mental grasp ⟨∼ knowledge⟩ — **com·pre·hen·sive·ly** adv — **com·pre·hen·sive·ness** n

¹**com·press** \kəm-ˈpres\ vb [ME, fr. LL compressare to press hard, freq. of L comprimere to compress, fr. com- + premere to press — more at PRESS] vt (14c) **1** : to press or squeeze together **2** : to reduce in size or volume as if by squeezing ∼ vi : to undergo compression syn see CONTRACT

²**com·press** \ˈkäm-ˌpres\ n [MF compresse, fr. compresser to compress, fr. LL compressare] (1599) **1** : a folded cloth or pad applied so as to press upon a body part **2** : a machine for compressing

com·pressed \kəm-ˈprest also ˈkäm-ˌ\ adj (14c) **1** : pressed together : reduced in size or volume (as by pressure) **2** : flattened as though subjected to compression: **a** : flattened laterally ⟨petioles ∼⟩ **b** : narrow from side to side and deep in a dorsoventral direction — **com·pressed·ly** \kəm-ˈprest-lē, -ˈpre-səd-lē\ adv

compressed air n (1669) : air under pressure greater than that of the atmosphere

com·press·ible \kəm-ˈpre-sə-bəl\ adj (ca. 1691) : capable of being compressed — **com·press·ibil·i·ty** \-ˌpre-sə-ˈbi-lə-tē\ n

com·pres·sion \kəm-ˈpre-shən\ n (15c) **1 a** : the act, process, or result of compressing **b** : the state of being compressed **2 a** : the process of compressing the fuel mixture in a cylinder of an internal combustion engine (as in an automobile) **3** : a much compressed fossil plant — **com·pres·sion·al** \-ˈpresh-nəl, -ˈpre-shə-nᵊl\ adj

compressional wave n (1887) : a longitudinal wave (as a sound wave) propagated by the elastic compression of the medium — called also compression wave

com·pres·sive \kəm-ˈpre-siv\ adj (1572) **1** : of or relating to compression **2** : tending to compress — **com·pres·sive·ly** adv

com·pres·sor \-ˈpre-sər\ n (1839) : one that compresses: as **a** : a muscle that compresses a part **b** : a machine that compresses gases

com·prise \kəm-ˈprīz\ vt comprised; com·pris·ing [ME, fr. MF compris, pp. of comprendre, fr. L comprehendere] (15c) **1** : to include esp. within a particular scope ⟨civilization as Lenin used the term would then certainly have comprised the changes that are now associated in our minds with "developed" rather than "developing" states —Times Lit. Supp.⟩ **2** : to be made up of ⟨a vast installation, comprising fifty buildings —Jane Jacobs⟩ **3** : COMPOSE, CONSTITUTE ⟨a misconception as to what ∼s a literary generation —William Styron⟩ ⟨about 8 percent of our military forces are comprised of women —Jimmy Carter⟩ usage Although it has been in use since the late 18th century, sense 3 is still attacked as wrong. Why it has been singled out is not clear, but until comparatively recent times it was found chiefly in scientific or technical writing rather than belles lettres. Our current evidence shows a slight shift in usage: sense 3 is somewhat more frequent in recent literary use than the earlier senses. You should be aware, however, that if you use sense 3 you may be subject to criticism for doing so, and you may want to choose a safer synonym such as compose or make up.

¹**com·pro·mise** \ˈkäm-prə-ˌmīz\ n [ME, mutual promise to abide by an arbiter's decision, fr. MF compromis, fr. L compromissum, fr. neut. of compromissus, pp. of compromittere to promise mutually, fr. com- + promittere to promise — more at PROMISE] (15c) **1 a** : settlement of differences by arbitration or by consent reached by mutual concessions **b** : something intermediate between or blending qualities of two different things **2** : a concession to something derogatory or prejudicial ⟨∼ of principles⟩

²**compromise** vb -mised; -mis·ing vt (1598) **1** obs : to bind by mutual agreement **2** : to adjust or settle by mutual concessions **3 a** : to expose to suspicion, discredit, or mischief **b** : to reveal or expose to an unauthorized person and esp. to an enemy ⟨confidential information was compromised⟩ **c** : to cause the impairment of ⟨a compromised immune system⟩ ⟨a seriously compromised patient⟩ ∼ vi **1 a** : to come to agreement by mutual concession **b** : to find or follow a way between extremes **2** : to make a shameful or disreputable concession ⟨wouldn't ∼ with their principles⟩ — **com·pro·mis·er** n

compt \ˈkaúnt, ˈkäm(p)t\ archaic var of COUNT

comp·trol·ler \kən-ˈtrō-lər, ˈkäm(p)-, käm(p)-ˈt-ˈ\ n [ME, alter. of conterroller controller] (15c) **1** : a royal-household official who examines and supervises expenditures **2** : a public official who audits government accounts and sometimes certifies expenditures **3** : CONTROLLER 1c — **comp·trol·ler·ship** \-ˌship\ n

com·pul·sion \kəm-ˈpəl-shən\ n [ME, fr. MF or LL; MF, fr. LL com-

pulsion-, compulsio, fr. L compellere to compel] (15c) **1 a** : an act of compelling : the state of being compelled **b** : a force that compels **2** : an irresistible impulse to perform an irrational act

com·pul·sive \-ˈpəl-siv\ adj (1588) **1** : having power to compel **2** : of, relating to, caused by, or suggestive of psychological compulsion or obsession ⟨∼ actions⟩ — **com·pul·sive·ly** adv — **com·pul·sive·ness** n — **com·pul·siv·i·ty** \kəm-ˌpəl-ˈsi-və-tē, ˌkäm-\ n

com·pul·so·ry \kəm-ˈpəls-rē, -ˈpal-sə-\ adj (1581) **1** : MANDATORY, ENFORCED **2** : COERCIVE, COMPELLING — **com·pul·so·ri·ly** \-rə-lē\ adv

com·punc·tion \kəm-ˈpəŋ(k)-shən\ n [ME compunccioun, fr. MF componction, fr. LL compunction-, compunctio, fr. L compungere to prick hard, sting, fr. com- + pungere to prick — more at PUNGENT] (14c) **1 a** : anxiety arising from awareness of guilt ⟨∼s of conscience⟩ **b** : distress of mind over an anticipated action or result ⟨showed no ∼ in planning devilish engines of ... destruction —Havelock Ellis⟩ **2** : a twinge of misgiving : SCRUPLE ⟨cheated without ∼⟩ syn see PENITENCE, QUALM — **com·punc·tious** \-shəs\ adj

com·pur·ga·tion \ˌkäm-(ˌ)pər-ˈgā-shən\ n [LL compurgation-, compurgatio, fr. L compurgare to clear completely, fr. com- + purgare to purge] (ca. 1658) : the clearing of an accused person by oaths of others who swear to the veracity or innocence of the accused

com·pur·ga·tor \ˈkäm-(ˌ)pər-ˌgā-tər\ n (1533) : one that under oath vouches for the character or conduct of an accused person

com·put·able \kəm-ˈpyü-tə-bəl\ adj (1646) : capable of being computed — **com·put·abil·i·ty** \-ˌpyü-tə-ˈbi-lə-tē\ n

com·pu·ta·tion \ˌkäm-pyü-ˈtā-shən\ n (15c) **1 a** : the act or action of computing : CALCULATION **b** : the use or operation of a computer **2** : a system of reckoning **3** : an amount computed — **com·pu·ta·tion·al** \-shnəl, -shə-nᵊl\ adj — **com·pu·ta·tion·al·ly** adv

com·pute \kəm-ˈpyüt\ vb com·put·ed; com·put·ing [L computare — more at COUNT] vt (1616) : to determine esp. by mathematical means ⟨∼ your income tax⟩; also : to determine or calculate by means of a computer ∼ vi **1** : to make calculation : RECKON **2** : to use a computer

computed tomography n (1975) : radiography in which a three-dimensional image of a body structure is constructed by computer from a series of plane cross-sectional images made along an axis — called also computed axial tomography, computerized axial tomography, computerized tomography

com·put·er \kəm-ˈpyü-tər\ n, often attrib (1646) : one that computes; specif : a programmable electronic device that can store, retrieve, and process data — **com·put·er·dom** \-dəm\ n — **com·put·er·less** \-ləs\ adj — **com·put·er·like** \-ˌlīk\ adj

com·put·er·ese \-ˌpyü-tə-ˈrēz, -ˈrēs\ n (ca. 1960) : jargon used by computer technologists

com·put·er·ise chiefly Brit var of COMPUTERIZE

com·put·er·ist \kəm-ˈpyü-tə-rist\ n (1973) : a person who uses or operates a computer

com·put·er·ize \kəm-ˈpyü-tə-ˌrīz\ vt -ized; -iz·ing (1957) **1** : to carry out, control, or produce by means of a computer **2** : to equip with computers **3 a** : to store in a computer **b** : to put in a form that a computer can use — **com·put·er·iz·able** \-ˌpyü-tə-ˈrī-zə-bəl\ adj — **com·put·er·i·za·tion** \-ˌpyü-tə-rə-ˈzā-shən\ n

com·put·er·nik \kəm-ˈpyü-tər-ˌnik\ n (1968) : a computer enthusiast or expert

com·put·er·phobe \-ˌfōb\ n (1976) : a person who experiences anxiety about computers and esp. about their use — **com·put·er·pho·bia** \-ˌpyü-tər-ˈfō-bē-ə\ n — **com·put·er·pho·bic** \-ˈfō-bik\ adj

com·rade \ˈkäm-ˌrad, -rəd, esp Brit -ˌrād\ n [MF camarade group sleeping in one room, roommate, companion, fr. OSp camarada, fr. cámara room, fr. LL camera, camara — more at CHAMBER] (1544) **1 a** : an intimate friend or associate : COMPANION **b** : a fellow soldier **2** [fr. its use as a form of address by communists] : COMMUNIST — **com·rade·li·ness** \-lē-nəs\ n — **com·rade·ly** adj — **com·rade·ship** \-ˌship\ n

com·rad·ery \ˈkäm-ˌra-d(ə-)rē, -rə-drē, -ˌrä-d(ə-)rē\ n (1879) : CAMARADERIE

Comsat \ˈkäm-ˌsat\ service mark — used for communications services involving an artificial satellite

Com·stock·ery \ˈkäm-ˌstä-kə-rē also ˈkəm-\ n [Anthony Comstock + E -ery] (1905) **1** : strict censorship of materials considered obscene **2** : censorious opposition to alleged immorality (as in literature)

Com·stock·ian \käm-ˈstä-kē-ən also ˌkəm-\ adj (1921) : of or relating to Comstockery

com·symp \ˈkäm-ˌsimp\ n [communist + sympathizer] (ca. 1961) : a person sympathetic to communist causes — usu. used disparagingly

Comt·ian or **Comt·ean** \ˈkäm(p)-tē-ən, ˈkōⁿ(n)-tē-\ adj (1846) : of or relating to Auguste Comte or his doctrines — **Comt·ism** \ˈkäm(p)-ˌtizəm, ˈkōⁿ(n)-\ n — **Comt·ist** \ˈkäm(p)-tist, ˈkōⁿ(n)-\ adj or n

¹**con** \ˈkän\ vt conned; con·ning [ME connen to know, learn, study, alter. of cunnen to know, infin. of can — more at CAN] (13c) **1** : to commit to memory **2** : to study or examine closely

²**con** var of CONN

³**con** adv [ME, short for contra] (15c) : on the negative side : in opposition ⟨so much has been written pro and ∼⟩

⁴**con** n (1589) **1** : an argument or evidence in opposition **2** : the negative position or one holding it ⟨an appraisal of the pros and ∼s⟩

⁵**con** adj [by shortening] (1889) : CONFIDENCE

⁶**con** vt conned; con·ning (1896) **1** : SWINDLE **2** : MANIPULATE 2b **3** : PERSUADE, CAJOLE

⁷**con** n (1901) : something (as a ruse) used deceptively to gain another's confidence; also : a confidence game : SWINDLE

⁸**con** n [by shortening] (1893) : CONVICT

⁹**con** n [short for consumption] (1915) slang : a destructive disease of the lungs; esp : TUBERCULOSIS

con- — see COM-

\ə\ abut \ᵊ\ kitten, F table \ər\ further \a\ ash \ā\ ace \ä\ mop, mar \aú\ out \ch\ chin \e\ bet \ē\ easy \g\ go \i\ hit \ī\ ice \j\ job \ŋ\ sing \ō\ go \ò\ law \òi\ boy \th\ thin \t̲h̲\ the \ü\ loot \ú\ foot \y\ yet \zh\ vision \ä, ḵ, ⁿ, œ, œ̄, ᵫ, ᵫ̄, ᵞ\ see Guide to Pronunciation

con amo·re \ˌkän-ə-ˈmȯr-ē, ˌkōn-ə-ˈmȯr-(ˌ)ā, -ˈmȯr-\ *adv* [It] (1739) **1** : with love, devotion, or zest **2** : in a tender manner — used as a direction in music

con ani·ma \ˌkän-ˈä-nə-ˌmä, kōn-ˈä-ni-\ *adv* [It, lit., with spirit] (ca. 1906) : in a spirited manner — used as a direction in music

co·na·tion \kō-ˈnä-shən\ *n* [L *conation-, conatio* act of attempting, fr. *conari* to attempt — more at DEACON] (ca. 1837) : an inclination (as an instinct, a drive, a wish, or a craving) to act purposefully : IMPULSE 3 — **co·na·tive** \ˈkō-nə-tiv, ˈkä-, ˈkō-ˌnä-\ *adj*

con brio \kän-ˈbrē-(ˌ)ō, kän-\ *adv* [It, lit., with vigor] (ca. 1889) : in a vigorous or brisk manner — used as a direction in music

con·ca·nav·a·lin \ˌkän-kə-ˈna-və-lən\ *n* [*com-* + *canavalin*, a noncrystalline globulin found in the jack bean, fr. NL *Canavalia*, genus name of the jack bean] (1917) : either of two crystalline globulins occurring in the jack bean; *esp* : one that is a potent hemagglutinin

¹con·cat·e·nate \kän-ˈka-tə-nət, kən-\ *adj* [ME, fr. LL *concatenatus*, pp. of *concatenare* to link together, fr. L *com-* + *catena* chain] (15c) : linked together

²concatenate \-ˌnāt\ *vt* **-nat·ed; -nat·ing** (1598) : to link together in a series or chain — **con·cat·e·na·tion** \(ˌ)kän-ˌka-tə-ˈnä-shən, kən-\ *n*

¹con·cave \kän-ˈkāv, ˈkän-ˌ\ *adj* [ME, fr. MF, fr. L *concavus*, fr. *com-* + *cavus* hollow — more at CAVE] (15c) **1** : hollowed or rounded inward like the inside of a bowl **2** : arched in : curving in — used of the side of a curve or surface on which neighboring normals to the curve or surface converge and on which lies the chord joining two neighboring points of the curve or surface

²con·cave \ˈkän-ˌkāv\ *n* (1552) : a concave line or surface

con·cav·i·ty \kän-ˈka-və-tē\ *n, pl* **-ties** (15c) **1** : a concave line, surface, or space : HOLLOW **2** : the quality or state of being concave

con·ca·vo–con·vex \kän-ˌkā-vō-kän-ˈveks; ˈkän-, kän-\ *adj* (1676) **1** : concave on one side and convex on the other **2** : having the concave side curved more than the convex ⟨a ∼ lens⟩

con·ceal \kən-ˈsē(ə)l\ *vt* [ME *concelen*, fr. MF *conceler*, fr. L *concelare*, fr. *com-* + *celare* to hide — more at HELL] (14c) **1** : to prevent disclosure or recognition of **2** : to place out of sight **syn** see HIDE — **con·ceal·able** \-ˈsē-lə-bəl\ *adj* — **con·ceal·er** \-ˈsē-lər\ *n* — **con·ceal·ing·ly** \-ˈsē-liŋ-lē\ *adv* — **con·ceal·ment** \-ˈsē(ə)l-mənt\ *n*

con·cede \kən-ˈsēd\ *vb* **con·ced·ed; con·ced·ing** [F or L; F *concéder*, fr. L *concedere*, fr. *com-* + *cedere* to yield] *vt* (1632) **1** : to grant as a right or privilege **2** a : to accept as true, valid, or accurate ⟨the right of the state to tax is generally *conceded*⟩ **b** : to acknowledge grudgingly or hesitantly ∼ *vi* : to make concession : YIELD **syn** see GRANT — **con·ced·ed·ly** \-ˈsē-dəd-lē\ *adv* — **con·ced·er** *n*

¹con·ceit \kən-ˈsēt\ *n* [ME, fr. *conceiven*] (14c) **1** a (1) : a result of mental activity : THOUGHT (2) : individual opinion **b** : favorable opinion; *esp* : excessive appreciation of one's own worth or virtue **2** : a fancy article **3** a : a fanciful idea **b** : an elaborate or strained metaphor **c** : use or presence of such conceits in poetry **d** : an organizing theme or concept ⟨found his ∼ for the film early —Peter Wilkinson⟩

²conceit *vt* (1557) **1** *obs* : CONCEIVE, UNDERSTAND **2** *chiefly dial* : IMAGINE **3** *dial Brit* : to take a fancy to

con·ceit·ed \-ˈsē-təd\ *adj* [¹*conceit*] (1593) **1** : ingeniously contrived : FANCIFUL **2** : having an excessively high opinion of oneself — **con·ceit·ed·ly** *adv* — **con·ceit·ed·ness** *n*

con·ceiv·able \kən-ˈsē-və-bəl\ *adj* (15c) : capable of being conceived : IMAGINABLE — **con·ceiv·abil·i·ty** \kən-ˌsē-və-ˈbi-lə-tē\ *n* — **con·ceiv·able·ness** \-ˈsē-və-bəl-nəs\ *n*

con·ceiv·ably \-blē\ *adv* (1625) **1** : in a conceivable manner **2** : it may be conceived : POSSIBLY

con·ceive \kən-ˈsēv\ *vb* **con·ceived; con·ceiv·ing** [ME, fr. MF *conceivre*, fr. L *concipere* to take in, conceive, fr. *com-* + *capere* to take — more at HEAVE] *vt* (14c) **1** a : to become pregnant with ⟨young⟩ **b** : to cause to begin : ORIGINATE **2** a : to take into one's mind ⟨∼ a prejudice⟩ **b** : to form a conception of : IMAGINE **3** : to apprehend by reason or imagination : UNDERSTAND **4** : to be of the opinion ∼ *vi* **1** : to become pregnant **2** : to have a conception — usu. used with *of* ⟨∼s of death as emptiness⟩ **syn** see THINK — **con·ceiv·er** *n*

con·cel·e·brant \kən-ˈse-lə-brənt, kän-\ *n* (ca. 1931) : one that concelebrates a Eucharist or Mass

con·cel·e·brate \kən-ˈse-lə-ˌbrāt, kän-\ *vb* [ML *concelebratus*, pp. of *concelebrare*, fr. L, to frequent, celebrate, fr. *com-* + *celebrare* to celebrate] *vt* (1879) : to participate in (a Eucharist) as a joint celebrant who recites the canon in unison with other celebrants ∼ *vi* : to participate as a celebrant in a concelebrated Eucharist — **con·cel·e·bra·tion** \(ˌ)kän-ˌse-lə-ˈbrā-shən, kən-\ *n*

con·cent \kən-ˈsent\ *n* [L *concentus*, fr. *concinere* to sing together, fr. *com-* + *canere* to sing — more at CHANT] (1585) *archaic* : HARMONY

con·cen·ter \kən-ˈsen-tər, kän-\ *vb* [F *concentrer*, fr. *com-* + *centre* center] *vt* (1598) : to draw or direct to a common center : CONCENTRATE ∼ *vi* : to come to a common center

¹con·cen·trate \ˈkän(t)-sən-ˌtrāt, -ˌsen-\ *vb* **-trat·ed; -trat·ing** [*com-* + L *centrum* center] *vt* (1646) **1** a : to bring or direct toward a common center or objective : FOCUS **b** : to gather into one body, mass, or force ⟨power was *concentrated* in a few able hands⟩ **c** : to accumulate (a toxic substance) in bodily tissues ⟨fish ∼ mercury⟩ **2** a : to make less dilute ⟨∼ syrup⟩ **b** : to express or exhibit in condensed form ∼ *vi* **1** : to draw toward or meet in a common center **2** : GATHER, COLLECT **3** : to concentrate one's powers, efforts, or attention ⟨∼ on a problem⟩ — **con·cen·trat·ed·ly** \-ˌtrā-təd-lē; ˌkän(t)-sən-ˈtrā-\ *adv* — **con·cen·tra·tive** \-ˌtrā-tiv\ *adj*

²concentrate *n* (1883) **1** : something concentrated: as **a** : a mineral-rich product obtained after an initial processing of ore **b** : a food reduced in bulk by elimination of fluid ⟨orange juice ∼⟩ **2** : a feedstuff (as grains) relatively rich in digestible nutrients — compare FIBER

con·cen·tra·tion \ˌkän(t)-sən-ˈtrā-shən, -ˌsen-\ *n* (1634) **1** a : the act or process of concentrating : the state of being concentrated; *esp* : direction of attention to a single object **b** : MAJOR 4a **2** : a concentrated mass or thing **3** : the amount of a component in a given area or volume

concentration camp *n* (1901) : a camp where persons (as prisoners of war, political prisoners, or refugees) are detained or confined

con·cen·tra·tor \ˈkän(t)-sən-ˌtrā-tər\ *n* (1833) : one that concentrates: as **a** : an industrial plant that produces concentrates from ores **b** : a

mirror or group of mirrors that focus sunlight for use as an energy source **c** : a device in a computer network that collects data from separate low-volume transmission channels and retransmits it over a single high-volume channel

con·cen·tric \kən-ˈsen-trik, ˌkän-\ *adj* [ML *concentricus*, fr. L *com-* + *centrum* center] (14c) **1** : having a common center ⟨∼ circles⟩ **2** : having a common axis : COAXIAL — **con·cen·tri·cal·ly** \-tri-k(ə-)lē\ *adv* — **con·cen·tric·i·ty** \ˌkän-ˌsen-ˈtri-sə-tē\ *n*

con·cept \ˈkän-ˌsept\ *n* [L *conceptum*, neut. of *conceptus*, pp. of *concipere* to conceive — more at CONCEIVE] (1556) **1** : something conceived in the mind : THOUGHT, NOTION **2** : an abstract or generic idea generalized from particular instances **syn** see IDEA

con·cep·ta·cle \kən-ˈsep-ti-kəl\ *n* [NL *conceptaculum*, fr. L, receptacle, fr. *conceptus*, pp. of *concipere* to take in] (1835) : an external cavity containing reproductive cells in algae (as of the genus *Fucus*)

con·cep·tion \kən-ˈsep-shən\ *n* [ME *concepcioun*, fr. OF *conception*, fr. L *conception-, conceptio*, fr. *concipere*] (14c) **1** a (1) : the act of becoming pregnant : the state of being conceived (2) : EMBRYO, FETUS **b** : BEGINNING ⟨joy had the like ∼ in our eyes —Shak.⟩ **2** a : the capacity, function, or process of forming or understanding ideas or abstractions or their symbols **b** : a general idea : CONCEPT **c** : a complex product of abstract or reflective thinking **d** : the sum of a person's ideas and beliefs concerning something **3** : the originating of something in the mind **syn** see IDEA — **con·cep·tion·al** \-shnəl, -shə-n³l\ *adj* — **con·cep·tive** \-ˈsep-tiv\ *adj*

con·cep·tu·al \kən-ˈsep-chə-wəl, kän-, -chəl, -shwəl\ *adj* [ML *conceptualis* of thought, fr. LL *conceptus* act of conceiving, thought, fr. L *concipere*] (ca. 1834) : of, relating to, or consisting of concepts — **con·cep·tu·al·i·ty** \-ˌsep-chə-ˈwa-lə-tē, -shə-\ *n* — **con·cep·tu·al·ly** *adv*

conceptual art *n* (ca. 1969) : an art form in which the artist's intent is to convey a concept rather than to create an art object — **conceptual artist** *n*

con·cep·tu·al·ise *Brit var of* CONCEPTUALIZE

con·cep·tu·al·ism \-ˈsep-chə-wə-ˌli-zəm, -chə-ˌli-, -shwə-ˌli-\ *n* (ca. 1838) : a theory in philosophy intermediate between realism and nominalism that universals exist in the mind as concepts of discourse or as predicates which may be properly affirmed of reality — **con·cep·tu·al·is·tic** \-ˌsep-chə-wə-ˈlis-tik, -chə-ˈlis-, -shwə-ˈlis-\ *adj* — **con·cep·tu·al·is·ti·cal·ly** \-ti-k(ə-)lē\ *adv*

con·cep·tu·al·ist \-ˈsep-chə-wə-list, -chə-list, -shwə-list\ *n* (1785) : an adherent to the tenets of conceptualism or of conceptual art

con·cep·tu·al·ize \-ˈsep-chə-wə-ˌlīz, -chə-ˌlīz, -shwə-ˌlīz\ *vt* **-ized; -iz·ing** (1878) : to form a concept of; *esp* : to interpret conceptually — **con·cep·tu·al·i·za·tion** \-ˌsep-chə-wə-lə-ˈzā-shən, -chə-lə-', -shwə-lə-'\ *n* — **con·cep·tu·al·iz·er** \-ˈsep-chə-wə-ˌlī-zər, chə-ˌlī-, -shwə-\ *n*

con·cep·tus \kən-ˈsep-təs\ *n* [L, one conceived, fr. pp. of *concipere* to conceive] (ca. 1860) : a fertilized egg, embryo, or fetus

¹con·cern \kən-ˈsərn\ *vb* [ME, fr. MF & ML; MF *concerner*, fr. ML *concernere*, fr. LL, to sift together, mingle, fr. L *com-* + *cernere* to sift — more at CERTAIN] *vt* (15c) **1** a : to relate to : be about ⟨the novel ∼s three soldiers⟩ **b** : to bear on **2** : to have an influence on : INVOLVE; *also* : to be the business or affair of ⟨the problem ∼s us all⟩ **3** : to be a care, trouble, or distress to ⟨her ill health ∼s me⟩ **4** : ENGAGE, OCCUPY ⟨he ∼s himself with trivia⟩ ∼ *vi, obs* : to be of importance : MATTER

²concern *n* (1655) **1** a : marked interest or regard usu. arising through a personal tie or relationship **b** : an uneasy state of blended interest, uncertainty, and apprehension **2** : something that relates or belongs to one : AFFAIR **3** : matter for consideration **4** : an organization or establishment for business or manufacture **5** : CONTRIVANCE, GADGET **syn** see CARE

concerned *adj* (1656) **1** a : ANXIOUS, WORRIED ⟨∼ for their safety⟩ **b** : INTERESTED ⟨∼ to prove the point⟩ **2** a : interestedly engaged ⟨∼ with books and music⟩ **b** : culpably involved : IMPLICATED ⟨arrested all ∼⟩

concerning *prep* (15c) : relating to : REGARDING

con·cern·ment \kən-ˈsərn-mənt\ *n* (1610) **1** : something in which one is concerned **2** : IMPORTANCE, CONSEQUENCE **3** *archaic* : INVOLVEMENT, PARTICIPATION **4** : SOLICITUDE, ANXIETY

¹con·cert \ˈkän(t)-sərt, -ˌsərt\ *n* [F, fr. It *concerto*, fr. *concertare*] (1674) **1** *obs* : musical harmony : CONCORD **2** a : agreement in design or plan : union formed by mutual communication of opinion and views **b** : a concerted action ⟨the sacrifice was hailed with a ∼ of praise⟩ **3** : a public performance (as of music or dancing) — **concert** *adj* — **in concert** : TOGETHER

²con·cert \kən-ˈsərt\ *vb* [MF *concerter*, fr. OIt *concertare*, perh. fr. *com-* + *certo* certain, decided, fr. L *certus* — more at CERTAIN] *vt* (1694) **1** : to settle or adjust by conferring and reaching an agreement ⟨∼ed their differences⟩ **2** : to make a plan for ⟨∼ measures for aiding the poor⟩ ∼ *vi* : to act in harmony or conjunction

con·cert·ed \kən-ˈsər-təd\ *adj* (1716) **1** a : mutually contrived or agreed on ⟨a ∼ effort⟩ **b** : performed in unison ⟨∼ artillery fire⟩ **2** : arranged in parts for several voices or instruments — **con·cert·ed·ly** *adv* — **con·cert·ed·ness** *n*

con·cert·go·er \ˈkän(t)-sərt-ˌgō(-ə)r, ˈkän-ˌsərt-\ *n* (1855) : one who frequently attends concerts — **con·cert·go·ing** \-ˌgō-iŋ, -ˌgō(-)iŋ\ *n or adj*

concert grand *n* (ca. 1891) : a grand piano of the largest size adapted in volume, timbre, and brilliance of tone to concert use

con·cer·ti·na \ˌkän(t)-sər-ˈtē-nə\ *n* [prob. fr. ¹*concert* + It *-ina*, dim. suffix] (1837) **1** : a musical instrument of the accordion family **2** : a coiled barbed wire for use as an obstacle — called also *concertina wire*

con·cer·ti·no \ˌkän-chər-ˈtē-(ˌ)nō\ *n, pl* **-nos** [It, dim. of *concerto*] (ca. 1801) **1** : the solo instruments in a concerto grosso **2** : a short concerto

con·cert·ize \ˈkän(t)-sər-ˌtīz\ *vi* **-ized; -iz·ing** (1883) : to perform professionally in concerts

con·cert·mas·ter \ˈkän(t)-sərt-ˌmas-tər\ *or* **con·cert·meis·ter** \-ˌmī-stər\ *n* [G *Konzertmeister*, fr. *Konzert* concert + *Meister* master] (ca. 1889) : the leader of the first violins of an orchestra and by custom usu. the assistant to the conductor

con·cer·to \kən-ˈcher-(ˌ)tō *also* -ˈchər-\ *n, pl* **-ti** \-(ˌ)tē\ *or* **-tos** [It, fr. *concerto* concert] (1730) : a piece for one or more soloists and orchestra with three contrasting movements

concerto gros·so \-'grō-(,)sō, -'grò-\ n, pl **concerti gros·si** \-(,)sē\ [It, lit., big concerto] (1724) : a baroque orchestral composition featuring a small group of solo instruments contrasting with the full orchestra

concert pitch n (1767) **1** : INTERNATIONAL PITCH **2** : a high state of fitness, tension, or readiness

con·ces·sion \kən-'se-shən\ n [ME, fr. MF or L; MF, fr. L concession-, concessio, fr. concedere to concede] (15c) **1 a** : the act or an instance of conceding **b** : the admitting of a point claimed in argument **2** : something conceded: **a** : ACKNOWLEDGMENT, ADMISSION **b** : GRANT **c** (1) : a grant of land or property esp. by a government in return for services or for a particular use (2) : a right to undertake and profit by a specified activity (3) : a lease of a portion of premises for a particular purpose; also : the portion leased or the activities carried on — **con·ces·sion·al** \-'sesh-nəl, -'se-shə-nᵊl\ adj — **con·ces·sion·ary** \-'se-shə-,ner-ē\ adj

con·ces·sion·aire \kən-,se-shə-'nar, -'ner\ n [F concessionnaire, fr. concession] (1862) : the owner or operator of a concession; esp : one that operates a refreshment stand at a recreational center

con·ces·sion·er \kən-'se-sh(ə-)nər\ n (ca. 1891) : CONCESSIONAIRE

con·ces·sive \kən-'se-siv\ adj (1711) **1** : denoting concession ⟨a ~ clause⟩ **2** : making for or being a concession — **con·ces·sive·ly** adv

conch \'käŋk, 'känch, 'köŋk\ n, pl **conchs** \'käŋks, 'köŋks\ or **conches** \'kän-chəz\ [ME, fr. L concha mussel, mussel shell, fr. Gk konchē; akin to Skt śaṅkha conch shell] (15c) **1** : any of various large spiral-shelled marine gastropod mollusks (as of the genus Strombus; also : its shell used esp. for cameos **2** often cap : a native or resident of the Florida Keys **3** : CONCHA 2

con·cha \'kän-kə\ n, pl **con·chae** \-,kē, -,kī\ [It & L; It conca semidome, apse, fr. LL concha, fr. L, shell] (ca. 1639) **1 a** : the plain semidome of an apse **b** : APSE **2** : something shaped like a shell; esp : the largest and deepest concavity of the external ear — **con·chal** \-kəl\ adj

conch 1

con·choi·dal \käŋ-'köi-dᵊl, kän-\ adj [Gk konchoeidēs like a mussel, fr. konchē] (1666) : having elevations or depressions shaped like the inside surface of a bivalve shell — **con·choi·dal·ly** \-dᵊl-ē\ adv

con·chol·o·gy \käŋ-'kä-lə-jē\ n [Gk konchē] (1776) **1** : a branch of zoology that deals with shells **2** : a treatise on shells — **con·chol·o·gist** \-jist\ n

con·cierge \kōⁿ-'syerzh\ n, pl **con·cierges** \-'syerzh, -'syer-zhəz\ [F, fr. OF, prob fr. (assumed) VL conservius, alter. of L conservus fellow slave, fr. com- + servus slave] (ca. 1697) **1** : a resident in an apartment building esp. in France who serves as doorkeeper, landlord's representative, and janitor **2** : a usu. multilingual hotel staff member who handles luggage and mail, makes reservations, and arranges tours

con·cil·i·ar \kən-'si-lē-ər\ adj [L concilium council] (ca. 1677) : of, relating to, or issued by a council — **con·cil·i·ar·ly** adv

con·cil·i·ate \kən-'si-lē-,āt\ vb **-at·ed; -at·ing** [L conciliatus, pp. of conciliare to assemble, unite, win over, fr. concilium assembly, council — more at COUNCIL] vt (1545) **1** : to gain (as goodwill) by pleasing acts **2** : to make compatible : RECONCILE **3** : APPEASE ~ vi : to become friendly or agreeable **syn** see PACIFY — **con·cil·i·a·tion** \-,si-lē-'ā-shən\ n — **con·cil·i·a·tive** \-'si-lē-,ā-tiv\ adj — **con·cil·i·a·tor** \-,ā-tər\ n — **con·cil·i·a·to·ry** \-si-lē-ə-,tòr-ē, -'si-lē-ə-, -,tòr-\ adj

con·cin·ni·ty \kən-'si-nə-tē\ n, pl **-ties** [L concinnitas, fr. concinnus skillfully put together] (1531) : harmony or elegance of design esp. of literary style in adaptation of parts to a whole or to each other

con·cise \kən-'sīs\ adj [L concisus, fr. pp. of concidere to cut up, fr. com- + caedere to cut, strike] (ca. 1590) **1** : marked by brevity of expression or statement : free from all elaboration and superfluous detail **2** : cut short : BRIEF — **con·cise·ly** adv — **con·cise·ness** n **syn** CONCISE, TERSE, SUCCINCT, LACONIC, SUMMARY, PITHY, COMPENDIOUS mean very brief in statement or expression. CONCISE suggests the removal of all that is superfluous or elaborative ⟨a concise description⟩. TERSE implies pointed conciseness ⟨a terse reply⟩. SUCCINCT implies the greatest possible compression ⟨a succinct letter of resignation⟩. LACONIC implies brevity to the point of seeming rude, indifferent, or mysterious ⟨an aloof and laconic stranger⟩. SUMMARY suggests the statement of main points with no elaboration or explanation ⟨a summary listing of the year's main events⟩. PITHY adds to SUCCINCT or TERSE the implication of richness of meaning or substance ⟨a comedy sharpened by pithy one-liners⟩. COMPENDIOUS applies to what is at once full in scope and brief and concise in treatment ⟨a compendious dictionary⟩.

con·ci·sion \kən-'si-zhən\ n [ME, fr. MF, fr. L concision-, concisio, fr. concidere] (14c) **1** archaic : a cutting up or off **2** : the quality or state of being concise

con·clave \'kän-,klāv\ n [ME, fr. MF or ML; MF, fr. ML, fr. L, room that can be locked up, fr. com- + clavis key — more at CLAVICLE] (1524) **1** : a private meeting or secret assembly; esp : a meeting of Roman Catholic cardinals secluded continuously while choosing a pope **2** : a gathering of a group or association

con·clude \kən-'klüd\ vb **con·clud·ed; con·clud·ing** [ME, fr. L concludere to shut up, end, infer, fr. com- + claudere to shut — more at CLOSE] vt (14c) **1** obs : to shut up : ENCLOSE **2** : to bring to an end esp. in a particular way or with a particular action ⟨~ a meeting with a prayer⟩ **3 a** : to reach as a logically necessary end by reasoning : infer on the basis of evidence ⟨concluded that her argument was sound⟩ **b** : to make a decision about : DECIDE ⟨concluded he would wait a little longer⟩ **c** : to come to an agreement on : EFFECT ⟨~ a sale⟩ **4** : to bring about as a result : COMPLETE ~ vi **1** : END **2 a** : to form a final judgment **b** : to reach a decision or agreement **syn** see CLOSE, INFER — **con·clud·er** n

con·clu·sion \kən-'klü-zhən\ n [ME, fr. MF, fr. L conclusion-, conclusio, fr. concludere] (14c) **1 a** : a reasoned judgment : INFERENCE **b** : the necessary consequence of two or more propositions taken as premises; esp : the inferred proposition of a syllogism **2** : the last part of something: as **a** : RESULT, OUTCOME **b** pl : trial of strength or skill — used in the phrase try conclusions **c** : a final summation **d** : the final decision in a law case **e** : the final part of a pleading in law **3** : an act or instance of concluding

con·clu·sion·ary \kən-'klü-zhə-,ner-ē\ adj (1948) : CONCLUSORY

con·clu·sive \-'klü-siv, -ziv\ adj (1536) **1** : of, relating to, or being a conclusion **2** : putting an end to debate or question esp. by reason of irrefutability — **con·clu·sive·ly** adv — **con·clu·sive·ness** n **syn** CONCLUSIVE, DECISIVE, DETERMINATIVE, DEFINITIVE mean bringing to an end. CONCLUSIVE applies to reasoning or logical proof that puts an end to debate or questioning ⟨conclusive evidence⟩. DECISIVE may apply to something that ends a controversy, a contest, or any uncertainty ⟨a decisive battle⟩. DETERMINATIVE adds an implication of giving a fixed character or direction ⟨the determinative factor in the court's decision⟩. DEFINITIVE applies to what is put forth as final and permanent ⟨the definitive biography⟩.

con·clu·so·ry \kən-'klüs-rē, -'klü-sə-\ adj (1923) : consisting of or relating to a conclusion or assertion for which no supporting evidence is offered ⟨~ allegations⟩

con·coct \kən-'käkt, kän-\ vt [L concoctus, pp. of concoquere to cook together, fr. com- + coquere to cook — more at COOK] (1675) **1** : to prepare by combining raw materials **2** : DEVISE, FABRICATE — **con·coct·er** n — **con·coc·tion** \-'käk-shən\ n — **con·coc·tive** \-'käk-tiv\ adj

con·com·i·tance \kən-'kä-mə-tən(t)s, kän-\ n (ca. 1535) : ACCOMPANIMENT; esp : a conjunction that is regular and is marked by correlative variation of accompanying elements

¹con·com·i·tant \-mə-tənt\ adj [L concomitant-, concomitans, prp. of concomitari to accompany, fr. com- + comitari to accompany, fr. comit-, comes companion — more at COUNT] (1607) : accompanying esp. in a subordinate or incidental way — **con·com·i·tant·ly** adv

²concomitant n (1621) : something that accompanies or is collaterally connected with something else : ACCOMPANIMENT

con·cord \'kän-,kórd, 'käŋ-\ n [ME, fr. MF concorde, fr. L concordia, fr. concord-, concors agreeing, fr. com- + cord-, cor heart — more at HEART] (14c) **1 a** : a state of agreement : HARMONY **b** : a simultaneous occurrence of two or more musical tones that produces an impression of agreeableness or resolution on a listener — compare DISCORD **2** : agreement by stipulation, compact, or covenant **3** : grammatical agreement

con·cor·dance \kən-'kór-dᵊn(t)s, kän-\ n [ME, fr. MF, fr. ML concordantia, fr. L concordant-, concordans, prp. of concordare to agree, fr. concord-, concors] (14c) **1** : an alphabetical index of the principal words in a book or the works of an author with their immediate contexts **2** : CONCORD, AGREEMENT

con·cor·dant \-dᵊnt\ adj [ME, fr. MF, fr. L concordant-, concordans] (15c) : CONSONANT, AGREEING — **con·cor·dant·ly** adv

con·cor·dat \kən-'kór-,dat\ n [F, fr. ML concordatum, fr. L, neut. of concordatus, pp. of concordare] (1616) : COMPACT, COVENANT; specif : an agreement between a pope and a sovereign or government for the regulation of ecclesiastical matters

con·cours d'e·le·gance \(,)kōⁿ-,kür-,dā-lā-'gäⁿs\ n [F concours d'élégance, lit., competition of elegance] (1950) : a show or contest of vehicles and accessories in which the entries are judged chiefly on excellence of appearance and turnout

con·course \'kän-,kōrs, 'käŋ-, -,kórs\ n [ME, fr. MF & L; MF concours, fr. L concursus, fr. concurrere to run together — more at CONCUR] (14c) **1** : an act or process of coming together and merging **2** : a meeting produced by voluntary or spontaneous coming together **3 a** : an open space where roads or paths meet **b** : an open space or hall (as in a railroad terminal) where crowds gather

con·cres·cence \kən-'kre-sᵊn(t)s, kän-\ n [L concrescentia, fr. concrescent-, concrescens, prp. of concrescere to grow together, fr. com- + crescere to grow — more at CRESCENT] (1614) **1** : increase by the addition of particles **2** : a growing together : COALESCENCE; esp : convergence and fusion of the lateral lips of the blastopore to form the primordium of an embryo — **con·cres·cent** \-sᵊnt\ adj

¹con·crete \(,)kän-'krēt, 'kän-,, kən-\ adj [ME, fr. L concretus, fr. pp. of concrescere] (14c) **1** : naming a real thing or class of things (the word poem is ~, poetry is abstract) **2** : formed by coalition of particles into one solid mass **3 a** : characterized by or belonging to immediate experience of actual things or events **b** : SPECIFIC, PARTICULAR **c** : REAL, TANGIBLE **4** : relating to or made of concrete — **con·crete·ly** adv — **con·crete·ness** n

²con·crete \'kän-,krēt, kän-'\ vb **con·cret·ed; con·cret·ing** vt (1590) **1 a** : to form into a solid mass : SOLIDIFY **b** : COMBINE, BLEND **2** : to make actual or real : cause to take on the qualities of reality **3** : to cover with, form of, or set in concrete ~ vi : to become concreted

³con·crete \'kän-,krēt, (,)kän-'\ n (1656) **1** : a mass formed by concretion or coalescence of separate particles of matter in one body **2** : a hard strong building material made by mixing a cementing material (as portland cement) and a mineral aggregate (as sand and gravel) with sufficient water to cause the cement to set and bind the entire mass **3** : a waxy essence of flowers prepared by extraction and evaporation and used in perfumery

concrete music n (1953) : MUSIQUE CONCRÈTE

concrete poetry n (1958) : poetry in which the poet's intent is conveyed by the graphic patterns of letters, words, or symbols rather than by the conventional arrangement of words

con·cre·tion \kän-'krē-shən, kən-\ n (1541) **1** : something concreted: as **a** : a hard usu. inorganic mass (as a bezoar or tophus) formed in a living body **b** : a mass of mineral matter found generally in rock of a composition different from its own and produced by deposition from aqueous solution in the rock **2** : the act or process of concreting : the state of being concreted ⟨~ of ideas in an hypothesis⟩ — **con·cre·tion·ary** \-shə-,ner-ē\ adj

con·cret·ism \'kän-krē-,ti-zəm, 'kän-,\ n (1865) : representation of abstract things as concrete; esp : the theory or practice of concrete poetry — **con·cret·ist** \-'krē-tist, -,krē-\ n

con·cret·ize \-,tīz\ vb **-ized; -iz·ing** vt (1884) : to make concrete, specific, or definite ⟨tried to ~ his ideas⟩ ~ vi : to become concrete — **con·cret·i·za·tion** \(,)kän-,krē-tə-'zā-shən\ n

---

\ə\ abut \ᵊ\ kitten, F table \ər\ further \a\ ash \ā\ ace \ä\ mop, mar \aú\ out \ch\ chin \e\ bet \ē\ easy \g\ go \i\ hit \ī\ ice \j\ job \ŋ\ sing \ō\ go \ò\ law \òi\ boy \th\ thin \t̲h̲\ the \ü\ loot \ú\ foot \y\ yet \zh\ vision \ä, k̲, ⁿ, œ, œ̄, ue, ūe, ᵞ\ see Guide to Pronunciation

con·cu·bi·nage \kän-'kyü-bə-nij, kən-\ n (14c) **1** : cohabitation of persons not legally married **2** : the state of being a concubine

con·cu·bine \'käŋ-kyü-ˌbīn, 'kän-\ n [ME, fr. MF, fr. L concubina, fr. com- + cubare to lie] (14c) : a woman with whom a man cohabits without being married: as **a** : one having a recognized social status in a household below that of a wife **b** : MISTRESS 4a

con·cu·pis·cence \kän-'kyü-bə-sən(t)s, kən-\ n [ME, fr. MF, fr. LL concupiscentia, fr. L concupiscent-, concupiscens, prp. of concupiscere to desire ardently, fr. com- + cupere to desire] (14c) : strong desire; esp : sexual desire — **con·cu·pis·cent** \-sənt\ adj

con·cu·pis·ci·ble \-'kyü-pə-sə-bəl\ adj [ME, fr. MF or LL; MF, fr. LL concupiscibilis, fr. L concupiscere] (14c) : LUSTFUL, DESIROUS

con·cur \kən-'kər, kän-\ vi **con·curred; con·cur·ring** [ME concurren, fr. L concurrere, fr. com- + currere to run — more at CAR] (15c) **1** : to act together to a common end or single effect **2 a** : APPROVE ⟨~ in a statement⟩ **b** : to express agreement ⟨~ with an opinion⟩ **3** obs : to come together : MEET **4** : to happen together : COINCIDE **syn** see AGREE

con·cur·rence \-'kər-ən(t)s, -'kə-rən(t)s\ n (15c) **1 a** : the simultaneous occurrence of events or circumstances **b** : the meeting of concurrent lines in a point **2 a** : agreement or union in action : COOPERATION **b** (1) : agreement in opinion or design **2** : CONSENT **3** : a coincidence of equal powers in law

con·cur·ren·cy \-ən(t)-sē, -rən(t)-sē\ n (1597) : CONCURRENCE

con·cur·rent \-'kər-ənt, -'kə-rənt\ adj [ME, fr. MF & L; MF, fr. L concurrent-, concurrens, prp. of concurrere] (14c) **1** : operating or occurring at the same time **2 a** : running parallel **b** : CONVERGENT; specif : meeting or intersecting in a point **3** : acting in conjunction **4** : exercised over the same matter or area by two different authorities ⟨~ jurisdiction⟩ — **concurrent** n — **con·cur·rent·ly** adv

concurrent resolution n (1802) : a resolution passed by both houses of a legislative body that lacks the force of law

con·cuss \kən-'kəs\ vt [L concussus, pp.] (1597) : to affect with or as if with concussion

con·cus·sion \kən-'kə-shən\ n [ME concussioun, fr. MF or L; MF concussion, fr. L concussion-, concussio, fr. concutere to shake violently, fr. com- + quatere to shake] (14c) **1 a** : a stunning, damaging, or shattering effect from a hard blow; esp : a jarring injury of the brain resulting in disturbance of cerebral function **b** : a hard blow or collision **2** : AGITATION, SHAKING — **con·cus·sive** \-'kə-siv\ adj

con·demn \kən-'dem\ vt [ME, fr. MF condemner, fr. L condemnare, fr. com- + damnare to condemn — more at DAMN] (14c) **1** : to declare to be reprehensible, wrong, or evil usu. after weighing evidence and without reservation **2 a** : to pronounce guilty : CONVICT **b** : SENTENCE, DOOM **3** : to adjudge unfit for use or consumption **4** : to declare convertible to public use under the right of eminent domain **syn** see CRITICIZE — **con·dem·na·ble** \-'dem-nə-bəl, -'dem-\ adj — **con·dem·nor** \-'dem-ər\ or **con·dem·nor** \'dem-ˌnor; kən-ˌdem-'nór, kän-\ n

con·dem·na·tion \ˌkän-ˌdem-'nā-shən, -dəm-\ n (14c) **1** : CENSURE, BLAME **2** : the act of judicially condemning **3** : the state of being condemned **4** : a reason for condemning

con·den·sate \'kän-dən-ˌsāt, -ˌden-; kən-'den-\ n (1889) : a product of condensation; esp : a liquid obtained by condensation of a gas or vapor ⟨steam ~⟩

con·den·sa·tion \ˌkän-ˌden-'sā-shən, -dən-\ n (1603) **1** : the act or process of condensing: as **a** : a chemical reaction involving union between molecules often with elimination of a simple molecule (as water) to form a new more complex compound of often greater molecular weight **b** : the conversion of a substance (as water) from the vapor state to a denser liquid or solid state usu. initiated by a reduction in temperature of the vapor **c** : compression of a written or spoken work into more concise form **2** : the quality or state of being condensed **3** : a product of condensing — **con·den·sa·tion·al** \-shnəl, -shə-nᵊl\ adj

con·dense \kən-'den(t)s\ vb **con·densed; con·dens·ing** [ME, fr. MF condenser, fr. L condensare, fr. com- + densare to make dense, fr. densus dense] vt (15c) : to make denser or more compact; esp : to subject to condensation ~ vi : to undergo condensation **syn** see CONTRACT — **con·dens·able** also **con·dens·ible** \-'den(t)-sə-bəl\ adj

condensed adj (1863) : reduced to a more compact or dense form; also : having a face narrower than that of a standard typeface

condensed milk n (1863) : evaporated milk with sugar added

con·dens·er \kən-'den(t)-sər\ n (1686) **1** : one that condenses: as **a** : a lens or mirror used to concentrate light on an object **b** : an apparatus in which gas or vapor is condensed **2** : CAPACITOR

con·de·scend \ˌkän-di-'send\ vi [ME, fr. MF condescendre, fr. LL condescendere, fr. L com- + descendere to descend] (14c) **1** : to descend to a less formal or dignified level : UNBEND **b** : to waive the privileges of rank **2** : to assume an air of superiority

con·de·scen·dence \-'sen-dən(t)s\ n (1638) : CONDESCENSION

condescending adj (1707) : showing or characterized by condescension : PATRONIZING — **con·de·scend·ing·ly** \-'sen-diŋ-lē\ adv

con·de·scen·sion \ˌkän-di-'sen(t)-shən\ n [LL condescension-, condescensio, fr. condescendere] (1647) **1** : voluntary descent from one's rank or dignity in relations with an inferior **2** : patronizing attitude or behavior

con·dign \kən-'dīn, 'kän-\ adj [ME condigne, fr. MF, fr. L condignus very worthy, fr. com- + dignus worthy — more at DECENT] (15c) : DESERVED, APPROPRIATE ⟨~ punishment⟩ — **con·dign·ly** adv

con·di·ment \'kän-də-mənt\ n [ME, fr. MF, fr. L condimentum, fr. condire to season] (15c) : something used to enhance the flavor of food; esp : a pungent seasoning — **con·di·men·tal** \ˌkän-də-'men-tᵊl\ adj

¹con·di·tion \kən-'di-shən\ n [ME condicion, fr. MF, fr. L condicion-, condicio terms of agreement, condition, fr. condicere to agree, fr. com- + dicere to say, determine — more at DICTION] (14c) **1 a** : a premise upon which the fulfillment of an agreement depends : STIPULATION **b** obs : COVENANT **c** : a provision making the effect of a legal instrument contingent upon an uncertain event; also : the event itself **2** : something essential to the appearance or occurrence of something else : PREREQUISITE: as **a** : an environmental requirement ⟨available oxygen is an essential ~ for animal life⟩ **b** : the subordinate clause of a conditional sentence **3 a** : a restricting or modifying factor : QUALIFICATION **b** : an unsatisfactory academic grade that may be raised by doing additional work **4 a** : a state of being **b** : social status

: RANK **c** : a usu. defective state of health ⟨a serious heart ~⟩ **d** : a state of physical fitness or readiness for use ⟨the car was in good ~⟩ ⟨exercising to get into ~⟩ **e** pl : attendant circumstances **5 a** obs : temper of mind **b** obs : TRAIT **c** pl, archaic : MANNERS, WAYS

²condition vb **con·di·tioned; con·di·tion·ing** \-'di-sh(ə-)niŋ\ vi (15c) archaic : to make stipulations ~ vt **1** : to agree by stipulating **2** : to make conditional **3 a** : to put into a proper state for work or use **b** : AIR-CONDITION **4** : to give a grade of condition to **5 a** : to adapt, modify, or mold so as to conform to an environing culture **b** : to modify so that an act or response previously associated with one stimulus becomes associated with another — **con·di·tion·able** \-sh(ə-)nə-bəl\ adj — **con·di·tion·er** \-sh(ə-)nər\ n

¹con·di·tion·al \kən-'dish-nəl, -'di-shə-nᵊl\ adj (14c) **1** : subject to, implying, or dependent upon a condition ⟨a ~ promise⟩ **2** : expressing, containing, or implying a supposition ⟨the ~ clause if he speaks⟩ **3 a** : true only for certain values of the variables or symbols involved ⟨~ equations⟩ **b** : stating the case when one or more random variables are fixed or one or more events are known ⟨~ frequency distribution⟩ **4 a** : CONDITIONED **2** ⟨~ reflex⟩ ⟨~ response⟩ **b** : established by conditioning as the stimulus eliciting a conditional response — **con·di·tion·al·i·ty** \-ˌdi-shə-'na-lə-tē\ n — **con·di·tion·al·ly** \-'dish-nə-lē, -'di-shə-nᵊl-ē\ adv

²conditional n (1828) **1** : a conditional word, clause, verb form, or morpheme **2** : IMPLICATION 2b

conditional probability n (1961) : the probability that a given event will occur if it is certain that another event has taken place or will take place

conditioned adj (1537) **1** : brought or put into a specified state **2** : determined or established by conditioning

con·do \'kän-(ˌ)dō\ n (1964) : CONDOMINIUM 3

con·dole \kən-'dōl\ vb **con·doled; con·dol·ing** [LL condolēre, fr. L com- + dolēre to feel pain] vi (1590) **1** obs : GRIEVE **2** : to express sympathetic sorrow ~ vt, archaic : LAMENT, GRIEVE — **con·do·la·to·ry** \-'dō-lə-ˌtōr-ē, -ˌtor-\ adj

con·do·lence \kən-'dō-lən(t)s also 'kän-də-\ n (1603) **1** : sympathy with another in sorrow **2** : an expression of sympathy **syn** see PITY

con·dom \'kän-dəm, 'kən-, dial -drəm\ n [origin unknown] (ca. 1706) : a sheath commonly of rubber worn over the penis (as to prevent conception or venereal infection during coitus); also : a similar device inserted into the vagina

con·do·min·i·um \ˌkän-də-'mi-nē-əm\ n, pl **-ums** [NL, fr. L com- + dominium domain] (ca. 1714) **1 a** : joint dominion; esp : joint sovereignty by two or more nations **b** : a government operating under joint rule **2** : a politically dependent territory under condominium **3 a** : individual ownership of a unit in a multiunit structure (as an apartment building) or on land owned in common (as a town house complex); also : a unit so owned **b** : a building containing condominiums

con·do·na·tion \ˌkän-dō-'nā-shən, -də-\ n (1625) : implied pardon of an offense by treating the offender as if it had not been committed

con·done \kən-'dōn\ vt **con·doned; con·don·ing** [L condonare to absolve, fr. com- + donare to give — more at DONATION] (1857) : to pardon or overlook voluntarily; esp : to treat as if trivial, harmless, or of no importance ⟨~ corruption in politics⟩ **syn** see EXCUSE — **con·don·able** \-'dō-nə-bəl\ adj

con·dor \'kän-dər, -ˌdór\ n [Sp cóndor, fr. Quechua kuntur] (1604) **1 a** : a very large American vulture (Vultur gryphus) of the high Andes having the head and neck bare and the plumage dull black with a downy white neck ruff and white patches on the wings **b** : CALIFORNIA CONDOR **2** pl **condors** or **con·do·res** \kən-'dōr-ˌās, -'dór-\ : a coin (the centesimo of Chile) bearing the picture of a condor

con·dot·tie·re \ˌkän-də-'tyer-ē, ˌälä-dē-'er-\ n, pl **-tie·ri** \-ē\ [It, fr. condotta troop of mercenaries, fr. fem. of condotto, pp. of condurre to conduct, hire, fr. L conducere] (1794) **1** : a leader of a band of mercenaries common in Europe between the 14th and 16th centuries; also : a member of such a band **2** : a mercenary soldier

con·duce \kən-'düs, -'dyüs\ vi **con·duced; con·duc·ing** [ME, to conduct, fr. L conducere to conduct, conduce, fr. com- + ducere to lead — more at TOW] (1586) : to lead or tend to a particular and usu. desirable result : CONTRIBUTE

con·du·cive \-'dü-siv, -'dyü-\ adj (1646) : tending to promote or assist ⟨an atmosphere ~ to education⟩ — **con·du·cive·ness** n

¹con·duct \'kän-(ˌ)dəkt\ n [ME, alter. of conduit, fr. MF, act of leading, escort, fr. ML conductus, fr. L conducere] (15c) **1** obs : ESCORT, GUIDE **2** : the act, manner, or process of carrying on : MANAGEMENT **3** : a mode or standard of personal behavior esp. as based on moral principles

²con·duct \kən-'dəkt also 'kän-ˌdəkt\ vt (15c) **1** : to bring by or as if by leading : GUIDE ⟨~ tourists through a museum⟩ **2 a** : to lead from a position of command ⟨~ a siege⟩ ⟨~ a class⟩ **b** : to direct or take part in the operation or management of ⟨~ an experiment⟩ ⟨~ a business⟩ ⟨~ an investigation⟩ **c** : to direct the performance of ⟨~ an orchestra⟩ ⟨~ an opera⟩ **3 a** : to convey in a channel **b** : to act as a medium for conveying or transmitting **4** : to cause (oneself) to act or behave in a particular and esp. in a controlled manner ~ vi **1** of a road or passage : to show the way : LEAD **2 a** : to act as leader or director **b** : to have the quality of transmitting light, heat, sound, or electricity — **con·duct·ibil·i·ty** \kən-ˌdək-tə-'bi-lə-tē\ n — **con·duct·ible** \-'dək-tə-bəl\ adj

syn CONDUCT, MANAGE, CONTROL, DIRECT mean to use one's powers to lead, guide, or dominate. CONDUCT implies taking responsibility for the acts and achievements of a group ⟨conducted negotiations⟩. MANAGE implies direct handling and manipulating or maneuvering toward a desired result ⟨manages a meat market⟩. CONTROL implies a regulating or restraining in order to keep within bounds or on a course ⟨controlling his appetite⟩. DIRECT implies constant guiding and regulating so as to achieve smooth operation ⟨directs the store's day-to-day business⟩. **syn** see in addition BEHAVE

con·duc·tance \kən-'dək-tən(t)s\ n (1885) **1** : conducting power **2** : the readiness with which a conductor transmits an electric current expressed as the reciprocal of electrical resistance

con·duc·tion \kən-'dək-shən\ n (1534) **1** : the act of conducting or conveying **2 a** : transmission through or by means of a conductor; also : the transfer of heat through matter by communication of kinetic energy from particle to particle with no net displacement of the parti-

cles — compare CONVECTION, RADIATION **b** : CONDUCTIVITY **3** : the transmission of excitation through living tissue and esp. nervous tissue
conduction band *n* (1953) : the range of permissible energy values that allow an electron of an atom to dissociate from the atom and become a free charge carrier — compare VALENCE BAND
con·duc·tive \kən-'dək-tiv\ *adj* (1528) : having conductivity : relating to conduction (as of electricity)
con·duc·tiv·i·ty \ˌkän-ˌdək-'ti-və-tē, kən-\ *n, pl* **-ties** (1837) : the quality or power of conducting or transmitting: as **a** : the reciprocal of electrical resistivity **b** : the quality of living matter responsible for the transmission of and progressive reaction to stimuli
con·duc·to·met·ric *also* **con·duc·ti·met·ric** \ˌkən-ˌdək-tə-'me-trik\ *adj* (ca. 1926) **1** : of or relating to the measurement of conductivity **2** : being or relating to titration based on determination of changes in the electrical conductivity of the solution
con·duc·tor \kən-'dək-tər\ *n* (15c) : one that conducts: as **a** : GUIDE **b** : a collector of fares in a public conveyance **c** : the leader of a musical ensemble **d** (1) : a material or object that permits an electric current to flow easily — compare INSULATOR, SEMICONDUCTOR (2) : a material capable of transmitting another form of energy (as heat or sound) — **con·duc·to·ri·al** \ˌkän-ˌdək-'tōr-ē-əl, kən-, -'tor-\ *adj*
con·duc·tress \kən-'dək-trəs\ *n* (1624) : a woman who is a conductor
con·duit \'kän-ˌdü-ət, -ˌdyü- *also* -dwət, -dət\ *n* [ME — more at CONDUCT] (14c) **1** : a natural or artificial channel through which something (as a fluid) is conveyed **2** *archaic* : FOUNTAIN **3** : a pipe, tube, or tile for protecting electric wires or cables **4** : a means of transmitting or distributing ⟨a ~ for illicit payments⟩ ⟨a ~ of information⟩
con·du·pli·cate \(ˌ)kän-'dü-pli-kət, -'dyü-\ *adj* [L *conduplicatus*, pp. of *conduplicare* to double, fr. *com-* + *duplic-, duplex* double — more at DUPLEX] (1777) : folded lengthwise ⟨~ petals in the bud⟩
con·dy·lar \'kän-də-lər\ *adj* (1876) : of or relating to a condyle
con·dyle \'kän-ˌdīl *also* -d°l\ *n* [F & L; F, fr. L *condylus* knuckle, fr. Gk *kondylos*] (1634) : an articular prominence of a bone; *esp* : one resembling a pair of knuckles — **con·dy·loid** \-də-ˌlȯid\ *adj*
con·dy·lo·ma \ˌkän-də-'lō-mə\ *n, pl* **-ma·ta** \-mə-tə\ *also* **-mas** [NL, fr. Gk *kondylōma*, fr. *kondylos*] (ca. 1526) : a warty growth on the skin or adjoining mucous membrane usu. near the anus and genital organs — **con·dy·lo·ma·tous** \-mə-təs\ *adj*
¹cone \'kōn\ *n* [MF or L; MF, fr. L *conus*, fr. Gk *kōnos*] (1545) **1 a** : a solid generated by rotating a right triangle about one of its legs — called also *right circular cone* **b** : a solid bounded by a circular or other closed plane base and the surface formed by line segments joining every point of the boundary of the base to a common vertex — see VOLUME table **c** : a surface traced by a moving straight line passing through a fixed vertex **2 a** : a mass of ovule-bearing or pollen-bearing scales or bracts in trees of the pine family or in cycads that are arranged usu. on a somewhat elongated axis **b** : any of several flower or fruit clusters suggesting a cone **3** : something that resembles a cone in shape: as **a** : any of the conical photosensitive receptor cells of the vertebrate retina that function in color vision — compare ROD 3 **b** : any of a family (Conidae) of tropical marine gastropod mollusks that inject their prey with a potent toxin **c** : the apex of a volcano **d** : a crisp usu. cone-shaped wafer for holding ice cream
²cone *vt* **coned; con·ing** (ca. 1859) **1** : to make cone-shaped **2** : to bevel like the slanting surface of a cone ⟨~ a tire⟩
cone·flow·er \'kōn-ˌflaú(-ə)r\ *n* (ca. 1818) : any of several composite plants having cone-shaped flower disks; *esp* : RUDBECKIA
cone·nose \'kōn-ˌnōz\ *n* (ca. 1891) : any of various large bloodsucking bugs and esp. some assassin bugs (genus *Triatoma*) including some capable of inflicting painful bites — called also *kissing bug*
con es·pres·sio·ne \ˌkän-ˌes-(ˌ)pre-sē-'ō-nē, ˌkōn-, -'ō-(ˌ)nā\ *adv* [It, lit., with expression] (ca. 1891) : with feeling — used as a direction in music
Con·es·to·ga wagon \ˌkä-nə-'stō-gə-\ *n* [*Conestoga*, Pa.] (1717) : a broad-wheeled covered wagon drawn usu. by six horses and used esp. for transporting freight across the prairies — called also *Conestoga*
co·ney \'kō-nē, *I also* 'kə-nē\ *n, pl* **coneys** [ME *conies*, pl., fr. OF *conis*, pl. of *conil*, fr. L *cuniculus*] (12c) **a** : a rabbit fur **b** (1) : RABBIT; *esp* : the European rabbit (*Oryctolagus cuniculus*) (2) : PIKA **c** : HYRAX **2** *archaic* : DUPE **3** : any of several fishes; *esp* : a dusky black-spotted reddish-finned grouper (*Epinephelus fulvus*) of the tropical Atlantic
con·fab \kən-'fab, 'kän-ˌ\ *vi* **con·fabbed; con·fab·bing** (1741) : CONFABULATE — **con·fab** \'kän-ˌfab, kən-'\ *n*
con·fab·u·late \kən-'fa-byə-ˌlāt\ *vi* **-lat·ed; -lat·ing** [L *confabulatus*, pp. of *confabulari*, fr. *com-* + *fabulari* to talk, fr. *fabula* story — more at FABLE] (ca. 1604) **1** : CHAT **2** : to hold a discussion : CONFER **3** : to fill in gaps in memory by fabrication — **con·fab·u·la·tion** \kən-ˌfa-byə-'lā-shən\ *n* — **con·fab·u·la·tor** \kən-'fa-byə-ˌlā-tər\ *n* — **con·fab·u·la·to·ry** \-lə-ˌtȯr-ē, -ˌtȯr-\ *adj*
con·fect \kən-'fekt\ *vt* [ME, fr. L *confectus*, pp. of *conficere* to prepare — more at COMFIT] (14c) **1** : to put together from varied material **2 a** : PREPARE **b** : PRESERVE — **con·fect** \'kän-ˌ\ *n*
con·fec·tion \kən-'fek-shən\ *n* (15c) **1** : the act or process of confecting **2** : something confected: as **a** : a fancy dish or sweetmeat; *also* : a sweet food **b** : a medicinal preparation usu. made with sugar, syrup, or honey **c** : a piece of fine craftsmanship
con·fec·tion·ary \-shə-ˌner-ē\ *n, pl* **-ar·ies** (1605) **1** *archaic* : CONFECTIONER **2** : CONFECTIONERY **3** : SWEETS — **confectionary** *adj*
con·fec·tion·er \-sh(ə-)nər\ *n* (1591) : a manufacturer of or dealer in confections
confectioners' sugar *n* (ca. 1889) : a refined finely powdered sugar

con·fec·tion·ery \-shə-ˌner-ē\ *n, pl* **-er·ies** (1769) **1** : sweet foods (as candy or pastry) **2** : the confectioner's art or business **3** : a confectioner's shop
con·fed·er·a·cy \kən-'fe-d(ə-)rə-sē\ *n, pl* **-cies** (14c) **1** : a league or compact for mutual support or common action : ALLIANCE **2** : a combination of persons for unlawful purposes : CONSPIRACY **3** : the body formed by persons, states, or nations united by a league; *specif, cap* : the 11 southern states seceding from the U.S. in 1860 and 1861
con·fed·er·al \-d(ə-)rəl\ *adj* (1782) : of or relating to a confederation
¹con·fed·er·ate \kən-'fe-d(ə-)rət\ *adj* [ME *confederat*, fr. LL *confoederatus*, pp. of *confoederare* to unite by a league, fr. L *com-* + *foeder-, foedus* compact — more at FEDERAL] (14c) **1** : united in a league : ALLIED **2** *cap* : of or relating to the Confederate States of America
²confederate *n* (15c) **1** : ALLY, ACCOMPLICE **2** *cap* : an adherent of the Confederate States of America or their cause
³con·fed·er·ate \-'fe-də-ˌrāt\ *vb* **-at·ed; -at·ing** *vt* (1531) : to unite in a confederacy ~ *vi* : to band together — **con·fed·er·a·tive** \-'fe-d(ə-)rə-tiv, -də-ˌrā-\ *adj*
Confederate Memorial Day *n* (1899) : any of several days appointed for the commemoration of servicemen of the Confederacy
con·fed·er·a·tion \kən-ˌfe-də-'rā-shən\ *n* (15c) **1** : an act of confederating : a state of being confederated : ALLIANCE **2** : LEAGUE
con·fer \kən-'fər\ *vb* **con·ferred; con·fer·ring** [L *conferre* to bring together, fr. *com-* + *ferre* to carry — more at BEAR] *vt* (1570) **1** : to bestow from or as if from a position of superiority ⟨*conferred* an honorary degree on her⟩ ⟨knowing how to read was a gift *conferred* with manhood —Murray Kempton⟩ **2** : to give (as a property or characteristic) to someone or something ⟨a reputation for power will ~ power —John Spanier⟩ ~ *vi* : to compare views or take counsel : CONSULT *syn* see GIVE — **con·fer·ment** \-'fər-mənt\ *n* — **con·fer·ra·ble** \-'fər-ə-bəl\ *adj* — **con·fer·ral** \-'fər-əl\ *n* — **con·fer·rer** \-'fər-ər\ *n*
con·fer·ee \ˌkän-fə-'rē\ *n* (1771) : one taking part in a conference
con·fer·ence \'kän-f(ə-)rən(t)s, -fərn(t)s, *for 2 usu* kän-'fər-ən(t)s\ *n* (1527) **1 a** : a meeting of two or more persons for discussing matters of common concern **b** : a usu. formal interchange of views : CONSULTATION **c** : a meeting of members of the two branches of a legislature to adjust differences **d** : CAUCUS **2** *also* **con·fer·rence** \kən-'fər-ən(t)s\ : BESTOWAL, CONFERMENT **3 a** : a representative assembly or administrative organization of a religious denomination **b** : a territorial division of a religious denomination **4** : an association of athletic teams — **con·fer·en·tial** \ˌkän-fə-'ren(t)-shəl\ *adj*
conference call *n* (1941) : a telephone call by which a caller can speak with several people at the same time
con·fer·enc·ing \'kän-f(ə-)rən(t)-siŋ, -fərn(t)-\ *n* (1865) : the holding of conferences esp. by means of an electronic communications system ⟨computer ~⟩
con·fess \kən-'fes\ *vb* [ME, fr. MF *confesser*, fr. OF, fr. *confes* having confessed, fr. L *confessus*, pp. of *confitēri* to confess, fr. *com-* + *fatēri* to confess; akin to L *fari* to speak — more at BAN] *vt* (14c) **1** : to tell or make known (as something wrong or damaging to oneself) : ADMIT **2 a** : to acknowledge (sin) to God or to a priest **b** : to receive the confession of (a penitent) **3** : to declare faith in or adherence to : PROFESS **4** : to give evidence of ~ *vi* **1 a** : to disclose one's faults; *specif* : to unburden one's sins or the state of one's conscience to God or to a priest **b** : to hear a confession **2** : ADMIT, OWN *syn* see ACKNOWLEDGE — **con·fess·able** \-'fe-sə-bəl\ *adj*
con·fessed·ly \-'fe-səd-lē, -'fest-lē\ *adv* (1640) : by confession
con·fes·sion \kən-'fe-shən\ *n* (14c) **1** : an act of confessing; *esp* : a disclosure of one's sins in the sacrament of reconciliation **2** : a statement of what is confessed: as **a** : a written acknowledgment of guilt by a party accused of an offense **b** : a formal statement of religious beliefs : CREED **3** : an organized religious body having a common creed
¹con·fes·sion·al \-'fesh-nəl, -'fe-shə-n°l\ *n* (1727) **1** : a place where a priest hears confessions **2** : the practice of confessing to a priest
²confessional *adj* (1817) **1** : of, relating to, or being a confession esp. of faith **2** : of, relating to, or being intimately autobiographical ⟨~ fiction⟩ — **con·fes·sion·al·ism** \-nə-ˌli-zəm\ *n* — **con·fes·sion·al·ist** \-list\ *n* — **con·fes·sion·al·ly** \-nə-lē, -n°l-ē\ *adv*
con·fes·sor \kən-'fe-sər, *1 & 3 also* 'kän-ˌfe-sər, *3 also* 'kän-fə-sər, 'kän-fe-ˌsȯr\ *n* (12c) **1** : one who shows heroic evidence of faith but does not suffer martyrdom **2** : one that confesses **3 a** : a priest who hears confessions **b** : a priest who is one's regular spiritual guide
con·fet·ti \kən-'fe-tē\ *n* [It, pl. of *confetto* sweetmeat, fr. ML *confectum*, fr. L, neut. of *confectus*, pp. of *conficere* to prepare — more at COMFIT] (1815) : small bits or streamers of brightly colored paper made for throwing (as at weddings)
con·fi·dant \'kän-fə-ˌdänt *also* -ˌdant, -dänt\ *n* [F *confident*, fr. It *confidente*, fr. *confidente* confident, trustworthy, fr. L *confident-, confidens*] (1646) : one to whom secrets are entrusted; *esp* : INTIMATE
con·fi·dante *same as* CONFIDANT\ *n* [F *confidente*, fem. of *confident*] (1696) : CONFIDANT; *esp* : one who is a woman
con·fide \kən-'fīd\ *vb* **con·fid·ed; con·fid·ing** [ME, fr. MF or L; MF *confider*, fr. L *confidere*, fr. *com-* + *fidere* to trust — more at BIDE] *vi* (15c) **1** : to have confidence : TRUST **2** : to show confidence by imparting secrets ~ *vt* **1** : to tell confidentially **2** : to give to the care or protection of another : ENTRUST *syn* see COMMIT — **con·fid·er** *n*
¹con·fi·dence \'kän-fə-dən(t)s, -ˌden(t)s\ *n* (14c) **1 a** : a feeling or consciousness of one's powers or of reliance on one's circumstances ⟨had perfect ~ in her ability to succeed⟩ ⟨met the risk with brash ~⟩ **b** : faith or belief that one will act in a right, proper, or effective way ⟨have ~ in a leader⟩ **2** : the quality or state of being certain : CERTITUDE ⟨they had every ~ of success⟩ **3 a** : a relation of trust or intimacy ⟨took his friend into his ~⟩ **b** : reliance on another's discretion ⟨their story was told in strictest ~⟩ **c** : support esp. in a legislative body ⟨vote of ~⟩ **4** : a communication made in confidence : SECRET *syn* CONFIDENCE, ASSURANCE, SELF-POSSESSION, APLOMB mean a state of

\ə\ abut \ᵊ\ kitten, F table \ər\ further \a\ ash \ā\ ace \ä\ mop, mar \aú\ out \ch\ chin \e\ bet \ē\ easy \g\ go \i\ hit \ī\ ice \j\ job \ŋ\ sing \ō\ go \ȯ\ law \ȯi\ boy \th\ thin \t͟h\ the \ü\ loot \ú\ foot \y\ yet \zh\ vision \ä, k̲, ⁿ, œ, œ̄, ᵫ, ᵫ̄, ᵞ\ *see* Guide to Pronunciation mind or a manner marked by easy coolness and freedom from uncertainty, diffidence, or embarrassment. CONFIDENCE stresses faith in oneself and one's powers without any suggestion of conceit or arrogance ⟨the *confidence* that comes from long experience⟩. ASSURANCE carries a stronger implication of certainty and may suggest arrogance or lack of objectivity in assessing one's own powers ⟨handled the cross-examination with complete *assurance*⟩. SELF-POSSESSION implies an ease or coolness under stress that reflects perfect self-control and command of one's powers ⟨answered the insolent question with complete *self-possession*⟩. APLOMB implies a manifest self-possession in trying or challenging situations ⟨handled the reporters with great *aplomb*⟩.

²**confidence** *adj* (1849) : of, relating to, or adept at swindling by false promises ⟨a ∼ game⟩ ⟨a ∼ man⟩

confidence interval *n* (1934) : a group of continuous or discrete adjacent values that is used to estimate a statistical parameter (as a mean or variance) and that tends to include the true value of the parameter a predetermined proportion of the time if the process of finding the group of values is repeated a number of times

confidence limits *n pl* (1939) : the end points of a confidence interval

con·fi·dent \'kän-fə-dənt, -,dent\ *adj* [L *confident-, confidens*, fr. prp. of *confidere*] (1576) **1** : characterized by assurance; *esp* : SELF-RELIANT **2** *obs* : TRUSTFUL, CONFIDING **3 a** : full of conviction : CERTAIN **b** : COCKSURE — **con·fi·dent·ly** *adv*

con·fi·den·tial \,kän-fə-'den(t)-shəl\ *adj* (1759) **1** : marked by intimacy or willingness to confide ⟨a ∼ tone⟩ **2** : PRIVATE, SECRET ⟨∼ information⟩ **3** : entrusted with confidences ⟨∼ clerk⟩ **4** : containing information whose unauthorized disclosure could be prejudicial to the national interest — compare SECRET, TOP SECRET — **con·fi·den·ti·al·i·ty** \-,den(t)-shē-'a-lə-tē\ *n* — **con·fi·den·tial·ly** \-'den(t)-sh(ə-)lē\ *adv*

con·fid·ing \kən-'fī-diŋ\ *adj* (1829) : tending to confide : TRUSTFUL — **con·fid·ing·ly** \-diŋ-lē\ *adv* — **con·fid·ing·ness** *n*

con·fig·u·ra·tion \kən-,fi-gyə-'rā-shən, ,kän-, -gə-\ *n* [LL *configuration-, configuratio* similar formation, fr. L *configurare* to form from or after, fr. *com-* + *figurare* to form, fr. *figura* figure] (1646) **1 a** : relative arrangement of parts or elements: as **(1)** : SHAPE **(2)** : contour of land ⟨∼ of the mountains⟩ **(3)** : functional arrangement ⟨a small business computer system in its simplest ∼⟩ **b** : something (as a figure, contour, pattern, or apparatus) that results from a particular arrangement of parts or components **c** : the stable structural makeup of a chemical compound esp. with reference to the space relations of the constituent atoms **2** : GESTALT ⟨personality ∼⟩ — **con·fig·u·ra·tion·al** \-shnəl, -shə-n³l\ *adj* — **con·fig·u·ra·tion·al·ly** *adv* — **con·fig·u·ra·tive** \-'fi-gyə-rə-tiv, -'fi-gə-\ *adj*

con·fig·ure \kən-'fi-gyər, *esp Brit* -'fi-gər\ *vt* **-ured; -ur·ing** (1677) : to set up for operation esp. in a particular way ⟨a fighter plane *configured* for the Malaysian air force⟩

¹**con·fine** \'kän-,fīn *also* kän-'\ *n* [ME, fr. MF or L; MF *confines*, pl., fr. L *confine* border, fr. neut. of *confinis* adjacent, fr. *com-* + *finis* end] (15c) **1** *pl* **a** : something (as borders or walls) that encloses ⟨outside the ∼s of the office or hospital — W. A. Nolen⟩; *also* : something that restrains ⟨escape from the ∼s of soot and clutter —E. S. Muskie⟩ **b** : SCOPE 3 ⟨work within the ∼s of a small group —Frank Newman⟩ **2 a** *archaic* : RESTRICTION **b** *obs* : PRISON

²**con·fine** \kən-'fīn\ *vb* **con·fined; con·fin·ing** *vi* (1523) *archaic* : BORDER ∼ *vt* **1 a** : to hold within a location **b** : IMPRISON **2** : to keep within limits ⟨will ∼ my remarks to one subject⟩ **syn** see LIMIT — **con·fin·er** *n*

con·fined \kən-'fīnd\ *adj* (1772) : undergoing childbirth

con·fine·ment \kən-'fīn-mənt\ *n* (1646) : an act of confining : the state of being confined ⟨solitary ∼⟩; *esp* : LYING-IN

con·firm \kən-'fərm\ *vt* [ME, fr. OF *confirmer*, fr. L *confirmare*, fr. *com-* + *firmare* to make firm, fr. *firmus* firm] (13c) **1** : to give approval to : RATIFY **2** : to make firm or firmer : STRENGTHEN **3** : to administer the rite of confirmation to **4** : to give new assurance of the validity of : remove doubt about by authoritative act or indisputable fact — **con·firm·abil·i·ty** \-,fər-mə-'bi-lə-tē\ *n* — **con·firm·able** \-'fər-mə-bəl\ *adj*

syn CONFIRM, CORROBORATE, SUBSTANTIATE, VERIFY, AUTHENTICATE, VALIDATE mean to attest to the truth or validity of something. CONFIRM implies the removing of doubts by an authoritative statement or indisputable fact ⟨*confirmed* the reports⟩. CORROBORATE suggests the strengthening of what is already partly established ⟨witnesses *corroborated* his story⟩. SUBSTANTIATE implies the offering of evidence that sustains the contention ⟨the claims have yet to be *substantiated*⟩. VERIFY implies the establishing of correspondence of actual facts or details with those proposed or guessed at ⟨all statements of fact in the article have been *verified*⟩. AUTHENTICATE implies establishing genuineness by adducing legal or official documents or expert opinion ⟨handwriting experts *authenticated* the diaries⟩. VALIDATE implies establishing validity by authoritative affirmation or by factual proof ⟨*validated* the hypothesis by experiments⟩.

con·fir·mand \,kän-fər-'mand\ *n* [L *confirmandus*, gerundive of *confirmare*] (1884) : a candidate for religious confirmation

con·fir·ma·tion \,kän-fər-'mā-shən\ *n* (14c) **1** : an act or process of confirming: as **a (1)** : a Christian rite conferring the gift of the Holy Spirit and among Protestants full church membership **(2)** : a ceremony esp. of Reform Judaism confirming youths in their faith **b** : the ratification of an executive act by a legislative body **2 a** : confirming proof : CORROBORATION **b** : the process of supporting a statement by evidence — **con·fir·ma·tion·al** \-shnəl, -shə-n³l\ *adj*

con·fir·ma·to·ry \kən-'fər-mə-,tōr-ē, -,tor-\ *adj* (1636) : serving to confirm : CORROBORATIVE

con·firmed \kən-'fərmd\ *adj* (14c) **1 a** : marked by long continuance and likely to persist ⟨a ∼ habit⟩ **b** : fixed in habit and unlikely to change ⟨a ∼ do-gooder⟩ **2** : having received the rite of confirmation **syn** see INVETERATE — **con·firm·ed·ly** \-'fər-məd-lē\ *adv* — **con·firmed·ness** \-'fər-məd-nəs, -'fərm(d)-nəs\ *n*

con·fis·ca·ble \kən-'fis-kə-bəl\ *adj* (ca. 1736) : liable to confiscation

con·fis·cat·able \'kän-fə-,skā-tə-bəl\ *adj* (1863) : CONFISCABLE

¹**con·fis·cate** \'kän-fə-,skāt, kən-'fis-kət\ *adj* [L *confiscatus*, pp. of *confiscare* to confiscate, fr. *com-* + *fiscus* treasury] (ca. 1533) **1** : appro-

---

priated by the government : FORFEITED **2** : deprived of property by confiscation

²**con·fis·cate** \'kän-fə-,skāt\ *vt* **-cat·ed; -cat·ing** (1552) **1** : to seize as forfeited to the public treasury **2** : to seize by or as if by authority — **con·fis·ca·tion** \,kän-fə-'skā-shən\ *n* — **con·fis·ca·tor** \'kän-fə-,skā-tər\ *n* — **con·fis·ca·to·ry** \kən-'fis-kə-,tōr-ē, -,tor-\ *adj*

con·fit \kōn-'fē, kōn-, kän-\ *n* [F, fr. OF, preparation, preserves, fr. pp. of *confire* to prepare — more at COMFIT] (1951) : meat (as goose, duck, or pork) that has been cooked and preserved in its own fat

con·fi·te·or \kən-'fē-tē-,ōr, -ər\ *n* [ME, fr. L, lit., I confess, fr. the opening words — more at CONFESS] (13c) : a liturgical form in which sinfulness is acknowledged and intercession for God's mercy requested

con·fi·ture \'kän-fə-,chùr, -,tyùr, -,tùr\ *n* [F, fr. MF, fr. *confit*] (1802) : preserved or candied fruit : JAM

con·fla·grant \kən-'flā-grənt\ *adj* [L *conflagrant-, conflagrans*, prp. of *conflagrare* to burn, fr. *com-* + *flagrare* to burn — more at BLACK] (ca. 1656) : BURNING, BLAZING

con·fla·gra·tion \,kän-flə-'grā-shən\ *n* [L *conflagration-, conflagratio*, fr. *conflagrare*] (ca. 1656) **1** : FIRE; *esp* : a large disastrous fire **2** : CONFLICT, WAR

con·flate \kən-'flāt\ *vt* **con·flat·ed; con·flat·ing** [L *conflatus*, pp. of *conflare* to blow together, fuse, fr. *com-* + *flare* to blow — more at BLOW] (1610) **1 a** : to bring together : FUSE **b** : CONFUSE **2** : to combine (as two readings of a text) into a composite whole

con·fla·tion \-'flā-shən\ *n* (15c) : BLEND, FUSION; *esp* : a composite reading or text

¹**con·flict** \'kän-,flikt\ *n* [ME, fr. L *conflictus* act of striking together, fr. *confligere* to strike together, fr. *com-* + *fligere* to strike — more at PROFLIGATE] (15c) **1** : FIGHT, BATTLE, WAR **2 a** : competitive or opposing action of incompatibles : antagonistic state or action (as of divergent ideas, interests, or persons) **b** : mental struggle resulting from incompatible or opposing needs, drives, wishes, or external or internal demands **3** : the opposition of persons or forces that gives rise to the dramatic action in a drama or fiction **syn** see DISCORD — **con·flict·ful** \'kän-,flikt-fəl\ *adj* — **con·flic·tu·al** \kän-'flik-chə-wəl, kən-, -chəl, -shwəl\ *adj*

²**con·flict** \kən-'flikt, 'kän-,\ *vi* (15c) **1** *archaic* : to contend in warfare **2** : to show antagonism or irreconcilability — **con·flic·tion** \kən-'flik-shən, kän-\ *n* — **con·flic·tive** \kən-'flik-tiv, 'kän-,\ *adj*

con·flict·ed \kən-'flik-təd, 'kän-,\ *adj* (1967) : having or experiencing an emotional conflict ⟨this unhappy and ∼ modern woman —John Updike⟩

conflicting *adj* (1607) : being in conflict, collision, or opposition : INCOMPATIBLE — **con·flict·ing·ly** \-'flik-tiŋ-lē, -,flik-\ *adv*

conflict of interest (1951) : a conflict between the private interests and the official responsibilities of a person in a position of trust

con·flu·ence \'kän-,flü-ən(t)s, kən-'\ *n* (15c) **1** : a coming or flowing together, meeting, or gathering at one point ⟨a happy ∼ of weather and scenery⟩ **2 a** : the flowing together of two or more streams **b** : the place of meeting of two streams **c** : the combined stream formed by conjunction

¹**con·flu·ent** \-ənt\ *adj* [L *confluent-, confluens*, prp. of *confluere* to flow together, fr. *com-* + *fluere* to flow — more at FLUID] (15c) **1** : flowing or coming together; *also* : run together ⟨∼ pustules⟩ **2** : characterized by confluent lesions ⟨∼ smallpox⟩

²**confluent** *n* (1850) : a confluent stream; *broadly* : TRIBUTARY

con·flux \'kän-,fləks\ *n* [ML *confluxus*, fr. L *confluere*] (1606) : CONFLUENCE

con·fo·cal \(,)kän-'fō-kəl\ *adj* (1867) : having the same foci ⟨∼ ellipses⟩ ⟨∼ lenses⟩ — **con·fo·cal·ly** \-kə-lē\ *adv*

con·form \kən-'form\ *vb* [ME, fr. MF *conformer*, fr. L *conformare*, fr. *com-* + *formare* to form, fr. *forma* form] *vt* (14c) : to give the same shape, outline, or contour to : bring into harmony or accord ⟨∼ furrows to the slope of the land⟩ ∼ *vi* **1** : to be similar or identical; *also* : to be in agreement or harmony — used with *to* or *with* **2 a** : to be obedient or compliant — usu. used with *to* **b** : to act in accordance with prevailing standards or customs **syn** see ADAPT — **con·form·er** *n* — **con·form·ism** \-'for-,mi-zəm\ *n* — **con·form·ist** \-mist\ *n or adj*

con·form·able \kən-'for-mə-bəl\ *adj* (1511) **1** : corresponding in form or character : SIMILAR — usu. used with *to* **2** : SUBMISSIVE, COMPLIANT **3** : following in unbroken sequence — used of geologic strata formed under uniform conditions — **con·form·ably** \-blē\ *adv*

con·for·mal \kən-'for-məl, (,)kän-\ *adj* [LL *conformalis* having the same shape, fr. L *com-* + *formalis* formal, fr. *forma*] (1893) **1** : leaving the size of the angle between corresponding curves unchanged ⟨∼ transformation⟩ **2** *of a map* : representing small areas in their true shape

con·for·mance \kən-'for-mən(t)s\ *n* (1606) : CONFORMITY

con·for·ma·tion \,kän-(,)for-'mā-shən, -fər-\ *n* (1511) **1** : the act of conforming or producing conformity : ADAPTATION **2** : formation of something by appropriate arrangement of parts or elements : an assembling into a whole ⟨the gradual ∼ of the embryo⟩ **3 a** : correspondence to a model or plan **b** : STRUCTURE **c** : the shape or proportionate dimensions esp. of an animal **d** : any of the spatial arrangements of a molecule that can be obtained by rotation of the atoms about a single bond — **con·for·ma·tion·al** \-shnəl, -shə-n³l\ *adj*

con·for·mi·ty \kən-'for-mə-tē\ *n, pl* **-ties** (15c) **1** : correspondence in form, manner, or character : AGREEMENT ⟨behaved in ∼ with her beliefs⟩ **2** : an act or instance of conforming **3** : action in accordance with some specified standard or authority ⟨∼ to social custom⟩

con·found \kən-'faùnd, kän-\ *vt* [ME, fr. MF *confondre*, fr. L *confundere* to pour together, confuse, fr. *com-* + *fundere* to pour — more at FOUND] (14c) **1** *archaic* : to bring to ruin : DESTROY **b** : BAFFLE, FRUSTRATE ⟨conferences . . . are not for accomplishment but to ∼ knavish tricks —J. K. Galbraith⟩ **2** *obs* : CONSUME, WASTE **3 a** : to put to shame : DISCOMFIT ⟨a performance that ∼ed the critics⟩ **b** : REFUTE ⟨sought to ∼ his arguments⟩ **4** : DAMN **5** : to throw (a person) into confusion or perplexity **6 a** : to fail to discern differences between : mix up **b** : to increase the confusion of **syn** see PUZZLE — **con·found·er** \-'faùn-dər\ *n* — **con·found·ed·ly** \-din-lē\ *adv*

con·found·ed \kən-'faùn-dəd, (,)kän-', 'kän-,\ *adj* (14c) **1** : CONFUSED, PERPLEXED **2** : DAMNED — **con·found·ed·ly** *adv*

con·fra·ter·ni·ty \,kän-frə-'tər-nə-tē\ *n* [ME *confraternite*, fr. MF *confraternité*, fr. ML *confraternitat-, confraternitas*, fr. *confrater* fellow, brother, fr. L *com-* + *frater* brother — more at BROTHER] (15c)   **1** : a society devoted esp. to a religious or charitable cause   **2** : fraternal union

con·frere *also* **con·frère** \'kän-ˌfrer, kōⁿ-ˌ, kän-', kōⁿ-', kən-'\ *n* [ME, fr. MF, trans. of ML *confrater*] (15c) : COLLEAGUE, COMRADE

con·front \kən-'frənt\ *vt* [MF *confronter* to border on, confront, fr. ML *confrontare* to bound, fr. L *com-* + *front-*, *frons* forehead, front] (ca. 1568)   **1** : to face esp. in challenge : OPPOSE   **2 a** : to cause to meet : bring face-to-face ⟨~ a reader with statistics⟩   **b** : to meet face-to-face : ENCOUNTER ⟨~ed the possibility of failure⟩ — **con·front·al** \-'frən-t°l\ *n* — **con·front·er** *n*

con·fron·ta·tion \ˌkän-(ˌ)frən-'tā-shən\ *n* (1632) : the act of confronting : the state of being confronted: as   **a** : a face-to-face meeting   **b** : the clashing of forces or ideas : CONFLICT   **c** : COMPARISON ⟨the flashbacks bring into meaningful ~ present and past, near and far —R. J. Clements⟩ — **con·fron·ta·tion·al** \-shnəl, -shə-n°l\ *adj* — **con·fron·ta·tion·ist** \-sh(ə-)nist\ *n or adj*

Con·fu·cian \kən-'fyü-shən\ *adj* (1837) : of or relating to the Chinese philosopher Confucius or his teachings or followers — **Confucian** *n* — **Con·fu·cian·ism** \-shə-ˌni-zəm\ *n* — **Con·fu·cian·ist** \-nist\ *n or adj*

con·fuse \kən-'fyüz\ *vt* **con·fused**; **con·fus·ing** [back-formation fr. ME *confused* perplexed, fr. MF *confus*, fr. L *confusus*, pp. of *confundere*] (14c)   **1** *archaic* : to bring to ruin   **2 a** : to make embarrassed : ABASH   **b** : to disturb in mind or purpose : THROW OFF   **3 a** : to make indistinct : BLUR ⟨stop *confusing* the issue⟩   **b** : to mix indiscriminately : JUMBLE   **c** : to fail to differentiate from an often similar or related other ⟨~ money with comfort⟩ — **con·fus·ing·ly** \-'fyü-ziŋ-lē\ *adv*

con·fused \-'fyüzd\ *adj* (14c)   **1** : being perplexed or disconcerted ⟨the ~ students⟩   **2** : INDISTINGUISHABLE ⟨a zigzag, crisscross, ~ trail — Harry Hervey⟩   **3** : being disordered or mixed up ⟨a contradictory and often ~ story⟩ — **con·fused·ly** \-'fyü-zəd-lē, -'fyüzd-\ *adv* — **con·fused·ness** \-'fyü-zəd-nəs, -'fyüzd-\ *n*

con·fu·sion \kən-'fyü-zhən\ *n* (14c)   **1** : an act or instance of confusing   **2 a** : the quality or state of being confused   **b** : a confused mass or mixture ⟨a ~ of voices⟩ — **con·fu·sion·al** \-'fyüzh-nəl, -'fyü-zhə-n°l\ *adj*

con·fu·ta·tion \ˌkän-fyü-'tā-shən\ *n* (15c)   **1** : the act or process of confuting : REFUTATION   **2** : something (as an argument or statement) that confutes — **con·fu·ta·tive** \kən-'fyü-tə-tiv\ *adj*

con·fute \kən-'fyüt\ *vt* **con·fut·ed**; **con·fut·ing** [L *confutare* to check, silence] (1529)   **1** : to overwhelm in argument : refute conclusively ⟨Elijah . . . *confuted* the prophets of Baal —G. B. Shaw⟩   **2** *obs* : CONFOUND — **con·fut·er** *n*

con·ga \'käŋ-gə\ *n* [AmerSp, prob. fr. fem. of *congo* Negro, fr. *Congo*, region in Africa] (1935)   **1** : a Cuban dance of African origin involving three steps followed by a kick and performed by a group usu. in single file   **2** : a tall barrel-shaped or tapering drum of Afro-Cuban origin that is played with the hands

conga line *n* (1947) : SNAKE DANCE 2

con·gé \kōⁿ-'zhā, 'kän-ˌzhā\ *n* [F, fr. L *commeatus* going back and forth, leave, fr. *commeare* to go back and forth, fr. *com-* + *meare* to go — more at PERMEATE] (1702)   **1 a** : a formal permission to depart   **b** : DISMISSAL   **2** : a ceremonious bow   **3** : FAREWELL   **4** : an architectural molding of concave profile — see MOLDING illustration

con·geal \kən-'jē(ə)l\ *vb* [ME *congelen*, fr. MF *congeler*, fr. L *congelare*, fr. *com-* + *gelare* to freeze — more at COLD] *vt* (14c)   **1** : to change from a fluid to a solid state by or as if by cold   **2** : to make viscid or curdled : COAGULATE   **3** : to make rigid, fixed, or immobile ~ *vi* : to become congealed : SOLIDIFY — **con·geal·ment** \-mənt\ *n*

con·gee \'kän-(ˌ)jē, -(ˌ)zhē\ *n* (14c) : CONGÉ

con·ge·la·tion \ˌkän-jə-'lā-shən\ *n* (15c) : the process or result of congealing

conga 2

con·ge·ner \'kän-jə-nər, kən-'jē-\ *n* [L, of the same kind, fr. *com-* + *gener-*, *genus* kind — more at KIN] (ca. 1736)   **1** : a member of the same taxonomic genus as another plant or animal   **2** : a person or thing resembling another in nature or action ⟨the New England private schools and their ~s west of the Alleghenies —Oliver La Farge⟩ — **con·ge·ner·ic** \ˌkän-jə-'ner-ik\ *adj* — **con·ge·ner·ous** \kən-'jē-nə-rəs, -'jē-nə-, (ˌ)kän-\ *adj*

con·ge·nial \kən-'jē-nē-əl, -'jēn-yəl\ *adj* [*com-* + *genius*] (ca. 1625)   **1** : having the same nature, disposition, or tastes : KINDRED   **2 a** : existing or associated together harmoniously   **b** : PLEASANT; *esp* : agreeably suited to one's nature, tastes, or outlook   **c** : SOCIABLE, GENIAL — **con·ge·nial·i·ty** \-ˌjē-nē-'a-lə-tē, -ˌjēn-'ya-\ *n* — **con·ge·nial·ly** \-'jē-nē-ə-lē, -'jēn-yə-\ *adv*

con·gen·i·tal \kən-'je-nə-t°l, kän-\ *adj* [L *congenitus*, fr. *com-* + *geni-tus*, pp. of *gignere* to bring forth — more at KIN] (1796)   **1 a** : existing at or dating from birth ⟨~ deafness⟩   **b** : constituting an essential characteristic : INHERENT ⟨~ fear of snakes⟩   **c** : acquired during development in the uterus and not through heredity ⟨~ syphilis⟩   **2** : being such by nature ⟨~ liar⟩   *syn* see INNATE — **con·gen·i·tal·ly** \-t°l-ē\ *adv*

con·ger eel \'käŋ-gər-\ *n* [ME *congre*, fr. OF, fr. L *congr-*, *conger*, prob. fr. Gk *gongros*] (1602) : a large strictly marine scaleless eel (*Conger oceanicus*) of the Atlantic; *broadly* : any of various related eels (family Congridae)

con·ge·ries \'kän-jə-(ˌ)rēz\ *n*, *pl* **congeries** *same*\ [L, fr. *congerere*] (ca. 1619) : AGGREGATION, COLLECTION

con·gest \kən-'jest\ *vb* [L *congestus*, pp. of *congerere* to bring together, fr. *com-* + *gerere* to bear] *vt* (1758)   **1** : to cause an excessive fullness of the blood vessels of (as an organ)   **2** : CLOG ⟨traffic ~ed the highways⟩   **3** : to concentrate in a small or narrow space ~ *vi* : to become congested — **con·ges·tion** \-'jes-chən, -'jesh-\ *n* — **con·ges·tive** \-'jes-tiv\ *adj*

congestive heart failure *n* (1930) : heart failure in which the heart is unable to maintain an adequate circulation of blood in the bodily tissues or to pump out the venous blood returned to it by the veins

con·glo·bate \kän-'glō-ˌbāt, kən-\ *vt* **-bat·ed**; **-bat·ing** [L *conglobatus*, pp. of *conglobare*, fr. *com-* + *globus* globe] (1635) : to form into a round compact mass — **con·glo·bate** \-bət, -ˌbāt\ *adj* — **con·glo·ba·tion** \ˌkän-(ˌ)glō-'bā-shən\ *n*

con·globe \kän-'glōb, kən-\ *vt* **con·globed**; **con·glob·ing** (1535) : CONGLOBATE

¹con·glom·er·ate \kən-'gläm-rət, -'glä-mə-\ *adj* [L *conglomeratus*, pp. of *conglomerare* to roll together, fr. *com-* + *glomerare* to wind into a ball, fr. *glomer-*, *glomus* ball — more at CLAM] (1572) : made up of parts from various sources or of various kinds

²con·glom·er·ate \-ˌrāt\ *vb* **-at·ed**; **-at·ing** *vi* (1642) : to gather into a mass or coherent whole ⟨numbers of dull people *conglomerated* round her —Virginia Woolf⟩ ~ *vt* : ACCUMULATE — **con·glom·er·a·tive** \-'gläm-rə-tiv, -'glä-mə-, -mə-ˌrā-\ *adj* — **con·glom·er·a·tor** \-'glä-mə-ˌrā-tər\ *n*

³con·glom·er·ate \-'gläm-rət, -'glä-mə-\ *n* (1818)   **1** : a composite mass or mixture; *esp* : rock composed of rounded fragments varying from small pebbles to large boulders in a cement (as of hardened clay)   **2** : a widely diversified corporation — **con·glom·er·at·ic** \kən-ˌglä-mə-'ra-tik, ˌkän-\ *adj*

con·glom·er·a·teur \kən-ˌglä-mə-rə-'tər, -'tyùr, -'tùr\ *n* [³*conglomerate* + *-eur* (as in *entrepreneur*)] (1969) : a person who forms or heads a conglomerate : CONGLOMERATOR

con·glom·er·a·tion \kən-ˌglä-mə-'rā-shən, ˌkän-\ *n* (1626)   **1** : the act of conglomerating : the state of being conglomerated   **2** : something conglomerated : a mixed mass or collection

con·glu·ti·nate \kən-'glü-t°n-ˌāt, kän-\ *vb* **-nat·ed**; **-nat·ing** [L *conglutinatus*, pp. of *conglutinare* to glue together, fr. *com-* + *glutin-*, *gluten* glue — more at GLUTEN] *vt* (1546) : to unite by or as if by a glutinous substance ~ *vi* : to become conglutinated ⟨blood platelets ~ in blood clotting⟩ — **con·glu·ti·na·tion** \kən-ˌglü-t°n-'ā-shən, kän-\ *n*

Congo red *n* [*Congo*, territory in Africa] (1885) : an azo dye $C_{32}H_{22}N_6Na_2O_6S_2$ that is red in alkaline and blue in acid solution and that is used esp. as an indicator and as a biological stain

con·gou \'käŋ-(ˌ)gō, -(ˌ)gü\ *n* [prob. fr. Chin (Xiamen) *kong-hu* pains taken] (1725) : a black tea from China

con·grat·u·late \kən-'gra-chə-ˌlāt, -'gra-jə-\ *vt* **-lat·ed**; **-lat·ing** [L *congratulatus*, pp. of *congratulari* to wish joy, fr. *com-* + *gratulari* to wish joy, fr. *gratus* pleasing — more at GRACE] (1539)   **1** *archaic* : to express sympathetic pleasure at (an event)   **2** : to express vicarious pleasure to (a person) on the occasion of success or good fortune; *also* : to feel pleased with ⟨*congratulating* herself for a job well done⟩   **3** *obs* : SALUTE, GREET — **con·grat·u·la·tor** \-ˌlā-tər\ *n* — **con·grat·u·la·to·ry** \-lə-ˌtōr-ē, -ˌtór-\ *adj*

con·grat·u·la·tion \kən-ˌgra-chə-'lā-shən, -ˌgra-jə-\ *n* (15c)   **1** : the act of congratulating   **2** : a congratulatory expression — usu. used in pl.

con·gre·gant \'kän-gri-gənt\ *n* (1886) : one that congregates; *specif* : a member of a congregation

¹con·gre·gate \-ˌgāt\ *vb* **-gat·ed**; **-gat·ing** [ME, fr. L *congregatus*, pp. of *congregare*, fr. *com-* + *greg-*, *grex* flock] *vt* (15c) : to collect into a group or crowd : ASSEMBLE ~ *vi* : to come together into a group, crowd, or assembly   *syn* see GATHER — **con·gre·ga·tor** \-ˌgā-tər\ *n*

²con·gre·gate \-gət\ *adj* (1900) : providing or being group services or facilities designed esp. for elderly persons requiring supportive services ⟨~ housing⟩

con·gre·ga·tion \ˌkäŋ-gri-'gā-shən\ *n* (14c)   **1 a** : an assembly of persons : GATHERING; *esp* : an assembly of persons met for worship and religious instruction   **b** : a religious community: as   (1) : an organized body of believers in a particular locality   (2) : a Roman Catholic religious institute with only simple vows   (3) : a group of monasteries forming an independent subdivision of an order   **2** : the act or an instance of congregating or bringing together : the state of being congregated   **3** : a body of cardinals and officials forming an administrative division of the papal curia

con·gre·ga·tion·al \-shnəl, -shə-n°l\ *adj* (1639)   **1** : of or relating to a congregation   **2** *cap* : of or relating to a body of Protestant churches deriving from the English Independents of the 17th century and affirming the essential importance and the autonomy of the local congregation   **3** : of or relating to church government placing final authority in the assembly of the local congregation — **con·gre·ga·tion·al·ism** \-shnə-ˌli-zəm, -shə-n°l-ˌi-\ *n*, *often cap* — **con·gre·ga·tion·al·ist** \-shnə-list, -shə-n°l-ist\ *n or adj*, *often cap*

con·gress \'käŋ-grəs *also* -rəs, *Brit usu* 'käŋ-ˌgres\ *n* [L *congressus*, fr. *congredi* to come together, fr. *com-* + *gradi* to go — more at GRADE] (1528)   **1 a** : the act or action of coming together and meeting   **b** : COITUS   **2** : a formal meeting of delegates for discussion and usu. action on some question   **3** : the supreme legislative body of a nation and esp. of a republic   **4** : an association usu. made up of delegates from constituent organizations   **5** : a single meeting or session of a group — **con·gres·sio·nal** \kən-'gresh-nəl, kän-, -'gre-shə-n°l\ *adj* — **con·gres·sio·nal·ly** *adv*

congressional district *n* (1812) : a territorial division of a state from which a member of the U.S. House of Representatives is elected

Congressional Medal *n* (1910) : MEDAL OF HONOR

con·gress·man \'käŋ-grəs-mən\ *n* (1780) : a member of a congress; *esp* : a member of the U.S. House of Representatives

con·gress·peo·ple \-(g)rəs-ˌpē-pəl\ *n pl* (1973) : congressmen or congresswomen

con·gress·per·son \-(g)rəs-ˌpər-sən\ *n* (1972) : a congressman or congresswoman

con·gress·wom·an \-(g)rəs-ˌwù-mən\ *n* (1917) : a female member of a congress; *esp* : a female member of the U.S. House of Representatives

con·gru·ence \kən-'grü-ən(t)s, 'käŋ-grü-ən(t)s\ *n* (1533)   **1** : the quality or state of agreeing, coinciding, or being congruent   **2** : a statement that two numbers or geometric figures are congruent

con·gru·en·cy \-ən(t)-sē\ *n*, *pl* **-cies** (15c) : CONGRUENCE

con·gru·ent \kən-'grü-ənt, 'käŋ-grü-ənt\ *adj* [ME, fr. L *congruent-*,

---

\ə\ abut \ᵊ\ kitten, F table \ər\ further \a\ ash \ā\ ace \ä\ mop, mar \aú\ out \ch\ chin \e\ bet \ē\ easy \g\ go \i\ hit \ī\ ice \j\ job \ŋ\ sing \ō\ go \ó\ law \ói\ boy \th\ thin \t̲h̲\ the \ü\ loot \ú\ foot \y\ yet \zh\ vision \å, k̲, ⁿ, œ, œ̄, ᵫ, ū̄, ᵿ\ *see* Guide to Pronunciation

congruens, prp. of *congruere* (15c) **1** : CONGRUOUS **2** : superposable so as to be coincident throughout **3** : having the difference divisible by a given modulus ⟨12 is ∼ to 2 (modulo 5) since 12−2=2·5⟩ — **con·gru·ent·ly** *adv*

con·gru·i·ty \kən-'grü-ə-tē, kän-\ *n, pl* **-ties** (14c) **1** : the quality or state of being congruent or congruous **2** : a point of agreement

con·gru·ous \'käŋ-grü-əs\ *adj* [L *congruus*, fr. *congruere* to come together, agree] (1599) **1 a** : being in agreement, harmony, or correspondence **b** : conforming to the circumstances or requirements of a situation : APPROPRIATE ⟨a ∼ room to work in —G. B. Shaw⟩ **2** : marked or enhanced by harmonious agreement among constituent elements ⟨a ∼ theme⟩ — **con·gru·ous·ly** *adv* — **con·gru·ous·ness** *n*

¹con·ic \'kä-nik\ *adj* (1570) **1** : of or relating to a cone **2** : CONICAL — **co·nic·i·ty** \kō-'ni-sə-tē\ *n*

²conic *n* (1879) : CONIC SECTION

con·i·cal \'kä-ni-kəl\ *adj* (1570) : resembling a cone esp. in shape — **con·i·cal·ly** \-k(ə-)lē\ *adv*

conic section *n* (1664) **1** : a plane curve, line, pair of intersecting lines, or point that is the intersection of or bounds the intersection of a plane and a cone with two nappes **2** : a curve generated by a point which always moves so that the ratio of its distance from a fixed point to its distance from a fixed line is constant

conic section 1: *1* straight lines, *2* circle, *3* ellipse, *4* parabola, *5* hyperbola

co·nid·i·o·phore \kə-'ni-dē-ə-ˌfȯr, -ˌför\ *n* [NL *conidium* + ISV *-phore*] (1874) : a structure that bears conidia; *specif* : a specialized hyphal branch of some fungi that produces conidia usu. by the successive cutting off of parts of the sporophore through the growth of septa

co·nid·i·um \kə-'ni-dē-əm\ *n, pl* **-ia** \-dē-ə\ [NL, fr. Gk *konis* dust — more at INCINERATE] (1856) : an asexual spore produced on a conidiophore — **co·nid·i·al** \-dē-əl\ *adj*

co·ni·fer \'kä-nə-fər *also* 'kō-\ *n* [ultim. fr. L *conifer* cone-bearing, fr. *conus* cone + *-fer*] (ca. 1841) : any of an order (Coniferales) of mostly evergreen trees and shrubs including forms (as pines) with true cones and others (as yews) with an arillate fruit — **co·nif·er·ous** \kō-'ni-f(ə-)rəs, kə-\ *adj*

co·ni·ine \'kō-nē-ˌēn\ *n* [G *Koniin*, fr. LL *conium* hemlock, fr. Gk *kō·neion*] (1831) : a poisonous alkaloid $C_8H_{17}N$ found in poison hemlock (*Conium maculatum*)

con·jec·tur·al \kən-'jek-chə-rəl, -'jek-shrəl\ *adj* (1553) **1** : of the nature of or involving or based on conjecture **2** : given to conjectures — **con·jec·tur·al·ly** *adv*

¹con·jec·ture \kən-'jek-chər\ *n* [ME, fr. MF or L; MF, fr. L *conjectura*, fr. *conjectus*, pp. of *conicere*, lit., to throw together, fr. *com-* + *jacere* to throw — more at JET] (14c) **1** *obs* **a** : interpretation of omens **b** : SUPPOSITION **2 a** : inference from defective or presumptive evidence **b** : a conclusion deduced by surmise or guesswork **c** : a proposition (as in mathematics) before it has been proved or disproved

²conjecture *vb* **-tured; -tur·ing** \-'jek-chə-riŋ, -'jek-shriŋ\ *vt* (15c) **1** : to arrive at by conjecture **2** : to make conjectures as to ∼ *vi* : to form conjectures — **con·jec·tur·er** \-'jek-chər-ər\ *n*

con·join \kən-'jȯin, kän-\ *vb* [ME, fr. MF *conjoindre*, fr. L *conjungere*, fr. *com-* + *jungere* to join — more at YOKE] *vt* (14c) : to join together (as separate entities) for a common purpose ∼ *vi* : to join together for a common purpose

con·joined \-'jȯind\ *adj* (1570) : being, coming, or brought together so as to meet, touch, or overlap ⟨∼ heads on a coin⟩

con·joint \-'jȯint\ *adj* [ME, fr. MF, pp. of *conjoindre*] (1725) **1** : UNITED, CONJOINED **2** : related to, made up of, or carried on by two or more in combination : JOINT — **con·joint·ly** *adv*

con·ju·gal \'kän-ji-gəl *also* kən-'jü-\ *adj* [MF or L; MF, fr. L *conjugalis*, fr. *conjug-, conjux* husband, wife, fr. *conjungere* to join, unite in marriage] (1545) : of or relating to the married state or to married persons and their relations : CONNUBIAL — **con·ju·gal·i·ty** \ˌkän-ji-'ga-lə-tē, -jü-\ *n* — **con·ju·gal·ly** \'kän-ji-gə-lē *also* kən-'jü-\ *adv*

conjugal rights *n pl* (ca. 1891) : the sexual rights or privileges implied by and involved in the marriage relationship : the right of sexual intercourse between husband and wife

con·ju·gant \'kän-ji-gənt\ *n* (1910) : either of a pair of conjugating gametes or organisms

¹con·ju·gate \'kän-ji-gət, -jə-ˌgāt\ *adj* [ME *conjugat*, fr. L *conjugatus*, pp. of *conjugare* to unite, fr. *com-* + *jugare* to join, fr. *jugum* yoke — more at YOKE] (15c) **1 a** : joined together esp. in pairs : COUPLED **b** : acting or operating as if joined **2 a** : having features in common but opposite or inverse in some particular **b** : relating to or being conjugate complex numbers ⟨complex roots occurring in ∼ pairs⟩ **3** *of an acid or base* : related by the difference of a proton ⟨the acid NH_4 and the base NH_3 are ∼ to each other⟩ **4** : having the same derivation and therefore usu. some likeness in meaning ⟨∼ words⟩ **5** *of two leaves of a book* : forming a single piece — **con·ju·gate·ly** *adv* — **con·ju·gate·ness** *n*

²con·ju·gate \-jə-ˌgāt\ *vb* **-gat·ed; -gat·ing** *vt* (1530) **1** : to give in prescribed order the various inflectional forms of — used esp. of a verb **2** : to join together ∼ *vi* **1** : to become joined together **2 a** : to pair and fuse in conjugation **b** : to pair in synapsis

³conjugate *same as* ¹\ *n* (ca. 1586) **1** : something conjugate : a product of conjugating **2** : CONJUGATE COMPLEX NUMBER **3** : an element of a mathematical group that is equal to a given element of the group multiplied on the right by another element and on the left by the inverse of the latter element

conjugate complex number *n* (ca. 1909) : one of two complex numbers differing only in the sign of the imaginary part

con·ju·gat·ed \-ˌgā-təd\ *adj* (1882) **1** : formed by the union of two compounds or united with another compound ⟨∼ bile acids⟩ **2** : relating to or containing a system of two double bonds separated by a single bond ⟨∼ fatty acids⟩

conjugated protein *n* (ca. 1909) : a compound of a protein with a nonprotein ⟨hemoglobin is a *conjugated protein*⟩ — compare SIMPLE PROTEIN

con·ju·ga·tion \ˌkän-jə-'gā-shən\ *n* (15c) **1 a** : a schematic arrangement of the inflectional forms of a verb **b** : verb inflection **c** : a class of verbs having the same type of inflectional forms ⟨the weak ∼⟩ **d** : a set of the simple or derivative inflectional forms of a verb esp. in Sanskrit or the Semitic languages ⟨the causative ∼⟩ **2** : the act of conjugating : the state of being conjugated **3 a** : fusion of usu. similar gametes with ultimate union of their nuclei that among lower thallophytes replaces the typical fertilization of higher forms **b** : temporary cytoplasmic union with exchange of nuclear material that is the usual sexual process in ciliated protozoans **c** : the one-way transfer of DNA between bacteria in cellular contact — **con·ju·ga·tion·al** \-shnəl, -shə-nᵊl\ *adj* — **con·ju·ga·tion·al·ly** *adv*

¹con·junct \kən-'jəŋ(k)t, kän-\ *adj* [ME, fr. L *conjunctus*, pp. of *conjungere*] (15c) **1** : UNITED, JOINED **2** : JOINT **3** : relating to melodic progression by intervals of no more than a major second — compare DISJUNCT

²con·junct \'kän-jəŋ(k)t\ *n* (1667) **1** : something joined or associated with another; *specif* : one of the components of a conjunction **2** : an adverb or adverbial (as *so, in addition, however, secondly*) that indicates the speaker's or writer's assessment of the connection between linguistic units (as clauses)

con·junc·tion \kən-'jəŋ(k)-shən\ *n* (14c) **1** : the act or an instance of conjoining : the state of being conjoined : COMBINATION **2** : occurrence together in time or space : CONCURRENCE **3 a** : the apparent meeting or passing of two or more celestial bodies in the same degree of the zodiac **b** : a configuration in which two celestial bodies have their least apparent separation **4** : an uninflected linguistic form that joins together sentences, clauses, phrases, or words **5** : a complex sentence in logic true if and only if each of its components is true — **con·junc·tion·al** \-shnəl, -shə-nᵊl\ *adj* — **con·junc·tion·al·ly** *adv*

con·junc·ti·va \ˌkän-jəŋ(k)-'tī-və, kən-\ *n, pl* **-vas** *or* **-vae** \-(ˌ)vē\ [NL, fr. LL, fem. of *conjunctivus* conjoining, fr. L *conjunctus*] (14c) : the mucous membrane that lines the inner surface of the eyelids and is continued over the forepart of the eyeball — see EYE illustration — **con·junc·ti·val** \-vəl\ *adj*

con·junc·tive \kən-'jəŋ(k)-tiv\ *adj* (1581) **1** : CONNECTIVE **2** : CONJUNCT, CONJOINED **3** : being or functioning like a conjunction **4** : COPULATIVE 1a — **conjunctive** *n* — **con·junc·tive·ly** *adv*

con·junc·ti·vi·tis \kən-ˌjəŋ(k)-ti-'vī-təs\ *n* (1835) : inflammation of the conjunctiva

con·junc·ture \kən-'jəŋ(k)-chər\ *n* (1605) **1** : CONJUNCTION, UNION **2** : a combination of circumstances or events usu. producing a crisis : JUNCTURE

con·ju·ra·tion \ˌkän-jù-'rā-shən, ˌkən-\ *n* (14c) **1** : the act or process of conjuring : INCANTATION **2** : an expression or trick used in conjuring **3** : a solemn appeal : ADJURATION

con·jure *vt* 2 & *vi senses* 'kän-jər *also* 'kən-; *vt 1* kən-'jür\ *vb* **conjured; con·jur·ing** \'känj-riŋ, 'kän-jə-, 'kənj-; 'kən-jə-, kən-'jür-iŋ\ [ME, fr. OF *conjurer*, fr. L *conjurare* to swear together, fr. *com-* + *jurare* to swear — more at JURY] *vt* (13c) **1** : to charge or entreat earnestly or solemnly **2 a** : to summon by or as if by invocation or incantation **b** (1) : to affect or effect by or as if by magic (2) : IMAGINE, CONTRIVE — often used with *up* ⟨we ∼ up our own metaphors for our own needs —R. J. Kaufmann⟩ (3) : to bring to mind ⟨words that ∼ pleasant images⟩ ∼ *vi* **1 a** : to summon a devil or spirit by invocation or incantation **b** : to practice magical arts **c** : to use a conjurer's tricks : JUGGLE

con·jur·er *or* **con·ju·ror** \'kän-jər-ər, 'kən-\ *n* (14c) **1** : one that practices magic arts : WIZARD **2** : one that performs feats of sleight of hand and illusion : MAGICIAN, JUGGLER

¹conk \'käŋk, 'kȯŋk\ *vt* [E slang *conk* head] (1821) : to hit esp. on the head : KNOCK OUT

²conk *n* [prob. alter. of *conch*] (1851) : the visible fruiting body of a bracket fungus; *also* : decay caused by such a fungus — **conky** \'käŋ-kē, 'kȯŋ-\ *adj*

³conk *vi* [prob. imit.] (1918) **1** : BREAK DOWN; *esp* : STALL — usu. used with *out* ⟨the motor suddenly ∼*ed* out⟩ **2 a** : FAINT **b** : to go to sleep — usu. used with *off* or *out* ⟨∼*ed* out for a while after lunch⟩ **c** : DIE ⟨I caught pneumonia. I almost ∼*ed* —Truman Capote⟩

⁴conk *vt* [prob. by shortening & alter. fr. *congolene* preparation used for straightening hair] (1950) : to straighten out (hair) usu. by the use of chemicals

⁵conk *n* (1965) : a hairstyle in which the hair is straightened out and flattened down or lightly waved — called also *process*

conk·er \'käŋ-kər\ *n* [*conch* + ²*-er*, fr. the original use of a snail shell on a string in the game] (ca. 1886) **1** : a horse chestnut esp. when used in conkers **2** *pl* : a game in which each player swings a horse chestnut on a string to try to break one held by the opponent

con mo·to \kän-'mō-(ˌ)tō, kōn-\ *adv* [It] (ca. 1854) : with movement : in a spirited manner — used as a direction in music

¹conn \'kän\ *vt* [alter. of ME *condien* to conduct, fr. MF *conduire*, fr. L *conducere* — more at CONDUCE] (1626) : to conduct or direct the steering of (as a ship)

²conn *n* (1825) : the control exercised by one who conns a ship

con·nate \kä-'nāt, 'kä-\ *adj* [LL *connatus*, pp. of *connasci* to be born together, fr. L *com-* + *nasci* to be born — more at NATION] (1641) **1** : AKIN, CONGENIAL **2** : INNATE, INBORN **3** : congenitally or firmly united ⟨∼ leaves⟩ **4** : born or originated together **5** : entrapped in sediments at the time of their deposition ⟨∼ water⟩ — **con·nate·ly** *adv*

con·nat·u·ral \kä-'nach-rəl, kə-, 'na-chə-\ *adj* [ML *connaturalis*, fr. L *com-* + *naturalis* natural] (1592) **1** : connected by nature : INBORN **2** : of the same nature — **con·nat·u·ral·i·ty** \ˌna-chə-'ra-lə-tē\ *n* — **con·nat·u·ral·ly** \-'nach-rə-lē, -'na-chə-\ *adv*

con·nect \kə-'nekt\ *vb* [ME, fr. L *conectere, connectere*, fr. *com-* + *nectere* to bind] *vi* (15c) **1** : to become joined ⟨the two rooms ∼ by a hallway⟩ ⟨ideas that ∼ easily to form a theory⟩ **2** : to make a successful hit, shot, or throw ⟨∼*ed* for a home run⟩ ⟨∼*ed* on 60 percent of his shots —*N.Y. Times*⟩ **3** : to have or establish a rapport ⟨tried to ∼ with the younger generation⟩ ∼ *vt* **1** : to join or fasten together usu. by something intervening **2** : to place or establish in relationship *syn* see JOIN — **con·nect·able** *also* **con·nect·ible** \-'nek-tə-bəl\ *adj* — **con·nec·tor** *also* **con·nect·er** \-'nek-tər\ *n*

connected *adj* (1712) **1** : joined or linked together **2** : having the parts or elements logically linked together ⟨presented a thoroughly ∼ view of the problem⟩ **3** : related by blood or marriage **4** : having social, professional, or commercial relationships ⟨a well-*connected* lawyer⟩ **5** *of a set* : having the property that any two of its points can be joined by a line completely contained in the set; *also* : incapable of being separated into two or more closed disjoint subsets — **con·nect·ed·ly** *adv* — **con·nect·ed·ness** *n*

connecting rod *n* (1839) : a rod that transmits motion from a reciprocating part of a machine (as a piston) to a rotating part or vice versa

con·nec·tion \kə-'nek-shən\ *n* [L *connexion-, connexio,* fr. *conectere*] (14c) **1** : the act of connecting : the state of being connected: as **a** : causal or logical relation or sequence ⟨the ~ between two ideas⟩ **b** (1) : contextual relation or association ⟨in this ~ the word has a different meaning⟩ (2) : relationship in fact ⟨wanted in ~ with a robbery⟩ **c** : a relation of personal intimacy (as of family ties) **d** : COHERENCE, CONTINUITY **2 a** : something that connects : LINK ⟨a loose ~ in the wiring⟩ **b** : a means of communication or transport **3** : a person connected with another esp. by marriage, kinship, or common interest ⟨has powerful ~s⟩ **4** : a political, social, professional, or commercial relationship : as **a** : POSITION, JOB **b** : an arrangement to execute orders or advance interests of another ⟨a firm's foreign ~s⟩ **c** : a source of contraband (as illegal drugs) **5** : a set of persons associated together: as **a** : DENOMINATION **b** : CLAN — **con·nec·tion·al** \-shnəl, -shə-nᵊl\ *adj*

¹**con·nec·tive** \kə-'nek-tiv\ *adj* (ca. 1660) : serving to connect — **con·nec·tive·ly** *adv*

²**connective** *n* (1751) : something that connects: as **a** : a linguistic form that connects words or word groups **b** : the tissue connecting the pollen sacs of an anther **c** : a logical term (as *or, if-then, and, not*) or a symbol for it that relates propositions in such a way that the truth or falsity of the resulting statement is determined by the truth or falsity of the components

connective tissue *n* (1846) : a tissue of mesodermal origin rich in intercellular substance or interlacing processes with little tendency for the cells to come together in sheets or masses; *specif* : connective tissue of stellate or spindle-shaped cells with interlacing processes that pervades, supports, and binds together other tissues and forms ligaments, tendons, and aponeuroses

con·nec·tiv·i·ty \(,)kä-,nek-'ti-və-tē, kə-\ *n, pl* **-ties** (1893) : the quality or state of being connective or connected ⟨~ of a surface⟩; *esp* : the ability to connect to or communicate with another computer or computer system

Con·ne·ma·ra \,kä-nə-'mär-ə, ,kö-\ *n* [*Connemara,* Ireland] (ca. 1952) : any of a breed of rugged ponies developed in Ireland

con·nex·ion \kə-'nek-shən\ *chiefly Brit var of* CONNECTION

con·ning tower \'kä-niŋ-\ *n* (1886) : a raised structure on the deck of a submarine used esp. formerly for navigation and attack direction

con·nip·tion \kə-'nip-shən\ *n* [origin unknown] (1833) : a fit of rage, hysteria, or alarm ⟨went into ~s⟩

con·niv·ance \kə-'nī-vən(t)s\ *n* (1593) : the act of conniving; *esp* : knowledge of and active or passive consent to wrongdoing

con·nive \kə-'nīv\ *vi* **con·nived; con·niv·ing** [F or L; F *conniver,* fr. L *conivēre, connivēre* to close the eyes, connive, fr. *com-* + *-nivēre* (akin to *nictare* to wink); akin to OE & OHG *hnigan* to bow] (1601) **1** : to pretend ignorance of or fail to take action against something one ought to oppose **2 a** : to be indulgent or in secret sympathy : WINK **b** : to cooperate secretly or have a secret understanding **3** : CONSPIRE, INTRIGUE — **con·niv·er** *n*

conning tower

con·ni·vent \-'nī-vənt\ *adj* [L *conivent-, conivens,* prp. of *conivēre*] (1757) : converging but not fused ⟨~ stamens⟩

con·nois·seur \,kä-nə-'sər *also* -'sùr\ *n* [obs. F (now *connaisseur*), fr. OF *connoisseor,* fr. *connoistre* to know, fr. L *cognoscere* — more at COGNITION] (1714) **1** : EXPERT; *esp* : one who understands the details, technique, or principles of an art and is competent to act as a critical judge **2** : one who enjoys with discrimination and appreciation of subtleties ⟨a ~ of fine wines⟩ — **con·nois·seur·ship** \-,ship\ *n*

con·no·ta·tion \,kä-nə-'tā-shən\ *n* (1532) **1 a** : the suggesting of a meaning by a word apart from the thing it explicitly names or describes **b** : something suggested by a word or thing : IMPLICATION ⟨the ~s of comfort that surrounded that old chair⟩ **2** : the signification of something ⟨that abuse of logic which consists in moving counters about as if they were known entities with a fixed ~ —W. R. Inge⟩ **3** : an essential property or group of properties of a thing named by a term in logic — compare DENOTATION — **con·no·ta·tion·al** \-shnəl, -shə-nᵊl\ *adj*

con·no·ta·tive \'kä-nə-,tā-tiv, kə-'nō-tə-tiv\ *adj* (1614) **1** : connoting or tending to connote **2** : relating to connotation — **con·no·ta·tive·ly** *adv*

con·note \kə-'nōt, kä-\ *vt* **con·not·ed; con·not·ing** [ML *connotare,* fr. L *com-* + *notare* to note] (1665) **1** : to be associated with or inseparable from as a consequence or concomitant ⟨the remorse so often *connoted* by guilt⟩ **2 a** : to convey in addition to exact explicit meaning ⟨all the misery that poverty ~s⟩ **b** : to imply as a logical connotation

con·nu·bi·al \kə-'nü-bē-əl, -'nyü-\ *adj* [L *conubialis,* fr. *conubium, connubium* marriage, fr. *com-* + *nubere* to marry — more at NUPTIAL] (ca. 1656) : of or relating to the married state : CONJUGAL — **con·nu·bi·al·ism** \-bē-ə-,li-zəm\ *n* — **con·nu·bi·al·i·ty** \-,nü-bē-'a-lə-tē, -,nyü-\ *n* — **con·nu·bi·al·ly** \-'nü-bē-ə-lē, -'nyü-\ *adv*

co·no·dont \'kō-nə-,dänt, 'kä-\ *n* [ISV *con-* (fr. Gk *kōnos* cone) + *-odont*] (1859) : a Paleozoic toothlike fossil that is prob. the remains of an extinct marine invertebrate

co·noid \'kō-,nòid\ *or* **co·noi·dal** \kō-'nòi-dᵊl\ *adj* (1668) : shaped like or nearly like a cone ⟨~ shells⟩ ⟨~ pottery⟩ — **conoid** *n*

con·quer \'käŋ-kər\ *vb* **con·quered; con·quer·ing** \-k(ə-)riŋ\ [ME, to acquire, conquer, fr. OF *conquerre,* fr. (assumed) VL *conquaerere,* alter. of L *conquirere* to search for, collect, fr. *com-* + *quaerere* to ask, search] *vt* (14c) **1** : to gain or acquire by force of arms : SUBJUGATE **2** : to overcome by force of arms : VANQUISH **3** : to gain mastery over or

win by overcoming obstacles or opposition ⟨~ed the mountain⟩ **4** : to overcome by mental or moral power : SURMOUNT ⟨~ed her fear⟩ ~ *vi* : to be victorious — **con·quer·or** \-kər-ər\ *n*

syn CONQUER, VANQUISH, DEFEAT, SUBDUE, REDUCE, OVERCOME, OVERTHROW mean to get the better of by force or strategy. CONQUER implies gaining mastery of ⟨Caesar *conquered* Gaul⟩. VANQUISH implies a complete overpowering ⟨*vanquished* the enemy and ended the war⟩. DEFEAT does not imply the finality or completeness of VANQUISH which it otherwise equals ⟨the Confederates *defeated* the Union forces at Manassas⟩. SUBDUE implies a defeating and suppression ⟨*subdued* the native tribes after years of fighting⟩. REDUCE implies a forcing to capitulate or surrender ⟨the city was *reduced* after a month-long siege⟩. OVERCOME suggests getting the better of with difficulty or after hard struggle ⟨*overcame* a host of bureaucratic roadblocks⟩. OVERTHROW stresses the bringing down or destruction of existing power ⟨violently *overthrew* the old regime⟩.

con·quest \'kän-,kwest, 'käŋ-; 'käŋ-kwəst\ *n* [ME, fr. MF, fr. (assumed) VL *conquaesitus,* alter. of L *conquisitus,* pp. of *conquirere*] (14c) **1** : the act or process of conquering **2 a** : something conquered; *esp* : territory appropriated in war **b** : a person whose favor or hand has been won

con·qui·an \'käŋ-kē-ən\ *n* [MexSp *conquián* — more at COONCAN] (ca. 1911) : a card game for two played with 40 cards from which all games of rummy developed

con·quis·ta·dor \kän-'kēs-tə-,dòr, kən- *also* -'kwis-, -'kis-\ *n, pl* **con·quis·ta·do·res** \(,)kän-,kēs-tə-'dòr-ēz, -'dòr-,ās, kən-; (,)käŋ-,kwis-, -,kis-\ *or* **con·quis·ta·dors** [Sp, ultim. fr. L *conquirere*] (1830) : one that conquers; *specif* : a leader in the Spanish conquest of America and esp. of Mexico and Peru in the 16th century

con·san·guine \kän-'saŋ-gwən, kən-\ *adj* (1610) : CONSANGUINEOUS

con·san·guin·e·ous \,kän-,san-'gwi-nē-əs, -,saŋ-\ *adj* [L *consanguineus,* fr. *com-* + *sanguin-, sanguis* blood] (1601) : of the same blood or origin; *specif* : descended from the same ancestor — **con·san·guin·e·ous·ly** *adv*

con·san·guin·i·ty \-'gwi-nə-tē\ *n, pl* **-ties** (14c) **1** : the quality or state of being consanguineous **2** : a close relation or connection

con·science \'kän(t)-shən(t)s\ *n* [ME, fr. OF, fr. L *conscientia,* fr. *conscient-, consciens,* prp. of *conscire* to be conscious, be conscious of guilt, fr. *com-* + *scire* to know — more at SCIENCE] (13c) **1 a** : the sense or consciousness of the moral goodness or blameworthiness of one's own conduct, intentions, or character together with a feeling of obligation to do right or be good **b** : a faculty, power, or principle enjoining good acts **c** : the part of the superego in psychoanalysis that transmits commands and admonitions to the ego **2** *archaic* : CONSCIOUSNESS **3** : conformity to the dictates of conscience : CONSCIENTIOUSNESS **4** : sensitive regard for fairness or justice : SCRUPLE — **con·science·less** \-ləs\ *adj* — **in all conscience** *or* **in conscience** : in all fairness

conscience money *n* (1848) : money paid usu. anonymously to relieve the conscience by restoring what has been wrongfully acquired

con·sci·en·tious \,kän(t)-shē-'en(t)-shəs\ *adj* (1611) **1** : governed by or conforming to the dictates of conscience : SCRUPULOUS ⟨a ~ public servant⟩ **2** : METICULOUS, CAREFUL ⟨a ~ listener⟩ *syn* see UPRIGHT — **con·sci·en·tious·ly** *adv* — **con·sci·en·tious·ness** *n*

conscientious objection *n* (1916) : objection on moral or religious grounds (as to service in the armed forces or to bearing arms)

conscientious objector *n* (1899) : a person who refuses to serve in the armed forces or bear arms on moral or religious grounds

con·scio·na·ble \'kän(t)-sh(ə-)nə-bəl\ *adj* [irreg. fr. *conscience*] (1549) : CONSCIENTIOUS

¹**con·scious** \'kän(t)-shəs\ *adj* [L *conscius,* fr. *com-* + *scire* to know] (1592) **1** : perceiving, apprehending, or noticing with a degree of controlled thought or observation **2** *archaic* : sharing another's knowledge or awareness of an inward state or outward fact **3** : personally felt ⟨~ guilt⟩ **4** : capable of or marked by thought, will, design, or perception **5** : SELF-CONSCIOUS **6** : having mental faculties undulled by sleep, faintness, or stupor : AWAKE ⟨became ~ after the anesthesia wore off⟩ **7** : done or acting with critical awareness ⟨a ~ effort to do better⟩ **8 a** : likely to notice, consider, or appraise ⟨a bargain-*conscious* shopper⟩ **b** : being concerned or interested ⟨a budget-*conscious* businessman⟩ **c** : marked by strong feelings or notions ⟨a race-*conscious* society⟩ *syn* see AWARE — **con·scious·ly** *adv*

²**conscious** *n* (1919) : CONSCIOUSNESS 5

con·scious·ness \-nəs\ *n* (1632) **1 a** : the quality or state of being aware esp. of something within oneself **b** : the state or fact of being conscious of an external object, state, or fact **c** : AWARENESS; *esp* : concern for some social or political cause **2** : the state of being characterized by sensation, emotion, volition, and thought : MIND **3** : the totality of conscious states of an individual **4** : the normal state of conscious life ⟨regained ~⟩ **5** : the upper level of mental life of which the person is aware as contrasted with unconscious processes

consciousness–raising *n* (1971) : an increasing of concerned awareness esp. of some social or political issue

con·scribe \kən-'skrīb\ *vt* **con·scribed; con·scrib·ing** [L *conscribere*] (1613) **1** : LIMIT, CIRCUMSCRIBE ⟨ill-health . . . *conscribed* the force of his intentions —*Times Lit. Supp.*⟩ **2** : to enlist forcibly : CONSCRIPT

¹**con·script** \'kän-,skript\ *n* (1800) : a conscripted person (as a military recruit)

²**con·script** \kən-'skript\ *vt* (1813) : to enroll into service by compulsion : DRAFT ⟨was ~ed into the army⟩

³**con·script** \'kän-,skript\ *adj* [alter. of F *conscrit,* fr. L *conscriptus,* pp. of *conscribere* to enroll, enlist, fr. *com-* + *scribere* to write — more at SCRIBE] (1823) **1** : enrolled into service by compulsion : DRAFTED **2** : made up of conscripted persons

con·scrip·tion \kən-'skrip-shən\ *n* (1800) : compulsory enrollment of persons esp. for military service : DRAFT

¹**con·se·crate** \'kän(t)-sə-,krāt\ *adj* (14c) : dedicated to a sacred purpose

\ə\ abut \ᵊ\ kitten, F table \ər\ further \a\ ash \ā\ ace \ä\ mop, mar \aú\ out \ch\ chin \e\ bet \ē\ easy \g\ go \i\ hit \ī\ ice \j\ job \ŋ\ sing \ō\ go \ò\ law \òi\ boy \th\ thin \ṯh\ the \ü\ loot \ù\ foot \y\ yet \zh\ vision \à, ḵ, ⁿ, œ, œ̄, ue, ūe, ᵞ\ *see* Guide to Pronunciation

²**con·se·crate** *vt* **-crat·ed; -crat·ing** [ME, fr. L *consecratus*, pp. of *consecrare*, fr. *com-* + *sacrare* to consecrate — more at SACRED] (14c) **1 :** to induct (a person) into a permanent office with a religious rite; *esp* : to ordain to the office of bishop **2 a :** to make or declare sacred; *esp* : to devote irrevocably to the worship of God by a solemn ceremony **b :** to effect the liturgical transubstantiation of (eucharistic bread and wine) **c :** to devote to a purpose with or as if with deep solemnity or dedication **3 :** to make inviolable or venerable ⟨principles *consecrated* by the weight of history⟩ *syn* see DEVOTE — **con·se·cra·tive** \-,krā-tiv\ *adj* — **con·se·cra·tor** \-,krā-tər\ *n* — **con·se·cra·to·ry** \'kän(t)-si-krə-,tōr-ē, -,tŏr-, -,krā-tə-rē\ *adj*

con·se·cra·tion \,kän(t)-sə-'krā-shən\ *n* (14c) **1 :** the act or ceremony of consecrating **2 :** the state of being consecrated **3** *cap* : the part of a Communion rite in which the bread and wine are consecrated

con·se·cu·tion \,kän(t)-si-'kyü-shən\ *n* [L *consecution-, consecutio,* fr. *consequi* to follow along — more at CONSEQUENT] (1651) : SEQUENCE

con·sec·u·tive \kən-'se-kyə-tiv, -kə-tiv\ *adj* (1611) : following one after the other in order : SUCCESSIVE — **con·sec·u·tive·ly** *adv* — **con·sec·u·tive·ness** *n*

con·sen·su·al \kən-'sen(t)-sh(ə-)wəl, -shəl\ *adj* [L *consensus* + E *-al*] (1754) **1 a :** existing or made by mutual consent without an act of writing ⟨a ~ contract⟩ **b :** involving or based on mutual consent ⟨~ acts⟩ **2 :** relating to or being the constrictive pupillary response of an eye that is covered when the other eye is exposed to light — **con·sen·su·al·ly** *adv*

con·sen·sus \kən-'sen(t)-səs\ *n, often attrib* [L, fr. *consentire*] (1858) **1 a :** general agreement : UNANIMITY ⟨the ~ of their opinion, based on reports . . . from the border —John Hersey⟩ **b :** the judgment arrived at by most of those concerned ⟨the ~ was to go ahead⟩ **2 :** group solidarity in sentiment and belief

usage The phrase *consensus of opinion,* which is not actually redundant (see sense 1a; the sense that takes the phrase is slightly older), has been so often claimed to be a redundancy that many writers avoid it. You are safe in using *consensus* alone when it is clear you mean consensus of opinion, and most writers in fact do so.

¹**con·sent** \kən-'sent\ *vi* [ME, fr. L *consentire,* fr. *com-* + *sentire* to feel — more at SENSE] (13c) **1 :** to give assent or approval : AGREE **2** *archaic* : to be in concord in opinion or sentiment *syn* see ASSENT — **con·sent·ing·ly** \-'sen-tip-lē\ *adv*

²**consent** *n* (14c) **1 :** compliance in or approval of what is done or proposed by another : ACQUIESCENCE ⟨he shall have power, by and with the advice and ~ of the Senate, to make treaties —*U.S. Constitution*⟩ **2 :** agreement as to action or opinion; *specif* : voluntary agreement by a people to organize a civil society and give authority to the government — **con·sent·er** *n*

con·sen·ta·ne·ous \,kän(t)-sən-'tā-nē-əs, ,kän-,sen-\ *adj* [L *consentaneus,* fr. *consentire* to agree] (1625) **1 :** expressing agreement : SUITED **2 :** done or made by the consent of all — **con·sen·ta·ne·ous·ly** *adv*

consent decree *n* (1904) : a judicial decree that sanctions a voluntary agreement between parties in dispute

con·se·quence \'kän(t)-sə-,kwen(t)s, -si-kwən(t)s\ *n* (14c) **1 :** a conclusion derived through logic : INFERENCE **2 :** something produced by a cause or necessarily following from a set of conditions **3 a :** importance with respect to power to produce an effect : MOMENT **b :** social importance **4 :** the appearance of importance; *esp* : SELF-IMPORTANCE *syn* see IMPORTANCE — **in consequence** : as a result : CONSEQUENTLY

¹**con·se·quent** \-kwənt, -,kwent\ *n* (14c) **1 a :** DEDUCTION 2b **b :** the conclusion of a conditional sentence **2 :** the second term of a ratio

²**consequent** *adj* [ME, fr. MF, fr. L *consequent-, consequens,* prp. of *consequi* to follow along, fr. *com-* + *sequi* to follow — more at SUE] (15c) **1 :** following as a result or effect ⟨her new job and ~ relocation⟩ **2 :** observing logical sequence : RATIONAL

con·se·quen·tial \,kän(t)-sə-'kwen(t)-shəl\ *adj* (1626) **1 :** of the nature of a secondary result : INDIRECT **2 :** CONSEQUENT **3 :** having significant consequences : IMPORTANT ⟨a grave and ~ event⟩ **4 :** SELF-IMPORTANT — **con·se·quen·ti·al·i·ty** \-,kwen(t)-shē-'a-lə-tē\ *n* — **con·se·quen·tial·ly** \-'kwen(t)-sh(ə-)lē\ *adv* — **con·se·quen·tial·ness** \-'kwen(t)-shəl-nəs\ *n*

con·se·quent·ly \'kän(t)-sə-,kwent-lē, -si-kwənt-\ *adv* (15c) : as a result : in view of the foregoing : ACCORDINGLY

con·ser·van·cy \kən-'sər-vən(t)-sē\ *n, pl* **-cies** [alter. of obs. *conservacy* conservation, fr. AF *conservacie,* fr. ML *conservatia,* fr. L *conservare*] (1755) **1** *Brit* : a board regulating fisheries and navigation in a river or port **2 a :** CONSERVATION **b :** an organization or area designated to conserve and protect natural resources

con·ser·va·tion \,kän(t)-sər-'vā-shən\ *n* [ME, fr. MF, fr. L *conservation-, conservatio,* fr. *conservare*] (14c) **1 :** a careful preservation and protection of something; *esp* : planned management of a natural resource to prevent exploitation, destruction, or neglect **2 :** the preservation of a physical quantity during transformations or reactions — **con·ser·va·tion·al** \-shnəl, -shə-nᵊl\ *adj*

con·ser·va·tion·ist \-sh(ə-)nist\ *n* (1870) : a person who advocates conservation esp. of natural resources

conservation of charge (1949) : a principle in physics: the total electric charge of an isolated system remains constant irrespective of whatever internal changes may take place

conservation of energy (1853) : a principle in physics: the total energy of an isolated system remains constant irrespective of whatever internal changes may take place with energy disappearing in one form reappearing in another

conservation of mass (1884) : a principle in classical physics: the total mass of any material system is neither increased nor diminished by reactions between the parts — called also *conservation of matter*

con·ser·va·tism \kən-'sər-və-,ti-zəm\ *n* (1835) **1** *cap* **a :** the principles and policies of a Conservative party **b :** the Conservative party **2 a :** disposition in politics to preserve what is established **b :** a political philosophy based on tradition and social stability, stressing established institutions, and preferring gradual development to abrupt change **3 :** the tendency to prefer an existing or traditional situation to change

¹**con·ser·va·tive** \kən-'sər-və-tiv\ *adj* (14c) **1 :** PRESERVATIVE **2 a :** of or relating to a philosophy of conservatism **b** *cap* : of or constituting a political party professing the principles of conservatism: as

(1) : of or constituting a party of the United Kingdom advocating support of established institutions (2) : PROGRESSIVE CONSERVATIVE **3 a :** tending or disposed to maintain existing views, conditions, or institutions : TRADITIONAL **b :** marked by moderation or caution ⟨a ~ estimate⟩ **c :** marked by or relating to traditional norms of taste, elegance, style, or manners ⟨a ~ suit⟩ **4 :** of or relating to Conservative Judaism — **con·ser·va·tive·ly** *adv* — **con·ser·va·tive·ness** *n*

²**conservative** *n* (1831) **1 a :** an adherent or advocate of political conservatism **b** *cap* : a member or supporter of a conservative political party **2 a :** one who adheres to traditional methods or views **b** : a cautious or discreet person

Conservative Judaism *n* (1946) : Judaism as practiced esp. among some U.S. Jews with adherence to the Torah and Talmud but with allowance for some departures in keeping with differing times and circumstances — compare ORTHODOX JUDAISM, REFORM JUDAISM

con·ser·va·tize \-,tīz\ *vb* **-tized; -tiz·ing** *vi* (1849) : to grow conservative — *vt* : to make conservative

con·ser·va·toire \kən-'sər-və-,twär\ *n* [F, fr. It *conservatorio*] (1845) : CONSERVATORY 2

con·ser·va·tor \kən-'sər-və-tər, -və-,tŏr; 'kän(t)-sər-,vā-tər\ *n* (15c) **1 a :** one that preserves from injury or violation : PROTECTOR **b :** one that is responsible for the care, restoration, and repair of archival or museum articles **2 :** a person, official, or institution designated to take over and protect the interests of an incompetent **3 :** an official charged with the protection of something affecting public welfare and interests — **con·ser·va·to·ri·al** \kən-,sər-və-'tōr-ē-əl, (,)kän-, -'tŏr-\ *adj* — **con·ser·va·tor·ship** \kən-'sər-və-tər-,ship, -və-,tŏr-; 'kän(t)-sər-,vā-tər-\ *n*

con·ser·va·to·ry \kən-'sər-və-,tōr-ē, -,tŏr-\ *n, pl* **-ries** (1664) **1 :** a greenhouse for growing or displaying plants **2** [It *conservatorio* home for foundlings, music school, fr. L *conservare*] : a school specializing in one of the fine arts ⟨music ~⟩

¹**con·serve** \kən-'sərv\ *vt* **con·served; con·serv·ing** [ME, fr. MF *conserver,* fr. L *conservare,* fr. *com-* + *servare* to keep, guard, observe; akin to Av *haurvaiti* he guards] (14c) **1 :** to keep in a safe or sound state ⟨he *conserved* his inheritance⟩; *esp* : to avoid wasteful or destructive use of ⟨~ natural resources⟩ **2 :** to preserve with sugar **3 :** to maintain (a quantity) constant during a process of chemical, physical, or evolutionary change — **con·serv·er** *n*

²**con·serve** \'kän(t),sərv\ *n* (15c) **1 :** SWEETMEAT; *esp* : a candied fruit **2** : PRESERVE; *specif* : one prepared from a mixture of fruits

con·sid·er \kən-'si-dər\ *vb* **con·sid·ered; con·sid·er·ing** \-d(ə-)rin\ [ME, fr. MF *considerer,* fr. L *considerare* to observe, think about, fr. *com-* + *sider-, sidus* star] *vt* (14c) **1 :** to think about carefully: as **a :** to think of esp. with regard to taking some action ⟨is ~*ing* you for the job⟩ ⟨~*ed* moving to the city⟩ **b :** to take into account ⟨defendant's age must be ~*ed*⟩ **2 :** to regard or treat in an attentive or kindly way ⟨he ~*ed* her every wish⟩ **3 :** to gaze on steadily or reflectively **4 :** to come to judge or classify ⟨~ thrift essential⟩ **5 :** REGARD ⟨his works are well ~*ed* abroad⟩ **6 :** SUPPOSE ~ *vi* : REFLECT, DELIBERATE ⟨paused a moment to ~⟩

syn CONSIDER, STUDY, CONTEMPLATE, WEIGH mean to think about in order to arrive at a judgment or decision. CONSIDER may suggest giving thought to in order to reach a suitable conclusion, opinion, or decision ⟨refused even to *consider* my proposal⟩. STUDY implies sustained purposeful concentration and attention to details and minutiae ⟨*study* the plan closely⟩. CONTEMPLATE stresses focusing one's thoughts on something but does not imply coming to a conclusion or decision ⟨*contemplate* the consequences of refusing⟩. WEIGH implies attempting to reach the truth or arrive at a decision by balancing conflicting claims or evidence ⟨*weigh* the pros and cons of the case⟩.

¹**con·sid·er·able** \-'si-d(ə)r(-ə)-bəl, -'si-drə-bəl\ *adj* (ca. 1619) **1 :** worth consideration : SIGNIFICANT **2 :** large in extent or degree ⟨a ~ number⟩ — **con·sid·er·ably** \-blē\ *adv*

²**considerable** *n* (1685) : a considerable amount, degree, or extent

con·sid·er·ate \kən-'si-d(ə-)rət\ *adj* (1572) **1 :** marked by or given to careful consideration : CIRCUMSPECT **2 :** thoughtful of the rights and feelings of others — **con·sid·er·ate·ly** *adv* — **con·sid·er·ate·ness** *n*

con·sid·er·a·tion \kən-,si-də-'rā-shən\ *n* (14c) **1 :** continuous and careful thought ⟨after long ~ he agreed to their requests⟩ **2 a :** a matter weighed or taken into account when formulating an opinion or plan ⟨economic ~s forced her to leave college⟩ **b :** a taking into account **3 :** thoughtful and sympathetic regard **4 :** an opinion obtained by reflection **5 :** ESTEEM, REGARD ⟨the family built themselves a large, ugly villa . . . and became people of ~ —V. S. Pritchett⟩ **6 a** : RECOMPENSE, PAYMENT **b :** the inducement to a contract or other legal transaction; *specif* : an act or forbearance or the promise thereof done or given by one party in return for the act or promise of another — **in consideration of :** as payment or recompense for ⟨a small fee *in consideration of* many kind services⟩

con·sid·ered \kən-'si-dərd\ *adj* (ca. 1677) **1 :** matured by extended deliberative thought ⟨a ~ opinion⟩ **2 :** viewed with respect or esteem

¹**con·sid·er·ing** \-d(ə-)rin\ *prep* (14c) : in view of : taking into account ⟨he did well ~ his limitations⟩

²**considering** *conj* (15c) : INASMUCH AS ⟨~ he was new at the job, he did quite well⟩

con·sig·li·e·re \kōn-(,)sil-'ye-re, -'yer-ē; kän-(,)si-glē-'ye-rā, -rē, -'yer\ *n, pl* **-ri** \-rē\ [It, fr. *consiglio* advice, counsel, fr. L *consilium* — more at COUNSEL] (1615) : COUNSELOR, ADVISER ⟨~ of a Mafia family⟩

con·sign \kən-'sīn\ *vb* [MF *consigner,* fr. L *consignare,* fr. *com-* + *signum* sign, mark, seal — more at SIGN] *vt* (1528) **1 :** to give over to another's care **2 :** to give, transfer, or deliver into the hands or control of another; *also* : to commit esp. to a final destination or fate ⟨a writer ~*ed* to oblivion⟩ **3 :** to send or address to an agent to be cared for or sold ~ *vi, obs* : AGREE, SUBMIT *syn* see COMMIT — **con·sign·able** \-'sī-nə-bəl\ *adj* — **con·sig·na·tion** \,kän-,sī-'nā-shən, ,kän-sī-; sig-\ *n* — **con·sign·or** \,kän-,sī-'nŏr, kən-\ *n*

con·sign·ee \,kän(t)-sə-'nē, ,kän-,sī-, kən-,sī-\ *n* (1789) : one to whom something is consigned or shipped

¹**con·sign·ment** \kən-'sīn-mənt\ *n* (ca. 1668) **1 :** the act or process of consigning **2 :** something consigned esp. in a single shipment — **on consignment :** shipped to a dealer who pays only for what he sells and who may return what is unsold ⟨goods shipped *on consignment*⟩

²**consignment** *adj* (1913) : of, relating to, or received as goods on consignment ⟨a ~ sale⟩

¹**con·sist** \kən-'sist\ *vi* [MF & L; MF *consister*, fr. L *consistere*, lit., to stop, stand still, fr. *com-* + *sistere* to take a stand; akin to L *stare* to stand — more at STAND] (1526) **1** : LIE, RESIDE — usu. used with *in* ⟨liberty ~s in the absence of obstructions —A. E. Housman⟩ **2** *archaic* **a** : EXIST, BE **b** : to be capable of existing **3** : to be composed or made up — usu. used with *of* ⟨breakfast ~ed of cereal, milk, and fruit⟩ **4** : to be consistent ⟨it ~s with the facts⟩

²**con·sist** \'kän-,sist\ *n* (1898) : makeup or composition (as of coal sizes or a railroad train) by classes, types, or grades and arrangement

con·sis·tence \kən-'sis-tən(t)s\ *n* (1601) : CONSISTENCY

con·sis·ten·cy \kən-'sis-tən(t)-sē\ *n, pl* **-cies** (1594) **1 a** *archaic* : condition of adhering together : firmness of material substance **b** : firmness of constitution or character : PERSISTENCY **2** : degree of firmness, density, viscosity, or resistance to movement or separation of constituent particles ⟨boil the juice to the ~ of a thick syrup⟩ **3 a** : agreement or harmony of parts or features to one another or a whole : CORRESPONDENCE; *specif* : ability to be asserted together without contradiction **b** : harmony of conduct or practice with profession ⟨followed her own advice with ~⟩

con·sis·tent \kən-'sis-tənt\ *adj* [L *consistent-, consistens*, prp. of *consistere*] (1647) **1** *archaic* : possessing firmness or coherence **2 a** : marked by harmony, regularity, or steady continuity : free from variation or contradiction ⟨a ~ style in painting⟩ **b** : COMPATIBLE — usu. used with *with* **c** : showing steady conformity to character, profession, belief, or custom ⟨a ~ patriot⟩ **3** : tending to be arbitrarily close to the true value of the parameter estimated as the sample becomes large ⟨a ~ statistical estimator⟩ — **con·sis·tent·ly** \-lē\ *adv*

con·sis·to·ry \kən-'sis-t(ə-)rē\ *n, pl* **-ries** [ME *consistorie*, fr. MF, fr. ML & LL; ML *consistorium* church tribunal, fr. LL, imperial council, fr. L *consistere*] (14c) **1** : a solemn assembly : COUNCIL **2** : a church tribunal or governing body: as **a** : a solemn meeting of Roman Catholic cardinals convoked and presided over by the pope **b** : a church session in some Reformed churches **3** : the organization that confers the degrees of the Ancient and Accepted Scottish Rite of Freemasonry usu. from the 19th to the 32d inclusive; *also* : a meeting of such an organization — **con·sis·to·ri·al** \,kän-si-'stōr-ē-əl, -'stor-\ *adj*

con·so·ci·ate \kən-'sō-sē-,āt, -shē-,āt\ *vb* **-at·ed; -at·ing** [L *consociatus*, pp. of *consociare*, fr. *com-* + *socius* companion — more at SOCIAL] *vt* (1566) : to bring into association ~ *vi* : to associate esp. in fellowship or partnership

con·so·ci·a·tion \-,sō-sē-'ā-shən, -shē-\ *n* (1593) **1** : association in fellowship or alliance **2** : an association of churches or religious societies **3** : an ecological community with a single dominant species — **con·so·ci·a·tion·al** \-shnəl, -shə-n⁴l\ *adj*

con·so·la·tion \,kän(t)-sə-'lā-shən\ *n* (14c) **1** : the act or an instance of consoling : the state of being consoled : COMFORT **2** : something that consoles; *specif* : a contest held for those who have lost early in a tournament ⟨the losers met in a ~ game⟩ — **con·so·la·to·ry** \kən-'sō-lə-,tōr-ē, -'sä-, -,tōr-\ *adj*

consolation prize *n* (1886) : a prize given to a runner-up or a loser in a contest

¹**con·sole** \'kän-,sōl\ *n* [F] (1664) **1** : an architectural member projecting from a wall to form a bracket or from a keystone for ornament **2** : CONSOLE TABLE **3 a** : an upright case which houses the keyboards and controlling mechanisms of an organ and from which the organ is played **b** : a combination of readouts or displays and an input device (as a keyboard or switches) by which an operator can monitor and interact with a system (as a computer or dubber) **4 a** : a cabinet (as for a radio or television set) designed to rest directly on the floor **b** : a small storage cabinet between bucket seats in an automobile

²**con·sole** \kən-'sōl\ *vt* **con·soled; con·sol·ing** [F *consoler*, fr. L *consolari*, fr. *com-* + *solari* to console] (1693) : to alleviate the grief, sense of loss, or trouble of : COMFORT ⟨~ a widow⟩ — **con·sol·ing·ly** \-'sō-liŋ-lē\ *adv*

console table *n* (1813) : a table fixed to a wall with its top supported by consoles or front legs; *broadly* : a table designed to fit against a wall

con·sol·i·date \kən-'sä-lə-,dāt\ *vb* **-dat·ed; -dat·ing** [L *consolidatus*, pp. of *consolidare* to make solid, fr. *com-* + *solidus* solid] *vt* (ca. 1512) **1** : to join together into one whole : UNITE ⟨~ several small school districts⟩ **2** : to make firm or secure : STRENGTHEN ⟨~ their hold on first place⟩ **3** : to form into a compact mass ~ *vi* : to become consolidated; *specif* : MERGE ⟨the two companies *consolidated*⟩ — **con·sol·i·da·tor** \-,dā-tər\ *n*

consolidated school *n* (1911) : a public school formed by merging other schools

con·sol·i·da·tion \kən-,sä-lə-'dā-shən\ *n* (15c) **1** : the act or process of consolidating : the state of being consolidated **2** : the process of uniting : the quality or state of being united; *specif* : the unification of two or more corporations by dissolution of existing ones and creation of a single new corporation **3** : pathological alteration of lung tissue from an aerated condition to one of solid consistency

con·som·mé \,kän(t)-sə-'mā\ *n* [F, fr. pp. of *consommer* to complete, boil down, fr. L *consummare* to complete — more at CONSUMMATE] (1815) : clear soup made from well-seasoned stock

con·so·nance \'kän(t)-s(ə-)nən(t)s\ *n* (15c) **1** : harmony or agreement among components **2 a** : correspondence or recurrence of sounds esp. in words; *specif* : recurrence or repetition of consonants esp. at the end of stressed syllables without the similar correspondence of vowels (as in the final sounds of "stroke" and "luck") **b** : CONCORD 1b **c** : SYMPATHETIC VIBRATION, RESONANCE

con·so·nan·cy \-s(ə-)nən(t)-sē\ *n, pl* **-cies** (14c) : CONSONANCE 1

¹**con·so·nant** \'kän(t)-s(ə-)nənt\ *adj* [MF, fr. L *consonant-, consonans*, prp. of *consonare* to sound together, agree, fr. *com-* + *sonare* to sound — more at SOUND] (15c) **1** : being in agreement or harmony : free from elements making for discord **2** : marked by musical consonances **3** : having similar sounds ⟨~ words⟩ **4** : relating to or exhibiting consonance : RESONANT — **con·so·nant·ly** *adv*

²**consonant** *n* [ME, fr. L *consonant-, consonans*, fr. prp. of *consonare*] (14c) : one of a class of speech sounds (as\p\, \g\, \n\, \l\, \s\, \r\) characterized by constriction or closure at one or more points in the breath channel; *also* : a letter representing a consonant — usu. used in English of any letter except *a, e, i, o,* and *u*

con·so·nan·tal \,kän(t)-sə-'nan-t⁴l\ *adj* (1795) : relating to, being, or marked by a consonant or group of consonants

consonant shift *n* (1888) : a set of regular changes in consonant articulation in the history of a language or dialect: **a** : such a set affecting the Indo-European stops and distinguishing the Germanic languages from the other Indo-European languages — compare GRIMM'S LAW **b** : such a set affecting the Germanic stops and distinguishing High German from the other Germanic languages

¹**con·sort** \'kän-,sort\ *n* [ME, fr. MF, fr. L *consort-, consors* partner, sharer, fr. *com-* + *sort-, sors* lot, share — more at SERIES] (15c) **1** : ASSOCIATE **2** : a ship accompanying another **3** : SPOUSE — compare PRINCE CONSORT

²**consort** *n* [MF *consorte*, fr. *consort*] (1584) **1** : GROUP, ASSEMBLY ⟨a ~ of specialists⟩ **2** : CONJUNCTION, ASSOCIATION ⟨he ruled in ~ with his father⟩ **3 a** : a group of singers or instrumentalists performing together **b** : a set of musical instruments of the same family

³**consort** \kən-'sort, kän-\ *vb* (1588) **1** : UNITE, ASSOCIATE **2** *obs* : ESCORT ~ *vi* **1** : to keep company ⟨~ing with criminals⟩ **2** *obs* : to make harmony : PLAY **3** : ACCORD, HARMONIZE ⟨the illustrations ~ admirably with the text —*Times Lit. Supp.*⟩

con·sor·tium \kən-'sòr-sh(ē-)əm, -'sòr-tē-əm\ *n, pl* **-sor·tia** \-'sòr-sh(ē-)ə, -'sòr-tē-ə\ *also* **-sortiums** [L, fellowship, fr. *consort-, consors*] (1829) **1** : an agreement, combination, or group (as of companies) formed to undertake an enterprise beyond the resources of any one member **2** : ASSOCIATION, SOCIETY **3** : the legal right of one spouse to the company, affection, and assistance of and to sexual relations with the other

con·spe·cif·ic \,kän(t)-spi-'si-fik\ *adj* (1859) : of the same species — **conspecific** *n*

con·spec·tus \kən-'spek-təs\ *n* [L, fr. *conspectus*, fr. *conspicere*] (ca. 1837) **1** : a usu. brief survey or summary (as of an extensive subject) often providing an overall view **2** : OUTLINE, SYNOPSIS

con·spi·cu·i·ty \,kän(t)-spə-'kyü-ə-tē\ *n* (1601) : the quality or state of being conspicuous : CONSPICUOUSNESS

con·spic·u·ous \kən-'spi-kyə-wəs\ *adj* [L *conspicuus*, fr. *conspicere* to get sight of, fr. *com-* + *specere* to look — more at SPY] (1545) **1** : obvious to the eye or mind **2** : attracting attention : STRIKING **3** : marked by a noticeable violation of good taste *syn* see NOTICEABLE — **con·spic·u·ous·ly** *adv* — **con·spic·u·ous·ness** \-nəs\ *n*

conspicuous consumption *n* (1899) : lavish or wasteful spending thought to enhance social prestige

con·spir·a·cy \kən-'spir-ə-sē\ *n, pl* **-cies** [ME *conspiracie*, fr. L *conspirare*] (14c) **1** : the act of conspiring together **2 a** : an agreement among conspirators **b** : a group of conspirators *syn* see PLOT

conspiracy of silence (1865) : a secret agreement to keep silent about an occurrence, situation, or subject esp. in order to promote or protect selfish interests

con·spi·ra·tion \,kän(t)-spə-'rā-shən, ,kän-(,)spi-'rā-\ *n* (14c) **1** : the act or action of plotting or secretly combining **2** : a joint effort toward a particular end — **con·spi·ra·tion·al** \-shnəl, -shə-n⁴l\ *adj*

con·spir·a·tor \kən-'spir-ə-tər\ *n* (15c) : one that conspires : PLOTTER

con·spir·a·to·ri·al \kən-,spir-ə-'tōr-ē-əl, -'tòr-\ *adj* (1855) : of, relating to, or suggestive of a conspiracy — **con·spir·a·to·ri·al·ly** \-ē-ə-lē\ *adv*

con·spire \kən-'spīr\ *vb* **con·spired; con·spir·ing** [ME, fr. MF *conspirer*, fr. L *conspirare* to be in harmony, conspire, fr. *com-* + *spirare* to breathe] *vt* (14c) : PLOT, CONTRIVE ~ *vi* **1 a** : to join in a secret agreement to do an unlawful or wrongful act or an act which becomes unlawful as a result of the secret agreement **b** : SCHEME **2** : to act in harmony toward a common end ⟨circumstances *conspired* to defeat his efforts⟩

con spi·ri·to \kän-'spir-ə-,tō, kōn-\ *adv* [It] (ca. 1891) : with spirit or animation — used as a direction in music

con·sta·ble \'kän(t)-stə-bəl, 'kən(t)-\ *n* [ME *conestable*, fr. OF, fr. LL *comes stabuli*, lit., officer of the stable] (13c) **1** : a high officer of a medieval royal or noble household **2** : the warden or governor of a royal castle or a fortified town **3 a** : a public officer usually of a town or township responsible for keeping the peace and for minor judicial duties **b** *Brit* : POLICE OFFICER; *esp* : one ranking below sergeant

¹**con·stab·u·lary** \kən-'sta-byə-,ler-ē\ *adj* (1824) : of or relating to a constable or constabulary

²**constabulary** *n, pl* **-lar·ies** (1837) **1** : the organized body of constables of a particular district or country **2** : an armed police force organized on military lines but distinct from the regular army

con·stan·cy \'kän(t)-stən(t)-sē\ *n, pl* **-cies** (15c) **1 a** : steadfastness of mind under duress : FORTITUDE **b** : FIDELITY, LOYALTY **2** : a state of being constant or unchanging

¹**con·stant** \'kän(t)-stənt\ *adj* [ME, fr. MF, fr. L *constant-, constans*, fr. prp. of *constare* to stand firm, be consistent, fr. *com-* + *stare* to stand — more at STAND] (14c) **1** : marked by firm steadfast resolution or faithfulness : exhibiting constancy of mind or attachment **2** : INVARIABLE, UNIFORM **3** : continually occurring or recurring : REGULAR *syn* see FAITHFUL, CONTINUAL — **con·stant·ly** *adv*

²**constant** *n* (1832) : something invariable or unchanging: as **a** : a number that has a fixed value in a given situation or universally or that is characteristic of some substance or instrument **b** : a number that is assumed not to change value in a given mathematical discussion **c** : a term in logic with a fixed designation

con·stan·tan \'kän(t)-stən-,tan\ *n* [fr. the fact that its resistance remains constant under change of temperature] (1903) : an alloy of copper and nickel used for electrical resistors and in thermocouples

---

\ə\ abut \'\ kitten, F table \ər\ further \a\ ash \ā\ ace \ä\ mop, mar \au̇\ out \ch\ chin \e\ bet \ē\ easy \g\ go \i\ hit \ī\ ice \j\ job \ŋ\ sing \ō\ go \o̊\ law \o̊i\ boy \th\ thin \t͟h\ the \ü\ loot \u̇\ foot \y\ yet \zh\ vision \á, k̲, ⁿ, œ, œ̄, ᴜᴇ, ɪē, ʸ\ *see* Guide to Pronunciation

con·sta·tive \kən-'stā-tiv, 'kän-stə-tiv\ *adj* [*constate* to assert positively, fr. F *constater*, fr. L *constat* it is certain, 3d sing. pres. indic. of *constare*] (1901) **1** : of, relating to, or being a verbal form that expresses past completed action **2** : being or relating to an utterance (as an assertion, question, or command) that is capable of being judged true or false — **constative** *n*

con·stel·late \'kän(t)-stə-,lāt\ *vb* **-lat·ed; -lat·ing** *vt* (1643) **1** : to unite in a cluster **2** : to set or adorn with or as if with constellations ~ *vi* : CLUSTER

con·stel·la·tion \,kän(t)-stə-'lā-shən\ *n* [ME *constellacioun*, fr. MF *constellation*, fr. LL *constellation-*, *constellatio*, fr. L *com-* + *stella* star — more at STAR] (14c) **1** : the configuration of stars esp. at one's birth **2** : any of 88 arbitrary configurations of stars or an area of the celestial sphere covering one of these configurations **3** : an assemblage, collection, or gathering of usu. related persons, qualities, or things ⟨a ~ of . . . relatives, friends, and hangers-on —Brendan Gill⟩ **4** : PATTERN, ARRANGEMENT ⟨taking advantage of the shifting ~ of power throughout the known world —H. D. Lasswell⟩ — **con·stel·la·to·ry** \kän-'ste-lə-,tōr-ē, -,tor-\ *adj*

con·ster·nate \'kän(t)-stər-,nāt\ *vt* **-nat·ed; -nat·ing** (1651) : to fill with consternation

con·ster·na·tion \,kän(t)-stər-'nā-shən\ *n* [F or L; F, fr. L *consternation-*, *consternatio*, fr. *consternare* to throw into confusion, fr. *com-* + *-sternare*, prob. fr. *sternere* to spread, strike down — more at STREW] (ca. 1611) : amazement or dismay that hinders or throws into confusion ⟨the two . . . stared at each other in ~, and neither knew what to do —Pearl Buck⟩

con·sti·pate \'kän(t)-stə-,pāt\ *vt* **-pat·ed; -pat·ing** [ML *constipatus*, pp. of *constipare*, fr. L, to crowd together, fr. *com-* + *stipare* to pack tight — more at STIFF] (1533) **1** : to cause constipation in **2** : to make immobile, inactive, or dull : STULTIFY ⟨so much clutter . . . will tend to ~ the novel's working order —*Times Lit. Supp.*⟩

con·sti·pat·ed \-,pā-təd\ *adj* (1547) **1** : affected with constipation **2** : stilted or stodgy in appearance, expression, or action

con·sti·pa·tion \,kän(t)-stə-'pā-shən\ *n* (15c) **1** : abnormally delayed or infrequent passage of usu. dry hardened feces **2** : STULTIFICATION

con·stit·u·en·cy \kən-'stich-wən(t)-sē, -'sti-chə-\ *n, pl* **-cies** (1831) **1 a** : a body of citizens entitled to elect a representative (as to a legislative or executive position) **b** : the residents in an electoral district **c** : an electoral district **2 a** : a group or body that patronizes, supports, or offers representation ⟨creating . . . a grass-roots ~ for continuing the project —Fred Reed⟩ **b** : the people involved in or served by an organization (as a business or institution) ⟨regards its corporate customers as its prime ~ —Andrew Hacker⟩

¹con·stit·u·ent \-wənt\ *n* [F *constituant*, fr. MF, fr. prp. of *constituer* to constitute, fr. L *constituere*] (1622) **1** : one who authorizes another to act as agent : PRINCIPAL **2** : a member of a constituency **3** : an essential part : COMPONENT, ELEMENT **4** : a structural unit of a definable syntactic, semantic, or phonological category that consists of one or more linguistic elements (as words, morphemes, or features) and that can occur as a component of a larger construction *syn* see ELEMENT

²constituent *adj* [L *constituent-*, *constituens*, prp. of *constituere*] (1660) **1** : serving to form, compose, or make up a unit or whole : COMPONENT **2** : having the power to create a government or frame or amend a constitution ⟨a ~ assembly⟩ — **con·stit·u·ent·ly** *adv*

con·sti·tute \'kän(t)-stə-,tüt, -,tyüt\ *vt* **-tut·ed; -tut·ing** [ME, fr. L *constitutus*, pp. of *constituere* to set up, constitute, fr. *com-* + *statuere* to set — more at STATUTE] (15c) **1** : to appoint to an office, function, or dignity **2** : SET UP, ESTABLISH: as **a** : ENACT **b** : FOUND **c** (1) : to give due or lawful form to (2) : to legally process **3** : MAKE UP, FORM, COMPOSE ⟨12 months ~ a year⟩ ⟨high school dropouts who ~ a major problem in large city slums —J. B. Conant⟩

con·sti·tu·tion \,kän(t)-stə-'tü-shən, -'tyü-\ *n* (14c) **1** : an established law or custom : ORDINANCE **2 a** : the physical makeup of the individual comprising inherited qualities modified by environment **b** : the structure, composition, physical makeup, or nature of something **3** : the act of establishing, making, or setting up **4** : the mode in which a state or society is organized; *esp* : the manner in which sovereign power is distributed **5 a** : the basic principles and laws of a nation, state, or social group that determine the powers and duties of the government and guarantee certain rights to the people in it **b** : a written instrument embodying the rules of a political or social organization — **con·sti·tu·tion·less** \-ləs\ *adj*

¹con·sti·tu·tion·al \-shnəl, -shə-n³l\ *adj* (1682) **1** : relating to, inherent in, or affecting the constitution of body or mind **2** : of, relating to, or entering into the fundamental makeup of something : ESSENTIAL **3** : being in accordance with or authorized by the constitution of a state or society ⟨a ~ government⟩ **4** : regulated by or ruling according to a constitution ⟨a ~ monarchy⟩ **5** : of or relating to a constitution **6** : loyal to or supporting an established constitution or form of government

²constitutional *n* (1829) : a walk taken for one's health

con·sti·tu·tion·al·ism \-sh(ə-)nə-,li-zəm\ *n* (1832) : adherence to or government according to constitutional principles; *also* : a constitutional system of government — **con·sti·tu·tion·al·ist** \-list\ *n*

con·sti·tu·tion·al·i·ty \-,tü-shə-'na-lə-tē, -,tyü-\ *n* (1787) : the quality or state of being constitutional; *esp* : accordance with the provisions of a constitution ⟨questioned the ~ of the law⟩

con·sti·tu·tion·al·ize \-'tü-shnə-,līz, -shə-n³l-,īz\ *vt* **-ized; -iz·ing** (1831) : to provide with a constitution : organize along constitutional principles — **con·sti·tu·tion·al·i·za·tion** \-,tü-shnə-lə-'zā-shən, -shə-n³l-ə-\ *n*

con·sti·tu·tion·al·ly \-'tü-shnə-lē, -'tyü-, -shə-n³l-ē\ *adv* (1742) **1 a** : in accordance with one's constitution ⟨~ unable to grasp subtleties⟩ **b** : in structure, composition, or constitution ⟨despite repeated heatings the material remained ~ the same⟩ **2** : in accordance with a political constitution ⟨was not ~ eligible to fill the office⟩

con·sti·tu·tive \'kän(t)-stə-,tü-tiv, -,tyü-; kən-'sti-chə-tiv\ *adj* (1592) **1** : having the power to enact or establish : CONSTRUCTIVE **2** : CONSTITUENT, ESSENTIAL **3** : relating to or dependent on constitution ⟨a ~ property of all electrolytes⟩ — **con·sti·tu·tive·ly** *adv*

con·strain \kən-'strān\ *vt* [ME, fr. MF *constraindre*, fr. L *constringere* to constrict, constrain, fr. *com-* + *stringere* to draw tight — more at STRAIN] (14c) **1 a** : to force by imposed stricture, restriction, or limi-

tation **b** : to restrict the motion of (a mechanical body) to a particular mode **2** : COMPRESS; *also* : to clasp tightly **3** : to secure by or as if by bonds : CONFINE; *broadly* : LIMIT **4** : to force or produce in an unnatural or strained manner ⟨a ~ed smile⟩ **5** : to hold back by or as if by force ⟨~ing my mind not to wander from the task —Charles Dickens⟩ *syn* see FORCE — **con·strained·ly** \-'strā-nəd-lē, -'strānd-lē\ *adv*

con·straint \kən-'strānt\ *n* [ME, fr. MF *constrainte*, fr. *constraindre*] (15c) **1 a** : the act of constraining **b** : the state of being checked, restricted, or compelled to avoid or perform some action ⟨the ~ and monotony of a monastic life —Matthew Arnold⟩ **c** : a constraining condition, agency, or force : CHECK ⟨put legal ~s on the board's activities⟩ **2 a** : repression of one's own feelings, behavior, or actions **b** : a sense of being constrained : EMBARRASSMENT

con·strict \kən-'strikt\ *vb* [L *constrictus*, pp. of *constringere*] *vt* (1732) **1 a** : to make narrow or draw together **b** : COMPRESS, SQUEEZE ⟨~ a nerve⟩ **2** : to stultify, stop, or cause to falter : INHIBIT ~ *vi* : to become constricted *syn* see CONTRACT — **con·stric·tive** \-'strik-tiv\ *adj*

con·stric·tion \-'strik-shən\ *n* (15c) **1** : an act or product of constricting **2** : the quality or state of being constricted **3** : something that constricts

con·stric·tor \-'strik-tər\ *n* (1735) **1** : a muscle that contracts a cavity or orifice or compresses an organ **2** : a snake (as a boa constrictor) that kills prey by compression in its coils **3** : one that constricts

con·stringe \kən-'strinj\ *vt* **con·stringed; con·string·ing** [L *constringere*] (1604) **1** : to cause to shrink ⟨cold ~s the pores⟩ **2** : CONSTRICT — **con·strin·gent** \-'strin-jənt\ *adj*

¹con·struct \kən-'strəkt\ *vt* [L *constructus*, pp. of *construere*, fr. *com-* + *struere* to build — more at STRUCTURE] (1663) **1** : to make or form by combining or arranging parts or elements : BUILD; *also* : CONTRIVE, DEVISE **2** : to draw (a geometrical figure) with suitable instruments and under specified conditions **3** : to set in logical order — **con·struct·ible** \-'strək-tə-bəl\ *adj* — **con·struc·tor** \-tər\ *n*

²con·struct \'kän-,strəkt\ *n* (1933) **1** : something constructed by the mind: as **a** : a theoretical entity ⟨the deductive study of abstract ~s —Daniel J. Boorstin⟩ **b** : a working hypothesis or concept ⟨a point of view which made "abroad" singularly containable as a literary ~ —Jonathan Raban⟩ **c** : a product of mental invention ⟨the novel . . . a verbal ~ in which invented human characters appear —Anthony Burgess⟩ **2** : something produced by human effort ⟨the East bloc was always an unnatural ~ —Walter Isaacson⟩

con·struc·tion \kən-'strək-shən\ *n* (14c) **1** : the act or result of construing, interpreting, or explaining **2 a** : the process, art, or manner of constructing something; *also* : a thing constructed **b** : the construction industry ⟨working in ~⟩ **3** : the arrangement and connection of words or groups of words in a sentence : syntactical arrangement **4** : a sculpture that is put together out of separate pieces of often disparate materials — **con·struc·tion·al** \-shnəl, -shə-n³l\ *adj* — **con·struc·tion·al·ly** *adv*

con·struc·tion·ist \-sh(ə-)nist\ *n* (1838) : one who construes a legal document (as the U.S. Constitution) in a specific way ⟨a strict ~⟩

construction paper *n* (ca. 1924) : a thick groundwood paper available in many colors and used esp. for school artwork

con·struc·tive \kən-'strək-tiv\ *adj* (ca. 1680) **1** : declared such by judicial construction or interpretation ⟨~ fraud⟩ **2** : of or relating to construction or creation **3** : promoting improvement or development ⟨~ criticism⟩ — **con·struc·tive·ly** *adv* — **con·struc·tive·ness** *n*

con·struc·tiv·ism \kən-'strək-ti-,vi-zəm\ *n, often cap* (1925) : a nonobjective art movement originating in Russia and concerned with formal organization of planes and expression of volume in terms of modern industrial materials (as glass and plastic) — **con·struc·tiv·ist** \-vist\ *adj or n, often cap*

¹con·strue \kən-'strü\ *vb* **con·strued; con·stru·ing** [ME, fr. LL *construere*, fr. L, to construct] *vt* (14c) **1** : to analyze the arrangement and connection of words in (a sentence or sentence part) **2** : to understand or explain the sense or intention of usu. in a particular way or with respect to a given set of circumstances ⟨construed my actions as hostile⟩ ~ *vi* : to construe a sentence or sentence part esp. in connection with translating — **con·stru·able** \-'strü-ə-bəl\ *adj*

²con·strue \'kän-,strü\ *n* (1844) : an act or result of construing esp. by piecemeal translation

con·sub·stan·tial \,kän(t)-səb-'stan(t)-shəl\ *adj* [LL *consubstantialis*, fr. L *com-* + *substantia* substance] (14c) : of the same substance

con·sub·stan·ti·a·tion \,kän(t)-səb-,stan(t)-shē-'ā-shən\ *n* (1597) : the actual substantial presence and combination of the body and blood of Christ with the eucharistic bread and wine according to a teaching associated with Martin Luther — compare TRANSUBSTANTIATION

con·sue·tude \'kän(t)-swi-,tüd, kən-'sü-ə-, -,tyüd\ *n* [ME, fr. L *consuetudo* — more at CUSTOM] (14c) : social usage : CUSTOM — **con·sue·tu·di·nary** \,kän(t)-swi-'tü-də-,ner-ē, kən-,sü-ə-, -'tyü-\ *adj*

con·sul \'kän(t)-səl\ *n* [ME, fr. L; perh. akin to L *consulere* to consult] (14c) **1 a** : either of two annually elected chief magistrates of the Roman republic **b** : one of three chief magistrates of the French republic from 1799 to 1804 **2** : an official appointed by a government to reside in a foreign country to represent the commercial interests of citizens of the appointing country — **con·sul·ar** \-s(ə-)lər\ *adj* — **con·sul·ship** \-səl-,ship\ *n*

con·sul·ate \-s(ə-)lət\ *n* (14c) **1** : a government by consuls **2** : the office, term of office, or jurisdiction of a consul **3** : the residence or official premises of a consul

consulate general *n, pl* **consulates general** (1883) : the residence, office, or jurisdiction of a consul general

consul general *n, pl* **consuls general** (1753) : a consul of the first rank stationed in an important place or having jurisdiction in several places or over several consuls

¹con·sult \kən-'səlt\ *vb* [MF or L; MF *consulter*, fr. L *consultare*, freq. of *consulere* to deliberate, counsel, consult] *vt* (1527) **1** : to have regard to : CONSIDER **2 a** : to ask the advice or opinion of ⟨~ a doctor⟩ **b** : to refer to ⟨~ a dictionary⟩ ~ *vi* **1** : to consult an individual **2** : to deliberate together : CONFER **3** : to serve as a consultant — **con·sult·er** *n*

²con·sult \kən-'səlt, 'kän-,\ *n* (1560) : CONSULTATION

con·sul·tan·cy \kən-'səl-t²n(t)-sē\ *n, pl* **-cies** (1955) **1** : CONSULTATION **2** : an agency that provides consulting services **3** : the position of a consultant

con·sul·tant \kən-'səl-t²nt\ *n* (1697) **1** : one who consults another **2** : one who gives professional advice or services : EXPERT — **con·sul·tant·ship** \-;ship\ *n*

con·sul·ta·tion \ˌkän(t)-səl-'tā-shən\ *n* (15c) **1** : COUNCIL, CONFERENCE; *specif* : a deliberation between physicians on a case or its treatment **2** : the act of consulting or conferring

con·sul·ta·tive \kən-'səl-tə-tiv, 'kän(t)-səl-ˌtā-tiv\ *adj* (1583) : of, relating to, or intended for consultation : ADVISORY ⟨~ committee⟩

con·sult·ing \kən-'səl-tiŋ\ *adj* (1801) **1** : providing professional or expert advice ⟨a ~ architect⟩ **2** : of or relating to consultation or a consultant ⟨the ~ room of a psychiatrist⟩

con·sul·tive \kən-'səl-tiv\ *adj* (1616) : CONSULTATIVE

con·sul·tor \kən-'səl-tər\ *n* (1611) : one that consults or advises; *esp* : an adviser to a Roman Catholic bishop, provincial, or sacred congregation

¹**con·sum·able** \kən-'sü-mə-bəl\ *adj* (1641) : capable of being consumed

²**consumable** *n* (1802) : something (as food or fuel) that is consumable — usu. used in pl.

con·sume \kən-'süm\ *vb* **con·sumed; con·sum·ing** [ME, fr. MF or L; MF *consumer*, fr. L *consumere*, fr. *com-* + *sumere* to take up, take, fr. *sub-* up + *emere* to take — more at SUB, REDEEM] *vt* (14c) **1** : to do away with completely : DESTROY ⟨fire *consumed* several buildings⟩ **2 a** : to spend wastefully : SQUANDER **b** : USE UP ⟨writing *consumed* much of his time⟩ **3** : to eat or drink esp. in great quantity ⟨*consumed* several kegs of beer⟩ **4** : to engage fully : ENGROSS ⟨*consumed* with curiosity⟩ ~ *vi* **1** : to waste or burn away : PERISH **2** : to utilize economic goods

con·sum·ed·ly \-'sü-məd-lē\ *adv* (1707) : as if consumed : EXCESSIVELY

con·sum·er \kən-'sü-mər\ *n, often attrib* (15c) : one that consumes: as **a** : one that utilizes economic goods **b** : an organism requiring complex organic compounds for food which it obtains by preying on other organisms or by eating particles of organic matter — compare PRODUCER **4** — **con·sum·er·ship** \-ˌship\ *n*

consumer credit *n* (1927) : credit granted to an individual esp. to finance the purchase of consumer goods or to defray personal expenses

consumer goods *n pl* (1890) : goods that directly satisfy human wants

con·sum·er·ism \kən-'sü-mə-ˌri-zəm\ *n* (1944) **1** : the promotion of the consumer's interests **2** : the theory that an increasing consumption of goods is economically desirable; *also* : a preoccupation with and an inclination toward the buying of consumer goods — **con·sum·er·ist** \-rist\ *n* — **con·sum·er·is·tic** \kən-ˌsü-mə-'ris-tik\ *adj*

consumer price index *n* (1948) : an index measuring the change in the cost of typical wage-earner purchases of goods and services expressed as a percentage of the cost of these same goods and services in some base period — called also *cost-of-living index*

con·sum·ing \kən-'sü-miŋ\ *adj* (1920) : deeply felt : ARDENT ⟨a ~ interest⟩; *also* : ENGROSSING

¹**con·sum·mate** \'kän(t)-sə-mət, kən-'sə-mət\ *adj* [ME *consummat* fulfilled, fr. L *consummatus*, pp. of *consummare* to sum up, finish, fr. *com-* + *summa* sum] (1527) **1** : complete in every detail : PERFECT **2** : extremely skilled and accomplished ⟨a ~ liar⟩ **3** : of the highest degree ⟨~ skill⟩ ⟨~ cruelty⟩ — **con·sum·mate·ly** *adv*

²**con·sum·mate** \'kän(t)-sə-ˌmāt\ *vb* **-mat·ed; -mat·ing** *vt* (1530) **1 a** : FINISH, COMPLETE ⟨~ a business deal⟩ **b** : to make perfect **c** : ACHIEVE **2** : to make (marital union) complete by sexual intercourse ⟨~ a marriage⟩ ~ *vi* : to become perfected — **con·sum·ma·tive** \'kän(t)-sə-ˌmā-tiv, kən-'sə-mə-tiv\ *adj* — **con·sum·ma·tor** \'kän(t)-sə-ˌmāt-ər\ *n*

con·sum·ma·tion \ˌkän-sə-'mā-shən\ *n* (14c) **1** : the act of consummating ⟨the ~ of a contract by mutual signature⟩; *specif* : the consummating of a marriage **2** : the ultimate end : FINISH

con·sum·ma·to·ry \kən-'sə-mə-ˌtōr-ē, -ˌtȯr-\ *adj* (1648) **1** : of or relating to consummation : CONCLUDING **2** : of, relating to, or being a response or act (as eating or copulating) that terminates a period of usu. goal-directed behavior

con·sump·tion \kən-'səm(p)-shən\ *n* [ME *consumpcioun*, fr. L *consumption-, consumptio*, fr. *consumere*] (14c) **1 a** : a progressive wasting away of the body esp. from pulmonary tuberculosis **b** : TUBERCULOSIS **2** : the act or process of consuming **3** : the utilization of economic goods in the satisfaction of wants or in the process of production resulting chiefly in their destruction, deterioration, or transformation

¹**con·sump·tive** \-'səm(p)-tiv\ *adj* (1664) **1** : tending to consume **2** : of, relating to, or affected with consumption — **con·sump·tive·ly** *adv*

²**consumptive** *n* (1666) : a person affected with consumption

¹**con·tact** \'kän-ˌtakt\ *n* [F or L; F, fr. L *contactus*, fr. *contingere* to have contact with — more at CONTINGENT] (1626) **1 a** : union or junction of surfaces **b** : the apparent touching or mutual tangency of the limbs of two celestial bodies or of the disk of one body with the shadow of another during an eclipse, transit, or occultation **c** (1) : the junction of two electrical conductors through which a current passes (2) : a special part made for such a junction **2 a** : ASSOCIATION, RELATIONSHIP **b** : CONNECTION, COMMUNICATION **c** : an establishing of communication with someone or an observing or receiving of a significant signal from a person or object ⟨radar ~ with Mars⟩ **3** : a person serving as a go-between, messenger, connection, or source of special information ⟨business ~s⟩ **4** : CONTACT LENS

²**con·tact** \'kän-ˌtakt, kən-'\ *vi* (1834) : to make contact ~ *vt* **1** : to bring into contact **2 a** : to enter or be in contact with : JOIN **b** : to get in communication with ⟨~ your local dealer⟩
    usage The use of *contact* as a verb, esp. in sense 2b, is accepted as standard by almost all commentators except those who write college handbooks.

³**con·tact** \'kän-ˌtakt\ *adj* (1859) : maintaining, involving, or activated or caused by contact ⟨~ poisons⟩ ⟨~ sports⟩

contact binary *n* (1952) : a binary star system in which the two stars are close enough together for material to pass between them

contact hitter *n* (1982) : a hitter in baseball who seldom strikes out

contact inhibition *n* (1965) : cessation of cellular undulating movements upon contact with other cells with accompanying cessation of cell growth and division

contact language *n* (1950) : PIDGIN

contact lens *n* (1888) : a thin lens designed to fit over the cornea and usu. worn to correct defects in vision

contact print *n* (1890) : a photographic print made with the negative in contact with the sensitized paper, plate, or film

con·ta·gion \kən-'tā-jən\ *n* [ME, fr. MF & L; MF, fr. L *contagion-, contagio*, fr. *contingere* to have contact with, pollute] (14c) **1 a** : a contagious disease **b** : the transmission of a disease by direct or indirect contact **c** : a disease-producing agent (as a virus) **2 a** : POISON **b** : contagious influence, quality, or nature **c** : corrupting influence or contact **3 a** : rapid communication of an influence (as a doctrine or emotional state) **b** : an influence that spreads rapidly

con·ta·gious \-jəs\ *adj* (14c) **1** : communicable by contact : CATCHING ⟨~ diseases⟩ **2** : bearing contagion **3** : used for contagious diseases ⟨a ~ ward⟩ **4** : exciting similar emotions or conduct in others ⟨~ enthusiasm⟩ — **con·ta·gious·ly** *adv* — **con·ta·gious·ness** *n*

contagious abortion *n* (1910) : a contagious or infectious disease (as a brucellosis) of domestic animals characterized by abortion

con·ta·gium \kən-'tā-j(ē-)əm\ *n, pl* **-gia** \-j(ē-)ə\ [L, contagion, fr. *contingere*] (1870) : a virus or living organism capable of causing a communicable disease

con·tain \kən-'tān\ *vb* [ME *conteinen*, fr. OF *contenir*, fr. L *continēre* to hold together, hold in, contain, fr. *com-* + *tenēre* to hold — more at THIN] *vt* (14c) **1** : to keep within limits: as **a** : RESTRAIN, CONTROL **b** : CHECK, HALT **c** : to follow successfully a policy of containment toward **d** : to prevent (as an enemy or opponent) from advancing or from making a successful attack **2 a** : to have within : HOLD **b** : COMPRISE, INCLUDE **3 a** : to be divisible by usu. without a remainder **b** : ENCLOSE, BOUND ~ *vi* : to restrain oneself — **con·tain·able** \-'tā-nə-bəl\ *adj*
    syn CONTAIN, HOLD, ACCOMMODATE mean to have or be capable of having within. CONTAIN implies the actual presence of a specified substance or quantity within something ⟨the can *contains* a quart of oil⟩. HOLD implies the capacity of containing or the usual or permanent function of containing or keeping ⟨the bookcase will *hold* all my textbooks⟩. ACCOMMODATE stresses holding without crowding or inconvenience ⟨the hall can *accommodate* 500 people⟩.

contained *adj* (1653) : RESTRAINED; *also* : CALM

con·tain·er \kən-'tā-nər\ *n* (15c) : one that contains; *esp* : a receptacle (as a box or jar) for holding goods — **con·tain·er·less** \-ləs\ *adj*

con·tain·er·board \-ˌbȯrd, -ˌbȯrd\ *n* (ca. 1924) : corrugated or solid paperboard used for making containers

con·tain·er·i·sa·tion, con·tain·er·ise Brit *var of* CONTAINERIZATION, CONTAINERIZE

con·tain·er·i·za·tion \kən-ˌtā-nə-rə-'zā-shən\ *n* (1956) : a shipping method in which a large amount of material (as merchandise) is packaged into large standardized containers

con·tain·er·ize \kən-'tā-nə-ˌrīz\ *vt* **-ized; -iz·ing** (1956) **1** : to ship by containerization **2** : to pack in containers

con·tain·er·port \-nər-ˌpȯrt, -ˌpȯrt\ *n* (1970) : a shipping port specially equipped to handle containerized cargo

con·tain·er·ship \-nər-ˌship\ *n* (1966) : a ship specially designed or equipped for carrying containerized cargo

con·tain·ment \kən-'tān-mənt\ *n* (1655) **1** : the act, process, or means of containing **2** : the policy, process, or result of preventing the expansion of a hostile power or ideology

con·tam·i·nant \kən-'ta-mə-nənt\ *n* (1922) : something that contaminates

con·tam·i·nate \kən-'ta-mə-ˌnāt\ *vt* **-nat·ed; -nat·ing** [ME, fr. L *contaminatus*, pp. of *contaminare*; akin to L *contagio* contagion] (15c) **1 a** : to soil, stain, corrupt, or infect by contact or association ⟨bacteria *contaminated* the wound⟩ **b** : to make inferior or impure by admixture ⟨iron *contaminated* with phosphorus⟩ **2** : to make unfit for use by the introduction of unwholesome or undesirable elements — **con·tam·i·na·tive** \-ˌnā-tiv\ *adj* — **con·tam·i·na·tor** \-ˌnā-tər\ *n*
    syn CONTAMINATE, TAINT, POLLUTE, DEFILE mean to make impure or unclean. CONTAMINATE implies intrusion of or contact with dirt or foulness from an outside source ⟨water *contaminated* by industrial wastes⟩. TAINT stresses the loss of purity or cleanliness that follows contamination ⟨*tainted* meat⟩ ⟨a politician's *tainted* reputation⟩. POLLUTE, sometimes interchangeable with *contaminate*, distinctively may imply that the process which begins with contamination is complete and that what was pure or clean has been made foul, poisoned, or filthy ⟨the *polluted* waters of the river⟩. DEFILE implies befouling of what could or should have been kept clean and pure or held sacred and commonly suggests violation or desecration ⟨*defile* a hero's memory with slanderous innuendo⟩.

con·tam·i·na·tion \kən-ˌta-mə-'nā-shən\ *n* (15c) **1** : a process of contaminating : a state of being contaminated **2** : CONTAMINANT

conte \'kōⁿ(n)t\ *n* [F] (1891) : a usu. short tale of adventure

con·temn \kən-'tem\ *vt* [ME *contempnen*, fr. MF *contempner*, fr. L *contemnere*, fr. *com-* + *temnere* to despise] (15c) **1** : to view or treat with contempt : SCORN *syn* see DESPISE — **con·tem·ner** *also* **con·tem·nor** \-'tem-nər, -'te-mər\ *n*

con·tem·plate \'kän-təm-ˌplāt, -ˌtem-\ *vb* **-plat·ed; -plat·ing** [L *contemplatus*, pp. of *contemplari*, fr. *com-* + *templum* space marked out for observation of auguries — more at TEMPLE] *vt* (1537) **1** : to view or consider with continued attention : meditate on **2** : to view as contingent or probable or as an end or intention ~ *vi* : PONDER, MEDITATE *syn* see CONSIDER — **con·tem·pla·tor** \-ˌplā-tər\ *n*

con·tem·pla·tion \ˌkän-təm-'plā-shən, -ˌtem-\ *n* (13c) **1 a** : concentration on spiritual things as a form of private devotion **b** : a state of mystical awareness of God's being **2** : an act of considering with

\ə\ abut \ᵊ\ kitten, F table \ər\ further \a\ ash \ā\ ace \ä\ mop, mar \au̇\ out \ch\ chin \e\ bet \ē\ easy \g\ go \i\ hit \ī\ ice \j\ job \ŋ\ sing \ō\ go \o̩\ law \o̩i\ boy \th\ thin \t̲h̲\ the \ü\ loot \u̇\ foot \y\ yet \zh\ vision \á, k̲, ⁿ, œ, œ̄, ᵫ, ᵫ̄, �\ *see* Guide to Pronunciation attention : STUDY **3** : the act of regarding steadily **4** : INTENTION, EXPECTATION

¹con·tem·pla·tive \kən-'tem-plə-tiv; 'kän-təm-ˌplā-, -ˌtem-\ *adj* (14c) : marked by or given to contemplation; *specif* : of or relating to a religious order devoted to prayer and penance — **con·tem·pla·tive·ly** *adv* — **con·tem·pla·tive·ness** *n*

²contemplative *n* (14c) : a person who practices contemplation

con·tem·po·ra·ne·i·ty \kən-ˌtem-p(ə-)rə-'nē-ə-tē, -'nā-\ *n* (1772) : the quality or state of being contemporaneous or contemporary

con·tem·po·ra·ne·ous \kən-ˌtem-pə-'rā-nē-əs\ *adj* [L *contemporaneus*, fr. *com-* + *tempor-, tempus* time] (ca. 1656) : existing, occurring, or originating during the same time *syn* see CONTEMPORARY — **con·tem·po·ra·ne·ous·ly** *adv* — **con·tem·po·ra·ne·ous·ness** *n*

¹con·tem·po·rary \kən-'tem-pə-ˌrer-ē\ *adj* [*com-* + L *tempor-, tempus*] (1631) **1** : happening, existing, living, or coming into being during the same period of time **2 a** : SIMULTANEOUS **b** : marked by characteristics of the present period : MODERN, CURRENT — **con·tem·po·rar·i·ly** \-ˌtem-pə-'rer-ə-lē\ *adv*

syn CONTEMPORARY, CONTEMPORANEOUS, COEVAL, SYNCHRONOUS, SIMULTANEOUS, COINCIDENT mean existing or occurring at the same time. CONTEMPORARY is likely to apply to people and what relates to them ⟨Abraham Lincoln was *contemporary* with Charles Darwin⟩. CONTEMPORANEOUS applies to events ⟨*contemporaneous* accounts of the kidnapping⟩. COEVAL refers usu. to periods, ages, eras, eons ⟨two stars thought to be *coeval*⟩. SYNCHRONOUS implies exact correspondence in time and esp. in periodic intervals ⟨*synchronous* timepieces⟩. SIMULTANEOUS implies correspondence in a moment of time ⟨the two shots were *simultaneous*⟩. COINCIDENT is applied to events and may be used in order to avoid implication of causal relationship ⟨the end of World War II was *coincident* with a great vintage year⟩.

²contemporary *n, pl* **-rar·ies** (1646) **1** : one that is contemporary with another **2** : one of the same or nearly the same age as another

con·tem·po·rize \kən-'tem-pə-ˌrīz\ *vt* **-rized; -riz·ing** (1646) : to make contemporary

con·tempt \kən-'tem(p)t\ *n* [ME, fr. L *contemptus*, fr. *contemnere*] (14c) **1 a** : the act of despising : the state of mind of one who despises : DISDAIN **b** : lack of respect or reverence for something **2** : the state of being despised **3** : willful disobedience to or open disrespect of a court, judge, or legislative body ⟨~ of court⟩

con·tempt·ible \kən-'tem(p)-tə-bəl\ *adj* (14c) **1** : worthy of contempt **2** *obs* : SCORNFUL, CONTEMPTUOUS — **con·tempt·i·bil·i·ty** \-ˌtem(p)-tə-'bi-lə-tē\ *n* — **con·tempt·ible·ness** *n* — **con·tempt·ibly** \-'tem(p)-tə-blē\ *adv*

syn CONTEMPTIBLE, DESPICABLE, PITIABLE, SORRY, SCURVY mean arousing or deserving scorn. CONTEMPTIBLE may imply any quality provoking scorn or a low standing in any scale of values ⟨a *contemptible* liar⟩. DESPICABLE may imply utter worthlessness and usu. suggests arousing an attitude of moral indignation ⟨a *despicable* crime⟩. PITIABLE applies to what inspires mixed contempt and pity ⟨a *pitiable* attempt at tragedy⟩. SORRY may stress pitiable inadequacy or may suggest wretchedness or sordidness ⟨this rattletrap is a *sorry* excuse for a car⟩. SCURVY adds to DESPICABLE an implication of arousing disgust ⟨a *scurvy* crew of hangers-on⟩.

con·temp·tu·ous \-'tem(p)-chə-wəs, -chəs, -shwəs\ *adj* [L *contemptus*] (1595) : manifesting, feeling, or expressing contempt — **con·temp·tu·ous·ly** *adv* — **con·temp·tu·ous·ness** *n*

con·tend \kən-'tend\ *vb* [ME, fr. MF or L; MF *contendre*, fr. L *contendere*, fr. *com-* + *tendere* to stretch — more at THIN] *vi* (15c) **1** : to strive or vie in contest or rivalry or against difficulties : STRUGGLE **2** : to strive in debate : ARGUE ~ *vt* **1** : MAINTAIN, ASSERT ⟨~ed that he was right⟩ **2** : to struggle for : CONTEST

con·tend·er \-'ten-dər\ *n* (1547) : one that contends; *esp* : a competitor for a championship or high honor ⟨a heavyweight title ~⟩

¹con·tent \kən-'tent\ *adj* [ME, fr. MF, fr. L *contentus*, fr. pp. of *continēre* to hold in, contain — more at CONTAIN] (15c) : CONTENTED, SATISFIED

²content *vt* (15c) **1** : to appease the desires of **2** : to limit (oneself) in requirements, desires, or actions

³content *n* (1579) : CONTENTMENT ⟨ate to his heart's ~⟩

⁴con·tent \'kän-ˌtent\ *n* [ME, fr. L *contentus*, pp. of *continēre* to contain] (15c) **1 a** : something contained — usu. used in pl. ⟨the jar's ~s⟩ ⟨the drawer's ~s⟩ **b** : the topics or matter treated in a written work ⟨table of ~s⟩ **2 a** : SUBSTANCE, GIST **b** : MEANING, SIGNIFICANCE **c** : the events, physical detail, and information in a work of art — compare FORM 10b **3 a** : the matter dealt with in a field of study **b** : a part, element, or complex of parts **4** : the amount of specified material contained : PROPORTION

content analysis *n* (1945) : analysis of the manifest and latent content of a body of communicated material (as a book or film) through a classification, tabulation, and evaluation of its key symbols and themes in order to ascertain its meaning and probable effect

con·tent·ed \kən-'ten-təd\ *adj* (1526) : feeling or manifesting satisfaction with one's possessions, status, or situation ⟨a ~ smile⟩ — **con·tent·ed·ly** *adv* — **con·tent·ed·ness** *n*

con·ten·tion \kən-'ten(t)-shən\ *n* [ME *contencioun*, fr. MF, fr. L *contention-, contentio*, fr. *contendere*] (14c) **1** : an act or instance of contending **2** : a point advanced or maintained in a debate or argument **3** : RIVALRY, COMPETITION *syn* see DISCORD

con·ten·tious \kən-'ten(t)-shəs\ *adj* (15c) **1** : likely to cause contention ⟨a ~ argument⟩ **2** : exhibiting an often perverse and wearisome tendency to quarrels and disputes ⟨a man of a most ~ nature⟩ *syn* see BELLIGERENT — **con·ten·tious·ly** *adv* — **con·ten·tious·ness** *n*

con·tent·ment \kən-'tent-mənt\ *n* (15c) **1** : the quality or state of being contented **2** : something that contents

content word \'kän-ˌtent-\ *n* (1940) : a word that primarily expresses lexical meaning — compare FUNCTION WORD

con·ter·mi·nous \kän-'tər-mə-nəs, kən-\ *adj* [L *conterminus*, fr. *com-* + *terminus* boundary — more at TERM] (1631) **1** : having a common boundary **2** : COTERMINOUS **3** : enclosed within one common boundary ⟨the 48 ~ states⟩ — **con·ter·mi·nous·ly** *adv*

¹con·test \kən-'test, 'kän-\ *vb* [MF *contester*, fr. L *contestari* (litem) to bring an action at law, fr. *contestari* to call to witness, fr. *com-* + *testis* witness — more at TESTAMENT] *vi* (1603) : STRIVE, VIE ~ *vt* : to make

the subject of dispute, contention, or litigation; *esp* : DISPUTE, CHALLENGE — **con·test·able** \-'tes-tə-bəl\ *adj* — **con·test·er** *n*

²con·test \'kän-ˌtest\ *n* (1647) **1** : a struggle for superiority or victory : COMPETITION **2** : a competition in which each contestant performs without direct contact with or interference from his competitors

con·tes·tant \kən-'tes-tənt *also* 'kän-\ *n* (1665) **1** : one that participates in a contest **2** : one that contests an award or decision

con·tes·ta·tion \ˌkän-ˌtes-'tā-shən\ *n* (1580) : CONTROVERSY, DEBATE

con·text \'kän-ˌtekst\ *n* [ME, weaving together of words, fr. L *contextus* connection of words, coherence, fr. *contexere* to weave together, fr. *com-* + *texere* to weave — more at TECHNICAL] (ca. 1568) **1** : the parts of a discourse that surround a word or passage and can throw light on its meaning **2** : the interrelated conditions in which something exists or occurs : ENVIRONMENT, SETTING — **con·text·less** \-ˌtekst-ləs\ *adj* — **con·tex·tu·al** \kän-'teks-chə-wəl, kən-, -chəl\ *adj* — **con·tex·tu·al·ly** *adv*

con·text–free \'kän-ˌtekst-'frē\ *adj* (1964) : of, relating to, or being a grammar or language based on rules that describe a change in a string without reference to elements outside of the string; *also* : being such a rule

con·tex·tu·al·ize \kän-'teks-chə-wə-ˌlīz, -chə-ˌlīz\ *vt* **-ized; -iz·ing** (1934) : to place (as a word or activity) in a context

con·tex·ture \kən-'teks-chər, 'kän-ˌ, kän-\ *n* [F, fr. L *contextus*, pp. of *contexere*] (1603) **1** : the act, process, or manner of weaving parts into a whole; *also* : a structure so formed ⟨a ~ of lies⟩ **2** : CONTEXT

con·ti·gu·i·ty \ˌkän-tə-'gyü-ə-tē\ *n, pl* **-ties** (1612) : the quality or state of being contiguous : PROXIMITY

con·tig·u·ous \kən-'ti-gyə-wəs\ *adj* [L *contiguus*, fr. *contingere* to have contact with — more at CONTINGENT] (ca. 1609) **1** : being in actual contact : touching along a boundary or at a point **2** *of angles* : ADJACENT **2 3** : next or near in time or sequence **4** : touching or connected throughout in an unbroken sequence ⟨~ row houses⟩ *syn* see ADJACENT — **con·tig·u·ous·ly** *adv* — **con·tig·u·ous·ness** *n*

con·ti·nence \'kän-t²n-ən(t)s\ *n* (14c) **1** : SELF-RESTRAINT; *esp* : a refraining from sexual intercourse **2** : the ability to retain a bodily discharge voluntarily ⟨fecal ~⟩

¹con·ti·nent \'kän-t²n-ənt\ *adj* [ME, fr. MF, fr. L *continent-, continens*, fr. prp. of *continēre* to hold in — more at CONTAIN] (14c) **1** : exercising continence **2** *obs* : RESTRICTIVE — **con·ti·nent·ly** *adv*

²con·ti·nent \'kän-t²n-ənt, 'känt-nənt\ *n* [in senses 1 & 2, fr. L *continent-, continens*, prp. of *continēre*, to hold together, contain; in senses 3 & 4, fr. L *continent-, continens* continuous mass of land, mainland, fr. *continent-, continens*, prp.] (1541) **1** *archaic* : CONTAINER, CONFINES **2** *archaic* : EPITOME **3** : MAINLAND **4 a** : one of the six or seven great divisions of land on the globe **b** *cap* : the continent of Europe — used with *the*

¹con·ti·nen·tal \ˌkän-t²n-'en-t²l\ *adj* (1760) **1 a** : of, relating to, or characteristic of a continent ⟨~ waters⟩; *specif, often cap* : of or relating to the continent of Europe excluding the British Isles **b** *often cap* : of, relating to, or being a cuisine derived from the classic dishes of Europe and esp. France **2 a** *often cap* : of or relating to the colonies later forming the U.S. ⟨*Continental* Congress⟩ **b** : being the part of the U.S. on the No. American continent; *also* : being the part of the U.S. comprising the lower 48 states — **con·ti·nen·tal·ly** \-t²l-ē\ *adv*

²continental *n* (1777) **1 a** *often cap* : an American soldier of the Revolution in the Continental army **b** (1) : a piece of Continental paper currency (2) : the least bit ⟨not worth a ~⟩ **2** : an inhabitant of a continent and esp. the continent of Europe

continental breakfast *n, often cap C* (1911) : a light breakfast (as of rolls or toast and coffee)

continental drift *n* (1926) : a hypothetical slow movement of the continents on a deep-seated viscous zone within the earth — compare PLATE TECTONICS

continental shelf *n* (1892) : a shallow submarine plain of varying width forming a border to a continent and typically ending in a steep slope to the oceanic abyss

continental slope *n* (1900) : the usu. steep slope from a continental shelf to the ocean floor

con·tin·gence \kən-'tin-jən(t)s\ *n* (ca. 1530) **1** : CONTINGENCY **2** : TANGENCY

con·tin·gen·cy \kən-'tin-jən(t)-sē\ *n, pl* **-cies** (1561) **1** : the quality or state of being contingent **2** : a contingent event or condition: as **a** : an event (as an emergency) that may but is not certain to occur ⟨trying to provide for every ~⟩ **b** : something liable to happen as an adjunct to or result of something else *syn* see JUNCTURE

contingency fee *n* (1945) : a fee for services (as of a lawyer) paid upon successful completion of the services and usu. calculated as a percentage of the gain realized for the client — called also *contingent fee*

contingency table *n* (ca. 1947) : a table of data in which the row entries tabulate the data according to one variable and the column entries tabulate it according to another variable and which is used esp. in the study of the correlation between variables

¹con·tin·gent \kən-'tin-jənt\ *adj* [ME, fr. MF, fr. L *contingent-, contingens*, prp. of *contingere* to have contact with, befall, fr. *com-* + *tangere* to touch — more at TANGENT] (14c) **1** : likely but not certain to happen : POSSIBLE **2** : not logically necessary; *esp* : EMPIRICAL **3 a** : happening by chance or unforeseen causes **b** : subject to chance or unseen effects : UNPREDICTABLE **c** : intended for use in circumstances not completely foreseen **4** : dependent on or conditioned by something else **5** : not necessitated : determined by free choice *syn* see ACCIDENTAL — **con·tin·gent·ly** *adv*

²contingent *n* (1548) **1** : something contingent : CONTINGENCY **2** : a representative group : DELEGATION, DETACHMENT

con·tin·u·al \kən-'tin-yü-əl, -yəl\ *adj* [ME, fr. MF, fr. L *continuus* continuous] (14c) **1** : continuing indefinitely in time without interruption ⟨~ fear⟩ **2** : recurring in steady usu. rapid succession ⟨a history of ~ invasions⟩ — **con·tin·u·al·ly** *adv*

syn CONTINUAL, CONTINUOUS, CONSTANT, INCESSANT, PERPETUAL, PERENNIAL mean characterized by continued occurrence or recurrence. CONTINUAL often implies a close prolonged succession or recurrence ⟨*continual* showers the whole weekend⟩. CONTINUOUS usu. implies an uninterrupted flow or spatial extension ⟨football's oldest *continuous* rivalry⟩. CONSTANT implies uniform or persistent occurrence or recurrence ⟨lived in *constant* pain⟩. INCESSANT implies ceaseless or uninterrupted activity ⟨annoyed by the *incessant* quarreling⟩. PERPETUAL suggests unfailing repetition or lasting duration ⟨a land of *perpetual* snowfall⟩. PERENNIAL implies enduring existence often through constant renewal ⟨a *perennial* source of controversy⟩.

con·tin·u·ance \kən-'tin-yü-ən(t)s\ *n* (14c) **1** : CONTINUATION **2** : the extent of continuing : DURATION **3** : the quality of enduring : PERMANENCE **4** : an adjournment of a court case to a future day

con·tin·u·ant \-yü-ənt\ *n* (1861) **1** : something that continues or serves as a continuation **2** : a speech sound (as a fricative or vowel) that is produced without a complete closure of the breath passage — compare STOP — **continuant** *adj*

continuate *adj* (1555) *obs* : CONTINUOUS, UNINTERRUPTED

con·tin·u·a·tion \kən-,tin-yə-'wā-shən\ *n* (14c) **1** : the act or fact of continuing in or the prolongation of a state or activity **2** : resumption after an interruption **3** : something that continues, increases, or adds

con·tin·u·a·tive \kən-'tin-yə-,wā-tiv, -wə-tiv\ *adj* (1684) : expressing continuity or continuation (as of an idea or action)

con·tin·u·a·tor \-,wā-tər\ *n* (1646) : one that continues

con·tin·ue \kən-'tin-(,)yü\ *vb* **-tin·ued; -tinu·ing** [ME, fr. MF *continuer*, fr. L *continuare*, fr. *continuus*] *vi* (14c) **1** : to maintain without interruption a condition, course, or action **2** : to remain in existence : ENDURE **3** : to remain in a place or condition : STAY **4** : to resume an activity after interruption ~ *vt* **1 a** : KEEP UP, MAINTAIN ⟨~s walking⟩ **b** : to keep going or add to : PROLONG; *also* : to resume after intermission **2** : to cause to continue **3** : to allow to remain in a place or condition : RETAIN **4** : to postpone (a legal proceeding) by a continuance — **con·tinu·er** \-yü-ər\ *n*

syn CONTINUE, LAST, ENDURE, ABIDE, PERSIST mean to exist over a period of time or indefinitely. CONTINUE applies to a process going on without ending ⟨the search for peace will *continue*⟩. LAST, esp. when unqualified, may stress existing beyond what is normal or expected ⟨buy shoes that will *last*⟩. ENDURE adds an implication of resisting destructive forces or agencies ⟨in spite of everything, her faith *endured*⟩. ABIDE implies stable and constant existing esp. as opposed to mutability ⟨a love that *abides* through 40 years of marriage⟩. PERSIST suggests outlasting the normal or appointed time and often connotes obstinacy or doggedness ⟨the sense of guilt *persisted*⟩ .

continued *adj* (15c) **1** : lasting or extending without interruption ⟨~ success⟩ **2** : resumed after interruption ⟨a ~ story⟩

continued fraction *n* (ca. 1856) : a fraction whose numerator is an integer and whose denominator is an integer plus a fraction whose numerator is an integer and whose denominator is an integer plus a fraction and so on

contin·uing *adj* (14c) **1** : CONTINUOUS, CONSTANT ⟨~ poverty⟩ **2** : needing no renewal : ENDURING ⟨~ fame⟩ — **con·tin·u·ing·ly** *adv*

continuing education *n* (1954) : formal courses of study for adult part-time students

con·ti·nu·i·ty \,kän-t⁸n-'ü-ə-tē, -'yü-\ *n, pl* **-ties** (15c) **1 a** : uninterrupted connection, succession, or union **b** : uninterrupted duration or continuation esp. without essential change **2** : something that has, exhibits, or provides continuity: as **a** : a script or scenario in the performing arts **b** : transitional spoken or musical matter esp. for a radio or television program **c** : the story and dialogue of a comic strip **3** : the property of being mathematically continuous

con·tin·uo \kən-'tin-yə-,wō, -'ti-nə-\ *n, pl* **-u·os** [It, fr. *continuo* continuous, fr. L *continuus*] (1724) : a bass part (as for a keyboard or stringed instrument) used esp. in baroque ensemble music and consisting of a succession of bass notes with figures that indicate the required chords — called also *figured bass, thoroughbass*

con·tin·u·ous \kən-'tin-yü-əs\ *adj* [L *continuus*, fr. *continēre* to hold together — more at CONTAIN] (1673) **1** : marked by uninterrupted extension in space, time, or sequence **2** *of a function* : having the property that the absolute value of the numerical difference between the value at a given point and the value at any point in a neighborhood of the given point can be made as close to zero as desired by choosing the neighborhood small enough *syn* see CONTINUAL — **con·tin·u·ous·ly** *adv* — **con·tin·u·ous·ness** *n*

con·tin·u·um \kən-'tin-yü-əm\ *n, pl* **-ua** \-yü-ə\ *also* **-u·ums** [L, neut. of *continuus*] (1646) **1** : a coherent whole characterized as a collection, sequence, or progression of values or elements varying by minute degrees ⟨"good" and "bad" . . . stand at opposite ends of a ~ instead of describing the two halves of a line —Wayne Shumaker⟩ **2** : the set of real numbers including both the rationals and the irrationals; *broadly* : a compact set which cannot be separated into two sets neither of which contains a limit point of the other

con·tort \kən-'tȯrt\ *vb* [ME, fr. L *contortus*, pp. of *contorquēre*, fr. *com-* + *torquēre* to twist — more at TORTURE] *vt* (15c) : to twist in a violent manner ⟨features ~ed with fury⟩ ~ *vi* : to twist into or as if into a strained shape or expression *syn* see DEFORM — **con·tor·tion** \-'tȯr-shən\ *n* — **con·tor·tive** \-'tȯr-tiv\ *adj*

con·tor·tion·ist \kən-'tȯr-sh(ə-)nist\ *n* (1859) : one who contorts; *specif* : an acrobat able to twist the body into unusual postures — **con·tor·tion·is·tic** \-,tȯr-shə-'nis-tik\ *adj*

¹con·tour \'kän-,tu̇r\ *n* [F, fr. *contorno* to round off, fr. ML, to turn around, fr. L *com-* + *tornare* to turn on a lathe — more at TURN] (1662) **1** : an outline esp. of a curving or irregular figure : SHAPE; *also* : the line representing this outline **2** : the general form or structure of something : CHARACTERISTIC — often used in pl. ⟨~s of a melody⟩ ⟨to delineate the tortured psychological ~s of the tribal past —B. J. Phillips⟩ **3** : a usu. meaningful change in intonation in speech *syn* see OUTLINE

²contour *adj* (1844) **1** : following contour lines or forming furrows or ridges along them ⟨~ flooding⟩ ⟨~ farming⟩ **2** : made to fit the contour of something ⟨a ~ couch⟩ ⟨~ sheets⟩

³contour *vt* (1871) **1 a** : to shape the contour of **b** : to shape so as to fit contours **2** : to construct (as a road) in conformity to a contour

contour feather *n* (1867) : one of the medium-sized feathers that form the general covering of a bird and determine the external contour

contour line *n* (1844) : a line (as on a map) connecting the points on a land surface that have the same elevation

contour map *n* (1862) : a map having contour lines

¹con·tra \'kän-trə\ *prep* [L] (15c) **1** : AGAINST — used chiefly in the phrase *pro and contra* **2** : in opposition or contrast to — used before a proper name

²con·tra \'kän-trə, 'kȯn-, -,trä\ *n* [AmerSp, short for *contra-revolucionario* counterrevolutionary] (1981) : a member of a guerrilla group opposed to the Sandinista government in Nicaragua

contra- *prefix* [ME, fr. L, fr. *contra* against, opposite — more at COUNTER] **1** : against : contrary : contrasting ⟨*contra*distinction⟩ **2** : pitched below normal bass ⟨*contra*octave⟩

contour map

con·tra·band \'kän-trə-,band\ *n* [It *contrabbando*, fr. ML *contrabannum*, fr. *contra-* + *bannus, bannum* decree, of Gmc origin; akin to OHG *bannan* to command — more at BAN] (ca. 1529) **1** : illegal or prohibited traffic in goods : SMUGGLING **2** : goods or merchandise whose importation, exportation, or possession is forbidden; *also* : smuggled goods **3** : a slave who during the Civil War escaped to or was brought within the Union lines — **contraband** *adj*

con·tra·band·ist \-,ban-dist\ *n* (ca. 1818) : SMUGGLER

con·tra·bass \'kän-trə-,bäs\ *n* [It *contrabbasso*, fr. *contra-* + *basso* bass] (ca. 1611) : DOUBLE BASS — **con·tra·bass·ist** \-,bä-sist\ *n*

con·tra·bas·soon \,kän-trə-bə-'sün, -ba-\ *n* (1891) : a double-reed woodwind instrument having a range an octave lower than that of the bassoon — called also *double bassoon*

con·tra·cep·tion \,kän-trə-'sep-shən\ *n* [*contra-* + conception] (1886) : deliberate prevention of conception or impregnation — **con·tra·cep·tive** \-'sep-tiv\ *adj or n*

¹con·tract \'kän-,trakt\ *n* [ME, fr. L *contractus*, fr. *contrahere* to draw together, make a contract, reduce in size, fr. *com-* + *trahere* to draw] (14c) **1 a** : a binding agreement between two or more persons or parties; *esp* : one legally enforceable **b** : a business arrangement for the supply of goods or services at a fixed price ⟨make parts on ~⟩ **c** : the act of marriage or an agreement to marry **2** : a document describing the terms of a contract **3** : the final bid to win a specified number of tricks in bridge **4** : an order or arrangement for a hired assassin to kill someone

²con·tract *vt* 2a & *vi* 1 *usu* 'kän-,trakt, *others usu* kən-'\ *vb* [ME, fr. MF or L; MF *contracter* to agree upon, fr. L *contractus*] (14c) **1 a** : to bring on oneself esp. inadvertently : INCUR ⟨~ing debts⟩ **b** : to become affected with ⟨~ pneumonia⟩ **2 a** : to establish or undertake by contract **b** : BETROTH; *also* : to establish (a marriage) formally **c** (1) : to hire by contract (2) : to purchase (as goods or services) on a contract basis — often used with *out* **3 a** : LIMIT, RESTRICT **b** : KNIT, WRINKLE ⟨frown ~ed his brow⟩ **c** : to draw together : CONCENTRATE **4** : to reduce to smaller size by or as if by squeezing or forcing together **5** : to shorten (as a word) by omitting one or more sounds or letters ~ *vi* **1** : to make a contract **2** : to draw together so as to become diminished in size ⟨metal ~s on cooling⟩; *also* : to become less in compass, duration, or length ⟨muscle ~s in tetanus⟩ — **con·tract·ibil·i·ty** \kən-,trak-tə-'bi-lə-tē, ,kän-\ *n* — **con·tract·ible** \kən-'trak-tə-bəl, 'kän-,\ *adj*

syn CONTRACT, SHRINK, CONDENSE, COMPRESS, CONSTRICT, DEFLATE mean to decrease in bulk or volume. CONTRACT applies to a drawing together of surfaces or particles or a reduction of area or length ⟨caused her muscles to *contract*⟩. SHRINK implies a contracting or a loss of material and stresses a falling short of original dimensions ⟨the sweater will *shrink* when washed⟩. CONDENSE implies a reducing of something homogeneous to greater compactness without significant loss of content ⟨*condense* the essay into a paragraph⟩. COMPRESS implies a pressing into a small compass and definite shape usu. against resistance ⟨*compressed* cotton into bales⟩. CONSTRICT implies a tightening that reduces diameter ⟨the throat is *constricted* by a tight collar⟩. DEFLATE implies a contracting by reducing the internal pressure of contained air or gas ⟨*deflate* the balloon⟩.

contract bridge \'kän-,trakt-\ *n* (1924) : a bridge game distinguished by the fact that overtricks do not count toward game or slam bonuses

con·trac·tile \kən-'trak-t⁸l, -,tīl\ *adj* (ca. 1706) : having or concerned with the power or property of contracting ⟨~ proteins of muscle fibrils⟩ — **con·trac·til·i·ty** \,kän-,trak-'ti-lə-tē\ *n*

contractile vacuole *n* (1877) : a vacuole in a unicellular organism that contracts regularly to discharge fluid from the body

con·trac·tion \kən-'trak-shən\ *n* (15c) **1 a** : the action or process of contracting : the state of being contracted **b** : the shortening and thickening of a functioning muscle or muscle fiber **c** : a reduction in business activity or growth **2** : a shortening of a word, syllable, or word group by omission of a sound or letter; *also* : a form produced by such shortening — **con·trac·tion·al** \-shnəl, -shə-n⁸l\ *adj* — **con·trac·tive** \kən-'trak-tiv, 'kän-,\ *adj* — **con·trac·tion·ary** \kən-'trak-shə-,ner-ē\ *adj*

con·trac·tor *1 usu* 'kän-,trak-tər, *2 usu* kən-'\ *n* (1548) **1** : one that contracts or is party to a contract: as **a** : one that contracts to perform work or provide supplies **b** : one that contracts to erect buildings **2** : something (as a muscle) that contracts or shortens

con·trac·tu·al \kən-'trak-chə-wəl, -chəl, -shwəl\ *adj* (1861) : of, relating to, or constituting a contract — **con·trac·tu·al·ly** *adv*

con·trac·ture \kən-'trak-chər\ *n* (1601) : a permanent shortening (as of muscle, tendon, or scar tissue) producing deformity or distortion

con·tra·dict \,kän-trə-'dikt\ *vt* [L *contradictus*, pp. of *contradicere*, fr. *contra-* + *dicere* to say, speak — more at DICTION] (ca. 1576) **1** : to assert the contrary of : take issue with **2** : to imply the opposite or a denial of ⟨your actions ~ your words⟩ *syn* see DENY — **con·tra·dict·able** \-'dik-tə-bəl\ *adj* — **con·tra·dic·tor** \-'dik-tər\ *n*

con·tra·dic·tion \,kän-trə-'dik-shən\ *n* (14c) **1** : act or an instance of contradicting **2 a** : a proposition, statement, or phrase that asserts or implies both the truth and falsity of something **b** : a statement or phrase whose parts contradict each other ⟨a round square is a ~ in terms⟩ **3 a** : logical incongruity **b** : a situation in which inherent

\ə\ abut \'\ kitten, F table \ər\ further \a\ ash \ā\ ace \ä\ mop, mar \au̇\ out \ch\ chin \e\ bet \ē\ easy \g\ go \i\ hit \ī\ ice \j\ job \ŋ\ sing \ō\ go \ȯ\ law \ȯi\ boy \th\ thin \t͟h\ the \ü\ loot \u̇\ foot \y\ yet \zh\ vision \á, k̲, ⁿ, œ, œ̄, ᴜe, ᴜ̄e, ᵞ\ see Guide to Pronunciation factors, actions, or propositions are inconsistent or contrary to one another

con·tra·dic·tious \-shəs\ *adj* (1604) **1** : CONTRADICTORY, OPPOSITE **2** : given to or marked by contradiction : CONTRARY

¹**con·tra·dic·to·ry** \ˌkän-trə-'dik-t(ə-)rē\ *n, pl* **-ries** (14c) : a proposition so related to another that if either of the two is true the other is false and if either is false the other must be true

²**contradictory** *adj* (1534) : involving, causing, or constituting a contradiction **syn** see OPPOSITE — **con·tra·dic·to·ri·ly** \-t(ə-)rə-lē\ *adv* — **con·tra·dic·to·ri·ness** \-t(ə-)rē-nəs\ *n*

con·tra·dis·tinc·tion \ˌkän-trə-dis-'tiŋ(k)-shən\ *n* (1647) : distinction by means of contrast ⟨painting in ~ to sculpture⟩ — **con·tra·dis·tinc·tive** \-'tiŋ(k)-tiv\ *adj* — **con·tra·dis·tinc·tive·ly** *adv*

con·tra·dis·tin·guish \-'tiŋ-gwish\ *vt* (1622) : to distinguish by contrasting qualities

con·trail \'kän-ˌtrāl\ *n* [*condensation trail*] (1943) : streaks of condensed water vapor created in the air by an airplane or rocket at high altitudes

con·tra·in·di·cate \ˌkän-trə-'in-də-ˌkāt\ *vt* (1666) : to make (a treatment or procedure) inadvisable

con·tra·in·di·ca·tion \-ˌin-də-'kā-shən\ *n* (1623) : something (as a symptom or condition) that makes a particular treatment or procedure inadvisable

con·tra·lat·er·al \-'la-t(ə-)rəl\ *adj* [ISV] (1882) : occurring on or acting in conjunction with a part on the opposite side of the body

con·tral·to \kən-'tral-(ˌ)tō\ *n, pl* **-tos** [It, fr. *contra-* + *alto*] (1730) **1 a** : a singing voice having a range between tenor and mezzo-soprano **b** : a person having this voice **2** : the part sung by a contralto

con·tra·oc·tave \ˌkän-trə-'äk-tiv, -təv, -ˌtäv\ *n* (ca. 1891) : the musical octave that begins on the third C below middle C — see PITCH illustration

con·tra·po·si·tion \-pə-'zi-shən\ *n* [LL *contraposition-, contrapositio*, fr. L *contraponere* to place opposite, fr. *contra-* + *ponere* to place — more at POSITION] (1551) : the relationship between two propositions when the subject and predicate of one are respectively the negation of the predicate and the negation of the subject of the other

con·tra·pos·i·tive \-'pä-zə-tiv, -'päz-tiv\ *n* (1870) : a proposition resulting from an operation of immediate inference in which the terms of a given proposition are permuted and negated ⟨"all not-*P* is not-*S*" is the ~ of "all *S* is *P*"⟩

con·trap·tion \kən-'trap-shən\ *n* [perh. blend of *contrivance, trap,* and *invention*] (ca. 1825) : DEVICE, GADGET

con·tra·pun·tal \ˌkän-trə-'pən-t³l\ *adj* [It *contrappunto* counterpoint, fr. ML *contrapunctus* — more at COUNTERPOINT] (1845) **1** : POLYPHONIC **2** : of, relating to, or marked by counterpoint — **con·tra·pun·tal·ly** \-t³l-ē\ *adv*

con·tra·pun·tist \-'pən-tist\ *n* (1776) : one who writes counterpoint

con·trar·i·an \kən-'trer-ē-ən, kän-\ *n* (1657) : a person who takes a contrary position or attitude; *specif* : an investor who buys shares of stock when most others are selling and sells when others are buying — **contrarian** *adj*

con·tra·ri·ety \ˌkän-trə-'rī-ə-tē\ *n, pl* **-eties** [ME *contrariete*, fr. MF *contrarieté*, fr. LL *contrarietat-, contrarietas*, fr. L *contrarius* contrary] (14c) **1** : the quality or state of being contrary **2** : something contrary

con·trar·i·ous \kən-'trer-ē-əs, kän-\ *adj* (13c) : PERVERSE, ANTAGONISTIC

con·trari·wise \'kän-ˌtrer-ē-ˌwīz, kən-'\ *adv* (14c) **1** : on the contrary **2** : VICE VERSA **3** : in a contrary manner

¹**con·trary** \'kän-ˌtrer-ē\ *n, pl* **-trar·ies** (13c) **1** : a fact or condition incompatible with another : OPPOSITE — usu. used with *the* **2** : one of a pair of opposites **3 a** : a proposition so related to another that though both may be false they cannot both be true — compare SUBCONTRARY **b** : either of two terms (as *good* and *evil*) that cannot both be affirmed of the same subject — **by contraries** *obs* : in a manner opposite to what is logical or expected — **on the contrary** : just the opposite — **to the contrary** **1** : on the contrary **2** : NOTWITHSTANDING

²**con·trary** *same as* ²\ *adv* (15c) : CONTRARIWISE, CONTRARILY

contrary to *prep* (14c) : in conflict with : DESPITE ⟨*contrary to* orders, he set out alone⟩

¹**con·trast** \kən-'trast, 'kän-ˌ\ *vb* [F *contraster*, fr. MF, to oppose, resist, alter. of *contrester*, fr. (assumed) VL *contrastare*, fr. L *contra-* + *stare* to stand — more at STAND] (1695) : to set off in contrast : compare or appraise in respect to differences ⟨~ European and American manners⟩ — often used with *to* or *with* ⟨~ing her with other women — Victoria Sackville-West⟩ ~ *vi* : to form a contrast **syn** see COMPARE — **con·trast·able** \-'tras-tə-bəl, -ˌtras-\ *adj*

²**con·trast** \'kän-ˌtrast\ *n* (1711) **1 a** : juxtaposition of dissimilar elements (as color, tone, or emotion) in a work of art **b** : degree of difference between the lightest and darkest parts of a picture **2 a** : the difference or degree of difference between things having similar or comparable natures ⟨the ~ between the two forms of government⟩ **b** : comparison of similar objects to set off their dissimilar qualities : the state of being so compared ⟨the enforced simplicity in this diary . . . is

in ~ to the intensity of his former life —*Times Lit. Supp.*⟩ **3** : a person or thing that exhibits differences when compared with another

con·tras·tive \kən-'tras-tiv, 'kän-ˌ\ *adj* (1841) : forming or consisting of a contrast — **con·tras·tive·ly** *adv*

con·trasty \'kän-ˌtras-tē\ *adj* (1891) : having or producing in photography great contrast between highlights and shadows

con·tra·vene \ˌkän-trə-'vēn\ *vt* **-vened; -ven·ing** [MF or LL; MF *contrevenir*, fr. LL *contravenire*, fr. L *contra-* + *venire* to come — more at COME] (1567) **1** : to go or act contrary to : VIOLATE ⟨~ a law⟩ **2** : to oppose in argument : CONTRADICT ⟨~ a proposition⟩ **syn** see DENY — **con·tra·ven·er** *n*

con·tra·ven·tion \ˌkän-trə-'ven(t)-shən\ *n* [MF, fr. LL *contravenire*] (1579) : the act of contravening : VIOLATION

con·tre·danse \'kän-trə-ˌdan(t)s, kō⁻-trə-ˈdä⁻s\ *or* **con·tra dance** \'kän-trə-ˌdan(t)s\ *n* [F *contredanse*, by folk etymology fr. E *country-dance*] (1803) **1** : a folk dance in which couples face each other in two lines or in a square **2** : a piece of music for a contredanse

con·tre·temps \'kän-trə-ˌtä⁻, kō⁻-trə-tä⁻\ *n, pl* **con·tre·temps** \-(ˌ)tä⁻(z)\ [F, *contre-* counter- + *temps* time, fr. L *tempus*] (1769) : an inopportune or embarrassing occurrence or situation

con·trib·ute \kən-'tri-byət, -(ˌ)byüt *also & esp before -ed or -ing* 'tri-bət; *chiefly Brit also* 'kän-trə-ˌbyüt\ *vb* **-ut·ed; -ut·ing** [L *contributus*, pp. of *contribuere*, fr. *com-* + *tribuere* to grant — more at TRIBUTE] *vt* (1530) **1** : to give or supply in common with others **2** : to supply (as an article) for a publication ~ *vi* **1 a** : to give a part to a common fund or store **b** : to play a significant part in bringing about an end or result **2** : to submit articles to a publication — **con·trib·u·tor** \-byə-tər, -bə-, -ˌbyü-\ *n*

con·tri·bu·tion \ˌkän-trə-'byü-shən\ *n* (14c) **1** : a payment (as a levy or tax) imposed by military, civil, or ecclesiastical authorities usu. for a special or extraordinary purpose **2** : the act of contributing; *also* : the thing contributed — **con·trib·u·tive** \kən-'tri-byə-tiv\ *adj* — **con·trib·u·tive·ly** *adv*

con·trib·u·to·ry \kən-'tri-byə-ˌtōr-ē, -ˌtȯr-\ *adj* (15c) **1 a** : subject to a levy of supplies, money, or men **b** : contributing to a common fund or enterprise **2** : of, relating to, or forming a contribution

con·trite \'kän-ˌtrīt, kən-\ *adj* [ME *contrit*, fr. MF, fr. ML *contritus*, fr. L, pp. of *conterere* to grind, bruise, fr. *com-* + *terere* to rub — more at THROW] (14c) **1** : grieving and penitent for sin or shortcoming **2** : proceeding from contrition ⟨~ sighs⟩ — **con·trite·ly** *adv* — **con·trite·ness** *n*

con·tri·tion \kən-'tri-shən\ *n* (14c) : the state of being contrite : REPENTANCE **syn** see PENITENCE

con·triv·ance \kən-'trī-vən(t)s\ *n* (ca. 1628) **1 a** : a thing contrived; *esp* : a mechanical device **b** : an artificial arrangement or development **2** : the act or faculty of contriving : the state of being contrived

con·trive \kən-'trīv\ *vb* **con·trived; con·triv·ing** [ME *controven, contreven*, fr. MF *controver*, fr. ML *contropare* to compare, fr. L *com-* + (assumed) VL *tropare* to compose, find — more at TROUBADOUR] *vt* (14c) **1 a** : DEVISE, PLAN ⟨~ ways of handling the situation⟩ **b** : to form or create in an artistic or ingenious manner ⟨*contrived* household utensils from stone⟩ **2** : to bring about by stratagem or with difficulty : MANAGE ~ *vi* : to make schemes — **con·triv·er** *n*

contrived *adj* (15c) : ARTIFICIAL, LABORED

¹**con·trol** \kən-'trōl\ *vt* **con·trolled; con·trol·ling** [ME *controllen*, fr. MF *contreroller*, fr. *contrerolle* copy of an account, audit, fr. ML *contrarotulus*, fr. L *contra-* + ML *rotulus* roll — more at ROLL] (15c) **1 a** *archaic* : to check, test, or verify by evidence or experiments **b** : to incorporate suitable controls in ⟨a *controlled* experiment⟩ **2 a** : to exercise restraining or directing influence over : REGULATE **b** : to have power over : RULE **c** : to reduce the incidence or severity of esp. to innocuous levels ⟨~ an insect population⟩ ⟨~ a disease⟩ **syn** see CONDUCT — **con·trol·la·bil·i·ty** \-ˌtrō-lə-'bi-lə-tē\ *n* — **con·trol·la·ble** \-'trō-lə-bəl\ *adj* — **con·trol·ment** \-'trōl-mənt\ *n*

²**control** *n, often attrib* (1590) **1 a** : an act or instance of controlling; *also* : power or authority to guide or manage **b** : skill in the use of a tool, instrument, technique, or artistic medium **c** : the regulation of economic activity esp. by government directive — usu. used in pl. ⟨price ~s⟩ **2** : RESTRAINT, RESERVE **3** : one that controls: as **a** (1) : an experiment in which the subjects are treated as in a parallel experiment except for omission of the procedure or agent under test and which is used as a standard of comparison in judging experimental effects — called also *control experiment* (2) : one (as an organism, culture, or group) that is part of a control **b** : a device or mechanism used to regulate or guide the operation of a machine, apparatus, or system **c** : an organization that directs a spaceflight ⟨mission ~⟩ **d** : a personality or spirit believed to actuate the utterances or performances of a spiritualist medium **syn** see POWER

con·trolled \kən-'trōld\ *adj* (1586) **1** : RESTRAINED **2** : regulated by law with regard to possession and use ⟨~ drugs⟩

con·trol·ler \kən-'trō-lər, 'kän-ˌ\ *n* [ME *contreroller*, fr. MF *contrerolleur*, fr. *contrerolle*] (15c) **1 a** : COMPTROLLER 1 **b** : COMPTROLLER 2 **c** : the chief accounting officer of a business enterprise or an institution (as a college) **2 a** : one that controls or has power or authority to control ⟨air traffic ~⟩ **b** : CONTROL 3b — **con·trol·ler·ship** \-ˌship\ *n*

controlling interest *n* (ca. 1924) : sufficient stock ownership in a corporation to exert control over policy

control surface *n* (1917) : a movable airfoil designed to change the attitude of an aircraft

con·tro·ver·sial \ˌkän-trə-'vər-shəl, -'vər-sē-əl\ *adj* (1583) **1** : of, relating to, or arousing controversy : DISPUTATIOUS — **con·tro·ver·sial·ism** \-shə-ˌli-zəm, -sē-ə-\ *n* — **con·tro·ver·sial·ist** \-list\ *n* — **con·tro·ver·sial·ly** *adv*

con·tro·ver·sy \'kän-trə-ˌvər-sē, *Brit also* kən-'trä-vər-sē\ *n, pl* **-sies** [ME *controversie*, fr. L *controversia*, fr. *controversus* disputable, lit., turned against, fr. *contro-* (akin to *contra-*) + *versus*, pp. of *vertere* to turn — more at WORTH] (14c) **1** : a discussion marked esp. by the expression of opposing views : DISPUTE **2** : QUARREL, STRIFE

con·tro·vert \'kän-trə-ˌvərt, ˌkän-trə-'\ *vb* [*controversy*] *vt* (1609) : to dispute or oppose by reasoning ⟨~ a point in a discussion⟩ ~ *vi* : to engage in controversy — **con·tro·vert·er** \-ˌvər-tər, -'vər-\ *n* — **con·tro·vert·ible** \-tə-bəl\ *adj*

con·tu·ma·cious \ˌkän-tü-'mā-shəs, -tyü-', -chə-\ *adj* (ca. 1600) : stubbornly disobedient : REBELLIOUS — **con·tu·ma·cious·ly** *adv*

con·tu·ma·cy \ˈkän-tü-mə-sē, -ˈtyü-; ˈkän-tü-, -tyü-, -chə-\ *n* [ME *contumacie*, fr. L *contumacia*, fr. *contumac-*, *contumax* rebellious] (13c) : stubborn resistance to authority; *specif* : willful contempt of court

con·tu·me·li·ous \ˌkän-tü-ˈmē-lē-əs, -tyü-ˈ, -chə-ˈ\ *adj* (15c) : insolently abusive and humiliating — **con·tu·me·li·ous·ly** *adv*

con·tume·ly \ˈkän-ˈtü-mə-lē, kən-, -ˈtyü-; ˈkän-tü-ˌmē-lē, -tyü-ˌ, -chə-ˌ; in "*Hamlet*" ˈkän-(ˌ)tyüm-lē *or* ˈkän-chəm-\ *n, pl* **-lies** [ME *contumelie*, fr. MF, fr. L *contumelia*] (14c) : harsh language or treatment arising from haughtiness and contempt; *also* : an instance of such language or treatment

con·tu·sion \kən-ˈtü-zhən, -ˈtyü-\ *n* [ME *conteschown*, fr. MF *contusion*, fr. L *contusion-*, *contusio*, fr. *contundere* to pound, bruise, fr. *com-* + *tundere* to beat; akin to Goth *stautan* to strike, Skt *tudati* he pushes] (15c) : injury to tissue usu. without laceration : BRUISE 1a — **con·tuse** \-ˈtüz, -ˈtyüz\ *vt*

co·nun·drum \kə-ˈnən-drəm\ *n* [origin unknown] (1645) **1** : a riddle whose answer is or involves a pun **2** **a** : a question or problem having only a conjectural answer **b** : an intricate and difficult problem

con·ur·ba·tion \ˌkä-(ˌ)nər-ˈbā-shən\ *n* [*com-* + L *urb-*, *urbs* city] (1915) : an aggregation or continuous network of urban communities

co·nus ar·te·ri·o·sus \ˈkō-nəs-är-ˌtir-ē-ˈō-səs\ *n, pl* **co·ni ar·te·ri·o·si** \-ˌnī-är-ˌtir-ē-ˈō-ˌsī\ [NL, lit., arterial cone] (ca. 1860) **1** : a conical prolongation of the right ventricle in mammals from which the pulmonary arteries emerge — called also *conus* **2** : a prolongation of the ventricle of amphibians and some fishes that has a spiral valve separating venous blood going to the respiratory arteries from blood going to the aorta and systemic arteries

con·va·lesce \ˌkän-və-ˈles\ *vi* **-lesced; -lesc·ing** [L *convalescere*, fr. *com-* + *valescere* to grow strong, fr. *valēre* to be strong, be well — more at WIELD] (15c) : to recover health and strength gradually after sickness or weakness — **con·va·les·cence** \-ˈle-sᵊn(t)s\ *n* — **con·va·les·cent** \-sᵊnt\ *adj or n*

con·vect \kən-ˈvekt\ *vb* [back-formation fr. *convection*] *vi* (1881) : to transfer heat by convection ~ *vt* : to circulate (as air) by convection — **con·vec·tive** \-ˈvek-tiv\ *adj*

con·vec·tion \kən-ˈvek-shən\ *n* [LL *convection-*, *convectio*, fr. L *convehere* to bring together, fr. *com-* + *vehere* to carry — more at WAY] (ca. 1623) **1** : the action or process of conveying **2** **a** : the circulatory motion that occurs in a fluid at a nonuniform temperature owing to the variation of its density and the action of gravity **b** : the transfer of heat by convection — compare CONDUCTION, RADIATION — **con·vec·tion·al** \-shnəl, -shə-nᵊl\ *adj*

convection oven *n* (1973) : an oven having a fan that circulates hot air uniformly and continuously around food

con·vec·tor \-ˈvek-tər\ *n* (1907) : a heating unit in which air heated by contact with a heating device (as a radiator or a tube with fins) in a casing circulates by convection

con·vene \kən-ˈvēn\ *vb* **con·vened; con·ven·ing** [ME, fr. MF *convenir* to come together, fr. L *convenire*] *vi* (15c) : to come together in a body ~ *vt* **1** : to summon before a tribunal **2** : to cause to assemble **syn** see SUMMON — **con·ven·er** *or* **con·ve·nor** \-ˈvē-nər\ *n*

¹con·ve·nience \kən-ˈvēn-yən(t)s\ *n* (14c) **1** : fitness or suitability for performing an action or fulfilling a requirement **2** **a** : something (as an appliance, device, or service) conducive to comfort or ease **b** *chiefly Brit* : TOILET **3** **3** : a suitable or convenient time ⟨at your ~⟩ **4** : freedom from discomfort : EASE

²convenience *adj* (1917) : designed for quick and easy preparation or use ⟨~ foods⟩

convenience store *n* (1965) : a small often franchised market that is open long hours

con·ve·nien·cy \-yən(t)-sē\ *n* (1601) *archaic* : CONVENIENCE

con·ve·nient \kən-ˈvēn-yənt\ *adj* [ME, fr. L *convenient-*, *conveniens*, fr. prp. of *convenire* to come together, be suitable, fr. *com-* + *venire* to come — more at COME] (14c) **1** *obs* : SUITABLE, PROPER **2** **a** : suited to personal comfort or to easy performance **b** : suited to a particular situation **c** : affording accommodation or advantage **3** : being near at hand : HANDY — **con·ve·nient·ly** *adv*

¹con·vent \ˈkän-vənt, -ˌvent\ *n* [ME *covent*, fr. OF, fr. ML *conventus*, fr. L, assembly, fr. *convenire*] (13c) : a local community or house of a religious order or congregation; *esp* : an establishment of nuns

²con·vent \kən-ˈvent\ *vb* [L *conventus*, pp. of *convenire*] (1514) *obs* : CONVENE

con·ven·ti·cle \kən-ˈven-ti-kəl\ *n* [ME, fr. L *conventiculum*, dim. of *conventus* assembly] (14c) **1** : ASSEMBLY, MEETING **2** : an assembly of an irregular or unlawful character **3** : an assembly for religious worship; *esp* : a secret meeting for worship not sanctioned by law **4** : MEETINGHOUSE — **con·ven·ti·cler** \-k(ə-)lər\ *n*

con·ven·tion \kən-ˈven(t)-shən\ *n* [ME, fr. MF *or* L; MF, fr. L *convention-*, *conventio*, fr. *convenire*] (15c) **1** **a** : AGREEMENT, CONTRACT **b** : an agreement between states for regulation of matters affecting all of them **c** : a compact between opposing commanders esp. concerning prisoner exchange or armistice **d** : a general agreement about basic principles or procedures; *also* : a principle or procedure accepted as true or correct by convention **2** **a** : the summoning or convening of an assembly **b** : an assembly of persons met for a common purpose; *esp* : a meeting of the delegates of a political party for the purpose of formulating a platform and selecting candidates for office **c** : the usu. state or national organization of a religious denomination **3** **a** : usage or custom esp. in social matters **b** : a rule of conduct or behavior **c** : a practice in bidding or playing that conveys information between partners in a card game (as bridge) **4** : an established technique, practice, or device (as in literature or the theater)

con·ven·tion·al \-ˈvench-nəl, -ˈven(t)-shə-nᵊl\ *adj* (15c) **1** : formed by agreement or compact **2** : according with, sanctioned by, or based on convention **3** : lacking originality or individuality : TRITE **c** (1) : ORDINARY, COMMONPLACE (2) : NONNUCLEAR 1 ⟨~ warfare⟩ **3** **a** : according with a mode of artistic representation that simplifies or provides symbols or substitutes for natural forms **b** : of traditional design **4** : of, resembling, or relating to a convention, assembly, or public meeting **syn** see CEREMONIAL — **con·ven·tion·al·ism** \-nə-ˌli-zəm, -nᵊl-ˌi-zəm\ *n* — **con·ven·tion·al·ist** \-list\ *n or adj* — **con·ven·tion·al·i·za·tion** \-ˌvench-nə-lə-ˈzā-shən, -ˌven(t)-shə-nᵊl-ə-ˈzā-\ *n* — **con·ven·tion·al·ize** \-ˈvench-nə-ˌlīz, -ˈven(t)-shə-nᵊl-ˌīz\ *vt* — **con·ven·tion·al·ly** *adv*

con·ven·tion·al·i·ty \-ˌven(t)-shə-ˈna-lə-tē\ *n, pl* **-ties** (ca. 1834) **1** : conventional usage, practice, or thing **2** : the quality or state of being conventional; *esp* : adherence to conventions

con·ven·tion·eer \kən-ˌven(t)-shə-ˈnir\ *n* (1926) : a person attending a convention

¹con·ven·tu·al \kən-ˈven-chə-wəl, kän-, -ˈvench-wəl\ *adj* [ME, fr. MF or ML; MF, fr. ML *conventualis*, fr. *conventus* convent] (15c) **1** : of, relating to, or befitting a convent or monastic life : MONASTIC **2** *cap* : of or relating to the Conventuals — **con·ven·tu·al·ly** *adv*

²conventual *n* (1533) **1** *cap* : a member of the Order of Friars Minor Conventual forming a branch of the first order of St. Francis of Assisi under a mitigated rule **2** : a member of a conventual community

con·verge \kən-ˈvərj\ *vb* **con·verged; con·verg·ing** [LL *convergere*, fr. L *com-* + *vergere* to bend, incline — more at WRENCH] *vi* (1691) **1** : to tend or move toward one point or one another : come together : MEET **2** : to come together and unite in a common interest or focus **3** : to approach a limit as the number of terms increases without limit ~ *vt* : to cause to converge

con·ver·gence \kən-ˈvər-jən(t)s\ *n* (1713) **1** : the act of converging and esp. moving toward union or uniformity; *esp* : coordinated movement of the two eyes so that the image of a single point is formed on corresponding retinal areas **2** : the state or property of being convergent **3** : independent development of similar characters (as of bodily structure or cultural traits) often associated with similarity of habits or environment

con·ver·gen·cy \-jən(t)-sē\ *n* (1709) : CONVERGENCE

con·ver·gent \-jənt\ *adj* (ca. 1751) **1** : tending to move toward one point or to approach each other : CONVERGING ⟨~ lines⟩ **2** : exhibiting convergence in form, function, or development ⟨~ evolution⟩ **3** **a** *of an improper integral* : having a value that is a real number **b** : characterized by having the *n*th term or the sum of the first *n* terms approach a finite limit ⟨a ~ sequence⟩ ⟨a ~ series⟩

converging lens *n* (1860) : a lens that causes parallel rays (as of light) to come to a focus

con·vers·able \kən-ˈvər-sə-bəl\ *adj* (ca. 1631) **1** *archaic* : relating to or suitable for social interaction **2** : pleasant and easy to converse with

con·ver·sance \kən-ˈvər-sᵊn(t)s *also* ˈkän-vər-sən(t)s\ *n* (1609) : the quality or state of being conversant

con·ver·san·cy \-sᵊn(t)-sē, -sən(t)-\ *n* (1798) : CONVERSANCE

con·ver·sant \kən-ˈvər-sᵊnt *also* ˈkän-vər-sənt\ *adj* (14c) **1** *archaic* : having frequent or familiar association **2** *archaic* : CONCERNED, OCCUPIED **3** : having knowledge or experience — used with *with*

con·ver·sa·tion \ˌkän-vər-ˈsā-shən\ *n* [ME *conversacioun*, fr. MF *conversation*, fr. L *conversation-*, *conversatio*, fr. *conversari* to associate with, freq. of *convertere* to turn around] (14c) **1** *obs* : CONDUCT, BEHAVIOR **2** **a** (1) : oral exchange of sentiments, observations, opinions, or ideas (2) : an instance of such exchange : TALK **b** : an informal discussion of an issue by representatives of governments, institutions, or groups **c** : an exchange similar to conversation — **con·ver·sa·tion·al** \-shnəl, -shə-nᵊl\ *adj* — **con·ver·sa·tion·al·ly** *adv*

con·ver·sa·tion·al·ist \-shnə-list, -shə-nᵊl-ist\ *n* (1836) : one who converses a great deal or who excels in conversation

conversation piece *n* (1712) **1** : a painting of a group of persons in their customary surroundings **2** : something (as a novel or unusual object) that stimulates conversation

con·ver·sa·zi·o·ne \ˌkän-vər-ˌsät-sē-ˈō-nē, ˌkōn-\ *n, pl* **-o·nes** *or* **-o·ni** \-ˈō-(ˌ)nē\ [It, lit., conversation, fr. L *conversation-*, *conversatio*] (1739) : a meeting for conversation esp. about art, literature, or science

¹con·verse \ˈkän-ˌvərs\ *n* (15c) **1** *obs* : social interaction **2** : CONVERSATION

²con·verse \kən-ˈvərs\ *vi* **con·versed; con·vers·ing** [ME, to live (with), fr. MF *converser*, fr. L *conversari*] (1586) **1** *archaic* **a** : to become occupied or engaged **b** : to have acquaintance or familiarity **2** **a** : to exchange thoughts and opinions in speech : TALK **b** : to carry on an exchange similar to a conversation (as with a computer) — **con·vers·er** \-ˈvər-sər\ *n*

³con·verse \ˈkän-ˌvərs\ *n* [L *conversus*, pp. of *convertere*] (1570) : something reversed in order, relation, or action: as **a** : a theorem formed by interchanging the hypothesis and conclusion of a given theorem **b** : a proposition obtained by interchange of the subject and predicate of a given proposition ("no *P* is *S*" is the ~ of "no *S* is *P*")

⁴con·verse \kən-ˈvərs, ˈkän-ˌ\ *adj* (1794) **1** : reversed in order, relation, or action **2** : being a logical or mathematical converse ⟨the ~ theorem⟩ — **con·verse·ly** *adv*

con·ver·sion \kən-ˈvər-zhən, -shən\ *n* [ME, fr. MF, fr. L *conversion-*, *conversio*, fr. *convertere*] (14c) : the act of converting : the process of being converted — compare GENE CONVERSION **2** : an experience associated with a definite and decisive adoption of religion **3** **a** : the operation of finding a converse in logic or mathematics **b** : reduction of a mathematical expression by clearing of fractions **4** : a successful try for point or free throw **5** : something converted from one use to another — **con·ver·sion·al** \-ˈvərzh-nəl, -ˈvər-zhə-, -ˈvər-shnəl, -shə-nᵊl\ *adj*

conversion reaction *n* (1945) : a psychoneurosis in which bodily symptoms (as paralysis of the limbs) appear without physical basis — called also *conversion hysteria*

¹con·vert \kən-ˈvərt\ *vb* [ME, fr. MF *convertir*, fr. L *convertere* to turn around, transform, convert, fr. *com-* + *vertere* to turn — more at WORTH] *vt* (14c) **1** **a** : to bring over from one belief, view, or party to another **b** : to bring about a religious conversion in **2** **a** : to alter the physical or chemical nature or properties of esp. in manufacturing **b** (1) : to change from one form or function to another (2) : to alter for more effective utilization (3) : to appropriate without right **c** : to exchange for an equivalent **3** *obs* : TURN **4** : to subject to logical conversion **5** **a** : to make a goal after receiving (a pass) from a teammate **b** : to score on (as a try for point or free throw) **c** : to make (a

---

\ə\ abut \ˈə\ kitten, F table \ər\ further \a\ ash \ā\ ace \ä\ mop, mar \aů\ out \ch\ chin \e\ bet \ē\ easy \g\ go \i\ hit \ī\ ice \j\ job \ŋ\ sing \ō\ go \ȯ\ law \ȯi\ boy \th\ thin \t͟h\ the \ü\ loot \ů\ foot \y\ yet \zh\ vision \ä, k̲, ⁿ, œ, œ̄, ս, ս̄, ʸ\ see Guide to Pronunciation spare) in bowling ~ *vi* **1** : to undergo conversion **2** : to make good on a try for point, field goal, or free throw *syn* see TRANSFORM

²**con·vert** \'kän-ˌvərt\ *n* (1561) : one that is converted

con·vert·er \kən-'vər-tər\ *n* (1533) : one that converts: as **a** : the furnace used in the Bessemer process **b** *or* **con·ver·tor** \-'vər-tər\ : a device employing mechanical rotation for changing electrical energy from one form to another (as from direct current to alternating current or vice versa); *also* : a radio device for converting one frequency to another **c** : a device for adapting a television or radio receiver to receive channels or frequencies for which it was not orig. designed ⟨a cable ~⟩ ⟨FM ~⟩ **d** : a device that accepts data in one form and converts it to another ⟨analog-digital ~⟩ **e** : CATALYTIC CONVERTER

¹**con·vert·ible** \kən-'vər-tə-bəl\ *adj* (14c) **1** : capable of being converted **2** : having a top that may be lowered or removed ⟨~ coupe⟩ **3** : capable of being exchanged for a specified equivalent (as another currency or security) ⟨a bond ~ to 12 shares of common stock⟩ — **con·vert·ibil·i·ty** \-ˌvər-tə-'bi-lə-tē\ *n* — **con·vert·ible·ness** \-'vər-tə-bəl-nəs\ *n* — **con·vert·ibly** \-blē\ *adv*

²**convertible** *n* (1615) : something convertible; *esp* : a convertible automobile

con·verti·plane *also* **con·verta·plane** \kən-'vər-tə-ˌplän\ *n* (1949) : an aircraft that takes off and lands like a helicopter and is convertible to a fixed-wing configuration for forward flight

con·vex \kän-'veks, 'kän-ˌ, kən-'\ *adj* [MF *or* L; MF *convexe*, fr. L *convexus* vaulted, concave, convex, fr. *com-* + *-vexus*; perh. akin to L *vehere* to carry — more at WAY] (1571) **1 a** : curved or rounded like the exterior of a sphere or circle **b** : being a continuous function or part of a continuous function with the property that a line joining any two points on its graph lies on or above the graph **2 a** *of a set of points* : containing all points in a line joining any two constituent points **b** *of a geometric figure* : comprising a convex set when combined with its interior ⟨a ~ polygon⟩

con·vex·i·ty \kən-'vek-sət-ē, kän-\ *n, pl* **-ties** (1599) **1** : the quality or state of being convex **2** : a convex surface or part

con·vexo–con·cave \kän-ˌvek-(ˌ)sō-kän-'kāv, kän-ˌvek-, -'kän-ˌkāv\ *adj* (1693) **1** : CONCAVO-CONVEX **2** : having the convex side of greater curvature than the concave

con·vey \kən-'vā\ *vt* **con·veyed; con·vey·ing** [ME, fr. MF *conveier* to accompany, escort, fr. (assumed) VL *conviare*, fr. L *com-* + *via* way — more at WAY] (14c) **1** *obs* : LEAD, CONDUCT **2 a** : to bear from one place to another; *esp* : to move in a continuous stream or mass **b** : to impart or communicate by statement, suggestion, gesture, or appearance **c** (1) *archaic* : STEAL (2) *obs* : to carry away secretly **d** : to transfer or deliver to another esp. by a sealed writing **e** : to cause to pass from one place or person to another

con·vey·ance \kən-'vā-ən(t)s\ *n* (15c) **1** : the action of conveying **2** : a means or way of conveying: as **a** : an instrument by which title to property is conveyed **b** : a means of transport : VEHICLE

con·vey·anc·er \-ən(t)-sər\ *n* (1650) : one whose business is conveyancing

con·vey·anc·ing \-ən(t)-siŋ\ *n* (1714) : the act or business of drawing deeds, leases, or other writings for transferring the title to property

con·vey·or *also* **con·vey·er** \kən-'vā-ər\ *n* (ca. 1514) : one that conveys: as **a** : a person who transfers property **b** *usu conveyor* : a mechanical apparatus for moving articles or bulk material from place to place (as by an endless moving belt or a chain of receptacles)

con·vey·or·ise *Brit var of* CONVEYORIZE

con·vey·or·ize \-ə-ˌrīz\ *vt* **-ized; -iz·ing** (1941) : to equip with a conveyor — **con·vey·or·i·za·tion** \-ˌvā-ə-rə-'zā-shən\ *n*

¹**con·vict** \kən-'vikt\ *adj* (14c) *archaic* : having been convicted

²**con·vict** \kən-'vikt\ *vt* [ME, fr. L *convictus*, pp. of *convincere* to refute, convict] (14c) **1** : to find or prove to be guilty **2** : to convince of error or sinfulness

³**con·vict** \'kän-ˌvikt\ *n* (15c) **1** : a person convicted of and under sentence for a crime **2** : a person serving a usu. long prison sentence

con·vic·tion \kən-'vik-shən\ *n* (15c) **1** : the act or process of convicting of a crime esp. in a court of law **2 a** : the act of convincing a person of error or of compelling the admission of a truth **b** : the state of being convinced of error or compelled to admit the truth **3 a** : a strong persuasion or belief **b** : the state of being convinced *syn* see CERTAINTY, OPINION

con·vince \kən-'vin(t)s\ *vt* **con·vinced; con·vinc·ing** [L *convincere* to refute, convict, prove, fr. *com-* + *vincere* to conquer — more at VICTOR] (1530) **1** *obs* : to overcome by argument **b** : OVERPOWER, OVERCOME **2** *obs* : DEMONSTRATE, PROVE **3** : to bring (as by argument) to belief, consent, or a course of action : PERSUADE ⟨*convinced* himself that she was all right —William Faulkner⟩ ⟨something I could never ~ him to read —John Lahr⟩ — **con·vinc·er** *n*

con·vinc·ing \kən-'vin(t)-siŋ\ *adj* (1624) **1** : satisfying or assuring by argument or proof ⟨a ~ test of a new product⟩ **2** : having power to convince of the truth, rightness, or reality of something : PLAUSIBLE ⟨told a ~ story⟩ *syn* see VALID — **con·vinc·ing·ly** \-siŋ-lē\ *adv* — **con·vinc·ing·ness** *n*

con·viv·ial \kən-'viv-yəl, -'vi-vē-əl\ *adj* [LL *convivialis*, fr. L *convivium* banquet, fr. *com-* + *vivere* to live — more at QUICK] (ca. 1668) : relating to, occupied with, or fond of feasting, drinking, and good company — **con·viv·i·al·i·ty** \-ˌvi-vē-'a-lə-tē\ *n* — **con·viv·ial·ly** \-'viv-yə-lē, -'vi-vē-ə-lē\ *adv*

con·vo·ca·tion \ˌkän-və-'kā-shən\ *n* [ME, fr. MF, fr. L *convocation-, convocatio*, fr. *convocare*] (14c) **1 a** : an assembly of persons convoked **b** (1) : an assembly of bishops and representative clergy of the Church of England (2) : a consultative assembly of clergy and lay delegates from one part of an Episcopal diocese; *also* : a territorial division of an Episcopal diocese **c** : a ceremonial assembly of members of a college or university **2** : the act or process of convoking — **con·vo·ca·tion·al** \-shnəl, -shə-nᵊl\ *adj*

con·voke \kən-'vōk\ *vt* **con·voked; con·vok·ing** [MF *convoquer*, fr. L *convocare*, fr. *com-* + *vocare* to call, fr. *voc-, vox* voice — more at VOICE] (1598) : to call together to a meeting *syn* see SUMMON

con·vo·lute \'kän-və-ˌlüt\ *vb* **-lut·ed; -lut·ing** [L *convolutus*, pp. of *convolvere*] (1698) : TWIST, COIL

con·vo·lut·ed \-ˌlü-təd\ *adj* (1766) **1** : having convolutions **2** : INVOLVED, INTRICATE

convoluted tubule *n* (1923) : all or part of the coiled sections of a nephron: **a** : PROXIMAL CONVOLUTED TUBULE **b** : DISTAL CONVOLUTED TUBULE

con·vo·lu·tion \ˌkän-və-'lü-shən\ *n* (1545) **1** : a form or shape that is folded in curved or tortuous windings **2** : one of the irregular ridges on the surface of the brain and esp. of the cerebrum of higher mammals **3** : a complication or intricacy of form, design, or structure

con·volve \kən-'välv, -'vȯlv *also* -'väv *or* -'vȯv\ *vb* **con·volved; con·volv·ing** [L *convolvere*, fr. *com-* + *volvere* to roll — more at VOLUBLE] *vt* (1650) : to roll together : WRITHE ~ *vi* : to roll together or circulate involvedly

con·vol·vu·lus \kən-'väl-vyə-ləs, -'vȯl- *also* -'väv-yə- *or* -'vȯv-yə-\ *n, pl* **-lus·es** *or* **-li** \-ˌlī, -ˌlē\ [NL, fr. L *convolvere*] (1548) : any of a genus (*Convolvulus*) of erect, trailing, or twining herbs and shrubs of the morning-glory family

¹**con·voy** \'kän-ˌvȯi, kən-'\ *vt* [ME, fr. MF *conveier, convoier* — more at CONVEY] (14c) : to escort for protection

²**con·voy** \'kän-ˌvȯi\ *n* (1523) **1** : one that convoys; *esp* : a protective escort (as for ships) **2** : the act of convoying **3** : a group convoyed or organized for convenience or protection in moving

con·vul·sant \kən-'vəl-sənt\ *adj* (1875) : causing convulsions : CONVULSIVE 1a — **convulsant** *n*

con·vulse \kən-'vəls\ *vb* **con·vulsed; con·vuls·ing** [L *convulsus*, pp. of *convellere* to pluck up, convulse, fr. *com-* + *vellere* to pluck — more at VULNERABLE] *vt* (1643) : to shake or agitate violently; *esp* : to shake with or as if with irregular spasms ~ *vi* : to become affected with convulsions *syn* see SHAKE

con·vul·sion \kən-'vəl-shən\ *n* (1547) **1** : an abnormal violent and involuntary contraction or series of contractions of the muscles **2 a** : a violent disturbance **b** : an uncontrolled fit : PAROXYSM — **con·vul·sion·ary** \-shə-ˌner-ē\ *adj*

con·vul·sive \kən-'vəl-siv\ *adj* (1615) **1 a** : constituting or producing a convulsion **b** : attended or affected with convulsions **2** : resembling a convulsion in being violent, sudden, frantic, or spasmodic *syn* see FITFUL — **con·vul·sive·ly** *adv* — **con·vul·sive·ness** *n*

cony *var of* CONEY

coo \'kü\ *vi* [imit.] (1670) **1** : to make the low soft cry of a dove or pigeon or a similar sound **2** : to talk fondly, amorously, or appreciatively ⟨an album that will be ~ed over by condescending classical music critics —Ellen Sander⟩ — **coo** *n*

¹**cook** \'kuk\ *n* [ME, fr. OE *cōc*, fr. L *coquus*, fr. *coquere* to cook; akin to OE *āfigen* fried, Gk *pessein* to cook] (bef. 12c) **1** : a person who prepares food for eating **2** : a technical or industrial process comparable to cooking food; *also* : a substance so processed

²**cook** *vi* (14c) **1** : to prepare food for eating by means of heat **2** : to undergo the action of being cooked ⟨the rice is ~ing now⟩ **3** : OCCUR, HAPPEN ⟨find out what was ~ing in the committee⟩ **4** : to perform, do, or proceed well ⟨the jazz quartet was ~ing along⟩ ⟨the party ~ed right through the night⟩ ~ *vt* **1** : CONCOCT, FABRICATE — usu. used with *up* ⟨~ed up a scheme⟩ **2** : to prepare for eating by a heating process **3** : FALSIFY, DOCTOR ⟨~ed the books with phony spending cuts and accounting gimmickry —Colleen O'Connor⟩ **4** : to subject to the action of heat or fire — **cook·able** \'ku-kə-bəl\ *adj* — **cook one's goose** : to ruin one irretrievably

¹**cook·book** \-ˌbuk\ *n* (1809) **1** : a book of cooking directions and recipes; *broadly* : a book of detailed instructions

²**cookbook** *adj* (1944) : involving or using step-by-step procedures whose rationale is usu. not explained ⟨a ~ approach⟩

cook cheese *n* (1941) : an unripened cheese made from curd that has been cooked to a soft consistency — called also *cooked cheese*

cook·er \'ku-kər\ *n* (1869) : one that cooks: as **a** : a utensil, device, or apparatus for cooking **b** : a person who tends a cooking process : COOK **c** *Brit* : STOVE

cook·ery \'ku-k(ə-)rē\ *n, pl* **-er·ies** (14c) **1** : the art or practice of cooking **2** : an establishment for cooking

cookery book *n* (1639) *chiefly Brit* : COOKBOOK

cook·house \'kuk-ˌhaus\ *n* (1795) : a building for cooking

cook·ie *or* **cooky** \'ku-kē\ *n, pl* **cook·ies** [D *koekje*, dim. of *koek* cake] (1703) **1** : a small flat or slightly raised cake **2 a** : an attractive woman ⟨a buxom French ~ who haunts the . . . colony's one night spot —*Newsweek*⟩ **b** : PERSON, GUY ⟨a tough ~⟩

cookie–cutter *adj* (1963) : marked by lack of originality or distinction ⟨~ shopping malls⟩

cookie cutter *n* (1903) : a device used to cut rolled cookie dough into shapes before baking

cookie sheet *n* (1926) : a flat rectangle of metal with at least one rolled edge used esp. for the baking of cookies or biscuits

cooking *adj* (ca. 1813) : suitable for or used in cooking ⟨~ apples⟩

cook–off \'kuk-ˌȯf, -ˌäf\ *n* (1937) : a cooking competition

cook off *vi* (1945) *of a cartridge* : to fire as a result of overheating

cook·out \'kuk-ˌaut\ *n* (1947) : an outing at which a meal is cooked and served in the open; *also* : the meal cooked

cook·shack \-ˌshak\ *n* (1909) : a shack used for cooking

cook·shop \-ˌshäp\ *n* (ca. 1552) : a shop supplying or serving cooked food

Cook's tour \'kuks-\ *n* [Thomas Cook & Son, Eng. travel agency] (ca. 1909) : a rapid or cursory survey or review

cook·stove \'kuk-ˌstōv\ *n* (1824) : a stove for cooking

cook·top \'kuk-ˌtäp\ *n* (1948) **1** : the flat top of a range **2** : a built-in cabinet-top cooking apparatus containing usu. four heating units

cook·ware \'kuk-ˌwar, -ˌwer\ *n* (1953) : utensils used in cooking

¹**cool** \'kül\ *adj* [ME *col*, fr. OE *cōl*; akin to OHG *kuoli* cool, OE *ceald* cold — more at COLD] (bef. 12c) **1** : moderately cold : lacking in warmth **2 a** : marked by steady dispassionate calmness and self-control ⟨a ~ and calculating administrator —*Current Biog.*⟩ **b** : lacking ardor or friendliness ⟨a ~ impersonal manner⟩ **c** *of jazz* : marked by restrained emotion and the frequent use of counterpoint **d** : free from tensions or violence ⟨meeting with minority groups in an attempt to keep the city ~⟩ **3** — used as an intensive ⟨a ~ million dollars⟩ **4** : marked by deliberate effrontery or lack of due respect or discretion ⟨a ~ reply⟩ **5** : facilitating or suggesting relief from heat ⟨a ~ dress⟩ **6 a** *of a color* : producing an impression of being cool; *specif* : of a hue in the range violet through blue to green **b** *of a musical tone* : relatively lacking in timbre or resonance **7** *slang* **a** : very good : EXCELLENT;

also : ALL RIGHT **b** : FASHIONABLE 1 — **cool·ish** \'kü-lish\ *adj* — **cool·ly** *also* **cooly** \'kü(l)-lē\ *adv* — **cool·ness** \'kül-nəs\ *n*
syn COOL, COMPOSED, COLLECTED, UNRUFFLED, IMPERTURBABLE, NONCHALANT mean free from agitation or excitement. COOL may imply calmness, deliberateness, or dispassionateness ⟨kept a *cool* head⟩. COMPOSED implies freedom from agitation as a result of self-discipline or a sedate disposition ⟨the *composed* pianist gave a flawless concert⟩. COLLECTED implies a concentration of mind that eliminates distractions esp. in moments of crisis ⟨the nurse stayed calm and *collected*⟩. UNRUFFLED suggests apparent serenity and poise in the face of setbacks or in the midst of excitement ⟨harried but *unruffled*⟩. IMPERTURBABLE implies coolness or assurance even under severe provocation ⟨the speaker remained *imperturbable* despite the heckling⟩. NONCHALANT stresses an easy coolness of manner or casualness that suggests indifference or unconcern ⟨a *nonchalant* driver⟩.
²**cool** *vi* (bef. 12c) **1** : to become cool : lose heat or warmth ⟨placed the pie in the window to ~⟩ — sometimes used with *off* or *down* **2** : to lose ardor or passion ⟨his anger ~ed⟩ ~ *vt* **1** : to make cool : impart a feeling of coolness to ⟨~ed the room with a fan⟩ — often used with *off* or *down* ⟨a swim ~ed us off a little⟩ **2** : to moderate the heat, excitement, or force of : CALM ⟨~ed her growing anger⟩. **b** : to slow or lessen the growth or activity of — usu. used with *off* or *down* ⟨wants to ~ off the economy without freezing it —*Newsweek*⟩ — **cool it** : to calm down : go easy ⟨the world went out to the young to *cool it* —W. M. Young⟩ — **cool one's heels** : to wait or be kept waiting for a long time esp. from or as if from disdain or discourtesy
³**cool** *n* (15c) **1** : a cool time, place, or situation ⟨the ~ of the evening⟩ **2 a** : absence of excitement or emotional involvement : DETACHMENT ⟨must surrender his fine ~ and enter the closed crazy world of suicide —Wilfred Sheed⟩ **b** : POISE, COMPOSURE ⟨press questions . . . seemed to rattle him and he lost his ~ —*New Republic*⟩
⁴**cool** *adv* (1951) : in a casual and nonchalant manner ⟨play it ~⟩
cool·ant \'kü-lənt\ *n* (1926) : a usu. fluid cooling agent
cool·down \'kül-,daůn\ *n* (1980) : the act or an instance of allowing physiological activity to return to normal gradually after strenuous exercise by engaging in less strenuous exercise
cool·er \'kü-lər\ *n* (1575) **1** : one that cools: as **a** : a container for cooling liquids **b** : REFRIGERATOR **2** : LOCKUP, JAIL; *esp* : a cell for violent or unmanageable prisoners **3** : an iced drink usu. with an alcoholic beverage as a base
Coo·ley's anemia \'kü-lēz-\ *n* [Thomas B. *Cooley* †1945 Am. pediatrician] (ca. 1935) : a severe thalassemic anemia that is associated with the presence of microcytes, enlargement of the liver and spleen, increase in the erythroid bone marrow, and jaundice and that occurs esp. in children of Mediterranean parents
cool-head·ed \'kül-,he-dəd\ *adj* (1777) : not easily excited
coo·lie \'kü-lē\ *n* [Hindi *kulī*] (1638) : an unskilled laborer or porter usu. in or from the Far East hired for low or subsistence wages
coolie hat *n* (1924) : a conical-shaped usu. straw hat worn esp. to protect the head from the heat of the sun
cool·ing–off \'kü-liŋ-'ȯf\ *adj* (1926) : designed to allow passions to cool or to permit negotiation between parties ⟨a ~ period⟩
cooling tower *n* (1901) : a structure over which circulated water is trickled to reduce its temperature by partial evaporation
coombe *or* **coomb** \'küm\ *var of* COMBE
coon \'kün\ *n* (1742) **1** : RACCOON **2** : BLACK 4 — usu. taken to be offensive
coon·can \'kün-,kan\ *n* [by folk etymology fr. MexSp *conquián* conquian, fr. Sp *¿con quién?* with whom?] (1889) : a game of rummy played with two packs including two jokers
coon cat *n* (1901) : MAINE COON
coon cheese \'kün-\ *n* [prob. fr. *coon* (black person); fr. the color of the coating] (1953) : a sharp cheddar cheese that has been cured at higher than usual temperature and humidity and that is usu. coated with black wax
coon·hound \'kün-,haůnd\ *n* (1920) : a sporting dog trained to hunt raccoons; *esp* : BLACK-AND-TAN COONHOUND
coon's age *n* (1844) : a long while ⟨best fried chicken I've tasted for a *coon's age* —Sinclair Lewis⟩
coon·skin \'kün-,skin\ *n* (1818) **1** : the skin or pelt of the raccoon **2** : an article (as a cap or coat) made of coonskin
coon·tie \'kün-tē\ *n* [Creek (Florida dial.) *kuntí*] (1791) : any of several tropical American woody plants (genus *Zamia*) of the cycad family whose roots and stems yield a starchy foodstuff — called also *arrowroot*
¹**coop** \'küp, 'kůp\ *n* [ME *cupe*; akin to OE *cype* basket] (14c) **1** : a cage or small enclosure (as for poultry); *also* : a small building for housing poultry **2 a** : a confined area **b** : JAIL
²**coop** *vt* (1583) **1** : to confine in a restricted and often crowded area — usu. used with *up* **2** : to place or keep in a coop : PEN — often used with *up*
co–op \'kō-,äp, kō-'\ *n* (1869) : COOPERATIVE
¹**coo·per** \'kü-pər, 'ků-\ *n* [ME *couper, cowper*, fr. MD *cūper* (fr. *cūpe* cask) or MLG *kūper*, fr. *kūpe* cask; MD *cūpe* & MLG *kūpe*, fr. L *cupa*; akin to Gk *kypellon* cup — more at HIVE] (14c) : one that makes or repairs wooden casks or tubs
²**cooper** *vb* **coo·pered; coo·per·ing** \'kü-p(ə-)riŋ, 'ků-\ *vt* (1742) : to work as a cooper on ~ *vi* : to work at or do coopering
coo·per·age \'kü-p(ə-)rij, 'ků-\ *n* (1705) **1** : a cooper's work or products **2** : a cooper's place of business
co·op·er·ate \kō-'ä-pə-,rāt\ *vi* [LL *cooperatus*, pp. of *cooperari*, fr. L *co-* + *operari* to work — more at OPERATE] (1582) **1** : to act or work with another or others : act together **2** : to associate with another or others for mutual benefit — **co·op·er·a·tor** \-,rā-tər\ *n*
co·op·er·a·tion \(,)kō-,ä-pə-'rā-shən\ *n* (14c) **1** : the action of cooperating : common effort **2** : association of persons for common benefit — **co·op·er·a·tion·ist** \-sh(ə-)nist\ *n*
¹**co·op·er·a·tive** \kō-'ä-p(ə-)rə-tiv, -'ä-pə-,rā-\ *adj* (1603) **1 a** : marked by cooperation ⟨~ efforts⟩ **b** : marked by a willingness and ability to work with others ⟨~ neighbors⟩ **2** : of, relating to, or organized as a cooperative **3** : relating to or comprising a program of combined liberal arts and technical studies at different schools — **co·op·er·a·tive·ly** *adv* — **co·op·er·a·tive·ness** *n*

²**cooperative** *n* (1883) : an enterprise or organization owned by and operated for the benefit of those using its services
Coo·per's hawk \'kü-pərz-, 'ků-\ *n* [William *Cooper* †1864 Am. naturalist] (1828) : an American hawk (*Accipiter cooperii*) that is larger than the similarly colored sharp-shinned hawk and has a more rounded tail
co–opt \kō-'äpt\ *vt* [L *cooptare*, fr. *co-* + *optare* to choose] (1651) **1 a** : to choose or elect as a member **b** : to appoint as a colleague or assistant **2 a** : to take into a group (as a faction, movement, or culture) : ABSORB, ASSIMILATE ⟨the students are ~ed by a system they serve even in their struggle against it —A. C. Danto⟩ **b** : TAKE OVER, APPROPRIATE — **co·op·ta·tion** \,kō-,äp-'tā-shən\ *n* — **co·op·ta·tive** \kō-'äp-tə-tiv\ *adj* — **co·op·tion** \-'äp-shən\ *n* — **co·op·tive** \-'äp-tiv\ *adj*
¹**co·or·di·nate** \kō-'ȯrd-nət; -'ȯr-d°n-ət, -də-,nät\ *adj* [prob. back-formation fr. *coordination*] (1641) **1 a** : equal in rank, quality, or significance **b** : being of equal rank in a sentence ⟨~ clauses⟩ **2** : relating to or marked by coordination **3 a** : being a university that awards degrees to men and women taught usu. by the same faculty but attending separate classes often on separate campuses **b** : being one of the colleges and esp. the women's branch of a coordinate university **4** : of, relating to, or being a system of indexing by two or more terms so that documents may be retrieved through the intersection of index terms — **co·or·di·nate·ly** *adv* — **co·or·di·nate·ness** *n*
²**co·or·di·nate** \kō-'ȯr-d°n-,āt\ *vb* **-nat·ed; -nat·ing** *vt* (1665) **1** : to put in the same order or rank **2** : to bring into a common action, movement, or condition : HARMONIZE **3** : to attach so as to form a coordination complex ~ *vi* **1** : to be or become coordinate esp. so as to act together in a smooth concerted way **2** : to combine by means of a coordinate bond — **co·or·di·na·tive** \kō-'ȯrd-nə-tiv; -'ȯr-d°n-ə-tiv, -də-,nā-\ *adj* — **co·or·di·na·tor** \-'ȯr-d°n-,ā-tər\ *n*
³**co·or·di·nate** *same as* ¹\ *n* (ca. 1823) **1 a** : any of a set of numbers used in specifying the location of a point on a line, on a surface, or in space **b** : any one of a set of variables used in specifying the state of a substance or the motion of a particle or momentum **2** : one who is of equal rank, authority, or importance with another **3** *pl* : articles (as of clothing) designed to be used together and to attain their effect through pleasing contrast (as of color, material, or texture)
coordinate bond *n* (1947) : a covalent bond that consists of a pair of electrons supplied by only one of the two atoms it joins
co·or·di·nat·ed \-'ȯr-d°n-,nā-təd\ *adj* (1939) : able to use more than one set of muscle movements to a single end ⟨a well-*coordinated* athlete⟩
Coordinated Universal Time *n* (1969) : the international standard of time that is kept by atomic clocks around the world — abbr. UTC
coordinate geometry *n* (1855) : ANALYTIC GEOMETRY
coordinating conjunction *n* (1916) : a conjunction that joins together words or word groups of equal grammatical rank
co·or·di·na·tion \(,)kō-,ȯr-də-'nā-shən\ *n* [LL *coordination-, coordinatio*, fr. L *co-* + *ordination-, ordinatio* arrangement, fr. *ordinare* to arrange — more at ORDAIN] (ca. 1643) **1** : the act or action of coordinating **2** : the harmonious functioning of parts for effective results
coordination complex *n* (1951) : a compound or ion with a central usu. metallic atom or ion combined by coordinate bonds with a definite number of surrounding ions, groups, or molecules — called also *coordination compound*
coordination number *n* (1908) **1** : the number of attachments to the central atom in a coordination complex **2** : a number used in specifying the spatial arrangement of the constituent groups of crystals
coot \'küt\ *n* [ME *coote*; akin to D *koet* coot] (15c) **1** : any of various sluggish slow-flying slaty-black birds (genus *Fulica*) of the rail family that somewhat resemble ducks and have lobed toes and the upper mandible prolonged on the forehead as a horny frontal shield **2** : any of several No. American scoters **3** : a harmless simple person; *broadly* : FELLOW 4c
coo·ter \'kü-tər *also* 'ků-tə\ *n* [of African origin; akin to Bambara & Malinke *kuta* turtle] (1832) *chiefly Southern* : any of several turtles (genus *Pseudemys* and esp. *P. concinna*) esp. of the southern and eastern U.S.
coo·tie \'kü-tē\ *n* [perh. modif. of Malay *kutu*] (1917) : BODY LOUSE
¹**cop** \'käp\ *n* [ME, fr. OE *copp*] (bef. 12c) **1** *dial chiefly Eng* : TOP, CREST **2** : a cylindrical or conical mass of thread, yarn, or roving wound on a quill or tube; *also* : a quill or tube upon which it is wound
²**cop** *vt* **copped; cop·ping** [perh. fr. D *kapen* to steal, fr. Fris *kāpia* to take away; akin to OHG *kouf* trade — more at CHEAP] (1704) **1** *slang* : to get hold of : CATCH, CAPTURE; *also* : PURCHASE **2** *slang* : STEAL, SWIPE — **cop a plea** : to plead guilty to a lesser charge in order to avoid standing trial for a more serious one; *broadly* : to admit fault and plead for mercy
³**cop** *n* [short for ³*copper*] (1859) : POLICE OFFICER
co·pa·cet·ic *or* **co·pe·set·ic** *also* **co·pa·set·ic** \,kō-pə-'se-tik\ *adj* [origin unknown] (1919) : very satisfactory
co·pai·ba \kō-'pī-bə, -'pā-\ *n* [Sp & Pg; Sp, fr. Pg *copaíba*, fr. Tupi] (1712) : a stimulant oleoresin obtained from several pinnate-leaved So. American leguminous trees (genus *Copaifera*); *also* : one of these trees
co·pal \'kō-pəl, -,pal; kō-'pal\ *n* [Sp, fr. Nahuatl *copalli* resin] (1577) : a recent or fossil resin from various tropical trees
co·par·ce·nary \kō-'pär-s°n-,er-ē\ *n, pl* **-nar·ies** (ca. 1504) **1** : joint heirship **2** : joint ownership
co·par·ce·ner \-'pärs-nər, -'pär-s°n-ər\ *n* (15c) : a joint heir
co–pay·ment \'kō-,pā-mənt, ,kō-'\ *n* (1975) : a relatively small fixed fee required by a health insurer (as an HMO) to be paid by the patient at the time of each office visit, outpatient service, or filling of a prescription
¹**cope** \'kōp\ *n* [ME, fr. OE *-cāp*, fr. LL *cappa* head covering] (13c) **1** : a long enveloping ecclesiastical vestment **2 a** : something resembling a cope (as by concealing or covering) ⟨the dark sky's starry ~ — P. B. Shelley⟩ **b** : COPING
²**cope** *vt* **coped; cop·ing** (14c) : to cover or furnish with a cope
³**cope** *vb* **coped; cop·ing** [ME *copen, coupen*, fr. MF *couper* to strike,

\ə\ abut \ʼ\ kitten, F table \ər\ further \a\ ash \ā\ ace \ä\ mop, mar \aů\ out \ch\ chin \e\ bet \ē\ easy \g\ go \i\ hit \ī\ ice \j\ job \ŋ\ sing \ō\ go \ȯ\ law \ȯi\ boy \th\ thin \t͟h\ the \ü\ loot \ů\ foot \y\ yet \zh\ vision \à, k̵, ⁿ, œ, œ̄, ᵫ, ᵫ̄, ʸ\ *see* Guide to Pronunciation cut, fr. OF, fr. *coup* blow, fr. LL *colpus*, alter. of L *colaphus*, fr. Gk *kolaphos* buffet] *vi* (14c)   **1** *obs* : STRIKE, FIGHT   **2 a** : to maintain a contest or combat usu. on even terms or with success — used with *with*   **b** : to deal with and attempt to overcome problems and difficulties — often used with *with*   **3** *archaic* : MEET, ENCOUNTER ~ *vt*   **1** *obs* : to meet in combat   **2** *obs* : to come in contact with   **3** *obs* : MATCH

⁴cope *vt* **coped; cop·ing** [prob. fr. F *couper* to cut] (ca. 1901)   **1** : to shape (a structural member) to fit a coping or conform to the shape of another member   **2** : NOTCH

co·peck *var of* KOPECK

co·pe·pod \'kō-pə-ˌpäd\ *n* [ultim. fr. Gk *kōpē* oar, handle + *pod-, pous* foot; prob. akin to L *capere* to take — more at HEAVE, FOOT] (1836) : any of a large subclass (Copepoda) of usu. minute freshwater and marine crustaceans — **copepod** *adj*

cop·er \'kō-pər\ *n* [E dial. *cope* to trade] (1825) *Brit* : a horse dealer; *esp* : a dishonest one

Co·per·ni·can \kə-'pər-ni-kən, kō-\ *adj* [Nicolaus *Copernicus*] (1667)   **1** : of or relating to Copernicus or the belief that the earth rotates daily on its axis and the planets revolve in orbits around the sun   **2** : of radical or major importance or degree ⟨effected a ~ revolution in philosophy —*Times Lit. Supp.*⟩ — **Copernican** *n* — **Co·per·ni·can·ism** \-kə-ˌni-zəm\ *n*

cope·stone \'kōp-ˌstōn\ *n* (1567)   **1** : a stone forming a coping   **2** : a finishing touch : CROWN

copi·er \'kä-pē-ər\ *n* (1597) : one that copies; *specif* : a machine for making copies of graphic matter (as printing, drawings, or pictures)

co·pi·lot \'kō-ˌpī-lət\ *n* (1927) : a qualified pilot who assists or relieves the pilot but is not in command

cop·ing \'kō-piŋ\ *n* (1601) : the covering course of a wall usu. with a sloping top

cop·ing saw \'kō-piŋ-\ *n* [fr. prp. of ⁴*cope*] (1925) : a handsaw with a very narrow blade held under tension in a U-shaped frame and used esp. for cutting curves in wood

coping saw

cop·ing·stone \'kō-piŋ-ˌstōn\ *n* (1778) *chiefly Brit* : COPESTONE

co·pi·ous \'kō-pē-əs\ *adj* [ME, fr. L *copiosus*, fr. *copia* abundance, fr. *co-* + *ops* wealth — more at OPULENT] (14c)   **1 a** : yielding something abundantly ⟨a ~ harvest⟩ ⟨~ springs⟩   **b** : plentiful in number ⟨~ references to other writers⟩   **2 a** : full of thought, information, or matter   **b** : profuse or exuberant in words, expression, or style ⟨a ~ talker⟩   **3** : present in large quantity : taking place on a large scale ⟨~ weeping⟩ ⟨~ food and drink⟩   *syn* see PLENTIFUL — **co·pi·ous·ly** *adv* — **co·pi·ous·ness** *n*

co·pla·nar \(ˌ)kō-'plā-nər, -ˌnär\ *adj* (1862) : lying or acting in the same plane — **co·pla·nar·i·ty** \ˌkō-plā-'nar-ə-tē\ *n*

co·pol·y·mer \(ˌ)kō-'pä-lə-mər\ *n* (1936) : a product of copolymerization — **co·pol·y·mer·ic** \ˌkō-ˌpä-lə-'mer-ik\ *adj*

co·po·ly·mer·i·za·tion \ˌkō-pə-ˌli-mə-rə-'zā-shən, ˌkō-ˌpä-lə-mə-\ *n* (1936) : the polymerization of two substances (as different monomers) together — **co·po·ly·mer·ize** \ˌkō-pə-'li-mə-ˌrīz, ˌkō-'pä-lə-mə-\ *vb*

cop–out \'käp-ˌaút\ *n* (ca. 1942)   **1** : the act or an instance of copping out   **2** : an excuse or means for copping out : PRETEXT   **3** : a person who cops out

cop out *vi* (ca. 1961)   **1** : to back out (as of an unwanted responsibility) ⟨*cop out* on jury duty⟩   **2** : to avoid or neglect problems, responsibilities, or commitments ⟨accused the mayor of *copping out* on the issue of homelessness⟩

¹cop·per \'kä-pər\ *n, often attrib* [ME *coper*, fr. OE, fr. LL *cuprum* copper, fr. L (*aes*) *Cyprium*, lit., Cyprian metal] (bef. 12c)   **1** : a common reddish metallic element that is ductile and malleable and is one of the best conductors of heat and electricity — see ELEMENT table   **2** : a coin or token made of copper or bronze   **3** *chiefly Brit* : a large boiler (as for cooking)   **4** : any of a subfamily (Lycaeninae of the family Lycaenidae) of small butterflies with usu. copper-colored wings

²copper *vt* **cop·pered; cop·per·ing** \'kä-p(ə-)riŋ\ (1530) : to coat or sheathe with or as if with copper

³copper *n* [²*cop*] (1846) : POLICE OFFICER

cop·per·as \'kä-p(ə-)rəs\ *n* [ME *coperas*, fr. OF *couperose*, fr. ML *cuprosa*, fr. *aqua cuprosa*, lit., copper water, fr. LL *cuprum*] (14c) : a green hydrated ferrous sulfate $FeSO_4 \cdot 7H_2O$ used esp. in making inks and pigments

cop·per·head \'kä-pər-ˌhed\ *n* (1775)   **1** : a common pit viper (*Agkistrodon contortrix*) of the eastern and central U.S. usu. having a copper-colored head and often a reddish brown hourglass pattern on the body   **2** : a person in the northern states who sympathized with the South during the Civil War

cop·per·plate \'kä-pər-ˌplāt\ *n* (1663)   **1** : an engraved or etched copper printing plate; *also* : a print made from such a plate   **2** : a neat script handwriting based on engraved models

copper pyrites *n* (1776) : CHALCOPYRITE

cop·per·smith \'kä-pər-ˌsmith\ *n* (14c) : a worker in copper

copper sulfate *n* (ca. 1893) : a sulfate of copper; *esp* : the normal sulfate that is white in the anhydrous form but blue in the crystalline hydrous form $CuSO_4 \cdot 5H_2O$ and that is often used as an algicide and fungicide

cop·pery \'kä-p(ə-)rē\ *adj* (ca. 1775) : resembling or suggesting copper; *esp* : having the reddish to brownish orange color of copper ⟨~ leaves⟩

¹cop·pice \'kä-pəs\ *n* [MF *copeiz*, fr. *couper* to cut — more at COPE] (1534)   **1** : a thicket, grove, or growth of small trees   **2** : forest originating mainly from shoots or root suckers rather than seed

²coppice *vb* **cop·piced; cop·pic·ing** *vt* (1538) : to cut back so as to regrow in the form of a coppice ~ *vi* : to form a coppice; *specif, of a tree* : to sprout freely from the base

copr– or **copro–** *comb form* [NL, fr. Gk *kopr-, kopro-*, fr. *kopros* akin to Skt *śakṛt* dung] : dung : feces ⟨*coprolite*⟩

co·pra \'kō-prə *also* 'kä-\ *n* [Pg, fr. Malayalam *koppara*] (1584) : dried coconut meat yielding coconut oil

co·pro·ces·sor \(ˌ)kō-'prä-se-sər, -'prō-\ *n* (1980) : an extra processor in a computer that is designed to perform specialized tasks (as mathematical calculations)

co·prod·uct \(ˌ)kō-'prä-(ˌ)dəkt\ *n* (1942) : BY-PRODUCT 1

cop·ro·lite \'kä-prə-ˌlīt\ *n* (1829) : fossilized excrement — **cop·ro·lit·ic** \ˌkä-prə-'li-tik\ *adj*

co·proph·a·gous \kə-'prä-fə-gəs\ *adj* [Gk *koprophagos*, fr. *kopr-* + *-phagos* -phagous] (1826) : feeding on dung — **co·proph·a·gy** \-fə-jē\ *n*

cop·ro·phil·ia \ˌkä-prə-'fi-lē-ə\ *n* [NL] (1923) : marked interest in excrement; *esp* : the use of feces or filth for sexual excitement — **cop·ro·phil·i·ac** \-lē-ˌak\ *n*

cop·roph·i·lous \kə-'prä-fə-ləs\ *adj* (ca. 1900) : growing or living on dung ⟨~ fungi⟩

copse \'käps\ *n* [by alter.] (1578) : COPPICE 1

Copt \'käpt\ *n* [Ar *qubṭ* Copts, fr. Coptic *gyptios* Egyptian, fr. Gk *Aigyptios*] (1615)   **1** : a member of the traditional Monophysite Christian church originating and centering in Egypt   **2** : a member of a people descended from the ancient Egyptians

cop·ter \'käp-tər\ *n* (1943) : HELICOPTER

¹Cop·tic \'käp-tik\ *adj* (1677) : of or relating to the Copts, their liturgical language, or their church

²Coptic *n* (1711) : an Afro-Asiatic language descended from ancient Egyptian and used as the liturgical language of the Coptic church

cop·u·la \'kä-pyə-lə\ *n* [L, bond — more at COUPLE] (1619) : something that connects: as   **a** : the connecting link between subject and predicate of a proposition   **b** : LINKING VERB

cop·u·late \'kä-pyə-ˌlāt\ *vi* **-lat·ed; -lat·ing** [L *copulatus*, pp. of *copulare* to join, fr. *copula*] (1632) : to engage in sexual intercourse — **cop·u·la·tion** \ˌkä-pyə-'lā-shən\ *n* — **cop·u·la·to·ry** \'kä-pyə-lə-ˌtōr-ē, -ˌtȯr-\ *adj*

¹cop·u·la·tive \'kä-pyə-lə-tiv, -ˌlā-\ *adj* (14c)   **1 a** : joining together coordinate words or word groups and expressing addition of their meanings ⟨a ~ conjunction⟩   **b** : functioning as a copula   **2** : relating to or serving for copulation

²copulative *n* (1530) : a copulative word

¹copy \'kä-pē\ *n, pl* **cop·ies** [ME *copie*, fr. MF, fr. ML *copia*, fr. L, abundance — more at COPIOUS] (14c)   **1** : an imitation, transcript, or reproduction of an original work (as a letter, a painting, a table, or a dress)   **2** : one of a series of esp. mechanical reproductions of an original impression; *also* : an individual example of such a reproduction   **3** *archaic* : something to be imitated : MODEL   **4** : matter to be set esp. for printing   **b** : something considered printable or newsworthy — used without an article ⟨remarks that made good ~ —Norman Cousins⟩   **c** : text esp. of an advertisement   *syn* see REPRODUCTION

²copy *vb* **cop·ied; copy·ing** *vt* (14c)   **1** : to make a copy of   **2** : to model oneself on ~ *vi*   **1** : to make a copy   **2** : to undergo copying ⟨the document did not ~ well⟩

syn COPY, IMITATE, MIMIC, APE, MOCK mean to make something so that it resembles an existing thing. COPY suggests duplicating an original as nearly as possible ⟨copied the painting and sold the fake as an original⟩. IMITATE suggests following a model or a pattern but may allow for some variation ⟨imitate a poet's style⟩. MIMIC implies a close copying (as of voice or mannerism) often for fun, ridicule, or lifelike imitation ⟨pupils mimicking their teacher⟩. APE may suggest presumptuous, slavish, or inept imitating of a superior original ⟨American fashion designers aped their European colleagues⟩. MOCK usu. implies imitation with derision ⟨mocking a vain man's pompous manner⟩.

copy·book \'kä-pē-ˌbuk\ *n* (1588) : a book formerly used in teaching penmanship and containing models for imitation

copy·boy \-ˌbȯi\ *n* (1888) : one who carries copy and runs errands

¹copy·cat \-ˌkat\ *n, often attrib* (1896)   **1** : one who imitates or adopts the behavior or practices of another   **2** : an imitative act or product ⟨~ board games⟩

²copycat *vb* **copy·cat·ted; copy·cat·ting** *vi* (1926) : to act as a copycat ~ *vt* : IMITATE

copy·desk \-ˌdesk\ *n* (1921) : the desk at which newspaper copy is edited

copy editor *n* (1899) : an editor who prepares copy for the printer; *also* : one who edits and headlines newspaper copy — **copy·ed·it** \'kä-pē-ˌe-dət\ *vt*

copy·hold \'kä-pē-ˌhōld\ *n* (15c)   **1** : a former tenure of land in England and Ireland by right of being recorded in the court of the manor   **2** : an estate held by copyhold

copy·hold·er \-ˌhōl-dər\ *n* (1874)   **1** : a device for holding copy esp. for a typesetter   **2** : one who reads copy for a proofreader

copy·ist \'kä-pē-ist\ *n* (1699)   **1** : one who makes copies   **2** : IMITATOR

copy·read·er \-ˌrē-dər\ *n* (1892) : COPY EDITOR — **copy·read** \-ˌrēd\ *vt*

¹copy·right \-ˌrīt\ *n* (1735) : the exclusive legal right to reproduce, publish, and sell the matter and form (as of a literary, musical, or artistic work)

²copyright *vt* (ca. 1806) : to secure a copyright on — **copy·right·able** \-ˌrī-tə-bəl\ *adj*

³copyright *adj* (1870) : secured by copyright

copy·writ·er \'kä-pē-ˌrī-tər\ *n* (1911) : a writer of advertising or publicity copy

coq au vin \ˌkōk-ō-'vaⁿ, ˌkäk-ō-\ *n* [F, cock with wine] (ca. 1938) : chicken cooked in usu. red wine

¹co·quet \kō-'ket\ *n* [F, dim. of *coq* cock] (1691) \kō-'ket, -'kā\ : a man who indulges in coquetry   **2** \-'ket\ : COQUETTE

²co·quet \kō-'ket\ *adj* (1697) : characteristic of a coquette : COQUETTISH

³co·quet or **co·quette** \-'ket\ *vi* **co·quet·ted; co·quet·ting** (1701)   **1** : to play the coquette : FLIRT   **2** : to deal with something playfully rather than seriously   *syn* see TRIFLE

co·que·try \'kō-kə-trē, kō-'ke-trē\ *n, pl* **-tries** (ca. 1656) : a flirtatious act or attitude

co·quette \kō-'ket\ *n* [F, fem. of *coquet*] (ca. 1611) : a woman who endeavors without sincere affection to gain the attention and admiration of men — **co·quett·ish** \-'ke-tish\ *adj* — **co·quett·ish·ly** *adv* — **co·quett·ish·ness** *n*

co·qui·na \kō-'kē-nə\ *n* [Sp, prob. dim. of *coca* head, alter. of *coco* bogeyman, coconut] (1837)   **1** : a soft whitish limestone formed of broken shells and corals cemented together and used for building   **2** : a small clam (*Donax variabilis*) used for broth or chowder and occurring in the intertidal zone of sandy Atlantic beaches from Delaware to the Gulf of Mexico

cor \'kor\ *n* [ME, fr. LL *corus*, fr. Heb *kōr*] (14c) : an ancient Hebrew and Phoenician unit of measure of capacity

cor·a·cle \'kor-ə-kəl, 'kär-\ *n* [W *corwgl*] (ca. 1547) : a small boat used in Britain from ancient times and made of a frame (as of wicker) covered usu. with hide or tarpaulin

cor·a·coid \'kor-ə-ˌkȯid, 'kär-\ *adj* [NL *coracoides*, fr. Gk *korakoeidēs*, lit., like a raven, fr. *korak-, korax* raven — more at RAVEN] (1741) : of, relating to, or being a process of the scapula in most mammals or a well-developed cartilage bone of many lower vertebrates that extends from the scapula to or toward the sternum — **coracoid** *n*

cor·al \'kor-əl, 'kär-\ *n* [ME, fr. MF, fr. L *corallium*, fr. Gk *korallion*] (14c) **1 a** : the calcareous or horny skeletal deposit produced by anthozoan or rarely hydrozoan polyps; *esp* : a richly red precious coral secreted by a gorgonian (genus *Corallium*) **b** : a polyp or polyp colony together with its membranes and skeleton **2** : a piece of coral and esp. of red coral **3 a** : a bright reddish ovary (as of a lobster or scallop) **b** : a deep pink — **coral** *adj* — **cor·al·loid** \-ə-ˌlȯid\ *adj*

cor·al·bells \'kor-əl-ˌbelz, 'kär-\ *n pl but sing or pl in constr* (ca. 1900) : a perennial alumroot (*Heuchera sanguinea*) widely cultivated for its feathery spikes of tiny bright red campanulate flowers

cor·al·ber·ry \-ˌber-ē\ *n* (ca. 1859) : an American dwarf shrub (*Symphoricarpos orbiculatus*) that bears clusters of small flowers succeeded by red berries

¹cor·al·line \'kor-ə-ˌlīn, 'kär-\ *n* (1543) **1** : a coralline red alga **2** : a bryozoan or hydroid that resembles a coral

²coralline *adj* [MF, fr. fem. of *corallin* coral-like, fr. LL *corallinus*, fr. L *corallium*] (ca. 1633) **1** : of, relating to, or resembling coral **2** : of, relating to, or being any of a family (Corallinaceae) of calcareous red algae

coral snake *n* (ca. 1772) **1** : any of several venomous chiefly tropical New World elapid snakes (genus *Micrurus*) brilliantly banded in red, black, and yellow or white that include two (*M. fulvius* and *M. euryxanthus*) ranging northward into the southern U.S. **2** : any of several harmless snakes resembling the coral snakes

co·ran·to \kə-'ran-(ˌ)tō\ *n, pl* **-tos** *or* **-toes** [modif. of F *courante*] (1564) : COURANTE

cor·ban \'kor-ˌban\ *n* [Heb *qorbān* offering] (14c) : a sacrifice or offering to God among the ancient Hebrews

cor·beil *or* **cor·beille** \'kor-bəl, kor-'bā\ *n* [F *corbeille*, lit., basket, fr. LL *corbicula*] (ca. 1734) : a sculptured basket of flowers or fruit as an architectural decoration

¹cor·bel \'kor-bəl\ *n* [ME, fr. MF, fr. dim. of *corp* raven, fr. L *corvus* — more at RAVEN] (15c) : an architectural member that projects from within a wall and supports a weight; *esp* : one that is stepped upward and outward from a vertical surface

²corbel *vt* **-beled** *or* **-belled; -bel·ing** *or* **-bel·ling** (1843) : to furnish with or make into a corbel

corbeling *n* (1548) **1** : corbel work **2** : the construction of a corbel

cor·bic·u·la \kor-'bi-kyə-lə\ *n, pl* **-lae** \-(ˌ)lē, -ˌlī\ [LL, dim. of L *corbis* basket] (1816) : POLLEN BASKET

cor·bie \'kor-bē\ *n* [ME, modif. of MF *corbin*, fr. L *corvinus* of a raven — more at CORVINE] (15c) *chiefly Scot* : CARRION CROW; *also* : RAVEN

cor·bi·na \kor-'bē-nə\ *n* [MexSp, fr. Sp *corvina*, a marine fish (*Argyrosomus regius*), fr. fem. of *corvino* of a raven, fr. L *corvinus*] (1901) : a coastal marine croaker (*Menticirrhus undulatus*) favored by surf casters along the California coast

¹cord \'kord\ *n* [ME, fr. MF *corde*, fr. L *chorda* string, fr. Gk *chordē* — more at YARN] (14c) **1 a** : a long slender flexible material usu. consisting of several strands (as of thread or yarn) woven or twisted together **b** : the hangman's rope **2** : a moral, spiritual, or emotional bond **3 a** : an anatomical structure (as a nerve or the umbilical cord) resembling a cord **b** : a small flexible insulated electrical cable having a plug at one or both ends used to connect a lamp or other appliance with a receptacle **4** : a unit of wood cut for fuel equal to a stack 4 x 4 x 8 feet or 128 cubic feet **5 a** : a rib like a cord on a textile **b** (1) : a fabric made with such ribs or a garment made of such a fabric (2) *pl* : trousers made of such a fabric

²cord *vt* (15c) **1** : to furnish, bind, or connect with a cord **2** : to pile up (wood) in cords — **cord·er** *n*

cord·age \'kor-dij\ *n* (1598) **1** : ropes or cords; *esp* : the ropes in the rigging of a ship **2** : the number of cords (as of wood) on a given area

cor·date \'kor-ˌdāt\ *adj* [NL *cordatus*, fr. L *cord-, cor*] (1769) : shaped like a heart ⟨a ~ leaf⟩ — see LEAF illustration — **cor·date·ly** *adv*

cord·ed \'kor-dəd\ *adj* (14c) **1 a** : made of or provided with cords or ridges; *specif* : muscled in ridges **b** *of a muscle* : TENSE, TAUT **2** : bound, fastened, or wound about with cords **3** : striped or ribbed with or as if with cord : TWILLED

cord·grass \'kord-ˌgras\ *n* (1857) : any of a genus (*Spartina*) of chiefly salt-marsh grasses of coastal regions of Europe, northern Africa, and the New World that have stiff culms and panicled spikelets

¹cor·dial \'kor-jəl\ *adj* [ME, fr. ML *cordialis*, fr. L *cord-, cor* heart — more at HEART] (14c) **1** *obs* : of or relating to the heart : VITAL **2** : tending to revive, cheer, or invigorate **3 a** : sincerely or deeply felt ⟨a ~ dislike for each other⟩ **b** : warmly and genially affable ⟨~ relations⟩ *syn* see GRACIOUS — **cor·dial·ly** \'kor-jə-lē, 'kor-jə-\ *adv* — **cor·dial·ness** \'kor-jəl-nəs\ *n*

²cordial *n* (14c) **1** : a stimulating medicine or drink **2** : LIQUEUR

cor·dial·i·ty \kor-jē-'a-lə-tē, kor-'ja- *also* kor-'dya-\ *n* (1611) : sincere affection and kindness : cordial regard

cordia pulmonalia *pl of* COR PULMONALE

cor·di·er·ite \'kor-dē-ə-ˌrīt\ *n* [F, fr. Pierre L. A. *Cordier* †1861 Fr. geologist] (ca. 1814) : a blue mineral of vitreous luster and strong dichroism that consists of a silicate of aluminum, iron, and magnesium

cor·di·form \'kor-də-ˌform\ *adj* [F *cordiforme*, fr. L *cord-, cor* + *-iforme* -iform] (1828) : shaped like a heart ⟨a ~ sea-urchin shell⟩

cor·dil·le·ra \ˌkor-də-'l-'yer-ə, -də-'ler- *also* kor-'di-lə-rə\ *n* [Sp] (1704) : a system of mountain ranges often consisting of a number of more or less parallel chains — **cor·dil·le·ran** \-'yer-ən, -'ler-, -'di-lə-rən\ *adj*

cord·ite \'kor-ˌdīt\ *n* (1889) : a smokeless powder composed of nitroglycerin, guncotton, and a petroleum substance usu. gelatinized by addition of acetone and pressed into cords resembling brown twine

cord·less \'kor-dləs\ *adj* (1906) : having no cord; *esp* : powered by a battery ⟨~ tools⟩

cor·do·ba \'kor-də-bə, -və\ *n* [Sp *córdoba*, fr. Francisco Fernández de *Córdoba* †1526 Span. explorer] (1913) — see MONEY table

¹cor·don \'kor-dⁿn, -ˌdän\ *n* [F, dim. of *corde* cord] (15c) **1 a** : an ornamental cord or ribbon **b** : STRINGCOURSE **2 a** : a line of troops or objects around a person or place ⟨a ~ of police⟩ **3 a** : an espalier esp. of a fruit tree trained as a single horizontal shoot or two diverging horizontal shoots in a single line

²cordon *vt* (1561) : to form a protective or restrictive cordon around — usu. used with *off*

cor·don sa·ni·taire \ˌkor-ˌdōⁿ-sä-nē-'ter\ *n* [F, lit., sanitary cordon (quarantine line)] (1920) : a protective barrier (as of buffer states) against a potentially aggressive nation or a dangerous influence (as an ideology)

¹cor·do·van \'kor-də-vən\ *adj* [OSp *cordovano*, fr. *Córdova* (now *Córdoba*), Spain] (1591) **1** *cap* : of or relating to Córdoba and esp. Córdoba, Spain **2** : made of cordovan leather

²cordovan *n* (ca. 1625) **1** : a soft fine-grained colored leather **2** : dense nonporous leather tanned from the inner layer of horsehide

¹cor·du·roy \'kor-də-ˌroi\ *n, pl* **-roys** [origin unknown] (ca. 1791) **1 a** : trousers of corduroy fabric **b** : a durable usu. cotton pile fabric with vertical ribs or wales **2** : logs laid side by side transversely to make a road surface

²corduroy *vt* **-royed; -roy·ing** (1854) : to build (a road) of logs laid side by side transversely; *also* : to build a corduroy road across

cord·wain \'kord-ˌwān\ *n* [ME *cordwane*, fr. MF *cordoan*, fr. OSp *cordovano, cordován*] (14c) *archaic* : cordovan leather

cord·wain·er \-ˌwā-nər\ *n* (14c) **1** *archaic* : a worker in cordovan leather **2** : SHOEMAKER — **cord·wain·ery** \-ˌwā-nə-rē\ *n*

cord·wood \'kord-ˌwud\ *n* (ca. 1639) : wood piled or sold in cords

¹core \'kor, 'kor\ *n, often attrib* [ME] (14c) **1** : a central and often foundational part usu. distinct from the enveloping part by a difference in nature ⟨~ of the city⟩: as **a** : the usu. inedible central part of some fruits (as a pineapple); *esp* : the papery or leathery carpels composing the ripened ovary in a pome fruit **b** : the portion of a foundry mold that shapes the interior of a hollow casting **c** : a vertical space (as for elevator shafts, stairways, or plumbing apparatus) in a multistory building **d** (1) : a mass of iron serving to concentrate and intensify the magnetic field resulting from a current in a surrounding coil (2) : a tiny doughnut-shaped piece of magnetic material (as ferrite) used in computer memories (3) : a computer memory consisting of an array of cores strung on fine wires; *broadly* : the internal memory of a computer **e** : the central part of a celestial body (as the earth or sun) usu. having different physical properties from the surrounding parts **f** : a nodule of stone (as flint or obsidian) from which flakes have been struck for making implements **g** : the conducting wire with its insulation in an electric cable **h** : an arrangement of a course of studies that combines under basic topics material from subjects conventionally separated and aims to provide a common background for all students ⟨~ curriculum⟩ : the place in a nuclear reactor where fission occurs **2 a** : a basic, essential, or enduring part (as of an individual, a class, or an entity) ⟨the staff had a ~ of experts⟩ ⟨the ~ of her beliefs⟩ **b** : the essential meaning : GIST ⟨the ~ of the argument⟩ **c** : the inmost or most intimate part ⟨honest to the ~⟩ **3** : a part (as a thin cylinder of material) removed from the interior of a mass esp. to determine composition

²core *vt* **cored; cor·ing** (15c) : to remove a core from — **cor·er** *n*

³core *n* [perh. alter. of ME *chore* chorus, company, perh. fr. L *chorus*] (1622) *chiefly Scot* : a group of people

core city *n* (1965) : INNER CITY

cored \'kord, 'kord\ *adj* (1945) : having a core of a specified kind — usu. used in combination

co·re·li·gion·ist \ˌkō-ri-'li-jə-nist, -'li-jə-\ *n* (1826) : a person of the same religion

co·re·mi·um \kə-'rē-mē-əm\ *n, pl* **-mia** \-mē-ə\ [NL, fr. Gk *korēma* broom, fr. *korein* to sweep] (1929) : a fruiting body characteristic of some fungi (as the one causing Dutch elm disease) that consists of a sterile stalk of parallel or fascicled hyphae and a terminal fertile or spore-bearing head

co·re·op·sis \ˌkor-ē-'äp-səs, ˌkor-\ *n, pl* **coreopsis** [NL, genus name, fr. Gk *koris* bedbug + NL *-opsis*; akin to Gk *keirein* to cut — more at SHEAR] (ca. 1753) : any of a genus (*Coreopsis*) of widely cultivated composite herbs with showy flower heads and pinnately lobed or dissected leaves

co·re·pres·sor \ˌkō-ri-'pre-sər\ *n* (1963) : a substance that activates a particular genetic repressor by combining with it

co·req·ui·site \kō-'re-kwə-zət\ *n* (ca. 1948) : a formal course of study required to be taken simultaneously with another

co·re·spon·dent \ˌkō-ri-'spän-dənt\ *n* (1857) : a person named as guilty of adultery with the defendant in a divorce suit

corf \'korf\ *n, pl* **corves** \'korvz\ [ME, basket, fr. MD *corf* or MLG *korf*, fr. L *corbis* basket] (1653) *Brit* : a basket, tub, or truck used in a mine

cor·gi \'kor-gē\ *n, pl* **corgis** [W, fr. *cor* dwarf + *ci* dog; akin to OIr *cú* dog, OE *hund* — more at HOUND] (1926) **1** : CARDIGAN WELSH CORGI **2** : PEMBROKE WELSH CORGI

co·ri·a·ceous \ˌkor-ē-'ā-shəs, ˌkor-\ *adj* [LL *coriaceus* — more at CUIRASS] (1674) : resembling leather ⟨~ foliage⟩

co·ri·an·der \'kor-ē-ˌan-dər, ˌkor-ē-', 'kor-, ˌkor-\ *n* [ME *coriandre*, fr. OF, fr. L *coriandrum*, fr. Gk *koriandron, koriannon*] (14c) **1** : an Old World herb (*Coriandrum sativum*) of the carrot family with aromatic fruits **2** : the ripened dried fruit of coriander used as a flavoring — called also *coriander seed*

¹Co·rin·thi·an \kə-'rin(t)-thē-ən\ *n* (1526) **1** : a native or resident of Corinth, Greece **2** : a merry profligate man

²Corinthian *adj* (1594) **1** : of, relating to, or characteristic of Corinth or Corinthians **2** : of or relating to the lightest and most ornate of the

\ə\ abut \ᵊ\ kitten, F table \ər\ further \a\ ash \ā\ ace \ä\ mop, mar \au̇\ out \ch\ chin \e\ bet \ē\ easy \g\ go \i\ hit \ī\ ice \j\ job \ŋ\ sing \ō\ go \o\ law \oi\ boy \th\ thin \t̲h̲\ the \ü\ loot \u̇\ foot \y\ yet \zh\ vision \à, k̲, ⁿ, œ, œ̄, ᵫ, ᵫ̄, ᵞ\ see Guide to Pronunciation three ancient Greek architectural orders distinguished esp. by its large capitals decorated with carved acanthus leaves — see ORDER illustration

Co·rin·thi·ans \-thē-ənz\ *n pl but sing in constr* : either of two letters written by St. Paul to the Christians of Corinth and included as books in the New Testament — see BIBLE table

Co·ri·o·lis effect \,kȯr-ē-'ō-ləs-, ,kȯr-\ *n* (ca. 1946) : the apparent deflection of a moving object that is the result of the Coriolis force

Coriolis force *n* [Gaspard G. *Coriolis* †1843 Fr. civil engineer] (1923) : an apparent force that as a result of the earth's rotation deflects moving objects (as projectiles or air currents) to the right in the northern hemisphere and to the left in the southern hemisphere

co·ri·um \'kȯr-ē-əm, 'kȯr-\ *n, pl* **co·ria** \-ē-ə\ [NL, fr. L, leather — more at CUIRASS] (1836) : DERMIS

¹cork \'kȯrk\ *n* [ME, cork, bark, prob. fr. Ar *qurq,* fr. L *cortic-, cortex* bark — more at CUIRASS] (14c) **1 a** : the elastic tough outer tissue of the cork oak that is used esp. for stoppers and insulation **b** : PHELLEM **2** : a usu. cork stopper for a bottle or jug **3** : a fishing float

²cork *vt* (1535) **1** : to furnish or fit with cork or a cork **2** : to stop up with a cork **3** : to blacken with burnt cork

cork·age \'kȯr-kij\ *n* (1838) : a charge (as by a restaurant) for opening a bottle of wine bought elsewhere

cork·board \'kȯrk-,bȯrd, -,bȯrd\ *n* (ca. 1893) : a heat-insulating material made of compressed granulated cork; *also* : a bulletin board made with this material

cork cambium *n* (1878) : PHELLOGEN

corked \'kȯrkt\ *adj* (1830) : CORKY 2

cork·er \'kȯr-kər\ *n* (1881) **1** : one that corks containers (as bottles) **2** : one that is excellent or remarkable

cork·ing \'kȯr-kiŋ\ *adj or adv* (1895) : extremely fine — often used as an intensive esp. before *good* ⟨had a ~ good time⟩

cork oak *n* (1873) : an oak (*Quercus suber*) of southern Europe and northern Africa that is the source of the cork of commerce

¹cork·screw \'kȯrk-,skrü\ *n* (1720) : a device for drawing corks from bottles that has a pointed spiral piece of metal turned by a handle

²corkscrew *adj* (1815) : resembling a corkscrew : SPIRAL

³corkscrew *vt* (1837) **1** : WIND **2** : to draw out with difficulty **3** : to twist into a spiral ~ *vi* **1** : to move in a winding course

cork·wood \'kȯrk-,wu̇d\ *n* (1756) : any of several trees having light or corky wood; *esp* : a small or shrubby tree (*Leitneria floridana*) of the southeastern U.S. that has extremely light soft wood

corky \'kȯr-kē\ *adj* **cork·i·er; -est** (1756) **1** : resembling cork **2** : having an unpleasant odor and taste (as from a tainted cork) ⟨~ wine⟩ — **cork·i·ness** \-kē-nəs\ *n*

corm \'kȯrm\ *n* [NL *cormus,* fr. Gk *kormos* tree trunk, fr. *keirein* to cut — more at SHEAR] (1830) : a rounded thick modified underground stem base bearing membranous or scaly leaves and buds and acting as a vegetative reproductive structure — compare BULB, TUBER

corm·el \'kȯr-məl, kȯr-'mel\ *n* [dim. of *corm*] (ca. 1900) : a small or secondary corm produced by a larger corm

cor·mo·rant \'kȯrm-rənt, 'kȯr-mə-, 'kȯr-mə-,rant\ *n* [ME *cormeraunt,* fr. MF *cormorant,* fr. OF *cormareng,* fr. *corp* raven + *marenc* of the sea, fr. L *marinus* — more at CORBEL, MARINE] (14c) **1** : any of a family (Phalacrocoracidae) of dark-colored web-footed water birds that have a long neck, hooked bill, and distensible throat pouch **2** : a gluttonous, greedy, or rapacious person

¹corn \'kȯrn\ *n, often attrib* [ME, fr. OE; akin to OHG & ON *korn* grain, L *granum*] (bef. 12c) **1** *chiefly dial* : a small hard particle : GRAIN **2** : a small hard seed **3 a** : the seeds of a cereal grass and esp. of the important cereal crop of a particular region as wheat in Britain, oats in Scotland and Ireland, and Indian corn in the New World and Australia) **b** : the kernels of sweet corn served as a vegetable while still soft and milky **4** : a plant that produces corn **5** : CORN WHISKEY **6 a** : something (as writing, music, or acting) that is corny **b** : the quality or state of being corny : CORNINESS

²corn *vt* (1560) **1** : to form into grains : GRANULATE **2 a** : to preserve or season with salt in grains **b** : to cure or preserve in brine containing preservatives and often seasonings ⟨~ed beef⟩ **3** : to feed with corn ⟨~ the horses⟩

³corn *n* [ME *corne,* fr. MF, horn, corner, fr. L *cornu* horn, point — more at HORN] (15c) : a local hardening and thickening of epidermis (as on a toe)

¹corn·ball \'kȯrn-,bȯl\ *n* (ca. 1949) : an unsophisticated person; *also* : something corny

²cornball *adj* (1951) : CORNY

corn borer *n* (1919) : any of several insects that bore in maize: as **a** : EUROPEAN CORN BORER **b** : SOUTHWESTERN CORN BORER

corn bread *n* (1750) : bread made with cornmeal

corn chip *n* (1950) : a piece of a dry crisp snack food prepared from a seasoned cornmeal batter

corn·cob \'kȯrn-,käb\ *n* (1793) **1** : the axis on which the kernels of Indian corn are arranged **2** : an ear of Indian corn

corncob pipe *n* (1832) : a tobacco pipe with a bowl made of a corncob

corn cockle *n* (1713) : an annual hairy weed (*Agrostemma githago*) of the pink family with purplish red flowers that is found in grainfields

corn·crake \'kȯrn-,krāk\ *n* (15c) : a common Eurasian short-billed rail (*Crex crex*) that frequents grainfields

corn·crib \-,krib\ *n* (1681) : a crib for storing ears of Indian corn

corn dodger *n* (1834) *chiefly Southern & Midland* : a cake of corn bread that is fried, baked, or boiled as a dumpling

corn dog *n* (1967) : a frankfurter dipped in cornmeal batter, fried, and served on a stick

cor·nea \'kȯr-nē-ə\ *n* [ME, fr. ML, fr. L, fem. of *corneus* horny, fr. *cornu*] (14c) : the transparent part of the coat of the eyeball that covers the iris and pupil and admits light to the interior — see EYE illustration — **cor·ne·al** \-əl\ *adj*

corn ear·worm \-'ir-,wərm\ *n* (1802) : a noctuid moth (*Heliothis zea*) whose large striped yellow-headed larva is esp. destructive to Indian corn, tomatoes, tobacco, and cotton bolls

cor·nel \'kȯr-n²l, -,nel\ *n* [ultim. fr. L *cornus* cornel cherry tree; akin to Gk *kranon* cornel cherry tree] (1551) : any of various shrubs or trees (genus *Cornus*) of the dogwood family with very hard wood and perfect flowers; *specif* : DOGWOOD

cor·ne·lian \kȯr-'nēl-yən\ *n* (15c) : CARNELIAN

cor·ne·ous \'kȯr-nē-əs\ *adj* [L *corneus*] (1646) : of a horny texture

¹cor·ner \'kȯr-nər\ *n* [ME, fr. OF *cornere,* fr. *corne* horn, corner] (13c) **1 a** : the point where converging lines, edges, or sides meet : ANGLE **b** : the place of intersection of two streets or roads **c** : a piece designed to form, mark, or protect a corner **2** : the angular part or space between meeting lines, edges, or borders near the vertex of the angle ⟨the southwest ~ of the state⟩ ⟨the ~s of the tablecloth⟩: as **a** : the area of a playing field or court near the intersection of the sideline and the goal line or baseline **b** (1) : either of the four angles of a boxing ring; *esp* : the area in which a boxer rests or is worked on by his seconds during periods between rounds (2) : a group of supporters, well-wishers, or adherents associated esp. with a contestant **c** : the side of home plate nearest to or farthest from a batter ⟨a fast ball over the outside ~⟩ **d** : CORNER KICK **e** (1) : the outside of a football formation (2) : CORNERBACK **3 a** : a private, secret, or remote place ⟨a quiet ~ of New England⟩ ⟨to every ~ of the earth⟩ ⟨dark ~s of the mind⟩ **b** : a difficult or embarrassing situation : a position from which escape or retreat is difficult or impossible ⟨was backed into a ~⟩ **4** : control or ownership of enough of the available supply of a commodity or security esp. to permit manipulation of the price **5** : a point at which significant change occurs — often used in the phrase *turn the corner* — **cor·nered** \-nərd\ *adj* — **around the corner** : at hand : IMMINENT ⟨good times are just *around the corner*⟩

²corner *adj* (13c) **1** : situated at a corner ⟨the ~ drugstore⟩ **2** : used or fitted for use in or on a corner ⟨a ~ table⟩

³corner *vt* (1824) **1 a** : to drive into a corner ⟨the animal is dangerous when ~ed⟩ **b** : to catch and hold the attention of esp. to force an interview **2** : to get a corner on ⟨~ the market⟩ ~ *vi* **1** : to meet or converge at a corner or angle **2** : to turn a corner ⟨the car ~s well⟩

cor·ner·back \'kȯr-nər-,bak\ *n* (1955) : a defensive halfback in football who defends the flank

corner kick *n* (1882) : a free kick from a corner of a soccer field awarded to an attacker when a defender plays the ball out-of-bounds over the end line

cor·ner·man \'kȯr-nər-,man\ *n* (1957) **1** : one who plays in or near the corner: as **a** : CORNERBACK **b** : a basketball forward **2** : a boxer's second

cor·ner·stone \-,stōn\ *n* (13c) **1** : a stone forming a part of a corner or angle in a wall; *specif* : such a stone laid at a formal ceremony as a basic element : FOUNDATION ⟨a ~ of foreign policy⟩

cor·ner·ways \-,wāz\ *adv* (1922) : DIAGONALLY

cor·ner·wise \-,wīz\ *adv* (15c) : DIAGONALLY

cor·net \kȯr-'net, *Brit usu* 'kȯr-nit\ *n* [ME, fr. MF, dim. of *corn* horn, fr. L *cornu*] (14c) **1** : a valved brass instrument resembling a trumpet in design and range but having a shorter partly conical tube and less brilliant tone **2** : something shaped like a cone: as **a** : a piece of paper twisted for use as a container **b** : a cone-shaped pastry shell that is often filled with whipped cream **c** *Brit* : an ice-cream cone — **cor·net·ist** *or* **cor·net·tist** \kȯr-'ne-tist, 'kȯr-ni-\ *n*

corn-fed \'kȯrn-,fed\ *adj* (14c) **1** : fed or fattened on grain (as corn) ⟨~ hogs⟩ **2** : looking well-fed : PLUMP **3** : rustically wholesome or corny

corn·field \-,fēld\ *n* (14c) : a field in which corn is grown

corn·flakes \-,flāks\ *n pl* (1907) : toasted flakes made from the coarse meal of hulled corn for use as a breakfast cereal

corn flour *n* (1791) *Brit* : CORNSTARCH

corn·flow·er \'kȯrn-,flau̇(-ə)r\ *n* (1527) **1** : CORN COCKLE **2** : BACHELOR'S BUTTON

cornflower blue *n* (1907) : a moderate purplish blue

Corn·husk·er \'kȯrn-,həs-kər\ *n* (ca. 1948) : a native or resident of Nebraska — used as a nickname

corn·husk·ing \-,həs-kiŋ\ *n* (1692) : a social gathering esp. of farm families to husk corn

¹cor·nice \'kȯr-nəs, -nish\ *n* [MF, fr. It, frame, cornice, fr. L *cornic-, cornix* crow; akin to Gk *korax* raven — more at RAVEN] (1563) **1 a** : the molded and projecting horizontal member that crowns an architectural composition **b** : a top course that crowns a wall **2** : a decorative band of metal or wood used to conceal curtain fixtures **3** : an overhanging mass of snow, ice, or rock usu. on a ridge

c cornice 1a

²cornice *vt* **cor·niced; cor·nic·ing** (1744) : to furnish or crown with a cornice

cor·niche \kȯr-'nēsh\ *n* [F *cornice, corniche,* lit., cornice, fr. It *cornice*] (1837) : a road built along a coast and esp. along the face of a cliff

cor·nic·u·late cartilage \kȯr-'ni-kyə-lət-\ *n* [L *corniculatus* horned, fr. *corniculum,* dim. of *cornu* horn] (ca. 1909) : a small nodule of yellow elastic cartilage articulating with the apex of the arytenoid

cor·ni·fi·ca·tion \,kȯr-nə-fə-'kā-shən\ *n* [L *cornu* horn] (ca. 1843) **1** : conversion into horn or a horny substance or tissue **2** : the conversion of the vaginal epithelium from the columnar to the squamous type

¹Cor·nish \'kȯr-nish\ *adj* [ME *Cornysshe,* fr. *Cornwaile* Cornwall, England] (14c) : of, relating to, or characteristic of Cornwall, Cornishmen, or Cornish

²Cornish *n* (1547) **1** : a Celtic language of Cornwall extinct since the late 18th century **2** : any of an English breed of domestic fowls much used in crossbreeding for meat production

Cor·nish·man \-mən\ *n* (15c) : a native or resident of Cornwall, England

Corn Law *n* (1766) : one of a series of laws in force in Great Britain before 1846 prohibiting or discouraging the importation of grain

corn leaf aphid *n* (ca. 1939) : a dusky greenish or brownish aphid (*Rhopalosiphum maidis*) that feeds on the flowers and foliage of various commercially important grasses (as Indian corn)

corn·meal \'kȯrn-,mēl\ *n* (1749) : meal ground from corn

corn oil *n* (1900) : a yellow fatty oil obtained from the germ of Indian corn kernels and used chiefly as salad oil, in soft soap, and in margarine

corn·pone \'kȯrn-,pōn\ *adj* (1972) : DOWN-HOME, COUNTRIFIED ⟨~ humor⟩

corn pone *n* (1859) *Southern & Midland* : corn bread often made without milk or eggs and baked or fried

corn poppy *n* (ca. 1859) : an annual red-flowered Eurasian poppy (*Papaver rhoeas*) common in fields and cultivated in several varieties

corn rootworm *n* (1892) : any of several chrysomelid beetles (genus *Diabrotica*) whose root-eating larvae are pests esp. of corn

corn·row \'kȯrn-ˌrō\ *n* (1946) **1** : a section of hair which is braided usu. flat to the scalp **2** : a hairstyle in which the hair is divided into cornrow sections arranged in rows — **cornrow** *vb*

corn salad *n* [fr. its occurrence as a weed in fields of grain] (1597) : any of several herbs (genus *Valerianella*) of the valerian family; *esp* : a low European herb (*V. locusta* syn. *V. olitoria*) that is widely cultivated as a salad plant and potherb

cornrow 2

corn silk *n* (1861) : the silky styles on an ear of Indian corn

corn snow *n* (1935) : granular snow formed by alternate thawing and freezing

corn·stalk \'kȯrn-ˌstȯk\ *n* (1645) : a stalk of Indian corn

corn·starch \-ˌstärch\ *n* (1853) : starch made from corn and used in foods as a thickening agent, in making corn syrup and sugars, and in the manufacture of adhesives and sizes for paper and textiles

corn sugar *n* (1850) : DEXTROSE

corn syrup *n* (1903) : a syrup containing dextrins, maltose, and dextrose that is obtained by partial hydrolysis of cornstarch

cor·nu \'kȯr-(ˌ)nü, -(ˌ)nyü\ *n, pl* **cor·nua** \-nü-ə, -nyü-\ [L] (1691) : a horn-shaped anatomical part (as of the uterus) — **cor·nu·al** \-nü-əl, -nyü-\ *adj*

cor·nu·co·pia \ˌkȯr-nə-ˈkō-pē-ə, -nyə-\ *n* [LL, fr. L *cornu copiae* horn of plenty] (1508) **1** : a curved goat's horn overflowing with fruit and ears of grain that is used as a decorative motif emblematic of abundance **2** : an inexhaustible store : ABUNDANCE **3** : a receptacle shaped like a horn or cone — **cor·nu·co·pi·an** \-pē-ən\ *adj*

cor·nu·to \kȯr-ˈnü-(ˌ)tō, -ˈnyü-\ *n, pl* **-tos** [It, fr. L *cornutus* having horns, fr. *cornu*] (1598) : CUCKOLD

corn whiskey *n* (1780) : whiskey distilled from a mash made up of not less than 80 percent corn — compare BOURBON

¹corny \'kȯr-nē\ *adj* **corn·i·er; -est** (14c) **1** *archaic* : tasting strongly of malt **2** : of or relating to corn **3** : mawkishly old-fashioned : tiresomely simple and sentimental — **corn·i·ly** \'kȯr-nᵊl-ē\ *adv* — **corn·i·ness** \'kȯr-nē-nəs\ *n*

²corny *adj* **corn·i·er; -est** (1707) : relating to or having corns on the feet

cor·o·dy \'kȯr-ə-dē, 'kär-\ *n, pl* **-dies** [ME *corrodie*, fr. ML *corrodium*] (15c) : an allowance of provisions for maintenance dispensed as a charity

co·rol·la \kə-ˈrä-lə, -ˈrō-\ *n* [NL, fr. L, dim. of *corona*] (ca. 1753) : the part of a flower that consists of the separate or fused petals and constitutes the inner whorl of the perianth — **co·rol·late** \kə-ˈrä-lət; 'kȯr-ə-ˌlāt, 'kär-\ *adj*

cor·ol·lary \'kȯr-ə-ˌler-ē, 'kär-; *Brit* kə-ˈrä-lə-rē\ *n, pl* **-lar·ies** [ME *corolarie*, fr. LL *corollarium*, fr. L, money paid for a garland, gratuity, fr. *corolla*] (14c) **1** : a proposition inferred immediately from a proved proposition with little or no additional proof **2 a** : something that naturally follows : RESULT **b** : something that incidentally or naturally accompanies or parallels — **corollary** *adj*

cor·o·man·del \ˌkȯr-ə-ˈman-dᵊl, ˌkär-\ *n* [*Coromandel* coast region, India] (1845) : CALAMANDER

coromandel screen *n, often cap C* (1926) : a Chinese lacquered folding screen

co·ro·na \kə-ˈrō-nə\ *n* [L, garland, crown, cornice — more at CROWN] (1563) **1** : the projecting part of a classic cornice **2 a** : a usu. colored circle often seen around and close to a luminous body (as the sun or moon) caused by diffraction produced by suspended droplets or occas. particles of dust **b** : the tenuous outermost part of the atmosphere of a star (as the sun) **c** : a circle of light made by the apparent convergence of the streamers of the aurora borealis **d** : the upper portion of a bodily part (as a tooth or the skull) **e** : an appendage or series of united appendages on the inner side of the corolla in some flowers (as the daffodil, jonquil, or milkweed) **f** : a faint glow adjacent to the surface of an electrical conductor at high voltage **3** [fr. *La Corona*, a trademark] : a long cigar having the sides straight to the end to be lit and being roundly blunt at the other end

a corona 2e

Corona Aus·tra·lis \-ȯ-ˈstrā-ləs, -ä-\ *n* [NL (gen. *Coronae Australis*), lit., southern crown] : a southern constellation adjoining Sagittarius on the south

Corona Bo·re·al·is \-ˌbȯr-ē-ˈa-ləs, -ˌbȯr-\ *n* [NL (gen. *Coronae Borealis*), lit., northern crown] : a northern constellation between Hercules and Boötes

cor·o·nach \'kȯr-ə-nək, 'kär-\ *n* [ScGael *corranach* & Ir *coránach*] (1530) : a funeral dirge sung or played on the bagpipes in Scotland and Ireland

co·ro·na·graph *also* **co·ro·no·graph** \kə-ˈrō-nə-ˌgraf\ *n* (1885) : a telescope for observation of the sun's corona

¹cor·o·nal *also* **cor·o·nel** \'kȯr-ə-nᵊl, 'kär-\ *n* [ME *coronal*, fr. AF, fr. L *coronalis* of a crown, fr. *corona*] (14c) : a circlet for the head usu. implying rank or dignity

²co·ro·nal \'kȯr-ə-nᵊl, 'kär-; kə-ˈrō-\ *adj* (14c) **1 a** : lying in the direction of the coronal suture **b** : of or relating to the frontal plane that passes through the long axis of the body **2** : of or relating to a corona or crown

coronal suture *n* (1615) : a suture extending across the skull between the parietal and frontal bones

co·ro·na ra·di·a·ta \kə-ˈrō-nə-ˌrä-dē-ˈä-tə, -ˈä-tə\ *n, pl* **co·ro·nae ra·di·a·tae** \-(ˌ)nē-ˌrä-dē-ˈä-(ˌ)tē, -ˈä-(ˌ)tē\ [NL, lit., crown with rays] (1892) : the zone of small follicular cells immediately surrounding the ovum

in the graafian follicle and accompanying the ovum on its discharge from the follicle

¹cor·o·nary \'kȯr-ə-ˌner-ē, 'kär-\ *adj* (1610) **1** : of, relating to, resembling, or being a crown or coronal **2** : of, relating to, or being the coronary arteries or veins of the heart; *broadly* : of or relating to the heart

²coronary *n, pl* **-nar·ies** (1893) **1 a** : CORONARY ARTERY **b** : CORONARY VEIN **2** : CORONARY THROMBOSIS; *broadly* : HEART ATTACK

coronary artery *n* (1741) : either of two arteries that arise one from the left and one from the right side of the aorta immediately above the semilunar valves and supply the tissues of the heart itself

coronary occlusion *n* (1946) : the partial or complete blocking (as by a thrombus, by spasm, or by sclerosis) of a coronary artery

coronary sinus *n* (1831) : a venous channel that is derived from the sinus venosus, is continuous with the largest of the cardiac veins, receives most of the blood from the walls of the heart, and empties into the right atrium

coronary thrombosis *n* (1926) : the blocking of a coronary artery of the heart by a thrombus

coronary vein *n* (ca. 1828) : any of several veins that drain the tissues of the heart and empty into the coronary sinus

cor·o·nate \'kȯr-ə-ˌnāt, 'kär-\ *vt* **-nat·ed; -nat·ing** [L *coronatus*, pp. of *coronare* to crown, fr. *corona*] (ca. 1623) : CROWN 1a

cor·o·na·tion \ˌkȯr-ə-ˈnā-shən, ˌkär-\ *n* [ME *coronacion*, fr. MF *coronation*, fr. *coroner* to crown] (14c) : the act or occasion of crowning; *also* : accession to the highest office

cor·o·ner \'kȯr-ə-nər, 'kär-\ *n* [ME, an officer of the crown, fr. AF, fr. OF *corone* crown, fr. L *corona*] (ca. 1630) : a public officer whose principal duty is to inquire into the cause of any death which there is reason to suppose is not due to natural causes

cor·o·net \ˌkȯr-ə-ˈnet, ˌkär-\ *n* [MF *coronette*, fr. OF *coronete*, fr. *corone*] (15c) **1 a** : a small or lesser crown usu. signifying a rank below that of a sovereign **2 a** : an ornamental wreath or band for the head usu. for wear by women on formal occasions **3** : the lower part of a horse's pastern where the horn terminates in skin — see HORSE illustration

co·ro·tate \(ˌ)kō-ˈrō-ˌtāt\ *vi* (1962) : to rotate in conjunction with or at the same rate as another rotating body — **co·ro·ta·tion** \ˌkō-rō-ˈtā-shən\ *n*

corpora *pl of* CORPUS

¹cor·po·ral \'kȯr-p(ə-)rəl\ *n* [ME, fr. MF, fr. ML *corporale*, fr. L, neut. of *corporalis*; fr. the doctrine that the bread of the Eucharist becomes or represents the body of Christ] (14c) : a linen cloth on which the eucharistic elements are placed

²corporal *adj* [ME, fr. MF, fr. L *corporalis*, fr. *corpor-, corpus* body — more at MIDRIFF] (14c) **1** *obs* : CORPOREAL, PHYSICAL **2** : of, relating to, or affecting the body ⟨~ punishment⟩ — **cor·po·ral·ly** \-p(ə-)rə-lē\ *adv*

³corporal *n* [MF, fr. OIt *caporale*, fr. *capo* head, fr. L *caput* — more at HEAD] (1579) : a noncommissioned officer ranking in the army above a private first class and below a sergeant and in the marine corps above a lance corporal and below a sergeant

cor·po·ral·i·ty \ˌkȯr-pə-ˈra-lə-tē\ *n, pl* **-ties** (14c) : the quality or state of being or having a body or a material or physical existence

corporal's guard *n* (1844) **1** : the small detachment commanded by a corporal **2** : a small group

cor·po·rate \'kȯr-p(ə-)rət\ *adj* [L *corporatus*, pp. of *corporare* to make into a body, fr. *corpor-, corpus*] (1512) **1 a** : formed into an association and endowed by law with the rights and liabilities of an individual : INCORPORATED **b** : of or relating to a corporation ⟨a plan to reorganize the ~ structure⟩ **2** : of, relating to, or formed into a unified body of individuals ⟨human law arises by the ~ action of a people —G. H. Sabine⟩ **3** : CORPORATIVE 2 — **cor·po·rate·ly** *adv*

cor·po·ra·tion \ˌkȯr-pə-ˈrā-shən\ *n* (15c) **1 a** *obs* : a group of merchants or traders united in a trade guild **b** : the municipal authorities of a town or city **2** : a body formed and authorized by law to act as a single person although constituted by one or more persons and legally endowed with various rights and duties including the capacity of succession **3** : an association of employers and employees in a basic industry or of members of a profession organized as an organ of political representation in a corporative state **4** : POTBELLY 1

cor·po·rat·ism \'kȯr-p(ə-)rə-ˌti-zəm\ *n* (1890) : the organization of a society into industrial and professional corporations serving as organs of political representation and exercising some control over persons and activities within their jurisdiction — **cor·po·rat·ist** \-p(ə-)rə-tist\ *adj*

cor·po·ra·tive \'kȯr-pə-ˌrā-tiv, -p(ə-)rə-\ *adj* (1833) **1** : of or relating to a corporation **2** : of or relating to corporatism ⟨a ~ state⟩

cor·po·ra·tiv·ism \'kȯr-pə-ˌrā-ti-ˌvi-zəm, -p(ə-)rə-\ *n* (1930) : CORPORATISM

cor·po·ra·tor \'kȯr-pə-ˌrā-tər\ *n* (1784) : a corporation organizer, member, or stockholder

cor·po·re·al \kȯr-ˈpōr-ē-əl, -ˈpȯr-\ *adj* [L *corporeus* of the body, fr. *corpor-, corpus*] (15c) **1** : having, consisting of, or relating to a physical material body: as **a** : not spiritual **b** : not immaterial or intangible : SUBSTANTIAL **2** *archaic* : CORPORAL *syn* see MATERIAL — **cor·po·re·al·ly** \-ē-ə-lē\ *adv* — **cor·po·re·al·ness** *n*

cor·po·re·al·i·ty \(ˌ)kȯr-ˌpōr-ē-ˈa-lə-tē, -ˌpȯr-\ *n, pl* **-ties** (1651) : corporeal existence

cor·po·re·i·ty \ˌkȯr-pə-ˈrē-ə-tē, -ˈrā-\ *n, pl* **-ties** (1621) : the quality or state of having or being a body : MATERIALITY

cor·po·sant \'kȯr-pə-ˌsant, -ˌzant\ *n* [Pg *corpo-santo*, lit., holy body] (1655) : SAINT ELMO'S FIRE

corps \'kȯr, 'kȯr\ *n, pl* **corps** \'kȯrz, 'kȯrz\ [F, fr. L *corpus* body] (1711) **1 a** : an organized subdivision of the military establishment ⟨Marine *Corps*⟩ ⟨Signal *Corps*⟩ **b** : a tactical unit usu. consisting of

---

\ə\ abut \ᵊ\ kitten, F table \ər\ further \a\ ash \ā\ ace \ä\ mop, mar \aú\ out \ch\ chin \e\ bet \ē\ easy \g\ go \i\ hit \ī\ ice \j\ job \ŋ\ sing \ō\ go \ȯ\ law \ȯi\ boy \th\ thin \t̲h̲\ the \ü\ loot \ú\ foot \y\ yet \zh\ vision \á, k̲, ⁿ, œ, œ̄, ue, ūe, ᵞ\ *see* Guide to Pronunciation two or more divisions and auxiliary arms and services **2** : a group of persons associated together or acting under common direction; *esp* : a body of persons having a common activity or occupation ⟨the press ~⟩ **3** : CORPS DE BALLET

corps de bal·let \ˌkȯr-də-(ˌ)ba-ˈlā, ˌkȯr-\ *n, pl* **corps de ballet** *same or* ˌkȯrz-də-, ˌkȯrz-\ [F] (1826) : the ensemble of a ballet company

corps d'elite \ˌkȯr-dā-ˈlēt, ˌkȯr-\ *n, pl* **corps d'elite** *same or* ˌkȯrz-dā-, ˌkȯrz-\ [F *corps d'élite*] (1884) **1** : a body of picked troops **2** : a group of the best people in a category

corpse \ˈkȯrps\ *n* [ME *corps*, fr. MF, fr. L *corpus*] (13c) **1** *obs* : a human or animal body whether living or dead **2 a** : a dead body esp. of a human being **b** : the remains of something discarded or defunct ⟨the ~s of rusting cars⟩

corps·man \ˈkȯr(z)-mən, ˈkȯr(z)-\ *n* (1901) **1** : an enlisted man trained to give first aid and minor medical treatment **2** : a member of a government-sponsored service corps

cor·pu·lence \ˈkȯr-pyə-lən(t)s\ *n* (1581) : the state of being corpulent

cor·pu·len·cy \-lən(t)-sē\ *n, pl* **-cies** (1577) : CORPULENCE

cor·pu·lent \-lənt\ *adj* [ME, fr. L *corpulentus*, fr. *corpus*] (14c) : having a large bulky body : OBESE — **cor·pu·lent·ly** *adv*

cor pul·mo·na·le \ˌkȯr-ˌpu̇l-mə-ˈnä-lē, -ˌpȯl-, -ˈnä-\ *n, pl* **cor·dia pul·mo·na·lia** \ˈkȯr-dē-ə-ˌpu̇l-mə-ˈnä-lē-ə, -ˌpȯl-, -ˈnä-\ [NL, lit., pulmonary heart] (1857) : disease of the heart characterized by hypertrophy and dilatation of the right ventricle and secondary to disease of the lungs or their blood vessels

cor·pus \ˈkȯr-pəs\ *n, pl* **cor·po·ra** \-p(ə-)rə\ [ME, fr. L] (15c) **1** : the body of a human or animal body esp. when dead **2 a** : the main part or body of a bodily structure or organ ⟨the ~ of the uterus⟩ **b** : the main body or corporeal substance of a thing; *specif* : the principal of a fund or estate as distinct from income or interest **3 a** : all the writings or works of a particular kind or on a particular subject; *esp* : the complete works of an author **b** : a collection or body of knowledge or evidence; *esp* : a collection of recorded utterances used as a basis for the descriptive analysis of a language

corpus al·la·tum \-ə-ˈlä-təm, -ˈlä-\ *n, pl* **corpora al·la·ta** \-ˈlä-tə, -ˈlä-tə\ [NL, lit., applied body] (1947) : one of a pair of separate or fused bodies in many insects that are sometimes closely associated with the corpora cardiaca and that secrete hormones (as juvenile hormone)

corpus cal·lo·sum \-ka-ˈlō-səm\ *n, pl* **corpora cal·lo·sa** \-sə\ [NL, lit., callous body] (1706) : the great band of commissural fibers uniting the cerebral hemispheres of higher mammals including humans — see BRAIN illustration

corpus car·di·a·cum \-kär-ˈdī-ə-kəm\ *n, pl* **corpora car·di·a·ca** \-ə-kə\ [NL, lit., cardiac body] (1960) : one of a pair of separate or fused bodies of nervous tissue in many insects that lie posterior to the brain and dorsal to the esophagus and that function in the storage and secretion of brain hormone

Cor·pus Chris·ti \ˈkȯr-pəs-ˈkris-tē\ *n* [ME, fr. ML, lit., body of Christ] (14c) : the Thursday after Trinity observed as a Roman Catholic festival in honor of the Eucharist

cor·pus·cle \ˈkȯr-(ˌ)pə-səl\ *n* [L *corpusculum*, dim. of *corpus*] (1660) **1** : a minute particle **2 a** : a living cell; *esp* : one (as a red or white blood cell or a cell in cartilage or bone) not aggregated into continuous tissues **b** : any of various small circumscribed multicellular bodies — **cor·pus·cu·lar** \kȯr-ˈpəs-kyə-lər\ *adj*

cor·pus de·lic·ti \ˈkȯr-pəs-di-ˈlik-ˌtī, -(ˌ)tē\ *n, pl* **corpora delicti** [NL, lit., body of the crime] (1832) **1** : the substantial and fundamental fact necessary to prove the commission of a crime **2** : the material substance (as the body of the victim of a murder) upon which a crime has been committed

corpus lu·te·um \-ˈlü-tē-əm\ *n, pl* **corpora lu·tea** \-tē-ə\ [NL, lit., yellowish body] (1788) : a yellowish mass of progesterone-secreting endocrine tissue that forms immediately after ovulation from the ruptured graafian follicle in the mammalian ovary

corpus stri·a·tum \-(ˌ)strī-ˈā-təm\ *n, pl* **corpora stri·a·ta** \-ˈā-tə\ [NL, lit., striated body] (1851) : either of a pair of masses of nervous tissue within the brain that contain two large nuclei of gray matter separated by sheets of white matter

cor·rade \kə-ˈrād\ *vb* **cor·rad·ed; cor·rad·ing** [L *corradere* to scrape together, fr. *com-* + *radere* to scrape — more at RODENT] *vt* (1646) : to wear away by abrasion ~ *vi* : to crumble away through abrasion — **cor·ra·sion** \-ˈrā-zhən\ *n* — **cor·ra·sive** \-ˈrā-siv, -ziv\ *adj*

¹**cor·ral** \kə-ˈral, -ˈrel\ *n* [Sp, fr. (assumed) VL *currale* enclosure for vehicles, fr. L *currus* cart, fr. *currere* to run — more at CAR] (1582) **1** : a pen or enclosure for confining or capturing livestock **2** : an enclosure made with wagons for defense of an encampment

²**corral** *vt* **cor·ralled; cor·ral·ling** (1847) **1** : to enclose in a corral **2** : to arrange (wagons) so as to form a corral **3** : COLLECT, GATHER ⟨*corralling* votes for the upcoming election⟩

¹**cor·rect** \kə-ˈrekt\ *vt* [ME, fr. L *correctus*, pp. of *corrigere*, fr. *com-* + *regere* to lead straight — more at RIGHT] (14c) **1 a** : to make or set right : AMEND **b** : COUNTERACT, NEUTRALIZE **c** : to alter or adjust so as to bring to some standard or required condition ⟨~ a lens for spherical aberration⟩ **2 a** : to punish (as a child) with a view to reforming or improving **b** : to point out usu. for amendment the errors or faults of ⟨spent the day ~*ing* tests⟩ — **cor·rect·able** \-ˈrek-tə-bəl\ *adj* — **cor·rec·tor** \-ˈrek-tər\ *n*

syn CORRECT, RECTIFY, EMEND, REMEDY, REDRESS, AMEND, REFORM, REVISE mean to make right what is wrong. CORRECT implies taking action to remove errors, faults, deviations, defects ⟨*correct* your spelling⟩. RECTIFY implies a more essential changing to make something right, just, or properly controlled or directed ⟨*rectify* a misguided policy⟩. EMEND specif. implies correction of a text or manuscript ⟨*emend* a text⟩. REMEDY implies removing or making harmless a cause of trouble, harm, or evil ⟨set out to *remedy* the evils of the world⟩. REDRESS implies making compensation or reparation for an unfairness, injustice, or imbalance ⟨*redress* past social injustices⟩. AMEND, REFORM, REVISE imply an improving by making corrective changes, AMEND usu. suggesting slight changes ⟨*amend* a law⟩, REFORM implying drastic change ⟨plans to *reform* the court system⟩, and REVISE suggesting a careful examination of something and the making of necessary changes ⟨*revise* the schedule⟩. **syn** see in addition PUNISH

²**correct** *adj* [ME, corrected, fr. L *correctus*, fr. pp. of *corrigere*] (1676) **1** : conforming to an approved or conventional standard **2** : con-

forming to or agreeing with fact, logic, or known truth **3** : conforming to a set figure ⟨enclosed the ~ return postage⟩ — **cor·rect·ly** \kə-ˈrek(t)-lē\ *adv* — **cor·rect·ness** \-ˈrek(t)-nəs\ *n*

syn CORRECT, ACCURATE, EXACT, PRECISE, NICE, RIGHT mean conforming to fact, standard, or truth. CORRECT usu. implies freedom from fault or error ⟨*correct* answers⟩ ⟨socially *correct* dress⟩. ACCURATE implies fidelity to fact or truth attained by exercise of care ⟨an *accurate* description⟩. EXACT stresses a very strict agreement with fact, standard, or truth ⟨*exact* measurements⟩. PRECISE adds to EXACT an emphasis on sharpness of definition or delimitation ⟨*precise* calibration⟩. NICE stresses great precision and delicacy of adjustment or discrimination ⟨makes *nice* distinctions⟩. RIGHT is close to CORRECT but has a stronger positive emphasis on conformity to fact or truth rather than mere absence of error or fault ⟨the *right* thing to do⟩.

corrected time *n* (ca. 1891) : a boat's elapsed time less its time allowance in yacht racing

cor·rec·tion \kə-ˈrek-shən\ *n* (14c) **1** : the action or an instance of correcting: as **a** : AMENDMENT, RECTIFICATION **b** : REBUKE, PUNISHMENT **c** : a bringing into conformity with a standard **d** : NEUTRALIZATION, COUNTERACTION ⟨~ of acidity⟩ **2** : a decline in market price or business activity following and counteracting a rise **3 a** : something substituted in place of what is wrong ⟨marking ~s on the students' papers⟩ **b** : a quantity applied by way of correcting (as for adjustment of an instrument) **4** : the treatment and rehabilitation of offenders through a program involving penal custody, parole, and probation; *also* : the administration of such treatment as a matter of public policy — usu. used in pl. — **cor·rec·tion·al** \-shnəl, -shə-nᵊl\ *adj*

cor·rec·ti·tude \kə-ˈrek-tə-ˌtüd, -ˌtyüd\ *n* [blend of *correct* and *rectitude*] (1893) : correctness or propriety of conduct

cor·rec·tive \kə-ˈrek-tiv\ *adj* (1531) : intended to correct ⟨~ lenses⟩ ⟨~ punishment⟩ — **corrective** *n* — **cor·rec·tive·ly** *adv*

¹**cor·re·late** \ˈkȯr-ə-lət, ˌkär-, -ˌlāt\ *n* [back-formation fr. *correlation*] (1643) **1** : either of two things so related that one directly implies or is complementary to the other (as husband and wife) **2** : a phenomenon (as brain activity) that accompanies another phenomenon (as behavior), is usu. parallel to it (as in form, type, development, or distribution), and is related in some way to it — **correlate** *adj*

²**cor·re·late** \-ˌlāt\ *vb* **-lat·ed; -lat·ing** *vi* (ca. 1742) **1** : to bear reciprocal or mutual relations : CORRESPOND ~ *vt* **1 a** : to establish a mutual or reciprocal relation between ⟨~ activities in the lab and the field⟩ **b** : to show correlation or a causal relationship between **2** : to present or set forth so as to show relationship ⟨he ~s the findings of the scientists, the psychologists, and the mystics —Eugene Exman⟩ — **cor·re·lat·able** \-ˌlā-tə-bəl\ *adj* — **cor·re·la·tor** \-ˌlā-tər\ *n*

cor·re·la·tion \ˌkȯr-ə-ˈlā-shən, ˌkär-\ *n* [ML *correlation-, correlatio*, fr. L *com-* + *relation-, relatio* relation] (1561) **1** : the state or relation of being correlated; *specif* : a relation existing between phenomena or things or between mathematical or statistical variables which tend to vary, be associated, or occur together in a way not expected on the basis of chance alone ⟨the obviously high positive ~ between scholastic aptitude and college entrance —J. B. Conant⟩ **2** : the act of correlating — **cor·re·la·tion·al** \-shnəl, -shə-nᵊl\ *adj*

correlation coefficient *n* (ca. 1909) : a number or function that indicates the degree of correlation between two sets of data or between two random variables and that is equal to their covariance divided by the product of their standard deviations

cor·rel·a·tive \kə-ˈrel-ə-tiv\ *adj* (1530) **1** : naturally related : CORRESPONDING **2** : reciprocally related **3** : regularly used together but typically not adjacent ⟨the ~ conjunctions *either . . . or*⟩ — **correlative** *n* — **cor·rel·a·tive·ly** *adv*

cor·re·spond \ˌkȯr-ə-ˈspänd, ˌkär-\ *vi* [MF or ML; MF *correspondre*, fr. ML *correspondēre*, fr. L *com-* + *respondēre* to respond] (1529) **1 a** : to be in conformity or agreement ⟨the ideal hated . . . to ~ with the reality —James Sutherland⟩ **b** : to compare closely : MATCH — usu. used with *to* or *with* **c** : to be equivalent or parallel **2** : to communicate with a person by exchange of letters

cor·re·spon·dence \-ˈspän-dən(t)s\ *n* (15c) **1 a** : the agreement of things with one another **b** : a particular similarity **c** : a relation between sets in which each member of one set is associated with one or more members of the other — compare FUNCTION 5a **2 a** : communication by letters; *also* : the letters exchanged **b** : the news, information, or opinion contributed by a correspondent to a newspaper or periodical

correspondence course *n* (1902) : a course offered by a correspondence school

correspondence school *n* (1889) : a school that teaches nonresident students by mailing them lessons and exercises which upon completion are returned to the school for grading

cor·re·spon·den·cy \ˌkȯr-ə-ˈspän-dən(t)-sē, ˌkär-\ *n, pl* **-cies** (1589) : CORRESPONDENCE

¹**cor·re·spon·dent** \ˌkȯr-ə-ˈspän-dənt, ˌkär-\ *adj* [ME, fr. MF or ML; MF, fr. ML *correspondent-, correspondens*, prp. of *correspondēre*] (15c) **1** : CORRESPONDING **2** : FITTING, CONFORMING — used with *with* or *to* ⟨the outcome was entirely ~ with my wishes⟩

²**correspondent** *n* (ca. 1630) **1 a** : one who communicates with another by letter **b** : one who has regular commercial relations with another **c** : one who contributes news or commentary to a publication (as a newspaper) or a radio or television network often from a distant place ⟨a war ~⟩ **2** : something that corresponds

corresponding *adj* (1579) **1 a** : having or participating in the same relationship (as kind, degree, position, correspondence, or function) esp. with regard to the same or like wholes (as geometric figures or sets) ⟨~ parts of similar triangles⟩ **b** : RELATED, ACCOMPANYING ⟨all rights carry with them ~ responsibilities —W. P. Paepcke⟩ **2 a** : charged with the duty of writing letters ⟨~ secretary⟩ **b** : participating or serving at a distance and by mail ⟨a ~ member of the society⟩ — **cor·re·spond·ing·ly** \-ˈspän-diŋ-lē\ *adv*

corresponding angles *n pl* (ca. 1804) : any pair of angles each of which is on the same side of one of two lines cut by a transversal and on the same side of the transversal

cor·re·spon·sive \ˌkȯr-ə-ˈspän(t)-siv, ˌkär-\ *adj* (1606) : mutually responsive

cor·ri·da \kȯ-ˈrē-thə\ *n* [Sp, lit., act of running] (1898) : BULLFIGHT

cor·ri·dor \ˈkȯr-ə-dər, ˈkär-, -ˌdȯr\ *n* [MF, fr. OIt *corridore*, fr. *correre* to run, fr. L *currere* — more at CAR] (1814) **1 :** a passageway (as in a hotel) into which compartments or rooms open **2 :** a usu. narrow passageway or route: as **a :** a narrow strip of land through foreign-held territory **b :** a restricted lane for air traffic **3 :** a densely populated strip of land including two or more major cities ⟨the Northeast ~ stretching from Washington into New England —S. D. Browne⟩

cor·rie \'kȯr-ē, 'kär-ē\ *n* [ScGael *coire*, lit., kettle] (1795) **:** CIRQUE 3

Cor·rie·dale \-ˌdāl\ *n* [*Corriedale*, ranch in New Zealand] (1902) **:** any of a dual-purpose breed of rather large usu. hornless sheep developed in New Zealand

cor·ri·gen·dum \ˌkȯr-ə-'jen-dəm, ˌkär-\ *n, pl* **-da** \-də\ [L, neut. of *corrigendus*, gerundive of *corrigere* to correct] (ca. 1850) **:** an error in a printed work discovered after printing and shown with its correction on a separate sheet

cor·ri·gi·ble \'kȯr-ə-jə-bəl, 'kär-\ *adj* [ME, fr. MF, fr. ML *corrigibilis*, fr. L *corrigere*] (15c) **:** capable of being set right **:** REPARABLE ⟨a ~ defect⟩ — **cor·ri·gi·bil·i·ty** \ˌkȯr-ə-jə-'bi-lə-tē, ˌkär-\ *n*

cor·ri·val \kə-'rī-vəl, kȯ-, kō-\ *n* [MF, fr. L *corrivalis*, fr. *com-* + *rivalis* rival] (1579) **:** RIVAL, COMPETITOR — **corrival** *adj*

cor·rob·o·rant \kə-'rä-bə-rənt\ *adj* (1626) *archaic* **:** having an invigorating effect — used of a medicine

cor·rob·o·rate \kə-'rä-bə-ˌrāt\ *vt* **-rat·ed; -rat·ing** [L *corroboratus*, pp. of *corroborare*, fr. *com-* + *robor-, robur* strength] (1530) **:** to support with evidence or authority **:** make more certain **syn** see CONFIRM — **cor·rob·o·ra·tion** \-ˌrä-bə-'rā-shən\ *n* — **cor·rob·o·ra·tive** \-'rä-bə-ˌrā-tiv, -'rä-b(ə-)rə-\ *adj* — **cor·rob·o·ra·to·ry** \-'rä-b(ə-)rə-ˌtȯr-ē, -ˌtōr-\ *adj*

cor·rob·o·ree \kə-'rä-bə-rē, -'rä-\ *n* [Dharuk (Australian aboriginal language of the Port Jackson area) *garaabara*] (1811) **1 :** a nocturnal festivity with songs and symbolic dances by which the Australian aborigines celebrate events of importance **2** *Austral* **a :** a noisy festivity **b :** TUMULT

cor·rode \kə-'rōd\ *vb* **cor·rod·ed; cor·rod·ing** [ME, fr. L *corrodere* to gnaw to pieces, fr. *com-* + *rodere* to gnaw — more at RODENT] *vt* (14c) **1 :** to eat away by degrees as if by gnawing; *esp* **:** to wear away gradually usu. by chemical action ⟨the metal was *corroded* beyond repair⟩ **2 :** to weaken or destroy gradually **:** UNDERMINE ⟨manners and miserliness that ~ the human spirit —Bernard DeVoto⟩ ~ *vi* **:** to undergo corrosion — **cor·rod·ible** \-'rō-də-bəl\ *adj*

cor·ro·dy *var of* CORODY

cor·ro·sion \kə-'rō-zhən\ *n* [ME, fr. LL *corrosion-, corrosio* act of gnawing, fr. L *corrodere*] (14c) **1 :** the action, process, or effect of corroding **2 :** a product of corroding

cor·ro·sive \-'rō-siv, -ziv\ *adj* (14c) **1 :** tending or having the power to corrode ⟨~ acids⟩ ⟨~ action⟩ ⟨the ~ effects of alcoholism⟩ **2 :** bitingly sarcastic ⟨~ satire⟩ — **corrosive** *n* — **cor·ro·sive·ly** *adv* — **cor·ro·sive·ness** *n*

corrosive sublimate *n* (ca. 1751) **:** MERCURIC CHLORIDE

cor·ru·gate \'kȯr-ə-ˌgāt, 'kär-\ *vb* **-gat·ed; -gat·ing** [L *corrugatus*, pp. of *corrugare*, fr. *com-* + *ruga* wrinkle; prob. akin to Lith *raukas* wrinkle — more at ROUGH] *vt* (1620) **:** to form or shape into wrinkles or folds or into alternating ridges and grooves **:** FURROW ~ *vi* **:** to become corrugated

corrugated *adj* (1590) **:** having corrugations ⟨~ paper⟩; *also* **:** made of corrugated material (as paperboard) ⟨~ boxes⟩

cor·ru·ga·tion \ˌkȯr-ə-'gā-shən, ˌkär-\ *n* (1528) **1 :** the act of corrugating **2 :** a ridge or groove of a surface that has been corrugated

¹cor·rupt \kə-'rəpt\ *vb* [ME, fr. L *corruptus*, pp. of *corrumpere*, fr. *com-* + *rumpere* to break — more at REAVE] *vt* (14c) **1 a :** to change from good to bad in morals, manners, or actions; *also* **:** BRIBE **b :** to degrade with unsound principles or moral values **2 :** ROT, SPOIL **3 :** to subject (a person) to corruption of blood **4 :** to alter from the original or correct form or version ~ *vi* **1 :** to become tainted or rotten **b :** to become morally debased **2 :** to cause disintegration or ruin **syn** see DEBASE — **cor·rupt·er** *also* **cor·rup·tor** \-'rəp-tər\ *n* — **cor·rupt·ibil·i·ty** \-ˌrəp-tə-'bi-lə-tē\ *n* — **cor·rupt·ible** \-'rəp-tə-bəl\ *adj* — **cor·rupt·ibly** \-blē\ *adv*

²corrupt *adj* [ME, fr. MF or L; MF, fr. L *corruptus*] (14c) **1 a :** morally degenerate and perverted **:** DEPRAVED **b :** characterized by improper conduct (as bribery or the selling of favors) ⟨~ judges⟩ **2 :** PUTRID, TAINTED **3 :** adulterated or debased by change from an original or correct condition **syn** see VICIOUS — **cor·rupt·ly** \-'rəp(t)-lē\ *adv* — **cor·rupt·ness** \-'rəp(t)-nəs\ *n*

cor·rup·tion \kə-'rəp-shən\ *n* (14c) **1 a :** impairment of integrity, virtue, or moral principle **:** DEPRAVITY **b :** DECAY, DECOMPOSITION **c :** inducement to wrong by improper or unlawful means (as bribery) **2 :** a departure from the original or from what is pure or correct **2** *archaic* **:** an agency or influence that corrupts **3** *chiefly dial* **:** PUS

cor·rup·tion·ist \-sh(ə-)nist\ *n* (1810) **:** one who practices or defends corruption esp. in politics

corruption of blood (1563) **:** the effect of an attainder which bars a person from inheriting, retaining, or transmitting any estate, rank, or title

cor·rup·tive \kə-'rəp-tiv\ *adj* (15c) **:** producing or tending to produce corruption — **cor·rup·tive·ly** *adv*

cor·sage \kȯr-'säzh, -'säj, 'kȯr-\ *n* [F, bust, bodice, fr. OF, bust, fr. *cors* body, fr. L *corpus*] (1843) **1 :** the waist or bodice of a dress **2 :** an arrangement of flowers worn as a fashion accessory

cor·sair \'kȯr-ˌsar, -ˌser; kȯr-'\ *n* [MF & OIt; MF *corsaire* pirate, fr. OProv *corsari*, fr. OIt *corsaro*, fr. ML *cursarius*, fr. L *cursus* course — more at COURSE] (1549) **:** PIRATE; *esp* **:** a privateer of the Barbary Coast

corse \'kȯrs\ *n* [ME *cors*, fr. MF] (13c) *archaic* **:** CORPSE

corse·let \for 1 'kȯr-slət, for 2 ˌkȯr-sə-'let\ *n* (1563) **1** *or* **cors·let** [MF, dim. of *cors* body, bodice] **:** a piece of armor covering the trunk **2** *or* **cor·se·lette** [fr. *Corselette*, a trademark] **:** an undergarment combining girdle and brassiere

¹cor·set \'kȯr-sət\ *n* [ME, fr. OF, dim. of *cors*] (13c) **1 :** a usu. close-fitting and often laced medieval jacket **2 :** a woman's close-fitting boned supporting undergarment that is often hooked and laced and that extends from above or beneath the bust or from the waist to below the hips and has garters attached

²corset *vt* (ca. 1847) **1 :** to dress in or fit with a corset **2 :** to restrict closely **:** control rigidly

cor·se·tiere \ˌkȯr-sə-'tir, -'tyer\ *n* [F *corsetière*, fem. of *corsetier*, fr. *corset*] (1848) **:** one who makes, fits, or sells corsets, girdles, or brassieres

cor·tege *also* **cor·tège** \kȯr-'tezh, 'kȯr-ˌ\ *n* [F *cortège*, fr. It *corteggio*, fr. *corteggiare* to court, fr. *corte* court, fr. L *cohort-, cohors* enclosure — more at COURT] (1648) **1 :** a train of attendants **:** RETINUE **2 :** PROCESSION; *esp* **:** a funeral procession

cor·tex \'kȯr-ˌteks\ *n, pl* **cor·ti·ces** \'kȯr-tə-ˌsēz\ *or* **cor·tex·es** [L *cortic-, cortex* bark — more at CUIRASS] (1677) **1 a :** the outer or superficial part of an organ or bodily structure (as the kidney, adrenal gland, or a hair); *esp* **:** the outer layer of gray matter of the cerebrum and cerebellum **b :** the outer part of some organisms (as paramecia) **2 a :** a plant bark or rind (as cinchona) used medicinally **3 a :** the typically parenchymatous layer of tissue external to the vascular tissue and internal to the corky or epidermal tissues of a green plant; *broadly* **:** all tissues external to the xylem **b :** an outer or investing layer of various algae, lichens, or fungi

cor·ti·cal \'kȯr-ti-kəl\ *adj* (1671) **1 :** of, relating to, or consisting of cortex **2 :** involving or resulting from the action or condition of the cerebral cortex — **cor·ti·cal·ly** \-k(ə-)lē\ *adv*

cortico- *comb form* **:** cortex ⟨*corticotropin*⟩

cor·ti·coid \'kȯr-ti-ˌkȯid\ *n* (1941) **:** CORTICOSTEROID — **corticoid** *adj*

cor·ti·co·ste·roid \ˌkȯr-ti-kō-'stir-ˌȯid *also* -'ster-\ *n* (1944) **:** any of various adrenal-cortex steroids (as corticosterone, cortisone, and aldosterone) used medically esp. as anti-inflammatory agents

cor·ti·co·ste·rone \ˌkȯr-tə-'käs-tə-ˌrōn, -ti-kō-stə-'; ˌkȯr-ti-kō-'stir-ˌōn, -'ster-\ *n* (1937) **:** a colorless crystalline corticosteroid $C_{21}H_{30}O_4$ that is important in protein and carbohydrate metabolism

cor·ti·co·tro·pin \ˌkȯr-ti-kō-'trō-pən\ *also* **cor·ti·co·tro·phin** \-fən\ *n* (1946) **:** ACTH; *also* **:** a preparation of ACTH that is used esp. in the treatment of rheumatoid arthritis and rheumatic fever

cor·tin \'kȯr-t³n\ *n* (1928) **:** the active principle of the adrenal cortex

cor·ti·sol \'kȯr-tə-ˌsȯl, -ˌzȯl, -ˌsōl, -ˌzōl\ *n* [*cortisone* + *¹-ol*] (1951) **:** HYDROCORTISONE

cor·ti·sone \-ˌsōn, -ˌzōn\ *n* [alter. of *corticosterone*] (1949) **:** a glucocorticoid $C_{21}H_{28}O_5$ of the adrenal cortex used esp. in the treatment of rheumatoid arthritis

co·run·dum \kə-'rən-dəm\ *n* [Tamil *kuruntam;* akin to Skt *kuruvinda* ruby] (1804) **:** a very hard mineral that consists of aluminum oxide and occurs in massive form and as variously colored crystals (as ruby and sapphire), that can be synthesized, and that is used as an abrasive

co·rus·cant \kə-'rəs-kənt\ *adj* (15c) **:** SHINING, GLITTERING

cor·us·cate \'kȯr-ə-ˌskāt, 'kär-\ *vi* **-cat·ed; -cat·ing** [L *coruscatus*, pp. of *coruscare* to flash] (1705) **1 :** to give off or reflect light in bright beams or flashes **:** SPARKLE **2 :** to be brilliant or showy in technique or style

cor·us·ca·tion \ˌkȯr-ə-'skā-shən, ˌkär-\ *n* (15c) **1 :** GLITTER, SPARKLE **2 :** a flash of wit

cor·vée \'kȯr-ˌvā, kȯr-'\ *n* [ME *corvee*, fr. MF, fr. ML *corrogata*, fr. L, fem. of *corrogatus*, pp. of *corrogare* to collect, requisition, fr. *com-* + *rogare* to ask — more at RIGHT] (14c) **1 :** unpaid labor (as toward constructing roads) due from a feudal vassal to his lord **2 :** labor exacted in lieu of taxes by public authorities esp. for highway construction or repair

corves *pl of* CORF

cor·vette \kȯr-'vet\ *n* [F, fr. MF, prob. fr. MD *corf*, a kind of ship, lit., basket — more at CORF] (1636) **1 :** a warship ranking in the old sailing navies next below a frigate **2 :** a highly maneuverable armed escort ship that is smaller than a destroyer

cor·vi·na \kȯr-'vē-nə\ *var of* CORBINA

cor·vine \'kȯr-ˌvīn\ *adj* [L *corvinus*, fr. *corvus* raven — more at RAVEN] (ca. 1656) **:** of or relating to the crows **:** resembling a crow

Cor·vus \'kȯr-vəs\ *n* [L (gen. *Corvi*), lit., raven] **:** a small constellation adjoining Virgo on the south

Cor·y·bant \'kȯr-ə-ˌbant, 'kär-\ *n, pl* **Cor·y·bants** \-ˌban(t)s\ *or* **Cor·y·ban·tes** \ˌkȯr-ə-'ban-tēz, ˌkär-\ [MF *Corybante*, fr. L *Corybas*, fr. Gk *Korybas*] (14c) **:** one of the attendants or priests of Cybele noted for wildly emotional processions and rites

cor·y·ban·tic \ˌkȯr-ē-'ban-tik, ˌkär-\ *adj* (1642) **:** like or in the spirit of a Corybant; *esp* **:** WILD, FRENZIED

co·ryd·a·lis \kə-'ri-d³l-əs\ *n* [NL, genus name, fr. Gk *korydallis* crested lark (*Galerida cristata*), fr. *korydos* crested lark] (1818) **:** any of a large genus (*Corydalis*) of chiefly temperate herbs of the fumitory family with racemose irregular flowers and dissected leaves

cor·ymb \'kȯr-ˌim(b), 'kär-, -əm(b)\ *n, pl* **corymbs** \-ˌimz, -əmz\ [F *corymbe*, fr. L *corymbus* cluster of fruit or flowers, fr. Gk *korymbos*] (1776) **:** a flat-topped inflorescence; *specif* **:** one in which the flower stalks arise at different levels on the main axis and reach about the same height and in which the outer flowers open first and the inflorescence is indeterminate — **cor·ymbed** \-ˌimd, -əmd\ *adj* — **cor·ym·bose** \-əm-ˌbōs\ *adj* — **cor·ym·bose·ly** *adv*

co·ry·ne·bac·te·ri·um \ˌkȯr-ə-(ˌ)nē-bak-'tir-ē-əm, kə-ˌrī-nə-\ *n* [NL, fr. Gk *korynē* club] (1909) **:** any of a large genus (*Corynebacterium*) of usu. gram-positive nonmotile bacteria that occur as irregular or branching rods and numerous important animal and plant parasites — **co·ry·ne·bac·te·ri·al** \-ē-əl\ *adj*

co·ryn·e·form \kə-'ri-nə-ˌfȯrm\ *adj* (1952) **:** being or resembling corynebacteria

cor·y·phae·us \ˌkȯr-ə-'fē-əs, ˌkär-\ *n, pl* **-phaei** \-'fē-ˌī\ [L, leader, fr. Gk *koryphaios*, fr. *koryphē* summit] (1610) **1 :** the leader of a party or school of thought **2 :** the leader of a chorus

co·ry·phée \ˌkȯr-i-'fā\ *n* [F, fr. L *coryphaeus*] (1828) **:** a ballet dancer who dances in a small group instead of in the corps de ballet or as a soloist

co·ry·za \kə-'rī-zə\ *n* [LL, fr. Gk *koryza* nasal mucus; akin to OE *hrot* nasal mucus, Skt *kardama* mud] (1634) **:** an acute inflammatory conta-

---

\ə\ abut \³\ kitten, F table \ər\ further \a\ ash \ā\ ace \ä\ mop, mar \au̇\ out \ch\ chin \e\ bet \ē\ easy \g\ go \i\ hit \ī\ ice \j\ job \ŋ\ sing \ō\ go \ȯ\ law \ȯi\ boy \th\ thin \t̲h̲\ the \ü\ loot \u̇\ foot \y\ yet \zh\ vision \ə̄, k̲, ⁿ, œ, œ̄, ᵫ, ᵫ̄, ᵞ\ *see* Guide to Pronunciation gious disease involving the upper respiratory tract; *esp* : COMMON COLD — **co·ry·zal** \-zəl\ *adj*

co·se·cant \(ˌ)kō-ˈsē-ˌkant, -kənt\ *n* [NL *cosecant-, cosecans,* fr. *co-* + *secant-, secans* secant] (ca. 1706) **1** : a trigonometric function that for an acute angle is the ratio between the hypotenuse of a right triangle of which the angle is considered part and the leg opposite the angle **2** : a trigonometric function csc θ that is the reciprocal of the sine for all real numbers θ for which the sine is not zero and that is exactly equal to the cosecant of an angle of measure θ in radians

co·set \ˈkō-ˌset\ *n* (1910) : a subset of a mathematical group that consists of all the products obtained by multiplying either on the right or the left a fixed element of the group by each of the elements of a given subgroup

¹cosh \ˈkäsh\ *n* [perh. fr. Romany *kaš, kašt* stick, piece of wood] (1869) *chiefly Brit* : a weighted weapon similar to a blackjack

²cosh *vt* (1896) *chiefly Brit* : to strike or assault with or as if with a cosh

co·sig·na·to·ry \(ˌ)kō-ˈsig-nə-ˌtōr-ē, -ˌtȯr-\ *n* (1865) : a joint signer

co·sign·er \ˈkō-ˌsi-nər\ *n* (ca. 1903) : COSIGNATORY; *esp* : a joint signer of a promissory note — **co-sign** \ˈkō-ˌsīn\ *vb*

co·sine \ˈkō-ˌsīn\ *n* [NL *cosinus,* fr. *co-* + ML *sinus* sine] (1635) **1** : a trigonometric function that for an acute angle is the ratio between the leg adjacent to the angle when it is considered part of a right triangle and the hypotenuse **2** : a trigonometric function cos θ that for all real numbers θ is given by the sum of the alternating series

$$\cos \theta = 1 - \frac{\theta^2}{2!} + \frac{\theta^4}{4!} - \frac{\theta^6}{6!} + \frac{\theta^8}{8!} - \cdots$$

and that is exactly equal to the cosine of an angle of measure θ in radians

cos lettuce \ˈkäs-, ˈkȯs-\ *n* [*Kos, Cos,* Greek island] (1699) : ROMAINE

¹cos·met·ic \käz-ˈme-tik\ *adj* [Gk *kosmētikos* skilled in adornment, fr. *kosmein* to arrange, adorn, fr. *kosmos* order] (1650) **1** : of, relating to, or making for beauty esp. of the complexion : BEAUTIFYING 〈~ salves〉 **2** : done or made for the sake of appearance: as **a** : correcting defects esp. of the face 〈~ surgery〉 **b** : DECORATIVE, ORNAMENTAL **c** : not substantive : SUPERFICIAL 〈~ changes〉 **3** : visually appealing — **cos·met·i·cal·ly** \-ti-k(ə-)lē\ *adv*

²cosmetic *n* (1650) : something that is cosmetic: as **a** : a cosmetic preparation for external use **b** *pl* : superficial features 〈a poem without rhetorical ~s〉 —Guy Davenport〉

cosmetic case *n* (1948) : a small piece of luggage esp. for cosmetics

cos·me·ti·cian \ˌkäz-mə-ˈti-shən\ *n* (1924) : a person who is professionally trained in the use of cosmetics

cos·met·i·cize \käz-ˈme-tə-ˌsīz\ *vt* **-cized; -ciz·ing** (1824) : to make (something unpleasant or ugly) superficially attractive

cos·me·tol·o·gist \ˌkäz-mə-ˈtä-lə-jist\ *n* (1926) : a person who gives beauty treatments (as to skin and hair) — called also *beautician*

cos·me·tol·o·gy \-jē\ *n* [F *cosmétologie,* fr. *cosmétique* cosmetic (fr. E *cosmetic*) + *-logie* *-logy*] (1926) : the cosmetic treatment of the skin, hair, and nails

cos·mic \ˈkäz-mik\ *also* **cos·mi·cal** \-mi-kəl\ *adj* [Gk *kosmikos,* fr. *kosmos* order, universe] (1685) **1** : of or relating to the cosmos, the extraterrestrial vastness, or the universe in contrast to the earth alone **2** : characterized by greatness esp. in extent, intensity, or comprehensiveness 〈a ~ thinker〉 〈~ boredom〉 — **cos·mi·cal·ly** \-mi-k(ə-)lē\ *adv*

cosmic background radiation *n* (ca. 1976) : BACKGROUND RADIATION

cosmic dust *n* (1881) : very fine particles of solid matter found in any part of the universe

cosmic noise *n* (1947) : unidentified celestial radio-frequency radiation; *esp* : such radiation originating from outside the Milky Way

cosmic ray *n* (1925) : a stream of atomic nuclei of extremely penetrating character that enter the earth's atmosphere from outer space at speeds approaching that of light

cosmic string *n* (1984) : any of a class of hypothetical supermassive astronomical objects that are extremely thin but are millions of light years long and that are postulated to have formed very early in the history of the universe

cos·mo·chem·is·try \ˌkäz-mō-ˈke-mə-strē\ *n* [Gk *kosmos* universe] (1940) : a branch of chemistry that deals with the chemical composition of and changes in the universe — **cos·mo·chem·i·cal** \-ˈke-mi-kəl\ *adj* — **cos·mo·chem·ist** \-ˈmist\ *n*

cos·mo·gen·ic \ˌkäz-mə-ˈje-nik\ *adj* [*cosmic ray* + *-o-* + *-genic*] (1962) : produced by the action of cosmic rays 〈~ carbon 14〉

cos·mog·o·ny \käz-ˈmä-gə-nē\ *n, pl* **-nies** [NL *cosmogonia,* fr. Gk *kosmogonia,* fr. *kosmos* + *gonos* offspring; akin to Gk *genos* race — more at KIN] (1766) **1** : the creation or origin of the world or universe **2** : a theory of the origin of the universe — **cos·mo·gon·ic** \ˌkäz-mə-ˈgä-nik\ *or* **cos·mo·gon·i·cal** \-ni-kəl\ *adj* — **cos·mog·o·nist** \käz-ˈmä-gə-nist\ *n*

cos·mog·ra·phy \käz-ˈmä-grə-fē\ *n, pl* **-phies** [ME *cosmographie,* fr. LL *cosmographia,* fr. Gk *kosmographia,* fr. *kosmos* + *-graphia* *-graphy*] (14c) **1** : a general description of the world or of the universe **2** : the science that deals with the constitution of the whole order of nature — **cos·mog·ra·pher** \-fər\ *n* — **cos·mo·graph·ic** \ˌkäz-mə-ˈgra-fik\ *or* **cos·mo·graph·i·cal** \-fi-kəl\ *adj*

Cos·mo·line \ˈkäz-mə-ˌlēn\ *trademark* — used for petroleum jelly

cos·mol·o·gy \käz-ˈmä-lə-jē\ *n, pl* **-gies** [NL *cosmologia,* fr. Gk *kosmos* + NL *-logia* *-logy*] (ca. 1656) **1 a** : a branch of metaphysics that deals with the nature of the universe **b** : a theory or doctrine describing the natural order of the universe **2** : a branch of astronomy that deals with the origin, structure, and space-time relationships of the universe; *also* : a theory dealing with these matters — **cos·mo·log·i·cal** \ˌkäz-mə-ˈlä-ji-kəl\ *adj* — **cos·mo·log·i·cal·ly** \-ji-k(ə-)lē\ *adv* — **cos·mol·o·gist** \käz-ˈmä-lə-jist\ *n*

cos·mo·naut \ˈkäz-mə-ˌnȯt, -ˌnät\ *n* [Russ *kosmonavt,* fr. Gk *kosmos* + Russ *-navt* (as in *aeronavt* aeronaut)] (1959) : an astronaut of the Soviet or Russian space program

cos·mop·o·lis \käz-ˈmä-pə-ləs\ *n* [NL, back-formation fr. *cosmopolites*] (1849) : a cosmopolitan city

¹cos·mo·pol·i·tan \ˌkäz-mə-ˈpä-lə-t²n\ *n* (ca. 1645) : COSMOPOLITE

²cosmopolitan *adj* (1844) **1** : having worldwide rather than limited or provincial scope or bearing **2** : having wide international sophistication : WORLDLY **3** : composed of persons, constituents, or elements

from all or many parts of the world **4** : found in most parts of the world and under varied ecological conditions 〈a ~ herb〉 — **cos·mo·pol·i·tan·ism** \-tə-ˌni-zəm\ *n*

cos·mop·o·lite \käz-ˈmä-pə-ˌlīt\ *n* [NL *cosmopolites,* fr. Gk *kosmopolitēs,* fr. *kosmos* + *politēs* citizen] (ca. 1618) : a cosmopolitan person or organism — **cos·mo·po·li·tism** \käz-ˈmä-pə-ˌli-ˌti-zəm, -lə-ˌti-; ˌkäz-mə-ˈpä-lə-ˌti-\ *n*

cos·mos \ˈkäz-məs, *1 & 2 also* -ˌmōs, -ˌmäs\ *n* [Gk *kosmos*] (1650) **1 a** (1) : an orderly harmonious systematic universe — compare CHAOS (2) : ORDER, HARMONY **b** : UNIVERSE 1 **2** : a complex orderly self‑inclusive system **3** *pl* **cosmos** \-məs, -məz\ *also* **cos·mos·es** \-məˌsəz\ [NL, genus name, fr. Gk *kosmos*] : any of a genus (*Cosmos*) of tropical American composite herbs; *esp* : a widely cultivated tall annual (*C. bipinnatus*) with yellow or red disks and showy ray flowers

cos·sack \ˈkä-ˌsak, -sək\ *n, often cap* [Pol & Ukrainian *kozak,* of Turkic origin; akin to Volga Tatar *kazak* free person] (1589) : a member of a group of frontiersmen of southern Russia organized as cavalry in the czarist army

¹cos·set \ˈkä-sət\ *n* [origin unknown] (1579) : a pet lamb; *broadly* : PET

²cosset *vt* (1659) : to treat as a pet : PAMPER

¹cost \ˈkȯst\ *n* (13c) **1 a** : the amount or equivalent paid or charged for something : PRICE **b** : the outlay or expenditure (as of effort or sacrifice) made to achieve an object **2** : loss or penalty incurred esp. in gaining something **3** *pl* : expenses incurred in litigation; *esp* : those given by the law or the court to the prevailing party against the losing party — **cost·less** \-ləs\ *adj* — **cost·less·ly** *adv*

²cost *vb* **cost; cost·ing** [ME, fr. MF *coster,* fr. L *constare* to stand firm, cost — more at CONSTANT] *vi* (14c) **1** : to require expenditure or payment 〈the best goods ~ more〉 **2** : to require effort, suffering, or loss 〈~ *vt* **1** : to have a price of **2** : to cause to pay, suffer, or lose something 〈frequent absences ~ him his job〉 **3** *past* **cost·ed** : to estimate or set the cost of — often used with *out*

cos·ta \ˈkäs-tə\ *n, pl* **cos·tae** \-(ˌ)tē, -ˌtī\ [L — more at COAST] (ca. 1864) **1** : ¹RIB 1a **2** : a part (as the midrib of a leaf or the anterior vein of an insect wing) that resembles a rib — **cos·tal** \-t²l\ *adj*

cost accountant *n* (1918) : a specialist in cost accounting

cost accounting *n* (1913) : the systematic recording and analysis of the costs of material, labor, and overhead incident to production

cos·tard \ˈkäs-tərd\ *n* [ME] (13c) **1** : any of several large English cooking apples **2** *archaic* : NODDLE, PATE

cost–ben·e·fit \ˈkȯs(t)-ˈbe-nə-ˌfit\ *adj* (1928) : of, relating to, or being economic analysis that assigns a numerical value to the cost‑effectiveness of an operation, procedure, or program

cost–ef·fec·tive \ˈkȯst-ə-ˈfek-tiv, -ˌfek-\ *adj* (1967) : economical in terms of tangible benefits produced by money spent 〈~ measures to combat poverty〉 — **cost–ef·fec·tive·ness** *n*

cost–ef·fi·cient \-i-ˈfi-shənt, -ˌfi-\ *adj* (1979) : COST-EFFECTIVE

cos·ter \ˈkäs-tər\ *n* (1851) *Brit* : COSTERMONGER

cos·ter·mon·ger \-ˌmən-gər, -ˌmäŋ-\ *n* [*costard* + *monger*] (1514) *Brit* : a hawker of fruit or vegetables

cos·tive \ˈkäs-tiv, ˈkȯs-\ *adj* [ME, fr. MF *costivé,* pp. of *costiver* to constipate, fr. L *constipare*] (14c) **1 a** : affected with constipation **b** : causing constipation **2** : slow in action or expression **3** : NIGGARDLY, STINGY — **cos·tive·ly** *adv* — **cos·tive·ness** *n*

cost·ly \ˈkȯs(t)-lē\ *adj* **cost·li·er; -est** (14c) **1** : commanding a high price esp. because of intrinsic worth 〈~ gems〉 **b** : RICH, SPLENDID **2** : made or done at heavy expense or sacrifice 〈a ~ mistake〉 — **cost·li·ness** *n*

cost·mary \ˈkȯst-ˌmer-ē, ˈkäst-\ *n, pl* **-mar·ies** [ME *costmarie,* fr. *coste* costmary (fr. OE *cost,* fr. L *costum,* fr. Gk *kostos,* a fragrant root) + *Marie* the Virgin Mary] (14c) : an aromatic composite herb (*Chrysanthemum balsamita*) used as a potherb and in flavoring

cost of living (1896) : the cost of purchasing those goods and services which are included in an accepted standard level of consumption

cost–of–living index *n* (1913) : CONSUMER PRICE INDEX

cost–plus \ˈkȯs(t)-ˈpləs\ *adj* (1918) **1** : paid on the basis of a fixed fee or a percentage added to actual cost 〈a ~ contract〉 **2** : of or relating to a cost-plus contract

cost–push \ˈkȯs(t)-ˌpùsh\ *n* (1951) : an increase or upward trend in production costs (as wages) that tends to result in increased consumer prices irrespective of the level of demand — compare DEMAND-PULL — **cost–push** *adj*

cos·trel \ˈkäs-trəl\ *n* [ME, fr. MF *costerel,* fr. *costier* at the side, fr. *coste* rib, side — more at COAST] (14c) : a flat usu. earthenware container for liquids with through which a belt or cord may be passed for easy carrying — called also *pilgrim bottle*

¹cos·tume \ˈkäs-ˌtüm, -ˌtyüm *also* -təm *or* -ˌchüm\ *n* [F, fr. It, custom, dress, fr. L *consuetudin-, consuetudo* custom — more at CUSTOM] (1715) **1** : the prevailing fashion in coiffure, jewelry, and apparel of a period, country, or class **2** : an outfit worn to create the appearance characteristic of a particular period, person, place, or thing 〈Halloween ~s〉 **3** : a person's ensemble of outer garments; *esp* : a woman's ensemble of dress with coat or jacket — **cos·tum·ey** *adj*

²costume \ˈkäs-ˌtüm, -ˌtyüm *also* -ˈchüm; *or* ˈkäs-, *or* -təm\ *vt* **cos·tumed; cos·tum·ing** (1823) **1** : to provide with a costume **2** : to design costumes for 〈~ a play〉

³costume *same as* ¹\ *adj* (1884) **1** : characterized by the use of costumes 〈a ~ ball〉 〈a ~ drama〉 **2** : suitable for or enhancing the effect of a particular costume 〈a ~ handbag〉

costume jewelry *n* (1933) : jewelry designed for wear with current fashions and usu. made of inexpensive materials

cos·tum·er \ˈkäs-ˌtü-mər, -ˌtyü- *also* -ˌchü-; käs-ˈ\ *n* (ca. 1859) **1** : one that deals in or makes costumes **2** : an upright stand with hooks or pegs on which to hang clothes

cos·tum·ery \-mə-rē\ *n* (1838) **1** : articles of costume **2** : the art of costuming

cos·tu·mi·er \käs-ˈtü-mē-ˌā, -ˈtyü-, -mē-ər\ *n* [F] (1831) *chiefly Brit* : COSTUMER 1

co·sy \ˈkō-zē\ *var of* COZY

¹cot \ˈkät\ *n* [ME, fr. OE; akin to ON *kot* small hut] (bef. 12c) **1** : a small house **2** : COVER, SHEATH; *esp* : STALL 4

²cot *n* [Hindi *khāt* bedstead, fr. Skt *khatvā,* perh. of Dravidian origin; akin to Tamil *kaṭṭil* bedstead] (1634) **1** : a small usu. collapsible bed often of fabric stretched on a frame **2** *Brit* : CRIB 2b

co·tan·gent \(,)kō-'tan-jənt, 'kō-,\ *n* [NL *cotangent-, cotangens,* fr. *co- + tangent-, tangens* tangent] (1635) **1** : a trigonometric function that for an acute angle is the ratio between the leg adjacent to the angle when it is considered part of a right triangle and the leg opposite **2** : a trigonometric function cot θ that is equal to the cosine divided by the sine for all real numbers θ for which the sine is not equal to zero and is exactly equal to the cotangent of an angle of measure θ in radians

¹**cote** \'kōt, 'kät\ *n* [ME, fr. OE] (bef. 12c) **1** *dial Eng* : ¹COT 1 **2** : a shed or coop for small domestic animals and esp. pigeons

²**cote** \'kōt\ *vt* [prob. fr. MF *cotoyer*] (1555) *obs* : to pass by

co·te·rie \'kō-tə-(,)rē, ,kō-tə-'\ *n* [F, fr. MF, tenants, fr. OF *cotier* cotter, of Gmc origin; akin to OE *cot* hut] (1738) : an intimate and often exclusive group of persons with a unifying common interest or purpose

co·ter·mi·nous \(,)kō-'tər-mə-nəs\ *adj* [alter. of *conterminous*] (1799) **1** : having the same or coincident boundaries ⟨~ states⟩ **2** : coextensive in scope or duration ⟨an experience of life ~ with the years of his father —Elizabeth Hardwick⟩ — **co·ter·mi·nous·ly** *adv*

co·thur·nus \kō-'thər-nəs\ *n, pl* **-ni** \-,nī, -,(,)nē\ [L, fr. Gk *kothornos*] (1606) **1** : a high thick-soled laced boot worn by actors in Greek and Roman tragic drama — called also **co·thurn** \'kō-,thərn, kō-'\ **2** : the dignified somewhat stilted style of ancient tragedy

co·tid·al \(,)kō-'ti-d²l\ *adj* (1833) : indicating equality in the tides or a coincidence in the time of high or low tide

co·til·lion \kō-'til-yən, kə-\ *also* **co·til·lon** \kō-'til-yən, kə-, kò-tē-(y)ōⁿ\ *n* [F *cotillon,* lit., petticoat, fr. OF, fr. *cote* coat] (1766) **1** : a ballroom dance for couples that resembles the quadrille **2** : an elaborate dance with frequent changing of partners carried out under the leadership of one couple at formal balls **3** : a formal ball

co·to·ne·as·ter \kə-'tō-nē-,as-tər, 'kä-t²n-,ēs-\ *n* [NL, genus name, fr. L *cotoneum* quince + NL *-aster*] (1796) : any of a genus (*Cotoneaster*) of Old World flowering shrubs of the rose family

cot·quean \'kät-,kwēn\ *n* [¹*cot* + *quean*] (1547) **1** *archaic* : a coarse masculine woman **2** *archaic* : a man who busies himself with women's work or affairs

Cots·wold \'kät-,swōld, -swəld\ *n* [*Cotswold* Hills, England] (ca. 1658) : any of an English breed of large long-wooled sheep

cot·ta \'kä-tə\ *n* [ML, of Gmc origin; akin to OHG *kozza* coarse mantle — more at COAT] (1848) : a waist-length surplice

cot·tage \'kä-tij\ *n* [ME *cotage,* fr. (assumed) AF, fr. ME *cot* — more at COT] (14c) **1** : the dwelling of a farm laborer or small farmer **2** : a usu. small frame one-family house **3** : a small detached dwelling unit at an institution **4** : a usu. small house for vacation use — **cot·tag·ey** \-ti-jē\ *adj*

cottage cheese *n* (1848) : a bland soft white cheese made from the curds of skim milk — called also *Dutch cheese, pot cheese, smearcase*

cottage curtains *n pl* (1943) : a double set of upper and lower straight-hanging window curtains

cottage industry *n* (1921) **1** : an industry whose labor force consists of family units or individuals working at home with their own equipment **2** : a small and often informally organized industry

cottage pie *n* (1791) : a shepherd's pie made esp. with beef

cottage pudding *n* (ca. 1854) : plain cake covered with a hot sweet sauce

cot·tag·er \'kä-ti-jər\ *n* (1550) : a person who lives in a cottage

cottage tulip *n* (1928) : any of various tall late-flowering tulips

cot·tar *or* **cot·ter** \'kä-tər\ *n* [ME *cottar,* fr. ML *cotarius,* fr. ME *cot*] (14c) : a peasant or farm laborer who occupies a cottage and sometimes a small holding of land usu. in return for services

cot·ter \'kä-tər\ *n* [origin unknown] (14c) **1** : a wedge-shaped or tapered piece used to fasten together parts of a structure **2** : COTTER PIN — **cot·tered** \-tərd\ *adj* — **cot·ter·less** \-tər-ləs\ *adj*

cotter pin *n* (1881) : a half-round metal strip bent into a pin whose ends can be flared after insertion through a slot or hole

¹**cot·ton** \'kä-t²n\ *n, often attrib* [ME *coton,* fr. MF, fr. Ar *qutun*] (14c) **1 a** : a soft usu. white fibrous substance composed of the hairs surrounding the seeds of various erect freely branching tropical plants (genus *Gossypium*) of the mallow family **b** : a plant producing cotton; *esp* : one grown for its cotton **c** : a crop of cotton **2 a** : fabric made of cotton **b** : yarn spun from cotton **3** : a downy cottony substance produced by various plants (as the cottonwood)

²**cotton** *vi* **cot·toned; cot·ton·ing** \'kät-niŋ, 'ka-t²n-iŋ\ (1605) **1** : to take a liking — used with *to* ⟨~s to people easily⟩ **2** : to come to understand — used with *to* or *on to* ⟨~ed on to the fact that our children work furiously —H. M. McLuhan⟩

cotton candy *n* (1926) **1** : a candy made of spun sugar **2** : something attractive but insubstantial

cotton: *1 flowering branch; 2 fruit, unopened; 3 fruit, partly opened*

cotton gin *n* (1796) : a machine that separates the seeds, hulls, and foreign material from cotton

cotton grass *n* (1597) : any of a genus (*Eriophorum*) of sedges with tufted spikes

cot·ton·mouth \'kä-t²n-,maúth\ *n* [fr. the white interior of its mouth] (1832) : WATER MOCCASIN

cottonmouth moccasin *n* (1879) : WATER MOCCASIN

cot·ton–pick·ing \'kä-t²n-,pi-kiŋ, -,pi-kən\ *adj* (ca. 1952) **1** : DAMNED — used as a generalized expression of disapproval ⟨a ~ hypocrite⟩ **2** : DAMNED — used as an intensive ⟨out of his ~ mind —Irving Kristol⟩

cot·ton·seed \'kä-t²n-,sēd\ *n* (1774) : the seed of the cotton plant

cottonseed oil *n* (1833) : a pale yellow semidrying fatty oil that is obtained from the cottonseed and is used chiefly in salad and cooking oils and after hydrogenation in shortenings and margarine

cotton stainer *n* (1856) : any of several bugs (genus *Dysdercus*) that damage and stain the lint of developing cotton; *esp* : a red and brown bug (*D. suturellus*) that attacks cotton in the southern U.S.

cot·ton·tail \'kä-t²n-,tāl\ *n* (1869) : any of several rather small No. American rabbits (genus *Sylvilagus*) sandy to grayish brown in color with a white-tufted underside of the tail

cot·ton·weed \-,wēd\ *n* (1562) : any of various weedy plants (as cudweed) with hoary pubescence or cottony seeds

cot·ton·wood \-,wúd\ *n* (1802) : any of several poplars having seeds with cottony hairs; *esp* : one (*Populus deltoides*) of the eastern and central U.S. often cultivated for its rapid growth and luxuriant foliage

cotton wool *n* (14c) : raw cotton; *esp* : cotton batting

cot·tony \'kät-nē, 'kä-t²n-ē\ *adj* (1578) **1** : resembling cotton in appearance or character: **as a** : covered with hairs or pubescence **b** : SOFT

cot·tony–cush·ion scale \-'kú-shən-\ *n* (1886) : a scale insect (*Icerya purchasi*) introduced into the U.S. from Australia that infests citrus and other plants

-cotyl *n comb form* [*cotyledon*]: cotyledon ⟨hypocotyl⟩

cot·y·le·don \,kä-tə-'lē-d²n\ *n* [NL, fr. Gk *kotylēdōn* cup-shaped hollow, fr. *kotylē* cup, anything hollow] (1540) **1** : a lobule of the mammalian placenta **2** : the first leaf or one of the first pair or whorl of leaves developed by the embryo of a seed plant or of some lower plants (as ferns) — see PLUMULE illustration — **cot·y·le·don·ary** \-'lē-də-,ner-ē\ *adj*

co·ty·lo·saur \'kä-t²l-ō-,sòr, kə-'ti-lə-\ *n* [ultim. fr. Gk *kotylē* + *sauros* lizard] (ca. 1909) : any of an order (Cotylosauria) of extinct primitive reptiles with short legs and massive bodies that were prob. the earliest truly terrestrial vertebrate animals

¹**couch** \'kaúch\ *vb* [ME, fr. MF *coucher,* fr. L *collocare* to set in place — more at COLLOCATE] *vt* (14c) **1** : to lay (oneself) down for rest or sleep **2** : to embroider (a design) by laying down a thread and fastening it with small stitches at regular intervals **3** : to place or hold level and pointed forward ready for use **4** : to phrase or express in a specified manner ⟨the comments were ~ed in strong terms⟩ **5** : to treat (a cataract) by displacing the lens of the eye into the vitreous humor ~ *vi* **1** : to lie down or recline for sleep or rest **2** : to lie in ambush

²**couch** *n* [ME *couche* bed, fr. MF, fr. *coucher*] (14c) **1 a** : an article of furniture for sitting or reclining **b** : a couch on which a patient reclines when undergoing psychoanalysis **2** : the den of an animal (as an otter) — **on the couch** : receiving psychiatric treatment

couch·ant \'kaù-chənt\ *adj* [ME, fr. MF, prp. of *coucher*] (15c) : lying down esp. with the head up ⟨a heraldic lion ~⟩

couch grass \'kaúch-, 'kúch-\ *n* [alter. of *quitch*] (1578) **1** : QUACK GRASS **2** : any of several grasses that resemble quack grass in spreading by creeping rhizomes

couch potato *n* (1982) : a lazy and inactive person; *esp* : one who spends a great deal of time watching television

cou·dé \kü-'dā\ *adj* [F *coudé* bent like an elbow, fr. *coude* elbow, fr. L *cubitum*] (ca. 1889) : of, relating to, or being a telescope constructed so that the light is reflected along the polar axis to come to a focus at a point where the holder for a photographic plate or a spectrograph may be mounted

cou·gar \'kü-gər *also* -,gär\ *n, pl* **cougars** *also* **cougar** [F *couguar,* modif. of NL *cuguacuarana,* fr. Tupi *síwasuarána,* fr. *síwasú* deer + *-rana* resembling] (1774) : a large powerful tawny brown cat (*Felis concolor*) formerly widespread in the Americas but now reduced in number or extinct in many areas — called also *catamount, mountain lion, panther, puma*

cougar

¹**cough** \'kòf\ *vb* [ME, fr. (assumed) OE *cohhian;* akin to MHG *kūchen* to breathe heavily] *vi* (14c) **1** : to expel air from the lungs suddenly with an explosive noise **2** : to make a noise like that of coughing ~ *vt* : to expel by coughing — often used with *up* ⟨~ up mucus⟩

²**cough** *n* (14c) **1** : a condition marked by repeated or frequent coughing **2** : an act or sound of coughing

cough drop *n* (1831) : a lozenge or troche used to relieve coughing

cough syrup *n* (1877) : any of various sweet usu. medicated liquids used to relieve coughing

cough up *vt* (1894) : HAND OVER, DELIVER ⟨cough up the money⟩

could \kəd, 'kúd\ [ME *couthe, coude,* fr. OE *cūthe;* akin to OHG *konda* could] *past of* CAN — used in auxiliary function in the past ⟨we found we ~ go⟩, in the past conditional ⟨we said we would go if we ~⟩, and as an alternative to *can* suggesting less force or certainty or as a polite form in the present ⟨if you ~ come we would be pleased⟩

could·est \'kú-dəst\ *archaic past 2d sing of* CAN

couldn't \'kú-d²nt, -d²n, *dial also* 'kút-²n(t) *or* 'kúnt\ (1646) : could not

couldst \kədst, 'kúdst, kətst, 'kútst\ *archaic past 2d sing of* CAN

cou·lee \'kü-lē\ *n* [CanF *coulée,* fr. F, flowing, flow of lava, fr. *couler* to flow, fr. OF, fr. L *colare* to strain, fr. *colum* sieve] (1807) **1 a** : a small stream **b** : a dry streambed **c** : a usu. small or shallow ravine : GULLY **2** : a thick sheet or stream of lava

cou·lis \kü-'lē\ *n* [F, fr. OF *coleïs, coleïs* flowing] (1978) : a thick sauce made with pureed vegetable or fruit and often used as a garnish

cou·lisse \kü-'lēs, -'lis\ *n* [F, fr. OF *coulice* portcullis, fr. fem. of *coleïz* flowing, sliding, fr. *couler*] (1819) **1 a** : side scene of a stage; *also* : the space between the side scenes **b** : a backstage area **c** : HALLWAY **2** : a piece of timber having a groove in which something glides

cou·loir \kül-'wär\ *n* [F, lit., passage, fr. *couler*] (1822) : a steep mountainside gorge

¹**cou·lomb** \'kü-,läm, -,lōm\ *n* [Charles A. de *Coulomb*] (1881) : the practical meter-kilogram-second unit of electric charge equal to the quantity of electricity transferred by a current of one ampere in one second

\ə\ abut \²\ kitten, F table \ər\ further \a\ ash \ā\ ace \ä\ mop, mar \aú\ out \ch\ chin \e\ bet \ē\ easy \g\ go \i\ hit \ī\ ice \j\ job \ŋ\ sing \ō\ go \ò\ law \òi\ boy \th\ thin \th\ the \ü\ loot \ú\ foot \y\ yet \zh\ vision \ä, k, ⁿ, œ, œ, ue, ūe, ²\ *see* Guide to Pronunciation

²**coulomb** *or* **cou·lom·bic** \kü-'läm-bik, -'lōm-, -'lä-mik, -'lō-\ *adj* (1930) : of, relating to, or being the electrostatic force of attraction or repulsion between charged particles

Cou·lomb's law \'kü-,lämz-, -,lōmz-\ *n* (1854) : a statement in physics: the force of attraction or repulsion acting along a straight line between two electric charges is directly proportional to the product of the charges and inversely to the square of the distance between them

cou·lo·me·ter \kü-'lä-mə-tər, 'kü-lə-,mē-tər\ *n* [alter. of *coulombmeter*, fr. *coulomb* + *-meter*] (ca. 1889) : an instrument of chemical analysis that determines the amount of a substance released in electrolysis by measurement of the quantity of electricity used — **cou·lo·met·ric** \,kü-lə-'me-trik\ *adj* — **cou·lo·met·ri·cal·ly** \-tri-k(ə-)lē\ *adv* — **cou·lom·e·try** \kü-'lä-mə-trē\ *n*

coul·ter \'kōl-tər\ *n* [ME *colter*, fr. OE *culter* & OF *coltre*, both fr. L *culter* plowshare; akin to Gk *skallein* to hoe — more at SHELL] (bef. 12c) : a cutting tool (as a knife or sharp disc) that is attached to the beam of a plow, makes a vertical cut in the surface, and permits clean separation and effective covering of the soil and materials being turned under

cou·ma·rin \'kü-mə-rən\ *n* [F *coumarine*, fr. *coumarou* tonka bean tree, fr. Sp *or* Pg; Sp *cumarú*, fr. Pg, fr. Tupi *kumarú*] (1830) : a toxic white crystalline lactone $C_9H_6O_2$ with an odor of new-mown hay found in plants or made synthetically and used esp. in perfumery; *also* : a derivative of this compound

¹**coun·cil** \'kaún(t)-səl\ *n* [ME *counceil*, fr. OF *concile*, fr. L *concilium*, fr. *com-* + *calare* to call — more at LOW] (12c) 1 : an assembly or meeting for consultation, advice, or discussion 2 : a group elected or appointed as an advisory or legislative body 3 a : a usu. administrative body b : an executive body whose members are equal in power and authority c : a governing body of delegates from local units of a federation 4 : deliberation in a council 5 a : a federation of or a central body uniting a group of organizations b : a local chapter of an organization c : CLUB, SOCIETY

²**council** *adj* (14c) 1 : used for councils esp. by or with No. American Indians ⟨a ~ ground⟩ 2 *Brit* : built, maintained, or operated by a local governing agency ⟨~ housing⟩ ⟨~ flats⟩

coun·cil·lor *or* **coun·cil·or** \'kaún(t)-s(ə-)lər\ *n* (15c) : a member of a council — **coun·cil·lor·ship** \-,ship\ *n*

coun·cil·man \'kaún(t)-səl-mən\ *n* (1659) : a member of a council (as of a town or city) — **coun·cil·man·ic** \,kaún(t)-səl-'ma-nik\ *adj*

council of ministers *often cap C&M* (ca. 1909) : CABINET 3b

coun·cil·wom·an \'kaún(t)-səl-,wú-mən\ *n* (ca. 1928) : a woman who is a member of a council

¹**coun·sel** \'kaún(t)-səl\ *n* [ME *conseil*, fr. OF, fr. L *consilium*, fr. *consulere* to consult] (13c) 1 a : advice given esp. as a result of consultation b : a policy or plan of action or behavior 2 : DELIBERATION, CONSULTATION 3 *archaic* : PURPOSE b : guarded thoughts or intentions 4 a *pl* **counsel** (1) : a lawyer engaged in the trial or management of a case in court (2) : a lawyer appointed to advise and represent an individual client or a corporate and esp. a public body b : CONSULTANT 2

²**counsel** *vb* **-seled** *or* **-selled**; **-sel·ing** *or* **-sel·ling** \-s(ə-)liŋ\ *vt* (14c) : ADVISE ⟨~ed them to avoid rash actions —George Orwell⟩ ~ *vi* : CONSULT ⟨~ed with her husband⟩

coun·sel·ee \,kaún(t)-sə-'lē\ *n* (1923) : one who is being counseled

counseling *or* **counselling** *n* (1927) : professional guidance of the individual by utilizing psychological methods esp. in collecting case history data, using various techniques of the personal interview, and testing interests and aptitudes

coun·sel·or *or* **coun·sel·lor** \'kaún(t)-s(ə-)lər\ *n* (13c) 1 : a person who gives advice or counseling ⟨marriage ~⟩ 2 : LAWYER; *specif* : one that gives advice in law and manages cases for clients in court 3 : one who has supervisory duties at a summer camp — **coun·sel·or·ship** \-,ship\ *n*

counselor–at–law *n, pl* **counselors–at–law** (1617) : COUNSELOR 2

¹**count** \'kaúnt, *dial* 'kyaúnt\ *vb* [ME, fr. MF *conter, compter*, fr. L *computare*, fr. *com-* + *putare* to consider] *vt* (14c) 1 a : to indicate or name by units or groups so as to find the total number of units involved : NUMBER b : to name the numbers in order up to and including ⟨~ ten⟩ c : to include in a tallying and reckoning ⟨about 100 present, ~ing children⟩ d : to call aloud (beats or time units) ⟨~ cadence⟩ ⟨~ eighth notes⟩ 2 a : CONSIDER, ACCOUNT ⟨~ oneself lucky⟩ b : to record as of an opinion or persuasion ⟨~ me as uncommitted⟩ 3 : to include or exclude by or as if by counting ⟨~ me in⟩ ~ *vi* 1 a : to recite or indicate the numbers in order by units or groups ⟨~ by fives⟩ b : to count the units in a group 2 : to rely or depend on someone or something ⟨~ed on his parents to help with the expenses⟩ 3 : ADD, TOTAL ⟨it ~s up to a sizable amount⟩ 4 : to have value or significance ⟨these are the people who really ~⟩ — **count heads** *or* **count noses** : to count the number present — **count on** : to look forward to as certain : ANTICIPATE ⟨*counted on* winning⟩

²**count** *n* (14c) 1 a : the action or process of counting b : a total obtained by counting : TALLY 2 *archaic* a : RECKONING, ACCOUNT b : CONSIDERATION, ESTIMATION 3 a : ALLEGATION, CHARGE; *specif* : one separately stating the cause of action or prosecution in a legal declaration or indictment ⟨guilty on all ~s⟩ b : a specific point under consideration : ISSUE 4 : the total number of individual things in a given unit or sample obtained by counting all or a subsample of them ⟨bacteria ~⟩ 5 a : the calling off of the seconds from one to ten when a boxer has been knocked down b : the number of balls and strikes charged to a baseball batter during one turn ⟨the ~ stood at 3 and 2⟩ c : SCORE ⟨tied the ~ with a minute to play⟩ 6 : a measurement of the thickness or fineness of yarn by determining the number of hanks or yards per pound it produces

³**count** *n* [ME, fr. MF *comte*, fr. LL *comit-, comes*, fr. L, companion, one of the imperial court, fr. *com-* + *ire* to go — more at ISSUE] (15c) : a European nobleman whose rank corresponds to that of a British earl

count·able \'kaún-tə-bəl\ *adj* (1581) : capable of being counted : DENUMERABLE ⟨a ~ set⟩ — **count·abil·i·ty** \,kaún-tə-'bi-lə-tē\ *n* — **count·ably** \'kaún-tə-blē\ *adv*

count·down \'kaúnt-,daún\ *n* (ca. 1952) : an audible backward counting in fixed units (as seconds) from an arbitrary starting number to

mark the time remaining before an event; *also* : preparations carried on during such a count — **count down** \-'daún\ *vi*

¹**coun·te·nance** \'kaún-tⁿn-ən(t)s, 'kaúnt-nən(t)s\ *n* [ME *contenance*, fr. MF, fr. ML *continentia*, fr. L, restraint, fr. *continent-, continens*, prp. of *continēre* to hold together — more at CONTAIN] (13c) 1 *obs* : BEARING, DEMEANOR 2 a : calm expression b : mental composure c : LOOK, EXPRESSION 3 *archaic* a : ASPECT, SEMBLANCE b : PRETENSE 4 : FACE, VISAGE; *esp* : the face as an indication of mood, emotion, or character 5 : bearing or expression that offers approval or sanction : moral support

²**countenance** *vt* **-nanced; -nanc·ing** (1568) : to extend approval or toleration to : SANCTION — **coun·te·nanc·er** *n*

¹**count·er** \'kaún-tər\ *n* [ME *countour*, fr. MF *comptouer*, fr. ML *computorium* computing place, fr. L *computare*] (14c) 1 : a piece (as of metal or plastic) used in reckoning or in games 2 : something of value in bargaining : ASSET 3 : a level surface (as a table, shelf or display case) over which transactions are conducted or food is served or on which goods are displayed or work is conducted ⟨jewelry ~⟩ ⟨a lunch ~⟩ — **over the counter** 1 : in or through a broker's office rather than through a stock exchange ⟨stock bought *over the counter*⟩ 2 : without a prescription ⟨drugs available *over the counter*⟩ — **under the counter** : by surreptitious means : in an illicit and private manner

²**count·er** \'kaún-tər\ *n* [ME, fr. MF *conteor*, fr. *compter* to count] (14c) : one that counts; *esp* : a device for indicating a number or amount

³**count·er** *vb* **coun·tered; coun·ter·ing** \'kaún-t(ə-)riŋ\ *n* [ME *countren*, fr. MF *contre* against, opposite, fr. L *contra*; akin to L *com-* with, together — more at CO-] *vt* (14c) 1 a : to act in opposition to : OPPOSE b : OFFSET, NULLIFY ⟨tried to ~ the trend toward depersonalization⟩ 2 : to adduce in answer ⟨we ~ed that our warnings had been ignored⟩ ~ *vi* : to meet attacks or arguments with defensive or retaliatory steps

⁴**coun·ter** *adv* [ME *contre*, fr. MF] (15c) 1 : in an opposite or wrong direction 2 : to or toward a different or opposite direction, result, or effect ⟨values that run ~ to those of society⟩

⁵**coun·ter** *n* (15c) 1 : CONTRARY, OPPOSITE 2 : the after portion of a boat from the waterline to the extreme outward swell or stern overhang 3 a : the act of making an attack while parrying one (as in boxing or fencing); *also* : a blow thus given in boxing b : an agency or force that offsets : CHECK 4 : a stiffener to give permanent form to a boot or shoe upper around the heel 5 : an area within the face of a letter wholly or partly enclosed by strokes 6 : a football play in which the ballcarrier goes in a direction opposite to the movement of the play

⁶**coun·ter** *adj* (1596) 1 : marked by or tending toward or in an opposite direction or effect 2 : given to or marked by opposition, hostility, or antipathy 3 : situated or lying opposite ⟨the ~ side⟩ 4 : recalling or ordering back by a superseding contrary order : COUNTERMANDING ⟨~ orders from the colonel⟩

counter- *prefix* [ME *contre-*, fr. MF, fr. *contre*] 1 a : contrary : opposite ⟨counterclockwise⟩ ⟨countermarch⟩ b : opposing : retaliatory ⟨counterforce⟩ ⟨counteroffensive⟩ 2 : complementary : corresponding ⟨counterweight⟩ ⟨counterpart⟩ 3 : duplicate : substitute ⟨counterfoil⟩

coun·ter·ac·cu·sa·tion	coun·ter·fire	coun·ter·re·form
coun·ter·ad·ap·ta·tion	coun·ter·force	coun·ter·re·form·er
coun·ter·ad·ver·tis·ing	coun·ter·gov·ern·ment	coun·ter·re·sponse
coun·ter·agent	coun·ter·hy·poth·e·sis	coun·ter·re·tal·i·a·tion
coun·ter·ar·gue	coun·ter·im·age	coun·ter·sci·en·tif·ic
coun·ter·ag·gres·sion	coun·ter·in·cen·tive	coun·ter·shot
coun·ter·ar·gu·ment	coun·ter·in·fla·tion	coun·ter·snip·er
coun·ter·as·sault	coun·ter·in·fla·tion·ary	coun·ter·spell
coun·ter·at·tack	coun·ter·in·flu·ence	coun·ter·state
coun·ter·at·tack·er	coun·ter·in·stance	coun·ter·state·ment
coun·ter·bid	coun·ter·in·sti·tu·tion	coun·ter·step
coun·ter·blast	coun·ter·in·ter·pre·ta·tion	coun·ter·strat·e·gist
coun·ter·block·ade	coun·ter·memo	coun·ter·strat·e·gy
coun·ter·blow	coun·ter·mo·bi·li·za·tion	coun·ter·stream
coun·ter·cam·paign	coun·ter·move	coun·ter·strike
coun·ter·charge	coun·ter·move·ment	coun·ter·stroke
coun·ter·com·mer·cial	coun·ter·myth	coun·ter·style
coun·ter·com·plaint	coun·ter·or·der	coun·ter·sue
coun·ter·con·spir·a·cy	coun·ter·pe·ti·tion	coun·ter·sug·ges·tion
coun·ter·con·ven·tion	coun·ter·pick·et	coun·ter·suit
coun·ter·coun·ter·mea·sure	coun·ter·play	coun·ter·sur·veil·lance
coun·ter·coup	coun·ter·play·er	coun·ter·tac·tics
coun·ter·crit·i·cism	coun·ter·ploy	coun·ter·ten·den·cy
coun·ter·cry	coun·ter·pow·er	coun·ter·ter·ror
coun·ter·de·mand	coun·ter·pres·sure	coun·ter·ter·ror·ism
coun·ter·dem·on·strate	coun·ter·pro·ject	coun·ter·ter·ror·ist
coun·ter·dem·on·stra·tion	coun·ter·pro·pa·gan·da	coun·ter·threat
coun·ter·dem·on·stra·tor	coun·ter·pro·test	coun·ter·thrust
coun·ter·de·ploy·ment	coun·ter·ques·tion	coun·ter·tra·di·tion
coun·ter·ed·u·ca·tion·al	coun·ter·raid	coun·ter·trend
coun·ter·ef·fort	coun·ter·ral·ly	coun·ter·vi·o·lence
coun·ter·ev·i·dence	coun·ter·re·ac·tion	coun·ter·world

coun·ter·act \,kaún-tər-'rakt\ *vt* (1678) : to make ineffective or restrain or neutralize the usu. ill effects of by an opposite force — **coun·ter·ac·tion** \-'rak-shən\ *n* — **coun·ter·ac·tive** \-'rak-tiv\ *adj*

¹**coun·ter·bal·ance** \'kaún-tər-,ba-lən(t)s, ,kaún-tər-'\ *n* (1611) 1 : a weight that balances another 2 : a force or influence that offsets or checks an opposing force

²**counterbalance** \,kaún-tər-', 'kaún-tər-,\ *vt* (1611) 1 : to oppose or balance with an equal weight or force 2 : to equip with counterbalances

coun·ter·change \'kaún-tər-,chānj\ *vt* (ca. 1604) 1 : INTERCHANGE, TRANSPOSE 2 : CHECKER 1a

¹**coun·ter·check** \-,chek\ *n* (1559) : a check or restraint often operating against something that is itself a check

²**countercheck** *vt* (1587) 1 : CHECK, COUNTERACT 2 : to check a second time for verification

counter check *n* (1856) : a check obtainable at a bank usu. to be cashed only at the bank by the drawer

¹**coun·ter·claim** \'kaún-tər-,klām\ *n* (1784) : an opposing claim; *esp* : a claim brought by a defendant against a plaintiff in a legal action

²counterclaim *vi* (1881) : to enter or plead a counterclaim ~ *vt* : to ask in a counterclaim

coun·ter·clock·wise \ˌkaun-tər-'kläk-ˌwīz\ *adv* (1888) : in a direction opposite to that in which the hands of a clock rotate as viewed from in front — **counterclockwise** *adj*

coun·ter·con·di·tion·ing \-kən-'di-sh(ə-)niŋ\ *n* (1962) : conditioning in order to replace an undesirable response (as fear) to a stimulus (as an engagement in public speaking) by a favorable one

coun·ter·cul·ture \'kaun-tər-ˌkəl-chər\ *n* (1968) : a culture with values and mores that run counter to those of established society — **coun·ter·cul·tur·al** \ˌkaun-tər-'kəlch-rəl, -'kəl-chə-\ *adj* — **coun·ter·cul·tur·al·ism** \-rə-ˌli-zəm\ *n* — **coun·ter·cul·tur·ist** \-'rist\ *n*

¹coun·ter·cur·rent \'kaun-tər-ˌkər-ənt, -ˌkə-rənt\ *n* (1684) : a current flowing in a direction opposite that of another current

²countercurrent \ˌkaun-tər-'\ *adj* (1799) **1** : flowing in an opposite direction **2** : involving flow of materials in opposite directions ⟨~ dialysis⟩ — **coun·ter·cur·rent·ly** *adv*

coun·ter·cy·cli·cal \-'si-kli-kəl, -'si-\ *adj* (1944) : calculated to check excessive developments in a business cycle : COMPENSATORY ⟨~ budget policies⟩ — **coun·ter·cy·cli·cal·ly** \-k(ə-)lē\ *adv*

coun·ter·es·pi·o·nage \ˌkaun-tər-'es-pē-ə-ˌnäzh, -ˌnäj, -nij, *Canad also* -ˌnazh; -ˌes-pē-ə-'näzh; -ə-'spē-ə-nij\ *n* (1899) : the activity concerned with detecting and thwarting enemy espionage

coun·ter·ex·am·ple \'kaun-tər-ig-ˌzam-pəl\ *n* (1957) : an example that disproves a proposition or theory

coun·ter·fac·tu·al \ˌkaun-tər-'fak-chə-wəl, -chəl, -shwəl\ *adj* (1946) : contrary to fact ⟨~ assumptions⟩

¹coun·ter·feit \'kaunt-ər-ˌfit\ *adj* [ME *countrefet*, fr. MF *contrefait*, fr. pp. of *contrefaire* to imitate, fr. *contre-* + *faire* to make, fr. L *facere* — more at DO] (14c) **1** : made in imitation of something else with intent to deceive : FORGED ⟨~ money⟩ **2 a** : INSINCERE, FEIGNED ⟨~ sympathy⟩ **b** : IMITATION ⟨~ Georgian houses⟩

²counterfeit *vt* (14c) : to imitate or feign esp. with intent to deceive; *also* : to make a fraudulent replica of ⟨~ing $20 bills⟩ ~ *vi* **1** : to try to deceive by pretense or dissembling **2** : to engage in counterfeiting something of value *syn* see ASSUME — **coun·ter·feit·er** *n*

³counterfeit *n* (15c) **1** : something counterfeit : FORGERY **2** : something likely to be mistaken for something of higher value ⟨pity was a ~ of love —Harry Hervey⟩ *syn* see IMPOSTURE

coun·ter·flow \'kaun-tər-ˌflō\ *n* (1870) : the flow of a fluid in opposite directions (as in an apparatus)

coun·ter·foil \-ˌfoil\ *n* (1706) : a detachable stub (as on a check or ticket) usu. serving as a record or receipt

coun·ter·guer·ril·la *also* **coun·ter·gue·ril·la** \ˌkaun-tər-gə-'ri-lə, -gi-, -gyi-, -ge-\ *n* (1901) : a guerrilla who is trained to thwart enemy guerrilla operations

coun·ter·in·sur·gen·cy \ˌkaun-tər-in-'sər-jən(t)-sē\ *n* (1962) : organized military activity designed to combat insurgency — **coun·ter·in·sur·gent** \-jənt\ *n*

coun·ter·in·tel·li·gence \ˌkaun-tər-in-'te-lə-jən(t)s\ *n* (1940) : organized activity of an intelligence service designed to block an enemy's sources of information, to deceive the enemy, to prevent sabotage, and to gather political and military information

coun·ter·in·tu·i·tive \-in-'tü-ə-tiv, -'tyü-\ *adj* (1955) : contrary to what one would intuitively expect — **coun·ter·in·tu·i·tive·ly** \-lē\ *adv*

coun·ter·ion \'kaun-tər-ˌi-ən, -ˌän\ *n* (1940) : an ion having a charge opposite to that of the substance with which it is associated

coun·ter·ir·ri·tant \ˌkaun-tər-'ir-ə-tənt\ *n* (1854) **1** : an agent applied locally to produce superficial inflammation with the object of reducing inflammation in deeper adjacent structures **2** : an irritation or discomfort that diverts attention from another — **counterirritant** *adj*

count·er·man \'kaun-tər-ˌman, -mən\ *n* (1853) : one who tends a counter

¹coun·ter·mand \'kaun-tər-ˌmand, ˌkaun-tər-'\ *vt* [ME *countermaunden*, fr. MF *contremander*, fr. *contre-* counter- + *mander* to command, fr. L *mandare* — more at MANDATE] (15c) **1** : to revoke (a command) by a contrary order **2** : to recall or order back by a superseding contrary order ⟨~ reinforcements⟩

²coun·ter·mand \'kaun-tər-ˌmand\ *n* (1548) **1** : a contrary order **2** : the revocation of an order or command

coun·ter·march \'kaun-tər-ˌmärch\ *n* (1598) **1** : a marching back; *specif* : a movement in marching by which a unit of troops reverses direction while marching but keeps the same order **2** : a march (as of political demonstrators) designed to counter the effect of another march — **countermarch** *vi*

coun·ter·mea·sure \-ˌme-zhər, -ˌmā-\ *n* (1923) : an action or device designed to negate or offset another; *esp* : a military system or device intended to thwart a sensing mechanism (as radar) ⟨electronic ~s⟩

coun·ter·mel·o·dy \-ˌme-lə-dē\ *n* (1926) : a secondary melody that is sounded simultaneously with the principal one

coun·ter·mine \-ˌmīn\ *n* (1548) : a tunnel for intercepting an enemy mine

coun·ter·of·fen·sive \'kaun-tər-ə-ˌfen(t)-siv\ *n* (1909) : a large-scale military offensive undertaken by a force previously on the defensive

coun·ter·of·fer \-ˌo-fər, -ˌä-fər\ *n* (1788) : a return offer made by one who has rejected an offer

coun·ter·pane \'kaun-tər-ˌpān\ *n* [alter. of ME *countrepointe*, modif. of MF *coute pointe*, lit., embroidered quilt] (15c) : BEDSPREAD

coun·ter·part \-ˌpärt\ *n* (15c) **1** : one of two corresponding copies of a legal instrument : DUPLICATE **2 a** : a thing that fits another perfectly **b** : something that completes : COMPLEMENT **3 a** : one remarkably similar to another **b** : one having the same function or characteristics as another ⟨college presidents and their ~s in business⟩

coun·ter·plan \'kaun-tər-ˌplan\ *n* (1788) **1** : a plan designed to counter another plan **2** : an alternate or substitute plan

coun·ter·plea \-ˌplē\ *n* (1523) : a replication to a legal plea

¹coun·ter·plot \-ˌplät\ *n* (ca. 1611) : a plot designed to thwart an opponent's plot

²counterplot *vt* (1662) : to intrigue against : foil with a plot

¹coun·ter·point \'kaun-tər-ˌpoint\ *n* [MF *contrepoint*, fr. ML *contrapunctus*, fr. L *contra-* counter- + ML *punctus* musical note, melody, fr. L, act of pricking, fr. *pungere* to prick — more at PUNGENT] (15c) **1 a** : one or more independent melodies added above or below a given melody **b** : the combination of two or more independent melodies

into a single harmonic texture in which each retains its linear character : POLYPHONY **2 a** : a complementing or contrasting item : OPPOSITE **b** : use of contrast or interplay of elements in a work of art (as a drama)

²counterpoint *vt* (1875) **1** : to compose or arrange in counterpoint **2** : to set off or emphasize by juxtaposition : set in contrast ⟨~s the public and the private man —Tom Bishop⟩

¹coun·ter·poise \-ˌpoiz\ *vt* [ME *countrepesen*, fr. MF *contrepeser*, fr. *contre-* + *peser* to weigh — more at POISE] (14c) : COUNTERBALANCE

²counterpoise *n* (15c) **1** : COUNTERBALANCE **2** : an equivalent power or force acting in opposition **3** : a state of balance

coun·ter·pose \ˌkaun-tər-'pōz\ *vt* [*counter-* + *-pose* (as in *compose*)] (1594) : to place in opposition, contrast, or equilibrium ⟨~ a positive view to the negative assessment⟩

coun·ter·pro·duc·tive \-ˌprə-'dək-tiv\ *adj* (1959) : tending to hinder the attainment of a desired goal ⟨violence as a means to achieve an end is ~ —W. E. Brock *b*1930⟩

coun·ter·pro·gram·ming \ˌkaun-tər-'prō-gra-miŋ, -grə-\ *n* (ca. 1966) : the scheduling of programs by television networks so as to attract audiences away from simultaneously telecast programs of competitors

coun·ter·pro·pos·al \'kaun-tər-prə-ˌpō-zəl\ *n* (1885) : a return proposal made by one who has rejected a proposal

coun·ter·punch \'kaun-tər-ˌpənch\ *n* (1942) : a counter in boxing; *also* : a countering blow or attack — **counterpunch** *vi* — **coun·ter·punch·er** \-ˌpən-chər\ *n*

coun·ter·ref·or·ma·tion \ˌkaun-tər-ˌre-fər-'mā-shən\ *n* (1840) **1** *usu* **Counter–Reformation** : the reform movement in the Roman Catholic Church following the Reformation **2** : a reformation designed to counter the effects of a previous reformation

coun·ter·rev·o·lu·tion \-ˌre-və-'lü-shən\ *n* (1793) **1** : a revolution directed toward overthrowing a government or social system established by a previous revolution **2** : a movement to counteract revolutionary trends — **coun·ter·rev·o·lu·tion·ary** \-shə-ˌner-ē\ *adj or n*

coun·ter·shad·ing \'kaun-tər-ˌshā-diŋ\ *n* (1896) : cryptic coloration of an animal with parts normally in shadow being light and parts normally illuminated being dark thereby reducing shadows and contours

coun·ter·sign \-ˌsīn\ *n* (1591) **1** : a signature attesting the authenticity of a document already signed by another **2** : a sign given in reply to another; *specif* : a military secret signal that must be given by one wishing to pass a guard — **countersign** *vt* — **coun·ter·sig·na·ture** \ˌkaun-tər-'sig-nə-ˌchur, -chər, -ˌtyur, -ˌtur\ *n*

¹coun·ter·sink \'kaun-tər-ˌsiŋk\ *vt* **-sunk** \-ˌsəŋk\; **-sink·ing** (1816) **1** : to make a countersink on **2** : to set the head of (as a screw) at or below the surface

²countersink *n* (1816) **1** : a bit or drill for making a funnel-shaped enlargement at the outer end of a drilled hole **2** : the enlargement made by a countersink

countersink

coun·ter·spy \'kaun-tər-ˌspī\ *n* (1939) : a spy engaged in counterespionage

coun·ter·stain \-ˌstān\ *vt* (1895) : to stain (as a microscopy specimen) so as to color parts (as the cytoplasm of cells) not colored by another stain (as a nuclear stain) — **counterstain** *n*

coun·ter·ten·or \-ˌte-nər\ *n* [ME *countretenour*, fr. MF *contreteneur*, fr. *contre-* + *teneur* tenor] (15c) : a tenor with an unusually high range (as an alto range)

coun·ter·top \-ˌtäp\ *n* [¹*counter* + ¹*top*] (1897) : the flat working surface on waist-level kitchen cabinets

coun·ter·trade \-ˌtrād\ *n* (1978) : a form of international trade in which purchases made by an importing nation are linked to offsetting purchases made by the exporting nation

coun·ter·trans·fer·ence \ˌkaun-tər-(ˌ)tran(t)s-'fər-ən(t)s, -'tran(t)s-(ˌ)\ *n* (1920) **1** : psychological transference esp. by a psychotherapist during the course of treatment; *esp* : the psychotherapist's reactions to the patient's transference **2** : the complex of feelings of a psychotherapist toward the patient

coun·ter·vail \ˌkaun-tər-'vā(ə)l\ *vb* [ME *countrevailen*, fr. MF *contrevaloir*, fr. *contre-* counter- + *valoir* to be worth, fr. L *valēre* — more at WIELD] *vt* (14c) **1** : to compensate for **2** *archaic* : EQUAL, MATCH **3** : to exert force against : COUNTERACT ~ *vi* : to exert force against an opposing and often bad or harmful force or influence

coun·ter·view \'kaun-tər-ˌvyü\ *n* (1590) **1** *archaic* : CONFRONTATION **2** : an opposite point of view

coun·ter·weight \-ˌwāt\ *n* (1693) : an equivalent weight or force : COUNTERBALANCE — **counterweight** *vt*

count·ess \'kaun-təs\ *n* (12c) **1** : the wife or widow of an earl or count **2** : a woman who holds in her own right the rank of earl or count

coun·ti·an \'kaun-tē-ən\ *n* (15c) : a native or resident of a usu. specified county

count·ing·house \'kaun-tiŋ-ˌhaus\ *n* (15c) : a building, room, or office used for keeping books and transacting business

counting number *n* (ca. 1965) : NATURAL NUMBER

counting room *n* (1712) : COUNTINGHOUSE

count·less \'kaunt-ləs\ *adj* (1588) : too numerous to be counted : MYRIAD, MANY — **count·less·ly** *adv*

count noun *n* (1952) : a noun (as *bean* or *sheet*) that forms a plural and is used with a numeral, with words such as *many* or *few*, or with the indefinite article *a* or *an* — compare MASS NOUN

count palatine *n* (1539) **1 a** : a count of the Holy Roman Empire having imperial powers in his own domain **b** : a high judicial official in the Holy Roman Empire **2** : the proprietor of a county palatine in England or Ireland

coun·tri·fied *also* **coun·try·fied** \'kən-tri-ˌfid\ *adj* [*country* + *-fied* (as in *glorified*)] (1653) **1** : RURAL, RUSTIC **2** : UNSOPHISTICATED **3** : played or sung in the manner of country music ⟨~ rock⟩

\ə\ abut \ᵊ\ kitten, F table \ər\ further \a\ ash \ā\ ace \ä\ mop, mar \au\ out \ch\ chin \e\ bet \ē\ easy \g\ go \i\ hit \ī\ ice \j\ job \ŋ\ sing \ō\ go \o\ law \oi\ boy \th\ thin \th\ the \ü\ loot \u\ foot \y\ yet \zh\ vision \ä, k̲, ⁿ, œ, œ̄, ue, ūe, ᵌ\ *see* Guide to Pronunciation

¹coun·try \'kən-trē\ *n, pl* **countries** [ME *contree,* fr. OF *contrée,* fr. ML *contrata,* fr. L *contra* against, on the opposite side] (13c) **1 :** an indefinite usu. extended expanse of land **: REGION 2 a :** the land of a person's birth, residence, or citizenship **b :** a political state or nation or its territory **3 a :** the people of a state or district **: POPULACE b : JURY c : ELECTORATE 2 4 :** rural as distinguished from urban areas **5 : COUNTRY MUSIC — coun·try·ish** \-trē-ish\ *adj*

²country *adj* (14c) **1 :** of, relating to, or characteristic of the country **2 a :** of or relating to a decorative style associated with life in the country ⟨an English ~ look⟩; *also* **:** possessing a style of rustic simplicity ⟨~ furniture⟩ **b :** prepared or processed with farm supplies and procedures ⟨~ ham⟩ **3 :** of, relating to, suitable for, or featuring country music ⟨~ singers⟩

country and western *n* (1960) **: COUNTRY MUSIC —** usu. hyphenated in attributive use

country club *n* (1867) **:** a suburban club for social life and recreation; *esp* **:** one having a golf course — usu. hyphenated in attributive use

coun·try–dance \'kən-trē-dan(t)s\ *n* (1579) **:** any of various native English dances in which partners face each other esp. in rows

country gentleman *n* (1632) **1 :** a well-to-do country resident **:** an owner of a country estate **2 :** one of the English landed gentry

country house *n* (14c) **:** a house and esp. a mansion in the country

coun·try·man \'kən-trē-mən, *3 often* -,man\ *n* (14c) **1 :** an inhabitant or native of a specified country **2 : COMPATRIOT 3 :** one living in the country or marked by country ways **: RUSTIC**

country mile *n* (1950) **:** a long distance

country music *n* (1952) **:** music derived from or imitating the folk style of the Southern U.S. or of the Western cowboy

country rock *n* (1968) **: ROCKABILLY**

coun·try·seat \,kən-trē-'sēt\ *n* (1583) **:** a house or estate in the country

coun·try·side \'kən-trē-,sīd\ *n* (1727) **1 :** a rural area **2 :** the inhabitants of a countryside

coun·try·wide \'kən-trē-'wīd\ *adj* (1915) **:** extending throughout a country

coun·try·wom·an \'kən-trē-,wu̇-mən\ *n* (15c) **1 :** a woman compatriot **2 :** a woman resident of the country

¹coun·ty \'kau̇n-tē\ *n, pl* **counties** [ME *counte,* fr. MF *conté,* fr. ML *comitatus,* fr. LL, office of a count, fr. *comit-, comes* count — more at **COUNT**] (14c) **1 :** the domain of a count **2 a :** one of the territorial divisions of England and Wales and formerly also of Scotland and Northern Ireland constituting the chief units for administrative, judicial, and political purposes **b** (1) **:** the people of a county (2) *Brit* **:** the gentry of a county **3 :** the largest territorial division for local government within a state of the U.S. **4 :** the largest local administrative unit in various countries — **county** *adj*

²county *n, pl* **counties** [modif. of MF *comte*] (1550) *archaic* **: ³COUNT**

county agent *n* (1705) **:** a consultant employed jointly by federal and state governments to provide information about agriculture and home economics

county court *n* (1639) **:** a court in some states that has a designated jurisdiction usu. both civil and criminal within the limits of a county

county fair *n* (1856) **:** a fair usu. held annually at a set location in a county esp. to exhibit local agricultural products and livestock

county palatine *n* (15c) **:** the territory of a count palatine

county seat *n* (1803) **:** a town that is the seat of county administration

county town *n* (1670) *chiefly Brit* **: COUNTY SEAT**

¹coup \'kōp\ *vb* [ME, to strike, fr. MF *couper* — more at **COPE**] (ca. 1572) *chiefly Scot* **: OVERTURN, UPSET**

²coup \'kü\ *n, pl* **coups** \'küz\ [F, blow, stroke — more at **COPE**] (1791) **1 :** a brilliant, sudden, and usu. highly successful stroke or act **2 : COUP D'ÉTAT**

coup de grâce *or* **coup de grace** \,kü-də-'gräs\ *n, pl* **coups de grâce** *or* **coups de grace** \,kü-də-\ [F *coup de grâce,* lit., stroke of mercy] (1699) **1 :** a death blow or shot administered to end the suffering of one mortally wounded **2 :** a decisive finishing blow, act, or event

coup de main \-'maⁿ\ *n, pl* **coups de main** \,kü-də-\ [F, lit., hand stroke] (1758) **:** a sudden attack in force

coup d'état *or* **coup d'etat** \,kü-(,)dä-'tä, 'kü-(,)dä-,, -dä-\ *n, pl* **coups d'état** *or* **coups d'etat** \-'tä(z), -,tä(z)\ [F, lit., stroke of state] (1646) **:** a sudden decisive exercise of force in politics; *esp* **:** the violent overthrow or alteration of an existing government by a small group

coup de thé·âtre *or* **coup de the·atre** \,kü-də-tā-'ätrᵉ\ *n, pl* **coups de théâtre** *or* **coups de theatre** \,kü-də-\ [F *coup de théâtre,* lit., stroke of theater] (1747) **1 :** a sudden sensational turn in a play; *also* **:** a sudden dramatic effect or turn of events **2 :** a theatrical success

coup d'oeil \kü-'də(r), -'dəi\ *n, pl* **coups d'oeil** *same*\ [F, lit., stroke of the eye] (1739) **:** a brief survey **: GLANCE**

cou·pé *or* **coupe** \kü-'pā, *2 often* 'küp\ *n* [F *coupé,* fr. pp. of *couper* to cut, strike] (1834) **1 :** a four-wheeled closed horse-drawn carriage for two persons inside with an outside seat for the driver in front **2** *usu* *coupe* **:** a 2-door automobile often seating only two persons; *also* **:** one with a tight-spaced rear seat — compare **SEDAN**

¹cou·ple \'kə-pəl; "*couple of*" *is often* ,kə-plə(v)\ *n* [ME, pair, bond, fr. OF *cople,* fr. L *copula* bond, fr. *co-* + *apere* to fasten — more at **APT**] (13c) **1 a :** a man and woman married, engaged, or otherwise paired **b :** two persons paired together **2 : PAIR, BRACE 3 :** something that joins or links two things together: as **a :** two equal and opposite forces that act along parallel lines **b :** a pair of substances that in contact with an electrolyte participate in a transfer of electrons which causes an electric current to flow **4 :** an indefinite small number **: FEW** ⟨a ~ of days ago⟩

²cou·ple \'kə-pəl\ *vb* **cou·pled; cou·pling** \-p(ə-)liŋ\ *vt* (13c) **1 a :** to connect for consideration together **b :** to join for combined effect **2 a :** to fasten together **: LINK b :** to bring (two electric circuits) into such close proximity as to permit mutual influence **3 :** to join in marriage or sexual union **~** *vi* **1 :** to unite in sexual union **2 : JOIN 3 :** to unite chemically

³couple *adj* (1924) **: TWO;** *also* **: FEW** — used with *a* ⟨a ~ drinks⟩

   usage The adjective use of *a couple,* without *of,* has been called nonstandard, but it is not. In both British and American English it is standard before a word (as *more* or *less*) indicating degree ⟨a *couple* more examples of Middle English writing —Charles Barber⟩. Its use before an ordinary plural noun is an Americanism, common in speech and in writing that is not meant to be formal or elevated ⟨the first

couple chapters are pretty good —E. B. White (letter)⟩ ⟨still operated a *couple* wagons for hire —Garrison Keillor⟩. It is most frequently used with periods of time ⟨a *couple* weeks⟩ and numbers ⟨a *couple* hundred⟩ ⟨a *couple* dozen⟩.

cou·ple·ment \'kə-pəl-mənt\ *n* [MF, fr. *coupler* to join, fr. L *copulare,* fr. *copula*] (1548) *archaic* **:** the act or result of coupling

cou·pler \'kə-p(ə-)lər\ *n* (1552) **1 :** one that couples **2 :** a contrivance on a keyboard instrument by which keyboards or keys are connected to play together

cou·plet \'kə-plət\ *n* [MF, dim. of *cople*] (1580) **1 :** two successive lines of verse forming a unit marked usu. by rhythmic correspondence, rhyme, or the inclusion of a self-contained utterance **: DISTICH 2 : COUPLE 3 :** one of the musical episodes alternating with the main theme (as in a rondo)

cou·pling \'kə-pliŋ *(usual for 2),* -pə-liŋ\ *n* (14c) **1 :** the act of bringing or coming together **: PAIRING;** *specif* **:** sexual union **2 :** a device that serves to connect the ends of adjacent parts or objects **3 :** the joining of or the part of the body that joins the hindquarters to the forequarters of a quadruped **4 :** a means of electric connection of two electric circuits by having a part common to both

cou·pon \'kü-,pän, 'kyü-\ *n* [F, fr. OF, piece, fr. *couper* to cut — more at **COPE**] (1822) **1 :** a statement of due interest to be cut from a bearer bond when payable and presented for payment; *also* **:** the interest rate of a coupon **2 :** a form surrendered in order to obtain an article, service, or accommodation: as **a :** one of a series of attached tickets or certificates often to be detached and presented as needed **b :** a ticket or form authorizing purchases of rationed commodities **c :** a certificate or similar evidence of a purchase redeemable in premiums **d :** a part of a printed advertisement to be cut off to use as an order blank or inquiry form or to obtain a discount on merchandise

cou·pon·ing \'kü-,pä-niŋ, 'kyü-\ *n* (1954) **:** the distribution or redemption of coupons

cour·age \'kər-ij, 'kə-rij\ *n* [ME *corage,* fr. OF, fr. *cuer* heart, fr. L *cor* — more at **HEART**] (14c) **:** mental or moral strength to venture, persevere, and withstand danger, fear, or difficulty

   syn COURAGE, METTLE, SPIRIT, RESOLUTION, TENACITY mean mental or moral strength to resist opposition, danger, or hardship. COURAGE implies firmness of mind and will in the face of danger or extreme difficulty ⟨the *courage* to support unpopular causes⟩. METTLE suggests an ingrained capacity for meeting strain or difficulty with fortitude and resilience ⟨a challenge that will test your *mettle*⟩. SPIRIT also suggests a quality of temperament enabling one to hold one's own or keep up one's morale when opposed or threatened ⟨her *spirit* was unbroken by failure⟩. RESOLUTION stresses firm determination to achieve one's ends ⟨the *resolution* of pioneer women⟩. TENACITY adds to RESOLUTION implications of stubborn persistence and unwillingness to admit defeat ⟨held to their beliefs with great *tenacity*⟩.

cou·ra·geous \kə-'rā-jəs\ *adj* (14c) **:** having or characterized by courage **: BRAVE — cou·ra·geous·ly** *adv* **— cou·ra·geous·ness** *n*

cou·rante \ku̇-'ränt, -'rant\ *n* [MF, fr. *courir* to run, fr. L *currere*] (1586) **1 :** a dance of Italian origin marked by quick running steps **2 :** music in quick triple time or in a mixture of ³/₂ and ⁶/₄ time

cou·reur de bois \ku̇-,rər-də-'bwä\ *n, pl* **coureurs de bois** *same*\ [CanF, lit., woods runner] (1700) **:** a French or métis trapper of No. America and esp. of Canada

cour·gette \ku̇r-'zhet\ *n* [F, dim. of *courge* gourd, fr. L *cucurbita*] (1931) *chiefly Brit* **: ZUCCHINI**

cou·ri·er \'ku̇r-ē-ər, 'kər-ē-, 'kə-rē-\ *n* [MF *courrier,* fr. OIt *corriere,* fr. *correre* to run, fr. L *currere*] (1579) **1 : MESSENGER: as a :** a member of a diplomatic service entrusted with bearing messages **b** (1) **:** an espionage agent transferring secret information (2) **:** a runner of contraband **c :** a member of the armed services whose duties include carrying mail, information, or supplies **2 :** a traveler's paid attendant; *esp* **:** a tourists' guide employed by a travel agency

¹course \'kōrs, 'kȯrs\ *n* [ME, fr OF, fr. L *cursus,* fr. *currere* to run — more at **CAR**] (14c) **1 :** the act or action of moving in a path from point to point **2 :** the path over which something moves or extends: as **a : RACECOURSE b** (1) **:** the direction of travel of a vehicle (as a ship or airplane) usu. measured as a clockwise angle from north; *also* **:** the projected path of travel (2) **:** a point of the compass **c : WATERCOURSE d : GOLF COURSE 3 a :** accustomed procedure or normal action ⟨the law taking its ~⟩ **b :** a chosen manner of conducting oneself **:** way of acting ⟨our wisest ~ is to retreat⟩ **c** (1) **:** progression through a development or period or a series of acts or events (2) **: LIFE HISTORY, CAREER 4 :** an ordered process or succession: as **a :** a number of lectures or other matter dealing with a subject; *also* **:** a series of such courses constituting a curriculum ⟨a premed ~⟩ **b :** a series of doses or medications administered over a designated period **5 a :** a part of a meal served at one time **b : LAYER;** *esp* **:** a continuous level range of brick or masonry throughout a wall **c :** the lowest sail on a square-rigged mast — **in due course :** after a normal passage of time **:** in the expected or allotted time — **of course 1 :** following the ordinary way or procedure **2 :** as might be expected

²course *vb* **coursed; cours·ing** *vt* (15c) **1 :** to follow close upon **: PURSUE 2 a :** to hunt or pursue (game) with hounds **b :** to cause (dogs) to run (as after game) **3 :** to run or move swiftly through or over **: TRAVERSE** ⟨jets *coursed* the area daily⟩ **~** *vi* **:** to run or pass rapidly along or as if along an indicated path ⟨blood *coursing* through the veins⟩

course of study (1781) **1 : CURRICULUM 2 : COURSE 4a**

¹cours·er \'kōr-sər, 'kȯr-\ *n* [ME, fr. MF *coursier,* fr. OF *course* course, run] (14c) **:** a swift or spirited horse **: CHARGER**

²courser *n* (1600) **1 :** a dog for coursing **2 :** one that courses **: HUNTSMAN 3 :** any of various Old World birds (subfamily Cursoriinae of the family Glareolidae) noted for their speed in running

course·ware \'kōrs-,war, 'kȯrs-, -,wer\ *n* (1972) **:** educational software

coursing *n* (1538) **1 :** the pursuit of running game with dogs that follow by sight instead of by scent **2 :** the act of one that courses

¹court \'kōrt, 'kȯrt\ *n, often attrib* [ME, fr. OF, fr. L *cohort-, cohors* enclosure, group, retinue, cohort, fr. *co-* + *-hort-, -hors* (akin to *hortus* garden) — more at **YARD**] (12c) **1 a :** the residence or establishment of a sovereign or similar dignitary **b :** a sovereign's formal assembly of councillors and officers **c :** the sovereign and officers and advisers who are the governing power **d :** the family and retinue of a sovereign e : a reception held by a sovereign **2 a** (1) : a manor house or large building surrounded by usu. enclosed grounds (2) : MOTEL **b** : an open space enclosed wholly or partly by buildings or circumscribed by a single building **c** : a quadrangular space walled or marked off for playing one of various games with a ball (as lawn tennis, handball, or basketball); *also* : a division of such a court **d** : a wide alley with only one opening onto a street **3 a** : an official assembly for the transaction of judicial business **b** : a session of such a court ⟨~ is now adjourned⟩ **c** : a place (as a chamber) for the administration of justice **d** : a judge or judges in session; *also* : a faculty or agency of judgment or evaluation ⟨rest our case in the ~ of world opinion —L. H. Marks⟩ **4 a** : an assembly or board with legislative or administrative powers **b** : PARLIAMENT, LEGISLATURE **5** : conduct or attention intended to win favor or dispel hostility : HOMAGE ⟨pay ~ to the king⟩

²**court** *vt* (1571) **1 a** : to seek to gain or achieve **b** (1) : ALLURE, TEMPT (2) : to act so as to invite or provoke ⟨~s disaster⟩ **2 a** : to seek the affections of; *esp* : to seek to win a pledge of marriage from **b** *of an animal* : to perform actions in order to attract for mating **3 a** : to seek to attract (as by solicitous attention or offers of advantages) ⟨college teams ~ing high school basketball stars⟩ **b** : to seek an alliance with ~ *vi* **1** : to engage in social activities leading to engagement and marriage **2** *of an animal* : to engage in activity leading to mating

court bouil·lon \'kŭr-(,)bü-'yòⁿ, -(,)bwē-, 'kōr-, 'kòr-\ *n* [F *court= bouillon*, lit., short bouillon] (1723) : a liquid made usu. with water, white wine, vegetables, and seasonings and used to poach fish

cour·te·ous \'kər-tē-əs, *Brit also* 'kòr-\ *adj* [ME *corteis*, fr. OF, fr. *court*] (13c) **1** : marked by polished manners, gallantry, or ceremonial usage of a court **2** : marked by respect for and consideration of others **syn** see CIVIL — **cour·te·ous·ly** *adv* — **cour·te·ous·ness** *n*

cour·te·san \'kōr-tə-zən, 'kòr-, -,zan *also* 'kər-, -,zän; *esp Brit* ,kòr-tə-'zan\ *n* [MF *courtisane*, fr. northern It dial. form of It *cortigiana* woman courtier, fem. of *cortigiano* courtier, fr. *corte* court, fr. L *cohort-, cohors*] (1533) : a prostitute with a courtly, wealthy, or upper-class clientele

¹**cour·te·sy** \'kər-tə-sē, *Brit also* 'kòr-\ *n, pl* **-sies** [ME *corteisie*, fr. OF, fr. *corteis*] (13c) **1 a** : courteous behavior **b** : a courteous act or expression **2 a** : general allowance despite facts : INDULGENCE ⟨hills called mountains by ~ only⟩ **b** : consideration, cooperation, and generosity in providing (as a gift or privilege); *also* : AGENCY, MEANS — used chiefly in the phrases *through the courtesy of* or *by courtesy of* or sometimes simply *courtesy of*

²**courtesy** *adj* (1613) : granted, provided, or performed as a courtesy or by way of courtesy ⟨made a ~ call on the ambassador⟩

courtesy card *n* (1934) : a card entitling its holder to some special privilege

courtesy title *n* (1865) **1** : a title (as "Lord" added to the Christian name of a peer's younger son) used in addressing certain lineal relatives of British peers **2** : a title (as "Professor" for any teacher) taken by the user and commonly accepted without consideration of official right

court·house \'kōrt-,haus, 'kòrt-\ *n* (15c) **1 a** : a building in which courts of law are regularly held **b** : the principal building in which county offices are housed **2** : COUNTY SEAT

cour·tier \'kōr-tē-ər, 'kòr-; 'kōrt-yər, 'kòrt-; 'kōr-chər, 'kòr-\ *n* (14c) **1** : one in attendance at a royal court **2** : one who practices flattery

¹**court·ly** \'kōrt-lē, 'kòrt-\ *adj* **court·li·er; -est** (15c) **1 a** : of a quality befitting the court : ELEGANT **b** : insincerely flattering **2** : favoring the policy or party of the court — **court·li·ness** *n*

²**courtly** *adv* (ca. 1592) : in a courtly manner : POLITELY

courtly love *n* (1896) : a late medieval conventionalized code prescribing conduct and emotions of ladies and their lovers

¹**court–mar·tial** \'kōrt-,mär-shəl, 'kòrt-, -'mär-\ *n, pl* **courts–martial** *also* **court–martials** (1651) **1** : a court consisting of commissioned officers and in some instances enlisted personnel for the trial of members of the armed forces or others within its jurisdiction **2** : a trial by court-martial

²**court–martial** *vt* **–mar·tialed** *also* **–mar·tialled; –mar·tial·ing** *also* **–mar·tial·ling** \-,mär-sh(ə-)liŋ, -'mär-\ (1859) : to subject to trial by court-martial

court of appeals *often cap C&A* (1777) : a court hearing appeals from the decisions of lower courts — called also *court of appeal*

court of claims (1691) : a court that has jurisdiction over claims (as against a government)

court of common pleas (1687) **1** : a former English superior court having civil jurisdiction **2** : an intermediate court in some American states that usu. has civil and criminal jurisdiction

court of domestic relations (1926) : a court that has jurisdiction and often special advisory powers over family disputes involving the rights and duties of husband, wife, parent, or child esp. in matters affecting the support, custody, and welfare of children

court of honor (1687) : a tribunal (as a military court) for investigating questions of personal honor

court of inquiry (1757) : a military court that inquires into and reports on some military matter (as an officer's questionable conduct)

court of law (14c) : a court that hears cases and decides them on the basis of statutes or the common law

court of record (15c) : a court whose acts and proceedings are kept on permanent record

Court of St. James's \-sənt-'jämz, -'jäm-zəz, -,sänt-\ [fr. *St. James's* Palace, London, former seat of the British court] (1848) : the British court

court of sessions (ca. 1889) : any of various state criminal courts of record

court order *n* (1650) : an order issuing from a competent court that requires a party to do or abstain from doing a specified act

court plaster *n* [fr. its use for beauty spots by ladies at royal courts] (1772) : an adhesive plaster esp. of silk coated with isinglass and glycerin

court reporter *n* (1894) : a stenographer who records and transcribes a verbatim report of all proceedings in a court of law

court·room \'kōrt-,rüm, 'kòrt-, -,rum\ *n* (1677) : a room in which a court of law is held

court·ship \-,ship\ *n* (1596) : the act, process, or period of courting

court·side \-,sīd\ *n* (1969) : the area at the edge of a court (as for tennis or basketball)

court tennis *n* (ca. 1890) : a game played with a ball and racket in an enclosed court divided by a net

court·yard \'kōrt-,yärd, 'kòrt-\ *n* (1552) : a court or enclosure adjacent to a building (as a house or palace)

cous·cous \'küs-,küs\ *n* [F *couscous, couscoussou*, fr. Ar *kuskus, kuskusū*] (1759) : a No. African dish of steamed semolina usu. served with meat or vegetables; *also* : the semolina itself

cous·in \'kə-zən\ *n* [ME *cosin*, fr. OF, fr. L *consobrinus*, fr. *com-* + *sobrinus* second cousin, fr. *soror* sister — more at SISTER] (13c) **1 a** : a child of one's uncle or aunt **b** : a relative descended from one's grandparent or more remote ancestor by two or more steps and in a different line **c** : KINSMAN, RELATIVE ⟨a distant ~⟩ **2** : one associated with or related to another : COUNTERPART **3** — used as a title by a sovereign in addressing a nobleman **4** : a person of a race or people ethnically or culturally related ⟨our English ~s⟩ — **cous·in·hood** \-,hůd\ *n* — **cous·in·ly** *adj* — **cous·in·ship** \-,ship\ *n*

cous·in·age \'kə-zə-nij\ *n* (14c) **1** : relationship of cousins : KINSHIP **2** : a collection of cousins : KINFOLK

cous·in–ger·man \,kə-zən-'jər-mən\ *n, pl* **cous·ins–ger·man** \-zənz-\ [ME *cosin germain*, fr. MF, fr. OF, fr. *cosin* + *germain* german] (14c) : COUSIN 1a

Cousin Jack \,kə-zən-'jak\ *n* (1890) : CORNISHMAN; *esp* : a Cornish miner

¹**couth** \'küth\ *adj* [back-formation fr. *uncouth*] (1896) : SOPHISTICATED, POLISHED

²**couth** *n* (1956) : POLISH, REFINEMENT ⟨I expected kindness and gentility . . . but there is such a thing as too much ~ —S. J. Perelman⟩

couth·ie \'kü-thē\ *adj* [ME *couth* familiar, fr. OE *cūth* — more at UNCOUTH] (1719) *chiefly Scot* : PLEASANT, KINDLY

cou·ture \kü-'tůr, -'tŭer\ *n* [F, fr. OF *couture* sewing, fr. (assumed) VL *consutura*, fr. L *consutus*, pp. of *consuere* to sew together, fr. *com-* + *suere* to sew — more at SEW] (1908) **1** : the business of designing, making, and selling fashionable custom-made women's clothing **2** : the designers and establishments engaged in couture **3** : the clothes created by couture

cou·tu·ri·er \kü-'tůr-ē-ər, -ē-,ā\ *n* [F, dressmaker, fr. OF *cousturier* tailor's assistant, fr. *couture*] (1899) : an establishment engaged in couture; *also* : the proprietor of or designer for such an establishment

cou·tu·ri·ere \kü-'tůr-ē-ər, -ē-,er\ *n* [F *couturière*, fr. OF *couturiere*, fem. of *couturier*] (1818) : a woman who is a couturier

cou·vade \kü-'väd\ *n* [F, fr. MF, cowardly inactivity, fr. *cover* to sit on, brood over — more at COVEY] (1865) : a custom in some cultures in which when a child is born the father takes to bed as if bearing the child and submits himself to fasting, purification, or taboos

co·va·lence \,kō-'vā-lən(t)s, 'kō-,\ *n* (1919) : valence characterized by the sharing of electrons

co·va·len·cy \-lən(t)-sē\ *n* (1919) : COVALENCE

co·va·lent \,kō-'vā-lənt, 'kō-,\ *adj* (ca. 1926) : of, relating to, or characterized by covalent bonds — **co·va·lent·ly** \-lē\ *adv*

covalent bond (1939) : a chemical bond formed between atoms by the sharing of electrons

co·vari·ance \,kō-'ver-ē-ən(t)s, -'var-; 'kō-,\ *n* (1931) **1** : the expected value of the product of the deviations of two random variables from their respective means **2** : the arithmetic mean of the products of the deviations of corresponding values of two quantitative variables from their respective means

co·vari·ant \-ənt\ *adj* [ISV] (1893) : varying with something else so as to preserve certain mathematical interrelations

co·vari·a·tion \,kō-,ver-ē-'ā-shən, -,var-\ *n* (1906) : correlated variation of two or more variables

¹**cove** \'kōv\ *n* [ME, den, fr. OE *cofa*; akin to OHG *chubisi* hut] (bef. 12c) **1** : a recessed place : CONCAVITY: as **a** : an architectural member with a concave cross section **b** : a trough for concealed lighting at the upper part of a wall **2** : a small sheltered inlet or bay **3 a** : a deep recess or small valley in the side of a mountain **b** : a level area sheltered by hills or mountains

²**cove** *vt* **coved; cov·ing** (1756) : to make in a hollow concave form

³**cove** *n* [Romany *kova* thing, person] (1567) *Brit* : MAN, FELLOW

co·vel·lite \kō-'ve-,līt, 'kō-və-,\ *also* **co·vel·line** \-,lēn\ *n* [F *covelline*, fr. Niccolò Covelli †1829 Ital. chemist] (1850) : a native copper sulfide

co·ven \'kə-vən *also* 'kō-\ *n* [ME *covin* band, fr. MF, fr. ML *convenium* agreement, fr. L *convenire* to agree — more at CONVENIENT] (ca. 1520) **1** : a collection of individuals with similar interests or activities ⟨a ~ of intellectuals⟩ **2** : an assembly or band of usu. 13 witches

¹**cov·e·nant** \'kəv-nənt, 'kə-və-\ *n* [ME, fr. MF, fr. prp. of *covenir* to agree, fr. L *convenire*] (14c) **1** : a usu. formal, solemn, and binding agreement : COMPACT **2 a** : a written agreement or promise usu. under seal between two or more parties esp. for the performance of some action **b** : the common-law action to recover damages for breach of such a contract — **cov·e·nan·tal** \,kə-və-'nan-t³l\ *adj*

²**cov·e·nant** \-nənt, -,nant\ *vt* (14c) : to promise by a covenant : PLEDGE ~ *vi* : to enter into a covenant : CONTRACT

cov·e·nan·tee \,kə-və-,nan-'tē, -nən-\ *n* (1649) : the person to whom a promise in the form of a covenant is made

cov·e·nan·ter \'kə-və-,nan-tər, *1 also* ,kə-və-'\ *n* (1638) **1** *cap* : a signer or adherent of the Scottish National Covenant of 1638 **2** : one that makes a covenant

cov·e·nan·tor \'kə-və-,nan-tər; ,kə-və-,nan-'tòr, -nən-\ *n* (1649) : a party bound by a covenant

Cov·en·try \'kə-vən-trē *also* 'kä-\ *n* [*Coventry*, England] (1765) : a state of ostracism or exclusion ⟨sent to ~⟩

¹**cov·er** \'kə-vər\ *vb* **cov·ered; cov·er·ing** \'kəv-riŋ, 'kə-və-\ [ME, fr. OF *covrir*, fr. L *cooperire*, fr. *co-* + *operire* to close, cover] *vt* (13c) **1 a** : to guard from attack **b** (1) : to have within the range of one's guns : COMMAND (2) : to hold within range of an aimed firearm **c** (1) : to

---

\ə\ abut \ᵊ\ kitten, F table \ər\ further \a\ ash \ā\ ace \ä\ mop, mar \aů\ out \ch\ chin \e\ bet \ē\ easy \g\ go \i\ hit \ī\ ice \j\ job \ŋ\ sing \ō\ go \ò\ law \òi\ boy \th\ thin \t͟h\ the \ü\ loot \ů\ foot \y\ yet \zh\ vision \à, k̲, ⁿ, œ, œ̄, ŭe, ūe, ᵞ\ see Guide to Pronunciation afford protection or security to : INSURE (2) : to afford protection against or compensation for **d** (1) : to guard (an opponent) in order to obstruct a play (2) : to be in position to receive a throw to (a base in baseball) **e** (1) : to make provision for (a demand or charge) by means of a reserve or deposit ⟨your balance is insufficient to ~ the check⟩ (2) : to maintain a check on esp. by patrolling (3) : to protect by contrivance or expedient **2 a** : to hide from sight or knowledge : CONCEAL ⟨~ up a scandal⟩ **b** : to lie over : ENVELOP **3** : to lay or spread something over : OVERLAY **4 a** : to spread over **b** : to appear here and there on the surface of **5** : to place or set a cover or covering over **6 a** : to copulate with (a female animal) ⟨a horse ~s a mare⟩ **b** : to sit on and incubate (eggs) **7** : to invest with a large or excessive amount of something ⟨~ed herself with glory⟩ **8** : to play a higher-ranking card on (a previously played card) **9** : to have sufficient scope to include or take into account : COMPRISE **10** : to deal with : TREAT **11 a** : to have as one's territory or field of activity ⟨one sales rep ~s the whole state⟩ **b** : to report news about **12** : to pass over : TRAVERSE **13** : to place one's stake in equal jeopardy with in a bet **14** : to buy securities or commodities for delivery against (an earlier short sale) **15** : to record a cover of (a song) ~ *vi* **1** : to conceal something illicit, blameworthy, or embarrassing from notice — usu. used with *up* **2** : to act as a substitute or replacement during an absence — **cov·er·able** \'kəv-rə-bəl, 'kə-və-\ *adj* — **co·ver·er** \'kə-vər-ər\ *n* — **cover one's tracks** : to conceal traces in order to elude pursuers — **cover the ground** *or* **cover ground** : to deal with a subject or assignment in a particular manner ⟨the new book *covers* a lot of *ground*⟩

²**cover** *n, often attrib* (14c) **1** : something that protects, shelters, or guards: as **a** : natural shelter for an animal; *also* : the factors that provide such shelter **b** (1) : a position or situation affording protection from enemy fire (2) : the protection offered by airplanes in tactical support of a military operation **c** *Brit* : COVERAGE 1a, b, 2a **2** : something that is placed over or about another thing: **a** : LID, TOP **b** : a binding or case for a book or the analogous part of a magazine; *also* : the front or back of such a binding **c** : an overlay or outer layer esp. for protection ⟨a mattress ~⟩ **d** : a tablecloth and the other table accessories **e** : COVER CHARGE **f** : ROOF **g** : a cloth used on a bed **h** : something (as vegetation or snow) that covers the ground **i** : the extent to which clouds obscure the sky **3** : something that conceals or obscures ⟨under ~ of darkness⟩ **b** : a masking device : PRETEXT ⟨the project was a ~ for intelligence operations⟩ **4** : an envelope or wrapper for mail **5** : one who substitutes for another during an absence **6** : a recording of a song previously recorded usu. by another performer — **cov·er·less** \'kə-vər-ləs\ *adj* — **under cover** **1** : in an envelope or wrapper **2** : under concealment : in secret

cov·er·age \'kəv-rij, 'kə-və-\ *n* (1912) **1** : something that covers: as **a** : inclusion within the scope of an insurance policy or protective plan : INSURANCE **b** : the amount available to meet liabilities **c** : inclusion within the scope of discussion or reporting ⟨the news ~ of the trial⟩ **2** : the total group covered : SCOPE: as **a** : all the risks covered by the terms of an insurance contract **b** : the number or percentage of persons reached by a communications medium **3** : the act or fact of covering

cov·er·all \'kə-və-ˌról\ *n* (1824) : a one-piece outer garment worn to protect other garments — usu. used in pl. — **cov·er·alled** \-ˌróld\ *adj*

cov·er-all \'kə-və-ˌról\ *adj* (1895) : COMPREHENSIVE ⟨~ provisions⟩

cover charge *n* (1921) : a charge made by a restaurant or nightclub in addition to the charge for food and drink

cover crop *n* (1899) : a crop planted to prevent soil erosion and to provide humus

covered bridge *n* (1809) : a bridge that has its roadway protected by a roof and enclosing sides

covered smut *n* (1900) : a smut disease of grains in which the spore masses are held together by the persistent grain membrane and glumes

covered wagon *n* (1745) : a wagon with a canvas top supported by bowed strips of wood or metal

cover girl *n* (1915) : an attractive young woman whose picture appears on a magazine cover

cover glass *n* (1881) : a piece of very thin glass used to cover material on a glass microscope slide

¹**cov·er·ing** \'kəv-riŋ, 'kə-və-\ *n* (14c) : something that covers or conceals

²**covering** *adj* (1887) : containing explanation of or additional information about an accompanying communication ⟨a ~ letter⟩

cov·er·let \'kə-vər-lət, -(ˌ)lid\ *n* [ME, alter. of *coverlite*, fr. AF *coverelyth*, fr. OF *covrir* + *lit* bed, fr. L *lectus* — more at LIE] (14c) : BEDSPREAD

cov·er·slip \'kə-vər-ˌslip\ *n* (1875) : COVER GLASS

cover story *n* (1948) : a story accompanying a magazine-cover illustration

¹**co·vert** \'kō-(ˌ)vərt, kō-'; 'kə-vərt\ *adj* [ME, fr. MF, pp. of *covrir* to cover] (14c) **1** : not openly shown, engaged in, or avowed : VEILED ⟨a ~ alliance⟩ **2** : covered over : SHELTERED *syn* see SECRET — **co·vert·ly** *adv* — **co·vert·ness** *n*

²**co·vert** \'kə-vərt, 'kō-vərt *also* 'kə-vər\ *n* (14c) **1 a** : hiding place : SHELTER **b** : a thicket affording cover for game **c** : a masking or concealing device **2** : a feather covering the bases of the quills of the wings and tail of a bird — see BIRD illustration **3** : a firm durable twilled sometimes waterproofed cloth usu. of mixed-color yarns

cov·er·ture \'kə-vər-ˌchúr, -chər, -ˌtyúr, -ˌtúr\ *n* (13c) **1 a** : COVERING **b** : SHELTER **2** : the status a woman acquires upon marriage under common law

cov·er-up \'kə-və-ˌrəp\ *n* (1927) **1** : a device or stratagem for masking or concealing ⟨his garrulousness is a ~ for insecurity⟩; *also* : a usu. concerted effort to keep an illegal or unethical act or situation from being made public **2** : a loose outer garment

cov·et \'kə-vət\ *vb* [ME *coveiten*, fr. OF *coveitier*, fr. *coveitié* desire, modif. of L *cupiditat-, cupiditas*, fr. *cupidus* desirous, fr. *cupere* to desire] *vt* (14c) **1** : to wish for enviously **2** : to desire (what belongs to another) inordinately or culpably ~ *vi* : to feel inordinate desire for what belongs to another *syn* see DESIRE — **cov·et·able** \-və-tə-bəl\ *adj* — **cov·et·er** \-tər\ *n* — **cov·et·ing·ly** \-tiŋ-lē\ *adv*

cov·et·ous \'kə-və-təs\ *adj* (13c) **1** : marked by inordinate desire for wealth or possessions or for another's possessions **2** : having a crav-

ing for possession ⟨~ of power⟩ — **cov·et·ous·ly** *adv* — **cov·et·ous·ness** *n*

  syn COVETOUS, GREEDY, ACQUISITIVE, GRASPING, AVARICIOUS mean having or showing a strong desire for esp. material possessions. COVETOUS implies inordinate desire often for another's possessions ⟨*covetous* of his brother's country estate⟩. GREEDY stresses lack of restraint and often of discrimination in desire ⟨*greedy* for status symbols⟩. ACQUISITIVE implies both eagerness to possess and ability to acquire and keep ⟨an eagerly *acquisitive* mind⟩. GRASPING adds to COVETOUS and GREEDY an implication of selfishness and often suggests unfair or ruthless means ⟨a hard *grasping* trader who cheated the natives⟩. AVARICIOUS implies obsessive acquisitiveness esp. of money and strongly suggests stinginess ⟨an *avaricious* miser⟩.

cov·ey \'kə-vē\ *n, pl* **coveys** [ME, fr. MF *covee*, fr. OF, fr. *cover* to sit on, brood over, fr. L *cubare* to lie] (14c) **1** : a mature bird or pair of birds with a brood of young; *also* : a small flock **2** : COMPANY, GROUP

¹**cow** \'kaù\ *n* [ME *cou*, fr. OE *cū*; akin to OHG *kuo* cow, L *bos* head of cattle, Gk *bous*, Skt *go*] (bef. 12c) **1 a** : the mature female of cattle (genus *Bos*) **b** : the mature female of various usu. large animals (as an elephant, whale, or moose) **2** : a domestic bovine animal regardless of sex or age — **cowy** \-ē\ *adj*

cow 1: *1* hoof, *2* pastern, *3* dewclaw, *4* switch, *5* hock, *6* rear udder, *7* flank, *8* thigh, *9* tail, *10* pinbone, *11* tail head, *12* thurl, *13* hip, *14* barrel, *15* ribs, *16* crops, *17* withers, *18* heart girth, *19* neck, *20* horn, *21* poll, *22* forehead, *23* bridge of nose, *24* muzzle, *25* jaw, *26* throat, *27* point of shoulder, *28* dewlap, *29* point of elbow, *30* brisket, *31* chest floor, *32* knee, *33* milk well, *34* milk vein, *35* fore udder, *36* teats, *37* rump, *38* loin

²**cow** *vt* [prob. of Scand origin; akin to Dan *kue* to subdue] (1605) : to destroy the resolve or courage of ⟨the party that Stalin had ~ed — *World Press Rev.*⟩; *also* : to bring to a state or an action by intimidation — used with *into* ⟨like too many Asian armies, adept at ~ing a population into feeding them —Edward Lansdale⟩ *syn* see INTIMIDATE — **cowed·ly** \'kaù-(ˌ)d-lē\ *adv*

cow·ard \'kaù-(ə)rd\ *n* [ME, fr. OF *coart*, fr. *coe* tail, fr. L *cauda*] (13c) : one who shows disgraceful fear or timidity — **coward** *adj*

cow·ard·ice \'kaù-(ə)r-dəs, *dial* -(ˌ)dīs\ *n* [ME *cowardise*, fr. MF *coardise*, fr. *coart*] (14c) : lack of courage or resolution

¹**cow·ard·ly** \-lē\ *adv* (14c) : in a cowardly manner

²**cowardly** *adj* (1551) : being, resembling, or befitting a coward ⟨a ~ retreat⟩ — **cow·ard·li·ness** *n*

  syn COWARDLY, PUSILLANIMOUS, CRAVEN, DASTARDLY mean having or showing a lack of courage. COWARDLY implies a weak or ignoble lack of courage ⟨a *cowardly* failure to stand up for principle⟩. PUSILLANIMOUS suggests a contemptible lack of courage ⟨the *pusillanimous* fear of a future full of possibility⟩. CRAVEN suggests extreme defeatism and complete lack of resistance ⟨secretly despised her own *craven* yesmen⟩. DASTARDLY often implies behavior that is both cowardly and treacherous or skulking or outrageous ⟨a *dastardly* attack on unarmed civilians⟩.

cow·bane \'kaù-ˌbān\ *n* (1776) : any of several poisonous plants (as a water hemlock) of the carrot family

cow·bell \-ˌbel\ *n* (1652) : a bell hung around the neck of a cow to make a sound by which the cow can be located

cow·ber·ry \-ˌber-ē\ *n* (1800) : MOUNTAIN CRANBERRY; *also* : its fruit

cow·bird \-ˌbərd\ *n* (1810) : a small No. American blackbird (*Molothrus ater*) that lays its eggs in the nests of other birds

cow·boy \-ˌbói\ *n* (1623) **1** : one who tends cattle or horses; *esp* : a usu. mounted cattle-ranch hand **2** : a rodeo performer

cowboy boot *n* (1895) : a boot made with a high arch, a high Cuban heel, and usu. fancy stitching

cowboy hat *n* (1895) : a wide-brimmed hat with a large soft crown — called also *ten-gallon hat*

cow·catch·er \'kaù-ˌka-chər, -ˌke-\ *n* (1838) : an inclined frame on the front of a railroad locomotive for throwing obstacles off the track

cow college *n* (ca. 1915) **1** : a college that specializes in agriculture **2** : a provincial college or university that lacks culture, sophistication, and tradition

cow·er \'kaù-(ə)r\ *vi* [ME *couren*, of Scand origin; akin to ON *kura* to cower] (14c) : to shrink away or crouch esp. for shelter from something that menaces, domineers, or dismays *syn* see FAWN

cow·fish \'kaù-ˌfish\ *n* (1870) : any of various small bright-colored fishes (family Ostraciidae) with hornlike projections over the eyes

cow·girl \-ˌgər(-ə)l\ *n* (1884) **1** : a girl or woman who tends cattle or horses **2** : a girl or woman who is a rodeo performer

cow·hage *also* **cow·age** \'kaù-ij\ *n* [Hindi *kavāc*] (1640) : a tropical leguminous woody vine (*Mucuna pruriens*) with crooked pods covered with barbed hairs that cause severe itching; *also* : these hairs formerly used as a vermifuge

cow·hand \'kaù-ˌhand\ *n* (1852) : COWBOY 1

cow·herd \-ˌhərd\ *n* (bef. 12c) : one who tends cows

¹**cow·hide** \-ˌhīd\ *n* (14c) **1** : the hide of a cow; *also* : leather made from this hide **2** : a coarse whip of rawhide or braided leather

²**cowhide** *vt* **cow·hid·ed; cow·hid·ing** (1794) : to flog with a cowhide whip

cow horse *n* (1853) : COW PONY

¹**cowl** \'kaủ(ə)l\ *n* [ME *cowle,* fr. OE *cugele,* fr. LL *cuculla* monk's hood, fr. L *cucullus* hood] (bef. 12c) **1 a** : a hood or long hooded cloak esp. of a monk **b** : a draped neckline on a woman's garment **2 a** : a chimney covering designed to improve the draft **b** : the top portion of the front part of an automobile body forward of the two front doors to which are attached the windshield and instrument board **c** : COWLING

²**cowl** *vt* (1536) : to cover with or as if with a cowl

cow·lick \'kaủ-ˌlik\ *n* (1598) : a lock or tuft of hair growing in a different direction from the rest of the hair

cowl·ing \'kaủ-liŋ\ *n* (1917) : a removable metal covering that houses the engine and sometimes a part of the fuselage or nacelle of an airplane; *also* : a metal cover for an engine

cowl·staff \'kōl-ˌstaf, 'kaủ(ə)l-, 'kül-\ *n* [ME *cuvelstaff,* fr. *cuvel* vessel (fr. OE *cȳfel,* fr. ONF *cuvele* small vat) + ¹*staff*] (13c) *archaic* : a staff from which a vessel is suspended and carried between two persons

cow·man \'kaủ-mən, -ˌman\ *n* (1677) **1** : COWHERD, COWBOY **2** : a cattle owner or rancher

cow parsnip *n* (1548) : a tall perennial No. American plant (*Heracleum lanatum*) of the carrot family with large compound leaves and broad umbels of white or purplish flowers; *also* : a related Eurasian plant (*H. sphondylium*) naturalized in the U.S.

cow·pat \'kaủ-ˌpat\ *n* (1937) : a dropping of cow dung

cow·pea \'kaủ-ˌpē\ *n* (1776) : a sprawling leguminous herb (*Vigna unguiculata* syn. *V. sinensis*) related to the bean and widely cultivated in the southern U.S. esp. for forage and green manure; *also* : its edible seed — called also *black-eyed pea*

Cow·per's gland \'kaủ-pərz-, 'kü-, 'kü-\ *n* [William *Cowper* †1709 Eng. surgeon] (1738) : either of two small glands lying on either side of the male urethra below the prostate gland and discharging a secretion into the semen — called also *bulbourethral gland;* compare BARTHOLIN'S GLAND

cow·poke \'kaủ-ˌpōk\ *n* (ca. 1881) : COWBOY 1

cow pony *n* (1874) : a strong and agile saddle horse trained for herding cattle

cow·pox \'kaủ-ˌpäks\ *n* (1798) : a mild eruptive disease of the cow that when communicated to humans protects against smallpox

cow·punch·er \-ˌpən-chər\ *n* (1878) : COWBOY 1

cow·rie or **cow·ry** \'kaủ-rē\ *n, pl* **cowries** [Hindi *kauṛī*] (1662) : any of various marine gastropods (family Cypraeidae) that are widely distributed in warm seas and have glossy and often brightly colored shells; *also* : the shell of a cowrie

cow·shed \'kaủ-ˌshed\ *n* (1835) : a shed for the housing of cows

cow·slip \'kaủ-ˌslip\ *n* [ME *cowslyppe,* fr. OE *cūslyppe,* lit., cow dung, fr. *cū* cow + *slypa, slyppe* paste] (bef. 12c) **1** : a common European primrose (*Primula veris*) with fragrant yellow flowers **2** : MARSH MARIGOLD

cow town *n* (1885) **1** : a town or city that serves as a market center or shipping point for cattle **2** : a small unsophisticated town within a cattle-raising area

¹**cox** \'käks\ *n* (1869) : COXSWAIN

²**cox** *vb* (1881) : COXSWAIN

coxa \'käk-sə\ *n, pl* **cox·ae** \-ˌsē, -ˌsī\ [L, hip; akin to OHG *hāhsina* hock, Skt *kakṣa* armpit] (1826) : the basal segment of a limb of various arthropods (as an insect) — **cox·al** \-səl\ *adj*

cox·comb \'käk-ˌkōm\ *n* [ME *cokkes comb,* lit., cock's comb] (1573) **1 a** *obs* : a jester's cap adorned with a strip of red **b** *archaic* : PATE, HEAD **2** : FOOL **3** : a conceited foolish person : FOP — **cox·comb·i·cal** \käk-'skō-mi-kəl, -'skä-\ *adj*

cox·comb·ry \'käk-skəm-rē, -ˌskōm-\ *n, pl* **-ries** (1608) : behavior that is characteristic of a coxcomb : FOPPERY

Cox·sack·ie virus \(ˌ)käk-'sa-kē-\ *n* [*Coxsackie,* N.Y.] (1949) : any of several enteroviruses associated with human diseases (as meningitis)

¹**cox·swain** \'käk-sən, -ˌswän\ *n* [ME *cokswayne,* fr. *cok* cockboat + *swain* servant] (15c) **1** : a sailor who has charge of a ship's boat and its crew and who usu. steers **2** : a steersman of a racing shell who usu. directs the rowers

²**coxswain** *vt* (1928) : to direct as coxswain ~ *vi* : to act as coxswain

¹**coy** \'kỏi\ *adj* [ME, quiet, shy, fr. MF *coi* calm, fr. L *quietus* quiet] (14c) **1 a** : shrinking from contact or familiarity **b** : marked by cute, coquettish, or artful playfulness **2** : showing reluctance to make a definite commitment *syn* see SHY — **coy·ly** *adv* — **coy·ness** *n*

²**coy** *vt* (1583) *obs* : CARESS ~ *vi,* archaic : to act coyly

coy·dog \'kỏi-ˌdog\ *n* [*coyote* + *dog*] (1950) : a hybrid between a coyote and a feral dog

coy·ote \'kī-ˌōt, kī-'ō-tē\ *n, pl* **coyotes** or **coyote** [MexSp, fr. Nahuatl *coyōtl*] (1759) **1** : a buff-gray to reddish gray No. American canid (*Canis latrans*) closely related to but smaller than the wolf **2** : one who smuggles immigrants into the U.S.

coy·o·til·lo \ˌkī-ə-'ti-(ˌ)lō, ˌkỏi-ə-, -'tē-(ˌ)yō\ *n* [MexSp, dim. of *coyote*] (ca. 1892) : a shrub (*Karwinskia humboldtiana*) of the buckthorn family of the southwestern U.S. and Mexico having poisonous berries

coy·pu \'kỏi-(ˌ)pü, kỏi-'\ *n* [AmerSp *coipú,* fr. Araucanian *coipu*] (1793) : NUTRIA

coz \'kəz\ *n* [by shortening & alter.] (1559) : COUSIN

coz·en \'kə-zən\ *vt* **coz·ened; coz·en·ing** \'kəz-niŋ, 'kə-zə-\ [perh. fr. obs. It *cozzonare,* fr. It *cozzone* horse trader, fr. L *cocion-, cocio* trader] (1573) **1** : to deceive, win over, or induce to do something by artful coaxing and wheedling or shrewd trickery **2** : to gain by cozening someone ⟨~ed his supper out of the old couple⟩ *syn* see CHEAT — **coz·en·er** \'kəz-nər, 'kə-zə-\ *n*

coz·en·age \'kəz-nij, 'kə-zə-\ *n* (1583) **1** : the art or practice of cozening : FRAUD **2** : an act or instance of cozening

¹**co·zy** \'kō-zē\ *adj* **co·zi·er; -est** [prob. fr. Scand origin; akin to Norw *koselig* cozy] (1709) **1** : enjoying or affording warmth and ease : SNUG **2 a** : marked by the intimacy of the family or a close group **b** : marked by or suggesting close association or connivance ⟨a ~ agreement⟩ **3** : marked by a discreet and cautious attitude or procedure

syn see COMFORTABLE — **co·zi·ly** \-zə-lē\ *adv* — **co·zi·ness** \-zē-nəs\ *n*

²**cozy** *n, pl* **co·zies** (1863) : a padded covering esp. for a teapot to keep the contents hot

³**cozy** *adv* (1946) : in a cautious manner ⟨play it ~ and wait for the other team to make a mistake —Bobby Dodd⟩

cozy up *vi* (1937) : to attain or try to attain familiarity, friendship, or intimacy : ingratiate oneself ⟨*cozying up* to the boss⟩

¹**crab** \'krab\ *n, often attrib* [ME *crabbe,* fr. OE *crabba;* akin to OHG *krebiz* crab, OE *ceorfan* to carve — more at CARVE] (bef. 12c) **1** : any of numerous chiefly marine broadly built decapod crustaceans: **a** : any of a group (Brachyura) with a short broad usu. flattened carapace, a small abdomen that curls forward beneath the body, short antennae, and the anterior pair of limbs modified as grasping pincers **b** : any of various crustaceans of a group (Anomura) resembling true crabs in the more or less reduced condition of the abdomen **2** *cap* : CANCER 1 **3** *pl* : infestation with crab lice **4** : the angular difference between an aircraft's course and the heading necessary to make that course in the presence of a crosswind

²**crab** *vb* **crabbed; crab·bing** (1918) **1** : to cause to move sideways or in an indirect or diagonal manner; *specif* : to head (an airplane) into a crosswind to counteract drift **2** : to subject to crabbing ~ *vi* **1 a** (1) : to move sideways indirectly or diagonally (2) : to crab an airplane **b** : to scuttle or scurry sideways **2** : to fish for crabs — **crab·ber** *n*

³**crab** *n* [ME *crabbe,* perh. fr. *crabbe* ¹crab] (14c) : CRAB APPLE

⁴**crab** *n* (1580) : an ill-tempered person : CROSSPATCH

⁵**crab** *vb* **crabbed; crab·bing** [ME *crabben,* prob. back-formation fr. *crabbed*] (1662) **1** : to make sullen ⟨SOUR ⟨old age has *crabbed* his nature⟩ **2** : to complain about peevishly **3** : SPOIL, RUIN ~ *vi* : CARP, GROUSE ⟨always ~s about the weather⟩ — **crab·ber** *n*

crab apple *n* [³*crab*] (1712) : any of various wild or cultivated trees (genus *Malus*) that are cultivars or relatives of the cultivated apple and that produce small sour fruit; *also* : the fruit

crab·bed \'kra-bəd\ *adj* [ME, partly fr. *crabbe* ¹crab, partly fr. *crabbe* crab apple] (14c) **1** : marked by a forbidding moroseness **2** : difficult to read or understand ⟨~ handwriting⟩ *syn* see SULLEN — **crab·bed·ness** *n*

crab·by \'kra-bē\ *adj* **crab·bi·er; -est** [⁴*crab*] (1776) : CROSS, ILL-NATURED

crab cactus *n* (1900) : CHRISTMAS CACTUS

crab·grass \'krab-ˌgras\ *n* (1743) : a grass (esp. *Digitaria sanguinalis*) that has creeping or decumbent stems which root freely at the nodes and that is often a pest in turf or cultivated lands

crab louse *n* (1547) : a sucking louse (*Phthirus pubis*) infesting the pubic region of the human body

crab·meat \'krab-ˌmēt\ *n* (1876) : the edible part of a crab

crab·stick \-ˌstik\ *n* (1703) **1** : a stick, cane, or cudgel of crab apple tree wood **2** : a crabbed ill-natured person

crab·wise \-ˌwīz\ *adv* (1898) **1** : SIDEWAYS **2** : in a sidling or cautiously indirect manner

¹**crack** \'krak\ *vb* [ME *crakken,* fr. OE *cracian;* akin to OHG *chrahhōn* to resound] *vi* (bef. 12c) **1** : to make a very sharp explosive sound ⟨the whip ~s through the air⟩ **2** : to break, split, or snap apart **3** : FAIL: as **a** : to lose control or effectiveness under pressure — usu. used with *up* **b** : to fail in tone ⟨his voice ~ed⟩ **4** : to go or travel at good speed — usu. used with *on* ⟨the steamboat ~ed *on*⟩ ~ *vt* **1 a** : to break so that fissures appear on the surface ⟨a ~ mirror⟩ **b** : to break with a sudden sharp sound ⟨~ nuts⟩ **2** : to tell esp. suddenly or strikingly ⟨~ a joke⟩ **3** : to strike with a sharp noise : RAP ⟨then ~s him over the head⟩ ⟨~ed a two-run homer in the fifth —*N.Y. Times*⟩ **4 a** (1) : to open (as a bottle) for drinking (2) : to open (a book) for studying **b** : to puzzle out and expose, solve, or reveal the mystery of ⟨~ a code⟩ **c** : to break into ⟨~ a safe⟩ **d** : to open slightly ⟨~ the throttle⟩ **e** : to break through (as a barrier) so as to gain acceptance or recognition **5 a** : to impair seriously or irreparably : WRECK ⟨~ a car up⟩ **b** : to destroy the tone of (a voice) : DISORDER, CRAZE **d** : to interrupt sharply or abruptly ⟨the criticism ~ed our complacency⟩ **6** : to cause to make a sharp noise ⟨~s his knuckles⟩ **7 a** (1) : to subject (hydrocarbons) to cracking (2) : to produce by cracking ⟨~ed gasoline⟩ **b** : to break up (chemical compounds) into simpler compounds by means of heat

²**crack** *n* (14c) **1 a** : a loud roll or peal ⟨a ~ of thunder⟩ **b** : a sudden sharp noise ⟨the ~ of rifle fire⟩ **2** : a sharp witty remark : QUIP **3 a** : a narrow break : FISSURE ⟨a ~ in the ice⟩ **b** : a narrow opening ⟨leave the door open a ~⟩ **4 a** : a weakness or flaw caused by decay, age, or deficiency : UNSOUNDNESS **b** : a broken tone of the voice : CRACKPOT **5** : MOMENT, INSTANT ⟨the ~ of dawn⟩ **6** : HOUSEBREAKING, BURGLARY **7** : a sharp resounding blow ⟨gave him a ~ on the head⟩ **8** : ATTEMPT, TRY ⟨her first ~ at writing a novel⟩ **9** : highly purified cocaine in small chips used illicitly usu. for smoking

³**crack** *adj* (1793) : of superior excellence or ability ⟨a ~ marksman⟩

crack·back \'krak-ˌbak\ *n* (1967) : a blind-side block on a defensive back in football by a pass receiver who starts downfield and then cuts back to the middle of the line

crack·brain \-ˌbrān\ *n* (ca. 1570) : an erratic person : CRACKPOT — **crack·brained** \-ˌbrānd\ *adj*

crack·down \-ˌdaủn\ *n* (1935) : an act or instance of cracking down

crack down *vi* (1939) : to take positive regulatory or disciplinary action

cracked \'krakt\ *adj* (1503) **1 a** : broken (as by a sharp blow) so that the surface is fissured ⟨~ china⟩ **b** : broken into coarse particles ⟨~ wheat⟩ **c** : marked by harshness, dissonance, or failure to sustain a tone ⟨a ~ voice⟩ **2** : mentally disturbed : CRAZY

crack·er \'kra-kər\ *n* (15c) **1** *chiefly dial* : a bragging liar : BOASTER **2** : something that makes a cracking or snapping noise: as **a** : FIRECRACKER **b** : the snapping end of a whiplash : SNAPPER **c** : a paper

\ə\ abut \ᵊ\ kitten, F table \ər\ further \a\ ash \ā\ ace \ä\ mop, mar
\aủ\ out \ch\ chin \e\ bet \ē\ easy \g\ go \i\ hit \ī\ ice \j\ job
\ŋ\ sing \ō\ go \ȯ\ law \ȯi\ boy \th\ thin \th̲\ the \ü\ loot \ủ\ foot
\y\ yet \zh\ vision \ä, k, ⁿ, œ, œ̄, ᵫ, ᵫ̄, ᵊ\ *see* Guide to Pronunciation

holder for a party favor that pops when the ends are pulled sharply **3** *pl* : NUTCRACKER **4** : a dry thin crispy baked bread product that may be leavened or unleavened **5 a** : a poor usu. Southern white — usu. used disparagingly **b** *cap* : a native or resident of Florida or Georgia — used as a nickname **6** : the equipment in which cracking (as of petroleum) is carried out

crack·er–bar·rel \-,bar-əl\ *adj* [fr. the cracker barrel in country stores around which customers lounged for informal conversation] (1916) : suggestive of the friendly homespun character of a country store ⟨a ~ philosopher⟩

crack·er·jack \'kra-kər-,jak\ *also* **crack·a·jack** \-kə-,jak\ *n* [prob. alter. of ³*crack* + *jack* (man)] (1895) : a person or thing of marked excellence — **crackerjack** *adj*

Cracker Jack *trademark* — used for a candied popcorn confection

crack·ers \'kra-kərz\ *adj* [prob. *cracked* + *-ers* (as in *starkers*)] (1928) : CRAZY

¹crack·ing \'kra-kiŋ\ *adj* (1830) : very impressive or effective : GREAT

²cracking *adv* (1903) : VERY, EXTREMELY ⟨a ~ good book⟩

³cracking *n* (1868) : a process in which relatively heavy hydrocarbons are broken up by heat into lighter products (as gasoline)

¹crack·le \'kra-kəl\ *vb* **crack·led; crack·ling** \-k(ə-)liŋ\ [freq. of ¹*crack*] *vi* (ca. 1560) **1 a** : to make small sharp sudden repeated noises ⟨the fire ~s on the hearth⟩ **b** : to show animation : SPARKLE ⟨the essays ~ with wit⟩ **2** : CRAZE **3** ~ *vt* : to crush or crack with snapping noises

²crackle *n* (1833) **1 a** : the noise of repeated small cracks or reports **b** : SPARKLE, EFFERVESCENCE **2** : a network of fine cracks on an otherwise smooth surface

crack·le·ware \'kra-kəl-,war, -,wer\ *n* (1881) : ceramic ware with a decorative crazed glaze

crack·ling \'kra-k(ə-)liŋ\ (1599) **1** : a series of small sharp cracks or reports ⟨the ~ of frozen snow as we walk⟩ **2** \'kra-klən, -kliŋ\ : the crisp residue left after the rendering of lard from fat or the frying or roasting of the skin (as of pork) — usu. used in pl.

crack·ly \'kra-k(ə-)lē\ *adj* (1859) : inclined to crackle : CRISP

crack·nel \'krak-nᵊl\ *n* [ME *krakenelle*] (14c) **1** : a hard brittle biscuit **2** : CRACKLING 2 — usu. used in pl.

crack·pot \'krak-,pät\ *n* (1883) : one given to eccentric or lunatic notions — **crackpot** *adj*

cracks·man \'krak-smən\ *n* (ca. 1812) : BURGLAR; *also* : SAFECRACKER

crack–up \'krak-,əp\ *n* (ca. 1926) **1** : CRASH, WRECK ⟨an automobile ~⟩ **2 a** : a mental collapse : NERVOUS BREAKDOWN ⟨his wife's death brought on his ~⟩ **b** : COLLAPSE, BREAKDOWN

crack up *vt* (1829) **1** : PRAISE, TOUT 4 ⟨wasn't all that it was *cracked up* to be⟩ **2** : to cause to laugh out loud ⟨that joke really *cracks* him *up*⟩ ~ *vi* **1** : to smash up a vehicle (as by losing control) ⟨*cracked up* on a curve⟩ **2** : to laugh out loud

-cracy *n comb form* [MF & LL; MF *-cratie*, fr. LL *-cratia*, fr. Gk *-kratia*, fr. *kratos* strength, power — more at HARD] **1** : form of government; *also* : state having such a form ⟨monocracy⟩ **2** : social or political class (as of powerful persons) ⟨mobocracy⟩ **3** : theory of social organization ⟨technocracy⟩

¹cra·dle \'krā-dᵊl\ *n* [ME *cradel*, fr. OE *cradol*; perh. akin to OHG *kratto* basket, Skt *grantha* knot] (bef. 12c) **1 a** : a bed or cot for a baby usu. on rockers or pivots **b** : a framework or support suggestive of a baby's cradle: as **(1)** : a framework of bars and rods **(2)** : the support for a telephone receiver or handset **c** : an implement with rods like fingers attached to a scythe and used formerly for harvesting grain **2 a** : a frame to keep the bedclothes from contact with an injured part of the body **2 a** : the earliest period of life : INFANCY ⟨from the ~ to the grave⟩ **b** : a place of origin ⟨the ~ of civilization⟩ **3** : a rocking device used in panning for gold

²cradle *vb* **cra·dled; cra·dling** \'krād-liŋ, 'krā-dᵊl-iŋ\ *vt* (15c) **1 a** : to place or keep in or as if in a cradle : SHELTER, REAR **c** : to support protectively or intimately ⟨*cradling* the injured man's head in her arms⟩ **2** : to cut (grain) with a cradle scythe **3** : to place, raise, support, or transport on a cradle ~ *vi, obs* : to rest in or as if in a cradle

cradle cap *n* (ca. 1890) : a seborrheic condition in infants that usu. affects the scalp and is characterized by greasy gray or dark brown adherent scaly crusts

cra·dle·song \'krā-dᵊl-,sȯŋ\ *n* (14c) : LULLABY

¹craft \'kraft\ *n* [ME, strength, skill, fr. OE *cræft*; akin to OHG *kraft* strength] (bef. 12c) **1** : skill in planning, making, or executing : DEXTERITY **2** : an occupation or trade requiring manual dexterity or artistic skill ⟨the carpenter's ~⟩ ⟨the ~ of writing plays⟩ ⟨~s such as pottery, carpentry, and sewing⟩ **3** : skill in deceiving to gain an end ⟨used ~ and guile to close the deal⟩ **4** : the members of a trade or trade association **5** *pl usu* **craft** **a** : a boat esp. of small size **b** : AIRCRAFT **c** : SPACECRAFT **syn** see ART

²craft *vt* (15c) : to make or produce with care, skill, or ingenuity ⟨is ~*ing* a new sculpture⟩ ⟨a carefully ~*ed* story⟩

crafts·man \'kraf(t)s-mən\ *n* (13c) **1** : a worker who practices a trade or handicraft **2** : one who creates or performs with skill or dexterity esp. in the manual arts ⟨jewelry made by European *craftsmen*⟩ — **crafts·man·like** \-,līk\ *adj* — **crafts·man·ly** \-lē\ *adj* — **crafts·man·ship** \-,ship\ *n*

crafts·peo·ple \-,pē-pəl\ *n pl* (1953) : workers who practice a trade or craft

crafts·per·son \-,pər-sᵊn\ *n* (1920) : a craftsman or craftswoman

crafts·wom·an \'kraf(t)s-,wu̇-mən\ *n* (1886) **1** : a woman artisan **2** : a woman who is skilled in a craft

craft union *n* (1922) : a labor union with membership limited to workers of the same craft — compare INDUSTRIAL UNION

crafty \'kraf-tē\ *adj* **craft·i·er; -est** (bef. 12c) **1** *dial chiefly Brit* : SKILLFUL, CLEVER **2 a** : adept in the use of subtlety and cunning **b** : marked by subtlety and guile ⟨a ~ scheme⟩ **syn** see SLY — **craft·i·ly** \'kraf-tə-lē\ *adv* — **craft·i·ness** \-tē-nəs\ *n*

¹crag \'krag\ *n* [ME, of Celt origin; akin to W *craig* rock] (14c) **1** : a steep rugged rock or cliff **2** *archaic* : a sharp detached fragment of rock — **crag·ged** \'kra-gəd\ *adj*

²crag *n* [ME, fr. MD *crāghe*; akin to OE *cræga* throat — more at CRAW] (14c) *chiefly Scot* : NECK, THROAT

crag·gy \'kra-gē\ *adj* **crag·gi·er; -est** (15c) **1** : full of crags ⟨~ slopes⟩ **2** : ROUGH, RUGGED ⟨a ~ face⟩ — **crag·gi·ly** \'kra-gə-lē\ *adv* — **crag·gi·ness** \'kra-gē-nəs\ *n*

crags·man \'kragz-mən\ *n* (1816) : one that is expert in climbing crags or cliffs

crake \'krāk\ *n* [ME, prob. fr. ON *krāka* crow or *krākr* raven; akin to OE *crāwan* to crow] (14c) **1** : any of various rails; *esp* : a short-billed rail (as the corncrake) **2** : the corncrake's cry

¹cram \'kram\ *vb* **crammed; cram·ming** [ME *crammen*, fr. OE *crammian*; akin to ON *kremja* to squeeze] *vt* (bef. 12c) **1** : to pack tight : JAM ⟨~ a suitcase with clothes⟩ **2 a** : to fill with food to satiety : STUFF **b** : to eat voraciously : BOLT ⟨the child ~s her food⟩ **3** : to thrust in or as if in a rough or forceful manner ⟨*crammed* the letters into his pocket⟩ **4** : to prepare hastily for an examination ⟨~ the students for the test⟩ ~ *vi* **1** : to eat greedily or to satiety : STUFF **2** : to study hastily for an imminent examination — **cram·mer** *n*

²cram *n* (1810) **1** : a compressed multitude or crowd : CRUSH **2** : last-minute study for an examination

cram·bo \'kram-(,)bō\ *n, pl* **cramboes** [alter. of earlier *crambe*, fr. L, cabbage, fr. Gk *krambē*] (1660) : a game in which one player gives a word or line of verse to be matched in rhyme by other players

cram·oi·sie *or* **cram·oi·sy** \'kra-,mȯi-zē, 'kra-mə-zē\ *n, pl* **-sies** [ME *crammassy*, fr. MF *cramoisi*, fr. *cramoisi* crimson] (15c) : crimson cloth

¹cramp \'kramp\ *n* [ME *crampe*, fr. MF, of Gmc origin; akin to MD *crampe*; akin to OHG *krampf* bent] (14c) **1** : a painful involuntary spasmodic contraction of a muscle **2** : a temporary paralysis of muscles from overuse — compare WRITER'S CRAMP **3 a** : sharp abdominal pain — usu. used in pl. **b** : persistent and often intense though dull lower abdominal pain associated with dysmenorrhea — usu. used in pl.

²cramp *n* [ME *crampe*, fr. MD] (15c) **1 a** : a usu. iron device bent at the ends and used to hold timbers or blocks of stone together **b** : CLAMP **2 a** : something that confines : SHACKLE **b** : the state of being confined

³cramp *vt* (15c) **1** : to affect with or as if with a cramp or cramps **2 a** : CONFINE, RESTRAIN ⟨was ~*ed* in the tiny apartment⟩ **b** : to restrain from free expression — used esp. in the phrase *cramp one's style* **3** : to turn (the front wheels of a vehicle) to right or left **4** : to fasten or hold with a cramp ~ *vi* : to suffer from cramps

⁴cramp *adj* (1674) **1** : hard to understand or figure out ⟨~ law terms⟩ ⟨~ handwriting⟩ **2** : being cramped ⟨a ~ corner⟩

cram·pon \'kram-,pän\ *n* [ME, fr. MF *crampon*, of Gmc origin; akin to MD *crampe*] (15c) **1** : a hooked clutch or dog for raising heavy objects — usu. used in pl. **2** : a climbing iron used esp. on ice and snow in mountaineering — usu. used in pl.

cran·ber·ry \'kran-,ber-ē, -b(ə-)rē\ *n* [part trans. of LG *kraanbere*, fr. *kraan* crane + *bere* berry] (1647) **1** : the red acid berry produced by some plants (as *Vaccinium oxycoccos* and *V. macrocarpon*) of the heath family; *also* : a plant producing these **2** : any of various plants with a fruit that resembles a cranberry

crampon 2

cranberry bush *n* (1778) : a shrubby or arborescent viburnum (*Viburnum opulus*) of No. America and Europe with prominently 3-lobed leaves and red fruit

cranch \'kranch\ *var of* CRAUNCH

¹crane \'krān\ *n* [ME *cran*, fr. OE; akin to OHG *krano* crane, Gk *geranos*, L *grus*] (bef. 12c) **1** : any of a family (Gruidae of the order Gruiformes) of tall wading birds superficially resembling the herons but structurally more nearly related to the rails **2** : any of several herons **3** : an often horizontal projection swinging about a vertical axis: as **a** : a machine for raising, shifting, and lowering heavy weights by means of a projecting swinging arm or with the hoisting apparatus supported on an overhead track **b** : an iron arm in a fireplace for supporting kettles **c** : a boom for holding a motion-picture or television camera

²crane *vb* **craned; cran·ing** *vt* (1570) **1** : to raise or lift by or as if by a crane **2** : to stretch (as the neck) toward an object of attention ⟨*craning* her neck to get a better view⟩ ~ *vi* **1** : to stretch one's neck toward an object of attention ⟨I *craned* out of the window of my compartment —Webb Waldron⟩ **2** : HESITATE

crane fly *n* (1658) : any of a family (Tipulidae) of long-legged slender dipteran flies that resemble large mosquitoes but do not bite

cranes·bill \'krānz-,bil\ *n* (1548) : GERANIUM 1

crani- *or* **cranio-** *comb form* [ML *cranium*] : cranium ⟨craniate⟩ : cranial and ⟨craniosacral⟩

cra·ni·al \'krā-nē-əl\ *adj* (1800) **1** : of or relating to the skull or cranium **2** : CEPHALIC — **cra·ni·al·ly** \-ə-lē\ *adv*

cranial index *n* (1868) : the ratio multiplied by 100 of the maximum breadth of the bare skull to its maximum length from front to back

cranial nerve *n* (1840) : any of the nerves that arise in pairs from the lower surface of the brain one on each side and pass through openings in the skull to the periphery of the body and that comprise 12 pairs in reptiles, birds, and mammals and usu. 10 in fishes and amphibians

cra·ni·ate \'krā-nē-ət, -,āt\ *adj* (1879) : having a cranium — **craniate** *n*

cra·nio·ce·re·bral \,krā-nē-ō-sə-'rē-brəl, -'ser-ə-\ *adj* (ca. 1903) : involving both cranium and brain ⟨~ injury⟩

cra·nio·fa·cial \-'fā-shəl\ *adj* (ca. 1859) : of, relating to, or involving both the cranium and the face

cra·ni·ol·o·gy \,krā-nē-'ä-lə-jē\ *n* [prob. fr. G *Kraniologie*, fr. *kranio-* *crani-* + *-logie* -logy] (1851) : a science dealing with variations in size, shape, and proportions of skulls among human races

cra·ni·om·e·try \-'ä-mə-trē\ *n* [ISV] (ca. 1828) : a science dealing with cranial measurement — compare CEPHALOMETRY

cra·nio·sa·cral \,krā-nē-ō-'sa-krəl, -'sā-\ *adj* (ca. 1923) : PARASYMPATHETIC

cra·ni·ot·o·my \,krā-nē-'ä-tə-mē\ *n* [ISV] (1855) : surgical opening of the skull

cra·ni·um \'krā-nē-əm\ *n, pl* **-ni·ums** *or* **-nia** \-nē-ə\ [ML, fr. Gk *kranion;* akin to Gk *kara* head — more at CEREBRAL] (15c) : SKULL; *specif* : the part that encloses the brain : BRAINCASE

¹**crank** \'kraŋk\ *n* [ME *cranke,* fr. OE *cranc-* (as in *crancstæf,* a weaving instrument); prob. akin to MHG *krank* weak, sick — more at CRINGE] (13c) **1** : a bent part of an axle or shaft or an arm keyed at right angles to the end of a shaft by which circular motion is imparted to or received from the shaft or by which reciprocating motion is changed into circular motion or vice versa **2 a** *archaic* : BEND **b** : a twist or turn of speech : CONCEIT — used esp. in the phrase *quips and cranks* **c** (1) : CAPRICE, CROTCHET (2) : an annoyingly eccentric person; *also* : one that is overly enthusiastic about a particular subject or activity **d** : a bad-tempered person : GROUCH **3** : CRYSTAL 7 — **crank·ish** \'kraŋ-kish\ *adj*

²**crank** *vi* (1592) **1** : to move with a winding course : ZIGZAG **2 a** : to turn a crank **b** : to get started by or as if by the turning of a crank **c** : to gain speed, momentum, or intensity — usu. used with *up* ⟨the campaign is ~*ing* up⟩ **~** *vt* **1** : to move or operate by or as if by a crank ⟨~ the window down⟩ **2 a** : to cause to start (as an automobile) **b** : to rotate the shaft (as a crankshaft) of esp. with a starter ⟨~ over an engine⟩ **c** : to use in trying to start an engine ⟨~ the starter⟩ **3 a** : to start as if by use of a crank — usu. used with *up* ⟨~ up an atom smasher⟩ **b** : TURN UP 2 — usu. used with *up* ⟨~ up the volume⟩

³**crank** *adj* (1924) : of, relating to, or being a cranky or eccentric person; *also* : made or sent by such a person ⟨~ calls⟩ ⟨a ~ letter⟩

⁴**crank** *adj* [ME *cranke,* of unknown origin] (15c) **1** *chiefly dial* : MERRY, HIGH-SPIRITED **2** *chiefly dial* : COCKY, CONFIDENT

⁵**crank** *adj* [short for *crank-sided* (easily tipped)] (ca. 1649) *of a boat* : easily tipped by an external force

crank·case \'kraŋk-ˌkās\ *n* (ca. 1878) : the housing of a crankshaft

crank out *vt* (1956) : to produce esp. in a mechanical manner

crank·pin \'kraŋk-ˌpin\ *n* (1839) : the cylindrical piece which forms the handle of a crank or to which a connecting rod is attached

crank·shaft \'kraŋk-ˌshaft\ *n* (1854) **1** : a shaft driven by or driving a crank **2** : a shaft consisting of a series of cranks and crankpins to which the connecting rods of an engine are attached

¹**cranky** \'kraŋ-kē\ *adj* **crank·i·er; -est** [¹*crank*] (1821) **1 a** : given to fretful fussiness : readily angered when opposed : CROTCHETY **b** : marked by eccentricity **2** : full of twists and turns : TORTUOUS ⟨a ~ road⟩ **3** : working erratically : UNPREDICTABLE ⟨a ~ old tractor⟩ **4** *dial* : CRAZY, IMBECILE — **crank·i·ly** \-kə-lē\ *adv* — **crank·i·ness** \-kē-nəs\ *n*

²**cranky** *adj* (1841) *of a boat* : ⁵CRANK

cran·nog \'kra-ˌnóg, kra-'nóg\ *n* [ScGael *crannag* & Ir *crannóg*] (1608) : an artificial fortified island constructed in a lake or marsh orig. in prehistoric Ireland and Scotland

cran·ny \'kra-nē\ *n, pl* **crannies** [ME *crany,* fr. MF *cren, cran* notch] (15c) **1** : a small break or slit : CREVICE **2** : an obscure nook or corner — **cran·nied** \-nēd\ *adj*

cran·reuch \'kran-ˌrük\ *n* [prob. modif. of ScGael *crannreotha*] (1682) *Scot* : HOARFROST, RIME

¹**crap** \'krap\ *vi* **crapped; crap·ping** (1846) : DEFECATE — usu. considered vulgar

²**crap** *n* [ME *crappe* chaff, residue from rendered fat, perh. fr. OF *crappe* chaff, residue, fr. ML *crappa*] (ca. 1897) **1 a** : EXCREMENT — usu. considered vulgar **b** : the act of defecating — usu. considered vulgar **2** : NONSENSE, RUBBISH; *also* : STUFF 4b — sometimes considered vulgar

³**crap** *n* [sing. of *craps*] (1885) **1** — used as an attributive form of *craps* ⟨~ game⟩ ⟨~ table⟩ **2** : a throw of 2, 3, or 12 in the game of craps losing the shooter his bet unless he has a point — called also *craps;* compare NATURAL

⁴**crap** *vi* **crapped; crap·ping** (ca. 1930) **1** : to throw a crap **2** : to throw a seven while trying to make a point — usu. used with *out*

¹**crape** \'krāp\ *n* [alter. of F *crêpe,* fr. MF *crespe,* fr. *crespe* curly, fr. L *crispus* — more at CRISP] (1633) **1** : CREPE **2** : a band of crepe worn on a hat or sleeve as a sign of mourning

²**crape** *vt* **craped; crap·ing** (1815) : to cover or shroud with or as if with crape

³**crape** *vt* **craped; crap·ing** [F *crêper,* fr. L *crispare,* fr. *crispus*] (1774) : to make (the hair) curly

crape myrtle *n* (1850) : an Asian shrub (*Lagerstroemia indica*) of the loosestrife family widely grown in warm regions for its flowers

crap·per \'kra-pər\ *n* [¹*crap*] (ca. 1932) : TOILET — usu. considered vulgar

crap·pie \'krä-pē\ *n* [CanF *crapet*] (ca. 1827) **1** : BLACK CRAPPIE **2** : WHITE CRAPPIE

crap·py \'kra-pē\ *adj* **crap·pi·er; -est** (1846) *slang* : markedly inferior in quality : LOUSY

craps \'kraps\ *n pl but sing or pl in constr* [LaF, fr. F *crabs, craps,* fr. E *crabs* lowest throw at hazard, fr. pl. of ¹*crab*] (1843) **1** : a gambling game played with two dice **2** : ³CRAP 2

crap·shoot \'krap-ˌshüt\ *n* (1971) : something (as a business venture) that has an unpredictable outcome

crap·shoot·er \'krap-ˌshü-tər\ *n* (1895) : one who plays craps

crap·u·lous \'kra-pyə-ləs\ *adj* [LL *crapulosus,* fr. L *crapula* intoxication, fr. Gk *kraipalē*] (1536) **1** : marked by intemperance esp. in eating or drinking **2** : sick from excessive indulgence in liquor

¹**crash** \'krash\ *vb* [ME *crasschen*] *vt* (15c) **1 a** : to break violently and noisily : SMASH **b** : to damage (an airplane) in landing **2 a** : to cause to make a loud noise ⟨~ the cymbals together⟩ **b** : to force (as one's way) through with loud crashing noises **3** : to enter or attend without invitation or without paying ⟨~ the party⟩ **~** *vi* **1 a** : to break or go to pieces with or as if with violence and noise **b** : to fall, land, or hit with destructive force **c** : to decline suddenly and steeply **d** *of a computer system or program* : to suffer a sudden major failure usu. with attendant loss of data **2** : to make a smashing noise ⟨thunder ~*ing* overhead⟩ **3** : to move or force one's way with or as if with a crash ⟨~*es* into the room⟩ **4** *slang* : to experience the aftereffects (as dysphoria or depression) of drug intoxication **5** *slang* : to go to bed or fall asleep; *also* : to reside temporarily : STAY ⟨~*ing* with friends for a few days⟩ — **crash·er** *n*

²**crash** *n* (ca. 1580) **1** : a loud sound (as of things smashing) ⟨a ~ of thunder⟩ **2 a** : a breaking to pieces by or as if by collision **b** : an instance of crashing ⟨a plane ~⟩ ⟨a system ~⟩ **3** : a sudden decline (as of a population) or failure (as of a business) ⟨a stockmarket ~⟩ **4** *slang* : the process of crashing after drug intoxication

³**crash** *adj* (1945) : marked by a concerted effort and effected in the shortest possible time ⟨a ~ program⟩

⁴**crash** *n* [prob. fr. Russ *krashenina* colored linen] (1812) : a coarse fabric used for draperies, toweling, and clothing and for strengthening joints of cased-in books

crash dive *n* (1918) : a dive made by a submarine in the least possible time — **crash–dive** *vi*

crash helmet *n* (ca. 1918) : a helmet that is worn (as by motorcyclists) as protection for the head in the event of an accident

crash·ing \'kra-shin\ *adj* (1924) **1** : UTTER, ABSOLUTE ⟨a ~ bore⟩ **2** : SUPERLATIVE ⟨a ~ effect⟩ — **crash·ing·ly** \-lē\ *adv*

crash–land \'krash-'land\ *vt* (1941) : to land (an airplane or spacecraft) under emergency conditions usu. with damage to the craft **~** *vi* : to crash-land an airplane or spacecraft — **crash landing** *n*

crash pad *n* (1939) **1** : protective padding (as on the inside of an automobile or a tank) **2** : a place to stay temporarily

crash·wor·thy \'krash-ˌwər-thē\ *adj* (1966) : resistant to the effects of collision ⟨~ cars⟩ — **crash·wor·thi·ness** *n*

crass \'kras\ *adj* [L *crassus* thick, gross] (1653) **1 a** : GROSS 6a; *esp* : having or indicating such grossness of mind as precludes delicacy and discrimination **b** : being beneath one's dignity ⟨~ concerns of daily life⟩ **c** — used as a pejorative intensifier ⟨~ flattery⟩ ⟨~ propaganda⟩ **2** : guided by or indicative of base or materialistic values ⟨~ commercialism⟩ ⟨~ measures of success⟩ *syn* see STUPID — **crass·ly** *adv* — **crass·ness** *n*

cras·si·tude \'kra-sə-ˌtüd, -ˌtyüd\ *n* (1679) : the quality or state of being crass : GROSSNESS; *also* : an instance of grossness

-crat *n comb form* [F *-crate,* back-formation fr. *-cratie* -cracy] **1** : advocate or partisan of a (specified) theory of government ⟨theo*crat*⟩ **2** : member of a (specified) dominant class ⟨pluto*crat*⟩ — **-cratic** *adj comb form*

cratch \'krach\ *n* [ME *cracche,* fr. OF *creche* manger — more at CRÈCHE] (13c) **1** *archaic* : MANGER : a crib or rack esp. for fodder; *also* : FRAME

¹**crate** \'krāt\ *n* [ME, fr. L *cratis*] (15c) **1** : an open box of wooden slats or a usu. wooden protective case or framework for shipping **2** : JALOPY

²**crate** *vt* **crat·ed; crat·ing** (1871) : to pack in a crate

¹**cra·ter** \'krā-tər\ *n* [L, mixing bowl, crater, fr. Gk *krater,* fr. *kerannynai* to mix; akin to Skt *śṛṇāti* he mixes] (1613) **1** \'krā-tər\ **a** : the bowl-shaped depression around the orifice of a volcano **b** : a depression formed by the impact of a meteorite **c** : a hole in the ground made by the explosion of a bomb or shell **d** : an eroded lesion **e** : a dimple in a painted surface **2** \'krā-tər, krā-'ter\ : KRATER — **cra·ter·like** \'krā-tər-ˌlīk\ *adj*

²**crater** *vi* (1884) : to exhibit or form craters **~** *vt* : to form craters in

cra·ter·let \'krā-tər-lət\ *n* (1881) : a small crater

C ration *n* (1942) : a canned field ration of the U.S. Army

cra·ton \'krā-ˌtän, 'kra-\ *n* [G *Kraton,* modif. of Gk *kratos* strength — more at HARD] (1944) : a stable relatively immobile area of the earth's crust that forms the nuclear mass of a continent or the central basin of an ocean — **cra·ton·ic** \krə-'tä-nik, krā-, kra-\ *adj*

craunch \'krónch, 'kränch\ *vb* [prob. imit.] (1631) : CRUNCH — **craunch** *n*

cra·vat \krə-'vat\ *n* [F *cravate,* fr. *Crabate, Cravate* Croatian] (ca. 1656) **1** : a band or scarf worn around the neck **2** : NECKTIE

crave \'krāv\ *vb* **craved; crav·ing** [ME, fr. OE *crafian;* akin to ON *krefja* to crave, demand] *vt* (bef. 12c) **1** : to ask for earnestly : BEG, DEMAND ⟨~ a pardon for neglect⟩ **2 a** : to want greatly : NEED ⟨~*s* drugs⟩ **b** : to yearn for ⟨~ a vanished youth⟩ **~** *vi* : to have a strong or inward desire ⟨~*s* after affection⟩ *syn* see DESIRE — **crav·er** *n*

cra·ven \'krā-vən\ *adj* [ME *cravant*] (13c) **1** *archaic* : DEFEATED, VANQUISHED **2** : lacking the least bit of courage : contemptibly fainthearted *syn* see COWARDLY — **craven** *n* — **cra·ven·ly** *adv* — **cra·ven·ness** \-vən-nəs\ *n*

crav·ing \'krā-vin\ *n* (1633) : an intense, urgent, or abnormal desire or longing

craw \'kró\ *n* [ME *crawe,* fr. (assumed) OE *cræga;* perh. akin to L *vorare* to devour — more at VORACIOUS] (14c) **1** : the crop of a bird or insect **2** : the stomach esp. of a lower animal

craw·dad \'kró-ˌdad\ *n* [alter. of *crawfish*] (ca. 1905) : CRAYFISH 1 — used chiefly west of the Appalachians

¹**craw·fish** \'kró-ˌfish\ *n* [by folk etymology fr. ME *crevis, kraveys*] (1624) **1** : CRAYFISH 1 **2** : SPINY LOBSTER

²**crawfish** *vi* (1842) : to retreat from a position : back out

¹**crawl** \'król\ *vb* [ME, fr. ON *krafla*] *vi* (14c) **1** : to move slowly in a prone position without or as if without the use of limbs ⟨the snake ~*ed* into its hole⟩ **2** : to move or progress slowly or laboriously ⟨traffic ~*s* along at 10 miles an hour⟩ **3** : to advance by guile or servility ⟨~*ing* into favor by toadying to his boss⟩ **4** : to spread by extending stems or tendrils **5 a** : to be alive or swarming with or as if with creeping things ⟨a kitchen ~*ing* with ants⟩ **b** : to have the sensation of insects creeping over one ⟨the story made her flesh ~⟩ **6** : to fail to stay evenly spread — used of paint, varnish, or glaze **~** *vt* **1** : to move upon or as if in a creeping manner **2** : to reprove harshly ⟨they got no good right to ~ me for what I wrote —Marjorie K. Rawlings⟩

²**crawl** *n* (1818) **1 a** : the act or action of crawling **b** : slow or laborious progress **c** *chiefly Brit* : a going from one pub to another **2 a** : a prone speed swimming stroke consisting of alternating overarm strokes and a flutter kick **3** : lettering that moves vertically or horizontally across a television or motion-picture screen to give information (as performer credits or news bulletins)

crawl·er \'kró-lər\ *n* (ca. 1629) **1** : one that crawls **2** : a vehicle (as a crane) that travels on endless chain belts

---

\ə\ abut \'\ kitten, F table \ər\ further \a\ ash \ā\ ace \ä\ mop, mar \aú\ out \ch\ chin \e\ bet \ē\ easy \g\ go \i\ hit \ī\ ice \j\ job \ŋ\ sing \ō\ go \ó\ law \ói\ boy \th\ thin \t͟h\ the \ü\ loot \ú\ foot \y\ yet \zh\ vision \à, k̲, n, œ, œ̄, ɷ, ūe, ᵹ\ *see* Guide to Pronunciation

crawl space *n* (1946) : a shallow unfinished space beneath the first floor or under the roof of a building esp. for access to plumbing or wiring

crawl·way \'krȯl-ˌwā\ *n* (1909) : a low passageway (as in a cave) that can be traversed only by crawling

crawly \'krȯ-lē\ *adj* (1857) **1** : CREEPY 1 **2** : marked by crawling or slow motion ⟨~ creatures⟩

cray·fish \'krā-ˌfish\ *n* [by folk etymology fr. ME *crevis*, fr. MF *crevice*, of Gmc origin; akin to OHG *krebiz* crab — more at CRAB] (14c) **1** : any of numerous freshwater decapod crustaceans (superfamily Astacoidea) resembling the lobster but usu. much smaller **2** : SPINY LOBSTER

crayfish 1

¹cray·on \'krā-ˌän, -ən *also* 'kran\ *n* [F, crayon, pencil, fr. dim. of *craie* chalk, fr. L *creta*] (1644) **1** : a stick of white or colored chalk or of colored wax used for writing or drawing **2** : a crayon drawing

²crayon *vt* (1662) : to draw with a crayon — **cray·on·ist** \'krā-ə-nist\ *n*

¹craze \'krāz\ *vb* **crazed; craz·ing** [ME *crasen* to crush, craze, of Scand origin; akin to OSw *krasa* to crush] *vt* (14c) **1** *obs* : BREAK, SHATTER **2** : to produce minute cracks on the surface or glaze of **3** : to make insane or as if insane ⟨*crazed* by pain and fear⟩ ~ *vi* **1** *archaic* : SHATTER, BREAK **2** : to become insane **3** : to develop a mesh of fine cracks

²craze *n* (1813) **1** : an exaggerated and often transient enthusiasm : MANIA **2** : a crack in a surface or coating (as of glaze or enamel) *syn* see FASHION

¹cra·zy \'krā-zē\ *adj* **cra·zi·er; -est** (1583) **1 a** : full of cracks or flaws : UNSOUND **b** : CROOKED, ASKEW **2 a** : MAD, INSANE **b** (1) : IMPRACTICAL (2) : ERRATIC **c** : being out of the ordinary : UNUSUAL ⟨a taste for ~ hats⟩ **3 a** : distracted with desire or excitement ⟨a thrill-*crazy* mob⟩ **b** : absurdly fond : INFATUATED ⟨he's ~ about the girl⟩ **c** : passionately preoccupied : OBSESSED ⟨~ about boats⟩ — **cra·zi·ly** \-zə-lē\ *adv* — **cra·zi·ness** \-zē-nəs\ *n* — **like crazy** : to an extreme degree ⟨everyone dancing *like crazy*⟩

²crazy *n, pl* **cra·zies** (1867) : one who is or acts crazy; *esp* : such a one associated with a radical or extremist political cause

crazy bone *n* (1876) : FUNNY BONE

crazy quilt *n* (1886) **1** : a patchwork quilt without a design **2** : JUMBLE, HODGEPODGE ⟨a *crazy quilt* of regulations⟩

cra·zy·weed \'krā-zē-ˌwēd\ *n* (ca. 1889) : LOCOWEED

C–re·ac·tive protein \'sē-rē-'ak-tiv-\ *n* [C-*polysaccharide*, a polysaccharide found in the cell wall of pneumococci and precipitated by this protein, fr. *carbohydrate*] (1955) : a protein present in blood serum in various abnormal states (as inflammation or neoplasia)

¹creak \'krēk\ *vi* [ME *creken* to croak, of imit. origin] (1583) : to make a prolonged grating or squeaking sound often as a result of being worn out; *also* : to proceed slowly with or as if with creaking wheels ⟨the story ~s along to a dull conclusion⟩

²creak *n* (1605) : a rasping or grating noise

creaky \'krē-kē\ *adj* **creak·i·er; -est** (1834) **1** : marked by creaking : SQUEAKY ⟨~ shoes⟩ **2** : showing signs of deterioration or decrepitude ⟨a ~ old house⟩ ⟨a ~ economy⟩ — **creak·i·ly** \-kə-lē\ *adv* — **creak·i·ness** \-nəs\ *n*

¹cream \'krēm\ *n, often attrib* [ME *creime, creme*, fr. MF *craime, cresme*, fr. LL *cramum*, of Celt origin; akin to W *cramen* scab, crust] (14c) **1** : the yellowish part of milk containing from 18 to about 40 percent butterfat **2 a** : a food prepared with cream **b** : something having the consistency of cream; *esp* : a usu. emulsified medicinal or cosmetic preparation **3** : the choicest part : BEST ⟨the ~ of the crop⟩ **4** : CREAMER 1 **5 a** : a pale yellow **b** : a cream-colored animal — **cream·i·ly** \'krē-mə-lē\ *adv* — **cream·i·ness** \-mē-nəs\ *n* — **creamy** \-mē\ *adj*

²cream *vi* (1596) **1** : to form cream or a surface layer like the cream on standing milk **2** : to break into or cause something to break into a creamy froth; *also* : to move like froth ~ *vt* **1 a** : SKIM 1c **b** : to remove (something choice) from an aggregate ⟨she has ~ed off her favorite stories from her earlier books —*Times Lit. Supp.*⟩ **2** : to furnish, prepare, or treat with cream; *also* : to dress with a cream sauce **3 a** : to beat into a creamy froth **b** : to work or blend to the consistency of cream ⟨~ butter and sugar together⟩ **c** : to cause to form a surface layer of or like cream **4 a** : to defeat decisively ⟨was ~ed in the first round⟩ **b** : WRECK ⟨~ed the car on the turnpike⟩

cream cheese *n* (1583) : a mild soft unripened cheese made from whole sweet milk enriched with cream

cream·cups \'krēm-ˌkəps\ *n pl but sing or pl in constr* (1888) : a California annual (*Platystemon californicus*) of the poppy family

cream·er \'krē-mər\ *n* (1858) **1** : a small vessel for serving cream **2** : a nondairy product used as a substitute for cream (as in coffee)

cream·ery \'krēm-rē, 'krē-mə-\ *n, pl* **-er·ies** (1872) : an establishment where butter and cheese are made or where milk and cream are prepared or sold

cream of tartar (1662) : a white crystalline salt $C_4H_5KO_6$ used esp. in baking powder and in certain treatments of metals

cream puff *n* (1880) **1** : a round shell of light pastry filled with whipped cream or a cream filling **2** : an ineffectual person **3** : something trifling, inconsiderable, or easily dealt with **4** : a usu. used motor vehicle that is in especially good condition

cream soda *n* (1854) : a carbonated soft drink flavored with vanilla

cream·ware \'krēm-ˌwar, -ˌwer\ *n* (1780) : earthenware having a cream-colored glaze

¹crease \'krēs\ *n* [prob. alter. of earlier *creaste*, fr. ME *creste* crest] (1578) **1** : a line, mark, or ridge made by or as if by folding a pliable substance **2** : a specially marked area in various sports; *esp* : an area surrounding or in front of a goal (as in lacrosse or hockey) — **crease·less** \-ləs\ *adj*

²crease *vb* **creased; creas·ing** *vt* (1588) **1** : to make a crease in or on : WRINKLE ⟨a smile *creased* her face⟩ **2** : to wound slightly esp. by grazing ~ *vi* : to become creased — **creas·er** *n*

¹cre·ate \krē-'āt, 'krē-ˌ\ *vb* **cre·at·ed; cre·at·ing** [ME, fr. L *creatus*, pp.

of *creare*; akin to L *crescere* to grow — more at CRESCENT] *vt* (14c) **1** : to bring into existence ⟨God *created* the heaven and the earth —Gen 1:1 (AV)⟩ **2 a** : to invest with a new form, office, or rank ⟨was *created* a lieutenant⟩ **b** : to produce or bring about by a course of action or behavior ⟨her arrival *created* a terrible fuss⟩ ⟨~ new jobs⟩ **3** : CAUSE, OCCASION ⟨famine ~s high food prices⟩ **4 a** : to produce through imaginative skill ⟨~ a painting⟩ **b** : DESIGN ⟨~s dresses⟩ ~ *vi* : to make or bring into existence something new

²create *adj* (15c) *archaic* : CREATED

cre·a·tine \'krē-ə-ˌtēn, -t'n\ *n* [F *créatine*, fr. Gk *kreat-, kreas* flesh — more at RAW] (1840) : a white crystalline nitrogenous substance $C_4H_9N_3O_2$ found esp. in the muscles of vertebrates either free or as phosphocreatine

creatine phosphate *n* (1945) : PHOSPHOCREATINE

cre·at·i·nine \krē-'a-t'n-ˌēn, -on\ *n* [G *Kreatinin*, fr. *Kreatin* creatine] (1851) : a white crystalline strongly basic compound $C_4H_7N_3O$ formed from creatine and found esp. in muscle, blood, and urine

cre·a·tion \krē-'ā-shən\ *n* (14c) **1** : the act of creating; *esp* : the act of bringing the world into ordered existence **2** : the act of making, inventing, or producing: as **a** : the act of investing with a new rank or office **b** : the first representation of a dramatic role **3** : something that is created: as **a** : WORLD **b** : creatures singly or in aggregate **c** : an original work of art **d** : a new usu. striking article of clothing

cre·a·tion·ism \-shə-ˌni-zəm\ *n* (1880) : a doctrine or theory holding that matter, the various forms of life, and the world were created by God out of nothing and usu. in the way described in Genesis — compare EVOLUTION 4b — **cre·a·tion·ist** \-shə-nist\ *n or adj*

creation science *n* (1979) : CREATIONISM; *also* : scientific evidence or arguments put forth in support of creationism

cre·a·tive \krē-'ā-tiv, 'krē-ˌ\ *adj* (1678) **1** : marked by the ability or power to create : given to creating ⟨the ~ impulse⟩ **2** : having the quality of something created rather than imitated : IMAGINATIVE ⟨the ~ arts⟩ **3** : managed so as to get around legal or conventional limits ⟨~ financing⟩; *also* : deceptively arranged so as to conceal or defraud ⟨~ accounting⟩ — **cre·a·tive·ly** *adv* — **cre·a·tive·ness** *n*

creative evolution *n* (1909) : evolution that is a creative product of a vital force rather than a spontaneous process explicable in terms of scientific laws — compare EMERGENT EVOLUTION

cre·a·tiv·i·ty \ˌkrē-(ˌ)ā-'ti-və-tē, ˌkrē-ə-\ *n* (1875) **1** : the quality of being creative **2** : the ability to create

cre·a·tor \krē-'ā-tər\ *n* (13c) : one that creates usu. by bringing something new or original into being; *esp, cap* : GOD 1

crea·ture \'krē-chər\ *n* [ME, fr. OF, fr. LL *creatura*, fr. L *creatus*, pp. of *creare*] (14c) **1** : something created either animate or inanimate: as **a** : a lower animal; *esp* : a farm animal **b** : a human being ⟨a being of anomalous or uncertain aspect or nature ⟨~s of fantasy⟩ **2** : one that is the servile dependent or tool of another : INSTRUMENT — **crea·tur·al** \'krē-chə-rəl\ *adj* — **crea·ture·hood** \'krē-chər-ˌhùd\ *n* — **crea·ture·li·ness** \-lē-nəs\ *n* — **crea·ture·ly** \-lē\ *adj*

creature comfort *n* (1659) : something (as food, warmth, or special accommodations) that gives bodily comfort

crèche \'kresh, 'krāsh\ *n* [F, fr. OF *creche* manger, crib, of Gmc origin; akin to OHG *krippa* manger — more at CRIB] (1792) **1** : a representation of the Nativity scene **2** : DAY NURSERY **3** : a foundling hospital

cre·dence \'krē-d'n(t)s\ *n* [ME, fr. MF or ML; MF, fr. ML *credentia*, fr. L *credent-, credens*, prp. of *credere* to believe, trust — more at CREED] (14c) **1** : mental acceptance as true or real ⟨give ~ to gossip⟩ **b** : CREDIBILITY 1 ⟨lends ~ to the theory⟩ **2** : CREDENTIALS — used in the phrase *letters of credence* **3** [MF, fr. OIt *credenza*] : a Renaissance sideboard used chiefly for valuable plate **4** : a small table where the bread and wine rest before consecration *syn* see BELIEF

cre·dent \'krē-d'nt\ *adj* [L *credent-, credens*, prp.] (1602) **1** *archaic* : giving credence : CONFIDING **2** *obs* : CREDIBLE

¹cre·den·tial \kri-'den(t)-shəl\ *adj* (15c) : warranting credit or confidence — used chiefly in the phrase *credential letters*

²credential *n* (ca. 1674) **1** : something that gives a title to credit or confidence **2** *pl* : testimonials showing that a person is entitled to credit or has a right to exercise official power **3** : CERTIFICATE, DIPLOMA

³credential *vt* **-tialed** *also* **-tialled; -tial·ing** *also* **-tial·ling** (1888) : to furnish with credentials ⟨to ~ adequate academic performance —K. Patricia Cross⟩

cre·den·tial·ism \-shə-ˌli-zəm\ *n* (1967) : undue emphasis on credentials (as college degrees) as prerequisites to employment

cre·den·za \kri-'den-zə\ *n* [It, lit., belief, confidence, fr. ML *credentia*] (1880) **1** : CREDENCE 3 **2** : a sideboard, buffet, or bookcase patterned after a Renaissance credence; *esp* : one without legs

cred·i·bil·i·ty \ˌkre-də-'bi-lə-tē\ *n* (1594) **1** : the quality or power of inspiring belief ⟨an account lacking in ~⟩ **2** : capacity for belief ⟨strains his reader's ~ —*Times Lit. Supp.*⟩

credibility gap *n* (1966) **1 a** : lack of trust ⟨a *credibility gap* between generations⟩ **b** : lack of believability ⟨a *credibility gap* created by contradictory official statements —Samuel Ellenport⟩ **2** : DISCREPANCY ⟨the *credibility gap* between the professed ideals . . . and their actual practices —Jeanne L. Noble⟩

cred·i·ble \'kre-də-bəl\ *adj* [ME, fr. L *credibilis*, fr. *credere*] (14c) **1** : offering reasonable grounds for being believed ⟨a ~ account of an accident⟩ ⟨~ witnesses⟩ **2** : of sufficient capability to be militarily effective ⟨a ~ deterrent⟩ ⟨~ forces⟩ — **cred·i·bly** \'kre-də-blē\ *adv*

¹cred·it \'kre-dit\ *n* [MF, fr. OIt *credito*, fr. L *creditum* something entrusted to another, loan, fr. neut. of *creditus*, pp. of *credere* to believe, entrust — more at CREED] (1537) **1** : reliance on the truth or reality of something ⟨gave ~ to everything he said⟩ **2 a** : the balance in a person's favor in an account **b** : an amount or sum placed at a person's disposal by a bank **c** : time given for payment for goods or services sold on trust ⟨long-term ~⟩ **d** (1) : an entry on the right-hand side of an account constituting an addition to a revenue, net worth, or liability account (2) : a deduction from an expense or asset account **e** : any one of or the sum of the items entered on the right-hand side of an account **f** : a deduction from an amount otherwise due **3 a** : influence or power derived from enjoying the confidence of another or others **b** : good name : ESTEEM; *also* : financial or commercial trustworthiness **4** *archaic* : CREDIBILITY **5** : a source of honor ⟨a ~ to the school⟩ **6 a** : something that gains or adds to reputation or esteem

: HONOR ⟨took no ~ for his kindly act⟩   **b** : RECOGNITION, ACKNOWL-EDGMENT ⟨quite willing to accept undeserved ~⟩   **7** : recognition by name of a person contributing to a performance (as a film or telecast) ⟨the opening ~s⟩   **8   a** : recognition by a school or college that a student has fulfilled a requirement leading to a degree   **b** : CREDIT HOUR   *syn* see BELIEF, INFLUENCE
²credit *vt* [partly fr. ¹*credit*; partly fr. L *creditus*, pp.] (1541)   **1** : to supply goods on credit to   **2** : to trust in the truth of : BELIEVE   **3** *archaic* : to bring credit or honor upon   **4   a** : to enter upon the credit side of an account   **b** : to place an amount to the credit of ⟨~ his account with ten dollars⟩   **5   a** : to consider usu. favorably as the source, agent, or performer of an action or the possessor of a trait ⟨~s him with an excellent sense of humor⟩   **b** : to attribute to some person ⟨they ~ the invention to him⟩   *syn* see ASCRIBE
cred·it·able \'kre-di-tə-bəl\ *adj* (1526)   **1** : worthy of belief   **2** : sufficiently good to bring esteem or praise   **3** : worthy of commercial credit   **4** : capable of being assigned — **cred·it·abil·i·ty** \,kre-di-tə-'bi-lə-tē\ *n* — **cred·it·able·ness** \'kre-di-tə-bəl-nəs\ *n* — **cred·it·ably** \-blē\ *adv*
credit card *n* (1888) : a card authorizing purchases on credit
credit hour *n* (ca. 1927) : the unit of measuring educational credit usu. based on the number of classroom hours per week throughout a term
credit line *n* (1914)   **1** : a line, note, or name that acknowledges the source of an item (as a news dispatch or television program)   **2** : LINE OF CREDIT
cred·i·tor \'kre-di-tər, -,tȯr\ *n* (15c) : one to whom a debt is owed; *esp* : a person to whom money or goods are due
credit union *n* (1881) : a cooperative association that makes small loans to its members at low interest rates
cred·it·wor·thy \'kre-dit-,wər-thē\ *adj* (1924) : financially sound enough to justify the extension of credit — **cred·it·wor·thi·ness** *n*
cre·do \'krē-(,)dō, 'krā-\ *n, pl* **credos** [ME, fr. L, I believe] (12c) : CREED
cre·du·li·ty \kri-'dü-lə-tē, -'dyü-\ *n* (15c) : readiness or willingness to believe esp. on slight or uncertain evidence
cred·u·lous \'kre-jə-ləs\ *adj* [L *credulus*, fr. *credere*] (1576)   **1** : ready to believe esp. on slight or uncertain evidence   **2** : proceeding from credulity — **cred·u·lous·ly** *adv* — **cred·u·lous·ness** *n*
Cree \'krē\ *n, pl* **Cree** *or* **Crees** [CanF *Cris*, pl., short for *Cristinaux*, fr. Ojibwa dial. *kirištino*, sing., member of a band living south of James Bay] (1744)   **1** : a member of an American Indian people of Quebec, Ontario, Manitoba, and Saskatchewan   **2** : the Algonquian language of the Cree people
creed \'krēd\ *n* [ME *crede*, fr. OE *crēda*, fr. L *credo* (first word of the Apostles' and Nicene Creeds), fr. *credere* to believe, trust, entrust; akin to OIr *cretid* he believes, Skt *śrad-dadhāti*] (bef. 12c)   **1** : a brief authoritative formula of religious belief   **2** : a set of fundamental beliefs; *also* : a guiding principle — **creed·al** *or* **cre·dal** \'krē-d⁰l\ *adj*
creek \'krēk, 'krik\ *n* [ME *crike, creke*, fr. ON *-kriki* bend] (13c)   **1** *chiefly Brit* : a small inlet or bay narrower and extending farther inland than a cove   **2** : a natural stream of water normally smaller than and often tributary to a river   **3** *archaic* : a narrow or winding passage — **up the creek** : in a difficult or perplexing situation
Creek \'krēk\ *n* (1725)   **1** : an American Indian confederacy of peoples chiefly of Muskogean stock of Alabama, Georgia, and Florida   **2** : a member of any of the Creek peoples   **3** : the Muskogean language of the Creek Indians
¹creel \'krē(ə)l\ *n* [ME *creille, crele*] (14c)   **1** : a wicker basket (as for carrying newly caught fish)   **2** : a bar with skewers for holding bobbins in a spinning machine
²creel *vt* (1844) : to put (caught fish) in a creel
¹creep \'krēp\ *vi* **crept** \'krept\; **creep·ing** [ME *crepen*, fr. OE *crēopan*; akin to ON *krjūpa* to creep] (bef. 12c)   **1   a** : to move along with the body prone and close to the ground   **b** : to move slowly on hands and knees   **2   a** : to go very slowly ⟨the hours *crept* by⟩   **b** : to go timidly or cautiously so as to escape notice ⟨she *crept* away from the festive scene⟩   **c** : to enter or advance gradually so as to be almost unnoticed ⟨age ~s up on us⟩ ⟨a note of irritation *crept* into her voice⟩   **3** : to have the sensation of being covered with creeping things ⟨the thought made his flesh ~⟩   **4** *of a plant* : to spread or grow over a surface rooting at intervals or clinging with tendrils, stems, or aerial roots   **5   a** : to slip or gradually shift position   **b** : to change shape permanently from prolonged stress or exposure to high temperatures
²creep *n* (1818)   **1** : a movement of or like creeping ⟨traffic moving at a ~⟩   **2** : a distressing sensation like that caused by the creeping of insects over one's flesh; *esp* : a feeling of apprehension or horror — usu. used in pl. with *the* ⟨that gives me the creeps⟩   **3** : a feed trough or enclosure that young animals can enter while adults are excluded   **4** : the slow change of dimensions of an object from prolonged exposure to high temperature or stress   **5** : an unpleasant or obnoxious person
creep·age \'krē-pij\ *n* (1903) : gradual movement : CREEP
creep·er \'krē-pər\ *n* (bef. 12c)   **1** : one that creeps: as   **a** : a creeping plant   **b** : a bird (as of the family Certhiidae) that creeps about on trees or bushes searching for insects   **c** : a creeping insect or reptile   **2** : any of various devices used for creeping: as   **a** : a fixture with iron points worn on the shoe to prevent slipping   **b** : a low wheeled platform for supporting the body when working under an automobile   **3** : a usu. one-piece garment for a child at the crawling age
creep·ing \'krē-piŋ\ *adj* (14c) : developing or advancing by slow imperceptible degrees ⟨a period of ~ inflation⟩
creeping eruption *n* (1926) : a skin disorder marked by a spreading red line of eruption and caused esp. by larvae (as of hookworms) not normally parasitic in humans) burrowing beneath the human skin
creepy \'krē-pē\ *adj* **creep·i·er; -est** (1883)   **1** : producing a nervous shivery apprehension ⟨~ things were crawling over us⟩ ⟨a ~ horror story⟩   **2** : of, relating to, or being a creep : annoyingly unpleasant — **creep·i·ly** \-pə-lē\ *adv* — **creep·i·ness** \-pē-nəs\ *n*
creese *var of* KRIS
cre·mains \kri-'mānz\ *n pl* [blend of *cremated* and *remains*] (1947) : the ashes of a cremated human body
cre·mate \'krē-,māt, kri-'\ *vt* **cre·mat·ed; cre·mat·ing** [L *crematus*, pp. of *cremare* to burn up, cremate] (1874) : to reduce (as a dead body) to ashes by burning — **cre·ma·tion** \kri-'mā-shən\ *n*

cre·ma·to·ri·um \,krē-mə-'tōr-ē-əm, ,kre-, -'tȯr-\ *n, pl* **-ri·ums** *or* **-ria** \-ē-ə\ (1880) : CREMATORY
cre·ma·to·ry \'krē-mə-,tōr-ē, 'kre-, -,tȯr-\ *n, pl* **-ries** (1876) : a furnace for cremating; *also* : an establishment containing such a furnace — **crematory** *adj*
crème *or* **creme** \'krem *also* 'krēm *or* 'kräm\ *n, pl* **crèmes** *or* **cremes** \'krem(z), 'krēmz\ [F, fr. OF *cresme* — more at CREAM] (ca. 1821)   **1** : a sweet liqueur   **2** : cream or a preparation made with or resembling cream used in cooking   **3** : CREAM 2b
crème an·glaise \-,äⁿ-'glāz, -aŋ-, -,äⁿ-'glez\ *n* [F, lit., English cream] (1975) : a vanilla-flavored custard sauce usu. served with desserts
crème brû·lée \-brü-'lā, -brü-\ *n* [F, lit., scorched cream] (1886) : a rich custard topped with caramelized sugar
crème car·a·mel \-,kár-ə-'mel, *or see* CARAMEL\ *n* [F, lit., caramel cream] (1906) : a custard that has been baked with caramel sauce
crème de ca·cao \'krem-də-'kō-(,)kō, ,krem-də-kə-'kaù, -kə-'kā-(,)ō\ *n* [F, lit., cream of cacao] (1904) : a sweet brown or colorless liqueur flavored with cacao beans and vanilla
crème de la crème \'krem-də-lä-'krem, -lə-\ *n* [F, lit., cream of the cream] (1848) : the very best
crème de menthe \'krem-də-'men(t)th, 'krēm-, -'mint, 'krem-də-'mänt\ *n* [F, lit., cream of mint] (1901) : a sweet green or colorless mint-flavored liqueur
crème fraîche *or* **crème fraiche** \'krem-'fresh *also* 'krēm- *or* 'kräm-\ *n* [F, lit., fresh cream] (1950) : heavy cream thickened and slightly soured with buttermilk and often served on fruit
cre·nate \'krē-,nāt\ *or* **cre·nat·ed** \-,nā-təd\ *adj* [NL *crenatus*, fr. ML *crena* notch] (1794) : having the margin or surface cut into rounded scallops ⟨a ~ leaf⟩
cre·na·tion \kri-'nā-shən\ *n* (1846)   **1   a** : a crenate formation; *esp* : one of the rounded projections on an edge (as of a coin)   **b** : the quality or state of being crenate   **2** : shrinkage of red blood cells resulting in crenate margins
cren·el·lat·ed *or* **cren·el·at·ed** \'kre-n⁰l-,ā-təd\ *adj* [F *créneler* to furnish with embrasures, fr. OF *querneler*, fr. *kernel, crenel* embrasure, dim. of *cren* notch, fr. *crener* to notch; akin to ML *crena*] (ca. 1823) : having crenellations
cren·el·la·tion *also* **cren·el·a·tion** \,kre-n⁰l-'ā-shən\ *n* (1849)   **1** : BATTLEMENT   **2** : any of the embrasures alternating with merlons in a battlement — see BATTLEMENT illustration
cren·u·lat·ed \'kre-nyə-,lā-təd\ *or* **cren·u·late** \-lət, -,lāt\ *adj* [NL *crenulatus*, fr. *crenula*, dim. of ML *crena*] (1794) : having an irregularly wavy or serrate outline ⟨a ~ shoreline⟩ — **cren·u·la·tion** \,kren-yə-'lā-shən\ *n*
cre·ole \'krē-,ōl\ *adj* (1748)   **1** *often cap* : of or relating to Creoles or their language   **2** *often cap* : relating to or being highly seasoned food typically prepared with rice, okra, tomatoes, and peppers ⟨shrimp ~⟩
Cre·ole \'krē-,ōl\ *n* [F *créole*, fr. Sp *criollo*, fr. Pg *crioulo* white person born in the colonies] (1737)   **1** : a person of European descent born esp. in the West Indies or Spanish America   **2   a** : white person descended from early French or Spanish settlers of the U.S. Gulf states and preserving their speech and culture   **3** : a person of mixed French or Spanish and black descent speaking a dialect of French or Spanish   **4   a** : a language evolved from pidginized French that is spoken by blacks in southern Louisiana   **b** : HAITIAN   **c** *not cap* : a language that has evolved from a pidgin but serves as the native language of a speech community
cre·ol·ise *Brit var of* CREOLIZE
cre·ol·ize \'krē-ə-,līz, 'krē-ō-\ *vt* **-ized; -iz·ing** (ca. 1932) : to cause (a pidginized language) to become a creole in a speech community — **cre·ol·i·za·tion** \,krē-ə-lə-'zā-shən, ,krē-(,)ō-\ *n*
¹cre·o·sote \'krē-ə-,sōt\ *n* [G *Kreosot*, fr. Gk *kreas* flesh + *sōtēr* preserver, fr. *sōzein* to preserve, fr. *sōs* safe (prob. akin to Skt *taviti* he is strong); fr. its antiseptic properties — more at RAW] (1835)   **1** : a clear or yellowish flammable oily liquid mixture of phenolic compounds obtained by the distillation of wood tar esp. from beech wood   **2** : a brownish oily liquid consisting chiefly of aromatic hydrocarbons obtained by distillation of coal tar and used esp. as a wood preservative   **3** : a dark brown or black flammable tar deposited from esp. wood smoke on the walls of a chimney
²creosote *vt* **-sot·ed; -sot·ing** (1846) : to treat with creosote
creosote bush *n* (1846) : a resinous desert shrub (*Larrea tridentata*) of the caltrop family found in the southwestern U.S. and Mexico
crepe *or* **crêpe** \'krāp\ *n* [F *crêpe* — more at CRAPE] (1797)   **1** : a light crinkled fabric woven of any of various fibers   **2** : CRAPE 2   **3** : crude rubber in the form of nearly white to brown crinkled sheets used esp. for shoe soles ⟨crepe-soled shoes⟩   **4** : a small very thin pancake — **crepe** *adj* — **crep·ey** *or* **crepy** \'krā-pē\ *adj*
crepe de chine *or* **crêpe de chine** \,krāp-də-'shēn\ *n, often cap 2d C* [F *crêpe de Chine*, lit., China crepe] (1872) : a soft fine or sheer clothing crepe esp. of silk
crepe myrtle *or* **crêpe myrtle** \-'mir-t⁰l\ *n* (1916) : CRAPE MYRTLE
crepe paper *n* (1897) : paper with a crinkled or puckered texture
crêpe su·zette \,krāp-sü-'zet\ *n, pl* **crêpes suzette** \,krāp(s)-sü-'zet\ *or* **crêpe suzettes** \-'zets\ *often cap S* [F *crêpe Suzette*, prob. fr. *Suzette*, nickname of Suzanne Reichenberg †1924 Fr. actress] (1922) : a thin folded or rolled pancake in a hot orange-butter sauce that is sprinkled with a liqueur (as cognac or curaçao) and set ablaze for serving
crep·i·tant \'kre-pə-tənt\ *adj* (1855) : having or making a crackling sound ⟨~ sounds in breathing⟩
crep·i·tate \'kre-pə-,tāt\ *vi* **-tat·ed; -tat·ing** [L *crepitatus*, pp. of *crepitare* to crackle, freq. of *crepare* to rattle, crack] (ca. 1828) : to make a crackling sound : CRACKLE — **crep·i·ta·tion** \,kre-pə-'tā-shən\ *n*
cre·pon \'krā-,pän\ *n* [F, fr. *crêpe*] (ca. 1864) : a heavy crepe fabric with lengthwise crinkles
crept *past and past part of* CREEP

\ə\ abut \ᵊ\ kitten, F table \ər\ further \a\ ash \ā\ ace \ä\ mop, mar \aù\ out \ch\ chin \e\ bet \ē\ easy \g\ go \i\ hit \ī\ ice \j\ job \ŋ\ sing \ō\ go \ò\ law \òi\ boy \th\ thin \t͟h\ the \ü\ loot \ù\ foot \y\ yet \zh\ vision \ā, ḵ, ⁿ, œ, œ̄, ᵫ, ᵫ̄, ᵞ\ *see* Guide to Pronunciation

cre·pus·cu·lar \kri-'pəs-kyə-lər\ *adj* (1668) **1** : of, relating to, or resembling twilight : DIM **2** : active in the twilight ⟨~ insects⟩

cre·pus·cule \kri-'pəs-(,)kyü(ə)l\ *or* **cre·pus·cle** \-'pə-səl\ *n* [L *crepusculum,* fr. *creper* dusky] (14c) : TWILIGHT

¹cre·scen·do \kri-'shen-(,)dō\ *n, pl* **-dos** *or* **-does** *also* **-di** \-dē\ [It, fr. *crescendo,* adj., increasing, gerund of *crescere* to grow, increase, fr. L] (1776) **1 a** : a gradual increase; *specif* : a gradual increase in volume of a musical passage **b** : the peak of a gradual increase : CLIMAX ⟨complaints about stifling smog conditions reach a ~ —*Down Beat*⟩ **2** : a crescendo musical passage — **crescendo** *vi*

²crescendo *adv or adj* (1859) : with an increase in volume — used as a direction in music

¹cres·cent \'kre-sᵊnt\ *n* [ME *cressant,* fr. MF *creissant,* fr. prp. of *creistre* to grow, increase, fr. L *crescere;* akin to OHG *hirsi* millet, Lith *šerti* to feed, Gk *koros* boy] (15c) **1 a** : the moon at any stage between new moon and first quarter and between last quarter and the succeeding new moon when less than half of the illuminated hemisphere is visible **b** : the figure of the moon at such a stage defined by a convex and a concave edge **2** : something shaped like a crescent — **cres·cen·tic** \kre-'sen-tik, krə-\ *adj*

²crescent *adj* [L *crescent-, crescens,* prp. of *crescere*] (1574) : marked by an increase

Cres·cent \'kre-sᵊnt\ *trademark* — used for an adjustable open-end wrench

cres·cive \'kre-siv\ *adj* [L *crescere* to grow] (1566) : marked by gradual spontaneous development — **cres·cive·ly** *adv*

cre·sol \'krē-,sòl, -,sōl\ *n* [ISV, irreg. fr. *creosote*] (ca. 1869) : any of three poisonous colorless crystalline or liquid isomeric phenols C_7H_8O

cress \'kres\ *n* [ME *cresse,* fr. OE *cærse, cressa;* akin to OHG *kressa* cress] (bef. 12c) : any of numerous crucifers (esp. genera *Lepidium* and *Nasturtium*) with moderately pungent leaves used esp. in salads

cres·set \'kre-sət\ *n* [ME, fr. MF, fr. OF *craisset,* fr. *craisse* grease — more at GREASE] (14c) : an iron vessel or basket used for holding an illuminant (as oil) and mounted as a torch or suspended as a lantern

Cres·si·da \'kre-sə-də\ *n* : a Trojan woman of medieval legend who pledges herself to Troilus but while a captive of the Greeks gives herself to Diomedes

¹crest \'krest\ *n* [ME *creste,* fr. MF, fr. L *crista;* prob. akin to L *crinis* hair] (14c) **1 a** : a showy tuft or process on the head of an animal and esp. a bird — see BIRD illustration **b** : the plume or identifying emblem worn on a knight's helmet; *also* : the top of a helmet **c** (1) : a heraldic representation of the crest (2) : a heraldic device depicted above the escutcheon but not upon a helmet (3) : COAT OF ARMS 2a **d** : a ridge or prominence on a part of an animal body **2** : something suggesting a crest esp. in being an upper prominence, edge, or limit: as **a** : PEAK; *esp* : the top line of a mountain or hill **b** : the ridge of a roof **c** : the top of a wave **3 a** : a high point of an action or process and esp. of one that is rhythmic **b** : CLIMAX, CULMINATION ⟨at the ~ of his fame⟩ — **crest·al** \'kres-tᵊl\ *adj* — **crest·less** \-ləs\ *adj*

²crest *vt* (15c) **1** : to furnish with a crest; *also* : CROWN **2** : to reach the crest of ⟨~ed the hill and looked around⟩ ~ *vi* : to rise to a crest ⟨waves ~ing in the storm⟩

crest·ed \'kres-təd\ *adj* (14c) : having a crest ⟨a ~ bird⟩

crested wheatgrass *n* (1923) : either of two Eurasian grasses (*Agropyron cristatum* or *A. sibericum* syn. *A. desertorum*) that are grown in the U.S. for forage and for erosion control

crest·fall·en \'krest-,fò-lən\ *adj* (1589) **1** : having a drooping crest or hanging head **2** : feeling shame or humiliation : DEJECTED — **crest·fall·en·ly** *adv* — **crest·fall·en·ness** \-lən-nəs\ *n*

crest·ing \'kres-tiŋ\ *n* (1908) : a decorative edging or railing (as on pottery or furniture)

cre·syl \'kre-səl, 'krē-,sil\ *n* [ISV *cresol* + *-yl*] (ca. 1872) : TOLYL

Cre·ta·ceous \kri-'tā-shəs\ *adj* [L *cretaceus* resembling chalk, fr. *creta* chalk] (1832) : of, relating to, or being the last period of the Mesozoic era characterized by continued dominance of reptiles, emergent dominance of angiosperms, diversification of mammals, and the extinction of many organisms at the close of the period; *also* : of, relating to, or being the corresponding system of rocks — see GEOLOGIC TIME table — **Cretaceous** *n*

cre·tin \'krē-tᵊn\ *n* [F *crétin,* fr. F dial. *cretin,* lit., wretch, innocent victim, fr. L *christianus* Christian] (1779) **1** : one afflicted with cretinism **2** : a stupid, vulgar, or insensitive person : CLOD, LOUT — **cre·tinous** \-tᵊn-əs\ *adj*

cre·tin·ism \-tᵊn-,i-zəm\ *n* (1801) : a usu. congenital abnormal condition marked by physical stunting and mental retardation and caused by severe hypothyroidism

cre·tonne \'krē-,tän, kri-'\ *n* [F, fr *Creton,* Normandy] (1870) : a strong cotton or linen cloth used esp. for curtains and upholstery

Creutz·feldt–Ja·kob disease *also* **Creutz·feld–Ja·kob disease** \'kròits-,felt-'yä-(,)kōb-\ *n* [Hans G. *Creutzfeldt* †1964 Ger. psychiatrist and Alfons M. *Jakob* †1931 Ger. psychiatrist] (1963) : a rare progressive fatal encephalopathy caused by a slow virus and marked by development of porous brain tissue, premature dementia in middle age, and gradual loss of muscular coordination

cre·val·le \kri-'va-lē\ *n* [by alter.] (1879) : CAVALLA 1; *esp* : JACK CREVALLE

cre·vasse \kri-'vas\ *n* [F, fr. OF *crevace*] (1813) **1** : a breach in a levee **2** : a deep crevice or fissure (as in a glacier or the earth)

crev·ice \'kre-vəs\ *n* [ME, fr. MF *crevace,* fr. OF, fr. *crever* to break, fr. L *crepare* to crack] (14c) : a narrow opening resulting from a split or crack (as in a cliff) : FISSURE

¹crew \'krü\ *chiefly Brit past of* CROW

²crew \'krü\ *n* [ME *crue,* lit., reinforcement, fr. MF *creue* increase, fr. *creistre* to grow — more at CRESCENT] (1455) **1** *archaic* : a band or force of armed men **2** : a group of people associated together in a common activity or by common traits or interests **3 a** : a company of people working on one job or under one foreman or operating a machine **b** : the whole company belonging to a ship sometimes including the officers and master; *also* : one who assists the skipper of a sailboat **c** : the persons who have duties on an aircraft in flight **d** : the rowers and coxswain of a racing shell; *also* : ROWING — **crew·less** \-ləs\ *adj*

³crew *vi* (1935) : to act as a member of a crew ~ *vt* : to serve as a crew member on (as a ship or aircraft)

crew cut *n* (1942) : a very short haircut usu. for men or boys in which the hair resembles the bristle surface of a brush

crew·el \'krü-əl\ *n* [ME *crule*] (15c) **1** : slackly twisted worsted yarn used for embroidery **2** : CREWELWORK

crew·el·work \-,wərk\ *n* (1863) : embroidery work with crewel

crew·man \'krü-mən\ *n* (ca. 1927) : a member of a crew

crew·mate \-,māt\ *n* (1938) : a fellow crewman

crew neck *n* [fr. the sweaters with this neckline worn by oarsmen] (1940) **1** : a round collarless neckline **2** *usu* **crew-neck** \'krü-,nek\ : a sweater with a crew neck

crew sock *n* (1948) : a short bulky usu. ribbed sock

¹crib \'krib\ *n* [ME, fr. OE *cribb;* akin to OHG *krippa* manger, and perh. to Gk *griphos* reed basket] (bef. 12c) **1** : a manger for feeding animals **2** : an enclosure esp. of framework: as **a** : a stall for a stabled animal **b** : a small child's bedstead with high enclosing usu. slatted sides **c** : any of various devices resembling a crate or framework in structure **d** : a building for storage : BIN **3 a** : a small narrow room or dwelling : HUT, SHACK **b** : a room or shack used for prostitution **4** : the cards discarded in cribbage for the dealer to use in scoring **5 a** : a small theft **b** : PLAGIARISM **c** : a literal translation; *esp* : PONY 3 **d** : a summary and key to understanding a literary work **e** : something used for cheating in an examination **6** : CRÈCHE 1

²crib *vb* **cribbed; crib·bing** *vt* (1605) **1** : CONFINE, CRAMP **2** : to provide with or put into a crib; *esp* : to line or support with a framework of timber **3** : PILFER, STEAL; *esp* : PLAGIARIZE ~ *vi* **1 a** : STEAL, PLAGIARIZE **b** : to use a crib : CHEAT **2** : to have the vice of cribbing — **crib·ber** *n*

crib·bage \'kri-bij\ *n* [¹*crib*] (1630) : a card game for two players in which each player tries to form various counting combinations of cards

crib·bing \'kri-biŋ\ *n* (1841) **1** : material for use in making a crib **2** : a vice of horses in which they gnaw (as at the manger) while slobbering and salivating

crib biting *n* (1831) : CRIBBING 2

crib death *n* (1965) : SUDDEN INFANT DEATH SYNDROME

crib·ri·form \'kri-brə-,fòrm\ *adj* [L *cribrum* sieve; akin to L *cernere* to sift — more at CERTAIN] (1741) : pierced with small holes

cri·ce·tid \krī-'sē-təd, -'se-\ *n* [ultim. fr. NL *Cricetus,* genus name, of Slav origin; akin to Czech *křeček* hamster] (1960) : any of a family (Cricetidae) of small rodents including the hamsters — **cricetid** *adj*

¹crick \'krik\ *n* [ME *cryk*] (15c) : a painful spasmodic condition of muscles (as of the neck or back)

²crick *vt* (1884) **1** : to cause a crick in (as the neck) **2** : to turn or twist (as the head) esp. into a strained position

¹crick·et \'kri-kət\ *n* [ME *criket,* fr. MF *criquet,* of imit. origin] (14c) **1** : any of a family (Gryllidae) of leaping orthopteran insects noted for the chirping notes produced by the male by rubbing together specially modified parts of the forewings **2** : a low wooden footstool **3** : a small metal toy or signaling device that makes a sharp click or snap when pressed

²cricket *n* [MF *criquet* goal stake in a bowling game] (1598) **1** : a game played with a ball and bat by two sides of usu. 11 players each on a large field centering upon two wickets each defended by a batsman **2** : fair and honorable behavior ⟨it wasn't ~ for her to break her contract —Gerry Nadel⟩

³cricket *vi* (ca. 1809) : to play the game of cricket — **crick·et·er** *n*

cri·coid \'krī-,kòid\ *adj* [NL *cricoides,* fr. Gk *krikoeidēs* ring-shaped, fr. *krikos* ring — more at CIRCLE] (1746) : of, relating to, or being a cartilage of the larynx with which arytenoid cartilages articulate

cri de coeur \krē-də-'kər\ *n, pl* **cris de coeur** *same*\ [F, lit., cry from the heart] (1904) : a passionate outcry (as of appeal or protest)

cri·er \'krī(-ə)r\ *n* (14c): one that cries: **a** : an officer who proclaims the orders of a court **b** : TOWN CRIER

cri·key \'krī-kē\ *or* **cri·key** \'krī-kē\ *interj* [euphemism for *Christ*] (1838) — used as a mild oath

crime \'krīm\ *n* [ME, fr. MF, fr. L *crimen* accusation, reproach, crime; prob. akin to L *cernere* to sift, determine] (14c) **1** : an act or the commission of an act that is forbidden or the omission of a duty that is commanded by public law and that makes the offender liable to punishment by that law; *esp* : a gross violation of law **2** : a grave offense esp. against morality **3** : criminal activity ⟨efforts to fight ~⟩ **4** : something reprehensible, foolish, or disgraceful ⟨it's a ~ to waste good food⟩ *syn* see OFFENSE — **crime·less** \-ləs\ *adj*

crime against humanity *n* (1945) : atrocity (as extermination or enslavement) that is directed esp. against an entire population or part of a population on specious grounds and without regard to individual guilt or responsibility even on such grounds

crime against nature *n* (1828) : SODOMY

¹crim·i·nal \'kri-mə-nᵊl, 'krim-nəl\ *adj* [ME, fr. MF or LL; MF *criminel,* fr. LL *criminalis,* fr. L *crimin- crimen* crime] (15c) **1** : relating to, involving, or being a crime ⟨~ neglect⟩ **2** : relating to crime or to the prosecution of suspects in a crime ⟨~ statistics⟩ ⟨brought ~ action⟩ **3** : guilty of crime; *also* : of or befitting a criminal ⟨a ~ mind⟩ **4** : DISGRACEFUL — **crim·i·nal·ly** *adv*

²criminal *n* (ca. 1626) **1** : one who has committed a crime **2** : a person who has been convicted of a crime

criminal conversation *n* (1768) : adultery considered as a tort

criminal court *n* (1678) : a court that has jurisdiction to try and punish offenders against criminal law

crim·i·nal·is·tics \,kri-mə-nᵊl-'is-tiks, ,krim-nə-'lis-\ *n pl but sing in constr* (1943) : application of scientific techniques in collecting and analyzing physical evidence in criminal cases

crim·i·nal·i·ty \,kri-mə-'na-lə-tē\ *n* (1611) **1** : the quality or state of being criminal **2** : criminal activity ⟨urban ~⟩

crim·i·nal·ize \'kri-mə-nᵊl-,īz, 'krim-nə-,līz\ *vt* **-ized; -iz·ing** (ca. 1956) : to make illegal : OUTLAW; *also* : to turn into or treat as a criminal — **crim·i·nal·i·za·tion** \,kri-mə-nᵊl-ᵊl-ə-'zā-shən, ,krim-nə-lə-'zā-\ *n*

criminal law *n* (1864) : the law of crimes and their punishments

criminal lawyer *n* (1869) : a lawyer who specializes in criminal law; *esp* : a lawyer who represents defendants in criminal cases

crim·i·nate \'kri-mə-,nāt\ *vt* **-nat·ed; -nat·ing** [L *criminatus,* pp. of *criminari,* fr. *crimin- crimen* accusation] (1645) : INCRIMINATE — **crim·i·na·tion** \,kri-mə-'nā-shən\ *n*

crim·i·nol·o·gy \,kri-mə-'nä-lə-jē\ *n* [It *criminologia,* fr. L *crimin- crimen* + It *-o-* + *-logia* -logy] (1890) : the scientific study of crime as a social phenomenon, of criminals, and of penal treatment — **crim·i·no·log·i·cal** \-mə-n⁻¹-'ä-ji-kəl\ *adj* — **crim·i·no·log·i·cal·ly** \-k(ə-)lē\ *adv* — **crim·i·nol·o·gist** \₁kri-mə-'nä-lə-jist\ *n*

crim·i·nous \'kri-mə-nəs\ *adj* (15c) : CRIMINAL

¹crimp \'krimp\ *vt* [D or LG *krimpen* to shrivel; akin to MD *crampe* hook, cramp] (1712) **1** : to cause to become wavy, bent, or pinched: as **a** : to form (leather) into a desired shape **b** : to give (synthetic fibers) a curl or wave like that of natural fibers **c** : to pinch or press together (as the margins of a pie crust) in order to seal **2** : to be an inhibiting or restraining influence on : CRAMP ⟨sales had been ~ed by credit controls —*Time*⟩ — **crimp·er** \'krim-pər\ *n*

²crimp *n* (1863) **1** : something produced by or as if by crimping: as **a** : a section of hair artificially waved or curled **b** : a succession of waves (as in wool fiber) **c** : a bend or crease formed in something **2** : something that cramps or inhibits : RESTRAINT, CURB

³crimp *n* [perh. fr. ¹crimp] (1758) : a person who entraps or forces men into shipping as sailors or into enlisting in an army or navy

⁴crimp *vt* (1812) : to trap into military or sea service : IMPRESS

crimpy \'krim-pē\ *adj* **crimp·i·er; -est** (1888) : FRIZZY

¹crim·son \'krim-zən\ *n* [ME *crimsin*, fr. OSp *cremesín*, fr. Ar *qirmizī*, fr. *qirmiz* kermes] (15c) : any of several deep purplish reds

²crimson *adj* (15c) : of the color crimson

³crimson *vt* (1601) : to make crimson ~ *vi* : to become crimson; *esp* : BLUSH

¹cringe \'krinj\ *vi* **cringed; cring·ing** [ME *crengen;* akin to OE *cringan* to yield, MHG *krank* weak] (13c) **1** : to draw in or contract one's muscles involuntarily (as from cold or pain) **2** : to shrink in fear or servility **3** : to behave in an excessively humble or servile way *syn* see FAWN — **cring·er** *n*

²cringe *n* (1597) : a cringing act; *specif* : a servile bow

crin·gle \'krin-gəl\ *n* [LG *kringel*, dim. of *kring* ring] (1627) : a loop or grommet at the corner of a sail to which a line is attached

¹crin·kle \'krin-kəl\ *vb* **crin·kled; crin·kling** \-k(ə-)liŋ\ [ME *crynkelen;* akin to OE *cringan* to yield] *vi* (14c) **1** : to form many short bends or ripples **b** : WRINKLE **2** : to give forth a thin crackling sound : RUSTLE ⟨*crinkling* silks⟩ ~ *vt* : to cause to crinkle : make crinkles in

²crinkle *n* (1596) **1** : WRINKLE, CORRUGATION, PUCKER **2** : any of several plant diseases marked by crinkling of leaves — **crin·kly** \-k(ə-)lē\ *adj*

cri·noid \'krī-₁nȯid\ *n* [ultim. fr. Gk *krinon* lily] (1847) : any of a large class (Crinoidea) of echinoderms usu. having a somewhat cup-shaped body with five or more feathery arms — **crinoid** *adj*

crin·o·line \'kri-n⁻¹-ən\ *n* [F, fr. It *crinolino*, fr. *crino* horsehair (fr. L *crinis* hair) + *lino* flax, linen, fr. L *linum* — more at CREST] (1830) **1** : an open-weave fabric of horsehair or cotton that is usu. stiffened and used esp. for interlinings and millinery **2** : a full stiff skirt or underskirt made of crinoline; *also* : HOOPSKIRT — **crinoline** *or* **crin·o·lined** \-ənd\ *adj*

cri·ol·lo \krē-'ōl-(₁)yō, -'ō-(₁)yō\ *n, pl* **-llos** [Sp — more at CREOLE] (1604) **1 a** : a person of pure Spanish descent born in Spanish America **b** : a person born and usu. raised in a Spanish-American country **2** : a domestic animal of a breed or strain developed in Latin America; *esp, often cap* : a hardy muscular pony of a breed orig. developed in Argentina — **criollo** *adj*

cripes \'krīps\ *interj* [euphemism for *Christ*] (1910) — used as a mild oath

¹crip·ple \'kri-pəl\ *n* [ME *cripel*, fr. OE *crypel;* akin to OE *crēopan* to creep — more at CREEP] (bef. 12c) **1 a** : a lame or partly disabled person or animal — sometimes taken to be offensive **b** : one that is disabled or deficient in a specified manner ⟨a social ~⟩ **2** : something flawed or imperfect

²cripple *adj* (13c) : being a cripple : LAME

³cripple *vt* **crip·pled; crip·pling** \-p(ə-)liŋ\ (14c) **1** : to deprive of the use of a limb and esp. a leg **2** : to deprive of capability for service or of strength, efficiency, or wholeness *syn* see MAIM, WEAKEN — **crip·pler** \-p(ə-)lər\ *n* — **crip·pling·ly** \-p(ə-)liŋ-lē\ *adv*

cri·sis \'krī-səs\ *n, pl* **cri·ses** \'krī-₁sēz\ [ME, fr. L, fr. Gk *krisis*, lit., decision, fr. *krinein* to decide — more at CERTAIN] (15c) **1 a** : the turning point for better or worse in an acute disease or fever **b** : a paroxysmal attack of pain, distress, or disordered function **c** : an emotionally significant event or radical change of status in a person's life ⟨a midlife ~⟩ **2** : the decisive moment (as in a literary plot) **3 a** : an unstable or crucial time or state of affairs in which a decisive change is impending; *esp* : one with the distinct possibility of a highly undesirable outcome ⟨a financial ~⟩ **b** : a situation that has reached a critical phase ⟨the environmental ~⟩ *syn* see JUNCTURE

¹crisp \'krisp\ *adj* [ME, fr. OE, fr. L *crispus;* akin to W *crych* curly] (bef. 12c) **1** : CURLY, WAVY; *also* : having close stiff or wiry curls or waves **2 a** : easily crumbled : BRITTLE **b** : being desirably firm and fresh ⟨~ lettuce⟩ **3 a** : being sharp, clean-cut, and clear ⟨a ~ illustration⟩; *also* : concise and to the point ⟨a ~ reply⟩ **b** : noticeably neat ⟨~ new clothes⟩ **c** : BRISK, LIVELY ⟨a ~ tale of intrigue⟩ ⟨~ musical tempi⟩ **d** : FROSTY, SNAPPY ⟨~ winter weather⟩; *also* : FRESH, INVIGORATING ⟨~ autumn air⟩ ⟨a ~ white wine⟩ *syn* see FRAGILE — **crisp·ly** *adv* — **crisp·ness** *n*

²crisp *vt* (14c) **1** : CURL, CRIMP **2** : to cause to ripple : WRINKLE **3** : to make or keep crisp ~ *vi* **1** : CURL **2** : RIPPLE **3** : to become crisp

³crisp *n* (14c) **1 a** : something crisp or brittle ⟨burned to a ~⟩ **b** *chiefly Brit* : POTATO CHIP — usu. used in pl. **2** : a baked dessert of fruit with crumb topping ⟨apple ~⟩

crisp·bread \'krisp-₁bred\ *n* (ca. 1927) : a plain dry unsweetened cracker made from crushed grain (as wheat or rye)

crisp·en \'kris-pən\ *vt* (1943) : to make crisp ~ *vi* : to become crisp

crisp·er \'kris-pər\ *n* (1835) : one that crisps; *specif* : a closed container in a refrigerator intended to prevent loss of moisture from fresh produce

crispy \'kris-pē\ *adj* **crisp·i·er; -est** (14c) : CRISP — **crisp·i·ness** *n*

¹criss·cross \'kris-₁krȯs\ *vb* [obs. *christcross, crisscross* mark of a cross] *vt* (1818) **1** : to mark with intersecting lines **2** : to pass back and forth through or over ~ *vi* : to go or pass back and forth

²crisscross *adj* (1846) : marked or characterized by crisscrossing — **crisscross** *adv*

³crisscross *n* (1876) **1** : a crisscross pattern : NETWORK **2** : the state of being at cross-purposes; *also* : a confused state

cris·ta \'kris-tə\ *n, pl* **cris·tae** \-₁tē, -₁tī\ [NL, fr. L, crest — more at CREST] (1959) : any of the inwardly projecting folds of the inner membrane of a mitochondrion

cri·te·ri·on \krī-'tir-ē-ən *also* krə-\ *n, pl* **-ria** \-ē-ə\ *also* **-ri·ons** [Gk *kritērion*, fr. *krinein* to judge, decide — more at CERTAIN] (1622) **1** : a standard on which a judgment or decision may be based **2** : a characterizing mark or trait *syn* see STANDARD

usage The plural *criteria* has been used as a singular for nearly half a century ⟨let me now return to the third *criteria* —R. M. Nixon⟩ ⟨that really is the *criteria* —Burt Lance⟩. Many of our examples, like the two foregoing, are taken from speech. But singular *criteria* is not uncommon in edited prose, and its use both in speech and writing seems to be increasing. Only time will tell whether it will reach the unquestioned acceptability of *agenda*.

cri·te·ri·um \krī-'tir-ē-əm, krē-ter-'yom\ *n* [F *critérium* competition, lit., criterion, fr. LL *criterium*, fr. Gk *kritērion*] (1970) : a bicycle race of a specified number of laps on a closed course over public roads closed to normal traffic

¹crit·ic \'kri-tik\ *n* [L *criticus*, fr. Gk *kritikos*, fr. *kritikos* able to discern or judge, fr. *krinein*] (1588) **1 a** : one who expresses a reasoned opinion on any matter esp. involving a judgment of its value, truth, righteousness, beauty, or technique **b** : one who engages often professionally in the analysis, evaluation, or appreciation of works of art or artistic performances **2** : one given to harsh or captious judgment

²critic *n* [Gk *kritikē* art of the critic, fr. fem. of *kritikos*] (1656) **1** *archaic* : CRITICISM **2** *archaic* : CRITIQUE

crit·i·cal \'kri-ti-kəl\ *adj* (1547) **1 a** : of, relating to, or being a turning point or specially important juncture ⟨~ phase⟩: as (1) : relating to or being the stage of a disease at which an abrupt change for better or worse may be expected; *also* : being or relating to an illness or condition involving danger of death ⟨~ care⟩ (2) : relating to or being a state in which or a measurement or point at which some quality, property, or phenomenon suffers a definite change ⟨~ temperature⟩ **b** : CRUCIAL, DECISIVE ⟨~ test⟩ **c** : INDISPENSABLE, VITAL ⟨a ~ waterfowl habitat⟩ ⟨a component ~ to the operation of a machine⟩ **d** : being in or approaching a state of crisis ⟨a ~ shortage⟩ ⟨a ~ situation⟩ **2 a** : inclined to criticize severely and unfavorably **b** : consisting of or involving criticism ⟨~ writings⟩; *also* : of or relating to the judgment of critics ⟨the play was a ~ success⟩ **c** : exercising or involving careful judgment or judicious evaluation **d** : including variant readings and scholarly emendations ⟨a ~ edition⟩ **3** : characterized by risk or uncertainty **4 a** : of sufficient size to sustain a chain reaction — used of a mass of fissionable material **b** : sustaining a chain reaction — used of a nuclear reactor — **crit·i·cal·i·ty** \₁kri-tə-'ka-lə-tē\ *n* — **crit·i·cal·ly** \'kri-ti-k(ə-)lē\ *adv* — **crit·i·cal·ness** \-kəl-nəs\ *n*

syn CRITICAL, HYPERCRITICAL, FAULTFINDING, CAPTIOUS, CARPING, CENSORIOUS mean inclined to look for and point out faults and defects. CRITICAL may also imply an effort to see a thing clearly and truly in order to judge it fairly ⟨a *critical* essay⟩. HYPERCRITICAL suggests a tendency to judge by unreasonably strict standards ⟨*hypercritical* disparagement of other people's work⟩. FAULTFINDING implies a querulous or exacting temperament ⟨a *faultfinding* reviewer⟩. CAPTIOUS suggests a readiness to detect trivial faults or raise objections on trivial grounds ⟨a *captious* critic⟩. CARPING implies an ill-natured or perverse picking of flaws ⟨a *carping* editorial⟩. CENSORIOUS implies a disposition to be severely critical and condemnatory ⟨the *censorious* tone of the review⟩. *syn* see in addition ACUTE

critical angle *n* (1873) : the least angle of incidence at which total reflection takes place

critical mass *n* (1964) : a size, number, or amount large enough to produce a particular result ⟨the *critical mass* of activity needed for a retail store⟩

critical point *n* (ca. 1889) : a point on the graph of a function where the derivative is zero or infinite

critical region *n* (1951) : the set of outcomes of a statistical test for which the null hypothesis is to be rejected

critical value *n* (ca. 1909) : the value of an independent variable corresponding to a critical point of a function

crit·ic·as·ter \'kri-ti-₁kas-tər\ *n* (1684) : an inferior or petty critic

crit·i·cise *Brit var of* CRITICIZE

crit·i·cism \'kri-tə-₁si-zəm\ *n* (1607) **1 a** : the act of criticizing usu. unfavorably **b** : a critical observation or remark **c** : CRITIQUE **2** : the art of evaluating or analyzing works of art or literature **3** : the scientific investigation of literary documents (as the Bible) in regard to such matters as origin, text, composition, or history

crit·i·cize \'kri-tə-₁sīz\ *vb* **-cized; -ciz·ing** *vi* (1649) : to act as a critic ~ *vt* **1** : to consider the merits and demerits of and judge accordingly : EVALUATE **2** : to find fault with : point out the faults of — **crit·i·ciz·able** \-₁sī-zə-bəl\ *adj* — **crit·i·ciz·er** *n*

syn CRITICIZE, REPREHEND, CENSURE, REPROBATE, CONDEMN, DENOUNCE mean to find fault with openly. CRITICIZE implies finding fault esp. with methods or policies or intentions ⟨*criticized* the police for using violence⟩. REPREHEND implies both criticism and severe rebuking ⟨*reprehends* the self-centeredness of today's students⟩. CENSURE carries a strong suggestion of authority and of reprimanding ⟨a Senator formally *censured* by his peers⟩. REPROBATE implies strong disapproval or firm refusal to sanction ⟨*reprobated* his son's unconventional lifestyle⟩. CONDEMN usu. suggests an unqualified and final unfavorable judgment ⟨*condemned* the government's racial policies⟩. DENOUNCE adds to CONDEMN the implication of a public declaration ⟨a pastoral letter *denouncing* abortion⟩.

critical angle: AOB, AO'B', AO"B" angles of incidence; AOC refracted ray; AO"C" totally reflected ray; AO'B' critical angle

\ə\ abut \ᵊ\ kitten, F table \ər\ further \a\ ash \ā\ ace \ä\ mop, mar \au̇\ out \ch\ chin \e\ bet \ē\ easy \g\ go \i\ hit \ī\ ice \j\ job \ŋ\ sing \ō\ go \ȯ\ law \ȯi\ boy \th\ thin \t͟h\ the \ü\ loot \u̇\ foot \y\ yet \zh\ vision \a̱, k̲, ⁿ, œ, œ̄, ᵫ, ᵲ, ᶣ\ *see* Guide to Pronunciation

¹**cri·tique** \krə-'tēk, kri-\ *n* [alter. of ²*critic*] (1702) : an act of criticizing; *esp* : a critical estimate or discussion

²**critique** *vt* **cri·tiqued; cri·tiqu·ing** (1751) : REVIEW, CRITICIZE

crit·ter \'kri-tər\ *n* [by alter.] (1815) : CREATURE

¹**croak** \'krōk\ *vb* [ME *croken*, of imit. origin] *vi* (15c) **1 a** : to make a deep harsh sound **b** : to speak in a hoarse throaty voice **2** : GRUMBLE 1 **3** *slang* : DIE ~ *vt* **1** : to utter in a hoarse raucous voice **2** *slang* : KILL

²**croak** *n* (1561) : a hoarse harsh cry or sound — **croaky** \'krō-kē\ *adj*

croak·er \'krō-kər\ *n* (1651) **1** : an animal that croaks **2** : any of various fishes (esp. family Sciaenidae) that produce croaking or grunting noises **3** *slang* : DOCTOR

Croat \'krō-ət *also* 'krō(-ə)t\ *n* [NL *Croata*, fr. Serbo-Croatian *Hrvat*] (ca. 1702) : CROATIAN

Cro·atian \krō-'ā-shən\ *n* (1555) **1** : a native or inhabitant of Croatia **2** : a south Slavic language spoken by the Croatian people and distinct from Serbian chiefly in its use of the Latin alphabet — **Croatian** *adj*

croc \'kräk\ *n* (1884) : CROCODILE

¹**cro·chet** \krō-'shā\ *n* [F, hook, crochet, fr. MF, dim. of *croche* hook, of Scand origin; akin to ON *krōkr* hook] (1846) : needlework consisting of the interlocking of looped stitches formed with a single thread and a hooked needle

²**crochet** *vt* (1858) : to make of crochet ⟨~ed a doily⟩ ~ *vi* : to work with crochet — **cro·chet·er** \-'shā-ər\ *n*

cro·cid·o·lite \krō-'si-d°l-,īt\ *n* [G *Krokydolith*, fr. Gk *krokyd-, krokys* nap on cloth (akin to Gk *krekein* to weave) + G *-lith* -lite — more at REEL] (1835) : a lavender-blue or light green mineral of the amphibole group that occurs in silky fibers and in massive form and is a type of asbestos — compare TIGEREYE

¹**crock** \'kräk\ *n* [ME, fr. OE *crocc;* akin to MHG *krūche* crock] (bef. 12c) **1** : a thick earthenware pot or jar **2** [fr. its formation on cooking pots] *dial* : SOOT, SMUT **3** : coloring matter that rubs off from cloth or dyed leather **4** : BUNKUM — usu. used with *a*

²**crock** *vt* (1594) **1** : to put or preserve in a crock **2** *dial* : to soil with crock : SMUDGE ~ *vi* : to transfer color (as when rubbed or washed) ⟨a suede that will not ~⟩

³**crock** *n* [ME *crok*, prob. of Scand origin; akin to Norw dial. *krokje* crock] (1528) **1** : one that is broken-down, disabled, or impaired **2** : a complaining medical patient whose illness is largely imaginary or psychosomatic

⁴**crock** *vt* (1896) : to cause to become disabled ~ *vi* : BREAK DOWN

crocked \'kräkt\ *adj* (ca. 1927) : DRUNK

crock·ery \'krä-k(ə-)rē\ *n* (ca. 1755) : EARTHENWARE

crock·et \'krä-kət\ *n* [ME *croket*, fr. ONF *croquet* crook, dim. of *croc* hook, of Scand origin; akin to ON *krōkr* hook] (1673) : an ornament usu. in the form of curved and bent foliage used on the edge of a gable or spire — **crock·et·ed** \-kə-təd\ *adj*

Crock–Pot \'kräk-,pät\ *trademark* — used for an electric cooking pot

croc·o·dile \'krä-kə-,dīl\ *n* [ME & L; ME *cocodrille*, fr. MF, fr. ML *cocodrillus*, alter. of L *crocodilus*, fr. Gk *krokodilos* lizard, crocodile, fr. *krokē* shingle, pebble + *drilos* worm; akin to Skt *śarkara* pebble] (1684) **1 a** : any of several large carnivorous thick-skinned long-bodied aquatic reptiles (family Crocodylidae) of tropical and subtropical waters; *broadly* : CROCODILIAN **b** : the skin or hide of a crocodile **2** *chiefly Brit* : a line of people (as schoolchildren) usu. walking in pairs

crocodile bird *n* (1868) : an African bird (*Pluvianus aegyptius*) that is related to the pratincoles and lights on the crocodile and eats its insect parasites

crocodile tears *n pl* (1563) : false or affected tears; *also* : hypocritical sorrow

croc·o·dil·ian \,krä-kə-'di-lē-ən, -'dil-yən\ *n* (1837) : any of an order (Crocodylia) of reptiles including the crocodiles, alligators, caimans, gavials, and related extinct forms — **crocodilian** *adj*

cro·cus \'krō-kəs\ *n, pl* **cro·cus·es** [ME, the saffron plant, fr. L, fr. Gk *krokos*, of Sem origin; akin to Akkadian *kurkānū* saffron] (14c) **1 a** *pl* *also* **crocus** *or* **cro·ci** \-,kē, -,kī, -,sī\ : any of a large genus (*Crocus*) of herbs of the iris family developing from corms and having solitary long-tubed flowers and slender linear leaves **b** : SAFFRON 1a **2** : a dark red ferric oxide used for polishing metals

Croe·sus \'krē-səs\ *n* [Croesus, king of Lydia, famed for his wealth] (1650) : a very rich man

croft \'krȯft\ *n* [ME, fr. OE; akin to MD *krocht* hill] (bef. 12c) **1** *chiefly Brit* : a small enclosed field usu. adjoining a house **2** *chiefly Brit* : a small farm worked by a tenant — **croft·er** \'krȯf-tər\ *n, chiefly Brit*

crois·sant \krȯ-'sänt, krə-; krwä-'sä°\ *n, pl* **croissants** \-'sänt(s), -'sän(z)\ [F, lit., crescent, fr. MF *creissant*] (1899) : a flaky rich crescent-shaped roll

Croix de Guerre \,krwä-di-'ger\ *n* [F, lit., war cross] (1915) : a French military decoration awarded for gallant action in war

cro·ker sack \'krō-kər-\ *n* [alter. of *crocus sack, crocus bag,* of unknown origin] (1895) *chiefly Southern* : a sack of a coarse material (as burlap)

Cro–Ma·gnon \krō-'mag-nən, -'man-yən\ *n* [Cro-Magnon, a cave near Les Eyzies, France] (1869) : a tall erect race of hominids of the Upper Paleolithic known from skeletal remains found chiefly in southern France and classified as the same species (*Homo sapiens*) as present day humans

crom·lech \'kräm-,lek\ *n* [W, lit., bent stone] (1695) **1** : DOLMEN **2** : a circle of monoliths usu. enclosing a dolmen or mound

crone \'krōn\ *n* [ME, fr. ONF *carogne*, lit., carrion, fr. (assumed) VL *caronia* — more at CARRION] (14c) : a withered old woman

Cro·nus \'krō-nəs, 'krä-\ *n* [L, fr. Gk *Kronos*] : a Titan dethroned by his son Zeus

cro·ny \'krō-nē\ *n, pl* **cronies** [perh. fr. Gk *chronios* long-lasting, fr. *chronos* time] (1663) : a close friend esp. of long standing : PAL

cro·ny·ism \-nē-,i-zəm\ *n* (1840) : partiality to cronies esp. as evidenced in the appointment of political hangers-on to office without regard to their qualifications

¹**crook** \'krük\ *vt* (12c) : BEND ~ *vi* : CURVE, WIND

²**crook** *n* [ME *crok*, fr. ON *krōkr* hook] (13c) **1** : an implement having a bent or hooked form: as **a** : POTHOOK **b** (1) : a shepherd's staff (2) : CROSIER 1 **2** : a part of something that is hook-shaped, curved, or

bent ⟨the ~ of an umbrella handle⟩ **3** : BEND, CURVE **4** : a person who engages in fraudulent or criminal practices

³**crook** *adj* [prob. short for *crooked*] (1898) *Austral & NewZeal* : not right: **a** : UNSATISFACTORY **b** : DISHONEST, CROOKED **c** : IRRITABLE, ANGRY — used esp. in the phrase *go crook* **d** : ILL, UNWELL

crook·back \'krük-,bak\ *n* (1508) **1** *obs* : a crooked back **2** *obs* : HUNCHBACK — **crook·backed** \-'bakt\ *adj*

crook·ed \'krü-kəd\ *adj* (13c) **1** : not straight ⟨a ~ road⟩ ⟨your tie is ~⟩ **2** : DISHONEST ⟨a ~ election⟩ ⟨~ politicians⟩ — **crook·ed·ly** *adv* — **crook·ed·ness** *n*

crook·ery \'krü-kə-rē\ *n* (1927) : crooked dealings or practices

crook·neck \'krük-,nek\ *n* (1784) : a squash with a long recurved neck

croon \'krün\ *vb* [ME *croynen*, fr. MD *cronen;* akin to OHG *crōnen* to chatter] *vi* (15c) **1** *chiefly Scot* : BELLOW, BOOM **2** : to sing or speak in a gentle murmuring manner; *esp* : to sing in a soft intimate manner adapted to amplifying systems ~ *vt* : to sing (as a popular song or a lullaby) in a crooning manner — **croon** *n*

croon·er \'krü-nər\ *n* (1930) : one that croons; *esp* : a singer of popular songs

¹**crop** \'kräp\ *n* [ME, craw, head of a plant, yield of a field, fr. OE *cropp* craw, head of a plant; akin to OHG *kropf* goiter, craw] (bef. 12c) **1 a** : a pouched enlargement of the gullet of many birds that serves as a receptacle for food and for its preliminary maceration; *also* : an enlargement of the gullet of another animal (as an insect) **2 a** (1) : a plant or animal or plant or animal product that can be grown and harvested extensively for profit or subsistence ⟨an apple ~⟩ ⟨a ~ of wool⟩ (2) : the total yearly production from a specified area **b** : the product or yield of something formed together ⟨the ice ~⟩ **c** : a batch or lot of something produced during a particular cycle ⟨the current ~ of films⟩ **d** : COLLECTION ⟨a ~ of lies⟩ **3** : the stock or handle of a whip; *also* : a riding whip with a short straight stock and a loop **4** [²*crop*] **a** : the part of the chine of a quadruped (as a domestic cow) lying immediately behind the withers — usu. used in pl.; see COW illustration **b** : an earmark on an animal; *esp* : one made by a straight cut squarely removing the upper part of the ear **c** : a close cut of the hair

²**crop** *vb* **cropped; crop·ping** *vt* (13c) **1 a** : to remove the upper or outer parts of ⟨~ a hedge⟩ ⟨~ a dog's ears⟩ **b** : HARVEST ⟨~ trout⟩ **c** : to cut off short : TRIM ⟨~ a photograph⟩ **2** : to cause (land) to bear a crop ⟨planned to ~ another 40 acres⟩; *also* : to grow as a crop ~ *vi* **1** : to feed by cropping something **2** : to yield or make a crop **3** : to appear unexpectedly or casually ⟨problems ~ up daily⟩

crop duster *n* (1939) : a person who sprays crops with fungicidal or insecticidal dusts from an airplane; *also* : the airplane used for such spraying

crop–eared \'kräp-,ird\ *adj* (1530) : having the ears cropped

crop·land \-,land\ *n* (1846) : land that is suited to or used for crops

¹**crop·per** \'krä-pər\ *n* (15c) **1** : one that crops **2** : one that raises crops; *specif* : SHARECROPPER

²**cropper** *n* [prob. fr. E dial. *crop* neck, fr. ¹*crop*] (1858) **1** : a severe fall **2** : a sudden or violent failure or collapse

crop rotation *n* (1909) : the practice of growing different crops in succession on the same land chiefly to preserve the productive capacity of the soil

cro·quet \krō-'kā\ *n* [F dial., hockey stick, fr. ONF, crook — more at CROCKET] (1858) **1** : a game in which players using mallets drive wooden balls through a series of wickets set out on a lawn **2** : the act of driving away an opponent's croquet ball by striking one's own ball placed against it — **croquet** *vt*

cro·quette \krō-'ket\ *n* [F, fr. *croquer* to crunch, of imit. origin] (1706) : a small often rounded mass consisting usu. of minced meat, fish, or vegetable coated with egg and bread crumbs and deep-fried

cro·qui·gnole \'krō-kə-,nōl *also* -kən-,yōl\ *n* [F, light blow, fillip] (1932) : a method used in waving the hair by winding it on curlers from the ends of the hair toward the scalp

cro·quis \krō-'kē\ *n, pl* **cro·quis** \-'kē(z)\ [F, fr. *croquer* to sketch, rough out, lit., to crunch] (1805) : a rough draft : SKETCH

crore \'krȯr, 'krȯr\ *n, pl* **crores** *also* **crore** [Hindi *karoṛ*] (1609) : a unit of value equal to ten million rupees or 100 lakhs

cro·sier \'krō-zhər\ *n* [ME *crocer* crosier bearer, fr. MF *crossier*, fr. *crosse* crosier, of Gmc origin; akin to OE *crycc* crutch — more at CRUTCH] (1500) **1** : a staff resembling a shepherd's crook carried by bishops and abbots as a symbol of office **2** : a plant structure with a coiled end

¹**cross** \'krȯs\ *n* [ME, fr. OE, fr. ON or OIr; ON *kross*, fr. OIr *cros*, fr. L *cruc-, crux*] (bef. 12c) **1 a** : a structure consisting of an upright with a transverse beam used esp. by the ancient Romans for execution **b** *often cap* : the cross on which Jesus was crucified **2 a** : CRUCIFIXION **b** : an affliction that tries one's virtue, steadfastness, or patience **3 a** : a cruciform sign made to invoke the blessing of Christ esp. by touching the forehead, breast, and shoulders **4 a** : a device composed of an upright bar traversed by a horizontal one; *specif* : one used as a Christian symbol **b** *cap* : the Christian religion **5** : a structure (as a monument) shaped like or surmounted by a cross **6** : a figure or mark formed by two intersecting lines crossing at their midpoints; *specif* : such a mark used as a signature **7** : a cruciform badge, emblem, or decoration **8** : the intersection of two ways or lines : CROSSING **9** : ANNOYANCE, THWARTING ⟨a ~ in love⟩ **10 a** : an act of crossing dissimilar individuals **b** : a crossbred individual or kind **c** : one that combines characteristics of two different types or individuals **11 a** : a fraudulent or dishonest contest **b** : dishonest or illegal practices — used esp. in the phrase *on the cross* **12** : a movement from one part of a theater stage to another **13** : a hook thrown over the opponent's lead in boxing **14** : a security transaction in which a broker acts for both buyer and seller (as in the placing of a large lot of common stock) — called also *cross-trade*

²**cross** *vt* (14c) **1 a** : to lie or be situated across **b** : INTERSECT **2** : to make the sign of the cross upon or over **3** : to cancel by marking a cross on or drawing a line through : strike out ⟨~ names off a list⟩ **4** : to place or fold crosswise one over the other ⟨~ the arms⟩ **5 a** (1) : to run counter to : OPPOSE (2) : to deny the validity of : CONTRADICT **b** : to confront in a troublesome manner : OBSTRUCT **c** : to spoil completely : DISRUPT — used with *up* ⟨his failure to appear ~ed up the whole program⟩ (2) : to turn against : BETRAY ⟨~ed me up on the deal⟩ **6 a** : to extend across or over : TRAVERSE ⟨a highway ~ing the

cross 4a: 1 Latin, 2 Calvary, 3 patriarchal, 4 papal, 5 Lorraine, 6 Greek, 7 Celtic, 8 Maltese, 9 Saint Andrew's, 10 tau, 11 pommée, 12 botonée, 13 fleury, 14 avellan, 15 moline, 16 formée, 17 fourchée, 18 crosslet, 19 quadrate, 20 potent

entire state⟩   **b** : REACH, ATTAIN ⟨only two ~ed the finish line⟩   **c** : to go from one side of to the other ⟨~ a street⟩ ⟨~es racial barriers⟩   **7 a** : to draw a line across   **b** : to mark or figure with lines : STREAK   **8** : to cause (an animal or plant) to interbreed with one of a different kind : HYBRIDIZE   **9** : to meet and pass on the way ⟨our letters must have ~ed each other⟩   **10** : to occur to ⟨it never ~ed my mind⟩   **11** : to carry or take across something ⟨~ed the children at the intersection⟩   ~ **vi 1 a** : to move, pass, or extend across something ⟨~ed through France⟩ ⟨~ed over to the other side of the river⟩   **b** : to move or pass from one character, condition, or allegiance to another — used with *over*   **2** : to lie or be athwart each other   **3** : to meet in passing esp. from opposite directions   **4** : INTERBREED, HYBRIDIZE — **cross·er** *n* — **cross swords** : to engage in a dispute

³**cross** *adj* (14c)   **1 a** : lying across or athwart   **b** : moving across ⟨~ traffic⟩   **2 a** : running counter : OPPOSITE   **b** : mutually opposed ⟨~ purposes⟩   **3** : involving mutual interchange : RECIPROCAL   **4** : marked by typically transitory bad temper   **5** : extending over or treating several groups or classes ⟨a ~ sample from 25 colleges⟩   **6** : CROSSBRED, HYBRID — **cross·ly** *adv* — **cross·ness** *n*

⁴**cross** *prep* (1551)   : ACROSS

⁵**cross** *adv* (1577)   : not parallel : CRISSCROSS, CROSSWISE

cross·abil·i·ty \ˌkro·sə-'bi-lə-tē\ *n* (1916)   : the ability of different species or varieties to cross with each other

cross·able \'kro-sə-bəl\ *adj* (1865)   : capable of being crossed

cross action *n* (1859)   : a legal action in which the defendant in an existing action files a suit against the plaintiff on the same subject matter : COUNTERSUIT

cross·band·ing \'kros-ˌban-diŋ\ *n* (1904)   : a veneer border (as on furniture) with its grain at right angles to the grain of the adjacent wood — **cross·band·ed** \-ˌban-dəd\ *adj*

cross·bar \'kros-ˌbär\ *n* (1562)   : a transverse bar or stripe

cross·bear·er \'kros-ˌbar-ər, -ˌber-\ *n* (1568)   : CRUCIFER 1

cross·bill \-ˌbil\ *n* (ca. 1672)   : any of a small genus (*Loxia*) of finches with strongly curved mandibles that cross each other

cross·bones \-ˌbōnz\ *n pl* (1798)   : two leg or arm bones placed or depicted crosswise — compare SKULL AND CROSSBONES

cross·bow \-ˌbō\ *n* (15c)   : a weapon for discharging quarrels and stones that consists chiefly of a short bow mounted crosswise near the end of a stock

cross·bow·man \-mən\ *n* (ca. 1500)   : a person (as a soldier or a hunter) whose weapon is a crossbow

cross·bred \'kros-'bred\ *adj* (1856)   : produced by crossbreeding — HYBRID — **cross·bred** \-ˌbred\ *n*

¹**cross·breed** \'kros-ˌbrēd, -'brēd\ *vb* -**bred** \-ˌbred, -'bred\; -**breed·ing** *vt* (1675)   : HYBRIDIZE, CROSS; *esp* : to cross (two varieties or breeds) within the same species   ~ *vi* : to engage in or undergo hybridization

²**cross·breed** \-ˌbrēd\ *n* (1774)   : HYBRID

¹**cross-check** \-ˌchek\ *vt* (ca. 1930)   **1** : to obstruct in ice hockey or lacrosse by thrusting one's stick held in both hands across an opponent's face or body   **2** : to check (as data or reports) from various angles or sources to determine validity or accuracy

²**cross-check** *n* (1937)   : an act or instance of cross-checking

cross-claim \-ˌklām\ *n* (1952)   : a claim against a party on the same side of a legal action

¹**cross-coun·try** \'kros-'kən-trē, -ˌkən-\ *adj* (1767)   **1** : extending or moving across a country ⟨a ~ concert tour⟩   **2** : proceeding over countryside (as across fields and through woods) and not by roads   **3** : of or relating to racing or skiing over the countryside instead of over a track or run — **cross-country** *adv*

²**cross-country** *n* (1925)   : cross-country racing or skiing

cross-court \'kros-ˌkort, -ˈkort\ *adv or adj* (1915)   : to or toward the opposite side of a court (as in tennis or basketball)

cross-cul·tur·al \'kros-ˈkəlch-rəl, -ˈkəl-chə-\ *adj* (ca. 1942)   : dealing with or offering comparison between two or more different cultures or cultural areas — **cross-cul·tur·al·ly** \-rə-lē\ *adv*

cross-cur·rent \'kros-ˌkər-ənt, -ˌkə-rənt\ *n* (1598)   **1** : a current running counter to the general forward direction   **2** : a conflicting tendency — usu. used in pl. ⟨political ~s⟩

¹**cross·cut** \'kros-ˌkət, -'kət\ *vt* (1590)   **1** : to cut, go, or move across or through   **2** : to cut with a crosscut saw   **3** : to subject (as movie scenes) to crosscutting

²**crosscut** *adj* (1645)   **1** : made or used for cutting transversely ⟨a saw with ~ teeth⟩   **2** : cut across or transversely ⟨a ~ incision⟩

³**cross·cut** \'kros-ˌkət\ *n* (1789)   **1** : something that cuts across or through; *specif* : a mine working driven horizontally and at right angles to an adit, drift, or level   **2** : CROSS SECTION   **3** : CROSSCUT SAW   **4** : an instance of crosscutting (as in a movie)

crosscut saw *n* (1645)   : a saw designed chiefly to cut across the grain of wood — compare RIPSAW

cross-cut·ting \'kros-ˌkə-tiŋ\ *n* (1930)   : a technique esp. in filmmaking of interweaving bits of two or more separate scenes

cross-dress·ing \'kros-ˌdre-siŋ\ *n* (1911)   : the wearing of clothes designed for the opposite sex — **cross-dress** *vi* — **cross-dress·er** *n*

crosse \'kros\ *n* [F, lit., crosier — more at CROSIER] (1867)   : a stick with a small net at one end that is used in lacrosse

cross-ex·am·i·na·tion \'kros-ig-ˌza-mə-'nā-shən\ *n* (1824)   : the examination of a witness who has already testified in order to check or discredit the witness's testimony, knowledge, or credibility — compare DIRECT EXAMINATION — **cross-ex·am·ine** \-ig-'za-mən\ *vt* — **cross-ex·am·in·er** \-'zam-nər, -'za-mə-\ *n*

cross-eye \'kro-ˌsī\ *n* (1826)   **1** : strabismus in which the eye turns inward toward the nose   **2** *pl* : eyes affected with cross-eye — **cross-eyed** \-ˌsīd\ *adj*

cross-fer·tile \'kros-'fər-tᵊl, -ˌfər-\ *adj* (1929)   : fertile in a cross or capable of cross-fertilization

cross-fer·til·i·za·tion \-ˌfər-tᵊl-ə-'zā-shən\ *n* (1876)   **1 a** : fertilization in which the gametes are produced by separate individuals or sometimes by individuals of different kinds   **b** : CROSS-POLLINATION   **2** : interchange or interaction (as between different ideas, cultures, or categories) esp. of a broadening or productive nature

cross-fer·til·ize \-'fər-tᵊl-ˌīz\ *vt* (1876)   : to accomplish cross-fertilization of   ~ *vi* : to undergo cross-fertilization

cross-file \-'fī(ə)l\ *vi* (1949)   : to register as a candidate in the primary elections of more than one political party   ~ *vt* : to register (a person) as a candidate for more than one party

cross fire *n* (ca. 1859)   **1 a** : firing (as in combat) from two or more points so that the lines of fire cross   **b** : a situation wherein the forces of opposing factions meet, cross, or clash ⟨caught in a political cross fire⟩   **2** : rapid or heated exchange of words

cross-grained \'kros-'grānd\ *adj* (1647)   **1** : difficult to deal with   **2** : having the grain or fibers running diagonally, transversely, or irregularly

cross·hair \-ˌhar, -ˌher\ *n* (ca. 1884)   : a fine wire or thread in the focus of the eyepiece of an optical instrument used as a reference line in the field or for marking the instrumental axis

cross·hatch \'kros-ˌhach\ *vt* (1822)   : to mark with two series of parallel lines that intersect — **crosshatch** *n* — **cross-hatch·ing** *n*

cross·head \-ˌhed\ *n* (1827)   **1** : a metal block to which one end of a piston rod is secured   **2** : a heading centered usu. between portions of text

cross-in·dex \'kros-'in-ˌdeks\ *vt* (1892)   **1** : to index (an item) under a second or under more than one heading   **2** : to supply (as a book) with a cross-referenced index — **cross-index** *n*

cross·ing \'kro-siŋ\ *n* (1575)   **1** : the act or action of crossing: as   **a** : a traversing or traveling across   **b** : an opposing, blocking, or thwarting esp. in an unfair or dishonest manner   **2 a** : a place or structure (as on a street or over a river) where pedestrians or vehicles cross; *esp* : CROSSWALK   **b** : the place in a cruciform church where the transept crosses the nave   **c** : a place where a railroad track crosses a street

cross·ing-over \ˌkro-siŋ-'ō-vər\ *n* (1912)   : an interchange of genes or segments between homologous chromosomes

cross-legged \'kros-ˌle-gəd, -ˌlā-; -ˌlegd, -ˌlāgd\ *adv or adj* (ca. 1530)   **1** : with legs crossed and knees spread wide apart   **2** : with one leg placed over and across the other

cross·let \'kros-lət\ *n* (15c)   : a small cross usu. with crossed arms; *esp* : one used as a heraldic bearing — see CROSS illustration

cross·lin·guis·tic \ˌkros-liŋ-'gwis-tik\ *adj* (1954)   : of or relating to languages of different families and types; *esp* : relating to the comparison of different languages — **cross·lin·guis·ti·cal·ly** \-ti-k(ə-)lē\ *adv*

cross-link \'kros-ˌliŋk\ *n* (1936)   : a crosswise connecting part (as an atom or group) that connects parallel chains in a complex chemical molecule (as a polymer) — **cross-link** *vb*

cross-link·age \'kros-'liŋ-kij\ *n* (1937)   : the process of forming cross-links; *also* : CROSS-LINK

cross multiply *vi* (1951)   : to find the two products obtained by multiplying the numerator of each of two fractions by the denominator of the other — **cross multiplication** *n*

cross-na·tion·al \'kros-'nash-nəl, -'na-shə-nᵊl\ *adj* (1965)   : of or relating to two or more nations

cross of Lor·raine \-lə-'rän, -lȯ-\ [*Lorraine*, France] (ca. 1889)   : a cross with two crossbars the lower one of which is longer than the upper one — see CROSS illustration

cros·sop·ter·yg·ian \ˌkro-ˌsäp-tə-'ri-j(ē-)ən\ *n* [NL *Crossopterygii*, subclass name, fr. *Gk krossoi* fringe + *pterygion*, dim. of *pteryg-, pteryx* wing, fin; akin to Gk *pteron* wing — more at FEATHER] (1861)   : any of a subclass (Crossopterygii) of fishes (as a coelacanth) that have paired fins suggesting limbs, that may be ancestral to the terrestrial vertebrates, and that are mostly extinct — called also *lobe-fin* — **crossopterygian** *adj*

¹**cross·over** \'kros-ˌō-vər\ *n* (1884)   **1** : CROSSING 2a   **2** : an instance or product of genetic crossing-over   **3** : a voter registered as a member of one political party who votes in the primary of the other party   **4** : a broadening of the popular appeal of an artist (as a musician) or an artist's work that is the result of a change of the artist's medium or style; *also* : an artist or artistic work that has achieved a crossover   **5** : an instance of breaking into another category ⟨trying to make the ~ to serious acting —Michael Neill⟩

\ə\ abut \ᵊ\ kitten, F table \ər\ further \a\ ash \ā\ ace \ä\ mop, mar
\aů\ out \ch\ chin \e\ bet \ē\ easy \g\ go \i\ hit \ī\ ice \j\ job
\ŋ\ sing \ō\ go \ȯ\ law \ȯi\ boy \th\ thin \t̲h̲\ the \ü\ loot \ů\ foot
\y\ yet \zh\ vision \à, k̲, ⁿ, œ, œ̄, ᵫ, ᵫ̄, ᵊ\ see Guide to Pronunciation

²**crossover** *adj* (1893)　**1** : having two pieces that cross esp. one over the other ⟨a ~ vest⟩　**2** : CRITICAL 1 ⟨the ~ point⟩

cross-own·er·ship \-'ō-nər-,ship\ *n* (1969) : single ownership of two or more related businesses (as a newspaper and a television station) that allows the owner to control competition

cross·patch \'krós-,pach\ *n* [³*cross* + ³*patch*] (ca. 1700) : GROUCH 2

cross·piece \'krós-,pēs\ *n* (1607) : a horizontal member (as of a structure)

cross-pol·li·nate \'krós-'pä-lə-,nāt\ *vt* (ca. 1900) : to subject to cross-pollination

cross-pol·li·na·tion \,krós-,pä-lə-'nā-shən\ *n* (1882)　**1** : the transfer of pollen from one flower to the stigma of another　**2** : CROSS-FERTILIZATION 2

cross product *n* (1929)　**1** : VECTOR PRODUCT　**2** : either of the two products obtained by multiplying the two means or the two extremes of a proportion

cross-pur·pose \'krós-'pər-pəs\ *n* (1681) : a purpose usu. unintentionally contrary to another purpose of oneself or of someone or something else — usu. used in pl. ⟨the two were always working at ~s⟩

cross-ques·tion \'krós-'kwes-chən, -'kwesh-\ *n* (ca. 1694) : a question asked in cross-examination — **cross-question** *vt*

cross-re·ac·tion \,krós-rē-'ak-shən\ *n* (1946) : reaction of one antigen with antibodies developed against another antigen — **cross-re·act** \-rē-'akt\ *vi* — **cross-re·ac·tive** \-'ak-tiv\ *adj* — **cross-re·ac·tiv·i·ty** \-(,)rē-,ak-'ti-və-tē\ *n*

cross-re·fer \,krós-ri-'fər\ *vt* (1879) : to refer (a reader) by a notation or direction from one place to another (as in a book, list, or catalog) — *vi* : to make a cross-reference

¹**cross-ref·er·ence** \'krós-'re-fərn(t)s, -'re-f(ə-)rən(t)s\ *n* (1834) : a notation or direction at one place (as in a book or filing system) to pertinent information at another place

²**cross-reference** *vt* (1902) : to supply with cross-references

cross-re·sis·tance \,krós-ri-'zis-tən(t)s\ *n* (1946) : tolerance (as of an insect population) to a normally toxic substance (as an insecticide) that is acquired not as a result of direct exposure but by exposure to a related substance

cross·road \'krós-,rōd *also* -'rōd\ *n* (1719)　**1** : a road that crosses a main road or runs cross-country between main roads　**2** *usu pl but sing or pl in constr*　**a** : the place of intersection of two or more roads　**b** (1) : a small community located at such a crossroads　(2) : a central meeting place　**c** : a crucial point esp. where a decision must be made

cross·ruff \'krós-,rəf, -'rəf\ *n* (1862) : a series of plays in a card game (as bridge) in which partners alternately trump different suits and lead to each other for that purpose — **crossruff** *vb*

cross section *n* (1835)　**1 a** : a cutting or piece of something cut off at right angles to an axis; *also* : a representation of such a cutting　**b** : SECTION 3b　**2** : a measure of the probability of an encounter between particles such as will result in a specified effect (as scattering or capture)　**3** : a composite representation typifying the constituents of a thing in their relations — **cross-section** *vt* — **cross-sec·tion·al** \'krós-'sek-shnəl, -shə-nᵊl\ *adj*

cross-stitch \'kró(s)-,stich\ *n* (ca. 1710)　**1** : a needlework stitch that forms an X　**2** : work taking cross-stitch — **cross-stitch** *vb*

cross talk *n* (1887) : unwanted signals in a communication channel (as in a telephone, radio, or computer) caused by transference of energy from another circuit (as by leakage or coupling)

cross-tol·er·ance \'krós-'täl-rən(t)s, -'tä-lə-\ *n* (ca. 1923) : tolerance or resistance to a drug that develops through continued use of another drug with similar pharmacological action

cross-town \'krós-'taün\ *adj* (1886)　**1** : situated at opposite points of a town　**2** : extending or running across a town ⟨a ~ street⟩ ⟨a ~ bus⟩

cross-trade \-,trād\ *n* (ca. 1923) : CROSS 14

cross·trees \-(,)trēz\ *n pl* (1626) : two horizontal crosspieces of timber or metal supported by trestletrees at a masthead that spread the upper shrouds in order to support the mast

cross vault *n* (1850) : a vault formed by the intersection of two or more simple vaults — called *also* cross vaulting

cross·walk \'krós-,wòk\ *n* (1744) : a specially paved or marked path for pedestrians crossing a street or road

cross·way \-,wā\ *n* (14c) : CROSSROAD — often used in pl.

cross·ways \-,wāz\ *adv* (1564) : CROSSWISE, DIAGONALLY

cross·wind \-,wind\ *n* (1677) : a wind blowing in a direction not parallel to a course (as of an airplane)

¹**cross·wise** \-,wīz\ *adv* (14c)　**1** *archaic* : in the form of a cross　**2** : so as to cross something : ACROSS ⟨logs laid ~⟩

²**crosswise** *adj* (1903) : TRANSVERSE, CROSSING

cross·word \-,wərd\ *n* (1914) : a puzzle in which words are filled into a pattern of numbered squares in answer to correspondingly numbered clues and in such a way that the words read across and down

crotch \'kräch\ *n* [prob. alter. of ¹*crutch*] (1573)　**1** : a pole with a forked end used esp. as a prop　**2** : an angle formed by the parting of two legs, branches, or members — **crotched** \'krächt\ *adj*

crotch·et \'krä-chət\ *n* [ME *crochet*, fr. MF — more at CROCHET] (14c)　**1** *obs* : a small hook or hooked instrument　**b** : BROOCH　**2 a** : a highly individual and usu. eccentric opinion or preference　**b** : a peculiar trick or device　**3** : QUARTER NOTE　*syn* see CAPRICE

crotch·ety \'krä-chə-tē\ *adj* (1825)　**1** : given to crotchets : subject to whims, crankiness, or ill temper ⟨a ~ old man⟩　**2** : full of or arising from crotchets — **crotch·et·i·ness** \-tē-nəs\ *n*

cro·ton \'krō-tᵊn\ *n* [NL, genus name, fr. Gk *krotōn* castor-oil plant] (1751)　**1** : any of a genus (*Croton*) of herbs, shrubs, and trees of the spurge family: as　**a** : one (*C. eluteria*) of the Bahamas yielding cascarilla bark　**b** : an Asian plant (*C. tiglium*) yielding croton oil　**2** : any of a genus (*Codiaeum*) of shrubs and trees related to the crotons

Cro·ton bug \'krō-tᵊn-\ *n* [*Croton* River, N.Y., used as a water supply for New York City] (1877) : GERMAN COCKROACH

croton oil *n* (ca. 1831) : a viscid acrid fixed oil from an Asian croton (*Croton tiglium*) formerly used as a drastic cathartic but now used esp. in pharmacological experiments as an irritant

crouch \'kraüch\ *vb* [ME] *vi* (14c)　**1 a** : to lower the body stance esp. by bending the legs ⟨a sprinter ~ed ready to go⟩　**b** : to lie close to the ground with the legs bent ⟨a pair of cats, ~ing on the brink of a fight —Aldous Huxley⟩　**2** : to bend or bow servilely : CRINGE ~ *vt* : to bow esp. in humility or fear : BEND — **crouch** *n*

¹**croup** \'krüp\ *n* [ME *croupe*, fr. OF, of Gmc origin; akin to OHG *kropf* craw — more at CROP] (14c) : the rump of a quadruped

²**croup** *n* [E dial. *croup* to cry hoarsely, cough, prob. of imit. origin] (1765) : a spasmodic laryngitis esp. of infants marked by episodes of difficult breathing and hoarse metallic cough — **croup·ous** \'krü-pəs\ *adj* — **croupy** \-pē\ *adj*

crou·pi·er \'krü-pē-ər, -pē-,ā\ *n* [F, lit., rider on the croup of a horse, fr. *croupe* croup] (1709) : an employee of a gambling casino who collects and pays bets and assists at the gaming tables

crouse \'krüs\ *adj* (15c) *chiefly Scot* : BRISK, LIVELY

crous·tade \krü-'städ\ *n* [F, prob. fr. It *crostata* tart, fr. *crosta* pastry shell, crust, fr. L *crusta* — more at CRUST] (ca. 1845) : a crisp shell (as of toast or puff pastry) in which to serve food

crou·ton \'krü-,tän, krü-'\ *n* [F *croûton*, dim. of *croûte* crust, fr. MF *crouste*, OF, fr. L *crusta*] (1806) : a small cube of toasted or crisply fried bread

¹**crow** \'krō\ *n* [ME *crowe*, fr. OE *crāwe*; akin to OHG *krāwa* crow, OE *crāwan* to crow] (bef. 12c)　**1** : any of various large usu. entirely glossy black passerine birds (family Corvidae and esp. genus *Corvus*)　**2** *cap*　**a** : a member of an American Indian people of the region between the Platte and Yellowstone rivers　**b** : the language of the Crow people　**3** *cap* : CORVUS — **as the crow flies** : in a straight line

²**crow** *vb* **crowed** \'krōd\ *also in sense 1 chiefly Brit* **crew** \'krü\; **crow·ing** [ME, fr. OE *crāwan*] *vi* (bef. 12c)　**1** : to make the loud shrill sound characteristic of a cock　**2** : to utter a sound expressive of pleasure　**3 a** : to exult gloatingly esp. over the distress of another　**b** : to brag exultantly or blatantly ~ *vt* : to say with self-satisfaction　*syn* see BOAST

³**crow** *n* (13c)　**1** : the cry of the cock　**2** : a triumphant cry

crow·bar \'krō-,bär\ *n* (1748) : an iron or steel bar that is usu. wedge-shaped at the working end for use as a pry or lever — **crowbar** *vt*

crow·ber·ry \'krō-,ber-ē\ *n* (1597)　**1** : an evergreen subshrub (*Empetrum nigrum* of the family Empetraceae) of arctic and alpine regions with an insipid black berry　**2** : the fruit of a crowberry

¹**crowd** \'kraüd\ *vb* [ME *crouden*, fr. OE *crūdan*; akin to MHG *kroten* to crowd, OE *crod* multitude, MIr *gruth* curds] *vi* (bef. 12c)　**1 a** : to press on : HURRY　**b** : to press close　**2** : to collect in numbers ~ *vt*　**1 a** : to fill by pressing or thronging together　**b** : to press, force, or thrust into a small space　**2** : PUSH, FORCE — often used with *off* or *out*　**3 a** : to urge on　**b** : to put on (sail) in excess of the usual for greater speed　**4** : to put pressure on ⟨don't ~ me, I'll pay⟩　**5** : THRONG, JOSTLE　**6** : to press or stand close to

²**crowd** *n* (1567)　**1** : a large number of persons esp. when collected together : THRONG　**2 a** : the great body of the people : POPULACE　**b** : most of one's peers ⟨follow the ~⟩　**3** : a large number of things close together　**4** : a group of people having something (as a habit, interest, or occupation) in common ⟨in with the wrong ~⟩

syn CROWD, THRONG, CRUSH, MOB, HORDE mean an assembled multitude usu. of people. CROWD implies a close gathering and pressing together ⟨a small *crowd* gathered⟩. THRONG strongly suggests movement and pushing ⟨a *throng* of reporters⟩. CRUSH emphasizes the compactness of the group, the difficulty of individual movement, and the attendant discomfort ⟨a *crush* of fans⟩. MOB implies a disorderly crowd with the potential for violence ⟨an angry *mob* outside the jail⟩. HORDE suggests a rushing or tumultuous crowd ⟨a *horde* of shoppers⟩.

³**crowd** \'kraüd, 'krüd\ *n* [ME *crowde*, fr. MW *crwth*] (14c)　**1** : an ancient Celtic stringed instrument that is plucked or bowed — called *also* crwth　**2** *dial Eng* : VIOLIN

³crowd 1

crowd·ed·ness \'kraü-dəd-nəs\ *n* (1823) : the quality or state of being crowded

crow·die \'kraü-dē\ *n* [alter. of *crud* curd] (1820) : a Scottish cottage cheese that is partially cooked

crow·foot \'krō-,füt\ *n, pl* **crow-feet** \-,fēt\ (14c)　**1** *pl usu* **crow-foots** : any of numerous plants having leaves with cleft lobes; *esp* : BUTTERCUP　**2** : CROW'S-FOOT 1 — usu. used in pl.

crow·keep·er \'krō-,kē-pər\ *n* (1562) *dial Eng* : a person employed to scare off crows

¹**crown** \'kraün\ *n, often attrib* [ME *coroune, crowne*, fr. OF *corone*, fr. L *corona* wreath, crown, fr. Gk *korōnē* culmination, something curved like a crow's beak, lit., crow; akin to L *cornix* crow, Gk *korax* raven — more at RAVEN] (12c)　**1** : a reward of victory or mark of honor; *esp* : the title representing the championship in a sport　**2** : a royal or imperial headdress or cap of sovereignty : DIADEM　**3** : the highest part: as　**a** : the topmost part of the skull or head　**b** : the summit of a mountain　**c** : the head of foliage of a tree or shrub　**d** : the part of a hat or other headgear covering the crown of the head　**e** : the part of a tooth external to the gum or an artificial substitute for this — see TOOTH illustration　**4** : a wreath, band, or circular ornament for the head　**5 a** : something resembling a wreath or crown　**b** : the knurled cap on top of a watch stem　**6** *often cap*　**a** (1) : imperial or regal power : SOVEREIGNTY　(2) : the government under a constitutional monarchy　**b** : MONARCH　**7** : something that imparts splendor, honor, or finish : CULMINATION　**8 a** : any of several old gold coins with a crown as part of the device　**b** : an old usu. silver British coin worth five shillings　**9** : KORUNA　**b** : KRONA　**c** : KRONE　**10 a** : the region of a seed plant at which stem and root merge　**b** : the thick arching end of the shank of an anchor where the arms join it — see ANCHOR illustration — **crowned** \'kraünd\ *adj* — **crown·less** \-ləs\ *adj*

²**crown** *vb* [ME *corounen*, fr. OF *coroner*, fr. L *coronare*, fr. *corona*] *vt* (12c)　**1 a** : to place a crown or wreath on the head of; *specif* : to invest with regal dignity and power　**b** : to recognize officially as ⟨they ~ed her athlete of the year⟩　**2** : to bestow something on as a mark of honor or recompense : ADORN　**3** : SURMOUNT, TOP; *esp* : to top (a checker) with a checker to make a king　**4** : to bring to a successful conclusion : CLIMAX　**5** : to provide with something like a crown: as　**a** : to fill so that the surface forms a crown　**b** : to put an artificial crown on (a tooth)　**6** : to hit on the head ~ *vi, of a forest fire* : to burn rapidly through the tops of trees

crown colony *n, often cap both Cs* (1845) : a colony of the Commonwealth over which the Crown retains some control

crown court *n* (1827) : a court in England and Wales that exercises jurisdiction over matters formerly heard by the quarter sessions and criminal matters formerly heard by the courts of assize

crow·ner \'krü-nər, 'kraú-\ *n* [ME, alter. of *coroner*] (14c) *dial chiefly Eng* : CORONER

crow·net \'kraú-nət\ *n* (15c) *archaic* : CORONET

crown gall *n* (1900) : a disease that affects many species of plants and is caused by a bacterium (*Agrobacterium tumefaciens*) which forms tumorous enlargements just below the ground on the stem

crown glass *n* (1706) **1** : a glass blown and whirled into the form of a disk with a center lump left by the worker's rod **2** : alkali-lime silicate optical glass having relatively low index of refraction and low dispersion value

crown jewel *n* (1649) **1** *pl* : the jewels (as crown and scepter) belonging to a sovereign's regalia **2** : the most attractive or valuable one of a collection or group

crown land *n* (ca. 1625) **1** : land belonging to the crown and yielding revenues that the reigning sovereign is entitled to **2** : public land in some British dominions or colonies

crown of thorns (1964) : a starfish (*Acanthaster planci*) of the Pacific region that is covered with long spines and is destructive to the coral of coral reefs — called also *crown-of-thorns starfish*

crown prince *n* (1791) : a male heir apparent to a crown or throne

crown princess *n* (1863) **1** : the wife of a crown prince **2** : a female heir apparent or heir presumptive to a crown or throne

crown roast *n* (ca. 1909) : a fancy roast of lamb, veal, or pork made from the rib portions of two loins skewered together at the ends to form a circle

crown rust *n* (ca. 1899) : a leaf rust of oats and other grasses that is caused by a fungus (*Puccinia coronata*) and is characterized by rounded light-orange uredinia and buried telia

crown vetch *n* (ca. 1900) : a European leguminous herb (*Coronilla varia*) that is naturalized in the eastern U.S. and has umbels of pink⹀ and-white flowers and sharp-angled pods

crow's-foot \'krŏz-,fút\ *n*, *pl* **crow's-feet** \-,fēt\ (14c) **1** : a wrinkle extending from the outer corner of the eye — usu. used in pl. **2** : CROWFOOT 1

crow's nest *n* (1818) : a partly enclosed platform high on a ship's mast for use as a lookout; *also* : a similar lookout (as for traffic control)

crow·step \'krŏ-,step\ *n* (1822) : any of a series of steps at the top of a gable wall — **crow-stepped** \-,stept\ *adj*

cro·zier *var of* CROSIER

CRT \,sē-(,)är-'tē\ *n*, *pl* **CRTs** *or* **CRT's** (ca. 1945) : CATHODE-RAY TUBE; *also* : a display device incorporating a cathode-ray tube

cruces *pl of* CRUX

cru·cial \'krü-shəl\ *adj* [F, fr. L *cruc-, crux* cross] (1706) **1** *archaic* : CRUCIFORM **2 a** : important or essential as resolving a crisis : DECISIVE ⟨a ~ step⟩ **b** : marked by final determination of a doubtful issue ⟨the ~ game of a series⟩ **c** : IMPORTANT, SIGNIFICANT ⟨what use we make of them will be the ~ question —Stanley Kubrick⟩ *syn* see ACUTE

cru·cial·ly \'krü-sh(ə-)lē\ *adv* (1879) **1** : in a crucial manner **2** : very importantly

cru·cian carp \'krü-shən-\ *n* [modif. of LG *karuse*, fr. MLG *karusse*, perh. of Baltic origin; akin to Lith *karušis* carp] (1836) : a European carp (*Carassius carassius*) — called also *crucian*

cru·ci·ate \'krü-shē-,āt\ *adj* [NL *cruciatus*, fr. L *cruc-, crux*] (1826) : cross-shaped : CRUCIFORM

cru·ci·ble \'krü-sə-bəl\ *n* [ME *corusible*, fr. ML *crucibulum* earthen pot for melting metals] (15c) **1** : a vessel of a very refractory material (as porcelain) used for melting and calcining a substance that requires a high degree of heat **2** : a severe test **3** : a place or situation in which concentrated forces interact to cause or influence change or development ⟨conditioned by having grown up within the ~ of Chinatown —Tom Wolfe⟩

crucible steel *n* (ca. 1879) : hard cast steel made in pots that are lifted from the furnace before the metal is poured into molds

cru·ci·fer \'krü-sə-fər\ *n* [LL, fr. L *cruc-, crux* + *-fer*] (1574) **1** : one who carries a cross esp. at the head of an ecclesiastical procession **2** : any of a family (Cruciferae) of plants including the cabbage, turnip, and mustard — **cru·cif·er·ous** \krü-'si-f(ə-)rəs\ *adj*

cru·ci·fix \'krü-sə-,fiks\ *n* [ME, fr. LL *crucifixus* the crucified Christ, fr. *crucifixus*, pp. of *crucifigere* to crucify, fr. L *cruc-, crux* + *figere* to fasten — more at FIX] (13c) : a representation of Christ on the cross

cru·ci·fix·ion \,krü-sə-'fik-shən\ *n* (15c) **1 a** *cap* : the crucifying of Christ **b** : the act of crucifying **2** : extreme and painful punishment, affliction, or suffering

cru·ci·form \'krü-sə-,fŏrm\ *adj* [L *cruc-, crux* + E *-form*] (1661) : forming or arranged in a cross — **cruciform** *n*

cru·ci·fy \'krü-sə-,fī\ *vt* **-fied; -fy·ing** [ME *crucifien*, fr. OF *crucifier*, fr. LL *crucifigere*] (14c) **1** : to put to death by nailing or binding the wrists or hands and feet to a cross **2** : to destroy the power of : MORTIFY ⟨~ the flesh⟩ **3 a** : to treat cruelly : TORMENT **b** : PILLORY 2

cruck \'krək\ *n* [prob. fr. dial. form of ²*crook* (curved timber)] (1888) : one of a pair of curved timbers forming a principal support of a roof in primitive English house construction

¹crud \'krəd\ *n* [ME *curd, crudd*] (14c) **1** *dial* : CURD **2 a** : a deposit or incrustation of filth, grease, or refuse **b** : something disagreeable or disgusting : RUBBISH **c** *slang* : a despicable or contemptible person **3** : a usu. ill-defined or imperfectly identified bodily disorder — **crud·dy** \'krə-dē\ *adj*

²crud *vb* **crud·ded; crud·ding** (14c) *dial* : ²CURD

¹crude \'krüd\ *adj* **crud·er; crud·est** [ME, fr. L *crudus* raw, crude, undigested — more at RAW] (14c) **1** : existing in a natural state and unaltered by cooking or processing ⟨~ oil⟩ **2** *archaic* : UNRIPE, IMMATURE **3** : marked by the primitive, gross, or elemental or by uncultivated simplicity or vulgarity ⟨a ~ stereotype⟩ **4** : rough or inexpert in plan or execution ⟨a ~ shelter⟩ **5** : lacking a covering, glossing, or concealing element : OBVIOUS ⟨~ facts⟩ **6** : tabulated without being broken down into classes ⟨the ~ death rate⟩ *syn* see RUDE — **crude·ly** *adv* — **crude·ness** *n*

²crude *n* (1904) : a substance in its natural unprocessed state; *esp* : unrefined petroleum

cru·di·tés \krǖ-dē-tā, ,krü-di-'tä\ *n pl* [F, fr. pl. of *crudité* rawness, fr. L *cruditas* indigestion, fr. *crudus*] (1960) : pieces of raw vegetables (as celery or carrot sticks) served as an hors d'oeuvre often with a dip

cru·di·ty \'krü-də-tē\ *n*, *pl* **-ties** (1547) **1** : the quality or state of being crude **2** : something that is crude

cru·el \'krü(-ə)l\ *adj* **cru·el·er** *or* **cru·el·ler; cru·el·est** *or* **cru·el·lest** [ME, fr. OF, fr. L *crudelis*, fr. *crudus*] (14c) **1** : disposed to inflict pain or suffering : devoid of humane feelings **2 a** : causing or conducive to injury, grief, or pain ⟨a ~ joke⟩ **b** : unrelieved by leniency *syn* see FIERCE — **cru·el·ly** \'krü-(ə-)lē\ *adv* — **cru·el·ness** *n*

cru·el·ty \'krü(-ə)l-tē\ *n*, *pl* **-ties** [ME *cruelte*, fr. OF *cr*uelté, fr. L *crudelitat-, crudelitas*, fr. *crudelis*] (13c) **1** : the quality or state of being cruel **2 a** : a cruel action **b** : inhuman treatment **3** : marital conduct held (as in a divorce action) to endanger life or health or to cause mental suffering or fear

cru·et \'krü-ət\ *n* [ME, fr. AF, dim. of OF *crue*, of Gmc origin; akin to OE *cruce*] (14c) **1** : a vessel to hold wine or water for the Eucharist **2** : a usu. glass bottle used to hold a condiment (as oil or vinegar) for use at the table

¹cruise \'krüz\ *vb* **cruised; cruis·ing** [D *kruisen* to make a cross, cruise, fr. MD *crucen*, fr. *crūce* cross, fr. L *cruc-, crux*] *vi* (1651) **1** : to sail about touching at a series of ports **2** : to move or proceed speedily, smoothly, or effortlessly ⟨I'll ~ over to her house to see if she's home⟩ **3** : to travel without destination or purpose **4 a** : to go about the streets at random but on the lookout for possible developments ⟨the cabdriver *cruised* for an hour before being hailed⟩ **b** : to search (as in public places) for a sexual partner **5 a** *of an airplane* : to fly at the most efficient operating speed **b** *of an automobile* : to travel at a speed suitable for being maintained for a long distance ~ *vt* **1** : to cruise over or about **2** : to inspect (as land) with reference to possible lumber yield **3 a** : to search in (a public place) for a sexual partner **b** : to approach and suggest sexual relations to

²cruise *n* (ca. 1706) : an act or an instance of cruising; *esp* : a tour by ship

cruise control *n* (1968) **1** : an electronic device in an automobile that controls the throttle so as to maintain a constant speed **2** : a relaxed and seemingly automatic pace that is easily maintained

cruise missile *n* (1959) : a guided missile that has a terrain-following radar system and that flies at moderate speed and low altitude

cruis·er \'krü-zər\ *n* (1695) **1** : a vehicle that cruises: as **a** : SQUAD CAR **b** : a powerboat with facilities (as a cabin and plumbing) necessary for living aboard — called also *cabin cruiser* **2** : a large fast moderately armored and gunned warship usu. of 6000 to 15,000 tons displacement **3** : a person who cruises

crul·ler \'krə-lər\ *n* [D *krulle*, a twisted cake, fr. *krul* curly, fr. MD *crul* — more at CURL] (1818) **1** : a small sweet cake in the form of a twisted strip fried in deep fat **2** *Northern & Midland* : an unraised doughnut

¹crumb \'krəm\ *n* [ME *crumme*, fr. OE *cruma*; akin to MHG *krume* crumb] (bef. 12c) **1 a** : a small fragment esp. of something baked (as bread) **b** : a porous aggregate of soil particles : BIT ⟨a ~ of good news⟩ **3** : the soft part of bread **4** *slang* : a worthless person

²crumb *vt* (14c) **1** : to break into crumbs **2** : to cover or thicken with crumbs **3** : to remove crumbs from ⟨~ a table⟩

¹crum·ble \'krəm-bəl\ *vb* **crum·bled; crum·bling** \-b(ə-)liŋ\ [alter. of ME *kremelen*, freq. of OE *gecrymian* to crumble, fr. *cruma*] *vt* (1570) : to break into small pieces ~ *vi* **1** : to fall into small pieces : DISINTEGRATE **2** : to break down completely : COLLAPSE ⟨marriages ~⟩

²crumble *n* (1820) **1** : something crumbled : fine debris **2** : CRISP 2

crum·blings \'krəm-b(ə-)liŋz\ *n pl* (1660) : crumbled particles : CRUMBS

crum·bly \-b(ə-)lē\ *adj* **crum·bli·er; -est** (1523) : easily crumbled : FRIABLE ⟨~ soil⟩ — **crum·bli·ness** *n*

crumb structure *n* (ca. 1906) : a soil condition suitable for farming in which the soil particles are aggregated into crumbs

crumhorn *var of* KRUMMHORN

crum·mie *or* **crum·my** \'krə-mē\ *n*, *pl* **crummies** [Sc *crumb* crooked, fr. ME, fr. OE] (1724) *chiefly Scot* : COW; *esp* : one with crumpled horns

crum·my *also* **crumby** \'krə-mē\ *adj* **crum·mi·er** *also* **crumb·i·er; -est** [ME *crumme*] (1567) **1** *obs* : CRUMBLY **2 a** : MISERABLE, FILTHY **b** : CHEAP, WORTHLESS — **crum·mi·ness** *n*

¹crump \'krəmp\ *vi* [imit.] (1646) **1** : CRUNCH **2** : to explode heavily

²crump *n* (1914) **1** : a crunching sound **2** : SHELL, BOMB

³crump *adj* [perh. alter. of *crimp* friable] (1787) *chiefly Scot* : BRITTLE

crum·pet \'krəm-pət\ *n* [perh. fr. ME *crompid* (*cake*) wafer, lit., curled⹀ up cake, fr. *crumped*, pp. of *crumpen* to curl up, fr. *crump, crumb* crooked, fr. OE *crumb*; akin to OHG *krump* crooked] (1769) : a small round unsweetened bread cooked on a griddle and usu. split and toasted before serving

¹crum·ple \'krəm-pəl\ *vb* **crum·pled; crum·pling** \-p(ə-)liŋ\ [ME *crumplen*, freq. of ME *crumpen*] *vt* (14c) **1** : to press, bend, or crush out of shape : RUMPLE **2** : to cause to collapse ~ *vi* **1** : to become crumpled **2** : COLLAPSE

²crumple *n* (15c) : a wrinkle or crease made by crumpling — **crum·ply** \'krəm-p(ə-)lē\ *adj*

¹crunch \'krənch\ *vb* [alter. of *craunch*] *vi* (1814) **1** : to chew or press with a crushing noise **2** : to make one's way with a crushing noise ~ *vt* **1** : to chew, press, or grind with a crunching sound **2** : PROCESS; *esp* : to perform mathematical computations on ⟨~ numbers⟩ — **crunch·able** \'krən-chə-bəl\ *adj*

²crunch *n* (1836) **1** : an act of crunching **2** : a sound made by crunching **3** : a tight or critical situation: as **a** : a critical point in the buildup of pressure between opposing elements : SHOWDOWN **b** : a severe economic squeeze (as on credit) **c** : SHORTAGE ⟨an energy ~⟩

crunch·er \'krən-chər\ *n* (1946) **1** : one that crunches **2** : a finishing blow

\ə\ abut \ʰ\ kitten, F table \ər\ further \a\ ash \ā\ ace \ä\ mop, mar \aú\ out \ch\ chin \e\ bet \ē\ easy \g\ go \i\ hit \ī\ ice \j\ job \ŋ\ sing \ō\ go \ò\ law \òi\ boy \th\ thin \t͟h\ the \ü\ loot \ú\ foot \y\ yet \zh\ vision \ä, k̲, ʰ, œ, œ̄, ᵫ, ᵫ̄, ʲ\ *see* Guide to Pronunciation

crunchy \'krən-chē\ *adj* **crunch·i·er; -est** (1913) : making a crunching sound when chewed or pressed — **crunch·i·ly** \-chə-lē\ *adv* — **crunch·i·ness** \-chē-nəs\ *n*

crup·per \'krə-pər, 'krú-\ *n* [ME *cruper*, fr. OF *crupiere*, fr. *croupe* hindquarters — more at CROUP] (14c) **1** : a leather loop passing under a horse's tail and buckled to the saddle **2** : ¹CROUP; *broadly* : BUTTOCKS

cru·ral \'krúr-əl\ *adj* [L *crur-, crus* leg] (1599) : of or relating to the thigh or leg; *specif* : FEMORAL ⟨∼ artery⟩

crus \'krüs, 'krəs\ *n, pl* **cru·ra** \'krúr-ə\ [L *crur-, crus*] (ca. 1751) : any of various anatomical parts that resemble a leg or a pair of legs

¹**cru·sade** \krü-'sād\ *n* [blend of MF *croisade* & Sp *cruzada;* both ultim. fr. L *cruc-, crux* cross] (ca. 1708) **1** *cap* : any of the military expeditions undertaken by Christian powers in the 11th, 12th, and 13th centuries to win the Holy Land from the Muslims **2** : a remedial enterprise undertaken with zeal and enthusiasm

²**crusade** *vi* **cru·sad·ed; cru·sad·ing** (1732) : to engage in a crusade — **cru·sad·er** *n*

cru·sa·do \krü-'sä-(,)dō\ *also* **cru·za·do** \-'zä-(,)dō, -(,)dü\ *n, pl* **-does** *or* **-dos** [Pg *cruzado*, lit., marked with a cross] (1544) : an old gold or silver coin of Portugal having a cross on the reverse

cruse \'krüz, 'krüs\ *n* [ME; akin to OE *crüse* pitcher] (13c) : a small vessel (as a jar or pot) for holding a liquid (as water or oil)

¹**crush** \'krəsh\ *vb* [ME *crusshen*, fr. MF *cruisir*, of Gmc origin; akin to MLG *krossen* to crush] *vt* (15c) **1 a** : to squeeze or force by pressure so as to alter or destroy structure **b** : to squeeze together into a mass **2** : HUG, EMBRACE **3** : to reduce to particles by pounding or grinding **4 a** : to suppress or overwhelm as if by pressure or weight **b** : to oppress or burden grievously ⟨∼ to subdue completely **5** : CROWD, PUSH **6** *archaic* : DRINK ∼ *vi* **1** *obs* : CRASH **2** : to become crushed **3** : to advance with or as if with crushing — **crush·able** \'krə-shə-bəl\ *adj* — **crush·er** *n* — **crush·ing·ly** *adv*

²**crush** *n* (1599) **1** : an act of crushing **2** : the quantity of material crushed **3 a** : a crowding together (as of people) **b** : CROWD, MOB, *esp* : a crowd of people pressing against one another **4** : an intense and usu. passing infatuation ⟨have a ∼ on someone⟩; *also* : the object of infatuation **syn** see CROWD — **crush-proof** \-,prüf\ *adj*

crust \'krəst\ *n* [ME, fr. L *crusta;* akin to OE *hrüse* earth, Gk *kryos* icy cold, *krystallos* ice, crystal] (14c) **1 a** : the hardened exterior or surface part of bread **b** : a piece of this or of bread grown dry or hard **2** : the pastry cover of a pie **3** : a hard or brittle external coat or covering: as **a** : a hard surface layer (as of soil or snow) **b** : the outer part of a planet, moon, or asteroid composed essentially of crystalline rocks **c** : a deposit built up on the interior surface of a wine bottle during long aging **d** : an encrusting deposit of dried secretions or exudate; *esp* : SCAB **4** : GALL, NERVE — **crust** *vb* — **crust·al** \'krəs-t³l\ *adj* — **crust·less** \'krəs(t)-ləs\ *adj*

crus·ta·cea \,krəs-'tā-sh(ē-)ə\ *n pl* [NL, group name, fr. neut. pl. of *crustaceus*] (1814) : arthropods that are crustaceans

crus·ta·cean \,krəs-'tā-shən\ *n* (1835) : any of a large class (Crustacea) of mostly aquatic mandibulate arthropods that have a chitinous or calcareous and chitinous exoskeleton, a pair of often much modified appendages on each segment, and two pairs of antennae and that include the lobsters, shrimps, crabs, wood lice, water fleas, and barnacles — **crustacean** *adj*

crus·ta·ceous \-shəs\ *adj* [NL *crustaceus*, fr. L *crusta* crust, shell] (ca. 1656) : of, relating to, having, or forming a crust or shell; *esp* : CRUSTOSE

crus·tose \'krəs-,tōs\ *adj* [L *crustosus* crusted, fr. *crusta*] (ca. 1879) : having a thin thallus adhering closely to a substrate (as of rock, bark, or soil) ⟨∼ lichens⟩ — compare FOLIOSE, FRUTICOSE

crusty \'krəs-tē\ *adj* **crust·i·er; -est** (14c) **1** : having or being a crust **2** : giving an effect of surly incivility in address or disposition **syn** see BLUFF — **crust·i·ly** \-tə-lē\ *adv* — **crust·i·ness** \-tē-nəs\ *n*

¹**crutch** \'krəch\ *n* [ME *crucche*, fr. OE *crycc;* akin to OHG *krucka* crutch] (bef. 12c) **1 a** : a support typically fitting under the armpit for use by the disabled in walking **b** : PROP, STAY **2** : a forked leg rest constituting the pommel of a sidesaddle **3** : the crotch of a human being or an animal **4** : a forked support

²**crutch** *vt* (1681) : to support on crutches : prop up

crux \'krəks, 'krúks\ *n, pl* **crux·es** *also* **cru·ces** \'krü-,sēz\ [L *cruc-, crux* cross, torture] (1718) **1** : a puzzling or difficult problem : an unsolved question **2** : an essential point requiring resolution or resolving an outcome ⟨the ∼ of the problem⟩ **3** : a main or central feature (as of an argument)

cru·za·do \krü-'zä-(,)dō, -(,)dü\ *n, pl* **-dos** [Pg] (1986) : the basic monetary unit of Brazil 1986–90

Cru·zan \krü-'zan\ *n* [(assumed) AmerSp *cruzano*, fr. Santa Cruz St. Croix] (1958) : a native or inhabitant of St. Croix — **Cruzan** *adj*

cru·zei·ro \krü-'zer-(,)ō, -(,)ü\ *n, pl* **-ros** [Pg] (1927) : the basic monetary unit of Brazil 1942–85 and 1991–93

crwth \'krüth\ *n* [W] (ca. 1837) : ³CROWD 1

¹**cry** \'krī\ *vb* **cried; cry·ing** [ME *crien*, fr. OF *crier*, fr. L *quiritare* to make a public outcry, perh. fr. *Quirit-, Quiris*, name for the Roman citizen] *vt* (13c) **1** : to utter loudly : SHOUT **2** *archaic* : BEG, BESEECH **3** : to proclaim publicly : ADVERTISE ⟨∼ their wares⟩ ∼ *vi* **1** : to call loudly : SHOUT **2** : to shed tears often noisily : WEEP, SOB **3** : to utter a characteristic sound or call **4** : to require or suggest strongly a remedy or disposition ⟨a hundred things which ∼ out for planning — Roger Burlingame⟩ — **cry havoc** : to sound an alarm — **cry over spilled milk** : to express vain regrets for what cannot be recovered or undone — **cry wolf** : to give alarm unnecessarily

²**cry** *n, pl* **cries** (13c) **1** : an instance of crying: as **a** : an inarticulate utterance of distress, rage, or pain **b** *obs* : OUTCRY, CLAMOR **2 a** *obs* : PROCLAMATION **b** *pl, Scot* : BANNS **3** : ENTREATY, APPEAL **4** : a loud shout **5** : WATCHWORD, SLOGAN **6 a** : common report **b** : a general opinion **7** : the public voice raised in protest or approval **8** : a fit of weeping **9** : the characteristic sound or call of an animal **10 a** : a pack of hounds **b** : PURSUIT — used in the phrase *in full cry* **11** : DISTANCE — usu. used in the phrase *a far cry*

cry- *or* **cryo-** *comb form* [G *kryo-*, fr. Gk, fr. *kryos* — more at CRUST] : cold : freezing ⟨cryonics⟩ ⟨cryogen⟩

cry·ba·by \'krī-,bā-bē\ *n* (1851) : one who cries or complains easily or often

cry down *vt* (1598) : DISPARAGE, DEPRECIATE

cry·ing \'krī-iŋ\ *adj* (1607) **1** : calling for notice ⟨a ∼ need⟩ **2** : NOTORIOUS, HEINOUS ⟨a ∼ shame⟩

cryo·bi·ol·o·gy \,krī-ō-bī-'ä-lə-jē\ *n* (1960) : the study of the effects of extremely low temperature on biological systems — **cryo·bi·o·log·i·cal** \-,bī-ə-'lä-ji-kəl\ *adj* — **cryo·bi·ol·o·gist** \-bī-'ä-lə-jist\ *n*

cry off *vt* (1928) : to call off (as a bargain) ∼ *vi, chiefly Brit* : to beg off

cryo·gen \'krī-ə-jən\ *n* (1875) : a substance for obtaining low temperatures : REFRIGERANT — called also *cryogenic*

cryo·gen·ic \,krī-ō-'je-nik\ *adj* (1896) **1 a** : of or relating to the production of very low temperatures **b** : being or relating to very low temperatures **2 a** : requiring or involving the use of a cryogenic temperature **b** : requiring cryogenic storage **c** : suitable for storage of a cryogenic substance — **cryo·gen·i·cal·ly** \-ni-k(ə-)lē\ *adv*

cryo·gen·ics \-niks\ *n pl but sing in constr* (ca. 1934) : a branch of physics that deals with the production and effects of very low temperatures

cryo·lite \'krī-ə-,līt\ *n* (1801) : a mineral consisting of a fluoride of sodium and aluminum found in Greenland usu. in white cleavable masses and used as a source of aluminum

cry·on·ics \krī-'ä-niks\ *n pl but usu sing in constr* [*cry-* + *-onics* (as in *electronics*)] (1967) : the practice of freezing a dead diseased human in hopes of restoring life at some future time when a cure for the disease has been developed — **cry·on·ic** \-nik\ *adj*

cryo·phil·ic \,krī-ə-'fi-lik\ *adj* (1942) : thriving at low temperatures

cryo·pres·er·va·tion \,krī-ō-,pre-zər-'vā-shən\ *n* (1968) : preservation (as of cells) by subjection to extremely low temperatures — **cryo·pre·serve** \,krī-ō-pri-'zərv, 'krī-ō-pri-,\ *vt*

cryo·probe \'krī-ə-,prōb\ *n* (1965) : a blunt chilled instrument used to freeze tissues in cryosurgery

cryo·pro·tec·tive \,krī-ō-prə-'tek-tiv\ *adj* (1967) : serving to protect from freezing ⟨an extracellular ∼ agent⟩ — **cryo·pro·tec·tant** \-'tek-tənt\ *n or adj*

cryo·scope \'krī-ə-,skōp\ *n* (1920) : an instrument for determining freezing points

cry·os·co·py \krī-'äs-kə-pē\ *n* [ISV] (ca. 1900) : the determination of the lowered freezing points produced in liquid by dissolved substances in order to determine molecular weights of solutes and various properties of solutions — **cryo·scop·ic** \,krī-ə-'skä-pik\ *adj*

cryo·stat \'krī-ə-,stat\ *n* [ISV] (1913) : an apparatus for maintaining a constant low temperature esp. below 0°C — **cryo·stat·ic** \,krī-ə-'sta-tik\ *adj*

cryo·sur·gery \,krī-ō-'sərj-rē, -'sər-jə-\ *n* (1962) : surgery in which the tissue to be treated or operated on is frozen (as by liquid nitrogen) — **cryo·sur·geon** \-'sər-jən\ *n* — **cryo·sur·gi·cal** \-ji-kəl\ *adj*

cryo·ther·a·py \-'ther-ə-pē\ *n* (1926) : the therapeutic use of cold

crypt \'kript\ *n* [L *crypta*, fr. Gk *kryptē*, fr. fem. of *kryptos* hidden, fr. *kryptein* to hide; perh. akin to Lith *krauti* to pile up] (1789) **1 a** : a chamber (as a vault) wholly or partly underground; *esp* : a vault under the main floor of a church **b** : a chamber in a mausoleum **2 a** : an anatomical pit or depression **b** : a simple tubular gland

crypt- *or* **crypto-** *comb form* [NL, fr. Gk *kryptos*] **1** : hidden : covered ⟨cryptogenic⟩ **2** : CRYPTOGRAPHIC ⟨cryptanalysis⟩

crypt·anal·y·sis \,krip-tə-'na-lə-səs\ *n* (1923) **1** : the solving of cryptograms or cryptographic systems **2** : the theory of solving cryptograms or cryptographic systems : the art of devising methods for this — **crypt·an·a·lyt·ic** \,krip-,tan-³l-'i-tik\ *also* **crypt·an·a·lyt·i·cal** \-ti-kəl\ *adj*

crypt·an·a·lyst \krip-'ta-n³l-ist\ *n* (1921) : a specialist in cryptanalysis

cryp·ta·rithm \'krip-tə-,ri-thəm\ *n* [*crypt-* + *-arithm* (as in *logarithm*)] (1943) : an arithmetic problem in which letters have been substituted for numbers and which is solved by finding all possible pairings of digits with letters that produce a numerically correct answer

cryp·tic \'krip-tik\ *adj* [LL *crypticus*, fr. Gk *kryptikos*, fr. *kryptos*] (ca. 1638) **1** : SECRET, OCCULT **2 a** : having or seeming to have a hidden or ambiguous meaning : MYSTERIOUS ⟨∼ messages⟩ **b** : marked by an often perplexing brevity ⟨∼ marginal notes⟩ **3** : serving to conceal ⟨∼ coloration in animals⟩; *also* : exhibiting cryptic coloration ⟨∼ animals⟩ **4** : UNRECOGNIZED ⟨a ∼ infection⟩ **5** : employing cipher or code **syn** see OBSCURE — **cryp·ti·cal·ly** \-ti-k(ə-)lē\ *adv*

¹**cryp·to** \'krip-(,)tō\ *n, pl* **cryptos** [*crypt-*] (1946) : a person who adheres or belongs secretly to a party, sect, or other group

²**crypto** *adj* (1952) **1** : CRYPTOGRAPHIC **2** : not openly avowed or declared : used in combination ⟨crypto-fascist⟩

cryp·to·coc·co·sis \,krip-tə-(,)kä-'kō-səs\ *n, pl* **-co·ses** \-(,)sēz\ [NL] (1938) : an infectious disease that is caused by a fungus (*Cryptococcus neoformans*) and is characterized by the production of nodular lesions or abscesses in the lungs, subcutaneous tissues, joints, and esp. the brain and meninges

cryp·to·coc·cus \-'kä-kəs\ *n, pl* **-coc·ci** \-'käk-,sī, -,sē, -'kä-,kī, -,kē\ [NL] (ca. 1902) : any of a genus (*Cryptococcus*) of budding imperfect fungi that resemble yeasts and include a number of saprophytes and a few serious pathogens — **cryp·to·coc·cal** \-'kä-kəl\ *adj*

cryp·to·crys·tal·line \,krip-tō-'kris-tə-lən\ *adj* [ISV] (1862) : having a crystalline structure so fine that no distinct particles are recognizable under the microscope ⟨∼ quartz⟩

cryp·to·gam \'krip-tə-,gam\ *n* [ultim. fr. Gk *kryptos* + *-gamia* -gamy] (1847) : a plant (as a fern, moss, alga, or fungus) reproducing by spores and not producing flowers or seed — **cryp·to·gam·ic** \,krip-tə-'ga-mik\ *or* **cryp·tog·a·mous** \krip-'tä-gə-məs\ *adj*

cryp·to·gen·ic \,krip-tə-'je-nik\ *adj* (1908) : of obscure or unknown origin ⟨a ∼ disease⟩

cryp·to·gram \'krip-tə-,gram\ *n* [F *cryptogramme*, fr. *crypt-* + *-gramme* -gram] (1880) **1** : a communication in cipher or code **2** : a figure or representation having a hidden significance

cryp·to·graph \'krip-tə-,graf\ *n* (1849) : CRYPTOGRAM

cryp·tog·ra·pher \krip-'tä-grə-fər\ *n* (1641) : a specialist in cryptography: as **a** : a clerk who enciphers and deciphers messages **b** : one who devises cryptographic methods or systems **c** : CRYPTANALYST

cryp·to·graph·ic \,krip-tə-'gra-fik\ *adj* (1824) : of, relating to, or using cryptography — **cryp·to·graph·i·cal·ly** \-fi-k(ə-)lē\ *adv*

cryp·tog·ra·phy \krip-'tä-grə-fē\ *n* [NL *cryptographia*, fr. *crypt-* + *-graphia* -graphy] (1658) **1** : secret writing **2** : the enciphering and deciphering of messages in secret code or cipher **3** : CRYPTANALYSIS

cryp·tol·o·gy \krip-'tä-lə-jē\ n (1935) : the scientific study of cryptography and cryptanalysis — **cryp·to·log·i·cal** \ˌkrip-tə-'lä-ji-kəl\ or **cryp·to·log·ic** \-jik\ adj — **cryp·tol·o·gist** \krip-'tä-lə-jist\ n

cryp·to·me·ria \ˌkrip-tə-'mir-ē-ə\ n [NL, genus name, fr. crypt- + Gk meros part — more at MERIT] (1841) : an evergreen tree (Cryptomeria japonica) of the pine family that is a valuable timber tree of Japan

cryp·to·nym \'krip-tə-ˌnim\ n (1876) : a secret name

cryp·tor·chid \krip-'tȯr-kəd\ n [NL cryptorchid-, cryptorchis, fr. crypt- + orchid-, orchis testicle, fr. Gk orchis — more at ORCHIS] (1874) : one affected with cryptorchidism — **cryptorchid** adj

crypt·or·chi·dism \-kə-ˌdi-zəm\ or **crypt·or·chism** \-ki-zəm\ n (ca. 1882) : a condition in which one or both testes fail to descend normally

cryp·to·zo·ol·o·gy \ˌkrip-tə-zō-'ä-lə-jē, -zə-'wä-\ n (1969) : the study of the lore concerning legendary animals (as Sasquatch) esp. in order to evaluate the possibility of their existence — **cryp·to·zo·ol·o·gist** \-'ä-lə-jist, -'wä-\ n

¹crys·tal \'kris-t³l\ n [ME cristal, fr. OF, fr. L crystallum, fr. Gk krystallos — more at CRUST] (13c) **1** : quartz that is transparent or nearly so and that is either colorless or only slightly tinged **2** : something resembling crystal in transparency and colorlessness **3** : a body that is formed by the solidification of a chemical element, a compound, or a mixture and has a regularly repeating internal arrangement of its atoms and often external plane faces **4** : a clear colorless glass of superior quality; also : objects or ware of such glass **5** : the glass or transparent plastic cover over a watch or clock dial **6** : a crystalline material used in electronics or for a frequency-determining element or for rectification **7** : powdered methamphetamine

²crystal adj (14c) **1** : consisting of or resembling crystal : CLEAR, LUCID **2** : relating to or using a crystal ⟨a ~ radio receiver⟩

crystal ball n (1855) **1** : a sphere esp. of quartz crystal traditionally used by fortune-tellers **2** : a means or method of predicting future events

crystal gazing n (1889) **1** : the art or practice of concentrating on a glass or crystal globe with the aim of inducing a psychic state in which divination can be performed **2** : the attempt to predict future events or make difficult judgments esp. without adequate data — **crystal gazer** n

crystall- or **crystallo-** comb form [Gk krystallos] : crystal ⟨crystallography⟩

crys·tal·line \'kris-tə-lən also -ˌlīn, -ˌlēn\ adj [ME cristallin, fr. MF & L; MF, fr. L crystallinus, fr. Gk krystallinos, fr. krystallos] (15c) **1** : resembling crystal: as **a** : strikingly clear or sparkling ⟨~ air⟩ ⟨a ~ lake⟩ **b** : CLEAR-CUT **2** : made of crystal : composed of crystals **3** : constituting or relating to a crystal — **crys·tal·lin·i·ty** \ˌkris-tə-'li-nə-tē\ n

crystalline lens n (1794) : the lens of the eye in vertebrates

crys·tal·lise Brit var of CRYSTALLIZE

crys·tal·lite \'kris-tə-ˌlīt\ n [G Kristallit, fr. Gk krystallos] (1805) **1 a** : a minute mineral form (as in glassy volcanic rocks) that marks the beginning of crystallization **b** : a single grain in a polycrystalline substance **2** : MICELLE

crys·tal·lize also **crys·tal·ize** \'kris-tə-ˌlīz\ vb **-lized; -liz·ing** vt (1598) **1** : to cause to form crystals or assume crystalline form **2** : to cause to take a definite form ⟨tried to ~ his thoughts⟩ **3** : to coat with crystals esp. of sugar ⟨~ grapes⟩ ~ vi **1** : to become crystallized — **crys·tal·liz·able** \-ˌlī-zə-bəl, ˌkris-tə-'\ adj — **crys·tal·li·za·tion** \ˌkris-tə-li-'zā-shən\ n — **crys·tal·liz·er** n

crys·tal·lo·graph·ic \ˌkris-tə-lə-'gra-fik\ adj (1804) : of or relating to crystals or crystallography — **crys·tal·lo·graph·i·cal·ly** \-fi-k(ə-)lē\ adv

crys·tal·log·ra·phy \ˌkris-tə-'lä-grə-fē\ n (1802) : a science that deals with the forms and structures of crystals — **crys·tal·log·ra·pher** \-fər\ n

crys·tal·loid \'kris-tə-ˌlȯid\ n (1861) : a substance that forms a true solution and is capable of being crystallized — **crystalloid** or **crys·tal·loi·dal** \ˌkris-tə-'lȯi-d³l\ adj

crystal pleat n (1976) : any of a series of narrow sharply pressed pleats all turned in one direction — **crystal pleated** adj

crystal violet n (ca. 1893) : a triphenylmethane dye found in gentian violet

cry up vt (1593) : to praise publicly in order to enhance in value or repute

CS \ˌsē-'es\ n [Ben B. Corson b1896 and Roger W. Staughton †1957 Am. chemists] (1960) : a potent tear gas used esp. for riot control

C–sec·tion \'sē-ˌsek-shən\ n (1973) : CESAREAN SECTION

cte·noid \'te-ˌnȯid, 'tē-\ adj [ISV, fr. Gk ktenoeidēs, fr. kten-, kteis comb — more at PECTINATE] (1872) : having the margin toothed ⟨~ scale⟩; also : having or consisting of ctenoid scales ⟨~ fishes⟩

cteno·phore \'te-nə-ˌfȯr, -ˌfȯr\ n [ultim. fr. Gk kten-, kteis + pherein to carry — more at BEAR] (ca. 1882) : any of a phylum (Ctenophora) of marine animals superficially resembling jellyfishes but having biradial symmetry and swimming by means of eight meridional bands of transverse ciliated plates — called also comb jelly — **cte·noph·o·ran** \tə-'nä-fə-rən\ n or adj

CT scan \ˌsē-'tē-\ n [computerized tomography] (1974) : CAT SCAN — **CT scanner** n

C–type \'sē-ˌtīp\ adj (1967) : relating to or being any of the oncornaviruses in which the structure containing the nucleic acid is spherical and centrally located ⟨~ virus particles⟩

cua·dri·lla \kwä-'drē-yə, -'drēl-\ n [Sp, dim. of cuadra square, fr. L quadra] (1893) : the team assisting the matador in the bullring

cub \'kəb\ n [origin unknown] (1530) **1 a** : a young carnivorous mammal (as a bear, fox, or lion) **b** : a young shark **2** : a young person **3** : APPRENTICE; esp : an inexperienced newspaper reporter

cub·age \'kyü-bij\ n (1840) : cubic content, volume, or displacement

Cu·ban heel \ˌkyü-bən-\ n [Cuba, West Indies] (1908) : a broad medium-high heel with a moderately curved back

cu·ba·ture \'kyü-bə-ˌchùr, -ˌchər, -ˌtyùr, -ˌtùr\ n [cube + -ature (as in quadrature)] (1679) : the process of determining the volume of a solid

cub·by \'kə-bē\ n, pl **cubbies** [obs. E cub pen, fr. D kub fish basket; akin to OE cofa den] (ca. 1859) : CUBBYHOLE

cub·by·hole \'kə-bē-ˌhōl\ n (ca. 1842) : a small snug place (as for hiding or storage); also : a cramped space

¹cube \'kyüb\ n [L cubus, fr. Gk kybos die, cube] (1551) **1 a** : the regular solid of six equal square sides — see VOLUME table **b** : something shaped like a cube ⟨ice ~⟩ **2** : the product got by taking a number three times as a factor

²cube adj (1570) : raised to the third power

³cube vt **cubed; cub·ing** (1588) **1** : to raise to the third power **2** : to form into a cube **3** : to cut partly through (a steak) in a checkered pattern to increase tenderness by breaking the fibers — **cub·er** n

⁴cu·be or **cu·bé** \'kyü-ˌbā, kyü-'\ n [AmerSp cubé] (1924) : any of several tropical American plants (genus Lonchocarpus) furnishing rotenone

cu·beb \'kyü-ˌbeb\ n [MF cubebe, fr. OF, fr. ML cubeba, fr. Ar kubābah] (14c) : the dried unripe berry of a tropical shrub (Piper cubeba) of the pepper family that is crushed and smoked in cigarettes for catarrh

cube root n (ca. 1696) : a number whose cube is a given number

cube steak n (1930) : a thin slice of beef that has been cubed

¹cu·bic \'kyü-bik\ adj (15c) **1** : having the form of a cube : CUBICAL **2 a** : relating to the cube considered as a crystal form **b** : ISOMETRIC 1 **3 a** : THREE-DIMENSIONAL **b** : being the volume of a cube whose edge is a specified unit ⟨~ inch⟩ **4** : of third degree, order, or power ⟨a ~ polynomial⟩

²cubic n (1799) : a cubic curve, equation, or polynomial

cu·bi·cal \'kyü-bi-kəl\ adj (15c) **1** : CUBIC **2** : relating to volume — **cu·bi·cal·ly** \-k(ə-)lē\ adv

cu·bi·cle \'kyü-bi-kəl\ n [L cubiculum, fr. cubare to lie, recline] (15c) **1** : a sleeping compartment partitioned off from a large room **2** : a small partitioned space; esp : CARREL

cubic measure n (1660) : a unit (as cubic inch or cubic centimeter) for measuring volume — see METRIC SYSTEM table, WEIGHT table

cub·ism \'kyü-bi-zəm\ n, often cap (1911) : a style of art that stresses abstract structure at the expense of other pictorial elements esp. by displaying several aspects of the same object simultaneously and by fragmenting the form of depicted objects — **cub·ist** \-bist\ n or adj, often cap — **cu·bis·tic** \kyü-'bis-tik\ adj

cu·bit \'kyü-bət\ n [ME, fr. L cubitum elbow, cubit] (14c) : any of various ancient units of length based on the length of the forearm from the elbow to the tip of the middle finger and usu. equal to about 18 inches (45.7 centimeters)

¹cu·boid \'kyü-ˌbȯid\ adj (ca. 1828) **1** : approximately cubical in shape **2** : relating to or being the cuboid

²cuboid n (1839) : the outermost bone in the distal row of tarsal bones of many higher vertebrates

cu·boi·dal \kyü-'bȯi-d³l\ adj (1803) **1** : somewhat cubical **2** : composed of nearly cubical elements ⟨~ epithelium⟩

Cub Scout n (ca. 1935) : a member of the scouting program of the Boy Scouts for boys in the first through fifth grades in school

cuck·ing stool \'kə-kiŋ-\ n [ME cucking stol, lit., defecating chair] (12c) : a chair formerly used for punishing offenders (as dishonest tradesmen) by public exposure or ducking in water

cuck·old \'kə-kəld, -(ˌ)kōld\ n [ME cokewold] (13c) : a man whose wife is unfaithful — **cuckold** vt

cuck·old·ry \-kəl-drē\ n (1529) **1** : the practice of making cuckolds **2** : the state of being a cuckold

¹cuck·oo \'kü-(ˌ)kü, 'kü-\ n, pl **cuckoos** [ME cuccu, of imit. origin] (13c) **1** : a largely grayish brown European bird (Cuculus canorus) that is a parasite given to laying its eggs in the nests of other birds which hatch them and rear the offspring; broadly : any of a large family (Cuculidae of the order Cuculiformes) to which this bird belongs **2** : the call of the cuckoo **3** : a silly or slightly crackbrained person

²cuckoo vt (1648) : to repeat monotonously as a cuckoo does its call

³cuckoo adj (1627) **1** : of, relating to, or resembling the cuckoo **2** : deficient in sense or intelligence : SILLY

cuckoo clock n (1789) : a wall or shelf clock that announces the hours by sounds resembling a cuckoo's call

cuckoo 1

cuck·oo-flow·er \'kü-(ˌ)kü-ˌflaù(-ə)r, 'kü-\ n (1578) **1** : a bitter cress (Cardamine pratensis) of Eurasia and No. America **2** : RAGGED ROBIN

cuck·oo-pint \-ˌpint\ n [ME cuccupintel, fr. cuccu + pintel pintle] (1551) : a European arum (Arum maculatum) with erect spathe and short purple spadix

cuckoo spit n (1592) **1** : a frothy secretion exuded on plants by the nymphs of spittle insects **2** : SPITTLEBUG

cu·cul·late \'kyü-kə-ˌlāt, kyü-'kə-lət\ adj [ML cucullatus, fr. L cucullus hood] (1794) : having the shape of a hood ⟨a ~ leaf⟩

cu·cum·ber \'kyü-(ˌ)kəm-bər\ n [ME, fr. MF coombre, fr. L cucumer-, cucumis] (14c) : the fruit of a vine (Cucumis sativus) of the gourd family cultivated as a garden vegetable; also : this vine

cucumber mosaic n (1916) : a virus disease esp. of cucumbers that is transmitted chiefly by an aphid and produces mottled foliage and often pale warty fruits

cucumber tree n (ca. 1782) : a magnolia (Magnolia acuminata) of the eastern U.S. having fruit resembling a small cucumber

cu·cur·bit \kyü-'kər-bət\ n [ME cucurbite, fr. MF, fr. L cucurbita gourd] (14c) **1** : a vessel or flask for distillation used with or forming part of an alembic **2** : a plant of the gourd family

cud \'kəd, chiefly Southern 'kùd or 'kùd\ n [ME cudde, fr. OE cwudu; akin to OHG kuti glue, Skt jatu gum] (bef. 12c) **1** : food brought up into the mouth by a ruminating animal from its first stomach to be chewed again **2** : ²QUID

\ə\ abut \ᵊ\ kitten, F table \ər\ further \a\ ash \ā\ ace \ä\ mop, mar \aù\ out \ch\ chin \e\ bet \ē\ easy \g\ go \i\ hit \ī\ ice \j\ job \ŋ\ sing \ō\ go \ȯ\ law \ȯi\ boy \th\ thin \t̲h̲\ the \ü\ loot \ù\ foot \y\ yet \zh\ vision \á, ḵ, ⁿ, œ, œ̄, ᵫ, ᵫ̄, ᵞ\ see Guide to Pronunciation

cud·bear \'kəd-ˌbar, -ˌber\ n [irreg. fr. Dr. *Cuthbert* Gordon, 18th cent. Scot. chemist] (1764) : a reddish coloring matter from lichens

¹cud·dle \'kə-d⁹l\ vb **cud·dled; cud·dling** \'kəd-liŋ, 'kə-d⁹l-iŋ\ [origin unknown] vt (1520) : to hold close for warmth or comfort or in affection ～ vi : to lie close or snug : NESTLE, SNUGGLE — **cud·dler** \'kəd-lər, 'kə-d⁹l-ər\ n

²cuddle n (1825) : a close embrace

cud·dle·some \'kə-d⁹l-səm\ adj (1876) : CUDDLY

cud·dly \'kəd-lē, 'kə-d⁹l-ē\ adj **cud·dli·er; -est** (1863) : fit for or inviting cuddling

¹cud·dy \'kə-dē\ n, pl **cuddies** [origin unknown] (1660) 1 : a usu. small cabin or shelter (as on a sailboat) 2 : a small room or cupboard

²cud·dy or **cud·die** \'kù-dē, 'kə-\ n, pl **cuddies** [perh. fr. *Cuddy*, nickname for *Cuthbert*] (ca. 1715) 1 dial Brit : DONKEY 2 dial Brit : BLOCKHEAD

¹cud·gel \'kə-jəl\ n [ME *kuggel*, fr. OE *cycgel*; perh. akin to MHG *kugele* ball] (bef. 12c) : a short heavy club

²cudgel vt **-geled** or **-gelled; -gel·ing** or **-gel·ling** \'kəj-liŋ, 'kə-jə-\ (1596) : to beat with or as if with a cudgel — **cudgel one's brains** : to think hard (as for a solution to a problem)

cud·weed \'kəd-ˌwēd, chiefly Southern 'kùd- or 'küd-\ n (1548) : any of several composite plants (as of the genus *Gnaphalium*) with silky or woolly foliage

¹cue \'kyü\ n [ME *cu* half a farthing (spelled form of q, abbr. for L *quadrans* quarter of an as)] (ca. 1755) : the letter q

²cue n [prob. fr. qu, abbr. (used as a direction in actors' copies of plays) of L *quando* when] (1553) 1 a : a signal (as a word, phrase, or bit of stage business) to a performer to begin a specific speech or action b : something serving a comparable purpose : HINT 2 : a feature indicating the nature of something perceived 3 archaic : the part one has to perform in or as if in a play 4 archaic : MOOD, HUMOR

³cue vt **cued; cu·ing** or **cue·ing** (1922) 1 : to give a cue to : PROMPT 2 : to insert into a continuous performance (～ in sound effects)

⁴cue n [F *queue*, lit., tail, fr. L *cauda*] (ca. 1749) 1 a : a leather-tipped tapering rod for striking the cue ball (as in billiards and pool) b : a long-handled instrument with a concave head for shoving disks in shuffleboard 2 : QUEUE 2

⁵cue vb **cued; cu·ing** or **cue·ing** vt (ca. 1784) 1 : QUEUE 2 : to strike with a cue ～ vi 1 : QUEUE 2 : to use a cue

cue ball n (1881) : the ball a player strikes with the cue in billiards and pool

cues·ta \'kwes-tə\ n [Sp, fr. L *costa* side, rib — more at COAST] (1818) : a hill or ridge with a steep face on one side and a gentle slope on the other

¹cuff \'kəf\ n [ME *coffe, cuffe* mitten] (1522) 1 : something (as a part of a sleeve or glove) encircling the wrist 2 : the turned-back hem of a trouser leg 3 a : HANDCUFF — usu. used in pl. b : a usu. wide metal band worn as a bracelet 4 : an inflatable band that is wrapped around an extremity to control the flow of blood through the part when recording blood pressure with a sphygmomanometer — **cuff·less** \'kə-fləs\ adj — **off the cuff** : without preparation : AD LIB — **on the cuff** : on credit

²cuff vt (1693) 1 : to furnish with a cuff 2 : HANDCUFF

³cuff vb [perh. fr. obs. E, glove, fr. ME] vt (1530) : to strike esp. with or as if with the palm of the hand : BUFFET ～ vi : FIGHT, SCUFFLE

⁴cuff n (1570) : a blow with the hand esp. when open : SLAP

cuff link n (1897) : a usu. ornamental device consisting of two parts joined by a shank, chain, or bar for passing through buttonholes to fasten shirt cuffs — usu. used in pl.

cui bo·no \'kwē-'bō-(ˌ)nō\ n [L, to whose advantage?] (1604) 1 : a principle that probable responsibility for an act or event lies with one having something to gain 2 : usefulness or utility as a principle in estimating the value of an act or policy

cui·rass \kwi-'ras, kyù-\ n [ME *curas*, fr. MF *curasse*, fr. LL *coreacea*, fem. of *coreaceus* leathern, fr. L *corium* skin, leather; akin to OE *heortha* deerskin, L *cortex* bark, Gk *keirein* to cut — more at SHEAR] (15c) 1 : a piece of armor covering the body from neck to waist; *also* : the breastplate of such a piece 2 : something (as bony plates covering an animal) resembling a cuirass — **cui·rassed** adj

cui·ras·sier \ˌkwir-ə-'sir, ˌkyùr-\ n (1625) : a mounted soldier wearing a cuirass

Cui·se·naire rod \ˌkwē-zə-'nar-, -'ner-\ n [fr. *Cuisenaire*, a trademark] (1954) : any of a set of colored rods usu. of 1 centimeter cross section and of 10 lengths from 1 to 10 centimeters that are used for teaching number concepts and the basic operations of arithmetic

cui·sine \kwi-'zēn, kwē-\ n [F, lit., kitchen, fr. LL *coquina* — more at KITCHEN] (1786) : manner of preparing food : style of cooking; *also* : the food prepared

cuisse \'kwis\ also **cuish** \'kwish\ n [ME *cusseis*, pl., fr. MF *cuissaux*, pl. of *cuissel*, fr. *cuisse* thigh, fr. L *coxa* hip — more at COXA] (15c) : a piece of plate armor for the front of the thigh — see ARMOR illustration

cuke \'kyük\ n (1903) : CUCUMBER

cul–de–sac \'kəl-di-ˌsak, 'kül-; ˌkəl-di-', ˌkül-\ n, pl **culs–de–sac** \'kəl(z)-, 'kül(z)-, ˌkəl(z)-, ˌkül(z)-\ also **cul–de–sacs** \-ˌsaks, -'saks\ [F, lit., bottom of the bag] (1738) 1 : a blind diverticulum or pouch 2 : a street or passage closed at one end 3 : BLIND ALLEY

cu·let \'kyü-lət, 'kə-lət\ n [F, fr. dim. of *cul* backside, fr. L *culus*; akin to OIr *cúl* back] (1678) 1 : the small flat facet at the bottom of a brilliant parallel to the table — see BRILLIANT illustration 2 : plate armor covering the buttocks

cu·lex \'kyü-ˌleks\ n [NL, fr. L, gnat; akin to OIr *cuil* fly] (15c) : any of a large cosmopolitan genus (*Culex*) of mosquitoes that includes the common house mosquito (*C. pipiens*) of Europe and No. America — **cu·li·cine** \'kyü-lə-ˌsīn\ adj or n

cu·li·nar·i·an \ˌkə-lə-'ner-ē-ən, ˌkyü-\ n (1949) : COOK, CHEF

cu·li·nary \'kə-lə-ˌner-ē, 'kyü-\ adj [L *culinarius*, fr. *culina* kitchen — more at KILN] (1638) : of or relating to the kitchen or cookery — **cu·li·nar·i·ly** \ˌkə-lə-'ner-ə-lē, ˌkyü-\ adv

¹cull \'kəl\ vt [ME, fr. MF *cuillir*, fr. L *colligere* to bind together — more at COLLECT] (13c) 1 : to select from a group : CHOOSE ⟨～ed the best passages from the poet's work⟩ 2 : to identify and remove the culls from — **cull·er** n

²cull n (1809) : something rejected esp. as being inferior or worthless ⟨how to separate good-looking pecans from ～s —*Washington Post*⟩

cul·len·der \'kə-lən-dər\ var of COLANDER

cul·let \'kə-lət\ n [perh. fr. F *cueillette* act of gathering, fr. L *collecta*, fr. fem. of *collectus*, pp. of *colligere*] (1817) : broken or refuse glass usu. added to new material to facilitate melting in making glass

cul·lion \'kəl-yən\ n [ME *coillon* testicle, fr. MF, fr. (assumed) VL *coleon-, coleo*, fr. L *coleus* scrotum] (1575) archaic : a mean or base fellow

¹cul·ly \'kə-lē\ n, pl **cullies** [perh. alter. of *cullion*] (1664) : one easily tricked or imposed on : DUPE

²cully vt **cul·lied; cul·ly·ing** (1676) archaic : CHEAT, DECEIVE

¹culm \'kəlm\ n [ME] (14c) : refuse coal screenings : SLACK

²culm n [L *culmus* stalk — more at HAULM] (ca. 1657) : a monocotyledonous stem (as of a grass or sedge)

cul·mi·nant \'kəl-mə-nənt\ adj (1605) 1 : being at greatest altitude or on the meridian 2 : fully developed

cul·mi·nate \'kəl-mə-ˌnāt\ vb **-nat·ed; -nat·ing** [ML *culminatus*, pp. of *culminare*, fr. LL, to crown, fr. L *culmin-, culmen* top — more at HILL] vi (1647) 1 of a celestial body : to reach its highest altitude; *also* : to be directly overhead 2 a : to rise to or form a summit b : to reach the highest or a climactic or decisive point ～ vt : to bring to a head or to the highest point

cul·mi·na·tion \ˌkəl-mə-'nā-shən\ n (1633) 1 : the action of culminating 2 : culminating position : CLIMAX *syn* see SUMMIT

cu·lotte \'kü-ˌlät, 'kyü-; kü-'lät, kyü-'\ n [F, breeches, fr. dim. of *cul* backside — more at CULET] (1911) : a divided skirt; *also* : a garment having a divided skirt — often used in pl.

cul·pa·ble \'kəl-pə-bəl\ adj [ME *coupable*, fr. MF, fr. L *culpabilis*, fr. *culpare* to blame, fr. *culpa* guilt] (14c) 1 archaic : GUILTY, CRIMINAL 2 : meriting condemnation or blame esp. as wrong or harmful ⟨～ negligence⟩ *syn* see BLAMEWORTHY — **cul·pa·bil·i·ty** \ˌkəl-pə-'bi-lə-tē\ n — **cul·pa·ble·ness** \'kəl-pə-bəl-nəs\ n — **cul·pa·bly** \-blē\ adv

cul·prit \'kəl-prət, -ˌprit\ n [AF *cul.* (abbr. of *culpable* guilty) + *prest, prit* ready (i.e., to prove it), fr. L *praestus* — more at PRESTO] (1678) 1 : one accused of or charged with a crime 2 : one guilty of a crime or a fault 3 : the source or cause of a problem

cult \'kəlt\ n, often attrib [F & L; F *culte*, fr. L *cultus* care, adoration, fr. *colere* to cultivate — more at WHEEL] (1617) 1 : formal religious veneration : WORSHIP 2 : a system of religious beliefs and ritual; *also* : its body of adherents 3 : a religion regarded as unorthodox or spurious; *also* : its body of adherents 4 : a system for the cure of disease based on dogma set forth by its promulgator ⟨health ～s⟩ 5 a : great devotion to a person, idea, object, movement, or work (as a film or book); *esp* : such devotion regarded as a literary or intellectual fad b : a usu. small group of people characterized by such devotion — **cul·tic** \'kəl-tik\ adj — **cult·ish** \-tish\ adj — **cult·ish·ly** \-lē\ adv — **cult·ish·ness** \-nəs\ n — **cult·ism** \'kəl-ˌti-zəm\ n — **cult·ist** \'kəl-tist\ n — **cult·like** \-ˌlīk\ adj

cultch also **culch** \'kəlch\ n [perh. fr. a F dial. form of F *couche* couch] (1667) 1 : material (as oyster shells) laid down on oyster grounds to furnish points of attachment for the spat 2 chiefly NewEng : CLUTTER, TRASH

cul·ti·gen \'kəl-tə-jən\ n [*cultivated* + *-gen*] (1924) 1 : a cultivated or domestic organism of a variety or species for which a wild ancestor is unknown 2 : CULTIVAR

cul·ti·va·ble \'kəl-tə-və-bəl\ adj (1682) : capable of being cultivated — **cul·ti·va·bil·i·ty** \ˌkəl-tə-və-'bi-lə-tē\ n

cul·ti·var \'kəl-tə-ˌvär, -ˌver, -ˌvär\ n [*cultivated* + *variety*] (1923) : an organism of a kind originating and persistent under cultivation

cul·ti·vate \'kəl-tə-ˌvāt\ vt **-vat·ed; -vat·ing** [ML *cultivatus*, pp. of *cultivare*, fr. *cultivus* cultivable, fr. L *cultus*, pp. of *colere*] (ca. 1655) 1 : to prepare or prepare and use for the raising of crops; *also* : to loosen or break up the soil about (growing plants) 2 a : to foster the growth of ⟨～ vegetables⟩ b : CULTURE 2a c : to improve by labor, care, or study : REFINE ⟨～ the mind⟩ 3 a : FURTHER, ENCOURAGE ⟨～ the arts⟩ 4 : to seek the society of : make friends with — **cul·ti·vat·able** \-ˌvā-tə-bəl\ adj

cultivated adj (1665) : REFINED, EDUCATED ⟨～ speech⟩ ⟨～ tastes⟩

cul·ti·va·tion \ˌkəl-tə-'vā-shən\ n (ca. 1716) 1 : CULTURE, REFINEMENT 2 : the act or art of cultivating or tilling

cul·ti·va·tor \'kəl-tə-ˌvā-tər\ n (1665) : one that cultivates; *esp* : an implement for loosening the soil while crops are growing

cul·tur·al \'kəlch-rəl, 'kəl-chə-\ adj (ca. 1864) 1 : of or relating to culture or culturing 2 : concerned with the fostering of plant or animal growth — **cul·tur·al·ly** \-rə-lē\ adv

cultural anthropology n (1933) : anthropology that deals with human culture esp. with respect to social structure, language, law, politics, religion, magic, art, and technology — compare PHYSICAL ANTHROPOLOGY — **cultural anthropologist** n

cul·tur·a·ti \ˌkəl-chə-'rä-(ˌ)tē\ n pl [¹*culture* + *-ati* (as in *literati*)] (1964) : people intensely interested in cultural affairs

¹cul·ture \'kəl-chər\ n [ME, fr. MF, fr. L *cultura*, fr. *cultus*, pp.] (15c) 1 : CULTIVATION, TILLAGE 2 : the act of developing the intellectual and moral faculties esp. by education 3 : expert care and training ⟨beauty ～⟩ 4 a : enlightenment and excellence of taste acquired by intellectual and aesthetic training b : acquaintance with and taste in fine arts, humanities, and broad aspects of science as distinguished from vocational and technical skills 5 a : the integrated pattern of human knowledge, belief, and behavior that depends upon man's capacity for learning and transmitting knowledge to succeeding generations b : the customary beliefs, social forms, and material traits of a racial, religious, or social group c : the set of shared attitudes, values, goals, and practices that characterizes a company or corporation 6 : cultivation of living material in prepared nutrient media; *also* : a product of such cultivation

²culture vt **cul·tured; cul·tur·ing** \'kəlch-riŋ, 'kəl-chə-\ (1510) 1 : CULTIVATE 2 a : to grow in a prepared medium b : to start a culture from

cultured adj (ca. 1746) 1 : CULTIVATED 2 : produced under artificial conditions ⟨～ viruses⟩ ⟨～ pearls⟩

culture shock n (ca. 1940) : a sense of confusion and uncertainty sometimes with feelings of anxiety that may affect people exposed to an alien culture or environment without adequate preparation

cul·tus \'kəl-təs\ n [L, adoration] (1640) : CULT

cul·ver \'kəl-vər, 'kúl-\ n [ME, fr. OE *culfer*, fr. (assumed) VL *columbra*, fr. L *columbula*, dim. of L *columba* dove — more at COLUMBINE] (bef. 12c) : PIGEON

cul·ver·in \'kəl-və-rən\ n [ME, fr. MF *couleuvrine*, fr. *couleuvre* snake, fr. L *colubra*] (15c) : an early firearm: **a** : a rude musket **b** : a long cannon (as an 18-pounder) of the 16th and 17th centuries

cul·vert \'kəl-vərt\ n [origin unknown] (1773) **1** : a transverse drain **2** : a conduit for a culvert **3** : a bridge over a culvert

cum \'kúm, 'kəm\ conj [L, with; akin to L *com*- — more at CO-] (ca. 1873) : along with being : AND — used to form usu. hyphenated phrases ⟨a credible mining camp elder-*cum*-publican —G. B. Shaw⟩ ⟨Christian and Christian-*cum*-voodoo churches —David Binder⟩

¹cum·ber \'kəm-bər\ vt cum·bered; cum·ber·ing \-b(ə-)riŋ\ [ME *combren*, perh. fr. OF *combrer* to prevent, fr. (assumed) OF *combre* abatis] (14c) **1** archaic : TROUBLE, HARASS **2 a** : to hinder or encumber by being in the way ⟨~ed with heavy clothing⟩ **b** : to clutter up ⟨rocks ~ing the yard⟩

²cumber n (14c) : something that cumbers; esp : HINDRANCE

cum·ber·some \'kəm-bər-səm\ adj (1535) **1** dial : BURDENSOME, TROUBLESOME **2** : unwieldy because of heaviness and bulk **3** : slow: moving : PONDEROUS syn see HEAVY — **cum·ber·some·ly** adv — **cum·ber·some·ness** n

cum·brous \'kəm-b(ə-)rəs\ adj (15c) : CUMBERSOME syn see HEAVY — **cum·brous·ly** adv — **cum·brous·ness** n

cum·in \'kə-mən, 'kyü-\ n [ME, fr. OE *cymen*, fr. L *cuminum*, fr. Gk *kyminon*, of Sem origin; akin to Akkadian *kamūnu* cumin] (bef. 12c) : a low plant (*Cuminum cyminum*) of the carrot family long cultivated for its aromatic seeds; also : the fruit or seed of cumin used as a spice

cum lau·de \'kúm-'laú-də, -,dā, ,kəm-'lò-dē\ adv or adj [NL, with praise] (1893) : with distinction ⟨graduated *cum laude*⟩ — compare MAGNA CUM LAUDE, SUMMA CUM LAUDE

cum·mer·bund \'kə-mər-,bənd, 'kəm-bər-\ also **cum·ber·bund** \'kəm-bər-\ n [Hindi *kamarband*, fr. Per, fr. *kamar* waist + *band* band] (1616) : a broad waistband usu. worn in place of a vest with men's dress clothes and adapted in various styles of women's clothes

cum·shaw \'kəm-,shò\ n [Chin (Xiamen) *kam siā* grateful thanks] (1839) : PRESENT, GRATUITY

cumul- or **cumuli-** or **cumulo-** comb form [NL, fr. L *cumulus*] : cumulus and ⟨*cumulonimbus*⟩

cu·mu·late \'kyü-myə-,lāt\ vb -lat·ed; -lat·ing [L *cumulatus*, pp. of *cumulare*, fr. *cumulus* mass] vt (1534) **1** : to gather or pile in a heap **2** : to combine into one **3** : to build up by addition of new material ~ vi : to become massed — cu·mu·late \-lət, -,lāt\ adj — **cu·mu·la·tion** \,kyü-myə-'lā-shən\ n

cu·mu·la·tive \'kyü-myə-lə-tiv, -,lā-\ adj (1605) **1 a** : made up of accumulated parts **b** : increasing by successive additions **2 a** : tending to prove the same point ⟨~ evidence⟩ **b** : additional rather than repeated ⟨~ legacy⟩ **3 a** : taking effect upon completion of another penal sentence ⟨~ sentence⟩ **b** : increasing in severity with repetition of the offense ⟨~ penalty⟩ **4** : formed by the addition of new material of the same kind ⟨~ book index⟩ **5** : summing or integrating overall data or values of a random variable less than or less than or equal to a specified value ⟨~ normal distribution⟩ ⟨~ frequency distribution⟩ — **cu·mu·la·tive·ly** adv — **cu·mu·la·tive·ness** n

cumulative distribution function n (ca. 1965) : DISTRIBUTION FUNCTION

cu·mu·li·form \'kyü-myə-lə-,form\ adj (1885) : of the form of a cumulus

cu·mu·lo·nim·bus \-'nim-bəs\ n [NL] (1887) : cumulus cloud often spread out in the shape of an anvil extending to great heights — see CLOUD illustration

cu·mu·lous \'kyü-myə-ləs\ adj (1815) : resembling cumulus

cu·mu·lus \-ləs\ n, pl -li \-,lī, -,lē\ [L] (1659) **1** : HEAP, ACCUMULATION **2** [NL, fr. L] : a massy cloud form having a flat base and rounded outlines often piled up like a mountain — see CLOUD illustration

cunc·ta·tion \,kəŋ(k)-'tā-shən\ n [L *cunctation-, cunctatio*, fr. *cunctari* to hesitate; akin to Skt *śaṅkate* he hangs, OE *hangian* to hang] (1585) : DELAY — **cunc·ta·tive** \'kəŋ(k)-,tā-tiv, -tə-tiv\ adj

cu·ne·ate \'kyü-nē-,āt, -ət\ adj [L *cuneatus*, fr. *cuneus* wedge] (1661) : narrowly triangular with the acute angle toward the base — see LEAF illustration

¹cu·nei·form \kyú-'nē-ə-,fórm, 'kyü-n(ē-)ə-\ adj [prob. fr. F *cunéiforme*, fr. MF, fr. L *cuneus* + MF *-iforme* -iform] (1677) **1** : having the shape of a wedge **2** : composed of or written in wedge-shaped characters ⟨~ syllabary⟩

²cuneiform n (1808) **1** : a cuneiform part; specif : a cuneiform bone or cartilage **2** : cuneiform writing

cun·ner \'kə-nər\ n [origin unknown] (1602) : either of two wrasses: **a** : a European wrasse (*Crenilabrus melops*) **b** : a wrasse (*Tautogolabrus adspersus*) common along the northeastern U.S. and adjacent Canadian coast

cun·ni·lin·gus \,kə-ni-'liŋ-gəs\ also **cun·ni·linc·tus** \-'liŋ(k)-təs\ n [cunnilingus, NL, fr. L, one who licks the vulva, fr. *cunnus* vulva + *lingere* to lick; cunnilinctus, NL, fr. L *cunnus* + *linctus*, act of licking, fr. *lingere* — more at LICK] (1887) : oral stimulation of the vulva or clitoris

¹cun·ning \'kə-niŋ\ adj [ME, fr. prp. of *can* know] (14c) **1** : dexterous or crafty in the use of special resources (as skill or knowledge) or in attaining an end ⟨a ~ plotter⟩ **2** : displaying keen insight ⟨a ~ observation⟩ **3** : characterized by wiliness and trickery ⟨~ schemes⟩ **4** : prettily appealing : CUTE syn see CLEVER, SLY — **cun·ning·ly** \-niŋ-lē\ adv — **cun·ning·ness** n

²cunning n (14c) **1** obs : KNOWLEDGE, LEARNING **b** : magic art **2** : dexterous skill and subtlety (as in inventing, devising, or executing) ⟨high-ribbed vault . . . with perfect ~ framed —William Wordsworth⟩ **3** : CRAFT, SLYNESS syn see ART

cuneiform 2

cunt \'kənt\ n [ME *cunte*; akin to MLG *kunte* female pudenda] (14c) **1** : the female pudenda; also : coitus with a woman — usu. considered obscene **2** : WOMAN 1a — usu. used disparagingly; usu. considered obscene

¹cup \'kəp\ n [ME *cuppe*, fr. OE, fr. LL *cuppa* cup, alter. of L *cupa* tub — more at HIVE] (bef. 12c) **1** : an open usu. bowl-shaped drinking vessel **2 a** : a drinking vessel and its contents **b** : the consecrated wine of the Communion **3** : something that falls to one's lot **4** : an ornamental cup offered as a prize (as in a championship) **5 a** : something resembling a cup **b** : a cup-shaped plant organ **c** : an athletic supporter reinforced usu. with plastic to provide extra protection to the wearer **d** : either of two parts of a brassiere that are shaped like and fit over the breasts **e** : the metal case inside a hole in golf; also : the hole itself **6 a** : usu. iced beverage resembling punch but served from a pitcher rather than a bowl **7 a** : a half pint : eight fluid ounces **8 a** : a food served in a cup-shaped usu. footed vessel ⟨fruit ~⟩ **9** : the symbol ∪ indicating the union of two sets — compare CAP 7 — **cup·like** \-,līk\ adj — **in one's cups** : DRUNK

²cup vt cupped; cup·ping (14c) **1** : to treat by cupping **2 a** : to curve into the shape of a cup ⟨*cupped* his hands around his mouth⟩ **b** : to place in or as if in a cup

cup·bear·er \'kəp-,bar-ər, -,ber-\ n (15c) : one who has the duty of filling and handing around the cups in which wine is served

cup·board \'kə-bərd\ n (1530) : a closet with shelves where dishes, utensils, or food is kept; also : a small closet

cup·cake \'kəp-,kāk\ n (1828) : a small cake baked in a cuplike mold

¹cu·pel \kyü-'pel, 'kyü-pəl\ n [F *coupelle*, dim. of *coupe* cup, fr. LL *cuppa*] (1605) : a small shallow porous cup esp. of bone ash used in assaying to separate precious metals from lead

²cupel vt -pelled or -peled; -pel·ling or -pel·ing (1644) : to refine by means of a cupel — **cu·pel·ler** n

cu·pel·la·tion \,kyü-pə-'lā-shən, -pe-\ n (ca. 1691) : refinement (as of gold or silver) in a cupel by exposure to high temperature in a blast of air by which the lead, copper, tin, and other unwanted metals are oxidized and partly sink into the porous cupel

cup·ful \'kəp-,fúl\ n, pl cup·fuls \-,fúlz\ also cups·ful \'kəps-,fúl\ (12c) **1** : as much as a cup will hold **2** : CUP 7

cup fungus n (ca. 1905) : any of an order (Pezizales) of mostly saprophytic fungi with a fleshy or horny apothecium that is often colored and is typically shaped like a cup, saucer, or disk

Cu·pid \'kyü-pəd\ n [L *Cupido*] **1** : the Roman god of erotic love — compare EROS **2** not cap : a figure that represents Cupid as a naked usu. winged boy often holding a bow and arrow

cu·pid·i·ty \kyú-'pi-də-tē\ n, pl -ties [ME *cupidite*, fr. MF *cupidité*, fr. L *cupiditat-, cupiditas* — more at COVET] (15c) **1** : inordinate desire for wealth : AVARICE, GREED **2** : strong desire : LUST

Cupid's bow n (1858) : a bow that consists of two convex curves usu. with recurved ends

cup of tea (1932) **1** : something one likes or excels in ⟨I see already that storytelling isn't my *cup of tea* —John Barth⟩; also : a person suited to one's taste **2** : a thing to be reckoned with : MATTER ⟨poltergeists are a different *cup of tea* —D. B. W. Lewis⟩

cu·po·la \'kyü-pə-lə, -₊-,lò\ n [It, fr. L *cupula*, dim. of *cupa* tub] (1549) **1 a** : a rounded vault resting on a usu. circular base and forming a roof or a ceiling **b** : a small structure built on top of a roof **2** : a vertical cylindrical furnace for melting iron in the foundry that has tuyeres and tapping spouts near the bottom **3** : a raised observation post in the roof of a railroad caboose — **cu·po·laed** \-ləd, -₊-,löd\ adj

cup·pa \'kə-pə\ n [short for *cuppa tea*, pronunciation spelling of *cup of tea*] (1934) chiefly Brit : a cup of tea

cup·ping n (14c) : an operation of drawing blood to the surface of the body by use of a glass vessel evacuated by heat

cup·py \'kə-pē\ adj (14c) and cup·pi·er; -est (1882) **1** : resembling a cup **2** : full of small depressions ⟨a ~ racetrack⟩

cupr- or **cupri-** or **cupro-** comb form [LL *cuprum* — more at COPPER] **1** : copper ⟨*cupriferous*⟩ **2** : copper and ⟨*cupronickel*⟩

cu·pric \'kyü-prik, 'kü-\ adj (1799) : of, relating to, or containing copper with a valence of two

cu·prif·er·ous \kyü-'pri-f(ə-)rəs, kü-\ adj (1784) : containing copper

cu·prite \'kyü-,prīt, 'kü-\ n [G *Kuprit*, fr. LL *cuprum*] (ca. 1850) : a mineral consisting of copper oxide and constituting an ore of copper

cu·pro·nick·el \,kyü-prō-'ni-kəl, ,kü-\ n (1900) : an alloy of copper and nickel; esp : one containing about 70 percent copper and 30 percent nickel

cu·prous \'kyü-prəs, 'kü-\ adj (1669) : of, relating to, or containing copper with a valence of one

cu·pu·late \'kyü-pyə-,lāt, -lət\ adj (1835) : shaped like, having, or bearing a cupule

cu·pule \'kyü-(,)pyü(ə)l\ n [NL *cupula*, fr. LL, dim. of L *cupa* tub — more at HIVE] (1826) : a cup-shaped anatomical structure: as **a** : an involucre characteristic of the oak in which the bracts are indurated and coherent **b** : an outer integument partially enclosing the seed of some seed ferns

cur \'kər\ n [ME, short for *curdogge*, fr. (assumed) ME *curren* to growl (perh. fr. ON *kurra* to grumble) + ME *dogge* dog] (13c) **1** : a mongrel or inferior dog **2** : a surly or cowardly fellow

cur·able \'kyúr-ə-bəl\ adj (14c) : capable of being cured — **cur·abil·i·ty** \,kyúr-ə-'bi-lə-tē\ n — **cur·able·ness** \'kyúr-ə-bəl-nəs\ n — **cur·ably** \-blē\ adv

cu·ra·çao \'kyúr-ə-,sō, -,saú, 'kúr-; ,k(y)úr-ə-'\ also **cu·ra·çoa** \same, or ,kyúr-ə-'sō-ə\ n [D *curaçao*, fr. *Curaçao*, Netherlands Antilles] (1813) : a liqueur flavored with the dried peel of the sour orange

cu·ra·cy \'kyúr-ə-sē\ n, pl -cies (1682) : the office or term of office of a curate

cu·ra·re also **cu·ra·ri** \kyü-'rär-ē, kú-\ n [Pg & Sp *curare*, fr. Carib *kurari*] (1777) : a dried aqueous extract esp. of a vine (as *Strychnos toxifera* of the family Loganiaceae or *Chondodendron tomentosum* of the family Menispermaceae) used by So. American Indians to poison arrow tips and in medicine to produce muscular relaxation

cu·ra·rine \-'rär-ən, -,ēn\ n (ca. 1872) : any of several alkaloids from curare

---

\ə\ abut \ʾ\ kitten, F table \ər\ further \a\ ash \ā\ ace \ä\ mop, mar \aú\ out \ch\ chin \e\ bet \ē\ easy \g\ go \i\ hit \ī\ ice \j\ job \ŋ\ sing \ō\ go \ò\ law \òi\ boy \th\ thin \t̲h̲\ the \ü\ loot \ú\ foot \y\ yet \zh\ vision \á, k̲, ⁿ, œ, œ̄, ue, ūe, ᵞ\ see Guide to Pronunciation

cu·ra·rize \-'rär-,īz\ vt **-rized; -riz·ing** (1875) : to treat with curare — **cu·ra·ri·za·tion** \-,rär-ə-'zā-shən\ n

cu·ras·sow \'kyùr-ə-,sō, 'kùr-\ n [alter. of Curaçao] (1685) : any of several large arboreal game birds (family Cracidae, esp. genus Crax) of So. and Central America related to the domestic fowls

¹cu·rate \'kyùr-ət also 'kyùr-,āt\ n [ME, fr. ML curatus, fr. cura cure of souls, fr. L, care] (14c) **1** : a clergyman in charge of a parish **2** : a clergyman serving as assistant (as to a rector) in a parish

²cu·rate \'kyùr-,āt, kyù-'rāt\ vt **cu·rat·ed; cu·rat·ing** (1909) : to act as curator of

curate's egg n [fr. the story of a curate who was given a stale egg by his bishop and declared that parts of it were excellent] (1905) Brit : something with both good and bad parts or qualities

cu·ra·tive \'kyùr-ə-tiv\ adj (15c) : relating to or used in the cure of diseases : tending to cure — **curative** n — **cu·ra·tive·ly** adv

cu·ra·tor \'kyùr-,ā-tər, kyù-'rā-, 'kyùr-ə-\ n [L, fr. curatus, pp. of curare to care, fr. cura care] (1632) : one that has the care and superintendence of something; esp : one in charge of a museum, zoo, or other place of exhibit — **cu·ra·to·ri·al** \,kyùr-ə-'tōr-ē-əl, -'tòr-\ adj — **cu·ra·tor·ship** \'kyùr-ə-tər-,ship, kyù-'rā-, 'kyùr-ə-\ n

¹curb \'kərb\ n [MF courbe curve, curved piece of wood or iron, fr. courbe curved, fr. L curvus] (15c) **1** : a bit that exerts severe pressure on a horse's jaws; also : the chain or strap attached to it **2** : an enclosing frame, border, or edging **3** : CHECK, RESTRAINT ⟨a price ~⟩ **4** : a raised edge or margin to strengthen or confine **5** : an edging (as of concrete) built along a street to form part of a gutter **6** [fr. the fact that it orig. transacted its business on the street] : a market for trading in securities not listed on a stock exchange

²curb vt (1530) **1** : to furnish with a curb **2** : to check or control with or as if with a curb ⟨trying to ~ her curiosity⟩ **3** : to lead (a dog) to a suitable place (as a gutter) for defecation syn see RESTRAIN

curb·ing \'kər-biŋ\ n (1838) **1** : the material for a curb **2** : CURB

curb service n (1931) : service extended (as by a restaurant) to persons sitting in parked automobiles

curb·side \'kərb-,sīd\ n (1946) **1** : the side of a pavement bordered by a curb **2** : SIDEWALK

¹curb·stone \-,stōn\ n (1791) : a stone or edging of concrete forming a curb

²curbstone adj (1848) **1** : operating on the street without maintaining an office ⟨a ~ broker⟩ **2** : not having the benefit of training or experience ⟨a ~ critic⟩

curb weight n (1949) : the weight of an automobile with standard equipment and fuel, oil, and coolant

curch \'kərch\ n [ME] (14c) Scot : KERCHIEF 1

cur·cu·lio \(,)kər-'kyü-lē-,ō\ n, pl **-li·os** [L, grain weevil] (1756) : any of various weevils; esp : one that injures fruit

curd \'kərd\ n [ME crud; prob. akin to OE crūdan to press — more at CROWD] (15c) **1** : the thick casein-rich part of coagulated milk **2** : something suggesting the curd of milk — **curdy** \'kər-dē\ adj

²curd vb (15c) : COAGULATE, CURDLE

cur·dle \'kər-d⁰l\ vb **cur·dled; cur·dling** \'kərd-liŋ, 'kər-d⁰l-iŋ\ [freq. of ²curd] vi (1590) **1** : to form curds; also : to congeal as if by forming curds ⟨a scream curdled in her throat⟩ **2** : to go bad or wrong : SPOIL ~ vt **1** : to cause curds to form in **2** : SPOIL, SOUR

¹cure \'kyùr\ n [ME, fr. OF, fr. ML & L; ML cura, cure of souls, fr. L, care] (14c) **1 a** : spiritual charge : CARE **b** : pastoral charge of a parish **2 a** : recovery or relief from a disease **b** : something (as a drug or treatment) that cures a disease **c** : a course or period of treatment ⟨take the ~ for alcoholism⟩ d : SPA **3** : a complete or permanent solution or remedy ⟨seeking a ~ for unemployment⟩ **4** : a process or method of curing — **cure·less** \-ləs\ adj

²cure vb **cured; cur·ing** vt (14c) **1 a** : to restore to health, soundness, or normality **b** : to bring about recovery from **2 a** : to deal with in a way that eliminates or rectifies ⟨his small size, which time would ~ for him —William Faulkner⟩ **b** : to free from something objectionable or harmful **3** : to prepare or alter esp. by chemical or physical processing for keeping or use ~ vi **1** : to undergo a curing process **b** : SET 11 **2** : to effect a cure — **cur·er** n

cu·ré \kyù-'rā, 'kyùr-,ā\ n [F, fr. OF, fr. ML curatus — more at CURATE] (1655) : a parish priest

cure–all \'kyùr-,ȯl\ n (1821) : a remedy for all ills : PANACEA

cu·ret·tage \,kyùr-ə-'täzh\ n (1897) : a surgical scraping or cleaning by means of a curette

¹cu·rette also **cu·ret** \kyù-'ret\ n [F curette, fr. curer to cure, fr. L curare, fr. cura] (1753) : a surgical instrument that has a scoop, ring, or loop at the tip and is used in performing curettage

²curette also **curet** vt **cu·rett·ed; cu·rett·ing** (1888) : to perform curettage on — **cu·rette·ment** \kyù-'ret-mənt\ n

cur·few \'kər-(,)fyü\ n [ME, fr. MF covrefeu, signal given to bank the hearth fire, curfew, fr. covrir to cover + feu fire, fr. L focus hearth] (14c) **1** : the sounding of a bell at evening ⟨the Curfew tolls the knell of parting day —Thomas Gray⟩ **2 a** : a regulation enjoining the withdrawal of usu. specified persons (as juveniles or military personnel) from the streets or the closing of business establishments or places of assembly at a stated hour **b** : a signal to announce the beginning of a curfew **c** : the hour at which a curfew becomes effective **d** : the period during which a curfew is in effect

cu·ria \'kyùr-ē-ə, 'kùr-\ n, pl **cu·ri·ae** \'kyùr-ē-,ē, 'kùr-ē-,ī\ [L, perh. fr. co- + vir man — more at VIRILE] (1600) **1 a** : a division of the ancient Roman people comprising several gentes of a tribe **b** : the place of assembly of one of these divisions **2 a** : the court of a medieval king **b** : a court of justice **3** often cap : the body of congregations, tribunals, and offices through which the pope governs the Roman Catholic Church — **cu·ri·al** \'kyùr-ē-əl, 'kùr-\ adj

cu·rie \'kyùr-(,)ē, kyù-'rē\ n [Marie & Pierre Curie] (1910) **1** : a unit quantity of any radioactive nuclide in which 3.7×10^{10} disintegrations occur per second **2** : a unit of radioactivity equal to 3.7×10^{10} disintegrations per second

Curie point n (1911) **1** : the temperature at which there is a transition between the ferromagnetic and paramagnetic phases **2** : a temperature at which the anomalies that characterize a ferroelectric substance disappear — called also Curie temperature

cu·rio \'kyùr-ē-,ō\ n, pl **cu·ri·os** [short for curiosity] (1851) : something (as a decorative object) considered novel, rare, or bizarre : CURIOSITY; also : an unusual or bizarre person

cu·ri·o·sa \,kyùr-ē-'ō-sə, -'ō-zə\ n pl [NL, fr. L, neut. pl. of curiosus] (1883) : CURIOSITIES, RARITIES; esp : unusual or erotic books

cu·ri·os·i·ty \,kyùr-ē-'ä-s(ə-)tē\ n, pl **-ties** (14c) **1** : desire to know: **a** : inquisitive interest in others' concerns : NOSINESS **b** : interest leading to inquiry ⟨intellectual ~⟩ **2** archaic : undue nicety or fastidiousness **3 a** : one that arouses interest esp. for uncommon or exotic characteristics **b** : an unusual knickknack : CURIO **c** : a curious trait or aspect

cu·ri·ous \'kyùr-ē-əs\ adj [ME, fr. MF curios, fr. L curiosus careful, inquisitive, fr. cura cure] (14c) **1 a** archaic : made carefully **b** obs : ABSTRUSE **c** archaic : precisely accurate **2 a** : marked by desire to investigate and learn **b** : marked by inquisitive interest in others' concerns : NOSY **3** : exciting attention as strange, novel, or unexpected : ODD — **cu·ri·ous·ness** n

syn CURIOUS, INQUISITIVE, PRYING mean interested in what is not one's personal or proper concern. CURIOUS, a neutral term, basically connotes an active desire to learn or to know ⟨children are curious about everything⟩. INQUISITIVE suggests impertinent and habitual curiosity and persistent quizzing ⟨dreaded the visits of their inquisitive relatives⟩. PRYING implies busy meddling and officiousness ⟨prying neighbors who refuse to mind their own business⟩.

cu·ri·ous·ly \-lē\ adv (1665) **1** : in a curious manner ⟨seemed ~ calm⟩ **2** : as is curious ⟨~, he continues to win reelection⟩

cu·ri·um \'kyùr-ē-əm\ n [NL, fr. Marie & Pierre Curie] (1946) : a metallic radioactive element produced artificially — see ELEMENT table

¹curl \'kər(-ə)l\ vb [ME, fr. crul curly, prob. fr. MD; akin to OHG krol curly] vt (14c) **1** : to form (as the hair) into coils or ringlets **2** : to form into a curved shape : TWIST ⟨~ed his lip in a sneer⟩ **3** : to furnish with curls ~ vi **1 a** : to grow in coils or spirals **b** : to form ripples or crinkles ⟨bacon ~ing in a pan⟩ **2** : to move or progress in curves or spirals : WIND ⟨the path ~ed along the mountainside⟩ **3** : TWIST, CONTORT **4** : to play the game of curling

²curl n (1602) **1** : a lock of hair that coils : RINGLET **2** : something having a spiral or winding form : COIL **3** : the action of curling : the state of being curled **4** : a curved or spiral marking in the grain of wood **5** : a hollow arch of water formed when the crest of a breaking wave spills forward

curl·er \'kər-lər\ n (1638) **1** : a player of curling **2** : one that curls; esp : a device on which hair is wound for curling

cur·lew \'kər-(,)lü, 'kərl-(,)yü\ n, pl **curlews** or **curlew** [ME, fr. MF corlieu, of imit. origin] (14c) : any of various largely brownish chiefly migratory birds (esp. genus Numenius) having long legs and a long slender down-curved bill and related to the sandpipers and snipes

¹cur·li·cue also **cur·ly·cue** \'kər-lē-,kyü, -li-\ n [curly + cue a braid of hair] (1843) : a fancifully curved or spiral figure : FLOURISH

²curlicue vb **-cued; -cu·ing** vi (1844) : to form curlicues ~ vt : to embellish with curlicues

curl·ing \'kər-liŋ\ n (1620) : a game in which two teams of four players each slide curling stones over a stretch of ice toward a target circle

curling iron n (1616) : a rod-shaped usu. metal instrument which is heated and around which a lock of hair is to be curled or waved is wound

curling stone n (1620) : an ellipsoid stone or occas. piece of iron with a gooseneck handle used in the game of curling

curl·pa·per \'kər(-ə)l-,pā-pər\ n (ca. 1817) : a strip or piece of paper around which a lock of hair is wound for curling

curl up vi (1861) : to arrange oneself in or as if in a ball or curl ⟨curl up by the fire⟩ ⟨curl up with a good book⟩

curly \'kər-lē\ adj **curl·i·er; -est** (ca. 1784) **1** : tending to curl; also : having curls **2** : having the grain composed of fibers that undulate without crossing and that often form alternating light and dark lines ⟨~ maple⟩ — **curl·i·ness** n

curly–coat·ed retriever \'kər-lē-'kō-təd-\ n (1885) : any of a breed of sporting dogs with a short curly black or liver-colored coat

curly top n (1901) : a destructive virus disease esp. of beets that kills young plants and causes curling and puckering of the leaves in older plants

cur·mud·geon \(,)kər-'mə-jən\ n [origin unknown] (1577) **1** archaic : MISER **2** : a crusty, ill-tempered, and usu. old man — **cur·mud·geon·li·ness** \-lē-nəs\ n — **cur·mud·geon·ly** \-lē\ adj

curn \'kərn\ or **cur·ran** \'kə-rən\ n [ME curn; akin to ME corn] (14c) **1** Scot : GRAIN **2** Scot : a small number : FEW

curr \'kər\ vi [imit.] (1677) : to make a murmuring sound (as of doves)

cur·ragh or **cur·rach** \'kə-rə, -rək\ n [ME currok, fr. Ir carrach, currach] (15c) : a usu. large coracle esp. on the west coast of Ireland

cur·rant \'kər-ənt, 'kə-rənt\ n [ME raison of Coraunte, lit., raisin of Corinth] (14c) **1** : a small seedless raisin grown chiefly in the Levant **2** : the acid edible fruit of several shrubs (genus Ribes) of the saxifrage family; also : a plant bearing currants

cur·ren·cy \'kər-ən(t)-sē, 'kə-rən(t)-\ n, pl **-cies** (1699) **1 a** : circulation as a medium of exchange **b** : general use, acceptance, or prevalence **c** : the quality or state of being current : CURRENTNESS **2 a** : something (as coins, treasury notes, and banknotes) that is in circulation as a medium of exchange **b** : paper money in circulation **c** : a common article for bartering **d** : a medium of verbal or intellectual expression

¹cur·rent \'kər-ənt, 'kə-rənt\ adj [ME curraunt, fr. OF curant, prp. of courre to run, fr. L currere — more at CAR] (14c) **1 a** archaic : RUNNING, FLOWING **b** (1) : presently elapsing (2) : occurring in or existing at the present time (3) : most recent ⟨the ~ issue⟩ **2** : used as a medium of exchange **3** : generally accepted, used, practiced, or prevalent at the moment — **cur·rent·ly** adv — **cur·rent·ness** n

²current n (14c) **1 a** : the part of a fluid body (as air or water) moving continuously in a certain direction **b** : the swiftest part of a stream **c** : a tidal or nontidal movement of lake or ocean water **2** : flow marked by force or strength **2 a** : a tendency or course of events that is usu. the result of an interplay of forces ⟨~s of public opinion⟩ **b** : a prevailing mood : STRAIN **3** : a flow of electric charge; also : the rate of such flow syn see TENDENCY

current assets n pl (ca. 1909) : assets of a short-term nature that are readily convertible to cash

cur·ri·cle \'kər-i-kəl, 'kə-ri-\ n [L curriculum running, chariot, fr. currere] (1752) : a 2-wheeled chaise usu. drawn by two horses cur·ric·u·lar \kə-'ri-kyə-lər\ adj (ca. 1909) : of or relating to a curriculum

cur·ric·u·lum \-ləm\ n, pl -la \-lə\ also -lums [NL, fr. L, running, course] (1633) 1 : the courses offered by an educational institution 2 : a set of courses constituting an area of specialization

cur·ric·u·lum vi·tae \kə-'ri-kyə-ləm-'vē-,tī, -kə-ləm-, -'wē-,tī, -'vī-,tē\ n, pl cur·ric·u·la vitae \-lə-\ [L, course of (one's) life] (1902) : a short account of one's career and qualifications prepared typically by an applicant for a position

cur·ri·ery \'kər-ē-ə-rē, 'kə-rē-\ n, pl -er·ies (ca. 1889) 1 : the trade of a currier of leather 2 : a place where currying is done

cur·rish \'kər-ish\ adj (15c) 1 : IGNOBLE 2 : resembling a cur : MONGREL — cur·rish·ly adv

¹cur·ry \'kər-ē, 'kə-rē\ vt cur·ried; cur·ry·ing [ME currayen, fr. OF correer to prepare, curry, fr. (assumed) VL conredare, fr. L com- + a base of Gmc origin; akin to Goth garaiths arrayed — more at READY] (13c) 1 : to clean the coat of (as a horse) with a currycomb 2 : to treat (tanned leather) esp. by incorporating oil or grease 3 : BEAT, THRASH — cur·ri·er n — curry favor [ME currayen favel to curry a chestnut horse] : to seek to gain favor by flattery or attention

²cur·ry also cur·rie \'kər-ē, 'kə-rē\ n, pl curries [Tamil kaṟi] (1681) 1 : a food, dish, or sauce in Indian cuisine seasoned with a mixture of pungent spices; also : a food or dish seasoned with curry powder 2 : CURRY POWDER

³curry vt cur·ried; cur·ry·ing (1839) : to flavor or cook with curry powder or a curry sauce

cur·ry·comb \-,kōm\ n (1573) : a comb made of rows of metallic teeth or serrated ridges and used esp. to curry horses — currycomb vt

curry powder n (1810) : a condiment consisting of several pungent ground spices (as cayenne pepper, fenugreek, and turmeric)

¹curse \'kərs\ n [ME curs, fr. OE] (bef. 12c) 1 : a prayer or invocation for harm or injury to come upon one : IMPRECATION 2 : something that is cursed or accursed 3 : evil or misfortune that comes as if in response to imprecation or as retribution 4 : a cause of great harm or misfortune : TORMENT 5 : MENSTRUATION — used with the

²curse vb cursed; curs·ing (bef. 12c) 1 : to use profanely insolent language against : BLASPHEME 2 a : to call upon divine or supernatural power to send injury upon b : to execrate in fervent and often profane terms 3 : to bring great evil upon : AFFLICT ~ vi : to utter imprecations : SWEAR syn see EXECRATE

cursed \'kər-səd, 'kərst\ also curst \'kərst\ adj (13c) : being under or deserving a curse — cursed·ly adv — cursed·ness n

¹cur·sive \'kər-siv\ adj [F or ML; F cursif, fr. ML cursivus, lit., running, fr. L cursus, pp. of currere to run] (1784) : RUNNING, COURSING: as a of writing : flowing often with the strokes of successive characters joined and the angles rounded b : having a flowing, easy, impromptu character — cur·sive·ly adv — cur·sive·ness n

²cursive n (1861) 1 : a manuscript written in cursive writing; also : cursive writing 2 : a style of printed letter resembling handwriting

cur·sor \'kər-sər, -,sȯr\ n [L, runner, fr. currere] (1594) : a movable item used to mark a position: as a : a transparent slide with a line attached to a slide rule b : a visual cue (as a flashing rectangle) on a video display that indicates position (as for data entry)

cur·so·ri·al \,kər-'sȯr-ē-əl, -'sȯr-\ adj (1836) : adapted to or involving running

cur·so·ry \'kərs-rē, 'kər-sə-\ adj [LL cursorius of running, fr. L currere] (1601) : rapidly and often superficially performed or produced : HASTY ⟨a ~ glance⟩ syn see SUPERFICIAL — cur·so·ri·ly \-rə-lē\ adv — cur·so·ri·ness \-rē-nəs\ n

curt \'kərt\ adj [L curtus shortened — more at SHEAR] (1630) 1 a : sparing of words : TERSE b : marked by rude or peremptory shortness : BRUSQUE 2 : shortened in linear dimension syn see BLUFF — curt·ly adv — curt·ness n

cur·tail \(,)kər-'tā(ə)l\ vt [by folk etymology fr. earlier curtal to dock an animal's tail, fr. curtal, n., animal with a docked tail, fr. MF courtault — more at CURTAL] (1580) : to make less by or as if by cutting off or away some part ⟨~ the power of the executive branch⟩ ⟨~ inflation⟩ syn see SHORTEN — cur·tail·er n

cur·tail·ment \-'tā(ə)l-mənt\ n (1794) : the act of curtailing : the state of being curtailed

¹cur·tain \'kər-t²n\ n [ME curtine, fr. OF, fr. LL cortina (trans. of Gk aulaia, fr. aulē court), fr. L cohort-, cohors enclosure, court — more at COURT] (14c) 1 : a hanging screen usu. capable of being drawn back or up; esp : window drapery 2 : a device or agency that conceals or acts as a barrier — compare IRON CURTAIN 3 a : the part of a bastioned front that connects two neighboring bastions b (1) : a similar stretch of plain wall (2) : a nonbearing exterior wall 4 a : the movable screen separating the stage from the auditorium of a theater b : the ascent or opening (as at the beginning of a play) of a stage curtain; also : its descent or closing (as at the end of an act) c : the final situation, line, or scene of an act or play d : the time at which a theatrical performance begins e pl : END; esp : DEATH ⟨it will be ~s for us if we're caught⟩ — cur·tain·less \-ləs\ adj

²curtain vt cur·tained; cur·tain·ing \'kərt-niŋ, -'kər-t²n-iŋ\ (14c) 1 : to furnish with or as if with curtains 2 : to veil or shut off with or as if with a curtain

curtain call n (1884) : an appearance by a performer (as after the final curtain of a play) in response to the applause of the audience

curtain lecture n [fr. its orig. being given behind the curtains of a bed] (1633) : a private lecture by a wife to her husband

cur·tain–rais·er \'kər-t²n-,rā-zər\ n (1886) 1 : a short play usu. of one scene that is presented before the main full-length drama 2 : a usu. short preliminary to a main event

curtain wall n (1853) : a nonbearing exterior wall between columns or piers

cur·tal \'kər-t²l\ adj [MF courtault, fr. court short, fr. L curtus] (1576) 1 obs : having a docked tail 2 obs : BRIEF, CURTAILED 3 archaic : wearing a short frock

cur·tal ax or cur·tle ax \'kər-t²l-\ n [modif. of MF coutelas] (ca. 1580) archaic : CUTLASS

cur·te·sy \'kər-tə-sē\ n, pl -sies [ME corteisie courtesy] (1523) : a husband's interest upon the death of his wife in the real property of an estate that she either solely owned or inherited provided they bore a child capable of inheriting the estate — compare DOWER

cur·ti·lage \'kər-t²l-ij\ n [ME, fr. MF cortillage, fr. cortil courtyard, fr. cort court] (14c) : a piece of ground (as a yard or courtyard) within the fence surrounding a house

¹curt·sy also curt·sey \'kərt-sē\ vi curt·sied also curt·seyed; curt·sy·ing also curt·sey·ing [alter. of courtesy] (ca. 1553) : to make a curtsy

²curtsy also curtsey n, pl curtsies also curtseys (1575) : an act of civility, respect, or reverence made mainly by women and consisting of a slight lowering of the body with bending of the knees

cu·rule \'kyur-,ül\ adj [L curulis, perh. alter. of currulis, fr. currus chariot, fr. currere to run] (1600) : privileged to sit in a seat reserved in ancient Rome for the use of the highest dignitaries; also : of or relating to a curule chair

cur·va·ceous also cur·va·cious \,kər-'vā-shəs\ adj (ca. 1935) : having curves suggestive of a well-proportioned feminine figure

cur·va·ture \'kər-və-,chur, -chər, -,tyur, -,tur\ n (1603) 1 : the act of curving : the state of being curved 2 : a measure or amount of curving; specif : the rate of change of the angle through which the tangent to a curve turns in moving along the curve and which for a circle is equal to the reciprocal of the radius 3 a : an abnormal curving (as of the spine) b : a curved surface of an organ

¹curve \'kərv\ adj [ME, fr. L curvus; akin to Gk kyrtos convex, MIr cruinn round] (15c) archaic : bent or formed into a curve

²curve vb curved; curv·ing [L curvare, fr. curvus] vi (1594) : to have or take a turn, change, or deviation from a straight line or plane surface without sharp breaks or angularity ~ vt 1 : to cause to curve 2 : to throw a curveball to (a batter) 3 : to grade (as an examination) on a curve

³curve n (1696) 1 a : a line esp. when curved: as (1) : the path of a moving point (2) : a line defined by an equation so that the coordinates of its points are functions of a single independent variable or parameter b : the graph of a variable 2 : something curved: as a : a curving line of the human body b pl : PARENTHESIS 3 a : CURVEBALL b : TRICK, DECEPTION 4 : a distribution indicating the relative performance of individuals measured against each other that is used esp. in assigning good, medium, or poor grades to usu. predetermined proportions of students rather than in assigning grades based on predetermined standards of achievement — curvy \'kər-vē\ adj

curve·ball \'kərv-,bȯl\ n (1936) : a slow or moderately fast baseball pitch thrown with spin to make it swerve downward and usu. to the left when thrown from the right hand or to the right when thrown from the left hand — curveball vb

curve fitting n (ca. 1924) : the empirical determination of a curve or function that approximates a set of data

¹cur·vet \(,)kər-'vet\ n [It corvetta, fr. MF courbette, fr. courber to curve, fr. L curvare] (1575) : a prancing leap of a horse in which the hind legs are raised just before the forelegs touch the ground

²curvet vi -vet·ted or -vet·ed; -vet·ting or -vet·ing (1592) : to make a curvet; also : PRANCE, CAPER

cur·vi·lin·ear \,kər-və-'li-nē-ər\ adj [L curvus + linea line] (1710) 1 : consisting of or bounded by curved lines : represented by a curved line 2 : marked by flowing tracery ⟨~ Gothic⟩ — cur·vi·lin·ear·i·ty \-,li-nē-'ar-ə-tē\ n

cu·sec \'kyü-,sek\ n [cubic foot per second] (ca. 1903) : a volumetric unit of flow equal to a cubic foot per second

cush·at \'kə-shət\ n [ME cowschote, fr. OE cūscote] (bef. 12c) chiefly Scot : RINGDOVE 1

cu·shaw \kü-'shȯ, 'kü-,\ n [origin unknown] (1698) : a squash of any of several cultivars of a winter squash (Cucurbita mixta)

Cush·ing's disease \'kü-shiŋz-\ n [Harvey Cushing] (ca. 1935) : Cushing's syndrome esp. when caused by excessive production of ACTH by the pituitary gland

Cushing's syndrome n (1937) : an abnormal bodily condition characterized by obesity and muscular weakness due to excess corticosteroids and esp. hydrocortisone from adrenal or pituitary hyperfunction

¹cush·ion \'kü-shən\ n [ME cusshin, fr. MF coissin, fr. (assumed) VL coxinus, fr. L coxa hip — more at COXA] (14c) 1 : a soft pillow or pad usu. used for sitting, reclining, or kneeling 2 : a bodily part resembling a pad 3 : something resembling a cushion: as a : PILLOW 2 b : RAT 3 c : a pad of springy rubber along the inside of the rim of a billiard table d : a padded insert in a shoe e : an elastic body for reducing shock f : a mat laid under a large rug to ease the effect of wear 4 a : something (as an economic factor or a medical procedure) serving to mitigate the effects of disturbances or disorders b : a reserve supply (as of money) c : a comfortable lead ⟨a 4–0 ~ in the ninth inning⟩ — cush·ion·less \-ləs\ adj — cush·iony \-shə-nē\ adj

²cushion vt cush·ioned; cush·ion·ing \'kü-sh(ə-)niŋ\ (ca. 1738) 1 : to seat or place on a cushion 2 : to suppress by ignoring 3 : to furnish with a cushion 4 a : to mitigate the effects of b : to protect against force or shock 5 : to check gradually so as to minimize shock of moving parts

Cush·it·ic \kə-'shi-tik, kü-\ n [Cush (Kush), Africa] (ca. 1903) : a subfamily of the Afro-Asiatic language family comprising various languages spoken in eastern Africa and esp. in Ethiopia, Djibouti, and Somalia — Cushitic adj

cushy \'kü-shē\ adj cush·i·er; cush·i·est [Hindi khush pleasant, fr. Per khūsh] (1915) : entailing little hardship or difficulty ⟨a ~ job with a high salary⟩ — cush·i·ly \'kü-shə-lē\ adv

cusk \'kəsk\ n, pl cusk or cusks [prob. alter. of tusk, a kind of codfish] (1616) 1 : a large edible No. Atlantic fish (Brosme brosme) of the cod family 2 : BURBOT

cusp \'kəsp\ n [L cuspis point] (1585) : POINT, APEX: as a : either horn of a crescent moon b : a fixed point on a mathematical curve at which a point tracing the curve would exactly reverse

1 cusp c

\ə\ abut \'ə\ kitten, F table \ər\ further \a\ ash \ā\ ace \ä\ mop, mar
\au̇\ out \ch\ chin \e\ bet \ē\ easy \g\ go \i\ hit \ī\ ice \j\ job
\ŋ\ sing \ō\ go \ȯ\ law \ȯi\ boy \th\ thin \t͟h\ the \ü\ loot \u̇\ foot
\y\ yet \zh\ vision \ä, k̲, ⁿ, œ, œ̄, ᵫ, ūᵉ, ᵞ\ see Guide to Pronunciation

its direction of motion **c** : an ornamental pointed projection formed by or arising from the intersection of two arcs or foils **d** (1) : a point on the grinding surface of a tooth (2) : a fold or flap of a cardiac valve **e** : a point of transition (as from one astrological sign to another or one historical period to the next) : TURNING POINT; *also* : EDGE, VERGE ⟨on the ~ of stardom⟩ — **cus·pate** \'kəs-ˌpāt, -pət\ *adj* — **cusped** \'kəspt\ *adj*

cus·pid \'kəs-pəd\ *n* [*bicuspid*] (1878) : CANINE 1
cus·pi·date \'kəs-pə-ˌdāt\ *adj* [L *cuspidatus*, pp. of *cuspidare* to make pointed, fr. *cuspid-, cuspis* point] (1692) : having a cusp : terminating in a point ⟨a ~ leaf⟩ ⟨~ molars⟩
cus·pi·da·tion \ˌkəs-pə-'dā-shən\ *n* (1848) : decoration with cusps
cus·pi·dor \'kəs-pə-ˌdȯr, -ˌdȯr\ *n* [Pg *cuspidouro* place for spitting, fr. *cuspir* to spit, fr. L *conspuere*, fr. *com-* + *spuere* to spit — more at SPEW] (1735) : SPITTOON
¹cuss \'kəs\ *n* [alter. of *curse*] (1775) **1** : FELLOW 4c **2** : CURSE 1, 2
²cuss (1815) : CURSE — **cuss·er** *n*
cuss·ed \'kə-səd\ *adj* (1840) **1** : CURSED **2** : OBSTINATE, CANTANKEROUS — **cuss·ed·ly** *adv* — **cuss·ed·ness** \-nəs\ *n*
cuss·word \'kəs-ˌwərd\ *n* (1872) **1** : SWEARWORD **2** : a term of abuse : a derogatory term
cus·tard \'kəs-tərd\ *n* [ME, a kind of pie, alter. of *crustarde, crustade*, prob. fr. (assumed) AF *crustade*, fr. OF *crouste* crust, fr. L *crusta* — more at CRUST] (1740) : a pudding-like usu. sweetened mixture made with eggs and milk — **cus·tardy** \-tər-dē\ *adj*
custard apple *n* (1657) **1 a** : any of several chiefly tropical American soft-fleshed edible fruits **b** : any of a genus (*Annona* of the family Annonaceae, the custard-apple family) of trees or shrubs bearing this fruit; *esp* : a small West Indian tree (*A. reticulata*) **2** : PAPAW 2
cus·to·di·al \ˌkəs-'tō-dē-əl\ *adj* (1772) : relating to guardianship; *specif* : marked by or given to watching and protecting rather than seeking to cure ⟨~ care⟩
cus·to·di·an \ˌkəs-'tō-dē-ən\ *n* (1781) : one that guards and protects or maintains; *esp* : one entrusted with guarding and keeping property or records or with custody or guardianship of prisoners or inmates — **cus·to·di·an·ship** \-ˌship\ *n*
cus·to·dy \'kəs-tə-dē\ *n, pl* **-dies** [ME *custodie*, fr. L *custodia* guarding, fr. *custod-, custos* guardian] (15c) : immediate charge and control (as over a ward or a suspect) exercised by a person or an authority; *also* : SAFEKEEPING
¹cus·tom \'kəs-təm\ *n* [ME *custume*, fr. OF, fr. L *consuetudin-, consuetudo*, fr. *consuescere* to accustom, fr. *com-* + *suescere* to accustom; akin to *suus* one's own — more at SUICIDE] (13c) **1 a** : a usage or practice common to many or to a particular place or class or habitual with an individual **b** : long-established practice considered as unwritten law **c** : repeated practice **2 a** : the whole body of usages, practices, or conventions that regulate social life **2** *pl* **a** : duties, tolls, or imposts imposed by the sovereign law of a country on imports or exports **b** *usu sing in constr* : the agency, establishment, or procedure for collecting such customs **3 a** : business patronage **b** : usu. habitual patrons : CUSTOMERS   *syn* see HABIT
²custom *adj* (1830) **1** : made or performed according to personal order **2** : specializing in custom work or operation ⟨a ~ tailor⟩
cus·tom·ary \'kəs-tə-ˌmer-ē\ *adj* (1535) **1** : based on or established by custom **2** : commonly practiced, used, or observed   *syn* see USUAL — **cus·tom·ar·i·ly** \ˌkəs-tə-'mer-ə-lē\ *adv* — **cus·tom·ar·i·ness** \'kəs-tə-ˌmer-ē-nəs\ *n*
cus·tom-built \'kəs-təm-'bilt\ *adj* (1925) : built to individual specifications
cus·tom·er \'kəs-tə-mər\ *n* [ME *customer*, fr. *custume*] (15c) **1** : one that purchases a commodity or service **2** : an individual usu. having some specified distinctive trait ⟨a real tough ~⟩
cus·tom·house \'kəs-təm-ˌhau̇s\ *also* **cus·toms·house** \-təmz-\ *n* (15c) : a building where customs and duties are paid or collected and where vessels are entered and cleared
cus·tom·ise *Brit var of* CUSTOMIZE
cus·tom·ize \'kəs-tə-ˌmīz\ *vt* **-ized; -iz·ing** (1926) : to build, fit, or alter according to individual specifications — **cus·tom·iz·er** *n*
cus·tom-made \'kəs-tə(m)-'mād\ *adj* (1855) : made to individual specifications
cus·tom-tai·lor \-'tā-lər\ *vt* (1895) : to alter, plan, or build according to individual specifications or needs
¹cut \'kət\ *vb* **cut; cut·ting** [ME *cutten*] *vt* (13c) **1 a** : to penetrate with or as if with an edged instrument **b** : to hurt the feelings of **c** : to strike sharply with a cutting effect **d** : to strike (a ball) with a glancing blow that imparts a reverse spin **e** : to experience the growth of (a tooth) through the gum **2 a** : TRIM, PARE ⟨~ one's nails⟩ **b** : to shorten by omissions **c** : DISSOLVE, DILUTE, ADULTERATE **d** : to reduce in amount ⟨~ costs⟩ **3 a** : MOW, REAP **b** (1) : to divide into parts with an edged tool ⟨~ bread⟩ (2) : FELL, HEW **c** (1) : to separate or discharge from an organization : DETACH (2) : to single out and isolate ⟨~ a calf out from the herd⟩ **d** : to change the direction of sharply **e** : to go or pass around or about **4 a** : to divide into segments **b** : INTERSECT, CROSS **c** : BREAK, INTERRUPT ⟨~ our supply lines⟩ **d** (1) : to divide (a deck of cards) into two portions (2) : to draw (a card) from the deck **e** : to divide into shares : SPLIT **5 a** : to make by or as if by cutting: as (1) : CARVE ⟨~ stone⟩ (2) : to shape by grinding ⟨~ a diamond⟩ (3) : ENGRAVE (4) : to shear or hollow out **b** : to record sounds (as speech or music) on ⟨~ a record⟩ **c** : to type on a stencil **6 a** : STOP, CEASE ⟨~ the nonsense⟩ **b** : to refuse to recognize (an acquaintance) : OSTRACIZE **c** : to absent oneself from (as a class) **d** : to stop (a motor) by opening a switch **e** : to stop the filming of (a motion-picture scene) **7 a** : to engage in (a frolicsome or mischievous action) ⟨on summer nights strange capers are ~ under the thin guise of a Christian festival —D. C. Peattie⟩ **b** : to give the appearance or impression of ⟨~ a fine figure⟩ **8** : to be able to manage or handle — usu. used in negative constructions ⟨can't ~ that kind of work anymore⟩ ~ *vi* **1 a** : to function as or as if as an edged tool **b** : to undergo incision or severance ⟨cheese ~s easily⟩ **c** : to perform the operation of dividing, severing, incising, or intersecting **d** : to make a stroke with a whip, sword, or other weapon **e** : to wound feelings or sensibilities **f** : to cause constriction or chafing **g** : to be of effect, influence, or significance ⟨an analysis that ~s deep⟩ **2 a** (1) : to divide a pack of cards esp. in order to decide the deal or settle a

bet (2) : to draw a card from the pack **b** : to divide spoils : SPLIT **3 a** : to proceed obliquely from a straight course ⟨~ across the yard⟩ **b** : to move swiftly ⟨a yacht *cutting* through the water⟩ **c** : to describe an oblique or diagonal line **d** : to change sharply in direction : SWERVE **e** : to make an abrupt transition from one sound or image to another in motion pictures, radio, or television **4** : to stop photographing motion pictures — **cut a deal** : to negotiate an agreement — **cut both ways** : to have both favorable and unfavorable results or implications — **cut corners** : to perform some action in the quickest, easiest, or cheapest way — **cut ice** : to be of importance — usu. used in negative constructions — **cut it** : to cut the mustard — **cut the mustard** : to achieve the standard of performance necessary for success
²cut *n* (1548) **1** : a product of cutting: as **a** : a creek, channel, or inlet made by excavation or worn by natural action **b** (1) : an opening made with an edged instrument (2) : a wound made by something sharp : GASH **c** : a surface or outline left by cutting **d** : a passage cut as a roadway **e** : a grade or step esp. in a social scale ⟨a ~ above the ordinary⟩ **f** : a subset of a set such that when it is subtracted from the set the remainder is not connected **g** : a pictorial illustration **h** : TRACK 1e(2) **2** : the act or an instance of cutting: as **a** : a gesture or expression that hurts the feelings ⟨made an unkind ~⟩ **b** : a straight passage or course **c** : a stroke or blow with the edge of a knife or other edged tool **d** : a lash with or as if with a whip **e** : the act of reducing or removing a part ⟨a ~ in pay⟩ **f** : an act or turn of cutting cards; *also* : the result of cutting **g** : the elimination of part of a large field from further competition (as in a golf tournament) — often used with *miss* or *make* to denote respectively being or not being among those eliminated ⟨played poorly and missed the ~⟩ **3** : something that is cut or cut off: as **a** : a length of cloth varying from 40 to 100 yards (36.6 to 91.4 meters) **b** : the yield of products cut esp. during one harvest **c** : a segment or section of a meat carcass or a part of one **d** : a group of animals selected from a herd **e** : SHARE ⟨took his ~ of the profits⟩ **4** : a voluntary absence from a class **5 a** : a stroke that cuts a ball; *also* : the spin imparted by such a stroke **b** : a swing by a batter at a pitched baseball **c** : an exchange of captures in checkers **6** : an abrupt transition from one sound or image to another in motion pictures, radio, or television **7 a** : the shape and style in which a thing is cut, formed, or made ⟨clothes of the latest ~⟩ **b** : PATTERN, TYPE **c** : HAIRCUT — **cut of one's jib** : APPEARANCE, STYLE
cut·abil·i·ty \ˌkət-ə-'bi-lə-tē\ *n* (1965) : the proportion of lean salable meat yielded by a carcass
cut-and-dried \ˌkət-ᵊn-'drīd\ *also* **cut-and-dry** \-'drī\ *adj* (1710) : being or done according to a plan, set procedure, or formula : ROUTINE
cut-and-paste \-'pāst\ *adj* (1953) : pieced together by excerpting and combining passages from many sources ⟨the book was a ~ job⟩
cut-and-try \-'trī\ *adj* (1903) : marked by experimental procedure : EMPIRICAL
cu·ta·ne·ous \kyu̇-'tā-nē-əs\ *adj* [NL *cutaneus*, fr. L *cutis* skin — more at HIDE] (1578) : of, relating to, or affecting the skin — **cu·ta·ne·ous·ly** *adv*
¹cut·away \'kə-tə-ˌwā\ *adj* (1841) : having or showing parts cut away
²cutaway *n* (1849) **1** : a coat with skirts tapering from the front waistline to form tails at the back **2 a** : a cutaway picture or representation **b** : a shot that interrupts the main action of a film or television program to take up a related subject or to depict action supposed to be going on at the same time as the main action **3** : a back dive in which the head is lowered toward the board after the takeoff
cut·back \'kət-ˌbak\ *n* (1897) **1** : something cut back **2** : REDUCTION
cut back *vt* (1871) **1** : to shorten by cutting : PRUNE ~ *vi* **1** : to interrupt the sequence of a plot (as of a movie) by introducing events prior to those last presented **2** : CUT DOWN ⟨*cut back* on sugar⟩
cutch \'kəch\ *n* [modif. of Malay *kachu*] (1759) : CATECHU
cut down *vt* (1821) **1 a** : to strike down and kill or incapacitate **b** : KNOCK DOWN **2 a** : to remodel by removing extras or unwanted furnishings and fittings **b** : to remake in a smaller size ~ *vi* : to reduce or curtail volume or activity ⟨*cut down* on smoking⟩ — **cut down to size** : to reduce from an inflated or exaggerated importance to true or suitable stature
cute \'kyüt\ *adj* **cut·er; cut·est** [short for *acute*] (ca. 1731) **1 a** : clever or shrewd often in an underhanded manner **b** : IMPERTINENT, SMART-ALECKY ⟨don't get ~ with me⟩ **2** : attractive or pretty esp. in a dainty or delicate way **3** : obviously straining for effect — **cute·ly** *adv* — **cute·ness** *n*
cute·sy \'kyüt-sē\ *adj* **cute·si·er; -est** [*cute* + *-sy* (as in *folksy*)] (1914) : self-consciously or excessively cute
cut glass *n* (1800) : glass ornamented with patterns cut into its surface by an abrasive wheel and polished
cut-grass \'kət-ˌgras\ *n* (ca. 1818) : a grass (esp. genus *Leersia*) with minute hooked bristles along the edges of the leaf blade
cu·ti·cle \'kyü-ti-kəl\ *n* [L *cuticula*, dim. of *cutis* skin — more at HIDE] (1615) **1** : SKIN, PELLICLE: as **a** : an external investment (as of an insect) secreted usu. by epidermal cells **b** : the outermost layer of animal integument (as in humans) when composed of epidermis **c** : a thin continuous fatty or waxy film on the external surface of many higher plants that consists chiefly of cutin **2** : dead or horny epidermis — **cu·tic·u·lar** \kyü-'ti-kyə-lər\ *adj*
cut·ie *or* **cut·ey** \'kyü-tē\ *n, pl* **cuties** *or* **cuteys** [*cute* + *-ie*] (1908) : an attractive person; *esp* : a pretty girl
cu·tin \'kyü-tᵊn\ *n* [ISV, fr. L *cutis*] (ca. 1872) : an insoluble mixture containing waxes, fatty acids, soaps, and resinous material that forms a continuous layer on the outer epidermal wall of a plant
cut-in \'kət-ˌin\ *n* (1883) : something cut in — **cut-in** *adj*
cut in *vi* (1612) **1** : to thrust oneself into a position between others or belonging to another **2** : to join in something suddenly ⟨*cut in* on the conversation⟩ **3** : to interrupt a dancing couple and take one as one's partner **4** : to become automatically connected or started in operation ~ *vt* **1** : to mix with cutting motions ⟨after sifting the flour into a mixing bowl, *cut* the lard *in*⟩ **2** : to introduce into a number, group, or sequence **3** : to connect into an electrical circuit so as to permit operation **4** : to include esp. among those benefiting or favored ⟨*cut* them *in* on the profits⟩

cu·tin·ized \'kyü-tᵊn-ˌīzd\ *adj* (1901) : infiltrated with cutin ⟨~ epidermal cells⟩

cu·tis \'kyü-təs\ *n, pl* **cu·tes** \'kyü-ˌtēz\ *or* **cu·tis·es** [L] (1603) : DERMIS

cut·lass \'kət-ləs\ *n* [MF *coutelas*, aug. of *coutel* knife, fr. L *cultellus*, dim. of *culter* knife, plowshare] (1594) **1** : a short curving sword formerly used by sailors on warships **2** : MACHETE

cut·ler \'kət-lər\ *n* [ME, fr. MF *coutelier*, fr. LL *cultellarius*, fr. L *cultellus*] (14c) : one who makes, deals in, or repairs cutlery

cut·lery \'kət-lə-rē\ *n* (15c) **1** : the business of a cutler **2** : edged or cutting tools; *specif* : implements for cutting and eating food

cut·let \'kət-lət\ *n* [F *côtelette*, fr. OF *costelette*, dim. of *coste* rib, side, fr. L *costa* — more at COAST] (ca. 1706) **1** : a small slice of meat ⟨a veal ~⟩ **2** : a flat croquette of chopped meat or fish

cut·line \'kət-ˌlin\ *n* (1943) : CAPTION, LEGEND

cut·off \'kət-ˌȯf\ *n* (1741) **1** : the act or action of cutting off **2 a** : the new and relatively short channel formed when a stream cuts through the neck of an oxbow **b** : SHORTCUT 1 **c** : a channel made to straighten a stream **3** : a device for cutting off **4 a** : something cut off **b** *pl* : shorts orig. made from jeans with the legs cut off at the knees or higher **5** : the point, date, or period for a cutoff — **cutoff** *adj*

cut off *vt* (14c) **1** : to bring to an untimely end **2** : to stop the passage of **3** : SHUT OFF, BAR **4** : DISCONTINUE, TERMINATE **5** : SEPARATE, ISOLATE **6** : DISINHERIT **7 a** : to stop the operation of : TURN OFF **b** : to stop or interrupt while in communication ⟨the operator *cut* me *off*⟩ ~ *vi* : to cease operating

cutoff man *n* (1967) : a player in baseball who relays a ball from an outfielder to the infield

cut·out \'kət-ˌaůt\ *n* (1851) **1** : something cut out or off from something else; *also* : the space or hole left after cutting **2** : one that cuts out **3** : one serving as an intermediary for clandestine operations — **cutout** *adj*

¹cut out *vt* (15c) **1** : to form by erosion **2** : to determine or assign through necessity ⟨you've got your work *cut out* for you⟩ **3** : to take the place of : SUPPLANT **4** : to put an end to : desist from **5** : DEPRIVE, DEFRAUD **6 a** : to remove from a series or circuit : DISCONNECT **b** : to make inoperative ~ *vi* **1** : to depart in haste **2** : to cease operating **3** : to swerve out of a traffic line

²cut out *adj* (1645) : naturally fitted or suited ⟨not *cut out* to be a vet⟩

cut·over \'kət-ˌō-vər\ *adj* (1899) : having most of the salable timber cut down

cut–price \-'prīs\ *adj* (1897) *chiefly Brit* : CUT-RATE

cut·purse \'kət-ˌpərs\ *n* (14c) : PICKPOCKET

cut–rate \'kət-'rāt\ *adj* (1881) **1** : marked by, offering, or making use of a reduced rate or price ⟨~ stores⟩ **2** : SECOND-RATE, CHEAP

cut·ta·ble \'kət-ə-bəl\ *adj* (15c) : capable of being cut : ready for cutting

cut·ter \'kət-ər\ *n* (15c) **1** : one that cuts: **a** : one whose work is cutting or involves cutting **b** (1) : an instrument, machine, machine part, or tool that cuts (2) : a device for vibrating a cutting stylus in disc recording; *also* : the stylus or its point **2 a** : a ship's boat for carrying stores or passengers **b** : a single-masted fore-and-aft rigged sailing vessel **c** : a small armed vessel in government service **3** : a light sleigh

¹cut·throat \'kət-ˌthrōt\ *n* (1535) **1** : KILLER, MURDERER **2** : a cruel unprincipled person

²cutthroat *adj* (1567) **1** : MURDEROUS, CRUEL **2** : marked by unprincipled practices : RUTHLESS ⟨~ competition⟩ **3** : characterized by each player playing independently rather than having a permanent partner — used esp. of partnership games adapted for three players ⟨~ bridge⟩

cutthroat contract *n* (ca. 1944) : contract bridge in which partnerships are determined by the bidding

cutthroat trout *n* (ca. 1891) : a large spotted trout (*Oncorhynchus clarki* syn. *Salmo clarki*) chiefly of northwestern No. America that has reddish streaks on the integument of the lower jaw — called also *cutthroat*

cutthroat trout

cut time *n* (1951) : duple or quadruple time with the beat represented by a half note

¹cut·ting \'kə-tiŋ\ *n* (14c) **1** : something cut or cut off or out: as **a** : a plant section originating from stem, leaf, or root and capable of developing into a new plant **b** : HARVEST **2** : something made by cutting; *esp* : RECORD 4

²cutting *adj* (15c) **1** : given to or designed for cutting; *esp* : SHARP, EDGED **2** : marked by sharp piercing cold **3** : inclined or likely to wound the feelings of others esp. because of a ruthless incisiveness ⟨a ~ remark⟩ **4** : INTENSE, PIERCING ⟨a ~ pain⟩ — **cut·ting·ly** \-tiŋ-lē\ *adv*

cutting board *n* (1825) : a board on which something (as food or cloth) is placed for cutting

cutting edge *n* (1951) **1** : the foremost part or place : VANGUARD **2** : a sharp effect or quality

cutting horse *n* (1881) : an agile saddle horse trained to separate individual animals from a cattle herd

cut·tle·bone \'kə-tᵊl-ˌbōn\ *n* [ME *cotul* cuttlefish (fr. OE *cudele*) + E *bone*] (1547) : the shell of cuttlefishes that is sometimes used for polishing powder or for supplying cage birds with lime and salts

cut·tle·fish \-ˌfish\ *n* [ME *cotul* + E *fish*] (ca. 1828) : any of various 10-armed marine cephalopod mollusks (order Sepioidea, esp. genus *Sepia*) differing from the related squid in having a calcified internal shell

cut·ty sark \'kə-tē-'särk\ *n* [E dial. *cutty* short + *sark*] (1779) *chiefly Scot* : a short garment; *esp* : a woman's short undergarment

cutty stool *n* (1820) **1** *chiefly Scot* : a low stool **2** : a seat in a Scottish church where offenders formerly sat for public rebuke

cut–up \'kət-ˌəp\ *n* (1843) : a person who clowns or acts boisterously

cut up *vt* (1580) **1 a** : to cut into parts or pieces **b** : to injure or damage by or as if by cutting : GASH, SLASH **2** : to subject to hostile criticism : CENSURE ~ *vi* **1** : to undergo being cut up **2** : to behave in a comic, boisterous, or unruly manner : CLOWN

cut·wa·ter \'kət-ˌwȯ-tər, -ˌwä-\ *n* (1644) : the forepart of a ship's stem

cut·work \-ˌwərk\ *n* (15c) : embroidery usu. on linen in which a design is outlined in buttonhole stitch and the enclosed material cut away

cut·worm \-ˌwərm\ *n* (1816) : any of various smooth-bodied chiefly nocturnal noctuid moth caterpillars which often feed on young plant stems near ground level

cu·vette \kyü-'vet\ *n* [F, dim. of *cuve* tub, fr. L *cupa* — more at HIVE] (ca. 1909) : a small often transparent laboratory vessel (as a tube)

cwm \'küm\ *n* [W, valley] (1853) *chiefly Brit* : CIRQUE 3

-cy *n suffix* [ME *-cie*, fr. OF, fr. L *-tia*, partly fr. *-t-* (final stem consonant) + *-ia* -y, partly fr. Gk *-tia*, *-teia*, fr. *-t-* (final stem consonant) + *-ia*, *-eia* -y] **1** : action : practice ⟨mendican*cy*⟩ **2** : rank : office ⟨baronet*cy*⟩ ⟨chaplain*cy*⟩ **3** : body : class ⟨magistra*cy*⟩ **4** : state : quality ⟨accura*cy*⟩ — often replacing a final *-t* or *-te* of the base word

cy·an \'sī-ˌan, -ən\ *n* [Gk *kyanos*] (ca. 1889) : a greenish blue color — used in photography and color printing of one of the primary colors

cyan- *or* **cyano-** *comb form* [G, fr. Gk *kyan-*, *kyano-*, fr. *kyanos* dark blue enamel] **1** : dark blue : blue ⟨*cyano*bacterium⟩ **2** : cyanogen ⟨*cyan*ide⟩ **3** : cyanide ⟨*cyano*genetic⟩

cy·an·a·mide \sī-'a-nə-məd\ *n* [ISV] (1838) **1** : a caustic acidic compound CH_2N_2 **2** : CALCIUM CYANAMIDE

cy·a·nate \'sī-ə-ˌnāt, -nət\ *n* [ISV] (ca. 1846) : a salt (as ammonium cyanate) or ester of cyanic acid

cy·an·ic acid \sī-ˌa-nik-\ *n* (1832) : a strong acid HOCN used to prepare cyanates

cy·a·nide \'sī-ə-ˌnīd, -nəd\ *n* [ISV] (1826) **1** : a compound of cyanogen with a more electropositive element or group: as **a** : POTASSIUM CYANIDE **b** : SODIUM CYANIDE **2** : CYANOGEN 1

cy·a·nine \'sī-ə-ˌnēn, -nən\ *n* [ISV] (ca. 1872) : any of various dyes that sensitize photographic film to light from the green, yellow, red, and infrared regions of the spectrum

cy·a·no \'sī-ə-(ˌ)nō, sī-'a-(ˌ)nō\ *adj* [*cyan-*] (1929) : relating to or containing the cyanogen group — often used in combination

cy·a·no·ac·ry·late \ˌsī-ə-nō-'a-krə-ˌlāt, sī-ˌa-nō-\ *n* (1963) : any of several liquid acrylate monomers that readily polymerize as anions and are used as adhesives in industry and in closing wounds in surgery

cy·a·no·bac·te·ri·um \-bak-'tir-ē-əm\ *n* [NL] (1974) : BLUE-GREEN ALGA

cy·a·no·co·bal·a·min \-kō-'ba-lə-mən\ *also* **cy·a·no·co·bal·a·mine** \-ˌmēn\ *n* [*cyan-* + *cobalt* + *vitamin*] (1950) : VITAMIN B₁₂ 1

cy·a·no·eth·yl·ate \-'e-thə-ˌlāt\ *vt* (1942) : to introduce a cyano-ethyl group CNC₂H₄ into (a compound) usu. by means of acrylonitrile ⟨~ cotton⟩ — **cy·a·no·eth·yl·ation** \-ˌe-thə-'lā-shən\ *n*

cy·an·o·gen \sī-'a-nə-jən\ *n* [F *cyanogène*, fr. *cyan-* + *gène* -gen] (1826) **1** : a univalent group —CN present in cyanides **2** : a colorless flammable poisonous gas (CN)₂

cy·a·no·ge·net·ic \ˌsī-ə-nō-jə-'ne-tik, sī-ˌa-nō-\ *or* **cy·a·no·gen·ic** \-'je-nik\ *adj* (1902) : capable of producing cyanide (as hydrogen cyanide) ⟨a ~ plant⟩ ⟨a ~ glucoside⟩ — **cy·a·no·gen·e·sis** \-'je-nə-səs\ *n*

cy·a·no·hy·drin \-'hī-drən\ *n* [ISV, fr. *cyan-* + *hydr-* + *¹-in*] (1925) : any of various compounds containing both cyano and hydroxyl groups

cy·a·no·sis \ˌsī-ə-'nō-səs\ *n* [NL, fr. Gk *kyanōsis* dark blue color, fr. *kyanos*] (1834) : a bluish or purplish discoloration (as of skin) due to deficient oxygenation of the blood — **cy·a·not·ic** \-'nä-tik\ *adj*

cy·an·uric acid \ˌsī-ə-'nùr-ik-, -'nyùr-\ *n* [*cyan-* + *urea*] (1838) : a crystalline weak acid C₃N₃(OH)₃ that yields cyanic acid when heated

Cyb·e·le \'si-bə-(ˌ)lē, -lē, fr. Gk *Kybelē*] : a nature goddess of the ancient peoples of Asia Minor

cy·ber·na·tion \ˌsī-bər-'nā-shən\ *n* [*cybernetics* + *-ation*] (1962) : the automatic control of a process or operation (as in manufacturing) by means of computers — **cy·ber·nat·ed** \'sī-bər-ˌnā-təd\ *adj*

cy·ber·ne·ti·cian \ˌsī-(ˌ)bər-nə-'ti-shən\ *n* (1951) : a specialist in cybernetics

cy·ber·net·i·cist \ˌsī-bər-'ne-tə-sist\ *n* (1948) : CYBERNETICIAN

cy·ber·net·ics \ˌsī-bər-'ne-tiks\ *n pl but sing in constr* [Gk *kybernētēs* pilot, governor (fr. *kybernan* to steer, govern) + E *-ics*] (1948) : the science of communication and control theory that is concerned esp. with the comparative study of automatic control systems (as the nervous system and brain and mechanical-electrical communication systems) — **cy·ber·net·ic** \-tik\ *also* **cy·ber·net·i·cal** \-ti-kəl\ *adj* — **cy·ber·net·i·cal·ly** \-ti-k(ə-)lē\ *adv*

cy·ber·punk \'sī-bər-ˌpəŋk\ *n* [*cybernetic* + *¹punk*] (1984) **1** : science fiction dealing with future urban societies dominated by computer technology **2** : an opportunistic computer hacker

cy·ber·space \-ˌspās\ *n* [*cybernetic* + *space*] (1986) : the on-line world of computer networks

cy·borg \'sī-ˌbȯrg\ *n* [*cybernetic* + *organism*] (1960) : a bionic human

cy·cad \'sī-kəd\ *n* [NL *Cycad-*, *Cycas*, genus name, fr. Gk *kykas*, MS var. of *koïkas*, acc. pl. of *koïx*, a kind of palm] (1845) : any of an order (Cycadales) of dioecious cycadophytes that are represented by a single surviving family (Cycadaceae) of palmlike tropical plants that reproduce by means of spermatozoids

cy·cad·e·oid \sī-'kad-ē-ˌȯid\ *n* [NL *Cycadeoidales*, group name, ultim. fr. *Cycad-*, *Cycas*] (1928) : any of an extinct order (Cycadeoidales or Bennettitales) of Mesozoic cycadophytes that differ from the cycads chiefly in having the reproductive organs on the trunk embedded in a thick external covering of persistent leaf bases

cy·cad·o·phyte \sī-'ka-də-ˌfīt\ *n* [ultim. fr. NL *Cycad-*, *Cycas* + Gk *phyton* plant — more at -PHYTE] (1911) : any of a subclass (Cycadophytae) of usu. unbranched gymnosperms with pinnate leaves, large pith, little xylem, and a thick cortex that includes the cycads, cycadeoids, and seed ferns

cy·ca·sin \'sī-kə-sən\ *n* [NL *Cycas* cycad + ISV ¹-*in*] (ca. 1965) : a glucoside C₈H₁₆N₂O₇ that occurs in cycads and results in toxic and carcinogenic effects when introduced into mammals

cycl- *or* **cyclo-** *comb form* [NL, fr. Gk *kykl-*, *kyklo-*, fr. *kyklos*] **1** : circle ⟨*cyclo*meter⟩ **2** : cyclic ⟨*cyclo*hexane⟩

\ə\ abut \ᵊ\ kitten, F table \ər\ further \a\ ash \ā\ ace \ä\ mop, mar \aů\ out \ch\ chin \e\ bet \ē\ easy \g\ go \i\ hit \ī\ ice \j\ job \ŋ\ sing \ō\ go \ȯ\ law \ȯi\ boy \th\ thin \t͟h\ the \ü\ loot \ů\ foot \y\ yet \zh\ vision \á, k̠, ⁿ, œ, œ̄, ue, ūe, ᵕ\ *see* Guide to Pronunciation

cy·cla·mate \'sī-klə-ˌmāt, -mət\ n [*cyclo*hexyl-sulf*amate*] (1954) : an artificially prepared salt of sodium or calcium used esp. formerly as a sweetener

cy·cla·men \'sī-klə-mən, 'si-\ n [NL, genus name, fr. Gk *kyklaminos*] (ca. 1550) : any of a genus (*Cyclamen*) of plants of the primrose family having showy nodding flowers

cy·clase \'sī-ˌklās, -ˌklāz\ n [*cycl*- + *-ase*] (1946) : an enzyme (as adenylate cyclase) that catalyzes cyclization of a compound

cy·claz·o·cine \sī-'kla-zə-ˌsēn, -sən\ n [*cycl*- + *azocine* (C_7H_7N), prob. fr. *az*- + *octa*- + [2]*-ine*] (1966) : an analgesic drug $C_{18}H_{25}NO$ that inhibits the effect of morphine and related addictive drugs and is used in the treatment of drug addiction

[1]cy·cle \'sī-kəl\ n [ME *cicle*, fr. LL *cyclus*, fr. Gk *kyklos* circle, wheel, cycle — more at WHEEL] (14c) **1** : an interval of time during which a sequence of a recurring succession of events or phenomena is completed **2 a** : a course or series of events or operations that recur regularly and usu. lead back to the starting point **b** : one complete performance of a vibration, electric oscillation, current alternation, or other periodic process **c** : a permutation of a set of ordered elements in which each element takes the place of the next and the last becomes first **3** : a circular or spiral arrangement: as **a** : an imaginary circle or orbit in the heavens **b** : WHORL **c** : RING 10 **4** : a long period of time : AGE **5 a** : a group of poems, plays, novels, or songs treating the same theme **b** : a series of narratives dealing typically with the exploits of a legendary hero **6 a** : BICYCLE **b** : TRICYCLE **c** : MOTORCYCLE **7** : the series of a single, double, triple, and home run hit in any order by one player during one baseball game

[2]cycle vb **cy·cled; cy·cling** \'sī-k(ə-)liŋ\ vi (1842) **1 a** : to pass through a cycle **b** : to recur in cycles **2** : to ride a cycle; *specif* : BICYCLE ~ vt : to cause to go through a cycle — **cy·cler** \'sī-k(ə-)lər\ n

cy·clic \'sī-klik *also* 'si-\ *or* **cy·cli·cal** \'sī-kli-kəl, 'si-\ *adj* (1794) **1 a** : of, relating to, or being a cycle **b** : moving in cycles ⟨~ time⟩ **c** : of, relating to, or being a chemical compound containing a ring of atoms **2** *cyclic* : being a mathematical group that has an element such that every element of the group can be expressed as one of its powers — **cy·cli·cal·ly** \-k(ə-)lē\ *also* **cy·clic·ly** \'sī-kli-klē, 'si-\ *adv*

cyclic AMP n (1966) : a cyclic mononucleotide of adenosine that is formed from ATP and is responsible for the intracellular mediation of hormonal effects on various cellular processes — called also *adenosine 3',5'-monophosphate*

cyclic GMP \-ˌjē-(ˌ)em-'pē\ n [*guanosine* + *mon*- + *phosphate*] (1969) : a cyclic mononucleotide of guanosine that acts similarly to cyclic AMP as a secondary messenger in response to hormones

cy·clic·i·ty \sī-'kli-sə-tē, si-\ n (1944) : the quality or state of being cyclic ⟨estrous ~⟩ — called also *cyclical·i·ty* \ˌsī-kli-'ka-lə-tē, ˌsi-\

cy·clist \'sī-k(ə-)ləst\ n (1882) : one who rides a cycle

cy·cli·tol \'sī-klə-ˌtȯl, -ˌtōl\ n [*cycl*- + *-itol* (as in *inositol*)] (1943) : an alicyclic polyhydroxy compound (as inositol)

cy·cli·za·tion \ˌsī-k(ə-)lə-'zā-shən, ˌsi-\ n (1909) : formation of one or more rings in a chemical compound — **cy·clize** \'sī-kə-ˌlīz, 'si-, -ˌklīz\ vb

cy·clo \'sē-(ˌ)klō, 'si-\ n, pl **cyclos** [F, bicycle, moped, fr. *cyclo*- (as in *cyclomoteur* moped), fr. *cycle* two- or three-wheeled vehicle] (1964) : a 3-wheeled often motor-driven taxi

cy·clo·ad·di·tion \ˌsī-klō-(ˌ)klō-ə-'di-shən\ n (1963) : a chemical reaction leading to ring formation in a compound

cy·clo·al·i·phat·ic \ˌsī-klō-ˌa-lə-'fa-tik\ *adj* (1936) : ALICYCLIC

cy·clo·dex·trin \-'dek-strən\ n (1960) : any of a class of complex cyclic sugars that are products of the enzymatic decomposition of starch and that can catalyze reactions between simpler molecules which come together within the cylindrical body of the sugar

cy·clo·di·ene \-'dī-ˌēn, -dī-'\ n (1942) : an organic insecticide (as dieldrin or chlordane) with a chlorinated methylene group forming a bridge across a 6-membered carbon ring

cy·clo·gen·e·sis \-'je-nə-səs\ n [*cyclone* + *genesis*] (ca. 1938) : the development or intensification of a cyclone

cy·clo·hex·ane \ˌsī-klō-'hek-ˌsān\ n [ISV] (ca. 1909) : a pungent saturated cyclic hydrocarbon C_6H_{12} found in petroleum or made synthetically and used chiefly as a solvent and in organic synthesis

cy·clo·hex·a·none \-'hek-sə-ˌnōn\ n (ca. 1909) : a liquid ketone $C_6H_{10}O$ used esp. as a solvent and in organic synthesis

cy·clo·hex·i·mide \-'hek-sə-ˌmid, -məd\ n [*cyclohexane* + *imide*] (1950) : an agricultural fungicide $C_{15}H_{23}NO_4$ that inhibits protein synthesis and is obtained from a soil bacterium (*Streptomyces griseus*)

cy·clo·hex·yl·amine \-hek-'si-lə-ˌmēn\ n [*cyclohexane* + *-yl* + *amine*] (1943) : a colorless liquid amine $C_6H_{11}NH_2$ that is used in organic synthesis and to prevent corrosion in boilers and that is believed to be harmful as a metabolic breakdown product of cyclamate

[1]cy·cloid \'sī-ˌklȯid\ n [F *cycloïde*, fr. Gk *kykloeidēs* circular, fr. *kyklos*] (1661) : a curve that is generated by a point on the circumference of a circle as it rolls along a straight line — **cy·cloi·dal** \sī-'klȯi-d⁹l\ *adj*

[2]cycloid *adj* (1847) **1** : smooth with concentric lines of growth ⟨~ scales⟩; *also* : having or consisting of cycloid scales **2** : relating to or being a personality characterized by alternating high and low moods — compare CYCLOTHYMIC

cycloid

cy·clom·e·ter \sī-'klä-mə-tər\ n (1880) : a device made for recording the revolutions of a wheel and often used for registering distance traversed by a wheeled vehicle

cy·clone \'sī-ˌklōn\ n [modif. of Gk *kyklōma* wheel, coil, fr. *kykloun* to go around, fr. *kyklos* circle] (1848) **1 a** : a storm or system of winds that rotates about a center of low atmospheric pressure, advances at a speed of 20 to 30 miles (about 30 to 50 kilometers) an hour, and often brings heavy rain **b** : TORNADO **c** : LOW 1b **2** : any of various centrifugal devices for separating materials (as solid particles from gases) — **cy·clon·ic** \sī-'klä-nik\ *adj* — **cy·clon·i·cal·ly** \-ni-k(ə-)lē\ *adv*

Cy·clone \'sī-ˌklōn\ *trademark* — used for a chain-link fence

cyclone cellar n (1887) : STORM CELLAR

cy·clo·ole·fin \ˌsī-klō-'ō-lə-fən\ n [ISV] (ca. 1929) : a hydrocarbon containing a ring having one or more double bonds — **cy·clo·ole·fin·ic** \-ˌō-lə-'fi-nik\ *adj*

cy·clo·par·af·fin \-'par-ə-fən\ n (1900) : a saturated cyclic hydrocarbon of the formula C_nH_{2n}

cy·clo·pe·an \ˌsī-klə-'pē-ən, sī-'klō-pē-\ *adj* (1626) **1** *often cap* : of, relating to, or characteristic of a Cyclops **2** : HUGE, MASSIVE **3** : of or relating to a style of stone construction marked typically by the use of large irregular blocks without mortar

cy·clo·pe·dia *also* **cy·clo·pae·dia** \ˌsī-klə-'pē-dē-ə\ n (1728) : ENCYCLOPEDIA — **cy·clo·pe·dic** \-'pē-dik\ *adj*

cy·clo·phos·pha·mide \ˌsī-klō-'fäs-fə-ˌmid\ n (1960) : an immunosuppressive and antineoplastic agent $C_7H_{15}Cl_2N_2O_2P$ used esp. in the treatment of lymphomas and some leukemias

cy·clo·pro·pane \ˌsī-klə-'prō-ˌpān\ n [ISV] (1894) : a flammable gaseous saturated cyclic hydrocarbon C_3H_6 sometimes used as a general anesthetic

cy·clops \'sī-ˌkläps\ n [L, fr. Gk *Kyklōps*, fr. *kykl*- cycl- + *ōps* eye] (1513) **1** *pl* **cy·clo·pes** \sī-'klō-(ˌ)pēz\ *cap* : any of a race of giants in Greek mythology with a single eye in the middle of the forehead **2** *pl* **cyclops** [NL, genus name, fr. L] : any of a genus (*Cyclops*) of freshwater predatory copepods having a median eye

cy·clo·ra·ma \ˌsī-klə-'ra-mə, -'rä-\ n [*cycl*- + *-orama* (as in *panorama*)] (1840) **1** : a large pictorial representation encircling the spectator and often having real objects as a foreground **2** : a curved curtain or wall used as a background of a stage set to suggest unlimited space — **cy·clo·ram·ic** \-'ra-mik\ *adj*

cy·clo·ser·ine \ˌsī-klō-'ser-ˌēn\ n (1952) : an amino antibiotic $C_3H_6N_2O_2$ produced by an actinomycete (*Streptomyces orchidaceus*) and used esp. in the treatment of tuberculosis

cy·clo·sis \sī-'klō-səs\ n [NL, fr. Gk *kyklōsis* encirclement, fr. *kykloun* to go around] (1835) : the streaming of protoplasm within a cell

cy·clo·spor·ine \ˌsī-klə-'spȯr-⁹n, -ˌēn\ n [ISV *cycl*- + *spor*- + [2]*-ine*] (1976) : an immunosuppressive polypeptide drug $C_{62}H_{111}N_{11}O_{12}$ obtained from various imperfect fungi and used esp. to prevent rejection of organ transplants

cy·clo·stome \'sī-klə-ˌstōm\ n [ultim. fr. Gk *kykl*- + *stoma* mouth — more at STOMACH] (1835) : any of a class (Cyclostomata) of jawless fishes having a large sucking mouth and comprising the hagfishes and lampreys

cy·clo·style \-ˌstīl\ n [fr. *Cyclostyle*, a trademark] (1883) : a machine for making multiple copies that utilizes a stencil cut by a graver whose tip is a small rowel — **cyclostyle** vt

cy·clo·thy·mic \ˌsī-klə-'thī-mik\ *adj* [NL *cyclothymia* (fr. G *Zyklothymie*, fr. *zykl*- cycl- + *-thymie* -thymia) + E *-ic*] (1923) : relating to or being an affective disorder characterized by the alternation of depressed moods with elevated, expansive, or irritable moods without psychotic features — compare CYCLOID 2 — **cy·clo·thy·mia** \-'thī-mē-ə\ n

cy·clo·tom·ic \-'tä-mik\ *adj* [*cyclotomy* mathematical theory of the division of the circle into equal parts, fr. *cycl*- + *-tomy*] (1879) : relating to, being, or containing a polynomial of the form $x^p - 1 + x^p - 2 + \ldots + x + 1$ where *p* is a prime number

cy·clo·tron \'sī-klə-ˌträn\ n [*cycl*- + *-tron*; fr. the circular movement of the particles] (1935) : an accelerator in which charged particles (as protons, deuterons, or ions) are propelled by an alternating electric field in a constant magnetic field

cy·der *Brit var of* CIDER

cyg·net \'sig-nət\ n [ME *sygnett*, fr. MF *cygne* swan, fr. L *cycnus*, *cygnus*, fr. Gk *kyknos*] (15c) : a young swan

Cyg·nus \'sig-nəs\ n [L (gen. *Cygni*), lit., swan] : a northern constellation between Lyra and Pegasus in the Milky Way

cyl·in·der \'si-lən-dər\ n [MF or L; MF *cylindre*, fr. L *cylindrus*, fr. Gk *kylindros*, fr. *kylindein* to roll; perh. akin to Gk *kyklos* wheel — more at WHEEL] (1570) **1 a** : the surface traced by a straight line moving parallel to a fixed straight line and intersecting a fixed planar closed curve **b** : the space bounded by a cylinder and two parallel planes cutting all its elements — see VOLUME table **2** : a cylindrical body or space: as **a** : the turning chambered breech of a revolver **b** (1) : the piston chamber in an engine (2) : a chamber in a pump from which the piston expels the fluid **c** : any of various rotating members in a press (as a printing press); *esp* : one that impresses paper on an inked form **d** : a cylindrical clay object inscribed with cuneiform inscriptions — **cyl·in·dered** \-dərd\ *adj*

cylinder head n (1884) : the closed end of an engine or pump cylinder

cylinder seal n (1887) : a cylinder (as of stone) engraved in intaglio and used esp. in ancient Mesopotamia to roll an impression on wet clay

cy·lin·dri·cal \sə-'lin-dri-kəl\ *also* **cy·lin·dric** \-drik\ *adj* (1646) : relating to or having the form or properties of a cylinder — **cy·lin·dri·cal·ly** \-dri-k(ə-)lē\ *adv*

cylindrical coordinate n (ca. 1934) : any of the coordinates in space obtained by constructing in a plane a polar coordinate system and on a line perpendicular to the plane a linear coordinate system

cy·ma \'sī-mə\ n [Gk *kyma*, lit., wave] (1563) **1** : a projecting molding whose profile is an S-shaped curve **2** : an S-shaped curve formed by the union of a concave line and a convex line

cy·ma·tium \sī-'mā-sh(ē-)əm\ n, pl **-tia** \-sh(ē-)ə\ [L, fr. Gk *kymation*, dim. of *kymat-, kyma*] (1563) : a crowning molding in classic architecture; *esp* : CYMA

cym·bal \'sim-bəl\ n [ME, fr. OE *cymbal* & MF *cymbale*, fr. L *cymbalum*, fr. Gk *kymbalon*, fr. *kymbē* bowl, boat] (bef. 12c) : a concave brass plate that produces a brilliant clashing tone and that is struck with a drumstick or is used in pairs struck glancingly together — **cym·bal·ist** \-bə-list\ n

cym·bid·i·um \sim-'bi-dē-əm\ n [NL, genus name, fr. L *cymba* boat, fr. Gk *kymbē*] (1815) : any of a genus (*Cymbidium*) of tropical Old World epiphytic orchids with showy flowers

cyme \'sīm\ n [NL *cyma*, fr. L, cabbage sprout, fr. Gk *kyma* swell, wave, cabbage sprout, fr. *kyein* to be pregnant; akin to Skt *śvayati* it swells, grows] (1794) : an inflorescence in which each floral axis terminates in a single flower; *esp* : a determinate inflorescence of this type containing several flowers with the first-opening central flower terminating the main axis and subsequent flowers developing from lateral buds — see INFLORESCENCE illustration

cym·ling \'sim-lən, -liŋ\ n [prob. alter. of *simnel*] (1779) : PATTYPAN

cy·mo·phane \'sī-mə-ˌfān\ n [F, fr. Gk *kyma* wave + F *-phane* -phane] (ca. 1804) : CHRYSOBERYL; *esp* : an opalescent chrysoberyl

cy·mose \'sī-₁mōs\ *adj* (1807) : of, relating to, being, or bearing a cyme

¹**Cym·ric** \'kəm-rik, 'kim-\ *adj* (1839) : of, relating to, or characteristic of the non-Gaelic Celtic people of Britain or their language; *specif* : WELSH

²**Cymric** *n* (ca. 1889) : BRYTHONIC; *specif* : the Welsh language

Cym·ry \-rē\ *n* [W] (1833) : WELSH 2

cyn·ic \'si-nik\ *n* [MF or L, MF *cynique*, fr. L *cynicus*, fr. Gk *kynikos*, lit., like a dog, fr. *kyn-, kyōn* dog — more at HOUND] (ca. 1554) **1** *cap* : an adherent of an ancient Greek school of philosophers who held the view that virtue is the only good and that its essence lies in self-control and independence **2** : a faultfinding captious critic; *esp* : one who believes that human conduct is motivated wholly by self-interest — **cynic** *adj*

cyn·i·cal \'si-ni-kəl\ *adj* (1584) **1** : CAPTIOUS, PEEVISH **2** : having or showing the attitude or temper of a cynic; *esp* : contemptuously distrustful of human nature and motives ⟨those ∼ men who say that democracy cannot be honest and efficient —F. D. Roosevelt⟩ — **cyn·i·cal·ly** \-k(ə-)lē\ *adv*
syn CYNICAL, MISANTHROPIC, PESSIMISTIC mean deeply distrustful. CYNICAL implies having a sneering disbelief in sincerity or integrity ⟨*cynical* about politicians' motives⟩. MISANTHROPIC suggests a rooted distrust and dislike of human beings and their society ⟨a solitary and *misanthropic* artist⟩. PESSIMISTIC implies having a gloomy, distrustful view of life ⟨*pessimistic* about the future⟩.

cyn·i·cism \'si-nə-₁si-zəm\ *n* (1672) **1** *cap* : the doctrine of the Cynics **2** : cynical character, attitude, or quality; *also* : an expression of such quality

cy·no·mol·gus monkey \₁si-nə-'mäl-gəs-\ *n* [NL, alter. of *cynamolgus*, fr. L, member of an ancient tribe in Africa, fr. Gk *Kynamolgoi*, lit., dog milkers] (1936) : a macaque (*Macaca fascicularis* syn. *M. cynomolgus*) of southeastern Asia, Borneo, and the Philippines that sometimes feeds on marine crustaceans and shellfish and is often used in medical research

cy·no·sure \'sī-nə-₁shùr, 'si-\ *n* [MF & L; MF, Ursa Minor, guide, fr. L *cynosura* Ursa Minor, fr. Gk *kynosoura*, fr. *kynos oura*, lit., dog's tail] **1** *cap* : the northern constellation Ursa Minor; *also* : NORTH STAR 2 : one that serves to direct or guide **3** : a center of attraction or attention

Cyn·thia \'sin(t)-thē-ə\ *n* [L, fr. fem. of *Cynthius* of Cynthus, fr. *Cynthus*, mountain on Delos where she was born, fr. Gk *Kynthos*] **1** : ARTEMIS 2 : MOON 1a

cy·pher *chiefly Brit var of* CIPHER

¹**cy pres** \₁si-'prā, ₁sē-\ *n* [AF, so near, as near (as may be)] (1802) : a rule providing for the interpretation of instruments in equity as nearly as possible in conformity to the intention of the testator when literal construction is illegal, impracticable, or impossible — called also *cy pres doctrine*

²**cy pres** *adv* (1885) : in accordance with the rule of cy pres

¹**cy·press** \'sī-prəs\ *n* [ME, fr. MF *ciprès*, fr. L *cyparissus*, fr. Gk *kyparissos*] (14c) **1 a** (1) : any of a genus (*Cupressus* of the family Cupressaceae, the cypress family) of evergreen trees and shrubs with small overlapping leaves resembling scales (2) : any of several coniferous trees of the cypress family or the bald cypress family; *esp* : BALD CYPRESS 1 **b** : the wood of a cypress tree **2** : branches of cypress used as a symbol of mourning

²**cypress** *n* [ME *ciprus, cipres,* fr. *Cyprus,* Mediterranean island] (15c) : a silk or cotton usu. black gauze formerly used for mourning

cypress vine *n* (1819) : a tropical American vine (*Ipomoea quamoclit* syn. *Quamoclit pennata*) of the morning-glory family with usu. red or white tubular flowers and finely dissected leaves

cyp·ri·an \'si-prē-ən\ *n, often cap* [L *cyprius* of Cyprus, fr. Gk *kyprios*, fr. *Kypros* Cyprus, birthplace of Aphrodite] (1819) : PROSTITUTE

cyp·ri·nid \'si-prə-nəd\ *n* [ultim. fr. L *cyprinus* carp, fr. Gk *kyprinos*] (ca. 1889) : any of a family (Cyprinidae) of soft-finned freshwater fishes including the carps and minnows — **cyprinid** *adj*

cyp·ri·pe·di·um \₁si-prə-'pē-dē-əm\ *n* [NL, genus name, fr. LL *Cypris*, a name for Venus + Gk *pedilon* sandal] (1813) **1** : any of a genus (*Cypripedium*) of Eurasian and No. American terrestrial orchids having large usu. showy drooping flowers with the lip inflated or pouched — compare LADY'S SLIPPER **2** : any of a genus (*Paphiopedalum*) of widely cultivated Asian orchids

cy·pro·hep·ta·dine \₁si-prō-'hep-tə-₁dēn\ *n* [*cyclic* + *propyl* + *hepta-* + *piperidine*] (1971) : a drug C₂₁H₂₁N that acts antagonistically to histamine and serotonin and is used esp. in the treatment of asthma

cy·prot·er·one \sī-'prä-tə-₁rōn\ *n* [prob. fr. *cycl-* + *progesterone*] (1966) : a synthetic steroid C₂₂H₂₇ClO₃ that inhibits androgenic secretions (as testosterone)

Cy·re·na·ic \₁sir-ə-'nā-ik, ₁sī-rə-\ *n* [L *cyrenaicus,* fr. Gk *kyrēnaikos,* fr. *Kyrēnē* Cyrene, Africa, home of Aristippus, author of the doctrine] (1586) : an adherent of the doctrine that pleasure is the chief end of life — **Cyrenaic** *adj* — **Cy·re·na·icism** \-'nā-ə₁si-zəm\ *n*

Cy·ril·lic \sə-'ri-lik\ *adj* [St. *Cyril,* reputed inventor of the Cyrillic alphabet] (1842) : of, relating to, or constituting an alphabet used for writing Old Church Slavonic and for Russian and a number of other languages of eastern Europe and Asia

cyst \'sist\ *n* [NL *cystis,* fr. Gk *kystis* bladder, pouch; akin to Skt *śvasiti* he blows, snorts — more at WHEEZE] (ca. 1720) **1** : a closed sac having a distinct membrane and developing abnormally in a cavity or structure of the body **2** : a body resembling a cyst: **a** : a resting spore of many algae **b** : a gas-filled vesicle (as of a rockweed or bladderwort) **c** : a capsule formed about a minute organism going into a resting or spore stage; *also* : this capsule with its contents **d** : a resistant cover about a parasite produced by the parasite or the host

cyst- *or* **cysti-** *or* **cysto-** *comb form* [F, fr. Gk *kyst-, kysto-,* fr. *kystis*] : bladder ⟨*cystitis*⟩ : sac ⟨*cystocarp*⟩
-cyst *n comb form* [NL *-cystis,* fr. Gk *kystis*] : bladder : sac ⟨*blastocyst*⟩

cys·te·amine \sis-'tē-ə-mən\ *n* [*cysteine* + *amine*] (1943) : a cysteine derivative C₂H₇NS that has been used experimentally in the prevention of radiation sickness (as of cancer patients)

cys·te·ine \'sis-tə-₁ēn\ *n* [ISV, fr. *cystine* + *-ein*] (1884) : a crystalline sulfur-containing amino acid C₃H₇NO₂S readily oxidizable to cystine

cys·tic \'sis-tik\ *adj* (1713) **1** : relating to, composed of, or containing cysts **2** : of or relating to the urinary bladder or the gallbladder **3** : enclosed in a cyst

cys·ti·cer·coid \₁sis-tə-'sər-₁kòid\ *n* (1858) : a tapeworm larva having an invaginated scolex and solid tailpiece

cys·ti·cer·co·sis \₁sis-tə-(₁)sər-'kō-səs\ *n, pl* **-co·ses** \-'kō-₁sēz\ [NL] (1905) : infestation with or disease caused by cysticerci

cys·ti·cer·cus \-'sər-kəs\ *n, pl* **-cer·ci** \-'sər-₁sī, -₁kī\ [NL, fr. *cyst-* + Gk *kerkos* tail] (ca. 1871) : a tapeworm larva that consists of a fluid-filled sac containing an invaginated scolex and is situated in the tissues of an intermediate host

cystic fibrosis *n* (1938) : a common hereditary disease esp. among whites that appears usu. in early childhood, involves functional disorder of the exocrine glands, and is marked esp. by faulty digestion due to a deficiency of pancreatic enzymes, by difficulty in breathing due to mucus accumulation in airways, and by excessive loss of salt in the sweat

cys·tine \'sis-₁tēn\ *n* [fr. its discovery in bladder stones] (1843) : a crystalline amino acid C₆H₁₂N₂O₄S₂ that is widespread in proteins (as keratins) and is a major metabolic sulfur source

cys·tin·uria \₁sis-tə-'nùr-ē-ə, -'nyùr-\ *n* [NL] (1853) : a metabolic defect characterized by excretion of excessive amounts of cystine in the urine and inherited as an autosomal recessive trait

cys·ti·tis \sis-'tī-təs\ *n* [NL] (ca. 1783) : inflammation of the urinary bladder

cys·to·carp \'sis-tə-₁kärp\ *n* [ISV] (1875) : the fruiting structure produced in the red algae after fertilization

cys·to·lith \'sis-tə-₁lith\ *n* [G *Zystolith,* fr. *zyst-* cyst- + *-lith*] (1857) : a calcium carbonate concretion arising from the cellulose wall of cells of higher plants

cys·to·scope \'sis-tə-₁skōp\ *n* [ISV] (1889) : a medical instrument for the visual examination of the bladder and for the passage of instruments under visual control — **cys·to·scop·ic** \₁sis-tə-'skä-pik\ *adj* — **cys·tos·co·py** \si-'stäs-kə-pē\ *n*

cyt- *or* **cyto-** *comb form* [F *zyt-, zyto-,* fr. Gk *kytos* hollow vessel — more at HIDE] **1** : cell ⟨*cytology*⟩ **2** : cytoplasm ⟨*cytokinesis*⟩
-cyte *n comb form* [NL *-cyta,* fr. Gk *kytos* hollow vessel] : cell ⟨*leukocyte*⟩

Cyth·er·ea \₁si-thə-'rē-ə\ *n* [L, fr. Gk *Kythereia,* fr. *Kythēra* Cythera, island associated with Aphrodite] : APHRODITE

Cyth·er·e·an \-'rē-ən\ *adj* (1885) : of or relating to the planet Venus

cy·ti·dine \'sī-tə-₁dēn, 'sī-\ *n* [*cytosine* + *-idine*] (1911) : a nucleoside containing cytosine

cy·ti·dyl·ic acid \₁sī-tə-'dil-ik-, ₁sī-\ *n* [*cytidine* + *-yl* + ¹*-ic*] (1936) : a nucleotide containing cytosine

cy·to·cha·la·sin \₁sī-tə-kə-'lā-sən\ *n* [*cyt-* + Gk *chalasis* slackening + E ¹*-in*] (1967) : any of a group of metabolites isolated from fungi (esp. *Helminthosporium dematioideum*) that inhibit various cell processes

cy·to·chem·is·try \-'ke-mə-strē\ *n* (ca. 1905) **1** : microscopical biochemistry **2** : the chemistry of cells — **cy·to·chem·i·cal** \-'ke-mi-kəl\ *adj*

cy·to·chrome \'sī-tə-₁krōm\ *n* (1925) : any of several intracellular hemoprotein respiratory pigments that are enzymes functioning in electron transport as carriers of electrons

cytochrome c *n, often ital 2d c* (1940) : the most abundant and stable of the cytochromes

cytochrome oxidase *n* (1942) : an iron-porphyrin enzyme important in cell respiration because of its ability to catalyze the oxidation of reduced cytochrome c in the presence of oxygen

cy·to·dif·fer·en·ti·a·tion \'sī-tō-₁di-fə-₁ren(t)-shē-'ā-shən\ *n* (1959) : the development of specialized cells (as muscle, blood, or nerve cells) from undifferentiated precursors

cy·to·ge·net·ics \₁sī-tō-jə-'ne-tiks\ *n pl but sing or pl in constr* [ISV] (1942) : a branch of biology that deals with the study of heredity and variation by the methods of both cytology and genetics — **cy·to·ge·net·ic** \-'ne-tik\ *or* **cy·to·ge·net·i·cal** \-ti-kəl\ *adj* — **cy·to·ge·net·i·cal·ly** \-ti-k(ə-)lē\ *adv* — **cy·to·ge·net·i·cist** \-'ne-tə-sist\ *n*

cy·to·kine \'sī-tə-₁kīn\ *n* [*cyt-* + *-kine* (as in *lymphokine*)] (1979) : any of a class of immunoregulatory substances (as lymphokines) that are secreted by cells of the immune system

cy·to·ki·ne·sis \₁sī-tō-kə-'nē-səs, -kī-\ *n* [NL] (1919) **1** : the cytoplasmic changes accompanying mitosis **2** : cleavage of the cytoplasm into daughter cells following nuclear division — **cy·to·ki·net·ic** \-'ne-tik\ *adj*

cy·to·ki·nin \₁sī-tə-'kī-nən\ *n* [*cyt-* + *kinin*] (1965) : any of various plant growth substances (as kinetin) that are usu. derivatives of adenine

cy·tol·o·gy \sī-'tä-lə-jē\ *n* [ISV] (1889) **1** : a branch of biology dealing with the structure, function, multiplication, pathology, and life history of cells **2** : the cytological aspects of a process or structure — **cy·to·log·i·cal** \₁sī-t'l-'ä-ji-kəl\ *or* **cy·to·log·ic** \-'ä-jik\ *adj* — **cy·to·log·i·cal·ly** \-ji-k(ə-)lē\ *adv* — **cy·tol·o·gist** \sī-'tä-lə-jist\ *n*

cy·to·ly·sin \₁sī-t'l-'ī-s'n\ *n* [ISV] (ca. 1903) : a substance (as an antibody that lyses bacteria) producing cytolysis

cy·tol·y·sis \sī-'tä-lə-səs\ *n* [NL] (1907) : the usu. pathologic dissolution or disintegration of cells — **cy·to·lyt·ic** \₁sī-t'l-'i-tik\ *adj*

cy·to·meg·al·ic \₁sī-tō-mi-'ga-lik\ *adj* [NL *cytomegalia* condition of having enlarged cells, fr. *cyt-* + *megal-* + *-ia*] (1952) : characterized by or causing the formation of enlarged cells

cy·to·meg·a·lo·vi·rus \₁sī-tə-₁me-gə-lō-'vī-rəs\ *n* [NL, fr. *cytomegalia* + *-o-* + *virus*] (1963) : any of several viruses that cause cellular enlargement and formation of eosinophilic inclusion bodies esp. in the nucleus and include some acting as opportunistic infectious agents in immunosuppressed conditions (as AIDS)

cy·to·mem·brane \₁sī-tō-'mem-₁brān\ *n* (1962) : one of the cellular membranes including those of the plasmalemma, endoplasmic reticulum, nuclear envelope, and Golgi apparatus; *specif* : UNIT MEMBRANE

cy·to·path·ic \₁sī-tə-'pa-thik\ *adj* (1952) : of, relating to, characterized by, or producing pathological changes in cells

---

\ə\ abut \ᵊ\ kitten, F table \ər\ further \a\ ash \ā\ ace \ä\ mop, mar \aù\ out \ch\ chin \e\ bet \ē\ easy \g\ go \i\ hit \ī\ ice \j\ job \ŋ\ sing \ō\ go \ò\ law \òi\ boy \th\ thin \t̸h\ the \ü\ loot \ù\ foot \y\ yet \zh\ vision \à, ḳ, ⁿ, œ, œ̄, ᴜᴇ, ᵫ, ᵜ\ *see* Guide to Pronunciation

cy·to·path·o·gen·ic \-ˌpa-thə-'je-nik\ *adj* (1952) : pathologic for or destructive to cells — **cy·to·path·o·ge·nic·i·ty** \-jə-'ni-sə-tē\ *n*

cy·to·phil·ic \ˌsī-tə-'fi-lik\ *adj* (ca. 1909) : having an affinity for cells ⟨~ antibodies⟩

cy·to·pho·tom·e·try \-fō-'tä-mə-trē\ *n* (1955) : photometry applied to the study of the cell or its constituents — **cy·to·pho·to·met·ric** \-ˌfō-tə-'me-trik\ *adj*

cy·to·plasm \'sī-tə-ˌpla-zəm\ *n* [ISV] (1874) : the organized complex of inorganic and organic substances external to the nuclear membrane of a cell and including the cytosol and membrane-bound organelles (as mitochondria or chloroplasts) — see CELL illustration — **cy·to·plas·mic** \ˌsī-tə-'plaz-mik\ *adj* — **cy·to·plas·mi·cal·ly** \-mi-k(ə-)lē\ *adv*

cy·to·sine \'sī-tə-ˌsēn\ *n* [ISV *cyt-* + *-ose* + *²-ine*] (1894) : a pyrimidine base C₄H₅N₃O that codes genetic information in the polynucleotide chain of DNA or RNA — compare ADENINE, GUANINE, THYMINE, URACIL

cy·to·skel·e·ton \ˌsī-tə-'ske-lə-t²n\ *n* (1940) : the network of protein filaments and microtubules in the cytoplasm that controls cell shape, maintains intracellular organization, and is involved in cell movement — **cy·to·skel·e·tal** \-t²l\ *adj*

cy·to·sol \'sī-tə-ˌsäl, -ˌsȯl\ *n* (1970) : the fluid portion of the cytoplasm exclusive of organelles and membranes — called also *hyaloplasm, ground substance* — **cy·to·sol·ic** \ˌsī-tə-'sä-lik, -'sō-\ *adj*

cy·to·stat·ic \ˌsī-tə-'sta-tik\ *adj* (1949) : tending to retard cellular activity and multiplication ⟨~ treatment of tumor cells⟩ — **cytostatic** *n* — **cy·to·stat·i·cal·ly** \-ti-k(ə-)lē\ *adv*

cy·to·tax·on·o·my \ˌsī-tō-(ˌ)tak-'sä-nə-mē\ *n* (1930) 1 : study of the relationships and classification of organisms using both classical systematic techniques and comparative studies of chromosomes 2 : the nuclear cytologic makeup of a kind of organism — **cy·to·tax·o·nom-ic** \-ˌtak-sə-'nä-mik\ *adj* — **cy·to·tax·o·nom·i·cal·ly** \-mi-k(ə-)lē\ *adv*

cy·to·tech·nol·o·gist \ˌsī-tə-tek-'nä-lə-jist\ *n* (1961) : a medical technician trained in the identification of cells and cellular abnormalities (as in cancer) — **cy·to·tech·nol·o·gy** \-lə-jē\ *n*

cy·to·tox·ic \ˌsī-tə-'täk-sik\ *adj* (1904) 1 : of or relating to a cytotoxin 2 : toxic to cells ⟨~ properties of platinum⟩ — **cy·to·tox·ic·i·ty** \-(ˌ)täk-'si-sə-tē\ *n*

cy·to·tox·in \-'täk-sən\ *n* (1902) : a substance (as a toxin or antibody) having a toxic effect on cells

czar \'zär, '(t)sär\ *n* [NL *czar,* fr. Russ *tsar',* fr. ORuss *tsĭsari,* fr. Goth *kaisar,* fr. Gk or L; Gk, fr. L *Caesar* — more at CAESAR] (1555) 1 : EMPEROR; *specif* : the ruler of Russia until the 1917 revolution 2 : one having great power or authority ⟨a banking ~⟩ — **czar·dom** \'zär-dəm, '(t)sär-\ *n*

czar·das \'chär-ˌdash, -ˌdäsh\ *n, pl* **czardas** [Hung *csárdás*] (1860) : a Hungarian dance to music in duple time in which the dancers start slowly and finish with a rapid whirl

czar·e·vitch \'zär-ə-ˌvich, '(t)sär-\ *n* [Russ *tsarevich,* fr. *tsar'* + *-evich,* patronymic suffix] (1710) : an heir apparent of a Russian czar

cza·ri·na \zä-'rē-nə, (t)sä-\ *n* [prob. modif. of G *Zarin,* fr. *Zar* czar, fr. Russ *tsar'*] (1717) : the wife of a czar

czar·ism \'zär-ˌi-zəm, '(t)sär-\ *n* (1855) 1 : the government of Russia under the czars 2 : autocratic rule — **czar·ist** \'zär-ist, '(t)sär-\ *n or adj*

Czech \'chek\ *n* [Czech *Čech*] (1841) 1 : a native or inhabitant of western Czechoslovakia including Bohemia and Moravia 2 : the Slavic language of the Czechs 3 : a native or inhabitant of Czechoslovakia or the Czech Republic — **Czech** *adj* — **Czech·ish** \'che-kish\ *adj*

---

d \'dē\ *n, pl* **d's** *or* **ds** \'dēz\ *often cap, often attrib* (bef. 12c) 1 a : the 4th letter of the English alphabet b : a graphic representation of this letter c : a speech counterpart of orthographic *d* 2 : 500 — see NUMBER table 3 : the 2d tone of a C-major scale 4 : a graphic device for reproducing the letter *d* 5 : one designated *d* esp. as the 4th in order or class 6 a : a grade rating a student's work as poor in quality b : one graded or rated with a D 7 : something shaped like the letter D; *specif* : a semicircle on a pool table about 23 inches in diameter for use esp. in snooker 8 : DEFENSE 2b, 4b ⟨play tough *D*⟩

d- \ˌdē, 'dē\ *prefix* [ISV, fr. *dextr-*] 1 : dextrorotatory ⟨*d*-tartaric acid⟩ 2 : having a similar configuration at a selected carbon atom to the configuration of dextrorotatory glyceraldehyde — usu. printed as a small capital ⟨D-fructose⟩

-d *symbol* — used after the figure 2 or 3 to indicate the ordinal number second or third ⟨2*d*⟩ ⟨53*d*⟩

'd \d, əd, id\ *vb* 1 : HAD 2 : WOULD 3 : DID

DA \ˌdē-'ā\ *n* [*duck's* *ass*; fr. its resemblance to the tail of a duck] (1951) : DUCKTAIL

¹dab \'dab\ *n* [ME *dabbe*] (14c) 1 : a sudden blow or thrust : POKE 2 : a small amount 3 : a gentle touch or stroke : PAT 4 : DAUB

²dab *vb* **dabbed; dab·bing** *vt* (1562) 1 : to strike or touch lightly : PAT 2 : to apply lightly or irregularly : DAUB ~ *vi* : to make a dab — **dab·ber** *n*

³dab *n* [AF *dabbe*] (15c) : FLATFISH; *esp* : any of several flounders (genus *Limanda*)

⁴dab *n* [origin unknown] (1691) *chiefly Brit* : a skillful person

dab·ble \'da-bəl\ *vb* **dab·bled; dab·bling** \-b(ə-)liŋ\ [perh. freq. of *²dab*] *vt* (1557) : to wet by splashing or by little dips or strokes : SPATTER ~ *vi* 1 a : to paddle, splash, or play in or as if in water b : to reach with the bill to the bottom of shallow water in order to obtain food 2 : to work or involve oneself superficially or intermittently esp. in a secondary activity or interest ⟨~s in art⟩

dab·bler \-b(ə-)lər\ *n* (1611) : one that dabbles: as a : one not deeply engaged in or concerned with something b : a duck (as a mallard or shoveler) that feeds by dabbling — called also *dabbling duck, puddle duck* **syn** see AMATEUR

dab·bling \-b(ə-)liŋ\ *n* (ca. 1847) : a superficial or intermittent interest, investigation, or experiment ⟨his ~s in philosophy and art⟩

dab·chick \'dab-ˌchik\ *n* [prob. irreg. fr. obs. E *dop* (to dive) + E *chick*] (ca. 1550) : any of several small grebes

dab hand *n* [⁴*dab*] (ca. 1828) *chiefly Brit* : EXPERT

da ca·po \dä-'kä-(ˌ)pō, də-\ *adv or adj* [It] (ca. 1724) : from the beginning — used as a direction in music to repeat

dace \'dās\ *n, pl* **dace** [ME *dace, darce,* fr. MF *dars,* fr. ML *darsus*] (15c) 1 : a small freshwater European cyprinid fish (*Leuciscus leuciscus*) 2 : any of various small No. American freshwater cyprinid fishes

da·cha \'dä-chə *also* 'da-\ *n* [Russ, fr. ORuss, land allotted by a prince; akin to L *dos* dowry — more at DATE] (1896) : a Russian country cottage used esp. in the summer

dachs·hund \'däks-ˌhu̇nt, -ˌhu̇nd; 'däk-sənt; *esp Brit* 'dak-sənd\ *n* [G, fr. *Dachs* badger + *Hund* dog] (1882) : any of a breed of long-bodied, short-legged dogs of German origin that occur in short-haired, long-haired, and wirehaired varieties

Da·cron \'dā-ˌkrän, 'da-\ *trademark* — used for a synthetic polyester textile fiber

dac·tyl \'dak-t²l, -ˌtil\ *n* [ME *dactile,* fr. L *dactylus,* fr. Gk *daktylos,* lit., finger; fr. the fact that the first of three syllables is the longest, like the joints of the finger] (14c) : a metrical foot consisting of one long and two short syllables or of one stressed and two unstressed syllables (as in *tenderly*) — **dac·tyl·ic** \dak-'ti-lik\ *adj or n*

dactyl- *or* **dactylo-** *comb form* [Gk *daktyl-, daktylo-,* fr. *daktylos*] : finger : toe : digit ⟨*dactylology*⟩

dac·ty·lol·o·gy \ˌdak-tə-'lä-lə-jē\ *n* (ca. 1656) : FINGER SPELLING

dad \'dad\ *n* [prob. baby talk] (15c) : FATHER 1a

Da·da \'dä-(ˌ)dä\ *n* [F] (1919) : a movement in art and literature based on deliberate irrationality and negation of traditional artistic values; *also* : the art and literature produced by this movement

da·da·ism \-ˌi-zəm\ *n, often cap* [F *dadaïsme*] (1919) : DADA — **da·da·ist** \-ist\ *n or adj, often cap* — **da·da·is·tic** \ˌdä-dä-'is-tik\ *adj, often cap*

dad·dy \'da-dē\ *n, pl* **daddies** (15c) 1 : FATHER 1a 2 : GRANDDADDY 2

dad·dy long·legs \ˌda-dē-'lȯŋ-ˌlegz, -ˌlägz\ *n, pl* **daddy longlegs** (ca. 1814) 1 : CRANE FLY 2 : HARVESTMAN

¹da·do \'dä-(ˌ)dō\ *n, pl* **dadoes** [It, die, plinth] (1664) 1 a : the part of a pedestal of a column between the base and the surbase b : the lower part of an interior wall when specially decorated or faced; *also* : the decoration adorning this part of a wall 2 : a rectangular groove cut to make a joint in woodworking; *specif* : one cut across the grain

²dado *vt* **da·doed; da·do·ing** (1881) 1 : to provide with a dado 2 a : to set into a groove b : to cut a dado in (as a plank)

dae·dal \'dē-d²l\ *adj* [L *daedalus,* fr. Gk *daidalos*] (1590) 1 a : SKILLFUL, ARTISTIC b : INTRICATE ⟨the computer's ~ circuitry⟩ 2 : adorned with many things ⟨visions of cloud and light and ~ earth are the airman's daily scene —Laurence Binyon⟩

Dae·da·lus \'de-d²l-əs, 'dē-\ *n* [L, fr. Gk *Daidalos*] : the legendary builder of the Cretan labyrinth who makes wings to enable himself and his son Icarus to escape imprisonment — **Dae·da·lian** *or* **Dae·da·lean** \di-'dāl-yən\ *adj*

dae·mon *var of* DEMON

daff \'daf\ *vt* [alter. of *doff*] (1596) 1 *archaic* : to thrust aside 2 *obs* : to put off (as with an excuse)

daf·fo·dil \'da-fə-ˌdil\ *n* [perh. fr. D *de affodil* the asphodel, fr. *de* the (fr. MD) + *affodil* asphodel, fr. MF *afrodile,* fr. L *asphodelus;* akin to OHG *thaz* the — more at THAT, ASPHODEL] (1548) : any of various bulbous herbs (genus *Narcissus*); *esp* : a plant whose flowers have a large corona elongated into a trumpet — compare JONQUIL

daf·fy \'da-fē\ *adj* **daf·fi·er; -est** [obs. E *daff,* n. (fool)] (ca. 1884) : CRAZY, FOOLISH — **daf·fi·ly** \'da-fə-lē\ *adv*

daft \'daft *also* 'däft\ *adj* [ME *dafte* gentle, stupid; akin to OE *gedæfte* mild, gentle, ME *defte* deft, OCS *podobati* to be fitting] (14c) 1 a : SILLY, FOOLISH b : MAD, INSANE 2 *Scot* : frivolously gay — **daft·ly** *adv* — **daft·ness** \'daft(t)-nəs\ *n*

dag \'dag\ *n* [ME *dagge*] (14c) 1 : a hanging end or shred 2 : matted or manure-coated wool

dag·ger \'da-gər\ *n* [ME] (14c) 1 : a sharp pointed knife for stabbing 2 a : something that resembles a dagger b : a character † used as a reference mark or to indicate a death date — **dag·ger·like** \-ˌlīk\ *adj* — **at daggers drawn** : in a state of open hostility or conflict

da·go \'dā-(,)gō\ *n, pl* **dagos** *or* **dagoes** [alter. of earlier *diego*, fr. *Diego*, a common Sp given name] (1832) : a person of Italian or Spanish birth or descent — usu. used disparagingly

da·guerre·o·type \də-'ger-ō-,tīp, -rə- *also* də-'ge-rē-ō-,tīp\ *n* [F *daguerréotype*, fr. L. J. M. *Daguerre* + F *-o-* + *type*] (1839) : an early photograph produced on a silver or a silver-covered copper plate; *also* : the process of producing such photographs — **daguerreotype** *vt* — **da·guerre·o·typ·ist** \-,tī-pist\ *n* — **da·guerre·o·typy** \-,tī-pē\ *n*

dah \'dä\ *n* [imit.] (1940) : DASH 7

dahl·ia \'dal-yə, 'däl-, *U.S. also & Brit usu* 'dāl-\ *n* [NL, genus name, fr. Anders *Dahl* †1789 Swed. botanist] (1840) : any of a genus (*Dahlia*) of American tuberous-rooted composite herbs having opposite pinnate leaves and rayed flower heads and including many that are cultivated as ornamentals

dai·kon \'dī-kən\ *n* [Jp, fr. *dai* big + *kon* root] (1876) : a large long hard white radish used esp. in Oriental cuisine; *also* : a plant (*Raphanus sativus longipinnatus*) whose root is a daikon

dai·li·ness \'dā-lē-nəs, -li-\ *n* (1596) : daily or routine quality : ORDINARINESS ⟨the ~ of family life⟩

¹**dai·ly** \'dā-lē\ *adj* (15c) **1 a** : occurring, made, or acted upon every day **b** : issued every day or every weekday **c** : of or providing for every day **2 a** : reckoned by the day ⟨average ~ wage⟩ **b** : covering the period of or based on a day ⟨~ statistics⟩

²**daily** *adv* (15c) **1** : every day **2** : every weekday

³**daily** *n, pl* **dai·lies** (1832) **1** : a newspaper published every weekday **2** *Brit* : a servant who works on a daily basis **3** *pl* : RUSH 6

daily double *n* (1942) : a system of betting (as on horse races) in which the bettor must pick the winners of two stipulated races in order to win

daily dozen *n* (1919) **1** : a series of physical exercises to be performed daily : WORKOUT **2** : a set of routine duties or tasks

dai·mon \'dī-,mōn\ *n, pl* **dai·mo·nes** \-mə-,nēz\ *or* **daimons** [Gk *daimōn*] (1852) : DEMON 2, 3 — **dai·mon·ic** \dī-'mä-nik\ *adj*

dai·myo *also* **dai·mio** \'dī-mē-,ō, -(,)myō\ *n, pl* **-myo** *or* **-myos** *also* **-mio** *or* **-mios** [Jp *daimyō*] (1727) : a Japanese feudal baron

¹**dain·ty** \'dān-tē\ *n, pl* **dain·ties** [ME *deinte*, fr. OF *deintié*, fr. L *dignitat-, dignitas* dignity, worth] (14c) **1 a** : something delicious to the taste **b** : something choice or pleasing **2** *obs* : FASTIDIOUSNESS

²**dainty** *adj* **dain·ti·er; -est** (14c) **1 a** : tasting good : TASTY **b** : attractively prepared and served **2** : marked by delicate or diminutive beauty, form, or grace **3** *obs* : CHARY, RELUCTANT **4 a** : marked by fastidious discrimination or finical taste **b** : showing avoidance of anything rough **syn** see CHOICE — **dain·ti·ly** \'dān-tə-lē\ *adv* — **dain·ti·ness** \'dān-tē-nəs\ *n*

dai·qui·ri \'da-kə-rē, 'dī-\ *n* [*Daiquirí*, Cuba] (1920) : a cocktail made of rum, lime juice, and sugar

dairy \'der-ē, 'dar-\ *n, pl* **dair·ies** *often attrib* [ME *deyerie*, fr. *deye* dairymaid, fr. OE *dæge* kneader of bread; akin to OE *dāg* dough — more at DOUGH] (14c) **1** : a room, building, or establishment where milk is kept and butter or cheese is made **2 a** : the department of farming or of a farm that is concerned with the production of milk, butter, and cheese **b** : a farm devoted to such production **3** : an establishment for the sale or distribution chiefly of milk and milk products

dairy cattle *n pl* (1895) : cattle kept for milk production

dairy·ing \'der-ē-iŋ\ *n* (1649) : the business of operating a dairy

dairy·maid \-,mād\ *n* (1599) : a woman employed in a dairy

dairy·man \-mən, -,man\ *n* (ca. 1617) : one who operates a dairy farm or works in a dairy

da·is \'dā-əs, ÷'dī-\ *n* [ME *deis*, fr. OF, fr. LL *discus* high table, fr. L, dish, quoit — more at DISH] (13c) : a raised platform (as in a hall or large room)

dai·shi·ki \dī-'shē-kē\ *var of* DASHIKI

dai·sy \'dā-zē\ *n, pl* **daisies** [ME *dayeseye*, fr. OE *dægesēage*, fr. *dæg* day + *ēage* eye] (bef. 12c) **1** : a composite plant (as of the genera *Bellis* or *Chrysanthemum*) having a flower head with well-developed ray flowers usu. arranged in one or a few whorls: as **a** : a low European herb (*Bellis perennis*) with white or pink ray flowers — called also *English daisy* **b** : a leafy-stemmed perennial herb (*Chrysanthemum leucanthemum*) with long white ray flowers and a yellow disk that was introduced into the U.S. from Europe — called also *oxeye daisy* **2** : the flower head of a daisy **3** : a first-rate person or thing **4** *cap* : a member of a program of the Girl Scouts for girls in kindergarten and first grade in school

daisy chain *n* (1841) **1** : a string of daisies with stems linked to form a chain **2** : an interlinked series

daisy ham *n* (ca. 1938) : a boned and smoked piece of pork from the shoulder

daisy wheel *n* [fr. its resemblance to the flower] (ca. 1977) : a disk with spokes bearing type that serves as the printing element of an electric typewriter or printer; *also* : a printer that uses such a disk

Da·ko·ta \də-'kō-tə\ *n, pl* **Dakotas** *also* **Dakota** (1804) **1** : a member of an American Indian people of the northern Mississippi valley **2** : the language of the Dakota people

dal *also* **dahl** \'däl\ *n* [Hindi *dāl*] (1673) : a dried legume (as lentils, beans, or peas); *also* : an Indian dish made of simmered and usu. pureed and spiced legumes

Da·lai La·ma \,dä-li-'lä-mə, ,däl-ā-, ,da-\ *n* [Mongolian *dalai* ocean] (1698) : the spiritual head of Lamaism

da·la·si \də-'lä-sē\ *n, pl* **dalasi** *or* **dalasis** [Wolof] (1966) — see MONEY table

dale \'dāl\ *n* [ME, fr. OE *dæl*; akin to OHG *tal* valley, W *dôl*] (bef. 12c) : VALLEY, VALE ⟨went riding over hill and ~⟩

dales·man \'dā(ə)lz-mən\ *n* (1769) *Brit* : one living or born in a dale

da·leth \'dä-,leth, -,let *also* -ləd\ *n* [Heb *dāleth*, fr. *deleth* door] (1823) : the 4th letter of the Hebrew alphabet — see ALPHABET table

dal·li·ance \'da-lē-ən(t)s\ *n* (14c) : an act of dallying: as **a** : PLAY; *esp* : amorous play **b** : frivolous action : TRIFLING

Dal·lis grass \'da-ləs-\ *n* [A. T. *Dallis*, 19th cent. Am. farmer] (1907) : a tall tufted tropical perennial grass (*Paspalum dilatatum*) introduced as a pasture and forage grass in the southern U.S.

Dall por·poise \'dȯl-\ *n* [William H. *Dall* †1927 Am. naturalist] (1951) : a black-and-white porpoise (*Phocoenoides dalli*) of temperate and arctic waters of the rim of the No. Pacific Ocean — called also *Dall's porpoise* \'dȯlz-\

Dall sheep *n* [W. H. *Dall*] (1887) : a large white wild sheep (*Ovis dalli*) of Alaska and northern British Columbia — called also *Dall's sheep*

dal·ly \'da-lē\ *vi* **dal·lied; dal·ly·ing** [ME *dalyen*, fr. AF *dalier*] (15c) **1 a** : to act playfully; *esp* : to play amorously **b** : to deal lightly : TOY ⟨accused him of ~*ing* with a serious problem⟩ **2 a** : to waste time **b** : LINGER, DAWDLE **syn** see TRIFLE, DELAY — **dal·li·er** *n*

dal·ma·tian \dal-'mā-shən\ *n, often cap* [fr. the supposed origin of the breed in Dalmatia] (1824) : any of a breed of medium-sized dogs having a white short-haired coat with black or brown spots

dalmatian

dal·mat·ic \dal-'ma-tik\ *n* [ME *dalmatyk*, fr. OE *dalmatice*, fr. LL *dalmatica*, fr. L, fem. of *dalmaticus* Dalmatian, fr. *Dalmatia*] (bef. 12c) **1** : a wide-sleeved overgarment with slit sides worn by a deacon or prelate **2** : a robe worn by a British sovereign at his or her coronation

dal se·gno \däl-'sā-(,)nyō\ *adv* [It, from the sign] (ca. 1854) — used as a direction in music to return to the sign that marks the beginning of a repeat

dal·ton \'dȯl-t°n\ *n* [John *Dalton* †1844 Eng. chemist] (ca. 1928) : ATOMIC MASS UNIT — used chiefly in biochemistry

¹**dam** \'dam\ *n* [ME *dam, dame* lady, dam — more at DAME] (13c) : a female parent — used esp. of a domestic animal

²**dam** *n* [ME, prob. fr. MD; akin to OE for*demman* to stop up] (14c) **1 a** : a barrier preventing the flow of water or of loose solid materials (as soil or snow); *esp* : a barrier built across a watercourse for impounding water **b** : a barrier to check the flow of liquid, gas, or air

³**dam** *vt* **dammed; dam·ming** (15c) **1** : to provide or restrain with a dam **2** : to stop up : BLOCK

¹**dam·age** \'da-mij\ *n* [ME, fr. MF, fr. L *damnum*] (14c) **1** : loss or harm resulting from injury to person, property, or reputation **2** *pl* : compensation in money imposed by law for loss or injury **3** : EXPENSE, COST ⟨"What's the ~?" he asked the waiter⟩

²**damage** *vt* **dam·aged; dam·ag·ing** (14c) : to cause damage to **syn** see INJURE — **dam·age·abil·i·ty** \,da-mi-jə-'bi-lə-tē\ *n* — **dam·ag·er** *n*

dam·ag·ing *adj* (ca. 1828) : causing or able to cause damage : INJURIOUS ⟨has a ~ effect on wildlife⟩ — **dam·ag·ing·ly** \'da-mi-jiŋ-lē\ *adv*

dam·ar *or* **dam·mar** \'da-mər\ *n* [Malay] (1698) : any of various resins used in varnishes and inks and obtained chiefly in Malaya and Indonesia from several timber trees (families Dipterocarpaceae and Burseraceae)

¹**dam·a·scene** \'da-mə-,sēn, ,da-mə-'\ *n* (14c) **1** *cap* : a native or inhabitant of Damascus **2** : the characteristic markings of Damascus steel

²**damascene** *adj* (14c) **1** *cap* : of, relating to, or characteristic of Damascus or the Damascenes **2** : of or relating to damask or the art of damascening

³**damascene** *vt* **-scened; -scen·ing** [MF *damasquiner*, fr. *damasquin* of Damascus] (1585) : to ornament (as iron or steel) with wavy patterns like those of watered silk or with inlaid work of precious metals

Da·mas·cus steel \də-'mas-kəs-\ *n* (ca. 1727) : hard elastic steel ornamented with wavy patterns and used esp. for sword blades

¹**dam·ask** \'da-məsk\ *n* [ME *damaske*, fr. ML *damascus*, fr. *Damascus*] (14c) **1** : a firm lustrous fabric (as of linen, cotton, silk, or rayon) made with flat patterns in a satin weave on a plain-woven ground on jacquard looms **2** : DAMASCUS STEEL; *also* : the characteristic markings of this steel **3** : a grayish red

²**damask** *adj* (15c) **1** : made of or resembling damask **2** : of the color damask

damask rose *n* [obs. *Damask* of Damascus, fr. obs. *Damask* Damascus] (1540) : a large hardy fragrant pink rose (*Rosa damascena*) widely introduced from Asia Minor and the major source of attar of roses

dame \'dām\ *n* [ME, fr. OF, fr. L *domina*, fem. of *dominus* master; akin to L *domus* house — more at DOME] (13c) **1** : a woman of rank, station, or authority: as **a** *archaic* : the mistress of a household **b** : the wife or daughter of a lord **c** : a female member of an order of knighthood — used as a title prefixed to the given name **2 a** : an elderly woman **b** : WOMAN

dame school *n* (1817) : a school in which the rudiments of reading and writing were taught by a woman in her own home

dame's rocket *n* (ca. 1900) : a Eurasian perennial plant (*Hesperis matronalis*) of the mustard family cultivated for its spikes of showy fragrant white or purple flowers — called also *dame's violet, rocket*

¹**damn** \'dam\ *vb* **damned; damn·ing** [ME *dampnen*, fr. OF *dampner*, fr. L *damnare*, fr. *damnum* damage, loss, fine] *vt* (13c) **1** : to condemn to a punishment or fate; *esp* : to condemn to hell **2 a** : to condemn vigorously and often irascibly for some real or fancied fault or defect ⟨~ the storm for their delay⟩ **b** : to condemn as a failure by public criticism **3** : to bring ruin on **4** : to swear at : CURSE — often used to express annoyance, disgust, or surprise ~ *vi* : CURSE, SWEAR **syn** see EXECRATE

²**damn** *n* (1619) **1** : the utterance of the word *damn* as a curse **2 a** : minimum amount or degree (as of care or consideration) : the least bit ⟨don't give a ~⟩

³**damn** *adj or adv* (1775) : DAMNED ⟨a ~ nuisance⟩ ⟨ran ~ fast⟩

damn well : beyond doubt or question : CERTAINLY ⟨knew damn well what would happen⟩

dam·na·ble \'dam-nə-bəl\ *adj* (14c) **1** : liable to or deserving condemnation **2** : very bad : DETESTABLE ⟨~ weather⟩ — **dam·na·ble·ness** *n* — **dam·na·bly** \-blē\ *adv*

\ə\ abut \ʼ\ kitten, F table \ər\ further \a\ ash \ā\ ace \ä\ mop, mar
\aú\ out \ch\ chin \e\ bet \ē\ easy \g\ go \i\ hit \ī\ ice \j\ job
\ŋ\ sing \ō\ go \ȯ\ law \ȯi\ boy \th\ thin \t̲h̲\ the \ü\ loot \ú\ foot
\y\ yet \zh\ vision \ä, ḵ, ⁿ, œ, œ̄, ᵫ, ᵫ̄, ᵞ\ see Guide to Pronunciation

dam·na·tion \dam-'nā-shən\ n (14c) : the act of damning : the state of being damned

dam·na·to·ry \'dam-nə-ˌtōr-ē, -ˌtȯr-\ adj (1682) : expressing, imposing, or causing condemnation : CONDEMNATORY

¹damned \'dam(d)\ adj **damned·er** \'dam-dər\; **damned·est** or **damnd·est** \-dəst\ (1563) 1 : DAMNABLE ⟨this ~ smog⟩ 2 : COMPLETE, UTTER — often used as an intensive 3 : EXTRAORDINARY — used in the superlative ⟨the ~est contraption you ever saw⟩

²damned \'dam(d)\ adv (1757) : EXTREMELY, VERY ⟨a ~ good job⟩

damned·est or **damnd·est** \'dam-dəst\ n (1830) : UTMOST, BEST — used chiefly in the phrase do one's damnedest ⟨doing my ~ to win⟩

dam·ni·fy \'dam-nə-ˌfī\ vt **-fied; -fy·ing** [MF damnifier, fr. OF, fr. LL damnificare, fr. L damnificus injurious, fr. damnum damage] (1512) : to cause loss or damage to

damn·ing \'da-miŋ\ adj (1599) 1 : bringing damnation ⟨a ~ sin⟩ 2 : causing or leading to condemnation or ruin ⟨presented some ~ testimony⟩ — **damn·ing·ly** \-miŋ-lē\ adv

Dam·o·cles \'da-mə-ˌklēz\ n [L, fr. Gk Damoklēs] : a courtier of ancient Syracuse held to have been seated at a banquet beneath a sword hung by a single hair — **Dam·o·cle·an** \ˌda-mə-'klē-ən\ adj

Da·mon \'dā-mən\ n [L, fr. Gk Damōn] : a legendary Sicilian who pledges his life for his condemned friend Pythias

¹damp \'damp\ n [MD or MLG, vapor; akin to OHG damph vapor] (14c) 1 : a noxious gas — compare BLACK DAMP, FIREDAMP 2 : MOISTURE: **a** : HUMIDITY, DAMPNESS **b** archaic : FOG, MIST 3 : **a** : DISCOURAGEMENT, CHECK **b** archaic : DEPRESSION, DEJECTION

²damp vt (14c) 1 **a** : to affect with or as if with a noxious gas : CHOKE **b** : to diminish the activity or intensity of ⟨~ing down the causes of inflation⟩ ⟨liquid ~s out compass oscillations⟩ **c** : to check the vibration or oscillation of (as a string or voltage) : DAMPEN ~ vi : to diminish progressively in vibration or oscillation

³damp adj (1590) 1 **a** archaic : being confused, bewildered, or shocked : STUPEFIED **b** : DEPRESSED, DULL 2 : slightly or moderately wet : MOIST; also : HUMID syn see WET — **damp·ish** \'dam-pish\ adj — **damp·ly** adv — **damp·ness** n

damp·en \'dam-pən\ vb **damp·ened; damp·en·ing** \'damp-niŋ, 'dam-pə-\ vt (1547) 1 : to check or diminish the activity or vigor of : DEADEN ⟨the heat ~ed our spirits⟩ 2 : to make damp ⟨the shower barely ~ed the ground⟩ 3 : DAMP 1c ~ vi : to become damp 2 : to become deadened or depressed — **damp·en·er** \-nər\ n

damp·er \'dam-pər\ n (1748) 1 : a dulling or deadening influence ⟨put a ~ on the celebration⟩ 2 : a device that damps: as **a** : a valve or plate (as in the flue of a furnace) for regulating the draft **b** : a small felted block to stop the vibration of a piano string **c** chiefly Brit : SHOCK ABSORBER

damp·ing–off \ˌdam-piŋ-'ȯf\ n (1890) : a diseased condition of seedlings or cuttings caused by fungi and marked by wilting or rotting

dam·sel \'dam-zəl\ also **dam·o·sel** or **dam·o·zel** \'da-mə-ˌzel\ n [ME damesel, fr. OF dameisele, fr. (assumed) VL domnicella young noblewoman, dim. of L domina lady] (13c) **a** : a young woman: **a** archaic : a young unmarried woman of noble birth **b** : GIRL

dam·sel·fish \'dam-zəl-ˌfish\ n (1904) : any of numerous often brilliantly colored marine fishes (family Pomacentridae) living esp. along coral reefs — called also demoiselle

dam·sel·fly \-ˌflī\ n (1815) : any of numerous odonate insects (suborder Zygoptera) distinguished from dragonflies by laterally projecting eyes and petiolate wings folded above the body when at rest

dam·son \'dam-zən\ n [ME, fr. L (prunum) damascenum, lit., plum of Damascus] (14c) : the small tart fruit of a widely cultivated Asian plum tree (Prunus insititia); also : this tree

¹Dan \'dan\ n [Heb Dān] : a son of Jacob and the traditional eponymous ancestor of one of the tribes of Israel

²Dan \'dan\ n [ME, title of members of religious orders, fr. MF, fr. L dominus master] (13c) archaic : MASTER, SIR

Dan·aë \'da-nə-ˌē\ n [L, fr. Gk Danaē] : a princess of Argos visited by Zeus in the form of a shower of gold and by him the mother of Perseus

¹dance \'dan(t)s, 'dȧn(t)s\ vb **danced; danc·ing** [ME dauncen, fr. OF dancier] vi (14c) 1 : to engage in or perform a dance 2 : to move or seem to move up and down or about in a quick or lively manner ~ vt 1 : to perform or take part in as a dancer 2 : to cause to dance 3 : to bring into a specified condition by dancing — **dance·able** \'dan(t)-sə-bəl\ adj — **danc·er** n

²dance n, often attrib (14c) 1 : an act or instance of dancing 2 : a series of rhythmic and patterned bodily movements usu. performed to music 3 : a social gathering for dancing 4 : a piece of music by which dancing may be guided 5 : the art of dancing

dan·de·li·on \'dan-də-ˌlī-ən, -dē-\ n [MF dent de lion, lit., lion's tooth] (14c) : any of a genus (Taraxacum) of yellow-flowered composite plants; esp : an herb (T. officinale) sometimes grown as a potherb and nearly cosmopolitan as a weed

dan·der \'dan-dər\ n [alter. of dandruff] (1786) 1 : DANDRUFF; specif : minute scales from hair, feathers, or skin that may be allergenic 2 : ANGER, TEMPER ⟨now don't get your ~ up⟩

dan·di·a·cal \dan-'dī-ə-kəl\ adj ['dandy + -acal (as in demoniacal)] (1831) : of, relating to, or suggestive of a dandy

Dan·die Din·mont terrier \'dan-dē-'din-ˌmänt-\ n [Dandie Dinmont, character owning six such dogs in the novel Guy Mannering by Sir Walter Scott] (1875) : any of a breed of terriers characterized by short legs, a long body, pendulous ears, a rough coat, and a full silky topknot

dan·di·fy \'dan-di-ˌfī\ vt **-fied; -fy·ing** (1823) : to cause to resemble a dandy — **dan·di·fi·ca·tion** \ˌdan-di-fə-'kā-shən\ n

dan·dle \'dan-dᵊl\ vt **dan·dled; dan·dling** \-d(ᵊ)liŋ, -dᵊl-iŋ\ [origin unknown] (1530) 1 : to move (as a baby) up and down in one's arms or on one's knee in affectionate play 2 : PAMPER, PET

dan·druff \'dan-drəf\ n [prob. fr. dand- (origin unknown) + -ruff, fr. ME rove scabby condition, fr. ON hrúfa scab; akin to OHG hruf scurf, Lith kraupus rough] (1545) : a scurf that forms on skin esp. of the scalp and comes off in small white or grayish scales — **dan·druffy** \-drə-fē\ adj

¹dan·dy \'dan-dē\ n, pl **dandies** [prob. short for jack-a-dandy, fr. ¹jack + a (of) + dandy (origin unknown)] (ca. 1780) 1 : a man who gives exaggerated attention to personal appearance 2 : something excellent in its class — **dan·dy·ish** \-dē-ish\ adj — **dan·dy·ish·ly** adv

²dandy adj **dan·di·er; -est** (1792) 1 : of, relating to, or suggestive of a dandy : FOPPISH 2 : very good : FIRST-RATE ⟨a ~ place to stay⟩

dan·dy·ism \'dan-dē-ˌi-zəm\ n (1819) 1 : the style or conduct of a dandy 2 : a literary and artistic style of the latter part of the 19th century marked by artificiality and excessive refinement

Dane \'dān\ n [ME Dan, fr. ON Danr] (14c) 1 : a native or inhabitant of Denmark 2 : a person of Danish descent 3 : GREAT DANE

dane·geld \'dān-ˌgeld\ n, often cap (bef. 12c) : an annual tax believed to have been imposed orig. to buy off Danish invaders in England or to maintain forces to oppose them but continued as a land tax

Dane·law \'dān-ˌlȯ\ n (bef. 12c) 1 : the law in force in the part of England held by the Danes before the Norman Conquest 2 : the part of England under the Danelaw

¹dang \'daŋ\ vt [euphemism] (1797) : DAMN 4

²dang adj or adv (1914) : DAMNED

¹dan·ger \'dān-jər\ n [ME daunger, fr. OF dangier, alter. of dongier, fr. (assumed) VL dominiarium, fr. L dominium ownership] (13c) 1 **a** archaic : JURISDICTION **b** obs : REACH, RANGE 2 obs : HARM, DAMAGE 3 : exposure or liability to injury, pain, harm, or loss ⟨a place where children could play without ~⟩ 4 : a case or cause of danger ⟨the ~s of mining⟩

²danger vt (14c) archaic : ENDANGER

dan·ger·ous \'dān-jə-rəs; 'dān-jərs, -zhrəs\ adj (15c) 1 : exposing to or involving danger 2 : able or likely to inflict injury or harm — **dan·ger·ous·ly** adv — **dan·ger·ous·ness** n
syn DANGEROUS, HAZARDOUS, PRECARIOUS, PERILOUS, RISKY mean bringing or involving the chance of loss or injury. DANGEROUS applies to something that may cause harm or loss unless dealt with carefully ⟨soldiers on a dangerous mission⟩. HAZARDOUS implies great and continuous risk of harm or failure ⟨claims that smoking is hazardous to your health⟩. PRECARIOUS suggests both insecurity and uncertainty ⟨earned a precarious living by gambling⟩. PERILOUS strongly implies the immediacy of danger ⟨perilous mountain roads⟩. RISKY often applies to a known and accepted danger ⟨shied away from risky investments⟩.

¹dan·gle \'daŋ-gəl\ vb **dan·gled; dan·gling** \-g(ə-)liŋ\ [prob. of Scand origin; akin to Dan dangle to dangle] vi (ca. 1590) 1 : to hang loosely and usu. so as to be able to swing freely 2 : to be a hanger-on or a dependent 3 : to occur in a sentence without having a normally expected syntactic relation to the rest of the sentence ⟨the word climbing in "Climbing the mountain the cabin came into view" is dangling⟩ ~ vt 1 : to cause to dangle : SWING 2 **a** : to keep hanging uncertainly **b** : to hold out as an inducement — **dan·gler** \-g(ə-)lər\ n

²dangle n (1756) 1 : the action of dangling 2 : something that dangles

Dan·iel \'da-nyəl also 'da-nᵊl\ n [Heb Dānī'ēl] 1 : the Jewish hero of the Book of Daniel who as an exile in Babylon interprets dreams, gives accounts of apocalyptic visions, and is divinely delivered from a den of lions 2 : a book of narratives, visions, and prophecies in canonical Jewish and Christian Scripture — see BIBLE table

da·nio \'dā-nē-ˌō\ n, pl **da·ni·os** [NL, genus name] (ca. 1889) : any of several small brightly colored Asian cyprinid fishes

¹Dan·ish \'dā-nish\ adj (14c) : of, relating to, or characteristic of Denmark, the Danes, or the Danish language

²Danish n (15c) 1 : the Germanic language of the Danes 2 pl **Danish** : a piece of Danish pastry

Danish pastry n (ca. 1928) : a pastry made of a rich raised dough

dank \'daŋk\ adj [ME danke] (1573) : unpleasantly moist or wet syn see WET — **dank·ly** adv — **dank·ness** n

dan·seur \dän-'sər, dän-\ n [F, fr. danser to dance] (1828) : a male ballet dancer

dan·seuse \dän-'sœz; dän-'sə(r)z, dän-'süz\ n [F, fem. of danseur] (1828) : a female ballet dancer

Dan·te·an \'dan-tē-ən, dän-\ n (ca. 1850) : a student or admirer of Dante

Dao·ism, Dao·ist, Dao·is·tic var of TAOISM, TAOIST, TAOISTIC

daph·ne \'daf-nē\ n [NL, genus name, fr. L, laurel, fr. Gk daphnē] (1862) : any of a genus (Daphne) of Eurasian shrubs of the mezereon family with apetalous flowers whose colored calyx resembles a corolla

Daph·ne \'daf-nē\ n [L, fr. Gk Daphnē] : a nymph who is transformed into a laurel tree to escape the pursuing Apollo

daph·nia \'daf-nē-ə\ n [NL, genus name] (1847) : any of a genus (Daphnia) of minute freshwater branchiopod crustaceans with biramous antennae used as locomotor organs — compare WATER FLEA

Daph·nis \'daf-nəs\ n [L, fr. Gk] : a Sicilian shepherd renowned in Greek mythology as the inventor of pastoral poetry

dap·per \'da-pər\ adj [ME dapyr, fr. MD dapper quick, strong; akin to OHG tapfar heavy, OCS debelŭ thick] (15c) 1 **a** : neat and trim in appearance **b** : excessively spruce and stylish 2 : alert and lively in movement and manners — **dap·per·ly** adv — **dap·per·ness** n

¹dap·ple \'da-pəl\ n [ME dappel-gray, adj., gray marked with spots of another color] (1580) 1 : any of numerous usu. cloudy and rounded spots or patches of a color or shade different from their background 2 : the quality or state of being dappled 3 : a dappled animal

²dapple vb **dap·pled; dap·pling** \-p(ə-)liŋ\ vt (1599) : to mark with dapples ~ vi : to produce a dappled pattern ⟨sun dappling through trees⟩

dap·pled also **dap·ple** adj (15c) : marked with small spots or patches contrasting with the background ⟨a ~ fawn⟩

dap·sone \'dap-ˌsōn\ n [diamine + phenyl + sulfone] (1952) : an antimicrobial agent $C_{12}H_{12}N_2O_2S$ used esp. against leprosy

Dar·by and Joan \ˌdär-bē-ən-'jōn\ n [prob. fr. Darby & Joan, couple in an 18th cent. song] (1857) : a happily married usu. elderly couple

Dard \'därd\ n (ca. 1885) : DARDIC

Dar·dan \'där-dᵊn\ adj or n [L Dardanus, fr. Gk Dardanos] (1606) archaic : TROJAN

Dar·da·ni·an \där-'dā-nē-ən\ adj (1596) : TROJAN

Dar·dic \'där-dik\ n (1910) : a complex of Indic languages spoken in the upper valley of the Indus

¹dare \'dar, 'der\ vb **dared; dar·ing; dares** or (auxiliary) **dare** [ME dar (1st & 3d sing. pres. indic.), fr. OE dear; akin to OHG gitar (1st & 3d sing. pres. indic.) dare, Gk tharsos courage] (bef. 12c) verbal auxiliary : to be sufficiently courageous to ⟨no one dared say a word⟩ ⟨she ~ not let herself love —G. B. Shaw⟩ ~ vi : to have sufficient courage ⟨try it if you ~⟩ ~ vt 1 **a** : to challenge to perform an action esp. as a proof of courage ⟨*dared* him to jump⟩ **b** : to confront boldly : DEFY ⟨*dared* the anger of his family⟩ **2** : to have the courage to contend against, venture, or try ⟨the actress *dared* a new interpretation of this classic role⟩ — **dar·er** \'dar-ər, 'der-\ *n*

²**dare** *n* (1594) **1** : an act or instance of daring : CHALLENGE ⟨foolishly took a ~⟩ **2** : imaginative or vivacious boldness : DARING

¹**dare·dev·il** \'dar-₁de-vᵊl, 'der-\ *n* (1794) : a recklessly bold person — **dare·dev·il·ry** \-vᵊl-rē\ *n* — **dare·dev·il·try** \-vᵊl-trē\ *n*

²**daredevil** *adj* (1832) : recklessly and often ostentatiously daring **syn** see ADVENTUROUS

dareful *adj* (1605) *obs* : DARING

daren't \'dar-ənt, 'der-\ : dare not : dared not

dare·say \₁dar-'sā, ₁der-\ *vt* (13c) : venture to say : think probable — used in pres. 1st sing. ~ *vi* : AGREE, SUPPOSE — used in pres. 1st sing.

¹**dar·ing** *adj* (1582) : venturesomely bold in action or thought **syn** see ADVENTUROUS — **dar·ing·ly** \-iŋ-lē\ *adv* — **dar·ing·ness** *n*

²**daring** *n* (1651) : venturesome boldness

Dar·jee·ling \där-'jē-liŋ\ *n* [*Darjeeling*, India] (1907) : a tea of high quality grown esp. in the mountainous districts of northern India

¹**dark** \'därk\ *adj* [ME *derk*, fr. OE *deorc*; akin to OHG *tarchannen* to hide] (bef. 12c) **1 a** : devoid or partially devoid of light : not receiving, reflecting, transmitting, or radiating light **b** : transmitting only a portion of light **2 a** : wholly or partially black **b** *of a color* : of low or very low lightness **3 a** : arising from or showing evil traits or desires : EVIL ⟨the ~ powers that lead to war⟩ **b** : DISMAL, GLOOMY ⟨had a ~ view of the future⟩ **c** : lacking knowledge or culture **4** : not clear to the understanding **5** : not fair in complexion : SWARTHY **6** : SECRET ⟨kept his plans ~⟩ **7** : possessing depth and richness ⟨a ~ voice⟩ **8** : closed to the public ⟨the theater is ~ in the summer⟩ **syn** see OBSCURE — **dark·ish** \'där-kish\ *adj* — **dark·ly** *adv* — **dark·ness** *n*

²**dark** *n* (13c) **1 a** : a place or time of little or no light : NIGHT, NIGHTFALL **b** : absence of light : DARKNESS **2** : a dark or deep color — **in the dark** **1** : in secrecy ⟨most of his dealings were done *in the dark*⟩ **2** : in ignorance ⟨kept the public *in the dark* about the agreement⟩

³**dark** *vi* (14c) *obs* : to grow dark ~ *vt* : to make dark

dark adaptation *n* (1909) : the phenomena including dilation of the pupil, increase in retinal sensitivity, shift of the region of maximum luminosity toward the blue, and regeneration of visual purple by which the eye adapts to conditions of reduced illumination — **dark–adapt·ed** \₁därk-ə-'dap-təd\ *adj*

dark age *n* (1730) **1** : a time during which a civilization undergoes a decline: as **a** *pl, cap D&A* : the European historical period from about A.D. 476 to about 1000; *broadly* : MIDDLE AGES **b** *often pl, often cap D&A* : the Greek historical period of three to four centuries from about 1100 B.C. **2 a** *often pl, often cap D&A* : the primitive period in the development of something ⟨in the 1890s, way back in baseball's *Dark Ages* —R. W. Creamer⟩ **b** *often pl, often cap D&A* : a state of stagnation or decline

dark·en \'där-kən\ *vb* **dark·ened; dark·en·ing** \'där-kə-niŋ\ *vi* (13c) **1** : to grow dark : become obscured **2** : to become gloomy ~ *vt* **1** : to make dark **2** : to make less clear : OBSCURE ⟨the financial crisis ~ed the future of the company⟩ **3** : TAINT, TARNISH **4** : to cast a gloom over **5** : to make of darker color — **dark·en·er** \'där-kə-nər\ *n*

dark field *n* (1865) : the dark area that serves as the background for objects viewed in an ultramicroscope

dark–field microscope *n* (1926) : ULTRAMICROSCOPE

dark horse *n* (1831) **1 a** : a usu. little known contender (as a racehorse) that makes an unexpectedly good showing **b** : an entrant in a contest that is judged unlikely to succeed **2** : a political candidate unexpectedly nominated usu. as a compromise between factions

dark lantern *n* (1650) : a lantern that can be closed to conceal the light

dar·kle \'där-kəl\ *vi* **dar·kled; dar·kling** \-k(ə-)liŋ\ [back-formation fr. *darkling*] (1800) **1 a** : to become clouded or gloomy **b** : to grow dark **2** : to become concealed in the dark

¹**dark·ling** \'där-kliŋ\ *adv* [ME *derkelyng*, fr. *derk* dark + *-lyng* -ling] (15c) : in the dark

²**dark·ling** *adj* (1739) **1** : DARK **2** : done or taking place in the dark

darkling beetle *n* (1816) : TENEBRIONID

dark matter *n* (1982) : nonluminous matter not yet directly detected by astronomers that is hypothesized to exist because the visible matter in the universe is insufficient to account for various observed gravitational effects

dark reaction *n* (1927) : any of a series of chemical reactions in photosynthesis not requiring the presence of light and involving the reduction of carbon dioxide to form carbohydrate; *also* : CALVIN CYCLE

dark·room \'därk-₁rüm, -₁rüm\ *n* (1841) : a room with no light or with a safelight for handling and processing light-sensitive photographic materials

dark·some \'därk-səm\ *adj* (ca. 1530) : gloomily somber : DARK

darky *or* **dark·ie** \'där-kē\ *n, pl* **darkies** (1775) : a black person — usu. taken to be offensive

¹**dar·ling** \'där-liŋ\ *n* [ME *derling*, fr. OE *dēorling*, fr. *dēore* dear] (bef. 12c) **1** : a dearly loved person **2** : FAVORITE

²**darling** *adj* (1509) **1** : dearly loved : FAVORITE **2** : very pleasing : CHARMING — **dar·ling·ly** \-liŋ-lē\ *adv* — **dar·ling·ness** *n*

¹**darn** \'därn\ *vb* [perh. fr. F dial. *darner*] *vt* (ca. 1600) **1** : to mend with interlacing stitches **2** : to embroider by filling in with long running or interlacing stitches ~ *vi* : to do darning — **darn·er** *n*

²**darn** *n* (1720) : a place that has been darned ⟨a sweater full of ~s⟩

³**darn** *adj or adv* [euphemism] (1781) : DAMNED

⁴**darn** *vb* (1781) : DAMN — **darned** \'därn(d)\ *adj or adv*

⁵**darn** *n* (1840) : DAMN

dar·nel \'där-nᵊl\ *n* [ME] (14c) : any of several usu. weedy grasses (genus *Lolium*)

darning needle *n* (1761) **1** : a long needle with a large eye for use in darning **2** : DRAGONFLY, DAMSELFLY

¹**dart** \'därt\ *n* [ME, fr. MF, fr. of Gmc origin; akin to OHG *tart* dart, OE *daroth*] (14c) **1 a** *archaic* : a light spear **b** (1) : a small missile usu. with a pointed shaft at one end and feathers at the other (2) *pl but sing in constr* : a game in which darts are thrown at a target **2 a** : something projected with sudden speed; *esp* : a sharp glance **b** : something causing sudden pain or distress ⟨~s of sarcasm⟩ **3** : something with a

slender pointed shaft or outline; *specif* : a stitched tapering fold in a garment **4** : a quick movement ⟨made a ~ for the door⟩

²**dart** *vt* (1580) **1** : to throw with a sudden movement **2** : to thrust or move with sudden speed **3** : to shoot with a dart containing a usu. tranquilizing drug ~ *vi* : to move suddenly or rapidly ⟨~ed across the street⟩

dart·board \'därt-₁bōrd, -₁bȯrd\ *n* (1901) : a usu. circular board (as of compressed bristles) used as a target in the game of darts

dart·er \'där-tər\ *n* (1813) **1** : ANHINGA **2** : any of numerous small American freshwater bony fishes (esp. genera *Ammocrypta, Etheostoma*, and *Percina* of the family Percidae)

Dar·win·i·an \där-'wi-nē-ən\ *adj* (1860) : of or relating to Charles Darwin, his theories esp. of evolution, or his followers — **Darwinian** *n*

Dar·win·ism \'där-wə-₁ni-zəm\ *n* (1864) : a theory of the origin and perpetuation of new species of animals and plants that offspring of a given organism vary, that natural selection favors the survival of some of these variations over others, that new species have arisen and may continue to arise by these processes, and that widely divergent groups of plants and animals have arisen from the same ancestors; *broadly* : biological evolutionism — **Dar·win·ist** \-wə-nist\ *n or adj*

Dar·win's finches \₁där-wənz-\ *n pl* [Charles *Darwin*] (1947) : finches of a subfamily (Geospizinae) having great variation in bill shape and confined mostly to the Galapagos islands

Dar·win tulip \₁där-wən-\ *n* (1889) : a tall late-flowering tulip with the flowers single and of one color

¹**dash** \'dash\ *vb* [ME *dasshen*] *vt* (13c) **1** : to break by striking or knocking **2** : to knock, hurl, or thrust violently **3** : SPLASH, SPATTER **4 a** : RUIN, DESTROY ⟨the news ~ed his hopes⟩ **b** : DEPRESS, SADDEN **c** : to make ashamed **5** : to affect by mixing in something different ⟨his delight was ~ed with bitterness over the delay⟩ **6** : to complete, execute, or finish off hastily — used with *down* or *off* ⟨~ed down a drink⟩ ⟨~ off a letter⟩ **7** [euphemism]: ¹DAMN 4 ~ *vi* **1** : to move with sudden speed ⟨~ed through the rain⟩ **2** : SMASH

²**dash** *n* (14c) **1 a** *archaic* : BLOW **b** (1) : a sudden burst or splash (2) : the sound produced by such a burst **2 a** : a stroke of a pen **b** : a punctuation mark — that is used esp. to indicate a break in the thought or structure of a sentence **3** : a small usu. distinctive addition ⟨a ~ of salt⟩ ⟨a ~ of humor⟩ **4** : flashy display **5** : animation in style and action **6 a** : a sudden onset, rush, or attempt **b** : a short fast race **7** : a long click or buzz forming a letter or part of a letter (as in Morse code) **8** : DASHBOARD 2

dash·board \'dash-₁bōrd, -₁bȯrd\ *n* (1846) **1** : a screen on the front of a usu. horse-drawn vehicle to intercept water, mud, or snow **2** : a panel extending across the interior of a vehicle (as an automobile) below the windshield and usu. containing dials and controls

dashed \'dasht\ *adj* (ca. 1889) : made up of a series of dashes

da·sheen \da-'shēn, də-\ *n* [origin unknown] (ca. 1899) : TARO

dash·er \'da-shər\ *n* (1790) **1** : a dashing person **2** : one that dashes; *specif* : a device having blades for agitating a liquid or semisolid

dashi \'dä-(₁)shē\ *n* [Jp, broth] (ca. 1961) : a fish broth made from dried bonito

da·shi·ki \də-'shē-kē, dä-, da-\ *n* [modif. of Yoruba *dàṇ̇síkí*] (ca. 1968) : a usu. brightly colored loose-fitting pullover garment

dash·ing *adj* (1796) **1** : marked by vigorous action : SPIRITED ⟨a ~ young horse⟩ **2** : marked by smartness esp. in dress and manners — **dash·ing·ly** \-iŋ-lē\ *adv*

dash·pot \'dash-₁pät\ *n* (1861) : a device for cushioning or damping a movement (as of a mechanical part) to avoid shock

das·sie \'da-sē\ *n* [Afrik] (1786) : HYRAX

das·tard \'das-tərd\ *n* [ME] (15c) **1** : COWARD **2** : a person who acts treacherously or underhandedly

das·tard·ly \-lē\ *adj* (1576) **1** : COWARDLY **2** : characterized by underhandedness or treachery ⟨a ~ attack⟩ ⟨a ~ villain⟩ **syn** see COWARDLY — **das·tard·li·ness** *n*

da·ta \'dā-tə, 'da- *also* 'dä-\ *n pl but sing or pl in constr, often attrib* [L, pl. of *datum*] (1646) **1** : factual information (as measurements or statistics) used as a basis for reasoning, discussion, or calculation ⟨the ~ is plentiful and easily available —H. A. Gleason, Jr.⟩ ⟨comprehensive ~ on economic growth have been published —N. H. Jacoby⟩ **2** : information output by a sensing device or organ that includes both useful and irrelevant or redundant information and must be processed to be meaningful **3** : information in numerical form that can be digitally transmitted or processed

usage Data leads a life of its own quite independent of *datum*, of which it was originally the plural. It occurs in two constructions: as a plural noun (like *earnings*), taking a plural verb and plural modifiers (as *these, many, a few*) but not cardinal numbers, and serving as a referent for plural pronouns (as *they, them*); and as an abstract mass noun (like *information*), taking a singular verb and singular modifiers (as *this, much, little*), and being referred to by a singular pronoun (*it*). Both constructions are standard. The plural construction is more common in print, evidently because the house style of several publishers mandates it.

data bank *n* (1966) : DATABASE

da·ta·base \'dā-tə-₁bās, 'da- *also* 'dä-\ *n* (ca. 1962) : a usu. large collection of data organized esp. for rapid search and retrieval (as by a computer)

data processing *n* (1954) : the converting of raw data to machine-readable form and its subsequent processing (as storing, updating, combining, rearranging, or printing out) by a computer — **data processor** *n*

data structure *n* (1963) : any of various methods of organizing data items (as records) in a computer

¹**date** \'dāt\ *n* [ME, fr. OF, ultim. fr. L *dactylus* — more at DACTYL] (14c) **1** : the oblong edible fruit of a palm (*Phoenix dactylifera*) **2** : the tall palm with pinnate leaves that yields the date

---

\ə\ abut \ᵊ\ kitten, F table \ər\ further \a\ ash \ā\ ace \ä\ mop, mar \aů\ out \ch\ chin \e\ bet \ē\ easy \g\ go \i\ hit \ī\ ice \j\ job \ŋ\ sing \ō\ go \ȯ\ law \ȯi\ boy \th\ thin \t̷h\ the \ü\ loot \ů\ foot \y\ yet \zh\ vision \à, k̲, ⁿ, œ, œ̄, ue, ūe, ᵊ\ *see* Guide to Pronunciation

²**date** n [ME, fr. MF, fr. LL *data*, fr. *data* (as in *data Romae* given at Rome), fem. of L *datus*, pp. of *dare* to give; akin to L *dos* gift, dowry, Gk *didonai* to give] (14c) **1 a** : the time at which an event occurs ⟨the ~ of his birth⟩ **b** : a statement of the time of execution or making ⟨the ~ on the letter⟩ **2** : DURATION **3** : the period of time to which something belongs **4 a** : an appointment to meet at a specified time; *esp* : a social engagement between two persons that often has a romantic character **b** : a person with whom one has a ~ ∙ romantic date **5** : an engagement for a professional performance (as of a dance band) — **to date** : up to the present moment

³**date** vb **dat·ed; dat·ing** vt (15c) **1** : to determine the date of ⟨~ an antique⟩ **2** : to record the date of : mark with the date **3 a** : to mark with characteristics typical of a particular period **b** : to show up plainly the age of **4** : to make or have a date with ~ vi **1** : to reckon chronologically **2** : ORIGINATE ⟨a friendship *dating* from college days⟩ **3** : to become dated — **dat·able** *also* **date·able** \'dā-tə-bəl\ adj — **dat·er** \'dā-tər\ n

dat·ed adj (1731) **1** : provided with a date ⟨a ~ document⟩ **2** : OUTMODED, OLD-FASHIONED ⟨~ formalities⟩ — **dat·ed·ly** adv — **dat·ed·ness** n

date·less \'dāt-ləs\ adj (1593) **1** : ENDLESS **2** : having no date **3** : too ancient to be dated **4** : TIMELESS ⟨the play's ~ theme⟩

date·line \'dāt-ˌlīn\ n (1888) **1** : a line in a written document or a printed publication giving the date and place of composition or issue **2** *usu* **date line** : INTERNATIONAL DATE LINE — **dateline** vt

date rape n (ca. 1983) : rape committed by someone known to the victim

¹**da·tive** \'dā-tiv\ adj [ME *datif*, fr. L *dativus*, fr. *datus*] (15c) : of, relating to, or being the grammatical case that marks typically the indirect object of a verb, the object of some prepositions, or a possessor

²**dative** n (15c) : a dative case or form

dative bond n [fr. the donation of electrons by one of the atoms] (ca. 1929) : COORDINATE BOND

da·tum \'dā-təm, 'da-, 'dä-\ n [L, fr. neut. of *datus*] (1646) **1** *pl* **da·ta** \-ə\ : something given or admitted esp. as a basis for reasoning or inference **2** *pl* **datums** : something used as a basis for calculating or measuring *usage* see DATA

da·tu·ra \də-'t(y)ùr-ə\ n [NL, genus name, fr. Hindi *dhatūrā* jimsonweed] (1598) : any of a genus (*Datura*) of widely distributed strong-scented herbs, shrubs, or trees of the nightshade family including some used as sources of medicinal alkaloids (as stramonium) or in folk rites or illicitly for their poisonous, narcotic, or hallucinogenic properties — compare JIMSONWEED

¹**daub** \'dòb, 'däb\ vb [ME, fr. MF *dauber*] vt (14c) **1** : to cover or coat with soft adhesive matter : PLASTER **2** : to coat with a dirty substance **3 a** : to apply coloring material crudely to **b** : to apply (as paint) crudely ~ vi **1** *archaic* : to put on a false exterior **2** : to apply colors crudely — **daub·er** n

²**daub** n (15c) **1** : material used to daub walls **2** : an act or instance of daubing **3** : something daubed on : SMEAR **4** : a crude picture

daube \'dōb\ n [F] (1723) : a stew of braised meat, vegetables, herbs, and spices

¹**daugh·ter** \'dò-tər, 'dä-\ n [ME, *doughter*, fr. OE *dohtor*; akin to OHG *tohter* daughter, Gk *thygatēr*] (bef. 12c) **1 a** (1) : a human female having the relation of child to parent (2) : a female offspring of a lower animal **b** : a human female having a specified ancestor or belonging to a group of common ancestry **2** : something considered as a daughter ⟨the United States is a ~ of Great Britain⟩ **3** : an atomic species that is the product of the radioactive decay of a given element — **daugh·ter·less** \-ləs\ adj

²**daughter** adj (1614) **1** : having the characteristics or relationship of a daughter **2** : belonging to the first generation of offspring, organelles, or molecules produced by reproduction, division, or replication ⟨~ cell⟩ ⟨~ DNA molecules⟩

daugh·ter–in–law \'dò-tər-in-ˌlò, 'dò-tərn-\ n, *pl* **daugh·ters–in–law** \-tər-zin-\ (14c) : the wife of one's son

dau·no·my·cin \ˌdò-nō-nə-'mī-sᵊn, ˌdaú-\ n [ISV *dauno-* (fr. L *Daunus* Apulian) + *-mycin*] (1964) : DAUNORUBICIN

dau·no·ru·bi·cin \-'rü-bə-sᵊn\ n [*dauno-* (as in *daunomycin*) + *rubido-mycin*, a substance found to be identical with daunomycin (fr. ISV *rubido-* — fr. L *rubidus* red — + *-mycin*)] (ca. 1968) : an antibiotic $C_{27}H_{29}NO_{10}$ that is a nitrogenous glycoside and is used esp. in the treatment of leukemia

daunt \'dònt, 'dänt\ vt [ME, fr. MF *danter*, alter. of *donter*, fr. L *domitare* to tame, freq. of *domare* — more at TAME] (14c) : to lessen the courage of : COW, SUBDUE *syn* see DISMAY — **daunt·ing·ly** \-iŋ-lē\ adv

daunt·less \-ləs\ adj (1593) : FEARLESS, UNDAUNTED ⟨a ~ hero⟩ — **daunt·less·ly** adv — **daunt·less·ness** n

dau·phin \'dò-fən, 'dō-; ˌdò-'faⁿ\ n, *often cap* [ME *dolphin*, fr. MF *dalfin*, fr. OF, title of lords of the Dauphiné, fr. *Dalfin*, a surname] (15c) : the eldest son of a king of France

dau·phine \dò-'fēn, dō-\ n, *often cap* [F] (ca. 1864) : the wife of the dauphin

da·ven \'dä-vən\ vi [Yiddish *davnen*] (ca. 1930) : to recite the prescribed prayers in a Jewish liturgy

dav·en·port \'da-vᵊn-ˌpōrt, 'da-vᵊm-, -ˌpòrt\ n [prob. fr. the name *Davenport*] (1853) **1** : a small compact writing desk **2** : a large upholstered sofa often convertible into a bed

Da·vid \'dā-vəd\ n [Heb *Dāwidh*] **1** : a Hebrew shepherd who became the second king of Israel in succession to Saul according to biblical accounts **2** : UNDERDOG 1 — **Da·vid·ic** \də-'vi-dik, dā-\ adj

da·vit \'dā-vət, 'da-\ n [prob. fr. the name *David*] (15c) : a crane that projects over the side of a ship or a hatchway and is used esp. for boats, anchors, or cargo

Da·vy Jones \ˌdā-vē-'jōnz\ n (1751) : the bottom of the sea personified

Da·vy Jones's locker \ˌdā-vē-ˌjōnz(-əz)-\ n (ca. 1777) : the bottom of the ocean

¹**daw** \'dò, 'dä\ n [ME *dawe*; akin to OHG *taha* jackdaw] (15c) : JACKDAW

²**daw** \'dò\ n [ME *dawe*; akin to OHG *tagēn* to dawn, OE *dæg* day] (13c) *chiefly Scot* : DAWN

daw·dle \'dò-dᵊl\ vb **daw·dled; daw·dling** \'dò-dliŋ, -dᵊl-iŋ\ [origin unknown] vi (ca. 1656) **1** : to spend time idly **2** : to move lackadaisi-

cally ⟨*dawdled* up the hill⟩ ~ vt : to spend fruitlessly or lackadaisically ⟨*dawdled* the day away⟩ *syn* see DELAY — **daw·dler** \'dò-dlər, -dᵊl-ər\ n

¹**dawn** \'dòn, 'dän\ vi [ME, prob. back-formation fr. *dawning* daybreak, alter. of *dawing*, fr. OE *dagung*, fr. *dagian*] (15c) **1** : to begin to grow light as the sun rises **2** : to begin to appear or develop **3** : to begin to be perceived or understood ⟨the truth finally ~ed on us⟩

²**dawn** n (1599) **1** : the first appearance of light in the morning followed by sunrise **2** : BEGINNING ⟨the ~ of the space age⟩

dawn horse n (1930) : EOHIPPUS

dawn redwood n (1948) : a metasequoia (*Metasequoia glyptostroboides*) of China resembling the coast redwood but having deciduous foliage

daw·son·ite \'dò-sə-ˌnīt\ n [Sir John W. *Dawson*] (1874) : a mineral consisting of a basic sodium aluminum carbonate

day \'dā\ n [ME, fr. OE *dæg*; akin to OHG *tag* day] (bef. 12c) **1 a** : the time of light between one night and the next **b** : DAYLIGHT 1, 2 **2** : the period of rotation of a planet (as earth) or a moon on its axis **3** : the mean solar day of 24 hours beginning at mean midnight **4 a** : a specified day or date **5** : a specified time or period : AGE ⟨in grandfather's ~⟩ **6** : the conflict or contention of the day ⟨played hard and won the ~⟩ **7** : the time established by usage or law for work, school, or business **8** : a period of existence or prominence of a person or thing — **day after day** : for an indefinite or seemingly endless number of days — **day in, day out** : for an indefinite number of successive days

Day·ak \'dī-ˌak\ n [Malay, lit., up-country] (1836) : a member of any of several Indonesian peoples of the interior of Borneo

day·bed \'dā-ˌbed\ n (1818) **1** : a chaise longue of a type made 1680–1780 **2** : a couch that can be converted into a bed

day·book \-ˌbùk\ n (1580) : DIARY, JOURNAL

day·break \-ˌbrāk\ n (1530) : DAWN

day care n (1947) **1** : supervision of and care for children or disabled adults that is provided during the day by a person or organization **2** : a program, facility, or organization offering day care

¹**day·dream** \'dā-ˌdrēm\ n (1685) : a pleasant visionary usu. wishful creation of the imagination — **day·dream·like** \-ˌlīk\ adj

²**daydream** vi (1820) : to have a daydream — **day·dream·er** n

day·flow·er \'dā-ˌflaù(-ə)r\ n (ca. 1688) : any of a genus (*Commelina*) of herbs of the spiderwort family having one petal smaller than the other two; *esp* : a blue-flowered weed (*C. communis*) with the smaller petal white

Day–Glo \'dā-ˌglō\ *trademark* — used for fluorescent materials or colors

day·glow \'dā-ˌglō\ n (ca. 1960) : airglow seen during the day

day laborer n (1548) : one who works for daily wages esp. as an unskilled laborer

day letter n (ca. 1913) : a telegram sent during the day that has a lower priority than a regular telegram

day·light \'dā-ˌlīt\ n (13c) **1** : the light of day **2** : DAYTIME **3** : DAWN **4 a** : knowledge or understanding of something that has been obscure ⟨began to see ~ on the problem⟩ **b** : the quality or state of being open : OPENNESS **5** *pl* **a** : CONSCIOUSNESS **b** : mental soundness or stability : WITS ⟨scared the ~s out of him⟩ **6** : an opening or opportunity esp. for action

day·light·ing \'dā-ˌlī-tiŋ\ n (1929) : illumination of indoor spaces by natural light

daylight saving time n (1919) : time usu. one hour ahead of standard time — called also **daylight saving, daylight time**

day·lily \'dā-ˌli-lē\ n (1597) : any of various Eurasian plants (genus *Hemerocallis*) of the lily family that have short-lived flowers resembling lilies and are widespread in cultivation and as escapes

day·long \'dā-ˌlòŋ\ adj (1855) : lasting all day ⟨a ~ tour⟩

day·mare \'dā-ˌmar, -ˌmer\ n [*day* + *-mare* (as in *nightmare*)] (1737) : a nightmarish fantasy experienced while awake

day–neutral adj (1941) : developing and maturing regardless of relative length of alternating exposures to light and dark periods — used esp. of a plant; compare LONG-DAY, SHORT-DAY

day nursery n (1844) : a public center for the care and training of young children; *specif* : NURSERY SCHOOL

Day of Atonement (1611) : YOM KIPPUR

day one n, *often cap D&O* (1971) : the first day or very beginning of something

day·room \'dā-ˌrüm, -ˌrùm\ n (1823) : a room (as in a hospital) equipped for reading, writing, and recreation

days \'dāz\ adv (bef. 12c) : in the daytime repeatedly : on any day

day school n (1838) : an elementary or secondary school held on weekdays; *specif* : a private school without boarding facilities

day·side \'dā-ˌsīd\ n (1963) : the side of a planet in sunlight

days of grace (1726) : the days allowed for payment of a note or an insurance premium after it becomes due

day·star \'dā-ˌstär\ n (bef. 12c) **1** : MORNING STAR **2** : SUN 1a

day student n (1883) : a student who attends regular classes at a college or preparatory school but does not live at the institution

day·time \'dā-ˌtīm\ n, *often attrib* (1535) : the time during which there is daylight

day·times \'dā-ˌtīmz\ adv (1854) : during the day or during the work-day repeatedly ⟨has a housekeeper ~⟩

day–to–day \ˌdā-tə-ˌdā\ adj (1883) **1** : taking place, made, or done in the course of successive days ⟨~ problems⟩ **2** : providing for a day at a time with little thought for the future ⟨lived an aimless ~ existence⟩

day–trip·per \'dā-ˌtri-pər\ n (1897) : one who takes a trip that does not last overnight

daze \'dāz\ vt **dazed; daz·ing** [ME *dasen*, fr. (assumed) ON *dasa;* akin to ON *dasask* to become exhausted] (14c) **1** : to stupefy esp. by a blow : STUN **2** : to dazzle with light — **daze** n — **dazed·ly** \'dā-zəd-lē\ adv — **dazed·ness** \'dā-zəd-nəs, 'dāzd-\ n

daz·zle \'da-zəl\ vb **daz·zled; daz·zling** \-z(ə-)liŋ\ [freq. of *daze*] vi (15c) **1** : to lose clear vision esp. from looking at bright light **2 a** : to shine brilliantly **b** : to arouse admiration by an impressive display ~ vt **1** : to overpower with light **2** : to impress deeply, overpower, or confound with brilliance ⟨*dazzled* us with her wit⟩ — **dazzle** n — **daz·zler** \-z(ə-)lər\ n — **daz·zling·ly** \-z(ə-)liŋ-lē\ adv

DBCP \dē-(ˌ)bē-(ˌ)sē-ˈpē\ *n* [*di*- + *brom*- + *chlor*- + *propane*] (1967) : a halocarbon compound $C_3H_5Br_2Cl$ used as an agricultural pesticide that is a suspected carcinogen and cause of sterility in human males

D day *n* [*D*, abbr. for *day*] (1918) : a day set for launching an operation; *specif* : June 6, 1944, on which Allied forces began the invasion of France in World War II

DDC \ˌdē-(ˌ)dē-ˈsē\ *n* [*di*- + *deoxy* + *cytidine*] (1987) : an antiviral drug $C_{10}H_{13}N_3O_3$ used to reduce virus growth and reproduction in AIDS and HIV infection

DDD \ˌdē-(ˌ)dē-ˈdē\ *n* [*di*chlor- + *di*phenyl + *dichlor*-] (1946) : an insecticide (ClC₆H₄)₂CHCHCl₂ closely related chemically and similar in properties to DDT

DDE \ˌdē-(ˌ)dē-ˈē\ *n* [*di*chlor- + *di*phenyl + *ethylene*] (1949) : a persistent organochlorine $C_{15}H_8Cl_4$ that is produced by the metabolic breakdown of DDT

DDI \ˌdē-(ˌ)dē-ˈī\ *n* [*di*- + *deoxy* + *inosine*, a nucleoside] (1988) : an antiviral drug $C_{10}H_{12}N_4O_3$ used to reduce virus growth and reproduction in AIDS and HIV infection

DDT \ˌdē-(ˌ)dē-ˈtē\ *n* [*di*chlor- + *di*phenyl + *trichlor*- (fr. *tri*- + *chlor*-)] (1943) : a colorless odorless water-insoluble crystalline insecticide $C_{14}H_9Cl_5$ that tends to accumulate in ecosystems and has toxic effects on many vertebrates

DDVP \ˌdē-(ˌ)dē-ˌvē-ˈpē\ *n* [*di*methyl + *di*chlor- + *vinyl* + *phos-phate*] (1954) : DICHLORVOS

de- *prefix* [ME, fr. OF *de-*, *des-*, partly fr. L *de-* from, down, away (fr. *de*, prep.) and partly fr. L *dis-*; L *de* akin to OIr *di* from, OE *tō* to — more at TO, DIS] **1 a** : do the opposite of ⟨*deactivate*⟩ **b** : reverse of ⟨*de*-emphasis⟩ **2 a** : remove ⟨a specified thing⟩ from ⟨*delouse*⟩ **b** : remove from ⟨a specified thing⟩ ⟨*dethrone*⟩ **3** : reduce ⟨*devalue*⟩ **4** : something derived from ⟨a specified thing⟩ ⟨*decompound*⟩ : derived from something ⟨of a specified nature⟩ ⟨*denominative*⟩ **5** : get off of ⟨a specified thing⟩ ⟨*detrain*⟩ **6** : having a molecule characterized by the removal of one or more atoms ⟨of a specified element⟩ ⟨*deoxy*-⟩

de·acid·i·fy \ˌdē-ə-ˈsi-də-ˌfī\ *vt* (1786) : to remove acid from : reduce the acidity of ⟨as by neutralization⟩ — **de·acid·i·fi·ca·tion** \-ˌsi-də-fə-ˈkā-shən\ *n*

dea·con \ˈdē-kən\ *n* [ME *dekene*, fr. OE *dēacon*, fr. LL *diaconus*, fr. Gk *diakonos*, lit., servant, fr. *dia*- + -*konos* (akin to en*konein* to be active); perh. akin to L *conari* to attempt] (bef. 12c) : a subordinate officer in a Christian church: as **a** : a Roman Catholic, Anglican, or Eastern Orthodox cleric ranking next below a priest **b** : one of the laymen elected by a church with congregational polity to serve in worship, in pastoral care, and on administrative committees **c** : a Mormon in the lowest grade of the Aaronic priesthood

dea·con·ess \ˈdē-kə-nəs\ *n* (15c) : a woman chosen to assist in the church ministry; *specif* : one in a Protestant order

deacon's bench *n* (1922) : a bench with usu. spindled arms and back

de·ac·ti·vate \(ˌ)dē-ˈak-tə-ˌvāt\ *vt* (1926) : to make inactive or ineffective — **de·ac·ti·va·tion** \(ˌ)dē-ˌak-tə-ˈvā-shən\ *n* — **de·ac·ti·va·tor** \(ˌ)dē-ˈak-tə-ˌvā-tər\ *n*

deacon's bench

¹**dead** \ˈded\ *adj* [ME *deed*, fr. OE *dēad*; akin to ON *dauthr* dead, *deyja* to die, OHG *tōt* dead — more at DIE] (bef. 12c) **1** : deprived of life : having died **2 a** (1) : having the appearance of death : DEATHLY ⟨in a ~ faint⟩ (2) : lacking power to move, feel, or respond : NUMB **b** : very tired **c** (1) : incapable of being stirred emotionally or intellectually : UNRESPONSIVE ⟨~ to pity⟩ (2) : grown cold : EXTINGUISHED ⟨~ coals⟩ **3 a** : INANIMATE, INERT ⟨~ matter⟩ **b** : BARREN, INFERTILE ⟨~ soil⟩ **c** : no longer producing or functioning : EXHAUSTED ⟨a ~ battery⟩ **4 a** (1) : lacking power or effect ⟨a ~ law⟩ (2) : no longer having interest, relevance, or significance ⟨a ~ issue⟩ **b** : no longer in use : OBSOLETE ⟨a ~ language⟩ **c** : no longer active : EXTINCT ⟨a ~ volcano⟩ **d** : lacking in gaiety or animation ⟨a ~ party⟩ **e** (1) : lacking in commercial activity : QUIET (2) : commercially idle or unproductive ⟨~ capital⟩ **f** : lacking elasticity ⟨a ~ tennis ball⟩ **g** : being out of action or out of use; *specif* : free from any connection to a source of voltage and free from electric charges **h** (1) : being out of play ⟨a ~ ball⟩ (2) : temporarily forbidden to play or to make a certain play in croquet **5 a** : not running or circulating : STAGNANT ⟨~ water⟩ **b** : not turning ⟨a ~ lathe center⟩ **c** : not imparting motion or power although otherwise functioning ⟨a ~ rear axle⟩ **d** : lacking warmth, vigor, or taste **6 a** : absolutely uniform ⟨a ~ level⟩ **b** (1) : UNERRING (2) : EXACT ⟨~ center of the target⟩ (3) : certain to be doomed ⟨he's ~ if he's late for curfew⟩ (4) : IRREVOCABLE ⟨a ~ loss⟩ **c** : ABRUPT ⟨brought to a ~ stop⟩ **d** (1) : COMPLETE, ABSOLUTE ⟨a ~ silence⟩ (2) : ALL-OUT ⟨caught it on the ~ run⟩ **7** : devoid of former occupants ⟨~ villages⟩ — **dead·ness** *n* — **dead in the water** : incapable of being effective : STALLED **2** : ¹DEAD 6b(3)
syn DEAD, DEFUNCT, DECEASED, DEPARTED, LATE mean devoid of life. DEAD applies literally to what is deprived of vital force but is used figuratively of anything that has lost any attribute (as energy, activity, radiance) suggesting life ⟨a *dead*, listless performance⟩. DEFUNCT stresses cessation of active existence or operation ⟨a *defunct* television series⟩. DECEASED, DEPARTED, and LATE apply to persons who have died recently. DECEASED is the preferred term in legal use ⟨the estate of the *deceased*⟩. DEPARTED is used usu. as a euphemism ⟨our *departed* sister⟩. LATE is used esp. with reference to a person in a specific relation or status ⟨the company's *late* president⟩.

²**dead** *n*, *pl* **dead** (bef. 12c) **1** : one that is dead — usu. used collectively **2** : the state of being dead ⟨raised him from the ~ —Col 2:12(RSV)⟩ **3** : the time of greatest quiet ⟨the ~ of night⟩

³**dead** *adv* (14c) **1** : ABSOLUTELY, UTTERLY ⟨~ certain⟩ **2** : suddenly and completely ⟨stopped ~⟩ **3** : DIRECTLY ⟨~ ahead⟩

dead air *n* (ca. 1943) : a period of silence esp. during a broadcast

dead–air space \ˈded-ˈar-, -ˈer-\ *n* (1902) : an unventilated air space

¹**dead·beat** \ˈded-ˌbēt\ *n* (1863) **1** : LOAFER **2** : one who persistently fails to pay personal debts or expenses

²**deadbeat** *adj* (ca. 1864) : having a pointer that gives a reading with little or no oscillation

dead bolt *n* (ca. 1902) : a lock bolt that is moved by turning the knob or key without action of a spring

dead duck *n* (1943) : one that is doomed

dead·en \ˈde-dᵊn\ *vb* **dead·ened; dead·en·ing** \ˈded-niŋ, ˈde-dᵊn-iŋ\ *vt* (1665) **1** : to impair in vigor or sensation : BLUNT ⟨~ed his enthusiasm⟩ **2 a** : to deprive of brilliance **b** : to make vapid or spiritless **c** : to make ⟨as a wall⟩ impervious to sound **3** : to deprive of life : KILL ~ *vi* : to become dead : lose life or vigor — **dead·en·er** \ˈded-nər, -dᵊn-ər\ *n* — **dead·en·ing·ly** \-niŋ-lē, -dᵊn-iŋ-\ *adv*

¹**dead–end** \ˈded-ˌend\ *adj* (1919) **1 a** : lacking opportunities esp. for advancement ⟨a ~ job⟩ **b** : lacking an exit ⟨a ~ street⟩ **2** : UNRULY ⟨~ kids⟩ — **dead–end·ed·ness** \ˌded-ˈen-dəd-nəs\ *n*

²**dead–end** \ˈded-ˈend\ *vi* (1944) : to come to a dead end : TERMINATE

dead end \ˈded-ˈend\ *n* (1886) **1** : an end (as of a street) without an exit **2** : a position, situation, or course of action that leads to nothing further

dead·en·ing *n* (ca. 1874) : material used to soundproof walls or floors

dead·eye \ˈded-ˌī\ *n* (1748) **1** : a rounded wood block encircled by a rope or an iron band and having holes to receive the lanyard that is used esp. to set up shrouds and stays **2** : an unerring marksman

dead·fall \-ˌfȯl\ *n* (1611) **1** : a trap so constructed that a weight ⟨as a heavy log⟩ falls on an animal and kills or disables it **2** : a tangled mass of fallen trees and branches

dead hand *n* (14c) **1** : MORTMAIN 1 **2** : the oppressive influence of the past

¹**dead·head** \ˈded-ˌhed\ *n* (1841) **1** : one who has not paid for a ticket **2** : a dull or stupid person

²**deadhead** *vi* (1911) : to make a return trip without a load ~ *vt* : to remove the faded flowers of ⟨a plant⟩ esp. to keep a neat appearance and to promote reblooming by preventing seed production

dead heat *n* (1796) : a tie with no single winner of a race

dead horse *n* (1830) : an exhausted or profitless topic or issue — usu. used in the phrases *beat a dead horse* and *flog a dead horse*

dead letter *n* (1663) **1** : something that has lost its force or authority without being formally abolished **2** : a letter that is undeliverable and unreturnable by the post office

dead lift *n* (1963) : a lift in weight lifting in which the weight is lifted from the floor to hip level — **dead·lift** \ˈded-ˌlift\ *vt*

dead·light \ˈded-ˌlīt\ *n* (1726) : a metal cover or shutter fitted to a port to keep out light and water

dead·line \-ˌlīn\ *n* (1864) **1** : a line drawn within or around a prison that a prisoner passes at the risk of being shot **2 a** : a date or time before which something must be done **b** : the time after which copy is not accepted for a particular issue of a publication

dead load *n* (ca. 1888) : a constant load in a structure ⟨as a bridge, building, or machine⟩ that is due to the weight of the members, the supported structure, and permanent attachments or accessories

dead·lock \ˈded-ˌläk\ *n* (1779) **1** : a state of inaction or neutralization resulting from the opposition of equally powerful uncompromising persons or factions : STANDSTILL **2** : a tie score — **deadlock** *vb*

¹**dead·ly** \ˈded-lē\ *adj* **dead·li·er; -est** (bef. 12c) **1** : likely to cause or capable of producing death **2 a** : aiming to kill or destroy : IMPLACABLE ⟨a ~ enemy⟩ **b** : highly effective ⟨a ~ exposé⟩ **c** : UNERRING ⟨a ~ marksman⟩ **d** : marked by determination or extreme seriousness **3 a** : tending to deprive of force or vitality ⟨a ~ habit⟩ **b** : suggestive of death esp. in dullness or lack of animation ⟨~ bores⟩ ⟨a ~ conversation⟩ **4** : very great : EXTREME — **dead·li·ness** *n*
syn DEADLY, MORTAL, FATAL, LETHAL mean causing or capable of causing death. DEADLY applies to an established or very likely cause of death ⟨a *deadly* disease⟩. MORTAL implies that death has occurred or is inevitable ⟨a *mortal* wound⟩. FATAL stresses the inevitability of what has in fact resulted in death or destruction ⟨*fatal* consequences⟩. LETHAL applies to something that is bound to cause death or exists for the destruction of life ⟨*lethal* gas⟩.

²**deadly** *adv* (bef. 12c) **1** *archaic* : in a manner to cause death : MORTALLY **2** : suggesting death **3** : EXTREMELY ⟨~ serious⟩

deadly nightshade *n* (1578) : BELLADONNA 1

deadly sin *n* (13c) : one of seven sins of pride, covetousness, lust, anger, gluttony, envy, and sloth held to be fatal to spiritual progress

dead man's float *n* (ca. 1946) : a prone floating position with the arms extended forward

dead march *n* (1603) : a solemn march for a funeral

dead metaphor *n* (1922) : a word or phrase ⟨as *time is running out*⟩ that has lost its metaphoric force through common usage

dead–on \ˈded-ˈȯn, -ˈän\ *adj* (ca. 1889) : exactly correct or accurate

¹**dead·pan** \ˈded-ˌpan\ *adj* (ca. 1928) : marked by an impassive matter-of-fact manner, style, or expression ⟨a ~ comedy⟩ — **deadpan** *adv*

²**deadpan** *n* (ca. 1930) **1** : a completely expressionless face **2** : a deadpan manner of behavior or presentation

³**deadpan** *vt* (ca. 1942) : to express in a deadpan manner — **dead·pan·ner** *n*

dead reckoning *n* (1613) **1** : the determination without the aid of celestial observations of the position of a ship or aircraft from the record of the courses sailed or flown, the distance made, and the known or estimated drift **2** : GUESSWORK — **dead reckon** *vb*

dead space *n* (ca. 1923) : the portion of the respiratory system which is external to the bronchioles and through which air must pass to reach the bronchioles and alveoli

dead–stick landing \ˈded-ˌstik-\ *n* (ca. 1917) : a landing of an airplane or spacecraft made without power

dead·weight \ˈded-ˈwāt\ *n* (1660) **1** : the unrelieved weight of an inert mass **2** : DEAD LOAD **3** : a ship's load including the total weight of cargo, fuel, stores, crew, and passengers

deadweight ton *n* (ca. 1917) : a long ton used in indicating a ship's gross capacity — abbr. *dwt*

\ə\ abut \ᵊ\ kitten, F table \ər\ further \a\ ash \ā\ ace \ä\ mop, mar \au̇\ out \ch\ chin \e\ bet \ē\ easy \g\ go \i\ hit \ī\ ice \j\ job \ŋ\ sing \ō\ go \ȯ\ law \ȯi\ boy \th\ thin \t̲h̲\ the \ü\ loot \u̇\ foot \y\ yet \zh\ vision \ȧ, k̲, ⁿ, œ, œ̄, ᵫ, ᵫ̄, ᵊ\ *see* Guide to Pronunciation

dead-wood \-,wu̇d\ *n* (15c) **1** : wood dead on the tree **2** : useless personnel or material **3** : solid timbers built in at the extreme bow and stern of a ship when too narrow to permit framing **4** : bowling pins that have been knocked down but remain on the alley

de-aer-ate \,dē-'ar-,āt, -'er-\ *vt* (1791) : to remove air or gas from — **de-aer-a-tion** \,dē-ar-'ā-shən, -,er-\ *n* — **de-aer-a-tor** \-'ar-,ā-tər, -'er-\ *n*

deaf \'def, *dial* 'dēf\ *adj* [ME *deef,* fr. OE *dēaf;* akin to Gk *typhlos* blind, *typhein* to smoke, L *fumus* smoke — more at FUME] (bef. 12c) **1** : lacking or deficient in the sense of hearing **2** : unwilling to hear or listen : not to be persuaded ⟨was overwrought and ∼ to reason⟩ — **deaf-ish** \'de-fish\ *adj* — **deaf-ly** *adv* — **deaf-ness** *n*

deaf-en \'de-fən\ *vt* **deaf-ened; deaf-en-ing** \-f-niŋ, 'def-niŋ\ (1597) : to make deaf

deaf-en-ing *adj* (1597) **1** : that deafens **2** : very loud : EARSPLITTING ⟨fell with a ∼ clap⟩ — **deaf-en-ing-ly** *adv*

deaf–mute \'def-'myüt\ *n* (ca. 1837) : a deaf person who cannot speak — **deaf–mute** *adj*

¹deal \'dē(ə)l\ *n* [ME *deel,* fr. OE *dæl;* akin to OE *dāl* division, portion, OHG *teil* part] (bef. 12c) **1** *obs* : PART, PORTION **2** : a usu. large or indefinite quantity or degree ⟨a great ∼ of support⟩ ⟨a good ∼ faster⟩ **3 a** : the act or right of distributing cards to players in a card game **b** : HAND 9b

²deal *vb* **dealt** \'delt\; **deal-ing** \'dē-liŋ\ *vt* (bef. 12c) **1 a** : to give as one's portion : APPORTION ⟨tried to ∼ justice to all⟩ ⟨dealt out three sandwiches apiece⟩ **b** : to distribute (playing cards) to players in a game **2** : ADMINISTER, DELIVER ⟨dealt him a blow⟩ **3** : SELL ⟨∼s marijuana⟩ **∼** *vi* **1** : to distribute the cards in a card game **2** : to concern oneself or itself ⟨the book ∼s with education⟩ **3 a** : to engage in bargaining : TRADE **b** : to sell or distribute something as a business ⟨∼ in insurance⟩ **4 a** : to take action with regard to someone or something ⟨∼ with an offender⟩ **b** : to reach or try to reach a state of acceptance or reconcilement ⟨trying to ∼ with her son's death⟩ *syn* see DISTRIBUTE — **deal-er** \'dē-lər\ *n*

³deal *n* (15c) **1 a** : an act of dealing : TRANSACTION **b** : BARGAIN **2** : PACKAGE DEAL **3** : treatment received ⟨a dirty ∼⟩ **4** : an arrangement for mutual advantage **5** : AFFAIR 2 ⟨dinner was an informal ∼⟩

⁴deal *n* [ME *dele,* fr. MD or MLG, plank; akin to OHG *dili* plank — more at THILL] (14c) **1 a** *Brit* : a board of fir or pine **b** : sawed yellow-pine lumber nine inches (22.5 centimeters) or wider and three, four, or five inches (7.6 to 12.4 centimeters) thick **2** : pine or fir wood — **deal** *adj*

de-alat-ed \(,)dē-'ā-,lā-təd\ *adj* (1904) : divested of the wings — used of postnuptial adults of insects (as ants) that drop their wings after a nuptial flight — **de-ala-tion** \,dē-(,)ā-'lā-shən\ *n*

deal-er-ship \'dē-lər-,ship\ *n* (1916) : an authorized sales agency ⟨an automobile ∼⟩

deal-fish \'dē(ə)l-,fish\ *n* [⁴deal] (1845) : any of several long thin fishes (genus *Trachipterus* esp. *T. arcticus* of the family Trachipteridae) inhabiting the deep sea

deal-ing *n* (15c) **1** : method of business : manner of conduct **2** *pl* : friendly or business interactions

dealing box *n* (1897) : a case that holds a deck of playing cards so that they may be dealt one by one

de-am-i-nase \(,)dē-'a-mi-,nās, -,nāz\ *n* [*de-* + *amino* + *-ase*] (1920) : an enzyme that hydrolyzes amino compounds (as amino acids) with removal of the amino group

de-am-i-nate \-,nāt\ *vt* **-nat-ed; -nat-ing** (1926) : to remove the amino group from (a compound) — **de-am-i-na-tion** \(,)dē-,a-mi-'nā-shən\ *n*

dean \'dēn\ *n* [ME *deen,* fr. OF *deien,* fr. LL *decanus* chief of ten, fr. Gk *dekanos,* fr. *deka* ten — more at TEN] (13c) **1 a** : the head of the chapter of a collegiate or cathedral church **b** : a Roman Catholic priest who supervises one district of a diocese **2 a** : the head of a division, faculty, college, or school of a university **b** : a college or secondary school administrator in charge of counseling and disciplining students **3** : DOYEN 1 — **dean** *vi* — **dean-ship** \-,ship\ *n*

dean-ery \'dēn-rē, 'dē-nə-rē\ *n, pl* **-er-ies** (15c) : the office, jurisdiction, or official residence of a clerical dean

dean's list *n* (ca. 1926) : a list of students receiving special recognition from the dean of a college because of superior scholarship

¹dear \'dir\ *adj* [ME *dere,* fr. OE *dēor*] (bef. 12c) **1** : SEVERE, SORE ⟨in our ∼ peril —Shak.⟩

²dear *adj* [ME *dere,* fr. OE *dēore;* akin to OHG *tiuri* distinguished, costly] (bef. 12c) **1** *obs* : NOBLE **2** : highly valued : PRECIOUS ⟨a ∼ friend⟩ — often used in a salutation ⟨∼ Sir⟩ **3** : AFFECTIONATE, FOND **4** : high or exorbitant in price : EXPENSIVE ⟨eggs are very ∼ just now⟩ **5** : HEARTFELT — **dear** *adv* — **dear-ly** *adv* — **dear-ness** *n*

³dear *n* (13c) **1** : a loved one : SWEETHEART **2** : a lovable person

⁴dear *interj* (1694) — used esp. to express annoyance or dismay

Dear John \-'jän\ *n* (1945) : a letter (as to a soldier) in which a wife asks for a divorce or a girlfriend breaks off an engagement or a friendship

dearth \'dərth\ *n* [ME *derthe,* fr. (assumed) OE *dierthe,* fr. *dēore* dear] (13c) **1** : scarcity that makes dear; *specif* : FAMINE **2** : an inadequate supply : LACK

dea-sil \'dē-zəl\ *adv* [ScGael *deiseil;* akin to L *dexter* right hand] (1771) : CLOCKWISE — compare WIDDERSHINS

death \'deth\ *n* [ME *deeth,* fr. OE *dēath;* akin to ON *dauthi* death, *deyja* to die — more at DIE] (bef. 12c) **1** : a permanent cessation of all vital functions : the end of life — compare BRAIN DEATH **2** : the cause or occasion of loss of life ⟨drinking was the ∼ of him⟩ **3** *cap* : the destroyer of life represented usu. as a skeleton with a scythe **4** : the state of being dead **5 a** : the passing or destruction of something inanimate ⟨the ∼ of vaudeville⟩ **b** : EXTINCTION **6** : CIVIL DEATH **7** : SLAUGHTER **8** *Christian Science* : the lie of life in matter : that which is unreal and untrue : ILLUSION — **at death's door** : close to death : critically ill — **to death** : beyond endurance : EXCESSIVELY ⟨bored *to death*⟩

death-bed \'deth-,bed\ *n* (bef. 12c) **1** : the bed in which a person dies **2** : the last hours of life — **on one's deathbed** : near the point of death

death benefit *n* (1921) : money payable to the beneficiary of a deceased

death-blow \'deth-,blō\ *n* (1795) : a destructive or killing stroke or event

death camas *n* (ca. 1889) : any of several plants (genus *Zigadenus*) of the lily family that cause poisoning of livestock in the western U.S.

death camp *n* (1944) : a concentration camp in which large numbers of prisoners are systematically killed

death cap *n* (1925) : a very poisonous mushroom (*Amanita phalloides*) of deciduous woods of No. America and Europe that varies in color from pure white to olive or yellow and has a prominent volva at the base — called also *death cup*

death duty *n* (1881) *chiefly Brit* : DEATH TAX

death instinct *n* (1922) : an innate and unconscious tendency toward self-destruction postulated in psychoanalytic theory to explain aggressive and destructive behavior not satisfactorily explained by the pleasure principle — called also *Thanatos;* compare EROS 2

death-less \'deth-ləs\ *adj* (1589) : IMMORTAL, IMPERISHABLE ⟨∼ fame⟩ — **death-less-ly** *adv* — **death-less-ness** *n*

death-ly \'deth-lē\ *adj* (bef. 12c) **1** : FATAL **2** : of, relating to, or suggestive of death ⟨a ∼ pallor⟩ — **deathly** *adv*

death mask *n* (1877) : a cast taken from the face of a dead person

death rattle *n* (1822) : a rattling or gurgling sound produced by air passing through mucus in the lungs and air passages of a dying person

death ray *n* (1919) : a weapon that generates an intense beam of particles or radiation by which it destroys its target

death row *n* (1950) : a prison area housing inmates sentenced to death

death's–head \'deths-,hed\ *n* (1596) : a human skull or a depiction of a human skull symbolizing death

death's–head hawkmoth *n* (1879) : a large dark hawkmoth (*Acherontia atropos*) with markings resembling a human skull on the back of the thorax — called also *death's-head moth*

deaths-man \'deths-mən\ *n* (1589) *archaic* : EXECUTIONER

death squad *n* (1969) : any of various right-wing vigilante groups in Latin America whose members kill suspected political adversaries and criminals

death tax *n* (1937) : a tax arising on the transmission of property after the owner's death; *esp* : ESTATE TAX

death trap *n* (1835) : a structure or situation that is potentially very dangerous to life

death warrant *n* (1692) **1** : a warrant for the execution of a death sentence **2** : DEATHBLOW

¹death-watch \'deth-,wäch\ *n* [*death* + *watch* (timepiece); fr. the superstition that its ticking presages death] (1646) : a small insect that makes a ticking sound; *esp* : DEATHWATCH BEETLE

²deathwatch *n* [*death* + *watch* (vigil)] (ca. 1890) **1** : a vigil kept over the dead or dying **2** : the guard set over a criminal to be executed

deathwatch beetle *n* (1877) : any of various small beetles (family Anobiidae) that are common in old houses where they bore in woodwork and furniture and make a tapping noise as a mating call

death wish *n* (1913) : the conscious or unconscious desire for the death of oneself or of another

deb \'deb\ *n* (1920) : DEBUTANTE

de-ba-cle \di-'bä-kəl, -'ba-; -̇'bə-bə-kəl\ *also* **dé-bâ-cle** *also* dā-'bäk(l⁹)\ *n* [F *débâcle,* fr. *débâcler* to clear, fr. MF *desbacler,* fr. *des-* de- + *bacler* to block, perh. fr. (assumed) VL *bacculare,* fr. L *baculum* staff] (1802) **1** : a tumultuous breakup of ice in a river **2** : a violent disruption (as of an army) : ROUT **3 a** : a great disaster **b** : a complete failure : FIASCO

de-bar \di-'bär, dē-\ *vt* [ME *debarren,* fr. MF *desbarrer* to unbar, fr. *des-* de- + *barrer* to bar] (15c) : to bar from having or doing something : PRECLUDE — **de-bar-ment** \-mənt\ *n*

¹de-bark \di-'bärk, dē-\ *vb* [F *debarquer,* fr. *de-* + *barque* bark (ship)] (1654) : DISEMBARK — **de-bar-ka-tion** \,dē-,bär-'kā-shən\ *n*

²de-bark \(,)dē-'bärk\ *vt* (1742) : to remove bark from

de-base \di-'bās, dē-\ *vt* (1565) **1** : to lower in status, esteem, quality, or character **2 a** : to reduce the intrinsic value of (a coin) by increasing the base-metal content **b** : to reduce the exchange value of (a monetary unit) — **de-base-ment** \-'bās-mənt\ *n* — **de-bas-er** \-'bā-sər\ *n*

syn DEBASE, VITIATE, DEPRAVE, CORRUPT, DEBAUCH, PERVERT mean to cause deterioration or lowering in quality or character. DEBASE implies a loss of position, worth, value, or dignity ⟨commercialism has *debased* the holiday⟩. VITIATE implies a destruction of purity, validity, or effectiveness by allowing entrance of a fault or defect ⟨a foreign policy *vitiated* by partisanship⟩. DEPRAVE implies moral deterioration by evil thoughts or influences ⟨the claim that society is *depraved* by pornography⟩. CORRUPT implies loss of soundness, purity, or integrity ⟨the belief that bureaucratese *corrupts* the language⟩. DEBAUCH implies a debasing through sensual indulgence ⟨the long stay on a tropical isle had *debauched* the ship's crew⟩. PERVERT implies a twisting or distorting from what is natural or normal ⟨*perverted* the original goals of the institute⟩.

de-bat-able \di-'bā-tə-bəl, dē-\ *adj* (1536) **1** : claimed by more than one country ⟨∼ border territory⟩ **2 a** : open to dispute : QUESTIONABLE **b** : open to debate **3** : capable of being debated

¹de-bate \di-'bāt, dē-\ *n* (13c) : a contention by words or arguments: as **a** : the formal discussion of a motion before a deliberative body according to the rules of parliamentary procedure **b** : a regulated discussion of a proposition between two matched sides

²debate *vb* **de-bat-ed; de-bat-ing** [ME, fr. MF *debatre,* fr. OF, fr. *de-* + *batre* to beat, fr. L *battuere*] *vi* (14c) **1** *obs* : FIGHT, CONTEND **2 a** : to contend in words **b** : to discuss a question by considering opposed arguments **3** : to participate in a debate **∼** *vt* **1 a** : to argue about **b** : to engage (an opponent) in debate **2** : to turn over in one's mind *syn* see DISCUSS — **de-bate-ment** \-'bāt-mənt\ *n* — **de-bat-er** *n*

¹de-bauch \di-'bȯch, -'bäch\ *vb* [MF *debaucher,* fr. OF *desbauchier* to scatter, disperse, fr. *des-* de- + *bauch* beam, of Gmc origin; akin to OHG *balko* beam — more at BALK] (1595) **1 a** *archaic* : to make disloyal **b** : to seduce from chastity **2 a** : to lead away from virtue or excellence **b** : to corrupt by intemperance or sensuality *syn* see DEBASE — **de-bauch-er** *n*

²debauch *n* (1603) **1** : an act or occasion of debauchery **2** : ORGY

de-bauch-ee \di-,bȯ-'chē, -,bä-; ,de-bȯ-'shē, -'shā\ *n* [F *débauché,* fr. pp. of *débaucher*] (1661) : one given to debauchery

de·bauch·ery \di-'bȯ-chə-rē, -chrē, -'bä-\ *n, pl* **-er·ies** (1642) **1 a** : extreme indulgence in sensuality **b** *pl* : ORGIES **2** *archaic* : seduction from virtue or duty

de·beak \(ˌ)dē-'bēk\ *vt* (1937) : to remove the tip of the upper mandible of (as a chicken) to prevent cannibalism and fighting

de·ben·ture \di-'ben-chər\ *n* [ME *debentur*, fr. L, they are due, 3d pl. pres. pass. of *debēre* to owe — more at DEBT] (15c) **1** *Brit* : a corporate security other than an equity security : BOND **2** : a bond backed by the general credit of the issuer rather than a specific lien on particular assets

de·bil·i·tate \di-'bi-lə-ˌtāt, dē-\ *vt* **-tat·ed; -tat·ing** [L *debilitatus*, pp. of *debilitare* to weaken, fr. *debilis* weak] (1533) : to impair the strength of : ENFEEBLE **syn** see WEAKEN — **de·bil·i·ta·tion** \-ˌbi-lə-'tā-shən\ *n*

de·bil·i·ty \di-'bi-lə-tē, dē-\ *n, pl* **-ties** [MF *debilité*, fr. L *debilitat-, debilitas*, fr. *debilis*, fr. *de-* de- + *-bilis*; akin to Skt *bala* strength] (15c) : WEAKNESS, INFIRMITY

¹deb·it \'de-bət\ *vt* (1682) : to enter upon the debit side of an account : charge with a debit

²debit *n* [L *debitum* debt] (1776) **1 a** : a record of an indebtedness; *specif* : an entry on the left-hand side of an account constituting an addition to an expense or asset account or a deduction from a revenue, net worth, or liability account **b** : the sum of the items entered as debits **2** : a charge against a bank deposit account **3** : DRAWBACK, SHORTCOMING

debit card *n* (1977) : a card like a credit card by which money may be withdrawn or the cost of purchases paid directly from the holder's bank account without the payment of interest

deb·o·nair \ˌde-bə-'nar, -'ner\ *adj* [ME *debonere*, fr. OF *debonaire*, fr. *de bon aire* of good family or nature] (13c) **1** *archaic* : GENTLE, COURTEOUS **2 a** : SUAVE, URBANE **b** : LIGHTHEARTED, NONCHALANT — **deb·o·nair·ly** *adv* — **deb·o·nair·ness** *n*

de·bone \(ˌ)dē-'bōn\ *vt* (1944) : BONE ⟨~ a roast⟩ — **de·bon·er** *n*

Deb·o·rah \'de-b(ə-)rə\ *n* [Heb *Dĕbhōrāh*] : a Hebrew prophetess who rallied the Israelites in their struggles against the Canaanites

de·bouch \di-'bau̇ch, -'büsh, dē-\ *vb* [F *déboucher*, fr. *dé-* de- + *bouche* mouth, fr. L *bucca* cheek] *vi* (1745) : to cause to emerge : DISCHARGE ~ *vi* **1** : to march out into open ground **2** : EMERGE, ISSUE — **de·bouch·ment** \-mənt\ *n*

de·bride·ment \di-'brēd-mənt, dā-, -ˌmänt, dā-brēd-'mäⁿ\ *n* [F *débridement*, fr. *débrider* to remove adhesions, lit., to unbridle, fr. MF *desbrider*, fr. *des-* de- + *bride* bridle, fr. MHG *brīdel* — more at BRIDLE] (ca. 1842) : the surgical removal of lacerated, devitalized, or contaminated tissue — **de·bride** \di-'brēd, dā-\ *vt*

de·brief \(ˌ)dē-'brēf\ *vt* (1945) : to interrogate (as a pilot) usu. upon return (as from a mission) in order to obtain useful information

de·bris \də-'brē, dā-', 'dā-, *Brit usu* 'de-(ˌ)brē\ *n, pl* **de·bris** \-'brēz, -ˌbrēz\ [F *débris*, fr. MF, fr. *debriser* to break to pieces, fr. OF *debrisier*, fr. *de-* + *brisier* to break — more at BRISANCE] (1708) **1** : the remains of something broken down or destroyed **2** : an accumulation of fragments of rock **3** : something discarded : RUBBISH

debt \'det\ *n* [ME *dette, debte*, fr. OF *dette* something owed, fr. (assumed) VL *debita*, fr. L pl. of *debitum* debt, fr. neut. of *debitus*, pp. of *debēre* to owe, fr. *de-* + *habēre* to have — more at GIVE] (13c) **1** : SIN, TRESPASS **2** : something owed : OBLIGATION **3** : a state of owing **4** : the common-law action for the recovery of money held to be due — **debt·less** \-ləs\ *adj*

debt·or \'de-tər\ *n* (13c) **1** : one guilty of neglect or violation of duty **2** : one who owes a debt

debt service *n* (1929) : the amount of interest and sinking fund payments due annually on long-term debt

de·bug \(ˌ)dē-'bəg\ *vt* (1944) **1** : to remove insects from **2** : to eliminate errors in or malfunctions of **3** : to remove a concealed microphone or wiretapping device from — **de·bug·ger** *n*

de·bunk \(ˌ)dē-'bəŋk\ *vt* (1923) : to expose the sham or falseness of ⟨~ a legend⟩ — **de·bunk·er** *n*

¹de·but *also* **dé·but** \'dā-ˌbyü, dā-'\ *n* [F *début*, fr. *débuter* to begin, fr. MF *desbuter* to play first, fr. *des-* de- + *but* starting point, goal — more at BUTT] (1751) **1** : a first appearance ⟨made her singing ~⟩ **2** : a formal entrance into society

²debut *vi* (1830) : to make a debut ~ *vt* : to present to the public for the first time : INTRODUCE

deb·u·tant \'de-byü-ˌtänt\ *n* [F *débutant*, fr. prp. of *débuter*] (1821) : one making a debut

deb·u·tante \'de-byü-ˌtänt\ *n* [F *débutante*, fem. of *débutant*] (1801) : DEBUTANT; *esp* : a young woman making her formal entrance into society

deca- *or* **dec-** *or* **deka-** *or* **dek-** *comb form* [ME, fr. L, fr. Gk *deka-, dek-*, fr. *deka* — more at TEN] : ten ⟨*deca*syllabic⟩ ⟨*deka*meter⟩

de·cade \'de-ˌkäd, de-'käd; *esp sense 1b* \de-kəd\ *n* [ME, fr. MF *décade*, fr. LL *decad-, decas*, fr. Gk *dekad-, dekas*, fr. *deka*] (15c) **1** : a group or set of 10: as **a** : a period of 10 years **b** : a division of the rosary that consists primarily of 10 Hail Marys **2** : a ratio of 10 to 1 : ORDER OF MAGNITUDE — **de·cad·al** \-d³l\ *adj*

dec·a·dence \'de-kə-dən(t)s *also* di-'kä-\ *n* [MF, fr. ML *decadentia*, fr. LL *decadent-, decadens*, prp. of *decadere* to fall, sink — more at DECAY] (1549) **1** : the process of becoming decadent : the quality or state of being decadent **2** : a period of decline **syn** see DETERIORATION

dec·a·den·cy \-d³n-sē\ *n* (1632) : DECADENCE 1

¹dec·a·dent \'de-kə-dənt *also* di-'kä-\ *adj* [back-formation fr. *decadence*] (1837) **1** : marked by decay or decline **2** : of, relating to, or having the characteristics of the decadents **3** : characterized by or appealing to self-indulgence — **dec·a·dent·ly** *adv*

²decadent *n* (1886) **1** : one of a group of late 19th century French and English writers tending toward artificial and unconventional subjects and subtilized style **2** : one that is decadent

de·caf \'dē-ˌkaf\ *n* [short for *decaffeinated*] (1984) : decaffeinated coffee

de·caf·fein·at·ed \(ˌ)dē-'ka-fə-ˌnā-təd, -fē-ə-\ *adj* (1921) : having the caffeine removed ⟨~ coffee⟩ ⟨~ tea⟩

deca·gon \'de-kə-ˌgän\ *n* [NL *decagonum*, fr. Gk *dekagōnon*, fr. *deka-* + *-gōnon* -gon] (1571) : a plane polygon of 10 angles and 10 sides

deca·gram \-ˌgram\ *n* [F *décagramme*, fr. *déca-* deca- + *gramme* gram] (1810) : DEKAGRAM

deca·he·dron \ˌde-kə-'hē-drən\ *n* [ISV] (ca. 1828) : a polyhedron of 10 faces

de·cal \'dē-ˌkal, di-'kal; *Canad usu* 'de-kəl\ *n* [short for *decalcomania*] (1937) : a picture, design, or label made to be transferred (as to glass) from specially prepared paper

de·cal·ci·fi·ca·tion \(ˌ)dē-ˌkal-sə-fə-'kā-shən\ *n* (1859) : the removal or loss of calcium or calcium compounds (as from bones or soil) — **de·cal·ci·fy** \(ˌ)dē-'kal-sə-ˌfī\ *vt*

de·cal·co·ma·nia \di-ˌkal-kə-'mā-nē-ə\ *n* [F *décalcomanie*, fr. *décalquer* to copy by tracing (fr. *dé-* de- + *calquer* to trace, fr. It *calcare*, lit., to tread, fr. L) + *manie* mania, fr. LL *mania*— more at CAULK] (1864) **1** : the art or process of transferring pictures and designs from specially prepared paper (as to glass) **2** : DECAL

deca·li·ter \'de-kə-ˌlē-tər\ *n* [F *décalitre*, fr. *déca-* + *litre* liter] (1810) : DEKALITER

deca·logue \'de-kə-ˌlȯg, -ˌläg\ *n* [ME *decaloge*, fr. LL *decalogus*, fr. Gk *dekalogos*, fr. *deka-* + *logos* word — more at LEGEND] (14c) **1** *cap* : TEN COMMANDMENTS **2** : a basic set of rules carrying binding authority

¹deca·me·ter \'de-kə-ˌmē-tər\ *n* [F *décamètre*, fr. *déca-* + *mètre* meter] (1810) : DEKAMETER

²de·cam·e·ter \de-'ka-mə-tər, də-\ *n* [Gk *dekametron*, fr. *deka-* + *metron* measure, meter] (1821) : a line of verse consisting of 10 metrical feet

deca·me·tho·ni·um \ˌde-kə-mə-'thō-nē-əm\ *n* [*deca-* + *methylene* + *-onium*] (ca. 1949) : a synthetic ion used in the form of its bromide or iodide salts ($C_{16}H_{38}Br_2N_2$ or $C_{16}H_{38}I_2N_2$) as a skeletal muscle relaxant; *also* : either of these salts

deca·met·ric \ˌde-kə-'me-trik\ *adj* [*decameter* + *-ic*; the wavelength range being between 1 and 10 dekameters] (1950) : of, relating to, or being a radio wave of high frequency

de·camp \di-'kamp, dē-\ *vi* [F *décamper*, fr. MF *descamper*, fr. *des-* de- + *camper* to camp] (1676) **1** : to break up a camp **2** : to depart suddenly : ABSCOND — **de·camp·ment** \-mənt\ *n*

dec·ane \'de-ˌkān\ *n* [ISV *deca-*] (ca. 1875) : any of several isomeric liquid alkanes $C_{10}H_{22}$

de·cant \di-'kant, dē-\ *vt* [NL *decantare*, fr. L *de-* + ML *cantus* edge, fr. L, iron ring round a wheel — more at CANT] (1633) **1** : to draw off (a liquid) without disturbing the sediment or the lower liquid layers **2** : to pour from one vessel into another **3** : to pour out, transfer, or unload as if by pouring — **de·can·ta·tion** \ˌdē-ˌkan-'tā-shən\ *n*

de·cant·er \di-'kan-tər, dē-\ *n* (1712) : a vessel used to decant or to receive decanted liquids; *esp* : an ornamental glass bottle used for serving wine

decanter

de·cap·i·tate \di-'ka-pə-ˌtāt, dē-\ *vt* **-tat·ed; -tat·ing** [LL *decapitatus*, pp. of *decapitare*, fr. L *de-* + *capit-, caput* head — more at HEAD] (ca. 1611) **1** : to cut off the head of : BEHEAD **2** : to make ineffective : DESTROY — **de·cap·i·ta·tion** \-ˌka-pə-'tā-shən\ *n* — **de·cap·i·ta·tor** \-'ka-pə-ˌtā-tər\ *n*

deca·pod \'de-kə-ˌpäd\ *n* [NL *Decapoda*, order name] (1836) **1** : any of an order (Decapoda) of crustaceans (as shrimps, lobsters, and crabs) with five pairs of thoracic appendages one or more of which are modified into pincers, with stalked eyes, and with the head and thorax fused into a cephalothorax and covered by a carapace **2** : any of the cephalopod mollusks (orders Sepioidea and Teuthoidea) with 10 arms including cuttlefishes, squids, and related forms — **decapod** *adj* — **de·cap·o·dan** \di-'ka-pə-dən\ *adj or n* — **de·cap·o·dous** \-ə-dəs\ *adj*

de·car·bon·ate \(ˌ)dē-'kär-bə-ˌnāt\ *vt* (1831) : to remove carbon dioxide or carbonic acid from — **de·car·bon·ation** \-ˌkär-bə-'nā-shən\ *n*

de·car·bon·ize \(ˌ)dē-'kär-bə-ˌnīz\ *vt* [ISV] (1825) : to remove carbon from — **de·car·bon·iz·er** *n*

de·car·box·yl·ase \ˌdē-ˌkär-'bäk-sə-ˌlās, -ˌlāz\ *n* (1940) : any of a group of enzymes that accelerate decarboxylation esp. of amino acids

de·car·box·yl·ation \-ˌbäk-sə-'lā-shən\ *n* (1922) : the removal or elimination of carboxyl from a molecule — **de·car·box·yl·ate** \-'bäk-sə-ˌlāt\ *vt*

de·car·bu·rize \(ˌ)dē-'kär-b(y)ə-ˌrīz\ *vt* (1856) : DECARBONIZE — **de·car·bu·ri·za·tion** \-ˌkär-b(y)ə-rə-'zā-shən\ *n*

de·care \'de-ˌkar, -ˌker, -ˌkär\ *n* [F *décare*, fr. *déca-* deca- + *are*] (1810) : a metric unit of area equal to 10 ares or 0.2471 acre

de·ca·su·al·iza·tion \(ˌ)dē-ˌka-zh(ə-)wə-lə-'zā-shən, -ˌka-zhə-lə-\ *n* (1892) : the process of eliminating the employment of casual workers in order to stabilize the work force

deca·syl·lab·ic \ˌde-kə-sə-'la-bik\ *adj* [prob. fr. F *décasyllabique*, fr. Gk *dekasyllabos*, fr. *deka-* deca- + *syllabē* syllable] (1771) : consisting of 10 syllables or composed of verses of 10 syllables — **decasyllabic** *n* — **deca·syl·la·ble** \'de-kə-ˌsi-lə-bəl, de-kə-'\ *n*

de·cath·lete \di-'kath-ˌlēt\ *n* [blend of *decathlon* and *athlete*] (1968) : an athlete who competes in the decathlon

de·cath·lon \di-'kath-lən, -ˌlän\ *n* [F *décathlon*, fr. *déca-* deca- + *-athlon* (as in *pentathlon*)] (1912) : a 10-event athletic contest; *specif* : a composite contest that consists of the 100-meter, 400-meter, and 1500-meter runs, the 110-meter high hurdles, the javelin and discus throws, shot put, pole vault, high jump, and long jump

¹de·cay \di-'kā\ *vb* [ME, fr. ONF *decair*, fr. LL *decadere* to fall, sink, fr. L *de-* + *cadere* to fall — more at CHANCE] *vi* (15c) **1** : to decline from a sound or prosperous condition **2** : to decrease gradually in quantity, activity, or force **3** : to fall into ruin **4** : to decline in health, strength, or vigor **5** : to undergo decomposition ~ *vt* **1** *obs* : to cause to decay : IMPAIR ⟨infirmity that ~s the wise —Shak.⟩ **2** : to destroy by decomposition — **de·cay·er** *n*

syn DECAY, DECOMPOSE, ROT, PUTREFY, SPOIL mean to undergo destructive dissolution. DECAY implies a slow change from a state of soundness or perfection ⟨a *decaying* mansion⟩. DECOMPOSE stresses a breaking down by chemical change and when applied to organic matter a corruption ⟨the strong odor of *decomposing* vegetation⟩. ROT is a close synonym of DECOMPOSE and often connotes foulness ⟨fruit was left to *rot* in warehouses⟩. PUTREFY implies the rotting of animal matter and offensiveness to sight and smell ⟨corpses *putrefying* on the battlefield⟩. SPOIL applies chiefly to the decomposition of foods ⟨keep the ham from *spoiling*⟩.

²**decay** n (15c) **1 :** gradual decline in strength, soundness, or prosperity or in degree of excellence or perfection **2 :** a wasting or wearing away **:** RUIN **3** *obs* **:** DESTRUCTION, DEATH **4 a :** ROT; *specif* : aerobic decomposition of proteins chiefly by bacteria **b :** the product of decay **5 :** a decline in health or vigor **6 :** decrease in quantity, activity, or force: as **a :** spontaneous decrease in the number of radioactive atoms in radioactive material **b :** spontaneous disintegration (as of an atom or a particle)

Dec·ca \'de-kə\ *n* [*Decca* Co., British firm which developed it] (1946) : a system of long-range navigation used chiefly in Europe that utilizes the phase differences of continuous-wave signals from synchronized ground transmitters to establish position

de·cease \di-'sēs\ *n* [ME *deces*, fr. MF, fr. L *decessus* departure, death, fr. *decedere* to depart, die, fr. *de-* + *cedere* to go] (14c) : departure from life : DEATH — **decease** *vi*

¹**de·ceased** \-'sēst\ *adj* (15c) : no longer living; *esp* : recently dead — used of persons *syn* see DEAD

²**deceased** *n, pl* **deceased** (1625) : a dead person ⟨the will of the ~⟩

de·ce·dent \di-'sē-dᵊnt\ *n* [L *decedent-, decedens*, prp. of *decedere*] (1599) : a deceased person — used chiefly in law

de·ceit \di-'sēt\ *n* [ME *deceite*, fr. MF, fr. L *decepta*, fem. of *deceptus*, pp. of *decipere*] (14c) **1 :** the act or practice of deceiving : DECEPTION **2 :** an attempt or device to deceive : TRICK **3 :** the quality of being deceitful : DECEITFULNESS

de·ceit·ful \-fəl\ *adj* (15c) : having a tendency or disposition to deceive: **a :** not honest ⟨a ~ child⟩ **b :** DECEPTIVE, MISLEADING *syn* see DISHONEST — **de·ceit·ful·ly** \-fə-lē\ *adv* — **de·ceit·ful·ness** *n*

de·ceiv·able \di-'sē-və-bəl\ *adj* (14c) **1** *archaic* : DECEITFUL, DECEPTIVE **2** *archaic* : capable of being deceived

de·ceive \di-'sēv\ *vb* **de·ceived; de·ceiv·ing** [ME, fr. MF *deceivre*, fr. L *decipere*, fr. *de-* + *capere* to take — more at HEAVE] *vt* (13c) **1** *archaic* : ENSNARE **2 a** *obs* : to be false to **b** *archaic* : to fail to fulfill **3** *obs* : CHEAT **4 :** to cause to accept as true or valid what is false or invalid **5** *archaic* : to while away ~ *vi* : to practice deceit; *also* : to give a false impression ⟨appearances can ~⟩ — **de·ceiv·er** *n* — **de·ceiv·ing·ly** \-'sē-viŋ-lē\ *adv*

syn DECEIVE, MISLEAD, DELUDE, BEGUILE mean to lead astray or frustrate usu. by underhandedness. DECEIVE implies imposing a false idea or belief that causes ignorance, bewilderment, or helplessness ⟨tried to *deceive* me about the cost⟩. MISLEAD implies a leading astray that may or may not be intentional ⟨I was *misled* by the confusing sign⟩. DELUDE implies deceiving so thoroughly as to obscure the truth ⟨we were *deluded* into thinking we were safe⟩. BEGUILE stresses the use of charm and persuasion in deceiving ⟨was *beguiled* by false promises⟩.

de·cel·er·ate \(ˌ)dē-'se-lə-ˌrāt\ *vb* **-at·ed; -at·ing** [*de-* + *accelerate*] *vt* (1899) **1 :** to reduce the speed of : slow down **2 :** to decrease the rate of progress of ~ *vi* : to move at decreasing speed — **de·cel·er·a·tion** \(ˌ)dē-ˌse-lə-'rā-shən\ *n* — **de·cel·er·a·tor** \(ˌ)dē-'se-lə-ˌrā-tər\ *n*

De·cem·ber \di-'sem-bər, dē-\ *n* [ME *Decembre*, fr. OE or OF, both fr. L *December* (tenth month), fr. *decem* ten — more at TEN] (bef. 12c) : the 12th month of the Gregorian calendar

De·cem·brist \-brist\ *n* (1877) : one taking part in the unsuccessful uprising against the Russian emperor Nicholas I in December 1825

de·cem·vir \di-'sem-vər\ *n* [ME, fr. L, back-formation fr. *decemviri*, pl., fr. *decem* + *viri*, pl. of *vir* man — more at VIRILE] (1579) : one of a ruling body of 10; *specif* : one of a body of 10 magistrates in ancient Rome — **de·cem·vi·ral** \-vər-əl\ *adj* — **de·cem·vi·rate** \-vər-ət\ *n*

de·cen·cy \'dē-sᵊn-sē\ *n, pl* **-cies** (1567) **1** *archaic* **a :** FITNESS **b** : ORDERLINESS **2 a :** the quality or state of being decent : PROPRIETY **b :** conformity to standards of taste, propriety, or quality **3 :** standard of propriety — usu. used in pl. **4** *pl* : conditions or services considered essential for a proper standard of living **5 :** literary decorum

de·cen·ni·al \di-'se-nē-əl\ *adj* (ca. 1656) **1 :** consisting of or lasting for 10 years **2 :** occurring or being done every 10 years ⟨the ~ census⟩ — **decennial** *n* — **de·cen·ni·al·ly** *adv*

de·cen·ni·um \-nē-əm\ *n, pl* **-ni·ums** *or* **-nia** \-nē-ə\ [L, fr. *decem* + *annus* year — more at ANNUAL] (1685) : a period of 10 years : DECADE

de·cent \'dē-sᵊnt\ *adj* [MF or L; MF, fr. L *decent-, decens*, prp. of *decēre* to be fitting; akin to L *decus* honor, *dignus* worthy, Gk *dokein* to seem, seem good] (1539) **1** *archaic* **a :** APPROPRIATE **b :** well-formed : HANDSOME **2 a :** conforming to standards of propriety, good taste, or morality **b :** modestly clothed **3 :** free from immodesty or obscenity **4 :** fairly good but not excellent : ADEQUATE, SATISFACTORY ⟨~ wages⟩ **5 :** marked by moral integrity, kindness, and goodwill ⟨hard-working and ~ folks⟩ *syn* see CHASTE — **de·cent·ly** *adv*

de·cen·tral·iza·tion \(ˌ)dē-ˌsen-trə-lə-'zā-shən⟩ *n* (1846) **1 :** the dispersion or distribution of functions and powers; *specif* : the delegation of power from a central authority to regional and local authorities **2** : the redistribution of population and industry from urban centers to outlying areas — **de·cen·tral·ize** \(ˌ)dē-'sen-trə-ˌliz\ *vb*

de·cep·tion \di-'sep-shən\ *n* [ME *decepcioun*, fr. MF *deception*, fr. LL *deception-, deceptio*, fr. L *decipere* to deceive] (15c) **1 a :** the act of deceiving **b :** the fact or condition of being deceived **2 :** something that deceives : TRICK — **de·cep·tion·al** \-shə-nəl\ *adj*

syn DECEPTION, FRAUD, DOUBLE-DEALING, SUBTERFUGE, TRICKERY mean the acts or practices of those who deliberately deceive. DECEPTION may or may not imply blameworthiness, since it may suggest cheating or merely tactical resource ⟨magicians are masters of *deception*⟩. FRAUD always implies guilt and often criminality in act or practice ⟨indicted for *fraud*⟩. DOUBLE-DEALING suggests treachery or at least action contrary to a professed attitude ⟨a go-between suspected of *double-dealing*⟩. SUBTERFUGE suggests the adoption of a stratagem or the telling of a lie in order to escape guilt or to gain an end ⟨obtained the papers by *subterfuge*⟩. TRICKERY implies ingenious acts intended to dupe or cheat ⟨resorted to *trickery* to gain their ends⟩.

de·cep·tive \di-'sep-tiv\ *adj* (ca. 1611) : tending or having power to deceive : MISLEADING — **de·cep·tive·ly** *adv* — **de·cep·tive·ness** *n*

¹**de·cer·e·brate** \(ˌ)dē-'ser-ə-brət, -ˌbrāt\ *adj* (1897) **1 :** characteristic of decerebration ⟨~ rigidity⟩ **2 :** having the cerebrum removed or made inactive

²**de·cer·e·brate** \(ˌ)dē-'ser-ə-ˌbrāt\ *vt* (ca. 1900) : to remove the cerebrum from; *also* : to make incapable of cerebral activity — **de·cer·e·bra·tion** \(ˌ)dē-ˌser-ə-'brā-shən\ *n*

de·cer·ti·fy \(ˌ)dē-'sər-tə-ˌfī\ *vt* (1918) : to withdraw or revoke the certification of — **de·cer·ti·fi·ca·tion** \(ˌ)dē-ˌsər-tə-fə-'kā-shən\ *n*

de·chlo·ri·nate \(ˌ)dē-'klōr-ə-ˌnāt, -'klór-\ *vt* (1941) : to remove chlorine from ⟨~ water⟩ — **de·chlo·ri·na·tion** \(ˌ)dē-ˌklōr-ə-'nā-shən, -ˌklór-\ *n*

deci- *comb form* [F *déci-*, fr. L *decimus* tenth, fr. *decem* ten — more at TEN] : tenth part ⟨*decimeter*⟩

deci·bel \'de-sə-ˌbel, -bəl\ *n* [ISV *deci-* + *bel*] (1928) **1 a :** a unit for expressing the ratio of two amounts of electric or acoustic signal power equal to 10 times the common logarithm of this ratio **:** a unit for expressing the ratio of the magnitudes of two electric voltages or currents or analogous acoustic quantities equal to 20 times the common logarithm of the voltage or current ratio **2 :** a unit for expressing the relative intensity of sounds on a scale from zero for the average least perceptible sound to about 130 for the average pain level **3 :** degree of loudness; *esp* : extremely loud sound — usu. used in pl.

de·cide \di-'sīd, dē-\ *vb* **de·cid·ed; de·cid·ing** [ME, fr. MF *decider*, fr. L *decidere*, lit., to cut off, fr. *de-* + *caedere* to cut] *vt* (14c) **1 a :** to arrive at a solution that ends uncertainty or dispute about ⟨~ what to do⟩ **b :** to select as a course of action — used with an infinitive ⟨*decided* to go⟩ **2 :** to bring to a definitive end ⟨one blow *decided* the fight⟩ **3 :** to induce to come to a choice ⟨her pleas *decided* him to help⟩ ~ *vi* : to make a choice or judgment — **de·cid·abil·i·ty** \di-ˌsī-də-'bi-lə-tē\ *n* — **de·cid·able** \-'sī-də-bəl\ *adj* — **de·cid·er** *n*

syn DECIDE, DETERMINE, SETTLE, RULE, RESOLVE mean to come or cause to come to a conclusion. DECIDE implies previous consideration of a matter causing doubt, wavering, debate, or controversy ⟨she *decided* to sell her house⟩. DETERMINE implies fixing the identity, character, scope, or direction of something ⟨*determined* the cause of the problem⟩. SETTLE implies a decision reached by someone with power to end all dispute or uncertainty ⟨the dean's decision *settled* the campus alcohol policy⟩. RULE implies a determination by judicial or administrative authority ⟨the judge *ruled* that the evidence was inadmissible⟩. RESOLVE implies an expressed or clear decision or determination to do or refrain from doing something ⟨he *resolved* to quit smoking⟩.

de·cid·ed *adj* (1790) **1 :** UNQUESTIONABLE ⟨a ~ advantage⟩ **2 :** free from doubt or wavering — **de·cid·ed·ly** *adv* — **de·cid·ed·ness** *n*

de·cid·ing *adj* (1658) : that decides : DECISIVE ⟨drive in the ~ run⟩

de·cid·ua \di-'si-jə-wə\ *n, pl* **-u·ae** \-jə-ˌwē\ [NL, fr. L, fem. of *deciduus*] (1785) **1 :** the part of the mucous membrane lining the uterus that in higher placental mammals undergoes special modifications in preparation for and during pregnancy and is cast off at parturition **2 :** the part of the mucous membrane of the uterus cast off in the process of menstruation — **de·cid·u·al** \-wəl\ *adj*

de·cid·u·ate \-wət\ *adj* (1868) : having the fetal and maternal tissues firmly interlocked so that a layer of maternal tissue is torn away at parturition and forms part of the afterbirth

de·cid·u·ous \di-'si-jə-wəs\ *adj* [L *deciduus*, fr. *decidere* to fall off, fr. *de-* + *cadere* to fall — more at CHANCE] (1688) **1 :** falling off or shed seasonally or at a certain stage of development in the life cycle ⟨~ leaves⟩ ⟨~ teeth⟩ **2 a :** having deciduous parts ⟨~ trees⟩ **b :** having the dominant plants deciduous ⟨a ~ forest⟩ **3 :** EPHEMERAL — **de·cid·u·ous·ness** *n*

deci·gram \'de-sə-ˌgram\ *n* [F *décigramme*, fr. *déci-* + *gramme* gram] (1810) — see METRIC SYSTEM table

dec·ile \'de-ˌsil, -səl\ *n* [L *decem* ten — more at TEN] (1882) : any one of nine numbers that divide a frequency distribution into 10 classes such that each contains the same number of individuals; *also* : any one of these 10 classes — **decile** *adj*

deci·li·ter \'de-sə-ˌlē-tər\ *n* [F *décilitre*, fr. *déci-* + *litre* liter] (1801) — see METRIC SYSTEM table

de·cil·lion \di-'sil-yən\ *n, often attrib* [L *decem* + E *-illion* (as in *million*)] (1847) — see NUMBER table

¹**dec·i·mal** \'de-sə-məl, 'des-məl\ *adj* [F *décimal*, fr. ML *decimalis* of a tithe, fr. L *decima* tithe — more at DIME] (1608) **:** numbered or proceeding by tens: **a :** based on the number 10; *also* : expressed in or utilizing a decimal system esp. with a decimal point **b :** subdivided into 10th or 100th units ⟨~ coinage⟩ — **dec·i·mal·ly** \-mə-lē\ *adv*

²**decimal** *n* (1651) : any real number expressed in base 10; *esp* : DECIMAL FRACTION

decimal fraction *n* (1660) : a fraction (as .25 = ²⁵/₁₀₀ or .025 = ²⁵/₁₀₀₀) or mixed number (as 3.025 = 3²⁵/₁₀₀₀) in which the denominator is a power of 10 usu. expressed by use of the decimal point

dec·i·mal·iza·tion \ˌde-sə-mə-lə-'zā-shən\ *n* (1855) : conversion (as of a currency) to a decimal system — **dec·i·mal·ize** \'de-sə-mə-ˌliz\ *vt*

decimal point *n* (ca. 1864) : a period, centered dot, or in some countries a comma at the left of a proper decimal fraction (as .678) or between the parts of a mixed number (as 3.678) expressed by a whole number and a decimal fraction

decimal system *n* (1864) **1 :** a number system that uses a notation in which each number is expressed in base 10 by using one of the first nine integers or 0 in each place and letting each place value be a power of 10 **2 :** a system of measurement or currency in which the basic units increase by powers of 10

dec·i·mate \'de-sə-ˌmāt\ *vt* **-mat·ed; -mat·ing** [L *decimatus*, pp. of *decimare*, fr. *decimus* tenth, fr. *decem* ten] (1660) **1 :** to select by lot and kill every tenth man of **2 :** to exact a tax of 10 percent from ⟨poor as a *decimated* Cavalier —John Dryden⟩ **3 a :** to reduce drastically esp. in number ⟨cholera *decimated* the population⟩ **b :** to destroy a large part of ⟨firebombs *decimated* large sections of the city⟩ — **dec·i·ma·tion** \ˌde-sə-'mā-shən\ *n*

deci·me·ter \'de-sə-ˌmē-tər\ *n* [F *décimètre*, fr. *déci-* deci- + *mètre* meter] (1809) — see METRIC SYSTEM table

de·ci·pher \dē-'si-fər\ *vt* (1545) **1 :** DECODE 1a **2** *obs* : DEPICT **3 a** : to make out the meaning of despite indistinctness or obscurity **b**

: to interpret the meaning of — **de·ci·pher·able** \-f(ə-)rə-bəl\ *adj* — **de·ci·pher·er** \-fər-ər\ *n* — **de·ci·pher·ment** \-fər-mənt\ *n*

¹de·ci·sion \di-'si-zhən\ *n* [MF, fr. L *decision-, decisio*, fr. *decidere* to decide] (15c) **1 a** : the act or process of deciding **b** : a determination arrived at after consideration : CONCLUSION **2** : a report of a conclusion **3** : promptness and firmness in deciding : DETERMINATION **4 a** : WIN; *specif* : a victory in boxing decided on points **b** : a win or loss officially credited to a pitcher in baseball — **de·ci·sion·al** \-'si-zhnəl, -'si-zhə-nᵊl\ *adj*

²decision *vt* (1943) : to win a decision over (a boxing opponent)

decision theory *n* (1961) : a branch of statistical theory concerned with quantifying the process of making choices between alternatives

decision tree *n* (1964) : a tree diagram which is used for making decisions in business or computer programming and in which the branches represent choices with associated risks, costs, results, or probabilities

de·ci·sive \di-'sī-siv\ *adj* (1611) **1** : having the power or quality of deciding **2** : RESOLUTE, DETERMINED **3** : UNMISTAKABLE, UNQUESTIONABLE ⟨a ~ superiority⟩ *syn* see CONCLUSIVE — **de·ci·sive·ly** *adv* — **de·ci·sive·ness** *n*

¹deck \'dek\ *n* [ME *dekke* covering of a ship, fr. (assumed) MD *dec* covering, prob. fr. MLG *vordeck*, fr. *vordecken* to cover, fr. *vor-* for- + *decken* to cover; akin to OHG *decchen* to cover — more at THATCH] (1509) **1** : a platform in a ship serving usu. as a structural element and forming the floor for its compartments **2** : something resembling the deck of a ship: as **a** : a story or tier of a building **b** : the roadway of a bridge **c** : a flat floored roofless area adjoining a house **d** : the lid of the compartment at the rear of the body of an automobile; *also* : the compartment **e** : a layer of clouds **3 a** : a pack of playing cards **b** : a packet of narcotics **4** : TAPE DECK — **on deck 1** : ready for duty **2** : next in line : next in turn

²deck *vt* [D *dekken* to cover; akin to OHG *decchen*] (1513) **1** *obs* : COVER **2 a** : to clothe elegantly ⟨*~ed* out in furs⟩ **b** : DECORATE ⟨*~* the halls with boughs of holly —*English carol*⟩ **c** : to portray or present with embellishments **3** [¹*deck*]: to furnish with or as if with a deck **4** [¹*deck*]: to knock down forcibly : FLOOR ⟨*~ed* him with one punch⟩ *syn* see ADORN

deck chair *n* (1884) : a folding chair often having an adjustable leg rest

deck·er \'de-kər\ *n* (1790) : something having a specified number of decks, levels, floors, or layers — used in combination ⟨many of the city's buses are double= *deckers*⟩

deck·hand \'dek-,hand\ *n* (1844) : a seaman who performs manual duties

deck·house \-,haüs\ *n* (1856) : a superstructure on a ship's upper deck

deck·ing \'de-kiŋ\ *n* (1580) : DECK; *also* : material for a deck

deck·le \'de-kəl\ *n* [G *Deckel*, lit., cover, fr. *decken* to cover, fr. OHG *decchen*] (1816) : a frame around the edges of a mold used in making paper by hand; *also* : either of the bands around the edge of the wire of a papermaking machine that determine the width of the web

deck chair

deckle edge *n* (ca. 1874) : the rough untrimmed edge of paper left by a deckle or produced artificially — **deck·le·edged** \-'ejd\ *adj*

deck tennis *n* [fr. its being played on the decks of ocean liners] (1927) : a game in which players toss a ring or quoit back and forth over a net stretched across a small court

de·claim \di-'klām, dē-\ *vb* [ME *declamen*, fr. L *declamare*, fr. *de-* + *clamare* to cry out; akin to L *calare* to call — more at LOW] *vi* (14c) **1** : to speak rhetorically; *specif* : to recite something as an exercise in elocution **2** : to speak pompously or bombastically : HARANGUE ~ *vt* : to deliver rhetorically; *specif* : to recite in elocution — **de·claim·er** *n* — **dec·la·ma·tion** \,de-klə-'mā-shən\ *n*

de·clam·a·to·ry \di-'kla-mə-,tōr-ē, -,tor-\ *adj* (1581) : of, relating to, or marked by declamation or rhetorical display

de·clar·ant \di-'klar-ənt, -'kler-\ *n* (1681) : a person who makes a statement or declaration esp. in connection with a legal proceeding

dec·la·ra·tion \,de-klə-'rā-shən\ *n* (15c) **1** : the act of declaring : ANNOUNCEMENT **2 a** : the first pleading in a common-law action **b** : a statement made by a party to a legal transaction usu. not under oath **3 a** : something that is declared **b** : the document containing such a declaration

de·clar·a·tive \di-'klar-ə-tiv, -'kler-\ *adj* (1628) : making a declaration : DECLARATORY ⟨a ~ sentence⟩ — **de·clar·a·tive·ly** *adv*

de·clar·a·to·ry \-ə-,tōr-ē, -,tor-\ *adj* (15c) **1** : serving to declare, set forth, or explain **2 a** : declaring what is the existing law ⟨~ statute⟩ **b** : declaring a legal right or interpretation ⟨a ~ judgment⟩

de·clare \di-'klar, -'kler\ *vb* **de·clared; de·clar·ing** [ME, fr. MF & L; MF *declarer*, fr. L *declarare*, fr. *de-* + *clarare* to make visible, fr. *clarus* clear — more at CLEAR] *vt* (14c) **1** : to make known formally, officially, or explicitly **2** *obs* : to make clear **3** : to make evident : SHOW **4** : to state emphatically : AFFIRM ⟨~s his innocence⟩ **5** : to make a full statement of (one's taxable or dutiable property) **6 a** : to announce (as a trump suit) in a card game **b** : MELD **7** : to make payable ⟨~ a dividend⟩ ~ *vi* **1** : to make a declaration **2** : to avow one's opinion or support — **de·clar·able** \-'klar-ə-bəl, -'kler-\ *adj*

syn DECLARE, ANNOUNCE, PROCLAIM, PROMULGATE mean to make known publicly. DECLARE implies explicitness and usu. formality in making known ⟨the referee *declared* the contest a draw⟩. ANNOUNCE implies the declaration of something for the first time ⟨*announced* their engagement at a party⟩. PROCLAIM implies declaring clearly, forcefully, and authoritatively ⟨the president *proclaimed* a national day of mourning⟩. PROMULGATE implies the proclaiming of a dogma, doctrine, or law ⟨*promulgated* an edict of religious toleration⟩. *syn* see in addition ASSERT

de·clar·er \di-'klar-ər, -'kler-\ *n* (14c) : one that declares; *specif* : the bridge player who names the trump and plays both his own hand and that of the dummy

de·class \(,)dē-'klas\ *vt* (1888) : to remove from a class; *esp* : to assign to a lower social status

dé·clas·sé \,dā-,kla-'sā, -,klä-\ *adj* [F, fr. pp. of *déclasser* to declass] (1887) **1** : fallen or lowered in class, rank, or social position **2** : of inferior status

de·clas·si·fy \(,)dē-'kla-sə-,fī\ *vt* (1945) : to remove or reduce the security classification of ⟨~ a secret document⟩ — **de·clas·si·fi·ca·tion** \(,)dē-,kla-sə-fə-'kā-shən\ *n*

de·claw \-'klo\ *vt* (1953) : to remove the claws of (as a cat) surgically

de·clen·sion \di-'klen(t)-shən\ *n* [ME *declenson*, modif. of MF *declinaison*, fr. L *declination-, declinatio* grammatical inflection, turning aside, fr. *declinare* to inflect, turn aside] (15c) **1 a** : noun, adjective, or pronoun inflection esp. in some prescribed order of the forms **b** : a class of nouns or adjectives having the same type of inflectional forms **2** : a falling off or away : DETERIORATION **3** : DESCENT, SLOPE — **de·clen·sion·al** \-'klen(t)-shə-nᵊl\ *adj*

dec·li·na·tion \,de-klə-'nā-shən\ *n* [ME *declinacioun*, fr. MF *declination*, fr. L *declination-, declinatio* angle of the heavens, turning aside] (14c) **1** : angular distance north or south from the celestial equator measured along a great circle passing through the celestial poles **2** : a turning aside or swerving **3** : DETERIORATION ⟨moral ~⟩ **4** : a bending downward : INCLINATION **5** : a formal refusal **6** : the angle formed between a magnetic needle and the geographical meridian — **dec·li·na·tion·al** \-shnəl, -shə-nᵊl\ *adj*

¹de·cline \di-'klīn, dē-\ *vb* **de·clined; de·clin·ing** [ME, fr. MF *decliner*, fr. L *declinare* to turn aside, inflect, fr. *de-* + *clinare* to incline — more at LEAN] *vi* (14c) **1** *archaic* : to turn from a straight course : STRAY **2 a** : to slope downward : DESCEND **b** : to bend down : DROOP **c** : to stoop to what is unworthy **3 a** *of a celestial body* : to sink toward setting **b** : to draw toward a close : WANE ⟨the day *declined*⟩ **4** : to tend toward an inferior state or weaker condition ⟨his health *declined*⟩ **5** : to withhold consent **6** : to become less in amount ⟨prices *declined*⟩ ~ *vt* **1** : to give in prescribed order the grammatical forms of (a noun, pronoun, or adjective) **2** *obs* **a** : AVERT **b** : AVOID **3** : to cause to bend or bow downward **4 a** : to refuse to undertake, undergo, engage in, or comply with **b** : to refuse esp. courteously ⟨~ an invitation⟩ — **de·clin·able** \-'klī-nə-bəl\ *adj* — **de·clin·er** \-'klī-nər\ *n*

syn DECLINE, REFUSE, REJECT, REPUDIATE, SPURN mean to turn away by not accepting, receiving, or considering. DECLINE often implies courteous refusal esp. of offers or invitations ⟨*declined* his party's nomination⟩. REFUSE suggests more positiveness or ungraciousness and often implies the denial of something asked for ⟨*refused* to lend them the money⟩. REJECT implies a peremptory refusal by sending away or discarding ⟨*rejected* the manuscript as unpublishable⟩. REPUDIATE implies a casting off or disowning as untrue, unauthorized, or unworthy of acceptance ⟨teenagers who *repudiate* the values of their parents⟩. SPURN stresses contempt or disdain in rejection or repudiation ⟨*spurned* his overtures of friendship⟩.

²decline *also* 'dē-,klīn\ *n* (14c) **1** : the process of declining: **a** : a gradual physical or mental sinking and wasting away **b** : a change to a lower state or level **2** : the period during which something is deteriorating or approaching its end **3** : a downward slope **4** : a wasting disease; *esp* : pulmonary tuberculosis *syn* see DETERIORATION

de·clin·ing \-niŋ\ *adj* (1593) : of or relating to the period during which something is deteriorating or nearing its end ⟨her ~ years⟩

de·cliv·i·tous \di-'kliv-ət-əs\ *adj* (1799) : moderately steep

de·cliv·i·ty \-ət-ē\ *n, pl* **-ties** [L *declivitat-, declivitas*, fr. *declivis* sloping down, fr. *de-* + *clivus* slope, hill; akin to L *clinare* (1612) **1** : downward inclination **2** : a descending slope

de·co \'dek-(,)kō, dā-'kō, 'dā-,\ *n, often cap* (1969) : ART DECO

de·coct \di-'käkt\ *vt* [L *decoctus*, pp. of *decoquere*, fr. *de-* + *coquere* to cook — more at COOK] (15c) **1** : to extract the flavor of by boiling **2** : BOIL DOWN, CONCENTRATE

de·coc·tion \di-'käk-shən\ *n* (15c) **1** : an extract obtained by decocting **2** : the act or process of decocting

de·code \(,)dē-'kōd\ *vt* (1896) **1 a** : to convert (as a coded message) into intelligible form **b** : to recognize and interpret (an electronic signal) **2 a** : DECIPHER 3a **b** : to discover the underlying meaning of ⟨~ the play's imagery⟩

de·cod·er \-'kō-dər\ *n* (1920) : one that decodes; *esp* : an electronic device for unscrambling a television transmission

de·col·late \di-'käl-,āt, -'ke-,lāt\ *vt* **-lat·ed; -lat·ing** [L *decollatus*, pp. of *decollare*, fr. *de-* + *collum* neck — more at COLLAR] (1599) : BEHEAD — **de·col·la·tion** \,dē-kä-'lā-shən\ *n*

dé·col·le·tage \(,)dā-,kä-lə-'täzh, (,)dā-,kol-'täzh, ,de-klə-\ *n* [F, action of cutting or wearing a low neckline, fr. *décolleter*] (1894) **1** : the low= cut neckline of a dress **2** : a décolleté dress **3** : ¹BUST 2

¹dé·col·le·té \(,)dā-,käl-'tā, -,kol-, -lə-'tā; *also* dā-'kol-tā\ *adj* [F, fr. pp. of *décolleter* to give a low neckline to, fr. *dé-* de- + *collet* collar, fr. OF *colet*, fr. *col* collar, neck, fr. L *collum* neck] (1831) **1** : wearing a strapless or low-necked dress **2** : having a low-cut neckline

²dé·col·le·té *also* **de·col·le·te** \(,)dā-,kä-lə-'tā\ *adj* (1900) : DÉCOLLETAGE

de·col·o·nize \(,)dē-'kä-lə-,nīz\ *vt* (1853) : to free from colonial status — **de·col·o·ni·za·tion** \(,)dē-,kä-lə-nə-'zā-shən\ *n*

de·col·or·ize \(,)dē-'kə-lə-,rīz\ *vt* **-ized; -iz·ing** (1839) : to remove color from ⟨~ vinegar by adsorption of impurities on activated charcoal⟩ — **de·col·or·iza·tion** \(,)dē-,kə-lə-rə-'zā-shən\ *n* — **de·col·or·iz·er** \(')dē-'kə-lə-,rī-zər\ *n*

de·com·mis·sion \,dē-kə-'mi-shən\ *vt* (1922) : to remove (as a ship or nuclear power plant) from service

de·com·pen·sa·tion \(,)dē-,käm-pən-'sā-shən, -,pen-\ *n* [ISV] (ca. 1903) : loss of physiological compensation or psychological balance; *esp* : inability of the heart to maintain adequate circulation — **de·com·pen·sate** \(,)dē-'käm-pən-,sāt, -,pen-\ *vb*

de·com·pose \,dē-kəm-'pōz\ *vb* [F *décomposer*, fr. *dé-* de + *composer* to compose] *vt* (ca. 1751) **1** : to separate into constituent parts or elements or into simpler compounds ⟨~ water by electrolysis⟩ ⟨~ a word into its base and affixes⟩ **2** : ROT ~ *vi* : to break up into constituent

\ə\ abut \ᵊ\ kitten, F table \ər\ further \a\ ash \ā\ ace \ä\ mop, mar
\aů\ out \ch\ chin \e\ bet \ē\ easy \g\ go \i\ hit \ī\ ice \j\ job
\ŋ\ sing \ō\ go \ò\ law \òi\ boy \th\ thin \t̲h̲\ the \ü\ loot \ů\ foot
\y\ yet \zh\ vision \å, k̲, ⁿ, œ, œ̄, ɵ, ue, ūe, ʸ\ see Guide to Pronunciation

parts by or as if by a chemical process : DECAY, ROT ⟨fruit ~s⟩ *syn* see DECAY — **de·com·pos·abil·i·ty** \-,pō-zə-'bi-lə-tē\ *n* — **de·com·pos·able** \-'pō-zə-bəl\ *adj* — **de·com·po·si·tion** \(,)dē-,käm-pə-'zi-shən\ *n*

de·com·pos·er \,dē-kəm-'pō-zər\ *n* (1959) : any of various organisms (as many bacteria and fungi) that return constituents of organic substances to ecological cycles by feeding on and breaking down dead protoplasm

de·com·pound \,dē-'käm-,paùnd, ,dē-kəm-'\ *adj* (ca. 1793) *of a leaf* : having divisions that are themselves compound

de·com·press \,dē-kəm-'pres\ *vt* (1905) : to release from pressure or compression ~ *vi* : to undergo release from pressure; *esp* : RELAX ⟨need a week off to ~⟩ — **de·com·pres·sion** \-'pre-shən\ *n*

decompression sickness *n* (ca. 1941) : [2]BEND 3, AEROEMBOLISM

de·con·cen·trate \(,)dē-'kän(t)-sən-,trāt\ *vt* (ca. 1889) : to reduce or abolish the concentration of — DECENTRALIZE — **de·con·cen·tra·tion** \(,)dē-,kän(t)-sən-'trā-shən\ *n*

de·con·di·tion \,dē-kən-'di-shən\ *vt* (1941) **1** : to cause extinction of (a conditioned response) **2** : to cause to lose physical fitness

de·con·ges·tant \,dē-kən-'jes-tənt\ *n* (1947) : an agent that relieves congestion (as of mucous membranes) — **decongestant** *adj*

de·con·ges·tion \,dē-kən-'jes(h)-chən\ *n* (1908) : the process of relieving congestion — **de·con·gest** \-'jest\ *vt* — **de·con·ges·tive** \-'jes-tiv\ *adj*

de·con·se·crate \(,)dē-'kän(t)-sə-,krāt\ *vt* (1876) : to remove the sacred character of ⟨~ a church⟩ — **de·con·se·cra·tion** \(,)dē-,kän(t)-sə-'krā-shən\ *n*

de·con·struct \,dē-kən-'strəkt\ *vt* (1973) : to discuss (as a work of literature) using the methods of deconstruction — **de·con·struc·tive** \-tiv\ *adj* — **de·con·struc·tor** \-tər\ *n*

de·con·struc·tion \,dē-kən-'strək-shən\ *n* [F *déconstruction*, fr. *dé-* de- + *construction*] (1973) : a method of literary criticism that assumes language refers only to itself rather than to an extratextual reality, that asserts multiple conflicting interpretations of a text, and that bases such interpretations on the philosophical, political, or social implications of the use of language in the text rather than on the author's intention — **de·con·struc·tion·ist** \-shə-nist\ *n*

de·con·tam·i·nate \,dē-kən-'ta-mə-,nāt\ *vt* (1936) : to rid of contamination (as radioactive material) — **de·con·tam·i·na·tion** \-,ta-mə-'nā-shən\ *n* — **de·con·tam·i·na·tor** \-'ta-mə-,nā-tər\ *n*

de·con·trol \,dē-kən-'trōl\ *vt* (1919) : to end control of — **decontrol** *n*

de·cor *or* **dé·cor** \dā-'kòr, di-'; 'dē-,kòr, 'dā-,\ \ *n* [F *décor*, fr. *décorer* to decorate, fr. L *decorare*] (1897) **1** : a stage setting **2 a** : DECORATION 2 **b** : the style and layout of interior furnishings

dec·o·rate \'de-kə-,rāt\ *vt* **-rat·ed; -rat·ing** [L *decoratus*, pp. of *decorare*, fr. *decor-, decus* ornament, honor — more at DECENT] (1530) **1** : to add honor to **2** : to furnish with something ornamental ⟨~ a room⟩ **3** : to award a mark of honor to *syn* see ADORN

dec·o·ra·tion \,de-kə-'rā-shən\ *n* (1530) **1** : the act or process of decorating **2** : something that adorns, enriches, or beautifies : ORNAMENT **3** : a badge of honor (as a U.S. military award)

Decoration Day *n* [fr. the custom of decorating graves on this day] (1871) : MEMORIAL DAY

dec·o·ra·tive \'de-k(ə-)rə-tiv, 'de-kə-,rā-\ *adj* (1791) : serving to decorate; *esp* : purely ornamental — **dec·o·ra·tive·ly** *adv* — **dec·o·ra·tive·ness** *n*

decorative art *n* (1967) **1** : an art concerned primarily with the creation of useful items (as furniture, ceramics, and textiles) — usu. used in pl. **2** : objects of decorative art

[1]dec·o·ra·tor \'de-kə-,rā-tər\ *n* (ca. 1755) : one that decorates; *esp* : one that designs or executes interiors and their furnishings

[2]decorator *adj* (1950) : suitable for interior decoration ⟨~ fabrics⟩

dec·o·rous \'de-kə-rəs *also* di-'kōr-əs *or* -'kòr-\ *adj* [L *decorus*, fr. *decor* beauty, grace; akin to L *decēre* to be fitting — more at DECENT] (1673) : marked by propriety and good taste : CORRECT ⟨~ conduct⟩ — **dec·o·rous·ly** *adv* — **dec·o·rous·ness** *n*

de·cor·ti·ca·tion \,dē-,kòr-tə-'kā-shən\ *n* [L *decortication-, decorticatio*, fr. *decorticare* to remove the bark from, fr. *de-* + *cortic-, cortex* bark — more at CUIRASS] (ca. 1623) **1** : the act or process of removing the outer coverings (as bark or husks) from something (as fiber or seed) **2** : the surgical removal of the cortex of an organ (as the brain), an enveloping membrane, or a constrictive fibrinous covering — **de·cor·ti·cate** \(,)dē-'kòr-tə-,kāt\ *vt* — **de·cor·ti·ca·tor** \-,kā-tər\ *n*

de·co·rum \di-'kòr-əm, -'kòr-\ *n* [L, fr. neut. of *decorus*] (1576) **1** : literary and dramatic propriety : FITNESS **2** : propriety and good taste in conduct or appearance **3** : ORDERLINESS **4** *pl* : the conventions of polite behavior

de·cou·page *or* **dé·cou·page** \dā-(,)kü-'päzh\ *n* [F *découpage*, lit., act of cutting out, fr. MF, fr. *decouper* to cut out, fr. *de-* + *couper* to cut — more at COPE] (1946) **1** : the art of decorating surfaces by applying cutouts (as of paper) and then coating with usu. several layers of finish (as lacquer or varnish) **2** : work produced by decoupage — **decoupage** *or* **découpage** *vt*

de·cou·ple \(,)dē-'kə-pəl\ *vt* (1953) : to eliminate the interrelationship of : SEPARATE

[1]de·coy \'dē-,kòi, di-'\ *n* [prob. fr. D *de kooi*, lit., the cage, fr. *de*, masc. def. art. (akin to OE *thæt*, neut. def. art.) + *kooi* cage, fr. L *cavea* — more at THAT, CAGE] (1641) **1** : a pond into which wildfowl are lured for capture **2** : someone or something used to lure or lead another into a trap; *esp* : an artificial bird used to attract live birds within shot **3** : someone or something used to draw attention away from another

[2]de·coy \'dē-,kòi, di-,\ *vt* (ca. 1674) : to lure by or as if by a decoy : ENTICE *syn* see LURE

[1]de·crease \di-'krēs, 'dē-,\ *vb* **de·creased; de·creas·ing** [ME *decreessen*, fr. (assumed) AF *decreistre*, fr. L *decrescere*, fr. *de-* + *crescere* to grow — more at CRESCENT] *vi* (14c) : to grow progressively less (as in size, amount, number, or intensity) ~ *vt* : to cause to decrease — **de·creas·ing·ly** \di-'krē-siŋ-lē, dē-\ *adv*

syn DECREASE, LESSEN, DIMINISH, REDUCE, ABATE, DWINDLE mean to grow or make less. DECREASE suggests a progressive decline in size, amount, numbers, or intensity ⟨slowly *decreased* the amount of pressure⟩. LESSEN suggests a decline in amount rather than in number ⟨has been unable to *lessen* her debt⟩. DIMINISH emphasizes a perceptible loss and implies its subtraction from a total ⟨his visual acuity has *diminished*⟩. REDUCE implies a bringing down or lowering ⟨you must *reduce*

your caloric intake⟩. ABATE implies a reducing of something excessive or oppressive in force or amount ⟨the storm *abated*⟩. DWINDLE implies progressive lessening and is applied to things growing visibly smaller ⟨their provisions *dwindled* slowly⟩.

[2]de·crease \'dē-,krēs, di-'\ *n* (14c) **1** : the process of decreasing **2** : an amount of diminution : REDUCTION

[1]de·cree \di-'krē\ *n* [ME, fr. MF *decré*, fr. L *decretum*, fr. neut. of *decretus*, pp. of *decernere* to decide, fr. *de-* + *cernere* to sift, decide — more at CERTAIN] (14c) **1** : an order usu. having the force of law **2 a** : a religious ordinance enacted by council or titular head **b** : a foreordaining will **3 a** : a judicial decision of the Roman emperor **b** : a judicial decision esp. in an equity or probate court

[2]de·cree *vb* **de·creed; de·cree·ing** *vt* (14c) **1** : to command or enjoin by or as if by decree ⟨~ an amnesty⟩ **2** : to determine or order judicially ⟨~ a punishment⟩ ~ *vi* : ORDAIN — **de·cre·er** \-'krē-ər\ *n*

de·cree–law \di-'krē-,lò\ *n* (1926) : a decree of a ruler or ministry having the force of a law enacted by the legislature

dec·re·ment \'de-krə-mənt\ *n* [L *decrementum*, fr. *decrescere*] (1610) **1** : a gradual decrease in quality or quantity **2 a** : the quantity lost by diminution or waste **b** : the amount of decrease (as of a variable) — **dec·re·men·tal** \,de-krə-'men-t[?]l\ *adj*

de·crep·it \di-'kre-pət\ *adj* [ME, fr. MF, fr. L *decrepitus*] (15c) **1** : wasted and weakened by or as if by the infirmities of old age **2 a** : impaired by use or wear : WORN-OUT **b** : fallen into ruin or disrepair **3** : DILAPIDATED, RUN-DOWN *syn* see WEAK — **de·crep·it·ly** *adv*

de·crep·i·tate \di-'kre-pə-,tāt\ *vb* **-tat·ed; -tat·ing** [prob. fr. (assumed) NL *decrepitatus*, pp. of *decrepitare*, fr. L *de-* + *crepitare* to crackle — more at CREPITATE] *vt* (1646) : to roast or calcine (as salt) so as to cause crackling or until crackling stops ~ *vi* : to become decrepitated — **de·crep·i·ta·tion** \-,kre-pə-'tā-shən\ *n*

de·crep·i·tude \di-'kre-pə-,tüd, -,tyüd\ *n* (1603) : the quality or state of being decrepit

[1]de·cre·scen·do \,dā-krə-'shen-(,)dō\ *n, pl* **-dos** [It, lit., decreasing, fr. L *decrescendum*, gerund of *decrescere*] (ca. 1880) **1** : a gradual decrease in volume of a musical passage **2** : a decrescendo musical passage

[2]decrescendo *adv or adj* (ca. 1890) : with a decrease in volume — used as a direction in music

de·cres·cent \di-'kre-s[?]nt\ *adj* [alter. of earlier *decressant*, prob. fr. AF, prp. of (assumed) AF *decreistre* to decrease] (1610) : becoming less by gradual diminution : DECREASING, WANING

de·cre·tal \di-'krē-t[?]l, dē-'kri-t[?]l\ *n* [ME, fr. MF, fr. LL *decretalis* of a decree, fr. L *decretum* decree] (14c) : DECREE; *esp* : a papal letter giving an authoritative decision on a point of canon law

de·cre·tive \-'krē-tiv\ *adj* (1609) : having the force of a decree : DECRETORY

de·cre·to·ry \'de-krə-,tòr-ē, -,tòr-; di-'krē-tər-ē\ *adj* (ca. 1631) : relating to or fixed by a decree or decision

de·crim·i·nal·ize \(,)dē-'kri-mə-nə-,līz, -'krim-nəl-\ *vt* (1969) : to remove or reduce the criminal classification or status of; *esp* : to repeal a strict ban on while keeping under some form of regulation ⟨~ the possession of marijuana⟩ — **de·crim·i·nal·iza·tion** \(,)dē-,kri-mə-nə-lə-'zā-shən, -,krim-nəl-\ *n*

de·cry \di-'krī, dē-\ *vt* [F *décrier*, fr. OF *descrier*, fr. *des-* de- + *crier* to cry] (1614) **1** : to depreciate (as a coin) officially or publicly **2** : to express strong disapproval of ⟨~ the emphasis on sex⟩ — **de·cri·er** \-'krī(-ə)r\ *n*

syn DECRY, DEPRECIATE, DISPARAGE, BELITTLE mean to express a low opinion of. DECRY implies open condemnation with intent to discredit ⟨*decried* their defeatist attitude⟩. DEPRECIATE implies a representing as being of less value than commonly believed ⟨critics *depreciate* his plays for being unabashedly sentimental⟩. DISPARAGE implies depreciation by indirect means such as slighting or invidious comparison ⟨*disparaged* polo as a game for the rich⟩. BELITTLE usu. suggests a contemptuous or envious attitude ⟨*belittled* the achievements of others⟩.

de·crypt \(,)dē-'kript\ *vt* [ISV *de-* + *cryptogram, cryptograph*] (1935) : DECODE 1a — **de·cryp·tion** \-'krip-shən\ *n*

de·cum·bent \di-'kəm-bənt, dē-\ *adj* [L *decumbent-, decumbens*, prp. of *decumbere* to lie down, fr. *de-* + *-cumbere* to lie down; akin to L *cubare* to lie] (1656) **1** : lying down **2** *of a plant* : reclining on the ground but with ascending apex or extremity

dec·u·ple \'de-kyə-pəl\ *adj* [F *décuple*, fr. MF, fr. LL *decuplus*, fr. L *decem* ten + *-uplus* (as in *quadruple* quadruple)] (1613) **1** : TENFOLD **2** : taken in groups of 10

de·cu·ri·on \di-'kyùr-ē-ən\ *n* [ME *decurioun*] (L *decurion-, decurio*, fr. *decuria* division of ten, fr. *decem*] (14c) **1** : a Roman cavalry officer in command of 10 men **2** : a member of a Roman senate

de·cur·rent \di-'kər-ənt, -'kə-rənt\ *adj* [L *decurrent-, decurrens*, prp. of *decurrere* to run down, fr. *de-* + *currere* to run — more at CAR] (ca. 1753) : running or extending downward along the stem ⟨~ leaves⟩

de·curved \(,)dē-'kərvd\ *adj* [part trans. of LL *decurvatus*, fr. L *de-* + *curvatus* curved] (1835) : curved downward : bent down

[1]de·cus·sate \'de-kə-,sāt, di-'kə-,sāt\ *vb* **-sat·ed; -sat·ing** [L *decussatus*, pp. of *decussare* to arrange crosswise, fr. *decussis* the number ten, numeral X, intersection, fr. *decem* + *ass-, as* unit — more at ACE] (1658) : INTERSECT, CROSS

[2]de·cus·sate \'de-kə-,sāt, di-'kə-sət\ *adj* (ca. 1823) : arranged in pairs each at right angles to the next pair above or below ⟨~ leaves⟩

de·cus·sa·tion \,de-kə-'sā-shən, ,dē-,kə-\ *n* (ca. 1656) **1** : the action of crossing (as of nerve fibers) esp. in the form of an X **2** : a crossed tract of nerve fibers passing between centers on opposite sides of the nervous system

[1]ded·i·cate \'de-di-kət\ *adj* [ME, fr. L *dedicatus*, pp. of *dedicare* to dedicate, fr. *de-* + *dicare* to proclaim, dedicate — more at DICTION] (14c) : DEDICATED

[2]ded·i·cate \'de-di-,kāt *also* 'dē-,dē-\ *vt* **-cat·ed; -cat·ing** (15c) **1** : to devote to the worship of a divine being; *specif* : to set apart (a church) to sacred uses with solemn rites **2 a** : to set apart to a definite use ⟨money *dedicated* to their vacation fund⟩ **b** : to commit to a goal or way of life ⟨ready to ~ his life to public service⟩ **3** : to inscribe or address by way of compliment ⟨~ a book to a friend⟩ **4** : to open to public use *syn* see DEVOTE — **ded·i·ca·tor** \-,kā-tər\ *n*

ded·i·cat·ed *adj* (ca. 1600) **1** : devoted to a cause, ideal, or purpose : ZEALOUS ⟨a ~ scholar⟩ **2** : given over to a particular purpose ⟨a ~ process control computer⟩ — **ded·i·cat·ed·ly** *adv*

ded·i·ca·tee \,de-di-kə-'tē\ *n* (1760) : one to whom a thing is dedicated

ded·i·ca·tion \,de-di-'kā-shən\ *n* (14c) **1** : an act or rite of dedicating to a divine being or to a sacred use **2** : a devoting or setting aside for a particular purpose **3** : a name and often a message prefixed to a literary, musical, or artistic production in tribute to a person or cause **4** : self-sacrificing devotion — **ded·i·ca·to·ry** \'de-di-kə-,tōr-ē, -,tor-\ *adj*

de·dif·fer·en·ti·a·tion \(,)dē-,di-fə-,ren-chē-'ā-shən\ *n* (1915) : reversion of specialized structures (as cells) to a more generalized or primitive condition often as a preliminary to major physiological or structural change — **de·dif·fer·en·ti·ate** \-'ren-chē-,āt\ *vi*

de·duce \di-'düs, dē-; *chiefly Brit* -'dyüs\ *vt* **de·duced; de·duc·ing** [ME, fr. L *deducere*, lit., to lead away, fr. *de-* + *ducere* to lead — more at TOW] (15c) **1** : to determine by deduction; *specif* : to infer from a general principle **2** : to trace the course of *syn* see INFER — **de·duc·ible** \-'d(y)ü-sə-bəl\ *adj*

de·duct \di-'dəkt, dē-\ *vt* [L *deductus*, pp. of *deducere*] (15c) **1** : to take away (an amount) from a total : SUBTRACT **2** : DEDUCE, INFER

[1]de·duct·ible \di-'dək-tə-bəl, dē-\ *adj* (1856) : allowable as a deduction — **de·duct·ibil·i·ty** \-,dək-tə-'bi-lə-tē\ *n*

[2]deductible *n* (1929) : a clause in an insurance policy that relieves the insurer of responsibility for an initial specified loss of the kind insured against; *also* : the amount of the loss specified in such a clause

de·duc·tion \di-'dək-shən, dē-\ *n* (15c) **1 a** : an act of taking away ⟨~ of legitimate business expenses⟩ **b** : something that is or may be subtracted ⟨~s from his taxable income⟩ **2 a** : the deriving of a conclusion by reasoning; *specif* : inference in which the conclusion about particulars follows necessarily from general or universal premises — compare INDUCTION **b** : a conclusion reached by logical deduction

de·duc·tive \di-'dək-tiv, dē-\ *adj* (1665) **1** : of, relating to, or provable by deduction **2** : employing deduction in reasoning — **de·duc·tive·ly** *adv*

dee \'dē\ *n* (13c) **1** : the letter *d* **2** : something shaped like the letter D

[1]deed \'dēd\ *n* [ME *dede*, fr. OE *dǣd*; akin to OE *dōn* to do] (bef. 12c) **1** : something that is done ⟨evil ~s⟩ **2** : a usu. illustrious act or action : FEAT, EXPLOIT **3** : the act of performing : ACTION ⟨righteous in word and in ~⟩ **4** : a signed and usu. sealed instrument containing some legal transfer, bargain, or contract — **deed·less** \-ləs\ *adj*

[2]deed *vt* (1806) : to convey or transfer by deed

deed poll \-'pōl\ *n, pl* **deeds poll** [[1]deed + poll, adj. (having the edges cut even rather than indented), fr. [2]poll] (1588) *Brit* : a deed (as to change one's name) made and executed by only one party

deedy \'dē-dē\ *adj* **deed·i·er; -est** (1615) *dial chiefly Eng* : INDUSTRIOUS

dee·jay \'dē-,jā\ *n* [*disc jockey*] (ca. 1949) : DISC JOCKEY

deem \'dēm\ *vb* [ME *demen*, fr. OE *dēman*; akin to OHG *tuomen* to judge, OE *dōm* doom] *vt* (bef. 12c) : to come to think or judge : CONSIDER ⟨~ed it wise to go slow⟩ ~ *vi* : to have an opinion : BELIEVE

de·em·pha·size \(,)dē-'em(p)-fə-,sīz\ *vt* (1938) : to reduce in relative importance; *also* : PLAY DOWN — **de·em·pha·sis** \-fə-səs\ *n*

de·en·er·gize \,dē-'e-nər-,jīz\ *vt* (1925) : to disconnect from a source of electricity : shut off the power to

[1]deep \'dēp\ *adj* [ME *dep*, fr. OE *dēop*; akin to OHG *tiof* deep, OE *dyppan* to dip — more at DIP] (bef. 12c) **1** : extending far from some surface or area: as **a** : extending far downward ⟨a ~ well⟩ **b** (1) : extending well inward from an outer surface ⟨a ~ gash⟩ ⟨a *deep*-chested animal⟩ (2) : not located superficially within the body ⟨~ pressure receptors in muscles⟩ **c** : extending well back from a surface accepted as front ⟨a ~ closet⟩ **d** : extending far laterally from the center ⟨~ borders of lace⟩ **e** : occurring or located near the outer limits of the playing area ⟨hit to ~ right field⟩ **f** : thrown deep ⟨a ~ pass⟩ **2** : having a specified extension in an implied direction usu. downward or backward ⟨a shelf 20 inches ~⟩ ⟨cars parked three-*deep*⟩ **3** : difficult to penetrate or comprehend : RECONDITE ⟨~ mathematical problems⟩ **b** : MYSTERIOUS, OBSCURE ⟨a ~ dark secret⟩ **c** : grave in nature or effect ⟨in ~*est* disgrace⟩ **d** : of penetrating intellect : WISE ⟨a ~ thinker⟩ **e** : INVOLVED, ENGROSSED ⟨~ in debt⟩ **f** : characterized by profundity of feeling or quality ⟨a ~ sleep⟩; *also* : DEEP-SEATED ⟨~ religious beliefs⟩ **4** *a* (of color) : high in saturation and low in lightness **b** : having a low musical pitch or pitch range ⟨a ~ voice⟩ **5 a** : situated well within the boundaries ⟨a house ~ in the woods⟩ **b** : remote in time or space **c** : being below the level of the conscious ⟨~ neuroses⟩ **d** : covered, enclosed, or filled to a specified degree — usu. used in combination ⟨ankle-*deep* in mud⟩ **6** : LARGE ⟨~ discounts⟩ **7** : having many good players ⟨a ~ bull pen⟩ *syn* see BROAD — **deep·ly** *adv* — **deep·ness** *n* — **in deep water** : in difficulty or distress

[2]deep *adv* (bef. 12c) **1** : to a great depth : DEEPLY ⟨still waters run ~⟩ **2** : far on : LATE ⟨danced ~ into the night⟩ **3** : near the outer limits of the playing area ⟨the shortstop was playing ~⟩ **b** : LONG 6

[3]deep *n* (bef. 12c) **1 a** : a vast or immeasurable extent : ABYSS **b** (1) : the extent of surrounding space or time (2) : OCEAN **2** : any of the deep portions of a body of water; *specif* : a generally long and narrow area in the ocean where the depth exceeds 3000 fathoms (5500 meters) **3** : the middle or most intense part ⟨the ~ of winter⟩ **4** : any of the fathom points on a sounding line other than the marks

deep–dish pie *n* (1918) : a pie usu. with a fruit filling and no bottom crust that is baked in a deep dish

deep·en \'dē-pən\ *vb* **deep·ened; deep·en·ing** \'dē-pə-niŋ, 'dēp-niŋ\ *vt* (1598) : to make deep or deeper ~ *vi* : to become deeper or more profound

deep fat *n* (1921) : hot fat or oil deep enough in a cooking utensil to cover the food to be fried

Deep·freeze \'dēp-,frēz\ *trademark* — used for a freezer for food storage

deep–freeze \'dēp-'frēz\ *vt* **-froze** \-'frōz\; **-fro·zen** \-'frō-z²n\ (1943) **1** : QUICK-FREEZE **2** : to store in a frozen state

deep freeze \'dēp-,frēz\ *n* (1948) **1** : COLD STORAGE 2 ⟨a bill presently in *deep freeze* awaiting a new congress —*Newsweek*⟩ **2** : intense cold

deep–fry \'dēp-'frī\ *vt* (1922) : to cook in deep fat

deep fryer *n* (1950) : a utensil suitable for deep-fat frying

deep pocket *n* (1976) **1** : a person or an organization having substantial financial resources **2** *pl* : substantial financial resources

deep–root·ed \'dēp-'rü-təd, -'rü-\ *adj* (15c) : deeply implanted or established ⟨a ~ loyalty⟩ *syn* see INVETERATE

deep–sea \'dēp-'sē\ *adj* (1626) : of, relating to, or occurring in the deeper parts of the sea ⟨~ fishing⟩

deep–seat·ed \'dēp-'sē-təd\ *adj* (1741) **1** : situated far below the surface ⟨a ~ inflammation⟩ **2** : firmly established ⟨a ~ tradition⟩ *syn* see INVETERATE

deep–six \'dēp-'siks\ *vt* (1952) **1** *slang* : to throw away : DISCARD **2** *slang* : to throw overboard

deep six *n* [fr. the leadsman's call *by the deep six* for a depth corresponding to the sixth deep on a sounding line] (1944) *slang* : a place of disposal or abandonment — used esp. in the phrase *give it the deep six*

deep–sky \'dēp-,skī\ *adj* (1968) : relating to or existing in space outside the solar system ⟨*deep-sky* objects⟩

deep space *n* (ca. 1952) : space well outside the earth's atmosphere and esp. that part lying beyond the earth-moon system

deep structure *n* (1964) : a formal representation of the underlying semantic content of a sentence; *also* : the structure which such a representation specifies

deep throat *n, often cap D&T* [fr. the nickname given to such an informant in the Watergate scandal by Bob Woodward *b*1943 U.S. journalist, fr. the title of a pornographic film (1972)] (1973) : an informant who divulges damaging information under cover of anonymity

deep–wa·ter \'dēp-,wȯ-tər, -,wä-\ *adj* (1795) : of, relating to, or characterized by water of considerable depth; *esp* : able to accommodate oceangoing vessels ⟨~ ports⟩

deer \'dir\ *n, pl* **deer** *also* **deers** [ME, deer, animal, fr. OE *dēor* beast; akin to OHG *tior* wild animal, Lith *dvasia* breath, spirit] (bef. 12c) **1** *archaic* : ANIMAL; *esp* : a small mammal **2** : any of numerous ruminant mammals (family Cervidae, the deer family) having two large and two small hooves on each foot and antlers borne by the males of nearly all and by the females of a few forms — **deer–like** \-,līk\ *adj*

deer·ber·ry \-,ber-ē\ *n* (1814) **1** : either of two shrubs (*Vaccinium stamineum* or *V. caesium*) of dry woods and scrub of the eastern U.S. **2** : the edible fruit of a deerberry

deer·fly \'dir-,flī\ *n* (1853) : any of numerous small horseflies (as of the genus *Chrysops*) that include important vectors of tularemia

deer·hound \-,haůnd\ *n* (1818) : SCOTTISH DEERHOUND

deer mouse *n* [fr. its agility] (1833) : WHITE-FOOTED MOUSE; *esp* : a mouse (*Peromyscus maniculatus*) widely distributed in forests and grasslands of No. America and Mexico

deer·skin \'dir-,skin\ *n* (14c) : leather made from the skin of a deer; *also* : a garment of this leather

deer·stalk·er \-,stȯ-kər\ *n* (1870) : a close-fitting hat with a visor at the front and the back and with earflaps that may be worn up or down — called also *deerstalker cap, deerstalker hat*

deer tick *n* (1982) : an ixodid tick (*Ixodes dammini*) that transmits the bacterium causing Lyme disease

deer·yard \'dir-,yärd\ *n* (1849) : a place where deer herd in winter

deerstalker

de·es·ca·late \(,)dē-'es-kə-,lāt, ÷-kyə-\ *vt* (1964) **1** : LIMIT 2b ~ *vi* : to decrease in extent, volume, or scope — **de·es·ca·la·tion** \(,)dē-,es-kə-'lā-shən, ÷-kyə-\ *n* — **de·es·ca·la·to·ry** \(,)dē-'es-kə-lə-,tōr-ē, -,tȯr-, ÷-kyə-\ *adj*

deet \'dēt\ *n, often all cap* [prob. fr. *d. e. t.*, fr. *di-* + *ethyl* + *toluamide* (C$_{12}$H$_{17}$NO)] (1962) : a colorless oily liquid insect repellent C$_{12}$H$_{17}$NO

de·face \di-'fās, dē-\ *vt* [ME, fr. MF *desfacier*, fr. OF, fr. *des-* de- + *face* front, face] (14c) **1** : to mar the external appearance of : injure by effacing significant details ⟨~ an inscription⟩ **2** : IMPAIR **3** *obs* : DESTROY — **de·face·ment** \-'fās-mənt\ *n* — **de·fac·er** *n*

[1]de fac·to \di-'fak-(,)tō, dā-, dē-\ *adv* [ML, lit., from the fact] (1601) : in reality : ACTUALLY

[2]de facto *adj* (1696) **1** : ACTUAL; *esp* : being such in effect though not formally recognized ⟨a *de facto* state of war⟩ **2** : exercising power as if legally constituted ⟨a *de facto* government⟩

de·fal·cate \di-'fal-,kāt, -'fȯl-, dē-; 'de-fal-\ *vb* **-cat·ed; -cat·ing** [ML *defalcatus*, pp. of *defalcare*, fr. L *de-* + *falc-, falx* sickle] *vt* (1540) *archaic* : DEDUCT, CURTAIL ~ *vi* : to engage in embezzlement — **de·fal·ca·tor** \-,kā-tər\ *n*

de·fal·ca·tion \,dē-,fal-'kā-shən, ,dē-,fȯl-, di-; ,de-fəl-\ *n* (15c) **1** *archaic* : DEDUCTION **2** : the act or an instance of embezzling **3** : a failure to meet a promise or an expectation

def·a·ma·tion \,de-fə-'mā-shən\ *n* (14c) : the act of defaming another : CALUMNY — **de·fam·a·to·ry** \di-'fa-mə-,tȯr-ē, dē-\ *adj*

de·fame \di-'fām, dē-\ *vt* **de·famed; de·fam·ing** [ME, fr. MF & ML; MF *defamer*, fr. ML *defamare*, alter. of L *diffamare*, fr. *dis-* + *fama* reputation, fame] (14c) **1** *archaic* : DISGRACE **2** : to harm the reputation of by libel or slander **3** *archaic* : ACCUSE *syn* see MALIGN — **de·fam·er** *n*

de·fang \(,)dē-'faŋ\ *vt* (1953) : to make harmless or less powerful

de·fat \(,)dē-'fat\ *vt* (1919) : to remove fat from

[1]de·fault \di-'fȯlt, dē-; 'dē-,fȯlt\ *n* [ME *defaute, defaulte*, fr. OF *defaute*, fr. *defaillir* to be lacking, fail, fr. *de-* + *faillir* to fail] (13c) **1** : failure to do something required by duty or law : NEGLECT **2** *archaic* : FAULT **3** : a failure to pay financial debts **4** *a* : failure to appear at the required time in a legal proceeding **b** : failure to compete in or to finish an appointed contest **5** : a selection automatically used by a computer program in the absence of a choice made by the user — **in default of** : in the absence of

[2]default *vi* (15c) : to fail to fulfill a contract, agreement, or duty: as **a** : to fail to meet a financial obligation **b** : to fail to appear in court **c**

\ə\ abut \ᵊ\ kitten, F table \ər\ further \a\ ash \ā\ ace \ä\ mop, mar \aů\ out \ch\ chin \e\ bet \ē\ easy \g\ go \i\ hit \ī\ ice \j\ job \ŋ\ sing \ō\ go \ȯ\ law \ȯi\ boy \th\ thin \t͟h\ the \ü\ loot \ů\ foot \y\ yet \zh\ vision \à, k̲, ⁿ, œ, œ̄, ᵫ, ᵫ̄, ᵞ\ *see* Guide to Pronunciation

: to fail to compete in or to finish an appointed contest; *also* : to forfeit a contest by such failure ~ *vt* **1** : to fail to perform, pay, or make good **2 a** : FORFEIT **b** : to exclude (a player or a team) from a contest by default — **de·fault·er** *n*

de·fea·sance \di-'fē-zən(t)s\ *n* [ME *defesance*, fr. AF, fr. OF *deffesant*, prp. of *deffaire*] (15c) **1 a** (1) : the termination of a property interest in accordance with stipulated conditions (as in a deed) (2) : an instrument stating such conditions of limitation **b** : a rendering null or void **2** : DEFEAT, OVERTHROW

de·fea·si·ble \di-'fē-zə-bəl\ *adj* (15c) : capable of being annulled or made void ⟨a ~ claim⟩ — **de·fea·si·bil·i·ty** \-,fē-zə-'bi-lə-tē\ *n*

¹de·feat \di-'fēt, dē-\ *vt* [ME *deffeten*, fr. MF *deffait*, pp. of *deffaire* to destroy, fr. OF *desfaire*, fr. ML *disfacere*, fr. L *dis-* + *facere* to do — more at DO] (14c) **1** *obs* : DESTROY **2 a** : NULLIFY ⟨~ an estate⟩ **b** : FRUSTRATE 2a(1) ⟨~ a hope⟩ **3** : to win victory over : BEAT ⟨~ the opposing team⟩ *syn* see CONQUER

²defeat *n* (1590) **1** : frustration by nullification or by prevention of success ⟨the bill suffered ~ in the Senate⟩ **2** *obs* : DESTRUCTION **3 a** : an overthrow esp. of an army in battle **b** : the loss of a contest

de·feat·ism \di-'fē-,ti-zəm, dē-\ *n* (1918) : acceptance or expectation of or resignation to defeat — **de·feat·ist** \-tist\ *n or adj*

de·fea·ture \di-'fē-chər, dē-\ *n* [prob. fr. *de-* + *feature*] (1590) **1** *archaic* : DISFIGUREMENT **2** *archaic* : DEFEAT

def·e·cate \'de-fi-,kāt\ *vb* **-cat·ed; -cat·ing** [L *defaecatus*, pp. of *defaecare*, fr. *de-* + *faec-, faex* dregs, lees] *vt* (1575) **1** : to free from impurity or corruption **2** : to discharge from the anus ~ *vi* : to discharge feces from the bowels — **def·e·ca·tion** \,de-fi-'kā-shən\ *n*

¹de·fect \'dē-,fekt, di-'\ *n* [ME, fr. MF, fr. L *defectus* lack, fr. *deficere* to desert, fail, fr. *de-* + *facere* to do — more at DO] (15c) **1 a** : an imperfection that impairs worth or utility : SHORTCOMING ⟨the grave ~s in our foreign policy⟩ **b** : an imperfection (as a vacancy or a foreign atom) in a crystal lattice **2** [L *defectus*] : a lack of something necessary for completeness, adequacy, or perfection : DEFICIENCY ⟨a hearing ~⟩

²de·fect \di-'fekt\ *vi* [L *defectus*, pp. of *deficere*] (1596) **1** : to forsake one cause, party, or nation for another often because of a change in ideology **2** : to leave one situation (as a job) often to go over to a rival ⟨the reporter ~ed to another network⟩ — **de·fec·tor** \-'fek-tər\ *n*

de·fec·tion \di-'fek-shən\ *n* (1552) **1** : conscious abandonment of allegiance or duty (as to a person, cause, or doctrine) : DESERTION

¹de·fec·tive \di-'fek-tiv\ *adj* (14c) **1** : imperfect in form or function : FAULTY ⟨a ~ pane of glass⟩ **b** : falling below the norm in structure or in mental or physical function ⟨~ eyesight⟩ **2** : lacking one or more of the usual forms of grammatical inflection ⟨*must* is a ~ verb⟩ — **de·fec·tive·ly** *adv* — **de·fec·tive·ness** *n*

²defective *n* (1881) : a person who is subnormal physically or mentally

de·fem·i·nize \(,)dē-'fe-mə-,nīz\ *vt* (1907) : to divest of feminine qualities or characteristics : MASCULINIZE — **de·fem·i·ni·za·tion** \(,)dē-,fe-mə-nə-'zā-shən\ *n*

de·fence, de·fence·man *chiefly Brit var of* DEFENSE, DEFENSEMAN

de·fend \di-'fend\ *vb* [ME, fr. OF *defendre*, fr. L *defendere*, fr. *de-* + *-fendere* to strike; akin to OE *gūth* battle, war, Gk *theinein* to strike] *vt* (14c) **1 a** : to drive danger or attack away from **b** (1) : to maintain or support in the face of argument or hostile criticism (2) : to prove (as a doctoral thesis) valid by answering questions in an oral exam **c** : to attempt to prevent an opponent from scoring at ⟨elects to ~ the south goal⟩ **2** *archaic* : PREVENT, FORBID **3** : to act as attorney for **4** : to deny or oppose the right of a plaintiff in regard to (a suit or a wrong charged) : CONTEST **5** : to seek to retain (as a title or position) against a challenge in a contest ~ *vi* **1** : to take action against attack or challenge ⟨couldn't fight back, could only ~⟩ **2** : to play or be on defense ⟨playing deep to ~ against a pass⟩ **3** : to play against the high bidder in a card game — **de·fend·able** \'fen-də-bəl\ *adj*

syn DEFEND, PROTECT, SHIELD, GUARD, SAFEGUARD mean to keep secure from danger or against attack. DEFEND denotes warding off actual or threatened attack ⟨*defend* the country⟩. PROTECT implies the use of something (as a covering) as a bar to the admission or impact of what may attack or injure ⟨a hard hat to *protect* your head⟩. SHIELD suggests protective intervention in imminent danger or actual attack ⟨*shielded* her eyes from the sun with her hand⟩. GUARD implies protecting with vigilance and force against expected danger ⟨White House entrances are well *guarded*⟩. SAFEGUARD implies taking precautionary protective measures against merely possible danger ⟨our civil liberties must be *safeguarded*⟩. *syn* see in addition MAINTAIN

¹de·fen·dant \di-'fen-dənt, *in legal circles often* -,dant\ *n* (14c) : a person required to make answer in a legal action or suit — compare PLAINTIFF

²defendant *adj* (15c) : being on the defensive : DEFENDING

de·fend·er \di-'fen-dər\ *n* (14c) **1** : one that defends **2** : a player in a sport (as football) assigned to a defensive position

de·fen·es·tra·tion \(,)dē-,fe-nə-'strā-shən\ *n* [*de-* + L *fenestra* window] (1620) : a throwing of a person or thing out of a window — **de·fen·es·trate** \(,)dē-'fe-nə-,strāt\ *vt*

¹de·fense \di-'fen(t)s; *as antonym of "offense," often* 'dē-,\ *n* [ME, fr. MF, fr. LL *defensa* vengeance, fr. L, fem. of *defensus*, pp. of *defendere*] (14c) **1 a** : the act or action of defending ⟨the ~ of our country⟩ ⟨speak out in ~ of justice⟩ **b** : a defendant's denial, answer, or plea **2 a** : capability of resisting attack **b** : defensive play or ability ⟨a player known for good ~⟩ **3 a** : means or method of defending or protecting oneself, one's team, or another; *also* : a defensive structure **b** : an argument in support or justification **c** : the collected facts and method adopted by a defendant to protect himself against a plaintiff's action **d** : a sequence of moves available in chess to the second player in the opening **4 a** : a defending party or group (as in a court of law) ⟨the ~ rests⟩ **b** : a defensive team **5** : the military and industrial aggregate that authorizes and supervises arms production ⟨appropriations for ~⟩ ⟨~ contract⟩ — **de·fense·less** \-ləs\ *adj* — **de·fense·less·ly** *adv* — **de·fense·less·ness** *n*

²defense *vt* **de·fensed; de·fens·ing** (1950) : to take specific defensive action against (an opposing team or player or an offensive play)

de·fense·man \-mən, -,man\ *n* (1895) : a player in a sport (as hockey) who is assigned to a defensive zone or position

defense mechanism *n* (1913) **1** : an often unconscious mental process (as repression) that makes possible compromise solutions to personal problems **2** : a defensive reaction by an organism

de·fen·si·ble \di-'fen(t)-sə-bəl\ *adj* (14c) : capable of being defended — **de·fen·si·bil·i·ty** \di-,fen(t)-sə-'bi-lə-tē, ,dē-\ *n* — **de·fen·si·bly** \-blē\ *adv*

¹de·fen·sive \di-'fen(t)-siv, 'dē-,\ *adj* (14c) **1** : serving to defend or protect **2 a** : devoted to resisting or preventing aggression or attack **b** : of or relating to the attempt to keep an opponent from scoring in a game or contest **3 a** : valuable in defensive play ⟨a ~ card in bridge⟩ **b** : designed to keep an opponent from being the highest bidder ⟨a ~ bid⟩ — **de·fen·sive·ly** *adv* — **de·fen·sive·ness** *n*

²defensive *n* (1601) : a defensive position — **on the defensive** : in the state or condition of being prepared for an expected aggression or attack

¹de·fer \di-'fər\ *vt* **de·ferred; de·fer·ring** [ME *deferren, differren*, fr. MF *differer*, fr. L *differre* to postpone, be different — more at DIFFER] (14c) **1** : PUT OFF, DELAY **2** : to postpone induction of (a person) into military service — **de·fer·rer** *n*

syn DEFER, POSTPONE, SUSPEND, STAY mean to delay an action or proceeding. DEFER implies a deliberate putting off to a later time ⟨*deferred* buying a car until next spring⟩. POSTPONE implies an intentional deferring usu. to a definite time ⟨the game is *postponed* until Saturday⟩. SUSPEND implies temporary stoppage with an added suggestion of waiting until some condition is satisfied ⟨business will be *suspended* while repairs are under way⟩. STAY often suggests the stopping or checking by an intervening agency or authority ⟨the governor *stayed* the execution⟩.

²defer *vb* **deferred; deferring** [ME *deferren, differren*, fr. MF *deferer, defferer*, fr. LL *deferre*, fr. L, to bring down, bring, fr. *de-* + *ferre* to carry — more at BEAR] *vt* (15c) : to delegate to another ⟨he could ~ his job to no one —J. A. Michener⟩ ~ *vi* : to submit to another's wishes, opinion, or governance usu. through deference or respect ⟨*deferred* to her father's wishes⟩ *syn* see YIELD

def·er·ence \'de-f(ə-)rən(t)s, 'def-rən(t)s\ *n* (1660) : respect and esteem due a superior or an elder; *also* : affected or ingratiating regard for another's wishes *syn* see HONOR — **in deference to** : in consideration of

def·er·ent \'de-fə-rənt, 'def-rənt\ *adj* [back-formation fr. *deference*] (1822) : DEFERENTIAL

def·er·en·tial \,de-fə-'ren-chəl\ *adj* (1822) : showing or expressing deference ⟨~ attention⟩ — **def·er·en·tial·ly** \-'ren-chə-lē\ *adv*

de·fer·ment \di-'fər-mənt\ *n* (1612) : the act of delaying or postponing; *specif* : official postponement of military service

de·fer·ra·ble \di-'fər-ə-bəl\ *adj* (1943) : capable of or suitable or eligible for being deferred — **deferrable** *n*

de·fer·ral \di-'fər-əl\ *n* (1895) : the act of delaying : POSTPONEMENT

de·ferred *adj* (1651) **1** : withheld for or until a stated time ⟨a ~ payment⟩ **2** : charged in cases of delayed handling ⟨a ~ rate⟩

de·fer·ves·cence \,dē-(,)fər-'ves-ᵊn(t)s, ,de-fər-\ *n* [G *Deferveszenz*, fr. L *defervescent-, defervescens*, prp. of *defervescere* to stop boiling, fr. *de-* + *fervescere* to begin to boil — more at EFFERVESCE] (1866) : the subsidence of a fever

de·fi·ance \di-'fī-ən(t)s, dē-\ *n* (15c) **1** : the act or an instance of defying : CHALLENGE **2** : disposition to resist : willingness to contend or fight — **in defiance of** : contrary to : DESPITE

de·fi·ant \-ənt\ *adj* [F *défiant*, fr. OF, prp. of *defier* to defy] (ca. 1837) : full of defiance : BOLD — **de·fi·ant·ly** *adv*

de·fi·bril·la·tor \(,)dē-'fi-brə-,lā-tər\ *n* (1952) : an electronic device that applies an electric shock to restore the rhythm of a fibrillating heart — **de·fi·bril·late** \-,lāt\ *vt* — **de·fi·bril·la·tion** \-,fi-brə-'lā-shən\ *n*

de·fi·bri·nate \(,)dē-'fi-brə-,nāt, -'fī-\ *vt* **-at·ed; -at·ing** (1845) : to remove fibrin from (blood) — **de·fi·bri·na·tion** \(,)dē-,fi-brə-'nā-shən, -,fī-\ *n*

de·fi·cien·cy \di-'fi-shən-sē\ *n, pl* **-cies** (1634) **1** : the quality or state of being deficient : INADEQUACY **2** : an amount that is lacking or inadequate : SHORTAGE: as **a** : a shortage of substances necessary to health **b** : DELETION 2b(1)

deficiency disease *n* (1912) : a disease (as scurvy) caused by a lack of essential dietary elements and esp. a vitamin or mineral

¹de·fi·cient \di-'fi-shənt\ *adj* [L *deficient-, deficiens*, prp. of *deficere* to be wanting — more at DEFECT] (1581) **1** : lacking in some necessary quality or element ⟨~ in judgment⟩ **2** : not up to a normal standard or complement : DEFECTIVE ⟨~ strength⟩ — **de·fi·cient·ly** *adv*

²deficient *n* (1906) : one that is deficient ⟨a mental ~⟩

def·i·cit \'de-fə-sət, *Brit also* di-'fis-ət *or* 'dē-fə-sət\ *n* [F *déficit*, fr. L *deficit* it is wanting, 3d sing. pres. indic. of *deficere*] (1782) **1 a** (1) : deficiency in amount or quality ⟨a ~ in rainfall⟩ (2) : a lack or impairment in a functional capacity ⟨cognitive ~s⟩ ⟨a hearing ~⟩ **b** : DISADVANTAGE ⟨scored two runs to overcome a 2–1 ~⟩ **2 a** : an excess of expenditure over revenue **b** : a loss in business operations

deficit spending *n* (1938) : the spending of public funds raised by borrowing rather than by taxation

de·fi·er \di-'fī-(ə)r\ *n* (1585) : one that defies

def·i·lade \'de-fə-,lād, -,läd\ *vt* **-lad·ed; -lad·ing** [prob. fr. *de-* + *-filade* (as in *enfilade*)] (1828) : to arrange (fortifications) so as to protect the lines from frontal or enfilading fire and the interior from fire from above or behind — **defilade** *n*

¹de·file \di-'fī(ə)l, dē-\ *vt* **de·filed; de·fil·ing** [ME, alter. (influenced by OE *fȳlan* to defile) of *defoulen* to trample, defile, fr. OF *defouler* to trample, fr. *de-* + *fouler* to trample, lit., to full — more at FULL] (14c) : to make unclean or impure: as **a** : to corrupt the purity or perfection of : DEBASE ⟨the countryside *defiled* by billboards⟩ **b** : to violate the chastity of : DEFLOWER **c** : to make physically unclean esp. with something unpleasant or contaminating ⟨boots *defiled* with blood⟩ **d** : to violate the sanctity of : DESECRATE ⟨~ a sanctuary⟩ **e** : SULLY, DISHONOR *syn* see CONTAMINATE — **de·file·ment** \-'fī(ə)l-mənt\ *n* — **de·fil·er** \-'fī-lər\ *n*

²de·file \di-'fī(ə)l, 'dē-,fīl\ *n* [F *défilé*, fr. pp. of *défiler*] (1685) : a narrow passage or gorge

³de·file \di-'fī(ə)l, 'dē-,fīl\ *vi* **de·filed; de·fil·ing** [F *défiler*, fr. *dé-* de- + *filer* to move in a column — more at FILE] (1705) : to march off in a line

de·fin·able \di-'fī-nə-bəl\ *adj* (ca. 1660) **1** : able to be defined **2** : able to be specified to have a particular function or operation ⟨~ keys⟩ — **de·fin·ably** \-'fī-nə-blē\ *adv*

de·fine \di-'fīn\ *vb* **de·fined; de·fin·ing** [ME, fr. MF & L; MF *definer*, fr. L *definire*, fr. *de-* + *finire* to limit, end, fr. *finis* boundary, end] *vt* (14c) **1 a** : to determine or identify the essential qualities or meaning of ⟨whatever ~s us as human⟩ **b** : to discover and set forth the meaning of (as a word) **c** : to create on a computer ⟨~ a window⟩ ⟨~ a procedure⟩ **2 a** : to fix or mark the limits of : DEMARCATE ⟨rigidly *defined* property lines⟩ **b** : to make distinct, clear, or detailed esp. in outline ⟨the issues aren't too well *defined*⟩ **3** : CHARACTERIZE, DISTINGUISH ⟨you ~ yourself by the choices you make —*Denison Univ. Bull.*⟩ ~ *vi* : to make a definition — **de·fine·ment** \-'fīn-mənt\ *n* — **de·fin·er** \-'fī-nər\ *n*

de·fin·i·en·dum \di-,fi-nē-'en-dəm\ *n, pl* **-da** \-də\ [L, something to be defined, neut. of *definiendus*, gerundive of *definire*] (1871) : an expression that is being defined

de·fin·i·ens \di-'fi-nē-,enz\ *n, pl* **de·fin·i·en·tia** \di-,fi-nē-'en(t)-shē-ə\ [L, prp. of *definire*] (1871) : an expression that defines : DEFINITION

def·i·nite \'de-fə-nit, 'def-nət\ *adj* [L *definitus*, pp. of *definire*] (1553) **1** : having distinct or certain limits ⟨set ~ standards for pupils to meet⟩ **2 a** : free of all ambiguity, uncertainty, or obscurity ⟨demanded a ~ answer⟩ **b** : UNQUESTIONABLE, DECIDED ⟨the quarterback was a ~ hero today⟩ **3** : typically designating an identified or immediately identifiable person or thing ⟨the ~ article *the*⟩ **4 a** : being constant in number, usu. less than 20, and occurring in multiples of the petal number ⟨stamens ~⟩ **b** : CYMOSE ⟨a ~ inflorescence⟩ *syn* see EXPLICIT — **def·i·nite·ly** *adv* — **def·i·nite·ness** *n*

definite integral *n* (1860) : the difference between the values of the integral of a given function *f(x)* for an upper value *b* and a lower value *a* of the independent variable *x*

def·i·ni·tion \,de-fə-'ni-shən\ *n* [ME *diffinicioun*, fr. MF *definition*, fr. L *definition-, definitio*, fr. *definire*] (14c) **1** : an act of determining; *specif* : the formal proclamation of a Roman Catholic dogma **2 a** : a statement expressing the essential nature of something **b** : a statement of the meaning of a word or word group or a sign or symbol ⟨dictionary ~s⟩ **c** : a product of defining **3** : the action or process of defining **4 a** : the action or the power of describing, explaining, or making definite and clear ⟨the ~ of a telescope⟩ ⟨her comic genius is beyond ~⟩ **b** (1) : clarity of visual presentation : distinctness of outline or detail ⟨high-*definition* television⟩ (2) : clarity esp. of musical sound in reproduction **c** : sharp demarcation of outlines or limits ⟨a jacket with distinct waist ~⟩ — **def·i·ni·tion·al** \-'ni-shə-nᵊl\ *adj*

¹de·fin·i·tive \di-'fi-nə-tiv\ *adj* [ME *diffinityf*, fr. MF *definitif*, fr. L *definitivus*, fr. *definitus*] (14c) **1** : serving to provide a final solution or to end a situation ⟨a ~ victory⟩ **2** : authoritative and apparently exhaustive ⟨a ~ edition⟩ **3 a** : serving to define or specify precisely ⟨~ laws⟩ **b** : serving as a perfect example : QUINTESSENTIAL ⟨a ~ bourgeois⟩ **4** : fully differentiated or developed ⟨a ~ organ⟩ **5** *of a postage stamp* : issued as a regular stamp for the country or territory in which it is to be used *syn* see CONCLUSIVE — **de·fin·i·tive·ly** *adv* — **de·fin·i·tive·ness** *n*

²definitive *n* (1951) : a definitive postage stamp — compare PROVISIONAL

definitive host *n* (1901) : the host in which the sexual reproduction of a parasite takes place — compare INTERMEDIATE HOST 1

de·fin·i·tize \'de-fə-nə-,tīz, di-'fi-\ *vt* **-tized; -tiz·ing** (1876) : to make definite

de·fin·i·tude \di-'fi-nə-,tüd, -,tyüd\ *n* [irreg. fr. *definite*] (1836) : PRECISION, DEFINITENESS

def·la·grate \'def-lə-,grāt\ *vb* **-grat·ed; -grat·ing** [L *deflagratus*, pp. of *deflagrare* to burn down, fr. *de-* + *flagrare* to burn — more at BLACK] *vt* (ca. 1727) : to cause to deflagrate — compare DETONATE 1 ~ *vi* : to burn rapidly with intense heat and sparks being given off — **def·la·gra·tion** \,def-lə-'grā-shən\ *n*

de·flate \di-'flāt, dē-\ *vb* **de·flat·ed; de·flat·ing** [*de-* + *-flate* (as in *inflate*)] *vt* (1891) **1** : to release air or gas from **2** : to reduce in size, importance, or effectiveness ⟨~ his ego with cutting remarks⟩ **3** : to reduce (a price level) or cause (a volume of credit) to contract ~ *vi* : to lose firmness through or as if through the escape of contained gas *syn* see CONTRACT — **de·fla·tor** *also* **de·fla·ter** \-'flā-tər\ *n*

de·fla·tion \di-'flā-shən, dē-\ *n* (1891) **1** : an act or instance of deflating : the state of being deflated **2** : a contraction in the volume of available money or credit that results in a general decline in prices **3** : the erosion of soil by the wind — **de·fla·tion·ary** \-shə-,ner-ē\ *adj*

de·flect \di-'flekt, dē-\ *vb* [L *deflectere* to bend down, turn aside, fr. *de-* + *flectere* to bend] *vt* (ca. 1555) : to turn aside esp. from a straight course or fixed direction ~ *vi* : to turn aside : DEVIATE — **de·flect·able** \-'flek-tə-bəl\ *adj* — **de·flec·tive** \-tiv\ *adj* — **de·flec·tor** \-tər\ *n*

de·flec·tion \di-'flek-shən, dē-\ *n* (1605) **1** : a turning aside or off course : DEVIATION **2** : the departure of an indicator or pointer from the zero reading on the scale of an instrument

de·flexed \'dē-,flekst, di-'\ *adj* [L *deflexus*, pp. of *deflectere*] (1826) : turned abruptly downward ⟨a ~ leaf⟩

de·flo·ra·tion \,def-lə-'rā-shən, ,dē-flō-\ *n* [ME *defloracioun*, fr. MF & LL; MF *defloracion*, fr. LL *defloration-, defloratio*, fr. *deflorare*] (15c) : rupture of the hymen

de·flow·er \(,)dē-'flaü(-ə)r\ *vt* [ME *deflouren*, fr. MF or LL; OF *des-florer*, fr. LL *deflorare*, fr. L *de-* + *flor-, flos* flower — more at BLOW] (14c) **1** : to deprive of virginity **2** : to take away the prime beauty of — **de·flow·er·er** *n*

de·fog \(,)dē-'fóg, -'fäg\ *vt* (1904) : to remove fog or condensed moisture from — **de·fog·ger** *n*

de·fo·li·ant \(,)dē-'fō-lē-ənt\ *n* (1943) : a chemical spray or dust applied to plants in order to cause the leaves to drop off prematurely

de·fo·li·ate \-lē-,āt\ *vt* [LL *defoliatus*, pp. of *defoliare*, fr. L *de-* + *folium* leaf — more at BLADE] (1791) : to deprive of leaves esp. prematurely — **de·fo·li·a·tion** \(,)dē-,fō-lē-'ā-shən\ *n* — **de·fo·li·a·tor** \(,)dē-'fō-lē-,ā-tər\ *n*

de·force \(,)dē-'fōrs, -'fórs\ *vt* [ME, fr. MF *deforcier*, fr. *de-* + *forcier* to force] (15c) **1** : to keep (as lands) by force from the rightful owner **2** : to eject (a person) from possession by force — **de·force·ment** \-'fōrs-mənt, -'fórs-\ *n*

de·for·es·ta·tion \(,)dē-,fór-ə-'stā-shən, -,fär-\ *n* (1874) : the action or process of clearing of forests; *also* : the state of having been cleared of forests — **de·for·est** \(')dē-'fór-əst, -'fär-\ *vt*

de·form \di-'fórm, dē-\ *vb* [ME, fr. MF or L; OF *deformer*, fr. L *deformare*, fr. *de-* + *formare* to form, fr. *forma* form] *vt* (15c) **1** : to spoil the form of **2 a** : to spoil the looks of : DISFIGURE ⟨a face ~ed by bitterness⟩ **b** : to mar the character of ⟨a marriage ~ed by jealousy⟩ **3** : to alter the shape of by stress ~ *vi* : to become misshapen or changed in shape — **de·form·able** \-mə-bəl\ *adj*

syn DEFORM, DISTORT, CONTORT, WARP means to mar or spoil by or as if by twisting. DEFORM may imply a change of shape through stress, injury, or some accident of growth ⟨his face was *deformed* by hatred⟩. DISTORT and CONTORT both imply a wrenching from the natural, normal, or justly proportioned, but CONTORT suggests a more involved twisting and a more grotesque and painful result ⟨the odd camera angle *distorts* the figure in the photograph⟩ ⟨disease had painfully *contorted* her body⟩. WARP indicates physically an uneven shrinking that bends or twists out of a flat plane ⟨*warped* floorboards⟩.

de·for·mal·ize \(,)dē-'fór-mə-,līz\ *vt* (1880) : to make less formal

de·for·ma·tion \,dē-,fór-'mā-shən, ,de-fór-\ *n* (15c) **1** : alteration of form or shape; *also* : the product of such alteration **2** : the action of deforming : the state of being deformed **3** : change for the worse — **de·for·ma·tion·al** \-shə-nᵊl\ *adj*

de·for·ma·tive \di-'fór-mə-tiv, dē-\ *adj* (1641) : tending to deform

de·formed *adj* (15c) : distorted or unshapely in form : MISSHAPEN

de·for·mi·ty \di-'fór-mə-tē, dē-\ *n, pl* **-ties** [ME *deformite*, fr. MF *defformeteit*, fr. L *deformitat-, deformitas*, fr. *deformis* deformed, fr. *de-* + *forma*] (15c) **1** : the state of being deformed **2** : IMPERFECTION, BLEMISH: as **a** : a physical blemish or distortion : DISFIGUREMENT **b** : a moral or aesthetic flaw or defect

de·fraud \di-'fród, dē-\ *vt* [ME, fr. MF *defrauder*, fr. L *defraudare*, fr. *de-* + *fraudare* to cheat, fr. *fraud-, fraus* fraud] (14c) : to deprive of something by deception or fraud *syn* see CHEAT — **de·fraud·er** \di-'fró-dər\ *n*

de·fray \di-'frā, dē-\ *vt* [MF *deffrayer*, fr. *des-* de- + *frayer* to expend, fr. OF, fr. (assumed) OF *frai* expenditure, lit., damage by breaking, fr. L *fractum*, neut. of *fractus*, pp. of *frangere* to break — more at BREAK] (1536) **1** : to provide for the payment of : PAY **2** *archaic* : to bear the expenses of — **de·fray·able** \-ə-bəl\ *adj* — **de·fray·al** \-'frā(-ə)l\ *n*

de·frock \(,)dē-'fräk\ *vt* (1581) **1** : to deprive (as a priest) of the right to exercise the functions of office **2** : to remove from a position of honor or privilege

de·frost \di-'fróst, dē-\ *vt* (1895) **1** : to release from a frozen state ⟨~ meat⟩ **2** : to free from ice ⟨~ the refrigerator⟩ ~ *vi* : to thaw out esp. from a deep-frozen state — **de·frost·er** *n*

deft \'deft\ *adj* [ME *defte* gentle — more at DAFT] (15c) : characterized by facility and skill *syn* see DEXTEROUS — **deft·ly** *adv* — **deft·ness** \'deft(t)-nəs\ *n*

de·funct \di-'fəŋkt, dē-\ *adj* [L *defunctus*, fr. pp. of *defungi* to finish, die, fr. *de-* + *fungi* to perform — more at FUNCTION] (1599) : no longer living, existing, or functioning ⟨the committee is now ~⟩ *syn* see DEAD

de·fund \(,)dē-'fənd\ *vt* (1948) : to withdraw funding from

de·fuse \(,)dē-'fyüz\ *vt* (1943) **1** : to remove the fuse from (as a mine or bomb) **2** : to make less harmful, potent, or tense ⟨~ the crisis⟩

¹de·fy \di-'fī, dē-\ *vt* **de·fied; de·fy·ing** [ME, to renounce faith in, challenge, fr. MF *defier*, fr. *de-* + *fier* to entrust, fr. (assumed) VL *fidare*, alter. of L *fidere* to trust — more at BIDE] (14c) **1** *archaic* : to challenge to combat **2** : to challenge to do something considered impossible : DARE **3** : to confront with assured power of resistance : DISREGARD ⟨~ public opinion⟩ **4** : to resist attempts at : WITHSTAND ⟨the paintings ~ classification⟩

²de·fy \di-'fī, 'dē-\ *n, pl* **defies** (1580) : CHALLENGE, DEFIANCE

dé·ga·gé \,dā-,gä-'zhā\ *adj* [F, fr. pp. of *dégager* to put at ease, fr. OF *desgagier* to redeem a pledge, free, fr. *des-* de- + *gage* pledge — more at GAGE] (1696) **1** : free of constraint : NONCHALANT **2** : being free and easy ⟨clothes with a ~ look⟩ **3** : extended with toe pointed in preparation for a ballet step

de·gas \(,)dē-'gas\ *vt* (1928) : to remove gas from ⟨~ an electron tube⟩

de Gaull·ism \di-'gō-,li-zəm, -'gò-\ *n* (1943) : GAULLISM — **de Gaull·ist** \-ləst\ *n*

de·gauss \(,)dē-'gaüs\ *vt* [*de-* + *gauss*, after Karl F. *Gauss*] (ca. 1940) : to remove or neutralize the magnetic field of ⟨~ a ship⟩ ⟨~ a magnetic tape⟩ — **de·gauss·er** *n*

de·gen·er·a·cy \di-'jen-rə-sē, -'je-nə-, dē-\ *n, pl* **-cies** (1664) **1** : the state of being degenerate **2** : the process of becoming degenerate **3** : sexual perversion **4** : the coding of an amino acid by more than one codon

¹de·gen·er·ate \di-'jen-rət, -'je-nə-, dē-\ *adj* [ME *degenerat*, fr. L *degeneratus*, pp. of *degenerare* to degenerate, fr. *de-* + *gener-, genus* race, kind — more at KIN] (15c) **1 a** : having declined (as in nature, character, structure, or function) from an ancestral or former state **b** : having sunk to a condition below that which is normal to a type; *esp* : having sunk to a lower and usu. corrupt and vicious state **c** : DEGRADED 2 **2** : being mathematically simpler (as by having a factor or constant equal to zero) than the typical case ⟨a ~ hyperbola⟩ **3** : characterized by atoms stripped of their electrons and by very great density ⟨~ matter⟩; *also* : consisting of degenerate matter ⟨a ~ star⟩ **4** : having two or more states or subdivisions ⟨~ energy level⟩ **5** : having more than one codon representing an amino acid; *also* : being such a codon *syn* see VICIOUS — **de·gen·er·ate·ly** *adv* — **de·gen·er·ate·ness** *n*

²de·gen·er·ate \di-'je-nə-,rāt, dē-\ *vi* (1545) **1** : to pass from a higher to a lower type or condition : DETERIORATE **2** : to sink into a low intellectual or moral state **3** : to decline in quality ⟨the poetry gradually ~s into jingles⟩ **4** : to decline from a condition or from the standards of a species, race, or breed **5** : to evolve or develop into a less autono-

\ə\ abut \ᵊ\ kitten, F table \ər\ further \a\ ash \ā\ ace \ä\ mop, mar \aü\ out \ch\ chin \e\ bet \ē\ easy \g\ go \i\ hit \ī\ ice \j\ job \ŋ\ sing \ō\ go \ò\ law \òi\ boy \th\ thin \ṫh\ the \ü\ loot \u̇\ foot \y\ yet \zh\ vision \à, k̲, ⁿ, œ, œ̄, ᴜe, ᵫ, ᵊ\ *see* Guide to Pronunciation mous or less functionally active form ⟨*degenerated* into dependent parasites⟩ ~ *vt* : to cause to degenerate

³**de·gen·er·ate** \-'jen-rət, -'je-nə-\ *n* (1555) : one that is degenerate: as **a** : one degraded from the normal moral standard **b** : a sexual pervert **c** : one showing signs of reversion to an earlier culture stage

de·gen·er·a·tion \di-ˌje-nə-'rā-shən, ˌdē-\ *n* (15c) **1** : degenerate condition **2** : a lowering of effective power, vitality, or essential quality to an enfeebled and worsened kind or state **3** : intellectual, moral, or artistic decline **4 a** : progressive deterioration of physical characters from a level representing the norm of earlier generations or forms **b** : deterioration of a tissue or an organ in which its function is diminished or its structure is impaired *syn* see DETERIORATION

de·gen·er·a·tive \di-'je-nə-rə-tiv, -ˌjen-rə-; -ˌje-nə-ˌrā-; dē-\ *adj* (ca. 1846) : of, relating to, involving, or causing degeneration ⟨a ~ disease⟩

de·gla·ci·a·tion \(ˌ)dē-ˌglā-s(h)ē-'ā-shən\ *n* (1895) : the melting of ice; *specif* : the retreat of a glacier or ice sheet — **de·gla·ci·at·ed** \-'glā-s(h)ē-ˌā-təd\ *adj*

de·glam·or·ize \(ˌ)dē-'gla-mə-ˌrīz\ *vt* (1938) : to remove the glamor from — **de·glam·or·iza·tion** \(ˌ)dē-ˌgla-mə-rə-'zā-shən\ *n*

¹**de·glaze** \(ˌ)dē-'glāz\ *vt* (ca. 1889) : to remove the glaze from

²**deglaze** *vt* [modif. of F *déglacer*, lit., to melt the ice from, fr. *dé-* + *glacer* to freeze — more at GLACÉ] (1968) : to dissolve the small particles of sautéed meat remaining in (a pan) by adding a liquid and heating

de·glu·ti·tion \ˌdē-glü-'ti-shən, ˌde-glü-\ *n* [F *déglutition*, fr. L *deglutire* to swallow down, fr. *de-* + *glutire, gluttire* to swallow — more at GLUTTON] (1650) : the act or process of swallowing

de·grad·able \di-'grā-də-bəl, dē-\ *adj* (ca. 1962) : capable of being chemically degraded ⟨~ detergents⟩ — compare BIODEGRADABLE

deg·ra·da·tion \ˌde-grə-'dā-shən\ *n* (ca. 1535) **1** : the act or process of degrading **2** : decline to a low, destitute, or demoralized state **b** : moral or intellectual decadence : DEGENERATION — **deg·ra·da·tive** \'de-grə-ˌdā-tiv\ *adj*

de·grade \di-'grād, dē-\ *vb* [ME, fr. OF *degrader*, fr. LL *degradare*, fr. L *de-* + *gradus* step, grade — more at GRADE] *vt* (14c) **1 a** : to lower in grade, rank, or status : DEMOTE **b** : to strip of rank or honors **c** : to lower to an inferior or less effective level **d** : to scale down in desirability or salability **2 a** : to bring to low esteem or into disrepute **b** : to drag down in moral or intellectual character : CORRUPT **3** : to impair in respect to some physical property **4** : to wear down by erosion **5** : to reduce the complexity of (a chemical compound) : DECOMPOSE ~ *vi* **1** : to pass from a higher grade or class to a lower **2** *of a chemical compound* : to become reduced in complexity — **de·grad·er** *n* — **de·grad·ing·ly** \-'grā-diŋ-lē\ *adv*

de·grad·ed *adj* (1643) **1** : reduced far below ordinary standards of civilized life and conduct **2** : characterized by degeneration of structure or function — **de·grad·ed·ly** *adv*

de·gran·u·la·tion \(ˌ)dē-ˌgra-nyə-'lā-shən\ *n* (ca. 1941) : the process of losing granules ⟨~ of leukocytes⟩

de·grease \(ˌ)dē-'grēs, -'grēz\ *vt* (ca. 1889) : to remove grease from — **de·greas·er** \-'grē-sər, -zər\ *n*

de·gree \di-'grē\ *n* [ME, fr. OF *degré*, fr. (assumed) VL *degradus*, fr. L *de-* + *gradus*] (13c) **1** : a step or stage in a process, course, or order of classification ⟨advanced by ~s⟩ **2 a** : a rank or grade of official, ecclesiastical, or social position ⟨people of low ~⟩ **b** *archaic* : a particular standing esp. as to dignity or worth **c** : the civil condition or status of a person **3** : a step in a direct line of descent or in the line of ascent to a common ancestor **4 a** *obs* : STEP, STAIR **b** *archaic* : a member of a series arranged in steps **5** : a measure of damage to tissue caused by injury or disease — compare FIRST-DEGREE BURN, SECOND-DEGREE BURN, THIRD-DEGREE BURN **6 a** : the extent, measure, or scope of an action, condition, or relation ⟨different in ~ but not in kind⟩ **b** : relative intensity ⟨a high ~ of stress⟩ **c** : one of the forms or sets of forms used in the comparison of an adjective or adverb **d** : a legal measure of guilt or negligence ⟨found guilty of robbery in the first ~⟩ **7 a** : a title conferred on students by a college, university, or professional school on completion of a program of study **b** : a grade of membership attained in a ritualistic order or society **c** : an academic title conferred to honor distinguished achievement or service **d** : the formal ceremonies observed in the conferral of such a distinction **8 a** : a unit of measure for angles equal to an angle with its vertex at the center of a circle and its sides cutting off ¹/₃₆₀ of the circumference; *also* : a unit of measure for arcs of a circle equal to the amount of arc that subtends a central angle of one degree **9** *archaic* : a position or space on the earth or in the heavens as measured by degrees of latitude **10 a** : a step, note, or tone of a musical scale **b** : a line or space of the musical staff **11** : one of the divisions or intervals marked on a scale of a measuring instrument; *specif* : any of various units for measuring temperature **12 a** : the sum of the exponents of the variables in the term of highest degree in a polynomial, polynomial function, or polynomial equation **b** : the sum of the exponents of the variable factors of a monomial **c** : the greatest power of the derivative of highest order in a differential equation after the equation has been rationalized and cleared of fractions with respect to the derivative — **de·greed** \-'grēd\ *adj* — **to a degree 1** : to a remarkable extent **2** : in a small way

de·gree–day \di-'grē-ˌdā\ *n* (1832) : a unit that represents one degree of difference from a given point (as 65°) in the mean daily outdoor temperature and that is used esp. to measure heat requirements

degree of freedom (1867) **1** : any of a limited number of ways in which a body may move or in which a dynamic system may change **2** : one of the capabilities of a statistic for variation of which there are as many as the number of unrestricted and independent variables determining its value

de·gres·sive \di-'gre-siv, 'dē-\ *adj* [*de-* + *-gressive* (as in *progressive*)] (1886) : tending to descend or decrease — **de·gres·sive·ly** *adv*

dé·grin·go·lade \ˌdā-ˌgraⁿ(ŋ)-gə-'läd\ *n* [F, fr. *dégringoler* to tumble down, fr. MF *desgringueler*, fr. *des-* + *gringueler* to tumble, fr. MD *crinkelen* to make curl, fr. *crinc, cring* ring, circle] (1883) : a rapid decline or deterioration (as in strength, position, or condition) : DOWNFALL

de·gum \(ˌ)dē-'gəm\ *vt* (1887) : to free from gum, a gummy substance, or sericin

de·gus·ta·tion \ˌdē-ˌgəs-'tā-shən, de-\ *n* [F *dégustation*, fr. L *degusta-tion-, degustatio*, fr. *degustare* to taste, fr. *de-* + *gustare* to taste — more at CHOOSE] (ca. 1656) : the action or an instance of tasting esp. in a series of small portions — **de·gust** \di-'gəst, dē-\ *vt*

de haut en bas \də-ō-tän-bä\ *adj or adv* [F, lit., from top to bottom] (1696) : of superiority : of or with condescension

de·hisce \di-'his\ *vi* **de·hisced; de·hisc·ing** [L *dehiscere* to split open, fr. *de-* + *hiscere* to gape; akin to L *hiare* to yawn — more at YAWN] (1657) : to split along a natural line; *also* : to discharge contents by so splitting ⟨seedpods *dehiscing* at maturity⟩

de·his·cence \di-'hi-sⁿ(t)s\ *n* [NL *dehiscentia*, fr. L *dehiscent-, dehiscens*, prp. of *dehiscere*] (ca. 1828) : an act or instance of dehiscing ⟨pollen freed by ~ of the anther⟩ — **de·his·cent** \-sⁿt\ *adj*

de·horn \(ˌ)dē-'hȯrn\ *vt* (1888) **1** : to deprive of horns **2** : to prevent the growth of the horns of — **de·horn·er** *n*

de·hu·man·ize \(ˌ)dē-'hyü-mə-ˌnīz, (ˌ)dē-'yü-\ *vt* (1818) : to deprive of human qualities, personality, or spirit — **de·hu·man·iza·tion** \(ˌ)dē-ˌhyü-mə-nə-'zā-shən, (ˌ)dē-ˌyü-\ *n*

de·hu·mid·i·fy \ˌdē-hyü-'mi-də-ˌfī, ˌdē-yü-\ *vt* (1927) : to remove moisture from (as air) — **de·hu·mid·i·fi·ca·tion** \-ˌmi-də-fə-'kā-shən\ *n* — **de·hu·mid·i·fi·er** \-'mi-də-ˌfī(-ə)r\ *n*

de·hy·drate \(ˌ)dē-'hī-ˌdrāt\ *vt* (1876) **1 a** : to remove bound water or hydrogen and oxygen from (a chemical compound) in the proportion in which they form water **b** : to remove water from (as foods) **2** : to deprive of vitality or savor ~ *vi* : to lose water or body fluids — **de·hy·dra·tor** \-ˌdrā-tər\ *n*

de·hy·dra·tion \ˌdē-ˌhī-'drā-shən\ *n* (1854) : the process of dehydrating; *esp* : an abnormal depletion of body fluids

de·hy·dro·chlo·ri·nase \(ˌ)dē-ˌhī-drə-'klȯr-ə-ˌnās, -'klȯr-, -ˌnāz\ *n* (1956) : an enzyme that dehydrochlorinates a chlorinated hydrocarbon (as DDT) and is found esp. in some DDT resistant insects

de·hy·dro·chlo·ri·na·tion \-ˌklȯr-ə-'nā-shən, -ˌklȯr-ə-, -ˌklȯr-\ *n* (1936) : the process of removing hydrogen and chlorine or hydrogen chloride from a compound — **de·hy·dro·chlo·ri·nate** \-'klȯr-ə-ˌnāt, -'klȯr-\ *vt*

de·hy·dro·ge·nase \(ˌ)dē-(ˌ)hī-'drä-jə-ˌnās, (ˌ)dē-'hī-drə-jə-, -ˌnāz\ *n* [ISV] (1923) : an enzyme that accelerates the removal of hydrogen from metabolites and its transfer to other substances ⟨succinic ~⟩

de·hy·dro·ge·na·tion \ˌdē-(ˌ)hī-ˌdrä-jə-'nā-shən, (ˌ)dē-ˌhī-drə-jə-\ *n* (1866) : the removal of hydrogen from a chemical compound — **de·hy·dro·ge·nate** \(ˌ)dē-(ˌ)hī-'drä-jə-ˌnāt, (ˌ)dē-'hī-drə-jə-\ *vt*

de·ice \(ˌ)dē-'īs\ *vt* (1934) : to rid or keep free of ice — **de·ic·er** *n*

de·i·cide \'dē-ə-ˌsīd, 'dā-ə-\ *n* [ultim. fr. L *deus* god + *-cidium, -cida* *-cide* — more at DEITY] (1611) **1** : the act of killing a divine being or a symbolic substitute of such a being **2** : the killer or destroyer of a god

deic·tic \'dīk-tik *also* 'dāk-\ *adj* [Gk *deiktikos* able to show, fr. *deiktos*, verbal of *deiknynai* to show — more at DICTION] (1876) : showing or pointing out directly ⟨the words *this, that,* and *those* have a ~ function⟩

de·i·fi·ca·tion \ˌdē-ə-fə-'kā-shən, ˌdā-\ *n* (14c) : the act or an instance of deifying

de·i·fy \'dē-ə-ˌfī, 'dā-\ *vt* **-fied; -fy·ing** [ME, fr. MF *deifier*, fr. LL *deificare*, fr. L *deus* god + *-ficare* *-fy*] (14c) **1** : to make a god of **2** : to take as an object of worship **2** : to glorify as of supreme worth

deign \'dān\ *vb* [ME, fr. OF *deignier*, fr. LL *dignare, dignari*, fr. *dignus* worthy — more at DECENT] *vi* (14c) : to condescend reluctantly and with a strong sense of the affront to one's superiority that is involved ~ *vt* : to condescend to give or offer

deil \'dē(ə)l\ *n* [ME *devel, del*] (15c) *Scot* : DEVIL

de·in·dus·tri·al·iza·tion \(ˌ)dē-in-ˌdəs-trē-ə-lə-'zā-shən\ *n* (1940) : the reduction or destruction of a nation's industrial capacity — **de·in·dus·tri·al·ize** \(ˌ)dē-in-'dəs-trē-ə-ˌlīz\ *vb*

dei·non·y·chus \(ˌ)dī-'nä-ni-kəs\ *n* [NL, fr. Gk *deinos* terrifying + *-onychos* -clawed (fr. *onych-, onyx* claw, nail) — more at DIRE, NAIL] (1969) : any of a genus (*Deinonychus*) of small bipedal carnivorous dinosaurs from the Cretaceous

de·in·sti·tu·tion·al·iza·tion \(ˌ)dē-ˌin(t)-stə-ˌtü-shə-nə-lə-'zā-shən, -ˌtyü-\ *n* (1955) **1** : the release of institutionalized individuals (as mental patients) from institutional care to care in the community **2** : the reform or modification of an institution to remove or disguise its institutional character — **de·in·sti·tu·tion·al·ize** \-'tü-shə-nə-ˌlīz, -'tyü-\ *vt*

de·ion·ize \(ˌ)dē-'ī-ə-ˌnīz\ *vt* (1906) : to remove ions from ⟨~ water by ion exchange⟩ — **de·ion·iza·tion** \(ˌ)dē-ˌī-ə-nə-'zā-shən\ *n* — **de·ion·iz·er** \-ˌnī-zər\ *n*

de·ism \'dē-ˌi-zəm, 'dā-\ *n, often cap* (1682) : a movement or system of thought advocating natural religion, emphasizing morality, and in the 18th century denying the interference of the Creator with the laws of the universe — **de·ist** \'dē-ist, 'dā-\ *n, often cap* — **de·is·tic** \dē-'is-tik, dā-\ *adj* — **de·is·ti·cal** \-ti-kəl\ *adj* — **de·is·ti·cal·ly** \-ti-k(ə-)lē\ *adv*

de·i·ty \'dē-ə-tē, 'dā-\ *n, pl* **-ties** [ME *deitee*, fr. OF *deité*, fr. LL *deitat-, deitas*, fr. L *deus* god; akin to OE *Tīw*, god of war, L *divus* god, *dies* day, Gk *dios* heavenly, Skt *deva* heavenly, god] (14c) **1 a** : the rank or essential nature of a god : DIVINITY **b** *cap* : GOD 1, SUPREME BEING **2** : a god or goddess ⟨the *deities* of ancient Greece⟩ **3** : one exalted or revered as supremely good or powerful

deix·is \'dīk-sis *also* 'dāk-\ *n* [Gk, lit., display, fr. *deiknynai* to show — more at DICTION] (1949) : the pointing or specifying function of some words (as definite articles and demonstrative pronouns) whose denotation changes from one discourse to another

dé·jà vu \ˌdā-ˌzhä-'vü, ˌdā-zhä-vᵫ\ *n* [F, adj., lit., already seen] (1903) **1 a** : the illusion of remembering scenes and events when experienced for the first time **b** : a feeling that one has seen or heard something before **2** : something overly or unpleasantly familiar

¹**de·ject** \di-'jekt, dē-\ *adj* (15c) *archaic* : DEJECTED

²**deject** *vt* [ME, to throw down, fr. L *dejectus*, pp. of *deicere*, fr. *de-* + *jacere* to throw — more at JET] (1581) : to make gloomy

de·jec·ta \di-'jek-tə, dē-\ *n pl* [NL, fr. L, neut. pl. of *dejectus*] (1887) : FECES, EXCREMENT

de·ject·ed \di-'jek-təd, dē-\ *adj* (1581) **1** : cast down in spirits : DEPRESSED **2 a** *obs, of the eyes* : DOWNCAST **b** *archaic* : thrown down **3** *obs* : lowered in rank or condition — **de·ject·ed·ly** *adv* — **de·ject·ed·ness** *n*

de·jec·tion \di-'jek-shən, dē-\ *n* (15c) : lowness of spirits

de ju·re \(ˌ)dē-'jūr-ē, (ˌ)dā-'yūr-\ *adv or adj* [ML] (1611) : by right : of right

deka- *or* **dek-** — see DECA-

deka·gram \'de-kə-ˌgram\ n (ca. 1879) — see METRIC SYSTEM table
deka·li·ter \-ˌlē-tər\ n (ca. 1879) — see METRIC SYSTEM table
deka·me·ter \-ˌmē-tər\ n (ca. 1879) — see METRIC SYSTEM table
deka·met·ric \ˌde-kə-'me-trik\ adj (1968) : DECAMETRIC
de·lam·i·na·tion \(ˌ)dē-ˌla-mə-'nā-shən\ n (1877) 1 : gastrula formation in which the endoderm is split off as a layer from the inner surface of the blastoderm and the archenteron is represented by the space between this endoderm and the yolk mass 2 : separation into constituent layers — **de·lam·i·nate** \(ˌ)dē-'la-mə-ˌnāt\ vi
de·late \di-'lāt, dē-\ vt **de·lat·ed; de·lat·ing** [L delatus (pp. of deferre to bring down, report, accuse), fr. de- + latus, pp. of ferre to bear — more at TOLERATE] (15c) 1 : ACCUSE, DENOUNCE 2 : REPORT, RELATE — **de·la·tion** \-'lā-shən\ n — **de·la·tor** \-'lā-tər\ n
Del·a·ware \'de-lə-ˌwar, -ˌwer, -wər\ n, pl **Delaware** or **Delawares** [Delaware River] (1721) 1 : a member of an American Indian people orig. of the Delaware valley 2 : the Algonquian language of the Delaware
¹**de·lay** \di-'lā, dē-\ n (13c) 1 a : the act of delaying : the state of being delayed b : an instance of being delayed 2 : the time during which something is delayed
²**delay** vb [ME, fr. OF delaier, fr. de- + laier to leave, perh. alter. of laissier, fr. L laxare to slacken, fr. laxus loose — more at SLACK] vt (14c) 1 : PUT OFF, POSTPONE 2 : to stop, detain, or hinder for a time ~ vi : to move or act slowly; also : to cause delay — **de·lay·er** n
syn DELAY, RETARD, SLOW, SLACKEN, DETAIN mean to cause to be late or behind in movement or progress. DELAY implies a holding back, usu. by interference, from completion or arrival ⟨bad weather delayed our arrival⟩. RETARD suggests reduction of speed without actual stopping ⟨language barriers retarded their progress⟩. SLOW and SLACKEN also imply a reduction of speed, SLOW often suggesting deliberate intention ⟨medication slowed the patient's heart rate⟩, SLACKEN an easing up or relaxing of power or effort ⟨on hot days runners slacken their pace⟩. DETAIN implies a holding back beyond a reasonable or appointed time ⟨unexpected business had detained her⟩.
syn DELAY, PROCRASTINATE, LAG, LOITER, DAWDLE, DALLY mean to move or act slowly so as to fall behind. DELAY usu. implies a putting off (as a beginning or departure) ⟨we cannot delay any longer⟩. PROCRASTINATE implies blameworthy delay esp. through laziness or apathy ⟨procrastinates about making decisions⟩. LAG implies failure to maintain a speed set by others ⟨lagging behind in technology⟩. LOITER and DAWDLE imply delay while in progress, esp. in walking, but DAWDLE more clearly suggests an aimless wasting of time ⟨loitered at several store windows⟩ ⟨children dawdling on their way home from school⟩. DALLY suggests delay through trifling or vacillation when promptness is necessary ⟨stop dallying and get to work⟩.
¹**de·le** \'dē-(ˌ)lē\ vt **de·led; de·le·ing** [L, imper. sing. of delēre] (1705) : to delete esp. from typeset matter
²**dele** n (ca. 1751) : a mark indicating that something is to be deled
¹**de·lec·ta·ble** \di-'lek-tə-bəl\ adj [ME, fr. OF, fr. L delectabilis, fr. delectare to delight — more at DELIGHT] (15c) 1 : highly pleasing : DELIGHTFUL 2 : DELICIOUS — **de·lec·ta·bil·i·ty** \-ˌlek-tə-'bi-lə-tē\ n — **de·lec·ta·bly** \-blē\ adv
²**delectable** n (1921) : something that is delectable
de·lec·ta·tion \ˌdē-ˌlek-'tā-shən, di-; ˌde-lək-\ n (14c) : DELIGHT, ENJOYMENT
del·e·ga·ble \'de-li-gə-bəl\ adj (1660) : capable of being delegated
del·e·ga·cy \-gə-sē\ n, pl **-cies** (15c) 1 : a body of delegates : BOARD 2 a : the act of delegating b : appointment as delegate
¹**del·e·gate** \'de-li-gət, -ˌgāt\ n [ME delegat, fr. ML delegatus, fr. L, pp. of delegare to delegate, fr. de- + legare to send — more at LEGATE] (15c) : a person acting for another: as a : a representative to a convention or conference b : a representative of a U.S. territory in the House of Representatives c : a member of the lower house of the legislature of Maryland, Virginia, or West Virginia
²**del·e·gate** \-ˌgāt\ vb **-gat·ed; -gat·ing** vt (1530) 1 : to entrust to another ⟨~ authority⟩ 2 : to appoint as one's representative ~ vi : to assign responsibility or authority — **del·e·ga·tee** \ˌde-li-gə-'tē\ n — **del·e·ga·tor** \'de-li-ˌgā-tər\ n
del·e·ga·tion \ˌde-li-'gā-shən\ n (1612) 1 : the act of empowering to act for another 2 : a group of persons chosen to represent others
de·le·git·i·ma·tion \ˌdē-lə-ˌji-tə-'mā-shən\ n (1968) : a decline in or loss of prestige or authority
de·lete \di-'lēt, dē-\ vt **de·let·ed; de·let·ing** [L deletus, pp. of delēre to wipe out, destroy] (ca. 1605) : to eliminate esp. by blotting out, cutting out, or erasing
del·e·te·ri·ous \ˌde-lə-'ti-rē-əs\ adj [Gk dēlētērios, fr. dēleisthai to hurt] (1643) : harmful often in a subtle or unexpected way ⟨~ effects⟩ ⟨~ to health⟩ **syn** see PERNICIOUS — **del·e·te·ri·ous·ly** adv — **del·e·te·ri·ous·ness** n
de·le·tion \di-'lē-shən, dē-\ n [L deletion-, deletio destruction, fr. delēre] (1590) 1 : the act of deleting 2 a : something deleted b (1) : the absence of a section of genetic material from a chromosome (2) : the mutational process that results in a deletion
delft \'delft\ n [Delft, Netherlands] (1723) 1 : tin-glazed Dutch earthenware with blue and white or polychrome decoration 2 : a ceramic ware resembling or imitative of Dutch delft
delft·ware \'delft-ˌwar, -ˌwer\ n (1714) : DELFT
deli \'de-lē\ n, pl **del·is** (ca. 1954) : DELICATESSEN
¹**de·lib·er·ate** \di-'li-bə-ˌrāt\ vb **-at·ed; -at·ing** vi (14c) : to think about or discuss issues and decisions carefully ~ vt : to think about deliberately and often with formal discussion before reaching a decision **syn** see THINK
²**de·lib·er·ate** \di-'li-bə-rət, -'lib-rət\ adj [L deliberatus, pp. of deliberare to consider carefully, perh. alter. of (assumed) delibrare, fr. de- + libra scale, pound] (15c) 1 : characterized by or resulting from careful and thorough consideration ⟨a ~ decision⟩ 2 : characterized by awareness of the consequences ⟨~ falsehood⟩ 3 : slow, unhurried, and steady as though allowing time for decision on each individual action involved ⟨a ~ pace⟩ **syn** see VOLUNTARY — **de·lib·er·ate·ly** adv — **de·lib·er·ate·ness** n
de·lib·er·a·tion \di-ˌli-bə-'rā-shən\ n (14c) 1 a : the act of deliberating b : a discussion and consideration by a group of persons of the reasons for and against a measure 2 : the quality or state of being

deliberate — **de·lib·er·a·tive** \-'li-bə-ˌrāt-iv, -'li-b(ə-)rət-\ adj — **de·lib·er·a·tive·ly** adv — **de·lib·er·a·tive·ness** n
del·i·ca·cy \'de-li-kə-sē\ n, pl **-cies** (14c) 1 obs a : the quality or state of being luxurious b : INDULGENCE 2 : something pleasing to eat that is considered rare or luxurious ⟨considered caviar a ~⟩ 3 a : the quality or state of being dainty : FINENESS ⟨lace of great ~⟩ b : FRAILTY 1 4 : fineness or subtle expressiveness of touch (as in painting or music) 5 a : precise and refined perception and discrimination b : extreme sensitivity : PRECISION ⟨an electronic instrument of great ~⟩ 6 a : refined sensibility in feeling or conduct b : the quality or state of being squeamish 7 : the quality or state of requiring delicate handling
¹**del·i·cate** \'de-li-kət\ adj [ME delicat, fr. L delicatus delicate, addicted to pleasure; akin to L delicere to allure] (14c) 1 : pleasing to the senses: a : generally pleasant ⟨the climate's ~, the air most sweet — Shak.⟩ b : pleasing to the sense of taste or smell esp. in a mild or subtle way ⟨a ~ aroma⟩ ⟨a robust wine will dominate ~ dishes⟩ c : marked by daintiness or charm of color, lines, or proportions ⟨a ~ floral print⟩ ⟨an ample tear trilled down her ~ cheek —Shak.⟩ d : marked by fineness of structure, workmanship, or texture ⟨a ~ tracery⟩ ⟨a ~ lace⟩ 2 a : marked by keen sensitivity or fine discrimination ⟨~ insights⟩ ⟨a more ~ syntactic analysis —R. H. Robins⟩ b : FASTIDIOUS, SQUEAMISH ⟨a person of ~ tastes⟩ 3 a : not robust in health or constitution : WEAK, SICKLY ⟨had been considered a ~ child⟩ b : easily torn or damaged : FRAGILE ⟨the ~ chain of life⟩ 4 a : requiring careful handling: (1) : easily unsettled or upset ⟨a ~ balance⟩ ⟨the ~ relationships defined by the Constitution —New Yorker⟩ (2) : requiring skill or tact ⟨in a ~ position⟩ ⟨~ negotiations⟩ ⟨a ~ operation⟩ (3) : involving matters of a deeply personal nature : SENSITIVE ⟨this is a ~ matter. Could I possibly speak to you alone —Daphne Du Maurier⟩ b : marked by care, skill, or tact ⟨~ handling of a difficult situation⟩ 5 : marked by great precision or sensitivity ⟨a ~ instrument⟩ **syn** see CHOICE — **del·i·cate·ly** adv
²**delicate** n (15c) : something delicate
del·i·ca·tes·sen \ˌde-li-kə-'te-s⁰n\ n pl [obs. G (now Delikatessen), pl. of Delicatesse delicacy, fr. F délicatesse, prob. fr. OIt delicatezza, fr. delicato delicate, fr. L delicatus] (1889) 1 : ready-to-eat food products (as cooked meats and prepared salads) 2 sing, pl **delicatessens** [delicatessen (store)] : a store where delicatessen are sold
de·li·cious \di-'li-shəs\ adj [ME, fr. MF, fr. LL deliciosus, fr. L deliciae delights, fr. delicere to allure] (14c) 1 : affording great pleasure : DELIGHTFUL ⟨~ anecdotes⟩ 2 : appealing to one of the bodily senses esp. of taste or smell — **de·li·cious·ly** adv — **de·li·cious·ness** n
Delicious n, pl **De·li·cious·es** or **Deliciouses** (ca. 1903) : an important red or yellow market apple of American origin that has a crown of five rounded prominences on the end opposite the stem
de·lict \di-'likt, dē-\ n [L delictum fault, fr. neut. of delictus, pp. of delinquere] (1523) : an offense against the law
¹**de·light** \di-'līt, dē-\ n (13c) 1 : a high degree of gratification : JOY; also : extreme satisfaction 2 : something that gives great pleasure 3 archaic : the power of affording pleasure
²**delight** vb [ME deliten, fr. OF delitier, fr. L delectare, freq. of delicere to allure, fr. de- + lacere to allure] vi (13c) 1 : to take great pleasure ⟨~ed in playing the guitar⟩ 2 : to give keen enjoyment ⟨a book certain to ~⟩ ~ vt : to give joy or satisfaction to — **de·light·er** n
de·light·ed adj (1603) 1 obs : DELIGHTFUL 2 : highly pleased — **de·light·ed·ly** adv — **de·light·ed·ness** n
de·light·ful \di-'līt-fəl, dē-\ adj (ca. 1530) : highly pleasing — **de·light·ful·ly** \-fə-lē\ adv — **de·light·ful·ness** n
de·light·some \-'līt-səm\ adj (1520) : very pleasing : DELIGHTFUL
De·li·lah \di-'lī-lə\ n [Heb Dĕlīlāh] : the mistress and betrayer of Samson in the book of Judges
de·lim·it \di-'li-mət\ vt [F délimiter, fr. L delimitare, fr. de- + limitare to limit, fr. limit-, limes boundary, limit] (1852) : to fix or define the limits of — **de·lim·i·ta·tion** \di-ˌli-mə-'tā-shən, ˌdē-\ n
de·lim·it·er \di-'li-mə-tər\ n (1960) : a character that marks the beginning or end of a unit of data
de·lin·eate \di-'li-nē-ˌāt\ vt **-at·ed; -at·ing** [L delineatus, pp. of delineare, fr. de- + linea line] (1559) 1 a : to indicate or represent by drawn or painted lines b : to mark the outline of ⟨lights delineating the narrow streets⟩ 2 : to describe, portray, or set forth with accuracy or in detail ⟨~ a character in the story⟩ ⟨~ the steps to be taken by the government⟩ — **de·lin·ea·tor** \-ē-ˌā-tər\ n
de·lin·ea·tion \di-ˌli-nē-'ā-shən\ n (1570) 1 : the act of delineating 2 : something made by delineating — **de·lin·ea·tive** \-'li-nē-ˌā-tiv\ adj
de·lin·quen·cy \di-'liŋ-kwən-sē, -'lin-\ n, pl **-cies** (1636) 1 a : a delinquent act b : conduct that is out of accord with accepted behavior or the law; esp : JUVENILE DELINQUENCY 2 : a debt on which payment is overdue
¹**de·lin·quent** \-kwənt\ n (15c) : a delinquent person
²**delinquent** adj [L delinquent-, delinquens, prp. of delinquere to fail, offend, fr. de- + linquere to leave — more at LOAN] (1603) 1 : offending by neglect or violation of duty or of law 2 : being overdue in payment ⟨a ~ charge account⟩ 3 : of, relating to, or characteristic of delinquents : marked by delinquency — **de·lin·quent·ly** adv
del·i·quesce \ˌde-li-'kwes\ vi **-quesced; -quesc·ing** [L deliquescere, fr. de- + liquescere, incho. of liquēre to be fluid — more at LIQUID] (1756) 1 : to dissolve or melt away 2 : to become soft or liquid with age — used of plant structures (as mushrooms)
del·i·ques·cent \-'kwe-s⁰nt\ adj [L deliquescent-, deliquescens, prp. of deliquescere] (1791) 1 : tending to melt or dissolve; esp : tending to undergo gradual dissolution and liquefaction by the attraction and absorption of moisture from the air 2 : having repeated division into branches ⟨elms are ~ trees⟩ — compare EXCURRENT 2a — **del·i·ques·cence** \-s⁰n(t)s\ n

---

\ə\ abut \ᵊ\ kitten, F table \ər\ further \a\ ash \ā\ ace \ä\ mop, mar
\aů\ out \ch\ chin \e\ bet \ē\ easy \g\ go \i\ hit \ī\ ice \j\ job
\ŋ\ sing \ō\ go \ȯ\ law \ȯi\ boy \th\ thin \t͟h\ the \ü\ loot \ů\ foot
\y\ yet \zh\ vision \à, k̲, ⁿ, œ, œ̄, ᵫ, ᵫ̄, ᵊ\ see Guide to Pronunciation

de·lir·i·ous \di-'lir-ē-əs\ *adj* (1599) **1 :** of, relating to, or characteristic of delirium **2 :** affected with or marked by delirium — **de·lir·i·ous·ly** *adv* — **de·lir·i·ous·ness** *n*

de·lir·i·um \di-'lir-ē-əm\ *n* [L, fr. *delirare* to be crazy, lit., to leave the furrow (in plowing), fr. *de-* + *lira* furrow — more at LEARN] (ca. 1563) **1 :** a mental disturbance characterized by confusion, disordered speech, and hallucinations **2 :** frenzied excitement ⟨he would stride about his room in a ~ of joy —Thomas Wolfe⟩

delirium tre·mens \-'trē-mənz, -'tre-\ *n* [NL, lit., trembling delirium] (1865) **:** a violent delirium with tremors that is induced by excessive and prolonged use of alcoholic liquors — called also *d.t.'s*

de·list \(,)dē-'list\ *vt* (1933) **:** to remove from a list; *esp* **:** to remove (a security) from the list of securities that may be dealt in on a particular exchange

de·liv·er \di-'li-vər, dē-\ *vb* de·liv·ered; de·liv·er·ing \-v(ə-)riŋ\ [ME, fr. OF *delivrer*, fr. LL *deliberare*, fr. L *de-* + *liberare* to liberate] *vt* (13c) **1 :** to set free ⟨and evil was not into temptation, but ~ us from evil — Mt 6:13 (AV)⟩ **2 a :** to take and hand over to or leave for another **:** CONVEY ⟨~ a package⟩ **b :** HAND OVER, SURRENDER ⟨~ed the prisoners to the sheriff⟩ ⟨~ed themselves over to God⟩ **3 a** (1) **:** to assist in giving birth (2) **:** to aid in the birth of **b :** to give birth to **c :** to cause (oneself) to produce as if by giving birth ⟨has ~ed himself of half an autobiography —H. C. Schonberg⟩ **4 :** SPEAK, SING, UTTER ⟨~ed their lines with style⟩ ⟨~ a song⟩ ⟨~ a speech⟩ **5 :** to send (something aimed or guided) to an intended target or destination ⟨ability to ~ nuclear warheads⟩ ⟨~ed a fastball⟩ **6 a :** to bring (as votes) to the support of a candidate or cause **b :** to come through with **:** PRODUCE ⟨can ~ the goods⟩ ⟨new car ~s high gas mileage⟩ ~ *vi* **:** to produce the promised, desired, or expected results **:** COME THROUGH ⟨can't ~ on all these promises⟩ *syn* see RESCUE — de·liv·er·abil·i·ty \-,li-v(ə-)rə-'bi-lə-tē\ *n* — de·liv·er·able \-'li-v(ə-)rə-bəl\ *adj* — de·liv·er·er \-'li-vər-ər\ *n* — **deliver the goods :** to give results that are promised, expected, or desired

de·liv·er·ance \di-'li-v(ə-)rən(t)s, dē-\ *n* (14c) **1 :** the act of delivering someone or something **:** the state of being delivered; *esp* **:** LIBERATION, RESCUE **2 :** something delivered; *esp* **:** an opinion or decision (as the verdict of a jury) expressed publicly

de·liv·ery \di-'li-v(ə-)rē, dē-\ *n, pl* -er·ies (15c) **:** the act of delivering something; *also* **:** something delivered

delivery boy *n* (1920) **:** a person employed by a retail store to deliver small orders to customers on call

de·liv·ery·man \-v(ə-)rē-mən, -,man\ *n* (1920) **:** a person who delivers wholesale or retail goods to customers usu. over a regular local route

dell \'del\ *n* [ME *delle*; akin to MHG *telle* ravine, OE *dæl* valley — more at DALE] (13c) **:** a secluded hollow or small valley usu. covered with trees or turf

delly *var of* DELI

Del·mon·i·co steak \del-'mä-ni-(,)kō-\ *n* [fr. the *Delmonico* restaurants, New York City, after Lorenzo Delmonico †1881 Am. restaurateur] (1925) **:** CLUB STEAK — called also *Delmonico*

de·lo·cal·ize \(,)dē-'lō-kə-,līz\ *vt* (1855) **:** to free from the limitations of locality; *specif* **:** to remove (a charge or charge carrier) from a particular position — de·lo·cal·iza·tion \(,)dē-,lō-kə-lə-'zā-shən\ *n*

de·louse \(,)dē-'laus, -'lauz\ *vt* (ca. 1919) **:** to remove lice from

Del·phi·an \'del-fē-ən\ *adj* (1625) **:** DELPHIC

Del·phic \'del-fik\ *adj* (ca. 1599) **1 :** of or relating to ancient Delphi or its oracle **2** *often not cap* **:** AMBIGUOUS, OBSCURE ⟨~ utterances⟩ — del·phi·cal·ly \-fi-k(ə-)lē\ *adv*

del·phin·i·um \del-'fi-nē-əm\ *n* [NL, genus name, fr. Gk *delphinion* larkspur, dim. of *delphin-, delphis* dolphin; prob. fr. the shape of the nectary] (1664) **:** any of a large genus (*Delphinium*) of the buttercup family that comprises chiefly perennial erect branching herbs with palmately divided leaves and irregular flowers in showy spikes and includes several that are poisonous — compare LARKSPUR

Del·phi·nus \del-'fi-nəs, -'fē-\ *n* [L (gen. *Delphini*), lit., dolphin, fr. Gk *delphin-, delphis*] **:** a northern constellation nearly west of Pegasus

¹del·ta \'del-tə\ *n* [ME *deltha*, fr. Gk *delta*, of Sem origin; akin to Heb *dāleth* daleth] (13c) **1 :** the fourth letter of the Greek alphabet — see ALPHABET table **2 :** something shaped like a capital Greek delta; *esp* **:** the alluvial deposit at the mouth of a river **3 :** an increment of a variable — symbol Δ — del·ta·ic \del-'tā-ik\ *adj*

²delta *adj* (ca. 1929) **:** fourth in position in the structure of an organic molecule from a particular group or atom — symbol δ

Delta (1952) — a communications code word for the letter *d*

delta ray *n* (1908) **:** an electron ejected by an ionizing particle in its passage through matter

delta wave *n* (1936) **:** a high amplitude electrical rhythm of the brain with a frequency of less than 6 cycles per second that occurs esp. in deep sleep, in infancy, and in many diseased conditions of the brain — called also *delta, delta rhythm*

delta wing *n* [¹*delta*; fr. its shape] (1946) **:** a triangular swept-back airplane wing with a usu. straight trailing edge

¹del·toid \'del-,tȯid\ *n* [NL *deltoides*, fr. Gk *deltoeidēs* shaped like a delta, fr. *delta*] (ca. 1681) **:** a large triangular muscle that covers the shoulder joint and serves to raise the arm laterally

²deltoid *adj* (ca. 1753) **1 :** having a triangular shape ⟨a ~ leaf⟩ — see LEAF illustration **2 :** relating to, associated with, or supplying the deltoid

del·toi·de·us \del-'tȯi-dē-əs\ *n, pl* del·toi·dei \-ē-,ī\ [NL, alter. of *deltoides*] (ca. 1860) **:** DELTOID

de·lude \di-'lüd, dē-\ *vt* de·lud·ed; de·lud·ing [ME, fr. L *deludere*, fr. *de-* + *ludere* to play — more at LUDICROUS] (15c) **1 :** to mislead the mind or judgment of **:** DECEIVE, TRICK **2** *obs* **a :** FRUSTRATE, DISAPPOINT **b :** EVADE, ELUDE *syn* see DECEIVE — de·lud·er *n*

¹del·uge \'del-,yüj, -,yüzh; ÷də-'lüj, 'dä-,lüj\ *n* [ME, fr. OF, fr. L *diluvium*, fr. *diluere* to wash away, fr. *dis-* + *lavere* to wash — more at

delphinium

LYE] (14c) **1 a :** an overflowing of the land by water **b :** a drenching rain **2 :** an overwhelming amount or number

²deluge *vt* del·uged; del·ug·ing (1593) **1 :** to overflow with water **:** INUNDATE **2 :** OVERWHELM, SWAMP

de·lu·sion \di-'lü-zhən, dē-\ *n* [ME, fr. LL *delusion-, delusio*, fr. *deludere*] (15c) **1 a :** the act of deluding **:** the state of being deluded **b :** an abnormal mental state characterized by the occurrence of psychotic delusions **2 a :** something that is falsely or delusively believed or propagated **b :** a persistent false psychotic belief regarding the self or persons or objects outside the self — de·lu·sion·al \-'lüzh-nəl, -'lü-zhə-n²l\ *adj* — de·lu·sion·ary \-zhə-,ner-ē\ *adj*

de·lu·sive \-'lü-siv, -'lü-ziv\ *adj* (1605) **1 :** likely to delude **2 :** constituting a delusion — de·lu·sive·ly *adv* — de·lu·sive·ness *n*

de·lu·so·ry \-sə-rē, -zə-\ *adj* (15c) **:** DECEPTIVE, DELUSIVE

de·lus·ter \(,)dē-'ləs-tər\ *vt* (1926) **:** to reduce the sheen of (as yarn or fabric)

de·luxe \di-'ləks, dē- *also* -'luks, -'lüks\ *adj* [F *de luxe*, lit., of luxury] (1819) **:** notably luxurious, elegant, or expensive ⟨a ~ edition⟩ ⟨~ hotels⟩

¹delve \'delv\ *vb* delved; delv·ing [ME, fr. OE *delfan*; akin to OHG *telban* to dig] *vt* (bef. 12c) *archaic* **:** EXCAVATE ~ *vi* **1 :** to dig or labor with or as if with a spade **2 :** to make a careful or detailed search for information ⟨*delved* into the past⟩ — delv·er *n*

²delve *n* (14c) *archaic* **:** CAVE, HOLLOW

de·mag·ne·tize \(,)dē-'mag-nə-,tīz\ *vt* (1839) **:** to deprive of magnetic properties — de·mag·ne·ti·za·tion \(,)dē-,mag-nə-tə-'zā-shən\ *n* — de·mag·ne·tiz·er \(,)dē-'mag-nə-,tī-zər\ *n*

dem·a·gog·ic \,de-mə-'gä-gik *also* -'gä-jik *or* -'gō-jik\ *adj* (1831) **:** of, relating to, or characteristic of a demagogue **:** employing demagoguery — dem·a·gog·i·cal·ly \-gä-k(ə-)lē, -ji-\ *adv*

¹dem·a·gogue *or* dem·a·gog \'de-mə-,gäg\ *n* [Gk *dēmagōgos*, fr. *dēmos* people (perh. akin to Gk *daiesthai* to divide) + *agōgos* leading, fr. *agein* to lead — more at TIDE, AGENT] (1648) **1 :** a leader who makes use of popular prejudices and false claims and promises in order to gain power **2 :** a leader championing the cause of the common people in ancient times — dem·a·gogu·ery \-,gä-g(ə-)rē\ *n* — dem·a·gogy \-,gä-gē, -,gä-jē, -,gō-jē\ *n*

²demagogue *or* demagog *vb* -gogued *or* -goged; -gogu·ing *or* -gog·ing *vi* (1656) **:** to behave like a demagogue ~ *vt* **:** to treat (as an issue) in a demogogic manner

¹de·mand \di-'mand, -'mȧnd, dē-\ *n* (13c) **1 a :** an act of demanding or asking esp. with authority **b :** something claimed as due **2** *archaic* **:** QUESTION **3 a :** willingness and ability to purchase a commodity or service **b :** the quantity of a commodity or service wanted at a specified price and time **4 a :** a seeking or state of being sought after ⟨in great ~ as an entertainer⟩ **b :** urgent need **5 :** the requirement of work or of the expenditure of a resource ⟨equal to the ~s of the office⟩ ⟨oxygen ~ for waste oxidation⟩ — on demand **:** upon presentation and request for payment; *also* **:** when requested or needed

²demand *vb* [ME *demaunden*, fr. OF *demander*, fr. ML *demandare*, fr. L, to entrust, charge, fr. *de-* + *mandare* to enjoin — more at MANDATE] *vi* (14c) **:** to make a demand **:** ASK ~ *vt* **1 :** to ask or call for with authority **:** claim as due or just ⟨~ed to see a lawyer⟩ **2 :** to call for urgently, peremptorily, or insistently ⟨~ed that the rioters disperse⟩ **3 a :** to ask authoritatively or earnestly to be informed of **b :** to require to come **:** SUMMON **4 :** to call for as useful or necessary — de·mand·able \-'man-də-bəl\ *adj* — de·mand·er *n*

syn DEMAND, CLAIM, REQUIRE, EXACT mean to ask or call for something as due or as necessary. DEMAND implies peremptoriness and insistence and often the right to make requests that are to be regarded as commands ⟨*demanded* payment of the debt⟩. CLAIM implies a demand for the delivery or concession of something due as one's own or one's right ⟨*claimed* the right to manage his own affairs⟩. REQUIRE suggests the imperativeness that arises from inner necessity, compulsion of law or regulation, or the exigencies of the situation ⟨the patient *requires* constant attention⟩. EXACT implies not only demanding but getting what one demands ⟨*exacts* absolute loyalty⟩.

de·man·dant \di-'man-dənt\ *n* (15c) **1** *archaic* **:** the plaintiff in a real action **2** *archaic* **:** one who makes a demand or claim

demand deposit *n* (1923) **:** a bank deposit that can be withdrawn without advance notice

de·mand·ing *adj* (1926) **:** requiring much time, effort, or attention **:** EXACTING — de·mand·ing·ly \-'man-diŋ-lē\ *adv* — de·mand·ing·ness *n*

demand loan *n* (1913) **:** CALL LOAN

demand note *n* (1862) **:** a note payable on demand

de·mand–pull \di-'mand(d)-,pul\ *n* (1952) **:** an increase or upward trend in spendable money that tends to result in increased competition for available goods and services and a corresponding increase in consumer prices — compare COST-PUSH — demand–pull *adj*

de·mand–side \di-'mand-,sid\ *adj* (1980) **:** of, relating to, or being an economic theory that advocates use of government spending and growth in the money supply to stimulate the demand for goods and services and therefore expand economic activity — compare SUPPLY-SIDE

dem·an·toid \'de-mən-,tȯid\ *n* [G, fr. obs. G *Demant* diamond, fr. MHG *diemant*, fr. OF *diamant* — more at DIAMOND] (ca. 1890) **:** a green garnet used as a gem

de·mar·cate \di-'mär-,kāt, 'dē-,\ *vt* -cat·ed; -cat·ing [back-formation fr. *demarcation*, fr. Sp *demarcación*, fr. *demarcar* to delimit, fr. *de-* + *marcar* to mark, prob. fr. It *marcare*, of Gmc origin; akin to OHG *marha* boundary — more at MARK] (1816) **1 :** DELIMIT **2 :** to set apart **:** SEPARATE — de·mar·ca·tion \,dē-,mär-'kā-shən\ *n*

de·marche *or* de·marche \dā-'märsh, di-', 'dā-,\ *n* [F *démarche*, lit., gait, fr. MF, fr. *demarcher* to march, fr. OF *demarchier*, fr. *de-* + *marchier* to march] (1658) **1 a :** a course of action **:** MANEUVER **b :** a diplomatic or political initiative or maneuver **2 :** a petition or protest presented through diplomatic channels

de·mark \di-'märk\ *vt* (1834) **:** DEMARCATE

de·ma·te·ri·al·ize \,dē-mə-'tir-ē-ə-,līz\ *vt* (ca. 1864) **:** to cause to become or appear immaterial ~ *vi* **:** to lose or appear to lose materiality — de·ma·te·ri·al·iza·tion \-,tir-ē-ə-lə-'zā-shən\ *n*

deme \'dēm\ n [Gk dēmos people, deme] (1833) 1 : a unit of local government in ancient Attica 2 : a local population of closely related interbreeding organisms

¹de·mean \di-'mēn\ vt **de·meaned; de·mean·ing** [ME demenen, fr. MF demener to conduct, fr. de- + mener to lead, fr. L minare to drive, fr. minari to threaten — more at MOUNT] (14c) : to conduct or behave (oneself) usu. in a proper manner

²demean vt **de·meaned; de·mean·ing** [de- + ¹mean] (1601) : to lower in character, status, or reputation

de·mean·or \di-'mē-nər\ n [¹demean] (ca. 1485) : behavior toward others : outward manner *syn* see BEARING

demeanour Brit var of DEMEANOR

de·ment·ed \di-'men-təd\ adj (1644) : MAD, INSANE — **de·ment·ed·ly** adv — **de·ment·ed·ness** n

de·men·tia \di-'men(t)-shə, -shē-ə\ n [L, fr. dement-, demens mad, fr. de- + ment-, mens mind — more at MIND] (1806) 1 : a condition of deteriorated mentality often with emotional apathy 2 : MADNESS, INSANITY ⟨a fanaticism bordering on ∼⟩ — **de·men·tial** \-shəl\ adj

dementia prae·cox \-'prē-,käks\ n [NL, lit., premature dementia] (1899) : SCHIZOPHRENIA

de·mer·it \di-'mer-ət, dē-\ n [ME, fr. MF & ML; MF demerite, fr. ML demeritum, fr. neut. of demeritus, pp. of demerēre to be undeserving of, fr. L, to earn, fr. de- + merēre to merit] (15c) 1 obs : OFFENSE 2 a : a quality that deserves blame or lacks merit : FAULT, DEFECT b : lack of merit 3 : a mark usu. entailing a loss of privilege given to an offender

De·mer·ol \'de-mə-,rȯl, -,rōl\ trademark — used for meperidine

de·mer·sal \di-'mər-səl\ adj [L demersus (pp. of demergere to sink, fr. de- + mergere to dip, sink) + E ¹-al — more at MERGE] (1889) : living near, deposited on, or sinking to the bottom of the sea ⟨∼ fish eggs⟩

de·mesne \di-'mān, -'mēn\ n [ME, fr. AF, modif. of OF demeine — more at DOMAIN] (14c) 1 : legal possession of land as one's own 2 : REALM 4b, DOMAIN 3 : manorial land actually possessed by the lord and not held by tenants 4 a : the land attached to a mansion b : landed property : ESTATE c : REGION 2, TERRITORY

De·me·ter \di-'mē-tər\ n [L, fr. Gk Dēmētēr] : the Greek goddess of agriculture — compare CERES

demi- prefix [ME, fr. demi, fr. MF, fr. (assumed) VL dimedius, modif. of L dimidius, fr. dis- + medius mid — more at MID] 1 : half ⟨demisemiquaver⟩ 2 : one that partly belongs to (a specified type or class) ⟨demigod⟩

demi·god \'de-mē-,gäd\ n (1530) 1 : a mythological being with more power than a mortal but less than a god 2 : a person so outstanding as to seem to approach the divine

demi·god·dess \'de-mē-,gä-dəs\ n (1603) : a female demigod

demi·john \'de-mē-,jän\ n [by folk etymology fr. F dame-jeanne, lit., Lady Jane] (1806) : a large narrow-necked bottle usu. enclosed in wickerwork

de·mil·i·ta·rize \(,)dē-'mi-lə-tə-,rīz, di-\ vt (1883) 1 a : to do away with the military organization or potential of b : to prohibit (as a zone or frontier area) from being used for military purposes 2 : to rid of military characteristics or uses — **de·mil·i·tar·iza·tion** \(,)dē-,mi-lə-t(ə-)rə-'zā-shən, di-\ n

demi·mon·daine \,de-mi-,män-'dän, -'män-,, -mē-\ n [F demi-mondaine, fr. fem. of demi-mondain, fr. demi-monde] (1894) : a woman of the demimonde

demi·monde \'de-mi-,mänd, -mē-\ n [F demi-monde, fr. demi- + monde world, fr. L mundus] (1855) 1 a : a class of women on the fringes of respectable society supported by wealthy lovers b : PROSTITUTES 2 : DEMIMONDAINE 3 : a distinctive class, group, or activity that is often an isolated part of a larger class, group, or activity ⟨the pop music ∼⟩ ⟨the literary ∼⟩; esp : one having little reputation or prestige

de·min·er·al·iza·tion \(,)dē-,mi-nə-rə-lə-'zā-shən, di-\ n (1903) 1 : loss of bodily minerals (as calcium salts) esp. in disease 2 : the process of removing mineral matter or salts (as from water) — **de·min·er·al·ize** \(,)dē-'mi-nə-rə-,līz\ vt — **de·min·er·al·iz·er** \-,lī-zər\ n

demi·rep \'de-mi-,rep, -mē-\ n [demi- + rep (reprobate)] (1749) : DEMIMONDAINE

¹de·mise \di-'mīz\ vb **de·mised; de·mis·ing** vt (15c) 1 : to convey (as an estate) by will or lease 2 obs : CONVEY, GIVE 3 : to transmit by succession or inheritance ∼ vi 1 : DIE, DECEASE 2 : to pass by descent or bequest ⟨the property has demised to the king⟩

²demise n [MF, fem. of demis, pp. of demettre to dismiss, fr. L demittere to send down, fr. de- + mittere to send] (15c) 1 : the conveyance of an estate 2 : transfer of the sovereignty to a successor 3 a : DEATH b : a cessation of existence or activity c : a loss of position or status

demi·sec \,de-mi-'sek, -mē-\ adj [F] (1926) of champagne : moderately sweet

demi·semi·qua·ver \,de-mē-'se-mē-,kwä-vər\ n (ca. 1706) : THIRTY-SECOND NOTE

de·mis·sion \di-'mi-shən\ n [MF, fr. L demission-, demissio lowering, fr. demittere] (15c) : RESIGNATION, ABDICATION

de·mit \di-'mit\ vb **de·mit·ted; de·mit·ting** [MF demettre] vt (15c) 1 archaic : DISMISS 2 : RESIGN ∼ vi : to withdraw from office or membership

demi·tasse \'de-mi-,tas, -,täs, -mē\ n [F demi-tasse, fr. demi- + tasse cup, fr. MF, fr. Ar tass, fr. Per tast] (1842) : a small cup of black coffee; also : the cup used to serve it

demi·urge \'de-mē-,ərj\ n [LL demiurgus, fr. Gk dēmiourgos, lit., artisan, one with special skill, fr. dēmios of the people (fr. dēmos people) + -ourgos worker (fr. ergon work) — more at DEMAGOGUE, WORK] (1678) 1 cap a : a Platonic subordinate deity who fashions the sensible world in the light of eternal ideas b : a Gnostic subordinate deity who is the creator of the material world 2 : one that is an autonomous creative force or decisive power — **demi·ur·gic** \-jik\ also **demi·ur·gi·cal** \-ji-kəl\ adj

demi·world \'de-mē-,wərld\ n (1862) : DEMIMONDE 3

demo \'de-(,)mō\ n, pl **dem·os** (1793) 1 cap a : DEMOCRAT 2 2 a : DEMONSTRATION 1b b Brit : DEMONSTRATION 4 3 a : DEMONSTRATOR a b : a recording intended to show off a song or performer to a record producer

¹de·mob \(,)dē-'mäb, di-\ vt (1919) chiefly Brit : DEMOBILIZE

²demob n (1945) chiefly Brit : the act or process of demobilizing

de·mo·bi·lize \di-'mō-bə-,līz, ,dē-\ vt (1882) 1 : DISBAND 2 : to discharge from military service — **de·mo·bi·li·za·tion** \di-,mō-bə-lə-'zā-shən, ,dē-\ n

de·moc·ra·cy \di-'mä-krə-sē\ n, pl **-cies** [MF democratie, fr. LL democratia, fr. Gk dēmokratia, fr. dēmos + -kratia -cracy] (1576) 1 a : government by the people; esp : rule of the majority b : a government in which the supreme power is vested in the people and exercised by them directly or indirectly through a system of representation usu. involving periodically held free elections 2 : a political unit that has a democratic government 3 cap : the principles and policies of the Democratic party in the U.S. 4 : the common people esp. when constituting the source of political authority 5 : the absence of hereditary or arbitrary class distinctions or privileges

dem·o·crat \'de-mə-,krat\ n (1740) 1 a : an adherent of democracy b : one who practices social equality 2 cap : a member of the Democratic party of the U.S.

dem·o·crat·ic \,de-mə-'kra-tik\ adj (1602) 1 : of, relating to, or favoring democracy 2 often cap : of or relating to one of the two major political parties in the U.S. evolving in the early 19th century from the anti-federalists and the Democratic-Republican party and associated in modern times with policies of broad social reform and internationalism 3 : relating to, appealing to, or available to the broad masses of the people ⟨∼ art⟩ 4 : favoring social equality : not snobbish — **dem·o·crat·i·cal·ly** \-ti-k(ə-)lē\ adv

democratic centralism n (1926) : a principle of Communist party organization by which members take part in policy discussions and elections at all levels but must follow decisions made at higher levels

Democratic–Republican adj (1818) : of or relating to a major American political party of the early 19th century favoring a strict interpretation of the constitution to restrict the powers of the federal government and emphasizing states' rights

de·moc·ra·tize \di-'mä-krə-,tīz\ vt **-tized; -tiz·ing** (1798) : to make democratic — **de·moc·ra·ti·za·tion** \-,mä-krə-tə-'zā-shən\ n — **de·moc·ra·tiz·er** \-'mä-krə-,tī-zər\ n

dé·mo·dé \,dā-mō-'dā\ adj [F, fr. dé- de- + mode] (1873) : no longer fashionable : OUT-OF-DATE

de·mod·ed \(,)dē-'mō-dəd\ adj (1887) : DÉMODÉ

de·mod·u·late \(,)dē-'mä-jə-,lāt\ vt (1927) : to extract the intelligence from (a modulated signal) — **de·mod·u·la·tion** \(,)dē-,mä-jə-'lā-shən\ n — **de·mod·u·la·tor** \(')dē-'mä-jə-,lā-tər\ n

De·mo·gor·gon \,dē-mə-'gȯr-gən, ,de-mə-\ n [LL] : a mysterious spirit or deity often explained as a primeval creator god who antedates the gods of Greek mythology

de·mo·graph·ic \,dē-mə-'gra-fik, ,de-mə-\ also **de·mo·graph·i·cal** \-fi-kəl\ adj (1882) 1 : of or relating to demography or demographics 2 : relating to the dynamic balance of a population esp. with regard to density and capacity for expansion or decline — **de·mo·graph·i·cal·ly** \-fi-k(ə-)lē\ adv

de·mo·graph·ics \-fiks\ n pl (ca. 1966) 1 : the statistical characteristics of human populations (as age or income) used esp. to identify markets 2 : the demographic profile of a market (as the viewers of a TV show)

de·mog·ra·phy \di-'mä-grə-fē\ n [F démographie, fr. Gk dēmos people + F -graphie -graphy] (1880) : the statistical study of human populations esp. with reference to size and density, distribution, and vital statistics — **de·mog·ra·pher** \-fər\ n

dem·oi·selle \,de-mwä-'zel\ n [F, fr. OF dameisele — more at DAMSEL] (1520) 1 : a young lady 2 : DAMSELFLY 3 : DAMSELFISH

De·Moi·vre's theorem \də-'mȯi-vərz-, -'mwäv(-rə)z-\ n [Abraham De Moivre †1754 Fr. mathematician] (ca. 1891) : a theorem of complex numbers: the nth power of a complex number has for its absolute value its nth power and for its argument respectively the nth power of the absolute value and n times the argument of the complex number

de·mol·ish \di-'mä-lish\ vt [MF demoliss-, stem of demolir, fr. L demoliri, fr. de- + moliri to construct, fr. moles mass — more at MOLE] (1570) 1 a : TEAR DOWN, RAZE b : to break to pieces : SMASH 2 a : to do away with : DESTROY b : to strip of any pretense of merit or credence — **de·mol·ish·er** n — **de·mol·ish·ment** \-lish-mənt\ n

de·mo·li·tion \,de-mə-'li-shən, ,dē-mə-\ n (1549) 1 : the act of demolishing; esp : destruction in war by means of explosives 2 pl : explosives for destruction in war — **de·mo·li·tion·ist** \-'li-sh(ə-)nəst\ n

demolition derby n (ca. 1953) : a contest in which skilled drivers ram old cars into one another until only one car remains running

de·mon or **dae·mon** \'dē-mən\ n [ME demon, fr. LL & L; LL daemon evil spirit, fr. L, divinity, spirit, fr. Gk daimōn, prob. fr. daiesthai to distribute — more at TIDE] (13c) 1 a : an evil spirit b : a source or agent of evil, harm, distress, or ruin 2 usu daemon : an attendant power or spirit : GENIUS 3 usu daemon : a supernatural being of Greek mythology intermediate between gods and men 4 : one that has exceptional enthusiasm, drive, or effectiveness ⟨a ∼ for work⟩ — **de·mo·ni·an** \di-'mō-nē-ən\ adj — **de·mon·iza·tion** \,dē-mə-nə-'zā-shən\ n — **de·mon·ize** \'dē-mə-,nīz\ vt

— \'de-mə-,nīz\ vt [F démonétiser, fr. dé- de- + L moneta coin — more at MINT] (1852) 1 : to stop using (a metal) as a monetary standard 2 : to deprive of value for official payment — **de·mon·e·ti·za·tion** \(,)dē-,mä-nə-tə-'zā-shən, -,mə-\ n

¹de·mo·ni·ac \di-'mō-nē-,ak\ also **de·mo·ni·a·cal** \,dē-mə-'nī-ə-kəl\ adj [ME demoniak, fr. LL daemoniacus, fr. Gk daimoniakos, fr. daimon-, daimōn] (14c) 1 : possessed or influenced by a demon 2 : of, relating to, or suggestive of a demon : FIENDISH ⟨∼ cruelty⟩ — **de·mo·ni·a·cal·ly** \,dē-mə-'nī-ə-k(ə-)lē\ adv

²demoniac n (14c) : one possessed by a demon

de·mon·ic \di-'mä-nik, dē-\ also **de·mon·i·cal** \-ni-kəl\ adj (1662) : DEMONIAC 2 — **de·mon·i·cal·ly** \-ni-k(ə-)lē\ adv

de·mon·ol·o·gy \,dē-mə-'nä-lə-jē\ n (1597) 1 : the study of demons or evil spirits 2 : belief in demons : a doctrine of evil spirits 3 : a catalog of enemies ⟨the liberal creed at that time put Big Business in a cen-

\ə\ abut \ᵊ\ kitten, F table \ər\ further \a\ ash \ā\ ace \ä\ mop, mar \au̇\ out \ch\ chin \e\ bet \ē\ easy \g\ go \i\ hit \ī\ ice \j\ job \ŋ\ sing \ō\ go \ȯ\ law \ȯi\ boy \th\ thin \t̲h̲\ the \ü\ loot \u̇\ foot \y\ yet \zh\ vision \à, ᵏ, ⁿ, œ, œ̄, ᵫ, ᵫ̄, ᵞ\ see Guide to Pronunciation tral place in its ~ —Carl Kaysen⟩ — **de·mon·olog·i·cal** \,dē-mə-nə-'lä-ji-kəl\ *adj* — **de·mon·ol·o·gist** \-'nä-lə-jist\ *n*

de·mon·stra·ble \di-'män(t)-strə-bəl\ *adj* (15c) **1** : capable of being demonstrated **2** : APPARENT, EVIDENT — **de·mon·stra·bil·i·ty** \-,män(t)-strə-'bil-ə-tē\ *n* — **de·mon·stra·bly** \-blē\ *adv*

dem·on·strate \'de-mən-,strāt\ *vb* **-strat·ed; -strat·ing** [L *demonstratus,* pp. of *demonstrare,* fr. *de-* + *monstrare* to show — more at MUSTER] *vt* (1552) **1** : to show clearly **2 a** : to prove or make clear by reasoning or evidence **b** : to illustrate and explain esp. with many examples **3** : to show or prove the value or efficiency of to a prospective buyer ~ *vi* : to make a demonstration **syn** see SHOW

dem·on·stra·tion \,de-mən-'strā-shən\ *n* (14c) **1** : an act, process, or means of demonstrating to the intelligence: as **a** (1) : conclusive evidence : PROOF (2) : DERIVATION 5 **b** : a showing of the merits of a product or service to a prospective consumer **2** : an outward expression or display **3** : a show of armed force **4** : a public display of group feelings toward a person or cause — **dem·on·stra·tion·al** \-shnəl, -shə-n⁰l\ *adj*

¹de·mon·stra·tive \di-'män(t)-strə-tiv\ *adj* (14c) **1 a** : demonstrating as real or true **b** : characterized or established by demonstration **2** : pointing out the one referred to and distinguishing it from others of the same class ⟨~ pronouns⟩ **3 a** : marked by display of feeling **b** : inclined to display feelings openly — **de·mon·stra·tive·ly** *adv* — **de·mon·stra·tive·ness** *n*

²demonstrative *n* (15c) : a demonstrative word or morpheme

dem·on·stra·tor \'de-mən-,strā-tər\ *n* (1611) : one that demonstrates: **a** : a product (as an automobile) used to demonstrate performance or merits to prospective buyers **b** : someone who engages in a public demonstration

de·mor·al·ize \di-'mȯr-ə-,līz, ,dē-, -'mär-\ *vt* (ca. 1793) **1** : to corrupt the morals of **2 a** : to weaken the morale of : DISCOURAGE, DISPIRIT **b** : to upset or destroy the normal functioning of **c** : to throw into disorder — **de·mor·al·iza·tion** \di-,mȯr-ə-lə-'zā-shən, ,dē-, -,mär-\ *n* — **de·mor·al·iz·er** \di-'mȯr-ə-,lī-zər, ,dē-, -'mär-\ *n* — **de·mor·al·iz·ing·ly** \-ziŋ-lē\ *adv*

de·mos \'dē-,mäs\ *n* [Gk *dēmos* — more at DEMAGOGUE] (1831) **1** : POPULACE **2** : the common people of an ancient Greek state

de·mote \di-'mōt, ,dē-\ *vt* **de·mot·ed; de·mot·ing** [*de-* + *-mote* (as in *promote*)] (ca. 1891) **1** : to reduce to a lower grade or rank **2** : to relegate to a less important position — **de·mo·tion** \-'mō-shən\ *n*

de·mot·ic \di-'mä-tik\ *adj* [Gk *dēmotikos,* fr. *dēmotēs* commoner, fr. *dēmos*] (1822) **1** : of, relating to, or written in a simplified form of the ancient Egyptian hieratic writing **2** : POPULAR, COMMON ⟨~ idiom⟩ **3** : of or relating to the form of Modern Greek that is based on everyday speech

de·mount \(,)dē-'maunt\ *vt* (ca. 1930) **1** : to remove from a mounted position **2** : DISASSEMBLE — **de·mount·able** \-tə-bəl\ *adj*

¹de·mul·cent \di-'məl-sənt\ *adj* [L *demulcent-, demulcens,* prp. of *demulcēre* to soothe, fr. *de-* + *mulcēre* to soothe] (1732) : SOOTHING

²demulcent *n* (1732) : a usu. mucilaginous or oily substance (as tragacanth) that can soothe or protect an abraded mucous membrane

de·mul·ti·plex·er \(,)dē-'məl-tə-,plek-sər\ *n* (1963) : an electronic device that separates a multiplex signal into its component parts

¹de·mur \di-'mər\ *vi* **de·murred; de·mur·ring** [ME *demeoren* to linger, fr. OF *demorer,* fr. L *demorari,* fr. *de-* + *morari* to linger, fr. *mora* delay — more at MORA] (13c) **1** *archaic* : DELAY, HESITATE **2** : to file a demurrer **3** : to take exception : OBJECT — often used with *to* or *at*

²demur *n* (13c) **1** : hesitation (as in doing or accepting) usu. based on doubt of the acceptability of something offered or proposed **2** : the act or an instance of objecting : PROTEST **syn** see QUALM

de·mure \di-'myur\ *adj* [ME] (14c) **1** : RESERVED, MODEST **2** : affectedly modest, reserved, or serious : COY — **de·mure·ly** *adv* — **de·mure·ness** *n*

de·mur·rage \di-'mər-ij, -'mə-rij\ *n* (1641) **1** : the detention of a ship by the freighter beyond the time allowed for loading, unloading, or sailing **2** : a charge for detaining a ship, freight car, or truck

de·mur·ral \di-'mər-əl, -'mə-rəl\ *n* (1810) : the act or an instance of demurring

¹de·mur·rer \di-'mər-ər, -'mə-rər\ *n* [MF *demorer,* v.] (ca. 1521) **1** : a response in a court proceeding in which the defendant does not dispute the truth of the allegation but claims it is not sufficient grounds to justify legal action **2** : OBJECTION

²de·mur·rer \-'mər-ər\ *n* [¹*demur*] (1711) : one that demurs

de·my·e·lin·at·ing \(,)dē-'mī-ə-lə-,nā-tiŋ\ *adj* (1939) : causing or characterized by the loss or destruction of myelin ⟨~ diseases⟩ ⟨a ~ agent⟩ — **de·my·e·lin·ation** \(,)dē-,mī-ə-lə-'nā-shən\ *n*

de·mys·ti·fy \(,)dē-'mis-tə-,fī\ *vt* (1963) : to eliminate the mystifying features of — **de·mys·ti·fi·ca·tion** \(,)dē-,mis-tə-fə-'kā-shən\ *n*

de·my·thol·o·gize \,dē-mi-'thä-lə-,jīz\ *vt* (1950) **1** : to divest of mythological forms in order to uncover the meaning underlying them ⟨~ the Gospels⟩ **2** : to divest of mythical elements or associations — **de·my·thol·o·gi·za·tion** \-,thä-lə-jə-'zā-shən\ *n* — **de·my·thol·o·giz·er** \-'thä-lə-,jī-zər\ *n*

¹den \'den\ *n* [ME, fr. OE *denn;* akin to OE *denu* valley, OHG *tenni* threshing floor] (bef. 12c) **1** : the lair of a wild usu. predatory animal **2 a** (1) : a hollow or cavern used esp. as a hideout (2) : a center of secret activity **b** : a small usu. squalid dwelling **3** : a comfortable usu. secluded room **4** : a subdivision of a Cub Scout pack made up of two or more boys

²den *vb* **denned; den·ning** *vi* (13c) : to live in or retire to a den ~ *vt* : to drive into a den

de·nar·i·us \di-'nar-ē-əs, 'ner-\ *n, pl* **de·nar·ii** \-ē-,ī, -ē-,ē\ [ME, fr. L — more at DENIER] (14c) **1** : a small silver coin of ancient Rome **2** : a gold coin of the Roman Empire equivalent to 25 denarii

de·na·tion·al·ize \(')dē-'nash-nə-,līz, -'na-shə-n⁰l-,īz\ *vt* (1807) **1** : to divest of national character or rights **2** : to remove from ownership

denarius of Julius Caesar, 44 B.C.

or control by the national government — **de·na·tion·al·iza·tion** \(,)dē-,nash-nə-lə-'zā-shən, -,na-shə-n⁰l-ə-'zā-\ *n*

de·nat·u·ral·ize \(,)dē-'na-ch(ə-)rə-,līz\ *vt* (1800) **1** : to make unnatural **2** : to deprive of the rights and duties of a citizen — **de·nat·u·ral·iza·tion** \(,)dē-,na-ch(ə-)rə-lə-'zā-shən\ *n*

de·na·ture \(,)dē-'nā-chər\ *vb* **de·na·tured; de·na·tur·ing** \-'nā-ch(ə-)riŋ\ *vt* (1685) **1** : DEHUMANIZE **2** : to deprive of natural qualities : change the nature of: as **a** : to make (alcohol) unfit for drinking (as by adding an obnoxious substance) without impairing usefulness for other purposes **b** : to modify the molecular structure of (as a protein or DNA) esp. by heat, acid, alkali, or ultraviolet radiation so as to destroy or diminish some of the original properties and esp. the specific biological activity ~ *vi* : to become denatured — **de·na·tur·ant** \(,)dē-'nā-chər-ənt\ *n* — **de·na·tur·ation** \(,)dē-,nā-chə-'rā-shən\ *n*

de·na·zi·fy \(,)dē-'nät-si-,fī, -'nat-\ *vt* **-fied; -fying** (1940) : to rid of Nazism and its influence — **de·na·zi·fi·ca·tion** \(,)dē-,nät-si-fə-'kā-shən, -,nat-\ *n*

dendr- *or* **dendro-** *comb form* [Gk, fr. *dendron;* akin to Gk *drys* tree — more at TREE] : tree ⟨*dendro*logy⟩ : resembling a tree ⟨*dendrite*⟩

den·dri·form \'den-drə-,fȯrm\ *adj* (ca. 1847) : resembling a tree in structure

den·drite \'den-,drīt\ *n* (1751) **1** : a branching treelike figure produced on or in a mineral by a foreign mineral; *also* : the mineral so marked **2** : a crystallized arborescent form **3** : any of the usu. branching protoplasmic processes that conduct impulses toward the body of a nerve cell — see NEURON illustration

den·drit·ic \(,)den-'dri-tik\ *adj* (1816) : resembling or having dendrites : branching like a tree ⟨a ~ drainage system⟩ ⟨~ cells⟩

den·dro·chro·nol·o·gy \,den-(,)drō-krə-'nä-lə-jē\ *n* (ca. 1928) : the science of dating events and variations in environment in former periods by comparative study of growth rings in trees and aged wood — **den·dro·chro·no·log·i·cal** \-,krä-nə-'lä-ji-kəl, -,krō-\ *adj* — **den·dro·chro·no·log·i·cal·ly** \-ji-k(ə-)lē\ *adv* — **den·dro·chro·nol·o·gist** \-krə-'nä-lə-jist\ *n*

den·dro·gram \'den-drə-,gram\ *n* (ca. 1953) : a branching diagram representing a hierarchy of categories based on degree of similarity or number of shared characteristics esp. in biological taxonomy — compare CLADOGRAM

den·droid \'den-,drȯid\ *adj* [Gk *dendroeidēs,* fr. *dendron*] (ca. 1828) : resembling a tree in form : ARBORESCENT

den·drol·o·gy \den-'drä-lə-jē\ *n* (ca. 1708) : the study of trees — **den·dro·log·ic** \,den-drə-'lä-jik\ *or* **den·dro·log·i·cal** \-ji-kəl\ *adj* — **den·drol·o·gist** \den-'drä-lə-jist\ *n*

dene \'dēn\ *n* [ME, fr. OE *denu*] (bef. 12c) *Brit* : VALLEY

Dé·né \de-'nā, dā-\ *n, pl* **Déné** *or* **Dé·nés** \-āz\ [CanF, fr. Athabascan; akin to Chipewyan *dene* person] (1891) : a member of any of the Athabascan-speaking peoples of the interior of Alaska and northwestern Canada; *also* : the languages of these peoples

Den·eb \'de-,neb, -,nəb\ *n* [Ar *dhanab al-dajāja,* lit., the tail of the hen] : a star of the first magnitude in Cygnus

den·e·ga·tion \,de-ni-'gā-shən\ *n* [ME *denegacioun,* fr. MF or L; MF *denegation,* fr. L *denegation-, denegatio,* fr. *denegare* to deny — more at DENY] (15c) : DENIAL

de·ner·vate \'dē-(,)nər-,vāt\ *vt* **-vat·ed; -vat·ing** (1905) : to deprive of a nerve supply (as by cutting a nerve) — **de·ner·va·tion** \,dē-(,)nər-'vā-shən\ *n*

den·gue \'deŋ-gē, -,gā\ *n* [AmerSp] (1828) : an acute infectious disease caused by an arbovirus, transmitted by aedes mosquitoes, and characterized by headache, severe joint pain, and a rash — called also *breakbone fever, dengue fever*

de·ni·abil·i·ty \dē,nī-ə-'bi-lə-tē\ *n* (1973) : the ability to deny something esp. on the basis of being officially uninformed

de·ni·able \di-'nī-ə-bəl, dē-\ *adj* (1548) : capable of being denied

de·ni·al \di-'nī(-ə)l, dē-\ *n* (1528) **1** : refusal to satisfy a request or desire **2 a** (1) : refusal to admit the truth or reality (as of a statement or charge) (2) : assertion that an allegation is false **b** : refusal to acknowledge a person or a thing : DISAVOWAL **3** : the opposing by the defendant of an allegation of the opposite party in a lawsuit **4** : SELF-DENIAL **5** : negation in logic **6** : a psychological defense mechanism in which confrontation with a personal problem or with reality is avoided by denying the existence of the problem or reality

¹de·ni·er \di-'nī(-ə)r, dē-\ *n* (15c) : one that denies

²de·nier *n* [ME *denere,* fr. MF *denier,* fr. L *denarius,* coin worth ten asses, fr. *denarius* containing ten, fr. *deni* ten each, fr. *decem* ten — more at TEN] (15c) **1** \də-'ni(ə)r, də-'nyä\ : a small orig. silver coin formerly used in western Europe **2** \'də-nyər\ : a unit of fineness for yarn equal to the fineness of a yarn weighing one gram for each 9000 meters ⟨100-*denier* yarn is finer than 150-*denier* yarn⟩

den·i·grate \'de-ni-,grāt\ *vt* **-grat·ed; -grat·ing** [L *denigratus,* pp. of *denigrare,* fr. *de-* + *nigrare* to blacken, fr. *nigr-, niger* black] (1526) **1** : to cast aspersions on : DEFAME **2** : to deny the importance or validity of : BELITTLE — **den·i·gra·tion** \,de-ni-'grā-shən\ *n* — **den·i·gra·tive** \'de-ni-,grā-tiv\ *adj* — **den·i·gra·tor** \-,grā-tər\ *n* — **den·i·gra·to·ry** \'de-ni-grə-,tȯr-ē, -,tȯr-\ *adj*

den·im \'de-nəm\ *n* [F *serge) de Nîmes* serge of Nîmes, France] (1695) **1 a** : a firm durable twilled usu. cotton fabric woven with colored warp and white filling threads **b** : a similar fabric woven in colored stripes **2** *pl* : overalls or trousers usu. of blue denim

de·ni·tri·fi·ca·tion \(,)dē-,nī-trə-fə-'kā-shən\ *n* (1883) : the loss or removal of nitrogen or nitrogen compounds; *specif* : reduction of nitrates or nitrites commonly by bacteria (as in soil) that usu. results in the escape of nitrogen into the air — **de·ni·tri·fi·er** \-'nī-trə-,fī-ər\ *n* — **de·ni·tri·fy** \-'nī-trə-,fī\ *vt*

den·i·zen \'de-nə-zən\ *n* [ME *denizeine,* fr. AF *denzein* inhabitant, inner part, inner, fr. OF *denz* within, fr. LL *deintus,* fr. L *de-* + *intus* within — more at ENT-] (15c) **1** : INHABITANT **2** : one admitted to residence in a foreign country; *esp* : an alien admitted to rights of citizenship **3** : one that frequents a place

den mother *n* (1946) : a female adult leader of a Cub Scout den; *also* : a person seen in the role of leader or protector of a group

de·nom·i·nal \dē-'nä-mə-n⁰l\ *adj* (1951) : derived from a noun

de·nom·i·nate \di-'nä-mə-,nāt, dē-\ *vt* [L *denominatus,* pp. of *denominare,* fr. *de-* + *nominare* to name — more at NOMINATE] (ca. 1552) **1**

: to give a name to : DESIGNATE **2** : to express or designate in some denomination ⟨will ~ prices in U.S. dollars⟩
de·nom·i·nate number \di-,näm-ə-nət-\ n [L *denominatus*] (1579) : a number (as 7 in 7 *feet*) that specifies a quantity in terms of a unit of measurement
de·nom·i·na·tion \di-,nä-mə-'nā-shən\ n (15c) **1** : an act of denominating **2** : a value or size of a series of values or sizes (as of money) **3** : NAME, DESIGNATION; *esp* : a general name for a category **4** : a religious organization uniting local congregations in a single legal and administrative body — **de·nom·i·na·tion·al** \-shnəl, -shə-n°l\ *adj*
de·nom·i·na·tion·al·ism \-shə-nə-,li-zəm\ n (ca. 1855) **1** : devotion to denominational principles or interests **2** : the emphasizing of denominational differences to the point of being narrowly exclusive : SECTARIANISM
de·nom·i·na·tive \di-'nä-mə-nə-tiv\ *adj* [L *de* from + *nomin-, nomen* name] (ca. 1783) : derived from a noun or adjective — **denominative** n
de·nom·i·na·tor \di-'nä-mə-,nā-tər\ n (ca. 1542) **1** : the part of a fraction below the line signifying division that functions as the divisor of the numerator and in fractions with 1 as the numerator indicates into how many parts the unit is divided **2 a** : a common trait **b** : the average level (as of taste or opinion) : STANDARD
de·no·ta·tion \,dē-nō-'tā-shən\ n (ca. 1532) **1** : an act or process of denoting **2** : MEANING; *esp* : a direct specific meaning as distinct from an implied or associated idea **3 a** : a denoting term : NAME **b** : SIGN, INDICATION ⟨visible ~s of divine wrath⟩ **4** : the totality of things to which a term is applicable esp. in logic — compare CONNOTATION
de·no·ta·tive \'dē-nō-,tā-tiv, di-'nōt-ə-tiv\ *adj* (ca. 1611) **1** : denoting or tending to denote **2** : relating to denotation
de·note \di-'nōt, dē-\ *vt* [MF *denoter*, fr. L *denotare*, fr. *de-* + *notare* to note] (1592) **1** : to serve as an indication of : BETOKEN ⟨the swollen bellies that ~ starvation⟩ **2** : to serve as an arbitrary mark for ⟨red flares *denoting* danger⟩ **3** : to make known : ANNOUNCE ⟨his crestfallen look *denoted* his distress⟩ **4** a : to serve as a linguistic expression of the notion of : MEAN **b** : to stand for : DESIGNATE — **de·note·ment** \-'nōt-mənt\ n
de·noue·ment *also* **dé·noue·ment** \,dā-,nü-'mäⁿ, dā-'nü-,\ n [F *dénouement*, lit., untying, fr. MF *desnouement*, fr. *desnouer* to untie, fr. OF *desnoer*, fr. *des-* de- + *noer* to tie, fr. L *nodare*, fr. *nodus* knot — more at NODE] (1752) **1** : the final outcome of the main dramatic complication in a literary work **2** : the outcome of a complex sequence of events
de·nounce \di-'nau̇n(t)s, dē-\ *vt* **de·nounced; de·nounc·ing** [ME, fr. OF *denoncier* to proclaim, fr. L *denuntiare*, fr. *de-* + *nuntiare* to report — more at ANNOUNCE] (13c) **1** : to pronounce esp. publicly to be blameworthy or evil **2** *archaic* **a** : PROCLAIM **b** : to announce threateningly **3** : to inform against : ACCUSE **4** *obs* : PORTEND **5** : to announce formally the termination of (as a treaty) *syn* see CRITICIZE — **de·nounce·ment** \-'nau̇n(t)-smənt\ n — **de·nounc·er** n
de no·vo \di-'nō-(,)vō, dā-, dē-\ *adv or adj* [L] (1536) : over again : ANEW
dense \'den(t)s\ *adj* **dens·er; dens·est** [L *densus*; akin to Gk *dasys* thick with hair or leaves] (15c) **1 a** : marked by compactness or crowding together of parts **b** : having a high mass per unit volume ⟨carbon dioxide is a ~ gas⟩ **2 a** : marked by a stupid imperviousness to ideas or impressions : THICKHEADED **b** : EXTREME ⟨~ ignorance⟩ **3** : having between any two elements at least one element ⟨the set of rational numbers is ~⟩ **4** : demanding concentration to follow or comprehend ⟨~ prose⟩ **5** : having high or relatively high opacity ⟨a ~ fog⟩ ⟨a ~ photographic negative⟩ *syn* see STUPID — **dense·ly** *adv* — **dense·ness** \'den(t)-snəs\ n
den·si·fy \'den(t)-sə-,fī\ *vt* **-fied; -fy·ing** (1820) : to make denser : COMPRESS — **den·si·fi·ca·tion** \,den(t)-sə-fə-'kā-shən\ n
den·si·tom·e·ter \,den(t)-sə-'tä-mə-tər\ n (1901) : an instrument for determining optical or photographic density — **den·si·to·met·ric** \,den(t)-sə-tə-'me-trik\ *adj* — **den·si·tom·e·try** \,den(t)-sə-'tä-mə-trē\ n
den·si·ty \'den(t)-sə-tē\ n, *pl* **-ties** (1603) **1** : the quality or state of being dense **2** : the quantity per unit volume, unit area, or unit length: as **a** : the mass of a substance per unit volume **b** : the distribution of a quantity (as mass, electricity, or energy) per unit usu. of space (as length, area, or volume) **c** : the average number of individuals or units per space unit ⟨a population ~ of 500 per square mile⟩ ⟨a housing ~ of 10 houses per acre⟩ **3 a** : the degree of opacity of a translucent medium **b** : the common logarithm of the opacity
density function n (ca. 1962) : PROBABILITY DENSITY FUNCTION
¹dent \'dent\ *vb* [ME, short for *indenten* to make dents in, indent] *vt* (14c) **1** : to make a dent in **2** : to have a weakening effect on ~ *vi* : to form a dent by sinking inward : become dented
²dent n (1565) **1** : a depression or hollow made by a blow or by pressure **2 a** : an impression or effect often made against resistance and usu. having a weakening effect **b** : initial progress : HEADWAY
³dent n [F, lit., tooth, fr. L *dent-, dens*] (1703) : TOOTH 3a
dent- *or* **denti-** *or* **dento-** *comb form* [ME *denti-*, fr. L, fr. *dent-, dens* tooth — more at TOOTH] : tooth : teeth ⟨*denti*form⟩
¹den·tal \'den-t°l\ *adj* [L *dentalis*, fr. *dent-, dens*] (1594) **1** : articulated with the tip or blade of the tongue against or near the upper front teeth **2** : of or relating to the teeth or dentistry — **den·tal·ly** \-ē\ *adv*
²dental n (ca. 1727) : a dental consonant
dental floss n (1910) : a thread used to clean between the teeth
dental hygienist n (ca. 1922) : a licensed dental professional who cleans and examines teeth
den·ta·li·um \den-'tā-lē-əm\ n, *pl* **-lia** \-lē-ə\ [NL, genus name, fr. L *dentalis*] (1864) : any of a genus (*Dentalium*) of widely distributed tooth shells; *broadly* : TOOTH SHELL
dental technician n (1946) : one who makes dental appliances
den·tate \'den-,tāt\ *adj* [L *dentatus*, fr. *dent-, dens*] (1810) : having teeth or pointed conical projections ⟨a ~ margin of a leaf⟩
dent corn n (1873) : an Indian corn having kernels that contain both hard and soft starch and that become indented at maturity
den·ti·cle \'den-ti-kəl\ n [ME, fr. L *denticulus*, dim. of *dent-, dens*] (14c) : a conical pointed projection (as a small tooth)

den·tic·u·late \den-'ti-kyə-lət\ *or* **den·tic·u·lat·ed** \-,lā-təd\ *adj* (1661) **1** : finely dentate or serrate ⟨a ~ shell⟩ ⟨a ~ margin of a leaf⟩ **2** : cut into dentils — **den·tic·u·la·tion** \(,)den-,ti-kyə-'lā-shən\ n
den·ti·form \'den-tə-,fȯrm\ *adj* (1708) : shaped like a tooth
den·ti·frice \'den-tə-frəs\ n [MF, fr. L *dentifricium*, fr. *denti-* + *fricare* to rub — more at FRICTION] (15c) : a powder, paste, or liquid for cleaning the teeth
den·til \'den-t°l, -,til\ n [obs. F *dentille*, fr. MF, dim. of *dent*] (1663) : one of a series of small projecting rectangular blocks forming a molding esp. under a cornice — **den·tiled** \-t°ld, -,tild\ *adj*
den·tin \'den-t°n\ *or* **den·tine** \'den-,tēn, den-\ n (1845) : a calcareous material similar to but harder and denser than bone that composes the principal mass of a tooth — see TOOTH illustration — **den·tin·al** \den-'tē-n°l, 'den-t°n-əl\ *adj*
den·tist \'den-təst\ n [F *dentiste*, fr. *dent*] (1752) : one who is skilled in and licensed to practice the prevention, diagnosis, and treatment of diseases, injuries, and malformations of the teeth, jaws, and mouth and who makes and inserts false teeth
den·tist·ry \'den-tə-strē\ n (1838) : the art or profession of a dentist
den·ti·tion \den-'ti-shən\ n [L *dentition-, dentitio*, fr. *dentire* to cut teeth, fr. *dent-, dens*] (1615) **1** : the development and cutting of teeth **2** : the character of a set of teeth esp. with regard to their number, kind, and arrangement — see TOOTH illustration **3** : TEETH
den·tu·lous \'den-chə-ləs\ *adj* [back-formation fr. *edentulous*] (1926) : having teeth
den·ture \'den-chər\ n [F, fr. MF, fr. *dent*] (1874) **1** : a set of teeth **2** : an artificial replacement for one or more teeth; *esp* : a set of false teeth
den·tur·ist \'den-chə-rist\ n (1965) : a dental technician who makes, fits, and repairs dentures directly for the public
de·nu·cle·ar·ize \(')dē-'n(y)ü-klē-ə-,rīz, ÷-n(y)ə-,rīz\ *vt* **-ized; -iz·ing** (1958) : to remove nuclear arms from : prohibit the use of nuclear arms in — **de·nu·cle·ar·iza·tion** \(,)dē-,n(y)ü-klē-ə-rə-'zā-shən, ÷-,kyə-lə-rə-\ n
de·nude \di-'n(y)üd, dē-\ *vt* **de·nud·ed; de·nud·ing** [L *denudare*, fr. *de-* + *nudus* bare — more at NAKED] (15c) **1** : to deprive of something important **2 a** : to strip of all covering or surface layers **b** : to lay bare by erosion **c** : to strip (land) of forests — **de·nu·da·tion** \,dē-(,)n(y)ü-'dā-shən, ,den-yü-\ n — **de·nude·ment** \di-'n(y)üd-mənt\ n
de·nu·mer·a·ble \di-'n(y)ü-mə-rə-bəl\ *adj* (1902) : capable of being put into one-to-one correspondence with the positive integers — **de·nu·mer·a·bil·i·ty** \-,n(y)ü-mə-rə-'bi-lə-tē\ n — **de·nu·mer·a·bly** \-'n(y)ü-mə-rə-blē\ *adv*
de·nun·ci·a·tion \di-,nən(t)-sē-'ā-shən\ n (1842) : an act of denouncing; *esp* : a public condemnation — **de·nun·ci·a·tive** \-'nən(t)-sē-,ā-tiv\ *adj* — **de·nun·ci·a·to·ry** \-sē-ə-,tȯr-ē, -,tȯr-\ *adj*
Den·ver boot \'den-vər-\ n [*Denver*, Colo.] (1968) : a metal clamp that is locked onto one of the wheels of an automobile to immobilize it esp. until its owner pays accumulated parking fines
Denver omelet n (1954) : WESTERN OMELET
Denver sandwich n (1950) : WESTERN SANDWICH
de·ny \di-'nī, dē-\ *vt* **de·nied; de·ny·ing** [ME, fr. MF *denier*, fr. L *denegare*, fr. *de-* + *negare* to deny — more at NEGATE] (14c) **1** : to declare untrue **2** : to disclaim connection with or responsibility for : DISAVOW **3 a** : to give a negative answer to **b** : to refuse to grant **c** : to restrain (oneself) from gratification of desires **4** *archaic* : DECLINE **5** : to refuse to accept the existence, truth, or validity of — **de·ny·ing·ly** \-'nī-iŋ-lē\ *adv*
syn DENY, GAINSAY, CONTRADICT, CONTRAVENE mean to refuse to accept as true or valid. DENY implies a firm refusal to accept as true, to grant or concede, or to acknowledge the existence or claims of ⟨*denied* the charges⟩. GAINSAY implies disputing the truth of what another has said ⟨no one can *gainsay* her claims⟩. CONTRADICT implies an open or flat denial ⟨her account *contradicts* his⟩. CONTRAVENE implies not so much an intentional opposition as some inherent incompatibility ⟨laws that *contravene* tradition⟩.
deoch an dor·is \,d(y)ȯk-°n-'dȯr-əs\ *Scot & Irish var of* DOCH-AN-DORRIS
de·o·dar \'dē-ə-,där\ *also* **de·o·da·ra** \,dē-ə-'där-ə\ n [Hindi *deodār*, fr. Skt *devadāru*, lit., timber of the gods, fr. *deva* god + *dāru* wood — more at DEITY, TREE] (1842) : an East Indian cedar (*Cedrus deodara*)
de·odor·ant \dē-'ō-də-rənt\ n (1869) : a preparation that destroys or masks unpleasant odors — **deodorant** *adj*
de·odor·ize \dē-'ō-də-,rīz\ *vt* (1856) **1** : to eliminate or prevent the offensive odor of **2** : to make (something unpleasant or reprehensible) more acceptable ⟨the movie ~s his scandalous career⟩ — **de·odor·iza·tion** \-,ō-də-rə-'zā-shən\ n — **de·odor·iz·er** n
de·on·tic \(,)dē-'än-tik\ *adj* [Gk *deont-, deon* that which is obligatory, fr. neut. of prp. of *dein* to lack, be needful — more at DEUTER-] (ca. 1866) : of or relating to moral obligation : DEONTOLOGICAL
de·on·tol·o·gy \,dē-,än-'tä-lə-jē\ n (1826) : the theory or study of moral obligation — **de·on·to·log·i·cal** \,dē-,än-tə-'lä-ji-kəl\ *adj* — **de·on·tol·o·gist** \,dē-,än-'tä-lə-jist\ n
Deo vo·len·te \,dā-(,)ō-vō-'len-tē, ,dē-\ [L] (1767) : God being willing
de·ox·i·dize \(,)dē-'äk-sə-,dīz\ *vt* (1794) **1** : to remove oxygen from — **de·ox·i·da·tion** \(,)dē-,äk-sə-'dā-shən\ n — **de·ox·i·diz·er** \(,)dē-'äk-sə-,dī-zər\ n
de·oxy \(,)dē-'äk-sē\ *also* **des·oxy** \(,)dē-'zäk-sē, -'säk-\ *adj* [ISV] : containing less oxygen in the molecule than the compound from which it is derived ⟨~ sugars⟩ — usu. used in combination ⟨*deoxy*ribonucleic acid⟩
de·ox·y·gen·ate \(,)dē-'äk-si-jə-,nāt, ,dē-äk-'si-jə-\ *vt* (1799) : to remove oxygen from — **de·ox·y·gen·ation** \(,)dē-,äk-si-jə-'nā-shən, ,dē-äk-,si-jə-\ n
de·ox·y·gen·at·ed *adj* (1799) : having the hemoglobin in the reduced state

\ə\ abut \ʹ\ kitten, F table \ər\ further \a\ ash \ā\ ace \ä\ mop, mar
\au̇\ out \ch\ chin \e\ bet \ē\ easy \g\ go \i\ hit \ī\ ice \j\ job
\ŋ\ sing \ō\ go \ȯ\ law \ȯi\ boy \th\ thin \th\ the \ü\ loot \u̇\ foot
\y\ yet \zh\ vision \a, k̲, ⁿ, œ, œ̄, ue, ūe, ʸ\ see Guide to Pronunciation

de·oxy·ri·bo·nu·cle·ase \(,)dē-'äk-si-,rī-bō-'n(y)ü-klē-,ās, -,āz\ n (1946) : an enzyme that hydrolyzes DNA to nucleotides — called also *DNase*

de·oxy·ri·bo·nu·cle·ic acid \(,)dē-'äk-si-,rī-bō-n(y)ù-,klē-ik-, -,klā-\ n [*deoxyribose* + *nucleic acid*] (1938) : DNA

de·oxy·ri·bo·nu·cle·o·tide \-'n(y)ü-klē-ə-,tīd\ n (1972) : a nucleotide that contains deoxyribose and is a constituent of DNA

de·oxy·ri·bose \(,)dē-,äk-si-'rī-,bōs, -,bōz\ n [ISV] (1957) : a pentose sugar $C_5H_{10}O_4$ that is a structural element of DNA

de·part \di-'pärt\ vb [ME, to divide, part company, fr. OF *departir*, fr. *de-* + *partir* to divide, fr. L *partire*, fr. *part-, pars* part] vi (13c) **1 a** : to go away : LEAVE **b** : DIE **2** : to turn aside : DEVIATE ~ vt : to go away from : LEAVE **syn** see SWERVE

de·part·ed adj (14c) **1** : BYGONE **2** : having died esp. recently ⟨mourning our ~ friend⟩ **syn** see DEAD

de·part·ment \di-'pärt-mənt\ n [F *département*, fr. OF, act of dividing, fr. *departir*] (1735) **1 a** : a distinct sphere : PROVINCE ⟨that's not my ~⟩ **b** : a category consisting esp. of a measurable activity or attribute ⟨lacking in the trustworthiness ~ —Garrison Keillor⟩ **2** : a functional or territorial division: as **a** : a major administrative division of a government **b** : a major territorial administrative subdivision **c** : a division of a college or school giving instruction in a particular subject **d** : a major division of a business **e** : a section of a department store handling a particular kind of merchandise **f** : a territorial subdivision made for the administration and training of military units — **de·part·men·tal** \di-,pärt-'men-t³l, ,dē-\ adj — **de·part·men·tal·ly** \-t³l-ē\ adv

de·part·men·tal·ize \di-,pärt-'men-t³l-,īz, ,dē-\ vt **-ized; -iz·ing** (ca. 1895) : to divide into departments — **de·part·men·tal·iza·tion** \-,men-t³l-ə-'zā-shən\ n

department store n (1887) : a store selling a wide variety of goods and arranged in several departments

de·par·ture \di-'pär-chər\ n (15c) **1 a** (1) : the act or an instance of departing (2) *archaic* : DEATH **b** : a setting out (as on a new course) **2** : DIVERGENCE

de·pau·per·ate \di-'pò-pə-rət\ adj [ME *depauperat*, fr. ML *depaupera-tus*, pp. of *depauperare* to impoverish, fr. L *de-* + *pauperare* to impoverish, fr. *pauper* poor — more at POOR] (1670) **1** : falling short of natural development or size **2** : IMPOVERISHED ⟨a ~ fauna⟩

de·pend \di-'pend\ vi [ME, fr. MF *dependre*, modif. of L *dependēre*, fr. *de-* + *pendēre* to hang — more at PENDANT] (15c) **1** : to be determined, based, or contingent ⟨life ~s on food⟩ ⟨the value of *Y* ~s on *X*⟩ **2** : to be pending or undecided **3 a** : to place reliance or trust ⟨you can ~ on me⟩ **b** : to be dependent esp. for financial support **4** : to hang down

de·pend·able \di-'pen-də-bəl\ adj (1735) : capable of being depended on : RELIABLE — **de·pend·abil·i·ty** \-,pen-də-'bi-lə-tē\ n — **de·pend·able·ness** n — **de·pend·ably** \-blē\ adv

de·pen·dence also **de·pen·dance** \di-'pen-dən(t)s\ n (15c) **1** : the quality or state of being dependent; *esp* : the quality or state of being influenced or determined by or subject to another **2** : RELIANCE, TRUST **3** : one that is relied on **4 a** : drug addiction **b** : HABITUATION 2b

de·pen·den·cy \-dən(t)-sē\ n, pl **-cies** (1594) **1** : DEPENDENCE 1 **2** : something that is dependent on something else; *esp* : a territorial unit under the jurisdiction of a nation but not formally annexed by it **3** : a building (as a stable) that is an adjunct to a main dwelling

¹de·pen·dent \di-'pen-dənt\ adj [ME *dependant*, fr. MF, prp. of *dependre*] (14c) **1** : hanging down **2 a** : determined or conditioned by another : CONTINGENT **b** (1) : relying on another for support (2) : affected with a drug dependence **c** : subject to another's jurisdiction **d** : SUBORDINATE 3a **3 a** : not mathematically or statistically independent ⟨a ~ set of vectors⟩ ⟨~ events⟩ **b** : EQUIVALENT 6a ⟨~ equations⟩ — **de·pen·dent·ly** adv

²dependent also **de·pen·dant** \-dənt\ n (1523) **1** *archaic* : DEPENDENCY **2** : one that is dependent; *esp* : a person who relies on another for support

dependent variable n (ca. 1852) : a mathematical variable whose value is determined by that of one or more other variables in a function

de·per·son·al·iza·tion \(,)dē-,pər-snə-lə-'zā-shən, -,pər-s³n-ə-lə-\ n (1906) **1 a** : an act or process of depersonalizing **b** : the quality or state of being depersonalized **2** : a psychopathological syndrome characterized by loss of identity and feelings of unreality and strangeness about one's own behavior

de·per·son·al·ize \(')dē-'pər-snə-,līz, -'pər-s³n-ə-\ vt (1866) **1** : to deprive of the sense of personal identity ⟨schools that ~ students⟩ **2** : to make impersonal

de·phos·phor·y·la·tion \(,)dē-,fäs-fòr-ə-'lā-shən\ n (1931) : the process of removing phosphate groups from an organic compound (as ATP) by hydrolysis; *also* : the resulting state — **de·phos·phor·y·late** \(,)dē-fäs-'fòr-ə-,lāt\ vt

de·pict \di-'pikt, dē-\ vt [L *depictus*, pp. of *depingere*, fr. *de-* + *pingere* to paint — more at PAINT] (15c) **1** : to represent by or as if by a picture **2** : DESCRIBE 1 — **de·pic·ter** \-'pik-tər\ n — **de·pic·tion** \-'pik-shən\ n

de·pig·men·ta·tion \(,)dē-,pig-mən-'tā-shən, -,men-\ n (1889) : loss of normal pigmentation

dep·i·la·tion \,de-pə-'lā-shən\ n [MF or ML; MF, fr. ML *depilation-, depilatio*, fr. L *depilare*, fr. *de-* + *pilus* hair — more at PILE] (1547) : the removal of hair, wool, or bristles by chemical or mechanical methods — **dep·i·late** \'de-pə-,lāt\ vt

de·pil·a·to·ry \di-'pi-lə-,tòr-ē, -,tòr-\ n, pl **-ries** (1606) : an agent for removing hair, wool, or bristles — **depilatory** adj

de·plane \(,)dē-'plān\ vi (1923) : to disembark from an airplane

de·plete \di-'plēt\ vt **de·plet·ed; de·plet·ing** [L *depletus*, pp. of *deplēre*, fr. *de-* + *plēre* to fill — more at FULL] (1807) **1** : to empty of a principal substance **2** : to lessen markedly in quantity, content, power, or value — **de·plet·able** \-'plē-tə-bəl\ adj — **de·ple·tion** \-'plē-shən\ n — **de·ple·tive** \-'plē-tiv\ adj

syn DEPLETE, DRAIN, EXHAUST, IMPOVERISH, BANKRUPT mean to deprive of something essential to existence or potency. DEPLETE implies a reduction in number or quantity so as to endanger the ability to function ⟨*depleting* our natural resources⟩. DRAIN implies a gradual withdrawal and ultimate deprivation of what is necessary to an existence ⟨personal tragedy had *drained* him of all spirit⟩. EXHAUST stresses a complete emptying ⟨her lecture *exhausted* the subject⟩. IMPOVERISH suggests a deprivation of something essential to richness or produc-

tiveness ⟨*impoverished* soil⟩. BANKRUPT suggests impoverishment to the point of imminent collapse ⟨war had *bankrupted* the nation of resources⟩.

de·plor·able \di-'plòr-ə-bəl, -'plòr-\ adj (1612) **1** : LAMENTABLE **2** : deserving censure or contempt : WRETCHED — **de·plor·able·ness** n — **de·plor·ably** \-blē\ adv

de·plore \di-'plòr, -'plòr\ vt **de·plored; de·plor·ing** [MF or L; MF *deplorer*, fr. L *deplorare*, fr. *de-* + *plorare* to wail] (1567) **1 a** : to feel or express grief for **b** : to regret strongly **2** : to consider unfortunate or deserving of deprecation — **de·plor·er** \-'plòr-ər\ n — **de·plor·ing·ly** \-iŋ-lē\ adv

syn DEPLORE, LAMENT, BEWAIL, BEMOAN mean to express grief or sorrow for something. DEPLORE implies regret for the loss or impairment of something of value ⟨*deplores* the breakdown in family values⟩. LAMENT implies a profound or demonstrative expression of sorrow ⟨*lamenting* the loss of their only child⟩. BEWAIL and BEMOAN imply sorrow, disappointment, or protest finding outlet in words or cries, BEWAIL commonly suggesting loudness, and BEMOAN lugubriousness ⟨fans *bewailed* the defeat⟩ ⟨purists *bemoaning* the corruption of the language⟩.

de·ploy \di-'plòi\ vb [F *déployer*, lit., to unfold, fr. OF *desdis-* + *ploier, plier* to fold — more at PLY] vt (1786) **1 a** : to extend (a military unit) esp. in width **b** : to place in battle formation or appropriate positions **2** : to spread out, utilize, or arrange esp. strategically ~ vi : to move in being deployed — **de·ploy·able** \-ə-bəl\ adj — **de·ploy·ment** \-mənt\ n

de·po·lar·ize \(,)dē-'pō-lə-,rīz\ vt (1818) **1** : to cause to become partially or wholly unpolarized **2** : to prevent or remove polarization of (as a dry cell or cell membrane) — **de·po·lar·iza·tion** \(,)dē-,pō-lə-rə-'zā-shən\ n — **de·po·lar·iz·er** \(,)dē-'pō-lə-,rī-zər\ n

de·po·lit·i·cize \,dē-pə-'li-tə-,sīz\ vt (1937) : to remove the political character of : take out of the realm of politics ⟨~ foreign aid⟩ — **de·po·lit·i·ci·za·tion** \,dē-pə-,li-tə-sə-'zā-shən\ n

de·po·ly·mer·ize \(,)dē-pə-'li-mə-,rīz, -'pä-lə-mə-\ vt (ca. 1909) : to decompose (macromolecules) into simpler compounds (as monomers) ~ vi : to undergo decomposition into simpler compounds — **de·po·ly·mer·iza·tion** \(,)dē-,li-mə-rə-'zā-shən, (,)dē-,pä-lə-mə-rə-\ n

de·pone \di-'pōn\ vb **de·poned; de·pon·ing** [ML *deponere*, fr. L, to put down, fr. *de-* + *ponere* to put — more at POSITION] (15c) : TESTIFY

¹de·po·nent \di-'pō-nənt\ adj [LL *deponent-, deponens*, fr. L, prp. of *deponere*] (15c) : occurring with passive or middle voice forms but with active voice meaning — used of verbs in Latin and Greek

²deponent n (1530) **1** : a deponent verb **2** : one who gives evidence

de·pop·u·late \(,)dē-'pä-pyə-,lāt\ vt [L *depopulatus*, pp. of *depopulari*, fr. *de-* + *populari* to ravage] (1548) **1** *obs* : RAVAGE **2** : to reduce greatly the population of — **de·pop·u·la·tion** \(,)dē-,pä-pyə-'lā-shən\ n

de·port \di-'pōrt, -'pòrt, dē-\ vt [MF *deporter*, fr. L *deportare* to carry away, fr. *de-* + *portare* to carry — more at FARE] (1598) **1** : to behave or comport (oneself) esp. in accord with a code **2** [L *deportare*] **a** : to carry away **b** : to send out of the country by legal deportation **syn** see BANISH, BEHAVE

de·port·able \di-'pòr-tə-bəl, -'pòr-, dē-\ adj (1891) **1** : punishable by deportation ⟨~ offenses⟩ **2** : subject to deportation ⟨~ aliens⟩

de·por·ta·tion \,dē-,pòr-'tā-shən, -,pòr-, -pər-\ n (1595) **1** : an act or instance of deporting **2** : the removal from a country of an alien whose presence is unlawful or prejudicial

de·por·tee \,dē-,pòr-'tē, di-, -,pòr-\ n (1865) : one who has been deported or is under sentence of deportation

de·port·ment \di-'pòrt-mənt, -'pòrt-, dē-\ n (1601) : the manner in which one conducts oneself : BEHAVIOR **syn** see BEARING

de·pos·al \di-'pō-zəl, dē-\ n (14c) : an act of deposing from office

de·pose \di-'pōz, dē-\ vb **de·posed; de·pos·ing** [ME, fr. MF *deposer*, fr. LL *deponere* (perf. indic. *deposui*), fr. L, to put down] vt (14c) **1** : to remove from a throne or other high position **2** : to put down : DEPOSIT **3 a** [ME, fr. ML *deponere*, fr. LL] : to testify to under oath or by affidavit **b** : AFFIRM, ASSERT ~ vi : to bear witness

¹de·pos·it \di-'pä-zət\ vb **de·pos·it·ed; de·pos·it·ing** \-'pä-zə-tiŋ, -'päz-tiŋ\ [L *depositus*, pp. of *deponere*] vt (1624) **1** : to place esp. for safekeeping or as a pledge; *esp* : to put in a bank **2 a** : to lay down : PLACE **b** : to let fall (as sediment) ~ vi : to become deposited — **de·pos·i·tor** \-'pä-zə-tər, -'päz-tər\ n

²deposit n (1624) **1** : the state of being deposited **2** : something placed for safekeeping: as **a** : money deposited in a bank **b** : money given as a pledge or down payment **3** : a place of deposit : DEPOSITORY **4** : an act of depositing **5 a** : something laid down; *esp* : matter deposited by a natural process **b** : a natural accumulation (as of iron ore, coal, or gas)

de·pos·i·tary \di-'pä-zə-,ter-ē\ n, pl **-tar·ies** (1605) **1** : a person to whom something is entrusted **2** : DEPOSITORY 2

de·po·si·tion \,de-pə-'zi-shən, ,dē-pə-\ n (14c) **1** : an act of removing from a position of authority **2 a** : a testifying esp. before a court **b** : DECLARATION; *specif* : testimony taken down in writing under oath **3** : an act or process of depositing **4** : something deposited : DEPOSIT — **de·po·si·tion·al** \-'zish-nəl, -shə-n³l\ adj

de·pos·i·to·ry \di-'pä-zə-,tōr-ē, -,tòr-\ n, pl **-ries** (1656) **1** : DEPOSITARY 1 **2** : a place where something is deposited esp. for safekeeping

depository library n (ca. 1930) : a library designated to receive U.S. government publications

de·pot \1 & 2 are 'de-(,)pō also 'dē-, 3 is 'dē- sometimes 'de-\ n [F *dépôt*, fr. MF *depost*, ML *depositum*, fr. L, neut. of *depositus*] (1795) **1 a** : a place for storing goods or motor vehicles : STORE, CACHE **2 a** : a place for the storage of military supplies **b** : a place for the reception and forwarding of military replacements **3** : a building for railroad or bus passengers or freight

de·prave \di-'prāv\ vt **de·praved; de·prav·ing** [ME, fr. MF *depraver*, fr. L *depravare* to pervert, fr. *de-* + *pravus* crooked, bad] (14c) **1** *archaic* : to speak ill of : MALIGN **2** : to make bad : CORRUPT; *esp* : to corrupt morally **syn** see DEBASE — **de·pra·va·tion** \,de-prə-'vā-shən, ,dē-,prā-\ n — **de·prave·ment** \di-'prāv-mənt\ n — **de·prav·er** \di-'prā-vər\ n

de·praved \di-'prāvd\ adj (14c) : marked by corruption or evil; *esp* : PERVERTED — **de·praved·ly** \-'prā-vəd-lē, -'prāvd-lē\ adv — **de·prav·ed·ness** \-'prā-vəd-nəs, -'prāvd-nəs\ n

de·prav·i·ty \di-'pra-və-tē *also* -'prā-\ *n, pl* **-ties** (1641) **1** : the quality or state of being depraved **2** : a corrupt act or practice

dep·re·cate \'de-pri-ˌkāt\ *vt* **-cat·ed; -cat·ing** [L *deprecatus,* pp. of *deprecari* to avert by prayer, fr. *de-* + *precari* to pray — more at PRAY] (1628) **1 a** *archaic* : to pray against (as an evil) **b** : to seek to avert ⟨~ the wrath . . . of the Roman people —Tobias Smollett⟩ **2** : to express disapproval of **3 a** : PLAY DOWN : make little of ⟨speaks five languages . . . but ~s this facility —*Time*⟩ **b** : BELITTLE, DISPARAGE ⟨the most reluctantly admired and least easily *deprecated* of . . . novelists —*New Yorker*⟩ — **dep·re·cat·ing·ly** \-ˌkā-tiŋ-lē\ *adv* — **dep·re·ca·tion** \ˌde-pri-'kā-shən\ *n*

dep·re·ca·to·ry \'de-pri-kə-ˌtōr-ē, -ˌtȯr-, 'de-prə-ˌkā-tə-rē\ *adj* (1586) **1** : seeking to avert disapproval : APOLOGETIC **2** : serving to deprecate : DISAPPROVING — **dep·re·ca·to·ri·ly** \ˌde-pri-kə-'tōr-ə-lē, -'tȯr-\ *adv*

de·pre·ci·ate \di-'prē-shē-ˌāt\ *vb* **-at·ed; -at·ing** [LL *depretiatus,* pp. of *depretiare,* fr. L *de-* + *pretium* price — more at PRICE] *vt* (15c) **1** : to lower in estimation or esteem **2** : to lower the price or estimated value of ~ *vi* : to fall in value *syn* see DECRY — **de·pre·cia·ble** \-shə-bəl\ *adj* — **de·pre·ci·at·ing·ly** \-shē-ˌā-tiŋ-lē\ *adv* — **de·pre·ci·a·tion** \-ˌprē-shē-'ā-shən\ *n* — **de·pre·ci·a·tive** \-'prē-shə-tiv, -shē-ˌā-tiv\ *adj* — **de·pre·ci·a·tor** \-shē-ˌā-tər\ *n* — **de·pre·cia·to·ry** \-shə-ˌtōr-ē, -ˌtȯr-\ *adj*

dep·re·date \'de-prə-ˌdāt\ *vb* **-dat·ed; -dat·ing** [LL *depraedatus,* pp. of *depraedari,* fr. L *de-* + *praedari* to plunder — more at PREY] *vt* (1626) : to lay waste : PLUNDER, RAVAGE ~ *vi* : to engage in plunder — **dep·re·da·tion** \ˌde-prə-'dā-shən\ *n* — **dep·re·da·tor** \'de-prə-ˌdā-tər, di-'pre-də-\ *n* — **dep·re·da·to·ry** \di-'pre-də-ˌtōr-ē, 'de-pri-də-, -ˌtȯr-\ *adj*

de·press \di-'pres, dē-\ *vt* [ME, fr. MF *depresser,* fr. L *depressus,* pp. of *deprimere* to press down, fr. *de-* + *premere* to press — more at PRESS] (14c) **1** *obs* : REPRESS, SUBJUGATE **2 a** : to press down ⟨~ a typewriter key⟩ **b** : to cause to sink to a lower position **4** : to lessen the activity or strength of **4** : SADDEN, DISCOURAGE **5** : to decrease the market value or marketability of — **de·press·ible** \-'pre-sə-bəl\ *adj*

de·pres·sant \di-'pre-sᵊnt, dē-\ *n* (1876) : one that depresses; *specif* : an agent that reduces a bodily functional activity or an instinctive desire (as appetite) — **depressant** *adj*

de·pressed *adj* (1621) **1** : low in spirits : SAD; *esp* : affected by psychological depression **2 a** : vertically flattened ⟨a ~ cactus⟩ **b** : having the central part lower than the margin **c** : lying flat or prostrate **d** : dorsoventrally flattened **3** : suffering from economic depression; *esp* : UNDERPRIVILEGED **4** : being below the standard

de·press·ing *adj* (1789) : that depresses; *esp* : causing emotional depression ⟨a ~ story⟩ — **de·press·ing·ly** \-siŋ-lē\ *adv*

de·pres·sion \di-'pre-shən, dē-\ *n* (14c) **1 a** : the angular distance of a celestial object below the horizon **b** : the size of an angle of depression **2** : an act of depressing or a state of being depressed: as **a** : a pressing down : LOWERING **b** (1) : a state of feeling sad : DEJECTION (2) : a psychoneurotic or psychotic disorder marked esp. by sadness, inactivity, difficulty in thinking and concentration, a significant increase or decrease in appetite and time spent sleeping, feelings of dejection and hopelessness, and sometimes suicidal tendencies **c** (1) : a reduction in activity, amount, quality, or force (2) : a lowering of vitality or functional activity **3** : a depressed place or part : HOLLOW **4** : LOW 1b **5** : a period of low general economic activity marked esp. by rising levels of unemployment

Depression glass *n* [Great *Depression* of 1929 to ca. 1939] (1971) : tinted glassware machine-produced during the 1930s

¹**de·pres·sive** \di-'pre-siv, dē-\ *adj* (1620) **1** : tending to depress **2** : of, relating to, marked by, or affected by psychological depression — **de·pres·sive·ly** *adv*

²**depressive** *n* (1937) : one who is affected with or prone to psychological depression

de·pres·sor \di-'pre-sər, dē-\ *n* [LL, fr. L *deprimere*] (1611) : one that depresses: as **a** : a muscle that draws down a part — compare LEVATOR **b** : a device for pressing down or aside **c** : a nerve or nerve fiber that decreases the activity or the tone of the organ or part it innervates

de·pres·sur·ize \ˌdē-'pre-shə-ˌrīz\ *vt* (1944) : to release pressure from — **de·pres·sur·iza·tion** \-ˌpre-shə-rə-'zā-shən\ *n*

dep·ri·va·tion \ˌde-prə-'vā-shən *also* ˌde-ˌprī-\ *n* (15c) **1** : the state of being deprived : PRIVATION; *esp* : removal from an office, dignity, or benefice **2** : an act or instance of depriving : LOSS

de·prive \di-'prīv\ *vt* **de·prived; de·priv·ing** [ME *depriven,* fr. ML *deprivare,* fr. L *de-* + *privare* to deprive — more at PRIVATE] (14c) **1** *obs* : REMOVE **2** : to take something away from ⟨*deprived* him of his professorship —J. M. Phalen⟩ **3** : to remove from office **4** : to withhold something from ⟨*deprived* a citizen of her rights⟩

de·prived *adj* (ca. 1522) : marked by deprivation esp. of the necessities of life or of healthful environmental influences ⟨culturally ~ children⟩

de·pro·gram \ˌdē-'prō-ˌgram, -grəm\ *vt* (1973) : to dissuade from convictions usu. of a religious nature often by coercive means — **de·pro·gram·mer** \-mər\ *n*

depth \'depth\ *n, pl* **depths** \'depths, 'dep(t)s\ [ME, prob. fr. *dep* deep] (14c) **1 a** (1) : a deep place in a body of water **b** : a part that is far from the outside or surface ⟨the ~s of the woods⟩ : ABYSS **2 b** (1) : a profound or intense state (as of thought or feeling) ⟨the ~s of misery⟩; *also* : a reprehensibly low condition ⟨hadn't realized that standards had fallen to such ~s⟩ (2) : the middle of a time (as winter) (3) : the worst part **2 a** : the perpendicular measurement downward from a surface **b** : the direct linear measurement from front to back **3** : the quality of being deep **4** : the degree of intensity ⟨~ of a color⟩; *also* : the quality of being profound (as in insight) or full (as of knowledge) **5** : the quality or state of being complete or thorough ⟨a study will be made in ~⟩ — **depth·less** \'depth-ləs\ *adj*

depth charge *n* (1917) : an antisubmarine weapon that consists essentially of a drum filled with explosives which is dropped near a target and descends to a predetermined depth where it explodes — called also **depth bomb**

depth of field (1911) : the range of distances of the object in front of an image-forming device (as a camera lens) measured along the axis of the device throughout which the image has acceptable sharpness

depth perception *n* (ca. 1911) : the ability to judge the distance of objects and the spatial relationship of objects at different distances

depth psychology *n* (1924) : PSYCHOANALYSIS; *also* : psychology concerned esp. with the unconscious mind

dep·u·ta·tion \ˌde-pyə-'tā-shən\ *n* (14c) **1** : the act of appointing a deputy **2** : a group of people appointed to represent others

de·pute \di-'pyüt\ *vt* **de·put·ed; de·put·ing** [ME, to appoint, fr. MF *deputer,* fr. LL *deputare* to assign, fr. L, to consider (as), fr. *de-* + *putare* to consider — more at PAVE] (14c) : DELEGATE

dep·u·tize \'de-pyə-ˌtīz\ *vb* **-tized; -tiz·ing** *vt* (ca. 1736) : to appoint as deputy ~ *vi* : to act as deputy — **dep·u·ti·za·tion** \ˌde-pyə-tə-'zā-shən\ *n*

dep·u·ty \'de-pyə-tē\ *n, pl* **-ties** [ME, fr. MF *député,* pp. of *deputer*] (15c) **1 a** : a person appointed as a substitute with power to act **b** : a second in command or assistant who usu. takes charge when his or her superior is absent **2** : a member of the lower house of some legislative assemblies

de·rac·i·nate \(ˌ)dē-'ra-sᵊn-ˌāt\ *vt* **-nat·ed; -nat·ing** [MF *desraciner,* fr. *des-* de- + *racine* root, fr. LL *radicina,* fr. L *radic-, radix* — more at ROOT] (1599) : UPROOT — **de·rac·i·na·tion** \(ˌ)dē-ˌra-sᵊn-'ā-shən\ *n*

de·rail \di-'rā(ə)l, dē-\ *vb* [F *dérailler* to throw off the track, fr. *dé-* de- + *rail,* fr. E] *vt* (1850) **1** : to cause to run off the rails **2** : to obstruct the progress of : FRUSTRATE ~ *vi* : to leave the rails — **de·rail·ment** \-mənt\ *n*

de·rail·leur \di-'rā-lər\ *n* [F *dérailleur,* fr. *dérailler*] (1930) : a mechanism for shifting gears on a bicycle that operates by moving the chain from one set of exposed gears to another

de·range \di-'rānj\ *vt* **de·ranged; de·rang·ing** [F *déranger,* fr. OF *desrengier,* fr. *des-* de- + *reng* line, row — more at RANK] (1776) **1** : to disturb the operation or functions of **2** : DISARRANGE ⟨hatless, with tie *deranged* —G. W. Stonier⟩ **3** : to make insane — **de·range·ment** \-mənt\ *n*

de·rate \(ˌ)dē-'rāt\ *vt* (1947) : to lower the rated capability of (as electrical or mechanical apparatus) because of deterioration or inadequacy

der·by \'dər-bē, *esp Brit* 'där-\ *n, pl* **derbies** [Edward Stanley †1834, 12th earl of *Derby*] (1844) **1** : any of several horse races held annually and usu. restricted to three-year-olds **2** : a race or contest open to all comers or to a specified category of contestants ⟨bicycle ~⟩ **3** : a man's stiff felt hat with dome-shaped crown and narrow brim

de·re·al·iza·tion \(ˌ)dē-ˌrē-ə-lə-'zā-shən, -ˌri-ə-\ *n* (1942) : a feeling of altered reality that occurs often in schizophrenia and in some drug reactions

de·reg·u·la·tion \(ˌ)dē-ˌre-gyə-'lā-shən\ *n* (1963) : the act or process of removing restrictions and regulations — **de·reg·u·late** \(ᐟ)dē-'re-gyə-ˌlāt\ *vt*

¹**der·e·lict** \'der-ə-ˌlikt\ *adj* [L *derelictus,* pp. of *derelinquere* to abandon, fr. *de-* + *relinquere* to leave — more at RELINQUISH] (1649) **1** : abandoned esp. by the owner or occupant : RUN-DOWN **2** : lacking a sense of duty : NEGLIGENT

²**derelict** *n* (1670) **1 a** : something voluntarily abandoned; *specif* : a ship abandoned on the high seas **b** : a tract of land left dry by receding water **2** : a destitute homeless social misfit : VAGRANT, BUM

der·e·lic·tion \ˌder-ə-'lik-shən\ *n* (1597) **1 a** : an intentional abandonment **b** : the state of being abandoned **2** : a recession of water leaving permanently dry land **3 a** : intentional or conscious neglect : DELINQUENCY ⟨~ of duty⟩ **b** : FAULT, SHORTCOMING

de·re·press \ˌdē-ri-'pres\ *vt* (1962) : to activate (a gene or enzyme) by releasing from a blocked state — **de·re·pres·sion** \-'pre-shən\ *n*

de·ride \di-'rīd, dē-\ *vt* **de·rid·ed; de·rid·ing** [L *deridēre,* fr. *de-* + *ridēre* to laugh] (1530) **1** : to laugh at contemptuously **2** : to subject to usu. bitter or contemptuous ridicule *syn* see RIDICULE — **de·rid·er** *n* — **de·rid·ing·ly** \-'rī-diŋ-lē\ *adv*

de ri·gueur \də-ˌ(ᐟ)rē-'gər\ *adj* [F] (1833) : prescribed or required by fashion, etiquette, or custom : PROPER

de·ri·sion \di-'ri-zhən\ *n* [ME, fr. MF, fr. LL *derision-, derisio,* fr. L *deridēre*] (14c) **1 a** : the use of ridicule or scorn to show contempt **b** : a state of being derided **2** : an object of ridicule or scorn

de·ri·sive \di-'rī-siv, -'ri-siv, -ziv; -'rī-ziv, -'ri-ziv\ *adj* (ca. 1662) : expressing or causing derision — **de·ri·sive·ly** *adv* — **de·ri·sive·ness** *n*

de·ri·so·ry \di-'rī-sə-rē, -zə-\ *adj* (1618) **1** : expressing derision : DERISIVE **2** : worthy of derision; *esp* : laughably small ⟨a ~ sum⟩

der·iv·able \di-'rī-və-bəl\ *adj* (1653) : capable of being derived

der·i·vate \'der-ə-vət\ *n* (1660) : DERIVATIVE

der·i·va·tion \ˌder-ə-'vā-shən\ *n* (15c) **1 a** (1) : the formation of a word from another word or base (as by the addition of a usu. noninflectional affix) (2) : an act of ascertaining or stating the derivation of a word (3) : ETYMOLOGY 1 **b** : the relation of a word to its base **2 a** : SOURCE, ORIGIN **b** : DESCENT, ORIGINATION **3** : something derived : DERIVATIVE **4** : an act or process of deriving **5** : a sequence of statements (as in logic or mathematics) showing that a result is a necessary consequence of previously accepted statements — **der·i·va·tion·al** \-shnəl, -shə-nᵊl\ *adj*

¹**de·riv·a·tive** \di-'ri-və-tiv\ *n* (15c) **1** : a word formed by derivation **2** : something derived **3** : the limit of the ratio of the change in a function to the corresponding change in its independent variable as the latter change approaches zero **4 a** : a chemical substance related structurally to another substance and theoretically derivable from it **b** : a substance that can be made from another substance

²**derivative** *adj* (ca. 1530) **1** : formed by derivation **2** : made up of or marked by derived elements **3** : lacking originality : BANAL — **de·riv·a·tive·ly** *adv* — **de·riv·a·tive·ness** *n*

de·riv·a·ti·za·tion \də-ˌri-və-tə-'zā-shən\ *n* (1967) : the conversion of a chemical compound into a derivative (as for identification) — **de·riv·a·tize** \də-'ri-və-ˌtīz\ *vt*

de·rive \di-'rīv, dē-\ *vb* **de·rived; de·riv·ing** [ME, fr. MF *deriver,* fr. L *derivare,* lit., to draw off (water), fr. *de-* + *rivus* stream — more at RUN] *vt* (14c) **1 a** : to take, receive, or obtain esp. from a specified source **b** : to obtain (a chemical substance) actually or theoretically from a parent substance **2** : INFER, DEDUCE **3** *archaic* : BRING **4** : to trace

\ə\ abut \ᵊ\ kitten, F table \ər\ further \a\ ash \ā\ ace \ä\ mop, mar \aů\ out \ch\ chin \e\ bet \ē\ easy \g\ go \i\ hit \ī\ ice \j\ job \ŋ\ sing \ō\ go \ȯ\ law \ȯi\ boy \th\ thin \t̲h̲\ the \ü\ loot \ů\ foot \y\ yet \zh\ vision \à, k̠, ⁿ, œ, œ̄, ŭe, ŭē, ᵞ\ see Guide to Pronunciation

the derivation of ∼ *vi* : to have or take origin : come as a derivative
syn see SPRING — **de·riv·er** *n*
derm- *or* **derma-** *or* **dermo-** *comb form* [NL, fr. Gk *derm-, dermo-*, fr. *derma*, fr. *derein* to skin — more at TEAR] : skin ⟨*dermal*⟩ : covering ⟨*ectoderm*⟩
-derm \ˌdərm\ *n comb form* [prob. fr. F *-derme*, fr. Gk *derma*] : skin : covering ⟨*ectoderm*⟩
-der·ma \ˈdər-mə\ *n comb form, pl* **-dermas** *or* **-der·ma·ta** \-mə-tə\ [NL, fr. Gk *dermat-, derma* skin] : skin or skin ailment of a (specified) type ⟨*scleroderma*⟩
derm·abra·sion \ˌdər-mə-ˈbrā-zhən\ *n* (ca. 1954) : surgical removal of skin blemishes or imperfections (as scars or tattoos) by abrasion (as with sandpaper or wire brushes)
der·mal \ˈdər-məl\ *adj* (ca. 1803) **1** : of or relating to skin and esp. to the dermis : CUTANEOUS **2** : EPIDERMAL
dermat- *or* **dermato-** *comb form* [Gk, fr. *dermat-, derma*] : skin ⟨*dermatitis*⟩ ⟨*dermatology*⟩
der·ma·ti·tis \ˌdər-mə-ˈtī-təs\ *n* (1876) : inflammation of the skin
der·mat·o·gen \(ˌ)dər-ˈma-tə-jən\ *n* [ISV] (1882) : PROTODERM
der·ma·to·glyph·ics \ˌdər-mə-tə-ˈgli-fiks\ *n pl but sing or pl in constr* [*dermat-* + Gk *glyphein* to carve + E *-ics* — more at CLEAVE] (1926) **1** : skin patterns; *esp* : patterns of the specialized skin of the inferior surfaces of the hands and feet **2** : the science of the study of skin patterns — **der·ma·to·glyph·ic** \-fik\ *adj*
der·ma·tol·o·gy \ˌdər-mə-ˈtä-lə-jē\ *n* (1819) : a branch of science dealing with the skin, its structure, functions, and diseases — **der·ma·to·log·ic** \-mə-tᵊl-ˈä-jik\ *or* **der·ma·to·log·i·cal** \-ji-kəl\ *adj* — **der·ma·tol·o·gist** \-mə-ˈtä-lə-jist\ *n*
der·ma·tome \ˈdər-mə-ˌtōm\ *n* [ISV *dermat-* + *-ome*] (1910) : the lateral wall of a somite from which the dermis is produced — **der·ma·to·mal** \ˌdər-mə-ˈtō-məl\ *adj*
der·ma·to·phyte \ˈdər-mə-tə-ˌfīt, ˌdər-mə-\ *n* [ISV] (1882) : a fungus parasitic on the skin or skin derivatives (as hair or nails)
der·ma·to·sis \ˌdər-mə-ˈtō-səs\ *n, pl* **-to·ses** \-ˌsēz\ (1866) : a disease of the skin
-der·ma·tous \ˈdər-mə-təs\ *adj comb form* [Gk *dermat-, derma* skin] : having a (specified) type of skin ⟨*pachydermatous*⟩
der·mes·tid \(ˌ)dər-ˈmes-təd\ *n* [ultim. fr. Gk *dermēstēs*, a leather=eating worm, lit., skin eater, fr. *derm-* + *edmenai* to eat — more at EAT] (ca. 1888) : any of a family (Dermestidae) of beetles with clubbed antennae that are very destructive to organic material of animal origin (as dried meat, wool, or museum specimens) — **dermestid** *adj*
der·mis \ˈdər-məs\ *n* [NL, fr. LL *-dermis*] (ca. 1830) : the sensitive vascular inner mesodermic layer of the skin — called also *corium, cutis*
-der·mis \ˈdər-məs\ *n comb form* [LL, fr. Gk, fr. *derma*] : layer of skin or tissue ⟨*endodermis*⟩
der·moid cyst \ˈdər-ˌmȯid-\ *n* (1872) : a cystic tumor often of the ovary that contains skin and skin derivatives (as hair or teeth) — called also *dermoid*
der·nier cri \ˌdern-ˌyā-ˈkrē\ *n* [F, lit., last cry] (1896) : the newest fashion
der·o·gate \ˈder-ə-ˌgāt\ *vb* **-gat·ed; -gat·ing** [ME, fr. LL *derogatus*, pp. of *derogare*, fr. L, to annul (a law), detract, fr. *de-* + *rogare* to ask, propose (a law) — more at RIGHT] *vt* (15c) : to cause to seem inferior : DISPARAGE ∼ *vi* **1** : to take away a part so as to impair : DETRACT **2** : to act beneath one's position or character — **der·o·ga·tion** \ˌder-ə-ˈgā-shən\ *n* — **de·rog·a·tive** \di-ˈrä-gə-tiv\ *adj*
de·rog·a·to·ry \di-ˈrä-gə-ˌtȯr-ē, -ˌtȯr-\ *adj* (1503) **1** : detracting from the character or standing of something — often used with *to, of,* or *from* **2** : expressive of a low opinion : DISPARAGING ⟨∼ remarks⟩ — **de·rog·a·to·ri·ly** \-ˌrä-gə-ˈtȯr-ə-lē, -ˌtȯr-\ *adv*
der·rick \ˈder-ik\ *n* [obs. *derrick* hangman, gallows, fr. *Derick*, name of 17th cent. Eng. hangman] (ca. 1752) **1** : a hoisting apparatus employing a tackle rigged at the end of a beam **2** : a framework or tower over a deep drill hole (as of an oil well) for supporting boring tackle or for hoisting and lowering
der·ri·ere *or* **der·ri·ère** \ˌder-ē-ˈer\ *n* [F *derrière*, fr. OF *derrier* back part, rear, fr. *derier*, adv., behind, fr. LL *deretro*, fr. L *de* from + *retro* back] (1774) : BUTTOCKS
der·ring-do \ˌder-iŋ-ˈdü\ *n* [ME *dorring don* daring to do, fr. *dorring* (gerund of *dorren* to dare) + *don* to do] (1579) : daring action : DARING ⟨deeds of ∼⟩
der·rin·ger \ˈder-ən-jər\ *n* [Henry *Deringer* †1869 Am. inventor] (1853) : a short-barreled pocket pistol
der·ris \ˈder-əs\ *n* [NL, genus name, fr. Gk, skin, fr. *derein* to skin — more at TEAR] (1919) **1** : a preparation of derris roots and stems used as an insecticide **2** : any of a large genus (*Derris*) of leguminous tropical Old World shrubs and woody vines including sources of poisons and esp. commercial sources of rotenone

derrick 2

der·vish \ˈdər-vish\ *n* [Turk *derviş*, lit., beggar, fr. Per *darvīsh*] (1585) **1** : a member of a Muslim religious order noted for devotional exercises (as bodily movements leading to a trance) **2** : one that whirls or dances with or as if with the abandonment of a dervish
des- *prefix* [F *dés-*, fr. OF *des-* — more at DE-] : DE- 6 — esp. before vowels ⟨*desoxy*⟩
DES \ˌdē-(ˌ)ē-ˈes\ *n* (1971) : DIETHYLSTILBESTROL
de·sa·cral·ize \(ˌ)dē-ˈsā-krə-ˌlīz, -ˈsa-\ *vt* **-ized; -iz·ing** (1911) : to divest of sacred qualities — **de·sa·cral·iza·tion** \(ˌ)dē-ˌsā-krə-lī-ˈzā-shən, -ˌsa-\ *n*
de·sa·li·nate \(ˈ)dē-ˈsa-lə-ˌnāt *also* -ˈsā-\ *vt* **-nat·ed; -nat·ing** (1949) : DESALT — **de·sa·li·na·tion** \(ˌ)dē-ˌsa-lə-ˈnā-shən *also* -ˌsā-\ *n* — **de·sa·li·na·tor** \(ˌ)dē-ˈsa-lə-ˌnā-tər *also* -ˈsā-\ *n*
de·sa·li·nize \(ˈ)dē-ˈsa-lə-ˌnīz *also* -ˈsā-\ *vt* **-nized; -niz·ing** (1963) : DESALT — **de·sa·li·ni·za·tion** \(ˌ)dē-ˌsa-lə-nə-ˈzā-shən *also* -ˌsā-\ *n*
de·salt \(ˌ)dē-ˈsȯlt\ *vt* (ca. 1904) : to remove salt from — **de·salt·er** *n*
¹des·cant \ˈdes-ˌkant\ *n* [ME *dyscant*, fr. ONF & ML; ONF *descant*, ML *discantus*, fr. L *dis-* + *cantus* song — more at CHANT] (14c) **1 a** : a melody or counterpoint sung above the plainsong of the tenor **b** : the art of composing or improvising contrapuntal part music; *also* : the music so composed or improvised **c** : SOPRANO, TREBLE **d** : a

superimposed counterpoint to a simple melody sung typically by some or all of the sopranos **2** : discourse or comment on a theme
²des·cant \ˈdes-ˌkant, des-ˈ, dis-ˈ\ *vi* (15c) **1** : to sing or play a descant; *broadly* : SING **2** : COMMENT, DISCOURSE
de·scend \di-ˈsend, dē-\ *vb* [ME, fr. OF *descendre*, fr. L *descendere*, fr. *de-* + *scandere* to climb — more at SCAN] *vi* (13c) **1** : to pass from a higher place or level to a lower one ⟨∼ed from the platform⟩ **2** : to pass in discussion from what is logically prior or more comprehensive **3 a** : to come down from a stock or source : DERIVE ⟨∼s from an old merchant family⟩ **b** : to pass by inheritance ⟨a desk that has ∼ed in the family⟩ **c** : to pass by transmission ⟨songs ∼ed from old ballads⟩ **4** : to incline, lead, or extend downward ⟨the road ∼s to the river⟩ **5 a** : to swoop or pounce down (as in a sudden attack) **b** : to appear suddenly and often disconcertingly as if from above ⟨reporters ∼ed on the candidate⟩ **6** : to proceed in a sequence or gradation from higher to lower or from more remote to nearer or more recent **7 a** : to lower oneself in status or dignity : STOOP **b** : to worsen and sink in condition or estimation ∼ *vt* **1** : to pass, move, or climb down or down along **2** : to extend down along — **de·scend·ible** \-ˈsen-də-bəl\ *adj*
¹de·scen·dant *or* **de·scen·dent** \di-ˈsen-dənt\ *adj* [MF & L; MF *descendant*, fr. L *descendent-, descendens*, prp. of *descendere*] (1572) **1** : moving or directed downward **2** : proceeding from an ancestor or source
²descendant *or* **descendent** *n* [F & L; F *descendant*, fr. LL *descendent-, descendens*, fr. L] (1600) **1** : one descended from another or from a common stock **2** : one deriving directly from a precursor or prototype
de·scend·er \di-ˈsen-dər, ˈdē-\ *n* (1802) : the part of a lowercase letter (as p) that descends below the main body of the letter; *also* : a letter that has such a part
de·scen·sion \di-ˈsen-chən\ *n* (15c) *archaic* : DESCENT 2
de·scent \di-ˈsent\ *n* [ME, fr. MF *descente*, fr. OF *descendre*] (14c) **1 a** : derivation from an ancestor : BIRTH, LINEAGE ⟨of French ∼⟩ **b** : transmission or devolution of an estate by inheritance usu. in the descending line **c** : the fact or process of originating from an ancestral stock **d** : the shaping or development in nature and character by transmission from a source : DERIVATION **2** : the act or process of descending **3 a** : a step downward in a scale of gradation; *specif* : one generation in an ancestral line or genealogical scale **4 a** : an inclination downward : SLOPE **b** : a descending way (as a downgrade or stairway) **c** *obs* : the lowest part **5 a** : ATTACK, INVASION **b** : a sudden disconcerting appearance (as for a visit) **6** : a downward step (as in station or value) : DECLINE ⟨∼ of the family to actual poverty⟩
de·scribe \di-ˈskrīb\ *vt* **de·scribed; de·scrib·ing** [ME, fr. L *describere*, fr. *de-* + *scribere* to write — more at SCRIBE] (15c) **1** : to represent or give an account of in words ⟨∼ a picture⟩ **2** : to represent by a figure, model, or picture : DELINEATE **3** *obs* : DISTRIBUTE **4** : to trace or traverse the outline of ⟨∼ a circle⟩ **5** *archaic* : OBSERVE, PERCEIVE — **de·scrib·able** \-ˈskrī-bə-bəl\ *adj* — **de·scrib·er** *n*
de·scrip·tion \di-ˈskrip-shən\ *n* [ME *descripcioun*, fr. MF & L; MF *description*, fr. L *description-, descriptio*, fr. *describere*] (14c) **1 a** : an act of describing; *specif* : discourse intended to give a mental image of something experienced **b** : a descriptive statement or account **2** : kind or character esp. as determined by salient features ⟨opposed to any tax of so radical a ∼⟩ *syn* see TYPE
de·scrip·tive \di-ˈskrip-tiv\ *adj* (1751) **1** : serving to describe ⟨a ∼ account⟩ **2 a** : referring to, constituting, or grounded in matters of observation or experience ⟨the ∼ basis of science⟩ **b** : factually grounded or informative rather than normative, prescriptive, or emotive ⟨∼ cultural studies⟩ **3** *of a modifier* **a** : expressing the quality, kind, or condition of what is denoted by the modified term ⟨*hot* in "hot water" is a ∼ adjective⟩ **b** : NONRESTRICTIVE **4** : of, relating to, or dealing with the structure of a language at a particular time usu. with exclusion of historical and comparative data ⟨∼ linguistics⟩ — **de·scrip·tive·ly** *adv* — **de·scrip·tive·ness** *n*
de·scrip·tor \di-ˈskrip-tər\ *n* (1933) : something (as a word or characteristic feature) that serves to describe or identify; *esp* : a word or phrase (as an index term) used to identify an item (as a subject or document) in an information retrieval system
¹de·scry \di-ˈskrī\ *vt* **de·scried; de·scry·ing** [ME *descrien*, fr. MF *descrier* to proclaim, decry] (14c) **1 a** : to catch sight of **b** : FIND OUT, DISCOVER **2** *obs* : to make known : REVEAL
²descry *n* (1605) *obs* : discovery or view from afar
Des·de·mo·na \ˌdez-də-ˈmō-nə\ *n* : the wife of Othello in Shakespeare's *Othello*
des·e·crate \ˈde-si-ˌkrāt\ *vt* **-crat·ed; -crat·ing** [*de-* + *-secrate* (as in *consecrate*)] (1677) **1** : to violate the sanctity of : PROFANE **2** : to treat disrespectfully, irreverently, or outrageously ⟨the kind of shore development . . . that has desecrated so many waterfronts —John Fischer⟩ — **des·e·crat·er** *or* **des·e·cra·tor** \-ˌkrā-tər\ *n*
des·e·cra·tion \ˌde-si-ˈkrā-shən\ *n* (ca. 1717) : an act or instance of desecrating : the state of being desecrated
de·seg·re·gate \(ˌ)dē-ˈse-gri-ˌgāt\ *vt* (1944) : to eliminate segregation in; *specif* : to free of any law, provision, or practice requiring isolation of the members of a particular race in separate units ∼ *vi* : to become desegregated
de·seg·re·ga·tion \(ˌ)dē-ˌse-gri-ˈgā-shən\ *n* (1951) **1** : the action or an instance of desegregating **2** : the state of being desegregated
de·se·lect \ˌdē-sə-ˈlekt\ *vt* (1965) : DISMISS, REJECT
de·sen·si·tize \(ˌ)dē-ˈsen(t)-sə-ˌtīz\ *vt* (1898) **1** : to make (a sensitized or hypersensitive individual) insensitive or nonreactive to a sensitizing agent **2** : to make emotionally insensitive or callous; *specif* : to extinguish an emotional response (as of fear, anxiety, or guilt) to stimuli that formerly induced it — **de·sen·si·ti·za·tion** \(ˌ)dē-ˌsen(t)-sə-tə-ˈzā-shən\ *n* — **de·sen·si·tiz·er** \(ˌ)dē-ˈsen-sə-ˌtī-zər\ *n*
¹des·ert \di-ˈzərt\ *n* [ME, fr. OF, fr. L *desertus*, pp. of *deserere* to desert, fr. *de-* + *serere* to join together — more at SERIES] (13c) **1 a** : arid barren land; *esp* : a tract incapable of supporting any considerable population without an artificial water supply **b** : an area of water apparently devoid of life **2** *archaic* : a wild uninhabited and uncultivated tract **3** : a desolate or forbidding area ⟨lost in a ∼ of doubt⟩ — **de·ser·tic** \de-ˈzər-tik\ *adj*

²**des·ert** \'de-zərt\ *adj* (13c) **1** : desolate and sparsely occupied or unoccupied ⟨a ~ island⟩ **2** : of or relating to a desert **3** *archaic* : FORSAKEN

³**de·sert** \di-'zərt\ *n* [ME *deserte*, fr. OF, fr. fem. of *desert*, pp. of *deservir* to deserve] (13c) **1** : the quality or fact of deserving reward or punishment **2** : deserved reward or punishment — usu. used in plural ⟨got their just ~s⟩ **2** : EXCELLENCE, WORTH

⁴**de·sert** \di-'zərt\ *vb* [F *déserter*, fr. LL *desertare*, freq. of L *deserere*] *vt* (1603) **1** : to withdraw from or leave usu. without intent to return **2 a** : to leave in the lurch ⟨~ a friend in trouble⟩ **b** : to abandon (military service) without leave ~ *vi* : to quit one's post, allegiance, or service without leave or justification; *esp* : to abandon military duty without leave and without intent to return *syn* see ABANDON — **de·sert·er** *n*

de·ser·ti·fi·ca·tion \di-ˌzər-tə-fə-'kā-shən\ *n* (1974) : the process of becoming desert (as from land mismanagement or climate change)

de·ser·tion \di-'zər-shən\ *n* (1591) **1** : an act of deserting; *esp* : the abandonment without consent or legal justification of a person, post, or relationship and the associated duties and obligations ⟨sued for divorce on grounds of ~⟩ **2** : a state of being deserted or forsaken

desert locust *n* (1944) : a destructive migratory locust (*Schistocerca gregaria*) of southwestern Asia and parts of northern Africa

desert soil *n* (ca. 1938) : a soil that develops under sparse shrub vegetation in warm to cool arid climates with a light-colored surface soil usu. underlain by calcareous material and a hardpan layer

desert varnish *n* (ca. 1898) : a dark coating which is found on rocks after long exposure in desert regions and whose color is due to iron and manganese oxides

de·serve \di-'zərv\ *vb* **de·served; de·serv·ing** [ME, fr. OF *deservir*, L *deservire* to devote oneself to, fr. *de-* + *servire* to serve] *vt* (13c) : to be worthy of : MERIT ⟨~s another chance⟩ ~ *vi* : to be worthy, fit, or suitable for some reward or requital ⟨have become recognized as they ~ —T. S. Eliot⟩ — **de·serv·er** *n*

de·served \-'zərvd\ *adj* (ca. 1552) : of, relating to, or being that which one deserves ⟨a ~ reputation⟩ — **de·served·ly** \-'zər-vəd-lē, -'zərvd-lē\ *adv* — **de·served·ness** \-'zər-vəd-nəs, -'zərvd-nəs\ *n*

¹**de·serv·ing** \-'zər-viŋ\ *n* (14c) : DESERT, MERIT ⟨reward the proud according to their ~s —Charles Kingsley⟩

²**deserving** *adj* (1576) : MERITORIOUS, WORTHY; *esp* : meriting financial aid ⟨scholarships for ~ students⟩

de·sex \(ˌ)dē-'seks\ *vt* (1911) **1** : CASTRATE, SPAY **2** : to eliminate perceived sexism from ⟨~ the language of church Bible study programs — R. M. Harley⟩

de·sex·u·al·ize \(ˌ)dē-'sek-sh(ə-)wə-ˌlīz, -'sek-shə-ˌlīz\ *vt* (1894) **1** : to deprive of sexual characters or power **2** : to divest of sexual quality — **de·sex·u·al·iza·tion** \(ˌ)dē-ˌsek-sh(ə-)wə-lə-'zā-shən, -'sek-shə-lə-\ *n*

des·ha·bille \ˌdez-ə-'bē(ə)l, -'bil, -'bē\ *var of* DISHABILLE

des·ic·cant \'de-si-kənt\ *n* (1676) : a drying agent (as calcium chloride)

des·ic·cate \'de-si-ˌkāt\ *vb* **-cat·ed; -cat·ing** [L *desiccatus*, pp. of *desiccare* to dry up, fr. *de-* + *siccare* to dry, fr. *siccus* dry — more at SACK] *vt* (1575) **1** : to dry up **2** : to preserve (a food) by drying : DEHYDRATE **3** : to drain of emotional or intellectual vitality ~ *vi* : to become dried up — **des·ic·ca·tion** \ˌde-si-'kā-shən\ *n* — **des·ic·ca·tive** \'de-si-ˌkā-tiv\ *adj* — **des·ic·ca·tor** \'de-si-ˌkā-tər\ *n*

de·sid·er·ate \di-'si-də-ˌrāt, -'zi-\ *vt* **-at·ed; -at·ing** [L *desideratus*, pp. of *desiderare* to desire] (1645) : to entertain or express a wish to have or attain — **de·sid·er·a·tion** \-ˌsi-də-'rā-shən, -ˌzi-\ *n* — **de·sid·er·a·tive** \-'si-də-ˌrā-tiv, -'si-d(ə-)rət-, -'zi-\ *adj*

de·sid·er·a·tum \di-ˌsi-də-'rä-təm, -ˌzi-, -'rā-\ *n, pl* **-ta** \-tə\ [L, neut. of *desideratus*] (1652) : something desired as essential

¹**de·sign** \di-'zīn\ *vb* [ME, to outline, indicate, mean, fr. MF & ML *designer* to designate, fr. ML *designare*, fr. L, to mark out, fr. *de-* + *signare* to mark — more at SIGN] *vt* (14c) **1** : to create, fashion, execute, or construct according to plan : DEVISE, CONTRIVE **2 a** : to conceive and plan out in the mind ⟨he ~ed the perfect crime⟩ **b** : to have as a purpose : INTEND ⟨she ~ed to excel in her studies⟩ **c** : to devise for a specific function or end ⟨a book ~ed primarily as a college textbook⟩ **3** *archaic* : to indicate with a distinctive mark, sign, or name **4 a** : to make a drawing, pattern, or sketch of **b** : to draw the plans for ~ *vi* **1** : to conceive or execute a plan **2** : to draw, lay out, or prepare a design — **de·sign·ed·ly** \-'zī-nəd-lē\ *adv*

²**design** *n* (1588) **1 a** : a particular purpose held in view by an individual or group ⟨he has ambitious ~s for his son⟩ **b** : deliberate purposive planning ⟨more by accident than ~⟩ **2** : a mental project or scheme in which means to an end are laid down **3 a** : a deliberate undercover project or scheme : PLOT **b** *pl* : aggressive or evil intent — used with *on* or *against* ⟨he has ~s on the money⟩ **4** : a preliminary sketch or outline showing the main features of something to be executed : DELINEATION **5 a** : an underlying scheme that governs functioning, developing, or unfolding : PATTERN, MOTIF ⟨the general ~ of the epic⟩ **b** : a plan or protocol for carrying out or accomplishing something (as a scientific experiment); *also* : the process of preparing this **6** : the arrangement of elements or details in a product or work of art **7** : a decorative pattern **8** : the creative art of executing aesthetic or functional designs *syn* see INTENTION, PLAN

¹**des·ig·nate** \'de-zig-ˌnāt, -nət\ *adj* [L *designatus*, pp. of *designare*] (1646) : chosen but not yet installed ⟨ambassador ~⟩

²**des·ig·nate** \-ˌnāt\ *vt* **-nat·ed; -nat·ing** (1791) **1** : to indicate and set apart for a specific purpose, office, or duty ⟨~ a group to prepare a plan⟩ **2 a** : to point out the location of ⟨a marker *designating* the battle⟩ **b** : to distinguish as to class ⟨the area we ~ as that of spiritual values —J. B. Conant⟩ **c** : SPECIFY, STIPULATE ⟨to be sent by a *designated* shipper⟩ **3** : DENOTE ⟨associate names with the people they ~⟩ **4** : to call by a distinctive title, term, or expression ⟨a particle *designated* the neutron⟩ — **des·ig·na·tive** \-ˌnā-tiv\ *adj* — **des·ig·na·tor** \-ˌnā-tər\ *n* — **des·ig·na·to·ry** \-nə-ˌtōr-ē, -ˌtòr-\ *adj*

designated hitter *n* (1973) : a baseball player designated at the start of the game to bat in place of the pitcher without causing the pitcher to be removed from the game

des·ig·na·tion \ˌde-zig-'nā-shən\ *n* (14c) **1** : the act of indicating or identifying **2** : appointment to or selection for an office, post, or service **3** : a distinguishing name, sign, or title **4** : the relation between a sign and the thing signified

des·ig·nee \ˌde-zig-'nē\ *n* (1925) : one who is designated

¹**de·sign·er** \di-'zī-nər\ *n* (1662) : one that designs: as **a** : one who creates and often executes plans for a project or structure ⟨urban ~s⟩ ⟨a theater set ~⟩ **b** : one that creates and manufactures a new product style or design; *esp* : one who designs and manufactures high-fashion clothing ⟨the ~'s new fall line⟩

²**designer** *adj* (1966) **1** : of, relating to, or produced by a designer ⟨~ wallpaper⟩ ⟨wearing a ~ original⟩; *also* : displaying the name, signature, or logo of a designer or manufacturer ⟨~ jeans⟩ **2** : intended to reflect the latest in sophisticated taste or fashion ⟨~ ice cream⟩ ⟨a ~ haircut⟩

designer drug *n* (1983) : a synthetic version of a controlled substance (as heroin) that is produced with a slightly altered molecular structure to avoid having it classified as an illicit drug

de·sign·ing \di-'zī-niŋ\ *adj* (1653) **1** : practicing forethought **2** : CRAFTY, SCHEMING

de·sign·ment \di-'zīn-mənt\ *n* (1583) *obs* : PLAN, PURPOSE

de·si·pra·mine \də-'zi-prə-ˌmēn\ *n* [desmethyl (fr. des- + methyl) + imipramine] (1965) : a tricyclic antidepressant $C_{18}H_{22}N_2$

de·sir·abil·i·ty \di-ˌzī-rə-'bi-lə-tē\ *n, pl* **-ties** (1824) **1** *pl* : desirable conditions ⟨had understood and studied certain *desirabilities* —D. D. Eisenhower⟩ **2** : the quality, fact, or degree of being desirable

¹**de·sir·able** \di-'zī-rə-bəl\ *adj* (14c) **1** : having pleasing qualities or properties : ATTRACTIVE ⟨a ~ woman⟩ **2** : worth seeking or doing as advantageous, beneficial, or wise : ADVISABLE ⟨~ legislation⟩ — **de·sir·able·ness** *n* — **de·sir·ably** \-blē\ *adv*

²**desirable** *n* (1645) : one that is desirable

¹**de·sire** \di-'zīr, dē-\ *vb* **de·sired; de·sir·ing** [ME, fr. OF *desirer*, fr. L *desiderare*, fr. *de-* + *sider-, sidus* heavenly body] *vt* (13c) **1** : to long or hope for : exhibit or feel desire for **2 a** : to express a wish for : REQUEST **b** *archaic* : to express a wish to : ASK **3** *obs* : INVITE **4** *archaic* : to feel the loss of ~ *vi* : to have or feel desire *syn* DESIRE, WISH, WANT, CRAVE, COVET mean to have a longing for. DESIRE stresses the strength of feeling and often implies strong intention or aim ⟨*desires* to start a new life⟩. WISH sometimes implies a general or transient longing esp. for the unattainable ⟨*wishes* for permanent world peace⟩. WANT specif. suggests a felt need or lack ⟨*wants* to have a family⟩. CRAVE stresses the force of physical appetite or emotional need ⟨*craves* sweets⟩. COVET implies strong envious desire ⟨*covets* his rise to fame⟩.

²**desire** *n* (14c) **1** : conscious impulse toward something that promises enjoyment or satisfaction in its attainment **2 a** : LONGING, CRAVING **b** : sexual urge or appetite **3** : a usu. formal request or petition for some action **4** : something desired

de·sir·ous \di-'zīr-əs\ *adj* (14c) : impelled or governed by desire ⟨~ of fame⟩ — **de·sir·ous·ly** *adv* — **de·sir·ous·ness** *n*

de·sist \di-'zist, -'sist, dē-\ *vi* [ME, fr. MF *desister*, fr. L *desistere*, fr. *de-* + *sistere* to stand, stop; akin to L *stare* to stand — more at STAND] (15c) : to cease to proceed or act *syn* see STOP — **de·sis·tance** \-'zis-tən(t)s, -'sis-\ *n*

desk \'desk\ *n* [ME *deske*, fr. ML *desca*, modif. of OIt *desco* table, fr. L *discus* dish, disc — more at DISH] (14c) **1 a** : a table, frame, or case with a sloping or horizontal surface esp. for writing and reading and often with drawers, compartments, and pigeonholes **b** : a reading table or lectern from which a liturgical service is read **c** : a table, counter, stand, or booth at which a person works **2 a** : a division of an organization specializing in a particular phase of activity ⟨the Russian ~ in the Department of State⟩ **b** : a seating position according to rank in an orchestra ⟨*first-desk* violinist⟩

desk·bound \'desk-ˌbaund\ *adj* (1944) : restricted to work at a desk

de·skill \ˌdē-'skil\ *vt* (1941) **1** : to reduce the level of skill needed for (a job) **2** : to reduce the level of skill needed for a job by (a worker)

desk·man \'desk-ˌman, -mən\ *n* (1913) : one that works at a desk; *specif* : a newspaperman who processes news and prepares copy

¹**desk·top** \'desk-ˌtäp\ *n* (1929) **1** : the top of a desk; *also* : an office desktop simulated by a computer program **2** : a desktop computer

²**desktop** *adj* (1958) : of a size that can be conveniently used on a desk or table ⟨~ computers⟩ — compare LAPTOP

desktop publishing *n* (1984) : the production of printed matter by means of a desktop computer having a layout program that integrates text and graphics

desm- *or* **desmo-** *comb form* [NL, fr. Gk, fr. *desmos*, fr. *dein* to bind — more at DIADEM] : bond : ligament ⟨*desmo*some⟩

des·mid \'dez-məd\ *n* [ultim. fr. Gk *desmos*] (1862) : any of numerous unicellular or colonial green algae (order Zygnematales)

des·mo·some \'dez-mə-ˌsōm\ *n* (ca. 1932) : a specialized localized thickening of the cell membrane of an epithelial cell that serves to anchor contiguous cells together — **des·mo·som·al** \-ˌsō-məl\ *adj*

¹**des·o·late** \'de-sə-lət, 'de-zə-\ *adj* [ME *desolat*, fr. L *desolatus*, pp. of *desolare* to abandon, fr. *de-* + *solus* alone] (14c) **1** : devoid of inhabitants and visitors : DESERTED **2** : joyless, disconsolate, and sorrowful through or as if through separation from a loved one **3 a** : showing the effects of abandonment and neglect : DILAPIDATED **b** : BARREN, LIFELESS ⟨a ~ landscape⟩ **c** : devoid of warmth, comfort, or hope : GLOOMY ⟨~ memories⟩ *syn* see ALONE — **des·o·late·ly** *adv* — **des·o·late·ness** *n*

²**des·o·late** \-ˌlāt\ *vt* **-lat·ed; -lat·ing** (14c) : to make desolate: **a** : to deprive of inhabitants **b** : to lay waste **c** : FORSAKE **d** : to make wretched — **des·o·lat·er** *or* **des·o·la·tor** \-ˌlā-tər\ *n* — **des·o·lat·ing·ly** \-ˌlā-tiŋ-lē\ *adv*

desmid

\ə\ abut \ᵊ\ kitten, F table \ər\ further \a\ ash \ā\ ace \ä\ mop, mar \aù\ out \ch\ chin \e\ bet \ē\ easy \g\ go \i\ hit \ī\ ice \j\ job \ŋ\ sing \ō\ go \ò\ law \òi\ boy \th\ thin \t͟h\ the \ü\ loot \ù\ foot \y\ yet \zh\ vision \ä, k̶, ⁿ, œ, œ̄, ᵫ, ᵫ̄, ᵞ\ *see* Guide to Pronunciation

des·o·la·tion \,de-sə-'lā-shən, ,de-zə-\ n (14c) **1** : the action of desolating **2 a** : GRIEF, SADNESS **b** : LONELINESS **3** : DEVASTATION, RUIN **4** : barren wasteland

de·sorb \(,)dē-'sȯrb, -'zȯrb\ vt (1924) : to remove (a sorbed substance) by the reverse of adsorption or absorption

de·sorp·tion \-'sȯrp-shən, -'zȯrp-\ n (1924) : the process of desorbing

desoxy- — see DEOXY-

des·oxy·ri·bo·nu·cle·ic acid \de-,zäk-sē-'rī-bō-n(y)ü-,klē-ik-, -,klā-\ n (1931) : DNA

1de·spair \di-'spar, -'sper\ vb [ME despeiren, fr. MF desperer, fr. L desperare, fr. de- + sperare to hope; akin to L spes hope — more at SPEED] vi (14c) : to lose all hope or confidence ⟨~ of winning⟩ ~ vt, obs : to lose hope for — **de·spair·er** n

2despair n (14c) **1** : utter loss of hope **2** : a cause of hopelessness ⟨an incorrigible child is the ~ of his parents⟩

de·spair·ing adj (1589) : given to, arising from, or marked by despair : devoid of hope syn see DESPONDENT — **de·spair·ing·ly** \-iŋ-lē\ adv

des·patch \dis-'pach\ var of DISPATCH

des·per·a·do \,des-pə-'rä-(,)dō, -'rā-\ n, pl **-does** or **-dos** [prob. alter. of obs. desperate desperado, fr. desperate, fr. L desperatus, pp. of desperare] (1647) : a bold or violent criminal; esp : a bandit of the western U.S. in the 19th century

des·per·ate \'des-p(ə-)rət, -pərt\ adj [L desperatus, pp. of desperare] (15c) **1 a** : having lost hope ⟨a ~ spirit crying for relief⟩ **b** : giving no ground for hope ⟨the outlook was ~⟩ **2 a** : moved by despair ⟨victims made ~ by abuse⟩ **b** : involving or employing extreme measures in an attempt to escape defeat or frustration ⟨made a ~ leap for the rope⟩ **3** : suffering extreme need or anxiety ⟨~ for money⟩ **4** : involving extreme danger or possible disaster ⟨a ~ situation⟩ **5** : of extreme intensity **6** : SHOCKING, OUTRAGEOUS syn see DESPONDENT — **des·per·ate·ly** adv — **des·per·ate·ness** n

des·per·a·tion \,des-pə-'rā-shən\ n (14c) **1** : loss of hope and surrender to despair **2** : a state of hopelessness leading to rashness

de·spi·ca·ble \di-'spi-kə-bəl, 'des-(,)pi-\ adj [LL despicabilis, fr. L despicari to despise] (1553) : deserving to be despised : so worthless or obnoxious as to rouse moral indignation ⟨~ behavior⟩ syn see CONTEMPTIBLE — **de·spi·ca·ble·ness** n — **de·spi·ca·bly** \-blē\ adv

de·spir·i·tu·al·ize \(,)dē-'spi-ri-ch(ə-)wə-,līz, -chə-,līz\ vt (1868) : to deprive of spiritual character or influence

de·spise \di-'spīz\ vt **de·spised; de·spis·ing** [ME, fr. OF despis-, stem of despire, fr. L despicere, fr. de- + specere to look — more at SPY] (14c) **1** : to look down on with contempt or aversion ⟨despised the weak⟩ **2** : to regard as negligible, worthless, or distasteful ⟨despise the ~⟩ — **de·spise·ment** \-'spīz-mənt\ n — **de·spis·er** \-'spī-zər\ n

syn DESPISE, CONTEMN, SCORN, DISDAIN mean to regard as unworthy of one's notice or consideration. DESPISE may suggest an emotional response ranging from strong dislike to loathing ⟨despises cowards⟩. CONTEMN implies a vehement condemnation of a person or thing as low, vile, feeble, or ignominious ⟨contemns the image of women promoted by advertisers⟩. SCORN implies a ready or indignant contempt ⟨scorns the very thought of retirement⟩. DISDAIN implies an arrogant or supercilious aversion to what is regarded as unworthy ⟨disdained popular music⟩.

1de·spite \di-'spīt\ n [ME, fr. OF despit, fr. L despicere] (13c) **1** : the feeling or attitude of despising : CONTEMPT **2** : MALICE, SPITE **3 a** : an act showing contempt or defiance **b** : DETRIMENT, DISADVANTAGE ⟨I know of no government which stands to its obligations, even in its own ~, more solidly —Sir Winston Churchill⟩ — **in despite of** : in spite of

2despite vt **de·spit·ed; de·spit·ing** (14c) **1** archaic : to treat with contempt **2** obs : to provoke to anger : VEX

3despite prep (15c) : in spite of ⟨played ~ an injury⟩

de·spite·ful \-'spīt-fəl\ adj (15c) : expressing malice or hate — **de·spite·ful·ly** \-fə-lē\ adv — **de·spite·ful·ness** n

de·spit·eous \dis-'pi-tē-əs\ adj (14c) archaic : feeling or showing despite : MALICIOUS — **de·spit·eous·ly** adv, archaic

de·spoil \di-'spȯi(ə)l\ vt [ME despoylen, fr. MF despoillier, fr. L despoliare, fr. de- + spoliare to strip, rob — more at SPOIL] (14c) : to strip of belongings, possessions, or value : PILLAGE syn see RAVAGE — **de·spoil·er** n — **de·spoil·ment** \-mənt\ n

de·spo·li·a·tion \di-,spō-lē-'ā-shən\ n [LL despoliation-, despoliatio, fr. despoliare] (ca. 1657) : the condition of being despoiled : SPOLIATION

1de·spond \di-'spänd\ vi [L despondēre, fr. de- + spondēre to promise solemnly — more at SPOUSE] (1655) : to become despondent

2despond n (1678) : DESPONDENCY

de·spon·dence \di-'spän-dən(t)s\ n (1676) : DESPONDENCY

de·spon·den·cy \-dən-sē\ n (1653) : the state of being despondent : DEJECTION, HOPELESSNESS

de·spon·dent \-dənt\ adj [L despondent-, despondens, prp. of despondēre] (ca. 1699) : feeling or showing extreme discouragement, dejection, or depression ⟨~ about his health⟩ — **de·spon·dent·ly** adv

syn DESPONDENT, DESPAIRING, DESPERATE, HOPELESS mean having lost all or nearly all hope. DESPONDENT implies a deep dejection arising from a conviction of the uselessness of further effort ⟨despondent about yet another rejection⟩. DESPAIRING suggests the slipping away of all hope and often despondency ⟨despairing appeals for the return of the kidnapped child⟩. DESPERATE implies despair that prompts reckless action or violence in the face of defeat or frustration ⟨one last desperate attempt to turn the tide of battle⟩. HOPELESS suggests despair and the cessation of effort or resistance and often implies acceptance or resignation ⟨the situation of the trapped miners is hopeless⟩.

des·pot \'des-pət, -,pät\ n [MF despote, fr. Gk despotēs master, lord, autocrat, fr. des- (akin to domos house) + -potēs (akin to posis husband); akin to Skt dampati lord of the house — more at DOME, POTENT] (1585) **1 a** : a Byzantine emperor or prince **b** : a bishop or patriarch of the Eastern Orthodox Church **c** : an Italian hereditary prince or military leader during the Renaissance **2 a** : a ruler with absolute power and authority **b** : a person exercising power tyrannically

des·pot·ic \des-'pä-tik, dis-\ adj (1650) : of, relating to, or characteristic of a despot — **des·pot·i·cal·ly** \-ti-k(ə-)lē\ adv

des·po·tism \'des-pə-,ti-zəm\ n (ca. 1727) **1 a** : rule by a despot **b** : despotic exercise of power **2 a** : a system of government in which the ruler has unlimited power : ABSOLUTISM **b** : a despotic state

des·qua·mate \'des-kwə-,māt\ vi **-mat·ed; -mat·ing** [L desquamatus, pp. of desquamare to scale, fr. de- + squama scale] (1828) : to peel off in scales — **des·qua·ma·tion** \,des-kwə-'mā-shən\ n

des·sert \di-'zərt\ n [MF, fr. desservir to clear the table, fr. des- de- + servir to serve, fr. L servire] (1600) **1** : a usu. sweet course or dish (as of pastry or ice cream) served at the end of a meal **2** Brit : a fresh fruit served after a sweet course

des·sert·spoon \-,spün\ n (1754) **1** : a spoon intermediate in size between a teaspoon and a tablespoon for use in eating dessert **2** : DESSERTSPOONFUL

des·sert·spoon·ful \di-'zərt-,spün-,fu̇l\ n (1875) **1** : as much as a dessertspoon will hold **2** chiefly Brit : a unit of measure equal to about 2½ fluidrams

dessert wine n (1773) : a usu. sweet wine typically served with dessert or afterward

de·sta·bi·lize \(,)dē-'stā-bə-,līz\ vt (1924) **1** : to make unstable **2** : to cause (a government) to be incapable of functioning or surviving — **de·sta·bi·li·za·tion** \(,)dē-,stā-bə-lə-'zā-shən\ n

de·stain \(,)dē-'stān\ vt (1927) : to selectively remove stain from (a specimen for microscopic study)

de–Sta·lin·iza·tion \(,)dē-,stä-lə-nə-'zā-shən, -,sta-\ n (1951) : the discrediting of Stalin and his policies

de Stijl \də-'sti(ə)l, -'stā(ə)l\ n [D De Stijl, lit., the style, magazine published by members of the school] (1934) : a school of art founded in Holland in 1917 typically using rectangular forms and the primary colors plus black and white and asymmetric balance

des·ti·na·tion \,des-tə-'nā-shən\ n (14c) **1** : the purpose for which something is destined **2** : an act of appointing, setting aside for a purpose, or predetermining **3** : a place to which one is journeying or to which something is sent ⟨kept their ~ secret⟩

des·tine \'des-tən\ vt **des·tined; des·tin·ing** [ME, fr. MF destiner, fr. L destinare, fr. de- + -stinare (akin to L stare to stand) — more at STAND] (14c) **1** : to decree beforehand : PREDETERMINE **2 a** : to designate, assign, or dedicate in advance ⟨the younger son was destined for the priesthood⟩ **b** : to direct, devise, or set apart for a specific purpose or place ⟨freight destined for European ports⟩

des·ti·ny \'des-tə-nē\ n, pl **-nies** [ME destinee, fr. MF, fr. fem. of destiné, pp. of destiner] (14c) **1** : something to which a person or thing is destined : FORTUNE **2** : a predetermined course of events often held to be an irresistible power or agency syn see FATE

des·ti·tute \'des-tə-,tüt, -,t(y)üt\ adj [ME, fr. L destitutus, pp. of destituere to abandon, deprive, fr. de- + statuere to set up — more at STATUTE] (14c) **1** : lacking something needed or desirable ⟨a lake ~ of fish⟩ **2** : lacking possessions and resources; esp : suffering extreme poverty ⟨a ~ old man⟩ — **des·ti·tute·ness** n

des·ti·tu·tion \,des-tə-'tü-shən, -'tyü-\ n (15c) : the state of being destitute; esp : such extreme want as threatens life unless relieved syn see POVERTY

des·trier \'des-trē-ər, də-'stri(ə)r\ n [ME, fr. MF, fr. destre right hand, fr. L dextra, fr. neut. of dexter] (14c) archaic : WAR-HORSE; also : a charger used esp. in medieval tournaments

de·stroy \di-'strȯi, dē-\ vb [ME, fr. OF destruire, fr. (assumed) VL destrugere, alter. of L destruere, fr. de- + struere to build — more at STRUCTURE] vt (13c) **1** : to ruin the structure, organic existence, or condition of ⟨~ed the files⟩; also : to ruin as if by tearing to shreds ⟨their reputation was ~ed⟩ **2 a** : to put out of existence : KILL **b** : NEUTRALIZE ⟨the moon ~s the light of the stars⟩ **c** : ANNIHILATE, VANQUISH ⟨armies had been crippled but not ~ed —W. L. Shirer⟩ ~ vi : to cause destruction

de·stroy·er \di-'strȯi(-ə)r, dē-\ n (14c) **1** : one that destroys **2** : a small fast warship used esp. to support larger vessels and usu. armed with 5-inch guns, depth charges, torpedoes, and often guided missiles

destroyer escort n (1924) : a warship similar to but smaller than a destroyer

destroying angel n (ca. 1900) : DEATH CAP; also : a related poisonous mushroom (Amanita verna)

de·struc·ti·ble \di-'strək-tə-bəl\ adj (ca. 1755) : capable of being destroyed — **de·struc·ti·bil·i·ty** \-,strək-tə-'bil-ə-tē\ n

de·struc·tion \di-'strək-shən\ n [ME destruccioun, fr. MF destruction, fr. L destruction-, destructio, fr. destruere] (14c) **1** : the state or fact of being destroyed : RUIN **2** : the action or process of destroying something **3** : a destroying agency

de·struc·tion·ist \-sh(ə-)nəst\ n (1833) : one who delights in or advocates destruction

de·struc·tive \di-'strək-tiv\ adj (15c) **1** : causing destruction : RUINOUS ⟨~ storm⟩ **2** : designed or tending to destroy ⟨~ criticism⟩ — **de·struc·tive·ly** adv — **de·struc·tive·ness** n

destructive distillation n (ca. 1831) : decomposition of a substance (as wood, coal, or oil) by heat in a closed container and collection of the volatile products produced

de·struc·tiv·i·ty \di-,strək-'ti-və-tē, ,dē-\ n (1902) : capacity for destruction

de·sue·tude \'de-swi-,tüd, -,tyüd, di-'sü-ə-, -'syü-\ n [ME dissuetude, fr. L desuetudo, fr. desuescere to become unaccustomed, fr. de- + suescere to become accustomed; akin to L sodalis comrade — more at SIB] (15c) : discontinuance from use or exercise : DISUSE

de·sul·fur·iza·tion \(,)dē-,səl-fər-ə-'zā-shən\ n (1854) : the removal of sulfur or sulfur compounds (as from coal or flue gas) — **de·sul·fur·ize** \(,)dē-'səl-fər-,īz\ vt

de·sul·to·ry \'de-səl-,tōr-ē, -,tȯr- also -zəl-\ adj [L desultorius, lit., of a circus rider who leaps from horse to horse, fr. desilire to leap down, fr. de- + salire to leap — more at SALLY] (1581) **1** : marked by lack of definite plan, regularity, or purpose ⟨a dragged-out ordeal of . . . ~ shopping —Herman Wouk⟩ **2** : not connected with the main subject **3** : disappointing in progress or performance : SLUGGISH — **des·ul·to·ri·ly** \,de-səl-'tōr-ə-lē, -'tȯr-\ adv — **des·ul·to·ri·ness** \'de-səl-,tōr-ē-nəs, -,tȯr-\ n

de·tach \di-'tach, dē-\ vt [F détacher, fr. OF destachier, fr. des- de- + -tachier (as in atachier to attach)] (1686) **1** : to separate esp. from a larger mass and usu. without violence or damage **2** : DISENGAGE, WITHDRAW — **de·tach·abil·i·ty** \-,ta-chə-'bi-lə-tē\ n — **de·tach·able** \-'ta-chə-bəl\ adj — **de·tach·ably** \-blē\ adv

de·tached \di-'tacht, dē-\ adj (ca. 1706) **1** : standing by itself : SEPARATE, UNCONNECTED; esp : not sharing any wall with another building

⟨a ~ house⟩ 2 : exhibiting an aloof objectivity usu. free from prejudice or self-interest ⟨a ~ observer⟩ **syn** see INDIFFERENT — **de-tached-ly** \-'ta-chəd-lē, -'tacht-lē\ adv — **de-tached-ness** \-'ta-chəd-nəs, -'tacht-nəs\ n

detached service n (ca. 1889) : military service away from one's assigned organization

de-tach-ment \di-'tach-mənt, dē-\ n (1669) 1 : the action or process of detaching : SEPARATION 2 a : the dispatch of a body of troops or part of a fleet from the main body for a special mission or service b : the part so dispatched c : a permanently organized separate unit usu. smaller than a platoon and of special composition 3 a : indifference to worldly concerns : ALOOFNESS b : freedom from bias or prejudice

¹**de-tail** \di-'tā(ə)l, 'dē-,tāl\ n [F détail, fr. OF detail slice, piece, fr. taillier to cut in pieces, fr. de- + taillier to cut — more at TAILOR] (1603) 1 : extended treatment of or attention to particular items 2 : a part of a whole: as a : a small and subordinate part : PARTICULAR; also : a reproduction of such a part of a work of art b : a part considered or requiring to be considered separately from the whole c : the small elements that collectively constitute a work of art d : the small elements of a photographic image corresponding to those of the subject 3 a : selection of a person or group for a particular task (as in military service) b (1) : the person or group selected (2) : the task to be performed **syn** see ITEM — **in detail** : with all the particulars

²**detail** vt (1650) 1 : to report minutely and distinctly : SPECIFY ⟨~ed their grievances⟩ 2 : to assign to a particular task 3 : to furnish with the smaller elements of design and finish ⟨trimmings that ~ slips and petticoats⟩ ~ vi : to make detail drawings — **de-tail-er** n

de-tailed \di-'tā(ə)ld, 'dē-,tāld\ adj (1740) : marked by abundant detail or by thoroughness in treating small items or parts ⟨the ~ study of history⟩ **syn** see CIRCUMSTANTIAL — **de-tailed-ly** \di-'tāld-lē, -'tā-ləd-, 'dē-,\ adv — **de-tailed-ness** \di-'tā-ləd-nəs, -'tāld-, 'dē,\ \ n

detail man n (1928) : a representative of a drug manufacturer who introduces new drugs esp. to physicians and pharmacists

de-tain \di-'tān, dē-\ vt [ME deteynen, fr. MF detenir, modif. of L detinēre, fr. de- + tenēre to hold — more at THIN] (15c) 1 : to hold or keep in or as if in custody 2 obs : to keep back (as something due) : WITHHOLD 3 : to restrain esp. from proceeding : STOP **syn** see KEEP, DELAY — **de-tain-ment** \-mənt\ n

de-tain-ee \di-,tā-'nē, dē-\ n (ca. 1928) : a person held in custody esp. for political reasons

de-tain-er \di-'tā-nər\ n [AF detener, fr. detener to detain, fr. L detinēre] (1619) 1 : the act of keeping something in one's possession; specif : the withholding from the rightful owner of something that has lawfully come into the possession of the holder 2 : detention in custody 3 : a writ authorizing the keeper of a prison to continue to hold a person in custody

de-tect \di-'tekt, dē-\ vb [ME, fr. L detectus, pp. of detegere to uncover, detect, fr. de- + tegere to cover — more at THATCH] vt (1581) 1 : to discover the true character of 2 : to discover or determine the existence, presence, or fact of ⟨~ alcohol in the blood⟩ 3 : DEMODULATE ~ vi : to work as a detective — **de-tect-abil-i-ty** \-,tek-tə-'bi-lə-tē\ n — **de-tect-able** \-'tek-tə-bəl\ adj

de-tec-tion \di-'tek-shən\ n (15c) 1 : the act of detecting : the state or fact of being detected 2 : the process of demodulating

¹**de-tec-tive** \di-'tek-tiv\ adj (1843) 1 : fitted for or used in detecting something ⟨had perfected his ~ sensibilities⟩ 2 : of or relating to detectives or their work ⟨a ~ novel⟩ — **de-tec-tive-like** \-,līk\ adj

²**detective** n (1850) : one employed or engaged in detecting lawbreakers or in getting information that is not readily or publicly accessible

de-tec-tor \di-'tek-tər\ n (1541) : one that detects: as a : a device for detecting the presence of electromagnetic waves or of radioactivity b : a rectifier of high-frequency current used esp. for extracting the intelligence from a radio signal

de-tent \'dē-,tent, di-'\ n [F détente, fr. MF destente, fr. destendre to slacken, fr. OF, fr. des- de- + tendre to stretch, fr. L tendere — more at THIN] (1688) : a device (as a catch, dog, or spring-operated ball) for positioning and holding one mechanical part in relation to another so that the device can be released by force applied to one of the parts

dé-tente or **detente** \dā-'tänt\ n [F] (1908) 1 : the relaxation of strained relations or tensions (as between nations); also : a policy promoting this 2 : a period of détente

de-ten-tion \di-'ten-chən\ n [ME detencion, fr. MF or L; MF, fr. L detention-, detentio, fr. detinēre to detain] (15c) 1 : the act or fact of detaining or holding back; esp : a holding in custody 2 : the state of being detained; esp : a period of temporary custody prior to disposition by a court

detention home n (ca. 1930) : a house of detention for juvenile delinquents usu. under the supervision of a juvenile court

de-ter \di-'tər, dē-\ vt de-terred; de-ter-ring [L deterrēre, fr. de- + terrēre to frighten — more at TERROR] (1579) 1 : to turn aside, discourage, or prevent from acting 2 : INHIBIT — **de-ter-ment** \-'tər-mənt\ n — **de-ter-ra-bil-i-ty** \-,tər-ə-'bi-lə-tē\ n — **de-ter-ra-ble** \-'tər-ə-bəl\ adj

de-terge \di-'tərj\ vt de-terged; de-terg-ing [F or L; F déterger, fr. L detergēre, fr. de- + tergēre to wipe] (ca. 1623) : to wash off : CLEANSE — **de-terg-er** n

de-ter-gen-cy \di-'tər-jən(t)-sē\ n (1710) : cleansing quality or power

¹**de-ter-gent** \-jənt\ adj (1616) : that cleanses : CLEANSING

²**detergent** n (1676) : a cleansing agent: as a : SOAP b : any of numerous synthetic water-soluble or liquid organic preparations that are chemically different from soaps but are able to emulsify oils, hold dirt in suspension, and act as wetting agents c : an oil-soluble substance that holds insoluble foreign matter in suspension and is used in lubricating oils and dry-cleaning solutions

de-te-ri-o-rate \di-'tir-ē-ə-,rāt, dē-\ vb -rat-ed; -rat-ing [LL deterioratus, pp. of deteriorare, fr. L deterior worse, fr. de- + -ter (suffix as in L uter which of two) + -ior (compar. suffix) — more at WHETHER, -ER] vt (1572) 1 : to make inferior in quality or value : IMPAIR 2 : DISINTEGRATE ~ vi : to become impaired in quality, functioning, or condition : DEGENERATE ⟨allowed a tradition of academic excellence to ~⟩ ⟨his health deteriorated⟩ — **de-te-ri-o-ra-tive** \-,rā-tiv\ adj

de-te-ri-o-ra-tion \di-,tir-ē-ə-'rā-shən, dē-\ n (ca. 1658) : the action or process of deteriorating : the state of having deteriorated

syn DETERIORATION, DEGENERATION, DECADENCE, DECLINE mean the falling from a higher to a lower level in quality, character, or vitality. DETERIORATION implies generally the impairment of value or usefulness ⟨the deterioration of the house through neglect⟩. DEGENERATION stresses physical, intellectual, or esp. moral retrogression ⟨the degeneration of their youthful idealism into cynicism⟩. DECADENCE presupposes a reaching and passing the peak of development and implies a turn downward with a consequent loss in vitality or energy ⟨cited love of luxury as a sign of cultural decadence⟩. DECLINE differs from DECADENCE in suggesting a more markedly downward direction and greater momentum as well as more obvious evidence of deterioration ⟨the meteoric decline of his career after the scandal⟩.

de-ter-min-able \-'tər-mə-nə-bəl\ adj (15c) 1 : capable of being determined, definitely ascertained, or decided upon 2 : liable to be terminated : TERMINABLE — **de-ter-min-able-ness** n — **de-ter-min-ably** \-blē\ adv

de-ter-mi-na-cy \di-'tər-mə-nə-sē\ n, pl -cies (1873) 1 : the quality or state of being determinate 2 a : the state of being definitely and unequivocally characterized : EXACTNESS b : the state of being determined or necessitated

de-ter-mi-nant \di-'tər-mə-nənt\ n (1686) 1 : an element that identifies or determines the nature of something or that fixes or conditions an outcome 2 : a square array of numbers bordered on the left and right by a vertical line and having a value equal to the algebraic sum of all possible products where the number of factors in each product is the same as the number of rows or columns, each factor in a given product is taken from a different row and column, and the sign of a product is positive or negative depending upon whether the number of permutations necessary to place the indices representing each factor's position in its row or column in the order of the natural numbers is odd or even 3 : GENE 4 : EPITOPE — **de-ter-mi-nan-tal** \-,tər-mə-'nan-tᵊl\ adj

de-ter-mi-nate \di-'tər-mə-nət\ adj [ME, fr. L determinatus, pp. of determinare] (14c) 1 : having defined limits 2 : definitely settled 3 : conclusively determined : DEFINITIVE 4 : characterized by sequential flowering from the central or uppermost bud to the lateral or basal buds; also : characterized by growth in which the main stem ends in an inflorescence and stops growing with only branches from the main stem having further and similarly restricted growth ⟨~ tomato plants⟩ — compare INDETERMINATE 4 5 : relating to, being, or undergoing egg cleavage in which each division irreversibly separates portions of the zygote with specific potencies for further development — **de-ter-mi-nate-ly** adv — **de-ter-mi-nate-ness** n

de-ter-mi-na-tion \di-,tər-mə-'nā-shən\ n (14c) 1 a : a judicial decision settling and ending a controversy b : the resolving of a question by argument or reasoning 2 archaic : TERMINATION 3 a : the act of deciding definitely and firmly; also : the result of such an act of decision b : the power or habit of deciding definitely and firmly 4 : a fixing or finding of the position, magnitude, value, or character of something: as a : the act, process, or result of an accurate measurement b : an identification of the taxonomic position of a plant or animal 5 a : the definition of a concept in logic by its essential constituents b : the addition of a differentia to a concept to limit its denotation 6 : direction or tendency to a certain end : IMPULSION 7 : the fixation of the destiny of undifferentiated embryonic tissue

de-ter-mi-na-tive \-'tər-mə-,nā-tiv, -'tər-mə-nə-\ adj (1655) : having power or tendency to determine : tending to fix, settle, or define something ⟨regard experiments as ~ of the principles from which deductions could be made—S. F. Mason⟩ **syn** see CONCLUSIVE — **determinative** n

de-ter-mi-na-tor \di-'tər-mə-,nā-tər\ n (1556) : DETERMINER

de-ter-mine \di-'tər-mən, dē-\ vb de-ter-mined; de-ter-min-ing [ME, fr. MF determiner, fr. L determinare, fr. de- + terminare to limit, fr. terminus boundary, limit — more at TERM] vt (14c) 1 a : to fix conclusively or authoritatively b : to decide by judicial sentence c : to settle or decide by choice of alternatives or possibilities d : RESOLVE 2 a : to fix the form, position, or character of beforehand : ORDAIN ⟨two points ~ a straight line⟩ b : to bring about as a result : REGULATE ⟨demand ~s the price⟩ 3 a : to fix the boundaries of b : to limit in extent or scope c : to put or set an end to : TERMINATE ⟨~ an estate⟩ 4 : to find out or come to a decision about by investigation, reasoning, or calculation ⟨~ the answer to the problem⟩ ⟨~ a position at sea⟩ 5 : to bring about the determination of ⟨~ the fate of a cell⟩ ~ vi 1 : to come to a decision 2 : to come to an end or become void **syn** see DECIDE, DISCOVER

de-ter-mined \-'tər-mənd\ adj (1513) 1 : having reached a decision : firmly resolved ⟨~ to be a pilot⟩ 2 a : showing determination ⟨a ~ effort⟩ b : characterized by determination ⟨will deter all but the most ~ thief—Security World⟩ — **de-ter-mined-ly** \-mənd-lē, -mə-nəd-lē\ adv — **de-ter-mined-ness** \-mənd-nəs\ n

de-ter-min-er \-'tər-mə-nər\ n (ca. 1530) : one that determines: as a : GENE b : a word (as an article, possessive, demonstrative, or quantifier) that makes specific the denotation of a noun phrase

de-ter-min-ism \di-'tər-mə-,ni-zəm, dē-\ n (1846) 1 a : a theory or doctrine that acts of the will, occurrences in nature, or social or psychological phenomena are causally determined by preceding events or natural laws b : a belief in predestination 2 : the quality or state of being determined — **de-ter-min-ist** \-nəst\ n or adj — **de-ter-min-is-tic** \-,tər-mə-'nis-tik\ adj — **de-ter-min-is-ti-cal-ly** \-ti-k(ə-)lē\ adv

de-ter-rence \di-'tər-ən(t)s, -'ter-; -'tə-rən(t)s, dē-\ n (1861) : the inhibition of criminal behavior by fear esp. of punishment; also : the maintenance of military power for the purpose of discouraging attack

de-ter-rent \-ənt, -rənt\ adj [L deterrent-, deterrens, prp. of deterrēre to deter] (1829) 1 : serving to deter 2 : relating to deterrence — **deterrent** n — **de-ter-rent-ly** adv

de-ter-sive \di-'tər-siv, -ziv\ adj [MF detersif, fr. L detersus, pp. of detergēre to deterge] (1586) : DETERGENT — **detersive** n

de-test \di-'test, dē-\ vt [MF detester or L detestari; MF detester, fr. L

\ə\ abut \ᵊ\ kitten, F table \ər\ further \a\ ash \ā\ ace \ä\ mop, mar \aú\ out \ch\ chin \e\ bet \ē\ easy \g\ go \i\ hit \ī\ ice \j\ job \ŋ\ sing \ō\ go \ò\ law \òi\ boy \th\ thin \t͟h\ the \ü\ loot \ù\ foot \y\ yet \zh\ vision \á, k̇, ⁿ, œ, œ̄, ᵫ, ᵫ̄, ᵞ\ see Guide to Pronunciation

detestari, lit., to curse while calling a deity to witness, fr. *de-* + *testari* to call to witness — more at TESTAMENT] (ca. 1535) **1 :** to feel intense and often violent antipathy toward : LOATHE **2** *obs* : CURSE, DENOUNCE *syn* see HATE — **de·test·er** *n*

de·test·able \di-'tes-tə-bəl, dē-\ *adj* (15c) : arousing or meriting intense dislike : ABOMINABLE — **de·test·able·ness** *n* — **de·test·ably** \-blē\ *adv*

de·tes·ta·tion \ˌdē-ˌtes-'tā-shən, di-\ *n* (15c) **1 :** extreme hatred or dislike : ABHORRENCE, LOATHING **2 :** an object of hatred or contempt

de·throne \di-'thrōn, dē-\ *vt* (1609) : to remove from a throne or place of power or prominence : DEPOSE — **de·throne·ment** \-mənt\ *n* — **de·thron·er** *n*

de·tick \(ˌ)dē-'tik\ *vt* (1925) : to remove ticks from — **de·tick·er** *n*

det·i·nue \'de-tᵊn-ˌ(y)ü\ *n* [ME *detenewe*, fr. MF *detenue* detention, fr. fem. of *detenu*, pp. of *detenir* to detain] (15c) **1 :** a common-law action for the recovery of a personal chattel wrongfully detained or of its value **2 :** detention of something due; *esp* : the unlawful detention of a personal chattel from another

det·o·na·ble \'de-tᵊn-ə-bəl, -tə-nə-\ *adj* (1884) : capable of being detonated — **det·o·na·bil·i·ty** \ˌdet-ᵊn-ə-'bil-ət-ē, ˌdet-ə-nə-\ *n*

det·o·nate \'de-tᵊn-ˌāt, 'de-tə-ˌnāt\ *vb* **-nat·ed; -nat·ing** [F *détoner* to explode, fr. L *detonare* to expend thunder, fr. *de-* + *tonare* to thunder — more at THUNDER] *vi* (1729) : to explode with sudden violence ~ *vt* **1 :** to cause to detonate ⟨~ a bomb⟩ — compare DEFLAGRATE **2 :** to set off in a burst of activity : SPARK ⟨programs that *detonated* controversies⟩ — **det·o·nat·able** \-ˌā-tə-bəl, -ˌnä-\ *adj* — **de·na·tive** \'de-tᵊn-ˌā-tiv, 'de-tə-ˌnä-\ *adj*

det·o·na·tion \ˌde-tᵊn-'ā-shən, ˌde-tə-'nā-\ *n* (1686) **1 :** the action or process of detonating **2 :** rapid combustion in an internal combustion engine that results in knocking

det·o·na·tor \'de-tᵊn-ˌā-tər, -tə-ˌnā-\ *n* (1822) : a device or small quantity of explosive used for detonating a high explosive

¹de·tour \'dē-ˌtur *also* di-'tuər\ *n* [F *détour*, fr. OF *destor*, fr. *destorner* to divert, fr. *des-* de- + *torner* to turn — more at TURN] (1738) : a deviation from a direct course or the usual procedure; *esp* : a roundabout way temporarily replacing part of a route

²detour *vi* (1836) : to proceed by a detour ⟨~ around road construction⟩ ~ *vt* **1 :** to send by a circuitous route **2 :** to avoid by going around : BYPASS

de·tox \'dē-ˌtäks, di-'täks\ *n, often attrib* (1973) : detoxification from an intoxicating or an addictive substance — **detox** *vb*

de·tox·i·cate \(ˌ)dē-'täk-sə-ˌkāt\ *vt* **-cat·ed; -cat·ing** [*de-* + ²intoxi*cate*] (1867) : DETOXIFY 1, 2 — **de·tox·i·cant** \-si-kənt\ *n* — **de·tox·i·ca·tion** \(ˌ)dē-ˌtäk-sə-'kā-shən\ *n*

de·tox·i·fy \(ˌ)dē-'täk-sə-ˌfi\ *vt* **-fied; -fy·ing** (ca. 1905) **1 a :** to remove a poison or toxin or the effect of such from **b :** to render (a harmful substance) harmless **2 :** to free (as a drug user or an alcoholic) from an intoxicating or an addictive substance in the body or from dependence on or addiction to such a substance **3 :** NEUTRALIZE 2 — **de·tox·i·fi·ca·tion** \(ˌ)dē-ˌtäk-sə-fə-'kā-shən\ *n*

de·tract \di-'trakt, dē-\ *vb* [ME, fr. L *detractus*, pp. of *detrahere* to pull down, disparage, fr. *de-* + *trahere* to draw] *vt* (15c) **1** *archaic* : to speak ill of **2** *archaic* : to take away **3 :** DIVERT ⟨~ attention⟩ ~ *vi* : to diminish the importance, value, or effectiveness of something — often used with *from* — **de·trac·tor** \-'trak-tər\ *n*

de·trac·tion \di-'trak-shən, dē-\ *n* (14c) **1 :** a lessening of reputation or esteem esp. by envious, malicious, or petty criticism : BELITTLING, DISPARAGEMENT **2 :** a taking away ⟨it is no ~ from its dignity or prestige —J. F. Golay⟩ — **de·trac·tive** \-'trak-tiv\ *adj* — **de·trac·tive·ly** *adv*

de·train \(ˌ)dē-'trān\ *vi* (1881) : to get off a railroad train ~ *vt* : to remove from a railroad train — **de·train·ment** \-mənt\ *n*

de·trib·al·ize \(ˌ)dē-'tri-bə-ˌliz\ *vt* **-ized; -iz·ing** (1920) : to cause to lose tribal identity : ACCULTURATE — **de·trib·al·iza·tion** \(ˌ)dē-ˌtri-bə-lə-'zā-shən\ *n*

det·ri·ment \'de-trə-mənt\ *n* [ME, fr. MF or L; MF, fr. L *detrimentum*, fr. *deterere* to wear away, impair, fr. *de-* + *terere* to rub — more at THROW] (15c) **1 :** INJURY, DAMAGE ⟨did hard work without ~ to his health⟩ **2 :** a cause of injury or damage ⟨a ~ to progress⟩

¹det·ri·men·tal \ˌde-trə-'men-tᵊl\ *adj* (1590) : obviously harmful : DAMAGING ⟨the ~ effects of pollution⟩ *syn* see PERNICIOUS — **det·ri·men·tal·ly** \-tᵊl-ē\ *adv*

²detrimental *n* (1831) : an undesirable or harmful person or thing

de·tri·tion \di-'tri-shən\ *n* (1674) : a wearing off or away

de·tri·tus \di-'trī-təs\ *n, pl* **de·tri·tus** \-'trī-təs, -'trī-ˌtüs\ [F *détritus*, fr. L *detritus*, pp. of *deterere*] (1802) **1 :** loose material (as rock fragments or organic particles) that results directly from disintegration **2 :** a product of disintegration, destruction, or wearing away : DEBRIS — **de·tri·tal** \-'trī-tᵊl\ *adj*

de trop \də-'trō\ *adj* [F] (1752) : too much or too many : SUPERFLUOUS

de·tu·mes·cence \ˌdē-t(y)ü-'mes-ᵊn(t)s\ *n* [L *detumescere* to become less swollen, fr. *de-* + *tumescere* to swell — more at TUMESCENT] (1678) : subsidence or diminution of swelling or erection — **de·tu·mes·cent** \-s°nt\ *adj*

Deu·ca·lion \d(y)ü-'kāl-yən\ *n* [L, fr. Gk *Deukaliōn*] : a survivor with his wife Pyrrha of a great flood by which Zeus destroys the rest of the human race

¹deuce \'düs *also* 'dyüs\ *n* [MF *deus* two, fr. L *duos*, acc. masc. of *duo* two — more at TWO] (15c) **1 a** (1) : the face of a die that bears two spots (2) : a playing card bearing an index number two **b :** a throw of the dice yielding two points **2 :** a tie in tennis after each side has scored 40 requiring two consecutive points by one side to win **3** [obs. E *deuce* bad luck] **a :** DEVIL, DICKENS — used chiefly as a mild oath ⟨what the ~ is he up to now⟩ **b :** something notable of its kind ⟨~ of a mess⟩

²deuce *vt* **deuced; deuc·ing** (1919) : to bring the score of (a tennis game or set) to deuce

deuc·ed \'dü-səd *also* 'dyü-\ *adj* (1782) : DAMNED, CONFOUNDED ⟨in a ~ fix⟩ — **deuc·ed** *or* **deuc·ed·ly** *adv*

deuces wild *n* (1927) : a card game (as poker) in which each deuce may represent any card designated by its holder

de·us ex ma·chi·na \ˌdā-əs-ˌeks-'mä-, -ˌma-, -ˌnä; -mə-'shē-nə\ *n* [NL, a god from a machine, trans. of Gk *theos ek mēchanēs*] (1697) **1 :** a god introduced by means of a crane in ancient Greek and Roman

drama to decide the final outcome **2 :** a person or thing (as in fiction or drama) that appears or is introduced suddenly and unexpectedly and provides a contrived solution to an apparently insoluble difficulty

deuter- *or* **deutero-** *comb form* [alter. of ME *deutro-*, modif. of LL *deuter-*, fr. Gk *deuter-*, *deutero-*, fr. *deuteros*; prob. akin to Gk *dein* to lack, Skt *dosa* fault, lack] : second : secondary ⟨*deuter*anopia⟩

deu·ter·ag·o·nist \ˌdü-tə-'ra-gə-nist *also* ˌdyü-\ *n* [Gk *deuteragōnistēs*, fr. *deuter-* + *agōnistēs* combatant, actor — more at PROTAGONIST] (1855) **1 :** the actor taking the part of second importance in a classical Greek drama **2 :** a person who serves as a foil to another

deu·ter·anom·a·lous \ˌdü-tə-rə-'nä-mə-ləs *also* ˌdyü-\ *adj* [NL *deuteranomalia* (fr. *deuter-* + L *anomalia* anomaly) abnormal trichromatism + E *-ous*] (ca. 1931) : exhibiting partial loss of green color vision so that an increased intensity of this color is required in a mixture of red and green to match a given yellow — **deu·ter·anom·a·ly** \-'nä-mə-lē\ *n*

deu·ter·an·ope \'dü-tə-rə-ˌnōp *also* 'dyü-\ *n* (1902) : an individual affected with deuteranopia

deu·ter·an·opia \ˌdü-tə-rə-'nō-pē-ə *also* ˌdyü-\ *n* [NL, fr. *deuter-* + ²*a-* + *-opia;* fr. the blindness to green, regarded as the second primary color] (ca. 1901) : color blindness marked by confusion of purplish red and green — **deu·ter·an·opic** \-'nō-pik, -'nä-pik\ *adj*

deu·ter·ate \'dü-tə-ˌrāt *also* 'dyü-\ *vt* **-at·ed; -at·ing** (1947) : to introduce deuterium into (a compound) — **deu·ter·a·tion** \ˌdü-tə-'rā-shən\ *n*

deu·te·ri·um \dü-'tir-ē-əm *also* dyü-\ *n* [NL, fr. Gk *deuteros* second] (1933) : an isotope of hydrogen that has one proton and one neutron in its nucleus and that has twice the mass of ordinary hydrogen — symbol *D;* called also *heavy hydrogen*

deuterium oxide *n* (1934) : HEAVY WATER 1

deu·tero·ca·non·i·cal \ˌdü-tə-rō-kə-'nä-ni-kəl *also* ˌdyü-\ *adj* [NL *deuterocanonicus*, fr. *deuter-* + LL *canonicus* canonical] (1684) : of, relating to, or constituting the books of Scripture contained in the Septuagint but not in the Hebrew canon

deu·ter·on \'dü-tə-ˌrän *also* 'dyü-\ *n* (1933) : a deuterium nucleus

Deu·ter·o·nom·ic \ˌdü-tə-rə-'nä-mik *also* ˌdyü-\ *adj* (1857) : of or relating to the book of Deuteronomy, its style, or its contents

Deu·ter·on·o·mist \ˌdü-tə-'rä-nə-mist *also* ˌdyü-\ *n* (1862) : any of the writers or editors of a Deuteronomic body of source material often distinguished in the earlier books of the Old Testament — **Deu·ter·on·o·mis·tic** \-ˌrä-nə-'mis-tik\ *adj*

Deu·ter·on·o·my \ˌdü-tə-'rä-nə-mē *also* ˌdyü-\ *n* [ME *Deutronomie*, fr. LL *Deuteronomium*, fr. Gk *Deuteronomion*, fr. *deuter-* + *nomos* law — more at NIMBLE] : the fifth book of canonical Jewish and Christian Scripture containing narrative and Mosaic laws — see BIBLE table

deu·tero·stome \'dü-tə-rō-ˌstōm *also* 'dyü-\ *n* [NL *Deuterostomia*, group name, fr. *deuter-* + Gk *stoma* mouth — more at STOMACH] (1950) : any of a major division (Deuterostomia) of the animal kingdom that includes the bilaterally symmetrical animals (as the chordates) with indeterminate cleavage and a mouth that does not arise from the blastopore

deu·to·plasm \'dü-tō-ˌpla-zəm *also* 'dyü-\ *n* [ISV *deuter-* + *-plasm*] (1884) : the nutritive inclusions of protoplasm; *esp* : the yolk reserves of an egg

deut·sche mark \'dòich-ˌmärk, 'doi-chə-ˌ\ *n* [G, German mark] (1948) — see MONEY table

deut·zia \'düt-sē-ə *also* 'dyüt-\ *n* [NL, fr. Jean *Deutz* †1784? Du. patron of botanical research] (1837) : any of a genus (*Deutzia*) of the saxifrage family of ornamental shrubs with white or pink flowers

de·val·u·ate \(ˌ)dē-'val-yə-ˌwāt\ *vb* (1898) : DEVALUE

de·val·u·a·tion \(ˌ)dē-ˌval-yə-'wā-shən\ *n* (1914) **1 :** an official reduction in the exchange value of a currency by a lowering of its gold equivalency or its value relative to another currency **2 :** a lessening esp. of status or stature : DECLINE

de·val·ue \(ˌ)dē-'val-(ˌ)yü, -yə(-w)\ *vt* (1918) **1 :** to institute the devaluation of (money) **2 :** to lessen the value of ~ *vi* : to institute devaluation

De·va·na·ga·ri \ˌdā-və-'nä-gə-rē\ *n* [Skt *devanāgarī*, fr. *deva* divine + *nāgarī* script of the city — more at DEITY] (1781) : an alphabet usu. employed for Sanskrit and also used as a literary hand for various modern languages of India — see ALPHABET table

dev·as·tate \'de-və-ˌstāt\ *vt* **-tat·ed; -tat·ing** [L *devastatus*, pp. of *devastare*, fr. *de-* + *vastare* to lay waste — more at WASTE] (1638) **1 :** to bring to ruin or desolation by violent action **2 :** to reduce to chaos, disorder, or helplessness : OVERWHELM ⟨*devastated* by grief⟩ ⟨her wisecrack *devastated* the class⟩ *syn* see RAVAGE — **dev·as·tat·ing·ly** \-ˌstā-tiŋ-lē\ *adv* — **dev·as·ta·tion** \ˌde-və-'stā-shən\ *n* — **dev·as·tat·ive** \'de-və-ˌstā-tiv\ *adj* — **dev·as·ta·tor** \-ˌstā-tər\ *n*

de·vein \(ˌ)dē-'vān\ *vt* (1953) : to remove the dark dorsal vein from (shrimp)

de·vel·op \di-'vel-əp, dē-\ *vb* [F *développer*, fr. OF *desveloper, desvoluper* to unwrap, expose, fr. *des-* + *en voloper* to enclose — more at ENVELOP] *vt* (1750) **1 a :** to set forth or make clear by degrees or in detail : EXPOUND **b :** to make visible or manifest **c :** to treat (as in dyeing) with an agent to cause the appearance of color **d :** to subject (exposed photograph material) esp. to chemicals in order to produce a visible image; *also* : to make visible by such a method **e :** to elaborate (a musical idea) by the working out of rhythmic and harmonic changes in the theme **2 :** to work out the possibilities of **3 a :** to make active or promote the growth of ⟨~ed his muscles⟩ **b** (1) : to make available or usable ⟨~ natural resources⟩ (2) : to make suitable for commercial or residential purposes **c :** to move (as a chess piece) from the original position to one providing more opportunity for effective use **4 a :** to cause to unfold gradually ⟨~ed his argument⟩ **b :** to expand by a process of growth ⟨~ed a strong organization⟩ **c :** to cause to grow and differentiate along lines natural to its kind ⟨rain and sun ~ the grain⟩ **d :** to have unfold or differentiate within one ⟨~ed pneumonia⟩ **5 :** to acquire gradually ⟨~ an appreciation for ballet⟩ ~ *vi* **1 a :** to go through a process of natural growth, differentiation, or evolution by successive changes ⟨a blossom ~s from a bud⟩ **b :** to acquire secondary sex characters **2 :** to become gradually manifest **3 :** to come into being gradually ⟨the situation ~ing in eastern Europe⟩; *also* : TURN OUT *vi* 2a ⟨it ~ed that no one had paid the bill⟩ — **de·vel·op·able** \-'ve-lə-pə-bəl\ *adj*

de·vel·oped \di-'ve-ləpt\ *adj* (1945) : having a relatively high level of industrialization and standard of living ⟨a ∼ country⟩
de·vel·op·er \-lə-pər\ *n* (1883) : one that develops: as **a** : a chemical used to develop exposed photographic materials **b** : a person who develops real estate
de·vel·op·ing \-lə-piŋ\ *adj* (1964) : UNDERDEVELOPED 2 ⟨∼ nations⟩
de·vel·op·ment \di-'ve-ləp-mənt, dē-\ *n* (1756) **1** : the act, process, or result of developing **2** : the state of being developed **3** : a developed tract of land; *esp* : one with houses built on it
de·vel·op·men·tal \dē-,ve-ləp-'men-tᵊl\ *adj* (1849) **1 a** : of, relating to, or being development ⟨∼ processes⟩; *broadly* : EXPERIMENTAL 2 ⟨∼ aircraft⟩ **b** : serving economic development ⟨∼ highways⟩ **2** : designed to assist growth or bring about improvement (as of a skill) ⟨∼ toys⟩ — **de·vel·op·men·tal·ly** \-tᵊl-ē\ *adv*
developmentally disabled *adj* (1975) : having a physical or mental handicap that impedes or prevents normal development
de·verb·al \(,)dē-'vər-bəl\ *adj* (1943) : DEVERBATIVE
de·verb·a·tive \(,)dē-'vər-bə-tiv\ *adj* (1930) **1** : derived from a verb ⟨the ∼ noun *developer* is derived from *develop*⟩ **2** : used in derivation from a verb ⟨the ∼ suffix *-er* in *developer*⟩ — **deverbative** *n*
de·vest \di-'vest\ *vt* [MF *desvestir*, fr. ML *disvestire*, fr. L *dis-* + *vestire* to clothe — more at VEST] (1563) : DIVEST
de·vi·ance \'dē-vē-ən(t)s\ *n* (1944) : deviant quality, state, or behavior
de·vi·an·cy \-ən-sē\ *n*, *pl* **-cies** (1947) : DEVIANCE
de·vi·ant \-ənt\ *adj* (15c) : deviating esp. from an accepted norm ⟨∼ behavior⟩ — **deviant** *n*
¹de·vi·ate \'dē-vē-,āt\ *vb* **-at·ed; -at·ing** [LL *deviatus*, pp. of *deviare*, fr. L *de-* + *via* way — more at WAY] *vi* (ca. 1633) **1** : to stray esp. from a standard, principle, or topic **2** : to depart from an established course or norm ∼ *vt* : to cause to turn out of a previous course *syn* see SWERVE — **de·vi·a·tor** \-,ā-tər\ *n* — **de·vi·a·to·ry** \-ə-,tōr-ē, -,tȯr-\ *adj*
²de·vi·ate \-vē-ət, -vē-,āt\ *n* (1912) **1** : one that deviates from a norm; *esp* : a person who differs markedly from a group norm **2** : a statistical variable that gives the deviation of another variable from a fixed value (as the mean)
³de·vi·ate \-vē-ət, -vē-,āt\ *adj* (1929) : departing significantly from the behavioral norms of a particular society
de·vi·a·tion \,dē-vē-'ā-shən\ *n* (15c) : an act or instance of deviating: as **a** : deflection of the needle of a compass caused by local magnetic influences (as in a ship) **b** : the difference between a value in a frequency distribution and a fixed number (as the mean) **c** : departure from an established ideology or party line **d** : noticeable or marked departure from accepted norms of behavior — **de·vi·a·tion·ism** \-shə-,ni-zəm\ *n* — **de·vi·a·tion·ist** \-sh(ə-)nist\ *n or adj*
de·vice \di-'vīs\ *n* [ME *devis, devise*, fr. MF, division, intention, fr. OF *deviser* to divide, regulate, tell — more at DEVISE] (14c) **1** : something devised or contrived: as **a** (1) : PLAN, PROCEDURE, TECHNIQUE (2) : a scheme to deceive : STRATAGEM, TRICK **b** : something fanciful, elaborate, or intricate in design **c** : something (as a figure of speech) in a literary work designed to achieve a particular artistic effect **d** *archaic* : MASQUE, SPECTACLE **e** : a conventional stage practice or means (as a stage whisper) used to achieve a particular dramatic effect **f** : a piece of equipment or a mechanism designed to serve a special purpose or perform a special function **2** : DESIRE, INCLINATION ⟨left to my own ∼s⟩ **3** : an emblematic design used esp. as a heraldic bearing
¹dev·il \'de-vᵊl, *dial* 'de-\ *n* [ME *devel*, fr. OE *dēofol*, fr. LL *diabolus*, fr. Gk *diabolos*, lit., slanderer, fr. *diaballein* to throw across, slander, fr. *dia-* + *ballein* to throw; prob. akin to Skt *gurate* he lifts up] (bef. 12c) **1** *often cap* : the personal supreme spirit of evil often represented in Jewish and Christian belief as the tempter of mankind, the leader of all apostate angels, and the ruler of hell — usu. used with *the*; often used as an interjection, an intensive, or a generalized term of abuse ⟨what the ∼ is this?⟩ ⟨the ∼ you say!⟩ **2** : an evil spirit : DEMON **3 a** : an extremely wicked person : FIEND **b** *archaic* : a great evil **4** : a person of notable energy, recklessness, and dashing spirit; *also* : one who is mischievous ⟨those kids are ∼s today⟩ **5** : FELLOW — usu. used in the phrases *poor devil, lucky devil* **6 a** : something very trying or provoking ⟨having a ∼ of a time with this problem⟩ **b** : severe criticism or rebuke : HELL — used with *the* ⟨I'll probably catch the ∼ for this⟩ **7** : DUST DEVIL **8** *Christian Science* : the opposite of Truth : a belief in sin, sickness, and death : EVIL, ERROR — **between the devil and the deep blue sea** : faced with two equally objectionable alternatives — **devil to pay** : severe consequences — used with *the*
²devil *vt* **-iled** *or* **-illed; -il·ing** *or* **-il·ling** \'de-vᵊl-iŋ, 'dev-liŋ\ (1800) **1** : to season highly ⟨∼ed eggs⟩ **2** : TEASE, ANNOY
dev·il·fish \'de-vᵊl-,fish\ *n* (1709) **1** : any of several extremely large rays (genera *Manta* and *Mobula*) widely distributed in warm seas **2** : OCTOPUS; *broadly* : any large cephalopod
dev·il·ish \'de-vᵊl-ish, 'dev-lish\ *adj* (15c) **1** : resembling or befitting a devil: as **a** : EVIL, SINISTER **b** : MISCHIEVOUS, ROGUISH **2** : EXTREME ⟨in a ∼ hurry⟩ — **devilish** *adv* — **dev·il·ish·ly** *adv* — **dev·il·ish·ness** *n*
dev·il-may-care \,de-vᵊl-(,)mā-'ker, -'kar\ *adj* (1837) : EASYGOING, CAREFREE
dev·il·ment \'de-vᵊl-mənt, -,ment\ *n* (1771) : MISCHIEF
dev·il·ry \'de-vᵊl-rē\ *or* **dev·il·try** \-vᵊl-trē\ *n, pl* **-ries** *or* **-tries** (14c) **1 a** : action performed with the help of the devil : WITCHCRAFT **b** : WICKEDNESS **c** : MISCHIEF **2** : an act of devilry
devil's advocate *n* [trans. of NL *advocatus diaboli*] (1760) **1** : a Roman Catholic official whose duty is to examine critically the evidence on which a demand for beatification or canonization rests **2** : a person who champions the less accepted cause for the sake of argument
devil's claw *n* (ca. 1900) : any of several herbs (genus *Proboscidea* syn. *Martynia* of the family Martyniaceae) of the southwestern U.S. and Mexico that have edible pods yielding a black sewing material used in basket making
devil's darning needle *n* (1809) **1** : DRAGONFLY **2** : DAMSELFLY
devil's food cake *n* (1905) : a rich chocolate cake

devilfish 1

devil's paintbrush *n* (1900) : ORANGE HAWKWEED; *broadly* : any of various hawkweeds that are naturalized weeds in the eastern U.S.
devil theory *n* (1937) : a theory of history: political and social crises arise from the deliberate actions of evil or misguided leaders rather than as a natural result of conditions
dev·il·wood \'de-vᵊl-,wúd\ *n* (1818) : a small tree (*Osmanthus americanus*) of the southern U.S. that is related to the olive
de·vi·ous \'dē-vē-əs, -vyəs\ *adj* [L *devius*, fr. *de* from + *via* way — more at DE-, WAY] (1599) **1** : OUT-OF-THE-WAY, REMOTE **2 a** : WANDERING, ROUNDABOUT ⟨a ∼ path⟩ **b** : moving without a fixed course : ERRANT ⟨∼ breezes⟩ **3 a** : deviating from a right, accepted, or common course **b** : not straightforward : CUNNING; *also* : DECEPTIVE — **de·vi·ous·ly** *adv* — **de·vi·ous·ness** *n*
¹de·vise \di-'vīz\ *vt* **de·vised; de·vis·ing** [ME, fr. OF *deviser* to divide, regulate, tell, modif. of (assumed) VL *divisare*, freq. of L *dividere* to divide] (13c) **1 a** : to form in the mind by new combinations or applications of ideas or principles : INVENT **b** : to plan to obtain or bring about : PLOT **2** : to give (real estate) by will — compare BEQUEATH — **de·vis·able** \-'vī-zə-bəl\ *adj* — **de·vis·er** *n*
²devise *n* (15c) **1** : the act of giving or disposing of real property by will **2** : a will or clause of a will disposing of real property **3** : property devised by will
de·vi·see \,de-və-'zē, di-,vī-'zē\ *n* (1543) : one to whom a devise of property is made
de·vi·sor \,de-və-'zȯr; di-'vī-zər, -,vī-'zȯr\ *n* (1543) : one who devises property in a will
de·vi·tal·ize \(,)dē-'vī-tᵊl-,īz\ *vt* (1849) : to deprive of life, vigor, or vitality
de·vit·ri·fy \(,)dē-'vi-trə-,fī\ *vt* [F *dévitrifier*, fr. *dé-* de- + *vitrifier* to vitrify] (1832) : to deprive of glassy luster and transparency; *esp* : to change (as a glass) from a vitreous to a crystalline condition — **de·vit·ri·fi·ca·tion** \(,)dē-,vi-trə-fə-'kā-shən\ *n*
de·vo·cal·ize \(,)dē-'vō-kə-,līz\ *vt* (1877) : DEVOICE
de·voice \(,)dē-'vȯis\ *vt* (1932) : to pronounce (as a sometimes or formerly voiced sound) without vibration of the vocal cords
de·void \di-'vȯid\ *adj* [ME, pp. of *devoiden* to dispel, fr. MF *desvuidier* to empty, fr. OF, fr. *des-* dis- + *vuidier* to empty — more at VOID] (15c) : being without a usual, typical, or expected attribute or accompaniment ⟨an argument ∼ of sense⟩
de·voir \də-'vwär, 'de-,\ *n* [ME, alter. of *dever*, fr. OF *devoir, deveir* to owe, be obliged, fr. L *debēre* — more at DEBT] (14c) **1** : DUTY, RESPONSIBILITY **2** : a usu. formal act of civility or respect
de·vo·lu·tion \,de-və-'lü-shən *also* ,dē-və-\ *n* [ML *devolution-, devolutio*, fr. L *devolvere*] (1545) **1** : transference (as of rights, powers, property, or responsibility) to another; *esp* : the surrender of powers to local authorities by a central government **2** : retrograde evolution : DEGENERATION — **de·vo·lu·tion·ary** \-shə-,ner-ē\ *adj* — **de·vo·lu·tion·ist** \-sh(ə-)nist\ *n*
de·volve \di-'välv, -'vȯlv, dē-\ *vb* **de·volved; de·volv·ing** [ME, fr. L *devolvere*, fr. *de-* + *volvere* to roll — more at VOLUBLE] *vt* (15c) : to pass on (as responsibility, rights, or powers) from one person or entity to another ⟨*devolving* to western Europe full responsibility for its own defense —Christopher Lane⟩ ∼ *vi* **1 a** : to pass by transmission or succession ⟨the estate *devolved* on a distant cousin⟩ **b** : to fall or be passed usu. as a responsibility or obligation ⟨the responsibility for breadwinning has *devolved* increasingly upon women —Barbara Ehrenreich⟩ **2** : to come by or as if by flowing down ⟨his allegedly subversive campaigns . . . ∼ from his belief in basic American rights — Frank Deford⟩ **3** : to degenerate through a gradual change or evolution ⟨where order ∼s into chaos —*Johns Hopkins Mag.*⟩
dev·on \'de-vən\ *n*, *often cap* [*Devon*, England] (1834) : any of a breed of vigorous red dual-purpose cattle of English origin
De·vo·ni·an \di-'vō-nē-ən\ *adj* [*Devon*, England] (1612) **1** : of or relating to Devonshire, England **2** : of, relating to, or being the period of the Paleozoic era between the Silurian and the Mississippian or the corresponding system of rocks — see GEOLOGIC TIME table — **Devonian** *n*
Dev·on·shire cream \,de-vən-,shir-, -shər-\ *n* (1825) : CLOTTED CREAM
de·vote \di-'vōt, dē-\ *vt* **de·vot·ed; de·vot·ing** [L *devotus*, pp. of *devovēre*, fr. *de-* + *vovēre* to vow] (1586) **1** : to commit by a solemn act ⟨*devoted* herself to serving God⟩ **2** : to give over or direct (as time, money, or effort) to a cause, enterprise, or activity — **de·vote·ment** \-'vōt-mənt\ *n*
syn DEVOTE, DEDICATE, CONSECRATE, HALLOW mean to set apart for a special and often higher end. DEVOTE is likely to imply compelling motives and often attachment to an objective ⟨*devoted* his evenings to study⟩. DEDICATE implies solemn and exclusive devotion to a sacred or serious use or purpose ⟨*dedicated* her life to medical research⟩. CONSECRATE stresses investment with a solemn or sacred quality ⟨*consecrate* a church to the worship of God⟩. HALLOW, often differing little from *dedicate* or *consecrate*, may distinctively imply an attribution of intrinsic sanctity ⟨battlegrounds *hallowed* by the blood of patriots⟩.
de·vot·ed *adj* (1593) : characterized by loyalty and devotion — **de·vot·ed·ly** *adv* — **de·vot·ed·ness** *n*
dev·o·tee \,de-və-'tē, -'tā; dē-,vō-'tē\ *n* (1645) : an ardent follower, supporter, or enthusiast (as of a religion, art form, or sport)
de·vo·tion \di-'vō-shən, dē-\ *n* (13c) **1 a** : religious fervor : PIETY **b** : an act of prayer or private worship — usu. used in pl. **c** : a religious exercise or practice other than the regular corporate worship of a congregation **2 a** : the act of devoting **b** : the fact or state of being ardently dedicated and loyal (as to an idea or person) **3** *obs* : the object of one's devotion *syn* see FIDELITY
¹de·vo·tion·al \-shnəl, -shə-nᵊl\ *adj* (1648) : of, relating to, or characterized by devotion — **de·vo·tion·al·ly** \-ē\ *adv*
²devotional *n* (1659) : a short worship service
de·vour \di-'vaú(ə)r, dē-\ *vt* [ME, fr. MF *devourer*, fr. L *devorare*, fr. *de-*

\ə\ abut \ᵊ\ kitten, F table \ər\ further \a\ ash \ā\ ace \ä\ mop, mar \aú\ out \ch\ chin \e\ bet \ē\ easy \g\ go \i\ hit \ī\ ice \j\ job \ŋ\ sing \ō\ go \ȯ\ law \ȯi\ boy \th\ thin \t͟h\ the \ü\ loot \ú\ foot \y\ yet \zh\ vision \á, k̲, ⁿ, œ, œ̄, ᵫ, ᵫ̄, ʸ\ see Guide to Pronunciation

+ *vorare* to devour — more at VORACIOUS⟩ (14c) **1** : to eat up greedily or ravenously **2** : to use up or destroy as if by eating ⟨we are ~*ing* the world's resources⟩ **3** : to prey upon ⟨~*ed* by guilt⟩ **4** : to enjoy avidly ⟨~*s* books⟩ — **de·vour·er** *n*

de·vout \di-'vaüt\ *adj* [ME *devot*, fr. OF, fr. LL *devotus*, fr. L, pp. of *devovēre*] (13c) **1** : devoted to religion or to religious duties or exercises **2** : expressing devotion or piety ⟨a ~ attitude⟩ **3** : devoted to a pursuit, belief, or mode of behavior : SERIOUS, EARNEST ⟨a ~ baseball fan⟩ ⟨born a ~ coward —G. B. Shaw⟩ — **de·vout·ly** *adv* — **de·vout·ness** *n*

dew \'dü *also* 'dyü\ *n* [ME, fr. OE *dēaw*; akin to OHG *tou* dew, Gk *thein* to run] (bef. 12c) **1** : moisture condensed upon the surfaces of cool bodies esp. at night **2** : something resembling dew in purity, freshness, or power to refresh **3** : moisture esp. when appearing in minute droplets: as **a** : TEARS **b** : SWEAT **c** : droplets of water produced by a plant in transpiration — **dew** *vt* — **dew·less** \-ləs\ *adj*

dew·ar \'dü-ər *also* 'dyü-\ *n*, *often cap* [Sir James *Dewar*] (ca. 1909) : a glass or metal container made like a vacuum bottle that is used esp. for storing liquefied gases — called also *Dewar flask*

de·wa·ter \(,)dē-'wȯt-ər, -'wät-\ *vt* (ca. 1909) : to remove water from — **de·wa·ter·er** *n*

dew·ber·ry \'dü-,ber-ē *also* 'dyü-\ *n* (ca. 1578) **1** : any of several sweet edible berries related to and resembling blackberries **2** : a trailing or decumbent bramble (genus *Rubus*) that bears dewberries

dew·claw \'dü-,klȯ *also* 'dyü-\ *n* (1576) : a vestigial digit not reaching to the ground on the foot of a mammal; *also* : a claw or hoof terminating such a digit — see COW illustration

dew·drop \'dü-,dräp *also* 'dyü-\ *n* (13c) : a drop of dew

Dew·ey decimal classification \'dü-ē- *also* 'dyü-\ *n* [Melvil *Dewey*] (1924) : a system of classifying books and other publications whereby main classes are designated by a three-digit number and subdivisions are shown by numbers after a decimal point — called also *Dewey decimal system*

dew·fall \'dü-,fȯl *also* 'dyü-\ *n* (1622) : formation of dew; *also* : the time when dew begins to deposit

dew·lap \'dü-,lap *also* 'dyü-\ *n* (14c) **1** : loose skin hanging under the neck of an animal — see COW illustration **2** : loose flesh on the human throat — **dew·lapped** \-,lapt\ *adj*

de·worm \(,)dē-'wȯrm\ *vt* (1926) : to rid (as a dog) of worms : WORM 4 — **de·worm·er** \(,)dē-'wər-mər\ *n*

dew point *n* (ca. 1833) : the temperature at which a vapor begins to condense

dew worm *n* (1599) : NIGHT CRAWLER

dewy \'dü-ē *also* 'dyü-\ *adj* **dew·i·er; -est** (bef. 12c) **1** : moist with, affected by, or suggestive of dew **2** : INNOCENT, UNSOPHISTICATED ⟨from a ~ bride to an ill-mannered, murderous courtesan —Melvin Gussow⟩ — **dew·i·ly** \'dü-ə-lē, 'dyü-\ *adv* — **dew·i·ness** \'dü-ē-nəs, 'dyü-\ *n*

dewy-eyed \'dü-ē-,īd *also* 'dyü-\ *adj* (1938) : naively credulous

dex \'deks\ *n* (ca. 1961) : the sulfate of dextroamphetamine

dexa·meth·a·sone \,dek-sə-'me-thə-,sōn, -,zōn\ *n* [*dexa-* (blend of *deca-* and *hexa-*) + *methyl* + *-a-* (perh. fr. *pregnane*, a parent compound of corticoid hormones) + *-sone* (as in *cortisone*)] (1958) : a synthetic glucocorticoid $C_{22}H_{29}FO_5$ used esp. as an anti-inflammatory agent

Dex·e·drine \'dek-sə-,drēn, -drən\ *trademark* — used for a preparation of the sulfate of dextroamphetamine

dex·ies \'dek-sēz\ *n pl* [*Dexedrine* + *-ie* + [1]*-s*] (1956) : tablets or capsules of the sulfate of dextroamphetamine

dex·ter \'dek-stər\ *adj* [L; akin to OHG *zeso* situated on the right, Gk *dexios*] (1562) **1** : relating to or situated on the right **2** : being or relating to the side of a heraldic shield at the right of the person bearing it — **dexter** *adv*

dex·ter·i·ty \dek-'ster-ə-tē\ *n*, *pl* **-ties** [MF or L; MF *dexterité*, fr. L *dexteritat-, dexteritas*, fr. *dexter*] (1527) **1** : mental skill or quickness : ADROITNESS **2** : readiness and grace in physical activity; *esp* : skill and ease in using the hands

dex·ter·ous *also* **dex·trous** \'dek-st(ə-)rəs\ *adj* [L *dextr-*, *dexter* on the right side, skillful] (1622) **1** : mentally adroit and skillful : CLEVER **2** : done with dexterity : ARTFUL **3** : skillful and competent with the hands — **dex·ter·ous·ly** *adv* — **dex·ter·ous·ness** *n*

syn DEXTEROUS, ADROIT, DEFT mean ready and skilled in physical movement. DEXTEROUS implies expertness with consequent facility and quickness in manipulation ⟨unrolled the sleeping bag with a *dexterous* toss⟩. ADROIT implies dexterity but usu. also stresses resourcefulness or artfulness or inventiveness ⟨the magician's *adroit* response to the failure of her prop won applause⟩. DEFT emphasizes lightness, neatness, and sureness of touch or handling ⟨a surgeon's *deft* manipulation of the scalpel⟩.

dextr- *or* **dextro-** *comb form* [L *dextr-, dexter*] **1** : right : on or toward the right ⟨*dextrorotatory*⟩ **2** *usu* **dextro-** : dextrorotatory ⟨*dextroamphetamine*⟩

dex·tral \'dek-strəl\ *adj* (1646) : of or relating to the right : inclined to the right: as **a** : RIGHT-HANDED **3 b** of a gastropod shell : having the whorls coiling clockwise down the spire when viewed with the apex toward the observer and having the aperture situated on the right of the axis when held with the spire uppermost and with the aperture opening toward the observer — compare SINISTRAL

dex·tran \'dek-stran, -,stran\ *n* [ISV] (1879) : any of numerous glucose biopolymers of variable molecular weight produced esp. by bacteria (as genus *Leuconostoc*), occurring in dental plaque, and used after chemical modification as blood plasma substitutes, as packing materials in chromatography, and as pharmaceutical agents

dex·tran·ase \-strə-,nās, -,nāz\ *n* (ca. 1949) : a hydrolase that prevents tooth decay by breaking down dextran and eliminating dental plaque

dex·trin \'dek-strən\ *also* **dex·trine** \-,strēn, -strən\ *n* [F *dextrine*, fr. *dextr-*] (1838) : any of various water-soluble gummy polysaccharides $(C_6H_{10}O_5)_n$ obtained from starch by the action of heat, acids, or enzymes and used as adhesives, as sizes for paper and textiles, as thickening agents (as in syrups), and in beer

dex·tro \'dek-(,)strō\ *adj* [*dextr-*] (ca. 1929) : DEXTROROTATORY

dex·tro·am·phet·amine \'dek-(,)strō-am-'fe-tə-,mēn, -mən\ *n* (1943) : dextrorotatory amphetamine sulfate

dex·tro·ro·ta·to·ry \-'rō-tə-,tȯr-ē, -,tȯr-\ *also* **dex·tro·ro·ta·ry** \-'rō-**

---

tə-rē\ *adj* (1878) : turning clockwise or toward the right; *esp* : rotating the plane of polarization of light toward the right ⟨~ crystals⟩ — compare LEVOROTATORY

dex·trose \'dek-,strōs, -,strōz\ *n* (ca. 1869) : dextrorotatory glucose

dey \'dā\ *n* [F, fr. Turk *dayı*, lit., maternal uncle] (1659) : a ruling official of the Ottoman Empire in northern Africa

[1]**DH** \,dē-'āch\ *n* (1973) : DESIGNATED HITTER

[2]**DH** \,dē-'āch, 'dē-,āch\ *vi* **DH-d; DH-ing** (1975) : to play the position of designated hitter

dhar·ma \'där-mə, 'dər-\ *n* [Skt; akin to L *firmus* firm] (1796) **1** *Hinduism* : an individual's duty fulfilled by observance of custom or law **2** *Hinduism & Buddhism* **a** : the basic principles of cosmic or individual existence : divine law **b** : conformity to one's duty and nature — **dhar·mic** \-mik\ *adj*

dhar·na \'dər-nə, 'där-\ *n* [Hindi *dharnā*, fr. Skt *dharana* support, prop; akin to L *firmus* firm] (1747) : a fast held at the door of an offender in India as an appeal for justice

dhole \'dōl\ *n* [perh. fr. Kannada *tōla* wolf] (ca. 1827) : a wild dog (*Cuon alpinus*) occurring from India to southern Siberia

dho·ti \'dō-tē\ *n*, *pl* **dhotis** [Hindi *dhotī*] (1614) : a loincloth worn by men in some parts of India

dhow \'daü\ *n* [Ar *dāwa*] (1785) : an Arab lateen-rigged boat usu. having a long overhang forward, a high poop, and a low waist

Dhu'l-Hij·ja \,dül-'hi-(,)jä, ,thül-\ *n* [Ar *Dhū-l-hijjah*, lit., the one of the pilgrimage] (ca. 1771) : the 12th month of the Islamic year — see MONTH table

Dhu'l-Qa'·dah \-'kä-(,)dä\ *n* [Ar *Dhū-l-qa'dah*, lit., the one of the sitting] (ca. 1771) : the 11th month of the Islamic year — see MONTH table

dhur·rie \'də-rē, 'dər-ē\ *n* [Hindi *darī*] (1880) : a thick flat-woven cotton or wool cloth or rug made in India

dhow

di- *comb form* [ME, fr. MF, fr. L, fr. Gk; akin to OE *twi-*] **1** : twice : twofold **2** : double ⟨*dichromatic*⟩ **2** : containing two atoms, radicals, or groups ⟨*dioxide*⟩

dia- *also* **di-** *prefix* [ME, fr. OF, fr. L, fr. Gk, through, apart, fr. *dia*; akin to L *dis-*] : through ⟨*diapositive*⟩ : across ⟨*diadromous*⟩

di·a·base \'dī-ə-,bās\ *n* [F, prob. fr. Gk *diabasis* act of crossing over, fr. *diabainein* to cross over, fr. *dia-* + *bainein* to go — more at COME] (ca. 1816) **1** *archaic* : DIORITE **2** *chiefly Brit* : an altered basalt **3** : a fine-grained rock of the composition of gabbro but with an ophitic texture — **di·a·ba·sic** \,dī-ə-'bā-sik\ *adj*

di·a·be·tes \,dī-ə-'bē-tēz, -'bē-təs\ *n* [L, fr. Gk *diabētēs* diabetes insipidus, fr. *diabainein* to walk with the legs apart, cross over] (15c) : any of various abnormal conditions characterized by the secretion and excretion of excessive amounts of urine; *esp* : DIABETES MELLITUS

diabetes in·sip·i·dus \-in-'si-pə-dəs\ *n* [NL, lit., bland diabetes] (ca. 1860) : a disorder of the pituitary gland characterized by intense thirst and by the excretion of large amounts of urine

diabetes mel·li·tus \-'me-lə-təs\ *n* [NL, lit., honey-sweet diabetes] (ca. 1860) : a variable disorder of carbohydrate metabolism caused by a combination of hereditary and environmental factors and usu. characterized by inadequate secretion or utilization of insulin, by excessive urine production, by excessive amounts of sugar in the blood and urine, and by thirst, hunger, and loss of weight

[1]**di·a·bet·ic** \,dī-ə-'be-tik\ *adj* (1799) **1** : of or relating to diabetes or diabetics **2** : affected with diabetes **3** : occurring in or caused by diabetes ⟨~ coma⟩ **4** : suitable for diabetics ⟨~ food⟩

[2]**diabetic** *n* (1840) : a person affected with diabetes

di·a·be·to·gen·ic \,dī-ə-,be-tə-'je-nik, -,bē-\ *adj* (ca. 1903) : producing diabetes

di·a·be·tol·o·gist \,dī-ə-(,)bē-'tä-lə-jist, -,bē-\ *n* (1970) : a specialist in diabetes

di·a·ble·rie \dē-'ä-blə-(,)rē, -'a-blə-\ *n* [F, fr. OF, fr. *diable* devil, fr. LL *diabolus* — more at DEVIL] (1751) **1** : black magic : SORCERY **2** **a** : representation in words or pictures of black magic or of dealings with the devil **b** : demon lore **3** : mischievous conduct or manner

di·a·bol·i·cal \,dī-ə-'bä-li-kəl\ *or* **di·a·bol·ic** \-'bä-lik\ *adj* [ME *deabolik*, fr. MF *diabolique*, fr. LL *diabolicus*, fr. *diabolus*] (14c) : of, relating to, or characteristic of the devil : DEVILISH — **di·a·bol·i·cal·ly** \-li-k(ə-)lē\ *adv* — **di·a·bol·i·cal·ness** \-li-kəl-nəs\ *n*

di·ab·o·lism \dī-'a-bə-,li-zəm\ *n* (1614) **1** : dealings with or possession by the devil **2** : belief in or worship of devils **3** : evil character or conduct — **di·ab·o·list** \-list\ *n*

di·ab·o·lize \-,līz\ *vt* **-lized; -liz·ing** (1702) : to represent as or make diabolic

dia·chron·ic \,dī-ə-'krä-nik\ *adj* (1927) : of, relating to, or dealing with phenomena (as of language or culture) as they occur or change over a period of time — **dia·chron·i·cal·ly** \-'krä-ni-k(ə-)lē\ *adv*

di·ach·ro·ny \,dī-'a-krə-nē\ *n* [ISV *dia-* + *-chrony* (as in *synchrony*)] (ca. 1939) **1** : diachronic analysis **2** : change extending through time

[1]**di·ac·id** \,dī-'a-səd\ *or* **di·acid·ic** \,dī-ə-'si-dik\ *adj* (1866) : able to react with two molecules of a monobasic acid or one of a dibasic acid to form a salt or ester — used esp. of bases

[2]**diacid** *n* [ISV] (ca. 1929) : an acid with two acid hydrogen atoms

di·ac·o·nal \dī-'a-kə-n°l, dē-\ *adj* [LL *diaconalis*, fr. *diaconus* deacon — more at DEACON] (ca. 1611) : of or relating to a deacon or deaconess

di·ac·o·nate \-'a-kə-nət, -,nāt\ *n* (ca. 1751) **1** : the office or period of office of a deacon or deaconess **2** : an official body of deacons

di·a·crit·ic \,dī-ə-'kri-tik\ *n* (1866) : an accent near or through an orthographic or phonetic character or combination of characters indicating a phonetic value different from that given the unmarked or otherwise marked element

di·a·crit·i·cal \,dī-ə-'kri-ti-kəl\ *also* **di·a·crit·ic** \-'kri-tik\ *adj* [Gk *diakritikos* separative, fr. *diakrinein* to distinguish, fr. *dia-* + *krinein* to separate — more at CERTAIN] (1749) **1** : serving as a diacritic **2** **a** : DISTINCTIVE ⟨the ~ elements in culture —S. F. Nadel⟩ **b** : capable of distinguishing ⟨students of superior ~ powers⟩

di·adel·phous \,dī-ə-'del-fəs\ *adj* [*di-* + *-adelphous*] (1807) : united by filaments into two fascicles — used of stamens

DIACRITICS

´	(é)	acute accent	˘	(ŭ)	breve
`	(è)	grave accent	ˇ	(č)	haček
^	(ô) *or* ^ *or* ~ circumflex		¨	(oö)	diaeresis
~	(ñ)	tilde	ˌ	(ç)	cedilla
¯	(ō)	macron			

di·a·dem \'dī-ə-ˌdem, -dəm\ *n* [ME *diademe*, fr. OF, fr. L *diadema*, fr. Gk *diadēma*, fr. *diadein* to bind around, fr. *dia-* + *dein* to bind; akin to Skt *dāman* rope] (13c) **1 a** : CROWN 1; *specif* : a royal headband **b** : CROWN 6a(1) **2** : something that adorns like a crown

di·ad·ro·mous \dī-'a-drə-məs\ *adj* (ca. 1949) *of a fish* : migratory between salt and fresh waters

di·aer·e·sis \dī-'er-ə-səs, *Brit also* -'ir-\ *n*, *pl* **-e·ses** \-ˌsēz\ [LL *diaeresis*, fr. Gk *diairesis*, lit., division, fr. *diairein* to divide, fr. *dia-* + *hairein* to take] (ca. 1611) **1** : a mark ¨ placed over a vowel to indicate that the vowel is pronounced in a separate syllable (as in *naïve* or *Brontë*) **2** : the break in a verse caused by the coincidence of the end of a foot with the end of a word — **di·ae·ret·ic** \ˌdī-ə-'re-tik\ *adj*

dia·gen·e·sis \ˌdī-ə-'je-nə-səs\ *n* [NL] (ca. 1886) **1** : recombination or rearrangement of constituents (as of a chemical or mineral) resulting in a new product **2** : the conversion (as by compaction or chemical reaction) of sediment into rock — **dia·ge·net·ic** \ˌdī-ə-jə-'ne-tik\ *adj* — **dia·ge·net·i·cal·ly** \-'ne-ti-k(ə-)lē\ *adv*

dia·geo·tro·pic \ˌdī-ə-ˌjē-ə-'trō-pik, -'trä-pik\ *adj* (1880) : tending to grow at right angles to the line of gravity ⟨~ branches and roots⟩

di·ag·nose \'dī-ig-ˌnōs, -ˌnōz, ˌdī-ig-', -əg-\ *vb* **-nosed; -nos·ing** [back-formation fr. *diagnosis*] *vt* (ca. 1859) **1 a** : to recognize (as a disease) by signs and symptoms **b** : to diagnose a disease or condition in ⟨*diagnosed* the patient⟩ **2** : to analyze the cause or nature of ⟨~ the problem⟩ ~ *vi* : to make a diagnosis — **di·ag·nos·able** *or* **di·ag·nose·able** \-ə-bəl\ *adj*

di·ag·no·sis \ˌdī-ig-'nō-səs, -əg-\ *n*, *pl* **-no·ses** \-ˌsēz\ [NL, fr. Gk *diagnōsis*, fr. *diagignōskein* to distinguish, fr. *dia-* + *gignōskein* to know — more at KNOW] (ca. 1681) **1 a** : the art or act of identifying a disease from its signs and symptoms **b** : the decision reached by diagnosis **2** : a concise technical description of a taxon **3 a** : investigation or analysis of the cause or nature of a condition, situation, or problem ⟨~ of engine trouble⟩ **b** : a statement or conclusion from such an analysis

¹di·ag·nos·tic \-'näs-tik\ *also* **di·ag·nos·ti·cal** \-ti-kəl\ *adj* (1625) **1 a** : of, relating to, or used in diagnosis **b** : using the methods of or yielding a diagnosis **2** : serving to distinguish or identify — **di·ag·nos·ti·cal·ly** \-ti-k(ə-)lē\ *adv*

²diagnostic *n* (1625) **1** : the art or practice of diagnosis — often used in pl. **2** : a distinguishing mark — **di·ag·nos·ti·cian** \-(ˌ)näs-'ti-shən\ *n*

¹di·ag·o·nal \dī-'a-gə-nᵊl, -'ag-nəl\ *adj* [L *diagonalis*, fr. Gk *diagōnios* from angle to angle, fr. *dia-* + *gōnia* angle; akin to Gk *gony* knee — more at KNEE] (1563) **1 a** : joining two vertices of a rectilinear figure that are nonadjacent or two vertices of a polyhedral figure that are not in the same face **b** : passing through two nonadjacent edges of a polyhedron ⟨a ~ plane⟩ **2 a** : inclined obliquely from a reference line (as the vertical) ⟨wood with a ~ grain⟩ **b** : having diagonal markings or parts ⟨a ~ weave⟩

²diagonal *n* (1571) **1** : a diagonal straight line or plane **2 a** (1) : a diagonal direction (2) : a diagonal row, arrangement, or pattern **b** : something oriented in a diagonal position **3** : a mark / used typically to denote "or" (as in *and/or*), "and or" (as in *straggler/deserter*), or "per" (as in *feet/second*) — called also *solidus*, *virgule* — **on the diagonal** : in an oblique direction : DIAGONALLY

di·ag·o·nal·ize \-nə-ˌlīz\ *vt* **-ized; -iz·ing** (1942) : to put (a matrix) in a form with all the nonzero elements along the diagonal from upper left to lower right — **di·ag·o·nal·iz·able** \-ˌlī-zə-bəl\ *adj* — **di·ag·o·nal·iza·tion** \-ə-gə-nᵊl-ə-'zā-shən, -ˌag-nə-lə-'zā-\ *n*

di·ag·o·nal·ly \dī-'a-gə-nᵊl-ē, -'ag-nə-lē\ *adv* (1541) : in a diagonal manner

diagonal matrix *n* (ca. 1928) : a diagonalized matrix

¹di·a·gram \'dī-ə-ˌgram\ *n* [Gk *diagramma*, fr. *diagraphein* to mark out by lines, fr. *dia-* + *graphein* to write — more at CARVE] (1619) **1 a** : a graphic design that explains rather than represents; *esp* : a drawing that shows arrangement and relations (as of parts) **2** : a line drawing made for mathematical or scientific purposes — **di·a·gram·ma·ble** \-ˌgra-mə-bəl\ *adj* — **di·a·gram·mat·i·cal** \ˌdī-ə-grə-'ma-tik\ *also* **di·a·gram·mat·i·cal** \-'ma-ti-kəl\ *adj* — **di·a·gram·mat·i·cal·ly** \-ti-k(ə-)lē\ *adv*

²diagram *vt* **-grammed** *or* **-gramed** \-ˌgramd\; **-gram·ming** *or* **-gram·ing** \-ˌgra-miŋ\ (1840) : to represent by or put into the form of a diagram

dia·ki·ne·sis \ˌdī-ə-kə-'nē-səs, -(ˌ)kī-\ *n*, *pl* **-ne·ses** \-ˌsēz\ [NL] (ca. 1902) : the final stage of the meiotic prophase marked by contraction of the bivalents

¹di·al \'dī(-ə)l\ *n* [ME *dyal*, fr. ML *dialis* clock wheel revolving daily, fr. L *dies* day — more at DEITY] (15c) **1** : the face of a sundial **2** *obs* : TIMEPIECE **3** : the graduated face of a timepiece **4 a** : a face upon which some measurement is registered usu. by means of graduations and a pointer ⟨the thermometer ~ reads 70°F⟩ **b** : a device that may be operated to make electrical connections or to regulate the operation of a machine ⟨a radio ~⟩ ⟨a telephone ~⟩

²dial *vb* **di·aled** *or* **di·alled; di·al·ing** *or* **di·al·ling** *vt* (1821) **1** : to measure with a dial **2 a** : to manipulate a device (as a dial) so as to operate, regulate, or select ⟨~ your favorite program⟩ ⟨~ed the wrong number⟩ **b** : CALL 1m(1) ⟨~ed the office⟩ ~ *vi* **1** : to manipulate a dial **2** : to make a telephone call or connection — **di·al·er** *n*

di·a·lect \'dī-ə-ˌlekt\ *n*, *often attrib* [MF *dialecte*, fr. L *dialectus*, fr. Gk *dialektos* conversation, dialect, fr. *dialegesthai* to converse — more at DIALOGUE] (1577) **1 a** : a regional variety of language distinguished by features of vocabulary, grammar, and pronunciation from other regional varieties and constituting together with them a single language ⟨the Doric ~ of ancient Greek⟩ **b** : one of two or more cognate languages ⟨French and Italian are Romance ~s⟩ **c** : a variety of a language used by the members of a group ⟨such ~s as politics and advertising —Philip Howard⟩ **d** : a variety of language whose identity is fixed by a factor other than geography (as social class) ⟨spoke a rough peasant ~⟩ **e** : REGISTER 4c **f** : a version of a computer programming language **2** : manner or means of expressing oneself : PHRASEOLOGY — **di·a·lec·tal** \ˌdī-ə-'lek-tᵊl\ *adj* — **di·a·lec·tal·ly** \-tᵊl-ē\ *adv*

dialect atlas *n* (1932) : LINGUISTIC ATLAS

dialect geography *n* (1929) : LINGUISTIC GEOGRAPHY

di·a·lec·tic \ˌdī-ə-'lek-tik\ *n* [ME *dialetik*, fr. MF *dialetique*, fr. L *dialectica*, fr. Gk *dialektikē*, fr. fem. of *dialektikos* of conversation, fr. *dialektos*] (14c) **1** : LOGIC 1a(1) **2 a** : discussion and reasoning by dialogue as a method of intellectual investigation; *specif* : the Socratic techniques of exposing false beliefs and eliciting truth **b** : the Platonic investigation of the eternal ideas **3** : the logic of fallacy **4 a** : the Hegelian process of change in which a concept or its realization passes over into and is preserved and fulfilled by its opposite; *also* : the critical investigation of this process **b** (1) *usu pl but sing or pl in constr* : development through the stages of thesis, antithesis, and synthesis in accordance with the laws of dialectical materialism (2) : the investigation of this process (3) : the theoretical application of this process esp. in the social sciences **5** *usu pl but sing or pl in constr* **a** : any systematic reasoning, exposition, or argument that juxtaposes opposed or contradictory ideas and usu. seeks to resolve their conflict **b** : an intellectual exchange of ideas **6** : the dialectical tension or opposition between two interacting forces or elements

di·a·lec·ti·cal \ˌdī-ə-'lek-ti-kəl\ *also* **di·a·lec·tic** \-tik\ *adj* (1548) **1 a** : of, relating to, or in accordance with dialectic ⟨~ method⟩ **b** : practicing, devoted to, or employing dialectic ⟨a ~ philosopher⟩ **2** : of, relating to, or characteristic of a dialect — **di·a·lec·ti·cal·ly** \-ti-k(ə-)lē\ *adv*

dialectical materialism *n* (1927) : the Marxist theory that maintains the material basis of a reality constantly changing in a dialectical process and the priority of matter over mind — compare HISTORICAL MATERIALISM

di·a·lec·ti·cian \ˌdī-ə-ˌlek-'ti-shən\ *n* (ca. 1693) **1** : one who is skilled in or practices dialectic **2** : a student of dialects

di·a·lec·tol·o·gist \ˌdī-ə-ˌlek-'tä-lə-jist\ *n* (1883) : a specialist in dialectology

di·a·lec·tol·o·gy \-jē\ *n* [ISV] (ca. 1864) **1** : the systematic study of dialect **2** : the body of data available for study of a dialect — **di·a·lec·to·log·i·cal** \-ˌlek-tə-'lä-ji-kəl\ *adj* — **di·a·lec·to·log·i·cal·ly** \-k(ə-)lē\ *adv*

di·al·lel \'dī-ə-ˌlel\ *adj* [Gk *diallēlos* reciprocating, fr. *dia* through + *allēlon* one another — more at ALLELO-] (1920) : relating to or being the crossing of each of several individuals with two or more others in order to determine the relative genetic contribution of each parent to specific characters in the offspring

di·a·log·ic \ˌdī-ə-'lä-jik\ *or* **di·a·log·i·cal** \-ji-kəl\ *adj* (1833) : of, relating to, or characterized by dialogue ⟨~ writing⟩ — **di·a·log·i·cal·ly** \-ji-k(ə-)lē\ *adv*

di·a·lo·gist \dī-'a-lə-jist; 'dī-ə-ˌlō-gist, -ˌlä-\ *n* (ca. 1660) **1** : a writer of dialogues **2** : one who participates in a dialogue — **di·a·lo·gis·tic** \(ˌ)dī-ˌa-lə-'jis-tik; ˌdī-ə-ˌlō-'gis-, -ˌlä-'gis-\ *adj*

¹di·a·logue *also* **di·a·log** \'dī-ə-ˌlòg, -ˌläg\ *n* [ME *dialoge*, fr. OF *dialogue*, fr. L *dialogus*, fr. Gk *dialogos*, fr. *dialegesthai* to converse, fr. *dia-* + *legein* to speak — more at LEGEND] (13c) **1** : a written composition in which two or more characters are represented as conversing **2 a** : a conversation between two or more persons; *also* : a similar exchange between a person and something else (as a computer) **b** : an exchange of ideas and opinions **c** : a discussion between representatives of parties to a conflict that is aimed at resolution **3** : the conversational element of literary or dramatic composition **4** : a musical composition for two or more parts suggestive of a conversation

²dialogue *vb* **-logued; -logu·ing** *vt* (1597) : to express in dialogue ~ *vi* : to take part in a dialogue

dial tone *n* (1923) : a tone emitted by a telephone as a signal that the system is ready for dialing

dial–up \'dī(-ə)l-ˌəp\ *adj* (1972) : relating to or being a standard telephone line used for computer communications; *also* : accessible via a standard telephone line ⟨a ~ information service⟩

di·al·y·sate \dī-'a-lə-ˌzāt, -ˌsät\ *also* **di·al·y·zate** \-ˌzāt\ *n* (ca. 1867) : the material that passes through the membrane in dialysis; *also* : the liquid into which this material passes

di·al·y·sis \dī-'a-lə-səs\ *n*, *pl* **-y·ses** \-ˌsēz\ [NL, fr. Gk, separation, fr. *dialyein* to dissolve, fr. *dia-* + *lyein* to loosen — more at LOSE] (1861) **1** : the separation of substances in solution by means of their unequal diffusion through semipermeable membranes; *esp* : such a separation of colloids from soluble substances **2** : HEMODIALYSIS — **di·a·lyt·ic** \ˌdī-ə-'li-tik\ *adj*

di·a·lyze \'dī-ə-ˌlīz\ *vb* **-lyzed; -lyz·ing** *vt* (1861) : to subject to dialysis ~ *vi* : to undergo dialysis — **di·a·lyz·able** \-ˌlī-zə-bəl\ *adj* — **di·a·lyz·er** \-ˌlī-zər\ *n*

dia·mag·net·ic \ˌdī-ə-mag-'ne-tik\ *adj* (1846) : having a magnetic permeability less than that of a vacuum : slightly repelled by a magnet — **dia·mag·ne·tism** \-'mag-nə-ˌti-zəm\ *n*

di·a·man·té \ˌdē-ə-ˌmän-'tā\ *n* [F, adj., like a diamond, fr. *diamant* diamond, fr. MF] (1904) : a sparkling decoration (as of sequins) or material decorated with this ⟨a gown trimmed with ~⟩

di·am·e·ter \dī-'a-mə-tər\ *n* [ME *diametre*, fr. MF, fr. L *diametros*, fr. Gk, fr. *dia-* + *metron* measure — more at MEASURE] (14c) **1** : a chord passing through the center of a figure or body **2** : the length of a straight line through the center of an object **3** : a unit of magnification for an optical instrument equal to the number of times the linear

\ə\ abut \ᵊ\ kitten, F table \ər\ further \a\ ash \ā\ ace \ä\ mop, mar \aù\ out \ch\ chin \e\ bet \ē\ easy \g\ go \i\ hit \ī\ ice \j\ job \ŋ\ sing \ō\ go \ò\ law \òi\ boy \th\ thin \t̲h̲\ the \ü\ loot \ù\ foot \y\ yet \zh\ vision \ə̄, k̲, ⁿ, œ, œ̄, ue, ūe, ᵞ\ see Guide to Pronunciation dimensions of an object are apparently increased ⟨a microscope magnifying 60 ~s⟩ — **di·am·e·tral** \-'a-mə-trəl\ *adj*

di·a·met·ric \ˌdī-ə-'me-trik\ *or* **di·a·met·ri·cal** \-tri-kəl\ *adj* (1553) **1** : of, relating to, or constituting a diameter : located at the diameter **2** : completely opposed : being at opposite extremes ⟨in ~ contradiction to his claims⟩ — **di·a·met·ri·cal·ly** \-tri-k(ə-)lē\ *adv*

di·amide \'dī-ə-ˌmīd, dī-'a-məd\ *n* (1866) : a compound containing two amido groups

di·amine \'dī-ə-ˌmēn, dī-'a-mən\ *n* [ISV] (1866) : a compound containing two amino groups

di·am·mo·ni·um phosphate \ˌdī-ə-'mō-nē-əm-\ *n* (ca. 1929) : a white crystalline compound (NH₄)₂HPO₄ used esp. as a fertilizer and as a fire retardant

¹di·a·mond \'dī-(ə-)mənd\ *n, often attrib* [ME *diamaunde, fr.* MF *diamant, fr.* OF, *fr.* LL *diamant-, diamas,* alter. of L *adamant-, adamas* hardest metal, diamond, fr. Gk] (14c) **1 a** : native crystalline carbon that is usu. nearly colorless, that when transparent and free from flaws is highly valued as a precious stone, and that is used industrially as an abrasive powder and in rock drills because of its great hardness; *also* : a piece of this substance **b** : crystallized carbon produced artificially **2** : something that resembles a diamond (as in brilliance, value, or fine quality) **3** : a square or rhombus-shaped figure usu. oriented with the long diagonal vertical **4 a** : a playing card marked with a stylized figure of a red diamond **b** *pl but sing or pl in constr* : the suit comprising cards marked with diamonds **5** : a baseball infield; *also* : the entire playing field

²diamond *vt* (1751) : to adorn with or as if with diamonds

³diamond *adj* (1872) : of, relating to, or being a 60th or 75th anniversary or its celebration ⟨~ jubilee⟩

di·a·mond·back \'dī-(ə-)mən(d)-ˌbak\ *adj* (1887) : having marks like diamonds or lozenges on the back

diamondback moth *n* (1891) : a nearly cosmopolitan moth (*Plutella xylostella* of the family Plutellidae) whose larva is a pest on cruciferous plants

diamondback rattlesnake *n* (1894) : either of two large and deadly rattlesnakes (*Crotalus adamanteus* of the southeastern U.S. and *C. atrox* of the south central and southwestern U.S. and Mexico) — called also **diamondback, diamondback rattler**

diamondback terrapin *n* (1887) : any of several terrapins (genus *Malaclemys*) formerly widely distributed in salt marshes along the Atlantic and Gulf coasts but now much restricted

di·a·mond·if·er·ous \ˌdī-(ə-)mən-'di-fə-rəs\ *adj* (1870) : containing diamonds ⟨~ earth⟩

diamond in the rough (ca. 1947) : a person of exceptional qualities or potential but lacking refinement or polish

Di·ana \dī-'a-nə\ *n* [L] : an ancient Italian goddess of the forest and of childbirth who was identified with Artemis by the Romans

di·an·thus \dī-'an(t)-thəs\ *n* [NL, genus name, fr. Gk *dios* heavenly + *anthos* flower — more at DEITY, ANTHOLOGY] (1849) : ²PINK 1

di·a·pa·son \ˌdī-ə-'pā-zᵊn, -sᵊn\ *n* [ME, fr. L, fr. Gk *(hē) dia pasōn (chordōn symphōnia),* lit., the concord through all the notes, fr. *dia* through + *pasōn,* gen. fem. pl. of *pas* all — more at DIA-, PAN-] (ca. 1501) **1 a** : a burst of sound ⟨~s of laughter⟩ **b** : the principal foundation stop in the organ extending through the complete range of the instrument **c** (1) : the entire compass of musical tones (2) : RANGE, SCOPE **2 a** : TUNING FORK **b** : a standard of pitch

dia·pause \'dī-ə-ˌpòz\ *n* [Gk *diapausis* pause, fr. *diapauein* to pause, fr. *dia-* + *pauein* to stop] (1893) : a period of physiologically enforced dormancy between periods of activity

dia·paus·ing \-ˌpò-ziŋ\ *adj* (1944) : undergoing diapause

di·a·pe·de·sis \ˌdī-ə-pə-'dē-səs\ *n, pl* **-de·ses** \-ˌsēz\ [NL, fr. Gk *diapēdēsis,* lit., act of leaping through, fr. *diapēdan* to leap through, fr. *dia-* + *pēdan* to leap] (1625) : the passage of blood cells through capillary walls into the tissues

¹di·a·per \'dī-pər *also* 'dī-ə-\ *n* [ME *diapre,* fr. MF, fr. ML *diasprum*] (14c) **1 a** : a fabric with a distinctive pattern: **a** : a rich silky fabric **b** : a soft usu. white linen or cotton fabric used for tablecloths or towels **2** : an allover pattern consisting of one or more small repeated units of design (as geometric figures) connecting with one another or growing out of one another with continuously flowing or straight lines **3** : a basic garment for infants consisting of a folded cloth or other absorbent material drawn up between the legs and fastened about the waist

²diaper *vt* **di·a·pered; di·a·per·ing** \-p(ə-)riŋ\ (14c) **1** : to ornament with diaper designs **2** : to put on or change the diaper of (an infant)

diaper rash *n* : skin irritation of the diaper-covered area of an infant esp. from excessive urinary ammonia

di·a·pha·ne·i·ty \(ˌ)dī-ˌa-fə-'nē-ə-tē, ˌdī-ə-fə-, -'nā-\ *n* (15c) : the quality or state of being diaphanous

di·aph·a·nous \dī-'a-fə-nəs\ *adj* [ML *diaphanus,* fr. Gk *diaphainein* to show through, fr. *dia-* + *phainein* to show — more at FANCY] (1614) **1** : characterized by such fineness of texture as to permit seeing through **2** : characterized by extreme delicacy of form : ETHEREAL ⟨painted ~ landscapes⟩ **3** : INSUBSTANTIAL, VAGUE ⟨had only a ~ hope of success⟩ — **di·aph·a·nous·ly** *adv* — **di·aph·a·nous·ness** *n*

dia·phone \'dī-ə-ˌfōn\ *n* (1906) : a fog signal similar to a siren but producing a blast of two tones

di·aph·o·rase \dī-'a-fə-ˌrās, -ˌrāz\ *n* [ISV *diaphor-* (fr. Gk *diaphoros* different, fr. *diapherein* to differ, fr. *dia-* + *pherein* to carry) + *-ase*— more at BEAR] (1938) : a flavoprotein enzyme capable of oxidizing the reduced form of NAD

di·a·pho·re·sis \ˌdī-ə-fə-'rē-səs, (ˌ)dī-ˌa-fə-\ *n, pl* **-re·ses** \-ˌsēz\ [LL, fr. Gk *diaphorēsis,* fr. *diaphorein* to dissipate by perspiration, fr. *dia-* + *phorein,* freq. of *pherein* to carry] (ca. 1681) : PERSPIRATION; *esp* : profuse perspiration artificially induced

di·a·pho·ret·ic \-'re-tik\ *adj* (15c) : having the power to increase perspiration — **diaphoretic** *n*

di·a·phragm \'dī-ə-ˌfram\ *n* [ME *diafragma,* fr. LL *diaphragma,* fr. Gk,

---

fr. *diaphrassein* to barricade, fr. *dia-* + *phrassein* to enclose] (14c) **1** : a body partition of muscle and connective tissue; *specif* : the partition separating the chest and abdominal cavities in mammals **2** : a dividing membrane or thin partition esp. in a tube **3 a** : a more or less rigid partition in the body or shell of an invertebrate **b** : a transverse septum in a plant stem **4** : a device that limits the aperture of a lens or optical system — compare IRIS DIAPHRAGM **5** : a thin flexible disk (as in a microphone or loudspeaker) that vibrates when struck by sound waves or that vibrates to generate sound waves **6** : a molded cap usu. of thin rubber fitted over the uterine cervix to act as a mechanical contraceptive barrier — **di·a·phrag·mat·ic** \ˌdī-ə-frə(g)'-ma-tik, -ˌfrag-\ *adj* — **di·a·phrag·mat·i·cal·ly** \-'ma-ti-k(ə-)lē\ *adv*

di·aph·y·sis \dī-'a-fə-səs\ *n, pl* **-y·ses** \-ˌsēz\ [NL, fr. Gk, spinous process of the tibia, fr. *diaphyesthai* to grow between, fr. *dia-* + *phyein* to bring forth — more at BE] (1831) : the shaft of a long bone — **di·aph·y·se·al** \(ˌ)dī-ˌa-fə-'sē-əl\ *or* **di·a·phys·i·al** \ˌdī-ə-'fi-zē-əl\ *adj*

di·a·pir \'dī-ə-ˌpir\ *n* [F, prob. fr. Gk *diapeirein* to drive through, fr. *dia-* + *peirein* to pierce; akin to Gk *poros* passage — more at FARE] (1918) : an anticlinal fold in which a mobile core has broken through brittle overlying rocks — **di·a·pir·ic** \ˌdī-ə-'pir-ik\ *adj*

di·a·pos·i·tive \ˌdī-ə-'pä-zə-tiv, -'päz-tiv\ *n* (1893) : a positive photographic image on transparent material (as glass or film)

di·ap·sid \dī-'ap-səd\ *adj* [ultim. fr. Gk *di-* + *hapsid-, hapsis* loop, arch — more at APSIS] (ca. 1909) : of, relating to, or including reptiles (as the crocodiles) with two pairs of temporal openings in the skull

di·ar·chy *var of* DYARCHY

di·a·rist \'dī-ə-rəst\ *n* (ca. 1818) : one who keeps a diary

di·ar·rhea \ˌdī-ə-'rē-ə\ *n* [ME *diaria, fr.* LL *diarrhoea, fr.* Gk *diarrhoia, fr. diarrhein* to flow through, fr. *dia-* + *rhein* to flow — more at STREAM] (14c) **1** : abnormally frequent intestinal evacuations with more or less fluid stools **2** : excessive flow ⟨verbal ~⟩ — **di·ar·rhe·ic** \-'rē-ik\ *adj* — **di·ar·rhe·al** \-'rē-əl\ *adj* — **di·ar·rhet·ic** \-'re-tik\ *adj*

di·ar·rhoea *chiefly Brit var of* DIARRHEA

di·ar·thro·sis \ˌdī-är-'thrō-səs\ *n, pl* **-thro·ses** \-ˌsēz\ [NL, fr. Gk *diarthrōsis,* fr. *diarthroun* to joint, fr. *dia-* + *arthroun* to fasten by a joint, fr. *arthron* joint — more at ARTHR-] (1578) **1** : articulation that permits free movement **2** : a freely movable joint

di·a·ry \'dī-(ə-)rē\ *n, pl* **-ries** [L *diarium,* fr. *dies* day — more at DEITY] (1581) **1** : a record of events, transactions, or observations kept daily or at frequent intervals : JOURNAL; *esp* : a daily record of personal activities, reflections, or feelings **2** : a book intended or used for a diary

di·as·po·ra \dī-'as-p(ə-)rə, dē-\ *n* [Gk, dispersion, fr. *diaspeirein* to scatter, fr. *dia-* + *speirein* to sow] (1881) **1** *cap* **a** : the settling of scattered colonies of Jews outside Palestine after the Babylonian exile **b** : the area outside Palestine settled by Jews **c** : the Jews living outside Palestine or modern Israel **2 a** : the breaking up and scattering of a people : MIGRATION ⟨the black ~ to northern cities⟩ **b** : people settled far from their ancestral homelands ⟨African ~⟩ **c** : the place where these people live

di·a·spore \'dī-ə-ˌspòr, -ˌspòr\ *n* [F, fr. Gk *diaspora*] (1805) : a mineral consisting of aluminum hydrogen oxide

di·a·stase \'dī-ə-ˌstās, -ˌstāz\ *n* [F, fr. Gk *diastasis* separation, interval, fr. *diistanai* to separate, fr. *dia-* + *histanai* to cause to stand — more at STAND] (1838) **1** : AMYLASE; *esp* : a mixture of amylases from malt **2** : ENZYME

di·a·stat·ic \ˌdī-ə-'sta-tik\ *adj* (1881) : relating to or having the properties of diastase; *esp* : converting starch into sugar

di·a·ste·ma \ˌdī-ə-'stē-mə\ *n, pl* **-ma·ta** \-mə-tə\ [NL, fr. LL, interval, fr. Gk *diastēma, fr. diistanai*] (1854) : a space between teeth in a jaw

di·a·ste·reo·mer \ˌdī-ə-'ster-ē-ō-(ˌ)mər, -'stir-\ *or* **di·a·ste·reo·iso·mer** \-ˌster-ē-ō-'ī-sə-mər, -stir-\ *n* (1936) : a stereoisomer of a compound having two or more chiral centers that is not a mirror image of another stereoisomer of the same compound — compare ENANTIOMORPH — **di·a·ste·reo·mer·ic** \-ˌster-ē-ō-'mer-ik, -stir-\ *or* **di·a·ste·reo·iso·mer·ic** \-ˌī-sō-'mer-ik\ *adj* — **di·a·ste·reo·isom·er·ism** \-ī-'sä-mə-ˌri-zəm\ *n*

di·as·to·le \dī-'as-tə-(ˌ)lē\ *n* [Gk *diastolē* dilatation, fr. *diastellein* to expand, fr. *dia-* + *stellein* to prepare, send] (ca. 1578) : a rhythmically recurrent expansion; *esp* : the dilatation of the cavities of the heart during which they fill with blood — **di·a·stol·ic** \ˌdī-ə-'stä-lik\ *adj*

di·as·tro·phism \dī-'as-trə-ˌfi-zəm\ *n* [Gk *diastrophē* twisting, fr. *diastrephein* to distort, fr. *dia-* + *strephein* to twist] (1890) : the process of deformation that produces in the earth's crust its continents and ocean basins, plateaus and mountains, folds of strata, and faults — **di·a·stroph·ic** \ˌdī-ə-'strä-fik\ *adj* — **di·a·stroph·i·cal·ly** \-fi-k(ə-)lē\ *adv*

di·a·tes·sa·ron \ˌdī-ə-'te-sə-rən\ *n* [Gk *(Euangelion) dia tessarōn,* lit., Gospel out of four, fr. *dia* through, out of + *tessarōn,* gen. of *tessares* four — more at DIA-, FOUR] (1803) : a harmony of the four Gospels edited and arranged into a single connected narrative

dia·ther·ma·nous \ˌdī-ə-'thər-mə-nəs\ *adj* [F *diathermane,* modif. of Gk *diathermainein* to heat through, fr. *dia-* + *thermainein* to heat, fr. *thermos* hot — more at THERM] (1834) : DIATHERMIC 1

dia·ther·mic \ˌdī-ə-'thər-mik\ *adj* (1840) **1** : transmitting infrared radiation **2** : of or relating to diathermy ⟨~ treatment⟩

dia·ther·my \'dī-ə-ˌthər-mē\ *n* [ISV] (1909) : the generation of heat in tissue by electric currents for medical or surgical purposes

di·ath·e·sis \dī-'a-thə-səs\ *n, pl* **-e·ses** \-ˌsēz\ [NL, fr. Gk, lit., arrangement, fr. *diatithenai* to arrange, fr. *dia-* + *tithenai* to set — more at DO] (1651) : a constitutional predisposition toward a particular state or condition and esp. one that is abnormal or diseased — **di·a·thet·ic** \ˌdī-ə-'the-tik\ *adj*

di·a·tom \'dī-ə-ˌtäm\ *n* [ultim. fr. Gk *diatomos* cut in half, fr. *diatemnein* to cut through, fr. *dia-* + *temnein* to cut — more at TOME] (1845) : any of a class (Bacillariophyceae) of minute planktonic unicellular or colonial algae with silicified skeletons that form diatomite

di·a·to·ma·ceous \ˌdī-ə-tə-'mā-shəs, (ˌ)dī-ˌa-tə-\ *adj* (1847) : consisting of or abounding in diatoms or their siliceous remains ⟨~ silica⟩

diatomaceous earth *n* (1883) : DIATOMITE

di·atom·ic \ˌdī-ə-'tä-mik\ *adj* [ISV] (ca. 1859) : consisting of two atoms : having two atoms in the molecule

di·at·o·mite \dī-'a-tə-ˌmīt\ *n* (1887) : a light friable siliceous material derived chiefly from diatom remains and used esp. as a filter

dia·ton·ic \ˌdī-ə-'tä-nik\ *adj* [LL *diatonicus,* fr. Gk *diatonikos,* fr. *diatonos* stretching, fr. *diateinein* to stretch out, fr. *dia-* + *teinein* to stretch — more at THIN] (1694) : of or relating to a major or minor musical

diaper 2

scale comprising intervals of five whole steps and two half steps — **di·a·ton·i·cal·ly** \-'tä-ni-k(ə-)lē\ *adv*

di·a·tribe \'dī-ə-ˌtrīb\ *n* [L *diatriba*, fr. Gk *diatribē* pastime, discourse, fr. *diatribein* to spend (time), wear away, fr. *dia-* + *tribein* to rub — more at THROW] (1581) **1** *archaic* : a prolonged discourse **2** : a bitter and abusive speech or writing **3** : ironical or satirical criticism

di·az·e·pam \dī-'a-zə-ˌpam\ *n* [benzo*diaze*pine + *-am* (of unknown origin)] (ca. 1961) : a tranquilizer $C_{16}H_{13}ClN_2O$ used esp. to relieve anxiety and tension and as a muscle relaxant — compare VALIUM

Di·az·i·non \dī-'a-zi-ˌnän\ *trademark* — used for a cholinesterase= inhibiting organophosphate insecticide

di·azo \dī-'a-(ˌ)zō, -'ā-\ *adj* [ISV *diaz-, diazo-,* fr. *di-* + *az-*] (1878) **1 a** : relating to or containing the group N_2 composed of two nitrogen atoms united to a single carbon atom of an organic radical — often used in combination **b** : relating to or containing diazonium — often used in combination **2** : of or relating to a photograph or photocopy whose production involves the use of a coating of a diazo compound that is decomposed by exposure to light

di·a·zo·ni·um \ˌdī-ə-'zō-nē-əm\ *n* [ISV *di-* + *az-* + *-onium*] (1895) : the univalent cation N_2^+ that is composed of two nitrogen atoms united to carbon in an organic radical and that usu. exists in salts used in the manufacture of azo dyes

di·az·o·tize \dī-'a-zə-ˌtīz\ *vt* **-tized; -tiz·ing** [ISV *di-* + *azote* nitrogen + *-ize* — more at AZ-] (ca. 1889) : to convert (a compound) into a diazo compound (as a diazonium salt) — **di·az·o·ti·za·tion** \-ˌa-zə-tə-'zā-shən\ *n*

di·ba·sic \(ˌ)dī-'bā-sik\ *adj* (1868) : having two replaceable hydrogen atoms — used of acids

dib·ber \'di-bər\ *n* (ca. 1736) : DIBBLE

1dib·ble \'di-bəl\ *n* [ME *debylle*] (15c) : a small hand implement used to make holes in the ground for plants, seeds, or bulbs

2dibble *vt* **dib·bled; dib·bling** \-b(ə-)liŋ\ (1583) **1** : to plant with a dibble **2** : to make holes in (soil) with or as if with a dibble

di·ben·zo·fu·ran \ˌdī-ˌben-zō-'fyù-ˌran, -fyə-'ran\ *n* (1940) : a highly toxic chemical compound $C_{12}H_8O$ that is used in chemical synthesis and as an insecticide and is a hazardous pollutant in its chlorinated form

dibs \'dibz\ *n pl* [short for *dibstones* (jacks), fr. obs. *dib* to dib] (1812) **1** *slang* : money esp. in small amounts **2** : CLAIM, RIGHTS ⟨I have ∼ on that piece of cake⟩

di·bu·tyl phthal·ate \ˌdī-ˌbyü-t°l-'tha-ˌlāt\ *n* [*phtha*lic acid + ¹-*ate*] (1925) : a colorless oily ester $C_{16}H_{22}O_4$ used chiefly as a solvent, plasticizer, pesticide, and repellent (as for chiggers and mites)

di·cal·ci·um silicate \(ˌ)dī-'kal-sē-əm-\ *n* (1925) : a calcium silicate $2CaO·SiO_2$ that is an essential ingredient of portland cement

di·car·box·yl·ic \ˌdī-ˌkär-ˌbäk-'si-lik\ *adj* (ca. 1890) : containing two carboxyl groups in the molecule ⟨∼ acids⟩

di·cast \'dī-ˌkast, 'di-\ *n* [Gk *dikastēs,* fr. *dikazein* to judge, fr. *dikē* judgment — more at DICTION] (1822) : an ancient Athenian performing the functions of both judge and juror at a trial

1dice \'dīs\ *n, pl* **dice** [ME *dyce,* fr. *dees, dyce,* pl. of *dee* die — more at DIE] (14c) **1 a** : DIE **1 b** : a gambling game played with dice **2** *pl also* **dic·es** : a small cubical piece (as of food) **3** : a close contest between two racing-car drivers for position during a race — **no dice 1** : of no avail : no use : FUTILE **2** : ¹NO 3 ⟨said *no dice* to my request⟩

2dice *vb* **diced; dic·ing** [ME *dycen,* fr. *dyce*] *vt* (14c) **1 a** : to cut into small cubes **b** : to ornament with square markings ⟨*diced* leather⟩ **2 a** : to bring by playing dice ⟨∼ himself into debt⟩ **b** : to lose by dicing ⟨∼ her money away⟩ ∼ *vi* **1** : to play games with dice ⟨∼ for drinks in the bar —Malcolm Lowry⟩ **2** : to take a chance ⟨the temptation to ∼ with death —*Newsweek*⟩ — **dic·er** *n*

di·cen·tric \(ˌ)dī-'sen-trik\ *adj* (1937) : having two centromeres ⟨a ∼ chromosome⟩ — **dicentric** *n*

dic·ey \'dī-sē\ *adj* **dic·i·er; -est** [¹*dice* + *-y*] (1950) : RISKY, UNPREDICTABLE ⟨a ∼ proposition⟩ ⟨∼ weather⟩

dich- *or* **dicho-** *comb form* [LL, fr. Gk, fr. *dicha;* akin to Gk *di-*] : in two : apart ⟨*dicho*gamous⟩

di·cha·sium \dī-'kā-z(h)ē-əm, -zhəm\ *n, pl* **-sia** \-z(h)ē-ə, -zhə\ [NL, fr. Gk *dichasis* halving, fr. *dichazein* to halve, fr. *dicha*] (1875) : a cymose inflorescence that produces two main axes

dichlor- *or* **dichloro-** *comb form* : containing two atoms of chlorine ⟨*dichloro*ethane⟩

di·chlo·ro·ben·zene \(ˌ)dī-ˌklōr-ə-'ben-ˌzēn, -ˌklōr-, -(ˌ)ben-'\ *n* (1873) : any of three isomeric compounds $C_6H_4Cl_2$; *esp* : PARADICHLOROBENZENE

di·chlo·ro·di·flu·o·ro·meth·ane \-ˌdī-ˌflùr-ə-'me-ˌthān\ *n* (1936) : a chlorofluoromethane CCl_2F_2

di·chlo·ro·eth·ane \(ˌ)dī-ˌklō-rō-'e-ˌthān\ *n* (1936) : a colorless toxic liquid compound $C_2H_4Cl_2$ that is used chiefly as a solvent

di·chlor·vos \(ˌ)dī-'klōr-ˌväs, -'klōr-, -vəs\ *n* [*dichlor-* + *vin*yl + *phos*phate] (1957) : an organophosphorus insecticide and anthelmintic $C_4H_7Cl_2O_4P$ used esp. in veterinary medicine — called also *DDVP*

di·chog·a·my \dī-'kä-gə-mē\ *n, pl* **-mies** [G *Dichogamie,* fr. *dich-* + *-gamie* -gamy] (1862) : the production of male and female reproductive elements at different times by a hermaphroditic organism in order to ensure cross-fertilization — **di·chog·a·mous** \-gə-məs\ *adj*

di·chon·dra \dī-'kän-drə\ *n* [NL, genus name, fr. *di-* + Gk *chondros* grain — more at GRIND] (1947) : any of a genus (*Dichondra*) of chiefly tropical perennial herbs of the morning glory family that includes some (esp. *D. repens* or its varieties) used as a ground cover and a substitute for lawn grasses in warmer parts of the U.S.

dich·ot·ic \(ˌ)dī-'kō-tik\ *adj* [*dich-* + ²*-otic*] (ca. 1911) : affecting or relating to the two ears differently in regard to a conscious aspect (as pitch or loudness) or a physical aspect (as frequency or energy) of sound — **dich·ot·i·cal·ly** \-ti-k(ə-)lē\ *adv*

di·chot·o·mist \dī-'kä-tə-məst *also* də-\ *n* (ca. 1592) : one that dichotomizes

di·chot·o·mize \-ˌmīz\ *vb* **-mized; -miz·ing** [LL *dichotomos*] *vt* (1606) : to divide into two parts, classes, or groups ∼ *vi* : to exhibit dichotomy — **di·chot·o·mi·za·tion** \-ˌkä-tə-mə-'zā-shən\ *n*

di·chot·o·mous \dī-'kä-tə-məs *also* də-\ *adj* [LL *dichotomos,* fr. Gk, fr. *dich-* + *temnein* to cut — more at TOME] (1752) **1** : dividing into two parts **2** : relating to, involving, or proceeding from dichotomy — **di·chot·o·mous·ly** *adv* — **di·chot·o·mous·ness** *n*

dichotomous key *n* (ca. 1889) : a key for the identification of organisms based on a series of choices between alternative characters

di·chot·o·my \dī-'kä-tə-mē *also* də-\ *n, pl* **-mies** [Gk *dichotomia,* fr. *dichotomos*] (1610) **1** : a division or the process of dividing into two esp. mutually exclusive or contradictory groups or entities **2** : the phase of the moon or an inferior planet in which half its disk appears illuminated **3 a** : BIFURCATION; *esp* : repeated bifurcation (as of a plant's stem) **b** : a system of branching in which the main axis forks repeatedly into two branches **c** : branching of an ancestral line into two equal diverging branches **4** : something with seemingly contradictory qualities

di·chro·ic \dī-'krō-ik\ *adj* [Gk *dichroos* two-colored, fr. *di-* + *chrōs* color, lit., skin] (ca. 1859) **1** : having the property of dichroism ⟨a ∼ crystal⟩ ⟨a ∼ mirror⟩ **2** : DICHROMATIC

di·chro·ism \'dī-(ˌ)krō-ˌi-zəm\ *n* (1819) : the property of some crystals and solutions of absorbing one of two plane-polarized components of transmitted light more strongly than the other; *also* : the property of exhibiting different colors by reflected or transmitted light — compare CIRCULAR DICHROISM

di·chro·mat \'dī-krō-ˌmat, (ˌ)dī-krō-\ *n* [back-formation fr. *dichromatic*] (ca. 1909) : one affected with dichromatism

di·chro·mate \(ˌ)dī-'krō-ˌmāt, 'dī-krō-\ *n* [ISV] (ca. 1864) : a usu. orange to red chromium salt containing the anion $Cr_2O_7^{2-}$ ⟨∼ of potassium⟩ — called also *bichromate*

di·chro·mat·ic \ˌdī-krō-'ma-tik\ *adj* (ca. 1847) **1** : having or exhibiting two colors **2** : of, relating to, or exhibiting dichromatism

di·chro·ma·tism \(ˌ)dī-'krō-mə-ˌti-zəm\ *n* (ca. 1901) : partial color blindness in which only two colors are perceptible

di·chro·scope \'dī-krə-ˌskōp\ *n* (1857) : an instrument for examining crystals for dichroism

dick \'dik\ *n* [*Dick,* nickname for *Richard*] (1553) **1** *chiefly Brit* : FELLOW, CHAP **2** : PENIS — usu. considered vulgar **3** [by shortening & alter.]: DETECTIVE

dick·cis·sel \dik-'si-səl, 'dik-ˌ\ *n* [imit.] (1886) : a common migratory black= throated finch (*Spiza americana*) of the central U.S.

dick·ens \'di-kənz\ *n* [euphemism] (1598) : DEVIL, DEUCE

1dick·er \'di-kər\ *n* [ME *dyker,* fr. L *decuria* quantity of ten, fr. *decem* ten — more at TEN] (14c) : the number or quantity of 10 esp. of hides or skins

2dicker *vi* **dick·ered; dick·er·ing** \'di-k(ə-)riŋ\ [origin unknown] (ca. 1802) : BARGAIN ⟨∼*ed* over the price⟩

3dicker *n* (1823) **1** : BARTER **2** : an act or session of bargaining

dickcissel

dick·ey *or* **dicky** *also* **dick·ie** \'di-kē\ *n, pl* **dickeys** *or* **dick·ies** [*Dicky,* nickname for *Richard*] (1753) **1** : any of various articles of clothing: as **a** : a man's separate or detachable shirtfront **b** : a small fabric insert used to fill in the neckline **2** *chiefly Brit* **a** : the driver's seat in a carriage **b** : a seat at the back of a carriage or automobile **3** : a small bird

Dick test \'dik-\ *n* [George F. *Dick* and Gladys H. *Dick*] (1925) : a test to determine susceptibility or immunity to scarlet fever by an injection of scarlet fever toxin

di·cli·nous \(ˌ)dī-'klī-nəs\ *adj* (1830) : having the stamens and pistils in separate flowers

di·cot \'dī-ˌkät\ *n* (1877) : DICOTYLEDON

di·cot·y·le·don \ˌdī-ˌkä-t°l-'ē-d°n\ *n* [NL] (ca. 1727) : any of a class or subclass (Magnoliopsida or Dicotyledoneae) of angiospermous plants that produce an embryo with two cotyledons and usu. have floral organs arranged in cycles of four or five and leaves with reticulate venation — compare MONOCOTYLEDON — **di·cot·y·le·don·ous** \-d°n-əs\ *adj*

di·cou·ma·rin \(ˌ)dī-'kü-mə-rən\ *n* (1886) : DICUMAROL

di·crot·ic \dī-'krä-tik\ *adj* [Gk *dikrotos,* fr. *di-* + *krotos* rattling noise, beat] (ca. 1811) **1** *of the pulse* : having a double beat **2** : being or relating to the second part of the arterial pulse occurring during diastole of the heart or of an arterial pressure recording made during the same period — **di·cro·tism** \'dī-krə-ˌti-zəm\ *n*

Dic·ta·phone \'dik-tə-ˌfōn\ *trademark* — used for a dictating machine

1dic·tate \'dik-ˌtāt, dik-'\ *vb* **dic·tat·ed; dic·tat·ing** [L *dictatus,* pp. of *dictare* to assert, dictate, freq. of *dicere* to say — more at DICTION] *vi* (1592) **1** : to give dictation **2** : to speak or act domineeringly : PRESCRIBE ∼ *vt* **1** : to speak or read for a person to transcribe or for a machine to record **2 a** : to issue as an order **b** : to impose, pronounce, or specify authoritatively **c** : to require or determine necessarily ⟨injuries *dictated* the choice of players⟩

2dic·tate \'dik-ˌtāt\ *n* (1594) **1 a** : an authoritative rule, prescription, or injunction **b** : a ruling principle ⟨according to the ∼s of your conscience⟩ **2** : a command by one in authority

dictating machine *n* (1907) : a machine used esp. for the recording of human speech for transcription

dic·ta·tion \dik-'tā-shən\ *n* (ca. 1656) **1 a** : PRESCRIPTION **b** : arbitrary command **2 a** (1) : the act or manner of uttering words to be transcribed (2) : material that is dictated or transcribed **b** (1) : the performing of music to be reproduced by a student (2) : music so reproduced

dic·ta·tor \'dik-ˌtā-tər, dik-'\ *n* [L, fr. *dictare*] (14c) **1 a** : a person granted absolute emergency power; *esp* : one appointed by the senate of ancient Rome **b** : one holding complete autocratic control **c** : one ruling absolutely and often oppressively **2** : one that dictates

dic·ta·to·ri·al \ˌdik-tə-'tōr-ē-əl, -'tòr-\ *adj* (1701) **1 a** : of, relating to, or befitting a dictator ⟨∼ power⟩ **b** : ruled by a dictator **2** : oppressive to or arrogantly overbearing toward others — **dic·ta·to·ri·al·ly** \-ē-ə-lē\ *adv* — **dic·ta·to·ri·al·ness** *n*

\ə\ abut \ᵊ\ kitten, F table \ər\ further \a\ ash \ā\ ace \ä\ mop, mar \aù\ out \ch\ chin \e\ bet \ē\ easy \g\ go \i\ hit \ī\ ice \j\ job \ŋ\ sing \ō\ go \ò\ law \òi\ boy \th\ thin \t͟h\ the \ü\ loot \ù\ foot \y\ yet \zh\ vision \á, k̲, ⁿ, œ, œ̄, ɶ, ūe, ʸ\ see Guide to Pronunciation *syn* DICTATORIAL, MAGISTERIAL, DOGMATIC, DOCTRINAIRE, ORACULAR mean imposing one's will or opinions on others. DICTATORIAL stresses autocratic, high-handed methods and a domineering manner ⟨exercised *dictatorial* control over the office⟩. MAGISTERIAL stresses assumption or use of prerogatives appropriate to a magistrate or schoolmaster in forcing acceptance of one's opinions ⟨the *magisterial* tone of his pronouncements⟩. DOGMATIC implies being unduly and offensively positive in laying down principles and expressing opinions ⟨*dogmatic* about what is art and what is not⟩. DOCTRINAIRE implies a disposition to follow abstract theories in framing laws or policies affecting people ⟨a *doctrinaire* approach to improving the economy⟩. ORACULAR implies the manner of one who delivers opinions in cryptic phrases or with pompous dogmatism ⟨a designer who is the *oracular* voice of fashion⟩.

dic·ta·tor·ship \dik-'tā-tər-,ship, 'dik-\ *n* (1542) **1** : the office of dictator **2** : autocratic rule, control, or leadership **3 a** : a form of government in which absolute power is concentrated in a dictator or a small clique **b** : a government organization or group in which absolute power is so concentrated **c** : a despotic state

dic·tion \'dik-shən\ *n* [L *diction-, dictio* speaking, style, fr. *dicere* to say; akin to OE *tēon* to accuse, L *dicare* to proclaim, dedicate, Gk *deiknynai* to show, *dikē* judgment, right] (1581) **1** *obs* : verbal description **2** : choice of words esp. with regard to correctness, clearness, or effectiveness **3 a** : vocal expression : ENUNCIATION **b** : pronunciation and enunciation of words in singing — **dic·tion·al** \-shnəl, -shə-nᵊl\ *adj* — **dic·tion·al·ly** \-ē\ *adv*

dic·tio·nary \'dik-shə-,ner-ē\ *n, pl* **-nar·ies** [ML *dictionarium,* fr. LL *diction-, dictio* word, fr. L, speaking] (1526) **1** : a reference book containing words usu. alphabetically arranged along with information about their forms, pronunciations, functions, etymologies, meanings, and syntactical and idiomatic uses **2** : a reference book listing alphabetically terms or names important to a particular subject or activity along with discussion of their meanings and applications **3** : a reference book giving for words of one language equivalents in another **4** : a list (as of items of data or words) stored in a computer for reference (as for information retrieval or word processing)

dic·tum \'dik-təm\ *n, pl* **dic·ta** \-tə\ *also* **dictums** [L, fr. neut. of *dictus,* ptp. of *dicere*] (1599) **1** : a noteworthy statement: as **a** : a formal pronouncement of a principle, proposition, or opinion **b** : an observation intended or regarded as authoritative **2** : a judicial opinion on a point other than the precise issue involved in determining a case

dicty- *or* **dictyo-** *comb form* [NL, fr. Gk *dikty-, diktyo-,* fr. *diktyon,* fr. *dikein* to throw]: net ⟨*dictyo*stele⟩ ⟨*dictyo*some⟩

dic·tyo·some \'dik-tē-ə-,sōm\ *n* (ca. 1930) : any of the membranous or vesicular structures making up the Golgi apparatus

dic·tyo·stele \'dik-tē-ə-,stēl, ,dik-tē-ə-'stē-lē\ *n* (ca. 1902) : a stele in which the vascular cylinder is broken up into a longitudinal series or network of vascular strands around a central pith (as in many ferns)

di·cu·ma·rol *also* **di·cou·ma·rol** \dī-'k(y)ü-mə-,ról, -,ról\ *n* [*di-* + *coumar*in + ¹*-ol*] (1943) : a crystalline compound $C_{19}H_{12}O_6$ orig. obtained from spoiled sweet clover hay and used to delay clotting of blood esp. in preventing and treating thromboembolic disease

di·cyn·o·dont \(,)dī-'si-nō-,dänt, -'si-\ *n* [ultim. fr. Gk *di-* + *kyn-, kyōn* dog + *odont-, odous* tooth — more at HOUND, TOOTH] (1854) : any of a suborder (Dicynodontia) of small herbivorous therapsid reptiles with reduced dentition — **dicynodont** *adj*

did *past of* DO

di·dact \'dī-,dakt\ *n* [back-formation fr. *didactic*] (1954) : a didactic person

di·dac·tic \dī-'dak-tik, də-\ *adj* [Gk *didaktikos,* fr. *didaskein* to teach] (1658) **1 a** : designed or intended to teach **b** : intended to convey instruction and information as well as pleasure and entertainment **2** : making moral observations — **di·dac·ti·cal** \-ti-kəl\ *adj* — **di·dac·ti·cal·ly** \-ti-k(ə-)lē\ *adv* — **di·dac·ti·cism** \-tə-,si-zəm\ *n*

di·dac·tics \-tiks\ *n pl but sing or pl in constr* (1644) : systematic instruction : PEDAGOGY

did·dle \'di-dᵊl\ *vb* **did·dled; did·dling** \'did-liŋ, -dᵊl-iŋ\ [origin unknown] *vt* (1786) **1** *chiefly dial* : to move with short rapid motions **2** : to waste (as time) in trifling **3** : HOAX, SWINDLE **4** : to copulate with — often considered vulgar ~ *vi* **1** : DAWDLE, FOOL **2** : FIDDLE, TOY usu. used with ⟨*diddled* with the machine until it broke⟩ — **did·dler** \'did-lər, -dᵊl-ər\ *n*

did·dly \'di-dᵊl-ē, 'did-lē\ *n* (1964) *slang* : DIDDLY-SQUAT

did·dly–squat \-,skwät\ *n* [prob. alter. of *doodly-squat*] (1974) *slang* : the least amount : anything at all ⟨didn't know ~ about sports — Sam Toperoff⟩

did·ger·i·doo *also* **did·jer·i·doo** \'di-jə-rē-,dü, ,di-jə-rē-'\ *n* [Yolngu (Australian aboriginal language group of Arnhem Land) *didjeridu*] (1919) : a large bamboo or wooden trumpet of the Australian Aborigines

didn't \'di-dᵊnt, -dᵊn, *dial also* 'dit-ᵊn(t) *or* 'dint\ (1705) : did not

di·do \'dī-(,)dō\ *n, pl* **didoes** *or* **didos** [origin unknown] (1807) **1** : a mischievous or capricious act : PRANK, ANTIC — often used in the phrase *cut didoes* **2** : something that is frivolous or showy

Di·do \'dī-(,)dō\ *n* [L, fr. Gk *Didō*] : a legendary queen of Carthage in Virgil's *Aeneid* who kills herself when Aeneas leaves her

didst \'didst, 'ditst\ *archaic past 2d sing of* DO

di·dym·i·um \dī-'di-mē-əm\ *n* [NL, fr. Gk *didymos* twin, fr. *dyo* two — more at TWO] (1842) : a mixture of rare-earth elements made up chiefly of neodymium and praseodymium and used esp. for coloring glass for optical filters

¹die \'dī\ *vi* **died; dy·ing** \'dī-iŋ\ [ME *dien,* fr. or akin to ON *deyja* to die; akin to OHG *touwen* to die] (12c) **1** : to pass from physical life : EXPIRE **2 a** : to pass out of existence : CEASE ⟨their anger *died* at these words⟩ **b** : to disappear or subside gradually — often used with *away, down,* or *out* ⟨the storm *died* down⟩ **3 a** : SINK, LANGUISH ⟨*dying* from fatigue⟩ **b** : to long keenly or desperately ⟨*dying* to go⟩ **c** : to be overwhelmed by emotion ⟨~ of embarrassment⟩ **4 a** : to cease functioning : STOP ⟨the motor *died*⟩ **b** : to end in failure ⟨the bill *died* in committee⟩ **5** : to become indifferent ⟨~ to worldly things⟩ — **die hard 1** : to be long in dying ⟨such rumors *die hard*⟩ **2** : to continue resistance against hopeless odds ⟨hard-shell conservatism *dies hard*⟩ — **die on the vine** : to fail esp. at an early stage through lack of support or enthusiasm ⟨let the proposal *die on the vine*⟩

²die \'dī\ *n, pl* **dice** \'dīs\ *or* **dies** \'dīz\ [ME *dee,* fr. MF *dé*] (14c) **1** *pl*

dice : a small cube marked on each face with from one to six spots and used usu. in pairs in various games and in gambling by being shaken and thrown to come to rest at random on a flat surface — often used figuratively in expressions concerning chance or the irrevocability of a course of action ⟨the ~ was cast⟩ **2** *pl* **dies** : DADO 1a **3** *pl* **dies** : any of various tools or devices for imparting a desired shape, form, or finish to a material or for impressing an object or material: as **a** (1) : the larger of a pair of cutting or shaping tools that when moved toward each other produce a desired form in or impress a desired device on an object by pressure or by a blow (2) : a device composed of a pair of such tools **b** : a hollow internally threaded screw-cutting tool used for forming screw threads **c** : a mold into which molten metal or other material is forced **d** : a perforated block through which metal or plastic is drawn or extruded for shaping

die-back \'dī-,bak\ *n* (ca. 1886) : a condition in woody plants in which peripheral parts are killed esp. by parasites

di·ecious *var of* DIOECIOUS

dief·fen·bach·ia \,dē-fən-'ba-kē-ə, ,di-, -'bä-\ *n* [NL, fr. Ernst *Dieffenbach* †1855 Ger. naturalist] (ca. 1900) : any of a genus (*Dieffenbachia* of the family Araceae) of erect poisonous tropical American plants that have oblong usu. variegated leaves and are often used as houseplants

die–hard \'dī-,härd\ *adj* (1922) : strongly or fanatically determined or devoted ⟨~ fans⟩; *esp* : strongly resisting change ⟨a ~ conservative⟩ — **die·hard** *n* — **die–hard·ism** \-,iz-əm\ *n*

di·el \'dī-əl, -,el\ *adj* [irreg. fr. L *dies* day + E *-al*] (ca. 1935) : involving a 24-hour period that usu. includes a day and the adjoining night ⟨~ fluctuations in temperature⟩

diel·drin \'dē(ə)l-drən\ *n* [*Diels*-Al*drin* reaction (an addition reaction forming a 6-membered ring), after Otto *Diels* & Kurt *Alder*] (ca. 1949) : a white crystalline persistent chlorinated hydrocarbon insecticide $C_{12}H_8Cl_6O$ that accumulates in and becomes toxic to vertebrates

di·elec·tric \,dī-ə-'lek-trik\ *n* [*dia-* + *electric*] (1837) : a nonconductor of direct electric current — **dielectric** *adj*

dielectric constant *n* (1875) : PERMITTIVITY

dielectric heating *n* (1944) : the rapid and uniform heating throughout a nonconducting material by means of a high-frequency electromagnetic field

di·en·ceph·a·lon \,dī-ən-'se-fə-,län, ,dī-(,)en-, -lən\ *n* [NL, fr. *dia-* + *encephalon*] (ca. 1883) : the posterior subdivision of the forebrain — called also *betweenbrain* — **di·en·ce·phal·ic** \-sə-'fa-lik\ *adj*

di·ene \'dī-,ēn\ *n* [*di-* + *-ene*] (1917) : a compound containing two double bonds between carbon atoms

die–off \'dī-,óf\ *n* (1936) : a sudden sharp decline of a population (as of rabbits) that is not caused directly by human activity (as hunting)

die off \'dī-'óf\ *vi* (1697) : to die sequentially either singly or in numbers so that the total number is greatly diminished

die out *vi* (1853) : to become extinct

di·er·e·sis *var of* DIAERESIS

die·sel \'dē-zəl, -səl\ *n* [Rudolf *Diesel*] (1894) **1** : DIESEL ENGINE **2** : a vehicle driven by a diesel engine

diesel–electric *adj* (1914) : of, relating to, or employing the combination of a diesel engine driving an electric generator ⟨a ~ locomotive⟩

diesel engine *n* (1894) : an internal combustion engine in which air is compressed to a temperature sufficiently high to ignite fuel injected into the cylinder where the combustion and expansion actuate a piston

die·sel·ing \'dē-zə-liŋ, -sə-\ *n* (ca. 1955) : the continued operation of an internal combustion engine after the ignition is turned off

die·sel·ize \'dē-zə-,līz, -sə-\ *vt* **-ized; -iz·ing** (1925) : to equip with a diesel engine or with electric locomotives having generators powered by diesel engines — **die·sel·iza·tion** \,dē-zə-lə-'zā-shən, -sə-\ *n*

Di·es Irae \,dē-(,)ās-'ē-,rā\ *n* [ML, day of wrath; fr. the first words of the hymn] (1860) : a medieval Latin hymn on the Day of Judgment sung in requiem masses

di·esis \'dī-ə-səs\ *n, pl* **di·eses** \-,sēz\ [prob. fr. It, sharp (in music), symbol for a sharp, fr. ML, quarter tone, fr. L, fr. Gk, fr. *diienai* to send through, fr. *dia-* + *hienai* to send — more at JET] (ca. 1706) : DOUBLE DAGGER

di·es·ter \'dī-,es-tər\ *n* (1935) : a compound containing two ester groups

die·stock \'dī-,stäk\ *n* (ca. 1859) : a stock to hold dies used for cutting threads

di·es·trus \(,)dī-'es-trəs\ *n* [NL, fr. *dia-* + *estrus*] (1942) : a period of sexual quiescence that intervenes between two periods of estrus — **di·es·trous** \-trəs\ *adj*

¹di·et \'dī-ət\ *n* [ME *diete,* fr. OF, fr. L *diaeta,* fr. Gk *diaita,* lit., manner of living, fr. *diaitasthai* to lead one's life] (13c) **1 a** : food and drink regularly provided or consumed **b** : habitual nourishment **c** : the kind and amount of food prescribed for a person or animal for a special reason **2** : something provided esp. habitually ⟨a ~ of Broadway shows and nightclubs —Frederick Wyatt⟩

²diet *vt* (14c) **1** : to cause to take food : FEED **2** : to cause to eat and drink sparingly or according to prescribed rules ~ *vi* : to eat sparingly or according to prescribed rules — **di·et·er** *n*

³diet *adj* (1969) : reduced in calories ⟨a ~ soft drink⟩

⁴diet *n* [ME *diete* day's journey, day set for a meeting, fr. ML *dieta,* lit., daily regimen, diet (taken as a derivative of L *dies* day), fr. L *diaeta*] (1565) **1** : a formal deliberative assembly of princes or estates **2** : any of various national or provincial legislatures

¹di·e·tary \'dī-ə-,ter-ē\ *n, pl* **di·e·tar·ies** (1838) : the kinds and amounts of food available to or eaten by an individual, group, or population

²dietary *adj* (1614) : of or relating to a diet or to the rules of a diet — **di·e·tar·i·ly** \,dī-ə-'ter-ə-lē\ *adv*

dietary law *n* (ca. 1930) : any of the laws observed by Orthodox Jews that permit or prohibit certain foods

di·e·tet·ic \,dī-ə-'te-tik\ *adj* (1579) **1** : of or relating to diet **2** : adapted for use in special diets — **di·e·tet·i·cal·ly** \-ti-k(ə-)lē\ *adv*

di·e·tet·ics \-'te-tiks\ *n pl but sing or pl in constr* (1799) : the science or art of applying the principles of nutrition to the diet

di·ether \(,)dī-'ē-thər\ *n* (1950) : a compound containing two atoms of oxygen with ether linkages

di·eth·yl·car·bam·a·zine \,dī-,e-thəl-kär-'ba-mə-,zēn, -zən\ *n* [*di-* + *ethyl* + *carboxy-* + *amide* + *azine*] (1948) : an anthelmintic administered in the form of its crystalline citrate $C_{10}H_{21}N_3O \cdot C_6H_8O_7$ esp. to control human filariasis and large roundworms in dogs and cats

di·eth·yl ether \(,)dī-,e-thəl-\ *n* (ca. 1930) : ETHER 3a

di·eth·yl·stil·bes·trol \-stil-'bes-,tról, -,trōl\ *n* [ISV] (1938) : a colorless crystalline synthetic compound $C_{18}H_{20}O_2$ used as a potent estrogen but contraindicated in pregnancy for its tendency to cause cancer or birth defects in offspring — called also *stilbestrol*

di·eth·yl zinc *n* (1952) : a volatile pyrophoric liquid organometallic compound $C_4H_{10}Zn$ used esp. to catalyze polymerization reactions and to deacidify paper

di·e·ti·tian *or* **di·e·ti·cian** \,dī-ə-'ti-shən\ *n* [*dietitian* irreg. fr. ¹*diet* + *-ician*] (ca. 1846) : a specialist in dietetics

dif·fer \'di-fər\ *vi* **dif·fered; dif·fer·ing** \-f(ə-)riŋ\ [ME, fr. MF or L; MF *differer* to postpone, be different, fr. L *differre*, fr. *dis-* + *ferre* to carry — more at BEAR] (14c) **1 a** : to be unlike or distinct in nature, form, or characteristics ⟨the law of one state ∼s from that of another⟩ **b** : to change from time to time or from one instance to another : VARY ⟨the number of cookies in a box may ∼⟩ **2** : to be of unlike or opposite opinion : DISAGREE ⟨they ∼ on religious matters⟩

¹**dif·fer·ence** \'di-fərn(t)s, 'di-f(ə-)rən(t)s\ *n* (14c) **1 a** : the quality or state of being different **b** : an instance of differing in nature, form, or quality **c** *archaic* : a characteristic that distinguishes one from another or from the average **d** : the element or factor that separates or distinguishes contrasting situations **2** : distinction or discrimination in preference **3 a** : disagreement in opinion : DISSENSION **b** : an instance or cause of disagreement **4** : the degree or amount by which things differ in quantity or measure; *specif* : REMAINDER 2b(1) **5** : a significant change in or effect on a situation

²**difference** *vt* **-enced; -enc·ing** (1576) : DIFFERENTIATE, DISTINGUISH

¹**dif·fer·ent** \'di-fərnt, 'di-f(ə-)rənt\ *adj* [MF, fr. L *different-, differens*, prp. of *differre*] (14c) **1** : partly or totally unlike in nature, form, or quality : DISSIMILAR ⟨could hardly be more ∼⟩ — often followed by *from, than,* or chiefly Brit. *to* ⟨small, neat hand, very ∼ from the captain's tottery characters —R. L. Stevenson⟩ ⟨vastly ∼ in size than it was twenty-five years ago —N. M. Pusey⟩ ⟨a very ∼ situation to the . . . one under which we live —Sir Winston Churchill⟩ **2** : not the same: as **a** : DISTINCT ⟨∼ age groups⟩ **b** : VARIOUS ⟨∼ members of the class⟩ **c** : ANOTHER ⟨switched to a ∼ TV program⟩ **3** : UNUSUAL, SPECIAL ⟨she was ∼ and superior⟩ — **dif·fer·ent·ness** *n*

syn DIFFERENT, DIVERSE, DIVERGENT, DISPARATE, VARIOUS mean unlike in kind or character. DIFFERENT may imply little more than separateness but it may also imply contrast or contrariness ⟨*different* foods⟩. DIVERSE implies both distinctness and marked contrast ⟨such *diverse* interests as dancing and football⟩. DIVERGENT implies movement away from each other and unlikelihood of ultimate meeting or reconciliation ⟨went on to pursue *divergent* careers⟩. DISPARATE emphasizes incongruity or incompatibility ⟨*disparate* notions of freedom⟩. VARIOUS stresses the number of sorts or kinds ⟨tried *various* methods⟩.

usage Numerous commentators have condemned *different than* in spite of its use since the 17th century by many of the best-known names in English literature. It is nevertheless standard and is even recommended in many handbooks when followed by a clause. *Different from,* the generally safe choice, is more common and is even used in constructions where *than* would work more smoothly.

²**different** *adv* (1744) : DIFFERENTLY

dif·fer·en·tia \,di-fə-'ren(t)-sh(ē-)ə\ *n, pl* **-ti·ae** \-shē-,ē, -shē-,ī\ [L, difference, fr. *different-, differens*] (1690) : an element, feature, or factor that distinguishes one entity, state, or class from another; *esp* : a characteristic trait distinguishing a species from other species of the same genus

¹**dif·fer·en·tial** \,di-fə-'ren(t)-shəl\ *adj* (1647) **1 a** : of, relating to, or constituting a difference : DISTINGUISHING **b** : making a distinction between individuals or classes **c** : based on or resulting from a differential **d** : functioning or proceeding differently or at a different rate **2** : being, relating to, or involving a differential or differentiation **3 a** : relating to quantitative differences **b** : producing effects by reason of quantitative differences — **dif·fer·en·tial·ly** \-'ren(t)-shə-lē\ *adv*

²**differential** *n* (1704) **1 a** : the product of the derivative of a function of one variable by the increment of the independent variable **b** : a sum of products in which each product consists of a partial derivative of a given function of several variables multiplied by the corresponding increment and which contains as many products as there are independent variables in the function **2** : a difference between comparable individuals or classes ⟨a price ∼⟩; *also* : the amount of such a difference **3 a** : DIFFERENTIAL GEAR **b** : a case covering a differential gear

differential calculus *n* (1702) : a branch of mathematics concerned chiefly with the study of the rate of change of functions with respect to their variables esp. through the use of derivatives and differentials

differential equation *n* (1763) : an equation containing differentials or derivatives of functions — compare PARTIAL DIFFERENTIAL EQUATION

differential gear *n* (ca. 1859) : an arrangement of gears forming an epicyclic train for connecting two shafts or axles in the same line, dividing the driving force equally between them, and permitting one shaft to revolve faster than the other — called also *differential gearing*

differential geometry *n* (ca. 1909) : a branch of mathematics using calculus to study the geometric properties of curves and surfaces

dif·fer·en·ti·ate \,di-fə-'ren(t)-shē-,āt\ *vb* **-at·ed; -at·ing** *vt* (1816) **1** : to obtain the mathematical derivative of **2** : to mark or show a difference in : constitute a difference that distinguishes **3** : to develop differential characteristics in **4** : to cause differentiation of in the course of development **5** : to express the specific distinguishing quality of : DISCRIMINATE ∼ *vi* **1** : to recognize or give expression to a difference **2** : to become distinct or different in character **3** : to undergo differentiation — **dif·fer·en·tia·bil·i·ty** \-,ren(t)-sh(ē-)ə-'bi-lə-tē\ *n* — **dif·fer·en·tia·ble** \-'ren(t)-sh(ē-)ə-bəl\ *adj*

dif·fer·en·ti·a·tion \-,ren(t)-shē-'ā-shən\ *n* (1802) **1** : the act or process of differentiating **2** : development from the one to the many, the simple to the complex, or the homogeneous to the heterogeneous **3 a** : modification of body parts for performance of particular functions **b** : the sum of the processes whereby apparently indifferent cells, tissues, and structures attain their adult form and function **4** : the processes by which various rock types are produced from a common magma

dif·fer·ent·ly \'di-fərnt-lē, 'di-f(ə-)rənt-\ *adv* (14c) **1** : in a different manner **2** : OTHERWISE

dif·fi·cile \,dē-fi-'sē(ə)l\ *adj* [F, lit., difficult] (1536) : STUBBORN, UNREASONABLE

dif·fi·cult \'di-fi-(,)kəlt\ *adj* [ME, back-formation fr. *difficulty*] (14c) **1** : hard to do, make, or carry out : ARDUOUS ⟨a ∼ climb⟩ **2 a** : hard to deal with, manage, or overcome ⟨a ∼ child⟩ **b** : hard to understand : PUZZLING ⟨∼ reading⟩ *syn* see HARD — **dif·fi·cult·ly** *adv*

dif·fi·cul·ty \-(,)kəl-tē\ *n, pl* **-ties** [ME *difficulte,* fr. L *difficultas,* fr. *difficilis* not easy, fr. *dis-* + *facilis* easy — more at FACILE] (14c) **1** : the quality or state of being difficult **2** : CONTROVERSY, DISAGREEMENT **3** : OBJECTION **4** : something difficult : IMPEDIMENT **5** : EMBARRASSMENT, TROUBLE — usu. used in pl.

dif·fi·dence \'di-fə-dən(t)s, -fə-,den(t)s\ *n* (14c) : the quality or state of being diffident

dif·fi·dent \-dənt, -,dent\ *adj* [ME, fr. L *diffident-, diffidens,* prp. of *diffidere* to distrust, fr. *dis-* + *fidere* to trust — more at BIDE] (15c) **1** : hesitant in acting or speaking through lack of self-confidence **2** *archaic* : DISTRUSTFUL **3** : RESERVED, UNASSERTIVE *syn* see SHY — **dif·fi·dent·ly** *adv*

dif·fract \di-'frakt\ *vt* [back-formation fr. *diffraction*] (1803) : to cause to undergo diffraction

dif·frac·tion \di-'frak-shən\ *n* [NL *diffraction-, diffractio,* fr. L *diffringere* to break apart, fr. *dis-* + *frangere* to break — more at BREAK] (1671) : a modification which light undergoes in passing by the edges of opaque bodies or through narrow slits or in being reflected from ruled surfaces and in which the rays appear to be deflected and to produce fringes of parallel light and dark or colored bands; *also* : a similar modification of other waves (as sound waves)

diffraction grating *n* (1867) : GRATING 3

dif·frac·tom·e·ter \,di-,frak-'tä-mə-tər\ *n* (ca. 1909) : an instrument for analyzing the structure of a usu. crystalline substance from the scattering pattern produced when a beam of radiation or particles (as X rays or neutrons) strikes it — **dif·frac·to·met·ric** \di-,frak-tə-'me-trik\ *adj* — **dif·frac·tom·e·try** \,di-,frak-'tä-mə-trē\ *n*

¹**dif·fuse** \di-'fyüs\ *adj* [ME, fr. L *diffusus,* pp. of *diffundere* to spread out, fr. *dis-* + *fundere* to pour — more at FOUND] (15c) **1** : being at once verbose and ill-organized **2** : not concentrated or localized ⟨∼ sclerosis⟩ *syn* see WORDY — **dif·fuse·ly** *adv* — **dif·fuse·ness** *n*

²**dif·fuse** \di-'fyüz\ *vb* **dif·fused; dif·fus·ing** [ME *diffused,* pp., fr. L *diffusus,* pp.] *vt* (14c) **1 a** : to pour out and permit or cause to spread freely **b** : EXTEND, SCATTER **c** : to spread thinly or wastefully **2** : to subject to diffusion; *esp* : to break up and distribute (incident light) by reflection ∼ *vi* **1** : to spread out or become transmitted esp. by contact **2** : to undergo diffusion — **dif·fus·ible** \di-'fyü-zə-bəl\ *adj*

dif·fuse–po·rous \di-,fyüs-'pōr-əs, -'pòr-\ *adj* [¹*diffuse*] (ca. 1902) : having vessels more or less evenly distributed throughout an annual ring and not varying greatly in size — compare RING-POROUS

dif·fus·er \di-'fyü-zər\ *n* (ca. 1679) **1** : one that diffuses: as **a** : a device (as a reflector) for distributing the light of a lamp evenly **b** : a screen (as of cloth or frosted glass) for softening lighting (as in photography) **c** : a device (as slats at different angles) for deflecting air from an outlet in various directions **2** : a device for reducing the velocity and increasing the static pressure of a fluid passing through a system

dif·fu·sion \di-'fyü-zhən\ *n* (14c) **1** : the action of diffusing : the state of being diffused **2** : PROLIXITY, DIFFUSENESS **3 a** : the process whereby particles of liquids, gases, or solids intermingle as the result of their spontaneous movement caused by thermal agitation and in dissolved substances move from a region of higher to one of lower concentration **b** (1) : reflection of light by a rough reflecting surface (2) : transmission of light through a translucent material : SCATTERING **4** : the spread of cultural elements from one area or group of people to others by contact **5** : the softening of sharp outlines in a photographic image — **dif·fu·sion·al** \-'fyü-zhə-nᵊl\ *adj*

dif·fu·sion·ist \-'fyü-zhə-nəst\ *n* (1938) : an anthropologist who emphasizes the role of diffusion in the history of culture rather than independent invention or discovery — **dif·fu·sion·ism** \-'fyü-zhə-,ni-zəm\ *n* — **diffusionist** *adj*

dif·fu·sive \di-'fyü-siv, -ziv\ *adj* (1614) : tending to diffuse : characterized by diffusion ⟨∼ motion of atoms⟩ — **dif·fu·sive·ly** *adv* — **dif·fu·sive·ness** *n* — **dif·fu·siv·i·ty** \di-,fyü-'si-və-tē, -'zi-\ *n*

di·func·tion·al \(,)dī-'fəŋ(k)-shnəl, -shə-nᵊl\ *adj* (1943) : of, relating to, or being a compound with two highly reactive sites in each molecule

¹**dig** \'dig\ *vb* **dug** \'dəg\; **dig·ging** [ME *diggen*] *vt* (13c) **1 a** : to break up, turn, or loosen (earth) with an implement **b** : to prepare the soil of ⟨∼ a garden⟩ **2 a** : to bring to the surface by digging : UNEARTH **b** : to bring to light or out of hiding ⟨∼ up facts⟩ **3** : to hollow out or form by removing earth : EXCAVATE **4** : to drive down so as to penetrate : THRUST **5** : POKE, PROD **6 a** : to pay attention to : NOTICE ⟨∼ that fancy hat⟩ **b** : UNDERSTAND, APPRECIATE ⟨if you . . . do something subtle . . . only one tenth of the audience will ∼ it —Nat Hentoff⟩ **c** : LIKE, ADMIRE ⟨high school students ∼ short poetry — David Burmester⟩ ∼ *vi* **1** : to turn up, loosen, or remove earth : DELVE **2** : to work hard or laboriously **3** : to advance by or as if by removing or pushing aside material

²**dig** *n* (1819) **1 a** : THRUST, POKE **b** : a cutting remark **2** *pl* **a** : living accommodations **b** *chiefly Brit* : LODGING, HOTEL **3** : an archaeological excavation site; *also* : the excavation itself

dig·a·my \'di-gə-mē\ *n, pl* **-mies** [LL *digamia,* fr. LGk, fr. Gk *digamos* married to two people, fr. *di-* + *-gamos* -gamous] (1635) : a second marriage after the termination of the first

di·gas·tric \(,)dī-'gas-trik\ *adj* [NL *digastricus,* fr. *di-* + *gastricus* gastric] (ca. 1721) : of, relating to, or being a muscle with two bellies separated by a median tendon

di·ge·net·ic \,dī-jə-'ne-tik\ *adj* [NL *Digenetica,* subclass name (syn. of *Digenea),* fr. *di-* + *genetica,* neut. pl. of *geneticus* genetic] (ca. 1883) : of or relating to a subclass (Digenea) of trematode worms in which sexual reproduction as an internal parasite of a vertebrate alternates with asexual reproduction in a mollusk

\ə\ abut \ᵊ\ kitten, F table \ər\ further \a\ ash \ā\ ace \ä\ mop, mar \aú\ out \ch\ chin \e\ bet \ē\ easy \g\ go \i\ hit \ī\ ice \j\ job \ŋ\ sing \ō\ go \ò\ law \òi\ boy \th\ thin \t̲h̲\ the \ü\ loot \ù\ foot \y\ yet \zh\ vision \à, k̲, ⁿ, œ, œ̄, ɶ, ūᴇ, ᵊ\ *see* Guide to Pronunciation

¹**di·gest** \'dī-ˌjest\ *n* [ME, systematic arrangement of laws, fr. L *digesta*, fr. neut. pl. of *digestus*, pp. of *digerere* to arrange, distribute, digest, fr. *dis-* + *gerere* to carry] (14c) **1 :** a summation or condensation of a body of information: as **a :** a systematic compilation of legal rules, statutes, or decisions **b :** a periodical devoted to condensed versions of previously published articles **2 :** a product of digestion
²**di·gest** \di-'jest, də-\ *vb* [ME, fr. L *digestus*] *vt* (14c) **1 :** to distribute or arrange systematically : CLASSIFY **2 :** to convert (food) into absorbable form **3 :** to take into the mind or memory; *esp* : to assimilate mentally **4 a :** to soften, decompose, or break down by heat and moisture or chemicals **b :** to extract soluble ingredients from by warming with a liquid **5 :** to compress into a short summary **6 :** ABSORB 1 ⟨the capacity of the U. S. to ∼ immigrants⟩ ∼ *vi* **1 :** to digest food **2 :** to become digested
di·gest·er \-'jes-tər\ *n* (1614) **1 :** one that digests or makes a digest **2 :** a vessel for digesting esp. plant or animal materials
di·gest·ibil·i·ty \-ˌjes-tə-'bi-lə-tē\ *n, pl* **-ties** (1740) **1 :** the fitness of something for digestion **2 :** the percentage of a foodstuff taken into the digestive tract that is absorbed into the body
di·gest·ible \-'jes-tə-bəl\ *adj* (14c) **:** capable of being digested
di·ges·tion \di-'jes-chən, də-, -'jesh-\ *n* (14c) **:** the action, process, or power of digesting: as **a :** the process of making food absorbable by dissolving it and breaking it down into simpler chemical compounds that occurs in the living body chiefly through the action of enzymes secreted into the alimentary canal **b :** the process in sewage treatment by which organic matter in sludge is decomposed by anaerobic bacteria with the release of a burnable mixture of gases
¹**di·ges·tive** \-'jes-tiv\ *n* (14c) **:** an aid to digestion esp. of food
²**digestive** *adj* (15c) **1 :** relating to or functioning in digestion ⟨the ∼ system⟩ **2 :** having the power to cause or promote digestion ⟨∼ enzymes⟩ — **di·ges·tive·ly** *adv*
digestive gland *n* (1940) **:** a gland secreting digestive enzymes
dig·ger \'di-gər\ *n* (15c) **1 a :** one that digs **b :** a tool or machine for digging **2** *cap* **:** a No. American Indian (as a Paiute) who dug roots for food — usu. used disparagingly esp. formerly **3** *often cap, chiefly Austral & NewZeal* **:** an Australian or New Zealand soldier
digger wasp *n* (1880) **:** a burrowing wasp; *esp* : a usu. solitary wasp (superfamily Sphecoidea) that digs nest burrows in the soil and provisions them with insects or spiders paralyzed by stinging
dig·gings *n pl* (1538) **1 :** a place of excavating esp. for ore, metals, or precious stones **2 :** material dug out **3 a :** QUARTERS, PREMISES **b** *chiefly Brit* **:** lodgings for a student
dight \'dīt\ *vt* **dight·ed** *or* **dight; dight·ing** [ME, fr. OE *dihtan* to arrange, compose, fr. L *dictare* to dictate, compose] (13c) *archaic* **:** DRESS, ADORN
dig in *vt* (1839) **1 :** to cover or incorporate by burying ⟨dig in compost⟩ **2 :** to establish in a dug defensive position ⟨the platoon was well *dug in*⟩ ∼ *vi* **1 :** to establish a defensive position esp. by digging trenches **2 a :** to go resolutely to work **b :** to begin eating **3 :** to hold stubbornly to a position **4 :** to scuff the ground for better footing while batting (as in baseball) — **dig in one's heels** : to take or persist in an uncompromising position or attitude despite opposition
dig·it \'di-jət\ *n* [ME, fr. L *digitus* finger, toe; perh. akin to Gk *deiknynai* to show — more at DICTION] (14c) **1 a :** any of the Arabic numerals 1 to 9 and usu. the symbol 0 **b :** one of the elements that combine to form numbers in a system other than the decimal system **2 :** a unit of length based on the breadth of a finger and equal in English measure to ³/₄ inch **3 :** any of the divisions in which the limbs of amphibians and all higher vertebrates terminate, which are typically five in number but may be reduced (as in the horse), and which typically have a series of phalanges bearing a nail, claw, or hoof at the tip — compare FINGER 1, TOE 1a
dig·i·tal \'di-jə-t²l\ *adj* [L *digitalis*] (ca. 1656) **1 :** of or relating to the fingers or toes : DIGITATE **2 :** done with a finger **3 :** of, relating to, or using calculation by numerical methods or by discrete units **4 :** of or relating to data in the form of numerical digits **5 :** providing a readout in numerical digits ⟨a ∼ voltmeter⟩ **6 :** relating to an audio recording method in which sound waves are represented digitally (as on magnetic tape) so that in the recording wow and flutter are eliminated and background noise is reduced — **dig·i·tal·ly** \-t²l-ē\ *adv*
digital computer *n* (1947) **:** a computer that operates with numbers expressed directly as digits — compare ANALOG COMPUTER, HYBRID COMPUTER
dig·i·tal·in \ˌdi-jə-'ta-lən *also* -'tā-\ *n* [NL *Digitalis*] (1837) **1 :** a white crystalline steroid glycoside C₃₆H₅₆O₁₄ obtained from seeds esp. of the common foxglove **2 :** a mixture of the glycosides of digitalis leaves or seeds
dig·i·tal·is \-'ta-ləs *also* -'tā-\ *n* [NL, genus name, fr. L, of a finger, fr. *digitus;* fr. its finger-shaped corolla] (1664) **1 :** FOXGLOVE **2 :** the dried powdered leaf of the common foxglove containing cardiac glycosides and serving as a powerful cardiac stimulant and a diuretic
dig·i·ta·li·za·tion \ˌdi-jə-t²l-ə-'zā-shən\ *n* [*digitalis*] (1882) **:** the administration of digitalis until the desired physiological adjustment is attained; *also* : the bodily state so produced
¹**dig·i·ta·lize** \'di-jə-t²l-ˌīz\ *vt* **-lized; -liz·ing** [*digitalis*] (1927) **:** to subject to digitalization
²**dig·i·tal·ize** \'di-jə-t²l-ˌīz\ *vt* **-ized; -iz·ing** [*digital*] (1962) **:** DIGITIZE
dig·i·tate \'di-jə-ˌtāt\ *adj* (1661) **:** having divisions arranged like those of a bird's foot ⟨∼ leaves⟩ — **dig·i·tate·ly** *adv*
digiti- *comb form* [F, fr. L *digitus*] **:** digit : finger ⟨digitigrade⟩
dig·i·ti·grade \'di-jə-tə-ˌgrād\ *adj* [F, fr. *digiti-* + *-grade*] (ca. 1833) **:** walking on the digits with the posterior of the foot more or less raised
dig·i·tize \'di-jə-ˌtīz\ *vt* **-tized; -tiz·ing** (1953) **:** to convert (as data or an image) to digital form — **dig·i·ti·za·tion** \ˌdi-jə-tə-'zā-shən\ *n* — **dig·i·tiz·er** \'di-jə-ˌtī-zər\ *n*
dig·i·to·nin \ˌdi-jə-'tō-nən\ *n* [ISV *digit-* (fr. NL *Digitalis*) + *saponin*] (1875) **:** a steroid saponin C₅₆H₉₂O₂₉ occurring in the leaves and seeds of foxglove
digi·toxi·gen·in \ˌdi-jə-ˌtäk-sə-'je-nən\ *n* [ISV, blend of *digitoxin* and *-gen*] (ca. 1909) **:** a steroid lactone C₂₃H₃₄O₄ obtained esp. by hydrolysis of digitoxin
digi·tox·in \ˌdi-jə-'täk-sən\ *n* [ISV, blend of NL *Digitalis* and ISV *toxin*] (ca. 1883) **:** a poisonous glycoside C₄₁H₆₄O₁₃ that is the most

active constituent of digitalis; *also* : a mixture of digitalis glycosides consisting chiefly of digitoxin
di·glyc·er·ide \ˌdī-'gli-sə-ˌrīd\ *n* (1918) **:** an ester formed from glycerol by reacting two of its alcohol hydroxy groups with fatty acids
dig·ni·fied \'dig-nə-ˌfīd\ *adj* (1763) **:** showing or expressing dignity
dig·ni·fy \'dig-nə-ˌfī\ *vt* **-fied; -fy·ing** [MF *dignifier*, fr. LL *dignificare*, fr. L *dignus* worthy — more at DECENT] (15c) **1 :** to give distinction to : ENNOBLE **2 :** to confer dignity upon; *also* : to give undue attention or status to ⟨won't ∼ that remark with a reply⟩
dig·ni·tary \'dig-nə-ˌter-ē\ *n, pl* **-tar·ies** (1673) **:** one who possesses exalted rank or holds a position of dignity or honor — **dignitary** *adj*
dig·ni·ty \'dig-nə-tē\ *n, pl* **-ties** [ME *dignete*, fr. OF *digneté*, fr. L *dignitat-, dignitas,* fr. *dignus*] (13c) **1 :** the quality or state of being worthy, honored, or esteemed **2 a :** high rank, office, or position **b :** a legal title of nobility or honor **3** *archaic* **:** DIGNITARY **4 :** formal reserve or seriousness of manner, appearance, or language
dig out *vt* (14c) **1 :** FIND, UNEARTH **2 :** to make hollow by digging ∼ *vi* : TAKE OFF 2a
di·gox·in \di-'jäk-sən, -'gäk-\ *n* [ISV *dig-* (fr. NL *Digitalis*) + *toxin*] (ca. 1930) **:** a poisonous cardiotonic steroid C₄₁H₆₄O₁₄ obtained from a foxglove (*Digitalis lanata*) and used similarly to digitalis
di·graph \'dī-ˌgraf\ *n* (1780) **1 :** a group of two successive letters whose phonetic value is a single sound (as *ea* in *bread* or *ng* in *sing*) or whose value is not the sum of a value borne by each in other occurrences (as *ch* in *chin* where the value is \t\ + \sh\) **2 :** a group of two successive letters **3 :** LIGATURE 4 — **di·graph·ic** \dī-'gra-fik\ *adj* — **di·graph·i·cal·ly** \-fi-k(ə-)lē\ *adv*
di·gress \dī-'gres, də-\ *vi* [L *digressus,* pp. of *digredi,* fr. *dis-* + *gradi* to step — more at GRADE] (1530) **:** to turn aside esp. from the main subject of attention or course of argument ***syn*** see SWERVE
di·gres·sion \-'gre-shən\ *n* (14c) **1 :** the act or an instance of digressing in a discourse or other usu. organized literary work **2** *archaic* **:** a going aside — **di·gres·sion·al** \-'gresh-nəl, -ən-²l\ *adj* — **di·gres·sion·ary** \-'gre-shə-ˌner-ē\ *adj*
di·gres·sive \-'gre-siv\ *adj* (ca. 1611) **:** characterized by digressions ⟨a ∼ talk⟩ — **di·gres·sive·ly** *adv* — **di·gres·sive·ness** *n*
dig up *vt* (14c) **:** FIND, UNEARTH
di·he·dral \(ˌ)dī-'hē-drəl\ *n* (ca. 1911) **1 :** DIHEDRAL ANGLE **2 :** the angle between an aircraft supporting surface (as a wing) and a horizontal transverse line
dihedral angle *n* [*di-* + *-hedral*] (1826) **:** a figure formed by two intersecting planes
di·hy·brid \(ˌ)dī-'hī-brəd\ *adj* [ISV] (1907) **:** of, relating to, involving, or being an individual or strain that is heterozygous at two genetic loci — **dihybrid** *n*
dihydr- *or* **dihydro-** *comb form* **:** combined with two atoms of hydrogen ⟨*dihydro*ergotamine⟩
di·hy·dro·er·got·a·mine \(ˌ)dī-ˌhī-drō-ˌər-'gä-tə-ˌmēn\ *n* (1945) **:** a hydrogenated derivative C₃₃H₃₇N₅O₅ of ergotamine that is used in the treatment of migraine
dihydroxy- *comb form* **:** containing two hydroxyl groups ⟨*dihydroxy*acetone⟩
di·hy·droxy·ac·e·tone \ˌdī-hī-ˌdräk-sē-'a-sə-ˌtōn\ *n* (1895) **:** a glyceraldehyde isomer C₃H₆O₃ used esp. to stain the skin to resemble a tan
dik–dik \'dik-ˌdik\ *n, pl* **dik–diks** *or* **dik–dik** [origin unknown] (1883) **:** any of a genus (*Madoqua*) of small eastern African antelopes
¹**dike** \'dīk\ *n* [ME, prob. fr. ON *dík* ditch and MLG *dīk* dam; akin to OE *dīc* ditch — more at DITCH] (13c) **1 :** an artificial watercourse : DITCH **2 a :** a bank usu. of earth constructed to control or confine water : LEVEE **b :** a barrier preventing passage esp. of something undesirable **3 a :** a raised causeway **b :** a tabular body of igneous rock that has been injected while molten into a fissure

dik-dik

²**dike** *vt* **diked; dik·ing** (14c) **1 :** to surround or protect with a dike **2 :** to drain by a dike — **dik·er** *n*
³**dike** *var of* ²DYKE
dik·tat \dik-'tät\ *n* [G, lit., something dictated, fr. NL *dictatum,* fr. L, neut. of *dictatus,* pp. of *dictare* to dictate] (1933) **1 :** a harsh settlement unilaterally imposed (as on a defeated nation) **2 :** DECREE, ORDER
Di·lan·tin \dī-'lan-t²n, də-\ *trademark* — used for phenytoin
di·lap·i·date \də-'la-pə-ˌdāt\ *vb* **-dat·ed; -dat·ing** [L *dilapidatus,* pp. of *dilapidare* to squander, destroy, fr. *dis-* + *lapidare* to pelt with stones, fr. *lapid-, lapis* stone] *vt* (ca. 1570) **1 :** to bring into a condition of decay or partial ruin ⟨furniture is *dilapidated* by use —Janet Flanner⟩ **2** *archaic* **:** SQUANDER ∼ *vi* **:** to become dilapidated — **di·lap·i·da·tion** \-ˌla-pə-'dā-shən\ *n*
di·lap·i·dat·ed *adj* (ca. 1806) **:** decayed, deteriorated, or fallen into partial ruin esp. through neglect or misuse ⟨a ∼ old house⟩
di·lat·an·cy \dī-'lat-²n-sē, di-\ *n* (1885) **:** the property of being dilatant
di·lat·ant \-t²nt\ *adj* (1885) **:** increasing in viscosity and setting to a solid as a result of deformation by expansion, pressure, or agitation
di·la·ta·tion \ˌdi-lə-'tā-shən, ˌdī-\ *n* (14c) **1 :** amplification in writing or speech **2 a :** the condition of being stretched beyond normal dimensions esp. as a result of overwork, disease, or abnormal relaxation ⟨∼ of the heart⟩ ⟨∼ of the stomach⟩ **b :** DILATION 2 **3 :** the action of expanding : the state of being expanded **4 :** a dilated part or formation — **di·la·ta·tion·al** \-shnəl, -shə-n²l\ *adj*
di·late \'dī-ˌlāt, dī-\ *vb* **di·lat·ed; di·lat·ing** [ME, fr. MF *dilater,* fr. L *dilatare,* lit., to spread wide, fr. *dis-* + *latus* wide — more at LATITUDE] *vt* (14c) **1** *archaic* **:** to describe or set forth at length or in detail **2 :** to enlarge or expand in bulk or extent : DISTEND, WIDEN ∼ *vi* **1 :** to comment at length : DISCOURSE — usu. used with *on* or *upon* **2 :** to become wide : SWELL ***syn*** see EXPAND — **di·lat·abil·i·ty** \(ˌ)dī-ˌlā-tə-'bi-lə-tē\ *n* — **di·lat·able** \dī-'lā-tə-bəl, 'dī-, -\ *adj* — **di·la·tor** \dī-'lā-tər, 'dī-\ *n*

di·lat·ed \adj (15c) **1** : expanded laterally; esp : being flat and widened ⟨~ leaves⟩ **2** : expanded normally or abnormally in all dimensions

di·la·tion \dī-'lā-shən\ n (15c) **1** : the act or action of dilating : the state of being dilated : EXPANSION, DILATATION **2** : the action of stretching or enlarging an organ or part of the body

di·la·tive \dī-'lā-tiv, 'dī-,\ adj (1634) : causing dilation : tending to dilate

di·la·tom·e·ter \,dī-lə-'tä-mə-tər, ,dī-\ n [ISV] (ca. 1883) : an instrument for measuring expansion — **di·la·to·met·ric** \-tō-'me-trik\ adj — **di·la·tom·e·try** \-'tä-mə-trē\ n

dil·a·to·ry \'di-lə-,tōr-ē, -,tȯr-\ adj [ME, fr. LL dilatorius, fr. L differre (pp. dilatus) to postpone, differ — more at DIFFER, TOLERATE] (15c) **1** : tending or intended to cause delay ⟨~ tactics⟩ **2** : characterized by procrastination : TARDY ⟨~ in answering letters⟩ — **dil·a·to·ri·ly** \,di-lə-'tōr-ə-lē, -'tȯr-\ adv — **dil·a·to·ri·ness** \'di-lə-,tōr-ē-nəs, -,tȯr-\ n

dil·do \'dil-(,)dō\ n, pl **dildos** also **dildoes** [origin unknown] (ca. 1593) : an object serving as a penis substitute for vaginal insertion

di·lem·ma \də-'le-mə also dī-\ n [LL, fr. LGk dilēmmat-, dilēmma, prob. back-formation fr. Gk dilēmmatos involving two assumptions, fr. di- + lēmmat-, lēmma assumption — more at LEMMA] (1523) **1** : an argument presenting two or more equally conclusive alternatives against an opponent **2 a** : a usu. undesirable or unpleasant choice ⟨faces this ~: raise interest rates and slow the economy or lower them and risk serious inflation⟩ **b** : a situation involving such a choice ⟨here am I brought to a very pretty ~; I must commit murder or commit matrimony —George Farquhar⟩; broadly : PREDICAMENT ⟨lords and bailiffs were in a terrible ~ —G. M. Trevelyan⟩ **3 a** : a problem involving a difficult choice ⟨the ~ of "liberty versus order"—J. M. Burns⟩ **b** : a difficult or persistent problem ⟨unemployment . . . the great central ~ of our advancing technology —August Heckscher⟩ — **dil·em·mat·ic** \,di-lə-'ma-tik also -,dī-\ adj

usage Although some commentators insist that dilemma be restricted to instances in which the alternatives to be chosen are equally unsatisfactory, their concern is misplaced; the unsatisfactoriness of the options is usu. a matter of how the author presents them. What is distressing or painful about a dilemma is having to make a choice one does not want to make. The use of such adjectives as terrible, painful, and irreconcilable suggests that dilemma is losing some of its unpleasant force. There also seems to be a tendency esp. in sense 3b toward applying the word to less weighty problems ⟨solved their goaltending ~ —Pat Calabria⟩.

dil·et·tante \'di-lə-,tänt, -,tant; ,di-lə-'\ n, pl **-tantes** or **-tan·ti** \-'tän-tē, -'tan-tē\ [It, fr. prp. of dilettare to delight, fr. L dilectare — more at DELIGHT] (1748) **1** : an admirer or lover of the arts **2** : a person having a superficial interest in an art or a branch of knowledge : DABBLER syn see AMATEUR — **dilettante** adj — **dil·et·tant·ish** \-'tän-tish, -,tan-, ,di-lə-'\ adj — **dil·et·tan·tism** \-,tän-,ti-zəm, -,tan-, ,di-lə-'\ n

¹dil·i·gence \'di-lə-jən(t)s\ n [ME, fr. MF, fr. L diligentia, fr. diligent-, diligens] (14c) **1 a** : persevering application : ASSIDUITY **b** obs : SPEED, HASTE **2** : the attention and care legally expected or required of a person (as a party to a contract)

²di·li·gence \'di-lə-,zhäⁿs, 'di-lə-jən(t)s\ n [F, lit., haste, fr. MF, persevering application] (1742) : STAGECOACH

dil·i·gent \'di-lə-jənt\ adj [ME, fr. MF, fr. L diligent-, diligens, fr. prp. of diligere to esteem, love, fr. di- (fr. dis- apart) + legere to select — more at LEGEND] (14c) : characterized by steady, earnest, and energetic effort : PAINSTAKING syn see BUSY — **dil·i·gent·ly** adv

dill \'dil\ n [ME dile, fr. OE; akin to OHG tilli dill] (bef. 12c) **1** : any of several plants of the carrot family; esp : a European herb (Anethum graveolens) with aromatic foliage and seeds both of which are used in flavoring foods and esp. pickles **2** : DILL PICKLE — **dilled** adj

dill pickle n (1904) : a pickle seasoned with fresh dill or dill juice

dil·ly \'di-lē\ n, pl **dillies** [obs. dilly, adj. (delightful), perh. by shortening & alter. fr. delightful] (1935) : one that is remarkable or outstanding ⟨had a ~ of a story⟩ ⟨for a practical joke, that was a ~⟩

dil·ly bag \'di-lē-\ n [Jagara (Australian aboriginal language of Queensland) dili coarse grass, fiber bag] (1867) : an Australian mesh bag made of native fibers

dil·ly·dal·ly \'di-lē-,da-lē\ vi [redupl. of dally] (1741) : to waste time by loitering or delaying : DAWDLE

dil·u·ent \'dil-yə-wənt\ n [L diluent-, diluens, prp. of diluere] (ca. 1721) : a diluting agent (as the vehicle in a medicinal preparation)

¹di·lute \dī-'lüt, də-\ vt **di·lut·ed; di·lut·ing** [L dilutus, pp. of diluere to wash away, dilute, fr. di- + lavere to wash — more at LYE] (ca. 1555) **1** : ATTENUATE **2** : to make thinner or more liquid by admixture **3** : to diminish the strength, flavor, or brilliance of by admixture **4** : to decrease the per share value of (common stock) by increasing the total number of shares — **di·lut·er** or **di·lu·tor** \-'lü-tər\ n — **di·lu·tive** \-'lü-tiv\ adj

²dilute adj (1605) : WEAK, DILUTED — **di·lute·ness** n

di·lu·tion \dī-'lü-shən, də-\ n (1646) **1** : the action of diluting : the state of being diluted **2** : something (as a solution) that is diluted **3** : a lessening of real value (as of equity) by a decrease in relative worth; specif : a decrease of per share value of common stock by an increase in the total number of shares

di·lu·vi·al \də-'lü-vē-əl, dī-\ or **di·lu·vi·an** \-vē-ən\ adj [LL diluvialis, fr. L diluvium deluge — more at DELUGE] (ca. 1656) : of, relating to, or brought about by a flood

¹dim \'dim\ adj **dim·mer; dim·mest** [ME, fr. OE dimm; akin to OHG timber dark] (bef. 12c) **1 a** : emitting a limited or insufficient amount of light **b** : DULL, LUSTERLESS **c** : lacking pronounced, clear-cut, or vigorous quality or character **2 a** : seen indistinctly or without clear outlines or details **b** : perceived by the senses or mind indistinctly or weakly : FAINT ⟨had only a ~ notion of what was going on⟩ **c** : having little prospect of favorable result or outcome ⟨a ~ future⟩ **d** : characterized by an unfavorable, skeptical, or pessimistic attitude — usu. used in the phrase take a dim view of **3** : not perceiving clearly and distinctly ⟨~ eyes⟩ **4** : DIM-WITTED — **dim·ly** adv — **dim·ma·ble** \'di-mə-bəl\ adj — **dim·ness** n

²dim vb **dimmed; dim·ming** vt (bef. 12c) **1** : to make dim or lusterless **2** : to reduce the light from ~ vi : to become dim

³dim n (14c) **1** archaic : DUSK, DIMNESS **2** : LOW BEAM

dim bulb n (1927) slang : DIMWIT

dime \'dīm\ n [ME, tenth part, tithe, fr. MF, fr. L decima, fr. fem. of decimus tenth, fr. decem ten — more at TEN] (1786) **1 a** : a coin of the U.S. worth ¹/₁₀ dollar **b** : a petty sum of money **2** : a Canadian 10-cent piece — **a dime a dozen** : so plentiful or commonplace as to be of little esteem or slight value — **on a dime 1** : in a very small area ⟨these cars can turn on a dime⟩ **2** : INSTANTLY

di·men·hy·dri·nate \,dī-,men-'hī-drə-,nāt\ n [dimethyl + amine + hydr- + amine + ¹-ate] (ca. 1950) : a crystalline antihistaminic compound C₂₄H₂₈ClN₅O₃ used esp. to prevent nausea

dime novel n (1864) : a usu. paperback melodramatic novel; esp : one popular in the U.S. from about the mid-19th century to the early 20th often featuring a Western theme

¹di·men·sion \də-'men(t)-shən also dī-\ n [ME, fr. MF, fr. L dimension-, dimensio, fr. dimetiri to measure out, fr. dis- + metiri to measure — more at MEASURE] (14c) **1 a** (1) : measure in one direction; specif : one of three coordinates determining a position in space or four coordinates determining a position in space and time (2) : one of a group of properties whose number is necessary and sufficient to determine uniquely each element of a system of usu. mathematical entities (as an aggregate of points in real or abstract space) ⟨the surface of a sphere has two ~s⟩; also : a parameter or coordinate variable assigned to such a property ⟨the three ~s of momentum⟩ (3) : the number of elements in a basis of a vector space **b** : the quality of spatial extension : MAGNITUDE, SIZE **c** : a lifelike or realistic quality **d** : the range over which or the degree to which something extends : SCOPE — usu. used in pl. **e** : one of the elements or factors making up a complete personality or entity : ASPECT **2** obs : bodily form or proportions **3** : any of the fundamental units (as of mass, length, or time) on which a derived unit is based; also : the power of such a unit **4** : wood or stone cut to pieces of specified size **5** : a level of existence or consciousness — **di·men·sion·al** \-'mench-nəl, -'men(t)-shən-n¹l\ adj — **di·men·sion·al·i·ty** \-,men(t)-shə-'na-lə-tē\ n — **di·men·sion·al·ly** \-'mench-nə-lē, -'men(t)-shə-n¹l-ē\ adv — **di·men·sion·less** \-'men(t)-shən-ləs\ adj

²dimension vt **di·men·sioned; di·men·sion·ing** \-'men(t)-shə-niŋ\ (1754) **1** : to form to the required dimensions **2** : to indicate the dimensions of (as on a drawing)

di·mer \'dī-mər\ n [ISV] (ca. 1926) : a compound formed by the union of two radicals or two molecules of a simpler compound; specif : a polymer formed from two molecules of a monomer — **di·mer·ic** \(,)dī-'mer-ik\ adj — **di·mer·iza·tion** \,dī-mə-rə-'zā-shən\ n — **di·mer·ize** \'dī-mə-,rīz\ vt

di·mer·cap·rol \,dī-mər-'ka-,prȯl, -,prōl\ n [di- + mercaptan + propane + ¹-ol] (1947) : a compound C₃H₈OS₂ developed as an antidote against lewisite and used against arsenic, mercury, and gold poisoning — called also BAL

dime–store \'dīm-,stȯr, -,stȯr\ adj (1938) **1** : INEXPENSIVE ⟨~ perfume⟩ **2** : TAWDRY, SECOND-RATE ⟨~ philosophy⟩

dime store n (ca. 1928) : FIVE-AND-TEN

dim·e·ter \'di-mə-tər\ n [LL, fr. Gk dimetros, adj., being a dimeter, fr. di- + metron measure — more at MEASURE] (1589) : a line of verse consisting of two metrical feet or of two dipodies

di·meth·o·ate \dī-'me-thə-,wāt\ n [dimethyl + thio acid + ¹-ate] (1960) : an insecticide C₅H₁₂NO₃PS₂ used in agriculture and animal husbandry

dimethyl \,dī-'me-thəl\ adj : containing two methyl groups in the molecule — often used in combination

di·meth·yl·hy·dra·zine \,dī-,me-thəl-'hī-drə-,zēn\ n (1961) : either of two flammable corrosive isomeric liquids C₂H₈N₂ which are methylated derivatives of hydrazine and of which one is used as a rocket fuel

di·meth·yl·ni·tro·sa·mine \-nī-'trō-sə-,mēn\ n (1965) : a carcinogenic nitrosamine C₂H₆N₂O that occurs esp. in tobacco smoke

di·meth·yl sulfoxide n (1964) : a compound (CH₃)₂SO obtained as a by-product in wood-pulp manufacture and used as a solvent and in veterinary medicine as an anti-inflammatory — called also DMSO

di·meth·yl·tryp·ta·mine \-'trip-tə-,mēn\ n (1966) : a naturally occurring or easily synthesized hallucinogenic drug C₁₂H₁₆N₂ that is chemically similar to but shorter acting than psilocybin — called also DMT

di·min·ish \də-'mi-nish\ vb [ME deminishen, alter. of diminue, fr. MF diminuer, fr. LL diminuere, alter. of L deminuere, fr. de- + minuere to lessen — more at MINOR] vt (15c) **1** : to make less or cause to appear less **2** : to lessen the authority, dignity, or reputation of : BELITTLE **3** : to cause to taper ~ vi **1** : to become gradually less (as in size or importance) : DWINDLE **2** : TAPER syn see DECREASE — **di·min·ish·able** \-ni-shə-bəl\ adj — **di·min·ish·ment** \-mənt\ n

di·min·ished adj (ca. 1751) of a musical interval : made one half step less than perfect or minor ⟨a ~ fifth⟩

diminishing returns n pl (1815) : a rate of yield that beyond a certain point fails to increase in proportion to additional investments of labor or capital

di·min·u·en·do \də-,min-yə-'wen-(,)dō also -,mi-nə-'\ adv or adj [It, lit., diminishing, fr. LL diminuendum, gerund of diminuere] (1775) : DECRESCENDO — **diminuendo** n

dim·i·nu·tion \,di-mə-'nü-shən also -'nyü-\ n [ME diminucioun, fr. MF diminution, fr. ML diminution-, diminutio, alter. of L deminution-, deminutio, fr. deminuere] (14c) : the act, process, or an instance of diminishing : DECREASE

¹di·min·u·tive \də-'min-yə-tiv\ n [ME diminutif, fr. ML diminutivum, alter. of LL deminutivum, fr. neut. of deminutivus, adj., fr. deminutus, pp. of deminuere] (14c) **1** : a diminutive word, affix, or name **2** : a diminutive individual

²diminutive adj (14c) **1** : indicating small size and sometimes the state or quality of being familiarly known, lovable, pitiable, or contemptible — used of affixes (as -ette, -kin, -ling) and of words formed with them (as kitchenette, manikin, duckling), of clipped forms (as Jim), and of altered forms (as Peggy); compare AUGMENTATIVE **2** : exceptionally or notably small : TINY syn see SMALL — **di·min·u·tive·ly** adv — **di·min·u·tive·ness** n

---

\ə\ abut \ᵊ\ kitten, F table \ər\ further \a\ ash \ā\ ace \ä\ mop, mar \au̇\ out \ch\ chin \e\ bet \ē\ easy \g\ go \i\ hit \ī\ ice \j\ job \ŋ\ sing \ō\ go \ȯ\ law \ȯi\ boy \th\ thin \t̠h\ the \ü\ loot \u̇\ foot \y\ yet \zh\ vision \á, k̟, ⁿ, œ, œ̄, ue, ūe, ʸ\ see Guide to Pronunciation

dim·i·ty \'di-mə-tē\ *n, pl* **-ties** [alter. of ME *demyt*, fr. ML *dimitum*, fr. MGk *dimitos* of double thread, fr. Gk *di-* + *mitos* warp thread] (1570) : a sheer woven. corded cotton fabric of plain weave in checks or stripes

dim·mer \'di-mər\ *n* (ca. 1896) **1** : a device for regulating the intensity of an electric lighting unit **2** : LOW BEAM

di·mor·phic \(,)dī-'mȯr-fik\ *adj* (1859) **1 a** : DIMORPHOUS 1 **b** : occurring in two distinct forms ⟨~ leaves of emergent plants⟩ ⟨sexually ~ coloration in birds⟩ **2** : combining qualities of two kinds of individuals in one

di·mor·phism \-,fi-zəm\ *n* (1832) : the condition or property of being dimorphic or dimorphous: as **a** : the existence of two different forms (as of color or size) of a species esp. in the same population ⟨sexual ~⟩ **b** : the existence of an organ (as the leaves of a plant) in two different forms

di·mor·phous \(,)dī-'mȯr-fəs\ *adj* [Gk *dimorphos* having two forms, fr. *di-* + *-morphos* -morphous] (1832) **1** : crystallizing in two different forms **2** : DIMORPHIC 1b

dim·out \'dim-,aut\ *n* (1942) : a restriction limiting the use or showing of lights at night esp. during the threat of an air raid; *also* : a condition of partial darkness produced by this restriction

¹dim·ple \'dim-pəl\ *n* [ME *dympull*; akin to OHG *tumphilo* whirlpool, OE *dyppan* to dip — more at DIP] (15c) **1** : a slight natural indentation in the surface of some part of the human body **2** : a depression or indentation on a surface (as of a golf ball) — **dim·ply** \-p(ə-)lē\ *adj*

²dimple *vb* **dim·pled; dim·pling** \-p(ə-)liŋ\ *vt* (1602) : to mark with dimples ~ *vi* : to exhibit or form dimples

dim sum \'dim-'səm\ *n* [Chin (Guangdong) *dímsām*, fr. *dím* dot, speck + *sām* heart] (1948) : traditional Chinese food consisting of a variety of items (as steamed or fried dumplings, pieces of cooked chicken, and rice balls) served in small portions

dim·wit \'dim-,wit\ *n* (ca. 1922) : a stupid or mentally slow person

dim–wit·ted \-'wi-təd\ *adj* (1934) : not mentally bright : STUPID — **dim–wit·ted·ly** *adv* — **dim–wit·ted·ness** *n*

¹din \'din\ *n* [ME, fr. OE *dyne*; akin to ON *dynr* din, Skt *dhvanati* it roars] (bef. 12c) **1** : a loud continued noise; *esp* : a welter of discordant sounds **2** : a situation or condition resembling a din

²din *vb* **dinned; din·ning** *vi* (bef. 12c) : to make a loud noise ~ *vt* **1** : to assail with loud continued noise **2** : to impress by insistent repetition — often used with *into*

di·nar \di-'när, 'dē-,\ *n* [Ar *dīnār*, fr. LGk *dēnarion* denarius, fr. L *denarius* — more at DENIER] (1634) **1** : a gold coin formerly used in countries of southwest Asia and north Africa **2 a** — see MONEY table **b** — see *rial* at MONEY table

¹dine \'dīn\ *vb* **dined; din·ing** [ME, fr. OF *diner*, fr. (assumed) VL *disjejunare* to break one's fast, fr. L *dis-* + LL *jejunare* to fast, fr. L *jejunus* fasting] *vi* (13c) : to take dinner ~ *vt* : to give a dinner to

²dine *n* (15c) *Scot* : DINNER

dine out *vi* (1816) : to eat a meal away from home — **dine out on** : to use as a subject for dining table conversation

din·er \'dī-nər\ *n* (1815) **1** : one that dines **2 a** : DINING CAR **b** : a restaurant usu. resembling a dining car in shape

din·er–out \,dī-nə-'raut\ *n, pl* **di·ners–out** \-nər-'zaut\ (1808) : one who dines out

di·nette \dī-'net\ *n* (1925) : a small space usu. off a kitchen used for informal dining; *also* : furniture for such a space

¹ding \'diŋ\ *vb* [prob. imit.] *vt* (1582) : to dwell on with tiresome repetition ⟨keeps ~*ing* it into him that the less he smokes the better —Samuel Butler †1902⟩ ~ *vi* **1** : to make a ringing sound : CLANG **2** : to speak with tiresome reiteration

²ding *n* [*ding* (to strike), fr. ME *dingen*] (ca. 1945) : an instance of minor surface damage (as a dent)

ding–a–ling \'diŋ-ə-,liŋ\ *n* [redupl. of ¹*ding*] (ca. 1935) : NITWIT, KOOK

ding·bat \'diŋ-,bat\ *n* [origin unknown] (1904) **1** : a typographical symbol or ornament (as *, ¶, or ✠) **2** : NITWIT, KOOK

¹ding·dong \'diŋ-,dȯŋ, -,däŋ\ *n* [imit.] (1611) : the ringing sound produced by repeated strokes esp. on a bell

²dingdong *vi* (1659) **1** : to make a dingdong sound **2** : to repeat a sound or action tediously or insistently

³dingdong *adj* (1792) **1** : of, relating to, or resembling the ringing sound made by a bell **2** : marked by a rapid exchange or alternation

dinge \'dinj\ *n* [back-formation fr. *dingy*] (1846) : the condition of being dingy

ding·er \'diŋ-ər\ *n* [perh. fr. *ding* (to strike) + -²*er*] (1974) : HOME RUN

din·ghy \'diŋ-ē, -gē\ *n, pl* **dinghies** [Bengali *diṅgi* & Hindi *diṅgī*] (1810) **1** : an East Indian rowboat or sailboat **2 a** : a small boat carried on or towed behind a larger boat as a tender or a lifeboat **b** : a small sailboat **3** : a rubber life raft

din·gle \'diŋ-gəl\ *n* [ME, deep hollow] (13c) : a small wooded valley : DELL

din·gle·ber·ry \'diŋ-gəl-,ber-ē\ *n* [origin unknown] (1955) : a piece of dried fecal matter clinging to the hair around the anus

din·go \'diŋ-(,)gō\ *n, pl* **dingoes** [Dharuk (Australian aboriginal language of the Port Jackson area) *dingu*] (1789) : a reddish brown wild dog (*Canis dingo*) of Australia

din·gus \'diŋ-(g)əs\ *n* [D or G; D *dinges*, prob. fr. G *Dings*, fr. gen. of *Ding* thing, fr. OHG — more at THING] (1876) : DOODAD

din·gy \'din-jē\ *adj* **din·gi·er; -est** [origin unknown] (ca. 1736) **1** : DIRTY, DISCOLORED **2** : SHABBY, SQUALID — **din·gi·ly** \-jə-lē\ *adv* — **din·gi·ness** *n*

dining car *n* (1838) : a railroad car in which meals are served

dining room *n* (1601) : a room used for eating meals

di·ni·tro \(,)dī-'nī-trō\ *adj* : containing two nitro groups — often used in combination

di·ni·tro·ben·zene \(,)dī-,nī-trō-'ben-,zēn, -(,)ben-'\ *n* [ISV] (1873) : any of three isomeric toxic compounds $C_6H_4(NO_2)_2$

di·ni·tro·phe·nol \-'fē-,nōl, -fi-'\ *n* (ca. 1897) : any of six isomeric crystalline compounds $C_6H_4N_2O_5$ some of whose derivatives are pesticides

¹dink \'diŋk\ *n* [by shortening & alter.] (1903) : DINGHY

dingo

²dink *n* [*dink* (to hit with a drop shot), prob. of imit. origin] (1939) : DROP SHOT

³dink *n* [perh. fr. *dink*, disparaging name for a Vietnamese] (1974) *slang* : NITWIT, JERK, NERD

Din·ka \'diŋ-kə\ *n, pl* **Dinkas** *also* **Dinka** (1861) **1** : a member of a pastoral people of the Nile Valley in south central Sudan **2** : the Nilotic language of the Dinkas

din·key *or* **din·ky** \'diŋ-kē\ *n, pl* **dinkeys** *or* **dinkies** [prob. fr. *dinky*] (1874) : a small locomotive

¹din·kum \'diŋ-kəm\ *adj* [E dial. *dinkum*, n., work, share of work] (1905) *Austral & NewZeal* : AUTHENTIC, GENUINE — often used with *fair*

²dinkum *adv* (1915) *Austral & NewZeal* : TRULY, HONESTLY — often used with *fair*, often used interjectionally

din·ky \'diŋ-kē\ *adj* **din·ki·er; -est** [Sc *dink* neat] (1880) : SMALL 1a; *also* : INSIGNIFICANT

din·ner \'di-nər\ *n, often attrib* [ME *diner*, fr. OF, fr. *diner* to dine] (13c) **1 a** : the principal meal of the day **b** : a formal feast or banquet **2** : TABLE D'HÔTE 2 **3** : the food prepared for a dinner ⟨eat your ~⟩ **4** : a packaged meal usu. for quick preparation ⟨warmed up a frozen ~⟩ — **din·ner·less** \-ləs\ *adj*

dinner jacket *n* (1891) : a jacket for formal evening wear

dinner theater *n* (1960) : a restaurant in which a play is presented after the meal is over

din·ner·time \'di-nər-,tīm\ *n* (14c) : the customary time for dinner

din·ner·ware \-,war, -,wer\ *n* (1895) : tableware other than flatware

di·no·fla·gel·late \,dī-nō-'fla-jə-lət, -,lāt; -flə-'je-lət\ *n* [ultim. fr. Gk *dinos* rotation, eddy + NL *flagellum*] (1889) : any of an order (Dinoflagellata) of chiefly marine planktonic usu. solitary unicellular phytoflagellates that include luminescent forms, forms important in marine food chains, and forms causing red tide

di·no·saur \'dī-nə-,sȯr\ *n* [NL *Dinosaurus*, genus name, fr. Gk *deinos* terrifying + *sauros* lizard — more at DIRE] (1841) **1** : any of a group (Dinosauria) of extinct chiefly terrestrial carnivorous or herbivorous reptiles of the Mesozoic era **2** : any of various large extinct reptiles other than the true dinosaurs **3** : one that is impractically large, outof-date, or obsolete — **di·no·sau·ri·an** \,dī-nə-'sȯr-ē-ən\ *adj*

¹dint \'dint\ *n* [ME, fr. OE *dynt*; akin to ON *dyntr* noise] (bef. 12c) **1** *archaic* : BLOW, STROKE **2** : FORCE, POWER **3** : ²DENT — **by dint of** : by force of : BECAUSE OF

²dint *vt* (1597) **1** : to make a dent in **2** : to impress or drive in with force

di·nu·cle·o·tide \(,)dī-'n(y)ü-klē-ə-,tīd\ *n* (ca. 1927) : a nucleotide consisting of two units each composed of a phosphate, a pentose, and a nitrogen base

di·oc·e·san \dī-'ä-sə-sən *also* 'dī-ə-,sē-s²n\ *n* (15c) : a bishop having jurisdiction over a diocese

di·o·cese \'dī-ə-səs, -,sēs, -,sēz\ *n, pl* **-ces·es** \'dī-ə-sə-səz, -,sē-zəz, ÷'dī-ə-,sēz\ [ME *diocise*, fr. MF, fr. LL *diocesis*, alter. of *dioecesis*, fr. L, administrative division, fr. Gk *dioikēsis* administration, administrative division, fr. *dioikein* to keep house, govern, fr. *dia-* + *oikein* to dwell, manage, fr. *oikos* house — more at VICINITY] (14c) : the territorial jurisdiction of a bishop — **di·oc·e·san** \dī-'ä-sə-sən *also* 'dī-ə-,sē-s²n\ *adj*

di·ode \'dī-,ōd\ *n* [ISV] (1919) : an electronic device that has two electrodes or terminals and is used esp. as a rectifier

di·oe·cious \(,)dī-'ē-shəs\ *adj* [ultim. fr. Gk *di-* + *oikos*] (1752) **1** : having male reproductive organs in one individual and female in another **2** : having staminate and pistillate flowers borne on different individuals — **di·oe·cism** \-'ē-,si-zəm\ *n* — **di·oe·cy** \'dī-,ē-sē\ *n*

di·ol \'dī-,ōl, -,ȯl\ *n* [ISV] (1923) : a compound containing two hydroxyl groups

di·ole·fin \dī-'ō-lə-fən\ *n* [ISV] (ca. 1909) : DIENE

Di·o·me·des \,dī-ə-'mē-dēz\ *n* [L, fr. Gk *Diomēdēs*] : one of the Greek heroes of the Trojan War

Di·o·ny·sia \,dī-ə-'ni-zhē-ə, -'nē-, -shē-, -zē-, -sē-\ *n pl* [L, fr. Gk, fr. neut. pl. of *dionysios* of Dionysus, fr. *Dionysos*] (ca. 1895) : ancient Greek festival observances held in seasonal cycles in honor of Dionysus; *esp* : such observances marked by dramatic performances

Di·o·ny·si·ac \-'ni-zhē-,ak, -'nē-, -shē-, -zē-, -sē-\ *adj* [L *dionysiacus*, fr. Gk *dionysiakos*, fr. *Dionysos*] (1844) : DIONYSIAN 2

Di·o·ny·sian \-'ni-zhē-ən, -'nē-, -shē-, -zē-, -zhən, -shən\ *adj* (1607) **1 a** : of or relating to Dionysius **b** : of or related to the theological writings once mistakenly attributed to Dionysius the Areopagite **2 a** : devoted to the worship of Dionysus **b** : characteristic of Dionysus or the cult of worship of Dionysus; *esp* : being of a frenzied or orgiastic character — compare APOLLONIAN

Di·o·ny·sus \,dī-ə-'ni-səs, -'nē-\ *n* [L, fr. Gk *Dionysos*] : BACCHUS

Di·o·phan·tine equation \,dī-ə-'fan-,tīn-, -'fan-t²n-\ *n* [*Diophantus*, 3d cent. A.D. Gk mathematician] (ca. 1928) : an indeterminate polynomial equation with integral coefficients for which it is required to find all integral solutions

di·op·side \dī-'äp-,sīd\ *n* [F, fr. *di-* + Gk *opsis* appearance — more at OPTIC] (ca. 1808) : a green to white mineral that consists of pyroxene containing little or no aluminum — **di·op·sid·ic** \,dī-,äp-'si-dik\ *adj*

di·op·ter \dī-'äp-tər, 'dī-,äp-\ *n* [*diopter* (an optical instrument), fr. MF *dioptre*, fr. L *dioptra*, fr. Gk, fr. *dia-* + *opsesthai* to be going to see — more at OPTIC] (ca. 1864) : a unit of measurement of the refractive power of lenses equal to the reciprocal of the focal length in meters

di·op·tric \dī-'äp-trik\ *adj* [Gk *dioptrikos* of a diopter (instrument), fr. *dioptra*] (1653) : REFRACTIVE; *specif* : assisting vision by refracting and focusing light

di·o·ra·ma \,dī-ə-'ra-mə, -'rä-\ *n* [F, fr. *dia-* + *-orama* (as in *panorama*, fr. E)] (1823) **1** : a scenic representation in which a partly translucent painting is seen from a distance through an opening **2 a** : a scenic representation in which sculptured figures and lifelike details are displayed usu. in miniature so as to blend indistinguishably with a realistic painted background **b** : a life-size exhibit (as of a wildlife specimen or scene) with realistic natural surroundings and a painted background — **di·oram·ic** \-'ra-mik\ *adj*

di·o·rite \'dī-ə-,rīt\ *n* [F, irreg. fr. Gk *diorizein* to distinguish, fr. *dia-* + *horizein* to define — more at HORIZON] (1826) : a granular crystalline igneous rock commonly of acid plagioclase and hornblende, pyroxene, or biotite — **di·o·rit·ic** \,dī-ə-'ri-tik\ *adj*

Di·os·cu·ri \,dī-əs-'kyu̇(ə)r-,ī, dī-'äs-kyə-,rī\ *n pl* [NL, fr. Gk *Dios-*

kouroi, lit., sons of Zeus, fr. *Dios* (gen. of *Zeus;* akin to L *divus* divine) + *kouroi,* pl. of *kouros, koros* boy — more at DEITY, CRESCENT] : the twins Castor and Pollux reunited as stars in the sky by Zeus after Castor's death and regarded as patrons of athletes and sailors

di·ox·ane \dī-ˈäk-ˌsān\ *also* **di·ox·an** \-ˌsan, -sən\ *n* [ISV] (1912) : a flammable toxic liquid diether $C_4H_8O_2$ used esp. as a solvent

di·ox·ide \(ˌ)dī-ˈäk-ˌsīd\ *n* [ISV] (ca. 1847) : an oxide (as carbon dioxide) containing two atoms of oxygen in the molecule

di·ox·in \(ˌ)dī-ˈäk-sən\ *n* (ca. 1919) : any of several heterocyclic hydrocarbons that occur esp. as persistent toxic impurities in herbicides; *esp* : TCDD

¹**dip** \ˈdip\ *vb* **dipped; dip·ping** [ME *dippen,* fr. OE *dyppan;* akin to OHG *tupfen* to wash, Lith *dubus* deep] *vt* (bef. 12c) **1 a** : to plunge or immerse momentarily or partially under the surface (as of a liquid) so as to moisten, cool, or coat ⟨~ candles⟩ **b** : to thrust in a way to suggest immersion **c** : to immerse (as a sheep or dog) in an antiseptic or parasiticidal solution **2 a** : to lift a portion of by reaching below the surface with something shaped to hold liquid : LADLE **b** : to take a portion of (snuff) **3 a** *archaic* : INVOLVE **b** : MORTGAGE **4 a** : to lower and then raise again ⟨~ a flag in salute⟩ **b** *chiefly Brit* : DIM 2 ~ *vi* **1 a** : to plunge into a liquid and quickly emerge **b** : to immerse something into a processing liquid or finishing material **2 a** : to suddenly drop down or out of sight **b** *of an airplane* : to drop suddenly before climbing **c** : to decline or decrease moderately and usu. temporarily ⟨prices *dipped*⟩ **d** : to lower the body momentarily esp. as part of an athletic or dancing motion **3 a** : to reach down inside or below or as if inside or below a surface esp. to withdraw a part of the contents — used with *into* ⟨*dipped* into the family's savings⟩ **4** : to examine or read something casually or superficially — used with *into* **5** : to incline downward from the plane of the horizon — **dip·pable** \ˈdi-pə-bəl\ *adj*

²**dip** *n* (1599) **1 a** : an act of dipping; *esp* : a brief plunge into the water for sport or exercise **2** : inclination downward: **a** : PITCH **b** : a sharp downward course : DROP **c** : the angle that a stratum or similar geological feature makes with a horizontal plane **3** : the angle formed with the horizon by a magnetic needle free to rotate in the vertical plane **4** : HOLLOW, DEPRESSION **5** : something obtained by or used in dipping **6 a** : a sauce or soft mixture into which food may be dipped **b** : a liquid preparation for the dipping of something; *esp* : an insecticide or parasiticide for the dipping of animals — compare SHEEP-DIP **7** *slang* : PICKPOCKET **8** : a stupid or unsophisticated person

di·pep·ti·dase \dī-ˈpep-tə-ˌdās, -ˌdāz\ *n* (1927) : any of various enzymes that hydrolyze dipeptides but not polypeptides

di·pep·tide \(ˌ)dī-ˈpep-ˌtīd\ *n* (1903) : a peptide that yields two molecules of amino acid on hydrolysis

di·pha·sic \(ˌ)dī-ˈfā-zik\ *adj* (1881) : having two phases

di·phen·hy·dra·mine \ˌdī-ˌfen-ˈhī-drə-ˌmēn\ *n* (1948) : an antihistamine $C_{17}H_{21}NO$ used esp. in the form of its hydrochloride to treat allergy symptoms and motion sickness

di·phe·nyl·amine \(ˌ)dī-ˌfe-nᵊl-ə-ˈmēn, -ˌfē-, -nᵊl-ˈa-mən\ *n* [ISV] (1872) : a crystalline pleasant-smelling compound $(C_6H_5)_2NH$ used chiefly in the manufacture of dyes and as an indicator

di·phe·nyl·hy·dan·to·in \-hī-ˈdan-tə-wən\ *n* [*di-* + *phenyl* + *hydrogen* + all*antoin*] (1937) : PHENYTOIN

di·phos·gene \(ˌ)dī-ˈfäz-ˌjēn\ *n* [ISV] (ca. 1922) : a liquid compound $C_2Cl_4O_2$ used as a poison gas in World War I

di·phos·phate \(ˌ)dī-ˈfäs-ˌfāt\ *n* (1826) : a phosphate containing two phosphate groups

di·phos·pho·gly·cer·ic acid \(ˌ)dī-ˌfäs-fō-gli-ˌser-ik-\ *n* (1959) : a diphosphate of glyceric acid that is an important intermediate in photosynthesis and in glycolysis and fermentation

di·phos·pho·pyr·i·dine nucleotide \-ˌpir-ə-ˌdēn-\ *n* (1938) : NAD

diph·the·ria \dif-ˈthir-ē-ə, *÷*dip-\ *n* [NL, fr. F *diphthérie,* fr. Gk *diphthera* leather; fr. the toughness of the false membrane] (ca. 1851) : an acute febrile contagious disease marked by the formation of a false membrane esp. in the throat and caused by a bacterium (*Corynebacterium diphtheriae*) that produces a toxin causing inflammation of the heart and nervous system — **diph·the·ri·al** \-ē-əl\ *adj* — **diph·the·rit·ic** \ˌdif-thə-ˈri-tik, *÷*ˌdip-\ *adj*

¹**diph·the·roid** \ˈdif-thə-ˌröid\ *adj* (1861) : resembling diphtheria

²**diphtheroid** *n* (1908) : a bacterium (esp. genus *Corynebacterium*) that resembles the bacterium of diphtheria but does not produce diphtheria toxin

diph·thong \ˈdif-ˌthȯŋ, ˈdip-\ *n* [ME *diptonge,* fr. MF *diptongue,* fr. LL *diphthongus,* fr. Gk *diphthongos,* fr. *di-* + *phthongos* voice, sound] (15c) **1** : a gliding monosyllabic speech sound (as the vowel combination at the end of *toy*) that starts at or near the articulatory position for one vowel and moves to or toward the position of another **2** : DIGRAPH **3** : the ligature æ or œ — **diph·thon·gal** \dif-ˈthȯŋ-(g)əl, dip-\ *adj*

diph·thong·i·za·tion \(ˌ)dif-ˌthȯŋ-ə-ˈzā-shən, (ˌ)dip-\ *n* (1874) : the act of diphthongizing : the state of being diphthongized

diph·thong·ize \ˈdif-ˌthȯŋ-ˌīz, ˈdip-\ *vb* **-ized; -iz·ing** *vi* (1867) *of a simple vowel* : to change into a diphthong ~ *vt* : to pronounce as a diphthong

diphy- *or* **diphyo-** *comb form* [NL, fr. Gk *diphy-,* fr. *diphyēs,* fr. *di-* + *phyein* to bring forth — more at BE] : double : bipartite ⟨*diphy*odont⟩

di·phy·let·ic \ˌdī-fī-ˈle-tik\ *adj* (1902) : derived from two lines of evolutionary descent ⟨~ dinosaurs⟩

di·phy·odont \(ˌ)dī-ˈfī-ə-ˌdänt\ *adj* [ISV] (1854) : marked by the successive development of deciduous and permanent sets of teeth

dipl- *or* **diplo-** *comb form* [Gk, fr. *diploos* — more at DOUBLE] **1** : double : twofold ⟨*diplopia*⟩ **2** : diploid ⟨*diplophase*⟩

di·ple·gia \dī-ˈplē-j(ē-)ə\ *n* [NL] (ca. 1881) : paralysis of corresponding parts on both sides of the body

dip·lo·blas·tic \ˌdip-lō-ˈblas-tik\ *adj* (ca. 1885) : having two germ layers — used of an embryo or lower invertebrate that lacks a true mesoderm

dip·lo·coc·cus \-ˈkä-kəs\ *n* (ca. 1881) : any of various encapsulated bacteria (as *Streptococcus pneumoniae,* a common cause of pneumonia) that usu. occur in pairs and that were formerly grouped in a single taxon (genus *Diplococcus*) but are now all assigned to other genera

di·plod·o·cus \də-ˈplä-də-kəs, dī-\ *n* [NL, genus name, fr. *dipl-* + Gk *dokos* beam, fr. *dekesthai, dechesthai* to receive; akin to L *decēre* to be

fitting — more at DECENT] (1928) : any of a genus (*Diplodocus*) of large herbivorous sauropod dinosaurs of the late Jurassic period in Colorado and Wyoming

dip·loe \ˈdi-plə-ˌwē\ *n* [NL, fr. Gk *diploē,* fr. *diploos* double] (ca. 1696) : cancellous bony tissue between the external and internal layers of the skull — **di·plo·ic** \di-ˈplō-ik, dī-\ *adj*

¹**dip·loid** \ˈdi-ˌplȯid\ *adj* [ISV] (1908) : having the basic chromosome number doubled — **dip·loi·dy** \-ˌplȯi-dē\ *n*

²**diploid** *n* (1908) : a single cell, individual, or generation characterized by the diploid chromosome number

di·plo·ma \də-ˈplō-mə\ *n, pl* **diplomas** [L, passport, diploma, fr. Gk *diplōma* folded paper, passport, fr. *diploun* to double, fr. *diploos*] (1622) **1** *pl also* **di·plo·ma·ta** \-mə-tə\ : an official or state document : CHARTER **2** : a writing usu. under seal conferring some honor or privilege **3** : a document bearing record of graduation from or of a degree conferred by an educational institution

di·plo·ma·cy \də-ˈplō-mə-sē\ *n* (1796) **1** : the art and practice of conducting negotiations between nations **2** : skill in handling affairs without arousing hostility : TACT

diploma mill *n* (1914) : a usu. unregulated institution of higher education granting degrees with few or no academic requirements

dip·lo·mat \ˈdi-plə-ˌmat\ *n* [F *diplomate,* back-formation fr. *diplomatique*] (1813) : one employed or skilled in diplomacy

dip·lo·mate \ˈdi-plə-ˌmāt\ *n* (1879) : one who holds a diploma; *esp* : a physician qualified to practice in a medical specialty by advanced training and experience in the specialty followed by passing an intensive examination by a national board of senior specialists

dip·lo·mat·ic \ˌdi-plə-ˈma-tik\ *adj* [in sense 1, fr. NL *diplomaticus,* fr. L *diplomat-, diploma;* in other senses, fr. F *diplomatique* connected with documents regulating international relations, fr. NL *diplomaticus*] (1711) **1 a** : PALEOGRAPHIC **b** : exactly reproducing the original ⟨a ~ edition⟩ **2** : of, relating to, or concerned with diplomacy or diplomats ⟨~ relations⟩ **3** : employing tact and conciliation esp. in situations of stress *syn* see SUAVE — **dip·lo·mat·i·cal·ly** \-ti-k(ə-)lē\ *adv*

di·plo·ma·tist \də-ˈplō-mə-tist\ *n* (1815) : DIPLOMAT

dip·lont \ˈdi-ˌplänt\ *n* [ISV] (1925) : an organism with somatic cells having the diploid chromosome number — compare HAPLONT — **dip·lon·tic** \dī-ˈplän-tik\ *adj*

dip·lo·phase \ˈdi-plə-ˌfāz\ *n* (ca. 1925) : a diploid phase in a life cycle

dip·lo·pia \di-ˈplō-pē-ə\ *n* [NL] (ca. 1811) : a disorder of vision in which two images of a single object are seen because of unequal action of the eye muscles — called also *double vision* — **dip·lo·pic** \-ˈplō-pik, -ˈplä-pik\ *adj*

dip·lo·pod \ˈdi-plə-ˌpäd\ *n* [ultim. fr. Gk *dipl-* + *pod-, pous* foot — more at FOOT] (ca. 1864) : MILLIPEDE

dip·lo·tene \ˈdi-plə-ˌtēn\ *n* [ISV] (1925) : a stage of meiotic prophase which follows the pachytene and during which the paired homologous chromosomes begin to separate and chiasmata become visible — **diplotene** *adj*

dip net *n* (1820) : a bag net with a handle that is used esp. to scoop fish from the water — **dip-net** \ˈdip-ˌnet\ *vt*

dip·no·an \ˈdip-nə-wən\ *adj* [ultim. fr. Gk *dipnoos* having two breathing apertures, fr. *di-* + *pnoē* breath, fr. *pnein* to breathe — more at SNEEZE] (1883) : of or relating to a group (Dipnoi) of fishes with pulmonary circulation, gills, and lungs — **dipnoan** *n*

dip·o·dy \ˈdi-pə-dē\ *n, pl* **-dies** [LL *dipodia,* fr. Gk, fr. *dipod-, dipous* having two feet, fr. *di-* + *pod-, pous*] (ca. 1844) : a prosodic unit or measure of two feet — **di·pod·ic** \dī-ˈpä-dik\ *adj*

di·pole \ˈdī-ˌpōl\ *n* [ISV] (1912) **1 a** : a pair of equal and opposite electric charges or magnetic poles of opposite sign separated esp. by a small distance **b** : a body or system (as a molecule) having such charges **2** : a radio antenna consisting of two horizontal rods in line with each other with their ends slightly separated — **di·po·lar** \ˈdī-ˌpō-lər, dī-ˈpō-\ *adj*

dipole moment *n* (1926) : the product of the distance between the two poles (as magnetic or electric) of a dipole and the magnitude of either pole

dip·per \ˈdi-pər\ *n* (1611) **1** : one that dips: as **a** : a worker who dips articles **b** : something (as a long-handled cup) used for dipping **c** *slang* : PICKPOCKET **2** : any of a genus (*Cinclus* and esp. *C. cinclus* of the Old World and *C. mexicanus* of No. America) of birds that comprise an oscine family (Cinclidae) related to the thrushes and including individuals that are not web-footed but dive into swift mountain streams and walk on the bottom in search of food — called also *water ouzel* **3** *cap* : a group of stars that resembles a dipper: as **a** : BIG DIPPER **b** : LITTLE DIPPER — **dip·per·ful** \-ˌfu̇l\ *n*

dip·py \ˈdi-pē\ *adj* **dip·pi·er; -est** [origin unknown] (1911) : FOOLISH

dip·so \ˈdi-p(ˌ)sō\ *n, pl* **dipsos** [by shortening] (1880) : one affected with dipsomania

dip·so·ma·nia \ˌdip-sə-ˈmā-nē-ə, -nyə\ *n* [NL, fr. Gk *dipsa* thirst + LL *mania*] (ca. 1844) : an uncontrollable craving for alcoholic liquors — **dip·so·ma·ni·ac** \-nē-ˌak\ *n* — **dip·so·ma·ni·a·cal** \ˌdip-sō-mə-ˈnī-ə-kəl\ *adj*

dip·stick \ˈdip-ˌstik\ *n* (1927) : a graduated rod for indicating depth (as of oil in a crankcase)

dip·ter·an \ˈdip-tə-rən\ *adj* [ultim. fr. Gk *dipteros* two-winged, fr. *di-* + *pteron* wing — more at FEATHER] (1842) : of, relating to, or being a fly (sense 2a) — **dipteran** *n* — **dip·ter·ous** \ˈdip-t(ə-)rəs\ *adj*

dip·tero·carp \ˈdip-tə-rō-ˌkärp\ *n* [ultim. fr. Gk *dipteros* + *-karpos* -carpous] (ca. 1876) : any of a family (Dipterocarpaceae) of tall hardwood trees of tropical Asia, Indonesia, and the Philippines that have a 2-winged fruit and are the source of valuable timber, aromatic oils, and resins; *esp* : a member of the type genus (*Dipterocarpus*)

dip·ter·on \ˈdip-tə-ˌrän\ *n, pl* **-tera** \-rə\ [Gk, neut. of *dipteros*] (ca. 1891) : ⁴FLY 2a

dip·tych \ˈdip-(ˌ)tik\ *n* [LL *diptycha,* pl., fr. Gk *diptycha,* neut. pl. of *diptychos* folded in two, fr. *di-* + *ptychē* fold] (1622) **1** : a 2-leaved hinged tablet

\ə\ abut \ᵊ\ kitten, F table \ər\ further \a\ ash \ā\ ace \ä\ mop, mar \au̇\ out \ch\ chin \e\ bet \ē\ easy \g\ go \i\ hit \ī\ ice \j\ job \ŋ\ sing \ō\ go \ȯ\ law \ȯi\ boy \th\ thin \t̲h̲\ the \ü\ loot \u̇\ foot \y\ yet \zh\ vision \ä, k̲, ⁿ, œ, œ̄, ᵫ, ᵫ̄, ᵊ\ see Guide to Pronunciation folding together to protect writing on its waxed surfaces **2** : a picture or series of pictures (as an altarpiece) painted or carved on two hinged tablets **3** : a work made up of two matching parts

di·quat \'dī-ˌkwät\ *n* [*di-* + *quaternary*] (1960) : a powerful nonpersistent herbicide $C_{12}H_{12}Br_2N_2$ that has been used to control water weeds (as the water hyacinth)

dir·dum \'dir-dəm, 'dər-\ *n* [ME (northern dial.) *durdan, durdum* uproar, fr. Celt; akin to W *dwrdd* noise, clamor, MIr *dordán* humming, droning] (ca. 1693) *Scot* : BLAME

dire \'dīr\ *adj* **dir·er; dir·est** [L *dirus*; akin to Gk *deinos* terrifying, Skt *dvesti* he hates] (1567) **1 a** : exciting horror ⟨~ suffering⟩ **b** : DISMAL, OPPRESSIVE ⟨~ days⟩ **2** : warning of disaster ⟨a ~ forecast⟩ **3 a** : desperately urgent ⟨~ need⟩ **b** : EXTREME ⟨~ poverty⟩ — **dire·ly** *adv* — **dire·ness** *n*

diptych 2

¹di·rect \də-'rekt, dī-\ *vb* [ME, fr. L *directus* straight, fr. pp. of *dirigere* to direct — more at DRESS] *vt* (14c) **1 a** *obs* : to write (a letter) to a person **b** : to mark with the name and address of the intended recipient **c** : to impart orally **d** : to adapt in expression so as to have particular applicability ⟨a lawyer who ~s his appeals to intelligence⟩ **2 a** : to regulate the activities or course of **b** : to carry out the organizing, energizing, and supervising of **c** : to dominate and determine the course of **d** : to train and lead performances of **3** : to cause to turn, move, or point undeviatingly or to follow a straight course ⟨X rays are ~ed through the body⟩ **4** : to point, extend, or project in a specified line or course **5** : to request or enjoin with authority **6** : to show or point out the way for ~ *vi* **1** : to point out, prescribe, or determine a course or procedure **2** : to act as director **syn** see COMMAND, CONDUCT

²direct *adj* [ME, fr. L *directus*] (15c) **1** *of a celestial body* : moving in the general planetary direction from west to east : not retrograde **2 a** : stemming immediately from a source ⟨~ result⟩ **b** : being or passing in a straight line of descent from parent to offspring : LINEAL ⟨~ ancestor⟩ **c** : having no compromising or impairing element ⟨~ insult⟩ **3 a** : proceeding from one point to another in time or space without deviation or interruption : STRAIGHT **b** : proceeding by the shortest way ⟨the ~ route⟩ **4** : NATURAL, STRAIGHTFORWARD ⟨~ manner⟩ **5 a** : marked by absence of an intervening agency, instrumentality, or influence **b** : effected by the action of the people or the electorate and not by representatives ⟨~ democracy⟩ **c** : consisting of or reproducing the exact words of a speaker or writer **6** : characterized by close logical, causal, or consequential relationship ⟨~ evidence⟩ **7** : capable of dyeing without the aid of a mordant

³direct *adv* (14c) : in a direct way: as **a** : from point to point without deviation : by the shortest way ⟨flew ~ to Miami⟩ **b** : from the source without interruption or diversion ⟨the writer must take his material ~ from life —Douglas Stewart⟩ **c** : without an intervening agency or step ⟨buy ~ from the manufacturer⟩

direct action *n* (1912) : action that seeks to attain an end directly and by the most immediately effective means (as boycott or strike)

direct current *n* (ca. 1889) : an electric current flowing in one direction only and substantially constant in value — abbr. *DC*

di·rect·ed *adj* (1891) **1** : subject to supervision or regulation ⟨a ~ reading program for students⟩ **2** : having a positive or negative sense ⟨~ line segment⟩ — **di·rect·ed·ness** *n*

direct examination *n* (ca. 1859) : the first examination of a witness by the party calling the witness — compare CROSS-EXAMINATION

di·rec·tion \də-'rek-shən, dī-\ *n* (15c) **1** : guidance or supervision of action or conduct : MANAGEMENT **2** *archaic* : SUPERSCRIPTION **3 a** : an explicit instruction : ORDER **b** : assistance in pointing out the proper route — usu. used in pl. ⟨asked for ~s to the beach⟩ **4** : the line or course on which something is moving or is aimed to move or along which something is pointing or facing **5** *archaic* : DIRECTORATE **1 6 a** : a channel or direct course of thought or action **b** : TENDENCY, TREND **c** : a guiding, governing, or motivating purpose **7 a** : the art and technique of directing an orchestra, band, or a show (as for stage or screen) **b** : a word, phrase, or sign indicating the appropriate tempo, mood, or intensity of a passage or movement in music — **di·rec·tion·less** \-ləs\ *adj* — **di·rec·tion·less·ness** \-nəs\ *n*

di·rec·tion·al \-shnəl, -shə-nⁿl\ *adj* (1881) **1** : of, relating to, or indicating direction in space: **a** : suitable for detecting the direction from which radio signals come or for sending out radio signals in one direction only **b** : operating most effectively in a particular direction **2** : relating to direction or guidance esp. of thought or effort — **di·rec·tion·al·i·ty** \-ˌrek-shə-'na-lə-tē\ *n*

direction angle *n* (ca. 1909) : an angle made by a given line with an axis of reference; *specif* : such an angle made by a straight line with the three axes of a rectangular Cartesian coordinate system — usu. used in pl.

direction cosine *n* (ca. 1889) : any of the cosines of the three angles between a directed line in space and the positive direction of the axes of a rectangular Cartesian coordinate system — usu. used in pl.

direction finder *n* (1913) : a radio receiving device for determining the direction of incoming radio waves that typically consists of a coil antenna rotating freely on a vertical axis

¹di·rec·tive \də-'rek-tiv, dī-\ *adj* (15c) **1** : serving or intended to guide, govern, or influence **2** : serving to point direction; *specif* : DIRECTIONAL **1b 3** : of or relating to psychotherapy or counseling in which the counselor introduces information, content, or attitudes not previously expressed by the client

²directive *n* (1902) : something that serves to direct, guide, and usu. impel toward an action or goal; *esp* : an authoritative instrument issued by a high-level body or official

di·rec·tiv·i·ty \də-ˌrek-'ti-və-tē, ˌ(ˌ)dī-\ *n* (1928) : the property of being directional

direct lighting *n* (1928) : lighting in which the greater part of the light goes directly from the source to the area lit

¹di·rect·ly \də-'rek(t)-lē, dī-; in sense 2 *esp* də-'rek-lē *or* 'drek-lē\ *adv* (15c) **1 a** : in a direct manner ⟨~ relevant⟩ ⟨the road runs ~ east

and west⟩ **b** : in immediate physical contact **c** : in the manner of direct variation **2 a** : without delay : IMMEDIATELY **b** : in a little while : SHORTLY

²di·rect·ly \də-'rek(t)-lē, dī-; 'drek-lē\ *conj* (1795) *chiefly Brit* : immediately after : AS SOON AS ⟨~ I received it I rang up the shipping company —F. W. Crofts⟩

directly proportional *n* (1796) : related by direct variation — compare INVERSELY PROPORTIONAL

direct mail *n* (ca. 1923) : printed matter (as circulars) prepared for soliciting business or contributions and mailed directly to individuals

di·rect·ness \də-'rek(t)-nəs, dī-\ *n* (1598) **1** : the character of being accurate in course or aim **2** : strict pertinence : STRAIGHTFORWARDNESS ⟨her ~ was disarming —Robin Cook⟩

direct object *n* (1879) : a word or phrase denoting the goal or the result of the action of a verb

Di·rec·toire \dē-ˌ(ˌ)rek-'twär⟩, -'rek-ˌ\ *adj* [F, fr. *Directoire*, the group of five officials who governed France from 1795–99, fr. *directeur* director] (1878) : of, relating to, or imitative of the style of clothing, furniture, or decoration prevalent in France during the period of the Directory

di·rec·tor \də-'rek-tər, dī-\ *n* (15c) : one that directs: as **a** : the head of an organized group or administrative unit (as a bureau or school) **b** : one of a group of persons entrusted with the overall direction of a corporate enterprise **c** : one that supervises the production of a show (as for stage or screen) usu. with responsibility for action, lighting, music, and rehearsals **d** : CONDUCTOR c — **di·rec·tor·ship** \-ˌship\ *n*

di·rec·tor·ate \də-'rek-t(ə-)rət, dī-\ *n* (1837) **1** : the office of director **2 a** : a board of directors (as of a corporation) **b** : membership on a board of directors **3** : an executive staff (as of a department)

di·rec·to·ri·al \də-ˌrek-'tōr-ē-əl, ˌ(ˌ)dī-, -'tòr-\ *adj* (1770) **1** : serving to direct **2** : of or relating to a director or to theatrical or motion-picture direction **3** : of, relating to, or administered by a directory

director's chair *n* [fr. its use by motion-picture directors on the set] (1953) : a lightweight folding armchair with a back and seat usu. of cotton duck

¹di·rec·to·ry \də-'rek-t(ə-)rē, dī-\ *adj* (15c) : serving to direct; *specif* : providing advisory but not compulsory guidance

²directory *n, pl* **-ries** [ME *directorie* guide, fr. ML *directorium*, fr. neut. of LL *directorius* directorial, fr. L *dirigere*] (1543) **1 a** : a book or collection of directions, rules, or ordinances **b** : an alphabetical or classified list (as of names and addresses) **2 a** : a body of directors

director's chair

direct primary *n* (1900) : a primary in which nominations of candidates for office are made by direct vote

direct product *n* (ca. 1925) : CARTESIAN PRODUCT; *esp* : a group that is the Cartesian product of two other groups

di·rec·tress \də-'rek-trəs, dī-\ *n* (1580) : a woman who is a director

di·rec·trice \də-ˌrek-'trēs\ *n* [F, fr. ML *directric-, directrix*] (1631) : DIRECTRESS

di·rec·trix \-'rek-triks\ *n, pl* **-trix·es** \-trik-səz\ *also* **-tri·ces** \-trə-ˌsēz\ [ML, fem. of LL *director*, fr. L *dirigere*] (1622) **1** *archaic* : DIRECTRESS **2** : a fixed curve with which a generatrix maintains a given relationship in generating a geometric figure; *specif* : a straight line the distance to which from any point of a conic section is in fixed ratio to the distance from the same point to a focus

direct sum *n* (ca. 1928) : CARTESIAN PRODUCT — compare DIRECT PRODUCT

direct tax *n* (1801) : a tax exacted directly from the taxpayer

direct variation *n* (1949) **1** : mathematical relationship between two variables that can be expressed by an equation in which one variable is equal to a constant times the other **2** : an equation or function expressing direct variation — compare INVERSE VARIATION

dire·ful \'dīr-fəl\ *adj* (1583) **1** : DREADFUL **2** : OMINOUS — **dire·ful·ly** \-fə-lē\ *adv*

dire wolf *n* (1925) : a large extinct lupine mammal (*Canis dirus*) known from Pleistocene deposits of No. America

dirge \'dərj\ *n* [ME *dirige*, the Office of the Dead, fr. the first word of a LL antiphon, fr. L, imper. of *dirigere* to direct — more at DRESS] (13c) **1** : a song or hymn of grief or lamentation; *esp* : one intended to accompany a funeral or memorial rites **2** : a slow, solemn, and mournful piece of music **3** : something (as a poem) that has the qualities of a dirge — **dirge·like** \-ˌlīk\ *adj*

dir·ham \'dir-həm\ *n* [Ar, fr. L *drachma* drachma] (1788) **1** — see MONEY table **2** — see *dinar, riyal* at MONEY table

¹di·ri·gi·ble \'dir-ə-jə-bəl, də-'ri-jə-\ *adj* [L *dirigere*] (1581) : capable of being steered

²dirigible *n* [*dirigible (balloon)*] (1885) : AIRSHIP

di·ri·gisme \ˌdir-i-'zhi-z⁰m, dē-rē-zhēs-m⁰\ *n* [F, fr. *diriger* to direct (fr. L *dirigere*) + *-isme* -ism] (1947) : economic planning and control by the state — **di·ri·giste** \di-ri-'zhēst, dē-rē-\ *adj*

¹dirk \'dərk\ *n* [Sc *durk*] (1557) : a long straight-bladed dagger

²dirk *vt* (1599) : to stab with a dirk

dirl \'dir(-ə)l, 'dərl\ *vi* [perh. alter. of *thirl*] (1715) *Scot* : TREMBLE, QUIVER

dirndl \'dərn-d⁰l\ *n* [short for G *Dirndlkleid*, fr. G dial. *Dirndl* girl + G *Kleid* dress] (1937) **1** : a dress style with tight bodice, short sleeves, low neck, and gathered skirt **2** : a full skirt with a tight waistband

dirt \'dərt\ *n* [ME *drit*, fr. ON; akin to OE *dritan* to defecate] (13c) **1 a** : EXCREMENT **b** : a filthy or soiling substance (as mud, dust, or grime) **c** *archaic* : something worthless **d** : a contemptible person **2** : loose or packed soil or sand : EARTH **3 a** : an abject or filthy state : SQUALOR **b** : CORRUPTION, CHICANERY **c** : licentiousness of language or theme **d** : scandalous or malicious gossip **e** : embarrassing or incriminating information

dirt·bag \'dərt-ˌbag\ *n* (ca. 1967) *slang* : a dirty, unkempt, or contemptible person

dirt bike *n* (1970) : a usu. lightweight motorcycle designed for operation on unpaved surfaces

dirt cheap *adj or adv* (1821) : exceedingly cheap

dirt farmer *n* (1920) : a farmer who earns his living by farming his own land esp. without the help of hired hands or tenants

dirt–poor \'dərt-'pür\ *adj* (1937) : suffering extreme poverty

¹dirty \'dər-tē\ *adj* **dirt·i·er; -est** (14c) **1 a** : not clean or pure ⟨~ clothes⟩ **b** : likely to befoul or defile with dirt ⟨~ jobs⟩ **c** : tedious, disagreeable, and unrecognized or thankless ⟨had to do the ~ work⟩ **d** : contaminated with infecting organisms ⟨~ wounds⟩ **e** : containing impurities ⟨~ coal⟩ **2 a** : morally unclean or corrupt: as (1) : INDECENT, VULGAR ⟨~ jokes⟩ ⟨a ~ movie⟩ (2) : DISHONORABLE, BASE ⟨~ tricks⟩ (3) : UNSPORTSMANLIKE ⟨~ players⟩ **b** : acquired by disreputable or illegal means : ILL-GOTTEN ⟨~ money⟩ **3 a** : ABOMINABLE, HATEFUL ⟨war is a ~ business⟩ **b** : highly regrettable ⟨a ~ shame⟩ **4** : FOGGY, STORMY ⟨~ weather⟩ **5 a** *of color* : not clear and bright : DULLISH ⟨~ blond⟩ **b** : characterized by a husky, rasping, or raw tonal quality ⟨~ trumpet tones⟩ **6** : conveying ill-natured resentment ⟨gave him a ~ look⟩ **7** : having considerable fallout ⟨~ bombs⟩ — **dirt·i·ly** \'dər-t³l-ē\ *adv* — **dirt·i·ness** \'dər-tē-nəs\ *n*

syn DIRTY, FILTHY, FOUL, NASTY, SQUALID mean conspicuously unclean or impure. DIRTY emphasizes the presence of dirt more than an emotional reaction to it ⟨a *dirty* littered street⟩. FILTHY carries a strong suggestion of offensiveness and typically of gradually accumulated dirt that begrimes and besmears ⟨a stained greasy floor, utterly *filthy*⟩. FOUL implies extreme offensiveness and an accumulation of what is rotten or stinking ⟨a *foul*-smelling open sewer⟩. NASTY applies to what is actually foul or is repugnant to one expecting freshness, cleanliness, or sweetness ⟨it's a *nasty* job to clean up after a sick cat⟩. In practice, *nasty* is often weakened to the point of being no more than a synonym of *unpleasant* or *disagreeable* ⟨had a *nasty* fall⟩ ⟨his answer gave her a *nasty* shock⟩. SQUALID adds to the idea of dirtiness and filth that of slovenly neglect ⟨*squalid* slums⟩. All these terms are also applicable to moral uncleanness or baseness or obscenity. DIRTY then stresses meanness or despicableness ⟨don't ask me to do your *dirty* work⟩, while FILTHY and FOUL describe disgusting obscenity or loathsome behavior ⟨*filthy* street language⟩ ⟨a *foul* story of lust and greed⟩, and NASTY implies a peculiarly offensive unpleasantness ⟨a stand-up comedian known for *nasty* humor⟩. Distinctively, SQUALID implies sordidness as well as baseness and dirtiness ⟨engaged in a series of *squalid* affairs⟩.

²dirty *adv* **dirt·i·er; -est** (ca. 1934) : in a dirty manner: as **a** : DECEPTIVELY, UNDERHANDEDLY ⟨fight ~⟩ **b** : INDECENTLY ⟨talk ~⟩

³dirty *vb* **dirt·ied; dirty·ing** *vt* (1591) **1** : to make dirty **2 a** : to stain with dishonor : SULLY **b** : to debase by distorting the real nature of ~ ~ *vi* : to become soiled

dirty linen *n* (1946) : private matters whose public exposure brings distress and embarrassment — called also *dirty laundry*

dirty old man *n* (1932) : a lecherous older man

dirty pool *n* (1940) : underhanded or unsportsmanlike conduct

dirty rice *n* (ca. 1967) : a Cajun dish of white rice cooked with chopped or ground giblets

dirty word *n* (1842) : a word, expression, or idea that is disagreeable or unpopular in a particular frame of reference

dis \'dis\ *vt* **dissed; dis·sing** [perh. short for *disrespect*] (1986) **1** *slang* : to treat with disrespect or contempt : INSULT **2** *slang* : to find fault with : CRITICIZE

Dis \'dis\ *n* [L] : the Roman god of the underworld — compare PLUTO

dis- *prefix* [ME *dis-, des-*, fr. OF & L; OF *des-, dis-*, fr. L *dis-*, lit., apart; akin to OE *te-* apart, L *duo* two — more at TWO] **1 a** : do the opposite of ⟨*disestablish*⟩ **b** : deprive of (a specified quality, rank, or object) ⟨*disfranchise*⟩ **c** : exclude or expel from ⟨*disbar*⟩ **2** : opposite or absence of ⟨*disunion*⟩ ⟨*disaffection*⟩ **3** : not ⟨*disagreeable*⟩ **4** : completely ⟨*disannul*⟩ **5** [by folk etymology]: DYS- ⟨*disfunction*⟩

dis·abil·i·ty \,di-sə-'bi-lə-tē\ *n* (1580) **1 a** : the condition of being disabled **b** : inability to pursue an occupation because of physical or mental impairment **2** : lack of legal qualification to do something **3** : a disqualification, restriction, or disadvantage

dis·able \di-'sā-bəl, dis-\ *vt* **dis·abled; dis·abling** \-b(ə-)liŋ\ (15c) **1** : to deprive of legal right, qualification, or capacity ⟨ ⟩ **2** : to make incapable or ineffective; *esp* : to deprive of physical, mental, or intellectual strength *syn* see WEAKEN — **dis·able·ment** \-bəl-mənt\ *n*

dis·abled *adj* (1633) : incapacitated by illness, injury, or wounds; *broadly* : physically or mentally impaired

dis·abuse \,di-sə-'byüz\ *vt* [F *désabuser*, fr. *dés-* dis- + *abuser* to abuse] (1611) : to free from error, fallacy, or misconception

di·sac·cha·ri·dase \(,)dī-'sa-kə-rə-,dās, -,dāz\ *n* (1961) : an enzyme (as maltase or lactase) that hydrolyzes disaccharides

di·sac·cha·ride \(,)dī-'sa-kə-,rīd\ *n* (1892) : any of a class of sugars (as sucrose) that yields on hydrolysis two monosaccharide molecules

dis·ac·cord \,di-sə-'körd\ *vi* [ME *disacorden*, fr. MF *desacorder*, fr. *desacorde* disagreement, fr. *des-* dis- + *acort* accord] (15c) : CLASH, DISAGREE — **disaccord** *n*

dis·ac·cus·tom \,di-sə-'kəs-təm\ *vt* [MF *desaccoustumer*, fr. OF *desacostumer*, fr. *des-* dis- + *acostumer* to accustom] (1530) : to free from a habit

¹dis·ad·van·tage \,di-səd-'van-tij\ *n* [ME *disavauntage*, fr. MF *desavantage*, fr. OF, fr. *des-* dis- + *avantage* advantage] (14c) **1** : loss or damage esp. to reputation, credit, or finances : DETRIMENT **2 a** : an unfavorable, inferior, or prejudicial condition ⟨we were at a ~⟩ **b** : HANDICAP ⟨it put us under a serious ~⟩

²disadvantage *vt* (ca. 1534) : to place at a disadvantage : HARM

dis·ad·van·taged \-tijd\ *adj* (1648) : lacking in the basic resources or conditions (as standard housing, medical and educational facilities, and civil rights) believed to be necessary for an equal position in society — **dis·ad·van·taged·ness** \-tijd-nəs\ *n*

dis·ad·van·ta·geous \(,)dis-,ad-,van-'tā-jəs, -vən-'tā-jəs, -vən-\ *adj* (1603) **1** : constituting a disadvantage **2** : DEROGATORY, DISPARAGING — **dis·ad·van·ta·geous·ly** *adv* — **dis·ad·van·ta·geous·ness** *n*

dis·af·fect \,di-sə-'fekt\ *vt* (1641) : to alienate the affection or loyalty of *syn* see ESTRANGE — **dis·af·fec·tion** \-'fek-shən\ *n*

dis·af·fect·ed *adj* (1632) : discontented and resentful esp. against authority : REBELLIOUS

dis·af·fil·i·ate \,di-sə-'fi-lē-,āt\ *vt* (1870) : DISASSOCIATE ~ ~ *vi* : to terminate an affiliation — **dis·af·fil·i·a·tion** \-,fil-ē-'ā-shən\ *n*

dis·af·firm \,di-sə-'fərm\ *vt* (1531) **1** : to refuse to confirm : ANNUL, REPUDIATE **2** : CONTRADICT — **dis·af·fir·mance** \-'fər-mən(t)s\ *n*

dis·ag·gre·gate \(,)dis-'a-gri-,gāt\ *vt* (ca. 1828) : to separate into component parts ⟨~ sandstone⟩ ⟨~ demographic data⟩ ~ *vi* : to break up or apart ⟨the molecules of a gel ~ to form a sol⟩ — **dis·ag·gre·ga·tion** \(,)dis-,a-gri-'gā-shən\ *n* — **dis·ag·gre·ga·tive** \(,)dis-'a-gri-,gā-tiv\ *adj*

dis·agree \,di-sə-'grē\ *vi* [ME, fr. MF *desagreer*, fr. *des-* dis- + *agreer* to agree] (15c) **1** : to fail to agree ⟨the two accounts ~⟩ **2** : to differ in opinion ⟨he *disagreed* with me on every topic⟩ **3** : to cause discomfort or distress ⟨fried foods ~ with me⟩

dis·agree·able \-ə-bəl\ *adj* (15c) **1** : causing discomfort : UNPLEASANT, OFFENSIVE **2** : marked by ill temper : PEEVISH — **dis·agree·able·ness** *n* — **dis·agree·ably** \-blē\ *adv*

dis·agree·ment \,di-sə-'grē-mənt\ *n* (15c) **1** : the act of disagreeing **2 a** : the state of being at variance : DISPARITY **b** : QUARREL

dis·al·low \,di-sə-'laů\ *vt* (14c) **1** : to deny the force, truth, or validity of **2** : to refuse to allow — **dis·al·low·ance** \-ən(t)s\ *n*

dis·am·big·u·ate \,di-sam-'bi-gyə-,wāt\ *vt* **-at·ed; -at·ing** (1963) : to establish a single semantic or grammatical interpretation for — **dis·am·big·u·a·tion** \-,bi-gyə-'wā-shən\ *n*

dis·an·nul \,di-sə-'nəl\ *vt* (15c) : ANNUL, CANCEL

dis·ap·pear \,di-sə-'pir\ *vi* (15c) **1** : to pass from view **2** : to cease to be : pass out of existence or notice ~ *vt* : to cause the disappearance of — **dis·ap·pear·ance** \-'pir-ən(t)s\ *n*

dis·ap·point \,di-sə-'point\ *vb* [ME *disapoynten*, fr. MF *desapointier*, fr. *des-* dis- + *apointier* to arrange — more at APPOINT] *vt* (15c) : to fail to meet the expectation or hope of : FRUSTRATE ~ *vi* : to cause disappointment ⟨where the show ~s most is in the work of the younger generation —John Ashbery⟩

dis·ap·point·ed *adj* (1537) **1** : defeated in expectation or hope **2** *obs* : not adequately equipped — **dis·ap·point·ed·ly** *adv*

dis·ap·point·ing *adj* (1530) : failing to meet expectations — **dis·ap·point·ing·ly** \-'poin-tiŋ-lē\ *adv*

dis·ap·point·ment \,di-sə-'point-mənt\ *n* (1614) **1** : the act or an instance of disappointing : the state or emotion of being disappointed **2** : one that disappoints

dis·ap·pro·ba·tion \(,)di-,sa-prə-'bā-shən\ *n* (1647) : the act or state of disapproving : the state of being disapproved : CONDEMNATION

dis·ap·prov·al \,di-sə-'prü-vəl\ *n* (1662) : DISAPPROBATION, CENSURE

dis·ap·prove \-'prüv\ *vt* (1647) **1** : to pass unfavorable judgment on **2** : to refuse approval to : REJECT ~ *vi* : to feel or express disapproval — **dis·ap·prov·er** *n* — **dis·ap·prov·ing·ly** \-'prü-viŋ-lē\ *adv*

dis·arm \dis-'ärm, -'zärm, -särm\ *vb* [ME *desarmen*, lit., to disarm, fr. MF *desarmer*, fr. OF, fr. *des-* dis- + *armer* to arm] *vt* (14c) **1 a** : to deprive of means, reason, or disposition to be hostile **b** : to win over **2 a** : to divest of arms **b** : to deprive of a means of attack or defense **c** : to make harmless ~ *vi* **1** : to lay aside arms **2** : to give up or reduce armed forces — **dis·ar·ma·ment** \-'sär-mə-mənt, -'zär-\ *n* — **dis·arm·er** *n*

dis·arm·ing *adj* (1839) : allaying criticism or hostility : INGRATIATING — **dis·arm·ing·ly** \-'sär-miŋ-lē-, -'zär-\ *adv*

dis·ar·range \,di-sə-'rānj\ *vt* (1744) : to disturb the arrangement or order of — **dis·ar·range·ment** \-mənt\ *n*

¹dis·ar·ray \,di-sə-'rā\ *n* (15c) **1** : a lack of order or sequence : CONFUSION, DISORDER **2** : disorderly dress : DISHABILLE

²disarray *vt* [ME *disarayen*, fr. MF *desarroyer*, fr. OF *desareer*, fr. *des-* dis- + *areer* to array] (14c) **1** : to throw into disorder **2** : UNDRESS

dis·ar·tic·u·late \,di-sär-'ti-kyə-,lāt\ *vi* (1830) : to become disjointed ~ *vt* : DISJOINT — **dis·ar·tic·u·la·tion** \-,ti-kyə-'lā-shən\ *n*

dis·as·sem·ble \,di-sə-'sem-bəl\ *vt* (1903) : to take apart ⟨~ a watch⟩ ~ *vi* **1** : to come apart ⟨the frame ~s into sections⟩ **2** : DISPERSE, SCATTER ⟨the crowd began to ~⟩ — **dis·as·sem·bly** \-blē\ *n*

dis·as·so·ci·ate \,di-sə-'sō-sē-,āt, -shē-\ *vt* (1603) : to detach from association : DISSOCIATE — **dis·as·so·ci·a·tion** \-,sō-sē-'ā-shən, -shē-\ *n*

di·sas·ter \di-'zas-tər, -'sas-\ *n* [MF & OIt; MF *desastre*, fr. OIt *disastro*, fr. dis- (fr. L) + *astro* star, fr. L *astrum* — more at ASTRAL] (1591) **1** : a sudden calamitous event bringing great damage, loss, or destruction; *broadly* : a sudden or great misfortune or failure **2** *obs* : an unfavorable aspect of a planet or star

disaster area *n* (1953) : an area officially declared to be the scene of an emergency created by a disaster and therefore qualified to receive certain types of governmental aid (as emergency loans and relief supplies)

di·sas·trous \di-'zas-trəs *also* -'sas-\ *adj* (1603) **1** : attended by or causing suffering or disaster : CALAMITOUS **2** : TERRIBLE, HORRENDOUS ⟨a ~ score⟩ — **di·sas·trous·ly** *adv*

dis·avow \,di-sə-'vaů\ *vt* [ME *desavowen*, fr. MF *desavouer*, fr. OF, fr. *des-* dis- + *avouer* to avow] (14c) **1** : to deny responsibility for : REPUDIATE **2** : to refuse to acknowledge : DISCLAIM — **dis·avow·able** \-ə-bəl\ *adj* — **dis·avow·al** \-'vaů(-ə)l\ *n*

dis·band \dis-'band\ *vb* [MF *desbander*, fr. *des-* dis- + *bande* band] *vt* (1591) : to break up the organization of : DISSOLVE ~ *vi* : to break up as an organization : DISPERSE — **dis·band·ment** \-'ban(d)-mənt\ *n*

dis·bar \dis-'bär\ *vt* (1633) : to expel from the bar or the legal profession : deprive (an attorney) of legal status and privileges — **dis·bar·ment** \-mənt\ *n*

dis·be·lief \,dis-bə-'lēf\ *n* (1672) : the act of disbelieving : mental rejection of something as untrue

dis·be·lieve \-'lēv\ *vt* (ca. 1644) : to hold as not worthy of belief : not believe ~ *vi* : to withhold or reject belief — **dis·be·liev·er** *n*

dis·ben·e·fit \(,)dis-'be-nə-fit\ *n* (1968) : something disadvantageous or objectionable : DRAWBACK

dis·bud \(,)dis-'bəd\ *vt* (1727) **1** : to thin out flower buds in order to improve the quality of bloom of **2** : to dehorn (cattle) by destroying the undeveloped horn bud

dis·bur·den \(,)dis-'bər-d³n\ *vt* (1532) **1 a** : to rid of a burden ⟨~ a pack animal⟩ **b** : UNBURDEN ⟨~ your conscience⟩ **2** : UNLOAD ⟨~ed their merchandise in the town square⟩ ~ *vi* : DISCHARGE ⟨the vessels ~ed at the dock⟩ — **dis·bur·den·ment** \-mənt\ *n*

dis·burse \dis-'bərs\ *vt* **dis·bursed; dis·burs·ing** [MF *desbourser*, fr.

\ə\ abut \³\ kitten, F table \ər\ further \a\ ash \ā\ ace \ä\ mop, mar \aů\ out \ch\ chin \e\ bet \ē\ easy \g\ go \i\ hit \ī\ ice \j\ job \ŋ\ sing \ō\ go \ò\ law \òi\ boy \th\ thin \th\ the \ü\ loot \ů\ foot \y\ yet \zh\ vision \ə, k, ⁿ, œ, œ̄, ᵫ, ᵫ̄, ᵉ\ see Guide to Pronunciation

OF *desborser*, fr. *des-* dis- + *borser* to get money, fr. *borse* burse] (1530) **1 a :** to pay out : expend esp. from a fund **b :** to make a payment in settlement of **2 :** DISTRIBUTE — **dis·burs·er** *n*
dis·burse·ment \-'bər-smənt\ *n* (1596) **:** the act of disbursing; *also* **:** funds paid out
disc *var of* DISK
disc- *or* **disci-** *or* **disco-** *comb form* [L, fr. Gk *disk-, disko-,* fr. *diskos*] **1 :** disk ⟨*discoid*⟩ **2 :** phonograph record ⟨*discophile*⟩
dis·calced \(ˌ)dis-'kalst\ *adj* [part trans. of L *discalceatus*, fr. *dis-* + *calceatus*, pp. of *calceare* to put on shoes, fr. *calceus* shoe, fr. *calc-, calx* heel] (1631) **:** UNSHOD, BAREFOOT ⟨~ friars⟩
dis·cant \'dis-ˌkant\ *var of* DESCANT
¹dis·card \dis-'kärd, 'dis-ˌ\ *vt* (ca. 1586) **1 :** to get rid of esp. as useless or unpleasant **2 a :** to remove (a playing card) from one's hand **b :** to play (any card except a trump) from a suit different from the one led ~ *vi* **:** to discard a playing card — **dis·card·able** \-də-bəl\ *adj* — **dis·card·er** *n*
syn DISCARD, CAST, SHED, SLOUGH, SCRAP, JUNK mean to get rid of. DIS-CARD implies the letting go or throwing away of something that has become useless or superfluous though often not intrinsically valueless ⟨*discard* old clothes⟩. CAST, esp. when used with *off, away,* or *out,* implies a forceful rejection or repudiation ⟨*cast* off her friends⟩. SHED and SLOUGH imply a throwing off of something both useless and encumbering and often suggest a consequent renewal of vitality or luster ⟨*shed* a bad habit⟩ ⟨finally *sloughed* off the depression⟩. SCRAP and JUNK imply throwing away or breaking up as worthless in existent form ⟨*scrap* all the old ways⟩ ⟨would *junk* our educational system⟩.
²dis·card \'dis-ˌkärd\ *n* (1744) **1 a :** the act of discarding in a card game **b :** a card discarded **2 :** one that is cast off or rejected
dis·car·nate \dis-'kär-nət, -ˌnāt\ *adj* [*dis-* + *-carnate* (as in *incarnate*)] (1895) **:** having no physical body **:** INCORPOREAL
disc brake *n* (1904) **:** a brake that operates by the friction of a caliper pressing against the sides of a rotating disc

disc brake: *1* caliper, *2* disc

dis·cern \di-'sərn, -'zərn\ *vb* [ME, fr. MF *discerner,* fr. L *discernere* to separate, distinguish between, fr. *dis-* apart + *cernere* to sift — more at DIS-, CERTAIN] *vt* (14c) **1 a :** to detect with the eyes **b :** to detect with senses other than vision **2 :** to recognize or identify as separate and distinct **:** DISCRIMINATE **3 :** to come to know or recognize mentally ~ *vi* **:** to see or understand the difference — **dis·cern·er** *n* — **dis·cern·ible** *also* **dis·cern·able** \-'sər-nə-bəl, -'zər-\ *adj* — **dis·cern·ibly** \-blē\ *adv*
dis·cern·ing *adj* (1589) **:** showing insight and understanding **:** DISCRIMINATING ⟨a ~ critic⟩ — **dis·cern·ing·ly** \-'sər-niŋ-lē, -'zər-\ *adv*
dis·cern·ment \di-'sərn-mənt, -'zərn-\ *n* (1586) **1 :** the quality of being able to grasp and comprehend what is obscure **:** skill in discerning **2 :** an act of discerning
syn DISCERNMENT, DISCRIMINATION, PERCEPTION, PENETRATION, INSIGHT, ACUMEN mean a power to see what is not evident to the average mind. DISCERNMENT stresses accuracy (as in reading character or motives or appreciating art) ⟨the *discernment* to know true friends⟩. DISCRIMINA-TION stresses the power to distinguish and select what is true or appropriate or excellent ⟨the *discrimination* that develops through listening to a lot of great music⟩. PERCEPTION implies quick and often sympathetic discernment (as of shades of feeling) ⟨a novelist of keen *perception* into human motives⟩. PENETRATION implies a searching mind that goes beyond what is obvious or superficial ⟨lacks the *penetration* to see the scorn beneath their friendly smiles⟩. INSIGHT suggests depth of discernment coupled with understanding sympathy ⟨a documentary providing *insight* into the plight of the homeless⟩. ACUMEN implies characteristic penetration combined with keen practical judgment ⟨a director of reliable box-office *acumen*⟩.
¹dis·charge \dis-'chärj, 'dis-ˌ\ *vb* [ME, fr. MF *descharger,* fr. LL *discarricare,* fr. L *dis-* + LL *carricare* to load — more at CHARGE] *vt* (14c) **1 :** to relieve of a charge, load, or burden : **a :** UNLOAD **b :** to release from an obligation **c :** to release electrical energy from (as a battery or capacitor) by a discharge **2 a :** to let or put off ⟨~ passengers⟩ ⟨~ cargo⟩ **b :** SHOOT ⟨~ an arrow⟩ **c :** to release from confinement, custody, or care ⟨~ a prisoner⟩ **d :** to give outlet or vent to **:** EMIT **3 a** (1) **:** to dismiss from employment (2) **:** to release from service or duty ⟨~ a soldier⟩ **b :** to get rid of (as a debt or obligation) by performing an appropriate action (as payment) **c :** to set aside : ANNUL **d :** to order (a legislative committee) to end consideration of a bill in order to bring it before the house for action **4 :** to bear and distribute (as the weight of a wall above an opening) **5 :** to bleach out or remove (color or dye) in dyeing and printing textiles **6 :** to cancel the record of the loan of (a library book) upon return ~ *vi* **1 a :** to throw off or deliver a load, charge, or burden **b :** to release electrical energy by a discharge **2 a :** GO OFF, FIRE — used of a gun **b :** SPREAD, RUN ⟨some dyes ~⟩ **c :** to pour forth fluid or other contents **syn** *see* PERFORM — **dis·charge·able** \-jə-bəl\ *adj* — **dis·charg·ee** \(ˌ)dis-ˌchär-'jē\ *n* — **dis·charg·er** \dis-'chär-jər, 'dis-ˌ\ *n*
²dis·charge \'dis-ˌchärj, dis-'\ *n* (14c) **1 :** the act of relieving of something that oppresses : RELEASE **b :** something that discharges or releases; *esp* **:** a certification of release or payment **2 :** the state of being discharged or relieved **3 :** the act of discharging or unloading **4 :** legal release from confinement **5 :** a firing off **6 a :** a flowing or issuing out ⟨a ~ of spores⟩; *also* **:** a rate of flow **b :** something that is emitted ⟨a purulent ~⟩ **7 :** the act of removing an obligation or liability **8 a :** release or dismissal esp. from an office or employment **b :** complete separation from military service **9 a :** the equalization of a difference of electric potential between two points **b :** the conversion of the chemical energy of a battery into electrical energy
discharge lamp *n* (1936) **:** an electric lamp in which an enclosed gas or vapor glows or causes a phosphor coating on the lamp's inner surface to glow

discharge tube *n* (1898) **:** an electron tube which contains gas or vapor at low pressure and through which conduction takes place when a high voltage is applied
disci- — *see* DISC-
dis·ci·form \'di-sə-ˌfȯrm\ *adj* (1830) **:** round or oval in shape
dis·ci·ple \di-'sī-pəl\ *n* [ME, fr. OE *discipul* & OF *deciple,* fr. LL and L; LL *discipulus* follower of Jesus Christ in his lifetime, fr. L, pupil] (bef. 12c) **1 :** one who accepts and assists in spreading the doctrines of another; *as* **a :** one of the twelve in the inner circle of Christ's followers according to the Gospel accounts **b :** a convinced adherent of a school or individual **2** *cap* **:** a member of the Disciples of Christ founded in the U.S. in 1809 that holds the Bible alone to be the rule of faith and practice, usu. baptizes by immersion, and has a congregational polity **syn** *see* FOLLOWER — **dis·ci·ple·ship** \-ˌship\ *n*
dis·ci·plin·able \ˌdi-sə-'pli-nə-bəl; 'di-sə-pli-\ *adj* (15c) **1 :** DOCILE, TEACHABLE **2 :** subject to or deserving discipline ⟨a ~ offense⟩
dis·ci·pli·nar·i·an \ˌdi-sə-plə-'ner-ē-ən\ *n* (1639) **:** one who disciplines or enforces order — **disciplinarian** *adj*
dis·ci·plin·ary \'di-sə-plə-ˌner-ē, *esp Brit* ˌdi-sə-'pli-nə-rē\ *adj* (1598) **1 a :** of or relating to discipline **b :** designed to correct or punish breaches of discipline ⟨took ~ action⟩ **2 :** of or relating to a particular field of study — **dis·ci·plin·ar·i·ly** \ˌdi-sə-plə-'ner-ə-lē\ *adv* — **dis·ci·plin·ar·i·ty** \-'nar-ə-tē\ *n*
¹dis·ci·pline \'di-sə-plən\ *n* [ME, fr. OF & L; OF, fr. L *disciplina* teaching, learning, fr. *discipulus* pupil] (13c) **1 :** PUNISHMENT **2** *obs* **:** INSTRUCTION **3 :** a field of study **4 :** training that corrects, molds, or perfects the mental faculties or moral character **5 a :** control gained by enforcing obedience or order **b :** orderly or prescribed conduct or pattern of behavior **c :** SELF-CONTROL **6 :** a rule or system of rules governing conduct or activity — **dis·ci·plin·al** \-plə-nᵊl\ *adj*
²discipline *vt* -plined; -plin·ing (14c) **1 :** to punish or penalize for the sake of discipline **2 :** to train or develop by instruction and exercise esp. in self-control **3 a :** to bring (a group) under control ⟨~ troops⟩ **b :** to impose order upon ⟨serious writers ~ and refine their writing styles⟩ **syn** *see* PUNISH, TEACH — **dis·ci·plin·er** *n*
dis·ci·plined *adj* (14c) **:** marked by or possessing discipline ⟨a ~ mind⟩
disc jockey *n* (1941) **:** an announcer of a radio show of popular recorded music; *also* **:** one who plays recorded music for dancing at a nightclub or party
dis·claim \dis-'klām\ *vb* [ME, fr. AF *disclaimer,* fr. *dis-* + *claimer* to claim, fr. OF *clamer*] *vi* (15c) **1 :** to make a disclaimer **2 a** *obs* **:** to disavow all part or share **b :** to utter denial ~ *vt* **1 :** to renounce a legal claim to **2 :** DENY, DISAVOW ⟨~ed any knowledge of the contents of the letter⟩
dis·claim·er \-'klā-mər\ *n* (15c) **1 a :** a denial or disavowal of legal claim **:** relinquishment of or formal refusal to accept an interest or estate **b :** a writing that embodies a legal disclaimer **2 a :** DENIAL, DISAVOWAL **b :** REPUDIATION
dis·cla·ma·tion \ˌdis-klə-'mā-shən\ *n* (1592) **:** RENUNCIATION, DISAVOWAL
dis·cli·max \(ˌ)dis-'klī-ˌmaks\ *n* (1935) **:** a relatively stable ecological community often including kinds of organisms foreign to the region and displacing the climax because of disturbance esp. by man
¹dis·close \dis-'klōz\ *vt* [ME, fr. MF *desclos-,* stem of *desclore* to disclose, fr. ML *disclaudere* to open, fr. L *dis-* + *claudere* to close — more at CLOSE] (14c) **1** *obs* **:** to open up **2 a :** to expose to view **b** *archaic* **:** HATCH **c :** to make known or public ⟨demands that politicians ~ the sources of their income⟩ **syn** *see* REVEAL — **dis·clos·er** *n*
²disclose *n* (1548) *obs* **:** DISCLOSURE
dis·clos·ing \-'klō-ziŋ\ *adj* (1965) **:** being or using an agent (as a tablet or liquid) that contains a usu. red dye that stains dental plaque
dis·clo·sure \dis-'klō-zhər\ *n* (ca. 1598) **1 :** the act or an instance of disclosing **:** EXPOSURE **2 :** something disclosed **:** REVELATION
¹dis·co \'dis-(ˌ)kō\ *n, pl* **discos** [short for *discotheque*] (1964) **1 :** a nightclub for dancing to live and recorded music **2 :** popular dance music characterized by hypnotic rhythm, repetitive lyrics, and electronically produced sounds
²disco *vi* (1979) **:** to dance to disco music
disco- — *see* DISC-
dis·cog·ra·pher \dis-'kä-grə-fər\ *n* (1941) **:** a person who compiles discographies
dis·cog·ra·phy \-fē\ *n, pl* **-phies** [F *discographie,* fr. *disc-* + *-graphie* -graphy] (1933) **1 :** a descriptive list of phonograph records by category, composer, performer, or date of release **2 :** the history of recorded music — **dis·co·graph·i·cal** \ˌdis-kə-'gra-fi-kəl\ *also* **dis·co·graph·ic** \-fik\ *adj*
dis·coid \'dis-ˌkȯid\ *adj* [LL *discoides* quoit-shaped, fr. Gk *diskoeidēs,* fr. *diskos* disk] (1794) **1 :** relating to or having a disk: *as* **a** *of a composite floret* **:** situated in the floral disk **b** *of a composite flower head* **:** having only tubular florets **2 :** flat and circular like a disc
dis·coi·dal \dis-'kȯi-dᵊl\ *adj* (ca. 1706) **:** of, resembling, or producing a disk
discoidal cleavage *n* (ca. 1909) **:** meroblastic cleavage in which a disk of cells is produced at the animal pole of the zygote (as in bird eggs)
dis·col·or \(ˌ)dis-'kə-lər\ *vb* [ME *discolouren,* fr. MF *descolourer,* fr. LL *discolorari,* fr. L *discolor* of another color, fr. *dis-* + *color* color] *vt* (14c) **:** to alter or change the hue or color of ~ *vi* **:** to change color esp. for the worse
dis·col·or·ation \(ˌ)dis-ˌkə-lə-'rā-shən\ *n* (1642) **1 :** the act of discoloring **:** the state of being discolored **2 :** a discolored spot or formation **:** STAIN
dis·com·bob·u·late \ˌdis-kəm-'bä-b(y)ə-ˌlāt\ *vt* -lat·ed; -lat·ing [prob. alter. of *discompose*] (ca. 1916) **:** UPSET, CONFUSE ⟨the offensive had *discombobulated* all the German defensive arrangements —A. J. Liebling⟩ — **dis·com·bob·u·la·tion** \-ˌbä-b(y)ə-'lā-shən\ *n*
¹dis·com·fit \dis-'kəm(p)-fət, *esp Southern* ˌdis-kəm-'fit\ *vt* [ME, fr. OF *desconfit,* pp. of *desconfire,* fr. *des-* dis- + *confire* to prepare — more at COMFIT] (13c) **1 a** *archaic* **:** to defeat in battle **b :** to frustrate the plans of **:** THWART **2 :** to put into a state of perplexity and embarrassment **:** DISCONCERT **syn** *see* EMBARRASS
²discomfit *n* (15c) **:** DISCOMFITURE
dis·com·fi·ture \dis-'kəm(p)-fə-ˌchu̇r, -chər, *esp Southern* -ˌt(y)u̇r\ *n* (14c) **:** the act of discomfiting **:** the state of being discomfited
¹dis·com·fort \dis-'kəm(p)-fərt\ *vt* [ME, fr. MF *desconforter,* fr. OF, fr.

des- dis- + *conforter* to comfort] (14c) **1** *archaic* : DISMAY **2** : to make uncomfortable or uneasy — **dis·com·fort·able** \-'kəm(p)-fər-tə-bəl, -'kəm(p)f-tər-bəl\ *adj*

²**discomfort** *n* (14c) **1** *archaic* : DISTRESS, GRIEF **2** : mental or physical uneasiness : ANNOYANCE

dis·com·mend \,dis-kə-'mend\ *vt* [ME *dyscommenden*] (15c) **1** : DISAPPROVE, DISPARAGE **2** : to cause to be viewed unfavorably

dis·com·mode \,dis-kə-'mōd\ *vt* **-mod·ed; -mod·ing** [MF *discommoder*, fr. *dis-* + *commode* convenient — more at COMMODE] (ca. 1721) : to cause inconvenience to : TROUBLE

dis·com·pose \,dis-kəm-'pōz\ *vt* [ME] (15c) **1** : to destroy the composure of **2** : to disturb the order of — **dis·com·po·sure** \-'pō-zhər\ *n*
syn DISCOMPOSE, DISQUIET, DISTURB, PERTURB, AGITATE, UPSET, FLUSTER mean to destroy capacity for collected thought or decisive action. DISCOMPOSE implies some degree of loss of self-control or self-confidence esp. through emotional stress ⟨*discomposed* by the loss of his beloved wife⟩. DISQUIET suggests loss of sense of security or peace of mind ⟨the *disquieting* news of factories closing⟩. DISTURB implies interference with one's mental processes caused by worry, perplexity, or interruption ⟨the discrepancy in accounts *disturbed* me⟩. PERTURB implies deep disturbance of mind and emotions ⟨*perturbed* by her husband's strange behavior⟩. AGITATE suggests obvious external signs of nervous or emotional excitement ⟨in his *agitated* state we could see he was unable to work⟩. UPSET implies the disturbance of normal or habitual functioning by disappointment, distress, or grief ⟨the family's constant bickering *upsets* the youngest child⟩. FLUSTER suggests bewildered agitation ⟨his declaration of love completely *flustered* her⟩.

dis·con·cert \,dis-kən-'sərt\ *vt* [obs. F *disconcerter*, alter. of MF *desconcerter*, fr. *des-* + *concerter* to concert] (1687) **1** : to throw into confusion **2** : to disturb the composure of **syn** see EMBARRASS — **dis·con·cert·ing** *adj* — **dis·con·cert·ing·ly** \-tiŋ-lē\ *adv* — **dis·con·cert·ment** \-mənt\ *n*

dis·con·firm \,dis-kən-'fərm\ *vt* (1936) : to deny the validity of

dis·con·for·mi·ty \,dis-kən-'for-mə-tē\ *n* (1587) **1** : NONCONFORMITY **2** : a break in a sequence of sedimentary rocks all of which have approximately the same dip

dis·con·nect \,dis-kə-'nekt\ *vt* (1770) : to sever the connection of or between ~ *vi* **1** : to terminate a connection **2** : to become detached or withdrawn ⟨~s into dark moods⟩ — **dis·con·nec·tion** \-'nek-shən\ *n*

dis·con·nect·ed *adj* (1783) : not connected : SEPARATE; *also* : INCOHERENT — **dis·con·nect·ed·ly** *adv* — **dis·con·nect·ed·ness** *n*

dis·con·so·late \dis-'kän(t)-sə-lət\ *adj* [ME, fr. ML *disconsolatus*, fr. L *dis-* + *consolatus*, pp. of *consolari* to console] (14c) **1** : CHEERLESS ⟨a clutch of ~ houses —D. H. Lawrence⟩ **2** : DEJECTED, DOWNCAST ⟨the team returned ~ from three losses⟩ — **dis·con·so·late·ly** *adv* — **dis·con·so·late·ness** *n* — **dis·con·so·la·tion** \(,)dis-,kän(t)-sə-'lā-shən\ *n*

¹**dis·con·tent** \,dis-kən-'tent\ *adj* (15c) : DISCONTENTED

²**discontent** *vt* (1549) : to make discontented — **dis·con·tent·ment** \-mənt\ *n*

³**discontent** *n* (1591) : lack of contentment: **a** : a sense of grievance : DISSATISFACTION ⟨the winter of our ~ —Shak.⟩ **b** : restless aspiration for improvement

⁴**discontent** *n* (1596) : one who is discontented : MALCONTENT

dis·con·tent·ed *adj* (1525) : DISSATISFIED, MALCONTENT — **dis·con·tent·ed·ly** *adv* — **dis·con·tent·ed·ness** *n*

dis·con·tin·u·ance \,dis-kən-'tin-yə-wən(t)s\ *n* (14c) **1** : the act or an instance of discontinuing **2** : the interruption or termination of a legal action by the plaintiff's not continuing it

dis·con·tin·ue \,dis-kən-'tin-(,)yü, -yə(-w)\ *vb* [ME, fr. MF *discontinuer*, fr. ML *discontinuare*, fr. L *dis-* + *continuare* to continue] *vt* (14c) **1** : to break the continuity of : cease to operate, administer, use, produce, or take **2** : to abandon or terminate by a legal discontinuance ~ *vi* : to come to an end **syn** see STOP — **dis·con·tin·u·a·tion** \-kən-,tin-yə-'wā-shən\ *n*

dis·con·ti·nu·ity \(,)dis-,kän-tə-'nü-ə-tē, -'nyü-\ *n* (1570) **1** : lack of continuity or cohesion **2** : GAP 5 **3** **a** : the property of being not mathematically continuous ⟨a point of ~⟩ **b** : an instance of being not mathematically continuous; *esp* : a value of an independent variable at which a function is not continuous

dis·con·tin·u·ous \,dis-kən-'tin-yə-wəs\ *adj* (1718) **1** **a** (1) : not continuous ⟨a ~ series of events⟩ (2) : not continued : DISCRETE ⟨~ features of terrain⟩ **b** : lacking sequence or coherence **2** : having one or more mathematical discontinuities — used of a variable or a function — **dis·con·tin·u·ous·ly** *adv*

dis·co·phile \'dis-kə-,fīl\ *n* (1940) : one who studies and collects phonograph records

¹**dis·cord** \'dis-,kȯrd\ *n* (13c) **1** **a** : lack of agreement or harmony (as between persons, things, or ideas) **b** : active quarreling or conflict resulting from discord among persons or factions : STRIFE **2** **a** (1) : a combination of musical sounds that strikes the ear harshly (2) : DISSONANCE **b** : a harsh or unpleasant sound
syn DISCORD, STRIFE, CONFLICT, CONTENTION, DISSENSION, VARIANCE mean a state or condition marked by a lack of agreement or harmony. DISCORD implies an intrinsic or essential lack of harmony producing quarreling, factiousness, or antagonism ⟨a political party long racked by *discord*⟩. STRIFE emphasizes a struggle for superiority rather than the incongruity or incompatibility of the persons or things involved ⟨during his brief reign the empire was never free of civil *strife*⟩. CONFLICT usu. stresses the action of forces in opposition but in static applications implies an irreconcilability as of duties or desires ⟨the *conflict* of freedom and responsibility⟩. CONTENTION applies to strife or competition that shows itself in quarreling, disputing, or controversy ⟨several points of *contention* about the new zoning law⟩. DISSENSION implies strife or discord and stresses a division into factions ⟨religious *dissension* threatened to split the colony⟩. VARIANCE implies a clash between persons or things owing to a difference in nature, opinion, or interest ⟨cultural *variances* that work against a national identity⟩.

²**dis·cord** \'dis-,kȯrd, dis-'\ *vi* [ME, fr. OF *discorder*, fr. L *discordare*, fr. *discord-, discors* discordant, fr. *dis-* + *cord-, cor* heart — more at HEART] (14c) : DISAGREE, CLASH

dis·cor·dance \dis-'kȯr-d°n(t)s\ *n* (14c) **1** : the state or an instance of being discordant **2** : DISSONANCE

dis·cor·dan·cy \-d°n-sē\ *n, pl* **-cies** (1607) : DISCORDANCE

dis·cor·dant \-d°nt\ *adj* (14c) **1** **a** : being at variance : DISAGREEING **b** : QUARRELSOME **2** : relating to a discord — **dis·cor·dant·ly** *adv*

dis·co·theque *or* **discothèque** \'dis-kə-,tek, ,dis-kə-'\ *n* [F *discothèque*, fr. *disque* disk, record + -*o*- + -*thèque* (as in *bibliothèque* library)] (1954) : DISCO 1

¹**dis·count** \'dis-,kau̇nt\ *n* (1622) **1** : a reduction made from the gross amount or value of something: as **a** (1) : a reduction made from a regular or list price (2) : a proportionate deduction from a debt account usu. made for cash or prompt payment **b** : a deduction made for interest in advancing money upon or purchasing a bill or note not due **2** : the act or practice of discounting **3** : a deduction taken or allowance made

²**dis·count** \'dis-,kau̇nt, dis-'\ *vb* [modif. of F *décompter*, fr. OF *desconter*, fr. ML *discomputare*, fr. L *dis-* + *computare* to count — more at COUNT] *vt* (1629) **1** **a** : to make a deduction from usu. for cash or prompt payment **b** : to sell or offer for sale at a discount **c** : to lend money on after deducting the discount **3** **a** : to leave out of account : DISREGARD **b** : to minimize the importance of **c** (1) : to make allowance for bias or exaggeration in (2) : to view with doubt **d** : to take into account (as a future event) in present calculations ~ *vi* : to give or make discounts — **dis·count·er** \-,kau̇n-tər, -'kau̇n-\ *n*

³**dis·count** \'dis-,kau̇nt\ *adj* (1889) **1** **a** : selling goods or services at a discount ⟨~ stores⟩ ⟨a ~ broker⟩ ⟨~ airlines⟩ **b** : offered or sold at a discount **2** : reflecting a discount ⟨~ prices⟩

dis·count·able \dis-'kau̇n-tə-bəl, 'dis-,\ *adj* (1800) **1** : set apart for discounting ⟨within the ~ period⟩ **2** : subject to being discounted ⟨a ~ note⟩

¹**dis·coun·te·nance** \dis-'kau̇n-t°n-ən(t)s, -'kau̇nt-nən(t)s\ *vt* (1580) **1** : ABASH, DISCONCERT **2** : to look with disfavor on : discourage by evidence of disapproval

²**discountenance** *n* (1580) : DISAPPROBATION, DISFAVOR

discount rate *n* (ca. 1927) **1** : the interest on an annual basis deducted in advance on a loan **2** : the charge levied by a central bank for advances and rediscounts

dis·cour·age \dis-'kər-ij, -'kə-rij\ *vt* **-aged; -ag·ing** [ME *discoragen*, fr. MF *descorager*, fr. OF *descoragier*, fr. *des-* dis- + *corage* courage] (15c) **1** : to deprive of courage or confidence : DISHEARTEN **2** **a** : to hinder by disfavoring **b** : to attempt to dissuade — **dis·cour·age·able** \-jə-bəl\ *adj* — **dis·cour·ag·er** *n* — **dis·cour·ag·ing·ly** \-jiŋ-lē\ *adv*

dis·cour·age·ment \-mənt\ *n* (1561) **1** : the act of discouraging : the state of being discouraged **2** : something that discourages

¹**dis·course** \'dis-,kȯrs, -,kȯrs, dis-'\ *n* [ME *discours*, fr. ML *discursus*; ML, argument, fr. LL, conversation, fr. L, act of running about, fr. *discurrere* to run about, fr. *dis-* + *currere* to run — more at CAR] (14c) **1** *archaic* : the capacity of orderly thought or procedure : RATIONALITY **2** : verbal interchange of ideas; *esp* : CONVERSATION **3** **a** : formal and orderly and usu. extended expression of thought on a subject **b** : connected speech or writing **c** : a linguistic unit (as a conversation or a story) larger than a sentence **4** *obs* : social familiarity

²**dis·course** \dis-'kȯrs, -'kȯrs, 'dis-,\ *vb* **dis·coursed; dis·cours·ing** *vi* (1559) **1** : to express oneself esp. in oral discourse **2** : TALK, CONVERSE ~ *vt, archaic* : to give forth : UTTER — **dis·cours·er** *n*

discourse analysis *n* (1952) : the study of linguistic relations and structures in discourse

dis·cour·te·ous \(,)dis-'kər-tē-əs\ *adj* (1578) : lacking courtesy : RUDE — **dis·cour·te·ous·ly** *adv* — **dis·cour·te·ous·ness** *n*

dis·cour·te·sy \-'kər-tə-sē\ *n* (1555) **1** : RUDENESS **2** : a rude act

dis·cov·er \dis-'kə-vər\ *vb* **dis·cov·ered; dis·cov·er·ing** \-'kə-v(ə-)riŋ\ [ME, fr. MF *descovrir*, fr. LL *discooperire*, fr. L *dis-* + *cooperire* to cover — more at COVER] *vt* (14c) **1** **a** : to make known or visible : EXPOSE **b** *archaic* : DISPLAY **2** **a** : to obtain sight or knowledge of for the first time : FIND ⟨~ the solution⟩ **b** : FIND OUT ⟨~ed he was out of gas⟩ ~ *vi* : to make a discovery — **dis·cov·er·able** \-'kə-v(ə-)rə-bəl\ *adj* — **dis·cov·er·er** \-ər-ər\ *n*
syn DISCOVER, ASCERTAIN, DETERMINE, UNEARTH, LEARN mean to find out what one did not previously know. DISCOVER may apply to something requiring exploration or investigation or to a chance encounter ⟨*discovered* the source of the river⟩. ASCERTAIN implies effort to find the facts or the truth proceeding from awareness of ignorance or uncertainty ⟨attempts to *ascertain* the population of the region⟩. DETERMINE emphasizes the intent to establish the facts definitely or precisely ⟨unable to *determine* the origin of the word⟩. UNEARTH implies bringing to light something forgotten or hidden ⟨*unearth* old records⟩. LEARN may imply acquiring knowledge with little effort or conscious intention (as by simply being told) or it may imply study and practice ⟨I *learned* her name only today⟩ ⟨*learning* Greek⟩.

dis·cov·ery \dis-'kə-v(ə-)rē\ *n, pl* **-er·ies** (1539) **1** **a** : the act or process of discovering **b** (1) *archaic* : DISCLOSURE (2) *obs* : DISPLAY **c** *obs* : EXPLORATION **2** : something discovered **3** : the usu. pretrial disclosure of pertinent facts or documents by one or both parties to a legal action or proceeding

Discovery Day *n* (ca. 1913) : COLUMBUS DAY

¹**dis·cred·it** \(,)dis-'kre-dət\ *vt* (1559) **1** : to refuse to accept as true or accurate : DISBELIEVE **2** : to cause disbelief in the accuracy or authority of **3** : to deprive of good repute : DISGRACE

²**discredit** *n* (1565) **1** **a** : loss of credit or reputation ⟨I knew stories to the ~ of England —W. B. Yeats⟩ **b** : lack or loss of belief or confidence : DOUBT ⟨contradictions cast ~ on his testimony⟩

dis·cred·it·able \-'kre-də-bəl\ *adj* (1640) : injurious to reputation : DISGRACEFUL — **dis·cred·it·ably** \-blē\ *adv*

dis·creet \di-'skrēt\ *adj* [ME, fr. MF *discret*, fr. ML *discretus*, fr. L, pp. of *discernere* to separate, distinguish between — more at DISCERN] (14c) **1** : having or showing discernment or good judgment in conduct and esp. in speech : PRUDENT; *esp* : capable of preserving prudent silence **2** : UNPRETENTIOUS, MODEST ⟨the warmth and ~ elegance of a civilized

\ə\ abut \ᵊ\ kitten, F table \ər\ further \a\ ash \ā\ ace \ä\ mop, mar \au̇\ out \ch\ chin \e\ bet \ē\ easy \g\ go \i\ hit \ī\ ice \j\ job \ŋ\ sing \ō\ go \ȯ\ law \ȯi\ boy \th\ thin \t̶h̶\ the \ü\ loot \u̇\ foot \y\ yet \zh\ vision \ā, k̲, ⁿ, œ, œ̄, ᵫ, ᵫ̄, ᶌ\ see Guide to Pronunciation home —Joseph Wechsberg⟩ **3** : UNOBTRUSIVE, UNNOTICEABLE ⟨followed at a ∼ distance⟩ — **dis·creet·ly** adv — **dis·creet·ness** n

dis·crep·an·cy \dis-ˈkre-pən-sē\ n, pl **-cies** (ca. 1623) **1** : the quality or state of being discrepant **2** : an instance of being discrepant

dis·crep·ant \-pənt\ adj [ME discrepaunt, fr. L discrepant-, discrepans, prp. of discrepare to sound discordantly, fr. dis- + crepare to rattle, creak — more at RAVEN] (15c) : being at variance : DISAGREEING ⟨widely ∼ conclusions⟩ — **dis·crep·ant·ly** adv

dis·crete \dis-ˈkrēt, ˈdis-,\ adj [ME, fr. L discretus] (14c) **1** : constituting a separate entity : individually distinct **2 a** : consisting of distinct or unconnected elements : NONCONTINUOUS **b** : taking on or having a finite or countably infinite number of values ⟨∼ probabilities⟩ ⟨a ∼ random variable⟩ syn see DISTINCT — **dis·crete·ly** adv — **dis·crete·ness** n

dis·cre·tion \dis-ˈkre-shən\ n (14c) **1** : the quality of being discreet : CIRCUMSPECTION; esp : cautious reserve in speech **2** : ability to make responsible decisions **3 a** : individual choice or judgment ⟨left the decision to his ∼⟩ **b** : power of free decision or latitude of choice within certain legal bounds ⟨reached the age of ∼⟩ **4** : the result of separating or distinguishing

dis·cre·tion·ary \-ˈkre-shə-ˌner-ē\ adj (1698) **1** : left to discretion : exercised at one's own discretion **2** : available for discretionary use ⟨∼ purchasing power⟩

discretionary account n (ca. 1920) : a security or commodity market account in which an agent (as a broker) is given power of attorney so as to be able to make independent decisions and buy and sell for the principal's account

dis·crim·i·na·bil·i·ty \-ˌkri-mə-nə-ˈbi-lə-tē\ n, pl **-ties** (ca. 1901) **1** : the quality of being discriminable **2** : the ability to discriminate

dis·crim·i·na·ble \dis-ˈkri-mə-nə-bəl\ adj (1736) : capable of being discriminated — **dis·crim·i·na·bly** \-blē\ adv

dis·crim·i·nant \-ˈkri-mə-nənt\ n (ca. 1948) : a mathematical expression providing a criterion for the behavior of another more complicated expression, relation, or set of relations

discriminant function n (ca. 1936) : a function of a set of variables (as measurements of taxonomic specimens) that is evaluated for samples of events or objects and used as an aid in discriminating between or classifying them

dis·crim·i·nate \dis-ˈkri-mə-ˌnāt\ vb **-nat·ed; -nat·ing** [L discriminatus, pp. of discriminare, fr. discrimin-, discrimen distinction, fr. discernere to distinguish between — more at DISCERN] vt (1628) **1 a** : to mark or perceive the distinguishing or peculiar features of **b** : DISTINGUISH, DIFFERENTIATE ⟨∼ hundreds of colors⟩ **2** : to distinguish by discerning or exposing differences; esp : to distinguish from another like object ∼ vi **1 a** : to make a distinction ⟨∼ among historical sources⟩ **b** : to use good judgment **2** : to make a difference in treatment or favor on a basis other than individual merit ⟨∼ in favor of your friends⟩ ⟨∼ against a certain nationality⟩

dis·crim·i·nat·ing adj (1647) **1** : making a distinction : DISTINGUISHING **2** : marked by discrimination: **a** : DISCERNING, JUDICIOUS **b** : DISCRIMINATORY — **dis·crim·i·nat·ing·ly** \-ˌnā-tiŋ-lē\ adv

dis·crim·i·na·tion \dis-ˌkri-mə-ˈnā-shən\ n (1648) **1 a** : the act of discriminating **b** : the process by which two stimuli differing in some aspect are responded to differently **2** : the quality or power of finely distinguishing **3 a** : the act, practice, or an instance of discriminating categorically rather than individually **b** : prejudiced or prejudicial outlook, action, or treatment ⟨racial ∼⟩ syn see DISCERNMENT — **dis·crim·i·na·tion·al** \-shnəl, -shə-nᵊl\ adj

dis·crim·i·na·tive \dis-ˈkri-mə-ˌnā-tiv, -ˈkri-mə-nət-\ adj (1677) **1** : making distinctions **2** : DISCRIMINATORY 2

dis·crim·i·na·tor \dis-ˈkri-mə-ˌnā-tər\ n (1828) : one that discriminates; esp : a circuit that can be adjusted to accept or reject signals of different characteristics (as amplitude or frequency)

dis·crim·i·na·to·ry \dis-ˈkri-mə-nə-ˌtōr-ē, -ˌtȯr-, -ˈkrim-nə-\ adj (1828) **1** : DISCRIMINATIVE 2 : applying or favoring discrimination in treatment — **dis·crim·i·na·to·ri·ly** \-ˌkri-mə-nə-ˈtōr-ə-lē, -ˈtȯr-, -ˌkrim-nə-\ adv

dis·cur·sive \dis-ˈkər-siv\ adj [ML discursivus, fr. L discursus, pp. of discurrere to run about — more at DISCOURSE] (1598) **1 a** : moving from topic to topic without order : RAMBLING **b** : proceeding coherently from topic to topic **2** : marked by analytical reasoning — **dis·cur·sive·ly** adv — **dis·cur·sive·ness** n

dis·cus \ˈdis-kəs\ n, pl **dis·cus·es** [L — more at DISH] (1656) : a disk (as of wood or plastic) that is thicker in the center than at the perimeter and that is hurled for distance as a track-and-field event; also : the event

dis·cuss \di-ˈskəs\ vt [ME, fr. L discussus, pp. of discutere to disperse, fr. dis- apart + quatere to shake — more at DIS-, QUASH] (14c) **1** obs : DISPEL **2 a** : to investigate by reasoning or argument **b** : to present in detail for examination or consideration ⟨∼ed plans for the party⟩ **c** : to talk about **3** obs : DECLARE — **dis·cuss·able** or **dis·cuss·ible** \-ˈskə-sə-bəl\ adj — **dis·cuss·er** n

discus

syn DISCUSS, ARGUE, DEBATE mean to discourse about in order to reach conclusions or to convince. DISCUSS implies a sifting of possibilities esp. by presenting considerations pro and con ⟨discussed the need for a new highway⟩. ARGUE implies the offering of reasons or evidence in support of convictions already held ⟨argued that the project would be too costly⟩. DEBATE suggests formal or public argument between opposing parties ⟨debated the merits of the amendment⟩; it may also apply to deliberation with oneself ⟨I'm debating whether I should go⟩.

dis·cus·sant \di-ˈskə-sᵊnt\ n (1926) : one who takes part in a formal discussion or symposium

dis·cus·sion \di-ˈskə-shən\ n (14c) **1** : consideration of a question in open and usu. informal debate **2** : a formal treatment of a topic in speech or writing

¹dis·dain \dis-ˈdān\ n [ME desdeyne, fr. OF desdeign, fr. desdeignier] (14c) : a feeling of contempt for what is beneath one : SCORN

²disdain vt [ME desdeynen, fr. MF desdeignier, fr. OF, fr. (assumed) VL

disdignare, fr. L dis- + dignare to deign — more at DEIGN] (14c) **1** : to look on with scorn **2** : to refuse or abstain from because of disdain **3** : to treat as beneath one's notice or dignity syn see DESPISE

dis·dain·ful \-fəl\ adj (ca. 1542) : full of or expressing disdain syn see PROUD — **dis·dain·ful·ly** \-fə-lē\ adv — **dis·dain·ful·ness** n

dis·ease \di-ˈzēz\ n [ME disese, fr. MF desaise, fr. des- dis- + aise ease] (14c) **1** obs : TROUBLE **2** : a condition of the living animal or plant body or of one of its parts that impairs normal functioning : SICKNESS, MALADY **3** : a harmful development (as in a social institution) — **dis·eased** \-ˈzēzd\ adj

dis·econ·o·my \ˌdi-si-ˈkä-nə-mē\ n (1937) **1** : a lack of economy **2** : a factor responsible for an increase in cost

dis·em·bark \ˌdi-səm-ˈbärk\ vb [MF desembarquer, fr. des- dis- + embarquer to embark] vt (1582) : to remove to shore from a ship ∼ vi **1** : to go ashore out of a ship **2** : to get out of a vehicle or craft — **dis·em·bar·ka·tion** \(ˌ)di-ˌsem-ˌbär-ˈkā-shən, -bər-\ n

dis·em·bar·rass \ˌdi-səm-ˈbar-əs\ vt (1726) : to free (as oneself) from something troublesome or superfluous syn see EXTRICATE

dis·em·body \ˌdi-səm-ˈbä-dē\ vt (1714) : to divest of a body, of corporeal existence, or of reality

dis·em·bogue \ˌdi-sim-ˈbōg\ vb **-bogued; -bogu·ing** [modif. of Sp desembocar, fr. des- dis- (fr. L dis-) + embocar to put into the mouth, fr. en in (fr. L in) + boca mouth, fr. L bucca] vi (1595) : to flow or come forth from or as if from a channel ∼ vt, archaic : to pour out from or as if from a container

dis·em·bow·el \ˌdi-səm-ˈbau̇(-ə)l\ vt (1618) **1** : to take out the bowels of : EVISCERATE **2** : to remove the substance of — **dis·em·bow·el·ment** \-mənt\ n

dis·en·chant \ˌdi-sᵊn-ˈchant\ vt [MF desenchanter, fr. des- dis- + enchanter to enchant] (ca. 1586) : to free from illusion — **dis·en·chant·er** n — **dis·en·chant·ing** adj — **dis·en·chant·ing·ly** \-ˈchan-tiŋ-lē\ adv — **dis·en·chant·ment** \-mənt\ n

dis·en·chant·ed \-ˈchan-təd\ adj (1838) : DISAPPOINTED, DISSATISFIED

dis·en·cum·ber \ˌdi-sᵊn-ˈkəm-bər\ vt [MF desencombrer, fr. des- dis- + encombrer to encumber] (1598) : to free from encumbrance : DISBURDEN syn see EXTRICATE

dis·en·dow \ˌdi-sᵊn-ˈdau̇\ vt (1861) : to strip of endowment — **dis·en·dow·er** \-ˈdau̇(-ə)r\ n — **dis·en·dow·ment** \-ˈdau̇-mənt\ n

dis·en·fran·chise \ˌdi-sᵊn-ˈfran-ˌchīz\ vt (1664) : DISFRANCHISE — **dis·en·fran·chise·ment** \-ˌchīz-mənt, -chəz-\ n

dis·en·gage \ˌdi-sᵊn-ˈgāj\ vb [F désengager, fr. MF, fr. des- dis- + engager to engage] vt (1611) : to release from something that engages or involves ∼ vi : to release or detach oneself : WITHDRAW — **dis·en·gage·ment** \-mənt\ n

dis·en·tail \ˌdi-sᵊn-ˈtā(ə)l\ vt (1641) : to free from entail

dis·en·tan·gle \ˌdi-sᵊn-ˈtaŋ-gəl\ vt (1598) : to free from entanglement : UNRAVEL ∼ vi : to become disentangled syn see EXTRICATE — **dis·en·tan·gle·ment** \-mənt\ n

dis·en·thral also **dis·en·thrall** \ˌdi-sᵊn-ˈthrȯl\ vt (1643) : to free from bondage : LIBERATE

dis·en·ti·tle \ˌdi-sᵊn-ˈtī-tᵊl\ vt (1654) : to deprive of title, claim, or right

dis·equil·i·brate \ˌdi-si-ˈkwi-lə-ˌbrāt\ vt (1891) : to put out of balance — **dis·equil·i·bra·tion** \-ˌkwi-lə-ˈbrā-shən\ n

dis·equi·lib·ri·um \(ˌ)di-ˌsē-kwə-ˈli-brē-əm, -ˌse-kwə-\ n (1840) : loss or lack of equilibrium

dis·es·tab·lish \ˌdi-sə-ˈstab-lish\ vt (1598) : to deprive of an established status; esp : to deprive of the status and privileges of an established church — **dis·es·tab·lish·ment** \-mənt\ n

dis·es·tab·lish·men·tar·i·an \ˌstab-lish-ˌmen-ˈter-ē-ən, -mən-\ n, often cap [disestablishment] (1885) : one who opposes an established order — **disestablishmentarian** adj, often cap

¹dis·es·teem \ˌdi-sə-ˈstēm\ vt (1594) : to regard with disfavor

²disesteem n (1603) : DISFAVOR, DISREPUTE

di·seuse \dē-ˈzüz, -ˈzœz\ n, pl **-seuses** \same\ [F, fem. of diseur, fr. OF, fr. dire to say, fr. L dicere — more at DICTION] (1896) : a skilled and usu. professional woman reciter

¹dis·fa·vor \(ˌ)dis-ˈfā-vər\ n [prob. fr. MF desfaveur, fr. des- dis- + faveur favor, fr. OF favor] (ca. 1533) **1** : DISAPPROVAL, DISLIKE ⟨practices looked upon with ∼⟩ **2** : the state or fact of being no longer favored ⟨fell into ∼⟩ **3** : DISADVANTAGE

²disfavor vt (1570) : to withhold or withdraw favor from

dis·fig·ure \dis-ˈfi-gyər, esp Brit -ˈfi-gər\ vt [ME, fr. MF desfigurer, fr. des- dis- + figure figure] (14c) **1** : to impair (as in beauty) by deep and persistent injuries ⟨a face disfigured by smallpox⟩ **2** obs : DISGUISE — **dis·fig·ure·ment** \-mənt\ n

dis·fran·chise \(ˌ)dis-ˈfran-ˌchīz\ vt (15c) : to deprive of a franchise, of a legal right, or of some privilege or immunity; esp : to deprive of the right to vote — **dis·fran·chise·ment** \-ˌchīz-mənt, -chəz-\ n

dis·frock \(ˌ)dis-ˈfräk\ vt (1837) : DEFROCK

dis·func·tion var of DYSFUNCTION

dis·fur·nish \(ˌ)dis-ˈfər-nish\ vt [MF desfourniss-, stem of desfournir, fr. des- dis- + fournir to furnish] (1531) : to make destitute of possessions : DIVEST — **dis·fur·nish·ment** \-mənt\ n

dis·gorge \(ˌ)dis-ˈgȯrj\ vb [ME, fr. MF desgorger, fr. des- dis- + gorge gorge] vt (15c) **1 a** : to discharge by the throat and mouth : VOMIT **b** : to discharge or let go of in a manner suggesting vomiting ⟨the train disgorged its passengers⟩ **c** : to give up on request or under pressure ⟨refused to ∼ his ill-gotten gains⟩ **2** : to discharge the contents of (as the stomach) ∼ vi : to discharge contents ⟨where the river ∼s into the sea⟩

¹dis·grace \di-ˈskrās, dis-ˈgrās\ vt (1580) **1** archaic : to humiliate by a superior showing **2** : to be a source of shame to ⟨your actions disgraced the family⟩ **3** : to cause to lose favor or standing ⟨was disgraced by the hint of scandal⟩ — **dis·grac·er** n

²disgrace n [MF, fr. OIt disgrazia, fr. dis- (fr. L) + grazia grace, fr. L gratia — more at GRACE] (1586) **1 a** : the condition of one fallen from grace or honor **b** : loss of grace, favor, or honor **2** : something that disgraces ⟨your manners are a ∼⟩

syn DISGRACE, DISHONOR, DISREPUTE, INFAMY, IGNOMINY mean the state or condition of suffering loss of esteem and of enduring reproach. DISGRACE often implies humiliation and sometimes ostracism ⟨sent home in disgrace⟩. DISHONOR emphasizes the loss of honor that one has enjoyed or the loss of self-esteem ⟨preferred death to life with dishonor⟩. DISREPUTE stresses loss of one's good name or the acquiring of a bad reputation ⟨a once proud name fallen into *disrepute*⟩. INFAMY usu. implies notoriety as well as exceeding shame ⟨a day that lives in *infamy*⟩. IGNOMINY stresses humiliation ⟨the *ignominy* of being arrested⟩.

dis·grace·ful \-fəl\ *adj* (1597) : bringing or involving disgrace — **dis·grace·ful·ly** \-fə-lē\ *adv* — **dis·grace·ful·ness** *n*

dis·grun·tle \dis-'grən-t⁰l\ *vt* **dis·grun·tled; dis·grun·tling** \-'grənt-liŋ, -'grən-t⁰l-iŋ\ [*dis-* + *gruntle* (to grumble), fr. ME *gruntlen*, freq. of *grunten* to grunt (1682)] : to make ill-humored or discontented — usu. used as a participial adjective ⟨has a very *disgruntled* crew — Flannery O'Connor⟩ — **dis·grun·tle·ment** \-t⁰l-mənt\ *n*

¹dis·guise \də-'skīz, dis-'gīz *also* diz-\ *vt* **dis·guised; dis·guis·ing** [ME *disgisen*, fr. MF *desguiser*, fr. OF, fr. *des-* + *guise* guise] (14c) **1 a** : to change the customary dress or appearance of **b** : to furnish with a false appearance or an assumed identity **2** *obs* : DISFIGURE **3** : to obscure the existence or true state or character of : CONCEAL — **dis·guised·ly** \-'gīz(-ə)d-lē, -'kīz(-ə)d-\ *adv* — **dis·guise·ment** \-'gīz-mənt, -'kīz-\ *n* — **dis·guis·er** *n*

syn DISGUISE, CLOAK, MASK mean to alter the dress or appearance of so as to conceal the identity or true nature. DISGUISE implies a change in appearance or behavior that misleads by presenting a different apparent identity ⟨*disguised* himself as a peasant⟩. CLOAK suggests a means of hiding a movement or an intention ⟨*cloaked* their maneuvers in secrecy⟩. MASK suggests some often obvious means of hiding or disguising something ⟨smiling to *mask* his discontent⟩.

²disguise *n* (14c) **1** : apparel assumed to conceal one's identity or counterfeit another's **2** : the act of disguising **3 a** : form misrepresenting the true nature of something ⟨blessings in ~⟩ **b** : an artificial manner ⟨threw off all ~⟩

¹dis·gust \di-'skəst, dis-'gəst *also* diz-\ *n* (1598) : marked aversion aroused by something highly distasteful : REPUGNANCE

²disgust *vb* [MF *desgouster*, fr. *des-* dis- + *goust* taste, fr. L *gustus*; akin to L *gustare* to taste — more at CHOOSE] *vt* (1616) **1** : to provoke to loathing, repugnance, or aversion : to be offensive to **2** : to cause (one) to lose an interest or intention ~ *vi* : to cause disgust — **dis·gust·ed·ly** *adj* — **dis·gust·ed·ly** *adv*

dis·gust·ful \-fəl\ *adj* (ca. 1616) **1** : provoking disgust **2** : full of or accompanied by disgust — **dis·gust·ful·ly** \-fə-lē\ *adv*

dis·gust·ing *adj* (1754) : causing disgust — **dis·gust·ing·ly** \di-'skəs-tiŋ-lē, dis-'gəs- *also* diz-\ *adv*

¹dish \'dish\ *n*, fr. OE *disc* plate, fr. L *discus* quoit, disk, dish, fr. Gk *diskos*, fr. *dikein* to throw] (bef. 12c) **1 a** : a more or less concave vessel from which food is served **b** : the contents of a dish ⟨a ~ of strawberries⟩ **2 a** : food prepared in a particular way **b** : something one particularly enjoys : CUP OF TEA **3 a** (1) : any of various shallow concave vessels; *broadly* : anything shallowly concave (2) : a directional receiver having a concave usu. parabolic reflector; *esp* : one used as a microwave antenna **b** : the state of being concave or the degree of concavity **4 a** : something that is favored ⟨entertainment that is just his ~⟩ **b** : an attractive or sexy person

²dish *vt* (14c) **1** : to put (as food for serving) into a dish — often used with *up* **2** : PRESENT — usu. used with *up* **3** : to make concave like a dish ~ *vi* : to pass to a teammate (as in basketball) — usu. used with *off*

dis·ha·bille \,dis-ə-'bē(ə)l, -'bil\ *n* [F *déshabillé*, fr. pp. of *déshabiller* to undress, fr. *dés-* dis- + *habiller* to dress — more at HABILIMENT] (1673) **1** *archaic* : NEGLIGEE **2** : the state of being dressed in a casual or careless style **2** : a deliberately careless or casual manner

dis·har·mo·ni·ous \,dis-(,)här-'mō-nē-əs\ *adj* (1659) : lacking in harmony

dis·har·mo·nize \(,)dis-'här-mə-,nīz\ *vt* (1801) : to make disharmonious

dis·har·mo·ny \-nē\ *n* (ca. 1602) : lack of harmony : DISCORD

dish·cloth \'dish-,klȯth\ *n* (ca. 1828) : a cloth for washing dishes

dish·clout \'dish-,klaȯt\ *n* (ca. 1530) *Brit* : DISHCLOTH

dis·heart·en \(,)dis-'här-t⁰n\ *vt* (1590) : to cause to lose spirit or morale — **dis·heart·en·ing·ly** \-'härt-niŋ-lē, -'härt-t⁰n-iŋ-\ *adv* — **dis·heart·en·ment** \-'härt-t⁰n-mənt\ *n*

dished \'disht\ *adj* (1737) : CONCAVE

di·shev·el \di-'shev-əl\ *vt* **di·shev·eled** *or* **di·shev·elled; di·shev·el·ing** *or* **di·shev·el·ling** \-'she-v(ə-)liŋ\ [back-formation fr. *disheveled*] (1598) : to throw into disorder or disarray

di·shev·eled *or* **di·shev·elled** *adj* [ME *discheveled* with disordered hair, part trans. of MF *deschevelé*, fr. pp. of *descheveler* to disarrange the hair, fr. *des-* dis- + *chevel* hair, fr. L *capillus*] (1583) : marked by disorder or disarray

dis·hon·est \(,)di-'sä-nəst *also* -'zä-\ *adj* [ME, fr. MF *deshoneste*, fr. *des-* dis- + *honeste* honest] (14c) **1** *obs* : SHAMEFUL, UNCHASTE **2** : characterized by lack of truth, honesty, or trustworthiness : UNFAIR, DECEPTIVE — **dis·hon·est·ly** *adv*

syn DISHONEST, DECEITFUL, MENDACIOUS, UNTRUTHFUL mean unworthy of trust or belief. DISHONEST implies a willful perversion of truth in order to deceive, cheat, or defraud ⟨a swindle usually involves two *dishonest* people⟩. DECEITFUL usu. implies an intent to mislead and commonly suggests a false appearance or double-dealing ⟨the secret affairs of a *deceitful* spouse⟩. MENDACIOUS may suggest bland or even harmlessly mischievous deceit and when used of people often suggests a habit of telling untruths ⟨*mendacious* tales of adventure⟩. UNTRUTHFUL stresses a discrepancy between what is said and fact or reality ⟨an *untruthful* account of their actions⟩.

dis·hon·es·ty \-nə-stē\ *n* (1599) **1** : lack of honesty or integrity : disposition to defraud or deceive **2** : a dishonest act : FRAUD

¹dis·hon·or \(,)di-'sä-nər *also* -'zä-\ *n* [ME *dishonour*, fr. MF *deshonor*, fr. *des-* dis- + *honor* honor] (13c) **1** : lack or loss of honor or reputation **2** : the state of one who has lost honor or prestige : SHAME **3** : a cause of disgrace **4** : the nonpayment or nonacceptance of commercial paper by the party on whom it is drawn **syn** see DISGRACE — **dis·hon·or·er** \-'sän-ər-ər *also* -'zä-\ *n*

²dishonor *vt* (13c) **1 a** : to treat in a degrading manner **b** : to bring shame on **2** : to refuse to accept or pay (as a bill or check)

dis·hon·or·able \(,)di-'sä-nə-rə-bəl, -'sä-nər-bəl\ *adj* (1534) **1** : lacking honor : SHAMEFUL ⟨~ conduct⟩ **2** *archaic* : not honored — **dis·hon·or·able·ness** *n* — **dis·hon·or·ably** \-blē\ *adv*

dish out *vt* (1641) : to give or dispense freely ⟨*dish out* gifts⟩ ⟨*dish out* advice⟩ ⟨*dish out* punishment⟩

dish·pan \'dish-,pan\ *n* (1872) : a large flat-bottomed pan used for washing dishes

dishpan hands *n pl but sing or pl in constr* (1944) : a condition of dryness, redness, and scaling of the hands that results typically from repeated exposure to, sensitivity to, or overuse of cleaning materials (as detergents) used in housework

dish·rag \'dish-,rag\ *n* (1839) : DISHCLOTH

dish·ware \'dish-,war, -,wer\ *n* (1946) : tableware (as of china) used in serving food

dish·wash·er \-,wȯ-shər, -,wä-\ *n* (15c) **1** : a worker employed to wash dishes **2** : a machine for washing dishes

dish·wa·ter \-,wȯ-tər, -,wä-\ *n* (15c) : water in which dishes have been or are to be washed

dishy \'di-shē\ *adj* **dish·i·er; -est** (1961) : ATTRACTIVE 2

¹dis·il·lu·sion \,di-sə-'lü-zhən\ *n* (1851) : the condition of being disenchanted

²disillusion *vt* **dis·il·lu·sioned; dis·il·lu·sion·ing** \-'lü-zhə-niŋ\ (1855) : to leave without illusion or naive faith and trust — **dis·il·lu·sion·ment** \-'lü-zhən-mənt\ *n*

disillusioned *adj* (1871) : DISAPPOINTED, DISSATISFIED

dis·in·cen·tive \,di-s⁰n-'sen-tiv\ *n* (1946) : DETERRENT

dis·in·cli·na·tion \(,)di-,sin-klə-'nä-shən, -,siŋ-\ *n* (1647) : a preference for avoiding something : slight aversion

dis·in·cline \,di-s⁰n-'klīn\ *vt* (1647) : to make unwilling

dis·in·clined *adj* (1647) : unwilling because of mild dislike or disapproval

syn DISINCLINED, HESITANT, RELUCTANT, LOATH, AVERSE mean lacking the will or desire to do something indicated. DISINCLINED implies lack of taste for or inclination ⟨*disinclined* to move again⟩ ⟨*disinclined* for reading⟩. HESITANT implies a holding back esp. through fear or uncertainty ⟨*hesitant* about asking for a date⟩. RELUCTANT implies a holding back through unwillingness ⟨a *reluctant* witness⟩. LOATH implies hesitancy because of conflict with one's opinions, predilections, or liking ⟨seems *loath* to trust anyone⟩. AVERSE implies a holding back from or avoiding because of distaste or repugnance ⟨*averse* to hard work⟩ ⟨not *averse* to an occasional drink⟩.

dis·in·fect \,dis-⁰n-'fekt\ *vt* [MF *desinfecter*, fr. *des-* dis- + *infecter* to infect] (1598) : to free from infection esp. by destroying harmful microorganisms; *broadly* : CLEANSE — **dis·in·fec·tion** \-'fek-shən\ *n*

dis·in·fec·tant \-'fek-tənt\ *n* (1837) : an agent that frees from infection; *esp* : a chemical that destroys vegetative forms of harmful microorganisms esp. on inanimate objects but that may be less effective in destroying bacterial spores

dis·in·fest \,dis-⁰n-'fest\ *vt* (ca. 1920) : to rid of small animal pests (as insects or rodents) — **dis·in·fes·ta·tion** \(,)dis-,in-,fes-'tā-shən\ *n*

dis·in·fes·tant \,dis-⁰n-'fes-tənt\ *n* (1943) : a disinfesting agent

dis·in·fla·tion \,dis-⁰n-'flā-shən\ *n* (1880) : a reversal of inflationary pressures — **dis·in·fla·tion·ary** \-shə-,ner-ē\ *adj*

dis·in·for·ma·tion \(,)di-,sin-fər-'mä-shən\ *n* (1939) : false information deliberately and often covertly spread (as by the planting of rumors) in order to influence public opinion or obscure the truth

dis·in·gen·u·ous \,di-s⁰n-'jen-yə-wəs\ *adj* (1655) : lacking in candor; *also* : giving a false appearance of simple frankness : CALCULATING — **dis·in·gen·u·ous·ly** *adv* — **dis·in·gen·u·ous·ness** *n*

dis·in·her·it \,di-s⁰n-'her-ət\ *vt* [ME] (15c) **1** : to prevent deliberately from inheriting something (as by making a will) **2** : to deprive of natural or human rights or of previously held special privileges — **dis·in·her·i·tance** \-'her-ə-tən(t)s\ *n*

dis·in·hi·bi·tion \(,)di-,sin-(h)ə-'bi-shən\ *n* (ca. 1927) : loss or reduction of an inhibition (as by the action of interfering stimuli or events) ⟨~ of a reflex⟩ ⟨~ of violent tendencies⟩ — **dis·in·hib·it** \(,)di-s⁰n-'hi-bət\ *vt*

dis·in·te·grate \(,)di-'sin-tə-,grāt\ *vt* (1796) **1** : to break or decompose into constituent elements, parts, or small particles **2** : to destroy the unity or integrity of ~ *vi* **1** : to break or separate into constituent elements or parts **2** : to lose unity or integrity by or as if by breaking into parts **3** : to undergo a change in composition ⟨an atomic nucleus that ~s because of radioactivity⟩ — **dis·in·te·gra·tion** \(,)di-,sin-tə-'grā-shən\ *n* — **dis·in·te·gra·tive** \(,)di-'sin-tə-,grā-tiv\ *adj* — **dis·in·te·gra·tor** \-,grā-tər\ *n*

dis·in·ter \,di-s⁰n-'tər\ *vt* (1611) **1** : to take out of the grave or tomb **2** : to bring back into awareness or prominence; *also* : to bring to light : UNEARTH — **dis·in·ter·ment** *n*

¹dis·in·ter·est \(,)dis-'in-trəst; -'in-tə-,rest, -tə-rəst, -tərst; -'in-,trest\ *n* (1612) : to cause to regard something with no interest or concern

²disinterest *n* (1658) **1** : DISINTERESTEDNESS **2** : lack of interest : INDIFFERENCE

dis·in·ter·est·ed \-təd\ *adj* (ca. 1612) **1 a** : not having the mind or feelings engaged : not interested ⟨telling them in a ~ voice —Tom Wicker⟩ ⟨Introverted. Unsocial . . . *Disinterested* in women —J. A. Brussel⟩ **b** : no longer interested ⟨husband and wife become ~ in each other —T. I. Rubin⟩ **2** : free from selfish motive or interest : UNBIASED ⟨a ~ decision⟩ ⟨~ intellectual curiosity is the lifeblood of real civilization —G. M. Trevelyan⟩ **syn** see INDIFFERENT — **dis·in·ter·est·ed·ly** *adv*

usage *Disinterested* and *uninterested* have a tangled history. *Uninterested* orig. meant impartial, but this sense fell into disuse during the 18th century. About the same time the original sense of *disinterested* also disappeared, with *uninterested* developing a new sense—the present meaning—to take its place. The original sense of *uninterested* is still out of use, but the original sense of *disinterested* revived in the early 20th century. The revival has since been under frequent attack as an illiterate and a blurring or loss of a useful distinction. Actual usage shows otherwise. Sense 2 of *disinterested* is still its most frequent sense, esp. in edited prose; it shows no sign of vanishing. A careful

\ə\ abut \ᵊ\ kitten, F table \ər\ further \a\ ash \ā\ ace \ä\ mop, mar \aȯ\ out \ch\ chin \e\ bet \ē\ easy \g\ go \i\ hit \ī\ ice \j\ job \ŋ\ sing \ō\ go \ȯ\ law \ȯi\ boy \th\ thin \t͟h\ the \ü\ loot \u̇\ foot \y\ yet \zh\ vision \á, k̠, ⁿ, œ, œ̄, ue, u̇e, ᵞ\ *see* Guide to Pronunciation writer may choose sense 1a of *disinterested* in preference to *uninterested* for emphasis ⟨teaching the letters of the alphabet to her wiggling and supremely *disinterested* little daughter —C. L. Sulzberger⟩ Further, *disinterested* has developed a sense (1b), perhaps influenced by sense 1 of the prefix *dis-*, that contrasts with *uninterested* ⟨when I grow tired or *disinterested* in anything, I experience a disgust —Jack London (letter, 1914)⟩ Still, use of senses 1a and 1b will incur the disapproval of some who may not fully appreciate the history of this word or the subtleties of its present use.

dis·in·ter·est·ed·ness \-təd-nəs\ *n* (ca. 1682) : the quality of being objective or impartial

dis·in·ter·me·di·a·tion \,di-,sin-tər-,mē-dē-'ā-shən\ *n* (1967) : the diversion of savings from accounts with low fixed interest rates to direct investment in high-yielding instruments

dis·in·tox·i·cate \,di-sᵊn-'täk-sə-,kāt\ *vt* (1685) : DETOXIFY 2 — **dis·in·tox·i·ca·tion** \-,täk-sə-'kā-shən\ *n*

dis·in·vest \,(,)di-sᵊn-'vest\ *vi* (1945) : to reduce or eliminate capital investment (as in an industry or area)

dis·in·vest·ment \-di-sᵊn-'ves(t)-mənt\ *n* (1936) : consumption of capital; *also* : the withdrawing of investment

dis·in·vite \(,)di-sᵊn-'vīt\ *vt* (1580) : to withdraw an invitation to

dis·join \(,)dis-'jöin\ *vb* [ME *disjoynen*, fr. MF *desjoindre*, fr. L *disjungere*, fr. *dis-* + *jungere* to join — more at YOKE] *vt* (15c) : to end the joining of ~ *vi* : to become detached

¹dis·joint \-'jöint\ *adj* [ME *disjoynt*, fr. MF *desjoint*, pp. of *desjoindre*] (15c) 1 *obs* : DISJOINTED 1a 2 : having no elements in common ⟨~ mathematical sets⟩

²disjoint *vt* (15c) 1 : to disturb the orderly structure or arrangement of 2 : to take apart at the joints ~ *vi* : to come apart at the joints

dis·joint·ed *adj* (ca. 1586) 1 a : being thrown out of orderly function ⟨a ~ society⟩ b : lacking coherence or orderly sequence ⟨an incomplete and ~ history⟩ 2 : separated at or as if at the joint — **dis·joint·ed·ly** *adv* — **dis·joint·ed·ness** *n*

¹dis·junct \dis-'jəŋ(k)t\ *adj* [ME, fr. L *disjunctus*, pp. of *disjungere* to disjoin] (15c) 1 : marked by separation of or from usu. contiguous parts or individuals: as a : DISCONTINUOUS b : relating to melodic progression by intervals larger than a major second — compare CONJUNCT

²dis·junct \'dis-,jəŋ(k)t, dis-'\ *n* (1921) 1 : any of the alternatives that make up a logical disjunction 2 : an adverb or adverbial (as *luckily* in "Luckily we had an extra set" or *in short* in "In short, there is nothing we can do") that is loosely connected to a sentence and conveys the speaker's or writer's comment on its content, truth, or manner — compare ADJUNCT 2b

dis·junc·tion \dis-'jəŋ(k)-shən\ *n* (14c) 1 : a sharp cleavage : DISUNION, SEPARATION ⟨the ~ between theory and practice⟩ 2 : a compound sentence in logic formed by joining two simple statements by *or*: a : INCLUSIVE DISJUNCTION b : EXCLUSIVE DISJUNCTION

¹dis·junc·tive \-'jəŋ(k)-tiv\ *adj* (15c) 1 a : relating to, being, or forming a logical disjunction b : expressing an alternative or opposition between the meanings of the words connected ⟨the ~ conjunction *or*⟩ c : expressed by mutually exclusive alternatives joined by *or* ⟨~ pleading⟩ 2 : marked by breaks or disunity ⟨a ~ narrative sequence⟩ 3 *of a pronoun form* : stressed and not attached to the verb as an enclitic or proclitic — **dis·junc·tive·ly** *adv*

²disjunctive *n* (1530) : a disjunctive conjunction

dis·junc·ture \-'jəŋ(k)-chər\ *n* [ME, modif. (influenced by L *disjunctus*) of MF *desjointure*, fr. *desjoint* disjoint] (14c) : DISJUNCTION 1

¹disk *or* **disc** \'disk\ *n, often attrib* [L *discus* — more at DISH] (1664) 1 a : the seemingly flat figure of a celestial body ⟨the solar ~⟩ b *archaic* : DISCUS 2 : any of various rounded and flattened animal anatomical structures (as an intervertebral disk) — compare SLIPPED DISK 3 : the central part of the flower head of a typical composite made up of closely packed tubular flowers 4 a : a thin circular object b *usu disc* : a phonograph record c : a round flat plate coated with a magnetic substance on which data for a computer is stored d *usu disc* : OPTICAL DISK: as (1) : VIDEODISC (2) : COMPACT DISC 5 *usu disc* : one of the concave circular steel tools with sharpened edge making up the working part of a disc harrow or plow; *also* : an implement employing such tools — **disk·like** \-,līk\ *adj*

²disk *or* **disc** *vt* (ca. 1884) : to cultivate with an implement (as a harrow or plow) that turns and loosens the soil with a series of disks

dis·kette \dis-'ket\ *n* (1973) : FLOPPY DISK

disk flower *n* (1870) : one of the tubular flowers in the disk of a composite plant — called also *disk floret*

dis·lik·able *also* **dis·like·able** \(,)dis-'lī-kə-bəl\ *adj* (1843) : easy to dislike

¹dis·like \(,)dis-'līk, 'dis-,\ *n* (1577) 1 : a feeling of aversion or disapproval 2 *obs* : DISCORD

²dislike *vt* (1579) 1 *archaic* : DISPLEASE 2 : to regard with dislike : DISAPPROVE 3 *obs* : to show aversion to — **dis·lik·er** *n*

dis·limn \(,)dis-'lim\ *vb* (1606) : DIM

dis·lo·cate \'dis-lō-,kāt, -lə-; (,)dis-'lō-\ *vt* [ML *dislocatus*, pp. of *dislocare*, fr. L *dis-* + *locare* to locate] (1605) 1 : to put out of place; *specif* : to displace (a bone) from normal connections with another bone 2 : to force a change in the usual status, relationship, or order of : DISRUPT

dis·lo·ca·tion \,dis-(,)lō-'kā-shən, -lə-\ *n* (14c) : the act of dislocating : the state of being dislocated: as a : displacement of one or more bones at a joint : LUXATION b : a discontinuity in the otherwise normal lattice structure of a crystal c : disruption of an established order

dis·lodge \(,)dis-'läj\ *vb* [ME *dislogen*, fr. MF *desloger*, fr. *des-* dis- + *loger* to lodge, fr. OF *loge* lodge] *vt* (15c) 1 : to drive from a position of hiding, defense, or advantage 2 : to force out of a secure or settled position ⟨*dislodged* the rock with a shovel⟩ ~ *vi* : to leave a lodging place — **dis·lodg·ment** *or* **dis·lodge·ment** *n*

dis·loy·al \(,)dis-'löi(-ə)l\ *adj* [ME, fr. MF *desloial*, fr. OF, fr. *des-* dis- + *loial* loyal] (15c) : lacking in loyalty; *also* : showing an absence of allegiance, devotion, obligation, faith, or support ⟨his ~ refusal to help his friend⟩ *syn* see FAITHLESS — **dis·loy·al·ly** \-'löi-ə-lē\ *adv*

dis·loy·al·ty \-'löi(-ə)l-tē\ *n* (15c) : lack of loyalty

dis·mal \'diz-məl\ *adj* [ME, fr. *dismal*, n., days marked as unlucky in medieval calendars, fr. AF, fr. ML *dies mali*, lit., evil days] (15c) 1 *obs* : DISASTROUS, DREADFUL 2 : showing or causing gloom or depression

3 : lacking merit : particularly bad — **dis·mal·ly** \-mə-lē\ *adv* — **dis·mal·ness** *n*

dis·man·tle \(,)dis-'man-tᵊl\ *vt* **dis·man·tled; dis·man·tling** \-'mant-liŋ, -'man-tᵊl-\ [MF *desmanteler*, fr. *des-* dis- + *mantel* mantle] (1602) 1 : to take to pieces; *also* : to destroy the integrity or functioning of 2 : to strip of dress or covering : DIVEST 3 : to strip of furniture and equipment — **dis·man·tle·ment** \-'man-tᵊl-mənt\ *n*

dis·mast \(,)dis-'mast\ *vt* (1747) : to remove or break off the mast of

¹dis·may \dis-'mā, diz-\ *vt* **dis·mayed; dis·may·ing** [ME, fr. (assumed) OF *desmaier*, fr. OF *des-* dis- + *-maier* (as in *esmaier* to dismay), fr. (assumed) VL *-magare*, of Gmc origin; akin to OHG *magan* to be able — more at MAY] (13c) : to deprive of courage, resolution, and initiative through the pressure of sudden fear or anxiety or great perplexity — **dis·may·ing·ly** \-iŋ-lē\ *adv*

syn DISMAY, APPALL, HORRIFY, DAUNT mean to unnerve or deter by arousing fear, apprehension, or aversion. DISMAY implies that one is disconcerted and at a loss as to how to deal with something ⟨*dismayed* at the size of the job⟩. APPALL implies that one is faced with that which perturbs, confounds, or shocks ⟨I am *appalled* by your behavior⟩. HORRIFY stresses a reaction of horror or revulsion ⟨was *horrified* by such wanton cruelty⟩. DAUNT suggests a cowing, disheartening, or frightening in a venture requiring courage ⟨a cliff that would *daunt* the most intrepid climber⟩.

²dismay *n* (14c) 1 : sudden loss of courage or resolution from alarm or fear 2 a : sudden disappointment b : PERTURBATION 1

disme \'dim\ *n* [obs. E, tenth, fr. obs. F, fr. MF *disme, dime* — more at DIME] (1792) : a U.S. 10-cent coin struck in 1792

dis·mem·ber \(,)dis-'mem-bər\ *vt* **-bered; -ber·ing** \-b(ə-)riŋ\ [ME *dismembren*, fr. OF *desmembrer*, fr. *des-* dis- + *membre* member] (14c) 1 : to cut off or disjoin the limbs, members, or parts of 2 : to break up or tear into pieces — **dis·mem·ber·ment** \-bər-mənt\ *n*

dis·miss \dis-'mis\ *vt* [ME, modif. of L *dimissus*, pp. of *dimittere*, fr. *dis-* apart + *mittere* to send — more at DIS-, SMITE] (15c) 1 : to permit or cause to leave ⟨~ed the visitors⟩ 2 : to remove from position or service : DISCHARGE 3 a : to reject serious consideration of ⟨~ed the thought⟩ b : to put out of judicial consideration ⟨~ed all charges⟩ — **dis·mis·sion** \-'mi-shən\ *n* — **dis·mis·sive** \-'mi-siv\ *adj* — **dis·mis·sive·ly** *adv*

dis·miss·al \-'mi-səl\ *n* (1816) : the act of dismissing : the fact or state of being dismissed

¹dis·mount \(,)dis-'maunt\ *vb* [prob. modif. of MF *desmonter*, fr. *des-* dis- + *monter* to mount] *vi* (1579) 1 *obs* : DESCEND 2 : to alight from an elevated position (as on a horse); *also* : to get out of an enclosed craft or vehicle ~ *vt* 1 : to throw down or remove from a mount or an elevated position; *esp* : UNHORSE 2 : DISASSEMBLE

²dismount *n* (1654) : the act of dismounting

dis·obe·di·ence \,di-sə-'bē-dē-ən(t)s\ *n* (15c) : refusal or neglect to obey

dis·obe·di·ent \-ənt\ *adj* [ME, fr. MF *desobedient*, fr. OF, fr. *des-* dis- + *obedient* obedient] (15c) : refusing or neglecting to obey — **dis·obe·di·ent·ly** *adv*

dis·obey \,di-sə-'bā\ *vb* [ME, fr. MF *desobeir*, fr. OF, fr. *des-* dis- + *obeir* to obey] *vi* (14c) : to be disobedient ~ *vt* : to fail to obey — **dis·obey·er** *n*

dis·oblige \,di-sə-'blīj\ *vt* [F *désobliger*, fr. MF, fr. *des-* dis- + *obliger* to oblige] (1632) 1 : to go counter to the wishes of 2 : INCONVENIENCE

di·so·di·um phosphate \(,)di-'sō-dē-əm-\ *n* (ca. 1928) : a sodium phosphate Na_2HPO_4

di·so·mic \(,)dī-'sō-mik\ *adj* [*di-* + *-somic*] (1924) : having one or more chromosomes present in twice the normal number but not having the entire genome doubled

¹dis·or·der \(,)di-'sör-dər, -'zor-\ *vt* (15c) 1 : to disturb the order of 2 : to disturb the regular or normal functions of

²disorder *n* (1530) 1 : lack of order ⟨clothes in ~⟩ 2 : breach of the peace or public order ⟨troubled times marked by social ~s⟩ 3 : an abnormal physical or mental condition : AILMENT ⟨a nervous ~⟩

dis·or·dered *adj* (1548) 1 *obs* a : morally reprehensible b : UNRULY 2 a : marked by disorder b : not functioning in a normal orderly healthy way — **dis·or·dered·ly** *adv* — **dis·or·dered·ness** *n*

¹dis·or·der·ly \-'sörd-ər-lē\ *adv* (1564) *archaic* : in a disorderly manner

²disorderly *adj* (1585) 1 : engaged in conduct offensive to public order ⟨charged with being drunk and ~⟩ 2 : characterized by disorder ⟨a ~ pile of clothes⟩ — **dis·or·der·li·ness** *n*

disorderly conduct *n* (ca. 1845) : a petty offense chiefly against public order and decency that falls short of an indictable misdemeanor

disorderly house *n* [euphemism] (ca. 1809) : BORDELLO

dis·or·ga·nize \(,)di-'sör-gə-,nīz\ *vt* [F *désorganiser*, fr. *dés-* dis- + *organiser* to organize] (1793) : to destroy or interrupt the orderly structure or function of — **dis·or·ga·ni·za·tion** \(,)di-,sör-gə-nə-'zā-shən\ *n*

dis·or·ga·nized *adj* (1812) : lacking coherence, system, or central guiding agency ⟨~ work habits⟩

dis·ori·ent \(,)di-'sör-ē-,ent, -'sòr-\ *vt* [F *désorienter*, fr. *dés-* dis- + *orienter* to orient] (1655) 1 a : to cause to lose bearings : displace from normal position or relationship b : to cause to lose the sense of time, place, or identity 2 : CONFUSE

dis·ori·en·tate \-ē-ən-,tāt, -ē-,en-\ *vt* (ca. 1704) : DISORIENT — **dis·ori·en·ta·tion** \(,)di-,sòr-ē-ən-'tā-shən, -,sòr-, -ē-,en-\ *n*

dis·own \(,)di-'sōn\ *vt* (1649) 1 : to refuse to acknowledge as one's own 2 a : to repudiate any connection or identification with b : to deny the validity or authority of — **dis·own·ment** \-mənt\ *n*

dis·par·age \di-'spar-ij\ *vt* **-aged; -ag·ing** [ME, to degrade by marriage below one's class, disparage, fr. MF *desparagier* to marry below one's class, fr. OF, fr. *des-* dis- + *parage* extraction, lineage, fr. *per* peer] (14c) 1 : to lower in rank or reputation : DEGRADE 2 : to depreciate by indirect means (as invidious comparison) : speak slightingly about *syn* see DECRY — **dis·par·age·ment** \-ij-mənt\ *n* — **dis·par·ag·er** *n* — **dis·par·ag·ing·ly** \-ij-iŋ-lē\ *adv*

dis·pa·rate \'dis-p(ə-)rət, di-'spar-ət\ *adj* [L *disparatus*, pp. of *disparare* to separate, fr. *dis-* + *parare* to prepare — more at PARE] (15c) 1 : containing or made up of fundamentally different and often incongruous elements 2 : markedly distinct in quality or character *syn* see DIFFERENT — **dis·pa·rate·ly** *adv* — **dis·pa·rate·ness** *n* — **dis·par·i·ty** \di-'spar-ə-tē\ *n*

dis·part \(,)dis-'pärt\ vb [It & L; It dispartire, fr. L, fr. dis- + partire to divide — more at PART] (1590) archaic : SEPARATE, DIVIDE

dis·pas·sion \(,)dis-'pa-shən\ n (1692) : absence of passion : COOLNESS

dis·pas·sion·ate \-sh(ə-)nət\ adj (1594) : not influenced by strong feeling; esp : not affected by personal or emotional involvement ⟨a ~ critic⟩ ⟨a ~ approach to an issue⟩ syn see FAIR — **dis·pas·sion·ate·ly** adv — **dis·pas·sion·ate·ness** n

¹dis·patch \di-'spach\ vb [Sp despachar or It dispacciare, fr. Prov despachar to get rid of, fr. MF despeechier to set free, fr. OF, fr. des- dis- + -peechier (as in empeechier to hinder) — more at IMPEACH] (1517) 1 : to send off or away with promptness or speed; esp : to send off on official business 2 a : to kill with quick efficiency b obs : DEPRIVE 3 : to dispose of (as a task) rapidly or efficiently 4 : DEFEAT 3 ~ vi, archaic : to make haste syn see KILL — **dis·patch·er** n

²dis·patch \di-'spach, 'dis-,pach\ n (1537) 1 a : a message sent with speed; esp : an important official message sent by a diplomatic, military, or naval officer b : a news item filed by a correspondent 2 : the act of dispatching: as a obs : DISMISSAL b : the act of killing c (1) : prompt settlement (as of an item of business) (2) : quick riddance d : a sending off : SHIPMENT 3 : promptness and efficiency in performance or transmission ⟨done with ~⟩ syn see HASTE

dispatch case n (ca. 1918) : a case for carrying papers

dis·pel \di-'spel\ vt **dis·pelled; dis·pel·ling** [ME, fr. L dispellere, fr. dis- + pellere to drive, beat — more at FELT] (15c) : to drive away or as if by scattering : DISSIPATE ⟨~ a rumor⟩ syn see SCATTER

dis·pens·able \di-'spen(t)-sə-bəl\ adj (1649) : capable of being dispensed with — **dis·pens·abil·i·ty** \-,spen(t)-sə-'bi-lə-tē\ n

dis·pen·sa·ry \di-'spen(t)s-(ə-)rē\ n, pl -ries (1699) : a place where medicine or medical or dental treatment is dispensed

dis·pen·sa·tion \,dis-pən-'sā-shən, -,pen-\ n (14c) 1 a : a general state or ordering of things; specif : a system of revealed commands and promises regulating human affairs b : a particular arrangement or provision esp. of providence or nature 2 a : an exemption from a law or from an impediment, vow, or oath b : a formal authorization 3 a : the act of dispensing b : something dispensed or distributed — **dis·pen·sa·tion·al** \-shnəl, -shə-nᵊl\ adj

dis·pen·sa·to·ry \di-'spen(t)-sə-,tōr-ē, -,tòr-\ n, pl -ries (1566) : a medicinal formulary

dis·pense \di-'spen(t)s\ vb **dis·pensed; dis·pens·ing** [ME, fr. ML & L; ML dispensare to exempt, fr. L, to distribute, fr. dis- + pensare to weigh, freq. of pendere to weigh, pay out — more at SPIN] vt (14c) 1 a : to deal out in portions b : ADMINISTER ⟨~ justice⟩ 2 : to give dispensation to : EXEMPT 3 : to prepare and distribute (medication) ~ vi, archaic : to grant dispensation syn see DISTRIBUTE — **dispense with** 1 : to set aside : DISCARD ⟨dispensing with the usual introduction⟩ 2 : to do without ⟨could dispense with such a large staff⟩

dis·pens·er \di-'spen(t)-sər\ n (14c) : one that dispenses: as a : a container that extrudes, sprays, or feeds out in convenient units b : a usu. mechanical device for vending merchandise

dis·peo·ple \(,)dis-'pē-pəl\ vt (15c) : DEPOPULATE

dis·per·sal \di-'spər-səl\ n (1821) : the act or result of dispersing; esp : the process or result of the spreading of organisms from one place to another

dis·per·sant \di-'spər-sənt\ n (1941) : a dispersing agent; esp : a substance for promoting the formation and stabilization of a dispersion of one substance in another — **dispersant** adj

dis·perse \di-'spərs\ vb **dis·persed; dis·pers·ing** [ME dysparsen, fr. MF disperser, fr. L dispersus, pp. of dispergere to scatter, fr. dis- + spargere to scatter — more at SPARK] vt (14c) 1 a : to cause to break up ⟨police dispersed the crowd⟩ b : to cause to become spread widely c : to cause to evaporate or vanish ⟨sunlight dispersing the mist⟩ 2 : to spread or distribute from a fixed or constant source: as a archaic : DISSEMINATE b : to subject (as light) to dispersion c : to distribute (as fine particles) more or less evenly throughout a medium ~ vi 1 : to break up in random fashion ⟨the crowd dispersed on request⟩ 2 a : to become dispersed b : DISSIPATE, VANISH ⟨the fog dispersed toward morning⟩ syn see SCATTER — **dis·persed·ly** \-'spər-səd-lē, -'spərst-lē\ adv — **dis·pers·er** n — **dis·pers·ible** \-'spər-sə-bəl\ adj

dis·per·sion \di-'spər-zhən, -shən\ n (14c) 1 cap : DIASPORA 1a 2 : the act or process of dispersing : the state of being dispersed 3 : the scattering of the values of a frequency distribution from an average 4 : the separation of light into colors by refraction or diffraction with formation of a spectrum; also : the separation of radiation into components in accordance with some varying characteristic (as energy) 5 a : a dispersed substance b : a system consisting of a dispersed substance and the medium in which it is dispersed : COLLOID 2b

dis·per·sive \-'spər-siv, -ziv\ adj (1677) 1 : of or relating to dispersion ⟨a ~ medium⟩ ⟨the ~ power of a lens⟩ 2 : tending to disperse — **dis·per·sive·ly** adv — **dis·per·sive·ness** n

dis·per·soid \-'spər-,sòid\ n (1911) : finely divided particles of one substance dispersed in another

dis·pir·it \(,)dis-'pir-ət\ vt [dis- + spirit] (1647) : to deprive of morale or enthusiasm — **dis·pir·it·ed** adj — **dis·pir·it·ed·ly** adv — **dis·pir·it·ed·ness** n

dis·pit·e·ous \di-'spi-tē-əs\ adj [alter. of despiteous] (1803) archaic : CRUEL

dis·place \(,)dis-'plās\ vt [prob. fr. MF desplacer, fr. des- dis- + place place] (1553) 1 a : to remove from the usual or proper place; specif : to expel or force to flee from home or homeland b : to remove from an office, status, or job c obs : to drive out : BANISH 2 a : to move physically out of position ⟨a floating object ~s water⟩ b : to take the place of (as in a chemical reaction) : SUPPLANT syn see REPLACE — **dis·place·able** \-'plā-sə-bəl\ adj

dis·place·ment \di-'splā-smənt\ n (1611) 1 : the act or process of displacing : the state of being displaced 2 a : the volume or weight of a fluid (as water) displaced by a floating body (as a ship) of equal weight b : the difference between the initial position of something (as a body or geometric figure) and any later position c : the volume displaced by a piston (as in a pump or an engine) in a single stroke; also : the total volume so displaced by all the pistons in an internal combustion engine (as in an automobile) 3 a : the redirection of an emotion or impulse from its original object to another (as an idea or person) to another b : the substitution of another form of behavior for what is usual or expected esp. when the usual response is nonadaptive

dis·plant \di-'splant\ vt [MF desplanter, fr. des- dis- + planter to plant, fr. LL plantare] (15c) 1 : DISPLACE, REMOVE 2 : SUPPLANT

¹dis·play \di-'splā\ vb [ME, fr. AF despleer, desploier, lit., to unfold — more at DEPLOY] vt (14c) 1 a : to put or spread before the view ⟨~ the flag⟩ b : to make evident ⟨~ed great skill⟩ c : to exhibit ostentatiously ⟨liked to ~ his erudition⟩ 2 obs : DESCRY ~ vi 1 obs : SHOW OFF 2 : to make a breeding display ⟨penguins ~ed and copulated⟩ syn see SHOW — **dis·play·able** \-'splā-ə-bəl\ adj

²display n, often attrib (1665) 1 a (1) : a setting or presentation of something in open view ⟨a fireworks ~⟩ (2) : a clear sign or evidence : EXHIBITION ⟨a ~ of courage⟩ b : ostentatious show c : type, composition, or printing designed to catch the eye d : an eye-catching arrangement by which something is exhibited e : an electronic device (as a cathode-ray tube) that temporarily presents information in visual form; also : the visual information 2 : a pattern of behavior exhibited esp. by male birds in the breeding season

dis·please \(,)dis-'plēz\ vb [ME displesen, fr. MF desplaisir, modif. of (assumed) VL displacēre, fr. L dis- + placēre to please — more at PLEASE] vt (14c) 1 : to incur the disapproval or dislike of esp. by annoying ⟨their gossip ~s her⟩ 2 : to be offensive to ⟨abstract art ~s him⟩ ~ vi : to give displeasure ⟨behavior calculated to ~⟩

dis·plea·sure \(,)dis-'ple-zhər, -'plā-\ n (15c) 1 : the feeling of one that is displeased : DISFAVOR 2 : DISCOMFORT, UNHAPPINESS 3 archaic : OFFENSE, INJURY

dis·plode \di-'splōd\ vb **dis·plod·ed; dis·plod·ing** [L displodere, fr. dis- + plaudere to clap, applaud] (1667) archaic : EXPLODE — **dis·plo·sion** \-'splō-zhən\ n

¹dis·port \di-'spōrt, -'spòrt\ n (14c) archaic : SPORT, PASTIME

²disport vb [ME, fr. MF desporter, fr. des- dis- + porter to carry, fr. L portare — more at FARE] vt (14c) 1 : DIVERT, AMUSE 2 : DISPLAY ~ vi : to amuse oneself in light or lively fashion : FROLIC — **dis·port·ment** \-mənt\ n

¹dis·pos·able \di-'spō-zə-bəl\ adj (1643) 1 : subject to or available for disposal; specif : remaining to an individual after deduction of taxes ⟨~ income⟩ 2 : designed to be used once and then thrown away ⟨~ diapers⟩ — **dis·pos·abil·i·ty** \-,spō-zə-'bi-lə-tē\ n

²disposable n (1963) : something that is disposable

dis·pos·al \di-'spō-zəl\ n (1630) 1 : the power or authority to dispose or make use of as one chooses ⟨the car was at my ~⟩ 2 : the act or process of disposing: as a : orderly placement or distribution b : REGULATION, ADMINISTRATION c : the act or action of presenting or bestowing something ⟨~ of favors⟩ d : systematic destruction; esp : destruction or transformation of garbage 3 [garbage disposal unit] : a device used to reduce waste matter (as by grinding)

¹dis·pose \di-'spōz\ vb **dis·posed; dis·pos·ing** [ME, fr. MF disposer, fr. L disponere to arrange (perf. indic. disposui), fr. dis- + ponere to put — more at POSITION] vt (14c) 1 : to give a tendency to : INCLINE ⟨faulty diet ~s one to sickness⟩ 2 a : to put in place : set in readiness : ARRANGE ⟨disposing troops for withdrawal⟩ b obs : REGULATE c : BESTOW ~ vi 1 : to settle a matter finally 2 obs : to come to terms syn see INCLINE — **dis·pos·er** n — **dispose of** 1 : to place, distribute, or arrange esp. in an orderly way 2 a : to transfer to the control of another ⟨disposing of personal property to a total stranger⟩ b (1) : to get rid of ⟨how to dispose of toxic waste⟩ (2) : to deal with conclusively ⟨disposed of the matter efficiently⟩

²dispose n (1590) 1 obs : DISPOSAL 2 obs : DISPOSITION b : DEMEANOR

dis·po·si·tion \,dis-pə-'zi-shən\ n [ME, fr. MF, fr. L disposition-, dispositio, fr. disponere] (14c) 1 : the act or the power of disposing or the state of being disposed: as a : ADMINISTRATION, CONTROL b : final arrangement : SETTLEMENT ⟨the ~ of the case⟩ c (1) : transfer to the care or possession of another (2) : the power of such transferal d : orderly arrangement 2 a : prevailing tendency, mood, or inclination b : temperamental makeup c : the tendency of something to act in a certain manner under given circumstances — **dis·po·si·tion·al** \-'zish-nəl, -'zi-shə-nᵊl\ adj
syn DISPOSITION, TEMPERAMENT, TEMPER, CHARACTER, PERSONALITY mean the dominant quality or qualities distinguishing a person or group. DISPOSITION implies customary moods and attitude toward the life around one ⟨a cheerful disposition⟩. TEMPERAMENT implies a pattern of innate characteristics associated with one's specific physical and nervous organization ⟨an artistic temperament⟩. TEMPER implies the qualities acquired through experience that determine how a person or group meets difficulties or handles situations ⟨a resilient temper⟩. CHARACTER applies to the aggregate of moral qualities by which a person is judged apart from intelligence, competence, or special talents ⟨strength of character⟩. PERSONALITY applies to an aggregate of qualities that distinguish one as a person ⟨a somber personality⟩.

dis·pos·i·tive \di-'spä-zə-tiv\ adj (1613) : directed toward or effecting disposition (as of a case) ⟨~ evidence⟩

dis·pos·sess \,dis-pə-'zes also -'ses\ vt [MF despossesser, fr. des- dis- + possesser to possess] (1555) : to put out of possession or occupancy ⟨~ed the nobles of their land⟩ — **dis·pos·ses·sion** \-'ze-shən also -'se-\ n — **dis·pos·ses·sor** \-'ze-sər also -'se-\ n

dis·pos·sessed adj (15c) : deprived of homes, possessions, and security

dis·po·sure \di-'spō-zhər\ n (1569) archaic : DISPOSAL, DISPOSITION

dis·praise \(,)dis-'prāz\ vt [ME dispraisen, fr. MF despreisier, fr. OF, fr. des- dis- + preisier to praise] (13c) : to comment on with disapproval or censure — **dispraise** n — **dis·prais·er** n — **dis·prais·ing·ly** \-'prā-ziŋ-lē\ adv

dis·pread \di-'spred\ vt (1590) : to spread abroad or out

dis·prize \(,)dis-'prīz\ vt [MF despriser, fr. OF despreisier] (15c) archaic : UNDERVALUE, SCORN

dis·proof \(,)dis-'prüf\ n (15c) 1 : the action of disproving 2 : evidence that disproves

---

\ə\ abut \ᵊ\ kitten, F table \ər\ further \a\ ash \ā\ ace \ä\ mop, mar \au̇\ out \ch\ chin \e\ bet \ē\ easy \g\ go \i\ hit \ī\ ice \j\ job \ŋ\ sing \ō\ go \ò\ law \ói\ boy \th\ thin \th\ the \ü\ loot \u̇\ foot \y\ yet \zh\ vision \ä, k, ⁿ, œ, œ̄, ᵫ, ᵫ̄, ᵜ\ see Guide to Pronunciation

¹dis·pro·por·tion \,dis-prə-'pōr-shən, -'pȯr-\ n (1555) : lack of proportion, symmetry, or proper relation : DISPARITY; also : an instance of such disparity — **dis·pro·por·tion·al** \-shnəl, -shə-nᵊl\ adj

²disproportion vt (1593) : to make out of proportion : MISMATCH

dis·pro·por·tion·ate \-sh(ə-)nət\ adj (1555) : being out of proportion ⟨a ~ share⟩ — **dis·pro·por·tion·ate·ly** adv

dis·pro·por·tion·ation \-,pōr-shə-'nā-shən, -,pȯr-\ n (ca. 1929) : the transformation of a substance into two or more dissimilar substances usu. by simultaneous oxidation and reduction — **dis·pro·por·tion·ate** \-'pōr-shə-,nāt, -'pȯr-\ vi

dis·prove \(,)dis-'prüv\ vt [ME, fr. MF desprover, fr. des- dis- + prover to prove] (14c) : to prove to be false or wrong : REFUTE — **dis·prov·able** \-'prü-və-bəl\ adj

dis·pu·tant \di-'spyü-tᵊnt \dis-pyə-tənt\ n (1593) : one that is engaged in a dispute

dis·pu·ta·tion \,dis-pyə-'tā-shən\ n (14c) 1 : the action of disputing : verbal controversy ⟨continuous ~ between them⟩ ⟨ideological ~s⟩ 2 : an academic exercise in oral defense of a thesis by formal logic

dis·pu·ta·tious \-shəs\ adj (1660) 1 a : inclined to dispute b : marked by disputation 2 : provoking debate : CONTROVERSIAL — **dis·pu·ta·tious·ly** adv — **dis·pu·ta·tious·ness** n

¹dis·pute \di-'spyüt\ vb **dis·put·ed; dis·put·ing** [ME, fr. OF desputer, fr. L disputare to discuss, fr. dis- + putare to think] vi (13c) : to engage in argument : DEBATE; esp : to argue irritably or with irritating persistence ~ vt 1 a : to make the subject of disputation b : to call into question ⟨her honesty was never disputed⟩ 2 a : to struggle against : OPPOSE ⟨disputed the advance of the invaders⟩ b : to contend over ⟨both sides disputed the bridgehead⟩ — **dis·put·able** \di-'spyü-tə-bəl, 'dis-pyə-\ adj — **dis·put·ably** \-blē\ adv — **dis·put·er** n

²dis·pute \di-'spyüt, 'dis-,pyüt\ n (1608) 1 a : verbal controversy : DEBATE b : QUARREL 2 obs : physical combat

dis·qual·i·fi·ca·tion \(,)dis-,kwä-lə-fə-'kā-shən\ n (1714) 1 : something that disqualifies or incapacitates 2 : the act of disqualifying : the state of being disqualified ⟨~ from office⟩

dis·qual·i·fy \(,)dis-'kwä-lə-,fī\ vt (1723) 1 : to deprive of the required qualities, properties, or conditions : make unfit 2 : to deprive of a power, right, or privilege 3 : to make ineligible for a prize or for further competition because of violations of the rules

dis·quan·ti·ty \(,)dis-'kwän-(t)ə-tē\ vt (1605) obs : DIMINISH, LESSEN

¹dis·qui·et \(,)dis-'kwī-ət\ vt (ca. 1530) : to take away the peace or tranquillity of : DISTURB, ALARM **syn** see DISCOMPOSE — **dis·qui·et·ing** adj — **dis·qui·et·ing·ly** \-'kwī-ə-tiŋ-lē\ adv

²disquiet n (1581) : lack of peace or tranquillity : ANXIETY

³disquiet adj (1587) archaic : UNEASY, DISQUIETED — **dis·qui·et·ly** adv

dis·qui·etude \(,)dis-'kwī-ə-,t(y)üd\ n (1709) : ANXIETY, AGITATION

dis·qui·si·tion \,dis-kwə-'zi-shən\ n [L disquisition-, disquisitio, fr. disquirere to investigate, fr. dis- + quaerere to seek] (1647) : a formal inquiry into or discussion of a subject : DISCOURSE

dis·rate \(,)dis-'rāt\ vt (1811) : to reduce in rank : DEMOTE

¹dis·re·gard \,dis-ri-'gärd\ vt (1641) : to pay no attention to : treat as unworthy of regard or notice **syn** see NEGLECT

²disregard n (1665) : the act of disregarding : the state of being disregarded : NEGLECT — **dis·re·gard·ful** \-fəl\ adj

dis·re·lat·ed \,dis-ri-'lā-təd\ adj (1894) : not related

dis·re·la·tion \-'lā-shən\ n (1893) : lack of a fitting or proportionate connection or relationship

¹dis·rel·ish \(,)dis-'re-lish\ vt (1604) : to find unpalatable or distasteful

²disrelish n (ca. 1625) : lack of relish : DISTASTE, DISLIKE

dis·re·mem·ber \,dis-ri-'mem-bər\ vt (1815) : FORGET

dis·re·pair \,dis-ri-'par, -'per\ n (1798) : the state of being in need of repair ⟨a building fallen into ~⟩

dis·rep·u·ta·ble \(,)dis-'re-pyə-tə-bəl\ adj (1772) : not reputable — **dis·rep·u·ta·bil·i·ty** \(,)dis-,re-pyə-tə-'bi-lə-tē\ n — **dis·rep·u·ta·ble·ness** \(,)dis-'re-pyə-tə-bəl-nəs\ n — **dis·rep·u·ta·bly** \-blē\ adv

dis·re·pute \,dis-ri-'pyüt\ n (1653) : lack or decline of good reputation : a state of being held in low esteem **syn** see DISGRACE

¹dis·re·spect \,dis-ri-'spekt\ vt (1614) : to have disrespect for

²disrespect n (1631) : lack of respect — **dis·re·spect·ful** \-fəl\ adj — **dis·re·spect·ful·ly** adv — **dis·re·spect·ful·ness** n

dis·re·spect·able \,dis-ri-'spek-tə-bəl\ adj (1813) : not respectable — **dis·re·spect·abil·i·ty** \-,spek-tə-'bi-lə-tē\ n

dis·robe \dis-'rōb\ vb [MF desrober, fr. des- dis- + robe garment, fr. OF] vi (1581) : to take off one's clothing ~ vt : to strip of clothing or covering

dis·rupt \dis-'rəpt\ vt [L disruptus, pp. of disrumpere, fr. dis- + rumpere to break — more at REAVE] (1817) 1 a : to break apart : RUPTURE b : to throw into disorder ⟨agitators trying to ~ the meeting⟩ 2 : to interrupt the normal course or unity of — **dis·rupt·er** n — **dis·rup·tion** \-'rəp-shən\ n — **dis·rup·tive** \-'rəp-tiv\ adj — **dis·rup·tive·ly** adv — **dis·rup·tive·ness** n

diss var of DIS

dis·sat·is·fac·tion \(,)di(s)-,sat-əs-'fak-shən\ n (1640) : the quality or state of being dissatisfied

dis·sat·is·fac·to·ry \-'fak-t(ə-)rē\ adj (ca. 1610) : causing dissatisfaction

dis·sat·is·fied \(,)di(s)-'sa-təs-,fīd\ adj (1675) : expressing or showing lack of satisfaction : not pleased or satisfied

dis·sat·is·fy \-,fī\ vt (1666) : to fail to satisfy : DISPLEASE

dis·save \(,)di(s)-'sāv\ vi (1936) : to use savings for current expenses

dis·seat \(,)di(s)-'sēt\ vt (1612) archaic : UNSEAT

dis·sect \di-'sekt; ÷dī-'sekt, ÷'dī-,\ vb [L dissectus, pp. of dissecare to cut apart, fr. dis- + secare to cut — more at SAW] vt (1607) 1 : to separate into pieces : expose the several parts of (as an animal) for scientific examination 2 : to analyze and interpret minutely ~ vi : to make a dissection **syn** see ANALYZE — **dis·sec·tor** \-'sek-tər\ n

dis·sect·ed adj (1652) 1 : cut deeply into fine lobes ⟨a ~ leaf⟩ 2 : divided into hills and ridges (as by gorges) ⟨a ~ plateau⟩

dis·sect·ing microscope n (ca. 1897) : a microscope with low magnification

dis·sec·tion \di-'sek-shən; ÷dī-'sek-, ÷'dī-,\ n (1605) 1 : the act or process of dissecting : the state of being dissected 2 : an anatomical specimen prepared by dissecting

dis·seise or **dis·seize** \(,)di(s)-'sēz\ vt **dis·seised** or **dis·seized; dis·seis·ing** or **dis·seiz·ing** [ME disseisen, fr. ML disseisiare & AF dis-

seisir, fr. OF dessaisir, fr. des- dis- + saisir to put in possession of — more at SEIZE] (14c) : to deprive esp. wrongfully of seisin : DISPOSSESS — **dis·sei·sor** \-'sē-zər\ n

dis·sei·sin or **dis·sei·zin** \-'sē-zᵊn\ n [ME dysseysyne, fr. AF disseisine, fr. OF dessaisine, fr. des- dis- + saisine seisin] (14c) : the act of disseising : the state of being disseised

dis·sem·ble \di-'sem-bəl\ vb **dis·sem·bled; dis·sem·bling** \-b(ə-)liŋ\ [ME dissymblen, alter. of dissimulen, fr. MF dissimuler, fr. L dissimulare — more at DISSIMULATE] vt (15c) 1 : to hide under a false appearance 2 : to put on the appearance of : SIMULATE ~ vi : to put on a false appearance : conceal facts, intentions, or feelings under some pretense — **dis·sem·bler** \-b(ə-)lər\ n

dis·sem·i·nate \di-'se-mə-,nāt\ vt **-nat·ed; -nat·ing** [L disseminatus, pp. of disseminare, fr. dis- + seminare to sow, fr. semin-, semen seed — more at SEMEN] (1603) 1 : to spread abroad as though sowing seed ⟨~ ideas⟩ 2 : to disperse throughout — **dis·sem·i·na·tion** \-,se-mə-'nā-shən\ n — **dis·sem·i·na·tor** \-'se-mə-,nā-tər\ n

dis·sem·i·nat·ed adj (1876) : widely dispersed in a tissue, organ, or the entire body ⟨~ gonococcal disease⟩

dis·sem·i·nule \di-'sem-ə-,nyül\ n (1904) : a part or organ (as a seed or spore) of a plant that ensures propagation

dis·sen·sion also **dis·sen·tion** \di-'sen(t)-shən\ n [ME, fr. MF, fr. L dissension-, dissensio, fr. dissentire] (14c) : DISAGREEMENT; esp : partisan and contentious quarreling **syn** see DISCORD

dis·sen·sus \(,)di(s)-'sen(t)-səs\ n [dis- + consensus] (1966) : difference of opinion

¹dis·sent \di-'sent\ vi [ME, fr. L dissentire, fr. dis- + sentire to feel — more at SENSE] (15c) 1 : to withhold assent 2 : to differ in opinion

²dissent n (1585) : difference of opinion: as a : religious nonconformity b : a justice's nonconcurrence with a decision of the majority — called also **dissenting opinion**

dis·sent·er \di-'sen-tər\ n (1639) 1 : one that dissents 2 cap : an English Nonconformist

dis·sen·tient \di-'sen(t)-sh(ē-)ənt\ adj [L dissentient-, dissentiens, prp. of dissentire] (1651) : expressing dissent — **dissentient** n

dis·sent·ing \di-'sen-tiŋ\ adj, often cap (1644) : of or relating to the English Nonconformists ⟨a ~ church⟩ ⟨~ merchants⟩

dis·sen·tious \di-'sen(t)-shəs\ adj (1560) : characterized by dissension or dissent

dis·sep·i·ment \di-'se-pə-mənt\ n [L dissaepimentum partition, fr. dissaepire to divide, fr. dis- + saepire to fence in — more at SEPTUM] (ca. 1727) : a dividing tissue : SEPTUM

dis·sert \di-'sərt\ vi [L dissertus, pp. of disserere, fr. dis- + serere to join, arrange — more at SERIES] (1657) : to speak or write at length

dis·ser·tate \'di-sər-,tāt\ vi **-tat·ed; -tat·ing** [L dissertatus, pp. of dissertare, fr. dissertus] (1766) : DISSERT; also : to write a dissertation — **dis·ser·ta·tor** \-,tā-tər\ n

dis·ser·ta·tion \,di-sər-'tā-shən\ n (1651) : an extended usu. written treatment of a subject; specif : one submitted for a doctorate — **dis·ser·ta·tion·al** \-'tāsh-nəl, -'tā-shə-nᵊl\ adj

dis·serve \(,)di(s)-'sərv\ vt (1629) : to serve badly or falsely : HARM

dis·ser·vice \(,)di(s)-'sər-vəs\ n (1599) : ill service : HARM; also : an unhelpful, unkind, or harmful act

dis·ser·vice·able \di(s)-'sər-və-sə-bəl\ adj (1644) : COUNTERPRODUCTIVE

dis·sev·er \di-'se-vər\ vb [ME, fr. OF dessevrer, fr. LL disseparare, fr. L dis- + separare to separate] vt (13c) : SEVER, SEPARATE ~ vi : to come apart : DISUNITE — **dis·sev·er·ance** \-'se-v(ə-)rən(t)s\ n — **dis·sev·er·ment** \-'se-vər-mənt\ n

dis·si·dence \'di-sə-dən(t)s\ n (ca. 1656) : DISSENT, DISAGREEMENT

dis·si·dent \-dənt\ adj [L dissident-, dissidens, prp. of dissidēre to sit apart, disagree, fr. dis- + sedēre to sit — more at SIT] (1837) : disagreeing esp. with an established religious or political system, organization, or belief — **dissident** n

dis·sim·i·lar \(,)di(s)-'si-mə-lər, -'sim-lər\ adj (1599) : UNLIKE — **dis·sim·i·lar·i·ty** \(,)di(s)-,si-mə-'lar-ə-tē\ n — **dis·sim·i·lar·ly** \(')'si-mə-lər-lē, -'sim-lər-\ adv — **dis·sim·i·lars** \-lərz\ n pl

dis·sim·i·late \(,)di(s)-'si-mə-,lāt\ vi **-lat·ed; -lat·ing** [dis- + -similate (as in assimilate)] (1841) : to undergo dissimilation — **dis·sim·i·la·to·ry** \-mə-lə-,tōr-ē, -,tȯr-\ adj

dis·sim·i·la·tion \(,)di-,si-mə-'lā-shən\ n (ca. 1874) : the change or omission of one of two identical or closely related sounds in a word

dis·si·mil·i·tude \(,)di(s)-sə-'mi-lə-,tüd, -,tyüd\ n [L dissimilitudo, fr. dissimilis unlike, fr. dis- + similis like — more at SAME] (15c) : lack of resemblance

dis·sim·u·late \(,)di-'sim-yə-,lāt\ vb **-lat·ed; -lat·ing** [L dissimulatus, pp. of dissimulare, fr. dis- + simulare to simulate] vt (15c) : to hide under a false appearance ⟨smiled to ~ her urgency —Alice Glenday⟩ ~ vi : DISSEMBLE — **dis·sim·u·la·tion** \(,)di-,sim-yə-'lā-shən\ n — **dis·sim·u·la·tor** \(')'sim-yə-,lā-tər\ n

dis·si·pate \'di-sə-,pāt\ vb **-pat·ed; -pat·ing** [L dissipatus, pp. of dissipare, dissupare, fr. dis- + supare to throw] vt (15c) 1 a : to break up and drive off (as a crowd) b : to cause to spread thin or scatter and gradually vanish ⟨one's sympathy is eventually dissipated —Andrew Feinberg⟩ c : to lose (as heat or electricity) irrecoverably 2 : to spend or use up wastefully or foolishly ⟨lifelong tendency to ~ his gifts in travel and pleasure —Edmund Morris⟩ ⟨his fortune is dissipated in imprudent political adventures —John Butt⟩ ~ vi 1 : to break up and scatter or vanish 2 : to be extravagant or dissolute in the pursuit of pleasure; esp : to drink to excess **syn** see SCATTER — **dis·si·pat·er** n

dis·si·pat·ed adj (1744) : given to or marked by dissipation : DISSOLUTE — **dis·si·pat·ed·ly** adv — **dis·si·pat·ed·ness** n

dis·si·pa·tion \,di-sə-'pā-shən\ n (15c) 1 : the action or process of dissipating; the state of being dissipated: a : DISPERSION, DIFFUSION b archaic : DISSOLUTION, DISINTEGRATION c : wasteful expenditure 2 : intemperate living; esp : excessive drinking 2 : an act of self-indulgence; esp : one that is not harmful : AMUSEMENT

dis·si·pa·tive \'di-sə-,pā-tiv\ adj (1684) : relating to dissipation esp. of heat

dis·so·cia·ble \(,)di-'sō-sh(ē-)ə-bəl, -sē-ə-\ adj (1833) : SEPARABLE — **dis·so·cia·bil·i·ty** \(,)di-,sō-sh(ē-)ə-'bi-lə-tē, -sē-ə-\ n

dis·so·cial \(,)di-'sō-shəl\ adj (1762) : UNSOCIAL, SELFISH

dis·so·ci·ate \(,)di-'sō-shē-,āt, -sē-\ vb **-at·ed; -at·ing** [L dissociatus, pp. of *dissociare*, fr. *dis-* + *sociare* to join, fr. *socius* companion — more at SOCIAL] *vt* (1590)   **1** : to separate from association or union with another   **2** : DISUNITE; *specif* : to subject to chemical dissociation ~ *vi*   **1** : to undergo dissociation   **2** : to mutate esp. reversibly

dis·so·ci·a·tion \(,)di-,sō-sē-'ā-shən, -shē-\ *n* (1611)   **1** : the act or process of dissociating : the state of being dissociated: as   **a** : the process by which a chemical combination breaks up into simpler constituents; *esp* : one that results from the action of energy (as heat) on a gas or of a solvent on a dissolved substance   **b** : the separation of whole segments of the personality (as in multiple personality) or of discrete mental processes (as in the schizophrenias) from the mainstream of consciousness or of behavior   **2** : the property inherent in some biological stocks (as of certain bacteria) of differentiating into two or more distinct and relatively permanent strains; *also* : such a strain — **dis·so·cia·tive** \(,)di-'sō-shē-,ā-tiv, -sē-, -sha-tiv\ *adj*

dis·sol·u·ble \di-'säl-yə-bəl\ *adj* [L *dissolubilis*, fr. *dissolvere* to dissolve] (1534) : capable of being dissolved or disintegrated

dis·so·lute \'dis-ə-,lüt, -lət\ *adj* [L *dissolutus*, fr. pp. of *dissolvere* to loosen, dissolve] (14c) : lacking restraint; *esp* : marked by indulgence in things (as drink or promiscuous sex) deemed vices ⟨the ~ and degrading aspects of human nature —Wallace Fowlie⟩ — **dis·so·lute·ly** *adv* — **dis·so·lute·ness** *n*

dis·so·lu·tion \,di-sə-'lü-shən\ *n* (14c)   **1** : the act or process of dissolving: as   **a** : separation into component parts   **b** (1) : DECAY, DISINTEGRATION   (2) : DEATH   **c** : termination or destruction by breaking down, disrupting, or dispersing ⟨the ~ of the republic⟩   **d** : the dissolving of an assembly or organization   **e** : LIQUEFACTION   **2** : a dissolute act or practice

¹dis·solve \di-'zälv, -'zòlv *also* -'zäv *or* -'zòv\ *vb* [ME, fr. L *dissolvere*, fr. *dis-* + *solvere* to loosen — more at SOLVE] *vt* (14c)   **1   a** : to cause to disperse or disappear : DESTROY   **b** : to separate into component parts : DISINTEGRATE   **c** : to bring to an end : TERMINATE ⟨~ parliament⟩   **d** : ANNUL ⟨~ an injunction⟩   **2   a** : to cause to pass into solution ⟨~ sugar in water⟩   **b** : MELT, LIQUEFY   **c** : to cause to be emotionally moved   **d** : to cause to fade out in a dissolve   **3** *archaic* : DETACH, LOOSEN   **4** : to clear up ⟨~ a problem⟩ ~ *vi*   **1   a** : to become dissipated or decomposed   **b** : BREAK UP, DISPERSE   **c** : to fade away   **2   a** : to become fluid : MELT   **b** : to pass into solution   **c** : to be overcome emotionally ⟨*dissolved* into tears⟩   **d** : to resolve itself as if by dissolution ⟨hate *dissolved* into fear⟩   **e** : to change by a dissolve ⟨the scene ~s to a Victorian parlor⟩ — **dis·solv·able** \-'zäl-və-bəl, -'zòl-\ *adj* — **dis·sol·vent** \-'zäl-vənt, -'zòl-\ *n or adj* — **dis·solv·er** *n*

²dissolve *n* (1916) : a gradual superimposing of one motion-picture or television shot upon another on a screen

dis·so·nance \'di-sə-nən(t)s\ *n* (15c)   **1   a** : lack of agreement; *esp* : inconsistency between the beliefs one holds or between one's actions and one's beliefs — compare COGNITIVE DISSONANCE   **b** : an instance of such inconsistency or disagreement   **2   a** : a mingling of discordant sounds; *esp* : a clashing or unresolved musical interval or chord

dis·so·nant \-nənt\ *adj* [MF or L; MF, fr. L *dissonant-, dissonans*, prp. of *dissonare* to be discordant, fr. *dis-* + *sonare* to sound — more at SOUND] (15c)   **1** : marked by dissonance : DISCORDANT   **2** : INCONGRUOUS   **3** : harmonically unresolved — **dis·so·nant·ly** *adv*

dis·suade \di-'swād\ *vt* **dis·suad·ed; dis·suad·ing** [MF or L; MF *dissuader*, fr. L *dissuadēre*, fr. *dis-* + *suadēre* to urge — more at SWEET] (15c)   **1** : to advise (a person) against something   **b** *archaic* : to advise against (an action)   **2** : to turn from something by persuasion — **dis·suad·er** *n*

dis·sua·sion \di-'swā-zhən\ *n* [MF or L; MF, fr. L *dissuasion-, dissuasio*, fr. *dissuadēre*] (15c) : the action of dissuading

dis·sua·sive \di-'swā-siv, -ziv\ *adj* (1609) : tending to dissuade — **dis·sua·sive·ly** *adv* — **dis·sua·sive·ness** *n*

dis·syl·la·ble \'di-,si-lə-bəl, (,)di(s)-'si-; 'dī-,si-, (,)dī-'si-\ *var of* DISYLLABLE

dis·sym·me·try \(,)di(s)-'si-mə-trē\ *n* (1845) : the absence of or the lack of symmetry — **dis·sym·met·ric** \(,)di(s)-sə-'me-trik\ *adj*

¹dis·taff \'dis-,taf\ *n, pl* **distaffs** \-,tafs, -,tavz\ [ME *distaf*, fr. OE *distæf*, fr. *dis-* (akin to MLG *dise* bunch of flax) + *stæf* staff] (bef. 12c)   **1   a** : a staff for holding the flax, tow, or wool in spinning   **b** : woman's work or domain   **2** : the female branch or side of a family

²distaff *adj* (ca. 1633)   **1** : MATERNAL ⟨the ~ side of the family⟩ — compare SPEAR ; *also* : FEMALE ⟨~ executives⟩

dis·tain \dis-'tān\ *vt* [ME *disteynen*, fr. MF *desteindre* to take away the color of, fr. OF, fr. *des-* dis- + *teindre* to dye, fr. L *tingere* to wet, dye — more at TINGE] (14c)   **1** *archaic* : STAIN   **2** *archaic* : DISHONOR

dis·tal \'dis-t³l\ *adj* [*distant* + *-al*] (1808)   **1** : situated away from the point of attachment or origin or a central point esp. of the body — compare PROXIMAL   **2** : of, relating to, or being the surface of a tooth that is next to the tooth behind it or that is farthest from the middle of the front of the jaw — compare MESIAL 2 — **dis·tal·ly** \-t³l-ē\ *adv*

distal convoluted tubule *n* (ca. 1901) : the convoluted portion of the vertebrate nephron that lies between the loop of Henle and the nonsecretory part of the nephron and that is concerned esp. with the concentration of urine

¹dis·tance \'dis-tən(t)s\ *n* (14c)   **1** *obs* : DISCORD   **2   a** : separation in time   **b** : the degree or amount of separation between two points, lines, surfaces, or objects   **c** (1) : an extent of area or an advance along a route measured linearly   (2) : an extent of space measured other than linearly ⟨within walking ~⟩   **d** : an extent of advance from a beginning   **e** : EXPANSE   **f** (1) : length of a race or contest ⟨won at all ~s⟩   (2) : the full length (as of a prizefight or ball game)   (3) : a long race ⟨~ training⟩   **3** : the quality or state of being distant: as   **a** : spatial remoteness   **b** : personal and esp. emotional separation; *also* : RESERVE, COLDNESS   **c** : DIFFERENCE, DISPARITY   **4** : a distant point or region   **5   a** : AESTHETIC DISTANCE   **b** : capacity to observe dispassionately — **go the distance** *also* **last the distance** : to complete a course of action

distaff 1a

²distance *vt* **dis·tanced; dis·tanc·ing** (1578)   **1** : to place or keep at a distance   **2** : to leave far behind : OUTSTRIP

dis·tant \'dis-tənt\ *adj* [ME, fr. MF, fr. L *distant-, distans*, prp. of *distare* to stand apart, be distant, fr. *dis-* + *stare* to stand — more at STAND] (14c)   **1   a** : separated in space : AWAY   **b** : situated at a great distance : FAR-OFF   **c** : separated by a great distance from each other : far apart   **d** : far behind ⟨finished a ~ third⟩   **2** : separated in a relationship other than spatial ⟨a ~ cousin⟩ ⟨the ~ past⟩   **3** : different in kind   **4** : reserved or aloof in personal relationship : COLD ⟨was ~ and distracted⟩   **5   a** : going a long distance ⟨~ voyages⟩   **b** : concerned with remote things ⟨~ thoughts⟩ — **dis·tant·ly** *adv* — **dis·tant·ness** *n*

¹dis·taste \(,)dis-'tāst\ *vt* (1592)   **1** *archaic* : to feel aversion to   **2** *archaic* : OFFEND, DISPLEASE ~ *vi, obs* : to have an offensive taste

²distaste *n* (1598)   **1** *archaic* : dislike of food or drink   **b** : AVERSION, DISINCLINATION ⟨a ~ for opera⟩   **2** *obs* : ANNOYANCE, DISCOMFORT

dis·taste·ful \(,)dis-'tāst-fəl\ *adj* (1607)   **1** : objectionable because offensive to one's personal taste : DISAGREEABLE   **2** : unpleasant to the taste : LOATHSOME — **dis·taste·ful·ly** \-fə-lē\ *adv* — **dis·taste·ful·ness** *n*

dis·tel·fink \'dish-t³l-,fiŋk, 'dis-\ *n* [PaG *dischdelfink*, lit., goldfinch, fr. *dischdel* thistle + *fink* finch] (1939) : a traditional Pennsylvania Dutch design motif in the form of a stylized bird

¹dis·tem·per \dis-'tem-pər\ *vt* [ME *distempren*, fr. LL *distemperare* to temper badly, fr. L *dis-* + *temperare* to temper] (14c)   **1** : to throw out of order   **2** *archaic* : DERANGE, UNSETTLE

²distemper *n* (ca. 1555)   **1** : bad humor or temper   **2** : a disordered or abnormal bodily state esp. of quadruped mammals: as   **a** : a highly contagious virus disease esp. of dogs marked by fever, leukopenia, and respiratory, gastrointestinal, and neurological symptoms — *see* STRANGLES   **c** : PANLEUKOPENIA   **3** : AILMENT, DISORDER ⟨political ~⟩ ⟨intellectual ~s⟩ — **dis·tem·per·ate** \-p(ə-)rət\ *adj*

³distemper *n* [obs. *distemper*, v., to dilute, mix to produce distemper, fr. ME, fr. MF *destemprer*, fr. L *dis-* + *temperare*] (1632)   **1** : a process of painting in which the pigments are mixed with an emulsion of egg yolk, white of egg, or with white of egg as a vehicle and which is used for painting scenery and murals   **2   a** : the paint or the prepared ground used in the distemper process   **b** : a painting done in distemper   **3** : any of various water-based paints

⁴distemper *vt* (ca. 1873) : to paint in or with distemper

dis·tem·per·a·ture \di-'stem-p(ə-)rə-,chur, -pə(r)-, -chər, *chiefly Southern* -,t(y)ú(ə)r\ *n* (1531) : a disordered condition

dis·tend \di-'stend\ *vb* [ME, fr. L *distendere*, fr. *dis-* + *tendere* to stretch — more at THIN] *vt* (15c)   **1** : EXTEND   **2** : to enlarge from internal pressure : SWELL ~ *vi* : to become expanded   *syn* see EXPAND

dis·ten·si·ble \-'sten(t)-sə-bəl\ *adj* [*distens-* (fr. L *distensus*, pp. of *distendere*) + *-ible*] (ca. 1828) : capable of being distended — **dis·ten·si·bil·i·ty** \-,sten(t)-sə-'bi-lə-tē\ *n*

dis·ten·sion *or* **dis·ten·tion** \di-'sten(t)-shən\ *n* [L *distention-, distentio*, fr. *distendere*] (15c) : the act of distending or the state of being distended esp. unduly or abnormally

dis·tich \'dis-(,)tik\ *n* [L *distichon*, fr. Gk, fr. neut. of *distichos* having two rows, fr. *di-* + *stichos* row, verse; akin to Gk *steichein* to go — more at STAIR] (1553) : a strophic unit of two lines

dis·ti·chous \'dis-ti-kəs\ *adj* [LL *distichus*, fr. Gk *distichos*] (ca. 1753) : disposed in two vertical rows ⟨~ leaves⟩

dis·till *also* **dis·til** \di-'stil\ *vb* **dis·tilled; dis·till·ing** [ME *distillen*, fr. MF *distiller*, fr. LL *distillare*, alter. of L *destillare*, fr. *de-* + *stillare* to drip, fr. *stilla* drop] *vt* (14c)   **1** : to let fall, exude, or precipitate in drops or in a wet mist   **2   a** : to subject to or transform by distillation   **b** : to obtain by or as if by distillation   **c** : to extract the essence of : CONCENTRATE ~ *vi*   **1   a** : to fall or materialize in drops or in a fine moisture   **b** : to appear slowly or in small quantities at a time   **2   a** : to undergo distillation   **b** : to perform distillation

dis·til·late \'dis-tə-,lāt, -lət; di-'sti-lət\ *n* (ca. 1859)   **1** : a liquid product condensed from vapor during distillation   **2** : something concentrated or extracted as if by distillation

dis·til·la·tion \,dis-tə-'lā-shən\ *n* (14c)   **1   a** : the process of purifying a liquid by successive evaporation and condensation   **b** : a process like distillation; *also* : an instance of distilling   **2** : something distilled : DISTILLATE 2

dis·till·er \di-'sti-lər\ *n* (1577) : one that distills esp. alcoholic liquors

dis·till·ery \di-'sti-lə-rē, -'stil-rē\ *n, pl* **-er·ies** (1759) : the works where distilling (as of alcoholic liquors) is done

dis·tinct \di-'stiŋ(k)t\ *adj* [ME, fr. MF, fr. L *distinctus*, fr. pp. of *distinguere*] (14c)   **1** : distinguishable to the eye or mind as discrete : SEPARATE ⟨a ~ cultural group⟩ ⟨teaching as ~ from research⟩   **2** : presenting a clear unmistakable impression ⟨a neat ~ handwriting⟩   **3** *archaic* : notably decorated   **4   a** : NOTABLE ⟨a ~ contribution to scholarship⟩   **b** : readily and unmistakably apprehended ⟨a ~ possibility of snow⟩ ⟨a ~ British accent⟩ — **dis·tinct·ly** \-'stiŋ(k)-tlē, -'stiŋ-klē\ *adv* — **dis·tinct·ness** \-'stiŋ(k)t-nəs, -'stiŋk-nəs\ *n*

syn DISTINCT, SEPARATE, DISCRETE mean not being each and every one the same. DISTINCT indicates that something is distinguished by the mind or eye as being apart or different from others ⟨two *distinct* versions⟩. SEPARATE often stresses lack of connection or a difference in identity between two things ⟨*separate* rooms⟩. DISCRETE strongly emphasizes individuality and lack of connection ⟨broke the job down into *discrete* stages⟩.   *syn* see in addition EVIDENT

dis·tinc·tion \di-'stiŋ(k)-shən\ *n* (13c)   **1   a** *archaic* : DIVISION   **b** : CLASS 4   **2** : the distinguishing of a difference ⟨without ~ as to race, sex, or religion⟩; *also* : the difference distinguished ⟨the ~ between *imply* and *infer*⟩   **3** : something that distinguishes ⟨regional ~s⟩   **4** : the quality or state of being distinguishable   **5   a** : the quality or state of being distinguished or worthy ⟨a politician of some ~⟩   **b** : special honor or recognition ⟨took a law degree with ~⟩ ⟨won many

\ə\ abut   \³\ kitten, F table   \ər\ further   \a\ ash   \ā\ ace   \ä\ mop, mar
\aú\ out   \ch\ chin   \e\ bet   \ē\ easy   \g\ go   \i\ hit   \ī\ ice   \j\ job
\ŋ\ sing   \ō\ go   \ò\ law   \òi\ boy   \th\ thin   \t͟h\ the   \ü\ loot   \ú\ foot
\y\ yet   \zh\ vision   \á, k̲, ⁿ, œ, œ̄, ue, ūe, ᵞ\ *see* Guide to Pronunciation

~s⟩ **c** : an accomplishment that sets one apart ⟨the ~ of being the oldest to win the title⟩

dis·tinc·tive \di-'stin(k)-tiv\ adj (15c) **1 a** : serving to distinguish **b** : having or giving style or distinction **2** : capable of making a segment of utterance different in meaning as well as in sound from an otherwise identical utterance **syn** see CHARACTERISTIC — **dis·tinc·tive·ly** adv — **dis·tinc·tive·ness** n

dis·tin·gué \,dēs-,taⁿ-'gā, (,)dis-; di-'staⁿ-,\ adj [F, fr. pp. of distinguer] (1813) : distinguished esp. in manner or bearing

dis·tin·guish \di-'stiŋ-(g)wish\ vb [MF distinguer, fr. L distinguere, lit., to separate by pricking, fr. dis- + -stinguere (akin to L instigare to urge on) — more at STICK] vt (1561) **1** : to perceive a difference in : mentally separate ⟨so alike they could not be ~ed⟩ **2 a** : to mark as separate or different **b** : to separate into kinds, classes, or categories **c** : to give prominence or distinction to ⟨~ed themselves in music⟩ **d** : CHARACTERIZE **3 a** : DISCERN ⟨~ed a light in the distance⟩ **b** : to single out : take special notice of ~ vi : to perceive a difference — **dis·tin·guish·abil·i·ty** \-,stiŋ-(g)wi-shə-'bi-lə-tē\ n — **dis·tin·guish·able** \-'stiŋ-(g)wi-shə-bəl\ adj — **dis·tin·guish·ably** \-blē\ adv

dis·tin·guished adj (1714) **1** : marked by eminence, distinction, or excellence **2** : befitting an eminent person **syn** see FAMOUS

Distinguished Conduct Medal n (1862) : a British military decoration awarded for distinguished conduct in the field

Distinguished Flying Cross n (1918) **1** : a British military decoration awarded for acts of gallantry when flying in operations against an enemy **2** : a U.S. military decoration awarded for heroism or extraordinary achievement while participating in an aerial flight

Distinguished Service Cross n (1914) **1** : a British military decoration awarded for distinguished service against the enemy **2** : a U.S. Army decoration awarded for extraordinary heroism during operations against an armed enemy

Distinguished Service Medal n (1914) **1** : a British military decoration awarded for distinguished conduct in war **2** : a U.S. military decoration awarded for exceptionally meritorious service to the government in a wartime duty of great responsibility

Distinguished Service Order n (1886) : a British military decoration awarded for special services in action

dis·tort \di-'stȯrt\ vb [L distortus, pp. of distorquēre, fr. dis- + torquēre to twist — more at TORTURE] vt (ca. 1586) **1** : to twist out of the true meaning or proportion ⟨~ed the facts⟩ **2** : to twist out of a natural, normal, or original shape or condition ⟨a face ~ed by pain⟩; also : to cause to be perceived unnaturally ⟨the new lights ~ed colors⟩ **3** : PERVERT ~ vi : to become distorted; also : to cause a twisting from the true, natural, or normal **syn** see DEFORM — **dis·tort·er** n

dis·tor·tion \di-'stȯr-shən\ n (1581) **1** : the act of distorting **2** : the quality or state of being distorted : a product of distorting: as **a** : a lack of proportionality in an image resulting from defects in the optical system **b** : falsified reproduction of an audio or video signal caused by change in the wave form of the original signal — **dis·tor·tion·al** \-shnəl, -shə-nᵊl\ adj

¹dis·tract \di-'strakt, 'dis-,trakt\ adj (14c) archaic : INSANE, MAD

²dis·tract \di-'strakt\ vt [ME, fr. L distractus, pp. of distrahere, lit., to draw apart, fr. dis- + trahere to draw] (14c) **1 a** : to turn aside : DIVERT **b** : to draw or direct (as one's attention) to a different object or in different directions at the same time **2** : to stir up or confuse with conflicting emotions or motives **syn** see PUZZLE — **dis·tract·i·bil·i·ty** \-,strak-tə-'bi-lə-tē\ n — **dis·tract·ible** or **dis·tract·able** \-'strak-tə-bəl\ adj — **dis·tract·ing·ly** \-tiŋ-lē\ adv

dis·tract·ed adj (1590) **1** : maddened or deranged esp. by grief or anxiety **2** : mentally confused, troubled, or remote — **dis·tract·ed·ly** adv

dis·trac·tion \di-'strak-shən\ n (15c) **1** : the act of distracting or the state of being distracted; esp : mental confusion **2** : something that distracts; esp : AMUSEMENT — **dis·trac·tive** \-'strak-tiv\ adj

dis·train \di-'strān\ vb [ME distreynen, fr. OF destreindre, fr. ML distringere, fr. L, to draw apart, detain, fr. dis- + stringere to bind tight — more at STRAIN] vt (14c) **1** : to force or compel to satisfy an obligation by means of a distress **2** : to seize by distress ~ vi : to levy a distress — **dis·train·able** \-'strā-nə-bəl\ adj — **dis·train·er** \-'strā-nər\ or **dis·train·or** \-'strā-nȯr, -,strā-'nȯr\ n

dis·traint \di-'strānt\ n [distrain + -t (as in constraint)] (ca. 1736) : the act or action of distraining

dis·trait \di-'strā\ adj [ME, fr. OF destrait, fr. L distractus] (15c) : apprehensively divided or withdrawn in attention : DISTRACTED 2

dis·traite \di-'strāt\ adj (15c) : DISTRAIT — used esp. of women

dis·traught \dis-'trȯt\ adj [ME, modif. of L distractus] (14c) **1** : agitated with doubt or mental conflict **2** : INSANE — **dis·traught·ly** adv

¹dis·tress \di-'stres\ n [ME destresse, fr. OF, fr. (assumed) VL districtia, fr. L districtus, pp. of distringere] (13c) **1 a** : seizure and detention of the goods of another as pledge or to obtain satisfaction of a claim by the sale of the goods seized **b** : something that is distrained **2 a** : pain or suffering affecting the body, a bodily part, or the mind : TROUBLE ⟨gastric ~⟩ **b** : a painful situation : MISFORTUNE **3 a** : a state of danger or desperate need ⟨a ship in ~⟩

syn DISTRESS, SUFFERING, MISERY, AGONY mean the state of being in great trouble. DISTRESS implies an external and usu. temporary cause of great physical or mental strain and stress ⟨the hurricane put everyone in great distress⟩. SUFFERING implies conscious endurance of pain or distress ⟨the suffering of famine victims⟩. MISERY stresses the unhappiness attending esp. sickness, poverty, or loss ⟨the homeless live with misery every day⟩. AGONY suggests pain too intense to be borne ⟨in agony over the death of their child⟩.

²distress vt (14c) **1** : to subject to great strain or difficulties **2** archaic : to force or overcome by inflicting pain **3** : to cause to worry or be troubled : UPSET **4** : to mar (as clothing or wood) deliberately to give an effect of age — **dis·tress·ing·ly** \-'stre-siŋ-lē\ adv

³distress adj (1926) **1** : offered for sale at a loss ⟨~ merchandise⟩ **2** : involving distress goods ⟨a ~ sale⟩

dis·tress·ful \di-'stres-fəl\ adj (1591) : causing distress : full of distress — **dis·tress·ful·ly** \-fə-lē\ adv — **dis·tress·ful·ness** n

dis·trib·u·tary \di-'stri-byə-,ter-ē\ n, pl **-tar·ies** (1863) : a river branch flowing away from the main stream

dis·trib·ute \di-'stri-byət, Brit also 'dis-tri-,byüt\ vb **-ut·ed**; **-ut·ing** [ME, fr. L distributus, pp. of distribuere, fr. dis- + tribuere to allot —

more at TRIBUTE] vt (15c) **1** : to divide among several or many : APPORTION ⟨~ expenses⟩ **2 a** : to spread out so as to cover something : SCATTER **b** : to give out or deliver esp. to members of a group ⟨~ newspapers⟩ ⟨~ leaflets⟩ **c** : to place or position so as to be properly apportioned over or throughout an area ⟨200 pounds distributed on a 6-foot frame⟩ **d** : to use (a term) so as to convey information about every member of the class named ⟨the proposition "all men are mortal" ~s "man" but not "mortal"⟩ **3 a** : to divide or separate esp. into kinds **b** : to return the units of (as typeset matter) to storage **4** : to use in or as an operation so as to be mathematically distributive ~ vi : to be mathematically distributive ⟨multiplication ~s over addition⟩ — **dis·trib·u·tee** \dis-,tri-byə-'tē\ n

syn DISTRIBUTE, DISPENSE, DIVIDE, DEAL, DOLE OUT mean to give out, usu. in shares, to each member of a group. DISTRIBUTE implies an apportioning by separation of something into parts, units, or amounts ⟨distributed food to the needy⟩. DISPENSE suggests the giving of a carefully weighed or measured portion to each of a group according to due or need ⟨dispensed wisdom to the students⟩. DIVIDE stresses the separation of a whole into parts and implies that the parts are equal ⟨three charitable groups divided the proceeds⟩. DEAL emphasizes the allotment of something piece by piece ⟨deal out equipment and supplies⟩. DOLE OUT implies a carefully measured portion that is often scant or niggardly ⟨doled out what little food there was⟩.

dis·trib·ut·ed adj (1968) **1** : characterized by a statistical distribution of a particular kind ⟨a normally ~ random variable⟩ **2** : of, relating to, or being a computer network in which at least some of the processing is done by the individual workstations and information is shared by and often stored at the workstations

dis·tri·bu·tion \,dis-trə-'byü-shən\ n (14c) **1 a** : the act or process of distributing **b** : the apportionment by a court of the personal property of an intestate **2 a** : the position, arrangement, or frequency of occurrence (as of the members of a group) over an area or throughout a space or unit of time **b** : the natural geographic range of an organism **3 a** : something distributed **b** (1) : FREQUENCY DISTRIBUTION (2) : PROBABILITY FUNCTION (3) : PROBABILITY DENSITY FUNCTION **2 4** : the pattern of branching and termination of a ramifying structure (as a nerve) **5** : the marketing or merchandising of commodities — **dis·tri·bu·tion·al** \-shnəl, -shə-nᵊl\ adj

distribution function n (ca. 1909) : a function that gives the probability that a random variable is less than or equal to the independent variable of the function

dis·trib·u·tive \di-'stri-byə-tiv\ adj (15c) **1** : of or relating to distribution: as **a** : dealing a proper share to each of a group **b** : diffusing more or less evenly **2** of a word : referring singly and without exception to the members of a group ⟨each, either, and none are ~⟩ **3 a** : being an operation (as multiplication in $a(b + c) = ab + ac$) that produces the same result when operating on the whole mathematical expression as when operating on each part and collecting the results **b** : being or relating to a rule or property concerning a distributive operation ⟨the ~ property of multiplication with respect to addition⟩ — **dis·trib·u·tive·ly** adv — **dis·trib·u·tiv·i·ty** \-,stri-byə-'ti-və-tē\ n

dis·trib·u·tor \di-'stri-byə-tər\ n (1526) **1** : one that distributes **2** : one that markets a commodity; esp : WHOLESALER **3** : an apparatus for directing the secondary current from the induction coil to the various spark plugs of an engine in their proper firing order

¹dis·trict \'dis-(,)trikt\ n, often attrib [F, fr. ML districtus jurisdiction, district, fr. distringere to distrain — more at DISTRAIN] (1611) **1 a** : a territorial division (as for administrative or electoral purposes) **b** : the basic administrative unit for local government in Northern Ireland **2** : an area, region, or section with a distinguishing character

²district vt (1792) : to divide or organize into districts

district attorney n (1789) : the prosecuting officer of a judicial district

district court n (1789) : a trial court that has jurisdiction over certain cases within a specific judicial district

¹dis·trust \(,)dis-'trəst\ n (1513) : the lack or absence of trust

²distrust vt (1548) : to have no trust or confidence in

dis·trust·ful \-'trəs(t)-fəl\ adj (1585) : having or showing distrust — **dis·trust·ful·ly** \-fə-lē\ adv — **dis·trust·ful·ness** n

dis·turb \di-'stərb\ vb [ME disturben, destourben, fr. OF & L; OF destourber, fr. L disturbare, fr. dis- + turbare to throw into disorder, fr. turba disorder — more at TURBID] vt (14c) **1 a** : to interfere with : INTERRUPT **b** : to alter the position or arrangement of **c** : to upset the natural and esp. the ecological balance or relations of ⟨land ~ed by dumping⟩ **2 a** : to destroy the tranquillity or composure of **b** : to throw into disorder **c** : ALARM **d** : to put to inconvenience ~ vi : to cause disturbance **syn** see DISCOMPOSE — **dis·turb·er** n — **dis·turb·ing·ly** \-'stər-biŋ-lē\ adv

dis·tur·bance \di-'stər-bən(t)s\ n (13c) **1** : the act of disturbing : the state of being disturbed **2** : a local variation from the average or normal wind conditions

dis·turbed adj (1904) : showing symptoms of emotional illness ⟨~ children⟩ ⟨~ behavior⟩

di·sub·sti·tut·ed \(,)dī-'səb-stə-,tü-təd, -,tyü-\ adj (ca. 1909) : having two substituent atoms or groups in a molecule

di·sul·fide \(,)dī-'səl-,fīd\ n (1872) **1** : a compound containing two atoms of sulfur combined with an element or radical **2** : an organic compound containing the bivalent group SS composed of two sulfur atoms

di·sul·fi·ram \dī-'səl-fə-,ram\ n [disulfide + thiourea + amyl] (1952) : a compound $C_{10}H_{20}N_2S_4$ that causes a severe physiological reaction to alcohol and is used esp. in the treatment of alcoholism

di·sul·fo·ton \di-'səl-fə-,tän\ n [di- + sulfo- + -ton (prob. fr. thion-)] (1965) : an organophosphorus systemic insecticide $C_8H_{19}O_2PS_3$

dis·union \(,)dis-'yü-nyən, dish-\ n (15c) **1** : the termination of union : SEPARATION **2** : DISUNITY — **dis·union·ist** \-nyə-nist\ n

dis·unite \(,)dis-yü-'nīt, -yə-, dish-\ vt (1598) : DIVIDE, SEPARATE

dis·uni·ty \(,)dis-'yü-nə-tē, dish-\ n (1632) : lack of unity; esp : DISSENSION

¹dis·use \(,)dis-'yüz, dish-\ vt (15c) : to discontinue the use or practice of

²dis·use \-'yüs\ n (15c) : cessation of use or practice

dis·util·i·ty \(,)dis-yü-'ti-lə-tē, -yə-, dish-\ n (1879) : the state or fact of being counterproductive

¹**dis·val·ue** \(,)dis-'val-(,)yü, -yə(-w)\ *vt* (1603) **1** *archaic* : UNDERVALUE, DEPRECIATE **2** : to consider of little value

²**disvalue** *n* (1603) **1** *obs* : DISREGARD, DISESTEEM **2** : a negative value

di·syl·la·ble \'dī-,si-lə-bəl, (,)dī-'sil-; 'dī-,sil-, (,)di(s)-'sil-\ *n* [part trans. of MF *dissilabe*, fr. L *disyllabus* having two syllables, fr. Gk *disyllabos*, fr. *di-* + *syllabē* syllable] (1589) : a linguistic form consisting of two syllables — **di·syl·lab·ic** \,dī-sə-'la-bik, ,di(s)-sə-\ *adj*

dit \'dit\ *n* [imit.] (1940) : a dot in radio or telegraphic code

¹**ditch** \'dich\ *n* [ME *dich*, fr. OE *dīc* dike, ditch; akin to MHG *tīch* pond, dike] (bef. 12c) : a long narrow excavation dug in the earth (as for drainage)

²**ditch** *vt* (14c) **1 a** : to enclose with a ditch **b** : to dig a ditch in **2** : to make a forced landing of (an airplane) on water **3** : to get rid of : DISCARD ~ *vi* **1** : to dig a ditch **2** : to crash-land at sea

ditch·dig·ger \-,di-gər\ *n* (ca. 1897) **1** : one that digs ditches **2** : one employed at menial and usu. hard physical labor

dite \'dīt\ *n* [var. of *doit*] (ca. 1877) *dial* : MITE, BIT

¹**dith·er** \'di-thər\ *vi* **dith·ered; dith·er·ing** \-th(ə-)riŋ\ [ME *didderen* (15c)] **1** : SHIVER, TREMBLE **2** : to act nervously or indecisively : VACILLATE — **dith·er·er** \-thər-ər\ *n*

²**dither** *n* (1819) : a highly nervous, excited, or agitated state : EXCITEMENT, CONFUSION — **dith·ery** \'di-thə-rē\ *adj*

dithi- *or* **dithio-** *comb form* [ISV *di-* + *thi-*] : containing two atoms of sulfur usu. in place of two oxygen atoms 〈*dithi*ocarbamate〉

di·thio·car·ba·mate \,di-,thī-ō-'kär-bə-,māt\ *n* (1929) : any of several sulfur analogues of the carbamates including some used as fungicides

dith·y·ramb \'di-thi-,ram(b)\ *n, pl* **-rambs** \-,ramz\ [Gk *dithyrambos*] (1656) **1** : a usu. short poem in an inspired wild irregular strain **2** : a statement or writing in an exalted or enthusiastic vein — **dith·y·ram·bic** \,di-thi-'ram-bik\ *adj* — **dith·y·ram·bi·cal·ly** \-bi-k(ə-)lē\ *adv*

di·tran·si·tive \,dī-'tran(t)-sə-tiv, -'tran-zə-\ *adj* (1972) : able to take both a direct and an indirect object 〈a ~ verb〉 — **ditransitive** *n*

dit·sy *or* **dit·zy** \'dit-sē\ *adj* **dits·i·er** *or* **ditz·i·er; -est** [origin unknown] (1973) : eccentrically silly, giddy, or inane : DIZZY

dit·ta·ny \'di-t*n-ē\ *n, pl* **-nies** [ME *ditoyne*, fr. OF *ditayne*, fr. L *dictamnum*, fr. Gk *diktamnon*] (12c) **1** : a pink-flowered herb (*Origanum dictamnus*) that is native to Crete **2** : an American herb (*Conila origanoides*) of the mint family that has much-branched stems

¹**dit·to** \'di-(,)tō\ *n, pl* **dittos** [It *ditto, detto*, pp. of *dire* to say, fr. L *dicere* — more at DICTION] (ca. 1678) **1** : a thing mentioned previously or above — used to avoid repeating a word; often symbolized by inverted commas or apostrophes **2** : a ditto mark

²**ditto** *adj* (1776) : having the same characteristics : SIMILAR

³**ditto** *vt* (1837) **1** : to repeat the action or statement of **2** [fr. *Ditto*, a trademark] : to copy (as printed matter) on a duplicator

⁴**ditto** *adv* (ca. 1864) : as before or aforesaid : in the same manner

dit·ty \'di-tē\ *n, pl* **ditties** [ME *ditee*, fr. MF *ditié* poem, fr. pp. of *ditier* to compose, fr. L *dictare* to dictate, compose] (14c) : an esp. simple and unaffected song

dit·ty bag \'di-tē-\ *n* [origin unknown] (ca. 1860) : a bag used esp. by sailors to hold small articles (as needles and thread)

ditty box *n* (ca. 1880) : a box used for the same purpose as a ditty bag

ditz \'dits\ *n* (1982) : a ditsy person

di·ure·sis \,dī-yə-'rē-səs\ *n, pl* **-ure·ses** \-,sēz\ [NL] (ca. 1681) : an increased excretion of urine

di·uret·ic \,dī-yə-'re-tik\ *adj* [ME, fr. MF or LL; MF *diuretique*, fr. LL *diureticus*, fr. Gk *diourētikos*, fr. *diourein* to urinate, fr. *dia-* + *ourein* to urinate — more at URINE] (14c) : tending to increase the flow of urine — **diuretic** *n* — **di·uret·i·cal·ly** \-ti-k(ə-)lē\ *adv*

¹**di·ur·nal** \dī-'ər-n³l\ *adj* [ME, fr. L *diurnalis* — more at JOURNAL] (14c) **1 a** : recurring every day 〈~ tasks〉 **b** : having a daily cycle 〈~ tides〉 **2 a** : of, relating to, or occurring in the daytime 〈the city's ~ noises〉 **b** : active chiefly in the daytime 〈~ animals〉 **c** : opening during the day and closing at night 〈~ flowers〉 — **di·ur·nal·ly** \-n³l-ē\ *adv*

²**diurnal** *n* (1600) **1** *archaic* : DIARY, DAYBOOK **2** : JOURNAL 2a

di·u·ron \'dī-yə-,rän\ *n* [*dichlor-* + *urea* + ¹*-on*] (1957) : a persistent herbicide C₉H₁₀Cl₂N₂O used esp. to control annual weeds

di·va \'dē-və\ *n, pl* **divas** *or* **di·ve** \-(,)vā\ [It, lit., goddess, fr. L, fem. of *divus* divine, god — more at DEITY] (1883) : PRIMA DONNA 1

di·va·gate \'dī-və-,gāt, 'di-\ *vi* **-gat·ed; -gat·ing** [LL *divagatus*, pp. of *divagari*, fr. L *dis-* + *vagari* to wander — more at VAGARY] (1599) : to wander or stray from a course or subject : DIVERGE, DIGRESS — **di·va·ga·tion** \,dī-və-'gā-shən, ,di-\ *n*

di·va·lent \(,)dī-'vā-lənt\ *adj* (1869) : having a chemical valence of two; *also* : bonded to two other atoms or groups

di·van \di-'van, 'di-,van, *esp in senses 1, 2, & 4 also* di-'vän, 'di-'van\ *n* [Turk, fr. Per *dīwān* account book] (1586) **1 a** : the privy council of the Ottoman Empire **b** : COUNCIL **2** : a council chamber **3** : a large couch usu. without back or arms often designed for use as a bed **4** : a collection of poems in Persian or Arabic usu. by one author

di·var·i·cate \dī-'var-ə-,kāt, də-\ *vi* **-cat·ed; -cat·ing** [L *divaricatus*, pp. of *divaricare*, fr. L *dis-* + *varicare* to straddle — more at PREVARICATE] (1673) : to spread apart : branch off : DIVERGE

di·var·i·ca·tion \(,)dī-,var-ə-'kā-shən, də-\ *n* (1578) **1** : the action, process, or fact of divaricating **2** : a divergence of opinion

¹**dive** \'dīv\ *vb* **dived** \'dīvd\ *or* **dove** \'dōv\; **dived** *also* **dove;** **div·ing** [ME *diven, duven,* fr. OE *dȳfan* to dip & *dūfan* to dive; akin to OE *dyppan* to dip — more at DIP] *vi* (bef. 12c) **1 a** : to plunge into water intentionally and esp. headfirst; *also* : to execute a dive **b** : SUBMERGE **2 a** : to come or drop down precipitously : PLUNGE **3 b** : to plunge one's hand into something **c** *of an airplane* : to descend in a dive **3 a** : to plunge into some matter or activity **b** : to plunge or dash for some place 〈dove for cover〉; *also* : to lunge esp. in order to seize something 〈dove for the ball〉 ~ *vt* **1** : to thrust into something **2** : to cause to dive

 usage Dive, which was orig. a weak verb, developed a past tense *dove*, prob. by analogy with verbs like *drive, drove*. Dove exists in some British dialects and has become the standard past tense esp. in speech in some parts of Canada. In the U.S. *dived* and *dove* are both widespread in speech as past tense and past participle, with *dove* less common than *dived* in the south Midland area, and *dived* less common than *dove* in the Northern and north Midland areas. In writing, the past tense *dived* is usual in British English and somewhat more common in

American English. *Dove* seems relatively rare as a past participle in writing.

²**dive** *n* (1700) **1** : the act or an instance of diving: as **a** (1) : a plunge into water executed in a prescribed manner (2) : a submerging of a submarine (3) : a steep descent of an airplane at greater than the maximum horizontal speed **b** : a sharp decline **2** : a disreputable entertainment establishment **3** : a faked knockout — usu. used in the phrase *take a dive* **4** : an offensive play in football in which the ball-carrier plunges into the line for short yardage

dive–bomb \'dīv-,bäm\ *vt* (1936) : to bomb from an airplane by making a steep dive toward the target before releasing the bomb — **dive-bomb·er** *n*

div·er \'dī-vər\ *n* (1506) **1** : one that dives **2 a** : a person who stays underwater for long periods by having air supplied from the surface or by carrying a supply of compressed air **b** : any of various birds that obtain food by diving in water; *esp* : LOON

di·verge \də-'vərj, dī-\ *vb* **di·verged; di·verg·ing** [ML *divergere*, fr. L *dis-* + *vergere* to incline — more at WRENCH] *vi* (1665) **1 a** : to move or extend in different directions from a common point : draw apart 〈*diverging* roads〉 **b** : to become or be different in character or form **c** : differ in opinion **2** : to turn aside from a path or course : DEVIATE **3** : to be mathematically divergent ~ *vt* : DEFLECT **syn** see SWERVE

di·ver·gence \-'vər-jən(t)s\ *n* (1656) **1 a** : a drawing apart (as of lines extending from a common center) **b** : DIFFERENCE, DISAGREEMENT **c** : the acquisition of dissimilar characters by related organisms in unlike environments **2** : a deviation from a course or standard **3** : the condition of being mathematically divergent

di·ver·gen·cy \-jən(t)-sē\ *n, pl* **-cies** (1709) : DIVERGENCE

di·ver·gent \-jənt\ *adj* [*divergent-, divergens*, prp. of *divergere*] (1696) **1 a** : diverging from each other **b** : differing from each other or from a standard : DEVIANT 〈the ~ interests of capital and labor〉 **2** : relating to or being an infinite sequence that does not have a limit or an infinite series whose partial sums do not have a limit **3** : causing divergence of rays 〈a ~ lens〉 **syn** see DIFFERENT — **di·ver·gent·ly** *adv*

di·vers \'dī-vərz\ *adj* [ME *divers, diverse*] (14c) : VARIOUS

di·verse \dī-'vərs, də-', 'dī-,\ *adj* [ME *divers, diverse*, fr. OF & L; OF *divers*, fr. L *diversus*, fr. pp. of *divertere*] (14c) **1** : differing from one another : UNLIKE **2** : composed of distinct or unlike elements or qualities **syn** see DIFFERENT — **di·verse·ly** *adv* — **di·verse·ness** *n*

di·ver·si·fy \də-'vər-sə-,fī, dī-\ *vb* **-fied; -fy·ing** *vt* (15c) **1** : to make diverse : give variety to 〈~ a course of study〉 **2** : to balance (as an investment portfolio) defensively among securities of different industries or of different classes **3** : to increase the variety of the products of ~ *vi* **1** : to produce variety **2** : to engage in varied operations — **di·ver·si·fi·ca·tion** \-,vər-sə-fə-'kā-shən\ *n* — **di·ver·si·fi·er** \-'vər-sə-,fī(-ə)r\ *n*

di·ver·sion \də-'vər-zhən, dī-, -shən\ *n* (1600) **1** : the act or an instance of diverting from a course, activity, or use : DEVIATION **2** : something that diverts or amuses : PASTIME **3** : an attack or feint that draws the attention and force of an enemy from the point of the principal operation

di·ver·sion·ary \də-'vər-zhə-,ner-ē, dī-, -shə-\ *adj* (1846) : tending to draw attention away from the principal concern : being a diversion

di·ver·sion·ist \-zhə-nəst, -shə-\ *n* (1937) **1** : one engaged in diversionary activities **2** : one characterized by political deviation

di·ver·si·ty \də-'vər-sə-tē, dī-\ *n, pl* **-ties** (14c) **1** : the condition of being diverse : VARIETY **2** : an instance of being diverse

di·vert \də-'vərt, dī-\ *vb* [ME, fr. MF & L; MF *divertir*, fr. L *divertere* to turn in opposite directions, fr. *dis-* + *vertere* to turn — more at WORTH] *vi* (15c) : to turn aside : DEVIATE 〈studied law but ~ed to diplomacy〉 ~ *vt* **1 a** : to turn from one course or use to another : DEFLECT **b** : DISTRACT **2** : to give pleasure to esp. by distracting the attention from what burdens or distresses **syn** see AMUSE

di·ver·tic·u·li·tis \,dī-vər-,ti-kyə-'lī-təs\ *n* [NL] (ca. 1900) : inflammation of a diverticulum

di·ver·tic·u·lo·sis \,dī-vər-,ti-kyə-'lō-səs\ *n* [NL] (1917) : an intestinal disorder characterized by the presence of many diverticula

di·ver·tic·u·lum \,dī-vər-'ti-kyə-ləm\ *n, pl* **-la** \-lə\ [NL, fr. L, bypath, prob. alter. of *deverticulum*, fr. *devertere* to turn aside, fr. *de-* + *vertere*] (ca. 1819) **1** : an abnormal pouch or sac opening from a hollow organ (as the intestine or bladder) **2** : a pocket or closed branch opening off a main passage — **di·ver·tic·u·lar** \-kyə-lər\ *adj*

di·ver·ti·men·to \di-,vər-tə-'men-(,)tō, -,ver-\ *n, pl* **-men·ti** \-'men-(,)tē\ *or* **-mentos** [It, lit., diversion, fr. *divertire* to divert, amuse, fr. L *divertere*] (1823) **1** : an instrumental chamber work in several movements usu. light in character **2** : DIVERTISSEMENT 1

di·ver·tisse·ment \di-'vər-təs-mənt, -,təz-, F dē-ver-tē-smäⁿ\ *n, pl* **di·vertissements** \-mən(t)s, -smäⁿ(z)\ [F, lit., diversion, fr. *divertiss-* (stem of *divertir*)] (1728) **1** : a dance sequence or short ballet usu. used as an interlude **2** : DIVERTIMENTO 1 **3** : DIVERSION, ENTERTAINMENT

Di·ves \'dī-(,)vēz\ *n* [ME, fr. L, rich, rich man; misunderstood as a proper name in Lk 16:19] (14c) : a rich man

di·vest \dī-'vest, də-\ *vt* [alter. of *devest*] (1563) **1 a** : to deprive or dispossess esp. of property, authority, or title **b** : to undress or strip esp. of clothing, ornament, or equipment **c** : RID, FREE **2** : to take away from a person — **di·vest·ment** \-'ves(t)-mənt\ *n*

di·ves·ti·ture \dī-'ves-tə-,chùr, -chər, də-, *chiefly Southern* -t(y)ù(ə)r\ *n* [*divest* + *-iture* (as in *investiture*)] (1601) **1** : the act of divesting **2** : the compulsory transfer of title or disposal of interests (as stock in a corporation) upon government order

¹**di·vide** \də-'vīd\ *vb* **di·vid·ed; di·vid·ing** [ME, fr. L *dividere*, fr. *dis-* + *-videre* to separate — more at WIDOW] *vt* (14c) **1 a** : to separate into two or more parts, areas, or groups **b** : to separate into classes, categories, or divisions **c** : CLEAVE, PART **2 a** : to separate into portions and give out in shares : DISTRIBUTE **b** : to possess, enjoy, or make use of in common **c** : APPORTION **3 a** : to cause to be separate,

---

\ə\ **abut** \³\ **kitten, F table** \ər\ **further** \a\ **ash** \ā\ **ace** \ä\ **mop, mar** \aù\ **out** \ch\ **chin** \e\ **bet** \ē\ **easy** \g\ **go** \i\ **hit** \ī\ **ice** \j\ **job** \ŋ\ **sing** \ō\ **go** \ò\ **law** \òi\ **boy** \th\ **thin** \t͟h\ **the** \ü\ **loot** \ù\ **foot** \y\ **yet** \zh\ **vision** \ā, k̟, ⁿ, œ, œ̄, ᵫ, ᵭ, ᵊ\ *see* Guide to Pronunciation distinct, or apart from one another **b** : to separate into opposing sides or parties **c** : to cause (a parliamentary body) to vote by division **4 a** : to subject (a number or quantity) to the operation of finding how many times it contains another number or quantity ⟨~ 42 by 14⟩ **b** : to be used as a divisor with respect to (a dividend) ⟨4 ~s 16 evenly⟩ **c** : to use as a divisor — used with *into* ⟨~ 14 into 42⟩ ~ *vi* **1** : to perform mathematical division **2 a** (1) : to undergo replication, multiplication, fission, or separation into parts (2) : to branch out **b** : to become separated or disunited esp. in opinion or interest *syn* see SEPARATE, DISTRIBUTE — **di·vid·able** \-'vī-də-bəl\ *adj*

²divide *n* (1642) **1** : an act of dividing **2 a** : a dividing ridge between drainage areas : WATERSHED **b** : a point or line of division

di·vid·ed *adj* (14c) **1 a** : separated into parts or pieces **b** *of a leaf* : cut into distinct parts by incisions extending to the base or to the midrib **c** : having a barrier (as a guardrail) to separate lanes of traffic going in opposite directions ⟨a ~ highway⟩ **2 a** : disagreeing with each other : DISUNITED **b** : directed or moved toward conflicting interests, states, or objects ⟨~ loyalties⟩ **3** : separated by distance ⟨familiar objects from which she had never dreamed of being —James Joyce⟩ — **di·vid·ed·ly** \də-'vī-dəd-lē\ *adv* — **di·vid·ed·ness** \-nəs\ *n*

div·i·dend \'di-və-,dend, -dənd\ *n* [ME *divident*, fr. L *dividendus*, gerundive of *dividere*] (15c) **1** : an individual share of something distributed: as **a** : a share in a pro rata distribution (as of profits) to stockholders **b** : a share of surplus allocated to a policyholder in a participating insurance policy **2 a** : a resultant return or reward **b** : BONUS **3 a** : a number to be divided **b** : a sum or fund to be divided and distributed — **div·i·dend·less** \-ləs\ *adj*

di·vid·er \də-'vī-dər\ *n* (1534) **1** : one that divides **2** *pl* : an instrument for measuring or marking (as in dividing lines) **3** : something serving as a partition between separate spaces within a larger area

di·vi-di·vi \,dē-vē-'dē-vē, ,di-vē-'di-vē\ *n* [AmerSp *dividivi*, prob. fr. Cumanagoto (extinct Cariban language of northern Venezuela)] (ca. 1837) : a small leguminous tree (*Caesalpinia coriaria*) of tropical America with twisted astringent pods that contain a large proportion of tannin

div·i·na·tion \,di-və-'nā-shən\ *n* [ME *divinacioun*, fr. L *divination-, divinatio*, fr. *divinare*] (14c) **1** : the art or practice that seeks to foresee or foretell future events or discover hidden knowledge usu. by the interpretation of omens or by the aid of supernatural powers **2** : unusual insight : intuitive perception — **di·vi·na·to·ry** \də-'vi-nə-,tōr-ē, də-'vī-nə-, 'di-və-nə-, -,tȯr-\ *adj*

¹di·vine \də-'vīn\ *adj* **di·vin·er; -est** [ME *divin*, fr. MF, fr. L *divinus*, fr. *divus* god — more at DEITY] (14c) **1 a** : of, relating to, or proceeding directly from God or a god ⟨~ love⟩ **b** : being a deity ⟨the ~ Savior⟩ **c** : directed to a deity ⟨~ worship⟩ **2 a** : supremely good : SUPERB ⟨the pie was ~⟩ **b** : HEAVENLY, GODLIKE — **di·vine·ly** *adv*

²divine *n* [ME, fr. ML *divinus*, fr. L, soothsayer, fr. *divinus*, adj.] (14c) **1** : CLERGYMAN **2** : THEOLOGIAN

³divine *vb* **di·vined; di·vin·ing** [ME, fr. MF & L; MF *diviner*, fr. L *divinare*, fr. *divinus*, n.] *vt* (14c) **1** : to discover intuitively : INFER **2** : to discover or locate (as water or minerals underground) usu. by means of a divining rod ~ *vi* **1** : to practice divination : PROPHESY **2** : to perceive intuitively *syn* see FORESEE

Divine Liturgy *n* (1870) : the eucharistic rite of Eastern churches

Divine Office *n* (15c) : the office for the canonical hours of prayer that priests and religious say daily

di·vin·er \də-'vī-nər\ *n* (14c) **1** : one who practices divination : SOOTHSAYER **2** : a person who divines the location of water or minerals

divine right *n* (ca. 1600) : the right of a sovereign to rule as set forth by the theory of government that holds that a monarch receives the right to rule directly from God and not from the people

divine service *n* (14c) : a service of Christian worship; *specif* : such a service that is not sacramental in character

diving beetle *n* (ca. 1889) : any of various predatory aquatic beetles (family Dytiscidae) that breathe while submerged using air trapped under their elytra

diving bell *n* (1661) : a diving apparatus consisting of a container open only at the bottom and supplied with compressed air by a hose

diving board *n* (1893) : SPRINGBOARD 1

diving duck *n* (1813) : any of various ducks (as a bufflehead) that frequent deep waters and obtain their food by diving

diving suit *n* (1908) : a waterproof suit with a removable helmet that is worn by a diver who is supplied with air pumped through a tube

divining rod *n* (1751) : a forked rod believed to indicate the presence of water or minerals esp. by dipping downward when held over a vein

di·vin·i·ty \də-'vi-nə-tē\ *n, pl* **-ties** (14c) **1** : THEOLOGY **2** : the quality or state of being divine **3** *often cap* : a divine being: as **a** : GOD 1 **b** (1) : GOD 2 (2) : GODDESS **4** : fudge made of whipped egg whites, sugar, and nuts

divinity school *n* (ca. 1555) : a professional school having a religious curriculum esp. for ministerial candidates

di·vis·i·ble \də-'vi-zə-bəl\ *adj* (14c) : capable of being divided — **di·vis·i·bil·i·ty** \də-,vi-zə-'bi-lə-tē\ *n*

di·vi·sion \də-'vi-zhən\ *n* [ME, fr. MF, fr. L *division-, divisio*, fr. *dividere* to divide] (14c) **1 a** : the act or process of dividing : the state of being divided **b** : the act, process, or an instance of distributing among a number : DISTRIBUTION **c** *obs* : a method of arranging or disposing (as troops) **2** : one of the parts or groupings into which a whole is divided or is divisible **3** : the condition or an instance of being divided in opinion or interest : DISAGREEMENT, DISUNITY ⟨exploited the ~s between the two countries⟩ **4 a** : something that divides, separates, or marks off : the act, process, or an instance of separating or keeping apart : SEPARATION **5** : the mathematical operation of dividing something **6 a** : a self-contained major military unit capable of independent action **b** : a tactical military unit composed of headquarters and usu. three to five brigades **c** (1) : the basic naval administrative unit (2) : a tactical subdivision of a squadron of ships **d** : a unit of the U.S. Air Force higher than a wing and lower than an air force **7** : a portion of a territorial unit marked off for a particu-

lar purpose (as administrative or judicial functions) **b** : an administrative or operating unit of a governmental, business, or educational organization **8** : the physical separation into different lobbies of the members of a parliamentary body voting for and against a question **9** : plant propagation by dividing parts and planting segments capable of producing roots and shoots **10** : a group of organisms forming part of a larger group; *specif* : a primary category of the plant kingdom **11** : a competitive class or category (as in boxing or wrestling) *syn* see PART — **di·vi·sion·al** \-'vizh-nəl, -'vi-zhə-n³l\ *adj*

di·vi·sion·ism \-'vi-zhən-,ni-zəm\ *n, often cap* (1901) : POINTILLISM — **di·vi·sion·ist** \-'vi-zhə-nəst\ *n or adj*

division of labor (1776) : the breakdown of labor into its components and their distribution among different persons, groups, or machines to increase productive efficiency

division sign *n* (ca. 1934) **1** : the symbol ÷ used to indicate division **2** : the diagonal / used to indicate a fraction

di·vi·sive \də-'vī-siv *also* -'vi- *or* -ziv\ *adj* (1642) : creating disunity or dissension — **di·vi·sive·ly** *adv* — **di·vi·sive·ness** *n*

di·vi·sor \də-'vī-zər\ *n* (15c) : the number by which a dividend is divided

¹di·vorce \də-'vōrs, -'vȯrs *also* dī-\ *n* [ME *divorse*, fr. MF, fr. L *divortium*, fr. *divertere, divortere* to divert, to leave one's husband] (14c) **1** : the action or an instance of legally dissolving a marriage **2** : SEPARATION, SEVERANCE

²divorce *vb* **di·vorced; di·vorc·ing** *vt* (15c) **1 a** : to end marriage with (one's spouse) by divorce **b** : to dissolve the marriage contract between **2** : to terminate an existing relationship or union : SEPARATE ⟨~ church from state⟩ ~ *vi* : to obtain a divorce *syn* see SEPARATE — **di·vorce·ment** \-'vȯrs-mənt, -'vȯr-\ *n*

di·vor·cé \də-,vōr-'sā, -,vȯr-, -'sē, -'vȯr-,, -'vȯr-,\ *n* (1877) : a divorced man

di·vor·cée \də-,vōr-'sā, -,vȯr-, -'sē, -'vȯr-,, -'vȯr-,\ *n* [F, fr. fem. of *divorcé*, pp. of *divorcer* to divorce, fr. MF *divorse*] (1813) : a divorced woman

div·ot \'di-vət\ *n* [alter. of earlier Sc *devat*, fr. ME (Sc dial.) *duvat*] (1586) **1** *Scot* : a square of turf or sod **2** : a loose piece of turf (as one dug from a golf fairway in making a shot)

di·vulge \də-'vəlj, dī-\ *vt* **di·vulged; di·vulg·ing** [ME, fr. L *divulgare*, fr. *dis-* + *vulgare* to make known, fr. *vulgus* mob] (15c) **1** *archaic* : to make public : PROCLAIM **2** : to make known (as a confidence or secret) *syn* see REVEAL — **di·vul·gence** \-'vəl-jən(t)s\ *n*

div·vy \'di-vē\ *vt* **div·vied; div·vy·ing** [by shortening & alter. fr *divide*] (1877) : DIVIDE, SHARE — usu. used with *up*

Dix·ie \'dik-sē\ *n* [name for the Southern states in the song *Dixie* (1859) by Daniel D. Emmett] (1859) : the Southern states of the U.S.

Dix·ie·crat \-,krat\ *n* (1948) : a dissident Southern Democrat; *specif* : a supporter of a 1948 presidential ticket opposing the civil rights stand of the Democrats — **Dix·ie·crat·ic** \,dik-sē-'kra-tik\ *adj*

Dix·ie·land \-,land\ *n* [prob. fr. the *Original Dixieland Jazz Band*] (1927) : jazz music in duple time usu. played by a small band and characterized by ensemble and solo improvisation

DIY \,dē-(,)ī-'wī\ *n, often attrib* (1955) *chiefly Brit* : DO-IT-YOURSELF

di·zen \'dī-z³n, 'di-\ *vt* [earlier *disen* to dress a distaff with flax, fr. MD] (1619) *archaic* : BEDIZEN

di·zy·got·ic \,dī-(,)zī-'gä-tik\ *also* **di·zy·gous** \(,)dī-'zī-gəs\ *adj* (1916) *of twins* : FRATERNAL 2

¹diz·zy \'di-zē\ *adj* **diz·zi·er; -est** [ME *disy*, fr. OE *dysig* stupid; akin to OHG *tusig* stupid] (bef. 12c) **1** : FOOLISH, SILLY **2 a** : having a whirling sensation in the head with a tendency to fall **b** : mentally confused **3 a** : causing giddiness or mental confusion **b** : caused by or marked by giddiness **c** : extremely rapid — **diz·zi·ly** \'di-zə-lē\ *adv* — **diz·zi·ness** \-zē-nəs\ *n*

²dizzy *vt* **diz·zied; diz·zy·ing** (1501) **1** : to make dizzy or giddy **2** : BEWILDER ⟨disasters that ~ the mind⟩ — **diz·zy·ing·ly** \-zē-iŋ-lē\ *adv*

DJ \'dē-,jā\ *n, often not cap* (1950) : DISC JOCKEY

dje·l·la·ba *also* **dje·l·la·bah** \jə-'lä-bə\ *n* [F *djellaba*, fr. Ar *jallābiya*] (1919) : a long loose garment with full sleeves and a hood

djin·ni \'jē-nē\ *or* **djinn** *or* **djin** \'jin\ *var of* JINNI

dl- \(,)dē-'el, 'dē-\ *prefix* **1** *also* **d,l-** : consisting of equal amounts of the dextro and levo forms of a specified compound ⟨*dl-*tartaric acid⟩ **2** : consisting of equal amounts of the D- and L- forms of a specified compound ⟨DL-fructose⟩

D layer *n* (ca. 1934) : a layer that may exist within the D region of the ionosphere; *also* : D REGION

D–mark \'dȯich-,märk, 'dȯi-chə-,\ *n* (1948) : DEUTSCHE MARK

DME \,dē-(,)em-'ē\ *n* [*distance measuring equipment*] (1947) : an electronic device that informs the pilot of an airplane of its distance from a particular ground station

DMSO \,dē-,em-,es-'ō\ *n* (1965) : DIMETHYL SULFOXIDE

DMT \,dē-(,)em-'tē\ *n* (ca. 1966) : DIMETHYLTRYPTAMINE

DNA \,dē-,en-'ā\ *n* [*deoxyribonucleic acid*] (1944) : any of various nucleic acids that are usu. the molecular basis of heredity, are localized esp. in cell nuclei, and are constructed of a double helix held together by hydrogen bonds between purine and pyrimidine bases which project inward from two chains containing alternate links of deoxyribose and phosphate — compare RECOMBINANT DNA

DNA fingerprinting *n* (1984) : a method of identification (as for forensic purposes) by determining the sequence of base pairs in the DNA esp. of a person — **DNA fingerprint** *n*

DNA polymerase *n* (ca. 1962) : any of several polymerases that promote replication or repair of DNA usu. using single-stranded DNA as a template

DN·ase \(,)dē-'en-,ās, -,āz\ *also* **DNA·ase** \(,)dē-,en-'ā-,ās, -,āz\ *n* (ca. 1956) : DEOXYRIBONUCLEASE

¹do \'dü, də-(w)\ *vb* **did** \'did, dəd\; **done** \'dən\; **do·ing** \'dü-iŋ\; **does** \'dəz\ [ME *don*, fr. OE *dōn*; akin to OHG *tuon* to do, L *-dere* to put, *facere* to make, do, Gk *tithenai* to place, set] *vt* (bef. 12c) **1** : to bring to pass : CARRY OUT **2** : PUT — used chiefly in *do to death* **3 a** : PERFORM, EXECUTE ⟨~ some work⟩ ⟨*did* his duty⟩ **b** : COMMIT ⟨crimes *done* deliberately⟩ **4 a** : BRING ABOUT, EFFECT ⟨trying to ~ good⟩ ⟨~ violence⟩ **b** : to give freely : PAY ⟨~ honor to her memory⟩ **5** : to bring to an end : FINISH — used in the past participle ⟨the job is finally *done*⟩ **6** : to put forth : EXERT ⟨*did* her best to win the race⟩ **7 a** : to

dividers

DNA: *A* molecular model: *1* hydrogen, *2* oxygen, *3* carbon in the helical phosphate ester chains, *4* carbon and nitrogen in the cross-linked purine and pyrimidine bases, *5* phosphorus; *B* double helix

wear out esp. by physical exertion : EXHAUST ⟨at the end of the race they were pretty well *done*⟩ **b** *Brit* : to attack physically : BEAT; *also* : KILL **8** : to bring into existence : PRODUCE ⟨~ a biography on the general⟩ **9** — used as a substitute verb esp. to avoid repetition ⟨if you must make such a racket, ~ it somewhere else⟩ **10 a** : to play the role or character of **b** : MIMIC; *also* : to behave like ⟨~ a Houdini and disappear⟩ **c** : to perform in or serve as producer of ⟨~ a play⟩ **11** : to treat unfairly; *esp* : CHEAT ⟨*did* him out of his inheritance⟩ **12** : to treat or deal with in any way typically with the sense of preparation or with that of care or attention : **a** (1) : to put in order : CLEAN ⟨was ~*ing* the kitchen⟩ (2) : WASH ⟨*did* the dishes after supper⟩ **b** : to prepare for use or consumption; *esp* : COOK ⟨like my steak *done* rare⟩ **c** : SET, ARRANGE ⟨had her hair *done*⟩ **d** : to apply cosmetics to ⟨wanted to ~ her face before the party⟩ **e** : DECORATE, FURNISH ⟨*did* the living room in Early American⟩ **13** : to be engaged in the study or practice of ⟨~ science⟩; *esp* : to work at as a vocation ⟨what to ~ after college⟩ **14 a** : to pass over (as distance) : TRAVERSE **b** : to travel at a speed of ⟨~*ing* 55 on the turnpike⟩ **15** : TOUR ⟨~*ing* 12 countries in 30 days⟩ **16** : to spend or serve out (a period of time) ⟨*did* ten years in prison⟩ **17** : to serve the needs of : SUIT, SUFFICE ⟨worms will ~ us for bait⟩ **18** : to approve esp. by custom, opinion, or propriety ⟨you oughtn't to say a thing like that . . . it's not *done* —Dorothy Sayers⟩ **19** : to treat with respect to physical comforts ⟨*did* themselves well⟩ **20** : USE *vt* **3** ⟨doesn't ~ drugs⟩ ~ *vi* **1** : ACT, BEHAVE ⟨~ as I say⟩ **2 a** : GET ALONG, FARE ⟨~ well in school⟩ **b** : to carry on business or affairs : MANAGE ⟨we can ~ without your help⟩ **3** : to take place : HAPPEN ⟨what's ~*ing* across the street⟩ **4** : to come to or make an end : FIN-ISH — used in the past participle **5** : to be active or busy ⟨let us then be up and ~*ing* —H. W. Longfellow⟩ **6** : to be adequate or sufficient : SERVE ⟨half of that will ~⟩ **7** : to be fitting : conform to custom or propriety ⟨won't ~ to be late⟩ **8** — used as a substitute verb to avoid repetition ⟨wanted to run and play as children ~⟩; used esp. in British English following a modal auxiliary or perfective *have* ⟨a great many people had died, or would ~ —Bruce Chatwin⟩ **9** — used in the imperative after an imperative to add emphasis ⟨be quiet ~⟩ ~ *verbal auxiliary* **1 a** — used with the infinitive without *to* to form present and past tenses in legal and parliamentary language ⟨~ hereby be-queath⟩ and in poetry ⟨give what she *did* crave —Shak.⟩ **b** — used with the infinitive without *to* to form present and past tenses in declarative sentences with inverted word order ⟨fervently ~ we pray —Abra-ham Lincoln⟩, in interrogative sentences ⟨*did* you hear that⟩, and in negative sentences ⟨we *don't* know⟩ ⟨*don't* go⟩ **2** — used with the infinitive without *to* to form present and past tenses expressing empha-sis ⟨I ~ say⟩ ⟨~ be careful⟩ — **do·able** \'dü-ə-bəl\ *adj* — **do a num-ber on** : to defeat or confound thoroughly esp. by indirect or decep-tive means — **do away with 1** : to put an end to : ABOLISH **2** : to put to death : KILL — **do by** : to deal with : TREAT — **do for** *chiefly Brit* **1** : to attend to the wants and needs of : take care of **2** : to bring about the death or ruin of — **do it** : to have sexual intercourse — **do justice 1 a** : to act justly **b** : to treat fairly or adequately **c** : to show due appreciation for **2** : to acquit in a way worthy of one's abilities — **do proud** : to give cause for pride or gratification — **do the trick** : to produce a desired result — **do with** : to m̄ake good use of : benefit by ⟨could *do with* a cup of coffee⟩ — **to do** : necessary to be done ⟨I've done my best and all's *to do* again —A. E. Housman⟩
²**do** \'dü\ *n, pl* **dos** *or* **do's** \'düz\ (1599) **1** *chiefly dial* : FUSS, ADO **2** *archaic* : DEED, DUTY **3 a** : a festive get-together : AFFAIR, PARTY **b** *chiefly Brit* : BATTLE **4** : a command or entreaty to do something ⟨a list of ~s and don'ts⟩ **5** *Brit* : CHEAT, SWINDLE **6** : HAIRDO
³**do** \'dō\ *n* [It] (ca. 1754) : the 1st tone of the diatonic scale in solmiza-tion
dob·bin \'dä-bən\ *n* [*Dobbin*, nickname for *Robert*] (1596) **1** : a farm horse **2** : a quiet plodding horse
dob·by \'dä-bē\ *n, pl* **dobbies** [perh. fr. *Dobby*, nickname for *Robert*] (1878) **1** : a loom attachment for weaving small figures **2** : a fabric or figured weave made with a dobby
Dobe \'dōb\ *n* (1946) : DOBERMAN PINSCHER
Do·ber·man pin·scher \,dō-bər-mən-'pin-chər\ *n* [G *Dobermann-pinscher*, fr. Ludwig *Dobermann*, 19th cent. Ger. dog breeder + G *Pinscher*, a breed of hunting dog] (1917) : any of a breed of short-haired medium-sized dogs of German origin — called also *Doberman*
do·bra \'dō-brə, 'dò-\ *n* [Pg, fr. fem. of obs. *dobro* double, fr. L *duplus* — more at DOUBLE] (1978) — see MONEY table
Do·bro \'dō-(,)brō\ *trademark* — used for an acoustic guitar having a metal resonator

dob·son·fly \'däb-sən-,flī\ *n* [origin unknown] (ca. 1904) : a winged insect (family Corydalidae) that has very long slender mandibles in the male and a large carnivorous aquatic larva and that is now usu. consid-ered a neuropteran — compare HELLGRAMMITE
doc \'däk\ *n* (ca. 1850) : DOCTOR
do·cent \'dō-s°nt, dō(t)-'sent\ *n* [obs. G (now *Dozent*), fr. L *docent-, docens*, prp. of *docēre*] (1880) **1** : a college or university teacher or lecturer **2** : a person who leads guided tours esp. through a museum or art gallery
do·ce·tic \dō-'sē-tik, -'se-\ *adj, often cap* [LGk *Dokētai* Docetists, fr. Gk *dokein* to seem — more at DECENT] (1846) : of or relating to Docetism or the Docetists
Do·ce·tism \dō-'sē-,ti-zəm, 'dō-sə-\ *n* (1846) : a belief opposed as her-esy in early Christianity that Christ only seemed to have a human body and to suffer and die on the cross — **Do·ce·tist** \-'sē-tist, -sə-\ *n*
doch·an·dor·ris *or* **doch–an–dor·is** \,däk-ən-'dór-əs\ *n* [ScGael *deoch an doruis* & Ir *deoch an doruis*, lit., drink of the door] (1691) *Scot & Irish* : a parting drink : STIRRUP CUP
doc·ile \'dä-səl *also* -,sil, *esp Brit* 'dō-,sīl\ *adj* [L *docilis*, fr. *docēre* to teach; akin to L *decēre* to be fitting — more at DECENT] (15c) **1** : eas-ily taught **2** : easily led or managed : TRACTABLE **syn** see OBEDIENT — **doc·ile·ly** \'dä-sə(l)-lē\ *adv* — **do·cil·i·ty** \dä-'si-lə-tē, dō-\ *n*
¹**dock** \'däk\ *n* [ME, fr. OE *docce*; akin to MD *docke* dock] (bef. 12c) **1** : any of a genus (*Rumex*) of the buckwheat family of coarse weedy plants that have long taproots and are sometimes used as potherbs **2** : any of several usu. broad-leaved weedy plants
²**dock** *n* [ME *dok*, perh. fr. OE *-docca* (as in *fingirdocca* finger muscle); akin to OHG *tocka* doll, ON *dokka* bundle] (14c) **1** : the solid part of an animal's tail as distinguished from the hair **2** : the part of an ani-mal's tail left after it has been shortened
³**dock** *vt* (14c) **1 a** : to cut off the end of a body part of; *specif* : to remove part of the tail of **b** : to cut (as ears or a tail) short **2 a** : to take away a part of : ABRIDGE **b** : to subject (as wages) to a deduction **c** : to penalize by depriving of a benefit ordinarily due; *esp* : to fine by a deduction of wages ⟨~ed him for tardiness⟩
⁴**dock** *n* [ME *dokke*, prob. fr. MD *dock*] (15c) **1** : a usu. artificial basin or enclosure for the reception of ships that is equipped with means for controlling the water height **2** : the waterway extending between two piers for the reception of ships **3** : a place (as a wharf or platform) for the loading or unloading of materials
⁵**dock** *vt* (1600) **1** : to haul or guide into a dock **2** : to join (as two spacecraft) mechanically while in space ~ *vi* **1** : to come into dock **2** : to become docked
⁶**dock** *n* [Flem *docke* cage] (1586) : the place in a criminal court where a prisoner stands or sits during trial — **in the dock** : on trial
dock·age \'dä-kij\ *n* (1648) **1** : a charge for the use of a dock **2** : the docking of ships **3** : docking facilities
¹**dock·er** \'dä-kər\ *n* (1810) : one that docks the tails of animals
²**docker** *n* (1887) : one connected with docks; *esp* : LONGSHOREMAN
¹**dock·et** \'dä-kət\ *n* [ME *doggette*] (15c) **1** : a brief written summary of a document : ABSTRACT **2 a** (1) : a formal abridged record of the proceedings in a legal action (2) : a register of such records **b** (1) : a list of legal causes to be tried (2) : a calendar of business matters to be acted on : AGENDA **3** : an identifying statement about a docu-ment placed on its outer surface or cover
²**docket** *vt* (1615) **1** : to place on the docket for legal action **2** : to make a brief abstract of (as a legal matter) and inscribe it in a list **3** : to inscribe (as a document) with an identifying statement
dock·hand \'däk-,hand\ *n* (1920) : LONGSHOREMAN
dock·land \-,land\ *n* (1904) *Brit* : the part of a port occupied by docks; *also* : a residential section adjacent to docks
dock·mas·ter \'däk-,mas-tər\ *n* (1736) : a person in charge of a dock or marina or of the docking of ships
dock·side \-,sīd\ *n, often attrib* (1887) : the shore or area adjacent to a dock
dock·work·er \-,wər-kər\ *n* (1921) : LONGSHOREMAN
dock·yard \-,yärd\ *n* (1704) **1** : SHIPYARD **2** *Brit* : NAVY YARD
¹**doc·tor** \'däk-tər\ *n* [ME *doctour* teacher, doctor, fr. MF & ML; MF, fr. ML *doctor*, fr. L, teacher, fr. *docēre* to teach — more at DOCILE] (14c) **1 a** : an eminent theologian declared a sound expounder of doctrine by the Roman Catholic Church — called also *doctor of the church* **b** : a learned or authoritative teacher **c** : a person who has earned one of the highest academic degrees (as a PhD) conferred by a university **d** : a person awarded an honorary doctorate (as an LLD or Litt D) by a college or university **2 a** : one skilled or specializing in healing arts; *esp* : a physician, surgeon, dentist, or veterinarian who is licensed to practice **b** : MEDICINE MAN **3 a** : material added (as to food) to produce a desired effect **b** : a blade (as of metal) for spread-ing a coating or scraping a surface **4** : a person who restores or re-pairs things — **doc·tor·al** \-t(ə-)rəl\ *adj* — **doc·tor·less** \-tər-ləs\ *adj* — **doc·tor·ship** \-,ship\ *n*
²**doctor** *vb* **doc·tored; doc·tor·ing** \-t(ə-)riŋ\ *vt* (1712) **1 a** : to give medical treatment to **b** : to restore to good condition : REPAIR ⟨~ an old clock⟩ **2 a** : to adapt or modify for a desired end by alteration or special treatment ⟨~ed the play to suit the audience⟩ ⟨the drink was ~ed⟩ **b** : to alter deceptively ⟨accused of ~*ing* the election returns⟩ ~ *vi* **1** : to practice medicine **2** *dial* : to take medicine
doc·tor·ate \'däk-t(ə-)rət\ *n* (1676) : the degree, title, or rank of a doctor
¹**doc·tri·naire** \,däk-trə-'nar, -'ner\ *n* [F, fr. *doctrine*] (1831) : one who attempts to put into effect an abstract doctrine or theory with little or no regard for practical difficulties
²**doctrinaire** *adj* (1834) : of, relating to, or characteristic of a doctri-naire : DOGMATIC **syn** see DICTATORIAL — **doc·tri·nair·ism** \-'nar-,i-zəm, -'ner-\ *n*
doc·tri·nal \'däk-trə-n°l, *esp Brit* däk-'trī-\ *adj* (15c) : of, relating to, or preoccupied with doctrine — **doc·tri·nal·ly** \-n°l-ē\ *adv*

\ə\ abut \ᵊ\ kitten, F table \ər\ further \a\ ash \ā\ ace \ä\ mop, mar
\au̇\ out \ch\ chin \e\ bet \ē\ easy \g\ go \i\ hit \ī\ ice \j\ job
\ŋ\ sing \ō\ go \ȯ\ law \ȯi\ boy \th\ thin \t̲h̲\ the \ü\ loot \u̇\ foot
\y\ yet \zh\ vision \ä, k̲, ⁿ, œ, œ̄, ᵫ, ūe, ūē, ᵋ\ *see* Guide to Pronunciation

doc·trine \'däk-trən\ *n* [ME, fr. MF & L; MF, fr. L *doctrina*, fr. *doctor*] (14c) **1** *archaic* : TEACHING, INSTRUCTION **2 a** : something that is taught **b** : a principle or position or the body of principles in a branch of knowledge or system of belief : DOGMA **c** : a principle of law established through past decisions **d** : a statement of fundamental government policy esp. in international relations

docu·dra·ma \'dä-kyə-ˌdrä-mə, -ˌdra-\ *n* [*documentary* + *drama*] (ca. 1961) : a drama for television, motion pictures, or theater dealing freely with historical events esp. of a recent and controversial nature

1doc·u·ment \'dä-kyə-mənt\ *n* [ME, fr. MF, fr. LL & L; LL *documentum* official paper, fr. L, lesson, proof, fr. *docēre* to teach — more at DOCILE] (15c) **1 a** *archaic* : PROOF, EVIDENCE **b** : an original or official paper relied on as the basis, proof, or support of something **c** : something (as a photograph or a recording) that serves as evidence or proof **2 a** : a writing conveying information **b** : a material substance (as a coin or stone) having on it a representation of thoughts by means of some conventional mark or symbol **c** : DOCUMENTARY — **doc·u·men·tal** \ˌdä-kyə-'men-t⁰l\ *adj*

2doc·u·ment \'dä-kyə-ˌment\ *vt* (1711) **1** : to furnish documentary evidence of **2** : to furnish with documents **3 a** : to provide with factual or substantial support for statements made or a hypothesis proposed; *esp* : to equip with exact references to authoritative supporting information **b** (1) : to construct or produce (as a movie or novel) with authentic situations or events (2) : to portray realistically **4** : to furnish (a ship) with ship's papers — **doc·u·ment·able** \-ˌmen-tə-bəl, ˌdäk-yə-'\ *adj* — **doc·u·ment·er** \'dä-kyə-ˌmen-tər\ *n*

doc·u·men·tal·ist \ˌdä-kyə-'men-t⁰l-ist\ *n* (1939) : a specialist in documentation

doc·u·men·tar·i·an \ˌdä-kyə-mən-'ter-ē-ən, -ˌmen-\ *n* [2*documentary*] (1943) : one who makes a documentary

doc·u·men·ta·rist \-'men-tə-rist\ *n* [2*documentary*] (1949) : DOCUMENTARIAN

1doc·u·men·ta·ry \ˌdä-kyə-'men-tə-rē, -'men-trē\ *adj* (1802) **1** : being or consisting of documents : contained or certified in writing ⟨∼ evidence⟩ **2** : of, relating to, or employing documentation in literature or art; *broadly* : FACTUAL, OBJECTIVE ⟨a ∼ film of the war⟩ — **doc·u·men·tar·i·ly** \-mən-'ter-ə-lē, -ˌmen-\ *adv*

2documentary *n, pl* **-ries** (1935) : a documentary presentation (as a film or novel)

doc·u·men·ta·tion \ˌdä-kyə-mən-'tā-shən, -ˌmen-\ *n* (1884) **1** : the act or an instance of furnishing or authenticating with documents **2 a** : the provision of documents in substantiation; *also* : documentary evidence **b** (1) : the use of historical documents (2) : conformity to historical or objective facts (3) : the provision of footnotes, appendices, or addenda referring to or containing documentary evidence **3** : INFORMATION SCIENCE **4** : the usu. printed instructions, comments, and information for using a particular piece or system of computer software or hardware — **doc·u·men·ta·tion·al** \-shnəl, -shə-n⁰l\ *adj*

1dod·der \'dä-dər\ *n* [ME *doder*; akin to MHG *toter* dodder, egg yolk] (13c) : any of a genus (*Cuscuta*) of parasitic wiry twining vines of the morning-glory family that are deficient in chlorophyll and have tiny scales instead of leaves

2dodder *vi* **dod·dered; dod·der·ing** \'dä-d(ə-)riŋ\ [ME *dadiren*] (14c) **1** : to tremble or shake from weakness or age **2** : to progress feebly and unsteadily ⟨was ∼*ing* down the walk⟩ — **dod·der·er** \-dər-ər\ *n*

dod·dered \'dä-dərd\ *adj* [prob. alter. of *dodded*, fr. pp. of E dial. *dod* to lop, fr. ME *dodden*] (1697) **1** : deprived of branches through age or decay ⟨a ∼ oak⟩ **2** : INFIRM, ENFEEBLED

dod·der·ing \'dä-d(ə-)riŋ\ *adj* (1898) : FEEBLE, SENILE

dod·dery \-d(ə-)rē\ *adj* (1866) **1** : DODDERED **2** : DODDERING

dodeca- *or* **dodec-** *comb form* [L, fr. Gk *dōdeka-, dōdek-*, fr. *dōdeka, dyōdeka*, fr. *dyō, dyo* two + *deka* ten] : twelve ⟨*dodecaphonic*⟩

do·deca·gon \dō-'de-kə-ˌgän\ *n* [Gk *dōdekagōnon*, fr. *dōdeka-* + *-gōnon* -gon] (ca. 1658) : a polygon of 12 angles and 12 sides

do·deca·he·dron \ˌ(ˌ)dō-ˌde-kə-'hē-drən\ *n, pl* **-drons** *or* **-dra** \-drə\ [Gk *dōdekaedron*, fr. *dōdeka-* + *-edron* -hedron] (ca. 1570) : a solid having 12 plane faces — **do·deca·he·dral** \-drəl\ *adj*

do·deca·phon·ic \ˌ(ˌ)dō-ˌde-kə-'fä-nik\ *adj* [*dodeca-* + *phon-* + *-ic*] (1949) : TWELVE-TONE — **do·deca·phon·i·cal·ly** \-ni-k(ə-)lē\ *adv* — **do·deca·pho·nist** \dō-'de-kə-fə-nist, -ˌfō-; ˌdō-di-'ka-fə-nist\ *n* — **do·deca·pho·ny** \-nē\ *n*

1dodge \'däj\ *n* [origin unknown] (1575) **1 a** : an artful device to evade, deceive, or trick **b** : EXPEDIENT **2** : an act of evading by sudden bodily movement

2dodge *vb* **dodged; dodg·ing** *vt* (1680) **1** : to evade (as a duty) usu. indirectly or by trickery ⟨*dodged* the draft by leaving the country⟩ ⟨*dodged* questions⟩ **2 a** : to evade by a sudden or repeated shift of position **b** : to avoid an encounter with ∼ *vi* **1 a** : to make a sudden movement in a new direction (as to evade a blow) ⟨*dodged* behind the door⟩ **b** : to move to and fro or from place to place usu. in an irregular course ⟨*dodged* through the crowd⟩ **2** : to evade a responsibility or duty esp. by trickery or deceit

dodge·ball \'däj-ˌbol\ *n* (ca. 1922) : a game in which players stand in a circle and try to hit opponents within the circle with a large inflated ball

dodg·em \'dä-jəm\ *n, often cap* (1921) : an amusement ride featuring bumper cars

dodgem car *n* (1945) : BUMPER CAR

dodg·er \'dä-jər\ *n* (1568) **1** : one that dodges; *esp* : one who uses tricky devices **2** : a small leaflet : CIRCULAR **3** : CORN DODGER **4** : a usu. canvas screen on a boat or ship that provides protection from spray

dodg·ery \'dä-jə-rē\ *n, pl* **-er·ies** (1670) : EVASION, TRICKERY

dodgy \'dä-jē\ *adj* (1861) **1** *chiefly Brit* : EVASIVE, TRICKY **2** *chiefly Brit* : not sound, stable, or reliable : SHAKY **3** *Brit* : requiring skill or care in handling; *also* : CHANCY, RISKY — **dodg·i·ness** \-nəs\ *n*

do·do \'dō-(ˌ)dō\ *n, pl* **dodoes** *or* **dodos** [Pg *doudo*, fr. *doudo* silly, stupid] (1628) **1 a** : an extinct heavy flightless bird (*Raphus cucullatus*, syn *Didus ineptus*) of the island of Mauritius that is related to the pigeon and larger than a turkey **b** : an extinct bird of the island of Réunion similar to and apparently closely related to the dodo **2 a** : one hopelessly behind the times **b** : a stupid person

do down *vt* (14c) *Brit* : to get the better of (as by trickery)

doe \'dō\ *n, pl* **does** *or* **doe** [ME *do*, fr. OE *dā*; akin to G dial. *tē* doe] (bef. 12c) : the adult female of various mammals (as a deer, rabbit, or kangaroo) of which the male is called buck

doe–eyed \'dō-ˌīd\ *adj* (1933) : having large innocent-looking eyes

do·er \'dü-ər\ *n* (14c) : one that takes an active part ⟨a thinker or a ∼⟩

does *pres 3d sing of* DO, *pl of* DOE

doe·skin \'dō-ˌskin\ *n* (15c) **1** : the skin of does or leather made of it; *also* : soft leather from sheep- or lambskins **2** : a compact coating and sportswear fabric napped and felted for a smooth surface

doesn't \'də-z⁰nt\ (1860) : does not

do·est \'dü-əst\ *archaic pres 2d sing of* DO

do·eth \'dü-əth\ *archaic pres 3d sing of* DO

doff \'däf, 'dȯf\ *vt* [ME, fr. *don* to do + *of* off] (14c) **1 a** : to remove (an article of wear) from the body **b** : to take off (the hat) in greeting or as a sign of respect **2** : to rid oneself of : put aside — **doff one's hat to** *or* **doff one's cap to** : to show respect to : SALUTE

1dog \'dȯg, 'däg\ *n, often attrib* [ME, fr. OE *docga*] (bef. 12c) **1 a** : CANID; *esp* : a highly variable domestic mammal (*Canis familiaris*) closely related to the common wolf (*Canis lupus*) **b** : a male dog; *also* : a male usu. carnivorous mammal **2 a** : a worthless person **b** : FELLOW, CHAP ⟨a lazy ∼⟩ ⟨you lucky ∼⟩ **3 a** : any of various usu. simple mechanical devices for holding, gripping, or fastening that consist of a spike, bar, or hook **b** : ANDIRON **4** : uncharacteristic or affected stylishness or dignity ⟨put on the ∼⟩ **5** *cap* : either of the constellations Canis Major or Canis Minor **6** *pl* : FEET **7** *pl* : RUIN ⟨going to the ∼s⟩ **8** : one inferior of its kind: as **a** : an investment not worth its price **b** : an undesirable piece of merchandise **9** : an unattractive person and esp. a girl or woman **10** : HOT DOG 1 — **dog·like** \'dȯg-ˌlīk\ *adj*

dog 1a: *1* pastern, *2* chest, *3* flews, *4* muzzle, *5* stop, *6* occiput, *7* leather, *8* crest, *9* withers, *10* loin, *11* point of rump, *12* hock *or* tarsus, *13* knee *or* stifle, *14* brisket, *15* elbow, *16* feathering

2dog *adj* (14c) **1** : CANINE **2** : SPURIOUS; *esp* : unlike that used by native speakers or writers ⟨∼ Latin⟩ ⟨∼ French⟩

3dog *vt* **dogged** \'dȯgd, 'dägd\; **dog·ging** (1519) **1 a** : to hunt or track like a hound **b** : to worry as if by pursuit with dogs : PLAGUE **2** : to fasten with a dog — **dog it** : to fail to do one's best : GOLDBRICK

4dog *adv* (ca. 1552) : EXTREMELY, UTTERLY ⟨*dog*-tired⟩

dog and pony show *n* (1965) : an often elaborate public relations or sales presentation

dog·bane \'dȯg-ˌbān\ *n* (1597) : any of a genus (*Apocynum* of the family Apocynaceae, the dogbane family) comprising chiefly tropical and often poisonous plants with milky juice and usu. showy flowers

dog biscuit *n* (ca. 1858) : a hard dry cracker for dogs

dog·cart \'dȯg-ˌkärt\ *n* (1668) **1** : a cart drawn by a dog **2** : a light two-wheeled carriage with two transverse seats set back to back

dog·catch·er \-ˌka-chər, -ˌke-\ *n* (1835) : a community official assigned to catch and dispose of stray dogs

dog collar *n* (1524) **1** : a collar for a dog **2** *slang* : CLERICAL COLLAR **3** : a wide flexible snug-fitting necklace

dog days *n pl* [fr. their being reckoned from the heliacal rising of the Dog Star (Sirius)] (1538) **1** : the period between early July and early September when the hot sultry weather of summer usu. occurs in the northern hemisphere **2** : a period of stagnation or inactivity

dog·dom \'dȯg-dəm\ *n* (1854) : the world of dogs or of dog fanciers

doge \'dōj\ *n* [It dial., fr. L *duc-, dux* leader — more at DUKE] (1549) : the chief magistrate in the republics of Venice and Genoa

dog–ear \'dȯ-ˌgir\ *n* (ca. 1725) : the turned-down corner of a page esp. of a book — **dog-ear** *vt*

dog–eared \'dȯ-ˌgird\ *adj* (1784) **1** : having dog-ears ⟨a ∼ book⟩ **2** : SHABBY, TIMEWORN ⟨a ∼ resort⟩ ⟨∼ myths⟩

dog–eat–dog \ˌdȯg-ˌēt-'dȯg\ *adj* (1834) : marked by ruthless self-interest ⟨∼ competition⟩

dog·face \'dȯg-ˌfās\ *n* (1917) : SOLDIER; *esp* : INFANTRYMAN

dog fennel *n* (14c) : a strong-scented chamomile (*Anthemis cotula*) of Europe and Asia naturalized along roadsides in the U.S.

dog·fight \'dȯg-ˌfīt\ *n* (1656) **1** : a fight between dogs; *broadly* : a fiercely disputed contest **2** : a fight between two or more fighter planes usu. at close quarters — **dogfight** *vi*

dog·fish \-ˌfish\ *n* (15c) : any of various usu. small bottom-dwelling sharks (as of the families Squalidae, Carcharhinidae, and Scyliorhinidae) that often appear in schools near shore, prey chiefly on fish and invertebrates, and are a valuable food source

dog·ged \'dȯ-gəd\ *adj* (1653) : marked by stubborn determination *syn* see OBSTINATE — **dog·ged·ly** *adv* — **dog·ged·ness** *n*

1dog·ger·el \'dȯ-g(ə-)rəl, 'dä-\ *adj* [ME *dogerel*, prob. dim. of *dogge* dog] (14c) : loosely styled and irregular in measure esp. for burlesque or comic effect; *also* : marked by triviality or inferiority

2doggerel *n* (1630) : doggerel verse

dog·gery \'dȯ-gə-rē\ *n, pl* **-ger·ies** (1830) : a cheap saloon : DIVE
dog·gie bag *or* **doggy bag** \'dȯ-gē-\ *n* [¹*doggy;* fr. the presumption that such leftovers are intended for a pet dog] (1963) : a container for carrying home leftover food and esp. meat from a restaurant meal
dog·gish \'dȯ-gish\ *adj* (15c) **1** : CANINE **2** : stylish in a showy way — **dog·gish·ly** *adv* — **dog·gish·ness** *n*
dog·go \'dȯ-(,)gō\ *adv* [prob. fr. ¹*dog*] (1893) : in hiding — used chiefly in the phrase *to lie doggo*
¹**dog·gone** \'däg-'gän, 'dȯg-'gȯn\ *vb* **dog-goned; dog-gon·ing** [euphemism for *God damn*] (1828) : DAMN
²**dog·gone** *or* **dog-goned** \,däg-,gän(d), ,dȯg-,gȯn(d)\ *adj or adv* (1851) : DAMNED
³**doggone** *n* (1928) : DAMN
¹**dog·gy** *or* **dog·gie** \'dȯ-gē\ *n, pl* **doggies** (1825) : a small dog
²**dog·gy** \'dȯ-gē\ *adj* **dog·gi·er; -est** (1859) **1** : concerned with or fond of dogs **2** : resembling or suggestive of a dog ⟨~ odor⟩ **3** : STYLISH, SHOWY **4** : not worthy or profitable : INFERIOR
dog·house \'dȯg-,hau̇s\ *n* (1594) : a shelter for a dog — **in the doghouse** : in a state of disfavor
do·gie \'dō-gē\ *n* [origin unknown] (1888) *chiefly West* : a motherless calf in a range herd
dog in the manger [fr. the fable of the dog who prevented an ox from eating hay which he did not want himself] (1573) : a person who selfishly withholds from others something useless to himself
¹**dog·leg** \'dȯg-,leg, -,lāg\ *adj* (1889) : crooked or bent like a dog's hind leg
²**dogleg** *n* (ca. 1909) **1 a** : something having an abrupt angle **b** : a sharp bend (as in a road) **2** : a golf hole having an angled fairway
³**dogleg** \'(1947) : to proceed along a dogleg course ⟨the single narrow street that ~s through town —Russ Leadabrand⟩
dog·ma \'dȯg-mə, 'däg-\ *n, pl* **dogmas** *also* **dog·ma·ta** \-mə-tə\ [L *dogmat-, dogma,* fr. Gk, fr. *dokein* to seem — more at DECENT] (1638) **1 a** : something held as an established opinion; *esp* : a definite authoritative tenet **b** : a code of such tenets ⟨pedagogical ~⟩ **c** : a point of view or tenet put forth as authoritative without adequate grounds **2** : a doctrine or body of doctrines concerning faith or morals formally stated and authoritatively proclaimed by a church
dog·mat·ic \dȯg-'ma-tik, däg-\ *also* **dog·mat·i·cal** \-ti-kəl\ *adj* (ca. 1681) **1** : characterized by or given to the use of dogmatism ⟨a ~ critic⟩ **2** : of or relating to dogma *syn* see DICTATORIAL — **dog·mat·i·cal·ly** \-ti-k(ə-)lē\ *adv* — **dog·mat·i·cal·ness** \-ti-kəl-nəs\ *n*
dog·mat·ics \-tiks\ *n pl but sing or pl in constr* (1845) : a branch of theology that seeks to interpret the dogmas of a religious faith
dogmatic theology *n* (1846) : DOGMATICS
dog·ma·tism \'dȯg-mə-,ti-zəm, 'däg-\ *n* (1603) **1** : positiveness in assertion of opinion esp. when unwarranted or arrogant **2** : a viewpoint or system of ideas based on insufficiently examined premises
dog·ma·tist \-mə-tist\ *n* (1541) : one who dogmatizes
dog·ma·tize \'dȯg-mə-,tīz, 'däg-\ *vb* **-tized; -tiz·ing** [F *dogmatiser,* fr. LL *dogmatizare,* fr. Gk *dogmatizein,* fr. *dogmat-, dogma*] *vi* (1611) : to speak or write dogmatically ~ *vt* : to state as a dogma or in a dogmatic manner — **dog·ma·ti·za·tion** \,dȯg-mə-tə-'zā-shən, ,däg-\ *n* — **dog·ma·tiz·er** *n*
dog·nap \'dȯg-,nap\ *vt* **-napped** *or* **-naped** \-,napt\; **-nap·ping** *or* **-nap·ing** \-,na-piŋ\ [¹*dog* + *-nap* (as in *kidnap*)] (1947) : to steal (a dog) esp. to obtain a reward for its return or to sell to a scientific laboratory — **dog·nap·per** *or* **dog·nap·er** *n*
Do·gon \'dō-,gän\ *n, pl* **Dogon** *or* **Dogons** (ca. 1931) **1** : a member of a people of Mali noted for their sculpture **2** : the language of the Dogon
do–good \'dü-,gu̇d\ *adj* (1952) : designed or disposed sometimes impractically and too zealously toward bettering the conditions under which others live — **do–good·ism** \-,i-zəm\ *n*
do–good·er \-,gu̇-dər\ *n* (1926) : an earnest often naive humanitarian or reformer — **do–good·ing** \-diŋ\ *n or adj*
dog paddle *n* (1904) : an elementary swimming stroke in which the arms paddle in the water and the legs maintain a kicking motion — **dog–pad·dle** *vi*
dog rose *n* (ca. 1597) : a common European wild rose (*Rosa canina*)
dogs·body \'dȯgz-,bä-dē\ *n* [Brit naval slang *dogsbody* pudding made of peas, junior officer] (1922) *chiefly Brit* : DRUDGE
dog's chance *n* (1902) : a bare chance in one's favor
dog·sled \'dȯg-,sled\ *n* (1810) : a sled drawn by dogs — **dogsled** *vi* — **dog·sled·der** \-,sle-dər\ *n*
Dog Star *n* : SIRIUS
dog tag *n* (1918) : an identification tag (as for military personnel or pets)
dog tick *n* (ca. 1552) : AMERICAN DOG TICK
dog·tooth \'dȯg-,tüth\ *n* (1552) **1** : CANINE 1, EYETOOTH **2** : an architectural ornament common in early English Gothic consisting usu. of four leaves radiating from a raised point at the center **3** *chiefly Brit* : HOUNDSTOOTH CHECK
dogtooth violet *n* (1629) : any of a genus (*Erythronium*) of small spring-flowering bulbous herbs of the lily family
¹**dog·trot** \'dȯg-,trät\ *n* (15c) **1** : a quick easy gait suggesting that of a dog **2** *chiefly Southern & Midland* : a roofed passage similar to a breezeway; *esp* : one connecting two parts of a cabin
²**dogtrot** *vi* (ca. 1900) : to move or progress at a dogtrot
dog·watch \'dȯg-,wäch\ *n* (1700) **1** : either of two watches of two hours on shipboard that extend from 4 to 6 and 6 to 8 p.m. **2** : any of various night shifts; *esp* : the last shift
dog·wood \'dȯg-,wu̇d\ *n* (1617) : any of various trees and shrubs (genus *Cornus* of the family Cornaceae, the dogwood family) with clusters of small flowers and often large white, pink, or red involucral bracts

dogtooth 2

doi·ly \'dȯi-lē\ *n, pl* **doilies** [*Doily* or *Doyley fl* 1711 London draper] (1711) **1** : a small napkin **2** : a small often decorative mat
do in *vt* (1905) **1 a** : to bring about the defeat or destruction of; *also* : KILL **b** : EXHAUST, WEAR OUT **2** : CHEAT

do·ing \'dü-iŋ\ *n* (14c) **1** : the act of performing or executing : ACTION ⟨that will take a great deal of ~⟩ **2** *pl* **a** : things that are done or that occur : GOINGS-ON ⟨everyday ~s⟩ **b** : social activities
doit \'dȯit\ *n* [D *duit;* akin to ON *thveiti* small coin, *thveita* to hew] (1592) **1** : an old Dutch coin equal to about ⅛ stiver **2** : TRIFLE 1
do–it–your·self \,dü-ə-chər-'self, -tyər-\ *n, often attrib* (1952) : the activity of doing or making something (as in woodworking or home repair) without professional training or assistance; *broadly* : an activity in which one does something oneself or on one's own initiative — **do–it–your·self·er** \-'sel-fər\ *n*
do·jo \'dō-(,)jō\ *n, pl* **dojos** [Jp *dōjō,* fr. *dō* way, art + *-jō* ground] (1942) : a school for training in various arts of self-defense (as judo or karate)
Dol·by \'dȯl-bē, 'dōl-\ *trademark* — used for an electronic device that eliminates noise from recorded sound or sound broadcast on FM radio
dol·ce \'dōl-(,)chā\ *adj or adv* [It, lit., sweet, fr. L *dulcis* — more at DULCET] (ca. 1847) : SOFT, SMOOTH — used as a direction in music
dol·ce far nien·te \'dōl-chē-,fär-nē-'en-tē\ *n* [It, lit., sweet doing nothing] (1814) : pleasant relaxation in carefree idleness
dol·ce vi·ta \,dōl-chā-'vē-(,)tä\ *n* [It, lit., sweet life] (1961) : a life of indolence and self-indulgence
dol·drums \'dōl-drəmz, 'däl-, 'dȯl-\ *n pl* [prob. akin to OE *dol* foolish] (1811) **1** : a spell of listlessness or despondency **2** *often cap* : a part of the ocean near the equator abounding in calms, squalls, and light shifting winds **3** : a state or period of inactivity, stagnation, or slump
¹**dole** \'dōl\ *n* [ME, fr. OE *dāl* portion — more at DEAL] (bef. 12c) **1** *archaic* : one's allotted share, portion, or destiny **2 a** (1) : a giving or distribution of food, money, or clothing to the needy (2) : a grant of government funds to the unemployed **b** : something distributed at intervals to the needy; *also* : HANDOUT 1 **c** : something portioned out bit by bit
²**dole** *vt* **doled; dol·ing** (15c) : to give or distribute as a charity — usu. used with *out*
³**dole** *n* [ME *dol,* fr. OF, fr. LL *dolus,* alter. of L *dolor*] (13c) *archaic* : GRIEF, SORROW
dole·ful \'dōl-fəl\ *adj* (13c) **1** : causing grief or affliction ⟨a ~ loss⟩ **2** : full of grief : CHEERLESS ⟨a ~ face⟩ **3** : expressing grief : SAD ⟨a ~ melody⟩ — **dole·ful·ly** \-fə-lē\ *adv* — **dole·ful·ness** *n*
dole out *vt* (1749) **1** : to give or deliver in small portions **2** : DISH OUT *syn* see DISTRIBUTE
dol·er·ite \'dä-lə-,rīt\ *n* [F *dolérite,* fr. Gk *doleros* deceitful, fr. *dolos* deceit; fr. its being easily mistaken for diorite] (1838) **1** : any of various coarse basalts **2** *chiefly Brit* : DIABASE **3** — **dol·er·it·ic** \,dä-lə-'ri-tik\ *adj*
dole·some \'dōl-səm\ *adj* (1533) : DOLEFUL
dol·i·cho·ce·phal·ic \,dä-li-kō-sə-'fa-lik\ *adj* [NL *dolichocephalus* long-headed, fr. Gk *dolichos* long + *-kephalos,* fr. *kephalē* head — more at CEPHALIC] (1852) : having a relatively long head with cephalic index of less than 75 — **dol·i·cho·ceph·a·ly** \-'se-fə-lē\ *n*
doll \'däl, 'dȯl\ *n* [prob. fr. *Doll,* nickname for *Dorothy*] (ca. 1700) **1** : a small-scale figure of a human being used esp. as a child's plaything **2 a** (1) : a pretty but often empty-headed young woman (2) : WOMAN **b** : DARLING, SWEETHEART **c** : an attractive person — **doll·ish** \'dä-lish, 'dȯ-\ *adj* — **doll·ish·ly** *adv* — **doll·ish·ness** *n*
dol·lar \'dä-lər\ *n, often attrib* [D or LG *daler,* fr. G *Taler,* short for *Joachimstaler,* fr. Sankt *Joachimsthal,* Bohemia, where talers were first made] (1553) **1** : TALER **2** : any of numerous coins patterned after the taler (as a Spanish peso) **3 a** : any of various basic monetary units (as in the U.S. and Canada) — see MONEY table **b** : a coin, note, or token representing one dollar **4** : RINGGIT
dollar cost averaging *n* (ca. 1957) : investment in a security at regular intervals of a uniform sum regardless of the price level in order to obtain an overall reduction in cost per unit — called also *dollar averaging*
dollar–a–year *adj* (1918) : compensated by a token salary usu. for government service ⟨a ~ man⟩
dollar day *n* (1949) : a day on which special low prices are offered — often used in pl.
dollar diplomacy *n* (1910) **1** : diplomacy used by a country to promote its financial or commercial interests abroad **2** : diplomacy that seeks to strengthen the power of a country or effect its purposes in foreign relations by the use of its financial resources
dollars–and–cents \'dä-lər-z²n-'sen(t)s\ *adj* (1899) : dealing with or expressed in terms of money, sales, or profits
dollar sign *n* (1881) : a mark $ placed before a number to indicate that it stands for dollars — called also *dollar mark*
doll·house \'däl-,hau̇s, 'dȯl-\ *also* **doll's house** *or* **dolls' house** *n* (1783) **1** : a child's small-scale toy house **2** : a dwelling so small as to suggest a house for dolls
¹**dol·lop** \'dä-ləp\ *n* [origin unknown] (ca. 1812) **1** *chiefly Brit* : an indefinite often large quantity esp. of something liquid ⟨out of heaven, as if a plug had been pulled, fell a jolly ~ of rain —E. M. Forster⟩ **2** : a lump or glob of something soft or mushy ⟨top it with a ~ of jam⟩ **3** : an amount given, spooned, or ladled out : PORTION ⟨hold out their mess tins for a ~ of gruel —Robert Craft⟩ **4** : a small lump, portion, or amount ⟨want just a ~ of catsup⟩ ⟨a ~ of brandy after dinner⟩ **5** : something added or served as if in dollops ⟨fantasy with a ~ of satire —Lee Rogow⟩ ⟨a delicious ~ of gossip —Leon Harris⟩
²**dollop** *vt* (ca. 1860) : to serve or dispense in dollops
doll up *vt* (1906) **1** : to dress elegantly or extravagantly **2** : to make more attractive (as by addition of decorative details) ~ *vi* : to get dolled up
¹**dol·ly** \'dä-lē, 'dȯ-lē\ *n, pl* **dollies** (1790) **1** : DOLL **2** : a wooden-pronged instrument for beating and stirring clothes in the process of washing them in a tub **3** : a compact narrow-gauge railroad locomotive for moving construction trains and for switching **4 a** : a plat-

\ə\ abut \ᵊ\ kitten, F table \ər\ further \a\ ash \ā\ ace \ä\ mop, mar
\au̇\ out \ch\ chin \e\ bet \ē\ easy \g\ go \i\ hit \ī\ ice \j\ job
\ŋ\ sing \ō\ go \ȯ\ law \ȯi\ boy \th\ thin \t̶h̶\ the \ü\ loot \u̇\ foot
\y\ yet \zh\ vision \à, k̟, ⁿ, œ, œ̄, ᵫ, ᵫ̄, ᶦ\ see Guide to Pronunciation

form on a roller or on wheels or casters for moving heavy objects **b** : a wheeled platform for a television or motion-picture camera
²**dolly** *vb* **dol·lied; dol·ly·ing** *vt* (1878) **1** : to treat with a dolly **2** : to move or convey on a dolly ~ *vi* : to move a motion-picture or television camera about on a dolly while shooting a scene; *also, of a camera* : to be moved on a dolly
dol·ly bird \'dä-lē-,bərd, 'dō-lē-\ *n* (1964) *Brit* : a pretty young woman
dolly shot *n* (1933) : TRACKING SHOT
Dol·ly Var·den trout \,dä-lē-'vär-dⁿn-\ *n* [*Dolly Varden,* gaily dressed coquette in *Barnaby Rudge* (1841), novel by Charles Dickens] (ca. 1876) : a large char (*Salvelinus malma*) widespread in streams of western No. America and Japan as well as in coastal salt waters — called also *Dolly Varden*
dol·ma \,dōl-'mä, 'dȯl-mə, 'däl-\ *n, pl* **dolmas** *or* **dol·ma·des** \dȯl-'mä-(,)thēz, dȯl-, däl-\ [Turk, lit., something stuffed] (ca. 1889) : a stuffed grape leaf or vegetable shell
dolman sleeve *n* [F *dolman* coat with dolman sleeves, fr. G *Dolman* or Hung *dolmány,* fr. Turk *dolama,* a Turkish robe] (1934) : a sleeve very wide at the armhole and tight at the wrist often cut in one piece with the bodice
dol·men \'dōl-mən, 'dȯl-, 'däl-\ *n* [F, fr. Bret *tolmen,* fr. *tol* table + *men* stone] (1859) : a prehistoric monument of two or more upright stones supporting a horizontal stone slab found esp. in Britain and France and thought to be a tomb

dolmen

do·lo·mite \'dō-lə-,mīt, 'dä-\ *n* [F, fr. Déodat de *Dolomieu* †1801 Fr. geologist] (1794) **1** : a mineral CaMg(CO₃)₂ consisting of a calcium magnesium carbonate found in crystals and in extensive beds as a compact limestone **2** : a limestone or marble rich in magnesium carbonate — **do·lo·mit·ic** \,dō-lə-'mi-tik, ,dä-\ *adj*
do·lo·mi·ti·za·tion \,dō-lə-,mī-tə-'zā-shən, ,dä-\ *n* (1862) : the process of converting into dolomite — **do·lo·mi·tize** \'dō-lə-mə-,tīz, 'dä-\ *vt*
do·lor \'dō-lər *also* 'dä-\ *n* [ME *dolour,* fr. MF, fr. L *dolor* pain, grief, fr. *dolēre* to feel pain, grieve] (14c) : mental suffering or anguish : SORROW
do·lor·ous \'dō-lə-rəs *also* 'dä-\ *adj* (15c) : causing, marked by, or expressing misery or grief — **do·lor·ous·ly** *adv* — **do·lor·ous·ness** *n*
do·lour *chiefly Brit var of* DOLOR
dol·phin \'däl-fən, 'dȯl-\ *n* [ME, fr. MF *dophin, daufin,* fr. OF *dalfin,* fr. OProv, fr. ML *dalfinus,* alter. of L *delphinus,* fr. Gk *delphin-, del-phis;* akin to Gk *delphys* womb, Skt *garbha*] (14c) **1 a** : any of various small toothed whales (family Delphinidae) with the snout more or less elongated into a beak and the neck vertebrae partially fused **b** : PORPOISE 1 **2** : either of two active pelagic bony food fishes (genus *Coryphaena* of the family Coryphaenidae) of tropical and temperate seas that are used for food — called also *dolphinfish* **3** *cap* : DELPHINUS **4** : a spar or buoy for mooring boats; *also* : a cluster of closely driven piles used as a fender for a dock or as a mooring or guide for boats
dolphin striker *n* (1833) : a vertical spar under the end of the bowsprit of a sailboat to extend and support the martingale
dolt \'dōlt\ *n* [prob. akin to OE *dol* foolish] (1553) : a stupid person — **dolt·ish** \'dōl-tish\ *adj* — **dolt·ish·ly** *adv* — **dolt·ish·ness** *n*
Dom [L *dominus* master] (1716) **1** \'däm\ — used as a title for some monks and canons regular **2** \'dōⁿ\ — used as a title prefixed to the Christian name of a Portuguese or Brazilian man of rank
-dom \dəm\ *n suffix* [ME, fr. OE *-dōm;* akin to OHG *-tuom* -dom, OE *dōm* judgment — more at DOOM] **1 a** : dignity : office ⟨duke*dom*⟩ **b** : realm : jurisdiction ⟨king*dom*⟩ **2** : state or fact of being ⟨free*dom*⟩ **3** : those having a (specified) office, occupation, interest, or character ⟨official*dom*⟩
do·main \dō-'mān, də-\ *n* [ME *domayne,* fr. MF *domaine, demaine,* fr. L *dominium,* fr. *dominus*] (15c) **1 a** : complete and absolute ownership of land — compare EMINENT DOMAIN **b** : land so owned **2 a** : territory over which dominion is exercised **3** : a region distinctively marked by some physical feature ⟨the ~ of rushing streams, tall trees, and lakes⟩ **4** : a sphere of knowledge, influence, or activity ⟨the ~ of art⟩ **5** : the set of elements to which a mathematical or logical variable is limited; *specif* : the set on which a function is defined **6** : any of the small randomly oriented regions of uniform magnetization in a ferromagnetic substance **7** : INTEGRAL DOMAIN
¹**dome** \'dōm\ *n* [F, It, & L; F *dôme* dome, cathedral, fr. It *duomo* cathedral, fr. ML *domus* church, fr. L, house; akin to Gk *domos* house, Skt *dam*] (1513) **1** *archaic* : a stately building : MANSION **2** : a large hemispherical roof or ceiling **3** : a natural formation or structure that resembles the dome or cupola of a building **4** : a form of crystal composed of planes parallel to a lateral axis that meet above in a horizontal edge like a roof **5** : an upward fold in rock whose sides dip uniformly in all directions **6** : a roofed sports stadium — **dom·al** \'dō-məl\ *adj*
²**dome** *vb* **domed; dom·ing** *vt* (1769) **1** : to cover with a dome **2** : to form into a dome ~ *vi* : to swell upward or outward like a dome
Domes·day Book \'dümz-,dā-, 'dōmz-\ *n* [ME, fr. *domesday* dooms-day] (1591) : a record of a survey of English lands and landholdings made by order of William the Conqueror about 1086
¹**do·mes·tic** \də-'mes-tik\ *adj* [ME, fr. MF *domestique,* fr. L *domesticus,* fr. *domus*] (15c) **1 a** : living near or about human habitations **b** : TAME, DOMESTICATED **2** : of, relating to, or originating within a country and esp. one's own country ⟨~ politics⟩ ⟨~ wines⟩ **3** : of or relating to the household or the family **4** : devoted to home duties and pleasures **5** : INDIGENOUS — **do·mes·ti·cal·ly** \-ti-k(ə-)lē\ *adv*
²**domestic** *n* (1613) **1** : a household servant **2** : an article of domestic manufacture — usu. used in pl.
domestic animal *n* (ca. 1855) : any of various animals (as the horse or sheep) domesticated so as to live and breed in a tame condition
¹**do·mes·ti·cate** \də-'mes-ti-,kāt\ *vt* **-cat·ed; -cat·ing** (ca. 1639) **1** : to bring into domestic use : ADOPT **2** : to adapt (an animal or plant) to life in intimate association with and to the advantage of humans **3** : to make domestic : fit for domestic life **4** : to bring to the level of

ordinary people : FAMILIARIZE — **do·mes·ti·ca·tion** \-,mes-ti-'kā-shən\ *n*
²**do·mes·ti·cate** \-kət, -,kāt\ *n* (1951) : a domesticated animal or plant
do·mes·tic·i·ty \,dō-,mes-'ti-sə-tē, -məs-; ,dä-\ *n, pl* **-ties** (1721) **1** : the quality or state of being domestic or domesticated **2** : domestic activities or life **3** *pl* : domestic affairs
domestic prelate *n* (1929) : a priest having permanent honorary membership in the papal household
domestic relations court *n* (ca. 1939) : COURT OF DOMESTIC RELATIONS
domestic science *n* (1869) : HOME ECONOMICS
dom·i·cal \'dō-mi-kəl, 'dä-\ *adj* (1846) : relating to, shaped like, or having a dome
¹**dom·i·cile** \'dä-mə-,sīl, 'dō-; 'dä-mə-sil\ *also* **dom·i·cil** \'däm-ə-səl\ *n* [ME, fr. MF, fr. L *domicilium,* fr. *domus*] (15c) **1** : a dwelling place : place of residence : HOME **2 a** : a person's fixed, permanent, and principal home for legal purposes **b** : RESIDENCE 2b
²**domicile** *vt* **-ciled; -cil·ing** (1809) : to establish in or provide with a domicile
do·mi·cil·i·ary \,dä-mə-'si-lē-,er-ē, ,dō-\ *adj* (1790) : of, relating to, or constituting a domicile: as **a** : provided or taking place in the home ⟨~ midwifery⟩ **b** : providing care and living space (as for disabled veterans)
do·mi·cil·i·ate \,dä-mə-'si-lē-,āt, ,dō-\ *vb* **-at·ed; -at·ing** [L *domicilium*] *vt* (1778) : DOMICILE ~ *vi* : RESIDE — **do·mi·cil·i·a·tion** \-,si-lē-'ā-shən\ *n*
dom·i·nance \'dä-mə-nən(t)s, 'däm-nən(t)s\ *n* (1819) **1** : the fact or state of being dominant: as **a** : dominant position esp. in a social hierarchy **b** : the property of one of a pair of alleles or traits that suppresses expression of the other in the heterozygous condition **c** : the influence or control over ecological communities exerted by a dominant **2** : functional asymmetry between a pair of bodily structures (as the right and left hands)
¹**dom·i·nant** \-nənt\ *adj* [MF or L; MF, fr. L *dominant-, dominans,* prp. of *dominari*] (ca. 1532) **1** : commanding, controlling, or prevailing over all others **2** : overlooking and commanding from a superior position **3** : of, relating to, or exerting ecological or genetic dominance **4** : being the one of a pair of bodily structures that is the more effective or predominant in action ⟨~ eye⟩ — **dom·i·nant·ly** *adv*
syn DOMINANT, PREDOMINANT, PARAMOUNT, PREPONDERANT mean superior to all others in influence or importance. DOMINANT applies to something that is uppermost because ruling or controlling ⟨a *dominant* social class⟩. PREDOMINANT applies to something that exerts, often temporarily, the most marked influence ⟨a *predominant* emotion⟩. PARAMOUNT implies supremacy in importance, rank, or jurisdiction ⟨unemployment was the *paramount* issue in the campaign⟩. PREPONDERANT applies to an element or factor that outweighs all others in influence or effect ⟨*preponderant* evidence in her favor⟩.
²**dominant** *n* (1819) **1** : the fifth tone of a diatonic scale **2 a** : a dominant genetic character or factor **b** : any of one or more kinds of organism (as a species) in an ecological community that exerts a controlling influence on the environment and thereby largely determines what other kinds of organisms are present **c** : a dominant individual in a social hierarchy
dom·i·nate \'dä-mə-,nāt\ *vb* **-nat·ed; -nat·ing** [L *dominatus,* pp. of *dominari,* fr. *dominus* master; akin to L *domus* house — more at DOME] *vt* (1611) **1** : RULE, CONTROL **2** : to exert the supreme determining or guiding influence on **3** : to overlook from a superior elevation or command because of superior height or position **4** : to have a commanding or preeminent place or position in ⟨name brands ~ the market⟩ ~ *vi* **1** : to have or exert mastery, control, or preeminence **2** : to occupy a more elevated or superior position — **dom·i·na·tive** \-,nā-tiv\ *adj* — **dom·i·na·tor** \-,nā-tər\ *n*
dom·i·na·tion \,dä-mə-'nā-shən\ *n* (14c) **1** : supremacy or preeminence over another **2** : exercise of mastery or ruling power **3** : exercise of preponderant, governing, or controlling influence **4** *pl* : DOMINION 3
do·mi·na·trix \,dä-mi-'nā-triks\ *n, pl* **-trices** \-'nā-trə-sēz, -nə-'trī-sēz\ [L, fem. of *dominator*] (1971) : a woman who physically and psychologically dominates and abuses her partner in sadomasochistic sex; *broadly* : a dominating woman
dom·i·neer \,dä-mə-'nir\ *vb* [D *domineren,* fr. F *dominer,* fr. L *dominari*] *vi* (1591) : to exercise arbitrary or overbearing control ~ *vt* : to tyrannize over
dom·i·neer·ing *adj* (1588) : inclined to domineer *syn* see MASTERFUL — **dom·i·neer·ing·ly** \-iŋ-lē\ *adv* — **dom·i·neer·ing·ness** *n*
do·min·i·cal \də-'mi-ni-kəl\ *adj* [LL *dominicalis,* fr. *dominicus* (*dies*) the Lord's day, fr. L *dominicus* of a lord, fr. *dominus* lord, master] (15c) **1** : of or relating to Jesus Christ as Lord **2** : of or relating to the Lord's day
Do·min·i·can \də-'mi-ni-kən\ *n* [St. *Dominic*] (ca. 1632) : a member of a mendicant order of friars founded by St. Dominic in 1215 and dedicated esp. to preaching — **Dominican** *adj*
dom·i·nick·er \'dä-mə-,ne-kər, -,ni-\ *also* **dom·i·nick** \-(,)nik, -,nek\ *n, often cap* (1806) : DOMINIQUE
do·mi·nie \1 *usu* 'dä-mə-nē, 2 *usu* 'dō-\ *n* [L *domine,* voc. of *dominus*] (1612) **1** *chiefly Scot* : SCHOOLMASTER **2** : CLERGYMAN
do·min·ion \də-'mi-nyən\ *n* [ME *dominioun,* fr. MF *dominion,* modif. of L *dominium,* fr. *dominus*] (14c) **1** : DOMAIN **2** : supreme authority : SOVEREIGNTY **3** *pl* : an order of angels — see CELESTIAL HIERARCHY **4** *often cap* : a self-governing nation of the Commonwealth other than the United Kingdom that acknowledges the British monarch as chief of state **5** : absolute ownership *syn* see POWER
Dominion Day *n* (1867) : CANADA DAY
dom·i·nique \'dä-mə-,nēk\ *n* [*Dominique* (Dominica), one of the Windward islands, West Indies] (1849) : any of an American breed of domestic fowl with a rose comb, yellow legs, and barred plumage; *broadly* : a barred fowl
dom·i·no \'dä-mə-,nō\ *n, pl* **-noes** *or* **-nos** [F, prob. fr. L (in the ritual formula *benedicamus Domino* let us bless the Lord)] (ca. 1694) **1 a** (1) : a long loose hooded cloak usu. worn with a half mask as a masquerade costume (2) : a half mask worn over the eyes with a masquerade costume **b** : a person wearing a domino **2 a** : a flat rectangular block (as of wood or plastic) whose face is divided into two equal

parts that are blank or bear usu. from one to six dots arranged as on dice faces **b** *pl but usu sing in constr*: any of several games played with a set of usu. 28 dominoes **3** : a member of a group (as of nations) expected to behave in accordance with the domino theory

domino effect *n* (1966) : a cumulative effect produced when one event initiates a succession of similar events — compare RIPPLE EFFECT

domino theory *n* [fr. the fact that if dominoes are stood on end one slightly behind the other, a slight push on the first will topple the others] (1965) **1** : a theory that if one nation becomes Communist-controlled the neighboring nations will also become Communist-controlled **2** : the theory that if one act or event is allowed to take place a series of similar acts or events will follow

¹**don** \'dän\ *vt* **donned; don·ning** [ME, contr. of *do on*] (14c) **1** : to put on (an article of clothing) **2** : to wrap oneself in : TAKE ON 3a

²**don** \'dän\ *n* [Sp, fr. L *dominus* master — more at DAME] (1523) **1** : a Spanish nobleman or gentleman — used as a title prefixed to the Christian name **2** *archaic* : a person of consequence : GRANDEE **3** : a head, tutor, or fellow in a college of Oxford or Cambridge University; *broadly* : a college or university professor **4** [It, title of respect, fr. *donno*, lit., lord, fr. L *dominus*]: a powerful Mafia leader

do·na \,dō-nə\ *n* [Pg, fr. L *domina* lady — more at DAME] (ca. 1897) : a Portuguese or Brazilian woman of rank — used as a title prefixed to the Christian name

do·ña \'dō-nyə\ *n* [Sp, fr. L *domina*] (1622) : a Spanish woman of rank — used as a title prefixed to the Christian name

do·nate \'dō-,nāt, dō-'\ *vb* **do·nat·ed; do·nat·ing** [back-formation fr. *donation*] *vt* (1785) **1** : to make a gift of; *esp* : to contribute to a public or charitable cause **2** : to transfer (as electrons) to another atom or molecule ~ *vi* : to make a donation *syn* see GIVE

do·na·tion \dō-'nā-shən\ *n* [ME *donayowne*, fr. L *donation-, donatio*, fr. *donare* to present, fr. *donum* gift; akin to L *dare* to give — more at DATE] (15c) : the act or an instance of donating: as **a** : the making of a gift esp. to a charity or public institution **b** : a free contribution : GIFT

Do·na·tism \'dō-nə-,ti-zəm, 'dä-\ *n* [*Donatus*, 4th cent. bishop of Carthage] (1588) : the doctrines of a Christian sect arising in No. Africa in 311 and holding that sanctity is essential for the administration of sacraments and church membership — **Do·na·tist** \-tist\ *n*

¹**do·na·tive** \'dō-nə-tiv, 'dä-\ *n* (15c) : a special gift or donation

²**do·na·tive** *same or* 'dō-,nā-, dō-'\ *adj* [L *donativus*, fr. *donatus*] (1559) : of or relating to donation

do·na·tor \'dō-,nā-tər, dō-'\ *n* (15c) : DONOR

¹**done** \'dən\ *past part of* DO

²**done** *adj* (14c) **1** : arrived at or brought to an end **2** : doomed to failure, defeat, or death **3** : gone by : OVER **4** : physically exhausted **5** : cooked sufficiently **6** : conformable to social convention

do·nee \dō-'nē\ *n* [*donor*] (1523) : a recipient of a gift

done for \'dən-,fȯr\ *adj* (1803) **1** : sunk in defeat : BEATEN **2** : mortally stricken : DOOMED

done·ness \'dən-nəs\ *n* (1927) : the condition of being cooked to the desired degree

¹**dong** \'dȯŋ, 'däŋ\ *n* [origin unknown] (ca. 1930) : PENIS — usu. considered vulgar

²**dong** *n, pl* **dong** [Vietnamese *dŏng*] (1948) — see MONEY table

don·jon \'dän-jən, 'dən-\ *n* [ME — more at DUNGEON] (14c) : a massive inner tower in a medieval castle

Don Juan \dän-'(h)wän, *chiefly Brit & in poetry* dän-'jü-ən\ *n* [Sp] **1** : a legendary Spaniard proverbial for his seduction of women **2** : a captivating man known as a great lover or seducer of women — **Don Juan·ism** \-'(h)wän-,i-zəm, -'jü-ə-,ni-\ *n*

don·key \'däŋ-kē, 'dȯŋ-, 'dəŋ-\ *n, pl* **donkeys** [origin unknown] (ca. 1785) **1** : the domestic ass (*Equus asinus*) **2** : a stupid or obstinate person

donkey engine *n* (1858) **1** : a small usu. portable auxiliary engine **2** : a small locomotive used in switching

donkey jacket *n* (1929) *Brit* : a jacket of heavy material worn esp. by laborers

donkey's years *n pl* (1927) *chiefly Brit* : a very long time

don·key·work \'däŋ-kē-,wərk, 'dȯŋ-, 'dəŋ-\ *n* (1920) : monotonous and routine work : DRUDGERY

don·na \,dä-nə, ,dȯ-\ *n, pl* **don·ne** \-(,)nä\ [It, fr. L *domina*] (1740) : an Italian woman esp. of rank — used as a title prefixed to the Christian name

don·née \dȯ-'nā, (,)dȯ-\ *n, pl* **données** \-'nā(z)\ [F, fr. fem. of *donné*, pp. of *donner* to give, fr. L *donare* to donate — more at DONATION] (1876) : the set of assumptions on which a work of fiction or drama proceeds

don·nick·er *or* **don·ni·ker** \'dä-ni-kər\ *n* [alter. of E dial. *dunnekin* toilet, cesspool] (ca. 1931) : TOILET 3a

don·nish \'dä-nish\ *adj* (1848) : of, relating to, or characteristic of a university don — **don·nish·ly** *adv* — **don·nish·ness** *n*

don·ny·brook \'dä-nē-,brůk\ *n, often cap* [*Donnybrook* Fair, annual Irish event known for its brawls] (1852) **1** : FREE-FOR-ALL, BRAWL **2** : a noisy public quarrel or dispute

do·nor \'dō-nər, -,nȯr\ *n* [MF *doneur*, fr. L *donator*, fr. *donare*] (15c) **1** : one that gives, donates, or presents something **2** : one used as a source of biological material (as blood or an organ) **3 a** : a compound capable of giving up a part (as an atom, chemical group, or subatomic particle) for combination with an acceptor **b** : an impurity added to a semiconductor to increase the number of mobile electrons

¹**do–noth·ing** \'dü-,nə-thiŋ\ *n* (1579) : a shiftless or lazy person

²**do–nothing** *adj* (1832) : marked by inactivity or failure to make positive progress — **do–noth·ing·ism** \-,i-zəm\ *n*

Don Qui·xote \,dän-kē-'(h)ō-tē, ,däŋ-; *chiefly Brit* dän-'kwik-sət\ *n* [Sp, hero of Cervantes' *Don Quixote*]: an impractical idealist

don·sie *or* **don·sy** \'dän(t)-sē\ *adj* [ScGael *donas* evil, harm + E *-ie*] (1720) **1** *dial Brit* : UNLUCKY **2** *Scot* **a** : RESTIVE **b** : SAUCY **3** *chiefly northern Midland* : slightly ill

¹**don't** \'dōnt\ (1639) **1** : do not **2** : does not

usage *Don't* is the earliest attested contraction of *does not* and until about 1900 was the standard spoken form in the U.S. (it survived as spoken standard longer in British English). Dialect surveys find it more common in the speech of the less educated than in that of the educated; in those places (as the Midland and southern Atlantic seaboard regions) where it has lasted in educated speech, it is most common with older informants. Surveys of attitudes toward usage show it more widely disapproved in 1971 than it had been 40 years earlier. Its chief use in edited prose is in fiction for purposes of characterization. It is sometimes used consciously, like *ain't*, to gain an informal effect.

²**don't** \'dōnt\ *n* (1894) : a command or entreaty not to do something

do·nut \'dō-(,)nət\ *var of* DOUGHNUT

doo·dad \'dü-,dad\ *n* [origin unknown] (1888) **1** : an ornamental attachment or decoration **2** : an often small article whose common name is unknown or forgotten : GADGET

¹**doo·dle** \'dü-d²l\ *vb* **doo·dled; doo·dling** \'düd-liŋ, 'dü-d²l-iŋ\ [perh. fr. *doodle* (to ridicule)] *vi* (1936) **1** : to make a doodle **2** : DAWDLE, TRIFLE ~ *vt* : to produce by doodling — **doo·dler** \'düd-lər, 'dü-d²l-ər\ *n*

²**doodle** *n* (1937) : an aimless or casual scribble, design, or sketch; *also* : a minor work

doo·dle·bug \'dü-d²l-,bəg\ *n* [prob. fr. *doodle* (fool) + *bug*] (ca. 1866) **1** : the larva of an ant lion; *also* : any of several other insects **2** : a device (as a divining rod) used in attempting to locate underground gas, water, oil, or ores **3** : BUZZ BOMB

doodley–squat *or* **doodly–squat** \'dü-d²l-ē-,skwät\ *n* [perh. fr. *doodle* + ⁴*-y* + *squat*, euphemism for *shit*] (1934) : DIDDLY-SQUAT

doo–doo \'dü-(,)dü\ *n* [baby talk] (1948) : EXCREMENT — **in deep doo–doo** : in trouble

doo·fus \'dü-fəs, -fis\ *n, pl* **doo·fus·es** \-fə-siz\ [perh. alter. of ¹*goof*] (1970) *slang* : a stupid, incompetent, or foolish person

doo·hick·ey \'dü-,hi-kē\ *n, pl* **-hickeys** *also* **-hickies** [prob. fr. *doodad* + *hickey*] (1914) : DOODAD 2

¹**doom** \'düm\ *n* [ME, fr. OE *dōm*; akin to OHG *tuom* condition, state, OE *dōn* to do] (bef. 12c) **1** : a law or ordinance esp. in Anglo-Saxon England **2 a** : JUDGMENT, DECISION; *esp* : a judicial condemnation or sentence **b** (1) : JUDGMENT 3a (2) : JUDGMENT DAY 1 **3 a** : DESTINY; *esp* : unhappy destiny **b** : DEATH, RUIN *syn* see FATE

²**doom** *vt* (15c) **1** : to give judgment against : CONDEMN **2 a** : to fix the fate of : DESTINE **b** : to make certain the failure or destruction of

doom·ful \'düm-fəl\ *adj* (1586) : presaging doom : OMINOUS — **doom·ful·ly** \-fə-lē\ *adv*

doom·say·er \'düm-,sā-ər\ *n* (1953) : one given to forebodings and predictions of impending calamity — **doom·say·ing** \-,sā-iŋ\ *n*

dooms·day \'dümz-,dā\ *n, often attrib* (bef. 12c) : a day of final judgment

dooms·day·er \-,dā-ər, -,de(ə)r\ *n* (1972) : DOOMSAYER

doom·ster \'düm(p)-stər\ *n* (15c) **1** : JUDGE **2** : DOOMSAYER

doomy \'dü-mē\ *adj* (1971) : suggestive of doom : DOOMFUL — **doom·i·ly** \'dü-mi-lē\ *adv*

door \'dōr, 'dȯr\ *n, often attrib* [ME *dure, dor*, fr. OE *duru* door & *dor* gate; akin to OHG *turi* door, L *fores*, Gk *thyra*] (bef. 12c) **1** : a usu. swinging or sliding barrier by which an entry is closed and opened; *also* : a similar part of a piece of furniture **2** : DOORWAY **3** : DOORWAY **4** : a means of access or participation : OPPORTUNITY ⟨opens new ~s⟩ ⟨~ to success⟩ — **door·less** \-ləs\ *adj* — **at one's door** : as a charge against one as being responsible ⟨laid the blame *at our door*⟩

door·bell \'dōr-,bel, 'dȯr-\ *n* (ca. 1815) : a bell or set of chimes to be rung usu. by a push button at an outer door

do–or–die \'dü-ər-'dī, -ȯr-\ *adj* (1879) **1** : doggedly determined to reach one's objective : INDOMITABLE **2** : presenting as the only alternatives complete success or complete ruin ⟨a ~ situation⟩

door·jamb \'dōr-,jam, 'dȯr-\ *n* (1837) : an upright piece forming the side of a door opening

door·keep·er \-,kē-pər\ *n* (1535) : a person who tends a door

door·knob \-,näb\ *n* (1846) : a knob that releases a door latch

door·man \-,man, -mən\ *n* (ca. 1897) : a usu. uniformed attendant at the door of a building (as a hotel or apartment house)

door·mat \-,mat\ *n* (1665) **1** : a mat placed before or inside a door for wiping dirt from the shoes **2** : one that submits without protest to abuse or indignities **3** : a team that regularly finishes last

door·nail \-,nāl, -'nā(ə)l\ *n* (14c) : a large-headed nail — used chiefly in the phrase *dead as a doornail*

door·plate \-,plāt\ *n* (1823) : a nameplate on a door

door·post \-,pōst\ *n* (1535) : DOORJAMB

door prize *n* (1951) : a prize awarded to the holder of a winning ticket passed out at the entrance to an entertainment or function

door·sill \'dōr-,sil, 'dȯr-\ *n* (1587) : SILL 1b

door·step \-,step\ *n* (1767) : a step before an outer door — **on one's doorstep** : close at hand; *esp* : too close to be overlooked

door·stop \-,stäp\ *n* (ca. 1895) **1** : a device (as a wedge or weight) for holding a door open **2** : a usu. rubber-tipped device attached to a wall or floor to prevent damaging contact between an opened door and the wall

door–to–door \,dōr-tə-'dōr, ,dȯr-tə-'dȯr\ *adj* (1902) : going or made by going to each house in a neighborhood ⟨~ salesmen⟩ ⟨a ~ canvass⟩ — **door–to–door** *adv*

door·way \'dōr-,wā, 'dȯr-\ *n* (1799) **1** : the opening that a door closes; *esp* : entrance into a building or room **2** : DOOR 3

door·yard \-,yärd\ *n* (ca. 1764) : a yard next to the door of a house

doo–wop \'dü-,wäp\ *n* [fr. nonsense syllables typical of the style] (1969) : a vocal style of rock and roll characterized by a cappella singing of nonsense syllables in rhythmical support of the melody

doo·zy *or* **doo·zie** \'dü-zē\ *also* **doo·zer** \-zər\ *n, pl* **doozies** *or* **doozers** [perh. alter. of *daisy*] (1916) : an extraordinary one of its kind

do·pa \'dō-pə, -(,)pä\ *n* [ISV *di*hydroxy- + *p*henylalanine] (1917) : an amino acid $C_9H_{11}NO_4$ that in the levorotatory form is found in the broad bean and is used in the treatment of Parkinson's disease

do·pa·mine \'dō-pə-,mēn\ *n* [*dopa* + *amine*] (1959) : a monoamine $C_8H_{11}NO_2$ that is a decarboxylated form of dopa and that occurs esp. as a neurotransmitter in the brain

\ə\ abut \ᵊ\ kitten, F table \ər\ further \a\ ash \ā\ ace \ä\ mop, mar
\aů\ out \ch\ chin \e\ bet \ē\ easy \g\ go \i\ hit \ī\ ice \j\ job
\ŋ\ sing \ō\ go \ȯ\ law \ȯi\ boy \th\ thin \t̲h̲\ the \ü\ loot \ů\ foot
\y\ yet \zh\ vision \à, k̲, ⁿ, œ, œ̄, ᵫ, ᵫ̄, ᶀ, ʸ\ see Guide to Pronunciation

do·pa·mi·ner·gic \,dō-pə-,mē-'nər-jik\ *adj* (1970) : relating to, participating in, or activated by dopamine or related substances

dop·ant \'dō-pənt\ *n* [²*dope*] (1962) : an impurity added usu. in minute amounts to a pure substance to alter its properties

¹dope \'dōp\ *n* [D *doop* sauce, fr. *dopen* to dip; akin to OE *dyppan* to dip] (1807) **1 a** : a thick liquid or pasty preparation **b** : a preparation for giving a desired quality to a substance or surface **2** : absorbent or adsorbent material used in various manufacturing processes (as the making of dynamite) **3 a** (1) : an illicit, habit-forming, or narcotic drug (2) : a preparation given to a racehorse to help or hinder its performance **b** *chiefly Southern* : a cola drink **c** : a stupid person **4** : information esp. from a reliable source (the inside ∼)

²dope *vb* **doped; dop·ing** *vt* (1889) **1** : to treat or affect with dope; *esp* : to give a narcotic to **2** : FIGURE OUT — usu. used with *out* **3** : to treat with a dopant ∼ *vi* : to take dope — **dop·er** *n*

dope·head \'dōp-,hed\ *n* (1903) : a drug addict

dope·ster \'dōp-stər\ *n* (1907) : a forecaster of the outcome of future events (as sports contests or elections)

dop·ey *also* **dopy** \'dō-pē\ *adj* **dop·i·er; -est** (1896) **1 a** : dulled by alcohol or a narcotic **b** : SLUGGISH, STUPEFIED **2** : STUPID, FATUOUS — **dop·i·ness** *n*

dop·pel·gäng·er *or* **dop·pel·gang·er** \'dä-pəl-,gaŋ-ər, -,geŋ-, ,dä-pəl-'\ *n* [G *Doppelgänger*, fr. *doppel-* double + *-gänger* goer] (1851) **1** : a ghostly counterpart of a living person **2 a** : DOUBLE 2a **b** : ALTER EGO b **c** : a person who has the same name as another

Dopp·ler \'dä-plər\ *adj* (1905) : of, relating to, being, or utilizing a shift in frequency in accordance with the Doppler effect; *also* : of or relating to Doppler radar

Doppler effect *n* [Christian J. *Doppler*] (1905) : a change in the frequency with which waves (as sound or light) from a given source reach an observer when the source and the observer are in motion with respect to each other so that the frequency increases or decreases according to the speed at which the distance is decreasing or increasing

Doppler radar *n* (1954) : a radar system that utilizes the Doppler effect for measuring velocity

Dor·cas \'dȯr-kəs\ *n* [Gk *Dorkas*] : a Christian woman of New Testament times who made clothing for the poor

Do·ri·an \'dȯr-ē-ən, 'dōr-\ *n* [L *Dorius* of Doris, fr. Gk *dōrios*, fr. *Dōris*, region of ancient Greece] (1662) : a member of an ancient Hellenic race that completed the overthrow of Mycenaean civilization and settled esp. in the Peloponnisos and Crete — **Dorian** *adj*

¹Dor·ic \'dȯr-ik, 'där-\ *adj* (1569) **1** : of, relating to, or characteristic of the Dorians **2** : belonging to the oldest and simplest Greek architectural order — see ORDER illustration **3** : of, relating to, or constituting Doric

²Doric *n* (1837) : a dialect of ancient Greek spoken esp. in the Peloponnisos, Crete, Sicily, and southern Italy

dork \'dȯrk\ *n* [perh. alter. of *dick*] (1972) *slang* : NERD; *also* : JERK 4

dorky \'dȯr-kē\ *adj* **dork·i·er; -est** (1983) *slang* : foolishly stupid : INEPT

dorm \'dȯrm\ *n* (1900) : DORMITORY

dor·man·cy \'dȯr-mən(t)-sē\ *n* (1789) : the quality or state of being dormant

dor·mant \'dȯr-mənt\ *adj* [ME, fixed, stationary, fr. MF, fr. prp. of *dormir* to sleep, fr. L *dormire*; akin to Skt *drāti* he sleeps] (1500) **1** : represented on a coat of arms in a lying position with the head on the forepaws **2** : marked by a suspension of activity: as **a** : temporarily devoid of external activity (a ∼ volcano) **b** : temporarily in abeyance yet capable of being activated **3 a** : ASLEEP, INACTIVE **b** : having the faculties suspended : SLUGGISH **c** : having biological activity suspended: as (1) : being in a state of suspended animation (2) : not actively growing but protected (as by bud scales) from the environment — used of plant parts **4** : associated with, carried out, or applied during a period of dormancy (∼ grafting) *syn* see LATENT

dor·mer \'dȯr-mər\ *n* [MF *dormeor* dormitory, fr. L *dormitorium*] (1592) : a window set vertically in a structure projecting through a sloping roof; *also* : the roofed structure containing such a window

dor·mie *or* **dor·my** \'dȯr-mē\ *adj* [origin unknown] (1847) : being ahead by as many holes in golf as remain to be played

dor·mi·to·ry \'dȯr-mə-,tȯr-ē, -,tōr-\ *n, pl* **-ries** [ME, fr. L *dormitorium*, fr. *dormitus*, pp. of *dormire*] (15c) **1** : a room for sleeping; *esp* : a large room containing numerous beds **2** : a residence hall providing rooms for individuals or for groups usu. without private baths **3** *chiefly Brit* : a residential community inhabited chiefly by commuters

dor·mouse \'dȯr-,maus\ *n, pl* **dor·mice** \-mīs\ [ME *dormowse*, perh. fr. MF *dormir* + ME *mous* mouse] (15c) : any of numerous small Old World rodents (families Gliridae and Seleviniidae) that are intermediate in form and behavior between mice and squirrels

dor·nick \'dȯr-nik, 'dä-nik\ *n* [prob. fr. Ir *dornóg*] (1840) : a stone small enough to throw; *also* : a large piece of rock

do·ron·i·cum \də-'rä-ni-kəm\ *n* [NL, genus name, fr. Ar *darūnaj*, a plant of this genus] (1892) : any of a genus (*Doronicum*) of Eurasian perennial composite herbs including several cultivated for their showy yellow flower heads

dorp \'dȯrp\ *n* [D, fr. MD; akin to OHG *dorf* village — more at THORP] (ca. 1576) : VILLAGE

dors- *or* **dorsi-** *or* **dorso-** *comb form* [LL *dors-*, fr. L *dorsum*] **1** : back (*dorsad*) **2** : dorsal and (*dorsolateral*)

dor·sad \'dȯr-,sad\ *adv* (ca. 1803) : toward the back : DORSALLY

¹dorsal *var of* DOSSAL

²dor·sal \'dȯr-səl\ *adj* [LL *dorsalis*, fr. L *dorsum* back] (1727) **1** : relating to or situated near or on the back esp. of an animal or of one of its parts **2** : ABAXIAL — **dor·sal·ly** \-sə-lē\ *adv*

³dorsal *n* (1834) : a dorsally located part; *esp* : a thoracic vertebra

dorsal lip *n* (1940) : the margin of the fold of blastula wall that delineates the dorsal limit of the blastopore, constitutes the primary organizer, and forms the point of origin of chordamesoderm

dorsal root *n* (ca. 1934) : the one of the two roots of a spinal nerve that passes dorsally to the spinal cord and consists of sensory fibers

Dor·set \'dȯr-sət\ *n* (1891) : any of a breed of domestic white-faced sheep orig. developed in Dorset, England

dor·si·ven·tral \,dȯr-si-'ven-trəl\ *adj* (ca. 1882) **1** : having distinct dorsal and ventral surfaces **2** : DORSOVENTRAL 1 — **dor·si·ven·tral·i·ty** \-ven-'tra-lə-tē\ *n* — **dor·si·ven·tral·ly** \-'ven-trə-lē\ *adv*

dor·so·lat·er·al \,dȯr-sō-'la-tə-rəl, -'la-trəl\ *adj* (1835) : of, relating to, or involving both the back and the sides

dor·so·ven·tral \-'ven-trəl\ *adj* [ISV] (1870) **1** : relating to, involving, or extending along the axis joining the dorsal and ventral sides **2** : DORSIVENTRAL 1 — **dor·so·ven·tral·i·ty** \-ven-'tra-lə-tē\ *n* — **dor·so·ven·tral·ly** \-trə-lē\ *adv*

dor·sum \'dȯr-səm\ *n, pl* **dor·sa** \-sə\ [L] (1840) **1** : the upper surface of an appendage or part **2** : BACK; *esp* : the entire dorsal surface of an animal

do·ry \'dȯr-ē, 'dōr-\ *n, pl* **dories** [Miskito *dóri* dugout] (1709) : a flat-bottomed boat with high flaring sides, sharp bow, and deep V-shaped transom

dos *or* **do's** *pl of* ²DO

dos·age \'dō-sij\ *n* (ca. 1867) **1 a** : the addition of an ingredient or the application of an agent in a measured dose **b** : the presence and relative representation or strength of a factor or agent **2 a** : DOSE 2 **b** (1) : the giving of a dose (2) : regulation or determination of doses **3** : an exposure to some experience in or as if in measured portions

¹dose \'dōs\ *n* [ME, fr. MF, fr. LL *dosis*, fr. Gk, lit., act of giving, fr. *didonai* to give — more at DATE] (15c) **1 a** : the measured quantity of a therapeutic agent to be taken at one time **b** : the quantity of radiation administered or absorbed **2** : a portion of a substance added during a process **3** : something experienced as if in a prescribed or measured amount (a daily ∼ of hard work) **4** : a gonorrheal infection

²dose *vt* **dosed; dos·ing** (1654) **1** : to give a dose to; *esp* : to give medicine to **2** : to divide (as a medicine) into doses **3** : to treat with an application or agent

do–si–do \,dō-(,)sē-'dō\ *n, pl* **do–si–dos** [F *dos-à-dos* back to back] (1926) : a square-dance figure: **a** : a figure in which the dancers pass each other right shoulder to right shoulder and circle each other back to back **b** : a figure in which the woman moves in a figure circling first her partner and then the man on her right

do·sim·e·ter \dō-'si-mə-tər\ *n* [L *dosis* + ISV *-meter*] (1938) : a device for measuring doses of radiations (as X rays) — **do·si·met·ric** \,dō-sə-'me-trik\ *adj* — **do·sim·e·try** \dō-'si-mə-trē\ *n*

¹doss \'dȯs, 'däs\ *vi* [origin unknown] (ca. 1785) *chiefly Brit* : to sleep or bed down in a convenient place — usu. used with *down*

²doss *n* (ca. 1789) *chiefly Brit* : a crude or makeshift bed

dos·sal \'dä-səl\ *or* **dor·sal** \'dȯr-səl\ *or* **dos·sel** \'dä-səl\ *n* [ML *dossale, dorsale,* fr. neut. of LL *dorsualis* dorsal] (1851) : an ornamental cloth hung behind and above an altar

doss–house \'dȯs-,haus, 'däs-\ *n* (1888) *chiefly Brit* : a cheap rooming house or hotel

dos·sier \'dȯs-,yā, 'däs-; 'dȯ-sē-,ā, 'dä-\ *n* [F, bundle of documents labeled on the back, dossier, fr. *dos* back, fr. L *dorsum*] (1880) : a file containing detailed records on a particular person or subject

dost \'dəst\ *archaic pres 2d sing of* DO

¹dot \'dät\ *n* [(assumed) ME, fr. OE *dott* head of a boil; akin to OHG *tutta* nipple] (1674) **1** : a small spot : SPECK **2 a** (1) : a small point made with a pointed instrument (a ∼ on the chart marked the ship's position) (2) : a small round mark used in orthography or punctuation (put a ∼ over the *i*) **b** : a centered point used as a multiplication sign (as in 6 · 5 = 30) **c** (1) : a point after a note or rest in music indicating augmentation of the time value by one half (2) : a point over or under a note indicating that it is to be played staccato **3** : a precise point esp. in time (arrived at six on the ∼) **4** : a short click or buzz forming a letter or part of a letter (as in the Morse code)

²dot *vb* **dot·ted; dot·ting** *vt* (ca. 1740) **1** : to mark with a dot **2** : to intersperse with dots or objects scattered at random (boats dotting the lake) ∼ *vi* : to make a dot — **dot·ter** *n*

³dot \'dȯt\ *n* [F, fr. L *dot-, dos* dowry] (1855) : DOWRY 2

dot·age \'dō-tij\ *n* [*dote*] (14c) : a state or period of senile decay marked by decline of mental poise and alertness

do·tal \'dō-t²l\ *adj* [L *dotalis,* fr. *dot-, dos*] (1513) : of or relating to a woman's marriage dowry

dot·ard \'dō-tərd\ *n* (14c) : a person in his or her dotage

dote \'dōt\ *vi* **dot·ed; dot·ing** [ME; akin to MLG *dotten* to be foolish] (13c) **1** : to exhibit mental decline of or like that of old age : be in one's dotage **2** : to be lavish or excessive in one's attention, fondness, or affection — usu. used with *on* (doted on her only grandchild) — **dot·er** *n* — **dot·ing·ly** \'dō-tiŋ-lē\ *adv*

doth \'dəth\ *archaic pres 3d sing of* DO

dot matrix *n* (1963) : a pattern of dots in a grid from which alphanumeric characters can be formed (a *dot matrix* printer)

dot product *n* [¹*dot*; fr. its being commonly written *A* · *B*] (1901) : SCALAR PRODUCT

dotted swiss *n* (ca. 1924) : a sheer light muslin ornamented with evenly spaced raised dots

dot·ter·el \'dä-tə-rəl, 'dä-trəl\ *n* [ME *dotrelle,* irreg. fr. *doten* to dote] (15c) : a Eurasian plover (*Eudromias morinellus*) formerly common in England; *also* : any of various related plovers chiefly of eastern Asia, Australia, and So. America

dot·tle \'dä-t²l, 'dȯ-\ *n* [ME *dottel* plug, fr. (assumed) ME *dot*] (ca. 1825) : unburned and partially burned tobacco in the bowl of a pipe

¹dot·ty \'dä-tē\ *adj* **dot·ti·er; -est** [alter. of Sc *dottle* fool, fr. ME *dotel,* fr. *doten*] (15c) **1 a** : mentally unbalanced : CRAZY **b** : amiably eccentric **2** : being obsessed or infatuated **3** : amusingly absurd : RIDICULOUS (some sublimely ∼ exchanges of letters) — **dot·ti·ly** \'dä-t²l-ē\ *adv* — **dot·ti·ness** \'dä-tē-nəs\ *n*

²dotty *adj* (1812) : composed of or marked by dots

Dou·ay Version \dü-'ā-\ *n* [*Douay,* France] (1837) : an English translation of the Vulgate used by Roman Catholics

¹dou·ble \'də-bəl\ *adj* [ME, fr. OF, fr. L *duplus* (akin to Gk *diploos*), fr. *duo* two + *-plus* multiplied by; akin to OE *-feald* -fold — more at TWO, -FOLD] (13c) **1** : having a twofold relation or character : DUAL **2** : consisting of two usu. combined members or parts (an egg with a ∼ yolk) **3 a** : being twice as great or as many (∼ the number of expected applicants) **b** : of a coin : worth two of the specified amount (a ∼ eagle) (a ∼ crown) **4** : marked by duplicity : DECEITFUL **5** : folded in two **6** : of extra size, strength, or value (a ∼ martini) **7** : having more than the normal number of floral leaves often at the expense of the sporophylls **8** *of rhyme* : involving correspondence of two syllables (as in *exciting* and *inviting*) **9** : designed for the use of two persons (a ∼ room) (a ∼ bed) — **dou·ble·ness** *n*

²**double** *vb* **dou·bled; dou·bling** \'də-b(ə-)liŋ\ *vt* (13c) **1 :** to make twice as great or as many: as **a :** to increase by adding an equal amount **b :** to amount to twice the number of **c :** to make a call in bridge that increases the value of odd tricks or undertricks at (an opponent's bid) **2 a :** to make of two thicknesses : FOLD **b :** CLENCH ⟨*doubled* his fist⟩ **c :** to cause to stoop **3 :** to avoid by doubling : ELUDE **4 a :** to replace in a dramatic role **b :** to play (dramatic roles) by doubling **5 a** (1) **:** to advance or score (a base runner) by a double (2) **:** to bring about the scoring of (a run) by a double **b :** to put out (a base runner) in completing a double play ~ *vi* **1 a :** to become twice as much or as many **b :** to double a bid (as in bridge) **2 a :** to turn sharply and suddenly; *esp* : to turn back on one's course **b :** to follow a circuitous course **3 :** to become bent or folded usu. in the middle — usu. used with *up* ⟨she *doubled* up in pain⟩ **4 a :** to serve an additional purpose or perform an additional duty **b :** to play a dramatic role as a double **5 :** to make a double in baseball — **dou·bler** \-b(ə-)lər\ *n*

³**double** *adv* (14c) **1 :** to twice the extent or amount **2 :** two together

⁴**double** *n* (14c) **1 :** something twice the usual size, strength, speed, quantity, or value: as **a :** a double amount **b :** a base hit that enables the batter to reach second base **2 :** one that is the counterpart of another : DUPLICATE: as **a :** a living person that closely resembles another living person **b :** WRAITH **c** (1) **:** UNDERSTUDY (2) **:** one who resembles an actor and takes his or her place esp. in scenes calling for special skills (3) **:** an actor who plays more than one role in a production **3 a :** a sharp turn (as in running) : REVERSAL **b :** an evasive shift **4 :** something consisting of two paired members: as **a :** FOLD **b :** a combined bet placed on two different contests **c :** two consecutive strikes in bowling **5** *pl* **:** a game between two pairs of players **6 :** an act of doubling in a card game **7 :** a room (as in a hotel) for two guests — compare SINGLE 4

double agent *n* (1935) **:** a spy pretending to serve one government while actually serving another

double bar *n* (ca. 1674) **:** two adjacent vertical lines or a heavy single line separating principal sections of a musical composition

dou·ble–bar·rel \,də-bəl-'bar-əl\ *n* (1811) **:** a double-barreled gun

dou·ble–bar·reled \-əld\ *adj* (1709) **1** *of a firearm* **:** having two barrels mounted side by side or one beneath the other **2 :** TWOFOLD; *esp* : having a double purpose ⟨asked a ~ question⟩

double bass *n* (1752) **:** the largest and lowest pitched of the stringed instruments tuned in fourths — **double bass·ist** \-'bā-sist\ *n*

double bassoon *n* (ca. 1876) **:** CONTRABASSOON

double bill *n* (1917) **:** a bill (as at a theater) offering two principal features

double bind *n* (1956) **:** a psychological predicament in which a person receives from a single source conflicting messages that allow no appropriate response to be made; *broadly* : DILEMMA 2

dou·ble–blind \,də-bəl-'blīnd\ *adj* (1950) **:** of, relating to, or being an experimental procedure in which neither the subjects nor the experimenters know the makeup of the test and control groups during the actual course of the experiments — compare SINGLE-BLIND

double boiler *n* (1879) **:** a cooking utensil consisting of two saucepans fitting together so that the contents of the upper can be cooked or heated by boiling water in the lower

double bond *n* (1889) **:** a chemical bond in which two pairs of electrons are shared by two atoms in a molecule — compare SINGLE BOND, TRIPLE BOND

dou·ble–breast·ed \,də-bəl-'bres-təd\ *adj* (1701) **1 :** having one half of the front lapped over the other and usu. a double row of buttons and a single row of buttonholes ⟨a ~ coat⟩ **2 :** having a double-breasted coat ⟨a ~ suit⟩

double–check \,də-bəl-'chek, 'də-bəl-,\ *vt* (1944) **:** to subject to a double check ⟨an article ~*ed* for accuracy⟩ ~ *vi* **:** to make a double check

double check *n* (1953) **:** a careful checking to determine accuracy, condition, or progress esp. of something already checked

dou·ble–clutch \,də-bəl-'kləch\ *vi* (1928) **:** to shift gears in an automotive vehicle by shifting into neutral and pumping the clutch before shifting to another gear

dou·ble–crop \,də-bəl-'kräp\ *vi* (1918) **:** to grow two or more crops on the same land in the same season or at the same time

dou·ble–cross \,də-bəl-'krös\ *vt* (1903) **:** to deceive by double-dealing : BETRAY — **dou·ble–cross·er** *n*

double cross *n* (1834) **1 a :** an act of winning or trying to win a fight or match after agreeing to lose it **b :** an act of betraying or cheating an associate **2 :** a cross between first-generation hybrids of four separate inbred lines (as in the production of hybrid seed corn)

double dagger *n* (1706) **:** the character ‡ used as a reference mark — called also *diesis*

double date *n* (ca. 1931) **:** a date participated in by two couples — **dou·ble–date** *vi*

¹**dou·ble–deal·ing** \,də-bəl-'dē-liŋ\ *n* (1529) **:** action contradictory to a professed attitude : DUPLICITY *syn* see DECEPTION — **dou·ble–deal·er** \-'dē-lər\ *n*

²**double–dealing** *adj* (1587) **:** given to or marked by duplicity

dou·ble–deck \,də-bəl-,dek\ *or* **dou·ble–decked** \-'dekt\ *adj* (1894) **:** having two decks, levels, or layers ⟨a ~ bus⟩ ⟨a ~ sandwich⟩

dou·ble–deck·er \-'de-kər\ *n* (1835) **:** something that is double-deck

dou·ble–dig·it \,də-bəl-'di-jət\ *adj* (1959) **:** amounting to 10 percent or more ⟨~ inflation⟩ ⟨~ price increases⟩

dou·ble–dip·per \-'di-pər\ *n* (ca. 1974) **:** a person who collects both a government pension and a government salary — **dou·ble–dip·ping** \-piŋ\ *n*

dou·ble–dome \'də-bəl-,dōm\ *n* (1938) **:** INTELLECTUAL

double door *n* (1840) **:** an opening with two vertical doors that meet in the middle of the opening when closed — compare DUTCH DOOR

double bass

double dribble *n* (ca. 1949) **:** an illegal action in basketball made when a player dribbles the ball with two hands simultaneously or continues to dribble after allowing the ball to come to rest in one or both hands

double Dutch *n* (1876) **1 :** unintelligible language : GIBBERISH **2 :** the jumping of two jump ropes rotating in opposite directions simultaneously

dou·ble–edged \,də-bəl-'ejd\ *adj* (15c) **1 :** having two cutting edges **2 a :** having two components or aspects ⟨a spy with a ~ mission⟩ **b :** capable of being taken in two ways ⟨a ~ remark⟩

double–edged sword *n* (15c) **:** something that has or can have both favorable and unfavorable consequences ⟨freedom of expression . . . can be a *double-edged sword* —Linda Connors⟩

dou·ble–end·ed \,də-bəl-'en-dəd\ *adj* (ca. 1874) **:** similar at both ends ⟨a ~ bolt⟩

dou·ble–end·er \-dər\ *n* (1864) **:** a ship or boat with bow and stern of similar shape

dou·ble en·ten·dre \'düb-°l-än-'tänd(-r°); 'də-bəl-än-'tänd(-rə)\ *n, pl* **double entendres** *same also* -'tä°z; -'tän-drəz\ [obs. F, lit., double meaning] (1673) **1 :** ambiguity of meaning arising from language that lends itself to more than one interpretation **2 :** a word or expression capable of two interpretations with one usu. risqué

double entry *n* (1741) **:** a method of bookkeeping that recognizes both sides of a business transaction by debiting the amount of the transaction to one account and crediting it to another account so the total debits equal the total credits

dou·ble–faced \,də-bəl-'fāst\ *adj* (1577) **1 :** HYPOCRITICAL, TWO-FACED **2 a :** having two faces or sides designed for use ⟨a ~ bookshelf⟩ **b** *also* **dou·ble–face** \-'fās\ **:** finished on both sides : REVERSIBLE — used of fabric

double fault *n* (ca. 1909) **:** two consecutive serving faults in tennis that result in the loss of a point — **dou·ble–fault** \,də-bəl-'fölt\ *vi*

double feature *n* (1928) **:** a movie program with two main films

double fertilization *n* (ca. 1909) **:** fertilization characteristic of seed plants in which one sperm nucleus fuses with the egg nucleus to form an embryo and another fuses with polar nuclei to form endosperm

double genitive *n* (1824) **:** a syntactic construction in English in which possession is marked both by the preposition *of* and a noun or pronoun in the possessive case (as in "A friend of Bob's is a friend of mine") — called also *double possessive*

double glazing *n* (1943) **:** two layers of glass set in a window to reduce heat flow in either direction

Double Glouces·ter \-'gläs-tər, -,glös-\ *n* [*Gloucester*, England] (1816) **:** a firm mild orange-colored English cheese similar to cheddar

dou·ble–head·er \,də-bəl-'he-dər\ *n* (1878) **1 :** a train pulled by two locomotives **2 :** two games, contests, or events held consecutively on the same program

double helix *n* (1954) **:** a helix or spiral consisting of two strands in the surface of a cylinder that coil around its axis; *esp* : the structural arrangement of DNA in space that consists of paired polynucleotide strands stabilized by cross-links between purine and pyrimidine bases — compare ALPHA-HELIX, WATSON-CRICK MODEL — **dou·ble–he·li·cal** \-'he-li-kəl, -'hē-\ *adj*

double–hung \,də-bəl-'həŋ\ *adj* (1823) *of a window* **:** having an upper and a lower sash that can slide vertically past each other

double hyphen *n* (1893) **:** a punctuation mark ⸗ used in place of a hyphen at the end of a line to indicate that the word so divided is normally hyphenated

double indemnity *n* (1924) **:** a provision in a life-insurance or accident policy whereby the company agrees to pay twice the face of the contract in case of accidental death

double jeopardy *n* (1910) **:** the putting of a person on trial for an offense for which he or she has previously been put on trial under a valid charge : two adjudications for one offense

dou·ble–joint·ed \,də-bəl-'jöin-təd\ *adj* (1831) **:** having a joint that permits an exceptional degree of freedom of motion of the parts joined

double knit *n* (1895) **:** a knitted fabric (as wool) made with a double set of needles to produce a double thickness of fabric with each thickness joined by interlocking stitches; *also* : an article of clothing made of such fabric

double negative *n* (1827) **:** a now substandard syntactic construction containing two negatives and having a negative meaning ⟨"I didn't hear nothing" is a *double negative*⟩

dou·ble–park \,də-bəl-'pärk\ *vt* (1936) **:** to park (a vehicle) beside a row of vehicles already parked parallel to the curb ~ *vi* **:** to double-park a vehicle

double play *n* (1867) **:** a play in baseball by which two players are put out

dou·ble–quick \'də-bəl-,kwik\ *n* (1834) **:** DOUBLE TIME 1; *broadly* : a rapid pace — **dou·ble–quick** *adj or adv*

double reed *n* (ca. 1876) **:** two reeds bound together with a slight separation between them so that air passing through them causes them to beat against one another and that are used as a sound-producing device in certain woodwind instruments (as members of the oboe family)

double refraction *n* (1831) **:** BIREFRINGENCE

dou·ble–ring \'də-bəl-,riŋ\ *adj* (ca. 1959) **:** of or relating to a wedding ceremony in which each partner ceremonially gives the other a wedding ring while reciting vows

double salt *n* (ca. 1849) **:** a salt (as an alum) yielding on hydrolysis two different cations or anions

dou·ble–space \,də-bəl-'spās\ *vt* (ca. 1937) **:** to type (text) leaving alternate lines blank ~ *vi* **:** to type on every other line

dou·ble·speak \'də-bəl-,spēk\ *n* (1952) **:** language used to deceive usu. through concealment or misrepresentation of truth; *also* : GOBBLEDYGOOK — **dou·ble·speak·er** \-,spē-kər\ *n*

double standard *n* (1894) **1 :** BIMETALLISM **2 :** a set of principles that applies differently and usu. more rigorously to one group of people or

\ə\ abut \°\ kitten, F table \ər\ further \a\ ash \ā\ ace \ä\ mop, mar \aú\ out \ch\ chin \e\ bet \ē\ easy \g\ go \i\ hit \ī\ ice \j\ job \ŋ\ sing \ō\ go \ó\ law \ói\ boy \th\ thin \t̲h̲\ the \ü\ loot \ú\ foot \y\ yet \zh\ vision \á, k̲, °, œ, œ̄, ǣ, ūe, ʸ\ *see* Guide to Pronunciation circumstances than to another; *esp* : a code of morals that applies more severe standards of sexual behavior to women than to men

double star *n* (1781) **1** : BINARY STAR **2** : two stars in very nearly the same line of sight but actually physically separate

dou·ble–stop \,də-bəl-'stäp\ *vt* (ca. 1889) : to produce two or more tones simultaneously on (as a violin) — **double–stop** *n*

double sugar *n* (1956) : DISACCHARIDE

dou·blet \'dəb-lət\ *n* [ME, fr. MF, fr. *double*] (14c) **1** : a man's close-fitting jacket worn in Europe esp. during the Renaissance **2** : something consisting of two identical or similar parts: as **a** : a lens consisting of two components; *esp* : a handheld magnifier consisting of two lenses in a metal cylinder **b** : a spectrum line having two close components **c** : a domino with the same number of spots on each end **3** : a set of two identical or similar things: as **a** : two thrown dice with the same number of spots on the upper face **b** : one of nine pairs of microtubules found in cilia and flagella **4** : one of a pair; *specif* : one of two or more words (as *guard* and *ward*) in the same language derived by different routes of transmission from the same source

dou·ble take \'də-bəl-,tāk\ *n* (1930) : a delayed reaction to a surprising or significant situation after an initial failure to notice anything unusual — usu. used in the phrase *do a double take*

dou·ble–talk \-,tȯk\ *n* (1936) **1** : language that appears to be earnest and meaningful but in fact is a mixture of sense and nonsense **2** : inflated, involved, and often deliberately ambiguous language — **double–talk** *vi* — **dou·ble–talk·er** *n*

dou·ble–team \,—,tēm\ *vt* (1860) : to block or guard (an opponent) with two players at one time

Double Ten *n* [trans. of Chin (Beijing) *shuāngshí;* fr. its being the tenth day of the tenth month] (1940) : October 10 observed by the Republic of China in commemoration of the revolution of 1911

dou·ble·think \'də-bəl-,thiŋk\ *n* (1949) : a simultaneous belief in two contradictory ideas

dou·ble–time \'də-bəl-,tīm\ *vi* (1943) : to move at double time

double time *n* (1853) **1** : a marching cadence of 180 36-inch steps per minute **2** : payment of a worker at twice the regular wage rate

dou·ble·ton \'də-bəl-tən\ *n* [*double* + *-ton* (as in *singleton*)] (ca. 1894) : two cards that are the only ones of their suit orig. dealt to a player — compare SINGLETON 1, VOID 4

dou·ble–tongue \,də-bəl-'təŋ\ *vi* (ca. 1900) : to cause the tongue to alternate rapidly between the positions for *t* and *k* so as to produce a fast succession of detached notes on a wind instrument

dou·ble–u \as at w\ *n* (1840) : the letter *w*

double up *vi* (1789) : to share accommodations designed for one

double vision *n* (ca. 1860) : DIPLOPIA

double whammy *n* (1951) : a combination of two usu. adverse forces, circumstances, or effects

double–wide \,də-bəl-'wīd\ *n* (1970) : a mobile home consisting of two units which have been fastened together along their length

dou·bloon \,də-'blün\ *n* [Sp *dobla,* aug. of *dobla,* an old Spanish coin, fr. L *dupla,* fem. of *duplus* double — more at DOUBLE] (1622) : an old gold coin of Spain and Spanish America

dou·bly \'də-b(ə-)lē\ *adv* (15c) **1** : in a twofold manner **2** : to twice the degree

¹doubt \'daut\ *vb* [alter. of ME *douten,* fr. OF *douter* to doubt, fr. L *dubitare;* akin to L *dubius* dubious] *vt* (13c) **1** *archaic* **a** : FEAR **b** : SUSPECT **2** : to be in doubt about ⟨he ~s everyone's word⟩ **3 a** : to lack confidence in : DISTRUST ⟨find myself ~ing him even when I know that he is honest —H. L. Mencken⟩ **b** : to consider unlikely ⟨I ~ if I can go⟩ ~ *vi* : to be uncertain — **doubt·able** \'daù-tə-bəl\ *adj* — **doubt·er** *n* — **doubt·ing·ly** \-tiŋ-lē\ *adv*

²doubt *n* (13c) **1** : uncertainty of belief or opinion that often interferes with decision-making **a** : a deliberate suspension of judgment **2** : a state of affairs giving rise to uncertainty, hesitation, or suspense **3 a** : a lack of confidence : DISTRUST **b** : an inclination not to believe or accept ⟨~ see UNCERTAINTY — **no doubt** : ¹DOUBTLESS

doubt·ful \'daùt-fəl\ *adj* (14c) **1** : giving rise to doubt : open to question ⟨it is ~ that they ever knew what happened⟩ **2 a** : lacking a definite opinion, conviction, or determination ⟨they were ~ about the advantages of the new system⟩ **b** : uncertain in outcome : UNDECIDED ⟨the outcome of the election remains ~⟩ **3** : marked by qualities that raise doubts about worth, honesty, or validity ⟨of ~ repute⟩ — **doubt·ful·ly** \-fə-lē\ *adv* — **doubt·ful·ness** *n*

syn DOUBTFUL, DUBIOUS, PROBLEMATIC, QUESTIONABLE mean not affording assurance of the worth, soundness, or certainty of something. DOUBTFUL implies little more than a lack of conviction or certainty ⟨*doubtful* about whether I said the right thing⟩. DUBIOUS stresses suspicion, mistrust, or hesitation ⟨*dubious* about the practicality of the scheme⟩. PROBLEMATIC applies esp. to things whose existence, meaning, fulfillment, or realization is highly uncertain ⟨whether the project will ever be finished is *problematic*⟩. QUESTIONABLE may imply no more than the existence of doubt but usu. suggests that the suspicions are well-grounded ⟨a man of *questionable* honesty⟩.

doubting Thom·as \-'tä-məs\ *n* [St. *Thomas,* apostle who doubted Jesus' resurrection until he had proof of it (Jn 20:24–29)] (1883) : a habitually doubtful person

¹doubt·less \'daùt-ləs\ *adv* (14c) **1** : without doubt **2** : PROBABLY

²doubtless *adj* (14c) : free from doubt : CERTAIN — **doubt·less·ly** *adv* — **doubt·less·ness** *n*

douce \'düs\ *adj* [ME, sweet, pleasant, fr. MF, fr. fem. of *douz,* fr. L *dulcis* sweet — more at DULCET] (1721) *chiefly Scot* : SOBER, SEDATE ⟨the ~ faces of the mourners —L. J. A. Bell⟩ — **douce·ly** *adv, chiefly Scot*

dou·ceur \dü-'sər\ *n* [F, pleasantness, fr. LL *dulcor* sweetness, fr. L *dulcis*] (1763) : a conciliatory gift

douche \'düsh\ *n* [F, fr. It *doccia,* fr. *docciare* to douche, fr. *doccia* water pipe, prob. back-formation fr. *doccione* conduit, fr. L * duction-, ductio* means of conveying water, fr. *ducere* to lead — more at TOW] (1766) **1 a** : a jet or current esp. of water directed against a part or into a cavity of the body **b** : an act of cleansing with a douche **2** : a device for giving douches **3** *Brit* : a rude awakening ⟨the icy ~ ⟨what he said about my father⟩ —John Fowles⟩ — **douche** *vb*

douche bag *n* (ca. 1963) *slang* : an unattractive or offensive person

dough \'dō\ *n* [ME *dogh,* fr. OE *dāg;* akin to OHG *teic* dough, L *fingere* to shape, Gk *teichos* wall] (bef. 12c) **1** : a mixture that consists essentially of flour or meal and a liquid (as milk or water) and is stiff enough

---

to knead or roll **2** : something resembling dough esp. in consistency **3** : MONEY **4** : DOUGHBOY — **dough·like** \-,līk\ *adj*

dough box *n* (ca. 1944) : a rectangular wooden box mounted on legs that is used as a worktable and storage space

dough·boy \-,bȯi\ *n* (1865) : an American infantryman esp. in World War I

dough–face \-,fās\ *n* (1830) : a Northern congressman not opposed to slavery in the South before or during the Civil War; *also* : a Northerner sympathetic to the South during the same period — **dough–faced** \-'fāst\ *adj*

dough·nut \-(,)nət\ *n* (ca. 1809) **1** : a small usu. ring-shaped cake fried in fat **2** : something (as a mathematical torus) that resembles a doughnut esp. in shape — **dough·nut·like** \-,līk\ *adj*

dough·ty \'daù-tē\ *adj* **dough·ti·er; -est** [ME, fr. OE *dohtig;* akin to OHG *toug* is useful, Gk *teuchein* to make] (bef. 12c) : marked by fearless resolution : VALIANT — **dough·ti·ly** \'daù-tᵊl-ē\ *adv* — **dough·ti·ness** \'daù-tē-nəs\ *n*

doughy \'dō-ē\ *adj* **dough·i·er; -est** (1601) : resembling dough: as **a** : not thoroughly baked **b** : unhealthily pale : PASTY

Doug·las fir \,də-gləs-\ *n* [David *Douglas* †1834 Scot. botanist] (1873) : any of a genus (*Pseudotsuga*) of tall evergreen timber trees having thick bark, pitchy wood, and pendulous cones; *esp* : one (*P. menziesii* syn. *P. taxifolia*) of the western U.S.

Dou·kho·bor \'dü-kə-,bȯr\ *n* [Russ *dukhobor, dukhoborets,* fr. *dukh* spirit + *borets* wrestler] (1876) : a member of a Christian sect of 18th century Russian origin emphasizing the duty of obeying the inner light and rejecting church or civil authority

do up *vt* (1666) **1** : to prepare (as by cleaning or repairing) for wear or use ⟨*do up* a shirt⟩ **2 a** : to wrap up ⟨*do up* a package⟩ **b** : PUT UP, CAN **3 a** : to deck out : CLOTHE **b** : to furnish with something ornamental : DECORATE **4** : EXHAUST, WEAR OUT

dour \'dú(-ə)r, 'daú(-ə)r\ *adj* [ME, fr. L *durus* hard — more at DURING] (14c) **1** : STERN, HARSH **2** : OBSTINATE, UNYIELDING **3** : GLOOMY, SULLEN — **dour·ly** *adv* — **dour·ness** *n*

dou·rou·cou·li \,dür-ə-'kü-lē\ *n* [F, fr. an unidentified American Indian language of Venezuela] (1842) : any of several small nocturnal monkeys (genus *Aotus*) of tropical America that have round heads, large eyes, and densely furred bodies

¹douse \'daús *also* 'daúz\ *vb* **doused; dous·ing** [perh. fr. obs. E *douse* (to smite)] *vt* (1600) **1** : to plunge into water **2 a** : to throw a liquid on : DRENCH **b** : SLUSH **3** : EXTINGUISH ⟨~ the lights⟩ ~ *vi* : to fall or become plunged into water — **dous·er** *n*

²douse \'daús *also* 'daúz\ *n* (1881) : a heavy drenching

³douse \'düs, 'daús\ *n* [origin unknown] (ca. 1625) *Brit* : BLOW, STROKE

⁴douse \'daús\ *vt* **doused; dous·ing** (1627) **1 a** : FURL ⟨~ a sail⟩ **b** : SLACKEN ⟨~ a rope⟩ **2** : TAKE OFF, DOFF

doux \'dü\ *adj* [F, lit., sweet, fr. OF *douz* — more at DOUCE] (ca. 1943) *of champagne* : very sweet

¹dove \'dəv\ *n* [ME, fr. (assumed) OE *dūfe;* akin to OHG *tūba* dove] (13c) **1** : any of numerous pigeons; *esp* : a small wild pigeon **2** : a gentle woman or child **3** : one who takes a conciliatory attitude and advocates negotiations and compromise; *esp* : an opponent of war — compare HAWK — **dov·ish** \'də-vish\ *adj* — **dov·ish·ness** *n*

²dove \'dōv\ *past of* DIVE

dove·cote \'dəv-,kōt, -,kät\ *also* **dove·cot** \-,kät\ *n* (15c) **1** : a small compartmented raised house or box for domestic pigeons **2** : a settled or harmonious group or organization

dove·kie \'dəv-kē\ *n* [dim. of *dove*] (1821) : a small short-billed auk (*Alle alle*) breeding on arctic coasts and ranging south in winter

doven *var of* DAVEN

Dover sole *n* [prob. fr. *Dover,* England] (ca. 1911) **1** : a common European sole (*Solea solea*) esteemed as a food fish **2** : a brownish blotched flatfish (*Microstomus pacificus*) of the Pacific coast of No. America that is a market fish in California

Do·ver's powder \,dō-vərz-\ *n* [Thomas *Dover* †1742 Eng. physician] (1801) : a powder of ipecac and opium used as a pain reliever and diaphoretic

¹dove·tail \'dəv-,tāl\ *n* (1573) : something resembling a dove's tail; *esp* : a flaring tenon and a mortise into which it fits tightly making an interlocking joint between two pieces (as of wood)

²dovetail *vt* (ca. 1656) **1 a** : to join by means of dovetails **b** : to cut to a dovetail **2 a** : to fit skillfully to form a whole **b** : to fit together with ~ *vi* : to fit together into a whole

dow \'daú\ *vi* **dought** \'daút\ *or* **dowed** \'daúd\; **dow·ing** [ME *dow, deih* have worth, am able, fr. OE *dēah, dēag;* akin to OHG *toug* is worthy, is useful — more at DOUGHTY] (bef. 12c) *chiefly Scot* : to be able or capable

dovetail: *1* mortises, *2* tenons, *3* joint

Dow \'daú\ *n* (1949) : DOW-JONES AVERAGE

dow·a·ger \'daú-i-jər\ *n* [MF *douagiere,* fr. *douage* dower, fr. *douer* to endow, fr. L *dotare,* fr. *dot-, dos* gift, dower — more at DATE] (1530) **1** : a widow holding property or a title from her deceased husband **2** : a dignified elderly woman

dowager's hump *n* (1948) : an abnormal curvature of the upper back with rounded shoulders and stooped posture caused esp. by bone loss and anterior compression of the vertebrae in osteoporosis

¹dow·dy \'daú-dē\ *n, pl* **dow·dies** [dim. of *dowd* (dowdy), fr. ME *doude*] (1581) *archaic* : a dowdy woman

²dowdy *adj* **dowd·i·er; -est** (1676) **1** : not neat or becoming in appearance : SHABBY **2** : lacking smartness or taste **b** : OLD-FASHIONED — **dowd·i·ly** \'daú-dᵊl-ē\ *adv* — **dowd·i·ness** \'daú-dē-nəs\ *n* — **dowdy·ish** \-ish\ *adj*

³dowdy *n* [origin unknown] (1936) : PANDOWDY

¹dow·el \'daú(-ə)l\ *n* [ME *dowle;* akin to OHG *tubili* plug, LGk *typhos* wedge] (14c) **1 a** : a pin fitting into a hole in an abutting piece to prevent motion or slipping; *also* : a round rod or stick used esp. for cutting up into dowels **2** : a piece of wood driven into a wall so that other pieces can be nailed to it

²**dowel** vt **-elled** also **-eled; -elling** also **-eling** (1713) : to fasten by or furnish with dowels

¹**dow·er** \'daù(-ə)r\ n [ME dowere, fr. MF douaire, modif. of ML dotarium — more at DOWRY] (14c) **1** : the part of or interest in the real estate of a deceased husband given by law to his widow during her life — compare CURTESY **2** : DOWRY 2, 3

²**dower** vt (1605) : to supply with a dower or dowry : ENDOW

dow·itch·er \'daù-i-chər\ n, pl **dowitchers** also **dowitcher** [prob. of Iroquoian origin; akin to Oneida tawístawis dowitcher] (1841) : any of several long-billed wading birds (esp. Limnodromus griseus and L. scolopaceus of the family Scolopacidae) related to the sandpipers

Dow–Jones average \ˌdaù-'jōnz-\ n [Charles H. Dow †1902 & Edward D. Jones †1920 Am. financial statisticians] (1922) : an index of the relative price of securities

¹**down** \'daùn\ adv [ME doun, fr. OE dūne, short for adūne, of dūne, fr. a- (fr. of), of off, from + dūne, dat. of dūn hill] (bef. 12c) **1 a** (1) : toward or in a lower physical position (2) : to a lying or sitting position (3) : toward or to the ground, floor, or bottom **b** : as a down payment ⟨paid $10 ~⟩ **c** : on paper ⟨put ~ what he says⟩ **2** : in a direction that is the opposite of up: as **a** : SOUTHWARD **b** : to or toward a point away from the speaker or the speaker's point of reference **3** : to a lesser degree, level, or rate ⟨cool ~ tensions⟩ **4** : to or toward a lower position in a series **5 a** : to or in a lower or worse condition or status **b** — used to indicate completion ⟨dusted ~ the house⟩ **6** : from a past time **7** : to or in a state of less activity or prominence **8** : to a concentrated state ⟨got the report ~ to three pages⟩ **9** : into the motion ~⟩ — **down to the ground** : PERFECTLY, COMPLETELY ⟨that suits me down to the ground⟩

²**down** prep (14c) : down along, around, through, toward, in, into, or on ⟨fell ~ the stairs⟩ ⟨~ the years⟩

³**down** vt (1562) **1** : to cause to go or come down **2** : to cause (a football) to be out of play **3** : DEFEAT ~ vi : to go down

⁴**down** adj (ca. 1565) **1 a** (1) : occupying a low position; specif : lying on the ground ⟨~ timber⟩ (2) : directed or going downward ⟨attendance is ~⟩ **b** : lower in price **c** : not being in play in football because of wholly stopped progress or because the officials stop the play **d** : defeated or trailing an opponent (as in points scored) ⟨~ by two runs⟩ **e** baseball : OUT **2 a** : reduced or low in activity or intensity ⟨a ~ economy⟩ **b** : not operating or able to function (the computer is ~⟩ **c** : DEPRESSED, DEJECTED; also : DEPRESSING ⟨a ~ movie⟩ **d** : SICK ⟨~ with flu⟩ **3** : DONE, FINISHED ⟨eight ~ and two to go⟩ **4** : completely mastered ⟨had her lines ~⟩ — often used with pat **5** slang : COOL 7 ⟨a ~ dude⟩ **6** : being a quark with an electric charge of −¹/₃, zero charm, and zero strangeness ⟨a ~ quark⟩ — compare ²UP 5 **7** : being on record ⟨you're ~ for two tickets⟩ — **down on** : having a low opinion of or dislike for

⁵**down** n (1710) **1** : DESCENT, DEPRESSION **2** : an instance of putting down **3 a** : a complete play to advance the ball in football **b** : one of a series of four attempts in American football or three attempts in Canadian football to advance the ball 10 yards **4** chiefly Brit : DISLIKE, GRUDGE **5** : DOWNER

⁶**down** n [ME doun hill, fr. OE dūn] (14c) **1** : an undulating usu. treeless upland with sparse soil — usu. used in pl. **2** often cap : a sheep of any breed originating in the downs of southern England

⁷**down** n [ME doun, fr. ON dūnn] (14c) **1** : a covering of soft fluffy feathers; also : these feathers **2** : something soft and fluffy like down

down and dirty adj or adv (1967) **1** : UNVARNISHED ⟨the down and dirty truth⟩ **2** : made or done hastily : not revised or polished **3** : marked by fierce competition **4** : BAWDY **5** : SEEDY 2

down-and-out \ˌdaù-nən-'(d)aùt\ adj (1901) **1** : DESTITUTE, IMPOVERISHED **2** : physically weakened or incapacitated — **down-and-out** or **down-and-out·er** \-'(d)aùt-ər\ n

down-at-the-heels \ˌdaù-nət-thə-'hē(ə)lz, -nat-\ or **down-at-heel** \-nət-'hē(ə)l\ also **down-at-the-heel** \-thə-'hē(ə)l\ or **down-at-heels** \-nət-'hē(ə)lz\ adj (1732) : SHABBY

¹**down·beat** \'daùn-ˌbēt\ n (1876) **1** : the downward stroke of a conductor indicating the principally accented note of a measure of music; also : the first beat of a measure **2** : a decline in activity or prosperity

²**downbeat** adj (1950) : PESSIMISTIC, GLOOMY

down–bow \'daùn-ˌbō\ n (ca. 1889) : a stroke in playing a bowed instrument (as a violin) in which the bow is drawn across the strings from the frog to the tip

down·burst \-ˌbərst\ n (1978) : a powerful downdraft usu. associated with a thunderstorm that strikes the ground and deflects in all directions and that constitutes a hazard esp. for low-flying aircraft; also : MICROBURST

down·cast \'daùn-ˌkast\ adj (14c) **1** : low in spirit : DEJECTED **2** : directed downward ⟨with ~ eyes⟩

down·court \-'kōrt, -'kòrt\ adv or adj (1952) : in or into the opposite end of the court (as in basketball)

down·draft \-ˌdraft\ n (1849) : a downward current of gas (as air during a thunderstorm)

down east adv, often cap D&E (1825) : in or into the northeast coastal section of the U.S. and parts of the Maritime Provinces of Canada; specif : in or into coastal Maine — **down east** adj, often cap D&E

down–east·er \daù-'nē-stər\ n, often cap D&E (1827) : one born or living down east

down·er \'daù-nər\ n (1966) **1** : a depressant drug; esp : BARBITURATE **2** : someone or something depressing

down·fall \'daùn-ˌfòl\ n (13c) **1 a** : a sudden fall (as from power) **b** : a fall (as of snow or rain) esp. when sudden or heavy **2** : something that causes a downfall (as of a person) — **down·fall·en** \-ˌfò-lən\ adj

down·field \-'fē(ə)ld\ adv or adj (1944) : in or into the part of the field toward which the offensive team is headed

¹**down·grade** \'daùn-ˌgrād\ n (1858) **1** : a downward grade (as of a road) **2** : a descent toward an inferior state ⟨a career on the ~⟩

²**downgrade** vt (1930) **1** : MINIMIZE, DEPRECIATE **2** : to lower in quality, value, status, or extent

down·haul \'daùn-ˌhòl\ n (1669) : a rope or line for hauling down or holding down a sail or spar

down·heart·ed \-'här-təd\ adj (ca. 1774) : DOWNCAST, DEJECTED — **down·heart·ed·ly** adv — **down·heart·ed·ness** n

down·hill \ˌdaùn-'hil\ adv (14c) **1** : toward the bottom of a hill **2** : toward a worsened or inferior state or level — used esp. in the phrase go downhill

²**down·hill** \'daùn-ˌhil\ n (1591) **1** : a descending slope **2** : a skiing race against time down a trail — often used attrib.

³**down·hill** \-ˌhil\ adj (1727) **1** : sloping downhill **2** : closer to the bottom of an incline ⟨your ~ ski⟩ **3** : not difficult : EASY ⟨after that problem the rest was ~⟩ **4** : progressively worse

down·hill·er \-'hi-lər\ n (1967) : a downhill skier

down–home \'daùn-ˌhōm\ adj (1938) : of, relating to, or having qualities (as informality and simplicity) associated with rural or small-town people esp. of the Southern U.S. ⟨~ country cooking⟩; broadly : SIMPLE, UNPRETENTIOUS

down in the mouth adj (1649) : DEJECTED 1

down·land \'daùn-ˌland\ n (bef. 12c) : ⁶DOWN 1

down·link \'daùn-ˌliŋk\ n (ca. 1969) : a communications channel for receiving transmissions from a spacecraft; also : such transmissions

down·load \'daùn-ˌlōd\ vt (1980) : to transfer (data) from a usu. large computer to the memory of another device (as a smaller computer) — **down·load·able** \-ˌlō-də-bəl\ adj

down–market \'daùn-ˌmär-kət\ adj (1970) : relating or appealing to lower-income consumers

down payment n (1926) : a part of the full price paid at the time of purchase or delivery with the balance to be paid later; broadly : the first step in a process

down·pipe \'daùn-ˌpīp\ n (1858) Brit : DOWNSPOUT

down·play \-ˌplā\ vt (1954) : PLAY DOWN, DE-EMPHASIZE

down·pour \-ˌpōr, -ˌpòr\ n (1811) : a pouring or streaming downward; esp : a heavy rain

down·range \-'rānj\ adv (1952) : away from a launching site

¹**down·right** \'daùn-ˌrīt\ adv (13c) **1** : straight down **2** : ABSOLUTELY 1 ⟨~ handsome⟩ ⟨~ mean⟩ **3** obs : FORTHRIGHT

²**downright** adj (1530) **1** archaic : directed vertically downward **2** : OUTRIGHT, THOROUGH ⟨a ~ lie⟩ **3** : PLAIN, BLUNT ⟨stories he had heard of her ~ tongue —Angus Wilson⟩ — **down·right·ly** adv — **down·right·ness** n

down–riv·er \'daùn-'ri-vər\ adv or adj (1852) : toward or at a point nearer the mouth of a river

¹**down·scale** \'daùn-ˌskāl\ vt **down·scaled; down·scal·ing** (1945) : to cut back in size or scope ⟨the recession forced us to ~ vacation plans⟩

²**downscale** adj (ca. 1966) : lower in class, income, or quality

down·shift \-ˌshift\ vi (1955) : to shift an automotive vehicle into a lower gear — **downshift** n

down·side \'daùn-ˌsīd\ n (1946) **1** : a downward trend (as of prices) **2** : a negative aspect ⟨the ~ of fame⟩

down·size \'daùn-ˌsīz\ vt (1975) : to reduce in size; esp : to design or produce in smaller size ~ vi : to undergo a reduction in size

down·slide \'daùn-ˌslīd\ n (1926) : a downward movement

down·slope \'daùn-ˌslōp\ adj or adv (1928) : toward the bottom of a slope

down·spout \'daùn-ˌspaùt\ n (ca. 1896) : a vertical pipe used to drain rainwater from a roof

Down's syndrome \'daùn(z)-\ n [J. L. H. Down †1896 Eng. physician] (1961) : a congenital condition characterized by moderate to severe mental retardation, slanting eyes, a broad short skull, broad hands with short fingers, and trisomy of the human chromosome numbered 21 — called also Down's, Down syndrome

¹**down·stage** \'daùn-ˌstāj\ adv or adj (1898) **1** : toward or at the front of a theatrical stage **2** : toward a motion-picture or television camera

²**downstage** \-ˌstāj\ n (ca. 1931) : the part of a stage that is nearest the audience or camera

¹**down·stairs** \'daùn-'sterz, -ˌsterz\ adv (1596) : down the stairs : on or to a lower floor

²**downstairs** \'daùn-ˌsterz, -ˌsterz\ adj (1819) : situated on the main, lower, or ground floor of a building

³**downstairs** \'daùn-, 'daùn-ˌ\ n pl but sing or pl in constr (1843) : the lower floor of a building

down·state \-ˌstāt\ n (1909) : the chiefly southerly sections of a state; also : the chiefly rural part of a state when the major metropolitan area is to the north — **down·state** \-'stāt\ adj or adv — **down·stat·er** \-'stā-tər\ n

down·stream \'daùn-'strēm\ adv or adj (1706) **1** : in the direction of or nearer to the mouth of a stream **2** : in or toward the latter stages of a usu. industrial process or the stages (as marketing) after manufacture

down·stroke \-ˌstrōk\ n (1852) : a downward stroke

down·swing \-ˌswiŋ\ n (1899) **1** : a downward swing **2** : DOWNTREND

down–the–line adj (1940) : COMPLETE ⟨a ~ union supporter⟩

down·time \'daùn-ˌtīm\ n (1928) **1** : time during which production is stopped esp. during setup for an operation or when making repairs **2** : break time between periods of work ⟨napping during our ~⟩

down–to–earth \ˌdaùn-tə-'(w)ərth\ adj (1932) **1** : PRACTICAL ⟨~ traveling tips⟩ **2** : UNPRETENTIOUS ⟨surprised to find the movie star so ~⟩

down–to–the–wire \'daùn-tə-thə-'wīr\ adj (1952) : full of suspense; esp : unsettled until the very end

down·town \ˌdaùn-'taùn, 'daùn-ˌ\ n (1851) : the lower part of a city; esp : the main business district — often used attrib. — **downtown** \ˌdaùn-'taùn\ adv — **down·town·er** \-'taù-nər\ n

down·trend \-ˌtrend\ n (1926) : a downturn esp. in business and economic activity

down·trod·den \'daùn-'trä-dᵊn\ adj (1595) : suffering oppression

down·turn \-ˌtərn\ n (1926) : a downward turn esp. toward a decline in business activity

down under adv or adj, often cap D&U (1886) : to or in Australia or New Zealand

¹**down·ward** \'daùn-wərd\ or **down·wards** \-wərdz\ adv (13c) **1 a**

\ə\ abut \ᵊ\ kitten, F table \ər\ further \a\ ash \ā\ ace \ä\ mop, mar \aù\ out \ch\ chin \e\ bet \ē\ easy \g\ go \i\ hit \ī\ ice \j\ job \ŋ\ sing \ō\ go \ò\ law \òi\ boy \th\ thin \t̲h̲\ the \ü\ loot \ù\ foot \y\ yet \zh\ vision \à, k, ⁿ, œ, œ̄, ue, ūe, ᵊ\ see Guide to Pronunciation

: from a higher to a lower place   **b** : toward a direction that is the opposite of up   **2** : from a higher to a lower condition   **3 a** : from an earlier time   **b** : from an ancestor or predecessor
²**downward** *adj* (ca. 1552)   **1** : moving or extending downward   **2** : descending from a head, origin, or source — **down·ward·ly** *adv* — **down·ward·ness** *n*
down-wash \'daún-ˌwȯsh, -ˌwäsh\ *n* (1915) : an airstream directed downward (as by an airfoil)
down-wind \'daún-'wind\ *adv or adj* (1855) : in the direction that the wind is blowing
downy \'daú-nē\ *adj* **down·i·er; -est** (1578)   **1** : resembling a bird's down   **2** : covered with down   **3** : made of down   **4** : SOFT, SOOTHING
downy mildew *n* (1886)   **1** : any of various parasitic lower fungi (family Peronosporaceae) that produce whitish masses of sporangiophores or conidiophores on the undersurface of the leaves of the host   **2** : a plant disease caused by a downy mildew
downy woodpecker *n* (1808) : a small black-and-white woodpecker (*Dendrocopos pubescens*) of No. America that has a white back and is smaller than the hairy woodpecker
dow·ry \'daú(-ə)-rē\ *n, pl* **dowries** [ME *dowarie*, fr. AF, irreg. fr. ML *dotarium*, fr. L *dot-, dos* gift, marriage portion — more at DATE] (14c)   **1** *archaic* : DOWER 1   **2** : the money, goods, or estate that a woman brings to her husband in marriage   **3** : a gift of money or property by a man to or for his bride   **4** : a natural talent
dowsabel *n* [*Dowsabel*, fem. name] (ca. 1652) *obs* : SWEETHEART
¹**dowse** *var of* DOUSE
²**dowse** \'daúz\ *vb* **dowsed; dows·ing** [origin unknown] *vi* (1894) : to use a divining rod   ~ *vt* : to find (as water) by dowsing
dows·er \'daú-zər\ *n* (1838) : DIVINING ROD; *also* : a person who uses it
dowsing rod *n* (1691) : DIVINING ROD
dox·ol·o·gy \däk-'sä-lə-jē\ *n, pl* **-gies** [ML *doxologia*, fr. LGk, fr. Gk *doxa* opinion, glory (fr. *dokein* to seem, seem good) + *-logia* -logy — more at DECENT] (1649) : a usu. liturgical expression of praise to God
doxo·ru·bi·cin \ˌdäk-sə-'rü-bə-sən\ *n* [*deoxy-* + *-orubicin* (as in *daunorubicin*)] (ca. 1977) : an antibiotic with broad antitumor activity that is obtained from a bacterium (*Streptomyces peucetius*) and is administered as the hydrochloride $C_{27}H_{29}NO_{11} \cdot HCl$
doxy *also* **dox·ie** \'däk-sē\ *n, pl* **dox·ies** [perh. modif. of obs. D *docke* doll, fr. MD] (ca. 1530)   **1** : FLOOZY, PROSTITUTE   **2** : MISTRESS 4a
doxy·cy·cline \ˌdäk-sə-'sī-ˌklēn\ *n* [*deoxy-* + *tetracycline*] (1966) : a broad-spectrum tetracycline antibiotic $C_{22}H_{24}N_2O_8$ with potent antibacterial activity that is often taken orally as a prophylactic against diarrhea by travelers
doy·en \'dȯi-ən, -ˌyēn; 'dwä-ˌyaⁿ(n)\ *n* [F, fr. LL *decanus* dean — more at DEAN] (1670)   **1 a** : the senior member of a body or group   **b** : a person considered to be knowledgeable or uniquely skilled as a result of long experience in some field of endeavor   **2** : the oldest example of a category
doy·enne \ˌdȯi-'(y)en, dwä-'yen\ *n* [F, fem. of *doyen*] (ca. 1897) : a woman who is a doyen
doy·ley *chiefly Brit var of* DOILY
¹**doze** \'dōz\ *vb* **dozed; doz·ing** [prob. of Scand origin; akin to ON *dúsa* to doze] *vt* (1693) : to pass (as time) drowsily   ~ *vi* **1 a** : to sleep lightly   **b** : to fall into a light sleep — usu. used with *off*   **2** : to be in a dull or stupefied condition — **doze** *n* — **doz·er** *n*
²**doze** *vt* **dozed; doz·ing** [prob. back-formation fr. *dozer* (bulldozer)] (1945) : BULLDOZE 2 — **doz·er** *n*
doz·en \'də-z²n\ *n, pl* **dozens** *or* **dozen** [ME *dozeine*, fr. MF *dozaine*, fr. *doze* twelve, fr. L *duodecim*, fr. *duo* two + *decem* ten — more at TWO, TEN] (13c)   **1** : a group of 12   **2** : an indefinitely large number ⟨~s of times⟩   **3** *pl but sing in constr* : a ritualized word game that consists of exchanging insults usu. about the members of the opponent's family — used with *the* — **dozen** *adj* — **doz·enth** \-z²n(t)th\ *adj*
dozy \'dō-zē\ *adj* **doz·i·er; -est** (1693) : DROWSY, SLEEPY — **doz·i·ly** \'dō-zə-lē\ *adv* — **doz·i·ness** *n*
DP \ˌdē-'pē\ *n, pl* **DP's** *or* **DPs** (ca. 1944) : a displaced person
DPN \ˌdē-ˌpē-'en\ *n* [*diphosphopyridine nucleotide*] (1938) : NAD
¹**drab** \'drab\ *n* [origin unknown] (ca. 1515)   **1** : SLATTERN   **2** : PROSTITUTE
²**drab** *vi* **drabbed; drab·bing** (1602) : to associate with prostitutes
³**drab** *n* [MF *drap* cloth, fr. LL *drappus*] (1541)   **1** : any of various cloths of a dull brown or gray color   **2 a** : a light olive brown   **b** : a dull, lifeless, or faded appearance or quality
⁴**drab** *adj* **drab·ber; drab·best** (1686)   **1 a** : of the dull brown color of drab   **b** : of the color drab   **2** : characterized by dullness and monotony : CHEERLESS — **drab·ly** *adv* — **drab·ness** *n*
⁵**drab** *n* [prob. alter. of *dribl*] (1828) : a small amount — usu. used in the phrase *dribs and drabs*
drab·ble \'dra-bəl\ *vb* **drab·bled; drab·bling** \-b(ə-)liŋ\ [ME *drabelen*; akin to LG *drabbelen*] *vt* (15c) : DRAGGLE   ~ *vi* : to become wet and muddy
dra·cae·na \drə-'sē-nə\ *n* [NL, fr. LL, she-serpent, fr. Gk *drakaina*, fem. of *drakōn* serpent — more at DRAGON] (ca. 1823) : any of two genera (*Dracaena* and *Cordyline*) of Old World tropical shrubs or trees of the agave family that have naked branches ending in tufts of sword-shaped leaves and include some used as houseplants
drachm \'dram\ *n* [alter. of ME *dragme* — more at DRAM] (14c)   **1** : DRACHMA   **2** *chiefly Brit* : DRAM
drach·ma \'drak-mə\ *n, pl* **drachmas** *or* **drach·mai** \-ˌmī\ *or* **drach·mae** \-(ˌ)mē, -ˌmī\ [L, fr. Gk *drachmē* — more at DRAM] (1525)   **1 a** : any of various ancient Greek units of weight   **b** : any of various modern units of weight; *esp* : DRAM 1   **2 a** : an ancient Greek silver coin equivalent to 6 obols   **b** — see MONEY table
Dra·co \'drā-(ˌ)kō\ *n* [L (gen. *Draconis*), lit., dragon — more at DRAGON] : a northern circumpolar constellation within which is the north pole of the ecliptic
dra·co·ni·an \drā-'kō-nē-ən, drə-\ *adj, often cap* [L *Dracon-, Draco*, fr. Gk *Drakōn* Draco (Athenian lawgiver)] (1876)   **1** : of, relating to, or characteristic of Draco or the severe code of laws held to have been framed by him   **2** : CRUEL; *also* : SEVERE ⟨~ littering fines⟩
¹**dra·con·ic** \drə-'kä-nik\ *adj* [L *dracon-, draco*] (1680) : of or relating to a dragon
²**dra·con·ic** \drā-'kä-nik, drə-\ *adj* (1708) : DRACONIAN

¹**draft** \'draft, 'dráft\ *n* [ME *draght*; akin to OE *dragan* to draw — more at DRAW] (13c)   **1** : the act of drawing a net; *also* : the quantity of fish taken at one drawing   **2 a** : the act or an instance of drinking or inhaling; *also* : the portion drunk or inhaled in one such act   **b** : a portion poured out or mixed for drinking : DOSE   **3 a** : the force required to pull an implement   **b** : load or load-pulling capacity   **4 a** : the act of moving loads by drawing or pulling : PULL   **b** : a team of animals together with what they draw   **5 a** : DELINEATION, REPRESENTATION   **b** : SCHEME, DESIGN   **c** : a preliminary sketch, outline, or version ⟨the author's first ~⟩ ⟨a ~ treaty⟩   **6** : the act, result, or plan of drawing out or stretching   **7 a** : the act of drawing (as from a cask)   **b** : a portion of liquid so drawn ⟨a ~ of ale⟩   **c** : draft beer ⟨a glass of ~⟩   **8** : the depth of water a ship draws esp. when loaded   **9 a** (1) : a system for or act of selecting individuals from a group (as for compulsory military service) (2) : an act or process of selecting an individual (as for political candidacy) without his expressed consent   **b** : a group of individuals selected esp. by military draft   **c** : a system whereby exclusive rights to selected new players are apportioned among professional teams   **10 a** : an order for the payment of money drawn by one person or bank on another   **b** : the act or an instance of drawing from or making demands upon something : DEMAND   **11 a** : a current of air in a closed-in space ⟨felt a ~⟩   **b** : a device for regulating the flow of air (as in a fireplace)   **12** : ANGLE, TAPER; *specif* : the taper given to a pattern or die so that the work can be easily withdrawn   **13** : a pocket of reduced air pressure behind a moving object; *also* : the use of such a draft to save energy — **on draft** : ready to be drawn from a receptacle ⟨beer *on draft*⟩
²**draft** *adj* (15c)   **1** : used or adapted for drawing loads ⟨~ horses⟩   **2** : being or having been on draft ⟨drinking ~ beer⟩
³**draft** *vt* (1714)   **1** : to select for some purpose: as   **a** : to conscript for military service   **b** : to select (a professional athlete) by draft   **2 a** : to draw the preliminary sketch, version, or plan of   **b** : COMPOSE, PREPARE   **3** : to draw off or away ⟨water ~ed by pumps⟩   **4** : to stay close behind (another racer) so as to take advantage of the reduced air pressure created by the leading racer   ~ *vi*   **1** : to practice draftsmanship   **2** : to draft another racer (as in car or bike racing) — **draft·able** \'draf-tə-bəl, 'dráf-\ *adj* — **draft·ee** \ˌdraf-'tē, ˌdráf-\ *n* — **draft·er** \'draf-tər, 'dráf-\ *n*
draft board *n* (1953) : a civilian board that registers, classifies, and selects men for compulsory military service
drafts·man \'draf(t)-smən, 'dráf(t)-\ *n* (1663)   **1** : a person who draws plans and sketches (as of machinery or structures)   **2** : a person who draws legal documents or other writings   **3** : an artist who excels in drawing — **drafts·man·ship** \-ˌship\ *n*
drafts·person \'draf(t)s-ˌpər-s²n\ *n* (1975) : DRAFTSMAN 1
drafty \'draf-tē, 'dráf-\ *adj* **draft·i·er; -est** (1846) : exposed to or abounding in drafts of air — **draft·i·ly** \-tə-lē\ *adv* — **draft·i·ness** \-tē-nəs\ *n*
¹**drag** \'drag\ *n* (14c)   **1** : something used to drag with; *esp* : a device for dragging under water to detect or obtain objects   **2** : something that is dragged, pulled, or drawn along or over a surface: as   **a** : HARROW   **b** : a sledge for conveying heavy bodies   **c** : CONVEYANCE   **3 a** : the act or an instance of dragging or drawing: as   (1) : a drawing along or over a surface with effort or pressure   (2) : motion effected with slowness or difficulty; *also* : the condition of having or seeming to have such motion   (3) : a draw on a pipe, cigarette, or cigar; *also* : a draft of liquid   **b** : a movement, inclination, or retardation caused by or as if by dragging   **c** *slang* : influence securing special favor : PULL   **4 a** : something that retards motion or action   **b** (1) : the retarding force acting on a body (as an airplane) moving through a fluid (as air) parallel and opposite to the direction of motion   (2) : friction between engine parts; *also* : retardation due to friction   **c** : BURDEN, ENCUMBRANCE ⟨the ~ of population growth on living standards⟩ ⟨maturity is a ~⟩   **d** : one that is boring or gets in the way of enjoyment ⟨this sickly kid is going to be a social ~ —Edmund Morris⟩   **5 a** : an object drawn over the ground to leave a scented trail   **b** : a clog fastened to a trap to prevent the escape of a trapped animal   **6** : STREET, ROAD ⟨the main ~⟩   **7 a** : COSTUME, OUTFIT ⟨in Victorian ~⟩   **b** : clothing typical of one sex worn by a person of the opposite sex — often used in the phrase *in drag*   **8** : DRAG RACE
²**drag** *vb* **dragged; drag·ging** [ME *draggen*, fr. ON *draga* — more at DRAW] *vt* (15c)   **1 a** (1) : to draw slowly or heavily : HAUL   (2) : to cause to move with painful or undue slowness or difficulty ⟨*dragging* the national anthem⟩   (3) : to cause to trail along a surface ⟨wandered off *dragging* the leash⟩   **b** (1) : to bring by or as if by force or compulsion ⟨had to ~ her husband to the opera⟩   (2) : to extract by or as if by pulling   **c** : PROTRACT ⟨~ a story out⟩   **2 a** : to explore with a drag   **b** : to catch with a dragnet   **3** : to hit (a drag bunt) while moving toward first base   ~ *vi*   **1** : to hang or lag behind   **2** : to fish or search with a drag   **3** : to trail along on the ground   ⟨the lawsuit *dragged* on for years⟩ ⟨was *dragging* after the long trip⟩   **5** : DRAW 4a ⟨~ on a cigarette⟩   **6** : to make a plucking or pulling movement   **7** : to participate in a drag race — **drag·gi·ly** \'dra-gi-lē\ *adv* — **drag one's feet** *also* **drag one's heels** : to act in a deliberately slow or dilatory manner
³**drag** *adj* (1887) : of, being, involving, or intended for a person in drag ⟨a ~ ball⟩
drag bunt *n* (ca. 1949) : a bunt in baseball made by a left-handed batter by trailing the bat while moving toward first base; *broadly* : a bunt made with the object of getting on base safely rather than sacrificing
drag coefficient *n* (ca. 1942) : a factor representing the drag acting on a body (as an automobile or airfoil)
dra·gée \dra-'zhā\ *n* [F, fr. MF *dragie* — more at DREDGE] (1853)   **1** : a sugar-coated nut   **2** : a small silver-colored ball for decorating cakes
drag·ger \'dra-gər\ *n* (ca. 1500) : one that drags; *specif* : a fishing boat operating a trawl or dragnet
drag·gle \'dra-gəl\ *vb* **drag·gled; drag·gling** \-g(ə-)liŋ\ [freq. of *drag*] *vt* (1513)   **1** : to make wet and dirty by dragging   ~ *vi*   **1** : to trail on the ground   **2** : STRAGGLE
drag·gle-tail \'dra-gəl-ˌtāl\ *n* (1596) : SLATTERN
drag·gy \'dra-gē\ *adj* **drag·gi·er; -est** (15c) : SLUGGISH, DULL

drag·line \'drag-ˌlīn\ *n* (ca. 1911) **1** : a line used in or for dragging **2** : an excavating machine in which the bucket is attached by cables and operates by being drawn toward the machine

drag·net \'drag-ˌnet\ *n* (ca. 1541) **1 a** : a net drawn along the bottom of a body of water **b** : a net used on the ground (as to capture small game) **2** : a network of measures for apprehension (as of criminals)

drag·o·man \'dra-gə-mən\ *n, pl* **-mans** *or* **-men** \-mən\ [ME *drogman*, fr. MF, fr. OIt *dragomanno*, fr. MGk *dragomanos*, fr. Ar *tarjumān*, fr. Aram *tūrgĕmānā*] (14c) : an interpreter chiefly of Arabic, Turkish, or Persian employed esp. in the Near East

drag·on \'dra-gən\ *n* [ME, fr. OF, fr. L *dracon-, draco* serpent, dragon, fr. Gk *drakōn* serpent; akin to OE *torht* bright, Gk *derkesthai* to see, look at] (13c) **1** *archaic* : a huge serpent **2** : a mythical animal usu. represented as a monstrous winged and scaly serpent or saurian with a crested head and enormous claws **3** : a violent, combative, or very strict person **4** *cap* : DRACO **5** : something or someone formidable or baneful — **drag·on·ish** \-gə-nish\ *adj*

drag·on·et \ˌdra-gə-'net, 'dra-gə-nət\ *n* (14c) **1** : a little dragon **2** : any of various small often brightly colored scaleless marine fishes constituting a family (Callionymidae); *esp* : a European fish (*Callionymus lyra*) sometimes used as food

drag·on·fly \'dra-gən-ˌflī\ *n* (1626) : any of a suborder (Anisoptera) of odonate insects that are larger and stouter than damselflies, hold the wings horizontal in repose, and have rectal gills during the naiad stage; *broadly* : ODONATE

drag·on·head \-ˌhed\ *n* (1784) : any of several mints (genus *Dracocephalum*) often grown for their showy flower heads; *esp* : a No. American plant (*D. parviflorum*)

dragon lady *n* [character in the comic strip "Terry and the Pirates" by Milton Caniff] (1973) : an overbearing or tyrannical woman; *also* : a glamorous often mysterious woman

dragon's blood *n* (1599) : any of several resinous mostly dark-red plant products; *specif* : a resin from the fruit of a palm (genus *Daemonorops*) used for coloring varnish and in photoengraving

dragonfly

dragon's teeth *n pl* [fr. the dragon's teeth sown by Cadmus which sprang up as armed warriors who killed one another off] (1853) **1** : seeds of strife **2** : wedge-shaped concrete antitank barriers laid in multiple rows

¹dra·goon \drə-'gün, dra-\ *n* [F *dragon* dragon, dragoon, fr. MF] (1622) : a member of a European military unit formerly composed of heavily armed mounted troops

²dragoon *vt* (1689) **1** : to subjugate or persecute by harsh use of troops **2** : to force or attempt to force into submission by violent measures : COERCE

drag queen *n* (ca. 1941) : a male homosexual who dresses as a woman

drag race *n* (1949) : an acceleration contest between vehicles (as automobiles) — **drag racing** *n*

drag·ster \'drag-stər\ *n* (ca. 1954) **1** : a vehicle built or modified for use in a drag race **2** : one who participates in a drag race

drag strip *n* (1952) : the site of a drag race; *specif* : a strip of pavement with a racing area at least ¼ mile long

¹drain \'drān\ *vb* [ME *draynen*, fr. OE *drēahnian* — more at DRY] *vt* (bef. 12c) **1** *obs* : FILTER **2 a** : to draw off (liquid) gradually or completely ⟨~*ed* all the water out⟩ **b** : to cause the gradual disappearance of **c** : to exhaust physically or emotionally **3 a** : to make gradually dry ⟨~ a swamp⟩ **b** : to carry away the surface water of ⟨the river that ~*s* the valley⟩ **c** : to deplete or empty by or as if by drawing off by degrees or in increments **d** : to empty by drinking the contents of **4** : DROP 7c, SINK ⟨~*ed* the putt⟩ **~** *vi* **1 a** : to flow off gradually **b** : to disappear gradually : DWINDLE **2** : to become emptied or freed of liquid by its flowing or dropping **3** : to discharge surface or surplus water *syn* see DEPLETE — **drain·er** *n*

²drain *n* (1552) **1 a** : a means (as a pipe) by which usu. liquid matter is drained **b** : a gradual outflow or withdrawal : DEPLETION **2** : something that causes depletion : BURDEN **3** : an electrode in a field-effect transistor toward which charge carriers move — compare GATE, SOURCE — **down the drain** : to a state of being wasted or irretrievably lost

drain·age \'drā-nij\ *n* (1652) **1** : the act, process, or mode of draining; *also* : something drained from **2** : a device for draining : DRAIN; *also* : a system of drains **3** : an area or district drained

drain·pipe \-ˌpīp\ *n* (1857) : a pipe for drainage

Draize test \'drāz-\ *n* [John H. *Draize* b1900 Am. pharmacologist] (1980) : a test for harmfulness of chemicals to the human eye that involves dropping the test substance into one eye of a rabbit without anesthesia using the other eye as a control — called also *Draize eye test*

drake \'drāk\ *n* [ME; akin to OHG an*trahho* drake] (14c) : a male duck

dram \'dram\ *n* [ME *dragme*, fr. MF & LL; MF, dram, drachma, fr. LL *dragma*, fr. L *drachma*, fr. Gk *drachmē*, lit., handful, fr. *drassesthai* to grasp] (14c) **1 a** — see WEIGHT table **b** : FLUID DRAM **2 a** : a small portion of something to drink **b** : a small amount

DRAM \'dram *also* 'dē-ˌram\ *n* [*dynamic* + *RAM* (random-access memory)] (1980) : a computer memory chip that must be continuously supplied with power in order to retain data

dra·ma \'drä-mə, 'dra-\ *n* [LL *dramat-, drama*, fr. Gk, deed, drama, fr. *dran* to do, act] (1515) **1** : a composition in verse or prose intended to portray life or character or to tell a story usu. involving conflicts and emotions through action and dialogue and typically designed for theatrical performance : PLAY — compare CLOSET DRAMA **2** : dramatic art, literature, or affairs **3** : a state, situation, or series of events involving interesting or intense conflict of forces **b** : dramatic state, effect, or quality ⟨the ~ of the courtroom proceedings⟩

Dram·a·mine \'dra-mə-ˌmēn\ *trademark* — used for dimenhydrinate

dra·mat·ic \drə-'ma-tik\ *adj* (1589) **1** : of or relating to the drama **2 a** : suitable to or characteristic of the drama **b** : striking in appearance or effect **3** *of an opera singer* : having a powerful voice and a

declamatory style — compare LYRIC — **dra·mat·i·cal·ly** \-ti-k(ə-)lē\ *adv*

syn DRAMATIC, THEATRICAL, HISTRIONIC, MELODRAMATIC mean having a character or an effect like that of acted plays. DRAMATIC applies to situations in life and literature that stir the imagination and emotions deeply ⟨a *dramatic* meeting of world leaders⟩. THEATRICAL implies a crude appeal through artificiality or exaggeration in gesture or vocal expression ⟨a *theatrical* oration⟩. HISTRIONIC applies to tones, gestures, and motions and suggests a deliberate affectation or staginess ⟨a *histrionic* show of grief⟩. MELODRAMATIC suggests an exaggerated emotionalism or an inappropriate theatricalism ⟨made a *melodramatic* plea⟩.

dramatic irony *n* (ca. 1907) : IRONY 3b

dramatic monologue *n* (ca. 1935) : a literary work in which a character reveals himself in a monologue usu. addressed to a second person

dra·mat·ics \drə-'ma-tiks\ *n pl but sing or pl in constr* (1796) **1** : the study or practice of theatrical arts (as acting and stagecraft) **2** : dramatic behavior or expression

dramatic unities *n pl* (ca. 1922) : the unities of time, place, and action that are observed in classical drama

dramatisation, dramatise *Brit var of* DRAMATIZATION, DRAMATIZE

dra·ma·tis per·so·nae \ˌdra-mə-təs-pər-'sō-(ˌ)nē, ˌdrä-, -ˌnī\ *n pl* [NL] (1730) **1** : the characters or actors in a drama **2** *sing in constr* : a list of the characters or actors in a drama **3** : the participants in an event

dra·ma·tist \'dra-mə-tist, 'drä-\ *n* (1678) : PLAYWRIGHT

dra·ma·ti·za·tion \ˌdra-mə-tə-'zā-shən, ˌdrä-\ *n* (1796) **1** : the action of dramatizing **2** : a dramatized version (as of a novel)

dra·ma·tize \'dra-mə-ˌtīz, 'drä-\ *vb* **-tized; -tiz·ing** *vt* (1783) **1** : to adapt (as a novel) for theatrical presentation **2** : to present or represent in a dramatic manner **~** *vi* **1** : to be suitable for dramatization **2** : to behave dramatically — **dra·ma·tiz·able** \-ˌtī-zə-bəl\ *adj*

dra·ma·turge *or* **dra·ma·turg** \'dra-mə-ˌtərj, 'drä-\ *n* (1870) : a specialist in dramaturgy

dra·ma·tur·gy \'dra-mə-ˌtər-jē, 'drä-\ *n* [G *Dramaturgie*, fr. Gk *dramatourgia* dramatic composition, fr. *dramat-, drama* + *-ourgia* -urgy] (1801) : the art or technique of dramatic composition and theatrical representation — **dra·ma·tur·gic** \ˌdra-mə-'tər-jik, ˌdrä-\ *or* **dra·ma·tur·gi·cal** \-ji-kəl\ *adj* — **dra·ma·tur·gi·cal·ly** \-ji-k(ə-)lē\ *adv*

dra·me·dy \'drä-mə-dē, 'dra-\ *n* [blend of *drama* and *comedy*] (1978) : a situation comedy having dramatic scenes

dram·mock \'dra-mək\ *n* [ScGael *dramag*] (1562) *chiefly Scot* : raw oatmeal mixed with cold water

dram·shop \'dram-ˌshäp\ *n* (1725) : BARROOM

drank *past and past part of* DRINK

¹drape \'drāp\ *vb* **draped; drap·ing** [prob. back-formation fr. *drapery*] *vt* (1847) **1** : to cover or adorn with or as if with folds of cloth **2** : to cause to hang or stretch out loosely or carelessly **3** : to arrange in flowing lines or folds **~** *vi* : to become arranged in folds ⟨this silk ~*s* beautifully⟩ — **drap·able** *also* **drape·able** \'drā-pə-bəl\ *adj* — **drap·abil·i·ty** *also* **drape·abil·i·ty** \ˌdrā-pə-'bi-lə-tē\ *n*

²drape *n* (1889) **1** : arrangement in or of folds **2 a** : a drapery esp. for a window : CURTAIN **b** : a sterile covering used in an operating room — usu. used in pl. **3** : the cut or hang of clothing — **drap·ey** \'drā-pē\ *adj*

drap·er \'drā-pər\ *n* [ME, weaver, clothier, fr. MF *drapier*, fr. OF, fr. *drap* cloth — more at DRAB] (14c) *chiefly Brit* : a dealer in cloth and sometimes also in clothing and dry goods

drap·ery \'drā-p(ə-)rē\ *n, pl* **-er·ies** (14c) **1** *Brit* : DRY GOODS **2 a** : a decorative piece of material usu. hung in loose folds and arranged in a graceful design **b** : hangings of heavy fabric for use as a curtain **3** : the draping or arranging of materials

dras·tic \'dras-tik\ *adj* [Gk *drastikos*, fr. *dran* to do] (ca. 1691) **1** : acting rapidly or violently ⟨a ~ purgative⟩ **2** : extreme in effect or action : SEVERE ⟨~ measures⟩ — **dras·ti·cal·ly** \-ti-k(ə-)lē\ *adv*

drat \'drat\ *vb* **drat·ted; drat·ting** [prob. euphemistic alter. of *God rot*] (1815) : DAMN — used as a mild oath

draught \'draft\, **draughty** \'draf-tē\ *chiefly Brit var of* DRAFT, DRAFTY

draughts \'draf(t)s\ *n pl but sing or pl in constr* [ME *draghtes*, fr. pl. of *draght* draft, move in chess] (15c) *Brit* : CHECKERS

draughts·man *chiefly Brit var of* DRAFTSMAN

Dra·vid·i·an \drə-'vi-dē-ən\ *n* [Skt *Drāvida*] (1856) **1** : a member of an ancient dark-skinned people of southern India **2** : DRAVIDIAN LANGUAGES — **Dravidian** *adj*

Dravidian languages *n pl* (1871) : a language family of India, Sri Lanka, and Pakistan that includes Tamil, Telugu, Kannada, and Malayalam

¹draw \'drȯ\ *vb* **drew** \'drü\; **drawn** \'drȯn, 'drän\; **draw·ing** [ME *drawen, dragen*, fr. OE *dragan*; akin to ON *draga* to draw, drag] *vt* (bef. 12c) **1** : to cause to move continuously toward or after a force applied in advance : PULL ⟨~ your chair up by the fire⟩: as **a** : to move (as a covering) over or to one side ⟨~ the drapes⟩ **b** : to pull up or out of a receptacle or place where seated or carried ⟨~ water from the well⟩ ⟨*drew* a gun⟩; *also* : to cause to come out of a container ⟨~ water for a bath⟩ **2** : to cause to go in a certain direction (as by leading) ⟨*drew* him aside⟩ **3 a** : to bring by inducement or allure : ATTRACT ⟨honey ~*s* flies⟩ **b** : to bring in or gather from a specified group or area ⟨a college that ~*s* its students from many states⟩ **c** : BRING ON, PROVOKE ⟨*drew* enemy fire⟩ **d** : to bring out by way of response : ELICIT ⟨*drew* cheers from the audience⟩ **e** : to receive in the course of play ⟨the batter *drew* a walk⟩ ⟨~ a foul⟩ **4** : INHALE ⟨*drew* a deep breath⟩ **5 a** : to extract the essence from ⟨~ tea⟩ **b** : EVISCERATE ⟨plucking and ~*ing* a goose before cooking⟩ **c** : to derive to one's benefit ⟨*drew* inspiration from the old masters⟩ **6** : to require (a specified depth) to float in ⟨a ship that ~*s* 12 feet of water⟩ **7 a** : ACCUMULATE, GAIN ⟨~*ing* interest⟩ **b** : to take (money) from a place of deposit **c** : to use in making a cash demand ⟨~*ing* a check against his account⟩ **d** : to receive regularly or in due course ⟨~ a salary⟩ **8 a** : to take (cards) from a stack or from the dealer **b** : to receive or take at random ⟨*drew*

\ə\ abut \ˌ, ˌə\ kitten, F table \ər\ further \a\ ash \ā\ ace \ä\ mop, mar \aú\ out \ch\ chin \e\ bet \ē\ easy \g\ go \i\ hit \ī\ ice \j\ job \ŋ\ sing \ō\ go \ȯ\ law \ȯi\ boy \th\ thin \t͟h\ the \ü\ loot \ú\ foot \y\ yet \zh\ vision \à, k̇, ⁿ, œ, œ̄, ᵫ, ᵬ, ᷓ\ *see* Guide to Pronunciation

a winning number〉 **9** : to bend (a bow) by pulling back the string **10** : to cause to shrink, contract, or tighten **11** : to strike (a ball) so as to impart a backward spin **12** : to leave (a contest) undecided : TIE **13 a** (1) : to produce a likeness or representation of by making lines on a surface 〈~ a picture〉 (2) : to give a portrayal of : DELINEATE 〈a writer who ~s characters well〉 **b** : to write out in due form 〈~ a will〉 **c** : to design or describe in detail : FORMULATE 〈~ comparisons〉 **14** : to infer from evidence or premises 〈~ a conclusion〉 **15** : to spread or elongate (metal) by hammering or by pulling through dies; *also* : to shape (as plastic) by stretching or by pulling through dies ~ *vi* **1** : to come or go steadily or gradually 〈night ~s near〉 **2 a** : to move something by pulling 〈~ing at the well〉 **b** : to exert an attractive force 〈the play is ~ing well〉 **3 a** : to pull back a bowstring **b** : to bring out a weapon 〈drew, aimed, and fired〉 **4 a** : to produce a draft 〈the chimney ~s well〉 〈~ on a cigar〉 **b** : to swell out in a wind 〈all sails ~ing〉 **5 a** : to wrinkle or tighten up : SHRINK **b** : to change shape by pulling or stretching **6** : to cause blood or pus to localize at one point **7** : to create a likeness or a picture in outlines : SKETCH **8** : to come out even in a contest **9 a** : to make a written demand for payment of money on deposit **b** : to obtain resources (as of information) 〈~ing from a common fund of knowledge〉 — **draw·able** \-ə-bəl\ *adj* — **draw a bead on** : to take aim at — **draw a blank** : to fail to gain a desired object (as information sought); *also* : to be unable to think of something — **draw on** *or* **draw upon** : to use as a source of supply 〈*drawing* on the whole community for support〉 — **draw straws** : to decide or assign something by lottery in which straws of unequal length are used — **draw the line** *or* **draw a line 1** : to fix an arbitrary boundary between things that tend to intermingle **2** : to fix a boundary excluding what one will not tolerate or engage in
²draw *n* (1663) **1** : the act or process of drawing: as **a** : a sucking pull on something held with the lips **b** : a removal of a handgun from its holster (quick on the ~) **c** : backward spin given to a ball by striking it below center — compare FOLLOW **2** : something that is drawn: as **a** : a card drawn to replace a discard in poker **b** : a lot or chance drawn at random **c** : the movable part of a drawbridge **3** : a contest left undecided or deadlocked : TIE **4** : one that draws attention or patronage **5 a** : the distance from the string to the back of a drawn bow **b** : the force required to draw a bow fully **6** : a gully shallower than a ravine **7** : the deal in draw poker to improve the players' hands after discarding **8** : a football play that simulates a pass play so a runner can go straight up the middle past the pass rushers
draw away *vi* (1670) : to move ahead (as of an opponent in a race)
draw·back \'drȯ-ˌbak\ *n* (1697) **1** : a refund of duties esp. on an imported product subsequently exported or used to produce a product for export **2** : an objectionable feature : DISADVANTAGE
draw back \drȯ-'bak\ *vi* (14c) : to avoid an issue or commitment
draw·bar \'drȯ-ˌbär\ *n* (1839) **1** : a railroad coupler **2** : a beam across the rear of a vehicle (as a tractor) to which implements are hitched
draw·bridge \-ˌbrij\ *n* (14c) : a bridge made to be raised up, let down, or drawn aside so as to permit or hinder passage
draw·down \-ˌdȧu̇n\ *n* (1918) **1** : a lowering of a water level (as in a reservoir) **2 a** : the process of depleting **b** : REDUCTION
draw down \drȯ-'dȧu̇n\ *vt* (1949) : to deplete by using or spending
draw·ee \drȯ-'ē\ *n* (1766) : the party on which an order or bill of exchange is drawn
draw·er \'drȯ(-ə)r\ *n* (14c) **1** : one that draws: as **a** : a person who draws liquor **b** : DRAFTSMAN **c** : one that draws a bill of exchange or order for payment or makes a promissory note **2** : a sliding box or receptacle opened by pulling out and closed by pushing in **3** *pl* : an article of clothing (as underwear) for the lower body — **drawer·ful** \-ˌfu̇l\ *n*
draw in *vt* (1558) **1** : to cause or entice to enter or participate **2** : to sketch roughly ~ *vi* **1 a** : to draw to an end 〈the day *drew in*〉 **b** : to shorten seasonally 〈the evenings are already *drawing in*〉 **2** : to become more cautious or economical
draw·ing \'drȯ(-)iŋ\ *n* (14c) **1** : an act or instance of drawing; *esp* : the process of deciding something by drawing lots **2** : the art or technique of representing an object or outlining a figure, plan, or sketch by means of lines **3** : something drawn or subject to drawing: as **a** : an amount drawn from a fund **b** : a representation formed by drawing : SKETCH
drawing account *n* (1920) : an account showing payments made to an employee in advance of actual earnings or for traveling expenses
drawing board *n* (1725) **1** : a board used as a base for drafting on paper **2** : a planning stage 〈a project still on the *drawing board*〉
drawing card *n* (1887) : one that attracts attention or patronage
drawing pin *n* (1859) *Brit* : THUMBTACK
drawing room *n* [short for *withdrawing room*] (1642) **1 a** : a formal reception room **b** : a private room on a railroad passenger car with three berths and an enclosed toilet **2** : a formal reception
drawing table *n* (1706) : a table with a surface adjustable for elevation and angle of incline
draw·knife \'drȯ-ˌnīf\ *n* (1703) : a woodworker's tool consisting of a blade with a handle at each end for use in shaving off surfaces
¹drawl \'drȯl\ *vb* [prob. freq. of *draw*] *vi* (1598) : to speak slowly with vowels greatly prolonged ~ *vt* : to utter in a slow lengthened tone — **drawl·er** *n* — **drawl·ing·ly** \'drȯ-liŋ-lē\ *adv*
²drawl *n* (1760) : a drawling manner of speaking — **drawly** \'drȯ-lē\ *adj*
¹drawn *past part of* DRAW
²drawn \'drȯn, 'drän\ *adj* (1613) : showing the effects of tension, pain, or illness : HAGGARD
drawn butter *n* (1826) : melted clarified butter
drawn·work \'drȯn-ˌwərk\ *n* (1595) : decoration on cloth made by drawing out threads according to a pattern
draw off *vt* (14c) : REMOVE, WITHDRAW ~ *vi* : to move apart or ahead
draw on *vi* (15c) : APPROACH 〈night *draws on*〉 ~ *vt* : BRING ON, CAUSE
draw out *vt* (14c) **1** : REMOVE, EXTRACT **2** : to extend beyond a minimum in time : PROTRACT **3** : to cause to speak freely 〈a reporter's ability to *draw* a person *out*〉
draw·plate \'drȯ-ˌplāt\ *n* (1832) : a die with holes through which wires are drawn

draw play *n* (1952) : DRAW 8
draw poker *n* (1849) : poker in which each player is dealt five cards face down and after betting may get replacements for discards
draw·shave \'drȯ-ˌshāv\ *n* (1828) : DRAWKNIFE
draw shot *n* (1897) : a shot in billiards or pool made by hitting the cue ball with draw so it moves back after striking the object ball
draw·string \'drȯ-ˌstriŋ\ *n* (1845) : a string, cord, or tape inserted into hems or casings or laced through eyelets for use in closing a bag or controlling fullness in garments or curtains
draw·tube \-ˌtüb, -ˌtyüb\ *n* (ca. 1891) : a telescoping tube (as for the eyepiece of a microscope)
draw up *vt* (1605) **1** : to bring (as troops) into array **2** : to prepare a draft or version of 〈*draw up* plans〉 **3** : to bring to a halt **4** : to straighten (oneself) to an erect posture esp. as an assertion of dignity or resentment ~ *vi* : to come to a halt
¹dray \'drā\ *n* [ME *draye*, a wheelless vehicle; akin to OE *dræge* drag-net, *dragan* to pull — more at DRAW] (14c) : a vehicle used to haul goods; *esp* : a strong cart or wagon without sides
²dray *vt* (1857) : to haul on a dray : CART
dray·age \'drā-ij\ *n* (1791) : the work or cost of hauling by dray
dray horse *n* (1709) : a horse adapted for drawing heavy loads
dray·man \'drā-mən\ *n* (1581) : one whose work is hauling by dray
¹dread \'dred\ *vb* [ME *dreden*, fr. OE *drǣdan*] *vt* (bef. 12c) **1 a** : to fear greatly **b** *archaic* : to regard with awe **2** : to feel extreme reluctance to meet or face ~ *vi* : to be apprehensive or fearful
²dread *n* (13c) **1 a** : great fear esp. in the face of impending evil **b** : extreme uneasiness in the face of a disagreeable prospect 〈~ of a social blunder〉 **c** *archaic* : AWE **2** : one causing fear or awe *syn* see FEAR
³dread *adj* (15c) **1** : causing great fear or anxiety **2** : inspiring awe
¹dread·ful \'dred-fəl\ *adj* (13c) **1 a** : inspiring dread : causing great and oppressive fear **b** : inspiring awe or reverence **2** : extremely bad, distasteful, unpleasant, or shocking **3** : EXTREME 〈~ disorder〉 — **dread·ful·ly** \-f(ə-)lē\ *adv* — **dread·ful·ness** \-fəl-nəs\ *n*
²dreadful *n* (1873) : a cheap and sensational story or periodical
dread·lock \'dred-ˌläk\ *n* (1960) **1** : a narrow ropelike strand of hair formed by matting or braiding **2** *pl* : a hairstyle consisting of dreadlocks
dread·nought \'dred-ˌnȯt, -ˌnät\ *n* (1806) **1** : a warm garment of thick cloth; *also* : the cloth **2** [*Dreadnought*, Brit. battleship] : BATTLESHIP **3** : one that is among the largest or most powerful of its kind
¹dream \'drēm\ *n, often attrib* [ME *dreem*, fr. OE *drēam* noise, joy, and ON *draumr* dream; akin to OHG *troum* dream] (13c) **1** : a series of thoughts, images, or emotions occurring during sleep — compare REM SLEEP **2** : an experience of waking life having the characteristics of a dream: as **a** : a visionary creation of the imagination : DAYDREAM **b** : a state of mind marked by abstraction or release from reality : REVERIE **c** : an object seen in a dreamlike state : VISION **3** : something notable for its beauty, excellence, or enjoyable quality 〈the new car is a ~ to operate〉 **4 a** : a strongly desired goal or purpose 〈a ~ of becoming president〉 **b** : something that fully satisfies a wish : IDEAL 〈a meal that was a gourmet's ~〉 — **dream·ful** \-fəl\ *adj* — **dream·ful·ly** \-fə-lē\ *adv* — **dream·ful·ness** *n* — **dream·less** *adj* — **dream·less·ly** *adv* — **dream·less·ness** *n* — **dream·like** \'drēm-ˌlīk\ *adj*
²dream *vb* **dreamed** \'drem(p)t, 'drēmd\ *or* **dreamt** \'drem(p)t\; **dream·ing** \'drē-miŋ\ *vi* (13c) **1** : to have a dream **2** : to indulge in daydreams or fantasies 〈~ing of a better future〉 **3** : to appear tranquil or dreamy 〈houses ~ in leafy shadows —Gladys Taber〉 ~ *vt* **1** : to have a dream of **2** : to consider as a possibility : IMAGINE **3** : to pass (time) in reverie or inaction 〈~ing the hours away〉 — **dream of** : to consider possible or fitting 〈wouldn't *dream of* disturbing you〉
dream·er \'drē-mər\ *n* (14c) **1** : one that dreams **2 a** : one who lives in a world of fancy and imagination **b** : one who has ideas or conceives projects regarded as impractical : VISIONARY
dream·land \'drēm-ˌland\ *n* (ca. 1834) : an unreal delightful country existing only in imagination or in dreams : NEVER-NEVER LAND
dream·time \-ˌtīm\ *n, often cap* (1896) : the time of creation in the mythology of the Australian aborigines
dream up *vt* (1941) : to form in the mind : DEVISE, CONCOCT
dream vision *n* (1906) : a usu. medieval poem having a framework in which the poet pictures himself as falling asleep and envisioning in his dream a series of allegorical people and events
dream·world \'drēm-ˌwərld\ *n* (1817) : a world of illusion or fantasy
dreamy \'drē-mē\ *adj* **dream·i·er; -est** (1567) **1 a** : full of dreams 〈a ~ night's sleep〉 **b** : pleasantly abstracted from immediate reality **2** : given to dreaming or fantasy 〈a ~ child〉 **3 a** : suggestive of a dream in vague or visionary quality **b** : quiet and soothing 〈~ : DELIGHTFUL, IDEAL 〈he's so handsome . . . real —Greg Foley〉 — **dream·i·ly** \-mə-lē\ *adv* — **dream·i·ness** \-mē-nəs\ *n*
drear \'drir\ *adj* (1629) : DREARY — **drear** *n*
drea·ry \'drir-ē\ *adj* **drea·ri·er; -est** [ME *drery*, fr. OE *drēorig* sad, bloody, fr. *drēor* gore; akin to OHG *trūrēn* to be sad, Goth *driusan* to fall] (bef. 12c) **1** : feeling, displaying, or reflecting listlessness or discouragement **2** : having nothing likely to provide cheer, comfort, or interest : GLOOMY, DISMAL — **drea·ri·ly** \'drir-ə-lē\ *adv* — **drea·ri·ness** \'drir-ē-nəs\ *n*
dreck *also* **drek** \'drek\ *n* [Yiddish *drek* & G *Dreck*, fr. MHG *drec*; akin to OE *threax* rubbish] (1922) : TRASH, RUBBISH
¹dredge \'drej\ *vb* **dredged; dredg·ing** *vt* (1508) **1 a** : to dig, gather, or pull out with or as if with a dredge — often used with *up* **b** : to deepen (as a waterway) with a dredging machine **2** : to bring to light by deep searching — often used with *up* 〈*dredging* up memories〉 ~ *vi* **1** : to use a dredge **2** : to search deeply — **dredg·er** *n*
²dredge *n* [perh. fr. (assumed) OE *drecge*; akin to OE *dræge* dragnet, *dragan* to draw] (1602) **1** : an apparatus usu. in the form of an oblong iron frame with an attached bag net used esp. for gathering fish and shellfish **2** : a machine for removing earth usu. by buckets on an endless chain or a suction tube **3** : a barge used in dredging
³dredge *vt* **dredged; dredg·ing** [obs. *dredge*, n., sweetmeat, fr. ME *drage, drege*, fr. MF *dragie*, modif. of L *tragemata* sweetmeats, fr. Gk *tragēmata*, pl. of *tragēma* sweetmeat, fr. *trōgein* to gnaw] (1596) : to coat (food) by sprinkling (as with flour) — **dredg·er** *n*

dree \'drē\ *vt* **dreed; dree·ing** [ME, fr. OE *drēogan;* akin to Goth *driugan* to perform military service] (bef. 12c) *chiefly Scot* : ENDURE, SUFFER

dreg \'dreg\ *n* [ME, fr. ON *dregg;* perh. akin to L *fraces* dregs of oil] (14c) **1** : sediment contained in a liquid or precipitated from it : LEES — usu. used in pl. **2** : the most undesirable part — usu. used in pl. **3** : the last remaining part : VESTIGE — **dreg·gy** \'dre-gē\ *adj*

D region *n* (1930) : the lowest part of the ionosphere occurring approximately between 30 and 55 miles (50 and 90 kilometers) above the surface of the earth

dreich \'drēk\ *adj* [ME, of Scand origin; akin to ON *drjūgr* lasting] (1813) *chiefly Scot* : DREARY

drei·del *also* **dreidl** \'drā-dªl\ *n* [Yiddish *dreydl,* fr. *dreyen* to turn, fr. MHG *dræjen,* fr. OHG *drāen* — more at THROW] (1926) **1** : a 4-sided toy marked with Hebrew letters and spun like a top in a game of chance **2** : a children's game of chance played esp. at Hanukkah with a dreidel

dreidel 1

¹drench \'drench\ *n* (bef. 12c) **1** : a poisonous or medicinal drink; *specif* : a large dose of medicine mixed with liquid and put down the throat of an animal **2 a** : something that drenches **b** : a quantity sufficient to drench or saturate

²drench *vt* [ME, fr. OE *drencan;* akin to OE *drincan* to drink] (bef. 12c) **1 a** *archaic* : to force to drink **b** : to administer a drench to (an animal) **2 a** : to wet thoroughly (as by soaking or immersing in liquid) **3** : to soak or cover thoroughly with liquid that falls or is precipitated **4** : to fill or cover completely as if by soaking or precipitation ⟨was ~ed in furs and diamonds —Richard Brautigan⟩ *syn* see SOAK — **drench·er** *n*

¹dress \'dres\ *vb* [ME, fr. MF *dresser,* fr. OF *drecier,* fr. (assumed) VL *directiare,* fr. L *directus* direct, pp. of *dirigere* to direct, fr. *dis-* + *regere* to lead straight — more at RIGHT] *vt* (14c) **1 a** : to make or set straight **b** : to arrange (as troops) in a straight line and at proper intervals **2** : to prepare for use or service; *specif* : to prepare for cooking or for the table **3** : to add decorative details or accessories to : EMBELLISH **4 a** : to put clothes on **b** : to provide with clothing **5** *archaic* : DRESS DOWN **6 a** : to apply dressings or medicaments to **b** (1) : to arrange (the hair) by combing, brushing, or curling (2) : to groom and curry (an animal) **c** : to kill and prepare for market or for consumption — often used with *out* **d** : CULTIVATE, TEND; *esp* : to apply manure or fertilizer to **e** : to put through a finishing process; *esp* : to trim and smooth the surface of (as lumber or stone) ~ *vi* **1 a** : to put on clothing **b** : to put on or wear formal, elaborate, or fancy clothes ⟨~ for dinner⟩ **2** *of a food animal* : to weigh after being dressed — often used with *out* **3** : to align oneself with the next soldier in a line to make the line straight — **dress ship** : to ornament a ship for a celebration by hoisting national ensigns at the mastheads and running a line of signal flags and pennants from bow to stern

²dress *n* (1606) **1** : APPAREL, CLOTHING **2** : an outer garment (as for a woman or girl) usu. consisting of a one-piece bodice and skirt **3** : covering, adornment, or appearance appropriate or peculiar to a particular time **4** : a particular form of presentation : GUISE

³dress *adj* (1767) **1** : suitable for a formal occasion **2** : requiring or permitting formal dress ⟨a ~ affair⟩ **3** : relating to or used for a dress

dres·sage \drə-'säzh, dre-\ *n, often attrib* [F, fr. *dresser* to train, drill, fr. MF] (1936) : the execution by a trained horse of precision movements in response to barely perceptible signals from its rider

dress circle *n* (1825) : the first or lowest curved tier of seats above the main floor in a theater or opera house

dress code *n* (1968) : formally or socially imposed standards of dress

dress down *vt* (ca. 1897) : to reprove severely ~ *vi* : to dress casually esp. for reasons of fashion

¹dress·er \'dre-sər\ *n* (15c) **1** *obs* : a table or sideboard for preparing and serving food **2** : a cupboard to hold dishes and cooking utensils **3** : a chest of drawers or bureau with a mirror

²dresser *n* (1520) : one that dresses ⟨a fashionable ~⟩

dresser set *n* (ca. 1934) : a set of toilet articles including hairbrush, comb, and mirror for use at a dresser or dressing table

dress·ing *n* (15c) **1 a** : the act or process of one who dresses **b** : an instance of such act or process **2 a** : a sauce for adding to a dish (as a salad) **b** : a seasoned mixture usu. used as a stuffing (as for poultry) **3** : material (as ointment or gauze) applied to cover a lesion **b** : fertilizing material (as manure or compost)

dress·ing–down \,dre-siŋ-'daůn\ *n* (ca. 1890) : a severe reprimand

dressing glass *n* (1714) : a small mirror set to swing in a standing frame and used at a dresser or dressing table

dressing gown *n* (1777) : a robe worn esp. while dressing or resting

dressing room *n* (1675) : a room used chiefly for dressing; *esp* : a room in a theater for changing costumes and makeup

dressing table *n* (1692) : a table often fitted with drawers and a mirror in front of which one sits while dressing and grooming oneself

¹dress·mak·er \'dres-,mā-kər\ *n* (1803) : one that makes dresses — **dress·mak·ing** \-,mā-kiŋ\ *n*

²dressmaker *adj* (1904) *of women's clothes* : having softness, rounded lines, and intricate detailing ⟨a ~ suit⟩

dress rehearsal *n* (1828) **1** : a full rehearsal (as of a play) in costume and with stage properties shortly before the first performance **2** : a practice exercise for something to come : DRY RUN

dress shield *n* (1884) : a pad worn inside a part of the clothing liable to be soiled by perspiration (as at the underarm)

dress shirt *n* (1892) : a man's shirt esp. for wear with evening dress; *broadly* : a shirt suitable for wear with a necktie

dress uniform *n* (ca. 1897) : a uniform for formal wear

dress up *vt* (1674) **1 a** : to attire in best or formal clothes **b** : to attire in clothes suited to a particular role **2 a** : to present in the most attractive or impressive light ⟨a fiasco *dressed up* as a triumph⟩ **b** : to make more attractive, glamorous, or fancy ⟨*dress up* a plain dessert with a rich chocolate sauce⟩ ~ *vi* : to get dressed up

dressy \'dre-sē\ *adj* **dress·i·er; -est** (1768) **1** : showy in dress **2** : STYLISH, SMART — **dress·i·ness** *n*

drew *past of* DRAW

Drey·fu·sard \,drī-f(y)ə-'sär(d), ,drā-, -'zär(d)\ *n* [F] (1898) : a defender or partisan of Alfred Dreyfus

drib \'drib\ *n* [prob. back-formation fr. *dribble & driblet*] (ca. 1730) : a small amount — usu. used in the phrase *dribs and drabs*

¹drib·ble \'dri-bəl\ *vb* **drib·bled; drib·bling** \-(ə-)liŋ\ [freq. of *drib* (to dribble)] *vt* (ca. 1589) **1** : to issue sporadically and in small bits **2** : to let or cause to fall in drops little by little **3 a** : to propel by successive slight taps or bounces with hand, foot, or stick **b** : to hit (as a baseball) so as to cause a slow bouncing ~ *vi* **1** : to fall or flow in drops or in a thin intermittent stream : TRICKLE **2** : to let saliva trickle from the corner of the mouth : DROOL **3** : to come or issue in piecemeal or desultory fashion **4 a** : to dribble a ball or puck **b** : to proceed by dribbling ⟨a *of a ball* : to move with short bounces — **drib·bler** \-b(ə-)lər\ *n*

²dribble *n* (ca. 1680) **1** : a tiny or insignificant bit or quantity **2** : a small trickling stream or flow **3** : an act, instance, or manner of dribbling a ball or puck — **drib·bly** \'dri-b(ə-)lē\ *adj*

drib·let \'dri-blət\ *n* (1678) **1** : a trifling or small sum or part **2** : a drop of liquid

dried–up \'drī-,dəp, ,drī-'\ *adj* (1885) : being wizened and shriveled

¹drier *comparative of* DRY

²dri·er *or* **dry·er** \'drī(-ə)r\ *n* (1528) **1** : something that extracts or absorbs moisture **2** : a substance that accelerates drying (as of oils, paints, and printing inks) **3** *usu* **dryer** : a device for drying

driest *superlative of* DRY

¹drift \'drift\ *n* [ME; akin to OE *drīfan* to drive — more at DRIVE] (14c) **1 a** : the act of driving something along **b** : the flow or the velocity of the current of a river or ocean stream **2 a** : something driven, propelled, or urged along or drawn together in a clump by or as if by a natural agency: as **a** : wind-driven snow, rain, cloud, dust, or smoke usu. at or near the ground surface **b** (1) : a mass of matter (as sand) deposited together by or as if by wind or water (2) : a helter-skelter accumulation **c** : DROVE, FLOCK **d** : something (as driftwood) washed ashore **e** : rock debris deposited by natural agents; *specif* : a deposit of clay, sand, gravel, and boulders transported by a glacier or by running water from a glacier **3 a** : a general underlying design or tendency **b** : the underlying meaning, import, or purport of what is spoken or written **4** : something (as a tool) driven down upon or forced into a body **5** : the motion or action of drifting esp. spatially and usu. under external influence: as **a** : the lateral motion of an aircraft due to air currents **b** : an easy moderate more or less steady flow or sweep along a spatial course **c** : a gradual shift in attitude, opinion, or position **d** : an aimless course; *esp* : a foregoing of any attempt at direction or control **e** : a deviation from a true reproduction, representation, or reading **6 a** : a nearly horizontal mine passageway driven on or parallel to the course of a vein or rock stratum **b** : a small crosscut in a mine connecting two larger tunnels **7 a** : an assumed trend toward a general change in the structure of a language over a period of time **b** : GENETIC DRIFT **c** : a gradual change in the zero reading of an instrument or in any quantitative characteristic that is supposed to remain constant *syn* see TENDENCY — **drifty** \'drif-tē\ *adj*

²drift *vi* (ca. 1600) **1 a** : to become driven or carried along (as by a current of water, wind, or air) **b** : to move or float smoothly and effortlessly **2 a** : to move along a line of least resistance **b** : to move in a random or casual way **c** : to become carried along subject to no guidance or control ⟨the talk ~ed from topic to topic⟩ **3 a** : to accumulate in a mass or become piled up in heaps by wind or water **b** : to become covered with a drift **4** : to vary or deviate from a set course or adjustment ~ *vt* **1** : to cause to be driven in a current **b** *West* : to drive (livestock) slowly esp. to allow grazing **2 a** : to pile in heaps **b** : to cover with drifts — **drift·ing·ly** \'drif-tiŋ-lē\ *adv*

drift·age \'drif-tij\ *n* (1768) : drifted material

drift·er \'drif-tər\ *n* (1897) : one that drifts; *esp* : one that travels or moves about aimlessly

drift fence *n* (1907) : a stretch of fence on rangeland esp. in the western U.S. for preventing cattle from drifting from their home range

drift net *n* (1848) : a fishing net often miles in extent arranged to drift with the tide or current and buoyed up by floats or attached to a boat

drift·wood \'drift-,wůd\ *n* (1633) **1** : wood drifted or floated by water **2** : FLOTSAM 2

¹drill \'dril\ *vb* [D *drillen*] *vt* (1622) **1 a** : to fix something in the mind or habit pattern by repetitive instruction ⟨~ pupils in spelling⟩ **b** : to impart or communicate by repetition ⟨impossible to ~ the simplest idea into some people⟩ **c** : to train or exercise in military drill **2 a** (1) : to bore or drive a hole in (2) : to make by piercing action **b** : to shoot with or as if with a gun **c** (1) : to propel (as a ball) with force or accuracy ⟨~ed a single to right field⟩ (2) : to hit with force ⟨~ed the batter with the first pitch⟩ ~ *vi* **1** : to make a hole with a drill **2** : to engage in an exercise — **drill·abil·i·ty** \,dri-lə-'bi-lə-tē\ *n* — **drill·able** \-lə-bəl\ *adj* — **drill·er** \'dri-lər\ *n*

²drill *n* (1611) **1** : an instrument with an edged or pointed end for making holes in hard substances by revolving or by a succession of blows; *also* : a machine for operating such an instrument **2** : the act or exercise of training soldiers in marching and in executing prescribed movements with a weapon **3 a** : a physical or mental exercise aimed at perfecting facility and skill esp. by regular practice **b** : a formal exercise by a team of marchers **c** *chiefly Brit* : the approved or correct procedure for accomplishing something efficiently **4 a** : a marine snail (*Urosalpinx cinerea*) destructive to oysters by boring through their shells and feeding on the soft parts **b** : any of several mollusks related to the drill **5** : a drilling sound

³drill *n* [origin unknown] (1644) : a western African baboon (*Papio leucophaeus* syn. *Mandrillus leucophaeus*) having a black face and brown coat and closely related to the typical mandrills

⁴drill *n* [perh. fr. *drill* (rill)] (1727) **1 a** : a shallow furrow or trench into which seed is sown **b** : a row of seed sown in such a furrow **2** : a planting implement that makes holes or furrows, drops in the seed and sometimes fertilizer, and covers them with earth

\ə\ abut \ª\ kitten, F table \ər\ further \a\ ash \ā\ ace \ä\ mop, mar \aů\ out \ch\ chin \e\ bet \ē\ easy \g\ go \i\ hit \ī\ ice \j\ job \ŋ\ sing \ō\ go \ȯ\ law \ȯi\ boy \th\ thin \<u>th</u>\ the \ü\ loot \ů\ foot \y\ yet \zh\ vision \à, k̲, ⁿ, œ, œ̄, ɷ, ūe, ᵛ\ *see* Guide to Pronunciation

⁵**drill** vt (ca. 1740) **1** : to sow (seeds) by dropping along a shallow furrow **2 a** : to sow with seed or set with seedlings inserted in drills **b** : to distribute seed or fertilizer in by means of a drill

⁶**drill** n [short for *drilling*] (1743) : a durable cotton twilled fabric

dril·ling \'dri-liŋ\ n [modif. of G *Drillich*, fr. MHG *drilich* fabric woven with a threefold thread, fr. OHG *drilih* made up of three threads, fr. L *trilic-, trilix*, fr. *tri-* + *licium* thread] (1640) : ⁶DRILL

drill·mas·ter \'dril-,mas-tər\ n (1869) **1** : an instructor in military drill **2** : an instructor or director who maintains severe discipline and often stresses method and detail

drill press n (ca. 1864) : an upright drilling machine in which the drill is pressed to the work by a hand lever or by power

drill team n (1928) : an exhibition marching team that engages in precision drill

drily var of DRYLY

D ring \'dē-,riŋ\ n (ca. 1899) : a usu. metal ring having the shape of a capital D

¹**drink** \'driŋk\ vb **drank** \'draŋk\; **drunk** \'drəŋk\ or **drank**; **drink·ing** [ME, fr. OE *drincan*; akin to OHG *trinkan* to drink] vt (bef. 12c) **1 a** : SWALLOW, IMBIBE **b** : to take in or suck up : ABSORB ⟨~ing air into his lungs⟩ **c** : to take in or receive avidly — usu. used with *in* ⟨*drank* in every word of the lecture⟩ **2** : to join in a toast to ⟨I'll ~ your good health⟩ **3** : to bring to a specified state by drinking alcoholic beverages ⟨*drank* himself into oblivion⟩ ~ vi **1 a** : to take liquid into the mouth for swallowing **b** : to receive into one's consciousness **2** : to partake of alcoholic beverages **3** : to make or join in a toast ⟨I'll ~ to that!⟩

²**drink** n (bef. 12c) **1 a** : a liquid suitable for swallowing **b** : alcoholic beverages **2** : a draft or portion of liquid **3** : excessive consumption of alcoholic beverages **4** : a sizable body of water — used with *the*

¹**drink·able** \'driŋ-kə-bəl\ adj (1611) : suitable or safe for drinking — **drink·abil·i·ty** \,driŋ-kə-bə-lə-tē\ n

²**drinkable** n (1708) : a liquid suitable for drinking : BEVERAGE

drink·er \'driŋ-kər\ n (bef. 12c) **1 a** : one that drinks **b** : a person who drinks alcoholic beverages esp. to a notable degree ⟨a heavy ~⟩ **2** : WATERER b

drinking fountain n (1860) : a fixture with nozzle that delivers a stream of water for drinking

drinking song n (1597) : a song on a convivial theme appropriate for a group engaged in social drinking

¹**drip** \'drip\ vb **dripped**; **drip·ping** [ME *drippen*, fr. OE *dryppan*; akin to OE *dropa* drop] vt (bef. 12c) **1** : to let fall in drops **2** : to let out or seem to spill copiously ⟨her voice *dripping* sarcasm⟩ ~ vi **1 a** : to let fall drops of moisture or liquid **b** : to overflow with or as if with moisture ⟨a uniform *dripping* with gold braid⟩ **2** : to fall in or as if in drops **3** : to waft or pass gently — **drip·per** n

²**drip** n (1664) **1** : a part of a cornice or other member that projects to throw off rainwater; *also* : an overlapping metal strip or an underneath groove for the same purpose **2 a** : a falling in drops **b** : liquid that falls, overflows, or is extruded in drops **3** : the sound made by or as if by falling drops **4** : a device for the administration of a fluid at a slow rate esp. into a vein; *also* : a material so administered **5** : a dull or unattractive person

³**drip** adj (1895) : of, relating to, or being coffee made by letting boiling water drip slowly through finely ground coffee ⟨~ coffee⟩ ⟨a ~ pot⟩

¹**drip–dry** \'drip-,drī\ adj (1953) : to dry with few or no wrinkles when hung wet ~ vt : to hang (as wet clothing) to drip-dry

²**drip–dry** adj (1957) : made of a washable fabric that drip-dries

³**drip–dry** n (1959) : a drip-dry garment

drip·less \'dri-pləs\ adj (1887) : designed not to drip ⟨~ candles⟩

drip·ping \'dri-piŋ\ n (15c) : fat and juices drawn from meat during cooking — often used in pl.

drip·py \'dri-pē\ adj **drip·pi·er; -est** (ca. 1718) **1** : characterized by dripping; *esp* : RAINY, DRIZZLY **2** : MAWKISH 2

drip·stone \'drip-,stōn\ n (ca. 1818) **1** : a stone drip (as over a window) **2** : calcium carbonate in the form of stalactites or stalagmites

¹**drive** \'drīv\ vb **drove** \'drōv\; **driv·en** \'dri-vən\; **driv·ing** \'drī-viŋ\ [ME, fr. OE *drīfan*; akin to OHG *triban* to drive] vt (bef. 12c) **1 a** : to frighten or prod (as game or cattle) into moving in a desired direction **b** : to go through (a district) driving game animals **2** : to carry on or through energetically ⟨~s a hard bargain⟩ **3 a** : to impart a forward motion to by physical force ⟨waves *drove* the boat ashore⟩ **b** : to repulse, remove, or cause to go by force, authority, or influence ⟨~ the enemy back⟩ **c** : to set or keep in motion or operation ⟨~ machinery by electricity⟩ **4 a** : to direct the motions and course of (a draft animal) **b** : to operate the mechanism and controls and direct the course of (as a vehicle) **c** : to convey in a vehicle **d** : to float (logs) down a stream **5 a** : to exert inescapable or coercive pressure on : FORCE **b** : to compel to undergo or suffer a change (as in situation or emotional state) ⟨*drove* him crazy⟩ ⟨*drove* her out of business⟩ **c** : to urge relentlessly to continuous exertion ⟨the sergeant *drove* his recruits⟩ **d** : to press or force into an activity, course, or direction ⟨the drug habit ~s addicts to steal⟩ **e** : to project, inject, or impress incisively ⟨*drove* her point home⟩ **6** : to force (a passage) by pressing or digging **7 a** : to propel (an object of play) swiftly **b** : to hit (a golf ball) from the tee esp. with a driver; *also* : to drive a golf ball onto (a green) **c** : to cause (a run or runner) to be scored in baseball — usu. used with *in* **8** : to give shape or impulse to ⟨factors that ~ the business cycle⟩ ~ vi **1 a** : to dash, plunge, or surge ahead rapidly or violently **b** : to progress with strong momentum ⟨the rain was *driving* hard⟩ **2 a** : to operate a vehicle **b** : to have oneself carried in a vehicle **3** : to drive a golf ball **syn** see MOVE — **driv·abil·i·ty** *also* **drive·abil·i·ty** \,drī-və-'bi-lə-tē\ n — **driv·able** *also* **drive·able** \'drī-və-bəl\ adj — **drive at** : to intend to express, convey, or accomplish ⟨did not understand what she was *driving at* —Eric Goldman⟩

²**drive** n, often attrib (1785) **1** : an act of driving: **a** : a trip in a carriage or automobile **b** : a collection and driving together of animals; *also* : the animals gathered **c** : a driving of cattle or sheep overland **d** : a hunt or shoot in which the game is driven within the hunter's range **e** : the guiding of logs downstream to a mill; *also* : the floating logs amassed in a drive **f** (1) : the act or an instance of driving an object of play (as a golf ball) (2) : the flight of a ball **2 a** : a private road : DRIVEWAY **b** : a public road for driving (as in a park) **3** : the

state of being hurried and under pressure **4 a** : a strong systematic group effort ⟨a fund-raising ~⟩ **b** : a sustained offensive effort ⟨the ~ ended in a touchdown⟩ **5 a** : the means for giving motion to a machine or machine part **b** : the means by which the propulsive power of an automobile is applied to the road ⟨front wheel ~⟩ **c** : the means by which the propulsion of an automotive vehicle is controlled and directed ⟨a left-hand ~⟩ **6** : an offensive, aggressive, or expansionist move; *esp* : a strong military attack against enemy-held terrain **7 a** : an urgent, basic, or instinctual need : a motivating physiological condition of an organism ⟨a sexual ~⟩ **b** : an impelling culturally acquired concern, interest, or longing **c** : dynamic quality **8 a** : a device for reading and writing on magnetic media (as tapes or disks)

drive–by \'drīv-,bī\ adj (1986) : carried out from a moving vehicle ⟨a ~ shooting⟩

drive–in \'drīv-,vin\ n (1937) : an establishment (as a theater or restaurant) so laid out that patrons can be accommodated while remaining in their automobiles — **drive–in** adj

¹**driv·el** \'dri-vəl\ vb **-eled** or **-elled; -el·ing** or **-el·ling** \-v(ə-)liŋ\ [ME, fr. OE *dreflian*; perh. akin to ON *draf* malt dregs] vi (bef. 12c) **1** : to let saliva dribble from the mouth : SLAVER **2** : to talk stupidly and carelessly ~ vt **1** : to utter in an infantile or imbecilic way **2** : to waste or fritter in a childish fashion — **driv·el·er** \-v(ə-)lər\ n

²**drivel** n (14c) **1** archaic : DROOL 1 **2** : NONSENSE

drive·line \'drīv-,līn\ n (1949) : DRIVETRAIN

driv·en adj (1925) : having a compulsive or urgent quality ⟨a ~ sense of obligation⟩ — **driv·en·ness** \'dri-vən-nəs\ n

driv·er \'drī-vər\ n (14c) : one that drives: as **a** : COACHMAN **b** : the operator of a motor vehicle **c** : an implement (as a hammer) for driving **d** : a mechanical piece for imparting motion to another piece **e** : a golf wood with a nearly straight face used in driving **f** : an electronic circuit that supplies input to another electronic circuit; *also* : LOUDSPEAKER **g** : a piece of computer software that controls input and output operations — **driv·er·less** \-ləs\ adj

driver ant n (1859) : ARMY ANT; *specif* : any of various African and Asian ants (*Dorylus* or related genera) that move in vast armies

driver's license n (1926) : a license issued under governmental authority that permits the holder to operate a motor vehicle

driver's seat n (1923) : the position of top authority or dominance

drive·shaft \'drīv-,shaft\ n (1895) : a shaft that transmits mechanical power

drive time n (1966) : a time during rush hour when radio audiences are swelled by commuters listening to car radios

drive·train \'drīv-,trān\ n (1954) : the parts (as the universal joint and the driveshaft) that connect the transmission with the driving axles of an automobile

drive·way \-,wā\ n (1871) : a private road giving access from a public way to a building on abutting grounds

driv·ing adj (14c) **1 a** : communicating force ⟨a ~ wheel⟩ **b** : exerting pressure ⟨a ~ influence⟩ **2 a** : having great force ⟨a ~ rain⟩ **b** : acting with vigor : ENERGETIC ⟨a hard-*driving* worker⟩

driving range n (ca. 1949) : an area equipped with distance markers, clubs, balls, and tees for practicing golf drives

¹**driz·zle** \'dri-zəl\ n (1554) : a fine misty rain — **driz·zly** \'driz-(ə-)lē\ adj

²**drizzle** vb **driz·zled; driz·zling** \-z(ə-)liŋ\ [perh. alter. of ME *drysnen* to fall, fr. OE *-drysnian* to disappear; akin to Goth *driusan* to fall] vt (1548) **1** : to shed or let fall in minute drops or particles **2** : to make wet with minute drops ~ vi : to rain in very small drops or very lightly : SPRINKLE — **driz·zling·ly** \-z(ə-)liŋ-lē\ adv

drogue \'drōg\ n [prob. alter. of *drag*] (1875) **1** : SEA ANCHOR **2 a** : a cylindrical or funnel-shaped device towed as a target by an airplane **b** : a small parachute for stabilizing or decelerating something (as an astronaut's capsule) or for pulling a larger parachute out of stowage **3** : a funnel-shaped device which is attached to the end of a long flexible hose suspended from a tanker airplane in flight and into which the probe of another airplane is fitted so as to receive fuel from the tanker

droit \'drȯit, 'drwä\ n [ME, fr. MF, fr. ML *directum*, fr. LL, neut. of *directus* just, fr. L, direct — more at DRESS] (15c) : a legal right

droit du sei·gneur \drwä-dü̅ē-se-n'œr\ n [F, right of the lord] (1825) : a supposed legal or customary right of a feudal lord to have sexual relations with a vassal's bride on her wedding night

¹**droll** \'drōl\ adj [F *drôle*, fr. *drôle* scamp, fr. MF *drolle*, fr. MD, imp] (1623) : having a humorous, whimsical, or odd quality — **droll·ness** n — **drol·ly** \'drō(l)-lē\ adv

²**droll** n (ca. 1645) : an amusing person : JESTER, COMEDIAN

³**droll** vi (1654) archaic : to make fun : JEST, SPORT

droll·ery \'drōl-rē, 'drō-lə-\ n, pl **-er·ies** (1597) **1** : something that is droll; *esp* : a comic picture or drawing **2** : the act or an instance of jesting or burlesquing **3** : whimsical humor

-drome \,drōm\ n comb form [hippodrome] **1** : racecourse ⟨motor-drome⟩ **2** : large specially prepared place ⟨aerodrome⟩

drom·e·dary \'drä-mə-,der-ē *also* 'drə-mə-\ n, pl **-dar·ies** [ME dromedarie, fr. OF dromedaire, fr. LL dromedarius, fr. L dromad-, dromas, fr. Gk, running; akin to Gk dramein to run, dromos racecourse, Skt dramati he runs about] (13c) : CAMEL 1a

-d·ro·mous \drə-məs\ adj comb form [NL -dromus, fr. Gk -dromos (akin to Gk dramein)] : running ⟨catadromous⟩

¹**drone** \'drōn\ n [ME, fr. OE drān; akin to OHG treno drone, Gk thrēnos dirge] (bef. 12c) **1** : the male of a bee (as the honeybee) that has no sting and gathers no honey **2** : one that lives on the labors of others : PARASITE **3** : an unmanned airplane, helicopter, or ship guided by remote control **4** : DRUDGE

²**drone** vb **droned; dron·ing** vi (ca. 1520) **1 a** : to make a sustained deep murmuring, humming, or buzzing sound **b** : to talk in a persistently dull or monotonous tone **2** : to pass, proceed, or act in a dull, drowsy, or indifferent manner ~ vt **1** : to utter or pronounce with a drone **2** : to pass or spend in dull or monotonous activity or in idleness — **dron·er** n — **dron·ing·ly** \'drō-niŋ-lē\ adv

³**drone** n (ca. 1520) **1** : a deep sustained or monotonous sound : HUM **2** : an instrument or part of an instrument (as one of the fixed-pitch pipes of a bagpipe) that sounds a continuous unvarying tone **3** : PEDAL POINT

¹**drool** \'drü(-ə)l\ vb [perh. alter. of *drivel*] vi (1802) **1 a** : to secrete saliva in anticipation of food **b** : DRIVEL 1 **2** : to make an effusive

show of pleasure or often envious or covetous appreciation 3 : to talk nonsense ~ vt : to express sentimentally or effusively

²**drool** n (1869) 1 : saliva trickling from the mouth 2 : NONSENSE

¹**droop** \'drüp\ vb [ME drupen, fr. ON drūpa; akin to OE dropa drop] vi (13c) 1 : to hang or incline downward 2 : to sink gradually 3 : to become depressed or weakened : LANGUISH ~ vt : to let droop — **droop·ing·ly** \'drü-piŋ-lē\ adv

²**droop** n (1647) : the condition or appearance of drooping

droopy \'drü-pē\ adj **droop·i·er; -est** (13c) 1 : GLOOMY 2 : drooping or tending to droop

¹**drop** \'dräp\ n, often attrib [ME, fr. OE dropa; akin to OHG tropfo drop] (bef. 12c) 1 a (1) : the quantity of fluid that falls in one spherical mass (2) pl : a dose of medicine measured by drops; esp : a solution for dilating the pupil of the eye b : a minute quantity or degree of something nonmaterial or intangible c : a small quantity of drink d : the smallest practical unit of liquid measure 2 : something that resembles a liquid drop: as a : a pendent ornament attached to a piece of jewelry; also : an earring with such a pendent b : a small globular cookie or candy 3 [²drop] a : the act or an instance of dropping : FALL b : a decline in quantity or quality c : a descent by parachute; also : the people or equipment dropped by parachute d : a place or central depository to which something (as mail, money, or stolen property) is brought for distribution or transmission; also : the act of depositing something at such a place (made the ~) 4 a : the distance from a higher to a lower level or through which something drops b : a fall of electric potential 5 : a slot into which something is to be dropped 6 [²drop] : something that drops, hangs, or falls: as a : a movable plate that covers the keyhole of a lock b : an unframed piece of cloth stage scenery; also : DROP CURTAIN c : a hinged platform on a gallows d : a fallen fruit 7 : the advantage of having an opponent covered with a firearm; broadly : ADVANTAGE, SUPERIORITY — usu. used in the phrase get the drop on — **at the drop of a hat** : as soon as the slightest provocation is given : IMMEDIATELY — **drop in the bucket** : a part so small as to be negligible

²**drop** vb **dropped; drop·ping** vi (bef. 12c) 1 : to fall in drops 2 a (1) : to fall unexpectedly or suddenly (2) : to descend from one line or level to another b : to fall in a state of collapse or death c of a card : to fall or roll into a hole or basket 3 : to enter or pass as if without conscious effort of will into some state, condition, or activity (dropped into sleep) 4 a : to cease to be of concern : LAPSE (let the matter ~) b : to pass from view or notice : DISAPPEAR — often used with out (~ out of sight) c : to become less (production dropped) — often used with off 5 : to move with a favoring wind or current — usu. used with down ~ vt 1 : to let fall : cause to fall 2 a : GIVE UP 2, ABANDON (~ an idea) (~ the charges) b : DISCONTINUE (dropped what she was doing) c : to break off an association or connection with : DISMISS (~ a failing student) 3 a : to utter or mention in a casual way (~ a suggestion) (~ names) b : WRITE (~ us a line soon) 4 a : to lower or cause to descend from one level or position to another b : to cause to lessen or decrease : REDUCE (dropped his speed) 5 of an animal : to give birth to 6 a : LOSE (dropped three games) (dropped $50 in a poker game) b : SPEND (~ $20 for lunch) 7 a : to bring down with a shot or a blow b : to cause (a high card) to fall c : to toss or roll into a hole or basket (~ a putt) 8 a : to deposit or deliver during a usu. brief stop — usu. used with off (~ the kids off at school) b : AIR-DROP 9 : to cause (the voice) to be less loud 10 a : to leave (a letter representing a speech sound) unsounded (~ the g in running) b : to leave out in writing : OMIT 11 : to draw from an external point (~ a perpendicular to the line) 12 : to take (a drug) orally : SWALLOW (~ acid) — **drop·pa·ble** \'drä-pə-bəl\ adj — **drop behind** : to fail to keep up

drop back vi (1927) 1 : RETREAT 2 : to move straight back from the line of scrimmage (the quarterback drops back to pass)

drop by vi (ca. 1905) : to pay a brief casual visit ~ vt : to visit casually or unexpectedly (drop by a friend's house)

drop cloth n (ca. 1928) : a protective sheet (as of cloth or plastic) used esp. by painters to cover floors and furniture

drop curtain n (1832) : a stage curtain that can be lowered and raised

drop-dead adj (1970) : sensationally striking, attractive, or impressive (a ~ evening gown) — **drop-dead** adv

drop-forge \'dräp-ˌförj, -ˌförj\ vt (1886) : to forge between dies by means of a drop hammer or punch press — **drop forger** n

drop front n (1925) : a hinged cover on the front of a desk that may be lowered to provide a surface for writing

drop hammer n (ca. 1864) : a power hammer raised and then released to drop (as on metal resting on an anvil or die)

drop-head \'dräp-ˌhed\ n, often attrib (1932) Brit : a convertible automobile

drop-in \'dräp-ˌin\ n (1819) 1 : a casual visit or brief stop 2 : one who drops in : a casual visitor

drop in vi (ca. 1600) : to pay an unexpected or casual visit — often used with on

drop-kick \-ˌkik\ n (1857) : a kick made by dropping a ball to the ground and kicking it at the moment it starts to rebound

drop-kick \-ˌkik\ vi (ca. 1909) : to make a dropkick ~ vt : to kick by means of a dropkick (~ a ball) (~ a field goal) — **drop-kick·er** n

drop leaf n (1882) : a hinged leaf on the side or end of a table that can be folded down

drop·let \'dräp-lət\ n (1607) : a tiny drop (as of a liquid)

drop·light \'dräp-ˌlīt\ n (1890) : an electric light suspended by a cord or on a portable extension

drop-off \'dräp-ˌöf\ n (1923) 1 : a very steep or perpendicular descent 2 : a marked dwindling or decline (a ~ in attendance)

drop off \ˌdräp-'öf\ vi (1820) : to fall asleep

drop·out \'dräp-ˌaut\ n (1930) 1 a : one who drops out of school b : one who drops out of conventional society c : one who abandons an attempt, activity, or chosen path (a corporate ~) 2 : a spot on a magnetic tape or disk from which data has disappeared

drop out \ˌdräp-'aut\ vi (1883) 1 : to withdraw from participation or membership : QUIT; esp : to withdraw from conventional society

drop pass n (1949) : a pass in ice hockey in which the passer skates past the puck leaving it for a teammate following close behind

dropped adj (1953) : designed to extend or begin lower than normal (a dress with a ~ waist) (~ shoulders)

dropped egg n (1824) : a poached egg

drop·per \'drä-pər\ n (ca. 1700) 1 : one that drops 2 : a short glass tube fitted with a rubber bulb and used to measure liquids by drops — called also eyedropper, medicine dropper — **drop·per·ful** \-ˌful\ n

drop·ping n (14c) 1 : something dropped 2 pl : DUNG

drop seat n (1926) 1 : a hinged seat (as in a taxi) that may be dropped down 2 : a seat (as in an undergarment) that can be unbuttoned

drop shot n (1908) : a delicately hit shot (as in tennis or squash) that drops quickly after crossing the net or dies after hitting a wall

drop·si·cal \'dräp-si-kəl\ adj (1678) 1 : relating to or affected with dropsy 2 : TURGID, SWOLLEN

drop·sy \'dräp-sē\ n [ME dropesie, short for ydropesie, fr. OF, fr. L hydropisis, modif. of Gk hydrōps, fr. hydōr water — more at WATER] (13c) : EDEMA

drop tank n (1943) : an auxiliary fuel tank for airplanes that can be jettisoned when empty

drop volley n (1907) : a drop shot made on a volley in tennis

drop zone n (ca. 1943) : the area in which troops, supplies, or equipment are to be air-dropped; also : the target on which a skydiver lands

drosh·ky \'dräsh-kē\ also **dros·ky** \'dräs-kē\ n, pl **droshkies** also **droskies** [Russ drozhki, fr. droga pole of a wagon] (1808) : any of various 2- or 4-wheeled carriages used esp. in Russia

dro·soph·i·la \drō-'sä-fə-lə\ n [NL, genus name, fr. Gk drosos dew + NL -phila, fem. of -philus -phil] (1910) : any of a genus (Drosophila) of small two-winged flies used in genetic research

dross \'dräs, 'dròs\ n [ME dros, fr. OE drōs dregs] (bef. 12c) 1 : the scum that forms on the surface of molten metal 2 : waste or foreign matter : IMPURITY 3 : something that is base, trivial, or inferior — **drossy** \'drä-sē, 'drò-\ adj

drought \'draut\ also **drouth** \'drauth\ n [ME, fr. OE drūgath, fr. drūgian to dry up; akin to OE drȳge dry — more at DRY] (bef. 12c) 1 : a period of dryness esp. when prolonged that causes extensive damage to crops or prevents their successful growth 2 : a prolonged or chronic shortage or lack of something expected or desired — **drought·i·ness** n — **droughty** \'drau-tē\ adj

¹**drove** \'drōv\ n [ME, fr. OE drāf, fr. drīfan to drive — more at DRIVE] (bef. 12c) 1 : a group of animals driven or moving in a body 2 : a large number : CROWD — usu. used in pl. esp. with in (tourists arriving in ~s) (stayed away in ~s)

²**drove** past of DRIVE

drov·er \'drō-vər\ n (15c) : one that drives cattle or sheep

drown \'draun\ vb **drowned** \'draund\; **drown·ing** \'drau-niŋ\ [ME drounen] vi (14c) 1 : to become drowned ~ vt 1 a : to suffocate by submersion esp. in water b : to submerge esp. by a rise in the water level c : to soak, drench, or cover with a liquid 2 : to engage (oneself) deeply and strenuously 3 : to cause (a sound) not to be heard by making a loud noise — usu. used with out 4 a : to drive out (as a sensation or an idea) (~ed his sorrows in liquor) b : OVERWHELM

drownd \'draund\ nonstand var of DROWN

¹**drowse** \'drauz\ vb **drowsed; drows·ing** [prob. akin to Goth driusan to fall — more at DREARY] vi (1573) 1 : to be inactive 2 : to fall into a light slumber ~ vt 1 : to make drowsy or inactive 2 : to pass (time) drowsily or in drowsing

²**drowse** n (1814) : the act or an instance of drowsing : DOZE

drowsy \'drau-zē\ adj **drows·i·er; -est** (1530) 1 a : ready to fall asleep b : inducing or tending to induce sleep c : INDOLENT, LETHARGIC 2 : giving the appearance of peaceful inactivity — **drows·i·ly** \-zə-lē\ adv — **drows·i·ness** \-zē-nəs\ n

drub \'drəb\ vb **drubbed; drub·bing** [perh. fr. Ar daraba] vt (1634) 1 : to beat severely 2 : to abuse with words : BERATE 3 : to defeat decisively ~ vi : DRUM, STAMP — **drub·ber** n — **drub·bing** n

¹**drudge** \'drəj\ vb **drudged; drudg·ing** [ME druggen] vi (14c) : to do hard, menial, or monotonous work ~ vt : to force to do hard, menial, or monotonous work — **drudg·er** n

²**drudge** n (15c) 1 : one who is obliged to do menial work 2 : one whose work is routine and boring

drudg·ery \'drəj-rē, 'drə-jə-rē\ n, pl **-er·ies** (1550) : dull, irksome, and fatiguing work : uninspiring or menial labor **syn** see WORK

drudg·ing \'drə-jiŋ\ adj (1548) : MONOTONOUS, TIRING — **drudg·ing·ly** \-jiŋ-lē\ adv

¹**drug** \'drəg\ n [ME drogge] (14c) 1 a obs : a substance used in dyeing or chemical operations b : a substance used as a medication or in the preparation of medication c according to the Food, Drug, and Cosmetic Act (1) : a substance recognized in an official pharmacopoeia or formulary (2) : a substance intended for use in the diagnosis, cure, mitigation, treatment, or prevention of disease (3) : a substance other than food intended to affect the structure or function of the body (4) : a substance intended for use as a component of a medicine but not a device or a component, part, or accessory of a device 2 : a commodity that is not salable or for which there is no demand — used in the phrase drug on the market 3 : something and often an illegal substance that causes addiction, habituation, or a marked change in consciousness — **drug·gy** also **drug·gie** \'drə-gē\ adj

²**drug** vb **drugged; drug·ging** vt (1605) 1 : to affect with a drug; esp : to stupefy by a narcotic drug 2 : to administer a drug to 3 : to lull or stupefy as if with a drug ~ vi : to take drugs for narcotic effect

³**drug** dial past of DRAG

drug·get \'drə-gət\ n [MF droguet, dim. of drogue trash, drug] (1580) 1 : a wool or partly wool fabric formerly used for clothing 2 : a coarse durable cloth used chiefly as a floor covering 3 : a rug having a cotton warp and a wool filling

drug·gie also **drug·gy** \'drə-gē\ n, pl **druggies** (1967) : one who habitually uses drugs

\ə\ abut \ᵊ\ kitten, F table \ər\ further \a\ ash \ā\ ace \ä\ mop, mar \aú\ out \ch\ chin \e\ bet \ē\ easy \g\ go \i\ hit \ī\ ice \j\ job \ŋ\ sing \ō\ go \ò\ law \òi\ boy \th\ thin \t͟h\ the \ü\ loot \ú\ foot \y\ yet \zh\ vision \á, k̲, ⁿ, œ, œ̄, ᵫ, ᵫ̄, ᵞ\ see Guide to Pronunciation

drug·gist \'drə-gist\ *n* (1611) : one who sells or dispenses drugs and medicines: as **a** : PHARMACIST **b** : one who owns or manages a drugstore

drug·mak·er \'drəg-‚mā-kər\ *n* (1964) : one that manufactures pharmaceuticals

drug·store \-‚stȯr, -‚stȯr\ *n* (1810) : a retail store where medicines and miscellaneous articles are sold : PHARMACY

drugstore cowboy *n* (1925) **1** : one who wears cowboy clothes but has had no experience as a cowboy **2** : one who loafs on street corners and in drugstores

dru·id \'drü-id\ *n, often cap* [L *druides, druidae*, pl., fr. Gaulish *druides*; akin to OIr *druí* druid, and perh. to OE *trēow* tree] (1563) : one of an ancient Celtic priesthood appearing in Irish and Welsh sagas and Christian legends as magicians and wizards — **dru·id·ic** \drü-'i-dik\ *or* **dru·id·i·cal** \-i-kəl\ *adj, often cap*

dru·id·ism \'drü-ə-‚di-zəm\ *n, often cap* (1715) : the system of religion, philosophy, and instruction of the druids

¹**drum** \'drəm\ *n* [prob. fr. D *trom*; akin to MHG *trumme* drum] (1539) **1** : a percussion instrument consisting of a hollow shell or cylinder with a drumhead stretched over one or both ends that is beaten with the hands or with some implement (as a stick or wire brush) **2** : TYMPANIC MEMBRANE **3** : the sound of a drum; *also* : a sound similar to that of a drum **4** : any of various bony fishes (family Sciaenidae) that make a drumming noise **5** : something resembling a drum in shape: as **a** : a cylindrical machine or mechanical device or part **b** : a cylindrical container; *specif* : a large usu. metal container for liquids ⟨a 55-gallon ∼⟩ **c** : a disk-shaped magazine for an automatic weapon — **drum·like** \-‚līk\ *adj*

drum 1: *1* bass, *2* snare (orchestra), *3* snare (parade)

²**drum** *vb* **drummed; drum·ming** *vi* (1583) **1** : to make a succession of strokes or vibrations that produce sounds like drumbeats **2** : to beat a drum **3** : to throb or sound rhythmically **4** : to stir up interest : SOLICIT ∼ *vt* **1** : to summon or enlist by or as if by beating a drum ⟨were *drummed* into service⟩ **2** : to dismiss ignominiously : EXPEL — usu. used with *out* **3** : to drive or force by steady effort or reiteration ⟨*drummed* the speech into her head⟩ **4 a** : to strike or tap repeatedly **b** : to produce (rhythmic sounds) by such action

³**drum** *n* [ScGael *druim* back, ridge, fr. OIr *druimm*] (1725) **1** *chiefly Scot* : a long narrow hill or ridge **2** : DRUMLIN

drum·beat \'drəm-‚bēt\ *n* (1855) **1** : a stroke on a drum or its sound; *also* : a series of such strokes **2** : vociferous advocacy of a cause **3** : DRUMFIRE **2** — **drum·beat·er** \-‚bē-tər\ *n* — **drum·beat·ing** \-tiŋ\ *n*

drum brake *n* (1950) : a brake that operates by the friction of usu. a pair of shoes pressing against the inner surface of the cylinder of a rotating drum — compare DISC BRAKE

drum·fire \'drəm-‚fīr\ *n* (1916) **1** : artillery firing so continuous as to sound like a drumroll **2** : something suggestive of drumfire in intensity : BARRAGE ⟨a ∼ of publicity⟩

drum·head \-‚hed\ *n* (1622) **1** : the material (as skin or plastic) stretched over one or both ends of a drum **2** : the top of a capstan that is pierced with sockets for the levers used in turning it

drumhead court-martial *n* [fr. the use of a drumhead as a table] (1835) : a summary court-martial that tries offenses on the battlefield

drum·lin \'drəm-lən\ *n* [Ir *druim* back, ridge (fr. OIr *druimm*) + E *-lin* (alter. of *-ling*)] (ca. 1833) : an elongate or oval hill of glacial drift

drum major *n* (1863) : the leader of a marching band

drum ma·jor·ette \‚drəm-‚mā-jə-'ret\ *n* (1938) **1** : a girl or woman who leads a marching band **2** : a baton twirler who accompanies a marching band

drum·mer \'drə-mər\ *n* (1580) **1 a** : one that plays a drum **b** — used figuratively in expressions denoting an unconventional way of behaving or thinking ⟨march to a different ∼⟩ **2** : TRAVELING SALESMAN

drum·roll \'drəm-‚rōl\ *n* (1887) : a roll on a drum or its sound

drum·stick \-‚stik\ *n* (1589) **1** : a stick for beating a drum **2** : the segment of a fowl's leg between the thigh and tarsus

drum up *vt* (1830) **1** : to bring about by persistent effort ⟨*drum up* some business⟩ **2** : INVENT, ORIGINATE ⟨*drum up* a new method⟩

¹**drunk** *past part of* DRINK

²**drunk** \'drəŋk\ *adj* [ME *drunke*, alter. of *drunken*] (14c) **1 a** : having the faculties impaired by alcohol **b** : having a level of alcohol in the blood that exceeds a maximum prescribed by law ⟨legally ∼⟩ **2** : dominated by an intense feeling ⟨∼ with rage⟩ **3** : of, relating to, or caused by intoxication : DRUNKEN

³**drunk** *n* (1779) **1** : a period of drinking to intoxication or of being intoxicated ⟨a 2-day ∼⟩ **2** : one who is drunk; *esp* : DRUNKARD

drunk·ard \'drəŋ-kərd\ *n* (15c) : one who is habitually drunk

drunk·en \'drəŋ-kən\ *adj* [ME, fr. OE *druncen*, fr. pp. of *drincan* to drink] (bef. 12c) **1** : DRUNK **1** ⟨a ∼ driver⟩ **2** *obs* : saturated with liquid **3 a** : given to habitual excessive use of alcohol **b** : of, relating to, or characterized by intoxication ⟨they come from . . . broken homes, ∼ homes —P. B. Gilliam⟩ **c** : resulting from or as if from intoxication ⟨a ∼ brawl⟩ **4** : unsteady or lurching as if from alcoholic intoxication — **drunk·en·ly** *adv* — **drunk·en·ness** \-kən-nəs\ *n*

drunk tank *n* (1947) : a large detention cell for arrested drunks

dru·pa·ceous \drü-'pā-shəs\ *adj* (1822) **1** : of or relating to a drupe **2** : bearing drupes

drupe \'drüp\ *n* [NL *drupa*, fr. L, overripe olive, fr. Gk *dryppa* olive] (ca. 1753) : a one-seeded indehiscent fruit having a hard bony endocarp, a fleshy mesocarp, and a thin exocarp that is flexible (as in the cherry) or dry and almost leathery (as in the almond)

drupe·let \'drü-plət\ *n* (1880) : a small drupe; *specif* : one of the individual parts of an aggregate fruit (as the raspberry)

druth·ers \'drə-thərz\ *n pl* [*bruther*, alter. of *would rather*] (1875) *dial* : free choice : PREFERENCE — used esp. in the phrase *if one had one's druthers*

Druze *or* **Druse** \'drüz\ *n, pl* **Druze** *or* **Druzes** *or* **Druse** *or* **Druses**

often attrib [Ar *Durūz*, pl., fr. Muḥammed ibn-Isma'īl al-*Darazīy* †1019 Muslim religious leader] (1786) : a member of a religious sect originating among Muslims and centered in the mountains of Lebanon and Syria

¹**dry** \'drī\ *adj* **dri·er** *also* **dry·er** \'drī-(-ə)r\; **dri·est** *also* **dry·est** \'drī-əst\ [ME, fr. OE *drȳge*; akin to OHG *truckan* dry, OE *drēahnian* to drain] (bef. 12c) **1 a** : free or relatively free from a liquid and esp. water **b** : not being in or under water ⟨∼ land⟩ **c** : lacking precipitation or humidity ⟨∼ climate⟩ **2 a** : characterized by exhaustion of a supply of liquid ⟨a ∼ well⟩ **b** : devoid of running water ⟨a ∼ ravine⟩ **c** : devoid of natural moisture ⟨my throat was ∼⟩ **d** : no longer sticky or damp ⟨the paint is ∼⟩ **e** : not giving milk ⟨a ∼ cow⟩ **f** : lacking freshness : STALE **g** : ANHYDROUS **3 a** : marked by the absence or scantiness of secretions ⟨a ∼ cough⟩ **b** : not shedding or accompanied by tears ⟨a ∼ sob⟩ **4** *obs* : involving no bloodshed or drowning ⟨I would fain die a ∼ death —Shak.⟩ **5 a** : marked by the absence of alcoholic beverages ⟨a ∼ party⟩ **b** : prohibiting the manufacture or distribution of alcoholic beverages **6** : served or eaten without butter or margarine ⟨∼ toast⟩ **7 a** : lacking sweetness : SEC ⟨∼ champagne⟩ **b** : having all or most sugar fermented to alcohol ⟨a ∼ wine⟩ ⟨∼ beer⟩ **8 a** : solid as opposed to liquid ⟨∼ groceries⟩ **b** : reduced to powder or flakes : DEHYDRATED ⟨∼ milk⟩ **9** : functioning without lubrication ⟨a ∼ clutch⟩ **10** *of natural gas* : containing no recoverable hydrocarbon (as gasoline) ⟨a ∼ photocopying process⟩ **12 a** : not showing or communicating warmth, enthusiasm, or tender feeling : SEVERE ⟨a ∼ style of painting⟩ **b** : WEARISOME, UNINTERESTING ⟨∼ passages of description⟩ **c** : lacking embellishment : PLAIN ⟨the ∼ facts⟩ **13 a** : not yielding what is expected or desired : UNPRODUCTIVE **b** : having no personal bias or emotional concern ⟨the ∼ light of reason⟩ **c** : RESERVED, ALOOF **14** : marked by matter-of-fact, ironic, or terse manner of expression ⟨∼ wit⟩ **15** : lacking smooth sound qualities ⟨a ∼ rasping voice⟩ **16** : being a dry run ⟨a ∼ rehearsal⟩ — **dry·ish** \'drī-ish\ *adj* — **dry·ly** *adv* — **dry·ness** *n*

²**dry** *vb* **dried; dry·ing** *vt* (bef. 12c) : to make dry ∼ *vi* : to become dry — **dry·able** \'drī-ə-bəl\ *adj*

³**dry** *n, pl* **drys** (13c) **1** : the condition of being dry : DRYNESS **2** : something dry; *esp* : a dry place **3** : PROHIBITIONIST

dry·ad \'drī-əd, -‚ad\ *n* [L *dryad-, dryas*, fr. Gk, fr. *drys* tree — more at TREE] (14c) : WOOD NYMPH

dry·as·dust \'drī-əz-‚dəst\ *adj* (ca. 1872) : BORING — **dryasdust** *n*

dry cell *n* (1893) : a voltaic cell whose contents are not spillable — called also *dry battery*

dry–clean \'drī-‚klēn\ *vt* (1817) : to subject to dry cleaning ∼ *vi* : to undergo dry cleaning — **dry–clean·able** \-‚klē-nə-bəl\ *adj*

dry cleaner *n* (1897) : one whose business is dry cleaning

dry cleaning *n* (1897) **1** : the cleansing of fabrics with substantially nonaqueous organic solvents **2** : something that is dry-cleaned

dry–dock \'drī-‚däk\ *vt* (1884) : to place in a dry dock

dry dock *n* (ca. 1627) : a dock that can be kept dry for use during the construction or repairing of ships

dry·er *var of* DRIER

dry–eyed \'drī-‚īd\ *adj* (1667) **1** : not moved to tears or to empathy **2** : marked by the absence of sentimentalism or romanticism

dry farming *n* (1878) : farming on nonirrigated land with little rainfall that relies on moisture-conserving tillage and drought-resistant crops — **dry farm** *n* — **dry–farm** *vt* — **dry farmer** *n*

dry fly *n* (1846) : an artificial angling fly designed to float

Dry·gas \'drī-‚gas\ *trademark* — used for fuel-line antifreeze for motor vehicles

dry goods \'drī-‚gu̇dz\ *n pl* (1657) : textiles, ready-to-wear clothing, and notions as distinguished esp. from hardware and groceries

dry hole *n* (1883) : a well (as for gas or oil) that proves unproductive

dry ice *n* (1925) : solidified carbon dioxide

drying oil *n* (ca. 1865) : an oil (as linseed oil) that changes readily to a hard tough elastic substance when exposed in a thin film to air

dry·land \'drī-‚land\ *adj* (1893) : of, relating to, or being a relatively arid region ⟨a ∼ wheat state⟩; *also* : of, adapted to, practicing, or being agricultural methods (as dry farming) suited to such a region

dry·lot \'drī-‚lät\ *n* (1924) : an enclosure of limited size usu. bare of vegetation and used for fattening livestock

dry measure *n* (1688) : a series of units of capacity for dry commodities — see METRIC SYSTEM table, WEIGHT table

dry mop *n* (1933) : a long-handled mop for dusting floors

dry–nurse *vt* (1581) **1** : to act as dry nurse to **2** : to give unnecessary supervision to

dry nurse *n* (1598) : a nurse who takes care of but does not breast-feed another woman's baby

dryo·pith·e·cine \‚drī-ō-'pi-thə-‚sīn\ *n* [ultim. fr. Gk *drys* tree + *pithēkos* ape] (1948) : any of a subfamily (Dryopithecinae) of Miocene and Pliocene Old World anthropoid apes sometimes regarded as ancestors of both man and modern anthropoids — **dryopithecine** *adj*

dry out *vi* (1892) : to undergo an extended period of withdrawal from alcohol or drug use esp. at a special clinic

dry·point \'drī-‚pȯint\ *n* (1883) : an engraving made with a steel or jeweled point directly into the metal plate without the use of acid as in etching; *also* : a print made from such an engraving

dry–rot *vt* (1870) : to affect with dry rot ∼ *vi* : to become affected with dry rot

dry rot *n* (1795) **1 a** : a decay of seasoned timber caused by fungi that consume the cellulose of wood leaving a soft skeleton which is readily reduced to powder **b** : a fungal rot of plant tissue in which the affected areas are dry and often firmer than normal or more or less mummified **2** : a fungus causing dry rot **3** : decay from within caused esp. by resistance to new forces

dry run *n* (ca. 1941) **1** : a practice exercise : REHEARSAL, TRIAL **2** : a practice firing without ammunition

dry·salt·er \'drī-‚sȯl-tər\ *n* (1707) *Brit* : a dealer in crude dry chemicals and dyes — **dry·salt·ery** \-tə-rē\ *n, Brit*

dry–shod \'drī-‚shäd\ *adj* (15c) : having dry shoes or feet

dry sink *n* (1951) : a wooden cabinet with a tray top for holding a wash basin

dry·stone \'drī-‚stōn\ *adj* (ca. 1702) *chiefly Brit* : constructed of stone without the use of mortar as an adhesive ⟨a ∼ wall⟩

dry suit *n* (1955) : a close-fitting air-insulated waterproof suit for divers

dry up *vt* (14c) : to cut off the supply of ∼ *vi* **1** : to disappear as if by evaporation, draining, or cutting off of a source of supply **2** : to wither or die through gradual loss of vitality **3** : to stop talking

dry·wall \'drī-,wȯl\ *n* (1952) : PLASTERBOARD

dry wash *n* (1872) *West* : WASH 1d

dry well *n* (ca. 1942) : a hole in the ground filled with gravel or rubble to receive drainage water and allow it to percolate away

d.t.'s \,dē-'tēz\ *n pl, often cap D&T* (1858) : DELIRIUM TREMENS

¹**du·al** \'dü(-ə)l *also* 'dyü-əl\ *adj* [L *dualis*, fr. *duo* two — more at TWO] (1607) **1** *of grammatical number* : denoting reference to two **2 a** : consisting of two parts or elements or having two like parts : DOUBLE **b** : having a double character or nature — **du·al·ly** \-ə(l)-lē\ *adv*

²**dual** *n* (1650) **1** : the dual number of a language **2** : a linguistic form in the dual

dual carriageway *n* (1933) *chiefly Brit* : a divided highway

dual citizenship *n* (ca. 1924) : the status of an individual who is a citizen of two or more nations

du·al·ism \'dü-ə-,li-zəm *also* 'dyü-\ *n* (1794) **1** : a theory that considers reality to consist of two irreducible elements or modes **2** : the quality or state of being dual or of having a dual nature **3 a** : a doctrine that the universe is under the dominion of two opposing principles one of which is good and the other evil **b** : a view of human beings as constituted of two irreducible elements (as matter and spirit) — **du·al·ist** \-list\ *n* — **du·al·is·tic** \,dü-ə-'lis-tik, ,dyü-\ *adj* — **du·al·is·ti·cal·ly** \-ti-k(ə-)lē\ *adv*

du·al·i·ty \dü-'a-lə-tē *also* dyü-\ *n, pl* **-ties** (15c) : DUALISM 2; *also* : DICHOTOMY

du·al·ize \'dü-ə-,līz *also* 'dyü-\ *vt* **-ized; -iz·ing** (1838) : to make dual

dual–purpose *adj* (1904) : having breed characteristics that serve two purposes ⟨∼ cattle that supply milk and meat⟩

¹**dub** \'dəb\ *vt* **dubbed; dub·bing** [ME *dubben*, fr. OE *dubbian;* akin to ON *dubba* to dub, OHG *tubili* plug] (bef. 12c) **1 a** : to confer knighthood on **b** : to call by a distinctive title, epithet, or nickname **2** : to trim or remove the comb and wattles of **3 a** : to hit (a golf ball) poorly **b** : to execute poorly — **dub·ber** *n*

²**dub** *n* (1887) : one who is inept or clumsy

³**dub** *n* [ME (Sc dial.) *dubbe*] (15c) *chiefly Scot* : POOL, PUDDLE

⁴**dub** *vt* **dubbed; dub·bing** [by shortening & alter. fr. *double*] (1930) **1** : to add (sound effects or new dialogue) to a film or to a radio or television production — usu. used with *in* **2** : to provide (a motion-picture film) with a new sound track and esp. dialogue in a different language **3** : to make a new recording of (sound or videotape already recorded); *also* : to mix (recorded sound or videotape from different sources) into a single recording — **dubber** *n*

⁵**dub** *n* (1974) : Jamaican pop music in which audio effects and spoken or chanted words are imposed on an instrumental reggae background

dub·bin \'də-bən\ *also* **dub·bing** \-bən, -biŋ\ *n* [*dubbing*, gerund of *dub* (to dress leather)] (1781) : a dressing of oil and tallow for leather

du·bi·ety \dü-'bī-ət-ē *also* dyü-\ *n, pl* **-eties** [LL *dubietas*, fr. L *dubius*] (1750) **1** : a usu. hesitant uncertainty or doubt that tends to cause vacillation **2** : a matter of doubt *syn* see UNCERTAINTY

du·bi·ous \'dü-bē-əs *also* dyü-\ *adj* [L *dubius*, fr. *dubare* to vacillate; akin to L *duo* two — more at TWO] (1548) **1** : giving rise to uncertainty: as **a** : of doubtful promise or outcome ⟨felt that our plan was a little ∼⟩ **b** : questionable or suspect as to true nature or quality ⟨the practice is of ∼ legality⟩ ⟨the ∼ honor of being the world's biggest polluter⟩ **2** : unsettled in opinion : DOUBTFUL ⟨I was ∼ about the plan⟩ *syn* see DOUBTFUL — **du·bi·ous·ly** *adv* — **du·bi·ous·ness** *n*

du·bi·ta·ble \'dü-bə-tə-bəl *also* 'dyü-\ *adj* [L *dubitabilis*, fr. *dubitare* to doubt — more at DOUBT] (ca. 1616) : open to doubt or question

du·bi·ta·tion \,d(y)ü-bə-'tā-shən\ *n* (15c) *archaic* : DOUBT

du·cal \'dü-kəl *also* 'dyü-\ *adj* [ME, fr. MF, fr. LL *ducalis* of a leader, fr. L *duc-, dux* leader — more at DUKE] (15c) : of or relating to a duke or dukedom — **du·cal·ly** \-kə-lē\ *adv*

duc·at \'də-kət\ *n* [ME, fr. MF, fr. OIt *ducato* coin with the doge's portrait on it, fr. *duca* doge, fr. LGk *douk-, doux* leader, fr. L *duc-, dux*] (14c) **1** : a usu. gold coin formerly used in various European countries **2** : TICKET 2

du·ce \'dü-(,)chā\ *n* [It (*Il*) *Duce*, lit., the leader, title of Benito Mussolini, fr. L *duc-, dux*] (1923) : LEADER — used esp. for the leader of the Italian Fascist party

Du·chenne \dü-'shen, də-\ *also* **Du·chenne's** \-'shenz\ *adj* [Guillaume Armand Duchenne †1875 Fr. neurologist] (ca. 1882) : relating to or being a severe form of muscular dystrophy of males that affects the muscles of the pelvic and shoulder girdles and the pectoral muscles first and is inherited as a sex-linked recessive trait

duch·ess \'də-chəs\ *n* [ME *duchesse*, fr. MF, fr. *duc* duke] (14c) **1** : the wife or widow of a duke **2 a** : a woman who holds the rank of duke in her own right

duchy \'də-chē\ *n, pl* **duch·ies** [ME *duche*, fr. MF *duché*, fr. *duc*] (14c) **1** : the territory of a duke or duchess : DUKEDOM **2** : special domain

¹**duck** \'dək\ *n, pl* **ducks** *often attrib* [ME *duk, doke*, fr. OE *dūce*] (bef. 12c) **1** *or pl* **duck a** : any of various swimming birds (family Anatidae, the duck family) in which the neck and legs are short, the body more or less depressed, the bill often broad and flat, and the sexes almost always different from each other in plumage **b** : the flesh of any of these birds used as food : a female duck — compare DRAKE **3** *chiefly Brit* : DARLING — often used in pl. but sing. in constr. **4** : PERSON, CREATURE

²**duck** *vb* [ME *douken;* akin to OHG *tūhhan* to dive, OE *dūce* duck] *vt* (14c) **1** : to thrust under water **2**

duck 1a (male): *1* bean, *2* bill, *3* nostril, *4* head, *5* eye, *6* auricular region, *7* neck, *8* cape, *9* shoulder, *10* wing coverts, *12* saddle, *13* secondaries, *14* primaries, *15* rump, *16* drake feathers, *17* tail, *18* tail coverts, *19* down, *20* shank, *21* web, *22* breast, *23* wing front, *24* wing bow

: to lower (as the head) quickly : BOW **3** : AVOID, EVADE ⟨∼ the issue⟩ ∼ *vi* **1 a** : to plunge under the surface of water **b** : to descend suddenly : DIP **2 a** : to lower the head or body suddenly : DODGE **b** : BOW, BOB **3** : to move quickly **b** : to evade a duty, question, or responsibility — **duck·er** *n*

³**duck** *n* (1554) : an instance of ducking

⁴**duck** *n* [D *doek* cloth; akin to OHG *tuoh* cloth] (1640) **1** : a durable closely woven usu. cotton fabric **2** *pl* : light clothes and esp. trousers made of duck

duck–bill \'dək-,bil\ *n* (1840) **1** : PLATYPUS **2** : HADROSAUR

duck–billed dinosaur *n* (ca. 1928) : HADROSAUR

duck–billed platypus *also* **duckbill platypus** *n* (1799) : PLATYPUS

duck–board \-,bȯrd, -,bȯrd\ *n* (1917) : a boardwalk or slatted flooring laid on a wet, muddy, or cold surface — usu. used in pl.

duck call *n* (1872) : a device for imitating the calls of ducks

duck hook *n* (1973) : a pronounced and unintended hook in golf

ducking stool *n* (1597) : a seat attached to a plank and formerly used to plunge culprits tied to it into water

duck·ling \'dək-liŋ, 'də-klin\ *n* (15c) : a young duck

duck·pin \-,pin\ *n* (ca. 1911) **1** : a small bowling pin shorter than a tenpin but proportionately wider at mid-diameter **2** *pl but sing in constr* : a bowling game using duckpins

ducks and drakes *or* **duck and drake** *n* (1583) : the pastime of skimming flat stones or shells along the surface of calm water — **play ducks and drakes with** *or* **make ducks and drakes of** : to use recklessly : SQUANDER ⟨played ducks and drakes with his money⟩

duck soup *n* (1912) : something easy to do

duck·tail \'dək-,tāl\ *n* [fr. its resemblance to the tail of a duck] (1948) : a hairstyle in which the hair on each side is slicked back to meet in a ridge at the back of the head

duck·walk \'dək-,wȯk\ *vi* (1950) : to walk while in a crouch or full squatting position

duck·weed \'dək-,wēd\ *n* (15c) : a small floating aquatic monocotyledonous plant (family Lemnaceae, the duckweed family)

ducky \'də-kē\ *adj* **duck·i·er; -est** (1897) **1** : DARLING, CUTE ⟨a ∼ little tearoom⟩ **2** : SATISFACTORY, FINE ⟨everything is just ∼⟩

ducktail

¹**duct** \'dəkt\ *n* [NL *ductus*, fr. ML, aqueduct, fr. L, act of leading, fr. *ducere* to lead — more at TOW] (1667) **1** : a bodily tube or vessel esp. when carrying the secretion of a gland **2 a** : a pipe, tube, or channel that conveys a substance **b** : a pipe or tubular runway for carrying an electric power line, telephone cables, or other conductors **3 a** : a continuous tube formed in plant tissue by a row of elongated cells that have lost their intervening end walls **b** : an elongated cavity (as a resin canal of a conifer) formed by disintegration or separation of cells **4** : a layer (as in the atmosphere or the ocean) which occurs under usu. abnormal conditions and in which radio or sound waves are confined to a restricted path — **duc·tal** \'dək-t²l\ *adj* — **duct·less** \'dək(t)-ləs\ *adj*

²**duct** *vt* (1936) **1** : to enclose in a duct **2** : to convey (as a gas) through a duct; *also* : to propagate (as radio waves) through a duct

duc·tile \'dək-t²l, -,til\ *adj* [ME & L; MF, fr. L *ductilis*, fr. *ducere*] (14c) **1** : capable of being drawn out or hammered thin ⟨∼ iron⟩ **2** : easily led or influenced **3** : capable of being fashioned into a new form *syn* see PLASTIC — **duc·til·i·ty** \,dək-'ti-lə-tē\ *n*

duct·ing \'dək-tiŋ\ *n* (1945) : a system of ducts; *also* : the material composing a duct

ductless gland *n* (ca. 1852) : ENDOCRINE GLAND

duct tape \'dək(t)-\ *n* (1970) : a wide silvery cloth adhesive tape designed for sealing joints in heating or air-conditioning ducts

duct·ule \'dək-(,)chül\ *n* (1883) : a small duct

duc·tus ar·te·ri·o·sus \'dək-təs-är-,tir-ē-'ō-səs\ *n* [NL, lit., arterial duct] (1811) : a short broad vessel in the fetus that connects the pulmonary artery with the aorta and conducts most of the blood directly from the right ventricle to the aorta bypassing the lungs

duct·work \'dək(t)-,wərk\ *n* (1934) : DUCTING

¹**dud** \'dəd\ *n* [ME *dudde*] (1567) **1** *pl* **a** : CLOTHING **b** : personal belongings **2 a** : one that is ineffectual; *also* : FAILURE ⟨a box-office ∼⟩ **b** : MISFIT **3** : a bomb or missile that fails to explode

²**dud** *adj* (1903) : of little or no worth : VALUELESS ⟨∼ checks⟩

dud–die *or* **dud·dy** \'də-dē\ *adj* (1718) *Scot* : RAGGED, TATTERED

¹**dude** \'düd *also* 'dyüd\ *n* [origin unknown] (1883) **1** : a man extremely fastidious in dress and manner : DANDY **2** : a city dweller unfamiliar with life on the range; *esp* : an Easterner in the West **3** : FELLOW, GUY — **dud·ish** \'dü-dish\ *adj* — **dud·ish·ly** *adv*

²**dude** *vt* **dud·ed; dud·ing** (1899) : DRESS UP — usu. used with *up*

du·deen \dü-'dēn\ *n* [Ir *dúidín*, dim. of *dúd* pipe] (1841) : a short tobacco pipe made of clay

dude ranch *n* (1921) : a vacation resort offering activities (as horseback riding) typical of western ranches

¹**dud·geon** \'də-jən\ *n* [ME *dogeon*, fr. AF *digeon*] (15c) **1** *obs* : a wood used esp. for dagger hilts **2** *archaic* : a dagger with a handle of dudgeon **b** *obs* : a haft made of dudgeon

²**dudgeon** *n* [origin unknown] (1573) : a fit or state of indignation — often used in the phrase *in high dudgeon syn* see OFFENSE

¹**due** \'dü, 'dyü\ *adj* [ME, fr. MF *deu*, pp. of *devoir* to owe, fr. L *debēre* — more at DEBT] (14c) **1** : owed or owing as a debt **2** : owed or owing as a natural or moral right ⟨everyone's right to dissent . . . is ∼ the full protection of the Constitution —Nat Hentoff⟩ **b** : according to accepted notions or procedures : APPROPRIATE **3 a** : satisfying or capable of satisfying a need, obligation, or duty : ADEQUATE **b** : REGULAR, LAWFUL ⟨∼ proof of loss⟩ **4** : capable of being attributed : ASCRIBABLE — used with *to* ⟨this advance is partly ∼ to a few men of genius —A. N. Whitehead⟩ **5** : having reached the date at which

\ə\ abut \'\ kitten, F table \ər\ further \a\ ash \ā\ ace \ä\ mop, mar \aù\ out \ch\ chin \e\ bet \ē\ easy \g\ go \i\ hit \ī\ ice \j\ job \ŋ\ sing \ō\ go \ȯ\ law \ȯi\ boy \th\ thin \th\ the \ü\ loot \ù\ foot \y\ yet \zh\ vision \ȧ, k̄, ⁿ, œ, œ̄, ᵫ, ᵫ̄, �\ *see* Guide to Pronunciation payment is required : PAYABLE **6** : required or expected in the prescribed, normal, or logical course of events : SCHEDULED; *also* : expected to give birth — **due·ness** *n*

²due *n* (15c) : something due or owed: as **a** : something that rightfully belongs to one **b** : a payment or obligation required by law or custom : DEBT **c** *pl* : FEES, CHARGES

³due *adv* (1582) **1** : DIRECTLY, EXACTLY ⟨∼ north⟩ **2** *obs* : DULY

due diligence *n* (1903) : the care that a reasonable person exercises under the circumstances to avoid harm to other persons or their property

¹du·el \'dü-əl *also* 'dyü-\ *n* [ME, fr. ML *duellum*, fr. OL, war] (15c) **1** : a combat between two persons; *specif* : a formal combat with weapons fought between two persons in the presence of witnesses **2** : a conflict between antagonistic persons, ideas, or forces; *also* : a hard-fought contest between two opponents

²duel *vb* **du·eled** *or* **du·elled; du·el·ing** *or* **du·el·ling** *vi* (ca. 1645) : to fight a duel ∼ *vt* : to encounter (an opponent) in a duel — **du·el·er** *or* **du·el·ler** *n* — **du·el·ist** *or* **du·el·list** \'dü-ə-list\ *n*

du·el·lo \d(y)ü-'e-(,)lō\ *n, pl* **-los** [It, fr. ML *duellum*] (1588) **1** : the rules or practice of dueling **2** : DUEL

du·en·de \dü-'en-(,)dā\ *n* [Sp dial., charm, fr. Sp, ghost, goblin, prob. fr. *duen de casa*, fr. *dueño de casa* owner of a house] (1964) : the power to attract through personal magnetism and charm

du·en·na \dü-'e-nə, dyü-\ *n* [Sp *dueña*, fr. L *domina* mistress — more at DAME] (1623) **1** : an elderly woman serving as governess and companion to the younger ladies in a Spanish or a Portuguese family **2** : CHAPERON — **du·en·na·ship** \-,ship\ *n*

due process *n* (1791) **1** : a course of formal proceedings (as legal proceedings) carried out regularly and in accordance with established rules and principles — called also *procedural due process* **2** : a judicial requirement that enacted laws may not contain provisions that result in the unfair, arbitrary, or unreasonable treatment of an individual — called also *substantive due process*

¹du·et \dü-'et *also* dyü-\ *n* [It *duetto*, dim. of *duo*] (ca. 1740) : a composition for two performers

²duet *vi* **du·et·ted; du·et·ting** (1822) : to perform a duet

due to *prep* (1897) : as a result of : BECAUSE OF ⟨*due to* the complaints of uptight parents . . . he lost his job —Herbert Gold⟩
 usage The objection to *due to* as a preposition is only a continuation of disagreements that began in the 18th century over the proper uses of *owing* and *due*. *Due to* is as grammatically sound as *owing to*, which is frequently recommended in its place. It has been and is used by reputable writers and has been recognized as standard for decades. There is no solid reason to avoid *due to*.

¹duff \'dəf\ *n* [E dial., alter. of *dough*] (1816) **1** : a boiled or steamed pudding often containing dried fruit **2** : the partly decayed organic matter on the forest floor **3** : fine coal : SLACK

²duff *n* [origin unknown] (ca. 1888) : BUTTOCKS ⟨get off your ∼⟩

³duff *adj* [*duff*, n., something worthless, fr. ¹*duff*] (ca. 1889) *Brit* : INFERIOR, WORTHLESS

duf·fel *or* **duf·fle** \'də-fəl\ *n* [D *duffel*, fr. *Duffel*, Belgium] (1677) **1** : a coarse heavy woolen material with a thick nap **2** : transportable personal belongings, equipment, and supplies **3** : DUFFEL BAG **4** : DUFFLE COAT

duffel bag *n* (1917) : a large cylindrical fabric bag for personal belongings

duf·fer \'də-fər\ *n* [perh. fr. *duff*, n., something worthless] (1756) **1 a** : a peddler esp. of cheap flashy articles **b** : something counterfeit or worthless **2** : an incompetent, ineffectual, or clumsy person; *esp* : a mediocre golfer **3** *Austral* : a cattle rustler

duffle coat \'də-fəl-\ *or* **duffel coat** *n* (1684) : a heavy usu. woolen medium-length coat with toggle fasteners and a hood

¹dug *past and past part of* DIG

²dug \'dəg\ *n* [perh. of Scand origin; akin to OSw *dæggia* to suckle; akin to OE *delu* nipple — more at FEMININE] (1530) : UDDER; *also* : TEAT — usu. used of a suckling animal; usu. considered vulgar when used of a woman

du·gong \'dü-,gäŋ, -,góŋ\ *n* [NL, genus name, modif. of Malay *duyong dugong*] (1800) : an aquatic herbivorous mammal of a monotypic genus (*Dugong*) that has a bilobed tail and in the male upper incisors altered into short tusks, is related to the manatee, and inhabits warm coastal regions — called also *sea cow*

dug·out \'dəg-,aůt\ *n* (1819) **1** : a boat made by hollowing out a large log **2 a** : a shelter dug in a hillside; *also* : a shelter dug in the ground and roofed with sod **b** : an area in the side of a trench for quarters, storage, or protection **3** : either of two low shelters on either side of and facing a baseball diamond that contain the players' benches

dui·ker \'dī-kər\ *n* [Afrik, lit., diver, fr. *duik* to dive, fr. MD *dūken*; akin to OHG *tūhhan* to dive — more at DUCK] (1777) : any of several small African antelopes comprising two genera (*Cephalophus* and *Sylvicapra*)

duit *var of* DOIT

du jour \dü-'zhər, də-, -'zhůr, -'zhür\ *adj* [F, lit., of the day] (1969) **1** : made for a particular day — used of an item not specified on the regular menu ⟨soup *du jour*⟩ **2** : popular, fashionable, or prominent at a particular time ⟨the buzzword *du jour*⟩

¹duke \'dük *also* 'dyük\ *n* [ME, fr. OF *duc*, fr. L *duc-, dux*, fr. *ducere* to lead — more at TOW] (12c) **1** : a sovereign male ruler of a continental European duchy **2** : a nobleman of the highest hereditary rank; *esp* : a member of the highest grade of the British peerage **3** [prob. fr. *dukes of York*, rhyming slang for *fork* (hand, fist)] *slang* : FIST, HAND — usu. used in pl. — **duke·dom** \-dəm\ *n*

²duke *vi* **duked; duk·ing** (ca. 1947) : FIGHT — **duke it out** : to engage in a fight and esp. a fistfight

Du·kho·bor *var of* DOUKHOBOR

dul·cet \'dəl-sət\ *adj* [ME *doucet*, fr. MF, fr. OF *douz* sweet, fr. L *dulcis*; perh. akin to Gk *glykys* sweet] (14c) **1** : sweet to the taste **2** : pleasing to the ear **3** : generally pleasing or agreeable — **dul·cet·ly** *adv*

dul·ci·fy \'dəl-sə-,fī\ *vt* **-fied; -fy·ing** [LL *dulcificare*, fr. L *dulcis*] (1599) **1** : to make sweet **2** : to make agreeable : MOLLIFY

dul·ci·mer \'dəl-sə-mər\ *n* [ME *dowcemere*, fr. MF *doulcemer*, fr. OIt *dolcimelo*, fr. *dolce* sweet, fr. L *dulcis*] (15c) **1** : a stringed instrument of trapezoidal shape played with light hammers held in the hands **2** *or* **dul·ci·more** \-,mōr, -,mór\ : an American folk instrument with three

or four strings stretched over an elongate fretted sound box that is held on the lap and played by plucking or strumming

dul·ci·nea \,dəl-sə-'nē-ə, -'si-nē-ə\ *n* [Sp, fr. *Dulcinea* del Toboso, beloved of Don Quixote] (1748) : MISTRESS, SWEETHEART

¹dull \'dəl\ *adj* [ME *dul*; akin to OE *dol* foolish, OIr *dall* blind] (13c) **1** : mentally slow : STUPID **2 a** : slow in perception or sensibility : INSENSIBLE **b** : lacking zest or vivacity : LISTLESS **3** : slow in action : SLUGGISH **4 a** : lacking in force, intensity, or sharpness **b** : not resonant or ringing ⟨a ∼ booming sound⟩ **5** : lacking sharpness of edge or point **6** : lacking brilliance or luster **7** *of a color* : low in saturation and low in lightness **8** : CLOUDY **9** : TEDIOUS, UNINTERESTING — **dull·ness** *or* **dul·ness** \'dəl-nəs\ *n* — **dul·ly** \'də(l)-lē\ *adv*
 syn DULL, BLUNT, OBTUSE mean not sharp, keen, or acute. DULL suggests a lack or loss of keenness, zest, or pungency ⟨a *dull* pain⟩ ⟨a *dull* mind⟩. BLUNT suggests an inherent lack of sharpness or quickness of feeling or perception ⟨a person of *blunt* sensibility⟩. OBTUSE implies such bluntness as makes one insensitive in perception or imagination ⟨too *obtuse* to realize the remark was offensive⟩. **syn** see in addition STUPID

²dull *vt* (13c) : to make dull ∼ *vi* : to become dull

dull·ard \'də-lərd\ *n* (15c) : a stupid or unimaginative person

dull·ish \'də-lish\ *adj* (14c) : somewhat dull — **dull·ish·ly** *adv*

dulls·ville \'dəlz-,vil\ *n* (ca. 1960) : something or some place that is dull or boring; *also* : BOREDOM

dulse \'dəls\ *n* [modif. of ScGael *duileasg*; akin to W *delysg* dulse] (ca. 1698) : any of several coarse red seaweeds (esp. *Palmaria palmata* syn. *Rhodymenia palmata*) found esp. in northern latitudes and used as a food condiment

du·ly \'dü-lē *also* 'dyü-\ *adv* (14c) : in a due manner or time : PROPERLY

du·ma \'dü-mə, -,(,)mä\ *n* [Russ, fr. ORuss, council, thought, prob. of Gmc origin; akin to OE *dōm* judgment — more at DOOM] (ca. 1870) : a representative council in Russia; *esp, often cap* : the principal legislative assembly in czarist Russia

¹dumb \'dəm\ *adj* [ME, fr. OE; akin to OHG *tumb* mute] (bef. 12c) **1** : lacking the power of speech ⟨deaf and ∼ from birth⟩ ⟨∼ animals⟩ **2** : temporarily unable to speak (as from shock or astonishment) ⟨struck ∼ with fear⟩ **3** : not expressed in uttered words ⟨∼ grief⟩ **4** : SILENT; *also* : TACITURN **5** : lacking some usual attribute or accompaniment; *esp* : having no means of self-propulsion ⟨∼ barge⟩ **6 a** : markedly lacking in intelligence : STUPID **b** : showing a lack of intelligence **c** : having little or no meaning — sometimes used in the phrase *dumb luck* **7** : not having the capability to process data ⟨a ∼ terminal⟩ — compare INTELLIGENT 3a **syn** see STUPID — **dumb·ly** \'dəm-lē\ *adv* — **dumb·ness** *n*
 usage There is evidence that, when applied to persons who cannot speak, *dumb* has come to be considered offensive.

²dumb *vt* (1608) : to make silent : DEADEN ⟨would lie around, ∼ed by the drugs —Norman Mailer⟩

dumb·bell \'dəm-,bel\ *n* (1785) **1** : a short bar with weights at each end that is used usu. in pairs for exercise **2** : one that is dull and stupid

dumb·cane \'dəm-,kān\ *n* [fr. the fact that chewing it causes the tongue and throat to swell] (1696) : DIEFFENBACHIA

dumb down *vt* (1980) : to lower the level of difficulty and the intellectual content of (as a textbook)

dumb·found *or* **dum·found** \,dəm-'fai̇nd, 'dəm-,\ *vt* [*dumb* + *-found* (as in *confound*)] (1653) : to confound briefly and usu. with astonishment **syn** see PUZZLE

dumb·foun·der \-'faün-dər\ *vt* (1710) *Brit* : DUMBFOUND

dumb·head \'dəm-,hed\ *n* [prob. trans. of G *dummkopf*] (1887) *slang* : a stupid person : BLOCKHEAD

dumb show *n* (1561) **1** : a part of a play presented in pantomime **2** : signs and gestures without words : PANTOMIME

dumb·struck \'dəm-,strək\ *adj* (1887) : made silent by astonishment

dumb·wait·er \'dəm-,wā-tər, ,dəm-'\ *n* (1749) **1** : a portable serving table or stand **2** : a small elevator used for conveying food and dishes from one story of a building to another

dum-dum \'dəm-,dəm\ *n* [*Dum Dum*, arsenal near Calcutta, India] (ca. 1889) : a bullet (as one with a hollow point) that expands more than usual upon hitting an object

dum–dum *n* [redupl. of ¹*dumb*] (1928) : a stupid person : DUMMY

dum·ka \'dům-kə\ *n, pl* **dum·ky** \-kē\ [Czech, elegy, fr. Ukrainian, dim. of *duma* narrative folk poem, fr. ORuss] (1895) : a musical composition containing alternating sad and gay passages

dumm·kopf \'dům-,köpf\ *n* [G, fr. *dumm* stupid + *Kopf* head] (1809) : BLOCKHEAD

¹dum·my \'də-mē\ *n, pl* **dummies** [¹*dumb* + ⁴*-y*] (1598) **1 a** : one who is incapable of speaking **b** : one who is habitually silent **c** : one who is stupid **2 a** : the exposed hand in bridge played by the declarer in addition to his own hand **b** : a bridge player whose hand is a dummy **3** : an imitation, copy, or likeness of something used as a substitute: as **a** : MANNEQUIN **b** : a stuffed figure or cylindrical bag used by football players for tackling and blocking practice **c** : a puppet usu. having movable features (as mouth and arms) manipulated by a ventriloquist **d** *chiefly Brit* : PACIFIER 2 **4** : one seeming to act independently but in reality controlled by another **5 a** : a mock-up of a proposed publication (as a book or magazine) **b** : a set of pages (as for a newspaper or magazine) with the position of text and artwork indicated for the printer

²dummy *adj* (1846) **1 a** : having the appearance of being real : ARTIFICIAL ⟨∼ foods in the display case⟩ **b** : existing in name only : FICTITIOUS ⟨∼ corporations⟩ **2** : apparently acting for oneself while really acting for or at the direction of another ⟨a ∼ director⟩

³dummy *vt* **dum·mied; dum·my·ing** (1925) : to make a dummy of (as a publication) — often used with *up* ⟨*dummied* up the front page⟩

dummy up *vi* (1926) : to say nothing : CLAM UP

dummy variable *n* (1957) : an arbitrary mathematical symbol or variable that can be replaced by another without affecting the value of the expression in which it occurs

du·mor·ti·er·ite \dü-'mȯr-tē-ə-,rīt *also* dyü-\ *n* [F *dumortiérite*, fr. Eugène *Dumortier* †1876 Fr. paleontologist] (1881) : a bright blue or greenish blue mineral consisting of a silicate of aluminum and used esp. for jewelry

¹dump \'dəmp\ *vb* [perh. fr. MD *dompen* to immerse, topple; akin to

ON *dumpa* to thump, fall suddenly] *vt* (14c) **1 a** : to let fall in or as if in a heap or mass **b** : to get rid of unceremoniously or irresponsibly **c** : JETTISON ⟨an airplane ∼*ing* gasoline⟩ **2** *slang* : to knock down : BEAT ⟨the man rushed out and ∼*ed* him —John Corry⟩ **3** : to sell in quantity at a very low price; *specif* : to sell abroad at less than the market price at home **4** : to copy (data in a computer's internal storage) to an external storage or output device **5** : to throw (as a pass) short and softly — often used with *off* ∼ *vi* **1** : to fall abruptly : PLUNGE **2** : to dump refuse — **dump·er** *n* — **dump on** : to treat disrespectfully; *esp* : BELITTLE, BAD-MOUTH

²dump *n* (1784) **1 a** : an accumulation of refuse and discarded materials **b** : a place where such materials are dumped **2 a** : a quantity of reserve materials accumulated at one place **b** : a place where such materials are stored ⟨ammunition ∼⟩ **3** : a disorderly, slovenly, or objectionable place **4** : an instance of dumping data stored in a computer **5** : an act of defecation — usu. used with *take*; often considered vulgar

dump·ing *n* (1857) : the act of one that dumps; *esp* : the selling of goods in quantity at below market price

dumping ground *n* (1857) : a place to which unwanted people or things are sent

dump·ish \'dəm-pish\ *adj* [*dumps*] (1519) : SAD, MELANCHOLY

dump·ling \'dəm-pliŋ\ *n* [perh. alter. of *lump*] (ca. 1600) **1 a** : a small mass of leavened dough cooked by boiling or steaming **b** : a usu. baked dessert of fruit wrapped in dough **2** : something soft and rounded like a dumpling; *esp* : a short fat person or animal

dumps \'dəm(p)s\ *n pl* [prob. fr. D *domp* haze, fr. MD *damp* — more at DAMP] (1529) : a gloomy state of mind : DESPONDENCY ⟨in the ∼⟩

Dump·ster \'dəm(p)-stər\ *trademark* — used for a large trash receptacle

dump truck *n* (1930) : an automotive truck for the transportation of bulk material that has a body which tilts to dump its contents

dumpy \'dəm-pē\ *adj* **dump·i·er; -est** [E dial. *dump* (lump)] (1750) **1** : being short and thick in build : SQUAT **2** : SHABBY, DINGY — **dump·i·ly** \-pə-lē\ *adv* — **dump·i·ness** \-pē-nəs\ *n*

dumpy level *n* (1838) : a surveyor's level with a short telescope rigidly fixed and rotating only in a horizontal plane

¹dun \'dən\ *adj* [ME, fr. OE *dunn* — more at DUSK] (bef. 12c) **1 a** : having the color dun ⟨*a* ∼ *horse*⟩ : having a grayish yellow coat with black mane and tail **2** : marked by dullness and drabness — **dun·ness** \'dən-nəs\ *n*

²dun *n* (14c) **1** : a dun horse **2** : a variable color averaging a nearly neutral slightly brownish dark gray **3** : a subadult mayfly; *also* : an artificial fly tied to imitate such an insect

³dun *vt* **dunned; dun·ning** [origin unknown] (ca. 1626) **1** : to make persistent demands upon for payment **2** : PLAGUE, PESTER

⁴dun *n* (1628) **1** : one who duns **2** : an urgent request; *esp* : a demand for payment

Dun·can Phyfe \,dən-kən-'fīf\ *adj* (1926) : of, relating to, or constituting furniture designed and built by or in the style of Duncan Phyfe

dunce \'dən(t)s\ *n* [John *Duns* Scotus, whose once accepted writings were ridiculed in the 16th cent.] (1587) : one who is slow-witted or stupid

dunce cap *n* (1840) : a conical cap formerly used as a punishment for slow learners at school — called also *dunce's cap*

dun·der·head \'dən-dər-,hed\ *n* [perh. fr. D *donder* thunder + E *head*; akin to OHG *thonar* thunder — more at THUNDER] (ca. 1625) : DUNCE, BLOCKHEAD — **dun·der·head·ed** \,dən-dər-'he-dəd\ *adj*

dun·drea·ries \,dən-'drir-ēz\ *n pl, often cap* [Lord *Dundreary*, character in the play *Our American Cousin* (1858), by Tom Taylor] (ca. 1922) : long flowing sideburns

dune \'dün *also* 'dyün\ *n* [F, fr. OF, fr. MD; akin to OE *dūn* down — more at DOWN] (1790) : a hill or ridge of sand piled up by the wind — **dune·like** \-,līk\ *adj*

dune buggy *n* (1956) : an off-road motor vehicle with oversize tires for use esp. on sand

dune·land \'dün-,land\ *n* (1922) : an area having many dunes

¹dung \'dəŋ\ *n* [ME, fr. OE; akin to ON *dyngja* manure pile] (bef. 12c) **1** : the excrement of an animal : MANURE **2** : something repulsive — **dungy** \'dəŋ-ē\ *adj*

²dung *vt* (bef. 12c) : to fertilize or dress with manure ∼ *vi* : DEFECATE

dun·ga·ree \,dəŋ-gə-'rē, 'dəŋ-gə-\ *n* [Hindi *dūgrī*] (1673) **1** : a heavy coarse durable cotton twill woven from colored yarns; *specif* : blue denim **2** : clothes made usu. of blue denim

dung beetle *n* (ca. 1634) : a beetle (as a tumblebug) that rolls balls of dung in which to lay eggs and on which the larvae feed

Dunge·ness crab \,dən-jə-,nes-\ *n* [*Dungeness*, village on the Strait of Juan de Fuca, Washington] (1925) : a large edible crab (*Cancer magister*) of the Pacific coast of No. America from Alaska to California

dun·geon \'dən-jən\ *n* [ME *donjon*, fr. MF, fr. (assumed) VL *domnion-, domnio* keep, mastery, fr. L *dominus* lord — more at DOMINATE] (14c) **1** : DONJON **2** : a dark usu. underground prison or vault

dung·hill \'dəŋ-,hil\ *n* (14c) **1** : a heap of dung **2** : something (as a situation or condition) that is repulsive or degraded

du·nite \'dü-,nīt, 'də-\ *n* [Mt. *Dun*, New Zealand] (ca. 1868) : a granitoid igneous rock consisting chiefly of olivine — **du·nit·ic** \dü-'ni-tik, ,də-\ *adj*

¹dunk \'dəŋk\ *vb* [PaG *dunke*, fr. MHG *dunken*, fr. OHG *dunkōn* — more at TINGE] *vt* (1919) **1** : to dip (as a piece of bread) into a beverage while eating **2** : to dip or submerge temporarily in liquid **3** : to throw (a basketball) into the basket from above the rim ∼ *vi* **1** : to submerge oneself in water **2** : to make a dunk shot in basketball

²dunk *n* (ca. 1944) : the act or action of dunking; *esp* : DUNK SHOT

Dun·ker \'dəŋ-kər\ *or* **Dun·kard** \-kərd\ *n* [PaG *Dunker*, fr. *dunke*] (1744) : a member of the Church of the Brethren or any of several other orig. German Baptist denominations practicing trine immersion and love feasts and refusing to take oaths or to perform military service

Dun·kirk \'dən-,kərk, ,dən-'\ *n* [*Dunkirk* or *Dunkerque*, France, scene of the evacuation of Allied forces in 1940] (1941) **1** : a retreat to avoid total defeat **2** : a crisis situation that requires a desperate last effort to forestall certain failure ⟨a ∼ for U.S. foreign policy —*Time*⟩

dunk shot *n* (ca. 1961) : a shot in basketball made by jumping high into the air and throwing the ball down through the basket

dun·lin \'dən-lən\ *n, pl* **dunlins** *or* **dunlin** ['*dun* + *-lin* (alter. of *-ling*)] (ca. 1532) : a small widely distributed sandpiper (*Calidris alpina*) largely cinnamon to rusty brown above and white below

Dun·lop \'dən-,läp, ,dən-'\ *n* [*Dunlop*, Ayrshire, Scotland] (ca. 1780) : a Scottish cheese similar to cheddar

dun·nage \'də-nij\ *n* [origin unknown] (15c) **1** : loose materials used to support and protect cargo in a ship's hold; *also* : padding in a shipping container **2** : BAGGAGE

duo \'dü-(,)ō *also* 'dyü-\ *n, pl* **du·os** [It, fr. L, two — more at TWO] (1590) **1** : DUET **2** : PAIR 2

duo- *comb form* [L *duo*] : two ⟨*duo*logue⟩

duo·de·cil·lion \,dü-ō-di-'sil-yən, ,dyü-\ *n, often attrib* [L *duodecim* twelve + E *-illion* (as in *million*)] (1875) — see NUMBER table

duo·dec·i·mal \,dü-ə-'de-sə-məl, ,dyü-\ *adj* [L *duodecim* — more at DOZEN] (1727) : of, relating to, or proceeding by twelve or the scale of twelves — **duodecimal** *n*

duo·dec·i·mo \-,mō\ *n, pl* **-mos** [L, abl. of *duodecimus* twelfth, fr. *duodecim*] (1658) : TWELVEMO

du·o·de·num \,dü-ə-'dē-nəm, dü-'ä-d³n-əm *also* (,)dyü-\ *n, pl* **-de·na** \-'dē-nə, -d³n-ə\ *or* **-denums** [ME, fr. ML, fr. L *duodeni* twelve each, fr. *duodecim* twelve; fr. its length, about 12 fingers' breadth] (14c) : the first part of the small intestine extending from the pylorus to the jejunum — **du·o·de·nal** \-'dē-n³l, -d³n-əl\ *adj*

duo·logue \'dü-ə-,lóg, -,läg *also* 'dyü-\ *n* (1864) : a dialogue between two persons

duo·mo \'dwó-(,)mō\ *n, pl* **duomos** [It, fr. L *domus* house — more at DOME] (1549) : CATHEDRAL

du·op·o·ly \dü-'ä-pə-lē *also* dyü-\ *n, pl* **-lies** [*duo-* + *-poly* (as in *monopoly*)] (1920) **1** : an oligopoly limited to two sellers **2** : preponderant influence or control by two political powers — **du·op·o·lis·tic** \-,ä-pə-'lis-tik\ *adj*

¹dup \'dəp\ *vt* [contr. of *do up*] (1547) *archaic* : OPEN

¹dupe \'düp *also* 'dyüp\ *n* [F, fr. MF *duppe*, prob. alter. of *huppe* hoopoe] (1681) : one that is easily deceived or cheated : FOOL

²dupe *vt* **duped; dup·ing** (1704) : to make a dupe of — **dup·er** *n*
syn DUPE, GULL, TRICK, HOAX mean to deceive by underhanded means. DUPE suggests unwariness in the person deluded. GULL stresses credulousness or readiness to be imposed on (as through greed) on the part of the victim. TRICK implies an intent to delude by means of a ruse or fraud but does not always imply a vicious intent. HOAX implies the contriving of an elaborate or adroit imposture in order to deceive.

³dupe *n or vb* (ca. 1900) : DUPLICATE

dup·ery \'dü-pə-rē *also* dyü-\ *n, pl* **-er·ies** (1759) **1** : the condition of being duped **2** : the act or practice of duping

du·ple \'dü-pəl *also* 'dyü-\ *adj* [L *duplus* double — more at DOUBLE] (15c) **1** : having two elements **2 a** : marked by two or a multiple of two beats per measure of music ⟨∼ *time*⟩ **b** *of rhythm* : consisting of a meter based on disyllabic feet

¹du·plex \'dü-,pleks *also* 'dyü-\ *adj* [L, fr. *duo* two + *-plex* -fold — more at TWO, -FOLD] (1567) **1 a** : having two principal elements or parts : DOUBLE, TWOFOLD **b** : having complementary polynucleotide strands ⟨∼ DNA⟩ **2** : allowing telecommunication in opposite directions simultaneously

²duplex *vt* (1833) : to make duplex

³duplex *n* (1922) : something duplex: as **a** : a 2-family house **b** : DUPLEX APARTMENT **c** : a duplex molecule of DNA or of RNA and DNA

duplex apartment *n* (ca. 1925) : an apartment having rooms on two floors

du·plex·er \'dü-,plek-sər *also* 'dyü-\ *n* (ca. 1932) : a switching device that permits alternate transmission and reception with the same radio antenna

¹du·pli·cate \'dü-pli-kət *also* 'dyü-\ *adj* [ME, fr. L *duplicatus*, pp. of *duplicare* to double, fr. *duplic-, duplex*] (15c) **1** : consisting of or existing in two corresponding or identical parts or examples ⟨∼ invoices⟩ **2** : being the same as another ⟨∼ copies⟩

²du·pli·cate \'dü-pli-,kāt *also* 'dyü-\ *vb* **-cat·ed; -cat·ing** (15c) **1** : to make double or twofold **2 a** : to make a copy of ⟨a cell ∼s itself when it divides⟩ **b** : to produce something equal to ⟨trying to ∼ last year's success⟩ **c** : to do over or again often needlessly ⟨*duplicated* effort⟩ ∼ *vi* : to become duplicated; *also* : REPEAT — **du·pli·ca·tive** \-,kā-tiv\ *adj*

³du·pli·cate \-kət\ *n* (1532) **1 a** : either of two things exactly alike and usu. produced at the same time or by the same process **b** : an additional copy of something (as a book or stamp) already in a collection **2** : one that resembles or corresponds to another : COUNTERPART **3** : two identical copies — used in the phrase *in duplicate* *syn* see REPRODUCTION

duplicate bridge *n* (1926) : a tournament form of contract bridge in which identical deals are played in order to compare individual scores

du·pli·ca·tion \,dü-pli-'kā-shən *also* ,dyü-\ *n* (15c) **1 a** : the act or process of duplicating **b** : the quality or state of being duplicated **2** : DUPLICATE, COUNTERPART **3** : a part of a chromosome in which the genetic material is repeated; *also* : the process of forming a duplication

du·pli·ca·tor \'dü-pli-,kā-tər *also* 'dyü-\ *n* (1893) : one that duplicates; *specif* : a machine for making copies of graphic matter

du·plic·i·tous \dü-'pli-sə-təs *also* dyü-\ *adj* (1928) : marked by duplicity — **du·plic·i·tous·ly** *adv*

du·plic·i·ty \dü-'pli-sə-tē *also* dyü-\ *n, pl* **-ties** [ME *duplicite*, fr. MF, fr. LL *duplicitat-, duplicitas*, fr. L *duplex*] (15c) **1** : contradictory doubleness of thought, speech, or action; *esp* : the belying of one's true intentions by deceptive words or action **2** : the quality or state of being double or twofold **3** : the technically incorrect use of two or more distinct items (as claims, charges, or defenses) in a single legal action

du·ra·ble \'dur-ə-bəl *also* 'dyur-\ *adj* [ME, fr. MF, fr. L *durabilis*, fr. *durare* to last — more at DURING] (14c) : able to exist for a long time without significant deterioration; *also* : designed to be durable ⟨∼

\ə\ abut \³\ kitten, F table \ər\ further \a\ ash \ā\ ace \ä\ mop, mar
\aú\ out \ch\ chin \e\ bet \ē\ easy \g\ go \i\ hit \ī\ ice \j\ job
\ŋ\ sing \ō\ go \ó\ law \ói\ boy \th\ thin \t̲h̲\ the \ü\ loot \ú\ foot
\y\ yet \zh\ vision \à, k̲, ⁿ, œ, œ̄, ᵫ, ᵫ̄, ᵞ\ see Guide to Pronunciation

goods⟩ *syn* see LASTING — **du·ra·bil·i·ty** \,dùr-ə-'bi-lə-tē, ,dyùr-\ *n* — **du·ra·ble·ness** \'dùr-ə-bəl-nəs, 'dyùr-\ *n* — **du·ra·bly** \-blē\ *adv*

durable press *n* (1966) : PERMANENT PRESS

du·ra·bles \'dùr-ə-bəlz *also* 'dyùr-\ *n pl* (1941) : consumer goods (as vehicles and household appliances) that are typically used repeatedly over a period of years — called also *durable goods*

du·ral·u·min \dù-'ral-yə-mən *also* dyù-\ *n* [fr. *Duralumin*, a trademark] (1910) : a light strong alloy of aluminum, copper, manganese, and magnesium

du·ra ma·ter \'dùr-ə-,mā-tər, 'dyùr-, -,mä-\ *n* [ME, fr. ML, lit., hard mother] (14c) : the tough fibrous membrane that envelops the brain and spinal cord external to the arachnoid and pia mater

du·rance \'dùr-ən(t)s *also* 'dyùr-\ *n* [ME, fr. MF, fr. *durer* to endure, fr. L *durare*] (15c) **1** *archaic* : ENDURANCE **2** : restraint by or as if by physical force — usu. used in the phrase *durance vile*

du·ra·tion \dù-'rā-shən *also* dyù-\ *n* (14c) **1** : continuance in time **2** : the time during which something exists or lasts

du·ra·tive \'dùr-ə-tiv, 'dyùr-\ *adj* (1889) : CONTINUATIVE — **durative** *n*

dur·bar \'dər-,bär, ,dər-\ *n* [Hindi *darbār*, fr. Per, fr. *dar* door + *bār* admission, audience] (1609) **1** : court held by an Indian prince **2** : a formal reception held by an Indian prince or an African ruler

du·ress \dù-'res *also* dyù-\ *n* [ME *duresse*, fr. MF *duresce* hardness, severity, fr. L *duritia*, fr. *durus*] (15c) **1** : forcible restraint or restriction **2** : compulsion by threat; *specif* : unlawful constraint

Dur·ham \'dər-əm, 'də-rəm, 'dùr-əm\ *n* [County *Durham*, England] (1810) : SHORTHORN

Durham Rule *n* [Monte *Durham*, 20th cent. Am. litigant] (1955) : a legal hypothesis under which a person is not judged responsible for a criminal act that is attributed to a mental disease or defect

du·ri·an \'dùr-ē-ən, -ē-,än *also* 'dyùr-\ *n* [Malay] (1588) **1** : a large oval tasty but foul-smelling fruit with a prickly rind **2** : an East Indian tree (*Durio zibethinus*) of the silk-cotton family that bears durians

dur·ing \'dùr-iŋ *also* 'dyùr-\ *prep* [ME, fr. prp. of *duren* to last, fr. OF *durer*, fr. L *durare* to harden, endure, fr. *durus* hard; perh. akin to Skt *dāru* wood — more at TREE] (14c) **1** : throughout the duration of ⟨swims every day ~ the summer⟩ **2** : at a point in the course of ⟨was offered a job ~ a visit to the capital⟩

dur·mast oak \'dər-,mast-\ *n* [perh. alter. of *dun mast*, fr. [1]*dun* + *mast*] (1791) : a European oak (*Quercus petraea*) valued esp. for its dark heavy tough elastic wood and for its tannin-rich bark

durn \'dərn\, **durned** \'dərn(d)\ *var of* DARN, DARNED

du·ro \'dùr-(,)ō\ *n, pl* **duros** [Sp, short for *peso duro* hard peso] (1832) : a Spanish or Spanish American peso or silver dollar

du·roc \'dùr-,äk *also* 'dyùr-\ *n, often cap* [*Duroc*, 19th cent. Am. stallion] (1883) : any of a breed of large vigorous red American hogs

du·rom·e·ter \dù-'rä-mə-tər *also* dyù-\ *n* [L *durus* hard] (ca. 1879) : an instrument for measuring hardness

dur·ra *also* **du·ra** \'dùr-ə\ *n* [Ar *dhurah*] (1798) : any of several grain sorghums widely grown in warm dry regions

durst \'dərst\ *archaic & dial past of* DARE

du·rum wheat \'dùr-əm-, 'dyùr-, 'dər-əm-, 'də-rəm-\ *n* [NL *durum*, fr. L, neut. of *durus* hard] (ca. 1903) : a wheat (*Triticum durum*) that yields a glutenous flour used esp. in pasta — called also *durum*

[1]**dusk** \'dəsk\ *adj* [ME *dosk*, alter. of OE *dox*; akin to L *fuscus* dark brown, OE *dunn* dun, *dūst* dust] (13c) : DUSKY

[2]**dusk** *vi* (13c) : to become dark ~ *vt* : to make dark or gloomy

[3]**dusk** *n* (1622) **1** : the darker part of twilight esp. at night **2** : darkness or semidarkness caused by the shutting out of light

dusky \'dəs-kē\ *adj* **dusk·i·er; -est** (1558) **1** : somewhat dark in color; *specif* : having dark skin **2** : marked by slight or deficient light : SHADOWY — **dusk·i·ly** \-kə-lē\ *adv* — **dusk·i·ness** \-kē-nəs\ *n*

[1]**dust** \'dəst\ *n* [ME, fr. OE *dūst*; akin to OHG *tunst* storm, and prob. to L *fumus* smoke — more at FUME] (bef. 12c) **1** : fine particles of matter (as of earth) **2** : the particles into which something disintegrates **3** : something worthless **b** : a state of humiliation **4 a** : the earth esp. as a place of burial **b** : the surface of the ground **5 a** : a cloud of dust **b** : CONFUSION, DISTURBANCE **6** *archaic* : a single particle (as of earth) **7** *Brit* : refuse ready for collection — **dust·less** \-ləs\ *adj* — **dust·like** \-,līk\ *adj*

[2]**dust** *vt* (1530) **1** *archaic* : to make dusty **2** : to make free of dust **3 a** : to sprinkle with fine particles **b** : to sprinkle in the form of dust ~ *vi* **1** *of a bird* : to work dust into the feathers **2** : to remove dust **3** : to give off dust

dust·bin \'dəs(t)-,bin\ *n* (1848) **1** *Brit* : a can for trash or garbage **2** : DUSTHEAP 2

dust bowl *n* (1936) : a region that suffers from prolonged droughts and dust storms

dust·cov·er \-,kə-vər\ *n* (1899) **1** : a cover (as of cloth or plastic) used to protect furniture or equipment from dust **2** : DUST JACKET

dust devil *n* (1888) : a small whirlwind containing sand or dust

dust·er \'dəs-tər\ *n* (1576) **1** : one that removes dust **2 a** (1) : a long lightweight overgarment to protect clothing from dust (2) : a long coat cut like a duster — called also *duster coat* **b** : a dress-length housecoat **3** : one that scatters fine particles; *specif* : a device for applying insecticidal or fungicidal dusts to crops **4** : DUST STORM

dust·heap \'dəst-,(h)ēp\ *n* (1599) **1** : a pile of refuse **2** : a category of forgotten items ⟨the ~ of history —*New Republic*⟩

dust jacket *n* (1926) : a paper cover for a book

dust·man \'dəs(t)-mən\ *n* (1707) *Brit* : a collector of trash or garbage

dust mop *n* (1953) : DRY MOP

dust off *vt* (1940) : to bring out or back to use again

dust·pan \'dəs(t)-,pan\ *n* (1783) : a shovel-shaped pan for sweepings

dust storm *n* (1879) **1** : a dust-laden whirlwind that moves across an arid region and is usu. associated with hot dry air and marked by high electrical tension **2** : strong winds bearing clouds of dust

dust-up \'dəs-,təp\ *n* (1897) : ROW, FIGHT

dust wrapper *n* (1932) : DUST JACKET

dusty \'dəs-tē\ *adj* **dust·i·er; -est** (13c) **1** : covered or abounding with dust **2** : consisting of dust : POWDERY **3** : resembling dust **4** : lacking vitality : DRY ⟨~ scholarship⟩ **5** *Brit* : UNSATISFACTORY — used esp. in the phrases *dusty answer* and *not so dusty* — **dust·i·ly** \'dəs-tə-lē\ *adv* — **dust·i·ness** \-tē-nəs\ *n*

dusty miller *n* (ca. 1825) : any of several plants having ashy-gray or white tomentose leaves; *esp* : an herbaceous artemisia (*Artemisia stelleriana*) with greyish foliage found along the eastern coast of the U.S.

dutch \'dəch\ *adv, often cap* (1914) : with each person paying his or her own way

[1]**Dutch** \'dəch\ *adj* [ME *Duch*, fr. MD *duutsch*; akin to OHG *diutisc* German, OE *thēod* nation, Goth *thiudisko* as a gentile, *thiuda* people, Oscan *touto* city] (14c) **1 a** *archaic* : of, relating to, or in any of the Germanic languages of Germany, Austria, Switzerland, and the Low Countries **b** : of, relating to, or in the Dutch of the Netherlands **2 a** *archaic* : of or relating to the Germanic peoples of Germany, Austria, Switzerland, and the Low Countries **b** : of or relating to the Netherlands or its inhabitants **c** : [2]GERMAN **3** : of or relating to the Pennsylvania Dutch or their language — **Dutch·ly** *adv*

[2]**Dutch** *n* (14c) **1 a** *archaic* (1) : any of the Germanic languages of Germany, Austria, Switzerland, and the Low Countries (2) : GERMAN **3 b** : the Germanic language of the Netherlands **2 Dutch** *pl* **a** *archaic* : the Germanic peoples of Germany, Austria, Switzerland, and the Low Countries **b** : GERMANS 2a, b **c** : the people of the Netherlands **3** : PENNSYLVANIA DUTCH **4** : DANDER ⟨her ~ is up⟩ **5** : DISFAVOR, TROUBLE ⟨in ~ with the boss⟩

Dutch cheese *n* (1829) *chiefly Northern* : COTTAGE CHEESE

Dutch clover *n* (1800) : WHITE CLOVER

Dutch Colonial *adj* (1922) : characterized by a gambrel roof with overhanging eaves

Dutch courage *n* (1809) : courage artificially stimulated esp. by drink; *also* : drink taken for courage

Dutch door *n* (ca. 1890) : a door divided horizontally so that the lower or upper part can be shut separately

Dutch elm disease *n* (1927) : a disease of elms caused by an ascomycetous fungus (*Ceratocystis ulmi*) and characterized by yellowing of the foliage, defoliation, and death

Dutch hoe *n* (1744) : SCUFFLE HOE

dutch·man \'dəch-mən\ *n* (14c) **1** *cap* **a** *archaic* : a member of any of the Germanic peoples of Germany, Austria, Switzerland, and the Low Countries **b** : a native or inhabitant of the Netherlands **c** : a person of Dutch descent **d** : GERMAN 1a, b **2** : a device for hiding or counteracting structural defects

Dutch·man's-breech·es \,dəch-mənz-'bri-chəz\ *n pl but sing or pl in constr* (1837) : a spring-flowering herb (*Dicentra cucullaria*) of the fumitory family occurring in the eastern U.S. and having finely divided leaves and cream-white double-spurred flowers

Dutchman's-pipe \-'pīp\ *n, pl* **Dutchman's-pipes** \-'pīps\ (1845) : a vine (*Aristolochia durior*) with large leaves and early summer flowers having the tube of the calyx curved like the bowl of a pipe

Dutch oven *n* (1769) **1** : a metal shield for roasting before an open fire **2** : a brick oven in which cooking is done by the preheated walls **3 a** : a cast-iron kettle with a tight cover that is used for baking in an open fire **b** : a heavy pot with a tight-fitting domed cover

Dutchman's-breeches

Dutch roll *n* (1913) : a combination of directional and lateral oscillation of an airplane

[1]**dutch treat** *n, often cap D* (1887) : a meal or other entertainment for which each person pays his or her own way

[2]**dutch treat** *adv, often cap D* (1942) : DUTCH ⟨go dutch treat⟩

Dutch uncle *n* (1837) : one who admonishes sternly and bluntly

du·te·ous \'dü-tē-əs *also* 'dyü-\ *adj* [irreg. fr. *duty*] (1593) : DUTIFUL, OBEDIENT

du·ti·able \'dü-tē-ə-bəl *also* 'dyü-\ *adj* (1774) : subject to a duty

du·ti·ful \'dü-ti-fəl *also* 'dyü-\ *adj* (1552) **1** : filled with or motivated by a sense of duty **2** : proceeding from or expressive of a sense of duty — **du·ti·ful·ly** \-f(ə-)lē\ *adv* — **du·ti·ful·ness** \-fəl-nəs\ *n*

[1]**du·ty** \'dü-tē *also* 'dyü-\ *n, pl* **duties** [ME *duete*, fr. AF *dueté*, fr. OF *deu* due] (13c) **1** : conduct due to parents and superiors : RESPECT **2 a** : obligatory tasks, conduct, service, or functions that arise from one's position (as in life or in a group) **b** (1) : assigned service or business (2) : active military service (3) : a period of being on duty **3 a** : a moral or legal obligation **b** : the force of moral obligation **4** : TAX; *esp* : a tax on imports **5 a** : WORK 1a **b** (1) : the service required (as of an electric machine) under specified conditions (2) : functional application : USE ⟨got double ~ out of the trip⟩ (3) : use as a substitute ⟨making the word do ~ for the thing —Edward Sapir⟩ *syn* see FUNCTION, TASK — **off duty** : free from assignment or responsibility — **on duty** : engaged in or responsible for an assigned task or duty

[2]**duty** *adj* (1806) **1** : done as a duty **2** : being on duty : assigned to specified tasks or functions ⟨the ~ officer⟩

duty-free \,dü-tē-'frē, ,dyü-, 'dü-tē-\ *adj or adv* (1689) **1** : without payment of customs duties : free from duties ⟨imported ~⟩ ⟨~ goods⟩ **2** : relating to or selling duty-free goods ⟨a ~ shop⟩

du·um·vir \dù-'əm-vər *also* dyù-\ *n* [L, fr. *duum* (gen. of *duo* two) + *vir* man] (1600) **1** : one of two Roman officers or magistrates constituting a board or court **2** : one of two people jointly holding power — **du·um·vi·rate** \-və-rət\ *n*

du·vet \d(y)ù-'vā, 'd(y)ü-,\ *n* [F] (1758) : COMFORTER 2b

duve·tyn \'dü-və-,tēn, 'dyü-, ,dəv-,tēn\ *n* [F *duvetine*, fr. *duvet* down, fr. MF, alter. of (assumed) MF *dumet*, dim. of OF *dun*, *dum* down, fr. ON *dūnn* — more at DOWN] (1913) : a smooth lustrous velvety fabric

dux·elles \dük-'sel, (,)dü-'sel\ *n* [Marquis Louis Chalon du Blé *d'Uxelles* †1658 Fr. nobleman] (1877) : a garnish or stuffing made esp. of finely chopped sautéed mushrooms

[1]**dwarf** \'dwórf\ *n, pl* **dwarfs** \'dwórfs\ *also* **dwarves** \'dwórvz\ *often attrib* [ME *dwerg*, *dwerf*, fr. OE *dweorg*, *dweorh*; akin to OHG *twerg* dwarf] (bef. 12c) **1 a** : a person of unusually small stature; *esp* : one whose bodily proportions are abnormal **b** : an insignificant person **2** : an animal or plant much below normal size **3** : a small legendary manlike being who is usu. misshapen and ugly and skilled as an artifi-

cer **4 :** a star (as the sun) of ordinary or low luminosity and relatively small mass and size — **dwarf·ish** \'dwȯr-fish\ *adj* — **dwarf·ish·ly** *adv* — **dwarf·ish·ness** *n* — **dwarf·like** \'dwȯr-ˌflīk\ *adj* — **dwarf·ness** \'dwȯrf-nəs\ *n*

²**dwarf** *vt* (ca. 1626) **1 :** to restrict the growth of : STUNT **2 :** to cause to appear smaller or to seem inferior ~ *vi* **:** to become smaller

³**dwarf** *adj* (1664) *of a plant* **:** low-growing in habit ⟨*~er* forms of citrus⟩

dwarf·ism \'dwȯrf-ˌfi-zəm\ *n* (1865) **:** the condition of stunted growth

dweeb \'dwēb\ *n* [origin unknown] (1983) *slang* **:** an unattractive, insignificant, or inept person

dwell \'dwel\ *vi* **dwelled** \'dweld, 'dwelt\ *or* **dwelt** \'dwelt\; **dwelling** [ME, fr. OE *dwellan* to go astray, hinder; akin to OHG *twellen* to tarry] (13c) **1 :** to remain for a time **2 a :** to live as a resident **b :** EXIST, LIE **3 a :** to keep the attention directed — used with *on* or *upon* ⟨tried not to ~ on my fears⟩ **b :** to speak or write insistently — used with *on* or *upon* ⟨leering reviewers *~ed* on a publicity photograph —James Atlas⟩ — **dwell·er** *n*

dwell·ing *n* (14c) **:** a shelter (as a house) in which people live

dwin·dle \'dwin-dᵊl\ *vb* **dwin·dled**; **dwin·dling** \-(d)liŋ, -dᵊl-iŋ\ [prob. freq. of *dwine* to waste away, fr. ME, fr. OE *dwinan;* akin to ON *dvina* to pine away, *deyja* to die — more at DIE] *vi* (1596) **:** to become steadily less : SHRINK ~ *vt* **:** to make steadily less *syn* see DECREASE

DX \(ˌ)dē-'eks\ *n* (ca. 1924) **:** DISTANCE — used of long-distance radio transmission

dy- *or* **dyo-** *comb form* [LL, fr. Gk, fr. *dyo* — more at TWO] **:** two ⟨*dyarchy*⟩

dy·ad \'dī-ˌad, -əd\ *n* [LL *dyad-, dyas,* fr. Gk, fr. *dyo*] (1675) **1 :** PAIR; *specif* **:** two individuals (as husband and wife) maintaining a sociologically significant relationship **2 :** a meiotic chromosome after separation of the two homologous members of a tetrad **3 :** a mathematical operator indicated by writing the symbols of two vectors without a dot or cross between (as AB) — **dy·ad·ic** \dī-'a-dik\ *adj* — **dy·ad·i·cal·ly** \-di-k(ə-)lē\ *adv*

dy·ad·ic \dī-'a-dik\ *n* (1884) **:** a mathematical expression formed by addition or subtraction of dyads

Dy·ak *var of* DAYAK

dy·ar·chy \'dī-ˌär-kē\ *n, pl* **-chies** (1640) **:** a government in which power is vested in two rulers or authorities

dyb·buk \'di-bək\ *n, pl* **dyb·bu·kim** \ˌdi-bú-'kēm\ *also* **dybbuks** [LHeb *dibbūq*] (ca. 1903) **:** a wandering soul believed in Jewish folklore to enter and control a living body until exorcised by a religious rite

¹**dye** \'dī\ *n* [ME *dehe,* fr. OE *dēah, dēag*] (bef. 12c) **1 :** color from dyeing **2 :** a soluble or insoluble coloring matter

²**dye** *vb* **dyed; dye·ing** *vt* (bef. 12c) **1 :** to impart a new and often permanent color to esp. by impregnating with a dye **2 :** to impart (a color) by dyeing ⟨*~ing* blue on yellow⟩ ~ *vi* **:** to take up or impart color in dyeing — **dye·abil·i·ty** \ˌdī-ə-'bi-lə-tē\ *n* — **dye·able** \'dī-ə-bəl\ *adj* — **dy·er** \'dī(-ə)r\ *n*

dyed–in–the–wool \ˌdīd-ᵊn-thə-'wúl\ *adj* (1580) **:** THOROUGHGOING, UNCOMPROMISING ⟨a ~ conservative⟩

dye·stuff \'dī-ˌstəf\ *n* (1837) **:** DYE 2

dye·wood \-ˌwúd\ *n* (1699) **:** a wood (as logwood or fustic) from which coloring matter is extracted for dyeing

dying *pres part of* DIE

¹**dyke** *chiefly Brit var of* DIKE

²**dyke** \'dīk\ *n* [origin unknown] (ca. 1942) **:** LESBIAN — often used disparagingly — **dykey** \'dī-kē\ *adj*

¹**dy·nam·ic** \dī-'na-mik\ *adj* [F *dynamique,* fr. Gk *dynamikos* powerful, fr. *dynamis* power, fr. *dynasthai* to be able] (1827) **1** *also* **dy·nam·i·cal** \-mi-kəl\ **a :** of or relating to physical force or energy **b :** of or relating to dynamics **2 a :** marked by usu. continuous and productive activity or change ⟨a ~ city⟩ **b :** ENERGETIC, FORCEFUL ⟨a ~ personality⟩ **3** *of random-access memory* **:** requiring periodic refreshment of charge in order to retain data — **dy·nam·i·cal·ly** \-mi-k(ə)lē\ *adv*

²**dynamic** *n* (1879) **1 :** a dynamic force **2 :** DYNAMICS 2; *also* **:** an underlying cause of change or growth

dynamic range *n* (1949) **:** the ratio of the strongest to the weakest sound intensity that can be transmitted or reproduced by an audio or broadcasting system

dy·nam·ics \dī-'na-miks\ *n pl but sing or pl in constr* (ca. 1789) **1 :** a branch of mechanics that deals with forces and their relation primarily to the motion but sometimes also to the equilibrium of bodies **2 :** a pattern or process of change, growth, or activity ⟨population ~⟩ **3** **:** variation and contrast in force or intensity (as in music)

dy·na·mism \'dī-nə-ˌmi-zəm\ *n* (ca. 1857) **1 a :** a theory that all phenomena (as matter or motion) can be explained as manifestations of force — compare MECHANISM **b :** DYNAMICS 2 **2 :** a dynamic or expansionist quality — **dy·na·mist** \-mist\ *n* — **dy·na·mis·tic** \ˌdī-nə-'mis-tik\ *adj*

¹**dy·na·mite** \'dī-nə-ˌmīt\ *n* (1867) **1 :** an explosive that is made of nitroglycerin absorbed in a porous material and that often contains ammonium nitrate or cellulose nitrate; *also* **:** an explosive (as a mixture of ammonium nitrate and nitrocellulose) that contains no nitroglycerin **2 :** one that has a powerful effect; *also* **:** something that has great potential to cause trouble or conflict — **dy·na·mit·ic** \ˌdī-nə-'mi-tik\ *adj*

²**dynamite** *vt* **-mit·ed; -mit·ing** (1881) **1 :** to blow up with dynamite **2 :** to cause the failure or destruction of — **dy·na·mit·er** *n*

³**dynamite** *adj* (1940) **:** TERRIFIC, WONDERFUL

dy·na·mo \'dī-nə-ˌmō\ *n, pl* **-mos** [short for *dynamoelectric machine*] (ca. 1882) **1 :** GENERATOR 3 **2 :** a forceful energetic individual

dy·na·mom·e·ter \ˌdī-nə-'mä-mə-tər\ *n* [F *dynamomètre,* fr. Gk *dynamis* power + F *-mètre* -meter] (1810) **1 :** an instrument for measuring mechanical force **2 :** an apparatus for measuring mechanical power (as of an engine) — **dy·na·mo·met·ric** \-ˌmō-'me-trik\ *adj* — **dy·na·mom·e·try** \-'mä-mə-trē\ *n*

dy·na·mo·tor \'dī-nə-ˌmō-tər\ *n* [*dyna*mo + *motor*] (1899) **:** a motor generator combining the electric motor and generator

dy·nast \'dī-ˌnast, -nəst\ *n* [L *dynastes,* fr. Gk *dynastēs,* fr. *dynasthai* to be able, have power] (1631) **:** RULER 1

dy·nas·ty \'dī-nə-stē *also* -ˌnas-tē, *esp Brit* 'di-nə-stē\ *n, pl* **-ties** (14c) **1** **:** a succession of rulers of the same line of descent **2 :** a powerful group or family that maintains its position for a considerable time — **dy·nas·tic** \dī-'nas-tik\ *adj* — **dy·nas·ti·cal·ly** \-ti-k(ə-)lē\ *adv*

dy·na·tron \'dī-nə-ˌträn\ *n* [Gk *dynamis* power] (1918) **:** a vacuum tube in which the secondary emission of electrons from the plate results in a decrease in the plate current as the plate voltage increases

dyne \'dīn\ *n* [F, fr. Gk *dynamis*] (ca. 1873) **:** the unit of force in the centimeter-gram-second system equal to the force that would give a free mass of one gram an acceleration of one centimeter per second per second

dy·ne·in \'dī-nē-in\ *n* [*dyne* (force) + *-in*] (1965) **:** an ATPase that is associated esp. with microtubules involved in the ciliary and flagellar movement of cells

dy·node \'dī-ˌnōd\ *n* [Gk *dynamis*] (1939) **:** an electrode in an electron tube that functions to produce secondary emission of electrons

dys- *prefix* [ME *dis-* bad, difficult, fr. MF & L; MF *dis-,* fr. L *dys-,* fr. Gk; akin to OE *tō-, te-* apart, Skt *dus-* bad, difficult] **1 :** abnormal ⟨*dys*plasia⟩ **2 :** difficult ⟨*dys*phagia⟩ — compare EU- **3 :** impaired ⟨*dys*function⟩ **4 :** bad ⟨*dys*logistic⟩ — compare EU-

dys·ar·thria \di-'sär-thrē-ə\ *n* [NL, fr. *dys-* + *arthr-* + *-ia*] (1878) **:** difficulty in articulating words due to disease of the central nervous system

dys·cra·sia \dis-'krā-zh(ē-)ə\ *n* [NL, fr. ML, bad mixture of humors, fr. Gk *dyskrasia,* fr. *dys-* + *krasis* mixture, fr. *kerannynai* to mix — more at CRATER] (14c) **:** an abnormal condition of the body and esp. the blood

dys·en·ter·ic \ˌdi-sᵊn-'ter-ik\ *adj* (1727) **:** of or relating to dysentery

dys·en·tery \'di-sᵊn-ˌter-ē\ *n, pl* **-ter·ies** [ME *dissenterie,* fr. L *dysenteria,* fr. Gk, fr. *dys-* + *enteron* intestine — more at INTER-] (14c) **1 :** a disease characterized by severe diarrhea with passage of mucus and blood and usu. caused by infection **2 :** DIARRHEA

dys·func·tion \(ˌ)dis-'fəŋ(k)-shən\ *n* (ca. 1916) **:** impaired or abnormal functioning — **dys·func·tion·al** \-shnəl, -shə-nᵊl\ *adj*

dys·gen·e·sis \(ˌ)dis-'je-nə-səs\ *n* [NL] (ca. 1883) **:** defective development esp. of the gonads (as in Klinefelter's syndrome)

dys·gen·ic \(ˌ)dis-'je-nik\ *adj* (1912) **1 :** tending to promote survival of or reproduction by less well-adapted individuals (as the weak or diseased) esp. at the expense of well-adapted individuals (as the strong or healthy) ⟨the ~ effect of war⟩ **2 :** biologically defective or deficient

dys·ki·ne·sia \dis-kə-'nē-zh(ē-)ə, -kī-\ *n* [NL, fr. Gk *dyskinēsia* difficulty in moving, fr. *dys-* + *-kinesia,* fr. *kinēsis* motion, fr. *kinein* to move — more at HIGHT] (ca. 1706) **:** impairment of voluntary movements resulting in fragmented or jerky motions (as in Parkinson's disease) — compare TARDIVE DYSKINESIA — **dys·ki·net·ic** \-'net-ik\ *adj*

dys·lex·ia \dis-'lek-sē-ə\ *n* [NL, fr. *dys-* + Gk *lexis* word, speech, fr. *legein* to say — more at LEGEND] (ca. 1888) **:** a disturbance of the ability to read; *broadly* **:** disturbance of the ability to use language — **dys·lex·ic** \-sik\ *adj or n*

dys·lo·gis·tic \ˌdis-lə-'jis-tik\ *adj* [*dys-* + *-logistic* (as in *eulogistic*)] (1812) **:** UNCOMPLIMENTARY — **dys·lo·gis·ti·cal·ly** \-ti-k(ə-)lē\ *adv*

dys·men·or·rhea \(ˌ)dis-ˌme-nə-'rē-ə\ *n* [NL] (ca. 1810) **:** painful menstruation — **dys·men·or·rhe·ic** \-'rē-ik\ *adj*

dys·pep·sia \dis-'pep-shə, -sē-ə\ *n* [L, fr. Gk, fr. *dys-* + *pepsis* digestion, fr. *peptein, pessein* to cook, digest — more at COOK] (ca. 1706) **1** **:** INDIGESTION **2 :** ill humor : DISGRUNTLEMENT — **dys·pep·tic** \-'pep-tik\ *adj or n* — **dys·pep·ti·cal·ly** \-ti-k(ə-)lē\ *adv*

dys·pha·gia \dis-'fā-j(ē-)ə\ *n* [NL] (1783) **:** difficulty in swallowing

dys·pha·sia \dis-'fā-zh(ē-)ə\ *n* [NL] (ca. 1883) **:** loss or deficiency in the power to use or understand language as a result of injury to or disease of the brain — **dys·pha·sic** \-'fā-zik\ *n or adj*

dys·phe·mism \'dis-fə-ˌmi-zəm\ *n* [*dys-* + *-phemism* (as in *euphemism*)] (1884) **:** the substitution of a disagreeable, offensive, or disparaging expression for an agreeable or inoffensive one; *also* **:** an expression so substituted — **dys·phe·mis·tic** \ˌdis-fə-'mis-tik\ *adj*

dys·pho·nia \dis-'fō-nē-ə\ *n* [NL] (ca. 1706) **:** defective use of the voice

dys·pho·ria \dis-'fȯr-ē-ə, -'fȯr-\ *n* [NL, fr. Gk, fr. *dysphoros* hard to bear, fr. *dys-* + *pherein* to bear — more at BEAR] (ca. 1842) **:** a state of feeling unwell or unhappy — **dys·phor·ic** \-'fȯr-ik, -'fär-\ *adj*

dys·pla·sia \dis-'plā-zh(ē-)ə\ *n* [NL] (ca. 1923) **:** abnormal growth or development (as of organs or cells); *broadly* **:** abnormal anatomic structure due to such growth — **dys·plas·tic** \-'plas-tik\ *adj*

dys·pnea \'dis(p)-nē-ə\ *n* [L *dyspnoea,* fr. Gk *dyspnoia,* fr. *dyspnoos* short of breath, fr. *dys-* + *pnein* to breathe — more at SNEEZE] (ca. 1681) **:** difficult or labored respiration — **dys·pne·ic** \-nē-ik\ *adj*

dyspnoea *chiefly Brit var of* DYSPNEA

dys·pro·si·um \dis-'prō-zē-əm, -zhē-əm\ *n* [NL, fr. Gk *dysprositos* hard to get at, fr. *dys-* + *prositos* approachable, fr. *prosienai* to approach, fr. *pros-* + *ienai* to go — more at ISSUE] (1886) **:** an element of the rare-earth group that forms highly magnetic compounds — see ELEMENT table

dys·rhyth·mia \dis-'rith-mē-ə\ *n* [NL, fr. *dys-* + L *rhythmus* rhythm] (ca. 1909) **:** an abnormal rhythm; *esp* **:** a disordered rhythm exhibited in a record of electrical activity of the brain or heart — **dys·rhyth·mic** \-mik\ *adj*

dys·to·cia \di-'stō-sh(ē-)ə\ *n* [NL, fr. Gk *dystokia,* fr. *dys-* + *tokos* childbirth; akin to Gk *tiktein* to give birth to — more at THANE] (ca. 1706) **:** slow or difficult labor or delivery

dys·to·pia \(ˌ)dis-'tō-pē-ə\ *n* [NL, fr. *dys-* + *-topia* (as in *utopia*)] (ca. 1950) **1 :** an imaginary place where people lead dehumanized and often fearful lives **2 :** ANTI-UTOPIA 2 — **dys·to·pi·an** \-pē-ən\ *adj*

dys·tro·phic \dis-'trō-fik\ *adj* (1893) **1 a :** relating to or caused by faulty nutrition **b :** relating to or affected with a dystrophy ⟨a ~ patient⟩ **2** *of a lake* **:** brownish with much dissolved humic matter, a sparse bottom fauna, and a high oxygen consumption

dys·tro·phy \'dis-trə-fē\ *n, pl* **-phies** [NL *dystrophia,* fr. *dys-* + *-trophia* -trophy] (1901) **1 :** a condition produced by faulty nutrition **2 :** any myogenic atrophy; *esp* **:** MUSCULAR DYSTROPHY

dys·uria \dis-'yūr-ē-ə, dish-\ *n* [NL, fr. Gk *dysouria,* fr. *dys-* + *-ouria* -uria] (14c) **:** difficult or painful discharge of urine — compare STRANGURY

\ə\ abut \ᵊ\ kitten, F table \ər\ further \a\ ash \ā\ ace \ä\ mop, mar \aú\ out \ch\ chin \e\ bet \ē\ easy \g\ go \i\ hit \ī\ ice \j\ job \ŋ\ sing \ō\ go \ȯ\ law \ȯi\ boy \th\ thin \th̲\ the \ü\ loot \ú\ foot \y\ yet \zh\ vision \à, k̲, ⁿ, œ, œ̄, ᵫ, ᵫ̄, ᵞ\ see Guide to Pronunciation

e \ˈē\ *n, pl* **e's** *or* **es** \ˈēz\ *often cap, often attrib* (bef. 12c) **1 a :** the 5th letter of the English alphabet **b :** a graphic representation of this letter **c :** a speech counterpart of orthographic *e* **2 :** the 3d tone of a C-major scale **3 :** a graphic device for reproducing the letter *e* **4 :** one designated *e* esp. as the 5th in order or class **5 a :** a grade rating a student's work as poor and usu. constituting a conditional pass **b :** a grade rating a student's work as failing **c :** one graded or rated with an E **6 :** a transcendental number having a value to eight decimal places of 2.71828183 that is the base of natural logarithms **7 :** something shaped like the letter E

e- \(ˈ)ē, i\ *prefix* [ME, fr. OF & L; OF, out, forth, away, fr. L, fr. *ex-*] **1 :** missing : absent ⟨edentulous⟩ **2 :** away ⟨eluviation⟩

¹each \ˈēch\ *adj* [ME *ech*, fr. OE *ǣlc*; akin to OHG *iogilīh* each; both fr. a prehistoric WGmc compound whose first and second constituents respectively are represented by OE *ā* always and by OE *gelīc* alike] (bef. 12c) : being one of two or more distinct individuals having a similar relation and often constituting an aggregate

²each *pron* (bef. 12c) : each one

³each *adv* (bef. 12c) : to or for each : APIECE

each other *pron* (bef. 12c) : each of two or more in reciprocal action or relation ⟨looked at *each other* in surprise⟩
    usage Some handbooks and textbooks recommend that *each other* be restricted to reference to two and *one another* to reference to three or more. The distinction, while neat, is not observed in actual usage. *Each other* and *one another* are used interchangeably by good writers and have been since at least the sixteenth century.

ea·ger \ˈē-gər\ *adj* [ME *egre*, fr. MF *aigre*, fr. L *acer* — more at EDGE] (14c) **1 a** *archaic* : SHARP **b** *obs* : SOUR **2 :** marked by enthusiastic or impatient desire or interest — **ea·ger·ly** *adv* — **ea·ger·ness** *n*
    syn EAGER, AVID, KEEN, ANXIOUS, ATHIRST mean moved by a strong and urgent desire or interest. EAGER implies ardor and enthusiasm and sometimes impatience at delay or restraint ⟨*eager* to get started⟩. AVID adds to EAGER the implication of insatiability or greed ⟨*avid* for new thrills⟩. KEEN suggests intensity of interest and quick responsiveness in action ⟨*keen* on the latest fashions⟩. ANXIOUS emphasizes fear of frustration or failure or disappointment ⟨*anxious* not to make a social blunder⟩. ATHIRST stresses yearning but not necessarily readiness for action ⟨*athirst* for adventure⟩.

eager beaver *n* (1943) : a person who is extremely zealous about performing duties and volunteering for more

ea·gle \ˈē-gəl\ *n* [ME *egle*, fr. OF *aigle*, fr. L *aquila*] (13c) **1 :** any of various large diurnal birds of prey of the accipiter family noted for their strength, size, keenness of vision, and powers of flight **2 a :** the eagle-bearing standard of the ancient Romans **b :** one of a pair of eagle-bearing silver insignia of rank worn by a military colonel or a navy captain **3 :** a gold coin of the U.S. bearing an eagle on the reverse and usu. having a value of ten dollars **4 :** a golf score of two strokes less than par on a hole — compare BIRDIE **5** *cap* [Fraternal Order of *Eagles*] : a member of a major fraternal order

eagle eye *n* (1802) **1 :** the ability to see or observe with exceptional keenness **2 :** one that sees or observes keenly — **eagle–eyed** \ˈē-gəl-ˌīd\ *adj*

eagle ray *n* (ca. 1856) : any of several widely distributed large active stingrays (family Myliobatidae) with broad pectoral fins like wings

Eagle Scout *n* (1913) **1 :** a Boy Scout who has reached the highest level of achievement in scouting **2 :** a straight-arrow and self-reliant man

ea·glet \ˈē-glət\ *n* (1572) : a young eagle

eal·dor·man \ˈal-dər-mən\ *n* [OE — more at ALDERMAN] (bef. 12c) : the chief officer in a district (as a shire) in Anglo-Saxon England

Eames chair \ˈēmz-, ˈāmz-\ *n* [Charles *Eames* †1978 Am. designer] (1946) : any of several chairs designed by Charles Eames to fit the contours of the body and to be made from modern materials

-ean — see -AN

¹ear \ˈir, ˈēr\ *n* [ME *ere*, fr. OE *ēare*; akin to OHG *ōra* ear, L *auris*, Gk *ous*] (bef. 12c) **1 a :** the characteristic vertebrate organ of hearing and equilibrium consisting in the typical mammal of a sound-collecting outer ear separated by the tympanic membrane from a sound-transmitting middle ear that in turn is separated from a sensory inner ear by membranous fenestrae **b :** any of various organs capable of detecting vibratory motion **2 :** the external ear of humans and most mammals **3 a :** the sense or act of hearing **b :** acuity of hearing **c :** sensitivity to musical tone and pitch; *also* : the ability to retain and reproduce music that has been heard **d :** sensitivity to nuances of language esp. as revealed in the command of verbal melody and rhythm or in the ability to render a spoken idiom accurately **4 :** something resembling a mammalian ear in shape, position, or function: as **a :** a projecting part (as a lug or handle) **b :** either of a pair of tufts of lengthened feathers on the head of some birds **5 a :** sympathetic attention **b :** ATTENTION, AWARENESS **c :** a space in the upper corner of the front page of a periodical (as a newspaper) usu. containing advertising for the periodical itself or a weather forecast — **by ear :** without reference to or memorization of written music ⟨plays *by ear*⟩ — **in one ear and out the other :** through one's mind without making an impression ⟨everything you say to him goes *in one ear and out the other*⟩ — **on one's ear :** in or into a state of irritation, shock, or discord ⟨set the racing world *on its ear* by breaking the record⟩ — **up to one's ears :** deeply involved : heavily implicated ⟨*up to his ears* in shady deals⟩

²ear *n* [ME *er*, fr. OE *ēar*; akin to OHG *ahir* ear, OE *ecg* edge — more at EDGE] (bef. 12c) : the fruiting spike of a cereal (as wheat or Indian corn) including both the seeds and protective structures

³ear *vi* (14c) : to form ears in growing ⟨the rye should be ~*ing* up⟩

ear·ache \ˈir-ˌāk\ *n* (1789) : an ache or pain in the ear

ear candy *n* (1977) : music that is pleasing to listen to but lacks depth

ear clip *n* (1945) : an earring with a clip fastener

ear·drop \-ˌdräp\ *n* (1720) : EARRING; *esp* : one with a pendant

ear·drum \-ˌdrəm\ *n* (1645) : TYMPANIC MEMBRANE

eared \ˈird\ *adj* (14c) : having ears esp. of a specified kind or number ⟨a big-*eared* man⟩ ⟨golden-*eared* corn⟩

ear 1a: *1* pinna, *2* lobe, *3* auditory meatus, *4* tympanic membrane, *5* eustachian tube, *6* auditory nerve, *7* cochlea, *8* semicircular canals, *9* stapes, *10* incus, *11* malleus, *12* bones of skull

eared seal *n* (1883) : any of a family (Otariidae) of seals including the sea lions and fur seals and having independent mobile hind limbs and small well-developed external ears — compare HAIR SEAL

ear-flap \ˈir-ˌflap\ *n* (1907) : a warm covering for the ears; *esp* : an extension on the lower edge of a cap that may be folded up or down

ear·ful \ˈir-ˌfül\ *n* (1911) **1 :** an outpouring of news or gossip **2 :** an outpouring of anger, abuse, or complaint

ear·ing \ˈir-iŋ\ *n* [perh. fr. ¹*ear*] (1626) : a line used to fasten a corner of a sail to the yard or gaff or to haul a reef cringle to the yard

earl \ˈər(-ə)l\ *n* [ME *erl*, fr. OE *eorl* warrior, nobleman; akin to ON *jarl* warrior, nobleman] (12c) : a member of the British peerage ranking below a marquess and above a viscount — **earl·dom** \-dəm\ *n*

earl marshal *n* (13c) : an officer of state in England serving chiefly as a royal attendant on ceremonial occasions, as marshal of state processions, and as head of the College of Arms

ear·lobe \ˈir-ˌlōb\ *n* (1859) : the pendent part of the ear of humans or some fowls

ear·lock \-ˌläk\ *n* (ca. 1775) : a curl of hair hanging in front of the ear

¹ear·ly \ˈər-lē\ *adv* **ear·li·er; -est** [ME *erly*, fr. OE *ǣrlice*, fr. *ǣr* early, soon — more at ERE] (bef. 12c) **1 a :** near the beginning of a period of time ⟨awoke ~ in the morning⟩ **b :** near the beginning of a course, process, or series ⟨~ in his senatorial career⟩ **2 a :** before the usual or expected time ⟨these apples bear ~⟩ **b** *archaic* : SOON **c :** sooner than related forms

²early *adj* **ear·li·er; -est** (13c) **1 a :** of, relating to, or occurring near the beginning of a period of time, a development, or a series **b** (1) : distant in past time (2) : PRIMITIVE **2 a :** occurring before the usual or expected time **b :** occurring in the near future ⟨at your *earliest* convenience⟩ **c :** maturing or producing sooner than related forms ⟨an ~ peach⟩ — **ear·li·ness** *n*

Early American *n* (1895) : a style (as of furniture, architecture, or fabric) originating in or characteristic of colonial America

early bird *n* [fr. the proverb, "the early bird catches the worm"] (ca. 1922) **1 :** an early riser **2 :** one that arrives early and esp. before possible competitors

early on *adv* (1928) : at or during an early point or stage ⟨the reasons were obvious *early on* in the experiment⟩
    usage This adverb is sometimes objected to in American writing as an obtrusive Briticism. It is a relative newcomer to the language, having arisen in British English around 1928. It seems to have filled a need, however. It came into frequent use in American English in the late 1960s and is now well established on both sides of the Atlantic in both speech and writing.

ear·ly·wood \ˈər-lē-ˌwüd\ *n* (ca. 1914) : SPRINGWOOD

¹ear·mark \ˈir-ˌmärk\ *n* (15c) **1 :** a mark of identification on the ear of an animal **2 :** a distinguishing mark ⟨all the ~s of poverty⟩

²earmark *vt* (1591) **1 a :** to mark (livestock) with an earmark **b :** to mark in a distinguishing manner **2 :** to designate (as funds) for a specific use or owner

ear·muff \ˈir-ˌməf\ *n* (1889) : one of a pair of ear coverings connected by a flexible band and worn as protection against cold or noises

¹earn \ˈərn\ *vt* [ME *ernen*, fr. OE *earnian*; akin to OHG *arnōn* to reap, Czech *jesen* autumn] (bef. 12c) **1 a :** to receive as return for effort and esp. for work done or services rendered **b :** to bring in by way of return ⟨bonds ~*ing* 10% interest⟩ **2 a :** to come to be duly worthy of or entitled or suited to ⟨she ~*ed* a promotion⟩ **b :** to make worthy of or obtain for ⟨the suggestion ~*ed* him a promotion⟩ — **earn·er** *n*

²earn *vi* [prob. alter. of *yearn*] (1599) *obs* : GRIEVE

earned run *n* (1886) : a run in baseball that scores without benefit of an error before the fielding team has had a chance to make the third putout of the inning

earned run average *n* (1947) : the average number of earned runs per game scored against a pitcher in baseball determined by dividing the total of earned runs scored against him by the total number of innings pitched and multiplying by nine

¹ear·nest \ˈər-nəst\ *n* [ME *ernest*, fr. OE *eornost*; akin to OHG *ernust* earnest] (bef. 12c) : a serious and intent mental state ⟨in ~⟩

²earnest *adj* (bef. 12c) **1 :** characterized by or proceeding from an intense and serious state of mind **2 :** GRAVE, IMPORTANT *syn* see SERIOUS — **ear·nest·ly** *adv* — **ear·nest·ness** \-nəs(t)-nəs\ *n*

³earnest *n* [ME *ernes*, *ernest*, fr. OF *erres*, pl. of *erre* earnest, fr. L *arra*, short for *arrabo*, fr. Gk *arrhabōn*, of Sem origin; akin to Heb *'ērābhōn* pledge] (13c) **1 :** something of value given by a buyer to a seller to bind a bargain **2 :** a token of what is to come : PLEDGE

earn·ings \ˈər-niŋz\ *n pl* (1732) **1 :** something (as wages) earned **2 :** the balance of revenue after deduction of costs and expenses

ear·phone \ˈir-ˌfōn\ *n* (1924) : a device that converts electrical energy into sound waves and is worn over or inserted into the ear

ear pick *n* (14c) : a device often of precious metal for removing wax or foreign bodies from the ear

ear·piece \'ir-ˌpēs\ *n* (1853) **1** : a part of an instrument (as a stethoscope or hearing aid) which is applied to the ear; *esp* : EARPHONE **2** : one of the two sidepieces that support eyeglasses by passing over or behind the ears

ear·plug \-ˌpləg\ *n* (1904) **1** : an ornament inserted in the lobe of the ear esp. to distend it **2** : a device of pliable material for insertion into the outer opening of the ear (as to keep out water or deaden sound)

ear·ring \'ir-(ˌ)iŋ, -ˌriŋ\ *n* (bef. 12c) : an ornament for the earlobe

ear rot *n* (1926) : a condition of Indian corn that is characterized by molding and decay of the ears and that is caused by fungi (genera *Diplodia, Fusarium,* or *Gibberella*)

ear shell *n* (ca. 1753) : ABALONE

ear·shot \'ir-ˌshät\ *n* (1607) : the range within which the unaided voice may be heard

ear·split·ting \-ˌspli-tiŋ\ *adj* (1884) : distressingly loud or shrill **syn** see LOUD

¹earth \'ərth\ *n* [ME *erthe,* fr. OE *eorthe;* akin to OHG *erda* earth, Gk *era*] (bef. 12c) **1** : the fragmental material composing part of the surface of the globe; *esp* : cultivable soil **2** : the sphere of mortal life as distinguished from spheres of spirit life — compare HEAVEN, HELL **3 a** : areas of land as distinguished from sea and air **b** : the solid footing formed of soil : GROUND **4** *often cap* : the planet on which we live that is third in order from the sun — see PLANET table **5 a** : the people of the planet Earth **b** : the mortal human body **c** : the pursuits, interests, and pleasures of earthly life as distinguished from spiritual concerns **6** : the lair of a burrowing animal **7** : an excessive amount of money — used with *the* ⟨real suede, which costs the ~ to clean —Joanne Winship⟩ — **earth·like** \-ˌlīk\ *adj* — **on earth** — used as an intensive ⟨to find out what *on earth* he was up to —Michael Holroyd⟩

²earth *vt* (1575) **1** : to drive to hiding in the earth **2** : to draw soil about (plants) — often used with *up* **3** *chiefly Brit* : GROUND **3** ~ *vi, of a hunted animal* : to hide in the ground

earth·born \'ərth-ˌbórn\ *adj* (1667) **1** : born on this earth : MORTAL **2** : associated with earthly life

earth·bound \-ˌbaůnd\ *adj* (1605) **1 a** : fast in or to the soil ⟨~ roots⟩ **b** : located on or restricted to land or to the surface of the earth **2 a** : bound by earthly interests **b** : PEDESTRIAN, UNIMAGINATIVE

earth color *n* (1931) : EARTH TONE

earth·en \'ər-thən, -thən\ *adj* (13c) **1** : made of earth **2** : EARTHLY

earth·en·ware \-ˌwar, -ˌwer\ *n* (1648) : ceramic ware made of slightly porous opaque clay fired at low heat

earth·i·ly \'ər-thə-lē, -thə-\ *adv* (1953) : in an earthy manner

earth·light \'ərth-ˌlīt\ *n* (1833) : EARTHSHINE

earth·ling \'ərth-liŋ\ *n* (1593) **1** : an inhabitant of the earth **2** : WORLDLING

earth·ly \'ərth-lē\ *adj* (bef. 12c) **1 a** : characteristic of or belonging to this earth **b** : relating to man's actual life on this earth **2** : POSSIBLE ⟨there is no ~ reason for such behavior⟩ — **earth·li·ness** *n* **syn** EARTHLY, WORLDLY, MUNDANE mean belonging to or characteristic of the earth. EARTHLY often implies a contrast with what is heavenly or spiritual ⟨abandoned *earthly* concerns and entered a convent⟩. WORLDLY and MUNDANE both imply a relation to the immediate concerns and activities of human beings, WORLDLY suggesting tangible personal gain or gratification ⟨*worldly* goods⟩ and MUNDANE suggesting reference to the immediate and practical ⟨a *mundane* discussion of finances⟩.

earth mother *n, often cap E&M* (1902) **1** : the earth viewed (as in primitive theology) as the divine source of terrestrial life **2** : the embodiment of the female principle of fertility : a nurturing maternal woman

earth·mov·er \'ərth-ˌmü-vər\ *n* (1941) : a machine (as a bulldozer) for excavating, pushing, or transporting large quantities of earth (as in road building) — **earth·mov·ing** \-ˌmü-viŋ\ *n*

earth·quake \'ərth-ˌkwāk\ *n* (14c) **1** : a shaking or trembling of the earth that is volcanic or tectonic in origin **2** : UPHEAVAL 2

earth·rise \'ərth-ˌrīz\ *n* (1968) : the rising of the earth above the horizon of the moon as seen from lunar orbit

earth science *n* (1939) : any of the sciences (as geology, meteorology, or oceanography) that deal with the earth or with one or more of its parts — compare GEOSCIENCE — **earth scientist** *n*

earth·shak·er \'ərth-ˌshā-kər\ *n* (1953) : one that is earthshaking

earth·shak·ing \-ˌkiŋ\ *adj* (1948) : of great importance : MOMENTOUS — **earth·shak·ing·ly** \-ˌkiŋ-lē\ *adv*

earth·shat·ter·ing \'ərth-ˌsha-tə-riŋ\ *adj* (1970) : EARTHSHAKING

earth·shel·tered \'ərth-ˌshel-tərd\ *adj* (1979) : built partly or mostly underground ⟨an ~ house⟩

earth·shine \'ərth-ˌshīn\ *n* (1876) : sunlight reflected by the earth that illuminates the dark part of the moon — called also *earthlight*

earth·star \-ˌstär\ *n* (1885) : any of a genus (*Geastrum*) of globose basidiomycetous fungi with an outer peridium that splits into the shape of a star

earth station *n* (1970) : DISH 3a(2); *esp* : one used primarily for receiving and transmitting television signals

earth tone *n* (1973) : any of various rich colors containing some brown

earth·ward \-wərd\ *also* **earth·wards** \-wərdz\ *adv* (14c) : toward the earth

earth·work \'ərth-ˌwərk\ *n* (1633) **1** : an embankment or other construction made of earth; *esp* : one used as a field fortification **2** : the operations connected with excavations and embankments of earth **3** : a work of art consisting of a portion of land modified by an artist

earth·worm \-ˌwərm\ *n* (14c) : a terrestrial annelid worm (class Oligochaeta); *esp* : any of a family (Lumbricidae) of numerous widely distributed hermaphroditic worms that move through the soil by means of setae

earthy \'ər-thē\ *adj* **earth·i·er; -est** (14c) **1 a** : of, relating to, or consisting of earth ⟨~ creatures like worms⟩ **b** : suggestive of earth (as in texture, odor, or color) ⟨an ~ yellow⟩ **c** : rough, coarse, or plain in taste ⟨~ flavors⟩ **2** *archaic* : EARTHLY, WORLDLY **b** : characteristic of or associated with mortal life on the earth ⟨prefers ~ to ethereal themes⟩ **3** : suggestive of plain or poor people or their ways: as **a** : PRACTICAL, DOWN-TO-EARTH ⟨~ problems of daily life⟩ **b**

: CRUDE, GROSS ⟨~ humor⟩ **c** : plain and simple in style : UNSOPHISTICATED ⟨~ peasant cookery⟩ ⟨~ decor⟩ ⟨~ clothes⟩ — **earth·i·ness** *n*

ear·wax \'ir-ˌwaks\ *n* (14c) : CERUMEN

¹ear·wig \-ˌwig\ *n* [ME *erwigge,* fr. OE *ēarwicga,* fr. *ēare* ear + *wicga* insect] (bef. 12c) : any of numerous insects (order Dermaptera) having slender many-jointed antennae and a pair of cerci resembling forceps at the end of the body

²earwig *vt* **ear·wigged; ear·wig·ging** (1837) : to annoy or attempt to influence by private talk

ear·wit·ness \'ir-'wit-nəs\ *n* (1594) : one who overhears something; *esp* : one who gives a report on what has been heard

¹ease \'ēz\ *n* [ME *ese,* fr. OF *aise* convenience, comfort, fr. L *adjacent-, adjacens* neighboring — more at ADJACENT] (13c) **1** : the state of being comfortable: as **a** : freedom from pain or discomfort **b** : freedom from care **c** : freedom from labor or difficulty **d** : freedom from embarrassment or constraint : NATURALNESS **e** : an easy fit **2** : relief from discomfort or obligation **3** : FACILITY, EFFORTLESSNESS **4** : an act of easing or a state of being eased — **ease·ful** \-fəl\ *adj* — **ease·ful·ly** \-fə-lē\ *adv* — **at ease 1** : free from pain or discomfort **2 a** : free from restraint or formality **b** : standing silently (as in a military formation) with the feet apart, the right foot in place, and one or both hands behind the body — often used as a command

²ease *vb* **eased; eas·ing** *vt* (14c) **1** : to free from something that pains, disquiets, or burdens **2** : to make less painful : ALLEVIATE ⟨~ his suffering⟩ **3 a** : to lessen the pressure or tension of esp. by slackening, lifting, or shifting **b** : to maneuver gently or carefully **c** : to moderate or reduce esp. in amount or intensity **4** : to make less difficult ⟨~ credit⟩ **5 a** : to put the helm of (a ship) alee **b** : to let (a helm or rudder) come back a little after having been put hard over ~ *vi* **1** : to give freedom or relief **2** : to move or pass with freedom or with little resistance **3** : MODERATE, SLACKEN

ea·sel \'ē-zəl\ *n* [D *ezel,* lit., ass, fr. MD *esel;* akin to OE *esol* ass; both fr. a prehistoric EGmc-WGmc word borrowed fr. L *asinus* ass] (1596) : a frame for supporting something (as an artist's canvas)

ease·ment \'ēz-mənt\ *n* (14c) **1** : an act or means of easing or relieving (as from discomfort) **2** : an interest in land owned by another that entitles its holder to a specific limited use or enjoyment

eas·i·ly \'ēz-lē, 'ē-zə-\ *adv* (13c) **1** : in an easy manner : without difficulty **2** : without question : by far **3** : WELL 10b ⟨it could ~ have been me⟩

¹east \'ēst\ *adv* [ME *est,* fr. OE *ēast;* akin to OHG *ōstar* to the east, L *aurora* dawn, Gk *ēōs, heōs*] (bef. 12c) : to, toward, or in the east

²east *adj* (bef. 12c) **1** : situated toward or at the east ⟨an ~ window⟩ **2** : coming from the east ⟨an ~ wind⟩

³east *n* (bef. 12c) **1 a** : the general direction of sunrise : the direction toward the right of one facing north **b** : the compass point directly opposite to west **2** *cap* **a** : regions lying to the east of a specified or implied point of orientation **b** : regions having a culture derived from ancient non-European esp. Asian areas **3** : the altar end of a church **4** *often cap* **a** : the one of four positions at 90-degree intervals that lies to the east or at the right of a diagram **b** : a person (as a bridge player) occupying this position in the course of a specified activity

east·bound \'ēs(t)-ˌbaůnd\ *adj* (1880) : traveling or heading east

east by north (1594) : a compass point that is one point north of due east : N78°45′E

east by south (14c) : a compass point that is one point south of due east : S78°45′E

East Caribbean dollar *n* (ca. 1974) : the basic monetary unit shared by a number of islands of the British West Indies

Eas·ter \'ē-stər\ *n* [ME *estre,* fr. OE *ēastre;* akin to OHG *ōstarun* (pl.) Easter, OE *ēast* east] (bef. 12c) : a feast that commemorates Christ's resurrection and is observed with variations of date due to different calendars on the first Sunday after the paschal full moon

EASTER DATES

YEAR	ASH WEDNESDAY		EASTER		YEAR	ASH WEDNESDAY		EASTER	
1993	Feb.	24	Apr.	11	2003	Mar.	5	Apr.	20
1994	Feb.	16	Apr.	3	2004	Feb.	25	Apr.	11
1995	Mar.	1	Apr.	16	2005	Feb.	9	Mar.	27
1996	Feb.	21	Apr.	7	2006	Mar.	1	Apr.	16
1997	Feb.	12	Mar.	30	2007	Feb.	21	Apr.	8
1998	Feb.	25	Apr.	12	2008	Feb.	6	Mar.	23
1999	Feb.	17	Apr.	4	2009	Feb.	25	Apr.	12
2000	Mar.	8	Apr.	23	2010	Feb.	17	Apr.	4
2001	Feb.	28	Apr.	15	2011	Mar.	9	Apr.	24
2002	Feb.	13	Mar.	31	2012	Feb.	22	Apr.	8

Easter egg *n* (1804) : an egg that is dyed and sometimes decorated and that is associated with the celebration of Easter

Easter lily *n* (1877) : any of several white cultivated lilies (esp. *Lilium longiflorum*) that bloom in early spring

¹east·er·ly \'ē-stər-lē\ *adj or adv* [obs. *easter* (eastern)] (1548) **1** : situated toward or belonging to the east ⟨the ~ shore of the lake⟩ **2** : coming from the east ⟨an ~ storm⟩

²easterly *n, pl* **-lies** (1901) : a wind from the east

Easter Monday *n* (14c) : the Monday after Easter observed as a legal holiday in some nations of the Commonwealth and in No. Carolina

east·ern \'ē-stərn\ *adj* [ME *estern,* fr. OE *ēasterne;* akin to OHG *ōstrōni* eastern, OE *ēast* east] (bef. 12c) **1** *cap* : of, relating to, or characteristic of a region conventionally designated East **2** *cap* **a** : of, relating to, or being the Christian churches originating in the church of the Eastern Roman Empire **b** : EASTERN ORTHODOX **3 a** : lying toward

\ə\ abut \ᵊ\ kitten, F table \ər\ further \a\ ash \ā\ ace \ä\ mop, mar \aů\ out \ch\ chin \e\ bet \ē\ easy \g\ go \i\ hit \ī\ ice \j\ job \ŋ\ sing \ō\ go \ó\ law \ói\ boy \th\ thin \t̷h\ the \ü\ loot \ů\ foot \y\ yet \zh\ vision \à, k̷, ⁿ, œ, œ̄, ᵫ, ᵫ̄, ᵉ\ see Guide to Pronunciation the east **b** : coming from the east ⟨an ~ wind⟩ — **east·ern·most** \-ˌmōst\ adj

East·ern·er \'ē-stə(r)-nər\ n (1840) : a native or inhabitant of the East; esp : a native or resident of the eastern part of the U.S.

eastern hemisphere n, often cap E&H (1624) : the half of the earth east of the Atlantic Ocean including Europe, Asia, Australia, and Africa

Eastern Orthodox adj (1909) : of or consisting of the Eastern churches that form a loose federation according primacy of honor to the patriarch of Constantinople and adhering to the decisions of the first seven ecumenical councils and to the Byzantine rite

eastern time n, often cap E (1883) : the time of the 5th time zone west of Greenwich that includes the eastern U.S. — see TIME ZONE illustration

eastern white pine n (1925) : WHITE PINE 1a

Eas·ter·tide \'ē-stər-ˌtīd\ n [ME estertide, fr. OE ēastortīd, fr. ēastor + tīd time — more at TIDE] (bef. 12c) : the period from Easter to Ascension Day, to Whitsunday, or to Trinity Sunday

East Germanic n (ca. 1901) : a subdivision of the Germanic languages that includes Gothic — see INDO-EUROPEAN LANGUAGES table

east·ing \'ē-stiŋ\ n (1628) **1** : easterly progress **2** : difference in longitude to the east from the last preceding point of reckoning

east–northeast n (1725) : a compass point that is two points north of due east : N67°30'E

east–southeast n (1555) : a compass point that is two points south of due east : S67°30'E

¹**east·ward** \'ēs-twərd\ adv or adj (bef. 12c) : toward the east — **east·wards** \-twərdz\ adv

²**eastward** n (1582) : eastward direction or part ⟨sail to the ~⟩

¹**easy** \'ē-zē\ adj **eas·i·er; -est** [ME esy, fr. OF aaisié, pp. of aaisier to ease, fr. a- ad- (fr. L ad-) + aise ease] (13c) **1 a** : causing or involving little difficulty or discomfort ⟨within ~ reach⟩ **b** : requiring or indicating little effort, thought, or reflection ⟨~ clichés⟩ **2 a** : not severe : LENIENT **b** : not steep or abrupt ⟨~ slopes⟩ **c** : not difficult to endure or undergo ⟨an ~ penalty⟩ **d** : readily taken advantage of ⟨an ~ target for takeovers⟩ **e** (1) : readily available : easily come by ⟨~ pickings⟩ (2) : plentiful in supply at low or declining interest rates ⟨~ money⟩ (3) : less in demand and usu. lower in price ⟨bonds were easier⟩ **f** : PLEASANT ⟨~ listening⟩ **3 a** : marked by peace and comfort ⟨the ~ life of a courtier⟩ **b** : not hurried or strenuous ⟨an ~ pace⟩ **4 a** : free from pain, annoyance, or anxiety ⟨did all she could to make him easier⟩ **b** : marked by social ease ⟨an air of ~ assurance⟩ **c** : EASYGOING ⟨an ~ disposition⟩ **5 a** : giving ease, comfort, or relaxation ⟨~ chairs⟩ **b** : not burdensome or straitened ⟨bought on ~ terms⟩ **c** : fitting comfortably : allowing freedom of movement ⟨~ jackets⟩ **d** : marked by ready facility ⟨an ~ flowing style⟩ **e** : felt or attained to readily, naturally, and spontaneously ⟨an ~ smile⟩ — **eas·i·ness** n

syn EASY, FACILE, SIMPLE, LIGHT, EFFORTLESS, SMOOTH mean not demanding effort or involving difficulty. EASY is applicable either to persons or things imposing tasks or to activity required by such tasks ⟨an easy college course⟩. FACILE often adds to EASY the connotation of undue haste or shallowness ⟨facile answers to complex questions⟩. SIMPLE stresses ease in understanding or dealing with because complication is absent ⟨a simple problem in arithmetic⟩. LIGHT stresses freedom from what is burdensome ⟨a light teaching load⟩. EFFORTLESS stresses the appearance of ease and usu. implies the prior attainment of artistry or expertness ⟨moving with effortless grace⟩. SMOOTH stresses the absence or removal of all difficulties, hardships, or obstacles ⟨a smooth ride⟩. **syn** see in addition COMFORTABLE

²**easy** adv **eas·i·er; -est** (14c) **1** : EASILY 1 ⟨promises come ~⟩ **2 a** : without undue speed or excitement ⟨take it ~⟩ **b** : in or with moderation ⟨go ~ on the mustard⟩ **3 a** : without worry or care ⟨rest ~⟩ **b** : without a severe penalty ⟨got off ~⟩ **c** : without violent movement ⟨the boat rode ~⟩ **4** : EASILY 2 ⟨cost $500 ~⟩

easy·go·ing \ˌē-zē-'gō-iŋ, -'gó(-)iŋ\ adj (1674) **1 a** : relaxed and casual in style or manner ⟨an ~ boss⟩ **b** : morally lax **2** : UNHURRIED, COMFORTABLE ⟨an ~ pace⟩ — **easy·go·ing·ness** n

easy mark n (ca. 1896) : one easily taken advantage of

easy street n (1900) : a situation with no worries

easy virtue n (1809) : sexually promiscuous behavior or habits ⟨ladies of easy virtue⟩

¹**eat** \'ēt\ vb **ate** \'āt, dial or Brit 'et\; **eat·en** \'ē-t°n\; **eat·ing** [ME eten, fr. OE etan; akin to OHG ezzan to eat, L edere, Gk edmenai] vt (bef. 12c) **1** : to take in through the mouth as food : ingest, chew, and swallow in turn **2 a** : to destroy, consume, or waste by or as if by eating ⟨expenses ate up the profits⟩ **b** : to bear the expense of : take a loss on **3 a** : to consume gradually : CORRODE **b** : to consume with vexation : BOTHER ⟨what's ~ing you now⟩ ~ vi **1** : to take food or a meal **2** : to affect something by gradual destruction or consumption — usu. used with into, away, or at — **eat·er** n — **eat another's lunch** : to deprive of profit, dominance, or success — **eat crow** : to accept what one has fought against — **eat humble pie** : to apologize or retract under pressure — **eat one's heart out 1** : to grieve bitterly **2** : to be jealous — **eat one's words** : to retract what one has said — **eat out of one's hand** : to accept the domination of another

²**eat** n [ME et, fr. OE ǣt; akin to OHG āz food; derivative fr. the root of ¹eat] (bef. 12c) : something to eat : FOOD — usu. used in pl.

¹**eat·able** \'ē-tə-bəl\ adj (14c) : fit or able to be eaten

²**eatable** n (1672) **1** : something to eat **2** pl : FOOD

eat·ery \'ē-tə-rē\ n, pl **-er·ies** (1901) : LUNCHEONETTE, RESTAURANT

eath \'ēth\ adv or adj [ME ethe, fr. OE ēathe; akin to OHG ōdi easy] (bef. 12c) Scot : EASY

eat·ing \'ē-tiŋ\ adj (15c) **1** : used for eating ⟨~ utensils⟩ **2** : suitable to eat ⟨the finest ~ fish⟩; also : suitable to eat raw ⟨an ~ apple⟩

eau de co·logne \ˌō-də-kə-'lōn\ n, pl **eaux de cologne** \ˌō(z)d-ə-\ [F, lit., Cologne water, fr. Cologne, Germany] (1802) : COLOGNE

eau–de–vie \ˌō-də-'vē\ n, pl **eaux–de–vie** \ˌō(z)-də-\ [F, lit., water of life, trans. of ML aqua vitae] (1748) : a clear brandy distilled from the fermented juice of fruit (as pears or raspberries)

eaves \'ēvz\ n pl [ME eves, alter. of eves (sing.), fr. OE efes; akin to OHG obasa portico, OE ūp up — more at UP] (bef. 12c) **1** : the lower border of a roof that overhangs the wall **2** : a projecting edge (as of a hill)

eaves·drop \'ēvz-ˌdräp\ vi [prob. back-formation fr. eavesdropper, lit., one standing under the drip from the eaves] (1606) : to listen secretly to what is said in private — **eaves·drop·per** n

eaves trough n (1878) : GUTTER 1a

¹**ebb** \'eb\ n [ME ebbe, fr. OE ebba; akin to MD ebbe ebb, OE of from — more at OF] (bef. 12c) **1** : the reflux of the tide toward the sea **2** : a point or condition of decline ⟨our spirits were at a low ~⟩

²**ebb** vi (bef. 12c) **1** : to recede from the flood **2** : to fall from a higher to a lower level or from a better to a worse state **syn** see ABATE

ebb tide n (1823) **1** : the tide while ebbing or at ebb **2** : a period or state of decline

EBCDIC \'ep-sə-ˌdik, 'eb-\ n [extended binary coded decimal interchange code] (ca. 1966) : a code for representing alphanumeric information (as on magnetic tape)

Ebo·la virus \ē-'bō-lə, i-, e-\ n [Ebola River, Zaire, site of an outbreak of the virus in 1976] (1977) : an RNA-containing virus of African origin that causes an often fatal hemorrhagic fever — called also Ebola

eb·on \'e-bən\ adj (15c) : EBONY

eb·o·nite \'e-bə-ˌnīt\ n (1861) : hard rubber esp. when black

eb·o·nize \-ˌnīz\ vt **-nized; -niz·ing** (ca. 1828) : to stain black in imitation of ebony

¹**eb·o·ny** \'e-bə-nē\ n, pl **-nies** [prob. fr. LL hebeninus of ebony, fr. Gk ebeninos, fr. ebenos ebony, fr. Egypt hbnj] (14c) **1** : a hard heavy wood yielded by various Old World tropical dicotyledonous trees ⟨genus Diospyros of the family Ebonaceae, the ebony family⟩ **2 a** : a tree yielding ebony **b** : any of several trees yielding wood like ebony

²**ebony** adj (1598) **1** : made of or resembling ebony **2** : BLACK, DARK

ebul·lience \i-'bùl-yən(t)s, -'bəl-\ n (1749) : the quality of lively or enthusiastic expression of thoughts or feelings : EXUBERANCE

ebul·lien·cy \-yən(t)-sē\ n (1676) : EBULLIENCE

ebul·lient \-yənt\ adj [L ebullient-, ebulliens, prp. of ebullire to bubble out, fr. e- + bullire to bubble, boil — more at BOIL] (1599) **1** : BOILING, AGITATED **2** : characterized by ebullience — **ebul·lient·ly** adv

eb·ul·li·tion \ˌe-bə-'li-shən\ n (1534) **1** : a sudden violent outburst or display **2** : the act, process, or state of boiling or bubbling up

EB virus \ˌē-'bē-\ n (1968) : EPSTEIN-BARR VIRUS

¹**ec·cen·tric** \ik-'sen-trik, ek-\ adj [ME, fr. ML eccentricus, fr. Gk ekkentros, fr. ex out of + kentron center] (ca. 1630) **1 a** : deviating from an established or usual pattern or style **b** : deviating from conventional or accepted usage or conduct esp. in odd or whimsical ways **2 a** : deviating from a circular path; esp : ELLIPTICAL 1 ⟨an ~ orbit⟩ **b** : located elsewhere than at the geometrical center; also : having the axis or support so located ⟨an ~ wheel⟩ **syn** see STRANGE — **ec·cen·tri·cal·ly** \-tri-k(ə-)lē\ adv

²**eccentric** n (1827) **1** : a mechanical device consisting of a disk through which a shaft is keyed eccentrically and a circular strap which works freely round the rim of the disk for communicating its motion to one end of a rod whose other end is constrained to move in a straight line so as to produce reciprocating motion **2** : an eccentric person

ec·cen·tric·i·ty \ˌek-(ˌ)sen-'tri-sə-tē\, n, pl **-ties** (1545) **1 a** : the quality or state of being eccentric **b** : deviation from an established pattern or norm; esp : odd or whimsical behavior **2 a** : a mathematical constant that for a given conic section is the ratio of the distances from any point of the conic section to a focus and the corresponding directrix **b** : the eccentricity of an astronomical orbit used as a measure of its deviation from circularity

ec·chy·mo·sis \ˌe-ki-'mō-səs\ n, pl **-mo·ses** \-ˌsēz\ [NL, fr. Gk ekchymōsis, fr. ekchymousthai to extravasate blood, fr. ex- + chymos juice — more at CHYME] (1541) : the escape of blood into the tissues from ruptured blood vessels — **ec·chy·mot·ic** \-'mä-tik\ adj

ecclesi- or **ecclesio-** comb form [ME ecclesi-, fr. LL ecclesia, fr. Gk ekklēsia assembly of citizens, church, fr. ekkalein to call forth, summon, fr. ex- + kalein to call — more at LOW] : church ⟨ecclesiology⟩

ec·cle·sia \i-'klē-zē-ə, e-\ adj (1641) : of or relating to a church

Ec·cle·si·as·tes \i-ˌklē-zē-'as-(ˌ)tēz, e-ˌklē-\ n [Gk Ekklēsiastēs, lit., preacher (trans. of Heb qōheleth), fr. ekklēsiastēs member of an assembly, fr. ekklēsia] : a book of wisdom literature in canonical Jewish and Christian Scripture — see BIBLE table

¹**ec·cle·si·as·tic** \-'as-tik\ adj (15c) : ECCLESIASTICAL

²**ecclesiastic** n (1651) : CLERGYMAN

ec·cle·si·as·ti·cal \-ti-kəl\ adj [ME, fr. LL ecclesiasticus, fr. LGk ekklēsiastikos, fr. Gk, of an assembly of citizens, fr. ekklēsiastēs] (15c) **1** : of or relating to a church esp. as an established institution **2** : suitable for use in a church — **ec·cle·si·as·ti·cal·ly** \-ti-k(ə-)lē\ adv

ec·cle·si·as·ti·cism \-tə-ˌsi-zəm\ n (ca. 1859) : excessive attachment to ecclesiastical forms and practices

Ec·cle·si·as·ti·cus \-ti-kəs\ n [LL, fr. ecclesiasticus] : a didactic book included in the Protestant Apocrypha and as Sirach in the Roman Catholic canon of the Old Testament

ec·cle·si·ol·o·gy \i-ˌklē-zē-'ä-lə-jē, e-ˌklē-\ n, pl **-gies** (ca. 1837) **1** : the study of church architecture and adornment **2** : theological doctrine relating to the church — **ec·cle·si·o·log·i·cal** \-zē-ə-'lä-ji-kəl\ adj — **ec·cle·si·ol·o·gist** \-zē-'ä-lə-jist\ n

ec·crine gland \'e-krən-, -ˌkrīn-, -ˌkrēn-\ n [Gk ekkrinein to secrete, fr. ek-, ex- out + krinein to separate — more at CERTAIN] (ca. 1927) : any of the rather small sweat glands in the human skin that produce a fluid secretion without removing cytoplasm from the secretory cells — called also eccrine sweat gland

ec·dys·i·ast \ek-'di-zē-ˌast, -ē-əst\ n [Gk ekdysis] (1940) : STRIPTEASER

ec·dy·sis \'ek-də-səs\ n, pl **ec·dy·ses** \-də-ˌsēz\ [NL, fr. Gk ekdysis act of getting out, fr. ekdyein to strip, fr. ex- + dyein to enter, don] (ca. 1854) : the act of molting or shedding an outer cuticular layer (as in insects and crustaceans)

ec·dy·sone \'ek-də-ˌsōn\ also **ec·dy·son** \-ˌsän\ n [ISV ecdysis + hormone] (1956) : any of several arthropod hormones that in insects are produced by the prothoracic gland and that trigger molting and metamorphosis

ece·sis \i-'sē-səs, -'kē-\ n [NL, fr. Gk oikēsis inhabitation, fr. oikein to inhabit — more at ECUMENICAL] (ca. 1904) : the establishment of a plant or animal in a new habitat

echelle \ā-'shel\ n [F, lit., ladder, fr. OF eschele] (1949) : a diffraction grating made by ruling a plane metallic mirror with lines having a relatively wide spacing

¹**ech·e·lon** \'e-shə-ˌlän\ n [F échelon, lit., rung of a ladder, fr. OF eschelon, fr. eschele ladder, fr. LL scala] (1796) **1 a** (1): an arrangement of a body of troops with its units each somewhat to the left or right of the one in the rear like a series of steps (2): a formation of units or individuals resembling such an echelon (3): a flight formation in which each airplane flies at a certain elevation above or below and at a certain distance behind and to the right or left of the airplane ahead **b** : any of several military units in echelon formation **2 a** : one of a series of levels or grades (as of leadership or responsibility) in an organization or field of activity **b** : a group of individuals at a particular level or grade in an organization

²**echelon** vt (ca. 1860) : to form or arrange in an echelon ~ vi : to take position in an echelon

ech·e·ve·ria \ˌe-chə-və-'rē-ə\ n [NL, genus name, after Atanasio Echeverría fl 1771 Mex. botanical illustrator] (1883) : any of a large genus (Echeveria) of tropical American succulent plants of the orpine family that have showy rosettes of often plushy basal leaves and axillary clusters of flowers with erect petals and that are often grown as ornamentals

echid·na \i-'kid-nə\ n [NL, fr. L, viper, fr. Gk — more at OPHITIC] (1832) : an oviparous spiny-coated toothless burrowing nocturnal monotreme mammal (Tachyglossus aculeatus) of Australia, Tasmania, and New Guinea that has a long extensile tongue and long heavy claws and that feeds chiefly on ants; also : a related mammal (Zaglossus bruijni) of New Guinea having a longer snout and shorter spines

echin- or **echino-** comb form [L, fr. Gk, fr. echinos sea urchin] **1** : prickle ⟨echinoderm⟩ **2** : sea urchin ⟨echinoid⟩

echi·no·coc·co·sis \i-ˌkī-nə-kä-'kō-səs\ n, pl **-co·ses** \-ˌsēz\ [NL] (1900) : infestation with or disease caused by an echinococcus (as Echinococcus granulosus)

echi·no·coc·cus \i-ˌkī-nə-'kä-kəs\ n, pl **-coc·ci** \-'käk-ˌ(s)ī, -'käk-ˌ(ˌ)s)ē\ [NL, genus name] (1839) : any of a genus (Echinococcus) of tapeworms that alternate a minute adult living as a commensal in the intestine of carnivores with a hydatid larva invading tissues esp. of the liver of cattle, sheep, swine, and humans and acting as a dangerous pathogen

echi·no·derm \i-'kī-nə-ˌdərm\ n [NL Echinodermata, phylum name, fr. echin- + -dermata (fr. Gk derma skin)] (1835) : any of a phylum (Echinodermata) of radially symmetrical coelomate marine animals including the starfishes, sea urchins, and related forms — **echi·no·der·ma·tous** \-ˌkī-nə-'dər-mə-təs\ adj

echi·noid \i-'kī-ˌnȯid, 'e-kə-ˌnȯid\ n (1864) : SEA URCHIN

echi·nus \i-'kī-nəs\ n, pl **-ni** \-ˌnī\ [ME, fr. L, fr. Gk echinos hedgehog, sea urchin — more at OPHITE] (14c) **1** : SEA URCHIN **2 a** : the rounded molding forming the bell of the capital in the Greek Doric order **b** : a similar member in other orders

echi·uroid \ˌe-ki-'yur-ˌȯid\ n [NL Echiuroidea or Echiura, ultim. fr. Gk echis viper + oura tail] (ca. 1889) : any of a taxon (class Echiuroidea or phylum Echiura) of marine worms of uncertain taxonomic affinities that have a sensitive but nonretractile proboscis above the mouth

¹**echo** \'e-(ˌ)kō\ n, pl **ech·oes** also **echos** [ME ecco, fr. MF & L; MF echo, fr. L, fr. Gk ēchō; akin to L vagire to wail, Gk ēchē sound] (14c) **1 a** : the repetition of a sound caused by reflection of sound waves **b** : the sound due to such reflection **2 a** : a repetition or imitation of another : REFLECTION **b** : REPERCUSSION, RESULT **c** : TRACE, VESTIGE **d** : RESPONSE **3** : one who closely imitates or repeats another's words, ideas, or acts **4** : a soft repetition of a musical phrase **5 a** : the repetition of a received radio signal due esp. to reflection of part of the wave from an ionized layer of the atmosphere **b** (1) : the reflection of transmitted radar signals by an object (2) : the visual indication of this reflection on a radarscope — **echo·ey** \'e-ˌkō-ē\ adj

²**echo** vb **ech·oed; echo·ing** \'e-(ˌ)kō-iŋ, 'e-kə-wiŋ\ vi (1596) **1** : to resound with echoes **2** : to produce an echo ~ vt **1** : REPEAT, IMITATE **2** : to send back (a sound) by the reflection of sound waves

¹**Echo** n [Gk Ēchō] : a nymph in Greek mythology who pines away for love of Narcissus until nothing is left of her but her voice

²**Echo** (ca. 1952) — a communications code word for the letter e

echo·car·dio·gram \ˌe-kō-'kär-dē-ə-ˌgram\ n (1967) : a visual record made by echocardiography

echo·car·di·og·ra·phy \-ˌkär-dē-'ä-grə-fē\ n, pl **-phies** (1965) : the use of ultrasound to examine the structure and functioning of the heart for abnormalities and disease — **echo·car·dio·graph·er** \-grə-fər\ n — **echo·car·dio·graph·ic** \-dē-ə-'gra-fik\ adj

echo chamber n (ca. 1937) : a room with sound-reflecting walls used for producing hollow or echoing sound effects

echo·ic \e-'kō-ik, e-\ adj (ca. 1880) **1** : formed in imitation of some natural sound : ONOMATOPOEIC **2** : of or relating to an echo

echo·la·lia \ˌe-kō-'lā-lē-ə\ n [NL] (ca. 1885) : the often pathological repetition of what is said by other people as if echoing them — **echo·lal·ic** \-'la-lik\ adj

echo·lo·ca·tion \ˌe-kō-lō-'kā-shən\ n (ca. 1944) : a physiological process for locating distant or invisible objects (as prey) by means of sound waves reflected back to the emitter (as a bat) by the objects

echo sounder n (1927) : an instrument for determining the depth of a body of water or of an object below the surface by sound waves

echo·vi·rus \'e-kō-ˌvī-rəs\ n [enteric cytopathogenic human orphan + virus] (1955) : any of a group of picornaviruses that are found in the gastrointestinal tract, that cause cytopathic changes in cells in tissue culture, and that are sometimes associated with respiratory ailments and meningitis

éclair \ā-'klar, i-, -'kler, 'ā-ˌ, 'ē-ˌ\ n [F, lit., lightning] (1861) : a usu. chocolate-frosted oblong light pastry with whipped cream or custard filling

éclair·cis·se·ment \ā-kler-sēs-(ə-)mäⁿ\ n, pl **-ments** \-mäⁿ(z)\ [F] (1667) : a clearing up of something obscure : ENLIGHTENMENT

eclamp·sia \i-'klam(p)-sē-ə\ n [NL, fr. Gk eklampsis sudden flashing, fr. eklampein to shine forth, fr. ex- out + lampein to shine] (ca. 1860) : a convulsive state; esp : an attack of convulsions during pregnancy or parturition — **eclamp·tic** \-'klam(p)-tik\ adj

éclat \ā-'klä, 'ā-ˌ, n [F, splinter, burst, éclat] (1672) **1** : ostentatious display : PUBLICITY **2** : dazzling effect : BRILLIANCE **3 a** : brilliant or conspicuous success **b** : PRAISE, APPLAUSE

¹**eclec·tic** \e-'klek-tik, i-\ adj [Gk eklektikos, fr. eklegein to select, fr. ex- out + legein to gather — more at LEGEND] (1683) **1** : selecting what

appears to be best in various doctrines, methods, or styles **2** : composed of elements drawn from various sources; also : HETEROGENEOUS — **eclec·ti·cal·ly** \-ti-k(ə-)lē\ adv

²**eclectic** n (1817) : one who uses an eclectic method or approach

eclec·ti·cism \-'klek-tə-ˌsi-zəm\ n (1798) **1** : the theory or practice of an eclectic method **2** : a mid-19th-century movement in architecture and design that revived the styles of various historical periods

¹**eclipse** \i-'klips\ n [ME, fr. OF, fr. L eclipsis, fr. Gk ekleipsis, fr. ekleipein to omit, fail, suffer eclipse, fr. ex- + leipein to leave — more at LOAN] (13c) **1 a** : the total or partial obscuring of one celestial body by another **b** : the passing into the shadow of a celestial body — compare OCCULTATION, TRANSIT **2** : a falling into obscurity or decline; also : the state of being eclipsed **3** : the state of being in eclipse plumage

eclipse 1a: S sun, E earth, M moon in solar eclipse, M¹ moon in lunar eclipse

²**eclipse** vt **eclipsed; eclips·ing** (13c) : to cause an eclipse of: as **a** : OBSCURE, DARKEN **b** : to reduce in importance or repute **c** : SURPASS

eclipse plumage n (1906) : comparatively dull plumage that is usu. of seasonal occurrence in birds exhibiting a distinct breeding plumage

¹**eclip·tic** \i-'klip-tik\ adj [ME ecliptik, fr. LL ecliptica linea, lit., line of eclipses] (14c) : of or relating to the ecliptic or an eclipse

²**ecliptic** n (15c) : the great circle of the celestial sphere that is the apparent path of the sun among the stars or of the earth as seen from the sun : the plane of the earth's orbit extended to meet the celestial sphere

ec·logue \'ek-ˌlȯg, -ˌläg\ n [ME eclog, fr. L Eclogae, title of Virgil's pastorals, lit., selections, pl. of ecloga, fr. Gk eklogē, fr. eklegein to select] (15c) : a poem in which shepherds converse

eclo·sion \i-'klō-zhən\ n [F éclosion, fr. éclore to hatch, fr. (assumed) VL exclaudere, alter. of L excludere to hatch out, exclude] (ca. 1889) of an insect : the act of emerging from the pupal case or hatching from the egg

eco- comb form [LL oeco- household, fr. Gk oik-, oiko-, fr. oikos house — more at VICINITY] **1** : habitat or environment ⟨ecospecies⟩ **2** : ecological or environmental ⟨ecocatastrophe⟩

eco·ca·tas·tro·phe \ˌē-(ˌ)kō-kə-'tas-trə-fē, ˌe-(ˌ)kō-\ n (1969) : a major destructive upset in the balance of nature esp. when caused by the intervention of humans

ecol·o·gy \i-'kä-lə-jē, e-\ n, pl **-gies** [G Ökologie, fr. öko- eco- + -logie -logy] (1873) **1** : a branch of science concerned with the interrelationship of organisms and their environments **2** : the totality or pattern of relations between organisms and their environment **3** : HUMAN ECOLOGY — **eco·log·i·cal** \ˌē-kə-'lä-ji-kəl, ˌe-kə-\ also **eco·log·ic** \-jik\ adj — **eco·log·i·cal·ly** \-ji-k(ə-)lē\ adv — **ecol·o·gist** \i-'kä-lə-jist, e-\ n

econo·box \i-'kä-nō-ˌbäks, ē-\ n [economical + ²box] (1980) : a small economical car

econo·met·rics \i-ˌkä-nə-'me-triks, ē-, kä-\ n pl but sing in constr [blend of economics and metric] (1933) : the application of statistical methods to the study of economic data and problems — **econo·met·ric** \-trik\ adj — **econo·met·ri·cal·ly** \-tri-k(ə-)lē\ adv — **econo·me·tri·cian** \-mə-'tri-shən\ n — **econo·met·rist** \-'me-trist\ n

eco·nom·ic \ˌe-kə-'nä-mik, ˌē-kə-\ adj (1592) **1** archaic : of or relating to a household or its management **2** : ECONOMICAL **2 3 a** : of or relating to economics **b** : of, relating to, or based on the production, distribution, and consumption of goods and services **c** : of or relating to an economy **4** : having practical or industrial significance or uses : affecting material resources **5** : PROFITABLE

econom·i·cal \-mi-kəl\ adj (15c) **1** archaic : ECONOMIC **1 2** : marked by careful, efficient, and prudent use of resources : THRIFTY **3** : operating with little waste or at a saving syn see SPARING — **econom·i·cal·ly** \-mi-k(ə-)lē\ adv

economic rent n (1889) : the return for the use of a factor in excess of the minimum required to bring forth its service

eco·nom·ics \ˌe-kə-'nä-miks, ˌē-kə-\ n pl but sing or pl in constr (1792) **1** : a social science concerned chiefly with description and analysis of the production, distribution, and consumption of goods and services **2** : economic aspect or significance

economise Brit var of ECONOMIZE

econ·o·mist \i-'kä-nə-mist\ n (1586) **1** archaic : one who practices economy **2** : a specialist in economics

econ·o·mize \-ˌmīz\ vb **-mized; -miz·ing** vi (1820) : to practice economy : be frugal ~ vt : to use more economically : SAVE — **econ·o·miz·er** n

¹**econ·o·my** \i-'kä-nə-mē, ə-, ē-\ n, pl **-mies** [MF yconomie, fr. ML oeconomia, fr. Gk oikonomia, fr. oikonomos household manager, fr. oikos house + nemein to manage — more at VICINITY, NIMBLE] (15c) **1** archaic : the management of household or private affairs and esp. expenses **2 a** : thrifty and efficient use of material resources : frugality in expenditures; also : an instance or a means of economizing : SAVING **b** : efficient and concise use of nonmaterial resources (as effort, language, or motion) **3** : the arrangement or mode of operation of something : ORGANIZATION **4** : the structure of economic life in a country, area, or period; specif : an economic system

²**economy** adj (ca. 1906) : designed to save money ⟨~ cars⟩

\ə\ abut \ᵊ\ kitten, F table \ər\ further \a\ ash \ā\ ace \ä\ mop, mar \au̇\ out \ch\ chin \e\ bet \ē\ easy \g\ go \i\ hit \ī\ ice \j\ job \ŋ\ sing \ō\ go \ȯ\ law \ȯi\ boy \th\ thin \t̲h̲\ the \ü\ loot \u̇\ foot \y\ yet \zh\ vision \a, k, ⁿ, œ, œ̄, ᵫ, ᵫ̄, ᵊ\ see Guide to Pronunciation

economy of scale (1957) : a reduction in unit costs brought about esp. by increased size of production facilities — usu. used in pl.

eco·phys·i·ol·o·gy \ˌē-kō-ˌfi-zē-'ä-lə-jē, ˌe-kō-\ n (1962) : the science of the interrelationships between the physiology of organisms and their environment — **eco·phys·i·o·log·i·cal** \-ē-ə-'lä-ji-kəl\ adj

eco·spe·cies \'ē-kō-ˌspē-(ˌ)shēz, 'e-kō-, -(ˌ)sēz\ n, pl **ecospecies** (1922) : a subdivision of a cenospecies comparable with a taxonomic species and composed of interbreeding individuals that are less capable of fertile crosses with individuals of other subdivisions

eco·sphere \'ē-kō-ˌsfir, 'e-kō-\ n (1953) : the parts of the universe habitable by living organisms; esp : BIOSPHERE 1

eco·sys·tem \-ˌsis-təm\ n (1935) : the complex of a community of organisms and its environment functioning as an ecological unit in nature

eco·tone \'ē-kə-ˌtōn, 'e-kə-\ n [eco- + Gk tonos tension — more at TONE] (1904) : a transition area between two adjacent ecological communities

eco·tour·ism \ˌē-kō-'tùr-ˌi-zəm, ˌe-kō-\ n (1989) : the practice of touring natural habitats in a manner meant to minimize ecological impact — **eco·tour·ist** \-'tùr-ist\ n

eco·type \'ē-kə-ˌtip, 'e-\ n (1922) : a subdivision of an ecospecies that survives as a distinct group through environmental selection and isolation and that is comparable with a taxonomic subspecies — **eco·typ·ic** \ˌē-kə-'ti-pik, ˌe-kə-\ adj

ecru \'e-(ˌ)krü, 'ā-(ˌ)krü\ n [F écru, lit., unbleached, raw, fr. OF escru, fr. es- completely (fr. L ex-) + cru raw, fr. L crudus — more at RAW] (1850) : BEIGE 2 — **ecru** adj

ec·sta·sy \'ek-stə-sē\ n, pl **-sies** [ME extasie, fr. MF, fr. LL ecstasis, fr. Gk ekstasis, fr. existanai to derange, fr. ex- out + histanai to cause to stand — more at EX-, STAND] (14c) **1 a** : a state of being beyond reason and self-control **b** archaic : SWOON **2** : a state of overwhelming emotion; esp : rapturous delight **3** : TRANCE; esp : a mystic or prophetic trance **4** : a synthetic amphetamine analogue $C_{11}H_{15}NO_2$ used illicitly for its mood-enhancing and hallucinogenic properties

syn ECSTASY, RAPTURE, TRANSPORT mean intense exaltation of mind and feelings. ECSTASY and RAPTURE both suggest a state of trance or near immobility produced by an overpowering emotion. ECSTASY may apply to any strong emotion (as joy, fear, rage, adoration) ⟨religious *ecstasy*⟩. RAPTURE usu. implies intense bliss or beatitude ⟨in speechless *rapture*⟩. TRANSPORT applies to any powerful emotion that lifts one out of oneself and usu. provokes vehement expression or frenzied action ⟨in a *transport* of rage⟩.

¹ec·stat·ic \ek-'sta-tik, ik-'sta-\ adj [ML ecstaticus, fr. Gk ekstatikos, fr. existanai] (1590) : of, relating to, or marked by ecstasy — **ec·stat·i·cal·ly** \-'sta-ti-k(ə-)lē\ adv

²ecstatic n (1659) : one that is subject to ecstasies

ect- or **ecto-** comb form [NL, fr. Gk ekto-, fr. ektos, fr. ex out — more at EX-] : outside : external ⟨ectoderm⟩ — compare END-, EXO-

ec·to·derm \'ek-tə-ˌdərm\ n [ISV] (1861) **1** : the outer cellular membrane of a diploblastic animal (as a jellyfish) **2 a** : the outermost of the three primary germ layers of an embryo **b** : a tissue (as neural tissue) derived from this germ layer — **ec·to·der·mal** \ˌek-tə-'dər-məl\ adj

ec·to·morph \'ek-tə-ˌmòrf\ n [ectoderm + -morph] (1940) : an ectomorphic individual

ec·to·mor·phic \ˌek-tə-'mòr-fik\ adj [ectoderm + -morphic; fr. the predominance in such types of structures developed from the ectoderm] (1940) **1** : of or relating to the component in W. H. Sheldon's classification of body types that measures the body's degree of slenderness, angularity, and fragility **2** : characterized by a light body build with slight muscular development

-ec·to·my \'ek-tə-mē\ n comb form [NL -ectomia, fr. Gk ektemnein to cut out, fr. ec-, ex- out + temnein to cut — more at TOME] : surgical removal ⟨gastrectomy⟩

ec·to·par·a·site \ˌek-tō-'par-ə-ˌsit\ n [ISV] (1861) : a parasite that lives on the exterior of its host — **ec·to·par·a·sit·ic** \-ˌpar-ə-'si-tik\ adj

ec·top·ic \ek-'tä-pik\ adj [Gk ektopos out of place, fr. ex- out + topos place] (1873) : occurring in an abnormal position or in an unusual manner or form ⟨~ lesions⟩ — **ec·top·i·cal·ly** \-pi-k(ə-)lē\ adv

ectopic pregnancy n (1929) : gestation elsewhere than in the uterus (as in a fallopian tube or in the peritoneal cavity)

ec·to·plasm \'ek-tə-ˌpla-zəm\ n (1883) **1** : the outer relatively rigid granule-free layer of the cytoplasm usu. held to be a gel reversibly convertible to a sol **2** : a substance held to produce spirit materialization and telekinesis — **ec·to·plas·mic** \ˌek-tə-'plaz-mik\ adj

ec·to·therm \'ek-tə-ˌthərm\ n (1945) : a cold-blooded animal : POIKILOTHERM — **ec·to·ther·mic** \ˌek-tə-'thər-mik\ adj

ec·to·tro·phic \ˌek-tə-'trō-fik\ adj (ca. 1889) of a mycorrhiza : growing in a close web on the surface of the associated root — compare ENDOTROPHIC

¹ecu \'ā-ˌkyü, ā-kū͞e\ n, pl **ecus** \-ˌkyüz, -kū͞e\ [MF, lit., shield, fr. OF escu, fr. L scutum; from the device of a shield on the coin — more at ESQUIRE] (ca. 1593) : any of various old French units of value; also : a coin representing an ecu

²ecu \ˌē-(ˌ)sē-'yü\ n, often cap E&C&U [European Currency Unit (influenced by F écu ecu)] (1970) : a money of account based on the currency units of members of the European Community

ec·u·men·i·cal \ˌe-kyə-'me-ni-kəl\ adj [LL oecumenicus, fr. LGk oikoumenikos, fr. Gk oikoumenē the inhabited world, fr. fem. of oikoumenos, pres. pass. part. of oikein to inhabit, fr. oikos house — more at VICINITY] (1587) **1** : worldwide or general in extent, influence, or application **2 a** : of, relating to, or representing the whole of a body of churches **b** : promoting or tending toward worldwide Christian unity or cooperation — **ec·u·men·i·cal·ly** \-k(ə-)lē\ adv

ec·u·men·i·cal·ism \-'me-ni-kə-ˌli-zəm\ n (1888) : ECUMENISM

ecumenical patriarch n (1862) : the patriarch of Constantinople as the dignitary given first honor in the Eastern Orthodox Church

ec·u·men·i·cism \ˌe-kyə-'me-nə-ˌsi-zəm\ n (1961) : ECUMENISM — **ec·u·men·i·cist** \-sist\ n

ec·u·me·nic·i·ty \ˌe-kyə-mə-'ni-sə-tē, ˌme-\ n (1840) : the quality or state of being drawn close to others esp. through Christian ecumenism

ec·u·men·ics \-'me-niks\ n pl but sing in constr (ca. 1937) : the study of the nature, mission, problems, and strategy of the Christian church from the perspective of its ecumenical character

ec·u·me·nism \e-'kyü-mə-ˌni-zəm, i- also 'e-kyə- or ˌe-kyə-'me-\ n (1948)

: ecumenical principles and practices esp. as shown among religious groups (as Christian denominations) — **ec·u·me·nist** \e-'kyü-mə-nist, i- also 'e-kyə-mə-nist or ˌe-kyə-'me-nist\ n

ec·ze·ma \ig-'zē-mə, 'eg-zə-mə, 'ek-sə-\ n [NL, fr. Gk ekzema, fr. ekzein to erupt, fr. ex- out + zein to boil — more at EX-, YEAST] (ca. 1753) : an inflammatory condition of the skin characterized by redness, itching, and oozing vesicular lesions which become scaly, crusted, or hardened — **ec·zem·a·tous** \ig-'ze-mə-təs\ adj

ed \'ed\ n (1954) : EDUCATION ⟨driver's ~⟩ ⟨adult ~⟩

¹-ed \d after a vowel or b, g, j, l, m, n, ŋ, r, th, v, z, or zh; əd, id after d or t; t after other sounds; exceptions are pronounced at their entries\ vb suffix or adj suffix [ME, fr. OE -ed, -od, -ad; akin to OHG -t, pp. ending, L -tus, Gk -tos, suffix forming verbals] **1** — used to form the past participle of regular weak verbs ⟨ended⟩ ⟨faded⟩ ⟨tried⟩ ⟨patted⟩ **2** — used to form adjectives of identical meaning from Latin-derived adjectives ending in -ate ⟨crenulated⟩ **3 a** : having : characterized by ⟨cultured⟩ ⟨two-legged⟩ **b** : having the characteristics of ⟨bigoted⟩

²-ed vb suffix [ME -ede, -de, fr. OE -de, -ede, -ode, -ade; akin to OHG -ta, past ending (1st sing.) and prob. to OHG -t, pp. ending] — used to form the past tense of regular weak verbs ⟨judged⟩ ⟨denied⟩ ⟨dropped⟩

eda·cious \i-'dā-shəs\ adj [L edac-, edax, fr. edere to eat — more at EAT] (ca. 1798) **1** archaic : of or relating to eating **2** : VORACIOUS — **edac·i·ty** \-'da-sə-tē\ n

Edam \'ē-dəm, 'ē-ˌdam\ n [Edam, Netherlands] (1836) : a yellow pressed cheese of Dutch origin usu. made in flattened balls and often coated with red wax

edaph·ic \i-'da-fik\ adj [Gk edaphos bottom, ground] (ca. 1900) **1** : of or relating to the soil **2** : resulting from or influenced by the soil rather than the climate — compare CLIMATIC 2 — **edaph·i·cal·ly** \-'da-fi-k(ə-)lē\ adv

edaphic climax n (ca. 1934) : an ecological climax resulting from soil factors and commonly persisting through cycles of climatic and physiographic change — compare CLIMATIC CLIMAX

Ed·dic \'e-dik\ adj [ON Edda, a 13th cent. collection of mythological, heroic, and aphoristic poetry] (1868) : of, relating to, or resembling the Old Norse Edda

¹ed·dy \'e-dē\ n, pl **eddies** [ME (Sc dial.) ydy, prob. fr. ON itha] (15c) **1 a** : a current of water or air running contrary to the main current; esp : a circular current : WHIRLPOOL **b** : something moving similarly **2** : a contrary or circular current (as of thought or policy)

²eddy vb **ed·died; ed·dy·ing** vt (1810) : to cause to move in an eddy ~ vi : to move in an eddy or in the manner of an eddy

eddy current n (1887) : an electric current induced by an alternating magnetic field

edel·weiss \'ā-dəl-ˌvis, -ˌwis\ n [G, fr. edel noble + weiss white] (1862) : a small alpine perennial composite herb (Leontopodium alpinum) of central and southeast Europe that has a dense woolly white pubescence

ede·ma \i-'dē-mə\ n [NL, fr. Gk oidēma swelling, fr. oidein to swell; akin to OE ātor poison] (15c) **1** : an abnormal infiltration and excess accumulation of serous fluid in connective tissue or in a serous cavity — called also dropsy **2 a** : watery swelling of plant organs or parts **b** : any of various plant diseases characterized by such swellings — **edem·a·tous** \-'de-mə-təs\ adj

Eden \'ē-dᵊn\ n [LL, fr. Heb 'Edhen] (13c) **1** : PARADISE **2** : the garden where according to the account in Genesis Adam and Eve first lived — **Eden·ic** \i-'de-nik, ē-\ adj

¹eden·tate \(ˌ)ē-'den-ˌtāt\ adj [L edentatus, pp. of edentare to make toothless, fr. e- + dent-, dens tooth — more at TOOTH] (1828) **1** : lacking teeth **2** : being an edentate

²edentate n (1835) : any of an order (Edentata) of mammals having few or no teeth and including the sloths, armadillos, and New World anteaters and formerly also the pangolins and the aardvark

eden·tu·lous \(ˌ)ē-'den-chə-ləs\ adj [L edentulus, fr. e- + dent-, dens] (1782) : TOOTHLESS

Ed·gar \'ed-gər\ n [Edgar Allan Poe, regarded as father of the detective story] (1947) : a statuette awarded annually by a professional organization for notable achievement in mystery-novel writing

¹edge \'ej\ n [ME egge, fr. OE ecg; akin to L acer sharp, Gk akmē point] (bef. 12c) **1 a** : the cutting side of a blade **b** : the sharpness of a blade **c** (1) : FORCE, EFFECTIVENESS ⟨blunted the ~ of the legislation⟩ (2) : vigor or energy esp. of body ⟨maintains his hard ~⟩ **d** (1) : incisive or penetrating quality ⟨writing with a satirical ~⟩ (2) : a noticeably harsh or sharp quality ⟨her voice had an ~ to it⟩ **e** : keenness of desire or enjoyment ⟨lost my competitive ~⟩ ⟨took the ~ off our appetites⟩ **2 a** : the line where an object or area begins or ends : BORDER ⟨on the ~ of a plain⟩ **b** : the narrow part adjacent to a border ⟨the ~ of the deck⟩ **c** : a point near the beginning or the end; esp : BRINK, VERGE ⟨on the ~ of disaster⟩ **d** : a favorable margin : ADVANTAGE ⟨has an ~ on the competition⟩ **3** : a line or line segment that is the intersection of two plane faces (as of a pyramid) or of two planes — **edge·less** adj — **on edge** : ANXIOUS, NERVOUS

²edge vb **edged; edg·ing** vt (14c) **1 a** : to give an edge to **b** : to be on an edge of ⟨trees edging the lake⟩ **2** : to move or force gradually ⟨edged him off the road⟩ **3** : to incline (a ski) sideways so that one edge cuts into the snow **4** : to defeat by a small margin — often used with out ⟨edged out her opponent⟩ ~ vi : to advance by short moves

edged \'ejd, 'e-jid\ adj (bef. 12c) **1** : having a specified kind of edge, boundary, or border or a specified number of edges ⟨rough-edged⟩ ⟨two-edged⟩ **2** : SHARP, CUTTING ⟨an ~ knife⟩ ⟨an ~ remark⟩

edge effect n (1933) : the effect of an abrupt transition between two quite different adjoining ecological communities on the numbers and kinds of organisms in the marginal habitat

edge-grain \'ej-ˌgrān\ or **edge-grained** \'ej-ˌgrānd\ adj (1906) : QUARTERSAWN

edge in vt (1683) : to work in : INTERPOLATE ⟨edged in a few remarks⟩

edg·er \'e-jər\ n (1591) : one that edges; esp : a tool used to trim the edge of a lawn along a sidewalk or curb

edge tool n (14c) : a tool with a sharp cutting edge

edge·ways \'ej-ˌwāz\ adv (1566) chiefly Brit : SIDEWAYS

edge·wise \-ˌwiz\ adv (1677) : SIDEWAYS

edg·ing n (1558) : something that forms an edge or border

edgy \'e-jē\ adj **edg·i·er; -est** (1775) **1** : having an edge : SHARP **2 a** : being on edge : TENSE, IRRITABLE **b** : characterized by tension ⟨~ negotiations⟩ — **edg·i·ly** \'e-jə-lē\ adv — **edg·i·ness** \'e-jē-nəs\ n

edh \'eth\ *n* [Icel *eth*] (1875) : the letter ð used in Old English and in Icelandic to represent either of the fricatives \th\ or \t̶h̶\ and in some phonetic alphabets to represent the fricative \th\

ed·i·ble \'e-də-bəl\ *adj* [LL *edibilis,* fr. L *edere* to eat — more at EAT] (1594) : fit to be eaten : EATABLE — **ed·i·bil·i·ty** \,e-də-'bi-lə-tē\ *n* — **edible** *n* — **ed·i·ble·ness** \'e-də-bəl-nəs\ *n*

edict \'ē-,dikt\ *n* [ME, fr. L *edictum,* fr. neut. of *edictus,* pp. of *edicere* to decree, fr. *e-* + *dicere* to say — more at DICTION] (14c) **1** : a proclamation having the force of law **2** : ORDER, COMMAND ⟨we held firm to Grandmother's ∼ —M. F. K. Fisher⟩ — **edic·tal** \i-'dik-t²l\ *adj*

ed·i·fi·ca·tion \,e-də-fə-'kā-shən\ *n* (14c) : an act or process of edifying

ed·i·fice \'e-də-fəs\ *n* [ME, fr. MF, fr. L *aedificium,* fr. *aedificare*] (14c) **1** : BUILDING; *esp* : a large or massive structure **2** : a large abstract structure ⟨holds together the social ∼ —R. H. Tawney⟩

ed·i·fy \'e-də-,fī\ *vt* **-fied; -fy·ing** [ME, fr. MF *edifier,* fr. LL & L; LL *aedificare* to instruct or improve spiritually, fr. L, to erect a house, fr. *aedes* temple, house; akin to OE *ād* funeral pyre, L *aestas* summer] (14c) **1** *archaic* **a** : BUILD **b** : ESTABLISH **2** : to instruct and improve esp. in moral and religious knowledge : UPLIFT; *also* : ENLIGHTEN 2, INFORM

¹ed·it \'e-dət\ *vt* [back-formation fr. *editor*] (1791) **1** **a** : to prepare (as literary material) for publication or public presentation **b** : to assemble (as a moving picture or tape recording) by cutting and rearranging **c** : to alter, adapt, or refine esp. to bring about conformity to a standard or to suit a particular purpose ⟨carefully ∼*ed* the speech⟩ **2** : to direct the publication of ⟨∼s the daily newspaper⟩ **3** : DELETE — usu. used with *out* — **ed·it·able** \'e-də-tə-bəl\ *adj*

²edit *n* (1955) : an instance of editing

edi·tion \i-'di-shən\ *n* [MF, fr. L *edition-, editio* publication, edition, fr. *edere* to bring forth, publish, fr. *e-* + *-dere* to put or *-dere* (fr. *dare* to give) — more at DO, DATE] (1555) **1** **a** : the form or version in which a text is published ⟨a paperback ∼⟩ ⟨the German ∼⟩ **b** (1) : the whole number of copies published at one time (2) : a usu. special issue of a newspaper (as for a particular day or purpose) ⟨Sunday ∼⟩ ⟨international ∼⟩ (3) : one of the usu. several issues of a newspaper in a single day ⟨city ∼⟩ ⟨late ∼⟩ **2** **a** : one of the forms in which something is presented ⟨this year's ∼ of the annual charity ball⟩ **b** : the whole number of articles of one style put out at one time ⟨a limited ∼ of collectors' pieces⟩ **3** : COPY, VERSION

edi·tio prin·ceps \ā-,di-tē-(,)ō-'priŋ-,keps, i-,di-shē-(,)ō-'prin-,seps\ *n, pl* **edi·ti·o·nes prin·ci·pes** \ā-,di-tē-'ō-,nās-'priŋ-kə-,pās, i-,di-shē-'ō-(,)nēz-'prin(t)-sə-,pēz\ [NL, lit., first edition] (1802) : the first printed edition esp. of a work that circulated in manuscript before printing became common

ed·i·tor \'e-də-tər\ *n* (1649) **1** : someone who edits esp. as an occupation **2** : a device used in editing motion-picture film or magnetic tape **3** : a computer program that permits the user to create or modify data (as text or graphics) esp. on a display screen — **ed·i·tor·ship** \-,ship\ *n*

¹ed·i·to·ri·al \,e-də-'tōr-ē-əl, -'tȯr-\ *adj* (1744) **1** : of or relating to an editor or editing ⟨an ∼ office⟩ **2** : being or resembling an editorial ⟨an ∼ statement⟩ — **ed·i·to·ri·al·ly** \-ē-ə-lē\ *adv*

²editorial *n* (1830) : a newspaper or magazine article that gives the opinions of the editors or publishers; *also* : an expression of opinion that resembles such an article ⟨a television ∼⟩

ed·i·to·ri·al·ist \-ē-ə-list\ *n* (1901) : a writer of editorials

ed·i·to·ri·al·ize \,e-də-'tōr-ē-ə-,līz, -'tȯr-\ *vi* **-ized; -iz·ing** (1856) **1** : to express an opinion in the form of an editorial **2** : to introduce opinion into the reporting of facts **3** : to express an opinion (as on a controversial issue) — **ed·i·to·ri·al·iza·tion** \-,tōr-ē-ə-lə-'zā-shən, -,tȯr-\ *n* — **ed·i·to·ri·al·iz·er** *n*

editor in chief *n* (1873) : an editor who heads an editorial staff

ed·i·tress \'e-də-trəs\ *n* (1799) : a woman who is an editor

Edom·ite \'ē-də-,mīt\ *n* [*Edom* (Esau), ancestor of the Edomites] (1534) : a member of a Semitic people living south of the Dead Sea in biblical times

EDTA \,ē-,dē-(,)tē-'ā\ *n* [*e*thylene*d*iamine*t*etra*a*cetic acid] (1954) : a white crystalline acid $C_{10}H_{16}N_2O_8$ used esp. as a chelating agent in medicine as an anticoagulant and in the treatment of lead poisoning

ed·u·ca·ble \'e-jə-kə-bəl\ *adj* (1845) : capable of being educated; *specif* : capable of some degree of learning — **ed·u·ca·bil·i·ty** \,e-jə-kə-'bi-lə-tē\ *n*

ed·u·cate \'e-jə-,kāt\ *vb* **-cat·ed; -cat·ing** [ME, to rear, fr. L *educatus,* pp. of *educare* to rear, educate, fr. *educere* to lead forth — more at EDUCE] *vt* (15c) **1** **a** : to provide schooling for **b** : to train by formal instruction and supervised practice esp. in a skill, trade, or profession **2** **a** : to develop mentally, morally, or aesthetically esp. by instruction **b** : to provide with information : INFORM **3** : to persuade or condition to feel, believe, or act in a desired way ⟨∼ the public to support our position⟩ ∼ *vi* : to educate a person or thing *syn* see TEACH

ed·u·cat·ed *adj* (1588) **1** : having an education; *esp* : having an education beyond the average **2** **a** : giving evidence of training or practice : SKILLED **b** : befitting one that is educated ⟨∼ taste⟩ **c** : based on some knowledge of fact ⟨an ∼ guess⟩ — **ed·u·cat·ed·ness** *n*

ed·u·ca·tion \,e-jə-'kā-shən\ *n* (1531) **1** **a** : the action or process of educating or of being educated; *also* : a stage of such a process **b** : the knowledge and development resulting from an educational process ⟨a man of little ∼⟩ **2** : the field of study that deals mainly with methods of teaching and learning in schools — **ed·u·ca·tion·al** \-shnəl, -shə-n²l\ *adj* — **ed·u·ca·tion·al·ly** \-ē\ *adv*

educational psychology *n* (1911) : psychology concerned with human maturation, school learning, teaching methods, guidance, and evaluation of aptitude and progress by standardized tests — **educational psychologist** *n*

educational television *n* (1951) **1** : television that provides instruction esp. for students **2** : PUBLIC TELEVISION

ed·u·ca·tion·ese \,e-jə-,kā-shə-'nēz, -'nēs\ *n* (1954) : the jargon used esp. by educational theorists

ed·u·ca·tion·ist \,e-jə-'kā-sh(ə-)nist\ *also* **ed·u·ca·tion·al·ist** \-shnə-list, -shə-n²l-ist\ *n* (1829) **1** *chiefly Brit* : a professional educator **2** : an educational theorist

ed·u·ca·tive \'e-jə-,kā-tiv\ *adj* (1856) **1** : tending to educate : INSTRUCTIVE **2** : of or relating to education

ed·u·ca·tor \'e-jə-,kā-tər\ *n* (1673) **1** : one skilled in teaching : TEACHER **2** **a** : a student of the theory and practice of education : EDUCATIONIST **2** **b** : an administrator in education

educe \i-'düs *also* -'dyüs\ *vt* **educed; educ·ing** [L *educere* to draw out, fr. *e-* + *ducere* to lead — more at TOW] (1603) **1** : to bring out (as something latent) **2** : DEDUCE — **educ·ible** \-'dü-sə-bəl *also* -'dyü-\ *adj* — **educ·tion** \-'dək-shən\ *n*

syn EDUCE, EVOKE, ELICIT, EXTRACT, EXTORT mean to draw out something hidden, latent, or reserved. EDUCE implies the bringing out of something potential or latent ⟨*educed* order out of chaos⟩. EVOKE implies a strong stimulus that arouses an emotion or an interest or recalls an image or memory ⟨a song that *evokes* warm memories⟩. ELICIT usu. implies some effort or skill in drawing forth a response ⟨careful questioning *elicited* the truth⟩. EXTRACT implies the use of force or pressure in obtaining answers or information ⟨*extracted* a confession from him⟩. EXTORT suggests a wringing or wresting from one who resists strongly ⟨*extorted* their cooperation by threatening to inform⟩.

educ·tor \i-'dək-tər\ *n* [LL, one that leads out, fr. L *educere*] (1796) : EJECTOR 2

edul·co·rate \i-'dəl-kə-,rāt\ *vt* **-rat·ed; -rat·ing** [NL *edulcoratus,* pp. of *edulcorare,* fr. L *e-* + *dulcor* sweetness, fr. *dulcis* sweet — more at DULCET] (1641) : to free from harshness (as of attitude) : SOFTEN

ed·u·tain·ment \,e-jə-'tān-mənt, ,e-dyü-\ *n* [*edu*cation + enter*tain*ment] (1973) : a form of entertainment (as by games, films, or shows) that is designed to be educational

Ed·war·di·an \e-'dwär-dē-ən, -'dwȯr-\ *adj* (1908) : of, relating to, or characteristic of Edward VII of England or his age; *esp, of clothing* : marked by the hourglass silhouette for women and long narrow fitted suits and high collars for men — **Edwardian** *n*

¹-ee \'ē, ,ē, ē\ *n suffix* [ME *-e,* fr. MF *-é,* fr. *-é,* pp. ending, fr. L *-atus*] **1** : recipient or beneficiary of (a specified action) ⟨appointee⟩ ⟨grantee⟩ **2** : person furnished with (a specified thing) ⟨patentee⟩ **3** : person that performs (a specified action) ⟨escapee⟩

²-ee *n suffix* [prob. alter. of *-y*] **1** : one associated with ⟨bargee⟩ **2** : a particular esp. small kind of ⟨bootee⟩ **3** : one resembling or suggestive of ⟨goatee⟩

eel \'ē(ə)l\ *n* [ME *ele,* fr. OE *ǣl;* akin to OHG *āl* eel] (bef. 12c) **1** **a** : any of numerous voracious elongate snakelike bony fishes (order Anguilliformes) that have a smooth slimy skin, lack pelvic fins, and have the median fins confluent around the tail — compare AMERICAN EEL **b** : any of numerous other elongate fishes (as of the order Symbranchii) **2** : any of various nematodes — **eel·like** \'ē(ə)l-,līk\ *adj* — **eely** \'ē-lē\ *adj*

eel 1a

eel·grass \'ē(ə)l-,gras\ *n* (1790) **1** : a submerged long-leaved monocotyledonous marine plant (*Zostera marina*) of the eelgrass family that is abundant along the Atlantic coast and has stems used esp. in woven products (as mats and hats) **2** : TAPE GRASS

eel·pout \-,paůt\ *n* (bef. 12c) **1** : any of various elongate tapered marine fishes (family Zoarcidae) usu. living on the bottom of cold seas **2** : BURBOT

eel·worm \-,wərm\ *n* (1888) : a nematode worm; *esp* : any of various small free-living or plant-parasitic roundworms

-een \'ēn\ *n suffix* [prob. fr. *ratteen*] : inferior fabric resembling (a specified fabric) : imitation ⟨velveteen⟩

e'en \'ēn\ *adv* (ca. 1553) : EVEN

-eer \'ir\ *n suffix* [MF *-ier,* fr. L *-arius* — more at -ARY] : one that is concerned with professionally, conducts, or produces ⟨auctioneer⟩ ⟨pamphleteer⟩ — often in words with derogatory meaning ⟨profiteer⟩

e'er \'er\ *adv* (13c) : EVER

ee·rie *also* **ee·ry** \'ir-ē, 'er-\ *adj* **ee·ri·er; -est** [ME (northern dial.) *eri*] (14c) **1** *chiefly Scot* : affected with fright : SCARED **2** : so mysterious, strange, or unexpected as to send a chill up the spine ⟨a coyote's ∼ howl⟩ ⟨the similarities were ∼⟩; *also* : seemingly not of earthly origin ⟨the flames cast an ∼ glow⟩ *syn* see WEIRD — **ee·ri·ly** \'ir-ə-lē, 'er-\ *adv* — **ee·ri·ness** \'ir-ē-nəs, 'er-\ *n*

ef \'ef\ *n* (bef. 12c) : the letter *f*

ef·face \i-'fās, e-\ *vt* **ef·faced; ef·fac·ing** [ME, fr. MF *effacer,* fr. OF *esfacier,* fr. *e-* + *face* face] (15c) **1** : to eliminate or make indistinct by or as if by wearing away a surface ⟨coins with dates *effaced* by wear⟩; *also* : to cause to vanish ⟨daylight *effaced* the stars⟩ **2** : to make (oneself) modestly or shyly inconspicuous — **ef·face·able** \-'fā-sə-bəl\ *adj* — **ef·face·ment** \-'fā-smənt\ *n* — **ef·fac·er** *n*

¹ef·fect \i-'fekt, e-\ *n* [ME, fr. MF & L; MF, fr. L *effectus,* fr. *efficere* to bring about, fr. *ex-* + *facere* to make, do — more at DO] (14c) **1** **a** : PURPORT, INTENT **b** : basic meaning : ESSENCE **2** : something that inevitably follows an antecedent (as a cause or agent) **3** : an outward sign : APPEARANCE **4** : ACCOMPLISHMENT, FULFILLMENT **5** : power to bring about a result : INFLUENCE ⟨the content itself of television . . . is therefore less important than its ∼ —*Current Biog.*⟩ **6** *pl* : movable property : GOODS ⟨personal ∼s⟩ **7** **a** : a distinctive impression ⟨the color gives the ∼ of being warm⟩ **b** : the creation of a desired impression ⟨her tears were purely for ∼⟩ **c** (1) : something designed to produce a distinctive or desired impression — usu. used in pl. (2) *pl* : SPECIAL EFFECTS **8** : the quality or state of being operative : OPERATION ⟨the law goes into ∼ next week⟩ — **in effect** : in substance : VIRTUALLY ⟨the . . . committee agreed to what was *in effect* a reduction in the hourly wage —*Current Biog.*⟩ — **to the effect** : with the meaning ⟨issued a statement *to the effect* that he would resign⟩

²effect *vt* (1533) **1** : to cause to come into being **2** **a** : to bring about often by surmounting obstacles : ACCOMPLISH ⟨∼ a settlement of a dispute⟩ **b** : to put into operation ⟨the duty of the legislature to ∼ the will of the citizens⟩ *syn* see PERFORM

\ə\ abut \²\ kitten, F table \ər\ further \a\ ash \ā\ ace \ä\ mop, mar \aů\ out \ch\ chin \e\ bet \ē\ easy \g\ go \i\ hit \ī\ ice \j\ job \ŋ\ sing \ō\ go \ȯ\ law \ȯi\ boy \th\ thin \t̶h̶\ the \ü\ loot \ů\ foot \y\ yet \zh\ vision \ä, k̲, ⁿ, œ, œ̄, ᵫ, ᵫ̄, ᵞ\ *see* Guide to Pronunciation *usage* The confusion of the verbs *affect* and *effect* is not only quite common but has a long history. *Effect* was used in place of [3]*affect* as early as 1494 and in place of [2]*affect* as early as 1652. If you think you want to use the verb *effect* but are not certain, check the definitions in this dictionary. The noun *affect* is sometimes mistakenly used for *effect*. Except when your topic is psychology, you will seldom need the noun *affect*.

[1]**ef·fec·tive** \i-'fek-tiv, e-, ē-\ *adj* (14c) **1 a :** producing a decided, decisive, or desired effect **b :** IMPRESSIVE, STRIKING ⟨a gold lamé fabric studded with ~ . . . precious stones —Stanley Marcus⟩ **2 :** ready for service or action ⟨~ manpower⟩ **3 :** ACTUAL ⟨the need to increase ~ demand for goods⟩ **4 :** being in effect : OPERATIVE ⟨the tax becomes ~ next year⟩ **5** *of a rate of interest* **:** equal to the rate of simple interest that yields the same amount when the interest is paid once at the end of the interest period as a quoted rate of interest does when calculated at compound interest over the same period — compare NOMINAL 4 — **ef·fec·tive·ness** *n* — **ef·fec·tiv·i·ty** \e-,fek-'ti-və-tē, i-, ē-\ *n*
syn EFFECTIVE, EFFECTUAL, EFFICIENT, EFFICACIOUS mean producing or capable of producing a result. EFFECTIVE stresses the actual production of or the power to produce an effect ⟨an *effective* rebuttal⟩. EFFECTUAL suggests the accomplishment of a desired result esp. as viewed after the fact ⟨the measures to stop the pilfering proved *effectual*⟩. EFFICIENT suggests an acting or a potential for action or use in such a way as to avoid loss or waste of energy in effecting, producing, or functioning ⟨an *efficient* small car⟩. EFFICACIOUS suggests possession of a special quality or virtue that gives effective power ⟨a detergent that is *efficacious* in removing grease⟩.

[2]**effective** *n* (1722) **:** one that is effective; *esp* **:** a soldier equipped for duty

ef·fec·tive·ly \-lē\ *adv* (ca. 1536) **1 :** in effect : VIRTUALLY **2 :** in an effective manner

ef·fec·tor \i-'fek-tər, -,tȯr\ *n* (1906) **1 :** a bodily organ (as a gland or muscle) that becomes active in response to stimulation **2 :** a substance (as an inducer or corepressor) that controls protein synthesis by combining allosterically with a genetic repressor

ef·fec·tu·al \i-'fek-chə-(wə)l, -'feksh-wəl\ *adj* (14c) **:** producing or able to produce a desired effect *syn* see EFFECTIVE — **ef·fec·tu·al·i·ty** \-,fek-chə-'wa-lə-tē\ *n* — **ef·fec·tu·al·ness** \-'fek-chə-(wə)l-nəs, -'feksh-wəl-\ *n*

ef·fec·tu·al·ly \i-'fek-chə-(wə)-lē, -'fek-shwə-\ *adv* (14c) **1 :** in an effectual manner **2 :** with great effect : COMPLETELY

ef·fec·tu·ate \i-'fek-chə-,wāt\ *vt* **-at·ed; -at·ing** (1580) **:** EFFECT 2 — **ef·fec·tu·a·tion** \-,fek-chə-'wā-shən\ *n*

ef·fem·i·na·cy \ə-'fe-mə-nə-sē\ *n* (1602) **:** the quality of being effeminate

[1]**ef·fem·i·nate** \-nət\ *adj* [ME, fr. L *effeminatus*, fr. pp. of *effeminare* to make effeminate, fr. *ex-* + *femina* woman — more at FEMININE] (15c) **1 :** having feminine qualities untypical of a man : not manly in appearance or manner **2 :** marked by an unbecoming delicacy or overrefinement ⟨~ art⟩ ⟨an ~ civilization⟩

[2]**effeminate** *n* (1597) **:** an effeminate person

ef·fen·di \e-'fen-dē, ə-\ *n* [Turk *efendi* master, fr. NGk *aphentēs*, alter. of Gk *authentēs* — more at AUTHENTIC] (1614) **:** a man of property, authority, or education in an eastern Mediterranean country

ef·fer·ent \'e-fər-ənt, -,fer-, 'ē-\ *adj* [F *efférent*, fr. L *efferent-, efferens*, prp. of *efferre* to carry outward, fr. *ex-* + *ferre* to carry — more at BEAR] (1856) **:** conducting outward from a part or organ; *specif* **:** conveying nervous impulses to an effector — compare AFFERENT — **efferent** *n* — **ef·fer·ent·ly** *adv*

ef·fer·vesce \,e-fər-'ves\ *vi* **-vesced; -vesc·ing** [L *effervescere*, fr. *ex-* + *fervescere* to begin to boil, incho. of *fervēre* to boil — more at BREW] (1784) **1 :** to bubble, hiss, and foam as gas escapes **2 :** to show liveliness or exhilaration — **ef·fer·ves·cence** \-'ve-s[superscript]n(t)s\ *n* — **ef·fer·ves·cent** \-s[superscript]nt\ *adj* — **ef·fer·ves·cent·ly** *adv*

ef·fete \e-'fēt, i-\ *adj* [L *effetus*, fr. *ex-* + *fetus* fruitful — more at FEMININE] (1660) **1 :** no longer fertile **2 a :** having lost character, vitality, or strength ⟨the ~ monarchies . . . of feudal Europe —G. M. Trevelyan⟩ **b :** marked by weakness or decadence ⟨the ~ East⟩ **c :** soft or delicate from or as if from a pampered existence ⟨peddled . . . trendy tweeds to ~ Easterners —William Helmer⟩ ⟨~ and snobbish : also : characteristic of an effete person ⟨a wool scarf . . . a bit ~ on an outdoorsman —Nelson Bryant⟩ **3 :** EFFEMINATE 1 ⟨a good-humored, ~ boy brought up by maiden aunts —Herman Wouk⟩ — **ef·fete·ly** *adv* — **ef·fete·ness** *n*

ef·fi·ca·cious \,e-fə-'kā-shəs\ *adj* [L *efficac-, efficax*, fr. *efficere*] (1528) **:** having the power to produce a desired effect *syn* see EFFECTIVE — **ef·fi·ca·cious·ly** *adv* — **ef·fi·ca·cious·ness** *n*

ef·fi·cac·i·ty \,e-fə-'ka-sə-tē\ *n* (15c) **:** EFFICACY

ef·fi·ca·cy \'e-fi-kə-sē\ *n, pl* **-cies** (13c) **:** the power to produce an effect

ef·fi·cien·cy \i-'fi-shən-sē\ *n, pl* **-cies** (1633) **1 :** the quality or degree of being efficient **2 a :** efficient operation **b** (1) **:** effective operation as measured by a comparison of production with cost (as in energy, time, and money) (2) **:** the ratio of the useful energy delivered by a dynamic system to the energy supplied to it **3 :** EFFICIENCY APARTMENT

efficiency apartment *n* (1930) **:** a small usu. furnished apartment with minimal kitchen and bath facilities

efficiency expert *n* (1913) **:** one who analyzes methods, procedures, and jobs in order to secure maximum efficiency — called also *efficiency engineer*

ef·fi·cient \i-'fi-shənt\ *adj* [ME, fr. MF or L; MF, fr. L *efficient-, efficiens*, fr. prp. of *efficere*] (14c) **1 :** being or involving the immediate agent in producing an effect ⟨the ~ action of heat in changing water to steam⟩ **2 :** productive of desired effects; *esp* **:** productive without waste *syn* see EFFECTIVE — **ef·fi·cient·ly** *adv*

ef·fi·gy \'e-fə-jē\ *n, pl* **-gies** [MF *effigie*, fr. L *effigies*, fr. *effingere* to form, fr. *ex-* + *fingere* to shape — more at DOUGH] (1539) **:** an image or representation esp. of a person; *esp* **:** a crude figure representing a hated person — **in effigy :** publicly in the form of an effigy ⟨the football coach was burned *in effigy*⟩

ef·flo·resce \,e-flə-'res\ *vi* **-resced; -resc·ing** [L *efflorescere*, fr. *ex-* + *florescere* to begin to blossom — more at FLORESCENCE] (1775) **1 :** to burst forth : BLOOM **2 a :** to change to a powder from loss of water of

crystallization **b :** to form or become covered with a powdery crust ⟨bricks may ~ owing to the deposition of soluble salts⟩

ef·flo·res·cence \-'re-s[superscript]n(t)s\ *n* (1626) **1 a :** the action or process of developing and unfolding as if coming into flower : BLOSSOMING ⟨periods of . . . intellectual and artistic ~ —Julian Huxley⟩ **b :** an instance of such development **c :** fullness of manifestation : CULMINATION 2 **:** the period or state of flowering **3 :** the process or product of efflorescing chemically — **ef·flo·res·cent** \-s[superscript]nt\ *adj*

ef·flu·ence \'e-,flü-ən(t)s; e-'flü-, ə-\ *n* (1603) **1 :** something that flows out **2 :** an action or process of flowing out

[1]**ef·flu·ent** \-ənt\ *adj* [L *effluent-, effluens*, prp. of *effluere* to flow out, fr. *ex-* + *fluere* to flow — more at FLUID] (1726) **:** flowing out : EMANATING, OUTGOING ⟨an ~ river⟩

[2]**effluent** *n* (1859) **:** something that flows out: as **a :** an outflowing branch of a main stream or lake **b :** waste material (as smoke, liquid industrial refuse, or sewage) discharged into the environment esp. when serving as a pollutant

ef·flu·vi·um \e-'flü-vē-əm\ *also* **ef·flu·via** \-vē-ə\ *n, pl* **-via** *or* **-vi·ums** [L *effluvium* act of flowing out, fr. *effluere*] (1651) **1 :** an invisible emanation; *esp* **:** an offensive exhalation or smell **2 :** a by-product esp. in the form of waste

ef·flux \'e-,fləks\ *n* [ML *effluxus*, fr. *effluere*] (1647) **1 :** something given off in or as if in a stream **2 a :** EFFLUENCE 2 **b :** a passing away : EXPIRATION — **ef·flux·ion** \e-'flək-shən\ *n*

ef·fort \'e-fərt, -,fȯrt\ *n* [ME, fr. MF, fr. OF *esfort*, fr. *esforcier* to force, fr. *ex-* + *forcier* to force] (15c) **1 :** conscious exertion of power : hard work **2 :** a serious attempt : TRY **3 :** something produced by exertion or trying ⟨the novel was her most ambitious ~⟩ **4 :** effective force as distinguished from the possible resistance called into action by such a force **5 :** the total work done to achieve a particular end ⟨the war ~⟩

ef·fort·ful \-fəl\ *adj* (ca. 1895) **:** showing or requiring effort — **ef·fort·ful·ly** \-fə-lē\ *adv*

ef·fort·less \-ləs\ *adj* (1801) **:** showing or requiring little or no effort *syn* see EASY — **ef·fort·less·ly** *adv* — **ef·fort·less·ness** *n*

ef·fron·tery \i-'frən-tə-rē, e-\ *n, pl* **-ter·ies** [F *effronterie*, ultim. fr. ML *effront-, effrons* shameless, fr. L *ex-* + *front-, frons* forehead] (1697) **:** shameless boldness : INSOLENCE *syn* see TEMERITY

ef·ful·gence \i-'fu̇l-jən(t)s, e-, -'fəl-\ *n* [LL *effulgentia*, fr. L *effulgent-, effulgens*, prp. of *effulgēre* to shine forth, fr. *ex-* + *fulgēre* to shine — more at FULGENT] (1667) **:** radiant splendor : BRILLIANCE — **ef·ful·gent** \-jənt\ *adj*

[1]**ef·fuse** \e-'fyüz, e-\ *vb* **ef·fused; ef·fus·ing** [L *effusus*, pp. of *effundere*, fr. *ex-* + *fundere* to pour — more at FOUND] *vt* (1526) **:** to pour out (a liquid) ~ *vi* **:** to flow out : EMANATE

[2]**ef·fuse** \-'fyüs\ *adj* (ca. 1530) **:** DIFFUSE; *specif* **:** spread out flat without definite form ⟨~ lichens⟩

ef·fu·sion \i-'fyü-zhən, e-\ *n* (15c) **1 :** an act of effusing **2 :** unrestrained expression of words or feelings ⟨greeted her with great ~ —Olive H. Prouty⟩ **3 a** (1) **:** the escape of a fluid from anatomical vessels by rupture or exudation (2) **:** the flow of a gas through an aperture whose diameter is small as compared with the distance between the molecules of the gas **b :** the fluid that escapes

ef·fu·sive \i-'fyü-siv, e-, -ziv\ *adj* (1662) **1 :** excessively demonstrative **2** *archaic* **:** pouring freely **3 :** characterized or formed by a nonexplosive outpouring of lava ⟨~ rocks⟩ — **ef·fu·sive·ly** *adv* — **ef·fu·sive·ness** *n*

Efik \'e-fik\ *n* (1849) **1 :** a member of a people of southeastern Nigeria **2 :** the language of the Efik people

eft \'eft\ *n* [ME *evete, ewte*, fr. OE *efete*] (bef. 12c) **:** NEWT; *esp* **:** the terrestrial phase of a predominantly aquatic newt

eft·soons \eft-'sünz\ *adv* [ME *eftsones*, alter. of OE *eftsōna*, fr. OE *eft* after + *sōna* soon; akin to OE *æfter* after] (bef. 12c) *archaic* **:** soon after

egad \i-'gad\ *or* **egads** \-'gadz\ *interj* [prob. euphemism for *oh God*] (1673) — used as a mild oath

egal \'ē-gəl\ *adj* [ME, fr. MF, fr. L *aequalis*] (14c) *obs* **:** EQUAL

egal·i·tar·i·an \i-,ga-lə-'ter-ē-ən\ *adj* [F *égalitaire*, fr. *égalité* equality, fr. L *aequalitat-, aequalitas*, fr. *aequalis* equal] (1885) **:** asserting, promoting, or marked by egalitarianism — **egalitarian** *n*

egal·i·tar·i·an·ism \-ē-ə-,ni-zəm\ *n* (1905) **1 :** a belief in human equality esp. with respect to social, political, and economic rights and privileges **2 :** a social philosophy advocating the removal of inequalities among people

éga·li·té \ā-gà-lē-tā\ *n* [F] (1794) **:** social or political equality

Ege·ria \i-'jir-ē-ə\ *n* [L, a nymph who advised the legendary Roman king Numa Pompilius] (1621) **:** a woman adviser or companion

eges·ta \i-'jes-tə\ *n pl* [NL, fr. L, neut. pl. of *egestus*] (1727) **:** something egested

eges·tion \i-'jes(h)-chən\ *n* [ME *egestioun*, fr. MF or L; MF *egestion*, fr. L *egestion-, egestio*, fr. *egerere* to carry outside, discharge, fr. *e-* + *gerere* to carry] (1547) **:** the act or process of discharging undigested or waste material from a cell or organism; *specif* **:** DEFECATION — **egest** \i-'jest\ *vt* — **eges·tive** \-'jes-tiv\ *adj*

[1]**egg** \'eg, 'āg\ *vt* [ME, fr. ON *eggja*; akin to OE *ecg* edge — more at EDGE] (13c) **:** to incite to action — usu. used with *on* ⟨~ed the mob on to riot⟩

[2]**egg** *n, often attrib* [ME *egge*, fr. ON *egg*; akin to OE *æg* egg, L *ovum*, Gk *ōion*] (14c) **1 a :** the hard-shelled reproductive body produced by a bird and esp. by the common domestic chicken; *also* **:** its contents used as food **b :** an animal reproductive body consisting of an ovum together with its nutritive and protective envelopes and having the capacity to develop into a new individual capable of independent existence **c :** OVUM 2 **:** something resembling an egg **3 :** PERSON, SORT ⟨a good ~⟩ — **egg·less** *adj* — **eggy** \-gē\ *adj* — **egg on one's face :** a state of embarrassment or humiliation

egg 1a: *1* shell, *2* shell membrane, *3* egg membrane, *4* air space, *5* chalaza, *6* albumen or white layers, *7* yolk layers, *8* blastodisc, *9* vitelline membrane

³**egg** *vt* (1833) **1** : to cover with egg **2** : to pelt with eggs
egg and dart *n* (ca. 1864) : a carved ornamental design in relief consisting of an egg-shaped figure alternating with a figure somewhat like an elongated javelin or arrowhead
egg·beat·er \'eg-₁bē-tər, 'äg-\ *n* (1828) **1** : a hand-operated kitchen utensil used for beating, stirring, or whipping; *esp* : a rotary device for these purposes **2** : HELICOPTER
egg case *n* (1847) : a protective case enclosing eggs — OOTHECA — called also *egg capsule*
egg cell *n* (1880) : OVUM
egg cream *n* (1954) : a drink consisting of milk, a flavoring syrup, and soda water
egg·cup \'eg-₁kəp, 'äg-\ *n* (1773) : a cup for holding an egg that is to be eaten from the shell
egg·head \-₁hed\ *n, often attrib* (1952) : INTELLECTUAL, HIGHBROW
egg·head·ed \-'he-dəd\ *adj* (1938) : having the characteristics of an egghead — **egg·head·ed·ness** *n*
egg·nog \-₁näg\ *n* (ca. 1775) : a drink consisting of eggs beaten with sugar, milk or cream, and often alcoholic liquor
egg·plant \-₁plant\ *n* (1767) **1 a** : a widely cultivated perennial herb (*Solanum melongena*) of the nightshade family yielding edible fruit **b** : the usu. smooth ovoid fruit of the eggplant **2** : a dark grayish or blackish purple
egg roll *n* (1947) : a thin egg-dough casing filled with minced vegetables and often bits of meat (as shrimp or chicken) and usu. deep-fried
eggs Ben·e·dict \-'be-nə-₁dikt\ *n pl but sing or pl in constr* [prob. fr. the name *Benedict*] (1898) : poached eggs and broiled ham placed on toasted halves of English muffin and covered with hollandaise
¹**egg·shell** \'eg-₁shel, 'äg-\ *n* (14c) **1** : the hard exterior covering of an egg **2** : something resembling an eggshell esp. in fragility
²**eggshell** *adj* (1835) **1** : thin and fragile **2** : slightly glossy **3** : yellowish white
egg timer *n* (1884) : a small sandglass for timing the boiling of eggs
egg tooth *n* (1893) : a hard sharp prominence on the beak of an unhatched bird or the nose of an unhatched reptile that is used to break through the eggshell
egis \'ē-jəs\ *var of* AEGIS
eg·lan·tine \'e-glən-₁tīn, -₁tēn\ *n* [ME *eglentyn*, fr. MF *aiglent*, fr. (assumed) VL *aculentum*, fr. L *acus* needle; akin to L *acer* sharp — more at EDGE] (14c) : SWEETBRIER
églo·mi·sé *also* **églo·mi·sé** \₁ā-glə-(₁)mē-'zā, ₁e-; 'ā-glə-(₁)mē-, 'e-\ *adj* [F, pp. of *églomiser* to decorate a glass panel by painting on its back, fr. Jean-Baptiste *Glomy* †1786 Fr. decorator] (1877) : made of glass on the back of which is a painted picture that shows through ⟨a clock with ~ panels⟩
ego \'ē-(₁)gō *also* 'e-\ *n, pl* **egos** [NL, fr. L, I — more at I] (1789) **1** : the self esp. as contrasted with another self or the world **2 a** : EGOTISM **2 b** : SELF-ESTEEM **1 3** : the one of the three divisions of the psyche in psychoanalytic theory that serves as the organized conscious mediator between the person and reality esp. by functioning both in the perception of and adaptation to reality — compare ID, SUPEREGO — **ego·less** *adj*
ego·cen·tric \₁ē-gō-'sen-trik *also* ₁e-\ *adj* (1894) **1** : concerned with the individual rather than society **2** : taking the ego as the starting point in philosophy **3 a** : limited in outlook or concern to one's own activities or needs **b** : SELF-CENTERED, SELFISH — **egocentric** *n* — **ego·cen·tri·cal·ly** \-tri-k(ə-)lē\ *adv* — **ego·cen·tric·i·ty** \-₁sen-'tri-sə-tē\ *n* — **ego·cen·trism** \-'sen-₁tri-zəm\ *n*
ego ideal *n* (1922) : the standards, ideals, and ambitions that according to psychoanalytic theory are assimilated from the superego
ego·ism \'ē-gə-₁wi-zəm *also* 'e-\ *n* (1785) **1 a** : a doctrine that individual self-interest is the actual motive of all conscious action **b** : a doctrine that individual self-interest is the valid end of all actions **2** : excessive concern for oneself with or without exaggerated feelings of self-importance — compare EGOTISM 2
ego·ist \-wist\ *n* (1785) **1** : a believer in egoism **2** : an egocentric or egotistic person — **ego·is·tic** \₁ē-gə-'wis-tik *also* ₁e-\ *also* **ego·is·ti·cal** \-ti-kəl\ *adj* — **ego·is·ti·cal·ly** \-ti-k(ə-)lē\ *adv*
egoistic hedonism *n* (1874) : the ethical theory that achieving one's own happiness is the proper goal of all conduct
ego·ma·nia \₁ē-gō-'mā-nē-ə, -nyə\ *n* (1825) : the quality or state of being extremely egocentric — **ego·ma·ni·ac** \-nē-₁ak\ *n* — **ego·ma·ni·a·cal** \-mə-'nī-ə-kəl\ *adj* — **ego·ma·ni·a·cal·ly** \-k(ə-)lē\ *adv*
ego·tism \'ē-gə-₁ti-zəm *also* 'e-\ *n* [L *ego* + E -*ism* (as in *idiotism*)] (1714) **1 a** : excessive use of the first person singular personal pronoun **b** : the practice of talking about oneself too much **2** : an exaggerated sense of self-importance : CONCEIT — compare EGOISM 2 — **ego·tist** \-tist\ *n* — **ego·tis·tic** \₁ē-gə-'tis-tik *or* **ego·tis·ti·cal** \-'tis-ti-kəl\ *adj* — **ego·tis·ti·cal·ly** \-k(ə-)lē\ *adv*
ego trip *n* (1967) : an act or course of action that enhances and satisfies one's ego — **ego—trip** *vi* — **ego—trip·per** *n*
egre·gious \i-'grē-jəs\ *adj* [L *egregius*, fr. *e-* + *greg-, grex* herd — more at GREGARIOUS] (ca. 1534) **1** *archaic* : DISTINGUISHED **2** : CONSPICUOUS; *esp* : conspicuously bad : FLAGRANT ⟨an ~ mistake⟩ — **egre·gious·ly** *adv* — **egre·gious·ness** *n*
¹**egress** \'ē-₁gres\ *n* [L *egressus*, fr. *egressus*, pp. of *egredi* to go out, fr. *e-* + *gradi* to go — more at GRADE] (1538) **1** : the action or right of going or coming out **2** : a place or means of going out : EXIT
²**egress** \ē-'gres\ *vi* (1578) : to go or come out
egres·sion \ē-'gre-shən\ *n* (15c) : EGRESS, EMERGENCE
egret \'ē-grət, -₁gret *also* i-'gret, 'eg-rət\ *n* [ME, fr. MF *aigrette*, fr. OProv *aigreta*, of Gmc origin; akin to OHG *heigaro* heron] (14c) : any of various herons that bear long plumes during the breeding season
¹**Egyp·tian** \i-'jip-shən\ *adj* (14c) : of, relating to, or characteristic of Egypt or the Egyptians
²**Egyptian** *n* (14c) **1** : a native or inhabitant of Egypt **2** : the Afro-Asiatic language of the ancient Egyptians from earliest times to about the 3d century A.D. **3** *often not cap* : a typeface having little contrast between thick and thin strokes and squared serifs
Egyptian alfalfa weevil *n* (1943) : an Old World weevil (*Hypera brunneipennis*) established in western No. America where it feeds on alfalfa and various clovers
Egyptian clover *n* (ca. 1900) : BERSEEM

Egyptian cotton *n* (1877) : a fine long-staple often somewhat brownish cotton grown chiefly in Egypt
Egyp·tol·o·gy \₁ē-₁jip-'tä-lə-jē\ *n* (1862) : the study of Egyptian antiquities — **Egyp·to·log·i·cal** \-tə-'lä-jə-kəl\ *adj* — **Egyp·tol·o·gist** \-'tä-lə-jist\ *n*
eh \'ā, 'e, 'a(i), *also with* h *preceding and/or with nasalization*\ *interj* [ME *ey*] (13c) — used to ask for confirmation or repetition or to express inquiry; used esp. in Canadian English in anticipation of the listener's or reader's agreement
ei·cos·a·noid \ī-'kō-sə-₁nȯid\ *n* [*eicosa-* containing 20 atoms (fr. Gk *eikosa-* twenty, fr. *eikosi*) + -*noic*, suffix used in names of fatty acids (fr. -*ane* + -*oic*) + ¹-*oid* — more at VIGESIMAL] (1980) : any of a class of compounds (as the prostaglandins) derived from polyunsaturated acids (as arachidonic acid) and involved in cellular activity
ei·der \'ī-dər\ *n* [D, G, or Sw, fr. Icel *æthur*, fr. ON *æthr*] (1743) **1** : any of several large northern sea ducks (genera *Somateria* and *Polysticta*) having fine soft down that is used by the female for lining the nest — called also *eider duck* **2** : EIDERDOWN 1
ei·der·down \-₁daün\ *n* [prob. fr. G *Eiderdaune*, fr. Icel *æthardūnn*, fr. *æthur* + *dūnn* ⁷down] (1774) **1** : the down of the eider **2** : a comforter filled with eiderdown **3** : a soft lightweight clothing fabric knitted or woven and napped on one or both sides
ei·det·ic \ī-'de-tik\ *adj* [Gk *eidētikos* of a form, fr. *eidos* form — more at WISE] (ca. 1924) : marked by or involving extraordinarily accurate and vivid recall esp. of visual images ⟨an ~ memory⟩ — **ei·det·i·cal·ly** \-ti-k(ə-)lē\ *adv*
ei·do·lon \ī-'dō-lən\ *n, pl* -**lons** \-lənz\ *or* -**la** \-lə\ [Gk *eidōlon* — more at IDOL] (1828) **1** : an unsubstantial image : PHANTOM **2** : IDEAL
ei·gen·mode \'ī-gən-₁mōd\ *n* [*eigen-* (as in *eigenvector*) + ¹*mode*] : a normal mode of vibration of an oscillating system
ei·gen·val·ue \'ī-gən-₁val-(₁)yü, -yə(-w)\ *n* [part trans. of G *Eigenwert*, fr. *eigen* own, peculiar + *Wert* value] (1927) : a scalar associated with a given linear transformation of a vector space and having the property that there is some nonzero vector which when multiplied by the scalar is equal to the vector obtained by letting the transformation operate on the vector; *esp* : a root of the characteristic equation of a matrix
ei·gen·vec·tor \-₁vek-tər\ *n* [ISV *eigen-* (fr. G *eigen*) + *vector*] (1941) : a nonzero vector that is mapped by a given linear transformation of a vector space onto a vector that is the product of a scalar multiplied by the original vector — called also *characteristic vector*
eight \'āt\ *n* [ME *eighte*, fr. *eighte*, adj., fr. OE *eahta*; akin to OHG *ahto* eight, L *octo*, Gk *oktō*] (bef. 12c) **1** — see NUMBER table **2** : the eighth in a set or series ⟨the ~ of spades⟩ **3** : something having eight units or members: as **a** : an 8-oared racing boat or its crew **b** : an 8-cylinder engine or automobile — **eight** *adj* — **eight** *pron, pl in constr*
eight ball *n* (1932) **1** : a black pool ball numbered 8 **2** : MISFIT — **behind the eight ball** : in a highly disadvantageous position
eigh·teen \(')ā(t)-'tēn\ *n* [ME *eightetene*, adj., fr. OE *eahtatīene*, fr. *eahta* + -*tiene*; akin to OE *tien* ten] (bef. 12c) — see NUMBER table — **eighteen** *adj* — **eighteen** *pron, pl in constr* — **eigh·teenth** \-'tēn(t)th\ *adj or n*
18—wheel·er *or* **eigh·teen—wheel·er** \₁ā(t)-(₁)tēn-'wē-lər\ *n* (1976) : a trucking rig consisting of a tractor and a trailer and typically having eighteen wheels
eight·fold \'āt-₁fōld, -'fōld\ *adj* (bef. 12c) **1** : having eight units or members **2** : being eight times as great or as many — **eight·fold** \-'fōld\ *adv*
eightfold way *n* (1961) : a unified theoretical scheme for classifying the relationship among strongly interacting elementary particles on the basis of isospin and hypercharge
eighth \'ātth, 'āth\ *n, pl* **eighths** \'āt(th)s, 'āth(th)s, 'āths\ (1557) **1** — see NUMBER table **2** : OCTAVE — **eighth** *adj or adv*
eighth note *n* (ca. 1864) : a musical note with the time value of ¹/₈ of a whole note — see NOTE illustration
eighth rest *n* (ca. 1890) : a musical rest corresponding in time value to an eighth note — see REST illustration
800 number \₁āt-'hən-drəd-, -dərd-\ *n* (1979) : a toll-free telephone number for long-distance calls (as to a business) that is prefixed by the number 800
eight·pen·ny nail \₁āt-₁pe-nē-\ *n* [fr. its original price per hundred] (15c) : a nail typically 2¹/₂ inches (6.35 centimeters) long
eighty \'ā-tē\ *n, pl* **eight·ies** [ME *eighty*, adj., fr. OE *eahtatig*, short for *hundeahtatig*, n., group of eighty, fr. *hund-*, lit., hundred + *eahta* eight + -*tig* group of ten; akin to OE *tien* ten] (bef. 12c) **1** — see NUMBER table **2** *pl* : the numbers 80 to 89; *specif* : the years 80 to 89 in a lifetime or century — **eight·i·eth** \'ā-tē-əth\ *adj or n* — **eighty** *adj* — **eighty** *pron, pl in constr*
eighty—six *or* **86** \₁ā-tē-'siks\ *vt* [prob. rhyming slang for ³*nix*] (1967) *slang* : to refuse to serve (a customer); *also* : to get rid of : THROW OUT
ein·korn \'īn-₁kȯrn\ *n* [G, fr. OHG, fr. *ein* one + *korn* grain — more at ONE, CORN] (ca. 1901) : a one-grained wheat (*Triticum monococcum*) sometimes considered the most primitive wheat and grown esp. in poor soils in central Europe — called also *einkorn wheat*
ein·stei·ni·um \īn-'stī-nē-əm\ *n* [NL, fr. Albert *Einstein*] (1955) : a radioactive element produced artificially — see ELEMENT table
ei·re·nic *chiefly Brit var of* IRENIC
eis·e·ge·sis \₁ī-sə-'jē-səs, 'ī-sə-₁\ *n, pl* -**ge·ses** \-₁sēz\ [Gk *eis* into (akin to Gk *en* in) + E *exegesis* — more at IN] (1892) : the interpretation of a text (as of the Bible) by reading into it one's own ideas — compare EXEGESIS
ei·stedd·fod \ī-'steth-₁vȯd, ā-\ *n, pl* -**fods** \-₁vȯdz\ *or* -**fod·au** \-₁steth-'vȯ-₁dī\ [W, lit., session, fr. *eistedd* to sit + *bod* being] (1822) : a usu. Welsh competitive festival of the arts esp. in poetry and singing — **ei·stedd·fod·ic** \₁ī-₁steth-'vȯ-dik, ā-\ *adj*
eis·wein \'īs-₁wīn, -₁vīn\ *n, often cap* [G, fr. *Eis* ice + *Wein* wine] (1967) : a sweet German wine made from grapes that have frozen on the vine
¹**ei·ther** \'ē-thər *also* 'ī-\ *adj* [ME, fr. OE *æghwæther* both, each, fr. *ā*

\ə\ abut \ᵊ\ kitten, F table \ər\ further \a\ ash \ā\ ace \ä\ mop, mar
\aü\ out \ch\ chin \e\ bet \ē\ easy \g\ go \i\ hit \ī\ ice \j\ job
\ŋ\ sing \ō\ go \ȯ\ law \ȯi\ boy \th\ thin \t̲h̲\ the \ü\ loot \u̇\ foot
\y\ yet \zh\ vision \à, k̲, ⁿ, œ, œ̄, ᵫ, ūᴇ, ʸ\ see Guide to Pronunciation

always + *ge*-, collective prefix + *hwæther* which of two, whether — more at AYE, CO-] (bef. 12c) **1** : being the one and the other of two : EACH ⟨flowers blooming on ∼ side of the walk⟩ **2** : being the one or the other of two ⟨take ∼ road⟩
²**either** *pron* (bef. 12c) : the one or the other
³**either** *conj* (bef. 12c) — used as a function word before two or more coordinate words, phrases, or clauses joined usu. by *or* to indicate that what immediately follows is the first of two or more alternatives
⁴**either** *adv* (15c) **1** : LIKEWISE, MOREOVER — used for emphasis after a negative ⟨not smart or handsome ∼⟩ **2** : for that matter — used for emphasis after an alternative following a question or conditional clause esp. where negation is implied ⟨who answers for the Irish parliament? or army ∼? —Robert Browning⟩
¹**ei·ther–or** \ˌē-thə-ˈrȯr *also* ˌi-\ *n* (1922) : an unavoidable choice or exclusive division between only two alternatives
²**either–or** *adj* (1926) : of or marked by either-or : BLACK-AND-WHITE
¹**ejac·u·late** \i-ˈja-kyə-ˌlāt\ *vb* **-lat·ed; -lat·ing** [L *ejaculatus,* pp. of *ejaculari* to throw out, fr. *e-* + *jaculari* to throw, fr. *jaculum* dart, fr. *jacere* to throw — more at JET] *vt* (1578) **1** : to eject from a living body; *specif* : to eject (semen) in orgasm **2** : to utter suddenly and vehemently ∼ *vi* : to eject a fluid — **ejac·u·la·tor** \-ˌlā-tər\ *n*
²**ejac·u·late** \-lət\ *n* (1927) : the semen released by one ejaculation
ejac·u·la·tion \i-ˌja-kyə-ˈlā-shən\ *n* (1603) **1** : an act of ejaculating; *specif* : a sudden discharging of a fluid from a duct **2** : something ejaculated; *esp* : a short sudden emotional utterance
ejac·u·la·to·ry \i-ˈja-kyə-lə-ˌtȯr-ē, -ˌtȯr-\ *adj* (1644) **1** : marked by or given to vocal ejaculation **2** : casting or throwing out; *specif* : associated with or concerned in physiological ejaculation ⟨∼ vessels⟩
ejaculatory duct *n* (1751) : a duct through which semen is ejaculated; *specif* : either of the paired ducts in the human male that are formed by the junction of the duct from the seminal vesicle with the vas deferens and that pass through the prostate to empty into the urethra by means of a small opening
eject \i-ˈjekt\ *vt* [ME, fr. L *ejectus,* pp. of *eicere,* fr. *e-* + *jacere*] (15c) **1 a** : to drive out esp. by physical force **b** : to evict from property **2** : to throw out or off from within ⟨∼s the empty cartridges⟩ — **eject·able** \-ˈjek-tə-bəl\ *adj* — **ejec·tion** \-ˈjek-shən\ *n* — **ejec·tive** \-ˈjek-tiv\ *adj*
   syn EJECT, EXPEL, OUST, EVICT mean to drive or force out. EJECT carries an esp. strong implication of throwing or thrusting out from within as a physical action ⟨*ejected* an obnoxious patron from the bar⟩. EXPEL stresses a thrusting out or driving away esp. permanently which need not be physical ⟨a student *expelled* from college⟩. OUST implies removal or dispossession by power of the law or by force or compulsion ⟨got the sheriff to *oust* the squatters⟩. EVICT chiefly applies to turning out of house and home ⟨*evicted* for nonpayment of rent⟩.
ejec·ta \i-ˈjek-tə\ *n pl but sing or pl in constr* [NL, fr. L, neut. pl. of *ejectus*] (1886) : material thrown out (as from a volcano)
ejection seat *n* (1945) : an emergency escape seat for propelling an occupant out and away from an airplane
eject·ment \i-ˈjekt\)t-mənt\ *n* (1523) **1** : the act or an instance of ejecting : DISPOSSESSION **2** : an action for the recovery of possession of real property and damages and costs
ejec·tor \i-ˈjek-tər\ *n* (1640) **1** : one that ejects; *esp* : a mechanism of a firearm that ejects an empty cartridge **2** : a jet pump for withdrawing a gas, fluid, or powdery substance from a space
eka- \ˌe-kə, ˌā-kə\ *comb form* [ISV, fr. Skt *eka* one — more at ONE] : standing or assumed to stand next in order beyond (a specified element) in the same family of the periodic table — in names of chemical elements esp. when not yet discovered ⟨*eka*-lead is the hypothetical element 114⟩
¹**eke** \ˈēk\ *adv* [ME, fr. OE *ēac;* akin to OHG *ouh* also, L *aut* or, Gk *au* again] (bef. 12c) *archaic* : ALSO
²**eke** *vt* **eked; ek·ing** [ME, fr. OE *īecan, ēcan;* akin to OHG *ouhhōn* to add, L *augēre* to increase, Gk *auxein*] (bef. 12c) **1** *archaic* : INCREASE, LENGTHEN **2** : to get with great difficulty — usu. used with *out* ⟨∼ out a living⟩
eke out *vt* (1596) **1** : to make up for the deficiencies of : SUPPLEMENT ⟨*eked* out his income by getting a second job⟩ **2** : to make (a supply) last by economy
ekis·tics \i-ˈkis-tiks\ *n pl but sing in constr* [NGk *oikistikē,* fr. fem. of *oikistikos* of settlement, fr. Gk, fr. *oikizein* to settle, colonize, fr. *oikos* house — more at VICINITY] (1958) : a science dealing with human settlements and drawing on the research and experience of professionals in various fields (as architecture, engineering, city planning, and sociology) — **ekis·tic** \-tik\ *adj*
Ek·man dredge \ˌek-mən-\ *n* [prob. fr. V. W. *Ekman* †1954 Swed. oceanographer] (1948) : a dredge that has opposable jaws operated by a messenger traveling down a cable to release a spring catch and that is used in ecology for sampling the bottom of a body of water
ekue·le \ā-ˈkwā-(ˌ)lā\ *also* **ek·pwe·le** \-ˈek-ˈpwā-\ *n, pl* **ekuele** *also* **ek·pweles** [Fang (Bantu language of western equatorial Africa)] (ca. 1973) : the basic monetary unit of Equatorial Guinea 1975–85
¹**el** \ˈel\ *n* (14c) : the letter *l*
²**el** *n, often cap* (ca. 1906) : an urban railway that operates chiefly on an elevated structure; *also* : a train belonging to such a railway
¹**elab·o·rate** \i-ˈla-b(ə-)rət\ *adj* [L *elaboratus,* fr. *e-* + *laborare* to work — more at LABORATORY] (1592) **1** : planned or carried out with great care ⟨took ∼ precautions⟩ **2** : marked by complexity, fullness of detail, or ornateness ⟨∼ prose⟩ — **elab·o·rate·ly** *adv* — **elab·o·rate·ness** *n*
²**elab·o·rate** \i-ˈla-bə-ˌrāt\ *vb* **-rat·ed; -rat·ing** *vt* (1611) **1** : to produce by labor **2** : to build up (as complex organic compounds) from simple ingredients **3** : to work out in detail : DEVELOP ∼ *vi* **1** : to become elaborate **2** : to expand something in detail ⟨would you care to ∼ on that statement⟩ — **elab·o·ra·tion** \-ˌla-bə-ˈrā-shən\ *n* — **elab·o·ra·tive** \-ˈla-bə-ˌrā-tiv\ *adj*
Elaine \i-ˈlān\ *n* : any of several women in Arthurian legend; *esp* : one who dies for unrequited love of Lancelot
Elam·ite \ˈē-lə-ˌmīt\ *n* (1874) : a language of unknown affinities used in Elam approximately from the 25th to the 4th centuries B.C.
élan \ā-ˈlä\ *n* [F, fr. MF *eslan* rush, fr. (s')*eslancer* to rush, fr. *ex-* + *lancer* to hurl — more at LANCE] (1864) : vigorous spirit or enthusiasm
eland \ˈē-lənd, -ˌland\ *n, pl* **eland** *also* **elands** [Afrik, elk, fr. D, fr. obs.

G *Elend,* prob. fr. obs. Lith *ellenis;* akin to OHG *elaho* elk — more at ELK] (1600) : either of two large African antelopes (*Tragelaphus oryx* and *T. derbianus*) bovine in form with short spirally twisted horns in both sexes
élan vi·tal \ā-ˌläⁿ-vē-ˈtál\ *n* [F] (1907) : the vital force or impulse of life; *esp* : a creative principle held by Bergson to be immanent in all organisms and responsible for evolution
el·a·pid \ˈe-lə-pəd\ *n* [NL *Elap-, Elaps,* genus of snakes, fr. MGk, a fish, alter. of Gk *elops*] (1885) : any of a family (Elapidae) of venomous snakes with grooved fangs
¹**elapse** \i-ˈlaps\ *vi* **elapsed; elaps·ing** [L *elapsus,* pp. of *elabi,* fr. *e-* + *labi* to slip — more at SLEEP] (1644) : to slip or glide away : PASS ⟨four years *elapsed* before he returned⟩
²**elapse** *n* (ca. 1677) : PASSAGE ⟨returned after an ∼ of 15 years⟩
elapsed time *n* (ca. 1909) : the actual time taken (as by a boat or automobile in traveling over a racecourse)
elas·mo·branch \i-ˈlaz-mə-ˌbraŋk\ *n, pl* **-branchs** [ultim. fr. Gk *elasmos* metal plate (fr. *elaunein*) + *branchia* gills] (1872) : any of a subclass (Elasmobranchii) of cartilaginous fishes that have five to seven lateral to ventral gill openings on each side and that comprise the sharks, rays, skates, and extinct related fishes — **elasmobranch** *adj*
elas·tase \i-ˈlas-ˌtās, -ˌtāz\ *n* [*elastin* + *-ase*] (1949) : an enzyme esp. of pancreatic juice that digests elastin
¹**elas·tic** \i-ˈlas-tik\ *adj* [NL *elasticus,* fr. LGk *elastos* ductile, beaten, fr. Gk *elaunein* to drive, beat out; prob. akin to Gk *ēlythe* he went, OIr *luid*] (1674) **1 a** *of a solid* : capable of recovering size and shape after deformation **b** : being a collision between particles in which the total kinetic energy of the particles remains unchanged **2** : capable of recovering quickly esp. from depression or disappointment **3** : capable of being easily stretched or expanded and resuming former shape : FLEXIBLE **4 a** : capable of ready change or easy expansion or contraction : not rigid or constricted **b** : receptive to new ideas : ADAPTABLE — **elas·ti·cal·ly** \-ti-k(ə-)lē\ *adv*
   syn ELASTIC, RESILIENT, SPRINGY, FLEXIBLE, SUPPLE mean able to endure strain without being permanently injured. ELASTIC implies the property of resisting deformation by stretching ⟨an *elastic* waistband⟩. RESILIENT implies the ability to recover shape quickly when the deforming force or pressure is removed ⟨a *resilient* innersole⟩. SPRINGY stresses both the ease with which something yields to pressure and the quickness of its return to original shape ⟨the cake is done when the top is *springy*⟩. FLEXIBLE applies to something which may or may not be resilient or elastic but which can be bent or folded without breaking ⟨*flexible* plastic tubing⟩. SUPPLE applies to something that can be readily bent, twisted, or folded without any sign of injury ⟨*supple* leather⟩.
²**elastic** *n* (1847) **1 a** : easily stretched rubber usu. prepared in cords, strings, or bands **b** : RUBBER BAND **2 a** : an elastic fabric usu. made of yarns containing rubber **b** : something made from this fabric
elastic fiber *n* (1849) : a thick very elastic smooth yellowish anastomosing fiber of connective tissue that contains elastin
elas·tic·i·ty \i-ˌlas-ˈti-sə-tē, ˌē-ˌlas-, -ˈtis-tē\ *n, pl* **-ties** (1664) : the quality or state of being elastic: as **a** : the capability of a strained body to recover its size and shape after deformation : SPRINGINESS **b** : RESILIENCE 2 **c** : the quality of being adaptable
elas·ti·cized \i-ˈlas-tə-ˌsīzd\ *adj* (ca. 1909) : made with elastic thread or inserts
elastic limit *n* (1898) : the greatest strain that an elastic solid can sustain without undergoing permanent deformation
elastic modulus *n* (1904) : the ratio of the stress in a body to the corresponding strain
elastic scattering *n* (1933) : a scattering of particles as the result of an elastic collision
elas·tin \i-ˈlas-tən\ *n* [ISV, fr. NL *elasticus*] (1875) : a protein that is similar to collagen and is the chief constituent of elastic fibers
elas·to·mer \i-ˈlas-tə-mər\ *n* [*elastic* + *-o-* + *-mer*] (ca. 1939) : any of various elastic substances resembling rubber ⟨polyvinyl ∼s⟩ — **elas·to·mer·ic** \i-ˌlas-tə-ˈmer-ik\ *adj*
¹**elate** \i-ˈlāt\ *vt* **elat·ed; elat·ing** [L *elatus* (pp. of *efferre* to carry out, elevate), fr. *e-* + *latus,* pp. of *ferre* to carry — more at TOLERATE, BEAR] (ca. 1619) : to fill with joy or pride
²**elate** *adj* (1647) : ELATED
elat·ed *adj* (ca. 1619) : marked by high spirits : EXULTANT — **elat·ed·ly** *adv* — **elat·ed·ness** *n*
ela·ter \ˈe-lə-tər\ *n* [NL, fr. Gk *elatēr* driver, fr. *elaunein* to drive] (1830) : a plant structure functioning in the distribution of spores: as **a** : one of the elongated filaments among the spores in the capsule of a liverwort **b** : one of the filamentous appendages of the spores in the scouring rushes
elat·er·ite \i-ˈla-tə-ˌrīt\ *n* [G *Elaterit,* fr. Gk *elatēr*] (1826) : a dark brown elastic mineral resin occurring in soft flexible masses
ela·tion \i-ˈlā-shən\ *n* (14c) **1** : the quality or state of being elated **2** : pathological euphoria
E layer *n* (1933) : a layer of the ionosphere occurring about 65 miles (110 kilometers) above the earth's surface during daylight hours that is capable of reflecting shortwave frequencies
El·ba \ˈel-bə\ *n* [*Elba* (Mediterranean island), residence of Napoléon Bonaparte after his first abdication May 14, 1814 to Feb. 26, 1815] (1924) : a place or state of exile
¹**el·bow** \ˈel-ˌbō\ *n* [ME *elbowe,* fr. OE *elboga,* fr. *el-* (akin to *eln* ell) + OE *boga* bow — more at ELL, BOW] (bef. 12c) **1 a** : the joint of the human arm **b** : a corresponding joint in the anterior limb of a lower vertebrate **2** : something (as macaroni or an angular pipe fitting) resembling an elbow — **at one's elbow** : at one's side — **out at elbows 1** : shabbily dressed **2** : short of funds
²**elbow** *vt* (1605) **1 a** : to push with the elbow : JOSTLE **b** : to shove aside by pushing with or as if with the elbow **2** : to force (as one's way) by pushing with or as if with the elbow ⟨∼*ing* our way through the crowd⟩ ⟨∼s her way into the best social circles⟩ ∼ *vi* **1** : to advance by pushing with the elbow **2** : to make an angle : TURN
elbow grease *n* (1672) : vigorously applied physical labor : hard work
el·bow·room \ˈel-ˌbō-ˌrüm, -ˌrùm\ *n* (ca. 1540) **1 a** : room for moving the elbows freely **b** : adequate space for work or operation ⟨the large house gives plenty of ∼⟩ **2** : free scope ⟨∼ to try new ideas⟩

el cheapo \(ˌ)el-'chē-(ˌ)pō, 'el-\ *adj* [Sp *el* the + E *cheap* + Sp *-o* (masc. n. ending)] (1969) : CHEAP 3a, b

eld \'eld\ *n* [ME, fr. OE *ieldo;* akin to OE *eald* old — more at OLD] (bef. 12c) **1** : old age **2** *archaic* : old times : ANTIQUITY

¹el·der \'el-dər\ *n* [ME *eldre,* fr. OE *ellærn;* perh. akin to OE *alor* alder — more at ALDER] (bef. 12c) : ELDERBERRY 2

²elder *adj* [ME, fr. OE *ieldra,* compar. of *eald* old] (bef. 12c) **1** : of earlier birth or greater age ⟨his ~ brother⟩ **2** : of or relating to earlier times : FORMER **3** *obs* : of or relating to a more advanced time of life **4** : prior or superior in rank, office, or validity

³elder *n* (bef. 12c) **1** : one living in an earlier period **2 a** : one who is older : SENIOR ⟨a child trying to please her ~s⟩ **b** : an aged person **3** : one having authority by virtue of age and experience ⟨the village ~s⟩ **4** : any of various officers of religious groups: as **a** : PRESBYTER 1 **b** : a permanent officer elected by a Presbyterian congregation and ordained to serve on the session and assist the pastor at communion **c** : MINISTER 2 **d** : a leader of the Shakers **e** : a Mormon ordained to the Melchizedek priesthood — **el·der·ship** \-ˌship\ *n*

el·der·ber·ry \'el-də(r)-ˌber-ē\ *n* (1589) **1** : the edible black or red berrylike drupe of any of a genus (*Sambucus*) of shrubs or trees of the honeysuckle family bearing flat clusters of small white or pink flowers **2** : a tree or shrub bearing elderberries

¹el·der·ly \'el-dər-lē\ *adj* (1611) **1 a** : rather old; *esp* : being past middle age **b** : OLD-FASHIONED **2** : of, relating to, or characteristic of later life or elderly persons — **el·der·li·ness** *n*

²elderly *n, pl* **-ly** *or* **-lies** (1865) : an elderly person

elder statesman *n* (1904) : an eminent senior member of a group or organization; *esp* : a retired statesman who unofficially advises current leaders

el·dest \'el-dəst\ *adj* (bef. 12c) : of the greatest age or seniority : OLDEST

eldest hand *n* (1599) : the card player who first receives cards in the deal

El Do·ra·do \ˌel-də-'rä-(ˌ)dō, -'rä-\ *n* [Sp, lit., the gilded one] **1** : a city or country of fabulous riches held by 16th century explorers to exist in So. America **2** : a place of fabulous wealth or opportunity

el·dress \'el-drəs\ *n* (1640) : a woman elder esp. of the Shakers

el·dritch \'el-drich\ *adj* [perh. fr. (assumed) ME *elfriche* fairyland, fr. ME *elf* + *riche* kingdom, fr. OE *rice* — more at RICH] (1508) : WEIRD, EERIE

El·e·at·ic \ˌel-ē-'a-tik\ *adj* [L *Eleaticus,* fr. Gk *Eleatikos,* fr. *Elea* (*Velia*), ancient town in southern Italy] (1695) : of or relating to a school of Greek philosophers founded by Parmenides and developed by Zeno and marked by belief in the unity of being and the unreality of motion or change — **Eleatic** *n* — **El·e·at·i·cism** \-'a-tə-ˌsi-zəm\ *n*

ele·cam·pane \ˌe-li-ˌkam-'pān\ *n* [ME *elena campana,* fr. ML *enula campana,* lit., field elecampane, fr. *inula, enula* elecampane + *campana* of the field] (14c) : a large coarse European composite herb (*Inula helenium*) that has yellow ray flowers and is naturalized in the U.S.

¹elect \i-'lekt\ *adj* [ME, fr. L *electus,* pp. of *eligere* to select, fr. *e-* + *legere* to choose — more at LEGEND] (15c) **1** : carefully selected : CHOSEN **2** : chosen for salvation through divine mercy **3 a** : chosen for office or position but not yet installed ⟨the president-*elect*⟩ **b** : chosen for marriage at some future time ⟨the bride-*elect*⟩

²elect *n, pl* **elect** (15c) **1** : one chosen or set apart (as by divine favor) **2** *pl* : a select or exclusive group of people

³elect *vb* [ME, fr. L *electus*] *vt* (15c) **1** : to select by vote for an office, position, or membership ⟨~ed her class president⟩ **2** : to make a selection ⟨*will* ~ an academic program⟩ **3** : to choose (as a course of action) esp. by preference ⟨*might* ~ to sell the business⟩ ~ *vi* : to make a selection

elect·able \i-'lek-tə-bəl\ *adj* (1879) : capable of being elected (as to public office) — **elect·abil·i·ty** \-ˌlek-tə-'bi-lə-tē\ *n*

elec·tion \i-'lek-shən\ *n* (13c) **1 a** : an act or process of electing **b** : the fact of being elected **2** : predestination to eternal life **3** : the right, power, or privilege of making a choice

Election Day *n* (15c) : a day legally established for the election of public officials; *esp* : the first Tuesday after the first Monday in November in an even year designated for national elections in the U.S. and observed as a legal holiday in many states

elec·tion·eer \i-ˌlek-shə-'nir\ *vi* [*election* + *-eer* (as in *privateer,* v.)] (1789) : to take an active part in an election; *specif* : to work for the election of a candidate or party — **elec·tion·eer·er** *n*

¹elec·tive \i-'lek-tiv\ *adj* (1531) **1 a** : chosen or filled by popular election ⟨an ~ official⟩ **b** : of or relating to election **c** : based on the right or principle of election ⟨the presidency is an ~ office⟩ **2 a** : permitting a choice : OPTIONAL ⟨an ~ course in school⟩ **b** : beneficial to the patient but not essential for survival ⟨~ surgery⟩ **3 a** : tending to operate on one substance rather than another ⟨~ absorption⟩ **b** : favorably inclined to one more than to another : SYMPATHETIC ⟨an ~ affinity⟩ — **elec·tive·ly** *adv* — **elec·tive·ness** *n*

²elective *n* (1850) : an elective course or subject

elec·tor \i-'lek-tər, -ˌtòr\ *n* (15c) **1** : one qualified to vote in an election **2** : one entitled to participate in an election: as **a** : any of the German princes entitled to take part in choosing the Holy Roman Emperor **b** : a member of the electoral college in the U.S.

elec·tor·al \i-'lek-t(ə-)rəl, ē-ˌlek-'tòr-əl\ *adj* (1675) **1** : of or relating to an elector ⟨the ~ vote⟩ **2** : of or relating to election ⟨an ~ system⟩ — **elec·tor·al·ly** \-t(ə-)rə-lē, -'tòr-ə-lē\ *adv*

electoral college *n* (ca. 1691) : a body of electors; *esp* : one that elects the president and vice president of the U.S.

elec·tor·ate \i-'lek-t(ə-)rət\ *n* (1675) **1** : the territory, jurisdiction, or dignity of a German elector **2** : a body of people entitled to vote

electr- *or* **electro-** *comb form* [NL *electricus*] **1 a** : electricity ⟨*elec*trometer⟩ **b** : electric ⟨*electrode*⟩ : electric and ⟨*electro*chemical⟩ : electrically ⟨*electro*positive⟩ **2** : electrolytic ⟨*electro*analysis⟩ **3** : electron ⟨*electro*philic⟩

Elec·tra \i-'lek-trə\ *n* [L, fr. Gk *Ēlektra*] : a sister of Orestes who aids him in killing their mother Clytemnestra

Electra complex *n* (1913) : the Oedipus complex when it occurs in a female

elec·tress \i-'lek-trəs\ *n* (1618) : the wife or widow of a German elector

elec·tret \i-'lek-trat, -ˌtret\ *n* [*electricity* + *magnet*] (1885) : a dielectric body in which a permanent state of electric polarization has been set up

¹elec·tric \i-'lek-trik, ē-\ *adj* [NL *electricus* produced from amber by friction, electric, fr. ML, of amber, fr. L *electrum* amber, electrum, fr. Gk *ēlektron;* akin to Gk *ēlektōr* beaming sun] (1675) **1** *or* **elec·tri·cal** \-tri-kəl\ : of, relating to, or operated by electricity **2** : exciting as if by electric shock ⟨an ~ performance⟩ ⟨an ~ personality⟩; *also* : charged with strong emotion ⟨the room was ~ with tension⟩ **3 a** : ELECTRONIC 3a **b** : amplifying sound by electronic means — used of a musical instrument ⟨an ~ guitar⟩ **4** : very bright ⟨~ blue⟩ ⟨~ orange⟩ — **elec·tri·cal·ly** \-tri-k(ə-)lē\ *adv*

²electric *n* (1646) **1** *archaic* : a nonconductor of electricity used to excite or accumulate electricity **2** : something (as a light, automobile, or train) operated by electricity

electrical storm *n* (1941) : THUNDERSTORM — called also *electric storm*

electric chair *n* (1889) **1** : a chair used in legal electrocution **2** : the penalty of death by electrocution

electric eel *n* (1794) : a large eel-shaped fish (*Electrophorus electricus*) of the Orinoco and Amazon basins that is capable of giving a severe shock with its electric organs

electric eye *n* (1898) : PHOTOELECTRIC CELL

electric field *n* (ca. 1889) : a region associated with a distribution of electric charge or a varying magnetic field in which forces due to that charge or field act upon other electric charges

elec·tri·cian \i-ˌlek-'tri-shən, ē-\ *n* (1869) : one who installs, maintains, operates, or repairs electrical equipment

elec·tric·i·ty \i-ˌlek-'tri-sə-tē, ē-, -'tris-tē\ *n, pl* **-ties** (1646) **1 a** : a fundamental entity of nature consisting of negative and positive kinds, observable in the attractions and repulsions of bodies electrified by friction and in natural phenomena (as lightning or the aurora borealis), and usu. utilized in the form of electric currents **b** : electric current or power **2** : a science that deals with the phenomena and laws of electricity **3** : keen contagious excitement

electric organ *n* (1773) : a specialized tract of tissue (as in the electric eel) in which electricity is generated

electric ray *n* (1774) : any of various round-bodied short-tailed rays (family Torpedinidae) of warm seas with a pair of electric organs

elec·tri·fi·ca·tion \i-ˌlek-trə-fə-'kā-shən, ē-\ *n* (1748) **1** : an act or process of electrifying **2** : the state of being electrified

elec·tri·fy \i-'lek-trə-ˌfī, ē-\ *vt* **-fied; -fy·ing** (1745) **1 a** : to charge with electricity **b** (1) : to equip for use of electric power (2) : to supply with electric power (3) : to amplify (music) electronically **2** : to excite intensely or suddenly as if by electric shock

elec·tro·acous·tics \i-ˌlek-trō-ə-'küs-tiks\ *n pl but sing in constr* (1927) : a science that deals with the transformation of acoustic energy into electric energy or vice versa — **elec·tro·acous·tic** \-tik\ *adj*

elec·tro·anal·y·sis \-ə-'na-lə-səs\ *n* (1903) : chemical analysis by electrolytic methods — **elec·tro·an·a·lyt·i·cal** \-ˌlit-i-kəl\ *adj*

elec·tro·car·dio·gram \-'kär-dē-ə-ˌgram\ *n* (ca. 1904) : the tracing made by an electrocardiograph

elec·tro·car·dio·graph \-ˌgraf\ *n* (1913) : an instrument for recording the changes of electrical potential occurring during the heartbeat used esp. in diagnosing abnormalities of heart action — **elec·tro·car·dio·graph·ic** \-ˌkär-dē-ə-'gra-fik\ *adj* — **elec·tro·car·dio·graph·i·cal·ly** \-fi-k(ə-)lē\ *adv* — **elec·tro·car·di·og·ra·phy** \-dē-'ä-grə-fē\ *n*

elec·tro·chem·is·try \-'ke-mə-strē\ *n* (1814) : a science that deals with the relation of electricity to chemical changes and with the interconversion of chemical and electrical energy — **elec·tro·chem·i·cal** \-'ke-mi-kəl\ *adj* — **elec·tro·chem·i·cal·ly** \-k(ə-)lē\ *adv*

elec·tro·con·vul·sive \i-ˌlek-trō-kən-'vəl-siv\ *adj* (1947) : of, relating to, or involving convulsive response to electroshock ⟨~ shocks⟩

electroconvulsive therapy *n* (1948) : ELECTROSHOCK THERAPY

elec·tro·cor·ti·co·gram \i-ˌlek-trō-'kòr-ti-kə-ˌgram\ *n* (1939) : an electrocorticogram made with the electrodes in direct contact with the brain

elec·tro·cute \i-'lek-trə-ˌkyüt\ *vt* **-cut·ed; -cut·ing** [*electr-* + *-cute* (as in *execute*)] (1889) **1** : to execute (a criminal) by electricity **2** : to kill by electric shock — **elec·tro·cu·tion** \-ˌlek-trə-'kyü-shən\ *n*

elec·trode \i-'lek-ˌtrōd\ *n* (1834) **1** : a conductor used to establish electrical contact with a nonmetallic part of a circuit **2** : an element in a semiconductor device (as a transistor) that emits or collects electrons or holes or controls their movements

¹elec·tro·de·pos·it \i-ˌlek-trō-di-'pä-zət\ *n* (1864) : a deposit formed in or at an electrode by electrolysis

²electrodeposit *vt* (1882) : to deposit (as a metal or rubber) by electrolysis — **elec·tro·de·po·si·tion** \-ˌde-pə-'zi-shən, -ˌdē-pə-\ *n*

elec·tro·der·mal \i-ˌlek-trō-'dər-məl\ *adj* (1946) : of or relating to electrical activity in or electrical properties of the skin

elec·tro·des·ic·ca·tion \i-ˌlek-trō-ˌde-si-'kā-shən\ *n* (1919) : the drying up of tissue by a high-frequency electric current applied with a needle-shaped electrode — called also *fulguration*

elec·tro·di·al·y·sis \i-ˌlek-trō-dī-'a-lə-səs\ *n* (1921) : dialysis accelerated by an electromotive force applied to electrodes adjacent to the membranes — **elec·tro·di·a·lyt·ic** \-ə-'li-tik\ *adj*

elec·tro·dy·nam·ics \-dī-'na-miks\ *n pl but sing in constr* (1827) : a branch of physics that deals with the effects arising from the interactions of electric currents with magnets, with other currents, or with themselves — **elec·tro·dy·nam·ic** \-mik\ *adj*

elec·tro·dy·na·mom·e·ter \-ˌdī-nə-'mä-mə-tər\ *n* [ISV] (1876) : an instrument that measures current by indicating the strength of the forces between a current flowing in fixed coils and one flowing in movable coils

elec·tro·en·ceph·a·lo·gram \-in-'se-f(ə-)lə-ˌgram\ *n* [ISV] (1934) : the tracing of brain waves made by an electroencephalograph

elec·tro·en·ceph·a·lo·graph \-ˌgraf\ *n* [ISV] (1936) : an apparatus for detecting and recording brain waves — **elec·tro·en·ceph·a·log·ra·**

\ə\ abut \ᵊ\ kitten, F table \ər\ further \a\ ash \ā\ ace \ä\ mop, mar \aů\ out \ch\ chin \e\ bet \ē\ easy \g\ go \i\ hit \ī\ ice \j\ job \ŋ\ sing \ō\ go \ò\ law \òi\ boy \th\ thin \t͟h\ the \ü\ loot \ů\ foot \y\ yet \zh\ vision \à, ᵏ, ⁿ, œ, œ̄, ᵫ, ᵬ, ᵲ\ *see* Guide to Pronunciation

pher \-ˌse-fə-ˈlä-grə-fər\ *n* — **elec·tro·en·ceph·a·lo·graph·ic** \-ˌse-f(ə-)lə-ˈgra-fik\ *adj* — **elec·tro·en·ceph·a·lo·graph·i·cal·ly** \-fi-k(ə-)lē\ *adv* — **elec·tro·en·ceph·a·log·ra·phy** \-ˈlä-grə-fē\ *n*

elec·tro·fish·ing \i-ˈlek-trō-ˌfi-shiŋ\ *n* (1950) : the taking of fish by a system based on their tendency to respond positively to a source of direct electric current

elec·tro·form \i-ˈlek-trə-ˌfȯrm\ *vt* (1931) : to form (shaped articles) by electrodeposition on a mold — **electroform** *n*

elec·tro·gen·ic \i-ˌlek-trə-ˈje-nik\ *adj* (ca. 1891) : of or relating to the production of electrical activity in living tissue ⟨an ~ pump⟩ — **elec·tro·gen·e·sis** \-ˈje-nə-sis\ *n*

elec·tro·gram \i-ˈlek-trə-ˌgram\ *n* (ca. 1935) : a tracing of the electrical potentials of a tissue (as the brain or heart) made by means of electrodes placed directly in the tissue instead of on the surface of the body

elec·tro·hy·drau·lic \i-ˌlek-trō-hi-ˈdrȯ-lik, -ˈdrä-\ *adj* (1922) **1** : of or relating to a combination of electric and hydraulic mechanisms **2** : involving or produced by the action of very brief but powerful pulse discharges of electricity under a liquid resulting in the generation of shock waves and highly reactive chemical species ⟨an ~ effect⟩

elec·tro·jet \i-ˈlek-trə-ˌjet\ *n* (1955) : an overhead concentration of electric current found in the regions of strong auroral displays and along the magnetic equator

elec·tro·ki·net·ic \i-ˌlek-trō-kə-ˈne-tik, -kī-\ *adj* (1881) : of or relating to the motion of particles or liquids that results from or produces a difference of electric potential

elec·tro·ki·net·ics \-tiks\ *n pl but sing in constr* (ca. 1925) : a branch of physics dealing with the motion of electric currents or charged particles

elec·tro·less \i-ˈlek-ˌtrō-ləs, -trə-\ *adj* (1947) : being or involving chemical deposition of metal instead of electrodeposition

elec·trol·o·gist \i-ˌlek-ˈträ-lə-jist\ *n* [blend of *electrolysis* and *-logist* (fr. *-logy* + *-ist*)] (ca. 1902) : one that removes hair, warts, moles, and birthmarks by means of an electric current applied to the body with a needle-shaped electrode — **elec·trol·o·gy** \-lə-jē\ *n*

elec·tro·lu·mi·nes·cent \i-ˌlek-trō-ˌlü-mə-ˈne-sᵊnt\ *adj* (ca. 1909) : of or relating to luminescence resulting from a high-frequency discharge through a gas or from application of an alternating current to a layer of phosphor — **elec·tro·lu·mi·nes·cence** \-sᵊn(t)s\ *n*

elec·trol·y·sis \i-ˌlek-ˈträ-lə-səs\ *n* (1834) **1 a** : the producing of chemical changes by passage of an electric current through an electrolyte **b** : subjection to this action **2** : the destruction of hair roots with an electric current

elec·tro·lyte \i-ˈlek-trə-ˌlīt\ *n* (1834) **1** : a nonmetallic electric conductor in which current is carried by the movement of ions **2** : a substance that when dissolved in a suitable solvent or when fused becomes an ionic conductor

elec·tro·lyt·ic \i-ˌlek-trə-ˈli-tik\ *adj* (1842) : of or relating to electrolysis or an electrolyte; *also* : involving, produced by, or used in electrolysis ⟨~ cell⟩ — **elec·tro·lyt·i·cal·ly** \-ti-k(ə-)lē\ *adv*

elec·tro·lyze \i-ˈlek-trə-ˌlīz\ *vt* **-lyzed; -lyz·ing** (1834) : to subject to electrolysis

elec·tro·mag·net \i-ˌlek-trō-ˈmag-nət\ *n* (1831) : a core of magnetic material surrounded by a coil of wire through which an electric current is passed to magnetize the core

elec·tro·mag·net·ic \-ˈmag-ˈne-tik\ *adj* (1821) : of, relating to, or produced by electromagnetism — **elec·tro·mag·net·i·cal·ly** \-ti-k(ə-)lē\ *adv*

electromagnetic pulse *n* (1981) : high-intensity electromagnetic radiation generated by a nuclear blast high above the earth's surface and held to disrupt electronic and electrical systems

electromagnetic radiation *n* (1939) : a series of electromagnetic waves

electromagnetic spectrum *n* (ca. 1934) : the entire range of wavelengths or frequencies of electromagnetic radiation extending from gamma rays to the longest radio waves and including visible light

electromagnetic unit *n* (ca. 1889) : any of a system of electrical units based primarily on the magnetic properties of electrical currents

electromagnetic wave *n* (1908) : one of the waves that are propagated by simultaneous periodic variations of electric and magnetic field intensity and that include radio waves, infrared, visible light, ultraviolet, X rays, and gamma rays

elec·tro·mag·ne·tism \i-ˌlek-trō-ˈmag-nə-ˌti-zəm\ *n* (1828) **1** : magnetism developed by a current of electricity **2 a** : a fundamental physical force that is responsible for interactions between charged particles which occur because of their charge and for the emission and absorption of photons, that is about 100 times weaker than the strong force, and that extends over infinite distances but is dominant over atomic and molecular distances — called also *electromagnetic force*; compare GRAVITY 3a(2), STRONG FORCE, WEAK FORCE **b** : a branch of physical science that deals with the physical relations between electricity and magnetism

elec·tro·me·chan·i·cal \-mə-ˈka-ni-kəl\ *adj* (1888) : of, relating to, or being a mechanical process or device actuated or controlled electrically; *esp* : being a transducer for converting electrical energy to mechanical energy — **elec·tro·me·chan·i·cal·ly** \-k(ə-)lē\ *adv*

elec·tro·met·al·lur·gy \-ˈme-tᵊl-ˌər-jē, *esp Brit* -mə-ˈta-lər-\ *n* (1840) : a branch of metallurgy that deals with the application of electric current either for electrolytic deposition or as a source of heat

elec·trom·e·ter \i-ˌlek-ˈträ-mə-tər\ *n* (1749) : any of various instruments for detecting or measuring electric-potential differences or ionizing radiations by means of the forces of attraction or repulsion between charged bodies

elec·tro·mo·tive force \i-ˌlek-trō-ˌmō-tiv-, -trə-\ *n* (1827) : something that moves or tends to move electricity : the potential difference derived from an electrical source per unit quantity of electricity passing through the source (as a cell or generator)

elec·tro·myo·gram \i-ˌlek-trō-ˈmī-ə-ˌgram\ *n* (1917) : a tracing made with an electromyograph

elec·tro·myo·graph \-ˌgraf\ *n* [*electr-* + *my-* + *-graph*] (1948) : an instrument that converts the electrical activity associated with functioning skeletal muscle into a visual record or into sound and used to diagnose neuromuscular disorders and in biofeedback training — **elec·tro·myo·graph·ic** \-ˌmī-ə-ˈgra-fik\ *adj* — **elec·tro·myo·graph·i·cal·ly** \-fi-k(ə-)lē\ *adv* — **elec·tro·my·og·ra·phy** \-mī-ˈä-grə-fē\ *n*

elec·tron \i-ˈlek-ˌträn\ *n* [*electr-* + ²*-on*] (1891) : an elementary particle consisting of a charge of negative electricity equal to about 1.602 × 10⁻¹⁹ coulomb and having a mass when at rest of about 9.109534 × 10⁻²⁸ gram or about ¹/₁₈₃₆ that of a proton

electron cloud *n* (1926) : the system of electrons surrounding the nucleus of an atom

elec·tro·neg·a·tive \i-ˌlek-trō-ˈne-gə-tiv\ *adj* (1834) : having a tendency to attract electrons — **elec·tro·neg·a·tiv·i·ty** \-ˌne-gə-ˈti-və-tē\ *n*

electron gas *n* (ca. 1929) : a population of free electrons in a vacuum or in a metallic conductor

electron gun *n* (1924) : an electron-emitting cathode and its surrounding assembly (as in a cathode-ray tube) for directing, controlling, and focusing a beam of electrons

elec·tron·ic \i-ˌlek-ˈträ-nik\ *adj* (1902) **1** : of or relating to electrons **2** : of, relating to, or utilizing devices constructed or working by the methods or principles of electronics; *also* : implemented on or by means of a computer ⟨~ food stamps⟩ ⟨~ banking⟩ **3 a** : generating musical tones by electronic means ⟨an ~ organ⟩ **b** : of, relating to, or being music that consists of sounds electronically generated or modified **4** : of, relating to, or being a medium (as television) by which information is transmitted electronically ⟨~ journalism⟩ — **elec·tron·i·cal·ly** \-ni-k(ə-)lē\ *adv*

electronic countermeasure *n* (1962) : the disruption of the operation of an enemy's equipment (as by jamming radio or radar signals)

electronic mail *n* (1977) : messages sent and received electronically (as between terminals linked by telephone lines or microwave relays)

electronic publishing *n* (1980) : publishing in which information is distributed by means of a computer network or is produced in a format for use with a computer

elec·tron·ics \i-ˌlek-ˈträ-niks\ *n pl* (1910) **1** *sing in constr* : a branch of physics that deals with the emission, behavior, and effects of electrons (as in electron tubes and transistors) and with electronic devices **2** : electronic devices or equipment

electron lens *n* (1931) : a device for focusing a beam of electrons by means of an electric or a magnetic field

electron micrograph *n* (1934) : a micrograph made with an electron microscope — **electron micrography** \-ˌmī-ˈkrä-grə-fē\ *n*

electron microscope *n* (1932) : an electron-optical instrument in which a beam of electrons focused by means of an electron lens is used to produce an enlarged image of a minute object on a fluorescent screen or photographic plate — **electron microscopist** *n* — **electron microscopy** *n*

electron multiplier *n* (1936) : a device utilizing secondary emission of electrons for amplifying a current of electrons

electron optics *n pl but sing in constr* (1916) : a branch of physics in which the principles of optics are applied to beams of electrons — **electron–op·ti·cal** \i-ˌlek-ˌträn-ˈäp-ti-kəl\ *adj*

electron probe *n* (1962) : a microprobe that uses an electron beam to induce X-ray emissions in a sample

electron transport *n* (1951) : the sequential transfer of electrons esp. by cytochromes in cellular respiration from an oxidizable substrate to molecular oxygen by a series of oxidation-reduction reactions

electron tube *n* (1922) : an electronic device in which conduction by electrons takes place through a vacuum or a gaseous medium within a sealed glass or metal container and which has various uses based on the controlled flow of electrons

electron volt *n* (1930) : a unit of energy equal to the energy gained by an electron in passing from a point of low potential to a point one volt higher in potential : 1.60 × 10⁻¹⁹ joule

elec·tro·oc·u·lo·gram \i-ˌlek-trō-ˈä-kyə-lə-ˌgram\ *n* [*electr-* + L *oculus* eye + E *-gram* — more at EYE] (1947) : a record of the standing voltage between the front and back of the eye that is correlated with eyeball movement (as in REM sleep) and obtained by electrodes placed on the skin near the eye

elec·tro·oc·u·log·ra·phy \-ˌä-kyə-ˈlä-grə-fē\ *n, pl* **-phies** (1951) : the preparation and study of electrooculograms

elec·tro–op·ti·cal \i-ˌlek-trō-ˈäp-ti-kəl\ *or* **elec·tro–op·tic** \-ˈäp-tik\ *adj* (1879) **1** : of or relating to electro-optics **2 a** : relating to or being a change in the refractive index of a material due to an electric field ⟨~ effect⟩ **b** : using or being a material that exhibits electro-optical properties ⟨an ~ crystal⟩ **3** : relating to or being an electronic device for emitting, modulating, transmitting, or sensing light — **elec·tro–op·ti·cal·ly** \-k(ə-)lē\ *adv*

elec·tro–op·tics \-trō-ˈäp-tiks\ *n pl* (ca. 1889) **1** *sing in constr* : a branch of physics that deals with the effects of an electric field on light traversing it **2** : electro-optical devices

elec·tro·os·mo·sis \i-ˌlek-trō-äz-ˈmō-səs, -äs-\ *n* (1906) : the movement of a liquid out of or through a porous material or a biological membrane under the influence of an electric field — **elec·tro·os·mot·ic** \-ˈmä-tik\ *adj*

elec·tro·phe·ro·gram \-trə-ˈfir-ə-ˌgram, -ˈfer-\ *n* [*electr-* + *phero-* (fr. Gk *pherein* to carry) + *-gram*] (1951) : ELECTROPHORETOGRAM

elec·tro·phile \i-ˈlek-trə-ˌfil\ *n* (1943) : an electrophilic substance (as an electron-accepting reagent)

elec·tro·phil·ic \i-ˌlek-trə-ˈfi-lik\ *adj* (1936) **1** *of an atom, ion, or molecule* : having an affinity for electrons : being an electron acceptor **2** : involving an electrophilic species ⟨an ~ reaction⟩ — compare NUCLEOPHILIC — **elec·tro·phi·lic·i·ty** \-ˌtrō-fi-ˈli-sə-tē\ *n*

elec·tro·pho·re·sis \i-ˌlek-trə-fə-ˈrē-səs\ *n* [NL] (1911) : the movement of suspended particles through a fluid or gel under the action of an electromotive force applied to electrodes in contact with the suspension — **elec·tro·pho·rese** \-ˈrēs, -ˈrēz\ *vt* — **elec·tro·pho·ret·ic** \-ˈre-tik\ *adj* — **elec·tro·pho·ret·i·cal·ly** \-ti-k(ə-)lē\ *adv*

elec·tro·pho·reto·gram \-ˈre-tə-ˌgram\ *n* [*electrophoretic* + *-o-* + *-gram*] (1954) : a record that consists of the separated components of a mixture (as of proteins) produced by electrophoresis in a supporting medium (as filter paper)

elec·troph·o·rus \i-ˌlek-ˈträ-fə-rəs\ *n, pl* **-ri** \-ˌrī, -ˌrē\ [NL, fr. *electr-* + *-phorus* -phore] (1778) : a device for producing electric charges consisting of a disk that is negatively electrified by friction and a metal plate that becomes charged by induction when placed on the disk

elec·tro·pho·tog·ra·phy \i-ˌlek-trō-fə-ˈtä-grə-fē\ *n* (1894) : photography in which images are produced by electrical means (as in xerography) — **elec·tro·pho·to·graph·ic** \-trə-ˌfō-tə-ˈgra-fik\ *adj*

elec·tro·phys·i·ol·o·gy \i-ˌlek-trō-ˌfi-zē-'ä-lə-jē\ n (1838) **1** : physiology that is concerned with the electrical aspects of physiological phenomena **2** : electrical phenomena associated with a physiological process (as the function of a body or bodily part) ⟨~ of the eye⟩ — **elec·tro·phys·i·o·log·i·cal** \-zē-ə-'lä-ji-kəl\ also **elec·tro·phys·i·o·log·ic** \-jik\ adj — **elec·tro·phys·i·o·log·i·cal·ly** \-ji-k(ə-)lē\ adv — **elec·tro·phys·i·ol·o·gist** \-zē-'äl-ə-jist\ n

elec·tro·plate \i-'lek-trə-ˌplāt\ vt (ca. 1859) : to plate with an adherent continuous coating by electrodeposition

elec·tro·pos·i·tive \i-ˌlek-trō-'pä-zə-tiv, -'päz-tiv\ adj (1834) : having a tendency to release electrons

elec·tro·ret·i·no·gram \-'re-t²n-ə-ˌgram\ n (1936) : a graphic record of electrical activity of the retina used esp. in the diagnosis of retinal conditions

elec·tro·ret·i·no·graph \-ˌgraf\ n (1962) : an instrument for recording electrical activity in the retina — **elec·tro·ret·i·no·graph·ic** \-ˌre-t²n-ə-'gra-fik\ adj — **elec·tro·ret·i·nog·ra·phy** \-t²n-'ä-grə-fē\ n

elec·tro·scope \i-'lek-trə-ˌskōp\ n [prob. fr. F électroscope] (1810) : any of various instruments for detecting the presence of an electric charge on a body, for determining whether the charge is positive or negative, or for indicating and measuring intensity of radiation

elec·tro·shock \-trō-ˌshäk\ n (1941) **1** : ³SHOCK 5 **2** : ELECTROSHOCK THERAPY

electroshock therapy n (1942) : the treatment of mental disorder and esp. depression by the induction of unconsciousness and convulsions through the use of an electric current now usu. on an anesthetized patient — called also *electroconvulsive therapy*

elec·tro·stat·ic \i-ˌlek-trə-'sta-tik\ adj [ISV] (1860) **1** : of or relating to static electricity or electrostatics **2** : of or relating to painting with a spray that utilizes electrically charged particles to ensure complete coating — **elec·tro·stat·i·cal·ly** \-'sta-ti-k(ə-)lē\ adv

electrostatic generator n (ca. 1931) : VAN DE GRAAFF GENERATOR

electrostatic precipitator n (1949) : an electrostatic device in chimney flues that removes particles from escaping gases

elec·tro·stat·ics \i-ˌlek-trə-'sta-tiks\ n pl but sing in constr (1827) : physics that deals with phenomena due to attractions or repulsions of electric charges but not dependent upon their motion

elec·tro·sur·gery \i-ˌlek-trō-'sər-jə-rē\ n (ca. 1903) : surgery by means of diathermy — **elec·tro·sur·gi·cal** \-'sər-ji-kəl\ adj

elec·tro·ther·a·py \-'ther-ə-pē\ n (1881) : treatment of disease by means of electricity (as in diathermy)

elec·tro·ther·mal \-'thər-məl\ adj (1884) : relating to or combining electricity and heat; specif : relating to the generation of heat by electricity — **elec·tro·ther·mal·ly** \-mə-lē\ adv

elec·tro·ton·ic \i-ˌlek-trə-'tä-nik\ adj (1832) **1** : of, induced by, relating to, or constituting electrotonus **2** : of, relating to, or being the spread of electrical activity through living tissue or cells in the absence of repeated action potentials ⟨an ~ junction between cells⟩ — **elec·tro·ton·i·cal·ly** \-ni-k(ə-)lē\ adv

elec·trot·o·nus \i-ˌlek-'trä-t²n-əs\ n [NL] (1878) : the altered sensitivity of a nerve when a constant current of electricity passes through any part of it

elec·tro·type \i-'lek-trə-ˌtīp\ n (1840) **1** : a duplicate printing surface made by an electroplating process **2** : a copy (as of a coin) made by an electroplating process — **electrotype** vt — **elec·tro·typ·er** \-ˌtī-pər\ n

elec·tro·weak \i-'lek-trō-ˌwēk\ adj (1978) : of, relating to, or being the unification of electromagnetism and the weak force

elec·tro·win·ning \i-'lek-trō-ˌwi-niŋ\ n (1924) : the recovery esp. of metals from solutions by electrolysis

elec·trum \i-'lek-trəm\ n [ME, fr. L — more at ELECTRIC] (14c) : a natural pale yellow alloy of gold and silver

elec·tu·ary \i-'lek-chə-ˌwer-ē\ n, pl **-ar·ies** [ME electuarie, fr. LL electuarium, prob. fr. Gk ekleikton, fr. ekleichein to lick up, fr. ex- + leichein to lick — more at LICK] (14c) : CONFECTION 2b

el·e·doi·sin \ˌe-lə-'dȯi-s²n\ n [irreg. fr. NL Eledone, fr. Gk eledōnē, a kind of octopus] (1963) : a small protein $C_{54}H_{85}N_{13}O_{15}S$ from the salivary glands of several octopuses (genus Eledone) that is a powerful vasodilator and hypotensive agent

el·ee·mo·sy·nary \ˌe-li-'mä-s²n-ˌer-ē, -'mō-; -'mä-z²n-\ adj [ML eleemosynarius, fr. LL eleemosyna alms — more at ALMS] (ca. 1616) : of, relating to, or supported by charity

el·e·gance \'e-li-gən(t)s\ n (ca. 1510) **1 a** : refined grace or dignified propriety : URBANITY **b** : tasteful richness of design or ornamentation ⟨the sumptuous ~ of the furnishings⟩ **c** : dignified gracefulness or restrained beauty of style : POLISH ⟨the essay is marked by lucidity, wit, and ~⟩ **d** : scientific precision, neatness, and simplicity ⟨the ~ of a mathematical proof⟩ **2** : something that is elegant

el·e·gan·cy \-gən(t)-sē\ n, pl **-cies** (15c) : ELEGANCE

el·e·gant \'e-li-gənt\ adj [MF or L; MF, fr. L elegant-, elegans; akin to L eligere to select — more at ELECT] (15c) **1** : marked by elegance **2** : of a high grade or quality : SPLENDID ⟨~ gems priced at hundreds of thousands of dollars⟩ syn see CHOICE — **el·e·gant·ly** adv

ele·gi·ac \ˌe-lə-'jī-ˌak, -ˌak also i-'lē-jē-ˌak\ also **ele·gi·a·cal** \ˌe-lə-'jī-ə-kəl\ adj [LL elegiacus, fr. Gk elegeiakos, fr. elegeion] (1542) **1 a** : of, relating to, or consisting of two dactylic hexameter lines the second of which lacks the arsis in the third and sixth feet **b** (1) : written in or consisting of elegiac couplets (2) : noted for having written poetry in such couplets **c** : of or relating to the period in Greece about the seventh century B.C. when poetry written in such couplets flourished **2** : of, relating to, or comprising elegy or an elegy; esp : expressing sorrow ⟨an ~ lament for departed youth⟩ — **elegiac** n — **ele·gi·a·cal·ly** \ˌe-lə-'jī-ə-k(ə-)lē\ adv

ele·git \i-'lē-jət\ n [L, lit., he has chosen, fr. eligere] (1504) : a judicial writ of execution by which a defendant's goods and if necessary his or her lands are delivered for debt to the plaintiff until the debt is paid

el·e·gize \'e-lə-ˌjīz\ vb **-gized; -giz·ing** vi (1702) : to write an elegy ~ vt : to write an elegy on

el·e·gy \'e-lə-jē\ n, pl **-gies** [L elegia poem in elegiac couplets, fr. Gk elegeia, elegeion, fr. elegos song of mourning] (1501) **1** : a poem in elegiac couplets **2 a** : a song or poem expressing sorrow or lamentation esp. for one who is dead **b** : something (as a speech) resembling such a song or poem **3 a** : a pensive or reflective poem that is usu. nostalgic or melancholy **b** : a short pensive musical composition

el·e·ment \'e-lə-mənt\ n [ME, fr. OF & L; OF, fr. L elementum] (13c) **1 a** : any of the four substances air, water, fire, and earth formerly believed to compose the physical universe **b** pl : weather conditions; esp : violent or severe weather ⟨battling the ~s⟩ **c** : the state or sphere natural or suited to a person or thing ⟨at school she was in her ~⟩ **2** : a constituent part: as **a** pl : the simplest principles of a subject of study : RUDIMENTS **b** (1) : a part of a geometric magnitude ⟨an infinitesimal ~ of volume⟩ (2) : a generator of a geometric figure; also : a line or line segment contained in the surface of a cone or cylinder (3) : a basic member of a mathematical or logical class or set (4) : one of the individual entries in a mathematical matrix or determinant **c** : one of a number of distinct groups composing a larger group or community ⟨the criminal ~ in the city⟩ **d** (1) : one of the necessary data or values on which calculations or conclusions are based (2) : one of the factors determining the outcome of a process **e** : any of more than 100 fundamental substances that consist of atoms of only one kind and that singly or in combination constitute all matter **f** : a distinct part of a composite device **g** : a subdivision of a military unit **3** pl : the bread and wine used in the Eucharist

syn ELEMENT, COMPONENT, CONSTITUENT, INGREDIENT mean one of the parts of a compound or complex whole. ELEMENT applies to any such part and often connotes irreducible simplicity ⟨the basic *elements* of geometry⟩. COMPONENT and CONSTITUENT may designate any of the substances (whether elements or compounds) or the qualities that enter into the makeup of a complex product; COMPONENT stresses its separate entity or distinguishable character ⟨the *components* of a stereo system⟩. CONSTITUENT stresses its essential and formative character ⟨the *constituents* of a chemical compound⟩. INGREDIENT applies to any of the substances which when combined form a particular mixture (as a medicine or alloy) ⟨the *ingredients* of a cocktail⟩.

CHEMICAL ELEMENTS

ELEMENT	SYMBOL	ATOMIC NUMBER	ATOMIC WEIGHT (C = 12)
actinium	Ac	89	227.0278
aluminum	Al	13	26.98154
americium	Am	95	
antimony	Sb	51	121.75
argon	Ar	18	39.948
arsenic	As	33	74.9216
astatine	At	85	
barium	Ba	56	137.33
berkelium	Bk	97	
beryllium	Be	4	9.01218
bismuth	Bi	83	208.9804
boron	B	5	10.81
bromine	Br	35	79.904
cadmium	Cd	48	112.41
calcium	Ca	20	40.08
californium	Cf	98	
carbon	C	6	12.011
cerium	Ce	58	140.12
cesium	Cs	55	132.9054
chlorine	Cl	17	35.453
chromium	Cr	24	51.996
cobalt	Co	27	58.9332
copper	Cu	29	63.546
curium	Cm	96	
dysprosium	Dy	66	162.50
einsteinium	Es	99	
erbium	Er	68	167.26
europium	Eu	63	151.96
fermium	Fm	100	
fluorine	F	9	18.998403
francium	Fr	87	
gadolinium	Gd	64	157.25
gallium	Ga	31	69.72
germanium	Ge	32	72.59
gold	Au	79	196.9665
hafnium	Hf	72	178.49
helium	He	2	4.00260
holmium	Ho	67	164.9304
hydrogen	H	1	1.0079
indium	In	49	114.82
iodine	I	53	126.9045
iridium	Ir	77	192.22
iron	Fe	26	55.847
krypton	Kr	36	83.80
lanthanum	La	57	138.9055
lawrencium	Lr	103	
lead	Pb	82	207.2
lithium	Li	3	6.941
lutetium	Lu	71	174.967
magnesium	Mg	12	24.305
manganese	Mn	25	54.9380
mendelevium	Md	101	
mercury	Hg	80	200.59
molybdenum	Mo	42	95.94
neodymium	Nd	60	144.24
neon	Ne	10	20.179
neptunium	Np	93	237.0482
nickel	Ni	28	58.69
niobium	Nb	41	92.9064
nitrogen	N	7	14.0067

\ə\ abut \²\ kitten, F table \ər\ further \a\ ash \ā\ ace \ä\ mop, mar \au̇\ out \ch\ chin \e\ bet \ē\ easy \g\ go \i\ hit \ī\ ice \j\ job \ŋ\ sing \ō\ go \ȯ\ law \ȯi\ boy \th\ thin \t͟h\ the \ü\ loot \u̇\ foot \y\ yet \zh\ vision \ȧ, k̲, ⁿ, œ, œ̄, ᵫ, ᵫ̄, ʸ\ see Guide to Pronunciation

ELEMENT	SYMBOL	ATOMIC NUMBER	ATOMIC WEIGHT (C = 12)
nobelium	No	102	
osmium	Os	76	190.2
oxygen	O	8	15.9994
palladium	Pd	46	106.42
phosphorus	P	15	30.97376
platinum	Pt	78	195.08
plutonium	Pu	94	
polonium	Po	84	
potassium	K	19	39.0983
praseodymium	Pr	59	140.9077
promethium	Pm	61	
protactinium	Pa	91	231.0359
radium	Ra	88	226.0254
radon	Rn	86	
rhenium	Re	75	186.207
rhodium	Rh	45	102.9055
rubidium	Rb	37	85.4678
ruthenium	Ru	44	101.07
samarium	Sm	62	150.36
scandium	Sc	21	44.9559
selenium	Se	34	78.96
silicon	Si	14	28.0855
silver	Ag	47	107.868
sodium	Na	11	22.98977
strontium	Sr	38	87.62
sulfur	S	16	32.06
tantalum	Ta	73	180.9479
technetium	Tc	43	
tellurium	Te	52	127.60
terbium	Tb	65	158.9254
thallium	Tl	81	204.383
thorium	Th	90	232.0381
thulium	Tm	69	168.9342
tin	Sn	50	118.69
titanium	Ti	22	47.88
tungsten	W	74	183.85
unnilhexium	Unh	106	
unnilpentium	Unp	105	
unnilquadium	Unq	104	
uranium	U	92	238.0289
vanadium	V	23	50.9415
xenon	Xe	54	131.29
ytterbium	Yb	70	173.04
yttrium	Y	39	88.9059
zinc	Zn	30	65.38
zirconium	Zr	40	91.22

elephant: *1* African, *2* Asian

of the family Phocidae) characterized by a long inflatable proboscis: **a** : one (*M. angustirostris*) found in Pacific coastal waters from southeastern Alaska to Baja California **b** : one (*M. leonina*) found in coastal waters of subantarctic islands and Patagonia

El·eu·sin·i·an \,el-yu̇-'si-nē-ən\ *adj* (1611) : of or relating to ancient Eleusis or to the religious mysteries celebrated there in worship of Demeter and Persephone

¹el·e·vate \'e-lə-,vāt, -vət\ *adj* (14c) *archaic* : ELEVATED

²el·e·vate \-,vāt\ *vb* **-vat·ed; -vat·ing** [ME, fr. L *elevatus*, pp. of *elevare*, fr. *e-* + *levare* to raise — more at LEVER] *vt* (15c) **1** : to lift up : RAISE **2** : to raise in rank or status : EXALT **3** : to improve morally, intellectually, or culturally **4** : to raise the spirits of : ELATE ~ *vi* : to become elevated ⟨his voice ~ed to a shout⟩ *syn* see LIFT

¹el·e·vat·ed \-,vā-təd\ *adj* (1553) **1 a** : raised esp. above the ground or other surface ⟨an ~ highway⟩ **b** : increased esp. abnormally (as in degree or amount) ⟨~ blood pressure⟩ **2 a** : being morally or intellectually on a high plane ⟨~ conversation⟩ **b** : FORMAL, DIGNIFIED ⟨~ diction⟩ **3** : exhilarated in mood or feeling

²elevated *n* (1881) : ²EL

el·e·va·tion \,e-lə-'vā-shən\ *n* (14c) **1** : the height to which something is elevated: as **a** : the angular distance of something (as a celestial object) above the horizon **b** : the degree to which a gun is aimed above the horizon **c** : the height above the level of the sea : ALTITUDE **2** : a ballet dancer's or a skater's leap and seeming suspension in the air; *also* : the ability to achieve an elevation **3** : an act or instance of elevating **4** : something that is elevated: as **a** : an elevated place **b** : a swelling esp. on the skin **5** : the quality or state of being elevated **6** : a geometrical projection (as of a building) on a vertical plane *syn* see HEIGHT

el·e·va·tor \'e-lə-,vā-tər\ *n* (1646) **1** : one that raises or lifts something up: as **a** : an endless belt or chain conveyor with cleats, scoops, or buckets for raising material **b** : a cage or platform and its hoisting machinery for conveying people or things to different levels **c** : GRAIN ELEVATOR **2** : a movable auxiliary airfoil usu. attached to the tail plane of an airplane for controlling pitch — see AIRPLANE illustration

elevator music *n* (1979) : instrumental arrangements of popular songs often piped in (as to an elevator or retail store)

elev·en \i-'le-vən\ *n* [ME *enleven*, fr. *enleven*, adj., fr. OE *endleofan*, fr. *end-* (alter. of *ān* one) + *-leofan*; akin to OE *lēon* to lend — more at ONE, LOAN] (bef. 12c) **1** — see NUMBER table **2** : the 11th in a set or series **3** : something having 11 units or members; *esp* : a football team — **eleven** *adj* — **eleven** *pron, pl in constr* — **elev·enth** \-vən(t)th\ *adj or n*

eleven–plus \i-,le-vən-'pləs\ *n* (1955) *Brit* : an examination taken by schoolchildren between the ages of 11 and 12 that determines the type of secondary education to which they are assigned

elev·ens·es \-vən-zəz\ *n pl but sometimes sing in constr* [double pl. of *eleven* (o'clock)] (ca. 1819) *Brit* : light refreshment (as a snack) taken in the middle of the morning

eleventh hour *n* (1826) : the latest possible time ⟨still making changes at the *eleventh hour*⟩

el·e·von \'e-lə-,vän\ *n* [*elevator* + *aileron*] (1944) : an airplane control surface that combines the functions of elevator and aileron

elf \'elf\ *n, pl* **elves** \'elvz\ [ME, fr. OE *ælf*; akin to ON *alfr* elf & perh. to L *albus* white — more at ALB] (bef. 12c) **1** : a small often mischievous fairy **2** : a small lively creature; *also* : a usu. lively mischievous or malicious person — **elf·ish** \'el-fish\ *adj* — **elf·ish·ly** *adv*

elf·in \'el-fən\ *adj* [irreg. fr. *elf*] (1596) **1** : of, relating to, or produced by an elf **b** : resembling an elf esp. in its tiny size ⟨~ portions⟩ **2** : having an otherworldly or magical quality or charm

elf·lock \'elf-,läk\ *n* (1592) : hair matted as if by elves — usu. used in pl.

elf owl *n* (1887) : a very small insectivorous owl (*Micrathene whitneyi*) of the Southwestern U.S. and Mexico that often roosts and nests in giant cacti

el·hi \(,)el-'hī\ *adj* [*elementary* (school) + *high* (school)] (ca. 1948) : of, relating to, or designed for use in grades 1 to 12

Eli \'ē-,lī\ *n* [Heb *'Ēlī*] : a judge and priest of Israel who according to the account in I Samuel was entrusted with the care of the boy Samuel

Eli·as \i-'lī-əs\ *n* [LL, fr. Gk *Ēlias*, fr. Heb *Ēliyāh*] : ELIJAH

elic·it \i-'li-sət\ *vt* [L *elicitus*, pp. of *elicere*, fr. *e-* + *lacere* to allure] (1605) **1** : to draw forth or bring out (something latent or potential) ⟨hypnotism ~ed his hidden fears⟩ **2** : to call forth or draw out (as information or a response) ⟨her performance ~ed wild applause⟩ *syn* see EDUCE — **elic·i·ta·tion** \i-,li-sə-'tā-shən, ,ē-\ *n* — **elic·i·tor** \i-'li-sə-tər\ *n*

elide \i-'līd\ *vt* **elid·ed; elid·ing** [L *elidere* to strike out, fr. *e-* + *laedere* to injure by striking] (1796) **1 a** : to suppress or alter (as a vowel or syllable) by elision **b** : to strike out (as a written word) **2 a** : to leave out of consideration : OMIT **b** : CURTAIL, ABRIDGE

el·i·gi·ble \'e-lə-jə-bəl\ *adj* [ME, fr. MF & LL; MF, fr. LL *eligibilis*, fr. L *eligere* to choose — more at ELECT] (15c) **1 a** : qualified to be chosen : ENTITLED ⟨~ to retire⟩ **b** : permitted under football rules to

el·e·men·tal \,e-lə-'men-t³l\ *adj* (15c) **1 a** : of, relating to, or being an element; *specif* : existing as an uncombined chemical element **b** (1) : of, relating to, or being the basic or essential constituent of something ⟨~ biological needs⟩ (2) : SIMPLE, UNCOMPLICATED ⟨~ food⟩ **c** : of, relating to, or dealing with the rudiments of something : ELEMENTARY ⟨taught ~ crafts to the children⟩ **d** : forming an integral part : INHERENT ⟨an ~ sense of rhythm⟩ **2** : of, relating to, or resembling a great force of nature ⟨the rains come with ~ violence⟩ ⟨~ passions⟩ — **el·e·men·tal·ly** \-t³l-ē\ *adv*

el·e·men·ta·ry \,e-lə-'men-tə-rē, -'men-trē\ *adj* (14c) **1 a** : of, relating to, or dealing with the simplest elements or principles of something ⟨avoids the most ~ decision-making⟩ **b** : of or relating to an elementary school ⟨an ~ curriculum⟩ **2** : ELEMENTAL 1a, 1b **3** : ELEMENTAL 2 — **el·e·men·ta·ri·ly** \-,men-'ter-ə-lē, -'men-trə-lē\ *adv* — **el·e·men·ta·ri·ness** \-'men-tə-rē-nəs, -'men-trē-\ *n*

elementary particle *n* (1934) : any of the particles of which matter and energy are composed or which mediate the fundamental forces of nature; *esp* : one whose existence has not been attributed to the combination of other more fundamental entities

elementary school *n* (1841) : a school including usu. the first four to the first eight grades and often a kindergarten

el·e·mi \'e-lə-mē\ *n* [NL *elimi*, prob. fr. Ar *al lāmi* the elemi] (1543) : any of various fragrant oleoresins obtained from tropical trees (family Burseraceae) and used chiefly in varnishes, lacquers, and printing inks

elen·chus \i-'leŋ-kəs\ *n, pl* **-chi** \-,kī, -(,)kē\ [L, fr. Gk *elenchos*] (1663) : REFUTATION; *esp* : one in syllogistic form

el·e·phant \'e-lə-fənt\ *n, pl* **elephants** *also* **elephant** *often attrib* [ME, fr. MF & L; MF *olifant*, fr. L *elephantus*, fr. Gk *elephant-, elephas*] (14c) **1** : any of a family (Elephantidae, the elephant family) of thickset usu. extremely large nearly hairless herbivorous mammals that have a snout elongated into a muscular trunk and two incisors in the upper jaw developed esp. in the male into large ivory tusks and that include two living forms and various extinct relatives: as **a** : a tall large-eared mammal (*Loxodonta africana*) of tropical Africa — called also *African elephant* **b** : a relatively small-eared mammal (*Elephas maximus*) of forests of southeastern Asia — called also *Asian elephant, Indian elephant* **2** : an animal or fossil related to the elephants **3** : one that is uncommonly large or hard to manage

elephant bird *n* (ca. 1889) : AEPYORNIS

elephant grass *n* (1832) **1** : an Old World cattail (*Typha elephantina*) used esp. in making baskets **2** : NAPIER GRASS

el·e·phan·ti·a·sis \,e-lə-fən-'tī-ə-səs, -,fan-\ *n, pl* **-a·ses** \-,sēz\ [NL, fr. L, a kind of leprosy, fr. Gk, fr. *elephant-, elephas*] (1581) **1** : enlargement and thickening of tissues; *specif* : the enormous enlargement of a limb or the scrotum caused by obstruction of lymphatics by filarial worms (esp. *Wuchereria bancrofti*) **2** : an undesirable usu. enormous growth, enlargement, or overdevelopment ⟨~ of intellect and atrophy of emotion —Michael Lerner⟩

el·e·phan·tine \,e-lə-'fan-,tēn, -,tīn, 'e-lə-fən-\ *adj* (1610) **1 a** : having enormous size or strength : MASSIVE **b** : CLUMSY, PONDEROUS ⟨~ verse⟩ **2** : of or relating to an elephant

elephant seal *n* (1841) : either of two very large seals (genus *Mirounga* catch a forward pass ⟨an ~ receiver⟩ **2** : worthy of being chosen : DE-SIRABLE ⟨an ~ young bachelor⟩ — **el·i·gi·bil·i·ty** \ˌe-lə-jə-'bi-lə-tē\ *n* — **eligible** *n* — **el·i·gi·bly** \'e-lə-jə-blē\ *adv*

Eli·jah \i-'lī-jə\ *n* [Heb *Ēlīyāh*] : a Hebrew prophet of the 9th century B.C. who according to the account in I Kings championed the worship of Jehovah as against Baal

elim·i·nate \i-'li-mə-ˌnāt\ *vt* **-nat·ed; -nat·ing** [L *eliminatus*, pp. of *eliminare*, fr. *e-* + *limin-*, *limen* threshold] (1568) **1 a** : to cast out or get rid of : REMOVE, ERADICATE ⟨the need to ~ poverty⟩ **b** : to set aside as unimportant : IGNORE **2** : to expel (as waste) from the living body **3** : to cause (as an unknown) to disappear by combining two or more mathematical equations — **elim·i·na·tive** \-'li-mə-ˌnā-tiv\ *adj* — **elim·i·na·tor** \-ˌnā-tər\ *n*

elim·i·na·tion \i-ˌli-mə-'nā-shən\ *n, often attrib* (1627) : the act, pro-cess, or an instance of eliminating or discharging: as **a** : the act of discharging or excreting waste products from the body **b** : the re-moval from a molecule of the constituents of a simpler molecule ⟨eth-ylene is formed by the ~ of water from ethanol⟩ — compare ADDITION 4

ELISA \ē-'lī-sə, -zə\ *n* (1978) : ENZYME-LINKED IMMUNOSORBENT ASSAY

Eli·sha \i-'lī-shə\ *n* [Heb *Elisha`*] : a Hebrew prophet and disciple and successor of Elijah

eli·sion \i-'li-zhən\ *n* [LL *elision-*, *elisio*, fr. L *elidere*] (1581) **1 a** : the use of a speech form that lacks a final or initial sound which a variant speech form has (as *'s* instead of *is* in *there's*) **b** : the omission of an unstressed vowel or syllable in a verse to achieve a uniform metrical pattern **2** : the act or an instance of omitting something : OMISSION

elite \ā-'lēt, i-, ē-\ *n* [F *élite*, fr. OF *eslite*, fr. fem. of *eslit*, pp. of *eslire* to choose, fr. L *eligere*] (1823) **1 a** *sing or pl in constr* : the choice part : CREAM ⟨the ~ of the entertainment world⟩ **b** *sing or pl in constr* : the best of a class ⟨superachievers who dominate the computer ~ —Marilyn Chase⟩ **c** *sing or pl in constr* : the socially superior part of society ⟨how the ~ live —*A P World*⟩ ⟨how the French-speaking ~ . . . was changing —*Economist*⟩ **d** : a group of persons who by virtue of posi-tion or education exercise much power or influence ⟨members of the ruling ~⟩ ⟨the intellectual ~s of the country⟩ **e** : a member of such an elite — usu. used in pl. ⟨the ~s . . . , pursuing their studies in Europe —Robert Wernick⟩ **2** : a typewriter type providing 12 characters to the linear inch — **elite** *adj*

élite, élitism *chiefly Brit var of* ELITE, ELITISM

elit·ism \ā-'lē-ˌti-zəm, i-, ē-\ *n* (1947) **1** : leadership or rule by an elite **2** : the selectivity of the elite; *esp* : SNOBBERY 1 ⟨~ in choosing new members⟩ **3** : consciousness of being or belonging to an elite — **elit·ist** \-'lē-tist\ *n or adj*

elix·ir \i-'lik-sər\ *n* [ME, fr. ML, fr. Ar *al-iksīr* the elixir, fr. *al* the + *iksīr* elixir, prob. fr. Gk *xērion* desiccative powder, fr. *xēros* dry] (14c) **1 a** (1) : a substance held capable of changing base metals into gold (2) : a substance held capable of prolonging life indefinitely **b** (1) : CURE-ALL (2) : a medicinal concoction **2** : a sweetened liquid usu. containing alcohol that is used in medication either for its medicinal ingredients or as a flavoring **3** : the essential principle

Eliz·a·be·than \i-ˌli-zə-'bē-thən\ *adj* (1807) : of, relating to, or charac-teristic of Elizabeth I of England or her reign — **Elizabethan** *n*

elk \'elk\ *n, pl* **elks** [ME, prob. fr. OE *eolh*; akin to OHG *elaho* elk, Gk *elaphos* deer] (bef. 12c) **1** *pl usu* **elk a** : MOOSE 1 — used for one of the Old World deer **b** : a large gregarious deer (*Cervus elaphus*) of No. America, Europe, Asia, and northwestern Africa — called also *red deer, wapiti* **c** : any of various large Asian deer **2** : soft tanned rug-ged leather **3** *cap* [Benevolent and Protective Order of *Elks*]: a mem-ber of a major benevolent and fraternal order

elk·hound \'elk-ˌhaůnd, 'el-ˌkaůnd\ *n* (1889) : NORWEGIAN ELKHOUND

¹ell \'el\ *n* [ME *eln*, fr. OE; akin to OHG *elina* ell, L *ulna* forearm, Gk *ōlenē* elbow, Skt *aratnī*] (bef. 12c) : a former English unit of length (as for cloth) equal to 45 inches (about 1.14 meters); *also* : any of various units of length used similarly

²ell *n* [alter. of ¹*el*] (1773) **1** : an extension at right angles to the length of a building **2** : an elbow in a pipe or conduit

el·lag·ic acid \ə-'la-jik-, e-\ *n* [F *ellagique*, fr. *ellag*, anagram of *galle* gall] (1810) : a crystalline phenolic compound $C_{14}H_6O_8$ with two lac-tone groupings that is obtained esp. from oak galls and some tannins and is used medicinally as a hemostatic

el·lipse \i-'lips, e-\ *n* [Gk *elleipsis*] (ca. 1753) **1 a** : OVAL **b** : a closed plane curve gener-ated by a point moving in such a way that the sums of its distances from two fixed points is a constant : a plane section of a right circular cone that is a closed curve **2** : ELLIPSIS

el·lip·sis \i-'lip-səs, e-\ *n, pl* **el·lip·ses** \-ˌsēz\ [L, fr. Gk *elleipsis* ellipsis, ellipse, fr. *elleipein* to leave out, fall short, fr. *en* in + *leipein* to leave — more at IN, LOAN] (1540) **1 a** : the omission of one or more words that are obvi-ously understood but that must be supplied to make a construction grammatically complete **b** : a sudden leap from one topic to another **2** : marks or a mark (as . . . or *** or —) indicating an omission (as of words) or a pause

ellipse 1b: F, F' foci; P, P', P'' any point on the curve; FP + PF' = FP'' + P''F' = FP' + P'F'

el·lip·soid \i-'lip-ˌsóid, e-\ *n* (1721) : a surface all plane sections of which are ellipses or circles — **el·lip·soi·dal** \i-ˌlip-'sói-d²l, (ˌ)e-\ *also* **ellipsoid** *adj*

el·lip·ti·cal \i-'lip-ti-kəl, e-\ *or* **el·lip·tic** \-'tik\ *adj* [Gk *elleiptikos* defec-tive, marked by ellipsis, fr. *elleipein*] (1656) **1** : of, relating to, or shaped like an ellipse **2 a** : of, relating to, or marked by ellipsis or an ellipsis **b** (1) : of, relating to, or marked by extreme economy of speech or writing (2) : of or relating to deliberate obscurity or ambiguity (as of literary or conversational style) — **el·lip·ti·cal·ly** \-ti-k(ə-)lē\ *adv*

elliptical galaxy *n* (1948) : a galaxy that has a generally elliptical shape and that has no apparent internal structure or spiral arms — called also *elliptical*; compare SPIRAL GALAXY

el·lip·tic·i·ty \i-ˌlip-'ti-sə-tē, (ˌ)e-\ *n* (1753) : deviation of an ellipse or a spheroid from the form of a circle or a sphere

elm \'elm\ *n* [ME, fr. OE; akin to OHG *elme* elm, L *ulmus*] (bef. 12c) **1** : any of a genus (*Ulmus* of the family Ulmaceae, the elm family)

comprising large trees with alternate stipulate leaves and small apetal-ous flowers **2** : the wood of an elm

elm bark beetle *n* (ca. 1909) : either of two beetles (family Scolytidae) that are vectors for the fungus causing Dutch elm disease: **a** : one (*Hylurgopinus rufipes*) native to eastern No. America **b** : one (*Scolytus multistriatus*) introduced from Europe into eastern No. America

elm leaf beetle *n* (1881) : a small orange-yellow black-striped Old World chrysomelid beetle (*Pyrrhalta luteola*) that in the larval and adult stage is a leaf-eating pest of elms in eastern No. America

El Ni·ño \el-'nē-nyō\ *n, pl* **El Niños** [Sp, lit., the child (i.e., the Christ child); fr. the appearance of the flow at the Christmas season] (1925) : an irregularly occurring flow of unusually warm surface water along the western coast of South America that is accompanied by abnormally high rainfall in usu. arid areas and that prevents upwelling of nutrient≠ rich cold deep water causing a decline in the regional fish population

el·o·cu·tion \ˌe-lə-'kyü-shən\ *n* [ME *elocucioun*, fr. L *elocution-*, *elo-cutio*, fr. *eloqui*] (15c) : a style of speaking esp. in public **2** : the art of effective public speaking — **el·o·cu·tion·ary** \-shə-ˌner-ē\ *adj* — **el·o·cu·tion·ist** \-sh(ə-)nist\ *n*

elo·dea \i-'lō-dē-ə\ *n* [NL, genus name, fr. Gk *helōdēs* marshy, fr. *helos* marsh; akin to Skt *saras* pond] (ca. 1868) : any of a small American genus (*Elodea*) of submerged aquatic monocotyledonous herbs

eloign \i-'lóin\ *vt* [ME *eloynen*, fr. MF *esloigner*, fr. OF, fr. *es-* ex- (fr. L *ex-*) + *loing* (adv.) far, fr. L *longe*, fr. *longus* long] (15c) **1** *archaic* : to take (oneself) far away **2** *archaic* : to remove to a distant or unknown place : CONCEAL

¹elon·gate \i-'lón-ˌgāt, (ˌ)ē-, 'ē-\ *vb* **-gat·ed; -gat·ing** [LL *elongatus*, pp. of *elongare*, to withdraw, fr. L *e-* + *longus*] *vt* (1578) : to extend the length of ~ *vi* : to grow in length

²elongate *or* **elon·gat·ed** *adj* (1751) **1** : stretched out **2** : SLENDER

elon·ga·tion \(ˌ)ē-ˌlón-'gā-shən\ *n* (14c) **1** : the angular distance of a celestial body from another around which it revolves or from a particu-lar point in the sky **2 a** : the state of being elongated or lengthened; *also* : the process of growing or increasing in length **b** : something that is elongated

elope \i-'lōp\ *vi* **eloped; elop·ing** [AF *aloper*] (1628) **1** : to slip away : ESCAPE **2 a** : to run away from one's husband with a lover **b** : to run away secretly with the intention of getting married usu. without parental consent — **elope·ment** \-'lōp-mənt\ *n* — **elop·er** *n*

el·o·quence \'e-lə-kwən(t)s\ *n* (14c) **1** : discourse marked by force and persuasiveness; *also* : the art or power of using such discourse **2** : the quality of forceful or persuasive expressiveness

el·o·quent \-kwənt\ *adj* [ME, fr. MF, fr. L *eloquent-*, *eloquens*, fr. prp. of *eloqui* to speak out, fr. *e-* + *loqui* to speak] (14c) **1** : marked by forceful and fluent expression ⟨an ~ preacher⟩ **2** : vividly or mov-ingly expressive or revealing ⟨an ~ monument⟩ — **el·o·quent·ly** *adv*

¹else \'el(t)s\ *adv* [ME *elles*, fr. OE; akin to L *alius* other, *alter* other of two, Gk *allos* other; (bef. 12c) **1 a** : in a different manner or place or at a different time ⟨how ~ could he have acted⟩ ⟨here and nowhere ~⟩ **b** : in an additional manner or place or an additional time ⟨where ~ is gold found⟩ **2** : if not : OTHERWISE ⟨leave or ~ you'll be sorry⟩ — used absolutely to express a threat ⟨do what I tell you or ~⟩

²else *adj* (bef. 12c) **1** : OTHER: **a** : being different in identity ⟨it must have been somebody ~⟩ **b** : being in addition ⟨what ~ did he say⟩

else·where \-,(h)wer, -,(h)war\ *adv* [ME *elleswher*, fr. OE *elles hwær*] (bef. 12c) : in or to another place ⟨took my business ~⟩

el·u·ant *or* **el·u·ent** \'el-yə-wənt\ *n* [L *eluent-*, *eluens*, prp. of *eluere*] (1941) : a solvent used in eluting

el·u·ate \'el-yə-wət, -ˌwāt\ *n* [L *eluere* + E ¹*-ate*] (1932) : the washings obtained by eluting

elu·ci·date \i-'lü-sə-ˌdāt\ *vb* **-dat·ed; -dat·ing** [LL *elucidatus*, pp. of *elucidare*, fr. L *e-* + *lucidus* lucid] *vt* (ca. 1568) : to make lucid esp. by explanation or analysis ~ *vi* : to give a clarifying explanation — **syn** see EXPLAIN — **elu·ci·da·tion** \i-ˌlü-sə-'dā-shən\ *n* — **elu·ci·da·tive** \-'lü-sə-ˌdā-tiv\ *adj* — **elu·ci·da·tor** \-ˌdā-tər\ *n*

elu·cu·brate \i-'lü-k(y)ə-ˌbrāt\ *vi* **-brat·ed; -brat·ing** [L *elucubratus*, pp. of *elucubrare* to work on far into the night, fr. *e-* + *lucubrare* to work by lamplight — more at LUCUBRATION] (ca. 1623) : to work out or express by studious effort — **elu·cu·bra·tion** \-ˌlü-k(y)ə-'brā-shən\ *n*

elude \ē-'lüd\ *vt* **elud·ed; elud·ing** [L *eludere*, fr. *e-* + *ludere* to play — more at LUDICROUS] (1667) **1** : to avoid adroitly : EVADE ⟨the mice eluded the traps⟩ ⟨managed to ~ capture⟩ **2** : to escape the percep-tion, understanding, or grasp of ⟨subtlety simply ~s them⟩ ⟨victory continued to ~ us⟩ **3** : DEFY 4 ⟨it ~s explanation⟩ — **syn** see ESCAPE

Elul \e-'lül\ *n* [Heb *Ělūl*] (1535) : the 12th month of the civil year or the 6th month of the ecclesiastical year in the Jewish calendar — see MONTH table

elu·sion \ē-'lü-zhən\ *n* [ML *elusion-*, *elusio*, fr. LL, deception, fr. L *eludere*] (1617) : an act of eluding

elu·sive \ē-'lü-siv, -'lü-ziv\ *adj* (1719) : tending to elude: as **a** : tend-ing to evade grasp or pursuit **b** : hard to comprehend or define ⟨an ~ concept⟩ **c** : hard to isolate or identify ⟨a haunting ~ aroma⟩ — **elu·sive·ly** *adv* — **elu·sive·ness** *n*

elute \ē-'lüt\ *vt* **elut·ed; elut·ing** [L *elutus*, pp. of *eluere* to wash out, fr. *e-* + *lavere* to wash — more at LYE] (1731) : EXTRACT; *specif* : to remove (adsorbed material) from an adsorbent by means of a solvent — **elu·tion** \-'lü-shən\ *n*

elu·tri·ate \ē-'lü-trē-ˌāt\ *vt* **-at·ed; -at·ing** [L *elutriatus*, pp. of *elutriare* to put in a vat, perh. fr. (assumed) *elutrum* vat, fr. Gk *elytron* reservoir, lit., covering] (ca. 1727) : to purify, separate, or remove by washing — **elu·tri·a·tion** \-ˌlü-trē-'ā-shən\ *n* — **elu·tri·a·tor** \ē-'lü-trē-ˌā-tər\ *n*

elu·vi·a·tion \(ˌ)ē-ˌlü-vē-'ā-shən\ *n* [*eluvial* of eluviation (fr. *e-* + *-luvial*—as in *alluvial*) + *-ation*] (1899) : the transportation of dis-solved or suspended material within the soil by the movement of water when rainfall exceeds evaporation — **elu·vi·al** \ē-'lü-vē-əl\ *adj* — **elu·vi·at·ed** \ē-'lü-vē-ā-təd\ *adj*

\ə\ abut \ᵊ\ kitten, F table \ər\ further \a\ ash \ā\ ace \ä\ mop, mar \aů\ out \ch\ chin \e\ bet \ē\ easy \g\ go \i\ hit \ī\ ice \j\ job \ŋ\ sing \ō\ go \ó\ law \ói\ boy \th\ thin \th\ the \ü\ loot \ů\ foot \y\ yet \zh\ vision \ä, k̲, ⁿ, œ, œ̄, ᵫ, ᵫ̄, ʸ\ see Guide to Pronunciation

el·ver \'el-vər\ *n* [alter. of *eelfare* (migration of eels)] (ca. 1640) : a young eel

elves *pl of* ELF

el·vish \'el-vish\ *adj* (13c) **1** : of or relating to elves **2** : MISCHIEVOUS

ely·sian \i-'li-zhən\ *adj, often cap* (1579) **1** : of or relating to Elysium **2** : BLISSFUL, DELIGHTFUL

elysian fields *n pl, often cap E* (1579) : ELYSIUM

Ely·si·um \i-'li-zhē-əm, -zē-\ *n, pl* **-si·ums** *or* **-sia** \-zhē-ə, -zē-\ [L, fr. Gk *Ēlysion*] **1** : the abode of the blessed after death in classical mythology **2** : PARADISE 2

el·y·tron \'e-lə-,trän\ *n, pl* **-tra** \-trə\ [NL, fr. Gk, sheath, wing cover, fr. *eilyein* to roll, wrap — more at VOLUBLE] (1774) : one of the anterior wings in beetles and some other insects that serve to protect the posterior pair of functional wings

em \'em\ *n* (13c) **1** : the letter *m* **2** : the width of a piece of type about as wide as it is tall used as a unit of measure of typeset matter

em- — see EN-

³em \əm; *after* p,b,f, *or* v *often* ²m\ *pron* [ME *hem*, fr. OE *heom*, *him*, dat. pl. of *hē* he] (bef. 12c) : THEM

ema·ci·ate \i-'mā-shē-,āt\ *vb* **-at·ed; -at·ing** [L *emaciatus*, pp. of *emaciare*, fr. *e-* + *macies* leanness, fr. *macer* lean — more at MEAGER] *vi* (1646) : to waste away physically ∼ *vt* **1** : to cause to lose flesh so as to become very thin **2** : to make feeble — **ema·ci·a·tion** \-,mā-s(h)ē-'ā-shən\ *n*

E–mail \'ē-,māl\ *n* (1982) : ELECTRONIC MAIL

emalangeni *pl of* LILANGENI

em·a·nate \'e-mə-,nāt\ *vb* **-nat·ed; -nat·ing** [L *emanatus*, pp. of *emanare*, fr. *e-* + *manare* to flow] *vi* (1756) : to come out from a source ∼ *vt* : EMIT **syn** see SPRING

em·a·na·tion \,e-mə-'nā-shən\ *n* (1570) **1 a** : the action of emanating **b** : the origination of the world by a series of hierarchically descending radiations from the Godhead through intermediate stages to matter **2 a** : something that emanates or is produced by emanation : EFFLUENCE **b** : an isotope of radon produced by radioactive disintegration ⟨radium ∼⟩— **em·a·na·tive** \'e-mə-,nā-tiv\ *adj*

eman·ci·pate \i-'man(t)-sə-,pāt\ *vt* **-pat·ed; -pat·ing** [L *emancipatus*, pp. of *emancipare*, fr. *e-* + *mancipare* to transfer ownership of, fr. *mancip-, manceps* contractor, fr. *manus* hand + *capere* to take — more at MANUAL, HEAVE] (1613) **1** : to free from restraint, control, or the power of another; *esp* : to free from bondage **2** : to release from paternal care and responsibility and make sui juris **3** : to free from any controlling influence (as traditional mores or beliefs) **syn** see FREE — **eman·ci·pa·tor** \-,pā-tər\ *n*

eman·ci·pa·tion \i-,man(t)-sə-'pā-shən\ *n* (1631) : the act or process of emancipating — **eman·ci·pa·tion·ist** \-sh(ə)nist\ *n*

emar·gin·ate \(,)ē-'mär-jə-nət, -,nāt\ *adj* [L *emarginatus*, pp. of *emarginare* to deprive of a margin, fr. *e-* + *margin-, margo* margin] (1794) : having the margin notched — **emar·gi·na·tion** \(,)ē-,mär-jə-'nā-shən\ *n*

emas·cu·late \i-'mas-kyə-,lāt\ *vt* **-lat·ed; -lat·ing** [L *emasculatus*, pp. of *emasculare*, fr. *e-* + *masculus* male — more at MALE] (1607) **1** : to deprive of strength, vigor, or spirit : WEAKEN **2** : to deprive of virility or procreative power : CASTRATE **3** : to remove the androecium of (a flower) in the process of artificial cross-pollination **syn** see UNNERVE — **emas·cu·late** \-lət\ *adj* — **emas·cu·la·tion** \-,mas-kyə-'lā-shən\ *n* — **emas·cu·la·tor** \-'mas-kyə-,lā-tər\ *n*

em·balm \im-'bä(l)m, *NewEng also* -'bám\ *vt* [ME *embaumen*, fr. MF *embaumer*, fr. OF *embasmer*, fr. *en-* + *basme* balm — more at BALM] (14c) **1** : to treat (a dead body) so as to protect from decay **2** : to fill with sweet odors : PERFUME **3** : to protect from decay or oblivion : PRESERVE **4** : to fix in a static condition — **em·balm·er** *n* — **em·balm·ment** \-'bä(l)m-mənt, -'bám-\ *n*

em·bank \im-'baŋk\ *vt* (1576) : to enclose or confine by an embankment

em·bank·ment \-mənt\ *n* (1786) **1** : a raised structure to hold back water or to carry a roadway **2** : the action of embanking

em·bar·ca·de·ro \(,)em-,bär-kə-'der-(,)ō, -'dā-\ *n, pl* **-ros** [Sp, fr. *embarcado*, pp. of *embarcar* to embark, fr. *en-* (fr. L *in-*) + *barca* bark, fr. LL] (1846) *West* : a landing place esp. on an inland waterway

¹em·bar·go \im-'bär-(,)gō\ *n, pl* **-goes** [Sp, fr. *embargar* to bar, fr. (assumed) VL *imbarricare*, fr. L *in-* + (assumed) VL *barra* bar] (1593) **1** : an order of a government prohibiting the departure of commercial ships from its ports **2** : a legal prohibition on commerce ⟨an ∼ on arms shipments⟩ **3** : STOPPAGE, IMPEDIMENT; *esp* : PROHIBITION ⟨I lay no ∼ on anybody's words —Jane Austen⟩ **4** : an order by a common carrier or public regulatory agency prohibiting or restricting freight transportation

²embargo *vt* **-goed; -go·ing** (1755) : to place an embargo on

em·bark \im-'bärk\ *vb* [MF *embarquer*, fr. OProv *embarcar*, fr. *em-* (fr. L *in-*) + *barca* bark] *vi* (1533) **1** : to go on board a vehicle for transportation **2** : to make a start ⟨∼ed on a new career⟩ ∼ *vt* **1** : to cause to go on board (as a boat or airplane) **2** : to engage, enlist, or invest in an enterprise — **em·bar·ka·tion** \,em-,bär-'kā-shən, -bər-\ *n* — **em·bark·ment** \im-'bärk-mənt\ *n*

em·bar·rass \im-'bar-əs\ *vt* [F *embarrasser*, fr. Sp *embarazar*, fr. Pg *embaraçar*, fr. *em-* (fr. L *in-*) + *baraça* noose] (1672) **1 a** : to place in doubt, perplexity, or difficulties **b** : to involve in financial difficulties **c** : to cause to experience a state of self-conscious distress ⟨bawdy stories ∼ed him⟩ **2 a** : to hamper the movement of **b** : HINDER, IMPEDE **3** : to make intricate : COMPLICATE **4** : to impair the activity of (a bodily function) or the function of (a bodily part) ⟨digestion ∼ed by overeating⟩ — **em·bar·rass·able** \-ə-bəl\ *adj*

syn EMBARRASS, DISCOMFIT, ABASH, DISCONCERT, RATTLE mean to distress by confusing or confounding. EMBARRASS implies some influence that impedes thought, speech, or action ⟨*embarrassed* to admit that she liked the movie⟩. DISCOMFIT implies a hampering or frustrating accompanied by confusion ⟨hecklers *discomfited* the speaker⟩. ABASH presupposes some initial self-confidence that receives a sudden check, producing shyness, shame, or a feeling of inferiority ⟨*abashed* by her swift and cutting retort⟩. DISCONCERT implies an upsetting of equanimity or assurance producing uncertainty or hesitancy ⟨*disconcerted* by finding so many in attendance⟩. RATTLE implies an agitation that impairs thought and judgment ⟨*rattled* by all the television cameras⟩.

em·bar·rassed·ly \-əst-lē, -ə-səd-lē\ *adv* (1883) : with embarrassment

em·bar·rass·ing·ly \-ə-siŋ-lē\ *adv* (ca. 1864) : to an embarrassing degree : so as to cause embarrassment

em·bar·rass·ment \im-'bar-ə-smənt\ *n* (1729) **1 a** : something that embarrasses : IMPEDIMENT **b** : an excessive quantity from which to select — used esp. in the phrase *embarrassment of riches* **2** : the state of being embarrassed: as **a** : confusion or disturbance of mind **b** : difficulty arising from the want of money to pay debts **c** : difficulty in functioning as a result of disease ⟨cardiac ∼⟩

em·bas·sage \'em-bə-sij\ *n* (1526) **1** : the message or commission entrusted to an ambassador : EMBASSY

em·bas·sy \'em-bə-sē\ *n, pl* **-sies** [MF *ambassee*, ultim. of Gmc origin; akin to OHG *ambaht* service] (1534) **1** : a body of diplomatic representatives; *specif* : one headed by an ambassador **2 a** : the function or position of an ambassador **b** : a mission abroad undertaken officially esp. by an ambassador **3** : EMBASSAGE 1 **4** : the official residence and offices of an ambassador

em·bat·tle \im-'ba-t⁰l\ *vt* **em·bat·tled; em·bat·tling** \-'bat-liŋ, -t⁰l-iŋ\ [ME *embatailen*, fr. MF *embatailler*, fr. *en-* + *batailler* to battle] (14c) **1** : to arrange in order of battle : prepare for battle **2** : FORTIFY

em·bat·tled *adj* (15c) **1 a** : ready to fight : prepared to give battle ⟨here once the ∼ farmers stood —R. W. Emerson⟩ **b** : engaged in battle, conflict, or controversy ⟨an ∼ official accused of extortion⟩ **2 a** : being a site of battle, conflict, or controversy ⟨the ∼ capital⟩ **b** : characterized by conflict or controversy ⟨his ... often ∼ experience as an educator —Nat Hentoff⟩

em·bat·tle·ment \-'ba-t⁰l-mənt\ *n* (15c) **1** : BATTLEMENT **2** : the state of being embattled

em·bay \im-'bā\ *vt* (1600) : to trap or catch in or as if in a bay ⟨an ∼ed sailing ship⟩

em·bay·ment \-'bā-mənt\ *n* (1815) **1** : formation of a bay **2** : a bay or a conformation resembling a bay

Emb·den \'em-dən\ *n* [*Emden*, Germany] (1903) : a breed of large white domestic geese with an orange bill and deep orange shanks and toes

em·bed \im-'bed\ *vb* **em·bed·ded; em·bed·ding** *vt* (ca. 1794) **1 a** : to enclose closely in or as if in a matrix ⟨fossils *embedded* in stone⟩ **b** : to make something an integral part of ⟨the prejudices *embedded* in our language⟩ **c** : to prepare (a microscopy specimen) for sectioning by infiltrating with and enclosing in a supporting substance **2** : to surround closely ⟨a sweet pulp ∼s the plum seed⟩ ∼ *vi* : to become embedded — **em·bed·ment** \-'bed-mənt\ *n*

em·bed·ded \im-'be-dəd\ *adj* (1961) : occurring as a grammatical constituent (as a verb phrase or clause) within a like constituent — **em·bed·ding** \-diŋ\ *n*

em·bel·lish \im-'be-lish\ *vt* [ME, fr. MF *embeliss-*, stem of *embelir*, fr. *en-* + *bel* beautiful — more at BEAUTY] (14c) **1** : to make beautiful with ornamentation : DECORATE **2** : to heighten the attractiveness of by adding ornamental details : ENHANCE ⟨∼ed our account of the trip⟩ **syn** see ADORN — **em·bel·lish·er** *n*

em·bel·lish·ment \-lish-mənt\ *n* (1591) **1** : the act or process of embellishing **2** : something serving to embellish **3** : ORNAMENT 5

em·ber \'em-bər\ *n* [ME *eymere*, fr. ON *eimyrja*; akin to OE *æmerge* ashes, L *urere* to burn] (14c) **1** : a glowing fragment (as of coal) from a fire; *esp* : one smoldering in ashes **2** *pl* : the smoldering remains of a fire **3** *pl* : slowly dying or fading emotions, memories, ideas, or responses still capable of being revived

ember day \'em-bər-\ *n* [ME, fr. OE *ymbrendæg*, fr. *ymbrene* circuit, anniversary + *dæg* day] (bef. 12c) : a Wednesday, Friday, or Saturday following the first Sunday in Lent, Whitsunday, September 14, or December 13 set apart for fasting and prayer in Western churches

em·bez·zle \im-'be-zəl\ *vt* **em·bez·zled; em·bez·zling** \-(ə-)liŋ\ [ME *embesilen*, fr. AF *embeseiller*, fr. MF *en-* + *besillier* to destroy] (15c) : to appropriate (as property entrusted to one's care) fraudulently to one's own use — **em·bez·zle·ment** \-zəl-mənt\ *n* — **em·bez·zler** \-z(ə-)lər\ *n*

em·bit·ter \im-'bi-tər\ *vt* (15c) **1** : to excite bitter feelings in **2** : to make bitter — **em·bit·ter·ment** \-mənt\ *n*

¹em·blaze \im-'blāz\ *vt* **em·blazed; em·blaz·ing** (15c) **1** : to illuminate esp. by a blaze **2** : to set ablaze

²emblaze *vt* **em·blazed; em·blaz·ing** [*en-* + *blaze* (to blazon)] (1593) **1** *archaic* : EMBLAZON 1 **2** : to adorn sumptuously ⟨with gems and golden luster rich *emblazed* —John Milton⟩

em·bla·zon \im-'blā-z⁰n\ *vt* **em·bla·zoned; em·bla·zon·ing** \-'blāz-niŋ, -'blā-z⁰n-iŋ\ (1589) **1 a** : to inscribe or adorn with or as if with heraldic bearings or devices **b** : to inscribe (as heraldic bearings) on a surface **2** : CELEBRATE, EXTOL ⟨have his ... deeds ∼ed by a poet —Thomas Nash⟩ — **em·bla·zon·er** \-'blāz-nər, -z⁰n-ər\ *n* — **em·bla·zon·ment** \-'blā-z⁰n-mənt\ *n*

em·bla·zon·ry \-z⁰n-rē\ *n* (1667) **1** : emblazoned figures : brilliant decoration **2** : the act or art of emblazoning

¹em·blem \'em-bləm\ *n* [ME, fr. L *emblema* inlaid work, fr. Gk *emblēmat-, emblēma*, fr. *emballein* to insert, fr. *en-* + *ballein* to throw — more at DEVIL] (15c) **1** : a picture with a motto or set of verses intended as a moral lesson **2** : an object or the figure of an object symbolizing and suggesting another object or an idea **3 a** : a symbolic object used as a heraldic device **b** : a device, symbol, or figure adopted and used as an identifying mark

²emblem *vt* (1584) : EMBLEMATIZE

em·blem·at·ic \,em-blə-'ma-tik\ *also* **em·blem·at·i·cal** \-ti-kəl\ *adj* (1645) : of, relating to, or constituting an emblem : SYMBOLIC, REPRESENTATIVE — **em·blem·at·i·cal·ly** \-ti-k(ə-)lē\ *adv*

em·blem·a·tize \em-'ble-mə-,tīz\ *vt* **-tized; -tiz·ing** (1615) : to represent by or as if by an emblem : SYMBOLIZE

em·ble·ments \'em-blə-mən(t)s\ *n pl* [ME *emblayment*, fr. MF *emblaement*, fr. *emblaer* to sow with grain, fr. *en-* + *blee* grain, of Gmc origin; akin to OE *blæd* fruit, growth, leaf — more at BLADE] (15c) : crops from annual cultivation legally belonging to the tenant

em·bodi·ment \im-'bä-di-mənt\ *n* (1828) **1** : one that embodies something ⟨the ∼ of all our hopes⟩ **2** : the act of embodying : the state of being embodied

em·body \im-'bä-dē\ *vt* **em·bod·ied; em·body·ing** (ca. 1548) **1** : to give a body to (a spirit) : INCARNATE **2 a** : to deprive of spirituality **b** : to make concrete and perceptible **3** : to cause to become a body or part of a body : INCORPORATE **4** : to represent in human or animal form : PERSONIFY ⟨men who greatly *embodied* the idealism of American life —A. M. Schlesinger *b*1917⟩ — **em·bod·i·er** *n*

em·bold·en \im-'bōl-dən\ *vt* (15c) : to instill with boldness or courage

em·bo·lec·to·my \₁em-bə-'lek-tə-mē\ *n, pl* **-mies** (1923) : surgical removal of an embolus

em·bol·ic \em-'bä-lik, im-\ *adj* (1866) : of or relating to an embolus or embolism

em·bo·lism \'em-bə-₁li-zəm\ *n* [ME *embolisme*, fr. ML *embolismus*, fr. Gk *embol-* (fr. *emballein* to insert, intercalate) — more at EMBLEM] (14c) 1 : the insertion of one or more days in a calendar : INTERCALATION 2 a : the sudden obstruction of a blood vessel by an embolus b : EMBOLUS — **em·bo·lis·mic** \₁em-bə-'liz-mik\ *adj*

em·bo·li·za·tion \₁em-bə-lə-'zā-shən\ *n* (1942) : the process or state in which a blood vessel or organ is obstructed by the lodgment of a material mass (as an embolus)

em·bo·lus \'em-bə-ləs\ *n, pl* **-li** \-₁lī\ [NL, fr. Gk *embolos* wedge-shaped object, stopper, fr. *emballein*] (1859) : an abnormal particle (as an air bubble) circulating in the blood — compare THROMBUS

em·bon·point \än-bōⁿ-pwanⁿ\ *n* [F, fr. MF, fr. *en bon point* in good condition] (1670) : plumpness of person : STOUTNESS

em·bos·om \im-'bu̇-zəm *also* -'bü-\ *vt* (ca. 1590) 1 *archaic* : to take into or place in the bosom 2 : to shelter closely : ENCLOSE ⟨his house ~ed in the grove —Alexander Pope⟩

¹**em·boss** \im-'bäs, -'bȯs\ *vt* [ME *embosen* to become exhausted from being hunted, ultim. fr. MF *bois* woods] (14c) *archaic* : to drive (as a hunted animal) to bay or to exhaustion

²**emboss** *vt* [ME *embosen*, fr. MF *embocer*, fr. *en-* + *boce* boss] (15c) 1 : to raise the surface of into bosses; *esp* : to ornament with raised work 2 : to raise in relief from a surface 3 : ADORN, EMBELLISH — **em·boss·able** \-'bä-sə-bəl, -'bȯ-\ *adj* — **em·boss·er** \-sər\ *n* — **em·boss·ment** \-mənt\ *n*

em·bou·chure \'äm-bu̇-₁shu̇r, ₁äm-bu̇-'\ *n* [F, fr. (s')*emboucher* to flow into, fr. *en-* + *bouche* mouth — more at DEBOUCH] (1760) 1 : the position and use of the lips, tongue, and teeth in playing a wind instrument 2 : the mouthpiece of a musical instrument

em·bour·geoise·ment \em-'bu̇rzh-₁wäz-mənt, äm-; än-₁bu̇rzh-wäz-mänⁿ\ *n* [F, fr. *embourgeoiser* to make bourgeois, fr. *em-* + *bourgeois*] (1937) : a shift to bourgeois values and practices

em·bowed \im-'bōd\ *adj* (15c) : bent like a bow : ARCHED

em·bow·el \im-'bau̇(-ə)l\ *vt* **-eled** *or* **-elled; -el·ing** *or* **-el·ling** (1521) 1 : DISEMBOWEL 2 *obs* : ENCLOSE

em·bow·er \im-'bau̇(-ə)r\ *vt* (1580) : to shelter or enclose in or as if in a bower ⟨like a rose ~ed in its own green leaves —P. B. Shelley⟩

¹**em·brace** \im-'brās\ *vb* **em·braced; em·brac·ing** [ME, fr. MF *embracer*, fr. OF *embracier*, fr. *en-* + *brace* two arms — more at BRACE] (14c) 1 a : to clasp in the arms : HUG b : CHERISH, LOVE 2 : ENCIRCLE, ENCLOSE 3 a : to take up esp. readily or gladly ⟨~ a cause⟩ b : to avail oneself of : WELCOME ⟨*embraced* the opportunity to study further⟩ 4 a : to take in or include as a part, item, or element of a more inclusive whole ⟨charity ~s all acts that contribute to human welfare⟩ b : to be equal or equivalent to ⟨his assets *embraced* $10⟩ ~ *vi* : to participate in an embrace *syn* see ADOPT, INCLUDE — **em·brace·able** \-'brā-sə-bəl\ *adj* — **em·brace·ment** \-'brā-smənt\ *n* — **em·brac·er** *n* — **em·brac·ing·ly** \-'brā-siŋ-lē\ *adv*

²**embrace** *n* (1592) 1 : a close encircling with the arms and pressure to the bosom esp. as a sign of affection : HUG 2 : GRIP, ENCIRCLEMENT ⟨in the ~ of terror⟩ 3 : ACCEPTANCE ⟨her ~ of death⟩

em·bra·ceor \im-'brā-sər\ *n* [AF, fr. MF *embraseor* instigator, fr. *embraser* to set on fire, fr. *en-* + *brase, brese* live coals] (15c) : one guilty of embracery

em·brac·ery \im-'brā-sə-rē\ *n, pl* **-er·ies** [ME, fr. AF *embraceor*] (15c) : an attempt to influence a jury corruptly

em·brac·ive \-'brā-siv\ *adj* (1855) 1 : disposed to embrace 2 : INCLUSIVE, COMPREHENSIVE

em·bran·gle \im-'braŋ-gəl\ *vt* **-gled; -gling** \-g(ə-)liŋ\ [*en-* + *brangle* (squabble)] (1664) : EMBROIL — **em·bran·gle·ment** \-gəl-mənt\ *n*

em·bra·sure \im-'brā-zhər\ *n* [F, fr. obs. *em·braser* to widen an opening] (1702) 1 : an opening with sides flaring outward in a wall or parapet of a fortification usu. for allowing the firing of cannon 2 : a recess of a door or window

em·brit·tle \im-'bri-t²l\ *vb* **brit·tled; brit·tling** \-'brit-liŋ, -t²l-iŋ\ *vt* (1902) : to make brittle ~ *vi* : to become brittle — **em·brit·tle·ment** \-'bri-t²l-mənt\ *n*

em·bro·ca·tion \₁em-brə-'kā-shən\ *n* [ME *embrocacioun*, fr. MF *embrocacion*, fr. ML *embrocacion-, embrocatio*, fr. LL *embrocare* to rub with lotion, fr. Gk *embroche* lotion, fr. *en-* + *brechein* to wet] (15c) : LINIMENT

em·broi·der \im-'brȯi-dər\ *vb* **em·broi·dered; em·broi·der·ing** \-d(ə-)riŋ\ [ME *em·broderen*, fr. MF *embroder*, fr. *en-* + Gmc origin; akin to OE *brord* point, *byrst* bristle] *vt* (14c) 1 a : to ornament with needlework b : to form with needlework 2 : to elaborate on : EMBELLISH ~ *vi* 1 : to make embroidery 2 : to provide embellishments : ELABORATE — **em·broi·der·er** \-'brȯi-dər-ər\ *n*

em·broi·dery \im-'brȯi-d(ə-)rē\ *n, pl* **-der·ies** (14c) 1 a : the art or process of forming decorative designs with hand or machine needlework b : a design or decoration formed by or as if by embroidery c : an object decorated with embroidery 2 : elaboration by use of decorative and often fictitious detail 3 : something pleasing or desirable but unimportant ⟨considered the humanities mere educational ~⟩

em·broil \im-'brȯi(ə)l\ *vt* [F *embrouiller*, fr. MF, fr. *en-* + *brouiller* to broil] (1603) 1 : to throw into disorder or confusion 2 : to involve in conflict or difficulties — **em·broil·ment** \-mənt\ *n*

em·brown \im-'brau̇n\ *vt* (1667) 1 : DARKEN 2 : to cause to turn brown

embrue *var of* IMBRUE

embry- *or* **embryo-** *comb form* [LL, fr. Gk, fr. *embryon*] : embryo ⟨*embryogeny*⟩

---

em·bryo \'em-brē-₁ō\ *n, pl* **em·bry·os** [ML *embryon-, embryo*, fr. Gk *embryon*, fr. *en-* + *bryein* to swell; akin to Gk *bryon* catkin] (1548) 1 a *archaic* : a vertebrate at any stage of development prior to birth or hatching b : an animal in the early stages of growth and differentiation that are characterized by cleavage, the laying down of fundamental tissues, and the formation of primitive organs and organ systems; *esp* : the developing human individual from the time of implantation to the end of the eighth week after conception 2 : the young sporophyte of a seed plant usu. comprising a rudimentary plant with plumule, radicle, and cotyledons 3 a : something as yet undeveloped b : a beginning or undeveloped state of something ⟨productions seen in ~ during their out-of-town tryout period —Henry Hewes⟩

em·bryo·gen·e·sis \₁em-brē-ō-'je-nə-səs\ *n* (1830) : the formation and development of the embryo — **em·bryo·ge·net·ic** \-jə-'ne-tik\ *adj*

em·bryo·ge·ny \₁em-brē-'ä-jə-nē\ *n, pl* **-nies** (1835) : EMBRYOGENESIS — **em·bryo·gen·ic** \-brē-ō-'je-nik\ *adj*

em·bry·oid \'em-brē-₁ȯid\ *n* (ca. 1970) : a mass of plant or animal tissue that resembles an embryo — **embryoid** *adj*

em·bry·ol·o·gy \₁em-brē-'ä-lə-jē\ *n* [F *embryologie*] (ca. 1847) 1 : a branch of biology dealing with embryos and their development 2 : the features and phenomena exhibited in the formation and development of an embryo — **em·bry·o·log·i·cal** \-brē-ə-'lä-ji-kəl\ *adj* — **em·bry·o·log·i·cal·ly** \-ji-k(ə-)lē\ *adv* — **em·bry·ol·o·gist** \-brē-'ä-lə-jist\ *n*

embryon- *or* **embryoni-** *comb form* [ML *embryon-, embryo*] : embryo ⟨*embryonic*⟩

em·bry·o·nal \em-'brī-ə-n²l\ *adj* (1652) : EMBRYONIC 1

em·bry·o·nat·ed \'em-brē-ə-₁nā-təd\ *adj* (1687) : having an embryo

em·bry·on·ic \₁em-brē-'ä-nik\ *adj* (ca. 1841) 1 : of or relating to an embryo 2 : being in an early stage of development : INCIPIENT, RUDIMENTARY — **em·bry·on·i·cal·ly** \-ni-k(ə-)lē\ *adv*

embryonic disk *n* (ca. 1938) 1 a : BLASTODISC b : BLASTODERM 2 : the part of the inner cell mass of a blastocyst from which the embryo of a placental mammal develops — called also *embryonic shield*

embryonic membrane *n* (1947) : a structure (as the amnion) that derives from the fertilized ovum but does not form a part of the embryo

em·bryo·phyte \'em-brē-ə-₁fīt\ *n* (ca. 1909) : any of a subkingdom (Embryophyta) of plants in which the embryo is retained within maternal tissue and which include the bryophytes and tracheophytes

embryo sac *n* (1872) : the female gametophyte of a seed plant consisting of a thin-walled sac within the nucellus that contains the egg nucleus and other nuclei which give rise to endosperm on fertilization

embryo transfer *n* (1969) : a procedure used esp. in animal breeding in which an embryo from a superovulated female is removed and reimplanted in the uterus of another female — called also *embryo transplant*

¹**em·cee** \₁em-'sē\ *n* [*MC*] (ca. 1933) : MASTER OF CEREMONIES

²**emcee** *vb* **em·ceed; em·cee·ing** *vt* (1937) : to act as master of ceremonies of ~ *vi* : to act as master of ceremonies

-eme \₁ēm\ *n suffix* [F *-ème* (fr. *phonème* speech sound, phoneme)] : significantly distinctive unit of language structure ⟨taxe*me*⟩

emend \ē-'mend\ *vt* [ME, fr. L *emendare* — more at AMEND] (15c) : to correct usu. by textual alterations *syn* see CORRECT — **emend·able** \-'men-də-bəl\ *adj* — **emend·er** *n*

emen·da·tion \₁ē-₁men-'dā-shən; ₁e-mən-, e-₁men-\ *n* (1536) 1 : the act or practice of emending 2 : an alteration designed to correct or improve

¹**em·er·ald** \'em-rəld, 'e-mə-\ *n* [ME *emeralde*, fr. MF *esmeralde*, fr. (assumed) VL *smaralda*, fr. L *smaragdus*, fr. Gk *smaragdos*] (14c) 1 : a rich green variety of beryl prized as a gemstone 2 : any of various green gemstones (as synthetic corundum or demantoid)

²**emerald** *adj* (1508) : brightly or richly green

emerald cut *n* (1926) : a rectangular cut for a gem having a series of parallel facets on each side and at each corner

emerald green *n* (1646) 1 : a clear bright green resembling that of the emerald 2 : any of various strong greens

emerge \i-'mərj\ *vi* **emerged; emerg·ing** [L *emergere*, fr. *e-* + *mergere* to plunge — more at MERGE] (1563) 1 : to become manifest 2 : to rise from or as if from an enveloping fluid : come out into view 3 : to rise from an obscure or inferior position or condition 4 : to come into being through evolution

emer·gence \i-'mər-jən(t)s\ *n* (1704) 1 : the act or an instance of emerging 2 : any of various superficial outgrowths of plant tissue usu. formed from both epidermis and immediately underlying tissues 3 : penetration of the soil surface by a newly germinated plant

emer·gen·cy \i-'mər-jənt-sē\ *n, pl* **-cies** *often attrib* (ca. 1631) 1 : an unforeseen combination of circumstances or the resulting state that calls for immediate action 2 : an urgent need for assistance or relief ⟨the governor declared a state of ~ after the flood⟩ *syn* see JUNCTURE

emergency brake *n* (1900) : a brake (as on an automobile) that can be used for stopping in the event of failure of the main brakes and to keep the vehicle from rolling when parked

emergency medical technician *n* (1980) : EMT

emergency room *n* (1964) : a hospital room or area staffed and equipped for the reception and treatment of persons requiring immediate medical care

¹**emer·gent** \i-'mər-jənt\ *adj* [ME, fr. L *emergent-, emergens*, prp. of *emergere*] (1593) 1 a : arising unexpectedly b : calling for prompt action : URGENT 2 : rising out of or as if out of a fluid 3 : arising as a natural or logical consequence 4 : newly formed or prominent

²**emergent** *n* (1620) 1 : something emergent 2 a : a tree that rises above the surrounding forest b : a plant rooted in shallow water and having most of the vegetative growth above water

emergent evolution *n* (1923) : evolution that according to some theories involves the appearance of new characters and qualities at complex levels of organization (as the cell or organism) which cannot be predicted solely from the study of less complex levels (as the atom or molecule) — compare CREATIVE EVOLUTION

\ə\ abut \ᵊ\ kitten, F table \ər\ further \a\ ash \ā\ ace \ä\ mop, mar \au̇\ out \ch\ chin \e\ bet \ē\ easy \g\ go \i\ hit \ī\ ice \j\ job \ŋ\ sing \ō\ go \ȯ\ law \ȯi\ boy \th\ thin \t̲h̲\ the \ü\ loot \u̇\ foot \y\ yet \zh\ vision \ā, k̲, ⁿ, œ, œ̄, ᵫ, ᵫ̄, ᵊ\ *see* Guide to Pronunciation

emerg·ing adj (1646) : EMERGENT 4 ⟨the ~ nations of Africa⟩

emer·i·ta \i-'mer-ə-tə\ adj [L, fem. of emeritus] (1928) : EMERITUS — used of a woman ⟨Professor Emerita Mary Smith⟩

¹emer·i·tus \i-'mer-ə-təs\ n, pl **-i·ti** \-ə-ˌtī, -ˌtē\ (1750) : one retired from professional life but permitted to retain as an honorary title the rank of the last office held

²emeritus adj [L, pp. of emereri to serve out one's term, fr. e- + mereri, merēre to earn, deserve, serve — more at MERIT] (1794) 1 : holding after retirement an honorary title corresponding to that held last during active service 2 : retired from an office or position ⟨professor ~⟩ — converted to emeriti after a plural ⟨professors emeriti⟩

emersed \(ˌ)ē-'mərst\ adj (1686) : standing out of or rising above a surface (as of a fluid) ⟨~ aquatic weeds⟩

emer·sion \(ˌ)ē-'mər-zhən, -shən\ n [L emersus, pp. of emergere] (1633) : an act of emerging : EMERGENCE

em·ery \'em-rē, 'e-mə-\ n, pl **em·er·ies** often attrib [ME, fr. MF emeri, fr. OIt smeriglio, fr. ML smiriglium, fr. Gk smyrid-, smyris] (15c) : a dark granular mineral that consists essentially of corundum and is used for grinding and polishing; also : a hard abrasive powder

emery board n (1725) : a cardboard nail file covered with emery

eme·sis \'e-mə-səs, i-'mē-\ n, pl **eme·ses** \-ˌsēz\ [NL, fr. Gk, fr. emein] (ca. 1847) : an act or instance of vomiting

emet·ic \i-'me-tik\ n [L emetica, fr. Gk emetikē, fr. fem. of emetikos causing vomiting, fr. emein to vomit — more at VOMIT] (1657) : an agent that induces vomiting — **emetic** adj — **emet·i·cal·ly** \-ti-k(ə-)lē\ adv

em·e·tine \'e-mə-ˌtēn\ n (1819) : an amorphous alkaloid $C_{29}H_{40}N_2O_4$ extracted from ipecac root and used as an emetic and expectorant

émeute \ā-mœt\ n, pl **émeutes** \same\ [F, fr. OF esmeute act of starting, fr. fem. of esmeut, pp. of esmovoir to start — more at EMOTION] (1782) : UPRISING

emf \ˌē-(ˌ)em-'ef\ n [electromotive force] (1868) : POTENTIAL DIFFERENCE

-emia \'ē-mē-ə\ n comb form [NL -emia, -aemia, fr. Gk -aimia, fr. haima blood] 1 : condition of having (such) blood ⟨leukemia⟩ 2 : condition of having (a specified thing) in the blood ⟨uremia⟩

emic \'ē-mik\ adj [phonemic] (1954) : of, relating to, or involving analysis of linguistic or behavioral phenomena in terms of the internal structural or functional elements of a particular system — compare ETIC

¹em·i·grant \'e-mi-grənt\ n (1754) 1 : one who emigrates 2 : a migrant plant or animal

²emigrant adj (1794) : departing or having departed from a country to settle elsewhere

em·i·grate \'e-mə-ˌgrāt\ vi **-grat·ed; -grat·ing** [L emigratus, pp. of emigrare, fr. e- + migrare to migrate] (1778) : to leave one's place of residence or country to live elsewhere — **em·i·gra·tion** \ˌe-mə-'grā-shən\ n

émi·gré \'e-mi-ˌgrā, ˌe-mi-'\ n, often attrib [F émigré, fr. pp. of émigrer to emigrate, fr. L emigrare] (1792) : EMIGRANT; esp : a person forced to emigrate for political reasons

em·i·nence \'e-mə-nən(t)s\ n (15c) 1 : a position of prominence or superiority 2 : one that is eminent, prominent, or lofty: as a : an anatomical protuberance (as on a bone) b : a person of high rank or attainments — often used as a title for a cardinal c : a natural elevation

émi·nence grise \ā-mē-näⁿs-grēz\ n, pl **éminences grises** \same\ [F, lit., gray eminence, nickname of Père Joseph (François du Tremblay) †1638 Fr. monk and diplomat, confidant of Cardinal Richelieu who was known as Éminence Rouge red eminence; fr. the colors of their respective habits] (1925) : a confidential agent; esp : one exercising unsuspected or unofficial power

em·i·nen·cy \'e-mə-nən(t)-sē\ n, pl **-cies** (1605) archaic : EMINENCE

em·i·nent \'e-mə-nənt\ adj [ME, fr. MF or L; MF, fr. L eminent-, eminens, prp. of eminēre to stand out, fr. e- + -minēre; akin to L mont-, mons mountain — more at MOUNT] (15c) 1 : standing out so as to be readily perceived or noted : CONSPICUOUS 2 : jutting out : PROJECTING 3 : exhibiting eminence esp. in standing above others in some quality or position : PROMINENT **syn** see FAMOUS

eminent domain n (1783) : a right of a government to take private property for public use by virtue of the superior dominion of the sovereign power over all lands within its jurisdiction

em·i·nent·ly \-lē\ adv (1641) : to a high degree : VERY ⟨~ worthy⟩ ⟨an ~ sensible plan⟩

emir \i-'mir, ā-\ n [Ar amīr commander] (1595) : a ruler, chief, or commander in Islamic countries

emir·ate \i-'mir-ət, -ˌrāt\ n (1863) : the state or jurisdiction of an emir

em·is·sary \'e-mə-ˌser-ē\ n, pl **-sar·ies** [L emissarius, fr. emissus, pp. of emittere] (1616) 1 : one designated as the agent of another : REPRESENTATIVE 2 : a secret agent

emis·sion \ē-'mi-shən\ n (1607) 1 a : an act or instance of emitting : EMANATION b archaic : PUBLICATION c : a putting into circulation 2 a : something sent forth by emitting: as (1) : electromagnetic waves radiated by an antenna or a celestial body (2) : substances discharged into the air (as by a smokestack or an automobile gasoline engine) b : EFFLUVIUM — **emis·sive** \-'mi-siv\ adj

emis·siv·i·ty \ˌe-mə-'si-və-tē, ˌē-ˌmi-'siv-\ n, pl **-ties** (1880) : the relative power of a surface to emit heat by radiation : the ratio of the radiant energy emitted by a surface to that emitted by a blackbody at the same temperature

emit \ē-'mit\ vt **emit·ted; emit·ting** [L emittere to send out, fr. e- + mittere to send] (1626) 1 a : to throw or give off or out (as light) b : to send out : EJECT 2 a : to issue with authority; esp : to put (as money) into circulation b obs : PUBLISH 3 : to give utterance or voice to ⟨emitted a groan⟩ — **emit·ter** n

emit·tance \ē-'mi-tⁿn(t)s\ n (1940) 1 : the energy radiated by the surface of a body per second per unit area 2 : EMISSIVITY

Emmanuel var of IMMANUEL

em·men·a·gogue \ə-'me-nə-ˌgäg, e-\ n [Gk emmēna menses (fr. neut. pl. of emmēnos monthly, fr. en- + mēn month) + E -agogue — more at MOON] (ca. 1732) : an agent that promotes the menstrual discharge

Em·men·ta·ler or **Em·men·tha·ler** \'e-mən-ˌtä-lər\ or **Em·men·tal** or **Em·men·thal** \-ˌtäl\ n [G, fr. Emmental, Switzerland] (1902) : SWISS CHEESE

em·mer \'e-mər\ n [G, fr. OHG amarī] (ca. 1900) : a wheat (Triticum dicoccum) having spikelets with two hard red kernels that remain in the glumes after threshing; broadly : a tetraploid wheat — called also emmer wheat

em·met \'e-mət\ n [ME emete, fr. OE ǣmette ant — more at ANT] (bef. 12c) chiefly dial : ANT

Em·my \'e-mē\ n, pl **Emmys** [fr. alter. of Immy, nickname for image orthicon (a camera tube used in television)] (1949) : a statuette awarded annually by a professional organization for notable achievement in television

em·o·din \'e-mə-dən\ n [ISV emodi- (fr. NL Rheum emodi, species of rhubarb) + -in] (1858) : an orange crystalline phenolic compound $C_{15}H_{10}O_5$ that is obtained from plants (as rhubarb and cascara buckthorn) and is used as a laxative

¹emol·lient \i-'mäl-yənt\ adj [L emollient-, emolliens, prp. of emollire to soften, fr. e- + mollis soft — more at MOLLIFY] (ca. 1640) 1 : making soft or supple; also : soothing esp. to the skin or mucous membrane 2 : making less intense or harsh : MOLLIFYING ⟨soothe us in our agonies with ~ words —H. L. Mencken⟩

²emollient n (1656) : something that softens or soothes

emol·u·ment \i-'mäl-yə-mənt\ n [ME, fr. L emolumentum advantage, fr. emolere to produce by grinding, fr. e- + molere to grind — more at MEAL] (15c) 1 : the returns arising from office or employment usu. in the form of compensation or perquisites 2 archaic : ADVANTAGE

emote \i-'mōt\ vi **emot·ed; emot·ing** [back-formation fr. emotion] (1917) : to give expression to emotion esp. in or as if in acting

emo·tion \i-'mō-shən\ n [MF, fr. emouvoir to stir up, fr. OF esmovoir, fr. L emovēre to remove, displace, fr. e- + movēre to move] (1579) 1 a obs : DISTURBANCE b : EXCITEMENT 2 a : the affective aspect of consciousness : FEELING b : a state of feeling c : a psychic and physical reaction (as anger or fear) subjectively experienced as strong feeling and physiologically involving changes that prepare the body for immediate vigorous action — more at FEELING

emo·tion·al \-shnəl, -shə-nᵊl\ adj (1834) 1 : of or relating to emotion ⟨an ~ disorder⟩ 2 : dominated by or prone to emotion ⟨an ~ person⟩ 3 : appealing to or arousing emotion ⟨an ~ sermon⟩ 4 : markedly aroused or agitated in feeling or sensibilities ⟨gets ~ at weddings⟩ — **emo·tion·al·i·ty** \-ˌmō-shə-'na-lə-tē\ n — **emo·tion·al·ly** \'-mō-shnə-lē, -shə-nᵊl-ē\

emo·tion·al·ism \i-'mō-shnə-ˌli-zəm, -shə-nᵊl-ˌiz-\ n (1865) 1 : a tendency to regard things emotionally 2 : undue indulgence in or display of emotion

emo·tion·al·ist \-shnə-list, -shə-nᵊl-ist\ n (ca. 1866) 1 : one who bases a theory or policy on an emotional conviction 2 : one prone to emotionalism — **emo·tion·al·is·tic** \-ˌmō-shnə-'lis-tik, -shə-nᵊl-'is-\ adj

emo·tion·al·ize \i-'mō-shnə-ˌliz, -shə-nᵊl-ˌiz\ vt **-ized; -iz·ing** (1879) : to give an emotional quality to

emo·tion·less \i-'mō-shən-ləs\ adj (1862) : showing, having, or expressing no emotion — **emo·tion·less·ness** n — **emo·tion·less·ly** adv

emo·tive \i-'mō-tiv\ adj (1830) 1 : of or relating to the emotions 2 : appealing to or expressing emotion ⟨the ~ use of language⟩ — **emo·tive·ly** \i-'mō-tiv-lē\ adv — **emo·tiv·i·ty** \i-ˌmō-'ti-və-tē, ˌē-ˌmō-\ n

em·pa·na·da \ˌem-pə-'nä-də\ n [AmSp, fr. Sp, fem. of empanado, pp. of empanar to bread, fr. en- (fr. L in-) + pan bread, fr. L panis — more at FOOD] (ca. 1922) : a turnover with a sweet or savory filling

empanel var of IMPANEL

em·pa·thet·ic \ˌem-pə-'the-tik\ adj (1932) : EMPATHIC — **em·pa·thet·i·cal·ly** \-ti-k(ə-)lē\ adv

em·path·ic \em-'pa-thik, im-\ adj (1909) : involving, eliciting, characterized by, or based on empathy — **em·path·i·cal·ly** \-thi-k(ə-)lē\ adv

em·pa·thise Brit var of EMPATHIZE

em·pa·thize \'em-pə-ˌthīz\ vi **-thized; -thiz·ing** (ca. 1921) : to experience empathy ⟨adults unable to ~ with a child's frustrations⟩

em·pa·thy \'em-pə-thē\ n [Gk empatheia, lit., passion, fr. empathēs emotional, fr. em- + pathos feelings, emotion — more at PATHOS] (1904) 1 : the imaginative projection of a subjective state into an object so that the object appears to be infused with it 2 : the action of understanding, being aware of, being sensitive to, and vicariously experiencing the feelings, thoughts, and experience of another of either the past or present without having the feelings, thoughts, and experience fully communicated in an objectively explicit manner; also : the capacity for this

em·pen·nage \ˌäm-pə-'näzh, ˌem-\ n [F, feathers of an arrow, empennage, fr. empenner to feather an arrow, fr. em- ¹en- + penne feather, fr. MF — more at PEN] (1909) : the tail assembly of an airplane

em·per·or \'em-pər-ər, -prər\ n [ME, fr. OF empereor, fr. L imperator, lit., commander, fr. imperare to command, fr. in- + parare to prepare, order — more at PARE] (13c) : the sovereign or supreme male monarch of an empire — **em·per·or·ship** \-ˌship\ n

emperor penguin n (1885) : a penguin (Aptenodytes forsteri) that is the largest known and that is noted for its habit of brooding the egg or young between the feet and a fold of abdominal skin resembling a pouch

em·pery \'em-p(ə-)rē\ n, pl **em·per·ies** [ME emperie, fr. OF, fr. emperer to command, fr. L imperare] (13c) : wide dominion : EMPIRE

em·pha·sise Brit var of EMPHASIZE

em·pha·sis \'em(p)-fə-səs\ n, pl **-pha·ses** \-ˌsēz\ [L, fr. Gk, exposition, emphasis, fr. emphainein to indicate, fr. en- + phainein to show — more at FANCY] (1573) 1 a : force or intensity of expression that gives impressiveness or importance to something b : a particular prominence given in reading or speaking to one or more words or syllables 2 : special consideration of or stress or insistence on something ⟨emphasize the need for reform⟩

em·pha·size \'em(p)-fə-ˌsīz\ vt **-sized; -siz·ing** (ca. 1806) : to place emphasis on : STRESS ⟨emphasized the need for reform⟩

em·phat·ic \im-'fa-tik, em-\ adj [Gk emphatikos, fr. emphainein] (ca. 1708) 1 : uttered with or marked by emphasis 2 : tending to express oneself in forceful speech or to take decisive action 3 : attracting special attention 4 : constituting or belonging to a set of tense forms in English consisting of the auxiliary do followed by an infinitive without to that are used to facilitate rhetorical inversion or to emphasize something — **em·phat·i·cal·ly** \-'fa-ti-k(ə-)lē\ adv

em·phy·se·ma \ˌem(p)-fə-'zē-mə, -'sē-\ n [NL, fr. Gk emphysēma, fr.

emphysan to inflate, fr. *em-* [2]*en-* + *physan* to blow, fr. *physa* breath — more at PUSTULE] (1661) : a condition characterized by air-filled expansions of body tissues; *specif* : a condition of the lung marked by abnormal dilation of its air spaces and distension of its walls and frequently by impairment of heart action — **em·phy·se·ma·tous** \-'ze-mə-təs, -'se-, -'zē-, -'sē-\ *adj* — **em·phy·se·mic** \-'zē-mik, -'sē-\ *adj*

em·pire \'em-,pīr\ *n* [ME, fr. OF *empire, empirie,* fr. L *imperium* absolute authority, empire, fr. *imperare*] (14c) **1 a** (1) : a major political unit having a territory of great extent or a number of territories or peoples under a single sovereign authority; *esp* : one having an emperor as chief of state (2) : the territory of such a political unit **b** : something resembling a political empire; *esp* : an extensive territory or enterprise under single domination or control **2** : imperial sovereignty, rule, or dominion

Em·pire \'äm-,pir, 'em-,pīr\ *adj* [F, fr. *(le premier) Empire* the first Empire of France] (1869) : of, relating to, or characteristic of a style (as of clothing or furniture) popular in early 19th century France

Em·pire Day \'em-,pīr-\ *n* (1902) : COMMONWEALTH DAY — used before the official adoption of *Commonwealth Day* in 1958

em·pir·ic \im-'pir-ik, em-\ *n* [L *empiricus,* fr. Gk *empeirikos* doctor relying on experience alone, fr. *empeiria* experience, fr. *em-* [2]*en-* + *peiran* to attempt — more at FEAR] (1562) **1** : CHARLATAN **2** : one who relies on practical experience

em·pir·i·cal \-i-kəl\ *also* **em·pir·ic** \-ik\ *adj* (1569) **1** : originating in or based on observation or experience ⟨~ data⟩ **2** : relying on experience or observation alone often without due regard for system and theory **3** : capable of being verified or disproved by observation or experiment ⟨~ laws⟩ **4** : of or relating to empiricism — **em·pir·i·cal·ly** \-i-k(ə-)lē\ *adv*

empirical formula *n* (1885) : a chemical formula showing the simplest ratio of elements in a compound rather than the total number of atoms in the molecule ⟨CH₂O is the *empirical formula* for glucose⟩

em·pir·i·cism \im-'pir-ə-,si-zəm, em-\ *n* (1657) **1 a** : a former school of medical practice founded on experience without the aid of science or theory **b** : QUACKERY, CHARLATANRY **2 a** : the practice of relying on observation and experiment esp. in the natural sciences **b** : a tenet arrived at empirically **3** : a theory that all knowledge originates in experience — **em·pir·i·cist** \-sist\ *n*

em·place \im-'plās\ *vt* [back-formation fr. *emplacement*] (1865) : to put into position ⟨missiles *emplaced* around the city⟩

em·place·ment \-'plā-smənt\ *n* [F, fr. MF *emplacer* to emplace, fr. *en-* + *place*] (1802) **1** : the situation or location of something **2** : a prepared position for weapons or military equipment ⟨radar ~s⟩ **3** : a putting into position : PLACEMENT

em·plane \im-'plān\ *var of* ENPLANE

1em·ploy \im-'ploi, em-\ *vt* [ME *emploien,* fr. MF *emploier,* fr. L *implicare* to enfold, involve, implicate, fr. *in-* + *plicare* to fold — more at PLY] (15c) **1 a** : to make use of (someone or something inactive) ⟨~ a pen for sketching⟩ **b** : to use (as time) advantageously **c** (1) : to use or engage the services of (2) : to provide with a job that pays wages or a salary **2** : to devote to or direct toward a particular activity or person ⟨~ed all her energies to help the poor⟩ *syn* see USE — **em·ploy·er** *n*

2em·ploy \im-'ploi, 'im-,, 'em-,\ *n* (1666) **1 a** : USE, PURPOSE **b** : OCCUPATION, JOB **2** : the state of being employed ⟨in the government's ~⟩

1em·ploy·able \im-'ploi-ə-bəl\ *adj* (1593) : capable of being employed — **em·ploy·abil·i·ty** \-,ploi-ə-'bi-lə-tē\ *n*

2employable *n* (1934) : one who is employable

em·ploy·ee *or* **em·ploye** \im-,ploi(-)-'ē, (,)em-; im-'plò(i)-,ē, em-\ *n* (1822) : one employed by another usu. for wages or salary and in a position below the executive level

em·ploy·ment \im-'ploi-mənt\ *n* (15c) **1** : USE, PURPOSE **2 a** : activity in which one engages or is employed **b** : an instance of such activity **3** : the act of employing : the state of being employed *syn* see WORK

employment agency *n* (1888) : an agency whose business is to find jobs for people seeking them or to find people to fill jobs that are open

em·poi·son \im-'pòi-z²n\ *vt* [ME *empoysonen,* fr. MF *empoisoner,* fr. *en-* + *poison* poison, fr. OF] (14c) **1** *archaic* : POISON **2** : EMBITTER ⟨a look of ~ed acceptance —Saul Bellow⟩ — **em·poi·son·ment** \-mənt\ *n*

em·po·ri·um \im-'pōr-ē-əm, em-, -'pòr-\ *n, pl* **-ri·ums** *also* **-ria** \-ē-ə\ [L, fr. Gk *emporion,* fr. *emporos* traveler, trader, fr. *em-* [2]*en-* + *poros* passage, journey — more at FARE] (1586) **1 a** : a place of trade; *esp* : a commercial center **b** : a retail outlet ⟨a hardware ~⟩ ⟨a pizza ~⟩ **2** : a store carrying a diversity of merchandise

em·pow·er \im-'pau(-ə)r\ *vt* (1648) **1** : to give official authority or legal power to **2** : ENABLE 1a **3** : to promote the self-actualization or influence of ⟨women's movement has been inspiring and ~ing women —Ron Hansen⟩ — **em·pow·er·ment** \-mənt\ *n*

em·press \'em-prəs\ *n* [ME *emperesse,* fr. OF, fem. of *empereor* emperor] (12c) **1** : the wife or widow of an emperor **2** : a woman who is the sovereign or supreme monarch of an empire

em·presse·ment \äⁿ-pres-mäⁿ\ *n* [F, fr. *(s')empresser* to hurry, fr. *en-* + *presser* to press] (1709) : demonstrative warmth or cordiality

em·prise \em-'prīz\ *n* [ME, fr. MF, fr. OF, fr. *emprendre* to undertake, fr. (assumed) VL *imprehendere,* fr. L *in-* + *prehendere* to seize — more at GET] (13c) : an adventurous, daring, or chivalric enterprise

1emp·ty \'em(p)-tē\ *adj* **emp·ti·er; -est** [ME, fr. OE *æmettig* unoccupied, fr. *æmetta* leisure, perh. fr. *æ-* without + *-metta* (prob. akin to *mōtan* to have to) — more at MUST] (bef. 12c) **1 a** : containing nothing **b** : not occupied or inhabited **c** : UNFREQUENTED **d** : not pregnant ⟨~ heifer⟩ **e** : NULL 4a ⟨the ~ set⟩ **2 a** : lacking reality, substance, meaning, or value : HOLLOW ⟨an ~ pleasure⟩ **b** : destitute of effect or force **c** : devoid of sense : FOOLISH **3** : HUNGRY **4 a** : IDLE ⟨~ hours⟩ **b** : having no purpose or result : USELESS **5** : marked by the absence of human life, activity, or comfort — **emp·ti·ly** \-tə-lē\ *adv* — **emp·ti·ness** \-tē-nəs\ *n*

syn EMPTY, VACANT, BLANK, VOID, VACUOUS mean lacking contents which could or should be present. EMPTY suggests a complete absence of contents ⟨an *empty* bucket⟩. VACANT suggests an absence of appropriate contents or occupants ⟨a *vacant* apartment⟩. BLANK stresses the absence of any significant, relieving, or intelligible features on a surface ⟨a *blank* wall⟩. VOID suggests absolute emptiness as far as the mind or senses can determine ⟨a statement *void* of meaning⟩. VACUOUS suggests the emptiness of a vacuum and esp. the lack of intelligence or significance ⟨a *vacuous* facial expression⟩. *syn* see in addition VAIN

2empty *vb* **emp·tied; emp·ty·ing** *vt* (1555) **1 a** : to make empty : remove the contents of **b** : DEPRIVE, DIVEST **c** : to discharge (itself) of contents **d** : to fire (a repeating firearm) until empty **2** : to remove from what encloses or holds ⟨~ the grain from sacks⟩ ~ *vi* **1** : to become empty **2** : to discharge contents ⟨the river *empties* into the ocean⟩

3empty *n, pl* **emp·ties** (1535) : something (as a container) that is empty

emp·ty–hand·ed \,em(p)-tē-'han-dəd\ *adj* (1589) **1** : having or bringing nothing **2** : having acquired or gained nothing ⟨came back ~⟩

emp·ty–head·ed \-'he-dəd\ *adj* (1650) : SCATTERBRAINED

empty nest·er \-'nes-tər\ *n* (1962) : a parent whose children have grown and moved away from home

emp·ty–nest syndrome \,em(p)-tē-'nest-\ *n* (1972) : the emotional letdown experienced by an empty nester

em·pur·ple \im-'pər-pəl\ *vb* **em·pur·pled; em·pur·pling** \-'pər-p(ə-)liŋ\ *vt* (1590) : to tinge or color purple ~ *vi* : to become purple

em·py·ema \,em-,pī-'ē-mə\ *n, pl* **-ema·ta** \-mə-tə\ *or* **-emas** [LL, fr. Gk *empyēma,* fr. *empyein* to suppurate, fr. *em-* [2]*en-* + *pyon* pus — more at FOUL] (ca. 1605) : the presence of pus in a bodily cavity — **em·py·emic** \-mik\ *adj*

em·py·re·al \,em-,pī-'rē-əl, -,pə-; em-'pir-ē-əl, -'pī-rē-\ *adj* [LL *empyrius, empyreus,* fr. LGk *empyrios,* fr. Gk *em-* [2]*en-* + *pyr* fire] (15c) **1** : of or relating to the empyrean : CELESTIAL **2** : SUBLIME

1em·py·re·an \-ən\ *adj* (15c) : EMPYREAL

2empyrean *n* (ca. 1610) **1 a** : the highest heaven or heavenly sphere in ancient and medieval cosmology usu. consisting of fire or light **b** : the true and ultimate heavenly paradise : FIRMAMENT, HEAVENS **3** : an ideal place or state

EMT \,ē-(,)em-'tē\ *n* [emergency medical technician] (1972) : a specially trained medical technician licensed to provide basic emergency services before and during transportation to a hospital — compare PARAMEDIC 2

emu \'ē-(,)myü\ *n* [modif. of Pg *ema* cassowary] (1656) **1** : any of various tall flightless birds (as the rhea) **2** : a swift-running Australian bird (*Dromaius novae-hollandiae*) with undeveloped wings that is related to and smaller than the ostrich

emu 2

1em·u·late \'em-yə-,lāt\ *vt* **-lat·ed; -lat·ing** [L *aemulatus,* pp. of *aemulari,* fr. *aemulus* rivaling] (1582) **1 a** : to strive to equal or excel **b** : IMITATE; *esp* : to imitate by means of an emulator **2** : to equal or approach equality with

2em·u·late \-lət\ *adj* (1602) *obs* : EMULOUS 1b ⟨pricked on by a moot ~ pride —Shak.⟩

em·u·la·tion \,em-yə-'lā-shən\ *n* (1542) **1** *obs* : ambitious or envious rivalry **2** : ambition or endeavor to equal or excel others (as in achievement) **3 a** : IMITATION **b** : the use or technique of using an emulator — **em·u·la·tive** \'em-yə-,lā-tiv\ *adj* — **em·u·la·tive·ly** *adv*

em·u·la·tor \'em-yə-,lā-tər\ *n* (1589) **1** : one that emulates **2** : hardware or software that permits programs written for one computer to be run on another usu. newer computer

em·u·lous \'em-yə-ləs\ *adj* (1535) **1 a** : inspired by or deriving from a desire to emulate **b** : ambitious or eager to emulate **2** *obs* : JEALOUS — **em·u·lous·ly** *adv* — **em·u·lous·ness** *n*

emul·si·fi·er \i-'məl-sə-,fī(-ə)r\ *n* (1888) : one that emulsifies; *esp* : a surface-active agent (as a soap) promoting the formation and stabilization of an emulsion

emul·si·fy \-,fī\ *vt* **-fied; -fy·ing** (1859) : to disperse (as an oil) in an emulsion; *also* : to convert (two or more immiscible liquids) into an emulsion — **emul·si·fi·able** \i-'məl-sə-,fī-ə-bəl\ *adj* — **emul·si·fi·ca·tion** \i-,məl-sə-fə-'kā-shən\ *n*

emul·sion \i-'məl-shən\ *n* [NL *emulsion-, emulsio,* fr. L *emulgēre* to milk out, fr. *e-* + *mulgēre* to milk; akin to OE *melcan* to milk, Gk *amelgein*] (1612) **1 a** : a system (as fat in milk) consisting of a liquid dispersed with or without an emulsifier in an immiscible liquid usu. in droplets of larger than colloidal size **b** : the state of such a system **2** : SUSPENSION 2b(3); *esp* : a suspension of a sensitive silver salt or a mixture of silver halides in a viscous medium (as a gelatin solution) forming a coating on photographic plates, film, or paper

emul·soid \i-'məl-,sòid\ *n* (ca. 1909) **1** : a colloidal system consisting of a liquid dispersed in a liquid **2** : a lyophilic sol (as a gelatin solution) — **emul·soi·dal** \-,məl-'sòi-d²l\ *adj*

en \'en\ *n* (1792) **1** : the width of a piece of type half the width of an em **2** : the letter n

1en- *also* **em-** \in *also* en; *sometimes only in* is shown when en is *infrequent\ prefix* [ME, fr. OF, fr. L *in-, im-,* fr. *in*] **1** : put into or onto ⟨enthrone⟩ : cover with ⟨enshroud⟩ : go into or onto ⟨enplane⟩ — in verbs formed from nouns **2** : cause to be ⟨enslave⟩ — in verbs formed from adjectives or nouns **3** : provide with ⟨empower⟩ — in verbs formed from nouns **4** : so as to cover ⟨enwrap⟩ : thoroughly ⟨entangle⟩ — in verbs formed from verbs; in all senses usu. *em-* before *b, m,* or *p*

2en- *also* **em-** *prefix* [ME, fr. L, fr. Gk, fr. *en* — more at IN] : in : within ⟨enzootic⟩ — usu. *em-* before *b, m,* or *p* ⟨empathy⟩

3en- *comb form* [ISV, fr. *-ene*] : chemically unsaturated; *esp* : having one double bond ⟨enamine⟩

1-en \ən, ²n\ *also* **-n** \n\ *adj suffix* [ME, fr. OE; akin to OHG *-īn* made of, L *-inus* of or belonging to, Gk *-inos* made of, of, or belonging to] : made of : consisting of ⟨earthen⟩ ⟨leathern⟩

\ə\ abut \'\ kitten, F table \ər\ further \a\ ash \ā\ ace \ä\ mop, mar \aú\ out \ch\ chin \e\ bet \ē\ easy \g\ go \i\ hit \ī\ ice \j\ job \ŋ\ sing \ō\ go \ò\ law \òi\ boy \th\ thin \th̯\ the \ü\ loot \u̇\ foot \y\ yet \zh\ vision \à, k̲, ⁿ, œ, œ̄, ᴜ, üᴇ, ᵛ\ see Guide to Pronunciation

²**-en** *vb suffix* [ME *-nen*, fr. OE *-nian*; akin to OHG *-inōn* -en] **1** **a** : cause to be ⟨sharp*en*⟩ **b** : cause to have ⟨length*en*⟩ **2** **a** : come to be ⟨steep*en*⟩ **b** : come to have ⟨length*en*⟩

en·able \i-'nā-bəl\ *vt* **en·abled; en·abling** \-b(ə-)liŋ\ (15c) **1** **a** : to provide with the means or opportunity ⟨training that ∼s people to earn a living⟩ **b** : to make possible, practical, or easy **c** : to cause to operate ⟨software that ∼s the keyboard⟩ **2** : to give legal power, capacity, or sanction to ⟨a law *enabling* admission of a state⟩

en·act \i-'nakt\ *vt* (15c) **1** : to establish by law and authoritative act; *specif* : to make (as a bill) into law **2** : ACT OUT ⟨∼ a role⟩ — **en·ac·tor** \-'nak-tər\ *n*

en·act·ment \-'nak(t)-mənt\ *n* (1817) **1** : the act of enacting : the state of being enacted **2** : something (as a law) that has been enacted

¹**enam·el** \i-'na-məl\ *vt* **-eled** *or* **-elled; -el·ing** *or* **-el·ling** \-'nam-liŋ, -'na-mə-\ [ME, fr. MF *enamailler*, fr. *en-* + *esmail* enamel, of Gmc origin; akin to OHG *smelzan* to melt — more at SMELT] (14c) **1** : to cover, inlay, or decorate with enamel **2** : to beautify with a colorful surface **3** : to form a glossy surface on (as paper, leather, or cloth) — **enam·el·er** *or* **enam·el·ist** \-mə-list\ *n*

²**enamel** *n* (15c) **1** : a usu. opaque vitreous composition applied by fusion to the surface of metal, glass, or pottery **2** : a surface or outer covering that resembles enamel **3** **a** : something that is enameled **b** : ENAMELWARE **4** : a cosmetic intended to give a smooth or glossy appearance **5** : a hard calcareous substance that forms a thin layer capping the teeth — see TOOTH illustration **6** : a paint that flows out to a smooth coat when applied and that dries with a glossy appearance

enam·el·ware \i-'na-məl-,war, -,wer\ *n* (1903) : metalware (as kitchen utensils) coated with enamel

en·amine \'e-nə-,mēn, 'ē-\ *n* (1942) : an amine containing the double bond linkage C=C—N

en·am·or \i-'na-mər\ *vt* **-ored; -or·ing** \-mə-riŋ, -'nam-riŋ\ [ME *enamouren*, fr. MF *enamourer*, fr. *en-* + *amour* love — more at AMOUR] (14c) **1** : to inflame with love — usu. used in the passive with *of* **2** : FASCINATE 2b — usu. used in the passive with *of* or *with*

en·am·our *chiefly Brit var of* ENAMOR

en·an·tio·mer \i-'nan-tē-ə-mər\ *n* [Gk *enantios* + E *-mer*] (ca. 1929) : either of a pair of chemical compounds whose molecular structures have a mirror-image relationship to each other — **en·an·tio·mer·ic** \-,nan-tē-ə-'mer-ik\ *adj*

en·an·tio·morph \i-'nan-tē-ə-,mórf\ *n* [Gk *enantios* opposite (fr. *enanti* facing, fr. *en* in + *anti* against) + ISV *-morph* -morph] (1885) : ENAN-TIOMER; *also* : either of a pair of crystals (as of quartz) that are structural mirror images — **en·an·tio·mor·phic** \-,nan-tē-ə-'mór-fik\ *adj* — **en·an·tio·mor·phism** \-'mór-,fi-zəm\ *n* — **en·an·tio·mor·phous** \-'mór-fəs\ *adj*

ena·tion \i-'nā-shən\ *n* [L *enatus*, pp. of *enasci* to rise out of, fr. *e-* + *nasci* to be born — more at NATION] (ca. 1842) : an outgrowth from the surface of an organ ⟨a plant virus forming ∼s on leaves⟩

en banc \än-'bän\ *adv or adj* [F, on the bench] (1863) : in full court : with full judiciary authority

en bloc \än-'bläk\ *adv or adj* [F] (1861) : as a whole : in a mass

en bro·chette \än-brō-'shet\ *adj* [F] (ca. 1909) *of food* : cooked or served on a skewer ⟨shrimp *en brochette*⟩

en·cae·nia \en-'sē-nyə\ *n pl but sing or pl in constr, often cap* [NL, fr. L, dedication festival, fr. Gk *enkainia*, fr. *en* + *kainos* new — more at RECENT] (1691) : an annual university ceremony (as at Oxford) of commemoration with recital of poems and essays and conferring of degrees

en·cage \in-'kāj, en-\ *vt* (1593) : CAGE 1

en·camp \in-'kamp, en-\ *vt* (1568) : to place or establish in a camp ∼ *vi* : to set up or occupy a camp

en·camp·ment \-mənt\ *n* (1598) **1** **a** : the place where a group (as a body of troops) is encamped **b** : the individuals that make up an encampment **2** : the act of encamping : the state of being encamped

en·cap·su·late \in-'kap-sə-,lāt, en-\ *vb* **-lat·ed; -lat·ing** *vt* (1876) **1** : to enclose in or as if in a capsule ⟨a pilot *encapsulated* in the cockpit⟩ **2** : EPITOMIZE, SUMMARIZE ⟨∼ an era in an aphorism⟩ ∼ *vi* : to become encapsulated — **en·cap·su·la·tion** \-,kap-sə-'lā-shən\ *n*

en·cap·su·lat·ed \-,lā-təd\ *adj* (1894) **1** : surrounded by a gelatinous or membranous envelope ⟨∼ water bacteria⟩ **2** : CONDENSED

en·cap·sule \in-'kap-səl, -,(,)sül, en-\ *vt* **-suled; -sul·ing** (1877) : ENCAPSULATE

en·case \in-'kās, en-\ *vt* (1633) : to enclose in or as if in a case

en·case·ment \in-'kā-smənt, en-\ *n* (1741) : the act or process of encasing : the state of being encased; *also* : CASE, COVERING

en·cash \in-'kash, en-\ *vt* (1861) *Brit* : CASH — **en·cash·able** \-'ka-shə-bəl\ *adj, chiefly Brit* — **en·cash·ment** \-mənt\ *n, chiefly Brit*

en·caus·tic \in-'kó-stik\ *n* [*encaustic*, adj., fr. L *encausticus*, fr. Gk *enkaustikos*, fr. *enkaiein* to burn in, fr. *en-* + *kaiein* to burn] (1601) **1** : a paint made from pigment mixed with melted beeswax and resin and after application fixed by heat **2** : the method involving the use of encaustic; *also* : a work produced by this method — **encaustic** *adj*

-ence \ən(t)s, ²n(t)s\ *n suffix* [ME, fr. OF, fr. L *-entia*, fr. *-ent-, -ens*, prp. ending + *-ia* ²-y] **1** : action or process ⟨emerg*ence*⟩ : instance of an action or process ⟨refer*ence*⟩ **2** : quality or state ⟨despond*ence*⟩

¹**en·ceinte** \än(n)-'sant\ *adj* [MF, perh. fr. (assumed) VL *incenta*, alter. of L *incient-, inciens* being with young, modif. of Gk *enkyos* pregnant, fr. *en-* + *kyein* to be pregnant — more at CYME] (1599) : PREGNANT 3

²**enceinte** *n* [F, fr. OF, enclosing wall, fr. *enceindre* to surround, fr. L *incingere*, fr. *in-* + *cingere* to gird — more at CINCTURE] (ca. 1708) : a line of fortification enclosing a castle or town; *also* : the area so enclosed

encephal- *or* **encephalo-** *comb form* [F *encéphal-*, fr. Gk *enkephal-*, fr. *enkephalos*, fr. *en* + *kephalē* head — more at CEPHALIC] : brain ⟨*en*cephalitis⟩ ⟨*encephalo*myocarditis⟩

en·ceph·a·li·tis \in-,se-fə-'lī-təs\ *n, pl* **-lit·i·des** \-'li-tə-,dēz\ (1843) : inflammation of the brain — **en·ceph·a·lit·ic** \-'li-tik\ *adj*

en·ceph·a·li·to·gen·ic \-,lī-tə-'je-nik\ *adj* (1923) : tending to cause encephalitis ⟨an ∼ virus⟩ — **en·ceph·a·li·to·gen** \-'lī-tə-jən, -,jen\ *n*

en·ceph·a·lo·gram \in-'se-fə-lə-,gram\ *n* (1928) : an X-ray picture of the brain made by encephalography

en·ceph·a·lo·graph \-,graf\ *n* (1928) **1** : ENCEPHALOGRAM **2** : ELECTROENCEPHALOGRAPH

en·ceph·a·log·ra·phy \in-,se-fə-'lä-grə-fē\ *n* (1922) : roentgenography of the brain after the cerebrospinal fluid has been replaced by a gas (or air)

en·ceph·a·lo·my·eli·tis \in-,se-fə-lō-,mī-ə-'lī-təs\ *n, pl* **-elit·i·des** \-ə-'li-tə-,dēz\ [NL] (1908) : concurrent inflammation of the brain and spinal cord; *specif* : any of several virus diseases of horses

en·ceph·a·lo·myo·car·di·tis \-,mī-ə-kär-'dī-təs\ *n* [NL] (1947) : an acute febrile virus disease characterized by degeneration and inflammation of skeletal and cardiac muscle and lesions of the central nervous system

en·ceph·a·lon \in-'se-fə-,län, -lən\ *n, pl* **-la** \-lə\ [NL, fr. Gk *enkephalos*] (1741) : the vertebrate brain

en·ceph·a·lop·a·thy \in-,se-fə-'lä-pə-thē\ *n* (1866) : a disease of the brain; *esp* : one involving alterations of brain structure — **en·ceph·a·lo·path·ic** \-lə-'pa-thik\ *adj*

en·chain \in-'chān\ *vt* [ME *encheynen*, fr. MF *enchainer*, fr. OF, fr. *en-* + *chaeine* chain] (14c) : to bind or hold with or as if with chains — **en·chain·ment** \-mənt\ *n*

en·chant \in-'chant, en-\ *vt* [ME, fr. MF *enchanter*, fr. L *incantare*, fr. *in-* + *cantare* to sing — more at CHANT] (14c) **1** : to influence by or as if by charms and incantation : BEWITCH **2** : to attract and move deeply : rouse to ecstatic admiration ⟨the scene ∼ed her to the point of tears —Elinor Wylie⟩ *syn* see ATTRACT

en·chant·er *n* (13c) : one that enchants; *esp* : SORCERER

en·chant·ing *adj* (1606) : CHARMING — **en·chant·ing·ly** \-'chan-tiŋ-lē\ *adv*

en·chant·ment \in-'chant-mənt, en-\ *n* (13c) **1** **a** : the act or art of enchanting **b** : the quality or state of being enchanted **2** : something that enchants

en·chant·ress \in-'chan-trəs, en-\ *n* (14c) **1** : a woman who practices magic : SORCERESS **2** : a fascinating woman

en·chase \in-'chās\ *vt* [ME, to emboss, fr. MF *enchasser* to enshrine, set, fr. *en-* + *chasse* reliquary, fr. L *capsa* case — more at CASE] (15c) **1** : ORNAMENT: as **a** : to cut or carve in relief **b** : INLAY **2** : SET ⟨∼ a gem⟩

en·chi·la·da \,en-chə-'lä-də\ *n* [AmerSp, fr. fem. of *enchilado*, pp. of *enchilar* to season with chili, fr. Sp *en-* ¹en- + *chile* chili] (1887) **1** : a rolled filled tortilla covered with chili sauce and usu. baked **2** : SCHMEAR, BALL OF WAX ⟨the whole ∼⟩

en·chi·rid·i·on \,en-,ki-'ri-dē-ən, -,ki-\ *n, pl* **-rid·ia** \-dē-ə\ [LL, fr. Gk *encheiridion*, fr. *en* in + *cheir* hand — more at IN, CHIR.] (15c) : HANDBOOK, MANUAL

-en·chy·ma \-(,)ki-mə\ *n comb form, pl* **-en·chy·ma·ta** \ən-'ki-mə-tə, -'kī-mə-\ *or* **-enchymas** [NL, fr. *parenchyma*] : cellular tissue ⟨collenchyma⟩

en·ci·pher \in-'sī-fər, en-\ *vt* (1577) : to convert (a message) into cipher — **en·ci·pher·er** \-fər-ər\ *n* — **en·ci·pher·ment** \-fər-mənt\ *n*

en·cir·cle \in-'sər-kəl, en-\ *vt* [ME *enserclen*] (15c) **1** : to form a circle around : SURROUND **2** : to pass completely around — **en·cir·cle·ment** \-mənt\ *n*

en clair \än-'kler\ *adv or adj* [F, in clear] (ca. 1897) : in plain language ⟨a message sent *en clair*⟩

en·clasp \in-'klasp, en-\ *vt* (1596) : to seize and hold : EMBRACE

en·clave \'en-,klāv, ÷än-,klāv, ÷'äŋ-\ *n* [F, fr. MF, fr. *enclaver* to enclose, fr. (assumed) VL *inclavare* to lock up, fr. L *in-* + *clavis* key — more at CLAVICLE] (1868) : a distinct territorial, cultural, or social unit enclosed within or as if within foreign territory ⟨ethnic ∼s⟩

en·clit·ic \en-'kli-tik\ *n* [LL *encliticos*, fr. Gk *enklitikos*, fr. *enklinesthai* to lean on, fr. *en-* + *klinein* to lean — more at LEAN] (ca. 1663) : a clitic that is associated with a preceding word — **enclitic** *adj*

en·close \in-'klōz, en-\ *vt* [ME, prob. fr. *enclos* enclosed, fr. MF, pp. of *enclore* to enclose, fr. (assumed) VL *inclaudere*, alter. of L *includere* — more at INCLUDE] (14c) **1** **a** (1): to close in : SURROUND ⟨a porch with glass⟩ (2): to fence off (common land) for individual use **b** : to hold in : CONFINE **2** : to include along with something else in a parcel or envelope ⟨a check is *enclosed* herewith⟩

en·clo·sure \in-'klō-zhər, en-\ *n* (15c) **1** : the act or action of enclosing : the quality or state of being enclosed **2** : something that encloses ⟨a letter with two ∼s⟩

en·code \in-'kōd, en-\ *vt* (ca. 1919) **1** : to convert (as a body of information) from one system of communication into another; *esp* : to convert (a message) into code **2** : to specify the genetic code for — **en·cod·er** *n*

en·co·mi·ast \en-'kō-mē-,ast, -mē-əst\ *n* [Gk *enkōmiastēs*, fr. *enkōmiazein* to praise, fr. *enkōmion*] (1610) : one that praises : EULOGIST — **en·co·mi·as·tic** \-,kō-mē-'as-tik\ *adj*

en·co·mi·um \en-'kō-mē-əm\ *n, pl* **-mi·ums** *or* **-mia** \-mē-ə\ [L, fr. Gk *enkōmion*, fr. *en* in + *kōmos* revel, celebration] (1589) : glowing and warmly enthusiastic praise; *also* : an expression of this

syn ENCOMIUM, EULOGY, PANEGYRIC, TRIBUTE, CITATION mean a formal expression of praise. ENCOMIUM implies enthusiasm and warmth in praising a person or a thing. EULOGY applies to a prepared speech or writing extolling the virtues and services of a person. PANEGYRIC suggests an elaborate often poetic compliment. TRIBUTE implies deeply felt praise conveyed either through words or through a significant act. CITATION applies to the formal praise accompanying the mention of a person in a military dispatch or in awarding an honorary degree.

en·com·pass \in-'kəm-pəs, en-\ *vt* [ME] (14c) **1** **a** : to form a circle about : ENCLOSE **b** *obs* : to go completely around **2** **a** : ENVELOP **b** : INCLUDE ⟨a plan that ∼es a number of aims⟩ **3** : BRING ABOUT, ACCOMPLISH ⟨∼ a task⟩ — **en·com·pass·ment** \-mənt\ *n*

¹**en·core** \'än-,kōr, -,kór\ *n* [F, still, again] (1712) : a demand for repetition or reappearance made by an audience; *also* : a reappearance or additional performance in response to such a demand

²**encore** *vt* **en·cored; en·cor·ing** (1748) : to request an encore of or by

¹**en·coun·ter** \in-'kaún-tər, en-\ *vb* **en·coun·tered; en·coun·ter·ing** \-'kaún-t(ə-)riŋ\ [ME *encountren*, fr. MF *encontrer*, fr. ML *incontrare*, fr. LL *incontra* toward, fr. L *in-* + *contra* against — more at COUNTER] *vt* (14c) **1** **a** : to meet as an adversary or enemy **b** : to engage in conflict with **2** : to come upon face-to-face **3** : to come upon esp. unexpectedly ∼ *vi* : to meet esp. by chance

²**encounter** *n* (14c) **1** **a** : a meeting esp. between hostile factions or persons **b** : a sudden often violent clash : COMBAT **2** **a** : a chance

meeting **b** : a direct often momentary meeting **3** : a coming into the vicinity of a celestial body ⟨the Martian ∼ of a spacecraft⟩
encounter group *n* (1967) : a usu. unstructured group that seeks to develop the capacity of the individual to express feelings and to form emotional ties by unrestrained confrontation of individuals
en·cour·age \in-'kər-ij, -'kə-rij, en-\ *vt* **-aged; -ag·ing** [ME *encoragen*, fr. MF *encoragier*, fr. OF, fr. *en-* + *corage* courage] (15c) **1** : to inspire with courage, spirit, or hope : HEARTEN **2** : to spur on : STIMULATE **3** : to give help or patronage to : FOSTER **syn** see HEARTEN — **en·cour·ag·er** *n*
syn ENCOURAGE, INSPIRIT, HEARTEN, EMBOLDEN mean to fill with courage or strength of purpose. ENCOURAGE suggests the raising of one's confidence esp. by an external agency ⟨the teacher's praise *encouraged* the students to greater efforts⟩. INSPIRIT, somewhat literary, implies instilling life, energy, courage, or vigor into something ⟨patriots *inspirited* the people to resist⟩. HEARTEN implies the lifting of dispiritedness or despondency by an infusion of fresh courage or zeal ⟨a hospital patient *heartened* by good news⟩. EMBOLDEN implies the giving of courage sufficient to overcome timidity or reluctance ⟨*emboldened* by her first success, she tried an even more difficult climb⟩.
en·cour·age·ment \-ij-mənt, -rij-\ *n* (1568) **1** : the act of encouraging : the state of being encouraged **2** : something that encourages
en·cour·ag·ing \-i-jiŋ, -ri-jiŋ\ *adj* (1593) : giving hope or promise : INSPIRITING — **en·cour·ag·ing·ly** \-jiŋ-lē\ *adv*
en·crim·son \in-'krim-zən\ *vt* (1597) : to make or dye crimson
en·croach \in-'krōch, en-\ *vi* [ME *encrochen* to get, seize, fr. MF *encrochier*, fr. OF, fr. *en-* + *croc, croche* hook — more at CROCHET] (ca. 1534) **1** : to enter by gradual steps or by stealth into the possessions or rights of another **2** : to advance beyond the usual or proper limits ⟨the gradually ∼*ing* sea⟩ **syn** see TRESPASS — **en·croach·er** *n* — **en·croach·ment** \-'krōch-mənt\ *n*
en·crust \in-'krəst, iŋ-\ *vb* [prob. fr. L *incrustare*, fr. *in-* + *crusta* crust] *vt* (1641) : to cover, line, or overlay with or as if with a crust ∼ *vi* : to form a crust
en·crus·ta·tion \(,)in-,krəs-'tā-shən, ,en-\ *var of* INCRUSTATION
en·crypt \in-'kript, en-\ *vt* [*en-* + *crypt-* (as in *cryptogram*)] (1944) **1** : ENCIPHER **2** : ENCODE 1 — **en·cryp·tion** \-'krip-shən\ *n*
en·cum·ber \in-'kəm-bər\ *vt* **-cum·bered; -cum·ber·ing** \-b(ə-)riŋ\ [ME *encombren*, fr. MF *encombrer*, fr. OF, fr. *en-* + (assumed) OF *combre* dam, weir] (14c) **1** : WEIGH DOWN, BURDEN **2** : to impede or hamper the function or activity of : HINDER **3** : to burden with a legal claim (as a mortgage) ⟨∼ an estate⟩
en·cum·brance \in-'kəm-brən(t)s\ *n* (1535) **1** : something that encumbers : IMPEDIMENT **2** : a claim (as a mortgage) against property
en·cum·branc·er \-brən(t)-sər\ *n* (1858) : one that holds an encumbrance
-en·cy \ən(t)-sē, ᵊn(t)-\ *n suffix* [ME -*encie*, fr. L -*entia* — more at -ENCE] : quality or state ⟨despond*ency*⟩
¹**en·cyc·li·cal** \in-'si-kli-kəl, en-\ *adj* [LL *encyclicus*, fr. Gk *enkyklios* circular, general, fr. *en* + *kyklos* circle — more at IN, WHEEL] (1647) : addressed to all the individuals of a group : GENERAL
²**encyclical** *n* (1837) : an encyclical letter; *specif* : a papal letter to the bishops of the church as a whole or to those in one country
en·cy·clo·pe·dia *also* **en·cy·clo·pae·dia** \in-,sī-klə-'pē-dē-ə\ *n* [ML *encyclopaedia* course of general education, fr. Gk *enkyklios* + *paideia* education, child rearing, fr. *paid-, pais* child — more at FEW] (1644) : a work that contains information on all branches of knowledge or treats comprehensively a particular branch of knowledge usu. in articles arranged alphabetically often by subject
en·cy·clo·pe·dic *also* **en·cy·clo·pae·dic** \-'pē-dik\ *adj* (1824) : of, relating to, or suggestive of an encyclopedia or its methods of treating or covering a subject : COMPREHENSIVE ⟨an ∼ mind⟩ ⟨an ∼ collection of armor⟩ — **en·cy·clo·pe·di·cal·ly** \-di-k(ə-)lē\ *adv*
en·cy·clo·pe·dism \-'pē-,di-zəm\ *n* (1833) : the quality or state of being encyclopedic
en·cy·clo·pe·dist \-'pē-dist\ *n* (1651) **1** : one who compiles or writes for an encyclopedia **2** *often cap* : one of the writers of a French encyclopedia (1751–80) who were identified with the Enlightenment and advocated deism and scientific rationalism
en·cyst \in-'sist, en-\ *vi* (1845) : to enclose in a cyst ∼ *vi* : to form or become enclosed in a cyst — **en·cyst·ment** \-'sist(t)-mənt\ *n*
¹**end** \'end\ *n* [ME *ende*, fr. OE; akin to OHG *enti* end, L *ante* before, Gk *anti* against] (bef. 12c) **1 a** : the part of an area that lies at the boundary **b** (1) : a point that marks the extent of something (2) : the point where something ceases to exist ⟨world without ∼⟩ **c** : the extreme or last part lengthwise : TIP **d** : the terminal unit of something spatial that is marked off by units **e** : a player stationed at the extremity of a line (as in football) **2 a** : cessation of a course of action, pursuit, or activity **b** : DEATH, DESTRUCTION **c** (1) : the ultimate state (2) : RESULT, ISSUE **3** : something incomplete, fragmentary, or undersized : REMNANT **4** : an outcome worked toward : PURPOSE ⟨the ∼ of poetry is to be poetry —R. P. Warren⟩ **b** : the object by virtue of or for the sake of which an event takes place **5 a** : a share in an undertaking ⟨kept your ∼ up⟩ **b** : a particular operation or aspect of an undertaking or organization ⟨the sales ∼ of the business⟩ **6** : something that is extreme : ULTIMATE — used with ∼ **7** : a period of action or turn in any of various sports events (as archery or lawn bowling) **syn** see INTENTION — **end·ed** \'en-dəd\ *adj* — **in the end** : AFTER ALL, ULTIMATELY — **no end** : EXCEEDINGLY — **on end** : without a stop or letup ⟨it rained for days *on end*⟩
²**end** *vt* (bef. 12c) **1 a** : to bring to an end **b** : DESTROY **2** : to make up the end of ∼ *vi* **1 a** : to come to an end **b** : to reach a specified ultimate rank or situation — usu. used with *up* ⟨∼*ed* up as a colonel⟩ **2** : DIE **syn** see CLOSE
³**end** *adj* (13c) : FINAL, ULTIMATE ⟨∼ results⟩ ⟨∼ markets⟩ ⟨∼ product⟩
⁴**end** *vt* [prob. alter. of E dial. *in* (to harvest)] (1607) *dial Eng* : to put (grain or hay) into a barn or stack
end- *or* **endo-** *comb form* [F, fr. Gk, fr. *endon* within; akin to Gk *en* in, OL *indu*, Hitt *andan* within — more at IN] **1** : within : inside ⟨*endo*skeleton⟩ — compare ECT-, EXO- **2** : taking in ⟨*endo*thermic⟩
en·dam·age \in-'da-mij\ *vt* [ME] (14c) : to cause loss or damage to
end·amoe·ba \,en-də-'mē-bə\ *n* [NL, genus name] (ca. 1879) : any of a genus (*Endamoeba*) comprising amoebas parasitic in the intestines of insects — compare ENTAMOEBA

en·dan·ger \in-'dān-jər\ *vb* **-dan·gered; -dan·ger·ing** \-'dānj-riŋ, -'dān-jə-\ *vt* (1509) : to bring into danger or peril ∼ *vi* : to create a dangerous situation ⟨driving to ∼⟩ — **en·dan·ger·ment** \-'dān-jər-mənt\ *n*
en·dan·gered *adj* (1964) : being or relating to an endangered species ⟨an ∼ bird⟩ ⟨put on the ∼ list⟩
endangered species *n* (1964) : a species threatened with extinction; *broadly* : anyone or anything whose continued existence is threatened
en·darch \'en-,därk\ *adj* (ca. 1900) : formed or taking place from inner cells outward ⟨∼ xylem⟩
end around *n* (1926) : a football play in which an offensive end comes behind the line of scrimmage to take a handoff and attempts to carry the ball around the opposite flank
end·ar·ter·ec·to·my \,en-,där-tə-'rek-tə-mē\ *n, pl* **-mies** [NL *endarterium* intima of an artery (fr. *end-* + *arteria* artery) + E -*ectomy*] (1950) : surgical removal of the inner layer of an artery when thickened and atheromatous or occluded (as by intimal plaques)
end·brain \'en(d)-,brān\ *n* (1927) : TELENCEPHALON
end brush *n* (ca. 1891) : END PLATE
en·dear \in-'dir\ *vt* (1580) **1** *obs* : to make higher in cost, value, or estimation **2** : to cause to become beloved or admired — **en·dear·ing·ly** \-iŋ-lē\ *adv*
en·dear·ment \in-'dir-mənt\ *n* (1610) **1** : a word or an act (as a caress) expressing affection **2** : the act or process of endearing
¹**en·deav·or** \in-'de-vər\ *vb* **en·deav·ored; en·deav·or·ing** \-v(ə-)riŋ\ [ME *endeveren* to exert oneself, fr. *en-* + *dever* duty — more at DEVOIR] *vt* (15c) **1** *archaic* : to strive to achieve or reach **2** : to attempt (as the fulfillment of an obligation) by exertion of effort ⟨∼*s* to finish the race⟩ ∼ *vi* : to work with set purpose **syn** see ATTEMPT
²**endeavor** *n* (15c) **1** : serious determined effort **2** : activity directed toward a goal : ENTERPRISE ⟨fields of ∼⟩
en·deav·our *chiefly Brit var of* ENDEAVOR
¹**en·dem·ic** \en-'de-mik, in-\ *adj* [F *endémique*, fr. *endémie* endemic disease, fr. Gk *endēmia* action of dwelling, fr. *endēmos* endemic, fr. *en* in + *dēmos* people, populace — more at DEMAGOGUE] (1759) **1 a** : belonging or native to a particular people or country **b** : characteristic of or prevalent in a particular field, area, or environment ⟨problems ∼ to translation⟩ ⟨the self-indulgence ∼ in the film industry⟩ **2** : restricted or peculiar to a locality or region ⟨∼ diseases⟩ ⟨an ∼ species⟩ **syn** see NATIVE — **en·dem·i·cal·ly** \-'de-mi-k(ə-)lē\ *adv* — **en·de·mic·i·ty** \,en-,de-'mi-sə-tē, -də-'mi-\ *n* — **en·de·mism** \'en-də-,mi-zəm\ *n*
²**endemic** *n* (1926) : an endemic organism
end·er·gon·ic \,en-,dər-'gä-nik\ *adj* [*end-* + Gk *ergon* work — more at WORK] (1940) : ENDOTHERMIC 1 ⟨an ∼ biochemical reaction⟩
end·ex·ine \(,)en-'dek-,sēn, -,sīn\ *n* (1947) : an inner membranous layer of the exine
end·game \'en(d)-,gām\ *n* (1884) : the stage of a chess game after major reduction of forces; *also* : the final stages of some action
end·ing \'en-diŋ\ *n* (bef. 12c) : something that constitutes an end: as **a** : CONCLUSION **b** : one or more letters or syllables added to a word base esp. in inflection
endite *var of* INDITE
en·dive \'en-,dīv, än-'dēv\ *n* [ME, fr. MF, fr. LL *endivia*, fr. LGk *entybion*, fr. L *intubus*] (14c) **1** : an annual or biennial composite herb (*Cichorium endivia*) widely cultivated as a salad plant — called also *escarole* **2** : the developing crown of chicory when blanched for use as a vegetable or in salads by growing in darkness or semidarkness
end·leaf \'end-,lēf\ *n* (1888) : ENDPAPER
end·less \'en(d)-ləs\ *adj* (bef. 12c) **1** : being or seeming to be without end ⟨an ∼ speech⟩ **2** : extremely numerous ⟨all the multiplied, ∼, nameless iniquities —Edmund Burke⟩ **3** : joined at the ends ⟨an ∼ chain⟩ — **end·less·ly** *adv* — **end·less·ness** *n*
end line *n* (1893) : a line marking an end or boundary esp. of a playing area: as **a** : a line at either end of a football field 10 yards beyond and parallel to the goal line **b** : a line at either end of a court (as in basketball or tennis) perpendicular to the sidelines
end·long \'end-,lȯŋ\ *adv* [ME *endelong*, alter. of *andlong*, fr. OE *andlang*, fr. *andlang*, prep. — more at ALONG] (13c) *archaic* : LENGTHWISE
end man *n* (1865) : a man at each end of the line of performers in a minstrel show who engages in comic repartee with the interlocutor
end·most \'en(d)-,mōst\ *adj* (bef. 12c) : situated at the very end
end·note \'en(d)-,nōt\ *n* (1926) : a note placed at the end of the text
en·do·bi·ot·ic \,en-dō-,bī-'ä-tik, -bē-\ *adj* [ISV] (ca. 1900) : dwelling within the cells or tissues of a host ⟨∼ fungi⟩
en·do·car·di·al \,en-dō-'kär-dē-əl\ *adj* (ca. 1849) **1** : situated within the heart **2** : of or relating to the endocardium
en·do·car·di·tis \-,kär-'dī-təs\ *n* [NL] (ca. 1839) : inflammation of the lining of the heart and its valves
en·do·car·di·um \-'kär-dē-əm\ *n, pl* **-dia** \-dē-ə\ [NL, fr. *end-* + Gk *kardia* heart] (ca. 1864) : a thin serous membrane lining the cavities of the heart
en·do·carp \'en-də-,kärp\ *n* [F *endocarpe*] (1830) : the inner layer of the pericarp of a fruit (as an apple or orange) when it consists of two or more layers of different texture or consistency
en·do·cast \'en-dō-,kast\ *n* (1949) : ENDOCRANIAL CAST
en·do·chon·dral \,en-də-'kän-drəl\ *adj* (1882) : relating to, formed by, or being ossification that takes place from centers arising in cartilage and involves deposition of lime salts in the carti-

endocarp (cross section of a cherry): *1* exocarp, *2* mesocarp, *3* endocarp, *4* seed; *1, 2,* and *3* together form the pericarp

---

\a\ abut \ᵊ\ kitten, F table \ər\ further \a\ ash \ā\ ace \ä\ mop, mar \au̇\ out \ch\ chin \e\ bet \ē\ easy \g\ go \i\ hit \ī\ ice \j\ job \ŋ\ sing \ō\ go \ȯ\ law \ȯi\ boy \th\ thin \th\ the \ü\ loot \u̇\ foot \y\ yet \zh\ vision \à, k̲, ⁿ, œ, œ̄, ᵾ, ᵫ, ᵞ\ see Guide to Pronunciation lage matrix followed by secondary absorption and replacement by true bony tissue

en·do·cra·ni·al cast \en-də-ˌkrā-nē-əl-\ n (1923) : a cast of the cranial cavity showing the approximate shape of the brain

¹en·do·crine \ˈen-də-krən, -ˌkrīn, -ˌkrēn\ adj [ISV end- + Gk krinein to separate — more at CERTAIN] (ca. 1911) **1** : secreting internally; specif : producing secretions that are distributed in the body by way of the bloodstream ⟨an ~ system⟩ **2** : of, relating to, affecting, or resembling an endocrine gland or secretion ⟨~ tumors⟩

²endocrine n (1922) **1** : HORMONE **2** : ENDOCRINE GLAND

endocrine gland n (1914) : a gland (as the thyroid or the pituitary) that produces an endocrine secretion — called also ductless gland

en·do·cri·no·log·ic \ˌen-də-ˌkri-nᵊl-ˈä-jik, -ˌkri-, -ˌkrē-\ or **en·do·cri·no·log·i·cal** \-ji-kəl\ adj (ca. 1934) : involving or relating to the endocrine glands or secretions or to endocrinology

en·do·cri·nol·o·gy \ˌen-də-kri-ˈnä-lə-jē, -ˌkri-\ n [ISV] (ca. 1913) : a science dealing with the endocrine glands — **en·do·cri·nol·o·gist** \-jist\ n

en·do·cy·to·sis \-sī-ˈtō-səs\ n [NL, fr. end- + -cytosis (as in phagocytosis)] (1963) : incorporation of substances into a cell by phagocytosis or pinocytosis — **en·do·cy·tot·ic** \-ˈtä-tik\ adj

en·do·derm \ˈen-də-ˌdərm\ n [F endoderme, fr. end- + Gk derma skin — more at DERM-] (1861) : the innermost of the germ layers of an embryo that is the source of the epithelium of the digestive tract and its derivatives; also : a tissue that is derived from this germ layer — compare HYPOBLAST — **en·do·der·mal** \ˌen-də-ˈdər-məl\ adj

en·do·der·mis \ˌen-də-ˈdər-məs\ n [NL] (1884) : the innermost tissue of the cortex in many roots and stems

end·odon·tics \ˈdän-tiks\ n pl but sing in constr [end- + odont- + -ics] (1946) : a branch of dentistry concerned with diseases of the pulp — **end·odon·tic** \-ˈdän-tik\ adj — **end·odon·ti·cal·ly** \-ˈdän-ti-k(ə-)lē\ adv — **end·odon·tist** \-ˈdän-tist\ n

en·do·en·zyme \ˌen-dō-ˈen-ˌzīm\ n [ISV] (ca. 1909) : an enzyme that functions inside the cell

en·do·er·gic \ˌen-dō-ˈər-jik\ adj (1940) : absorbing energy : ENDOTHERMIC ⟨~ nuclear reactions⟩

en·dog·a·my \en-ˈdä-gə-mē\ n (1865) : marriage within a specific group as required by custom or law — **en·dog·a·mous** \-məs\ adj

en·do·gen·ic \ˌen-də-ˈje-nik\ adj (ca. 1904) **1** : of or relating to metamorphism taking place within a planet or moon **2** : ENDOGENOUS

en·dog·e·nous \en-ˈdä-jə-nəs\ adj (1830) **1** : growing or produced by growth from deep tissue ⟨~ plant roots⟩ **2 a** : caused by factors inside the organism or system ⟨an ~ psychic depression⟩ ⟨~ business cycles⟩ **b** : produced or synthesized within the organism or system ⟨an ~ hormone⟩ — **en·dog·e·nous·ly** adv

en·do·lith·ic \ˌen-də-ˈli-thik\ adj (1886) : living within or penetrating deeply into stony substances (as rocks, coral, or mollusk shells) ⟨~ lichens⟩

en·do·lymph \ˈen-də-ˌlim(p)f\ n [ISV] (ca. 1839) : the watery fluid in the membranous labyrinth of the ear — **en·do·lym·phat·ic** \ˌen-də-lim-ˈfa-tik\ adj

en·do·me·tri·osis \ˌen-dō-ˌmē-trē-ˈō-səs\ n [NL] (1925) : the presence and growth of functioning endometrial tissue in places other than the uterus that often results in severe pain and infertility

en·do·me·tri·tis \ˌen-dō-mə-ˈtrī-təs\ n [NL] (1872) : inflammation of the endometrium

en·do·me·tri·um \-ˈmē-trē-əm\ n, pl **-tria** \-trē-ə\ [NL, fr. end- + Gk mētra uterus, fr. mētr-, mētēr mother — more at MOTHER] (ca. 1882) : the mucous membrane lining the uterus — **en·do·me·tri·al** \-trē-əl\ adj

en·do·mi·to·sis \-mī-ˈtō-səs\ n [NL] (1942) : division of chromosomes not followed by nuclear division that results in an increased number of chromosomes in the cell — **en·do·mi·tot·ic** \-mī-ˈtä-tik\ adj

en·do·mix·is \-ˈmik-səs\ n [NL, fr. end- + Gk mixis act of mixing, fr. mignynai to mix — more at MIX] (1914) : a periodic nuclear reorganization in ciliated protozoans

en·do·morph \ˈen-də-ˌmȯrf\ n [endoderm + -morph] (1940) : an endomorphic individual

en·do·mor·phic \ˌen-də-ˈmȯr-fik\ adj [endoderm + -morphic; fr. the predominance in such types of structures developed from the endoderm] (1940) **1** : of or relating to the component in W. H. Sheldon's classification of body types that measures the massiveness of the digestive viscera and the body's degree of roundedness and softness **2** : having a heavy rounded body build often with a marked tendency to become fat — **en·do·mor·phy** \ˈen-də-ˌmȯr-fē\ n

en·do·mor·phism \ˌen-də-ˈmȯr-ˌfi-zəm\ n (1909) : a homomorphism that maps a mathematical set into itself — compare ISOMORPHISM

en·do·nu·cle·ase \ˌen-dō-ˈnü-klē-ˌās, -ˌāz, -ˈnyü-\ n (1962) : an enzyme that breaks down a nucleotide chain into two or more shorter chains by cleaving it at points not adjacent to the end — compare EXONUCLEASE

en·do·nu·cleo·lyt·ic \-ˌnü-klē-ō-ˈli-tik, -ˌnyü-\ adj [end- + nucleo- + -lytic] (1967) : cleaving a nucleotide chain at an internal point ⟨~ nicks⟩

en·do·par·a·site \-ˈpar-ə-ˌsīt\ n [ISV] (ca. 1882) : a parasite that lives in the internal organs or tissues of its host — **en·do·par·a·sit·ic** \-ˌpar-ə-ˈsi-tik\ adj — **en·do·par·a·sit·ism** \-ˈpar-ə-ˌsī-ˌti-zəm, -sə-ˌti-\ n

en·do·pep·ti·dase \-ˈpep-tə-ˌdās, -ˌdāz\ n (1936) : any of a group of enzymes that hydrolyze peptide bonds within the long chains of protein molecules : PROTEASE — compare EXOPEPTIDASE

en·do·per·ox·ide \-pə-ˈräk-ˌsīd\ n (1962) : any of various biosynthetic intermediates in the formation of prostaglandins

en·do·phyte \ˈen-də-ˌfīt\ n [ISV] (1854) : a plant living within another plant — **en·do·phyt·ic** \ˌen-də-ˈfi-tik\ adj

en·do·plasm \ˈen-də-ˌpla-zəm\ n [ISV] (1882) : the inner relatively fluid part of the cytoplasm — **en·do·plas·mic** \ˌen-də-ˈplaz-mik\ adj

endoplasmic reticulum n (1947) : a system of interconnected vesicular and lamellar cytoplasmic membranes that functions esp. in the transport of materials within the cell and that is studded with ribosomes in some places — see CELL illustration

en·do·po·dite \en-ˈdä-pə-ˌdīt\ n [ISV] (1870) : the mesial or internal branch of a typical limb of a crustacean

en·do·poly·ploidy \ˌen-dō-ˈpä-li-ˌplȯi-dē\ n (1945) : a polyploid state in which the chromosomes have divided repeatedly without subsequent division of the nucleus or cell — **en·do·poly·ploid** \-ˌplȯid\ adj

end organ n (1878) : a structure forming the end of a neural path and consisting of an effector or a receptor with its associated nerve terminations

en·dor·phin \en-ˈdȯr-fən\ n [ISV endogenous + morphine] (1976) : any of a group of proteins with potent analgesic properties that occur naturally in the brain — compare ENKEPHALIN

en·dorse \in-ˈdȯrs, en-\ vt **en·dorsed; en·dors·ing** [alter. of obs. endoss, fr. ME endosen, fr. MF endosser, fr. OF, to put on the back, fr. en- + dos back, fr. L dorsum] (1581) **1 a** : to write on the back of; esp : to sign one's name as payee on the back of (a check) in order to obtain the cash or credit represented on the face **b** : to inscribe (one's signature) on a check, bill, or note **c** : to inscribe (as an official document) with a title or memorandum **d** : to make over to another (the value represented in a check, bill, or note) by inscribing one's name on the document **e** : to acknowledge receipt of (a sum specified) by one's signature on a document **2** : to approve openly ⟨~ an idea⟩; esp : to express support or approval of publicly and definitely ⟨~ a mayoral candidate⟩ syn see APPROVE — **en·dors·able** \-ˈdȯr-sə-bəl\ adj — **en·dors·ee** \in-ˌdȯr-ˈsē, ˌen-\ n — **en·dors·er** \in-ˈdȯr-sər\ n

en·dorse·ment \in-ˈdȯr-smənt, en-\ n (1547) **1** : the act or process of endorsing **2 a** : something that is written in the process of endorsing **b** : a provision added to an insurance contract altering its scope or application **3** : SANCTION, APPROVAL

en·do·scope \ˈen-də-ˌskōp\ n [ISV] (1861) : an instrument for visualizing the interior of a hollow organ (as the rectum or urethra) — **en·dos·co·py** \en-ˈdäs-kə-pē\ n

en·do·scop·ic \ˌen-də-ˈskä-pik\ adj (1861) : of, relating to, or performed by means of an endoscope or endoscopy — **en·do·scop·i·cal·ly** \-pi-k(ə-)lē\ adv

en·do·skel·e·ton \ˌen-dō-ˈske-lə-tᵊn\ n (ca. 1847) : an internal skeleton or supporting framework in an animal — **en·do·skel·e·tal** \-lə-tᵊl\ adj

en·do·sperm \ˈen-də-ˌspərm\ n [F endosperme, fr. end- + Gk sperma seed — more at SPERM] (ca. 1850) : a nutritive tissue in seed plants formed within the embryo sac

endosperm nucleus n (ca. 1902) : the triploid nucleus formed in the embryo sac of a seed plant by fusion of a sperm nucleus with two polar nuclei or with a nucleus formed by the prior fusion of the polar nuclei

en·do·spore \ˈen-dō-ˌspȯr, -ˌspȯr\ n [ISV] (1875) : an asexual spore developed within the cell esp. in bacteria

end·os·te·al \en-ˈdäs-tē-əl\ adj (ca. 1868) **1** : of or relating to the endosteum **2** : located within bone or cartilage — **end·os·te·al·ly** adv

end·os·te·um \en-ˈdäs-tē-əm\ n, pl **-tea** \-tē-ə\ [NL, fr. end- + Gk osteon bone — more at OSSEOUS] (ca. 1881) : the layer of vascular connective tissue lining the medullary cavities of bone

en·do·style \ˈen-dō-ˌstīl\ n [ISV end- + Gk stylos pillar — more at STEER] (1854) : a pair of parallel longitudinal folds projecting into the pharyngeal cavity and bounding a furrow lined with glandular ciliated cells in lower chordates (as the tunicates)

en·do·sul·fan \ˌen-dō-ˈsȯl-fən, -ˌfan\ n [endo- + sulf- + ³-an] (1962) : a brownish crystalline insecticide $C_9H_6Cl_6O_3S$ that is used in the control of numerous crop insects and some mites

en·do·sym·bi·o·sis \ˌen-dō-ˌsim-bī-ˈō-səs, -bē-\ n (ca. 1940) : symbiosis in which a symbiont dwells within the body of its symbiotic partner — **en·do·sym·bi·ont** \-ˈsim-bī-ˌänt, -bē-\ n — **en·do·sym·bi·ot·ic** \-ˌsim-bī-ˈä-tik, -bē-\ adj

en·do·the·ci·um \ˌen-dō-ˈthē-s(h)ē-əm\ n, pl **-cia** \-s(h)ē-ə\ [NL] (1832) : the inner lining of a mature anther

en·do·the·li·o·ma \-ˌthē-lē-ˈō-mə\ n, pl **-o·mas** or **-o·ma·ta** \-mə-tə\ [NL] (1880) : a tumor developing from endothelial tissue

en·do·the·li·um \ˌen-də-ˈthē-lē-əm\ n, pl **-lia** \-lē-ə\ [NL, fr. end- + -thelium (as in epithelium)] (1872) **1** : an epithelium of mesodermal origin composed of a single layer of thin flattened cells that lines internal body cavities **2** : the inner layer of the seed coat of some plants — **en·do·the·li·al** \-lē-əl\ adj

en·do·therm \ˈen-dō-ˌthərm\ n (1946) : a warm-blooded animal

en·do·ther·mic \ˌen-dō-ˈthər-mik\ adj [ISV] (1884) **1** : characterized by or formed with absorption of heat **2** : WARM-BLOODED

en·do·ther·my \ˈen-dō-ˌthər-mē\ n (1922) : physiological regulation of body temperature by metabolic means; esp : the property or state of being warm-blooded

en·do·tox·in \ˌen-dō-ˈtäk-sən\ n [ISV] (1904) : a toxin of internal origin; specif : a poisonous substance present in bacteria (as the causative agent of typhoid fever) but separable from the cell body only on its disintegration — **en·do·tox·ic** \-sik\ adj

en·do·tra·che·al \-ˈträ-kē-əl\ adj (1910) **1** : placed within the trachea ⟨an ~ tube⟩ **2** : applied or effected through the trachea

en·do·tro·phic \ˌen-də-ˈtrō-fik\ adj (1899) of a mycorrhiza : penetrating into the associated root and ramifying between the cells — compare ECTOTROPHIC

en·dow \in-ˈdau̇, en-\ vt [ME, fr. AF endouer, fr. MF en- + douer to endow, fr. L dotare, fr. dot-, dos gift, dowry — more at DATE] (15c) **1** : to furnish with an income; esp : to make a grant of money providing for the continuing support or maintenance of ⟨~ a hospital⟩ **2** : to furnish with a dower **3** : to provide with something freely or naturally ⟨~ed with a good sense of humor⟩

en·dow·ment \-mənt\ n (15c) **1** : the act or process of endowing **2** : something that is endowed; specif : the part of an institution's income derived from donations **3** : natural capacity, power, or ability

end·pa·per \ˈen(d)-ˌpā-pər\ n (1818) : a once-folded sheet of paper having one leaf pasted flat against the inside of the front or back cover of a book and the other pasted at the base to the first or last page

end plate n (1878) : a complex terminal treelike branching of a motor nerve cell

end point n (1899) **1** : a point marking the completion of a process or stage of a process; esp : a point in a titration at which a definite effect (as a color change) is observed **2** usu **end·point** : either of two points or values that mark the ends of a line segment or interval; also : a point that marks the end of a ray

en·drin \ˈen-drən\ n [end- + dieldrin] (1952) : a chlorinated hydrocarbon insecticide $C_{12}H_8Cl_6O$ that is a stereoisomer of dieldrin and resembles dieldrin in toxicity

end run n (1902) **1** : a football play in which the ballcarrier attempts to run wide around the end of the line; specif : SWEEP 3e **2** : an evasive trick or maneuver

end–stopped \'en(d)-ˌstäpt\ *adj* (1877) : marked by a logical or rhetorical pause at the end ⟨an ∼ line of verse⟩ — compare RUN-ON

end table *n* (1851) : a small table usu. about the height of the arm of a chair that is used beside a larger piece of furniture (as a sofa)

en·due \in-'dü, -'dyü, en-\ *vt* **en·dued; en·du·ing** [ME, fr. MF *enduire* to bring in, introduce, fr. L *inducere* — more at INDUCE] (15c) 1 : PROVIDE, ENDOW 2 : IMBUE, TRANSFUSE 3 [ME *induen;* influenced by L *induere* to put on] : PUT ON, DON

en·dur·able \in-'dúr-ə-bəl, -'dyúr-, en-\ *adj* (1800) : capable of being endured : BEARABLE — **en·dur·ably** \-blē\ *adv*

en·dur·ance \in-'dúr-ən(t)s, -'dyúr-, en-\ *n* (15c) 1 : PERMANENCE, DURATION 2 : the ability to withstand hardship or adversity; *esp* : the ability to sustain a prolonged stressful effort or activity ⟨a marathon runner's ∼⟩ 3 : the act or an instance of enduring or suffering ⟨∼ of many hardships⟩

en·dure \in-'dúr, -'dyúr, en-\ *vb* **en·dured; en·dur·ing** [ME, fr. MF *endurer,* fr. (assumed) VL *indurare,* fr. L, to harden, fr. *in-* + *durare* to harden, endure — more at DURING] *vt* (14c) 1 : to undergo (as a hardship) esp. without giving in : SUFFER 2 : to regard with acceptance or tolerance ⟨could not ∼ noisy children⟩ ∼ *vi* 1 : to continue in the same state : LAST 2 : to remain firm under suffering or misfortune without yielding — *syn* see BEAR, CONTINUE

en·dur·ing *adj* (15c) : LASTING, DURABLE — **en·dur·ing·ly** \-'d(y)úr-iŋ-lē\ *adv* — **en·dur·ing·ness** *n*

en·duro \in-'dúr-(ˌ)ō, -'dyúr-\ *n, pl* **en·dur·os** [*endurance* + *-o* (It or Sp masc. n. ending)] (1935) : a long race (as for automobiles or motorcycles) stressing endurance rather than speed

end user *n* (ca. 1945) : the ultimate consumer of a finished product

end·ways \'en-ˌdwāz\ *adv or adj* (ca. 1608) 1 : in or toward the direction of the ends : LENGTHWISE ⟨∼ pressure⟩ 2 : with the end forward (as toward the observer) 3 : on end : UPRIGHT ⟨boxes set ∼⟩

end·wise \'en-ˌdwīz\ *adv or adj* (1657) : ENDWAYS

En·dym·i·on \en-'di-mē-ən\ *n* [L, fr. Gk *Endymiōn*] : a beautiful youth loved by Selene in Greek mythology

end zone *n* (ca. 1916) : the area at either end of a football field between the goal line and the end line

-ene \ˌēn\ *n suffix* [ISV, fr. Gk *-ēnē,* fem. of *-ēnos,* adj. suffix] : unsaturated carbon compound ⟨benzene⟩; *esp* : carbon compound with one double bond ⟨ethylene⟩

en·e·ma \'e-nə-mə\ *n, pl* **enemas** *also* **ene·ma·ta** \e-nə-'mä-tə, 'e-nə-mə-tə\ [LL, fr. Gk, fr. *enienai* to inject, fr. *en-* + *hienai* to send — more at JET] (15c) 1 : the injection of liquid into the intestine by way of the anus 2 : material for injection as an enema

en·e·my \'e-nə-mē\ *n, pl* **-mies** [ME *enemi,* fr. OF, fr. L *inimicus,* fr. *in-* + *amicus* friend — more at AMIABLE] (13c) 1 : one that is antagonistic to another; *esp* : one seeking to injure, overthrow, or confound an opponent 2 : something harmful or deadly 3 **a** : a military adversary **b** : a hostile unit or force

en·er·get·ic \ˌe-nər-'je-tik\ *adj* [Gk *energētikos,* fr. *energein* to be active, fr. *energos*] (1651) 1 : operating with or marked by vigor or effect 2 : marked by energy : STRENUOUS 3 : of or relating to energy ⟨∼ equation⟩ *syn* see VIGOROUS — **en·er·get·i·cal·ly** \-ti-k(ə-)lē\ *adv*

en·er·get·ics \-tiks\ *n pl but sing in constr* (1855) 1 : a branch of mechanics that deals primarily with energy and its transformations 2 : the total energy relations and transformations of a physical, chemical, or biological system ⟨the ∼ of an ecological community⟩

en·er·gise *Brit var of* ENERGIZE

en·er·gize \'e-nər-ˌjīz\ *vb* **-gized; -giz·ing** *vi* (1752) : to put forth energy : ACT ∼ *vt* 1 : to make energetic, vigorous, or active 2 : to impart energy to 3 : to apply voltage to — **en·er·gi·za·tion** \ˌe-nər-ˌji-'zā-shən\ *n* — **en·er·giz·er** *n*

en·er·gy \'e-nər-jē\ *n, pl* **-gies** [LL *energia,* fr. Gk *energeia* activity, fr. *energos* active, fr. *en* in + *ergon* work — more at WORK] (1599) 1 **a** : dynamic quality ⟨narrative ∼⟩ **b** : the capacity of acting or being active ⟨intellectual ∼⟩ 2 : vigorous exertion of power : EFFORT ⟨investing time and ∼⟩ 3 : the capacity for doing work : usable power (as heat or electricity); *also* : the resources for producing such power *syn* see POWER

energy level *n* (1910) : one of the stable states of constant energy that may be assumed by a physical system — used esp. of the quantum states of electrons in atoms and of nuclei; called also *energy state*

[1]**ener·vate** \i-'nər-vət\ *adj* (1603) : lacking physical, mental, or moral vigor : ENERVATED

[2]**en·er·vate** \'e-nər-ˌvāt\ *vt* **-vat·ed; -vat·ing** [L *enervatus,* pp. of *enervare,* fr. *e-* + *nervus* sinew — more at NERVE] (1614) 1 : to reduce the mental or moral vigor of 2 : to lessen the vitality or strength of *syn* see UNNERVE — **en·er·va·tion** \ˌe-nər-'vā-shən\ *n*

en·fant ter·ri·ble \äⁿ-fäⁿ-te-rēblᵊ\ *n, pl* **enfants terribles** \same\ [F, lit., terrifying child] (1851) 1 **a** : a child whose inopportune remarks cause embarrassment **b** : a person known for shocking remarks or outrageous behavior 2 : a usu. young and successful person who is strikingly unorthodox, innovative, or avant-garde

en·fee·ble \in-'fē-bəl, en-\ *vt* **en·fee·bled; en·fee·bling** \-b(ə-)liŋ\ [ME *enfeblen,* fr. MF *enfeblir,* fr. OF, fr. *en-* + *feble* feeble] (14c) : to make feeble : deprive of strength *syn* see WEAKEN — **en·fee·ble·ment** \-mənt\ *n*

en·feoff \in-'fef, -'fēf, en-\ *vt* [ME *enfeoffen,* fr. AF *enfeoffer,* fr. OF *en-* + *fief* fief] (15c) : to invest with a fief or fee — **en·feoff·ment** \-mənt\ *n*

en·fet·ter \in-'fe-tər, en-\ *vt* (1599) : to bind in fetters : ENCHAIN

en·fe·ver \in-'fē-vər, en-\ *vt* (1647) : FEVER

En·field rifle \'en-ˌfēld-\ *n* [*Enfield,* England] (1854) : a .30 caliber bolt-action repeating rifle used by U.S. and British troops in World War I

[1]**en·fi·lade** \'en-fə-ˌlād, -ˌläd\ *n* [F, fr. *enfiler* to thread, enfilade, fr. OF, to thread, fr. *en-* + *fil* thread — more at FILE] (ca. 1730) 1 : an interconnected group of rooms arranged usu. in a row with each room opening into the next 2 : gunfire directed from a flanking position along the length of an enemy battle line

[2]**enfilade** *vt* **-lad·ed; -lad·ing** (1706) : to rake or be in a position to rake with gunfire in a lengthwise direction

enflame *var of* INFLAME

en·fleu·rage \ˌäⁿ-flər-'äzh\ *n* [F, fr. *enfleurer* to saturate with the perfume of flowers, fr. *en-* ¹*en-* + *fleur* flower, fr. OF *flor* — more at

FLOWER] (1855) : a process of extracting perfumes by exposing absorbents to the exhalations of flowers

en·fold \in-'fōld, en-\ *vt* (ca. 1674) 1 **a** : to cover with or as if with folds : ENVELOP **b** : to surround with a covering : CONTAIN 2 : to clasp within the arms : EMBRACE

en·force \in-'fōrs, -'fors, en-\ *vt* [ME, fr. MF *enforcier,* fr. OF, fr. *en-* + *force* force] (14c) 1 : to give force to : STRENGTHEN 2 : to urge with energy 3 : CONSTRAIN, COMPEL 4 *obs* : to effect or gain by force 5 : to carry out effectively ⟨∼ laws⟩ — **en·force·abil·i·ty** \-ˌfōr-sə-'bi-lə-tē, -ˌfor-\ *n* — **en·force·able** \-'fōr-sə-bəl, -'for-\ *adj* — **en·force·ment** \-'fōr-smənt, -'for-\ *n*

en·forc·er \in-'fōr-sər, -'for-\ *n* (1580) : one that enforces 2 **a** : a violent criminal employed by a crime syndicate; *esp* : HIT MAN 1 **b** : an aggressive player (as in ice hockey) known for rough play and fighting

en·frame \in-'frām, en-\ *vt* (1848) : FRAME 6 — **en·frame·ment** \-'frām-mənt\ *n*

en·fran·chise \in-'fran-ˌchīz, en-\ *vt* **-chised; -chis·ing** [ME, fr. MF *enfranchiss-,* stem of *enfranchir,* fr. OF, fr. *en-* + *franc* free — more at FRANK] (15c) 1 : to set free (as from slavery) 2 : to endow with a franchise: as **a** : to admit to the privileges of a citizen and esp. to the right of suffrage **b** : to admit (a municipality) to political privileges or rights — **en·fran·chise·ment** \-ˌchīz-mənt, -chəz-\ *n*

en·gage \in-'gāj, en-\ *vb* **en·gaged; en·gag·ing** [ME, fr. MF *engagier,* fr. OF, fr. *en-* + *gage* token, gage] *vt* (15c) 1 **a** : to offer (as one's word) as security for a debt or cause 2 **a** *obs* : to entangle or entrap in or as if in a snare or bog **b** : to attract and hold by influence or power **c** : to interlock with : MESH; *also* : to cause (mechanical parts) to mesh 3 : to bind (as oneself) to do something; *esp* : to bind by a pledge to marry 4 **a** : to provide occupation for : INVOLVE ⟨∼ him in a new project⟩ **b** : to arrange to obtain the use or services of : HIRE 5 **a** : to hold the attention of : ENGROSS ⟨her work ∼s her completely⟩ **b** : to induce to participate ⟨*engaged* the shy boy in conversation⟩ 6 **a** : to enter into contest with **b** : to bring together or interlock (weapons) 7 : to deal with esp. at length ∼ *vi* 1 **a** : to pledge oneself : PROMISE **b** : GUARANTEE ⟨he ∼s for the honesty of his brother⟩ 2 **a** : to begin and carry on an enterprise or activity ⟨*engaged* in trade for a number of years⟩ **b** : to take part : PARTICIPATE ⟨at college she *engaged* in gymnastics⟩ 3 : to enter into conflict 4 : to come together and interlock (as of machinery parts) : to be or become in gear

en·ga·gé \ˌäⁿ-ˌgä-'zhā\ *adj* [F, pp. of *engager* to engage, fr. MF *engagier*] (1946) : committed to or supportive of a cause

en·gaged \in-'gājd, en-\ *adj* (1665) 1 : involved in activity : OCCUPIED 2 : pledged to be married : BETROTHED 3 : greatly interested : COMMITTED 4 : involved esp. in a hostile encounter 5 : partly embedded in a wall ⟨an ∼ column⟩ 6 : being in gear : MESHED

en·gage·ment \in-'gāj-mənt, en-\ *n* (1601) 1 **a** : an arrangement to meet or be present at a specified time and place ⟨a dinner ∼⟩ **b** : a job or period of employment esp. as a performer 2 : something that engages : PLEDGE 3 **a** : the act of engaging : the state of being engaged **b** : emotional involvement or commitment ⟨seesaws between obsessive ∼ and ambiguous detachment —Gary Taylor⟩ **c** : BETROTHAL 4 : the state of being in gear 5 : a hostile encounter between military forces

en·gag·ing *adj* (1673) : tending to draw favorable attention : ATTRACTIVE — **en·gag·ing·ly** \-'gā-jiŋ-lē\ *adv*

en·gar·land \in-'gär-lənd, en-\ *vt* (1581) : to adorn with or as if with a garland

En·gel·mann spruce \ˌeŋ-gəl-mən-\ *n* [George *Engelmann* †1884 Am. botanist] (1908) : a large spruce (*Picea engelmannii*) of the Rocky mountain region and British Columbia that yields a light-colored wood

en·gen·der \in-'jen-dər, en-\ *vb* **en·gen·dered; en·gen·der·ing** \-d(ə-)riŋ\ [ME *engendren,* fr. MF *engendrer,* fr. L *ingenerare,* fr. *in-* + *generare* to generate] *vt* (14c) 1 : BEGET, PROCREATE 2 : to cause to exist or to develop : PRODUCE ⟨angry words ∼ strife⟩ ∼ *vi* : to assume form : ORIGINATE

en·gild \in-'gild, en-\ *vt* (15c) : to make bright with or as if with light

[1]**en·gine** \'en-jən\ *n* [ME *engin,* fr. MF, fr. L *ingenium* natural disposition, talent, fr. *in-* + *gignere* to beget — more at KIN] (13c) 1 *obs* **a** : INGENUITY **b** : evil contrivance : WILE 2 : something used to effect a purpose : AGENT, INSTRUMENT ⟨mournful and terrible ∼ of horror and of crime —E. A. Poe⟩ 3 **a** : a mechanical tool: as (1) : an instrument or machine of war (2) *obs* : a torture implement **b** : MACHINERY **c** : any of various mechanical appliances — often used in combination ⟨fire ∼⟩ 4 : a machine for converting any of various forms of energy into mechanical force and motion; *also* : a mechanism or object that serves as an energy source ⟨black holes may be the ∼s for quasars⟩ 5 : a railroad locomotive

[2]**engine** *vt* **en·gined; en·gin·ing** (1868) : to equip with engines

engine driver *n* (1828) *Brit* : ENGINEER 4

[1]**en·gi·neer** \ˌen-jə-'nir\ *n* [alter. of earlier *enginer,* fr. ME, alter. of *enginour,* fr. MF *engigneour,* fr. OF *enginier* to contrive, fr. *engin*] (14c) 1 : a member of a military group devoted to engineering work 2 *obs* : a crafty schemer : PLOTTER 3 **a** : a designer or builder of engines **b** : a person who is trained in or follows as a profession a branch of engineering **c** : a person who carries through an enterprise by skillful or artful contrivance 4 : a person who runs or supervises an engine or an apparatus

[2]**engineer** *vt* (1843) 1 : to lay out, construct, or manage as an engineer 2 : to contrive or plan out usu. with more or less subtle skill and craft **b** : to guide the course of 3 : to modify or produce by genetic engineering ⟨grain crops ∼ed to require fewer nutrients and produce higher yields⟩ *syn* see GUIDE

en·gi·neer·ing *n* (1720) 1 : the activities or function of an engineer 2 **a** : the application of science and mathematics by which the properties of matter and the sources of energy in nature are made useful to people **b** : the design and manufacture of complex products ⟨software ∼⟩ 3

\ə\ abut \ᵊ\ kitten, F table \ər\ further \a\ ash \ā\ ace \ä\ mop, mar \aú\ out \ch\ chin \e\ bet \ē\ easy \g\ go \i\ hit \ī\ ice \j\ job \ŋ\ sing \ō\ go \ó\ law \ói\ boy \th\ thin \t̷h\ the \ü\ loot \ú\ foot \y\ yet \zh\ vision \à, k̲, ⁿ, œ, œ̄, œ, ūe, ᵊ\ *see* Guide to Pronunciation

: calculated manipulation or direction (as of behavior) ⟨social ∼⟩ — compare GENETIC ENGINEERING

en·gine·ry \'en-jən-rē\ n (1641) : instruments of war

en·gird \in-'gərd, en-\ vt (1566) archaic : GIRD, ENCOMPASS

en·gir·dle \in-'gər-d²l, en-\ vt (1602) : to encircle with or as if with a girdle

¹**En·glish** \'iŋ-glish, 'iŋ-lish\ adj [ME, fr. OE englisc, fr. Engle (pl.) Angles] (bef. 12c) : of, relating to, or characteristic of England, the English people, or the English language — **En·glish·ness** n

²**English** n (bef. 12c) **1 a** : the language of the people of England and the U.S. and many areas now or formerly under British control **b** : a particular variety of English distinguished by peculiarities (as of pronunciation) **c** : English language, literature, or composition when a subject of study **2** pl in constr : the people of England **3 a** : an English translation **b** : idiomatic or intelligible English **4** : spin around the vertical axis deliberately imparted to a ball that is driven or rolled — compare DRAW, FOLLOW; BODY ENGLISH

³**English** vt (14c) **1** : to translate into English **2** : to adopt into English : ANGLICIZE

English breakfast n (1807) **1** : a substantial breakfast (as of eggs, ham or bacon, toast, and cereal) **2** : CONGOU; broadly : any similar black tea

English cocker spaniel n (1948) : any of a breed of spaniels that have square muzzles, wide well-developed noses, and distinctive heads which are ideally half muzzle and half skull with the forehead and skull arched and slightly flattened

English daisy n (ca. 1890) : DAISY 1a

English foxhound n (1929) : any of a breed of medium-sized foxhounds developed in England and characterized by a muscular body, bi- or tri-colored short coat, and lightly fringed tail

English cocker spaniel

English horn n [trans. of It corno inglese] (1838) : a double-reed wood-wind instrument resembling the oboe in design but having a longer tube and a range a fifth lower than that of the oboe

English ivy n (1624) : IVY 1

En·glish·man \'iŋ-glish-mən, 'iŋ-lish-\ n (bef. 12c) : a native or inhabitant of England

English muffin n (1902) : bread dough rolled and cut into rounds, baked on a griddle, and split and toasted just before eating

English pea n (1634) Southern : PEA 1a, b

En·glish·ry \'iŋ-glish-rē, 'iŋ-lish-\ n (1620) : the state, fact, or quality of being English : ENGLISHNESS

English saddle n (1817) : a saddle with long side bars, steel cantle and pommel, no horn, and a leather seat supported by webbing stretched between the saddlebow and cantle — see SADDLE illustration

English setter n (1859) : any of a breed of dogs often trained as bird dogs and characterized by a moderately long flat silky coat of white or white with color and by feathering on the tail and legs

English shepherd n (1950) : any of a breed of vigorous medium-sized working dogs with a long and glossy black coat usu. with tan to brown markings that was developed in England for herding sheep and cattle

English sonnet n (ca. 1903) : a sonnet consisting of three quatrains and a couplet with a rhyme scheme of abab cdcd efef gg — called also Shakespearean sonnet

English sparrow n (1876) : HOUSE SPARROW

English springer spaniel n (1929) : any of a breed of springer spaniels having a muscular build and a moderately long silky coat usu. of black and white or liver and white hair — called also English springer

English system n (1927) : the foot-pound-second system of units

English toy spaniel n (ca. 1934) : any of a breed of small blocky spaniels with well-rounded upper skull projecting forward toward the short turned-up nose

English walnut n (1772) : a Eurasian walnut (Juglans regia) valued for its large edible nut and its hard richly figured wood; also : its nut

En·glish·wom·an \'iŋ-glish-ˌwu̇-mən also 'iŋ-lish-\ n (15c) : a woman of English birth, nationality, or origin

English yew n (ca. 1887) : YEW 1a(1)

en·gorge \in-'gȯrj, en-\ vb [MF engorgier, fr. OF, to devour, fr. en- + gorge throat — more at GORGE] vt (1515) : GORGE, GLUT; esp : to fill with blood to the point of congestion ∼ vi : to suck blood to the limit of body capacity — **en·gorge·ment** \-mənt\ n

en·graft \in-'graft, en-\ vt (1585) **1** : to join or fasten as if by grafting **2** : GRAFT 1, 3 ⟨∼ed embryonic gill tissue into the back⟩ — **en·graft·ment** \-'graf(t)-mənt\ n

en·grailed \in-'grāld, en-\ adj [ME engreled, fr. MF engreslé, fr. en- + gresle slender, fr. L gracilis] (15c) **1** : indented with small concave curves ⟨an ∼ heraldic bordure⟩ **2** : made of or bordered by a circle of raised dots ⟨an ∼ coin⟩

en·grain \in-'grān\ vt (ca. 1641) : INGRAIN

en·gram also **en·gramme** \'en-ˌgram\ n [ISV] (1908) : a hypothetical change in neural tissue postulated in order to account for persistence of memory

en·grave \in-'grāv, en-\ vt **en·graved; en·grav·ing** [MF engraver, fr. en- + graver to grave, of Gmc origin; akin to OE grafan to grave] (1509) **1 a** : to form by incision (as on wood or metal) **b** : to impress deeply as if with a graver ⟨the incident was engraved in his memory⟩ **2 a** : to cut figures, letters, or designs on for printing; also : to print from an engraved plate **b** : PHOTOENGRAVE — **en·grav·er** n

en·grav·ing n (1601) **1** : the act or process of one that engraves **2** : something that is engraved: as **a** : an engraved printing surface **b** : engraved work **3** : an impression from an engraved printing surface

en·gross \in-'grōs, en-\ vt [ME, fr. AF engrosser, prob. fr. ML ingrossare, fr. L in + ML grossa large handwriting, fr. L, fem. of grossus thick] (15c) **1 a** : to copy or write in a large hand **b** : to prepare the usu. final handwritten or printed text of (an official document) **2** [ME, fr. MF en gros in large quantities] **a** : to purchase large quantities of (as for speculation) **b** archaic : AMASS, COLLECT **c** : to take or

engage the whole attention of : occupy completely ⟨ideas that have ∼ed the minds of scholars for generations⟩ — **en·gross·er** n

en·gross·ing \-'grō-siŋ\ adj (1820) : taking up the attention completely : ABSORBING — **en·gross·ing·ly** \-siŋ-lē\ adv

en·gross·ment \in-'grōs-mənt, en-\ n (1526) **1** : the act of engrossing **2** : the state of being absorbed or occupied : PREOCCUPATION

en·gulf \in-'gəlf, en-\ vt (1555) **1** : to flow over and enclose : OVER-WHELM ⟨the mounting seas threatened to ∼ the island⟩ **2** : to take in (food) by or as if by flowing over and enclosing — **en·gulf·ment** \-mənt\ n

en·ha·lo \in-'hā-(ˌ)lō, en-\ vt (1842) : to surround with or as if with a halo

en·hance \in-'han(t)s, en-\ vt **en·hanced; en·hanc·ing** [ME enhauncen, fr. AF enhaucer, alter. of OF enhaucier, fr. (assumed) VL inaltiare, fr. L in + altus high — more at OLD] (13c) **1** : RAISE **2** : HEIGHTEN, INCREASE; esp : to increase or improve in value, quality, desirability, or attractiveness — **en·hance·ment** \-'han(t)-smənt\ n

enhanced recovery n (1970) : the extraction of oil from a nearly exhausted well by methods more costly and complex than waterflooding alone

en·hanc·er \in-'han(t)-sər, en-\ n (14c) **1** : one that enhances **2** : a nucleotide sequence that increases the rate of genetic transcription by preferentially increasing the activity of the nearest promoter on the same DNA molecule

en·har·mon·ic \ˌen-(ˌ)här-'mä-nik\ adj [F enharmonique, fr. MF, of a scale employing quarter tones, fr. Gk enarmonios, fr. en + harmonia harmony, scale] (1794) : of, relating to, or being notes that are written differently (as A flat and G sharp) but sound the same in the tempered scale — **en·har·mon·i·cal·ly** \-ni-k(ə-)lē\ adv

enig·ma \i-'nig-mə, e-\ n [L aenigma, fr. Gk ainigmat-, ainigma, fr. ainissesthai to speak in riddles, fr. ainos fable] (15c) **1** : an obscure speech or writing **2** : something hard to understand or explain **3** : an inscrutable or mysterious person syn see MYSTERY

enig·mat·ic \ˌe-(ˌ)nig-'ma-tik also ˌē-(ˌ)nig-\ also **enig·mat·i·cal** \-ti-kəl\ adj (1677) : of, relating to, or resembling an enigma : MYSTERIOUS syn see OBSCURE — **enig·mat·i·cal·ly** \-ti-k(ə-)lē\ adv

en·isle \e-'ī(ə)l, en-\ vt (1612) **1** : to place apart : ISOLATE **2** : to make an island of

en·jamb·ment \in-'jam-mənt\ or **en·jambe·ment** \same or än-zhänb-mäⁿ\ n [F enjambement, fr. MF, encroachment, fr. enjamber to straddle, encroach on, fr. en- + jambe leg — more at JAMB] (1839) : the running over of a sentence from one verse or couplet into another so that closely related words fall in different lines — compare RUN-ON

en·join \in-'jȯin, en-\ vt [ME, fr. OF enjoindre, fr. L injungere, fr. in- + jungere to join — more at YOKE] (13c) **1** : to direct or impose by authoritative order or with urgent admonition ⟨∼ed us to be careful⟩ **2 a** : FORBID, PROHIBIT ⟨was ∼ed by conscience from telling a lie⟩ **b** : to prohibit by a judicial order : put an injunction on ⟨a book had been ∼ed prior to publication —David Margolick⟩ syn see COMMAND

en·joy \in-'jȯi, en-\ vb [ME enjoie, fr. MF enjoir, fr. OF, fr. en- + joir to enjoy, fr. L gaudēre to rejoice — more at JOY] vi (15c) : to have a good time ∼ vt **1** : to have for one's use, benefit, or lot : EXPERIENCE ⟨∼ed great success⟩ **2** : to take pleasure or satisfaction in — **en·joy·able** \-ə-bəl\ adj — **en·joy·able·ness** n — **en·joy·ably** \-blē\ adv — **en·joy·er** n — **enjoy oneself** : to have a good time

en·joy·ment \in-'jȯi-mənt\ n (1553) **1 a** : the action or state of enjoying **b** : possession and use ⟨the ∼ of civic rights⟩ **2** : something that gives keen satisfaction

en·keph·a·lin \in-'ke-fə-lən, -(ˌ)lin, en-\ n [enkephal- (alter. of encephal-) + -in] (1975) : either of two pentapeptides with opiate and analgesic activity that occur naturally in the brain and have a marked affinity for opiate receptors — compare ENDORPHIN

en·kin·dle \in-'kin-d²l, en-\ vt (1542) **1** : to set (as fuel) on fire **2** : to make bright and glowing ∼ vi : to take fire : FLAME

en·lace \in-'lās, en-\ vt [ME, fr. MF enlacier, fr. OF, fr. en- + lacier to lace] (14c) **1** : ENCIRCLE, ENFOLD **2** : ENTWINE, INTERLACE

en·lace·ment \in-'lā-smənt, en-\ n (1830) **1** : the process or result of interlacing **2** : a pattern of interlacing elements

en·large \in-'lärj, en-\ vb **en·larged; en·larg·ing** [ME, fr. MF enlargier, fr. OF, fr. en- + large large, abundant] vt (14c) **1** : to make larger : EXTEND **2** : to give greater scope to : EXPAND **3** : to set free (as a captive) ∼ vi **1** : to grow larger **2** : to speak or write at length : ELABORATE ⟨let me ∼ upon that point⟩ syn see INCREASE — **en·large·able** \-'lär-jə-bəl\ adj — **en·larg·er** n

en·large·ment \in-'lärj-mənt, en-\ n (1540) **1** : an act or instance of enlarging : the state of being enlarged **2** : a photographic print larger than the negative that is made by projecting the negative image through a lens onto a photographic printing surface

en·light·en \in-'lī-t²n, en-\ vt **en·light·ened; en·light·en·ing** \-'līt-niŋ, -t²n-iŋ\ (1587) **1** archaic : ILLUMINATE **2 a** : to furnish knowledge to : INSTRUCT **b** : to give spiritual insight to

en·light·ened adj (1652) **1** : freed from ignorance and misinformation ⟨an ∼ people⟩ **2** : based on full comprehension of the problems involved ⟨issued an ∼ ruling⟩

en·light·en·ment \in-'lī-t²n-mənt, en-\ n (1669) **1** : the act or means of enlightening : the state of being enlightened **2** cap : a philosophic movement of the 18th century marked by a rejection of traditional social, religious, and political ideas and an emphasis on rationalism — used with the **3** Buddhism : a final blessed state marked by the absence of desire or suffering

en·list \in-'list, en-\ vt (1599) **1 a** : to secure the support and aid of : employ in advancing an interest ⟨∼ all the available resources⟩ ⟨∼ the community in an experiment⟩ **b** : to win over : ATTRACT ⟨trying to ∼ my sympathies⟩ **2** : to engage (a person) for duty in the armed forces ∼ vi **1** : to enroll oneself in the armed forces **2** : to participate heartily (as in a cause, drive, or crusade) — **en·list·ee** \-ˌlis-'tē, -'lis-tē\ n — **en·list·ment** \-'lis(t)-mənt\ n

en·list·ed \in-'lis-təd\ adj (1724) : of, relating to, or constituting the part of a military or naval force below commissioned or warrant officers

enlisted man n (1724) : a man or woman in the armed forces ranking below a commissioned or warrant officer; specif : one ranking below a noncommissioned officer or petty officer

en·liv·en \in-'lī-vən, en-\ vt (1604) : to give life, action, or spirit to : ANIMATE syn see QUICKEN

en masse \äⁿ(n)-'mas, -'mäs, en-\ *adv* [F] (1795) : in a body : as a whole

en·mesh \in-'mesh, en-\ *vt* (1604) : to catch or entangle in or as if in meshes — **en·mesh·ment** \-mənt\ *n*

en·mi·ty \'en-mə-tē\ *n, pl* **-ties** [ME *enmite*, fr. MF *enemité*, fr. OF *enemisté*, fr. *enemi* enemy] (13c) : positive, active, and typically mutual hatred or ill will
syn ENMITY, HOSTILITY, ANTIPATHY, ANTAGONISM, ANIMOSITY, RANCOR, ANIMUS mean deep-seated dislike or ill will. ENMITY suggests positive hatred which may be open or concealed ⟨an unspoken *enmity*⟩. HOSTIL-ITY suggests an enmity showing itself in attacks or aggression ⟨*hostility* between the two nations⟩. ANTIPATHY and ANTAGONISM imply a natural or logical basis for one's hatred or dislike, ANTIPATHY suggesting repugnance, a desire to avoid or reject, and ANTAGONISM suggesting a clash of temperaments leading readily to hostility ⟨a natural *antipathy* for self-seekers⟩ ⟨*antagonism* between the brothers⟩. ANIMOSITY suggests intense ill will and vindictiveness that threaten to kindle hostility ⟨*animosity* that led to revenge⟩. RANCOR is esp. applied to bitter brooding over a wrong ⟨*rancor* filled every line of his letters⟩. ANIMUS adds to animosity the implication of strong prejudice ⟨objections devoid of personal *animus*⟩.

en·ne·ad \'e-nē-,ad\ *n* [Gk *ennead-, enneas*, fr. *ennea* nine — more at NINE] (1550) : a group of nine

en·no·ble \i-'nō-bəl, e-'nō-\ *vt* **en·no·bled; en·no·bling** \-b(ə-)liŋ\ [ME *ennobelen*, fr. MF *ennoblir*, fr. OF, fr. *en-* + *noble* noble] (15c) **1** : to make noble : ELEVATE ⟨seemed *ennobled* by suffering⟩ **2** : to raise to the rank of nobility — **en·no·ble·ment** \-bəl-mənt\ *n*

en·nui \,än-'wē\ *n* [F, fr. OF *enui* annoyance, fr. *enuier* to annoy — more at ANNOY] (1732) : a feeling of weariness and dissatisfaction : BOREDOM

Enoch \'ē-nək, -nik\ *n* [Gk *Enōch*, fr. Heb *Ḥănōkh*] : an Old Testament patriarch and father of Methuselah

eno·ki·da·ke \e-,nō-kē-'dä-kē\ *n* [Jp *enokitake*, fr. *enoki* Chinese hackberry (*Celtis sinensis*) + *take* mushroom] (1983) : ENOKI MUSHROOM

enoki mushroom \e-'nō-kē-\ *n* [Jp *enoki*] (ca. 1977) : a small white edible mushroom (*Flammulina velutipes* syn. *Collybia velutipes* of the family Agaricaceae) — called also *enoki*

enol \'ē-,nòl, -,nōl\ *n* [ISV *ene-* (fr. *-ene*) + *-ol*] (1904) : an organic compound that contains a hydroxyl group bonded to a carbon atom having a double bond and that is usu. characterized by the grouping C=C(OH) — **eno·lic** \ē-'nō-lik, -'nä-lik\ *adj*

eno·lase \'ē-nə-,lās, -,lāz\ *n* [ISV *enol* + *-ase*] (1942) : a crystalline enzyme that is found esp. in muscle and yeast and is important in the metabolism of carbohydrates

enol·o·gy \ē-'nä-lə-jē\ *n* [Gk *oinos* wine + E *-logy* — more at WINE] (1814) : a science that deals with wine and wine making — **eno·log·i·cal** \,ē-nə-'lä-ji-kəl\ *adj* — **enol·o·gist** \ē-'nä-lə-jist\ *n*

enor·mi·ty \i-'nòr-mə-tē\ *n, pl* **-ties** (15c) **1** : an outrageous, improper, vicious, or immoral act ⟨the *enormities* of state power —Susan Sontag⟩ ⟨other *enormities* too juvenile to mention —Richard Freedman⟩ **2** : the quality or state of being immoderate, monstrous, or outrageous; *esp* : great wickedness ⟨the ~ of the crimes committed during the Third Reich —G. A. Craig⟩ **3** : the quality or state of being huge : IMMENSITY **4** : a quality of momentous importance
usage *Enormity*, some people insist, is improperly used to denote large size. They insist on *enormousness* for this meaning, and would limit *enormity* to the meaning "great wickedness." Those who urge such a limitation may not recognize the subtlety with which *enormity* is actually used. It regularly denotes a considerable departure from the expected or normal ⟨they awakened; they sat up; and then the *enormity* of their situation burst upon them. "How did the fire start?" —John Steinbeck⟩. When used to denote large size, either literal or figurative, it usu. suggests something so large as to seem overwhelming ⟨no intermediate zone of study. Either the *enormity* of the desert or the sight of a tiny flower —Paul Theroux⟩ ⟨the *enormity* of the task of teachers in slum schools —J. B. Conant⟩ and may even be used to suggest both great size and deviation from morality ⟨the *enormity* of existing stockpiles of atomic weapons —*New Republic*⟩. It can also emphasize the momentousness of what has happened ⟨the sombre *enormity* of the Russian Revolution —George Steiner⟩ or of its consequences ⟨perceived as no one in the family could the *enormity* of the misfortune —E. L. Doctorow⟩.

enor·mous \i-'nòr-məs, ē-\ *adj* [L *enormis*, fr. *e, ex* out of + *norma* rule] (1531) **1 a** *archaic* : ABNORMAL, INORDINATE **b** : exceedingly wicked : SHOCKING ⟨an ~ sin⟩ **2** : marked by extraordinarily great size, number, or degree; *esp* : exceeding usual bounds of accepted notions — **enor·mous·ly** *adv* — **enor·mous·ness** *n*
syn ENORMOUS, IMMENSE, HUGE, VAST, GIGANTIC, COLOSSAL, MAMMOTH mean exceedingly large. ENORMOUS and IMMENSE both suggest an exceeding of all ordinary bounds in size or amount or degree, but ENOR-MOUS often adds an implication of abnormality or monstrousness ⟨an *enormous* expense⟩ ⟨an *immense* shopping mall⟩. HUGE commonly suggests an immensity of bulk or amount ⟨incurred a *huge* debt⟩. VAST usu. suggests immensity of extent ⟨the *vast* Russian steppes⟩. GIGANTIC stresses the contrast with the size of others of the same kind ⟨a *gigantic* sports stadium⟩. COLOSSAL applies esp. to a human creation of stupendous or incredible dimensions ⟨a *colossal* statue of Lincoln⟩. MAM-MOTH suggests both hugeness and ponderousness of bulk ⟨a *mammoth* boulder⟩.

eno·sis \i-'nō-səs\ *n* [NGk *henōsis*, fr. Gk, union, fr. *henoun* to unite, fr. *hen-, heis* one — more at SAME] (1928) : a movement to secure the political union of Greece and Cyprus

¹enough \i-'nəf; *after* t, d, s, z *often* ⁹n-'əf\ *adj* [ME *ynough*, fr. OE *genōg* (akin to OHG *ginuog* enough), fr. *ge-* (perfective prefix) + *-nōg*; akin to L *nancisci* to get, Gk *enenkein* to carry — more at CO-] (bef. 12c) : occurring in such quantity, quality, or scope as to fully meet demands, needs, or expectations **syn** see SUFFICIENT

²enough *adv* (bef. 12c) **1** : in or to a degree or quantity that satisfies or that is sufficient or necessary for satisfaction : SUFFICIENTLY **2** : FULLY, QUITE **3** : in a tolerable degree

³enough *pron* (bef. 12c) : a sufficient number, quantity, or amount ⟨~ were present to constitute a quorum⟩ ⟨had ~ of their foolishness⟩

enounce \ē-'naùn(t)s\ *vt* **enounced; enounc·ing** [F *énoncer*, fr. L *enuntiare* to report — more at ENUNCIATE] (1805) **1** : to set forth or state (as a proposition) **2** : to pronounce distinctly : ARTICULATE

enow \i-'naù, i-'nō\ *adv or adj* [ME *inow*, fr. OE *genōg*] (bef. 12c) *archaic* : ENOUGH

en pas·sant \,äⁿ-,pä-'säⁿ, -pə-\ *adv* [F] (1665) **1** : in passing **2** — used in chess of the capture of a pawn as it makes a first move of two squares by an enemy pawn that threatens the first of these squares

en·plane \in-'plān, en-\ *vi* (1941) : to board an airplane

en prise \äⁿ-prēz\ *adj* [F, lit., engaged, within grasp] (1899) *of a chess piece* : exposed to capture

en·quire \in-'kwīr\, **en·qui·ry** \'in-,kwīr-ē, in-'; 'in-kwə-rē, 'iŋ-\ *var of* INQUIRE, INQUIRY

en·rage \in-'rāj, en-\ *vt* [MF *enrager* to become mad, fr. OF *enragier*, fr. *en-* + *rage* rage] (1589) : to fill with rage : ANGER

en·rapt \in-'rapt, en-\ *adj* (1606) : wholly absorbed with rapture

en·rap·ture \in-'rap-chər, en-\ *vt* **en·rap·tured; en·rap·tur·ing** \-'rap-chə-riŋ, -'rap-shriŋ\ (1740) : to fill with delight

en·reg·is·ter \in-'re-jə-stər, en-\ *vt* [MF *enregistrer*, fr. OF, fr. *en-* + *registre* register] (1523) : to put on record : REGISTER

en·rich \in-'rich, en-\ *vt* [ME, fr. MF *enrichir*, fr. OF, fr. *en-* + *riche* rich] (14c) : to make rich or richer esp. by the addition or increase of some desirable quality, attribute, or ingredient ⟨the experience will ~ your life⟩: as **a** : to add beauty to : ADORN **b** : to enhance the taste of ⟨butter will ~ the sauce⟩ **c** : to make (a soil) more fertile **d** : to improve the nutritive value of (a food) by adding nutrients (as vitamins or amino acids) and esp. by restoring part of the nutrients lost in processing ⟨~ed flour⟩ **e** : to process so as to add or increase the proportion of a desirable ingredient ⟨~ed uranium⟩ ⟨~ed natural gas⟩ — **en·rich·er** *n* — **en·rich·ment** \'rich-mənt\ *n*

en·robe \in-'rōb, en-\ *vt* (1593) **1** : to cover with or as if with a robe **2** : COAT 2

en·roll *or* **en·rol** \in-'rōl, en-\ *vb* **en·rolled; en·roll·ing** [ME, fr. MF *enroller*, fr. *en-* + *rolle* roll, register] (14c) **1** : to insert, register, or enter in a list, catalog, or roll ⟨the school ~s about 800 pupils⟩ **2** : to prepare a final perfect copy of (a bill passed by a legislature) in written or printed form **3** : to roll or wrap up ~ *vi* : to enroll oneself or cause oneself to be enrolled ⟨we ~ed in the history course⟩ — **en·roll·ee** \-rō-'lē\ *n* — **en·roll·ment** \-'rōl-mənt\ *n*

en·root \in-'rüt, -'rùt\ *vt* [ME] (15c) : ESTABLISH, IMPLANT

en route \äⁿ-'rüt, en-, in-, -'raùt\ *adv or adj* [F] (1779) : on or along the way ⟨he reads *en route*⟩ ⟨arrived early despite *en route* delays⟩

en·sam·ple \in-'sam-pəl\ *n* [ME, fr. MF *ensample, example*] (13c) *archaic* : EXAMPLE, INSTANCE

en·san·guine \in-'saŋ-gwən\ *vt* **-guined; -guin·ing** (1667) **1** : to make bloody **2** : CRIMSON

en·sconce \in-'skän(t)s\ *vt* **en·sconced; en·sconc·ing** [*en-* + *²sconce*] (1598) **1** : SHELTER, CONCEAL **2** : ESTABLISH, SETTLE ⟨*ensconced* in a new job⟩

¹en·sem·ble \än-'säm-bəl, äⁿ-\ *n* [F, fr. *ensemble* together, fr. L *insimul* at the same time, fr. *in-* + *simul* at the same time — more at SAME] (1750) : a group producing a single effect: as **a** : concerted music of two or more parts **b** : a complete costume of harmonizing or complementary clothing and accessories **c** (1) : the musicians engaged in the performance of a musical ensemble (2) : a group of supporting players, singers, or dancers; *esp* : CORPS DE BALLET

²ensemble *adj* (ca. 1911) : emphasizing the roles of all performers as a whole rather than a star performance ⟨~ acting⟩

en·serf \in-'sərf, en-\ *vt* (1882) : to make a serf of : deprive of liberty and personal rights — **en·serf·ment** \-mənt\ *n*

en·sheathe \in-'shēth, en-\ *vt* (1593) : to cover with or as if with a sheath

en·shrine \in-'shrīn, en-, *esp Southern* -'srīn\ *vt* [ME] (14c) **1** : to enclose in or as if in a shrine **2** : to preserve or cherish as sacred — **en·shrine·ment** \-mənt\ *n*

en·shri·nee \in-'shrī-nē, -,shrī-'nē, en-\ *n* (1968) : a person inducted into a Hall of Fame

en·shroud \in-'shraùd, en-, *esp Southern* -'sraùd\ *vt* (1583) : to cover or enclose with or as if with a shroud

en·si·form \'en(t)-sə-,fòrm\ *adj* [F *ensiforme*, fr. L *ensis* sword + F *-forme* -form; akin to Skt *asi* sword] (1541) : having sharp edges and tapering to a slender point ⟨~ leaves of the gladiolus⟩ — see LEAF illustration

en·sign \'en(t)-sən, *also* 'en-,sīn *for 1, 2, & 3a*\ *n* [ME *ensigne*, fr. MF *enseigne*, fr. L *insignia* insignia, flags] (15c) **1** : a flag that is flown (as by a ship) as the symbol of nationality and that may also be flown with a distinctive badge added to its design **2 a** : a badge of office, rank, or power **b** : EMBLEM, SIGN **3 a** : an infantry officer of what was formerly the lowest commissioned rank **b** : a commissioned officer in the navy or coast guard ranking above a chief warrant officer and below a lieutenant junior grade

en·si·lage \'en(t)-sə-(s)-lij, *for 1 also* in-'sī-lij\ *n* [Fr, fr. *ensiler* to ensile, fr. *en-* + *silo* silo, fr. Sp] (1876) **1** : the process of preserving fodder by ensiling **2** : SILAGE

en·sile \in-'sī(ə)l, en-\ *vt* **en·siled; en·sil·ing** (1883) : to prepare and store (fodder) for silage

en·sky \in-'skī, en-\ *vt* (1603) : EXALT

en·slave \in-'slāv, en-\ *vt* (1630) : to reduce to or as if to slavery : SUB-JUGATE — **en·slave·ment** \-mənt\ *n* — **en·slav·er** *n*

en·snare \in-'snar, -'sner, en-\ *vt* (1576) : to take in or as if in a snare **syn** see CATCH

en·snarl \in-'snär(-ə)l, en-\ *vt* (1593) : to involve in a snarl

en·sor·cell *or* **en·sor·cel** \in-'sòr-səl\ *vt* **-celled** *or* **-celed; -cell·ing** *or* **-cel·ing** [MF *ensorceler*, alter. of OF *ensorcerer*, fr. *en-* + *sorcier* sorcerer — more at SORCERY] (ca. 1541) : BEWITCH, ENCHANT — **en·sor·cell·ment** \-mənt\ *n*

en·soul \in-'sōl, en-\ *vt* (1605) : to endow or imbue with a soul

\ə\ abut \ᵊ\ kitten, F table \ər\ further \a\ ash \ā\ ace \ä\ mop, mar
\aù\ out \ch\ chin \e\ bet \ē\ easy \g\ go \i\ hit \ī\ ice \j\ job
\ŋ\ sing \ō\ go \ò\ law \òi\ boy \th\ thin \t͟h\ the \ü\ loot \ù\ foot
\y\ yet \zh\ vision \à, ḵ, ⁿ, œ, œ̄, ɷ, ūē, ᵞ\ see Guide to Pronunciation

en·sphere \in-'sfir, en-\ *vt* (1612) : to enclose in or as if in a sphere

en·sue \in-'sü, en-\ *vb* **en·sued; en·su·ing** [ME, fr. MF *ensuivre*, fr. OF, fr. *en-* + *suivre* to follow — more at SUE] *vt* (14c) : to strive to attain : PURSUE ⟨I wander, seeking peace, and *ensuing* it —Rupert Brooke⟩ ~ *vi* : to take place afterward or as a result *syn* see FOLLOW

en suite \än-'swēt\ *adv or adj* [F] (1818) : so as to form a suite : CONNECTED ⟨bathroom *en suite*⟩; *also* : so as to make a matching set

en·sure \in-'shur\ *vt* **en·sured; en·sur·ing** [ME, fr. AF *enseurer*, prob. alter. of OF *aseürer* — more at ASSURE] (ca. 1704) : to make sure, certain, or safe : GUARANTEE
syn ENSURE, INSURE, ASSURE, SECURE mean to make a thing or person sure. ENSURE, INSURE, and ASSURE are interchangeable in many contexts where they indicate the making certain or inevitable of an outcome, but INSURE sometimes stresses the taking of necessary measures beforehand, and ASSURE distinctively implies the removal of doubt and suspense from a person's mind. SECURE implies action taken to guard against attack or loss.

en·swathe \in-'swäth, -'swoth, -'swāth, en-\ *vt* (1597) : to enfold or enclose with or as if with a covering : SWATHE

ent- *or* **ento-** *comb form* [NL, fr. Gk *entos* within; akin to L *intus* within, Gk *en* in — more at IN] : inner : within ⟨*ento*derm⟩

en·tab·la·ture \in-'ta-blə-,chur, -,char, -,t(y)ur\ *n* [obs. F, modif. of It *intavolatura*, fr. *intavolare* to put on a board or table, fr. *in-* (fr. L) + *tavola* board, table, fr. L *tabula*] (1611) : a horizontal part in classical architecture that rests on the columns and consists of architrave, frieze, and cornice

¹en·tail \in-'tā(ə)l, en-\ *vt* [ME *entailen*, *entaillen*, fr. ¹*en-* + *taile*, *taille* limitation — more at TAIL] (14c) **1** : to restrict (property) by limiting the inheritance to the owner's lineal descendants or to a particular class thereof **2 a** : to confer, assign, or transmit as if by entail : FASTEN ⟨~ed on them indelible disgrace —Robert Browning⟩ **b** : to fix (a person) permanently in some condition or status ⟨~ him and his heirs unto the crown —Shak.⟩ **3** : to impose, involve, or imply as a necessary accompaniment or result ⟨the project will ~ considerable expense⟩ — **en·tail·er** \-'tā-lər\ *n* — **en·tail·ment** \-'tāl-mənt\ *n*

1 entablature, *2* cornice, *3* frieze, *4* architrave

²en·tail \'en-,tāl, in-'tā(ə)l\ *n* (14c) **1 a** : an entailing esp. of lands **b** : an entailed estate **2** : something transmitted as if by entail

ent·amoe·ba \,en-tə-'mē-bə\ *n* [NL] (1914) : any of a genus (*Entamoeba*) comprising various amoebas parasitic in vertebrates and including one (*E. histolytica*) that causes amebic dysentery in humans — compare ENDAMOEBA

en·tan·gle \in-'taŋ-gəl, en-\ *vt* (15c) **1 a** : to wrap or twist together : INTERWEAVE **b** : ENSNARE **2 a** : to involve in a perplexing or troublesome situation ⟨became *entangled* in a lawsuit⟩ **b** : to make complicated ⟨the story is *entangled* with legends⟩ — **en·tan·gler** \-g(ə-)lər\ *n*

en·tan·gle·ment \in-'taŋ-gəl-mənt, en-\ *n* (1535) **1 a** : the action of entangling : the state of being entangled **b** : something that entangles, confuses, or ensnares **2** : the condition of being deeply involved

en·ta·sis \'en-tə-sis\ *n, pl* **-ta·ses** \-,sēz\ [Gk, lit., distension, stretching, fr. *enteinein* to stretch tight (fr. *en-* ²*en-* + *teinein* to stretch) — more at THIN] (1664) : a slight convexity esp. in the shaft of a column

en·tel·e·chy \en-'te-lə-kē, in-\ *n, pl* **-chies** [LL *entelechia*, fr. Gk *entelecheia*, fr. *enteles* complete (fr. *en-* ²*en-* + *telos* end) + *echein* to have — more at WHEEL, SCHEME] (1603) **1** : the actualization of form-giving cause as contrasted with potential existence **2** : a hypothetical agency not demonstrable by scientific methods that in some vitalist doctrines is considered an inherent regulating and directing force in the development and functioning of an organism

en·tente \än-'tänt\ *n* [F, fr. OF, intent, understanding — more at INTENT] (1854) **1** : an international understanding providing for a common course of action **2** [F *entente cordiale*] : a coalition of parties to an entente

en·tente cor·diale \(')än-'tänt-,kor-'dyäl\ *n* [F, lit., cordial understanding] (1844) **1** : ENTENTE 1 **2** : a friendly agreement or working relationship

en·ter \'en-tər\ *vb* **en·tered; en·ter·ing** \'en-t(ə-)riŋ\ [ME *entren*, fr. OF *entrer*, fr. L *intrare*, fr. *intra* within; akin to L *inter* between — more at INTER.] *vi* (13c) **1** : to go or come in **2** : to come or gain admission into a group : JOIN — often used with *into* **3 a** : to make a beginning ⟨~*ing* upon a career⟩ **b** : to begin to consider a subject — usu. used with *into* or *upon* **4** : to go upon land for the purpose of taking possession **5** : to play a part : be a factor ⟨other considerations ~ when money is involved⟩ ~ *vt* **1** : to come or go into ⟨~ a room⟩ **2** : INSCRIBE, REGISTER ⟨~ the names of qualified voters⟩ **3** : to cause to be received or admitted ⟨~ a child at a school⟩ **4** : to put in : INSERT ⟨~ the new data into the computer⟩ **5 a** : to make a beginning in ⟨~ politics⟩ **b** : to go into (a particular period of time) ⟨~ middle age⟩ **6** : to become a member of or an active participant in ⟨~ the university⟩ ⟨~ a race⟩ **7** : to make report of (a ship or its cargo) to customs authorities **8** : to place in proper form before a court of law or upon record ⟨~ a writ⟩ **9** : to go into or upon and take actual possession of (as land) **10** : to put formally on record ⟨~*ing* a complaint⟩ — **en·ter·able** \'en-t(ə-)rə-bəl\ *adj* — **enter into 1** : to make oneself a party to or enter in ⟨*enter into* an agreement⟩ **2** : to form or be part of ⟨your prejudices shouldn't *enter into* it⟩ **3** : to participate or share in ⟨*enter into* the spirit of the occasion⟩ — **enter the lists** : to engage in a fight or struggle
syn ENTER, PENETRATE, PIERCE, PROBE mean to make way into something. ENTER is the most general of these and may imply either going in or forcing a way in ⟨*entered* the city in triumph⟩. PENETRATE carries a strong implication of an impelling force or compelling power that achieves entrance ⟨the enemy *penetrated* the fortress⟩. PIERCE means an entering or cutting through with a sharp pointed instrument ⟨*pierced* the boil with a lancet⟩. PROBE implies penetration to investigate or explore something hidden from sight or knowledge ⟨*probed* the depths of the sea⟩.

enter- *or* **entero-** *comb form* [Gk, fr. *enteron* — more at INTER.] : intestine ⟨*enteritis*⟩

en·ter·al \'en-tə-rəl\ *adj* (1903) : ENTERIC — **en·ter·al·ly** \-rə-lē\ *adv*

en·ter·ic \en-'ter-ik, in-\ *adj* (ca. 1859) **1** : of or relating to the intestines; *broadly* : ALIMENTARY **2** : of, relating to, or being a medicinal preparation treated to pass through the stomach unaltered and disintegrate in the intestines

en·ter·i·tis \,en-tə-'rī-təs\ *n* (1808) **1** : inflammation of the intestines and esp. of the human ileum **2** : a disease of domestic animals (as panleucopenia of cats) marked by enteritis and diarrhea

en·tero·bac·te·ri·um \,en-tə-rō-bak-'tir-ē-əm\ *n* [NL] (ca. 1951) : any of a family (Enterobacteriaceae) of gram-negative straight rod bacteria (as a salmonella or a colon bacillus) that ferment glucose and usu. saprophytes as well as some serious plant and animal pathogens — **en·tero·bac·te·ri·al** \-ē-əl\ *adj*

en·tero·bi·a·sis \-'bī-ə-səs\ *n, pl* **-a·ses** \-,sēz\ [NL, fr. *Enterobius*, genus name (fr. Gk *enter-* + *bios* mode of life) + *-iasis*] (ca. 1927) : infestation with or disease caused by pinworms (genus *Enterobius*) that occurs esp. in children

en·tero·chro·maf·fin \-,krō-mə-fən\ *adj* (ca. 1941) : of or relating to epithelial cells of the intestinal mucosa that stain esp. with chromium salts and usu. contain serotonin

en·tero·coc·cus \-'kä-kəs\ *n, pl* **-coc·ci** \-'käk-,(s)ī, -'käk-(,)(s)ē\ [NL, genus name] (1908) : STREPTOCOCCUS; *esp* : a streptococcus (as *Streptococcus faecalis*) normally present in the intestine — **en·tero·coc·cal** \-'kä-kəl\ *adj*

en·tero·coele *or* **en·tero·coel** \'en-tə-rō-,sēl\ *n* (1877) : a coelom originating by outgrowth from the archenteron — **en·tero·coe·lous** \,en-tə-rō-'sē-ləs\ *adj* — **en·tero·coe·lic** \-lik\ *adj*

en·tero·co·li·tis \,en-tə-rō-kə-'lī-təs\ *n* [NL] (ca. 1857) : enteritis affecting both the large and small intestine

en·tero·gas·trone \-'gas-,trōn\ *n* [*enter-* + *gastr-* + *-one* (as in *hormone*)] (ca. 1930) : a hormone that is produced by the duodenal mucosa and has an inhibitory action on gastric motility and secretion

en·tero·ki·nase \,en-tə-rō-'ki-,nās, -,nāz\ *n* [ISV] (ca. 1902) : an enzyme esp. of the upper intestinal mucosa that activates trypsinogen by converting it to trypsin

en·ter·on \'en-tə-,rän, -rən\ *n* [NL, fr. Gk, intestine — more at INTER.] (ca. 1842) : the alimentary canal or system — used esp. of the embryo

en·tero·patho·gen·ic \,en-tə-rō-,pa-thə-'je-nik\ *adj* (1961) : tending to produce disease in the intestinal tract ⟨~ bacteria⟩

en·ter·op·a·thy \,en-tə-'rä-pə-thē\ *n* (ca. 1889) : a disease of the intestinal tract

en·ter·os·to·my \,en-tə-'räs-tə-mē\ *n, pl* **-mies** [ISV] (1878) : a surgical formation of an opening into the intestine through the abdominal wall — **en·ter·os·to·mal** \-tə-məl\ *adj*

en·tero·tox·in \,en-tə-rō-'täk-sən\ *n* (ca. 1928) : a toxin that is produced by microorganisms (as some staphylococci) and causes gastrointestinal symptoms (as in some forms of food poisoning or cholera)

en·tero·vi·rus \-'vī-rəs\ *n* [NL] (1957) : any of a group of picornaviruses (as the poliomyelitis virus) that typically occur in the gastrointestinal tract but may be involved in respiratory ailments, meningitis, and neurological disorders — **en·tero·vi·ral** \-rəl\ *adj*

en·ter·prise \'en-tə(r)-,prīz\ *n* [ME, fr. MF, fr. OF *entreprendre* to undertake, fr. *entre-* inter- + *prendre* to take — more at PRIZE] (15c) **1** : a project or undertaking that is esp. difficult, complicated, or risky **2** : readiness to engage in daring action : INITIATIVE **3 a** : a unit of economic organization or activity; *esp* : a business organization **b** : a systematic purposeful activity ⟨agriculture is the main economic ~ among these people⟩

en·ter·pris·er \-,prī-zər\ *n* (1523) : ENTREPRENEUR

en·ter·pris·ing \-,prī-ziŋ\ *adj* (1611) : marked by an independent energetic spirit and by readiness to undertake or experiment

en·ter·tain \,en-tər-'tān\ *vb* [ME *entertinen*, fr. MF *entretenir*, fr. *entre-* inter- + *tenir* to hold — more at TENABLE] *vt* (15c) **1 a** *archaic* : MAINTAIN **b** *obs* : RECEIVE **2** : to show hospitality to **3 a** : to keep, hold, or maintain in the mind ⟨I ~ grave doubts about her sincerity⟩ **b** : to receive and take into consideration ⟨refused to ~ our plea⟩ **4** : to provide entertainment for **5** : to play against (an opposing team) on one's home field or court ~ *vi* : to provide entertainment esp. for guests *syn* see AMUSE — **en·ter·tain·er** *n*

en·ter·tain·ing *adj* (1568) : providing entertainment : DIVERTING — **en·ter·tain·ing·ly** \-tä-niŋ-lē\ *adv*

en·ter·tain·ment \,en-tər-'tān-mənt\ *n* (15c) **1** : the act of entertaining **2 a** *archaic* : MAINTENANCE, PROVISION **b** *obs* : EMPLOYMENT **3** : something diverting or engaging: as **a** : a public performance **b** : a usu. light comic or adventure novel

en·thal·py \'en-,thal-pē, en-\ *n* [*en-* + Gk *thalpein* to heat] (ca. 1924) : the sum of the internal energy of a body and the product of its volume multiplied by the pressure

en·thrall *or* **en·thral** \in-'throl, en-\ *vt* **en·thralled; en·thrall·ing** [ME] (15c) **1** : to hold in or reduce to slavery **2** : to hold spellbound : CHARM — **en·thrall·ment** \-'throl-mənt\ *n*

en·throne \in-'thrōn, en-\ *vt* (1606) **1 a** : to seat ceremonially on a throne **b** : to seat in a place associated with a position of authority or influence **2** : to assign supreme virtue or value to : EXALT — **en·throne·ment** \-mənt\ *n*

en·thuse \in-'thüz, en-, *also* -'thyüz\ *vb* **en·thused; en·thus·ing** [back-formation fr. *enthusiasm*] *vt* (1827) **1** : to make enthusiastic **2** : to express with enthusiasm ~ *vi* : to show enthusiasm ⟨a splendid performance, and I was *enthusing* over it —Julian Huxley⟩
usage Enthuse is apparently American in origin, although the earliest known example of its use occurs in a letter written in 1827 by a young Scotsman who spent about two years in the Pacific Northwest. It has been disapproved since about 1870. Current evidence shows it to be flourishing nonetheless on both sides of the Atlantic esp. in journalistic prose.

en·thu·si·asm \in-'thü-zē-,a-zəm, en-, *also* -'thyü-\ *n* [Gk *enthousiasmos*, fr. *enthousiazein* to be inspired, irreg. fr. *entheos* inspired, fr. *en-* + *theos* god] (1603) **1 a** : belief in special revelations of the Holy Spirit **b** : religious fanaticism **2 a** : strong excitement of feeling : ARDOR **b** : something inspiring zeal or fervor *syn* see PASSION

en·thu·si·ast \-,ast, -əst\ *n* (1570) : a person filled with enthusiasm: as **a** : one who is ardently attached to a cause, object, or pursuit ⟨a sports car ~⟩ **b** : one who tends to become ardently absorbed in an interest

en·thu·si·as·tic \in-,thü-zē-'as-tik, en-, *also* -,thyü-\ *adj* (1603) : filled with or marked by enthusiasm — **en·thu·si·as·ti·cal·ly** \-ti-k(ə-)lē\ *adv*

en·thy·meme \'en(t)-thi-,mēm\ *n* [L *enthymema*, fr. Gk *enthymēma*, fr. *enthymeisthai* to keep in mind, fr. en- + *thymos* mind, soul] (1552) : a syllogism in which one of the premises is implicit

en·tice \in-'tīs, en-\ *vt* **en·ticed; en·tic·ing** [ME, fr. MF *enticier*, fr. (assumed) VL *initiare*, fr. L in- + *titio* firebrand] (14c) : to attract artfully or adroitly or by arousing hope or desire : TEMPT *syn* see LURE — **en·tice·ment** \-'tī-smənt\ *n* — **en·tic·ing·ly** \-'tī-siŋ-lē\ *adv*

¹en·tire \in-'tīr, 'en-,\ *adj* [ME, fr. MF *entir*, fr. L *integer*, lit., untouched, fr. in- + *tangere* to touch — more at TANGENT] (14c) **1** : having no element or part left out : WHOLE ⟨was alone the ~ day⟩ **2** : complete in degree : TOTAL ⟨their ~ devotion to their family⟩ **3 a** : consisting of one piece **b** : HOMOGENEOUS, UNMIXED **c** : INTACT ⟨strove to keep the collection ~⟩ **4** : not castrated **5** : having the margin continuous or free from indentations ⟨an ~ leaf⟩ *syn* see WHOLE, PERFECT — **entire** *adv* — **en·tire·ness** *n*

²entire *n* (1597) **1** *archaic* : the whole : ENTIRETY **2** : STALLION

en·tire·ly *adv* (14c) **1** : to the full or entire extent : COMPLETELY ⟨I agree ~⟩ ⟨you are ~ welcome⟩ **2** : to the exclusion of others : SOLELY ⟨~ by my own efforts⟩

en·tire·ty \in-'tī-rə-tē, -'tī(-ə)r-tē\ *n, pl* **-ties** (1548) **1** : the state of being entire or complete **2** : WHOLE

en·ti·tle \in-'tī-t°l, en-\ *vt* **en·ti·tled; en·ti·tling** \-'tīt-liŋ, -°l-iŋ\ [ME, fr. MF *entituler*, fr. LL *intitulare*, fr. L in- + *titulus* title] (14c) **1** : to give a title to : DESIGNATE **2** : to furnish with proper grounds for seeking or claiming something ⟨this ticket ~s the bearer to free admission⟩

en·ti·tle·ment \-'tī-t°l-mənt\ *n* (1944) **1 a** : the state or condition of being entitled : RIGHT **b** : a right to benefits specified esp. by law or contract **2** : a government program providing benefits to members of a specified group; *also* : funds supporting or distributed by such a program

en·ti·ty \'en-tə-tē, 'e-nə-\ *n, pl* **-ties** [ML *entitas*, fr. L *ent-, ens* existing thing, fr. coined prp. of *esse* to be — more at IS] (1596) **1 a** : BEING, EXISTENCE; *esp* : independent, separate, or self-contained existence **b** : the existence of a thing as contrasted with its attributes **2** : something that has separate and distinct existence and objective or conceptual reality

ento- see ENT-

en·to·derm \'en-tə-,dərm\ *n* (1879) : ENDODERM — **en·to·der·mal** \,en-tə-'dər-məl\ *adj* — **en·to·der·mic** \-mik\ *adj*

en·toil \in-'tȯi(ə)l\ *vt* (1581) : ENTRAP, ENMESH

entom- *or* **entomo-** *comb form* [F, fr. Gk *entomon*] : insect ⟨*entomophagous*⟩

en·tomb \in-'tüm, en-\ *vt* [ME *entoumben*, fr. MF *entomber*, fr. en- + *tombe* tomb] (1576) **1** : to deposit in a tomb : BURY **2** : to serve as a tomb for — **en·tomb·ment** \-'tüm-mənt\ *n*

en·to·mo·fau·na \,en-tə-mō-'fȯ-nə, -'fä-\ *n* [NL] (1951) : a fauna of insects : the insects of an environment or region

en·to·mol·o·gy \,en-tə-'mä-lə-jē\ *n* [F *entomologie*, fr. Gk *entomon* insect (fr. neut. of *entomos* cut up, fr. en- + *temnein* to cut) + *-logie* -logy — more at TOME] (1766) : a branch of zoology that deals with insects — **en·to·mo·log·i·cal** \,en-tə-'lä-ji-kəl\ *adj* — **en·to·mo·log·i·cal·ly** \-k(ə-)lē\ *adv* — **en·to·mol·o·gist** \,en-tə-'mä-lə-jist\ *n*

en·to·moph·a·gous \,en-tə-'mä-fə-gəs\ *adj* (1847) : feeding on insects

en·to·moph·i·lous \,en-tə-'mä-fə-ləs\ *adj* (1880) : normally pollinated by insects — compare ZOOPHILIC — **en·to·moph·i·ly** \-lē\ *n*

en·to·proct \'en-tə-,präkt\ *n* [ultim. fr. ent- + Gk *prōktos* anus] (1940) : any of a phylum (Entoprocta) of animals that are very similar to bryozoans but lack a true coelom and have the anus located near the mouth inside a crown of tentacles

en·tou·rage \,än-tù-'räzh\ *n* [F, fr. MF, fr. *entourer* to surround, fr. *entour* around, fr. en in (fr. L in) + *tour* circuit — more at TURN] (1834) **1** : one's attendants or associates **2** : SURROUNDINGS

en·tr'acte \'än(n)-trakt, -,träkt, än(n)-'\ *n* [F, fr. *entre-* inter- + *acte* act] (ca. 1842) **1** : a dance, piece of music, or interlude performed between two acts of a play **2** : the interval between two acts of a play

en·trails \'en-,trālz, -trəlz\ *n pl* [ME *entrailles*, fr. MF, fr. ML *intralia*, alter. of L *interanea*, pl. of *interaneum* intestine, fr. neut. of *interaneus* interior] (14c) **1** : BOWELS, VISCERA; *broadly* : internal parts **2** : the inner workings of something ⟨the ~ of the movie industry⟩

¹en·train \in-'trān\ *vt* [MF *entrainer*, fr. en- + *trainer* to draw, drag — more at TRAIN] (1568) **1** : to draw along with or after oneself **2** : to draw in and transport (as solid particles or gas) by the flow of a fluid **3** : to incorporate (air bubbles) into concrete **4** : to determine or modify the phase or period of ⟨circadian rhythms ~ed by a light cycle⟩ — **en·train·er** *n* — **en·train·ment** \-'trān-mənt\ *n*

²entrain *vt* (1881) : to put aboard a train ~ *vi* : to go aboard a train

¹en·trance \'en-trən(t)s\ *n* (15c) **1** : power or permission to enter : ADMISSION **2** : the act of entering **3** : the means or place of entry **4** : the point at which a voice or instrument part begins in ensemble music **5** : the first appearance of an actor in a scene

²en·trance \in-'tran(t)s, en-\ *vt* **en·tranced; en·tranc·ing** (1593) **1** : to carry away with delight, wonder, or rapture **2** : to put into a trance — **en·trance·ment** \-'tran(t)-smənt\ *n*

en·trance·way \'en-trən(t)s-,wā\ *n* (1865) : ENTRYWAY

en·trant \'en-trənt\ *n* (1635) : one that enters; *esp* : one that enters a contest

en·trap \in-'trap, en-\ *vt* [MF *entraper*, fr. en- + *trape* trap] (1534) **1** : to catch in or as if in a trap **2** : to lure into a compromising statement or act *syn* see CATCH

en·trap·ment \-mənt\ *n* (1597) **1 a** : the action or process of entrapping **b** : the condition of being entrapped **2** : the action of luring an individual into committing a crime in order to prosecute the person for it

en·treat \in-'trēt, en-\ *vb* [ME *entreten*, fr. MF *entraitier*, fr. en- + *traitier* to treat] *vi* (14c) **1** *obs* **a** : NEGOTIATE **b** : INTERCEDE **2** : to make an earnest request : PLEAD ~ *vt* **1** : to plead with esp. in order to persuade : ask urgently ⟨~ed his boss for another chance⟩ **2** *ar-*

chaic : to deal with : TREAT *syn* see BEG — **en·treat·ing·ly** \-'trē-tiŋ-lē\ *adv* — **en·treat·ment** \-mənt\ *n*

en·treaty \-'trē-tē\ *n, pl* **-treat·ies** (15c) : an act of entreating : PLEA

en·tre·chat \'än(n)-trə-,shä\ *n* [F, modif. of It (*capriola*) *intrecciata*, lit., intertwined caper] (1775) : a leap in which a ballet dancer repeatedly crosses the legs and sometimes beats them together

en·tre·côte *also* **en·tre·cote** \'än(n)-trə-,kōt\ *n* [F *entrecôte*, fr. *entre-* inter- + *côte* rib, fr. L *costa* — more at INTER-, COAST] (1841) : a steak cut from between the ribs

en·trée *or* **en·tree** \'än-,trä *also* än-'\ *n* [F *entrée*, fr. OF — more at ENTRY] (1761) **1 a** : the act or manner of entering : ENTRANCE **b** : freedom of entry or access **2** : the main course of a meal in the U.S.

en·tre·mets \as *sing* \än(n)-trə-'mä, *as pl* -'mä(z)\ *n pl but sing or pl in constr* [ME, fr. MF, fr. OF *entremes*, fr. L *intermissus*, pp. of *intermittere* to intermit] (15c) : dishes served in addition to the main course of a meal; *esp* : DESSERT

en·trench \in-'trench, en-\ *vt* (1555) **1 a** : to place within or surround with a trench esp. for defense **b** : to place (oneself) in a strong defensive position **c** : to establish solidly ⟨~ed themselves in the business⟩ **2** : to cut into : FURROW; *specif* : to erode downward so as to form a trench ~ *vi* **1** : to dig or occupy a trench for defensive purposes **2** : to enter upon or take over something unfairly, improperly, or unlawfully : ENCROACH — used with *on* or *upon* — **en·trench·ment** \-mənt\ *n*

en·tre·pôt \'än(n)-trə-,pō\ *n* [F, fr. MF *entrepost*, fr. *entreposer* to put between, fr. *entre-* inter- + *poser* to pose, put] (1758) : an intermediary center of trade and transshipment

en·tre·pre·neur \,än-trə-p(r)ə-'nər, -'n(y)ùr\ *n* [F, fr. OF, fr. *entreprendre* to undertake — more at ENTERPRISE] (1852) : one who organizes, manages, and assumes the risks of a business or enterprise — **en·tre·pre·neur·i·al** \-'n(y)ùr-ē-əl, -'nər-\ *adj* — **en·tre·pre·neur·i·al·ism** \-ē-ə-li-zəm\ *n* — **en·tre·pre·neur·i·al·ly** \-ē-ə-lē\ *adv* — **en·tre·pre·neur·ship** \-'nər-,ship, -'n(y)ùr-\ *n*

en·tre·sol \'än(n)-trə-,sȯl, -,sôl\ *n* [F, fr. Sp *entresuelo*, fr. *entre* between + *suelo* level, fr. (assumed) VL *sola*, fr. L *solea* sandal, sole, sill — more at SOLE] (1711) : MEZZANINE

en·tro·pi·on \en-'trō-pē-,än, -pē-ən\ *n* [NL, fr. en- ²en- + *ectropion* turning out of the eyelid, fr. Gk *ektropion*, fr. *ektrepein* to turn out, fr. ex- out + *trepein* to turn] (ca. 1860) : the inversion or turning inward of the border of the eyelid against the eyeball

en·tro·py \'en-trə-pē\ *n, pl* **-pies** [ISV en- + Gk *tropē* change, lit., turn, fr. *trepein* to turn] (1875) **1** : a measure of the unavailable energy in a closed thermodynamic system that is also usu. considered to be a measure of the system's disorder and that is a property of the system's state and is related to it in such a manner that a reversible change in heat in the system produces a change in the measure which varies directly with the heat change and inversely with the absolute temperature at which the change takes place; *broadly* : the degree of disorder or uncertainty in a system **2 a** : the degradation of the matter and energy in the universe to an ultimate state of inert uniformity **b** : a process of degradation or running down or a trend to disorder **3** : CHAOS, DISORGANIZATION, RANDOMNESS — **en·tro·pic** \en-'trō-pik, -'trä-pik\ *adj* — **en·tro·pi·cal·ly** \-pi-k(ə-)lē\ *adv*

en·trust \in-'trəst, en-\ *vt* (1602) **1** : to confer a trust on; *esp* : to deliver something in trust to **2** : to commit to another with confidence *syn* see COMMIT — **en·trust·ment** \-'trəs(t)-mənt\ *n*

en·try \'en-trē\ *n, pl* **entries** [ME *entre*, fr. OF *entree*, fr. fem. of *entré*, pp. of *entrer* to enter] (13c) **1** : the right or privilege of entering : ENTRÉE **2** : the act of entering : ENTRANCE **3** : a place of entrance: as **a** : VESTIBULE, PASSAGE **b** : DOOR, GATE **4 a** : the act of making or entering a record **b** : something entered: as **(1)** : a record or notation of an occurrence, transaction, or proceeding **(2)** : a descriptive record (as in a card catalog or an index) **(3)** : HEADWORD **(4)** : a headword with its definition or identification **(5)** : VOCABULARY ENTRY **5** : a person, thing, or group entered in a contest

en·try–lev·el \'en-trē-,le-vəl\ *adj* (1975) : of or being at the lowest level of a hierarchy ⟨~ jobs⟩

en·try·way \-,trē-,wā\ *n* (1746) : a passage for entrance

entry word *n* (ca. 1908) : HEADWORD

en·twine \in-'twīn, en-\ *vt* (1590) : to twine together or around ~ *vi* : to become twisted or twined

en·twist \in-'twist, en-\ *vt* (1590) : ENTWINE

enu·cle·ate \(,)ē-'nü-klē-,āt, -'nyü-\ *vt* **-at·ed; -at·ing** [L *enucleatus*, pp. of *enucleare*, lit., to remove the kernel from, fr. e- + *nucleus* kernel — more at NUCLEUS] (1548) **1** *archaic* : EXPLAIN **2** : to deprive of a nucleus **3** : to remove without cutting into ⟨~ a tumor⟩ ⟨~ the eyeball⟩ — **enu·cle·ation** \(,)ē-,n(y)ü-klē-'ā-shən\ *n*

enu·mer·a·ble \i-'n(y)üm-rə-bəl, -'n(y)ü-mə-\ *adj* (ca. 1889) : DENUMERABLE — **enu·mer·a·bil·i·ty** \-,n(y)üm-rə-'bi-lə-tē, -'n(y)ü-mə-rə-\ *n*

enu·mer·ate \i-'n(y)ü-mə-,rāt\ *vt* **-at·ed; -at·ing** [L *enumeratus*, pp. of *enumerare*, fr. e- + *numerare* to count, fr. *numerus* number] (1616) **1** : to ascertain the number of : COUNT **2** : to specify one after another : LIST — **enu·mer·a·tion** \-,n(y)ü-mə-'rā-shən\ *n* — **enu·mer·a·tive** \-'n(y)ü-mə-,rā-tiv, -'n(y)üm-rə-, -'n(y)ü-mə-rə-\ *adj*

enu·mer·a·tor \-'n(y)ü-mə-,rā-tər\ *n* (1856) : one that enumerates; *esp* : a census taker

enun·ci·ate \ē-'nən(t)-sē-,āt\ *vb* **-at·ed; -at·ing** [L *enuntiatus*, pp. of *enuntiare* to report, declare, fr. e- + *nuntiare* to report — more at ANNOUNCE] *vt* (1623) **1 a** : to make a definite or systematic statement of **b** : ANNOUNCE, PROCLAIM ⟨*enunciated* the new policy⟩ **2** : ARTICULATE, PRONOUNCE ⟨~ all the syllables⟩ ~ *vi* : to utter articulate sounds — **enun·ci·a·ble** \-'nən(t)-sē-ə-bəl, -'nən-ch(ē-)ə-\ *adj* — **enun·ci·a·tion** \-,nən(t)-sē-'ā-shən\ *n* — **enun·ci·a·tor** \-'nən(t)-sē-,ā-tər\ *n*

enure *var of* INURE

en·ure·sis \,en-yù-'rē-səs\ *n* [NL, fr. Gk *enourein* to urinate in, wet the bed, fr. en- + *ourein* to urinate — more at URINE] (ca. 1800) : the in-

\ə\ abut \ᵊ\ kitten, F table \ər\ further \a\ ash \ā\ ace \ä\ mop, mar \aù\ out \ch\ chin \e\ bet \ē\ easy \g\ go \i\ hit \ī\ ice \j\ job \ŋ\ sing \ō\ go \ȯ\ law \ȯi\ boy \th\ thin \t̲h̲\ the \ü\ loot \ù\ foot \y\ yet \zh\ vision \â, k̲, ⁿ, œ, œ̄, ᵫ, ᵳ̄, ʸ\ see Guide to Pronunciation

voluntary discharge of urine : incontinence of urine — **en·uret·ic**
\'-rə-tik\ *adj or n*

en·vel·op \in-'ve-ləp, en-\ *vt* [ME *envolupen*, fr. MF *envoluper, en·voleper*, fr. OF *envoloper*, fr. *en-* + *voloper* to wrap] (14c) **1 :** to enclose or enfold completely with or as if with a covering **2 :** to mount an attack on (an enemy's flank) — **en·vel·op·ment** \-mənt\ *n*

en·ve·lope \'en-və-,lōp, ÷'än-\ *n* (ca. 1714) **1 :** a flat usu. paper container (as for a letter) **2 :** something that envelops : WRAPPER ⟨the ~ of air around the earth⟩ **3 a :** the outer covering of an aerostat **b :** the bag containing the gas in a balloon or airship **4 :** a natural enclosing covering (as a membrane, shell, or integument) **5 a :** a curve tangent to each of a family of curves **b :** a surface tangent to each of a family of surfaces **6 :** a set of performance limits (as of an aircraft) that may not be safely exceeded; *also* : the set of operating parameters that exists within these limits

   usage The \'en-\ and \'än-\ pronunciations are used with about equal frequency, and both are fully acceptable, though the \'än-\ version is sometimes decried as "pseudo-French." Actually \'än-\ is exactly what one would expect to hear when a French word like *entrepreneur* is becoming anglicized. *Envelope*, however, has been in English for nearly 300 years, plenty of time for it to become completely anglicized and for both of its pronunciations to win respectability.

en·ven·om \in-'ve-nəm, en-\ *vt* [ME *envenimen*, fr. OF *envenimer*, fr. *en-* + *venim* venom] (13c) **1 :** to make poisonous **2 :** EMBITTER

en·ven·om·iza·tion \in-,ve-nə-mə-'zā-shən, en-\ *n* (1960) : a poisoning caused by a bite or sting

en·vi·able \'en-vē-ə-bəl\ *adj* (1602) : highly desirable — **en·vi·able·ness** *n* — **en·vi·ably** \-blē\ *adv*

en·vi·er \'en-vē-ər\ *n* (15c) : one that envies

en·vi·ous \'en-vē-əs\ *adj* (13c) **1 :** feeling or showing envy ⟨~ of their neighbor's new car⟩ ⟨~ looks⟩ **2** *archaic* **a :** EMULOUS **b :** ENVIABLE — **en·vi·ous·ly** *adv* — **en·vi·ous·ness** *n*

en·vi·ron \in-'vī-rən, -'vī(-ə)rn\ *vt* [ME *environen*, fr. MF *environner*, fr. *environ* around, fr. *en* in (fr. L *in*) + *viron* circle, fr. *virer* to turn — more at VEER] (14c) : ENCIRCLE, SURROUND

en·vi·ron·ment \in-'vī-rə(n)-mənt, -'vī(-ə)r(n)-\ *n* (1827) **1 :** the circumstances, objects, or conditions by which one is surrounded **2 a :** the complex of physical, chemical, and biotic factors (as climate, soil, and living things) that act upon an organism or an ecological community and ultimately determine its form and survival **b :** the aggregate of social and cultural conditions that influence the life of an individual or community **3 :** the position or characteristic position of a linguistic element in a sequence *syn* see BACKGROUND — **en·vi·ron·men·tal** \-,vī-rə(n)-'men-t⁰l, -,vī(-ə)r(n)-\ *adj* — **en·vi·ron·men·tal·ly** \-t⁰l-ē\ *adv*

en·vi·ron·men·tal·ism \-,vī-rə(n)-'men-t⁰l-,i-zəm, -,vī(-ə)r(n)-\ *n* (ca. 1922) **1 :** a theory that views environment rather than heredity as the important factor in the development and esp. the cultural and intellectual development of an individual or group **2 :** advocacy of the preservation or improvement of the natural environment; *esp* : the movement to control pollution

en·vi·ron·men·tal·ist \-t⁰l-əst\ *n* (1916) **1 :** an advocate of environmentalism **2 :** one concerned about environmental quality esp. of the human environment with respect to the control of pollution

en·vi·rons \in-'vī-rənz, -'vī(-ə)rnz\ *n pl* (1665) **1 :** the districts around a city **2 a :** environing things : SURROUNDINGS **b :** an adjoining region or space : VICINITY

en·vis·age \in-'vi-zij, en-\ *vt* -**aged; -ag·ing** [F *envisager*, fr. *en-* + *visage* face] (1837) **1 :** to view or regard in a certain way ⟨~s the slum as a hotbed of crime⟩ **2 :** to have a mental picture of esp. in advance of realization ⟨~s an entirely new system of education⟩ *syn* see THINK

en·vi·sion \in-'vi-zhən, en-\ *vt* (1919) : to picture to oneself ⟨~s a career dedicated to promoting peace⟩ *syn* see THINK

en·voi *or* **en·voy** \'en-,voi, 'än-\ *n* [ME *envoye*, fr. MF *envoi*, lit., message, fr. OF *envei*, fr. *envoier* to send on one's way, fr. (assumed) VL *inviare*, fr. L *in-* + *via* way — more at WAY] (14c) : the usu. explanatory or commendatory concluding remarks to a poem, essay, or book; *esp* : a short final stanza of a ballade serving as a summary or dedication

en·voy \'en-,voi, ÷'än-\ *n* [F *envoyé*, fr. pp. of *envoyer* to send, fr. OF *envoier*] (1635) **1 a :** a minister plenipotentiary accredited to a foreign government who ranks between an ambassador and a minister resident — called also *envoy extraordinary* **b :** a person delegated to represent one government in its dealings with another **2 :** MESSENGER, REPRESENTATIVE

¹en·vy \'en-vē\ *n, pl* **envies** [ME *envie*, fr. OF, fr. L *invidia*, fr. *invidus* envious, fr. *invidēre* to look askance at, envy, fr. *in-* + *vidēre* to see — more at WIT] (13c) **1 :** painful or resentful awareness of an advantage enjoyed by another joined with a desire to possess the same advantage **2** *obs* : MALICE **3 :** an object of envious notice or feeling ⟨his new car made him the ~ of his friends⟩

²envy *vb* **en·vied; en·vy·ing** *vt* (14c) **1 :** to feel envy toward or on account of **2** *obs* : BEGRUDGE ~ *vi, obs* : to feel or show envy — **en·vy·ing·ly** *adv*

en·wheel \in-'hwē(ə)l, -'wē(ə)l, en-\ *vt* (1604) *obs* : ENCIRCLE

en·wind \in-'wīnd, en-\ *vt* **en·wound** \-'waúnd\; **en·wind·ing** (1850) : to wind in or about : ENFOLD

en·womb \in-'wüm, en-\ *vt* (ca. 1591) : to shut up as if in a womb

en·wrap \in-'rap, en-\ *vt* (14c) **1 :** to wrap in a covering : ENFOLD **2 a :** ENVELOP **b :** to preoccupy or absorb mentally : ENGROSS

en·wreathe \in-'rēth, en-\ *vt* (15c) : to encircle with or as if with a wreath : ENVELOP

en·zo·ot·ic \,en-zə-'wä-tik\ *adj* [*en-* + *epizootic*] (1882) *of animal diseases* : peculiar to or constantly present in a locality — **enzootic** *n*

en·zy·mat·ic \,en-zə-'ma-tik\ *also* **en·zy·mic** \en-'zī-mik\ *adj* (1900) : of, relating to, or produced by an enzyme — **en·zy·mat·i·cal·ly** \,en-zə-'ma-ti-k(ə-)lē\ *also* **en·zy·mi·cal·ly** \en-'zī-mi-k(ə-)lē\ *adv*

en·zyme \'en-,zīm\ *n* [G *Enzym*, fr. MGk *enzymos* leavened, fr. Gk *en-* + *zymē* leaven — more at JUICE] (1881) : any of numerous complex proteins that are produced by living cells and catalyze specific biochemical reactions at body temperatures

enzyme–linked immunosorbent assay *n* (1977) : a quantitative in vitro test for an antibody or antigen in which the test material is adsorbed on a surface and exposed to a complex of an enzyme linked to

an antibody specific for the substance being tested for with a positive result indicated by a treatment yielding a color in proportion to the amount of antigen or antibody in the test material — called also *ELISA*

en·zy·mol·o·gy \,en-,zī-'mä-lə-jē, -zə-\ *n* [ISV] (ca. 1900) : a branch of biochemistry that deals with enzymes, their nature, activity, and significance — **en·zy·mol·o·gist** \-jist\ *n*

eo- *comb form* [Gk *ēo-* dawn, fr. *ēōs* — more at EAST] : earliest : oldest ⟨*eolithic*⟩

Eo·cene \'ē-ə-,sēn\ *adj* (1831) : of, relating to, or being an epoch of the Tertiary between the Paleocene and the Oligocene or the corresponding system of rocks — see GEOLOGIC TIME table — **Eocene** *n*

eo·hip·pus \,ē-ō-'hi-pəs\ *n* [NL, fr. *eo-* + Gk *hippos* horse — more at EQUINE] (ca. 1879) : any of a genus (*Hyracotherium* syn. *Eohippus*) of very small primitive horses from the Lower Eocene having four-toed forefeet and three-toed hind feet — called also *dawn horse*

eo·lian \ē-'ō-lē-ən, -'ōl-yən\ *adj* [L *Aeolus*, Aeolus] (1853) : borne, deposited, produced, or eroded by the wind

eo·lith \'ē-ə-,lith\ *n* (1895) : a very crudely chipped flint

Eo·lith·ic \,ē-ə-'li-thik\ *adj* (1890) : of or relating to the early period of the Stone Age marked by the use of eoliths

eon \'ē-ən, 'ē-,än\ *var of* AEON

eo no·mi·ne \,ē-ō-'nä-mə-nē\ [L] (1627) : by or under that name

Eos \'ē-,äs\ *n* [Gk *Eōs*] : the Greek goddess of dawn — compare AURORA

eo·sin \'ē-ə-sən\ *also* **eo·sine** \-sən, -,sēn\ *n* [ISV, fr. Gk *ēōs* dawn] (1866) **1 :** a red fluorescent dye $C_{20}H_8Br_4O_5$ obtained by the action of bromine on fluorescein and used esp. in cosmetics and as a toner; *also* : its red to brown sodium or potassium salt used esp. as a biological stain for cytoplasmic structures **2 :** any of several dyes related to eosin

¹eo·sin·o·phil \,ē-ə-'si·nə-,fil\ *adj* (ca. 1882) : EOSINOPHILIC 1

²eosinophil \-'fil\ *n* (ca. 1900) : a white blood cell or other granulocyte with cytoplasmic inclusions readily stained by eosin

eo·sin·o·phil·ia \-,si-nə-'fi-lē-ə\ *n* [NL] (ca. 1903) : abnormal increase in the number of eosinophils in the blood that is characteristic of allergic states and various parasitic infections

eo·sin·o·phil·ic \-,si-nə-'fi-lik\ *adj* (ca. 1900) **1 :** staining readily with eosin **2 :** of, relating to, or characterized by eosinophilia

epact \'ē-,pakt, 'ē-,pakt\ *n* [MF *epacte*, fr. LL *epacta*, fr. Gk *epaktē*, fr. *epagein* to bring in, intercalate, fr. *epi-* + *agein* to drive — more at AGENT] (1588) : a period added to harmonize the lunar with the solar calendar

ep·ar·chy \'e-,pär-kē\ *n, pl* **-chies** [Gk *eparchia* province, fr. *eparchos* prefect, fr. *epi-* + *archos* ruler — more at ARCH-] (1796) : a diocese of an Eastern church

ep·au·let *also* **ep·au·lette** \,e-pə-'let; 'e-pə-,let, -,lət\ *n* [F *épaulette*, dim. of *épaule* shoulder, fr. LL *spatula* shoulder blade, spoon, dim. of L *spatha* spoon, sword — more at SPADE] (1783) : something that ornaments or protects the shoulder: as **a :** an ornamental fringed shoulder pad formerly worn as part of a military uniform **b :** an ornamental strip or loop sewn across the shoulder of a dress or coat — **ep·au·let·ted** \,e-pə-'le-təd, 'e-pə-,\ *adj*

ep·a·zote \'e-pə-,zōt\ *n* [MexSp, fr. Nahuatl *epazōtl*] (1946) : WORMSEED b

épée \'e-,pā, ā-'pā\ *n* [F, fr. L *spatha*] (1889) **1 :** a fencing or dueling sword having a bowl–shaped guard and a rigid blade of triangular section with no cutting edge that tapers to a sharp point blunted for fencing — compare ⁴FOIL 1, SABER **2 :** the art or sport of fencing with the épée

E epaulet

épée·ist \-ist\ *n* (1910) : one who fences with an épée

epei·rog·e·ny \,e-,pī-'rä-jə-nē\ *n, pl* **-nies** [Gk *ēpeiros* mainland, continent + E *-geny*] (1890) : the deformation of the earth's crust by which the broader features of relief are produced — **epei·ro·gen·ic** \,i-,pī-rə-'je-nik\ *adj* — **epei·ro·gen·i·cal·ly** \-ni-k(ə-)lē\ *adv*

epen·the·sis \i-'pen(t)-thə-səs, e-\ *n, pl* **-the·ses** \-,sēz\ [LL, fr. Gk, fr. *epentithenai* to insert a letter, fr. *epi-* + *entithenai* to put in, fr. *en-* + *tithenai* to put — more at DO] (1543) : the insertion or development of a sound or letter in the body of a word (as \ə\ in \'a-thə-,lēt\ *athlete*) — **ep·en·thet·ic** \,e-pən-'the-tik\ *adj*

epergne \i-'pərn, ā-\ *n* [prob. fr. F *épargne* saving] (1761) : an often ornate tiered centerpiece consisting typically of a frame of wrought metal (as silver or gold) bearing dishes, vases, or candle holders or a combination of these

ep·ex·e·ge·sis \,e-,pek-sə-'jē-səs\ *n, pl* **-ge·ses** \-,sēz\ [Gk *epexēgēsis*, fr. *epi-* + *exēgēsis* exegesis] (ca. 1577) : additional explanation or explanatory matter — **ep·ex·e·get·i·cal** \-'je-ti-kəl\ *or* **ep·ex·e·get·ic** \-'je-tik\ *adj* — **ep·ex·e·get·i·cal·ly** \-'je-ti-k(ə-)lē\ *adv*

ephah \'ē-fə, 'e-fə\ *n* [ME *ephi*, fr. LL, fr. Heb *ēphāh*, fr. Egypt *'pt*] (1611) : an ancient Hebrew unit of dry measure equal to ¹/₁₀ homer or a little over a bushel

ephebe \'e-,fēb, i-'fēb\ *n* [L *ephebus*] (1880) : EPHEBUS; *also* : a young man : YOUTH

ephe·bic \i-'fē-bik\ *adj* (1865) : of, relating to, or characteristic of an ephebe or ephebus

ephe·bus \i-'fē-bəs, e-\ *n, pl* **-bi** \-,bī\ [L, fr. Gk *ephēbos*, fr. *epi-* + *hēbē* youth, puberty] (1697) : a youth of ancient Greece; *esp* : an Athenian 18 or 19 years old in training for full citizenship

ephe·dra \i-'fe-drə, 'e-fə-drə\ *n* [NL, genus name, fr. L, equisetum, fr. Gk, fr. *ephedros* sitting upon, fr. *epi-* + *hedra* seat — more at SIT] (ca. 1889) : any of a large genus (*Ephedra* of the family Gnetaceae) of jointed nearly leafless desert shrubs with the leaves reduced to scales at the nodes

ephed·rine \i-'fe-drən, *Brit also* 'e-fə-drən\ *n* [NL *Ephedra*] (1889) : a crystalline alkaloid $C_{10}H_{15}NO$ extracted from Chinese ephedras or synthesized and used in the form of a salt for relief of hay fever, asthma, and nasal congestion

ephem·era \i-'fe-mər-ə, -'fem-rə\ *n, pl* **ephemera** *also* **ephem·er·ae** \-mər-ē, -rē\ *or* **ephemeras** [NL, fr. Gk *ephēmera*, neut. pl. of *ephēmeros*] (1751) **1 :** something of no lasting significance — usu. used in pl. **2** *ephemera* pl **:** collectibles (as posters, broadsides, and tickets) not intended to have lasting value

¹ephem·er·al \i-'fem-rəl, -'fēm-; -'fe-mə-, -'fē-\ *adj* [Gk *ephēmeros* lasting a day, daily, fr. *epi-* + *hēmera* day] (1576) **1 :** lasting one day only ⟨an ∼ fever⟩ **2 :** lasting a very short time ⟨∼ pleasures⟩ *syn* see TRANSIENT — **ephem·er·al·ly** \-rə-lē\ *adv*

²ephemeral *n* (1817) **:** something ephemeral; *specif* **:** a plant that grows, flowers, and dies in a few days

ephem·er·al·i·ty \i-,fe-mə-'ra-lə-tē, -,fē-\ *n, pl* **-ties** (1822) **1 :** the quality or state of being ephemeral **2** *pl* **:** ephemeral things

ephem·er·id \i-'fe-mə-rəd\ *n* [ultim. fr. Gk *ephēmeron*] (1872) **:** MAYFLY

ephem·er·is \-mə-rəs\ *n, pl* **eph·e·mer·i·des** \,e-fə-'mer-ə-,dēz\ [L, diary, ephemeris, fr. Gk *ephēmeris*, fr. *ephēmeros*] (1508) **:** a tabular statement of the assigned places of a celestial body for regular intervals

ephemeris time *n* (1950) **:** a uniform measure of time defined by the orbital motions of the planets

Ephe·sians \i-'fē-zhənz\ *n pl but sing in constr* [short for *Epistle to the Ephesians*] **:** a letter addressed to early Christians and included as a book in the New Testament — see BIBLE table

eph·od \'e-,fäd, 'ē-,fäd\ *n* [ME, fr. LL, fr. Heb *ēphōdh*] (14c) **1 :** a linen apron worn in ancient Hebrew rites; *esp* **:** a vestment for the high priest **2 :** an ancient Hebrew instrument of priestly divination

eph·or \'e-fər, -,fȯr\ *n* [L *ephorus*, fr. Gk *ephoros*, fr. *ephoran* to oversee, fr. *epi-* + *horan* to see — more at WARY] (1579) **1 :** one of five ancient Spartan magistrates having power over the king **2 :** a government official in modern Greece; *esp* **:** one who oversees public works — **eph·or·ate** \'e-fə-,rāt\ *n*

Ephra·im \'ē-frē-əm\ *n* [Heb *Ephrayim*] **:** a son of Joseph and the traditional eponymous ancestor of one of the tribes of Israel

Ephra·im·ite \-frē-ə-,mit\ *n* (1611) **1 :** a member of the Hebrew tribe of Ephraim **2 :** a native or inhabitant of the biblical northern kingdom of Israel

epi- or **ep-** *prefix* [ME, fr. MF & L; MF, fr. L, fr. Gk, fr. *epi* on, at, besides, after; akin to OE *eofot* crime] **1 :** upon ⟨*epiphyte*⟩ **:** besides ⟨*epiphenomenon*⟩ **:** attached to ⟨*epididymis*⟩ **:** over ⟨*epicenter*⟩ **:** outer ⟨*epiblast*⟩ **:** after ⟨*epigenesis*⟩ **2 a :** chemical entity related to (such) another ⟨*epimer*⟩ **b :** chemical entity distinguished from (such) another by having a bridge connection ⟨*epichlorohydrin*⟩

epi·blast \'e-pə-,blast\ *n* (1875) **:** the outer layer of the blastoderm **:** ECTODERM — **epi·blas·tic** \,e-pə-'blas-tik\ *adj*

epib·o·ly \i-'pi-bə-lē\ *n, pl* **-lies** [Gk *epibolē* addition, fr. *epiballein* to throw on, fr. *epi-* + *ballein* to throw — more at DEVIL] (1875) **:** the growing of one part about another; *esp* **:** such growth of the dorsal lip area during gastrulation — **epi·bol·ic** \,e-pə-'bä-lik\ *adj*

¹ep·ic \'e-pik\ *adj* [L *epicus*, fr. Gk *epikos*, fr. *epos* word, speech, poem — more at VOICE] (1589) **1 :** of, relating to, or having the characteristics of an epic **2 a :** extending beyond the usual or ordinary esp. in size or scope ⟨his genius was ∼ —*Times Lit. Supp.*⟩ **b :** HEROIC — **ep·i·cal** \-pi-kəl\ *adj* — **ep·i·cal·ly** \-pi-k(ə-)lē\ *adv*

²epic *n* (1706) **1 :** a long narrative poem in elevated style recounting the deeds of a legendary or historical hero ⟨the *Iliad* and the *Odyssey* are ∼*s*⟩ **2 :** a work of art (as a novel or drama) that resembles or suggests an epic **3 :** a series of events or body of legend or tradition thought to form the proper subject of an epic ⟨the winning of the West was a great American ∼⟩

epi·ca·lyx \,e-pi-'kā-liks also -'ka-liks\ *n* (1870) **:** an involucre resembling the calyx but consisting of a whorl of bracts that is exterior to the calyx or results from the union of the sepal appendages

epi·can·thic fold \,e-pə-,kan(t)-thik-\ *n* [NL *epicanthus* epicanthic fold, fr. *epi-* + *canthus* canthus] (1913) **:** a prolongation of a fold of the skin of the upper eyelid over the inner angle or both angles of the eye

epi·car·di·um \,e-pə-'kar-dē-əm\ *n, pl* **-dia** \-dē-ə\ [NL] (ca. 1865) **:** the visceral part of the pericardium that closely envelops the heart — **epi·car·di·al** \-dē-əl\ *adj*

epi·carp \'e-pi-,kärp\ *n* [F *épicarpe*, fr. *épi-* fr. *epi-* + *-carpe* -carp] (1835) **:** EXOCARP

ep·i·cene \'e-pi-,sēn\ *adj* [ME, fr. L *epicoenus*, fr. Gk *epikoinos*, fr. *epi-* + *koinos* common — more at CO-] (15c) **1** *of a noun* **:** having but one form to indicate either sex **2 a :** having characteristics typical of the other sex **:** INTERSEXUAL **b :** EFFEMINATE **3 :** lacking characteristics of either sex — **epicene** *n* — **ep·i·cen·ism** \-,sē-,ni-zəm, ,e-pə-'\ *n*

epi·cen·ter \'e-pi-,sen-tər\ *n* [NL *epicentrum*, fr. *epi-* + L *centrum* center] (1887) **1 :** the part of the earth's surface directly above the focus of an earthquake — compare HYPOCENTER **1 2 :** CENTER 2a, b, c ⟨the ∼ of world finance⟩ — **epi·cen·tral** \,e-pi-'sen-trəl\ *adj*

epi·chlo·ro·hy·drin \,e-pi-,klōr-ə-'hī-drən, -,klȯr-\ *n* (ca. 1891) **:** a volatile liquid toxic epoxide C_3H_5ClO having a chloroform odor and used esp. in making epoxy resins and rubbers

epi·con·ti·nen·tal \,e-pi-,kän-t³n-'en-t³l\ *adj* (1900) **:** lying upon a continent or a continental shelf ⟨∼ seas⟩

epi·cot·yl \'e-pi-,kä-t³l\ *n* [*epi-* + *cotyledon*] (1880) **:** the portion of the axis of a plant embryo or seedling above the cotyledonary node

ep·i·crit·ic \,e-pə-'kri-tik\ *adj* [Gk *epikritikos* determinative, fr. *epikrinein* to decide, fr. *epi-* + *krinein* to judge — more at CERTAIN] (ca. 1905) **:** of, relating to, being, or mediating cutaneous sensory reception marked by accurate discrimination between small degrees of sensation

epic simile *n* (1931) **:** an extended simile that is used typically in epic poetry to intensify the heroic stature of the subject

ep·i·cure \'e-pi-,kyùr\ *n* [*Epicurus*] (1565) **1** *archaic* **:** one devoted to sensual pleasure **:** SYBARITE **2 :** one with sensitive and discriminating tastes esp. in food or wine

syn EPICURE, GOURMET, GOURMAND, GASTRONOME mean one who takes pleasure in eating and drinking. EPICURE implies fastidiousness and voluptuousness of taste. GOURMET implies being a connoisseur in food and drink and the discriminating enjoyment of them. GOURMAND implies a hearty appetite for good food and drink, not without discernment, but with less than a gourmet's. GASTRONOME implies that one has studied extensively the history and rituals of haute cuisine.

ep·i·cu·re·an \,e-pi-kyu-'rē-ən, -'kyùr-ē-\ *adj* (1586) **1** *cap* **:** of or relating to Epicurus or Epicureanism **2 :** of, relating to, or suited to an epicure

Epicurean *n* (14c) **1 :** a follower of Epicurus **2** *often not cap* **:** EPICURE 2

ep·i·cu·re·an·ism \-ə-,ni-zəm\ *n* (ca. 1751) **1** *cap* **a :** the philosophy of Epicurus who subscribed to a hedonistic ethics that considered an imperturbable emotional calm the highest good and whose followers held intellectual pleasures superior to transient sensualism **b :** a mode of life in consonance with Epicureanism **2 :** EPICURISM

ep·i·cur·ism \'e-pi-,kyùr-,i-zəm, ,e-pi-'\ *n* (1586) **:** the practices or tastes of an epicure or an epicurean

epi·cu·ti·cle \,e-pi-'kyü-ti-kəl\ *n* (1929) **:** an outermost waxy layer of the insect exoskeleton — **epi·cu·tic·u·lar** \-kyù-'ti-kyə-lər\ *adj*

epi·cy·cle \'e-pə-,sī-kəl\ *n* [ME *epicicle*, fr. LL *epicyclus*, fr. Gk *epikyklos*, fr. *epi-* + *kyklos* circle — more at WHEEL] (14c) **1** *in Ptolemaic astron* **:** a circle in which a planet moves and which has a center that is itself carried around at the same time on the circumference of a larger circle **2 :** a process going on within a larger one — **epi·cy·clic** \,e-pə-'sī-klik, -'si-klik\ *adj*

epicyclic train *n* (ca. 1890) **:** a train (as of gear wheels) designed to have one or more parts travel around the circumference of another fixed or revolving part

epi·cy·cloid \,e-pə-'sī-,klȯid\ *n* (ca. 1755) **:** a curve traced by a point on a circle that rolls on the outside of a fixed circle — **epi·cy·cloi·dal** \-sī-'klȯi-d³l\ *adj*

epicycloid *E,* traced by point *P,* on circle *R,* rolling on fixed circle *F*

¹epi·dem·ic \,e-pə-'de-mik\ *adj* [F *épidémique,* fr. MF, fr. *epidemie,* n., epidemic, fr. LL *epidemia,* fr. Gk *epidēmia* visit, epidemic, fr. *epidēmos* visiting, epidemic, fr. *epi-* + *dēmos* people — more at DEMAGOGUE] (1603) **1 :** affecting or tending to affect a disproportionately large number of individuals within a population, community, or region at the same time ⟨typhoid was ∼⟩ **2 a :** excessively prevalent **b :** CONTAGIOUS **4** ⟨∼ laughter⟩ **3 :** of, relating to, or constituting an epidemic ⟨the practice had reached ∼ proportions⟩ — **ep·i·dem·i·cal** \-'de-mi-kəl\ *adj* — **ep·i·dem·i·cal·ly** \-'de-mi-k(ə-)lē\ *adv* — **ep·i·de·mic·i·ty** \-də-'mi-sə-tē\ *n*

²epidemic *n* (1799) **1 :** an outbreak of epidemic disease **2 :** an outbreak or product of sudden rapid spread, growth, or development; *specif* **:** a natural population suddenly and greatly enlarged

ep·i·de·mi·ol·o·gy \,e-pə-,dē-mē-'ä-lə-jē, -,de-mē-\ *n* [LL *epidemia* + ISV *-logy*] (ca. 1860) **1 :** a branch of medical science that deals with the incidence, distribution, and control of disease in a population **2 :** the sum of the factors controlling the presence or absence of a disease or pathogen — **ep·i·de·mi·o·log·i·cal** \-,dē-mē-ə-'lä-ji-kəl, -,de-mē-\ *also* **ep·i·de·mi·o·log·ic** \-jik\ *adj* — **ep·i·de·mi·o·log·i·cal·ly** \-ji-k(ə-)lē\ *adv* — **ep·i·de·mi·ol·o·gist** \-,dē-mē-'ä-lə-jist, -,de-mē-\ *n*

ep·i·den·drum \,e-pə-'den-drəm\ *n* [NL, fr. Gk *epi-* + *dendron* tree — more at DENDR-] (1791) **:** any of a large genus (*Epidendrum*) of chiefly epiphytic orchids found esp. in tropical America

epi·der·mal \,e-pə-'dər-məl\ *also* **epi·der·mic** \-mik\ *adj* (1816) **:** of, relating to, or arising from the epidermis

epidermal growth factor *n* (1966) **:** a polypeptide hormone that stimulates cell proliferation

epi·der·mis \,e-pə-'dər-məs\ *n* [LL, fr. Gk, fr. *epi-* + *derma* skin — more at DERM-] (1626) **1 a :** the outer epithelial layer of the external integument of the animal body that is derived from the embryonic epiblast; *specif* **:** the outer nonsensitive and nonvascular layer of the skin of a vertebrate that overlies the dermis **b :** any of various animal integuments **2 :** a thin surface layer of tissue in higher plants formed by growth of a primary meristem

epi·der·moid \-,mȯid\ *adj* (1836) **:** resembling epidermis or epidermal cells **:** made up of elements like those of epidermis ⟨∼ cancer of the lung⟩

epi·dia·scope \,e-pə-'dī-ə-,skōp\ *n* [ISV] (1903) **1 :** a projector for images of both opaque objects and transparencies **2 :** EPISCOPE

ep·i·did·y·mis \,e-pə-'di-də-məs\ *n, pl* **-mi·des** \-mə-,dēz\ [NL, fr. Gk, fr. *epi-* + *didymos* testicle, twin, fr. *dyo* two — more at TWO] (1610) **:** a system of ductules emerging posteriorly from the testis that holds sperm during maturation and that forms a tangled mass before uniting into a single coiled duct which is continuous with the vas deferens — **ep·i·did·y·mal** \-məl\ *adj*

ep·i·did·y·mi·tis \,e-pə-,di-də-'mī-təs\ *n* [NL] (1852) **:** inflammation of the epididymis

ep·i·dote \'e-pə-,dōt\ *n* [F *épidote,* fr. Gk *epididonai* to give in addition, fr. *epi-* + *didonai* to give — more at DATE] (1808) **:** a yellowish green mineral $Ca_2(Al,Fe)_3Si_3O_{12}OH$ usu. occurring in grains or columnar masses and sometimes used as a gemstone

epi·du·ral \,e-pə-'d(y)ùr-əl\ *adj* (1882) **:** situated upon or administered outside the dura mater ⟨∼ anesthesia⟩ ⟨∼ structures⟩

epi·fau·na \'e-pə-,fȯ-nə, -'fä-\ *n* [NL] (ca. 1914) **:** benthic fauna living on the substrate (as a hard sea floor) or on other organisms — compare INFAUNA — **epi·fau·nal** \-,fȯ-n³l, -'fä-\ *adj*

epi·gas·tric \,e-pi-'gas-trik\ *adj* (ca. 1678) **1 :** lying upon or over the stomach **2 a :** of, relating to, supplying, or draining the anterior walls of the abdomen **b :** of or relating to the abdominal region

epi·ge·al \,e-pi-'jē-əl\ *or* **epi·ge·an** \-'jē-ən\ *also* **epi·ge·ous** \-'jē-əs\ *or* **epi·ge·ic** \-'jē-ik\ *adj* [Gk *epigaios* upon the earth, fr. *epi-* + *gaia* earth] (1861) **1** *of a cotyledon* **:** forced above ground by elongation of the hypocotyl **2 :** marked by the production of epigeal cotyledons ⟨∼ germination⟩ **3 :** living on or near the surface of the ground; *also* **:** relating to or being the environment near the surface of the ground

epi·gen·e·sis \,e-pə-'je-nə-səs\ *n* [NL] (1798) **1 :** development of a plant or animal from an egg or spore through a series of processes in which unorganized cell masses differentiate into organs and organ sys-

\ə\ abut \³\ kitten, F table \ər\ further \a\ ash \ā\ ace \ä\ mop, mar
\aù\ out \ch\ chin \e\ bet \ē\ easy \g\ go \i\ hit \ī\ ice \j\ job
\ŋ\ sing \ō\ go \ȯ\ law \ȯi\ boy \th\ thin \th̲\ the \ü\ loot \ù\ foot
\y\ yet \zh\ vision \á, k̲, ⁿ, œ, œ̄, ᵫ, ᵫ̄, ᵊ\ see Guide to Pronunciation

tems; *also* : the theory that plant and animal development proceeds in this way — compare PREFORMATION 2   **2** : change in the mineral character of a rock owing to outside influences

epi·ge·net·ic \,je-pə-'ne-tik\ *adj* (1883)   **1** : of, relating to, or produced by the chain of developmental processes in epigenesis that lead from genotype to phenotype after the initial action of the genes   **2** *of a deposit or structure* : formed after the laying down of the enclosing rock — **epi·ge·net·i·cal·ly** \-'ne-ti-k(ə)lē\ *adv*

epi·glot·tal \,e-pə-'glä-t°l\ *also* **epi·glot·tic** \-'glä-tik\ *adj* (1926) : of, relating to, or produced with the aid of the epiglottis

epi·glot·tis \-'glä-təs\ *n* [NL, fr. Gk *epiglōttis*, fr. *epi-* + *glōttis* glottis] (1615) : a thin plate of flexible cartilage in front of the glottis that folds back over and protects the glottis during swallowing

ep·i·gone \'e-pə-,gōn\ *n* [G, fr. L *epigonus* successor, fr. Gk *epigonos*, fr. *epigignesthai* to be born after, fr. *epi-* + *gignesthai* to be born — more at KIN] (1865) : FOLLOWER, DISCIPLE; *also* : an inferior imitator — **ep·i·gon·ic** \,e-pə-'gä-nik\ *or* **epig·o·nous** \i-'pi-gə-nəs, e-\ *adj* — **epig·o·nism** \-'pi-gə-,ni-zəm\ *n*

epig·o·nus \i-'pi-gə-nəs, e-\ *n, pl* **-ni** \-,nī, -,nē\ [L] (1922) : EPIGONE — usu. used in pl.

ep·i·gram \'e-pə-,gram\ *n* [ME *epigrame*, fr. L *epigrammat-, epigramma*, fr. Gk, fr. *epigraphein* to write on, inscribe, fr. *epi-* + *graphein* to write — more at CARVE] (15c)   **1** : a concise poem dealing pointedly and often satirically with a single thought or event and often ending with an ingenious turn of thought   **2** : a terse, sage, or witty and often paradoxical saying   **3** : epigrammatic expression — **ep·i·gram·ma·tism** \,e-pə-'gra-mə-,ti-zəm\ *n* — **ep·i·gram·ma·tist** \-'gra-mə-tist\ *n*

ep·i·gram·mat·ic \,e-pə-grə-'ma-tik\ *adj* (ca. 1704)   **1** : of, relating to, or resembling an epigram   **2** : marked by or given to the use of epigrams — **ep·i·gram·mat·i·cal·ly** \-'ma-ti-k(ə-)lē\ *adv*

ep·i·gram·ma·tize \-'gra-mə-,tīz\ *vb* **-tized; -tiz·ing** *vt* (1691)   **1** : to express in the form of an epigram   **2** : to make an epigram about ~ *vi* : to make an epigram — **ep·i·gram·ma·tiz·er** *n*

ep·i·graph \'e-pə-,graf\ *n* [Gk *epigraphē*, fr. *epigraphein*] (1624)   **1** : an engraved inscription   **2** : a quotation set at the beginning of a literary work or one of its divisions to suggest its theme

epig·ra·pher \i-'pi-grə-fər, e-\ *n* (1887) : EPIGRAPHIST

ep·i·graph·ic \,e-pə-'gra-fik\ *also* **ep·i·graph·i·cal** \-fi-kəl\ *adj* (1858) : of or relating to epigraphs or epigraphy — **ep·i·graph·i·cal·ly** \-fi-k(ə-)lē\ *adv*

epig·ra·phist \i-'pi-grə-fist, e-\ *n* (ca. 1864) : a specialist in epigraphy

epig·ra·phy \-fē\ *n* (1851)   **1** : EPIGRAPHS, INSCRIPTIONS   **2** : the study of inscriptions; *esp* : the deciphering of ancient inscriptions

epig·y·nous \i-'pi-jə-nəs, e-\ *adj* (1830)   **1** *of a floral organ* : adnate to the surface of the ovary and appearing to grow from the top of it   **2** : having epigynous floral organs — **epig·y·ny** \-nē\ *n*

ep·i·la·tion \,e-pə-'lā-shən\ *n* [F *épilation*, fr. *épiler* to remove hair, fr. *é-* + L *pilus* hair — more at PILE] (1878) : the loss or removal of hair

ep·i·lep·sy \'e-pə-,lep-sē\ *n, pl* **-sies** [MF *epilepsie*, fr. LL *epilepsia*, fr. Gk *epilēpsia*, fr. *epilambanein* to seize, fr. *epi-* + *lambanein* to take, seize — more at LATCH] (1543) : any of various disorders marked by disturbed electrical rhythms of the central nervous system and typically manifested by convulsive attacks usu. with clouding of consciousness

epilept- *or* **epilepti-** *or* **epilepto-** *comb form* [Gk *epilēpt-*, fr. *epilēptos* seized by epilepsy, fr. *epilambanein*] : epilepsy ⟨*epileptoid*⟩

ep·i·lep·tic \,e-pə-'lep-tik\ *adj* (1605) : relating to, affected with, or having the characteristics of epilepsy — **epileptic** *n* — **ep·i·lep·ti·cal·ly** \-ti-k(ə-)lē\ *adv*

ep·i·lep·ti·form \-'lep-tə-,fòrm\ *adj* (ca. 1859) : resembling that of epilepsy ⟨an ~ convulsion⟩

ep·i·lep·to·gen·ic \-,lep-tə-'je-nik\ *adj* (ca. 1882) : inducing or tending to induce epilepsy ⟨an ~ drug⟩

ep·i·lep·toid \-'lep-,tòid\ *adj* (ca. 1860)   **1** : EPILEPTIFORM   **2** : exhibiting symptoms resembling those of epilepsy ⟨the ~ person⟩

epi·lim·ni·on \,e-pə-'lim-nē-,än, -nə-ən\ *n* [NL, fr. *epi-* + Gk *limnion*, dim. of *limnē* marshy lake — more at LIMNETIC] (ca. 1910) : the water layer overlying the thermocline of a lake

ep·i·logue *also* **ep·i·log** \'e-pə-,lòg, -,läg\ *n* [ME *epiloge*, fr. MF *epilogue*, fr. L *epilogus*, fr. Gk *epilogos*, fr. *epilegein* to say in addition, fr. *epi-* + *legein* to say — more at LEGEND] (15c)   **1** : a concluding section that rounds out the design of a literary work   **2 a** : a speech often in verse addressed to the audience by an actor at the end of a play; *also* : the actor speaking such an epilogue   **b** : the final scene of a play that comments on or summarizes the main action   **3** : the concluding section of a musical composition : CODA

epi·mer \'e-pi-mər\ *n* [*epi-* + *isomer*] (ca. 1911) : either of the stereoisomers of a sugar or sugar derivative that differ in the arrangement of the hydrogen atom and the hydroxyl group on the first asymmetric carbon atom of a chain — **ep·i·mer·ic** \,e-pi-'mer-ik\ *adj*

epim·er·ase \i-'pi-mə-,rās, e-, -,rāz\ *n* (1960) : any of various isomerases that catalyze the inversion of asymmetric groups in a substrate with several centers of asymmetry

epi·my·si·um \,e-pə-'mi-zhē-əm, -zē-\ *n, pl* **-sia** \-zhē-ə, -zē-ə\ [NL, irreg. fr. *epi-* + Gk *mys* mouse, muscle — more at MOUSE] (1900) : the external connective-tissue sheath of a muscle

epi·nas·ty \'e-pə-,nas-tē\ *n* [ISV *epi-* + Gk *nastos* close-pressed (fr. *nassein* to press) + ISV *-y*] (1880) : a nastic movement in which a plant part (as a flower petal) is bent outward and often downward — **ep·i·nas·tic** \,e-pə-'nas-tik\ *adj* — **ep·i·nas·ti·cal·ly** \-ti-k(ə-)lē\ *adv*

epi·neph·rine *also* **epi·neph·rin** \,e-pə-'ne-frən\ *n* [ISV *epi-* + Gk *nephros* kidney — more at NEPHRITIS] (1899) : a colorless crystalline feebly basic sympathomimetic hormone $C_9H_{13}NO_3$ that is the principal blood-pressure raising hormone secreted by the adrenal medulla and is used medicinally esp. as a heart stimulant, a vasoconstrictor in controlling hemorrhages of the skin, and a muscle relaxant in bronchial asthma — called also *adrenalin*

epi·neu·ri·um \,e-pə-'n(y)ùr-ē-əm\ *n* [NL] (ca. 1882) : the external connective-tissue sheath of a nerve trunk

epi·pe·lag·ic \,e-pi-pə-'la-jik\ *adj* (1940) : of, relating to, or constituting the part of the oceanic zone into which enough light penetrates for photosynthesis

ep·i·phan·ic \,e-pə-'fa-nik\ *adj* (1951) : of or having the character of an epiphany

epiph·a·nous \i-'pi-fə-nəs\ *adj* (1823) : EPIPHANIC

epiph·a·ny \i-'pi-fə-nē\ *n, pl* **-nies** [ME *epiphanie*, fr. MF, fr. LL *epiphania*, fr. LGk, pl., prob. alter. of Gk *epiphaneia* appearance, manifestation, fr. *epiphainein* to manifest, fr. *epi-* + *phainein* to show — more at FANCY] (14c)   **1** *cap* : January 6 observed as a church festival in commemoration of the coming of the Magi as the first manifestation of Christ to the Gentiles or in the Eastern Church in commemoration of the baptism of Christ   **2** : an appearance or manifestation esp. of a divine being   **3 a** (1) : a usu. sudden manifestation or perception of the essential nature or meaning of something   (2) : an intuitive grasp of reality through something (as an event) usu. simple and striking   (3) : an illuminating discovery   **b** : a revealing scene or moment

epi·phe·nom·e·nal \,e-pi-fi-'nä-mə-n°l\ *adj* (1899) : of or relating to an epiphenomenon : DERIVATIVE — **epi·phe·nom·e·nal·ly** \-n°l-ē\ *adv*

epi·phe·nom·e·nal·ism \-n°l-,i-zəm\ *n* (1899) : a doctrine that mental processes are epiphenomena of brain processes

epi·phe·nom·e·non \-'nä-mə-,nän, -nən\ *n, pl* **-na** \-,nä, -nə\ (ca. 1706) : a secondary phenomenon accompanying another and caused by it

epi·phragm \'e-pə-,fram\ *n* [Gk *epiphragma* covering] (ca. 1854) : a closing membrane or septum (as of a snail shell or a moss capsule)

epiph·y·se·al \i-,pi-fə-'sē-əl\ *also* **epi·phys·i·al** \,e-pə-'fi-zē-əl\ *adj* (1842) : of or relating to an epiphysis

epiph·y·sis \i-'pi-fə-səs\ *n, pl* **-y·ses** \-,sēz\ [NL, fr. Gk, growth, fr. *epiphyesthai* to grow on, fr. *epi-* + *phyesthai* to grow, middle voice of *phyein* to bring forth — more at BE] (1634)   **1** : a part or process of a bone that ossifies separately and later becomes ankylosed to the main part of the bone; *esp* : an end of a long bone   **2** : PINEAL GLAND

epi·phyte \'e-pə-,fīt\ *n* (ca. 1847) : a plant that derives its moisture and nutrients from the air and rain and grows usu. on another plant

epi·phyt·ic \,e-pə-'fi-tik\ *adj* (1830)   **1** : of, relating to, or being an epiphyte   **2** : living on the surface of plants — **epi·phyt·i·cal·ly** \-'fi-ti-k(ə-)lē\ *adv* — **epi·phyt·ism** \'e-pə-,fī-,ti-zəm\ *n*

epi·phy·tol·o·gy \,e-pə-,fī-'tä-lə-jē\ *n* [*epiphytotic* + *-logy*] (1940)   **1** : a science that deals with character, ecology, and causes of outbreak of plant diseases   **2** : the sum of the factors controlling the occurrence of a disease or pathogen of plants

epi·phy·tot·ic \-'tä-tik\ *adj* [*epi-* + *-phyte* + *-otic* (as in *epizootic*)] (ca. 1899) : of, relating to, or being a plant disease that tends to recur sporadically and to affect large numbers of susceptible plants — **epiphytotic** *n*

epi·scia \i-'pi-sh(ē-)ə\ *n* [NL, fr. Gk *episkios* shaded, fr. *epi-* + *skia* shadow — more at SHINE] (ca. 1868) : any of a genus (*Episcia*) of tropical American herbs that have hairy foliage and are related to the African violet

epis·co·pa·cy \i-'pis-kə-pə-sē\ *n, pl* **-cies** (1647)   **1** : government of the church by bishops or by a hierarchy   **2** : EPISCOPATE

epis·co·pal \i-'pis-kə-pəl, -bəl\ *adj* [ME, fr. LL *episcopalis*, fr. *episcopus* bishop — more at BISHOP] (15c)   **1** : of or relating to a bishop   **2** : of, having, or constituting government by bishops   **3** *cap* : of or relating to the Protestant Episcopal Church representing the Anglican communion in the U.S. — **epis·co·pal·ly** \-p(ə-)lē\ *adv*

Episcopal *n* (1752) : EPISCOPALIAN

Epis·co·pa·lian \i-,pis-kə-'pāl-yən\ *n* (1690)   **1** : an adherent of the episcopal form of church government   **2** : a member of an episcopal church (as the Protestant Episcopal Church) — **Episcopalian** *adj* — **Epis·co·pa·lian·ism** \-yə-,ni-zəm\ *n*

epis·co·pate \i-'pis-kə-pət, -,pāt\ *n* (1641)   **1** : the rank, office, or term of bishop   **2** : DIOCESE   **3** : the body of bishops (as in a country)

epi·scope \'e-pə-,skōp\ *n* [ISV] (ca. 1909) : a projector for images of opaque objects (as photographs)

epi·si·ot·o·my \i-,pi-zē-'ä-tə-mē, -,pē-\ *n* [ISV *episio-* vulva (fr. Gk *epision* pubic region) + *-tomy*] (1878) : surgical enlargement of the vulval orifice for obstetrical purposes during parturition

ep·i·sode \'e-pə-,sōd *also* -,zōd\ *n* [Gk *epeisodion*, fr. neut. of *epeisodios* coming in besides, fr. *epi-* + *eisodios* coming in, fr. *eis* into (akin to Gk *en* in) + *hodos* road, journey — more at IN] (1678)   **1** : a usu. brief unit of action in a dramatic or literary work: as   **a** : the part of an ancient Greek tragedy between two choric songs   **b** : a developed situation that is integral to but separable from a continuous narrative : INCIDENT   **c** : one of a series of loosely connected stories or scenes   **d** : the part of a serial presented at one performance   **2** : an event that is distinctive and separate although part of a larger series   **3** : a digressive subdivision in a musical composition **syn** see OCCURRENCE

ep·i·sod·ic \,e-pə-'sä-dik *also* -'zä-\ *also* **ep·i·sod·i·cal** \-di-kəl\ *adj* (1711)   **1** : made up of separate esp. loosely connected episodes   **2** : having the form of an episode   **3** : of or limited in duration or significance to a particular episode : TEMPORARY ⟨may be able to establish whether the sea-floor spreading is continuous or ~ —A. I. Hammond⟩   **4** : occurring, appearing, or changing at usu. irregular intervals : OCCASIONAL ⟨an ~ illness⟩ — **ep·i·sod·i·cal·ly** \-di-k(ə-)lē\ *adv*

epi·some \'e-pə-,sōm, -,zōm\ *n* (ca. 1931) : a genetic determinant (as the DNA of some bacteriophages) that can replicate autonomously in bacterial cytoplasm or as an integral part of the chromosomes — **epi·som·al** \,e-pə-'sō-məl, -'zō-\ *adj* — **epi·som·al·ly** \-mə-lē\ *adv*

epis·ta·sis \i-'pis-tə-səs\ *n, pl* **-ta·ses** \-,sēz\ [NL, fr. Gk, act of stopping, fr. *ephistanai* to stop, fr. *epi-* + *histanai* to cause to stand — more at STAND] (ca. 1917) : suppression of the effect of a gene by a nonallelic gene — **ep·i·stat·ic** \,e-pə-'sta-tik\ *adj*

ep·i·stax·is \,e-pə-'stak-səs\ *n, pl* **-stax·es** \-,sēz\ [NL, fr. Gk, fr. *epistazein* to drip on, to bleed at the nose again, fr. *epi-* + *stazein* to drip] (1793) : NOSEBLEED

epi·ste·mic \,e-pə-'stē-mik, -'ste-mik\ *adj* (1922) : of or relating to knowledge or knowing : COGNITIVE — **ep·i·ste·mi·cal·ly** \-mi-k(ə-)lē\ *adv*

epis·te·mol·o·gy \i-,pis-tə-'mä-lə-jē\ *n* [Gk *epistēmē* knowledge, fr. *epistanai* to understand, know, fr. *epi-* + *histanai* to cause to stand — more at STAND] (ca. 1856) : the study or a theory of the nature and grounds of knowledge esp. with reference to its limits and validity — **epis·te·mo·log·i·cal** \-mə-'lä-ji-kəl\ *adj* — **epis·te·mo·log·i·cal·ly** \-k(ə-)lē\ *adv* — **epis·te·mol·o·gist** \-'mä-lə-jist\ *n*

epis·tle \i-'pi-səl\ *n* [ME, letter, Epistle, fr. OF, fr. L *epistula, epistola* letter, fr. Gk *epistolē* message, letter, fr. *epistellein* to send to, fr. *epi-* + *stellein* to send] (13c)   **1** *cap*   **a** : one of the letters adopted as books of the New Testament   **b** : a liturgical lection usu. from one of the New

Testament Epistles **2 a :** LETTER; *esp* : a formal or elegant letter **b** : a composition in the form of a letter — **epis·tler** \-'pis-lə-lər\ *n*

¹**epis·to·lary** \i-'pis-tə-ler-ē, ˌe-pi-'stō-lə-rē\ *adj* (ca. 1656) **1** : of, relating to, or suitable to a letter **2** : contained in or carried on by letters ⟨an endless sequence of ... ~ love affairs —*Times Lit. Supp.*⟩ **3** : written in the form of a series of letters ⟨~ novel⟩

²**epistolary** *n, pl* **-lar·ies** (ca. 1900) : a lectionary containing a body of liturgical epistles

epis·to·ler \i-'pis-tə-lər\ *n* (1530) : the reader of the liturgical Epistle esp. in Anglican churches

ep·i·stome \'e-pə-ˌstōm\ *n* [NL *epistoma*] (1852) : any of several structures or regions situated above or covering the mouth of various invertebrates

epis·tro·phe \i-'pis-trə-(ˌ)fē\ *n* [Gk *epistrophē*, lit., turning about, fr. *epi-* + *strophē* turning — more at STROPHE] (ca. 1584) : repetition of a word or expression at the end of successive phrases, clauses, sentences, or verses esp. for rhetorical or poetic effect (as Lincoln's "of the people, by the people, for the people") — compare ANAPHORA

ep·i·taph \'e-pə-ˌtaf\ *n* [ME *epitaphe*, fr. MF & ML; MF, fr. ML *epitaphium*, fr. L, funeral oration, fr. Gk *epitaphion*, fr. *epi-* + *taphos* tomb, funeral] (14c) **1** : an inscription on or at a tomb or a grave in memory of the one buried there **2** : a brief statement commemorating or epitomizing a deceased person or something past — **ep·i·taph·i·al** \ˌe-pə-'ta-fē-əl\ *adj* — **ep·i·taph·ic** \-'ta-fik\ *adj*

epit·a·sis \i-'pi-tə-səs\ *n, pl* **-a·ses** \-ˌsēz\ [Gk, increased intensity, fr. *epiteinein* to stretch tighter, fr. *epi-* + *teinein* to stretch — more at THIN] (1589) : the part of a play developing the main action and leading to the catastrophe

ep·i·taxy \'e-pə-ˌtak-sē\ *n* [ISV] (ca. 1931) : the growth on a crystalline substrate of a crystalline substance that mimics the orientation of the substrate — **ep·i·tax·i·al** \ˌe-pə-'tak-sē-əl\ *adj* — **ep·i·tax·i·al·ly** \-sē-ə-lē\ *adv*

ep·i·tha·la·mi·um \ˌe-pə-thə-'lā-mē-əm\ *or* **ep·i·tha·la·mi·on** \-mē-ən\ *n, pl* **-mi·ums** *or* **-mia** \-mē-ə\ [L & Gk; L *epithalamium*, fr. Gk *epithalamion*, fr. *epi-* + *thalamos* room, bridal chamber; perh. akin to Gk *tholos* rotunda] (ca. 1589) : a song or poem in honor of a bride and bridegroom — **ep·i·tha·lam·ic** \-'la-mik\ *adj*

ep·i·the·li·al \ˌe-pə-'thē-lē-əl\ *adj* (1845) : of or relating to epithelium

ep·i·the·li·oid \-lē-ˌȯid\ *adj* (1878) : resembling epithelium ⟨~ cells⟩

ep·i·the·li·o·ma \-ˌthē-lē-'ō-mə\ *n* (1872) : a tumor derived from epithelial tissue — **ep·i·the·li·o·ma·tous** \-mə-təs\ *adj*

ep·i·the·li·um \ˌe-pə-'thē-lē-əm\ *n, pl* **-lia** \-lē-ə\ [NL, fr. *epi-* + Gk *thēlē* nipple — more at FEMININE] (1748) **1** : a membranous cellular tissue that covers a free surface or lines a tube or cavity of an animal body and serves esp. to enclose and protect the other parts of the body, to produce secretions and excretions, and to function in assimilation **2** : a usu. thin layer of parenchyma that lines a cavity or tube of a plant

ep·i·the·li·za·tion \ˌe-pə-ˌthē-lə-'zā-shən\ *or* **ep·i·the·li·al·iza·tion** \-ˌthē-lē-ə-\ *n* (ca. 1934) : the process of becoming covered with or converted to epithelium — **ep·i·the·lize** \ˌe-pə-'thē-ˌlīz\ *or* **ep·i·the·li·al·ize** \-'thē-lē-ə-ˌlīz\ *vt*

ep·i·thet \'e-pə-ˌthet *also* -thət\ *n* [L *epitheton*, fr. Gk, fr. neut. of *epithetos* added, fr. *epitithenai* to put on, add, fr. *epi-* + *tithenai* to put — more at DO] (1579) **1 a** : a characterizing word or phrase accompanying or occurring in place of the name of a person or thing **b** : a disparaging or abusive word or phrase **c** : the part of a taxonomic name identifying a subordinate unit within a genus **2** *obs* : EXPRESSION — **ep·i·thet·ic** \ˌe-pə-'the-tik\ *or* **ep·i·thet·i·cal** \-ti-kəl\ *adj*

epit·o·me \i-'pi-tə-mē\ *n* [L, fr. Gk *epitomē*, fr. *epitemnein* to cut short, fr. *epi-* + *temnein* to cut — more at TOME] (1520) **1 a** : a summary of a written work **b** : a brief presentation or statement of something **2** : a typical or ideal example : EMBODIMENT ⟨the British monarchy itself is the ~ of tradition —Richard Joseph⟩ **3** : brief or miniature form — usu. used with *in* — **ep·i·tom·ic** \ˌe-pə-'tä-mik\ *or* **ep·i·tom·i·cal** \-mi-kəl\ *adj*

epit·o·mise *Brit var of* EPITOMIZE

epit·o·mize \-ˌmīz\ *vt* **-mized; -miz·ing** (1594) **1** : to make or give an epitome of **2** : to serve as the typical or ideal example of

epi·tope \'e-pə-ˌtōp\ *n* [ISV, fr. *epi-* + Gk *topos* place] (1960) : a molecular region on the surface of an antigen capable of eliciting an immune response and of combining with the specific antibody produced by such a response — called also *determinant, antigenic determinant*

epi·zo·ic \ˌe-pə-'zō-ik\ *adj* (ca. 1857) : living upon the body of an animal ⟨an ~ plant⟩ — **epi·zo·ite** \-ˌīt\ *n*

epi·zo·ot·ic \ˌe-pə-zə-'wä-tik\ *n* [F *épizootique*, fr. *épizootie* such an outbreak, fr. *épi-* (as in *épidemie* epidemic) + Gk *zōiotēs* animal nature, fr. *zōē* life — more at QUICK] (1748) : an outbreak of disease affecting many animals of one kind at the same time; *also* : the disease itself — **epizootic** *adj*

epi·zo·ot·i·ol·o·gy \ˌe-pə-zə-ˌwä-tē-'ä-lə-jē\ *n* (1910) **1** : the sum of the factors controlling the occurrence of a disease or pathogen of animals **2** : a science that deals with the character, ecology, and causes of outbreaks of animal diseases — **epi·zo·oti·o·log·i·cal** \-zə-ˌwä-tē-ə-'lä-ji-kəl\ *also* **epi·zo·oti·o·log·ic** \-jik\ *adj*

ep·och \'e-pək, 'e-ˌpäk, US *also & Brit usu* 'ē-ˌpäk\ *n* [ML *epocha*, fr. Gk *epochē* cessation, fixed point, fr. *epechein* to pause, hold back, fr. *epi-* + *echein* to hold — more at SCHEME] (1614) **1 a** : an event or a time marked by an event that begins a new period or development **b** : a memorable event or date **2 a** : an extended period of time usu. characterized by a distinctive development or by a memorable series of events **b** : a division of geologic time less than a period and greater than an age **3** : an instant of time or a date selected as a point of reference (as in astronomy) *syn* see PERIOD

ep·och·al \'e-pə-kəl, 'e-ˌpä-kəl\ *adj* (1685) **1** : of or relating to an epoch **2** : uniquely or highly significant : MOMENTOUS ⟨during his three ~ years in the assembly —C. G. Bowers⟩; *also* : UNPARALLELED ⟨~ stupidity⟩ — **ep·och·al·ly** *adv*

ep·ode \'e-ˌpōd\ *n* [L *epodos*, fr. Gk *epōidos* sung or said after, fr. *epi-* + *aidein* to sing — more at ODE] (1598) **1** : a lyric poem in which a long verse is followed by a shorter one **2** : the third part of a triadic Greek ode following the strophe and the antistrophe

ep·onym \'e-pə-ˌnim\ *n* [Gk *epōnymos*, fr. *epōnymos* eponymous, fr. *epi-* + *onyma* name — more at NAME] (1846) **1** : one for whom or which something is or is believed to be named **2** : a name (as of a drug or a

disease) based on or derived from an eponym — **ep·onym·ic** \ˌe-pə-'ni-mik\ *adj*

epon·y·mous \i-'pä-nə-məs, e-\ *adj* (1846) : of, relating to, or being an eponym

epon·y·my \-mē\ *n, pl* **-mies** (1865) : the explanation of a proper name (as of a town or tribe) by supposing a fictitious eponym

ep·o·pee \'e-pə-ˌpē\ *n* [F *épopée*, fr. Gk *epopoiia*, fr. *epos* + *poiein* to make — more at POET] (1697) : EPIC; *esp* : an epic poem

ep·os \'e-ˌpäs\ *n* [Gk, word, epic poem — more at VOICE] (ca. 1828) **1** : EPIC **2** : a number of poems that treat an epic theme but are not formally united

ep·ox·i·da·tion \(ˌ)e-ˌpäk-sə-'dā-shən\ *n* (1944) : a conversion of a usu. unsaturated compound into an epoxide

ep·ox·ide \(ˌ)e-'päk-ˌsīd\ *n* (1930) : an epoxy compound

ep·ox·i·dize \(ˌ)e-'päk-sə-ˌdīz\ *vt* **-dized; -diz·ing** (1945) : to convert into an epoxide ⟨*epoxidized* esters⟩

¹**ep·oxy** \i-'päk-sē\ *adj* [*epi-* + *oxy*] (1916) **1** : containing oxygen attached to two different atoms already united in some other way; *specif* : containing a 3-membered ring consisting of one oxygen and two carbon atoms **2** : of or relating to an epoxide

²**epoxy** *vt* **ep·ox·ied** *or* **ep·oxyed; ep·oxy·ing** (1966) : to glue with epoxy resin

epoxy resin *n* (1950) : a flexible usu. thermosetting resin made by copolymerization of an epoxide with another compound having two hydroxyl groups and used chiefly in coatings and adhesives — called also *epoxy*

EPROM \'ē-ˌpräm\ *n* [*e*rasable *p*rogrammable *r*ead-*o*nly *m*emory] (1977) : a programmable read-only memory that can be erased usu. by exposure to ultraviolet radiation

ep·si·lon \'ep-sə-ˌlän, -lən\ *n* [Gk *e psilon*, lit., simple e] (15c) **1** : the 5th letter of the Greek alphabet — see ALPHABET table **2** : an arbitrarily small positive quantity in mathematical analysis — **ep·si·lon·ic** \ˌep-sə-'lä-nik\ *adj*

Ep·som salt \'ep-səm-\ *n* (1770) : EPSOM SALTS

Epsom salts *n pl but sing in constr* [*Epsom*, England] (1876) : a bitter colorless or white crystalline salt $MgSO_4\cdot7H_2O$ that is a hydrated magnesium sulfate with cathartic properties

Ep·stein–Barr virus \ˌep-ˌstīn-'bär-\ *n* [Michael Anthony *Epstein* b1921 and Y. M. *Barr* b1932 Eng. pathologists] (1968) : a herpesvirus that causes infectious mononucleosis and is associated with Burkitt's lymphoma and nasopharyngeal carcinoma

equa·ble \'e-kwə-bəl, 'ē-\ *adj* [L *aequabilis*, fr. *aequare* to make level or equal, fr. *aequus*] (1677) **1** : marked by lack of variation or change : UNIFORM **2** : marked by lack of noticeable, unpleasant, or extreme variation or inequality *syn* see STEADY — **equa·bil·i·ty** \ˌe-kwə-'bi-lə-tē, ˌē-\ *n* — **equa·ble·ness** \'e-kwə-bəl-nəs, 'ē-\ *n* — **equa·bly** \-blē\ *adv*

¹**equal** \'ē-kwəl\ *adj* [ME, fr. L *aequalis*, fr. *aequus* level, equal] (14c) **1 a** (1) : of the same measure, quantity, amount, or number as another (2) : identical in mathematical value or logical denotation : EQUIVALENT **b** : like in quality, nature, or status **c** : like for each member of a group, class, or society ⟨provide ~ employment opportunities⟩ **2** : regarding or affecting all objects in the same way : IMPARTIAL **3** : free from extremes: as **a** : tranquil in mind or mood **b** : not showing variation in appearance, structure, or proportion **4 a** : capable of meeting the requirements of a situation or a task **b** : SUITABLE ⟨bored with work not ~ to his abilities⟩ *syn* see SAME

²**equal** *vt* **equaled** *or* **equalled; equal·ing** *or* **equal·ling** (1590) **1** : to be equal to; *esp* : to be identical in value to **2** *archaic* : EQUALIZE **3** : to make or produce something equal to

³**equal** *n* (1753) **1** : one that is equal ⟨insists that women can be absolute ~s with men —Anne Bernays⟩ **2** : an equal quantity

equal–area *adj* (ca. 1929) *of a map projection* : maintaining constant ratio of size between quadrilaterals formed by the meridians and parallels and the quadrilaterals of the globe thereby preserving true areal extent of forms represented

equal·ise, equal·is·er *Brit var of* EQUALIZE, EQUALIZER

equal·i·tar·i·an \i-ˌkwä-lə-'ter-ē-ən\ *adj or n* (1799) : EGALITARIAN — **equal·i·tar·i·an·ism** \-ē-ə-ˌni-zəm\ *n*

equal·i·ty \i-'kwä-lə-tē\ *n, pl* **-ties** (15c) **1** : the quality or state of being equal **2** : EQUATION 2a

equal·ize \'ē-kwə-ˌlīz\ *vb* **-ized; -iz·ing** *vt* (1622) **1** : to make equal **2 a** : to compensate for **b** : to make uniform; *esp* : to distribute evenly or uniformly ⟨~ the tax burden⟩ **c** : to adjust or correct the frequency characteristics of (an electronic signal) by restoring to their original level high frequencies that have been attenuated ~ *vi, chiefly Brit* : to tie the score — **equal·iza·tion** \ˌē-kwə-lə-'zā-shən\ *n*

equal·iz·er \-ˌlī-zər\ *n* (1792) : one that equalizes: as **a** : a score that ties a game **b** : an electronic device (as in a sound-reproducing system) used to adjust response to different audio frequencies

equal·ly \'ē-kwə-lē\ *adv* (14c) **1** : in an equal or uniform manner : EVENLY **2** : to an equal degree ⟨respected ~ by young and old⟩

equal opportunity employer *n* (1963) : an employer who agrees not to discriminate against any employee or job applicant because of race, color, religion, national origin, sex, physical or mental handicap, or age

equal sign *n* (ca. 1909) : a sign = indicating mathematical or logical equivalence — called also *equality sign, equals sign*

equa·nim·i·ty \ˌē-kwə-'ni-mə-tē, ˌe-kwə-\ *n, pl* **-ties** [L *aequanimitas*, fr. *aequo animo* with even mind] (ca. 1616) **1** : evenness of mind esp. under stress **2** : right disposition : BALANCE

syn EQUANIMITY, COMPOSURE, SANGFROID mean evenness of mind under stress. EQUANIMITY suggests a habit of mind that is only rarely disturbed under great strain ⟨accepted her troubles with *equanimity*⟩. COMPOSURE implies the controlling of emotional or mental agitation by an effort of will or as a matter of habit ⟨maintaining his *composure* even under hostile questioning⟩. SANGFROID implies great coolness and

---

\ə\ abut \ᵊ\ kitten, F table \ər\ further \a\ ash \ā\ ace \ä\ mop, mar
\aů\ out \ch\ chin \e\ bet \ē\ easy \g\ go \i\ hit \ī\ ice \j\ job
\ŋ\ sing \ō\ go \ȯ\ law \ȯi\ boy \th\ thin \th̲\ the \ü\ loot \ů\ foot
\y\ yet \zh\ vision \à, k̲, ⁿ, œ, œ̄, ᵫ, ᵫ̄, ᵊ\ *see* Guide to Pronunciation

steadiness under strain ⟨handled the situation with professional *sang-froid*⟩.

equate \i-'kwāt, 'ē-,\ *vb* **equat·ed; equat·ing** [ME, fr. L *aequatus*, pp. of *aequare*] *vt* (15c) **1 a** : to make equal : EQUALIZE **b** : to make such an allowance or correction in as will reduce to a common standard or obtain a correct result **2** : to treat, represent, or regard as equal, equivalent, or comparable ⟨~s disagreement with disloyalty⟩ ~ *vi* : to correspond as equal

equa·tion \i-'kwā-zhən *also* -shən\ *n* (14c) **1 a** : the act or process of equating **b** (1) : an element affecting a process : FACTOR (2) : a complex of variable factors **c** : a state of being equated; *specif* : a state of close association or identification ⟨bring governmental enterprises and payment for them into immediate ~ —R. G. Tugwell⟩ **2 a** : a usu. formal statement of the equality or equivalence of mathematical or logical expressions **b** : an expression representing a chemical reaction quantitatively by means of chemical symbols

equa·tion·al \i-'kwāzh-nəl, -'kwā-zhə-n°l *also* -'kwāsh-\ *adj* (1864) **1** : of, using, or involving equation or equations **2** : dividing into two equal parts — used esp. of the mitotic cell division usu. following reduction in meiosis — **equa·tion·al·ly** *adv*

equation of time (1726) : the difference between apparent time and mean time usu. expressed as a correction which is to be added to apparent time to give local mean time

equa·tor \i-'kwā-tər, 'ē-,\ *n* [ME, fr. ML *aequator*, lit., equalizer, fr. L *aequare*] (14c) **1** : the great circle of the celestial sphere whose plane is perpendicular to the axis of the earth **2** : a great circle of the earth or a celestial body that is everywhere equally distant from the two poles and divides the surface into the northern and southern hemispheres **3 a** : a circle or circular band dividing the surface of a body into two usu. equal and symmetrical parts **b** : EQUATORIAL PLANE ⟨the ~ of a dividing cell⟩ **4** : GREAT CIRCLE

equa·to·ri·al \,ē-kwə-'tȯr-ē-əl, ,e-kwə-, -'tȯr-\ *adj* (1664) **1 a** : of, relating to, or located at the equator or an equator; *also* : being in the plane of the equator ⟨a satellite in ~ orbit⟩ **b** : of, originating in, or suggesting the region around the geographic equator **2 a** : being or having a support that includes two axles at right angles to each other with one parallel to the earth's axis of rotation ⟨an ~ telescope⟩ **b** : extending in a direction essentially in the plane of a cyclic structure (as of cyclohexane) ⟨~ hydrogens⟩ — compare AXIAL

equatorial plane *n* (ca. 1892) : the plane perpendicular to the spindle of a dividing cell and midway between the poles

equatorial plate *n* (1887) **1** : METAPHASE PLATE **2** : EQUATORIAL PLANE

equa·tor·ward \i-'kwā-tər-wərd\ *adv or adj* (1875) : toward or near the equator ⟨currents flowing ~⟩ ⟨~ winds⟩

equer·ry \'e-kwə-rē, i-'kwer-ē\ *n, pl* **-ries** [obs. *escuirie, equerry* stable, fr. MF *escuirie* office of a squire, stable, fr. *escuier* squire — more at ESQUIRE] (1591) **1** : an officer of a prince or noble charged with the care of horses **2** : an officer of the British royal household in personal attendance on the sovereign or a member of the royal family

¹eques·tri·an \i-'kwes-trē-ən\ *adj* [L *equestr-, equester* of a horseman, fr. *eques* horseman, fr. *equus* horse — more at EQUINE] (ca. 1681) **1 a** : of, relating to, or featuring horseback riding **b** *archaic* : riding on horseback : MOUNTED **c** : representing a person on horseback ⟨an ~ statue⟩ **2** : of, relating to, or composed of knights

²equestrian *n* (1791) : one who rides on horseback

eques·tri·enne \i-,kwes-trē-'en\ *n* [²*equestrian* + -*enne* (as in *tragedienne*)] (ca. 1864) : a female rider on horseback

equi- *comb form* [ME, fr. MF, fr. L *aequi-*, fr. *aequus* equal] : equal ⟨*equipoise*⟩ : equally ⟨*equiprobable*⟩

equi·an·gu·lar \,ē-kwi-'aŋ-gyə-lər, ,e-kwi-\ *adj* (1660) : having all or corresponding angles equal ⟨mutually ~ parallelograms⟩

equi·ca·lor·ic \,ē-kwə-kə-'lȯr-ik, ,e-kwə-, -'lär-\ *adj* (1940) : capable of yielding equal amounts of energy in the body ⟨~ diets⟩

equid \'e-,kwid, 'ē-\ *n* [NL *Equidae*, family name, fr. *Equus*, genus name, fr. L, horse] (ca. 1889) : any of a family (Equidae) of perissodactyl mammals consisting of the horses, asses, zebras, and extinct related animals

equi·dis·tant \,ē-kwə-'dis-tənt, ,e-kwə-\ *adj* [MF or LL; MF, fr. LL *aequidistant-, aequidistans*, fr. L *aequi-* + *distant-, distans*, prp. of *distare* to stand apart — more at DISTANT] (1593) **1** : equally distant **2** : representing map distances true to scale in all directions — **equi·dis·tant·ly** *adv*

equi·lat·er·al \,ē-kwə-'la-tə-rəl, ,e-kwə-, -'la-trəl\ *adj* [LL *aequilateralis*, fr. L *aequi-* + *later-, latus* side — more at LATERAL] (1570) **1** : having all sides equal ⟨an ~ triangle⟩ ⟨an ~ polygon⟩ — see TRIANGLE illustration **2** : having all the faces equal ⟨an ~ polyhedron⟩

equilateral hyperbola *n* (1880) : a hyperbola with its asymptotes at right angles

equil·i·brant \i-'kwi-lə-brənt, ē-, *also* ,ē-kwə-'li-brənt\ *n* (1883) : a force that will balance one or more unbalanced forces

equil·i·brate \i-'kwi-lə-,brāt\ *vb* **-brat·ed; -brat·ing** *vt* (1635) : to bring into or keep in equilibrium : BALANCE ~ *vi* : to bring about, come to, or be in equilibrium — **equil·i·bra·tion** \-,kwi-lə-'brā-shən\ *n* — **equil·i·bra·tor** \-'kwi-lə-,brā-tər\ *n* — **equil·i·bra·to·ry** \-brə-,tȯr-ē, -,tȯr-\ *adj*

equi·li·brist \,ē-kwə-'li-brist, ,e-kwə-; i-'kwi-lə-brist\ *n* (1760) : one (as a rope dancer) who performs difficult feats of balancing — **equil·i·bris·tic** \i-,kwi-lə-'bris-tik\ *adj*

equi·lib·ri·um \,ē-kwə-'li-brē-əm, ,e-kwə-\ *n, pl* **-ri·ums** *or* **-ria** \-brē-ə\ [L *aequilibrium*, fr. *aequilibris* being in equilibrium, fr. *aequi-* + *libra* weight, balance] (1608) **1 a** : a state of intellectual or emotional balance : POISE **b** : a state of adjustment between opposing or divergent influences or elements **2** : a state of balance between opposing forces or actions that is either static (as in a body acted on by forces whose resultant is zero) or dynamic (as in a reversible chemical reaction when the velocities in both directions are equal) **3** : BALANCE 6a

equilibrium constant *n* (1929) : a number that expresses the relationship between the amounts of products and reactants present at equilibrium in a reversible chemical reaction at a given temperature

equi·mo·lar \,ē-'mō-lər\ *adj* (ca. 1909) **1** : of or relating to an equal number of moles ⟨an ~ mixture⟩ **2** : having equal molar concentration

equine \'ē-,kwīn, 'e-,kwīn\ *adj* [L *equinus*, fr. *equus* horse; akin to OE *eoh* horse, Gk *hippos*, Skt *aśva*] (1778) : of, relating to, or resembling a horse or the horse family — **equine** *n* — **equine·ly** *adv*

¹equi·noc·tial \,ē-kwə-'näk-shəl, ,e-kwə-\ *adj* (1545) **1** : relating to an equinox or to a state or the time of equal day and night **2** : relating to the regions or climate on or near the equator **3** : relating to the time when the sun passes an equinoctial point

²equinoctial *n* (1527) **1** : EQUATOR 1 **2** : an equinoctial storm

equi·nox \'ē-kwə-,näks, 'e-kwə-\ *n* [ME, fr. MF or ML; MF *equinoxe*, fr. ML *equinoxium*, alter. of L *aequinoctium*, fr. *aequi-* equi- + *noct-, nox* night — more at NIGHT] (14c) **1** : either of the two points on the celestial sphere where the celestial equator intersects the ecliptic **2** : either of the two times each year (as about March 21 and September 23) when the sun crosses the equator and day and night are everywhere of equal length

equip \i-'kwip\ *vt* **equipped; equip·ping** [MF *equiper*, fr. OF *esciper*, of Gmc origin; akin to OE *scip* ship] (1523) **1** : to furnish for service or action by appropriate provisioning **2** : DRESS, ARRAY **3** : to make ready : PREPARE *syn* see FURNISH

eq·ui·page \'e-kwə-pij\ *n* (1579) **1 a** : material or articles used in equipment : OUTFIT **b** *archaic* (1) : a set of small articles (as for table service) (2) : ETUI **c** : TRAPPINGS **2** *archaic* : RETINUE **3** : a horse-drawn carriage with its servants; *also* : such a carriage alone

equip·ment \i-'kwip-mənt\ *n* (1717) **1 a** : the set of articles or physical resources serving to equip a person or thing: as (1) : the implements used in an operation or activity : APPARATUS (2) : all the fixed assets other than land and buildings of a business enterprise (3) : the rolling stock of a railway **b** : a piece of such equipment **2 a** : the equipping of a person or thing **b** : the state of being equipped **3** : mental or emotional traits or resources : ENDOWMENT

¹equi·poise \'e-kwə-,pȯiz, 'ē-\ *n* (1658) **1** : a state of equilibrium **2** : COUNTERBALANCE

²equipoise *vt* (1664) **1** : to serve as an equipoise to **2** : to put or hold in equipoise

equi·pol·lence \,ē-kwə-'pä-lən(t)s, ,e-kwə-\ *n* (15c) : the quality of being equipollent

equi·pol·lent \-lənt\ *adj* [ME, fr. MF, fr. L *aequipollent-, aequipollens*, fr. *aequi-* equi- + *pollent-, pollens*, prp. of *pollēre* to be able] (15c) **1** : equal in force, power, or validity **2** : the same in effect or signification — **equipollent** *n* — **equi·pol·lent·ly** *adv*

equi·pon·der·ant \-'pän-d(ə-)rənt\ *adj* [ML *aequiponderant-, aequiponderans*, prp. of *aequiponderare*, fr. L *aequi-* + *ponderare* to weigh — more at PONDER] (1630) : evenly balanced

equi·po·ten·tial \,ē-kwə-pə-'ten(t)-shəl, ,e-kwə-\ *adj* (ca. 1865) : having the same potential : of uniform potential throughout ⟨~ points⟩

equi·prob·a·ble \-'prä-bə-bəl\ *adj* (1921) : having the same degree of logical or mathematical probability ⟨~ alternatives⟩

eq·ui·se·tum \,ē-kwə-'sē-təm\ *n, pl* **-se·tums** *or* **-se·ta** \-'sē-tə\ [NL, fr. L *equisaetum* horsetail plant, fr. *equus* horse + *saeta* bristle] (1830) : any of a genus (*Equisetum*) of lower tracheophytes comprising perennial plants that spread by creeping rhizomes and have leaves reduced to nodal sheaths on the hollow jointed ribbed shoots — called also *horsetail, scouring rush*

eq·ui·ta·ble \'e-kwə-tə-bəl\ *adj* (1646) **1** : having or exhibiting equity : dealing fairly and equally with all concerned **2** : existing or valid in equity as distinguished from law *syn* see FAIR — **eq·ui·ta·bil·i·ty** \,e-kwə-tə-'bi-lə-tē\ *n* — **eq·ui·ta·ble·ness** \'e-kwə-tə-bəl-nəs\ *n* — **eq·ui·ta·bly** \-blē\ *adv*

eq·ui·ta·tion \,e-kwə-'tā-shən\ *n* [MF, fr. L *equitation-, equitatio*, fr. *equitare* to ride on horseback, fr. *equit-, eques* horseman, fr. *equus* horse] (1562) : the act or art of riding on horseback

equisetum: *1* vegetative plant, *2* fertile plant

eq·ui·ty \'e-kwə-tē\ *n, pl* **-ties** [ME *equite*, fr. MF *equité*, fr. L *aequitat-, aequitas*, fr. *aequus* equal, fair] (14c) **1 a** : justice according to natural law or right; *specif* : freedom from bias or favoritism **b** : something that is equitable **2 a** : a system of law originating in the English chancery and comprising a settled and formal body of legal and procedural rules and doctrines that supplement, aid, or override common and statute law and are designed to protect rights and enforce duties fixed by substantive law **b** : trial or remedial justice under or by the rules and doctrines of equity **c** : a body of legal doctrines and rules developed to enlarge, supplement, or override a narrow rigid system of law **3 a** : a right, claim, or interest existing or valid in equity **b** : the money value of a property or of an interest in a property in excess of claims or liens against it **c** : a risk interest or ownership right in property **d** : the common stock of a corporation

equity capital *n* (1942) : VENTURE CAPITAL

equiv·a·lence \i-'kwiv-lən(t)s, -'kwi-və-\ *n* (ca. 1541) **1 a** : the state or property of being equivalent **b** : the relation holding between two statements if they are either both true or both false so that to affirm one and to deny the other would result in a contradiction **2** : a presentation of terms as equivalent **3** : equality in metrical value of a regular foot and one in which there are substitutions

equivalence class *n* (1952) : a set for which an equivalence relation holds between every pair of elements

equivalence relation *n* (ca. 1949) : a relation (as equality) between elements of a set (as the real numbers) that is symmetric, reflexive, and transitive and for any two elements either holds or does not hold

equiv·a·len·cy \i-'kwiv-lən(t)-sē, -'kwi-və-\ *n, pl* **-cies** (1535) **1** : EQUIVALENCE **2** : a level of achievement equivalent to completion of an educational or training program ⟨a high school ~ certificate⟩

equiv·a·lent \-lənt\ *adj* [ME, fr. MF or LL; MF, fr. LL *aequivalent-, aequivalens*, prp. of *aequivalēre* to have equal power, fr. L *aequi-* + *valēre* to be strong — more at WIELD] (15c) **1** : equal in force, amount, or value; *also* : equal in area or volume but not admitting of superposition ⟨a square ~ to a triangle⟩ **2 a** : like in signification or import **b** : having logical equivalence ⟨~ statements⟩ **3** : corresponding or virtually identical esp. in effect or function **4** *obs* : equal in might or authority **5** : having the same chemical combining capacity ⟨~ quantities of two elements⟩ **6 a** : having the same solution set ⟨~ equations⟩ **b** : capable of being placed in one-to-one correspondence ⟨~ sets⟩ **c** : related by an equivalence relation *syn* see SAME — **equivalent** *n* — **equiv·a·lent·ly** *adv*

equivalent weight *n* (1904) : the mass of a substance esp. in grams that combines with or is chemically equivalent to eight grams of oxygen or one gram of hydrogen : the atomic or molecular weight divided by the valence

equiv·o·cal \i-'kwi-və-kəl\ *adj* [LL *aequivocus*, fr. *aequi-* equi- + *voc-*, *vox* voice — more at VOICE] (1599) **1 a** : subject to two or more interpretations and usu. used to mislead or confuse **b** : uncertain as an indication or sign **2 a** : of uncertain nature or classification **b** : of uncertain disposition toward a person or thing : UNDECIDED **c** : of doubtful advantage, genuineness, or moral rectitude ⟨~ behavior⟩ *syn* see OBSCURE — **equiv·o·cal·i·ty** \-ˌkwi-və-'ka-lə-tē\ *n* — **equiv·o·cal·ly** \-'kwi-və-k(ə-)lē\ *adv* — **equiv·o·cal·ness** \-kəl-nəs\ *n*

equiv·o·cate \i-'kwi-və-ˌkāt\ *vi* **-cat·ed; -cat·ing** (1590) **1** : to use equivocal language esp. with intent to deceive **2** : to avoid committing oneself in what one says *syn* see LIE — **equiv·o·ca·tion** \-ˌkwi-və-'kā-shən\ *n* — **equiv·o·ca·tor** \-'kwi-və-ˌkā-tər\ *n*

equi·voque *also* **equi·voke** \'e-kwə-ˌvōk, 'ē-\ *n* [F *équivoque*, fr. *équivoque* equivocal, fr. LL *aequivocus*] (1599) **1** : an equivocal word or phrase; *specif* : PUN **2 a** : double meaning **b** : WORDPLAY

¹**-er** \ər; *after some vowels, often* r\ *adj suffix or adv suffix* [ME *-er, -ere, -re*, fr. OE *-ra* (in adjectives), *-or* (in adverbs); akin to OHG *-iro*, adj. compar. suffix, L *-ior*, Gk *-iōn*] — used to form the comparative degree of adjectives and adverbs of one syllable ⟨hotter⟩ ⟨drier⟩ and of some adjectives and adverbs of two syllables ⟨completer⟩ and sometimes of longer ones ⟨beautifuler⟩

²**-er** \ər; *after some vowels, often* r\ *also* **-ier** \ē-ər, yər\ *or* **-yer** \yər\ *n suffix* [ME *-er, -ier, -iere*; partly fr. OE *-ere* (fr. L *-arius*); partly fr. OF *-ier, -iere*, fr. L *-arius, -aria, -arium* -ary; partly fr. MF *-ere*, fr. L *-ator* — more at -ARY, -OR] **1 a** : person occupationally connected with ⟨hatter⟩ ⟨furrier⟩ ⟨lawyer⟩ **b** : person or thing belonging to or associated with ⟨header⟩ ⟨old-timer⟩ **c** : native of : resident of ⟨cottager⟩ ⟨New Yorker⟩ **d** : one that has ⟨three-decker⟩ **e** : one that produces or yields ⟨porker⟩ **2 a** : one that does or performs (a specified action) ⟨reporter⟩ — sometimes added to both elements of a compound ⟨builder-upper⟩ **b** : one that is a suitable object of (a specified action) ⟨broiler⟩ **3** : one that is ⟨foreigner⟩ — in all senses *-yer* in a few words after *w*, *-ier* in a few other words, otherwise *-er*

era \'ir-ə, 'er-ə, 'ē-rə\ *n* [LL *aera*, fr. L, counters, pl. of *aer-, aes* copper, money — more at ORE] (1615) **1 a** : a fixed point in time from which a series of years is reckoned **b** : a memorable or important date or event; *esp* : one that begins a new period in the history of a person or thing **2** : a system of chronological notation computed from a given date as basis **3 a** : a period identified by some prominent figure or characteristic feature **b** : a stage in development; *esp* : one of the four major divisions of geologic time ⟨Paleozoic ~⟩ *syn* see PERIOD

erad·i·cate \i-'ra-də-ˌkāt\ *vt* **-cat·ed; -cat·ing** [L *eradicatus*, pp. of *eradicare*, fr. *e-* + *radic-, radix* root — more at ROOT] (1578) **1** : to pull up by the roots **2** : to do away with as completely as if by pulling up by the roots ⟨programs to ~ illiteracy⟩ *syn* see EXTERMINATE — **erad·i·ca·ble** \-'ra-di-kə-bəl\ *adj* — **erad·i·ca·tion** \-ˌra-də-'kā-shən\ *n* — **erad·i·ca·tor** \-ˌkā-tər\ *n*

erase \i-'rās, Brit -'rāz\ *vb* **erased; eras·ing** [L *erasus*, pp. of *eradere*, fr. *e-* + *radere* to scratch, scrape — more at RODENT] *vt* (1605) **1 a** : to rub or scrape out (as written, painted, or engraved letters) **b** : to remove (recorded matter) from a magnetic medium; *also* : to remove recorded matter from ⟨~ a videotape⟩ **c** : to delete from a computer storage device **2 a** : to remove from existence or memory as if by erasing **b** : to nullify the effect or force of ⟨~⟩ *vi* : to yield to being erased — **eras·abil·i·ty** \-ˌrā-sə-'bi-lə-tē\ *n* — **eras·able** \-'rā-sə-bəl\ *adj*

eras·er \i-'rā-sər\ *n* (1790) : one that erases; *esp* : a device (as a piece of rubber, or a felt pad) used to erase marks (as of ink or chalk)

Eras·tian \i-'ras-tē-ən, -'ras-chən\ *adj* [Thomas *Erastus* †1583 Swiss physician and Zwinglian theologian] (1839) : of, characterized by, or advocating the doctrine of state supremacy in ecclesiastical affairs — **Erastian** *n* — **Eras·tian·ism** \-ˌni-zəm\ *n*

era·sure \i-'rā-shər *also* -zhər\ *n* (1734) : an act or instance of erasing

Er·a·to \'er-ə-ˌtō\ *n* [Gk *Eratō*] : the Greek Muse of lyric and love poetry

er·bi·um \'ər-bē-əm\ *n* [NL, fr. *Ytterby*, Sweden] (1843) : a metallic element of the rare-earth group that occurs with yttrium — see ELEMENT table

¹**ere** \'er, 'ar\ *prep* [ME *er*, fr. OE *ǣr*, fr. *ǣr*, adv., early, soon; akin to OHG *ēr* earlier, Gk *ēri* early] (bef. 12c) : ²BEFORE 2 ⟨contrived ~ the beginning of the world —Norman Douglas⟩

²**ere** *conj* (bef. 12c) : ³BEFORE

Er·e·bus \'er-ə-bəs\ *n* [L, fr. Gk *Erebos*] **1** : a personification of darkness in Greek mythology **2** : a place of darkness in the underworld on the way to Hades

¹**erect** \i-'rekt\ *adj* [ME, fr. L *erectus*, pp. of *erigere* to erect, fr. *e-* + *regere* to lead straight, guide — more at RIGHT] (14c) **1 a** : vertical in position; *also* : not spread out or decumbent ⟨an ~ plant stem⟩ **b** : standing up or out from the body ⟨~ hairs⟩ **c** : characterized by firm or rigid straightness in bodily posture ⟨an ~ bearing⟩ **2** *archaic* : directed upward **3** *obs* : ALERT, WATCHFUL **4** : being in a state of physiological erection — **erect·ly** \-'rek-(t)lē\ *adv* — **erect·ness** \-'rek(t)-nəs\ *n*

²**erect** *vt* (15c) **1 a** (1) : to put up by the fitting together of materials or parts : BUILD (2) : to fix in an upright position (3) : to cause to stand up or stand out **b** *archaic* : to direct upward **c** : to change (an image) from an inverted to a normal position **2** : to elevate in status **3** : SET UP, ESTABLISH **4** *obs* : ENCOURAGE, EMBOLDEN **5** : to draw or construct (as a perpendicular or figure) upon a given base — **erect·able** \-'rek-tə-bəl\ *adj*

erec·tile \i-'rek-t²l, -ˌtīl\ *adj* (1830) : capable of becoming erect ⟨~ tissue⟩ — compare CAVERNOUS 1b — **erec·til·i·ty** \-ˌrek-'ti-lə-tē\ *n*

erec·tion \i-'rek-shən\ *n* (15c) **1 a** : the state marked by firm turgid form and erect position of a previously flaccid bodily part containing cavernous tissue when that tissue becomes dilated with blood **b** : an occurrence of such a state in the penis or clitoris **2** : the act or process of erecting something : CONSTRUCTION **3** : something erected

erec·tor \i-'rek-tər\ *n* (1538) : one that erects; *esp* : a muscle that raises or keeps a part erect

Erector *trademark* — used for a metal toy construction set

E region *n* (1930) : the part of the ionosphere occurring between 55 and 80 miles (90 and 130 kilometers) above the surface of the earth and containing the daytime E layer and the sporadic E layer

ere·long \er-'lȯn, ar-\ *adv* (1577) *archaic* : before long : SOON

er·e·mite \'er-ə-ˌmīt\ *n* [ME — more at HERMIT] (13c) : HERMIT; *esp* : a religious recluse — **er·e·mit·ic** \ˌer-ə-'mi-tik\ *or* **er·e·mit·i·cal** \-ti-kəl\ *adj* — **er·e·mit·ism** \'er-ə-ˌmī-ˌti-zəm\ *n*

er·em·urus \ˌer-ə-'myu̇r-əs\ *n*, *pl* **-uri** \-'myu̇r-ˌī\ [NL, fr. Gk *erēmos* solitary + *oura* tail — more at ASS] (1829) : any of a genus (*Eremurus*) of perennial herbs of the lily family that produce tall racemes of showy blooms — called also *foxtail lily*

ere·now \er-'naù, ar-\ *adv* (14c) : before now : HERETOFORE

erep·sin \i-'rep-sən\ *n* [ISV *er-* (prob. fr. L *eripere* to snatch away, fr. *e-* + *rapere* to seize) + *pepsin* — more at RAPID] (1902) : a proteolytic fraction obtained esp. from the intestinal juice and known to be a mixture of exopeptidases

er·e·thism \'er-ə-ˌthi-zəm\ *n* [F *éréthisme*, fr. Gk *erethismos* irritation, fr. *erethizein* to irritate; akin to Gk *ornynai* to rouse — more at ORIENT] (1800) : abnormal irritability or responsiveness to stimulation

ere·while \er-'(h)wī(ə)l, ar-\ *also* **ere·whiles** \-'(h)wī(ə)lz\ *adv* (13c) *archaic* : HERETOFORE

erg \'ərg\ *n* [Gk *ergon* work — more at WORK] (ca. 1873) : a centimeter-gram-second unit of work equal to the work done by a force of one dyne acting through a distance of one centimeter and equivalent to 10^{-7} joule

erg- *or* **ergo-** *comb form* [Gk, fr. *ergon*] : work ⟨ergometer⟩

er·gas·tic \(ˌ)ər-'gas-tik\ *adj* [Gk *ergastikos* able to work, fr. *ergazesthai* to work, fr. *ergon* work] (ca. 1896) : constituting the nonliving by-products of protoplasmic activity ⟨~ substances⟩

er·gas·to·plasm \-tə-ˌpla-zəm\ *n* [ISV] (1902) : ribosome-studded endoplasmic reticulum — **er·gas·to·plas·mic** \-ˌgas-tə-'plaz-mik\ *adj*

er·ga·tive \'ər-gə-tiv\ *adj* [Gk *ergatēs* worker, fr. *ergon* work] (1939) : of, relating to, or being a language (as Inuit or Georgian) in which the objects of transitive verbs and subjects of intransitive verbs are typically marked by the same linguistic forms; *also* : being an inflectional morpheme that typically marks the subject of a transitive verb in an ergative language

-er·gic \(ˌ)ər-jik\ *adj comb form* [*-ergy* work (fr. LL *-ergia*, fr. Gk, fr. *ergon* work) + *-ic* — more at WORK] : exhibiting or stimulating activity of ⟨dopaminergic⟩

er·go \'er-(ˌ)gō, 'ȯr-\ *adv* [ME, fr. L, fr. OL, because of, fr. (assumed) OL *e rogo* from the direction (of)] (14c) : THEREFORE, HENCE

ergo- *comb form* [F, fr. *ergot*] : ergot ⟨ergosterol⟩

er·go·dic \(ˌ)ər-'gä-dik, -'gō-\ *adj* [ISV *erg-* + *-ode*] (1926) **1** : of or relating to a process in which every sequence or sizable sample is equally representative of the whole (as in regard to a statistical parameter) **2** : involving or relating to the probability that any state will recur; *esp* : having zero probability that any state will never recur — **er·go·dic·i·ty** \ˌər-gə-'di-sə-tē\ *n*

er·go·graph \'ər-gə-ˌgraf\ *n* [ISV] (1892) : an apparatus for measuring the work capacity of a muscle

er·gom·e·ter \(ˌ)ər-'gä-mə-tər\ *n* (ca. 1879) : an apparatus for measuring the work performed (as by a person exercising); *also* : an exercise machine equipped with an ergometer — **er·go·met·ric** \ˌər-gə-'me-trik\ *adj*

er·go·nom·ics \ˌər-gə-'nä-miks\ *n pl but sing or pl in constr* [*erg-* + *-nomics* (as in *economics*)] (1949) : an applied science concerned with designing and arranging things people use so that the people and things interact most efficiently and safely — called also *human engineering* — **er·go·nom·ic** \-mik\ *adj* — **er·go·nom·i·cal·ly** \-mi-k(ə-)lē\ *adv* — **er·go·no·mist** \(ˌ)ər-'gä-nə-mist\ *n*

er·go·no·vine \ˌər-gə-'nō-ˌvēn\ *n* [*ergo-* + L *novus* new — more at NEW] (ca. 1936) : an alkaloid $C_{19}H_{23}N_3O_2$ from ergot with similar pharmacological action but reduced toxicity

er·gos·ter·ol \(ˌ)ər-'gäs-tə-ˌrȯl, -ˌrōl\ *n* [ISV] (1906) : a crystalline steroid alcohol $C_{28}H_{44}O$ that occurs esp. in yeast, molds, and ergot and is converted by ultraviolet irradiation ultimately into vitamin D_2

er·got \'ər-gət, -ˌgät\ *n* [F, lit., cock's spur] (1683) **1** : the black or dark purple sclerotium of fungi (genus *Claviceps*) that occurs as a club-shaped body replacing the seed of a grass (as rye); *also* : a fungus bearing ergots **2** : a disease of rye and other cereals caused by an ergot fungus **3 a** : the dried sclerotia of an ergot fungus grown on rye and containing several alkaloids (as ergonovine and ergotamine) **b** : any of such alkaloids used medicinally for their contractile effect on smooth muscle (as of peripheral arterioles) — **er·got·ic** \(ˌ)ər-'gä-tik\ *adj*

er·got·a·mine \(ˌ)ər-'gä-tə-ˌmēn\ *n* [ISV] (1921) : an alkaloid $C_{33}H_{35}N_5O_5$ from ergot that is used chiefly in the form of its tartrate esp. in treating migraine

er·got·ism \'ər-gə-ˌti-zəm\ *n* (ca. 1841) : a toxic condition produced by eating grain, grain products (as rye bread), or grasses infected with ergot fungus or by chronic excessive use of an ergot drug

er·got·ized \-ˌtīzd\ *adj* (1860) : infected with ergot ⟨~ grain⟩; *also* : poisoned by ergot ⟨~ cattle⟩

er·i·ca \'er-i-kə\ *n* [NL, fr. L *erice* heather, fr. Gk *ereikē* — more at BRIER] (1826) : any of a large genus (*Erica*) of the heath family of low much-branched evergreen shrubs

\ə\ abut \ᵊ\ kitten, F table \ər\ further \a\ ash \ā\ ace \ä\ mop, mar \aù\ out \ch\ chin \e\ bet \ē\ easy \g\ go \i\ hit \ī\ ice \j\ job \ŋ\ sing \ō\ go \ȯ\ law \ȯi\ boy \th\ thin \th\ the \ü\ loot \ù\ foot \y\ yet \zh\ vision \á, k̲, ⁿ, œ, œ̄, ᵫ, ᵫ̄, ᷣ\ *see* Guide to Pronunciation er·i·ca·ceous \,er-ə-'kā-shəs\ adj (ca. 1859) : of, relating to, or being a heath or the heath family

er·i·coid \'er-ə-,kȯid\ adj (ca. 1900) : resembling heath ⟨~ foliage⟩

Erie \'ir-ē, 'ēr-ē\ n (ca. 1909) 1 : a member of an American Indian people living south of Lake Erie in the 17th century 2 : the extinct and prob. Iroquoian language of the Erie people

erig·er·on \ə-'ri-jə-,rän\ n [NL, fr. L, groundsel, fr. Gk ērigerōn, fr. ēri early + gerōn old man; fr. the hoary down of some species — more at ERE, GERONT-] (1601) : any of a widely distributed genus (Erigeron) of composite herbs with flower heads that resemble asters but have fewer and narrower involucral bracts

Erin·ys \i-'ri-nəs, -'rī-\ n, pl Erin·y·es \-'ri-nē-,ēz\ [Gk] (1590) : FURY 2a

er·i·o·phy·id \,er-ē-'ä-fē-əd, -ē-ō-'fī-əd\ n [ultim. fr. Gk erion wool + phyē growth; akin to Gk physis growth — more at PHYSICS] (1942) : any of a large family (Eriophyidae) of minute plant-feeding mites that have two pairs of legs placed far anterior and lack a respiratory system — eriophyid adj

1er·is·tic \i-'ris-tik, e-\ also eris·ti·cal \-ti-kəl\ adj [Gk eristikos fond of wrangling, fr. erizein to wrangle, fr. eris strife] (1637) : characterized by disputatious and often subtle and specious reasoning — eris·ti·cal·ly \-ti-k(ə-)lē\ adv

2eristic n (1659) 1 : a person devoted to logical disputation 2 : the art or practice of disputation and polemics

Er·len·mey·er flask \,ər-lən-,mī(-ə)r-, ,er-lən-\ n [Emil Erlenmeyer] (ca. 1890) : a flat-bottomed conical laboratory flask

er·mine \'ər-mən\ n, pl ermines [ME, fr. OF, of Gmc origin; akin to OHG harmo weasel] (12c) 1 or pl ermine a : any of several weasels whose coats become white in winter usu. with black on the tip of the tail; esp : a short-tailed weasel (Mustela erminea) of the forests and tundra of Eurasia and No. America b : the white fur of the ermine 2 : a rank or office whose ceremonial or official robe is ornamented with ermine

er·mined \-mənd\ adj (15c) : clothed or adorned with ermine

erne \'ərn, 'ern\ n [ME, fr. OE earn; akin to OHG arn eagle, Gk ornis bird] (bef. 12c) : EAGLE; esp : a long-winged sea eagle (Haliaetus albicilla) with a short white wedge-shaped tail

erode \i-'rōd\ vb erod·ed; erod·ing [L erodere to eat away, fr. e- + rodere to gnaw — more at RODENT] vt (1612) 1 : to diminish or destroy by degrees: a : to eat into or away by slow destruction of substance (as by acid, infection, or cancer) b : to wear away by the action of water, wind, or glacial ice ⟨eroding buying power⟩ 2 : to produce or form by eroding ⟨glaciers ~ U-shaped valleys⟩ ~ vi : to undergo erosion — erod·ibil·i·ty \-,rō-də-'bi-lə-tē\ n — erod·ible \-'rō-də-bəl\ adj

ermine 1a: winter coat

erog·e·nous \i-'rä-jə-nəs\ adj [Gk erōs + E -genous, -genic] (ca. 1889) 1 : producing sexual excitement or libidinal gratification when stimulated : sexually sensitive 2 : of, relating to, or arousing sexual feelings

Eros \'er-,äs, 'ir-\ n [Gk Erōs, fr. erōs sexual love; akin to Gk erasthai to love, desire] 1 : the Greek god of erotic love — compare CUPID 2 : the sum of life-preserving instincts that are manifested as impulses to gratify basic needs, as sublimated impulses, and as impulses to protect and preserve the body and mind — compare DEATH INSTINCT 3 a : love conceived in the philosophy of Plato as a fundamental creative impulse having a sensual element b often not cap : erotic love or desire

erose \i-'rōs\ adj [L erosus, pp. of erodere] (1793) : IRREGULAR, UNEVEN; specif : having the margin irregularly notched as if gnawed ⟨an ~ leaf⟩

ero·sion \i-'rō-zhən\ n (1541) 1 a : the action or process of eroding b : the state of being eroded 2 : an instance or product of erosive action — ero·sion·al \i-'rōzh-nəl, -'rō-zhə-nᵊl\ adj — ero·sion·al·ly \-ē\ adv

ero·sive \i-'rō-siv, -ziv\ adj (1830) : tending to erode or to induce or permit erosion — ero·sive·ness n — ero·siv·i·ty \i-,rō-'si-və-tē\ n

erot·ic \i-'rä-tik\ also erot·i·cal \-ti-kəl\ adj [Gk erōtikos, fr. erōt-, erōs] (1651) 1 : of, devoted to, or tending to arouse sexual love or desire ⟨~ art⟩ 2 : strongly marked or affected by sexual desire — erotic n — erot·i·cal·ly \-ti-k(ə-)lē\ adv

erot·i·ca \i-'rä-ti-kə\ n pl but sing or pl in constr [NL, fr. Gk erōtika, neut. pl. of erōtikos] (1854) 1 : literary or artistic works having an erotic theme or quality 2 : depictions of things erotic

erot·i·cism \i-'rä-tə-,si-zəm\ n (1881) 1 : an erotic theme or quality 2 : a state of sexual arousal 3 : insistent sexual impulse or desire — erot·i·cist \-sist\ n

erot·i·cize \-,sīz\ vt -cized; -ciz·ing (ca. 1914) : to make erotic — erot·i·ci·za·tion \i-,rä-tə-sə-'zā-shən\ n

er·o·tism \'er-ə-,ti-zəm\ n (1849) : EROTICISM

er·o·tize \'er-ə-,tīz\ vt -tized; -tiz·ing (1936) : to invest with erotic significance or sexual feeling — er·o·ti·za·tion \,er-ə-tə-'zā-shən\ n

eroto- comb form [NL, fr. Gk erōto-, fr. erōt-, eros] : sexual desire ⟨erotogenic⟩

ero·to·gen·ic \i-,rō-tə-'je-nik, -,rä-\ adj (ca. 1909) : EROGENOUS

err \'er, 'ər\ vi [ME, fr. MF errer, fr. L errare to wander, err; akin to OE ierre wandering, angry, ON rās race — more at RACE] (14c) 1 archaic : STRAY 2 a : to make a mistake b : to violate an accepted standard of conduct

er·ran·cy \'er-ən(t)-sē\ n, pl -cies (1621) : the state or an instance of erring

er·rand \'er-ənd\ n [ME erend message, business, fr. OE ǣrend; akin to OHG ārunti message] (bef. 12c) 1 archaic a : an oral message entrusted to a person b : EMBASSY, MISSION 2 a : a short trip taken to attend to some business often for another ⟨was on an ~ for his mother⟩ b : the object or purpose of such a trip

er·rant \'er-ənt\ adj [ME, fr. MF erraunt, prp. of errer to err & errer to travel, fr. LL iterare, fr. L iter road, journey — more at ITINERANT] (14c) 1 : traveling or given to traveling ⟨an ~ knight⟩ 2 a : straying outside the proper path or bounds ⟨an ~ calf⟩ b : moving about aimlessly or irregularly ⟨an ~ breeze⟩ c : deviating from a

standard (as of truth or propriety) ⟨an ~ child⟩ d : FALLIBLE — er·rant n — er·rant·ly adv

er·rant·ry \'er-ən-trē\ n, pl -ries (1654) : the quality, condition, or fact of wandering; esp : a roving in search of chivalrous adventure

er·ra·ta \e-'rä-tə, -'rä-, -'ra-\ n [L, pl. of erratum] (1589) : a list of corrigenda; also : a page bearing such a list

1er·rat·ic \ir-'a-tik\ adj [ME, fr. MF or L; MF erratique, fr. L erraticus, fr. erratus, pp. of errare] (14c) 1 a : having no fixed course : WANDERING ⟨an ~ comet⟩ b archaic : NOMADIC 2 : transported from an original resting place esp. by a glacier ⟨an ~ boulder⟩ 3 a : characterized by lack of consistency, regularity, or uniformity b : deviating from what is ordinary or standard : ECCENTRIC ⟨an ~ genius⟩ syn see STRANGE — er·rat·i·cal \-ti-kəl\ adj — er·rat·i·cal·ly \-ti-k(ə-)lē\ adv — er·rat·i·cism \-'a-tə-,si-zəm\ n

2erratic n (ca. 1623) : one that is erratic; esp : an erratic boulder or block of rock

er·ra·tum \e-'rä-təm, -'rä-, -'ra-\ n, pl -ta \-tə\ [L, fr. neut. of erratus] (1589) : ERROR; esp : CORRIGENDUM

er·ro·ne·ous \i-'rō-nē-əs, e-'rō-\ adj [ME, fr. L erroneus, fr. erron-, erro wanderer, fr. errare] (15c) 1 : containing or characterized by error : MISTAKEN ⟨~ assumptions⟩ 2 archaic : WANDERING — er·ro·ne·ous·ly adv — er·ro·ne·ous·ness n

er·ror \'er-ər\ n [ME errour, fr. MF, fr. L error, fr. errare] (13c) 1 a : an act or condition of ignorant or imprudent deviation from a code of behavior b : an act involving an unintentional deviation from truth or accuracy c : an act that through ignorance, deficiency, or accident departs from or fails to achieve what should be done: as (1) : a defensive misplay other than a wild pitch or passed ball made by a baseball player when normal play would have resulted in an out or prevented an advance by a base runner (2) : the failure of a player (as in tennis) to make a successful return of a ball during play d : a mistake in the proceedings of a court of record in matters of law or of fact 2 a : the quality or state of erring b Christian Science : illusion about the nature of reality that is the cause of human suffering : the contradiction of truth c : an instance of false belief 3 : something produced by mistake; esp : a postage stamp exhibiting a consistent flaw (as a wrong color) in its manufacture 4 a : the difference between an observed or calculated value and a true value; specif : variation in measurements, calculations, or observations of a quantity due to mistakes or to uncontrollable factors b : the amount of deviation from a standard or specification 5 : a deficiency or imperfection in structure or function ⟨an ~ of metabolism⟩ — er·ror·less \'er-ər-ləs\ adj

syn ERROR, MISTAKE, BLUNDER, SLIP, LAPSE mean a departure from what is true, right, or proper. ERROR suggests the existence of a standard or guide and a straying from the right course through failure to make effective use of this ⟨procedural errors⟩. MISTAKE implies misconception or inadvertence and usu. expresses less criticism than error ⟨dialed the wrong number by mistake⟩. BLUNDER regularly imputes stupidity or ignorance as a cause and connotes some degree of blame ⟨diplomatic blunders⟩. SLIP stresses inadvertence or accident and applies esp. to trivial but embarrassing mistakes ⟨a slip of the tongue⟩. LAPSE stresses forgetfulness, weakness, or inattention as a cause ⟨a lapse in judgment⟩.

er·satz \'er-,säts, -,zäts, er-'; 'ər-,sats\ adj [G ersatz, fr. Ersatz n., substitute] (1875) : being a usu. artificial and inferior substitute or imitation ⟨~ turf⟩ ⟨~ intellectuals⟩ — ersatz n

Erse \'ərs\ n [ME (Sc) Erisch, adj., Irish, alter. of Irish] (15c) 1 : SCOTTISH GAELIC 2 : IRISH GAELIC — Erse adj

erst \'ərst\ adv [ME erest earliest, formerly, fr. OE ǣrest, superl. of ǣr early — more at ERE] (12c) archaic : ERSTWHILE

1erst·while \'ərst-,(h)wīl\ adv (1569) : in the past : FORMERLY ⟨cultures, ~ unknown to each other —Robert Plank⟩

2erstwhile adj (1903) : FORMER, PREVIOUS ⟨her ~ students⟩

eru·cic acid \i-'rü-sik-\ n [NL Eruca, genus of herbs, fr. L, colewort] (1869) : a crystalline fatty acid $C_{22}H_{42}O_2$ found in the form of glycerides esp. in rapeseed oil

eruct \i-'rəkt\ vb [L eructare, freq. of erugere to belch, disgorge; akin to OE rocettan to belch, Gk ereugesthai] (1666) : BELCH

eruc·ta·tion \i-,rək-'tā-shən, ,ē-\ n (15c) : an act or instance of belching

er·u·dite \'er-ə-,dīt, 'er-yə-\ adj [ME erudit, fr. L eruditus, fr. pp. of erudire to instruct, fr. e- + rudis rude, ignorant] (15c) : possessing or displaying erudition : LEARNED ⟨an ~ scholar⟩ — er·u·dite·ly adv

er·u·di·tion \,er-ə-'di-shən, ,er-yə-\ n (15c) : extensive knowledge acquired chiefly from books : profound, recondite, or bookish learning syn see KNOWLEDGE

erum·pent \i-'rəm-pənt\ adj [L erumpent-, erumpens, prp. of erumpere] (1650) : bursting forth ⟨~ fungi⟩

erupt \i-'rəpt\ vb [L eruptus, pp. of erumpere to burst forth, fr. e- + rumpere to break — more at REAVE] vi (1657) 1 a (1) : to burst from limits or restraint (2) of a tooth : to emerge through the gum b : to force out or release suddenly and often violently something (as lava or steam) that is pent up c : to become active or violent esp. suddenly 2 : to break out with or as if with a skin eruption ~ vt : to force out or release usu. suddenly and violently — erupt·ible \-'rəp-tə-bəl\ adj — erup·tive \-tiv\ adj — erup·tive·ly adv

erup·tion \i-'rəp-shən\ n (1555) 1 a : an act, process, or instance of erupting b : the breaking out of a rash on the skin or mucous membrane 2 : a product of erupting (as a skin rash)

-ery \(ə-)rē\ n suffix, pl -er·ies [ME -erie, fr. OF, fr. -ier -er + -ie -y] 1 : qualities collectively : character ⟨-NESS ⟨snobbery⟩ 2 : art : practice ⟨quackery⟩ 3 : place of doing, keeping, producing, or selling ⟨the thing specified⟩ ⟨fishery⟩ ⟨bakery⟩ 4 : collection : aggregate ⟨finery⟩ 5 : state or condition ⟨slavery⟩

eryn·go \i-'riŋ-(,)gō\ n, pl -goes or -gos [modif. of L eryngion sea holly, fr. Gk ēryngion] (1543) 1 : any of various plants (genus Eryngium) of the carrot family that have elongate spinulose-margined leaves and flowers in dense bracted heads 2 obs : candied root of the sea holly made to be used as an aphrodisiac

ery·sip·e·las \,er-ə-'si-p(ə-)ləs, ,ir-\ n [ME erisipila, fr. L erysipelas, fr. Gk, fr. erysi- (prob. akin to Gk erythros red) + -pelas (prob. akin to L pellis skin — more at RED, FELL] (14c) : an acute febrile disease associated with intense edematous local inflammation of the skin and subcutaneous tissues caused by a hemolytic streptococcus

er·y·the·ma \‚er-ə-'thē-mə\ n [NL, fr. Gk erythēma, fr. erythainein to redden, fr. erythros] (ca. 1783) : abnormal redness of the skin due to capillary congestion — **er·y·them·a·tous** \-'the-mə-təs\ adj

er·y·thor·bate \-ə-'thȯr-‚bāt\ n (1963) : a salt of erythorbic acid that is used in foods as an antioxidant

er·y·thor·bic acid \-‚thȯr-bik-\ n [erythr- + ascorbic acid] (1963) : a diastereoisomer of ascorbic acid with optical activity

erythr- or **erythro-** comb form [Gk, fr. erythros — more at RED] 1 : red ⟨erythrocyte⟩ 2 : erythrocyte ⟨erythroid⟩

er·y·thre·mia \‚er-ə-'thrē-mē-ə\ n [NL] (1908) : POLYCYTHEMIA VERA

er·y·thrism \'er-ə-‚thri-zəm\ n (1864) : a condition marked by exceptional prevalence of red pigmentation (as in skin or hair) — **er·y·thris·tic** \‚er-ə-'thris-tik\ also **er·y·thris·mal** \-'thriz-məl\ adj

er·y·thrite \'er-ə-‚thrīt\ n (1844) : a usu. rose-colored mineral consisting of a hydrous cobalt arsenate occurring esp. in monoclinic crystals

eryth·ro·blast \i-'rith-rə-‚blast\ n [ISV] (ca. 1890) : a polychromatic nucleated cell of red marrow that synthesizes hemoglobin and that is an intermediate in the initial stage of red blood cell formation; broadly : a cell ancestral to red blood cells — **eryth·ro·blas·tic** \-‚rith-rə-'blas-tik\ adj

eryth·ro·blas·to·sis \i-‚rith-rə-‚blas-'tō-səs\ n, pl **-to·ses** \-‚sēz\ [NL] (ca. 1923) : abnormal presence of erythroblasts in the circulating blood; esp : ERYTHROBLASTOSIS FETALIS

erythroblastosis fe·ta·lis \-fi-'ta-ləs\ n [NL, fetal erythroblastosis] (ca. 1934) : a hemolytic disease of the fetus and newborn that occurs when the system of an Rh-negative mother produces antibodies to an antigen in the blood of an Rh-positive fetus which cross the placenta and destroy fetal erythrocytes and that is characterized by an increase in circulating erythroblasts and by jaundice

eryth·ro·cyte \i-'rith-rə-‚sīt\ n [ISV] (ca. 1894) : RED BLOOD CELL — **eryth·ro·cyt·ic** \-‚rith-rə-'si-tik\ adj

ery·throid \i-'rith-‚rȯid, 'er-ə-‚thrȯid\ adj (1927) : relating to erythrocytes or their precursors

eryth·ro·my·cin \i-‚rith-rə-'mī-s°n\ n (1952) : a broad-spectrum antibiotic $C_{37}H_{67}NO_{13}$ produced by an actinomycete (Streptomyces erythreus)

eryth·ro·poi·e·sis \i-‚rith-rō-pȯi-'ē-səs\ n [NL, fr. erythr- + Gk poiēsis creation — more at POESY] (1918) : the production of red blood cells (as from the bone marrow) — **eryth·ro·poi·et·ic** \-'e-tik\ adj

eryth·ro·poi·e·tin \-'pȯi-ə-t°n\ n (1948) : a hormonal substance that is formed esp. in the kidney and stimulates red blood cell formation

eryth·ro·sin \i-'rith-rə-sən\ also **eryth·ro·sine** \-sən, -‚sēn\ n [ISV erythr- + eosin] (ca. 1882) : any of several dyes made from fluorescein that yield reddish shades

¹-es \əz, iz after s, z, sh, ch; z after v or a vowel\ n pl suffix [ME -es, -s — more at ¹-s] — used to form the plural of most nouns that end in s ⟨glasses⟩, z ⟨fuzzes⟩, sh ⟨bushes⟩, ch ⟨peaches⟩, or a final y that changes to i ⟨ladies⟩ and of some nouns ending in f that changes to v ⟨loaves⟩; compare ¹-s

²-es vb suffix [ME — more at ³-s] — used to form the third person singular present of most verbs that end in s ⟨blesses⟩, z ⟨fizzes⟩, sh ⟨hushes⟩, ch ⟨catches⟩, or a final y that changes to i ⟨defies⟩; compare ³-s

Esau \'ē-(‚)sȯ\ n [L, fr. Gk Ēsau, fr. Heb 'Ēsāw] : the elder son of Isaac and Rebekah who sold his birthright to his twin brother Jacob

es·ca·drille \'es-kə-‚dril, -‚drē\ n [F, flotilla, escadrille, fr. Sp escuadrilla, dim. of escuadra squadron, squad — more at SQUAD] (1912) : a unit of a European air command containing usu. six airplanes

es·ca·lade \'es-kə-‚lād, -‚lād\ n [F, fr. It scalata, fr. scalare to scale, fr. scala ladder, fr. LL — more at SCALE] (1598) : an act of scaling esp. the walls of a fortification — **escalade** vt — **es·ca·lad·er** n

es·ca·late \'es-kə-‚lāt, -̇-kyə-\ vb **-lat·ed; -lat·ing** [back-formation fr. escalator] vi (1944) : to increase in extent, volume, number, amount, intensity, or scope ⟨a little war threatens to ~ into a huge ugly one — Arnold Abrams⟩ ~ vt : EXPAND 2 — **es·ca·la·tion** \‚es-kə-'lā-shən, -̇-kyə-\ n — **es·ca·la·to·ry** \‚es-lə-‚tȯr-ē, -‚tȯr-; -‚tȯr-, -̇-kyə-\ adj

¹es·ca·la·tor \'es-kə-‚lā-tər, -̇-kyə-\ n [fr. Escalator, a trademark] (1900) 1 a : a power-driven set of stairs arranged like an endless belt that ascend or descend continuously b : an upward course suggestive of an escalator ⟨a never-stopping ~ of economic progress —D. W. Brogan⟩ 2 : an escalator clause or provision

²escalator adj (1930) : providing for a periodic proportional upward or downward adjustment (as of prices or wages) ⟨an ~ arrangement tying the base pay . . . to living costs —N. Y. Times⟩

es·cal·lop \is-'kä-ləp, -'ka-\ var of SCALLOP

es·ca·pade \'es-kə-‚pād\ n [F, action of escaping, fr. Sp. escapada, fr. escapar to escape, fr. (assumed) VL excappare] (1672) : a usu. adventurous action that runs counter to approved or conventional conduct

¹es·cape \is-'kāp, es-, dial iks-'kāp\ vb **es·caped; es·cap·ing** [ME, fr. ONF escaper, fr. (assumed) VL excappare, fr. L ex- + LL cappa head covering, cloak] vi (13c) 1 a : to get away (as by flight) ⟨escaped from prison⟩ b : to issue from confinement ⟨gas is escaping⟩ c of a plant : to run wild from cultivation 2 : to avoid a threatening evil ~ vt 1 : to get free of : break away from ⟨~ the jungle⟩ ⟨~ the solar system⟩ 2 : to get or stay out of the way of : AVOID 3 : to fail to be noticed or recallable by ⟨his name ~s me⟩ 4 a : to issue from b : to be uttered involuntarily by — **es·cap·er** n

syn ESCAPE, AVOID, EVADE, ELUDE, SHUN, ESCHEW mean to get away or keep away from something. ESCAPE stresses the fact of getting away or being passed by not necessarily through effort or by conscious intent ⟨nothing escapes her sharp eyes⟩. AVOID stresses forethought and caution in keeping clear of danger or difficulty ⟨try to avoid past errors⟩. EVADE implies adroitness, ingenuity, or lack of scruple in escaping or avoiding ⟨evaded the question by changing the subject⟩. ELUDE implies a slippery or baffling quality in the person or thing that escapes ⟨what she sees in him eludes me⟩. SHUN often implies an avoiding as a matter of habitual practice or policy and may imply repugnance or abhorrence ⟨you have shunned your responsibilities⟩. ESCHEW implies an avoiding or abstaining from as unwise or distasteful ⟨a playwright who eschews melodrama⟩.

²escape n (14c) 1 : an act or instance of escaping: as a : flight from confinement b : evasion of something undesirable c : leakage or outflow esp. of a fluid d : distraction or relief from routine or reality 2 : a means of escape 3 : a cultivated plant run wild

³escape adj (1817) 1 : providing a means of escape ⟨~ literature⟩ 2 : providing a means of evading a regulation, claim, or commitment ⟨an ~ clause in a contract⟩

escape artist n (1943) : one (as a performer or criminal) unusually adept at escaping from confinement

es·cap·ee \is-‚kā-'pē, ‚es-(‚)kā-, ‚es-kə-\ n (ca. 1866) : one that has escaped; esp : an escaped prisoner

escape hatch n (1925) 1 : a hatch providing an emergency exit from an enclosed space 2 : a means of evading a difficulty, dilemma, or responsibility

escape mechanism n (1927) : a mode of behavior or thinking adopted to evade unpleasant facts or responsibilities

es·cape·ment \is-'kāp-mənt, es-\ n (1779) 1 a : a device in a timepiece which controls the motion of the train of wheelwork and through which the energy of the power source is delivered to the pendulum or balance by means of impulses that permit a tooth to escape from a pallet at regular intervals b : a ratchet device (as the spacing mechanism of a typewriter) that permits motion in one direction only in equal steps 2 a : the act of escaping b : a way of escape : VENT

escape velocity n (1934) : the minimum velocity that a moving body (as a rocket) must have to escape from the gravitational field of a celestial body (as the earth) and move outward into space

escapement 1a

es·cap·ism \is-'kā-‚pi-zəm\ n (1933) : habitual diversion of the mind to purely imaginative activity or entertainment as an escape from reality or routine — **es·cap·ist** \-pist\ adj or n

es·cap·ol·o·gy \is-‚kā-'pä-lə-jē, ‚es-(‚)\ n (1939) : the art or practice of escaping — **es·cap·ol·o·gist** \-jist\ n

es·car·got \‚es-‚kär-'gō\ n, pl **-gots** \-'gō(z)\ [F, snail, fr. MF, fr. OProv escaragol] (ca. 1892) : a snail prepared for use as food

es·ca·role \'es-kə-‚rōl\ n [F, fr. LL escariola, fr. L escarius of food, fr. esca food, fr. edere to eat — more at EAT] (1897) : ENDIVE 1

es·carp·ment \i-'skärp-mənt\ n [F escarpement, fr. escarper to scarp, fr. MF, fr. escarpe scarp, fr. OIt scarpa — more at SCARP] (ca. 1802) 1 : a steep slope in front of a fortification 2 : a long cliff or steep slope separating two comparatively level or more gently sloping surfaces and resulting from erosion or faulting

-es·cence \'e-s°n(t)s\ n suffix [MF, fr. L -escentia, fr. -escent-, -escens + -ia -y] : state or process of becoming ⟨obsolescence⟩

-es·cent \'e-s°nt\ adj suffix [MF, fr. L -escent-, -escens, prp. suffix of incho. verbs in -escere] 1 : beginning : beginning to be : slightly ⟨frutescent⟩ 2 : reflecting or emitting light (in a specified way) ⟨opalescent⟩

es·char \'es-‚kär\ n [ME escare — more at SCAR] (1543) : a scab formed esp. after a burn

es·cha·rot·ic \‚es-kə-'rä-tik\ adj [F or LL; F escharotique, fr. LL escharoticus, fr. Gk escharōtikos, fr. escharoun to form an eschar, fr. eschara eschar] (1612) : producing an eschar — **escharotic** n

es·cha·to·log·i·cal \(‚)es-‚kä-t°l-'ä-ji-kəl, ‚es-kə-\ adj (1854) 1 : of or relating to eschatology or an eschatology 2 : of or relating to the end of the world or the events associated with it in eschatology — **es·cha·to·log·i·cal·ly** \-ji-k(ə-)lē\ adv

es·cha·tol·o·gy \‚es-kə-'tä-lə-jē\ n, pl **-gies** [Gk eschatos last, farthest] (1844) 1 : a branch of theology concerned with the final events in the history of the world or of mankind 2 : a belief concerning death, the end of the world, or the ultimate destiny of mankind; specif : any of various Christian doctrines concerning the Second Coming, the resurrection of the dead, or the Last Judgment

¹es·cheat \is-'chēt, ish-'chēt\ n [ME eschete, fr. OF, reversion of property, fr. escheoir to fall, devolve, fr. (assumed) VL excadēre, fr. L ex- + (assumed) VL cadēre to fall, fr. L cadere — more at CHANCE] (14c) 1 : escheated property 2 a : the reversion of lands in English feudal law to the lord of the fee when there are no heirs capable of inheriting under the original grant b : the reversion of property to the crown in England or to the state in the U.S. when there are no legal heirs

²escheat vt (14c) : to revert by escheat ~ vi : to revert by escheat — **es·cheat·able** \-'chē-tə-bəl\ adj

es·chew \e-'shü, i-; es-'chü, is-; also e-'skyü\ vt [ME, fr. MF eschiuver, of Gmc origin; akin to OHG sciuhen to frighten off — more at SHY] (14c) : to avoid habitually esp. on moral or practical grounds : SHUN syn see ESCAPE — **es·chew·al** \-əl\ n

es·co·lar \‚es-kə-'lär\ n, pl **escolar** or **escolars** [Sp, lit., scholar, fr. ML scholaris — more at SCHOLAR] (ca. 1890) : a large widely distributed rough-scaled fish (Lepidocybium flavobrunneum) that resembles a mackerel

¹es·cort \'es-‚kȯrt\ n [F escorte, fr. It scorta, fr. scorgere to guide, fr. (assumed) VL excorrigere, fr. L ex- + corrigere to make straight, correct — more at CORRECT] (1745) 1 a (1) : a person or group of persons accompanying another to give protection or as a courtesy (2) : the man who goes on a date with a woman b : a protective screen of warships or fighter planes or a single ship or plane used to fend off enemy attack from one or more vulnerable craft 2 : accompaniment by a person or an armed protector (as a ship)

²es·cort \is-'kȯrt, es-, 'es-‚\ vt (1708) : to accompany as an escort

es·cot \is-'kät\ vt [MF escoter, fr. escot contribution, of Gmc origin; akin to ON skot contribution, shot — more at SHOT] (1602) obs : SUPPORT, MAINTAIN

es·cri·toire \'es-krə-‚twär\ n [obs. F, writing desk, scriptorium, fr. ML scriptorium] (1694) : a writing table or desk; specif : SECRETARY 4b

¹es·crow \'es-‚krō, es-'\ n [MF escroue scroll — more at SCROLL] (1594) 1 : a deed, a bond, money, or a piece of property held in trust by a third party to be turned over to the grantee only upon fulfillment of a condition 2 : a fund or deposit designed to serve as an escrow — **in escrow** : in trust as an escrow ⟨had $1000 in escrow to pay taxes⟩

\ə\ abut \ᵊ\ kitten, F table \ər\ further \a\ ash \ā\ ace \ä\ mop, mar \au̇\ out \ch\ chin \e\ bet \ē\ easy \g\ go \i\ hit \ī\ ice \j\ job \ŋ\ sing \ō\ go \ȯ\ law \ȯi\ boy \th\ thin \ṯẖ\ the \ü\ loot \u̇\ foot \y\ yet \zh\ vision \à, k̲, ⁿ, œ, œ̄, ᵫ, ᵫ̄, ʸ\ see Guide to Pronunciation

²es·crow \es-'krō, 'es-₁\ *vt* (1949) : to place in escrow

es·cu·do \is-'kü-(₁)dō\ *n, pl* **-dos** [Sp & Pg, lit., shield, fr. L *scutum*] (ca. 1821) **1** : any of various former gold or silver coins of Hispanic countries **2** — see MONEY table **3** : the basic monetary unit of Chile between 1960 and 1975 **4** : the peso of Guinea-Bissau

es·cu·lent \'es-kyə-lənt\ *adj* [L *esculentus*, fr. *esca* food, fr. *edere* to eat — more at EAT] (1626) : EDIBLE — **esculent** *n*

es·cutch·eon \is-'kə-chən\ *n* [ME *escochon*, fr. MF *escuchon*, fr. (assumed) VL *scution-, scutio*, fr. L *scutum* shield — more at ESQUIRE] (15c) **1** : a defined area on which armorial bearings are displayed and which usu. consists of a shield **2** : a protective or ornamental plate or flange (as around a keyhole) **3** : the part of a ship's stern on which the name is displayed

Es·dras \'ez-drəs\ *n* [LL, fr. Gk, fr. Heb *'Ezrā*] **1** : either of two books of the Roman Catholic canon of the Old Testament: **a** : EZRA 2 **b** : NEHEMIAH 2 **2** : either of two uncanonical books of Scripture included in the Protestant Apocrypha — see BIBLE table

¹-ese \'ēz, 'ēs\ *adj suffix* [Pg *-ês* & It *-ese*, fr. L *-ensis*] : of, relating to, or originating in (a certain place or country) ⟨Japan*ese*⟩

²-ese *n suffix, pl* **-ese** **1** : native or resident of (a specified place or country) ⟨Chin*ese*⟩ **2 a** : language of (a particular place, country, or nationality) ⟨Siam*ese*⟩ **b** : speech, literary style, or diction peculiar to (a specified place, person, or group) — usu. in words applied in depreciation ⟨journal*ese*⟩

es·em·plas·tic \₁e-₁sem-'plas-tik, -səm-\ *adj* [Gk *es hen* into one + E *plastic*] (1817) : shaping or having the power to shape disparate things into a unified whole ⟨the ∼ power of the poetic imagination —W. H. Gardner⟩

es·er·ine \'e-sə-₁rēn\ *n* [F *ésérine*] (1879) : PHYSOSTIGMINE

es·ker \'es-kər\ *n* [Ir *eiscir* ridge] (1848) : a long narrow ridge or mound of sand, gravel, and boulders deposited by a stream flowing on, within, or beneath a stagnant glacier

Es·ki·mo \'es-kə-₁mō\ *n* [obs. *Esquimawe*, prob. fr. Sp *esquimao*, fr. Montagnais (Algonquian language of eastern Canada) *aiachkime8* Micmac, Eskimo; prob. akin to modern Montagnais *assime'w* she laces a snowshoe, Ojibwa *aškime*] (1584) **1** *pl* **Eskimo** *or* **Eskimos** : a member of a group of peoples of northern Canada, Greenland, Alaska, and eastern Siberia **2** : any of the languages of the Eskimo peoples — **Es·ki·mo·an** \₁es-kə-'mō-ən\ *adj*

Eskimo curlew *n* (1813) : an extremely rare New World curlew (*Numenius borealis*) that breeds in northern No. America and winters in So. America

Eskimo dog *n* (1774) : a sled dog of American origin

ESOP \₁ē-₁es-(₁)ō-'pē, 'ē-₁säp\ *n* [*em*ployee *s*tock *o*wnership *p*lan] (1975) : a program by which a corporation's employees acquire its capital stock

esoph·a·gus \i-'sä-fə-gəs\ *n, pl* **-gi** \-₁gī, -₁jī\ [ME *ysophagus*, fr. Gk *oisophagos*, fr. *oisein* to be going to carry

Eskimo curlew

+ *phagein* to eat — more at BAKSHEESH] (14c) : a muscular tube that in humans is about nine inches long and passes from the pharynx down the neck between the trachea and the spinal column and behind the left bronchus where it pierces the diaphragm slightly to the left of the middle line and joins the cardiac end of the stomach — **esoph·age·al** \i-₁sä-fə-'jē-əl\ *adj*

es·o·ter·ic \₁e-sə-'ter-ik\ *adj* [LL *esotericus*, fr. Gk *esōterikos*, fr. *esōterō*, compar. of *eisō, esō* within, fr. *eis* into; akin to Gk *en* in — more at IN] (ca. 1660) **1 a** : designed for or understood by the specially initiated alone ⟨a body of ∼ legal doctrine —B. N. Cardozo⟩ **b** : of or relating to knowledge that is restricted to a small group **2 a** : limited to a small circle ⟨∼ pursuits⟩ **b** : PRIVATE, CONFIDENTIAL ⟨an ∼ purpose⟩ — **es·o·ter·i·cal·ly** \-i-k(ə-)lē\ *adv*

es·o·ter·i·ca \-i-kə\ *n pl* [NL, fr. Gk *esōterika*, neut. pl. of *esōterikos*] (ca. 1929) : esoteric items

es·o·ter·i·cism \-'ter-ə-₁si-zəm\ *n* (1846) **1** : esoteric doctrines or practices **2** : the quality or state of being esoteric

ESP \₁ē-₁es-'pē\ *n* [*e*xtra*s*ensory *p*erception] (1934) : EXTRASENSORY PERCEPTION

es·pa·drille \'es-pə-₁dril\ *n* [F, alter. of *espardille*, ultim. fr. L *spartum*] (1892) : a sandal usu. having a fabric upper and a flexible sole

¹es·pal·ier \is-'pal-yər, -₁yā\ *n* [F, ultim. fr. It *spalla* shoulder, fr. LL *spatula* shoulder blade — more at EPAULET] (1662) **1** : a plant (as a fruit tree) trained to grow flat against a support (as a wall) **2** : a railing or trellis on which fruit trees or shrubs are trained to grow flat

²espalier *vt* (1810) **1** : to train as an espalier **2** : to furnish with an espalier

es·par·to \is-'pär-(₁)tō\ *n, pl* **-tos** [Sp, fr. L *spartum*, fr. Gk *sparton* — more at SPIRE] (1845) **1** : either of two Spanish and Algerian grasses (*Stipa tenacissima* and *Lygeum spartum*) used esp. to make cordage, shoes, and paper — called also *esparto grass* **2** : the fiber of esparto

es·pe·cial \is-'pe-shəl\ *adj* [ME, fr. MF — more at SPECIAL] (14c) : being distinctive: as **a** : directed toward a particular individual, group, or end ⟨sent ∼ greetings to his son⟩ ⟨took ∼ care to speak clearly⟩ **b** : of special note or importance : unusually great or significant ⟨a decision of ∼ relevance⟩ **c** : highly distinctive or personal : PECULIAR ⟨had an ∼ dislike for music⟩ **d** : CLOSE, INTIMATE ⟨his ∼ crony⟩ **e** : SPECIFIC, PARTICULAR ⟨had no ∼ destination in mind⟩ *syn* see SPECIAL — **in especial** : in particular

es·pe·cial·ly \is-'pesh-lē, -'pe-shə-\ *adv* (15c) **1** : SPECIALLY 1 **2 a** : in particular : PARTICULARLY ⟨food seems cheaper, ∼ meats⟩ **b** : for a particular purpose ⟨built ∼ for research⟩ **3** — used as an intensive ⟨an ∼ good essay⟩ ⟨nothing ∼ radical in the remarks⟩

es·per·ance \'es-p(ə-)rən(t)s\ *n* [ME *esperaunce*, fr. MF *esperance*] (15c) *obs* : HOPE, EXPECTATION

Es·pe·ran·to \₁es-pə-'rän-(₁)tō, -'ran-(₁)tō\ *n* [Dr. *Esperanto*, pseudonym of L. L. Zamenhof †1917 Pol. oculist, its inventor] (1892) : an artificial international language based as far as possible on words common to the chief European languages — **Es·pe·ran·tist** \-'rän-tist, -'ran-\ *n or adj*

es·pi·al \is-'pī(-ə)l\ *n* (14c) **1** : OBSERVATION **2** : an act of noticing : DISCOVERY

es·piè·gle \es-pyegl'\ *adj* [F, after *Ulespiegle* (Till Eulenspiegel), peasant prankster] (1816) : FROLICSOME, ROGUISH

es·piè·gle·rie \es-pyeg-lə-rē\ *n* [F, fr. *espiègle*] (1816) : the quality or state of being roguish or frolicsome

es·pi·o·nage \'es-pē-ə-₁näzh, -₁näj, -nij, *Canad also* -₁nazh; ₁es-pē-ə-'näzh; is-'pē-ə-nij\ *n* [F *espionnage*, fr. MF, fr. *espionner* to spy, fr. *espion* spy, fr. OIt *spione* spy, fr. *spia*, of Gmc origin; akin to OHG *spehōn* to spy — more at SPY] (1793) : the practice of spying or using spies to obtain information about the plans and activities esp. of a foreign government or a competing company ⟨industrial ∼⟩

es·pla·nade \'es-plə-₁näd, -es-plə-'\ *also* -'näd *or* -₁näd\ *n* [MF, fr. It *spianata*, fr. *spianare* to level, fr. L *explanare* — more at EXPLAIN] (1591) : a level open stretch of paved or grassy ground; *esp* : one designed for walking or driving along a shore

es·pous·al \is-'paù-zəl *also* -səl\ *n* (14c) **1 a** : BETROTHAL **b** : WEDDING **c** : MARRIAGE **2** : a taking up or adopting of a cause or belief

es·pouse \is-'paùz *also* -'paùs\ *vt* **es·poused; es·pous·ing** [ME, fr. MF *espouser*, fr. LL *sponsare* to betroth, fr. L *sponsus* betrothed — more at SPOUSE] (15c) **1** : MARRY **2** : to take up and support as a cause : become attached to ⟨*syn* see ADOPT — **es·pous·er** *n*

espres·so \e-'spre-(₁)sō\ *n, pl* **-sos** [It (*caffè*) *espresso*, lit., pressed out coffee] (1945) **1** : coffee brewed by forcing steam through finely ground darkly roasted coffee beans **2** : a cup of espresso

es·prit \is-'prē\ *n* [F, fr. L *spiritus* spirit] (1591) **1** : vivacious cleverness or wit **2** : ESPRIT DE CORPS

es·prit de corps \is-₁prē-də-'kōr, -'kor\ *n* [F] (1780) : the common spirit existing in the members of a group and inspiring enthusiasm, devotion, and strong regard for the honor of the group

es·py \is-'pī\ *vt* **es·pied; es·py·ing** [ME *espien*, fr. OF *espier* — more at SPY] (14c) : to catch sight of ⟨among the several horses ... she espied the white mustang —Zane Grey⟩

-esque \'esk\ *adj suffix* [F, fr. It *-esco*, of Gmc origin; akin to OHG *-isc* *-ish* — more at -ISH] : in the manner or style of : like ⟨statu*esque*⟩

Es·qui·mau \'es-kə-₁mō\ *n, pl* **Esquimau** *or* **Es·qui·maux** \-₁mō(z)\ [F, fr. Montagnais (Algonquian language)] (1744) : ESKIMO

es·quire \'es-₁kwīr, is-'\ *n* [ME, fr. MF *escuier* squire, fr. LL *scutarius*, fr. L *scutum* shield; akin to OIr *sciath* shield] (15c) **1** : a member of the English gentry ranking below a knight **2** : a candidate for knighthood serving as shield bearer and attendant to a knight **3** — used as a title of courtesy usu. placed in its abbreviated form after the surname ⟨John R. Smith, *Esq.*⟩ **4** *archaic* : a landed proprietor

ess \'es\ *n* (1540) **1** : the letter *s* **2** : something resembling the letter *S* in shape; *esp* : an S-shaped curve in a road

-ess \əs, is *also* ₁es\ *n suffix* [ME *-esse*, fr. OF, fr. LL *-issa*, fr. Gk] : female ⟨giant*ess*⟩

¹es·say \e-'sā, ə-'sā, 'e-₁sā\ *vt* (14c) **1** : to put to a test **2** : to make an often tentative or experimental effort to perform : TRY *syn* see ATTEMPT — **es·say·er** *n*

²es·say \'e-₁sā; *senses 1, 2 & 4 also* e-'sā\ *n* [ME, fr. MF *essai*, ultim. fr. LL *exagium* act of weighing, fr. *ex-* + *agere* to drive — more at AGENT] (14c) **1** : TRIAL, TEST **2 a** : EFFORT, ATTEMPT; *esp* : an initial tentative effort **b** : the result or product of an attempt **3 a** : an analytic or interpretative literary composition usu. dealing with its subject from a limited or personal point of view **b** : something resembling such a composition ⟨a photographic ∼⟩ **4** : a proof of an unaccepted design for a stamp or piece of paper money

es·say·ist \'e-₁sā-ist\ *n* (1601) : a writer of essays

es·say·is·tic \₁e-(₁)sā-'is-tik\ *adj* (1862) **1** : of or relating to an essay or an essayist **2** : resembling an essay in quality or character

essay question *n* (1947) : an examination question that requires an answer in a sentence, paragraph, or short composition

es·sence \'e-s²n(t)s\ *n* [ME, fr. MF & L; MF, fr. L *essentia*, fr. *esse* to be — more at IS] (14c) **1 a** : the permanent as contrasted with the accidental element of being **b** : the individual, real, or ultimate nature of a thing esp. as opposed to its existence **c** : the properties or attributes by means of which something can be placed in its proper class or identified as being what it is **2** : something that exists : ENTITY **3 a** (1) : a volatile substance or constituent (as of perfume) (2) : a constituent or derivative possessing the special qualities (as of a plant or drug) in concentrated form; *also* : a preparation of such an essence by a synthetic substitute **b** : ODOR, PERFUME **4** : one that possesses or exhibits a quality in abundance as if in concentrated form ⟨she was the ∼ of punctuality⟩ — **in essence** : in or by its very nature : ESSENTIALLY, BASICALLY ⟨was *in essence* an honest person⟩ — **of the essence** : of the utmost importance ⟨time is *of the essence*⟩

Es·sene \i-'sēn, 'e-₁sēn\ *n* [Gk *Essēnos*] (1553) : a member of a monastic brotherhood of Jews in Palestine from the 2d century B.C. to the 2d century A.D. — **Es·se·ni·an** \i-'sē-nē-ən, e-'se-\ *or* **Es·se·nic** \-'se-nik, -'sē-nik\ *adj* — **Es·se·nism** \'se-₁ni-zəm\ *n*

¹es·sen·tial \i-'sen(t)-shəl\ *adj* (14c) **1** : of, relating to, or constituting essence : INHERENT **2** : of the utmost importance : BASIC, INDISPENSABLE, NECESSARY ⟨∼ foods⟩ ⟨an ∼ requirement for admission to college⟩ **3** : IDIOPATHIC ⟨∼ disease⟩ — **es·sen·tial·ly** \-'sench-lē, -'sen-chə-\ *adv* — **es·sen·tial·ness** \-'sen-chəl-nəs\ *n*

syn ESSENTIAL, FUNDAMENTAL, VITAL, CARDINAL mean so important as to be indispensable. ESSENTIAL implies belonging to the very nature of a thing and therefore being incapable of removal without destroying the thing itself or its character ⟨conflict is *essential* in drama⟩. FUNDAMENTAL applies to something that is a foundation without which an entire system or complex whole would collapse ⟨*fundamental* principles of algebra⟩. VITAL suggests something that is necessary to a thing's continued existence or operation ⟨cut off from *vital* supplies⟩. CARDINAL suggests something on which an outcome turns or depends ⟨a *cardinal* rule in buying a home⟩.

²essential *n* (15c) **1** : something basic ⟨the ∼s of astronomy⟩ **2** : something necessary, indispensable, or unavoidable

essential amino acid *n* (1935) : an amino acid (as lysine) required for normal health and growth, manufactured in the body in insufficient quantities or not at all, and usu. supplied by dietary protein

es·sen·tial·ism \-₁li-zəm\ *n* (1927) **1** : an educational theory that ideas and skills basic to a culture should be taught to all alike by time-tested methods — compare PROGRESSIVISM **2** : a philosophical theory ascribing ultimate reality to essence embodied in a thing perceptible to the senses — compare NOMINALISM — **es·sen·tial·ist** \-list\ *adj or n*

es·sen·ti·al·i·ty \i-ˌsen(t)-shē-ˈa-lə-tē\ *n, pl* **-ties** (1616) **1 a :** essential nature **:** ESSENCE **b :** an essential quality, property, or aspect **2 :** the quality or state of being essential ⟨the ~ of freedom and justice —P. G. Hoffman⟩

es·sen·tial·ize \i-ˈsen(t)-shə-ˌlīz\ *vt* **-ized; -iz·ing** (1913) **:** to express or formulate in essential form **:** reduce to essentials

essential oil *n* (1674) **:** any of a class of volatile oils that give plants their characteristic odors and are used esp. in perfumes and flavorings — compare FIXED OIL

es·soin \i-ˈsȯin\ *n* [ME *essoine*, fr. MF, fr. OF, fr. *essoinier* to offer an essoin, fr. *es-* ex- + *soine* legal excuse, of Gmc origin; akin to OS *sunnea* denial, OE *sōth* truth — more at SOOTH] (14c) **1 :** an excuse for not appearing in an English law court at the appointed time **2** *obs* **:** EXCUSE, DELAY

es·so·nite \ˈe-sᵊn-ˌit\ *n* [F, fr. Gk *hēsson* inferior; fr. its being less hard than true hyacinth] (1820) **:** a yellow to brown garnet

¹-est \əst, ist\ *adj suffix or adv suffix* [ME, fr. OE *-st, -est, -ost;* akin to OHG *-isto* (adj. superl. suffix), Gk *-istos*] — used to form the superlative degree of adjectives and adverbs of one syllable ⟨fatt*est*⟩ ⟨lat*est*⟩, of some adjectives and adverbs of two syllables ⟨luck*iest*⟩ ⟨often*est*⟩, and less often of longer ones ⟨beggarl*iest*⟩

²-est \əst, ist\ *or* **-st** \st\ *vb suffix* [ME, fr. OE *-est, -ast, -st;* akin to OHG *-ist, -ōst, -ēst,* 2d sing. ending] — used to form the archaic 2d person singular of English verbs (with *thou*) ⟨did*st*⟩

es·tab·lish \is-ˈta-blish\ *vt* [ME *establissen*, fr. MF *establiss-*, stem of *establir*, fr. L *stabilire*, fr. *stabilis* stable] (14c) **1 :** to institute (as a law) permanently by enactment or agreement **2** *obs* **:** SETTLE 7 **3 a :** to make firm or stable **b :** to introduce and cause to grow and multiply ⟨~ grass on pasturelands⟩ **4 a :** to bring into existence **:** FOUND ⟨~ed a republic⟩ **b :** BRING ABOUT, EFFECT ⟨~ed friendly relations⟩ **5 a :** to put on a firm basis **:** SET UP ⟨~ his son in business⟩ **b :** to put into a favorable position **c :** to gain full recognition or acceptance of ⟨the role ~ed her as a star⟩ **6 :** to make (a church) a national or state institution **7 :** to put beyond doubt **:** PROVE ⟨~ed my innocence⟩ — **es·tab·lish·able** \-shə-bəl\ *adj* — **es·tab·lish·er** \-shər\ *n*

established church *n* (1731) **:** a church recognized by law as the official church of a nation or state and supported by civil authority

es·tab·lish·ment \is-ˈta-blish-mənt\ *n* (15c) **1 :** something established: as **a :** a settled arrangement; *esp* **:** a code of laws **b :** ESTABLISHED CHURCH **c :** a permanent civil or military organization **d :** a place of business or residence with its furnishings and staff **e :** a public or private institution **2 :** an established order of society: as **a** *often cap* **:** a group of social, economic, and political leaders who form a ruling class (as of a nation) **b** *often cap* **:** a controlling group ⟨the literary ~⟩ **3 a :** the act of establishing **b :** the state of being established — **es·tab·lish·men·tar·i·an** \is-ˌta-blish-mən-ˈter-ē-ən, -ˌmen-\ *adj* (1847) **:** of, relating to, or favoring the social or political establishment — **establishmentarian** *n* — **es·tab·lish·men·tar·i·an·ism** \-ē-ə-ˌni-zəm\ *n*

es·ta·mi·net \e-stä-mē-nä\ *n, pl* **-nets** \-nä(z)\ [F] (1814) **:** a small café

es·tate \is-ˈtāt\ *n* [ME *estat*, fr. OF — more at STATE] (13c) **1 :** STATE, CONDITION **2 :** social standing or rank esp. of a high order **3 :** a social or political class; *specif* **:** one of the great classes (as the nobility, the clergy, and the commons) formerly vested with distinct political powers **4 a :** the degree, quality, nature, and extent of one's interest in land or other property **b** (1) **:** POSSESSIONS, PROPERTY; *esp* **:** a person's property in land and tenements ⟨a man of small ~⟩ (2) **:** the assets and liabilities left by a person at death **c :** a landed property usu. with a large house on it **d** *Brit* **:** PROJECT 4 **5** *Brit* **:** STATION WAGON

estate agent *n* (1880) *Brit* **:** a real estate broker or manager

estate car *n* (1950) *Brit* **:** STATION WAGON

estate tax *n* (1928) **:** an excise in the form of a percentage of the net estate that is levied on the privilege of an owner of property of transmitting the property to others after his or her death — compare INHERITANCE TAX 1

¹es·teem \is-ˈtēm\ *n* (14c) **1** *archaic* **:** WORTH, VALUE **2** *archaic* **:** OPINION, JUDGMENT **3 :** the regard in which one is held; *esp* **:** high regard ⟨the ~ we all feel for her⟩

²esteem *vt* [ME *estemen* to estimate, fr. MF *estimer*, fr. L *aestimare*] (15c) **1** *archaic* **:** APPRAISE **2 a :** to view as **:** CONSIDER ⟨~ it a privilege⟩ **b :** THINK, BELIEVE **3 :** to set a high value on **:** regard highly and prize accordingly **syn** see REGARD

es·ter \ˈes-tər\ *n* [G, fr. *Essigäther* ethyl acetate, fr. *Essig* vinegar + *Äther* ether] (ca. 1852) **:** any of a class of often fragrant compounds that can be represented by the formula RCOOR' and that are usu. formed by the reaction between an acid and an alcohol with elimination of water

es·ter·ase \ˈes-tə-ˌrās, -ˌrāz\ *n* (1910) **:** an enzyme that accelerates the hydrolysis or synthesis of esters

es·ter·i·fy \e-ˈster-ə-ˌfī\ *vt* **-fied; -fy·ing** (ca. 1905) **:** to convert into an ester — **es·ter·i·fi·ca·tion** \-ˌster-ə-fə-ˈkā-shən\ *n*

Es·ther \ˈes-tər\ *n* [L, fr. Heb *Estēr*] **1 :** the Jewish heroine of the Old Testament book of Esther **2 :** a narrative book of canonical Jewish and Christian Scripture — see BIBLE table

es·thete, es·thet·ic, es·the·ti·cian, es·the·ti·cism *var of* AESTHETE, AESTHETIC, AESTHETICIAN, AESTHETICISM

es·ti·ma·ble \ˈes-tə-mə-bəl\ *adj* (15c) **1 :** capable of being estimated **2** *archaic* **:** VALUABLE **3 :** worthy of esteem — **es·ti·ma·ble·ness** *n* — **es·ti·ma·bly** \-blē\ *adv*

¹es·ti·mate \ˈes-tə-ˌmāt\ *vt* **-mat·ed; -mat·ing** [L *aestimatus*, pp. of *aestimare* to value, estimate] (ca. 1532) **1** *archaic* **a :** ESTEEM **b :** APPRAISE **2 a :** to judge tentatively or approximately the value, worth, or significance of **b :** to determine roughly the size, extent, or nature of **c :** to produce a statement of the approximate cost of **3 :** JUDGE, CONCLUDE — **es·ti·ma·tive** \-ˌmā-tiv\ *adj*

syn ESTIMATE, APPRAISE, EVALUATE, VALUE, RATE, ASSESS mean to judge something with respect to its worth or significance. ESTIMATE implies a judgment, considered or casual, that precedes or takes the place of actual measuring or counting or testing out ⟨*estimated* the crowd at two hundred⟩. APPRAISE commonly implies the fixing by an expert of the monetary worth of a thing, but it may be used of any critical judgment ⟨having their house *appraised*⟩. EVALUATE suggests an attempt to

determine relative or intrinsic worth in terms other than monetary ⟨*evaluate* a student's work⟩. VALUE equals APPRAISE but without implying expertness of judgment ⟨a watercolor *valued* by the donor at $500⟩. RATE adds to ESTIMATE the notion of placing a thing according to a scale of values ⟨a highly *rated* restaurant⟩. ASSESS implies a critical appraisal for the purpose of understanding or interpreting, or as a guide in taking action ⟨officials are trying to *assess* the damage⟩.

²es·ti·mate \ˈes-tə-mət\ *n* (1563) **1 :** the act of appraising or valuing **:** CALCULATION **2 :** an opinion or judgment of the nature, character, or quality of a person or thing ⟨had a high ~ of his abilities⟩ **3 a :** a rough or approximate calculation **b :** a numerical value obtained from a statistical sample and assigned to a population parameter **4 :** a statement of the cost of work to be done

es·ti·ma·tion \ˌes-tə-ˈmā-shən\ *n* (14c) **1 :** JUDGMENT, OPINION **2 a :** the act of estimating something **b :** the value, amount, or size arrived at in an estimate **3 :** ESTEEM, HONOR

es·ti·ma·tor \ˈes-tə-ˌmā-tər\ *n* (1611) **1 :** one that estimates **2 :** ESTIMATE 3b; *also* **:** a statistical function whose value for a sample furnishes an estimate of a population parameter

es·ti·val \ˈes-tə-vəl\ *adj* [ME, fr. MF or L; MF, fr. L *aestivalis*, fr. *aestivus* of summer, fr. *aestas* summer — more at EDIFY] (14c) **:** of or relating to the summer

es·ti·vate \-ˌvāt\ *vi* **-vat·ed; -vat·ing** (1626) **1 :** to spend the summer usu. at one place **2 :** to pass the summer in a state of torpor — compare HIBERNATE

es·ti·va·tion \ˌes-tə-ˈvā-shən\ *n* (1625) **:** the state of one that estivates

Es·to·nian \e-ˈstō-nē-ən, -nyən\ *n* (1795) **1 :** a native or inhabitant of Estonia **2 :** the Finno-Ugric language of the Estonian people — **Estonian** *adj*

es·top \e-ˈstäp\ *vt* **es·topped; es·top·ping** [ME *estoppen*, fr. MF *estouper* (fr. assumed) VL *stuppare* to stop with a tow — more at STOP] (15c) **1** *archaic* **:** to stop up **2 :** BAR; *specif* **:** to impede by estoppel

es·top·pel \e-ˈstä-pəl\ *n* [prob. fr. MF *estoupail* bung, fr. *estouper*] (1531) **:** a legal bar to alleging or denying a fact because of one's own previous actions or words to the contrary

estr- *or* **estro-** *comb form* **:** estrus ⟨estrogen⟩

es·tra·di·ol \ˌes-trə-ˈdī-ˌȯl, -ˌōl\ *n* [ISV *estra-* (fr. *estrane* parent compound of estradiol, fr. NL *estrus* + E *-ane*) + ¹-*ol*] (1934) **:** an estrogenic hormone that is a phenolic steroid alcohol $C_{18}H_{24}O_2$ usu. made synthetically and that is often used combined as an ester esp. in treating menopausal symptoms

estral cycle \ˈes-trəl-\ *n* (1941) **:** ESTROUS CYCLE

es·trange \is-ˈtrānj\ *vt* **es·tranged; es·trang·ing** [ME, fr. MF *estranger*, fr. ML *extraneare*, fr. L *extraneus* strange — more at STRANGE] (15c) **1 :** to remove from customary environment or associations **2 :** to arouse esp. mutual enmity or indifference in where there had formerly been love, affection, or friendliness **:** ALIENATE — **es·trange·ment** \-ˈtrānj-mənt\ *n* — **es·trang·er** *n*

syn ESTRANGE, ALIENATE, DISAFFECT mean to cause one to break a bond of affection or loyalty. ESTRANGE implies the development of indifference or hostility with consequent separation or divorcement ⟨his *estranged* wife⟩. ALIENATE may or may not suggest separation but always implies loss of affection or interest ⟨managed to *alienate* all his coworkers⟩. DISAFFECT refers esp. to those from whom loyalty is expected and stresses the effects (as rebellion or discontent) of alienation without actual separation ⟨conservatives were *disaffected* by the new tax⟩.

¹es·tray \is-ˈtrā\ *n* (ca. 1523) **:** STRAY 1

²estray *n* [MF *estraier*] (1572) *archaic* **:** STRAY

es·tri·ol \ˈes-ˌtrī-ˌȯl, e-ˈstrī-, -ˌōl\ *n* [*estrane* + *tri-* + ¹-*ol*] (1933) **:** a crystalline estrogenic hormone that is a glycol $C_{18}H_{24}O_3$ usu. obtained from the urine of pregnant women

es·tro·gen \ˈes-trə-jən\ *n* [NL *estrus* + ISV *-o-* + *-gen*] (1927) **:** a substance (as a sex hormone) tending to promote estrus and stimulate the development of female secondary sex characteristics

es·tro·gen·ic \ˌes-trə-ˈje-nik\ *adj* (1930) **1 :** promoting estrus **2 :** of, relating to, caused by, or being an estrogen — **es·tro·gen·i·cal·ly** \-ni-k(ə-)lē\ *adv*

es·trone \ˈes-ˌtrōn\ *n* [*estrane*] (1933) **:** an estrogenic hormone that is a ketone $C_{18}H_{22}O_2$ usu. obtained from the urine of pregnant females and used similarly to estradiol

es·trous \ˈes-trəs\ *adj* (1900) **1 :** of, relating to, or characteristic of estrus **2 :** being in heat

estrous cycle *n* (1900) **:** the correlated phenomena of the endocrine and generative systems of a female mammal from the beginning of one period of estrus to the beginning of the next — called also *estral cycle, estrus cycle*

es·tru·al \ˈes-trə-wəl\ *adj* (ca. 1857) **:** ESTROUS

es·trus \ˈes-trəs\ *n* [NL, fr. L *oestrus* gadfly, frenzy, fr. Gk *oistros* — more at IRE] (1890) **:** a regularly recurrent state of sexual excitability during which the female of most mammals will accept the male and is capable of conceiving **:** HEAT; *also* **:** a single occurrence of this state

es·tu·ar·i·al \ˌes-chə-ˈwer-ē-əl, ˌesh-\ *adj* (1883) **:** ESTUARINE

es·tu·a·rine \ˈes-chə-(wə-)ˌrīn, -ˌrēn, -ˌrin, ˈesh-\ *adj* (1846) **:** of, relating to, or formed in an estuary ⟨~ currents⟩ ⟨~ animals⟩

es·tu·ary \ˈes-chə-ˌwer-ē, ˈesh-\ *n, pl* **-ar·ies** [L *aestuarium*, fr. *aestus* boiling, tide; akin to L *aestas* summer — more at EDIFY] (1538) **:** a water passage where the tide meets a river current; *esp* **:** an arm of the sea at the lower end of a river

esu·ri·ence \i-ˈsùr-ē-ən(t)s, -ˈzùr-\ *n* (1825) **:** the quality or state of being esurient

esu·ri·ent \-ənt\ *adj* [L *esurient-, esuriens,* prp. of *esurire* to be hungry; akin to L *edere* to eat — more at EAT] (ca. 1672) **:** HUNGRY, GREEDY — **esu·ri·ent·ly** *adv*

et \ˈet\ *dial past and past part of* EAT

¹-et \ət, ˌet, ət, it\ *n suffix* [ME, fr. OF *-et,* masc. & *-ete,* fem., fr. LL *-itus* & *-ita*] **:** small one ⟨baron*et*⟩ ⟨cellar*et*⟩

\ə\ abut \ᵊ\ kitten, F table \ər\ further \a\ ash \ā\ ace \ä\ mop, mar
\aù\ out \ch\ chin \e\ bet \ē\ easy \g\ go \i\ hit \ī\ ice \j\ job
\ŋ\ sing \ō\ go \ȯ\ law \ȯi\ boy \th\ thin \t̲h̲\ the \ü\ loot \ù\ foot
\y\ yet \zh\ vision \á, k̲, ⁿ, œ, œ̄, ᵫ, ū̇, ᵊ\ *see* Guide to Pronunciation

²**-et** n suffix [duet] : group ⟨octet⟩

eta \'ā-tə, chiefly Brit 'ē-tə\ n [ME, fr. LL, fr. Gk ēta, of Sem origin; akin to Heb hēth heth] (15c) : the 7th letter of the Greek alphabet — see ALPHABET table

éta·gère or **eta·gere** \ˌā-ˌtä-'zher, -tə-\ n [F, fr. MF estagiere, fr. estage floor of a building, station, fr. OF — more at STAGE] (1851) : a piece of furniture consisting of a set of open shelves for displaying small objects and sometimes having an enclosed cabinet as a base

et alia \(ˌ)et-'ā-l(ē-)yə, -'ä-, -'a-\ [L] (1953) : and others

eta·mine \'ā-tə-ˌmēn\ n [F étamine] (1714) : a light cotton or worsted fabric with an open mesh

etat·ism \ā-'tä-ˌti-zəm\ n [F étatisme, fr. état state, fr. OF estat — more at STATE] (1923) : STATE SOCIALISM — **etat·ist** \-'tä-tist\ adj

et·cet·era \et-'se-tə-rə, -'se-trə also it-, ÷ek-, ÷ik-\ n (1656) 1 : a number of unspecified additional persons or things 2 pl : unspecified additional items : ODDS AND ENDS

étagère

et cet·era \same\ [L] (12c) : and others esp. of the same kind : and so forth

¹**etch** \'ech\ vb [D etsen, fr. G ätzen to etch, corrode, fr. OHG azzen to feed; akin to OHG ezzan to eat — more at EAT] vt (1634) 1 a : to produce (as a pattern or design) on a hard material by eating into the material's surface (as by acid or laser beam) b : to subject to such etching 2 : to delineate or impress clearly ⟨scenes ~ed in our minds⟩ ⟨pain was ~ed on his features⟩ ~ vi : to practice etching — **etch·er** n

²**etch** n (1896) 1 : the action or effect of etching a surface 2 : a chemical agent used in etching

etch·ant \'e-chənt\ n (1904) : ETCH 2

etch·ing n (1634) 1 a : the action or process of etching b : the art of producing pictures or designs by printing from an etched metal plate 2 a : an etched design b : an impression made from an etched plate

¹**eter·nal** \i-'tər-nᵊl\ adj [ME, fr. MF, fr. LL aeternus eternal, fr. aevum age, eternity — more at AYE] (14c) 1 a : having infinite duration : EVERLASTING b : of or relating to eternity c : characterized by abiding fellowship with God ⟨good teacher, what must I do to inherit ~ life? —Mk 10:17 (RSV)⟩ 2 a : continued without intermission : PERPETUAL b : seemingly endless 3 archaic : INFERNAL ⟨some ~ villain ... devised this slander —Shak.⟩ 4 : valid or existing at all times : TIMELESS ⟨~ verities⟩ — **eter·nal·ize** \-nᵊl-ˌīz\ vt — **eter·nal·ly** \-nᵊl-ē\ adv — **eter·nal·ness** n

²**eternal** n (1582) 1 cap : GOD 1 — used with the 2 : something eternal

eterne \i-'tərn\ adj [ME, fr. MF, fr. L aeternus] (14c) archaic : ETERNAL

eter·ni·ty \i-'tər-nə-tē\ n, pl -ties [ME eternite, fr. MF eternité, fr. L aeternitat-, aeternitas, fr. aeternus] (14c) 1 : the quality or state of being eternal 2 : infinite time 3 pl : AGE 3b 4 : the state after death : IMMORTALITY 5 : a seemingly endless or immeasurable time

eter·nize \i-'tər-ˌnīz\ vt -nized; -niz·ing (1580) 1 a : to make eternal b : to prolong indefinitely 2 : IMMORTALIZE — **eter·ni·za·tion** \-ˌtər-nə-'zā-shən\ n

Ete·sian \i-'tē-zhən\ adj [L etesius, fr. Gk etēsios, fr. etos year — more at WETHER] (1601) : recurring annually — used of summer winds that blow over the Mediterranean — **Etesian** n

eth \'eth\ var of EDH

eth- comb form [ISV] : ethyl ⟨ethene⟩

¹**-eth** \əth, ith\ or **-th** \th\ vb suffix [ME, fr. OE -eth, -ath, -th; akin to OHG -it, -ōt, -ēt, 3d sing. ending, L -t, -it] — used to form the archaic third person singular present of verbs ⟨doth⟩

²**-eth** — see -TH

eth·a·cryn·ic acid \ˌe-thə-ˌkri-nik-\ n [perh. fr. eth- + acetic + butyryl + phenol] (1964) : a potent synthetic diuretic $C_{13}H_{12}Cl_2O_4$ used esp. in the treatment of edema

eth·am·bu·tol \e-'tham-byü-ˌtöl, -ˌtöl\ n [ethylene + amine + butanol] (1965) : a compound $C_{10}H_{24}N_2O_2$ used esp. in the treatment of tuberculosis

eth·ane \'e-ˌthān, Brit usu 'ē-\ n [ISV, fr. ethyl] (1873) : a colorless odorless gaseous alkane C_2H_6 found in natural gas and used as a fuel

eth·a·nol \'e-thə-ˌnöl, -ˌnöl, Brit also 'ē-\ n (1900) : a colorless volatile flammable liquid C_2H_5OH that is the intoxicating agent in liquors and is also used as a solvent — called also ethyl alcohol, grain alcohol

eth·a·nol·amine \ˌe-thə-'nä-lə-ˌmēn, -'nö-, Brit also ˌē-\ n (1897) : a colorless liquid amino alcohol C_2H_7NO used esp. as a solvent in the synthesis of detergents and in gas purification

eth·ene \'e-ˌthēn\ n (1873) : ETHYLENE

eth·e·phon \'e-thə-ˌfän\ n [ethyl + phosphonic acid (a dibasic organic acid)] (1971) : a synthetic plant growth regulator $C_2H_6ClO_3P$ that induces flowering and abscission by promoting the release of ethylene and has been used to cause early ripening (as of apples on the tree)

ether \'ē-thər\ n [ME, fr. L aether, fr. Gk aithēr, fr. aithein to ignite, blaze; akin to OE ād pyre — more at EDIFY] (14c) 1 a : the rarefied element formerly believed to fill the upper regions of space b : the upper regions of space : HEAVENS 2 a : a medium that in the wave theory of light permeates all space and transmits transverse waves b : AIRWAVES 2 a : a light volatile flammable liquid $C_4H_{10}O$ used chiefly as a solvent and anesthetic b : any of various organic compounds characterized by an oxygen atom attached to two carbon atoms — **ethe·ric** \i-'ther-ik, -'thir-\ adj

ethe·re·al \i-'thir-ē-əl\ adj (1513) 1 a : of or relating to the regions beyond the earth b : CELESTIAL, HEAVENLY c : UNWORLDLY, SPIRITUAL 2 a : lacking material substance : IMMATERIAL, INTANGIBLE b : marked by unusual delicacy or refinement ⟨this smallest, most ~, and daintiest of birds —William Beebe⟩ 3 : relating to, containing, or resembling a chemical ether — **ethe·re·al·i·ty** \-ˌthir-ē-'a-lə-tē\ n — **ethe·re·al·ize** \-'thir-ē-ə-ˌlīz\ vt — **ethe·re·al·ly** \-ē-ə-lē\ adv — **ethe·re·al·ness** n

ether extract n (ca. 1900) : the part of a complex organic material that is soluble in ether and consists chiefly of fats and fatty acids

ether·ize \'ē-thə-ˌrīz\ vt -ized; -iz·ing (1853) 1 : to treat or anesthetize with ether 2 : to make numb as if by anesthetizing — **ether·iza·tion** \ˌē-thə-rə-'zā-shən\ n — **ether·iz·er** n

eth·ic \'e-thik\ n [ME ethik, fr. MF ethique, fr. L ethice, fr. Gk ēthikē, fr. ēthikos] (14c) 1 pl but sing or pl in constr : the discipline dealing with what is good and bad and with moral duty and obligation 2 a : a set of moral principles or values b : a theory or system of moral values ⟨the present-day materialistic ~⟩ c pl but sing or pl in constr : the principles of conduct governing an individual or a group ⟨professional ~s⟩ d : a guiding philosophy

eth·i·cal \'e-thi-kəl\ also **eth·ic** \-thik\ adj [ME etik, fr. L ethicus, fr. Gk ēthikos, fr. ēthos character — more at SIB] (1607) 1 : of or relating to ethics 2 : involving or expressing moral approval or disapproval 3 : conforming to accepted professional standards of conduct 4 of a drug : restricted to sale only on a doctor's prescription syn see MORAL — **eth·i·cal·i·ty** \ˌe-thə-'ka-lə-tē\ n — **eth·i·cal·ly** \'e-thi-k(ə-)lē\ adv — **eth·i·cal·ness** \-kəl-nəs\ n

ethi·cian \e-'thi-shən\ n (1929) : ETHICIST

eth·i·cist \'e-thə-sist\ n (ca. 1890) : a specialist in ethics

ethid·ium bromide \e-'thi-dē-əm-\ n [ethyl + -id + -ium] (1963) : a biological dye used esp. to block nucleic acid synthesis (as in mitochondria) and to destroy trypanosomes

ethinyl var of ETHYNYL — used esp. in pharmacology

ethinyl estradiol n (1939) : a very potent synthetic estrogen $C_{20}H_{24}O_2$ used orally

eth·i·on \'e-thē-ˌän\ n [blend of eth- and thion-] (ca. 1960) : an organophosphate $C_9H_{22}O_4P_2S_4$ used as a pesticide

eth·i·on·amide \ˌe-thē-'ä-nə-ˌmīd\ n (1960) : a compound $C_8H_{10}N_2S$ used against mycobacteria (as in tuberculosis and leprosy)

ethi·o·nine \e-'thī-ə-ˌnēn\ n (1938) : an amino acid $C_6H_{13}NO_2S$ that is the ethyl homologue of methionine and is biologically antagonistic to methionine

Ethi·op \'ē-thē-ˌäp\ or **Ethi·ope** \-ˌōp\ n [ME Ethiope, fr. L Aethiops, fr. Gk Aithiops] (13c) archaic : ETHIOPIAN

¹**Ethi·o·pi·an** \ˌē-thē-'ō-pē-ən\ n (13c) 1 : a member of any of the mythical or actual peoples usu. described by the ancient Greeks as dark-skinned and living far to the south 2 archaic : a black person 3 : a native or inhabitant of Ethiopia

²**Ethiopian** adj (1578) 1 : of, relating to, or characteristic of the inhabitants or the country of Ethiopia 2 : of, relating to, or being the biogeographic region that includes Africa south of the Sahara, southern Arabia, and sometimes Madagascar and the adjacent islands

¹**Ethi·o·pic** \-'ä-pik, -'ō-pik\ adj (1654) 1 : ETHIOPIAN 2 a : of, relating to, or constituting Ethiopic b : of, relating to, or constituting a group of related Semitic languages spoken in Ethiopia

²**Ethiopic** n (1677) 1 : a Semitic language formerly spoken in Ethiopia and still used as the liturgical language of the Christian church in Ethiopia 2 : the Ethiopic group of Semitic languages

eth·moid \'eth-ˌmöid\ n [F ethmoïde, fr. Gk ēthmoeidēs, lit., like a strainer, fr. ēthmos strainer] (1842) : a light spongy cubical bone forming much of the walls of the nasal cavity and part of those of the orbits — **ethmoid** \same\ or **eth·moi·dal** \ˌeth-'möi-dᵊl\ adj

¹**eth·nic** \'eth-nik\ adj [ME, fr. LL ethnicus, fr. Gk ethnikos national, gentile, fr. ethnos nation, people; akin to Gk ēthos custom — more at SIB] (15c) 1 : HEATHEN 2 a : of or relating to large groups of people classed according to common racial, national, tribal, religious, linguistic, or cultural origin or background ⟨~ minorities⟩ ⟨~ enclaves⟩ b : being a member of an ethnic group ⟨~ of, relating to, or characteristic of ethnics ⟨~ neighborhoods⟩ ⟨~ foods⟩

²**ethnic** n (1941) : a member of an ethnic group; esp : a member of a minority group who retains the customs, language, or social views of the group

eth·ni·cal \'eth-ni-kəl\ adj (15c) 1 : ETHNIC 2 : of or relating to ethnology : ETHNOLOGIC — **eth·ni·cal·ly** \-k(ə-)lē\ adv

ethnic cleansing n (1992) : the expulsion, imprisonment, or killing of ethnic minorities by a dominant majority group

eth·nic·i·ty \eth-'ni-sə-tē\ n (1950) : ethnic quality or affiliation

ethno- comb form [Gk ethno-, ethn-, fr. ethnos] : race : people : cultural group ⟨ethnocentric⟩

eth·no·bot·a·ny \ˌeth-nō-'bä-tᵊn-ē, -'bät-nē\ n (1890) : the plant lore of a race or people; also : the systematic study of such lore — **eth·no·bo·tan·i·cal** \-bə-'ta-ni-kəl\ adj — **eth·no·bot·a·nist** \-'bä-tᵊn-ist, -'bät-nist\ n

eth·no·cen·tric \ˌeth-nō-'sen-trik\ adj (1900) : characterized by or based on the attitude that one's own group is superior — **eth·no·cen·tric·i·ty** \-sen-'tri-sə-tē\ n — **eth·no·cen·trism** \-'sen-ˌtri-zəm\ n

eth·nog·ra·phy \eth-'nä-grə-fē\ n [F ethnographie, fr. ethno- + -graphie -graphy] (1834) : the study and systematic recording of human cultures; also : a descriptive work produced from such research — **eth·nog·ra·pher** \-fər\ n — **eth·no·graph·ic** \ˌeth-nə-'gra-fik\ or **eth·no·graph·i·cal** \-fi-kəl\ adj — **eth·no·graph·i·cal·ly** \-fi-k(ə-)lē\ adv

eth·no·his·to·ry \ˌeth-nō-'his-t(ə-)rē\ n (1943) : a study of the development of cultures — **eth·no·his·to·ri·an** \-(ˌ)his-'tōr-ē-ən, -'tor-, -'tär-\ n — **eth·no·his·to·ric** \-(ˌ)his-'tör-ik, -'tär-\ or **eth·no·his·to·ri·cal** \-i-kəl\ adj

eth·nol·o·gy \eth-'nä-lə-jē\ n (ca. 1828) 1 : a science that deals with the division of human beings into races and their origin, distribution, relations, and characteristics 2 : anthropology dealing chiefly with the comparative and analytical study of cultures : CULTURAL ANTHROPOLOGY — **eth·no·log·i·cal** \ˌeth-nə-'lä-ji-kəl\ also **eth·no·log·ic** \-jik\ adj — **eth·no·log·i·cal·ly** \-ji-k(ə-)lē\ adv — **eth·nol·o·gist** \eth-'nä-lə-jist\ n

eth·no·meth·od·ol·o·gy \ˌeth-nō-ˌme-thə-'dä-lə-jē\ n (1967) : a branch of sociology dealing with nonspecialists' commonsense understanding of the structure and organization of society — **eth·no·meth·od·ol·o·gist** \-'dä-lə-jist\ n

eth·no·mu·si·col·o·gy \ˌeth-nō-ˌmyü-zi-'kä-lə-jē\ n (1950) 1 : the study of music that is outside the European art tradition 2 : the study of music in a sociocultural context — **eth·no·mu·si·co·log·i·cal** \-kə-'lä-ji-kəl\ adj — **eth·no·mu·si·col·o·gist** \-'kä-lə-jist\ n

eth·no·sci·ence \'eth-nō-ˌsī-ən(t)s\ n (1961) : the nature lore (as folk taxonomy of plants and animals) of primitive peoples

ethol·o·gy \ē-'thä-lə-jē\ n (ca. 1843) 1 : a branch of knowledge dealing with human ethos and with its formation and evolution **2** : the scientific and objective study of animal behavior esp. under natural conditions — **etho·log·i·cal** \ˌē-thə-ˈlä-ji-kəl, ˌe-thə-\ *adj* — **ethol·o·gist** \ē-ˈthä-lə-jist\ *n*

ethos \ˈē-ˌthäs\ *n* [NL, fr. Gk *ēthos* custom, character — more at SIB] (1851) : the distinguishing character, sentiment, moral nature, or guiding beliefs of a person, group, or institution

eth·oxy \e-ˈthäk-sē\ *adj* (ca. 1909) : relating to or containing the univalent group CH_3CH_2O— composed of ethyl united with oxygen

eth·yl \ˈe-thəl\ *n* [G *Ethyl* (now *Äthyl*), fr. *Äther* ether + -*yl*] (1838) : a univalent hydrocarbon group CH_3CH_2— — **eth·yl·ic** \e-ˈthi-lik\ *adj*

ethyl acetate *n* (1874) : a colorless fragrant volatile flammable liquid ester $C_4H_8O_2$ used esp. as a solvent

ethyl alcohol *n* (1869) : ETHANOL

eth·yl·ben·zene \ˌe-thil-ˈben-ˌzēn\ *n* [ISV] (1873) : a liquid hydrocarbon C_8H_{10} that is made usu. from benzene and ethylene and is used chiefly in the manufacture of styrene

ethyl cellulose *n* (1936) : any of various thermoplastic substances used esp. in plastics and lacquers

ethyl chloride *n* (ca. 1891) : a colorless pungent flammable gaseous or volatile liquid C_2H_5Cl used esp. as a local surface anesthetic

eth·yl·ene \ˈe-thə-ˌlēn\ *n* (ca. 1852) **1** : a colorless flammable gaseous unsaturated hydrocarbon C_2H_4 that is found in coal gas, can be produced by pyrolysis of petroleum hydrocarbons, and occurs in plants functioning esp. as a natural growth regulator that promotes the ripening of fruit **2** : a divalent hydrocarbon group C_2H_4 derived from ethane — **eth·yl·en·ic** \ˌe-thə-ˈle-nik, -ˈlē-nik\ *adj*

eth·yl·ene·di·amine·tet·ra·ac·e·tate \ˌe-thə-ˌlēn-ˌdī-ə-ˌmēn-ˌte-trə-ˈa-sə-ˌtāt, -di-ˌa-mēn-\ (1954) : a salt of EDTA

eth·yl·ene·di·amine·tet·ra·ace·tic acid \-(ə-)ˈsē-tik-\ *n* (1942) : EDTA

ethylene di·bro·mide \-(ˌ)dī-ˈbrō-ˌmīd\ *n* (ca. 1929) : a colorless toxic liquid compound $C_2H_4Br_2$ that is used chiefly as a fuel additive in leaded gasolines, that has been found to be strongly carcinogenic in laboratory animals, and that was used formerly in the U.S. as an agricultural pesticide — abbr. *EDB*

ethylene glycol *n* (1901) : a thick liquid diol $C_2H_6O_2$ used esp. as an antifreeze and in making polyester fibers

ethylene oxide *n* (1898) : a colorless flammable toxic compound C_2H_4O used esp. in synthesis (as of ethylene glycol) and in sterilization and fumigation

ethyl ether *n* (1878) : ETHER 3a

eth·yne \ˈe-ˌthin, e-ˈ\ *n* [*ethyl* + ²-*ine*] (ca. 1929) : ACETYLENE

ethy·nyl \e-ˈthi-nᵊl, ˈe-thə-ˌnil\ *n* (1929) : a univalent unsaturated group HC≡C— derived from acetylene by removal of one hydrogen atom

et·ic \ˈe-tik\ *adj* [phon*etic*] (1954) : of, relating to, or having linguistic or behavioral characteristics considered without regard to their structural significance — compare EMIC

-et·ic \ˈe-tik\ *adj suffix* [L & Gk; L -*eticus*, fr. Gk -*etikos*, -*ētikos*, fr. -*etos*, -*ētos*, ending of certain verbals] : -IC — often in adjectives corresponding to nouns ending in -*esis* ⟨gen*etic*⟩

eti·o·late \ˈē-tē-ə-ˌlāt\ *vt* -**lat·ed**; -**lat·ing** [F *étioler*] (1791) **1** : to bleach and alter the natural development of (a green plant) by excluding sunlight **2 a** : to make pale **b** : to deprive of natural vigor : make feeble — **eti·o·la·tion** \ˌē-tē-ə-ˈlā-shən\ *n*

eti·o·log·ic \ˌē-tē-ə-ˈlä-jik\ *or* **eti·o·log·i·cal** \-ji-kəl\ *adj* (ca. 1753) **1** : assigning or seeking to assign a cause **2** : of or relating to etiology — **eti·o·log·i·cal·ly** \-ji-k(ə-)lē\ *adv*

eti·ol·o·gy \ˌē-tē-ˈä-lə-jē\ *n, pl* -**gies** [ML *aetiologia* statement of causes, fr. Gk *aitiologia*, fr. *aitia* cause] (ca. 1555) **1** : CAUSE, ORIGIN; *specif* : all of the causes of a disease or abnormal condition **2** : a branch of knowledge concerned with causes; *specif* : a branch of medical science concerned with the causes and origins of diseases

et·i·quette \ˈe-ti-kət, -ˌket\ *n* [F *étiquette*, lit., ticket — more at TICKET] (1750) : the conduct or procedure required by good breeding or prescribed by authority to be observed in social or official life

Eton collar \ˌē-tᵊn-\ *n* [*Eton* College, English public school] (1887) : a large stiff turnover collar

Eto·ni·an \e-ˈtō-nē-ən\ *n* (ca. 1770) : a student or former student of Eton College — **Etonian** *adj*

Eton jacket *n* (1881) : a short black jacket with long sleeves, wide lapels, and an open front

étouf·fée *also* **etouf·fee** \ˌā-tü-ˈfā\ *n* [LaF, fr. F *à l'étouffée* braised, fr. fem. of *étouffer*, pp. of *étouffer* to smother, fr. OF *estofer*, alter. of *estoper* to plug up — more at ESTOP] (ca. 1933) : a Cajun stew of shellfish or chicken served over rice

Etru·ri·an \i-ˈtrür-ē-ən\ *n* (1623) : ETRUSCAN — **Etrurian** *adj*

¹Etrus·can \i-ˈtrəs-kən\ *adj* [L *etruscus*; akin to L *Etruria*, ancient country] (1706) : of, relating to, or characteristic of Etruria, the Etruscans, or the Etruscan language

²Etruscan *n* (1773) **1** : the language of the Etruscans which is of unknown affiliation **2** : a native or inhabitant of ancient Etruria

-ette \ˈet, ˌet, ət, it\ *n suffix* [ME, fr. MF, fem. dim. suffix, fr. OF -*ete* — more at -ET] **1** : little one ⟨kitchen*ette*⟩ **2** : female ⟨farmer*ette*⟩

étude \ˈā-ˌtüd, -ˌtyüd\ *n* [F, lit., study, fr. MF *estude*, *estudie*, fr. OF — more at STUDY] (ca. 1837) **1** : a piece of music for the practice of a point of technique **2** : a composition built on a technical motive but played for its artistic value

etui \ā-ˈtwē, ˈā-ˌ\ *n, pl* **etuis** [F *étui*] (1611) : a small ornamental case

et·y·mol·o·gise *Brit var of* ETYMOLOGIZE

et·y·mol·o·gist \ˌe-tə-ˈmä-lə-jist\ *n* (1635) : a specialist in etymology

et·y·mol·o·gize \-ˌjīz\ *vb* -**gized**; -**giz·ing** *vt* (1530) : to discover, formulate, or state an etymology for ~ *vi* : to study or formulate etymologies

et·y·mol·o·gy \-jē\ *n, pl* -**gies** [ME *ethimologie*, fr. L *etymologia*, fr. Gk, fr. *etymon* + -*logia* -logy] (14c) **1** : the history of a linguistic form (as a word) shown by tracing its development since its earliest recorded occurrence in the language in which it is found, by tracing its transmission from one language to another, by analyzing it into its component parts, by identifying its cognates in other languages, or by tracing it and its cognates to a common ancestral form in an ancestral language **2** : a branch of linguistics concerned with etymologies — **et·y·mo·log·i·cal** \-mə-ˈlä-ji-kəl\ *adj* — **et·y·mo·log·i·cal·ly** \-k(ə-)lē\ *adv*

et·y·mon \ˈe-tə-ˌmän\ *n, pl* -**ma** \-mə\ *also* -**mons** [L, fr. Gk, literal meaning of a word according to its origin, fr. *etymos* true; akin to Gk *eteos* true — more at SOOTH] (ca. 1576) **1 a** : an earlier form of a word in the same language or an ancestral language **b** : a word in a foreign language that is the source of a particular loanword **2** : a word or morpheme from which words are formed by composition or derivation

eu- *comb form* [ME, fr. L, fr. Gk, fr. *eu* well, fr. neut. of *eys* good; perh. akin to L *esse* to be] **1 a** : well : easily ⟨*euclase*⟩ — compare DYS- **b** : good ⟨*eudaemonism*⟩ — compare DYS- **2** : true ⟨*euchromatin*⟩

eu·ca·lypt \ˈyü-kə-ˌlipt\ *n* (1885) : EUCALYPTUS

eu·ca·lyp·tol *also* **eu·ca·lyp·tole** \ˌyü-kə-ˈlip-ˌtȯl, -ˌtōl\ *n* (1879) : CINEOLE

eu·ca·lyp·tus \ˌyü-kə-ˈlip-təs\ *n, pl* -**ti** \-ˌtī, -ˌtē\ *or* -**tus·es** [NL, genus name, fr. eu- + Gk *kalyptos* covered, fr. *kalyptein* to conceal; fr. the conical covering of the buds — more at HELL] (1801) : any of a genus (*Eucalyptus*) of mostly Australian evergreen trees or rarely shrubs of the myrtle family that have rigid entire leaves and umbellate flowers and are widely cultivated for their gums, resins, oils, and woods

eu·cary·ote *var of* EUKARYOTE

Eu·cha·rist \ˈyü-k(ə-)rəst\ *n* [ME *eukarist*, fr. MF *eucariste*, fr. LL *eucharistia*, fr. Gk, Eucharist, gratitude, fr. *eucharistos* grateful, fr. eu- + *charizesthai* to show favor, fr. *charis* favor, grace, gratitude; akin to Gk *chairein* to rejoice — more at YEARN] (14c) **1** : COMMUNION 2a **2** *Christian Science* : spiritual communion with God — **eu·cha·ris·tic** \ˌyü-kə-ˈris-tik\ *adj, often cap*

¹euchre \ˈyü-kər\ *n* [origin unknown] (1841) : a card game in which each player is dealt five cards and the player making trump must take three tricks to win a hand

²euchre *vt* **eu·chred; eu·chring** \-k(ə-)riŋ\ (1847) **1** : to prevent from winning three tricks in euchre **2** : CHEAT, TRICK ⟨euchred out of their life savings —Pete Martin⟩

eu·chro·ma·tin \(ˌ)yü-ˈkrō-mə-tən\ *n* [ISV] (1932) : the genetically active portion of chromatin that is largely composed of genes — **eu·chro·mat·ic** \ˌyü-krō-ˈma-tik\ *adj*

eu·clase \ˈyü-ˌklās, -ˌklāz\ *n* [F, fr. eu- (fr. L) + Gk *klasis* breaking, fr. *klan* to break] (1804) : a mineral that consists of a brittle silicate of beryllium and aluminum in pale-yellow, green, or blue prismatic crystals and is used esp. as a gemstone

eu·clid·e·an *also* **eu·clid·i·an** \yù-ˈkli-dē-ən\ *adj, often cap* (1660) : of, relating to, or based on the geometry of Euclid or a geometry with similar axioms

Euclidean algorithm *n* (ca. 1955) : a method of finding the greatest common divisor of two numbers by dividing the larger by the smaller, the smaller by the remainder, the first remainder by the second remainder, and so on until exact division is obtained whence the greatest common divisor is the exact divisor — called also *Euclid's algorithm*

euclidean geometry *n, often cap E* (ca. 1865) **1** : geometry based on Euclid's axioms **2** : the geometry of a euclidean space

euclidean space *n, often cap E* (1883) : a space in which Euclid's axioms and definitions (as of straight and parallel lines and angles of plane triangles) apply

eu·crite \ˈyü-ˌkrīt\ *n* [G *Eukrit*, fr. Gk *eukritos* easily discerned, fr. eu- + *kritos* separated, fr. *krinein* to separate — more at CERTAIN] (ca. 1899) **1** : a stony meteorite composed essentially of plagioclase and pigeonite **2** : a rock consisting of a very basic gabbro — **eu·crit·ic** \yü-ˈkri-tik\ *adj*

eu·dae·mo·nism \yü-ˈdē-mə-ˌni-zəm\ *or* **eu·dai·mo·nism** \-ˈdī-\ *n* [Gk *eudaimonia* happiness, fr. *eudaimōn* having a good attendant spirit, happy, fr. eu- + *daimōn* spirit — more at DEMON] (1827) : a theory that the highest ethical goal is happiness and personal well-being — **eu·dae·mo·nist** \-nist\ *n* — **eu·dae·mo·nis·tic** \-ˌdē-mə-ˈnis-tik\ *adj*

eu·di·om·e·ter \ˌyü-dē-ˈä-mə-tər\ *n* [modif. of It *eudiometro*, fr. Gk *eudia* fair weather (fr. eu- + *-dia* weather—akin to L *dies* day) + It *-metro* -meter, fr. Gk *metron* measure] (1777) : an instrument for the volumetric measurement and analysis of gases — **eu·dio·met·ric** \ˌyü-dē-ə-ˈme-trik\ *adj* — **eu·dio·met·ri·cal·ly** \-tri-k(ə-)lē\ *adv*

eu·gen·ic \yù-ˈje-nik\ *adj* [Gk *eugenēs* wellborn, fr. eu- + *genēs* born — more at -GEN] (1883) **1** : relating to or fitted for the production of good offspring **2** : of or relating to eugenics — **eu·gen·i·cal·ly** \-ni-k(ə-)lē\ *adv*

eu·gen·i·cist \-ˈje-nə-sist\ *n* (ca. 1909) : a student or advocate of eugenics

eu·gen·ics \yù-ˈje-niks\ *n pl but sing or pl in constr* (1883) : a science that deals with the improvement (as by control of human mating) of hereditary qualities of a race or breed

eu·gen·ist \ˈyü-je-nist\ *n* (1908) : EUGENICIST

eu·ge·nol \ˈyü-jə-ˌnȯl, -ˌnōl\ *n* [ISV *eugen*-, fr. NL *Eugenia*, genus of tropical trees] (1886) : a colorless aromatic liquid phenol $C_{10}H_{12}O_2$ found esp. in clove oil and used commercially in flavors and perfumes and in dentistry as an analgesic

eu·geo·syn·cline \(ˌ)yü-ˌjē-ō-ˈsin-ˌklīn\ *n* (1944) : a narrow rapidly subsiding geosyncline usu. with volcanic materials mingled with clastic sediments — **eu·geo·syn·cli·nal** \-(ˌ)sin-ˈklī-nᵊl\ *adj*

eu·gle·na \yü-ˈglē-nə\ *n* [NL, genus name, fr. eu- + Gk *glēnē* eyeball, socket of a joint] (ca. 1889) : any of a genus (*Euglena*) of green freshwater flagellates often classed as algae

eu·gle·noid \-ˌnȯid\ *n* (1885) : any of a taxon (Euglenoidina or Euglenophyta) of varied flagellates (as a euglena) that are typically green or colorless stigma-bearing solitary organisms with one or two flagella emerging from a well-defined gullet — **euglenoid** *adj*

euglenoid movement *n* (1940) : writhing usu. nonprogressive protoplasmic movement of plastic-bodied euglenoid flagellates

eu·glob·u·lin \yü-ˈglä-byə-lən\ *n* [ISV] (1904) : a simple protein that does not dissolve in pure water

eu·he·mer·ism \yü-ˈhē-mə-ˌri-zəm, -ˈhe-mə-\ *n* [*Euhemerus*, 4th cent. B.C. Greek mythographer] (1846) : interpretation of myths as tradi-

---

\ə\ abut \ᵊ\ kitten, F table \ər\ further \a\ ash \ā\ ace \ä\ mop, mar \au̇\ out \ch\ chin \e\ bet \ē\ easy \g\ go \i\ hit \ī\ ice \j\ job \ŋ\ sing \ō\ go \ȯ\ law \ȯi\ boy \th\ thin \t̲h̲\ the \ü\ loot \u̇\ foot \y\ yet \zh\ vision \à, k̲, ⁿ, œ, œ̄, ue, ūe, ᵞ\ *see* Guide to Pronunciation tional accounts of historical persons and events — **eu·he·mer·ist** \-rist\ *n* — **eu·he·mer·is·tic** \-,hē-mə-'ris-tik, -,he-mə-\ *adj*

eu·kary·ote \(,)yü-'kar-ē-,ōt, -ē-ət\ *n* [NL *Eukaryotes*, proposed subdivision of protists, fr. *eu-* + *kary-* + *-otes*, pl. n. suffix, fr. Gk *-ōtos* — more at -OTIC] (1943) : an organism composed of one or more cells containing visibly evident nuclei and organelles — compare PROKARYOTE — **eu·kary·ot·ic** \-,kar-ē-'ä-tik\ *adj*

eu·la·chon \'yü-lə-,kän, -li-kən\ *n, pl* **eulachon** *or* **eulachons** [Chinook Jargon *ulâkân*] (1807) : an anadromous marine food fish (*Thaleichthys pacificus*) of the north Pacific coast related to the smelt — called also *candlefish*

eulogise *Brit var of* EULOGIZE

eu·lo·gist \'yü-lə-jist\ *n* (1808) : one who eulogizes

eu·lo·gi·um \yu-'lō-jē-əm\ *n, pl* **-gia** \-jē-ə\ *or* **-gi·ums** [ML] (1621) : EULOGY

eu·lo·gize \'yü-lə-,jīz\ *vt* **-gized; -giz·ing** (1810) : to speak or write in high praise of : EXTOL — **eu·lo·giz·er** *n*

eu·lo·gy \'yü-lə-jē\ *n, pl* **-gies** [ME *euloge*, fr. ML *eulogium*, fr. Gk *eulogia* praise, fr. *eu-* + *-logia* -logy] (15c) **1** : a commendatory formal statement or set oration **2** : high praise *syn* see ENCOMIUM — **eu·lo·gis·tic** \,yü-lə-'jis-tik\ *adj* — **eu·lo·gis·ti·cal·ly** \-ti-k(ə-)lē\ *adv*

Eu·men·i·des \yu-'me-nə-,dēz\ *n pl* [L, fr. Gk, lit., the gracious ones] : the Furies in Greek mythology

eu·nuch \'yü-nək, -nik\ *n* [ME *eunuk*, fr. L *eunuchus*, fr. Gk *eunouchos*, fr. *eunē* bed + *echein* to have, have charge of — more at SCHEME] (15c) **1** : a castrated man placed in charge of a harem or employed as a chamberlain in a palace **2** : a man or boy deprived of the testes or external genitals **3** : one that lacks virility or power ⟨political ∼*s*⟩ — **eu·nuch·ism** \-nə-,ki-zəm, -ni-\ *n*

eu·nuch·oid \-nə-,k̇ȯid, -ni-\ *n* (1906) : a sexually deficient individual; *esp* : one lacking in sexual differentiation and tending toward the intersex state — **eunuchoid** *adj*

eu·on·y·mus \yü-'ä-nə-məs\ *n* [NL, genus name, fr. L *euonymos* spindle tree, fr. Gk *euōnymos*, fr. *euōnymos* having an auspicious name, fr. *eu-* + *onyma* name — more at NAME] (1767) : SPINDLE TREE

eu·pa·trid \yu-'pa-trəd, 'yü-pə-trəd\ *n, pl* **eu·pat·ri·dae** \yü-'pa-trə-,dē\ *often cap* [Gk *eupatridēs*, fr. *eu-* + *patr-, patēr* father — more at FATHER] (1836) : one of the hereditary aristocrats of ancient Athens

eu·pep·tic \yu-'pep-tik\ *adj* (1831) **1** : of, relating to, or having good digestion **2** : CHEERFUL, OPTIMISTIC

eu·phau·si·id \yu-'fȯ-zē-əd\ *n* [NL *Euphausia*, genus of crustaceans] (ca. 1893) : any of an order (Euphausiacea) of small usu. luminescent malacostracan crustaceans that resemble shrimps and in some areas form an important element in marine plankton — **euphausiid** *adj*

euphemise *Brit var of* EUPHEMIZE

eu·phe·mism \'yü-fə-,mi-zəm\ *n* [Gk *euphēmismos*, fr. *euphēmos* auspicious, sounding good, fr. *eu-* + *phēmē* speech, fr. *phanai* to speak — more at BAN] (ca. 1681) : the substitution of an agreeable or inoffensive expression for one that may offend or suggest something unpleasant; *also* : the expression so substituted — **eu·phe·mist** \-mist\ *n* — **eu·phe·mis·tic** \,yü-fə-'mis-tik\ *adj* — **eu·phe·mis·ti·cal·ly** \-ti-k(ə-)lē\ *adv*

eu·phe·mize \'yü-fə-,mīz\ *vt* **-mized; -miz·ing** (1857) : to express or describe euphemistically ⟨∼ death⟩ — **eu·phe·miz·er** \-,mī-zər\ *n*

eu·phen·ics \yu-'fe-niks\ *n pl but sing in constr* [*eu-* + *phen-* (fr. *phenotype*) + *-ics*; after E *genotype : eugenics*] (1963) : a science that deals with the biological improvement of human beings after birth — **eu·phen·ic** \-nik\ *adj*

eu·pho·ni·ous \yu-'fō-nē-əs\ *adj* (1774) : pleasing to the ear — **eu·pho·ni·ous·ly** *adv* — **eu·pho·ni·ous·ness** *n*

eu·pho·ni·um \yu-'fō-nē-əm\ *n* [Gk *euphōnos* + E *-ium* (as in *harmonium*)] (1865) : a brass instrument smaller than but resembling a tuba and having a range from B flat below the bass staff upward for three octaves

eu·pho·ny \'yü-fə-nē\ *n, pl* **-nies** [F *euphonie*, fr. LL *euphonia*, fr. Gk *euphōnia*, fr. *euphōnos* sweet≈ voiced, musical, fr. *eu-* + *phōnē* voice — more at BAN] (ca. 1616) **1** : pleasing or sweet sound; *esp* : the acoustic effect produced by words so formed or combined as to please the ear **2** : a harmonious succession of words having a pleasing sound — **eu·phon·ic** \yü-'fä-nik\ *adj* — **eu·phon·i·cal·ly** \-ni-k(ə-)lē\ *adv*

eu·phor·bia \yu-'fȯr-bē-ə\ *n* [NL, alter. of L *euphorbea*, fr. *Euphorbus*, 1st cent. A.D. Greek physician] (14c) : any of a large genus (*Euphorbia* of the family Euphorbiaceae) of plants that have a milky juice and flowers lacking a calyx and included in an involucre which surrounds a group of several staminate flowers and a central pistillate flower with 3-lobed pistils; *broadly* : SPURGE

euphonium

eu·pho·ria \yu-'fȯr-ē-ə, -'fȯr-\ *n* [NL, fr. Gk, fr. *euphoros* healthy, fr. *eu-* + *pherein* to bear — more at BEAR] (ca. 1751) : a feeling of well≈ being or elation — **eu·phor·ic** \-'fȯr-ik, -'fär-\ *adj* — **eu·phor·i·cal·ly** \-i-k(ə-)lē\ *adv*

eu·pho·ri·ant \yu-'fȯr-ē-ənt, -'fȯr-\ *n* (1947) : a drug that tends to induce euphoria — **euphoriant** *adj*

eu·pho·tic \yü-'fō-tik\ *adj* [ISV] (1909) : of, relating to, or constituting the upper layers of a body of water into which sufficient light penetrates to permit growth of green plants

Eu·phros·y·ne \yu-'frä-s⁀n-(,)ē, -z⁀n-\ *n* [L, fr. Gk *Euphrosynē*] : one of the three Graces

eu·phu·ism \'yü-fyə-,wi-zəm\ *n* [*Euphues*, character in prose romances by John Lyly] (1592) **1** : an elegant Elizabethan literary style marked by excessive use of balance, antithesis, and alliteration and by frequent use of similes drawn from mythology and nature **2** : artificial elegance of language — **eu·phu·ist** \-ist\ *n* — **eu·phu·is·tic** \,yü-fyə-'wis-tik\ *adj* — **eu·phu·is·ti·cal·ly** \-ti-k(ə-)lē\ *adv*

eu·ploid \'yü-,plȯid\ *adj* [ISV] (1926) : having a chromosome number that is an exact multiple of the monoploid number — compare ANEUPLOID — **euploid** *n* — **eu·ploi·dy** \-,plȯi-dē\ *n*

eup·nea *also* **eup·noea** \yùp-'nē-ə\ *n* [NL, fr. Gk *eupnoia*, fr. *eupnous* breathing freely, fr. *eu-* + *pnein* to breathe — more at SNEEZE] (ca. 1706) : normal respiration — **eup·ne·ic** \-'nē-ik\ *adj*

Eur- *or* **Euro-** *comb form* [*Europe*] : European and ⟨*Eur*american⟩ : European ⟨*Euro*centric⟩ : western European ⟨*Euro*communism⟩ : of the European Communities ⟨*Euro*crat⟩

Eur·amer·i·can \,yùr-ə-'mer-ə-kən\ *or* **Eu·ro-Amer·i·can** \,yùr-ō-ə-'mer-\ *adj* (1941) : common to Europe and America

Eur·asian \yu-'rā-zhən, -shən\ *adj* (1844) **1** : of a mixed European and Asian origin **2** : of or relating to Europe and Asia — **Eurasian** *n*

eu·re·ka \yù-'rē-kə\ *interj* [Gk *heurēka* I have found, fr. *heuriskein* to find; fr. the exclamation attributed to Archimedes on discovering a method for determining the purity of gold — more at HEURISTIC] (1603) — used to express triumph on a discovery

eu·ro \'yùr-(,)ō\ *n, pl* **euros** [Adnyamadhanha (Australian aboriginal language of South Australia) *yuru*] (1855) : WALLAROO

Eu·ro·bond \'yùr-ō-,bänd\ *n* (1966) : a bond of a U.S. corporation that is sold outside the U.S. and that is denominated and paid for in dollars and yields interest in dollars

Eu·ro·cen·tric \,yùr-ə-'sen-trik\ *adj* (1963) : centered on Europe or the Europeans; *esp* : reflecting a tendency to interpret the world in terms of western and esp. European values and experiences — **Eu·ro·cen·trism** \-,tri-zəm\ *n*

Eu·ro·com·mu·nism \,yùr-ō-'käm-yə-,ni-zəm\ *n* (1976) : the communism esp. of western European Communist parties that is marked by a willingness to reach power through coalitions and by independence from Soviet leadership — **Eu·ro·com·mu·nist** *n or adj*

Eu·ro·crat \'yùr-ə-,krat\ *n* (1961) : a staff member of the administrative commission of the European Communities

Eu·ro·cur·ren·cy \,yùr-ō-'kər-ən-sē, -'kə-rən-\ *n* (1963) : moneys (as of the U.S. and Japan) held outside their countries of origin and used in the money markets of Europe

Eu·ro·dol·lar \'yùr-ō-,dä-lər\ *n* (1960) : a U.S. dollar held as Eurocurrency

Eu·ro·pa \yù-'rō-pə\ *n* [L, fr. Gk *Europē*] : a Phoenician princess carried off by Zeus in the form of a white bull and by him mother of Minos, Rhadamanthus, and Sarpedon

¹Eu·ro·pe·an \,yùr-ə-'pē-ən, -'pēn\ *adj* (1603) : of, relating to, or characteristic of the continent of Europe or its people — **Eu·ro·pe·an·iza·tion** \-,pē-ə-nə-'zā-shən\ *n* — **Eu·ro·pe·an·ize** \-'pē-ə-,nīz\ *vt*

²European *n* (1632) **1** : a native or inhabitant of Europe **2** : a person of European descent

European bison *n* (1860) : WISENT

European chafer *n* (1947) : an Old World beetle (*Rhizotragus majalis* syn. *Amphimallon majalis*) established in parts of eastern No. America where its larva is a destructive pest on the roots of turf grasses

European corn borer *n* (1920) : an Old World moth (*Ostrinia nubilalis*) that is widespread in eastern No. America where its larva is a major pest esp. in the stems and crowns of Indian corn, dahlias, and potatoes

European plan *n* (1834) : a hotel plan whereby the daily rates cover only the cost of the room — compare AMERICAN PLAN

European red mite *n* (1940) : a small bright or brownish red oval mite (*Panonychus ulmi*) that is a destructive orchard pest

eu·ro·pi·um \yù-'rō-pē-əm\ *n* [NL, fr. *Europa*] (1901) : a bivalent and trivalent metallic element of the rare-earth group found in monazite sand — see ELEMENT table

Eu·ro·po·cen·tric \,yù-,rō-pə-'sen-trik\ *adj* (1926) : EUROCENTRIC — **Eu·ro·po·cen·trism** \-,tri-zəm\ *n*

eury- *comb form* [NL, fr. Gk, fr. *eurys*; akin to Skt *uru* broad, wide] : broad : wide ⟨*eury*haline⟩

eu·ry·bath·ic \,yùr-i-'ba-thik\ *adj* [*eury-* + Gk *bathos* depth] (1902) : capable of living on the bottom in both deep and shallow water

Eu·ryd·i·ce \yù-'ri-də-(,)sē\ *n* [L, fr. Gk *Eurydikē*] : the wife of Orpheus whom he attempts to bring back from Hades

eu·ry·ha·line \,yùr-i-'hā-,līn, -'ha-\ *adj* [ISV *eury-* + Gk *halinos* of salt, fr. *hals* salt — more at SALT] (1888) : able to live in waters of a wide range of salinity ⟨∼ crabs⟩

eu·ryp·ter·id \yù-'rip-tə-rəd\ *n* [ultim. fr. Gk *eury-* + *pteron* wing — more at FEATHER] (1871) : any of an order (Eurypterida) of usu. large aquatic Paleozoic arthropods related to the horseshoe crabs — **eurypterid** *adj*

eu·ry·ther·mal \,yùr-i-'thər-məl\ *adj* [ISV] (1881) : tolerating a wide range of temperature ⟨∼ animals⟩

eu·ry·ther·mic \-mik\ *adj* [ISV] (1903) : EURYTHERMAL

eu·ry·ther·mous \-məs\ *adj* [ISV] (1940) : EURYTHERMAL

eu·ryth·mic *or* **eu·rhyth·mic** \yü-'rith-mik\ *adj* (1921) **1** : HARMONIOUS **2** : of or relating to eurythmy or eurythmics

eu·ryth·mics *or* **eu·rhyth·mics** \-miks\ *n pl but sing or pl in constr* (1912) : the art of harmonious bodily movement esp. through expressive timed movements in response to improvised music

eu·ryth·my *or* **eu·rhyth·my** \-mē\ *n* [G *Eurhythmie*, fr. L *eurythmia* rhythmical movement, fr. Gk, fr. *eurythmos* rhythmical, fr. *eu-* + *rhythmos* rhythm] (1949) : a system of harmonious body movement to the rhythm of spoken words

eu·ry·top·ic \,yùr-i-'tä-pik\ *adj* [ISV *eury-* + Gk *topos* place] (ca. 1945) : tolerant of wide variation in one or more physical factors of the environment

eu·sta·chian tube \yù-'stā-sh(ē-)ən- *also* -'stā-kē-ən-\ *n, often cap E* [Bartolommeo *Eustachio*] (1741) : a bony and cartilaginous tube connecting the middle ear with the nasopharynx and equalizing air pressure on both sides of the tympanic membrane — called also *auditory tube;* see EAR illustration

eu·stat·ic \yù-'sta-tik\ *adj* [ISV] (1906) : relating to or characterized by worldwide change of sea level

eu·stele \'yü-,stēl, yù-'stē-lē\ *n* (ca. 1920) : a stele typical of dicotyledonous plants that consists of vascular bundles of xylem and phloem strands with parenchymal cells between the bundles

eu·tec·tic \yù-'tek-tik\ *adj* [Gk *eutēktos* easily melted, fr. *eu-* + *tēktos* melted, fr. *tēkein* to melt — more at THAW] (1884) **1** *of an alloy or solution* : having the lowest melting point possible **2** : of or relating to a eutectic alloy or solution or its melting or freezing point — **eutectic** *n* — **eu·tec·toid** \-,tȯid\ *adj or n*

Eu·ter·pe \yù-'tər-pē\ *n* [L, fr. Gk *Euterpē*] : the Greek Muse of music eu·tha·na·sia \,yü-thə-'nā-zh(ē-)ə\ n [Gk, easy death, fr. euthanatos, fr. eu- + thanatos death — more at THANATOS] (1869) : the act or practice of killing or permitting the death of hopelessly sick or injured individuals (as persons or domestic animals) in a relatively painless way for reasons of mercy — eu·tha·na·sic \-zik, -sik\ adj

eu·than·a·tize \yü-'than-ə-,tīz\ also eu·tha·nize \'yü-thə-,nīz\ vt -tized also -nized; -tiz·ing also -niz·ing [Gk euthanatos] (1873) : to subject to euthanasia

eu·then·ics \yü-'the-niks\ n pl but sing or pl in constr [Gk euthenein to thrive, fr. eu- + -thenein] (1905) : a science that deals with development of human well-being by improvement of living conditions — eu·the·nist \yü-'the-nist, 'yü-thə-\ n

eu·the·ri·an \yü-'thir-ē-ən\ adj [ultim. fr. NL eu- + Gk thērion beast — more at TREACLE] (1880) : of or relating to a major division (Eutheria) of mammals comprising the placental mammals — eutherian n

eu·thy·roid \(,)yü-'thī-,ròid\ adj (1924) : characterized by normal thyroid function

eu·tro·phic \yü-'trō-fik\ adj [prob. fr. G Eutroph eutrophic, fr. Gk eutrophos well-nourished, nourishing, fr. eu- + trephein to nourish] (1928) of a body of water : characterized by the state resulting from eutrophication — compare MESOTROPHIC, OLIGOTROPHIC — eu·tro·phy \'yü-trə-fē\ n

eu·tro·phi·ca·tion \yü-,trō-fə-'kā-shən, ,yü-trə-fə-\ n (1946) : the process by which a body of water becomes enriched in dissolved nutrients (as phosphates) that stimulate the growth of aquatic plant life usu. resulting in the depletion of dissolved oxygen

evac·u·ate \i-'va-kyə-,wāt\ vb -at·ed; -at·ing [ME, to draw off morbid humors, fr. L evacuatus, pp. of evacuare to empty, fr. e- + vacuus empty] vt (15c) 1 : to remove the contents of : EMPTY 2 : to discharge from the body as waste : VOID 3 : to remove something (as gas or water) from esp. by pumping 4 a : to remove esp. from a military zone or dangerous area b : to withdraw from military occupation of c : VACATE (were ordered to ~ the building) ~ vi 1 : to withdraw from a place in an organized way esp. for protection 2 : to pass urine or feces from the body — evac·u·a·tive \-,wā-tiv\ adj

evac·u·a·tion \i-,va-kyə-'wā-shən\ n (14c) 1 : the act or process of evacuating 2 : something evacuated or discharged

evac·u·ee \i-,va-kyə-'wē\ n (1918) : an evacuated person

evade \i-'vād\ vb evad·ed; evad·ing [MF & L; MF evader, fr. L evadere, fr. e- + vadere to go, walk — more at WADE] vi (1513) 1 : to slip away 2 : to take refuge in evasion ~ vt 1 : to elude by dexterity or stratagem 2 a : to avoid facing up to (evaded the real issues) b : to avoid the performance of : DODGE, CIRCUMVENT; esp : to fail to pay (taxes) c : to avoid answering directly : turn aside 3 : to be elusive to : BAFFLE (the simple, personal meaning evaded them —C. D. Lewis) syn see ESCAPE — evad·able \-'vā-də-bəl\ adj — evad·er n

evag·i·na·tion \i-,va-jə-'nā-shən\ n [LL evagination-, evaginatio, act of unsheathing, fr. L evaginatus, pp. of evaginare to unsheathe, fr. e- + vagina sheath] (ca. 1676) 1 : an act or instance of everting 2 : a product of eversion : OUTGROWTH

eval·u·ate \i-'val-yə-,wāt\ vt -at·ed; -at·ing [back-formation fr. evaluation] (1842) 1 : to determine or fix the value of 2 : to determine the significance, worth, or condition of usu. by careful appraisal and study syn see ESTIMATE — eval·u·a·tion \-,val-yə-'wā-shən\ n — eval·u·a·tive \-'val-yə-,wā-tiv\ adj — eval·u·a·tor \-,wā-tər\ n

ev·a·nesce \,e-və-'nes\ vi -nesced; -nesc·ing [L evanescere — more at VANISH] (1822) : to dissipate like vapor

ev·a·nes·cence \,e-və-'ne-s²n(t)s\ n (1751) : the process or fact of evanescing 2 : evanescent quality

ev·a·nes·cent \-s²nt\ adj [L evanescent-, evanescens, prp. of evanescere] (1717) : tending to vanish like vapor syn see TRANSIENT

¹evan·gel \i-'van-jəl\ n [ME evangile, fr. MF, fr. LL evangelium, fr. Gk euangelion good news, gospel, fr. euangelos bringing good news, fr. eu- + angelos messenger] (14c) : GOSPEL

²evangel n (1614) : EVANGELIST

evan·gel·i·cal \,ē-,van-'je-li-kəl, ,e-vən-\ also evan·gel·ic \-ik\ adj (1531) 1 : of, relating to, or being in agreement with the Christian gospel esp. as it is presented in the four Gospels 2 : PROTESTANT 3 : emphasizing salvation by faith in the atoning death of Jesus Christ through personal conversion, the authority of Scripture, and the importance of preaching as contrasted with ritual 4 a cap : of or relating to the Evangelical Church in Germany b often cap : of, adhering to, or marked by fundamentalism : FUNDAMENTALIST c often cap : LOW CHURCH 5 : marked by militant or crusading zeal : EVANGELISTIC (the ~ ardor of the movement's leaders —Amos Vogel) — Evan·gel·i·cal·ism \-li-kə-,li-zəm\ n — evan·gel·i·cal·ly \-li-k(ə-)lē\ adv

Evangelical n (1532) : one holding evangelical principles or belonging to an evangelical party or church

evan·ge·lism \i-'van-jə-,li-zəm\ n (ca. 1626) 1 : the winning or revival of personal commitments to Christ 2 : militant or crusading zeal — evan·ge·lis·tic \-,van-jə-'lis-tik\ adj — evan·ge·lis·ti·cal·ly \-ti-k(ə-)lē\ adv

evan·ge·list \i-'van-jə-list\ n (13c) 1 often cap : a writer of any of the four Gospels 2 : a person who evangelizes; specif : a Protestant minister or layman who preaches at special services

evan·ge·lize \i-'van-jə-,līz\ vb -lized; -liz·ing vt (14c) 1 : to preach the gospel to 2 : to convert to Christianity ~ vi : to preach the gospel — evan·ge·li·za·tion \-,van-jə-lə-'zā-shən\ n

evap·o·rate \i-'va-p(ə-),rāt\ vb -rat·ed; -rat·ing [ME, fr. L evaporatus, pp. of evaporare, fr. e- + vapor steam, vapor] vt (15c) 1 a : to convert into vapor; also : to dissipate or draw off in vapor or fumes b : to deposit (as a metal) in the form of a film by sublimation 2 a : to expel moisture from b : EXPEL (~ electrons from a hot wire) ~ vi 1 a : to pass off in vapor or in invisible minute particles b (1) : to pass off or away : DISAPPEAR (my despair evaporated —J. F. Wharton) (2) : to diminish quickly 2 : to give forth vapor — evap·o·ra·tion \-,va-pə-'rā-shən\ n — evap·o·ra·tive \-'va-pə-,rā-tiv\ adj — evap·o·ra·tor \-'va-pə-,rā-tər\ n

evaporated milk n (1870) : unsweetened milk concentrated by partial evaporation

evap·o·rite \i-'va-pə-,rīt\ n [evaporation + ¹-ite] (1924) : a sedimentary rock (as gypsum) that originates by evaporation of seawater in an enclosed basin — evap·o·rit·ic \-,va-pə-'ri-tik\ adj

evapo·trans·pi·ra·tion \i-'va-pō-,tran(t)-spə-'rā-shən\ n [evaporation + transpiration] (1938) : loss of water from the soil both by evaporation and by transpiration from the plants growing thereon

eva·sion \i-'vā-zhən\ n [ME, fr. MF or LL; MF, fr. LL evasion-, evasio, fr. L evadere to evade] (15c) 1 : a means of evading : DODGE 2 : the act or an instance of evading : ESCAPE (suspected of tax ~)

eva·sive \i-'vā-siv, -ziv\ adj (1725) : tending or intended to evade : EQUIVOCAL (~ answers) — eva·sive·ly adv — eva·sive·ness n

eve \'ēv\ n [ME eve, even] (13c) 1 : EVENING 2 : the evening or the day before a special day 3 : the period immediately preceding

Eve \'ēv\ n [OE Ēfe, fr. LL Eva, fr. Heb Ḥawwāh] : the first woman and wife of Adam

¹even \'ē-vən\ n [ME even, eve, fr. OE ǣfen] (bef. 12c) archaic : EVENING

²even \'ē-vən, -b²m\ adj [ME, fr. OE efen; akin to OHG eban even] (bef. 12c) 1 a : having a horizontal surface : FLAT (~ ground) b : being without break, indentation, or irregularity : SMOOTH c : being in the same plane or line 2 a : free from variation : UNIFORM (his disposition was ~) b : LEVEL 4 3 a : EQUAL, FAIR (an ~ exchange) b (1) : leaving nothing due on either side : SQUARE (we will not be ~ until you repay my visit) (2) : fully revenged c : being in equilibrium : BALANCED; specif : showing neither profit nor loss 4 a : being any of the integers (as −2, 0, and +2) that are exactly divisible by two b : marked by an even number c : being a mathematical function such that f(x) = f(−x) where the value remains unchanged if the sign of the independent variable is reversed 5 : EXACT, PRECISE (an ~ dollar) 6 : as likely as not : FIFTY-FIFTY (an ~ chance of winning) — syn see LEVEL, STEADY — even·ly adv — even·ness \-vən-nəs\ n — on an even keel also on even keel : in a sound or stable condition

³even adv [ME, fr. OE efne, fr. efen, adj.] (bef. 12c) 1 a : EXACTLY, PRECISELY b : to a degree that extends : FULLY, QUITE (faithful ~ unto death) c : at the very time 2 a — used as an intensive to emphasize the identity or character of something (he looked content, ~ happy) b — used as an intensive to stress an extreme or highly unlikely condition or instance (so simple ~ a child can do it) c — used as an intensive to stress the comparative degree (he did ~ better) d — used as an intensive to indicate a small or minimum amount (didn't ~ try)

⁴even vb evened; even·ing \'ēv-niŋ, 'ē-və-\ vt (13c) : to make even ~ vi : to become even — even·er \-nər\ n

even·fall \'ē-vən-,fòl\ n (1814) : the beginning of evening : DUSK

even·hand·ed \,ē-vən-'han-dəd\ adj (1605) : FAIR, IMPARTIAL — even·hand·ed·ly adv — even·hand·ed·ness n

¹eve·ning \'ēv-niŋ\ n, often attrib [ME, fr. OE ǣfnung, fr. ǣfnian to grow toward evening, fr. ǣfen evening; akin to OHG āband evening and perh. to Gk epi on] (bef. 12c) 1 a : the latter part and close of the day and early part of the night b chiefly Southern & Midland : AFTERNOON c : the period from sunset or the evening meal to bedtime 2 : the latter portion 3 : the period of an evening's entertainment

²evening adj (1797) : suitable for formal or semiformal evening social occasions (~ dress) (~ clothes)

evening prayer n, often cap E&P (1598) : the daily evening office of the Anglican liturgy

evening primrose n (1806) : any of several dicotyledonous plants of a family (Onagraceae, the evening-primrose family) and esp. of the type genus (Oenothera); esp : a coarse biennial herb (O. biennis) with yellow flowers that open in the evening

eve·nings \'ēv-niŋz\ adv (1652) : in the evening repeatedly : on any evening (goes bowling ~)

evening star n (1535) 1 : a bright planet (as Venus) seen esp. in the western sky at or after sunset 2 : a planet that rises before midnight

even money n (1891) : a situation in wagering in which the odds are even

even permutation n (ca. 1932) : a permutation that is produced by the successive application of an even number of interchanges of pairs of elements

even so adv (1948) : in spite of that : NEVERTHELESS

even·song \'ē-vən-,sòŋ\ n, often cap [ME, fr. OE ǣfensang, fr. ǣfen evening + sang song] (bef. 12c) 1 : VESPERS 1 2 : EVENING PRAYER

event \i-'vent\ n [MF or L; MF, fr. L eventus, fr. evenire to happen, fr. e- + venire to come — more at COME] (1573) 1 a archaic : OUTCOME b : the final outcome or determination of a legal action c : a postulated outcome, condition, or eventuality (in the ~ that I am not there, call the house) 2 a : something that happens : OCCURRENCE b : a noteworthy happening c : a social occasion or activity 3 : any of the contests in a program of sports 4 : the fundamental entity of observed physical reality represented by a point designated by three coordinates of place and one of time in the space-time continuum postulated by the theory of relativity 5 : a subset of the possible outcomes of an experiment syn see OCCURRENCE — event·less \-ləs\ adj — at all events : in any case — in any event : in any case — in the event Brit : as it turns out

event·ful \i-'vent-fəl\ adj (1600) 1 : full of or rich in events 2 : MOMENTOUS — event·ful·ly \-fə-lē\ adv — event·ful·ness n

event horizon n (1969) : the surface of a black hole : the boundary of a black hole at which the escape velocity equals the speed of light and beyond which nothing can escape from within it

even·tide \'ē-vən-,tīd\ n (bef. 12c) : the time of evening : EVENING

even·tu·al \i-'ven(t)-sh(ə-)wəl, -vən-chəl\ adj (1683) 1 archaic : CONTINGENT, CONDITIONAL 2 : taking place at an unspecified later time : ultimately resulting (they counted on our ~ success) syn see LAST

even·tu·al·i·ty \i-,ven-chə-'wa-lə-tē\ n, pl -ties (1759) : a possible event or outcome : POSSIBILITY

even·tu·al·ly \-ē\ adv (1680) : at an unspecified later time : in the end

even·tu·ate \i-'ven-chə-,wāt\ vi -at·ed; -at·ing (1789) : to come out finally : RESULT, COME ABOUT

ev·er \'e-vər\ adv [ME, fr. OE ǣfre] (bef. 12c) 1 : ALWAYS (~ striving

\ə\ abut \²\ kitten, F table \ər\ further \a\ ash \ā\ ace \ä\ mop, mar \aü\ out \ch\ chin \e\ bet \ē\ easy \g\ go \i\ hit \ī\ ice \j\ job \ŋ\ sing \ō\ go \ò\ law \òi\ boy \th\ thin \th̲\ the \ü\ loot \ù\ foot \y\ yet \zh\ vision \à, k̲, ⁿ, œ, œ̄, œ, ūe, ⁾\ see Guide to Pronunciation to improve) ⟨the *ever*-increasing population⟩ 2 a : at any time ⟨more than ~ before⟩ b : in any way ⟨how can I ~ thank you⟩ 3 — used as an intensive ⟨looks ~ so angry⟩ ⟨am I ~ happy to see you⟩

ev·er·bloom·ing \,e-vər-'blü-miŋ\ *adj* (ca. 1891) : blooming more or less continuously throughout the growing season

ev·er·dur·ing \,e-vər-'dür-iŋ, -'dyur-\ *adj* (15c) *archaic* : EVERLASTING

ev·er·glade \'e-vər-glād\ *n* [the *Everglades*, Fla.] (1823) : a swampy grassland esp. in southern Florida usu. containing saw grass and at least seasonally covered by slowly moving water — usu. used in pl.

¹ev·er·green \'e-vər-grēn\ *n* (1644) 1 : an evergreen plant; *also* : CO-NIFER 2 *pl* : twigs and branches of evergreen plants used for decoration 3 : something that retains its freshness, interest, or popularity

²evergreen *adj* (1671) 1 : having foliage that remains green and functional through more than one growing season — compare DECIDUOUS 1 2 : retaining freshness or interest : PERENNIAL

evergreen oak *n* (ca. 1682) : any of various oaks (as a live oak, a holm oak, or a tan oak) with foliage that persists for two years so that the plant is more or less continuously green

¹ev·er·last·ing \,e-vər-'las-tiŋ\ *adj* 1 : lasting or enduring through all time : ETERNAL 2 a (1) : continuing long or indefinitely (2) : having or being flowers or foliage that retain form or color for a long time when dried b : tediously persistent ⟨the ~ sympathy-seeker who demands attention —H. A. Overstreet⟩ 3 : wearing indefinitely — **ev·er·last·ing·ly** \-tiŋ-lē\ *adv* — **ev·er·last·ing·ness** *n*

²everlasting *n* (14c) 1 : ETERNITY ⟨from ~⟩ 2 *cap* : GOD 1 — used with *the* 3 a : any of several chiefly composite plants (as cudweed) with flowers that can be dried without loss of form or color — compare PEARLY EVERLASTING b : the flower of an everlasting

ev·er·more \,e-vər-'mōr, -'mòr\ *adv* (13c) 1 : FOREVER, ALWAYS 2 : in the future

ever·sion \i-'vər-zhən, -shən\ *n* (1751) 1 : the act of turning inside out : the state of being turned inside out ⟨~ of the bladder⟩ 2 : the condition (as of the foot) of being turned or rotated outward — **ever·si·ble** \-'vər-sə-bəl\ *adj*

evert \i-'vərt\ *vt* [L *evertere*, fr. *e-* + *vertere* to turn — more at WORTH] (1538) 1 : OVERTHROW, UPSET 2 : to subject to eversion

ev·ery \'ev-rē\ *adj* [ME *everich, every*, fr. OE *ǣfre ǣlc*, fr. *ǣfre* ever + *ǣlc* each] (bef. 12c) 1 a : being each individual or part of a group without exception b : being each in a series or succession ⟨~ few days⟩ 2 *obs* : being all taken severally 3 : being each within a range of possibilities ⟨was given ~ chance⟩ 4 : COMPLETE, ENTIRE ⟨we have ~ confidence in her⟩ — **every now and then** *or* **every now and again** *or* **every so often** : at intervals : OCCASIONALLY

ev·ery·body \'ev-ri-,bä-dē, -,bä-\ *pron* (1530) : every person : EVERY-ONE

ev·ery·day \,ev-rē-,dā\ *adj* (ca. 1623) : encountered or used routinely or typically ⟨~ clothes⟩ — **ev·ery·day·ness** \-'dā-nəs\ *n*

ev·ery·man \,ev-rē-,man\ *n, often cap* [*Everyman*, allegorical character in *The Summoning of Everyman*, 15th cent. Eng. morality play] (1906) : the typical or ordinary person

ev·ery·one \-(,) wən\ *pron* (14c) : EVERYBODY

ev·ery·place \-,plās\ *adv* (ca. 1917) : EVERYWHERE

ev·ery·thing \'ev-rē-,thiŋ\ *pron* (14c) 1 a : all that exists b : all that relates to the subject 2 : all that is important ⟨you mean ~ to me⟩ 3 : all sorts of other things — used to indicate related but unspecified events, facts, or conditions ⟨all the pains and colds and ~ —E. B. White⟩

ev·ery·where \'ev-rē-,(h)wer, -,(h)war\ *adv* (13c) : in every place or part

every which way *adv* [prob. by folk etymology fr. ME *everich way* every way] (1824) 1 : in every direction 2 : in a disorderly manner : IRREGULARLY ⟨toys scattered about *every which way*⟩

ev·ery·wom·an \'ev-rē-,wu-mən\ *n, often cap* [after *everyman*] (1945) : the typical or ordinary woman

evict \i-'vikt\ *vt* [ME, fr. LL *evictus*, pp. of *evincere*, fr. L to vanquish, win a point — more at EVINCE] (15c) 1 : to recover (property) from a person by legal process b : to put (a tenant) out by legal process 2 : to force out : EXPEL *syn* see EJECT — **evic·tion** \-'vik-shən\ *n* — **evic·tor** \-'vik-tər\ *n*

evict·ee \i-,vik-'tē\ *n* (1879) : an evicted person

¹ev·i·dence \'e-və-dən(t)s, -və-,den(t)s\ *n* (14c) 1 a : an outward sign : INDICATION b : something that furnishes proof : TESTIMONY; *specif* : something legally submitted to a tribunal to ascertain the truth of a matter 2 : one who bears witness; *esp* : one who voluntarily confesses a crime and testifies for the prosecution against his accomplices — **in evidence** 1 : to be seen : CONSPICUOUS ⟨trim lawns . . . are everywhere *in evidence* —Amer. Guide Series: N.C.⟩ 2 : as evidence

²evidence *vt* **-denced; -denc·ing** (ca. 1610) 1 : to offer evidence of : PROVE, EVINCE *syn* see SHOW

ev·i·dent \'e-və-dənt, -və-,dent\ *adj* [ME, fr. MF, fr. L *evident-, evidens*, fr. *e-* + *vident-, videns*, prp. of *vidēre* to see — more at WIT] (14c) : clear to the vision or understanding

syn EVIDENT, MANIFEST, PATENT, DISTINCT, OBVIOUS, APPARENT, PLAIN, CLEAR mean readily perceived or apprehended. EVIDENT implies presence of visible signs that lead one to a definite conclusion ⟨an *evident* fondness for sweets⟩. MANIFEST implies an external display so evident that little or no inference is required ⟨*manifest* hostility⟩. PATENT applies to a cause, effect, or significant feature that is clear and unmistakable once attention has been directed to it ⟨*patent* defects⟩. DISTINCT implies such sharpness of outline or definition that no unusual effort to see or hear or comprehend is required ⟨a *distinct* refusal⟩. OBVIOUS implies such ease in discovering that it often suggests conspicuousness or little need for perspicacity in the observer ⟨the *obvious* solution⟩. APPARENT is very close to EVIDENT except that it may imply more conscious exercise of inference ⟨for no *apparent* reason⟩. PLAIN suggests lack of intricacy, complexity, or elaboration ⟨her feelings about him are *plain*⟩. CLEAR implies an absence of anything that confuses the mind or obscures the pattern ⟨a *clear* explanation⟩.

ev·i·den·tial \,e-və-'den(t)-shəl\ *adj* (1641) : EVIDENTIARY 1 — **ev·i·den·tial·ly** *adv*

ev·i·den·tia·ry \,e-və-'den-chə-rē, -chē-,er-ē\ *adj* (1810) 1 : being, relating to, or affording evidence ⟨photographs of ~ value⟩ 2 : conducted so that evidence may be presented ⟨an ~ hearing⟩

ev·i·dent·ly \'e-və-dənt-lē, -ə-,dent-, *esp for 2 often* ,ev-ə-'dent-\ *adv*

(1690) 1 : in an evident manner : CLEARLY, OBVIOUSLY ⟨any style . . . so ~ bad or second-rate —T. S. Eliot⟩ 2 : on the basis of available evidence ⟨he was born . . . ~ in Texas —Robert Coughlan⟩

¹evil \'ē-vəl, Brit often & US also 'ē-(,)vil\ *adj* **evil·er** *or* **evil·ler; evil·est** *or* **evil·lest** [ME, fr. OE *yfel;* akin to OHG *ubil* evil] (bef. 12c) 1 a : morally reprehensible : SINFUL, WICKED ⟨an ~ impulse⟩ b : arising from actual or imputed bad character or conduct ⟨a man of ~ reputation⟩ 2 a *archaic* : INFERIOR b : causing discomfort or repulsion : OFFENSIVE ⟨an ~ odor⟩ c : DISAGREEABLE ⟨woke late and in an ~ temper⟩ 3 a : causing harm : PERNICIOUS ⟨the ~ institution of slavery⟩ b : marked by misfortune : UNLUCKY — **evil** *adv, archaic* — **evil·ly** \-(l)ē\ *adv* — **evil·ness** \-nəs\ *n*

²evil *n* (bef. 12c) 1 a : the fact of suffering, misfortune, and wrongdoing b : a cosmic evil force 2 : something that brings sorrow, distress, or calamity

evil·do·er \,ē-vəl-'dü-ər\ *n* (14c) : one who does evil

evil·do·ing \-'dü-iŋ\ *n* (14c) : the act or action of doing evil

evil eye *n* (bef. 12c) : an eye or glance held capable of inflicting harm; *also* : a person believed to have such an eye or glance

evil–mind·ed \,ē-vəl-'mīn-dəd, -vil-\ *adj* (1531) : having an evil disposition or evil thoughts — **evil–mind·ed·ly** *adv* — **evil–mind·ed·ness** *n*

evince \i-'vin(t)s\ *vt* **evinced; evinc·ing** [L *evincere* to vanquish, win a point, fr. *e-* + *vincere* to conquer — more at VICTOR] (1621) 1 : to constitute outward evidence of 2 : to display clearly : REVEAL *syn* see SHOW — **evinc·i·ble** \-'vin(t)-sə-bəl\ *adj*

evis·cer·ate \i-'vi-sə-,rāt\ *vb* **-at·ed; -at·ing** [L *evisceratus*, pp. of *eviscerare*, fr. *e-* + *viscera* viscera] *vt* (1621) 1 a : to take out the entrails of : DISEMBOWEL b : to deprive of vital content or force 2 : to remove an organ from (a patient) or the contents of (an organ) ~ *vi* : to protrude through a surgical incision or suffer protrusion of a part through an incision — **evis·cer·a·tion** \-,vi-sə-'rā-shən\ *n*

ev·i·ta·ble \'e-və-tə-bəl\ *adj* [L *evitabilis*, fr. *evitare* to avoid, fr. *e-* + *vitare* to shun] (1502) : capable of being avoided

evo·ca·ble \'e-və-kə-bəl, i-'vō-kə-\ *adj* (1886) : capable of being evoked

evo·ca·tion \,ē-vō-'kā-shən, ,e-və-\ *n* [L *evocation-, evocatio,* fr. *evocare*] (1633) 1 : the act or fact of evoking : SUMMONING; as a : the summoning of a spirit b : imaginative recreation ⟨an ~ of the past⟩ 2 : INDUCTION 4e — **evo·ca·tor** \'ē-vō-,kā-tər, 'e-və-\ *n*

evoc·a·tive \i-'vä-kə-tiv\ *adj* (1657) : evoking or tending to evoke an esp. emotional response ⟨settings . . . so ~ that they bring tears to the eyes —Eric Malpass⟩ — **evoc·a·tive·ly** *adv* — **evoc·a·tive·ness** *n*

evoke \i-'vōk\ *vt* **evoked; evok·ing** [F *évoquer*, fr. L *evocare*, fr. *e-* + *vocare* to call — more at VOCATION] (ca. 1626) 1 : to call forth or up: as a : CONJURE 2a ⟨~ evil spirits⟩ b : to cite esp. with approval or for support : INVOKE c : to bring to mind or recollection ⟨this place ~s memories⟩ 2 : to recreate imaginatively *syn* see EDUCE

evo·lute \'e-və-,lüt *also* 'ē-və-\ *n* (ca. 1736) : the locus of the center of curvature or the envelope of the normals of a curve

evo·lu·tion \,e-və-'lü-shən, ,ē-və-\ *n* [L *evolution-, evolutio* unrolling, fr. *evolvere*] (1622) 1 : one of a set of prescribed movements 2 a : a process of change in a certain direction : UNFOLDING b : the action or an instance of forming and giving something off : EMISSION c (1) : a process of continuous change from a lower, simpler, or worse to a higher, more complex, or better state : GROWTH (2) : a process of gradual and relatively peaceful social, political, and economic advance d : something evolved 3 : the process of working out or developing 4 a : the historical development of a biological group (as a race or species) : PHYLOGENY b : a theory that the various types of animals and plants have their origin in other preexisting types and that the distinguishable differences are due to modifications in successive generations 5 : the extraction of a mathematical root 6 : a process in which the whole universe is a progression of interrelated phenomena — **evo·lu·tion·ari·ly** \-shə-,ner-ə-lē\ *adv* — **evo·lu·tion·ary** \-shə-,ner-ē\ *adj* — **evo·lu·tion·ism** \-shə-,ni-zəm\ *n or adj* — **evo·lu·tion·ist** \-sh(ə-)nist\ *n or adj*

evolve \i-'välv, -'vòlv, ē- *also* -'väv *or* -'vòv\ *vb* **evolved; evolv·ing** [L *evolvere* to unroll, fr. *e-* + *volvere* to roll — more at VOLUBLE] *vt* (1641) 1 : EMIT 2 a : DERIVE, EDUCE b : to produce by natural evolutionary processes c : DEVELOP, WORK OUT ⟨~ social, political, and literary philosophies —L. W. Doob⟩ ~ *vi* : to undergo evolutionary change — **evolv·able** \-'väl-və-bəl, -'vòl- *also* -'väv-ə *or* -'vò-və-\ *adj* — **evolve·ment** \-'välv-mənt, -'vòlv- *also* -'väv- *or* -'vòv-\ *n*

evul·sion \i-'vəl-shən\ *n* [L *evulsion-, evulsio,* fr. *evellere* to pluck out, fr. *e-* + *vellere* to pluck — more at VULNERABLE] (ca. 1611) : EXTRACTION

ev·zone \'ev-,zōn\ *n* [NGk *euzōnos*, fr. Gk, active, lit., well girt, fr. *eu-* + *zōnē* girdle — more at ZONE] (1897) : a member of a select Greek infantry unit often serving as a palace guard

ewe \'yü, *in rural dials also* 'yō\ *n* [ME, fr. OE *ēowu;* akin to OHG *ouwi* ewe, L *ovis* sheep, Gk *ois*] (bef. 12c) : the female of the sheep esp. when mature; *also* : the female of various related animals

Ewe \'ā-,wā, 'ā-,vā\ *n, pl* **Ewe** *also* **Ewes** (1861) : a people of Ghana and Togo speaking a Kwa language; *also* : the language itself

ewe–neck \-'nek\ *n* (1820) : a thin neck with a concave arch occurring as a defect in dogs and horses — **ewe–necked** \-'nekt\ *adj*

ew·er \'yü-ər, 'yu(-ə)r\ *n* [ME, fr. AF, fr. OF *evier*, fr. L *aquarium* water source, neut. of *aquarius* of water, fr. *aqua* water — more at ISLAND] (14c) : a vase-shaped pitcher or jug

Ew·ing's sarcoma \'yü-iŋz-\ *n* [James *Ewing* †1943 Am. pathologist] (1951) : a tumor that invades the shaft of a long bone and that tends to recur but rarely metastasizes

¹ex \(')eks\ *prep* [L] (ca. 1755) 1 : out of : FROM: as a : from a specified place or source b : from a specified dam ⟨a promising calf by Eric XVI ~ Heatherbell⟩ 2 : free from : WITHOUT: as a : without an indicated value or right — used esp. of securities b : free of charges precedent to removal from the specified place with purchaser to

ewer

provide means of subsequent transportation ⟨∼ dock⟩
²**ex** n [¹ex-] (1827) : one that formerly held a specified position or place; esp : a former spouse
³**ex** n (ca. 1889) : the letter x
¹**ex-** \e also occurs in this prefix where only i is shown below (as in "express") and ks sometimes occurs where only gz is shown (as in "exact")\ prefix [ME, fr. OF & L; OF, fr. L (also, prefix with perfective and causative value), fr. ex out of, from; akin to Gk ex, ex- out of, from OCS iz] **1** : out of : outside ⟨exclave⟩ **2** : not ⟨exstipulate⟩ **3** \(,)eks, 'eks\ [ME, fr. LL, fr. L]: former ⟨ex-president⟩
²**ex-** — see EXO-
exa- comb form [ISV, modif. of Gk hexa- hexa-] : quintillion ⟨exajoules⟩
ex·ac·er·bate \ig-'za-sər-,bāt\ vt **-bat·ed; -bat·ing** [L exacerbatus, pp. of exacerbare, fr. ex- + acerbus harsh, bitter, fr. acer sharp — more at EDGE] (1660) : to make more violent, bitter, or severe ⟨the proposed shutdown . . . would ∼ unemployment problems —Science⟩ — **ex·ac·er·ba·tion** \-,za-sər-'bā-shən\ n
¹**ex·act** \ig-'zakt\ vt [ME, to require as payment, fr. L exactus, pp. of exigere to drive out, demand, measure, fr. ex- + agere to drive — more at AGENT] (1564) **1** : to call for forcibly or urgently and obtain ⟨from them has been ∼ed the ultimate sacrifice —D. D. Eisenhower⟩ **2** : to call for as necessary or desirable syn see DEMAND — **ex·act·able** \-'zak-tə-bəl\ adj — **ex·ac·tor** also **ex·act·er** \-'zak-tər\ n
²**exact** adj [L exactus] (1533) **1** : exhibiting or marked by strict, particular, and complete accordance with fact or a standard **2** : marked by thorough consideration or minute measurement of small factual details syn see CORRECT — **ex·act·ness** \-'zak(t)-nəs\ n
ex·ac·ta \ig-'zak-tə\ n [AmerSp (quiniela) exacta exact quiniela] (1964) : PERFECTA
exact differential n (1825) : a differential expression of the form $X_1 dx_1 + \ldots + X_n dx_n$ where the X's are the partial derivatives of a function $f(x_1, \ldots, x_n)$ with respect to $x_1, \ldots, x_n$ respectively
ex·act·ing \ig-'zak-tiŋ\ adj (1634) **1** : tryingly or unremittingly severe in making demands **2** : requiring careful attention and precision syn see ONEROUS — **ex·act·ing·ly** \-tiŋ-lē\ adv — **ex·act·ing·ness** n
ex·ac·tion \ig-'zak-shən\ n (15c) **1 a** : the act or process of exacting **b** : EXTORTION **2** : something exacted; esp : a fee, reward, or contribution demanded or levied with severity or injustice
ex·ac·ti·tude \ig-'zak-tə-,tüd, -,tyüd\ n (1734) : the quality or an instance of being exact : EXACTNESS
ex·act·ly \ig-'zak-(t)lē\ adv (1612) **1 a** : in a manner or measure or to a degree or number that strictly conforms to a fact or condition ⟨it's ∼ 3 o'clock⟩ ⟨these two pieces are ∼ the same size⟩ **b** : in every respect : ALTOGETHER, ENTIRELY ⟨that was ∼ the wrong thing to do⟩ ⟨not ∼ what I had in mind⟩ **2** : quite so — used to express agreement
exact science n (1843) : a science (as physics, chemistry, or astronomy) whose laws are capable of accurate quantitative expression
ex·ag·ger·ate \ig-'za-jə-,rāt\ vb **-at·ed; -at·ing** [L exaggeratus, pp. of exaggerare, lit., to heap up, fr. ex- + agger heap, fr. aggerere to carry toward, fr. ad- + gerere to carry] vt (ca. 1587) **1** : to enlarge beyond bounds or the truth : OVERSTATE ⟨a friend ∼s a man's virtues —Joseph Addison⟩ **2** : to enlarge or increase esp. beyond the normal : OVEREMPHASIZE ∼ vi : to make an overstatement — **ex·ag·ger·at·ed·ly** adv — **ex·ag·ger·at·ed·ness** n — **ex·ag·ger·a·tion** \-,za-jə-'rā-shən\ n — **ex·ag·ger·a·tive** \-'za-jə-,rā-tiv, -'zaj-rə-, -'za-jə-\ adj — **ex·ag·ger·a·tor** \-'za-jə-,rā-tər\ n — **ex·ag·ger·a·to·ry** \-'zaj-rə-,tōr-ē, -,tòr-, -'za-jə-\ adj
ex·alt \ig-'zólt\ vb [ME, fr. MF & L; MF exalter, fr. L exaltare, fr. ex- + altus high — more at OLD] vt (15c) **1** : to raise in rank, power, or character **2** : to elevate by praise or in estimation : GLORIFY **3** obs : ELATE **4** : to raise high : ELEVATE **5** : to enhance the activity of : INTENSIFY ⟨rousing and ∼ing the imagination —George Eliot⟩ ∼ vi : to induce exaltation — **ex·alt·ed·ly** adv — **ex·alt·er** n
ex·al·ta·tion \,eg-,zól-'tā-shən, ,ek-,sól-\ n (14c) **1** : an act of exalting : the state of being exalted **2** : an excessively intensified sense of wellbeing, power, or importance **3** : an increase in degree or intensity ⟨∼ of virulence of a virus⟩
ex·am \ig-'zam\ n (1877) : EXAMINATION
ex·a·men \ig-'zā-mən\ n [L, tongue of a balance, examination, fr. exigere to examine] n [MF] (1606) **1** : EXAMINATION **2** : a critical study
ex·am·i·nant \-'za-mə-nənt\ n (1588) **1** : EXAMINEE **2** : one who examines : EXAMINER
ex·am·i·na·tion \ig-,za-mə-'nā-shən\ n (14c) **1** : the act or process of examining : the state of being examined **2** : an exercise designed to examine progress or test qualification or knowledge **3** : a formal interrogation — **ex·am·i·na·tion·al** \-shnəl, -shə-n²l\ adj
ex·am·ine \ig-'za-mən\ vb **ex·am·ined; ex·am·in·ing** \-'zam-niŋ, -'za-mə-\ [ME, fr. MF examiner, fr. L examinare, fr. examen] vt (14c) **1 a** : to inspect closely **b** : to test the condition of **c** : to inquire into carefully : INVESTIGATE **2 a** : to interrogate closely ⟨∼ a prisoner⟩ **b** : to test by questioning in order to determine progress, fitness, or knowledge ∼ vi : to make or give an examination syn see SCRUTINIZE — **ex·am·in·able** \-'za-mə-nə-bəl\ adj — **ex·am·in·er** \-'zam-nər, -'za-mə-\ n
ex·am·in·ee \ig-,za-mə-'nē\ n (1788) : a person who is examined
¹**ex·am·ple** \ig-'zam-pəl\ n [ME, fr. MF, fr. L exemplum, fr. eximere to take out, fr. ex- + emere to take — more at REDEEM] (14c) **1** : one that serves as a pattern to be imitated or not to be imitated ⟨a good ∼⟩ ⟨a bad ∼⟩ **2** : a punishment inflicted on someone as a warning to others; also : an individual so punished **3** : one (as an item or incident) that is representative of all of a group or type **4** : a parallel or closely similar case esp. when serving as a precedent or model **5** : an instance (as a problem to be solved) serving to illustrate a rule or precept or to act as an exercise in the application of a rule syn see INSTANCE, MODEL — **for example** : as an example ⟨there are many sources of air pollution; exhaust fumes, for example⟩
²**example** vt **ex·am·pled; ex·am·pling** \-p(ə-)liŋ\ (15c) **1** : to serve as an example of **2** archaic : to be or set an example to
ex·an·i·mate \eg-'za-nə-mət\ adj [L exanimatus, pp. of exanimare to deprive of life or spirit, fr. ex- + anima breath, soul — more at ANIMATE] (ca. 1534) **1** : lacking animation : SPIRITLESS **2** : being or appearing lifeless
ex·an·them \eg-'zan(t)-thəm, 'ek-,san-,them\ also **ex·an·the·ma** \,eg-

,zan-'thē-mə\ n, pl **-thems** also **-them·a·ta** \,eg-,zan-'the-mə-tə\ or **-themas** [LL exanthema, fr. Gk exanthēma, fr. exanthein to bloom, break out, fr. ex- + anthos flower — more at ANTHOLOGY] (1656) : an eruptive disease (as measles) or its symptomatic eruption — **ex·an·them·a·tous** \,eg-,zan-'the-mə-təs\ or **ex·an·the·mat·ic** \-,zan-thə-'ma-tik\ adj
¹**ex·arch** \'ek-,särk\ n [LL exarchus, fr. LGk exarchos, fr. Gk, leader, fr. exarchein to begin, take the lead, fr. ex- + archein to rule, begin — more at ARCH-] (1588) **1** : a Byzantine viceroy **2** : an Eastern bishop ranking below a patriarch and above a metropolitan; specif : the head of an independent church — **ex·ar·chal** \ek-'sär-kəl\ adj — **ex·arch·ate** \'ek-,sär-kət\ n — **ex·ar·chy** \'ek-,sär-kē\ n
²**exarch** adj [exo- + -arch] (1891) : formed or taking place from the periphery toward the center ⟨∼ xylem⟩
¹**ex·as·per·ate** \ig-'zas-pə-,rāt\ vt **-at·ed; -at·ing** [L exasperatus, pp. of exasperare, fr. ex- + asper rough — more at ASPERITY] (1534) **1 a** : to excite the anger of : ENRAGE **b** : to cause irritation or annoyance to **2** obs : to make more grievous : AGGRAVATE syn see IRRITATE — **ex·as·per·at·ed·ly** adv — **ex·as·per·at·ing·ly** \-,rā-tiŋ-lē\ adv
²**ex·as·per·ate** \-p(ə-)rət\ adj (1541) **1** : irritated or annoyed esp. to the point of injudicious action : EXASPERATED **2** : roughened with irregular prickles or elevations ⟨∼ seed coats⟩
ex·as·per·a·tion \ig-,zas-pə-'rā-shən\ n (1547) **1** : the state of being exasperated **2** : the act or an instance of exasperating
Ex·cal·i·bur \ek-'ska-lə-bər\ n [ME Excalaber, fr. OF Escalibor, fr. ML Caliburnus] : the sword of King Arthur
ex ca·the·dra \,eks-kə-'thē-drə\ adv or adj [NL, lit., from the chair] (1818) : by virtue of or in the exercise of one's office or position ⟨ex cathedra pronouncements⟩
ex·ca·vate \'ek-skə-,vāt\ vb **-vat·ed; -vat·ing** [L excavatus, pp. of excavare, fr. ex- + cavare to make hollow — more at CAVATINA] vt (1599) **1** : to form a cavity or hole in **2** : to form by hollowing out **3** : to dig out and remove **4** : to expose to view by or as if by digging away a covering ⟨∼ the remains of a temple⟩ ⟨another writer whose work I excavated —William Zinsser⟩ ∼ vi : to make excavations
ex·ca·va·tion \,ek-skə-'vā-shən\ n (ca. 1611) **1** : the action or process of excavating **2** : a cavity formed by cutting, digging, or scooping — **ex·ca·va·tion·al** \-shnəl, -shə-n²l\ adj
ex·ca·va·tor \'ek-skə-,vā-tər\ n (ca. 1815) : one that excavates; esp : a power-operated shovel
ex·ceed \ik-'sēd\ vb [ME excedren, fr. MF exceder, fr. L excedere, fr. ex- + cedere to go] vt (14c) **1** : to extend outside of ⟨the river will ∼ its banks⟩ **2** : to be greater than or superior to **3** : to go beyond a limit set by ⟨∼ed his authority⟩ ∼ vi **1** obs : OVERDO **2** : PREDOMINATE syn EXCEED, SURPASS, TRANSCEND, EXCEL, OUTDO, OUTSTRIP mean to go or be beyond a stated or implied limit, measure, or degree. EXCEED implies going beyond a limit set by authority or established by custom or by prior achievement ⟨exceed the speed limit⟩. SURPASS suggests superiority in quality, merit, or skill ⟨the book surpassed our expectations⟩. TRANSCEND implies a rising or extending notably above or beyond ordinary limits ⟨transcended the values of their culture⟩. EXCEL implies preeminence in achievement or quality and may suggest superiority to all others ⟨excels in mathematics⟩. OUTDO applies to a bettering or exceeding what has been done before ⟨outdid herself this time⟩. OUTSTRIP suggests surpassing in a race or competition ⟨outstripped other firms in sales⟩.
ex·ceed·ing adj (15c) : exceptional in amount, quality, or degree
ex·ceed·ing·ly \-'sē-diŋ-lē\ also **ex·ceed·ing** adv (1535) : to an extreme degree : EXTREMELY
ex·cel \ik-'sel\ vb **-celled; -cel·ling** [ME excellen, fr. L excellere, fr. ex- + -cellere to rise, project; akin to L collis hill — more at HILL] vt (15c) : to be superior to : surpass in accomplishment or achievement ∼ vi : to be distinguishable by superiority : surpass others ⟨∼ in sports⟩ ⟨excelled at lipreading⟩ syn see EXCEED
ex·cel·lence \'ek-s(ə-)lən(t)s\ n (14c) **1** : the quality of being excellent **2** : an excellent or valuable quality : VIRTUE **3** : EXCELLENCY 2
ex·cel·len·cy \-s(ə-)lən(t)-sē\ n, pl **-cies** (15c) **1** : EXCELLENCE; esp : outstanding or valuable quality — usu. used in pl. ⟨so crammed, as he thinks, with excellencies —Shak.⟩ **2** — used as a title for high dignitaries of state (as a governor or an ambassador) or church (as a Roman Catholic archbishop or bishop)
ex·cel·lent \'ek-s(ə-)lənt\ adj [ME, fr. MF, fr. L excellent-, excellens, fr. prp. of excellere] (14c) **1** archaic : SUPERIOR **2** : very good of its kind : eminently good : FIRST-CLASS — **ex·cel·lent·ly** adv
ex·cel·si·or \ik-'sel-sē-ər, -ȯr\ n [trade name, fr. L, higher, compar. of excelsus high, fr. pp. of excellere] (1868) : fine curled wood shavings used esp. for packing fragile items
¹**ex·cept** \ik-'sept\ also **ex·cept·ing** \-'sep-tiŋ\ prep (14c) : with the exclusion or exception of ⟨daily ∼ Sundays⟩
²**except** vb [ME, fr. MF excepter, fr. L exceptare, fr. exceptus, pp. of excipere to take out, except, fr. ex- + capere to take — more at HEAVE] vt (14c) : to take or leave out from a number or a whole : EXCLUDE ∼ vi : to take exception : OBJECT — **ex·cep·tive** \-'sep-təv\ adj
³**except** also **excepting** conj (15c) **1** : on any other condition than that : UNLESS ⟨∼ you repent⟩ **2** : with this exception, namely ⟨was inaccessible ∼ by boat⟩ **3** : ONLY — often followed by that ⟨I would go ∼ that it's too far⟩
except for prep (1842) **1** : with the exception of ⟨everyone was gone except for me⟩ **2** : were it not for ⟨except for you I would be dead⟩
ex·cep·tion \ik-'sep-shən\ n (14c) **1** : the act of excepting : EXCLUSION **2** : one that is excepted; esp : a case to which a rule does not apply **3** : QUESTION, OBJECTION ⟨witnesses whose authority is beyond ∼ —T. B. Macaulay⟩ **4** : an oral or written legal objection
ex·cep·tion·able \ik-'sep-sh(ə-)nə-bəl\ adj (1691) : being likely to cause objection : OBJECTIONABLE ⟨visitors even drink the ∼ beer —W. D. Howells⟩ — **ex·cep·tion·abil·i·ty** \-,sep-sh(ə-)nə-'bi-lə-tē\ n — **ex·cep·tion·ably** \-'sep-sh(ə-)nə-blē\ adv

\ə\ abut \²\ kitten, F table \ər\ further \a\ ash \ā\ ace \ä\ mop, mar \aú\ out \ch\ chin \e\ bet \ē\ easy \g\ go \i\ hit \ī\ ice \j\ job \ŋ\ sing \ō\ go \ò\ law \òi\ boy \th\ thin \th\ the \ü\ loot \ú\ foot \y\ yet \zh\ vision \à, k̟, ⁿ, œ, œ̄, ᵫ, ᵫ̄, ᵧ\ see Guide to Pronunciation

ex·cep·tion·al \ik-'sep-shnəl, -shə-n²l\ *adj* (ca. 1846) **1** : forming an exception : RARE ⟨an ~ number of rainy days⟩ **2** : better than average : SUPERIOR ⟨~ skill⟩ **3** : deviating from the norm: as **a** : having above or below average intelligence **b** : physically handicapped — **ex·cep·tion·al·i·ty** \ik-,sep-shə-'na-lə-tē\ *n* — **ex·cep·tion·al·ness** *n*

ex·cep·tion·al·ism \ik-'sep-shnə-,li-zəm, -shə-n²l-,i-\ *n* (1937) : the condition of being different from the norm; *also* : a theory expounding the exceptionalism esp. of a nation or region

ex·cep·tion·al·ly \ik-'sep-shnə-lē, -shə-n²l-ē\ *adv* (1848) : in an exceptional manner : to an exceptional degree; *esp* : more than average or usual ⟨an ~ difficult task⟩

¹**ex·cerpt** \ek-'sərpt, eg-'zərpt, 'ek-,, 'eg-,\ *vt* [L *excerptus,* pp. of *excerpere,* fr. *ex-* + *carpere* to gather, pluck — more at HARVEST] (15c) **1** : to select (a passage) for quoting : EXTRACT **2** : to take or publish extracts from (as a book) — **ex·cerp·tor** *or* **ex·cerpt·er** *n* — **ex·cerp·tion** \ek-'sərp-shən, eg-'zərp-\ *n*

²**ex·cerpt** \'ek-,sərpt, 'eg-,zərpt\ *n* (1627) : a passage (as from a book or musical composition) selected, performed, or copied : EXTRACT

¹**ex·cess** \ik-'ses, 'ek-,\ *n* [ME, fr. MF or LL; MF *exces,* fr. LL *excessus,* fr. L, departure, projection, fr. *excedere* to exceed] (14c) **1 a** : the state or an instance of surpassing usual, proper, or specified limits : SUPERFLUITY **b** : the amount or degree by which one thing or quantity exceeds another ⟨an ~ of 10 bushels⟩ **2** : undue or immoderate indulgence : INTEMPERANCE; *also* : an act or instance of intemperance (prevent ~*es* and abuses by newly created local powers —Albert Shanker⟩ — **in excess of** : to an amount or degree beyond : OVER

²**excess** *adj* (15c) : more than the usual, proper, or specified amount

³**excess** *vt* (1974) : to eliminate the position of ⟨~*ed* several teachers because of budget cutbacks⟩

ex·ces·sive \ik-'se-siv\ *adj* (14c) : exceeding what is usual, proper, necessary, or normal — **ex·ces·sive·ly** *adv* — **ex·ces·sive·ness** *n*
  syn EXCESSIVE, IMMODERATE, INORDINATE, EXTRAVAGANT, EXORBITANT, EXTREME mean going beyond a normal limit. EXCESSIVE implies an amount or degree too great to be reasonable or acceptable ⟨*excessive* punishment⟩. IMMODERATE implies lack of desirable or necessary restraint ⟨*immoderate* spending⟩. INORDINATE implies an exceeding of the limits dictated by reason or good judgment ⟨*inordinate* pride⟩. EXTRAVAGANT implies an indifference to restraints imposed by truth, prudence, or good taste ⟨*extravagant* claims for the product⟩. EXORBITANT implies a departure from accepted standards regarding amount or degree ⟨*exorbitant* prices⟩. EXTREME may imply an approach to the farthest limit possible or conceivable but commonly means only to a notably high degree ⟨*extreme* shyness⟩.

¹**ex·change** \iks-'chānj, 'eks-,\ *n, often attrib* [ME *exchaunge,* fr. MF *eschange,* fr. *eschangier* to exchange, fr. (assumed) VL *excambiare,* fr. L *ex-* + *cambiare* to exchange — more at CHANGE] (14c) **1** : the act of giving or taking one thing in return for another : TRADE ⟨an ~ of prisoners⟩ **2 a** : the act or process of substituting one thing for another **b** : reciprocal giving and receiving **3** : something offered, given, or received in an exchange **4** : funds payable currently at a distant point either in a foreign currency or in domestic currency **b** (1) : interchange or conversion of the money of two countries or of current and uncurrent money with allowance for difference in value (2) : EXCHANGE RATE (3) : the amount of the difference in value between two currencies or between values of a particular currency at two places **c** : instruments (as checks or bills of exchange) presented in a clearinghouse for settlement **5** : a place where things or services are exchanged: as **a** : an organized market or center for trading in securities or commodities **b** : a store or shop specializing in merchandise usu. of a particular type **c** : a cooperative store or society **d** : a central office in which telephone lines are connected to permit communication — **in exchange** : as a substitute

²**exchange** *vb* **ex·changed; ex·chang·ing** *vt* (15c) **1 a** : to part with, give, or transfer in consideration of something received as an equivalent **b** : to have replaced by other merchandise ⟨*exchanged* the shirt for one in a larger size⟩ **2** : to part with for a substitute ⟨*exchanging* future security for immediate pleasure⟩ **3** : to give and receive reciprocally ⟨~ gifts⟩ ~ *vi* **1** : to pass or become received in exchange **2** : to engage in an exchange — **ex·change·abil·i·ty** \iks-,chān-jə-'bi-lə-tē, eks-,\ *n* — **ex·change·able** \iks-'chān-jə-bəl\ *adj* — **ex·chang·er** \iks-'chān-jər, eks-,\ *n*

exchange rate *n* (1896) : the ratio at which the principal unit of two currencies may be traded

exchange student *n* (ca. 1930) : a student from one country received into an institution in another country in exchange for one sent to an institution in the home country of the first

Ex·chang·ite \iks-'chān-,jīt\ *n* [(*National*) *Exchange* (*club*)] (ca. 1934) : a member of a major national service club

ex·che·quer \'eks-,che-kər, iks-'\ *n* [ME *escheker,* fr. AF, fr. OF *eschequier* chessboard, counting table — more at CHECKER] (14c) **1** *cap* : a department or office of state in medieval England charged with the collection and management of the royal revenue and judicial determination of all revenue causes **2** *cap* : a former superior court having jurisdiction in England and Wales primarily over revenue matters and now merged with King's Bench **3** *often cap* **a** : the department or office of state in Great Britain and Northern Ireland charged with the receipt and care of the national revenue **b** : the national banking account of this realm **4** : TREASURY; *esp* : a national or royal treasury **5** : pecuniary resources : FUNDS

ex·ci·mer laser \'ek-si-,mər-\ *n* [*excited* + *dimer*] (1973) : a laser that uses a noble-gas halide to generate radiation usu. in the ultraviolet region of the spectrum

ex·cip·i·ent \ik-'si-pē-ənt\ *n* [L *excipient-, excipiens,* prp. of *excipere* to take out, take up — more at EXCEPT] (1753) : a usu. inert substance (as gum arabic or starch) that forms a vehicle (as for a drug)

ex·ci·ple \'ek-sə-pəl\ *n* [NL *excipulum,* fr. L, receptacle, fr. *excipere*] (ca. 1866) : a saucer-shaped rim around the hymenium of various lichens

ex·cis·able \'ek-,sī-zə-bəl, -,sī-sə-, ek-'\ *adj* (1689) : subject to excise

¹**ex·cise** \'ek-,sīz, -,sīs\ *n* [obs. D *excijs* (now *accijus*), fr. MD, prob. modif. of OF *assise* session, assessment — more at ASSIZE] (15c) **1** : an internal tax levied on the manufacture, sale, or consumption of a commodity **2** : any of various taxes on privileges often assessed in the form of a license or fee

²**ex·cise** \'ek-,sīz, -,sīs, ik-'sīz\ *vt* **ex·cised; ex·cis·ing** (1652) : to impose an excise on

³**ex·cise** \ik-'sīz\ *vt* **ex·cised; ex·cis·ing** [L *excisus,* pp. of *excidere,* fr. *ex-* + *caedere* to cut] (1634) : to remove by or as if by excision

ex·cise·man \'ek-,sīz-mən, -,sīs-, -,man, ek-'\ *n* (1647) : an officer who inspects and rates articles liable to excise under British law

ex·ci·sion \ik-'si-zhən\ *n* [ME *excysion,* fr. MF *excision,* fr. L *excision-, excisio,* fr. *excidere*] (1541) : the act or procedure of removing by or as if by cutting out; *esp* : surgical removal or resection — **ex·ci·sion·al** \-'sizh-nəl, -ə-n°l\ *adj*

ex·cit·able \ik-'sī-tə-bəl\ *adj* (1609) **1** : capable of being readily roused into action or a state of excitement or irritability **2** : capable of being activated by and reacting to stimuli — **ex·cit·abil·i·ty** \-,sī-tə-'bi-lə-tē\ *n* — **ex·cit·able·ness** \-'sī-tə-bəl-nəs\ *n*

ex·ci·tant \ik-'sī-t²nt, 'ek-sə-tənt\ *adj* (1607) : tending to excite or augment ⟨~ drugs⟩ — **excitant** *n*

ex·ci·ta·tion \,ek-,sī-'tā-shən, ,ek-sə-\ *n* (14c) : EXCITEMENT; *esp* : the disturbed or altered condition resulting from stimulation of an individual, organ, tissue, or cell

ex·cit·ative \ik-'sī-tə-tiv\ *adj* (15c) : tending to induce excitation (as of a neuron) ⟨~ substances⟩

ex·cit·ato·ry \ik-'sī-tə-,tōr-ē, -,tȯr-\ *adj* (1803) : exhibiting, resulting from, related to, or producing excitement or excitation ⟨~ nerve fibers⟩

ex·cite \ik-'sīt, ek-\ *vt* **ex·cit·ed; ex·cit·ing** [ME, fr. MF *exciter,* fr. L *excitare,* fr. *ex-* + *citare* to rouse — more at CITE] (14c) **1 a** : to call to activity **b** : to rouse to an emotional response ⟨scenes to ~ the hardest man to pity⟩ **c** : to arouse (as a strong emotional response) by appropriate stimuli ⟨~ enthusiasm for the new regime —Arthur Knight⟩ **2 a** : ENERGIZE ⟨~ an electromagnet⟩ **b** : to produce a magnetic field in ⟨~ a dynamo⟩ **3** : to increase the activity of (as a living organism) : STIMULATE **4** : to raise (as an atomic nucleus, atom, or a molecule) to a higher energy level *syn* see PROVOKE — **ex·cit·ed·ly** \-'sī-təd-lē\ *adv*

excited state *n* (1927) : a state of a physical system (as an atomic nucleus, an atom, or a molecule) that is higher in energy than the ground state

ex·cite·ment \ik-'sīt-mənt\ *n* (1604) **1** : something that excites or rouses **2** : the action of exciting : the state of being excited

ex·cit·er \ik-'sī-tər\ *n* (14c) **1** : one that excites **2 a** : a generator or battery that supplies the electric current used to produce the magnetic field in another generator or motor **b** : an electrical oscillator that generates the carrier frequency (as for a radio transmitter)

ex·cit·ing \ik-'sī-tiŋ\ *adj* (ca. 1811) : producing excitement — **ex·cit·ing·ly** \-iŋ-lē\ *adv*

ex·ci·ton \'ek-sə-,tän, -,sī-\ *n* [ISV *excitation* + ²-*on*] (1936) : a mobile combination of an electron and a hole in an excited crystal (as of a semiconductor) — **ex·ci·ton·ic** \,ek-sə-'tä-nik, -,sī-\ *adj*

ex·ci·tor \ik-'sī-tər\ *n* (1816) : an afferent nerve arousing increased action of the part that it supplies

ex·claim \iks-'klām\ *vb* [MF *exclamer,* fr. L *exclamare,* fr. *ex-* + *clamare* to cry out — more at CLAIM] *vi* (ca. 1570) **1** : to cry out or speak in strong or sudden emotion ⟨~*ed* in delight⟩ **2** : to speak loudly or vehemently ⟨~*ed* against immorality⟩ ~ *vt* : to utter sharply, passionately, or vehemently : PROCLAIM — **ex·claim·er** *n*

ex·cla·ma·tion \,eks-klə-'mā-shən\ *n* (14c) **1** : a sharp or sudden utterance **2** : vehement expression of protest or complaint

exclamation point *n* (1824) : a mark ! used esp. after an interjection or exclamation to indicate forceful utterance or strong feeling — called also *exclamation mark*

ex·clam·a·to·ry \iks-'kla-mə-,tōr-ē, -,tȯr-\ *adj* (1593) : containing, expressing, using, or relating to exclamation ⟨an ~ phrase⟩

ex·clave \'eks-,klāv, -,kläv\ *n* [*ex-* + *-clave* (as in *enclave*)] (1888) : a portion of a country separated from the main part and constituting an enclave in respect to the surrounding territory

ex·clud·able *or* **ex·clud·ible** \iks-'klü-də-bəl\ *adj* (1916) : subject to exclusion ⟨~ income⟩ — **ex·clud·abil·i·ty** \-,klü-də-'bi-lə-tē\ *n*

ex·clude \iks-'klüd\ *vt* **ex·clud·ed; ex·clud·ing** [ME, fr. L *excludere,* fr. *ex-* + *claudere* to close — more at CLOSE] (14c) **1 a** : to prevent or restrict the entrance of **b** : to bar from participation, consideration, or inclusion **2** : to expel or bar esp. from a place or position previously occupied — **ex·clud·er** *n*

ex·clu·sion \iks-'klü-zhən\ *n* [L *exclusion-, exclusio,* fr. *excludere*] (15c) **1** : the act or an instance of excluding **2** : the state of being excluded — **ex·clu·sion·ary** \-zhə-,ner-ē\ *adj*

exclusionary rule *n* (1964) : a legal rule that bars unlawfully obtained evidence from being used in court proceedings

ex·clu·sion·ist \iks-'klüzh-nist, -'klü-zhə-\ *n* (1822) : one who would exclude another from some right or privilege — **exclusionist** *adj*

exclusion principle *n* (1926) : a principle in physics: no two particles (as electrons) in an atom or molecule can have the same set of quantum numbers

¹**ex·clu·sive** \iks-'klü-siv, -ziv\ *adj* (1515) **1 a** : excluding or having power to exclude **b** : limiting or limited to possession, control, or use by a single individual or group **2 a** : excluding others from participation **b** : snobbishly aloof **3 a** : accepting or soliciting only a socially restricted patronage (as of the upper class) : STYLISH, FASHIONABLE **c** : restricted in distribution, use, or appeal because of expense **4 a** : SINGLE, SOLE ⟨~ jurisdiction⟩ **b** : WHOLE, UNDIVIDED ⟨his ~ attention⟩ — **ex·clu·sive·ly** *adv* — **ex·clu·sive·ness** *n*

²**exclusive** *n* (15c) : something exclusive: as **a** : a newspaper story at first released to or printed by only one newspaper **b** : an exclusive right (as to talk a particular product in a certain area)

exclusive disjunction *n* (1942) : a compound proposition in logic that is true when one and only one of its constituent statements is true — see TRUTH TABLE table

exclusive of *prep* (1762) : not taking into account ⟨there were four of us *exclusive of* the guide⟩

ex·clu·siv·ism \iks-'klü-sə-,vi-zəm, -'klü-zə-\ *n* (ca. 1834) : the practice of excluding or of being exclusive — **ex·clu·siv·ist** \-vist\ *n or adj*

ex·clu·siv·i·ty \,eks-,klü-'si-və-tē, iks-, -'zi-\ *n, pl* **-ties** (1926) **1** : the quality or state of being exclusive **2** : exclusive rights or services

ex·cog·i·tate \ek-'skä-jə-,tāt\ *vt* [L *excogitatus,* pp. of *excogitare,* fr. *ex-* + *cogitare* to cogitate] (ca. 1530) : to think out : DEVISE — **ex·cog·i-**

ta·tion \(ˌ)ek-ˌskä-jə-'tā-shən\ n — **ex·cog·i·ta·tive** \ek-'skä-jə-ˌtā-tiv\ adj

¹**ex·com·mu·ni·cate** \ˌek-skə-'myü-nə-ˌkāt\ vt [ME, fr. LL excommunicatus, pp. of excommunicare, fr. L ex- + LL communicare to communicate] (15c) : to subject to excommunication — **ex·com·mu·ni·ca·tor** \-ˌkā-tər\ n

²**ex·com·mu·ni·cate** \-ni-kət\ adj (1551) : excluded from the rites of the church : EXCOMMUNICATED — **excommunicate** n

ex·com·mu·ni·ca·tion \-ˌmyü-nə-'kā-shən\ n (15c) 1 : an ecclesiastical censure depriving a person of the rights of church membership 2 : exclusion from fellowship in a group or community — **ex·com·mu·ni·ca·tive** \-'myü-nə-ˌkā-tiv, -ni-kət\ adj

ex·co·ri·ate \ek-'skōr-ē-ˌāt, -'skȯr-\ vt **-at·ed; -at·ing** [ME, fr. LL excoriatus, pp. of excoriare, fr. L ex- + corium skin, hide — more at CUIRASS] (15c) 1 : to wear off the skin of : ABRADE 2 : to censure scathingly — **ex·co·ri·a·tion** \(ˌ)ek-ˌskōr-ē-'ā-shən, -ˌskȯr-\ n

ex·cre·ment \'ek-skrə-mənt\ n [L excrementum, fr. excernere] (1533) : waste matter discharged from the body; esp : waste (as feces) discharged from the alimentary canal — **ex·cre·men·tal** \ˌek-skrə-'men-tᵊl\ adj — **ex·cre·men·ti·tious** \-ˌmen-'ti-shəs, -mən-\ adj

ex·cres·cence \ik-'skre-sᵊn(t)s, ek-\ n (15c) 1 : a projection or outgrowth esp. when abnormal ⟨warty ~s in the colon⟩ 2 : a disfiguring, extraneous, or unwanted mark or part : BLOT

ex·cres·cen·cy \-'sᵊn-sē\ n, pl **-cies** (1545) : EXCRESCENCE

ex·cres·cent \-s²nt\ adj [L excrescent-, excrescens, prp. of excrescere to grow out, fr. ex- + crescere to grow — more at CRESCENT] (1633) 1 : forming an abnormal, excessive, or useless outgrowth 2 : of, relating to, or constituting epenthesis — **ex·cres·cent·ly** adv

ex·cre·ta \ik-'skrē-tə\ n pl [NL, fr. L, neut. pl. of excretus] (1857) : waste matter eliminated or separated from an organism; esp : EXCRETIONS — **ex·cre·tal** \-'skrē-tᵊl\ adj

ex·crete \ik-'skrēt\ vt **-cret·ed; -cret·ing** [L excretus, pp. of excernere to sift out, discharge, fr. ex- + cernere to sift — more at CERTAIN] (1620) : to separate and eliminate or discharge (waste) from the blood or tissues or from the active protoplasm — **ex·cret·er** n

ex·cre·tion \ik-'skrē-shən\ n (1603) 1 : the act or process of excreting 2 : something excreted; esp : metabolic waste products (as urea and carbon dioxide) that are eliminated from the body and differ from a secretion in not being produced to perform a useful function

ex·cre·to·ry \'ek-skrə-ˌtōr-ē, -ˌtȯr-\ adj (ca. 1681) : of, relating to, or functioning in excretion ⟨~ ducts⟩

ex·cru·ci·ate \ik-'skrü-shē-ˌāt\ vt **-at·ed; -at·ing** [L excruciatus, pp. of excruciare, fr. ex- + cruciare to crucify, fr. cruc-, crux cross] (ca. 1570) 1 : to inflict intense pain on : TORTURE 2 : to subject to intense mental distress — **ex·cru·ci·a·tion** \-ˌskrü-shē-'ā-shən, -sē-\ n

ex·cru·ci·at·ing adj (1599) 1 : causing great pain or anguish : AGONIZING ⟨the nation's most ~ dilemma —W. H. Ferry⟩ 2 : very intense : EXTREME ⟨~ pain⟩ — **ex·cru·ci·at·ing·ly** \-ˌā-tiŋ-lē\ adv

ex·cul·pate \'ek-(ˌ)skəl-ˌpāt, (ˌ)ek-'\ vt **-pat·ed; -pat·ing** [ML exculpatus, pp. of exculpare, fr. L ex- + culpa blame] (ca. 1681) : to clear from alleged fault or guilt — **ex·cul·pa·tion** \ˌek-(ˌ)skəl-'pā-shən\ n

syn EXCULPATE, ABSOLVE, EXONERATE, ACQUIT, VINDICATE mean to free from a charge. EXCULPATE implies a clearing from blame or fault often in a matter of small importance ⟨exculpating himself from the charge of overenthusiasm⟩. ABSOLVE implies a release either from an obligation that binds the conscience or from the consequences of disobeying the law or committing a sin ⟨cannot be absolved of blame⟩. EXONERATE implies a complete clearance from an accusation or charge and from any attendant suspicion of blame or guilt ⟨exonerated by the investigation⟩. ACQUIT implies a formal decision in one's favor with respect to a definite charge ⟨voted to acquit the defendant⟩. VINDICATE may refer to things as well as persons that have been subjected to critical attack or imputation of guilt, weakness, or folly, and implies a clearing effected by proving the unfairness of such criticism or blame ⟨her judgment was vindicated⟩.

ex·cul·pa·to·ry \ek-'skəl-pə-ˌtōr-ē, -ˌtȯr-\ adj (1781) : tending or serving to exculpate

ex·cur·rent \(ˌ)ek-'skər-ənt, -'skə-rənt\ adj [L excurrent-, excurrens, prp. of excurrere to run out, extend, fr. ex- + currere to run — more at CAR] (1826) 1 : characterized by a current that flows outward ⟨~ canals of a sponge⟩ 2 a : having the axis prolonged to form an undivided main stem or trunk (as in conifers) — compare DELIQUESCENT 2 b : projecting beyond the apex — used esp. of the midrib of a mucronate leaf

ex·cur·sion \ik-'skər-zhən\ n [L excursion-, excursio, fr. excurrere] (1587) 1 a : a going out or forth : EXPEDITION b (1) : a usu. brief pleasure trip (2) : a trip at special reduced rates 2 : deviation from a direct, definite, or proper course; esp : DIGRESSION ⟨needless ~s into abstruse theory⟩ 3 a : a movement outward and back or from a mean position or axis; also : the distance traversed : AMPLITUDE ⟨the ~ of a piston⟩ b : one complete movement of expansion and contraction of the lungs and their membranes (as in breathing)

ex·cur·sion·ist \-'skərzh-nist, -'skər-zhə-\ n (1830) : a person who goes on an excursion

ex·cur·sive \-'skər-siv\ adj (1749) : constituting a digression : characterized by digression — **ex·cur·sive·ly** adv — **ex·cur·sive·ness** n

ex·cur·sus \ik-'skər-səs\ n, pl **ex·cur·sus·es** also **ex·cur·sus** \-səs, -ˌsüs\ [L, digression, fr. excurrere] (1803) : an appendix or digression that contains further exposition of some point or topic

ex·cus·a·to·ry \ik-'skyü-zə-ˌtōr-ē, -ˌtȯr-\ adj (1535) : making or containing excuse

¹**ex·cuse** \ik-'skyüz, imperatively often 'skyüz\ vt **ex·cused; ex·cus·ing** [ME, fr. OF excuser, fr. L excusare, fr. ex- + causa cause, explanation] (13c) 1 a : to make apology for b : to try to remove blame from 2 : to forgive entirely or disregard as of trivial import : regard as excusable ⟨graciously excused his tardiness⟩ 3 a : to grant exemption or release to ⟨was excused from jury duty⟩ b : to allow to leave ⟨excused the class⟩ 4 : to serve as excuse for : JUSTIFY ⟨nothing can ~ such neglect⟩ — **ex·cus·able** \ik-'skyü-zə-bəl\ adj — **ex·cus·able·ness** n — **ex·cus·ably** \-blē\ adv — **ex·cus·er** n

syn EXCUSE, CONDONE, PARDON, FORGIVE mean to exact neither punishment nor redress. EXCUSE may refer to specific acts esp. in social or conventional situations or the person responsible for these ⟨excuse an interruption⟩ ⟨excused them for interrupting⟩. Often the term implies extenuating circumstances ⟨injustice excuses strong responses⟩. CONDONE implies that one overlooks without censure behavior (as dishonesty or violence) that involves a serious breach of a moral, ethical, or legal code, and the term may refer to the behavior or to the agent responsible for it ⟨a society that condones alcohol but not narcotics⟩. PARDON implies that one remits a penalty due for an admitted or established offense ⟨pardon a criminal⟩. FORGIVE implies that one gives up all claim to requital and to resentment or vengeful feelings ⟨could not forgive their rudeness⟩.

²**ex·cuse** \ik-'skyüs\ n (14c) 1 : the act of excusing 2 a : something offered as justification or as grounds for being excused b pl : an expression of regret for failure to do something c : a note of explanation of an absence 3 : JUSTIFICATION, REASON **syn** see APOLOGY

ex·di·rec·to·ry \ˌeks-də-'rek-t(ə-)rē, -dī-\ adj [L ex out of — more at EX-] (1936) Brit : not listed in a telephone book : UNLISTED

ex·ec \ig-'zek\ n (1896) 1 : EXECUTIVE OFFICER 2 : EXECUTIVE

ex·e·cra·ble \'ek-si-krə-bəl\ adj (14c) 1 : deserving to be execrated : DETESTABLE ⟨~ crimes⟩ 2 : very bad : WRETCHED ⟨~ hotel food⟩ — **ex·e·cra·ble·ness** n — **ex·e·cra·bly** \-blē\ adv

ex·e·crate \'ek-sə-ˌkrāt\ vt **-crat·ed; -crat·ing** [L exsecratus, pp. of exsecrari to put under a curse, fr. ex + sacr-, sacer sacred] (1561) 1 : to declare to be evil or detestable : DENOUNCE 2 : to detest utterly — **ex·e·cra·tive** \-ˌkrā-tiv\ adj — **ex·e·cra·tor** \-ˌkrā-tər\ n

ex·e·cra·tion \ˌek-sə-'krā-shən\ n (14c) 1 : the act of cursing or denouncing; also : the curse so uttered 2 : an object of curses : something detested

ex·ec·u·tant \ig-'ze-k(y)ə-tənt\ n (1858) : one who executes or performs; esp : one skilled in the technique of an art : PERFORMER

ex·e·cute \'ek-si-ˌkyüt\ vb **-cut·ed; -cut·ing** [ME, fr. MF executer, back-formation fr. execution] vt (14c) 1 : to carry out fully : put completely into effect ⟨~ a command⟩ 2 : to do what is provided or required by ⟨~ a decree⟩ 3 : to put to death esp. in compliance with a legal sentence 4 : to make or produce (as a work of art) esp. by carrying out a design 5 : to perform what is required to give validity to ⟨~ a deed⟩ 6 : PLAY ⟨~ a piece of music⟩ ~ vi 1 : to perform properly or skillfully the fundamentals of a sport or of a particular play ⟨never had a team ~ better —Bobby Knight⟩ 2 : to perform indicated tasks according to encoded instructions — used of a computer program or routine **syn** see KILL, PERFORM — **ex·e·cut·able** \-ˌkyü-tə-bəl\ adj

ex·e·cu·tion \ˌek-si-'kyü-shən\ n [ME, fr. MF, fr. L exsecution-, exsecutio, fr. exsequi to execute, fr. ex- + sequi to follow — more at SUE] (14c) 1 : the act or process of executing : PERFORMANCE 2 : a putting to death esp. as a legal penalty 3 : the process of enforcing a legal judgment (as against a debtor); also : a judicial writ directing such enforcement 4 : the act or mode or result of performance 5 archaic : effective or destructive action ⟨his bra⟨dished steel, which smoked with bloody ~ —Shak.⟩ — usu. used wi⟨ n do ⟨as soon as day came, we went out to see what ~ we had do⟨ —Daniel Defoe⟩

ex·e·cu·tion·er \ˌ⟨⟩⟨-⟨-mər\ n (1536) : one who executes; esp : one who puts to death

¹**ex·ec·u·tive** \ig-'ze-k(y)ə-tiv\ adj (1649) 1 a : of or relating to the execution of the laws and the conduct of public and national affairs b : belonging to the branch of government that is charged with such powers as diplomatic representation, superintendence of the execution of the laws, and appointment of officials and that usu. has some power over legislation (as through veto) — compare JUDICIAL, LEGISLATIVE 2 a : designed for or relating to execution or carrying into effect ⟨~ board⟩ b : having administrative or managerial responsibility ⟨~ director⟩ 3 : of or relating to an executive ⟨the ~ offices⟩

²**executive** n (1774) 1 : the executive branch of a government; also : the person or persons who constitute the executive magistracy of a state 2 : a directing or controlling office of an organization 3 : one that exercises administrative or managerial control

executive agreement n (1942) : an agreement between the U.S. and a foreign government made by the executive branch of the government either alone or with Congressional approval and dealing usu. with routine matters

executive council n (1778) 1 : a council constituted to advise or share in the functions of a political executive 2 : a council that exercises supreme executive power

executive officer n (1881) : the officer second in command of a military or naval organization

executive order n (1883) : REGULATION 2b

executive privilege n (1940) : exemption from legally enforced disclosure of communications within the executive branch of government when such disclosure would adversely affect the functions and decision-making processes of the executive branch

executive secretary n (1950) : a secretary having administrative duties; esp : an official responsible for administering the activities and business affairs of an organization

executive session n (1840) : a usu. closed session (as of a legislative body) that functions as an executive council (as of the U.S. Senate when considering appointments or the ratification of treaties)

ex·ec·u·tor \ig-'ze-k(y)ə-tər or in sense 1 'ek-sə-ˌkyü-\ n [ME, fr. OF, fr. L exsecutor, fr. exsequi] (13c) 1 a : one who executes something b obs : EXECUTIONER 2 a : the person appointed by a testator to execute a will b : LITERARY EXECUTOR — **ex·ec·u·to·ri·al** \ig-ˌze-k(y)ə-'tōr-ē-əl, -'tȯr-\ adj

ex·ec·u·to·ry \ig-'ze-k(y)ə-ˌtōr-ē, -ˌtȯr-\ adj (1592) 1 : designed or of such a nature as to be executed in time to come or to take effect on a future contingency 2 : relating to administration

ex·ec·u·trix \ig-'ze-k(y)ə-(ˌ)triks\ n, pl **ex·ec·u·tri·ces** \-ˌze-k(y)ə-'trī-(ˌ)sēz\ or **ex·ec·u·trix·es** \-'ze-k(y)ə-ˌtrik-səz\ (15c) : a woman who is an executor

ex·e·dra \'ek-sə-drə\ n, pl **-drae** \-ˌdrē, -ˌdrī\ [L, fr. Gk, fr. ex- + hedra seat — more at SIT] (1706) 1 : a room (as in a temple or house) in ancient Greece and Rome used for conversation and formed by an

\ə\ abut \ᵊ\ kitten, F table \ər\ further \a\ ash \ā\ ace \ä\ mop, mar \aú\ out \ch\ chin \e\ bet \ē\ easy \g\ go \i\ hit \ī\ ice \j\ job \ŋ\ sing \ō\ go \ȯ\ law \ȯi\ boy \th\ thin \th̲\ the \ü\ loot \ú\ foot \y\ yet \zh\ vision \à, k̲, ⁿ, œ, œ̄, ᵫ, ᵫ̄, ᵊ\ see Guide to Pronunciation open or columned recess often semicircular in shape and furnished with seats **2 :** a large outdoor nearly semicircular seat with a solid back

ex·e·ge·sis \,ek-sə-'jē-səs, 'ek-sə-,\ *n, pl* **-ge·ses** \-'jē-(,)sēz\ [NL, fr. Gk *exēgēsis*, fr. *exēgeisthai* to explain, interpret, fr. *ex-* + *hēgeisthai* to lead — more at SEEK] (1619) : EXPOSITION, EXPLANATION; *esp* : an explanation or critical interpretation of a text

ex·e·gete \'ek-sə-,jēt\ *n* [Gk *exēgētēs*, fr. *exēgeisthai*] (ca. 1736) : one who practices exegesis

ex·e·get·i·cal \,ek-sə-'je-ti-kəl\ *also* **ex·e·get·ic** \-tik\ *adj* [Gk *exēgētikos*, fr. *exēgeisthai*] (1623) : of or relating to exegesis : EXPLANATORY

ex·e·get·ist \-'jē-tist, -'je-\ *n* (1848) : EXEGETE

ex·em·plar \ig-'zem-,plär, -plər, eg-\ *n* [ME, fr. L, fr. *exemplum* example] (15c) : one that serves as a model or example: as **a :** an ideal model **b :** a typical or standard specimen **c :** a copy of a book or writing **d :** IDEA 1a *syn* see MODEL

ex·em·pla·ry \ig-'zem-plə-rē\ *adj* (1589) **1 :** serving as a pattern **b :** deserving imitation : COMMENDABLE 〈his courage was ~〉; *also* : deserving imitation because of excellence 〈they serve ~ pastries —G. V. Higgins〉 **2 :** serving as a warning : MONITORY **3 :** serving as an example, instance, or illustration — **ex·em·plar·i·ly** \,eg-,zem-'pler-ə-lē\ *adv* — **ex·em·pla·ri·ness** \ig-'zem-plə-rē-nəs\ *n* — **ex·em·plar·i·ty** \,eg-,zem-'plar-ə-tē\ *n*

ex·em·pli·fi·ca·tion \ig-,zem-plə-fə-'kā-shən\ *n* (1510) **1 a :** the act or process of exemplifying **b :** EXAMPLE, CASE IN POINT **2 :** an exemplified copy of a document

ex·em·pli·fy \ig-'zem-plə-,fī\ *vt* **-fied; -fy·ing** [ME *exemplifien*, fr. MF *exemplifier*, fr. ML *exemplificare*, fr. L *exemplum*] (15c) **1 :** to show or illustrate by example **2 :** to make an attested copy or transcript of (a document) under seal **3 a :** to be an instance of or serve as an example : EMBODY **b :** to be typical of

ex·em·pli gra·tia \ig-,zem-(,)plē-'grä-tē-,ä, -'grä-sh(ē-)ə\ *adv* [L] (1602) : for example

ex·em·plum \ig-'zem-pləm, eg-\ *n, pl* **-pla** \-plə\ [L] (1890) **1 :** EXAMPLE, MODEL **2 :** an anecdote or short narrative used to point a moral or sustain an argument

1ex·empt \ig-'zem(p)t\ *adj* [ME, fr. L *exemptus*, pp. of *eximere* to take out — more at EXAMPLE] (14c) **1** *obs* : set apart **2 :** free or released from some liability or requirement to which others are subject 〈was ~ from jury duty〉 〈the estate was ~ from taxes〉

2exempt *vt* (15c) **1 :** to release or deliver from some liability or requirement to which others are subject : EXCUSE 〈a man ~ed from military service〉 **2** *obs* : to set apart

3exempt *n* (1670) : one exempted or freed from duty

ex·emp·tion \ig-'zem(p)-shən\ *n* (14c) **1 :** the act of exempting or state of being exempt : IMMUNITY **2 :** one that exempts or is exempted; *esp* : a source or amount of income exempted from taxation

ex·en·ter·ate \ig-'zen-tə-,rāt\ *vt* **-at·ed; -at·ing** [L *exenteratus*, pp. of *exenterare* to disembowel, modif. of Gk *exenterizein*, fr. *ex-* + *enteron* intestine — more at INTER-] (1607) : to remove the contents of (as the orbit or pelvis) — **ex·en·ter·a·tion** \-,zen-tə-'rā-shən\ *n*

1ex·er·cise \'ek-sər-,sīz\ *n* [ME, fr. MF *exercice*, fr. L *exercitium*, fr. *exercitare* to train, exercise, freq. of *exercēre* to train, occupy, fr. *ex-* + *arcēre* to enclose, hold off — more at ARK] (14c) **1 a :** the act of bringing into play or realizing in action : USE **b :** the discharge of an official function or professional occupation **c :** the act or an instance of carrying out the terms of an agreement (as an option) **2 a :** regular or repeated use of a faculty or bodily organ **b :** bodily exertion for the sake of developing and maintaining physical fitness **3 :** something performed or practiced in order to develop, improve, or display a specific power or skill 〈arithmetic ~s〉 **4 :** a performance having a strongly marked secondary or ulterior aspect 〈party politics has always been an ~ in compromise —H. S. Ashmore〉 **5 a :** a maneuver, operation, or drill carried out for training and discipline **b** *pl* : a program including speeches, announcements of awards and honors, and various traditional practices of secular or religious character 〈commencement ~s〉

2exercise *vb* **-cised; -cis·ing** *vt* (14c) **1 a :** to make effective in action : USE 〈didn't ~ good judgment〉 **b :** to bring to bear : EXERT 〈~ influence〉 **c :** to implement the terms of (as an option) **2 a :** to use repeatedly in order to strengthen or develop **b :** to train (as troops) by drills and maneuvers **c :** to put through exercises 〈~ the horses〉 **3 a :** to engage the attention and effort of **b :** to cause anxiety, alarm, or indignation in 〈the issues *exercising* voters this year〉 ~ *vi* **:** to take exercise — **ex·er·cis·able** \-,sī-zə-bəl\ *adj*

ex·er·cis·er \'ek-sər-,sī-zər\ *n* (1552) **1 :** one that exercises **2 :** an apparatus for use in physical exercise

ex·er·ci·ta·tion \ig-,zər-sə-'tā-shən\ *n* [ME *exercitacioun*, fr. L *exercitation-, exercitatio*, fr. *exercitare*] (14c) : EXERCISE

Ex·er·cy·cle \'ek-sər-,sī-kəl\ *trademark* — used for a stationary bicycle

ex·er·gon·ic \,ek-(,)sər-'gä-nik\ *adj* [*exo-* + Gk *ergon* work — more at WORK] (1940) : EXOTHERMIC 〈an ~ biochemical reaction〉

ex·ergue \'ek-,sərg, 'eg-,zərg\ *n* [F, fr. NL *exergum*, fr. Gk *ex* out of + *ergon* work] (1697) : a space on a coin, token, or medal usu. on the reverse below the central part of the design

ex·ert \ig-'zərt\ *vt* [L *exsertus*, pp. of *exserere* to thrust out, fr. *ex-* + *serere* to join — more at SERIES] (1681) **1 a :** to put forth (as strength) **b :** to put (oneself) into action or to tiring effort **2 :** to bring to bear esp. with sustained effort or lasting effect **3 :** EMPLOY, WIELD 〈~ed her leadership abilities intelligently〉

ex·er·tion \ig-'zər-shən\ *n* (1677) : the act or an instance of exerting; *esp* : a laborious or perceptible effort

ex·e·unt \'ek-sē-(,)ənt, -,ənt\ [L, they go out, fr. *exire* to go out — more at EXIT] (15c) — used as a stage direction to specify that all or certain named characters leave the stage

ex·fo·li·ate \(,)eks-'fō-lē-,āt\ *vb* **-at·ed; -at·ing** [LL *exfoliatus*, pp. of *exfoliare* to strip of leaves, fr. L *ex-* + *folium* leaf — more at BLADE] *vt* (1612) **1 :** to cast off in scales, laminae, or splinters **2 :** to remove the surface of in scales or laminae **3 :** to spread or extend by or as if by opening out leaves ~ *vi* **1 :** to split into or give off scales, laminae, or body cells **2 :** to come off in thin layers or scales **3 :** to grow by or as if by producing or unfolding leaves — **ex·fo·li·a·tion** \(,)eks-,fō-lē-'ā-shən\ *n* — **ex·fo·li·a·tive** \eks-'fō-lē-,ā-tiv\ *adj*

ex gra·tia \(,)eks-'grä-sh(ē-)ə\ *adj or adv* [NL] (1769) : as a favor : not compelled by legal right 〈*ex gratia* pension payments〉

ex·hal·ant *or* **ex·hal·ent** \eks-'hā-lənt, ek-'sā-\ *adj* (1771) : bearing out or outward : EMISSIVE 〈an ~ siphon of a clam〉

ex·ha·la·tion \,eks-hə-'lā-shən, ,ek-sə-\ *n* (14c) **1 :** something exhaled or given off : EMANATION **2 :** an act of exhaling

ex·hale \eks-'hā(ə)l, ek-'sā(ə)l\ *vb* **ex·haled; ex·hal·ing** [ME *exalen*, fr. L *exhalare*, fr. *ex-* + *halare* to breathe] *vi* (14c) **1 :** to rise or be given off as vapor **2 :** to emit breath or vapor ~ *vt* **1 a :** to breathe out **b :** to give forth (gaseous matter) : EMIT **2** *archaic* : to cause to be emitted in vapor

1ex·haust \ig-'zóst\ *vb* [L *exhaustus*, pp. of *exhaurire*, fr. *ex-* + *haurire* to draw; akin to MHG *œsen* to empty, Gk *auein* to take] *vt* (1533) **1 a :** to consume entirely : USE UP 〈~ed our funds in a week〉 **b :** to tire extremely or completely 〈~ed by overwork〉 **c :** to deprive of a valuable quality or constituent 〈~ a photographic developer〉 〈~ a soil of fertility〉 **2 a :** to draw off or let out completely **b :** to empty by drawing off the contents; *specif* : to create a vacuum in **3 a :** to develop (a subject) completely **b :** to try out the whole number of 〈~ed all the possibilities〉 ~ *vi* **:** DISCHARGE, EMPTY 〈the engine ~s through the muffler〉 *syn* see DEPLETE, TIRE — **ex·haust·er** *n* — **ex·haust·ibil·i·ty** \-,zó-stə-'bi-lə-tē\ *n* — **ex·haust·ible** \-'zó-stə-bəl\ *adj*

2exhaust *n* (1848) **1 a :** the escape of used gas or vapor from an engine **b :** the gas or vapor thus escaping **2 a :** the conduit through which used gases escape **b :** an arrangement for removing fumes, dusts, or odors from an enclosure **3 :** EXHAUSTION

ex·haus·tion \ig-'zós-chən\ *n* (1646) : the act or process of exhausting : the state of being exhausted

ex·haus·tive \ig-'zó-stiv\ *adj* (1786) : testing all possibilities or considering all elements : THOROUGH 〈conducted an ~ investigation〉 — **ex·haus·tive·ly** *adv* — **ex·haus·tive·ness** *n* — **ex·haus·tiv·i·ty** \-,zó-'sti-və-tē\ *n*

ex·haust·less \ig-'zóst-ləs\ *adj* (1712) : not to be exhausted : INEXHAUSTIBLE — **ex·haust·less·ly** *adv* — **ex·haust·less·ness** *n*

1ex·hib·it \ig-'zi-bət\ *vb* [ME, fr. L *exhibitus*, pp. of *exhibēre*, fr. *ex-* + *habēre* to have, hold — more at GIVE] *vt* (15c) **1 :** to submit (as a document) to a court or officer in course of proceedings; *also* : to present or offer officially or in legal form **2 :** to present to view: as **a :** to show or display outwardly esp. by visible signs or actions 〈~ed no fear〉 **b :** to have as a readily discernible quality or feature 〈in all cultures we know, men ~ an aesthetic sense —H. J. Muller〉 **c :** to show publicly esp. for purposes of competition or demonstration ~ *vi* **:** to display something for public inspection *syn* see SHOW — **ex·hib·i·tive** \-bə-tiv\ *adj* — **ex·hib·i·tor** \-bə-tər\ *n* — **ex·hib·i·to·ry** \-bə-,tór-ē, -,tór-\ *adj*

2exhibit *n* (1626) **1 :** a document or material object produced and identified in court or before an examiner for use as evidence **2 :** something exhibited **3 :** an act or instance of exhibiting

ex·hi·bi·tion \,ek-sə-'bi-shən\ *n* (14c) **1 :** an act or instance of exhibiting **2** *Brit* : a grant drawn from the funds of a school or university to help maintain a student **3 :** a public showing (as of works of art, objects of manufacture, or athletic skill) 〈a one-man ~〉 〈an art ~〉

ex·hi·bi·tion·er \-'bish-nər, -'bi-shə-\ *n* (1679) *Brit* : one who holds a grant from a school or university

ex·hi·bi·tion·ism \-'bi-shə-,ni-zəm\ *n* (1893) **1 a :** a perversion marked by a tendency to indecent exposure **b :** an act of such exposure **2 :** the act or practice of behaving so as to attract attention to oneself — **ex·hi·bi·tion·ist** \-'bish-nist, -'bi-shə-\ *n or adj* — **ex·hi·bi·tion·is·tic** \-,bi-shə-'nis-tik\ *adj* — **ex·hi·bi·tion·is·ti·cal·ly** \-ti-k(ə-)lē\ *adv*

ex·hil·a·rate \ig-'zi-lə-,rāt\ *vt* **-rat·ed; -rat·ing** [L *exhilaratus*, pp. of *exhilarare*, fr. *ex-* + *hilarare* to gladden, fr. *hilarus* cheerful — more at HILARIOUS] (1540) **1 a :** to make cheerful **b :** ENLIVEN, EXCITE **2 :** REFRESH, STIMULATE — **ex·hil·a·rat·ing·ly** \ig-'zi-lə-,rā-tiŋ-lē\ *adv* — **ex·hil·a·ra·tive** \-,rā-tiv\ *adj*

ex·hil·a·ra·tion \ig-,zi-lə-'rā-shən\ *n* (ca. 1626) **1 :** the action of exhilarating **2 :** the feeling or the state of being exhilarated

ex·hort \ig-'zórt\ *vb* [ME, fr. MF *exhorter*, fr. L *exhortari*, fr. *ex-* + *hortari* to incite — more at YEARN] *vt* (15c) : to incite by argument or advice : urge strongly ~ *vi* **:** to give warnings or advice : make urgent appeals — **ex·hort·er** *n*

ex·hor·ta·tion \,ek-,sór-'tā-shən, -sər-; ,eg-,zór-, -zər-\ *n* (14c) **1 :** an act or instance of exhorting **2 :** language intended to incite and encourage

ex·hor·ta·tive \ig-'zór-tə-tiv\ *adj* (15c) : serving to exhort

ex·hor·ta·to·ry \-tə-,tór-ē, -,tór\ *adj* (15c) : using exhortation : EXHORTATIVE 〈an ~ appeal〉

ex·hume \ig-'züm, igz-'yüm, iks-'(h)yüm\ *vt* **ex·humed; ex·hum·ing** [F or ML; F *exhumer*, fr. ML *exhumare*, fr. L *ex* out of + *humus* earth — more at EX-, HUMBLE] (15c) **1 :** DISINTER **2 :** to bring back from neglect or obscurity — **ex·hu·ma·tion** \,eks-(h)yü-'mā-shən, ,eg-zü-, ,egz-yü-, ,ek-sə-'hyü-\ *n*

ex hy·po·the·si \,eks-hī-'pä-thə-,sī\ *adv* [NL, from a hypothesis] (1603) : according to assumptions made : by hypothesis 〈regard . . . all elites as *ex hypothesi* incompatible with democracy —P. G. J. Pulzer〉

ex·i·gence \'ek-sə-jən(t)s\ *n* (15c) : EXIGENCY

ex·i·gen·cy \'ek-sə-jən(t)-sē, ig-'zi-jən(t)-\ *n, pl* **-cies** (1581) **1 :** that which is required in a particular situation — usu. used in pl. **2 a :** the quality or state of being exigent **b :** a state of affairs that makes urgent demands 〈a leader must act in any sudden ~〉 *syn* see JUNCTURE

ex·i·gent \'ek-sə-jənt\ *adj* [L *exigent-, exigens*, prp. of *exigere* to demand — more at EXACT] (1629) **1 :** requiring immediate aid or action **2 :** requiring or calling for much : DEMANDING — **ex·i·gent·ly** *adv*

ex·i·gu·ity \,eg-zi-'gyü-ə-tē\ *n, pl* **-ities** (ca. 1626) : the quality or state of being exiguous : SCANTINESS

ex·ig·u·ous \ig-'zi-gyə-wəs\ *adj* [L *exiguus*, fr. *exigere*] (1651) : excessively scanty : INADEQUATE 〈wrest an ~ existence from the land〉 〈~ evidence〉 — **ex·ig·u·ous·ly** *adv* — **ex·ig·u·ous·ness** *n*

1ex·ile \'eg-,zīl, 'ek-,sīl\ *n* [ME *exil*, fr. MF, fr. L *exilium* fr. *exul, exsul* an exile] (14c) **1 a :** the state or a period of forced absence from one's country or home **b :** the state or a period of voluntary absence from one's country or home **2 :** a person who is in exile — **ex·il·ic** \eg-'zi-lik\ *adj*

²exile vt **ex·iled; ex·il·ing** (14c) : to banish or expel from one's own country or home   syn see BANISH

ex·im·i·ous \eg-ˈzi-mē-əs\ adj [L eximius, fr. eximere to take out — more at EXAMPLE] (1547) archaic : CHOICE, EXCELLENT

ex·ine \ˈek-ˌsēn, -ˌsīn\ n [ISV ex- + in- fibrous tissue, fr. Gk in-, is tendon] (ca. 1884) : the outer of the two major layers forming the walls of some spores and esp. pollen grains

ex·ist \ig-ˈzist\ vi [L exsistere to come into being, exist, fr. ex- + sistere to stand, stop; akin to L stare to stand — more at STAND] (1602)   **1 a** : to have real being whether material or spiritual ⟨did unicorns ~⟩ ⟨the largest galaxy known to ~⟩   **b** : to have being in a specified place or with respect to understood limitations or conditions ⟨strange ideas ~ed in his mind⟩   **2** : to continue to be ⟨racism still ~s in society⟩   **3 a** : to have life or the functions of vitality ⟨we cannot ~ without oxygen⟩   **b** : to live at an inferior level or under adverse circumstances ⟨the hungry ~ing from day to day⟩

ex·is·tence \-ˈzis-tən(t)s\ n (14c)   **1 a** obs : reality as opposed to appearance   **b** : reality as presented in experience   **c** (1) : the totality of existent things   (2) : a particular being ⟨all the fair ~s of heaven — John Keats⟩   **d** : sentient or living being : LIFE   **2 a** : the state or fact of having being esp. independently of human consciousness and as contrasted with nonexistence   **b** : the manner of being that is common to every mode of being   **c** : being with respect to a limiting condition or under a particular aspect   **3** : continued or repeated manifestation

ex·is·tent \-tənt\ adj [L exsistent-, exsistens, prp. of exsistere] (1561)   **1** : having being : EXISTING   **2** : existing now : PRESENT — **existent** n

ex·is·ten·tial \ˌeg-(ˌ)zis-ˈten(t)-shəl, ˌek-(ˌ)sis-\ adj (1693)   **1** : of, relating to, or affirming existence ⟨~ propositions⟩   **2 a** : grounded in existence or the experience of existence : EMPIRICAL   **b** : having being in time and space   **3** [trans. of Dan eksistentiel & G existential] : EXISTENTIALIST — **ex·is·ten·tial·ly** adv

ex·is·ten·tial·ism \-ˈten(t)-shə-ˌli-zəm\ n (1941) : a chiefly 20th century philosophical movement embracing diverse doctrines but centering on analysis of individual existence in an unfathomable universe and the plight of the individual who must assume ultimate responsibility for his acts of free will without any certain knowledge of what is right or wrong or good or bad

¹ex·is·ten·tial·ist \-list\ n (1942) : an adherent of existentialism

²existentialist adj (1946) : of or relating to existentialism or existentialists — **ex·is·ten·tial·is·tic** \-ˌten(t)-shə-ˈlis-tik\ adj — **ex·is·ten·tial·is·ti·cal·ly** \-ˈdän-tist\ n

existential quantifier n (1940) : a quantifier (as for some in "for some x, 2x + 5 = 8") that asserts that there exists at least one value of a variable — called also existential operator

¹ex·it \ˈeg-zət, ˈek-sət\ [L, he goes out, fr. exire to go out, fr. ex- + ire to go — more at ISSUE] (1538) — used as a stage direction to specify who goes off stage

²exit n [L exitus, fr. exire] (1588)   **1** [¹exit] : a departure from a stage   **2 a** : the act of going out or going away   **b** : DEATH   **3** : a way out of an enclosed place or space   **4** : one of the designated points of departure from an expressway — **ex·it·less** adj

³exit vi (1607)   **1** : to go out or away : DEPART   **2** : DIE   ~ vt : LEAVE 3a

exit poll n (1980) : a poll taken (as by news media) of voters leaving the voting place that is usu. used for predicting the winners — **exit polling** n

ex li·bris \eks-ˈlē-brəs, -ˌbrēs\ n, pl **ex libris** [NL, from the books; used before the owner's name on bookplates] (1880) : BOOKPLATE

Ex·moor \ˈek-ˌsmu̇r, -ˌsmȯr, -ˌsmŏr\ n [Exmoor, England] (1808)   **1** : any of a breed of horned sheep of Devonshire in England valued esp. for mutton   **2** : any of a breed of hardy ponies native to the Exmoor district and having a mealy-colored muzzle

Exmoor 1

ex ni·hi·lo \(ˌ)eks-ˈnē-(h)ə-ˌlō, -ˈni-, -ˈnī-\ adv or adj [L] (1580) : from or out of nothing ⟨creation ex nihilo⟩

exo- or **ex-** comb form [Gk exō out, outside, fr. ex out of — more at EX-]   **1** : outside ⟨exogamy⟩ : outer ⟨exoskeleton⟩ — compare ECT-, END-   **2** : turning out ⟨exoergic⟩

exo·bi·ol·o·gy \ˌek-sō-bī-ˈä-lə-jē\ n (1960) : a branch of biology concerned with the search for life outside the earth and with the effects of extraterrestrial environments on living organisms — **exo·bi·o·log·i·cal** \-ˌbī-ə-ˈlä-ji-kəl\ adj — **exo·bi·ol·o·gist** \-bī-ˈä-lə-jist\ n

exo·carp \ˈek-sō-ˌkärp\ n [ISV] (ca. 1845) : the outermost layer of the pericarp of a fruit — see ENDOCARP illustration

exo·crine \ˈek-sə-krən, -ˌkrīn, -ˌkrēn\ adj [ISV exo- + Gk krinein to separate — more at CERTAIN] (ca. 1911) : producing, being, or relating to a secretion that is released outside its source ⟨~ pancreatic cells⟩

exocrine gland n (ca. 1927) : a gland (as a salivary gland or part of the pancreas) that releases a secretion external to or at the surface of an organ by means of a canal or duct

exo·cy·clic \ˌek-sō-ˈsī-klik, -ˈsi-\ adj (1888) : situated outside of a ring in a chemical structure

exo·cy·to·sis \ˌek-sō-sī-ˈtō-səs\ n, pl **-to·ses** \-ˌsēz\ [NL, fr. exo- + cyt- + -osis] (1963) : the release of cellular substances (as secretory products) contained in cell vesicles by fusion of the vesicular membrane with the plasma membrane and subsequent release of the contents to the exterior of the cell — **exo·cy·tot·ic** \-ˈtä-tik\ adj

exo·der·mis \ˌek-sō-ˈdər-məs\ n [NL] (ca. 1900) : a layer of the outer living cortical cells of plants that takes over the functions of the epidermis in roots lacking secondary thickening

ex·odon·tia \ˌek-sə-ˈdän(t)-sh(ē-)ə\ n [NL, fr. ex- + -odontia] (1913) : a branch of dentistry that deals with the extraction of teeth — **ex·odon·tist** \-ˈdän-tist\ n

ex·o·dus \ˈek-sə-dəs, ˈeg-zə-\ n [L, fr. Gk Exodos, lit., road out, fr. ex- + hodos road]   **1** cap : the mainly narrative second book of canonical Jewish and Christian Scripture — see BIBLE table   **2** : a mass departure : EMIGRATION

exo·en·zyme \ˌek-sō-ˈen-ˌzīm\ n [ISV] (ca. 1923) : an extracellular enzyme

exo·er·gic \ˌek-sō-ˈər-jik\ adj (1942) : releasing energy : EXOTHERMIC

exo·eryth·ro·cyt·ic \ˌek-sō-i-ˌri-thrə-ˈsi-tik\ adj (1942) : occurring outside the red blood cells — used esp. of stages of malaria parasites

ex of·fi·cio \ˌek-sə-ˈfi-shē-ˌō, -sē-\ adv or adj [LL] (1533) : by virtue or because of an office ⟨the Vice President serves ex officio as president of the Senate⟩

ex·og·a·my \ek-ˈsä-gə-mē\ n, pl **-mies** (1865) : marriage outside of a specific group esp. as required by custom or law — **ex·og·a·mous** \ek-ˈsä-gə-məs\ or **exo·gam·ic** \ˌek-sə-ˈga-mik\ adj

ex·og·e·nous \ek-ˈsä-jə-nəs\ adj [F exogène exogenous, fr. exo- + -gène (fr. Gk -genēs born) — more at -GEN] (1830)   **1** : produced by growth from superficial tissue ⟨~ roots produced by leaves⟩   **2 a** : caused by factors (as food or a traumatic factor) or an agent (as a disease-producing organism) from outside the organism or system ⟨~ obesity⟩ ⟨~ psychic depression⟩   **b** : introduced from or produced outside the organism or system; specif : not synthesized within the organism or system — **ex·og·e·nous·ly** adv

ex·on \ˈek-ˌsän\ n [expressed sequence + ²-on] (ca. 1978) : a polynucleotide sequence in a nucleic acid that codes information for protein synthesis and that is copied and spliced together with other such sequences to form messenger RNA — compare INTRON — **ex·on·ic** \ek-ˈsä-nik\ adj

ex·on·er·ate \ig-ˈzä-nə-ˌrāt, eg-\ vt **-at·ed; -at·ing** [ME, fr. L exoneratus, pp. of exonerare to unburden, fr. ex- + oner-, onus load] (1524)   **1** : to relieve of a responsibility, obligation, or hardship   **2** : to clear from accusation or blame   syn see EXCULPATE — **ex·on·er·a·tion** \-ˌzä-nə-ˈrā-shən\ n — **ex·on·er·a·tive** \-ˈzä-nə-ˌrā-tiv\ adj

exo·nu·cle·ase \ˌek-sō-ˈnü-klē-ˌās, -ˈnyü-, -ˌāz\ n (1963) : an enzyme that breaks down a nucleic acid by removing nucleotides one by one from the end of a chain — compare ENDONUCLEASE

exo·nu·mia \ˌek-sə-ˈnü-mē-ə, -ˈnyü-\ n pl [NL, fr. exo- + E numismatic + NL -ia] (1966) : numismatic items (as tokens, medals, or scrip) other than coins and paper money

exo·pep·ti·dase \ˈpep-tə-ˌdās, -ˌdāz\ n (1936) : any of a group of enzymes that hydrolyze peptide bonds formed by the terminal amino acids of peptide chains : PEPTIDASE — compare ENDOPEPTIDASE

ex·oph·thal·mos also **ex·oph·thal·mus** \ˌek-ˌsäf-ˈthal-məs, -ˌsəf-, -ˌsäp-\ n [NL, fr. Gk exophthalmos having prominent eyes, fr. ex out + ophthalmos eye; akin to Gk ōps eye — more at EYE] (1872) : abnormal protrusion of the eyeball — **ex·oph·thal·mic** \-mik\ adj

ex·or·bi·tance \ig-ˈzȯr-bə-tən(t)s\ n (1611)   **1** : an exorbitant action or procedure; esp : excessive or gross deviation from rule, right, or propriety   **2** : the tendency or disposition to be exorbitant

ex·or·bi·tant \-tənt\ adj [ME, fr. MF, fr. LL exorbitant-, exorbitans, prp. of exorbitare to deviate, fr. L ex- + orbita track of a wheel, rut, fr. orbis disk, hoop] (15c)   **1** : not coming within the scope of the law   **2** : exceeding in intensity, quality, or size the customary or appropriate limits   syn see EXCESSIVE — **ex·or·bi·tant·ly** adv

ex·or·cise also **ex·or·cize** \ˈek-ˌsȯr-ˌsīz, -sər-\ vt **-cised** also **-cized; -cis·ing** also **-ciz·ing** [ME, fr. MF exorciser, fr. LL exorcizare, fr. Gk exorkizein, fr. ex- + horkizein to bind by oath, adjure, fr. horkos oath] (1539)   **1 a** : to expel (an evil spirit) by adjuration   **b** : to get rid of (something troublesome, menacing, or oppressive)   **2** : to free of an evil spirit — **ex·or·cis·er** n

ex·or·cism \-ˌsi-zəm\ n (14c)   **1** : the act or practice of exorcising   **2** : a spell or formula used in exorcising — **ex·or·cist** \-ˌsist, -səst\ n — **ex·or·cis·tic** \ˌek-ˌsȯr-ˈsis-tik, -sər-\ or **ex·or·cis·ti·cal** \-ti-kəl\ adj

ex·or·di·um \eg-ˈzȯr-dē-əm\ n, pl **-diums** or **-dia** \-dē-ə\ [L, fr. exordiri to begin, fr. ex- + ordiri to begin — more at ORDER] (1577)   **1** : a beginning or introduction esp. to a discourse or composition — **ex·or·di·al** \-dē-əl\ adj

exo·skel·e·ton \ˌek-sō-ˈske-lə-tᵊn\ n (1847)   **1** : an external supportive covering of an animal (as an arthropod)   **2** : bony or horny parts of a vertebrate produced from epidermal tissues — **exo·skel·e·tal** \-lə-tᵊl\ adj

exo·sphere \ˈek-sō-ˌsfir\ n [ISV] (1949) : the outer fringe region of the atmosphere of the earth or a planet — **exo·spher·ic** \ˌek-sō-ˈsfir-ik, -ˈsfer-\ adj

exo·spore \ˈek-sə-ˌspȯr, -ˌspŏr\ n [ISV] (1859) : an asexual spore cut off from a parent sporophore by the formation of septa

ex·os·to·sis \ˌek-(ˌ)säs-ˈtō-səs\ n, pl **-to·ses** \-ˌsēz\ [NL, fr. Gk exostō-sis, fr. ex out of + osteon bone — more at EX-, OSSEOUS] (1736) : a spur or bony outgrowth from a bone or the root of a tooth

ex·o·ter·ic \ˌek-sə-ˈter-ik\ adj [L & Gk; L exotericus, fr. Gk exōterikos, lit., external, fr. exōterō more outside, compar. of exō outside — more at EXO-] (1660)   **1 a** : suitable to be imparted to the public ⟨the ~ doctrine⟩ — compare ESOTERIC   **b** : belonging to the outer or less initiate circle   **2** : relating to the outside : EXTERNAL — **ex·o·ter·i·cal·ly** \-i-k(ə-)lē\ adv

exo·ther·mal \ˌek-sō-ˈthər-məl\ (1906) : EXOTHERMIC — **exo·ther·mal·ly** \-mə-lē\ adv

exo·ther·mic \-mik\ adj [ISV] (1884) : characterized by or formed with evolution of heat — **exo·ther·mi·cal·ly** \-mi-k(ə-)lē\ adv — **exo·ther·mi·ci·ty** \-ˌthər-ˈmis-ə-tē\ n

¹ex·ot·ic \ig-ˈzä-tik\ adj [L exoticus, fr. Gk exōtikos, fr. exō] (1599)   **1** : introduced from another country : not native to the place where found   **2** archaic : FOREIGN, ALIEN   **3** : strikingly, excitingly, or mysteriously different or unusual   **4** : of or relating to striptease ⟨~ dancing⟩ — **ex·ot·i·cal·ly** \-ti-k(ə-)lē\ adv — **ex·ot·ic·ness** \-tik-nəs\ n

²exotic n (1645)   **1** : one (as a plant or animal) that is exotic   **2** : STRIPTEASER

ex·ot·i·ca \ig-ˈzä-ti-kə\ n pl [NL, fr. L, neut. pl. of exoticus] (1876) : things excitingly different or unusual; esp : literary or artistic items having an exotic theme or nature

\ə\ abut \ᵊ\ kitten, F table \ər\ further \a\ ash \ā\ ace \ä\ mop, mar \au̇\ out \ch\ chin \e\ bet \ē\ easy \g\ go \i\ hit \ī\ ice \j\ job \ŋ\ sing \ō\ go \ȯ\ law \ȯi\ boy \th\ thin \th\ the \ü\ loot \u̇\ foot \y\ yet \zh\ vision \à, ᴋ, ⁿ, œ, œ̄, ᵫ, ᵬ, ᵬ\ see Guide to Pronunciation

ex·ot·i·cism \ig-'zä-tə-,si-zəm\ *also* **ex·o·tism** \'eg-zə-,ti-zəm, 'ek-sə-\ *n* (1827) : the quality or state of being exotic

exo·tox·in \,ek-sō-'täk-sən\ *n* [ISV] (1920) : a soluble poisonous substance produced during growth of a microorganism and released into the surrounding medium

ex·pand \ik-'spand\ *vb* [ME *expaunden,* fr. L *expandere,* fr. *ex-* + *pandere* to spread — more at FATHOM] *vt* (15c) **1** : to open up : UNFOLD **2** : to increase the extent, number, volume, or scope of : ENLARGE **3 a** : to express at length or in greater detail **b** : to write out in full ⟨~ all abbreviations⟩ **c** : to subject to mathematical expansion ⟨~ a function in a power series⟩ ~ *vi* **1** : to open out : SPREAD **2** : to increase in extent, number, volume, or scope **3** : to speak or write fully or in detail ⟨~*ed* on the theme⟩ **4** : to feel generous or optimistic — **ex·pand·abil·i·ty** \-,span-də-'bi-lə-tē\ *n* — **ex·pand·able** \-'span-də-bəl\ *adj*

syn EXPAND, AMPLIFY, SWELL, DISTEND, INFLATE, DILATE mean to increase in size or volume. EXPAND may apply whether the increase comes from within or without and regardless of manner (as growth, unfolding, addition of parts). AMPLIFY implies the extension or enlargement of something inadequate. SWELL implies gradual expansion beyond a thing's original or normal limits. DISTEND implies outward extension caused by pressure from within. INFLATE implies expanding by introduction of air or something insubstantial and suggests a resulting vulnerability and liability to sudden collapse. DILATE applies esp. to expansion of circumference.

ex·pand·ed *adj* (1875) *of a typeface* : EXTENDED

expanded metal *n* (1890) : sheet metal cut and expanded into a lattice and used esp. as lath

expanded plastic *n* (1945) : lightweight cellular plastic used esp. as insulation and protective packing material — called also *foamed plastic, plastic foam*

ex·pand·er \ik-'span-dər\ *n* (1862) : one that expands; *specif* : any of several colloidal substances (as dextran) of high molecular weight used as a blood or plasma substitute for increasing the blood volume

ex·panse \ik-'span(t)s\ *n* [NL *expansum,* fr. L *expansus,* pp. of *expandere*] (1667) **1** : FIRMAMENT **2** : great extent of something spread out ⟨an ~ of calm ocean⟩

ex·pan·si·ble \ik-'span(t)-sə-bəl\ *adj* (ca. 1691) : capable of being expanded — **ex·pan·si·bil·i·ty** \-,span(t)-sə-'bi-lə-tē\ *n*

ex·pan·sion \ik-'span(t)-shən\ *n* (1611) **1** : EXPANSE **2** : the act or process of expanding ⟨territorial ~⟩ **3** : the quality or state of being expanded **4** : the increase in volume of working fluid (as steam) in an engine cylinder after cutoff or in an internal combustion engine after explosion **5 a** : an expanded part **b** : something that results from an act of expanding ⟨the book is an ~ of a lecture series⟩ **6** : the result of carrying out an indicated mathematical operation : the expression of a function in the form of a series — **ex·pan·sion·al** \-'panch-nəl, -chə-nᵊl\ *adj*

ex·pan·sion·ary \ik-'span(t)-shə-,ner-ē\ *adj* (1936) : tending toward expansion ⟨an ~ economy⟩

ex·pan·sion·ism \ik-'span-(t)-shə-,ni-zəm\ *n* (1899) : a policy or practice of expansion and esp. of territorial expansion by a nation — **ex·pan·sion·ist** \-'span(t)-sh(ə-)nist\ *n* — **expansionist** *also* **ex·pan·sion·is·tic** \-,span(t)-shə-'nis-tik\ *adj*

ex·pan·sive \ik-'span(t)-siv\ *adj* (1651) **1** : having a capacity or a tendency to expand **2** : causing or tending to cause expansion **3 a** : characterized by high spirits, generosity, or readiness to talk : OPEN ⟨grew ~ after dinner⟩ **b** : marked by or indicative of exaggerated euphoria and delusions of self-importance ⟨an ~ patient⟩ **4** : marked by expansion; *esp* : having a great expanse or extent : SIZABLE, EXTENSIVE **5** : characterized by richness, abundance, or magnificence ⟨~ living⟩ — **ex·pan·sive·ly** *adv* — **ex·pan·sive·ness** *n*

ex·pan·siv·i·ty \,ek-,span-'si-və-tē, ik-\ *n* (1837) : the quality or state of being expansive; *esp* : the capacity to expand

ex par·te \(,)eks-'pär-tē\ *adv or adj* (1672) **1** : on or from one side or party only — used of legal proceedings **2** : from a one-sided or partisan point of view

ex·pat \'eks-,pat\ *n* (1962) *chiefly Brit* : an expatriate person : EXPATRIATE

ex·pa·ti·ate \ek-'spā-shē-,āt\ *vi* -at·ed; -at·ing [L *exspatiatus,* pp. of *exspatiari* to wander, digress, fr. *ex-* + *spatium* space, course] (1538) **1** : to move about freely or at will : WANDER **2** : to speak or write at length or in detail ⟨expatiating upon the value of the fabric —Thomas Hardy⟩ — **ex·pa·ti·a·tion** \(,)ek-,spā-shē-'ā-shən\ *n*

¹ex·pa·tri·ate \ek-'spā-trē-,āt\ *vb* -at·ed; -at·ing [ML *expatriatus,* pp. of *expatriare* to leave one's own country, fr. L *ex-* + *patria* native country, fr. fem. of *patrius* of a father, fr. *pater-, pater* father — more at FATHER] *vt* (1784) **1** : to withdraw (oneself) from residence in or allegiance to one's native country **2** : BANISH, EXILE ~ *vi* : to leave one's native country to live elsewhere; *also* : to renounce allegiance to one's native country — **ex·pa·tri·ate** \-,āt, -ət\ *n* — **ex·pa·tri·a·tion** \(,)ek-,spā-trē-'ā-shən\ *n*

²ex·pa·tri·ate \ek-'spā-trē-ət, -,trē-,āt\ *adj* (1812) : living in a foreign land

ex·pa·tri·a·tism \ek-'spā-trē-ə-,ti-zəm\ *n* (1937) : the fact or state of being an expatriate

ex·pect \ik-'spekt\ *vb* [L *exspectare* to look forward to, fr. *ex-* + *spectare* to look at, fr. *spectus,* pp. of *specere* to look — more at SPY] *vi* (1560) **1** *archaic* : WAIT, STAY **2** : to look forward **3** : to be pregnant : await the birth of one's child — used in progressive tenses ⟨she's ~*ing* next month⟩ ~ *vt* **1** *archaic* : AWAIT **2** : SUPPOSE, THINK **3** : to anticipate or look forward to the coming or occurrence of ⟨we ~ them any minute now⟩ ⟨~*ed* a telephone call⟩ **4 a** : to consider probable or certain ⟨~ to be forgiven⟩ ⟨~ that things will improve⟩ **b** : to consider reasonable, due, or necessary ⟨~*ed* hard work from the students⟩ **c** : to consider bound in duty or obligated ⟨they ~ you to pay your bills⟩ — **ex·pect·able** \-'spek-tə-bəl\ *adj* — **ex·pect·ably** \-blē\ *adv* — **ex·pect·ed·ly** *adv* — **ex·pect·ed·ness** *n*

syn EXPECT, HOPE, LOOK mean to await some occurrence or outcome. EXPECT implies a high degree of certainty and usu. involves the idea of preparing or envisioning ⟨expects to be finished by Tuesday⟩. HOPE implies little certainty but suggests confidence or assurance in the possibility that what one desires or longs for will happen ⟨hopes to find a job soon⟩. LOOK, with *to,* implies assurance that expectations

will be fulfilled ⟨*looks* to a tidy profit from the sale⟩; with *for* it implies less assurance and suggests an attitude of expectancy and watchfulness ⟨*look* for rain when the wind shifts to the northeast⟩.

ex·pec·tance \ik-'spek-tən(t)s\ *n* (1603) : EXPECTANCY

ex·pec·tan·cy \-tən(t)-sē\ *n, pl* -cies (1600) **1 a** : the act, action, or state of expecting **b** : the state of being expected **2 a** : something expected **b** : the expected amount (as of the number of years of life) based on statistical probability ⟨life ~⟩

¹ex·pec·tant \-tənt\ *adj* (14c) **1** : characterized by expectation **2** : expecting the birth of a child ⟨~ mothers⟩ — **ex·pec·tant·ly** *adv*

²expectant *n* (1628) : one who is looking forward to something

ex·pec·ta·tion \,ek-,spek-'tā-shən, ik-\ *n* (1540) **1** : the act or state of expecting : ANTICIPATION **2 a** : something expected ⟨not up to ~s⟩ **b** : basis for expecting : ASSURANCE ⟨they have every ~ of success⟩ **c** : prospects of inheritance — usu. used in pl. **3** : the state of being expected **4** : EXPECTANCY 2b **b** : EXPECTED VALUE — **ex·pec·ta·tion·al** \-'tā-shə-nᵊl, -shnəl\ *adj*

ex·pec·ta·tive \ik-'spek-tə-tiv\ *adj* (15c) : of, relating to, or constituting an object of expectation

expected value *n* (1947) **1** : the sum of the values of a random variable with each value multiplied by its probability of occurrence **2** : the integral of the product of a probability density function of a continuous random variable and the random variable itself when taken over all possible values of the variable

ex·pec·to·rant \ik-'spek-t(ə-)rənt\ *n* (1782) : an agent that promotes the discharge or expulsion of mucus from the respiratory tract; *broadly* : an antitussive agent — **expectorant** *adj*

ex·pec·to·rate \-tə-,rāt\ *vb* -rat·ed; -rat·ing [L *expectoratus,* pp. of *expectorare* to banish from the mind (taken to mean lit. "to expel from the chest"), fr. *ex-* + *pector-, pectus* breast, soul — more at PECTORAL] *vt* (1601) **1** : to eject from the throat or lungs by coughing or hawking and spitting **2** : SPIT ~ *vi* **1** : to discharge matter from the throat or lungs by coughing or hawking and spitting **2** : SPIT — **ex·pec·to·ra·tion** \-,spek-tə-'rā-shən\ *n*

ex·pe·di·ence \ik-'spē-dē-ən(t)s\ *n* (1593) : EXPEDIENCY

ex·pe·di·en·cy \-dən-sē\ *n, pl* -cies (1612) **1** : the quality or state of being suited to the end in view : SUITABILITY, FITNESS **2** *obs* **a** : HASTE, DISPATCH **b** : an enterprise requiring haste or caution **3** : adherence to expedient means and methods ⟨put more emphasis on ~ than on principle —W. H. Jones⟩ **4** : a means of achieving a particular end : EXPEDIENT — **ex·pe·di·en·tial** \-,spē-dē-'en-chəl\ *adj*

¹ex·pe·di·ent \ik-'spē-dē-ənt\ *adj* [ME, fr. MF or L; MF, fr. L *expedient-, expediens,* prp. of *expedire* to extricate, prepare, be useful, fr. *ex-* + *ped-, pes* foot — more at FOOT] (14c) **1** : suitable for achieving a particular end in a given circumstance **2** : characterized by concern with what is opportune; *esp* : governed by self-interest — **ex·pe·di·ent·ly** *adv*

syn EXPEDIENT, POLITIC, ADVISABLE mean dictated by practical or prudent motives. EXPEDIENT usu. implies what is immediately advantageous without regard for ethics or consistent principles ⟨a politically *expedient* decision⟩. POLITIC stresses judiciousness and tactical value but usu. implies some lack of candor or sincerity ⟨a *politic* show of interest⟩. ADVISABLE applies to what is practical, prudent, or advantageous but lacks the derogatory implication of EXPEDIENT and POLITIC ⟨sometimes it's *advisable* to say nothing⟩.

²expedient *n* (1653) : something expedient : a temporary means to an end *syn* see RESOURCE

ex·pe·dite \'ek-spə-,dīt\ *vt* -dit·ed; -dit·ing [L *expeditus,* pp. of *expedire*] (15c) **1** : to execute promptly **2** : to accelerate the process or progress of : speed up **3** : ISSUE, DISPATCH

ex·pe·dit·er *also* **ex·pe·di·tor** \-,dī-tər\ *n* (1891) : one that expedites; *specif* : one employed to ensure efficient movement of goods or supplies in a business

ex·pe·di·tion \,ek-spə-'di-shən\ *n* (15c) **1 a** : a journey or excursion undertaken for a specific purpose **b** : the group of persons making such a journey **2** : efficient promptness : SPEED **3** : a sending or setting forth *syn* see HASTE

ex·pe·di·tion·ary \-'di-shə-,ner-ē\ *adj* (1817) : of, relating to, or being an expedition; *also* : sent on military service abroad ⟨an ~ force⟩

ex·pe·di·tious \,ek-spə-'di-shəs\ *adj* (1559) : characterized by or acting promptly and efficiently *syn* see FAST — **ex·pe·di·tious·ly** *adv* — **ex·pe·di·tious·ness** *n*

ex·pel \ik-'spel\ *vt* ex·pelled; ex·pel·ling [ME *expellen,* fr. L *expellere,* fr. *ex-* + *pellere* to drive — more at FELT] (14c) **1** : to force out : EJECT ⟨*expelled* the smoke from her lungs⟩ **2** : to force to leave (as a place or organization) by official action : take away rights or privileges of membership ⟨*expelled* from college⟩ *syn* see EJECT — **ex·pel·la·ble** \-'spe-lə-bəl\ *adj*

ex·pel·lee \,ek-,spe-'lē, ik-\ *n* (1888) : a person who is expelled esp. from a native or adopted country

ex·pend \ik-'spend\ *vt* [ME, fr. L *expendere* to weigh out, expend, fr. *ex-* + *pendere* to weigh — more at SPIN] (15c) **1** : to pay out : SPEND ⟨the social services upon which public revenue is ~*ed* —J. A. Hobson⟩ **2** : to make use of for a specific purpose : UTILIZE ⟨projects on which they ~*ed* great energy⟩; *also* : USE UP — **ex·pend·er** *n*

¹ex·pend·able \ik-'spen-də-bəl\ *adj* (1805) : that may be expended: as **a** : normally used up or consumed in service ⟨~ supplies like pencils and paper⟩ **b** : more easily or economically replaced than rescued, salvaged, or protected — **ex·pend·abil·i·ty** \-,spen-də-'bi-lə-tē\ *n*

²expendable *n* (1942) : one that is expendable — usu. used in pl.

ex·pen·di·ture \ik-'spen-di-chər, -də-,chùr, -də-,t(y)ùr\ *n* [irreg. fr. *expend*] (1769) **1** : the act or process of expending ⟨an ~ of energy⟩ **2** : something expended : DISBURSEMENT, EXPENSE ⟨income should exceed ~s⟩

¹ex·pense \ik-'spen(t)s\ *n* [ME, fr. AF or LL; AF, fr. LL *expensa,* fr. L, fem. of *expensus,* pp. of *expendere*] (14c) **1** *archaic* : the act or an instance of expending : EXPENDITURE **2 a** : something expended to secure a benefit or bring about a result **b** : financial burden or outlay : COST ⟨the monument at their own ~⟩ **c** : an item of business outlay chargeable against revenue for a specific period **3** : a cause or occasion of expenditure ⟨an estate is a great ~⟩ **4** : a loss, detriment, or embarrassment that results from some action or gain : SACRIFICE ⟨everyone had a good laugh at my ~⟩ — usu. used in the phrase *at the*

expense of ⟨develop a boy's physique at the ~ of his intelligence —Bertrand Russell⟩
²**expense** *vt* **ex·pensed; ex·pens·ing** (ca. 1909) **1** : to charge with expenses **2 a** : to charge to an expense account **b** : to write off as an expense
expense account *n* (1872) : an account of expenses reimbursable to an employee; *also* : the right of charging expenses to such an account
ex·pen·sive \ik-'spen(t)-siv\ *adj* (1634) **1** : involving high cost or sacrifice ⟨an ~ hobby⟩ **2 a** : commanding a high price and esp. one that is not based on intrinsic worth or is beyond a prospective buyer's means **b** : characterized by high prices ⟨~ shops⟩ — **ex·pen·sive·ly** *adv* — **ex·pen·sive·ness** *n*
¹**ex·pe·ri·ence** \ik-'spir-ē-ən(t)s\ *n* [ME, fr. MF, fr. L *experientia* act of trying, fr. *experient-, experiens*, prp. of *experiri* to try, fr. *ex-* + *-periri* (akin to *periculum* attempt) — more at FEAR] (14c) **1 a** : direct observation of or participation in events as a basis of knowledge **b** : the fact or state of having been affected by or gained knowledge through direct observation or participation **2 a** : practical knowledge, skill, or practice derived from direct observation of or participation in events or in a particular activity **b** : the length of such participation ⟨has 10 years ~ in the job⟩ **3 a** : the conscious events that make up an individual life **b** : the events that make up the conscious past of a community or nation or mankind generally **4** : something personally encountered, undergone, or lived through **5** : the act or process of directly perceiving events or reality
²**experience** *vt* **-enced; -enc·ing** (1580) **1** : to learn by experience ⟨I have *experienced* that a landscape and the sky unfold the deepest beauty —Nathaniel Hawthorne⟩ **2** : to have experience of : UNDERGO ⟨*experienced* severe hardships as a child⟩
ex·pe·ri·enced \-ən(t)st\ *adj* (1576) : made skillful or wise through experience : PRACTICED ⟨an ~ driver⟩
ex·pe·ri·en·tial \ik-,spir-ē-'en(t)-shəl\ *adj* (1816) : relating to, derived from, or providing experience : EMPIRICAL ⟨~ knowledge⟩ ⟨~ lessons⟩ — **ex·pe·ri·en·tial·ly** \-'en(t)-sh(ə-)lē\ *adv*
¹**ex·per·i·ment** \ik-'sper-ə-mənt *also* -'spir-\ *n* [ME, fr. MF, fr. L *experimentum*, fr. *experiri*] (14c) **1 a** : TEST, TRIAL ⟨make another ~ of his suspicion —Shak.⟩ **b** : a tentative procedure or policy **c** : an operation carried out under controlled conditions in order to discover an unknown effect or law, to test or establish a hypothesis, or to illustrate a known law **2** *obs* : EXPERIENCE **3** : the process of testing : EXPERIMENTATION
²**ex·per·i·ment** \-,ment\ *vi* (1787) : to carry out experiments : try out a new procedure, idea, or activity — **ex·per·i·men·ta·tion** \ik-,sper-ə-mən-'tā-shən, -,men- *also* -,spir-\ *n* — **ex·per·i·ment·er** \-'sper-ə-,men-tər *also* -'spir-\ *n*
ex·per·i·men·tal \ik-,sper-ə-'men-tᵊl *also* -,spir-\ *adj* (15c) **1** : of, relating to, or based on experience or experiment **2 a** : serving the ends of or used as a means of experimentation ⟨an ~ school⟩ **b** : relating to or having the characteristics of experiment : TENTATIVE ⟨still in the ~ stage⟩ — **ex·per·i·men·tal·ly** \-tᵊl-ē\ *adv*
ex·per·i·men·tal·ism \-tᵊl-,i-zəm\ *n* (ca. 1834) : reliance on or advocacy of experimental or empirical principles and procedures; *specif* : INSTRUMENTALISM
ex·per·i·men·tal·ist \-tᵊl-əst\ *n* (1762) : one who experiments; *specif* : a person conducting scientific experiments
experiment station *n* (1874) : an establishment for scientific research (as in agriculture) where experiments are carried out, studies of practical application are made, and information is disseminated
¹**ex·pert** \'ek-,spərt, ik-'\ *adj* [ME, fr. MF & L; MF, fr. L *expertus*, fr. pp. of *experiri*] (14c) **1** *obs* : EXPERIENCED **2** : having, involving, or displaying special skill or knowledge derived from training or experience *syn* see PROFICIENT — **ex·pert·ly** *adv* — **ex·pert·ness** *n*
²**ex·pert** \'ek-,spərt\ *n* [F, fr. *expert*, adj.] (1535) : one with the special skill or knowledge representing mastery of a particular subject
³**ex·pert** \'ek-,spərt\ *vi* (ca. 1889) : to serve as an expert
ex·per·tise \,ek-(,)spər-'tēz, -'tēs\ *n* [F, fr. MF, expertness, fr. *expert*] (1868) **1** : expert opinion or commentary **2** : the skill of an expert
ex·pert·ism \'ek-,spər-,ti-zəm\ *n* (1886) : EXPERTISE 2
ex·pert·ize \'ek-spər-,tiz\ *vb* **-ized; -iz·ing** *vi* (1889) : to give a professional opinion usu. after careful study ~ *vt* : to examine and give expert judgment on
expert system *n* (1977) : computer software that attempts to mimic the reasoning of a human specialist
ex·pi·ate \'ek-spē-,āt\ *vb* **-at·ed; -at·ing** [L *expiatus*, pp. of *expiare* to atone for, fr. *ex-* + *piare* to atone for, appease, fr. *pius* faithful, pious] *vt* (1594) **1** *obs* : to put an end to **2 a** : to extinguish the guilt incurred by **b** : to make amends for ⟨permission to ~ their offences by their assiduous labours —Francis Bacon⟩ ~ *vi* : to make expiation — **ex·pi·a·ble** \'ek-spē-ə-bəl\ *adj* — **ex·pi·a·tor** \-spē-,ā-tər\ *n*
ex·pi·a·tion \,ek-spē-'ā-shən\ *n* (15c) **1** : the act of making atonement **2** : the means by which atonement is made
ex·pi·a·to·ry \'ek-spē-ə-,tōr-ē, -,tor-ē\ *adj* (15c) : serving to expiate
ex·pi·ra·tion \,ek-spə-'rā-shən\ *n* (1526) **1 a** : the last emission of breath : DEATH **b** (1) : the act or process of releasing air from the lungs through the nose or mouth (2) : the escape of carbon dioxide from the body protoplasm (as through the blood and lungs or by diffusion) **2** : the fact of coming to an end or the point at which something ends : TERMINATION
ex·pi·ra·to·ry \ik-'spī-rə-,tōr-ē, ek-', -,tor-; 'ek-sp(ə-)rə-\ *adj* (ca. 1847) : of, relating to, or employed in the expiration of air from the lungs
ex·pire \ik-'spīr, *oftenest for vi 3 and vt 2* ek-\ *vb* **ex·pired; ex·pir·ing** [ME, fr. MF or L; MF *expirer*, fr. L *exspirare*, fr. *ex-* + *spirare* to breathe] *vi* (14c) **1** : to breathe one's last breath : DIE **2** : to come to an end **3** : to emit the breath ~ *vt* **1** *obs* : CONCLUDE **2** : to breathe out from or as if from the lungs **3** *archaic* : EMIT
ex·pi·ry \ik-'spīr-ē, 'ek-spə-rē\ *n, pl* **-ries** (1752) : EXPIRATION: as **a** : exhalation of breath **b** : DEATH **c** : TERMINATION; *esp* : the termination of a time or period fixed by law, contract, or agreement
ex·plain \ik-'splān\ *vb* [ME *explanen*, fr. L *explanare*, lit., to make level, fr. *ex-* + *planus* level, flat — more at FLOOR] *vt* (15c) **1 a** : to make known **b** : to make plain or understandable ⟨footnotes that ~ the terms⟩ **2** : to give the reason for or cause of **3** : to show the logical development or relationships of ~ *vi* : to make something plain or understandable — **ex·plain·able** \-'splā-nə-bəl\ *adj* — **ex·plain·er** *n*

— **explain oneself** : to clarify one's statements or the reasons for one's conduct
syn EXPLAIN, EXPOUND, EXPLICATE, ELUCIDATE, INTERPRET mean to make something clear or understandable. EXPLAIN implies a making plain or intelligible what is not immediately obvious or entirely known ⟨*explain* the rules⟩. EXPOUND implies a careful often elaborate explanation ⟨*expounding* a scientific theory⟩. EXPLICATE adds the idea of a developed or detailed analysis ⟨*explicate* a poem⟩. ELUCIDATE stresses the throwing of light upon as by offering details or motives previously unclear or only implicit ⟨*elucidate* an obscure passage⟩. INTERPRET adds to EXPLAIN the need for imagination or sympathy or special knowledge in dealing with something ⟨*interpreting* a work of art⟩.
explain away *vt* (1704) **1** : to get rid of by or as if by explanation **2** : to minimize the significance of by or as if by explanation
ex·pla·na·tion \,ek-splə-'nā-shən\ *n* (14c) **1** : the act or process of explaining **2** : something that explains ⟨gave no ~⟩
ex·plan·a·tive \ik-'spla-nə-tiv\ *adj* (ca. 1616) : EXPLANATORY — **explan·a·tive·ly** *adv*
ex·plan·a·to·ry \ik-'spla-nə-,tōr-ē, -,tor-\ *adj* (1618) : serving to explain ⟨~ notes⟩ — **ex·plan·a·to·ri·ly** \-,spla-nə-'tōr-ə-lē, -'tor-\ *adv*
¹**ex·plant** \(,)ek-'splant\ *vt* [*ex-* + *-plant* (as in *implant*)] (1915) : to remove (living tissue) esp. to a medium for tissue culture — **ex·plan·ta·tion** \,ek-,splan-'tā-shən\ *n*
²**ex·plant** \'ek-,splant\ *n* (1917) : living tissue removed from an organism and placed in a medium for tissue culture
¹**ex·ple·tive** \'ek-splə-tiv\ *n* (1612) **1 a** : a syllable, word, or phrase inserted to fill a vacancy (as in a sentence or a metrical line) without adding to the sense; *esp* : a word (as *it* in "make it clear which you prefer") that occupies the position of the subject or object of a verb in normal English word order and anticipates a subsequent word or phrase that supplies the needed meaningful content **b** : an exclamatory word or phrase; *esp* : one that is obscene or profane **2** : one that serves to fill out or as a filling
²**expletive** *adj* [LL *expletivus*, fr. L *expletus*, pp. of *explēre* to fill out, fr. *ex-* + *plēre* to fill — more at FULL] (1666) **1** : serving to fill up ⟨~ phrases⟩ **2** : marked by the use of expletives
ex·ple·to·ry \'ek-splə-,tōr-ē, -,tor-ē\ *adj* (1672) : EXPLETIVE
ex·pli·ca·ble \ek-'spli-kə-bəl, 'ek-(,)splik-\ *adj* (1556) : capable of being explained — **ex·pli·ca·bly** \-blē\ *adv*
ex·pli·cate \'ek-splə-,kāt\ *vt* **-cat·ed; -cat·ing** [L *explicatus*, pp. of *explicare*, lit., to unfold, fr. *ex-* + *plicare* to fold — more at PLY] (1531) **1** : to give a detailed explanation of **2** : to develop the implications of : analyze logically *syn* see EXPLAIN — **ex·pli·ca·tion** \,ek-splə-'kā-shən\ *n* — **ex·pli·ca·tor** \'ek-splə-,kā-tər\ *n*
ex·pli·ca·tion de texte \ek-splē-kä-syōⁿ-də-tekst\ *n, pl* **explications de texte** *same*\ [F, lit., explanation of text] (1935) : a method of literary criticism involving a detailed analysis of a work
ex·pli·ca·tive \ek-'spli-kə-tiv, 'ek-splə-,kāt-\ *adj* (1649) : serving to explicate; *specif* : serving to explain logically what is contained in the subject ⟨an ~ proposition⟩ — **ex·pli·ca·tive·ly** *adv*
ex·pli·ca·to·ry \ek-'spli-kə-,tōr-ē, -,tor-; 'ek-(,)spli-, -,tor-\ *adj* (1625) : EXPLICATIVE
ex·plic·it \ik-'spli-sət\ *adj* [F or ML; F *explicite*, fr. ML *explicitus*, fr. L, pp. of *explicare*] (ca. 1609) **1 a** : fully revealed or expressed without vagueness, implication, or ambiguity : leaving no question as to meaning or intent ⟨~ instructions⟩ **b** : open in the depiction of nudity or sexuality ⟨~ books and films⟩ **2** : fully developed or formulated ⟨an ~ plan⟩ ⟨an ~ notion of our objective⟩ **3** : unambiguous in expression ⟨was very ~ on how we are to behave⟩ **4** *of a mathematical function* : defined by an expression containing only independent variables — compare IMPLICIT 1c — **ex·plic·it·ly** *adv* — **ex·plic·it·ness** *n*
syn EXPLICIT, DEFINITE, EXPRESS, SPECIFIC mean perfectly clear in meaning. EXPLICIT implies such verbal plainness and distinctness that there is no need for inference and no room for difficulty in understanding ⟨*explicit* instructions⟩. DEFINITE stresses precise, clear statement or arrangement that leaves no doubt or indecision ⟨the law is *definite* in such cases⟩. EXPRESS implies both explicitness and direct and positive utterance ⟨her *express* wishes⟩. SPECIFIC applies to what is precisely and fully treated in detail or particular ⟨two *specific* criticisms⟩.
ex·plode \ik-'splōd\ *vb* **ex·plod·ed; ex·plod·ing** [L *explodere* to drive off the stage by clapping, fr. *ex-* + *plaudere* to clap] *vt* (ca. 1611) **1** *archaic* : to drive from the stage by noisy disapproval **2** : to bring into disrepute or discredit ⟨~ a theory⟩ **3** : to cause to explode or burst noisily ⟨~ a bomb⟩ ~ *vi* **1** : to burst forth with sudden violence or noise from internal energy: as **a** : to undergo a rapid chemical or nuclear reaction with the production of noise, heat, and violent expansion of gases ⟨dynamite ~s⟩ **b** : to burst violently as a result of pressure from within **2 a** : to give forth a sudden strong and noisy outburst of emotion ⟨*exploded* in anger⟩ **b** : to move with sudden speed and force ⟨*exploded* from the starting gate⟩ **3** : to increase rapidly ⟨the population of the city *exploded*⟩ — **ex·plod·er** *n*
ex·plod·ed *adj* (1944) : showing the parts separated but in correct relationship to each other ⟨an ~ view of a carburetor⟩
¹**ex·ploit** \'ek-,sploit, ik-'\ *n* [ME, outcome, success, fr. MF, fr. L *explicitum*, neut. of *explicitus*, pp.] (ca. 1538) : DEED, ACT; *esp* : a notable or heroic act *syn* see FEAT
²**ex·ploit** \ik-'sploit, 'ek-,\ *vt* (1838) **1** : to make productive use of : UTILIZE ⟨~*ing* your talents⟩ ⟨~ your opponent's weakness⟩ **2** : to make use of meanly or unjustly for one's own advantage ⟨~*ing* migrant farm workers⟩ — **ex·ploit·able** \-'sploi-tə-bəl\ *adj* — **ex·ploit·er** *n*
ex·ploi·ta·tion \,ek-,sploi-'tā-shən\ *n* (1803) : an act or instance of exploiting ⟨~ of natural resources⟩ ⟨~ of immigrant laborers⟩ ⟨clever ~ of the system⟩
ex·ploit·ative \ik-'sploi-tə-tiv, 'ek-,sploi-\ *adj* (1885) : exploiting or tending to exploit; *esp* : unfairly or cynically using another person or

---

\ə\ abut \ᵊ\ kitten, F table \ər\ further \a\ ash \ā\ ace \ä\ mop, mar
\aú\ out \ch\ chin \e\ bet \ē\ easy \g\ go \i\ hit \ī\ ice \j\ job
\ŋ\ sing \ō\ go \ò\ law \ òi\ boy \th\ thin \t͟h\ the \ü\ loot \ú\ foot
\y\ yet \zh\ vision \á, k̲, ⁿ, œ, œ̄, ue, ūe, ᵞ\ see Guide to Pronunciation

group for profit or advantage ⟨∼ terms of employment⟩ ⟨an ∼ film⟩ — **ex·ploit·ative·ly** *adv*

ex·ploit·ive \ik-'sploi-tiv\ *adj* (1921) : EXPLOITATIVE

ex·plo·ra·tion \,ek-splə-'rā-shən, -,splō-\ *n* (1537) : the act or an instance of exploring — **ex·plo·ra·tion·al** \-shnəl, -shə-n³l\ *adj*

ex·plor·ative \ik-'splōr-ə-tiv, -'splȯr-\ *adj* (1738) : EXPLORATORY — **ex·plor·ative·ly** *adv*

ex·plor·ato·ry \-ə-,tōr-ē, -,tȯr-\ *adj* (1620) : of, relating to, or being exploration ⟨∼ surgery⟩ ⟨∼ drilling for oil⟩

ex·plore \ik-'splōr, -'splȯr\ *vb* **ex·plored; ex·plor·ing** [L *explorare*, fr. *ex-* + *plorare* to cry out] *vt* (1585) **1 a** : to investigate, study, or analyze : look into ⟨∼ the relationship between social class and learning ability⟩ — sometimes used with indirect questions ⟨to ∼ where ethical issues arise —R. T. Blackburn⟩ **b** : to become familiar with by testing or experimenting ⟨∼ new cuisines⟩ **2** : to travel over (new territory) for adventure or discovery **3** : to examine minutely esp. for diagnostic purposes ⟨∼ the wound⟩ ∼ *vi* : to make or conduct a systematic search ⟨∼ for oil⟩

ex·plor·er \ik-'splōr-ər, -'splȯr-\ *n* (1685) **1** : one that explores; *esp* : a person who travels in search of geographical or scientific information **2** *cap* : a member of a coed scouting program of the Boy Scouts of America for young people ages 14 to 20 focusing on career awareness

ex·plo·sion \ik-'splō-zhən\ *n* [L *explosion-, explosio* act of driving off by clapping, fr. *explodere*] (ca. 1616) **1** : the act or an instance of exploding ⟨injured in a laboratory ∼⟩ **2** : a large-scale, rapid, or spectacular expansion or bursting out or forth ⟨the ∼ of suburbia⟩ ⟨an ∼ of red hair⟩ **3** : the release of occluded breath that occurs in one kind of articulation of stop consonants

¹ex·plo·sive \ik-'splō-siv, -ziv\ *adj* (1667) **1 a** : relating to, characterized by, or operated by explosion ⟨an ∼ hatch⟩ **b** : resulting from or as if from an explosion ⟨∼ population growth⟩ **2 a** : tending to explode ⟨an ∼ person⟩ **b** : likely to erupt in or produce hostile reaction or violence ⟨an ∼ ghetto situation⟩ — **ex·plo·sive·ly** *adv* — **ex·plo·sive·ness** *n*

²explosive *n* (1874) **1** : an explosive substance **2** : a consonant characterized by explosion in its articulation when it occurs in certain environments : STOP

ex·po \'ek-(,)spō\ *n, pl* **expos** (1913) : EXPOSITION 3

ex·po·nent \ik-'spō-nənt, 'ek-,\ *n* [L *exponent-, exponens*, prp. of *exponere*] (1706) **1** : a symbol written above and to the right of a mathematical expression to indicate the operation of raising to a power **2 a** : one that expounds or interprets **b** : one that champions, practices, or exemplifies

ex·po·nen·tial \,ek-spə-'nen-chəl\ *adj* (1704) **1** : of or relating to an exponent **2** : involving a variable in an exponent ⟨10ˣ is an ∼ expression⟩ **3** : expressible or approximately expressible by an exponential function; *esp* : characterized by or being an extremely rapid increase (as in size or extent) ⟨an ∼ growth rate⟩ — **ex·po·nen·tial·ly** \-'nench-(ə-)lē\ *adv*

exponential function *n* (ca. 1890) : a mathematical function in which an independent variable appears in one of the exponents — called also *exponential*

ex·po·nen·ti·a·tion \,ek-spə-,nen(t)-shē-'ā-shən\ *n* (1903) : the act or process of raising a quantity to a power — called also *involution*

¹ex·port \ek-'spōrt, -'spȯrt, 'ek-,\ *vb* [ME, fr. L *exportare*, fr. *ex-* + *portare* to carry — more at FARE] *vt* (15c) **1** : to carry away : REMOVE **2** : to carry or send (as a commodity) to some other place (as another country) ∼ *vi* : to export something abroad — **ex·port·abil·i·ty** \(,)ek-,spōr-tə-'bi-lə-tē, -,spȯr-\ *n* — **ex·port·able** \ek-'spōr-tə-bəl, -'spȯr-, 'ek-,\ *adj*

²ex·port \'ek-,spōrt, -,spȯrt\ *n* (1690) **1** : something exported; *specif* : a commodity conveyed from one country or region to another for purposes of trade **2** : the act of exporting : EXPORTATION ⟨the ∼ of wheat⟩

³ex·port \'ek-,\ *adj* (1795) : of or relating to exportation or exports ⟨∼ duties⟩

ex·por·ta·tion \,ek-,spōr-'tā-shən, -,spȯr-, -spər-\ *n* (1641) : the act of exporting; *also* : a commodity exported

ex·port·er \ek-'spōr-tər, -'spȯr-, 'ek-,\ *n* (1691) : one that exports; *specif* : a wholesaler who sells to merchants or industrial consumers in foreign countries

ex·pose \ik-'spōz\ *vt* **ex·posed; ex·pos·ing** [ME, fr. MF *exposer*, fr. L *exponere* to set forth, explain (perf. indic. *exposui*), fr. *ex-* + *ponere* to put, place — more at POSITION] (15c) **1 a** : to deprive of shelter, protection, or care : subject to risk from a harmful action or condition ⟨∼ troops needlessly⟩ ⟨has not yet been *exposed* to measles⟩ **b** : to submit or make accessible to a particular action or influence ⟨∼ children to good books; *esp* : to subject (a sensitive photographic film, plate, or paper) to radiant energy **c** : to abandon (an infant) esp. by leaving in the open **2 a** : to make known : bring to light (as something shameful) **b** : to disclose the faults or crimes of ⟨∼ a murderer⟩ **3** : to cause to be visible or open to view : DISPLAY: as **a** : to offer publicly for sale **b** : to exhibit for public veneration **c** : to reveal the face of (a playing card) or the cards of (a player's hand) **d** : to engage in indecent exposure of (oneself) *syn* see SHOW — **ex·pos·er** *n*

ex·po·sé *also* **ex·po·se** \,ek-spō-'zā, -spə-\ *n* [F *exposé*, fr. pp. of *exposer*] (1803) **1** : a formal statement of facts **2** : an exposure of something discreditable ⟨a newspaper ∼ of government corruption⟩

ex·posed \ik-'spōzd\ *adj* (ca. 1623) **1** : open to view **2** : not shielded or protected; *also* : not insulated ⟨an ∼ electric wire⟩ *syn* see LIABLE

ex·pos·it \ik-'spä-zət\ *vt* [L *expositus*, pp. of *exponere*] (1882) : EXPOUND

ex·po·si·tion \,ek-spə-'zi-shən\ *n* (14c) **1** : a setting forth of the meaning or purpose (as of a writing) **2 a** : discourse or an example of it designed to convey information or explain what is difficult to understand **b** (1) : the first part of a musical composition in sonata form in which the thematic material of the movement is presented (2) : the opening section of a fugue **3** : a public exhibition or show — **ex·po·si·tion·al** \-'zish-nəl, -'zi-shə-n³l\ *adj*

ex·pos·i·tive \ik-'spä-zə-tiv\ *adj* (15c) : DESCRIPTIVE, EXPOSITORY

ex·pos·i·tor \-zə-tər\ *n* [ME *expositour*, fr. MF *expositeur*, fr. LL *expositor*, fr. L *exponere*] (14c) : a person who explains : COMMENTATOR

ex·pos·i·to·ry \-zə-,tōr-ē, -,tȯr-\ *adj* (1628) : of, relating to, or containing exposition ⟨∼ writing⟩

¹ex post fac·to \,eks-,pōs(t)-'fak-(,)tō\ *adv* [LL, lit., from a thing done afterward] (1621) : after the fact : RETROACTIVELY

²ex post facto *adj* (1787) : done, made, or formulated after the fact : RETROACTIVE ⟨*ex post facto* approval⟩ ⟨*ex post facto* laws⟩

ex·pos·tu·late \ik-'späs-chə-,lāt\ *vb* [L *expostulatus*, pp. of *expostulare* to demand, dispute, fr. *ex-* + *postulare* to ask for — more at POSTULATE] *vt* (1573) *obs* : DISCUSS, EXAMINE ∼ *vi* : to reason earnestly with a person for purposes of dissuasion or remonstrance

ex·pos·tu·la·tion \-,späs-chə-'lā-shən\ *n* (1540) : an act or an instance of expostulating — **ex·pos·tu·la·to·ry** \-'späs-chə-lə-,tōr-ē, -,tȯr-\ *adj*

ex·po·sure \ik-'spō-zhər\ *n* (1606) **1** : the fact or condition of being exposed: as **a** : the condition of being presented to view or made known ⟨a politician seeks a lot of ∼⟩ **b** : the condition of being unprotected esp. from severe weather ⟨died of ∼⟩ **c** : the condition of being subject to some effect or influence ⟨risk ∼ to the flu⟩ **d** : the condition of being at risk of financial loss; *also* : an amount at risk **2** : the act or an instance of exposing: as **a** : disclosure of something secret ⟨tried to prevent ∼ of their past⟩ **b** : the treating of sensitized material (as film) to controlled amounts of radiant energy; *also* : the amount of such energy or length of such treatment ⟨a 3-second ∼⟩ **3 a** : the manner of being exposed **b** : the position (as of a house) with respect to weather influences or compass points ⟨a room with a southern ∼⟩ **4** : a piece or section of sensitized material (as film) on which an exposure is or can be made ⟨36 ∼s per roll⟩

exposure meter *n* (1891) : a device for indicating correct photographic exposure under varying conditions of illumination

ex·pound \ik-'spaund\ *vb* [ME, fr. MF *expondre*, fr. L *exponere* to explain — more at EXPOSE] *vt* (14c) **1 a** : to set forth : STATE **b** : to defend with argument **2** : to explain by setting forth in careful and often elaborate detail ⟨∼ a law⟩ ∼ *vi* : to make a statement : COMMENT *syn* see EXPLAIN — **ex·pound·er** *n*

¹ex·press \ik-'spres\ *adj* [ME, fr. MF *expres*, fr. L *expressus*, pp. of *exprimere* to press out, express, fr. *ex-* + *premere* to press — more at PRESS] (14c) **1 a** : directly, firmly, and explicitly stated ⟨my ∼ orders⟩ **b** : EXACT, PRECISE **2 a** : designed for or adapted to its purpose **b** : of a particular sort : SPECIFIC ⟨for that ∼ purpose⟩ **3 a** : traveling at high speed; *specif* : traveling with few or no stops along the way ⟨∼ train⟩ **b** : adapted or suitable for travel at high speed ⟨an ∼ highway⟩ **c** *Brit* : designated to be delivered without delay by special messenger *syn* see EXPLICIT

²express *adv* (14c) **1** *obs* : EXPRESSLY **2** : by express ⟨delivered ∼⟩

³express *n* (1619) **1 a** *Brit* : a messenger sent on a special errand **b** *Brit* : a dispatch conveyed by a special messenger **c** (1) : a system for the prompt and safe transportation of parcels, money, or goods at rates higher than standard freight charges (2) : a company operating such a merchandise freight service **d** *Brit* : SPECIAL DELIVERY **2** : an express vehicle

⁴express *vt* [ME, fr. MF & L; MF *expresser*, fr. OF, fr. *expres*, adj., fr. L *expressus*, pp.] (14c) **1 a** : DELINEATE, DEPICT **b** : to represent in words : STATE **c** : to give or convey a true impression of : SHOW, REFLECT **d** : to make known the opinions or feelings of (oneself) **e** : to give expression to the artistic or creative impulses or abilities of (oneself) **f** : to represent by a sign or symbol : SYMBOLIZE **2 a** : to force out (as the juice of a fruit) by pressure **b** : to subject to pressure so as to extract something **3** : to send by express **4** : to cause (a gene) to manifest its effects in the phenotype — **ex·press·er** *n* — **ex·press·ible** \-ə-bəl\ *adj*

syn EXPRESS, VENT, UTTER, VOICE, BROACH, AIR mean to make known what one thinks or feels. EXPRESS suggests an impulse to reveal in words, gestures, actions, or what one creates or produces ⟨*expressed* her feelings in music⟩. VENT stresses a strong inner compulsion to express esp. in words ⟨a tirade *venting* his frustration⟩. UTTER implies the use of the voice not necessarily in articulate speech ⟨*utter* a groan⟩. VOICE does not necessarily imply vocal utterance but does imply expression or formulation in words ⟨an editorial *voicing* their concerns⟩. BROACH adds the implication of disclosing for the first time something long thought over or reserved for a suitable occasion ⟨*broached* the subject of a divorce⟩. AIR implies an exposing or parading of one's views often in order to gain relief or sympathy or attention ⟨publicly *airing* their differences⟩.

ex·press·age \ik-'spre-sij\ *n* (1857) : a carrying of parcels by express; *also* : a charge for such carrying

ex·pres·sion \ik-'spre-shən\ *n* (15c) **1 a** : an act, process, or instance of representing in a medium (as words) : UTTERANCE ⟨freedom of ∼⟩ **b** (1) : something that manifests, embodies, or symbolizes something else ⟨this gift is an ∼ of my admiration for you⟩ (2) : a significant word or phrase (3) : a mathematical or logical symbol or a meaningful combination of symbols (4) : the detectable effect of a gene; *also* : EXPRESSIVITY 1 **2 a** : a mode, means, or use of significant representation or symbolism; *esp* : felicitous or vivid indication or depiction of mood or sentiment ⟨read the poem with ∼⟩ **b** (1) : the quality or fact of being expressive (2) : facial aspect or vocal intonation as indicative of feeling **3** : an act or product of pressing out — **ex·pres·sion·al** \-'spresh-nəl, -'spre-shə-n³l\ *adj*

ex·pres·sion·ism \ik-'spre-shə-,ni-zəm\ *n, often cap* (ca. 1901) : a theory or practice in art of seeking to depict the subjective emotions and responses that objects and events arouse in the artist — **ex·pres·sion·ist** \-'spre-shə-nist\ *n or adj, often cap* — **ex·pres·sion·is·tic** \-,spre-shə-'nis-tik\ *adj* — **ex·pres·sion·is·ti·cal·ly** \-ti-k(ə-)lē\ *adv*

ex·pres·sion·less \ik-'spre-shən-ləs\ *adj* (1831) : lacking expression ⟨an ∼ face⟩ — **ex·pres·sion·less·ly** *adv* — **ex·pres·sion·less·ness** *n*

ex·pres·sive \ik-'spre-siv\ *adj* (15c) **1** : of or relating to expression ⟨the ∼ function of language⟩ **2** : serving to express, utter, or represent ⟨foul and novel terms ∼ of rage —H. G. Wells⟩ **3** : effectively conveying meaning or feeling ⟨an ∼ silence⟩ ⟨∼ line drawings⟩ — **ex·pres·sive·ly** *adv* — **ex·pres·sive·ness** *n*

ex·pres·siv·i·ty \,ek-,spre-'si-və-tē\ *n, pl* **-ties** (1934) **1** : the relative capacity of a gene to affect the phenotype of the organism of which it is a part **2** : the quality of being expressive

ex·press·ly \ik-'spres-lē\ *adv* (14c) **1** : in an express manner : EXPLICITLY ⟨∼ rejected the proposal⟩ **2** : for the express purpose : PARTICULARLY, SPECIFICALLY ⟨made ∼ for me⟩

Express Mail *service mark* — used for overnight delivery of mail
ex·press·man \ik-'spres-ˌman, -mən\ *n* (1839) : a person employed in the express business
ex·pres·so \ik-'spre-(ˌ)sō\ *var of* ESPRESSO
ex·press·way \ik-'spres-ˌwā\ *n* (1944) : a high-speed divided highway for through traffic with access partially or fully controlled
ex·pro·pri·ate \ek-'sprō-prē-ˌāt\ *vt* **-at·ed; -at·ing** [ML *expropriatus*, pp. of *expropriare*, fr. L *ex-* + *proprius* own] (1611) **1** : to deprive of possession or proprietary rights **2** : to transfer (the property of another) to one's own possession — **ex·pro·pri·a·tor** \-ˌā-tər\ *n*
ex·pro·pri·a·tion \(ˌ)ek-ˌsprō-prē-'ā-shən\ *n* (15c) : the act of expropriating or the state of being expropriated; *specif* : the action of the state in taking or modifying the property rights of an individual in the exercise of its sovereignty
ex·pulse \ik-'spəls\ *vt* **ex·pulsed; ex·puls·ing** (15c) : EXPEL
ex·pul·sion \ik-'spəl-shən\ *n* [ME, fr. L *expulsion-, expulsio*, fr. *expellere* to expel] (15c) : the act of expelling : the state of being expelled — **ex·pul·sive** \-'spəl-siv\ *adj*
ex·punc·tion \ik-'spəŋ(k)-shən\ *n* [L *expunctus*] (1606) : the act of expunging : the state of being expunged : ERASURE
ex·punge \ik-'spənj\ *vt* **ex·punged; ex·pung·ing** [L *expungere* to mark for deletion by dots, fr. *ex-* + *pungere* to prick — more at PUNGENT] (1602) **1** : to strike out, obliterate, or mark for deletion **2** : to efface completely : DESTROY — **ex·pung·er** *n*
ex·pur·gate \'ek-spər-ˌgāt\ *vt* **-gat·ed; -gat·ing** [L *expurgatus*, pp. of *expurgare*, fr. *ex-* + *purgare* to purge] (1678) : to cleanse of something morally harmful, offensive, or erroneous; *esp* : to expunge objectionable parts from before publication or presentation (an *expurgated* edition of the letters) — **ex·pur·ga·tion** \ˌek-spər-'gā-shən\ *n* — **ex·pur·ga·tor** \'ek-spər-ˌgā-tər\ *n*
ex·pur·ga·to·ri·al \(ˌ)ek-ˌspər-gə-'tōr-ē-əl, -'tȯr-\ *adj* (1807) : relating to expurgation or an expurgator : EXPURGATORY
ex·pur·ga·to·ry \ek-'spər-gə-ˌtōr-ē, -ˌtȯr-\ *adj* (1625) : serving to purify from something morally harmful, offensive, or erroneous
¹ex·qui·site \ek-'skwi-zət, 'ek-(ˌ)\ *adj* [ME *exquisit*, fr. L *exquisitus*, pp. of *exquirere* to search out, fr. *ex-* + *quaerere* to seek] (15c) **1** : carefully selected : CHOICE **2** *archaic* : ACCURATE **3 a** : marked by flawless craftsmanship or by beautiful, ingenious, delicate, or elaborate execution **b** : marked by nice discrimination, deep sensitivity, or subtle understanding (an ~ taste) **c** : ACCOMPLISHED, PERFECTED (an ~ gentleman) **4 a** : pleasing through beauty, fitness, or perfection (an ~ white blossom) **b** : ACUTE, INTENSE (~ pain) **c** : having uncommon or esoteric appeal *syn* see CHOICE — **ex·qui·site·ly** *adv* — **ex·qui·site·ness** *n*
²exquisite *n* (1819) : one who is overly fastidious in dress or ornament
ex·san·gui·na·tion \(ˌ)ek(s)-ˌsaŋ-gwə-'nā-shən\ *n* [L *exsanguinatus* drained of blood, fr. *ex-* + *sanguin-, sanguis* blood] (ca. 1909) : the action or process of draining or losing blood — **ex·san·gui·nate** \ek(s)-'saŋ-gwə-ˌnāt\ *vt*
ex·scind \ek-'sind\ *vt* [L *exscindere*, fr. *ex-* + *scindere* to cut, tear — more at SHED] (1662) : to cut off or out : EXCISE
ex·sert \ek-'sərt\ *vt* [L *exsertus*, pp. of *exserere* — more at EXERT] (1836) : to thrust out — **ex·ser·tile** \-'sər-tᵊl, -'sər-ˌtīl\ *adj* — **ex·ser·tion** \-'sər-shən\ *n*
ex·sert·ed *adj* (1816) : projecting beyond an enclosing organ or part
ex·sic·cate \'ek-si-ˌkāt\ *vt* **-cat·ed; -cat·ing** [ME, fr. L *exsiccatus*, pp. of *exsiccare*, fr. *ex-* + *siccare* to dry, fr. *siccus* dry — more at SACK] (15c) : to remove moisture from : DRY — **ex·sic·ca·tion** \ˌek-si-'kā-shən\ *n*
ex·so·lu·tion \ˌek-sə-'lü-shən\ *n* (1929) : the process of separating or precipitating from a solid crystalline phase
ex·tant \'ek-stənt; ek-'stant, 'ek-\ *adj* [L *exstant-, exstans*, prp. of *exstare* to stand out, be in existence, fr. *ex-* + *stare* to stand — more at STAND] (1545) **1** *archaic* : standing out or above **2 a** : currently or actually existing (the most charming writer ~ —G. W. Johnson) **b** : not destroyed or lost (~ manuscripts)
ex·tem·po·ral \ek-'stem-p(ə-)rəl\ *adj* [L *extemporalis*, fr. *ex tempore*] (1570) *archaic* : EXTEMPORANEOUS — **ex·tem·po·ral·ly** \-ē\ *adv*
ex·tem·po·ra·ne·ity \(ˌ)ek-ˌstem-pə-rə-'nē-ə-tē, -'nā-\ *n* (1937) : the quality or state of being extemporaneous
ex·tem·po·ra·ne·ous \(ˌ)ek-ˌstem-pə-'rā-nē-əs\ *adj* [LL *extemporaneus*, fr. L *ex tempore*] (1673) **1 a** (1) : composed, performed, or uttered on the spur of the moment : IMPROMPTU (2) : carefully prepared but delivered without notes or text **b** : skilled at or given to extemporaneous utterance **c** : happening suddenly and often unexpectedly and usu. without clearly known causes or relationships (a great deal of criminal and delinquent behavior is . . . ~ —W. C. Reckless) **2** : provided, made, or put to use as an expedient : MAKESHIFT — **ex·tem·po·ra·ne·ous·ly** *adv* — **ex·tem·po·ra·ne·ous·ness** *n*
ex·tem·po·rary \ik-'stem-pə-ˌrer-ē\ *adj* (1596) : EXTEMPORANEOUS — **ex·tem·po·rar·i·ly** \-ˌstem-pə-'rer-ə-lē\ *adv*
ex·tem·po·re \ik-'stem-pə-(ˌ)rē\ *adv or adj* [L *ex tempore*, fr. *ex* + *tempore*, abl. of *tempus* time] (1553) : in an extemporaneous manner (speaking ~)
ex·tem·por·i·sa·tion, ex·tem·po·rise *Brit var of* EXTEMPORIZATION, EXTEMPORISE
ex·tem·po·ri·za·tion \ik-ˌstem-pə-rə-'zā-shən\ *n* (ca. 1860) **1** : the act of extemporizing : IMPROVISATION **2** : something extemporized
ex·tem·po·rize \ik-'stem-pə-ˌrīz\ *vb* **-rized; -riz·ing** *vi* (1644) **1** : to do something extemporaneously : IMPROVISE; *esp* : to speak extemporaneously **2** : to get along in a makeshift manner ~ *vt* : to compose, perform, or utter extemporaneously : IMPROVISE — **ex·tem·po·riz·er** *n*
ex·tend \ik-'stend\ *vb* [ME, fr. MF or L; MF *estendre*, fr. L *extendere*, fr. *ex-* + *tendere* to stretch — more at THIN] *vt* (14c) **1** : to spread or stretch forth : UNBEND (~ed both her arms) **2 a** : to stretch out to fullest length **b** : to cause (as a horse) to move at full stride **c** : to exert (oneself) to full capacity (could work long and hard without seeming to ~ himself) **d** (1) : to increase the bulk of (as by adding a cheaper substance or a modifier) (2) : ADULTERATE **3** [ME, fr. ML *extendere* (fr. L) or AF *extendre*, fr. OF] *a* *Brit* : to take possession of (as lands) by a writ of extent **b** *obs* : to take by force **4 a** : to make the offer of : PROFFER (~ing aid to the needy) **b** : to make available (~ing credit to customers) **5 a** : to cause to reach (as in distance or scope) (national authority was ~ed over new territories) **b** : to cause

to be longer : PROLONG (~ the side of a triangle) (~ed their visit another day); *also* : to prolong the time of payment of **c** : ADVANCE, FURTHER (~ing her potential through job training) **6 a** : to cause to be of greater area or volume : ENLARGE **b** : to increase the scope, meaning, or application of : BROADEN (beauty, I suppose, opens the heart, ~s the consciousness —Algernon Blackwood) **c** *archaic* : EXAGGERATE ~ *vi* **1** : to stretch out in distance, space, or time : REACH (their jurisdiction ~ed over the whole area) **2** : to reach in scope or application (his concern ~s beyond mere business to real service to his customers) — **ex·tend·abil·i·ty** \-ˌsten-də-'bi-lə-tē\ *n* — **ex·tend·able** *also* **ex·tend·ible** \-'sten-də-bəl\ *adj*
syn EXTEND, LENGTHEN, PROLONG, PROTRACT mean to draw out or add to so as to increase in length. EXTEND and LENGTHEN imply a drawing out in space or time but EXTEND may also imply increase in width, scope, area, or range (*extend* a vacation) (*extend* welfare services) (*lengthen* a skirt) (*lengthen* the workweek). PROLONG suggests chiefly increase in duration esp. beyond usual limits (*prolonged* illness). PROTRACT adds to PROLONG implications of needlessness, vexation, or indefiniteness (*protracted* litigation).
ex·tend·ed *adj* (15c) **1** : drawn out in length esp. of time (an ~ visit) **2 a** : fully stretched out (an ~ battle line) **b** *of a horse's gait* : performed with a greatly lengthened stride but without a break — compare COLLECTED **c** : INTENSIVE (~ efforts) **3** : having spatial magnitude : being larger than a point (an ~ source of light) **4** : EXTENSIVE 1 (made available ~ information —Ruth G. Strickland) **5** : DERIVATIVE 1, SECONDARY 2a (an ~ sense of a word) **6** *of a typeface* : having a wider face than that of a standard typeface — **ex·tend·ed·ly** *adv* — **ex·tend·ed·ness** *n*
extended family *n* (ca. 1935) : a family that includes in one household near relatives in addition to a nuclear family
ex·tend·er \ik-'sten-dər\ *n* (1611) : one that extends: as **a** : a substance added to a product esp. in the capacity of a diluent, adulterant, or modifier **b** : an added ingredient used to increase the bulk of a food (as soup or meat)
ex·ten·si·ble \ik-'sten(t)-sə-bəl\ *adj* (1611) : capable of being extended — **ex·ten·si·bil·i·ty** \-ˌsten(t)-sə-'bi-lə-tē\ *n*
ex·ten·sile \ik-'sten(t)-səl, -'sten-ˌsīl\ *adj* (1744) : EXTENSIBLE
ex·ten·sion \ik-'sten(t)-shən\ *n* [ME, fr. MF or LL; MF, fr. LL *extension-, extensio*, fr. L *extendere*] (15c) **1 a** : the action of extending : state of being extended **b** : an enlargement in scope or operation (tools are ~s of human hands) **2 a** : the total range over which something extends : COMPASS **b** : DENOTATION 4 **3 a** : the stretching of a fractured or dislocated limb so as to restore it to its natural position **b** : an unbending movement around a joint in a limb (as the knee or elbow) that increases the angle between the bones of the limb at the joint — compare FLEXION 4a : a property whereby something occupies space **5** : an increase in length of time; *specif* : an increase in time allowed under agreement or concession (was granted an ~) **6** : a program that geographically extends the educational resources of an institution by special arrangements (as correspondence courses) to persons otherwise unable to take advantage of such resources **7 a** : a part constituting an addition **b** : a section or line segment forming an additional length **c** : an extra telephone connected to the principal line **8** : a mathematical set (as a field or group) that includes a given and similar set as a subset
extension agent *n* (1949) : COUNTY AGENT
ex·ten·sion·al \ik-'stench-nəl, -'sten(t)-shə-nᵊl\ *adj* (1647) **1** : of, relating to, or marked by extension; *specif* : DENOTATIVE **2** : concerned with objective reality — **ex·ten·sion·al·i·ty** \-ˌsten(t)-shə-'na-lə-tē\ *n* — **ex·ten·sion·al·ly** \-'stench-nə-lē, -'sten(t)-shə-nᵊl-ē\ *adv*
extension cord *n* (1946) : an electric cord fitted with a plug at one end and a receptacle at the other
ex·ten·si·ty \ik-'sten(t)-sə-tē\ *n, pl* **-ties** (ca. 1834) **1 a** : the quality of having extension **b** : degree of extension : RANGE **2** : an attribute of sensation whereby space or size is perceived
ex·ten·sive \ik-'sten(t)-siv\ *adj* (1605) **1** : having wide or considerable extent (~ reading) **2** : EXTENSIONAL **3** : of, relating to, or constituting farming in which large areas of land are utilized with minimum outlay and labor — **ex·ten·sive·ly** *adv* — **ex·ten·sive·ness** *n*
ex·ten·som·e·ter \ˌek-ˌsten-'sä-mə-tər\ *n* [*extension* + *-o-* + *-meter*] (1887) : an instrument for measuring minute deformations of test specimens caused by tension, compression, bending, or twisting
ex·ten·sor \ik-'sten(t)-sər\ *n* (1713) : a muscle serving to extend a bodily part (as a limb)
ex·tent \ik-'stent\ *n* [ME, fr. AF & MF; AF *extente* land valuation, fr. MF, area, surveying of land, fr. *extendre, estendre* to extend] (14c) **1** *archaic* : valuation (as of land) in Great Britain esp. for taxation **2 a** : seizure (as of land) in execution of a writ of extent in Great Britain : the condition of being so seized **b** : a writ giving to a creditor temporary possession of his debtor's property **3 a** : the range over which something extends : SCOPE (the ~ of her jurisdiction) **b** : the point, degree, or limit to which something extends (using talents to the greatest ~) **c** : the amount of space or surface that something occupies or the distance over which it extends : MAGNITUDE (the ~ of the forest)
ex·ten·u·ate \ik-'sten-yə-ˌwāt\ *vt* **-at·ed; -at·ing** [L *extenuatus*, pp. of *extenuare*, fr. *ex-* + *tenuis* thin — more at THIN] (1529) **1 a** *archaic* : to make light of **b** : to lessen or to try to lessen the seriousness or extent of by making partial excuses : MITIGATE **2** *obs* : DISPARAGE **3 a** *archaic* : to make thin or emaciated **b** : to lessen the strength or effect of — **ex·ten·u·a·tor** \-ˌwā-tər\ *n* — **ex·ten·u·a·to·ry** \-wə-ˌtōr-ē, -ˌtȯr-\ *adj*
ex·ten·u·a·tion \ik-ˌsten-yə-'wā-shən\ *n* (ca. 1543) **1** : the act of extenuating or state of being extenuated; *esp* : partial justification **2** : something extenuating; *esp* : a partial excuse
¹ex·te·ri·or \ek-'stir-ē-ər\ *adj* [L, compar. of *exter, exterus* being on the outside, foreign, fr. *ex*] (1528) **1** : being on an outside surface : situ-

\ə\ abut \ᵊ\ kitten, F table \ər\ further \a\ ash \ā\ ace \ä\ mop, mar \au̇\ out \ch\ chin \e\ bet \ē\ easy \g\ go \i\ hit \ī\ ice \j\ job \ŋ\ sing \ō\ go \ȯ\ law \ȯi\ boy \th\ thin \t͟h\ the \ü\ loot \u̇\ foot \y\ yet \zh\ vision \ä, k̲, ⁿ, œ, œ̄, ᵫ, ᵬ, ʸ\ see Guide to Pronunciation

ated on the outside   **2** : observable by outward signs ⟨his ~ quietness is belied by an occasional nervous twitch —*Current Biog.*⟩   **3** : suitable for use on outside surfaces — **ex·te·ri·or·ly** *adv*
²exterior *n* (1591)   **1 a** : an exterior part or surface : OUTSIDE   **b** : outward manner or appearance   **2** : a representation (as on stage or film) of an outdoor scene; *also* : a scene filmed outdoors

exterior angle *n* (ca. 1864)   **1** : the angle between a side of a polygon and an extended adjacent side   **2** : an angle formed by a transversal as it cuts one of two lines and situated on the outside of the line

ega, egb, fhc, fhd exterior angle 2

ex·te·ri·or·ise *Brit var of* EXTERIORIZE
ex·te·ri·or·i·ty \(,)ek-,stir-ē-'ȯr-ə-tē, -'är-\ *n* (1611) : the quality or state of being exterior or exteriorized : EXTERNALITY
ex·te·ri·or·ize \ek-'stir-ē-ə-,rīz\ *vt* **-ized; -iz·ing** (1879)   **1** : EXTERNALIZE   **2** : to bring out of the body (as for surgery) — **ex·te·ri·or·iza·tion** \-,stir-ē-ə-rə-'zā-shən\ *n*
ex·ter·mi·nate \ik-'stər-mə-,nāt\ *vt* **-nat·ed; -nat·ing** [L *exterminatus*, pp. of *exterminare*, fr. *ex-* + *terminus* boundary — more at TERM] (1591) : to get rid of completely usu. by killing off ⟨~ crabgrass from a lawn⟩ — **ex·ter·mi·na·tion** \-,stər-mə-'nā-shən\ *n* — **ex·ter·mi·na·tor** \-'stər-mə-,nā-tər\ *n*
syn EXTERMINATE, EXTIRPATE, ERADICATE, UPROOT mean to effect the destruction or abolition of something. EXTERMINATE implies complete and immediate extinction by killing off all individuals ⟨*exterminate* cockroaches⟩. EXTIRPATE implies extinction of a race, family, species, or sometimes an idea or doctrine by destruction or removal of its means of propagation ⟨many species have been *extirpated* from the area⟩. ERADICATE implies the driving out or elimination of something that has established itself ⟨a campaign to *eradicate* illiteracy⟩. UPROOT implies a forcible or violent removal and stresses displacement or dislodgment rather than immediate destruction ⟨the war *uprooted* thousands⟩.
ex·ter·mi·na·to·ry \ik-'stər-mə-nə-,tōr-ē, -,tȯr-\ *adj* (1790) : of, relating to, or marked by extermination
ex·ter·mine \ik-'stər-mən\ *vt* **-mined; -min·ing** (1539) *obs* : EXTERMINATE
¹ex·tern \ek-'stərn, 'ek-,\ *adj* [MF or L; MF *externe*, fr. L *externus*] (1530) *archaic* : EXTERNAL
²ex·tern *also* **ex·terne** \'ek-,stərn\ *n* (ca. 1610) : a person connected with an institution but not living or boarding in it; *specif* : a nonresident doctor or medical student at a hospital
¹ex·ter·nal \ek-'stər-n³l\ *adj* [L *externus* external, fr. *exter*] (1556)   **1 a** : capable of being perceived outwardly ⟨~ signs of a disease⟩ ⟨~ reality⟩   **b** (1) : having merely the outward appearance of something : SUPERFICIAL   (2) : not intrinsic or essential ⟨~ circumstances⟩   **2 a** : of, relating to, or connected with the outside or an outer part   **b** : applied or applicable to the outside   **3 a** (1) : situated outside, apart, or beyond; *specif* : situated near or toward the surface of the body   (2) : arising or acting from outside ⟨~ force⟩   **b** : of or relating to dealings or relationships with foreign countries   **c** : having existence independent of the mind ⟨~ reality⟩ — **ex·ter·nal·ly** \-n³l-ē\ *adv*
²external *n* (ca. 1635) : something that is external: as   **a** : an outer part   **b** : an external feature or aspect — usu. used in pl.
external combustion engine *n* (1915) : a heat engine (as a steam engine) that derives its heat from fuel consumed outside the engine cylinder
external degree *n* (1928) : a degree conferred on a student who has not attended the university but has passed the qualifying examination
ex·ter·nal·isa·tion, ex·ter·nal·ise *Brit var of* EXTERNALIZATION, EXTERNALIZE
ex·ter·nal·ism \ek-'stər-n³l-,i-zəm\ *n* (1856)   **1** : attention to externals; *esp* : excessive preoccupation with externals   **2** : EXTERNALITY 1
ex·ter·nal·i·ty \,ek-stər-'na-lə-tē\ *n, pl* **-ties** (1673)   **1** : the quality or state of being external or externalized   **2** : something that is external   **3** : a secondary or unintended consequence ⟨pollution and other *externalities* of manufacturing⟩
ex·ter·nal·iza·tion \ek-,stər-n³l-ə-'zā-shən\ *n* (1803)   **1 a** : the action or process of externalizing   **b** : the quality or state of being externalized   **2** : something externalized : EMBODIMENT
ex·ter·nal·ize \ek-'stər-n³l-,īz\ *vt* **-ized; -iz·ing** (1852)   **1** : to make external or externally manifest   **2** : to attribute to causes outside the self : RATIONALIZE
external respiration *n* (1940) : exchange of gases between the external environment and a distributing system of the animal body (as the lungs of higher vertebrates or the tracheal tubes of insects) or between the alveoli of the lungs and the blood — compare INTERNAL RESPIRATION
ex·tern·ship \'ek-,stərn-,ship\ *n* (1945) : a training program that is part of a course of study of an educational institution and is taken in private business
ex·tero·cep·tive \,ek-stə-rō-'sep-tiv\ *adj* [*exterior* + *-o-* + *-ceptive* (as in *receptive*)] (ca. 1921) : activated by, relating to, or being stimuli received by an organism from outside
ex·tero·cep·tor \-tər\ *n* (1906) : a sense organ excited by exteroceptive stimuli
ex·ter·ri·to·ri·al \,ek-,ster-ə-'tōr-ē-əl, -'tȯr-\ *adj* (ca. 1880) : EXTRATERRITORIAL — **ex·ter·ri·to·ri·al·i·ty** \-,tōr-ē-'a-lə-tē, -,tȯr-\ *n*
¹ex·tinct \ik-'stiŋ(k)t, 'ek-,\ *adj* [ME, fr. L *exstinctus*, pp. of *exstinguere*] (15c)   **1 a** : no longer burning   **b** : no longer active ⟨an ~ volcano⟩   **2** : no longer existing ⟨an ~ animal⟩   **3 a** : gone out of use : SUPERSEDED   **b** : having no qualified claimant ⟨an ~ title⟩
²extinct *vt* (15c) *archaic* : EXTINGUISH
ex·tinc·tion \ik-'stiŋ(k)-shən\ *n* (15c)   **1** : the act of making extinct or causing to be extinguished   **2** : the condition or fact of being extinct or extinguished; *also* : the process of becoming extinct ⟨~ of a species⟩   **3** : the process of eliminating or reducing a conditioned response by not reinforcing it
extinction coefficient *n* (1902) : a measure of the rate of diminution of transmitted light via scattering and absorption for a medium
ex·tinc·tive \ik-'stiŋ(k)-tiv\ *adj* (1600) : tending or serving to extinguish or make extinct

ex·tin·guish \ik-'stiŋ-(g)wish\ *vt* [L *exstinguere* (fr. *ex-* + *stinguere* to extinguish) + E *-ish* (as in *abolish*); akin to L *instigare* to incite — more at STICK] (1551)   **1 a** : to cause to cease burning : QUENCH   **b** (1) : to bring to an end : make an end of ⟨hope for their safety was slowly ~ed⟩   (2) : to reduce to silence or ineffectiveness   **c** : to cause extinction of (a conditioned response)   **d** : to dim the brightness of : ECLIPSE   **2 a** : to cause to be void : NULLIFY ⟨~ a claim⟩   **b** : to get rid of usu. by payment ⟨~ a debt⟩ — **ex·tin·guish·able** \-(g)wi-shə-bəl\ *adj* — **ex·tin·guish·er** \-shər\ *n* — **ex·tin·guish·ment** \-mənt\ *n*
ex·tir·pate \'ek-stər-,pāt\ *vt* **-pat·ed; -pat·ing** [L *exstirpatus*, pp. of *exstirpare*, fr. *ex-* + *stirp-, stirps* trunk, root — more at TORPID] (1535)   **1 a** : to destroy completely : WIPE OUT   **b** : to pull up by the root   **2** : to cut out by surgery   **syn** see EXTERMINATE — **ex·tir·pa·tion** \,ek-stər-'pā-shən\ *n* — **ex·tir·pa·tor** \'ek-stər-,pā-tər\ *n*
ex·tol *also* **ex·toll** \ik-'stōl\ *vt* **ex·tolled; ex·tol·ling** [ME, fr. L *extollere*, fr. *ex-* + *tollere* to lift up — more at TOLERATE] (15c) : to praise highly : GLORIFY — **ex·tol·ler** \-'stōl-mənt\ *n*
ex·tort \ik-'stȯrt\ *vt* [L *extortus*, pp. of *extorquēre* to wrench out, extort, fr. *ex-* + *torquēre* to twist — more at TORTURE] (1529) : to obtain from a person by force, intimidation, or undue or illegal power : WRING; *also* : to gain esp. by ingenuity or compelling argument   **syn** see EDUCE — **ex·tort·er** *n* — **ex·tor·tive** \-'stȯr-tiv\ *adj*
ex·tor·tion \ik-'stȯr-shən\ *n* (14c)   **1** : the act or practice of extorting esp. money or other property; *esp* : the offense committed by an official engaging in such practice   **2** : something extorted; *esp* : a gross overcharge — **ex·tor·tion·er** \-sh(ə-)nər\ *n* — **ex·tor·tion·ist** \-sh(ə-)nist\ *n*
ex·tor·tion·ary \-shə-,ner-ē\ *adj* (1805) *archaic* : EXTORTIONATE 1
ex·tor·tion·ate \ik-'stȯr-sh(ə-)nət\ *adj* (1789)   **1** : characterized by extortion   **2** : EXCESSIVE, EXORBITANT ⟨~ prices⟩ — **ex·tor·tion·ate·ly** *adv*
¹ex·tra \'ek-strə\ *adj* [prob. short for *extraordinary*] (1776)   **1 a** : more than is due, usual, or necessary : ADDITIONAL ⟨~ work⟩   **b** : subject to an additional charge ⟨room service is ~⟩   **2** : SUPERIOR ⟨~ quality⟩
²extra *n* (1793)   **1** : one that is extra or additional: as   **a** : a special edition of a newspaper   **b** : an added charge   **c** : an additional worker; *specif* : one hired to act in a group scene in a motion picture or stage production   **2** : something of superior quality or grade
³extra *adv* (1823) : beyond the usual size, extent, or degree ⟨~ large⟩
extra- *prefix* [ME, fr. L, fr. *extra*, adv. & prep., outside, except, beyond, fr. *exter* being on the outside — more at EXTERIOR] : outside : beyond ⟨*extra*judicial⟩
extra–base hit *n* (ca. 1949) : a hit in baseball that lets the batter take more than one base
ex·tra·cel·lu·lar \,ek-strə-'sel-yə-lər\ *adj* (1867) : situated or occurring outside a cell or the cells of the body ⟨~ digestion⟩ ⟨~ enzymes⟩ — **ex·tra·cel·lu·lar·ly** *adv*
ex·tra·chro·mo·som·al \-,krō-mə-'sō-məl, -'zō-\ *adj* (1940) : situated or controlled by factors outside the chromosome ⟨~ inheritance⟩
ex·tra·cor·po·re·al \-kȯr-'pōr-ē-əl, -'pȯr-\ *adj* (1865) : occurring or based outside the living body ⟨heart surgery employing ~ circulation⟩ — **ex·tra·cor·po·re·al·ly** \-ē-ə-lē\ *adv*
ex·tra·cra·ni·al \-'krā-nē-əl\ *adj* (ca. 1884) : situated or occurring outside the cranium
¹ex·tract \ik-'strakt, *oftenest in sense 5* 'ek-,\ *vt* [ME, fr. L *extractus*, pp. of *extrahere*, fr. *ex-* + *trahere* to draw] (15c)   **1 a** : to draw forth (as by research) ⟨~ data⟩   **b** : to pull or take out forcibly ⟨~ed a wisdom tooth⟩   **c** : to obtain by much effort from someone unwilling ⟨~ed a confession⟩   **2** : to withdraw (as a juice or fraction) by physical or chemical process; *also* : to treat with a solvent so as to remove a soluble substance   **3** : to separate (a metal) from an ore   **4** : to determine (a mathematical root) by calculation   **5** : to select (excerpts) and copy out or cite   **syn** see EDUCE — **ex·tract·abil·i·ty** \ik-,strak-tə-'bi-lə-tē, (,)ek-\ *n* — **ex·tract·able** \ik-'strak-tə-bəl, 'ek-,\ *adj*
²ex·tract \'ek-,strakt\ *n* (15c)   **1** : a selection from a writing or discourse : EXCERPT   **2** : a product (as an essence or concentrate) prepared by extracting; *esp* : a solution (as in alcohol) of essential constituents of a complex material (as meat or an aromatic plant)
ex·trac·tion \ik-'strak-shən\ *n* (15c)   **1** : the act or process of extracting something   **2** : ANCESTRY, ORIGIN   **3** : something extracted
¹ex·trac·tive \ik-'strak-tiv, 'ek-,\ *adj* (1599)   **1 a** : of, relating to, or involving extraction   **b** : tending toward or resulting in withdrawal of natural resources by extraction with no provision for replenishment ⟨~ agriculture⟩   **2** : capable of being extracted — **ex·trac·tive·ly** *adv*
²extractive *n* (1847) : something extracted or extractable : EXTRACT
ex·trac·tor \ik-'strak-tər\ *n* (1611) : one that extracts; *esp* : the mechanism in a firearm that dislodges a spent cartridge from the chamber
ex·tra·cur·ric·u·lar \,ek-strə-kə-'ri-kyə-lər\ *adj* (1925)   **1** : not falling within the scope of a regular curriculum; *specif* : of or relating to officially or semiofficially approved and usu. organized student activities (as athletics) connected with school and usu. carrying no academic credit   **2 a** : lying outside one's regular duties or routine   **b** : EXTRAMARITAL — **extracurricular** *n*
ex·tra·dit·able \'ek-strə-,dī-tə-bəl\ *adj* (1881)   **1** : subject or liable to extradition   **2** : making one liable to extradition ⟨an ~ offense⟩
ex·tra·dite \'ek-strə-,dīt\ *vt* **-dit·ed; -dit·ing** [back-formation fr. *extradition*] (1864)   **1** : to deliver up to extradition   **2** : to obtain the extradition of
ex·tra·di·tion \,ek-strə-'di-shən\ *n* [F, fr. *ex-* + L *tradition-, traditio* act of handing over — more at TREASON] (1839) : the surrender of an alleged criminal usu. under the provisions of a treaty or statute by one authority (as a state) to another having jurisdiction to try the charge
ex·tra·dos \'ek-strə-,däs, -,dō; ek-'strā-däs\ *n, pl* **-dos·es** \-,dä-səz\ *or* **-dos** \-,dōz, -,däs\ [F, fr. L *extra* + F *dos* back — more at DOSSIER] (1772) : the exterior curve of an arch — see ARCH illustration
ex·tra·em·bry·on·ic \,ek-strə-,em-brē-'ä-nik\ *adj* (ca. 1903) : situated outside the embryo; *esp* : developed from the zygote but not part of the embryo ⟨~ membranes⟩
ex·tra·ga·lac·tic \,ek-strə-gə-'lak-tik\ *adj* [ISV] (1851) : lying or coming from outside the Milky Way; *also* : of or relating to extragalactic space ⟨~ space⟩
ex·tra·he·pat·ic \-hi-'pa-tik\ *adj* (ca. 1923) : situated or originating outside the liver

ex·tra·ju·di·cial \-jü-'di-shəl\ *adj* (1630) **1 a :** not forming a valid part of regular legal proceedings ⟨an ~ investigation⟩ **b :** delivered without legal authority : PRIVATE 2a(2) ⟨the judge's ~ statements⟩ **2** : done in contravention of due process of law ⟨an ~ execution⟩ — **ex·tra·ju·di·cial·ly** \-'dish-lē, -'di-shə-\ *adv*

ex·tra·le·gal \ˌek-strə-'lē-gəl\ *adj* (1644) : not regulated or sanctioned by law — **ex·tra·le·gal·ly** \-gə-lē\ *adv*

ex·tra·lim·it·al \-'li-mə-t³l\ *adj* (1874) : not present in a given area — used of kinds of organisms (as species)

ex·tra·lin·guis·tic \-liŋ-'gwis-tik\ *adj* (1927) : lying outside the province of linguistics — **ex·tra·lin·guis·ti·cal·ly** \-ti-kə-lē\ *adv*

ex·tra·lit·er·ary \-'li-tə-ˌrer-ē\ *adj* (1945) : lying outside the field of literature

ex·tral·i·ty \ek-'stra-lə-tē\ *n* [by contr.] (1925) : EXTRATERRITORIALITY

ex·tra·log·i·cal \ˌek-strə-'lä-ji-kəl\ *adj* (1833) : not guided or determined by considerations of logic

ex·tra·mar·i·tal \ˌek-strə-'mar-ə-t³l\ *adj* (1925) : of, relating to, or being sexual intercourse between a married person and someone other than his or her spouse : ADULTEROUS

ex·tra·mun·dane \ˌek-strə-ˌmən-'dān, -'mən-\ *adj* [LL *extramundanus*, fr. L *extra* + *mundus* the world] (1665) : situated in or relating to a region beyond the material world

ex·tra·mu·ral \-'myùr-əl\ *adj* (1854) **1 :** existing or functioning outside or beyond the walls, boundaries, or precincts of an organized unit (as a school or hospital) **2** *chiefly Brit* : of, relating to, or taking part in extension courses or facilities — **ex·tra·mu·ral·ly** \-ə-lē\ *adv*

ex·tra·mu·si·cal \-'myü-zi-kəl\ *adj* (1923) : lying outside the province of music

ex·tra·ne·ous \ek-'strā-nē-əs\ *adj* [L *extraneus* — more at STRANGE] (1638) **1 :** existing on or coming from the outside **2 a :** not forming an essential or vital part ⟨~ ornamentation⟩ **b :** having no relevance ⟨an ~ digression⟩ **3 :** being a number obtained in solving an equation that is not a solution of the equation ⟨~ roots⟩ *syn* see EXTRINSIC — **ex·tra·ne·ous·ly** *adv* — **ex·tra·ne·ous·ness** *n*

ex·tra·nu·cle·ar \ˌek-strə-'nü-klē-ər, -'nyü-, -ˌkyə-lər\ *adj* (1887) **1** : situated in or affecting the parts of a cell external to the nucleus : CYTOPLASMIC **2** : situated outside the nucleus of an atom

ex·tra·oc·u·lar muscle \ˌek-strə-'ä-kyə-lər-\ *n* (1939) : any of six small voluntary muscles that pass between the eyeball and the orbit and control the movement of the eyeball in relation to the orbit

ex·traor·di·naire \ik-ˌströ(r)-d³n-'er, ek-\ *adj* [F] (1940) : EXTRAORDINARY — used postpositively ⟨a chef ~⟩

ex·traor·di·nary \ik-'strör-d³n-ˌer-ē, ˌek-strə-'ör-\ *adj* [ME *extraordinarie*, fr. L *extraordinarius*, fr. *extra ordinem* out of course, fr. *extra* + *ordinem*, acc. of *ordin-, ordo* order] (15c) **1 a :** going beyond what is usual, regular, or customary ⟨~ powers⟩ **b :** exceptional to a very marked extent ⟨~ beauty⟩ *c of a financial transaction* : NONRECURRING **2 :** employed for or sent on a special function or service ⟨an ambassador ~⟩ — **ex·traor·di·nari·ly** \ik-ˌströr-d³n-'er-ə-lē, ˌek-strə-ˌör-\ *adv* — **ex·traor·di·nari·ness** \ik-'strör-d³n-ˌer-ē-nəs, ˌek-strə-'ör-\ *n*

extra point *n* (ca. 1949) : a point gained on a conversion in football

ex·trap·o·late \ik-'stra-pə-ˌlāt\ *vb* **-lat·ed; -lat·ing** [L *extra* outside + E *-polate* (as in *interpolate*) — more at EXTRA-] *vt* (1874) **1 :** to infer (values of a variable in an unobserved interval) from values within an already observed interval **2 a :** to project, extend, or expand (known data or experience) into an area not known or experienced so as to arrive at a usu. conjectural knowledge of the unknown area ⟨~s present trends to construct an image of the future⟩ **b :** to predict by projecting past experience or known data ⟨~ public sentiment on one issue from known public reaction on others⟩ ~ *vi* : to perform the act or process of extrapolating — **ex·trap·o·la·tion** \-ˌstra-pə-'lā-shən\ *n* — **ex·trap·o·la·tive** \-'stra-pə-ˌlā-tiv\ *adj* — **ex·trap·o·la·tor** \-ˌlā-tər\ *n*

ex·tra·py·ra·mi·dal \ˌek-strə-pə-'ra-mə-d³l, -ˌpir-ə-'mi-d³l\ *adj* (ca. 1902) : situated outside of and esp. involving descending nerve tracts other than the pyramidal tracts

ex·tra·sen·so·ry \ˌek-strə-'sen(t)s-rē, -'sen(t)-sə-\ *adj* (1934) : residing beyond or outside the ordinary senses

extrasensory perception *n* (1934) : perception (as in telepathy, clairvoyance, and precognition) that involves awareness of information about events external to the self not gained through the senses and not deducible from previous experience — called also ESP

ex·tra·sys·to·le \-'sis-tə-(ˌ)lē\ *n* [NL] (ca. 1900) : a premature beat of one of the chambers of the heart that leads to momentary arrhythmia

¹ex·tra·ter·res·tri·al \-tə-'res-trē-əl, -'res(h)-chəl\ *adj* (1868) : originating, existing, or occurring outside the earth or its atmosphere ⟨~ life⟩

²extraterrestrial *n* (1960) : an extraterrestrial being

ex·tra·ter·ri·to·ri·al \-ˌter-ə-'tör-ē-əl, -'tör-\ *adj* (1869) : existing or taking place outside the territorial limits of a jurisdiction

ex·tra·ter·ri·to·ri·al·i·ty \-ˌtör-ē-ˌa-lə-tē, -ˌtör-\ *n* (1836) : exemption from the application or jurisdiction of local law or tribunals

ex·tra·tex·tu·al \ˌek-strə-'teks-chə-wəl, -chəl\ *adj* (1900) : of, relating to, or being something outside a literary text

ex·tra·trop·i·cal cyclone \ˌek-strə-ˌträ-pi-kəl-\ *n* (1923) : a cyclone in the middle latitudes often being 1500 miles (2400 kilometers) in diameter and usu. containing a cold front that extends toward the equator for hundreds of miles

ex·tra·uter·ine \ˌek-strə-'yü-tə-rən, -ˌrīn\ *adj* (1709) : situated or occurring outside the uterus ⟨~ pregnancy⟩

ex·trav·a·gance \ik-'stra-vi-gən(t)s\ *n* (1650) **1 a :** an instance of excess or prodigality; *specif* : an excessive outlay of money **b :** something extravagant **2 :** the quality or fact of being extravagant

ex·trav·a·gan·cy \-gən(t)-sē\ *n, pl* **-cies** (1625) : EXTRAVAGANCE

ex·trav·a·gant \ik-'stra-vi-gənt\ *adj* [ME, fr. MF, fr. ML *extravagant-, extravagans*, fr. L *extra-* + *vagant-, vagans*, prp. of *vagari* to wander about, fr. *vagus* wandering] (15c) **1 a** *obs* : STRANGE, CURIOUS **b** *archaic* : WANDERING **2 a :** exceeding the limits of reason or necessity ⟨~ claims⟩ **b :** lacking in moderation, balance, and restraint ⟨~ praise⟩ **c :** extremely or excessively elaborate **3 a :** spending much more than necessary **b :** PROFUSE, LAVISH **4 :** unreasonably high in price *syn* see EXCESSIVE — **ex·trav·a·gant·ly** *adv*

ex·trav·a·gan·za \ik-ˌstra-və-'gan-zə\ *n* [It *estravaganza*, lit., extrava-

gance, fr. *estravagante* extravagant, fr. ML *extravagant-, extravagans*] (1754) **1 :** a literary or musical work marked by extreme freedom of style and structure and usu. by elements of burlesque or parody **2 :** a lavish or spectacular show or event **3 :** something extravagant

ex·trav·a·gate \ik-'stra-və-ˌgāt\ *vi* **-gat·ed; -gat·ing** (ca. 1755) *archaic* : to go beyond proper limits

ex·trav·a·sate \ik-'stra-və-ˌsāt, -ˌzāt\ *vb* **-sat·ed; -sat·ing** [L *extra* + *vas* vessel] *vt* (1668) : to force out or cause to escape from a proper vessel or channel ~ *vi* : to pass by infiltration or effusion from a proper vessel or channel (as a blood vessel) into surrounding tissue — **ex·trav·a·sa·tion** \-ˌstra-və-'sā-shən, -'zā-\ *n*

ex·tra·vas·cu·lar \ˌek-strə-'vas-kyə-lər\ *adj* (1804) : not occurring or contained in body vessels ⟨~ tissue fluids⟩

ex·tra·ve·hic·u·lar \-vē-'hi-kyə-lər\ *adj* (1965) : taking place outside a vehicle (as a spacecraft) ⟨~ activity⟩

¹ex·treme \ik-'strēm\ *adj* [ME, fr. MF, fr. L *extremus*, superl. of *exter, exterus* being on the outside — more at EXTERIOR] (15c) **1 a :** existing in a very high degree ⟨~ poverty⟩ **b :** going to great or exaggerated lengths : RADICAL ⟨went on an ~ diet⟩ **c :** exceeding the ordinary, usual, or expected ⟨~ weather conditions⟩ **2** *archaic* : LAST **3** : situated at the farthest possible point from a center ⟨the country's ~ north⟩ **4 a :** most advanced or thoroughgoing ⟨the ~ political left⟩ **b :** MAXIMUM *syn* see EXCESSIVE — **ex·treme·ness** *n*

²extreme *n* (1555) **1 a :** something situated at or marking one end or the other of a range ⟨~s of heat and cold⟩ **b :** the first term or the last term of a mathematical proportion **c :** the major term or minor term of a syllogism **2 a :** a very pronounced or excessive degree **b :** highest degree : MAXIMUM **3 :** an extreme measure or expedient ⟨going to ~s⟩ — **in the extreme** : to the greatest possible extent

ex·treme·ly *adv* (1531) **1 :** in an extreme manner **2 :** to an extreme extent

extremely high frequency *n* (1952) : a radio frequency in the highest range of the radio spectrum — see RADIO FREQUENCY table

extremely low frequency *n* (1966) : a radio frequency in the lowest range of the radio spectrum — see RADIO FREQUENCY table

extreme unction \ik-ˌstrēm-'əŋ(k)-shən, ˌek-(ˌ)strēm-\ *n* (15c) : a sacrament in which a priest anoints and prays for the recovery and salvation of a critically ill or injured person

ex·trem·ism \ik-'strē-ˌmi-zəm\ *n* (1865) **1 :** the quality or state of being extreme **2 :** advocacy of extreme political measures : RADICALISM — **ex·trem·ist** \-mist\ *n or adj*

ex·trem·i·ty \ik-'stre-mə-tē\ *n, pl* **-ties** (14c) **1 a :** the farthest or most remote part, section, or point **b :** a limb of the body; *esp* : a human hand or foot **2 a :** extreme danger or critical need **b :** a moment marked by imminent destruction or death **3 a :** an intense degree ⟨the ~ of his participation —*Saturday Rev.*⟩ **b :** the utmost degree (as of emotion or pain) **4 :** a drastic or desperate act or measure ⟨driven to *extremities*⟩

ex·tre·mum \ik-'strē-məm\ *n, pl* **-ma** \-mə\ [NL, fr. L, neut. of *extremus*] (1904) : a maximum or a minimum of a mathematical function — called also *extreme value*

ex·tri·cate \'ek-strə-ˌkāt\ *vt* **-cat·ed; -cat·ing** [L *extricatus*, pp. of *extricare*, fr. *ex-* + *tricae* trifles, perplexities] (1614) **1 a** *archaic* : UNRAVEL **b :** to distinguish from a related thing **2 :** to free or remove from an entanglement or difficulty — **ex·tri·ca·ble** \ik-'stri-kə-bəl, ek-\', 'ek-(ˌ)\ *adj* — **ex·tri·ca·tion** \ˌek-strə-'kā-shən\ *n*

syn EXTRICATE, DISENTANGLE, UNTANGLE, DISENCUMBER, DISEMBARRASS mean to free from what binds or holds back. EXTRICATE implies the use of care or ingenuity in freeing from a difficult position or situation ⟨*extricated* himself from financial difficulties⟩. DISENTANGLE and UNTANGLE suggest painstaking separation of a thing from other things ⟨*disentangling* fact from fiction⟩ ⟨*untangle* a web of deceit⟩. DISENCUMBER implies a release from something that clogs or weighs down ⟨an article *disencumbered* of jargon⟩. DISEMBARRASS suggests a release from something that impedes or hinders ⟨*disembarrassed* herself of her advisers⟩.

ex·trin·sic \ek-'strin-zik, -'strin(t)-sik\ *adj* [F & LL; F *extrinsèque*, fr. LL *extrinsecus*, fr. L, adv., from without; akin to L *exter* outward and to L *sequi* to follow — more at EXTERIOR, SUE] (1613) **1 a :** not forming part of or belonging to a thing : EXTRANEOUS **b :** originating from or on the outside; *esp* : originating outside a part and acting upon the part as a whole ⟨~ muscles of the tongue⟩ **2 :** EXTERNAL — **ex·trin·si·cal·ly** \-zi-k(ə-)lē, -si-\ *adv*

syn EXTRINSIC, EXTRANEOUS, FOREIGN, ALIEN mean external to a thing, its essential nature, or its original character. EXTRINSIC applies to what is distinctly outside the thing in question or is not contained in or derived from its essential nature ⟨sentimental value that is *extrinsic* to the house's market value⟩. EXTRANEOUS applies to what is on or comes from the outside and may or may not be capable of becoming an essential part ⟨arguments *extraneous* to the issue⟩. FOREIGN applies to what is so different as to be rejected or repelled or to be incapable of becoming assimilated ⟨techniques *foreign* to French cuisine⟩. ALIEN is stronger than FOREIGN in suggesting opposition, repugnance, or irreconcilability ⟨a practice totally *alien* to her nature⟩.

extrinsic factor *n* (1938) : VITAMIN B₁₂

extro- *prefix* [alter. of L *extra-*] : outward ⟨*extrovert*⟩ — compare INTRO-

ex·trorse \'ek-ˌströrs\ *adj* [prob. fr. (assumed) NL *extrorsus*, fr. LL, adv., outward, fr. L *extra-* + *-orsus* (as in *introrsus*) — more at INTRORSE] (1858) : facing outward ⟨an ~ anther⟩

ex·tro·ver·sion *or* **ex·tra·ver·sion** \ˌek-strə-'vər-zhən, -shən\ *n* [G *Extraversion*, fr. L *extra-* + *versus*, pp. of *vertere* to turn — more at WORTH] (1915) : the act, state, or habit of being predominantly concerned with and obtaining gratification from what is outside the self

ex·tro·vert *also* **ex·tra·vert** \'ek-strə-ˌvərt\ *n* [modif. of G *extravertiert*, fr. L *extra-* + *vertere*] (1918) : one whose personality is characterized by extroversion; *broadly* : a gregarious and unreserved person —

\ə\ abut \'ə\ kitten, F table \ər\ further \a\ ash \ā\ ace \ä\ mop, mar
\aü\ out \ch\ chin \e\ bet \ē\ easy \g\ go \i\ hit \ī\ ice \j\ job
\ŋ\ sing \ō\ go \ò\ law \òi\ boy \th\ thin \t̲h̲\ the \ü\ loot \ù\ foot
\y\ yet \zh\ vision \á, k̲, ⁿ, œ, œ̄, ᵫ, īᴇ, ʸ\ see Guide to Pronunciation

extrovert *also* **extravert** *adj* — **ex·tro·vert·ed** *also* **ex·tra·vert·ed**
\-,vər-təd, ,ek-strə-'vər-\ *adj*
ex·trude \ik-'strüd\ *vb* **ex·trud·ed; ex·trud·ing** [L *extrudere,* fr. *ex-*
+ *trudere* to thrust — more at THREAT] *vt* (1566) **1** : to force, press,
or push out **2** : to shape (as metal or plastic) by forcing through a die
~ *vi* : to become extruded — **ex·trud·abil·i·ty** \-,strü-də-'bi-lə-tē\ *n*
— **ex·trud·able** \-'strü-də-bəl\ *adj* — **ex·trud·er** \-'strü-dər\ *n*
ex·tru·sion \ik-'strü-zhən\ *n* [ML *extrusion-, extrusio,* fr. L *extrudere*]
(1540) : the act or process of extruding; *also* : a form or product produced by this process
ex·tru·sive \ik-'strü-siv, -ziv\ *adj* (1816) : relating to or formed by geological extrusion from the earth in a molten state or as volcanic ash
ex·u·ber·ance \ig-'zü-b(ə-)rən(t)s\ *n* (1631) **1** : the quality or state of
being exuberant **2** : an exuberant act or expression
ex·u·ber·ant \-b(ə-)rənt\ *adj* [ME, fr. MF, fr. L *exuberant-, exuberans,*
prp. of *exuberare* to be abundant, fr. *ex-* + *uber* fruitful, fr. *uber* udder
— more at UDDER] (15c) **1** : extreme or excessive in degree, size, or
extent **2 a** : joyously unrestrained and enthusiastic **b** : unrestrained or elaborate esp. in style : FLAMBOYANT ⟨~ architecture⟩ **3**
: produced in extreme abundance : PLENTIFUL **syn** see PROFUSE —
ex·u·ber·ant·ly *adv*
ex·u·ber·ate \-bə-,rāt\ *vi* **-at·ed; -at·ing** (15c) **1** *archaic* : to have
something in abundance : OVERFLOW **2** : to become exuberant : show
exuberance ⟨*exuberated* over his victory⟩
ex·u·date \'ek-s(y)ù-,dāt, -shù-\ *n* (1876) : exuded matter
ex·u·da·tion \,ek-s(y)ù-'dā-shən, -shù-\ *n* (1612) **1** : the process of
exuding **2** : EXUDATE — **ex·u·da·tive** \ig-'zü-də-tiv; 'ek-s(y)ù-,dā-tiv,
-shù-\ *adj*
ex·ude \ig-'züd\ *vb* **ex·ud·ed; ex·ud·ing** [L *exsudare,* fr. *ex-* + *sudare*
to sweat — more at SWEAT] *vi* (1574) **1** : to ooze out **2** : to undergo
diffusion ~ *vt* **1** : to cause to ooze or spread out in all directions **2**
: to display conspicuously or abundantly ⟨~*s* charm⟩
ex·ult \ig-'zəlt\ *vi* [MF *exulter,* fr. L *exsultare,* lit., to leap up, fr. *ex-* +
saltare to leap — more at SALTATION] (1570) **1** *obs* : to leap for joy **2**
: to be extremely joyful : REJOICE — **ex·ult·ing·ly** \-'zəl-tiŋ-lē\ *adv*
ex·ul·tance \ig-'zəl-t³n(t)s\ *n* (1650) : EXULTATION
ex·ul·tan·cy \-'zəl-t³n(t)-sē\ *n* (1621) : EXULTATION
ex·ul·tant \ig-'zəl-t³nt\ *adj* (1653) : filled with or expressing great joy
or triumph : JUBILANT — **ex·ul·tant·ly** *adv*
ex·ul·ta·tion \,ek-(,)zəl-'tā-shən, ,eg-(,)zəl-\ *n* (15c) : the act of exulting
: the state of being exultant
ex·urb \'ek-,sərb, 'eg-,zərb\ *n* [*ex-* + sub*urb*] (1955) : a region or settlement that lies outside a city and usu. beyond its suburbs and that
often is inhabited chiefly by well-to-do families — **ex·ur·ban** \ek-'sər-
bən; eg-'zər-, ig-\ *adj*
ex·ur·ban·ite \ek-'sər-bə-,nīt; eg-'zər-, ig-\ *n* (1955) : one who lives in
an exurb
ex·ur·bia \-bē-ə\ *n* (1955) : the generalized region of exurbs
ex·u·vi·ae \ig-'zü-vē-,ē, -vē-,ī\ *n pl* [L, fr. *exuere* to take off, fr. *ex-* +
-uere to put on; akin to OCS *obuti* to put on (footwear)] (1653)
: sloughed off natural animal coverings (as the skins of snakes) — **ex-
u·vi·al** \-vē-əl\ *adj*
ex·u·vi·a·tion \-,zü-vē-'ā-shən\ *n* (1839) : the process of molting
¹**ex·vo·to** \(,)eks-'vō-(,)tō\ *n, pl* **ex–votos** [L *ex voto* according to a
vow] (1787) : a votive offering
²**ex–voto** *adj* (1823) : VOTIVE
-ey — see -Y
ey·as \'ī-əs\ *n* [ME, alter. (by incorrect division of *a neias*) of *neias,* fr.
MF *niais* fresh from the nest, fr. (assumed) VL *nidax* nestling, fr. L
nidus nest — more at NEST] (15c) : an unfledged bird; *specif* : a nestling hawk
¹**eye** \'ī\ *n* [ME, fr. OE *ēage;* akin to
OHG *ouga* eye, L *oculus,* Gk *ōps* eye,
face, Skt *aksi* eye] (bef. 12c) **1 a**
: an organ of sight; *esp* : a nearly
spherical hollow organ that is lined
with a sensitive retina, is lodged in a
bony orbit in the skull, is the vertebrate organ of sight, and is normally
paired **b** : all the visible structures
within and surrounding the orbit and
including eyelids, eyelashes, and eyebrows **c** (1) : the faculty of seeing
with eyes (2) : the faculty of intellectual or aesthetic perception or appreciation ⟨an ~ for beauty⟩ **2** : LOOK,
GLANCE ⟨cast an eager ~⟩ **e** (1) : an
attentive look ⟨kept an ~ on his valu-
ables⟩ (2) : ATTENTION, NOTICE
⟨caught his ~⟩ (3) : close observation : SCRUTINY ⟨works under the ~
of her boss⟩ ⟨in the public ~⟩ **f**
: POINT OF VIEW, JUDGMENT ⟨beauty is
in the ~ of the beholder⟩ — often used in pl. ⟨an offender in the ~*s* of
the law⟩ **g** : VIEW 5 ⟨with an ~ to the future⟩ **2** : something having
an appearance suggestive of an eye: as **a** : the hole through the head
of a needle **b** : a usu. circular marking (as on a peacock's tail) **c**
: LOOP; *esp* : a loop or catch to receive a hook **d** : an undeveloped bud
(as on a potato) **e** : an area like a hole in the center of a tropical cyclone marked by only light winds or complete calm with no precipitation **f** : the center of a flower esp. when differently colored or marked;
specif : the disk of a composite **g** (1) : a triangular piece of beef cut
from between the top and bottom of a round (2) : the chief muscle of
a chop (3) : a compact mass of muscular tissue usu. embedded in fat
in a rib or loin cut of meat **h** : a device (as a photoelectric cell) that
functions in a manner analogous to human vision **3** : something central : CENTER ⟨the ~ of the problem —Norman Mailer⟩ **4** : the direction from which the wind is blowing — **eye·less** \'ī-ləs\ *adj* — **eyelike** \-,līk\ *adj* — **an eye for an eye** : retribution in kind — **my eye**
— used to express mild disagreement or sometimes surprise ⟨a
diamond, *my eye!* That's glass⟩
²**eye** *vb* **eyed; eye·ing** *or* **ey·ing** *vt* (15c) **1 a** : to fix the eyes on
: look at **b** : to watch closely **2** : to furnish with an eye ~ *vi, obs*
: SEEM, LOOK — **ey·er** \'ī-(-ə)r\ *n*

eye 1a: *1* optic nerve, *2* blind
spot, *3* fovea, *4* sclera, *5* choroid, *6* retina, *7* ciliary body, *8*
posterior chamber, *9* anterior
chamber, *10* cornea, *11* lens,
12 iris, *13* suspensory ligament, *14* conjunctiva, *15* vitreous humor

¹**eye·ball** \'ī-,bȯl\ *n* (1590) : the more or less globular capsule of the
vertebrate eye formed by the sclera and cornea together with their contained structures
²**eyeball** *vt* (1901) : to look at intently
³**eyeball** *adj* (1971) : based on observation ⟨~ judgment⟩
eyeball–to–eyeball *adv or adj* (1962) : FACE-TO-FACE
eye bank *n* (1944) : a storage place for human corneas from the newly
dead for transplanting to the eyes of those blind through corneal defects
eye·bar \'ī-,bär\ *n* (ca. 1889) : a metal bar having a closed loop at one
or both ends
eye·bolt \'ī-,bōlt\ *n* (1769) : a bolt with a looped head
eye·bright \'ī-,brīt\ *n* (1533) : any of a genus (*Euphrasia*) of herbs of
the snapdragon family with opposite toothed or cut leaves
eye·brow \'ī-,braù\ *n* (15c) : the ridge over the eye or the hair growing
on it
eyebrow pencil *n* (1881) : a cosmetic pencil for the eyebrows
eye–catch·er \'ī-,ka-chər, -,ke-\ *n* (1923) : something that arrests the
eye — **eye–catch·ing** \-chiŋ\ *adj* — **eye–catch·ing·ly** \-chiŋ-lē\ *adv*
eye chart *n* (1943) : a chart read at a fixed distance for purposes of
testing sight; *esp* : one with rows of letters or objects of decreasing size
eye contact *n* (1955) : visual contact with another person's eyes
eye·cup \'ī-,kəp\ *n* (ca. 1874) **1** : a small oval cup with a rim curved
to fit the orbit of the eye used for applying liquid remedies to the eyes
2 : OPTIC CUP **3** : a usu. rubber cup at the eyepiece of an optical instrument (as binoculars) for keeping out extraneous light
eyed \'īd\ *adj* (14c) : having an eye or eyes esp. of a specified kind or
number — often used in combination ⟨an almond-*eyed* girl⟩
eyed·ness \'īd-nəs\ *n* [-*eyed* (as in *right-eyed, left-eyed*)] (1924) : preference for the use of one eye instead of the other (as in using a monocular
microscope)
eye·drop·per \'ī-,drä-pər\ *n* (1937) : DROPPER 2
eye·drops \-,dräps\ *n pl* (1926) : a medicated solution for the eyes applied in drops
eye·ful \'ī-,fùl\ *n* (ca. 1864) **1** : a full or completely satisfying view **2**
: one that is visually attractive; *esp* : a strikingly beautiful woman
eye·glass \'ī-,glas\ *n* (1664) **1 a** : EYEPIECE **b** : a lens worn to aid
vision; *specif* : MONOCLE **c** *pl* : GLASSES, SPECTACLES **2** : EYECUP 1
eye·hole \'ī-,hōl\ *n* (1637) **1** : ORBIT **2** : PEEPHOLE
eye·lash \'ī-,lash\ *n* (1752) **1** : the fringe of hair edging the eyelid —
usu. used in pl. **2** : a single hair of the eyelashes
eye lens *n* (1871) : the lens nearest the eye in an eyepiece
eye·let \'ī-lət\ *n* [alter. of ME *oilet,* fr. MF *oillet,* dim. of *oil* eye, fr. L
oculus] (14c) **1 a** : a small hole designed to receive a cord or used for
decoration (as in embroidery) **b** : a small typically metal ring to reinforce an eyelet : GROMMET **2** : PEEPHOLE, LOOPHOLE
eye·lid \'ī-,lid\ *n* (13c) : either of the movable folds of skin and muscle
that can be closed over the eyeball
eye·lin·er \'ī-,lī-nər\ *n* (1947) : makeup used to emphasize the contour
of the eyes
eye·en \'ī(-ə)n\ *archaic pl of* EYE
eye–open·er \'ī-,ōp-nər, -,ō-pə-\ *n* (1818) **1** : a drink intended to
wake one up **2** : something startling, surprising, or enlightening —
eye–open·ing \-niŋ\ *adj*
eye·piece \'ī-,pēs\ *n* (1790) : the lens or combination of lenses at the
eye end of an optical instrument
eye–pop·per \'ī-,pä-pər\ *n* (1941) : something that excites, astonishes,
or attracts the eye — **eye–pop·ping** \-,pä-piŋ\ *adj*
eye rhyme *n* (1871) : an imperfect rhyme that appears to have identical vowel sounds from similarity of spelling (as *move* and *love*)
eye·shade \'ī-,shād\ *n* (1845) : a visor that shields the eyes from strong
light and is fastened on with a headband
eye shadow *n* (1930) : a cosmetic cream or powder in one of various
colors that is applied to the eyelids to accent the eyes
eye·shot \'ī-,shät\ *n* (1573) : the range of the eye : VIEW
eye·sight \'ī-,sīt\ *n* (13c) **1** : SIGHT 4a **2** *archaic* : OBSERVATION 1
eye socket *n* (ca. 1844) : ORBIT
eyes only *adj* (1972) : to be read by only the person addressed
eye·sore \'ī-,sȯr, -,sōr\ *n* (1530) : something offensive to view
eye·spot \'ī-,spät\ *n* (1877) **1 a** : a simple visual organ of pigment or
pigmented cells covering a sensory termination : OCELLUS **b** : a small
pigmented body of various unicellular algae **2** : a spot of color **3**
: any of several fungal diseases of plants characterized by yellowish
oval lesions on the leaves and stem; *esp* : a disease of various grasses
(as sugarcane) caused by a fungus (*Helminthosporium sacchari*)
eye·stalk \'ī-,stȯk\ *n* (1854) : one of the movable peduncles bearing an
eye at the tip in a decapod crustacean
eye·strain \'ī-,strān\ *n* (1874) : weariness or a strained state of the eye
eye·strings \'ī-,striŋz\ *n pl* (1590) *obs* : organic eye attachments formerly believed to break at death or blindness
eye·tooth \'ī-'tüth\ *n* (ca. 1545) : a canine tooth of the upper jaw
eye view *n* (ca. 1771) : POINT OF VIEW ⟨an alien *eye view*⟩
eye·wash \'ī-,wȯsh, -,wäsh\ *n* (ca. 1859) **1** : an eye lotion **2** : misleading or deceptive statements, actions, or procedures
eye·wear \'ī-,war, -,wer\ *n* (1926) : corrective or protective devices (as
glasses or contact lenses) for the eyes
eye·wink \'ī-,wiŋk\ *n* (1598) : LOOK, GLANCE
eye·wit·ness \'ī-'wit-nəs\ *n* (1539) : one who sees an occurrence or an
object; *esp* : one who gives a report on what he or she has seen
eyre \'ar, 'er\ *n* [ME *eire,* fr. AF, fr. OF *erre* trip, fr. *errer* to travel —
more at ERRANT] (14c) : a circuit traveled by an itinerant justice in
medieval England or the court he presided over
ey·rie \'ir-ē, *or same as* AERIE\ *var of* AERIE
ey·rir \'ā-,rir\ *n, pl* **au·rar** \'aù-,rär, 'ȯi-\ [Icel, fr. ON, money (in pl.),
prob. fr. L *aureus* a gold coin] (ca. 1927) — see *krona* at MONEY table
Eze·chiel \i-'zē-kyəl, -kē-əl\ *n* [LL]: EZEKIEL
Eze·kiel \i-'zē-kyəl, -kē-əl\ *n* [LL *Ezechiel,* fr. Heb *Yĕḥezqēl*] **1** : a
Hebrew priest and prophet of the 6th century B.C. **2** : a prophetic book
of canonical Jewish and Christian Scripture written by Ezekiel — see
BIBLE table
Ez·ra \'ez-rə\ *n* [LL, fr. Heb *'Ezrā*] **1** : a Hebrew priest, scribe, and
reformer of Judaism of the 5th century B.C. in Babylon and Jerusalem
2 : a narrative book of canonical Jewish and Christian Scripture — see
BIBLE table

F

f \'ef\ *n, pl* **f's** *or* **fs** \'efs\ *often cap, often attrib* (bef. 12c) **1 a** : the 6th letter of the English alphabet **b** : a graphic representation of this letter **c** : a speech counterpart of orthographic *f* **2** : the 4th tone of a C-major scale **3** : a graphic device for reproducing the letter *f* **4** : one designated *f* esp. as the 6th in order or class **5 a** : a grade rating a student's work as failing **b** : one graded or rated with an F **6** : something shaped like the letter F

fa \'fä\ *n* [ME, fr. ML, fr. the syllable sung to this note in a medieval hymn to St. John the Baptist] (13c) : the 4th tone of the diatonic scale in solmization

Fa·bi·an \'fā-bē-ən\ *adj* (1777) **1 a** : of, relating to, or in the manner of the Roman general Quintus Fabius Maximus known for his defeat of Hannibal in the Second Punic War by the avoidance of decisive contests **b** : CAUTIOUS, DILATORY [the *Fabian* Society; fr. the members' belief in slow rather than revolutionary change in government] : of, relating to, or being a society of socialists organized in England in 1884 to spread socialist principles gradually — **Fabian** *n* — **Fa·bi·an·ism** \-ə-ˌni-zəm\ *n*

¹**fa·ble** \'fā-bəl\ *n* [ME, fr. MF, fr. L *fabula* conversation, story, play, fr. *fari* to speak — more at BAN] (14c) **1** : a fictitious narrative or statement: as **a** : a legendary story of supernatural happenings **b** : a narration intended to enforce a useful truth; *esp* : one in which animals speak and act like human beings **c** : FALSEHOOD, LIE

²**fable** *vb* **fa·bled; fa·bling** \-b(ə-)liŋ\ *vi* (14c) *archaic* : to tell fables ~ *vt* : to talk or write about as if true — **fa·bler** \-b(ə-)lər\ *n*

fa·bled \'fā-bəld\ *adj* (1606) **1** : told or celebrated in fables **3** : RENOWNED, FAMOUS

fab·li·au \'fa-blē-ˌō\ *n, pl* **-aux** \-ˌō(z)\ [F, fr. OF, dim. of *fable*] (1804) : a short, usu. comic, frankly coarse, and often cynical tale in verse popular esp. in the 12th and 13th centuries

fab·ric \'fa-brik\ *n* [MF *fabrique*, fr. L *fabrica* workshop, structure] (15c) **1 a** : STRUCTURE, BUILDING **b** : underlying structure : FRAMEWORK ⟨the ~ of society⟩ **2** : an act of constructing : ERECTION; *specif* : the construction and maintenance of a church building **3 a** : structural plan or style of construction **b** : TEXTURE, QUALITY — used chiefly of textiles **c** : the arrangement of physical components (as of soil) in relation to each other **4 a** : CLOTH 1a **b** : a material that resembles cloth **5** : the appearance or pattern produced by the shapes and arrangement of the crystal grains in a rock

fab·ri·cant \'fa-bri-kənt\ *n* (1757) : MANUFACTURER

fab·ri·cate \'fa-bri-ˌkāt\ *vt* **-cat·ed; -cat·ing** [ME, fr. L *fabricatus*, pp. of *fabricari*, fr. *fabrica*] (15c) **1 a** : INVENT, CREATE **b** : to make up for the purpose of deception **2** : CONSTRUCT, MANUFACTURE; *specif* : to construct from diverse and usu. standardized parts — **fab·ri·ca·tor** \'fa-bri-ˌkā-tər\ *n*

fab·ri·ca·tion \ˌfa-bri-'kā-shən\ *n* (15c) **1** : the act or process of fabricating **2** : a product of fabrication; *esp* : LIE, FALSEHOOD

fabric softener *n* (1965) : a product used to make laundered fabrics softer and fluffier

fab·u·lar \'fa-byə-lər\ *adj* (1684) : of, relating to, or having the form of a fable

fab·u·list \'fa-byə-list\ *n* (1593) **1** : a creator or writer of fables **2** : LIAR — **fabulist** *or* **fab·u·lis·tic** \ˌfa-byə-'lis-tik\ *adj*

fab·u·lous \'fa-byə-ləs\ *adj* [ME, fr. L *fabulosus*, fr. *fabula*] (15c) **1 a** : resembling or suggesting a fable : of an incredible, astonishing, or exaggerated nature ⟨~ wealth⟩ **b** : WONDERFUL, MARVELOUS ⟨had a ~ time⟩ **2** : told in or based on fable *syn* see FICTITIOUS — **fab·u·lous·ly** *adv* — **fab·u·lous·ness** *n*

fa·cade *also* **fa·çade** \fə-'säd\ *n* [F *façade*, fr. It *facciata*, fr. *faccia* face, fr. (assumed) VL *facia*] (ca. 1681) **1** : the front of a building; *also* : any face of a building given special architectural treatment ⟨a museum's east ~⟩ **2** : a false, superficial, or artificial appearance or effect

¹**face** \'fās\ *n, often attrib* [ME, fr. OF, fr. (assumed) VL *facia*, fr. L *facies* mien, form, face, fr. *facere* to make, do — more at DO] (13c) **1 a** : the front part of the human head including the chin, mouth, nose, cheeks, eyes, and usu. the forehead **b** : the face as a means of identification : COUNTENANCE ⟨would know that ~ anywhere⟩ **2** *archaic* : PRESENCE, SIGHT **3 a** : facial expression **b** : GRIMACE **c** : MAKEUP 3a(1) **4 a** : outward appearance ⟨suspicious on the ~ of it⟩ **b** : DISGUISE, PRETENSE **c** (1) : ASSURANCE, CONFIDENCE ⟨maintaining a firm ~ in spite of adversity⟩ (2) : EFFRONTERY ⟨how anyone could have the ~ to ask that question⟩ **d** : DIGNITY, PRESTIGE ⟨afraid to lose ~⟩ **5** : SURFACE: **a** (1) : a front, upper, or outer surface (2) : the front of something having two or four sides (3) : FACADE (4) : the exposed surface of rock **5** : any of the plane surfaces that bound a geometric solid **b** : a surface specially prepared: as (1) : the principal dressed surface (as of a disk) (2) : the right side (as of cloth or leather) (3) : an inscribed, printed, or marked side **c** (1) : the surface (as of type) that receives the ink and transfers it to the paper (2) : a style of type **6** : the end or wall of a mine tunnel, drift, or excavation at which work is progressing **7** : FACE VALUE **8** : PERSON ⟨lots of new ~s around here⟩ — **in the face of** *also* **in face of** : in the face of ⟨succeed *in the face of* great difficulties⟩ — **to one's face** : in one's presence or so that one is fully aware of what is going on : FRANKLY

²**face** *vb* **faced; fac·ing** *vt* (15c) **1** : to confront impudently **2 a** : to line near the edge esp. with a different material **b** : to cover the front or surface of ⟨*faced* the building with marble⟩ **3** : to meet face-to-face or in competition **4 a** : to stand or sit with the face toward **b** : to have the front oriented toward ⟨a house *facing* the park⟩ **5 a** : to recognize and deal with straightforwardly ⟨~ the facts⟩ **b** : to master by confronting with determination — used with *down* ⟨*faced* down his critics⟩ **6 a** : to have as a prospect : be confronted by ⟨~ a grim

future⟩ **b** : to be a prospect or a source of concern for ⟨the problems that ~ us⟩ **c** : to bring face-to-face ⟨he was *faced* with ruin⟩ **7** : to make the surface of (as a stone) flat or smooth **8** : to cause (troops) to face in a particular direction on command ~ *vi* **1** : to have the face or front turned in a specified direction **2** : to turn the face in a specified direction — **face the music** : to meet an unpleasant situation, a danger, or the consequences of one's actions

face angle *n* (1913) : an angle formed by two edges of a polyhedral angle

face card *n* (1826) : a king, queen, or jack in a deck of cards

face–cen·tered \'fās-ˌsen-tərd\ *adj* (1913) : relating to or being a crystal space lattice in which each cubic unit cell has an atom at the center and at the corners of each face — compare BODY-CENTERED

face·cloth \'fās-ˌklȯth\ *n* (1602) : WASHCLOTH

face cord *n* (ca. 1926) : a unit of wood cut for fuel equal to a stack 4 × 8 feet with lengths of pieces from about 12 to 16 inches

-faced \ˌfāst\ *adj comb form* : having (such) a face or (so many) faces ⟨rosy-*faced*⟩ ⟨two-*faced*⟩

face·down \ˌfās-'dau̇n\ *adv* (1949) : with the face down ⟨sliding ~⟩

face fly *n* (1961) : a European fly (*Musca autumnalis*) that is similar to the housefly, is widely established in No. America, and causes distress to livestock by clustering about the face

face·less \'fās-ləs\ *adj* (1596) **1** : lacking a face **2 a** : lacking character or individuality : NONDESCRIPT ⟨the ~ masses⟩ **b** : not identified : ANONYMOUS ⟨a ~ accuser⟩ — **face·less·ness** *n*

face–lift \'fās-ˌlift\ *n* (1934) **1** : a cosmetic operation for removal of facial defects (as wrinkles) typical of aging **2** : an alteration, restoration, or restyling (as of a building) intended esp. to modernize — **face–lift** *vt*

face mask *n* (1906) : a mask covering the face (as in football or scuba diving) : MASK 3

face–off \'fās-ˌȯf\ *n* (1896) **1** : a method of beginning play (as in hockey or lacrosse) in which two opponents face each other and attempt to gain control of a puck or ball dropped between them **2** : CONFRONTATION

face·plate \'fās-ˌplāt\ *n* (1841) **1** : a disk fixed with its face at right angles to the live spindle of a lathe for the attachment of the work **2 a** : a protective plate for a machine or device **b** : a protective cover for the human face (as of a diver) **3** : the glass front of a cathode-ray tube on which the image is seen

fac·er \'fā-sər\ *n* (15c) **1** : one that faces **2** *Brit* : a sudden often stunning check or obstacle

face–sav·er \'fā(s)-ˌsā-vər\ *n* (1923) : something (as a compromise) that saves face — **face–sav·ing** \-ˌsā-viŋ\ *adj or n*

fac·et \'fa-sət\ *n* [F *facette*, dim. of *face*] (1625) **1** : a small plane surface (as on a cut gem) — see BRILLIANT illustration **2** : any of the definable aspects that make up a subject (as of contemplation) or an object (as of consideration) **3** : the external corneal surface of an ommatidium **4** : a smooth flat circumscribed anatomical surface (as of a bone) — **fac·et·ed** *or* **fac·et·ted** \'fa-sə-təd\ *adj*

fa·cete \fə-'sēt\ *adj* [L *facetus*] (1603) *archaic* : FACETIOUS, WITTY

fa·ce·ti·ae \fə-'sē-shē-ˌē, -ˌī\ *n pl* [L, fr. pl. of *facetia* jest, fr. *facetus* elegant, witty] (1529) : witty or humorous writings or sayings

fa·ce·tious \fə-'sē-shəs\ *adj* [MF *facetieux*, fr. *facetie* jest, fr. L *facetia*] (1599) **1** : joking or jesting often inappropriately ⟨just being ~⟩ **2** : meant to be humorous or funny : not serious ⟨a ~ remark⟩ *syn* see WITTY — **fa·ce·tious·ly** *adv* — **fa·ce·tious·ness** *n*

face–to–face *adv or adj* (14c) **1** : within each other's sight or presence ⟨met and talked ~⟩ ⟨a ~ consultation⟩ **2** : in or into direct contact or confrontation ⟨came ~ with the problem⟩

face·up \'fā-ˌsəp\ *adv* (1897) : with the face up

face up *vi* (1920) : to confront or deal directly with someone or something previously avoided — usu. used with *to* ⟨*faced up* to the situation⟩

face value *n* (1876) **1** : the value indicated on the face (as of a postage stamp or a stock certificate) **2** : the apparent value or significance ⟨if their remarks may be taken at *face value*⟩

facia *var of* FASCIA

¹**fa·cial** \'fā-shəl\ *adj* (ca. 1818) **1** : of or relating to the face **2** : concerned with or used in improving the appearance of the face — **fa·cial·ly** \-shə-lē\ *adv*

²**facial** *n* (1914) : a facial treatment

facial index *n* (ca. 1889) : the ratio of the breadth of the face to its length multiplied by 100

facial nerve *n* (ca. 1818) : either of the 7th pair of cranial nerves that supply motor fibers esp. to the muscles of the face and jaw and sensory and parasympathetic fibers to the tongue, palate, and fauces

-fa·cient \'fā-shənt\ *adj comb form* [L *-facient-, -faciens* (as in *calefacient-, calefaciens* making warm, prp. of *calefacere* to warm)] : making : causing ⟨*somnifacient*⟩

fa·cies \'fā-sh(ē-)ˌēz\ *n, pl* **facies** [NL, fr. L, face] (ca. 1736) **1** : an appearance and expression of the face characteristic of a particular condition esp. when abnormal ⟨adenoid ~⟩ **2** : general appearance ⟨a plant species with a particularly distinct ~⟩ **3** : a part of a rock or group of rocks that differs from the whole formation (as in composition, age, or fossil content)

fac·ile \'fa-səl\ *adj* [MF, fr. L *facilis*, fr. *facere* to do — more at DO] (15c) **1 a** : easily accomplished or attained ⟨a ~ victory⟩ (2) : SPECIOUS, SUPERFICIAL ⟨I am not concerned ... with offering any ~ solution for so complex a problem —T. S. Eliot⟩ **b** : used or comprehended with ease **c** : readily manifested and often lacking sincerity or depth ⟨~ tears⟩ **2** *archaic* : mild or pleasing in manner or disposition **3 a** : READY, FLUENT ⟨~ prose⟩ **b** : POISED, ASSURED *syn* see EASY — **fac·ile·ly** \-s(ə)l-lē\ *adv* — **fac·ile·ness** \-səl-nəs\ *n*

fa·cil·i·tate \fə-'si-lə-ˌtāt\ *vt* **-tat·ed; -tat·ing** (1611) : to make easier : help bring about ⟨~ economic recovery⟩ — **fa·cil·i·ta·tive** \-ˌtā-tiv\ *adj* — **fa·cil·i·ta·tor** \-ˌtā-tər\ *n*

facade 1

\ə\ abut \ᵊ\ kitten, F table \ər\ further \a\ ash \ā\ ace \ä\ mop, mar \au̇\ out \ch\ chin \e\ bet \ē\ easy \g\ go \i\ hit \ī\ ice \j\ job \ŋ\ sing \ō\ go \ȯ\ law \ȯi\ boy \th\ thin \th\ the \ü\ loot \u̇\ foot \y\ yet \zh\ vision \à, ᴋ, ⁿ, œ, œ̄, ᵫ, ᵫ̄, ʸ\ see Guide to Pronunciation

fa·cil·i·ta·tion \fə-ˌsi-lə-'tā-shən\ n (1619) **1** : the act of facilitating : the state of being facilitated **2 a** : the lowering of the threshold for reflex conduction along a particular neural pathway esp. from repeated use of that pathway **b** : the increasing of the ease or intensity of a response by repeated stimulation

fa·cil·i·ta·to·ry \fə-'si-lə-tə-ˌtōr-ē, -ˌtor-\ adj (1944) : inducing or involved in facilitation esp. of a reflex action

fa·cil·i·ty \fə-'si-lə-tē\ n, pl **-ties** (1531) **1** : the quality of being easily performed **2** : ease in performance : APTITUDE **3** : readiness of compliance **4 a** (1) : something that makes an action, operation, or course of conduct easier — usu. used in pl. ⟨facilities for study⟩ (2) : LAVATORY **2** — often used in pl. **b** : something (as a hospital) that is built, installed, or established to serve a particular purpose

fac·ing \'fā-siŋ\ n (1566) **1 a** : a lining at the edge esp. of a garment **b** pl : the collar, cuffs, and trimmings of a uniform coat **2** : an ornamental or protective layer **3** : material for facing

fac·sim·i·le \fak-'si-mə-lē\ n [L fac simile make similar] (1691) **1** : an exact copy **2** : a system of transmitting and reproducing graphic matter (as printing or still pictures) by means of signals sent over telephone lines **syn** see REPRODUCTION

fact \'fakt\ n [L factum, fr. neut. of factus, pp. of facere] (15c) **1** : a thing done: as **a** obs : FEAT **b** : CRIME ⟨accessory after the ~⟩ **c** archaic : ACTION **2** archaic : PERFORMANCE, DOING **3** : the quality of being actual : ACTUALITY ⟨a question of ~ hinges on evidence⟩ **4 a** : something that has actual existence ⟨space exploration is now a ~⟩ **b** : an actual occurrence ⟨prove the ~ of damage⟩ **5** : a piece of information presented as having objective reality — **in fact** : in truth

fact finder n (1926) : one that tries to determine the realities of a case, situation, or relationship; esp : an impartial examiner designated by a government agency to appraise the facts underlying a particular matter (as a labor dispute) — **fact-find·ing** n or adj

fac·tic·i·ty \fak-'ti-sə-tē\ n [F or G; F facticité, fr. G Faktizität, fr. Factum fact, fr. L factum] (1945) : the quality or state of being a fact

fac·tion \'fak-shən\ n [MF & L; MF, fr. L faction-, factio act of making, faction — more at FASHION] (1509) **1** : a party or group (as within a government) that is often contentious or self-seeking : CLIQUE **2** : party spirit esp. when marked by dissension — **fac·tion·al** \-shnəl, -shə-nᵊl\ adj — **fac·tion·al·ism** \-shnə-ˌli-zəm, -shə-nᵊl-ˌiz-\ n — **fac·tion·al·ly** \-ē\ adv

-fac·tion \'fak-shən\ n comb form [ME -faccioun, fr. MF & L; MF -faction, fr. L -faction-, -factio (as in satisfaction-, satisfactio satisfaction)] : making : -FICATION ⟨petrifaction⟩

fac·tious \'fak-shəs\ adj [MF or L; MF factiosus, fr. L factiosus, fr. factio] (1532) : of or relating to faction: as **a** : caused by faction ⟨~ disputes⟩ **b** : inclined to faction or the formation of factions **c** : SEDITIOUS — **fac·tious·ly** adv — **fac·tious·ness** n

fac·ti·tious \fak-'ti-shəs\ adj [L facticius, fr. factus, pp. of facere to make, do — more at DO] (1646) **1** : produced by humans rather than by natural forces **2** : formed by or adapted to an artificial or conventional standard **b** : produced by special effort : SHAM ⟨created a ~ demand by spreading rumors of shortage⟩ — **fac·ti·tious·ly** adv — **fac·ti·tious·ness** n

fac·ti·tive \'fak-tə-tiv\ adj [prob. fr. L factitare to do habitually, freq. of facere] (1846) : of, relating to, or being a transitive verb that in some constructions requires an objective complement as well as an object — **fac·ti·tive·ly** adv

-fac·tive \'fak-tiv\ adj comb form [MF -factif, fr. -faction] : making : causing ⟨putrefactive⟩

fact of life (1854) **1** : something that exists and must be taken into consideration **2** pl : the fundamental physiological processes and behavior involved in sex and reproduction

fac·toid \'fak-ˌtóid\ n (1973) **1** : an invented fact believed to be true because of its appearance in print **2** : a brief and usu. trivial news item

¹fac·tor \'fak-tər\ n [ME, fr. MF facteur, fr. L factor doer, fr. facere] (15c) **1** : one who acts or transacts business for another: as **a** : BROKER 1b **b** : one that lends money to producers and dealers (as on the security of accounts receivable) **2 a** (1) : one that actively contributes to the production of a result : INGREDIENT ⟨price wasn't a ~ in the decision⟩ (2) : a substance that functions in or promotes the function of a particular physiological process or bodily system **b** : a good or service used in the process of production **3** : GENE **4 a** : any of the numbers or symbols in mathematics that when multiplied together form a product; also : a number or symbol that divides another number or symbol **b** : a quantity by which a given quantity is multiplied or divided in order to indicate a difference in measurement ⟨costs increased by a ~ of 10⟩ — **fac·tor·ship** \-ˌship\ n

²factor vb **fac·tored; fac·tor·ing** \-t(ə-)riŋ\ vi (1621) : to work as a factor ~ vt **1** : to resolve into factors **2 a** : to include or admit as a factor — used with in or into ⟨~ inflation into our calculations⟩ **b** : to exclude as a factor — used with out — **fac·tor·able** \-t(ə-)rə-bəl\ adj

fac·tor·age \-t(ə-)rij\ n (1613) **1** : the charges made by a factor for services **2** : the business of a factor

factor analysis n (1931) : the analytical process of transforming statistical data (as measurements) into linear combinations of usu. independent variables — **factor analytic** adj

factor VIII \-'āt\ n (1954) : a glycoprotein of blood plasma that is essential for blood clotting and is absent or inactive in hemophilia — called also antihemophilic factor

factor group n (1897) : QUOTIENT GROUP

¹fac·to·ri·al \fak-'tōr-ē-əl, -'tor-\ adj (1837) : of, relating to, or being a factor or a factorial

²factorial n (1869) **1** : the product of all the positive integers from 1 to n — symbol n! **2** : the quantity 0! arbitrarily defined as equal to 1

fac·tor·iza·tion \ˌfak-tə-rə-'zā-shən\ n (1886) : the operation of resolving a quantity into factors; also : a product obtained by factorization — **fac·tor·ize** \'fak-tə-ˌrīz\ vt

fac·to·ry \'fak-t(ə-)rē\ n, pl **-ries** (1582) **1** : a station where resident factors trade **2 a** : a building or set of buildings with facilities for manufacturing **b** : the seat of some kind of production ⟨the vice factories of the slums⟩ — **fac·to·ry-like** \-ˌlīk\ adj

factory ship n (1927) : a ship equipped to process a whale or fish catch at sea

fac·to·tum \fak-'tō-təm\ n [NL, lit., do everything, fr. L fac (imper. of facere do) + totum everything] (1566) **1** : a person having many diverse activities or responsibilities **2** : a general servant

fac·tu·al \'fak-chə-wəl, -chəl, 'faksh-wəl\ adj [fact + -ual (as in actual)] (ca. 1834) **1** : of or relating to facts **2** : restricted to or based on fact — **fac·tu·al·i·ty** \ˌfak-chə-'wa-lə-tē\ n — **fac·tu·al·ly** \'fak-chə-wə-lē, -chə-lē, 'faksh-wə-\ adv — **fac·tu·al·ness** n

fac·tu·al·ism \'fak-chə-wə-ˌli-zəm, -chə-ˌli-, 'faksh-wə-\ n (1936) : adherence or dedication to facts — **fac·tu·al·ist** \-list\ n

fac·ture \'fak-chər\ n [ME, fr. MF, fr. L factura action of making, fr. factus] (15c) : the manner in which something (as an artistic work) is made : EXECUTION

fac·u·la \'fa-kyə-lə\ n, pl **-lae** \-ˌlē, -ˌlī\ [NL, fr. L, dim. of fac-, fax torch] (1706) : any of the bright regions of the sun's photosphere seen most easily near the sun's edge

fac·ul·ta·tive \'fa-kəl-ˌtā-tiv, Brit -tə-tiv\ adj (1820) **1 a** : of or relating to the grant of permission, authority, or privilege ⟨~ legislation⟩ **b** : OPTIONAL **2** : of or relating to a mental faculty **3 a** : taking place under some conditions but not under others ⟨~ diapause⟩ **b** : exhibiting an indicated lifestyle under some environmental conditions but not under others ⟨~ anaerobes⟩ — **fac·ul·ta·tive·ly** adv

fac·ul·ty \'fa-kəl-tē\ n, pl **-ties** [ME faculte, fr. MF faculté, fr. ML & L; ML facultat-, facultas branch of learning or teaching, fr. L, ability, abundance, fr. facilis facile] (14c) **1** : ABILITY, POWER: as **a** : innate or acquired ability to act or do **b** : an inherent capability, power, or function ⟨the ~ of hearing⟩ **c** : any of the powers of the mind formerly held by psychologists to form a basis for the explanation of all mental phenomena **d** : natural aptitude ⟨has a ~ for saying the right things⟩ **2 a** : a branch of teaching or learning in an educational institution **b** archaic : something in which one is trained or qualified **3 a** : the members of a profession **b** : the teaching and administrative staff and those members of the administration having academic rank in an educational institution **c** faculty pl : faculty members ⟨many ~ were present⟩ **4** : power, authority, or prerogative given or conferred **syn** see GIFT

fad \'fad\ n [origin unknown] (1867) : a practice or interest followed for a time with exaggerated zeal : CRAZE **syn** see FASHION — **fad·dish** \'fa-dish\ adj — **fad·dish·ness** n — **fad·dism** \'fa-ˌdi-zəm\ n — **fad·dist** \'fa-dist\ n — **fad·dy** \-dē\ adj

FAD \ˌef-ˌā-'dē\ n (1944) : FLAVIN ADENINE DINUCLEOTIDE

¹fade \'fād\ vb **fad·ed; fad·ing** [ME, fr. MF fader, fr. fade feeble, insipid, fr. (assumed) VL fatidus, alter. of L fatuus fatuous, insipid] vi (14c) **1** : to lose freshness, strength, or vitality : WITHER **2** : to lose freshness or brilliance of color **3** : to sink away : VANISH **4** : to change gradually in loudness, strength, or visibility — used of a motion-picture image or of an electronics signal and usu. with in or out **5** of an automobile brake : to lose braking power gradually **6** : to move back from the line of scrimmage — used of a quarterback ~ vt : to cause to fade — **fad·er** n

²fade n (1918) **1 a** : FADE-OUT **b** : a gradual changing of one picture to another in a motion-picture or television sequence **2** : a fading of an automobile brake **3** : a slight to moderate and usu. intentional slice in golf

³fade \'fād\ adj [ME, fr. MF] (15c) : INSIPID, COMMONPLACE

fade·away \'fā-də-ˌwā\ n (1909) **1 a** : SCREWBALL 1 **b** : a slide in which a base runner throws his body sideways to avoid the tag **2** : an act or instance of fading away

fade–in \'fā-ˌdin\ n (1917) : a gradual increase in a motion-picture or television image's visibility at the beginning of a sequence

fade·less \'fād-ləs\ adj (1652) : not susceptible to fading

fade–out \'fā-ˌdaút\ n (1917) : an act or instance of fading out; esp : a gradual decrease in a motion-picture or television image's visibility at the end of a sequence

fa·do \'fā-(ˌ)thü, 'fa-\ n, pl **fados** [Pg, lit., fate, fr. L fatum] (1902) : a plaintive Portuguese folk song

fae·cal, fae·ces var of FECAL, FECES

fa·e·na \fä-'ā-(ˌ)nä\ n [Sp, lit., task, fr. obs. Catal, fr. L facienda things to be done, fr. facere to do — more at DO] (1927) : a series of final passes leading to the kill made by the matador in a bullfight

fa·er·ie also **fa·ery** \'fā-(ə-)rē, 'far-ē, 'fer-ē\ n, pl **fa·er·ies** [MF faerie — more at FAIRY] (1590) **1** : FAIRYLAND **2** : FAIRY — **faery** adj

Faer·o·ese \ˌfar-ə-'wēz, ˌfer-, -'wēs\ n, pl **Faeroese** (1855) **1** : a member of the people inhabiting the Faeroes **2** : the North Germanic language of the Faeroese people — **Faeroese** adj

Faf·nir \'fäv-nər, 'fäf-, -ˌnir\ n [ON Fáfnir] : a dragon in Norse mythology that guards the Nibelungs' gold hoard until slain by Sigurd

¹fag \'fag\ vb **fagged; fag·ging** [obs. fag to droop, perh. fr. fag (fag end)] vi (1772) **1** : to work hard : TOIL **2** : to act as a fag esp. in an English public school ⟨fagging for older boys during his first year⟩ ~ vt : to tire by strenuous activity : EXHAUST **syn** see TIRE

²fag n (1780) **1** chiefly Brit : TOIL, DRUDGERY **2 a** : an English public school boy who acts as servant to an older schoolmate **b** : DRUDGE

³fag n [fag end] (ca. 1888) : CIGARETTE

⁴fag n [prob. by shortening] (ca. 1931) : FAGGOT — usu. used disparagingly — **fag·gy** \'fa-gē\ adj

fag end n [earlier fag, fr. ME fagge flap] (1613) **1 a** : a poor or worn-out end : REMNANT **b** : the extreme end **2 a** : the last part or coarser end of a web of cloth **b** : the untwisted end of a rope

fag·got \'fa-gət\ n [origin unknown] (1914) : a male homosexual — usu. used disparagingly — **fag·got·ry** \-gə-trē\ n — **fag·goty** \-gə-tē\ adj

fa·gin \'fā-gən\ n, often cap [Fagin, character in Charles Dickens' Oliver Twist 1839] (1847) : an adult who instructs others (as children) in crime

¹fag·ot or **fag·got** \'fa-gət\ n [ME fagot, fr. MF] (14c) : BUNDLE: as **a** : a bundle of sticks **b** : a bundle of pieces of wrought iron to be shaped by rolling or hammering at high temperature

²fagot or **faggot** vt (ca. 1598) : to make a fagot of : bind together into a bundle ⟨~ed sticks⟩

fagoting 1

fag·ot·ing or **fag·got·ing** n (1885) **1** : an embroidery produced by pulling out horizontal threads from a fabric and tying the remaining cross threads into groups of an hourglass shape **2 :** an openwork stitch joining hemmed edges

Fahr·en·heit \'far-ən-ˌhīt, 'fer-\ *adj* [Gabriel D. *Fahrenheit*] (1753) **:** relating or conforming to a thermometric scale on which under standard atmospheric pressure the boiling point of water is at 212 degrees above the zero of the scale, the freezing point is at 32 degrees above zero, and the zero point approximates the temperature produced by mixing equal quantities by weight of snow and common salt — abbr. *F*

fa·ience *or* **fa·ience** \fä-'än(t)s, fī-, -'äⁿs\ *n* [F, fr. *Faenza*, Italy] (1714) **:** earthenware decorated with opaque colored glazes

¹fail \'fā(ə)l\ *vb* [ME *failen*, fr. OF *faillir*, fr. (assumed) VL *fallire*, alter. of L *fallere* to deceive, disappoint] *vi* (13c) **1 a :** to lose strength **:** WEAKEN ⟨her health was ~*ing*⟩ **b :** to fade or die away ⟨until our family line ~*s*⟩ **c :** to stop functioning ⟨the patient's heart ~*ed*⟩ **2 a :** to fall short ⟨~*ed* in his duty⟩ **b :** to be or become absent or inadequate ⟨the water supply ~*ed*⟩ **c :** to be unsuccessful (as in passing an examination) **d :** to become bankrupt or insolvent ~ *vt* **1 a :** to disappoint the expectations or trust of ⟨her friends ~*ed* her⟩ **b :** to miss performing an expected service or function for ⟨his wit ~*ed* him⟩ **2 :** to be deficient in **:** LACK ⟨never ~*ed* an invincible courage —Douglas MacArthur⟩ **3 :** to leave undone **:** NEGLECT ⟨~ to lock the door⟩ **4 a :** to be unsuccessful in passing (as a test) **b :** to grade (as a student) as not passing — **fail·ing·ly** \'fā-liŋ-lē\ *adv*

²fail *n* (13c) **1 :** FAILURE — usu. used in the phrase *without fail* **2 :** a failure (as by a security dealer) to deliver or receive securities within a prescribed period after purchase or sale

¹fail·ing \'fā-liŋ\ *n* (1590) **:** a usu. slight or insignificant defect in character, conduct, or ability *syn* see FAULT

²failing *prep* (1810) **:** in absence or default of ⟨~ specific instructions, use your own judgment⟩

faille \'fī(ə)l\ *n* [F, fr. OF] (1869) **:** a somewhat shiny closely woven silk, rayon, or cotton fabric characterized by slight ribs in the weft

fail–safe \'fā(ə)l-ˌsāf\ *adj* (1946) **1 :** incorporating some feature for automatically counteracting the effect of an anticipated possible source of failure **2 :** being or relating to a safeguard that prevents continuing on a bombing mission according to a preconceived plan **3 :** having no chance of failure **:** infallibly problem-free

fail·ure \'fā(ə)l-yər\ *n* [alter. of earlier *failer*, fr. AF, fr. OF *faillir* to fail] (1643) **1 a :** omission of occurrence or performance; *specif* **:** a failing to perform a duty or expected action **b :** a state of inability to perform a normal function ⟨kidney ~⟩ — compare HEART FAILURE **c :** a fracturing or giving way under stress ⟨structural ~⟩ **2 a :** lack of success **b :** a failing in business **:** BANKRUPTCY **3 a :** a falling short **:** DEFICIENCY ⟨a crop ~⟩ **b :** DETERIORATION, DECAY **4 :** one that has failed

¹fain \'fān\ *adj* [ME *fagen*, *fayn*, fr. OE *fægen*; akin to ON *feginn* happy, OE *fæger* fair] (bef. 12c) **1** *archaic* **:** HAPPY, PLEASED **2** *archaic* **:** INCLINED, DESIROUS **3 a :** WILLING ⟨he was very ~, for the young widow was "altogether fair and lovely . . . " —Amy Kelly⟩ **b :** being obliged or constrained **:** COMPELLED ⟨Great Britain was ~ to devote its whole energy . . . to the business of slaying and being slain —G. M. Trevelyan⟩

²fain *adv* (12c) **1 :** with pleasure **:** GLADLY ⟨a speech of fire that ~ would blaze —Michael Billington⟩ **2 a :** by preference ⟨knew it, too, though he would ~ not admit it publicly —John Lukacs⟩ **b :** by desire ⟨I would ~ consult you —W. S. Gilbert⟩

¹fai·né·ant \fā-nā-'äⁿ\ *n, pl* **fainéants** \-'äⁿ(z)\ [F, fr. MF *fait-nient*, lit., does nothing, by folk etymology fr. *faignant*, fr. prp. of *faindre*, *feindre* to feign] (1619) **:** an irresponsible idler

²fai·né·ant \fā-nā-'äⁿ\ *or* **fai·ne·ant** \'fā-nē-ənt\ *adj* (1855) **:** idle and ineffectual **:** INDOLENT

¹faint \'fānt\ *adj* [ME *faint*, *feint*, fr. MF, fr. pp. of *faindre*, *feindre* to feign, shirk — more at FEIGN] (14c) **1 :** lacking courage and spirit **:** COWARDLY **2 :** weak, dizzy, and likely to faint **3 :** lacking strength or vigor **:** performed, offered, or accomplished weakly or languidly **4 :** producing a sensation of faintness **:** OPPRESSIVE ⟨the ~ atmosphere of a tropical port⟩ **5 :** lacking distinctness **:** DIM — **faint·ish** \'fān-tish\ *adj* — **faint·ish·ness** *n* — **faint·ly** *adv* — **faint·ness** *n*

²faint *vi* (14c) **1** *archaic* **:** to lose courage or spirit **2** *archaic* **:** to become weak **3 :** to lose consciousness because of a temporary decrease in the blood supply to the brain

³faint *n* (1808) **:** the physiological action of fainting; *also* **:** the resulting condition **:** SYNCOPE 1

faint·heart·ed \'fānt-'här-təd\ *adj* (15c) **:** lacking courage or resolution **:** TIMID — **faint·heart·ed·ly** *adv* — **faint·heart·ed·ness** *n*

¹fair \'far, 'fer\ *adj* [ME *fager*, *fair*, fr. OE *fæger*; akin to OHG *fagar* beautiful] (bef. 12c) **1 :** pleasing to the eye or mind esp. because of fresh, charming, or flawless quality **2 :** superficially pleasing **:** SPECIOUS ⟨he trusted his ~ promises⟩ **3 a :** CLEAN, PURE ⟨~ sparkling water⟩ **b :** CLEAR, LEGIBLE **4 :** not stormy or foul **:** FINE ⟨~ weather⟩ **5 :** AMPLE ⟨a ~ estate⟩ **6 a :** marked by impartiality and honesty **:** free from self-interest, prejudice, or favoritism ⟨a very ~ person to do business with⟩ **b** (1) **:** conforming with the established rules **:** ALLOWED (2) **:** consonant with merit or importance **:** DUE ⟨a ~ share⟩ **c :** open to legitimate pursuit, attack, or ridicule ⟨~ game⟩ **7 a :** PROMISING, LIKELY ⟨in a ~ way to win⟩ **b :** favorable to a ship's course ⟨a ~ wind⟩ **8** *archaic* **:** free of obstacles **9 :** not dark **:** BLOND **10 :** sufficient but not ample **:** ADEQUATE ⟨a ~ understanding of the work⟩ **11 :** being such to the utmost **:** UTTER ⟨a ~ treat to watch him —*New Republic*⟩ — **fair·ness** *n*

syn FAIR, JUST, EQUITABLE, IMPARTIAL, UNBIASED, DISPASSIONATE, OBJECTIVE mean free from favor toward either or any side. FAIR implies an elimination of one's own feelings, prejudices, and desires so as to achieve a proper balance of conflicting interests ⟨a *fair* decision⟩. JUST implies an exact following of a standard of what is right and proper ⟨a *just* settlement of territorial claims⟩. EQUITABLE implies a less rigorous standard than JUST and usu. suggests equal treatment of all concerned ⟨the *equitable* distribution of the property⟩. IMPARTIAL stresses an absence of favor or prejudice ⟨an *impartial* third party⟩. UNBIASED implies even more strongly an absence of all prejudice ⟨your *unbiased* opinion⟩. DISPASSIONATE suggests freedom from the influence of strong feeling and often implies cool or even cold judgment ⟨a *dispassionate* summation of the facts⟩. OBJECTIVE stresses a tendency to view events

or persons as apart from oneself and one's own interest or feelings ⟨I can't be *objective* about my own child⟩. *syn* see in addition BEAUTIFUL

²fair *n* (bef. 12c) **1** *obs* **:** BEAUTY, FAIRNESS **2 :** something that is fair or fortunate **3** *archaic* **:** WOMAN; *esp* **:** SWEETHEART — **for fair :** to the greatest extent or degree **:** FULLY ⟨the rush is on *for fair*⟩ — **no fair :** something that is not according to the rules ⟨that's *no fair*⟩

³fair *adv* (bef. 12c) *chiefly Brit* **:** FAIRLY 5

⁴fair *vi* (1836) *of the weather* **:** CLEAR ~ *vt* **:** to join so that the external surfaces blend smoothly

⁵fair *n* [ME *feire*, fr. OF, fr. ML *feria* weekday, fair, fr. LL, festal day, fr. L *feriae* (pl.) holidays — more at FEAST] (13c) **1 :** a gathering of buyers and sellers at a particular place and time for trade **2 a :** a competitive exhibition (as of farm products) usu. with accompanying entertainment and amusements **b :** an exhibition designed to acquaint prospective buyers or the general public with a product **3 :** a sale of assorted articles usu. for a charitable purpose

fair ball *n* (1856) **:** a batted baseball that lands within the foul lines or that is within the foul lines when bounding to the outfield past first or third base or when going beyond the outfield for a home run

fair catch *n* (ca. 1876) **:** a catch of a kicked football by a player who gives a prescribed signal, may not advance the ball, and may not be tackled

fair copy *n* (1709) **:** a neat and exact copy esp. of a corrected draft

fair-ground \'far-ˌgraůnd, 'fer-\ *n* (1741) **:** an area where outdoor fairs, circuses, or exhibitions are held — often used in pl. with sing. constr. ⟨what a spot for a ~*s* —W. L. Gresham⟩

fair–haired \'far-'hard, 'fer-'herd\ *adj* (1909) **:** specially favored **:** WHITE-HEADED — used esp. in the phrase *fair-haired boy*

¹fair·ing \'far-iŋ, 'fer-\ *n* (1574) **1** *Brit* **:** a present bought or given at a fair **b :** GIFT **2** *Brit* **:** ³DESERT 2

²fairing *n* (1914) **:** a member or structure whose primary function is to produce a smooth outline and to reduce drag (as on an airplane)

fair·ish \'far-ish, 'fer-\ *adj* (1611) **:** fairly good ⟨a ~ wage for those days⟩ — **fair·ish·ly** *adv*

Fair Isle *n* (1851) **:** a style of knitting originating in the Shetland Islands that is characterized by bands of multicolored geometric patterns; *also* **:** an article of clothing knitted in this style

fair–lead \'far-ˌlēd, 'fer-\ *n* (ca. 1841) **1** *also* **fair–lead·er** \-ˌlē-dər\ **:** a block, ring, or strip of plank with holes that serves as a guide for the running rigging or any ship's rope and keeps it from chafing **2 :** a course of running ship's rope that avoids all chafing

fair·ly \'far-lē, 'fer-\ *adv* (12c) **1 :** in a handsome manner ⟨a table ~ set⟩ **2** *obs* **a :** in a gentle manner **:** QUIETLY **b :** in a courteous manner **3 :** in a manner of speaking ⟨~ bursting with pride⟩ **4 a :** in a proper or legal manner ⟨~ priced stocks⟩ **b :** without bias or distortion **:** IMPARTIALLY ⟨a story told ~ and objectively⟩ **5 :** to a full degree or extent **:** PLAINLY, DISTINCTLY ⟨had ~ caught sight of him⟩ **6 :** RATHER 5, MODERATELY ⟨a ~ easy job⟩

fair market value *n* (1901) **:** a price at which both buyers and sellers are willing to do business

fair–mind·ed \'far-ˌmīn-dəd, 'fer-\ *adj* (1874) **:** marked by impartiality and honesty **:** JUST, UNPREJUDICED — **fair–mind·ed·ness** *n*

fairness doctrine *n* (1967) **:** a tenet of licensed broadcasting that ensures a reasonable opportunity for the airing of conflicting viewpoints on controversial issues

fair play *n* (1595) **:** equitable or impartial treatment **:** JUSTICE

fair shake *n* (1830) **:** a fair chance or fair treatment ⟨give the negative side a *fair shake* —S. L. Payne⟩

fair–spo·ken \'far-ˌspō-kən, 'fer-\ *adj* (15c) **:** pleasant and courteous in speech ⟨a ~ youth⟩

fair–trade \'far-'trād, 'fer-\ *vt* (1947) **:** to market (a commodity) in compliance with the provisions of a fair-trade agreement — **fair trade** *n* — **fair trader** *n*

fair–trade agreement *n* (1937) **:** an agreement between a producer and a seller that commodities bearing a trademark, label, or brand name belonging to the producer be sold at or above a specified price

fair·way \'far-ˌwā, 'fer-\ *n* (1584) **1 a :** a navigable part of a river, bay, or harbor **b :** an open path or space **2 :** the closely mowed part of a golf course between a tee and a green

fair–weather *adj* (1736) **1 :** loyal only during a time of success ⟨a ~ friend⟩ **2 :** suitable for or done during fair weather ⟨a ~ sail⟩

fairy \'far-ē, 'fer-\ *n, pl* **fair·ies** [ME *fairie*, fairyland, fairy people, fr. OF *faerie*, fr. *feie*, *fee* fairy, fr. L *Fata*, goddess of fate, fr. *fatum* fate] (14c) **1 :** a mythical being of folklore and romance usu. having diminutive human form and magic powers **2 :** a male homosexual — usu. used disparagingly — **fairy** *adj* — **fairy–like** \-ˌlīk\ *adj*

fairy godmother *n* (1851) **:** a generous friend or benefactor

fairy·ism \-ˌi-zəm\ *n* (1715) *archaic* **:** the power to enchant

fairy·land \-ˌland\ *n* (1590) **1 :** the land of fairies **2 :** a place of delicate beauty or magical charm

fairy ring *n* [fr. the folk belief that such rings were dancing places of the fairies] (1599) **1 :** a ring of basidiomycetous mushrooms produced at the periphery of a body of mycelium which has grown outward from an initial growth point; *also* **:** a ring of luxuriant vegetation esp. when associated with these mushrooms **2 :** a mushroom (esp. *Marasmius oreades*) that commonly grows in fairy rings

fairy shrimp *n* (1857) **:** any of several delicate transparent freshwater branchiopod crustaceans (order Anostraca)

fairy–tale *adj* (1924) **:** characteristic of or suitable to a fairy tale; *esp* **:** marked by seemingly unreal beauty, perfection, luck, or happiness

fairy tale *n* (1749) **1 :** a story (as for children) involving fantastic forces and beings (as fairies, wizards, and goblins) — called also *fairy story* **2 :** a made-up story usu. designed to mislead

fait ac·com·pli \ˌfä-tə-ˌkäm-'plē, ˌfe-, ˌfe-ˌta-, -ˌkōⁿ(m)-, *Brit usu* -'käm-(ˌ)plē\ *n, pl* **faits accomplis** *same*, *or* -'plēz\ [F, accomplished fact] (1845) **:** a thing accomplished and presumably irreversible

\ə\ abut \ᵊ\ kitten, F table \ər\ further \a\ ash \ā\ ace \ä\ mop, mar \aů\ out \ch\ chin \e\ bet \ē\ easy \g\ go \i\ hit \ī\ ice \j\ job \ŋ\ sing \ō\ go \ò\ law \òi\ boy \th\ thin \t͟h\ the \ü\ loot \ů\ foot \y\ yet \zh\ vision \à, k̲, ⁿ, œ, œ̄, ų, ūᴇ, ᵊ\ *see* Guide to Pronunciation

¹faith \'fāth\ *n, pl* **faiths** \'fāths, *sometimes* 'fāthz\ [ME *feith,* fr. OF *feid, foi,* fr. L *fides;* akin to L *fidere* to trust — more at BIDE] (13c) **1 a** : allegiance to duty or a person : LOYALTY **b** (1) : fidelity to one's promises (2) : sincerity of intentions **2 a** (1) : belief and trust in and loyalty to God (2) : belief in the traditional doctrines of a religion **b** (1) : firm belief in something for which there is no proof (2) : complete trust **3** : something that is believed esp. with strong conviction; *esp* : a system of religious beliefs **syn** see BELIEF — **in faith** : without doubt or question : VERILY

²faith *vt* (15c) *archaic* : BELIEVE, TRUST

¹faith·ful \'fāth-fəl\ *adj* (14c) **1** *obs* : full of faith **2** : steadfast in affection or allegiance : LOYAL **3** : firm in adherence to promises or in observance of duty : CONSCIENTIOUS **4** : given with strong assurance : BINDING ⟨~ promise⟩ **5** : true to the facts, to a standard, or to an original ⟨a ~ copy⟩ — **faith·ful·ly** \-fə-lē\ *adv* — **faith·ful·ness** *n*
syn FAITHFUL, LOYAL, CONSTANT, STAUNCH, STEADFAST, RESOLUTE mean firm in adherence to whatever one owes allegiance. FAITHFUL implies unswerving adherence to a person or thing or to the oath or promise by which a tie was contracted ⟨*faithful* to her promise⟩. LOYAL implies a firm resistance to any temptation to desert or betray ⟨remained *loyal* to the czar⟩. CONSTANT stresses continuing firmness of emotional attachment without necessarily implying strict obedience to promises or vows ⟨*constant* friends⟩. STAUNCH suggests fortitude and resolution in adherence and imperviousness to influences that would weaken it ⟨a *staunch* defender of free speech⟩. STEADFAST implies a steady and unwavering course in love, allegiance, or conviction ⟨*steadfast* in their support⟩. RESOLUTE implies firm determination to adhere to a cause or purpose ⟨a *resolute* ally⟩.

²faithful *n* (1558) **1** *pl in constr* **a** : church members in full communion and good standing — used with *the* **b** : the body of believers in Islam — used with *the* **2** *pl* **faithful** *or* **faithfuls** : one who is faithful; *esp* : a loyal follower, member, or fan ⟨party ~s⟩
faith healing *n* (1885) : a method of treating diseases by prayer and exercise of faith in God — **faith healer** *n*
faith·less \'fāth-ləs\ *adj* (14c) **1** : not true to allegiance or duty : TREACHEROUS, DISLOYAL ⟨a ~ servant⟩ **2** : not to be relied on : UNTRUSTWORTHY ⟨a ~ tool⟩ — **faith·less·ly** *adv* — **faith·less·ness** *n*
syn FAITHLESS, FALSE, DISLOYAL, TRAITOROUS, TREACHEROUS, PERFIDIOUS mean untrue to what should command one's fidelity or allegiance. FAITHLESS applies to any failure to keep a promise or pledge or any breach of allegiance or loyalty ⟨*faithless* allies⟩. FALSE stresses the fact of failing to be true in any manner ranging from fickleness to cold treachery ⟨betrayed by *false* friends⟩. DISLOYAL implies a lack of complete faithfulness to a friend, cause, leader, or country ⟨*disloyal* to their country⟩. TRAITOROUS implies either actual treason or a serious betrayal of trust ⟨*traitorous* acts punishable by death⟩. TREACHEROUS implies readiness to betray trust or confidence ⟨a *treacherous* adviser⟩. PERFIDIOUS adds to FAITHLESS the implication of an incapacity for fidelity or reliability ⟨a *perfidious* double-crosser⟩.

fai·tour \'fā-tər\ *n* [ME, fr. AF, fr. OF *faitor* perpetrator, fr. L *factor* doer — more at FACTOR] (14c) *archaic* : CHEAT, IMPOSTER
fa·ji·ta \fə-'hē-tə, fä-\ *n* [AmerSp, dim. of Sp *faja* sash, belt, prob. fr. Catal *faixa,* fr. L *fascia* band — more at FASCIA] (1984) : a marinated strip usu. of beef or chicken grilled or broiled and served usu. with a flour tortilla and various savory fillings — usu. used in pl.
¹fake \'fāk\ *vt* **faked; fak·ing** (15c) : to coil in fakes
²fake *n* (1627) : one loop of a coil (as of ship's rope or a fire hose) coiled free for running
³fake *adj* [origin unknown] (1775) : COUNTERFEIT, SHAM
⁴fake *n* (1827) : one that is not what it purports to be: as **a** : a worthless imitation passed off as genuine **b** : IMPOSTOR, CHARLATAN **c** : a simulated movement in a sports contest (as a pretended kick, pass, or jump or a quick movement in one direction before going in another) designed to deceive an opponent **d** : a device or apparatus used by a magician to achieve the illusion of magic in a trick **syn** see IMPOSTURE
⁵fake *vb* **faked; fak·ing** *vt* (1851) **1** : to alter, manipulate, or treat so as to give a spuriously genuine appearance to : DOCTOR ⟨*faked* the lab results⟩ **2** : COUNTERFEIT, SIMULATE, CONCOCT **3** : to deceive (an opponent) in a sports contest by means of a fake **4** : IMPROVISE, AD-LIB ⟨whistle a few bars . . . and I'll ~ the rest —Robert Sylvester⟩ ~ *vi* **1** : to engage in faking something : PRETEND **2** : to give a fake to an opponent — **fak·er** *n* — **fak·ery** \'fā-k(ə-)rē\ *n*
fake out *vt* (1968) : to deliberately mislead : FOOL, TRICK
fa·kir *n* [Ar *faqīr,* lit., poor man] (1609) **1** \fə-'kir, fä-, fa-; 'fā-kər\ **a** : a Muslim mendicant : DERVISH **b** : an itinerant Hindu ascetic or wonder-worker **2** \'fā-kər\ : IMPOSTOR; *esp* : SWINDLER
fa la \fä-'lä\ *n* [*fa-la,* meaningless syllables often occurring in its refrain] (1597) : a 16th and 17th century part-song
fa·la·fel \fə-'lä-fəl\ *n, pl* **falafel** [Ar *falāfil*] (1950) : a spicy mixture of ground vegetables (as chick-peas or fava beans) formed into balls or patties and then fried
Fa·lan·gist \fə-'lan-jist, 'fā-,\ *n* [Sp *falangista,* fr. *Falange española* Spanish Phalanx, a fascist organization] (1936) : a member of the fascist political party governing Spain after the civil war of 1936–39
Fa·la·sha \fə-'lä-shə\ *n, pl* **-sha** *or* **-shas** [Amharic *fälaša*] (1710) : a member of a people of highland Ethiopia who practice a variety of Judaism
fal·cate \'fal-,kāt, 'föl-\ *adj* [L *falcatus,* fr. *falc-, falx* sickle, scythe] (1826) : hooked or curved like a sickle
fal·chion \'föl-chən\ *n* [ME *fauchoun,* fr. MF *fauchon,* fr. *fauchier* to mow, fr. (assumed) VL *falcare,* fr. L *falc-, falx*] (14c) **1** : a broad-bladed slightly curved sword of medieval times **2** *archaic* : SWORD
fal·ci·form \'fal-sə-,förm, 'föl-\ *adj* [L *falc-, falx* + E *-iform*] (1766) : having the shape of a scythe or sickle
fal·con \'fal-kən, 'föl- *also* 'fö-kən\ *n* [ME, fr. OF, fr. LL *falcon-, falco,* prob. fr. L *falc-, falx*] (13c) **1** : any of various hawks trained for use in falconry; *esp* : PEREGRINE — used technically only of a female; compare TIERCEL **2** : any of various hawks (family Falconidae) that have long pointed wings, a long tail, and a notched beak and that usu. inhabit open areas
fal·con·er \-kə-nər\ *n* (14c) : a person who breeds, trains, or hunts with hawks

fal·con·et \,fal-kə-'net, ,föl- *also* ,fö-\ *n* (1559) **1** : a very small cannon used in the 16th and 17th centuries **2** : any of several very small falcons (genera *Microhierax, Prolihierax,* and *Spiziapteryx*)
fal·con-gen·tle \,fal-kən-'jen-t°l\ *n* [ME *faucon gentil* peregrine falcon, fr. MF, lit., noble falcon] (15c) : the female peregrine falcon
fal·co·nine \'fal-kə-,nīn, 'föl- *also* 'fö-\ *adj* (ca. 1889) : of or resembling a falcon ⟨a ~ face⟩
fal·con·ry \'fal-kən-rē, 'föl- *also* 'fö-kən-\ *n* (1575) **1** : the art of training hawks to hunt in cooperation with a person **2** : the sport of hunting with hawks
fal·de·ral \'fal-də-,räl\ *var of* FOLDEROL
fald·stool \'föl(d)-,stül\ *n* [ML *faldistolium,* of Gmc origin; akin to OHG *faltistuol* folding chair, fr. *falt* (akin to OHG *faldan* to fold) + *stuol* chair — more at FOLD, STOOL] (1603) **1** : a folding stool or chair; *specif* : one used by a bishop **2** : a folding stool or small desk at which one kneels during devotions; *esp* : one used by the sovereigns of England at their coronation **3** : the desk from which the litany is read in Anglican churches

faldstool 1

¹fall \'föl\ *vb* **fell** \'fel\; **fall·en** \'fö-lən\; **fall·ing** [ME, fr. OE *feallan;* akin to OHG *fallan* to fall and perh. to Lith *pulti*] *vi* (bef. 12c) **1 a** : to descend freely by the force of gravity **b** : to hang freely ⟨her hair ~s over her shoulders⟩ **c** : to drop oneself to a lower position ⟨*fell* to his knees⟩ **d** : to come or go as if by falling ⟨darkness ~s early in the winter⟩ **2** : to become born — usu. used of lambs **3 a** : to become lower in degree or level ⟨the temperature *fell* 10°⟩ **b** : to drop in pitch or volume ⟨their voices *fell* to a whisper⟩ **c** : ISSUE 1a,b ⟨wisdom that *fell* from his lips⟩ **d** : to become lowered ⟨her eyes *fell*⟩ **4 a** : to leave an erect position suddenly and involuntarily ⟨slipped and *fell* on the ice⟩ **b** : to enter as if unawares : STUMBLE, STRAY ⟨*fell* into error⟩ **c** : to drop down wounded or dead; *esp* : to die in battle **d** : to suffer military capture ⟨after a long siege the city *fell*⟩ **e** : to lose office ⟨the party *fell* from power⟩ **f** : to suffer ruin, defeat, or failure ⟨the deal *fell* through⟩ **5** : to commit an immoral act; *esp* : to lose one's chastity **6 a** : to move or extend in a downward direction ⟨the land ~s away to the east⟩ **b** : SUBSIDE, ABATE ⟨the wind is ~ing⟩ **c** : to decline in quality, activity, or quantity ⟨production *fell* off⟩ **d** : to lose weight — used with *off* or *away* **e** : to assume a look of shame, disappointment, or dejection ⟨his face *fell*⟩ **f** : to decline in financial value or price ⟨stocks *fell* sharply⟩ **7 a** : to occur at a certain time **b** : to come by chance ⟨*fell* in with a fast crowd⟩ **c** : to come or pass by lot, assignment, or inheritance : DEVOLVE ⟨it *fell* to him to break the news⟩ **d** : to have a certain or proper position, place, or station ⟨the accent ~s on the second syllable⟩ **8** : to come within the limits, scope, or jurisdiction of something ⟨this word ~s into the class of verbs⟩ **9** : to pass suddenly and passively into a state of body or mind or a new state or condition ⟨~ asleep⟩ ⟨~ in love⟩ **10** : to set about heartily or actively ⟨*fell* to work⟩ **11** : STRIKE, IMPINGE ⟨music ~ing on the ear⟩ ~ *vt* : FELL 1 — **fall apart 1** : DISINTEGRATE **2** : to succumb to mental or emotional stress : BREAK DOWN — **fall behind 1** : to lag behind **2** : to be in arrears — **fall between two stools** : to fail because of inability to choose between or reconcile two alternative or conflicting courses of action — **fall flat** : to produce no response or result ⟨the joke *fell* flat⟩ — **fall for 1** : to fall in love with **2** : to become a victim of ⟨*fell* for the trick⟩ — **fall foul** : to have a quarrel : CLASH — often used with *of* — **fall from grace** : BACKSLIDE 1 — **fall home** : to curve inward — used of the timbers or upper parts of a ship's side — **fall into line** : to comply with a certain course of action — **fall on** *or* **fall upon** : to meet with ⟨*fell* on hard times⟩ — **fall over oneself** *or* **fall over backward** : to display excessive eagerness — **fall short 1** : to be deficient **2** : to fail to attain something (as a goal or target)
²fall *n* (13c) **1** : the act of falling by the force of gravity **2 a** : a falling out, off, or away : DROPPING ⟨the ~ of leaves⟩ ⟨a ~ of snow⟩ **b** : the season when leaves fall from trees : AUTUMN **c** : a thing or quantity that falls or has fallen ⟨a ~ of rock at the base of the cliff⟩; *esp* : one or more meteorites or their fragments that have fallen together **d** (1) : BIRTH (2) : the quantity born — usu. used of lambs **3 a** : a costume decoration of lace or thin fabric arranged to hang loosely and gracefully **b** : a very wide turned-down collar worn in the 17th century **c** : the part of a turnover collar from the crease to the outer edge **d** : a wide front flap on trousers (as those worn by sailors) **e** : the freely hanging lower edge of the skirt of a coat **f** : one of the three outer and often drooping segments of the flower of an iris **g** : long hair overhanging the face of dogs of some breeds **h** : a usu. long straight portion of hair that is attached to a person's own hair **4 a** : a hoisting-tackle rope or chain; *esp* : the part of it to which the power is applied **5 a** : loss of greatness : COLLAPSE ⟨the ~ of the Roman Empire⟩ **b** : the surrender or capture of a besieged place ⟨the ~ of Troy⟩ **c** : lapse or departure from innocence or goodness **d** : loss of a woman's chastity **6 a** : the downward slope (as of a hill) : DECLIVITY **b** : a precipitous descent of water : WATERFALL — usu. used in pl. but sing. or pl. in constr. **c** : a musical cadence **d** : a falling-pitch intonation in speech **7** : a decrease in size, quantity, degree, or value **8 a** : the distance which something falls **b** : INCLINATION, PITCH **9 a** : the act of felling something **b** : the quantity of trees cut down ⟨c⟩ (1) : an act of forcing a wrestler's shoulders to the mat for a specified time (as one second) (2) : a bout of wrestling **10** *Scot* : DESTINY, LOT
³fall *adj* (1677) : of, relating to, or suitable for autumn ⟨a new ~ coat⟩
fal·la·cious \fə-'lā-shəs\ *adj* (1509) **1** : embodying a fallacy **2** : tending to deceive or mislead : DELUSIVE — **fal·la·cious·ly** *adv* — **fal·la·cious·ness** *n*
fal·la·cy \'fa-lə-sē\ *n, pl* **-cies** [L *fallacia,* fr. *fallac-, fallax* deceitful, fr. *fallere* to deceive] (14c) **1 a** *obs* : GUILE, TRICKERY **b** : deceptive appearance : DECEPTION **2 a** : a false or mistaken idea ⟨popular *fallacies*⟩ **b** : erroneous character : ERRONEOUSNESS **3** : an often plausible argument using false or invalid inference
fal–lal \fa-'lal, 'fa(l)-,lal\ *n* [perh. alter. of *falbala* furbelow, fr. F, fr. F dial. *ferbelà, farbélla*] (ca. 1706) : a fancy ornament esp. in dress — **fal·lal·ery** \fa-'la-lə-rē\ *n*

fall armyworm n (1881) : a migratory American moth (*Spodoptera frugiperda*) that is esp. destructive to small grains and grasses as a larva
fall-away \'fȯ-lə-ˌwā\ adj (1966) : made while moving away from the basket in basketball ⟨a ~ jumper⟩ — **fallaway** n
fall away vi (1535) **1 a** : to withdraw friendship or support **b** : to renounce one's faith **2 a** : to diminish gradually in size **b** : to drift off a course
fall-back \'fȯl-ˌbak\ n (1851) **1** : something on which one can fall back : RESERVE **2** : a falling back : RETREAT **3** : something that falls back ⟨the ~ from an explosion⟩
fall back vi (1607) : RETREAT, RECEDE — **fall back on** or **fall back upon** : to have recourse in ⟨had to *fall back on* their reserves⟩
fall down vi (1873) : to fail to meet expectations or requirements ⟨*fell down* on the job⟩
fall-er \'fȯ-lər\ n (1677) **1** : a machine part that acts by falling **2** : a logger who fells trees
fall-fish \'fȯl-ˌfish\ n (ca. 1811) : a common cyprinid fish (*Semotilus corporalis*) of the streams of northeastern No. America
fall guy n (1906) **1** : one that is easily duped **2** : SCAPEGOAT
fal-li-bil-i-ty \ˌfa-lə-'bi-lə-tē\ n (1634) : liability to err
fal-li-ble \'fa-lə-bəl\ adj [ME, fr. ML *fallibilis*, fr. L *fallere*] (15c) **1** : liable to be erroneous ⟨a ~ generalization⟩ **2** : capable of making a mistake ⟨all men are ~⟩ — **fal-li-bly** \-blē\ adv
fall in vi (1719) **1** : to sink inward ⟨the roof *fell in*⟩ **2** : to take one's proper place in a military formation — **fall in with 1** : to concur with ⟨had to *fall in* with her wishes⟩ **2** : to harmonize with ⟨it *falls in* exactly with my views⟩
falling diphthong n (1888) : a diphthong (as \ȯi\ in \'nȯiz\ *noise*) composed of a vowel followed by a less sonorous glide
fall-ing–out \ˌfȯ-liŋ-'aut\ n, pl **fallings–out** or **falling–outs** (1568) : an instance of falling out : QUARREL
falling rhythm n (1918) : rhythm with stress occurring regularly on the first syllable of each foot — compare RISING RHYTHM
falling star n (1563) : METEOR 2a
fall line n (1882) **1** : a line joining the waterfalls on numerous rivers that marks the point where each river descends from the upland to the lowland and the limit of the navigability of each river **2** : the natural downhill course (as for skiing) between two points on a slope
fall-off \'fȯ-ˌlȯf\ n (1880) : a decline esp. in quantity or quality ⟨a ~ in exports⟩ ⟨a ~ of light intensity⟩
fall off vi (1613) **1** : TREND 1b **2** *of a ship* : to deviate to leeward of the point to which the bow was directed
fal-lo-pi-an tube \fə-'lō-pē-ən-\ n, often cap F [Gabriel *Fallopius* †1562 Ital. anatomist] (ca. 1706) : either of the pair of tubes conducting the egg from the ovary to the uterus
fall-out \'fȯ-ˌlaut\ n (1949) **1 a** : the often radioactive particles stirred up by or resulting from a nuclear explosion and descending through the atmosphere; *also* : other polluting particles (as volcanic ash) descending likewise **b** : descent (as of fallout) through the atmosphere **2** : a secondary and often lingering effect, result, or set of consequences ⟨have to take a position and accept the political ~ — Andy Logan⟩
fall out vi (15c) **1** : QUARREL; *also* : to cut off relations over a quarrel ⟨former friends who have *fallen out*⟩ **2** : TURN OUT, HAPPEN ⟨expected to be in the States . . . , but things *fell out* otherwise —Mark Twain⟩ **3 a** : to leave one's place in the ranks **b** : to leave a building in order to take one's place in a military formation
¹**fal-low** \'fa-(ˌ)lō, -lə-(ˌ)w\ adj [ME *falow*, fr. OE *fealu*; akin to OHG *falo* pale, fallow, L *pallēre* to be pale, Gk *polios* gray] (bef. 12c) : of a light yellowish brown color
²**fallow** n [ME *falwe*, *falow*, fr. OE *fealg* — more at FELLY] (bef. 12c) **1** : usu. cultivated land that is allowed to lie idle during the growing season **2** obs : plowed land **3** : the state or period of being fallow **4** : the tilling of land without sowing it for a season
³**fallow** vt (15c) : to plow, harrow, and break up (land) without seeding to destroy weeds and conserve soil moisture
⁴**fallow** adj (15c) **1** : left untilled or unsown after plowing **2** : DORMANT, INACTIVE — used esp. in the phrase *to lie fallow* ⟨at this very moment there are probably important inventions lying ~ —*Harper's*⟩ — **fal-low-ness** n
fallow deer n [¹*fallow*] (15c) : a deer (*Cervus dama* syn. *Dama dama*) of variable color with broad antlers and typically a yellow-brown coat spotted with white in the summer that was orig. found in Europe and Asia Minor but has been introduced elsewhere
fall to vi (1593) : to begin doing something (as working or eating) esp. vigorously — often used in invitation or command
¹**false** \'fȯls\ adj **fals-er; fals-est** [ME *fals*, fr. OF & L; OF, fr. L *falsus*, fr. pp. of *fallere* to deceive] (12c) **1** : not genuine ⟨~ documents⟩ ⟨~ teeth⟩ **2 a** : intentionally untrue ⟨~ testimony⟩ **b** : adjusted or made so as to deceive ⟨~ scales⟩ ⟨a trunk with a ~ bottom⟩ **c** : intended or tending to mislead ⟨a ~ promise⟩ ⟨~ not true ⟨~ concepts⟩ **4 a** : not faithful or loyal : TREACHEROUS ⟨a ~ friend⟩ **b** : lacking naturalness or sincerity ⟨~ sympathy⟩ **5 a** : not essential or permanent — used of parts of a structure that are temporary or supplemental **b** : fitting over a main part to strengthen it, to protect it, or to disguise its appearance ⟨a ~ ceiling⟩ **6** : inaccurate in pitch ⟨a ~ note⟩ **7 a** : based on mistaken ideas ⟨~ pride⟩ **b** : inconsistent with the facts ⟨a ~ position⟩ ⟨a ~ sense of security⟩ **8** : threateningly sudden or deceptive ⟨don't make a ~ move⟩ **syn** see FAITHLESS — **false-ly** adv — **false-ness** n
²**false** adv (13c) : in a false or faithless manner : TREACHEROUSLY ⟨his friends played him ~⟩
false alarm n (1579) **1** : one causing alarm or excitement that proves to be unfounded **2** : an alarm (as a fire or burglar alarm) that is set off needlessly
false arrest n (1926) : an arrest not justifiable under law
false color n (1968) : color in an image (as a photograph) of an object that does not actually appear in the object but is used to enhance, contrast, or distinguish details which are evident solely or chiefly from differences in the absorption and reflection of electromagnetic radiation at wavelengths outside the visual spectrum
false-hood \'fȯls-ˌhud\ n (13c) **1** : an untrue statement : LIE **2** : absence of truth or accuracy **3** : the practice of lying : MENDACITY

false imprisonment n (14c) : imprisonment of a person contrary to law
false mi-ter-wort \-'mī-tər-ˌwȯrt, -ˌwȯrt\ n [*miterwort* fr. the resemblance of the plant's capsule to a bishop's miter] (1868) : FOAMFLOWER
false morel n (1942) : any of a genus (*Gyromitra*) of fungi that are often poisonous and have a cap with convolutions resembling a brain
false pregnancy n (ca. 1860) : PSEUDOCYESIS, PSEUDOPREGNANCY
false rib n (15c) : a rib whose cartilages unite indirectly or not at all with the sternum — compare FLOATING RIB
false Solomon's seal n (ca. 1856) : any of a genus (*Smilacina*) of herbs of the lily family that differ from Solomon's seal in having flowers in a terminal raceme or panicle — called also *false Solomonseal*
false start n (1815) **1** : a premature start (as of a race) **2** : an unsuccessful attempt to begin something (as a career)
¹**fal-set-to** \fȯl-'se-(ˌ)tō\ n, pl **-tos** [It, fr. dim. of *falso* false, fr. L *falsus*] (1774) **1** : an artificially high voice; *esp* : an artificially produced singing voice that overlaps and extends above the range of the full voice esp. of a tenor **2** : a singer who uses falsetto
²**falsetto** adv (1940) : in falsetto
false-work \'fȯls-ˌwərk\ n (ca. 1874) : temporary construction work on which a main work is wholly or partly built and supported until the main work is strong enough to support itself
fals-ie \'fȯl-sē\ n (ca. 1943) : an artificial addition to a bodily part worn to enhance appearance; *specif* : a breast-shaped usu. fabric or rubber cup used to pad a brassiere — usu. used in pl.
fal-si-fy \'fȯl-sə-ˌfī\ vb **-fied; -fy-ing** [ME *falsifien*, fr. MF *falsifier*, fr. ML *falsificare*, fr. L *falsus*] vt (15c) **1** : to prove or declare false **2** : to make false: as **a** : to make false by mutilation or addition ⟨the accounts were *falsified* to conceal a theft⟩ **b** : to represent falsely : MISREPRESENT **3** : to prove unsound by experience ~ vi : to tell lies : LIE — **fal-si-fi-abil-i-ty** \ˌfȯl-sə-ˌfī-ə-'bi-lə-tē\ n — **fal-si-fi-able** \-'fī-ə-bəl\ adj — **fal-si-fi-ca-tion** \ˌfȯl-sə-fə-'kā-shən\ n — **fal-si-fi-er** \'fȯl-sə-ˌfī-(ə)r\ n
fal-si-ty \'fȯl-sə-tē\ n, pl **-ties** (13c) **1** : something false : LIE **2** : the quality or state of being false
Fal-staff \'fȯl-ˌstaf\ n : a fat, convivial, roguish character in Shakespeare's *Merry Wives of Windsor* and *Henry IV* — **Fal-staff-ian** \fȯl-'sta-fē-ən\ adj
¹**fal-ter** \'fȯl-tər\ vb **fal-tered; fal-ter-ing** \-t(ə-)riŋ\ [ME] vi (14c) **1 a** : to walk unsteadily : STUMBLE **b** : to give way : TOTTER ⟨could feel my legs ~ing⟩ **c** : to move waveringly or hesitatingly **2 a** : to speak brokenly or weakly : STAMMER **3 a** : to hesitate in purpose or action : WAVER **b** : to lose drive or effectiveness ⟨the business was ~ing⟩ ~ vt : to utter hesitatingly or brokenly **syn** see HESITATE — **fal-ter-er** \-tər-ər\ n — **fal-ter-ing-ly** \-t(ə-)riŋ-lē\ adv
²**falter** n (1834) : an act or instance of faltering
¹**fame** \'fām\ n [ME, fr. OF, fr. L *fama* report, fame; akin to L *fari* to speak — more at BAN] (13c) **1 a** : public estimation : REPUTATION **b** : popular acclaim : RENOWN **2** *archaic* : RUMOR
²**fame** vt **famed; fam-ing** (14c) **1** *archaic* : REPORT, REPUTE **2** : to make famous
famed \'fāmd\ adj (ca. 1533) : known widely and well : FAMOUS
fa-mil-ial \fə-'mil-yəl, -'mi-lē-əl\ adj [F, fr. L *familia*] (ca. 1900) **1** : tending to occur in more members of a family than expected by chance alone ⟨a ~ disorder⟩ **2** : of, relating to, or suggestive of a family
¹**fa-mil-iar** \fə-'mil-yər\ n (13c) **1** : a member of the household of a high official **2** : one that is familiar; *esp* : an intimate associate : COMPANION **3** : a spirit often embodied in an animal and held to attend and serve or guard a person **4 a** : one who is well acquainted with something **b** : one who frequents a place
²**familiar** adj [ME *familier*, fr. MF, fr. L *familiaris*, fr. *familia*] (14c) **1** : closely acquainted : INTIMATE ⟨a ~ family friend⟩ **2** obs : AFFABLE, SOCIABLE **3 a** : of or relating to a family ⟨remembering past ~ celebrations⟩ **b** : frequented by families ⟨a ~ resort⟩ **4 a** : being free and easy ⟨the ~ association of old friends⟩ **b** : marked by informality ⟨a ~ essay⟩ **c** : overly free and unrestrained : PRESUMPTUOUS ⟨grossly ~ behavior⟩ **d** : moderately tame ⟨~ animals⟩ **5 a** : frequently seen or experienced : easily recognized ⟨a ~ theme⟩ **b** : of everyday occurrence **c** : possibly known but imperfectly remembered ⟨her face looked ~⟩ **6** : having personal or intimate knowledge — used with ⟨~ with the facts of the case⟩ **syn** see COMMON — **fa-mil-iar-ly** adv — **fa-mil-iar-ness** n
fa-mil-iar-ise Brit var of FAMILIARIZE
fa-mil-iar-i-ty \fə-ˌmi-lē-'(y)ar-ə-tē, -ˌmil-'yar-\ n, pl **-ties** (13c) **1 a** : the quality or state of being familiar **b** : a state of close relationship : INTIMACY **2 a** : absence of ceremony : INFORMALITY **b** : an unduly informal act or expression : IMPROPRIETY **c** : a sexual liberty **3** : close acquaintance with something ⟨my ~ with American history⟩
fa-mil-iar-ize \fə-'mil-yə-ˌrīz\ vt **-ized; -iz-ing** (1608) **1** : to make known or familiar ⟨Shakespeare . . . ~s the wonderful —Samuel Johnson⟩ **2** : to make well acquainted ⟨~ students with good literature⟩ — **fa-mil-iar-iza-tion** \-ˌmil-yə-rə-'zā-shən\ n
familiar spirit n (1565) **1** : a spirit or demon that serves or prompts an individual **2** : the spirit of a dead person invoked by a medium to advise or prophesy
fam-i-lism \'fa-mə-ˌli-zəm\ n (1925) : a social pattern in which the family assumes a position of ascendance over individual interests — **fam-i-lis-tic** \ˌfa-mə-'lis-tik\ adj
fa-mille rose \fə-ˌmē-\ n [F, lit., rose family] (ca. 1898) : Chinese porcelain in the decoration of which a rose color predominates
fa-mille verte \fə-'mē-'vert\ n [F, lit., green family] (1872) : Chinese porcelain in the decoration of which green predominates
¹**fam-i-ly** \'fam-lē, 'fa-mə-\ n, pl **-lies** [ME *familie*, fr. L *familia* household (including servants as well as kin of the householder), fr. *famulus* servant] (15c) **1** : a group of individuals living under one roof and usu. under one head : HOUSEHOLD **2 a** : a group of persons of com-

\ə\ abut \ᵊ\ kitten, F table \ər\ further \a\ ash \ā\ ace \ä\ mop, mar \aú\ out \ch\ chin \e\ bet \ē\ easy \g\ go \i\ hit \ī\ ice \j\ job \ŋ\ sing \ō\ go \ȯ\ law \ȯi\ boy \th\ thin \t̲h̲\ the \ü\ loot \ú\ foot \y\ yet \zh\ vision \à, k̇, ⁿ, œ, œ̄, ᵫ, ᵫ̄, ʸ\ see Guide to Pronunciation mon ancestry : CLAN **b** : a people or group of peoples regarded as deriving from a common stock : RACE **3 a** : a group of people united by certain convictions or a common affiliation : FELLOWSHIP **b** : the staff of a high official (as the President) **4** : a group of things related by common characteristics: as **a** : a closely related series of elements or chemical compounds **b** : a group of soils that have similar profiles and include one or more series **c** : a group of related languages descended from a single ancestral language **5 a** : the basic unit in society traditionally consisting of two parents rearing their own or adopted children; *also* : any of various social units differing from but regarded as equivalent to the traditional family ⟨a single-parent ∼⟩ **b** : spouse and children ⟨want to spend more time with my ∼⟩ **6 a** : a group of related plants or animals forming a category ranking above a genus and below an order and usu. comprising several to many genera **b** *in livestock breeding* (1) : the descendants or line of a particular individual esp. of some outstanding female (2) : an identifiable strain within a breed **7** : a set of curves or surfaces whose equations differ only in parameters **8** : a unit of a crime syndicate (as the Mafia) operating within a geographical area

²**family** *adj* (1602) **1** : of or relating to a family **2** : designed or suitable for both children and adults ⟨∼ restaurants⟩ ⟨∼ movies⟩

family Bible *n* (1740) : a large Bible usu. having special pages for recording births, marriages, and deaths

family court *n* (ca. 1931) : COURT OF DOMESTIC RELATIONS

family doctor *n* (1846) **1** : a doctor regularly consulted by a family **2** : a doctor specializing in family practice

family jewels *n pl* (ca. 1946) *slang* : a man's testicles

family man *n* (1856) **1** : a man with a wife and children dependent on him **2** : a responsible man of domestic habits

family name *n* (1699) : SURNAME 2

family physician *n* (1807) : FAMILY DOCTOR

family planning *n* (1939) : planning intended to determine the number and spacing of one's children through birth control

family practice *n* (1969) : a medical practice or specialty which provides continuing general medical care for the individual and family — called also *family medicine*

family practitioner *n* (1846) : FAMILY DOCTOR

family room *n* (1853) : a large room designed as a recreation center for members of a family

family style *adv or adj* (1932) : with the food placed on the table in serving dishes from which those eating may help themselves

family tree *n* (1807) **1** : a genealogical diagram **2** : GENEALOGY

family way *n* (1796) : condition of being pregnant — used with *in* and *the* or *a* ⟨she is in a *family* way⟩

fam·ine \'fa-mən\ *n* [ME, fr. MF, fr. *faim* hunger, fr. L *fames*] (14c) **1** : an extreme scarcity of food **2** *archaic* : STARVATION **3** *archaic* : a ravenous appetite **4** : a great shortage

fam·ish \'fa-mish\ *vb* [ME, prob. alter. of *famen*, fr. MF *afamer*, fr. (assumed) VL *affamare*, fr. L *ad-* + *fames*] *vt* (15c) **1** : to cause to suffer severely from hunger **2** *archaic* : to cause to starve to death ∼ *vi* **1** *archaic* : to suffer for lack of something necessary ⟨a moment when French poetry in particular was ∼ing for such invention —T. S. Eliot⟩ — **fam·ish·ment** \-mənt\ *n*

fam·ished \'fa-misht\ *adj* (15c) : intensely hungry; *also* : NEEDY

fa·mous \'fā-məs\ *adj* [ME, fr. MF *fameux*, fr. L *famosus*, fr. *fama* fame] (14c) **1 a** : widely known **b** : honored for achievement **2** : EXCELLENT, FIRST-RATE ⟨∼ weather for a walk⟩ — **fa·mous·ness** *n* *syn* FAMOUS, RENOWNED, CELEBRATED, NOTED, NOTORIOUS, DISTINGUISHED, EMINENT, ILLUSTRIOUS mean known far and wide. FAMOUS implies little more than the fact of being, sometimes briefly, widely and popularly known ⟨a *famous* actress⟩. RENOWNED implies more glory and acclamation ⟨one of the most *renowned* figures in sports history⟩. CELEBRATED implies notice and attention esp. in print ⟨the most *celebrated* beauty of her day⟩. NOTED suggests well-deserved public attention ⟨the *noted* mystery writer⟩. NOTORIOUS frequently adds to FAMOUS an implication of questionableness or evil ⟨a *notorious* gangster⟩. DISTINGUISHED implies acknowledged excellence or superiority ⟨a *distinguished* scientist who won the Nobel Prize⟩. EMINENT implies even greater conspicuousness for outstanding quality or character ⟨the country's most *eminent* writers⟩. ILLUSTRIOUS stresses enduring honor and glory attached to a deed or person ⟨our *illustrious* national heroes⟩.

fa·mous·ly *adv* (1579) **1** : in a celebrated manner **2** : in a superlative fashion **3** : to an unusual degree : VERY

fam·u·lus \'fam-yə-ləs\ *n, pl* **-li** \-ˌlī, -ˌlē\ [G, assistant to a professor, fr. L, servant] (1837) : a private secretary or attendant

¹**fan** \'fan\ *n* [ME, fr. OE *fann*, fr. L *vannus* — more at WINNOW] (bef. 12c) **1** : any of various devices for winnowing grain **2** : an instrument for producing a current of air: as **a** : a device for cooling the person that is usu. shaped like a segment of a circle and is composed of material (as feathers or paper) mounted on thin rods or slats moving about a pivot so that the device may be closed compactly when not in use **b** : a device that consists of a series of vanes radiating from a hub rotated on its axle by a motor ⟨an airplane propeller⟩ **3 a** : an airplane propeller **b** : something resembling an open fan **b** : a gently sloping fan-shaped body of detritus; *esp* : ALLUVIAL FAN — **fan-like** \-ˌlīk\ *adj*

²**fan** *vb* **fanned; fan·ning** *vt* (bef. 12c) **1 a** : to drive away the chaff of (grain) by means of a current of air **b** : to eliminate (as chaff) by winnowing **2** : to move or impel (air) with a fan **3** : to blow or breathe upon ⟨the breeze *fanning* her hair⟩ **4 a** : to direct a current of air upon with a fan **b** : to stir up to activity as if by fanning : STIMULATE ⟨*fanning* the fires of nationalism⟩ **5** *archaic* : WAVE **6** *slang* : SPANK **7** : to spread like a fan ⟨the peacock *fanned* his tail⟩ **8** : to strike (a batter) out in baseball **9** : to fire a series of shots from (a single-action revolver) by holding the trigger back and successively striking the hammer to the rear with the free hand ∼ *vi* **1** : to move like a fan : FLUTTER **2** : to spread like a fan — often used with *out* ⟨deputies *fanning* out on the hunt⟩ **3** : STRIKE OUT **3** — **fan·ner** \'fa-nər\ *n*

³**fan** *n* [prob. short for *fanatic*] (1682) **1** : an enthusiastic devotee (as of a sport or a performing art) usu. as a spectator **2** : an ardent admirer or enthusiast ⟨as of a celebrity or a pursuit⟩ ⟨science-fiction ∼s⟩

fa·nat·ic \fə-'na-tik\ *or* **fa·nat·i·cal** \-ti-kəl\ *adj* [L *fanaticus* inspired by a deity, frenzied, fr. *fanum* temple — more at FEAST] (1550)

: marked by excessive enthusiasm and often intense uncritical devotion ⟨they're ∼ about politics⟩ — **fanatic** *n* — **fa·nat·i·cal·ly** \fə-'na-ti-k(ə-)lē\ *adv* — **fa·nat·i·cal·ness** \-kəl-nəs\ *n*

fa·nat·i·cism \fə-'na-tə-ˌsi-zəm\ *n* (1652) : fanatic outlook or behavior

fa·nat·i·cize \-ˌsīz\ *vt* **-cized; -ciz·ing** (1812) : to cause to become fanatic

fan·ci·er \'fan(t)-sē-ər\ *n* (1765) **1** : one that has a special liking or interest **2** : a person who breeds or grows a particular animal or plant for points of excellence ⟨a pigeon ∼⟩

fan·ci·ful \'fan(t)-si-fəl\ *adj* (ca. 1627) **1** : marked by fancy or unrestrained imagination rather than by reason and experience ⟨a ∼ person⟩ **2** : existing in fancy only ⟨a ∼ notion⟩ **3** : marked by or as if by fancy or whim ⟨gave their children ∼ names⟩ *syn* see IMAGINARY — **fan·ci·ful·ly** \-f(ə-)lē\ *adv* — **fan·ci·ful·ness** \-fəl-nəs\ *n*

fan·ci·fy \'fan(t)-sə-ˌfī\ *vt* **-fied; -fy·ing** (1890) : to make ornate, elaborate, or fancy ⟨a *fancified* hamburger⟩

¹**fan·cy** \'fan(t)-sē\ *vt* **fan·cied; fan·cy·ing** (14c) **1** : to have a fancy for : LIKE **2** : to form a conception of : IMAGINE ⟨∼ our embarrassment⟩ **3 a** : to believe mistakenly or without evidence **b** : to believe without being certain ⟨she *fancied* she had met him before⟩ **4** : to visualize or interpret as ⟨*fancied* myself a child again⟩ *syn* see THINK

²**fancy** *n, pl* **fancies** [ME *fantasie, fantsy* fantasy, fancy, fr. MF *fantasie*, fr. L *phantasia*, fr. Gk, appearance, imagination, fr. *phantazein* to present to the mind (middle voice, to imagine), fr. *phainein* to show; akin to OE *gebōned* polished, Gk *phōs* light] (15c) **1 a** : a liking formed by caprice rather than reason : INCLINATION ⟨took a ∼ to the strange little animal⟩ **b** : amorous fondness : LOVE **2 a** : NOTION, WHIM **b** : an image or representation of something formed in the mind **3** *archaic* : fantastic quality or state **4 a** : imagination esp. of a capricious or delusive sort **b** : the power of conception and representation used in artistic expression (as by a poet) **5** : TASTE, JUDGMENT **6 a** : devotees of some particular art, practice, or amusement **b** : the object of interest of such a fancy; *esp* : ²BOXING

³**fancy** *adj* **fan·ci·er; -est** (1646) **1** : dependent or based on fancy : WHIMSICAL **2 a** (1) : not plain : ORNAMENTAL ⟨a ∼ hairdo⟩ (2) : SWANKY 2, POSH ⟨a ∼ restaurant⟩ **b** (1) : of particular excellence or highest grade ⟨∼ tuna⟩ (2) : IMPRESSIVE ⟨posted some ∼ numbers⟩ **c** *of an animal or plant* : bred esp. for bizarre or ornamental qualities that lack practical utility **3** : based on conceptions of the fancy ⟨∼ sketches⟩ **4 a** : dealing in fancy goods **b** : EXTRAVAGANT ⟨paying ∼ prices⟩ **5** : executed with technical skill and style ⟨∼ footwork⟩ ⟨∼ diving⟩ **6** : PARTI-COLOR ⟨∼ carnations⟩ — **fan·ci·ly** \'fan(t)-sə-lē\ *adv* — **fan·ci·ness** \-sē-nəs\ *n*

fancy–dan \'fan(t)-sē-ˈdan, -ˌdan\ *adj, often cap D* (1938) : SHOWY 2, FANCY

fancy Dan *n, often cap F* (ca. 1943) : one given to flamboyant display esp. of technique or dress

fancy dress *n* (1770) : a costume (as for a masquerade) chosen to suit the wearer's fancy

fan·cy–free \ˌfan(t)-sē-ˈfrē\ *adj* (1590) **1** : free from amorous attachment or engagement **2** : free to imagine or fancy

fancy man *n* (ca. 1811) : a woman's paramour; *also* : PIMP

fancy–pants *adj* (1945) : overly elegant or refined : LA-DI-DA

fancy up *vt* (1934) : to add superficial adornment to

fancy woman *n* (1812) : a woman of questionable morals; *specif* : PROSTITUTE

fan·cy·work \'fan(t)-sē-ˌwərk\ *n* (1810) : decorative needlework

fan·dan·go \fan-'daŋ-(ˌ)gō\ *n, pl* **-gos** [Sp] (1774) **1** : a lively Spanish or Spanish-American dance in triple time that is usu. performed by a man and a woman to the accompaniment of guitar and castanets; *also* : music for this dance **2** : TOMFOOLERY

fan·dom \'fan-dəm\ *n* (1903) : all the fans (as of a sport)

fane \'fān\ *n* [ME, fr. L *fanum* — more at FEAST] (15c) **1** : TEMPLE **2** : CHURCH

fan·fare \'fan-ˌfar, -ˌfer\ *n* [F] (1676) **1** : a showy outward display **2** : a short and lively sounding of trumpets

fan·far·o·nade \ˌfan-ˌfar-ə-'nād, -'näd\ *n* [F *fanfaronnade*, fr. Sp *fanfarronada*, fr. *fanfarrón* braggart] (1652) : empty boasting : BLUSTER

fan·fold \'fan-ˌfōld\ *n* (1925) : paper (as business forms or tape) made from a web and folded like a fan lengthwise and sometimes crosswise — **fanfold** *vt*

fang \'faŋ\ *n* [ME, that which is taken, fr. OE; akin to OHG *fang* seizure, OE *fōn* to seize — more at PACT] (1555) **1 a** : a long sharp tooth: as (1) : one by which an animal's prey is seized and held or torn (2) : one of the long hollow or grooved and often erectile teeth of a venomous snake **b** : one of the chelicerae of a spider at the tip of which a poison gland opens **2** : the root of a tooth or one of the processes or prongs into which a root divides **3** : a projecting tooth or prong — **fanged** \'faŋd\ *adj*

Fang \'faŋ, 'fäŋ\ *also* **Fan** \'fän, 'fän\ *n, pl* **Fang** *or* **Fangs** *also* **Fan** *or* **Fans** (1861) **1** : a member of a Bantu-speaking people of northern Gabon, mainland Equatorial Guinea, and southern Cameroon **2** : the language of the Fang people

fan–jet \'fan-ˌjet\ *n* (1962) : a jet engine having a fan that operates in a duct and draws in extra air whose compression and expulsion provide extra thrust; *also* : an airplane powered by a fan-jet engine

fan letter *n* (1932) : a letter sent to a public figure by an admirer

fan·light \'fan-ˌlīt\ *n* (1819) : a semicircular window with radiating bars like the ribs of a fan that is placed over a door or window

fan mail *n* (1924) : FAN LETTERS

fan·ny \'fa-nē\ *n, pl* **fannies** [perh. fr. *Fanny*, nickname of *Frances*] (1928) **1** : BUTTOCKS **2** *chiefly Brit* : VULVA

fanny pack *n* (1967) : a pack for carrying personal articles that straps to the waist

fan·tab·u·lous \fan-'ta-byə-ləs\ *adj* [blend of *fantastic* and *fabulous*] (1959) *slang* : marvelously good

fan·tail \'fan-ˌtāl\ *n* (1728) **1** : a fan-shaped tail or end **2** : a domestic pigeon having a broad rounded tail often with 30 or 40 feathers **3** : an architectural part resembling a fan **4** : a counter or after overhang of a ship shaped like a duck's bill

fan–tan \'fan-ˌtan\ *n* [Chin (Guangdong) *fāantāan*] (1878) **1** : a Chinese gambling game in which the banker divides a pile of objects (as beans) into fours and players bet on what number will be left at the end of the count **2** : a card game in which players must build in sequence upon sevens and attempt to be the first one out of cards

fan·ta·sia \fan-'tä-zhə, -z(h)ē-ə; ˌfan-tə-'zē-ə\ *n* [It, lit., fancy, fr. L *phantasia* — more at FANCY] (1724) **1** : a free usu. instrumental composition not in strict form **2 a** : a work (as a poem or play) in which the author's fancy roves unrestricted **b** : something possessing grotesque, bizarre, or unreal qualities

fan·ta·sie \ˌfan-tə-'zē, ˌfän-\ *n* [G *Phantasie*, fr. L *phantasia*] (ca. 1859) : FANTASIA

fan·ta·sied \'fan-tə-sēd, -zēd\ *adj* (1561) **1** : existing only in the imagination : FANCIED **2** *obs* : full of fancies or strange whims

fan·ta·sise *Brit var of* FANTASIZE

fan·ta·sist \-sist, -zist\ *n* (1896) : one who creates fantasias or fantasies

fan·ta·size \-ˌsīz\ *vb* **-sized; -siz·ing** *vi* (1926) : to indulge in reverie : create or develop imaginative and often fantastic views or ideas ⟨doing things I'd *fantasized* about in my sheltered childhood —Diane Arbus⟩ ∼ *vt* : to portray in the mind : FANCY ⟨likes to ∼ herself as very wealthy⟩ — **fan·ta·siz·er** \-ˌsī-zər\ *n*

fan·tasm *var of* PHANTASM

fan·tast \'fan-ˌtast\ *n* [G, fr. ML *fantasta*, prob. back-formation fr. LL *phantasticus*] (1588) **1** : VISIONARY **2** : a fantastic or eccentric person **3** : FANTASIST

¹fan·tas·tic \fan-'tas-tik, fən-\ *also* **fan·tas·ti·cal** \-ti-kəl\ *adj* [ME *fantastic, fantastical,* fr. MF & LL; MF *fantastique,* fr. LL *phantasticus,* fr. Gk *phantastikos* producing mental images, fr. *phantazein* to present to the mind] (14c) **1 a** : based on fantasy : not real **b** : conceived or seemingly conceived by unrestrained fancy **c** : so extreme as to challenge belief : UNBELIEVABLE; *broadly* : exceedingly large or great **2** : marked by extravagant fantasy or extreme individuality : ECCENTRIC **3** *fantastic* : EXCELLENT, SUPERLATIVE ⟨a ∼ dinner⟩ — **fan·tas·ti·cal·i·ty** \ˌ(ˌ)fan-ˌtas-tə-'ka-lə-tē, fən-\ *n* — **fan·tas·ti·cal·ness** \-'tas-tə-kəl-nəs\ *n*

syn FANTASTIC, BIZARRE, GROTESQUE mean conceived, made, or carried out without adherence to truth or reality. FANTASTIC may connote unrestrained extravagance in conception or merely ingenuity of decorative invention ⟨dreamed up *fantastic* rumors to spread⟩. BIZARRE applies to the sensationally queer or strange and implies violence of contrast or incongruity of combination ⟨a *bizarre* medieval castle built in the heart of a modern city⟩. GROTESQUE may apply to what is conventionally ugly but artistically effective or it may connote ludicrous awkwardness or incongruity often with sinister or tragic overtones ⟨*grotesque* statues adorn the cathedral⟩ ⟨though grief-stricken, she made a *grotesque* attempt at a smile⟩. **syn** see in addition IMAGINARY

²fantastic *n* (1598) : ECCENTRIC 2

fan·tas·ti·cal·ly \fan-'tas-ti-k(ə-)lē, fən-\ *adv* (1543) **1** : in a fantastic manner **2** : to a fantastic degree : EXTREMELY ⟨∼ expensive clothes⟩

fan·tas·ti·cate \fan-'tas-tə-ˌkāt, fən-\ *vt* **-cat·ed; -cat·ing** (1600) : to make fantastic — **fan·tas·ti·ca·tion** \ˌ(ˌ)fan-ˌtas-tə-'kā-shən, fən-\ *n*

fan·tas·ti·co \fan-'tas-ti-ˌkō, fən-\ *n, pl* **-coes** [It, fantastic (adj.), fr. LL *phantasticus*] (1596) : a ridiculously fantastic individual

¹fan·ta·sy \'fan-tə-sē, -zē\ *n, pl* **-sies** [ME *fantasie* — more at FANCY] (14c) **1** *obs* : HALLUCINATION **2** : FANCY; *esp* : the free play of creative imagination **3** : a creation of the imaginative faculty whether expressed or merely conceived: as **a** : a fanciful design or invention **b** : a chimerical or fantastic notion **c** : FANTASIA 1 **d** : imaginative fiction featuring esp. strange settings and grotesque characters — called also *fantasy fiction* **4** : CAPRICE **5** : the power or process of creating esp. unrealistic or improbable mental images in response to psychological need ⟨an object of ∼⟩; *also* : a mental image or a series of mental images (as a daydream) so created ⟨sexual *fantasies* of adolescence⟩ **6** : a coin usu. not intended for circulation as currency and often issued by a dubious authority (as a government-in-exile)

²fantasy *vb* **-sied; -sy·ing** (15c) : FANTASIZE

fan·ta·sy·land \-ˌland\ *n* (1967) : an imaginary or ideal place or situation

fan·toc·ci·ni \ˌfän-tə-'chē-nē, ˌfan-\ *n pl* [It, pl. of *fantoccino,* dim. of *fantoccio* doll, aug. of *fante* child, fr. L *infant-, infans* infant] (1771) : a puppet show using puppets operated by strings or mechanical devices; *also* : such puppets

fan·tod \'fan-ˌtäd\ *n* [perh. alter. of E dial. *fantique, fanteeg*] (1839) **1** *pl* **a** : a state of irritability and tension **b** : FIDGETS **2** : an emotional outburst : FIT

fan·tom *var of* PHANTOM

fan vault *n* (ca. 1901) : a Gothic vault in which the ribs from each springer spread out like the sticks of a fan — **fan vaulting** *n*

fan·wise \'fan-ˌwīz\ *adv or adj* (1882) : in the manner or position of the slats of an open fan ⟨boats anchored ∼ at the pier⟩

fan·zine \'fan-ˌzēn\ *n* [³*fan* + magazine] (1949) : a magazine written by and for fans esp. of science fiction or fantasy writing

¹far \'fär\ *adv* **far·ther** \-thər\ *or* **fur·ther** \'fər-\; **far·thest** *or* **fur·thest** \-thəst\ [ME *fer,* fr. OE *feorr;* akin to OHG *ferro* far, OE *faran* to go — more at FARE] (bef. 12c) **1** : at or to a considerable distance in space ⟨wandered ∼ from home⟩ **2** : to a great extent : MUCH ⟨∼ better methods⟩ **b** : by a broad interval : WIDELY ⟨the ∼ distant future⟩ **3** : to or at a definite distance, point, or degree ⟨as ∼ as I know⟩ **4** : to an advanced point or extent ⟨a bright student will go ∼⟩ ⟨worked ∼ into the night⟩ **5** : at a considerable distance in time ⟨not ∼ from the year 1870⟩ — **by far** : far and away ⟨is *by far* the best runner⟩ — **far be it from** : it would be inappropriate or impossible for ⟨*far be it from* God, that he should do wickedness —Job 34:10 (AV)⟩ — **far from** : of a distinctly different and esp. opposite quality than ⟨the trip was *far from* a failure⟩ — **how far** : to what extent, degree, or distance ⟨didn't know *how far* to trust them⟩ — **so far 1** : to a certain extent, degree, or distance ⟨when the water rose *so far,* the villagers sought higher ground⟩ **2** : up to the present ⟨has written just one novel *so far*⟩ — **thus far** : so far ⟨*thus far* our findings have been negative⟩

²far *adj* **farther** *or* **further; farthest** *or* **furthest** (bef. 12c) **1 a** : remote in space **b** : distinctly different in quality or relationship **c** : remote in time **2 a** : LONG ⟨a ∼ journey⟩ **b** : of notable extent : COMPREHENSIVE ⟨a man of ∼ vision⟩ **3** : the more distant of two **4** : EXTREME ⟨the ∼ left⟩ ⟨a ∼ right political organization⟩

far·ad \'far-ˌad, 'far-əd\ *n* [Michael *Faraday*] (1873) : the unit of capacitance equal to the capacitance of a capacitor between whose plates

there appears a potential of one volt when it is charged by one coulomb of electricity

far·a·day \'far-ə-ˌdā, -ə-dē\ *n* [Michael *Faraday*] (1904) : the quantity of electricity transferred in electrolysis per equivalent weight of an element or ion equal to about 96,500 coulombs

fa·rad·ic \fə-'ra-dik, fa-'ra-\ *also* **far·a·da·ic** \ˌfar-ə-'dā-ik\ *adj* (1875) : of or relating to an asymmetric alternating current of electricity produced by an induction coil ⟨∼ stimulation of the muscles⟩

far·a·dism \'far-ə-ˌdi-zəm\ *n* (1876) : the application of a faradic current of electricity (as for therapeutic purposes)

far and away *adv* (1852) : by a considerable margin ⟨was *far and away* the better team⟩

far·an·dole \'far-ən-ˌdōl\ *n* [F *farandole,* fr. Prov *farandoulo*] (1863) **1** : a lively Provençal dance in which men and women hold hands, form a chain, and follow a leader through a serpentine course **2** : music in sextuple time for a farandole

far and wide *adv* (bef. 12c) : in every direction : EVERYWHERE ⟨searched *far and wide*⟩

far·away \'fär-ə-ˌwä\ *adj* (1735) **1** : lying at a great distance : REMOTE **2** : DREAMY, ABSTRACTED ⟨a ∼ look in her eyes⟩

¹farce \'färs\ *vt* **farced; farc·ing** [ME *farsen,* fr. MF *farcir,* fr. L *farcire*] (14c) **1** : STUFF **2** : to improve as if by stuffing

²farce *n* [ME *farse,* fr. MF *farce,* fr. (assumed) VL *farsa,* fr. L, fem. of *farsus,* pp. of *farcire*] (14c) **1** : a savory stuffing : FORCEMEAT **2** : a light dramatic composition marked by broadly satirical comedy and improbable plot **3** : the broad humor characteristic of farce or pretense **4 a** : ridiculous or empty show **b** : MOCKERY ⟨the enforcement of this law became a ∼⟩

far·ceur \fär-'sər\ *n* [F, fr. MF, fr. *farcer* to joke, fr. OF, fr. *farce*] (1781) **1** : JOKER, WAG **2** : a writer or actor of farce

far·ci *or* **far·cie** \fär-'sē\ *adj* [F, fr. pp. of *farcir*] (1903) : stuffed esp. with forcemeat ⟨oysters ∼⟩

far·ci·cal \'fär-si-kəl\ *adj* (1716) **1** : of, relating to, or resembling farce : LUDICROUS **2** : laughably inept : ABSURD — **far·ci·cal·i·ty** \ˌfär-sə-'ka-lə-tē\ *n* — **far·ci·cal·ly** \'fär-si-k(ə-)lē\ *adv*

far·cy \'fär-sē\ *n* [ME *farsin, farsi,* fr. MF *farcin,* fr. LL *farcimen,* fr. L, sausage, fr. *farcire*] (15c) : GLANDERS; *esp* : cutaneous glanders

fard \'färd\ *vt* [ME, fr. MF *farder,* of Gmc origin; akin to OHG *faro* colored — more at PERCH] (15c) **1** : to paint (the face) with cosmetics **2** *archaic* : to gloss over — **fard** *n, archaic*

far·del \'fär-dᵊl\ *n* [ME, fr. MF, prob. fr. Ar *fardah*] (14c) **1** : BUNDLE **2** : BURDEN

¹fare \'far, 'fer\ *vi* **fared; far·ing** [ME *faren,* fr. OE *faran;* akin to OHG *faran* to go, L *portare* to carry, Gk *poros* passage through, *poros* passage, journey] (bef. 12c) **1** : GO, TRAVEL **2** : GET ALONG, SUCCEED ⟨how did you ∼ on your exam?⟩ **3** : EAT, DINE

²fare *n* [ME, journey, passage, supply of food, fr. OE *faru, fær;* akin to OE *faran* to go] (15c) **1 a** : range of food : DIET **b** : material provided for use, consumption, or enjoyment **2 a** : the price charged to transport a person **b** : a paying passenger on a public conveyance

fare-thee-well \'far-(ˌ)thē-ˌwel, 'fer-\ *also* **fare-you-well** \-yə-, -yü-, -yē-\ *n* (1884) **1** : the utmost degree ⟨researched the story to a ∼⟩ **2** : a state of perfection ⟨imitated the speaker's pompous manner to a ∼⟩

¹fare·well \far-'wel, fer-\ *vb imper* (14c) : get along well — used interjectionally to or by one departing

²farewell *n* (14c) **1** : a wish of well-being at parting : GOOD-BYE **2 a** : an act of departure : LEAVE-TAKING **b** : a formal occasion honoring a person about to leave or retire

³fare·well *vt* (1580) *chiefly Austral & NewZeal* : to bid farewell to

⁴fare·well \'far-ˌwel, 'fer-\ *adj* (1669) : of or relating to leave-taking : FINAL ⟨a ∼ appearance⟩

far·fel *or* **far·fal** \'fär-fəl\ *n* [Yiddish *farfl* (pl.), fr. MHG *varveln* noodles, noodle soup] (1892) : noodles in the form of small pellets or granules

far-fetched \'fär-'fecht\ *adj* (1583) **1** : brought from a remote time or place **2** : not easily or naturally deduced or introduced : IMPROBABLE ⟨a ∼ story⟩ — **far-fetched·ness** \-'fech(t)-nəs, -'fe-chəd-nəs\ *n*

far-flung \-'fləŋ\ *adj* (1895) **1** : widely spread or distributed ⟨a ∼ empire⟩ **2** : REMOTE ⟨a ∼ correspondent⟩

fa·ri·na \fə-'rē-nə\ *n* [L, meal, flour, fr. *far* spelt — more at BARLEY] (14c) **1** : a fine meal of vegetable matter (as cereal grains) used chiefly for puddings or as a breakfast cereal **2** : any of various powdery or mealy substances

far·i·na·ceous \ˌfar-ə-'nā-shəs\ *adj* (1646) **1** : having a mealy texture or surface **2** : containing or rich in starch

far-in·fra·red \ˌfär-ˌin-frə-'red\ *adj* (1923) : of or relating to the longer wavelengths of radiation in the infrared spectrum and esp. to those between 10 and 1000 micrometers

fa·ri·nha \fə-'rēn-yə\ *n* [Pg, flour, cassava meal, fr. L *farina*] (1726) : cassava meal

far·kle·ber·ry \'fär-kəl-ˌber-ē\ *n* [origin unknown] (1765) : a shrub or small tree (*Vaccinium arboreum*) of the heath family of the southeastern U.S. having a black berry with stony seeds

farl \'färl\ *n* [contr. of Sc *fardel,* lit., fourth part, fr. ME (Sc), fr. *ferde del;* fr. *ferde* fourth + *del* part] (1686) *Scot* : a small thin triangular cake or biscuit made esp. with oatmeal or wheat flour

¹farm \'färm\ *n, often attrib* [ME *ferme* rent, lease, fr. OF, lease, fr. *fermer* to fix, make a contract, fr. L *firmare* to make firm, fr. *firmus* firm] (14c) **1** *obs* : a sum or due fixed in amount and payable at fixed intervals **2** : a letting out of revenues or taxes for a fixed sum to one authorized to collect and retain them **3** : a district or division of a country leased out for the collection of government revenues **4** : a tract of land devoted to agricultural purposes **5 a** : a plot of land devoted to the raising of animals and esp. domestic livestock **b** : a tract of water reserved for the artificial cultivation of some aquatic life form **6** : a minor-league team (as in baseball) associated with a major-

\ə\ abut \ᵊ\ kitten, F table \ər\ further \a\ ash \ā\ ace \ä\ mop, mar \aů\ out \ch\ chin \e\ bet \ē\ easy \g\ go \i\ hit \ī\ ice \j\ job \ŋ\ sing \ō\ go \ȯ\ law \ȯi\ boy \th\ thin \t̲h̲\ the \ü\ loot \ů\ foot \y\ yet \zh\ vision \à, k̲, ⁿ, œ, œ̄, ǔ, ᵫ, ᵫ̄, �验\ *see* Guide to Pronunciation league team as a subsidiary   **7** : an area containing a number of similar structures (as radio antennas or storage tanks)

²farm *vt* (15c)   **1** *obs* : RENT   **2** : to collect and take the fees or profits of (an occupation or business) on payment of a fixed sum   **3** : to give up (as an estate or a business) to another on condition of receiving in return a fixed sum   **4 a** : to devote to agriculture   **b** : to manage and cultivate as a farm   **c** : to grow or cultivate in quantity ⟨∼ trees for fuel⟩ ⟨∼ salmon⟩ ∼ *vi* : to engage in raising crops, animals, or fish

farm·er \'fär-mər\ *n* (14c)   **1** : a person who pays a fixed sum for some privilege or source of income   **2** : a person who cultivates land or crops or raises animals or fish   **3** : YOKEL, BUMPKIN

farmer cheese *n* (1949) : a pressed unripened cheese similar to but drier and firmer than cottage cheese

farm·er·ette \,fär-mə-'ret\ *n* (1902) : a woman who is a farmer or farmhand

farmer's lung *n* (1945) : an acute pulmonary disorder characterized by sudden onset, fever, cough, expectoration, and breathlessness that results from the inhalation of dust from moldy hay or straw

farm·hand \'färm-,hand\ *n* (1843)   **1** : a farm laborer; *esp* : a hired laborer on a farm   **2** : a player on a farm team

farm·house \-,haùs\ *n* (1598) : a dwelling on a farm

farm·ing *n* (1733) : the practice of agriculture or aquaculture

farm·land \'färm-,land\ *n* (1638) : land used or suitable for farming

farm out *vt* (1607)   **1** : to turn over (as a job) for performance by another usu. under contract   **2 a** : to put (as children) into the hands of another for care   **b** : to send (as a baseball player) to a farm team   **3** : to exhaust (land) by farming esp. by continuously raising one crop

farm·stead \'färm-,sted\ *n* (1807) : the buildings and adjacent service areas of a farm; *broadly* : a farm with its buildings

farm·wife \'färm-,wīf\ *n* (1880) : a farmer's wife

farm·work·er \'färm-,wər-kər\ *n* (1946) : FARMHAND 1 — **farm·work** \-,wərk\ *n*

farm·yard \-,yärd\ *n* (1748) : land around or enclosed by farm buildings; *esp* : BARNYARD

faro \'far-(,)ō, 'fer-\ *n*, *pl* **far·os** [prob. alter. of earlier *pharoah*, trans. of F *pharaon*] (ca. 1735) : a gambling game in which players bet on cards drawn from a dealing box

Faro·ese *var of* FAEROESE

far–off \'fär-,óf\ *adj* (15c) : remote in time or space

fa·rouche \fə-'rüsh\ *adj* [F, wild, shy, fr. LL *forasticus* living outside, fr. L *foras* outdoors; akin to L *fores* door — more at DOOR] (1765)   **1** : WILD   **2** : marked by shyness and lack of social graces

far–out \'fär-,aùt\ *adj* (1954) : marked by a considerable departure from the conventional or traditional ⟨∼ clothes⟩ — **far–out·ness** *n*

far·rag·i·nous \fə-'ra-jə-nəs\ *adj* (1615) : consisting of a farrago

far·ra·go \fə-'rä-(,)gō, -'rā-\ *n*, *pl* **-goes** [L *farragin-*, *farrago* mixed fodder, mixture, fr. *far* spelt — more at BARLEY] (1632) : a confused mixture : HODGEPODGE

far–reach·ing \'fär-,rē-chiŋ\ *adj* (1824) : having a wide range or effect

far–red \-'red\ *adj* (1951) : NEAR-INFRARED

far·ri·er \'fär-ē-ər\ *n* [alter. of ME *ferrour*, fr. MF *ferrour* blacksmith, fr. OF *ferreor*, fr. *ferrer* to fit with iron, fr. (assumed) VL *ferrare*, fr. L *ferrum* iron] (15c) : a person who shoes horses

¹far·row \'far-(,)ō, -ə(-w)\ *vb* [ME *farwen*, fr. (assumed) OE *feargian*, fr. OE *fearh* young pig; akin to OHG *farah* young pig, L *porcus* pig] *vt* (13c) : to give birth to (a farrow) ∼ *vi*, *of swine* : to bring forth young — often used with *down*

²farrow *n* (1577)   **1** : a litter of pigs   **2** : an act of farrowing

³farrow *adj* [ME (Sc) *ferow*] (15c) *of a cow* : not pregnant

far·see·ing \'fär-,sē-iŋ\ *adj* (1837) : FARSIGHTED 1

Far·si \'fär-sē\ *n* [Per *fārsi*, fr. *Fārs* Persia] (1878) : PERSIAN 2b

far·side *n* (15c) : the farther side; *esp* : the side of the moon away from the earth — **on the far side of** : BEYOND ⟨just *on the far side of* 40⟩

far·sight·ed \'fär-,sīt-əd\ *adj* (1609)   **1 a** : seeing or able to see to a great distance   **b** : having or showing foresight or good judgment : SAGACIOUS   **2** : affected with hyperopia — **far·sight·ed·ly** *adv* — **far·sight·ed·ness** *n* (ca. 1829) : the quality or state of being farsighted   **2** : HYPEROPIA

¹fart \'färt\ *vi* [ME *ferten*, *farten*; akin to OHG *ferzan* to break wind, ON *freta*, Gk *perdesthai*, Skt *pardate* he breaks wind] (13c) : to expel intestinal gas from the anus — often considered vulgar

²fart *n* (14c)   **1** : an expulsion of intestinal gas — often considered vulgar   **2** : a foolish or contemptible person ⟨couldn't stand the old ∼⟩ — seldom in polite use

¹far·ther \'fär-thər\ *adv* [ME *ferther*, alter. of *further*] (14c)   **1** : at or to a greater distance or more advanced point ⟨got no ∼ than the first page⟩ ⟨nothing could be ∼ from the truth⟩   **2** : to a greater degree or extent ⟨see to it that I do not have to act any ∼ in the matter —Bernard DeVoto⟩

usage **Farther** and *further* have been used more or less interchangeably throughout most of their history, but currently they are showing signs of diverging. As adverbs they continue to be used interchangeably whenever spatial, temporal, or metaphorical distance is involved. But where there is no notion of distance, *further* is used ⟨our techniques can be *further* refined⟩. *Further* is also used as a sentence modifier ⟨*further*, the workshop participants were scarcely optimistic —L. B. Mayhew⟩, but *farther* is not. A polarizing process appears to be taking place in their adjective use. *Farther* is taking over the meaning of distance ⟨the *farther* shore⟩ and *further* the meaning of addition ⟨needed no *further* invitation⟩.

²farther *adj* (14c)   **1** : more distant : REMOTER ⟨the ∼ side of town⟩   **2** : FURTHER 2 ⟨clearing his throat preparatory to ∼ revelations —Edith Wharton⟩

far·ther·most \-,mōst\ *adj* (15c) : most distant : FARTHEST

¹far·thest \'fär-thəst\ *adj* (14c) : most distant esp. in space or time

²farthest *adv* (15c)   **1** : to or at the greatest distance in space or time ⟨who can jump the ∼⟩   **2** : to the most advanced point ⟨goes ∼ toward answering the question⟩   **3** : by the greatest degree or extent : MOST ⟨the painting ∼ removed from reality⟩

far·thing \'fär-thiŋ\ *n* [ME *ferthing*, fr. OE *fēorthung* (akin to MHG *vierdunc* fourth part), fr. OE *fēortha* fourth] (bef. 12c)   **1 a** : a former British monetary unit equal to ¼ of a penny   **b** : a coin representing this unit   **2** : something of small value : MITE

far·thin·gale \'fär-thən-,gāl, -thiŋ-\ *n* [modif. of MF *verdugale*, fr. OSp

verdugado, fr. *verdugo* young shoot of a tree, fr. *verde* green, fr. L *viridis* — more at VERDANT] (1552) : a support (as of hoops) worn esp. in the 16th century beneath a skirt to expand it at the hipline

far ultraviolet *adj* (1947) : of, relating to, or being the shortest wavelengths of radiation in the ultraviolet spectrum and esp. those between 100 and 300 nanometers

fas·ces \'fas-,ēz\ *n pl but sing or pl in constr* [L, fr. pl. of *fascis* bundle; akin to L *fascia*] (1598) : a bundle of rods and among them an ax with projecting blade borne before ancient Roman magistrates as a badge of authority

fas·cia \l & 3 *are usu* 'fä-sh(ē-)ə, 2 *is usu* 'fa-\ *n*, *pl* **-ci·ae** \-shē-,ē\ *or* **-cias** [It, fr. L, band, bandage; akin to MIr *basc* necklace] (1563)   **1** : a flat usu. horizontal member of a building having the form of a flat band or broad fillet: as   **a** : a flat piece used as a molding   **b** : a horizontal piece (as a board) covering the joint between the top of a wall and the projecting eaves — called also *fascia board*   **c** : a nameplate over the front of a shop   **2** : a sheet of connective tissue covering or binding together body structures; *also* : tissue of this character   **3** *or* **fa·cia** \'fä-sh(ē-)ə\ *Brit* : the dashboard of an automobile — **fas·cial** \'fa-sh(ē-)əl\ *adj*

fas·ci·at·ed \'fa-shē-,ā-təd\ *adj* (ca. 1835)   **1** : exhibiting fasciation   **2** : arranged in fascicles

fas·ci·a·tion \,fa-s(h)ē-'ā-shən\ *n* (1677) : a malformation of plant stems commonly manifested as enlargement and flattening as if several stems were fused

fas·ci·cle \'fa-si-kəl\ *n* [L *fasciculus*, dim. of *fascis*] (15c)   **1** : a small or slender bundle (as of pine needles or nerve fibers)   **2** : one of the divisions of a book published in parts — **fas·ci·cled** \-kəld\ *adj*

fas·cic·u·lar \fə-'si-kyə-lər, fa-\ *adj* (1816) : of, relating to, or consisting of fascicles or fasciculi — **fas·cic·u·lar·ly** *adv*

fas·cic·u·late \-lət\ *also* **fas·cic·u·lat·ed** \-,lā-təd\ *adj* (1794) : FASCICULAR

fas·cic·u·la·tion \fə-,si-kyə-'lā-shən, fa-\ *n* (1938) : muscular twitching involving the simultaneous contraction of contiguous groups of muscle fibers

fas·ci·cule \'fa-si-,kyü(ə)l\ *n* [F, fr. L *fasciculus*] (1880) : FASCICLE 2

fas·cic·u·lus \fə-'si-kyə-ləs, fa-\ *n*, *pl* **-li** \-,lī\ [NL, fr. L] (1713)   **1** : a slender bundle of anatomical fibers   **2** : FASCICLE 2

fas·ci·nate \'fa-sⁿn-,āt\ *vb* **fas·ci·nat·ed; fas·ci·nat·ing** \'fas-,nā-tiŋ, 'fa-sⁿn-,ā-\ [L *fascinatus*, pp. of *fascinare*, fr. *fascinum* evil spell] *vt* (1598)   **1** *obs* : BEWITCH   **2 a** : to transfix and hold spellbound by an irresistible power ⟨believed that the serpent could ∼ its prey⟩   **b** : to command the interest of : ALLURE ⟨was *fascinated* by carnivals⟩ ∼ *vi* : to be irresistibly attractive ⟨the novel's flamboyant cover ∼s⟩   *syn* see ATTRACT

fas·ci·nat·ing *adj* (1648) : extremely interesting or charming : CAPTIVATING — **fas·ci·nat·ing·ly** \-,ā-tiŋ-lē\ *adv*

fas·ci·na·tion \,fa-sⁿn-'ā-shən\ *n* (1605)   **1 a** : the quality or power of fascinating   **b** : something fascinating   **2** : the state of being fascinated

fas·ci·na·tor \'fa-sⁿn-,ā-tər\ *n* (1750)   **1** : one that fascinates   **2** : a woman's lightweight head scarf usu. of crochet or lace

fas·cine \fa-'sēn, fə-\ *n* [F, fr. L *fascina*, fr. *fascis*] (ca. 1688) : a long bundle of sticks of wood bound together and used for such purposes as filling ditches and making revetments for riverbanks

fa·sci·o·li·a·sis \fə-,sē-ə-'lī-ə-səs, -,si-\ *n*, *pl* **-a·ses** \-,sēz\ [NL, fr. *Fasciola*, genus of flukes + *-iasis*] (1890) : infestation with or disease caused by liver flukes (genus *Fasciola*)

fas·cism \'fa-,shi-zəm *also* 'fa-,si-\ *n* [It *fascismo*, fr. *fascio* bundle, fasces, group, fr. L *fascis* bundle & *fasces* fasces] (1921)   **1** *often cap* : a political philosophy, movement, or regime (as that of the Fascisti) that exalts nation and often race above the individual and that stands for a centralized autocratic government headed by a dictatorial leader, severe economic and social regimentation, and forcible suppression of opposition   **2** : a tendency toward or actual exercise of strong autocratic or dictatorial control ⟨early instances of army ∼ and brutality — J. W. Aldridge⟩ — **fas·cist** \-shist *also* -sist\ *n or adj*, *often cap* — **fas·cis·tic** \fa-'shis-tik *also* -'sis-\ *adj*, *often cap* — **fas·cis·ti·cal·ly** \-ti-k(ə-)lē\ *adv*, *often cap*

Fa·sci·sta \fä-'shē-(,)stä\ *n*, *pl* **-sti** \-(,)stē\ [It, fr. *fascio*] (1921) : a member of an Italian political organization under Mussolini governing Italy 1922–1943 according to the principles of fascism

fash \'fash\ *vb* [MF *fascher*, fr. (assumed) VL *fastidiare* to disgust, fr. L *fastidium* disgust — more at FASTIDIOUS] (1533) *chiefly Scot* : VEX — **fash** *n*, *chiefly Scot*

¹fash·ion \'fa-shⁿn\ *n* [ME *facioun*, *fasoun* shape, manner, fr. MF *façon*, fr. L *faction-*, *factio* act of making, faction, fr. *facere* to make — more at DO] (14c)   **1 a** : the make or form of something   **b** *archaic* : KIND, SORT   **2 a** : a distinctive or peculiar and often habitual manner or way ⟨he will, after his sour ∼, tell you —Shak.⟩   **b** : mode of action or operation ⟨assembled in an orderly ∼⟩   **3 a** : a prevailing custom, usage, or style   **b** (1) : the prevailing style (as in dress) during a particular time   (2) : a garment in such a style ⟨always wears the latest ∼s⟩   **c** : social standing or prominence esp. as signalized by dress or conduct ⟨men and women of ∼⟩ — **after a fashion** : in an approximate or rough way ⟨became an artist *after a fashion*⟩

syn FASHION, STYLE, MODE, VOGUE, FAD, RAGE, CRAZE mean the usage accepted by those who want to be up-to-date. FASHION is the most general term and applies to any way of dressing, behaving, writing, or performing that is favored at any one time or place ⟨the current *fashion*⟩. STYLE often implies a distinctive fashion adopted by people of taste ⟨a media baron used to traveling in *style*⟩. MODE suggests the fashion of the moment among those anxious to appear elegant and sophisticated ⟨slim bodies are the *mode* at this resort⟩. VOGUE stresses the wide acceptance of a fashion ⟨short skirts are back in *vogue*⟩. FAD suggests caprice in taking up or in dropping a fashion ⟨last year's *fad* is over⟩. RAGE and CRAZE stress intense enthusiasm in adopting a fad ⟨Cajun food was the *rage* nearly everywhere for a time⟩ ⟨crossword puzzles once seemed just a passing *craze* but have lasted⟩.   *syn* see in addition METHOD

²fashion *vt* **fash·ioned; fash·ion·ing** \'fash-niŋ, 'fa-shⁿn-iŋ\ (15c)   **1 a** : to give shape or form to : MOLD   **b** : ALTER, TRANSFORM   **c** : to mold into a particular character by influencing or training **d** : to make or construct usu. with the use of imagination and ingenuity ⟨∼ a lamp from an old churn⟩ **2** : FIT, ADAPT **3** *obs* : CONTRIVE — **fash-ion-er** \'fash-nər, 'fa-sh°n-ər\ *n*

¹**fash-ion-able** \'fash-nə-bəl, 'fa-sh°n-ə-\ *adj* (1606) **1** : conforming to the custom, fashion, or established mode **2** : of or relating to the world of fashion — **fash-ion-abil-i-ty** \ˌfash-nə-'bi-lə-tē, ˌfa-sh°n-ə-\ *n* — **fash-ion-able-ness** \'fash-nə-bəl-nəs, 'fa-shə-\ *n* — **fash-ion-ably** \-blē\ *adv*

²**fashionable** *n* (ca. 1800) : a fashionable person

fash-ion-mon-ger \'fash°n-ˌmäŋ-gər, -ˌməŋ-\ *n* (1599) : one that studies, imitates, or sets the fashion

fashion plate *n* (1851) **1** : an illustration of a clothing style **2** : a person who dresses in the latest fashions

¹**fast** \'fast\ *adj* [ME, fr. OE *fæst;* akin to OHG *festi* firm, ON *fastr,* Arm *hast*] (bef. 12c) **1 a** : firmly fixed ⟨roots ∼ in the ground⟩ **b** : tightly shut ⟨the drawers were ∼⟩ **c** : adhering firmly **d** : not easily freed : STUCK ⟨a ball ∼ in the mouth of the cannon⟩ **e** : STABLE ⟨movable items were made ∼ to the deck⟩ **2** : firmly loyal ⟨became ∼ friends⟩ **3 a** : characterized by quick motion, operation, or effect: (1) : moving or able to move rapidly : SWIFT (2) : taking a comparatively short time (3) : imparting quickness of motion ⟨a ∼ bowler⟩ (4) : accomplished quickly (5) : agile of mind; *esp* : quick to learn ⟨a class for ∼ students⟩ **b** : conducive to rapidity of play or action **c** (1) *of a timepiece or weighing device* : indicating in advance of what is correct (2) : according to or being daylight saving time **d** : contributing to a shortening of exposure time ⟨∼ film⟩ **e** : acquired with unusually little effort and often by shady or dishonest methods ⟨had a keen eye for a ∼ buck —R. A. Keith⟩ **4 a** : securely attached ⟨a rope ∼ to the wharf⟩ **b** : TENACIOUS ⟨a ∼ hold on her purse⟩ **5 a** *archaic* : sound asleep **b** *of sleep* : not easily disturbed **6** : not fading or changing color readily **7 a** : WILD ⟨a pretty ∼ crowd⟩ **b** : sexually promiscuous **8** : resistant to change (as from destructive action or fading) ⟨∼ dyes⟩ — often used in combination ⟨sun*fast*⟩ ⟨acid-*fast* bacteria⟩

syn FAST, RAPID, SWIFT, FLEET, QUICK, SPEEDY, HASTY, EXPEDITIOUS mean moving, proceeding, or acting with celerity. FAST and RAPID are very close in meaning, but FAST applies particularly to the thing that moves ⟨*fast* horses⟩ and RAPID to the movement itself ⟨*rapid* current⟩. SWIFT suggests great rapidity coupled with ease of movement ⟨returned the ball with one *swift* stroke⟩. FLEET adds the implication of lightness and nimbleness ⟨*fleet* runners⟩. QUICK suggests promptness and the taking of little time ⟨a *quick* wit⟩. SPEEDY implies quickness of successful accomplishment ⟨*speedy* delivery of mail⟩ and may also suggest unusual velocity. HASTY suggests hurry and precipitousness and often connotes carelessness ⟨a *hasty* inspection⟩. EXPEDITIOUS suggests efficiency together with rapidity of accomplishment ⟨the *expeditious* handling of an order⟩.

²**fast** *adv* (bef. 12c) **1** : in a firm or fixed manner ⟨stuck ∼⟩ **2** : in a sound manner : DEEPLY ⟨∼ asleep⟩ **3 a** : in a rapid manner : QUICKLY **b** : in quick succession ⟨kaleidoscopic impressions that come so thick and ∼ —M. B. Tucker⟩ **4** : in a reckless or dissipated manner **5** : ahead of a correct time or schedule **6** *archaic* : CLOSE, NEAR

³**fast** *vi* [ME, fr. OE *fæstan*] (bef. 12c) **1** : to abstain from food **2** : to eat sparingly or abstain from some foods

⁴**fast** *n* (bef. 12c) **1** : the practice of fasting **2** : a time of fasting

⁵**fast** *n* [alter. of ME *fest,* fr. ON *festr* rope, mooring cable, fr. *fastr* firm] (15c) : something that fastens (as a mooring line) or holds a fastening

fast and loose *adv* (1557) **1** : in a reckless or irresponsible manner ⟨played *fast and loose* with the public purse strings —Paul Stuewe⟩ **2** : in a craftily deceitful way ⟨manipulated evidence . . . and played *fast and loose* with the truth —C. V. Woodward⟩

fast-back \'fas(t)-ˌbak\ *n* (1954) : an automobile with a roof having a long curving downward slope to the rear; *also* : the back of such an automobile

fast-ball \'fas(t)-ˌból\ *n* (1912) : a baseball pitch thrown at full speed and often rising slightly as it nears the plate — **fast-ball-er** \-ˌbó-lər\ *n*

fast break *n* (ca. 1949) : a quick offensive drive toward a goal (as in basketball) in an attempt to score before the opponent's defense is set up — **fast–break** *vi*

fas-ten \'fa-s°n\ *vb* **fas-tened; fas-ten-ing** \'fas-niŋ, 'fa-s°n-iŋ\ [ME *fastnen,* fr. OE *fæstnian* to make fast; akin to OHG *festinōn* to make fast, OE *fæst* fast] *vt* (bef. 12c) **1 a** : to attach esp. by pinning, tying, or nailing **b** : to make fast and secure **c** : to fix firmly or securely **d** : to secure against opening **2** : to fix or set steadily ⟨∼ed her attention on the main problem⟩ **3** : to take a firm grip with ⟨the dog ∼ed its teeth in the shoe⟩ **4 a** : to attach (oneself) persistently and usu. objectionably **b** : IMPOSE ⟨∼ed the blame on the wrong person⟩ ∼ *vi* **1** : to become fast or fixed **2 a** : to take a firm grip or hold **b** : to focus attention — **fas-ten-er** \'fas-nər, 'fa-s°n-ər\ *n*

syn FASTEN, FIX, ATTACH, AFFIX mean to make something stay firmly in place. FASTEN implies an action such as tying, buttoning, nailing, locking, or otherwise securing ⟨*fasten* the reins to a post⟩. FIX usu. implies a driving in, implanting, or embedding ⟨*fixed* the stake in the ground⟩. ATTACH suggests a connecting or uniting by a bond, link, or tie in order to keep things together ⟨*attach* the W-2 form here⟩. AFFIX implies an imposing of one thing on another by gluing, impressing, or nailing ⟨*affix* your address label here⟩.

fas-ten-ing *n* (12c) : something that fastens : FASTENER

fast–food \'fas(t)-ˌfüd\ *adj* (1951) **1** : of, relating to, or specializing in food that can be prepared and served quickly ⟨a ∼ restaurant⟩ **2** : designed for ready availability, use, or consumption and with little consideration given to quality or significance ⟨∼ TV programming⟩ — **fast food** *n*

¹**fast–for-ward** \ˌfas(t)-'fór-wərd\ *n, often attrib* (1948) **1** : a function of a tape player by which the tape is advanced at a higher speed than when it is playing normally **2** : a state or an instance of rapid advancement ⟨put her career in *fast-forward*⟩

²**fast–forward** *vt* (1974) **1** : to advance (a magnetic tape) using the fast-forward of a tape player **2** : to bypass (as a commercial) by fast forwarding ∼ *vi* **1** : to advance a magnetic tape using the fast forward **2** : to proceed rapidly esp. in time ⟨∼ to the future⟩

fas-tid-i-ous \fa-'sti-dē-əs, fə-\ *adj* [ME, fr. L *fastidiosus,* fr. *fastidium*

disgust, prob. fr. *fastus* arrogance (prob. akin to L *fastigium* top) + *taedium* irksomeness — more at TEDIUM] (15c) **1** *archaic* : SCORNFUL **2 a** : having high and often capricious standards : difficult to please ⟨critics . . . so ∼ that they can talk only to a small circle of initiates — Granville Hicks⟩ **b** : showing or demanding excessive delicacy or care **c** : reflecting a meticulous, sensitive, or demanding attitude ⟨∼ workmanship⟩ **3** : having complex nutritional requirements ⟨∼ microorganisms⟩ — **fas-tid-i-ous-ly** *adv* — **fas-tid-i-ous-ness** *n*

fas-ti-gi-ate \fa-'sti-jē-ət\ *adj* [prob. fr. (assumed) NL *fastigiatus,* fr. L *fastigium* — more at BRISTLE] (1662) **1** : narrowing toward the top; *esp* : having upright usu. clustered branches ⟨∼ trees⟩

fast lane *n* (1966) **1** : a traffic lane intended for vehicles traveling at higher speeds **2** : a way of life marked by a fast pace and usu. the pursuit of immediate gratification **3** : FAST TRACK — **fast–lane** *adj*

fast-ness \'fas(t)-nəs\ *n* (bef. 12c) **1** : the quality or state of being fast: as **a** : the quality or state of being fixed **b** : the quality or state of being swift **c** : colorfast quality **d** : resistance (as of an organism) to the action of a usu. toxic substance **2 a** : a fortified or secure place **b** : a remote and secluded place ⟨vacationed in their mountain ∼⟩

Fast of Esther (1887) : a Jewish fast day observed the day before Purim in commemoration of a fast proclaimed by Queen Esther

fast–talk \'fas(t)-ˌtók\ *vt* (1946) : to influence or persuade by fluent, facile, and usu. deceptive or tricky talk ⟨∼ed him into buying a lemon⟩

¹**fast–track** \'fas(t)-ˌtrak\ *adj* (1967) **1** : of, relating to, or moving along a fast track ⟨∼ executives⟩ **2** : of, relating to, or being a construction procedure in which work on a building begins before designs are completed

²**fast–track** *vt* (1971) : to speed up the processing, production, or construction of in order to meet a goal — **fast–track-er** *n*

fast track *n* (1980) : a course leading to rapid advancement or success

fast–twitch \'fas(t)-ˌtwich\ *adj* (1970) : of, relating to, or being muscle fiber that contracts quickly esp. during brief high-intensity physical activity requiring strength — compare SLOW-TWITCH

fas-tu-ous \'fas-chə-wəs\ *adj* [L *fastuosus,* fr. *fastus* arrogance] (1638) **1** : HAUGHTY, ARROGANT ⟨a ∼ air of finality —Carl Van Vechten⟩ **2** : OSTENTATIOUS, SHOWY ⟨disdained ∼ ceremonies⟩

¹**fat** \'fat\ *adj* **fat-ter; fat-test** [ME, fr. OE *fætt,* pp. of *fǣtan* to cram; akin to OHG *feizit* fat] (bef. 12c) **1** : notable for having an unusual amount of fat: **a** : PLUMP **b** : OBESE **c** *of a meat animal* : fattened for market **d** *of food* : OILY, GREASY **2 a** : well filled out : THICK, BIG ⟨a ∼ book⟩ **b** : full in tone and quality : RICH ⟨a gorgeous ∼ bass voice —*Irish Digest*⟩ **c** : well stocked ⟨a ∼ larder⟩ **d** : PROSPEROUS, WEALTHY ⟨grew ∼ on the war —*Time*⟩ **e** : being substantial and impressive ⟨a ∼ bank account⟩ **3 a** : richly rewarding or profitable ⟨a ∼ part in a movie⟩ ⟨a ∼ contract⟩ **b** : practically nonexistent ⟨a ∼ chance⟩ **4** : PRODUCTIVE, FERTILE ⟨a ∼ year for crops⟩ **5** : STUPID, FOOLISH **6** : being swollen ⟨got a ∼ lip from the fight⟩ **7** *of a baseball pitch* : easy to hit — **fat-ness** *n*

²**fat** *vt* **fat-ted; fat-ting** (bef. 12c) : to make fat : FATTEN

³**fat** *n* (14c) **1** : animal tissue consisting chiefly of ⟨∼⟩us d⟨∼⟩ended with greasy or oily matter **2 a** : oily or greasy ma⟨∼⟩r making u⟨∼⟩ the bulk of adipose tissue and often abundant in s⟨∼⟩us **b** : any of n⟨∼⟩erous compounds of carbon, hydrogen, and⟨∼⟩xygen that are glyceri⟨∼⟩s of fat⟨∼⟩ ⟨∼⟩ids, are the chief constit⟨∼⟩s of plant and animal fat, are ∼ major cla⟨∼⟩s of energy-rich food and are soluble in organic solvents but not in water **c** : a solid or ⟨∼⟩misolid fat as distinguished from an oil **3** : the best or richest p⟨∼⟩ **4** : OBESITY **5** : something in excess : SUPERFLUITY ⟨trim the ∼ from the news operation —Ray Olson⟩ — **fat-less** \-ləs\ *adj*

fa-tal \'fā-t°l\ *adj* [ME, fr. MF & L; MF, fr. L *fatalis,* fr. *fatum*] (14c) **1** *obs* : FATED **2** : FATEFUL ⟨a ∼ hour⟩ **3 a** : of or relating to fate **b** : resembling fate in proceeding according to a fixed sequence **c** : determining one's fate **4 a** : causing death **b** : bringing ruin ***syn*** see DEADLY

fa-tal-ism \-ˌi-zəm\ *n* (1678) : a doctrine that events are fixed in advance so that human beings are powerless to change them; *also* : a belief in or attitude determined by this doctrine — **fa-tal-ist** \-ist\ *n* — **fa-tal-is-tic** \ˌfā-t°l-'is-tik\ *adj* — **fa-tal-is-ti-cal-ly** \-ti-k(ə-)lē\ *adv*

fa-tal-i-ty \fā-'ta-lə-tē, fə-\ *n, pl* **-ties** [ME, fr. MF *fatalité,* fr. LL *fatalitat-, fatalitas,* fr. L *fatalis*] (15c) **1 a** : the quality or state of causing death or destruction **b** : the quality or condition of being destined for disaster **2** : something established by fate **3 a** : FATE 1 **b** : FATALISM **4** : the agent or agency of fate **5 a** : death resulting from a disaster **b** : one that experiences a fatal outcome

fa-tal-ly \'fā-t°l-ē\ *adv* (15c) **1** : in a way determined by fate **2** : in a manner suggesting fate or an act of fate: as **a** : in a manner resulting in death : MORTALLY ⟨∼ wounded⟩ **b** : beyond repair : IRREVOCABLY **c** : in a manner resulting in ruin or evil ⟨it is ∼ easy to pass off our prejudices as our opinions —W. F. Hambly⟩ **d** : in a manner that cannot be easily resisted ⟨thinks she is ∼ attractive —J. W. Krutch⟩

fa-ta mor-ga-na \ˌfä-tə-mór-'gä-nə, -ˌga-\ *n* [It, lit., Morgan le Fay (sorceress of Arthurian legend)] (1818) : MIRAGE

fat-back \'fat-ˌbak\ *n* (1903) : the strip of fat from the back of a hog carcass usu. cured by drying and salting

fat body *n* (1869) : a fatty tissue esp. of nearly mature insect larvae that serves as a food reserve

fat cat *n* (1928) **1 a** : a wealthy contributor to a political campaign fund **b** : a wealthy and privileged person **c** : BIG SHOT **2** : a lethargic complacent person — **fat–cat** \'fat-ˌkat\ *adj*

fat cell *n* (1845) : one of the fat-laden cells making up adipose tissue

fat depot *n* (1946) : ADIPOSE TISSUE

¹**fate** \'fāt\ *n* [ME, fr. MF or L; MF, fr. L *fatum,* lit., what has been spoken, fr. neut. of *fatus,* pp. of *fari* to speak — more at BAN] (14c) **1** : the principle or determining cause or will by which things in general are believed to come to be as they are or events to happen as they do : DESTINY **2 a** : an inevitable and often adverse outcome, condition, or end **b** : DISASTER; *esp* : DEATH **3 a** : final outcome **b** : the ex-

\ə\ abut \ᵊ\ kitten, F table \ər\ further \a\ ash \ā\ ace \ä\ mop, mar \aú\ out \ch\ chin \e\ bet \ē\ easy \g\ go \i\ hit \ī\ ice \j\ job \ŋ\ sing \ō\ go \ó\ law \ói\ boy \th\ thin \th\ the \ü\ loot \ú\ foot \y\ yet \zh\ vision \ä, k, ⁿ, œ, œ̄, ᵫ, ᵫ̄, ʸ\ *see* Guide to Pronunciation pected result of normal development ⟨prospective ~ of embryonic cells⟩ **4** *pl, cap* : the three goddesses who determine the course of human life in classical mythology

syn FATE, DESTINY, LOT, PORTION, DOOM mean a predetermined state or end. FATE implies an inevitable and usu. an adverse outcome ⟨the *fate* of the submarine is unknown⟩. DESTINY implies something foreordained and often suggests a great or noble course or end ⟨the country's *destiny* to be a model of liberty to the world⟩. LOT and PORTION imply a distribution by fate or destiny, LOT suggesting blind chance ⟨it was her *lot* to die childless⟩, PORTION implying the apportioning of good and evil ⟨remorse was his daily *portion*⟩. DOOM distinctly implies a grim or calamitous fate ⟨if the rebellion fails, his *doom* is certain⟩.

²fate *vt* **fat·ed; fat·ing** (1601) : DESTINE; *also* : DOOM

fat·ed *adj* (ca. 1606) : decreed, controlled, or marked by fate

fate·ful \'fāt-fəl\ *adj* (ca. 1720) **1** : having a quality of ominous prophecy ⟨a ~ remark⟩ **2 a** : involving momentous consequences : DECISIVE ⟨made his ~ decision to declare war —W. L. Shirer⟩ **b** : DEADLY, CATASTROPHIC **3** : controlled by fate : FOREORDAINED **syn** see OMINOUS — **fate·ful·ly** \-fə-lē\ *adv* — **fate·ful·ness** *n*

fat farm *n* (1969) : a health spa that specializes in weight reduction

fat·head \'fat-,hed\ *n* (1842) : a stupid person — **fat·head·ed** \-'he-dəd\ *adj* — **fat·head·ed·ly** *adv* — **fat·head·ed·ness** *n*

¹fa·ther \'fä-thər, 'fā-\ *n* [ME *fader*, fr. OE *fæder*; akin to OHG *fater* father, L *pater*, Gk *patēr*] (bef. 12c) **1 a** : a man who has begotten a child; *also* : SIRE 3 **b** *cap* (1) : GOD 1 (2) : the first person of the Trinity **2** : FOREFATHER **3 a** : one related to another in a way suggesting that of father to child **b** : an old man — used as a respectful form of address **4** *often cap* : a pre-Scholastic Christian writer accepted by the church as an authoritative witness to its teaching and practice — called also *church father* **5 a** : one that originates or institutes ⟨the ~ of modern science⟩ **b** : SOURCE ⟨the sun, the ~ of warmth and light —Lena M. Whitney⟩ **c** : PROTOTYPE **6** : a priest of the regular clergy; *broadly* : PRIEST — used esp. as a title **7** : one of the leading men (as of a city) — usu. used in pl. — **fa·ther·hood** \-,hu̇d\ *n* — **fa·ther·less** \-ləs\ *adj* — **fa·ther·like** \-,līk\ *adj or adv*

²father *vb* **fa·thered; fa·ther·ing** \'fäth-riŋ, 'fäth-; 'fä-thə-, 'fā-\ *vt* (15c) **1 a** : BEGET **b** : to make oneself the founder, producer, or author of ⟨~ed the improvement plan⟩ **c** : to accept responsibility for **2 a** : to fix the paternity or origin of **b** : to place responsibility for the origin or cause of ⟨collected gossip and ~ed it on responsible men —J. A. Williamson⟩ **3** : FOIST, IMPOSE ~ *vi* : to care for or look after someone as a father might

Father Christmas *n, Brit* : SANTA CLAUS

father figure *n* (1934) : one often of particular power or influence who serves as an emotional substitute for a father

father image *n* (1937) : an idealization of one's father often projected onto someone to whom one looks for guidance and protection

fa·ther–in–law \'fä-thə-rən-,lȯ, -thərn-,lȯ, 'fä-\ *n, pl* **fa·thers–in–law** \-thər-zən-\ (14c) **1** : the father of one's spouse **2** *archaic* : STEPFATHER

fa·ther·land \'fä-thər-,land, 'fä-\ *n* (12c) **1** : the native land or country of one's father or ancestors **2** : one's native land or country

fa·ther·ly \'fä-thər-lē, 'fä-\ *adj* (15c) **1** : of, relating to, or befitting a father ⟨~ responsibilities⟩ **2** : resembling a father (as in affection or care) ⟨a ~ old man⟩ — **fa·ther·li·ness** \-lē-nəs\ *n* — **fatherly** *adv*

Father's Day *n* (1927) : the third Sunday in June appointed for the honoring of fathers

¹fath·om \'fa-thəm\ *n* [ME *fadme*, fr. OE *fæthm* outstretched arms, length of the outstretched arms; akin to ON *fathmr* fathom, L *patēre* to be open, *pandere* to spread out, Gk *petannynai*] (bef. 12c) **1** : a unit of length equal to six feet (1.83 meters) used esp. for measuring the depth of water **2** : COMPREHENSION

²fathom *vi* (1607) **1** : PROBE **2** : to take soundings — *vt* **1** : to measure by a sounding line **2** : to penetrate and come to understand ⟨couldn't ~ the problem⟩ — **fath·om·able** \'fa-thə-mə-bəl\ *adj*

Fa·thom·e·ter \fa-'thä-mə-tər, 'fa-thə-,mē-\ *trademark* — used for a sonic depth finder

fath·om·less \'fa-thəm-ləs\ *adj* (1638) : incapable of being fathomed — **fath·om·less·ly** *adv* — **fath·om·less·ness** *n*

fa·tid·ic \fā-'ti-dik, fə-\ *or* **fa·tid·i·cal** \-di-kəl\ *adj* [L *fatidicus*, fr. *fatum* fate + *dicere* to say — more at DICTION] (1607) : of or relating to prophecy

fa·ti·ga·ble \fə-'tē-gə-bəl, 'fa-ti-gə-\ *adj* (1608) : susceptible to fatigue — **fa·ti·ga·bil·i·ty** \fə-,tē-gə-'bi-lə-tē, ,fa-ti-gə-\ *n*

¹fa·tigue \fə-'tēg\ *n* [F, fr. MF, fr. *fatiguer* to fatigue, fr. L *fatigare*; akin to L *af·fatim* sufficiently] (1669) **1 a** : LABOR **b** : manual or menial work performed by military personnel **c** *pl* : the uniform or work clothing worn on fatigue and in the field **2 a** : weariness or exhaustion from labor, exertion, or stress **b** : the temporary loss of power to respond induced in a sensory receptor or motor end organ by continued stimulation **3** : the tendency of a material to break under repeated stress

²fatigue *vb* **fa·tigued; fa·tigu·ing** *vt* (1693) **1** : to weary with labor or exertion **2** : to induce a condition of fatigue in ~ *vi* : to suffer fatigue **syn** see TIRE — **fa·tigu·ing·ly** \-'tē-giŋ-lē\ *adv*

³fatigue *adj* (1774) **1** : consisting of, done, or used in fatigue ⟨~ detail⟩ **2** : belonging to fatigues ⟨a ~ cap⟩

fat·ling \'fat-liŋ\ *n* (ca. 1534) : a young animal fattened for slaughter

fat·ly *adv* (15c) **1** : RICHLY **2** : in the manner of one that is fat ⟨waddled ~⟩ **3** : in a smug manner : COMPLACENTLY ⟨snickered ~⟩

fats·hed·era \fats-'he-d(ə-)rə, ,fat-'se-\ *n* [NL *Fatsia*, genus of shrubs + *Hedera*, genus of vines (fr. L, ivy)] (1948) : a vigorous upright hybrid ornamental foliage plant (*Hedera helix* × *Aralia elata*) with glossy deeply lobed palmate leaves

fat·so \'fat-(,)sō\ *n, pl* **fat·soes** [prob. fr. *Fats*, nickname for a fat person + -o] (1944) : a fat person — often used disparagingly

fat·stock \-,stäk\ *n* (1880) *chiefly Brit* : livestock that is fat and ready for market

fat–tailed sheep \'fat-,tāld-\ *n* (1842) : a coarse-wooled mutton sheep that has great quantities of fat on each side of the tail bones

fat·ten \'fa-tᵊn\ *vb* **fat·tened; fat·ten·ing** \'fat-niŋ, 'fa-tᵊn-iŋ\ *vt* (1552) **1 a** : to make fat, fleshy, or plump; *esp* : to feed (as a stock animal) for slaughter **b** : to make more substantial **2** : to make fertile ~ *vi* : to become fat — **fat·ten·er** \'fat-nər, 'fa-tᵊn-ər\ *n*

fat·tish \'fa-tish\ *adj* (14c) : somewhat fat

¹fat·ty \'fa-tē\ *adj* **fat·ti·er; -est** (14c) **1** : containing fat esp. in unusual amounts; *also* : unduly stout : CORPULENT **2** : GREASY **3** : derived from or chemically related to fat — **fat·ti·ness** *n*

²fatty *n, pl* **fat·ties** (1797) : one that is fat; *esp* : an overweight person

fatty acid *n* (ca. 1872) **1** : any of numerous saturated aliphatic monocarboxylic acids $C_nH_{2n+1}COOH$ (as acetic acid) including many that occur naturally usu. in the form of esters in fats, waxes, and essential oils **2** : any of the saturated or unsaturated monocarboxylic acids (as palmitic acid) usu. with an even number of carbon atoms that occur naturally in the form of glycerides in fats and fatty oils

fa·tu·ity \fə-'tü-ət-ē, fa-, -'chü-, -'tyü-\ *n, pl* **-ities** [MF *fatuité* foolishness, fr. L *fatuitat-, fatuitas*, fr. *fatuus*] (1538) **1 a** : something foolish or stupid **b** : STUPIDITY, FOOLISHNESS **2** *archaic* : IMBECILITY, DEMENTIA

fat·u·ous \'fa-chü-əs, -tyü-\ *adj* [L *fatuus* foolish] (1633) : complacently or inanely foolish : SILLY **syn** see SIMPLE — **fat·u·ous·ly** *adv* — **fat·u·ous·ness** *n*

fat·wa \'fät-wə\ *n* [Ar *fatwā*] (1947) : a legal opinion or decree handed down by an Islamic religious leader

fat–wit·ted \'fat-,wi-təd\ *adj* (1596) : STUPID, IDIOTIC

fat·wood \'fat-,wu̇d\ *n* (1904) *chiefly Southern* : LIGHTWOOD

fau·bourg \fō-'bu̇r\ *n* [ME *fabour*, fr. MF *fauxbourg*, alter. of *forsbourg*, fr. OF *forsborc*, fr. *fors* outside + *borc* town — more at BOURG] (15c) **1** : SUBURB; *esp* : a suburb of a French city **2** : a city quarter

fau·ces \'fȯ-,sēz\ *n pl but sing or pl in constr* [L, pl., throat, fauces] (1541) : the narrow passage from the mouth to the pharynx situated between the soft palate and the base of the tongue — **fau·cial** \'fȯ-shəl\ *adj*

fau·cet \'fȯ-sət, 'fäs-\ *n* [ME, bung, faucet, fr. MF *fausset* bung, perh. fr. *fausser* to damage, fr. LL *falsare* to falsify, fr. L *falsus* false] (15c) : a fixture for drawing or regulating the flow of liquid esp. from a pipe

faugh *a strong p-sound or lip trill; often read as* 'fȯ(k)\ *interj* (1542) — used to express contempt, disgust, or abhorrence

¹fault \'fȯlt, *in poetry also* 'fȯt\ *n* [ME *faute*, fr. MF, fr. (assumed) VL *fallita*, fr. fem. of *fallitus*, pp. of L *fallere* to deceive, disappoint] (14c) **1** *obs* : LACK **2 a** : WEAKNESS, FAILING; *esp* : a moral weakness less serious than a vice **b** : a physical or intellectual imperfection or impairment : DEFECT **c** : an error esp. in service in a net or racket game **3 a** : MISDEMEANOR **b** : MISTAKE **4** : responsibility for wrongdoing or failure ⟨the accident was the driver's ~⟩ **5** : a fracture in the crust of a planet (as the earth) or

fault 5: *1* fault with displaced strata *a, b, c, d, e*; *2* scarp

moon accompanied by a displacement of one side of the fracture with respect to the other usu. in a direction parallel to the fracture — **at fault 1** : unable to find the scent and continue chase **2** : open to blame : RESPONSIBLE ⟨couldn't determine who was really *at fault*⟩ — **to a fault** : to an excessive degree ⟨precise *to a fault*⟩

syn FAULT, FAILING, FRAILTY, FOIBLE, VICE mean an imperfection or weakness of character. FAULT implies a failure, not necessarily culpable, to reach some standard of perfection in disposition, action, or habit ⟨a writer of many virtues and few *faults*⟩. FAILING suggests a minor shortcoming in character ⟨being late is a *failing* of mine⟩. FRAILTY implies a general or chronic proneness to yield to temptation ⟨human *frailties*⟩. FOIBLE applies to a harmless or endearing weakness or idiosyncrasy ⟨an eccentric's charming *foibles*⟩. VICE can be a general term for any imperfection or weakness, but it often suggests violation of a moral code or the giving of offense to the moral sensibilities of others ⟨compulsive gambling was his *vice*⟩.

²fault *vi* (15c) **1** : to commit a fault : ERR **2** : to fracture so as to produce a geologic fault ~ *vt* **1** : to find a fault in ⟨easy to praise this book and to ~ it —H. G. Roepke⟩ **2** : to produce a geologic fault in **3** : BLAME, CENSURE ⟨can't ~ them for not coming⟩

fault·find·er \'fȯlt-,fīn-dər\ *n* (1561) : one given to faultfinding

¹fault·find·ing \-diŋ\ *adj* (1622) : disposed to find fault : captiously critical **syn** see CRITICAL

²faultfinding *n* (1626) : petty, nagging, or unreasonable criticism

fault·less \'fȯlt-ləs\ *adj* (14c) : having no fault : IRREPROACHABLE ⟨~ workmanship⟩ — **fault·less·ly** *adv* — **fault·less·ness** *n*

fault line *n* (1869) : something resembling a fault : SPLIT, RIFT ⟨a major conceptual *fault line* in foreign policy —Morton Kondrake⟩

faulty \'fȯl-tē\ *adj* **fault·i·er; -est** (14c) : marked by fault or defect : IMPERFECT — **fault·i·ly** \-tə-lē\ *adv* — **fault·i·ness** \-tē-nəs\ *n*

faun \'fȯn, 'fän\ *n* [ME, fr. L *faunus*, fr. *Faunus*] (14c) : a figure in Roman mythology similar to but gentler than the satyr

fau·na \'fȯ-nə, 'fä-\ *n, pl* **faunas** *also* **fau·nae** \-,nē, -,nī\ [NL, fr. L *Fauna*, sister of Faunus] (1771) : animal life; *esp* : the animals characteristic of a region, period, or special environment — compare FLORA — **fau·nal** \-nᵊl\ *adj* — **fau·nal·ly** \-nᵊl-ē\ *adv*

fau·nis·tic \fȯ-'nis-tik, fä-\ *adj* (1881) : of or relating to zoogeography : FAUNAL — **fau·nis·ti·cal·ly** \-ti-k(ə-)lē\ *adv*

Fau·nus \'fȯ-nəs, 'fä-\ *n* [L] : the Roman god of animals

Faust \'fau̇st\ *or* **Fau·stus** \'fau̇-stəs, 'fȯ-\ *n* [G] : a magician of German legend who enters into a compact with the devil

Faust·ian \'fau̇-stē-ən, 'fȯ-\ *adj* (1876) : of, relating to, resembling, or suggesting Faust; *esp* : made or done for present gain without regard for future cost or consequences ⟨a ~ bargain⟩

faute de mieux \,fōt-də-'myə(r), -'myœ\ *adv* [F] (1766) : for lack of something better or more desirable ⟨sherry made him dopey but he drank it *faute de mieux* —F. T. Marsh⟩

fau·teuil \fō-'tœy, 'fō-,til\ *n, pl* **fau·teuils** \fō-'tœy, -,tilz\ [F, fr. OF *faudestuel*, of Gmc origin; akin to OHG *faltstuol* folding chair — more at FALDSTOOL] (1744) : ARMCHAIR; *esp* : an upholstered chair with open arms

¹fauve \'fōv\ *n, often cap* [F, lit., wild animal, fr. *fauve* tawny, wild, fr. OF *falve* tawny, of Gmc origin; akin to OHG *falo* fallow — more at FALLOW] (1931) : a painter practicing fauvism : FAUVIST

²fauve *adj* (1945) **1** *often cap* : of or relating to the fauves **2** : vivid in color

fau·vism \'fō-,vi-zəm\ *n, often cap* (1922) : a movement in painting typified by the work of Matisse and characterized by vivid colors, free treatment of form, and a resulting vibrant and decorative effect — **fau·vist** \-vist\ *n, often cap*

faux \'fō\ *adj* [F, false] (1975) : IMITATION, ERSATZ ⟨~ marble⟩

faux pas \'fō-,pä, fō-'\ *n, pl* **faux pas** \-,pä(z), -'pä(z)\ [F, lit., false step] (1676) : BLUNDER; *esp* : a social blunder

fa·va \'fä-və\ *n* [It, fr. L *faba* bean] (1928) : BROAD BEAN — called also *fava bean*

fave \'fāv\ *n* (1938) : FAVORITE 1 — **fave** *adj*

fa·ve·la *also* **fa·vel·la** \fə-'ve-lə\ *n* [Brazilian Pg *favela,* perh. fr. *Favela,* hill outside Rio de Janeiro] (1946) : a settlement of jerry-built shacks lying on the outskirts of a Brazilian city

fa·vism \'fä-,vi-zəm\ *n* (ca. 1927) : a hereditary condition esp. of males of Mediterranean descent that involves a severe allergic reaction to the broad bean or its pollen which is characterized by hemolytic anemia, fever, and jaundice

fa·vo·ni·an \fə-'vō-nē-ən\ *adj* [L *favonianus,* fr. *Favonius,* the west wind] (ca. 1681) : of or relating to the west wind : MILD

¹**fa·vor** \'fā-vər\ *n* [ME, friendly regard, attractiveness, fr. OF *favor* friendly regard, fr. L, fr. *favēre* to be favorable; perh. akin to OHG *gouma* attention, OCS *gověti* to revere] (14c) **1 a** (1) : friendly regard shown toward another esp. by a superior (2) : approving consideration or orientation : APPROBATION **b** : PARTIALITY **c** *archaic* : LENIENCY **d** *archaic* : PERMISSION **e** : POPULARITY **2** *archaic* **a** : APPEARANCE **b** (1) : FACE (2) : a facial feature **3 a** : gracious kindness; *also* : an act of such kindness **b** *archaic* : AID, ASSISTANCE **c** *pl* : effort in one's behalf or interest : ATTENTION **4 a** : a token of love (as a ribbon) usu. worn conspicuously **b** : a small gift or decorative item given out at a party **c** : BADGE **5 a** : a special privilege or right granted or conceded **b** : sexual privileges — usu. used in pl. **6** *archaic* : LETTER **7** : BEHALF, INTEREST — **in favor of**   of **1 a** : in accord or sympathy with **b** : for the acquittal of ⟨a verdict *in favor of* the accused⟩ **c** : in support of **2** : to the order of **3** : in order to choose : out of preference for ⟨turned down the scholarship *in favor of* a pro career⟩ — **in one's favor 1** : in one's good graces **2** : to one's advantage ⟨the odds were *in my favor*⟩ — **out of favor** : UNPOPULAR, DISLIKED ⟨was *out of favor* with his neighbors⟩

²**favor** *vt* **fa·vored; fa·vor·ing** \'fā-v(ə-)riŋ\ (14c) **1 a** : to regard or treat with favor **b** (1) : to do a kindness for : OBLIGE (2) : ENDOW **c** : to treat gently or carefully ⟨~ed his injured leg⟩ **2** : to show partiality toward : PREFER **3 a** : to give support or confirmation to : SUSTAIN **b** : to afford advantages for success to : FACILITATE ⟨good weather ~ed the outing⟩ **4** : to bear a resemblance to ⟨he ~s his father⟩ — **fa·vor·er** \'fā-vər-ər\ *n*

fa·vor·able \'fā-v(ə-)rə-bəl, 'fā-vər-bəl\ *adj* (14c) **1 a** : disposed to favor : PARTIAL **b** : expressing approval : COMMENDATORY **c** : giving a result that is in one's favor ⟨a ~ comparison⟩ **d** : AFFIRMATIVE **2 a** : winning approval : PLEASING **3 a** : tending to promote or facilitate : ADVANTAGEOUS ⟨a ~ wind⟩ **b** : marked by success — **fa·vor·able·ness** *n* — **fa·vor·ably** \-blē\ *adv*
  syn FAVORABLE, AUSPICIOUS, PROPITIOUS mean pointing toward a happy outcome. FAVORABLE implies that the persons involved are approving or helpful or that the circumstances are advantageous ⟨*favorable* weather conditions⟩. AUSPICIOUS applies to something taken as a sign or omen promising success before or at the start of an event ⟨an *auspicious* beginning⟩. PROPITIOUS may also apply to beginnings but often implies a continuing favorable condition ⟨a *propitious* time for starting a business⟩.

fa·vored \'fā-vərd\ *adj* (15c) **1** : having an appearance or features of a particular kind ⟨hard-*favored*⟩ **2** : endowed with special advantages or gifts **3** : providing preferential treatment

¹**fa·vor·ite** \'fā-v(ə-)rət, 'fā-vərt, *chiefly dial* 'fā-və-,rīt\ *n* [It *favorito,* pp. of *favorire* to favor, fr. *favore* favor, fr. L *favor*] (1583) **1** : one that is treated or regarded with special favor or liking; *esp* : one unusually loved, trusted, or provided with favors by a person of high rank or authority **2** : a competitor judged most likely to win

²**favorite** *adj* (1711) : constituting a favorite; *esp* : markedly popular

favorite son *n* (1788) **1** : one favored by the delegates of his state as presidential candidate at a national political convention **2** : a famous person who is popular with hometown people

fa·vor·it·ism \'fā-v(ə-)rə-,ti-zəm, 'fā-vər-\ *n* (1763) **1** : the showing of special favor : PARTIALITY **2** : the state or fact of being a favorite

fa·vour *chiefly Brit var of* FAVOR

fa·vus \'fā-vəs\ *n* [NL, fr. L, honeycomb] (ca. 1543) : a contagious skin disease caused by a fungus (as *Trichophyton schoenleinii*) and occurring in humans and many domestic animals and fowls

¹**fawn** \'fȯn, 'fän\ *vi* [ME *faunen,* fr. OE *fagnian* to rejoice, fr. *fægen, fagan* glad — more at FAIN] (13c) **1** : to show affection — used esp. of a dog **2** : to court favor by a cringing or flattering manner — **fawn·er** *n* — **fawn·ing·ly** \'fȯ-niŋ-lē, 'fä-\ *adv*
  syn FAWN, TOADY, TRUCKLE, CRINGE, COWER mean to behave abjectly before a superior. FAWN implies seeking favor by servile flattery or exaggerated attention ⟨waiters *fawning* over a celebrity⟩. TOADY suggests the attempt to ingratiate oneself by an abjectly menial or subservient attitude ⟨*toadying* to his boss⟩. TRUCKLE implies the subordination of oneself and one's desires or judgment to those of a superior ⟨*truckling* to a powerful lobbyist⟩. CRINGE suggests a bowing or shrinking in fear or servility ⟨a *cringing* sycophant⟩. COWER suggests a display of abject fear in the company of threatening or domineering people ⟨*cowering* before a bully⟩.

²**fawn** *n* [ME *foun,* fr. MF *feon, faon* young of an animal, fr. (assumed) VL *feton-, feto,* fr. L *fetus* offspring — more at FETUS] (14c) **1** : a young deer; *esp* : one still unweaned or retaining a distinctive baby coat **2** : KID 1 **3** : a light grayish brown

fawn lily *n* (ca. 1894) : DOGTOOTH VIOLET

fawny \'fȯ-nē, 'fä-\ *adj* (1849) : of a color approximating fawn

fax \'faks\ *n* [by shortening & alter.] (1948) **1** : FACSIMILE 2 **2** : a machine used to send or receive facsimile communications **3** : a facsimile communication — **fax** *vt*

¹**fay** \'fā\ *vb* [ME *feien,* fr. OE *fēgan;* akin to OHG *fuogen* to fit, L *pangere* to fasten — more at PACT] (bef. 12c) : to fit or join closely or tightly

²**fay** *n* [ME *fai, fei,* fr. OF *feid, fei* — more at FAITH] (13c) *obs* : FAITH

³**fay** *n* [ME *faie,* fr. MF *feie, fee* — more at FAIRY] (14c) : FAIRY, ELF

⁴**fay** *adj* (14c) : resembling an elf

⁵**fay** *n* (1927) : OFAY

faze \'fāz\ *vt* **fazed; faz·ing** [alter. of *feeze* (to drive away, frighten), fr. ME *fesen,* fr. OE *fēsian* to drive away] (1830) : to disturb the composure of : DISCONCERT, DAUNT ⟨nothing *fazed* her⟩

F clef *n* (1596) : BASS CLEF

F distribution *n* [Sir Ronald Fisher †1962 Eng. geneticist and statistician] (1947) : a probability density function that is used esp. in analysis of variance and is a function of the ratio of two independent random variables each of which has a chi-square distribution and is divided by its number of degrees of freedom

fe·al·ty \'fē(-ə)l-tē\ *n, pl* **-ties** [alter. of ME *feute,* fr. OF *feelté, fealté,* fr. L *fidelitat-, fidelitas* — more at FIDELITY] (14c) **1 a** : the fidelity of a vassal or feudal tenant to his lord **b** : the obligation of such fidelity **2** : intense fidelity   *syn* SEE FIDELITY

¹**fear** \'fir\ *vt* (bef. 12c) **1** *archaic* : FRIGHTEN **2** *archaic* : to feel fear in (oneself) **3** : to have a reverential awe of ⟨~ God⟩ **4** : to be afraid of : expect with alarm ~ *vi* : to be afraid or apprehensive — **fear·er** *n*

²**fear** *n* [ME *fer,* fr. OE *fǣr* sudden danger; akin to L *periculum* attempt, peril, Gk *peiran* to attempt] (12c) **1 a** : an unpleasant often strong emotion caused by anticipation or awareness of danger **b** (1) : an instance of this emotion (2) : a state marked by this emotion **2** : anxious concern : SOLICITUDE **3** : profound reverence and awe esp. toward God **4** : reason for alarm : DANGER
  syn FEAR, DREAD, FRIGHT, ALARM, PANIC, TERROR, TREPIDATION mean painful agitation in the presence or anticipation of danger. FEAR is the most general term and implies anxiety and usu. loss of courage ⟨*fear* of the unknown⟩. DREAD usu. adds the idea of intense reluctance to face or meet a person or situation and suggests aversion as well as anxiety ⟨faced the meeting with *dread*⟩. FRIGHT implies the shock of sudden, startling fear ⟨*fright* at being awakened suddenly⟩. ALARM suggests a sudden and intense awareness of immediate danger ⟨view the situation with *alarm*⟩. PANIC implies unreasoning and overmastering fear causing hysterical activity ⟨the news caused widespread *panic*⟩. TERROR implies the most extreme degree of fear ⟨immobilized with *terror*⟩. TREPIDATION adds to DREAD the implications of timidity, trembling, and hesitation ⟨raised the subject with *trepidation*⟩.

fear·ful \'fir-fəl\ *adj* (14c) **1** : causing or likely to cause fear, fright, or alarm esp. because of dangerous quality ⟨a ~ storm⟩ **2 a** : full of fear **b** : indicating or arising from fear ⟨a ~ glance⟩ **c** : inclined to fear : TIMOROUS **3** : very great or bad — used as an intensive ⟨a ~ waste⟩ ⟨~ slum conditions⟩ — **fear·ful·ly** \-f(ə-)lē\ *adv* — **fear·ful·ness** \-fəl-nəs\ *n*
  syn FEARFUL, APPREHENSIVE, AFRAID mean disturbed by fear. FEARFUL implies often a timorous or worrying temperament ⟨the child is *fearful* of loud noises⟩. APPREHENSIVE suggests a state of mind and implies a premonition of evil or danger ⟨*apprehensive* of being found out⟩. AFRAID often suggests weakness or cowardice and regularly implies inhibition of action or utterance ⟨*afraid* to speak the truth⟩.

fear·less \'fir-ləs\ *adj* (1591) : free from fear : BRAVE — **fear·less·ly** *adv* — **fear·less·ness** *n*

fear·some \'fir-səm\ *adj* (1768) **1** : causing fear **2** : TIMID, TIMOROUS — **fear·some·ly** *adv* — **fear·some·ness** *n*

fea·si·ble \'fē-zə-bəl\ *adj* [ME *faisible,* fr. MF, fr. *fais-,* stem of *faire* to make, do, fr. L *facere* — more at DO] (15c) **1** : capable of being done or carried out ⟨a ~ plan⟩ **2** : capable of being used or dealt with successfully : SUITABLE **3** : REASONABLE, LIKELY   *syn* SEE POSSIBLE — **fea·si·bil·i·ty** \,fē-zə-'bi-lə-tē\ *n* — **fea·si·bly** \'fē-zə-blē\ *adv*

¹**feast** \'fēst\ *n* [ME *feste* festival, feast, fr. MF, festival, fr. L *festa,* pl. of *festum* festival, fr. neut. of *festus* solemn, festal; akin to L *feriae* holidays, *fanum* temple] (13c) **1** : an elaborate meal often accompanied by a ceremony or entertainment : BANQUET **2** : something that gives unusual or abundant pleasure **2** : a periodic religious observance commemorating an event or honoring a deity, person, or thing

²**feast** *vi* (14c) **1** : to take part in a feast **2** : to enjoy some unusual pleasure or delight ~ *vt* **1** : to give a feast for **2** : DELIGHT, GRATIFY — **feast·er** *n*

Feast of Tabernacles (14c) : SUKKOTH

¹**feat** \'fēt\ *n* [ME *fait,* fr. MF, fr. L *factum,* fr. neut. of *factus,* pp. of *facere* to make, do — more at DO] (14c) **1** : ACT, DEED **2 a** : a deed notable esp. for courage **b** : an act or product of skill, endurance, or ingenuity

  syn FEAT, EXPLOIT, ACHIEVEMENT mean a remarkable deed. FEAT implies strength or dexterity or daring ⟨an acrobatic *feat*⟩. EXPLOIT suggests an adventurous or heroic act ⟨his *exploits* as a spy⟩. ACHIEVEMENT implies hard-won success in the face of difficulty or opposition ⟨her *achievements* as a chemist⟩.

²**feat** *adj* [ME *fete, fayt,* fr. MF *fait,* pp. of *faire*] (15c) **1** *archaic* : BECOMING, NEAT **2** *archaic* : SMART, DEXTEROUS

¹**feath·er** \'fe-thər\ *n* [ME *fether,* fr. OE; akin to OHG *federa* wing, L *petere* to go to, seek, Gk *petesthai* to fly, *piptein* to fall, *pteron* wing] (bef. 12c) **1 a** : any of the light horny epidermal outgrowths that form the external covering of the body of birds and that consist of a shaft bearing on each side a series of barbs which bear barbules which in turn bear barbicels commonly ending in hooked hamuli and interlock-

feather 1a: *A: 1* quill, *2* vane; *B: 1* barb, *2* barbule, *3* barbicel with hamulus

\ə\ abut \ᵊ\ kitten, F table \ər\ further \a\ ash \ā\ ace \ä\ mop, mar \aú\ out \ch\ chin \e\ bet \ē\ easy \g\ go \i\ hit \ī\ ice \j\ job \ŋ\ sing \ō\ go \ȯ\ law \ȯi\ boy \th\ thin \th\ the \ü\ loot \ú\ foot \y\ yet \zh\ vision \à, k̟, ⁿ, œ, œ̄, ᵫ, ᵢᴇ, ʸ\ see Guide to Pronunciation

ing with the barbules of an adjacent barb to link the barbs into a continuous vane **b** : PLUME **c** : the vane of an arrow **2 a** : PLUMAGE **b** : KIND, NATURE ⟨birds of a ~ flock together⟩ **c** : ATTIRE, DRESS **d** : CONDITION, MOOD **3** : FEATHERING 2 **4** : a projecting strip, rib, fin, or flange **5** : a feathery flaw in the eye or in a precious stone **6** : the act of feathering an oar — **feath·ered** \-thərd\ *adj* — **feath·er·less** *adj* — **a feather in one's cap** : a mark of distinction : HONOR
²**feather** *vb* **feath·ered; feath·er·ing** \'feth-riŋ, 'fe-thə-\ *vt* (13c) **1 a** : to furnish (as an arrow) with a feather **b** : to cover, clothe, or adorn with or as if with feathers **2 a** : to turn (an oar blade) almost horizontal when lifting from the water at the end of a stroke to reduce air resistance **b** (1) : to change the angle of (airplane propeller blades) so that the chords become approximately parallel to the line of flight; *also* : to change the angle of airplane propeller blades of (an engine) in such a manner (2) : to change the angle of (a rotor blade of a rotorcraft) periodically in forward flight **3** : to reduce the edge of to a featheredge **4** : to cut (as air) with or as if with a wing **5** : to join by a tongue and groove ~ *vi* **1** : to grow or form feathers **2** : to have or take on the appearance of a feather or something feathered **3** : to soak in and spread : BLUR — used of ink or a printed impression **4** : to feather an oar or an airplane propeller blade — **feather one's nest** : to provide for oneself esp. while in a position of trust
¹**feath·er·bed** \'fe-thər-,bed\ *adj* (1938) : calling for, sanctioning, or resulting from featherbedding
²**featherbed** *vi* (1949) **1 a** : to require that more workers be hired than are needed **b** : to limit production under a featherbed rule **2** : to do featherbed work or put in time under a featherbed rule ~ *vt* **1** : to bring under a featherbed rule **2** : to assist (as an industry) by government aid
feather bed *n* (bef. 12c) **1** : a feather mattress **2** : a bed having a feather mattress
feath·er·bed·ding *n* (1921) : the requiring of an employer usu. under a union rule or safety statute to hire more employees than are needed or to limit production
feath·er·brain \-,brān\ *n* (1839) : a foolish scatterbrained person — **feath·er·brained** \-,brānd\ *adj*
feath·er·edge \'fe-thə-,rej, ,fe-thə-'\ *n* (1616) : a very thin sharp edge; *esp* : one that is easily broken or bent over — **featheredge** *vt*
feath·er·head \'fe-thər-,hed\ *n* (1831) : FEATHERBRAIN — **feath·er·head·ed** \,fe-thər-'he-dəd\ *adj*
feath·er·ing \'feth-riŋ, 'fe-thə-\ *n* (1721) **1** : a covering of feathers : PLUMAGE **2** : a fringe of hair (as on the legs of a dog) — see DOG illustration
feath·er·light \'fe-thər-'līt\ *adj* (ca. 1837) : extremely light
feather star *n* (1862) : any of an order (Comatulida) of free-swimming stalkless crinoids
feath·er·stitch \'fe-thər-,stich\ *n* (1835) : an embroidery stitch consisting of a line of diagonal blanket stitches worked alternately to the left and right — **featherstitch** *vb*

featherstitch

feath·er·weight \-,wāt\ *n, often attrib* (1812) **1** : one that is very light in weight; *esp* : a boxer in a weight division having a maximum limit of 126 pounds for professionals and 125 pounds for amateurs — compare BANTAMWEIGHT, LIGHTWEIGHT **2** : LIGHTWEIGHT 2
feath·ery \'feth-rē, 'fe-thə-\ *adj* (1580) : resembling, suggesting, or covered with feathers; *esp* : extremely light
¹**feat·ly** \'fēt-lē\ *adv* [ME *fetly*, fr. *fete* feat (adj.)] (14c) **1** : in a graceful manner : NIMBLY **2** : in a suitable manner : PROPERLY **3** : with skill and ingenuity
²**featly** *adj* (1801) : GRACEFUL, NEAT
¹**fea·ture** \'fē-chər\ *n* [ME *feture*, fr. MF, fr. L *factura* act of making, fr. *factus*, pp. of *facere* to make — more at DO] (14c) **1 a** : the structure, form, or appearance esp. of a person **b** *obs* : physical beauty **2 a** : the makeup or appearance of the face or its parts **b** : a part of the face : LINEAMENT **3 a** : a prominent part or characteristic **b** : any of the properties (as voice or gender) that are characteristic of a grammatical element (as a phoneme or morpheme); *esp* : one that is distinctive **4** : a special attraction: as **a** : the principal motion picture shown on a program with other pictures **b** : a featured article, story, or department in a newspaper or magazine **c** : something offered to the public or advertised as particularly attractive — **fea·ture·less** \-ləs\ *adj*
²**feature** *vb* **fea·tured; fea·tur·ing** \'fēch-riŋ, 'fē-chə-\ *vt* (ca. 1755) **1** *chiefly dial* : to resemble in features **2** : to picture or portray in the mind : IMAGINE **3 a** : to give special prominence to **b** : to have as a characteristic or feature ~ *vi* : to play an important part
fea·tured \'fē-chərd\ *adj* (15c) **1** : having facial features of a particular kind — used in combination ⟨a heavy-*featured* lout⟩ **2** : displayed, advertised, or presented as a special attraction
fea·tur·ette \,fē-chə-,ret, ,fē-chə-\ *n* (1940) : a short film
feaze \'fēz, 'fāz\ *var of* FAZE
febri- *comb form* [LL, fr. L *febris*] : fever ⟨*febrific*⟩
fe·brif·ic \fi-'brif-ik\ *adj* (1710) *archaic* : FEVERISH
feb·ri·fuge \'fe-brə-,fyüj\ *n* [F *fébrifuge*, prob. fr. (assumed) NL *febrifuga*, fr. LL *febrifuga*, *febrifugia* centaury, fr. *febri-* + LL *-fuga* -fuge] (1686) : ANTIPYRETIC — **febrifuge** *adj*
fe·brile \'fe-,bril *also* 'fē-\ *adj* [ML *febrilis*, fr. L *febris* fever] (1651) : FEVERISH
Feb·ru·ary \ ÷ 'fe-b(y)ə-,wer-ē, 'fe-brə-\ *n, pl* **-ar·ies** *or* **-ar·ys** [ME *Februarie*, fr. OE *Februarius*, fr. L, fr. *Februa*, pl., feast of purification] (bef. 12c) : the 2d month of the Gregorian calendar
  usage Dissimilation may occur when a word contains two identical or closely related sounds, resulting in the change or loss of one of them. This happens regularly in *February*, which is more often pronounced \'fe-b(y)ə-,wer-ē\ than \'fe-brə-,wer-ē\, though all of these variants are in frequent use and widely accepted. The \y\ heard from many speakers is not an intrusion but rather a common pronunciation of the vowel *u* after a consonant, as in *January* and *annual*.
fe·cal \'fē-kəl\ *adj* (1541) : of, relating to, or constituting feces
fe·ces \'fē-(,)sēz\ *n pl* [ME, fr. L *faec-, faex* (sing.) dregs] (14c) : bodily waste discharged through the anus : EXCREMENT

feck·less \'fek-ləs\ *adj* [Sc, fr. *feck* effect, majority, fr. ME (Sc) *fek*, alter. of ME *effect*] (ca. 1585) **1** : WEAK, INEFFECTIVE **2** : WORTHLESS, IRRESPONSIBLE — **feck·less·ly** *adv* — **feck·less·ness** *n*
feck·ly \'fek-lē\ *adv* [*feck* + *-ly*] (1768) *chiefly Scot* : ALMOST, NEARLY
fec·u·lent \'fe-kyə-lənt\ *adj* [ME, fr. L *faeculentus*, fr. *faec-, faex*] (15c) : foul with impurities : FECAL
fe·cund \'fe-kənd, 'fē-\ *adj* [ME, fr. MF *fecond*, fr. L *fecundus* — more at FEMININE] (15c) **1** : fruitful in offspring or vegetation : PROLIFIC **2** : intellectually productive or inventive to a marked degree *syn* see FERTILE — **fe·cun·di·ty** \fi-'kən-də-tē, fe-\ *n*
fe·cun·date \'fe-kən-,dāt, 'fē-\ *vt* **-dat·ed; -dat·ing** [L *fecundatus*, pp. of *fecundare*, fr. *fecundus*] (ca. 1631) **1** : to make fecund **2** : IMPREGNATE — **fe·cun·da·tion** \,fe-kən-'dā-shən, ,fē-\ *n*
fed \'fed\ *n, often cap* (1916) : a federal agent, officer, or official — usu. used in pl.
fe·da·yee \fi-,da-'(y)ē, -,dä-\ *n, pl* **fe·da·yeen** \-'(y)ēn\ [Ar *fidā'ī,* lit., one who sacrifices himself] (1955) : a member of an Arab commando group operating esp. against Israel — usu. used in pl.
fed·er·al \'fe-d(ə-)rəl\ *adj* [L *foeder-, foedus* compact, league; akin to L *fidere* to trust — more at BIDE] (1660) **1** *archaic* : of or relating to a compact or treaty **2 a** : formed by a compact between political units that surrender their individual sovereignty to a central authority but retain limited residuary powers of government **b** : of or constituting a form of government in which power is distributed between a central authority and a number of constituent territorial units **c** : of or relating to the central government of a federation as distinguished from the governments of the constituent units **3** *cap* : advocating or friendly to the principle of a federal government with strong centralized powers; *esp* : of or relating to the American Federalists **4** *cap* : of, relating to, or loyal to the federal government or the Union armies of the U.S. in the American Civil War **5** *cap* : being or belonging to a style of architecture and decoration current in the U.S. following the Revolution — **fed·er·al·ly** \-d(ə-)rə-lē\ *adv*
Federal *n* (1861) **1** : a supporter of the U.S. government in the Civil War; *esp* : a soldier in the federal armies **2** : FED — usu. used in pl.
federal case *n* (1955) : BIG DEAL ⟨don't make a *federal case* out of it⟩
federal court *n* (1789) : a court established by a federal government; *esp* : one established under the constitution and laws of the U.S.
federal district *n* (ca. 1934) : a district set apart as the seat of the central government of a federation
federal district court *n* (1948) : a district trial court of law and equity that hears cases under federal jurisdiction
fed·er·al·ese \,fe-d(ə-)rə-'lēz, -'lēs; 'fe-d(ə-)rə-,\ *n* (1944) : BUREAUCRATESE
federal funds *n pl* (1950) : reserve funds lent overnight by one Federal Reserve bank to another
fed·er·al·ism \'fe-d(ə-)rə-,li-zəm\ *n* (1789) **1** *often cap* : the distribution of power in an organization (as a government) between a central authority and the constituent units — compare CENTRALISM **b** : support or advocacy of this principle **2** *cap* : Federalist principles
fed·er·al·ist \-list\ *n* (1787) **1** : an advocate of federalism: as **a** *often cap* : an advocate of a federal union between the American colonies after the Revolution and of the adoption of the U.S. Constitution **b** *often cap* : WORLD FEDERALIST **2** *cap* : a member of a major political party in the early years of the U.S. favoring a strong centralized national government — **federalist** *adj, often cap*
fed·er·al·iza·tion \,fe-d(ə-)rə-lə-'zā-shən\ *n* (ca. 1860) **1** : the act of federalizing **2** : the state of being federalized
fed·er·al·ize \'fe-d(ə-)rə-,līz\ *vt* **-ized; -iz·ing** (1801) **1** : to unite in or under a federal system **2** : to bring under the jurisdiction of a federal government
Federal Reserve bank *n* (1914) : one of 12 reserve banks set up under the Federal Reserve Act to hold reserves and discount commercial paper for affiliated banks in their respective districts
¹**fed·er·ate** \'fe-d(ə-)rət\ *adj* [L *foederatus*, fr. *foeder-, foedus*] (1710) : united in an alliance or federation : FEDERATED
²**fed·er·ate** \'fe-də-,rāt\ *vt* **-at·ed; -at·ing** (1837) : to join in a federation
federated church *n* (ca. 1926) : a local church uniting two or more congregations that maintain different denominational ties — compare UNION CHURCH
fed·er·a·tion \,fe-də-'rā-shən\ *n* (1791) **1** : something formed by federation: as **a** : a federal government **b** : a union of organizations **2** : the act of federating; *esp* : the forming of a federal union
fed·er·a·tive \'fe-də-,rā-tiv, 'fe-d(ə-)rə-\ *adj* (1690) : FEDERAL — **fed·er·a·tive·ly** *adv*
fe·do·ra \fi-'dōr-ə, -'dȯr-\ *n* [*Fédora* (1882), drama by V. Sardou] (1895) : a low soft felt hat with the crown creased lengthwise
fed up *adj* (1900) : tired, sated, or disgusted beyond endurance
¹**fee** \'fē\ *n* [ME, fr. MF *fé, fief,* fr. OF, of Gmc origin; akin to OE *feoh* cattle, property, OHG *fihu* cattle; akin to L *pecus* cattle, *pecunia* money] (14c) **1 a** (1) : an estate in land held in feudal law from a lord on condition of homage and service (2) : a piece of land so held **b** : an inherited or heritable estate in land **2 a** : a fixed charge **b** : a sum paid or charged for a service — **in fee** : in absolute and legal possession
²**fee** *vt* **feed; fee·ing** (15c) **1** *chiefly Scot* : HIRE **2** : ⁹TIP 2
fee·ble \'fē-bəl\ *adj* **fee·bler** \-b(ə-)lər\; **fee·blest** \-b(ə-)ləst\ [ME *feble,* fr. OF, fr. L *flebilis* lamentable, wretched, fr. *flēre* to weep — more at BLEAT] (12c) **1 a** : markedly lacking in strength **b** : indicating weakness **2 a** : deficient in qualities or resources that indicate vigor, authority, force, or efficiency **b** : INADEQUATE, INFERIOR *syn* see WEAK — **fee·ble·ness** \-bəl-nəs\ *n* — **fee·bly** \-blē\ *adv*
fee·ble·mind·ed \,fē-bəl-'mīn-dəd\ *adj* (1534) **1** *obs* : IRRESOLUTE, VACILLATING **2** : mentally deficient **3** : FOOLISH, STUPID — **fee·ble·mind·ed·ly** *adv* — **fee·ble·mind·ed·ness** *n*
fee·blish \'fē-b(ə-)lish\ *adj* (1674) : somewhat feeble
¹**feed** \'fēd\ *vb* **fed** \'fed\; **feed·ing** [ME *feden,* fr. OE *fēdan;* akin to OE *fōda* food — more at FOOD] *vt* (bef. 12c) **1 a** : to give food to **b** : to give as food **2 a** : to furnish something essential to the growth, sustenance, maintenance, or operation of **b** : to supply (material to be operated on) to a machine **3** : to produce or provide food for **4 a** : SATISFY, GRATIFY **b** : SUPPORT, ENCOURAGE **5 a** (1) : to supply for use or consumption (2) : CHANNEL, ROUTE **b** (1) : to supply (a sig-

nal) to an electronic circuit (2) : to send (as by wire or satellite) to a transmitting station for broadcast **6** : to supply (a fellow actor) with cues and situations that make a role more effective **7** : to pass a ball or puck to (a teammate) esp. for a shot at the goal ∼ *vi* **1 a** : to consume food : EAT **b** : PREY — used with *on, upon,* or *off* **2 a** : to become nourished or satisfied or sustained as if by food **3 a** : to become channeled or directed **b** : to move into a machine or opening in order to be used or processed

²**feed** *n* (1576) **1 a** : an act of eating **b** : MEAL; *esp* : a large meal **2 a** : food for livestock; *specif* : a mixture or preparation for feeding livestock **b** : the amount given at each feeding **3 a** : material supplied (as to a furnace or machine) **b** : a mechanism by which the action of feeding is effected **c** : the motion or process of carrying forward the material to be operated upon (as in a machine) **d** : the process of feeding a television program (as to a local station) **4** : the action of passing a ball or puck to a team member who is in position to score

feed·back \'fēd-ˌbak\ *n* (1920) **1 a** : the return to the input of a part of the output of a machine, system, or process (as for producing changes in an electronic circuit that improve performance or in an automatic control device that provide self-corrective action) **2 a** : the partial reversion of the effects of a process to its source or to a preceding stage **b** : the transmission of evaluative or corrective information to the original or controlling source about an action, event, or process; *also* : the information so transmitted

feedback inhibition *n* (1960) : inhibition of an enzyme controlling an early stage of a series of biochemical reactions by the end product when it reaches a critical concentration

feed dog *n* (ca. 1939) : a notched piece of metal on a sewing machine that feeds material into position under the needle

feed·er \'fē-dər\ *n* (14c) **1** : one that feeds: as **a** : one that fattens livestock for slaughter **b** : a device or apparatus for supplying food **2** : one that eats or takes nourishment; *esp* : an animal being fattened or one suitable for fattening **3 a** : one that supplies, replenishes, or connects **b** : TRIBUTARY **c** : a heavy wire conductor supplying electricity at some point of an electric distribution system (as from a substation) **d** : BRANCH; *esp* : a branch transportation line **e** : FEEDER ROAD

feeder road *n* (1938) : a road that provides access to a major artery

feeding frenzy *n* (1973) : a frenzy of eating; *also* : the excited pursuit of something by a group

feed·lot \'fēd-ˌlät\ *n* (1889) : a plot of land on which livestock are fattened for market

feed·stock \-ˌstäk\ *n* (1932) : raw material supplied to a machine or processing plant

feed·stuff \-ˌstəf\ *n* (1856) : FEED 2a; *also* : any of the constituent nutrients of an animal ration

¹**feel** \'fē(ə)l\ *vb* **felt** \'felt\; **feel·ing** [ME *felen,* fr. OE *fēlan;* akin to OHG *fuolen* to feel, L *palpare* to caress] *vt* (bef. 12c) **1 a** : to handle or touch in order to examine, test, or explore some quality **b** : to perceive by a physical sensation coming from discrete end organs (as of the skin or muscles) **2 a** : to undergo passive experience of **b** : to have one's sensibilities markedly affected by **3** : to ascertain by cautious trial — usu. used with *out* ∼ *vi* **1 a** : to receive or be able to receive a tactile sensation **b** : to search for something by using the sense of touch **2 a** : to be conscious of an inward impression, state of mind, or physical condition **b** : to have a marked sentiment or opinion ⟨∼s strongly about it⟩ **3** : SEEM ⟨it ∼s like spring today⟩ **4** : to have sympathy or pity ⟨I ∼ for you⟩ — **feel like** : to have an inclination for ⟨*feel like* a walk?⟩

²**feel** *n* (13c) **1** : SENSATION, FEELING **2** : the sense of touch **3 a** : the quality of a thing as imparted through or as if through touch **b** : typical or peculiar quality or atmosphere; *also* : an awareness of such a quality or atmosphere **4** : intuitive knowledge or ability

feel·er \'fē-lər\ *n* (1526) : one that feels: as **a** : a tactile process (as a tentacle) of an animal **b** : something (as a proposal) ventured to ascertain the views of others

feeler gauge *n* (1925) : a thin metal strip or wire of known thickness used as a gauge

feel–good \'fē(ə)l-ˌgud\ *adj* (1978) : relating to or promoting an often specious sense of satisfaction or well-being

¹**feel·ing** \'fē-liŋ\ *n* (12c) **1 a** (1) : the one of the basic physical senses of which the skin contains the chief end organs and of which the sensations of touch and temperature are characteristic : TOUCH (2) : a sensation experienced through this sense **b** : generalized bodily consciousness or sensation **c** : appreciative or responsive awareness or recognition **2 a** : an emotional state or reaction ⟨had a kindly ∼ toward the child⟩ **b** *pl* : susceptibility to impression : SENSITIVITY ⟨the remark hurt her ∼s⟩ **3 a** : the undifferentiated background of one's awareness considered apart from any identifiable sensation, perception, or thought **b** : the overall quality of one's awareness **c** : conscious recognition : SENSE **4 a** : often unreasoned opinion or belief : SENTIMENT **b** : PRESENTIMENT **5** : capacity to respond emotionally esp. with the higher emotions **6** : the character ascribed to something : ATMOSPHERE **7 a** : the quality of a work of art that conveys the emotion of the artist **b** : sympathetic aesthetic response : FEEL 4

syn FEELING, EMOTION, AFFECTION, SENTIMENT, PASSION mean a subjective response to a person, thing, or situation. FEELING denotes any partly mental, partly physical response marked by pleasure, pain, attraction, or repulsion; it may suggest the mere existence of a response but imply nothing about the nature or intensity of it ⟨the *feelings* that once moved me are gone⟩. EMOTION carries a strong implication of excitement or agitation but, like FEELING, encompasses both positive and negative responses ⟨the drama portrays the *emotions* of adolescence⟩. AFFECTION applies to feelings that are also inclinations or likings ⟨a memoir of childhood filled with *affection* for her family⟩. SENTIMENT often implies an emotion inspired by an idea ⟨her feminist *sentiments* are well known⟩. PASSION suggests a very powerful or controlling emotion ⟨revenge became his ruling *passion*⟩.

²**feeling** *adj* (14c) **1 a** : SENTIENT, SENSITIVE **b** : easily moved emotionally **2** *obs* : deeply felt **3** : expressing emotion or sensitivity — **feel·ing·ly** \-liŋ-lē\ *adv* — **feel·ing·ness** *n*

feel up *vt* (1930) : to touch or fondle (someone) for sexual pleasure

fee simple *n, pl* **fees simple** (14c) : a fee without limitation to any class of heirs or restrictions on transfer of ownership

fee splitting *n* (1943) : payment by a specialist (as a doctor or a lawyer) of a part of his fee to the person who made the referral

feet *pl of* FOOT

fee tail *n, pl* **fees tail** (15c) : a fee limited to a particular class of heirs

feet-first \ˌfēt-'fərst\ *adv* (ca. 1901) : with the feet foremost

feet of clay [fr. the feet of the idol in Dan 2:33] (1814) : a flaw of character that is usu. not readily apparent

feeze \'fēz, 'fāz\ *n* [ME *veze,* fr. *fesen, vesen* to drive away — more at FAZE] (14c) **1** *chiefly dial* : RUSH **2** *dial* : a state of alarm or excitement

Feh·ling's solution \'fā-liŋ(z)-\ *n* [Hermann *Fehling* †1885 Ger. chemist] (1873) : a blue solution of Rochelle salt and copper sulfate used as an oxidizing agent in a test for sugars and aldehydes

feign \'fān\ *vb* [ME, fr. OF *feign-,* stem of *feindre,* fr. L *fingere* to shape, feign — more at DOUGH] *vi* (13c) : PRETEND, DISSEMBLE ∼ *vt* **1 a** : to give a false appearance of : induce as a false impression ⟨∼ death⟩ **b** : to assert as if true : PRETEND **2** *archaic* **a** : INVENT, IMAGINE **b** : to give fictional representation to **3** *obs* : DISGUISE, CONCEAL *syn* see ASSUME — **feign·er** *n*

feigned *adj* (14c) **1** : FICTITIOUS **2** : not genuine or real

fei·joa \fā-'yō-ə, -'hō-ə\ *n* [NL, genus name, fr. João da Silva *Feijó* †1824 Brazilian naturalist] (1898) : the green edible fruit of a shrub or small tree (*Feijoa sellowiana*) of the myrtle family that is native to So. America and is grown commercially esp. in New Zealand; *also* : the tree or shrub

¹**feint** \'fānt\ *n* [F *feinte,* fr. OF, fr. *feint,* pp. of *feindre*] (1679) : something feigned; *specif* : a mock blow or attack on or toward one part in order to distract attention from the point one really intends to attack *syn* see TRICK

²**feint** *vi* (1810) : to make a feint ∼ *vt* **1** : to lure or deceive with a feint **2** : to make a pretense of

fei·rie \'fē-rē\ *adj* [ME (Sc) *fery,* fr. ME *fere* strong, fr. OE *fēre* able to go; akin to OE *faran* to travel, fare] (bef. 12c) *Scot* : NIMBLE, STRONG

feist \'fīst\ *n* [obs. *fisting hound,* fr. obs. *fist* (to break wind)] (1770) *chiefly dial* : a small dog

feisty \'fī-stē\ *adj* **feist·i·er; -est** (1896) **1** *chiefly Southern & Midland* **a** : full of nervous energy : FIDGETY **b** : being touchy and quarrelsome **c** : being frisky and exuberant **2** : having or showing a lively aggressiveness : SPUNKY — **feist·i·ness** *n*

fe·la·fel \fə-'lä-fəl\ *var of* FALAFEL

feld·sher \'fel(d)-shər\ *n* [Russ *fel'dsher,* fr. G *Feldscher, Feldscherer* field surgeon, fr. *Feld* field + *Scherer* barber, surgeon] (1877) : a medical or surgical practitioner without full professional qualifications or status in some east European countries and esp. Russia

feld·spar \'fel(d)-ˌspär\ *n* [modif. of obs. G *Feldspath* (now *Feldspat*), fr. G *Feld* field + obs. G *Spath* (now *Spat*) spar] (1772) : any of a group of crystalline minerals that consist of aluminum silicates with either potassium, sodium, calcium, or barium and that are an essential constituent of nearly all crystalline rocks

feld·spath·ic \fel(d)-'spa-thik\ *adj* [*feldspath* (var. of *feldspar*), fr. obs. G] (ca. 1828) : relating to or containing feldspar — used esp. of a porcelain glaze

fe·li·cif·ic \ˌfē-lə-'si-fik\ *adj* [L *felic-, felix*] (1865) : causing or intended to cause happiness

felicific calculus *n* (1945) : a method of determining the rightness of an action by balancing the probable pleasures and pains that it would produce

¹**fe·lic·i·tate** \fi-'li-sə-ˌtāt\ *adj* [LL *felicitatus,* pp. of *felicitare* to make happy, fr. L *felicitas*] (1605) *obs* : made happy

²**felicitate** *vt* **-tat·ed; -tat·ing** (1628) **1** *archaic* : to make happy **2 a** : to consider happy or fortunate **b** : to offer congratulations to — **fe·lic·i·ta·tion** \-ˌli-sə-'tā-shən\ *n* — **fe·lic·i·ta·tor** \-'li-sə-ˌtā-tər\ *n*

fe·lic·i·tous \fi-'li-sə-təs\ *adj* (1789) **1** : very well suited or expressed : APT ⟨a ∼ remark⟩ **2** : PLEASANT, DELIGHTFUL *syn* see FIT — **fe·lic·i·tous·ly** *adv* — **fe·lic·i·tous·ness** *n*

fe·lic·i·ty \fi-'li-sə-tē\ *n, pl* **-ties** [ME *felicite,* fr. MF *felicité,* fr. L *felicitat-, felicitas,* fr. *felic-, felix* fruitful, happy — more at FEMININE] (14c) **1 a** : the quality or state of being happy; *esp* : great happiness **b** : an instance of happiness **2** : something that causes happiness **3 a** : a pleasing manner or quality esp. in art or language **4** : an apt expression

fe·lid \'fē-ləd\ *n* [NL *Felidae,* family name, fr. *Felis,* genus of cats, fr. L, cat] (ca. 1889) : CAT 1b — **felid** *adj*

fe·line \'fē-ˌlīn\ *adj* [L *felinus,* fr. *felis*] (1681) **1** : of, relating to, or affecting cats or the cat family **2** : resembling a cat: as **a** : sleekly graceful **b** : SLY, TREACHEROUS **c** : STEALTHY — **feline** *n* — **fe·line·ly** *adv* — **fe·lin·i·ty** \fē-'li-nə-tē\ *n*

feline distemper *n* (1942) : PANLEUKOPENIA

feline panleukopenia *n* (ca. 1943) : PANLEUKOPENIA

¹**fell** \'fel\ *n* [ME, fr. OE; akin to OHG *fel* skin, L *pellis*] (bef. 12c) **1** : SKIN, HIDE, PELT **2** : a thin tough membrane covering a carcass directly under the hide

²**fell** *vt* [ME, fr. OE *fellan;* akin to OE *feallan* to fall — more at FALL] (bef. 12c) **1 a** : to cut, knock, or bring down **b** : KILL **2** : to sew (a seam) by folding one raw edge under the other and sewing flat on the wrong side — **fell·able** \'fe-lə-bəl\ *adj* — **fell·er** *n*

³**fell** *past of* FALL

⁴**fell** *adj* [ME *fel,* fr. MF, fr. OF — more at FELON] (14c) **1 a** : FIERCE, CRUEL, TERRIBLE **b** : SINISTER, MALEVOLENT ⟨a ∼ purpose⟩ **c** : very destructive : DEADLY ⟨a ∼ disease⟩ **2** *Scot* : SHARP, PUNGENT — **fell·ness** *n* — **fell·ly** \'fel-lē\ *adv* — **at one fell swoop** *or* **in one fell swoop** : all at once; *also* : with a single concentrated effort

⁵**fell** *n* [ME, fr. ON *fell, fjall* mountain; akin to OHG *felis* rock] (14c) *dial Brit* : a high barren field or moor

---

\ə\ abut, \ᵊ\ kitten, F table \ər\ further \a\ ash \ā\ ace \ä\ mop, mar \aú\ out \ch\ chin \e\ bet \ē\ easy \g\ go \i\ hit \ī\ ice \j\ job \ŋ\ sing \ō\ go \ò\ law \òi\ boy \th\ thin \t̶h\ the \ü\ loot \ù\ foot \y\ yet \zh\ vision \à, k̲, ⁿ, œ, œ̄, ᵫ, ᵫ̄, ᵊ\ *see* Guide to Pronunciation

fel·lah \'fe-lə, fə-'lä\ *n, pl* **fel·la·hin** *or* **fel·la·heen** \,fel-ə-'hēn, fə-,lä-'hēn\ [Ar *fallāḥ*] (1743) : a peasant or agricultural laborer in an Arab country (as Egypt)

fel·late \'fe-,lāt, fə-'lāt\ *vb* **fel·lat·ed; fel·lat·ing** [back-formation fr. *fellatio*] *vt* (1948) : to perform fellatio on ~ *vi* : to fellate someone — **fel·la·tor** \-,lā-tər, -'lā-tər\ *n*

fel·la·tio \fə-'lā-shē-,ō, fe-\ *also* **fel·la·tion** \-'lā-shən\ *n* [NL *fellation-, fellatio,* fr. L *felare, fellare,* lit., to suck — more at FEMININE] (ca. 1893) : oral stimulation of the penis

fell·mon·ger \'fel-,mən-gər, -,mäŋ-\ *n* [¹*fell*] (1530) *Brit* : one who removes hair or wool from hides in preparation for leather making — **fell·mon·gered** \-gərd\ *adj, Brit* — **fell·mon·ger·ing** \-g(ə-)riŋ\ *n, Brit* — **fell·mon·gery** \-g(ə-)rē\ *n, Brit*

fel·low \'fe-(,)lō, -lə(-w)\ *n, often attrib* [ME *felawe,* fr. OE *fēolaga,* fr. ON *fēlagi,* fr. *fēlag* partnership, fr. *fē* cattle, money + *lag* act of laying] (bef. 12c) **1 a** : COMRADE, ASSOCIATE **2 a** : an equal in rank, power, or character : PEER **b** : one of a pair : MATE **3** : a member of a group having common characteristics; *specif* : a member of an incorporated literary or scientific society **4 a** *obs* : a person of one of the lower social classes **b** : a worthless man or boy **c** : MAN, BOY **d** : BOYFRIEND, BEAU **5** : an incorporated member of a college or collegiate foundation esp. in a British university **6** : a person appointed to a position granting a stipend and allowing for advanced study or research

fellow feeling *n* (1712) : a feeling of community of interest or of mutual understanding

fel·low·ly \-lō-lē, -lə-lē\ *adj* (13c) : SOCIABLE — **fellowly** *adv*

fel·low·man \,fe-lō-'man, -lə-\ *n* (1667) : a kindred human being

fellow servant *n* (1900) : an employee working with another employee under such circumstances that each one if negligent may expose the other to harm which the employer cannot reasonably be expected to guard against or be held legally liable for

¹fel·low·ship \'fe-lə-,ship, -lō-\ *n* (bef. 12c) **1** : COMPANIONSHIP, COMPANY **2 a** : community of interest, activity, feeling, or experience **b** : the state of being a fellow or associate **3** : a company of equals or friends : ASSOCIATION **4** : the quality or state of being comradely **5** *obs* : MEMBERSHIP, PARTNERSHIP **6 a** : the position of a fellow (as of a university) **b** : the stipend of a fellow **c** : a foundation for the providing of such a stipend

²fellowship *vb* **-shipped** *also* **-shiped** \-,shipt\; **-ship·ping** *also* **-ship·ing** \-,shi-piŋ\ *vi* (14c) : to join in fellowship esp. with a church member ~ *vt* : to admit to fellowship (as in a church)

fellow traveler *n* [trans. of Russ *poputchik*] (1925) : one that sympathizes with and often furthers the ideals and program of an organized group (as the Communist party) without membership in the group or regular participation in its activities — **fel·low-trav·el·ing** *adj*

fel·ly \'fe-lē\ *or* **fel·loe** \-(,)lō\ *n, pl* **fellies** *or* **felloes** [ME *fely, felive,* fr. OE *felg;* akin to OHG *felga* felly, OE *fealg* piece of plowed land] (bef. 12c) : the exterior rim or a segment of the rim of a wheel supported by the spokes

felo-de-se \,fe-lō-də-'sā, -'sē\ *n, pl* **fe·lo·nes-de-se** \fə-,lō-(,)nēz-də-\ *or* **felos-de-se** \,fe-lōz-də-\ [ML *felo de se, fello de se,* lit., evildoer in respect to oneself] (1607) **1** : one who deliberately kills himself or who dies from the effects of his commission of an unlawful malicious act **2** : an act of deliberate self-destruction : SUICIDE

¹fel·on \'fe-lən\ *n* [ME, fr. MF *felon, fel* evildoer, prob. of Gmc origin; akin to OHG *fillen* to beat, whip, *fel* skin — more at FELL] (13c) **1** : one who has committed a felony **2** *archaic* : VILLAIN **3** : WHITLOW

²felon *adj* (13c) **1** *archaic* **a** : CRUEL **b** : EVIL **2** *archaic* : WILD

fe·lo·ni·ous \fə-'lō-nē-əs\ *adj* (1575) **1** *archaic* : very evil : VILLAINOUS **2** : of, relating to, or having the nature of a felony — **fe·lo·ni·ous·ly** *adv* — **fe·lo·ni·ous·ness** *n*

fel·on·ry \'fe-lən-rē\ *n* (1837) : FELONS; *esp* : the convict population of a penal colony

fel·o·ny \'fe-lə-nē\ *n, pl* **-nies** (14c) **1** : an act on the part of a feudal vassal involving the forfeiture of his fee **2 a** : a grave crime formerly differing from a misdemeanor under English common law by involving forfeiture in addition to any other punishment **b** : a grave crime declared to be a felony by the common law or by statute regardless of the punishment actually imposed **c** : a crime declared a felony by statute because of the punishment imposed **d** : a crime for which the punishment in federal law may be death or imprisonment for more than one year

fel·site \'fel-,sīt\ *n* [*fels*par + *-ite*] (1794) : a dense igneous rock consisting almost entirely of feldspar and quartz — **fel·sit·ic** \fel-'si-tik\ *adj*

fel·spar *chiefly Brit var of* FELDSPAR

¹felt \'felt\ *n* [ME, fr. OE; akin to OHG *filz* felt, L *pellere* to drive, beat] (bef. 12c) **1 a** : a cloth made of wool and fur often mixed with natural or synthetic fibers through the action of heat, moisture, chemicals, and pressure **b** : a firm woven cloth of wool or cotton heavily napped and shrunk **2** : an article made of felt **3** : a material resembling felt: as **a** : a heavy paper of organic or asbestos fibers impregnated with asphalt and used in building construction **b** : semirigid pressed fiber insulation used in building — **felt·like** *adj*

²felt *vt* (14c) **1** : to make out of or cover with felt **2** : to cause to adhere and mat together **3** : to make into felt or a similar substance

³felt *past and past part of* FEEL

felt·ing \'fel-tiŋ\ *n* (1686) **1** : the process of making felt **2** : FELT

fe·luc·ca \fə-'lü-kə, -'lə-kə\ *n* [It *feluca*] (1615) : a narrow fast lateen-rigged sailing vessel chiefly of the Mediterranean area

¹fe·male \'fē-,māl\ *adj* (14c) **1 a** : of, relating to, or being the sex that bears young or produces eggs **2** : PISTILLATE **3** : having some quality (as gentleness) associated with the female sex **3** : designed with a hollow or groove into which a corresponding male part fits ⟨~ coupling of a hose⟩ — **fe·male·ness** *n*

felucca

²female *n* [ME, alter. of *femel, femelle,* fr. MF & ML; MF *femelle,* fr. ML *femella,* fr. L, girl, dim. of *femina*] (14c) **1 a** : a female person : WOMAN, GIRL **b** : an individual that bears young or produces large usu. immobile gametes (as eggs) that are fertilized by small usu. motile gametes of a male **2** : a pistillate plant

¹fem·i·nine \'fe-mə-nən\ *adj* [ME, fr. MF *feminin,* fr. L *femininus,* fr. *femina* woman; akin to OE *delu* nipple, L *filius* son, *felix, fetus,* & *fecundus* fruitful, *felare* to suck, Gk *thēlē* nipple] (14c) **1** : FEMALE 1a **2** : characteristic of or appropriate or unique to women **3** : of, relating to, or constituting the gender that ordinarily includes most words or grammatical forms referring to females ⟨a ~ noun⟩ **4 a** : being an unstressed and usu. hypermetric final syllable ⟨~ ending⟩ **b** *of rhyme* : having an unstressed final syllable **c** : having the final chord occurring on a weak beat ⟨music in ~ cadences⟩ — **fem·i·nine·ly** *adv* — **fem·i·nine·ness** \-nə(n)-nəs\ *n*

²feminine *n* (15c) **1 a** : a noun, pronoun, adjective, or inflectional form or class of the feminine gender **b** : the feminine gender **2** : the female principle ⟨eternal ~⟩

fem·i·nin·i·ty \,fe-mə-'ni-nə-tē\ *n* (14c) **1** : the quality or nature of the female sex **2** : EFFEMINACY **3** : WOMEN, WOMANKIND

fem·i·nise *Brit var of* FEMINIZE

fem·i·nism \'fe-mə-,ni-zəm\ *n* (1895) **1** : the theory of the political, economic, and social equality of the sexes **2** : organized activity on behalf of women's rights and interests — **fem·i·nist** \-nist\ *n or adj* — **fem·i·nis·tic** \,fe-mə-'nis-tik\ *adj*

fem·in·i·ty \fe-'mi-nə-tē, fə-\ *n* (14c) : FEMININITY

fem·i·nize \'fe-mə-,nīz\ *vt* **-nized; -niz·ing** (1652) **1** : to give a feminine quality to **2** : to cause (a male or castrate) to take on feminine characters (as by implantation of ovaries or administration of estrogenic substances) — **fem·i·ni·za·tion** \,fe-mə-nə-'zā-shən\ *n*

femme *also* **fem** \'fem\ *n* [prob. fr. F *femme* woman, fr. L *femina*] (1958) : a lesbian who plays the female role in a homosexual relationship

femme fa·tale \,fem-fə-'tal, ,fam-, -'täl\ *n, pl* **femmes fa·tales** \-'tal(z), -'täl(z)\ [F, lit., disastrous woman] (1912) **1 a** : a seductive woman who lures men into dangerous or compromising situations **2** : a woman who attracts men by an aura of charm and mystery

fem·o·ral \'fe-mə-rəl, 'fem-rəl\ *adj* (ca. 1771) : of or relating to the femur or thigh

femoral artery *n* (ca. 1771) : the chief artery of the thigh lying in its anterior inner part

fem·to- \,fem(p)-tō\ *comb form* [ISV, fr. Dan or Norw *femten* fifteen, fr. ON *fimmtān;* akin to OE *fīftēne* fifteen] : one quadrillionth (10^{-15}) part of ⟨*femto*second⟩

fem·to·sec·ond \'fem(p)-tə-,se-kənd, -kənt, -tō-\ *n* (1976) : one quadrillionth of a second

fe·mur \'fē-mər\ *n, pl* **fe·murs** *or* **fem·o·ra** \'fe-mə-rə, 'fem-rə\ [NL *femor-, femur,* fr. L, thigh] (ca. 1771) **1** : the proximal bone of the hind or lower limb — called also *thighbone* **2** : the segment of an insect's leg that is third from the body

¹fen \'fen\ *n* [ME, fr. OE *fenn;* akin to OHG *fenna* fen, Skt *paṅka* mud] (bef. 12c) : low land covered wholly or partly with water unless artificially drained

²fen \'fən\ *n, pl* **fen** [Chin (Beijing) *fēn*] (1916) — see *yuan* at MONEY table

¹fence \'fen(t)s\ *n, often attrib* [ME *fens,* short for *defens* defense] (14c) **1** *archaic* : a means of protection : DEFENSE **2** : a barrier intended to prevent escape or intrusion or to mark a boundary; *esp* : such a barrier made of posts and wire or boards **3** : FENCING I **4 a** : a receiver of stolen goods **b** : a place where stolen goods are bought — **fence·less** \-ləs\ *adj* — **fence·less·ness** *n* — **on the fence** : in a position of neutrality or indecision

²fence *vb* **fenced; fenc·ing** *vt* (15c) **1 a** : to enclose with a fence **b** (1) : to keep in or out with a fence (2) : to ward off **2** : to provide a defense for **3** : to sell (stolen property) to a fence ~ *vi* **1 a** : to practice fencing **b** (1) : to use tactics of attack and defense resembling those of fencing (2) : to parry arguments by shifting ground **2** *archaic* : to provide protection — **fenc·er** *n*

fence-mend·ing \'fen(t)s-,men-diŋ\ *n* (1947) : the rehabilitating of a deteriorated political relationship

fence-row \'fen(t)s-,rō\ *n* (1842) : the land occupied by a fence including the uncultivated area on each side

fence-sit·ting \'fen(t)s-,si-tiŋ\ *n* (1904) : a state of indecision or neutrality with respect to conflicting positions — **fence-sit·ter** *n*

fenc·ing \'fen(t)s\ *n* (1581) **1** : the art or practice of attack and defense with the foil, épee, or saber **2 a** (1) : FENCE 2 (2) : the fences of a property or region **b** : material used for building fences

¹fend \'fend\ *vb* [ME *fenden,* short for *defenden*] *vt* (14c) **1** : DEFEND **2** : to keep or ward off : REPEL — often used with *off* **3** *dial Brit* : to provide for : SUPPORT ~ *vi* **1** *dial Brit* : to make an effort : STRUGGLE **2 a** : to try to get along without help : SHIFT ⟨had to ~ for themselves⟩ **b** : to provide a livelihood

²fend *n* (1721) *chiefly Scot* : an effort or attempt esp. for oneself

fend·er \'fen-dər\ *n* (13c) : a device that protects: as **a** (1) : a cushion (as foam rubber or a wood float) between a boat and a dock or between two boats that lessens shock and prevents chafing (2) : a pile or a row or cluster of piles placed to protect a dock or bridge pier from damage by ships or floating objects **b** : RAILING **c** : a device in front of locomotives and streetcars to lessen injury to animals or pedestrians in case of collision **d** : a guard over the wheel of a motor vehicle **e** : a low metal frame or a screen before an open fireplace **f** : an oblong or triangular shield of leather attached to the stirrup leather of a saddle to protect a rider's legs — **fend·ered** \-dərd\ *adj* — **fend·er·less** *adj*

fender bender *n* (ca. 1962) : a minor automobile accident

fe·nes·tra \fə-'nes-trə\ *n, pl* **-trae** \-,trē, -,trī\ [NL, fr. L, window] (ca. 1737) **1** : a small anatomical opening (as in a bone): as **a** : an oval opening between the middle ear and the vestibule having the base of the stapes or columella attached to its membrane — called also *fenestra ova·lis* \-ō-'vā-ləs\, *fenestra ves·tib·u·li* \-ves-'ti-byə-(,)lē\, *oval window* **b** : a round opening between the middle ear and the cochlea — called also *fenestra cochleae, fenestra ro·tun·da* \-rō-'tən-də\, *round window* **2** : an opening cut in bone — **fe·nes·tral** \-trəl\ *adj*

fe·nes·trate \fə-'nes-,trāt, 'fe-nə-,strāt\ *adj* [L *fenestratus,* fr. *fenestra*] (1835) : FENESTRATED

fen·es·trat·ed \'fe-nə-ˌstrā-təd\ *adj* (ca. 1852) : having one or more openings or pores ⟨~ blood capillaries⟩

fen·es·tra·tion \ˌfe-nə-'strā-shən\ *n* (1846) **1** : the arrangement, proportioning, and design of windows and doors in a building **2** : an opening in a surface (as a wall or membrane) **3** : the operation of cutting an opening in the bony labyrinth between the inner ear and tympanum to replace natural fenestrae that are not functional

Fe·ni·an \'fē-nē-ən\ *n* [Ir *féinne*, pl. of *fiann*, legendary band of Irish warriors] (1816) **1** : a member of a legendary band of warriors defending Ireland in the 2d and 3d centuries A.D. **2** : a member of a secret 19th century Irish and Irish-American organization dedicated to the overthrow of British rule in Ireland — **Fenian** *adj* — **Fe·ni·an·ism** \-ə-ˌni-zəm\ *n*

fen·land \'fen-ˌland\ *n* (bef. 12c) : an area of low often marshy ground

fen·nec \'fe-nik\ *n* [Ar *fanak*] (1790) : a small pale-fawn fox (*Vulpes zerda* syn. *Fennecus zerda*) with large ears that inhabits the deserts of northern Africa and Arabia

fen·nel \'fe-n²l\ *n* [ME *fenel*, fr. OE *finugl*, fr. (assumed) VL *fenuculum*, fr. L *feniculum* fennel, irreg. dim. of *fenum* hay] (bef. 12c) : a perennial European herb (*Foeniculum vulgare*) of the carrot family introduced into No. America and cultivated for its foliage and aromatic seeds

fen·ny \'fe-nē\ *adj* (bef. 12c) **1** : having the characteristics of a fen : BOGGY **2** *archaic* : peculiar to or found in a fen

fenu·greek \'fen-yə-ˌgrēk\ *n* [ME *fenugrek*, fr. MF *fenugrec*, fr. L *fenum Graecum*, lit., Greek hay] (14c) : a leguminous annual Asian herb (*Trigonella foenumgraecum*) with aromatic seeds

feoff·ee \fe-'fē, fē-'fē\ *n* (15c) : one to whom a feoffment is made

feoff·ment \'fef-mənt, 'fēf-\ *n* [ME *feoffement*, fr. AF, fr. *feoffer* to invest with a fee, fr. OF *fief* fee] (14c) : the granting of a fee

feof·for \'fe-fər, 'fē-; fe-'fôr, fē-\ *or* **feoff·er** \'fef-ər, 'fēf-\ *n* (15c) : one who makes a feoffment

-fer \fər\ *n comb form* [F & L; F *-fère*, fr. L *-fer* bearing, one that bears, fr. *ferre* to carry — more at BEAR] : one that bears ⟨aqui*fer*⟩

fe·rae na·tu·rae \'fer-ˌī-nə-'tūr-ˌī\ *adj* [L, of a wild nature] (ca. 1661) : wild by nature and not usu. tamed

fe·ral \'fir-əl, 'fer-\ *adj* [ML *feralis*, fr. L *fera* wild animal, fr. fem. of *ferus* wild — more at FIERCE] (1604) **1** : of, relating to, or suggestive of a wild beast : SAVAGE **2** **a** : not domesticated or cultivated : WILD **b** : having escaped from domestication and become wild *syn* see BRUTAL

fer–de–lance \'fer-d²l-'an(t)s, -'än(t)s\ *n, pl* **fer–de–lance** [F, lit., lance iron, spearhead] (1880) : a large extremely venomous pit viper (*Bothrops atrox*) of Central and So. America

fere \'fir\ *n* [ME, fr. OE *gefēra*; akin to OE *faran* to go, travel — more at FARE] (bef. 12c) **1** *archaic* : COMPANION, COMRADE **2** *archaic* : SPOUSE

¹fe·ria \'fir-ē-ə, 'fer-\ *n* [ML — more at FAIR] (15c) : a weekday of a church calendar on which no feast falls — **fe·ri·al** \-ē-əl\ *adj*

²fe·ria \'fer-ē-ə, -ˌä\ *n* [Sp, fair, market, fr. ML — more at FAIR] (1844) : an Hispanic market festival often in observance of a religious holiday

fe·rine \'fir-ˌīn\ *adj* [L *ferinus*, fr. *fera*] (1640) : FERAL

fer·i·ty \'fer-ət-ē\ *n, pl* **-ties** [L *feritas*, fr. *ferus*] (1534) *archaic* : the quality or state of being feral; *also* : BARBARITY

fer·lie *also* **fer·ly** \'fer-lē\ *n, pl* **fer·lies** [ME, fr. *ferly* strange, fr. OE *fǣrlic* unexpected, fr. *fǣr* sudden danger — more at FEAR] (13c) *Scot* : WONDER

fer·ma·ta \fer-'mä-tə\ *n* [It, lit., stop, fr. *fermare* to stop, fr. L *firmare* to make firm] (ca. 1859) : a prolongation at the discretion of the performer of a musical note, chord, or rest beyond its given time value; *also* : the sign ꓴ denoting such a prolongation — called also *hold*

¹fer·ment \(ˌ)fər-'ment\ *vi* (14c) **1** : to undergo fermentation **2** : to be in a state of agitation or intense activity ⟨~ *vt* **1** : to cause to undergo fermentation **2** : to work up (as into a state of agitation) : FOMENT ⟨quick-spreading rumors ~*ed* the city and violence then broke out⟩ — **fer·ment·able** \-'men-tə-bəl\ *adj*

²fer·ment \'fər-ˌment *also* (ˌ)fər-'\ *n* [ME, fr. L *fermentum* yeast — more at BARM] (15c) **1 a** : a living organism (as a yeast) that causes fermentation by virtue of its enzymes : ENZYME **2 a** : a state of unrest : AGITATION **b** : a process of active often disorderly development ⟨the great period of creative ~ in literature —William Barrett⟩

fer·men·ta·tion \ˌfər-mən-'tā-shən, -ˌmen-\ *n* (1601) **1 a** : a chemical change with effervescence **b** : an enzymatically controlled anaerobic breakdown of an energy-rich compound (as a carbohydrate to carbon dioxide and alcohol or to an organic acid); *broadly* : an enzymatically controlled transformation of an organic compound **2** : FERMENT 2

fer·men·ta·tive \(ˌ)fər-'men-tə-tiv\ *adj* (1661) **1** : causing or producing a substance that causes fermentation ⟨~ organisms⟩ **2** : of, relating to, or produced by fermentation

fer·men·ter \(ˌ)fər-'men-tər\ *n* (1918) **1** : an organism that causes fermentation **2** *or* **fer·men·tor** : an apparatus for carrying out fermentation

fer·mi \'fer-(ˌ)mē, 'fər-\ *n* [Enrico *Fermi*] (1955) : a unit of length equal to 10⁻¹³ centimeter

fer·mi·on \'fer-mē-ˌän, 'fər-\ *n* [Enrico *Fermi* + E ²-*on*] (1947) : a particle (as an electron, proton, or neutron) whose spin quantum number is an odd multiple of $\frac{1}{2}$ — compare BOSON

fer·mi·um \'fer-mē-əm, 'fər-\ *n* [Enrico *Fermi*] (1955) : a radioactive metallic element artificially produced (as by bombardment of plutonium with neutrons) — see ELEMENT table

fern \'fərn\ *n* [ME, fr. OE *fearn*; akin to OHG *farn* fern, Skt *parṇa* wing, leaf] (bef. 12c) : any of a large class (Filicopsida) of flowerless spore-producing vascular plants; *esp* : any of an order (Filicales) of homosporous plants possessing roots, stems, and leaflike fronds — **fern·like** \-ˌlīk\ *adj* — **ferny** \'fər-nē\ *adj*

fern bar *n* (1976) : a bar or restaurant fashionably decorated with green plants and esp. ferns

fern·ery \'fər-nə-rē\ *n, pl* **-er·ies** (1840) **1** : a place or stand where ferns grow **2** : a collection of growing ferns

fern seed *n* (1596) : the dustlike asexual spores of ferns formerly thought to be seeds and believed to make the possessor invisible

fe·ro·cious \fə-'rō-shəs\ *adj* [L *feroc-, ferox*, lit., fierce looking, fr. *ferus* + -*oc-, -ox* (akin to Gk *ōps* eye) — more at EYE] (1646) **1** : exhibiting or given to extreme fierceness and unrestrained violence and brutality **2** : extremely intense ⟨~ heat⟩ *syn* see FIERCE — **fe·ro·cious·ly** *adv* — **fe·ro·cious·ness** *n*

fe·roc·i·ty \fə-'rä-sə-tē\ *n* (1606) : the quality or state of being ferocious

-ferous *adj comb form* [ME, fr. MF & L; MF -*fere* -fer, fr. L -*fer*] : bearing : producing ⟨carboni*ferous*⟩

fer·re·dox·in \ˌfer-ə-'däk-sən\ *n* [L *ferrum* + E *redox* + -*in*] (1962) : any of a group of iron-containing plant proteins that function as electron carriers in photosynthetic organisms and in some anaerobic bacteria

¹fer·ret \'fer-ət\ *n* [ME *furet, ferret*, fr. MF *furet*, fr. (assumed) VL *furittus*, lit., little thief, dim. of L *fur* thief — more at FURTIVE] (14c) **1** : a partially domesticated usu. albino European polecat that is sometimes classed as a separate species (*Mustela furo*) **2** : an active and persistent searcher — **fer·rety** \-ə-tē\ *adj*

²ferret *vi* (15c) **1** : to hunt with ferrets **2** : to search about ⟨~ *vt* **1 a** (1) : to hunt (as rabbits) with ferrets (2) : to force out of hiding : FLUSH **b** : to find and bring to light by searching — usu. used with *out* ⟨~ out the answers⟩ **2** : HARRY, WORRY — **fer·ret·er** *n*

³ferret *n* [prob. modif. of It *fioretti* floss silk, fr. pl. of *fioretto*, dim. of *fiore* flower, fr. L *flor-, flos* — more at BLOW] (1649) : a narrow cotton, silk, or wool tape — called also *ferreting*

ferri- *comb form* [L, fr. *ferrum*] **1** : iron ⟨*ferri*ferous⟩ **2** : ferric iron ⟨*ferri*cyanide⟩

fer·ri·age \'fer-ē-ij\ *n* [ME] (14c) **1** : the fare paid for a ferry passage **2** : the act or business of transporting by ferry

fer·ric \'fer-ik\ *adj* (1799) **1** : of, relating to, or containing iron **2** : being or containing iron usu. with a valence of three

ferric ammonium citrate *n* (ca. 1924) : a complex salt containing varying amounts of iron and used esp. for making blueprints

ferric chloride *n* (1885) : a deliquescent dark salt $FeCl_3$ that readily hydrates to the yellow-orange form and that is used in sewage treatment and as an astringent

ferric hydroxide *n* (1885) : a hydrate $Fe_2O_3 \cdot nH_2O$ of ferric oxide that is capable of acting both as a base and as a weak acid

ferric oxide *n* (1882) : the red or black oxide of iron Fe_2O_3 found in nature as hematite and as rust and also obtained synthetically and used as a pigment and for polishing

fer·ri·cy·a·nide \ˌfer-ˌi-'sī-ə-ˌnīd, ˌfer-i-\ *n* [ISV] (1845) **1** : the trivalent anion $Fe(CN)_6^{3-}$ **2** : a compound containing the ferricyanide anion; *esp* : the red salt $K_3Fe(CN)_6$ used in making blue pigments

fer·rif·er·ous \fə-'ri-f(ə-)rəs, fe-\ *adj* (1811) : containing or yielding iron

fer·ri·mag·net·ic \'fer-ˌi-mag-'ne-tik, ˌfer-i-\ *adj* (1951) : of or relating to a substance (as ferrite) characterized by magnetization in which one group of magnetic ions is polarized in a direction opposite to the other — **fer·ri·mag·net** \'fer-ˌi-ˌmag-nət, 'fer-i-\ *n* — **fer·ri·mag·net·i·cal·ly** \'fer-ˌi-mag-'ne-ti-k(ə-)lē, ˌfer-i-\ *adv* — **fer·ri·mag·ne·tism** \-'mag-nə-ˌti-zəm\ *n*

Fer·ris wheel \'fer-əs-\ *n* [G. W. G. *Ferris* †1896 Am. engineer] (1893) : an amusement device consisting of a large upright power-driven wheel carrying seats that remain horizontal around its rim

fer·rite \'fer-ˌīt\ *n* (1851) **1** : any of several magnetic substances that consist essentially of ferric oxide combined with the oxides of one or more metals (as manganese, nickel, or zinc), have high magnetic permeability and high electrical resistivity, and are used esp. in electronic devices **2** : a solid solution in which alpha iron is the solvent — **fer·rit·ic** \fə-'ri-tik, fe-\ *adj*

fer·ri·tin \'fer-əs-t²n\ *n* [ISV, alter. of *ferratin*, iron-containing protein, fr. L *ferratus* bound with iron (fr. *ferrum*) + ISV -*in*] (1937) : a crystalline iron-containing protein that functions in the storage of iron and is found esp. in the liver and spleen

ferro- *comb form* [ML, fr. L *ferrum*] **1** : iron ⟨*ferro*concrete⟩ **2** : ferrous iron ⟨*ferro*cyanide⟩

fer·ro·ce·ment \ˌfer-ō-si-'ment\ *n* (1956) : a building material made of thin cement slabs reinforced with steel mesh

fer·ro·cene \'fer-ō-ˌsēn\ *n* [*ferro-* + *cycl-* + -*ene*] (1952) : a crystalline stable organometallic coordination compound $(C_5H_5)_2Fe$; *also* : an analogous compound with a heavy metal (as chromium)

fer·ro·con·crete \ˌfer-ō-'kän-ˌkrēt, -kän-\ *n* (1900) : REINFORCED CONCRETE

fer·ro·cy·a·nide \-'sī-ə-ˌnīd\ *n* (ca. 1826) **1** : the tetravalent anion $Fe(CN)_6^{4-}$ **2** : a compound containing the ferrocyanide anion; *esp* : the salt $K_4Fe(CN)_6$ used in making blue pigments (as Prussian blue)

fer·ro·elec·tric \ˌfer-ō-i-'lek-trik\ *adj* (1935) : of or relating to crystalline substances having spontaneous electric polarization reversible by an electric field — **ferroelectric** *n* — **fer·ro·elec·tric·i·ty** \-ˌlek-'tri-sə-tē, -'tris-tē\ *n*

fer·ro·mag·ne·sian \ˌmag-'nē-zhən, -shən\ *adj* (1899) : containing iron and magnesium ⟨~ minerals⟩

fer·ro·mag·net·ic \-'ne-tik\ *adj* (1896) : of or relating to substances with an abnormally high magnetic permeability, a definite saturation point, and appreciable residual magnetism and hysteresis — **fer·ro·mag·net** \'fer-ə-ˌmag-nət\ *n* — **fer·ro·mag·ne·tism** \ˌfer-ō-'mag-nə-ˌti-zəm\ *n*

fer·ro·man·ga·nese \-'maŋ-gə-ˌnēz, -ˌnēs, -ˌnēs\ *n* (1864) : an alloy of iron and manganese containing usu. about 80 percent manganese and used in the manufacture of steel

fer·ro·sil·i·con \-'si-li-kən, -lə-ˌkän\ *n* (1882) : an alloy of iron and silicon containing 15 to 95 percent silicon and used for deoxidizing molten steel and making silicon steel and high-silicon cast iron

fer·ro·type \'fer-ə-ˌtīp\ *n* (1844) **1** : a positive photograph made by a collodion process on a thin iron plate having a darkened surface **2** : the process by which a ferrotype is made

---

\ə\ abut \²\ kitten, F table \ər\ further \a\ ash \ā\ ace \ä\ mop, mar \aů\ out \ch\ chin \e\ bet \ē\ easy \g\ go \i\ hit \ī\ ice \j\ job \ŋ\ sing \ō\ go \ô\ law \ȯi\ boy \th\ thin \t͟h\ the \ü\ loot \ů\ foot \y\ yet \zh\ vision \à, k̲, ⁿ, œ, œ̄, ᵫ, ᵫ̄, ᵊ\ *see* Guide to Pronunciation

fer·rous \'fer-əs\ *adj* [NL *ferrosus*, fr. L *ferrum*] (1865) **1** : of, relating to, or containing iron **2** : being or containing divalent iron
ferrous oxide *n* (1873) : a black easily oxidizable powder FeO that is the monoxide of iron
ferrous sulfate *n* (1865) : a salt FeSO₄; *esp* : COPPERAS
fer·ru·gi·nous \fə-'rü-jə-nəs, fe-\ *adj* [L *ferrugineus, ferruginus,* fr. *ferrugin-, ferrugo* iron rust, fr. *ferrum*] (ca. 1661) **1** : of, relating to, or containing iron ⟨a ~ soil⟩ **2** : resembling iron rust in color
fer·rule \'fer-əl\ *n* [alter. of ME *virole,* fr. MF, fr. L *viriola,* dim. of *viria* bracelet, of Celtic origin; akin to OIr *fiar* oblique] (1611) **1** : a ring or cap usu. of metal put around a slender shaft (as a cane or a tool handle) to strengthen it or prevent splitting **2** : a usu. metal sleeve used esp. for joining or binding one part to another (as pipe sections or the bristles and handle of a brush) — **fer·ruled** *adj*
¹fer·ry \'fer-ē\ *vb* **fer·ried; fer·ry·ing** [ME *ferien,* fr. OE *ferian* to carry, convey; akin to OE *faran* to go — more at FARE] *vt* (bef. 12c) **1 a** : to carry by boat over a body of water **b** : to cross by a ferry **2 a** : to convey (as by aircraft or motor vehicle) from one place to another : TRANSPORT **b** : to fly (an airplane) from the factory or other shipping point to a designated delivery point or from one base to another ~ *vi* : to cross water in a boat
²ferry *n, pl* **fer·ries** (15c) **1** : a place where persons or things are carried across a body of water (as a river) in a boat **2** : FERRYBOAT **3** : a franchise or right to operate a ferry service across a body of water **4** : an organized service and route for flying airplanes esp. across a sea or continent for delivery to the user
fer·ry·boat \'fer-ē-,bōt\ *n* (15c) : a boat used to ferry passengers, vehicles, or goods
fer·ry·man \-mən\ *n* (15c) : a person who operates a ferry
fer·tile \'fər-tʰl\ *adj* [ME, fr. MF & L; MF, fr. L *fertilis,* fr. *ferre* to carry, bear — more at BEAR] (15c) **1 a** : producing or bearing fruit in great quantities : PRODUCTIVE **b** : characterized by great resourcefulness of thought or imagination : INVENTIVE ⟨a ~ mind⟩ **c** *obs* : PLENTIFUL **2 a** (1) : capable of sustaining abundant plant growth ⟨~ soil⟩ (2) : affording abundant possibilities for development ⟨a ~ area for research⟩ **b** : capable of growing or developing ⟨~ egg⟩ **c** (1) : capable of producing fruit (2) *of an anther* : containing pollen (3) : developing spores or spore-bearing organs **d** : capable of breeding or reproducing **3** : capable of being converted into fissionable material ⟨~ uranium 238⟩ — **fer·tile·ly** \-tʰl-(l)ē\ *adv* — **fer·tile·ness** \-tʰl-nəs\ *n*
syn FERTILE, FECUND, FRUITFUL, PROLIFIC mean producing or capable of producing offspring or fruit. FERTILE implies the power to reproduce in kind or to assist in reproduction and growth ⟨fertile soil⟩; applied figuratively, it suggests readiness of invention and development ⟨a fertile imagination⟩. FECUND emphasizes abundance or rapidity in bearing fruit or offspring ⟨a fecund herd⟩. FRUITFUL adds to FERTILE and FECUND the implication of desirable or useful results ⟨fruitful research⟩. PROLIFIC stresses rapidity of spreading or multiplying by or as if by natural reproduction ⟨a prolific writer⟩.
fer·til·i·ty \(,)fər-'til-ə-tē\ *n* (15c) **1** : the quality or state of being fertile **2** : the birthrate of a population
fer·til·iza·tion \,fər-tʰl-ə-'zā-shən\ *n* (ca. 1787) : an act or process of making fertile: as **a** : the application of fertilizer **b** (1) : an act or process of fecundation, insemination, or pollination — not used technically (2) : the process of union of two gametes whereby the somatic chromosome number is restored and the development of a new individual is initiated
fertilization membrane *n* (1931) : a resistant membranous layer in eggs of many animals that forms following fertilization by the thickening and separation of the vitelline membrane from the cell surface and that prevents multiple fertilization
fer·til·ize \'fər-tʰl-,īz\ *vt* **-ized; -iz·ing** (1648) : to make fertile: as **a** : to apply a fertilizer to ⟨~ land⟩ **b** : to cause the fertilization of — **fer·til·iz·able** \-,ī-zə-bəl\ *adj*
fer·til·iz·er \-,ī-zər\ *n* (ca. 1661) : one that fertilizes; *specif* : a substance (as manure or a chemical mixture) used to make soil more fertile
fer·ule \'fer-əl\ *also* **fer·u·la** \'fer-(y)ə-lə\ *n* [L *ferula* giant fennel, ferule] (1580) **1** : an instrument (as a flat piece of wood like a ruler) used to punish children ⟨~ school discipline
fe·ru·lic acid \fə-'rü-lik-\ *n* [*ferula*] (1876) : a white crystalline acid that is structurally related to vanillin and is obtained esp. from plant sources (as aspen bark)
fer·ven·cy \'fər-vən-sē\ *n, pl* **-cies** (15c) : FERVOR
fer·vent \'fər-vənt\ *adj* [ME, fr. MF & L; MF, fr. L *fervent-, fervens,* prp. of *fervēre* to boil, froth — more at BARM] (14c) **1** : very hot : GLOWING **2** : exhibiting or marked by great intensity of feeling : ZEALOUS ⟨~ prayers⟩ **syn** see IMPASSIONED — **fer·vent·ly** *adv*
fer·vid \'fər-vəd\ *adj* [L *fervidus,* fr. *fervēre*] (1599) **1** : very hot : BURNING **2** : marked by often extreme fervor ⟨a ~ crusader⟩ **syn** see IMPASSIONED — **fer·vid·ly** *adv* — **fer·vid·ness** *n*
fer·vor \'fər-vər\ *n* [ME *fervour,* fr. MF & L; MF *ferveur,* fr. L *fervor,* fr. *fervēre*] (14c) **1** : intensity of feeling or expression ⟨booing and cheering with almost equal ~ —Alan Rich⟩ **2** : intense heat **syn** see PASSION
fer·vour *chiefly Brit var of* FERVOR
fes·cen·nine \'fe-sᵊn-,īn, -,ēn\ *adj* [L *fescennini* (versus), ribald songs sung at rustic weddings, prob. fr. *Fescinninus* of Fescennium, fr. *Fescennium,* town in Etruria] (1601) : SCURRILOUS, OBSCENE
fes·cue \'fes-(,)kyü\ *n* [ME *festu* stalk, straw, fr. MF, fr. LL *festucum,* fr. L *festuca*] (1513) **1** : a small pointer (as a stick) used to point out letters to children learning to read **2** : any of a genus (*Festuca*) of tufted perennial grasses with panicled spikelets
fescue foot *n* (1949) : a disease of the feet of cattle resembling ergotism that is associated with feeding on fescue grass and esp. tall fescue
¹fess *also* **fesse** \'fes\ *n* [ME *fesse,* fr. MF *faisse,* fr. L *fascia* band — more at FASCIA] (15c) **1** : a broad horizontal bar across the middle of a heraldic field **2** : the center point of an armorial escutcheon
²fess \'fes\ *vi* [short for *confess*] (1840) : to own up : CONFESS — usu. used with *up*
-fest \,fest\ *n comb form* [G, fr. *Fest* celebration, fr. L *festum* — more at FEAST] : meeting or occasion marked by (such) activity ⟨songfest⟩
fes·tal \'fes-tʰl\ *adj* [L *festum*] (15c) : of or relating to a feast or festival : FESTIVE — **fes·tal·ly** \-tʰl-ē\ *adv*

¹fes·ter \'fes-tər\ *n* [ME, fr. MF *festre,* fr. L *fistula* pipe, fistulous ulcer] (14c) : a suppurating sore : PUSTULE
²fester *vb* **fes·tered; fes·ter·ing** \-t(ə-)riŋ\ *vi* (14c) **1** : to generate pus **2** : PUTREFY, ROT **3 a** : to cause increasing poisoning, irritation, or bitterness : RANKLE ⟨dissent ~ed unchecked⟩ **b** : to undergo or exist in a state of progressive deterioration (allowed slums to ~) ~ *vt* : to make inflamed or corrupt
¹fes·ti·nate \'fes-tə-,nāt\ *vb* **-nat·ed; -nat·ing** (1596) : HASTEN
²fes·ti·nate \-nət, -,nāt\ *adj* [L *festinatus,* pp. of *festinare* to hasten; perh. akin to MIr *bras* forceful, W *brys* haste] (1605) : HASTY — **fes·ti·nate·ly** *adv*
¹fes·ti·val \'fes-tə-vəl\ *adj* [ME, fr. MF, fr. L *festivus* festive] (14c) : of, relating to, appropriate to, or set apart as a festival
²festival *n* (1589) **1 a** : a time of celebration marked by special observances **b** : FEAST **2** : a periodic season or program of cultural events or entertainment **3** : GAIETY, CONVIVIALITY
fes·ti·val·go·er \-,gō(-ə)r\ *n* (1959) : one who attends a festival
fes·tive \'fes-tiv\ *adj* [L *festivus,* fr. *festum*] (1651) **1** : of, relating to, or suitable for a feast or festival **2** : JOYFUL, GAY — **fes·tive·ly** *adv* — **fes·tive·ness** *n*
fes·tiv·i·ty \fes-'ti-və-tē, fəs-\ *n, pl* **-ties** (14c) **1** : FESTIVAL 1 **2** : the quality or state of being festive : GAIETY **3** : festive activity
fes·toon \fes-'tün\ *n* [F *feston,* fr. It *festone,* fr. *festa* festival, fr. L — more at FEAST] (1630) **1** : a decorative chain or strip hanging between two points **2** : a carved, molded, or painted ornament representing a decorative chain
²festoon *vt* (1800) **1** : to hang or form festoons on **2** : to shape into festoons **3** : DECORATE, ADORN
fes·toon·ery \fes-'tü-nə-rē\ *n* (1836) : an arrangement of festoons
Fest·schrift \'fes(t)-,shrift\ *n, pl* **Fest·schrif·ten** \-,shrif-tən\ *or* **Fest·schrifts** [G, fr. *Fest* celebration + *Schrift* writing] (1898) : a volume of writings by different authors presented as a tribute or memorial esp. to a scholar
fe·ta \'fe-tə, 'fe-,tä\ *n, often cap* [NGk (tyri) *pheta,* fr. *tyri* cheese + *pheta* slice, fr. It *fetta* — more at FETTUCCINE] (1940) : a white moderately hard and crumbly Greek cheese made from sheep's or goat's milk and cured in brine
fe·tal \'fē-tʰl\ *adj* (1811) : of, relating to, or being a fetus
fetal alcohol syndrome *n* (1974) : a highly variable group of birth defects including mental retardation, deficient growth, and defects of the skull, face, and brain that tend to occur in the infants of women who consume large amounts of alcohol during pregnancy
fetal hemoglobin *n* (1950) : a hemoglobin variant that predominates in the blood of a newborn and persists in increased proportions in some forms of anemia (as thalassemia)
fetal position *n* (1963) : a position (as of a sleeping person) in which the body lies on one side, curled up with the arms and legs drawn up toward the chest and the head bowed forward
¹fetch \'fech\ *vb* [ME *fecchen,* fr. OE *fetian, feccan;* perh. akin to OE *fōt* foot — more at FOOT] *vt* (bef. 12c) **1 a** : to go or come after and bring or take back **b** : DERIVE, DEDUCE **2 a** : to cause to come **b** : to bring in (as a price) : REALIZE **c** : INTEREST, ATTRACT **3 a** : to give (a blow) by striking : DEAL **b** *chiefly dial* : BRING ABOUT, ACCOMPLISH **c** (1) : to take in (as a breath) : DRAW (2) : to bring forth (as a sound) : HEAVE ⟨~ a sigh⟩ **4 a** : to reach by sailing esp. against the wind or tide **b** : to arrive at : REACH ~ *vi* **1** : to get and bring something; *specif* : to retrieve killed game **2** : to take a roundabout way : CIRCLE **3 a** : to hold a course on a body of water **b** : VEER — **fetch·er** *n*
²fetch *n* (ca. 1530) **1** : TRICK, STRATAGEM **2** : an act or instance of fetching **3 a** : the distance along open water or land over which the wind blows **b** : the distance traversed by waves without obstruction
³fetch *n* [origin unknown] (ca. 1787) : DOPPELGÄNGER 1
fetch·ing \'fe-chiŋ\ *adj* (1880) : ATTRACTIVE, PLEASING — **fetch·ing·ly** \-chiŋ-lē\ *adv*
fetch up *vt* (1599) **1** : to bring up or out : PRODUCE **2** : to make up (as lost time) **3** : to bring to a stop ~ *vi* : to reach a standstill, stopping place, or goal : end up ⟨may have *fetched up* running a village store —Geoffrey Household⟩
¹fete *or* **fête** \'fāt, 'fet\ *n* [ME *fete,* fr. MF, fr. OF *feste* — more at FEAST] (15c) **1** : FESTIVAL **2 a** : a lavish often outdoor entertainment **b** : a large elaborate party
²fete *or* **fête** *vt* **fet·ed** *or* **fêt·ed; fet·ing** *or* **fêt·ing** (1819) **1** : to honor or commemorate with a fete **2** : to pay high honor to
fête cham·pê·tre \,fāt-,shäⁿ(m)-'petrᵊ, ,fet-\ *n, pl* **fêtes champêtres** \same\ [F, lit., rural festival] (1774?) : an outdoor entertainment
fe·ti·cide \'fē-tə-,sīd\ *n* (ca. 1844) : the act of causing the death of a fetus
fet·id \'fe-təd, *esp Brit* 'fē-tid\ *adj* [ME, fr. L *foetidus,* fr. *foetēre* to stink] (15c) : having a heavy offensive smell **syn** see MALODOROUS — **fet·id·ly** *adv* — **fet·id·ness** *n*
fe·tish *also* **fe·tich** \'fe-tish *also* 'fē-\ *n* [F & Pg; F *fétiche,* Pg *feitiço,* fr. *feitiço* artificial, false, fr. L *facticius* factitious] (1613) **1 a** : an object (as a small stone carving of an animal) believed to have magical power to protect or aid its owner; *broadly* : a material object regarded with superstitious or extravagant trust or reverence **b** : an object of irrational reverence or obsessive devotion : PREPOSSESSION **c** : an object or bodily part whose real or fantasied presence is psychologically necessary for sexual gratification and that is an object of fixation to the extent that it may interfere with complete sexual expression **2** : a rite or cult of fetish worshipers **3** : FIXATION
fe·tish·ism *also* **fe·tich·ism** \-tish-,i-zəm\ *n* (1801) **1** : belief in magical fetishes **2** : extravagant irrational devotion **3** : the pathological displacement of erotic interest and satisfaction to a fetish — **fe·tish·ist** \-tish-ist\ *n* — **fe·tish·is·tic** \,fe-ti-'shis-tik *also* ,fē-\ *adj* — **fe·tish·is·ti·cal·ly** \-ti-k(ə-)lē\ *adv*
fet·lock \'fet-,läk\ *n* [ME *fitlok, fetlak;* akin to OE *fōt* foot] (14c) **1 a** : a projection bearing a tuft of hair on the back of the leg above the hoof of a horse or similar animal — see HORSE illustration **b** : the tuft of hair itself **2** : the joint of the limb at the fetlock
feto- *or* **feti-** *comb form* [NL *fetus*] : fetus ⟨feticide⟩
fe·tol·o·gy \fē-'tä-lə-jē\ *n* (1965) : a branch of medical science concerned with the study and treatment of the fetus in the uterus — **fe·tol·o·gist** \-jist\ *n*

fe·to·pro·tein \,fē-tō-'prō-,tēn, -'prō-tē-ən\ n (1965) : any of several fetal antigens present in the adult in some abnormal conditions

fe·tor \'fē-tər, 'fē-,tór\ n [ME *fetoure*, fr. L *foetor*, fr. *foetēre*] (15c) : a strong offensive smell : STENCH

fe·tos·co·py \fē-'täs-kə-pē\ n, pl **-pies** (1971) : examination of the pregnant uterus by means of a fiber-optic tube — **fe·to·scope** \'fē-tə-,skōp\ n

¹fet·ter \'fet-ər\ n [ME *feter*, fr. OE; akin to OE *fōt* foot] (bef. 12c) 1 : a chain or shackle for the feet 2 : something that confines : RESTRAINT

²fetter vt (bef. 12c) 1 : to put fetters on : SHACKLE 2 : to restrain from motion, action, or progress *syn* see HAMPER

¹fet·tle \'fet-ᵊl\ n (1740) : state or condition of health, fitness, wholeness, spirit, or form — often used in the phrase *in fine fettle*

²fettle vt **fet·tled; fet·tling** \'fet-liŋ, 'fe-tᵊl-iŋ\ [ME *fetlen* to shape, prepare; perh. akin to OE *fæt* vessel — more at VAT] (1881) : to cover or line the hearth of (as a reverberatory furnace) with loose material (as sand or gravel)

fet·tuc·ci·ne or **fet·tuc·ci·ni** or **fet·tu·ci·ne** or **fet·tu·ci·ni** \,fe-tə-'chē-nē\ n pl but sing or pl in constr [It, pl. of *fettuccina*, dim. of *fettuccia* small slice, ribbon, dim. of *fetta* slice, prob. alter. of (assumed) *offetta*, fr. *offa* flour cake, fr. L] (1912) : pasta in the form of narrow ribbons; *also* : a dish of which fettuccine forms the base

fettuccine Al·fre·do \-(,)al-'frā-(,)dō, -(,)äl-\ n [fr. *Alfredo all'-Augusteo*, restaurant in Rome where it originated] (1961) : a dish consisting of fettuccine with butter, Parmesan cheese, cream, and seasonings — called also *fettuccine all'Alfredo* \-,al-(,)al-, -,äl-(,)äl-\

fe·tus \'fē-təs\ n [ME, fr. L, act of bearing young, offspring; akin to L *fetus* newly delivered, fruitful — more at FEMININE] (14c) : an unborn or unhatched vertebrate esp. after attaining the basic structural plan of its kind; *specif* : a developing human from usu. three months after conception to birth

¹feud \'fyüd\ n [alter. of ME *feide*, fr. MF, of Gmc origin; akin to OHG *fēhida* hostility, feud, OE *fāh* hostile — more at FOE] (15c) : a mutual enmity or quarrel that is often prolonged or inveterate; *esp* : a lasting state of hostilities between families or clans marked by violent attacks for revenge — **feud** vi

²feud n [ML *feodum, feudum*, of Gmc origin; akin to OE *feoh* cattle, property — more at FEE] (1614) : FEE 1a

feu·dal \'fyü-dᵊl\ adj (1612) 1 : of, relating to, or having the characteristics of a medieval fee 2 : of, relating to, or suggestive of feudalism ⟨~ law⟩ — **feu·dal·ly** \-dᵊl-ē\ adv

feu·dal·ism \'fyü-dᵊl-,i-zəm\ n (ca. 1818) 1 : the system of political organization prevailing in Europe from the 9th to about the 15th centuries having as its basis the relation of lord to vassal with all land held in fee and as chief characteristics homage, the service of tenants under arms and in court, wardship, and forfeiture 2 : any of various political or social systems similar to medieval feudalism — **feu·dal·ist** \-dᵊl-ist\ n — **feu·dal·is·tic** \,fyü-dᵊl-'is-tik\ adj

feu·dal·i·ty \fyü-'da-lə-tē\ n, pl **-ties** (1790) 1 : the quality or state of being feudal 2 : a feudal holding, domain, or concentration of power

feu·dal·ize \'fyü-dᵊl-,iz\ vt **-ized; -iz·ing** (1828) : to make feudal — **feu·dal·iza·tion** \,fyü-dᵊl-ə-'zā-shən\ n

¹feu·da·to·ry \'fyü-də-,tōr-ē, -,tór-\ adj [ML *feudatorius*, fr. *feudatus*, pp. of *feudare* to enfeoff, fr. *feudum*] (1592) 1 : owing feudal allegiance 2 : being under the overlordship of a foreign state

²feudatory n, pl **-ries** (1644) 1 : a dependent lordship : FEE 2 : one holding lands by feudal tenure

¹feud·ist \'fyü-dist\ n (1607) : a specialist in feudal law

²feudist n (1901) : one who feuds

feuil·le·ton \,fə-yə-'tō⁽ⁿ⁾, ,fər-, ,fœ-\ n [F, fr. *feuillet* sheet of paper, fr. OF *foillet*, dim. of *foille* leaf — more at FOIL] (1845) 1 : a part of a European newspaper or magazine devoted to material designed to entertain the general reader 2 : something (as an installment of a novel) printed in a feuilleton 3 : a novel printed in installments **b** : a work of fiction catering to popular taste 4 : a short literary composition often having a familiar tone and reminiscent content — **feuil·le·ton·ism** \-'tō⁽ⁿ⁾-,ni-zəm\ n — **feuil·le·ton·ist** \-nist\ n

Feul·gen \'fóil-gən\ adj (1928) : of, relating to, utilizing, or staining by the Feulgen reaction (positive ~ mitochondria)

Feulgen reaction n [Robert *Feulgen* †1955 Ger. physiologist] (1928) : the development of a brilliant purple color by DNA in a microscopic preparation stained with modified Schiff's reagent

¹fe·ver \'fē-vər\ n [ME, fr. OE *fēfer*, fr. L *febris*] (bef. 12c) 1 **a** : a rise of body temperature above the normal **b** : any of various diseases of which fever is a prominent symptom 2 **a** : a state of heightened or intense emotion or activity **b** : a contagious usu. transient enthusiasm : CRAZE

²fever vb **fe·vered; fe·ver·ing** \'fē-v(ə-)riŋ\ vt (1606) : to throw into a fever : AGITATE ~ vi : to contract or be in a fever : become feverish

fever blister n (ca. 1860) : COLD SORE

fe·ver·few \'fē-vər-,fyü\ n [ME, fr. OE *feferfuge*, fr. LL *febrifugia* centaury — more at FEBRIFUGE] (15c) : a perennial European composite herb (*Chrysanthemum parthenium*) widely cultivated as an ornamental

fe·ver·ish \'fē-v(ə-)rish\ adj (14c) 1 **a** : tending to cause fever **b** : having the symptoms of a fever **c** : indicating or relating to fever 2 : marked by intense emotion, activity, or instability — **fe·ver·ish·ly** adv — **fe·ver·ish·ness** n

fe·ver·ous \'fē-v(ə-)rəs\ adj (14c) : FEVERISH

fever pitch n (1915) : a state of intense excitement and agitation

fever tree n (1868) : any of several shrubs or trees that are thought to indicate regions free from fever or that yield remedies for fever; *esp* : an African acacia (*Acacia xanthlophloea*)

fe·ver·wort \'fē-vər-,wərt, -,wórt\ n (ca. 1814) : a coarse American herb (*Triosteum perfoliatum*) of the honeysuckle family — called also *horse gentian*

¹few \'fyü\ pron, pl in constr [ME *fewe*, pron. & adj., fr. OE *fēawa*; akin to OHG *fō* little, L *paucus* little, *pauper* poor, Gk *paid*-, *pais* child, Skt *putra* son] (bef. 12c) : not many persons or things ⟨~ were present⟩ ⟨~ of his stories are true⟩

²few adj (bef. 12c) 1 : consisting of or amounting to only a small number ⟨one of our ~ pleasures⟩ 2 : at least some but indeterminately small in number — used with *a* ⟨caught a ~ fish⟩ — **few·ness** n

few and far between : few in number and infrequently met : RARE

³few n, pl in constr (bef. 12c) 1 : a small number of units or individuals ⟨a ~ of them⟩ 2 : a special limited number ⟨the discriminating ~⟩

¹few·er \'fyü-ər, 'fyúr\ pron, pl in constr (bef. 12c) : a smaller number of persons or things

²fewer adj, comparative of FEW   *usage* see LESS

few·trils \'fyü-trəlz\ n pl [origin unknown] (ca. 1750) *dial Eng* : things of little value : TRIFLES

fey \'fā\ adj [ME *feye*, fr. OE *fǣge*; akin to OHG *feigi* fey and perh. to OE *fāh* hostile, outlawed — more at FOE] (bef. 12c) 1 **a** *chiefly Scot* : fated to die : DOOMED **b** : marked by a foreboding of death or calamity 2 **a** : able to see into the future : VISIONARY **b** : marked by an otherworldly air or attitude **c** : CRAZY, TOUCHED 3 **a** : PRECIOUS 3 **b** : UNCONVENTIONAL, CAMPY — **fey·ly** adv — **fey·ness** n

fez \'fez\ n, pl **fez·zes** also **fez·es** [F, fr. *Fez*, Morocco] (ca. 1803) : a brimless cone-shaped flat-crowned hat that usu. has a tassel, is usu. made of red felt, and is worn esp. by men in eastern Mediterranean countries — **fezzed** \'fezd\ adj

fi·acre \fē-'äkr⁵\ n, pl **fi·acres** \same, or -'äk-rəz\ [F, fr. the Hotel St. *Fiacre*, Paris] (1699) : a small hackney coach

fi·an·cé \,fē-,än-'sā, fē-'än-,\ n [F, fr. MF, fr. pp. of *fiancer* to promise, betroth, fr. OF *fiancier*, fr. *fiance* promise, trust, fr. *fier* to trust, fr. (assumed) VL *fidare*, alter. of L *fidere* — more at BIDE] (1864) : a man engaged to be married

fi·an·cée \,fē-,än-'sā, fē-'än-,\ n [F, fem. of *fiancé*] (1853) : a woman engaged to be married

fi·an·chet·to \,fē-ən-'ke-(,)tō, -'che-\ vb [fianchetto (an opening in chess), fr. It, dim. of *fianco* side, flank, fr. OF *flanc* — more at FLANK] vt (1927) : to develop (a bishop) in a chess game to the second square on the adjacent knight's file ~ vi : to fianchetto a bishop in a chess game

¹fi·as·co \fē-'as-(,)kō also -'äs-\ n, pl **-coes** [F, fr. It, fr. *fare fiasco*, lit., to make a bottle] (ca. 1854) : a complete failure

²fi·as·co \fē-'äs-(,)kō, -'as-\ n, pl **-coes** also **fi·as·chi** \-(,)kē\ [It, fr. LL *flasco* bottle — more at FLASK] (1887) : BOTTLE, FLASK; *esp* : a bulbous long-necked straw-covered bottle for wine

fi·at \'fē-ət, -,at, -,ät; 'fī-ət, -,at\ n [L, let it be done, 3d sing. pres. subj. of *fieri* to become, be done — more at BE] (ca. 1631) 1 : a command or act of will that creates something without or as if without further effort 2 : an authoritative determination : DICTATE ⟨a ~ of conscience⟩ 3 : an authoritative or arbitrary order : DECREE ⟨government by ~⟩

fiat money n (1876) : money (as paper currency) not convertible into coin or specie of equivalent value

¹fib \'fib\ n [perh. by shortening & alter. fr. *fable*] (1611) : a trivial or childish lie

²fib vi **fibbed; fib·bing** (1690) : to tell a fib *syn* see LIE — **fib·ber** n

³fib vb **fibbed; fib·bing** [origin unknown] (ca. 1665) *Brit* : BEAT, PUMMEL

fi·ber or **fi·bre** \'fī-bər\ n [F *fibre*, fr. L *fibra*] (1540) 1 : a thread or a structure or object resembling a thread: as **a** (1) : a slender root (as of a grass) (2) : an elongated tapering thick-walled plant cell void at maturity that imparts elasticity, flexibility, and tensile strength **b** (1) : a strand of nerve tissue : AXON, DENDRITE (2) : one of the filaments composing most of the intercellular matrix of connective tissue (3) : one of the elongated contractile cells of muscle tissue **c** : a slender and greatly elongated natural or synthetic filament (as of wool, cotton, asbestos, gold, glass, or rayon) typically capable of being spun into yarn **d** : indigestible material in human food that stimulates the intestine to peristalsis — called also *bulk, roughage* 2 : material made of fibers; *esp* : VULCANIZED FIBER 3 **a** : an element that gives texture or substance **b** : basic toughness : STRENGTH, FORTITUDE **c** : essential structure or character ⟨the very ~ of a person's being⟩ — **fi·bered** \-bərd\ adj

fi·ber·board also **fi·bre·board** \-,bōrd, -,bórd\ n (1897) : a material made by compressing fibers (as of wood) into stiff sheets; *also* : PAPERBOARD

fi·ber·fill also **fi·bre·fill** \-,fil\ n (1962) : synthetic fibers used as a filling material (as for cushions)

¹fi·ber·glass also **fi·bre·glass** \-,glas\ n (1937) 1 : glass in fibrous form used in making various products (as glass wool for insulation) 2 : a composite structural material of plastic and fiberglass

²fiberglass vt (1967) : to protect or repair by the application of fiberglass

fi·ber·ize \'fī-bə-,rīz\ vt **-ized; -iz·ing** (1925) : to make or break down into fibers — **fi·ber·iza·tion** \,fī-b(ə-)rə-'zā-shən\ n

fi·ber–op·tic \'fī-bə-,räp-tik\ adj (1961) : of, relating to, or using fiber optics

fiber optics n pl (1956) 1 : thin transparent fibers of glass or plastic that are enclosed by material of a lower index of refraction and that transmit light throughout their length by internal reflections; *also* : a bundle of such fibers used in an instrument (as for viewing body cavities) 2 sing in constr : the technique of the use of fiber optics

fi·ber·scope \'fī-bər-,skōp\ n (1954) : a flexible instrument utilizing fiber optics and used for examination of inaccessible areas

Fi·bo·nac·ci number \,fē-bə-,nä-chē-, ,fi-bə-\ n [Leonardo *Fibonacci* †ab 1250 Ital. mathematician] (1914) : an integer in the infinite sequence 1, 1, 2, 3, 5, 8, 13, . . . of which the first two terms are 1 and 1 and each succeeding term is the sum of the two immediately preceding

fibr- or **fibro-** comb form [L *fibra*] : fiber : fibrous tissue ⟨*fibroid*⟩ : fibrous and ⟨*fibrovascular*⟩

fi·branne \'fē-,bran, fi-'\ n [F, viscose rayon, fr. *fibre*] (1941) : a fabric made of spun-rayon yarn

fi·bril \'fī-brəl, 'fi-\ n [NL *fibrilla*, dim. of L *fibra*] (1664) : a small filament or fiber: as **a** : ROOT HAIR **b** (1) : one of the fine threads into which a striated muscle fiber can be longitudinally split (2) : NEUROFIBRIL — **fi·bril·lar** \'fī-brə-lər, 'fi-\ adj

---

\ə\ abut \ᵊ\ kitten, F table \ər\ further \a\ ash \ā\ ace \ä\ mop, mar \aú\ out \ch\ chin \e\ bet \ē\ easy \g\ go \i\ hit \ī\ ice \j\ job \ŋ\ sing \ō\ go \ó\ law \ói\ boy \th\ thin \t̲h̲\ the \ü\ loot \ú\ foot \y\ yet \zh\ vision \á, k̲, ⁿ, œ, œ̄, ᵫ, ᵫ̄, ᵊ\ see Guide to Pronunciation

fi·bril·late \'fi-brə-ˌlāt, 'fī-\ *vb* **-lat·ed; -lat·ing** *vi* (ca. 1847) : to undergo or exhibit fibrillation ~ *vt* : to cause to undergo fibrillation

fi·bril·la·tion \ˌfi-brə-'lā-shən, ˌfī-\ *n* (1845) **1** : an act or process of forming fibers or fibrils **2 a** : a muscular twitching involving individual muscle fibers acting without coordination **b** : very rapid irregular contractions of the muscle fibers of the heart resulting in a lack of synchronism between heartbeat and pulse

fi·brin \'fī-brən\ *n* (1800) : a white insoluble fibrous protein formed from fibrinogen by the action of thrombin esp. in the clotting of blood

fi·brin·o·gen \fī-'bri-nə-jən\ *n* [ISV] (1872) : a plasma protein that is produced in the liver and is converted into fibrin during blood clot formation

fi·bri·noid \'fī-brə-ˌnoid, 'fī-\ *n, often attrib* (1910) : a homogeneous acidophilic refractile material that somewhat resembles fibrin and is formed in the walls of blood vessels and in connective tissue in some pathological conditions and normally in the placenta

fi·bri·no·ly·sin \ˌfī-brə-nᵊl-'ī-sᵊn\ *n* [ISV] (1915) : any of several proteolytic enzymes that promote the dissolution of blood clots; *esp* : PLASMIN

fi·bri·no·ly·sis \-'ī-səs, -brə-'nä-lə-səs\ *n* [NL] (1907) : the usu. enzymatic breakdown of fibrin — **fi·bri·no·lyt·ic** \-brə-nᵊl-'i-tik\ *adj*

fi·bri·no·pep·tide \ˌfī-brə-nō-'pep-ˌtīd\ *n* (1960) : any of the vertebrate polypeptides that are cleaved from fibrinogen by thrombin during blood clot formation

fi·bro·blast \'fī-brə-ˌblast, 'fi-\ *n* [ISV] (1876) : a connective-tissue cell of mesenchymal origin that secretes proteins and esp. molecular collagen from which the extracellular fibrillar matrix of connective tissue forms — **fi·bro·blas·tic** \ˌfī-brə-'blas-tik, ˌfi-\ *adj*

fi·bro·cys·tic \ˌfī-brə-'sis-tik, ˌfi-\ *adj* (1854) : characterized by the presence or development of fibrous tissue and cysts

¹fi·broid \'fī-ˌbroid, 'fi-\ *adj* (1852) : resembling, forming, or consisting of fibrous tissue

²fibroid *n* (ca. 1860) : a benign tumor that consists of fibrous and muscular tissue and occurs esp. in the uterine wall

fi·bro·in \'fī-brə-wən, 'fi-\ *n* [F *fibroïne*, fr. *fibr-* + *-ine* -in] (1878) : an insoluble protein comprising the filaments of the raw silk fiber

fi·bro·ma \fī-'brō-mə\ *n, pl* **-mas** *also* **-ma·ta** \-mə-tə\ (ca. 1849) : a benign tumor consisting mainly of fibrous tissue — **fi·bro·ma·tous** \-mə-təs\ *adj*

fi·bro·nec·tin \ˌfī-brə-'nek-tən\ *n* [*fibr-* + L *nectere* to tie, bind + E *-in*] (1976) : any of a group of glycoproteins of cell surfaces, blood plasma, and connective tissue that promote cellular adhesion and migration

fi·bro·sar·co·ma \ˌfī-brə-sär-'kō-mə, ˌfi-\ *n* (1878) : a sarcoma of relatively low malignancy consisting chiefly of spindle-shaped cells that tend to form collagenous fibrils

fi·bro·sis \fī-'brō-səs\ *n* [NL] (1873) : a condition marked by increase of interstitial fibrous tissue — **fi·brot·ic** \-'brä-tik\ *adj*

fi·bro·si·tis \ˌfī-brə-'sī-təs, ˌfi-\ *n* [NL, fr. *fibrosus* fibrous, fr. ISV *fibrous*] (1904) : a rheumatic disorder of fibrous tissue

fi·brous \'fī-brəs\ *adj* [modif. of F *fibreux*, fr. *fibre* fiber] (1626) **1 a** : containing, consisting of, or resembling fibers **b** : characterized by fibrosis **c** : capable of being separated into fibers ⟨a ~ mineral⟩ **2** : TOUGH, SINEWY ⟨~ texture⟩

fibrous root *n* (1626) : a root (as in most grasses) that has no prominent central axis and that branches in all directions

fi·bro·vas·cu·lar \'fī-brō-'vas-kyə-lər, ˌfi-\ *adj* (1845) : having or consisting of fibers and conducting cells

fibrovascular bundle *n* (ca. 1889) : VASCULAR BUNDLE

fib·u·la \'fi-byə-lə\ *n, pl* **-lae** \-ˌlē, -ˌlī\ *or* **-las** [L, pin, clasp; akin to L *figere* to fasten] (1615) **1** : the outer and usu. smaller of the two bones between the knee and ankle in the hind or lower limbs of vertebrates **2** : a clasp resembling a safety pin used esp. by the ancient Greeks and Romans — **fib·u·lar** \-lər\ *adj*

-fic \fik\ *adj suffix* [MF & L; MF *-fique*, fr. L *-ficus*, fr. *facere* to make — more at DO] : making : causing ⟨felici*fic*⟩

-fi·ca·tion \fə-'kā-shən\ *n comb form* [ME *-ficacioun*, fr. MF & L; MF *-fication*, fr. L *-fication-*, *-ficatio*, fr. *-ficare* to make, fr. *-ficus*] : making : production ⟨rei*fication*⟩

fice \'fīs\ *var of* FEIST

fiche \'fēsh *also* 'fish\ *n, pl* **fiche** *also* **fiches** (1951) : MICROFICHE

fi·chu \'fi-(ˌ)shü, 'fē-\ *n* [F, fr. pp. of *ficher* to stick in, throw on, fr. (assumed) VL *figicare*, fr. L *figere* to fasten, pierce] (1803) : a woman's light triangular scarf that is draped over the shoulders and fastened in front or worn to fill in a low neckline

fi·cin \'fī-sᵊn\ *n* [L *ficus* fig] (1930) : a protease obtained from the latex of fig trees and used as an anthelmintic and protein digestive

fick·le \'fi-kəl\ *adj* [ME *fikel*, fr. OE *ficol* deceitful, inconstant, fr. OE *ficol* deceitful; akin to OE be*fician* to deceive, and prob. to OE *fāh* hostile — more at FOE] (13c) : marked by lack of steadfastness, constancy, or stability : given to erratic changeableness   *syn* see INCONSTANT — **fick·le·ness** *n* — **fick·ly** \'fi-k(ə-)lē\ *adv*

fi·co \'fē-(ˌ)kō\ *n, pl* **ficoes** [obs. *fico*, obscene gesture of contempt, modif. of It *fica* fig, vulva, gesture of contempt, fr. (assumed) VL *fica* fig — more at FIG] (1598) *archaic* : FIG 2

fic·tile \'fik-tᵊl, -ˌtīl\ *adj* [L *fictilis* molded of clay, fr. *fingere*] (1626) **1** *archaic* : PLASTIC 2a   **2** : of or relating to pottery   **3** : MALLEABLE 2a

fic·tion \'fik-shən\ *n* [ME *ficcioun*, fr. MF *fiction*, fr. L *fiction-*, *fictio* act of fashioning, fiction, fr. *fingere* to shape, fashion, feign — more at DOUGH] (14c) **1 a** : something invented by the imagination or feigned; *specif* : an invented story **b** : fictitious literature (as novels or short stories) **c** : a work of fiction; *esp* : NOVEL **2 a** : an assumption of a possibility as a fact irrespective of the question of its truth ⟨a legal ~⟩ **b** : a useful illusion or pretense **3** : the action of feigning or of creating with the imagination — **fic·tion·al** \-shnəl, -shə-nᵊl\ *adj* — **fic·tion·al·i·ty** \ˌfik-shə-'na-lə-tē\ *n* — **fic·tion·al·ly** \'fik-shnə-lē, -shə-nᵊl-ē\ *adv*

fictionalise *Brit var of* FICTIONALIZE

fic·tion·al·ize \'fik-shnə-ˌlīz, -shə-nᵊl-ˌīz\ *vt* **-ized; -iz·ing** (1918) : to make into or treat in the manner of fiction ⟨~ a biography⟩ — **fic·tion·al·iza·tion** \ˌfik-shnə-lə-'zā-shən, -shə-nᵊl-ə-\ *n*

fic·tion·eer \ˌfik-shə-'nir\ *n* (1923) : one who writes fiction esp. in quantity and without high standards — **fic·tion·eer·ing** *n*

fic·tion·ist \'fik-sh(ə-)nist\ *n* (1829) : a writer of fiction; *esp* : NOVELIST

fic·tion·ize \'fik-shə-ˌnīz\ *vt* **-ized; -iz·ing** (1831) : FICTIONALIZE — **fic·tion·iza·tion** \ˌfik-shə-nə-'zā-shən, -shə-nᵊl-ə-\ *n*

fic·ti·tious \fik-'ti-shəs\ *adj* [L *ficticius* artificial, feigned, fr. *fictus*] (1634) **1** : of, relating to, or characteristic of fiction : IMAGINARY **2 a** : conventionally or hypothetically assumed or accepted ⟨a ~ concept⟩ **b** *of a name* : FALSE, ASSUMED **3** : not genuinely felt — **fic·ti·tious·ly** *adv* — **fic·ti·tious·ness** *n*

syn FICTITIOUS, FABULOUS, LEGENDARY, MYTHICAL, APOCRYPHAL mean having the nature of something imagined or invented. FICTITIOUS implies fabrication and suggests artificiality or contrivance more than deliberate falsification or deception ⟨*fictitious* characters⟩. FABULOUS stresses the marvelous or incredible character of something without necessarily implying impossibility or actual nonexistence ⟨a land of *fabulous* riches⟩. LEGENDARY suggests the elaboration of invented details and distortion of historical facts produced by popular tradition ⟨the *legendary* exploits of Davy Crockett⟩. MYTHICAL implies a purely fanciful explanation of facts or the creation of beings and events out of the imagination ⟨*mythical* creatures⟩. APOCRYPHAL implies an unknown or dubious source or origin or may imply that the thing itself is dubious or inaccurate ⟨a book that repeats many *apocryphal* stories⟩.

fic·tive \'fik-tiv\ *adj* (1612) **1** : not genuine : FEIGNED **2** : of, relating to, or capable of imaginative creation **3** : of, relating to, or having the characteristics of fiction : FICTIONAL — **fic·tive·ly** *adv* — **fic·tive·ness** *n*

fi·cus \'fī-kəs\ *n, pl* **ficus** *or* **fi·cus·es** [NL, fr. L, fig] (1864) : FIG 1b

fid \'fid\ *n* [origin unknown] (1615) : a tapered usu. wooden pin used in opening the strands of a rope

-fid \fəd, ˌfid\ *adj comb form* [L *-fidus*, fr. *findere* to split — more at BITE] : divided into (so many) parts or (such) parts ⟨pinnati*fid*⟩

¹fid·dle \'fi-dᵊl\ *n* [ME *fidel*, fr. (assumed) OE *fithele*, prob. fr. ML *vitula*] (13c) **1** : VIOLIN **2** : a device (as a slat, rack, or light railing) to keep dishes from sliding off a table aboard ship **3** : FIDDLESTICKS — used as an interjection **4** [²*fiddle*] *chiefly Brit* : SWINDLE

²fiddle *vb* **fid·dled; fid·dling** \'fid-liŋ, 'fi-dᵊl-iŋ\ *vi* (14c) **1** : to play on a fiddle **2 a** : to move the hands or fingers restlessly **b** : to spend time in aimless or fruitless activity : PUTTER, TINKER ⟨*fiddled* around with the engine for hours⟩ **c** : MEDDLE, TAMPER ~ *vt* **1** : to play (as a tune) on a fiddle **2** : CHEAT, SWINDLE **3** : to alter or manipulate deceptively for fraudulent gain ⟨accountants *fiddling* the books —Stanley Cohen⟩ — **fid·dler** \'fid-lər, 'fi-dᵊl-ər\ *n*

fiddle away *vt* (1667) : to fritter away ⟨*fiddling away* the time⟩

fid·dle·back \'fi-dᵊl-ˌbak\ *n* (1890) : something resembling a fiddle

fid·dle–fad·dle \'fi-dᵊl-ˌfa-dᵊl\ *n* [redupl. of *fiddle* (fiddlesticks)] (1577) : NONSENSE — often used as an interjection

fid·dle–foot·ed \ˌfi-dᵊl-'fu-təd\ *adj* (1941) **1** : SKITTISH, JUMPY ⟨a ~ horse⟩ **2** : prone to wander ⟨the nameless ~ drifters, the shifty riders who traveled the back trails —Luke Short⟩

fid·dle·head \'fi-dᵊl-ˌhed\ *n* (1882) : one of the young unfurling fronds of some ferns that are often eaten as greens

fiddler crab *n* (1843) : any of a genus (*Uca*) of burrowing crabs in which the male has one claw that is greatly enlarged

fid·dle·stick \'fi-dᵊl-ˌstik\ *n* (15c) **1** : a violin bow **2 a** : something of little value : TRIFLE ⟨didn't care a ~ for that⟩ **b** *pl* : NONSENSE — used as an interjection

fiddler crab

fid·dling \'fid-liŋ, -lən\ *adj* (1652) : TRIFLING, PETTY ⟨a ~ excuse⟩

fid·dly \'fi-dᵊl-ē\ *adj* (1926) *chiefly Brit* : requiring close attention to detail : FUSSY

fi·de·ism \'fē-(ˌ)dā-ˌi-zəm\ *n* [prob. fr. F *fidéisme*, fr. L *fides*] (1885) : reliance upon faith rather than reason in pursuit of religious truth — **fi·de·ist** \-ˌdā-ist\ *n* — **fi·de·is·tic** \ˌfē-(ˌ)dā-'is-tik\ *adj*

Fi·del·is·ta \ˌfē-dᵊl-'ē-stə\ *n* [AmerSp, fr. *Fidel* Castro + *-ista* -ist] (1960) : an adherent of Castroism

fi·del·i·ty \fə-'de-lə-tē, fī-\ *n, pl* **-ties** [ME *fidelite*, fr. MF *fidelité*, fr. L *fidelitat-*, *fidelitas*, fr. *fidelis* faithful, fr. *fides* faith, fr. *fidere* to trust — more at BIDE] (15c) **1 a** : the quality or state of being faithful **b** : accuracy in details : EXACTNESS **2** : the degree to which an electronic device (as a record player, radio, or television) accurately reproduces its effect (as sound or picture)

syn FIDELITY, ALLEGIANCE, FEALTY, LOYALTY, DEVOTION, PIETY mean faithfulness to something to which one is bound by pledge or duty. FIDELITY implies strict and continuing faithfulness to an obligation, trust, or duty ⟨marital *fidelity*⟩. ALLEGIANCE suggests an adherence like that of citizens to their country ⟨pledging *allegiance*⟩. FEALTY implies a fidelity acknowledged by the individual and as compelling as a sworn vow ⟨*fealty* to the truth⟩. LOYALTY implies a faithfulness that is steadfast in the face of any temptation to renounce, desert, or betray ⟨valued the *loyalty* of his friends⟩. DEVOTION stresses zeal and service amounting to self-dedication ⟨a painter's *devotion* to her art⟩. PIETY stresses fidelity to obligations regarded as natural and fundamental ⟨filial *piety*⟩.

fidge \'fij\ *vi* **fidged; fidg·ing** [prob. alter. of E dial. *fitch*, fr. ME *fichen*] (1575) *chiefly Scot* : FIDGET

¹fidg·et \'fi-jət\ *n* [irreg. fr. *fidge*] (1674) **1** : uneasiness or restlessness as shown by nervous movements — usu. used in pl. **2** [²*fidget*] : one that fidgets

²fidget *vi* (1754) : to move or act restlessly or nervously ~ *vt* : to cause to move or act nervously

fidg·ety \'fi-jə-tē\ *adj* (ca. 1736) **1** : inclined to fidget **2** : making unnecessary fuss : FUSSY — **fidg·et·i·ness** *n*

fi·do \'fī-(ˌ)dō\ *n, pl* **fidos** [*freaks* + *irregulars* + *defects* + *oddities*] (1967) : a coin having a minting error

fi·du·cial \fə-'dü-shəl, -'dyü-, fĭ-\ *adj* (1571)   **1** : taken as standard of reference ⟨a ~ mark⟩   **2** : founded on faith or trust   **3** : having the nature of a trust : FIDUCIARY — **fi·du·cial·ly** \-shə-lē\ *adv*

¹fi·du·cia·ry \-'dü-shē-,er-ē, -shə-rē, -'dyü-\ *n, pl* **-ries** (1631) : one that holds a fiduciary relation or acts in a fiduciary capacity

²fiduciary *adj* [L *fiduciarius*, fr. *fiducia* confidence, trust, fr. *fidere*] (ca. 1641) : of, relating to, or involving a confidence or trust: as   **a** : held or founded in trust or confidence   **b** : holding in trust   **c** : depending on public confidence for value or currency ⟨~ fiat money⟩

fie \'fī\ *interj* [ME *fi*, fr. OF] (14c) — used to express disgust or disapproval

fief \'fēf\ *n* [F, fr. OF — more at FEE] (ca. 1611)   **1** : a feudal estate : FEE   **2** : something over which one has rights or exercises control ⟨a politician's ~⟩ — **fief·dom** \-dəm\ *n*

¹field \'fē(ə)ld\ *n* [ME, fr. OE *feld*; akin to OHG *feld* field, OE *flōr* floor — more at FLOOR] (bef. 12c)   **1 a** (1) : an open land area free of woods and buildings   (2) : an area of land marked by the presence of particular objects or features ⟨dune ~⟩   **b** (1) : an area of cleared enclosed land used for cultivation or pasture ⟨a ~ of wheat⟩   (2) : land containing a natural resource   **c** : the place where a battle is fought; *also* : BATTLE   **d** : a large unbroken expanse (as of ice)   **2 a** : an area or division of an activity   **b** : the sphere of practical operation outside a base (as a laboratory, office, or factory) ⟨geologists working in the ~⟩   **c** : an area for military exercises or maneuvers   **d** (1) : an area constructed, equipped, or marked for sports   (2) : the portion of an indoor or outdoor sports area enclosed by the running track and on which field events are conducted   (3) : any of the three sections of a baseball outfield ⟨hits to all ~s⟩   **3** : a space on which something is drawn or projected: as   **a** : the space on the surface of a coin, medal, or seal that does not contain the design   **b** : the ground of each division in a flag   **c** : the whole surface of an escutcheon   **4** : the individuals that make up all or part of the participants in a sports activity; *esp* : all participants with the exception of the favorite or the winner in a contest where more than two are entered   **5** : the area visible through the lens of an optical instrument   **6 a** : a region or space in which a given effect (as magnetism) exists   **b** : a region of embryonic tissue capable of a particular type of differentiation ⟨a morphogenetic ~⟩   **7** : a set of mathematical elements that is subject to two binary operations the second of which is distributive relative to the first and that constitutes a commutative group under the first operation and also under the second if the zero or unit element under the first is omitted   **8** : a complex of forces that serve as causative agents in human behavior   **9** : a series of drain tiles and an absorption area for septic-tank overflow   **10** : a particular area (as of a record in a database) in which the same type of information is regularly recorded

²field *adj* (12c) : of or relating to a field: as   **a** : growing in or inhabiting the fields or open country   **b** : made, conducted, or used in the field   **c** : operating or active in the field

³field *vt* (1823)   **1 a** : to catch or pick up ⟨a batted ball⟩ and usu. throw to a teammate   **b** : to take care of or respond to ⟨as a telephone call or a request⟩   **c** : to give an impromptu answer or solution to ⟨the senator ~ed the reporters' questions⟩   **2 a** : to put into the field ⟨~ an army⟩ ⟨~ a team⟩; *also* : to enter in competition ~ *vi* : to play as a fielder

field artillery *n* (1644) : artillery other than antiaircraft artillery used with armies in the field

field bed *n* (1926) : a four-poster with a canopy arched at the center

field corn *n* (1856) : an Indian corn (as dent corn or flint corn) with starchy kernels grown for feeding stock or for market grain

field crop *n* (1860) : an agricultural crop (as hay, grain, or cotton) grown on large areas

field day *n* (1747)   **1 a** : a day for military exercises or maneuvers   **b** : an outdoor meeting or social gathering   **c** : a day of sports and athletic competition   **2** : a time of extraordinary pleasure or opportunity ⟨the newspaper had a *field day* with the scandal⟩

field–ef·fect transistor \'fēl-də-,fekt-\ *n* (1959) : a transistor in which the output current is controlled by a variable electric field

field·er \'fēl-dər\ *n* (1832) : one that fields; *esp* : a defensive player stationed in the field (as in baseball)

fielder's choice *n* (1902) : a situation in baseball in which a batter reaches base safely because the fielder attempts to put out another base runner on the play

field event *n* (1899) : an event (as weight-throwing or jumping) in a track-and-field meet other than a race

field·fare \'fēl(d)-,far, -,fer\ *n* [ME *feldefare*, fr. OE, fr. *feld* + *-fare*; prob. akin to OE *fara* companion; akin to OE *faran* to go — more at FARE] (bef. 12c) : a medium-sized Eurasian thrush (*Turdus pilaris*) with an ash-colored head and chestnut wings

field glass *n* (1836) : a binocular without prisms esp. for use outdoors — usu. used in pl.

field goal *n* (1902)   **1** : a score of three points in football made by drop-kicking or place-kicking the ball over the crossbar from ordinary play   **2** : a goal in basketball made while the ball is in play

field grade *n* (1944) : the rank of a field officer

field guide *n* (1934) : a manual for identifying natural objects, flora, or fauna in the field

field hand *n* (1826) : an outdoor farm laborer

field hockey *n* (1903) : a game played on a turfed field between two teams of 11 players each whose object is to direct a ball into the opponent's goal with a hockey stick

field house *n* (1895)   **1** : a building at an athletic field for housing equipment or providing dressing facilities   **2** : a building enclosing a large area suitable for various forms of athletics and usu. providing seats for spectators

fielding average *n* (1947) : the average (as of a baseball fielder) determined by dividing the number of putouts and assists by the number of chances — compare BATTING AVERAGE

field judge *n* (ca. 1929) : a football official whose duties include covering action on kicks and forward passes and timing intermission periods and time-outs

field lens *n* (1837) : the lens in a compound eyepiece that is nearer the objective

field magnet *n* (1883) : a magnet for producing and maintaining a magnetic field esp. in a generator or electric motor

field marshal *n* (1614) : the highest ranking military officer (as in the British army)

field mouse *n* (15c) : any of various mice and voles that inhabit fields

field officer *n* (1656) : a commissioned officer in the army, air force, or marine corps of the rank of colonel, lieutenant colonel, or major — compare COMPANY OFFICER, GENERAL OFFICER

field of force (1850) : FIELD 6a

field of honor (1824)   **1** : BATTLEFIELD   **2** : a place where a duel is fought

field of view (ca. 1816) : FIELD 5

field of vision (1862) : VISUAL FIELD

field pea *n* (1709) : a small-seeded pea (*Pisum sativum* var. *arvense*) widely grown for forage and food

field·piece \'fē(ə)l(d)-,pēs\ *n* (1590) : a gun or howitzer for use in the field

field spaniel *n* (1867) : any of a breed of medium-sized hunting and retrieving spaniels that have a flat dense usu. black, liver, red, or roan coat

field·stone \'fē(ə)l(d)-,stōn\ *n* (1799) : stone (as in building) in usu. unaltered form as taken from the field

field·strip \-,strip\ *vt* (1947) : to take apart ⟨a weapon⟩ to the extent authorized for routine cleaning, lubrication, and minor repairs

field–test \-,test\ *vt* (1948) : to test ⟨as a procedure or product⟩ in a natural environment — **field test** *n*

field theory *n* (1901) : a detailed mathematical description of the assumed physical properties of a region under some influence (as gravitation)

field trial *n* (1895)   **1** : a trial of sporting dogs in actual performance   **2** : a trial of a new product in actual situations for which it is intended

field trip *n* (1926) : a visit (as to a factory, farm, or museum) made (as by students and a teacher) for purposes of firsthand observation

field winding *n* (1893) : the winding of a field magnet

field·work \'fē(ə)l-,dwərk\ *n* (1819)   **1** : a temporary fortification thrown up by an army in the field   **2** : work done in the field (as by students) to gain practical experience and knowledge through firsthand observation   **3** : the gathering of anthropological or sociological data through the interviewing and observation of subjects in the field — **field–work·er** *n*

fiend \'fēnd\ *n* [ME, fr. OE *fiend*; akin to OHG *fiant* enemy, Skt *pīyati* he scorns] (bef. 12c)   **1 a** : DEVIL 1   **b** : DEMON   **c** : a person of great wickedness or maliciousness   **2** : a person extremely devoted to a pursuit or study : FANATIC ⟨a golf ~⟩   **3** : ADDICT 1 ⟨a dope ~⟩   **4** : WIZARD 3 ⟨a ~ at mathematics⟩

fiend·ish \'fēn-dish\ *adj* (1529)   **1** : perversely diabolical ⟨took a ~ pleasure in hurting people⟩   **2** : extremely cruel or wicked   **3** : excessively bad, unpleasant, or difficult ⟨~ weather⟩ — **fiend·ish·ly** *adv* — **fiend·ish·ness** *n*

fierce \'firs\ *adj* **fierc·er; fierc·est** [ME *fiers*, fr. MF, fr. L *ferus* wild, savage; akin to Gk *thēr* wild animal] (14c)   **1 a** : violently hostile or aggressive in temperament   **b** : given to fighting or killing : PUGNACIOUS   **2 a** : marked by unrestrained zeal or vehemence ⟨a ~ argument⟩   **b** : extremely vexatious, disappointing, or intense ⟨~ pain⟩   **3** : furiously active or determined ⟨make a ~ effort⟩   **4** : wild or menacing in appearance — **fierce·ly** *adv* — **fierce·ness** *n*
syn FIERCE, FEROCIOUS, BARBAROUS, SAVAGE, CRUEL mean showing fury or malignity in looks or actions. FIERCE applies to humans and animals that inspire terror because of their wild and menacing aspect or fury in attack ⟨*fierce* warriors⟩. FEROCIOUS implies extreme fierceness and unrestrained violence and brutality ⟨a *ferocious* dog⟩. BARBAROUS implies a ferocity or mercilessness regarded as unworthy of civilized people ⟨*barbarous* treatment of prisoners⟩. SAVAGE implies the absence of inhibitions restraining civilized people filled with rage, lust, or other violent passion ⟨a *savage* criminal⟩. CRUEL implies indifference to suffering and even positive pleasure in inflicting it ⟨the *cruel* jokes of schoolboys⟩.

fi·eri fa·cias \,fī-(ə-)rē-'fā-sh(ē-)əs\ *n* [L, cause (it) to be done] (15c) : a writ authorizing the sheriff to obtain satisfaction of a judgment in debt or damages from the goods and chattels of the defendant

fi·ery \'fī(-ə)-rē\ *adj* **fi·er·i·er; -est** [ME, fr. *fire, fier* fire] (13c)   **1 a** : consisting of fire   **b** : BURNING, BLAZING   **c** : using or carried out with fire   **d** : liable to catch fire or explode : FLAMMABLE ⟨a ~ vapor⟩   **2 a** : hot like a fire   **b** (1) : being in an inflamed state or condition ⟨a ~ boil⟩   (2) : feverish and flushed ⟨a ~ forehead⟩   **3** : of the color of fire : RED ⟨a ~ sunset⟩   **4** : full of or exuding emotion or spirit ⟨a ~ sermon⟩   **b** : easily provoked : IRRITABLE — **fi·eri·ly** \'fī-rə-lē\ *adv* — **fi·eri·ness** \'fī-rē-nəs\ *n* — **fiery** *adv*

fi·es·ta \fē-'es-tə\ *n* [Sp, fr. L *festa* — more at FEAST] (1844) : FESTIVAL; *specif* : a saint's day celebrated in Spain and Latin America with processions and dances

fife \'fīf\ *n* [G *Pfeife* pipe, fife, fr. OHG *pfīfa*, fr. (assumed) VL *pipa* pipe — more at FIFE] (1539) : a small transverse flute with six to eight finger holes and usu. no keys

fife rail *n* (ca. 1800) : a rail about the mast near the deck to which rigging is belayed

fif·teen \,fif-'tēn, 'fif-,\ *n* [ME *fiftene*, adj., fr. OE *fīftēne*, fr. *fīf* five + *-tiene* (akin to OE *tien* ten) — more at FIVE, TEN] (bef. 12c)   **1** — see NUMBER table   **2** : the first point scored by a side in a game of tennis — called also *five* — **fifteen** *adj* — **fifteen** *pron, pl in constr* — **fif·teenth** \-'tēn(t)th, -,tēn(t)th\ *adj or n*

fifth \'fith, 'fif(t)th, 'fift\ *n, pl* **fifths** \'fiths, 'fif(t)ths, 'fif(t)s\ (bef. 12c)   **1** — see NUMBER table   **2 a** : the musical interval embracing five diatonic degrees   **b** : a tone at this interval; *specif* : DOMINANT 1   **c** : the harmonic combination of two tones at this interval   **3** : a unit of measure for liquor equal to one fifth of a U.S. gallon (0.757 liter)   **4** *cap*

\ə\ abut \ʰ\ kitten, F table \ər\ further \a\ ash \ā\ ace \ä\ mop, mar
\aú\ out \ch\ chin \e\ bet \ē\ easy \g\ go \i\ hit \ī\ ice \j\ job
\ŋ\ sing \ō\ go \ò\ law \òi\ boy \th\ thin \t̲h\ the \ü\ loot \ù\ foot
\y\ yet \zh\ vision \à, k̲, ⁿ, œ, œ̄, ue, ūe, ᵞ\ *see* Guide to Pronunciation

: the Fifth Amendment of the U.S. Constitution — **fifth** *adj or adv* — **fifth·ly** *adv*

fifth column *n* [name applied to rebel sympathizers in Madrid in 1936 when four rebel columns were advancing on the city] (1936) : a group of secret sympathizers or supporters of an enemy that engage in espionage or sabotage within defense lines or national borders — **fifth col·um·nism** \-'kä-ləm-,(n)i-zəm\ *n* — **fifth col·um·nist** \-(n)ist\ *n*

fifth wheel *n* (ca. 1874) **1 a** : a horizontal wheel or segment of a wheel that consists of two parts rotating on each other above the fore axle of a carriage and that forms support to prevent tipping **b** : a similar coupling between tractor and trailer of a semitrailer **2** : one that is superfluous, unnecessary, or burdensome

fif·ty \'fif-tē\ *n, pl* **fifties** [ME, fr. *fifty,* adj., fr. OE *fīftig,* fr. *fīftig,* n., group of 50, fr. *fīf* five + *-tig* group of ten; akin to *tien* ten] (bef. 12c) **1** — see NUMBER table **2** *pl* : the numbers 50 to 59; *specif* : the years 50 to 59 in a lifetime or century **3** : a 50-dollar bill — **fif·ti·eth** \-tē-əth\ *adj or n* — **fifty** *adj* — **fifty** *pron, pl in constr* — **fif·ty·ish** \-tē-ish\ *adj*

fif·ty–fif·ty \,fif-tē-'fif-tē\ *adj* (1913) **1** : shared, assumed, or borne equally ⟨a ~ proposition⟩ **2** : half favorable and half unfavorable ⟨a ~ chance⟩ — **fifty–fifty** *adv*

¹fig \'fig\ *n* [ME *fige,* fr. OF, fr. OProv *figa,* fr. (assumed) VL *fica,* fr. L *ficus* fig tree, fig] (13c) **1 a** : an oblong or pear-shaped fruit that is a syconium **b** : any of a genus (*Ficus*) of trees of the mulberry family bearing fruits that are syconia; *esp* : a widely cultivated tree (*F. carica*) that produces edible figs **2** : a worthless trifle : the least bit ⟨doesn't care a ~⟩

²fig *n* [*fig,* vb. (to adorn)] (1835) : DRESS, ARRAY ⟨a young woman in dazzling royal full ~ —Mollie Panter-Downes⟩

¹fight \'fīt\ *vb* **fought** \'fȯt\; **fight·ing** [ME, fr. OE *feohtan;* akin to OHG *fehtan* to fight and perh. to L *pectere* to comb — more at PECTINATE] *vi* (bef. 12c) **1 a** : to contend in battle or physical combat; *esp* : to strive to overcome a person by blows or weapons **b** : to engage in boxing **2** : to put forth a determined effort ~ *vt* **1 a** (1) : to contend against in or as if in battle or physical combat (2) : to box against in the ring **b** (1) : to attempt to prevent the success or effectiveness of ⟨the company *fought* the takeover attempt⟩ (2) : to oppose the passage or development of ⟨~ a bill in Congress⟩ **2 a** : WAGE, CARRY ON ⟨~ a battle⟩ **b** : to take part in (as a boxing match) **3** : to struggle to endure or surmount ⟨~ a cold⟩ **4 a** : to gain by struggle ⟨~s his way through⟩ **b** : to resolve by struggle ⟨*fought* out their differences in court⟩ **5 a** : to manage (a ship) in a battle or storm **b** : to cause to struggle or contend **c** : to manage in an unnecessarily rough or awkward manner — **fight shy of** : to avoid facing or meeting

²fight *n* (bef. 12c) **1 a** : a hostile encounter : BATTLE, COMBAT **b** : a boxing match **c** : a verbal disagreement : ARGUMENT **2** : a struggle for a goal or an objective ⟨a ~ for justice⟩ **3** : strength or disposition for fighting : PUGNACITY ⟨still full of ~⟩

fight·er \'fī-tər\ *n* (13c) : one that fights: as **a** (1) : WARRIOR, SOLDIER (2) : a pugnacious or game individual (3) : ¹BOXER 1 **b** : an airplane of high speed and maneuverability with armament designed to destroy enemy aircraft

fight·er–bomb·er \-'bä-mər\ *n* (1936) : a fighter aircraft fitted to carry bombs and rockets in addition to its normal armament

fighting chair *n* (1950) : a chair from which a salt-water angler plays a hooked fish

fighting chance *n* (1889) : a chance that may be realized by a struggle ⟨the patient had a *fighting chance* to live⟩

fighting word *n* (1917) : a word likely to provoke a fight

fight song *n* (1954) : a song used to inspire enthusiasm usu. during an athletic competition

fig leaf *n* (14c) **1** : the leaf of a fig tree **2** [fr. the use by Adam and Eve of fig leaves to cover their nakedness after eating the forbidden fruit (Gen. 3:7)] : something that conceals or camouflages usu. inadequately or dishonestly

fig marigold *n* (1731) : any of several herbs (genus *Mesembryanthemum*) of the carpetweed family with showy white or pink flowers

fig·ment \'fig-mənt\ *n* [ME, fr. L *figmentum,* fr. *fingere* to shape — more at DOUGH] (15c) : something made up or contrived

fig·ur·al \'fi-g(y)ə-rəl\ *adj* (1813) : of, relating to, or consisting of human or animal figures ⟨a ~ composition⟩

fig·u·ra·tion \,fi-g(y)ə-'rä-shən\ *n* (14c) **1** : FORM, OUTLINE **2** : the act or process of creating or providing a figure **3** : an act or instance of representation in figures and shapes ⟨cubism was explained as a synthesis of colored ~s of objects —Janet Flanner⟩ **4** : ornamentation of a musical passage by using decorative and usu. repetitive figures

fig·u·ra·tive \'fi-g(y)ə-rə-tiv\ *adj* (14c) **1 a** : representing by a figure or resemblance : EMBLEMATIC **b** : of or relating to representation of form or figure in art ⟨~ sculpture⟩ **2 a** : expressing one thing in terms normally denoting another with which it may be regarded as analogous : METAPHORICAL ⟨~ language⟩ **b** : characterized by figures of speech ⟨a ~ description⟩ — **fig·u·ra·tive·ly** *adv* — **fig·u·ra·tive·ness** *n*

¹fig·ure \'fi-gyər, *Brit & often US* 'fi-gər\ *n* [ME, fr. OF, fr. L *figura,* fr. *fingere*] (13c) **1 a** : a number symbol : NUMERAL, DIGIT ⟨a salary running into six ~s⟩ **b** *pl* : arithmetical calculations ⟨good at ~s⟩ **c** : a written or printed character **d** : value esp. as expressed in numbers : SUM, PRICE ⟨sold at a low ~⟩ **2 a** : a geometric form (as a line, triangle, or sphere) esp. when considered as a set of geometric elements (as points) in space of a given number of dimensions ⟨a square is a plane ~⟩ **b** : bodily shape or form esp. of a person ⟨a slender ~⟩ **c** : an object noticeable only as a shape or form ⟨~s moving in the dusk⟩ **3 a** : the graphic representation of a form esp. of a person or geometric entity **b** : a diagram or pictorial illustration of textual matter **4** : a person, thing, or action representative of another **5 a** : FIGURE OF SPEECH **b** : an intentional deviation from the ordinary form or syntactical relation of words **6** : the form of a syllogism with respect to the relative position of the middle term **7** : an often repetitive pattern or design in a manufactured article (as cloth) or natural product (as wood) ⟨a polka-dot ~⟩ **8** : appearance made : impression produced ⟨the couple cut quite a ~⟩ **9 a** : a series of movements in a dance **b** : an outline representation of a form traced by a series of evolutions (as with skates on an ice surface or by an airplane in the air) **10** : a prom-

inent personality : PERSONAGE ⟨great ~s of history⟩ **11** : a short coherent group of notes or chords that may constitute part of a phrase, theme, or composition

²figure *vb* **fig·ured; fig·ur·ing** \'fi-gyə-riŋ, 'fi-g(ə-)riŋ\ *vt* (14c) **1** : to represent by or as if by a figure or outline **2** : to decorate with a pattern; *also* : to write figures over or under (the bass) in order to indicate the accompanying chords **3** : to indicate or represent by numerals **4 a** : CALCULATE **b** : CONCLUDE, DECIDE ⟨*figured* there was no use in further effort⟩ **c** : REGARD, CONSIDER **d** : to appear likely ⟨~s to win⟩ ~ *vi* **1 a** : to be or appear important or conspicuous **b** : to be involved or implicated ⟨*figured* in a robbery⟩ **2** : to perform a figure in dancing **3** : COMPUTE, CALCULATE **4** : to seem rational, normal, or expected ⟨that ~s⟩ — **fig·ur·er** \-g(y)ər-ər\ *n* — **figure on 1** : to take into consideration ⟨*figuring on* the extra income⟩ **2** : to rely on **3** : PLAN ⟨*I figure on* going into town⟩

fig·ured \-g(y)ərd\ *adj* (15c) **1** : adorned with, formed into, or marked with a figure ⟨~ muslin⟩ ⟨~ wood⟩ **2** : being represented : PORTRAYED **3** : indicated by figures

figured bass *n* (1801) : CONTINUO

figure eight *n* (1887) : something resembling the Arabic numeral eight in form or shape: as **a** : a small knot — see KNOT illustration **b** : an embroidery stitch **c** : a dance pattern **d** : a skater's figure — called also *figure-of-eight*

fig·ure·head \'fi-g(y)ər-,hed\ *n* (1765) **1** : the figure on a ship's bow **2** : a head or chief in name only

figure in *vt* (ca. 1934) : to include esp. in a reckoning

figure of merit *n* (ca. 1865) : a numerical quantity based on one or more characteristics of a system or device that represents a measure of efficiency or effectiveness

figure of speech (1824) : a form of expression (as a simile or metaphor) used to convey meaning or heighten effect often by comparing or identifying one thing with another that has a meaning or connotation familiar to the reader or listener

figure out *vt* (1833) **1** : DISCOVER, DETERMINE ⟨try to *figure out* a way to do it⟩ **2** : SOLVE, FATHOM ⟨*figure out* a problem⟩

figure skating *n* (1852) : skating characterized by the performance of various jumps, spins, and dance movements and formerly by the tracing of prescribed figures — **figure skater** *n*

fig·u·rine \,fi-g(y)ə-'rēn\ *n* [F, fr. It *figurina,* dim. of *figura* figure, fr. L — more at FIGURE] (1854) : a small carved or molded figure : STATUETTE

fig wasp *n* (1883) : a minute wasp (*Blastophaga psenes* of the family Agaontidae) that breeds in the caprifig and is the agent of caprification; *broadly* : any wasp of the same family

fig·wort \'fig-,wȯrt, -,wərt\ *n* (1548) : any of a genus (*Scrophularia*) of chiefly herbaceous plants of the snapdragon family with leaves having no stipules, an irregular bilabiate corolla, and a 2-celled ovary

Fi·ji·an \'fē-(,)jē-ən, fi-'\ *n* (1809) **1** : a member of a Melanesian people of Fiji **2** : the Austronesian language of the Fijians — **Fijian** *adj*

fil·a·ment \'fi-lə-mənt\ *n* [MF, fr. ML *filamentum,* fr. LL *filare* to spin — more at FILE] (1594) : a single thread or a thin flexible threadlike object, process, or appendage: as **a** : a tenuous conductor (as of carbon or metal) made incandescent by the passage of an electric current; *specif* : a cathode in the form of a metal wire in an electron tube **b** (1) : a thin and fine elongated constituent part of a gill (2) : an elongated thin series of cells attached one to another or a very long thin cylindrical single cell (as of some algae, fungi, or bacteria) **c** : the anther-bearing stalk of a stamen — see FLOWER illustration — **fil·a·men·ta·ry** \,fil-ə-'men-t(ə-)rē\ *adj* — **fil·a·men·tous** \-'men-təs\ *adj*

fi·lar \'fī-lər\ *adj* [L *filum* thread] (ca. 1859) : of or relating to a thread or line; *esp* : having threads across the field of view ⟨a ~ eyepiece⟩

fi·lar·ia \fə-'lar-ē-ə, -'ler-\ *n, pl* **-i·ae** \-ē-,ē, -ē-,ī\ [NL, genus name, fr. L *filum*] (1834) : any of numerous slender filamentous nematodes (*Filaria* and related genera) that as adults are parasites in the blood or tissues of mammals and as larvae usu. develop in biting insects — **fi·lar·i·al** \-ē-əl\ *adj or n* — **fi·lar·i·id** \-ē-əd\ *adj or n*

fil·a·ri·a·sis \,fi-lə-'rī-ə-səs\ *n, pl* **-a·ses** \-,sēz\ [NL] (1879) : infestation with or disease caused by filariae

fil·a·ture \'fil-ə-,chú(ə)r, -,chər, -,t(y)ú(ə)r\ *n* [F, fr. LL *filatus,* pp. of *filare*] (1759) : a factory where silk is reeled

fil·bert \'fil-bərt\ *n* [ME, fr. AF *philber,* fr. St. *Philibert* †684 Frankish abbot whose feast day falls in the nutting season] (14c) **1** : either of two European hazels (*Corylus avellana* and *C. maxima*); *also* : the sweet thick-shelled nut of the filbert **2** : HAZELNUT

filch \'filch\ *vt* (1561) : to appropriate furtively or casually ⟨~ a cookie⟩ **syn** see STEAL

¹file \'fi(ə)l\ *n* [ME, fr. OE *fēol;* akin to OHG *fīla* file] (bef. 12c) **1** : a tool usu. of hardened steel with cutting ridges for forming or smoothing surfaces esp. of metal **2** : a shrewd or crafty person

²file *vt* **filed; fil·ing** (13c) : to rub, smooth, or cut away with or as if with a file

³file *vt* **filed; fil·ing** [ME, fr. OE *fȳlan,* fr. *fūl* foul] (bef. 12c) *chiefly dial* : DEFILE, CORRUPT

⁴file *vb* **filed; fil·ing** [ME, fr. MF *filer* to string documents on a string or wire, fr. *fil* thread, fr. OF, fr. L *filum;* akin to Arm *jil* sinew] *vt* (15c) **1** : to arrange in order for preservation and reference ⟨~ letters⟩ **2 a** : to place among official records as prescribed by law ⟨~ a mortgage⟩ **b** : to send (copy) to a newspaper ⟨*filed* a story⟩ **c** : to return to the office of the clerk of a court without action on the merits **3** : to initiate (as a legal action) through proper formal procedure ⟨threatened to ~ charges⟩ ~ *vi* **1** : to register as a candidate esp. in a primary election **2** : to place items in a file — **fil·er** \'fī-lər\ *n*

⁵file *n* (1525) **1** : a device (as a folder, case, or cabinet) by means of which papers are kept in order **2** *archaic* : ROLL, LIST **3 a** : a collection of papers or publications usu. arranged or classified **c** (1) : a collection of related data records (as for a computer) (2) : a complete collection of data (as text or a program) treated by a computer as a unit esp. for purposes of input and output — **on file** : in or as if in a file for ready reference

⁶file *n* [MF, fr. *filer* to spin, fr. LL *filare,* fr. L *filum*] (1598) **1** : a row of persons, animals, or things arranged one behind the other **2** : any of the rows of squares that extend across a chessboard from one player's side to the other player's side

⁷file *vi* **filed; fil·ing** (1616) : to march or proceed in file

filé *also* **file** \fə-'lā, (,)fē-'lā, 'fē-(,)lā\ *n* [LaF, fr. F, pp. of *filer* to twist, spin] (1806) : powdered young leaves of sassafras used to thicken soups or stews

file clerk *n* (1919) : a clerk who works on files

file-fish \'fī(ə)l-,fish\ *n* (1814) : any of various bony fishes (order Tetraodontiformes and esp. genera *Aluterus, Cantherhines,* and *Monacanthus* of the family Balistidae) with rough granular leathery skins

fi-let \fi-'lā\ *n* [F, lit., net] (1881) : a lace with a square mesh and geometric designs

fi-let mi-gnon \,fi-(,)lā-mēn-'yōⁿ, fi-,lā-\ *n, pl* **filets mignons** \,fi-(,)lā-mēn-'yōⁿz, fi-,lā-\ [F, lit., dainty fillet] (1906) : a thick slice of beef cut from the narrow end of a beef tenderloin

fili- *or* **filo-** *comb form* [L *filum*] : thread 〈*fili*form〉

fil-ial \'fi-lē-əl, 'fil-yəl\ *adj* [ME, fr. LL *filialis,* fr. L *filius* son — more at FEMININE] (14c) **1** : of, relating to, or befitting a son or daughter 〈~ obedience〉 **2** : having or assuming the relation of a child or offspring — **fil-ial-ly** \-lē-ə-lē, -yə-lē\ *adv*

filial generation *n* (1909) : a generation in a breeding experiment that is successive to a mating between parents of two distinctively different but usu. relatively pure genotypes

fil-i-a-tion \,fi-lē-'ā-shən\ *n* (15c) **1 a** : filial relationship esp. of a son to his father **b** : the adjudication of paternity **2 a** : descent or derivation esp. from a culture or language **b** : the act or process of determining such relationship

¹fil-i-bus-ter \'fi-lə-,bəs-tər\ *n* [Sp *filibustero,* lit., freebooter] (1851) **1** : an irregular military adventurer; *specif* : an American engaged in fomenting insurrections in Latin America in the mid-19th century **2** [²*filibuster*] **a** : the use of extreme dilatory tactics in an attempt to delay or prevent action esp. in a legislative assembly **b** : an instance of this practice

²filibuster *vb* **-tered; -ter-ing** \-t(ə-)riŋ\ *vi* (1853) **1** : to carry out insurrectionist activities in a foreign country **2** : to engage in a filibuster ~ *vt* : to subject to a filibuster — **fil-i-bus-ter-er** \-tər-ər\ *n*

fi-li-form \'fi-lə-,form, 'fī-\ *adj* (1757) : shaped like a filament

¹fil-i-gree \'fi-lə-,grē\ *n* [modif. of F *filigrane,* fr. It *filigrana,* fr. L *filum* + *granum* grain — more at CORN] (1693) **1** : ornamental work esp. of fine wire of gold, silver, or copper applied chiefly to gold and silver surfaces **2 a** : ornamental openwork of delicate or intricate design **b** : a pattern or design resembling such openwork 〈a ~ of frost〉 **c** : ORNAMENTATION, EMBELLISHMENT 〈*writings* . . . heavy with late Victorian ~ —Jack Beatty〉

filigree 2a

²filigree *vt* **fil-i-greed; fil-i-gree-ing** (1831) : to adorn with or as if with filigree

fil-ing \'fī-liŋ\ *n* (14c) **1** : an act or instance of using a file **2** : a fragment rubbed off in filing 〈iron ~s〉

fil-io-pi-etis-tic \'fi-lē-ō-,pī-ə-'tis-tik\ *adj* [*filial* + *-o-* + *pietistic*] (1893) : of or relating to an often excessive veneration of ancestors or tradition

Fil-i-pi-na \,fi-lə-'pē-nə\ *n* [Sp] (1899) : a Filipino girl or woman

Fil-i-pi-no \-'pē-(,)nō\ *n, pl* **Filipinos** [Sp] (ca. 1889) **1** : a native of the Philippine islands **2** : a citizen of the Republic of the Philippines — **Filipino** *adj*

¹fill \'fil\ *vb* [ME, fr. OE *fyllan;* akin to OE *full* full] *vt* (bef. 12c) **1 a** : to put into as much as can be held or conveniently contained 〈~ a cup with water〉 **b** : to supply with a full complement 〈the class is already ~ed〉 **c** (1) : to cause to swell or billow 〈wind ~ed the sails〉 (2) : to trim (a sail) to catch the wind **d** : to raise the level of with fill 〈~ed land〉 **e** : to repair the cavities of (teeth) **f** : to stop up : OBSTRUCT, PLUG 〈wreckage ~ed the channel〉 **g** : to stop up the interstices, crevices, or pores of (as cloth, wood, or leather) with a foreign substance **2 a** : FEED, SATIATE **b** : SATISFY, FULFILL 〈~s all requirements〉 **c** : MAKE OUT, COMPLETE — used with *out* or *in* 〈~ out a form〉 〈~ in the blanks〉 **d** : to draw the playing cards necessary to complete (as a straight or flush in poker) **3 a** : to occupy the whole of 〈smoke ~ed the room〉 **b** : to spread through **c** : to make full 〈a mind ~ed with fantasies〉 **4 a** : to possess and perform the duties of : HOLD 〈~ an office〉 **b** : to place a person in 〈~ a vacancy〉 **5** : to supply as directed 〈~ a prescription〉 **6** : to cover the bottom of a layer of precious metal ~ *vi* : to become full — **fill one's shoes** : to take over one's job, position, or responsibilities

²fill *n* (bef. 12c) **1** : a full supply; *esp* : a quantity that satisfies or satiates 〈eat your ~〉 **2** : something that fills: as **a** : material used to fill a receptacle, cavity, passage, or low place **b** : a bit of instrumental music that fills the pauses between phrases (as of a vocalist or soloist)

fill away *vi* (1840) **1** : to trim a sail to catch the wind **2** : to proceed on the course esp. after being brought up in the wind

¹fill-er \'fil-ər\ *n* (15c) : one that fills: as **a** : a substance added to a product (as to increase bulk, weight, viscosity, opacity, or strength) **b** : a composition used to fill the pores and grain esp. of a wood surface before painting or varnishing **c** : a piece used to cover or fill in a space between two parts of a structure **d** : tobacco used to form the core of a cigar **e** : material used to fill extra space in a column or page of a newspaper or magazine **f** : a pack of paper for a loose-leaf notebook **g** : a sound, word, or phrase (as "you know?") used to fill pauses in speaking

²fil-ler \'fi-,ler\ *n, pl* **fillers** *or* **filler** [Hung *fillér*] (1904) — see *forint* at MONEY table

¹fil-let \'fi-lət, *in sense 2b also* fi-'lā, 'fi-(,)lā\ *also* **fi-let** \fi-'lā, 'fi-(,)lā\ *n* [ME *filet,* fr. MF, dim. of *fil* thread — more at FILE] (14c) **1** : a ribbon or narrow strip of material used esp. as a headband **2 a** : a thin narrow strip of material **b** : a piece or slice of boneless meat or fish; *esp* : the tenderloin of beef **3 a** : a concave junction formed where two surfaces meet (as at an angle) **b** : a strip that gives a rounded appearance to such a junction; *also* : a strip to reinforce the corner where two surfaces meet **4** : a narrow flat architectural member: **a** : a flat molding separating others — see BASE illustration **b** : the space between two flutings in a shaft

²fil-let \'fi-lət, *in sense 2 also* fi-'lā, 'fi-(,)lā\ *vt* (1604) **1** : to bind, furnish, or adorn with or as if with a fillet **2** : to cut into fillets

fillet weld *n* (1926) : a weld of approximately triangular cross section used to join two pieces esp. perpendicularly

fill-in \'fil-,in\ *n* (1917) : someone or something that fills in

fill in *vt* (1840) **1** : to give necessary or recently acquired information to 〈I'll *fill* you *in*〉 **2** : to enrich (as a design) with detail ~ *vi* : to fill a vacancy usu. temporarily

fill-ing \'fi-liŋ\ *n* (14c) **1** : an act or instance of filling **2** : something used to fill a cavity, container, or depression **3** : something that completes: as **a** : the yarn interlacing the warp in a fabric; *also* : yarn for the shuttle **b** : a food mixture used to fill pastry or sandwiches

filling station *n* (1921) : SERVICE STATION 1

¹fil-lip \'fi-ləp\ *vt* [prob. of imit. origin] (15c) **1 a** : to make a filliping motion with **b** : to strike or tap with a fillip 〈~ed him on the nose〉 **2** : to project quickly by or as if by a fillip 〈~ crumbs off the table〉 **3** : STIMULATE 〈with this to ~ his spirits —Robert Westerby〉

²fillip *n* (1519) **1 a** : a blow or gesture made by the sudden forcible straightening of a finger curled up against the thumb **b** : a short sharp blow : BUFFET **2** : something tending to arouse or excite: as **a** : STIMULUS 〈just the ~ my confidence needed〉 〈lent a ~ of danger to the sport〉 **b** : a trivial addition : EMBELLISHMENT 〈showy ~s of language〉 **c** : a significant and often unexpected development : WRINKLE 〈plot twists and ~s〉

fill out *vi* (1888) : to put on flesh

fill-up \'fil-,əp\ *n* (1853) : an action or instance of filling up something (as a gas tank)

fil-ly \'fi-lē\ *n, pl* **fillies** [ME *fyly,* fr. ON *fylja;* akin to OE *fola* foal] (15c) **1** : a young female horse usu. of less than four years **2** : a young woman : GIRL

¹film \'film, *Southern also* 'fi(ə)m\ *n, often attrib* [ME *filme,* fr. OE *filmen;* akin to Gk *pelma* sole of the foot, OE *fell* skin — more at FELL] (bef. 12c) **1 a** : a thin skin or membranous covering : PELLICLE **b** : an abnormal growth on or in the eye **2** : a thin covering or coating 〈a ~ of ice〉 **3 a** : an exceedingly thin layer : LAMINA **b** (1) : a thin flexible transparent sheet (as of plastic) used esp. as a wrapping (2) : such a sheet of cellulose acetate or nitrocellulose coated with a radiation-sensitive emulsion for taking photographs **4** : MOTION PICTURE

²film *vt* (1602) **1** : to cover with or as if with a film **2** : to make a motion picture of or from 〈~ a scene〉 ~ *vi* **1** : to become covered or obscured with or as if with a film **2** : to make a motion picture — **film-able** \'fil-mə-bəl\ *adj*

film badge *n* (1945) : a small pack of sensitive photographic film worn as a badge for indicating exposure to radiation

film-dom \'film-dəm\ *n* (1914) : the motion-picture industry

film-go-er \-,gō(-ə)r\ *n* (1919) : one who frequently attends films

film-ic \'fil-mik\ *adj* (ca. 1930) : of, relating to, or resembling motion pictures — **film-i-cal-ly** \-mi-k(ə-)lē\ *adv*

film-land \'film-,land\ *n* (1913) : FILMDOM

film-mak-er \'film-,mā-kər\ *n* (1908) : one who makes motion pictures

film-mak-ing \-,mā-kiŋ\ *n* (1913) : the making of motion pictures

film noir \-'nwär\ *n* [F, lit., black film] (1958) : a type of crime film featuring cynical malevolent characters in a sleazy setting and an ominous atmosphere that is conveyed by shadowy photography and foreboding background music; *also* : a film of this type

film-og-ra-phy \fil-'mä-grə-fē\ *n, pl* **-phies** [*film* + *-ography* (as in *bibliography*)] (1962) : a list of motion pictures featuring the work of a prominent film figure or relating to a particular topic

film-set-ting \'film-,se-tiŋ\ *n* (1954) : PHOTOCOMPOSITION — **film-set** *adj* — **filmset** *vt* — **film-set-ter** *n*

film-strip \'film-,strip\ *n* (1930) : a strip of film bearing a sequence of images for projection as still pictures

filmy \'fil-mē\ *adj* **film-i-er; -est** (1604) **1** : of, resembling, or composed of film : GAUZY 〈~ draperies〉 **2** : covered with a haze or film — **film-i-ly** \-mə-lē\ *adv* — **film-i-ness** \-mē-nəs\ *n*

filo *also* **fil-lo** *var of* PHYLLO

filo- — see FILI-

fils \'fils\ *n, pl* **fils** [Ar] (1931) — see *dinar, dirham, rial* at MONEY table

¹fil-ter \'fil-tər\ *n* [ME *filtre,* fr. ML *filtrum* piece of felt used as a filter, of Gmc origin; akin to OHG *filz* felt — more at FELT] (1563) **1 a** : a porous article or mass (as of paper or sand) through which a gas or liquid is passed to separate out matter in suspension **b** : something that has the effect of a filter **2** : an apparatus containing a filter medium **3 a** : a device or material for suppressing or minimizing waves or oscillations of certain frequencies (as of electricity, light, or sound) **b** : a transparent material (as colored glass) that absorbs light of certain wavelengths or colors selectively and is used for modifying light that reaches a sensitized photographic material — called also *color filter*

²filter *vb* **fil-tered; fil-ter-ing** \-t(ə-)riŋ\ *vt* (1576) **1** : to subject to the action of a filter **2** : to remove by means of a filter ~ *vi* **1** : to pass or move through or as if through a filter **2** : to come or go in small units over a period of time 〈people began ~ing in〉

fil-ter-able *also* **fil-tra-ble** \'fil-t(ə-)rə-bəl\ *adj* (1908) : capable of being filtered or of passing through a filter — **fil-ter-abil-i-ty** \,fil-t(ə-)'bi-lə-tē\ *n*

filterable virus *n* (1911) : any of the infectious agents that pass through a filter of diatomite or unglazed porcelain with the filtrate and remain virulent and that include the viruses as presently understood and various other groups (as the mycoplasmas and rickettsias) which were orig. considered viruses before their cellular nature was established

filter bed *n* (ca. 1874) : a sand or gravel bed for filtering water or sewage

filter feeder *n* (1928) : an animal that obtains its food by filtering organic matter or minute organisms from a current of water that passes through some part of its system

filter paper *n* (ca. 1846) : porous unsized paper used esp. for filtering

---

\ə\ abut \ᵊ\ kitten, F table \ər\ further \a\ ash \ā\ ace \ä\ mop, mar \aú\ out \ch\ chin \e\ bet \ē\ easy \g\ go \i\ hit \ī\ ice \j\ job \ŋ\ sing \ō\ go \ò\ law \òi\ boy \th\ thin \t̲h̲\ the \ü\ loot \ù\ foot \y\ yet \zh\ vision \à, k̲, ⁿ, œ, œ̄, ue, ūe, ᵊ\ *see* Guide to Pronunciation

filter tip n (1932) : a cigar or cigarette tip designed to filter the smoke before it enters the smoker's mouth; *also* : a cigar or cigarette provided with such a tip — **fil·ter–tipped** \,fil-tər-'tipt\ *adj*

filth \'filth\ n [ME, fr. OE *fylth,* fr. *fūl* foul] (bef. 12c) **1** : foul or putrid matter; *esp* : loathsome dirt or refuse **2 a** : moral corruption or defilement **b** : something that tends to corrupt or defile

filthy \'fil-the\ *adj* **filth·i·er; -est** (14c) **1** : covered with or containing filth : offensively dirty **2 a** : UNDERHAND, VILE **b** : OBSCENE *syn* see DIRTY — **filth·i·ly** \-thə-lē\ *adv* — **filth·i·ness** \-thē-nəs\ n

fil·trate \'fil-,trāt\ n (ca. 1846) : material that has passed through a filter

fil·tra·tion \fil-'trā-shən\ n (1605) **1** : the process of filtering **2** : the process of passing through or as if through a filter; *also* : DIFFUSION

fim·bria \'fim-brē-ə\ n, pl **fim·bri·ae** \-brē-,ē, -,ī\ [NL, fr. L, fringe] (1752) : a bordering fringe esp. at the entrance of the fallopian tubes — **fim·bri·al** \-brē-əl\ *adj*

fim·bri·at·ed \'fim-brē-,ā-təd\ *also* **fim·bri·ate** \-,āt\ *adj* (15c) : having the edge or extremity bordered by slender processes : FRINGED — **fim·bri·a·tion** \,fim-brē-'ā-shən\ n

¹fin \'fin\ n [ME *finn,* fr. OE] (bef. 12c) **1** : an external membranous process of an aquatic animal (as a fish) used in propelling or guiding the body — see FISH illustration **2** : something resembling a fin: as **a** : HAND, ARM **b** (1) : an appendage of a boat (as a submarine) (2) : an airfoil attached to an airplane for directional stability **c** : FLIPPER 1b **d** : any of the projecting ribs on a radiator or an engine cylinder — **fin·like** \-,līk\ *adj* — **finned** \'find\ *adj*

²fin vb **finned; fin·ning** vt (1933) : to equip with fins ~ vi **1** : to show the fins above the water **2** : to move through the water propelled by fins

³fin n [Yiddish *finf* five, fr. MHG, fr. OHG — more at FIVE] (1925) *slang* : a 5-dollar bill

fi·na·gle \fə-'nā-gəl\ vb **fi·na·gled; fi·na·gling** \-g(ə-)liŋ\ [perh. alter. of *fainaigue* (to renege)] vt (ca. 1924) **1** : to obtain by indirect or involved means **2** : to obtain by trickery ~ vi : to use devious or dishonest methods to achieve one's ends — **fi·na·gler** \-g(ə-)lər\ n

¹fi·nal \'fīn-ᵊl\ *adj* [ME, fr. MF, fr. L *finalis,* fr. *finis* boundary, end] (14c) **1 a** : not to be altered or undone ⟨all sales are ~⟩ **b** : of or relating to a concluding court action or proceeding ⟨~ decree⟩ **2** : coming at the end : being the last in a series, process, or progress ⟨the ~ chapter⟩ **3** : of or relating to the ultimate purpose or result of a process ⟨our ~ goal⟩ *syn* see LAST — **fi·nal·ly** \'fīn-ᵊl-ē, 'fīn-lē\ *adv*

²final n (1609) : something that is final: as **a** : a deciding match, game, heat, or trial — usu. used in pl. **b** : the last examination in a course — often used in pl.

fi·na·le \fə-'na-lē, fi-'nä-\ n [It, fr. *finale,* adj., final, fr. L *finalis*] (1783) : the close or termination of something: as **a** : the last section of an instrumental musical composition **b** : the closing part, scene, or number in a public performance **c** : the last and often climactic event or item in a sequence

fi·nal·ise *Brit var of* FINALIZE

fi·nal·ist \'fīn-ᵊl-ist\ n (1898) : a contestant in the finals of a competition

fi·nal·i·ty \fī-'na-lə-tē, fə-\ n, pl **-ties** (1833) **1 a** : the character or condition of being final, settled, irrevocable, or complete **b** : the condition of being at an ultimate point esp. of development or authority **2** : something final; *esp* : a fundamental fact, action, or belief

fi·nal·ize \'fīn-ᵊl-,īz\ vt **-ized; -iz·ing** (1901) **1** : to put in final or finished form ⟨soon my conclusion will be *finalized* —D. D. Eisenhower⟩ **2** : to give final approval to ⟨*finalizing* the papers prepared . . . by his staff —*Newsweek*⟩ — **fi·nal·iza·tion** \,fī-nᵊl-ə-'zā-shən\ n

usage *Finalize* has been frequently castigated as an unnecessary neologism or as U.S. government gobbledygook. It appears to have first gained currency in Australia (where it has been acceptable all along) in the early 1920s. The U.S. Navy picked it up in the late 20s, and from there it came into widespread use. It is a standard formation (see -IZE). Our current evidence indicates it is most frequently used in government, business dealings, and child adoption; it usu. is not found in belles-lettres.

final solution n, *often cap F&S* (1947) : the Nazi program for extermination of all Jews in Europe

¹fi·nance \fə-'nan(t)s, 'fī-, fī-\ n [ME, payment, ransom, fr. MF, fr. *finer* to end, pay, fr. *fin* end — more at FINE] (1739) **1** pl : money or other liquid resources of a government, business, group, or individual **2** : the system that includes the circulation of money, the granting of credit, the making of investments, and the provision of banking facilities **3** : the science or study of the management of funds **4** : the obtaining of funds or capital : FINANCING

²finance vt **fi·nanced; fi·nanc·ing** (1866) **1 a** : to raise or provide funds or capital for ⟨~ a new house⟩ **b** : to furnish with necessary funds ⟨~ a son through college⟩ **2** : to sell something to on credit

finance company n (ca. 1924) : a company that makes usu. small short-term loans usu. to individuals

fi·nan·cial \fə-'nan(t)-shəl, fī-\ *adj* (1769) : relating to finance or financiers — **fi·nan·cial·ly** \-'nan(t)-sh(ə-)lē\ *adv*

fi·nan·cier \,fi-nən-'sir; fə-,nan-, ,fī-\ n (1618) **1** : one who specializes in raising and expending public moneys **2** : one who deals with finance and investment on a large scale

fi·nanc·ing n (1827) : the act or process or an instance of raising or providing funds; *also* : the funds thus raised or provided

fin–back \'fin-,bak\ n (1725) : FIN WHALE

finch \'finch\ n [ME, fr. OE *finc;* akin to OHG *fincho* finch and perh. to Gk *spiza* chaffinch] (bef. 12c) : any of numerous songbirds (esp. families Fringillidae, Estrildidae, and Emberizidae) having a short stout usu. conical bill adapted for crushing seeds — compare BUNTING, CROSSBILL, GOLDFINCH, GROSBEAK, LINNET, SPARROW

¹find \'find\ vb **found** \'faùnd\; **find·ing** [ME, fr. OE *findan;* akin to OHG *findan* to find, L *pont-, pons* bridge, Gk *pontos* sea, Skt *patha* way, course] vt (bef. 12c) **1 a** : to come upon often accidentally : ENCOUNTER **b** : to meet with (a particular reception) ⟨hoped to ~ favor⟩ **2 a** : to come upon by searching or effort ⟨must ~ a suitable person for the job⟩ **b** : to discover by study or experiment ⟨~ an answer⟩ **c** : to obtain by effort or management ⟨~ the time to study⟩ **d** : ATTAIN, REACH ⟨the bullet *found* its mark⟩ **3 a** : to discover by the intellect or the feelings : EXPERIENCE ⟨~ much pleasure in your com-

pany⟩ **b** : to perceive (oneself) to be in a certain place or condition : to gain or regain the use or power of ⟨trying to ~ his tongue⟩ **d** : to bring (oneself) to a realization of one's powers or of one's proper sphere of activity ⟨must help the student to ~ himself as an individual —N. M. Pusey⟩ **4 a** : PROVIDE, SUPPLY **b** : to furnish (room and board) esp. as a condition of employment **5** : to determine and make a statement about ⟨~ a verdict⟩ ⟨*found* her guilty⟩ ~ vi : to determine a case judicially by a verdict ⟨~ for the defendant⟩ — **find·able** \'fīn-də-bəl\ *adj* — **find fault** : to criticize unfavorably

²find n (1825) **1** : an act or instance of finding **2** : something found: as **a** : a valuable discovery ⟨an archaeological ~⟩ **b** : a person whose ability proves to be unexpectedly good

find·er \'fīn-dər\ n (14c) **1** : one that finds **2** : a small astronomical telescope of low power and wide field attached to a larger telescope for finding an object **3** : VIEWFINDER

fin de siè·cle \,fan-də-sē-'e-k³l; faⁿ-də-syekl'\ *adj* [F, end of the century] (1890) : of, relating to, or characteristic of the close of the 19th century and esp. its literary and artistic climate of sophistication, world-weariness, and fashionable despair

find·ing \'fīn-diŋ\ n (14c) **1 a** : the act of one that finds **b** : FIND 2 **2** pl : small tools and supplies used by an artisan (as a dressmaker, jeweler, or shoemaker) **3 a** : the result of a judicial examination or inquiry **b** : the results of an investigation — usu. used in pl.

find out vt (13c) **1** : to learn by study, observation, or search : DISCOVER **2 a** : to catch in an offense (as a crime) ⟨the culprits were soon *found out*⟩ **b** : to ascertain the true character or identity of ⟨the informer was *found out*⟩ ~ vi : to discover, learn, or verify something ⟨I don't know, but I'll *find out* for you⟩

¹fine \'fīn\ n [ME, fr. OF *fin,* fr. L *finis* boundary, end] (13c) **1** *obs* : END, CONCLUSION **2** : a compromise of a fictitious suit used as a form of conveyance of lands **3 a** : a sum imposed as punishment for an offense **b** : a forfeiture or penalty paid to an injured party in a civil action — **in fine** : in short

²fine vt **fined; fin·ing** (1559) : to impose a fine on : punish by a fine

³fine *adj* **fin·er; fin·est** [ME *fin,* fr. OF, fr. L *finis,* n., end, limit] (13c) **1 a** : free from impurity **b** *of a metal* : having a stated proportion of pure metal in the composition expressed in parts per thousand ⟨a gold coin .9166 ~⟩ **2 a** (1) : very thin in gauge or texture ⟨~ thread⟩ (2) : not coarse ⟨~ sand⟩ (3) : very small ⟨~ print⟩ (4) : KEEN ⟨a knife with a ~ edge⟩ (5) : very precise or accurate ⟨a ~ adjustment⟩ ⟨trying to be too ~ with his pitches⟩ **b** : physically trained or hardened close to the limit of efficiency — used of an athlete or animal **3** : delicate, subtle, or sensitive in quality, perception, or discrimination ⟨a ~ distinction⟩ **4** : superior in kind, quality, or appearance : EXCELLENT ⟨a ~ job⟩ ⟨a ~ day⟩ ⟨~ wines⟩ **5 a** : ORNATE 1 ⟨~ writing⟩ **b** : marked by or affecting elegance or refinement ⟨~ manners⟩ **6 a** : very well ⟨feel ~⟩ **b** : ALL RIGHT ⟨that's ~ with me⟩ **7** — used as an intensive ⟨the leader, in a ~ frenzy, beheaded one of his wives —Brian Crozier⟩ — **fine·ness** \'fīn-nəs\ n

⁴fine *adv* (14c) **1 a** : FINELY: as **a** : very well **b** : ALL RIGHT **2** : with a very narrow margin of time or space ⟨she had not intended to cut her escape so ~ —Melinda Beck *et al.*⟩

⁵fine vb **fined; fin·ing** vt (14c) **1** : PURIFY, CLARIFY ⟨~ and filter wine⟩ **2** : to make finer in quality or size ~ vi **1** : to become pure or clear ⟨the ale will ~⟩ **2** : to become smaller in lines or proportions

⁶fi·ne \'fē-(,)nä\ n [It, fr. L *finis* end] (ca. 1798) : END — used as a direction in music to mark the closing point after a repeat

fine art n (1767) **1 a** : art (as painting, sculpture, or music) concerned primarily with the creation of beautiful objects — usu. used in pl. **b** : objects of fine art **2** : an activity requiring a fine skill

fine·ly \'fīn-lē\ *adv* (14c) : in a fine manner: as **a** : extremely well : EXCELLENTLY ⟨plays the hero very ~ —*New Yorker*⟩ **b** : with close discrimination : PRECISELY **c** : with delicacy or subtlety : SENSITIVELY ⟨a leader ~ attuned to the needs of the people⟩ **d** : MINUTELY ⟨~ ground meal⟩

fine print n (1951) : something thoroughly and often deliberately obscure; *esp* : a part of an agreement or document spelling out restrictions and limitations often in small type or obscure language

fin·ery \'fīn-rē, 'fī-nə-\ n, pl **-er·ies** (1680) : ORNAMENT, DECORATION; *esp* : dressy or showy clothing and jewels

fines \'fīnz\ n pl [²*fine*] (ca. 1903) : finely crushed or powdered material (as ore); *also* : very small particles in a mixture of various sizes

fines herbes \fēn-'zerb, fē-'nerb\ n pl [F, lit., fine herbs] (1846) : a mixture of herbs used as a seasoning or garnish

fine–spun \'fīn-'spən\ *adj* (1647) : developed with extreme care or delicacy; *also* : developed in excessively fine or subtle detail

¹fi·nesse \fə-'nes\ n [ME, fr. MF, fr. *fin*] (1528) **1** : refinement or delicacy of workmanship, structure, or texture **2** : skillful handling of a situation : adroit maneuvering **3** : the withholding of one's highest card or trump in the hope that a lower card will take the trick because the only opposing higher card is in the hand of an opponent who has already played

²finesse vb **fi·nessed; fi·ness·ing** vi (1746) : to make a finesse in playing cards ~ vt **1** : to play (a card) in a finesse **2 a** : to bring about or manage by adroit maneuvering ⟨~ his way through tight places —Marquis James⟩ **b** : EVADE, TRICK

fin·est \'fī-nəst\ n, pl in constr [superl. of ³*fine*] (1951) : POLICE OFFICERS — usu. used with the possessive form of a city or area ⟨the city's ~⟩

fine structure n (1935) : microscopic structure of a biological entity or one of its parts esp. as studied in preparations for the electron microscope — **fine structural** *adj*

fine–tooth comb \'fīn-,tüth-\ n (1839) **1** : a comb with close-set teeth used esp. for clearing parasites or foreign matter from the hair **2** : an attitude or system of thorough searching or scrutinizing ⟨went over the report with a *fine-tooth comb*⟩

fine–tune \'fīn-'tün\ vt (1967) **1 a** : to adjust precisely so as to bring to the highest level of performance or effectiveness ⟨~ a TV set⟩ ⟨~ the format⟩ **b** : to improve through minor alteration or revision ⟨~ the temperature of the room⟩ **2** : to stabilize (an economy) by small-scale fiscal and monetary manipulations

fin·fish \'fin-,fish\ n (ca. 1890) : FISH 1b — compare SHELLFISH

¹fin·ger \'fiŋ-gər\ n [ME, fr. OE; akin to OHG *fingar* finger] (bef. 12c) **1** : any of the five terminating members of the hand : a digit of the forelimb; *esp* : one other than the thumb **2 a** : something that resembles a finger ⟨a narrow ∼ of land⟩   **b** : a part of a glove into which a finger is inserted   **c** : a projecting piece (as a pawl for a ratchet) brought into contact with an object to affect its motion   **3** : the breadth of a finger   **4** : INTEREST, SHARE — often used in the phrase *have a finger in the pie*   **5** : BIRD 10 — usu. used with *the* — **fin·ger·like** \-,līk\ *adj*

²**finger** *vb* **fin·gered; fin·ger·ing** \-g(ə-)riŋ\ *vt* (15c)   **1** : to touch or feel with the fingers   **2   a** : to play (a musical instrument) with the fingers   **b** : to play (as notes or chords) with a specific fingering   **c** : to mark the notes of (a music score) as a guide in playing   **3** : to point out : IDENTIFY   **4** : to extend into or penetrate in the shape of a finger   ∼ *vi*   **1** : to touch or handle something   **2   a** : to use the fingers in playing a musical instrument   **b** : to have a certain fingering — used of a musical instrument   **3** : to extend in the shape or manner of a finger

fin·ger·board \'fiŋ-gər-,bōrd, -,bȯrd\ *n* (ca. 1672) : the part of a stringed instrument against which the fingers press the strings to vary the pitch — see VIOLIN illustration

finger bowl *n* (ca. 1860) : a small water bowl for rinsing the fingers at the table

fin·gered \'fiŋ-gərd\ *adj* (ca. 1529)   **1** : having fingers esp. of a specified kind or number — used in combination ⟨stubby-*fingered*⟩ ⟨five-*fingered*⟩   **2** : having projections or processes like fingers ⟨the ∼ roots of giant trees⟩

finger food *n* (1928) : a food that is to be held with the fingers for eating

fin·ger·hold \'fiŋ-gər-,hōld\ *n* (1909)   **1** : a hold or place of support for the fingers   **2** : a tenuous hold or support

finger hole *n* (1854)   **1** : any of several holes in the side of a wind instrument (as a recorder) which may be covered or left open by the fingers to change the pitch of the tone   **2** : a hole (as in a telephone dial or a bowling ball) into which the finger is placed to provide a grip

fin·ger·ing \'fiŋ-g(ə-)riŋ\ *n* (14c)   **1   a** : the act or method of using the fingers in playing an instrument   **b** : the marking (as by figures on a musical score) of the method of fingering   **2** : the act or process of handling or touching with the fingers

fin·ger·ling \'fiŋ-gər-liŋ\ *n* (1836) : a small fish esp. up to one year of age

fin·ger·nail \'fiŋ-gər-,nāl, ,fiŋ-gər-'nā(ə)l\ *n* (13c) : the nail of a finger

finger painting *n* (1937) : a technique of spreading pigment on wet paper chiefly with the fingers; *also* : a picture so produced

fin·ger·pick·ing \'fiŋ-gər-,pi-kiŋ\ *n* (1969) : a method of playing a stringed instrument (as a guitar) with the thumb and tips of the fingers rather than with a pick — **fin·ger·pick** *vb*

fin·ger·point·ing \-,pȯin-tiŋ\ *n* (1949) : the act of making explicit and often unfair accusations of blame

fin·ger·post \'fiŋ-gər-,pōst\ *n* (1785)   **1** : a post bearing one or more signs often terminating in a pointing finger   **2** : something serving as a guide to understanding or knowledge

fin·ger·print \-,print\ *n* (1859)   **1** : the impression of a fingertip on any surface; *also* : an ink impression of the lines upon the fingertip taken for the purpose of identification   **2** : something that identifies: as   **a** : a trait, trace, or characteristic revealing origin or responsibility   **b** : analytical evidence (as a spectrogram) that characterizes an object or substance; *esp* : the chromatogram or electrophoretogram obtained by cleaving a protein by enzymatic action and subjecting the resulting collection of peptides to two-dimensional chromatography or electrophoresis — **fingerprint** *vt* — **fin·ger·print·ing** *n*

finger spelling *n* (1918) : communication by signs made with the fingers — called also *dactylology*

fingerprint: *1* arch, *2* loop, *3* whorl, *4* composite

¹**fin·ger·tip** \-,tip\ *n* (1842)   **1** : the tip of a finger   **2** : a protective covering for the end of a finger — **at one's fingertips** : instantly or readily available

²**fingertip** *adj* (1926)   **1** : readily accessible : being within easy reach ⟨∼ information⟩ ⟨∼ controls⟩   **2** : extending from head or shoulders to mid-thigh — used of clothing

finger wave *n* (ca. 1934) : a method of setting hair by dampening with water or wave solution and forming waves or curls with the fingers and a comb

fin·i·al \'fi-nē-əl\ *n* [ME, fr. *final, finial* final] (15c)   **1** : a usu. foliated ornament forming an upper extremity esp. in Gothic architecture   **2** : a crowning ornament or detail (as a decorative knob)

fin·i·cal \'fi-ni-kəl\ *adj* [prob. fr. ³*fine*] (1592) : FINICKY — **fin·i·cal·ly** \-k(ə-)lē\ *adv* — **fin·i·cal·ness** \-kəl-nəs\ *n*

fin·ick·ing \-kiŋ, -kən\ *adj* [alter. of *finical*] (1661) : FINICKY

fin·icky \'fi-ni-kē\ *adj* [alter. of *finicking* (ca. 1825)   **1** : extremely or excessively nice, exacting, or meticulous in taste or standards   **2** : requiring much care, precision, or attentive effort ⟨a ∼ recipe⟩ — **fin·ick·i·ness** *n*

fi·nis \'fi-nəs, 'fī-nəs; fə-'nē\ *n* [ME, fr. L] (15c) : END, CONCLUSION

¹**fin·ish** \'fi-nish\ *vb* [ME *finisshen*, fr. MF *finiss-*, stem of *finir*, fr. L *finire*, fr. *finis*] *vi* (14c)   **1   a** : to come to an end : TERMINATE   **b** : END   **1b**   **2** : to come to the end of a course, task, or undertaking   **c** : to end relations — used with *with* ⟨decided to ∼ with him for good⟩   **3** : to end a competition in a specified manner or position ⟨∼*ed* third in the race⟩   ∼ *vt*   **1   a** : to bring to an end : TERMINATE ⟨∼*ed* the speech and sat down⟩   **b** : to use or dispose of entirely ⟨her sandwich ∼*ed* the loaf⟩   **2   a** : to bring to completion or issue ⟨hope to ∼ their new home before winter⟩   **b** : to provide with a finish; *esp* : to put a final coat or surface on ⟨∼ a table with varnish⟩   **3   a** : to defeat or ruin utterly and finally ⟨the scandal ∼*ed* his career⟩   **b** : to bring about the death of   *syn* see CLOSE — **fin·ish·er** *n*

²**finish** *n* (1779)   **1** : something that completes or perfects: as   **a** : the

fine or decorative work required for a building or one of its parts   **b** : finishing material used in painting   **c** : the final treatment or coating of a surface   **d** : the taste in the mouth after swallowing a beverage (as wine)   **2   a** : final stage : END   **b** : the cause of one's ruin   **3** : the result or product of a finishing process   **4** : the quality or state of being perfected

fin·ished *adj* (1709) : marked by the highest quality : CONSUMMATE

finishing school *n* (ca. 1837) : a private school for girls that emphasizes cultural studies and prepares students esp. for social activities

finish line *n* (1899) : a line marking the end of a racecourse

fi·nite \'fi-,nīt\ *adj* [ME *finit*, fr. L *finitus*, pp. of *finire*] (15c)   **1   a** : having definite or definable limits ⟨∼ number of possibilities⟩   **b** : having a limited nature or existence ⟨∼ beings⟩   **2** : completely determinable in theory or in fact by counting, measurement, or thought ⟨the ∼ velocity of light⟩   **3   a** : less than an arbitrary positive integer and greater than the negative of that integer   **b** : having a finite number of elements ⟨a ∼ set⟩   **4** : of, relating to, or being a verb or verb form that can function as a predicate or as the initial element of one and that is limited (as in tense, person, and number) — **finite** *n* — **fi·nite·ly** *adv* — **fi·nite·ness** *n*

finite difference *n* (1807) : any of a sequence of differences obtained by incrementing successively the dependent variable of a function by a fixed amount; *esp* : any of such differences obtained from a polynomial function using successive integral values of its dependent variable

fi·ni·tude \'fi-nə-,tüd, -,tyüd, 'fin-ə-\ *n* (1644) : finite quality or state

¹**fink** \'fiŋk\ *n* [origin unknown] (1903)   **1** : one who is disapproved of or is held in contempt   **2** : STRIKEBREAKER   **3** : INFORMER 2

²**fink** *vi* (ca. 1925) : to turn informer : SQUEAL

fink out *vi* (1956) : BACK OUT, COP OUT

Fin·land·isa·tion *Brit var of* FINLANDIZATION

Fin·land·iza·tion \,fin-lən-də-'zā-shən, (,)fin-,lan-\ *n* [*Finland*] (1969) : a foreign policy of neutrality under the influence of the Soviet Union; *also* : the conversion to such a policy — **Fin·land·ize** \'fin-lən-,dīz, (,)fin-'lan-\ *vt*

Finn \'fin\ *n* [Sw *Finne*] (bef. 12c)   **1** : a member of a people speaking Finnish or a Finnic language   **2   a** : a native or inhabitant of Finland   **b** : one who is of Finnish descent

fin·nan had·die \,fi-nən-'ha-dē\ *n* [alter. of *findon haddock*, fr. *Findon*, village in Scotland] (1811) : smoked haddock — called also *finnan haddock*

Finn·ic \'fi-nik\ *adj* (1668)   **1** : of or relating to the Finns   **2** : of, relating to, or constituting the branch of the Finno-Ugric subfamily that includes Finnish, Estonian, and Lapp

¹**Finn·ish** \'fi-nish\ *adj* (1699) : of, relating to, or characteristic of Finland, the Finns, or Finnish

²**Finnish** *n* (ca. 1845) : a Finno-Ugric language spoken in Finland, Karelia, and small areas of Sweden and Norway

Fin·no-Ugri·an \,fi-(,)nō-'(y)ü-grē-ən\ *adj* (1880) : FINNO-UGRIC — **Finno-Ugrian** *n*

Fin·no-Ugric \,fi-nō-'(y)ü-grik\ *adj* (1879)   **1** : of, relating to, or constituting a subfamily of the Uralic family of languages comprising various languages spoken in Hungary, Lapland, Finland, Estonia, and parts of western Russia   **2** : of or relating to any of the peoples speaking Finno-Ugric languages — **Finno-Ugric** *n*

fin·ny \'fi-nē\ *adj* (1590)   **1** : provided with or characterized by fins   **2** : relating to or being fish

fino \'fē-(,)nō\ *n, pl* **finos** [Sp, fr. *fino* fine, fr. *fin* end, fr. L *finis*] (1846) : a very dry Spanish sherry

fin whale *n* (1885) : a baleen whale (*Balaenoptera physalus*) that attains a length of over 60 feet (18.3 meters) and is found in arctic to tropical waters worldwide — called also *finback*

fin whale

fiord *var of* FJORD

fio·ri·tu·ra \fē-,ȯr-ə-'tur-ə\ *n, pl* **-tu·re** \-'tur-ē\ [It, lit., flowering, fr. *fiorito*, pp. of *fiorire* to flower, fr. (assumed) VL *florire* — more at FLOURISH] (1841) : ORNAMENT 5

fip·ple flute \'fi-pəl-\ *n* [origin unknown] (1911) : any of a group of wind instruments (as a flageolet or recorder) having a straight tubular shape, a whistle mouthpiece, and finger holes

fir \'fər\ *n* [ME, fr. OE *fyrh*; akin to OHG *forha* fir, L *quercus* oak] (bef. 12c)   **1** : any of a genus (*Abies*) of north temperate evergreen trees of the pine family that have flattish leaves, circular leaf scars, and erect female cones and are valued for their wood; *also* : any of various conifers (as the Douglas fir) of other genera   **2** : the wood of a fir

¹**fire** \'fīr\ *n, often attrib* [ME, fr. OE *fyr*; akin to OHG *fiur* fire, Gk *pyr*] (bef. 12c)   **1   a** (1) : the phenomenon of combustion manifested in light, flame, and heat   (2) : one of the four elements of the alchemists   **b** (1) : burning passion : ARDOR   (2) : liveliness of imagination : INSPIRATION   **2   a** : fuel in a state of combustion (as on a hearth)   **b** *Brit* : a small gas or electric space heater   **3   a** : a destructive burning (as of a building)   **b** (1) : death or torture by fire   (2) : severe trial or ordeal   **4** : BRILLIANCY, LUMINOSITY ⟨the ∼ of a gem⟩   **5   a** : the firing of weapons (as firearms, artillery, or missiles)   **b** : intense verbal attack or criticism   **c** : a rapidly delivered series (as of remarks) — **fire·less** \-ləs\ *adj* — **on fire**   **1** : being consumed by fire : AFLAME   **2**

\ə\ abut   \ᵊ\ kitten, F table   \ər\ further   \a\ ash   \ā\ ace   \ä\ mop, mar
\au̇\ out   \ch\ chin   \e\ bet   \ē\ easy   \g\ go   \i\ hit   \ī\ ice   \j\ job
\ŋ\ sing   \ō\ go   \ȯ\ law   \ȯi\ boy   \th\ thin   \t̲h̲\ the   \ü\ loot   \u̇\ foot
\y\ yet   \zh\ vision   \à, k̲, ⁿ, œ, œ̄, ᵾ, ᵫ, ᵞ\ *see* Guide to Pronunciation

: EAGER, BURNING — **under fire 1 :** exposed to fire from an enemy's weapons **2 :** under attack

²fire *vb* **fired; fir-ing** *vt* (13c) **1 a :** to set on fire : KINDLE; *also* : IGNITE ⟨~ a rocket engine⟩ **b** (1) : to give life or spirit to : INSPIRE (2) : to fill with passion or enthusiasm — often used with *up* **c :** to light up as if by fire **d :** to cause to start operating — usu. used with *up* **2 a :** to drive out or away by or as if by fire **b :** to dismiss from a position **3 a** (1) : to cause to explode : DETONATE (2) : to propel from or as if from a gun : DISCHARGE, LAUNCH ⟨~ a rocket⟩ (3) : SHOOT 1b ⟨~ a gun⟩ (4) : to score (a number) in a game or contest **b :** to throw with speed or force ⟨*fired* the ball to first base⟩ ⟨~ a left jab⟩ **c :** to utter with force and rapidity **4 :** to apply fire or fuel to: as **a :** to process by applying heat **b :** to feed or serve the fire of ~ *vi* **1 a :** to take fire : KINDLE, IGNITE **b :** to begin operation : START ⟨the engine *fired*⟩ **c :** to operate esp. as the result of the application of an electrical impulse ⟨the spark plug ~s⟩ **2 a :** to become irritated or angry — often used with *up* **b :** to become filled with excitement or enthusiasm **3 a :** to discharge a firearm **b :** to emit or let fly an object **4 :** to tend a fire **5 :** to transmit a nerve impulse — **fire-able** \'fīr-ə-bəl, 'fī-rə-\ *adj* — **fir-er** *n*

fire and brimstone *n* (13c) : the torments suffered by sinners in hell — **fire–and–brimstone** *adj*

fire ant *n* (1796) : any of a genus (*Solenopsis*) of fiercely stinging omnivorous ants; *esp* : IMPORTED FIRE ANT

fire-arm \'fīr-,ärm\ *n* (1646) : a weapon from which a shot is discharged by gunpowder — usu. used of small arms

fire away *vi* (1840) : to speak without hesitation — usu. used as an imperative

fire-back \-,bak\ *n* (1847) : an often decorated cast-iron plate lining the back wall of a fireplace

fire-ball \'fīr-,bȯl\ *n* (1555) **1 :** a ball of fire; *also* : something resembling such a ball ⟨the primordial ~ associated with the beginning of the universe —*Scientific American*⟩ **2 :** a brilliant meteor that may trail bright sparks **3 :** the highly luminous cloud of vapor and dust created by a nuclear explosion **4 :** a highly energetic person

fire-ball-er \-,bȯ-lər\ *n* (1946) : a baseball pitcher known for throwing fastballs — **fire-ball-ing** \-liŋ\ *adj*

fire-base \-,bās\ *n* (1968) : a secured site from which field artillery can lay down interdicting fire

fire blight *n* (1817) : a destructive infectious disease esp. of apples, pears, and related fruits caused by a bacterium (*Erwinia amylovora*)

fire-boat \'fīr-,bōt\ *n* (1849) : a ship equipped with fire-fighting apparatus

fire-bomb \-,bäm\ *n* (1895) : an incendiary bomb — **firebomb** *vt*

fire-box \-,bäks\ *n* (1791) **1 :** a chamber (as of a furnace or steam boiler) that contains a fire **2 :** a box containing an apparatus for transmitting an alarm to a fire station

fire-brand \-,brand\ *n* (13c) **1 :** a piece of burning wood **2 :** one that creates unrest or strife (as in aggressively promoting a cause) : AGITATOR

fire-brat \-,brat\ *n* (1895) : a wingless insect (*Thermobia domestica*) related to the silverfish and found in warm moist places

fire-break \-,brāk\ *n* (1841) : a barrier of cleared or plowed land intended to check a forest or grass fire

fire–breath-ing \-,brē-thiŋ\ *adj* (1933) : intimidatingly or violently aggressive in speech and manner ⟨a ~ orator⟩

fire-brick \-,brik\ *n* (1793) : a refractory brick capable of sustaining high temperatures that is used esp. for lining furnaces or fireplaces

fire brigade *n* (1838) : a body of firefighters: as **a :** a usu. private or temporary fire-fighting organization **b** *Brit* : FIRE DEPARTMENT

fire-bug \'fīr-,bəg\ *n* (1872) : INCENDIARY, PYROMANIAC

fire chief *n* (1889) : the head of a fire department

fire-clay \'fīr-,klā\ *n* (1819) : clay capable of withstanding high temperatures that is used esp. for firebrick and crucibles

fire control *n* (1864) : the planning, preparation, and delivery of fire on targets

fire-crack-er \'fīr-,kra-kər\ *n* (1829) : a usu. paper cylinder containing an explosive and a fuse and set off to make a noise

fired \'fīrd\ *adj* (1889) : using a specified fuel — usu. used in combination ⟨oil-*fired* power plant⟩

fire-damp \'fīr-,damp\ *n* (1677) : a combustible mine gas that consists chiefly of methane; *also* : the explosive mixture of this gas with air

fire department *n* (1825) **1 :** an organization for preventing or extinguishing fires; *esp* : a government division (as in a municipality) having these duties **2 :** the members of a fire department

fire-dog \-,dȯg\ *n* (1792) *chiefly Southern & Midland* : ANDIRON

fire-drake \'fīr-,drāk\ *n* [ME *firdrake*, fr. OE *fyrdraca*, fr. *fyr* + *draca* dragon, fr. L *draco* — more at DRAGON] (bef. 12c) : a fire-breathing dragon esp. in Germanic mythology

fire drill *n* (ca. 1890) : a practice drill in extinguishing fires or in the conduct and manner of exit in case of fire

fire–eat-er \'fīr-,ē-tər\ *n* (1672) **1 :** a performer who pretends to eat fire **2 a :** a violent or pugnacious person **b :** a person who displays very militant or aggressive partisanship

fire–eat-ing \-,ē-tiŋ\ *adj* (1819) : violent or highly militant in disposition, bearing, or policy ⟨a ~ radical⟩

fire engine *n* (ca. 1680) : a usu. mobile apparatus for directing an extinguishing agent upon fires; *esp* : FIRE TRUCK

fire–en-gine red \'fīr-,en-jən-\ *n* (1954) : a bright red

fire escape *n* (1788) : a device for escape from a burning building; *esp* : a metal stairway attached to the outside of a building

fire extinguisher *n* (1849) : a portable or wheeled apparatus for putting out small fires by ejecting extinguishing chemicals

fire-fight \'fīr-,fīt\ *n* (1899) **1 a :** a usu. brief intense exchange of fire between opposing military units **b :** a hostile confrontation that involves gunfire **2 :** SKIRMISH 2b

fire-fight-er \-,fī-tər\ *n* (1903) : a person who fights fires : FIREMAN 2 — **fire fighting** *n*

fire-fly \-,flī\ *n* (1658) : any of various winged nocturnal beetles (esp. family Lampyridae) that produce a bright soft intermittent light by oxidation of luciferin esp. for courtship purposes

fire-guard \-,gärd\ *n* (1833) **1 :** a person who watches for the outbreak of fire; *also* : a person whose duty is to extinguish fires **2 :** FIRE SCREEN **3 :** FIREBREAK

fire hall *n* (1881) *chiefly Canad* : FIRE STATION

fire-house \'fīr-,haus\ *n* (1901) : FIRE STATION

fire irons *n pl* (1648) : utensils (as tongs) for tending a fire esp. in a fireplace

fire-light \'fīr-,līt\ *n* (bef. 12c) : the light of a fire (as in a fireplace) — **fire-lit** \-,lit\ *adj*

fire-lock \-,läk\ *n* (1547) **1 :** a gun's lock employing a slow match to ignite the powder charge; *also* : a gun having such a lock **2 a :** FLINTLOCK **b :** WHEEL LOCK

fire-man \-mən\ *n* (14c) **1 :** a person who tends or feeds fires : STOKER **2 :** a member of a fire department : FIREFIGHTER **3 :** an enlisted man in the navy who works with engineering machinery **4 :** a relief pitcher in baseball

fire-man-ic \-,ma-nik\ *adj* [*fireman* + ¹-*ic*] (1902) : of or relating to firefighters or fire fighting

fire off *vt* (1888) : to write and send usu. in haste or anger ⟨*fired off* a memo⟩

fire opal *n* (1816) : GIRASOLE 2

fire-place \'fīr-,plās\ *n* (1698) **1 :** a framed opening made in a chimney to hold an open fire : HEARTH; *also* : a metal container such as a smoke pipe used for the same purpose **2 :** an outdoor structure of brick, stone, or metal for an open fire — **fire-placed** \-,plāst\ *adj*

fire-plug \-,pləg\ *n* (1713) : HYDRANT

fire-pot \-,pät\ *n* (1627) **1 :** a clay pot filled with combustibles formerly used as a missile in war **2 :** a vessel used in Oriental cuisine for cooking foods in broth at the table; *also* : the food cooked in it

fire-pow-er \-,pau̇-(ə)r\ *n* (1913) **1 a :** the capacity (as of a military unit) to deliver effective fire on a target **b :** effective fire **2 a :** effective power or force ⟨intellectual ~⟩ **b :** the scoring action or potential of a team or player

¹fire-proof \-,prüf\ *adj* (ca. 1638) : proof against or resistant to fire

²fireproof *vt* (1867) : to make fireproof

fire sale *n* (1891) : a sale of merchandise damaged in a fire; *also* : a sale at very low prices

fire screen *n* (15c) : a protective screen before a fireplace

fire ship *n* (1588) : a ship carrying combustibles or explosives sent among the enemy's ships or works to set them on fire

¹fire-side \'fīr-,sīd\ *n* (1563) **1 :** a place near the fire or hearth **2 :** HOME

²fireside *adj* (1740) : having an informal or intimate quality ⟨a ~ chat⟩

fire station *n* (1877) : a building housing fire apparatus and usu. firefighters

fire-stone \'fīr-,stōn\ *n* (bef. 12c) **1 :** pyrite formerly used for striking fire; *also* : FLINT **2 :** a stone that will endure high heat

fire–stop \-,stäp\ *n* (1897) : material used to close open parts esp. of a building for preventing the spread of fire — **fire–stop** *vt*

fire-storm \-,stȯrm\ *n* (1945) **1 :** a large usu. stationary fire characterized by very high temperatures in which the central column of rising heated air induces strong inward winds which supply oxygen to the fire **2 :** a sudden or violent outburst ⟨a ~ of public protest⟩

fire-thorn \-,thȯrn\ *n* (ca. 1900) : any of a genus (*Pyracantha*) of usu. thorny ornamental shrubs of the rose family; *esp* : a European semievergreen shrub (*P. coccinea*) with orange-red berries

fire tower *n* (1827) : a tower (as in a forest) from which a watch for fires is maintained

fire-trap \'fīr-,trap\ *n* (1881) : a place (as a building) apt to catch on fire or difficult to escape from in case of fire

fire truck *n* (1935) : an automotive vehicle equipped with fire-fighting apparatus

fire wall *n* (1759) : a wall constructed to prevent the spread of fire

fire-wa-ter \'fīr-,wȯ-tər, -,wä-\ *n* (1817) : strong alcoholic liquor

fire-weed \-,wēd\ *n* (1784) : any of several plants that grow esp. in clearings or burned districts: as **a :** a weedy composite (*Erechtites hieracifolia*) of the eastern U.S. and Canada that has clusters of brush-shaped flower heads with no ray flowers **b :** a tall perennial (*Epilobium angustifolium*) of the evening-primrose family that has long spikes of pinkish purple flowers and is an important honey plant in some areas — called also *willow herb*

fire-wood \-,wud\ *n* (14c) : wood used for fuel

fire-work \-,wərk\ *n* (1575) **1 :** a device for producing a striking display by the combustion of explosive or flammable compositions **2** *pl* : a display of fireworks **3** *pl* **a :** a display of temper or intense conflict **b :** a spectacular display ⟨the ~s of autumn leaves⟩

fir-ing \'fīr-iŋ\ *n* (14c) **1 :** the act or process of one that fires **2 :** the process of maturing ceramic products by the application of heat

firing line *n* (1881) **1 :** a line from which fire is delivered against a target **2 :** the forefront of an activity — used esp. in the phrase *on the firing line*

firing pin *n* (1874) : the pin that strikes the cartridge primer in the breech mechanism of a firearm

firing squad *n* (1904) **1 :** a detachment detailed to fire volleys over the grave of one buried with military honors **2 :** a detachment detailed to carry out a sentence of death by shooting

fir-kin \'fər-kən\ *n* [ME, ultim. fr. MD *veerdel* fourth, fr. *veer* four; akin to OE *fēower* — more at FOUR] (14c) **1 :** a small wooden vessel or cask **2 :** any of various British units of capacity usu. equal to ¼ barrel

¹firm \'fərm\ *adj* [ME *ferm*, fr. MF, fr. L *firmus*; akin to Gk *thronos* chair, throne] (14c) **1 a :** securely or solidly fixed in place **b :** not weak or uncertain : VIGOROUS **c :** having a solid or compact structure that resists stress or pressure **2 a** (1) : not subject to change or revision (2) : not subject to price weakness : STEADY **b :** not easily moved or disturbed : STEADFAST **c :** WELL-FOUNDED **3 :** indicating firmness or resolution ⟨a ~ mouth⟩ — **firm-ly** *adv* — **firm-ness** *n*

²firm *adv* (14c) : in a firm manner : STEADFASTLY, FIXEDLY

³firm *vt* (14c) **1 a :** to make secure or fast : TIGHTEN ⟨~ing her grip on the racquet⟩ — often used with *up* **b :** to make solid or compact ⟨~ the soil⟩ **2 :** to put into final form : SETTLE ⟨~ a contract⟩ — often used with *up* **3 :** to give additional support to : STRENGTHEN — usu. used with *up* ~ *vi* **1 :** to become firm : HARDEN — often used with *up* **2 :** to recover from a decline : IMPROVE ⟨the market is ~ing⟩

⁴firm *n* [G *Firma*, fr. It, signature, ultim. fr. L *firmare* to make firm, confirm, fr. *firmus*] (1744) **1 :** the name or title under which a company transacts business **2 :** a partnership of two or more persons that is not recognized as a legal person distinct from the members composing it **3** : a business unit or enterprise

fir·ma·ment \'fər-mə-mənt\ *n* [ME, fr. LL & L; LL *firmamentum*, fr. L, support, fr. *firmare*] (13c) **1** : the vault or arch of the sky : HEAVENS **2** *obs* : BASIS **3** : the field or sphere of an interest or activity ⟨the international fashion ∼⟩ — **fir·ma·men·tal** \,fər-mə-'men-t²l\ *adj*

fir·mer chisel \'fər-mər-\ *n* [F *fermoir* chisel, alter. of MF *formoir*, fr. *former* to form, fr. OF *forme* form] (1823) : a woodworking chisel with a thin flat blade

firm·ware \'fərm-,war, -,wer\ *n* (1967) : computer programs contained permanently in a hardware device (as a read-only memory)

firn \'firn\ *n* [G, fr. OHG *firni* old; akin to OE *faran*] (1853) : NÉVÉ

¹first \'fərst\ *adj* [ME, fr. OE *fyrst*; akin to OHG *furist* first, OE *faran* to go — more at FARE] (bef. 12c) : preceding all others in time, order, or importance: as **a** : EARLIEST **b** : being the lowest forward gear or speed of a motor vehicle **c** : having the highest or most prominent part among a group of similar voices or instruments ⟨∼ tenor⟩ ⟨∼ violins⟩

²first *adv* (bef. 12c) **1 a** : before another in time, space, or importance **b** : in the first place — often used with *of all* **c** : for the first time **2** : in preference to something else : SOONER

³first *n* (13c) **1** — see NUMBER table **2** : something that is first: as **a** : the first occurrence or item of a kind **b** : the first forward gear or speed of a motor vehicle **c** : the highest or chief voice or instrument of a group **d** : an article of commerce of the finest grade **e** : the winning or highest place in a competition, examination, or contest **3** : FIRST BASE — **at first** : at the beginning : INITIALLY

first aid *n* (1882) : emergency care or treatment given to an ill or injured person before regular medical aid can be obtained

first base *n* (1845) **1** : the base that must be touched first by a base runner in baseball **2** : the player position for defending the area around first base **3** : the first step or stage in a course of action ⟨plans never got to *first base*⟩ — **first base·man** \-'bā-smən\ *n*

first·born \'fərs(t)-'bórn\ *adj* (14c) : first brought forth : ELDEST — **firstborn** *n*

first cause *n* (14c) : the self-created ultimate source of all being

first–class \'fərs(t)-'klas\ *adj* (ca. 1838) **1** : of or relating to first class **2** : of the highest quality ⟨a ∼ meal⟩ — **first–class** *adv*

first class *n* (1750) : the first or highest group in a classification: as **a** : the highest of usu. three classes of travel accommodations **b** : a class of mail that comprises letters, postcards, or matter sealed against inspection

first cousin *n* (1661) : COUSIN 1a

first day cover *n* (1932) : a philatelic cover franked with a newly issued postage stamp and postmarked on the first day of issue at a city officially chosen for first day sale

first–degree burn *n* (ca. 1929) : a mild burn characterized by heat, pain, and reddening of the burned surface but not exhibiting blistering or charring of tissues

first down *n* (1897) **1** : the first of a series of usu. four downs in which a football team must net a 10-yard gain to retain possession of the ball **2** : a gain of a total of 10 or more yards within usu. four downs giving the team the right to start a new series of downs

first edition *n* (ca. 1828) : the copies of a literary work first printed from the same type and issued at the same time; *also* : a single copy from a first edition

first estate *n*, *often cap F&E* (1935) : the first of the traditional political estates; *specif* : CLERGY

first floor *n* (15c) **1** : GROUND FLOOR 1 **2** *chiefly Brit* : the floor next above the ground floor

first–fruits \'fərs(t)-'früts\ *n pl* (14c) **1** : the earliest gathered fruits offered to the Deity in acknowledgment of the gift of fruitfulness **2** : the earliest products or results of an endeavor

first·hand \'fərst-'hand\ *adj* (1748) : obtained by, coming from, or being direct personal observation or experience ⟨a ∼ account of the war⟩ — **firsthand** *adv*

first lady *n*, *often cap F&L* (1834) **1** : the wife or hostess of the chief executive of a country or jurisdiction **2** : the leading woman of an art or profession

first lieutenant *n* (1782) **1** : a commissioned officer in the army, air force, or marine corps ranking above a second lieutenant and below a captain **2** : a naval officer responsible for a ship's upkeep

first·ling \'fərst-liŋ\ *n* (1535) **1** : the first of a class or kind **2** : the first produce or result of something

first·ly \-lē\ *adv* (ca. 1532) : in the first place : FIRST

first mortgage *n* (1855) : a mortgage that has priority as a lien over all mortgages and liens except those imposed by law

first name *n* (13c) : the name that stands first in one's full name

first night *n* (1711) : the night on which a theatrical production is first performed at a given place; *also* : the performance itself

first–night·er \'fərs(t)-'nī-tər\ *n* (1882) : a spectator at a first-night performance

first off *adv* (1880) : in the first place : before anything else

first offender *n* (1849) : one convicted of an offense for the first time

first papers *n pl* (1912) : papers declaring intention filed by an applicant for citizenship as the first step in the naturalization process

first person *n* (1520) **1 a** : a set of linguistic forms (as verb forms, pronouns, and inflectional affixes) referring to the speaker or writer of the utterance in which they occur **b** : a linguistic form belonging to such a set **c** : reference of a linguistic form to the speaker or writer of the utterance in which it occurs **2** : a style of discourse marked by general use of verbs and pronouns of the first person

¹first–rate \'fərs(t)-'rāt\ *adj* (1671) : of the first order of size, importance, or quality — **first–rate·ness** *n* — **first–rat·er** \-'rā-tər\ *n*

²first–rate *adv* (1844) : very well ⟨is getting along ∼, now —Mark Twain⟩

First Reader *n* (1895) : a Christian Scientist chosen to conduct meetings for a specified time and specif. to read aloud from the writings of Mary Baker Eddy

first reading *n* (ca. 1703) : the first submitting of a bill before a quorum of a legislative assembly usu. by title or number only

first–run \'fərs(t)-'rən\ *adj* (1912) : available for public viewing for the first time ⟨∼ movies⟩; *also* : exhibiting first-run movies ⟨∼ theaters⟩

first sergeant *n* (ca. 1860) **1** : a noncommissioned officer serving as

the chief assistant to the commander of a military unit (as a company or squadron) **2** : the rank of a first sergeant; *specif* : a rank in the army above a platoon sergeant and below a command sergeant major and in the marine corps above a gunnery sergeant and below a sergeant major

first strike *n* (1960) : a preemptive nuclear attack — **first–strike** *adj*

first–string \'fərs(t)-'striŋ\ *adj* (1917) **1** : being a regular as distinguished from a substitute (as on a team) **2** : FIRST-RATE

first water *n* (1753) **1** : the purest luster — used of gems **2** : the highest grade, degree, or quality

first world *n*, *often cap F&W* [after *third world*] (1967) : the highly developed industrialized nations often considered the westernized countries of the world

firth \'fərth\ *n* [ME, fr. ON *fjǫrthr* — more at FORD] (14c) : ESTUARY

fisc \'fisk\ *n* [L *fiscus*] (1598) : a state or royal treasury

¹fis·cal \'fis-kəl\ *adj* [L *fiscalis*, fr. *fiscus* basket, treasury] (1563) **1** : of or relating to taxation, public revenues, or public debt ⟨∼ policy⟩ **2** : of or relating to financial matters — **fis·cal·ly** \-kə-lē\ *adv*

²fiscal *n* (1929) **1** : REVENUE STAMP **2** : FISCAL YEAR

fiscal year *n* (1843) : an accounting period of 12 months

¹fish \'fish\ *n, pl* **fish** *or* **fish·es** *often attrib* [ME, fr. OE *fisc*; akin to OHG *fisc* fish, L *piscis*] (bef. 12c) **1 a** : an aquatic animal — usu. used in combination ⟨star*fish*⟩ ⟨cuttle*fish*⟩ **b** : any of numerous cold‑blooded strictly aquatic craniate vertebrates that include the bony fishes and usu. the cartilaginous and jawless fishes and that have typically an elongated somewhat spindle-shaped body terminating in a broad caudal fin, limbs in the form of fins when present at all, and a 2-chambered heart by which blood is sent through thoracic gills to be oxygenated **2** : the flesh of fish used as food **3 a** : a person who is caught or is wanted (as in a criminal investigation) **b** : FELLOW, PERSON ⟨an odd ∼⟩ **c** : SUCKER 5a **4** : something that resembles a fish: as **a** *pl, cap* : PISCES 1, 2a **b** : TORPEDO 2b — **fish·less** \'fish-ləs\ *adj* — **fish·like** \-,līk\ *adj* — **fish out of water** : a person who is in an unnatural or uncomfortable sphere or situation — **fish to fry** : concerns or interests to pursue — usu. used with *other* — **neither fish nor fowl** : one that does not belong to a particular class or category

fish 1b: *1* mandible, *2* nasal opening, *3* eye, *4* cheek, *5* operculum, *6* dorsal fins, *7* lateral line, *8* caudal fin, *9* scales, *10* anal fin, *11* anus, *12* pectoral fin, *13* pelvic fin, *14* maxilla, *15* premaxilla, *16* upper jaw

²fish *vi* (bef. 12c) **1** : to attempt to catch fish **2** : to seek something by roundabout means ⟨∼ing for a compliment⟩ **3 a** : to search for something underwater ⟨∼ for pearls⟩ **b** : to engage in a search by groping or feeling ⟨∼ing around in her purse for her keys⟩ ∼ *vt* **1 a** : to try to catch fish in **b** : to fish with : use (as a boat, net, or bait) in fishing **2 a** : to go fishing for ⟨∼ salmon⟩ **b** : to pull or draw as if fishing ⟨∼ed the ball from under the car⟩ ⟨∼ wires through a conduit⟩ — **fish·abil·i·ty** \,fish-ə-'bi-lə-tē\ *n* — **fish·able** \'fi-shə-bəl\ *adj* — **fish or cut bait** : to make a choice between alternatives

fish–and–chips \,fi-sh²n-'chips\ *n pl* (1876) : fried fish and french fried potatoes

fish·bowl \'fish-,bōl\ *n* (1906) **1** : a bowl for the keeping of live fish **2** : a place or condition that affords no privacy

fish cake *n* (1854) : a round fried cake made of shredded fish and mashed potato

fish duck *n* (1858) : MERGANSER

fish·er \'fi-shər\ *n* (bef. 12c) **1** : one that fishes **2 a** : a large dark brown No. American carnivorous mammal (*Martes pennanti*) related to the weasels **b** : the fur or pelt of this animal

fish·er·folk \'fi-shər-,fōk\ *n pl* (1854) : people who fish esp. for a living

fish·er·man \-mən\ *n* (15c) **1** : one who engages in fishing as an occupation or for pleasure **2** : a ship used in commercial fishing

fisherman's bend *n* (1823) : a knot made by passing the end twice round a spar or through a ring and then back under both turns — see KNOT illustration

fish·er·wo·man \'fi-shər-,wu̇-mən\ *n* (1816) : a woman who fishes as an occupation or for pleasure

fish·ery \'fi-shə-rē\ *n, pl* **-er·ies** (1528) **1** : the occupation, industry, or season of taking fish or other sea animals (as sponges, shrimp, or seals) : FISHING **2** : a place for catching fish or taking other sea animals **3** : a fishing establishment; *also* : its fishermen **4** : the legal right to take fish at a particular place or in particular waters **5** : the technology of fishery — usu. used in pl.

fish–eye \'fish-,ī\ *adj* (1943) : being, having, or produced by a wide‑angle photographic lens that has a highly curved protruding front, that covers an angle of about 180 degrees, and that gives a circular image

fish farm *n* (1865) : a commercial facility for raising aquatic animals for human food — **fish–farm** \'fish-,färm\ *vt*

fish finger *n* (1962) *Brit* : FISH STICK

\ə\ abut \²\ kitten, F table \ər\ further \a\ ash \ā\ ace \ä\ mop, mar \au̇\ out \ch\ chin \e\ bet \ē\ easy \g\ go \i\ hit \ī\ ice \j\ job \ŋ\ sing \ō\ go \ȯ\ law \ȯi\ boy \th\ thin \t͟h\ the \ü\ loot \u̇\ foot \y\ yet \zh\ vision \ä, k̲, ⁿ, œ, œ̄, ᵫ, ᵫ̄, ᵊ\ *see* Guide to Pronunciation

fish fry *n* (1824) **1** : a picnic or supper featuring fried fish **2** : fried fish

fish hawk *n* (1709) : OSPREY 1

fish·hook \'fish-,hůk\ *n* (14c) : a usu. barbed hook for catching fish

fish·ing *n* (13c) **1** : the sport or business of catching fish **2** : a place for catching fish

fishing expedition *n* (ca. 1925) **1** : a legal interrogation or examination to discover information for a later proceeding **2** : an investigation that does not stick to a stated objective but hopes to uncover incriminating or newsworthy evidence

fish ladder *n* (1865) : a series of pools arranged like steps by which fish can pass over a dam in going upstream

fish meal *n* (1854) : ground dried fish and fish waste used as fertilizer and animal food

fish·mong·er \'fish-,män-gər, -,mən-\ *n* (15c) *chiefly Brit* : a fish dealer

fish·net \-,net\ *n* (bef. 12c) **1** : netting fitted with floats and weights or a supporting frame for catching fish **2** : a coarse open-mesh fabric

fish out *vt* (1892) : to exhaust the supply of fish in by fishing

fish·plate \-,plāt\ *n* (1855) : a steel plate used to lap a butt joint

fish·pond \-,pänd\ *n* (14c) : a pond stocked with fish

fish protein concentrate *n* (1961) : a protein-rich food additive made from ground whole fish

fish stick *n* (1953) : a small elongated breaded fillet of fish

fish story *n* [fr. the traditional exaggeration by fishermen of the size of fish almost caught] (1819) : an extravagant or incredible story

fish·tail \'fish-,tāl\ *vi* (1927) **1** : to swing the tail of an airplane from side to side to reduce speed esp. when landing **2** : to have the rear end slide from side to side out of control while moving forward ⟨the car ~ed on the icy curve⟩

fish·way \-,wā\ *n* (1845) : a contrivance for enabling fish to pass around a fall or dam in a stream; *specif* : FISH LADDER

fish·wife \-,wīf\ *n* [ME] (15c) **1** : a woman who sells fish **2** : a vulgar abusive woman

fishy \'fi-shē\ *adj* **fish·i·er; -est** (15c) **1** : of or resembling fish esp. in taste or odor **2** : creating doubt or suspicion : QUESTIONABLE

fis·sile \'fi-səl, 'fi-,sil\ *adj* [L *fissilis*, fr. *findere*] (1661) **1** : capable of being split or divided in the direction of the grain or along natural planes of cleavage ⟨~ wood⟩ ⟨~ crystals⟩ **2** : capable of undergoing fission — **fis·sil·i·ty** \fi-'si-lə-tē\ *n*

1fis·sion \'fi-shⁿn, -zhⁿn\ *n* [L *fission-, fissio*, fr. *findere* to split — more at BITE] (ca. 1617) **1** : a splitting or breaking up into parts **2** : reproduction by spontaneous division of the body into two or more parts each of which grows into a complete organism **3** : the splitting of an atomic nucleus resulting in the release of large amounts of energy — **fis·sion·al** \-ⁿl\ *adj*

2fission *vi* (1929) : to undergo fission ~ *vt* : to cause to undergo fission

fis·sion·able \'fi-shⁿn-ə-bəl, -zhⁿn-; 'fish-nə-, 'fizh-\ *adj* (1945) : FISSILE 2 — **fis·sion·abil·i·ty** \,fi-shⁿn-ə-'bi-lə-tē, -zhⁿn-; ,fish-nə-, ,fizh-\ *n* — **fissionable** *n*

fis·sip·a·rous \fi-'si-p(ə-)rəs\ *adj* [L *fissus*, pp. of *findere* + E *-parous*] (1874) : tending to break up into parts : DIVISIVE — **fis·sip·a·rous·ness** *n*

1fis·sure \'fi-shər\ *n* [ME, fr. MF, fr. L *fissura*, fr. *fissus*] (14c) **1** : a narrow opening or crack of considerable length and depth usu. occurring from some breaking or parting **2 a** : a natural cleft between body parts or in the substance of an organ **b** : a break or slit in tissue usu. at the junction of skin and mucous membrane **3** : a separation or disagreement in thought or viewpoint : SCHISM ⟨~s in a political party⟩

2fissure *vb* **fis·sured; fis·sur·ing** *vt* (1656) : to break into fissures : CLEAVE ~ *vi* : CRACK, DIVIDE

1fist \'fist\ *n* [ME, fr. OE *fȳst*; akin to OHG *fūst* fist, Pol *pięść*, and prob. to OE *fīf* five] (bef. 12c) **1** : the hand clenched with the fingers doubled into the palm and the thumb doubled inward across the fingers **2** : the hand closed as in grasping : CLUTCH **3** : INDEX 5

2fist *vt* (1607) **1** : to grip with the fist : HANDLE **2** : to clench into a fist

-fist·ed \'fis-təd\ *comb form* : having (such or so many) fists ⟨two-fisted⟩ ⟨tight*fisted*⟩

fist·fight \'fist-,fīt\ *n* (1603) : a usu. spontaneous fight with bare fists

fist·ful \-,fůl\ *n* (1611) **1** : HANDFUL ⟨a ~ of coins⟩ **2** : a considerable number or amount ⟨a whole ~ of musicians —Thomas Lask⟩

fist·ic \'fis-tik\ *adj* (1806) : of or relating to boxing or to fighting with the fists

fist·i·cuffs \'fis-ti-,kəfs\ *n pl* [alter. of *fisty cuff*, fr. *fisty* (fistic) + *cuff*] (1605) : a fight with the fists

fist·note \'fis(t)-,nōt\ *n* (ca. 1934) : matter in a text to which attention is directed by means of an index mark

fis·tu·la \'fis(h)-chə-lə\ *n, pl* **-las** *or* **-lae** \-,lē, -,lī\ [ME, fr. L, pipe, fistula] (14c) : an abnormal passage leading from an abscess or hollow organ to the body surface or from one hollow organ to another and permitting passage of fluids or secretions

fis·tu·lous \-ləs\ *adj* (15c) **1** : of, relating to, or having the form or nature of a fistula **2** : hollow like a pipe or reed

fistulous withers *n pl but sing or pl in constr* (ca. 1900) : a deep-seated chronic inflammation of the withers of the horse in which bloody fluid is discharged

1fit \'fit\ *n* [ME, fr. OE *fitt*; akin to OS *fittea* division of a poem, OHG *fizza* skein] (bef. 12c) *archaic* : a division of a poem or song

2fit *adj* **fit·ter; fit·test** [ME; akin to ME *fitten*] (14c) **1 a** (1) : adapted to an end or design : suitable by nature or by art (2) : adapted to the environment so as to be capable of surviving **b** : acceptable from a particular viewpoint (as of competence or morality) : PROPER ⟨a movie ~ for the whole family⟩ **2 a** : put into a suitable state : made ready ⟨get the house ~ for company⟩ **b** : being in such a state as to be or seem ready to do or suffer something ⟨fair ~ to cry I was —Bryan MacMahon⟩ ⟨laughing ~ to burst⟩ **3** : sound physically and mentally : HEALTHY — **fit·ly** *adv* — **fit to be tied** : extremely angry or irritated — **fit to kill** : in a striking manner ⟨dressed *fit to kill*⟩

syn FIT, SUITABLE, MEET, PROPER, APPROPRIATE, FITTING, APT, HAPPY, FELICITOUS mean right with respect to some end, need, use, or circumstance. FIT stresses adaptability and sometimes special readiness for use or action ⟨*fit* for battle⟩. SUITABLE implies an answering to require-

ments or demands ⟨clothes *suitable* for camping⟩. MEET suggests a just proportioning ⟨*meet* payment⟩. PROPER suggests a suitability through essential nature or accordance with custom ⟨*proper* acknowledgement⟩. APPROPRIATE implies eminent or distinctive fitness ⟨an *appropriate* gift⟩. FITTING implies harmony of mood or tone ⟨a *fitting* end⟩. APT connotes a fitness marked by nicety and discrimination ⟨*apt* quotations⟩. HAPPY suggests what is effectively or successfully appropriate ⟨a *happy* choice of words⟩. FELICITOUS suggests an aptness that is opportune, telling, or graceful ⟨a *felicitous* phrase⟩.

3fit *n* [ME, fr. OE *fitt* strife] (ca. 1541) **1 a** : a sudden violent attack of a disease (as epilepsy) esp. when marked by convulsions or unconsciousness : PAROXYSM **b** : a sudden but transient attack of a physical disturbance **2 a** : a sudden burst or flurry (as of activity) ⟨cleaned the whole house in a ~ of efficiency⟩ **3** : an emotional reaction (as in anger or frustration) ⟨has a ~ when I show up late⟩ — **by fits** *or* **by fits and starts** *or* **in fits and starts** : in an impulsive and irregular manner

4fit *vb* **fit·ted** *also* **fit; fit·ting** [ME *fitten* to marshal troops, fr. or akin to MD *vitten* to be suitable; akin to OHG *fizza* skein] *vt* (15c) **1 a** : to be suitable for or to : harmonize with **b** *archaic* : to be seemly or proper for ⟨it ~s us then to be as provident as fear may teach us — Shak.⟩ **2 a** : to conform correctly to the shape or size of ⟨it doesn't ~ me anymore⟩ **b** (1) : to insert or adjust until correctly in place ⟨~ the mechanism into the box⟩ (2) : to make or adjust to the right shape and size ⟨*fitting* the jacket to the customer⟩ (3) : to measure for determining the specifications of something to be worn by ⟨*fitted* him for a new suit⟩ **c** : to make a place or room for : ACCOMMODATE **3** : to be in agreement or accord with ⟨the theory ~s all the facts⟩ **4 a** : to put into a condition of readiness **b** : to cause to conform to or suit something **5** : SUPPLY, EQUIP ⟨*fitted* the ship with new engines⟩ — often used with *out* **6** : to adjust ⟨a smooth curve of a specified type⟩ to a given set of points ~ *vi* **1** *archaic* : to be seemly, proper, or suitable **2** : to conform to a particular shape or size; *also* : to be accommodated ⟨will we all ~ into the car?⟩ **3** : to be in harmony or accord : BELONG — often used with *in* — **fit·ter** *n*

5fit *n* (1823) : the fact, condition, or manner of fitting or being fitted: as **a** : the way clothing fits the wearer **b** : the degree of closeness between surfaces in an assembly of parts **c** : GOODNESS OF FIT

6fit *dial past and past part of* FIGHT

fitch \'fich\ *or* **fitch·ew** \'fich-(,)ü\ *n* [ME *fiche, ficheux*, fr. MF or MD; MF *fichau*, fr. MD *vitsau*] (15c) **1** : POLECAT 1 **2** : the fur or pelt of the polecat

fitch·et \'fi-chət\ *n* (1535) : POLECAT 1

fit·ful \'fit-fəl\ *adj* (1592) **1** *obs* : characterized by fits or paroxysms **2** : having an erratic or intermittent character : IRREGULAR — **fit·ful·ly** \-fə-lē\ *adv* — **fit·ful·ness** *n*

syn FITFUL, SPASMODIC, CONVULSIVE mean lacking steadiness or regularity in movement. FITFUL implies intermittence, a succession of starts and stops or risings and fallings ⟨*fitful* sleep⟩. SPASMODIC adds to FITFUL the implication of rapid or violent activity alternating with inactivity ⟨*spasmodic* growth⟩. CONVULSIVE suggests the breaking of regularity or quiet by uncontrolled movement ⟨*convulsive* shocks⟩.

fit·ment \'fit-mənt\ *n* [⁴fit] (1851) *chiefly Brit* : FURNISHING 2, FIXTURE, CABINETRY — usu. used in pl.

fit·ness \'fit-nəs\ *n* (1580) **1** : the quality or state of being fit **2** : the capacity of an organism to survive and transmit its genotype to reproductive offspring as compared to competing organisms; *also* : the contribution of an allele or genotype to the gene pool of subsequent generations as compared to that of other alleles or genotypes

fit·ted \'fi-təd\ *adj* (ca. 1666) **1** : FIT, SUITABLE **2** : shaped for a precise fit ⟨a ~ sheet⟩; *esp* : shaped to conform to the lines of the body ⟨a ~ shirt⟩

1fit·ting \'fi-tiŋ\ *adj* (15c) : of a kind appropriate to the situation : SUITABLE **syn** see FIT — **fit·ting·ly** \-tiŋ-lē\ *adv* — **fit·ting·ness** *n*

2fitting *n* (1607) **1** : an action or act of one that fits; *specif* : a trying on of clothes which are in the process of being made or altered **2** : a small often standardized part ⟨an electrical ~⟩

five \'fiv\ *n* [ME, fr. *five*, adj., fr. OE *fīf*; akin to OHG *finf* five, L *quinque*, Gk *pente*] (bef. 12c) **1** — see NUMBER table **2** *pl* : a British handball game **3** : the fifth in a set or series ⟨the ~ of clubs⟩ **4** : something having five units or members; *esp* : a basketball team **5** : a 5-dollar bill **6** : FIFTEEN 2 — **five** *adj* — **five** *pron, pl in constr*

five–and–ten \,fi-vən-'ten\ *n* [fr. the fact that all articles in such stores were formerly priced at either 5 or 10 cents] (1880) : a retail store that carries chiefly inexpensive merchandise (as notions and household goods) — called also *five-and-dime*

five–fin·ger \'fiv-,fiŋ-gər\ *n* (bef. 12c) : CINQUEFOIL 1

five·fold \'fiv-,fōld, -'fōld\ *adj* (bef. 12c) **1** : having five units or members **2** : being five times as great or as many — **five·fold** \-'fōld\ *adv*

five of a kind (1897) : four cards of the same rank plus a wild card in one hand — see POKER illustration

fiv·er \'fī-vər\ *n* (1843) **1** *slang* : a 5-dollar bill **2** *Brit* : a 5-pound note

five–spice powder \'fiv-'spis-\ *n* (1970) : a blend of spices typically including anise, pepper, fennel, cloves, and cinnamon that is used in Chinese cooking

five–star \'fiv-'stär\ *adj* (1913) : of first class or quality

1fix \'fiks\ *vb* [ME, fr. L *fixus*, pp. of *figere* to fasten; akin to Lith *dygti* to sprout, break through] *vt* (14c) **1 a** : to make firm, stable, or stationary **b** : to give a permanent or final form to: as (1) : to change into a stable compound or available form ⟨bacteria that ~ nitrogen⟩ (2) : to kill, harden, and preserve for microscopic study (3) : to make the image of (a photographic film) permanent by removing unused salts **c** : AFFIX, ATTACH **2 a** : to hold or direct steadily ⟨~es his eyes on the horizon⟩ **b** : to capture the attention of ⟨~ed her with a stare⟩ **3 a** : to set or place definitely : ESTABLISH **b** : to make an accurate determination of : DISCOVER ⟨~ing our location on the chart⟩ **c** : ASSIGN ⟨~ the blame⟩ **4** : to set in order : ADJUST **5** : to get ready : PREPARE ⟨~ lunch⟩ **6 a** : REPAIR, MEND ⟨~ the clock⟩ **b** : RESTORE, CURE ⟨the doctor ~ed him up⟩ **c** : SPAY, CASTRATE **7 a** : to get even with **b** : to influence the actions, outcome, or effect of by improper or illegal methods ⟨the race had been ~ed⟩ ~ *vi* **1** : to become firm, stable, or fixed **2** : to get set : be on the verge ⟨we're ~ing to leave soon⟩ **3**

: to direct one's attention or efforts : FOCUS; *also* : DECIDE, SETTLE — usu. used with *on* *syn* see FASTEN — **fix·able** \'fik-sə-bəl\ *adj*

²**fix** *n* (1809) **1** : a position of difficulty or embarrassment : PREDICAMENT **2 a** : the position (as of a ship) determined by bearings, observations, or radio; *also* : a determination of one's position **b** : an accurate determination or understanding esp. by observation or analysis **3** : an act or instance of improper or illegal fixing ⟨the ~ was in⟩ **4 :** a supply or dose of something strongly desired or craved; *esp* : a shot of a narcotic **5** : FIXATION **6** : something that fixes or restores ⟨a quick ~⟩

fix·ate \'fik-ˌsāt\ *vb* **fix·at·ed; fix·at·ing** *vt* (1885) **1** : to make fixed, stationary, or unchanging **2** : to focus one's gaze on **3** : to direct (the libido) toward an infantile form of gratification ~ *vi* **1** : to focus or concentrate one's gaze or attention intently or obsessively **2** : to undergo arrestment at a stage of development

fix·at·ed *adj* (1926) : arrested in development or adjustment; *esp* : arrested at a pregenital level of psychosexual development

fix·a·tion \fik-'sā-shən\ *n* (14c) : the act, process, or result of fixing, fixating, or becoming fixated: as **a** : a persistent concentration of libidinal energies upon objects characteristic of psychosexual stages of development preceding the genital stage **b** : stereotyped behavior (as in response to frustration) **c** : an obsessive or unhealthy preoccupation or attachment

fix·a·tive \'fik-sə-tiv\ *n* (ca. 1859) : something that fixes or sets: as **a** : a substance added to a perfume esp. to prevent too rapid evaporation **b** : a substance used to fix living tissue **c** : a varnish used esp. for the protection of drawings (as in pastel or charcoal) — **fixative** *adj*

fixed \'fikst\ *adj* (14c) **1 a** : securely placed or fastened : STATIONARY **b** (1) : NONVOLATILE (2) : formed into a chemical compound **c** (1) : not subject to change or fluctuation ⟨a ~ income⟩ (2) : firmly set in the mind ⟨a ~ idea⟩ (3) : having a final or crystallized form or character (4) : recurring on the same date from year to year ⟨~ holidays⟩ **d** : IMMOBILE, CONCENTRATED ⟨a ~ stare⟩ **2** : supplied with something (as money) needed ⟨comfortably ~⟩ — **fixed·ly** \'fik-səd-lē, 'fiks-tlē\ *adv* — **fixed·ness** \'fik-səd-nəs, 'fiks(t)-nəs\ *n*

fixed charge *n* (ca. 1901) : a regularly recurring expense (as rent, taxes, or interest) that must be met when due

fixed oil *n* (ca. 1800) : a nonvolatile oil; *esp* : a fatty oil — compare ESSENTIAL OIL

fixed–point *adj* (1960) : involving or being a mathematical notation (as in a decimal system) in which the point separating whole numbers and fractions is fixed — compare FLOATING-POINT

fixed star *n* (1561) : a star so distant that its motion can be measured only by very precise observations over long periods

fix·er \'fik-sər\ *n* (1849) : one that fixes: as **a** : one who intervenes to enable a person to circumvent the law or obtain a political favor **b** : one who adjusts matters or disputes by negotiation **c** : ²HYPO

fix·ing \-siŋ\ *n* (1605) **1** : the act or process of one that fixes **2** *pl* *often* -sənz\ : customary accompaniments : TRIMMINGS ⟨a turkey dinner with all the ~s⟩

fix·i·ty \'fik-sə-tē\ *n, pl* **-ties** (1666) **1** : the quality or state of being fixed or stable **2** : something that is fixed

fix·ture \'fiks-chər\ *n* [modif. of LL *fixura*, fr. L *fixus*] (1598) **1** : the act or process of fixing : the state of being fixed **2 a** : something that is fixed or attached (as to a building) as a permanent appendage or as a structural part ⟨a plumbing ~⟩ **b** : a device for supporting work during machining **c** : an item of movable property so incorporated into real property that it may be regarded as legally a part of it **3** : a familiar or invariably present element or feature in some particular setting; *esp* : a person long associated with a place or activity **4** : a settled date or time esp. for a sporting or festive event; *also* : such an event esp. as a regularly scheduled affair

fix up *vt* (1831) **1** : REFURBISH ⟨*fix up* the attic⟩ **2** : to set right : SETTLE ⟨*fixed up* their dispute⟩ **3** : to provide with something needed or wanted; *esp* : to arrange a date for

¹**fizz** \'fiz\ *vi* [prob. of imit. origin] (1685) **1** : to make a hissing or sputtering sound : EFFERVESCE **2** : to show excitement or exhilaration

²**fizz** *n* (1842) **1 a** : a hissing sound **b** : SPIRIT, LIVELINESS **2** : an effervescent beverage — **fizzy** \'fi-zē\ *adj*

¹**fiz·zle** \'fi-zəl\ *vi* **fiz·zled; fiz·zling** \-z(ə-)liŋ\ [prob. alter. of *fist* (to break wind)] (ca. 1841) **1** : FIZZ **2** : to fail or end feebly esp. after a promising start — often used with *out*

²**fizzle** *n* (1842) : an abortive effort : FAILURE

fjord \fē-'ȯrd, 'fē-ˌ; 'fyȯrd\ *n* [Norw *fjord*, fr. ON *fjorthr* — more at FORD] (1674) : a narrow inlet of the sea between cliffs or steep slopes

flab \'flab\ *n* [back-formation fr. *flabby*] (1951) : soft flabby body tissue

flab·ber·gast \'fla-bər-ˌgast\ *vt* [origin unknown] (1772) **1** : to overwhelm with shock, surprise, or wonder : DUMBFOUND *syn* see SURPRISE — **flab·ber·gast·ing·ly** \-ˌgas-tiŋ-lē\ *adv*

flab·by \'fla-bē\ *adj* **flab·bi·er; -est** [alter. of *flappy*] (1697) **1** : lacking resilience or firmness : FLACCID **2** : weak and ineffective : FEEBLE — **flab·bi·ly** \-bə-lē\ *adv* — **flab·bi·ness** \'fla-bē-nəs\ *n*

fla·bel·late \flə-'be-lət, 'fla-bə-ˌlāt\ *adj* [L *flabellum* fan] (1819) : shaped like a fan

fla·bel·li·form \flə-'be-lə-ˌfȯrm\ *adj* (1777) : FLABELLATE

flac·cid \ ÷ 'fla-səd *also* 'flak-səd\ *adj* [L *flaccidus*, fr. *flaccus* flabby] (1620) **1 a** : not firm or stiff; *also* : lacking normal or youthful firmness ⟨~ muscles⟩ **b** *of a plant part* : deficient in turgor **2** : lacking vigor or force ⟨~ leadership⟩ — **flac·cid·i·ty** \fla(k)-'si-də-tē\ *n* — **flac·cid·ly** \'fla(k)-səd-lē\ *adv*

¹**flack** \'flak\ *n* [origin unknown] (1939) : one who provides publicity; *esp* : PRESS AGENT — **flack·ery** \'fla-k(ə-)rē\ *n*

²**flack** *var of* FLAK

³**flack** *vi* (1965) : to provide publicity : engage in press-agentry

fla·con \'fla-kən, -ˌkän; fla-'kōⁿ\ *n* [F, fr. MF, bottle — more at FLAGON] (1824) : a small usu. ornamental bottle with a tight cap

[illustration caption:] fjord

¹**flag** \'flag *also* 'flāg\ *n* [ME *flagge* reed, rush] (14c) : any of various monocotyledonous plants with long ensiform leaves: as **a** : IRIS; *esp* : a wild iris **b** : SWEET FLAG

²**flag** *n, often attrib* [perh. fr. ¹*flag*] (1530) **1** : a usu. rectangular piece of fabric of distinctive design that is used as a symbol (as of a nation), as a signaling device, or as a decoration **2 a** : the tail of some dogs (as a setter or hound); *also* : the long hair fringing a dog's tail **b** : the tail of a deer **3 a** : something used like a flag to signal or attract attention **b** : one of the cross strokes of a musical note less than a quarter note in value **4** : something represented by a flag: as **a** : FLAGSHIP **b** : an admiral functioning in his office of command **c** : NATIONALITY; *esp* : the nationality of registration of a ship or aircraft

³**flag** *vt* **flagged; flag·ging** (1856) **1** : to signal with or as if with a flag; *esp* : to signal to stop ⟨*flagged* the train⟩ — often used with *down* **2** : to put a flag on (as for identification) **3** : to call a penalty on : PENALIZE ⟨a lineman *flagged* for being offside⟩

⁴**flag** *vi* **flagged; flag·ging** [prob. fr. ²*flag*] (1545) **1** : to hang loose without stiffness **2 a** : to become unsteady, feeble, or spiritless **b** : to decline in interest or attraction

⁵**flag** *n* [ME *flagge* turf, fr. ON *flaga* slab; akin to OE *flōh* chip] (1604) : a hard evenly stratified stone that splits into flat pieces suitable for paving; *also* : a piece of such stone

⁶**flag** *vt* **flagged; flag·ging** (1615) : to lay (as a pavement) with flags

flag day *n* (1894) **1** *cap F&D* : June 14 observed in various states in commemoration of the adoption in 1777 of the official U.S. flag **2** *Brit* : a day on which charitable contributions are solicited in exchange for small flags

fla·gel·lant \'fla-jə-lənt, flə-'je-lənt\ *n* (ca. 1587) **1** : a person who scourges himself as a public penance **2** : a person who responds sexually to being beaten by or to beating another person — **flagellant** *adj* — **fla·gel·lant·ism** \-lən-ˌti-zəm\ *n*

fla·gel·lar \flə-'je-lər, 'fla-jə-lər\ *adj* (ca. 1889) : of or relating to a flagellum

¹**fla·gel·late** \'fla-jə-ˌlāt\ *vt* **-lat·ed; -lat·ing** [L *flagellatus*, pp. of *flagellare*, fr. *flagellum*, dim. of *flagrum* whip; perh. akin to ON *blaka* to wave] (ca. 1623) **1** : WHIP, SCOURGE **2** : to drive or punish as if by whipping

²**fla·gel·late** \flə-'je-lət, -ˌlāt; 'fla-jə-lət\ *adj* [NL *flagellatus*, fr. *flagellum*] (ca. 1859) **1** *a or* **flag·el·lat·ed** \'fla-jə-ˌlā-təd\ : having flagella **b** : shaped like a flagellum **2** [³*flagellate*] : of, relating to, or caused by flagellates ⟨~ diarrhea⟩

³**flagellate** *same as* ²\ *n* [NL *Flagellata*, class of unicellular organisms, fr. neut. pl. of *flagellatus*] (1879) : a flagellate protozoan or alga

flag·el·la·tion \ˌfla-jə-'lā-shən\ *n* (15c) : the act or practice of flagellating; *esp* : the practice of a flagellant

fla·gel·lin \flə-'je-lən\ *n* [*flagellum* + ¹*-in*] (1955) : a polymeric protein that is the chief constituent of bacterial flagella and is responsible for the specificity of their flagellar antigens

fla·gel·lum \flə-'je-ləm\ *n, pl* **-la** \-lə\ *also* **-lums** [NL, fr. L, whip, shoot of a plant] (1852) : any of various elongated filiform appendages of plants or animals: as **a** : the slender distal part of an antenna **b** : a long tapering process that projects singly or in groups from a cell and is the primary organ of motion of many microorganisms

¹**fla·geo·let** \ˌfla-jə-'let, -'lā\ *n* [F, fr. OF *flajolet*, fr. *flajol* flute, fr. (assumed) VL *flabeolum*, fr. L *flare* to blow — more at BLOW] (1659) : a small fipple flute resembling the treble recorder

²**flageolet** *n* [F, dim. of *flageolle* kidney bean, modif. of It *fagiolo*, fr. L *phaseolus* — more at FRIJOLE] (1877) : a green kidney bean used in French cuisine

flag football *n* (1954) : a variation of football in which a player must remove a flag attached to the ballcarrier's clothing to stop the play

flag·ging \'fla-giŋ, *also* 'flā-\ *adj* (1545) **1** : LANGUID, WEAK **2** : becoming progressively less : DWINDLING — **flag·ging·ly** \-giŋ-lē\ *adv*

fla·gi·tious \flə-'ji-shəs\ *adj* [ME *flagicious*, fr. L *flagitiosus*, fr. *flagitium* shameful thing] (14c) : marked by scandalous crime or vice : VILLAINOUS — **fla·gi·tious·ly** *adv* — **fla·gi·tious·ness** *n*

flag·man \'flag-mən\ *n* (1832) : a person who signals with a flag

flag of convenience (1956) : registry of a merchant ship under a foreign flag in order to profit from less restrictive regulations

flag officer *n* [fr. his being entitled to display a flag with one or more stars indicating his rank] (1665) : any of the officers in the navy or coast guard above captain — compare GENERAL OFFICER

flag of truce (1627) : a white flag carried or displayed to an enemy as an invitation to conference or parley

flag·on \'fla-gən\ *n* [ME, fr. MF *flascon, flacon* bottle, fr. LL *flascon-, flasco* — more at FLASK] (15c) **1 a** : a large usu. metal or pottery vessel (as for wine) with handle and spout and often a lid **b** : a large bulging short-necked bottle **2** : the contents of a flagon

flag·pole \'flag-ˌpōl\ *n* (1884) : a pole on which to raise a flag

fla·grance \'flā-grən(t)s *also* 'fla-\ *n* (ca. 1615) : FLAGRANCY

fla·gran·cy \'flā-grən(t)-sē *also* 'fla-\ *n* (1599) : the quality or state of being flagrant

flag rank *n* (1894) : the rank of a flag officer

fla·grant \'flā-grənt *also* 'fla-\ *adj* [L *flagrant-, flagrans*, prp. of *flagrare* to burn — more at BLACK] (1513) **1** *archaic* : fiery hot : BURNING **2** : conspicuously offensive ⟨~ errors⟩; *esp* : so obviously inconsistent with what is right or proper as to appear to be a flouting of law or morality ⟨~ violations of human rights⟩ — **fla·grant·ly** *adv*

syn FLAGRANT, GLARING, GROSS, RANK mean conspicuously bad or objectionable. FLAGRANT applies usu. to offenses or errors so bad that they can neither escape notice nor be condoned ⟨*flagrant* abuse of the office of president⟩. GLARING implies painful or damaging obtrusiveness of something that is conspicuously wrong, faulty, or improper ⟨*glaring* errors⟩. GROSS implies the exceeding of reasonable or excusable limits ⟨*gross* carelessness⟩. RANK applies to what is openly and extremely objectionable and utterly condemned ⟨*rank* heresy⟩.

\ə\ abut \ᵊ\ kitten, F table \ər\ further \a\ ash \ā\ ace \ä\ mop, mar
\aú\ out \ch\ chin \e\ bet \ē\ easy \g\ go \i\ hit \ī\ ice \j\ job
\ŋ\ sing \ō\ go \ȯ\ law \ȯi\ boy \th\ thin \th\ the \ü\ loot \ú\ foot
\y\ yet \zh\ vision \ä, k̩, ⁿ, œ, œ̄, ᵫ, ᵫ̄, �\ see Guide to Pronunciation

fla·gran·te de·lic·to \flə-,grän-tē-di-'lik-(,)tō, -,gran-\ *adv or adj* [ML, lit., while the crime is blazing] (1826) : in the very act of committing a misdeed : RED-HANDED; *also* : in the midst of sexual activity

flag·ship \'flag-,ship\ *n* (1672) **1** : the ship that carries the commander of a fleet or subdivision of a fleet and flies his flag **2** : the finest, largest, or most important one of a series, network, or chain

flag·staff \-,staf\ *n* (ca. 1613) : a staff on which a flag is hoisted

flag·stick \-,stik\ *n* (1926) : a staff for a flag marking the location of the cup on a golf putting green

flag·stone \-,stōn\ *n* (1730) : ²FLAG

flag stop *n* (1941) : a point at which a vehicle in public transportation stops only on prearrangement or signal

flag–wav·er \'flag-,wā-vər\ *n* (1894) **1** : one who is intensely and conspicuously patriotic **2** : one who waves a flag in signaling **3** : a song intended to rouse patriotic sentiment

flag–wav·ing \-viŋ\ *n* (1892) : passionate appeal to patriotic or partisan sentiment — CHAUVINISM

¹flail \'flā(ə)l\ *n* [ME *fleil, flail*, partly fr. (assumed) OE *flegel* (whence OE *fligel*), fr. LL *flagellum* flail, fr. L, whip & partly fr. MF *flaiel*, fr. LL *flagellum* — more at FLAGELLATE] (bef. 12c.) : a hand threshing implement consisting of a wooden handle at the end of which a stouter and shorter stick is so hung as to swing freely

²flail *vt* (15c) **1 a** : to strike with or as if with a flail ⟨arms ~ing the water⟩ **b** : to move, swing, or beat as if wielding a flail ⟨~ing a club to drive away the insects⟩ **2** : to thresh (grain) with a flail ~ *vi* : to move, swing, or beat like a flail

flair \'flar, 'fler\ *n* [F, lit., sense of smell, fr. OF, odor, fr. *flairier* to give off an odor, fr. LL *flagrare*, alter. of L *fragrare*] (1881) **1** : a skill or instinctive ability to appreciate or make good use of something : TALENT ⟨a ~ for color⟩; *also* : INCLINATION, TENDENCY ⟨a ~ for the dramatic⟩ **2** : a uniquely attractive quality : STYLE ⟨fashionable dresses with a ~ all their own⟩

flak \'flak\ *n pl* **flak** [G, fr. *Fliegerabwehrkanonen*, fr. *Flieger* flyer + *Abwehr* defense + *Kanonen* cannons] (1938) **1** : antiaircraft guns **2** : the bursting shells fired from flak **3** : CRITICISM, OPPOSITION

¹flake \'flāk\ *n* [ME, of Scand origin; akin to Norw *flak* disk] (14c) **1** : a small loose mass or bit ⟨snow ~s⟩ **2** : a thin flattened piece or layer : CHIP **3** *slang* : COCAINE

²flake *vb* **flaked; flak·ing** *vi* (1627) : to separate into flakes; *also* : to peel in flakes ~ *vt* **1** : to form or break into flakes : CHIP **2** : to cover with or as if with flakes — **flak·er** *n*

³flake *n* [ME, hurdle, fr. ON *flaki*] (1623) : a stage, platform, or tray for drying fish or produce

⁴flake *n* [perh. fr. *flake out*] (1964) : a person who is flaky : ODDBALL

flake out *vi* [prob. fr. dial. *flake* to lie, bask] (1939) **1** *slang* : to fall asleep **2** *slang* : to become esp. by exhaustion

flake tool *n* (ca. 1947) : a Stone-Age tool that is a flake of stone struck off from a larger piece

flak jacket *n* (1950) : a jacket containing metal plates for protection against flak; *broadly* : a bulletproof vest — called also *flak vest*

¹flaky *also* **flak·ey** \'flā-kē\ *adj* **flak·i·er; -est** (1580) **1** : consisting of flakes ⟨~ snow⟩ **2** : tending to flake ⟨a ~ crust⟩ — **flak·i·ness** *n*

²flaky *adj* **flak·i·er; -est** [⁴*flake*] (ca. 1963) : markedly odd or unconventional : OFFBEAT, WACKY — **flak·i·ness** *n*

flam \'flam\ *n* [prob. imit.] (1819) : a drumbeat of two strokes of which the first is a very quick grace note

¹flam·bé \fläm-'bā, flän-\ *adj* [F *flambé*, fr. pp. of *flamber* to flame, singe, fr. OF, fr. *flambe* flame] (1914) : dressed or served covered with flaming liquor — usu. used postpositively ⟨crepes suzette ~⟩

²flambé *vt* **flam·béed; flam·bé·ing** (ca. 1946) : to douse with a liquor (as brandy, rum, or cognac) and ignite

flam·beau \'flam-,bō\ *n, pl* **flam·beaux** \-,bōz\ *or* **flambeaus** [F, fr. MF, fr. *flambe* flame] (1632) : a flaming torch; *broadly* : TORCH

flam·boy·ance \flam-'bȯi-ən(t)s\ *n* (1891) : the quality or state of being flamboyant

flam·boy·an·cy \-ən(t)-sē\ *n* (ca. 1889) : FLAMBOYANCE

¹flam·boy·ant \-ənt\ *adj* [F, fr. prp. of *flamboyer* to flame, fr. OF, fr. *flambe*] (1832) **1** *often cap* : characterized by waving curves suggesting flames ⟨~ tracery⟩ ⟨~ architecture⟩ **2** : marked by or given to strikingly elaborate or colorful display or behavior — **flam·boy·ant·ly** *adv*

²flamboyant *n* (1879) : ROYAL POINCIANA

¹flame \'flām\ *n* [ME *flaume, flaumbe*, fr. MF *flamme* (fr. L *flamma*) & *flambe*, fr. OF, fr. *flamble*, fr. L *flammula*, dim. of *flamma* flame; akin to L *flagrare* to burn — more at BLACK] (14c) **1** : the glowing gaseous part of a fire **2 a** : a state of blazing combustion ⟨the car burst into ~⟩ **b** : a condition or appearance suggesting a flame or burning: as (1) : burning zeal or passion (2) : a strong reddish orange color **3** : BRILLIANCE, BRIGHTNESS **4** : SWEETHEART **5** : an angry, hostile, or abusive electronic message

²flame *vb* **flamed; flam·ing** *vi* (14c) **1** : to burn with a flame : BLAZE **2 a** : to burst or break out violently or passionately ⟨*flaming* with indignation⟩ **b** : to send an angry, hostile, or abusive electronic message **3** : to shine brightly : GLOW ⟨color *flaming* up in her cheeks⟩ ~ *vt* **1** : to send or convey by means of flame ⟨~ a message by signal fires⟩ **2** : to treat or affect with flame: as **a** : to sear, sterilize, or destroy by fire **b** : FLAMBÉ **3** : to send an angry, hostile, or abusive electronic message to or about — **flam·er** *n*

flame cell *n* (1888) : a hollow cell that has a tuft of vibratile cilia and is part of some lower invertebrate excretory systems (as of a flatworm)

fla·men \'flā-mən\ *n, pl* **flamens** *or* **flam·i·nes** \'fla-mə-,nēz\ [ME *flamin*, fr. L *flamin-, flamen*] (14c) : a priest esp. in ancient Rome

fla·men·co \flə-'men-(,)kō\ *n, pl* **-cos** [Sp, fr. *flamenco* of the Gypsies, lit., Flemish, fr. MD *Vlaminc* Fleming] (1896) **1** : a vigorous rhythmic dance style of the Andalusian Gypsies; *also* : a dance in flamenco style **2** : music or song suitable to accompany a flamenco dance

flame-out \'flā-,maut\ *n* (1950) **1** : the unintentional cessation of operation of a jet airplane engine **2** : a sudden or spectacular failure **3** : a person whose successful career ends abruptly

flame photometer *n* (1945) : a spectrophotometer in which a spray of metallic salts in solution is vaporized in a very hot flame and subjected to quantitative analysis by measuring the intensities of the spectral lines of the metals present — **flame photometric** *adj* — **flame photometry** *n*

flame-proof \'flām-,prüf\ *adj* (1886) : resistant to damage or burning on contact with flame — **flameproof** *vt* — **flame-proof·er** *n*

flame–retardant *adj* (1947) : made or treated so as to resist burning

flame stitch *n* (1936) : a needlepoint stitch that produces a pattern resembling flames

flame–throw·er \-,thrō(-ə)r\ *n* (1917) **1** : a device that expels from a nozzle a burning stream of liquid or semiliquid fuel under pressure **2** : a pitcher who throws hard : a fastball pitcher

flame tree *n* (1860) : any of several trees or shrubs with showy scarlet or yellow flowers: as **a** : a tree (*Brachychiton acerifolium* of the family Sterculiaceae) of southern Australia with panicles of brilliant scarlet flowers **b** : ROYAL POINCIANA

flam·ing \'flā-miŋ\ *adj* (14c) **1** : resembling or suggesting a flame in color, brilliance, or wavy outline ⟨the ~ sunset sky⟩ ⟨~ red hair⟩ **2** : being on fire : BLAZING **3** : INTENSE, PASSIONATE ⟨~ youth⟩ **4** — used as an intensive ⟨you ~ idiot⟩ — **flam·ing·ly** \-miŋ-lē\ *adv*

fla·min·go \flə-'miŋ-(,)gō\ *n, pl* **-gos** *also* **-goes** [obs. Sp *flamengo* (now *flamenco*), lit., Fleming, German (conventionally thought of as ruddy-complexioned)] (1565) : any of several large aquatic birds (family Phoenicopteridae) with long legs and neck, webbed feet, a broad lamellate bill resembling that of a duck but abruptly bent downward, and usu. rosy-white plumage with scarlet wing coverts and black wing quills

flamingo

flam·ma·bil·i·ty \,fla-mə-'bi-lə-tē\ *n* (1646) : ability to support combustion; *esp* : a high capacity for combustion

flam·ma·ble \'fla-mə-bəl\ *adj* [L *flammare* to flame, set on fire, fr. *flamma*] (1813) : capable of being easily ignited and of burning quickly — **flammable** *n*

flan \'flan, 'flä(n)\ *n* [F, fr. OF *flaon*, fr. LL *fladon-, flado* flat cake, of Gmc origin; akin to OHG *flado* flat cake] (1846) **1 a** : an open pie containing any of various sweet or savory fillings **b** : custard baked with a caramel glaze **2** : the metal disk of a coin, token, or medal as distinguished from the design and lettering stamped on it

fla·neur \flä-'nər\ *n* [F *flâneur*] (1854) : an idle man-about-town

¹flange \'flanj\ *n* [perh. alter. of *flanch* (a curving charge on a heraldic shield)] (ca. 1735) **1** : a rib or rim for strength, for guiding, or for attachment to another object ⟨a ~ on a pipe⟩ ⟨a ~ on a wheel⟩ **2** : a projecting edge of cloth used for decoration on clothing ⟨a jacket with ~ shoulders⟩

²flange *vt* **flanged; flang·ing** (ca. 1859) : to furnish with a flange

¹flank \'flaŋk\ *n* [ME, fr. OF *flanc*, of Gmc origin; akin to OHG *hlanca* loin, flank — more at LANK] (bef. 12c) **1 a** : the fleshy part of the side between the ribs and the hip; *broadly* : the side of a quadruped **b** : a cut of meat from this part of an animal — see BEEF illustration **2 a** : SIDE **b** : the right or left of a formation **3** : the area along either side of a heraldic shield

²flank *vt* (1596) **1** : to protect a flank of **2** : to attack or threaten the flank of (as a body of troops) **3 a** : to be situated at the side of; *esp* : to be situated on both sides of ⟨a road ~ed with linden trees⟩ **b** : to place something on each side of

flan·ken \'flän-kən\ *n* [Yiddish, pl. of *flank*, lit., flank, ultim. fr. F *flanc*] (1950) : beef flank cooked esp. by boiling

flank·er \'flan-kər\ *n* (1940) : a football player stationed wide of the formation slightly behind the line of scrimmage as a pass receiver — called also *flanker back*

flank steak *n* (1902) : a pear-shaped muscle of the beef flank; *also* : a steak cut from this muscle — see BEEF illustration

flan·nel \'fla-n⁹l\ *n* [ME *flaunneol* woolen cloth or garment] (1503) **1 a** : a soft twilled wool or worsted fabric with a loose texture and a slightly napped surface **b** : a napped cotton fabric of soft yarns simulating the texture of wool flannel **c** : a stout cotton fabric usu. napped on one side **2** *pl* **a** : flannel underwear **b** : outer garments of flannel; *esp* : men's trousers **3** *Brit* : WASHCLOTH **4** *Brit* : flattering or evasive talk; *also* : NONSENSE, RUBBISH — **flannel** *adj* — **flan·nel·ly** \-n⁹l-ē\ *adj*

flan·nel·ette \,fla-n⁹l-'et\ *n* (ca. 1882) : a lightweight cotton flannel

flan·nel–mouthed \'fla-n⁹l-,mauṫht, -,mauṫhd\ *adj* (ca. 1893) **1** : speaking indistinctly **2** : speaking in a tricky or ingratiating way

¹flap \'flap\ *n* [ME *flappe*] (14c) **1** : a stroke with something broad : SLAP **2** *obs* : something broad and flat used for striking **3** : something that is broad, limber, or flat and usu. thin and that hangs loose or projects freely: as **a** : a piece on a garment that hangs free **b** : a part of a book jacket that folds under the book's cover **c** : a piece of tissue partly severed from its place of origin for use in surgical grafting **d** : an extended part forming the closure (as of an envelope or carton) **4** : the motion of something broad and limber (as a sail or wing) **5** : a movable auxiliary airfoil usu. attached to an airplane wing's trailing edge to increase lift or drag — see AIRPLANE illustration **6 a** : a state of excitement or agitation : TIZZY, UPROAR **b** : something (as an incident or remark) that generates an uproar **7** : a consonant (as the sound \d\ in *ladder* and \t\ in *latter*) characterized by a single rapid contact of the tongue or lower lip against another point in the mouth — called also *tap*

²flap *vb* **flapped; flap·ping** *vt* (14c) **1** : to beat with or as if with a flap **2** : to toss sharply : FLING **3** : to move or cause to move in flaps ~ *vi* **1** : to sway loosely usu. with a noise of striking and esp. when moved by wind **2 a** : to beat or pulsate wings or something suggesting wings **b** : to progress by flapping **c** : to flutter ineffectively **3** : to talk foolishly and persistently

flap·doo·dle \'flap-,dü-d⁹l\ *n* [origin unknown] (1878) : NONSENSE

flap·jack \-,jak\ *n* (ca. 1600) : PANCAKE

flap·pa·ble \'fla-pə-bəl\ *adj* (1968) : easily upset

flap·per \'fla-pər\ *n* (ca. 1570) **1 a** : one that flaps **b** : something used in flapping or striking **c** : FLIPPER 1 **2** : a young woman; *specif* : a young woman of the period of World War I and the following decade who showed freedom from conventions (as in conduct)

flap·py \'fla-pē\ *adj* (1905) : flapping or tending to flap

¹flare \'flar, 'fler\ *vb* **flared; flar·ing** [origin unknown] *vi* (ca. 1700) **1 a :** to burn with an unsteady flame **b :** to stream in the wind **2 a :** to shine with a sudden light ⟨a match ~s in the darkness⟩ **b** (1) **:** to become suddenly excited or angry — usu. used with *up* (2) **:** to break out or intensify suddenly. suddenly or violently — often used with *up* ⟨fighting *flared* up after a two-week lull⟩ **c :** to express strong emotion (as anger) ⟨*flaring* out at such abuses⟩ **3 a :** to open or spread outward ⟨the pants ~ at the bottom⟩ ~ *vt* **1 :** to display conspicuously ⟨*flaring* her scarf to attract attention⟩ **2 :** to cause to flare ⟨the breeze ~s the candle⟩ **3 :** to signal with a flare or by flaring **4 :** to burn (a jet of waste gas) in the open air

²flare *n* (1814) **1 :** an unsteady glaring light **2 a :** a fire or blaze of light used esp. to signal, illuminate, or attract attention; *also* **:** a device or composition to produce such a flare **b :** SOLAR FLARE; *also* **:** a sudden increase and decrease in the brightness of a star often amounting to a difference of several magnitudes **3 :** a sudden outburst (as of excitement or anger) **4 a :** a spreading outward; *also* **:** a place or part that spreads **b :** an area of skin flush **5 :** light resulting from reflection (as between lens surfaces) or an effect of this light (as a fogged or dense area in a photographic negative)

flare–up \-,əp\ *n* (1839) **1 :** a sudden outburst or intensification **2 :** a sudden bursting (as of a smoldering fire) into flame or light

flar·ing \'flar-iŋ, 'fler-\ *adj* (1593) **1 :** opening or spreading outward ⟨~ nostrils⟩ **2 a :** flaming or as if flaming brightly or unsteadily **b :** GAUDY ⟨a ~ resort hotel⟩ — **flar·ing·ly** \-iŋ-lē\ *adv*

¹flash \'flash\ *vb* [ME *flaschen*, of imit. origin] *vi* (13c) **1 :** RUSH, DASH — used of flowing water **2 :** to break forth in or like a sudden flame or flare **3 a :** to appear suddenly ⟨an idea ~es into her mind⟩ **b :** to move with great speed ⟨the days ~ by⟩ **4 a :** to break forth or out so as to make a sudden display ⟨the sun ~ed from behind a cloud⟩ **b :** to act or speak vehemently and suddenly esp. in anger **5 a :** to give off light suddenly or in transient bursts **b :** to glow or gleam esp. with animation or passion ⟨her eyes ~ed with anger⟩ **6 :** to change suddenly or violently into vapor ⟨hot water ~ing to steam under reduced pressure⟩ **7 :** to expose one's genitals usu. suddenly and briefly in public **8 :** to have sudden insight — often used with *on* ~ *vt* **1 a** *archaic* **:** SPLASH **b :** to fill by a sudden inflow of water **2 a :** to cause the sudden appearance of (light) **b :** to cause to burst violently into flame **c** (1) **:** to cause (light) to reflect (2) **:** to cause (as a mirror) to reflect light (3) **:** to cause (a lamp) to flash **d :** to convey by means of flashes of light **3 a :** to make known or cause to appear with great speed ⟨~ a message on the screen⟩ **b :** to display obtrusively and ostentatiously ⟨always ~*ing* a roll of bills⟩ **c :** to expose to view suddenly and briefly ⟨~*ed* a badge⟩ **4 :** to cover with or form into a thin layer: as **a :** to protect against rain by covering with sheet metal or a substitute **b :** to coat (as glass) with a thin layer (as of metal or a differently colored glass) **5 :** to subject (an exposed photographic negative or positive) to a supplementary uniform exposure to light before development in order to modify detail or tone

syn FLASH, GLEAM, GLINT, SPARKLE, GLITTER, GLISTEN, GLIMMER, SHIMMER mean to send forth light. FLASH implies a sudden and transient outburst of bright light ⟨lightning *flashed*⟩. GLEAM suggests a steady light seen through an obscuring medium or against a dark background ⟨lights *gleamed* in the valley⟩. GLINT implies a cold glancing light ⟨*glinting* steel⟩. SPARKLE suggests innumerable moving points of bright light ⟨the *sparkling* waters of the gulf⟩. GLITTER connotes a brilliant sparkling or gleaming ⟨*glittering* diamonds⟩. GLISTEN applies to the soft sparkle from a wet or oily surface ⟨*glistening* rain-drenched sidewalks⟩. GLIMMER suggests a faint or wavering gleam ⟨a distant *glimmering* light⟩. SHIMMER implies a soft tremulous gleaming or a blurred reflection ⟨a *shimmering* satin dress⟩.

²flash *n* (1566) **1 a :** a sudden burst of light **b :** a movement of a flag in signaling **2 :** a sudden and often brilliant burst ⟨a ~ of wit⟩ **3 :** a brief time ⟨I'll be back in a ~⟩ **4 a :** SHOW, DISPLAY; *esp* **:** a vulgar ostentatious display **b** *archaic* **:** a showy ostentatious person **c :** one that attracts notice; *esp* **:** an outstanding athlete **d :** PIZZAZZ **5** *obs* **:** thieves' slang **6 :** something flashed: as **a :** GLIMPSE, LOOK **b :** SMILE **c :** a first brief news report **d :** FLASHLIGHT 1,2 **e :** a quick-spreading flame or momentary intense outburst of radiant heat **f :** a device for producing a brief and very bright flash of light for taking photographs **7 :** RUSH 7a **8 :** the rapid conversion of a liquid into vapor

³flash *adj* (ca. 1700) **1 a :** FLASHY, SHOWY **b :** of, relating to, or characteristic of flashy people or things ⟨~ behavior⟩ **c :** of, relating to, or characteristic of persons considered social outcasts ⟨~ language⟩ **2 a :** of sudden origin and short duration ⟨a ~ fire⟩ **b :** involving very brief exposure to an intense altering agent (as heat or cold) ⟨~ drying of milk⟩ ⟨~ freezing of food⟩

flash·back \'flash-,bak\ *n* (1903) **1 :** a recession of flame to an unwanted position (as into a blowpipe) **2 a :** interruption of chronological sequence (as in a film or literary work) by interjection of events of earlier occurrence; *also* **:** an instance of flashback **b :** a past incident recurring vividly in the mind

flash back *vi* (1944) **1 :** to focus one's mind on or vividly remember a past time or incident — usu. used with *to* **2 :** to employ a flashback (as in a film) — usu. used with *to*

flash·board \-,bōrd, -,bȯrd\ *n* (ca. 1774) **:** one or more boards projecting above the top of a dam to increase the depth of the water

flash·bulb \-,bəlb\ *n* (1935) **:** an electric bulb that can be used only once to produce a brief and very bright flash of light for taking photographs

flash card *n* (1923) **:** a card bearing words, numbers, or pictures that is briefly displayed (as by a teacher to a class) usu. as a learning aid

flash·cube \'flash-,kyüb\ *n* (1965) **:** a cubical device incorporating four flashbulbs

flash·er \'fla-shər\ *n* (1686) **:** one that flashes: as **a :** a light (as a traffic signal or automobile light) that catches the attention by flashing **b :** a device for automatically flashing a light **c :** an exhibitionist who flashes

flash flood *n* (1940) **:** a local flood of great volume and short duration generally resulting from heavy rainfall in the immediate vicinity — **flash flood** *vb*

flash–for·ward \'flash-'fȯr-wərd\ *n* (1949) **:** interruption of chronological sequence (as in a film or literary work) by interjection of events of future occurrence; *also* **:** an instance of flash-forward

flash–gun \-,gən\ *n* (1925) **:** a device for producing a bright flash of light for photography

flash·ing \'fla-shiŋ\ *n* (1742) **:** sheet metal used in waterproofing (as at roof valleys or hips or the angle between a chimney and a roof)

flash in the pan [fr. the firing of the priming in the pan of a flintlock musket without discharging the piece] (1901) **1 :** a sudden spasmodic effort that accomplishes nothing **2 :** one that appears promising but turns out to be disappointing or worthless

flash–lamp \'flash-,lamp\ *n* (1890) **:** a lamp for producing a brief but intense flash of light (as for taking photographs)

flash·light \'flash-,līt\ *n* (1886) **1 a :** a sudden bright artificial light used in taking photographic pictures **b :** a photograph taken by such a light **2 :** a small battery-operated portable electric light

flash·over \-,ō-vər\ *n* (1892) **1 :** an abnormal electrical discharge (as through the air to the ground from a high potential source or between two conducting portions of a structure) **2 :** the sudden spread of flame over an area when it becomes heated to the flash point

flash point *n* (1878) **1 :** the lowest temperature at which vapors above a volatile combustible substance ignite in air when exposed to flame **2 :** a point at which someone or something bursts suddenly into action or being **3 :** TINDERBOX 2

flash–tube \'flash-,t(y)üb\ *n* (1945) **:** a gas discharge tube that produces very brief intense flashes of light and is used esp. in photography

flashy \'fla-shē\ *adj* **flash·i·er; -est** (ca. 1598) **1** *chiefly dial* **:** lacking in substance or flavor **:** INSIPID **2 :** momentarily dazzling **3 a :** superficially attractive or impressive **b :** ostentatious or showy often beyond the bounds of good taste; *esp* **:** marked by gaudy brightness **syn** see GAUDY — **flash·i·ly** \'fla-shə-lē\ *adv* — **flash·i·ness** \'fla-shē-nəs\ *n*

flask \'flask, flȧsk\ *n* [MF *flasque* powder flask, ultim. fr. LL *flascon-, flasco* bottle, prob. of Gmc origin; akin to OHG *flaska* bottle] (1549) **:** a container often somewhat narrowed toward the outlet and often fitted with a closure: as **a :** a broad flattened necked vessel used esp. to carry alcoholic beverages on the person **b** *Brit* **:** VACUUM BOTTLE

¹flat \'flat\ *adj* **flat·ter; flat·test** [ME, fr. ON *flatr*; akin to OHG *flaz* flat, and prob. Gk *platys* broad — more at PLACE] (14c) **1 a :** lying at full length or spread out upon the ground **:** PROSTRATE **b :** utterly ruined or destroyed **c :** resting with a surface against something **2 a :** having a continuous horizontal surface **b :** being or characterized by a horizontal line or tracing without peaks or depressions ⟨a ~ EEG⟩ **3 :** having a relatively smooth or even surface **4 :** arranged or laid out so as to be level or even **5 a :** having the major surfaces essentially parallel and distinctly greater than the minor surfaces ⟨a ~ piece of wood⟩ **b** *of a heel* **:** very low and broad **6 a :** clearly unmistakable **:** DOWNRIGHT ⟨a ~ denial⟩ **b** (1) **:** not varying **:** FIXED ⟨a ~ rate⟩ (2) **:** having no fraction either lacking or in excess **:** EXACT ⟨in a ~ 10 seconds⟩ (3) *of a frequency response* **:** not varying significantly throughout its range **7 a :** lacking in animation, zest, or vigor **:** DULL ⟨life seemed ~ without her⟩ **b :** lacking flavor **:** TASTELESS **c :** lacking effervescence or sparkle ⟨~ ginger ale⟩ **d :** commercially inactive; *also* **:** characterized by no significant rise or decline from one period to another ⟨sales were ~⟩ **e** *of a tire* **:** lacking air **:** DEFLATED **f** *chiefly Brit, of a battery* **:** DEAD 3c, DISCHARGED **8 a** (1) *of a tone* **:** lowered a half step in pitch (2) **:** lower than the proper pitch **b** *of the vowel a* **:** pronounced as in *bad* or *bat* **9 a :** having a low trajectory ⟨a ~ tennis stroke⟩ **:** made so as to give little or no spin to the ball **10** *of a sail* **:** TAUT **11 a :** uniform in hue or shade **b :** having little or no illusion of depth **c** *of a photograph or negative* **:** lacking contrast **d** *of lighting conditions* **:** lacking shadows or contours **e :** free from gloss ⟨a ~ paint⟩ **f :** TWO-DIMENSIONAL 2 **12 :** of, relating to, or used in competition on the flat ⟨a ~ horse⟩ **syn** see LEVEL, INSIPID — **flat·ly** *adv* — **flat·ness** *n* — **flat·tish** \'fla-tish\ *adj*

²flat *n* (14c) **1 a :** a level surface of land — usu. used in pl. ⟨sagebrush ~s⟩ ⟨tidal ~s⟩ **b :** a stretch of land without obstacles; *esp* **:** a track or course for a flat race — usu. used with *the* ⟨has won twice on the ~⟩ **2 :** a flat part or surface ⟨the ~ of one's hand⟩ **3 a :** a musical note or tone one half step lower than a specified note or tone **b :** a character ♭ on a line or space of the musical staff indicating a half step drop in pitch **4 :** something flat: as **a :** a shallow container for shipping produce **b :** a shallow box in which seedlings are started **c :** a flat piece of theatrical scenery **d :** a shoe or slipper having a flat heel or no heel **5** *chiefly Brit* **:** an apartment on one floor **6 :** a deflated tire **7 :** the area to either side of an offensive football formation

³flat *adv* (1531) **1 :** in a flat manner **:** DIRECTLY, POSITIVELY **2 :** in a complete manner **:** ABSOLUTELY ⟨~ broke⟩ **3 :** below the proper musical pitch **4 :** without interest charge; *esp* **:** without allowance or charge for accrued interest ⟨bonds sold ~⟩

⁴flat *vb* **flat·ted; flat·ting** *vt* (ca. 1604) **1 :** FLATTEN **2 :** to lower in pitch esp. by a half step ~ *vi* **:** to sing or play below the true pitch

¹flat–bed \'flat-,bed\ *adj* (1892) **:** having a horizontal bed on which the work rests ⟨a ~ printing press⟩ ⟨a ~ plotter⟩

²flatbed *n* (1944) **:** a motortruck or trailer with a body in the form of a platform or shallow box

flat·boat \-,bōt\ *n* (1660) **:** a boat with a flat bottom and square ends used for transportation of bulky freight esp. in shallow waters

flat·car \-,kär\ *n* (1881) **:** a railroad freight car without permanent raised sides, ends, or covering

flat–coated retriever \'flat-,kō-tad-\ *n* (1929) **:** any of an English breed of medium-sized sporting dogs that have a dense smooth black or liver-colored coat

flat–earth·er \,flat-'ər-thər\ *also* **flat–earth·ist** \-thist\ *n* (1926) **:** a person who believes that the Earth is flat

flat·fish \'flat-,fish\ *n* (1710) **:** any of an order (Heterosomata) of marine typically bottom-dwelling bony fishes (as the halibuts, flounders, turbots, and soles) that as adults swim on one side of the laterally compressed body and have both eyes on the upper side

flat-foot \-ˌfut (*always so in sense 3*), ˌflat-\ *n, pl* **flat-feet** \-ˌfēt, -ˈfēt\ (1860) **1 :** a condition in which the arch of the instep is flattened so that the entire sole rests upon the ground **2 :** a foot affected with flatfoot **3** *a or pl* **flatfoots** *slang* **:** POLICE OFFICER; *esp* **:** a patrolman walking a regular beat **b** *slang* **:** SAILOR

¹flat-foot-ed \ˈflat-ˌfu̇-tad, ˈflat-\ *adj* (1601) **1 :** affected with flatfoot; *broadly* **:** walking with a dragging or shambling gait **2 a :** firm and well balanced on the feet **b :** free from reservation **:** FORTHRIGHT ⟨had an honest ~ way of saying a thing⟩ **3 :** not ready **:** UNPREPARED — used chiefly in the phrase *catch one flat-footed* **4 :** proceeding in a plodding or unimaginative way **:** PEDESTRIAN ⟨~ prose⟩ — **flat-foot-ed-ly** *adv* — **flat-foot-ed-ness** *n*

²flat-footed *adv* (1828) **1 :** in an open and determined manner **:** FLATLY **2 :** with the feet flat on a surface (as the ground)

flat-hat \ˈflat-ˌhat\ *vi* [fr. an alleged incident in which a pedestrian's hat was crushed by a low-flying plane] (1940) **:** to fly low in an airplane in a reckless manner **:** HEDGEHOP — **flat-hat-ter** *n*

Flat-head \-ˌhed\ *n, pl* **Flatheads** *or* **Flathead** (1709) **1 :** a member of any of several No. American Indian peoples that practiced head-flattening **2 :** an American Indian people of Montana **3** *not cap* **:** any of a family (Platycephalidae) of mostly Australian and East Indian marine fishes that resemble the sculpins

flat-head catfish \ˈflat-ˌhed-\ *n* (1945) **:** a large yellowish brown-mottled catfish (*Pylodictis olivaris*) of the central and Gulf states of the U.S.

flat-iron \ˈflat-ˌī(-ə)rn\ *n* (1744) **:** IRON 2c

flat-land \ˈflat-ˌland\ *n* (1735) **1 :** a region in which the land is predominantly flat — usu. used in pl. **2 :** land that lacks significant variation in elevation — **flat-land-er** \-ˌlan-dər\ *n*

flat-let \ˈflat-lət\ *n* (1925) *Brit* **:** EFFICIENCY APARTMENT

flat-ling \ˈflat-liŋ\ *or* **flat-lings** \-liŋz\ *adv* (15c) *dial Brit* **:** with a flat side or edge

flat-mate \ˈflat-ˌmāt\ *n* (1955) *chiefly Brit* **:** one of two or more persons sharing the same flat

flat-out \ˈflat-ˌau̇t\ *adj* (1906) **1 :** being or going at maximum effort or speed **2 :** OUT-AND-OUT, DOWNRIGHT ⟨it was a ~ lie⟩

flat out *adv* (1932) **1 :** in a blunt and direct manner **:** OPENLY ⟨called *flat out* for revolution —*Nat'l Review*⟩ **2 :** at top speed or peak performance ⟨the car does 180 m.p.h. *flat out*⟩ **3** *usu* **flat-out :** to the greatest degree **:** COMPLETELY — usu. used as an intensive ⟨is just *flat-out* confusing⟩

flat-pick-ing \ˈflat-ˌpi-kiŋ\ *n* (1970) **:** a method of playing a stringed instrument (as a guitar) with a plectrum held between the thumb and forefinger

flat race *n* (1848) **:** a race (as for horses) on a level course without obstacles (as hurdles) — compare STEEPLECHASE — **flat racing** *n*

flat-ten \ˈflat-ᵊn\ *vb* **flat-tened; flat-ten-ing** \ˈflat-niŋ, ˈfla-tə-\ *vt* (1630) **1 :** to make flat: as **a :** to make level or smooth **b :** to knock down; *also* **:** to defeat decisively **c :** to make dull or uninspired — often used with *out* **d :** to make (as paint) lusterless **e :** to stabilize esp. at a lower level ~ *vi* **:** to become flat or flatter: as **a :** to become dull or spiritless **b :** to extend in or into a flat position or form **c :** to become uniform or stabilized often at a new lower level — usu. used with *out* — **flat-ten-er** \-nər\ *n*

¹flat-ter \ˈfla-tər\ *vb* [ME *flateren*, fr. OF *flater* to lick, flatter, of Gmc origin; akin to OHG *flaz* flat] *vt* (13c) **1 :** to praise excessively esp. from motives of self-interest **2** *a archaic* **:** BEGUILE **4 b :** to encourage or gratify esp. with the assurance that something is right ⟨I ~ myself that my interpretation is correct⟩ **3 a :** to portray too favorably ⟨the portrait ~*s* him⟩ **b :** to display to advantage ⟨candlelight often ~*s* the face⟩ ~ *vi* **:** to use flattery — **flat-ter-er** \-tər-ər\ *n* — **flat-ter-ing-ly** \-tə-riŋ-lē\ *adv*

²flatter *n* (1714) **:** one that flattens; *esp* **:** a flat-faced swage used in smithing

flat-tery \ˈfla-tə-rē\ *n, pl* **-ter-ies** (14c) **1 a :** the act or practice of flattering **b** (1) **:** something that flatters (2) **:** insincere or excessive praise **2** *obs* **:** a pleasing self-deception

flat-top \ˈflat-ˌtäp\ *n* (1940) **:** something with a flat or flattened upper surface: as **a :** AIRCRAFT CARRIER **b :** a modified crew cut

flat-u-lence \ˈfla-chə-lən(t)s\ *n* (1711) **:** the quality or state of being flatulent

flat-u-len-cy \-lən(t)-sē\ *n* (1660) **:** FLATULENCE

flat-u-lent \-lənt\ *adj* [MF, fr. L *flatus* act of blowing, wind, fr. *flare* to blow — more at BLOW] (1599) **1 a :** marked by or affected with gas generated in the intestine or stomach **b :** likely to cause gas **2 :** pompously or portentously overblown **:** INFLATED — **flat-u-lent-ly** *adv*

fla-tus \ˈflā-təs\ *n* [L, act of blowing, act of breaking wind] (1651) **:** gas generated in the stomach or bowels

flat-ware \ˈflat-ˌwar, -ˌwer\ *n* (1851) **:** tableware more or less flat and usu. formed or cast in a single piece; *esp* **:** eating and serving utensils (as knives, forks, and spoons) — compare HOLLOWWARE

flat-ways \-ˌwāz\ *adv* (1692) **:** FLATWISE

flat-wise \-ˌwīz\ *adv* (1601) **:** with the flat surface presented in some expressed or implied position

flat-work \-ˌwərk\ *n* (1925) **:** laundry that can be finished mechanically and does not require hand ironing

flat-worm \-ˌwərm\ *n* (ca. 1889) **:** PLATYHELMINTH; *esp* **:** TURBELLARIAN

flaunt \ˈflȯnt, ˈflänt\ *vb* [perh. of Scand origin; akin to ON *flana* to rush around — more at PLANET] *vi* (1566) **1 :** to display or obtrude oneself to public notice **2 :** to wave or flutter showily ⟨the flag ~*s* in the breeze⟩ ~ *vt* **1 :** to display ostentatiously or impudently **:** PARADE ⟨~*ing* his superiority⟩ **2 :** to treat contemptuously ⟨~*ed* the rules —Louis Untermeyer⟩ *syn* see SHOW — **flaunt** *n* — **flaunt-ing-ly** \ˈflȯn-tiŋ-lē, ˈflän-\ *adv* — **flaunty** \-tē\ *adj*

usage Although transitive sense 2 of *flaunt* undoubtedly arose from confusion with *flout*, the contexts in which it appears cannot be called substandard ⟨meting out punishment to the occasional mavericks who operate rigged games, tolerate rowdyism, or otherwise *flaunt* the law —Oscar Lewis⟩ ⟨observed with horror the *flaunting* of their authority in the suburbs, where men . . . put up buildings that had no place at

all in a Christian commonwealth —Marchette Chute⟩ ⟨in our profession . . . very rarely do we publicly chastise a colleague who has *flaunted* our most basic principles —R. T. Blackburn, *AAUP Bull.*⟩. If you use it, however, you should be aware that many people will consider it a mistake. Use of *flout* in the sense of *flaunt* is found occasionally ⟨"The proper pronunciation," the blonde said, *flouting* her refined upbringing, "is pree feeks" —Mike Royko⟩.

flau-tist \ˈflȯ-tist, ˈflau̇-\ *n* [It *flautista*, fr. *flauto* flute, fr. OProv *flaut*] (1860) **:** FLUTIST

fla-va-none \ˈflā-və-ˌnōn\ *n* [L *flavus* + ISV -*ane* + -*one*] (1949) **:** a colorless crystalline ketone $C_{15}H_{12}O_2$; *also* **:** any of the derivatives of this ketone many of which occur in plants often in the form of glycosides

fla-vin \ˈflā-vən\ *n* [ISV, fr. L *flavus* yellow — more at BLUE] (1933) **:** any of a class of yellow water-soluble nitrogenous pigments derived from isoalloxazine and occurring in the form of nucleotides as coenzymes of flavoproteins; *esp* **:** RIBOFLAVIN

flavin adenine dinucleotide *n* (1960) **:** a coenzyme $C_{27}H_{33}N_9O_{15}P_2$ of some flavoproteins

fla-vine \ˈflā-ˌvēn\ *n* [ISV, fr. L *flavus*] (ca. 1853) **:** any of a series of yellow acridine dyes (as acriflavine) often used medicinally for their antiseptic properties

flavin mononucleotide *n* (ca. 1953) **:** FMN

fla-vone \ˈflā-ˌvōn\ *n* [ISV, fr. L *flavus*] (1897) **:** a colorless crystalline ketone $C_{15}H_{10}O_2$ found in the leaves, stems, and seed capsules of many primroses; *also* **:** any of the derivatives of this ketone many of which occur as yellow plant pigments in the form of glycosides and are used as dyestuffs

fla-vo-noid \ˈflā-və-ˌnȯid\ *n* [*flavone* + -*oid*] (1947) **:** any of a group of aromatic compounds that includes many common pigments (as the anthocyanins and flavones)

fla-vo-nol \ˈflā-və-ˌnȯl, -ˌnōl\ *n* (1898) **:** any of various hydroxy derivatives of flavone

fla-vo-pro-tein \ˌflā-vō-ˈprō-ˌtēn, -ˈprō-tē-ən\ *n* [ISV *flavin* + -*o*- + *protein*] (1934) **:** a dehydrogenase that contains a flavin and often a metal and plays a major role in biological oxidations

¹fla-vor \ˈflā-vər\ *n* [ME, fr. MF *flaor, flavor*, fr. (assumed) VL *flator*, alter. of L *flatus* breath, act of blowing — more at FLATULENT] (14c) **1 a** *archaic* **:** ODOR, FRAGRANCE **b :** the quality of something that affects the sense of taste **c :** the blend of taste and smell sensations evoked by a substance in the mouth ⟨the ~ of apples⟩ **2 :** a substance that flavors ⟨artificial ~*s*⟩ **3 :** characteristic or predominant quality ⟨the ethnic ~ of a neighborhood⟩ **4 a :** VARIETY 3a **b :** a property that distinguishes different types of elementary particles (as quarks and neutrinos); *also* **:** any of the different types of particles that are distinguished by flavor — **fla-vored** \-vərd\ *adj* — **fla-vor-ful** \-vər-fəl\ *adj* — **fla-vor-ful-ly** \-fə-lē\ *adv* — **fla-vor-less** \-vər-ləs\ *adj* — **fla-vor-some** \-səm\ *adj*

²flavor *vt* **fla-vored; fla-vor-ing** \ˈflā-v(ə-)riŋ\ (1542) **:** to give or add flavor to

fla-vor-ing *n* (1845) **:** FLAVOR 2

fla-vor-ist \ˈflā-vər-ist\ *n* (1964) **:** a specialist in the creation of artificial flavors

fla-vour *chiefly Brit var of* FLAVOR

¹flaw \ˈflȯ\ *n* [of Scand origin; akin to Norw *flaga* gust] (1513) **1 :** a sudden brief burst of wind; *also* **:** a spell of stormy weather **2** *obs* **:** an outburst esp. of passion

²flaw *n* [ME, flake, prob. of Scand origin; akin to Sw *flaga* flake, flaw; akin to OE *flōh* flat stone] (1586) **1 a :** a defect in physical structure or form **b :** an imperfection or weakness and esp. one that detracts from the whole or hinders effectiveness ⟨vanity was the ~ in his character⟩ ⟨a ~ in the book's plot⟩ **2** *obs* **:** FRAGMENT — **flawed** \ˈflȯd\ *adj* — **flaw-less** \-ləs\ *adj* — **flaw-less-ly** *adv* — **flaw-less-ness** *n*

³flaw *vt* (1610) **:** to make flaws in **:** MAR ~ *vi* **:** to become defective

flax \ˈflaks\ *n, often attrib* [ME, fr. OE *fleax*; akin to OHG *flahs* flax, L *plectere* to braid — more at PLY] (bef. 12c) **1 :** any of a genus (*Linum* of the family Linaceae, the flax family) of herbs; *esp* **:** a slender erect annual (*L. usitatissimum*) with blue flowers commonly cultivated for its bast fiber and seed **2 :** the fiber of the flax plant esp. when prepared for spinning **3 :** any of several plants resembling flax

flax-en \ˈflak-sən\ *adj* (15c) **1 :** made of flax **2 :** resembling flax esp. in pale soft strawy color ⟨~ hair⟩

flax-seed \ˈflak-(s)ˌsēd\ *n* (1562) **:** the seed of flax used as a source of oil and medicinally as a demulcent and emollient

flaxy \ˈflak-sē\ *adj* **flax-i-er; -est** (1634) **:** resembling flax esp. in texture

flay \ˈflā\ *vt* [ME *flen*, fr. OE *flēan*; akin to ON *flā* to flay, Lith *plēšti* to tear] (bef. 12c) **1 :** to strip off the skin or surface of **:** SKIN **2 :** to criticize harshly **:** EXCORIATE **3 :** LASH 1b ⟨the wind whipped up to gale fury, ~*ing* his face —Richard Kent⟩

F layer *n* (1928) **:** the highest and most densely ionized regular layer of the ionosphere occurring at night within the F region

flea \ˈflē\ *n* [ME *fle*, fr. OE *flēa*; akin to OHG *flōh* flea] (bef. 12c) **:** any of an order (Siphonaptera) of small wingless bloodsucking insects that have a hard laterally compressed body and legs adapted to leaping and that feed on warm-blooded animals — **flea in one's ear :** REBUKE ⟨sent him away with a *flea in his ear*⟩

flea-bag \ˈflē-ˌbag\ *n* (1839) **:** an inferior hotel or rooming house

flea-bane \-ˌbān\ *n* (1548) **:** any of various composite plants (as of the genus *Erigeron*) that were once believed to drive away fleas

flea beetle *n* (1842) **:** any of a subfamily (Alticinae, esp. genera *Alticia* and *Epitrix*) of small chrysomelid beetles with legs adapted for leaping that feed on foliage and sometimes serve as vectors of virus diseases of plants

flea-bite \ˈflē-ˌbīt\ *n* (ca. 1570) **1 :** the bite of a flea; *also* **:** the red spot caused by such a bite **2 :** a trifling pain or annoyance

flea-bit-ten \-ˌbi-tᵊn\ *adj* (1570) **1** *of a horse* **:** having a white or gray coat flecked with a darker color **2 :** bitten by or infested with fleas

flea collar *n* (1953) **:** a collar for animals (as dogs and cats) that contains insecticide for killing fleas

flea-flick-er \-ˌfli-kər\ *n* (1927) **:** any of various deceptive football plays in which the ball is quickly transferred between players (as by a lateral) before or after a forward pass

flea·hop·per \-ˌhä-pər\ *n* (1902) : any of various small jumping bugs that feed on cultivated plants

flea market *n* [trans. of F *Marché aux Puces*, a market in Paris] (1922) : a usu. open-air market for secondhand articles and antiques

flea-pit \-ˌpit\ *n* (1937) *Brit* : a dilapidated building usu. housing a movie theater

flea-wort \ˈflē-ˌwərt, -ˌwȯrt\ *n* (bef. 12c) : any of three Old World plantains (esp. *Plantago psyllium*) whose seeds are sometimes used as a mild laxative — compare PSYLLIUM SEED

flèche \ˈflāsh, ˈflesh\ *n* [F, lit., arrow, fr. OF *fleche*, fr. Gmc origin; akin to MD *vlieke* arrow, OE *flēogan* to fly] (1848) : SPIRE; *esp* : a slender spire above the intersection of the nave and transepts of a church

flé·chette \flā-ˈshet, fle-\ *n* [F, fr. dim. of *flèche* arrow] (1915) : a small dart-shaped projectile that is clustered in an explosive warhead, dropped as a missile from an airplane, or fired from a handheld gun

¹fleck \ˈflek\ *vt* [back-formation fr. *flecked* spotted, fr. ME, prob. fr. ON *flekkōttr*, fr. *flekkr* spot] (14c) 1 : STREAK, SPOT ⟨whitecaps ~ed the blue sea⟩ 2 : to color as if by sprinkling with flecks ⟨his wit is ~ed with sarcasm —James Atlas⟩

²fleck *n* (1598) 1 : SPOT, MARK ⟨a brown tweed with ~s of yellow⟩ 2 : FLAKE, PARTICLE ⟨~s of snow drifted down⟩

fledge \ˈflej\ *vb* **fledged; fledg·ing** [*fledge* capable of flying, fr. ME *flegge*, fr. OE *-flycge*; akin to OHG *flucki* capable of flying, OE *flēogan* to fly — more at FLY] *vi* (1566) *of a bird* : to acquire the feathers necessary for flight or independent activity ~ *vt* 1 : to rear until ready for flight or independent activity 2 : to cover with or as if with feathers or down 3 : to furnish (as an arrow) with feathers

fledg·ling \ˈflej-liŋ\ *n* (1830) 1 : a young bird just fledged 2 : an immature or inexperienced person 3 : one that is new ⟨a ~ company⟩

flee \ˈflē\ *vb* **fled** \ˈfled\; **flee·ing** [ME *flen*, fr. OE *flēon*; akin to OHG *fliohan* to flee] *vi* (bef. 12c) 1 a : to run away often from danger or evil : FLY b : to hurry toward a place of security 2 : to pass away swiftly : VANISH ~ *vt* : to run away from : SHUN

¹fleece \ˈflēs\ *n* [ME *flees*, fr. OE *flēos*; akin to MHG *vlius* fleece and perh. to L *pluma* feather, down] (bef. 12c) 1 a : the coat of wool covering a wool-bearing animal (as a sheep) b : the wool obtained from a sheep at one shearing 2 a : any of various soft or woolly coverings b : a soft bulky deep-piled knitted or woven fabric used chiefly for clothing

²fleece *vt* **fleeced; fleec·ing** (1537) 1 a : to strip of money or property by fraud or extortion b : to charge excessively for goods or services 2 : to remove the fleece from : SHEAR 3 : to dot or cover with fleecy masses

fleeced \ˈflēst\ *adj* (1580) 1 : covered with or as if with a fleece 2 *of a textile* : having a soft nap

fleech \ˈflēch\ *vb* [ME (Sc) *flechen*] (14c) *dial* : COAX, WHEEDLE

fleecy \ˈflē-sē\ *adj* **fleec·i·er; -est** (1590) : covered with, made of, or resembling fleece ⟨a ~ winter coat⟩

¹fleer \ˈflir\ *vi* [ME *fleryen*, of Scand origin; akin to Norw *flire* to giggle] (15c) : to laugh or grimace in a coarse derisive manner : SNEER *syn* see SCOFF — **fleer·ing·ly** \-iŋ-lē\ *adv*

²fleer *n* (1604) : a word or look of derision or mockery

¹fleet \ˈflēt\ *vb* [ME *fleten*, fr. OE *flēotan* to float, OE *flōwan* to flow] *vi* (bef. 12c) 1 *obs* : DRIFT 2 a *archaic* : FLOW b : to fade away : VANISH 3 [²*fleet*] : to fly swiftly ~ *vt* : to cause (time) to pass usu. quickly or imperceptibly

²fleet *n* [ME *flete*, fr. OE *flēot* ship, fr. *flēotan*] (13c) 1 : a number of warships under a single command; *specif* : an organization of ships and aircraft under the command of a flag officer : GROUP 2a, b; *esp* : a group (as of ships, planes, or trucks) operated under unified control

³fleet *adj* [prob. fr. ¹*fleet*] (ca. 1529) 1 : swift in motion : NIMBLE 2 : EVANESCENT, FLEETING *syn* see FAST — **fleet·ly** *adv* — **fleet·ness** *n*

fleet admiral *n* (1946) : an admiral of the highest rank in the navy whose insignia is five stars

fleet–foot·ed \-ˌfu̇-təd\ *adj* (ca. 1743) : able to run fast

fleet·ing \ˈflē-tiŋ\ *adj* (1563) : passing swiftly : TRANSITORY *syn* see TRANSIENT — **fleet·ing·ly** \ˈflē-tiŋ-lē\ *adv* — **fleet·ing·ness** *n*

Fleet Street \ˈflēt-\ *n* [*Fleet Street*, London, England, center of the London newspaper district] (1882) : the London press

flei·shig \ˈflā-shik\ *adj* [Yiddish *fleyshik*, fr. MHG *vleischic* meaty, fr. *vleisch* flesh, meat, fr. OHG *fleisk*] (1943) : made of, prepared with, or used for meat or meat products — compare MILCHIG, PAREVE

Flem·ing \ˈfle-miŋ\ *n* [ME, fr. MD *Vlaminc* (akin to MD *Vlander* Flanders)] (12c) : a member of the Germanic people inhabiting northern Belgium and a small section of northern France

¹Flem·ish \ˈfle-mish\ *adj* (14c) : of, relating to, or characteristic of Flanders or the Flemings or their language

²Flemish *n* (ca. 1714) 1 : the Germanic language of the Flemings that is made up of dialects of Dutch 2 *pl in constr* : FLEMINGS

Flemish giant *n* (1898) : any of a breed of very large solid-colored rabbits prob. of Belgian origin

flense \ˈflen(t)s\ *vt* **flensed; flens·ing** [D *flensen* or Dan & Norw *flense*] (1820) : to strip (as a whale) of blubber or skin

¹flesh \ˈflesh\ *n* [ME, fr. OE *flǣsc*; akin to OHG *fleisk* flesh and perh. to ON *flā* to flay — more at FLAY] (bef. 12c) 1 a : the soft parts of the body of an animal and esp. of a vertebrate; *esp* : the parts composed chiefly of skeletal muscle as distinguished from visceral structures, bone, and integuments b : sleek well-fatted condition of body c : SKIN 2 a : edible parts of an animal b : flesh of a mammal or fowl eaten as food 3 a : the physical nature of human beings ⟨the spirit indeed is willing, but the ~ is weak —Mt 26:41 (AV)⟩ b : HUMAN NATURE c : human beings : MANKIND b : living beings c : STOCK, KINDRED 5 : a fleshy plant part used as food; *also* : the fleshy part of a fruit 6 *Christian Science* : an illusion that matter has sensation 7 : SUBSTANCE ⟨insights buried in the ~ of the narrative —Jan Carew⟩ — **in the flesh** : in person and alive

²flesh *vt* (1530) 1 : to initiate or habituate esp. by giving a foretaste 2 *archaic* : GRATIFY 3 : to clothe or cover with or as if with flesh; *broadly* : to give substance to — usu. used with *out* 4 : to free from flesh ~ *vi* : to become fleshy — often used with *up* or *out*

flesh and blood *n* (bef. 12c) 1 : corporeal nature as composed of flesh and of blood 2 : near kindred — used chiefly in the phrase *one's own flesh and blood* 3 : SUBSTANCE, REALITY

fleshed \ˈflesht\ *adj* (15c) : having flesh esp. of a specified kind — often used in combination ⟨pink-*fleshed*⟩ ⟨thick-*fleshed*⟩

flesh fly *n* (14c) : a dipteran fly whose maggots feed on flesh; *esp* : any of a family (Sarcophagidae) of flies some of which cause myiasis

flesh-ings \ˈfle-shiŋz\ *n pl* (1860) : material removed in fleshing a hide

flesh·ly \ˈflesh-lē\ *adj* (bef. 12c) 1 a : CORPOREAL, BODILY b : of, relating to, or characterized by indulgence of bodily appetites; *esp* : LASCIVIOUS ⟨~ desires⟩ c : not spiritual : WORLDLY 2 : FLESHY, PLUMP 3 : having a sensuous quality ⟨~ art⟩ *syn* see CARNAL

flesh·ment \ˈflesh-mənt\ *n* [²*flesh*] (1605) *obs* : excitement associated with a successful beginning

flesh out *vt* (1886) : to make fuller or more nearly complete ⟨museums *fleshing out* their collections with borrowed works⟩ — **fleshed–out** *adj*

flesh·pot \ˈflesh-ˌpät\ *n* (1592) 1 *pl* : bodily comfort : LUXURY 2 : a place of lascivious entertainment — usu. used in pl.

flesh wound *n* (ca. 1674) : an injury involving penetration of the body musculature without damage to bones or internal organs

fleshy \ˈfle-shē\ *adj* **flesh·i·er; -est** (14c) 1 a : marked by, consisting of, or resembling flesh b : marked by abundant flesh; *esp* : CORPULENT 2 a : SUCCULENT, PULPY ⟨the ~ texture of a melon⟩ b : not thin, dry, or membranous ⟨~ fungi⟩ — **flesh·i·ness** *n*

fleshy fruit *n* (1929) : a fruit (as a berry, drupe, or pome) consisting largely of soft succulent tissue

fletch \ˈflech\ *vt* [back-formation fr. *fletcher*] (ca. 1656) : FEATHER ⟨~ an arrow⟩

fletch·er \ˈfle-chər\ *n* [ME *fleccher*, fr. OF *flechier*, fr. *fleche* arrow — more at FLÈCHE] (14c) : a maker of arrows

fletch·ing \-chiŋ\ *n* (ca. 1930) : the feathers on an arrow; *also* : the arrangement of such feathers

fleur de coin \ˌflər-də-ˈkwaⁿ\ *adj* [F *à fleur de coin*, lit., with the bloom of the die] (ca. 1889) : being in the preserved mint condition

fleur–de–lis *or* **fleur–de–lys** \ˌflər-d°l-ˈē, ˌflu̇r-\ *n, pl* **fleurs–de–lis** *or* **fleur–de–lis** *or* **fleurs–de–lys** *or* **fleur–de–lys** \ˌflər-d°l-ˈē(z), ˌflu̇r-\ [ME *flourdelis*, fr. MF *flor de lis*, lit., lily flower] (14c) 1 : IRIS 3 2 : a conventionalized iris in artistic design and heraldry

fleu·ry \ˈflu̇r-ē\ *adj* [alter. of ME *flory*, fr. OF *floré*, fr. *flor* flower — more at FLOWER] (15c) *of a heraldic cross* : having the ends of the arms broadening out into the heads of fleurs-de-lis — see CROSS illustration

flew *past of* FLY

flews \ˈflüz\ *n pl* [origin unknown] (1575) : the pendulous lateral parts of a dog's upper lip — see DOG illustration

¹flex \ˈfleks\ *vb* [L *flexus*, pp. of *flectere* to bend] *vt* (ca. 1521) 1 : to bend esp. repeatedly 2 a : to move muscles so as to cause flexion of (a joint) b : to move or tense (a muscle) by contraction ~ *vi* : BEND — **flex one's muscles** : to demonstrate one's strength ⟨an exaggerated need to *flex his* political muscles —J. P. Lash⟩

²flex *n* [short for *flexible cord*] (1905) *chiefly Brit* : an electric cord

³flex *n* (ca. 1934) : an act or instance of flexing

flex·i·ble \ˈflek-sə-bəl\ *adj* (15c) 1 : capable of being flexed : PLIANT 2 : yielding to influence : TRACTABLE 3 : characterized by a ready capability to adapt to new, different, or changing requirements ⟨a ~ foreign policy⟩ ⟨a ~ schedule⟩ *syn* see ELASTIC — **flex·i·bil·i·ty** \ˌflek-sə-ˈbi-lə-tē\ *n* — **flex·i·bly** \ˈflek-sə-blē\ *adv*

flex·ile \ˈflek-səl, -ˌsīl\ *adj* (1633) : FLEXIBLE

flex·ion \ˈflek-shən\ *n* [L *flexion-, flexio*, fr. *flectere*] (1615) 1 : the act of flexing or bending 2 : a part bent : BEND 3 : INFLECTION 3 4 a : a bending movement around a joint in a limb (as the knee or elbow) that decreases the angle between the bones of the limb at the joint — compare EXTENSION 3b b : a forward raising of the arm or leg by a movement at the shoulder or hip joint

flex·og·ra·phy \flek-ˈsä-grə-fē\ *n* [*flexible* + -*o*- + -*graphy*] (1954) : a process of rotary letterpress printing using flexible plates and fast-drying inks — **flexo·graph·ic** \ˌflek-sə-ˈgra-fik\ *adj* — **flexo·graph·i·cal·ly** \-fi-k(ə-)lē\ *adv*

flex·or \ˈflek-sər, -ˌsȯr\ *n* (1615) : a muscle serving to bend a body part (as a limb)

flex·time \ˈflek-ˌstīm\ *or* **flexi·time** \ˈflek-si-ˌtīm\ *n* (1972) : a system that allows employees to choose their own times for starting and finishing work within a broad range of available hours

flex·u·ous \ˈflek-sh(ə-)wəs\ *adj* [L *flexuosus*, fr. *flexus* bend, fr. *flectere*] (1605) 1 : having curves, turns, or windings 2 : lithe or fluid in action or movement

flex·ur·al \ˈflek-sh(ə-)rəl\ *adj* (1879) 1 : of, relating to, or resulting from flexure 2 : characterized by flexure

flex·ure \ˈflek-shər\ *n* (1592) 1 : the quality or state of being flexed : FLEXION 2 : TURN, BEND, FOLD

fley \ˈflā\ *vt* [ME *flayen*, fr. OE *āflīgan*, fr. *ā-*, perfective prefix + *-flīgan* to put to flight] (13c) *Scot* : FRIGHTEN

flib·ber·ti·gib·bet \ˌfli-bər-tē-ˈji-bət\ *n* [ME *flepergebet*] (15c) : a silly flighty person — **flib·ber·ti·gib·bety** \-bə-tē\ *adj*

flic \ˈflek\ *n* [F] (1899) : a French police officer

¹flick \ˈflik\ *n* [imit.] (15c) 1 : a light sharp jerky stroke or movement 2 : a sound produced by a flick 3 : FLICKER 1

²flick *vt* (1816) 1 a : to move or propel with or as if with a flick ⟨~ed her hair back over her shoulder⟩ ⟨~ a switch⟩ b : to activate, deactivate, or change by or as if by flicking a switch ⟨~ on a cigarette lighter⟩ ⟨~ off the radio⟩ 2 a : to strike lightly with a quick sharp motion ⟨~ed the horse with a whip⟩ b : to remove with light blows ⟨~ed an

\ə\ abut \ᵊ\ kitten, F table \ər\ further \a\ ash \ā\ ace \ä\ mop, mar
\au̇\ out \ch\ chin \e\ bet \ē\ easy \g\ go \i\ hit \ī\ ice \j\ job
\ŋ\ sing \ō\ go \ȯ\ law \ȯi\ boy \th\ thin \t͟h\ the \ü\ loot \u̇\ foot
\y\ yet \zh\ vision \å, k̲, ⁿ, œ, œ̄, ᵫ, ᵫ̄, ᵊ\ *see* Guide to Pronunciation

ash off her sleeve⟩ ~ *vi* **1** : to go or pass quickly or abruptly ⟨a bird ~*ed* by⟩ ⟨~*ing* through some papers⟩ **2** : to direct flicks at something
³**flick** *n* [short for ²*flicker*] (1926) : MOVIE
¹**flick·er** \'fli-kər\ *vb* **flick·ered; flick·er·ing** \-k(ə-)riŋ\ [ME *flikeren*, fr. OE *flicorian*] *vi* (bef. 12c) **1** : to move irregularly or unsteadily : FLUTTER **2** : to burn or shine fitfully or with a fluctuating light **3** : to appear briefly ~ *vt* **1** : to cause to flicker **2** : to produce by flickering — **flick·er·ing·ly** \-k(ə-)riŋ-lē\ *adv*
²**flicker** *n* (1849) **1 a** : an act of flickering **b** : a sudden brief movement **c** : a momentary quickening ⟨a ~ of anger⟩ **d** : a slight indication : HINT ⟨a ~ of recognition⟩ **2** : a wavering light **3** : MOVIE — often used in pl.
³**flicker** *n* [prob. imit. of its call] (1809) : a large barred and spotted No. American woodpecker (*Colaptes auratus*) with a brown back that commonly forages on the ground for ants — compare RED-SHAFTED FLICKER, YELLOW-SHAFTED FLICKER
flick–knife \'flik-ˌnīf\ *n* (1957) *Brit* : SWITCHBLADE
flied *past and past part of* ³FLY
fli·er \'flī(-ə)r\ *n* (15c) **1** : one that flies; *specif* : AIRMAN **2** : a reckless or speculative venture — usu. used in the phrase *take a flier* **3** *usu* **fly·er** : an advertising circular
¹**flight** \'flīt\ *n, often attrib* [ME, fr. OE *flyht*; akin to MD *vlucht* flight, OE *flēogan* to fly] (bef. 12c) **1 a** : an act or instance of passing through the air by the use of wings ⟨the ~ of a bee⟩ **b** : the ability to fly ⟨~ is natural to birds⟩ **2 a** : a passing through the air or through space outside the earth's atmosphere ⟨~ of an arrow⟩ ⟨~ of a rocket to the moon⟩ **b** : the distance covered in such a flight **c** : swift movement **3 a** : a trip made by or in an airplane or spacecraft **b** : a scheduled airplane trip **4** : a group of similar beings or objects flying through the air together **5** : a brilliant, imaginative, or unrestrained exercise or display ⟨a ~ of fancy⟩ **6 a** : a continuous series of stairs from one landing or floor to another **b** : a series (as of terraces or conveyors) resembling a flight of stairs **7** : a unit of the U.S. Air Force below a squadron — **flight·less** \-ləs\ *adj*
²**flight** *vi* (1873) : to rise, settle, or fly in a flock ⟨geese ~*ing* on the marsh⟩ ~ *vt* : ¹FLUSH
³**flight** *n* [ME *fluht, fliht*; akin to OHG *fluht* flight, OE *flēon* to flee] (13c) : an act or instance of running away
flight attendant *n* (1947) : a person who attends passengers on an airplane
flight bag *n* [¹*flight*] (1943) **1** : a lightweight traveling bag with zippered outside pockets **2** : a small canvas satchel
flight deck *n* (1924) **1** : the uppermost complete deck of an aircraft carrier **2** : the forward compartment in some airplanes
flight engineer *n* (1938) : a flight crewman responsible for mechanical operation
flight feather *n* (1735) : one of the quills of a bird's wing or tail that support it in flight — compare CONTOUR FEATHER
flight lieutenant *n* (1914) : a commissioned officer in the British air force who ranks with a captain in the army
flight line *n* (1943) : a parking and servicing area for airplanes
flight path *n* (1911) : the path in the air or space made or followed by something (as a particle, an airplane, or a spacecraft) in flight
flight pay *n* (1928) : an additional allowance paid to military personnel who take part in regular authorized aircraft flights
flight plan *n* (ca. 1936) : a usu. written statement (as by a pilot) of the details of an intended flight (as of an airplane or spacecraft) usu. filed with an authority
flight recorder *n* (1939) : a crashworthy instrument for recording flight data (as airspeed and altitude)
flight suit *n* (1944) : a usu. one-piece garment esp. of fire-resistant fabric worn esp. by military aircrews
flight surgeon *n* (1925) : a military medical officer trained in aerospace medicine
flight–test \'flīt-ˌtest\ *vt* (1930) : to test (as an airplane or spacecraft) in flight
flighty \'flī-tē\ *adj* **flight·i·er; -est** (1552) **1** : SWIFT **2** : lacking stability or steadiness: **a** : easily upset : VOLATILE ⟨a ~ temper⟩ **b** : easily excited : SKITTISH ⟨a ~ horse⟩ **c** : CAPRICIOUS, SILLY — **flight·i·ly** \'flī-t³l-ē\ *adv* — **flight·i·ness** \'flī-tē-nəs\ *n*
¹**flim·flam** \'flim-ˌflam\ *n* [prob. of Scand origin; akin to ON *flim* mockery] (ca. 1538) **1** : DECEPTION, FRAUD **2** : deceptive nonsense
²**flimflam** *vt* **flim·flammed; flim·flam·ming** (1660) : to subject to a flimflam — **flim·flam·mer** *n* — **flim·flam·mery** \-ˌfla-mə-rē\ *n*
¹**flim·sy** \'flim-zē\ *adj* **flim·si·er; -est** [perh. alter. of ¹*film* + *-sy* (as in *tricksy*)] (1702) **1** : lacking in physical strength or substance ⟨~ silks⟩ **b** : of inferior materials and workmanship **2** : having little worth or plausibility — **flim·si·ly** \-zə-lē\ *adv* — **flim·si·ness** \-zē-nəs\ *n*
²**flimsy** *n, pl* **flim·sies** (1857) *chiefly Brit* : a lightweight paper used esp. for multiple copies; *also* : a document printed on flimsy
flinch \'flinch\ *vi* [MF *flenchir* to bend, of Gmc origin; akin to MHG *lenken* to bend, OHG *hlanca* flank — more at LANK] (1579) : to withdraw or shrink from or as if from pain : WINCE; *also* : to tense the muscles involuntarily in anticipation of discomfort **syn** see RECOIL — **flinch** *n* — **flinch·er** *n*
flin·ders \'flin-dərz\ *n pl* [ME *flendris*] (15c) : SPLINTERS, FRAGMENTS
¹**fling** \'fliŋ\ *vb* **flung** \'fləŋ\; **fling·ing** \'fliŋ-iŋ\ [ME, perh. of Scand origin; akin to ON *flengja* to whip] *vi* (14c) **1** : to move in a brusque or headlong manner ⟨*flung* out of the room in a rage⟩ **2** *of an animal* : to kick or plunge vigorously **3** *Scot* : CAPER ~ *vt* **1 a** : to throw forcefully, impetuously, or casually ⟨*flung* herself down on the sofa⟩ ⟨clothes were *flung* on the floor⟩ **b** : to cast as if by throwing ⟨*flung* off all restraint⟩ **2** : to place or send suddenly and unceremoniously ⟨was arrested and *flung* into prison⟩ **3** : to give unrestrainedly ⟨*flung* himself into music⟩ **syn** see THROW — **fling·er** \'fliŋ-ər\ *n*
²**fling** *n* (1589) **1** : an act or instance of flinging **2 a** : a casual try or involvement **b** : a casual or brief love affair **3** : a period devoted to self-indulgence
flint \'flint\ *n* [ME, fr. OE; akin to OHG *flins* pebble, hard stone] (bef. 12c) **1** : a massive hard quartz that produces a spark when struck by steel **2** : an implement of flint used in prehistoric cultures **3 a** : a piece of flint **b** : a material used for producing a spark; *esp* : an alloy

(as of iron and cerium) used in lighters **4** : something resembling flint in hardness — **flint·like** \-ˌlīk\ *adj*
flint corn *n* (1705) : an Indian corn (*Zea mays indurata*) having hard horny usu. rounded kernels with the soft endosperm enclosed by a hard outer layer
flint glass *n* (1683) : heavy brilliant glass that contains lead oxide, has a relatively high index of refraction, and is used in lenses and prisms
flint·lock \'flint-ˌläk\ *n* (1683) **1** : a lock for a gun or pistol having a flint in the hammer for striking a spark to ignite the charge **2** : a firearm fitted with a flintlock
flinty \'flin-tē\ *adj* **flint·i·er; -est** (1536) **1** : resembling flint; *esp* : STERN, UNYIELDING **2** : composed of or covered with flint — **flint·i·ly** \'flin-t³l-ē\ *adv* — **flint·i·ness** \'flin-tē-nəs\ *n*
¹**flip** \'flip\ *vb* **flipped; flip·ping** [prob. imit.] *vt* (1616) **1** : to toss so as to cause to turn over in the air ⟨~ a coin⟩; *also* : TOSS ⟨~ me the ball⟩ ⟨~ one end of the scarf over your shoulder⟩ **2 a** : to cause to turn and esp. to turn over ⟨*flipping* the car⟩ ⟨*flipping* the pages of⟩ **b** : to move with a small quick motion ⟨~ a switch⟩ ~ *vi* **1** : to make a twitching or flicking movement ⟨the fish *flipped* and flopped on the deck⟩; *also* : to change from one position to another and esp. turn over ⟨the car *flipped*⟩ **2** : LEAF 2 ⟨*flipped* through the pages⟩ **3** *slang* **a** : to lose one's mind or composure — often used with *out* **b** : to become very enthusiastic
²**flip** *n* (1695) **1** : a mixed drink usu. consisting of a sweetened spiced liquor with beaten eggs **2** : an act or instance of flipping **3** : the motion used in flipping **4** : a somersault esp. in the air
³**flip** *adj* (ca. 1847): FLIPPANT, IMPERTINENT
flip–flop \'flip-ˌfläp\ *n* (1600) **1** : the sound or motion of something flapping loosely **2 a** : a backward handspring **b** : a sudden reversal (as of direction or point of view) **3** : a usu. electronic device or a circuit (as in a computer) capable of assuming either of two stable states **4** : a rubber sandal loosely fastened to the foot by a thong — **flip–flop** *vi*
flip·pan·cy \'fli-pən(t)-sē\ *n, pl* **-cies** (1746) : unbecoming levity or pertness esp. in respect to grave or sacred matters
flip·pant \'fli-pənt\ *adj* [prob. fr. ¹*flip*] (1605) **1** *archaic* : GLIB, TALKATIVE **2** : lacking proper respect or seriousness — **flip·pant·ly** *adv*
flip·per \'fli-pər\ *n* (1822) **1 a** : a broad flat limb (as of a seal or cetacean) adapted for swimming **b** : a flat rubber shoe with the front expanded into a paddle used in skin diving **2** : one that flips
flip·py \'fli-pē\ *adj* (1967) : loose and flaring at the bottom ⟨a ~ skirt⟩
flip side *n* (1949) **1** : the reverse and usu. less popular side of a phonograph record **2** : a reverse or opposite side, aspect, or result ⟨the *flip side* of deficient saving . . . is overconsumption —R. S. Gay⟩
¹**flirt** \'flərt\ *vb* [origin unknown] *vt* (1583) **1** : FLICK **2** : to move in a jerky manner ~ *vi* **1** : to move erratically : FLIT **2 a** : to behave amorously without serious intent **b** : to show superficial or casual interest or liking ⟨~*ed* with the idea⟩; *also* : EXPERIMENT ⟨a novelist ~*ing* with poetry⟩ **3** : to come close to — used with *with* ⟨the temperature ~*ed* with 100°⟩ **syn** see TRIFLE — **flir·ta·tion** \ˌflər-'tā-shən\ *n* — **flirt·er** *n* — **flirty** \'flər-tē\ *adj*
²**flirt** *n* (ca. 1590) **1** : an act or instance of flirting **2** : a person who flirts
flir·ta·tious \ˌflər-'tā-shəs\ *adj* (1834) : inclined to flirt : COQUETTISH — **flir·ta·tious·ly** *adv* — **flir·ta·tious·ness** *n*
flit \'flit\ *vi* **flit·ted; flit·ting** [ME *flitten*, of Scand origin; akin to ON *flytjask* to move, OE *flēotan* to float] (13c) **1** : to pass quickly or abruptly from one place or condition to another **2** *archaic* : ALTER, SHIFT **3** : to move in an erratic fluttering manner — **flit** *n*
flitch \'flich\ *n* [ME *flicche*, fr. OE *flicce*; akin to OHG *fleisk* flesh — more at FLESH] (bef. 12c) **1** : a side of cured meat; *esp* : a side of bacon **2 a** : a longitudinal section of a log **b** : a bundle of sheets of veneer laid together in sequence
¹**flit·ter** \'fli-tər\ *vi* [freq. of *flit*] (1534) : FLUTTER, FLICKER
²**flitter** *n* (1554) : one that flits
fliv·ver \'fli-vər\ *n* [origin unknown] (1910) : a small cheap usu. old automobile
¹**float** \'flōt\ *n* [ME *flote* boat, float, fr. OE *flota* ship; akin to OHG *flōz* raft, stream, OE *flēotan* to float — more at FLEET] (bef. 12c) **1** : an act or instance of floating **2** : something that floats in or on the surface of a fluid: as **a** : a device (as a cork) buoying up the baited end of a fishing line **b** : a floating platform anchored near a shoreline for use by swimmers or boats **c** : a hollow ball that floats at the end of a lever in a cistern, tank, or boiler and regulates the liquid level **d** : a sac containing air or gas and buoying up the body of a plant or animal — compare PNEUMATOPHORE 1 **e** : a watertight structure giving an airplane buoyancy on water **2 a** : a tool or apparatus for smoothing a surface (as of wet concrete) **b** : a government grant of a fixed amount of land not yet located by survey out of a larger specific tract **5 a** : a vehicle with a platform used to carry an exhibit in a parade **b** : the vehicle and exhibit together **6 a** : an amount of money represented by checks outstanding and in process of collection **b** : the time between a transaction (as the writing of a check or a purchase on credit) and the actual withdrawal of funds to cover it **c** : the volume of a company's shares available for active trading in the auction market **7** : a soft drink with ice cream floating in it — **floaty** \'flō-tē\ *adj*
²**float** *vi* (bef. 12c) **1** : to rest on the surface of or be suspended in a fluid **2 a** : to drift on or through or as if on or through a fluid ⟨yellow leaves ~*ed* down⟩ **b** : WANDER **3** *of a currency* : to find a level in the international exchange market in response to the law of supply and demand and without any restrictive effect of artificial support or control ~ *vt* **1 a** : to cause to float in or on the surface of a fluid **b** : to cause to float as if in a fluid **2** : FLOOD ⟨~ a cranberry bog⟩ **3** : to smooth (as plaster or cement) with a float **4 a** : to put forth (as a proposal) for acceptance **b** : to place (an issue of securities) on the market **c** : to obtain money for the establishment or development of (an enterprise) by issuing and selling securities **d** : NEGOTIATE ⟨~ a loan⟩
floa·ta·tion *var of* FLOTATION
float·er \'flō-tər\ *n* (1717) **1 a** : one that floats **b** : a person who floats something **2** : a person who votes illegally in various polling places **3 a** : a person without a permanent residence or regular employment **b** : a worker who moves from job to job; *esp* : one without

fixed duties   **4** : a policy insuring specific items of personal property (as jewelry or art)

float glass *n* (1959) : flat glass produced by solidifying molten glass on the surface of a bath of molten tin

float·ing *adj* (1600)   **1** : buoyed on or in a fluid   **2** : located out of the normal position ⟨a ~ kidney⟩   **3 a** : continually drifting or changing position ⟨the ~ population⟩   **b** : not presently committed or invested ⟨~ capital⟩   **c** : short-term and usu. not funded ⟨~ debt⟩   **d** : having no fixed value or rate ⟨~ currencies⟩ ⟨~ interest rates⟩   **4** : connected or constructed so as to operate and adjust smoothly ⟨a ~ axle⟩

floating dock *n* (1866) : a dock that floats on the water and can be partly submerged to permit entry of a ship and raised to keep the ship high and dry — called also *floating drydock*

floating island *n* (1771) : a dessert consisting of custard with floating masses of beaten egg whites

floating–point *adj* (1948) : expressed in, using, or being a mathematical notation in which a number is represented (as in a computer display) by an integer or a decimal fraction multiplied by a power of the number base indicated by an exponent (as in 4.52E2 for 452) — compare FIXED-POINT

floating rib *n* (1831) : a rib (as one of either of the last two pairs in humans) that has no attachment to the sternum — compare FALSE RIB

float·plane \'flōt-,plān\ *n* (1922) : a seaplane supported on the water by one or more floats

floc \'fläk\ *n* [short for *floccule*] (1921) : a flocculent mass formed by the aggregation of a number of fine suspended particles

floc·cu·late \'flä-kyə-,lāt\ *vb* **-lat·ed; -lat·ing** *vt* (1877) : to cause to aggregate into a flocculent mass ⟨~ clay⟩   ~ *vi* : to become flocculent — **floc·cu·lant** \-lənt\ *n* — **floc·cu·la·tion** \,flä-kyə-'lā-shən\ *n* — **floc·cu·la·tor** \'flä-kyə-,lā-tər\ *n*

floc·cule \'flä-(,)kyü(ə)l\ *n* [LL *flocculus*] (ca. 1846) : FLOC

floc·cu·lent \-lənt\ *adj* [L *floccus* + E *-ulent*] (1800)   **1** : resembling wool esp. in loose fluffy organization : made up of flocs or floccules ⟨a ~ precipitate⟩

floc·cu·lus \-ləs\ *n, pl* **-li** \-,lī, -,lē\ [LL, dim. of L *floccus* tuft of wool] (1799)   **1** : a small loosely aggregated mass   **2** : a bright or dark patch on the sun

¹flock \'fläk\ *n* [ME, fr. OE *flocc* crowd, band; akin to ON *flokkr* crowd, band] (13c)   **1** : a group of birds or mammals assembled or herded together   **2** : a group under the guidance of a leader; *esp* : a church congregation   **3** : a large number ⟨a ~ of tourists⟩

²flock *vi* (14c) : to gather or move in a flock ⟨they ~ed to the beach⟩

³flock *n* [ME *flok*, fr. OF *floc*, fr. L *floccus*] (13c)   **1** : a tuft of wool or cotton fiber   **2** : woolen or cotton refuse used for stuffing furniture and mattresses   **3** : very short or pulverized fiber used esp. to form a velvety pattern on cloth or paper or a protective covering on metal   **4** : FLOC

⁴flock *vt* (1530)   **1** : to fill with flock   **2** : to decorate with flock

flock·ing \'flä-kiŋ\ *n* (ca. 1874) : a design in flock

floe \'flō\ *n* [prob. fr. Norw *flo* flat layer] (1817)   **1** : floating ice formed in a large sheet on the surface of a body of water   **2** : ICE FLOE

flog \'fläg\ *vb* **flogged; flog·ging** [perh. modif. of L *flagellare* to whip — more at FLAGELLATE] *vt* (ca. 1676)   **1 a** : to beat with or as if with a rod or whip   **b** : to criticize harshly   **2** : to force or urge into action : DRIVE   **3 a** *chiefly Brit* : to sell ⟨as stolen goods⟩ illegally ⟨*flogged* their employers' petrol to ordinary motorists —*Economist*⟩   **b** : SELL 7 ⟨traveled by horse, *flogging* encyclopedias —Robert Darnton⟩   **c** : to promote aggressively : PLUG ⟨flying around the world *flogging* your movies —Peter Bogdanovich⟩   **4** *Brit* : STEAL 1   ~ *vi*   **1** : FLAP, FLUTTER ⟨sails *flogging*⟩   **2** *Brit* : to move along with difficulty : SLOG — **flog·ger** *n*

flo·ka·ti \flō-'kä-tē\ *n* [NGk *phlokatē*] (1967) : a hand-woven Greek woolen rug with a thick shaggy pile

¹flood \'fləd\ *n* [ME, fr. OE *flōd*; akin to OHG *fluot* flood, OE *flōwan* to flow] (bef. 12c)   **1 a** : a rising and overflowing of a body of water esp. onto normally dry land; *also* : a condition of overflowing ⟨rivers in ~⟩   **b** *cap* : a flood described in the Bible as covering the earth in the time of Noah   **2** : the flowing in of the tide   **3** : an overwhelming quantity or volume; *also* : a state of abundant flow or volume ⟨a debate in full ~⟩   **4** : FLOODLIGHT

²flood *vt* (1663)   **1** : to cover with a flood : INUNDATE   **2 a** : to fill abundantly or excessively ⟨~ the market⟩   **b** : to supply to (the carburetor of an internal combustion engine) an excess of fuel so that engine operation is hampered   ~ *vi*   **1** : to pour forth, go, or come in a flood   **2** : to become filled with a flood — **flood·er** *n*

flood·gate \'fləd-,gāt\ *n* [ME *flodgate*] (13c)   **1** : a gate for shutting out, admitting, or releasing a body of water : SLUICE   **2** : something serving to restrain an outburst ⟨opened the ~s⟩

¹flood·light \-,līt\ *vt* **-lit** \-,lit\ **or -light·ed; -light·ing** (1923) : to illuminate by means of one or more floodlights

²floodlight *n* (1924)   **1 a** : artificial illumination in a broad beam   **b** : a source of such illumination   **2** : a lighting unit for projecting a beam of light

flood·plain \'fləd-,plān\ *n* (1873)   **1** : level land that may be submerged by floodwaters   **2** : a plain built up by stream deposition

flood tide *n* (1719)   **1** : a rising tide   **2 a** : an overwhelming quantity   **b** : a high point : PEAK

flood·wa·ter \-,wo̅-tər, -,wä-\ *n* (1791) : the water of a flood

flood·way \-,wā\ *n* (1928) : a channel for diverting floodwaters

floo·ey \'flü-ē\ *adj* [origin unknown] (1920) : AWRY, ASKEW ⟨go ~⟩

¹floor \'flōr, 'flor\ *n, often attrib* [ME *flor*, fr. OE *flōr*; akin to OHG *fluor* meadow, L *planus* level, and perh. to Gk *planasthai* to wander] (bef. 12c)   **1** : the level base of a room   **2 a** : the lower inside surface of a hollow structure (as a cave or bodily part)   **b** : a ground surface ⟨the ocean ~⟩   **3 a** : a structure dividing a building into stories; *also* : STORY   **b** : the occupants of such a floor   **4** : the surface of a structure on which one travels ⟨the ~ of a bridge⟩   **5 a** : a main level space (as in a stock exchange or legislative chamber) distinguished from a platform or gallery   **b** : the members of an assembly ⟨took questions from the ~⟩   **c** : the right to address an assembly ⟨the senator from Utah has the ~⟩   **6** : a lower limit : BASE — **floored** *adj*

²floor *vt* (15c)   **1** : to cover with a floor or flooring   **2 a** : to knock or bring down   **b** : FLABBERGAST, DUMBFOUND   **3** : to press (the accelera-

tor of a vehicle) to the floorboard; *also* : to accelerate rapidly ⟨~ed the van⟩ — **floor·er** *n*

floor·board \'flōr-,bōrd, 'flor-,bord\ *n* (1881)   **1** : a board in a floor   **2** : the floor of an automobile

floor·cloth \-,kloth\ *n, pl* **-cloths** \-,klothz, -,kloths\ (1746) : a usu. decorated heavy cloth (as of canvas) used for a floor covering

floor exercise *n* (1961) : an event in gymnastics competition consisting of various ballet and tumbling movements (as jumps, somersaults, and handstands) performed without apparatus

floor·ing \'flōr-iŋ, 'flor-\ *n* (1624)   **1** : FLOOR, BASE   **2** : material for floors

floor lamp *n* (1892) : a tall lamp that stands on the floor

floor leader *n* (1899) : a member of a legislative body chosen by a party to have charge of its organization and strategy on the floor

floor–length *adj* (1939) : reaching to the floor ⟨a ~ gown⟩

floor manager *n* (1887) : a person who directs something from the floor (as of a nominating convention)

floor show *n* (1927) : a series of acts presented in a nightclub

floor–through \'flōr-,thrü, 'flor-\ *n* (1967) : an apartment that occupies an entire floor of a building

floor·walk·er \'flōr-,wo̅-kər, 'flor-\ *n* (1876) : a person employed in a retail store to oversee the salespeople and aid customers

floo·zy *or* **floo·zie** \'flü-zē\ *n, pl* **floozies** [origin unknown] (1911) : a usu. young woman of loose morals

¹flop \'fläp\ *vb* **flopped; flop·ping** [alter. of ²*flap*] *vi* (1602)   **1** : to swing or move loosely : FLAP   **2** : to throw or move oneself in a heavy, clumsy, or relaxed manner ⟨*flopped* into the chair⟩   **3** : to change or turn suddenly   **4** : to go to bed ⟨a place to ~ at night⟩   **5** : to fail completely ⟨the play *flopped*⟩   ~ *vt* : to move or drop heavily or noisily : cause to flop ⟨*flopped* the bundles down⟩ ⟨~ the rag over⟩ — **flop·per** *n*

²flop *adv* (1728) : RIGHT, SQUARELY ⟨fell ~ on my face⟩

³flop *n* (1823)   **1** : an act or sound of flopping   **2** : a complete failure   **3** *slang* : a place to sleep; *esp* : FLOPHOUSE   **4** : DUNG ⟨cow ~⟩; *also* : a piece of dung

flop·house \'fläp-,haus\ *n* (1916) : a cheap rooming house or hotel

¹flop·py \'flä-pē\ *adj* **flop·pi·er; -est** (1858) : tending to flop; *esp* : being both soft and flexible — **flop·pi·ly** \'flä-pə-lē\ *adv* — **flop·pi·ness** \'flä-pē-nəs\ *n*

²floppy *n, pl* **-pies** (1974) : FLOPPY DISK

floppy disk *n* (1972) : a small flexible plastic disk coated with magnetic material on which data for a computer can be stored

flo·ra \'flōr-ə, 'flor-\ *n, pl* **floras** *also* **flo·rae** \'flōr-,ē, 'flor-, -,ī\ [NL, fr. L *Flora*, Roman goddess of flowers, fr. L *flor-, flos*] (1777)   **1** : a treatise on or list of the plants of an area or period   **2** : plant or bacterial life; *esp* : such life characteristic of a region, period, or special environment ⟨fossil ~⟩ ⟨intestinal ~⟩ — compare FAUNA

¹flo·ral \'flōr-əl, 'flor-\ *adj* [L *flor-, flos* flower — more at BLOW] (1753) : of or relating to flowers or a flora

²floral *n* (1897) : a design, pattern, or picture in which flowers predominate

floral envelope *n* (ca. 1829) : PERIANTH

Flor·ence flask \'flōr-ən(t)s-, 'flär-\ *n* [*Florence*, Italy; fr. the use of flasks of this shape for certain Italian wines] (1744) : a round usu. flat-bottomed laboratory vessel with a long neck

Flor·en·tine \'flōr-ən-,tēn, 'flär-, -tin\ *adj* [ML *Florentinus*] (1597)   **1 a** : of or relating to Florence, Italy   **b** : MACHIAVELLIAN ⟨~ politics⟩   **2** : served or dressed with spinach ⟨poached eggs ~⟩   **3** : having a matte brushed finish ⟨~ gold⟩

flo·res·cence \flō-'re-s⁰n(t)s, flə-\ *n* [NL *florescentia*, fr. L *florescent-, florescens*, prp. of *florescere*, incho. of *florēre* to blossom, flourish — more at FLOURISH] (1793) : a state or period of flourishing — **flo·res·cent** \-s⁰nt\ *adj*

flo·ret \'flōr-ət, 'flor-\ *n* [ME *flourette*, fr. MF *flouret*, dim. of *flour* flower] (1671)   **1** : a small flower; *esp* : one of the small flowers forming the head of a composite plant   **2** : a cluster of flower buds separated from a head esp. when used as food ⟨cauliflower ~s⟩

flori- *comb form* [L, fr. *flor-, flos*] : flower or flowers ⟨*floriculture*⟩

flo·ri·at·ed \'flōr-ē-,ā-təd, 'flor-\ *adj* (1845) : having floral ornaments or a floral form — **flo·ri·a·tion** \,flōr-ē-'ā-shən, ,flor-\ *n*

flo·ri·bun·da \,flōr-ə-'bən-də, ,flor-\ *n* [NL, fem. of *floribundus* flowering freely] (1898) : any of various bush roses with large flowers in open clusters that derive from crosses of polyantha and tea roses

flo·ri·cul·ture \'flōr-ə-,kəl-chər, 'flor-\ *n* (1822) : the cultivation and management of ornamental and esp. flowering plants — **flo·ri·cul·tur·al** \,flōr-ə-'kəlch-rəl, ,flor-\ *adj* — **flo·ri·cul·tur·ist** \-'kəlch-ə-, 'flor-\ *adj*

flor·id \'flōr-əd, 'flär-\ *adj* [L *floridus* blooming, flowery, fr. *florēre*] (ca. 1656)   **1** *a obs* : covered with flowers   **b** : very flowery in style : ORNATE ⟨~ prose⟩ ⟨~ declamations⟩; *also* : having a florid style ⟨a ~ writer⟩   **c** : elaborately decorated ⟨~ interior⟩   **2 a** : tinged with red : RUDDY ⟨a ~ complexion⟩   **b** : marked by emotional or sexual fervor ⟨a ~ secret life⟩ ⟨a ~ sensibility⟩   **3** *archaic* : HEALTHY   **4** : fully developed : manifesting a complete and typical clinical syndrome ⟨the ~ stage of a disease⟩ — **flo·rid·i·ty** \flə-'ri-də-tē, flō-\ *n* — **flor·id·ly** \'flōr-əd-lē, 'flär-\ *adv* — **flor·id·ness** \-nəs\ *n*

flo·rif·er·ous \flō-'ri-f(ə-)rəs\ *adj* [L *florifer*, fr. *flori-* + *-fer*] (1678) : bearing flowers; *esp* : blooming freely — **flo·rif·er·ous·ness** *n*

flo·ri·gen \'flōr-ə-jən, 'flor-\ *n* [ISV] (1936) : a hormone or hormonal agent that promotes flowering — **flo·ri·gen·ic** \,flōr-ə-'je-nik, ,flor-\ *adj*

flo·ri·le·gium \,flōr-ə-'lē-j(ē-)əm, ,flor-\ *n, pl* **-gia** \-j(ē-)ə\ [NL, fr. L *florilegus* culling flowers, fr. *flori-* + *legere* to gather — more at LEGEND] (1647) : a volume of writings : ANTHOLOGY

flo·rin \'flōr-ən, 'flor-\ *n* [ME, fr. MF, fr. OIt *fiorino*, fr. *fiore* flower, fr. L *flor-, flos*; fr. the lily on the coins] (14c)   **1 a** : an old gold coin first struck at Florence in 1252   **b** : any of various European gold coins patterned after the Florentine florin   **2 a** : a British silver coin

---

\ə\ abut \ᵊ\ kitten, F table \ər\ further \a\ ash \ā\ ace \ä\ mop, mar
\aù\ out \ch\ chin \e\ bet \ē\ easy \g\ go \i\ hit \ī\ ice \j\ job
\ŋ\ sing \ō\ go \ò\ law \òi\ boy \th\ thin \th\ the \ü\ loot \ù\ foot
\y\ yet \zh\ vision \à, k̲, ⁿ, œ, œ̄, ᵫ, ᵫ̄, ᵞ\ see Guide to Pronunciation

worth two shillings **b** : any of several similar coins issued in Commonwealth countries **3** : GULDEN **4** : FORINT

flo·rist \'flōr-ist, 'flȯr-, 'flär-\ *n* (1623) : one who sells or grows for sale flowers and ornamental plants — **flo·rist·ry** \-ə-strē\ *n*

flo·ris·tic \flō-'ris-tik\ *adj* (1898) : of or relating to flowers, a flora, or the phytogeographical study of plants and plant groups — **flo·ris·ti·cal·ly** \-ti-k(ə-)lē\ *adv*

flo·ru·it \'flōr-(y)ə-wət, 'flär-\ *n* [L, he flourished, fr. *florēre* to flourish] (1843) : a period of flourishing (as of a person or movement)

¹floss \'fläs, 'flȯs\ *n* [prob. modif. of F *floche* soft, weak (of silk fiber), fr. Gascon, fr. L *fluxus*, lit., loose, flowing, pp. of *fluere* to flow — more at FLUID] (1759) **1 a** : soft thread of silk or mercerized cotton for embroidery **b** : DENTAL FLOSS **2** : fluffy fibrous material

²floss *vt* (1974) : to use dental floss on ∼ *vi* : to use dental floss

flossy \'fläs-ē, 'flȯs-\ *adj* **floss·i·er; -est** (1839) **1** : of, relating to, or having the characteristics of floss **2** : stylish or glamorous esp. at first impression ⟨∼ new hotels⟩ — **floss·i·ly** \'fläs-ə-lē\ *adv*

flo·ta \'flō-tə\ *n* [Sp] (1527) : a fleet of Spanish ships

flo·ta·tion \flō-'tā-shən\ *n* [²*float*] (1806) **1** : the act, process, or state of floating **2** : an act or instance of financing (as an issue of stock) **3** : the separation of the particles of a mass of pulverized ore according to their relative capacity for floating on a given liquid; *also* : any of various similar processes involving the relative capacity of materials for floating **4** : the ability (as of a tire or snowshoes) to stay on the surface of soft ground or snow

flo·til·la \flō-'til-ə\ *n* [Sp, dim. of *flota* fleet, fr. OF *flote*, fr. ON *floti*; akin to OE *flota* ship, fleet — more at FLOAT] (1711) **1** : a fleet of ships or boats; *esp* : a navy organizational unit consisting of two or more squadrons of small warships **2** : an indefinite large number ⟨a ∼ of changes⟩

flot·sam \'flät-səm\ *n* [AF *floteson*, fr. OF *floter* to float, of Gmc origin; akin to OE *flotian* to float, *flota* ship] (ca. 1607) **1** : floating wreckage of a ship or its cargo; *broadly* : floating debris **2 a** : a floating population (as of emigrants or castaways) **b** : an accumulation of miscellaneous or unimportant stuff

¹flounce \'flaůn(t)s\ *vi* **flounced; flounc·ing** [perh. of Scand origin; akin to Norw *flunsa* to hurry] (1542) **1 a** : to move with exaggerated jerky or bouncy motions ⟨*flounced* about the room, jerking her shoulders, gesticulating —Agatha Christie⟩; *also* : to move so as to draw attention to oneself ⟨*flounced* into the lobby⟩ **b** : to go with sudden determination ⟨*flounced* out of the room in a huff⟩ **2** : FLOUNDER, STRUGGLE

²flounce *n* (1583) : an act or instance of flouncing — **flouncy** \'flaůn(t)-sē\ *adj*

³flounce *vt* **flounced; flounc·ing** [alter. of earlier *frounce*, fr. ME *frouncen* to curl] (1711) : to trim with flounces

⁴flounce *n* (1713) : a strip of fabric attached by one edge; *also* : a wide ruffle — **flouncy** \'flaůn(t)-sē\ *adj*

flounc·ing \'flaůn(t)-siŋ\ *n* (1865) : material used for flounces

¹floun·der \'flaůn-dər\ *n, pl* **flounder** *or* **flounders** [ME, fr. AF *floundre*, of Scand origin; akin to ON *flythra* flounder] (15c) : FLATFISH; *esp* : a fish of either of two families (Pleuronectidae and Bothidae) that include important marine food fishes

²flounder *vi* **floun·dered; floun·der·ing** \-d(ə-)riŋ\ [prob. alter. of *founder*] (1592) **1** : to struggle to move or obtain footing : thrash about wildly **2** : to proceed or act clumsily or ineffectually

¹flour \'flaů(-ə)r\ *n* [ME — more at FLOWER] (13c) **1** : finely ground meal of wheat usu. largely freed from bran; *also* : a similar meal of another material (as a cereal grain, an edible seed, or dried processed fish) **2** : a fine soft powder — **flour·less** *adj* — **floury** \-ē\ *adj*

²flour *vt* (ca. 1657) : to coat with or as if with flour ∼ *vi* : to break up into particles

¹flour·ish \'flər-ish, 'flə-rish\ *vb* [ME *florisshen*, fr. MF *floriss-*, stem of *florir*, fr. (assumed) VL *florire*, alter. of L *florēre* fr. *flor-*, *flos* flower] (14c) **1** : to grow luxuriantly : THRIVE **2 a** : to achieve success : PROSPER **b** : to be in a state of activity or production ⟨∼ed around 1850⟩ **c** : to reach a height of development or influence **3** : to make bold and sweeping gestures ∼ *vt* : to wield with dramatic gestures : BRANDISH **syn** see SWING — **flour·ish·er** *n* — **flour·ish·ing·ly** \-i-shiŋ-lē\ *adv*

²flourish *n* (1597) **1 a** : a period of thriving **b** : a luxuriant growth or profusion ⟨a ∼ of white hair⟩ ⟨a springtime ∼ of color⟩ **2 a** : a florid bit of speech or writing ⟨rhetorical ∼es⟩ **b** : an ornamental stroke in writing or printing ⟨: a decorative or finishing detail ⟨a house with clever little ∼es⟩ **3** : FANFARE **4** : an act or instance of brandishing or waving **5** : showiness in the doing of something ⟨opened the door with a ∼⟩ **6** : a sudden burst (as of activity) ⟨the week ends with a ∼ of tests⟩

¹flout \'flaůt\ *vb* [prob. fr. ME *flouten* to play the flute, fr. *floute* flute] *vt* (1551) : to treat with contemptuous disregard : SCORN ⟨∼ing the rules⟩ ∼ *vi* : to indulge in scornful behavior **syn** see SCOFF **usage** see FLAUNT — **flout·er** *n*

²flout *n* (ca. 1570) : JEER

¹flow \'flō\ *vb* [ME, fr. OE *flōwan*; akin to OHG *flouwen* to rinse, wash, L *pluere* to rain, Gk *plein* to sail, float] *vi* (bef. 12c) **1 a** (1): to issue or move in a stream (2) : CIRCULATE **b** : to move with a continual change of place among the constituent particles ⟨molasses ∼s slowly⟩ **2** : RISE ⟨the tide ebbs and ∼s⟩ **3** : ABOUND **4 a** : to proceed smoothly and readily ⟨conversation ∼ed easily⟩ **b** : to have a smooth continuity **5** : to hang loose and billowing **6** : to derive from a source : COME ⟨the wealth that ∼s from trade⟩ **7** : to deform under stress without cracking or rupturing — used esp. of minerals and rocks **8** : MENSTRUATE ∼ *vt* **1** : to cause to flow **2** : to discharge in a flow **syn** see SPRING — **flow·ing·ly** \-iŋ-lē\ *adv*

²flow *n* (15c) **1** : an act of flowing **2** : FLOOD 1a, 2 **3 a** : a smooth uninterrupted movement or progress ⟨a ∼ of information⟩ **b** : STREAM; *also* : a mass of material which has flowed when molten ⟨an old lava ∼⟩ **c** : the direction of movement or development ⟨go with the ∼⟩ **4** : the quantity that flows in a certain time **5** : MENSTRUATION **6 a** : the motion characteristic of fluids **b** : a continuous transfer of energy

flow·age \'flō-ij\ *n* (1830) **1 a** : an overflowing onto adjacent land **b** : a body of water formed by overflowing or damming **c** : floodwa-

ter esp. of a stream **2** : gradual deformation of a body of plastic solid (as rock) by intermolecular shear

flow·chart \-,chärt\ *n* (1920) : a diagram that shows step-by-step progression through a procedure or system esp. using connecting lines and a set of conventional symbols — **flow·chart·ing** \-,chär-tiŋ\ *n*

flow cy·tom·e·try \-sī-'tä-mə-trē\ *n* (1978) : a technique for identifying and sorting cells and their components (as DNA) by staining with a fluorescent dye and detecting the fluorescence usu. by laser beam illumination

flow diagram *n* (1943) : FLOWCHART

¹flow·er \'flaů-(ə)r\ *n* [ME *flour* flower, best of anything, flour, fr. OF *flor, flour, flur*, fr. L *flor-, flos* — more at BLOW] (13c) **1 a** : BLOSSOM, INFLORESCENCE **b** : a shoot of the sporophyte of a higher plant that is modified for reproduction and consists of a shortened axis bearing modified leaves; *esp* : one of a seed plant differentiated into a calyx, corolla, stamens, and carpels **c** : a plant cultivated for its blossoms **2 a** : the best part or example ⟨the ∼ of our youth⟩ **b** : the finest most vigorous period **c** : a state of blooming or flourishing ⟨in full ∼⟩ **3** *pl* : a finely divided powder produced esp. by condensation or sublimation ⟨∼s of sulfur⟩ — **flow·ered** \'flaů(-ə)rd\ *adj* — **flow·er·ful** \'flaů(-ə)r-fəl\ *adj* — **flow·er·less** \-ləs\ *adj* — **flow·er·like** \-,līk\ *adj*

cross section of flower 1b: *1* filament, *2* anther, *3* stigma, *4* style, *5* petal, *6* ovary, *7* sepal, *8* pedicel, *9* stamen, *10* pistil, *11* perianth

²flower *vi* (13c) **1 a** : DEVELOP ⟨∼ed into young womanhood⟩ **b** : FLOURISH **2** : to produce flowers : BLOSSOM ∼ *vt* **1** : to cause to bear flowers **2** : to decorate with flowers or floral designs — **flow·er·er** \'flaů(-ə)r-ər\ *n*

flow·er·age \'flaů(-ə)r-ij\ *n* (1840) : a flowering process, state, or condition

flower bud *n* (1828) : a plant bud that produces only a flower

flower bug *n* (ca. 1889) : any of various small mostly black-and-white predaceous bugs (family Anthocoridae) that frequent flowers and feed on pest insects (as aphids and thrips)

flower child *n* (1967) : a hippie who advocates love, beauty, and peace

flow·er·et *also* **flow·er·ette** \'flaů(-ə)r-ət\ *n* (15c) : FLORET 1

flower girl *n* (1925) : a little girl who carries flowers at a wedding

flower head *n* (1845) : a capitulum (as of a composite) having sessile flowers so arranged that the whole inflorescence looks like a single flower

flowering dogwood *n* (1843) : a common spring-flowering white-bracted dogwood (*Cornus florida*)

flowering plant *n* (1745) : ANGIOSPERM

flower people *n pl* (1967) : FLOWER CHILDREN

flow·er·pot \'flaů(-ə)r-,pät\ *n* (1598) : a pot in which to grow plants

flow·ery \'flaů(-ə)r-ē\ *adj* (14c) **1** : of, relating to, or resembling flowers **2** : marked by or given to rhetorical elegance — **flow·er·i·ly** \'flaů(-ə)r-ə-lē\ *adv* — **flow·er·i·ness** *n*

flow·me·ter \'flō-,mē-tər\ *n* (1915) : an instrument for measuring one or more properties (as velocity or pressure) of a flow (as of a liquid in a pipe)

¹flown \'flōn\ *past part of* FLY

²flown *adj* [archaic pp. of ¹*flow*] (1626) : filled to excess

flow sheet *n* (1912) : FLOWCHART

flow·stone \'flō-,stōn\ *n* (1925) : calcite deposited by a thin sheet of flowing water usu. along the walls or floor of a cave

flu \'flü\ *n* [by shortening] (1839) **1** : INFLUENZA **2** : any of several virus diseases marked esp. by respiratory symptoms

¹flub \'fləb\ *vb* **flubbed; flub·bing** [origin unknown] *vt* (1904) : to make a mess of ⟨*flubbed* my lines⟩ ∼ *vi* : BLUNDER

²flub *n* (1948) : an act or instance of flubbing

flub·dub \'fləb-,dəb\ *n* [origin unknown] (1888) : BUNKUM, BALDERDASH

fluc·tu·ant \'flək-chə-wənt\ *adj* (1560) **1** : moving in waves **2** : VARIABLE, UNSTABLE **3** : being movable and compressible ⟨a ∼ abscess⟩

fluc·tu·ate \'flək-chə-,wāt\ *vb* **-at·ed; -at·ing** [L *fluctuatus*, pp. of *fluctuare*, fr. *fluctus* flow, wave, fr. *fluere* — more at FLUID] *vi* (1634) **1** : to shift back and forth uncertainly **2** : to ebb and flow in waves ∼ *vt* : to cause to fluctuate **syn** see SWING — **fluc·tu·a·tion** \,flək-chə-'wā-shən\ *n* — **fluc·tu·a·tion·al** \-'wā-shnəl, -shə-nᵊl\ *adj*

flue \'flü\ *n* [origin unknown] (1582) : an enclosed passageway for directing a current: as **a** : a channel in a chimney for conveying flame and smoke to the outer air **b** : a pipe for conveying flame and hot gases around or through water in a steam boiler **c** : an air channel leading to the lip of a wind instrument **d** : FLUE PIPE

flue-cured \-,kyůrd\ *adj* (1905) : cured with heat transmitted through a flue without exposure to smoke or fumes ⟨∼ tobacco⟩

flu·en·cy \'flü-ənt-sē\ *n* (1636) : the quality or state of being fluent

flu·ent \'flü-ənt\ *adj* [L *fluent-, fluens*, prp. of *fluere*] (1599) **1 a** : capable of flowing : FLUID **b** : capable of moving with ease and grace ⟨the ∼ body of a dancer⟩ **2 a** : ready or facile in speech ⟨∼ in Spanish⟩ **b** : effortlessly smooth and rapid : POLISHED ⟨a ∼ performance⟩ — **flu·ent·ly** *adv*

flue pipe *n* (1852) : an organ pipe whose tone is produced by an air current striking the lip and causing the air within to vibrate — compare REED PIPE

flue stop *n* (1855) : an organ stop made up of flue pipes

¹fluff \'fləf\ *n* [perh. blend of *flue* (fluff) and *puff*] (1790) **1** : NAP, DOWN **2** : something fluffy **3** : something inconsequential **4** : BLUNDER; *esp* : an actor's lapse of memory

²fluff *vi* (1875) **1** : to become fluffy **2** : to make a mistake; *esp* : to forget or bungle one's lines in a play ∼ *vt* **1** : to make fluffy **2 a** : to spoil by a mistake : BOTCH **b** : to deliver badly or forget (one's lines) in a play

fluffy \'flə-fē\ *adj* **fluff·i·er; -est** (ca. 1825) **1 a** : covered with or resembling fluff **b** : being light and soft or airy ⟨a ∼ omelet⟩ **2**

: lacking in meaning or substance : SUPERFICIAL 2c — **fluff·i·ly** \'flə-fə-lē\ *adv* — **fluff·i·ness** \'flə-fē-nəs\ *n*

flü·gel·horn *or* **flue·gel·horn** \'flü-gəl-,hȯrn, 'flüē-\ *n* [G, fr. *Flügel* wing, flank + *Horn* horn; fr. its use to signal the flanking drivers in a battue] (1854) : a valved brass instrument resembling a cornet but having a larger bore — **flü·gel·horn·ist** \-,hȯr-nist\ *n*

¹flu·id \'flü-əd\ *adj* [F or L; F *fluide*, fr. L *fluidus*, fr. *fluere* to flow; akin to Gk *phlyzein* to boil over] (1603) **1 a** : having particles that easily move and change their relative position without a separation of the mass and that easily yield to pressure : capable of flowing **b** : subject to change or movement ⟨boundaries became ~⟩ **2** : characterized by or employing a smooth easy style ⟨the ballerina's ~ movements⟩ **3 a** : available for a different use **b** : LIQUID 4 ⟨~ assets⟩ — **flu·id·ly** *adv* — **flu·id·ness** *n*

²fluid *n* (1661) : a substance (as a liquid or gas) tending to flow or conform to the outline of its container — **flu·id·al** \'flü-ə-dᵊl\ *adj* — **flu·id·al·ly** \-dᵊl-ē\ *adv*

fluid dram *or* **flu·i·dram** \,flü-ə(d)-'dram\ *n* (ca. 1860) : a unit of liquid capacity equal to ⅛ fluid ounce — see WEIGHT table

flu·id·ex·tract \,flü-ə-'dek-,strakt\ *n* (1851) : an alcohol preparation of a vegetable drug containing the active constituents of one gram of the dry drug in each milliliter

flu·id·ic \flü-'i-dik\ *adj* (1960) : of, relating to, or being a device (as an amplifier or control) that depends for operation on the pressures and flows of a fluid in precisely shaped channels — **fluidic** *n* — **flu·id·ics** \-diks\ *n pl but sing in constr*

flu·id·i·ty \flü-'i-də-tē\ *n* (1603) **1** : the quality or state of being fluid **2** : the physical property of a substance that enables it to flow

flu·id·ize \'flü-ə-,dīz\ *vt* **-ized; -iz·ing** (ca. 1855) **1** : to cause to flow like a fluid **2** : to suspend (as solid particles) in a rapidly moving stream of gas or vapor to induce flowing motion of the whole — **flu·id·iza·tion** \,flü-ə-də-'zā-shən\ *n* — **flu·id·iz·er** \'flü-ə-,dī-zər\ *n*

fluidized bed *n* (1949) : a bed of small solid particles (as in a coal burning furnace) suspended and kept in motion by an upward flow of a fluid (as a gas) — called also *fluid bed*

fluid mechanics *n pl but sing or pl in constr* (1937) : a branch of mechanics dealing with the properties of liquids and gases

fluid ounce *n* (ca. 1860) **1** : a U.S. unit of liquid capacity equal to ¹⁄₁₆ pint — see WEIGHT table **2** : a British unit of liquid capacity equal to ¹⁄₂₀ pint — see WEIGHT table

¹fluke \'flük\ *n* [ME, fr. OE *flōc*; akin to OE *flōh* chip, OHG *flah* smooth, Gk *plax* flat surface, and prob. to OE *flōr* floor — more at FLOOR] (bef. 12c) **1** : FLATFISH **2** : a flattened digenetic trematode worm; *broadly* : TREMATODE — compare LIVER FLUKE

²fluke *n* [perh. fr. ¹*fluke*] (1561) **1** : the part of an anchor that fastens in the ground — see ANCHOR illustration **2** : one of the lobes of a whale's tail

³fluke *n* [origin unknown] (1857) **1** : an accidentally successful stroke at billiards or pool **2** : a stroke of luck ⟨the discovery was a ~⟩

fluky *also* **fluk·ey** \'flü-kē\ *adj* **fluk·i·er; -est** (1867) **1** : happening by or depending on chance **2** : being unsteady or uncertain — used esp. of wind

flume \'flüm\ *n* [prob. fr. ME *flum* river, fr. OF, fr. L *flumen*, fr. *fluere* — more at FLUID] (1748) **1** : an inclined channel for conveying water (as for power) **2** : a ravine or gorge with a stream running through it

flum·mery \'fləm-rē, 'flə-mə-\ *n, pl* **-mer·ies** [W *llymru*] (1623) **1 a** : a soft jelly or porridge made with flour or meal **b** : any of several sweet desserts **2** : MUMMERY, MUMBO JUMBO

flum·mox \'flə-məks, -miks\ *vt* [origin unknown] (1837) : CONFUSE

¹flump \'fləmp\ [imit.] *vi* (1816) : to move or fall suddenly and heavily ⟨~ed down into the chair⟩ ~ *vt* : to place or drop with a flump

²flump *n* (1832) : a dull heavy sound (as of a fall)

flung *past and past part of* FLING

¹flunk \'fləŋk\ *vb* [perh. blend of *flinch* and *funk*] *vi* (1823) : to fail esp. in an examination or course ~ *vt* **1** : to give a failing grade to **2** : to get a failing grade in — **flunk·er** *n*

²flunk *n* (1846) : an act or instance of flunking

flunk out *vi* (1920) : to be dismissed from a school or college for failure ~ *vt* : to dismiss from a school or college for failure

flun·ky *or* **flun·key** \'fləŋ-kē\ *n, pl* **flunkies** *or* **flunkeys** [Sc, of unknown origin] (ca. 1782) **1 a** : a liveried servant **b** : one performing menial or miscellaneous duties **2** : YES-MAN

flu·o·cin·o·lone ac·e·to·nide \,flü-ə-'sin-ᵊl-,ōn-,a-sə-'tō-,nīd\ *n* [*fluor-* + *-cinolone*, prob. alter. of *-nisolone* (as in *prednisolone*)] (1963) : a glucocorticoid steroid $C_{24}H_{30}F_2O_6$ used esp. as an anti-inflammatory agent in the treatment of skin diseases

flu·or \'flü-,ȯr, 'flü-ər\ *n* [NL, mineral belonging to a group used as fluxes and including fluorite, fr. L, flow, fr. *fluere* — more at FLUID] (1661) : FLUORITE

fluor- *or* **fluoro-** *comb form* [F] **1** : fluorine ⟨*fluoride*⟩ **2** *also* **fluori-** : fluorescence ⟨*fluoroscope*⟩ ⟨*fluorimeter*⟩

fluo·resce \flü-'res, flō-, flȯ-\ *vi* **-resced; -resc·ing** [back-formation fr. *fluorescence*] (1874) : to produce, undergo, or exhibit fluorescence — **fluo·resc·er** *n*

fluo·res·ce·in \-'re-sē-ən\ *n* (1876) : a yellow or red crystalline dye $C_{20}H_{12}O_5$ with a bright yellow-green fluorescence in alkaline solution

fluo·res·cence \-'re-sᵊn(t)s\ *n* [*fluor*spar + *opal*escence] (1852) : luminescence that is caused by the absorption of radiation at one wavelength followed by nearly immediate reradiation usu. at a different wavelength and that ceases almost immediately when the incident radiation stops; *also* : the radiation emitted — compare PHOSPHORESCENCE

fluo·res·cent \-'sᵊnt\ *adj* (1853) **1** : having or relating to fluorescence **2** : bright and glowing as a result of fluorescence ⟨~ inks⟩; *broadly* : very bright in color — **fluorescent** *n*

fluorescent lamp *n* (1896) : a tubular electric lamp having a coating of fluorescent material on its inner surface and containing mercury vapor whose bombardment by electrons from the cathode provides ultraviolet light which causes the material to emit visible light

fluo·ri·date \'flür-ə-,dāt, 'flȯr-, 'flōr-\ *vt* **-dat·ed; -dat·ing** (1949) : to add a fluoride to (as drinking water) to reduce tooth decay — **fluo·ri·da·tion** \,flür-ə-'dā-shən, ,flȯr-, ,flōr-\ *n*

fluo·ride \'flȯr-,īd, 'flür-\ *n, often attrib* (1826) **1** : a compound of fluorine **2** : the monovalent anion of flourine

fluo·ri·nate \'flȯr-ə-,nāt, 'flōr-, 'flür-\ *vt* **-nat·ed; -nat·ing** (ca. 1929) : to treat or cause to combine with fluorine or a compound of fluorine — **fluo·ri·na·tion** \,flȯr-ə-'nā-shən, ,flōr-, ,flür-\ *n*

fluo·rine \'flür-,ēn, 'flȯr-, 'flōr-\ *n* [F, fr. NL *fluor*] (1813) : a nonmetallic halogen element that is isolated as a pale yellowish flammable irritating toxic diatomic gas — see ELEMENT table

fluo·rite \'flür-,īt, 'flȯr-, 'flōr-\ *n* [It, fr. NL *fluor*] (1868) : a transparent or translucent mineral of different colors that consists of the fluoride of calcium and is used as a flux and in the making of opalescent and opaque glasses

fluo·ro·car·bon \,flür-ō-'kär-bən, ,flȯr-, ,flōr-\ *n* (1937) : any of various chemically inert compounds containing carbon and fluorine used chiefly as lubricants, refrigerants, nonstick coatings, and formerly aerosol propellants and in making resins and plastics; *also* : CHLOROFLUOROCARBON

fluo·ro·chrome \'flür-ə-,krōm, ,flȯr-, ,flōr-\ *n* (1943) : any of various fluorescent substances used in biological staining to produce fluorescence in a specimen

fluo·rog·ra·phy \flü-'rä-grə-fē, flō-, flȯ-\ *n* (1941) : PHOTOFLUOROGRAPHY — **fluo·ro·graph·ic** \,flür-ə-'gra-fik, ,flȯr-, ,flōr-\ *adj*

fluo·rom·e·ter \flü-'rä-mə-tər, flō-, flȯ-\ *or* **fluo·rim·e·ter** \-'ri-ə-\ *n* (1897) : an instrument for measuring fluorescence and related phenomena (as intensity of radiation) — **fluo·ro·met·ric** *or* **fluo·ri·met·ric** \,flür-ə-'me-trik, ,flȯr-, ,flōr-\ *adj* — **fluo·rom·e·try** \flü-'rä-mə-trē, flō-, flȯ-\ *or* **fluo·rim·e·try** \-'ri-mə-trē\ *n*

¹fluo·ro·scope \'flür-ə-,skōp, 'flȯr-, 'flōr-\ *n* [ISV] (1896) : an instrument used for observing the internal structure of an opaque object (as the living body) by means of X rays — **fluo·ro·scop·ic** \,flür-ə-'skä-pik, ,flȯr-, ,flōr-\ *adj* — **fluo·ro·scop·i·cal·ly** \-pi-k(ə-)lē\ *adv* — **fluo·ros·co·pist** \flü-'räs-kə-pist, flō-, flȯ-\ *n* — **fluo·ros·co·py** \-pē\ *n*

²fluoroscope *vt* **-scoped; -scop·ing** (1898) : to examine by fluoroscopy

fluo·ro·sis \flü-'rō-səs, flō-\ *n* [NL] (1927) : an abnormal condition (as mottling of the teeth) caused by fluorine or its compounds — **fluo·rot·ic** \-'rä-tik\ *adj*

fluo·ro·ura·cil \,flür-ō-'yur-ə-,sil, -,səl, ,flȯr-, ,flōr-\ *n* [*fluor-* + *uracil*] (ca. 1958) : a fluorine-containing pyrimidine base $C_4H_3FN_2O_2$ used to treat some kinds of cancer

fluor·spar \'flür-,spär, 'flȯr-, 'flōr-\ *n* (1794) : FLUORITE

flu·phen·azine \flü-'fe-nə-,zēn\ *n* [*fluor-* + *phenazine*] (ca. 1960) : a tranquilizing compound $C_{22}H_{26}F_3N_3OS$ used esp. combined as a salt

flur·ry \'flər-ē, 'flə-rē\ *n, pl* **flurries** [prob. fr. *flurr* (to throw scatteringly)] (1686) **1 a** : a gust of wind **b** : a brief light snowfall **2 a** : a brief period of commotion or excitement **b** : a sudden occurrence of many things at once : BARRAGE 2 ⟨a ~ of insults⟩ **3** : a brief advance or decline in prices : a short-lived outburst of trading activity

²flurry *vb* **flur·ried; flur·ry·ing** *vt* (1757) : to cause to become agitated and confused ~ *vi* : to move in an agitated or confused manner

¹flush \'fləsh\ *vb* [ME *flusshen*] *vi* (13c) : to take wing suddenly ~ *vt* **1** : to cause (a bird) to flush **2** : to expose or chase from a place of concealment ⟨~ed the boys from their hiding place⟩

²flush *n* [MF *flus, fluz*, fr. L *fluxus* flow, flux] (ca. 1529) **1** : a hand of playing cards all of the same suit; *specif* : a poker hand containing five cards of the same suit but not in sequence — see POKER illustration **2** : a series of three or more slalom gates set vertically on a slope

³flush *n* [perh. modif. of L *fluxus*] (1529) **1** : a sudden flow (as of water); *also* : a rinsing or cleansing with or as if with a flush of water **2 a** : a sudden increase or expansion; *esp* : sudden and usu. abundant new plant growth **b** : a surge of emotion ⟨felt a ~ of anger at the insult⟩ **3 a** : a tinge of red : BLUSH **b** : a fresh and vigorous state ⟨in the first ~ of womanhood⟩ **4** : a transitory sensation of extreme heat — compare HOT FLASH

⁴flush *vi* (1548) **1** : to flow and spread suddenly and freely **2 a** : to glow brightly **b** : BLUSH **3** : to produce new growth ⟨the plants ~ twice during the year⟩ ~ *vt* **1 a** : to cause to flow **b** : to pour liquid over or through; *esp* : to cleanse or wash out with or as if with a rush of liquid ⟨~ the toilet⟩ ⟨~ the lungs with air⟩ **2** : INFLAME, EXCITE — usu. used passively ⟨~ed with pride⟩ **3** : to cause to blush

⁵flush *adj* (1594) **1 a** : of a ruddy healthy color **b** : full of life and vigor : LUSTY **2** : filled to overflowing : AFFLUENT **3** : readily available : ABUNDANT **4 a** : having or forming a continuous plane or unbroken surface ⟨~ paneling⟩ **b** : directly abutting or immediately adjacent: as **(1)** : set even with an edge of a type page or column : having no indentation **(2)** : arranged edge to edge so as to fit snugly — **flush·ness** *n*

⁶flush *adv* (1700) **1** : in a flush manner **2** : SQUARELY ⟨hit him ~ on the chin⟩

⁷flush *vt* (ca. 1842) : to make flush ⟨~ the headings on a page⟩

flush·able \'flə-shə-bəl\ *adj* (1973) : suitable for disposal by flushing down a toilet

¹flus·ter \'fləs-tər\ *vb* **flus·tered; flus·ter·ing** \-t(ə-)riŋ\ [prob. of Scand origin; akin to Icel *flaustur* hurry] *vt* (1604) **1** : to make tipsy **2** : to put into a state of agitated confusion : UPSET ~ *vi* : to move or behave in an agitated or confused manner **syn** see DISCOMPOSE — **flus·tered·ly** *adv*

²fluster *n* (1728) : a state of agitated confusion

flute \'flüt\ *n* [ME *floute*, fr. MF *fleute*, fr. *flaüte*, prob. fr. OProv *flaut*] (14c) **1 a** : RECORDER 3 **b** : a keyed woodwind instrument consisting of a cylindrical tube which is stopped at one end and which has a side hole over which air is blown to produce the tone and having a range from middle C upward for three octaves **2** : something

flute 1b

\ə\ abut \ᵊ\ kitten, F table \ər\ further \a\ ash \ā\ ace \ä\ mop, mar \au̇\ out \ch\ chin \e\ bet \ē\ easy \g\ go \i\ hit \ī\ ice \j\ job \ŋ\ sing \ō\ go \ȯ\ law \ȯi\ boy \th\ thin \t̲h̲\ the \ü\ loot \u̇\ foot \y\ yet \zh\ vision \à, k̲, ⁿ, œ, œ̄, ue, ūe, ᵞ\ *see* Guide to Pronunciation long and slender: as **a** : a tall slender wineglass **b** : a grooved pleat (as on a hat brim) **3** : a rounded groove; *specif* : one of the vertical parallel grooves on a classical architectural column — **flute-like** \-,līk\ *adj* — **fluty** *or* **flut-ey** \'flü-tē\ *adj*

²**flute** *vb* **flut-ed; flut-ing** *vi* (14c) **1** : to play a flute **2** : to produce a flutelike sound ~ *vt* **1** : to utter with a flutelike sound **2** : to form flutes in — **flut-er** *n*

flut-ed *adj* (1611) : having or marked by grooves

flut-ing \'flü-tiŋ\ *n* (1611) **1** : a series of flutes (the ~ of a column) **2** : fluted material

flut-ist \'flü-tist\ *n* (1603) : one who plays a flute

¹**flut-ter** \'flə-tər\ *vb* [ME *floteren* to float, flutter, fr. OE *floterian*, freq. of *flotian* to float; akin to OE *flēotan* to float — more at FLEET] *vi* (bef. 12c) **1** : to flap the wings rapidly **2 a** : to move with quick wavering or flapping motions **b** : to vibrate in irregular spasms **3** : to move about or behave in an agitated aimless manner ~ *vt* : to cause to flutter — **flut-ter-er** \-tər-ər\ *n* — **flut-tery** \-tə-rē\ *adj*

²**flutter** *n* (1641) **1** : an act of fluttering **2 a** : a state of nervous confusion or excitement **b** : FLURRY, COMMOTION **c** : abnormal spasmodic fluttering of a body part (treatment of atrial ~) **3 a** : a distortion in reproduced sound similar to but of a higher pitch than wow **b** : fluctuation in the brightness of a television image **4** : an unwanted oscillation (as of an aileron or a bridge) set up by natural forces **5** *chiefly Brit* : a small speculative venture or gamble

flut-ter-board \'flə-tər-,bȯrd, -,bȯrd\ *n* (1950) : a rectangular board used by swimmers in practicing leg strokes

flutter kick *n* (ca. 1934) : an alternating whipping motion of the legs used in various swimming styles (as the crawl)

flutter sleeve *n* (1973) : a loose-fitting tapered sleeve falling in folds over the upper arm

flu-vi-al \'flü-vē-əl\ *adj* [L *fluvialis*, fr. *fluvius* river, fr. *fluere*] (14c) **1** : of, relating to, or living in a stream or river **2** : produced by the action of a stream

flu-vi-a-tile \'flü-vē-ə-,tīl\ *adj* [MF, fr. L *fluviatilis*, fr. *fluvius*] (1599) : FLUVIAL

¹**flux** \'fləks\ *n* [ME, fr. MF & ML; MF, fr. ML *fluxus*, fr. L, flow, fr. *fluere* to flow — more at FLUID] (14c) **1** : a flowing of fluid from the body; *esp* : an excessive abnormal discharge from the bowels **2 a** : continuous moving on or passing by (as of a stream) **3** : a continued flow : FLOOD **4 a** : INFLUX **b** : CHANGE, FLUCTUATION (in a state of ~) **5** : a substance used to promote fusion (as of metals or minerals); *esp* : one (as rosin) applied to surfaces to be joined by soldering, brazing, or welding to clean and free them from oxide and promote their union **6** : the rate of transfer of fluid, particles, or energy across a given surface

²**flux** *vt* (15c) **1** : to cause to become fluid **2** : to treat with a flux ~ *vi* : to become fluid : FUSE

flux-gate \'fləks-,gāt\ *n* (1944) : a device used to indicate the direction and intensity of the magnetic field (as on a planet)

flux-ion \'flək-shən\ *n* (1599) **1** : the action of flowing or changing; *also* : something subjected to such action **2** : DERIVATIVE **3** — compare METHOD OF FLUXIONS — **flux-ion-al** \-shnəl, -shə-nᵊl\ *adj*

¹**fly** \'flī\ *vb* **flew** \'flü\; **flown** \'flōn\; **fly-ing** [ME *flien*, fr. OE *flēogan*; akin to OHG *fliogan* to fly and prob. OE *flōwan* to flow] *vi* (bef. 12c) **1 a** : to move in or pass through the air with wings **b** : to move through the air or before the wind or through outer space **c** : to float, wave, or soar in the air (flags ~*ing* at half-mast) **2 a** : to take flight : FLEE **b** : to fade and disappear : VANISH **3 a** : to move, pass, or spread quickly (rumors were ~*ing*) **b** : to be moved with sudden extreme emotion (*flew* into a rage) **c** : to seem to pass quickly (the time simply *flew*) **4** : to become expended or dissipated rapidly **5** : to operate or travel in an airplane or spacecraft **6** : to work successfully : win popular acceptance (knew . . . a pure human-rights approach would not ~ —Charles Brydon) ~ *vt* **1 a** : to cause to fly, float, or hang in the air (~*ing* a kite) **b** : to operate (as a balloon, aircraft, rocket, or spacecraft) in flight **c** : to journey over or through by flying **2 a** : to flee or escape from **b** : AVOID, SHUN **3** : to transport by aircraft or spacecraft — **fly at** : to assail suddenly and violently — **fly blind** : to fly an airplane solely by instruments — **fly high** : to be elated — **fly in the face of** *or* **fly in the teeth of** : to stand or act forthrightly or brazenly in defiance or contradiction of

²**fly** *n*, *pl* **flies** (bef. 12c) **1** : the action or process of flying : FLIGHT **2 a** : a device consisting of two or more radial vanes capable of rotating on a spindle to act as a fan or to govern the speed of clockwork or very light machinery **b** : FLYWHEEL **3** *pl* : the space over a theater stage where scenery and equipment can be hung **4** : something attached by one edge: as **a** : a garment closing concealed by a fold of cloth extending over the fastener **b** (1) : the length of an extended flag from its staff or support (2) : the outer or loose end of a flag **5** : a baseball hit high into the air **6** : FLYLEAF **7** : a sheet of material (as canvas) that is attachable to a tent for use as a double top or as a rooflike extension **8** : a football pass pattern in which the receiver runs straight downfield — **on the fly** **1** : in motion : BUSY **2** : while still in the air : without the ball bouncing (the home run carried 450 feet *on the fly*)

³**fly** *vi* **flied; fly-ing** (1893) : to hit a fly in baseball

⁴**fly** *n*, *pl* **flies** [ME *flie*, fr. OE *flēoge*; akin to OHG *flioga* fly, OE *flēogan* to fly] (bef. 12c) **1** : a winged insect — used chiefly in combination (may*flies*) (butter*fly*) **2 a** : any of a large order (Diptera) of winged or rarely wingless insects (as the housefly, mosquito, or gnat) that have segmented often headless, eyeless, and legless larvae, the anterior wings functional, and the posterior wings reduced to halteres **b** : a large stout-bodied fly **3** : a fishhook dressed (as with feathers or tinsel) to suggest an insect — **fly in the ointment** : a detracting factor or element

⁵**fly** *adj* [prob. fr. ¹*fly*] (1811) *chiefly Brit* : KEEN, ARTFUL

fly-able \'flī-ə-bəl\ *adj* (ca. 1909) : suitable for flying or for being flown

fly agaric *n* (1788) : a poisonous mushroom (*Amanita muscaria*) with a usu. bright red cap

fly ash *n* (1931) : fine solid particles of ashes, dust, and soot carried out from burning fuel (as coal or oil) by the draft

fly-away \'flī-ə-,wā\ *adj* (1844) **1** : loose and flowing esp. because of unconfined fullness at the back (a ~ jacket) **2** : of, relating to, or being an aircraft that is ready to fly (a ~ price)

fly ball *n* (1865) : ²FLY 5

¹**fly-blow** \-,blō\ *vt* **-blew; -blown** [⁴*fly* + ¹*blow*] (1603) **1** : TAINT, CONTAMINATE **2** : to deposit eggs or young larvae of a flesh fly or blowfly in

²**flyblow** *n* (1825) : FLY-STRIKE

fly-blown \'flī-,blōn\ *adj* (ca. 1529) **1 a** : not pure : TAINTED (a world ~ with the vices of irresponsible power —V. L. Parrington) **b** : not bright and new : SEEDY, MOTH-EATEN (a list of ~ metaphors —*Horizon*) **2 a** : infested with eggs or young larvae of a flesh fly or blowfly **b** : covered with flyspecks

fly-boat \-,bōt\ *n* [modif. of D *vlieboot*, fr. *Vlie*, channel between North Sea & Wadden Zee + *boot* boat] (1577) : any of various fast boats

fly-boy \'flī-,bȯi\ *n* (1946) : a member of the air force; *broadly* : an aircraft pilot

fly-bridge \'flī-,brij\ *n* (1965) : an open deck on a cabin cruiser located above the bridge on the cabin roof and usu. having a duplicate set of navigating equipment

fly-by \'flī-,bī\ *n*, *pl* **flybys** (1953) **1** : a prearranged usu. low-altitude flight by one or more airplanes over a public gathering (as in an air show) **2 a** : a flight of a spacecraft past a celestial body (as Mars) close enough to obtain scientific data **b** : a spacecraft that makes a flyby

¹**fly-by-night** \'flī-bī-,nīt\ *n* (1822) **1** : one that seeks to evade responsibilities and esp. creditors by flight **2** : one without established reputation or standing; *esp* : a shaky business enterprise

²**fly-by-night** *adj* (1914) **1** : given to making a quick profit usu. by shady or irresponsible acts **2** : TRANSITORY, PASSING (~ fashions)

fly-by-night-er \,flī-bī-'nīt-ər\ *n* (1946) : FLY-BY-NIGHT

fly-by-wire \'flī-bī-,wīr\ *adj* (1968) : of, relating to, being, or utilizing a flight-control system in which controls are operated electrically rather than mechanically

fly casting *n* (ca. 1889) : the casting of artificial flies in fly-fishing or as a competitive sport

fly-catch-er \'flī-,ka-chər, -,ke-\ *n* (1678) : any of various passerine birds (families Muscicapidae and Tyrannidae) that feed on insects taken on the wing

fly dope *n* (1897) : an insect repellent

fly-er *var of* FLIER

fly fisherman *n* (1886) : an angler who uses the technique of fly-fishing

fly-fish-ing \'flī-,fi-shiŋ\ *n* (1653) : a method of fishing in which an artificial fly is cast by use of a fly rod, a reel, and a relatively heavy oiled or treated line

fly front *n* (1893) : a concealed closing on the front of a coat, skirt, shirt, dress, or pants — **fly-front** \'flī-,frənt\ *adj*

fly gallery *n* (1888) : a narrow raised platform at the side of a theater stage from which flying scenery lines are operated

¹**fly-ing** \'flī-iŋ\ *adj* (bef. 12c) **1 a** : moving or capable of moving in the air **b** : moving or made by moving rapidly (~ feet) (a ~ leap) **c** : very brief **2** : intended for ready movement or action (a ~ squad car) **3** : having stylized wings — used esp. of livestock brand marks **4** : of or relating to the operation of aircraft (a ~ club) **5** : traversed or to be traversed (as in speed-record trials) after a running start (a ~ kilometer) — **with flying colors** : with complete or eminent success

²**flying** *n* (1548) **1** : travel by air **2** : the operation of an aircraft or spacecraft

flying boat *n* (1913) : a seaplane with a hull designed for floating

flying bomb *n* (1944) *chiefly Brit* : BUZZ BOMB

flying bridge *n* (ca. 1909) **1** : the highest navigational bridge on a ship **2** : FLYBRIDGE

flying buttress *n* (1669) : a masonry structure that typically consists of a straight inclined bar carried on an arch and a solid pier or buttress against which it abuts and that receives the thrust of a roof or vault

Flying Dutchman *n* **1** : a legendary Dutch mariner condemned to sail the seas until Judgment Day **2** : a spectral ship that according to legend haunts the seas near the Cape of Good Hope

flying fish *n* (ca. 1511) : any of numerous fishes (family Exocoetidae) chiefly of tropical and warm seas that are capable of long gliding flights out of water by spreading their large pectoral fins like wings

flying fox *n* (1759) : FRUIT BAT

flying gurnard *n* (1884) : any of several marine fishes (family Dactylopteridae) that resemble gurnards and have large pectoral fins allowing them to glide above the water for short distances

1 flying buttress

flying jib *n* (1711) : a sail outside the jib on an extension of the jibboom — see SAIL illustration

flying lemur *n* (1883) : either of two East Indian or Philippine arboreal nocturnal mammals (*Cynocephalus volans* and *C. variegatus*) that are about the size of a cat, that make long gliding leaps using a broad fold of skin on each side attached to and extending between the limbs, and that are placed in a separate order (Dermoptera)

flying machine *n* (1736) : an apparatus for navigating the air

flying mare *n* (1754) : a wrestling maneuver in which the aggressor seizes his opponent's wrist, turns about, and jerks him over his back

flying officer *n* (1913) : a commissioned officer in the British air force who ranks with a first lieutenant in the army

flying saucer *n* (1947) : any of various unidentified flying objects usu. described as being saucer-shaped or disk-shaped

flying spot *n* (1933) : a spot of light moved over a surface (as one bearing printing or an image) so that light reflected from or transmitted by different parts of the surface is translated into electrical signals for transmission (as in television or computers)

flying squad *n* (1927) : a usu. small standby group of people ready to move or act swiftly; *esp* : a police unit formed to respond quickly in an emergency

flying squirrel *n* (1624) : either of two small nocturnal No. American squirrels (*Glaucomys volans* and *G. sabrinus*) with folds of skin connecting the forelegs and hind legs that enable it to make long gliding leaps; *also* : any of various squirrels that possess a patagium

flying start *n* (1851) **1** : a start in racing in which the participants are already moving when they cross the starting line or receive the starting signal **2** : a favorable start of something

flying wedge *n* (1909) : a moving formation (as of guards or police) resembling a wedge

fly·leaf \'flī-,lēf\ *n, pl* **fly·leaves** \-,lēvz\ (1832) : one of the free end-papers of a book

fly·man \-mən, -,man\ *n* (1883) : a worker in the flies of a theater who manipulates curtains and scenery

fly net *n* (bef. 12c) : a net to exclude or keep off insects (as from a harness horse)

fly·over \'flī-,ō-vər\ *n* (1931) **1** : FLYBY 1 **2** *Brit* : OVERPASS

fly·pa·per \-,pā-pər\ *n* (1847) : paper coated with a sticky often poisonous substance for killing flies

fly·past \-,past\ *n* (1914) *chiefly Brit* : FLYBY 1

fly rod *n* (1684) : a light springy fishing rod used in fly casting

flysch \'flish\ *n* [G dial.] (1853) : a thick and extensive deposit largely of sandstone that is formed in a geosyncline adjacent to a rising mountain belt and is esp. common in the Alpine region of Europe

fly sheet *n* (1833) **1** : a small loose advertising sheet : HANDBILL **2** : a sheet of a folder, booklet, or catalog giving directions for the use of or information about the material that follows

fly·speck \'flī-,spek\ *n* (ca. 1847) **1** : a speck made by fly excrement **2** : something small and insignificant — **flyspeck** *vt*

fly–strike \-,strīk\ *n* (1940) : infestation with fly maggots — **fly-struck** \-,strək\ *adj*

fly·swat·ter \-,swä-tər\ *n* (1917) : a device for killing insects that consists of a flat piece of perforated rubber or plastic or fine-mesh wire netting attached to a handle

fly·ti·er \'flī-,tī(-ə)r\ *n* [*fly* + *tier* (one that ties)] (1881) : a person who makes flies for fishing

flyt·ing \'flī-tiŋ\ *n* [Sc, lit., contention, gerund of *flyte* to contend, argue, fr. ME *flītan*, fr. OE *flītan* to argue] (1508) : a dispute or exchange of personal abuse in verse form

fly·way \'flī-,wā\ *n* (1891) : an established air route of migratory birds

fly·weight \-,wāt\ *n* (1911) : a boxer in a weight division having a maximum limit of 112 pounds — compare BANTAMWEIGHT

fly·wheel \-,hwēl, -,wēl\ *n* (1784) : a heavy wheel for opposing and moderating by its inertia any fluctuation of speed in the machinery with which it revolves; *also* : a similar wheel used for storing kinetic energy (as for motive power)

fly whisk *n* (1841) : a whisk for brushing away flies

FM \'ef-,em\ *n, often attrib* [*frequency modulation*] (1940) : a broadcasting system using frequency modulation; *also* : a radio receiver of such a system

FMN \,ef-,em-'en\ *n* [*flavin mononucleotide*] (ca. 1953) : a yellow crystalline phosphoric ester $C_{17}H_{21}N_4O_9P$ of riboflavin that is a coenzyme of several flavoprotein enzymes

f–num·ber \'ef-,nəm-bər\ *n* [*focal length*] (ca. 1903) **1** : the ratio of the focal length to the aperture in an optical system **2** : a number following the symbol f/ that expresses the effectiveness of the aperture of a camera lens in relation to brightness of image so that the smaller the number the brighter the image and therefore the shorter the exposure required

¹foal \'fōl\ *n* [ME *fole*, fr. OE *fola*; akin to L *pullus* young of an animal, Gk *pais* child — more at FEW] (bef. 12c) : a young animal of the horse family; *esp* : one under one year — **in foal** : PREGNANT 3

²foal *vi* (14c) : to give birth to a foal

¹foam \'fōm\ *n* [ME *fome*, fr. OE *fām*; akin to OHG *feim* foam, L *spuma* foam, *pumex* pumice] (bef. 12c) **1** : a light frothy mass of fine bubbles formed in or on the surface of a liquid: as **a** : a frothy mass formed in salivating or sweating **b** : a stabilized froth produced chemically or mechanically and used esp. in fighting oil fires **c** : a material in a lightweight cellular form resulting from introduction of gas bubbles during manufacture **2** : SEA **3** : something resembling foam — **foam·less** \-ləs\ *adj*

²foam *vi* (bef. 12c) **1 a** : to produce or form foam **b** : to froth at the mouth esp. in anger; *broadly* : to be angry **2** : to gush out in foam **3** : to become covered with or as if with foam (streets . . . ~ing with life —Thomas Wolfe) ~ *vt* **1** : to cause to foam; *specif* : to cause air bubbles to form in **2** : to convert (as a plastic) into a foam — **foam·able** \'fō-mə-bəl\ *adj* — **foam·er** \'fō-mər\ *n*

foamed plastic *n* (1945) : EXPANDED PLASTIC

foam-flow·er \'fōm-,flaú(-ə)r\ *n* (1895) : an American woodland spring-flowering herb (*Tiarella cordifolia*) that has white flowers with very long stamens and no stem leaves — called also *false miterwort*

foam rubber *n* (ca. 1939) : spongy rubber of fine texture made from latex by foaming (as by whipping) before vulcanization

foamy \'fō-mē\ *adj* **foam·i·er; -est** (bef. 12c) **1** : covered with foam : FROTHY **2** : full of, consisting of, or resembling foam — **foam·i·ly** \-mə-lē\ *adv* — **foam·i·ness** \-mē-nəs\ *n*

¹fob \'fäb\ *vt* **fobbed; fob·bing** [ME *fobben*] (14c) *archaic* : DECEIVE, CHEAT

²fob *n* [perh. akin to G dial. *Fuppe* pocket] (1653) **1** : WATCH POCKET **2** : a short strap, ribbon, or chain attached esp. to a pocket watch **3** : an ornament attached to a fob chain

fob off *vt* (1597) **1** : to put off with a trick, excuse, or inferior substitute **2** : to pass or offer (something spurious) as genuine **3** : to put aside (now *fob off* what once they would have welcomed eagerly —Walter Lippmann)

fo·cac·cia \fō-'kä-ch(ē-)ə\ *n* [It, fr. LL *focacia* (neut. pl.), fr. L *focus* hearth] (1969) : a flat Italian bread typically seasoned with herbs and olive oil

fo·cal \'fō-kəl\ *adj* (1693) : of, relating to, being, or having a focus — **fo·cal·ly** \-kə-lē\ *adv*

focal infection *n* (ca. 1923) : a persistent bacterial infection of some organ or region; *esp* : one causing symptoms elsewhere in the body

fo·cal·ize \'fō-kə-,līz\ *vb* **-ized; -iz·ing** *vt* (1845) **1** : to bring to a focus **2** : LOCALIZE ~ *vi* **1** : to come to a focus : CONCENTRATE **2** : LOCALIZE — **fo·cal·iza·tion** \,fō-kə-lə-'zā-shən\ *n*

focal length *n* (1753) : the distance of a focus from the surface of a lens or curved mirror

focal plane *n* (1889) : a plane that is perpendicular to the axis of a lens or mirror and passes through the focus

focal point *n* (1713) : FOCUS 1a, 5a

focal ratio *n* (1926) : F-NUMBER

fo'·c'sle *var of* FORECASTLE

¹fo·cus \'fō-kəs\ *n, pl* **fo·ci** \'fō-,sī *also* -,kī\ *also* **fo·cus·es** [NL, fr. L, hearth] (1644) **1 a** : a point at which rays (as of light, heat, or sound) converge or from which they diverge or appear to diverge; *specif* : the point where the geometrical lines or their prolongations conforming to the rays diverging from or converging toward another point intersect and give rise to an image after reflection by a mirror or refraction by a lens or optical system **b** : a point of convergence of a beam of particles (as electrons) **2 a** : FOCAL LENGTH **b** : adjustment for distinct vision; *also* : the area that may be seen distinctly or resolved into a clear image **c** : a state or condition permitting clear perception or understanding (tried to bring the issues into ~) **d** : DIRECTION 6c **3** : one of the fixed points that with the corresponding directrix defines a conic section **4** : a localized area of disease or the chief site of a generalized disease or infection **5 a** : a center of activity, attraction, or attention (the ~ of the meeting was drug abuse) **b** : a point of concentration **6** : the place of origin of an earthquake or moonquake **7** : directed attention : EMPHASIS — **fo·cus·less** \-ləs\ *adj* — **in focus** : having or giving the proper sharpness of outline due to good focusing — **out of focus** : not in focus

²focus *vb* **fo·cused** *also* **fo·cussed; fo·cus·ing** *also* **fo·cus·sing** *vt* (1775) **1 a** : to bring into focus **b** : to adjust the focus of (as the eye or a lens) **2** : to cause to be concentrated (~ed their attention on the most urgent problems) **3** : to bring (as light rays) to a focus : CONCENTRATE ~ *vi* **1** : to come to a focus : CONVERGE **2** : to adjust one's eye or a camera to a particular range **3** : to concentrate attention or effort — **fo·cus·able** \-kə-sə-bəl\ *adj* — **fo·cus·er** *n*

fod·der \'fä-dər\ *n* [ME, fr. OE *fōdor*; akin to OHG *fuotar* food — more at FOOD] (bef. 12c) **1** : something fed to domestic animals; *esp* : coarse food for cattle, horses, or sheep **2** : inferior or readily available material used to supply a heavy demand (routine entertainment ~) (~ for gossip columnists) — **fodder** *vt*

fod·gel \'fä-jəl\ *adj* [origin unknown] (1724) *Scot* : BUXOM

foe \'fō\ *n* [ME *fo*, fr. OE *fāh, fr. fāh,* adj., hostile; akin to OHG *gifēh* hostile] (bef. 12c) **1** : one who has personal enmity for another **2 a** : an enemy in war **b** : ADVERSARY, OPPONENT **3** : one who opposes on principle (a ~ of needless expenditures) **4** : something prejudicial or injurious

foehn *or* **föhn** \'fə(r)n, 'fœn, 'fān\ *n* [G *Föhn*] (1861) : a warm dry wind blowing down the side of a mountain

foe·man \'fō-mən\ *n* (bef. 12c) : FOE 2

foe·tal, foe·tus *chiefly Brit var of* FETAL, FETUS

foe·tid *var of* FETID

foeto- *or* **foeti-** *chiefly Brit var of* FETO-

¹fog \'fóg, fäg\ *n* [prob. of Scand origin; akin to Dan *fog* spray, shower] (1544) **1 a** : vapor condensed to fine particles of water suspended in the lower atmosphere that differs from cloud only in being near the ground **b** : a fine spray or a foam for fire fighting **2** : a murky condition of the atmosphere or a substance causing it **3 a** : a state of confusion or bewilderment **b** : something that confuses or obscures (hid behind a ~ of rhetoric) **4** : cloudiness or partial opacity in a developed photographic image caused by chemical action or stray radiation — **fog·less** \-ləs\ *adj*

²fog *vb* **fogged; fog·ging** *vt* (1599) **1** : to cover, envelop, or suffuse with or as if with fog (~ the barns with pesticide) **2** : to make obscure or confusing (accusations which fogged the real issues) **3** : to make confused **4** : to produce fog on (as a photographic film) during development ~ *vi* **1** : to become covered or thick with fog **2 a** : to become blurred by a covering of fog or mist **b** : to become indistinct through exposure to light or radiation

fog·bound \-,baúnd, 'fäg-\ *adj* (ca. 1855) **1** : unable to move because of fog (~ ship) **2** : covered with or surrounded by fog (~ coast)

fog·bow \-,bō\ *n* (1831) : a nebulous arc or circle of white or yellowish light sometimes seen in fog

fog·gage \'fó-gij, 'fä-\ *n* [Sc, fr. ME (Sc) *fogage*, fr. AL *fogagium*, fr. ME *fogge* second growth of grass + ML *-agium -age*] (1786) *Scot* : a second growth of grass

fog·gy \'fó-gē, 'fä-\ *adj* **fog·gi·er; -est** (15c) **1 a** : filled or abounding with fog **b** : covered or made opaque by moisture or grime **2** : blurred or obscured as if by fog (hadn't the *foggiest* notion) — **fog·gi·ly** \'fó-gə-lē, 'fä-\ *adv* — **fog·gi·ness** \'fó-gē-nəs, 'fä-\ *n*

Foggy Bottom *n* [*Foggy Bottom*, district in Washington, D.C.] (1951) : the U.S. Department of State

fog·horn \'fóg-,hórn, 'fäg-\ *n* (1858) **1** : a horn (as on a ship) sounded in a fog to give warning **2** : a loud hoarse voice

fo·gy *also* **fo·gey** \'fō-gē\ *n, pl* **fogies** *also* **fogeys** [origin unknown] (1780) : a person with old-fashioned ideas — usu. used with *old* — **fo·gy·ish** \-gē-ish\ *adj* — **fo·gy·ism** \-gē-,i-zəm\ *n*

foi·ble \'fói-bəl\ *n* [obs. F (now *faible*), fr. obs. *foible* weak, fr. OF *feble* feeble] (ca. 1648) **1** : the part of a sword or foil blade between the middle and point **2** : a minor flaw or shortcoming in character or behavior : WEAKNESS *syn* see FAULT

foie gras \'fwä-'grä\ *n* [F, lit., fat liver] (1818) : the fatted liver of an animal and esp. of a goose usu. served as a pâté

¹foil \'fói(ə)l\ *vt* [ME, to trample, full cloth, fr. MF *fouler* — more at FULL] (14c) **1** *obs* : TRAMPLE **2 a** : to prevent from attaining an end : DEFEAT **b** : to bring to naught : THWART *syn* see FRUSTRATE

²foil *n* [ME, leaf, fr. MF *foille* (fr. L *folia*, pl. of *folium*) & *foil,* fr. L *folium* — more at BLADE] (14c) **1** : very thin sheet metal (aluminum ~) **2** : a thin piece of material (as metal) put under an inferior or paste stone to add color or brilliance **3** : someone or something that serves as a contrast to another (acted as a ~ for a comedian) **4 a** : an indentation between cusps in Gothic tracery **b** : one of several arcs that enclose a complex figure **5** : HYDROFOIL 1

\ə\ abut \ᵊ\ kitten, F table \ər\ further \a\ ash \ā\ ace \ä\ mop, mar \aú\ out \ch\ chin \e\ bet \ē\ easy \g\ go \i\ hit \ī\ ice \j\ job \ŋ\ sing \ō\ go \ò\ law \òi\ boy \th\ thin \t͟h\ the \ü\ loot \ú\ foot \y\ yet \zh\ vision \ä, k̲, ⁿ, œ, œ̄, ʊe, ᵫ, ᵊ\ *see* Guide to Pronunciation

³foil n (15c) **1** archaic : DEFEAT **2** archaic : the track or trail of an animal

⁴foil n [origin unknown] (1594) **1 a** : a light fencing sword having a usu. circular guard and a flexible blade of rectangular section tapering to a blunted point — compare ÉPÉE, SABER **2** : the art or sport of fencing with the foil — often used in pl.

⁵foil vt (1611) **1** : to back or cover with foil **2** : to enhance by contrast

foiled \'fȯi(ə)ld\ adj (1835) : ornamented with foils ⟨a ~ arch⟩

foils·man \'fȯi(ə)lz-mən\ n (1927) : one who fences with a foil

¹foin \'fȯin\ n [ME, fr. MF foin fork for spearing fish, fr. MF foisne] (14c) archaic : to thrust with a pointed weapon : LUNGE

²foin n (15c) archaic : a pass in fencing : LUNGE

foi·son \'fȯi-zᵊn\ n [ME foisoun, fr. MF foison, fr. L fusion-, fusio pouring, effusion — more at FUSION] (14c) **1** archaic : rich harvest **2** chiefly Scot : physical energy or strength **3** pl, obs : RESOURCES

foist \'fȯist\ vt [prob. fr. obs. D vuisten to take into one's hand, fr. MD vuysten, fr. vuyst fist; akin to OE fȳst fist] (ca. 1587) **1 a** : to introduce or insert surreptitiously or without warrant **b** : to force another to accept esp. by stealth or deceit **2** : to pass off as genuine or worthy ⟨~ costly and valueless products on the public —Jonathan Spivak⟩

fo·la·cin \'fō-lə-sən\ n [folic acid + -in] (1949) : FOLIC ACID

fo·late \'fō-ˌlāt\ n (1951) : FOLIC ACID

¹fold \'fōld\ n [ME, fr. OE falod; akin to OS faled enclosure] (bef. 12c) **1** : an enclosure for sheep **2 a** : a flock of sheep **b** : a group of people or institutions that share a common faith, belief, activity, or enthusiasm

²fold vt (bef. 12c) : to pen up or confine (as sheep) in a fold

³fold vb [ME, fr. OE fealdan; akin to OHG faldan to fold, Gk diplasios twofold] vt (bef. 12c) **1** : to lay one part over another part of ⟨~ a letter⟩ **2** : to reduce the length or bulk of by doubling over ⟨~ a tent⟩ **3** : to clasp together : ENTWINE ⟨~ the hands⟩ **4** : to clasp or enwrap closely : EMBRACE **5** : to bend (as a layer of rock) into folds **6 a** : to incorporate (a food ingredient) into a mixture by repeated gentle over-turnings without stirring or beating **b** : to incorporate closely ⟨7 a : to concede defeat by withdrawing (one's cards) from play (as in poker)⟩ **b** : to bring to an end ~ vi **1** : to become doubled or pleated **2** : to fail completely : COLLAPSE; esp : to go out of business **3** : to fold one's cards (as in poker) — **fold·able** \'fōl-də-bəl\ adj

⁴fold n (13c) **1** : a part doubled or laid over another part : PLEAT **2** : something that is folded together or that enfolds **3 a** : a bend or flexure produced in rock by forces operative after the depositing or consolidation of the rock **b** chiefly Brit : an undulation in the landscape **4** : a margin apparently formed by the doubling upon itself of a flat anatomical structure (as a membrane) **5** : a crease made by folding something (as a newspaper)

-fold \ˌfōld, 'fōld\ suffix [ME, fr. OE -feald; akin to OHG -falt -fold, L -plex, -plus, OE fealdan] **1** : multiplied by (a specified number) : times — in adjectives ⟨a sixfold increase⟩ and adverbs ⟨repay you tenfold⟩ **2** : having (so many) parts ⟨threefold aspect of the problem⟩

fold·a·way \'fōl-də-ˌwā\ adj (1948) : designed to be folded for storage or portability ⟨~ doors⟩ ⟨~ bed⟩ ⟨a ~ table⟩

fold·boat \'fōl(d)-ˌbōt\ n [trans. of G Faltboot] (1938) : a small collapsible canoe made of rubberized sailcloth stretched over a framework

fold·er \'fōl-dər\ n (1552) **1** : one that folds **2** : a folded printed circular **3** : a folded cover or large envelope for holding or filing loose papers

fol·de·rol \'fäl-də-ˌräl\ n [fol-de-rol, a nonsense refrain in songs] (1820) **1** : a useless ornament or accessory : TRIFLE **2** : NONSENSE

fold·ing \'fōl-diŋ\ adj (15c) : capable of being folded into a more compact shape ⟨~ chairs⟩ ⟨a ~ door⟩

folding money n (ca. 1930) : PAPER MONEY

fold·out \'fōl-ˌdau̇t\ n, often attrib (1950) : a folded leaf in a publication (as a book) that is larger in some dimension than the page ⟨a ~ map⟩

fo·li·a·ceous \ˌfō-lē-'ā-shəs\ adj [L foliaceus, fr. folium leaf + -aceus -aceous] (1658) : of, relating to, or resembling an ordinary green leaf as distinguished from a modified leaf (as a petal, bract, or scale)

fo·li·age \'fō-lē-ij also -lyij; ÷'fō-lij, ÷'fȯi-lij\ n [MF fuellage, fr. foille leaf — more at FOIL] (1598) **1** : a representation of leaves, flowers, and branches for architectural ornamentation **2** : the aggregate of leaves of one or more plants **3** : a cluster of leaves, flowers, and branches — **fo·liaged** \-lē-ijd also -lyijd; ÷'fō-lijd, ÷'fȯi-lijd\ adj
    usage The disyllabic pronunciation \'fō-lij\ is very common. Some commentators insist that foliage requires a trisyllabic pronunciation because of its spelling, but words of a similar pattern such as carriage and marriage do not fall under their prescription. The pronunciation \'fȯi-lij\ is disapproved because it suggests the transposition of the l and i in the spelling. It is not as common as \'fō-lij\ and may be associated with the nonstandard spelling foilage.

foliage plant n (1862) : a plant grown primarily for its decorative foliage

fo·li·ar \'fō-lē-ər\ adj [F foliaire, fr. L folium leaf + F -aire -ar] (ca. 1859) : of, relating to, or applied to leaves ⟨~ sprays⟩

fo·li·ate \'fō-lē-ət, -ˌāt\ adj [L foliatus leafy, fr. folium leaf — more at BLADE] (ca. 1658) **1** : shaped like a leaf ⟨a ~ sponge⟩ **2** : FOLIATED

fo·li·at·ed \-ˌā-təd\ adj (1650) **1** : composed of or separable into layers ⟨a ~ rock⟩ **2** : ornamented with foils or a leaf design

fo·li·a·tion \ˌfō-lē-'ā-shən\ n (ca. 1623) **1 a** : the process of forming into a leaf **b** : the state of being in leaf : VERNATION **2** : the numbering of the leaves of a manuscript or early printed book **3 a** : ornamentation with foliage **b** : a decoration resembling a leaf **4** : the enrichment of an opening by foils **5** : foliated texture

fo·lic acid \ˌfō-lik-\ n [L folium] (1941) : a crystalline vitamin C₁₉H₁₉N₇O₆ of the B complex that is used esp. in the treatment of nutritional anemias — called also pteroylglutamic acid

fo·lie à deux \fȯ-lē-ä-ˈdœ, ˌfä-lē-, ä-ˈdə(r)\ n [F, lit., double madness] (ca. 1892) : the presence of the same or similar delusional ideas in two persons closely associated with one another

¹fo·lio \'fō-lē-ˌō\ n, pl fo·li·os [ME, fr. L, abl. of folium] (1447) **1 a** : a leaf esp. of a manuscript or book **b** : a leaf number **c** : a page number **d** : an identifying reference in accounting used in posting **2 a** : a sheet of paper folded once **b** : a case or folder for loose papers **3 a** : the size of a piece of paper cut two from a sheet; also : paper or a page of this size **b** : a book printed on folio pages **c** : a book of the largest size **4** : a certain number of words taken as a unit or division in a document for purposes of measurement or reference

²folio vt (1858) : to put a serial number on each leaf or page of

fo·li·ose \'fō-lē-ˌōs\ adj [L foliosus leafy] (1758) : having a flat, thin, and usu. lobed thallus attached to the substratum ⟨~ lichens⟩ — compare CRUSTOSE, FRUTICOSE

¹folk \'fōk\ n, pl folk or folks [ME, fr. OE folc; akin to OHG folc people] (bef. 12c) **1** archaic : a group of kindred tribes forming a nation : PEOPLE **2** : the great proportion of the members of a people that determines the group character and that tends to preserve its characteristic form of civilization and its customs, arts and crafts, legends, traditions, and superstitions from generation to generation **3** pl : a certain kind, class, or group of people ⟨old ~s⟩ ⟨just plain ~⟩ ⟨country ~⟩ ⟨media ~⟩ **4** folks pl : people generally ⟨~s say⟩ **5** folks pl : the persons of one's own family; esp : PARENTS

²folk adj (bef. 12c) **1** : originating or traditional with the common people of a country or region and typically reflecting their lifestyle ⟨~ hero⟩ ⟨~ music⟩ **2** : of or relating to the common people or to the study of the common people ⟨~ sociology⟩

folk etymology n (1882) : the transformation of words so as to give them an apparent relationship to other better-known or familiar understood words (as in the change of Spanish cucaracha to English cockroach)

¹folk·ie also folky \'fō-kē\ n, pl folkies (1965) : a folk singer or instrumentalist

²folkie or folky adj (1965) : of or relating to folk music

folk·ish \'fō-kish\ adj (1938) : FOLKLIKE — **folk·ish·ness** n

folk·life \'fōk-ˌlīf\ n (1864) : the traditions, activities, skills, and products (as handicrafts) of a particular people or group

folk·like \'fō-ˌklīk\ adj (1939) : having a folk character

folk·lore \'fō-ˌklȯr, -ˌklȯr\ n (1846) **1** : traditional customs, tales, sayings, dances, or art forms preserved among a people **2** : a branch of knowledge that deals with folklore **3** : an often unsupported notion, story, or saying that is widely circulated — **folk·lor·ic** \-ˌklȯr-ik, -ˌklȯr-\ adj — **folk·lor·ish** \-ish\ adj — **folk·lor·ist** \-ist\ n — **folk·lor·is·tic** \ˌfō-ˌklȯr-'is-tik, -ˌklȯr-\ adj

folk mass n (1966) : a mass in which traditional liturgical music is replaced by folk music

folk medicine n (1878) : traditional medicine as practiced nonprofessionally esp. by people isolated from modern medical services and usu. involving the use of plant-derived remedies on an empirical basis

folk·moot \'fōk-ˌmüt\ or folk·mote \-ˌmōt\ n [alter. of OE folcmōt, folcgemōt, fr. folc people + mōt, gemōt meeting — more at MOOT] (bef. 12c) : a general assembly of the people (as of a shire) in early England

folk·sing·er \-ˌsiŋ-ər\ n (1884) : one who sings folk songs or sings in a style associated with folk songs — **folk·sing·ing** \-ˌsiŋ-iŋ\ n

folk song n (1847) : a traditional or composed song typically characterized by stanzaic form, refrain, and simplicity of melody

folksy \'fōk-sē\ adj folks·i·er; -est (1852) **1** : SOCIABLE, FRIENDLY **2** : informal, casual, or familiar in manner or style ⟨~ humor⟩ — **folks·i·ly** \-sə-lē\ adv — **folks·i·ness** \-sē-nəs\ n

folk·tale \'fōk-ˌtāl\ n (1852) : a characteristically anonymous, timeless, and placeless tale circulated orally among a people

folk·way \'fō-ˌkwā\ n (ca. 1906) : a mode of thinking, feeling, or acting common to a given group of people; esp : a traditional social custom

fol·li·cle \'fä-li-kəl\ n [NL folliculus, fr. L, dim. of follis bag — more at FOOL] (1646) **1 a** : a small anatomical cavity or deep narrow-mouthed depression **b** : a small lymph node **c** : a vesicle in the mammalian ovary that contains a developing egg surrounded by a covering of cells; esp : GRAAFIAN FOLLICLE **2 a** : a dry dehiscent one-celled many-seeded fruit (as of the milkweed) that has a single carpel and opens along one suture — **fol·lic·u·lar** \fə-'li-kyə-lər, fä-\ adj

follicle mite n (1925) : any of several minute mites (genus Demodex) parasitic in hair follicles

follicle–stimulating hormone n (ca. 1943) : a hormone produced by the anterior lobe of the pituitary gland that stimulates the growth of the ovum-containing follicles in the ovary and activates sperm-forming cells

fol·lic·u·li·tis \fə-ˌli-kyə-'lī-təs\ n [NL, fr. folliculus + -itis] (ca. 1860) : inflammation of one or more follicles esp. of the hair

¹fol·low \'fä-(ˌ)lō, -lə-(ˌw)\ vb [ME folwen, fr. OE folgian; akin to OHG folgēn to follow] vt (bef. 12c) **1** : to go, proceed, or come after ⟨~ed the guide⟩ **2 a** : to engage in as a calling or way of life : PURSUE ⟨wheat-growing is generally ~ed here⟩ **b** : to walk or proceed along ⟨~ a path⟩ **3 a** : to be or act in accordance with ⟨~ directions⟩ **b** : to accept as authority : OBEY ⟨~ed his conscience⟩ **4 a** : to pursue in an effort to overtake **b** : to seek to attain ⟨~ knowledge⟩ **5** : to come into existence or take place as a result or consequence of ⟨disaster ~ed the blunder⟩ **6 a** : to come or take place after in time, sequence, or order **b** : to cause to be followed ⟨~ed dinner with a liqueur⟩ **7** : to copy after : IMITATE **8 a** : to watch steadily ⟨~ed the flight of the ball⟩ **b** : to keep the mind on ⟨~ a speech⟩ **c** : to attend closely to : keep abreast of ⟨~ed his career with interest⟩ **d** : to understand the sense or logic of (as a line of thought) ~ vi **1** : to go or come after a person or thing in place, time, or sequence **2** : to result or occur as a consequence, effect, or inference — **as follows** : as comes next — used impersonally — **follow one's nose 1** : to go in a straight or obvious course **2** : to proceed without plan or reflection : obey one's instincts — **follow suit 1** : to play a card of the same suit as the card led **2** : to follow an example set
    syn FOLLOW, SUCCEED, ENSUE, SUPERVENE mean to come after something or someone. FOLLOW may apply to a coming after in time, position, or logical sequence ⟨speeches followed the dinner⟩. SUCCEED implies a coming after immediately in a sequence determined by natural order, inheritance, election, or laws of rank ⟨she succeeded her father as head of the business⟩. ENSUE commonly suggests a logical consequence or naturally expected development ⟨after the talk a general discussion ensued⟩. SUPERVENE suggests the following or beginning of something unforeseen or unpredictable ⟨supervening events brought unhappiness to him⟩. **syn** see in addition CHASE

²follow n (1870) **1** : the act or process of following **2** : forward spin given to a ball by striking it above center — compare DRAW, ENGLISH

fol·low·er \'fä-lə-wər\ n (bef. 12c) **1 a** : one in the service of another : RETAINER **b** : one that follows the opinions or teachings of another

c : one that imitates another **2** *archaic* : one that chases **3** : a sheet added to the first sheet of an indenture or other deed **4** : a machine part that receives motion from another part **5** : a spring-loaded plate at the bottom of a firearm's magazine that angles cartridges for proper insertion into the chamber **6** : FAN, DEVOTEE

syn FOLLOWER, ADHERENT, DISCIPLE, PARTISAN mean one who gives full loyalty and support to another. FOLLOWER may apply to people who attach themselves either to the person or beliefs of another ⟨an evangelist and his *followers*⟩. ADHERENT suggests a close and persistent attachment ⟨*adherents* to Marxism⟩. DISCIPLE implies a devoted allegiance to the teachings of one chosen as a master ⟨*disciples* of Gandhi⟩. PARTISAN suggests a zealous often prejudiced attachment ⟨*partisans* of the President⟩.

fol·low·er·ship \-,ship\ *n* (ca. 1928) **1** : FOLLOWING **2** : the capacity or willingness to follow a leader

¹fol·low·ing \'fä-lə-wiŋ\ *adj* (15c) **1** : being next in order or time ⟨the ~ day⟩ **2** : listed or shown next ⟨trains will leave at the ~ times⟩

²following *n* (15c) : a group of followers, adherents, or partisans

³following *prep* (ca. 1926) : SUBSEQUENT TO ⟨~ the lecture tea was served⟩

fol·low–on \'fä-lə-,wȯn, -,wän\ *adj* (1960) : being or relating to something that follows as a natural or logical consequence, development, or progression — **follow–on** *n*

follow out *vt* (1762) **1** : to follow to the end or to a conclusion **2** : CARRY OUT, EXECUTE ⟨*followed out* their orders⟩

follow shot *n* (ca. 1909) **1** : a shot in billiards or pool made by striking the cue ball above its center to cause it to continue forward after striking the object ball **2** : a camera shot in which the camera follows the movement of the subject

fol·low–through \'fä-lō-,thrü, ,fä-lō-', -lə-\ *n* (ca. 1899) **1** : the act or an instance of following through **2** : the part of the stroke following the striking of a ball

follow through *vi* (1895) **1** : to continue a stroke or motion to the end of its arc **2** : to press on in an activity or process esp. to a conclusion

¹fol·low–up \'fä-lə-,wəp\ *n* (1916) **1 a** : the act or an instance of following up **b** : something that follows up **2** : maintenance of contact with or reexamination of a person (as a patient) esp. following treatment **3** : a news story presenting new information on a story published earlier

²follow–up *adj* (1912) **1** : of, relating to, or being something that follows up ⟨~ action by the police —Frank Faulkner⟩ **2** : done, conducted, or administered in the course of following up persons ⟨~ care for discharged hospital patients⟩

follow up *vt* (1792) **1** : to follow with something similar, related, or supplementary ⟨*following up* his convictions with action —G. P. Merrill⟩ **2** : to maintain contact with (a person) so as to monitor the effects of earlier activities or treatments **3** : to pursue in an effort to take further action ⟨the police *follow up* leads⟩ ~ *vi* : to take appropriate action ⟨*follow up* on complaints⟩

fol·ly \'fä-lē\ *n, pl* **follies** [ME *folie*, fr. OF, fr. *fol* fool] (13c) **1** : lack of good sense or normal prudence and foresight **2 a** : criminally or tragically foolish actions or conduct **b** *obs* : EVIL, WICKEDNESS; *esp* : lewd behavior **3** : a foolish act or idea **4** : an excessively costly or unprofitable undertaking **5** : an often extravagant picturesque building erected to suit a fanciful taste

Fol·som \'fōl-səm\ *adj* [*Folsom*, town in New Mexico] (1928) : of, relating to, or characteristic of a prehistoric culture of No. America on the east side of the Rocky Mountains that is characterized by flint projectile points having a concave base with side projections and a longitudinal groove on each face

fo·ment \'fō-,ment, fō-'\ *vt* [ME *fomenten* to apply a warm substance to, fr. LL *fomentare*, fr. L *fomentum* compress, fr. *fovēre* to heat, soothe; akin to Lith *degti* to burn, Skt *dahati* it burns] (ca. 1613) **1** : to promote the growth or development of : ROUSE, INCITE ⟨~ a rebellion⟩ **syn** see INCITE — **fo·ment·er** *n*

fo·men·ta·tion \,fō-mən-'tā-shən, -,men-\ *n* (14c) **1 a** : the application of hot moist substances to the body to ease pain **b** : the material so applied **2** : the act of fomenting : INSTIGATION

¹fond \'fänd\ *adj* [ME, fr. *fonne* fool] (14c) **1** : FOOLISH, SILLY ⟨~ pride⟩ **2 a** : prizing highly : DESIROUS ⟨~ of praise⟩ **b** : having an affection or liking — used with *of* ⟨~ of music⟩ **3 a** : foolishly tender : INDULGENT ⟨a ~ mother⟩ **b** : AFFECTIONATE, LOVING ⟨absence makes the heart grow ~er⟩ **4** : cherished with great affection : doted on ⟨our ~est hopes⟩

²fond *vi* (1530) *obs* : to lavish affection : DOTE

³fond \'fōⁿ\ *n, pl* **fonds** \'fōⁿ(z)\ [F, fr. L *fundus* bottom, piece of property — more at BOTTOM] (1664) **1** : BACKGROUND, BASIS **2** *obs* : FUND

fon·dant \'fän-dənt\ *n* [F, fr. prp. of *fondre* to melt — more at FOUND] (1877) **1** : a soft creamy preparation of sugar, water, and flavorings that is used as a basis for candies or icings **2** : a candy consisting chiefly of fondant

fon·dle \'fän-d³l\ *vb* **fon·dled; fon·dling** \-(d)liŋ, -d³l-iŋ\ [freq. of obs. *fond* to fondle] *vt* (1694) **1** : to handle tenderly, lovingly, or lingeringly : CARESS ~ *vi* : to show affection or desire by caressing — **fon·dler** \-(d)lər, -d³l-ər\ *n*

fond·ly \'fän-(d)lē\ *adv* (14c) **1** *archaic* : in a foolish manner : FOOLISHLY **2** : in a fond manner : AFFECTIONATELY **3** : in a willingly credulous manner ⟨it would stun, I ~ hoped, the reader —Annie Dillard⟩

fond·ness \'fän(d)-nəs\ *n* (14c) **1** *obs* : FOOLISHNESS, FOLLY **2** : tender affection **3** : APPETITE, RELISH ⟨had a ~ for argument⟩

fon·due *also* **fon·du** \fän-'dü, -'dyü, 'fän-,\ *n* [F *fondue*, fr. fem. of *fondu*, pp. of *fondre* to melt] (1878) **1 a** (1) : a preparation of melted cheese (as Swiss cheese and Gruyère) usu. flavored with white wine and kirsch (2) : a dish that consists of small pieces of food (as meat or fruit) cooked in or dipped into a hot liquid ⟨beef ~⟩ ⟨chocolate ~⟩ **b** : a chafing dish in which fondue is made **2** : a dish similar to a soufflé usu. made with cheese and bread crumbs

F₁ layer \'ef-'wən-\ *n* (1933) : the lower of the two layers into which the F region of the ionosphere splits in the daytime that occurs at varying heights from about 80 to 120 miles (130 to 200 kilometers) above the earth's surface

¹font \'fänt\ *n* [ME, fr. OE, fr. LL *font-, fons*, fr. L, fountain] (bef. 12c) **1 a** : a receptacle for baptismal water **b** : a receptacle for holy water

c : a receptacle for various liquids **2** : SOURCE, FOUNTAIN ⟨a ~ of information⟩ — **font·al** \'fän-t³l\ *adj*

²font *n* [MF *fonte* act of founding, fr. (assumed) VL *fundita*, fem. of *funditus*, pp. of L *fundere* to found, pour — more at FOUND] (ca. 1688) : an assortment or set of type all of one size and style

fon·ta·nel *or* **fon·ta·nelle** \,fän-t³n-'el, 'fän-t³n-,\ *n* [ME *fontinelle* a bodily hollow or pit, fr. MF *fontenele*, dim. of *fontaine* fountain] (1741) : a membrane-covered opening in bone or between bones; *specif* : any of the spaces closed by membranous structures between the uncompleted angles of the parietal bones and the neighboring bones of a fetal or young skull

fon·ti·na \fän-'tē-nə\ *n, often cap* [It] (1938) : a cheese that is semisoft to hard in texture and mild to medium sharp in flavor

food \'füd\ *n, often attrib* [ME *fode*, fr. OE *fōda*; akin to OHG *fuotar* food, fodder, L *panis* bread, *pascere* to feed] (bef. 12c) **1 a** : material consisting essentially of protein, carbohydrate, and fat used in the body of an organism to sustain growth, repair, and vital processes and to furnish energy; *also* : such food together with supplementary substances (as minerals, vitamins, and condiments) **b** : inorganic substances absorbed by plants in gaseous form or in water solution **2** : nutriment in solid form **3** : something that nourishes, sustains, or supplies ⟨~ for thought⟩ — **food·less** \-ləs\ *adj* — **food·less·ness** *n*

food chain *n* (1926) : an arrangement of the organisms of an ecological community according to the order of predation in which each uses the next usu. lower member as a food source

food·ie \'fü-dē\ *n* (1982) : a person having an avid interest in the latest food fads

foo dog \'fü-\ *n, often cap* F [Chin (Beijing) *fó* Buddha; fr. the use of such figures in ceramic or stone as guardians of Buddhist temples] (1953) : a mythical lion-dog used as a decorative motif in Far Eastern art

food poisoning *n* (1887) : an acute gastrointestinal disorder caused by bacteria or their toxic products or by chemical residues in food

food processor *n* (1974) : an electric kitchen appliance with a set of interchangeable blades revolving inside a container

food pyramid *n* (1949) : an ecological hierarchy of food relationships in which a chief predator is at the top, each level preys on the next lower level, and usu. green plants are at the bottom

food stamp *n* (1940) : a government-issued coupon that is sold or given to low-income persons and is redeemable for food

food·stuff \'füd-,stəf\ *n* (1872) : a substance with food value; *specif* : the raw material of food before or after processing

food vacuole *n* (ca. 1889) : a membrane-bound vacuole (as in an amoeba) in which ingested food is digested — see AMOEBA illustration

food·ways \'füd-,wāz\ *n pl* (1946) : the eating habits and culinary practices of a people, region, or historical period

food web *n* (1949) : the totality of interacting food chains in an ecological community

foo·fa·raw \'fü-fə-,rȯ\ *n* [origin unknown] (1934) **1** : frills and flashy finery **2** : a disturbance or to-do over a trifle : FUSS

¹fool \'fül\ *n* [ME, fr. OF *fol*, fr. LL *follis*, fr. L, bellows, bag; akin to OHG *bolla* blister, *balg* bag — more at BELLY] (13c) **1** : a person lacking in judgment or prudence **2 a** : a retainer formerly kept in great households to provide casual entertainment and commonly dressed in motley with cap, bells, and bauble **b** : one who is victimized or made to appear foolish : DUPE **3 a** : a harmlessly deranged person or one lacking in common powers of understanding **b** : one with a marked propensity or fondness for something ⟨a dancing ~⟩ ⟨a ~ for candy⟩ **4** : a cold dessert of pureed fruit mixed with whipped cream or custard

²fool *adj* (13c) : FOOLISH, SILLY ⟨barking its ~ head off⟩

³fool *vi* (1593) **1 a** : to behave foolishly ⟨why old men ~ and children calculate —Shak.⟩ — often used with *around* **b** : to meddle, tamper, or experiment esp. thoughtlessly or ignorantly ⟨don't ~ with that gun⟩ — often used with *around* **2 a** : to play or improvise a comic role **b** : to speak in jest : JOKE ⟨I was only ~ing⟩ **3** : to contend or fight without serious intent or with less than full strength : TOY ⟨a dangerous man to ~ with⟩ ~ *vt* **1** : to make a fool of : DECEIVE **2** *obs* : INFATUATE **3** : to spend on trifles or without advantage : FRITTER — used with *away*

fool around *vi* (1837) **1** : to spend time idly, aimlessly, or frivolously **2** : to engage in casual sexual activity

fool·ery \'fül-rē, 'fü-lə-\ *n, pl* **-er·ies** (1552) **1** : a foolish act, utterance, or belief **2** : foolish behavior

fool·har·dy \'fül-,här-dē\ *adj* (13c) : foolishly adventurous and bold : RASH **syn** see ADVENTUROUS — **fool·har·di·ly** \-,här-d³l-ē\ *adv* — **fool·har·di·ness** \-,här-dē-nəs\ *n*

fool·ish \'fü-lish\ *adj* (13c) **1** : lacking in sense, judgment, or discretion **2 a** : ABSURD, RIDICULOUS **b** : marked by a loss of composure : NONPLUSSED, ABASHED **3** : INSIGNIFICANT, TRIFLING, HUMBLE **syn** see SIMPLE — **fool·ish·ly** *adv*

fool·ish·ness *n* (15c) **1** : foolish behavior : FOLLY **2** : a foolish act or idea

fool·proof \'fül-,prüf\ *adj* (1902) : so simple, plain, or reliable as to leave no opportunity for error, misuse, or failure ⟨a ~ plan⟩

fools·cap *also* **fool's cap** \'fül-,skap\ *n* (1632) **1** : a cap or hood usu. with bells worn by jesters **2** : a conical cap for slow or lazy students **3** *usu* *foolscap* [fr. the watermark of a foolscap formerly applied to such paper] : a size of paper formerly standard in Great Britain; *broadly* : a piece of writing paper

fool's gold *n* (1872) : PYRITE; *broadly* : any of various pyritic minerals resembling gold

fool's paradise *n* (15c) : a state of delusory happiness

foolscap 1

\ə\ abut \³\ kitten, F table \ər\ further \a\ ash \ā\ ace \ä\ mop, mar \au̇\ out \ch\ chin \e\ bet \ē\ easy \g\ go \i\ hit \ī\ ice \j\ job \ŋ\ sing \ō\ go \ȯ\ law \ȯi\ boy \th\ thin \t͟h\ the \ü\ loot \u̇\ foot \y\ yet \zh\ vision \à, k̲, ⁿ, œ, œ̄, ᵫ, ūᷠ, ᵊ\ see Guide to Pronunciation

fool's parsley n (1755) : a poisonous European weed (*Aethusa cynapium*) of the carrot family that resembles parsley and is naturalized in the northern U.S. and southern Canada

¹foot \'fut\ n, pl **feet** \'fēt\ also **foot** [ME *fot*, fr. OE *fōt*; akin to OHG *fuot* foot, L *ped-*, *pes*, Gk *pod-*, *pous*] (bef. 12c) **1** : the terminal part of the vertebrate leg upon which an individual stands **2** : an invertebrate organ of locomotion or attachment; *esp* : a ventral muscular surface or process of a mollusk — see CLAM illustration **3** : any of various units of length based on the length of the human foot; *esp* : a unit equal to ¹/₃ yard and comprising 12 inches — pl. *foot* used between a number and a noun ⟨a 10-*foot* pole⟩; pl. *feet* or *foot* used between a number and an adjective ⟨6 *feet* tall⟩; see WEIGHT table **4** : the basic unit of verse meter consisting of any of various fixed combinations or groups of stressed and unstressed or long and short syllables **5 a** : motion or power of walking or running : STEP ⟨fleet of ~⟩ **b** : SPEED, SWIFTNESS ⟨showed early ~⟩ **6** : something resembling a foot in position or use: as **a** : the lower end of the leg of a chair or table **b** (1) : the basal portion of the sporogonium in mosses (2) : a specialized outgrowth by which the embryonic sporophyte of many ferns and related plants and some seed plants absorbs nourishment from the gametophyte **c** : a piece on a sewing machine that presses the cloth against the feed **7** *foot pl*, *chiefly Brit* : INFANTRY **8** : the lower edge (as of a sail) **9** : the lowest part : BOTTOM ⟨the ~ of the hill⟩ **10 a** : the end that is lower or opposite the head ⟨the ~ of the bed⟩ **b** : the part (as of a stocking) that covers the foot **11 foots** *pl but sing or pl in constr* : material deposited esp. in aging or refining : DREGS **12 foots** *pl* : FOOTLIGHTS — **at one's feet** : under one's spell or influence — **foot in the door** : the initial step toward a goal — **off one's feet** : in a sitting or lying position — **on foot** : by walking or running ⟨tour the campus *on foot*⟩ — **on one's feet 1** : in a standing position **2** : in an established position or state **3** : in a recovered condition (as from illness) ⟨back *on my feet*⟩ **4** : in an extemporaneous manner ⟨while in action ⟨good debaters can think *on their feet*⟩ — **to one's feet** : to a standing position ⟨brought the crowd *to its feet*⟩

²foot vi (15c) **1** : DANCE **2** : to go on foot **3** *of a sailboat* : to make speed : MOVE ~ vt **1 a** : to perform the movements of (a dance) **b** : to walk, run, or dance on, over, or through **2** *archaic* **a** : KICK **b** : REJECT **3** *archaic* : ESTABLISH **4 a** : to add up **b** : to pay or stand credit for ⟨~ the bill⟩ **5** : to make or renew the foot of (as a stocking)

foot·age \'fu-tij\ n (1892) : length or quantity expressed in feet: as **a** : BOARD FEET **b** : the total number of running feet of motion-picture film used (as for a scene or subject); *also* : the material contained on such footage

foot–and–mouth disease n (1862) : an acute contagious febrile virus disease esp. of cloven-footed animals marked by ulcerating vesicles in the mouth, about the hooves, and on the udder and teats — called also *foot-and-mouth*, *hoof-and-mouth disease*

foot·ball \'fut-,bol\ n (15c) **1** : any of several games played between two teams on a rectangular field having two goalposts at each end and whose object is to get the ball over a goal line or between goalposts by running, passing, or kicking: as **a** *Brit* : SOCCER **b** *Brit* : RUGBY **c** : an American game played between two teams of 11 players each in which the ball is in possession of one side at a time and is advanced by running or passing **d** *Austral* : AUSTRALIAN RULES FOOTBALL **e** *Canad* : CANADIAN FOOTBALL **2 a** : an inflated oval ball used in the game of football **b** *Brit* : a soccer ball **3** : something treated roughly esp. as the subject of a prolonged dispute ⟨the issue became a political ~ in Congress⟩ — **foot·ball·er** \-,bo-lər\ n

foot·bath \'fut-,bath, -,bàth\ n (1599) : a bath (as at the entrance to an indoor swimming pool) for cleansing, warming, or disinfecting the feet

foot·board \'fut-,bōrd, -,bȯrd\ n (1766) **1** : a narrow platform on which to stand or brace the feet **2** : a board forming the foot of a bed

foot·boy \'fut-,boi\ n (1590) : a serving boy : PAGE, ATTENDANT

foot·bridge \'fut-,brij\ n (14c) : a bridge for pedestrians

foot–can·dle \-'kan-d²l\ n (1906) : a unit of illuminance on a surface that is everywhere one foot from a uniform point source of light of one candle and equal to one lumen per square foot

foot·cloth \-,klȯth\ n (14c) **1** *archaic* : an ornamental cloth draped over the back of a horse to reach the ground on each side **2** : CARPET

foot·drag·ger \-,dra-gər\ n (1957) : one who engages in foot-dragging

foot–drag·ging \-,dra-giŋ\ n (1952) : failure to act with the necessary promptness or vigor

foot·ed \'fu-təd\ adj (14c) : having a foot or feet esp. of a specified kind or number — often used in combination ⟨a four-*footed* animal⟩

foot·er \'fu-tər\ n (1608) *archaic* : PEDESTRIAN

-foot·er \'fu-tər\ n comb form : one that is a specified number of feet in height, length, or breadth ⟨a six-*footer*⟩

foot·fall \'fut-,fȯl\ n (1610) : the sound of a footstep

foot fault n (1886) : an infraction of the service rules (as in tennis, racquetball, or volleyball) that results from illegal placement of the server's feet — **foot·fault** \'fut-,fȯlt\ vi

foot·gear \'fut-,gir\ n (1837) : FOOTWEAR

foot·hill \-,hil\ n (1850) **1** : a hill at the foot of higher hills **2** *pl* : a hilly region at the base of a mountain range

foot·hold \-,hōld\ n (1625) **1** : a hold for the feet : FOOTING **2** : a position usable as a base for further advance

foot·ing \'fu-tiŋ\ n (14c) **1** : a stable position or placing of the feet **2** : a surface or its condition with respect to one walking or running on it; *esp* : the condition of a racetrack **3** : the act of moving on foot : STEP, TREAD **4 a** : a place or space for standing : FOOTHOLD **b** : established position : STATUS; *esp* : position or rank in relation to others ⟨they all started off on an equal ~⟩ **5** : BASIS **6** : terms of social intercourse **7** : an enlargement at the lower end of a foundation wall, pier, or column to distribute the load **8** : the sum of a column of figures

foot·lam·bert \'fut-,lam-bərt\ n (1925) : a unit of luminance equal to the luminance of a perfectly diffusing surface that emits or reflects one lumen per square foot

foo·tle \'fü-t²l\ vi **foo·tled; foo·tling** \-t²l-iŋ, 'füt-liŋ\ [alter. of *footer* (to footle)] (1892) **1** : to talk or act foolishly : TRIFLE, FOOL — **footle** n — **foo·tler** \-t²l-ər, 'füt-lər\ n

foot·less \'fut-ləs\ adj (14c) **1 a** : having no feet **b** : lacking foundation : UNSUBSTANTIAL **2** : STUPID, INEPT — **foot·less·ly** adv — **foot·less·ness** n

foot·lights \-,līts\ n pl (ca. 1839) **1** : a row of lights set across the front of a stage floor **2** : the stage as a profession

foo·tling \'fü-t²l-iŋ, 'füt-liŋ\ adj [*footle*] (ca. 1897) **1** : lacking judgment or ability : INEPT ⟨~ amateurs who understand nothing —E. R. Bentley⟩ **2** : lacking use or value : TRIVIAL

foot·lock·er \'fut-,lä-kər\ n (ca. 1942) : a small trunk designed to be placed at the foot of a bed (as in a barracks)

foot·loose \-,lüs\ adj (1873) : having no ties : free to move about

foot·man \-mən\ n (14c) **1 a** *archaic* : a traveler on foot : PEDESTRIAN **b** : INFANTRYMAN **2 a** : a servant in livery formerly attending a rider or required to run in front of his master's carriage **b** : a servant who serves at table, tends the door, and runs errands

foot·mark \-,märk\ n (1826) : FOOTPRINT

¹foot·note \-,nōt\ n (1822) **1** : a note of reference, explanation, or comment usu. placed below the text on a printed page **2** : something that is subordinately related to a larger event or work : COMMENTARY ⟨that biography is an illuminating ~ to our times⟩

²footnote vt (1864) : to furnish with a footnote : ANNOTATE

foot·pace \'fut-,pās\ n (1538) **1** : a walking pace **2** : PLATFORM, DAIS

¹foot·pad \-,pad\ n [*foot* + *pad* (highwayman)] (1683) : one who robs a pedestrian

²footpad n [*foot* + ¹*pad*] (1966) : a flattish foot on the leg of a spacecraft for distributing weight to minimize sinking into a surface

foot·path \'fut-,path, -,pàth\ n (1526) : a narrow path for pedestrians

foot–pound \-'paùnd\ n, pl **foot–pounds** (1850) : a unit of work equal to the work done by a force of one pound acting through a distance of one foot in the direction of the force

foot–pound–second adj (1892) : being or relating to a system of units based upon the foot as the unit of length, the pound as the unit of weight and the second as the unit of time — abbr. *fps*

foot·print \'fut-,print\ n (1552) **1** : an impression of the foot on a surface **2** : the area on a surface covered by something ⟨a tire with a wide ~⟩ ⟨the ~ of a laser beam on the surface of a planet⟩

foot·race \-,rās\ n (1663) : a race run by humans on foot

foot·rest \-,rest\ n (1861) : a support for the feet

foot·rope \-,rōp\ n (1772) **1** : the part of a boltrope sewed to the lower edge of a sail **2** : a rope rigged below a yard for men to stand on

foot rot n (1807) **1** : a progressive inflammation of the feet of sheep or cattle that is associated with bacterial infection **2** : a plant disease marked by rot of the stem near the ground

foot·sie or **foot·sy** \'fut-sē\ n [dim. of ¹*foot*] (1944) **1** : a furtive flirtatious caressing with the feet (as under a table) **2** : a usu. surreptitious cooperation or negotiation with someone supposed hostile to one's own interests — usu. used with *play*

foot·slog \'fut-,släg\ vi (1899) : to march or tramp through mud — **foot·slog·ger** n

foot soldier n (1622) : INFANTRYMAN

foot·sore \'fut-,sōr, -,sȯr\ adj (1719) : having sore or tender feet (as from much walking) — **foot·sore·ness** n

foot·step \-,step\ n (13c) **1** : the mark of the foot : TRACK **2 a** : TREAD **b** : distance covered by a step : PACE **3** : a step on which to ascend or descend **4** : a way of life, conduct, or action ⟨followed in his father's ~s⟩

foot·stone \-,stōn\ n (1724) : a stone placed at the foot of a grave

foot·stool \-,stül\ n (1530) : a low stool used to support the feet

foot·wall \-,wȯl\ n (1860) **1** : the lower underlying wall of a vein, ore deposit, or coal seam in a mine **2** : the lower wall of an inclined fault

foot·way \-,wā\ n (15c) : a narrow way or path for pedestrians

foot·wear \-,war, -,wer\ n (1881) : wearing apparel (as shoes or boots) for the feet

foot·work \-,wərk\ n (1895) **1** : the management of the feet (as in boxing); *also* : the work done with them **2** : the activity of moving from place to place ⟨the investigation entailed a lot of ~⟩ **3** : active and adroit maneuvering to achieve an end ⟨fancy political ~⟩

¹foo·zle \'fü-zəl\ n (1890) : an act of foozling; *esp* : a bungling golf stroke

²foozle vt **foo·zled; foo·zling** \'füz-liŋ, 'fü-zə-\ [perh. fr. G dial. *fuseln* to work carelessly] (1892) : to manage or play awkwardly : BUNGLE

¹fop \'fäp\ n [ME; akin to ME *fobben* to deceive, MHG *voppen*] (15c) **1** *obs* : a foolish or silly person **2** : a man who is devoted to or vain about his appearance or dress : COXCOMB, DANDY

²fop vt **fopped; fop·ping** (1602) *obs* : FOOL, DUPE

fop·pery \'fä-p(ə-)rē\ n, pl **-per·ies** (1546) **1** : foolish character or action : FOLLY **2** : the behavior or dress of a fop

fop·pish \'fä-pish\ adj (1599) **1** *obs* : FOOLISH, SILLY **2 a** : characteristic of a fop ⟨a ~ dressing gown⟩ **b** : behaving or dressing in the manner of a fop — **fop·pish·ly** adv — **fop·pish·ness** n

¹for \fər, (')fȯr, *Southern also* (')fär\ prep [ME, fr. OE; akin to L *per* through, *prae* before, *pro* before, for, ahead, Gk *pro*, OE *faran* to go — more at FARE] (bef. 12c) **1 a** — used as a function word to indicate purpose ⟨a grant ~ studying medicine⟩ **b** — used as a function word to indicate an intended goal ⟨left ~ home⟩ ⟨acted ~ the best⟩ **c** — used as a function word to indicate the object or recipient of a perception, desire, or activity ⟨now ~ a good rest⟩ ⟨run ~ your life⟩ ⟨an eye ~ a bargain⟩ **2** : as being or constituting ⟨taken ~ a fool⟩ ⟨eggs ~ breakfast⟩ **b** — used as a function word to indicate an actual or implied enumeration or selection ⟨~ one thing, the price is too high⟩ **3** : because of ⟨can't sleep ~ the heat⟩ **4** — used as a function word to indicate suitability or fitness ⟨it is not ~ you to choose⟩ ⟨ready ~ action⟩ **5 a** : in place of ⟨go to the store ~ me⟩ **b** (1) : on behalf of : REPRESENTING ⟨speaks ~ the court⟩ (2) : in favor of ⟨all ~ the plan⟩ **6** : in spite of — usu. used with *all* ⟨~ all his large size, he moves gracefully⟩ **7** : with respect to : CONCERNING ⟨a stickler ~ detail⟩ ⟨heavy ~ its size⟩ **8 a** — used as a function word to indicate equivalence in exchange ⟨$10 ~ a hat⟩, equality in number or quantity ⟨point ~ point⟩, or correspondence or correlation ⟨~ every one that works, you'll find five that don't⟩ **b** — used as a function word to indicate number of attempts ⟨0 ~ 4⟩ **9** — used as a function word to indicate duration of time or extent of space ⟨gone ~ two days⟩ **10** : in honor of : AFTER ⟨named ~ her grandmother⟩

²for conj (12c) : for the reason that : on this ground : BECAUSE

for- prefix [ME, fr. OE; akin to OHG *far-* for-, OE *for*] **1** : so as to involve prohibition, exclusion, omission, failure, neglect, or refusal

⟨*forbid*⟩ **2** : destructively or detrimentally ⟨*for*do⟩ **3** : completely : excessively : to exhaustion : to pieces ⟨*for*spent⟩

fora *pl of* FORUM

¹for·age \'fòr-ij, 'fär-\ *n* [ME, fr. OF, fr. *forre* fodder, of Gmc origin; akin to OHG *fuotar* food, fodder — more at FOOD] (14c) **1** : food for animals esp. when taken by browsing or grazing **2** ⟨*forage*⟩ : the act of foraging : search for provisions

²forage *vb* **for·aged; for·ag·ing** *vt* (15c) **1** : to strip of provisions : collect forage from **2** : to secure by foraging ⟨*foraged* a chicken for the feast⟩ ~ *vi* **1** : to wander in search of forage or food **2** : to secure forage (as for horses) by stripping the country **3** : RAVAGE, RAID **4** : to make a search : RUMMAGE — **for·ag·er** *n*

fo·ram \'fòr-əm, 'fòr-\ *n* (1927) : FORAMINIFER

fo·ra·men \fə-'rā-mən\ *n, pl* **fo·ram·i·na** \-'ra-mə-nə\ *or* **fo·ra·mens** \-'rā-mənz\ [L *foramin-, foramen,* fr. *forare* to bore — more at BORE] (1671) : a small opening, perforation, or orifice : FENESTRA — **fo·ram·i·nal** \fə-'ra-mə-nᵊl\ *or* **fo·ram·i·nous** \-mə-nəs\ *adj*

fo·ra·men mag·num \fə-,rā-mən-'mag-nəm\ *n* [NL, lit., large opening] (1860) : the opening in the skull through which the spinal cord passes to become the medulla oblongata

foramen ova·le \-ō-'va-lē, -'vä-, -'vā-\ *n* [NL, lit., oval opening] (ca. 1860) : an opening in the septum between the two atria of the heart that is normally present only in the fetus

for·a·min·i·fer \,fòr-ə-'mi-nə-fər, ,fär-\ *n* (ca. 1842) : any of an order (Foraminifera) of large chiefly marine rhizopod protozoans usu. having calcareous shells that often are perforated with minute holes for protrusion of slender pseudopodia and form the bulk of chalk and nummulitic limestone — **fo·ra·mi·nif·er·al** \fə-,ra-mə-'ni-f(ə-)rəl, ,fòr-ə-mə-'ni-, ,fär-\ *adj*

fo·ra·mi·nif·era \fə-,ra-mə-'ni-f(ə-)rə; ,fòr-ə-mə-'ni-, ,fär-\ *n pl* [NL, fr. L *foramin-, foramen* + *-fera*, neut. pl. of *-fer* -fer] (ca. 1836) : organisms that are foraminifers

fo·ra·min·i·fer·an \-f(ə-)rən\ *n* (1920) : FORAMINIFER

for·as·much as \'fòr-əz-,mə-chəz\ *conj* (13c) : in view of the fact that

¹for·ay \'fòr-,ā, 'fòr-, 'fär- *also* fò-'rā *or* fə-\ *vb* [ME *forrayen,* fr. MF *forrer,* fr. *forre* fodder — more at FORAGE] *vt* (14c) *archaic* : to ravage in search of spoils : PILLAGE ~ *vi* : to make a raid or brief invasion ⟨~ed into enemy territory⟩ — **for·ay·er** *n*

²foray *n* (14c) **1** : a sudden or irregular invasion or attack for war or spoils : RAID **2** : a brief excursion or attempt esp. outside one's accustomed sphere ⟨~ into nonfiction⟩

forb \'fòrb\ *n* [Gk *phorbē* fodder, food, fr. *pherbein* to graze] (1924) : an herb other than grass

¹for·bear \fòr-'bar, fər-, -'ber\ *vb* **-bore** \-'bōr, -'bòr\; **-borne** \-'bōrn, -'bòrn\; **-bear·ing** [ME *forberen,* fr. OE *forberan* to endure, do without, fr. *for-* + *beran* to bear] *vt* (bef. 12c) **1** *obs* : to do without **2** : to hold oneself back from esp. with an effort **3** *obs* : to leave alone : SHUN ⟨~ his presence —Shak.⟩ ~ *vi* **1** : HOLD BACK, ABSTAIN ⟨can write with ease what I ~ to read —Flannery O'Connor⟩ **2** : to control oneself when provoked : be patient — **for·bear·er** *n*

²forbear *var of* FOREBEAR

for·bear·ance \fòr-'bar-ən(t)s, fər-, -'ber-\ *n* (1576) **1** : a refraining from the enforcement of something (as a debt, right, or obligation) that is due **2** : the act of forbearing : PATIENCE **3** : the quality of being forbearing : LENIENCY

¹for·bid \fər-'bid, fòr-\ *vt* **-bade** \-'bad, -'bād\ *also* **-bad** \-'bad\; **-bidden** \-'bi-dᵊn\; **-bid·ding** [ME *forbidden,* fr. OE *forbēodan,* fr. *for-* + *bēodan* to bid — more at BID] (bef. 12c) **1** : to proscribe from or as if from the position of one in authority : command against ⟨the law ~s stores to sell liquor to minors⟩ ⟨her mother ~s her to go⟩ **2** : to hinder or prevent as if by an effectual command ⟨space ~s further treatment here⟩ — **for·bid·der** *n*

syn FORBID, PROHIBIT, INTERDICT, INHIBIT mean to debar one from doing something or to order that something not be done. FORBID implies that the order is from one in authority and that obedience is expected ⟨smoking is *forbidden* in the building⟩. PROHIBIT suggests the issuing of laws, statutes, or regulations ⟨*prohibited* the sale of liquor⟩. INTERDICT implies prohibition by civil or ecclesiastical authority usu. for a given time or a declared purpose ⟨practices *interdicted* by the church⟩. INHIBIT implies the imposition of restraints or restrictions that amount to prohibitions, not only by authority but also by the exigencies of the time or situation ⟨conditions *inhibiting* the growth of free trade⟩.

²forbid *adj* (1606) *archaic* : ACCURSED ⟨he shall live a man ~ —Shak.⟩

for·bid·dance \fər-'bi-dᵊn(t)s, fòr-\ *n* (ca. 1611) : the act of forbidding

for·bid·den \-'bi-dᵊn\ *adj* (13c) **1** : not permitted or allowed **2** : not conforming to the usual selection principles — used of quantum phenomena ⟨~ transition⟩ ⟨~ radiation⟩ ⟨~ spectral line⟩

forbidden fruit *n* [fr. the forbidden fruit of the Garden of Eden in Gen 3:2–19] (1662) : an immoral or illegal pleasure

for·bid·ding *adj* (1712) **1** : such as to make approach or passage difficult or impossible ⟨~ walls⟩ **2** : DISAGREEABLE, REPELLENT ⟨a ~ task⟩ **3** : GRIM, MENACING ⟨a dark ~ sky⟩ — **for·bid·ding·ly** \-'bi-diŋ-lē\ *adv*

forbode *var of* FOREBODE

¹for·by *or* **for·bye** \fòr-'bī\ *prep* [ME *forby,* prep. & adv., fr. *fore-* + *by*] (14c) **1** *archaic* **a** : PAST **b** : NEAR **2** *chiefly Scot* : BESIDES

²forby *or* **forbye** *adv* (1590) *chiefly Scot* : BESIDES : in addition

¹force \'fòrs, 'fòrs\ *n* [ME, fr. MF, fr. (assumed) VL *fortia,* fr. L *fortis* strong] (14c) **1 a** **(1)** : strength or energy exerted or brought to bear : cause of motion or change : active power ⟨the ~s of nature⟩ ⟨the motivating ~ in her life⟩ **(2)** *usu cap* — used with a number to indicate the strength of the wind according to the Beaufort scale ⟨a *Force* 10 hurricane⟩ **b** : moral or mental strength **c** : capacity to persuade or convince ⟨the ~ of the argument⟩ **2 a** : military strength **b** **(1)** : a body (as of troops or ships) assigned to a military purpose **(2)** *pl* : the whole military strength (as of a nation) **c** : a body of persons or things available for a particular end ⟨a labor ~⟩ ⟨the missile ~⟩ **d** : an individual or group having the power of effective action ⟨join ~s to prevent violence⟩ ⟨a ~ in politics⟩ **e** *often cap* : POLICE FORCE — usu. used with *the* **3** : violence, compulsion, or constraint exerted upon or against a person or thing **4 a** : an agency or influence that if applied to a free body results chiefly in an acceleration of the body and sometimes in elastic deformation and other effects

b : any of the natural influences (as electromagnetism, gravity, the strong force, and the weak force) that exist esp. between particles and determine the structure of the universe **5** : the quality of conveying impressions intensely in writing or speech **syn** see POWER — **force·less** \-ləs\ *adj* — **in force 1** : in great numbers ⟨picnickers were out *in force*⟩ **2** : VALID, OPERATIVE ⟨the ban remains *in force*⟩

²force *vt* **forced; forc·ing** (14c) **1** : to do violence to; *esp* : RAPE **2** : to compel by physical, moral, or intellectual means **3** : to make or cause esp. through natural or logical necessity ⟨*forced* to admit my error⟩ **4 a** : to press, drive, attain to, or effect against resistance or inertia ⟨~ your way through⟩ **b** : to impose or thrust urgently, importunately, or inexorably ⟨~ unwanted attentions on a woman⟩ **5** : to achieve or win by strength in struggle or violence: as **a** : to win one's way into ⟨~ a castle⟩ ⟨*forced* the mountain passes⟩ **b** : to break open or through ⟨~ a lock⟩ **6 a** : to raise or accelerate to the utmost ⟨*forcing* the pace⟩ **b** : to produce only with unnatural or unwilling effort ⟨*forced* a smile⟩ **c** : to wrench, strain, or use (language) with marked unnaturalness and lack of ease **7 a** : to hasten the rate of progress or growth of **b** : to bring (as plants) to maturity out of the normal season ⟨*forcing* lilies for Easter⟩ **8** : to induce (as a particular bid or play by another player) in a card game by some conventional act, play, bid, or response **9 a** : to cause (a runner in baseball) to be put out on a force-out **b** : to cause (a run) to be scored in baseball by giving a base on balls when the bases are full — **forc·er** *n* — **force one's hand** : to cause one to act precipitously : force one to reveal one's purpose or intention

syn FORCE, COMPEL, COERCE, CONSTRAIN, OBLIGE mean to make someone or something yield. FORCE is the general term and implies the overcoming of resistance by the exertion of strength, power, or duress ⟨*forced* to flee for their lives⟩. COMPEL typically suggests overcoming of resistance or unwillingness by an irresistible force ⟨*compelled* to admit my mistake⟩. COERCE suggests overcoming resistance or unwillingness by actual or threatened violence or pressure ⟨*coerced* into signing over the rights⟩. CONSTRAIN suggests the effect of a force or circumstance that limits freedom of action or choice ⟨*constrained* by conscience⟩. OBLIGE implies the constraint of necessity, law, or duty ⟨felt *obliged* to go⟩.

forced \'fòrst, 'fòrst\ *adj* (ca. 1537) **1** : compelled by force or necessity : INVOLUNTARY ⟨a ~ landing⟩ **2** : done or produced with effort, exertion, or pressure ⟨a ~ laugh⟩ — **forced·ly** \'fòr-səd-lē, 'fòrst-\ *adv*

force–feed *vt* **-fed; -feed·ing** (1901) **1** : to feed (as an animal) by forcible administration of food **2** : to force to take in ⟨~ students the classics⟩ — also used with a single object ⟨~ the classics to students⟩ ⟨~ students with the classics⟩

force·ful \'fòrs-fəl, 'fòrs-\ *adj* (1571) : possessing or filled with force : EFFECTIVE — **force·ful·ly** \-fə-lē\ *adv* — **force·ful·ness** *n*

force ma·jeure \,fòr-smä-'zhər, ,fòr-, -sma-\ *n* [F, superior force] (1883) **1** : superior or irresistible force **2** : an event or effect that cannot be reasonably anticipated or controlled — compare ACT OF GOD

force·meat \'fòrs-,mēt, 'fòrs-\ *n* [*force* (alter. of ³*farce*) + *meat*] (ca. 1688) : finely chopped and highly seasoned meat or fish that is either served alone or used as a stuffing — called also *farce*

force of habit (ca. 1925) : behavior made involuntary or automatic by repeated pleasure

force of nature (1981) : FORCE 4b

force–out \'fòrs-,aùt, 'fòrs-\ *n* (1896) : a play in baseball in which a runner is put out by being forced to advance to the next base but failing to do so safely

force play *n* (1912) : FORCE-OUT

for·ceps \'fòr-səps, -,seps\ *n, pl* **forceps** [L, tongs, perh. fr. *formus* warm + *capere* to take — more at THERM, HEAVE] (1634) : an instrument for grasping, holding firmly, or exerting traction upon objects esp. for delicate operations (as by jewelers or surgeons) — **for·ceps-like** \-,līk\ *adj*

force pump *n* (1659) : a pump with a solid piston for drawing and forcing through valves a liquid (as water) to a considerable height above the pump or under a considerable pressure

forc·ible \'fòr-sə-bəl, 'fòr-\ *adj* (15c) **1** : effected by force used against opposition or resistance **2** : characterized by force, efficiency, or energy : POWERFUL — **forc·ible·ness** *n* — **forc·ibly** \-blē\ *adv*

¹ford \'fòrd, 'fòrd\ *n* [ME, fr. OE; akin to ON *fjorthr* fjord, L *portus* port, OE *faran* to go — more at FARE] (bef. 12c) : a shallow part of a body of water that may be crossed by wading

²ford *vt* (1614) : to cross (a body of water) by wading — **ford·able** \'fòr-də-bəl, 'fòr-\ *adj*

for·do \fòr-'dü, fòr-\ *vt* **-did** \-'did\; **-done** \-'dən\; **-do·ing** \-'dü-iŋ\ [ME *fordon,* fr. OE *fordon,* fr. *for-* + *dōn* to do] (bef. 12c) **1** *archaic* : to do away with : DESTROY **2** : to overcome with fatigue — used only as past participle ⟨quite *fordone* with the heat⟩

¹fore \'fòr, 'fòr\ *adv* [ME, fr. OE; akin to OE *for*] (bef. 12c) **1** *obs* : at an earlier time or period **2** : in, toward, or adjacent to the front : FORWARD

²fore *also* **'fore** *prep* (bef. 12c) **1** *chiefly dial* : BEFORE **2** : in the presence of

³fore *adj* [*fore-*] (15c) **1** : situated in front of something else : FORWARD **2** : prior in order of occurrence : FORMER

⁴fore *n* (1842) : something that occupies a front position — **to the fore** : in or into a position of prominence : FORWARD

⁵fore *interj* [prob. short for *before*] (ca. 1878) — used by a golfer to warn anyone within range of the probable line of flight of the ball

fore- *comb form* [ME *for-, fore-,* fr. OE *fore-, fr. fore,* adv.] **1 a** : earlier : beforehand ⟨*foresee*⟩ **b** : occurring earlier : occurring beforehand ⟨*foreshock*⟩ **2 a** : situated at the front : in front ⟨*foreleg*⟩ **b** : front part of (something specified) ⟨*forearm*⟩ **c** : foremast ⟨*foretop*⟩

fore–and–aft \,fòr-ə-'naft, ,fòr-\ *adj* (1820) **1** : lying, running, or acting in the general line of the length of a construction (as a ship or a house) : LONGITUDINAL **2** : having no square sails

---

\ə\ abut \ᵊ\ kitten, F table \ər\ **f**ur**ther** \a\ **a**sh \ā\ **a**ce \ä\ m**o**p, m**a**r \aù\ **ou**t \ch\ **ch**in \e\ b**e**t \ē\ **ea**sy \g\ **g**o \i\ h**i**t \ī\ **i**ce \j\ **j**ob \ŋ\ si**ng** \ō\ g**o** \ò\ l**a**w \òi\ b**oy** \th\ **th**in \t̲h̲\ **th**e \ü\ l**oo**t \ù\ f**oo**t \y\ **y**et \zh\ vi**s**ion \ä, k̲, ⁿ, œ, œ̄, ᴜᴇ, ᵫ, ʸ\ *see* Guide to Pronunciation

fore and aft *adv* (ca. 1618) **1** : lengthwise of a ship : from stem to stern **2** : in, at, or toward both the bow and stern **3** : in or at the front and back or the beginning and end

fore-and-aft-er \-'naf-tər\ *n* (1823) : a ship with a fore-and-aft rig; *esp* : SCHOONER

fore-and-aft rig *n* (1879) : a sailing-ship rig in which most or all of the sails are not attached to yards but are bent to gaffs or set on the masts or on stays in a fore-and-aft line

¹**fore-arm** \(,)fōr-'ärm, (,)for-\ *vt* (1592) : to arm in advance : PREPARE

²**fore-arm** \'fōr-,ärm, 'for-\ *n* (1741) : the part of the arm between the elbow and the wrist; *also* : the corresponding part in other vertebrates

fore-bay \'fōr-,bā, 'for-\ *n* (1770) : a reservoir or canal from which water is taken to run equipment (as a waterwheel or turbine)

fore-bear \-,bar, -,ber\ *n* [ME (Sc), fr. *fore-* + *-bear* (fr. *been* to be)] (15c) : ANCESTOR, FOREFATHER; *also* : PRECURSOR — usu. used in pl.

fore-bode \(,)fōr-'bōd, (,)for-\ *vt* (1603) **1** : to have an inward conviction of (as coming ill or misfortune) **2** : FORETELL, PORTEND ∼ *vi* : AUGUR, PREDICT — **fore-bod-er** *n*

¹**fore-bod-ing** \-'bō-diŋ\ *n* (14c) : the act of one who forebodes; *also* : an omen, prediction, or presentiment esp. of coming evil : PORTENT

²**foreboding** *adj* (1679) : indicative of or marked by foreboding — **fore-bod-ing-ly** \-diŋ-lē\ *adv* — **fore-bod-ing-ness** *n*

fore-brain \'fōr-,brān, 'for-\ *n* (1879) : the anterior of the three primary divisions of the developing vertebrate brain or the corresponding part of the adult brain that includes esp. the cerebral hemispheres, the thalamus, and the hypothalamus and that esp. in higher vertebrates is the main control center for sensory and associative information processing, visceral functions, and voluntary motor functions — called also *prosencephalon*; compare DIENCEPHALON, TELENCEPHALON

fore-cad-die \-,ka-dē\ *n* (1792) : a golf caddie who is stationed in the fairway and who indicates the position of balls on the course

¹**fore-cast** \-,kast; fōr-'kast, for-\ *vb* **forecast** *also* **fore-cast-ed; fore-cast-ing** *vt* (15c) **1 a** : to calculate or predict (some future event or condition) usu. as a result of study and analysis of available pertinent data; *esp* : to predict (weather conditions) on the basis of correlated meteorological observations **b** : to indicate as likely to occur **2** : to serve as a forecast of : PRESAGE ⟨such events may ∼ peace⟩ ∼ *vi* : to calculate the future **syn** see FORETELL — **fore-cast-able** \-,kas-tə-bəl\ *adj* — **fore-cast-er** *n*

²**fore-cast** \'fōr-,kast, 'for-\ *n* (ca. 1541) **1** *archaic* : foresight of consequences and provision against them : FORETHOUGHT **2** : a prophecy, estimate, or prediction of a future happening or condition

fore-cas-tle \'fōk-səl; 'fōr-,ka-səl, 'for-\ *n* (15c) **1** : the forward part of the upper deck of a ship **2** : the crew's quarters usu. in a ship's bow

fore-check \'fōr-,chek, 'for-\ *vi* (1951) : to check an opponent in ice hockey in his own defensive zone — **fore-check-er** \-,che-kər\ *n*

fore-close \(,)fōr-'klōz, (,)for-\ *vb* [ME, fr. MF *forclos*, pp. of *forclore*, fr. *fors* outside (fr. L *foris*) + *clore* to close — more at FORUM] *vt* (15c) **1** : to shut out : PRECLUDE **2** : to hold exclusively **3** : to deal with or close in advance **4** : to subject to foreclosure proceedings ∼ *vi* : to foreclose a mortgage

fore-clo-sure \-'klō-zhər\ *n* (1728) : an act or instance of foreclosing; *specif* : a legal proceeding that bars or extinguishes a mortgagor's right of redeeming a mortgaged estate

fore-court \'fōr-,kōrt, 'for-, -,kört\ *n* (1535) **1** : an open court in front of a building **2** : the area near the net in a court game

fore-deck \'fōr-,dek, 'for-\ *n* (1565) : the forepart of a ship's main deck

fore-do *var of* FORDO

fore-doom \(,)fōr-'düm, (,)for-\ *vt* (1603) : DOOM 2

fore-face \'fōr-,fās, 'for-\ *n* (1545) : the part of the head of a quadruped that is in front of the eyes

fore-fa-ther \-,fä-thər, -,fä-\ *n* (14c) **1** : ANCESTOR 1a **2** : a person of an earlier period and common heritage

fore-feel \(,)fōr-'fēl, (,)for-\ *vt* **-felt** \-'felt\; **-feel-ing** (1580) : to have a presentiment of

fore-fend *var of* FORFEND

fore-fin-ger \'fōr-,fiŋ-gər, 'for-\ *n* (15c) : the finger next to the thumb — called also *index finger*

fore-foot \-,fút\ *n* (14c) **1 a** : one of the anterior feet esp. of a quadruped **b** : the front part of the human foot **2** : the forward part of a ship where the stem and keel meet

fore-front \-,frənt\ *n* (15c) : the foremost part or place

fore-gath-er *var of* FORGATHER

¹**fore-go** \fōr-'gō, for-\ *vt* **-went** \-'went\; **-gone** \-'gòn *also* -'gän\; **-go-ing** \-'gō-iŋ, -'gò(-)iŋ\ (bef. 12c) : to go before : PRECEDE — **fore-go-er** \-'gō(-ə)r\ *n*

²**forego** *var of* FORGO

fore-go-ing \-'gō-iŋ, -'gò(-)iŋ\ *adj* (15c) : listed, mentioned, or occurring before ⟨the ∼ statement can be proven⟩ **syn** see PRECEDING

fore-gone \'fōr-,gòn, 'for- *also* -,gän\ *adj* (ca. 1600) : PREVIOUS, PAST

foregone conclusion *n* (1604) **1** : a conclusion that has preceded argument or examination **2** : an inevitable result : CERTAINTY ⟨the victory was a *foregone conclusion*⟩

¹**fore-ground** \'fōr-,graùnd, 'for-\ *n* (1695) **1** : the part of a scene or representation that is nearest to and in front of the spectator **2** : a position of prominence : FOREFRONT

²**foreground** *vt* (1892) : to bring to the foreground; *esp* : to give prominence or emphasis to

fore-gut \'fōr-,gət, 'for-\ *n* (ca. 1889) : the anterior part of the alimentary canal of a vertebrate embryo that develops into the pharynx, esophagus, stomach, and extreme anterior part of the intestine

¹**fore-hand** \-,hand\ *n* (1557) **1** *archaic* : superior position : ADVANTAGE **2** : the part of a horse that is before the rider **3** : a forehand stroke (as in tennis or racquets); *also* : the side on which such strokes are made

²**forehand** *adj* (1599) **1** *obs* : done or given in advance : PRIOR **2** : made with the palm of the hand turned in the direction in which the hand is moving ⟨a ∼ tennis stroke⟩

forehand 3

³**forehand** *adv* (1925) : with a forehand stroke

fore-hand-ed \(,)fōr-'han-dəd, (,)for-\ *adj* (1650) **1 a** : mindful of the future : PRUDENT **b** : WELL-TO-DO **2** : FOREHAND 2 — **fore-hand-ed-ly** *adv* — **fore-hand-ed-ness** *n*

fore-head \'fär-əd, 'for-; 'fōr-,hed, 'for- *also* -,ed\ *n* (bef. 12c) **1** : the part of the face above the eyes **2** : the front or forepart of something ⟨flames in the morning sky —John Milton⟩

fore-hoof \'fōr-,húf, 'for-, -,hüf\ *n* (1770) : the hoof of a forefoot

for-eign \'fòr-ən, 'fär-\ *adj* [ME *forein*, fr. OF, fr. LL *foranus* on the outside, fr. L *foris* outside — more at FORUM] (13c) **1** : situated outside a place or country; *esp* : situated outside one's own country **2** : born in, belonging to, or characteristic of some place or country other than the one under consideration **3** : of, relating to, or proceeding from some other person or material thing than the one under consideration **4** : alien in character : not connected or pertinent **5** : related to or dealing with other nations **6** : occurring in an abnormal situation in the living body and often introduced from outside **7** : not being within the jurisdiction of a political unit (as a state) **syn** see EXTRINSIC — **for-eign-ness** \-ən-nəs\ *n*

foreign affairs *n pl* (1611) : matters having to do with international relations and with the interests of the home country in foreign countries

foreign aid *n* (1949) : assistance (as economic aid) provided by one nation to another

foreign bill *n* (1682) : a bill of exchange that is not both drawn and payable within a particular jurisdiction

for-eign-born \,fòr-ən-'bórn, ,fär-\ *adj* (1856) : foreign by birth

foreign correspondent *n* (1948) : a correspondent employed to send news or comment from a foreign country

for-eign-er \'fòr-ə-nər, 'fär-\ *n* (15c) **1** : a person belonging to or owing allegiance to a foreign country **2** *chiefly dial* : one not native to a place or community : STRANGER 1c

foreign exchange *n* (1691) **1** : a process of settling accounts or debts between persons residing in different countries **2** : foreign currency or current short-term credit instruments payable in such currency

for-eign-ism \'fòr-ə-,ni-zəm, 'fär-\ *n* (1855) : something peculiar to a foreign language or people; *specif* : a foreign idiom or custom

foreign minister *n* (1709) : a governmental minister for foreign affairs

foreign office *n* (1859) : a government office (as a ministry) that deals with foreign affairs

foreign policy *n* (1859) : the policy of a sovereign state in its interaction with other sovereign states

foreign service *n* (1927) : the field force of a foreign office comprising diplomatic and consular personnel

¹**fore-judge** \fòr-'jəj, fōr-\ *vt* [ME *forjuggen*, fr. MF *forjugier*, fr. *fors* outside (fr. L *foris*) + *jugier* to judge] (15c) : to expel, oust, or put out by judgment of a court

²**fore-judge** \(,)fōr-'jəj, (,)for-\ *vt* (1561) : PREJUDGE

fore-know \(,)fōr-'nō, (,)for-\ *vt* **-knew** \-'nü, -'nyü\; **-known** \-'nōn\; **-know-ing** (14c) : to have previous knowledge of : known beforehand esp. by paranormal means or by revelation **syn** see FORESEE — **fore-knowl-edge** \-'nä-lij\ *n*

fore-la-dy \'fōr-,lā-dē, 'for-\ *n* (ca. 1889) : FOREWOMAN

fore-land \'fōr-lənd, 'for-\ *n* (14c) : PROMONTORY, HEADLAND

fore-leg \'fōr-,leg, 'for-, -,lāg\ *n* (15c) : a front leg

fore-limb \-,lim\ *n* (ca. 1796) : a limb (as an arm, wing, fin, or leg) that is situated anteriorly ⟨the ∼ of a bat⟩

fore-lock \-,läk\ *n* (1589) : a lock of hair growing from the front of the head

fore-man \'fōr-mən, 'for-\ *n* (15c) : a first or chief person: as **a** : a member of a jury who acts as chairman and spokesman **b** (1) : a chief and often specially trained worker who works with and commonly leads a gang or crew (2) : a person in charge of a group of workers, a particular operation, or a section of a plant — **fore-man-ship** \-,ship\ *n*

fore-mast \'fōr-,mast, 'for-, -məst\ *n* (1582) : the mast nearest the bow of a ship

¹**fore-most** \-,mōst\ *adj* [ME *formest*, fr. OE, superl. of *forma* first; akin to OHG *fruma* advantage, OE *fore* fore] (bef. 12c) **1** : first in a series or progression **2** : of first rank or position : PREEMINENT

²**foremost** *adv* (bef. 12c) **1** : in the first place **2** : most importantly ⟨first and ∼⟩

fore-moth-er \'fōr-,mə-thər, 'for-\ *n* (1582) : a female ancestor

fore-name \-,nām\ *n* (1533) : a name that precedes one's surname

fore-named \-,nāmd\ *adj* (13c) : named previously : AFORESAID

fore-noon \'fōr-,nün, 'for-,, fōr-\ *n* (15c) : the early part of the day ending with noon : MORNING

¹**fo-ren-sic** \fə-'ren(t)-sik, -'ren-zik\ *adj* [L *forensic* public, forensic, fr. *forum* forum] (1659) **1** : belonging to, used in, or suitable to courts of judicature or to public discussion and debate **2** : ARGUMENTATIVE, RHETORICAL **3** : relating to or dealing with the application of scientific knowledge to legal problems ⟨∼ medicine⟩ ⟨∼ science⟩ ⟨∼ pathologist⟩ ⟨∼ experts⟩ — **fo-ren-si-cal-ly** \-si-k(ə-)lē, -zi-\ *adv*

²**forensic** *n* (1814) **1** : an argumentative exercise **2** *pl but sing or pl in constr* : the art or study of argumentative discourse

fore-or-dain \,fòr-òr-'dān, ,fōr-\ *vt* (15c) : to dispose or appoint in advance : PREDESTINE — **fore-or-di-na-tion** \-,òr-d°n-'ā-shən\ *n*

fore-part \'fōr-,pärt, 'for-\ *n* (14c) **1** : the anterior part of something **2** : the earlier part of a period of time

fore-passed *or* **fore-past** \-,past\ *adj* (1557) : BYGONE

fore-paw \-,pó\ *n* (1825) : the paw of a foreleg

fore-peak \-,pēk\ *n* (1693) : the extreme forward lower compartment or tank usu. used for trimming or storage in a ship

fore-play \-,plā\ *n* (1929) **1** : erotic stimulation preceding sexual intercourse **2** : action or behavior that precedes an event

fore-quar-ter \-,kwó(r)-tər, -,kòr-\ *n* (15c) : the front half of a lateral half of the body or carcass of a quadruped ⟨a ∼ of beef⟩

fore-reach \fōr-'rēch, for-\ *vi* (1644) *of a ship* : to gain ground in tacking ∼ *vt* : to gain on or go ahead of (a ship) when close-hauled

fore-run \-'rən\ *vt* **-ran** \-'ran\; **-run-ning** (bef. 12c) **1** : to run before **2** : to come before as a token of something to follow **3** : FORESTALL, ANTICIPATE

fore-run-ner \'fōr-,rə-nər, 'for-\ *n* (13c) **1** : one that precedes and indicates the approach of another: as **a** : a premonitory sign or symptom **b** : a skier who runs the course before the start of a race **2** : PREDECESSOR, ANCESTOR

syn FORERUNNER, PRECURSOR, HARBINGER, HERALD mean one that goes before or announces the coming of another. FORERUNNER is applicable to anything that serves as a sign or presage ⟨the blockade was the *forerunner* of war⟩. PRECURSOR applies to a person or thing paving the way for the success or accomplishment of another ⟨18th-century poets like Burns were *precursors* of the Romantics⟩. HARBINGER and HERALD both apply, chiefly figuratively, to one that proclaims or announces the coming or arrival of a notable event ⟨their early victory was the *harbinger* of a winning season⟩ ⟨the *herald* of a new age in medicine⟩.

fore·said \-ˌsed\ *adj* (bef. 12c) *archaic* : AFORESAID

fore·sail \ˈfōr-ˌsāl, ˈfȯr-, -səl\ *n* (15c) **1** : the lowest sail set on the foremast of a square-rigged ship or schooner — see SAIL illustration **2** : the sole or principal headsail (as of a sloop, cutter, or schooner)

fore·see \fōr-ˈsē, fȯr-\ *vt* **-saw** \-ˈsȯ\; **-seen** \-ˈsēn\; **-see·ing** (bef. 12c) : to see (as a development) beforehand — **fore·seer** \fōr-ˈsē-ər, fȯr-, -ˈsi(-ə)r\ *n*

syn FORESEE, FOREKNOW, DIVINE, ANTICIPATE mean to know beforehand. FORESEE implies nothing about how the knowledge is derived and may apply to ordinary reasoning and experience ⟨economists should have *foreseen* the recession⟩. FOREKNOW usu. implies supernatural assistance, as through revelation ⟨if only we could *foreknow* our own destinies⟩. DIVINE adds to FORESEE the suggestion of exceptional wisdom or discernment ⟨was able to *divine* Europe's rapid recovery from the war⟩. ANTICIPATE implies taking action about or responding emotionally to something before it happens ⟨the waiter *anticipated* our every need⟩.

fore·see·able \-ˈsē-ə-bəl\ *adj* (1804) **1** : being such as may be reasonably anticipated ⟨~ problems⟩ **2** : lying within the range for which forecasts are possible ⟨in the ~ future⟩ — **fore·see·abil·i·ty** \-ˌsē-ə-ˈbi-lə-tē\ *n*

fore·shad·ow \fōr-ˈsha-(ˌ)dō, -də(-w)\ *vt* (1577) : to represent, indicate, or typify beforehand : PREFIGURE — **fore·shad·ow·er** \-də-wər\ *n*

fore·shank \ˈfōr-ˌshaŋk, ˈfȯr-\ *n* (1924) : the upper part of the foreleg of cattle; *also* : meat cut from this part

fore·sheet \-ˌshēt\ *n* (1667) **1** : one of the sheets of a foresail **2** *pl* : the forward part of an open boat

fore·shock \-ˌshäk\ *n* (1902) : any of the usu. minor tremors commonly preceding the principal shock of an earthquake

fore·shore \-ˌshȯr, -ˌshōr\ *n* (1764) **1** : a strip of land margining a body of water **2** : the part of a seashore between high-water and low-water marks

fore·short·en \fōr-ˈshȯr-tᵊn, fȯr-\ *vt* (1606) **1** : to shorten by proportionately contracting in the direction of depth so that an illusion of projection or extension in space is obtained **2** : to make more compact : ABRIDGE, SHORTEN

fore·side \ˈfōr-ˌsīd, ˈfȯr-\ *n* (14c) : the front side or part : FRONT

fore·sight \ˈfōr-ˌsīt, ˈfȯr-\ *n* (14c) **1** : an act or the power of foreseeing : PRESCIENCE **2** : provident care : PRUDENCE ⟨had the ~ to invest his money wisely⟩ **3** : an act of looking forward; *also* : a view forward — **fore·sight·ed** \-ˌsī-təd\ *adj* — **fore·sight·ed·ly** *adv* — **fore·sight·ed·ness** *n* — **fore·sight·ful** \-ˌsīt-fəl\ *adj*

fore·skin \-ˌskin\ *n* (1535) : a fold of skin that covers the glans of the penis — called also *prepuce*

fore·speak \fōr-ˈspēk, fȯr-\ *vt* **-spoke** \-ˈspōk\; **-spo·ken** \-ˈspō-kən\; **-speak·ing** (14c) **1** : FORETELL, PREDICT **2** : to arrange for in advance

¹for·est \ˈfȯr-əst, ˈfär-\ *n, often attrib* [ME, fr. OF, fr. LL *forestis* (*silva*) unenclosed (woodland), fr. L *foris* outside — more at FORUM] (13c) **1** : a dense growth of trees and underbrush covering a large tract **2** : a tract of wooded land in England formerly owned by the sovereign and used for game **3** : something resembling a forest esp. in profusion ⟨a ~ of microphones⟩ — **for·est·al** \-əs-tᵊl\ *or* **fo·res·tial** \fə-ˈres-tē-əl, fȯ-, -ˈres(h)-chəl\ *adj* — **for·est·ed** \ˈfȯr-ə-stəd, ˈfär-\ *adj*

²forest *vt* (ca. 1828) : to cover with trees or forest — **for·es·ta·tion** \ˌfȯr-ə-ˈstā-shən, ˌfär-\ *n*

fore·stage \ˈfōr-ˌstāj, ˈfȯr-\ *n* (1923) : APRON 2e

fore·stall \fōr-ˈstȯl, fȯr-\ *vt* [ME, fr. *forstall* act of waylaying, fr. OE *foresteall*, fr. *fore-* + *steall* position, stall] (bef. 12c) **1** : to prevent the normal trading in by buying or diverting goods or by persuading persons to raise prices **2** *archaic* : INTERCEPT **3** *obs* : OBSTRUCT, BESET **4** : to exclude, hinder, or prevent by prior occupation or measures **5** : to get ahead of : ANTICIPATE *syn* see PREVENT — **fore·stall·er** *n* — **fore·stall·ment** \-ˈstȯl-mənt\ *n*

fore·stay \ˈfōr-ˌstā, ˈfȯr-\ *n* (13c) : a stay from the foremast to the foredeck or bow of a ship

fore·stay·sail \-ˌsāl, -səl\ *n* (1742) : the triangular aftermost headsail of a schooner, ketch, or yawl set on the forestay — see SAIL illustration

for·est·er \ˈfȯr-ə-stər, ˈfär-\ *n* [ME *forster, forester*, fr. OF *forestier*, fr. *forest*] (14c) **1** : a person trained in forestry **2** : an inhabitant of a forest **3** : any of various woodland moths (family Agaristidae) **4** *cap* : a member of a major benevolent and fraternal order

forest floor *n* (1849) : the richly organic layer of soil and debris characteristic of forested land

forest green *n* (1810) : a dark yellowish or moderate olive green

for·est·land \ˈfȯr-əst-ˌland, ˈfär-\ *n* (1649) : land covered with forest or reserved for the growth of forests

forest ranger *n* (1830) : an officer charged with the patrolling and guarding of a forest; *esp* : one in charge of the management and protection of a portion of a public forest

for·est·ry \ˈfȯr-ə-strē, ˈfär-\ *n* (1823) **1** : FORESTLAND **2 a** : the science of developing, caring for, or cultivating forests **b** : the management of growing timber

forest tent caterpillar *n* (1854) : a moth (*Malacosoma disstria* of the family Lasiocampidae) whose orange-marked larva is a tent caterpillar and a serious defoliator of deciduous trees

fore·swear, fore·sworn *var of* FORSWEAR, FORSWORN

¹fore·taste \ˈfōr-ˌtāst, ˈfȯr-\ *n* (15c) **1** : a small anticipatory sample **2** : an advance indication or warning *syn* see PROSPECT

²fore·taste \fōr-ˈtāst, fȯr-ˈ, ˈfōr-ˌ, ˈfȯr-\ *vt* (15c) : to taste beforehand : ANTICIPATE

fore·tell \fōr-ˈtel, fȯr-\ *vt* **-told** \-ˈtōld\; **-tell·ing** (14c) : to tell beforehand : PREDICT — **fore·tell·er** *n*

syn FORETELL, PREDICT, FORECAST, PROPHESY, PROGNOSTICATE mean to tell beforehand. FORETELL applies to the telling of the coming of a future event by any procedure or any source of information ⟨seers *foretold* the calamity⟩. PREDICT commonly implies inference from facts or accepted laws of nature ⟨astronomers *predicted* an eclipse⟩. FORECAST adds the implication of anticipating eventualities and differs from PREDICT in being usually concerned with probabilities rather than certainties ⟨*forecast* snow⟩. PROPHESY connotes inspired or mystic knowledge of the future esp. as the fulfilling of divine threats or promises ⟨*prophesying* a new messiah⟩. PROGNOSTICATE is used less often than the other words; it may suggest learned or skilled interpretation, but more often it is simply a colorful substitute for PREDICT or PROPHESY ⟨*prognosticating* the future⟩.

¹fore·thought \ˈfōr-ˌthȯt, ˈfȯr-\ *n* (14c) **1** : a thinking or planning out in advance : PREMEDITATION **2** : consideration for the future

²forethought *adj* (15c) *archaic* : AFORETHOUGHT

fore·thought·ful \-fəl\ *adj* (1809) : full of or having forethought — **fore·thought·ful·ly** \-fə-lē\ *adv* — **fore·thought·ful·ness** *n*

fore·time \ˈfōr-ˌtīm, ˈfȯr-\ *n* (ca. 1540) : former or past time : the time before the present

¹fore·to·ken \ˈfōr-ˌtō-kən, ˈfȯr-\ *n* (bef. 12c) : a premonitory sign

²fore·to·ken \fōr-ˈtō-kən, fȯr-\ *vt* **fore·to·kened; fore·to·ken·ing** \-ˈtōk-niŋ, -ˈtō-kə-\ (15c) : to indicate or warn of in advance

fore·top \ˈfōr-ˌtäp, ˈfȯr-; -təp\ *n* (1509) : the platform at the head of a ship's foremast

fore·top·man \ˈfōr-ˌtäp-mən, ˈfȯr-; -təp-\ *n* (1816) : a sailor on duty on the foremast and above

fore–top–mast \-ˈtäp-məst, ˈfȯr-; -təp-ˌmast\ *n* (1626) : a mast next above the foremast

¹for·ev·er \fə-ˈrev-ər, fȯ-; *Southern often* fə-ˈe-və\ *adv* (1629) **1** : for a limitless time ⟨wants to live ~⟩ **2** : at all times : CONTINUALLY ⟨is ~ making bad puns⟩

²forever *n* (1858) : a seemingly interminable time : excessively long ⟨it took her ~ to find the answer⟩

for·ev·er·more \-ˌre-və(r)-ˈmȯr, -ˈmōr\ *adv* (1837) : FOREVER 1

for·ev·er·ness \-ˈre-vər-nəs\ *n* (1945) : ETERNITY

fore·warn \fōr-ˈwȯrn, fȯr-\ *vt* (14c) : to warn in advance

fore·wing \ˈfōr-ˌwiŋ, ˈfȯr-\ *n* (ca. 1889) : either of the anterior wings of a 4-winged insect

fore·wom·an \ˈfōr-ˌwu̇-mən, ˈfȯr-\ *n* (1709) : a woman who is a foreman

fore·word \ˈfōr-(ˌ)wərd, ˈfȯr-\ *n* (1842) : prefatory comments (as for a book) esp. when written by someone other than the author

fore·worn *archaic var of* FORWORN

¹for·feit \ˈfȯr-fət\ *n* [ME *forfait*, fr. MF, fr. pp. of *forfaire* to commit a crime, forfeit, fr. *fors* outside (fr. L *foris*) + *faire* to do, fr. L *facere* — more at FORUM, DO] (14c) **1** : something forfeited or subject to being forfeited for a crime, offense, or neglect of duty) : PENALTY **2** : forfeiture esp. of civil rights **3 a** : something deposited (as for making a mistake in a game) and then redeemed on payment of a fine **b** *pl* : a game in which forfeits are exacted

²forfeit *vt* (14c) **1** : to lose or lose the right to by some error, offense, or crime **2** : to subject to confiscation as a forfeit — **for·feit·able** \-fə-tə-bəl\ *adj* — **for·feit·er** *n*

³forfeit *adj* (14c) : forfeited or subject to forfeiture

for·fei·ture \ˈfȯr-fə-ˌchu̇r, -chər, -ˌt(y)u̇r\ *n* (14c) **1** : the act of forfeiting : the loss of property or money because of a breach of a legal obligation **2** : something (as money or property) that is forfeited : PENALTY

for·fend \fȯr-ˈfend, fōr-\ *vt* (14c) **1 a** *archaic* : FORBID **b** : to ward off : PREVENT **2** : PROTECT, PRESERVE

for·gath·er \fȯr-ˈga-thər, fōr-\ *vi* (1513) **1** : to come together : ASSEMBLE **2** : to meet someone usu. by chance

¹forge \ˈfōrj, ˈfȯrj\ *n* [ME, fr. OF, fr. L *fabrica*, fr. *fabr-, faber* smith] (13c) **1** : a furnace or a shop with its furnace where metal is heated and wrought : SMITHY **2** : a workshop where wrought iron is produced or where iron is made malleable

forge 1

²forge *vb* **forged; forg·ing** *vt* (14c) **1 a** : to form (as metal) by heating and hammering **b** : to form (metal) by a mechanical or hydraulic press with or without heat **2** : to make or imitate falsely esp. with intent to defraud : COUNTERFEIT **3** : to form or bring into being esp. by an expenditure of effort ⟨working to ~ party unity⟩ ~ *vi* **1** : to work at a forge **2** : to commit forgery — **forge·abil·i·ty** \ˌfȯr-jə-ˈbi-lə-tē, ˌfōr-\ *n* — **forge·able** \ˈfȯr-jə-bəl, ˈfōr-\ *adj*

³forge *vi* **forged; forg·ing** [origin unknown] (1611) **1** : to move forward slowly and steadily ⟨the ship *forged* ahead through heavy seas⟩ **2** : to move with a sudden increase of speed and power ⟨*forged* into the lead⟩ ⟨*forged* ahead in marketing the product⟩

forg·er \ˈfȯr-jər, ˈfōr-\ *n* [²*forge*] (14c) **1** : one that forges metals **2 a** : one that falsifies; *esp* : a creator of false tales **b** : a person guilty of forgery

forg·ery \ˈfȯrj-rē, ˈfȯr-jə-, ˈfōrj-, ˈfōr-\ *n, pl* **-er·ies** (1583) **1** *archaic* : INVENTION **2** : something forged **3** : an act of forging; *esp* : the crime of falsely and fraudulently making or altering a document (as a check)

for·get \fər-ˈget, fȯr-\ *vb* **-got** \-ˈgät\; **-got·ten** \-ˈgä-tᵊn\ *or* **-got; -get·ting** [ME, fr. OE *forgietan*, fr. *for-* + *-gietan* (akin to ON *geta* to get)] *vt* (bef. 12c) **1 a** : to lose the remembrance of : be unable to think of

\ə\ abut \ᵊ\ kitten, F table \ər\ further \a\ ash \ā\ ace \ä\ mop, mar \au̇\ out \ch\ chin \e\ bet \ē\ easy \g\ go \i\ hit \ī\ ice \j\ job \ŋ\ sing \ō\ go \ȯ\ law \ȯi\ boy \th\ thin \th\ the \ü\ loot \u̇\ foot \y\ yet \zh\ vision \ä, k, ⁿ, œ, œ̄, ue, ūe, ᵜ\ *see* Guide to Pronunciation or recall ⟨I ~ his name⟩ **b** *obs* : to cease from doing **2** : to treat with inattention or disregard ⟨*forgot* their old friends⟩ **3** : to disregard intentionally — OVERLOOK — usu. used in the imperative ⟨~ it⟩ **~** *vi* **1** : to cease remembering or noticing ⟨forgive and ~⟩ **2** : to fail to become mindful at the proper time ⟨~ about paying the bill⟩ *syn* see NEGLECT — **for·get·ter** *n* — **forget oneself** : to lose one's dignity, temper, or self-control

for·get·ful \-'get-fəl\ *adj* (14c) **1** : likely to forget **2** : characterized by negligent failure to remember : NEGLECTFUL **3** : inducing oblivion ⟨~ sleep⟩ — **for·get·ful·ly** \-fə-lē\ *adv* — **for·get·ful·ness** *n*

for·ge·tive \'fȯr-jə-tiv, 'fȯr-\ *adj* [prob. fr. ²*forge* + *-tive* (as in *inventive*)] (1597) *archaic* : INVENTIVE, IMAGINATIVE

for·get-me-not \fər-'get-mē-ˌnät, fȯr-\ *n* (1532) : any of a genus (*Myosotis*) of small herbs of the borage family having bright-blue or white flowers usu. arranged in a curving spike

for·get·ta·ble \fər-'ge-tə-bəl, fȯr-\ *adj* (1845) : fit or likely to be forgotten ⟨a ~ movie⟩

forg·ing \'fȯr-jiŋ, 'fȯr-\ *n* (14c) **1** : the art or process of forging **2** : a piece of forged work **3** : FORGERY 3

for·give \fər-'giv, fȯr-\ *vb* **-gave** \-'gāv\; **-giv·en** \-'gi-vən\; **-giv·ing** [ME, fr. OE *forgifan*, fr. *for-* + *gifan* to give] *vt* (bef. 12c) **1 a** : to give up resentment of or claim to requital for ⟨~ an insult⟩ **b** : to grant relief from payment of ⟨~ a debt⟩ **2** : to cease to feel resentment against (an offender) : PARDON ⟨~ one's enemies⟩ **~** *vi* : to grant forgiveness *syn* see EXCUSE — **for·giv·able** \-'gi-və-bəl\ *adj* — **for·giv·ably** \-blē\ *adv* — **for·giv·er** *n*

for·give·ness \-'giv-nəs\ *n* (bef. 12c) : the act of forgiving

for·giv·ing (1690) **1** : willing or able to forgive **2** : allowing room for error or weakness ⟨designed to be a ~ tennis racquet⟩ — **for·giv·ing·ly** \-'gi-viŋ-lē\ *adv* — **for·giv·ing·ness** *n*

for·go \fȯr-'gō, fȯr-\ *vt* **-went** \-'went\; **-gone** \-'gȯn *also* -'gän\; **-go·ing** \-'gō-iŋ, -'gȯ(-)iŋ\ [ME, fr. OE *forgān* to pass by, forgo, fr. *for-* + *gān* to go] (bef. 12c) **1** : to give up the enjoyment or advantage of : do without **2** *archaic* : FORSAKE — **for·go·er** \-'gō-(ə)r\ *n*

forgotten man *n* (1925) : a person or category of persons that receives less attention than is merited

for instance \fə-'rin(t)-stənts, 'frin(t)-\ *n* (1959) : EXAMPLE ⟨I'll give you a *for instance*⟩

fo·rint \'fȯr-ˌint\ *n*, *pl* **forints** *also* **forint** [Hung] (ca. 1916) — see MONEY table

for·judge *var of* FOREJUDGE

¹fork \'fȯrk\ *n* [ME *forke*, fr. OE & ONF; OE *forca* & ONF *forque*, fr. L *furca*] (bef. 12c) **1** : an implement with two or more prongs used esp. for taking up (as in eating), pitching, or digging **2** : a forked part, tool, or piece of equipment **3 a** : a division into branches or the place where something divides into branches **b** : CONFLUENCE **4** : one of the branches into which something forks **5** : an attack by one chess piece (as a knight) on two pieces simultaneously — **fork·ful** \-ˌfu̇l\ *n*

²fork *vi* (15c) **1** : to divide into two or more branches ⟨where the road ~s⟩ **2 a** : to use or work with a fork **b** : to turn into a fork **~** *vt* **1** : to give the form of a fork to ⟨~*ing* her fingers⟩ **2** : to attack (two chessmen) simultaneously **3** : to raise, pitch, dig, or work with a fork ⟨~ hay⟩ **4** : PAY, CONTRIBUTE — used with *over*, *out*, or *up* ⟨had to ~ over $5000⟩ — **fork·er** *n*

fork·ball \'fȯrk-ˌbȯl\ *n* (1936) : a baseball pitch in which the ball is gripped between the forked index and middle fingers

forked \'fȯrkt, 'fȯr-kəd\ *adj* (13c) **1** : resembling a fork esp. in having one end divided into two or more branches or points ⟨~ lightning⟩ **2** : shaped like a fork or having a forked part ⟨a ~ road⟩

forked tongue *n* (1836) : intent to mislead or deceive — usu. used in the phrase *to speak with forked tongue*

fork·lift \'fȯr-ˌklift\ *n* (1944) : a self-propelled machine for hoisting and transporting heavy objects by means of steel fingers inserted under the load

fork-ten·der \'fȯrk-'ten-dər\ *adj* (1973) : tender enough to be easily pierced or cut with a fork ⟨~ filet mignon⟩

forky \'fȯr-kē\ *adj* **fork·i·er; -est** (1573) : FORKED ⟨a ~ beard⟩

for·lorn \fər-'lȯrn, fȯr-\ *adj* [ME *forloren*, fr. OE, pp. of *forlēosan* to lose, fr. *for-* + *lēosan* to lose — more at LOSE] (bef. 12c) **1 a** : BEREFT, FORSAKEN ⟨left quite ~ of hope⟩ **b** : sad and lonely because of isolation or desertion : DESOLATE **2** : being in poor condition : MISERABLE, WRETCHED ⟨~ tumbledown buildings⟩ **3** : nearly hopeless ⟨a ~ attempt⟩ *syn* see ALONE — **for·lorn·ly** *adv* — **for·lorn·ness** \-'lȯrn-nəs\ *n*

forlorn hope *n* [by folk etymology fr. D *verloren hoop*, lit., lost band] (1579) **1** : a body of men selected to perform a perilous service **2** : a desperate or extremely difficult enterprise

¹form \'fȯrm\ *n* [ME *forme*, fr. OF, fr. L *forma* form, beauty] (13c) **1 a** : the shape and structure of something as distinguished from its material **b** : a body (as of a person) esp. in its external appearance as distinguished from the face : FIGURE **c** *archaic* : BEAUTY **2** : the essential nature of a thing as distinguished from its matter: as **a** : IDEA 1a **b** : the component of a thing that determines its kind **3 a** : established method of expression or proceeding : procedure according to rule or rote **b** : a prescribed and set order of words : FORMULA ⟨the ~ of the marriage service⟩ **4** : a printed or typed document with blank spaces for insertion of required or requested information ⟨tax ~s⟩ **5 a** (1) : conduct regulated by extraneous controls (as of custom or etiquette) : CEREMONY (2) : show without substance **b** : manner or conduct as tested by a prescribed or accepted standard ⟨rudeness is simply bad ~⟩ **c** : manner or style of performing or accomplishing according to recognized standards of technique ⟨a strong swimmer but weak on ~⟩ **6 a** : the resting place or nest of a hare **b** : a long seat : BENCH **7 a** : a supporting frame model of the human figure or part (as the torso) of the human figure usu. used for displaying apparel **b** : a proportioned and often adjustable model for fitting clothes **c** : a mold in which concrete is placed to set **8** : the printing type or other matter arranged and secured in a chase ready for printing **9 a** : one of the different modes of existence, action, or manifestation of a particular thing or substance : KIND ⟨one ~ of respiratory disorder⟩ ⟨a ~ of art⟩ **b** : a distinguishable group of organisms **c** : LINGUISTIC FORM **d** : one of the different aspects a word may take as a result of inflection or change of spelling or pronunciation ⟨verbal ~s⟩ **e** : a mathematical expression of a particular type ⟨a bilinear ~⟩ ⟨a polynomial ~⟩ **10 a**

(1) : orderly method of arrangement (as in the presentation of ideas) : manner of coordinating elements (as of an artistic production or course of reasoning) (2) : a particular kind or instance of such arrangement ⟨the sonnet is a poetical ~⟩ **b** : PATTERN, SCHEMA ⟨arguments of the same logical ~⟩ **c** : the structural element, plan, or design of a work of art — compare CONTENT 2c **d** : a visible and measurable unit defined by a contour : a bounded surface or volume **11** : a grade in a British school or in some American private schools **12 a** (1) : the past performance of a race horse (2) : RACING FORM **b** : known ability to perform ⟨a singer at the top of her ~⟩ **c** : condition suitable for performing (as in athletic competition) ⟨back on ~⟩

²form *vt* (13c) **1 a** : to give a particular shape to : shape or mold into a certain state or after a particular model ⟨~ the dough into a ball⟩ ⟨a state ~ed along republican lines⟩ **b** : to arrange themselves in ⟨the dancers ~ed a line⟩ **c** : to model by instruction and discipline ⟨a mind ~ed by classical education⟩ **2** : to give form or shape to : FASHION, CONSTRUCT **3** : to serve to make up or constitute : be an essential or basic element of **4** : DEVELOP, ACQUIRE ⟨~ a habit⟩ **5** : to arrange in order : DRAW UP **6 a** : to assume an inflection so as to produce (as a tense) ⟨~s the past in *-ed*⟩ **b** : to combine to make (a compound word) **~** *vi* **1** : to become formed or shaped **2** : to take form : come into existence : ARISE **3** : to take on a definite form, shape, or arrangement — **form·abil·i·ty** \ˌfȯr-mə-'bi-lə-tē\ *n* — **form·able** \'fȯr-mə-bəl\ *adj* — **form on** : to take up a formation next to

form- *or* **formo-** *comb form* [*formic*] : formic acid ⟨*formate*⟩

-form \ˌfȯrm\ *adj comb form* [MF & L; MF *-forme*, fr. L *-formis*, fr. *forma*] : in the form or shape of : resembling ⟨filiform⟩

¹for·mal \'fȯr-məl\ *adj* [ME, fr. MF or L; MF, fr. L *formalis*, fr. *forma*] (14c) **1 a** : belonging to or constituting the form or essence of a thing ⟨~ cause⟩ **b** : relating to or involving the outward form, structure, relationships, or arrangement of elements rather than content ⟨~ logic⟩ ⟨~ style of painting⟩ ⟨~ approach to comparative linguistics⟩ **2 a** : following or according with established form, custom, or rule ⟨lacked ~ schooling⟩ ⟨a ~ dinner party⟩ ⟨~ attire⟩ **b** : done in due or lawful form ⟨a ~ contract⟩ ⟨received ~ recognition⟩ **3 a** : characterized by punctilious respect for form : METHODICAL ⟨very ~ in all his dealings⟩ **b** : rigidly ceremonious : PRIM **4** : having the appearance without the substance ⟨~ Christians who go to church only at Easter⟩ *syn* see CEREMONIAL — **for·mal·ly** \-mə-lē\ *adv* — **for·mal·ness** *n*

²formal *n* (1605) : something (as a dance or a dress) formal in character

³formal *adj* [*formula* + ¹*-al*] (ca. 1934) : ³MOLAR

form·al·de·hyde \fȯr-'mal-də-ˌhīd, fər-\ *n* [ISV *form-* + *aldehyde*] (1872) : a colorless pungent irritating gas CH_2O used chiefly as a disinfectant and preservative and in chemical synthesis

for·ma·lin \'fȯr-mə-lən, -ˌlēn\ *n* [*Formalin*, a trademark] (1893) : a clear aqueous solution of formaldehyde containing a small amount of methanol

for·mal·ise *Brit var of* FORMALIZE

for·mal·ism \'fȯr-mə-ˌli-zəm\ *n* (ca. 1840) **1** : the practice or the doctrine of strict adherence to prescribed or external forms (as in religion or art); *also* : an instance of this **2** : marked attention to arrangement, style, or artistic means (as in art or literature) usu. with corresponding de-emphasis of content — **for·mal·ist** \-list\ *n or adj* — **for·mal·is·tic** \ˌfȯr-mə-'lis-tik\ *adj*

for·mal·i·ty \fȯr-'ma-lə-tē\ *n*, *pl* **-ties** (1597) **1** : compliance with formal or conventional rules : CEREMONY **2** : the quality or state of being formal **3** : an established form or procedure that is required or conventional

for·mal·ize \'fȯr-mə-ˌlīz\ *vt* **-ized; -iz·ing** (1646) **1** : to give a certain or definite form to : SHAPE **2 a** : to make formal **b** : to give formal status or approval to — **for·mal·iz·able** \-ˌlī-zə-bəl\ *adj* — **for·mal·iza·tion** \ˌfȯr-mə-lə-'zā-shən\ *n* — **for·mal·iz·er** \'fȯr-mə-ˌlī-zər\ *n*

form·am·ide \fȯr-'ma-ˌmīd; 'fȯr-mə-ˌmīd, -məd\ *n* (1852) : a colorless hygroscopic liquid $CHONH_2$ used chiefly as a solvent

for·mant \'fȯr-mənt, -ˌmant\ *n* (1901) : a characteristic component of the quality of a speech sound; *specif* : any of several resonance bands held to determine the phonetic quality of a vowel

¹for·mat \'fȯr-ˌmat\ *n* [F or G; F, fr. G, fr. L *formatus*, pp. of *formare* to form, fr. *forma*] (1840) **1** : the shape, size, and general makeup (as of something printed) **2** : general plan of organization, arrangement, or choice of material (as for a television show)

²format *vt* **for·mat·ted; for·mat·ting** (1964) : to arrange (as material to be printed or stored data) in a particular format — **for·mat·ter** *n*

for·mate \'fȯr-ˌmāt\ *n* (1807) : a salt or ester of formic acid

for·ma·tion \fȯr-'mā-shən\ *n* (15c) **1** : an act of giving form or shape to something or of taking form : DEVELOPMENT **2** : something that is formed ⟨new word ~s⟩ **3** : the manner in which a thing is formed : STRUCTURE ⟨the peculiar ~ of the heart⟩ **4** : the largest unit in an ecological community comprising two or more associations and their precursors ⟨grassland ~⟩ **5 a** : any igneous, sedimentary, or metamorphic rock represented as a unit **b** : any sedimentary bed or consecutive series of beds sufficiently homogeneous or distinctive to be a unit **6** : an arrangement of a body or group of persons or things in some prescribed manner or for a particular purpose

¹for·ma·tive \'fȯr-mə-tiv\ *adj* (15c) **1 a** : giving or capable of giving form : CONSTRUCTIVE ⟨a ~ influence⟩ **b** : used in word formation or inflection **2** : capable of alteration by growth and development; *also* : producing new cells and tissues **3** : of, relating to, or characterized by formative effects or formation ⟨~ years⟩ — **for·ma·tive·ly** *adv*

²formative *n* (1816) : the element (as a suffix) in a word that serves to give the word appropriate form and is not part of the base

form class *n* (1921) : a class of linguistic forms that can be used in the same position in a construction and that have one or more morphological or syntactical features in common

form-critical (1933) : based on or applying form criticism

form criticism *n* (1928) : a method of criticism for determining the sources and historicity of biblical writings through analysis of the writings in terms of ancient literary forms and oral traditions (as love poems, parables, and proverbs) — **form critic** *n*

forme \'fȯm, 'fȯrm\ *n* (15c) *Brit* : FORM 8

formed \'fȯrmd\ *adj* (1605) : organized in a way characteristic of living matter ⟨mitochondria are ~ bodies of the cell⟩

for·mée \'fȯr-ˌmā, fȯr-'\ *adj* [F, fem. pp. of *former* to form, fr. L *formare*] (15c) *of a heraldic cross* : having the arms narrow at the center and expanding toward the ends — see CROSS illustration

¹for·mer \'fȯr-mər\ *adj* [ME, fr. *forme* first, fr. OE *forma* — more at FOREMOST] (12c) **1 a** : coming before in time **b** : of, relating to, or occurring in the past ⟨~ correspondence⟩ **2** : preceding in place or arrangement : FOREGOING ⟨~ part of the chapter⟩ **3** : first in order of two or more things cited or understood ⟨of the two given, the ~ spelling is more common⟩ ⟨of the two spellings, the ~ is more common⟩ **4** : having been previously : ONETIME ⟨a ~ athlete⟩ *syn* see PRECEDING

²form·er \'fȯr-mər\ *n* (14c) **1** : one that forms **2** *chiefly Brit* : a member of a school form — usu. used in combination ⟨sixth ~⟩

for·mer·ly \'fȯr-mə(r)-lē\ *adv* (1534) **1** : at an earlier time : PREVIOUSLY **2** *obs* : just before

form·fit·ting \'fȯrm-ˌfi-tiŋ\ *adj* (1897) : conforming to the outline of the body : fitting snugly ⟨a ~ sweater⟩

form·ful \'fȯrm-fəl\ *adj* (1832) : exhibiting or notable for form

form genus *n* (1873) : an artificial taxonomic category established for organisms (as imperfect fungi) of obscure true relationships

For·mi·ca \fȯr-'mī-kə, fər-\ *trademark* — used for any of various laminated plastic products used esp. for surface finish

for·mic acid \'fȯr-mik-\ *n* [irreg. fr. L *formica* ant — more at PISMIRE] (1791) : a colorless pungent fuming vesicant liquid acid CH_2O_2 found esp. in ants and in many plants and used chiefly in dyeing and finishing textiles

for·mi·cary \'fȯr-mə-ˌker-ē\ *n, pl* **-car·ies** [ML *formicarium*, fr. L *formica*] (1816) : an ant nest

for·mi·da·ble \'fȯr-mə-də-bəl; fȯr-'mi-, fər-'mi-\ *adj* [ME, fr. L *formidabilis*, fr. *formidare* to fear, fr. *formido* terror, bogey; akin to Gk *mormō* bogey] (15c) **1** : causing fear, dread, or apprehension ⟨a ~ prospect⟩ **2** : having qualities that discourage approach or attack **3** : tending to inspire awe or wonder — **for·mi·da·bil·i·ty** \ˌfȯr-mə-də-'bi-lə-tē; fȯr-ˌmi-, fər-\ *n* — **for·mi·da·ble·ness** \'fȯr-mə-də-bəl-nəs; fȯr-'mi-, fər-\ *n* — **for·mi·da·bly** \-blē\ *adv*

form·less \'fȯrm-ləs\ *adj* (1591) **1** : having no regular form or shape **2** : lacking order or arrangement **3** : having no physical existence — **form·less·ly** *adv* — **form·less·ness** *n*

form letter *n* (1909) **1** : a letter on a subject of frequent recurrence that can be sent to different people without essential change except in the address **2** : a letter for mass circulation that is printed in many copies and has a very general salutation (as *Dear Friend*)

formo- — see FORM-

¹for·mu·la \'fȯr-myə-lə\ *n, pl* **-las** *or* **-lae** \-ˌlē, -ˌlī\ [L, dim. of *forma* form] (1618) **1 a** : a set form of words for use in a ceremony or ritual **b** : a conventionalized statement intended to express some fundamental truth or principle esp. as a basis for negotiation or action **2 a** (1) : RECIPE (2) : PRESCRIPTION **b** : a milk mixture or substitute for feeding an infant **3 a** : a general fact, rule, or principle expressed in usu. mathematical symbols **b** : a symbolic expression of the chemical composition or constitution of a substance **c** : a group of symbols (as letters and numbers) associated to express concisely facts or data (as the number and kinds of teeth in the jaw) **d** : a combination of signs in a logical calculus **4** : a customary or set form or method allowing little room for originality — **for·mu·la·ic** \ˌfȯr-myə-'lā-ik\ *adj* — **for·mu·la·ical·ly** \-'lā-ə-k(ə-)lē\ *adv*

²formula *adj* (1927) : of, relating to, or being an open-wheel open-cockpit rear-engine racing car conforming to prescribed specifications as to size, weight, and engine displacement

for·mu·la·rize \'fȯr-myə-lə-ˌrīz\ *vt* **-rized; -riz·ing** (1852) : to state in or reduce to a formula : FORMULATE — **for·mu·la·ri·za·tion** \ˌfȯr-myə-lə-rə-'zā-shən\ *n* — **for·mu·la·riz·er** \'fȯr-myə-lə-ˌrī-zər\ *n*

for·mu·lary \'fȯr-myə-ˌler-ē\ *n, pl* **-lar·ies** (1541) **1** : a collection of prescribed forms (as oaths or prayers) **2** : FORMULA 1 **3** : a book listing medicinal substances and formulas — **formulary** *adj*

for·mu·late \'fȯr-myə-ˌlāt\ *vt* **-lat·ed; -lat·ing** (1860) **1 a** : to reduce to or express in a formula **b** : to put into a systematized statement or expression **c** : DEVISE ⟨~ a policy⟩ **2 a** : to develop a formula for the preparation of (as a soap or plastic) **b** : to prepare according to a formula — **for·mu·la·tor** \-ˌlā-tər\ *n*

for·mu·la·tion \ˌfȯr-myə-'lā-shən\ *n* (1876) : an act or the product of formulating

formula weight *n* (ca. 1920) : MOLECULAR WEIGHT — used esp. of ionic compounds

for·mu·lize \'fȯr-myə-ˌlīz\ *vt* **-lized; -liz·ing** (1842) : FORMULATE 1

form word *n* (1875) : FUNCTION WORD

form·work \'fȯrm-ˌwərk\ *n* (1918) : a set of forms in place to hold wet concrete until it sets

for·myl \'fȯr-ˌmil\ *n* [ISV] (ca. 1859) : the radical HCO of formic acid that is also characteristic of aldehydes

for·ni·cate \'fȯr-nə-ˌkāt\ *vb* **-cat·ed; -cat·ing** [LL *fornicatus*, pp. of *fornicare* to have intercourse with prostitutes, fr. L *fornic-, fornix* arch, vault, brothel] *vi* (1552) : to commit fornication ~ *vt* : to commit fornication with — **for·ni·ca·tor** \-ˌkā-tər\ *n*

for·ni·ca·tion \ˌfȯr-nə-'kā-shən\ *n* (14c) : consensual sexual intercourse between two persons not married to each other — compare ADULTERY

for·nix \'fȯr-niks\ *n, pl* **for·ni·ces** \-nə-ˌsēz\ [NL, fr. L] (1681) : an anatomical arch or fold

for·rad·er *also* **for·rard·er** \'fär-ə-dər\ *adv* [E dial., compar. of E *forward*] (1888) *chiefly Brit* : further ahead

for·sake \fər-'sāk, fȯr-\ *vt* **for·sook** \-'sūk\; **for·sak·en** \-'sā-kən\; **for·sak·ing** [ME, fr. OE *forsacan*, fr. *for-* + *sacan* to dispute; akin to OE *sacu* action at law — more at SAKE] (bef. 12c) : to renounce or turn away from entirely ⟨friends have *forsaken* her⟩ ⟨*forsook* the theater for politics⟩ *syn* see ABANDON

for·sooth \fər-'süth\ *adv* [ME *for soth*, fr. OE *forsōth*, fr. *for* + *sōth* sooth] (bef. 12c) : in truth : INDEED — often used to imply contempt or doubt

for·spent \fȯr-'spent, fȯr-\ *adj* (1563) *archaic* : WORN-OUT, EXHAUSTED

for·swear \fȯr-'swar, fȯr-\ *vb* **swore** \-'swōr, -'swȯr\; **-sworn** \-'swōrn, -'swȯrn\; **-swear·ing** [ME *forsweren*, fr. OE *forswerian*, fr. *for-* + *swerian* to swear] *vt* (bef. 12c) **1** : to make a liar of (oneself) under or as if under oath **2** : to reject or renounce under oath **b**

: to renounce earnestly **3** : to deny under oath ~ *vi* : to swear falsely *syn* see ABJURE

for·sworn \-'swōrn, -'swȯrn\ *adj* (bef. 12c) **1** : guilty of perjury **2** : marked by perjury

for·syth·ia \fər-'si-thē-ə, chiefly Brit -'sī-\ *n* [NL, genus name, fr. William *Forsyth* †1804 Brit. botanist] (ca. 1814) : any of a genus (*Forsythia*) of ornamental shrubs of the olive family with opposite leaves and yellow bell-shaped flowers appearing before the leaves in early spring

forsythia

fort \'fȯrt, 'fȯrt\ *n* [ME *forte*, fr. MF *fort*, fr. *fort*, adj., strong, fr. L *fortis*] (15c) **1** : a strong or fortified place; *esp* : a fortified place occupied only by troops and surrounded with such works as a ditch, rampart, and parapet : FORTIFICATION **2** : a permanent army post — often used in place names

for·ta·lice \'fȯr-tᵊl-əs\ *n* [ME, fr. ML *fortalitia* — more at FORTRESS] (15c) **1** *archaic* : FORTRESS **2** *archaic* : a small fort

¹forte \'fȯrt, 'fȯrt; **2** *is often* 'fȯr-ˌtā *or* fȯr-'tā *or* 'fȯr-tē\ *n* [F *fort*, fr. *fort*, adj., strong] (ca. 1648) **1** : the part of a sword or foil blade that is between the middle and the hilt and that is the strongest part of the blade **2** : one's strong point

usage In *forte* we have a word derived from French that in its "strong point" sense has no entirely satisfactory pronunciation. Usage writers have denigrated \'fȯr-ˌtā\ and \'fȯr-tē\ because they reflect the influence of the Italian-derived ²*forte*. Their recommended pronunciation \'fȯrt\, however, does not exactly reflect French either: the French would write the word *le fort* and would rhyme it with English *for*. So you can take your choice, knowing that someone somewhere will dislike whichever variant you choose. All are standard, however. In British English \'fȯ-ˌtā\ and \'fȯt\ predominate; \'fȯr-ˌtā\ and \fȯr-'tā\ are prob. the most frequent pronunciations in American English.

²for·te \'fȯr-ˌtā, 'fȯr-tē\ *adv or adj* [It, fr. *forte* strong, fr. L *fortis*] (ca. 1724) : LOUD — used as a direction in music

³for·te \'fȯr-ˌtā, 'fȯr-tē\ *n* (1759) : a tone or passage played forte

for·te·pia·no \ˌfȯr-ˌtā-pē-'a-(ˌ)nō *also* -ä-(ˌ)nō\ *n* [F or It; F, fr. It, fr. *forte* loud + *piano* soft] (1771) : an early form of the piano originating in the 18th and early 19th centuries and having a smaller range and softer timbre than a modern piano

for·te–pia·no \ˌfȯr-ˌtā-pē-'a-(ˌ)nō, -ˌfȯr-tē-\ *adv or adj* (ca. 1889) : loud then immediately soft — used as a direction in music

¹forth \'fȯrth, 'fȯrth\ *adv* [ME, fr. OE; akin to OE *for*] (bef. 12c) **1** : onward in time, place, or order : FORWARD ⟨from that day ~⟩ **2** : out into notice or view ⟨put ~ leaves⟩ **3** *obs* : AWAY, ABROAD

²forth *prep* (ca. 1577) *archaic* : forth from: OUT OF

forth·com·ing \fȯrth-'kə-miŋ, fȯrth-; 'fȯrth-ˌ, 'fȯrth-\ *adj* [obs. *forthcome* (to come forth)] (ca. 1532) **1** : being about to appear or to be produced or made available ⟨the ~ holidays⟩ ⟨your ~ novel⟩ ⟨funds are ~⟩ **2 a** : RESPONSIVE, OUTGOING ⟨a ~ and courteous man⟩ **b** : characterized by openness, candidness, and forthrightness ⟨not ~ about his memories of medical school —Mark Kramer⟩

forth of *prep* (13c) *archaic* : out from: OUT OF

¹forth·right \'fȯr-ˌthrīt, 'fȯr-\ *adv* [ME, fr. OE *forthriht*, fr. *forth* + *riht* right] (bef. 12c) **1** *archaic* : directly forward **b** : without hesitation : FRANKLY **2** *archaic* : at once

²forthright *adj* (bef. 12c) **1** *archaic* : proceeding straight on **2** : free from ambiguity or evasiveness : going straight to the point ⟨a ~ critic⟩ ⟨was ~ in appraising the problem⟩ **3** : notably simple in style or quality ⟨~ furniture⟩ — **forth·right·ly** *adv* — **forth·right·ness** *n*

³forthright *n* (1606) *archaic* : a straight path

forth·with \(ˌ)fȯrth-'with, (ˌ)fȯrth- *also* -'with\ *adv* (14c) : IMMEDIATELY

for·ti·fi·ca·tion \ˌfȯr-tə-fə-'kā-shən\ *n* (15c) **1** : an act or process of fortifying **2** : something that fortifies, defends, or strengthens; *esp* : works erected to defend a place or position

fortified wine *n* (1906) : a wine (as sherry) to which alcohol usu. in the form of grape brandy has been added during or after fermentation

for·ti·fi·er \'fȯr-tə-ˌfī(-ə)r\ *n* (ca. 1552) : one that fortifies

for·ti·fy \-ˌfī\ *vb* **-fied; -fy·ing** [ME *fortifien*, fr. MF *fortifier*, fr. LL *fortificare*, fr. L *fortis* strong] *vt* (15c) **1** : to make strong: as **a** : to strengthen and secure (as a town) by forts or batteries **b** : to give physical strength, courage, or endurance to **c** : to add mental or moral strength to : ENCOURAGE ⟨*fortified* by prayer⟩ **d** : to add material to for strengthening or enriching ~ *vi* : to erect fortifications

for·tis \'fȯr-təs\ *adj* [NL, fr. L, strong] (1897) : produced with relatively great articulatory tenseness and strong expiration ⟨\t\ in *toe* is ~, \d\ in *doe* is lenis⟩

¹for·tis·si·mo \fȯr-'ti-sə-ˌmō\ *adv or adj* [It, superl. of *forte*] (1724) : very loud — used esp. as a direction in music

²fortissimo *n, pl* **-mos** *or* **-mi** \-ˌmē\ (1856) : a very loud passage, sound, or tone

for·ti·tude \'fȯr-tə-ˌtüd, -ˌtyüd\ *n* [ME, fr. L *fortitudin-, fortitudo*, fr. *fortis*] (12c) **1** : strength of mind that enables a person to encounter danger or bear pain or adversity with courage **2** *obs* : STRENGTH

fort·night \'fȯrt-ˌnīt, 'fȯrt-\ *n* [ME *fourtenight*, alter. of *fourtene night*, fr. OE *fēowertȳne niht* fourteen nights] (bef. 12c) : a period of 14 days : two weeks

¹fort·night·ly \-lē\ *adj* (1800) : occurring or appearing once in a fortnight

²fortnightly *adv* (1820) : once in a fortnight : every fortnight

³fortnightly *n, pl* **-lies** (1940) : a publication issued fortnightly

FOR·TRAN *or* **For·tran** \'fȯr-ˌtran\ *n* [*formula translation*] (1956) : a computer programming language that resembles algebra in its notation and is widely used for scientific applications

---

\ə\ abut \ᵊ\ kitten, F table \ər\ further \a\ ash \ā\ ace \ä\ mop, mar
\au̇\ out \ch\ chin \e\ bet \ē\ easy \g\ go \i\ hit \ī\ ice \j\ job
\ŋ\ sing \ō\ go \o̧\ law \o̧i\ boy \th\ thin \t̶h̶\ the \ü\ loot \u̇\ foot
\y\ yet \zh\ vision \à, k̲, ⁿ, œ, œ̄, ᵫ, ᵮ, ᵞ\ *see* Guide to Pronunciation

for·tress \'fȯr-trəs\ *n* [ME *forteresse*, fr. MF *forteresce*, fr. ML *fortalitia*, fr. L *fortis* strong] (14c) : a fortified place : STRONGHOLD; *esp* : a large and permanent fortification sometimes including a town — **for·tress-like** \-līk\ *adj*

for·tu·itous \fȯr-'tü-ə-təs, -'tyü-, fər-\ *adj* [L *fortuitus*; akin to L *fort-, fors*] (1653) **1** : occurring by chance **2 a** : FORTUNATE, LUCKY ⟨from a cost standpoint, the company's timing is ~ —*Business Week*⟩ **b** : coming or happening by a lucky chance ⟨belted down the stairs, and there was a ~ train —Doris Lessing⟩ *syn* see ACCIDENTAL — **for·tu·itous·ly** *adv* — **for·tu·itous·ness** *n*

usage Sense 2a has been influenced in meaning by *fortunate*. It has been in standard if not elevated use for some 70 years, but is still disdained by some critics. Sense 2b, a blend of 1 and 2a, is virtually unnoticed by the critics. Sense 1 is the only sense commonly used in negative constructions.

for·tu·ity \-ə-tē\ *n, pl* **-ities** (ca. 1747) **1** : the quality or state of being fortuitous **2** : a chance event or occurrence

for·tu·nate \'fȯrch-nət, 'fȯr-chə-\ *adj* (14c) **1** : bringing some good thing not forseen as certain : AUSPICIOUS **2** : receiving some unexpected good *syn* see LUCKY — **for·tu·nate·ness** *n*

for·tu·nate·ly \-lē\ *adv* (1548) **1** : in a fortunate manner **2** : it is fortunate that

¹for·tune \'fȯr-chən\ *n* [ME, fr. MF, fr. L *fortuna*; akin to L *fort-, fors* chance, luck, and perh. to *ferre* to carry — more at BEAR] (14c) **1** *often cap* : a hypothetical force or personified power that unpredictably determines events and issues favorably or unfavorably **2** *obs* : ACCIDENT, INCIDENT **3 a** : prosperity attained partly through luck : SUCCESS **b** : LUCK **1** *pl* : the turns and courses of luck accompanying one's progress (as through life) ⟨her ~s varied but she never gave up⟩ **4** : DESTINY, FATE ⟨can tell your ~⟩; *also* : a prediction of fortune **5 a** : RICHES, WEALTH ⟨a man of ~⟩ **b** : a store of material possessions ⟨the family ~⟩ **c** : a very large sum of money ⟨spent a ~ redecorating⟩

²fortune *vb* **for·tuned; for·tun·ing** *vt* (14c) **1** *obs* : to give good or bad fortune to **2** *archaic* : to endow with a fortune ~ *vi, archaic* : HAPPEN, CHANCE

fortune cookie *n* (1962) : a thin cookie folded to contain a slip of paper on which is printed a fortune, proverb, or humorous statement

fortune hunter *n* (1689) : a person who seeks wealth esp. by marriage

for·tune–tell·er \-₁te-lər\ *n* (1590) : one that professes to foretell future events — **for·tune–tell·ing** \-liŋ\ *n or adj*

for·ty \'fȯr-tē\ *n, pl* **forties** [ME *fourty*, adj., fr. OE *fēowertig*, fr. *fēowertig* group of 40, fr. *fēower* four + *-tig* group of 10; akin to OE *tīen* ten] (bef. 12c) **1** — see NUMBER table **2** *pl* : the numbers 40 to 49; *specif* : the years 40 to 49 in a lifetime or century **3** : the third point scored by a side in a game of tennis — **for·ti·eth** \'fȯr-tē-əth\ *adj or n* — **forty** *adj* — **forty** *pron, pl in constr* — **for·ty·ish** \-tē-ish\ *adj*

for·ty–five \₁fȯr-tē-'fīv\ *n* (1904) **1** — see NUMBER table **2** : a .45 caliber handgun — usu. written .45 **3** : a phonograph record designed to be played at 45 revolutions per minute — usu. written 45 — **forty–five** *adj* — **forty–five** *pron, pl in constr*

Forty Hours *n pl but sing or pl in constr* (1759) : a Roman Catholic devotion in which the churches of a diocese in two-day turns have the Blessed Sacrament exposed on the altar for continuous daytime veneration

for·ty–nin·er \₁fȯr-tē-'nī-nər\ *n* (1853) : one taking part in the rush to California for gold in 1849

forty winks *n pl but sing or pl in constr* (1872) : a short sleep : NAP

fo·rum \'fȯr-əm, 'fȯr-\ *n, pl* **forums** *also* **fo·ra** \-ə\ [L; akin to L *foris* outside, *fores* door — more at DOOR] (15c) **1 a** : the marketplace or public place of an ancient Roman city forming the center of judicial and public business **b** : a public meeting place for open discussion **c** : a medium (as a newspaper) of open discussion or expression of ideas **2** : a judicial body or assembly : COURT **3 a** : a public meeting or lecture involving audience discussion **b** : a program (as on radio or television) involving discussion of a problem usu. by several authorities

¹for·ward \'fȯr-wərd, *also* 'fō- or 'fȯ-, *Southern also* 'fär-\ *adj* [ME, fr. OE *foreweard*, fr. *fore-* + *-weard* -ward] (bef. 12c) **1 a** : near, belonging to, or situated at the forepart **b** : situated in advance **2 a** : strongly inclined : READY **b** : lacking modesty or reserve : BRASH **3** : notably advanced or developed : PRECOCIOUS **4** : moving, tending, or leading toward a position in front; *also* : moving toward an opponent's goal **5 a** : advocating an advanced policy in the direction of what is considered progress **b** : EXTREME, RADICAL **6** : of, relating to, or getting ready for the future ⟨~ buying of produce⟩ — **for·ward·ly** *adv* — **for·ward·ness** *n*

²forward *adv* (bef. 12c) : to or toward what is ahead or in front ⟨from that time ~⟩ ⟨moved slowly ~⟩

³forward *vt* (1596) **1** : to help onward : PROMOTE ⟨~ed his friend's career⟩ **2 a** : to send forward : TRANSMIT ⟨will ~ the goods on receipt of your check⟩ **b** : to send or ship onward from an intermediate post or station in transit ⟨~ mail⟩ *syn* see ADVANCE

⁴forward *n* (1879) : a player who plays at the front of his team's formation near the goal at which his team is attempting to score

for·ward·er \-wər-dər\ *n* (1549) : one that forwards; *esp* : an agent who performs services (as receiving, transshipping, or delivering) designed to move goods to their destination

for·ward–look·ing \'fȯr-wərd-₁lu̇-kiŋ\ *adj* (1800) : concerned with or planning for the future

forward pass *n* (1903) : a pass (as in football) made in the direction of the opponents' goal

for·wards \'fȯr-wərdz\ *adv* (15c) : FORWARD

for·worn \fȯr-'wȯrn, -'wȯrn\ *adj* (1528) *archaic* : WORN-OUT

for·zan·do \fȯrt-'sän-(₁)dō\ *adj or adv* [It] (ca. 1828) : SFORZANDO

¹fos·sa \'fä-sə\ *n, pl* **fos·sae** \-₁sē, -₁sī\ [NL, fr. L, ditch] (1771) : an anatomical pit, groove, or depression

²fossa *n* [Malagasy] (1838) : a slender lithe carnivorous mammal (*Cryptoprocta ferox*) of Madagascar that resembles a cat esp. in having retractile claws but is usu. considered a viverrid

fosse *or* **foss** \'fäs\ *n* [ME *fosse*, fr. OF, fr. L *fossa*, fr. fem. of *fossus*] (15c) : DITCH, MOAT

fos·sick \'fä-sik\ *vb* [E dial. *fossick* to ferret out] *vi* (1852) **1** *Austral & NewZeal* : to search for gold or gemstones typically by picking over abandoned workings **2** *chiefly Austral & NewZeal* : to search about : RUMMAGE ~ *vt, chiefly Austral & NewZeal* : to search for by or as if

by rummaging : ferret out — **fos·sick·er** *n, chiefly Austral & NewZeal*

¹fos·sil \'fä-səl\ *adj* [L *fossilis* obtained by digging, fr. *fodere* to dig — more at BED] (1665) **1** : preserved from a past geologic age ⟨~ plants⟩ ⟨~ water in an underground reservoir⟩ **2** : being or resembling a fossil **3** : of or relating to fossil fuel

²fossil *n* (1736) **1** : a remnant, impression, or trace of an organism of past geologic ages that has been preserved in the earth's crust — compare LIVING FOSSIL **2 a** : one whose views are outmoded : FOGY **b** : something (as a theory) that has become rigidly fixed **3** : an old word or word element preserved only by idiom (as *fro* in *to and fro*)

fossil fuel *n* (1835) : a fuel (as coal, oil, or natural gas) that is formed in the earth from plant or animal remains — **fos·sil–fueled** \-₁fyü(-ə)ld\ *adj*

fos·sil·if·er·ous \₁fä-sə-'li-f(ə-)rəs\ *adj* (ca. 1846) : containing fossils

fos·sil·ise *chiefly Brit var of* FOSSILIZE

fos·sil·ize \'fä-sə-₁līz\ *vb* **-ized; -iz·ing** *vt* (1794) **1** : to convert into a fossil **2** : to make outmoded, rigid, or fixed ~ *vi* : to become changed into a fossil — **fos·sil·iza·tion** \₁fä-sə-lə-'zā-shən\ *n*

fos·so·ri·al \fä-'sȯr-ē-əl, -'sȯr-\ *adj* [ML *fossorius* used for digging, fr. L *fossor* digger, fr. *fodere*] (1837) : adapted to digging ⟨a ~ foot⟩

¹fos·ter \'fȯs-tər, 'fäs-\ *adj* [ME, fr. OE *fōstor-*, fr. *fōstor* food, feeding; akin to OE *fōda* food] (bef. 12c) : affording, receiving, or sharing nurture or parental care though not related by blood or legal ties

²foster *vt* **fos·tered; fos·ter·ing** \-t(ə-)riŋ\ (12c) **1** : to give parental care to : NURTURE **2** : to promote the growth or development of : ENCOURAGE — **fos·ter·er** \-tər-ər\ *n*

fos·ter·age \-tə-rij\ *n* (1614) **1** : the act of fostering **2** : a custom once prevalent in Ireland, Wales, and Scotland of entrusting one's child to foster parents to be brought up

foster home *n* (1886) : a household in which an orphaned, neglected, or delinquent child is placed for care

fos·ter·ling \-tər-liŋ\ *n* (bef. 12c) : a foster child

fou \'fü\ *adj* [ME (Sc) *fow* full, fr. ME *full*] (1535) *Scot* : DRUNK 1a

Fou·cault pendulum \₁fü-'kō-\ *n* [J.B.L. *Foucault*] (1931) : a freely swinging pendulum that consists of a heavy weight hung by a long wire and that swings in a constant direction which appears to change showing that the earth rotates

fouet·té \(₁)fwe-'tā\ *n* [F, fr. pp. of *fouetter* to whip, fr. MF, fr. *fouet* whip, fr. OF, fr. *fou* beech, fr. L *fagus* — more at BEECH] (1830) : a quick whipping movement of the raised leg in ballet usu. accompanying a pirouette

fought *past and past part of* FIGHT

¹foul \'fau̇(ə)l\ *adj* [ME, fr. OE *fūl*; akin to OHG *fūl* rotten, L *pus* pus, *putēre* to stink, Gk *pyon* pus] (bef. 12c) **1 a** : offensive to the senses : LOATHSOME **b** : filled or covered with offensive matter **2** : full of dirt or mud **3 a** : morally or spiritually odious : DETESTABLE ⟨a ~ crime⟩ **b** : notably unpleasant or distressing : WRETCHED, HORRID ⟨in a ~ mood⟩ **4** : OBSCENE, ABUSIVE ⟨~ language⟩ **5 a** : being wet and stormy **b** : obstructive to navigation ⟨a ~ tide⟩ **6** *dial Brit* : HOMELY, UGLY **7 a** : TREACHEROUS, DISHONORABLE ⟨fair means or ~⟩ **b** : constituting an infringement of rules in a game or sport ⟨a ~ blow in boxing⟩ **8** : containing marked-up corrections ⟨~ manuscript⟩ ⟨~ proofs⟩ **9** : encrusted, clogged, or choked with a foreign substance ⟨the chimney was ~ and smoked badly⟩ **10** : being odorous and impure : POLLUTED ⟨~ air⟩ **11** : placed in a situation that impedes physical movement : ENTANGLED **12** : being outside the foul lines in baseball *syn* see DIRTY — **foul·ly** \'fau̇(l)-lē\ *adv* — **foul·ness** *n*

²foul *n* (bef. 12c) **1** *archaic* : something foul **2** : an entanglement or collision esp. in angling or sailing **3 a** : an infringement of the rules in a game or sport **b** : FREE THROW **4** : FOUL BALL

³foul *vi* (bef. 12c) **1** : to become or be foul: as **a** : DECOMPOSE, ROT **b** : to become encrusted, clogged, or choked with a foreign substance **c** : to become entangled or come into collision **2** : to commit a violation of the rules in a sport or game **3** : to hit a foul ball ~ *vt* **1** : to make foul: as **a** : to make dirty : POLLUTE **b** : to tangle or come into collision with **c** : to encrust with a foreign substance ⟨a ship's bottom ~ed with barnacles⟩ **d** : OBSTRUCT, BLOCK **2** : DISHONOR, DISCREDIT **3** : to commit a foul against ~ **4** : to hit (a baseball) foul

⁴foul *adv* (13c) : in a foul manner : so as to be foul

fou·lard \fu̇-'lärd\ *n* [F] (1830) **1 a** : a lightweight plain-woven or twilled silk usu. decorated with a printed pattern **b** : an imitation of this fabric **2** : an article of clothing made of foulard

foul ball *n* (1860) : a baseball batted into foul territory

foul·brood \'fau̇l-₁brüd\ *n* (1863) : a destructive disease of honeybee larvae caused by bacteria (as *Bacillus larvae*)

foul·ing *n* (14c) : DEPOSIT, INCRUSTATION ⟨~ on a ship's bottom⟩

foul line *n* (1878) **1** : either of two straight lines extending from the rear corner of home plate through the outer corners of first and third base respectively and prolonged to the boundary of a baseball field **2** : a line across a bowling alley that a player must not step over when delivering the ball **3** : either of two lines on a basketball court parallel to and 15 feet from the backboards behind which a player must stand while shooting a free throw

foul–mouthed \'fau̇l-₁mau̇thd, -₁mau̇tht\ *adj* (1596) : given to the use of obscene, profane, or abusive language

foul out *vi* (1948) : to be put out of a basketball game for exceeding the number of fouls permitted

foul play *n* (15c) : VIOLENCE; *esp* : MURDER

foul shot *n* (ca. 1949) : FREE THROW

foul tip *n* [*foul* + *tip* (tap)] (1870) : a pitched ball in baseball that is slightly deflected by the bat; *specif* : a tipped pitch legally caught by the catcher and counting as a full strike with the ball remaining in play

foul–up \'fau̇l-₁əp\ *n* (1950) **1** : a state of confusion or an error caused by ineptitude, carelessness, or mismanagement ⟨~s in transportation⟩ **2** : a mechanical difficulty

foul up *vt* (1947) **1** : to make dirty : CONTAMINATE **2** : to spoil by making mistakes or using poor judgment : CONFUSE **3** : ENTANGLE, BLOCK ⟨*fouled up* communications⟩ ~ *vi* : to cause a foul-up : BUNGLE ⟨it was his fault. He had *fouled* up —Pat Frank⟩

¹found \'fau̇nd\ *past and past part of* FIND

²found *adj* (1793) **1** : having all usual, standard, or reasonably expected equipment ⟨the boat comes fully ~, ready to go —Holiday⟩ **2**

: presented as or incorporated into an artistic work essentially as found ⟨sculpture of fabric, wood, and other ~ materials —Hilton Kramer⟩
³**found** n (1830) : free food and lodging in addition to wages ⟨they're paid $175 a month and ~ —*New Yorker*⟩
⁴**found** vt [ME, fr. OF *fonder*, fr. L *fundare*, fr. *fundus* bottom — more at BOTTOM] (13c) **1** : to take the first steps in building **2** : to set or ground on something solid : BASE **3** : to establish (as an institution) often with provision for future maintenance
⁵**found** vt [MF *fondre* to pour, melt, fr. L *fundere;* akin to OE *gēotan* to pour, Gk *chein*] (1562) : to melt (as metal) and pour into a mold
foun·da·tion \faun-'dā-shən\ n (14c) **1** : the act of founding **2** : a basis (as a tenet, principle, or axiom) upon which something stands or is supported ⟨the ~s of geometry⟩ ⟨the rumor is without ~ in fact⟩ **3 a** : funds given for the permanent support of an institution : ENDOW-MENT **b** : an organization or institution established by endowment with provision for future maintenance **4** : an underlying base or support; *esp* : the whole masonry substructure of a building **5 a** : a body or ground upon which something is built up or overlaid **b** : a woman's supporting undergarment : CORSET **c** : a cosmetic usu. used as a base for makeup — **foun·da·tion·al** \-shnəl, -shə-n³l\ adj — **foun·da·tion·less** \-shən-ləs\ adj
foundation stone n (1651) **1** : BASIS, GROUNDWORK **2** : a stone in the foundation of a building; *esp* : such a stone laid with public ceremony — compare CORNERSTONE
¹**found·er** \'faun-dər\ n [⁴*found*] (14c) : one that founds or establishes
²**found·er** \'faun-dər\ vb **foun·dered; foun·der·ing** \-d(ə-)riŋ\ [ME *foundren* to send to the bottom, collapse, fr. MF *fondrer*, ultim. fr. L *fundus*] (14c) **1** : to become disabled; *esp* : to go lame **2** : to give way : COLLAPSE **3** : to sink below the surface of the water **4** : to come to grief : FAIL ~ vt : to disable (an animal) esp. by excessive feeding
³**found·er** n (ca. 1547) : LAMINITIS
⁴**found·er** n [⁵*found*] (15c) : one that founds metal; *esp* : TYPEFOUNDER
founding father n (1914) **1** : an originator of an institution or move-ment : FOUNDER **2** *often cap both Fs* : a leading figure in the founding of the U.S.; *specif* : a member of the American Constitutional Conven-tion of 1787
found·ling \'faun(d)-liŋ\ n (14c) : an infant found after its unknown parents have abandoned it
found object n (1950) : OBJET TROUVÉ
found poem n (1966) : a poem consisting of words found in a nonpo-etic context (as a product label) and usu. broken into lines that convey a verse rhythm
found·ry \'faun-drē\ n, pl **foundries** (1536) **1** : an establishment where founding is carried on **2** : the act, process, or art of casting metals
¹**fount** \'faunt\ n [ME, fr. MF *font*, fr. L *font-, fons*] (15c) : FOUNTAIN, SOURCE
²**fount** \'fänt, 'faunt\ n [F *fonte*, fr. MF — more at FONT] (ca. 1683) *Brit* : a type font
¹**foun·tain** \'faun-t³n\ n [ME, fr. MF *fontaine*, fr. LL *fontana*, fr. L, fem. of *fontanus* of a spring, fr. *font-, fons*] (14c) **1** : the source from which something proceeds or is supplied **2** : a spring of water issuing from the earth **3** : an artificially produced jet of water; *also* : the structure from which it rises **4** : a reservoir containing a liquid that can be drawn off as needed **5** : SODA FOUNTAIN 2
²**fountain** vi (1903) : to flow or spout like a fountain ~ vt : to cause to flow like a fountain
foun·tain·head \-,hed\ n (1585) **1** : a spring that is the source of a stream **2** : principal source : ORIGIN
fountain pen n (1710) : a pen containing a reservoir that automatically feeds the writing point with ink
four \'fōr, 'fȯr\ n [ME, fr. OE *fēower;* akin to OHG *fior* four, L *quattuor*, Gk *tessares, tettares*] (bef. 12c) **1** — see NUMBER table **2** : the fourth in a set or series ⟨the ~ of hearts⟩ **3** : something having four units or members: as **a** : a 4-oared racing shell or its crew **b** : a 4-cylinder engine or automobile — **four** adj — **four** pron, pl in constr
four–bag·ger \-'ba-gər\ n (1926) : HOME RUN
four–ball \-,bȯl\ adj (1904) : relating to or being a golf match in which the best individual score of one partnership is matched against the best individual score of another partnership for each hole
four–chée \fur-'shā\ adj [F (fem.), lit., forked] (1706) *of a heraldic cross* : having the end of each arm forked — see CROSS illustration
four–dimensional adj (1880) : relating to or having four dimensions ⟨~ space-time continuum⟩; *esp* : consisting of or relating to elements requiring four coordinates to determine them
four–dri·nier \'fȯr-drə-'nir, ,fȯr-; fur-'drin-ē-ər, fȯr-, fȯr-\ n, often cap [Henry & Sealy *Fourdrinier*] (1839) : a machine for making paper in an endless web
four–eyed \'fōr-,īd, 'fȯr-\ adj (1926) : wearing glasses
4–F \'fȯr-'ef, 'fȯr-\ n (1944) : classification as unfit for military service; *also* : a person having this classification
four–flush vi (1896) : to bluff in poker holding a four flush; *broadly* : to make a false claim : BLUFF — **four–flush·er** \-'flə-shər\ n
four flush n (1887) : four cards of the same suit in a 5-card poker hand
four·fold \'fȯr-,fōld, 'fȯr-, -'fōld\ adj [ME, fr. OE *fēowerfeald*, fr. *fēower* + *-feald* -fold] (bef. 12c) **1** : being four times as great or as many **2** : having four units or members — **fourfold** \-'fōld\ adv
four–foot·ed \'fu-təd\ adj (14c) : having four feet : QUADRUPED
four·gon \fur-'gōn\ n, pl **fourgons** \-'gōn(z)\ [F] (1848) : a wagon for carrying baggage
4–H \'fōr-'āch, 'fȯr-\ adj [fr. the fourfold aim of improving the head, heart, hands, and health] (1926) : of or relating to a program set up by the U.S. Department of Agriculture orig. in rural areas to help young people become productive citizens by instructing them in useful skills (as in agriculture, animal husbandry, and carpentry), community ser-vice, and personal development — **4–H'er** *also* **4–H–er** \-'ā-chər\ n
four–hand \'fȯr-,hand, 'fȯr-\ adj (ca. 1909) : FOUR-HANDED
four–hand·ed \-'han-dəd\ adj (1824) **1** : engaged in by four persons ⟨a ~ card game⟩ **2** : designed for four hands ⟨a ~ musical composi-tion⟩
Four Horsemen n pl [fr. the apocalyptic vision in Rev 6:2–8] (1918) : war, famine, pestilence, and death personified as the four major plagues of mankind

Four Hundred or **400** n (1888) : the exclusive social set of a commu-nity — used with *the*
Fou·ri·er analysis \'fur-ē-,ā-\ n [Baron J.B.J. *Fourier* †1830 Fr. geo-metrician & physicist] (ca. 1928) : the process of using the terms of a Fourier series to find a function that approximates periodic data
Fou·ri·er·ism \'fur-ē-ə-,ri-zəm, -ē-,ā-,i-\ n [F *fouriérisme*, fr. F.M.C. *Fourier*] (1843) : a system for reorganizing society into cooperative communities of small self-sustaining groups — **Fou·ri·er·ist** \-ē-ə-rist, -ē-,ā-ist\ n
Fou·ri·er series \'fur-ē-,ā-\ n [Baron J.B.J. *Fourier*] (1877) : an infinite series in which the terms are constants multiplied by sine or cosine functions of integer multiples of the variable and which is used in the analysis of periodic functions
Fourier's theorem n (1834) : a theorem in mathematics: under suit-able conditions any periodic function can be represented by a Fourier series
Fourier transform n (1923) : any of various functions (as $F(u)$) that under suitable conditions can be obtained from given functions (as $f(x)$) by multiplying by e^{iux} and integrating over all values of x and that in scientific instrumentation describe the dependence of the average of a series of measurements (as of a spectrum) on a quantity of interest (as brightness) esp. of a very small magnitude — called also *Fourier trans-formation*
four–in–hand \'fōr-ən-,hand, 'fȯr-\ n (1793) **1 a** : a team of four horses driven by one person **b** : a vehicle drawn by such a team **2** : a necktie tied in a slipknot with long ends overlapping vertically in front
four–letter adj (1897) : of, relating to, or being four-letter words
four–letter word n (1897) : any of a group of vulgar or obscene words typically made up of four letters
four–line octave n [fr. the four accent marks appended to the letters representing its notes] (1931) : the musical octave that begins on the third C above middle C — see PITCH illustration
four–o'clock \'fōr-ə-,kläk, 'fȯr-\ n (1756) : any of a genus (*Mirabilis*) of chiefly American annual or perennial herbs (family Nyctaginaceae, the four-o'clock family) having apetalous flowers with a showy involu-cre simulating a calyx; *esp* : a garden plant (*M. jalapa*) with fragrant yellow, red, or white flowers opening late in the afternoon
four of a kind (ca. 1934) : four cards of the same rank in one hand — see POKER illustration
four·plex \'fōr-,pleks, 'fȯr-\ n (1952) : a building that contains four separate apartments
four–post·er \,fōr-'pō-stər, ,fȯr-\ n (1836) : a bed with tall often carved corner posts orig. designed to support curtains or a canopy
four–ra·gère \,fur-ə-'zher\ n [F, fr. fem. of *fourrager* of forage, fr. *fourrage* forage] (1919) : a braided cord worn usu. around the left shoulder; *esp* : such a cord awarded as a decoration to a military unit
four·score \'fōr-'skōr, 'fȯr-'skȯr\ adj (13c) : being four times twenty : EIGHTY
four·some \'fōr-səm, 'fȯr-\ n (14c) **1 a** : a group of four persons or things : QUARTET **b** : two couples **2 a** : a golf match in which two players compete against two others with players on each side taking turns playing one ball; *broadly* : any golf match involving four players

four-poster

four·square \-'skwar, -'skwer\ adj (14c) **1** : SQUARE **2** : marked by boldness and conviction : FORTHRIGHT — **foursquare** adv
four–star \-'stär\ adj [fr. the number of asterisks used to denote rela-tive excellence in guidebooks] (1921) : of a superior degree of excel-lence ⟨a ~ French restaurant⟩
four·teen \fōr-'tēn, fȯr-\ n [ME *fourtene*, fr. *fēowertiene*, fr. OE *fēowertiene*, adj., fr. *fēower* + *-tiene;* akin to OE *tien* ten] (bef. 12c) — see NUMBER table — **fourteen** adj or pron, pl in constr — **four·teenth** \-'tēn(t)th; -,tēn(t)th\ adj or n
four·teen·er \-'tē-nər\ n (1884) : a verse consisting of 14 syllables or esp. of 7 iambic feet
fourth \'fōrth, 'fȯrth\ n, pl **fourths** \'fōr(th)s, 'fȯr(th)s\ (bef. 12c) **1** — see NUMBER table **2 a** : a musical interval embracing four tones of the diatonic scale **b** : a tone at this interval; *specif* : SUBDOMINANT 1 **c** : the harmonic combination of two tones a fourth apart **3** : the 4th forward gear or speed of a motor vehicle **4** cap : INDEPENDENCE DAY — used with *the* — **fourth** adj or adv — **fourth·ly** adv
fourth class n (1862) **1** : a class or group ranking fourth in a series **2** : a class of mail in the U.S. that comprises merchandise and non-second-class printed matter and is not sealed against inspection
fourth dimension n (1875) **1** : a dimension in addition to length, breadth, and depth; *specif* : a coordinate in addition to three rectangu-lar coordinates esp. when interpreted as the time coordinate in a space-time continuum **2** : something outside the range of ordinary experi-ence — **fourth–dimensional** adj
fourth estate n, *often cap F&E* (1752) : the public press
Fourth of July (1779) : INDEPENDENCE DAY
fourth world n, *often cap F&W* (1974) : a group of nations esp. in Africa and Asia characterized by extremely low per capita income and an absence of valuable natural resources
four–way \'fōr-,wā, 'fȯr-\ adj (1824) **1** : allowing or affecting passage in any of four directions **2** : including four participants
four–wheel \'fōr-,hwēl, 'fȯr-, -,wēl\ or **four–wheeled** \-,hwē(ə)ld, -,wē(ə)ld\ adj (1740) **1** : having four wheels **2** : acting on or by means of four wheels of an automotive vehicle ⟨~ drive⟩
four–wheel·er \-,hwē-lər, -,wē-\ n (1846) : a vehicle with four wheels
fo·vea \'fō-vē-ə\ n, pl **fo·ve·ae** \-vē-,ē, -vē-,ī\ [NL, fr. L, pit] (1849) **1** : a small fossa **2** : a small rodless area of the retina that affords acute

\ə\ abut \³\ kitten, F table \ər\ further \a\ ash \ā\ ace \ä\ mop, mar
\aú\ out \ch\ chin \e\ bet \ē\ easy \g\ go \i\ hit \ī\ ice \j\ job
\ŋ\ sing \ō\ go \ȯ\ law \ȯi\ boy \th\ thin \th\ the \ü\ loot \ú\ foot
\y\ yet \zh\ vision \ə, k, ⁿ, œ, œ̄, ᵫ, ūe, ᵞ\ see Guide to Pronunciation

vision — see EYE illustration — **fo·ve·al** \-vē-əl\ *adj* — **fo·ve·ate** \-vē-ˌāt, -ət\ *adj*

fovea cen·tra·lis \-sen-'tra-ləs, -'trä-, -'trä-\ *n* [NL, central fovea] (1858) : FOVEA 2

¹fowl \'faü(ə)l\ *n, pl* **fowl** or **fowls** [ME *foul*, fr. OE *fugel; akin to OHG *fogal* bird, and prob. to OE *flēogan* to fly — more at FLY] (bef. 12c) **1** : a bird of any kind — compare WATERFOWL, WILDFOWL **2 a** : a cock or hen of the domestic chicken (*Gallus gallus*); *esp* : an adult hen **b** : any of several domesticated or wild gallinaceous birds — compare GUINEA FOWL, JUNGLE FOWL **3** : the meat of fowls used as food

²fowl *vi* (bef. 12c) : to seek, catch, or kill wildfowl — **fowl·er** *n*

fowling piece *n* (1596) : a shotgun for shooting birds or small quadrupeds

¹fox \'fäks\ *n, pl* **fox·es** also **fox** *often attrib* [ME, fr. OE; akin to OHG *fuhs* fox and perh. to Skt *puccha* tail] (bef. 12c) **1 a** : any of various carnivorous mammals (esp. genus *Vulpes*) of the dog family related to but smaller than wolves with shorter legs, more pointed muzzle, large erect ears, and long bushy tail **b** : the fur of a fox **2** : a clever crafty person **3** *archaic* : SWORD **4** *cap* : a member of an American Indian people formerly living in what is now Wisconsin **5** : a good-looking young woman or man

²fox *vt* (1611) **1** *obs* : INTOXICATE **2 a** : to trick by ingenuity or cunning : OUTWIT **b** : BAFFLE

foxed \'fäkst\ *adj* (1847) : discolored with yellowish brown stains

fox fire *n* (15c) : an eerie phosphorescent light (as of decaying wood); *also* : a luminous fungus (as *Armillaria mellea*) that causes decaying wood to glow

fox·glove \'fäks-ˌgləv\ *n* (bef. 12c) : any of a genus (*Digitalis*) of erect herbs of the snapdragon family; *esp* : a common European biennial or perennial (*D. purpurea*) cultivated for its showy racemes of dotted white or purple tubular flowers and as a source of digitalis

fox grape *n* (1657) : any of several native grapes (esp. *Vitis labrusca*) of eastern No. America with sour or musky fruit

fox·hole \'fäks-ˌhōl\ *n* (1919) : a pit dug usu. hastily for individual cover from enemy fire

fox·hound \-ˌhaünd\ *n* (ca. 1763) : any of various large swift powerful hounds of great endurance used in hunting foxes and developed to form several breeds and many distinctive strains — compare AMERICAN FOXHOUND, ENGLISH FOXHOUND

fox-hunt·er \-ˌhən-tər\ *n* (1692) **1** : one who engages in foxhunting **2** : HUNTER 1c

fox-hunt·ing \-ˌhən-tiŋ\ *n* (1674) : a pastime in which participants on horseback ride over the countryside following a pack of hounds on the trail of a fox — **fox-hunt** \-ˌhənt\ *vi*

fox·tail \'fäks-ˌtāl\ *n* (14c) **1 a** : the tail of a fox **b** : something resembling the tail of a fox **2** : any of several grasses (esp. genera *Alopecurus, Hordeum,* and *Setaria*) with spikes resembling brushes — called also *foxtail grass*

foxtail lily *n* (1946) : EREMURUS

foxtail millet *n* (ca. 1899) : a coarse drought-resistant but frost-sensitive annual grass (*Setaria italica*) grown for grain, hay, and forage

fox terrier *n* (1823) : any of a smooth-haired or a wirehaired breed of small lively terriers formerly used to dig out foxes

Fox·trot \'fäks-ˌträt\ (1952) : a communications code word for the letter *f*

¹fox–trot \'fäks-ˌträt\ *n* (1872) **1** : a short broken slow trotting gait in which the hind foot of the horse hits the ground a trifle before the diagonally opposite forefoot **2** : a ballroom dance in duple time that includes slow walking steps, quick running steps, and the step of the two-step

²fox–trot *vi* (1916) : to dance the fox-trot

foxy \'fäk-sē\ *adj* **fox·i·er; -est** (1528) **1** : resembling or suggestive of a fox ⟨a narrow ~ face⟩: as **a** : cunningly shrewd **b** : of a warm reddish brown color ⟨~ eyebrows⟩ **2** : having a sharp brisk flavor ⟨~ grapes⟩ **3** : physically attractive ⟨a ~ lady⟩ *syn* see SLY — **fox·i·ly** \'fäk-sə-lē\ *adv* — **fox·i·ness** \-sē-nəs\ *n*

foy \'föi\ *n* [D dial. *fooi* feast at end of the harvest] (ca. 1645) *chiefly Scot* : a farewell feast or gift

foy·er \'föi-(ə)r, 'föi-ˌ(y)ā *also* 'fwä-ˌyā\ *n* [F, lit., fireplace, fr. (assumed) VL *focarium*, fr. L *focus* hearth] (1859) : an anteroom or lobby esp. of a theater; *also* : an entrance hallway : VESTIBULE

Fra \'frä\ *n* [It, short for *frate*, fr. L *frater* — more at BROTHER] (ca. 1890) — used as a title equivalent to *brother* preceding the name of an Italian monk or friar

fra·cas \'frā-kəs, 'fra-, *Brit* 'fra-ˌkä\ *n, pl* **fra·cas·es** \-kə-səz\ *or Brit* **frac·as** \-ˌkäz\ [F, din, row, fr. It *fracasso*, fr. *fracassare* to shatter] (1727) : a noisy quarrel : BRAWL

frac·tal \'frak-t³l\ *n* [F *fractale*, fr. L *fractus* broken, uneven (pp. of *frangere* to break) + *-ale* -al (n. suffix)] (1975) : any of various extremely irregular curves or shapes for which any suitably chosen part is similar in shape to a given larger or smaller part when magnified or reduced to the same size — **fractal** *adj*

fract·ed \'frak-təd\ *adj* [L *fractus*] (1547) *obs* : BROKEN

frac·tion \'frak-shən\ *n* [ME *fraccioun*, fr. LL *fraction-, fractio* act of breaking, fr. L *frangere* to break — more at BREAK] (14c) **1 a** : a numerical representation (as ¾, ⅝, 3.234) indicating the quotient of two numbers **b** (1) : a piece broken off : FRAGMENT (2) : a discrete unit : PORTION **2** : one of several portions (as of a distillate) separable by fractionation **3** : BIT, LITTLE ⟨a ~ closer⟩

frac·tion·al \-shnəl, -shə-n³l\ *adj* (1675) **1** : of, relating to, or being a fraction **2** : of, relating to, or being fractional currency **3** : relatively small : INCONSIDERABLE **4** : of, relating to, or involving a process for separating components of a mixture through differences in physical or chemical properties ⟨~ distillation⟩ — **frac·tion·al·ly** *adv*

fractional currency *n* (1862) **1** : paper money in denominations of less than one dollar issued by the U.S. 1863–76 **2** : currency in denominations less than the basic monetary unit

frac·tion·al·ize \'frak-shnə-ˌlīz, -shə-n³l-ˌiz\ *vt* **-ized; -iz·ing** (1924) : to break up into parts or sections — **frac·tion·al·iza·tion** \ˌfrak-shnə-lə-'zā-shən, -shə-n³l-ə-'zā-\ *n*

frac·tion·ate \'frak-shə-ˌnāt\ *vt* **-at·ed; -at·ing** (1867) **1** : to separate (as a mixture) into different portions **2** : to divide or break up — **frac·tion·ation** \ˌfrak-shə-'nā-shən\ *n* — **frac·tion·ator** \'frak-shə-ˌnā-tər\ *n*

frac·tious \'frak-shəs\ *adj* [*fraction* (discord) + *-ous*] (1725) **1** : tending to be troublesome : UNRULY **2** : QUARRELSOME, IRRITABLE — **frac·tious·ly** *adv* — **frac·tious·ness** *n*

¹frac·ture \'frak-chər, -shər\ *n* [ME, fr. L *fractura,* fr. *fractus*] (15c) **1** : the result of fracturing : BREAK **2** : the act or process of breaking or the state of being broken; *esp* : the breaking of hard tissue (as bone) **b** : the rupture (as by tearing) of soft tissue ⟨kidney ~⟩ **3** : the general appearance of a freshly broken surface of a mineral

²fracture *vb* **frac·tured; frac·tur·ing** \-chə-riŋ, -shriŋ\ *vt* (1612) **1 a** : to cause a fracture in : BREAK ⟨~ a rib⟩ **b** : RUPTURE, TEAR **2 a** : to damage or destroy as if by rupturing **b** : to cause great disorder in **c** : to break up : FRACTIONATE **d** : to go beyond the limits of (as rules) : VIOLATE ⟨*fractured* the English language with malaprops —Goodman Ace⟩ ~ *vi* : to undergo fracture

fracture zone *n* (1946) : an area of suboceanic crust characterized by fractures

frae \'frä\ *prep* [ME (northern) *fra, frae,* fr. ON *frā;* akin to OE *fram* from] (1700) *Scot* : FROM

frag·ile \'fra-jəl, -ˌjīl\ *adj* [MF, fr. L *fragilis* — more at FRAIL] (1607) **1** : easily broken or destroyed **b** : constitutionally delicate : lacking in physical vigor **2** : TENUOUS, SLIGHT — **fra·gil·i·ty** \frə-'ji-lə-tē\ *n*

syn FRAGILE, FRANGIBLE, BRITTLE, CRISP, FRIABLE mean breaking easily. FRAGILE implies extreme delicacy of material or construction and need for careful handling ⟨a *fragile* antique chair⟩. FRANGIBLE implies susceptibility to being broken without implying weakness or delicacy ⟨*frangible* stone used for paving⟩. BRITTLE implies hardness together with lack of elasticity or flexibility or toughness ⟨patients with *brittle* bones⟩. CRISP implies a firmness and brittleness desirable esp. in some foods ⟨*crisp* lettuce⟩. FRIABLE applies to substances that are easily crumbled or pulverized ⟨*friable* soil⟩. *syn* see in addition WEAK

¹frag·ment \'frag-mənt\ *n* [ME, fr. L *fragmentum,* fr. *frangere* to break — more at BREAK] (15c) : a part broken off, detached, or incomplete *syn* see PART

²frag·ment \-ˌment\ *vi* (1818) : to fall to pieces ~ *vt* : to break up or apart into fragments

frag·men·tal \frag-'men-t³l\ *adj* (1798) : FRAGMENTARY — **frag·men·tal·ly** \-t³l-ē\ *adv*

frag·men·tary \'frag-mən-ˌter-ē\ *adj* (1611) : consisting of fragments : INCOMPLETE — **frag·men·tari·ly** \ˌfrag-mən-'ter-ə-lē\ *adv* — **frag·men·tari·ness** \-ˌter-ē-nəs\ *n*

frag·men·ta·tion \ˌfrag-mən-'tā-shən, -ˌmen-\ *n* (1881) **1** : the act or process of fragmenting or making fragmentary **2** : the state of being fragmented or fragmentary — **frag·men·tate** \'frag-mən-ˌtāt\ *vb*

fragmentation bomb *n* (1918) : a bomb or shell whose relatively thick casing is splintered upon explosion and thrown in fragments in all directions

frag·men·tize \'frag-mən-ˌtīz\ *vt* **-tized; -tiz·ing** (1815) : FRAGMENT

fra·grance \'frā-grən(t)s\ *n* (1667) **1 a** : a sweet or delicate odor (as of fresh flowers, pine trees, or perfume) **b** : something (as a perfume) compounded to give off a sweet or pleasant odor **2** : the quality or state of having a sweet odor

syn FRAGRANCE, PERFUME, SCENT, REDOLENCE mean a sweet or pleasant odor. FRAGRANCE suggests the odors of flowers or other growing things ⟨the *fragrance* of pine⟩. PERFUME may suggest a stronger or heavier odor ⟨the *perfume* of lilacs⟩. SCENT is very close to PERFUME but of wider application because more neutral in connotation ⟨*scent*-free soaps⟩. REDOLENCE implies a mixture of fragrant or pungent odors ⟨the *redolence* of a forest after a rain⟩.

fra·gran·cy \-grən(t)-sē\ *n* (1578) : FRAGRANCE

fra·grant \'frā-grənt\ *adj* [ME *fragrant,* fr. L *fragrant-, fragrans,* fr. prp. of *fragrare* to be fragrant] (15c) : marked by fragrance *syn* see ODOROUS — **fra·grant·ly** *adv*

frail \'frā(ə)l\ *adj* [ME, fr. MF *fraile,* fr. L *fragilis* fragile, fr. *frangere*] (14c) **1** : easily led into evil ⟨~ humanity⟩ **2** : easily broken or destroyed : FRAGILE **3 a** : physically weak **b** : SLIGHT, UNSUBSTANTIAL *syn* see WEAK — **frail·ly** \'frā(ə)l)-lē\ *adv* — **frail·ness** *n*

frail·ty \'frā(-ə)l-tē\ *n, pl* **frailties** (14c) **1** : the quality or state of being frail **2** : a fault due to weakness esp. of moral character *syn* see FAULT

fraise \'frāz\ *n* [F] (1775) : an obstacle of pointed stakes driven into the ramparts of a fortification in a horizontal or inclined position

Frak·tur *also* **Frac·tur** \fräk-'tür\ *n* [G, fr. L *fractura* fracture] (1904) **1** : a German style of black letter **2** *often not cap* : a Pennsylvania German document (as a birth or wedding certificate) that is written in calligraphy and illuminated with decorative motifs (as tulips, birds, and scrolls)

fram·be·sia \fram-'bē-zh(ē-)ə\ *n* [NL, fr. F *framboise* raspberry; fr. the appearance of the lesions] (1803) : YAWS

fram·boise \frä-'bwäz\ *n* [F, lit., raspberry, fr. OF, of Gmc origin; akin to D *braambes* blackberry, lit., bramble berry, OHG *brāmberi* — more at BROOM, BERRY] (ca. 1945) : a brandy or liqueur made from raspberries

¹frame \'frām\ *vb* **framed; fram·ing** [ME, to benefit, construct, fr. OE *framian* to benefit, make progress; akin to ON *fram* forward, OE *fram* from] *vt* (14c) **1** : to construct by fitting and uniting the parts of the skeleton of (a structure) **2 a** : PLAN, CONTRIVE ⟨*framed* a new method of achieving their purpose⟩ **b** : SHAPE, CONSTRUCT **c** : to give expression to : FORMULATE **d** : to draw up (as a document) **3 a** : to devise falsely (as a criminal charge) **b** : to contrive the evidence against (an innocent person) so that a verdict of guilty is assured ⟨~ : FIX 7b **4** : to fit or adjust esp. to something or for an end : ARRANGE **5** *obs* : PRODUCE **6** : to enclose in a frame; *also* : to enclose as if in a frame ~ *vi* **1** *archaic* : PROCEED, GO **2** *obs* : MANAGE — **fram·able** *or* **frame·able** \'frā-mə-bəl\ *adj* — **fram·er** *n*

²frame *n* (14c) **1 a** : something composed of parts fitted together and united **b** : the physical makeup of an animal and esp. a human body : PHYSIQUE, FIGURE **2 a** : the constructional system that gives shape or strength (as to a building); *also* : a frame dwelling **b** : such a skeleton not filled in or covered **3** *obs* : the act or manner of framing **4 a** : a machine built upon or within a framework ⟨a spinning ~⟩ **b** : an open case or structure made for admitting, enclosing, or supporting something ⟨a window ~⟩ **c** (1) : a part of a pair of glasses that holds one of the lenses (2) *pl* : that part of a pair of glasses other than the lenses **d** : a structural unit in an automobile chassis supported on the axles and supporting the rest of the chassis and the body **5 a** : an enclosing border **b** : the matter or area enclosed in such a border: as (1) : one of the squares in which scores for each round are recorded (as in bowling); *also* : a round in bowling (2) : an individual drawing in a comic strip usu. enclosed by a bordering line (3) : one picture of the series on a length of film (4) : a complete image for display (as on a television set) **c** : an inning in baseball **d** (1) : FRAMEWORK 1a (2) : CONTEXT, FRAME OF REFERENCE **e** : an event that forms the background for the action of a novel or play **6** : FRAME-UP

³**frame** *adj* (1775) : having a wood frame ⟨~ houses⟩

frame of mind (1665) : mental attitude or outlook : MOOD

frame of reference (1897) **1** : an arbitrary set of axes with reference to which the position or motion of something is described or physical laws are formulated **2** : a set of ideas, conditions, or assumptions that determine how something will be approached, perceived, or understood ⟨a Marxian *frame of reference*⟩

frame·shift \'frām-,shift\ *adj* (1967) : relating to, being, or causing a mutation in which a number of nucleotides not divisible by three is inserted or deleted so as to change the reading frame of some triplet codons during genetic translation — **frameshift** *n*

frame–up \'frā-,məp\ *n* (1889) **1** : an act or series of actions in which someone is framed **2** : an action that is framed

frame·work \'frām-,wərk\ *n* (1644) **1 a** : a basic conceptional structure (as of ideas) ⟨the ~ of the constitution⟩ **b** : a skeletal, openwork, or structural frame **2** : FRAME OF REFERENCE **3** : the larger branches of a tree that determine its shape

fram·ing \'frā-miŋ\ *n* (1703) **1** : FRAME, FRAMEWORK

franc \'fraŋk\ *n* [F] (14c) — see MONEY table

¹**fran·chise** \'fran-,chīz\ *n* [ME, fr. MF, fr. *franchir* to free, fr. OF *franc* free — more at FRANK] (14c) **1** : freedom or immunity from some burden or restriction vested in a person or group **2 a** : a special privilege granted to an individual or group; *esp* : the right to be and exercise the powers of a corporation **b** : a constitutional or statutory right or privilege; *esp* : the right to vote **c** (1) : the right or license granted to an individual or group to market a company's goods or services in a particular territory; *also* : a business granted such a right or license (2) : the territory involved in such a right **3 a** : the right of membership in a professional sports league **b** : a team and its operating organization having such membership

²**franchise** *vt* **fran·chised; fran·chis·ing** (14c) **1** *archaic* : FREE **2** : to grant a franchise

fran·chi·see \,fran-,chī-'zē, -chə-\ *n* (1954) : one granted a franchise

fran·chis·er \'fran-,chī-zər\ *n* [in sense 1, fr. ¹*franchise*; in sense 2, fr. ²*franchise*] (1843) **1** : FRANCHISEE **2** : FRANCHISOR

fran·chi·sor \,fran-,chī-'zȯr, -chə-\ *n* [²*franchise* + ¹*-or*] (1967) : one that grants a franchise

Fran·cis·can \fran-'sis-kən\ *n* [ML *Franciscus* Francis] (1599) : a member of the Order of Friars Minor founded by St. Francis of Assisi in 1209 and dedicated esp. to preaching, missions, and charities — **Franciscan** *adj*

fran·ci·um \'fran(t)-sē-əm\ *n* [NL, fr. *France*] (1946) : a radioactive element of the alkali-metal group discovered as a disintegration product of actinium and obtained artificially by the bombardment of thorium with protons — see ELEMENT table

Fran·co- *comb form* [ML, fr. *Francus* Frenchman, fr. LL, Frank] **1** : French and ⟨*Franco*-American⟩ **2** : French ⟨*Franco*phile⟩

Fran·co–Amer·i·can \,fran-kō-ə-'mer-ə-kən\ *n* (1859) : an American of French or esp. French-Canadian descent — **Franco–American** *adj*

fran·co·lin \'fran-k(ə-)lən\ *n* [F, fr. It *francolino*] (1653) : any of a genus (*Francolinus*) of partridges of southern Asia and Africa

Fran·co·phile \'fran-kə-,fīl, -kō-\ *or* **Fran·co·phil** \-,fil\ *adj* (1889) : markedly friendly to France or French culture — **Francophile** *n* — **Fran·co·phil·ia** \,fran-kə-'fi-lē-ə, -lyə, -kō-\ *n*

Fran·co·phobe \-,fōb\ *adj* (1891) : marked by a fear or strong dislike of France or French culture or customs — **Francophobe** *n* — **Fran·co·pho·bia** \,fran-kə-'fō-bē-ə, -,kō-\ *n*

fran·co·phone \-,fōn\ *adj, often cap* (1962) : of, having, or belonging to a population using French as its first or sometimes second language — **Francophone** *n*

franc–ti·reur \,frä⁼-(,)tē-'rər\ *n* [F, fr. *franc* free + *tireur* shooter] (1808) : a civilian fighter or sniper

fran·gi·ble \'fran-jə-bəl\ *adj* [ME, fr. MF & ML; MF, fr. ML *frangibilis*, fr. L *frangere* to break — more at BREAK] (15c) : readily or easily broken **syn** see FRAGILE — **fran·gi·bil·i·ty** \,fran-jə-'bi-lə-tē\ *n*

fran·gi·pane \'fran-jə-,pān, frä⁼-zhē-pán\ *n* [F, frangipani (perfume), fragipane, fr. It] (1858) : a custard usu. flavored with almonds

fran·gi·pa·ni *also* **fran·gi·pan·ni** \,fran-jə-'pa-nē, -'pä-\ *n, pl* **-pani** *also* **-panni** [modif. of It *frangipane*, fr. Muzio *Frangipane*, 16th cent. Ital. nobleman] (1676) **1** : a perfume derived from or imitating the odor of the flower of a frangipani (*Plumeria rubra*) **2** : any of a genus (*Plumeria*) of shrubs or small trees of the dogbane family that are native to the American tropics and widely cultivated as ornamentals

fran·glais \frä⁼-'glä\ *n, often cap* [F, blend of *français* French and *anglais* English] (1964) : French marked by a considerable number of borrowings from English

¹**frank** \'fraŋk\ *adj* [ME, free, fr. OF *franc*, fr. ML *francus*, fr. LL *Francus* Frank] (1548) **1** : marked by free, forthright, and sincere expression ⟨a ~ reply⟩ **2 a** : unmistakably evident ⟨~ materialism⟩ **b** : clinically evident and unmistakable ⟨~ pus⟩ — **frank·ness** *n*
syn FRANK, CANDID, OPEN, PLAIN mean showing willingness to tell what one feels or thinks. FRANK stresses lack of shyness or secretiveness or of evasiveness from considerations of tact or expedience ⟨*frank* discussions⟩. CANDID suggests expression marked by sincerity and honesty esp. in offering unwelcome criticism or opinion ⟨a *candid* appraisal⟩. OPEN implies frankness but suggests more indiscretion than FRANK and less earnestness than CANDID ⟨*open* in saying what they think⟩. PLAIN suggests outspokenness and freedom from affectation or subtlety in expression ⟨*plain* talk⟩.

²**frank** *vt* (1708) **1 a** : to mark (a piece of mail) with an official signature or sign indicating the right of the sender to free mailing **b** : to mail free **c** : to affix to (mail) a stamp or a marking indicating the payment of postage **2** : to enable to pass or go freely or easily — **frank·able** \'fraŋ-kə-bəl\ *adj* — **frank·er** *n*

³**frank** *n* (1713) **1 a** : the signature of the sender on a piece of franked mail serving in place of a postage stamp **b** : a mark or stamp on a piece of mail indicating postage paid **c** : a franked envelope **2** : the privilege of sending mail free of charge

⁴**frank** *n* (1904) : FRANKFURTER

Frank \'fraŋk\ *n* [ME, partly fr. OE *Franca*; partly fr. OF *Franc*, fr. LL *Francus*, of Gmc origin; akin to OHG *Franko* Frank, OE *Franca*] (bef. 12c) : a member of a West Germanic people that entered the Roman provinces in A.D. 253, occupied the Netherlands and most of Gaul, and established themselves along the Rhine

Fran·ken·stein \'fran-kən-,stīn *also* -,stēn\ *n* **1 a** : the title character in Mary W. Shelley's novel *Frankenstein* who creates a monster by which he is eventually killed **b** : a monster in the shape of a man esp. in popularized versions of the Frankenstein story **2** : a monstrous creation; *esp* : a work or agency that ruins its originator — **Fran·ken·stein·ian** \,fran-kən-'stī-nē-ən, -'stī-\ *adj*

frank·furt·er \'fraŋk-fə(r)t-ər, -,fərt-\ *or* **frank·furt** \-,fərt\ *n* [G *Frankfurter* of Frankfurt, fr. *Frankfurt am Main*, Germany] (1894) : a cured cooked sausage (as of beef or beef and pork) that may be skinless or stuffed in a casing

frank·in·cense \'fraŋ-kən-,sen(t)s\ *n* [ME *fraunk encense*, fr. OF *franc encens*, fr. *franc* (perh. in sense "of high quality") + *encens* incense] (14c) : a fragrant gum resin from trees of a genus (*Boswellia* of the family Burseraceae) of Somalia and southern coastal Arabia that is an important incense resin and was used in ancient times in religious rites and in embalming

¹**Frank·ish** \'fran-kish\ *adj* (14c) : of or relating to the Franks

²**Frankish** *n* (1863) : the Germanic language of the Franks

frank·lin \'fran-klən\ *n* [ME *frankeleyn*, fr. AF *fraunclein*, fr. OF *franc*] (14c) : a medieval English landowner of free but not noble birth

Frank·lin·ite \-klə-,nīt\ *n* [*Franklin*, N.J.] (1820) : a black slightly magnetic mineral consisting of an oxide of iron and zinc

Frank·lin stove \'fran-klən-\ *n* [Benjamin *Franklin*, its inventor] (1787) : a metal heating stove resembling an open fireplace but designed to be set out in a room

Franklin stove

frank·ly \'fran-klē\ *adv* (1537) **1** : in a frank manner **2** : in truth : INDEED
usage see HOPEFULLY

frank·pledge \'fraŋk-,plej\ *n* [ME *frankeplegge*, fr. AF *fraunc plege* (prob. trans. of MF *friborg* peace pledge), fr. *fraunc* free (fr. OF *franc*) + *plege* pledge] (15c) : an Anglo-Saxon system under which each adult male member of a tithing was responsible for the good conduct of the others; *also* : the member himself or the tithing

fran·tic \'fran-tik\ *adj* [ME *frenetik, frantik* — more at FRENETIC] (14c) **1 a** *archaic* : mentally deranged **b** : emotionally out of control ⟨~ with anger and frustration⟩ **2** : marked by fast and nervous, disordered, or anxiety-driven activity ⟨made a ~ search for the lost child⟩ — **fran·ti·cal·ly** \-ti-k(ə-)lē\ *adv* — **fran·tic·ness** \-tik-nəs\ *n*

frap \'frap\ *vt* **frapped; frap·ping** [ME, to strike, beat, fr. MF *fraper*] (1548) : to draw tight (as with ropes or cables) ⟨~ a sail⟩

¹**frap·pé** \fra-'pā\ *adj* [F, fr. pp. of *frapper* to strike, chill, fr. MF *fraper* to strike] (1848) : chilled or partly frozen

²**frap·pé** \fra-'pā\ *or* **frappe** \'frap, fra-'pā\ *n* (1903) **1 a** : a partly frozen drink (as of fruit juice) **b** : a liqueur served over shaved ice **2** : a thick milk shake

Fra·ser fir \'frā-zər-\ *n* [John *Fraser* †1811 Brit. botanist] (1897) : a southern Appalachian fir (*Abies fraseri*) that resembles the balsam fir

frass \'fras\ *n* [G, insect damage, lit., eating away, fr. OHG *vrāz* food, fr. *frezzan* to devour — more at FRET] (1854) : debris or excrement produced by insects

frat \'frat\ *n* (ca. 1895) : FRATERNITY 1c

fra·ter·nal \frə-'tər-n³l\ *adj* [ME, fr. ML *fraternalis*, fr. L *fraternus*, fr. *frater* brother — more at BROTHER] (15c) **1 a** : of, relating to, or involving brothers **b** : of, relating to, or being a fraternity or society ⟨a ~ order⟩ **2** : derived from two ova : DIZYGOTIC ⟨~ twins⟩ **3** : FRIENDLY, BROTHERLY — **fra·ter·nal·ism** \-n³l-,iz-əm\ *n* — **fra·ter·nal·ly** \-n³l-ē\ *adv*

fra·ter·ni·ty \frə-'tər-nə-tē\ *n, pl* **-ties** (14c) **1** : a group of people associated or formally organized for a common purpose, interest, or pleasure: as **a** : a fraternal order **b** : GUILD **c** : a men's student organization formed chiefly for social purposes having secret rites and a name consisting of Greek letters **d** : a student organization for scholastic, professional, or extracurricular activities ⟨a debating ~⟩ **2** : the quality or state of being brothers : BROTHERLINESS **3** : persons of the same class, profession, character, or tastes ⟨the racetrack ~⟩

frat·er·nize \'fra-tər-,nīz\ *vi* **-nized; -niz·ing** (1611) **1** : to associate or mingle as brothers or on fraternal terms **2 a** : to associate on close terms with members of a hostile group esp. when contrary to military orders **b** : to be friendly or amiable — **frat·er·ni·za·tion** \,fra-tər-nə-'zā-shən\ *n* — **frat·er·niz·er** \'fra-tər-,nī-zər\ *n*

frat·ri·cide \'fra-trə-,sīd\ *n* [in sense 1, fr. ME, fr. MF or L; MF, fr. L *fratricida*, fr. *fratr-, frater* brother + *-cida* -cide; in sense 2, fr. MF or L; MF, fr. L *fratricidium*, fr. *fratr-, frater* + *-cidium* -cide] (15c) **1** : one that murders or kills his or her own brother or sister or an individual (as a countryman) having a relationship like that of a brother or sister **2** : the act of a fratricide — **frat·ri·cid·al** \,fra-trə-'sī-d³l\ *adj*

Frau \'fraȯ\ *n, pl* **Frau·en** \'fraȯ(-ə)n\ [G, woman, wife, fr. OHG *frouwa* mistress, lady; akin to OE *frēa* lord, OHG *fruma* advantage — more at FOREMOST] (ca. 1813) : a German married woman : WIFE — used as a title equivalent to *Mrs.*

fraud \'frȯd\ *n* [ME *fraude*, fr. MF, fr. L *fraud-, fraus*] (14c) **1 a** : DECEIT, TRICKERY; *specif* : intentional perversion of truth in order to

---

\ə\ abut \ᵊ\ kitten, F table \ər\ further \a\ ash \ā\ ace \ä\ mop, mar \aȯ\ out \ch\ chin \e\ bet \ē\ easy \g\ go \i\ hit \ī\ ice \j\ job \ŋ\ sing \ō\ go \ȯ\ law \ȯi\ boy \th\ thin \t͟h\ the \ü\ loot \u̇\ foot \y\ yet \zh\ vision \ä, ᵏ, ⁿ, œ, œ̄, ᵫ, ᵬ, ᵞ\ see Guide to Pronunciation induce another to part with something of value or to surrender a legal right **b :** an act of deceiving or misrepresenting : TRICK **2 a :** a person who is not what he or she pretends to be : IMPOSTOR; *also :* one who defrauds : CHEAT **b :** one that is not what it seems or is represented to be — **syn** see DECEPTION, IMPOSTURE

fraud·u·lence \'frȯ-jə-lən(t)s\ *n* (1601) **:** the quality or state of being fraudulent

fraud·u·lent \-lənt\ *adj* (15c) **:** characterized by, based on, or done by fraud : DECEITFUL — **fraud·u·lent·ly** *adv* — **fraud·u·lent·ness** *n*

¹fraught \'frȯkt\ *n* [ME, freight, load, fr. MD or MLG *vracht, vrecht*] (14c) *chiefly Scot* **:** LOAD, CARGO

²fraught *vt* **fraught·ed** *or* **fraught; fraught·ing** [ME *fraughten,* fr. ¹*fraught*] (14c) *chiefly Scot* **:** LOAD, FREIGHT

³fraught \'frȯt\ *adj* [ME, fr. pp. of *fraughten*] (14c) **1** *archaic* **a :** LADEN **b :** well supplied or provided **2 :** full of or accompanied by something specified — used with *with* ⟨a situation ~ with danger⟩ **3** *chiefly Brit* **:** causing or characterized by emotional distress or tension **:** UNEASY

fräu·lein \'froi-,līn\ *n* [G, dim. of *Frau*] (ca. 1689) **1** *cap* **:** an unmarried German woman — used as a title equivalent to *Miss* **2 :** a German governess

frax·i·nel·la \,frak-sə-'ne-lə\ *n* [NL, dim. of L *fraxinus* ash tree — more at BIRCH] (1664) **:** a Eurasian perennial herb (*Dictamnus albus*) of the rue family with flowers that exhale a flammable vapor in hot weather — called also *gas plant*

¹fray \'frā\ *vt* [ME *fraien,* short for *affraien* to affray] (14c) *archaic* **:** SCARE; *also :* to frighten away

²fray *n* (14c) **1 :** usu. disorderly or protracted fight, struggle, or dispute

³fray *vb* [ME *fraien,* fr. MF *froyer, frayer* to rub, fr. L *fricare* — more at FRICTION] *vt* (15c) **1 a :** to wear (as an edge of cloth) by or as if by rubbing : FRET **b :** to separate the threads at the edge of **2 :** STRAIN, IRRITATE ⟨tempers became a bit ~*ed*⟩ ~ *vi* **1 :** to wear out or into shreds **2 :** to show signs of strain ⟨~*ing* nerves⟩

⁴fray *n* (1630) **:** a raveled place or worn spot (as on fabric)

fray·ing *n* (1637) **:** something rubbed or worn off by fraying

¹fraz·zle \'fra-zəl\ *vb* **fraz·zled; fraz·zling** \'fraz-liŋ, 'fra-zə-\ [alter. of E dial. *fazle* (to tangle, fray)] *vt* (ca. 1825) **1 :** ³FRAY **2 a :** to put in a state of extreme physical or nervous fatigue **b :** UPSET ~ *vi* **:** to become frazzled

²frazzle *n* (1865) **1 :** the state of being frazzled **2 :** a condition of fatigue or nervous exhaustion ⟨worn to a ~⟩

¹freak \'frēk\ *n* [origin unknown] (1563) **1 a :** a sudden and odd or seemingly pointless idea or turn of the mind **b :** a seemingly capricious action or event **2** *archaic* **:** a whimsical quality or disposition **3 :** one that is markedly unusual or abnormal: as **a :** a person or animal with a physical oddity who appears in a circus sideshow **b** *slang* (1) **:** a sexual deviate (2) **:** a person who uses an illicit drug **c :** HIPPIE **d :** an atypical postage stamp usu. caused by a unique defect in paper (as a crease) or a unique event in the manufacturing process (as a speck of dirt on the plate) that does not produce a constant or systematic effect **4 :** an ardent enthusiast ⟨film ~s⟩

²freak *adj* (ca. 1887) **:** having the character of a freak ⟨a ~ accident⟩

³freak *vi* (1965) **1 :** to withdraw from reality esp. by taking drugs — often used with *out* **2 :** to experience nightmarish hallucinations as a result of taking drugs — often used with *out* **3 a :** to behave irrationally or unconventionally under the influence of drugs — often used with *out* **b :** to react with extreme or irrational distress or discomposure — often used with *out* ~ *vt* **1 :** to put under the influence of a psychedelic drug — often used with *out* **2 :** to make greatly distressed, astonished, or discomposed — often used with *out* ⟨the news ~*ed* them out⟩ — **freaked** *adj* — **freaked–out** *adj*

⁴freak *vt* [perh. fr. or akin to ¹*freckle*] (1637) **:** to streak esp. with color ⟨silver and mother-of-pearl ~*ing* the intense azure —Robert Bridges †1930⟩

freak·ing \'frē-kᵊn, -kiŋ\ *adj or adv* [euphemism for *frigging* or *fucking*] (1963) **:** DAMNED — used as an intensive

freak·ish \'frē-kish\ *adj* (1653) **1 :** WHIMSICAL, CAPRICIOUS **2 :** markedly strange or abnormal — **freak·ish·ly** *adv* — **freak·ish·ness** *n*

freak of nature (1883) **:** FREAK 3a

freak–out \'frē-,kaut\ *n* (1966) **1 :** an act or instance of freaking out **2 :** a gathering of hippies

freak show *n* (1887) **:** an exhibition (as a sideshow) featuring freaks of nature

freaky \'frē-kē\ *adj* **freak·i·er; -est** (1824) **:** FREAKISH — **freak·i·ness** *n*

¹freck·le \'fre-kəl\ *n* [ME *freken, frekel,* of Scand origin; akin to ON *freknōttr* freckled] (14c) **:** any of the small brownish spots in the skin usu. due to precipitation of pigment that increase in number and intensity on exposure to sunlight — **freck·ly** \'fre-k(ə-)lē\ *adj*

²freckle *vb* **freck·led; freck·ling** \'fre-k(ə-)liŋ\ *vt* (1613) **:** to sprinkle or mark with freckles or small spots ~ *vi* **:** to become marked with freckles

¹free \'frē\ *adj* **fre·er; free·est** [ME, fr. OE *frēo;* akin to OHG *frī* free, W *rhydd,* Skt *priya* own, dear] (bef. 12c) **1 a :** having the legal and political rights of a citizen **b :** enjoying civil and political liberty ⟨~ citizens⟩ **c :** enjoying political independence or freedom from outside domination **d :** enjoying personal freedom : not subject to the control or domination of another **2 a :** not determined by anything beyond its own nature or being : choosing or capable of choosing for itself **b :** determined by the choice of the actor or performer ⟨~ actions⟩ **c :** made, done, or given voluntarily or spontaneously **3 a :** relieved from or lacking something unpleasant or burdensome ⟨~ from pain⟩ ⟨a speech ~ of political rhetoric⟩ **b :** not bound, confined, or detained by force **4 a :** having no trade restrictions **b :** not subject to government regulation **c** *of foreign exchange* **:** not subject to restriction or official control **5 a :** having no obligations (as to work) or commitments ⟨I'll be ~ this evening⟩ **b :** not taken up with commitments or obligations ⟨a ~ evening⟩ **6 :** having a scope not restricted by qualification ⟨a ~ variable⟩ **7 a** (1) **:** not obstructed or impeded : CLEAR (2) **:** not being used or occupied ⟨waved with his ~ hand⟩ **b :** not hampered or restricted in its normal operation **8 a :** not fastened ⟨the ~ end of the rope⟩ **b :** not confined to a particular position or place; *also :* not having a specific opponent to cover in football ⟨a ~ safety⟩ **c :** capable of moving or turning in any direction ⟨a ~ particle⟩ **d :** performed without apparatus ⟨~ tumbling⟩ **e :** done with artificial aids (as pitons) used only for protection against falling and not for support ⟨a ~ climb⟩ **9 a :** not parsimonious ⟨~ spending⟩ **b :** OUTSPOKEN **c :** availing oneself of something without stint **d :** FRANK, OPEN **e :** overly familiar or forward in action or attitude **f :** LICENTIOUS **10 :** not costing or charging anything **11 a** (1) **:** not united with, attached to, combined with, or mixed with something else : SEPARATE ⟨~ ores⟩ ⟨a ~ surface of a bodily part⟩ (2) **:** FREESTANDING ⟨a ~ column⟩ **b :** chemically uncombined ⟨~ oxygen⟩ ⟨~ acids⟩ **c :** not permanently attached but able to move about ⟨a ~ electron in a metal⟩ **d :** capable of being used alone as a meaningful linguistic form (the word *hats* is a ~ form) — compare ⁵BOUND 7 **12 a :** not literal or exact ⟨~ translation⟩ **b :** not restricted by or conforming to conventional forms ⟨~ skating⟩ **13 :** FAVORABLE — used of a wind blowing from a direction more than six points from dead ahead **14 :** not allowing slavery **15 :** open to all comers — **free·ness** \-nəs\ *n* — **for free :** without charge

syn FREE, INDEPENDENT, SOVEREIGN, AUTONOMOUS mean not subject to the rule or control of another. FREE stresses the complete absence of external rule and the full right to make all of one's own decisions ⟨you're *free* to do as you like⟩. INDEPENDENT implies a standing alone; applied to a state it implies lack of connection with any other having power to interfere with its citizens, laws, or policies ⟨the colony's struggle to become *independent*⟩. SOVEREIGN stresses the absence of a superior power and implies supremacy within a thing's own domain or sphere ⟨separate and *sovereign* armed services⟩. AUTONOMOUS stresses independence in matters pertaining to self-government ⟨in this denomination each congregation is regarded as *autonomous*⟩.

²free *vt* **freed; free·ing** (bef. 12c) **1 a :** to cause to be free **b :** to relieve or rid of what restrains, confines, restricts, or embarrasses ⟨~ a person from debt⟩ **c :** DISENTANGLE, CLEAR **2** *obs* **:** BANISH — **fre·er** *n*

syn FREE, RELEASE, LIBERATE, EMANCIPATE, MANUMIT mean to set loose from restraint or constraint. FREE implies a usu. permanent removal from whatever binds, confines, entangles, or oppresses ⟨*freed* the animals from their cages⟩. RELEASE suggests a setting loose from confinement, restraint, or a state of pressure or tension, often without implication of permanent liberation ⟨*released* his anger on a punching bag⟩. LIBERATE stresses particularly the resulting state of liberty ⟨*liberated* their country from the tyrant⟩. EMANCIPATE implies the liberation of a person from subjection or domination ⟨labor-saving devices *emancipated* us from household drudgery⟩. MANUMIT implies emancipation from slavery ⟨the document *manumitted* the slaves⟩.

³free *adv* (1559) **1 :** in a free manner **2 :** without charge **3 :** with the wind more than six points from dead ahead ⟨sailing ~⟩

free agent *n* (1955) **:** a professional athlete (as a baseball player) who is free to negotiate a contract with any team — **free agency** *n*

free alongside ship *adv or adj* (ca. 1903) **:** with delivery at the side of the ship free of charges and the buyer's liability then beginning

free and easy *adj* (1699) **1 :** marked by informality and lack of constraint ⟨the *free and easy,* open-air life of the plains —Allan Murray⟩ **2 :** not observant of strict demands ⟨too *free and easy* in accepting political contributions⟩ — **free–and–eas·i·ness** \,frē-ən-'(d)ē-zē-nəs\ *n* — **free and easy** *adv*

free association *n* (1899) **1 a :** the expression (as by speaking or writing) of the content of consciousness without censorship as an aid in gaining access to unconscious processes esp. in psychoanalysis **b :** the reporting of the first thought that comes to mind in response to a given stimulus (as a word) **2 :** an idea or image elicited by free association **3 :** a method using free association — **free–as·so·ci·ate** \,frē-ə-'sō-s(h)ē-,āt\ *vi* — **free–as·so·ci·a·tive** \-s(h)ē-,ā-tiv, -shə-tiv\ *adj*

¹free·base \'frē-,bās\ *vi* (1980) **:** to prepare or use freebase cocaine ~ *vt* **:** to prepare or use (cocaine) as freebase — **free·bas·er** *n*

²freebase *n* (1980) **:** cocaine freed from impurities by treatment (as with ether) and heated to produce vapors for inhalation or smoked as crack

free beach *n* (1975) **:** a beach at which nudity is permitted

free·bie *or* **free·bee** \'frē-bē\ *n* [by alter. fr. obs. *freeby* gratis, irreg. fr. *free*] (1942) **:** something (as a theater ticket) given without charge

free·board \'frē-,bȯrd, -,bōrd\ *n* (1726) **1 :** the distance between the waterline and the main deck or weather deck of a ship or between the level of the water and the upper edge of the side of a small boat **2 :** the height above the recorded high-water mark of a structure (as a dam) associated with the water

free·boo·ter \'frē-,bü-tər\ *n* [by folk etymology fr. D *vrijbuiter,* fr. *vrijbuit* plunder, fr. *vrij* free + *buit* booty] (1570) **:** PIRATE, PLUNDERER — **free·boot** \-,büt\ *vi*

free·born \'frē-'bȯrn\ *adj* (13c) **1 :** not born in vassalage or slavery **2 :** of, relating to, or befitting one that is freeborn

free diver *n* (1953) **:** one who engages in skin diving — **free diving** *n*

freed·man \'frēd-mən, -,man\ *n* (1601) **:** a man freed from slavery

free·dom \'frē-dəm\ *n* (bef. 12c) **1 :** the quality or state of being free: as **a :** the absence of necessity, coercion, or constraint in choice or action **b :** liberation from slavery or restraint or from the power of another : INDEPENDENCE **c :** the quality or state of being exempt or released usu. from something onerous ⟨~ from care⟩ **d :** EASE, FACILITY ⟨spoke the language with ~⟩ **e :** the quality of being frank, open, or outspoken ⟨answered with ~⟩ **f :** improper familiarity **g :** boldness of conception or execution ⟨gave him the ~ of their home⟩ **2 a :** a political right **b :** FRANCHISE, PRIVILEGE

syn FREEDOM, LIBERTY, LICENSE mean the power or condition of acting without compulsion. FREEDOM has a broad range of application from total absence of restraint to merely a sense of not being unduly hampered or frustrated ⟨*freedom* of the press⟩. LIBERTY suggests release from former restraint or compulsion ⟨the released prisoner had difficulty adjusting to his new *liberty*⟩. LICENSE implies freedom specially granted or conceded and may connote an abuse of freedom ⟨freedom without responsibility may degenerate into *license*⟩.

freedom of the seas (1917) **:** the right of a merchant ship to travel any waters except territorial waters either in peace or war

freedom ride *n, often cap F&R* (1961) **:** a ride made by civil rights workers through states of the southern U.S. to ascertain whether public facilities (as bus terminals) are desegregated — **freedom rider** *n*

freed·wom·an \'frēd-,wu̇-mən\ *n* (1866) **:** a woman freed from slavery

free–elec·tron laser \'frē-i-'lek-,trän-\ *n* (1979) **:** a laser that can be tuned over a wide range of frequencies and that produces electromagnetic radiation by the motion of electrons moving at relativistic velocities in a magnetic field

free enterprise *n* (1890) : freedom of private business to organize and operate for profit in a competitive system without interference by government beyond regulation necessary to protect public interest and keep the national economy in balance

free enterpriser *n* (1943) : a supporter or advocate of free enterprise

free fall *n* (1919) **1** : the condition of unrestrained motion in a gravitational field; *also* : such motion **2 a** : the part of a parachute jump before the parachute opens **b** : a rapid and continuing drop or decline ⟨a *free fall* in stock prices⟩ — **free–fall** *vi*

free–fire zone \'frē-,fir-\ *n* (1967) : a combat area in which any moving thing is a legitimate target

free–float·ing \-'flō-tiŋ\ *adj* (1921) **1 a** : floating freely ⟨~ vegetation⟩ **b** : lacking specific attachment, direction, or purpose ⟨~ ideas⟩ **2** : felt as an emotion without apparent cause ⟨~ anxiety⟩

free–flow·ing \-,flō-iŋ\ *adj* (1920) : characterized by easy freedom in movement, progression, or style ⟨a ~ essay⟩

free–for–all \'frē-fə-,rȯl\ *n* (1881) : a competition, dispute, or fight open to all comers and usu. with no rules : BRAWL — **free–for–all** *adj*

free–form \'frē-,fȯrm\ *adj* (1950) **1** : having or being an irregular or asymmetrical shape or design ⟨~ furniture⟩ **2** : FREE 12b ⟨~ dancing⟩

free·hand \'frē-,hand\ *adj* (ca. 1862) : done without mechanical aids or devices ⟨~ drawing⟩ — **freehand** *adv*

free hand \-'hand\ *n* (1929) : freedom of action or decision

free·hand·ed \'frē-'han-dəd\ *adj* (ca. 1656) : GENEROUS, OPENHANDED — **free·hand·ed·ly** *adv* — **free·hand·ed·ness** *n*

free·heart·ed \-'här-təd\ *adj* (14c) **1** : FRANK, UNRESERVED **2** : GENEROUS — **free·heart·ed·ly** *adv*

free·hold \'frē-,hōld\ *n* (15c) **1** : a tenure of real property by which an estate of inheritance in fee simple or fee tail or an estate for life is held; *also* : an estate held by such tenure — compare FEE 1 **2** *Brit* : an estate held in fee simple — **freehold** *adj or adv* — **free·hold·er** \-,hōl-dər\ *n*

free kick *n* (1882) : a kick (as in football, soccer, or rugby) with which an opponent may not interfere; *esp* : such a kick in any direction awarded because of an infraction of the rules by an opponent

¹free·lance \'frē-,lan(t)s\ *n* (1820) **1** *a usu* **free lance** : a mercenary soldier esp. of the Middle Ages : CONDOTTIERE **b** : a person who acts independently without being affiliated with or authorized by an organization **2** : a person who pursues a profession without a long-term commitment to any one employer

²freelance *adj* (1901) **1 a** : of, relating to, or being a freelance : INDEPENDENT ⟨a ~ photographer⟩ ⟨~ fees⟩ **b** : done by a freelance ⟨~ reviewing⟩ ⟨~ jobs⟩ **2** : not sponsored by an organization ⟨~ terrorists⟩ ⟨a ~ demonstration⟩ — **freelance** *adv*

³freelance *vi* (1902) : to act or work as a freelance ~ *vt* : to produce as a freelance ⟨*freelancing* magazine articles⟩

free·lanc·er \'frē-,lan(t)-sər\ *n* (1937) : FREELANCE 1b, 2

free–liv·ing \'frē-'li-viŋ\ *adj* (1818) **1** : marked by more than usual freedom in the gratification of appetites **2 a** : not fixed to the substrate but capable of motility ⟨a ~ protozoan⟩ **b** : being metabolically independent : neither parasitic nor symbiotic

free·load \-,lōd\ *vi* (ca. 1934) : to impose upon another's generosity or hospitality without sharing in the cost or responsibility involved : SPONGE — **free·load·er** *n*

free love *n* (1822) **1** : the practice of living openly with one of the opposite sex without marriage **2** : sexual relations without any commitments by either partner

free lunch *n* (1975) : something one does not have to pay for; *also* : FREE RIDE

free·ly \'frē-lē\ *adv* (bef. 12c) : in a free manner: as **a** : of one's own accord ⟨left home ~⟩ **b** : with freedom from external control ⟨a ~ elected government⟩ **c** : without restraint or reservation ⟨spent ~ on clothes⟩ **d** : without hindrance ⟨a gate swinging ~⟩ ⟨currencies are ~ convertible⟩ **e** : not strictly following a model, convention, or rule ⟨~ translated⟩

free·man \'frē-mən, -,man\ *n* (bef. 12c) **1** : one enjoying civil or political liberty **2** : one having the full rights of a citizen

free market *n* (1907) : an economic market operating by free competition

free–mar·ke·teer \'frē-,mär-kə-'tir\ *n* (1954) : a proponent of a free-market economy

free–mar·tin \'frē-,mär-t²n\ *n* [origin unknown] (1681) : a sexually imperfect usu. sterile female calf twinborn with a male

Free·ma·son \-'mā-s²n\ *n* (1646) : a member of a major fraternal organization called Free and Accepted Masons or Ancient Free and Accepted Masons that has certain secret rituals

free·ma·son·ry \-rē\ *n* (1741) **1** *cap* : the principles, institutions, or practices of Freemasons — called also *Masonry* **2** : natural fellowship based on some common experience

free on board *adv or adj* (1924) : without charge for delivery to and placing on board a carrier at a specified point

free port *n* (1711) : an enclosed port or section of a port where goods are received and shipped free of customs duty

freer *comparative of* FREE

free radical *n* (1900) : an esp. reactive atom or group of atoms that has one or more unpaired electrons

free–range \'frē-'rānj\ *adj* (1912) : allowed to range and forage with relative freedom ⟨~ chickens⟩; *also* : of, relating to, or produced by free-range poultry ⟨~ eggs⟩

free reed *n* (1855) : a reed in a musical instrument (as a harmonium) that vibrates in an air opening just large enough to allow the reed to move freely — compare BEATING REED

free rein *n* (1952) : unrestricted liberty of action or decision

free ride *n* (1899) : a benefit obtained at another's expense or without the usual cost or effort — **free ride** *vi* — **free rider** *n*

free safety *n* (1973) : a safety in football who has no particular receiver to cover in a man-to-man defense

free·sia \'frē-zh(ē-)ə, -zē-ə\ *n* [NL, fr. F. H. T. *Freese* †1876 Ger. physician] (ca. 1882) : any of a genus (*Freesia*) of the iris family of sweet-scented African herbs with red, pink, white, or yellow flowers

free–soil *adj* (1846) **1** : characterized by free soil ⟨~ states⟩ **2** *cap*

F&S : opposing the extension of slavery into U.S. territories and the admission of slave states into the Union prior to the Civil War; *specif* : of, relating to, or constituting a minor U.S. political party having these aims — **Free–Soil·er** \-'sȯi-lər\ *n* — **Free–Soil·ism** \-'sȯi(ə)-,li-zəm\ *n*

free soil *n* (1848) : U.S. territory where prior to the Civil War slavery was prohibited

free–spo·ken \'frē-'spō-kən\ *adj* (1625) : speaking freely : OUTSPOKEN

freest *superlative of* FREE

free·stand·ing \'frē-'stan-diŋ\ *adj* (1876) **1** : standing alone or on its own foundation free of support or attachment ⟨a ~ wall⟩ **2** : being independent; *esp* : not part of or affiliated with another organization ⟨a ~ clinic⟩ ⟨a ~ city⟩ ⟨a ~ computer store⟩

Free State *n* (1819) : a state of the U.S. in which slavery was prohibited before the Civil War

free·stone \'frē-,stōn\ *n* (13c) **1** : a stone that may be cut freely without splitting **2 a** : a fruit stone to which the flesh does not cling **b** : a fruit having such a stone

free·style \'frē-,stīl\ *n, often attrib* (ca. 1934) **1** : a competition in which the contestant is given more latitude than in related events; *esp* : swimming competition in which the swimmer may use any stroke **2** : CRAWL **2** — **free·styl·er** *n*

free–swim·ming \-'swi-miŋ\ *adj* (ca. 1890) : able to swim about : not attached ⟨the ~ larva of the barnacle⟩

free–swing·ing \-'swiŋ-iŋ\ *adj* (1949) : bold, forthright, and heedless of personal consequences ⟨a ~ soldier of fortune —Will Herberg⟩

free–tailed bat \'frē-,tāld-\ *n* (1895) : any of a family (Molossidae) of bats characterized by a tail that projects beyond the posterior part of the flight membrane and found in warm regions of the world

free·think·er \-'thiŋ-kər\ *n* (1692) : one that forms opinions on the basis of reason independently of authority; *esp* : one who doubts or denies religious dogma — **free·think·ing** \-kiŋ\ *n or adj*

free thought *n* (1711) : unorthodox attitudes or beliefs; *specif* : 18th century deism

free throw *n* (ca. 1929) : an unhindered shot in basketball made from behind a set line and awarded because of a foul by an opponent

free throw lane *n* (ca. 1929) : a 12 or 16 foot wide lane on a basketball court that extends from underneath the goal to a line 15 feet in front of the backboard and that players may not enter during a free throw

free trade *n* (1823) : trade based on the unrestricted international exchange of goods with tariffs used only as a source of revenue

free trader *n* (1832) : one that practices or advocates free trade

free verse *n* (1908) : verse whose meter is irregular in some respect or whose rhythm is not metrical

free·way \'frē-,wā\ *n* (1930) **1** : an expressway with fully controlled access **2** : a toll-free highway

¹free·wheel \-'(h)wē(ə)l\ *n* (1930) **1** : a clutch fitted in the rear hub of a bicycle that permits the rear wheel to run on free from the rear sprocket when the pedals are stopped **2** : a power-transmission system in a motor vehicle with a device that permits the propeller shaft to run freely when its speed is greater than that of the engine shaft

²freewheel *vi* (1903) **1** : to roll along freely independent of a gear **2** : to move, live, or play freely or irresponsibly — **free·wheel·er** *n*

free·wheel·ing \-'hwē-liŋ, -'wē-\ *adj* (1931) : free and loose in form or manner: as **a** : heedless of social norms or niceties ⟨the raider style of his ~ father —Garry Wills⟩ **b** : not repressed or restrained ⟨~ promiscuity⟩ ⟨a ~ competitive spirit⟩ **c** : not bound by formal rules, procedures, or guidelines ⟨a ~ investigation⟩ ⟨~ improvisation⟩ **d** : loose and undisciplined : not defensive ⟨a ~ style of hockey⟩ — **free·wheel·ing·ly** *adv*

free·will \'frē-,wil\ *adj* (1535) : VOLUNTARY, SPONTANEOUS

free will *n* (13c) **1** : voluntary choice or decision ⟨I do this of my own *free will*⟩ **2** : freedom of humans to make choices that are not determined by prior causes or by divine intervention

Freewill Baptist *n* (1732) : a member of a Baptist group holding to Arminian doctrine and practicing open communion

free world *n, often cap F&W* (1949) : the part of the world where democracy and capitalism or moderate socialism rather than totalitarian or Communist political and economic systems prevail

free·writ·ing \'frē-,rī-tiŋ\ *n* (1980) : automatic writing done esp. as a classroom exercise

¹freeze \'frēz\ *vb* **froze** \'frōz\; **fro·zen** \'frō-z²n\; **freez·ing** [ME *fresen*, fr. OE *frēosan*; akin to OHG *friosan* to freeze, L *pruina* hoarfrost, OE *frost* frost] *vi* (bef. 12c) **1 a** : to become congealed into ice by cold **b** : to solidify as a result of abstraction of heat **c** : to withstand freezing ⟨the bread ~s well⟩ **2** : to become chilled with cold ⟨almost *froze* to death⟩ **3** : to adhere solidly by or as if by freezing ⟨pressure caused the metals to ~⟩ **4** : to become fixed or motionless; *esp* : to become incapable of acting or speaking **5** : to become clogged with ice ⟨the water pipes *froze*⟩ ~ *vt* **1 a** : to harden into ice **b** : to convert from a liquid to a solid by cold **2** : to make extremely cold : CHILL **3 a** : to act on usu. destructively by frost **b** : to anesthetize by cold **4** : to cause to grip tightly or remain in immovable contact **5 a** : to cause to become fixed, immovable, unavailable, or unalterable ⟨~ interest rates⟩ **b** : to immobilize by governmental regulation the expenditure, withdrawal, or exchange of ⟨~ foreign assets⟩ **c** : to render motionless ⟨a fake *froze* the defender⟩ **6** : to attempt to retain continuous possession of (a ball or puck) without an attempt to score usu. in order to protect a small lead — **freez·ing·ly** *adv*

²freeze *n* (15c) **1 a** : an act or instance of freezing **b** : the state of being frozen **2** : a state of weather marked by low temperature esp. when below the freezing point **3** : a halt in the production, testing, and deployment of military weapons ⟨a nuclear ~⟩

freeze–dried \-'drīd\ *adj* (1946) : being in a state produced by or as if by freeze-drying

freeze–dry \-'drī\ *vt* (1949) : to dry (as food) in a frozen state under high vacuum esp. for preservation

\ə\ abut \ᵊ\ kitten, F table \ər\ further \a\ ash \ā\ ace \ä\ mop, mar \au̇\ out \ch\ chin \e\ bet \ē\ easy \g\ go \i\ hit \ī\ ice \j\ job \ŋ\ sing \ō\ go \ȯ\ law \ȯi\ boy \th\ thin \t͟h\ the \ü\ loot \u̇\ foot \y\ yet \zh\ vision \à, k̠, ⁿ, œ, œ̄, ᴜᵉ, ᵫ, ᴿ\ *see* Guide to Pronunciation

freeze–etch·ing \'frē-ˌze-chiŋ\ *n* (1968) : preparation of a specimen (as of tissue) for electron microscopic examination by freezing, fracturing along natural structural lines, and preparing a replica (as by simultaneous vapor deposition of carbon and platinum) — **freeze–etch** \-'zech\ *adj* — **freeze–etched** \-'zecht\ *adj*

freeze fracture *n* (1973) : FREEZE-ETCHING

freeze–frame \'frēz-'frām\ *n* (1948) **1 a :** a frame of a motion-picture film that is repeated so as to give the illusion of a static picture **b :** a static picture produced from a videodisc or videotape recording **2 :** something resembling a freeze-frame esp. in unchanging quality

freeze out *vt* (1861) : EXCLUDE — **freeze–out** \'frē-ˌzaut\ *n*

freez·er \'frē-zər\ *n* (1847) : one that freezes or keeps cool; *esp* : a compartment, room, or device for freezing food or keeping it frozen

freezer burn *n* (1926) : light-colored spots developed in frozen foods as a result of surface evaporation and drying when inadequately wrapped or packaged

freezing point *n* (1747) : the temperature at which a liquid solidifies

free zone *n* (1900) : an area within which goods may be received and stored without payment of duty

F region *n* (1923) : the highest region of the ionosphere occurring from 80 miles (130 kilometers) to more than 300 miles (500 kilometers)

¹freight \'frāt\ *n, often attrib* [ME, fr. MD or MLG *vracht, vrecht*] (15c) **1 a :** the compensation paid for the transportation of goods **b :** COST ⟨help pay the ~⟩ **2 a :** goods to be shipped : CARGO **b :** LOAD, BURDEN **c :** MEANING 3, SIGNIFICANCE **3 a :** the ordinary transportation of goods by a common carrier and distinguished from express **b :** a train designed or used for such transportation

²freight *vt* (15c) **1 a :** to load with goods for transportation **b :** BURDEN, CHARGE ⟨~ed with memories⟩ **2 :** to transport or ship by freight

freight·age \'frā-tij\ *n* (1694) : FREIGHT

freight·er \-tər\ *n* (1622) **1 :** one that loads or charters and loads a ship **2 :** SHIPPER **3 :** a ship or airplane used chiefly to carry freight

frem·i·tus \'fre-mə-təs\ *n* [NL, fr. L, murmur, fr. *fremere* to murmur; akin to OE *bremman* to roar] (1879) : a sensation felt by a hand placed on a part of the body (as the chest) that vibrates during speech

french \'french\ *vt, often cap* (1941) **1 :** to trim the meat from the end of the bone of (as a chop) **2 :** to cut (green beans) in thin lengthwise strips before cooking

¹French \'french\ *adj* [ME, fr. OE *frencisc*, fr. *Franca* Frank] (bef. 12c) **1 :** of, relating to, or characteristic of France, its people, or their language **2 :** of or relating to the overseas descendents of the French people — **French·ness** *n*

²French *n* (12c) **1 :** a Romance language that developed out of the Vulgar Latin spoken in northern and central Transalpine Gaul and that became the literary and official language of France **2** *pl in constr* : the French people **3 :** strong language ⟨pardon my ~⟩

French bean *n* (1632) **1** *chiefly Brit* : a bean (as a green bean) of which the whole young pod is eaten **2** *chiefly Brit* : KIDNEY BEAN 2

French bread *n* (15c) : a crusty white bread baked usu. in long thin loaves

French bulldog *n* (1875) : any of a breed of small compact heavy-boned dogs developed in France and having erect ears

French Canadian *n* (1758) : one of the descendants of French settlers in Lower Canada — **French–Canadian** *adj*

French chalk *n* (ca. 1728) : a soft white granular variety of steatite used esp. for drawing lines on cloth and for removing grease in dry cleaning

French cuff *n* (1916) : a soft double cuff that is made by turning back half of a wide cuff band and fastening with cuff links

french curve *n, often cap F* (1885) : a curved piece of flat often plastic material used as a guide in drawing curves

French door *n* (1923) : a door with rectangular glass panes extending the full length; *also* : FRENCH WINDOW

French dressing *n* (1876) **1 :** a salad dressing made with oil and vinegar or lemon juice, and spices **2 :** a commercial salad dressing that is tomato-flavored and of creamy consistency

¹French fry *n, often cap 1st F* (1918) : a strip of potato fried in deep fat — usu. used in pl.

²french fry *vt, often cap 1st F* (ca. 1930) : to fry (as strips of potato) in deep fat until brown

French horn *n* (1682) : a circular valved brass instrument having a conical bore, a funnel-shaped mouthpiece, and a usual range from B below the bass staff upward for more than three octaves

french·ify \'fren-chə-ˌfi\ *vt -ified; -ify·ing often cap* (1592) : to make French in qualities, traits, or typical practices — **french·i·fi·ca·tion** \ˌfren-chə-fi-'kā-shən\ *n, often cap*

French kiss *n* (ca. 1923) : an open-mouth kiss usu. involving tongue-to-tongue contact — **French–kiss** *vb*

French leave *n* [fr. an 18th cent. French custom of leaving a reception without taking leave of the host or hostess] (1771) : an informal, hasty, or secret departure

French horn

French letter *n* (ca. 1856) *chiefly Brit* : CONDOM

French·man \'french-mən\ *n* (bef. 12c) **1 :** a native or inhabitant of France **2 :** one who is of French descent

French pastry *n* (1922) : a rich pastry filled esp. with custard or fruit

French provincial *n, often cap P* (1945) : a style of furniture, architecture, or fabric originating in or characteristic of the 17th and 18th century French provinces

French seam *n* (ca. 1890) : a strong seam stitched on both sides of the fabric to enclose all raw edges

French telephone *n* (1932) : HANDSET

French toast *n* (1871) : bread dipped in a mixture of egg and milk and sautéed

French window *n* (1801) : a pair of casement windows that reaches to the floor, opens in the middle, and is placed in an exterior wall

French·wom·an \'french-ˌwu̇-mən\ *n* (1593) **1 :** a woman who is a native or inhabitant of France **2 :** a woman of French descent

fre·net·ic \fri-'ne-tik\ *adj* [ME *frenetik* insane, fr. MF *frenetique*, fr. L

phreneticus, modif. of Gk *phrenitikos*, fr. *phrenitis* inflammation of the brain, fr. *phren-, phrēn* diaphragm, mind] (14c) : FRENZIED, FRANTIC — **fre·net·i·cal·ly** \-ti-k(ə-)lē\ *adv* — **fre·net·i·cism** \-'ne-tə-ˌsi-zəm\ *n*

fren·u·lum \'fren-yə-ləm\ *n, pl* **-la** \-lə\ [NL, dim. of L *frenum*] (ca. 1706) **1 :** a connecting fold of membrane serving to support or restrain a part (as the tongue) **2 :** a bristle or group of bristles on the front edge of the posterior wings of some lepidoptera that unites the wings by interlocking with the retinaculum of the forewings

fre·num \'frē-nəm\ *n, pl* **frenums** *or* **fre·na** \-nə\ [NL, fr. L, bridle, reins, and bit; prob. akin to L *frendere* to grind — more at GRIND] (1741) : FRENULUM 1

fren·zied \'fren-zēd\ *adj* (1796) : marked by frenzy — **fren·zied·ly** *adv*

¹fren·zy \'fren-zē\ *n, pl* **frenzies** [ME *frenesie*, fr. MF, fr. ML *phrenesia*, alter. of L *phrenesis*, fr. *phreneticus*] (14c) **1 a :** a temporary madness **b :** a violent mental or emotional agitation **2 :** intense usu. wild and often disorderly compulsive or agitated activity

²frenzy *vt* **fren·zied; fren·zy·ing** (1791) : to affect with frenzy

Fre·on \'frē-ˌän\ *trademark* — used for any of various nonflammable fluorocarbons used as refrigerants and as propellants for aerosols

fre·quence \'frē-kwən(t)s\ *n* (1603) : FREQUENCY

fre·quen·cy \'frē-kwən(t)-sē\ *n, pl* **-cies** (1600) **1 :** the fact or condition of occurring frequently **2 a :** the number of times that a periodic function repeats the same sequence of values during a unit variation of the independent variable **b :** the number of individuals in a single class when objects are classified according to variations in a set of one or more specified attributes **3 :** the number of repetitions of a periodic process in a unit of time: as **a :** the number of complete alternations per second of an alternating current **b :** the number of complete oscillations per second of energy (as sound or electromagnetic radiation) in the form of waves

frequency distribution *n* (1895) : an arrangement of statistical data that exhibits the frequency of the occurrence of the values of a variable

frequency modulation *n* (1922) : modulation of the frequency of the carrier wave in accordance with speech or a signal; *also* : FM

frequency response *n* (1926) : the ability of a device (as an audio amplifier) to handle the frequencies applied to it; *also* : a graph representing this ability

¹fre·quent \frē-'kwent, 'frē-kwənt\ *vt* (15c) **1 :** to associate with, be in, or resort to often or habitually **2** *archaic* : to read systematically or habitually — **fre·quen·ta·tion** \ˌfrē-ˌkwen-'tā-shən, -kwən-\ *n* — **fre·quent·er** *n*

²fre·quent \'frē-kwənt\ *adj* [ME, ample, fr. MF or L; MF, crowded, fr. L *frequent-, frequens*] (1531) **1 a :** COMMON, USUAL **b :** happening at short intervals : often repeated or occurring **2** *obs* : FULL, THRONGED **3 :** HABITUAL, PERSISTENT **4** *archaic* : INTIMATE, FAMILIAR — **fre·quent·ness** *n*

fre·quen·ta·tive \frē-'kwen-tə-tiv\ *adj* (1533) : denoting repeated or recurrent action or state — used of a verb aspect, verb form, or meaning — **frequentative** *n*

fre·quent·ly \'frē-kwənt-lē\ *adv* (1531) : at frequent or short intervals

fres·co \'fres-(ˌ)kō\ *n, pl* **frescoes** [It, fr. *fresco* fresh, of Gmc origin; akin to OHG *frisc* fresh] (1598) **1 :** the art of painting on freshly spread moist lime plaster with water-based pigments **2 :** a painting executed in fresco — **fresco** *vt*

¹fresh \'fresh\ *adj* [ME, fr. OF *freis*, of Gmc origin; akin to OHG *frisc* fresh, OE *fersc* fresh] (13c) **1 a :** having its original qualities unimpaired: as (1) : full of or renewed in vigor : REFRESHED ⟨rose ~ from a good night's sleep⟩ (2) : not stale, sour, or decayed ⟨~ bread⟩ (3) : not faded ⟨the lessons remain ~ in her memory⟩ (4) : not worn or rumpled ⟨a ~ white shirt⟩ **b :** not altered by processing ⟨~ vegetables⟩ **2 a :** not salt **b** (1) : free from taint : PURE ⟨~ air⟩ (2) *of wind* : moderately strong **3 a** (1) : experienced, made, or received newly or anew ⟨form ~ friendships⟩ (2) : ADDITIONAL, ANOTHER ⟨a ~ start⟩ **b :** ORIGINAL, VIVID ⟨a ~ portrayal⟩ **c :** lacking experience : RAW **d :** newly or just come or arrived ⟨~ from school⟩ **e :** having the milk flow recently established ⟨a ~ cow⟩ **4** [prob. by folk etymology fr. G *frech*] : disposed to take liberties : IMPUDENT **syn** see NEW — **fresh·ly** *adv* — **fresh·ness** *n*

²fresh *adv* (14c) : just recently : NEWLY ⟨we're ~ out of eggs⟩ ⟨~ caught fish⟩

³fresh *n* (1538) **1 :** an increased flow or rush (as of water) : FRESHET **2** *archaic* : a stream, spring, or pool of freshwater

fresh breeze *n* (ca. 1881) : wind having a speed of 19 to 24 miles per hour (30 to 38 kilometers per hour) — see BEAUFORT SCALE table

fresh·en \'fre-shən\ *vb* **fresh·ened; fresh·en·ing** \-sh(ə-)niŋ\ *vi* (1697) **1 :** to grow or become fresh: as **a** *of wind* : to increase in strength **b :** to become fresh in appearance or vitality — usu. used with *up* ⟨~ up with a shower⟩ **c** *of a milk animal* : to begin lactating ~ *vt* : to make fresh; *also* : REFRESH, REVIVE — **fresh·en·er** \-sh(ə-)nər\ *n*

fresh·et \'fre-shət\ *n* (1596) **1** *archaic* : STREAM 1 **2 a :** a great rise or overflowing of a stream caused by heavy rains or melted snow **b :** something resembling or suggesting a freshet ⟨a ~ of visitors⟩

fresh gale *n* (1582) : wind having a speed of 39 to 46 miles per hour (62 to 74 kilometers per hour) — see BEAUFORT SCALE table

fresh·man \'fresh-mən\ *n, often attrib* (1550) **1 :** a first-year student **2 :** BEGINNER, NEWCOMER

¹fresh·wa·ter \'fresh-'wȯ-tər, -'wä-\ *n* (14c) : water that is not salty esp. when considered as a natural resource

²freshwater *adj* (1528) **1 :** of, relating to, being, or living in freshwater **2 :** accustomed to navigating only in inland waters ⟨a ~ sailor⟩; *also* : UNSKILLED **3 :** inland and usu. provincial ⟨a ~ college⟩

freshwater drum *n* (1879) : a croaker (*Aplodinotus grunniens*) of the Great Lakes and Mississippi valley that may attain a weight of 50 pounds (23 kilograms) or more — called also *sheepshead, white perch*

freshwater pearl *n* (1918) : a usu. very small pearl produced by a freshwater mollusk

Fres·nel lens \'frez-nəl-, frā-'nel-\ *n* [Augustin J. Fresnel] (ca. 1884) : a lens that has a surface consisting of a concentric series of simple lens sections so that a thin lens with a short focal length and large diameter is possible and that is used esp. for spotlights

¹fret \'fret\ *vb* **fret·ted; fret·ting** [ME, to devour, fret, fr. OE *fretan* to devour; akin to OHG *frezzan* to devour, *ezzan* to eat — more at EAT] *vt* (12c) **1 a :** to eat or gnaw into : CORRODE; *also* : FRAY **b :** RUB,

CHAFE **c** : to make by wearing away a substance ⟨the stream *fretted* a channel⟩ **2** : to cause to suffer emotional strain : VEX **3** : to pass (as time) in fretting **4** : AGITATE, RIPPLE ~ *vi* **1 a** : to eat into something **b** : to affect something as if by gnawing or biting : GRATE **2 a** : WEAR, CORRODE **b** : CHAFE **c** : FRAY 1 **3 a** : to become vexed or worried **b** *of running water* : to become agitated
²**fret** *n* (15c) **1 a** : the action of wearing away : EROSION **b** : a worn or eroded spot **2** : an agitation of mind : IRRITATION
³**fret** *vt* **fret·ted; fret·ting** [ME, back-formation fr. *fret, fretted* adorned, interwoven, fr. MF *freté*, fr. OF, pp. of *freter, ferter* to tie, bind, prob. fr. (assumed) VL *firmitare*, fr. L *firmus* firm] (14c) **1 a** : to decorate with interlaced designs **b** : to form a pattern upon **2** : to enrich with embossed or pierced carved patterns
⁴**fret** *n* (14c) **1** : an ornamental network; *esp* : a medieval metallic or jeweled net for a woman's headdress **2** : an ornament or ornamental work often in relief consisting of small straight bars intersecting one another in right or oblique angles
⁵**fret** *n* [perh. fr. MF *frete* ferrule, fr. *freter*] (ca. 1500) : one of a series of ridges fixed across the fingerboard of a stringed musical instrument (as a guitar) — **fret·less** *adj* — **fret·ted** *adj*
⁶**fret** *vt* **fret·ted; fret·ting** (1602) : to press (the strings of a stringed instrument) against the frets
fret·ful \'fret-fəl\ *adj* (1602) : disposed to fret : IRRITABLE — **fret·ful·ly** \-fə-lē\ *adv* — **fret·ful·ness** *n*

fret 2

fret·saw \'fret-ˌsȯ\ *n* (1865) : a narrow-bladed fine-toothed saw held under tension in a frame and used for cutting curved outlines
fret·work \-ˌwərk\ *n* (1601) **1** : decoration consisting of work adorned with frets **2** : ornamental openwork or work in relief
Freud·ian \'frȯi-dē-ən\ *adj* (1910) : of, relating to, or according with the psychoanalytic theories or practices of Freud — **Freudian** *n* — **Freud·ian·ism** \-ə-ˌni-zəm\ *n*
Freudian slip *n* (1953) : a slip of the tongue that is motivated by and reveals some unconscious aspect of the mind
Frey \'frā\ *n* [ON *Freyr*] : the Norse god of fertility, crops, peace, and prosperity
Freya \'frā-ə\ *n* [ON *Freyja*] : the Norse goddess of love and beauty
fri·a·ble \'frī-ə-bəl\ *adj* [MF or L; MF, fr. L *friabilis*, fr. *friare* to crumble — more at FRICTION] (1563) : easily crumbled or pulverized ⟨~ soil⟩ *syn* see FRAGILE — **fri·a·bil·i·ty** \ˌfrī-ə-'bi-lə-tē\ *n*
fri·ar \'frī(-ə)r\ *n* [ME *frere, fryer*, fr. OF *frere*, lit., brother, fr. L *fratr-, frater* — more at BROTHER] (13c) : a member of a mendicant order
fri·ar·ly \-lē\ *adj* (1549) : resembling a friar : relating to friars
friar's lantern *n* (1632) *obs* : IGNIS FATUUS
fri·ary \'frī(-ə)-rē\ *n, pl* **-ar·ies** (1538) : a monastery of friars
¹**frib·ble** \'fri-bəl\ *vb* **frib·bled; frib·bling** \-b(ə-)liŋ\ [origin unknown] *vi* (1633) **1** : TRIFLE **2** *obs* : DODDER ~ *vt* : to trifle or fool away
²**fribble** *n* (1664) : a frivolous person, thing, or idea : TRIFLER — **frib·ble** *adj*
fric·an·deau \'fri-kən-ˌdō\ *n* [F, fr. MF, prob. fr. *fricasser* + *-ande* (as in *viande* meat) + *-eau*, n. suffix] (1706) : larded veal roasted and glazed in its own juices
¹**fric·as·see** *also* **fric·as·sée** \'fri-kə-ˌsē, ˌfri-kə-'\ *n* [MF, fr. fem. of *fricassé*, pp. of *fricasser* to fricassee] (1568) : a dish of cut-up pieces of meat (as chicken) stewed in stock and served in a white sauce
²**fricassee** *vt* **-seed; -see·ing** (1657) : to cook as a fricassee
fric·a·tive \'fri-kə-tiv\ *n* [L *fricatus*, pp. of *fricare*] (1863) : a consonant characterized by frictional passage of the expired breath through a narrowing at some point in the vocal tract — **fricative** *adj*
fric·tion \'frik-shən\ *n* [ME, fr. MF or L; MF, fr. L *friction-, frictio*, fr. *fricare* to rub; akin to L *friare* to crumble, and perh. to Skt *bhrīnanti* they injure] (1704) **1 a** : the rubbing of one body against another **b** : the force that resists relative motion between two bodies in contact **2** : the clashing between two persons or parties of opposed views : DISAGREEMENT — **fric·tion·less** \-ləs\ *adj* — **fric·tion·less·ly** *adv*
fric·tion·al \'frik-shnəl, -shə-n⁹l\ *adj* (1850) **1** : of or relating to friction **2** : moved or produced by friction — **fric·tion·al·ly** *adv*
friction clutch *n* (ca. 1842) : a clutch in which connection is made through sliding friction
friction drive *n* (1907) : a power-transmission system that transmits motion by surface friction instead of teeth
friction tape *n* (1920) : a usu. cloth tape impregnated with water-resistant insulating material and an adhesive and used esp. to protect, insulate, and support electrical conductors
Fri·day \'frī-dē, -(ˌ)dā\ *n* [ME, fr. OE *frigedæg* (akin to OHG *friatag* Friday), fr. (assumed) *Frīg* Frigga + *dæg* day, prehistoric trans. of L *dies Veneris* Venus' day] (bef. 12c) : the sixth day of the week — **Fri·days** \-dēz, -(ˌ)dāz\ *adv*
fridge *also* **frig** \'frij\ *n* [by shortening & alter.] (1926) : REFRIGERATOR
fried \'frīd\ *adj* (1926) : INTOXICATED
fried-cake \'frīd-ˌkāk\ *n* (1839) : DOUGHNUT, CRULLER
¹**friend** \'frend\ *n* [ME *frend*, fr. OE *frēond*; akin to OHG *friunt* friend, OE *frēon* to love, *frēo* free] (bef. 12c) **1 a** : one attached to another by affection or esteem **b** : ACQUAINTANCE **2 a** : one that is not hostile **b** : one that is of the same nation, party, or group **3** : one that favors or promotes something (as a charity) **4** : a favored companion **5** *cap* : a member of a Christian sect that stresses Inner Light, rejects sacraments and an ordained ministry, and opposes war — called also *Quaker* — **friend·less** \'fren(d)-ləs\ *adj* — **friend·less·ness** *n* — **be friends with** : to have a friendship or friendly relationship with — **make friends with** : to establish a friendship or friendly relations with
²**friend** *vt* (13c) : to act as the friend of : BEFRIEND
¹**friend·ly** \'fren(d)-lē\ *adj* **friend·li·er; -est** (bef. 12c) **1** : of, relating to, or befitting a friend: as **a** : showing kindly interest and goodwill **b** : not hostile ⟨a ~ merger offer⟩; *also* : involving or coming from actions of one's own forces ⟨~ fire⟩ **c** : CHEERFUL, COMFORTING ⟨the ~ glow of the fire⟩ **2** : serving a beneficial or helpful purpose **3** : easy to use or understand ⟨~ computer software⟩ *syn* see AMICABLE — **friend·li·ly** \'fren(d)-lə-lē\ *adv* — **friend·li·ness** *n*
²**friendly** *adv* (bef. 12c) : in a friendly manner : AMICABLY

³**friendly** *n, pl* **friendlies** (1861) **1** : one that is friendly; *esp* : a native who is friendly to settlers or invaders **2** *Brit* : a match between sports teams and esp. international teams that has no connection with league or championship play
friendly society *n* (1703) *Brit* : a mutual association for providing life and health insurance and old-age pension benefits to members
friend of the court (1944) : AMICUS CURIAE
friend·ship \'fren(d)-ˌship\ *n* (bef. 12c) **1** : the state of being friends **2** : the quality or state of being friendly : FRIENDLINESS **3** *obs* : AID
fri·er *var of* FRYER
Frie·sian \'frē-zhən\ *n* [var. of *Frisian*] (1923) *chiefly Brit* : HOLSTEIN
¹**frieze** \'frēz *or* frē-'zā\ *n* [ME *frise*, fr. MF, fr. MD *vriese*] (15c) **1** : a heavy durable coarse wool and shoddy fabric with a rough surface **2** : a pile surface of uncut loops or of patterned cut and uncut loops
²**frieze** \'frēz\ *n* [MF *frise*, perh. fr. ML *phrygium, frisium* embroidered cloth, fr. L *phrygium*, fr. neut. of *Phrygius* Phrygian, fr. *Phrygia*] (1563) **1** : the part of an entablature between the architrave and the cornice — see ENTABLATURE illustration **2** : a sculptured or richly ornamented band (as on a building or piece of furniture) **3** : a band, line, or series suggesting a frieze ⟨a constant ~ of visitors wound its way around the . . . ruins —Mollie Panter-Downes⟩ — **frieze·like** *adj*
frig \'frig\ *vi* **frigged; frig·ging** [ME *fryggen* to wriggle] (1598) : COPULATE — usu. considered vulgar; sometimes used in present participle as a meaningless intensive
frig·ate \'fri-gət\ *n* [MF, fr. OIt *fregata*] (1585) **1** : a light boat propelled orig. by oars but later by sails **2** : a square-rigged war vessel intermediate between a corvette and a ship of the line **3** : a warship that is smaller than a destroyer
frigate bird *n* (1738) : any of a family (Fregatidae) of tropical seabirds having a forked tail and large wingspans that are noted for aggressively taking food from other birds
Frig·ga \'fri-gə\ *n* [ON *Frigg*] : the wife of Odin and Norse goddess of married love and of the hearth
¹**fright** \'frīt\ *n* [ME, fr. OE *fyrhto, fryhto*; akin to OHG *forhta* fear] (bef. 12c) **1** : fear excited by sudden danger : ALARM **2** : something strange, ugly, or shocking *syn* see FEAR
²**fright** *vt* (bef. 12c) : to alarm suddenly : FRIGHTEN
fright·en \'frī-t⁹n\ *vb* **fright·ened; fright·en·ing** \'frī-t⁹n-iŋ, 'frīt-niŋ\ *vt* (1666) **1** : to make afraid : TERRIFY **2** : to drive or force by frightening ⟨~ed the boy into confessing⟩ ~ *vi* : to become frightened — **fright·en·ing·ly** \-t⁹n-iŋ-lē, -niŋ-lē\ *adv*
fright·ful \'frīt-fəl\ *adj* (1607) **1** : causing intense fear or alarm : TERRIFYING **2** : startling esp. in being bad or objectionable ⟨a ~ novel⟩ **3** : EXTREME ⟨~ thirst⟩ — **fright·ful·ly** \-fə-lē\ *adv* — **fright·ful·ness** *n*
fright wig *n* (1886) : a wig with hair that stands out from the head
frig·id \'fri-jəd\ *adj* [L *frigidus*, fr. *frigēre* to be cold; akin to L *frigus* frost, cold, Gk *rhigos*] (1622) **1 a** : intensely cold **b** : lacking warmth or ardor : INDIFFERENT **2** : lacking imaginative qualities : INSIPID **3 a** : abnormally averse to sexual intercourse — used esp. of women **b** *of a female* : unable to achieve orgasm during sexual intercourse — **frig·id·ly** *adv* — **frig·id·ness** *n*
Frig·i·daire \ˌfri-jə-'dar, -'der\ *trademark* — used for a mechanical refrigerator
fri·gid·i·ty \fri-'ji-də-tē\ *n* (15c) : the quality or state of being frigid; *specif* : marked or abnormal sexual indifference esp. in a woman
frigid zone *n* (1622) : the area or region between the arctic circle and the north pole or between the antarctic circle and the south pole
frig·o·rif·ic \ˌfri-gə-'ri-fik\ *adj* [L *frigorificus*, fr. *frigor-, frigus* frost] (1667) : causing cold : CHILLING
fri·jo·le \frē-'hō-lē\ *also* **fri·jol** \frē-'hōl, 'frē-\, *n, pl* **fri·jo·les** \frē-'hō-lēz, 'frē-\, [AmerSp *frijol*, fr. Sp, kidney bean, fr. earlier *fesol, fresol*, prob. modif. of Galician *feijoo*, fr. L *phaseolus*, dim. of *phaselus* cowpea, fr. Gk *phasēlos*] (1577) : any of various beans used in Mexican style cooking — usu. used in pl.
¹**frill** \'fril\ *vt* (1574) : to provide or decorate with a frill
²**frill** *n* [perh. fr. Flem *frul*] (1591) **1 a** : a gathered, pleated, or bias-cut fabric edging used on clothing **b** : a strip of paper curled at one end and rolled to be slipped over the bone end (as of a chop) in serving **2** : a ruff of hair or feathers or a bony projection about the neck of an animal **3 a** : AFFECTATION, AIR — usu. used in pl. ⟨an honest . . . man who had no ~s, . . . no nonsense about him —W. A. White⟩ **b** : something decorative or useful and desirable but not essential : LUXURY — **frilly** \'fri-lē\ *adj*
¹**fringe** \'frinj\ *n, often attrib* [ME *frenge*, fr. MF, fr. (assumed) VL *frimbia*, fr. L *fimbriae* (pl.)] (14c) **1** : an ornamental border consisting of short straight or twisted threads or strips hanging from cut or raveled edges or from a separate band **2** : something resembling a fringe : EDGE, PERIPHERY — often used in pl. ⟨operated on the ~s of the law⟩ **b** : one of various light or dark bands produced by the interference or diffraction of light **c** : an area bordering a putting green on a golf course with grass trimmed longer than on the green itself **3 a** : something that is marginal, additional, or secondary to some activity, process, or subject **b** : a group with marginal or extremist views **c** : FRINGE BENEFIT — **fringy** \'frin-jē\ *adj*
²**fringe** *vt* **fringed; fring·ing** \'frin-jiŋ\ (15c) **1** : to furnish or adorn with a fringe **2** : to serve as a fringe for : BORDER
fringe area *n* (1950) : a region in which reception from a given broadcasting station is weak or subject to serious distortion
fringe benefit *n* (1948) **1** : an employment benefit (as a pension, a paid holiday, or health insurance) granted by an employer that has a monetary value but does not affect basic wage rates **2** : any additional benefit
fringe tree *n* (ca. 1730) : a small tree (*Chionanthus virginicus*) of the olive family that has clusters of white flowers and is native to the southern U.S. but is widely cultivated as an ornamental
frip·pery \'fri-p(ə-)rē\ *n, pl* **-per·ies** [MF *friperie*, alter. of OF *freperie*, fr. *frepe* old garment] (1568) **1** *obs* **a** : cast-off clothes **b** *archaic* : a

---

\ə\ abut \ᵊ\ kitten, F table \ər\ further \a\ ash \ā\ ace \ä\ mop, mar \aù\ out \ch\ chin \e\ bet \ē\ easy \g\ go \i\ hit \ī\ ice \j\ job \ŋ\ sing \ō\ go \ȯ\ law \ȯi\ boy \th\ thin \t͟h\ the \ü\ loot \ù\ foot \y\ yet \zh\ vision \à, k̲, ⁿ, œ, œ̄, ᵫ, ᵫ̄, ᵛ\ *see* Guide to Pronunciation place where old clothes are sold   **2**   **a** : FINERY; *also* : an elegant or showy garment   **b** : something showy, frivolous, or nonessential : LUXURY, TRIFLE   **c** : OSTENTATION; *esp* : something foolish or affectedly elegant

Fris·bee \'friz-bē\ *trademark* — used for a plastic disk several inches in diameter sailed between players by a flip of the wrist

fri·sé \frē-'zā\ *n* [F, fr. pp. of *friser* to curl] (1884) : ¹FRIEZE

Frise aileron \'frēz-\ *n* [Leslie George *Frise b*1897 Eng. engineer] (ca. 1934) : an aileron having a nose portion projecting ahead of the hinge axis and a lower surface in line with the lower surface of the wing

fri·seur \frē-'zər\ *n* [F, fr. *friser*] (1750) : HAIRDRESSER

¹Fri·sian \'fri-zhən, 'frē-\ *adj* [L *Frisius* Frisian; akin to OE *Frisa, Frēsa* a Frisian] (1598) : of, relating to, or characteristic of Friesland, the Frisians, or Frisian

²Frisian *n* (1601)   **1** : a member of a people that inhabit principally the Netherlands province of Friesland and the Frisian islands in the North Sea   **2** : the Germanic language of the Frisian people

¹frisk \'frisk\ *vb* [obs. *frisk* (lively)] *vi* (1519) : to leap, skip, or dance in a lively or playful way : GAMBOL   *~ vt* : to search (a person) for something (as a concealed weapon) by running the hand rapidly over the clothing and through the pockets — **frisk·er** *n*

²frisk *n* (1525)   **1 a** *archaic* : CAPER   **b** : GAMBOL, ROMP   **c** : DIVERSION   **2** : an act of frisking

fris·ket \'fris-kət\ *n* [F *frisquette*, fr. MF] (ca. 1898) : a masking device or material used esp. in printing or graphic arts

frisky \'fris-kē\ *adj* **frisk·i·er; -est** (ca. 1500) : inclined to frisk : PLAYFUL; *also* : LIVELY — **frisk·i·ly** \'fris-kə-lē\ *adv* — **frisk·i·ness** \-kē-nəs\ *n*

fris·son \frē-'sōⁿ\ *n, pl* **frissons** \-'sōⁿ(z)\ [F, shiver, fr. OF *friçon*, fr. LL *friction-, frictio*, fr. L, lit., friction (taken in LL as derivative of *frigēre* to be cold)] (1777) : a brief moment of emotional excitement : SHUDDER, THRILL

¹frit \'frit\ *n* [It *fritta*, fem. of *fritto*, pp. of *friggere* to fry, fr. L *frigere* to roast — more at FRY] (1662)   **1** : the calcined or partly fused materials of which glass is made   **2** : any of various chemically complex glasses used ground esp. to introduce soluble or unstable ingredients into glazes or enamels

²frit *vt* **frit·ted; frit·ting** (1832)   **1** : to prepare (materials for glass) by heat : FUSE   **2** : to convert into a frit

frith \'frith\ *n* (14c) *archaic* : ESTUARY

frit·il·lar·ia \,frit-ᵊl-'er-ē-ə, -'ar-\ *n* [NL, fr. L *fritillus* dice cup; fr. the markings of the petals] (1664) : any of a widespread genus (*Fritillaria*) of bulbous herbs of the lily family with variably colored and often mottled or checkered flowers

frit·il·lary \'frit-ᵊl-,er-ē\ *n, pl* **-lar·ies** [NL *fritillaria*] (1633)   **1** : FRITILLARIA   **2** : any of numerous nymphalid butterflies (*Argynnis, Speyeria,* and related genera) that usu. are orange with black spots on the upper side of both wings and silver spotted on the underside of the hind wing

frit·ta·ta \frē-'tä-tə\ *n* [It, fr. *fritto*] (1931) : an unfolded omelet often containing chopped vegetables or meats

fritillaria

frit·ted *adj* [²frit] (1879) : being porous glass made of sintered powdered glass or fiberglass

¹frit·ter \'fri-tər\ *n* [ME *fritour*, fr. MF *friture*, fr. (assumed) VL *frictura*, fr. L *frictus*, pp. of *frigere* to roast] (14c) : a small mass of fried or sautéed batter often containing fruit or meat

²fritter *vb* [*fritter*, n. (fragment, shred)] *vt* (1728)   **1** : to spend or waste bit by bit, on trifles, or without commensurate return — usu. used with *away*   **2** : to break into small fragments *~ vi* : DISSIPATE, DWINDLE — **frit·ter·er** \-tar-ər\ *n*

frit·to mi·sto \'frē-(,)tō-'mē-(,)stō\ *n* [It, lit., mixed fried (food)] (1903) : small morsels of meat, seafood, or vegetables coated with batter and deep fried

fritz \'fritz\ *n* [origin unknown] (1902) : a state of disorder or disrepair — used in the phrase *on the fritz*

friv·ol \'fri-vᵊl\ *vi* **-oled** *or* **-olled; -ol·ing** *or* **-ol·ling** \-vᵊl-iŋ, -və-liŋ\ [back-formation fr. *frivolous*] (1866) : to act frivolously : TRIFLE — **friv·ol·er** *or* **friv·ol·ler** \-vᵊl-ər, -və-lər\ *n*

fri·vol·i·ty \fri-'vä-lə-tē\ *n, pl* **-ties** (1796)   **1** : the quality or state of being frivolous   **2** : a frivolous act or thing

friv·o·lous \'fri-vᵊl-əs, -və-ləs\ *adj* [ME, fr. L *frivolus*] (15c)   **1 a** : of little weight or importance   **b** : having no sound basis (as in fact or law) ⟨a ~ lawsuit⟩   **2** : lacking in seriousness   **b** : marked by unbecoming levity — **friv·o·lous·ly** *adv* — **friv·o·lous·ness** *n*

¹frizz \'friz\ *vb* [F *friser*] *vt* (1660) : to form into small tight curls *~ vi, of hair* : to form a mass of tight curls

²frizz *n* (1668)   **1** : a tight curl   **2** : hair that is tightly curled

³frizz *vb* [alter. of ¹*fry*] *vt* (1835) : to fry or sear with a sizzling noise *~ vi* : SIZZLE

¹friz·zle \'fri-zᵊl\ *vb* **friz·zled; friz·zling** \-zᵊl-iŋ, -zə-liŋ\ [prob. akin to OFris *frisle* curl] (1573) : FRIZZ, CURL

²frizzle *n* (1613) : a crisp curl

³frizzle *vb* **friz·zled; friz·zling** [¹*fry* + *sizzle*] *vt* (1839)   **1** : to fry until crisp and curled   **2** : BURN, SCORCH *~ vi* : to cook with a sizzling noise

frizzy \'fri-zē\ *adj* **frizz·i·er; -est** (ca. 1864) : tightly curled — **frizz·i·ness** *n*

¹fro \fra, 'frō\ *prep* [ME, fr. ON *frā;* akin to OE *fram* from] (13c) *dial Brit* : FROM

²fro \'frō\ *adv* (14c) : BACK, AWAY — used in the phrase *to and fro*

¹frock \'fräk\ *n* [ME *frok*, fr. MF *froc*, of Gmc origin; akin to OHG *hroch* mantle, coat] (14c)   **1** : an outer garment worn by monks and friars : HABIT   **2** : an outer garment worn chiefly by men : **a** : a long loose mantle   **b** : a workman's outer shirt; *esp* : SMOCK FROCK   **c** : a woolen jersey worn esp. by sailors   **3** : a woman's dress

²frock *vt* (1828)   **1** : to clothe in a frock   **2** : to make a cleric of

frock coat *n* (1823) : a man's knee-length usu. double-breasted coat

froe \'frō\ *n* [perh. alter. of obs. *froward* turned away, fr. ME; fr. the position of the handle] (1574) : a cleaving tool for splitting cask staves and shingles from the block

frog \'frȯg, 'fräg\ *n* [ME *frogge*, fr. OE *frogga;* akin to OHG *frosk* frog; senses 2, 3, 5, 7, 8 unclearly derived & perh. of distinct origin] (bef. 12c)   **1** : any of various smooth-skinned web-footed largely aquatic tailless agile leaping amphibians (as a ranid) — compare TOAD   **2** : the triangular elastic horny pad in the middle of the sole of the foot of a horse — see HOOF illustration   **3 a** : a loop attached to a belt to hold a weapon or tool   **b** : an ornamental braiding for fastening the front of a garment that consists of a button and a loop through which it passes   **4** *often cap* : FRENCHMAN — usu. taken to be offensive   **5** : a device permitting the wheels on one rail of a track to cross an intersecting rail   **6** : a condition in the throat that produces hoarseness ⟨had a ~ in his throat⟩   **7** : the nut of a violin bow   **8** : a small holder (as of metal, glass, or plastic) with perforations or spikes for holding flowers in place in a bowl or vase

frog·eye \-,ī\ *n* (ca. 1909) : any of numerous leaf diseases characterized by concentric rings about the diseased spots

frog·hop·per \-,hä-pər\ *n* (1711) : SPITTLEBUG

frog kick *n* (1940) : a breaststroke kick executed with the knees turned outward and the legs separated and then swung together

frog·man \'frȯg-,man, 'fräg-, -mən\ *n* (1945) : a person equipped (as with face mask, flippers, and air supply) for extended periods of underwater swimming; *esp* : a person so equipped for military reconnaissance and demolition

frog·march \-,märch\ *vt* (1923) : to seize from behind roughly and forcefully propel forward ⟨~ed him out the door⟩

frog spit *n* (ca. 1825) : CUCKOO SPIT 1

¹frol·ic \'frä-lik\ *adj* [D *vroolijk*, fr. MD *vrolijc*, fr. *vro* happy; akin to OHG *frō* happy] (1538) : full of fun : MERRY

²frolic *vi* **frol·icked; frol·ick·ing** (1593)   **1** : to amuse oneself : make merry   **2** : to play and run about happily : ROMP

³frolic *n* (1616)   **1** : a playful or mischievous action   **2 a** : an occasion or scene of fun : PARTY   **b** : FUN, MERRIMENT

frol·ic·some \'frä-lik-səm\ *adj* (1699) : full of gaiety : SPORTIVE, PLAYFUL

from \'frəm, 'främ *also* fəm\ *prep* [ME, fr. OE *from, fram;* akin to OHG *fram,* adv., forth, away, OE *faran* to go — more at FARE] (bef. 12c)   **1** — used as a function word to indicate a starting point of a physical movement or a starting point in measuring or reckoning or in a statement of limits ⟨came here ~ the city⟩ ⟨a week ~ today⟩ ⟨cost ~ $5 to $10⟩   **2** — used as a function word to indicate physical separation or an act or condition of removal, abstention, exclusion, release, subtraction, or differentiation ⟨protection ~ the sun⟩ ⟨relief ~ anxiety⟩   **3** — used as a function word to indicate the source, cause, agent, or basis ⟨we conclude ~ this⟩ ⟨a call ~ my lawyer⟩ ⟨inherited a love of music ~ his father⟩ ⟨worked hard ~ necessity⟩

frond \'fränd\ *n* [L *frond-, frons* foliage] (1785)   **1** : a large leaf (esp. of a palm or fern) usu. with many divisions   **2** : a thallus or thalloid shoot (as of a lichen or seaweed) resembling a leaf — **frond·ed** \'frän-dəd\ *adj*

fron·deur \frōⁿ-'dər\ *n* [F, lit., slinger, participant in a 17th cent. revolt in which the rebels were compared to schoolboys using slings only when the teacher was not looking] (1798) : REBEL, MALCONTENT

¹front \'frənt\ *n* [ME, fr. OF, fr. L *front-, frons*] (13c)   **1 a** : FOREHEAD; *also* : the whole face   **b** : external and often feigned appearance esp. in the face of danger or adversity   **2 a** (1) : VANGUARD (2) : a line of battle (3) : a zone of conflict between armies   **b** (1) : a stand on an issue (2) : POLICY (2) : an area of activity (as study or debate) ⟨progress on the educational ~⟩ (3) : a movement linking divergent elements to achieve common objectives; *esp* : a political coalition   **3** : a side of a building; *esp* : the side that contains the principal entrance   **4 a** : the forward part or surface   **b** (1) : FRONTAGE (2) : a beach promenade at a seaside resort   **c** : DICKEY 1a   **d** : the boundary between two dissimilar air masses   **5** *archaic* : BEGINNING   **6 a** (1) : a position ahead of a person or of the foremost part of a thing   (2) — used as a call by a hotel desk clerk in summoning a bellhop   **b** : a position of leadership or superiority   **7 a** : a person, group, or thing used to mask the identity or true character or activity of the actual controlling agent   **b** : a person who serves as the nominal head or spokesman of an enterprise or group to lend it prestige — **in front of** : directly before or ahead of — **out front** : in the audience

²front *vi* (1523)   **1** : to have the front or principal side adjacent to something; *also* : to have frontage on something ⟨a ten-acre plot ~ing on a lake — *Current Biog.*⟩   **2** : to serve as a front ⟨~ing for special interests⟩   *~ vt*   **1 a** : CONFRONT ⟨went to the woods because I wished . . . to ~ only the essential facts of life —H. D. Thoreau⟩   **b** : to appear before ⟨daily ~ed him in some fresh splendor —Alfred Tennyson⟩   **2 a** : to be in front of ⟨lawn ~ing the house⟩   **b** : to be the leader of (a musical group) ⟨appeared as a soloist and ~ed bands⟩   **3** : to face toward or have frontage on ⟨the house ~s the street⟩   **4** : to supply a front to ⟨~ed the building with bricks⟩   **5 a** : to articulate (a sound) with the tongue farther forward   **b** : to move (a word or phrase) to the beginning of a sentence   **6** *basketball* : to play in front of (an opposing player) rather than between the player and the basket

³front *adj* (1600)   **1 a** : of, relating to, or situated at the front   **b** : acting as a front ⟨~ company⟩   **2** : articulated at or toward the front of the oral passage ⟨~ vowels⟩   **3** : constituting the first nine holes of an 18-hole golf course — **front** *adv*

front·age \'frən-tij\ *n* (1622)   **1 a** : a piece of land that lies adjacent (as to a street or the ocean)   **b** : the land between the front of a building and the street   **c** : the length of a frontage   **2** : the act or fact of facing a given way   **3** : the front side of a building

frontage road *n* (1949) : a local street that parallels an expressway or through street and that provides access to property near the expressway — called also *service road*

¹fron·tal \'frən-tᵊl\ *n* (14c)   **1** [ME *frontel,* fr. ML *frontellum,* dim. of L *front-, frons*] : a cloth hanging over the front of an altar   **2** : FACADE 1

²frontal *adj* [NL *frontalis,* fr. L *front-, frons*] (1656)   **1** : of, relating to, or adjacent to the forehead or the frontal bone   **2 a** : of, relating to, or situated at the front   **b** : directed against the front or at the main point or issue : DIRECT ⟨~ assault⟩   **3** : parallel to the main axis of the body and at right angles to the sagittal plane   **4** : of or relating to a meteorological front — **fron·tal·ly** \-tᵊl-ē\ *adv*

frontal bone *n* (1741) : a bone that forms the forehead and roofs over most of the orbits and nasal cavity and that at birth consists of two halves separated by a suture

fron·tal·i·ty \,frən-'ta-lə-tē\ *n* (1905) **1** *sculpture* : a schematic composition of the front view that is complete without lateral movement **2** *painting* : the depiction of an object, figure, or scene in a plane parallel to the plane of the picture surface

frontal lobe *n* (1879) : the anterior division of each cerebral hemisphere

front and center *adv* (1951) : in or to the forefront of activity or consideration

front bench *n* (ca. 1889) : either of the two benches nearest the chair in a British legislature (as the House of Commons) occupied by government and opposition leaders; *also* : the leaders themselves — compare BACKBENCH — **front-bench·er** \-'ben-chər\ *n*

front burner *n* (1973) : the condition of being in active consideration or development — compare BACK BURNER

front-court \'frənt-,kȯrt, -'kȯrt\ *n* (ca. 1949) : a basketball team's offensive half of the court; *also* : the positions of forward and center on a basketball team

front dive *n* (ca. 1934) : a dive from a position facing the water

front–end *adj* (1962) : relating to or required at the beginning of an undertaking ⟨no ~ charge at the time of investment⟩

front end *n* (1973) : a unit in a computer system devoted to controlling the data communications link between terminals and the main computer and often to the preliminary processing of data

front–end load *n* (1962) : the part of the total commission and expenses taken out of early payments under a contract plan for the periodic purchase of investment-company shares

front–end loader *n* (1954) : a usu. wheeled vehicle with a hydraulically operated scoop in front for excavating and loading loose material — called also *front loader*

fron·tier \,frən-'tir, 'frən-,, frän-', 'frän-,\ *n* [ME *fronter*, fr. MF *frontiere*, fr. *front*] (15c) **1 a** : a border between two countries **b** *obs* : a stronghold on a frontier **2 a** : a region that forms the margin of settled or developed territory **b** : the farthermost limits of knowledge or achievement in a particular subject **c** : a line of division between different or opposed things ⟨the ~s separating science and the humanities —R. W. Clark⟩ **d** : a new field for exploitative or developmental activity — **frontier** *adj*

fron·tiers·man \,frən-'tirz-mən, frän-\ *n* (1782) : one who lives or works on a frontier

fron·tis·piece \'frən-tə-,spēs\ *n* [MF *frontispice*, fr. LL *frontispicium* facade, fr. L *front-, frons* + *-i-* + *specere* to look at — more at SPY] (ca. 1598) **1 a** : the principal front of a building **b** : a decorated pediment over a portico or window **2** : an illustration preceding and usu. facing the title page of a book or magazine

front·less \'frənt-ləs\ *adj* (1605) *archaic* : SHAMELESS

front·let \-lət\ *n* [ME *frontlette*, fr. MF *frontelet*, dim. of *frontel*, fr. L *frontale*, fr. *front-, frons*] (15c) **1** : a band or phylactery worn on the forehead **2** : the forehead esp. of an animal

front-line \'frənt-,līn\ *adj* (1915) **1** : relating to, being, or involved in a front line ⟨~ ambulances⟩ **2** : FIRST-RATE ⟨~ teachers⟩; *also* : FIRST-STRING ⟨~ goalie⟩

front line *n* (1917) **1 a** : a military line formed by the most advanced tactical combat units; *also* : FRONT 2a(2) **b** : an area of potential or actual conflict or struggle **2** : the most advanced, responsible, or visible position in a field or activity

front–load *vt* (1976) : to assign costs or benefits to the early stages of (as a contract, project, or time period)

front man *n* (1927) **1** : a person serving as a front or figurehead **2** : the lead performer in a musical group

front matter *n* (ca. 1909) : matter preceding the main text of a book

front money *n* (ca. 1928) : money that is paid in advance for a promised service or product

fronto- *comb form* [*front*] : boundary of an air mass ⟨*fronto*genesis⟩

front office *n*, *often attrib* (1900) : the policy-making officials of an organization

front-o·gen·e·sis \,frən-tō-'je-nə-səs\ *n* [NL] (1931) : the coming together into a distinct front of two dissimilar air masses that commonly react upon each other to induce cloud and precipitation

front·ol·y·sis \,frən-'tä-lə-səs\ *n* [NL] (ca. 1938) : a process tending to destroy a meteorological front

fron·ton \'frän-,tän\ *n* [Sp *frontón* gable, wall of a pelota court, fronton, fr. aug. of *frente* forehead, fr. L *front-, frons*] (1896) : a jai alai arena

¹**front–page** \'frənt-'pāj\ *adj* (1917) : printed on the front page of a newspaper; *also* : very newsworthy

²**front-page** *vt* (1929) : to print or report on the front page

front room *n* (1853) : LIVING ROOM, PARLOR

front–run·ner \'frənt-,rə-nər\ *n* (1914) **1** : a contestant who runs best when in the lead **2** : a leading contestant in or as if in a rivalry or competition ⟨a political ~⟩ ⟨dubbed . . . ~ for the title of "worst Senator" —Edward Roeder⟩

front·ward \'frənt-wərd\ *or* **front·wards** \-wərdz\ *adv or adj* (1865) : toward the front

frore \'frōr, 'frȯr\ *adj* [ME *froren*, fr. OE, pp. of *frēosan* to freeze] (13c) : FROSTY, FROZEN

frosh \'fräsh\ *n, pl* **frosh** [by shortening & alter.] (1915) : FRESHMAN

¹**frost** \'frȯst\ *n* [ME, fr. OE; akin to OHG *frost* — more at FREEZE] (bef. 12c) **1 a** : the process of freezing **b** : a covering of minute ice crystals on a cold surface; *also* : ice particles formed from a gas **c** : the temperature that causes freezing **2 a** : coldness of deportment or temperament : an indifferent, reserved, or unfriendly manner **b** : FAILURE ⟨the play was . . . a most dreadful ~ —Arnold Bennett⟩

²**frost** *vt* (1635) **1 a** : to cover with or as if with frost; *esp* : to put icing on (cake) **b** : to produce a fine-grained slightly roughened surface on (as metal or glass) **2** : to injure or kill (as plants) by frost **3** : to make angry or irritated ⟨your attitude really ~s me⟩ ~ *vi* : to become frosted

¹**frost·bite** \'frȯs(t)-,bīt\ *vt* -**bit** \-,bit\; -**bit·ten** \-,bi-t*ə*n\; -**bit·ing** \-,bī-tiŋ\ (1601) : to affect or injure by frost or frostbite

²**frostbite** *n* (1813) : the freezing or the local effect of a partial freezing of some part of the body

³**frostbite** *adj* (1953) : done in cold weather ⟨~ sailing⟩; *also* : of or relating to cold-weather sailing ⟨~ sailors⟩

frost·bit·ing \-,bī-tiŋ\ *n* (1965) : the sport of sailing in cold weather

frost·ed \'frȯ-stəd\ *adj* (1947) : having undergone frosting ⟨~ hair⟩

frost heave *n* (1941) : an upthrust of ground or pavement caused by freezing of moist soil — called also *frost heaving*

frost·ing \'frȯ-stiŋ\ *n* (1858) **1 a** : ICING **b** : TRIMMING, ORNAMENTATION **2** : lusterless finish of metal or glass : MAT; *also* : a white finish produced on glass (as by etching) **3** : the lightening (as by chemicals) of small strands of hair throughout the entire head to produce a two-tone effect — compare STREAKING

frost·work \'frȯs(t)-,wərk\ *n* (1729) : the figures that moisture sometimes forms in freezing (as on a windowpane)

frosty \'frȯ-stē\ *adj* **frost·i·er; -est** (bef. 12c) **1 a** : attended with or producing frost **b** : FREEZING **b** : briskly cold : CHILLY **2** : covered or appearing as if covered with frost : HOARY ⟨a man of 65, with ~ eyebrows and hair —Nan Robertson⟩ **3** : marked by coolness or extreme reserve in manner ⟨his smile was distinctly ~ —Erle Stanley Gardner⟩ — **frost·i·ly** \-stə-lē\ *adv* — **frost·i·ness** \-stē-nəs\ *n*

¹**froth** \'frȯth\ *n, pl* **froths** \'frȯths, 'frȯthz\ [ME, fr. ON *frotha*; akin to OE *āfrēothan* to froth] (14c) **1 a** : bubbles formed in or on a liquid : FOAM **b** : a foamy slaver sometimes accompanying disease or exhaustion **2** : something resembling froth (as in being unsubstantial, worthless, or light and airy)

²**froth** \'frȯth, 'frȯth\ *vi* (14c) **1** : to foam at the mouth **2** : to throw froth out or up **3** : to become covered with or as if with froth ⟨whole groves ~ with nodding blossoms —Amy Lovejoy⟩ ~ *vt* **1** : to cause to foam **2** : to cover with froth **3** : VENT, VOICE

frothy \'frȯ-thē, -thē\ *adj* **froth·i·er; -est** (15c) **1** : full of or consisting of froth **2 a** : gaily frivolous or light in content or treatment : INSUBSTANTIAL ⟨a ~ comedy⟩ **b** : made of light thin material — **froth·i·ly** \-thə-lē, -thə-\ *adv* — **froth·i·ness** \-thē-nəs, -thē-\ *n*

frot·tage \frȯ-'täzh\ *n* [F, fr. *frotter* to rub] (1935) : the technique of creating a design by rubbing (as with a pencil) over an object placed underneath the paper; *also* : a composition so made

frou-frou \'frü-(,)frü\ *n* [F, of imit. origin] (1870) **1** : a rustling esp. of a woman's skirts **2** : showy or frilly ornamentation

frow \'frō\ *var of* FROE

fro·ward \'frō-(w)ərd\ *adj* [ME, turned away, froward, fr. *fro* from + *-ward* -ward] (13c) **1** : habitually disposed to disobedience and opposition **2** *archaic* : ADVERSE — **fro·ward·ly** *adv* — **fro·ward·ness** *n*

¹**frown** \'fraủn\ *vb* [ME *frounen*, fr. MF *froigner* to snort, frown, of Celt origin; akin to W *ffroen* nostril, OIr *srón* nose] *vi* (14c) **1** : to contract the brow in displeasure or concentration **2** : to give evidence of displeasure or disapproval by or as if by facial expression ⟨critics ~ on the idea⟩ ~ *vt* : to show displeasure with or disapproval of esp. by facial expression — **frown·er** *n* — **frown·ing·ly** \'fraủ-niŋ-lē\ *adv*

²**frown** *n* (1581) **1** : an expression of displeasure **2** : a wrinkling of the brow in displeasure or concentration

frows·ty \'fraủ-stē\ *adj* **frowst·i·er; -est** [alter. of *frowsy*] (1865) **1** *chiefly Brit* : MUSTY **2** *chiefly Brit* : FROWSY

frow·sy *or* **frow·zy** \'fraủ-zē\ *adj* **frow·si·er** *or* **frow·zi·er; -est** [origin unknown] (1681) **1** : MUSTY, STALE ⟨a ~ smell of stale beer and stale smoke —W. S. Maugham⟩ **2** : having a slovenly or uncared-for appearance ⟨a couple of ~ stuffed chairs —R. M. Williams⟩

froze *past of* FREEZE

fro·zen \'frō-z*ə*n\ *adj* (14c) **1 a** : treated, affected, or crusted over by freezing **b** : subject to long and severe cold ⟨~ north⟩ **2 a** : incapable of being changed, moved, or undone : FIXED; *specif* : debarred by official action from movement or from change in status ⟨~ wages⟩ **b** : not available for present use ⟨~ capital⟩ **c** (1) : drained or incapable of emotion (2) : expressing or characterized by cold unfriendliness — **fro·zen·ly** *adv* — **fro·zen·ness** \-z*ə*n-(n)əs\ *n*

fruc·ti·fi·ca·tion \,frək-tə-fə-'kā-shən, ,frůk-\ *n* (1764) : the reproductive organs or fruit of a plant; *esp* : SPOROPHORE

fruc·ti·fy \'frək-tə-,fī, 'frůk-\ *vb* -**fied; -fy·ing** [ME *fructifien*, fr. MF *fructifier*, fr. L *fructificare*, fr. *fructus* fruit] *vi* (14c) : to bear fruit ⟨its seeds shall ~ —Amy Lowell⟩ ⟨no partnership can ~ without candor on both sides —D. M. Ogilvy⟩ ~ *vt* : to make fruitful or productive

fruc·tose \'frək-,tōs, 'frůk-, 'frůk-, -,tōz\ *n* (ca. 1864) **1** : an optically active sugar $C_6H_{12}O_6$ that differs from glucose in having a ketonic rather than aldehydic carbonyl group **2** : the very sweet soluble levorotatory D-form of fructose that occurs esp. in fruit juices and honey — called also *levulose*

fruc·tu·ous \'frək-chə-wəs, 'frůk-\ *adj* (14c) : FRUITFUL ⟨a ~ land⟩

fru·gal \'frü-gəl\ *adj* [MF or L; MF, fr. L *frugalis* virtuous, frugal, fr. *frug-, frux* fruit, value; akin to L *frui* to enjoy] (1598) : characterized by or reflecting economy in the use of resources **syn** see SPARING — **fru·gal·i·ty** \frü-'ga-lə-tē\ *n* — **fru·gal·ly** \'frü-gə-lē\ *adv*

fru·giv·o·rous \frü-'ji-və-rəs\ *adj* [L *frug-, frux* + E *-vorous*] (1713) : feeding on fruit — **fru·gi·vore** \'frü-ji-,vȯr, -,vȯr\ *n*

¹**fruit** \'früt\ *n, often attrib* [ME, fr. OF, fr. L *fructus* fruit, use, fr. *frui* to enjoy, have the use of — more at BROOK] (12c) **1 a** : a product of plant growth (as grain, vegetables, or cotton) ⟨the ~s of the field⟩ **b** (1) : the usu. edible reproductive body of a seed plant; *esp* : one having a sweet pulp associated with the seed ⟨the ~ of the tree⟩ (2) : a succulent plant part (as the petioles of a rhubarb plant) used chiefly in a dessert or sweet course **c** : a dish, quantity, or diet of fruits (live on ~⟩ **d** : a product of fertilization in a plant with its modified envelopes or appendages; *specif* : the ripened ovary of a seed plant and its contents **e** : the flavor or aroma of fresh fruit in mature wine **2** : OFFSPRING, PROGENY **3 a** : the state of bearing fruit ⟨a tree in ~⟩ **b** : the effect or consequence of an action or operation : PRODUCT, RESULT ⟨the ~s of our labor⟩ **4** : a male homosexual — often used disparagingly — **fruit·ed** \'frü-təd\ *adj*

²**fruit** *vi* (14c) : to bear fruit ~ *vt* : to cause to bear fruit

\ə\ abut \ᵊ\ kitten, F table \ər\ further \a\ ash \ā\ ace \ä\ mop, mar \aủ\ out \ch\ chin \e\ bet \ē\ easy \g\ go \i\ hit \ī\ ice \j\ job \ŋ\ sing \ō\ go \ȯ\ law \ȯi\ boy \th\ thin \th\ the \ü\ loot \ů\ foot \y\ yet \zh\ vision \à, ᵏ, ⁿ, œ, œ̄, ᵫ, ᵫ̄, ᵞ\ see Guide to Pronunciation

fruit·age \'früt-ij\ *n* (15c) **1 a :** FRUIT **b :** the condition or process of bearing fruit **2 :** the product or result of an action

fruit·tar·i·an \(,)frü(t)-'ter-ē-ən\ *n* (1893) **:** a person who lives on fruit

fruit bat *n* (1877) **:** any of a family (Pteropodidae of the suborder Megachiroptera) of often large tropical and subtropical Old World bats that feed on ripe fruit, pollen, and nectar and that usu. use visual navigation rather than echolocation — called also *flying fox*

fruit·cake \'früt-,kāk\ *n* (1848) **1 :** a rich cake containing nuts, dried or candied fruits, and spices **2 :** NUT 6a

fruit·er·er \'früt-ər-ər\ *n* [ME, modif. of MF *fruitier*, fr. *fruit*] (15c) *chiefly Brit* **:** a person who deals in fruit

fruit fly *n* (ca. 1753) **:** any of various small dipteran flies (as a drosophila) whose larvae feed on fruit or decaying vegetable matter

fruit·ful \'früt-fəl\ *adj* (14c) **1 a :** yielding or producing fruit **b :** conducive to an abundant yield **2 :** abundantly productive *syn* see FERTILE — **fruit·ful·ly** \-fə-lē\ *adv* — **fruit·ful·ness** *n*

fruiting body *n* (1918) **:** a plant organ specialized for producing spores; *esp* **:** SPOROPHORE

fru·ition \frü-'i-shən\ *n* [ME *fruicioun*, fr. MF or LL; MF *fruition*, fr. LL *fruition-, fruitio*, fr. L *frui*] (15c) **1 :** pleasurable use or possession **:** ENJOYMENT **2 a :** the state of bearing fruit **b :** REALIZATION

fruit·less \'früt-ləs\ *adj* (14c) **1 :** UNSUCCESSFUL **2 :** lacking or not bearing fruit *syn* see FUTILE — **fruit·less·ly** *adv* — **fruit·less·ness** *n*

fruit·let \-lət\ *n* (1882) **1 :** a small fruit **2 :** a unit of a collective fruit

fruit machine *n* (1933) *Brit* **:** SLOT MACHINE 2

fruit sugar *n* (ca. 1889) **:** FRUCTOSE 2

fruit·wood \'früt-,wud\ *n, often attrib* (1927) **:** the wood of a fruit tree (as the apple, cherry, or pear) ⟨~ furniture⟩

fruity \'früt-ē\ *adj* **fruit·i·er; -est** (1657) **1 :** relating to, made with, or resembling fruit **2 :** having the flavor or aroma of ripe fruit **2 a :** extremely effective, interesting, or enjoyable **b :** sweet or sentimental esp. to excess **c** *of a voice* **:** rich and deep **3 a** *slang* **:** CRAZY, SILLY **b :** HOMOSEXUAL — often used disparagingly — **fruit·i·ness** *n*

fru·men·ty \'frü-mən-tē\ *n, pl* **-ties** [ME, fr. MF *frumentee*, fr. *frument* grain, fr. L *frumentum*, fr. *frui* to enjoy — more at BROOK] (14c) **:** a dish of wheat boiled in milk and usu. sweetened and spiced

frump \'frəmp\ *n* [prob. fr. *frumple* (to wrinkle)] (1817) **1 :** a dowdy unattractive girl or woman **2 :** a staid, drab, old-fashioned person

frump·ish \'frəm-pish\ *adj* (ca. 1847) **:** DOWDY, DRAB

frumpy \'frəm-pē\ *adj* **frump·i·er; -est** (ca. 1840) **:** DOWDY, DRAB

¹frus·trate \'frəs-,trāt\ *vt* **frus·trat·ed; frus·trat·ing** [ME, fr. L *frustratus*, pp. of *frustrare* to deceive, frustrate, fr. *frustra* in error, in vain] (15c) **1 a :** to balk or defeat in an endeavor **b :** to induce feelings of discouragement in **2 a** (1) **:** to make ineffectual **:** bring to nothing (2) **:** IMPEDE, OBSTRUCT **b :** to make invalid or of no effect

syn FRUSTRATE, THWART, FOIL, BAFFLE, BALK mean to check or defeat another's plan or block achievement of a goal. FRUSTRATE implies making vain or ineffectual all efforts however vigorous or persistent ⟨*frustrated* attempts at government reform⟩. THWART suggests frustration or checking by crossing or opposing ⟨the army *thwarted* his attempt at a coup⟩. FOIL implies checking or defeating so as to discourage further effort ⟨*foiled* by her parents, he stopped trying to see her⟩. BAFFLE implies frustration by confusing or puzzling ⟨*baffled* by the maze of rules and regulations⟩. BALK suggests the interposing of obstacles or hindrances ⟨officials felt that legal restrictions had *balked* their efforts to control crime⟩.

²frustrate *adj* (15c) **:** characterized by frustration

frus·trat·ing \-,trā-tiŋ\ *adj* (1871) **:** tending to produce or characterized by frustration — **frus·trat·ing·ly** \-tiŋ-lē\ *adv*

frus·tra·tion \(,)frəs-'trā-shən\ *n* (1555) **1 :** the act of frustrating **2 a :** the state or an instance of being frustrated **b :** a deep chronic sense or state of insecurity and dissatisfaction arising from unresolved problems or unfulfilled needs **2 :** something that frustrates

frus·tule \'frəs-(,)chü(ə)l, -(,)t(y)ü(ə)l\ *n* [F, fr. L *frustulum*, dim. of *frustum*] (1857) **:** the 2-valved siliceous shell of a diatom

frus·tum \'frəs-təm\ *n, pl* **frustums** or **frus·ta** \-tə\ [NL, fr. L, piece, bit — more at BRUISE] (1658) **:** the basal part of a solid cone or pyramid formed by cutting off the top by a plane parallel to the base; *also* **:** the part of a solid intersected between two usu. parallel planes

fru·tes·cent \frü-'tes-ᵊnt\ *adj* [L *frutex* + E *-escent*] (1709) **:** having or approaching the habit or appearance of a shrub **:** SHRUBBY

fru·ti·cose \'früt-i-,kōs\ *adj* [L *fruticosus*, fr. *frutic-, frutex* shrub] (1882) **:** having a shrubby often branched thallus that grows perpendicular to the substrate ⟨~ lichens⟩ — compare CRUSTOSE, FOLIOSE

¹fry \'frī\ *vb* **fried; fry·ing** [ME *frien*, fr. OF *frire*, fr. L *frigere* to roast; akin to Gk *phrygein* to roast, fry, Skt *bhrjjati* he roasts] *vt* (13c) **:** to cook in a pan or on a griddle over heat esp. with the use of fat **~** *vi* **1 :** to undergo frying **2 :** to get very hot or burn as if being fried ⟨bodies ~*ing* on the beach⟩

²fry *n, pl* **fries** (1833) **1 :** a social gathering or picnic where food is fried and eaten ⟨a fish ~⟩ **2 a :** a dish of something fried **b :** FRENCH FRY — usu. used in pl.

³fry *n, pl* **fry** [ME, prob. fr. ONF *fri*, fr. OF *frier, froyer* to rub, spawn — more at FRAY] (14c) **1 a :** recently hatched or juvenile fishes **b :** the young of other animals **2 :** very small adult fishes **3 :** members of a group or class **:** INDIVIDUALS ⟨small ~s⟩ ⟨a great part of the earth is peopled with these ~ —Katherine Mansfield⟩

fry bread *n* (1950) **:** quick bread cooked (as by American Indians) by deep-frying

fry·er \'frī-(ə)r\ *n* (1851) **:** something intended for or used in frying: as **a :** a young chicken; *esp* **:** one weighing 2½ to 4 pounds (1.1 to 1.8 kilograms) when dressed **b :** a deep utensil for frying foods

frying pan *n* (14c) **:** a metal pan with a handle that is used for frying foods — called also *fry pan* — **out of the frying pan into the fire :** clear of one difficulty only to fall into a greater one

fry–up \'frī-,əp\ *n* (1967) *Brit* **:** a dish or meal of fried food

f–stop \'ef-,stäp\ *n* (1946) **:** a camera lens aperture setting indicated by an f-number

F₂ layer \'ef-'tü-\ *n* (1933) **:** the upper of the two layers into which the F region of the ionosphere splits in the daytime at varying heights from about 120 miles (200 kilometers) to more than 300 miles (500 kilometers) above the earth

fubsy \'fəb-zē\ *adj* [obs. E *fubs* (chubby person)] (1780) **:** chubby and somewhat squat

fuch·sia \'fyü-shə\ *n* [NL, fr. Leonhard *Fuchs* †1566 Ger. botanist] (1846) **1 :** any of a genus (*Fuchsia*) of decorative shrubs of the evening-primrose family having showy nodding flowers usu. in deep pinks, reds, and purples **2 :** a vivid reddish purple

fuch·sin or **fuch·sine** \'fyük-sən, -,sēn\ *n* [F *fuchsine*, prob. fr. NL *Fuchsia*; fr. its color] (1865) **:** a dye that is produced by oxidation of a mixture of aniline and toluidines and yields a brilliant bluish red

¹fuck \'fək\ *vb* [akin to D *fokken* to breed (cattle), Sw dial. *fokka* to copulate] *vi* (15c) **1 :** COPULATE — usu. considered obscene; sometimes used in the present participle as a meaningless intensive **2 :** MESS 3 — used with *with*; usu. considered vulgar **~** *vt* **1 :** to engage in coitus with — usu. considered obscene; sometimes used interjectionally with an object (as a personal or reflexive pronoun) to express anger, contempt, or disgust **2 :** to deal with unfairly or harshly **:** CHEAT, SCREW — usu. considered vulgar

fuchsia 1

²fuck *n* (1680) **1 :** an act of copulation — usu. considered obscene **2 :** a sexual partner — usu. considered obscene **3 a :** DAMN 2 — usu. considered vulgar **b :** used esp. with *the* as a meaningless intensive; usu. considered vulgar ⟨what the ~ do they want from me⟩

fucked–up \'fək-'təp\ *adj* (1966) **:** thoroughly confused or disordered — usu. considered vulgar

fuck·er \'fə-kər\ *n* (1598) **:** one that fucks — often used as a generalized term of abuse; usu. considered vulgar

fuck off *vi* (1929) **:** SCRAM — usu. used as a command; usu. considered vulgar

fuck up *vi* (1951) **:** to act foolishly or stupidly **:** BLUNDER — usu. considered vulgar **~** *vt* **:** to ruin or spoil esp. through stupidity or carelessness **:** BUNGLE — usu. considered vulgar — **fuck–up** \'fək-,əp\ *n*

¹fu·coid \'fyü-,kȯid\ *adj* [NL *Fucus*, fr. L] (1839) **:** relating to or resembling the brown algae

²fucoid *n* (ca. 1841) **:** a fucoid seaweed or fossil

fu·cose \'fyü-,kōs, -,kōz\ *n* [ISV *fuc-* (fr. L *fucus*) + *-ose*] (ca. 1909) **:** an aldose sugar that occurs in bound form in the dextrorotatory form in various glycosides and in the levorotatory form in some brown algae and in mammalian polysaccharides typical of some blood groups

fu·co·xan·thin \,fyü-kō-'zan-thən\ *n* (1873) **:** a brown carotenoid pigment $C_{40}H_{60}O_6$ occurring esp. in the chloroplasts of brown algae

fu·cus \'fyü-kəs\ *n* [L, seaweed, archil, dye obtained from archil, fr. Gk *phykos*] (1599) **1** *obs* **:** a face paint **2** [NL, genus name, fr. L] **:** any of a genus (*Fucus*) of cartilaginous brown algae used in the kelp industry; *broadly* **:** any of various brown algae

fud \'fəd\ *n* (1913) **:** FUDDY-DUDDY

fud·dle \'fə-d°l\ *vb* **fud·dled; fud·dling** \'fəd-liŋ, 'fə-d°l-iŋ\ [origin unknown] *vi* (1588) **:** BOOZE, TIPPLE **~** *vt* **1 :** to make drunk **:** INTOXICATE **2 :** to make confused **:** MUDDLE

fud·dy–dud·dy \'fə-dē-,də-dē\ *n, pl* **-dies** [origin unknown] (ca. 1904) **:** one that is old-fashioned, unimaginative, or conservative — **fuddy–duddy** *adj*

¹fudge \'fəj\ *vb* **fudged; fudg·ing** [origin unknown] *vt* (1674) **1 a :** to devise as a substitute **:** FAKE **b :** FALSIFY ⟨*fudged* the figures⟩ **2 :** to fail to come to grips with **:** DODGE ⟨*fudged* the issue⟩ **~** *vi* **1 :** to exceed the proper bounds or limits of something ⟨feel that the author has *fudged* a little on the ... rules for crime fiction —*Newsweek*⟩; *also* **:** CHEAT ⟨*fudging* on an exam⟩ **2 :** to fail to perform as expected **3 :** to avoid commitment **:** HEDGE ⟨the government's tendency to ~ on delicate matters of policy —Claire Sterling⟩

²fudge *n* (1766) **1 :** foolish nonsense — often used interjectionally to express annoyance, disappointment, or disbelief **2 :** a soft creamy candy made typically of sugar, milk, butter, and flavoring **3 :** something that is fudged; *esp* **:** a bending of rules or a compromise

fudge factor *n* (1962) **:** an arbitrary mathematical term inserted into a calculation in order to arrive at an expected solution or to allow for errors esp. of underestimation; *broadly* **:** any arbitrary unspecified factor

fu dog *often cap* F, *var of* FOO DOG

¹fu·el \'fyü(-ə)l\ *n, often attrib* [ME *fewel*, fr. OF *fouaille*, fr. (assumed) VL *focalia*, fr. L *focus* hearth] (13c) **1 a :** a material used to produce heat or power by burning **b :** nutritive material **c :** a material from which atomic energy can be liberated esp. in a reactor **2 :** a source of sustenance or incentive **:** REINFORCEMENT

²fuel *vb* **-eled** or **-elled; -el·ing** or **-el·ling** *vt* (1592) **1 :** to provide with fuel **2 :** SUPPORT, STIMULATE ⟨movement is ~*ed* by massive grants-in-aid —Allen Schick⟩ **~** *vi* **:** to take in fuel — often used with *up*

fuel cell *n* (1922) **:** a device that continuously changes the chemical energy of a fuel (as hydrogen) and an oxidant directly into electrical energy

fuel oil *n* (1893) **:** an oil that is used for fuel and that usu. has a higher flash point than kerosene

fuel·wood \'fyü(-ə)l-,wud\ *n* (14c) **:** wood grown or used for fuel

¹fug \'fəg\ *n* [perh. alter. of ¹*fog*] (1888) **:** the stuffy atmosphere of a poorly ventilated space; *also* **:** a stuffy or malodorous emanation — **fug·gy** \'fə-gē\ *adj*

²fug *vb* **fugged; fug·ging** *vi* (ca. 1889) **:** to loll indoors in a stuffy atmosphere **~** *vt* **:** to make stuffy and odorous

fu·ga·cious \fyü-'gā-shəs\ *adj* [L *fugac-, fugax*, fr. *fugere*] (1634) **1 :** lasting a short time **:** EVANESCENT **2 :** disappearing before the usual time — used chiefly of plant parts (as stipules) other than floral organs

fu·gac·i·ty \fyü-'ga-sə-tē\ *n* [*fugacious*] (ca. 1929) **:** the vapor pressure of a vapor assumed to be an ideal gas obtained by correcting the determined vapor pressure and useful as a measure of the escaping tendency of a substance from a heterogeneous system

fu·gal \'fyü-gəl\ *adj* (1854) **:** of, relating to, or being in the style of a musical fugue — **fu·gal·ly** \-gə-lē\ *adv*

-fuge *n comb form* [F, fr. L *fuga*, fr. L *fugare* to put to flight, fr. *fuga*] **:** one that drives away ⟨febri*fuge*⟩

¹fu·gi·tive \'fyü-jə-tiv\ *adj* [ME, fr. MF & L; MF *fugitif*, fr. L *fugitivus*, fr. *fugitus*, pp. of *fugere* to flee; akin to Gk *pheugein* to flee] (14c) **1**

: running away or intending flight ⟨~ slave⟩ ⟨~ debtor⟩ **2** : moving from place to place : WANDERING **3 a** : being of short duration **b** : difficult to grasp or retain : ELUSIVE **c** : likely to evaporate, deteriorate, change, fade, or disappear ⟨dyed with ~ colors⟩ **4** : being of transient interest ⟨~ essays⟩ **syn** see TRANSIENT — **fu·gi·tive·ly** *adv* — **fu·gi·tive·ness** *n*

²**fugitive** *n* (14c) **1** : a person who flees or tries to escape; *esp* : REFUGEE **2** : something elusive or hard to find

fu·gle·man \'fyü-gəl-mən\ *n* [modif. of G *Flügelmann*, fr. *Flügel* wing + *Mann* man] (1804) **1** : a trained soldier formerly posted in front of a line of soldiers at drill to serve as a model in their exercises **2** : one at the head or forefront of a group or movement

fu·gu \'f(y)ü-(,)gü\ *n* [Jp] (1909) : any of various very poisonous puffers (sense 2a) that contain tetrodotoxin and that are used as food in Japan after the toxin-containing organs are removed

fugue \'fyüg\ *n* [prob. fr. It *fuga* flight, fugue, fr. L, flight, fr. *fugere*] (1597) **1 a** : a musical composition in which one or two themes are repeated or imitated by successively entering voices and contrapuntally developed in a continuous interweaving of the voice parts **b** : something that resembles a fugue esp. in interweaving repetitive elements **2** : a disturbed state of consciousness in which the one affected seems to perform acts in full awareness but upon recovery cannot recollect the deeds — **fugue** *vb* — **fu·gu·ist** \'fyü-gist\ *n*

füh·rer *or* **fueh·rer** \'fyür-ər, 'fir-\ *n* [G (*der*) *Führer*, lit., the leader (title assumed by Adolf Hitler), fr. MHG *vüerer*, fr. *vüeren* to lead, bear, fr. OHG *fuoren* to lead; akin to OE *faran* to go — more at FARE] (1934) : LEADER 2; *esp* : TYRANT

fu·ji \'fü-(,)jē\ *n* [*Fuji*, mountain in Japan] (1925) : a spun silk clothing fabric in plain weave orig. made in Japan

¹**-ful** *adj suffix*, *sometimes* **-ful·ler**; *sometimes* **-ful·lest** [ME, fr. OE, fr. *full*, adj] **1** : full of ⟨pride*ful*⟩ **2** : characterized by ⟨peace*ful*⟩ **3** : having the qualities of ⟨master*ful*⟩ **4** : tending, given, or liable to ⟨help*ful*⟩

²**-ful** *n suffix* : number or quantity that fills or would fill ⟨room*ful*⟩

Fu·la *or* **Fu·lah** \'fü-lə\ *n*, *pl* **Fula** *or* **Fulas** *or* **Fulah** *or* **Fulahs** (1832) **1** : a member of a mainly pastoral African people dispersed over savanna and desert from Senegal to eastern Sudan **2** : the language of the Fula people

Fu·la·ni \'fü-,lä-nē, fü-'\ *n*, *pl* **-ni** *or* **-nis** (1860) **1** : FULA 1; *esp* : the Fula of northern Nigeria and adjacent areas **2** : FULA 2

ful·crum \'ful-krəm, 'fəl-\ *n*, *pl* **fulcrums** *or* **ful·cra** \-krə\ [LL, fr. L, bedpost, fr. *fulcire* to prop — more at BALK] (1674) **1 a** : PROP; *specif* : the support about which a lever turns **b** : one that supplies capability for action **2** : a part of an animal that serves as a hinge or support

ful·fill *or* **ful·fil** \ful(l)-'fil *also* fə(l)-\ *vt* **ful·filled**; **ful·fill·ing** [ME *fulfillen*, fr. OE *fullfyllan*, fr. *full* + *fyllan* to fill] (bef. 12c) **1** *archaic* : to make full : FILL ⟨her subtle, warm, and golden breath . . . ~s him with beatitude —Alfred Tennyson⟩ **2 a** : to put into effect : EXECUTE **b** : to bring to an end **c** : to measure up to : SATISFY **3 a** : to convert into reality **b** : to develop the full potentialities of *syn* see PERFORM — **ful·fill·er** *n* — **ful·fill·ment** \-mənt\ *n*

ful·gent \'ful-jənt, 'fəl-\ *adj* [ME, fr. L *fulgent-, fulgens*, prp. of *fulgēre* to shine; akin to L *flagrare* to burn — more at BLACK] (15c) : dazzlingly bright : RADIANT — **ful·gent·ly** *adv*

ful·gu·rant \'ful-g(y)ə-rənt, 'ful-jə-, 'fəl-\ *adj* (1647) : flashing like lightning; *also* : BRILLIANT

ful·gu·ra·tion \,ful-g(y)ə-'rā-shən, ,ful-jə-, fəl-\ *n* [L *fulguration-, fulguratio* sheet lightning, fr. *fulgurare* to flash with lightning, fr. *fulgur* lightning, fr. *fulgēre*] (1633) **1** : the act or process of flashing like lightning **2** : ELECTRODESICCATION — **ful·gu·rate** \'ful-g(y)ə-,rāt, 'ful-jə-, 'fəl-\ *vt*

ful·gu·rite \'ful-g(y)ə-,rīt, 'ful-jə-, 'fəl-\ *n* [ISV, fr. L *fulgur*] (1834) : an often tubular vitrified crust produced by the fusion of sand or rock by lightning

ful·gu·rous \-rəs\ *adj* [L *fulgur*] (1865) : flashing with lightning

ful·ham \'fu-ləm\ *n* [alter. of earlier *fullan*, perh. fr. ¹*full* + ³*one*] (ca. 1592) *archaic* : a loaded die

fu·lig·i·nous \fyu̇-'li-jə-nəs\ *adj* [LL *fuliginosus*, fr. L *fuligin-, fuligo* soot; akin to Lith *dūlis* cloud, vapor, and prob. to L *fumus* smoke — more at FUME] (1621) **1 a** : SOOTY **b** : OBSCURE, MURKY **2** : having a dark or dusky color — **fu·lig·i·nous·ly** *adv*

¹**full** \'ful *also* 'fol\ *adj* [ME, fr. OE; akin to OHG *fol* full, L *plenus* full, *plēre* to fill, Gk *plērēs* full, *plēthein* to be full] (bef. 12c) **1** : containing as much or as many as is possible or normal ⟨a bin ~ of corn⟩ **2 a** : complete esp. in detail, number, or duration ⟨a ~ report⟩ ⟨my ~ share⟩ ⟨gone a ~ hour⟩ **b** : lacking restraint, check, or qualification ⟨~ retreat⟩ ⟨~ support⟩ **c** : having all distinguishing characteristics : enjoying all authorized rights and privileges ⟨~ member⟩ ⟨~ professor⟩ **d** : not lacking in any essential : PERFECT ⟨in ~ control of your senses⟩ **3 a** : being at the highest or greatest degree : MAXIMUM ⟨~ speed⟩ **b** : being at the height of development ⟨~ bloom⟩ **4** : rounded in outline ⟨a ~ figure⟩ **5 a** : possessing or containing a great number or amount — used with *of* ⟨a room ~ of pictures⟩ ⟨~ of hope⟩ **b** : having an abundance of material esp. in the form of gathered, pleated, or flared parts ⟨a ~ skirt⟩ **c** : rich in experience ⟨a ~ life⟩ **6 a** : satisfied esp. with food or drink **b** : large enough to satisfy ⟨a ~ meal⟩ **7** *archaic* : completely weary **8** : having both parents in common ⟨~ sisters⟩ **9** : having volume or depth of sound ⟨~ tones⟩ **10** : completely occupied esp. with a thought or plan ⟨~ of their own concerns⟩ **11** : possessing a rich or pronounced quality ⟨a food of ~ flavor⟩ — **full·ness** *also* **ful·ness** \'ful-nəs\ *n* — **full of it** : not to be believed

syn FULL, COMPLETE, PLENARY, REPLETE mean containing all that is wanted or needed or possible. FULL implies the presence or inclusion of everything that is wanted or required by something or that can be held, contained, or attained by it ⟨a *full* schedule⟩. COMPLETE applies when all that is needed is present ⟨a *complete* picture of the situation⟩. PLENARY adds to COMPLETE the implication of fullness without qualification ⟨given *plenary* power⟩. REPLETE implies being filled to the brim or to satiety ⟨*replete* with delightful details⟩.

²**full** *adv* (bef. 12c) **1 a** : VERY, EXTREMELY ⟨knew ~ well they had lied to me⟩ **b** : ENTIRELY ⟨swung ~ around —Morley Callaghan⟩ **2** : STRAIGHT, SQUARELY ⟨got hit ~ in the face⟩ **3** — used as an intensive ⟨wound up winning by a ~ four strokes —William Johnson⟩

³**full** *n* (14c) **1 a** : the highest or fullest state or degree ⟨the ~ of the moon⟩ **b** : the utmost extent ⟨enjoy to the ~⟩ **2** : the requisite or complete amount ⟨paid in ~⟩

⁴**full** *vi* (1794) *of the moon* : to become full ~ *vt* : to make full in sewing

⁵**full** *vt* [ME, fr. MF *fouler* to trample under foot, fr. ML *fullare* to walk, trample, full, fr. L *fullo* fuller] (14c) : to shrink and thicken (woolen cloth) by moistening, heating, and pressing

full·back \'ful-,bak\ *n* (1887) **1** : an offensive football back used primarily for line plunges and blocking **2** : a primarily defensive player usu. stationed nearest the defended goal (as in soccer or field hockey)

full blast *adv* (1909) : at full capacity : with great intensity

¹**full–blood** \'ful-,bləd\ *adj* (1812) : FULL-BLOODED 1

²**full–blood** *n* (1846) : a full-blooded individual

full–blood·ed \'ful-,blə-dəd\ *adj* (1774) **1** : of unmixed ancestry : PUREBRED **2** : FLORID, RUDDY ⟨of ~ face⟩ **3** : FORCEFUL ⟨~ prose style⟩ **4 a** : lacking no particulars : GENUINE **b** : containing fullness of substance : RICH — **full–blood·ed·ness** *n*

full–blown \-'blōn\ *adj* (1601) **1 a** : fully mature **b** : being at the height of bloom **c** : FULL-FLEDGED **2** : possessing all the usual or necessary features ⟨a general philosophy, if not a ~ ideology, is emerging —W. H. Jones⟩

full–bod·ied \-,bä-dēd\ *adj* (1686) **1** : having a large body **2** *of a beverage* : imparting to the palate the general impression of substantial weight and rich texture **3** : having importance, significance, or meaningfulness ⟨~ study of literature⟩

full circle *adv* (1879) : through a series of developments that lead back to the original source, position, or situation or to a complete reversal of the original position — usu. used in the phrase *come full circle*

full–dress *adj* (1761) : involving attention to every detail in preparation or execution ⟨a ~ rehearsal⟩ ⟨a ~ investigation⟩

full dress *n* (1790) : the style of dress prescribed for ceremonial or formal social occasions

¹**full·er** \'ful-ər\ *n* [ME, fr. OE *fullere*, fr. L *fullo*] (bef. 12c) : one that fulls cloth

²**full·er** \'ful-ər\ *n* [*fuller* (to form a groove in)] (ca. 1864) : a blacksmithing hammer for grooving and spreading iron

ful·ler·ene \,ful-ə-'rēn\ *n* [R. Buckminster *Fuller*; fr. the resemblance of the molecules to the geodesic domes designed by Fuller] (1988) : any of a class of closed hollow aromatic carbon compounds that are made up of twelve pentagonal and differing numbers of hexagonal faces

fuller's earth *n* [¹*fuller*; fr. its earlier use as fulling agent] (15c) : an earthy substance that consists chiefly of clay mineral but lacks plasticity and that is used as an adsorbent, a filter medium, and a carrier for catalysts

ful·ler's teasel *n* (15c) : TEASEL 1a

full–fash·ioned \'ful-'fa-shənd\ *adj* (1883) : employing or produced by a knitting process for shaping to conform to body lines ⟨~ hosiery⟩

full–fledged \-'flejd\ *adj* (1883) **1** : fully developed : TOTAL, COMPLETE ⟨a ~ war⟩ **2** : having attained complete status ⟨~ lawyer⟩

full house *n* (1887) : a poker hand containing three of a kind and a pair — see POKER illustration

full–length \'ful-,len(k)th\ *adj* (1760) **1** : showing or adapted to the entire length esp. of the human figure ⟨a ~ mirror⟩ ⟨a ~ dress⟩ **2** : having a length as great as that which is normal or standard for an object of its kind ⟨a ~ play⟩

full marks *n pl* (1916) *chiefly Brit* : due credit or commendation

full moon *n* (bef. 12c) : the moon with its whole apparent disk illuminated

full–mouthed \'ful-'mautḥd, -'mautht\ *adj* (1577) **1** : having a full complement of teeth ⟨~ ewes⟩ **2** : uttered loudly

full nelson *n* (ca. 1922) : a wrestling hold gained from behind an opponent by thrusting the arms under the opponent's arms and clasping the hands behind the opponent's head — compare HALF NELSON

full–out \-,aut\ *adj* (14c) : COMPLETE, TOTAL

full–scale \-,skā(ə)l\ *adj* (1933) **1** : identical to an original in proportion and size ⟨~ drawing⟩ **2 a** : involving full use of available resources ⟨a ~ biography⟩ ⟨~ war⟩ **b** : TOTAL, COMPLETE ⟨a ~ musical renaissance —*Current Biog.*⟩

full–ser·vice \-'sər-vəs\ *adj* (1957) : providing comprehensive service of a particular kind ⟨a ~ bank⟩

full–size \-,sīz\ *adj* (1832) **1** : having the usual or normal size of its kind **2** : having the dimensions 54 inches by 75 inches ⟨about 1.4 by 1.9 meters⟩ — used of a bed; compare KING-SIZE, QUEEN-SIZE, TWIN-SIZE

full stop *n* (1596) : PERIOD 5a

full tilt *adv* [³*tilt*] (1600) : at high speed

full–time \'ful-'tīm\ *adj* (1898) **1** : employed for or involving full time ⟨~ employees⟩ **2** : devoting one's full attention and energies to something ⟨a ~ gambler⟩ — **full–time** *adv*

full time *n* (1898) : the amount of time considered the normal or standard amount for working during a given period

full–tim·er \'ful-'tī-mər\ *n* (1864) : a person who works full-time

ful·ly \'fu̇(l)-lē\ *adv* (bef. 12c) **1** : in a full manner or degree : COMPLETELY **2** : at least ⟨~ nine tenths of us⟩ *usage* see PLENTY

ful·mar \'ful-mər, -,mär\ *n* [of Scand origin; akin to ON *fūlmār* fulmar, fr. *fūll* foul + *mār* gull — more at MEW] (1698) : a seabird (*Fulmarus glacialis*) of colder northern seas closely related to the petrels; *also* : a related bird (*F. glacialoides*) of circumpolar distribution in colder southern seas

ful·mi·nant \'ful-mə-nənt, 'fəl-\ *adj* (1602) : FULMINATING 3

¹**ful·mi·nate** \-,nāt\ *vb* **-nat·ed; -nat·ing** [ME, fr. ML *fulminatus*, pp. of *fulminare*, fr. L, to strike (of lightning), fr. *fulmin-, fulmen* lightning; akin to L *flagrare* to burn — more at BLACK] *vt* (15c) : to utter or send out with denunciation ~ *vi* : to send forth censures or invectives — **ful·mi·na·tion** \,ful-mə-'nā-shən, ,fəl-\ *n*

²**fulminate** *n* [*fulminic acid*, fr. L *fulmin-, fulmen*] (1826) : an often explosive salt (as mercury fulminate) containing the group —CNO

\ə\ abut \ᵊ\ kitten, F table \ər\ further \a\ ash \ā\ ace \ä\ mop, mar \au̇\ out \ch\ chin \e\ bet \ē\ easy \g\ go \i\ hit \ī\ ice \j\ job \ŋ\ sing \ō\ go \ȯ\ law \ȯi\ boy \th\ thin \th̵\ the \ü\ loot \u̇\ foot \y\ yet \zh\ vision \a, k̄, ⁿ, œ, œ̄, ᴜᴇ, ᵫ, ʸ\ *see* Guide to Pronunciation

ful·mi·nat·ing adj (1626) **1** : hurling denunciations or menaces **2** : EXPLOSIVE **3** : coming on suddenly with great severity

ful·mine \'fûl-mən, 'fəl-\ vb (1590) archaic : FULMINATE

ful·some \'fûl-səm\ adj [ME fulsom copious, cloying, fr. full + -som -some] (13c) **1 a** : characterized by abundance : COPIOUS ⟨describes in ~ detail —G. N. Shuster⟩ ⟨~ bird life. The feeder overcrowded —Maxine Kumin⟩ **b** : generous in amount, extent, or spirit ⟨the passengers were ~ in praise of the plane's crew —Don Oliver⟩ ⟨a ~ victory for the far left —Bruce Rothwell⟩ ⟨the greetings have been ~, the farewells tender —Simon Gray⟩ **c** : being full and well developed ⟨she was in generally ~, limpid voice —Thor Eckert, Jr.⟩ **2** : aesthetically, morally, or generally offensive ⟨~ lies and nauseous flattery —William Congreve⟩ ⟨the devil take thee for a . . . ~ rogue —George Villiers⟩ **3** : exceeding the bounds of good taste : OVERDONE ⟨the ~ chromium glitter of the escalators dominating the central hall —Lewis Mumford⟩ **4** : excessively complimentary or flattering : EFFUSIVE ⟨an admiration whose extent I did not express, lest I be thought ~ —A. J. Liebling⟩ — **ful·some·ly** adv — **ful·some·ness** n

usage The senses shown above are the chief living senses of fulsome. Sense 2, which was a generalized term of disparagement in the late 17th century, is the least common of these. Fulsome became a point of dispute when sense 1, thought to be obsolete in the 19th century, began to be revived in the 20th. The dispute was exacerbated by the fact that the large dictionaries of the first half of the century missed the beginnings of the revival. Sense 1 has not only been revived but has spread in its application and continues to do so. The chief danger for the user of fulsome is ambiguity. Unless the context is made very clear, the reader or hearer can't be sure whether such an expression as "fulsome praise" or "a fulsome tribute" is meant in sense 1b or in sense 4.

ful·vous \'fûl-vəs, 'fəl-\ adj [L fulvus; perh. akin to L flavus yellow — more at BLUE] (1664) : of a dull brownish yellow : TAWNY

Fu Man·chu mustache \,fü-(,)man-'chü-\ n [Fu Manchu, Chinese villain in stories by "Sax Rohmer" (A. S. Ward †1955)] (1968) : a long mustache with ends that turn down to the chin

fu·ma·rase \'fyü-mə-,rās, -,rāz\ n (1936) : an enzyme that catalyzes the interconversion (as in the Krebs cycle) of fumaric acid and malic acid or their salts

fu·ma·rate \-,rāt\ n (1864) : a salt or ester of fumaric acid

fu·mar·ic acid \fyü-'mar-ik-\ n [ISV, fr. NL Fumaria, genus of herbs, fr. LL, fumitory, fr. L fumus] (ca. 1864) : a crystalline acid $C_4H_4O_4$ found in various plants or made synthetically and used esp. in making resins

fu·ma·role \'fyü-mə-,rōl\ n [It fumarola, fr. It dial. (Neapolitan), fr. LL fumariolum vent, fr. L fumarium smoke chamber for aging wine, fr. fumus] (1811) : a hole in a volcanic region from which hot gases and vapors issue — **fu·ma·rol·ic** \,fyü-mə-'rō-lik\ adj

¹fum·ble \'fəm-bəl\ vb **fum·bled; fum·bling** \-b(ə-)liŋ\ [prob. of Scand origin; akin to Sw fumla to fumble] vi (1534) **1 a** : to grope for or handle something clumsily or aimlessly **b** : to make awkward attempts to do or find something ⟨fumbled in his pocket for a coin⟩ **c** : to search by trial and error **d** : BLUNDER **2** : to feel one's way or move awkwardly **3 a** : to drop or juggle or fail to play cleanly a grounder **b** : to lose hold of a football while handling or running with it ~ vt **1** : to bring about by clumsy manipulation **2 a** : to feel or handle clumsily **b** : to deal with in a blundering way : BUNGLE **3 :** to make (one's way) in a clumsy manner **4 a** : MISPLAY ⟨~ a grounder⟩ **b** : to lose hold of (a football) while handling or running — **fum·bler** \-b(ə-)lər\ n — **fum·bling·ly** \-b(ə-)liŋ-lē\ adv

²fumble n (1634) **1** : an act or instance of fumbling **2** : a fumbled ball

¹fume \'fyüm\ n [ME, fr. MF fum, fr. L fumus; akin to OHG toumen to be fragrant, Skt dhūma smoke, OCS dymŭ] (14c) **1 a** : a smoke, vapor, or gas esp. when irritating or offensive ⟨engine exhaust ~s⟩ **b** : an often noxious suspension of particles in a gas (as air) **2** : something (as an emotion) that impairs one's reasoning ⟨sometimes his head gets a little hot with the ~s of patriotism —Matthew Arnold⟩ **3 a** : state of excited irritation or anger — usu. used in the phrase in a fume — **fumy** \'fyü-mē\ adj

²fume vb **fumed; fum·ing** vt (14c) **1** : to expose to or treat with fumes **2** : to give off in fumes ⟨fuming thick black smoke⟩ **3** : to utter while in a state of excited irritation or anger ~ vi **1 a** : to emit fumes **b** : to be in a state of excited irritation or anger ⟨fretted and fumed over the delay⟩ **2** : to rise in or as if in fumes

fu·met \fyü-'mā, 'fyü-mət\ n [F, lit., pleasant aroma (of meat cooking), fr. MF, fr. fumer to give off smoke or steam, fr. L fumare, fr. fumus] (1906) : a reduced and seasoned fish, meat, or vegetable stock

fu·mi·gant \'fyü-mi-gənt\ n (1890) : a substance used in fumigating

fu·mi·gate \'fyü-mə-,gāt\ vt **-gat·ed; -gat·ing** [L fumigatus, pp. of fumigare, fr. fumus + -igare (akin to L agere to drive) — more at AGENT] (1781) : to apply smoke, vapor, or gas to esp. for the purpose of disinfecting or of destroying pests — **fu·mi·ga·tion** \,fyü-mə-'gā-shən\ n — **fu·mi·ga·tor** \'fyü-mə-,gā-tər\ n

fu·mi·to·ry \'fyü-mə-,tōr-ē, -,tōr-\ n [ME fumeterre, fr. MF, fr. ML fumus terrae, lit., smoke of the earth, fr. L fumus + terrae, gen. of terra earth — more at TERRACE] (14c) : any of a genus (Fumaria of the family Fumariaceae, the fumitory family) of erect or climbing herbs; esp : a common European herb (F. officinalis)

¹fun \'fən\ n [E dial. fun to hoax, perh. alter. of ME fonnen, fr. fonne dupe] (1727) **1** : what provides amusement or enjoyment; specif : playful often boisterous action or speech ⟨full of ~⟩ **2** : a mood for finding or making amusement ⟨all in ~⟩ **3 a** : AMUSEMENT, ENJOYMENT ⟨sickness takes all the ~ out of life⟩ **b** : derisive jest : SPORT, RIDICULE ⟨a figure of ~⟩ **4** : violent or excited activity or argument ⟨let a snake loose in the classroom; then the ~ began⟩

syn FUN, JEST, SPORT, GAME, PLAY mean action or speech that provides amusement or arouses laughter. FUN usu. implies laughter or gaiety but may imply merely a lack of serious or ulterior purpose ⟨played cards just for fun⟩. JEST implies lack of earnestness in what is said or done and may suggest a hoaxing or teasing ⟨flung by remarks said only in jest⟩. SPORT applies esp. to the arousing of laughter against someone ⟨teasing begun in sport led to anger⟩. GAME is close to SPORT, and often stresses mischievous or malicious fun ⟨made game of their poor relations⟩. PLAY stresses the opposition to earnest without implying any

element of malice or mischief ⟨pretended to strangle his brother in play⟩.

²fun vi **funned; fun·ning** (1833) : to indulge in banter or play : JOKE

³fun adj, sometimes **fun·ner**; sometimes **fun·nest** (ca. 1846) **1** : providing entertainment, amusement, or enjoyment ⟨a ~ party⟩ ⟨a ~ person to be with⟩ **2** : full of fun : PLEASANT ⟨a ~ night⟩ ⟨have a ~ time⟩

fu·nam·bu·lism \fyù-'nam-byə-,li-zəm\ n [L funambulus ropewalker, fr. funis rope + ambulare to walk] (1824) **1** : tightrope walking **2** : a show esp. of mental agility — **fu·nam·bu·list** \-list\ n

fun and games n pl but sing or pl in constr (1920) : light amusement

¹func·tion \'fəŋ(k)-shən\ n [L function-, functio performance, fr. fungi to perform; prob. akin to Skt bhuṅkte he enjoys] (1533) **1** : professional or official position : OCCUPATION **2** : the action for which a person or thing is specially fitted or used or for which a thing exists : PURPOSE **3** : any of a group of related actions contributing to a larger action; esp : the normal and specific contribution of a bodily part to the economy of a living organism **4** : an official or formal ceremony or social gathering **5 a** : a mathematical correspondence that assigns exactly one element of one set to each element of the same or another set **b** : a variable (as a quality, trait, or measurement) that depends on and varies with another ⟨height is a ~ of age⟩; also : RESULT ⟨illnesses that are a ~ of stress⟩ **6** : characteristic behavior of a chemical compound due to a particular reactive unit; also : FUNCTIONAL GROUP **7** : a computer subroutine; specif : one that performs a calculation with variables provided by a program and supplies the program with a single result — **func·tion·less** \-ləs\ adj

syn FUNCTION, OFFICE, DUTY, PROVINCE mean the acts or operations expected of a person or thing. FUNCTION implies a definite end or purpose that the one in question serves or a particular kind of work it is intended to perform ⟨the function of language is two-fold: to communicate emotion and to give information —Aldous Huxley⟩. OFFICE is typically applied to the function or service expected of a person by reason of his trade or profession or his special relationship to others ⟨they exercise the offices of the judge, the priest, the counsellor —W. E. Gladstone⟩. DUTY applies to a task or responsibility imposed by one's occupation, rank, status, or calling ⟨it is the judicial duty of the court, to examine the whole case —R. B. Taney⟩. PROVINCE applies to a function, office, or duty that naturally or logically falls to one ⟨nursing does not belong to a man; it is not his province —Jane Austen⟩.

²function vi **func·tioned; func·tion·ing** \-sh(ə-)niŋ\ (1856) **1** : to have a function : SERVE ⟨an attributive noun ~s as an adjective⟩ **2** : to carry on a function or be in action : OPERATE ⟨a government ~s through numerous divisions⟩

func·tion·al \'fəŋ(k)-shnəl, -shə-n³l\ adj (1631) **1 a** : of, connected with, or being a function **b** : affecting physiological or psychological functions but not organic structure ⟨~ heart disease⟩ **2** : used to contribute to the development or maintenance of a larger whole ⟨~ and practical school courses⟩; also : designed or developed chiefly from the point of view of use ⟨~ clothing⟩ **3** : performing or able to perform a regular function — **func·tion·al·i·ty** \,fəŋ(k)-shə-'na-lə-tē\ n — **func·tion·al·ly** \'fəŋ(k)-shnə-lē, -shə-n³l-ē\ adv

functional calculus n (1933) : PREDICATE CALCULUS

functional group n (1943) : a characteristic reactive unit of a chemical compound esp. in organic chemistry

functional illiterate n (1946) : a person having had some schooling but not meeting a minimum standard of literacy — **functionally illiterate** adj

func·tion·al·ism \'fəŋ(k)-shnə-,li-zəm, -shə-n³l-,i-\ n (1914) **1** : a philosophy of design (as in architecture) holding that form should be adapted to use, material, and structure **2** : a theory that stresses the interdependence of the patterns and institutions of a society and their interaction in maintaining cultural and social unity **3** : a doctrine or practice that emphasizes practical utility or functional relations — **func·tion·al·ist** \-shnə-list, -shə-n³l-ist\ n — **functionalist** or **func·tion·al·is·tic** \,fəŋ(k)-shnə-'lis-tik, -shə-n³l-'is-\ adj

functional shift n (1942) : the process by which a word or form comes to be used in another grammatical function

func·tion·ary \'fəŋ(k)-shə-,ner-ē\ n, pl **-ar·ies** (1791) **1** : one who serves in a certain function **2** : one holding office in a government or political party

function word n (1940) : a word (as a preposition, auxiliary verb, or conjunction) expressing primarily grammatical relationship

func·tor \'fəŋ(k)-tər\ n (1935) : something that performs a function or an operation

¹fund \'fənd\ n [L fundus bottom, country estate — more at BOTTOM] (1694) **1 a** : a sum of money or other resources whose principal or interest is set apart for a specific objective **b** : money on deposit on which checks or drafts can be drawn — usu. used in pl. **c** : CAPITAL **2** pl : the stock of the British national debt — usu. used with the **2** : an available quantity of material or intangible resources : SUPPLY **3** pl : available pecuniary resources **4** : an organization administering a special fund

²fund vt (1789) **1 a** : to make provision of resources for discharging the interest or principal of **b** : to provide funds for ⟨a science program federally ~ed⟩ **2** : to place in a fund : ACCUMULATE **3** : to convert into a debt that is payable either at a distant date or at no definite date and that bears a fixed interest ⟨~ a floating debt⟩

fun·da·ment \'fən-də-mənt\ n [ME, fr. OF fondement, fr. L fundamentum, fr. fundare to found, fr. fundus] (13c) **1** : an underlying ground, theory, or principle **2 a** : BUTTOCKS **b** : ANUS **3** : the part of a land surface that has not been altered by human activities

¹fun·da·men·tal \,fən-də-'men-t³l\ adj (15c) **1 a** : serving as an original or generating source : PRIMARY ⟨a discovery ~ to modern computers⟩ **b** : serving as a basis supporting existence or determining essential structure or function : BASIC **2 a** : of or relating to essential structure, function, or facts : RADICAL ⟨~ change⟩; also : of or dealing with general principles rather than practical application ⟨~ science⟩ **b** : adhering to fundamentalism **3** : of, relating to, or produced by the lowest component of a complex vibration **4** : of central importance : PRINCIPAL ⟨~ purpose⟩ **5** : belonging to one's innate or ingrained characteristics : DEEP-ROOTED ⟨her ~ good humor⟩ **syn** see ESSENTIAL — **fun·da·men·tal·ly** \-t³l-ē\ adv

²fundamental n (1637) **1** : something fundamental; esp : one of the minimum constituents without which a thing or a system would not be what it is   **2 a :** the principal musical tone produced by vibration (as of a string or column of air) on which a series of higher harmonics is based   **b :** the root of a chord   **3 :** the harmonic component of a complex wave that has the lowest frequency and commonly the greatest amplitude

fundamental group *n* (1957) **:** a set that is a subset of all paths defined on a set of points each pair of which is joined by a path and that is the quotient group of the group of all paths beginning and ending with a given point

fun·da·men·tal·ism \-t⁰l-,i-zəm\ *n* (1922)   **1 a** *often cap* **:** a movement in 20th century Protestantism emphasizing the literally interpreted Bible as fundamental to Christian life and teaching   **b :** the beliefs of this movement   **c :** adherence to such beliefs   **2 :** a movement or attitude stressing strict and literal adherence to a set of basic principles — **fun·da·men·tal·ist** \-t⁰l-ist\ *n* — **fundamentalist** *or* **fun·da·men·tal·is·tic** \-,men-t⁰l-'is-tik\ *adj*

fundamental law *n* (ca. 1914) **:** the organic or basic law of a political unit as distinguished from legislative acts; *specif* **:** CONSTITUTION

fundamental particle *n* (1947) **:** ELEMENTARY PARTICLE

fun·dic \'fən-dik\ *adj* (ca. 1927) **:** of or relating to a fundus

fund–rais·er \'fən-,drā-zər\ *n* (1957)   **1 :** a person employed to raise funds   **2 :** a social event (as a cocktail party) held for the purpose of raising funds

fund–rais·ing \-ziŋ\ *n, often attrib* (1940) **:** the organized activity of raising funds (as for an institution or political cause)

fun·dus \'fən-dəs\ *n, pl* **fun·di** \-,dī, -,dē\ [NL, fr. L, bottom] (1764) **:** the bottom of or part opposite the aperture of the internal surface of a hollow organ: as   **a :** the greater curvature of the stomach   **b :** the lower back part of the bladder   **c :** the large upper end of the uterus   **d :** the part of the eye opposite the pupil

¹fu·ner·al \'fyün-rəl, 'fyü-nə-\ *adj* [ME, fr. LL *funeralis,* fr. L *funer-, funus* funeral (n.)] (14c)   **1 :** of, relating to, or constituting a funeral   **2 :** FUNEREAL 2

²funeral *n* [ME *funerelles* (pl.), fr. MF *funerailles* (pl.), fr. ML *funeralia* (pl.), fr. LL, neut. pl. of *funeralis,* adj.] (ca. 1512)   **1 :** the observances held for a dead person usu. before burial or cremation   **2** *chiefly dial* **:** a funeral sermon   **3 :** a funeral procession   **4 :** an end of something's existence   **5 :** a matter of concern to one **:** WORRY ⟨if you flunk, that's your ∼⟩

funeral director *n* (1886) **:** one whose profession is the management of funerals and who is usu. an embalmer

funeral home *n* (1926) **:** an establishment with facilities for the preparation of the dead for burial or cremation, for the viewing of the body, and for funerals — called also *funeral parlor*

fu·ner·ary \'fyü-nə-,rer-ē\ *adj* (ca. 1693) **:** of, used for, or associated with burial ⟨a pharaoh's ∼ chamber⟩

fu·ne·re·al \fyù-'nir-ē-əl\ *adj* [L *funereus,* fr. *funer-, funus*] (1725)   **1 :** of or relating to a funeral   **2 :** befitting or suggesting a funeral (as in solemnity) — **fu·ne·re·al·ly** \-ə-lē\ *adv*

fun·fair \'fən-,far, -,fer\ *n* (1925) *chiefly Brit* **:** AMUSEMENT PARK

fun·gal \'fən-gəl\ *adj* (1835)   **1 :** of, relating to, or having the characteristics of fungi   **2 :** caused by a fungus

fungi- *comb form* [L *fungus*]: fungus ⟨*fungi*form⟩

¹fun·gi·ble \'fən-jə-bəl\ *n* (ca. 1765) **:** something that is fungible — usu. used in pl.

²fungible *adj* [NL *fungibilis,* fr. L *fungi* to perform — more at FUNCTION] (1818)   **1 :** being of such a nature that one part or quantity may be replaced by another equal part or quantity in the satisfaction of an obligation ⟨oil, wheat, and lumber are ∼ commodities⟩   **2 :** INTERCHANGEABLE — **fun·gi·bil·i·ty** \,fən-jə-'bi-lə-tē\ *n*

fun·gi·cid·al \,fən-jə-'sī-d⁰l, ,fən-gə-\ *adj* (1905) **:** ANTIFUNGAL — **fun·gi·cid·al·ly** \-d⁰l-ē\ *adv*

fun·gi·cide \'fən-jə-,sīd, 'fən-gə-\ *n* [ISV] (1889) **:** an agent that destroys fungi or inhibits their growth

fun·gi·form \'fən-jə-,form, 'fən-gə-\ *adj* (1823) **:** shaped like a mushroom

fun·gi·stat·ic \,fən-jə-'sta-tik\ *adj* (1922) **:** inhibiting the growth of fungi without destroying them

fun·go \'fən-(,)gō\ *n, pl* **fungoes** [origin unknown] (ca. 1867)   **1 :** a fly ball hit esp. for practice fielding by a player who tosses a ball in the air and hits it as it comes down   **2 :** FUNGO BAT

fungo bat *n* (1926) **:** a long thin bat used for hitting fungoes

fun·goid \'fəŋ-,góid\ *adj* (ca. 1836) **:** resembling, characteristic of, caused by, or being a fungus ⟨a ∼ growth⟩ — **fungoid** *n*

fun·gous \'fəŋ-gəs\ *adj* (15c) **:** FUNGAL

fun·gus \'fəŋ-gəs\ *n, pl* **fun·gi** \'fən-,jī, 'fəŋ-,gī\ *also* **fun·gus·es** \'fəŋ-gə-səz\ *often attrib* [L] (1527) **:** any of a major group (Fungi) of saprophytic and parasitic spore-producing organisms usu. classified as plants that lack chlorophyll and include molds, rusts, mildews, smuts, mushrooms, and yeasts

fun house *n* (1948) **:** a building in an amusement park that contains various devices designed to startle or amuse

¹fu·nic·u·lar \fyu̇-'ni-kyə-lər, fə-\ *adj* [L *funiculus*] (1664)   **1 :** having the form of or associated with a cord usu. under tension   **2** [NL *funiculus*] **:** of, relating to, or being a funiculus   **3 :** of, relating to, or being a funicular ⟨a ∼ system⟩

²funicular *n* (1911) **:** a cable railway ascending a mountain; *esp* **:** one in which an ascending car counterbalances a descending car

fu·nic·u·lus \-ləs\ *n, pl* **-li** \-,lī, -,lē\ [NL, fr. L, dim. of *funis* rope] (1826)   **1 :** a bodily structure suggesting a cord; *esp* **:** a bundle of nerve fibers   **2 :** the stalk of a plant ovule

¹funk \'fəŋk\ *vi* (ca. 1739)   **1 :** to become frightened and shrink back ∼ *vt*   **1 :** to be afraid of **:** DREAD   **2 :** to shrink from undertaking or facing

²funk *n* [prob. fr. obs. Flem *fonck*] (1743)   **1 a :** a state of paralyzing fear   **b :** a depressed state of mind   **2 :** one that funks **:** COWARD

³funk *n* [back-formation fr. ²*funky*] (1959)   **1 :** music that combines traditional forms of black music (as blues, gospel, or soul) and is characterized by a strong backbeat   **2 :** the quality or state of being funky ⟨jeans . . . have lost much of their ∼ —Tom Wolfe⟩

funk hole *n* (1900)   **1 :** DUGOUT 2   **2 :** a place of safe retreat

fun·kia \'fəŋ-kē-ə, 'fùŋ-\ *n* [NL, genus name, fr. C. H. *Funck* †1839 Ger. botanist] (1839) **:** PLANTAIN LILY

¹funky \'fəŋ-kē\ *adj* (1845) **:** being in a funk **:** PANICKY

²funky *adj* **funk·i·er; -est** [*funk* (offensive odor)] (ca. 1899)   **1 :** having an offensive odor **:** FOUL   **2 :** having an earthy unsophisticated style and feeling; *esp* **:** having the style and feeling of older black American music (as blues or gospel) or of funk ⟨a slick, heavy beat that is unmistakably contemporary and irresistibly ∼ —Jay Cocks⟩   **3 a :** odd or quaint in appearance or feeling   **b :** lacking style or taste   **c :** unconventionally stylish **:** HIP — **funk·i·ness** *n*

¹fun·nel \'fə-n⁰l\ *n* [ME *fonel,* fr. OProv *fonilh,* fr. ML *fundibulum,* short for L *infundibulum,* fr. *infundere* to pour in, fr. *in-* + *fundere* to pour — more at FOUND] (15c)   **1 a :** a utensil that is usu. a hollow cone with a tube extending from the smaller end and that is designed to catch and direct a downward flow   **b :** something shaped like a funnel   **2 :** a stack or flue for the escape of smoke or for ventilation (as on a ship)

²funnel *vb* **-neled** *also* **-nelled; -nel·ing** *also* **-nel·ling** *vi* (1594)   **1 :** to have or take the shape of a funnel   **2 :** to pass through or as if through a funnel or conduit ∼ *vt*   **1 :** to form in the shape of a funnel ⟨∼ed his hands and shouted through them⟩   **2 :** to move to a focal point or into a conduit or central channel ⟨contributions were ∼ed into one account⟩

funnel cloud *n* (ca. 1909) **:** a funnel-shaped cloud that projects from the base of a thundercloud and that often betokens the formation of a tornado; *also* **:** TORNADO 2b

fun·nel·form \'fə-n⁰l-,form\ *adj* (ca. 1828) **:** INFUNDIBULIFORM

¹fun·ny \'fə-nē\ *adj* **fun·ni·er; -est** (1756)   **1 a :** affording light mirth and laughter **:** AMUSING   **b :** seeking or intended to amuse **:** FACETIOUS   **2 :** differing from the ordinary in a suspicious, perplexing, quaint, or eccentric way **:** PECULIAR — often used as a sentence modifier ⟨∼, things didn't turn out the way we planned⟩   **3 :** involving trickery or deception ⟨told his prisoner not to try anything ∼⟩ — **fun·ni·ly** \'fə-n⁰l-ē\ *adv* — **fun·ni·ness** \'fə-nē-nəs\ *n* — **funny** *adv*

²funny *n, pl* **funnies** (1852)   **1 :** one that is funny; *esp* **:** JOKE   **2** *pl* **:** comic strips or the comic section of a periodical — usu. used with *the*

funny bone *n* [fr. the tingling felt when it is struck] (1840)   **1 :** the place at the back of the elbow where the ulnar nerve rests against a prominence of the humerus   **2 :** a sense of humor

funny book *n* (1947) **:** COMIC BOOK

funny car *n* (1969) **:** a specialized dragster that has a one-piece molded body resembling the body of a mass-produced car

funny farm *n* (1963) *slang* **:** a psychiatric hospital

fun·ny·man \'fə-nē-,man\ *n* (1852) **:** COMEDIAN 2, HUMORIST

funny money *n* (1943)   **1 :** artificially inflated currency   **2 :** counterfeit money

funny paper *n* (1924) **:** a comic section of a newspaper

¹fur \'fər\ *vb* **furred; fur·ring** [ME *furren,* fr. MF *fourrer,* fr. OF *forrer,* fr. *fuerre* sheath, of Gmc origin; akin to OHG *fuotar* sheath; akin to Gk *pōma* lid, cover, Skt *pāti* he protects] *vt* (14c)   **1 :** to cover, line, trim, or clothe with fur   **2 :** to coat or clog as if with fur   **3 :** to apply furring to ∼ *vi* **:** to become coated or clogged as if with fur

²fur *n, often attrib* (14c)   **1 :** a piece of the dressed pelt of an animal used to make, trim, or line wearing apparel   **2 :** an article of clothing made of or with fur   **3 :** the hairy coat of a mammal esp. when fine, soft, and thick; *also* **:** such a coat with the skin   **4 :** a coating resembling fur: as   **a :** a coat of epithelial debris on the tongue   **b :** the thick pile of a fabric (as chenille) — **fur·less** \'fər-ləs\ *adj*

fu·ran \'fyu̇r-,an, fyü-'ran\ *also* **fu·rane** \'fyu̇r-,ān, fyù-'rān\ *n* [ISV, fr. *furfural*] (1894) **:** a flammable liquid C_4H_4O that is obtained from wood oils of pines or made synthetically and is used esp. in organic synthesis; *also* **:** a derivative of furan

fu·ra·nose \'fyu̇r-ə-,nōs, -,nōz\ *n* (1927) **:** a sugar having an oxygen-containing ring of five atoms

fu·ran·o·side \fyù-'ra-nə-,sīd\ *n* (1932) **:** a glycoside containing the ring characteristic of furanose

fu·ra·zol·i·done \,fyu̇r-ə-'zä-lə-,dōn\ *n* [*furfural* + *azole* + *-ide* + *-one*] (1955) **:** an antimicrobial drug $C_8H_7N_3O_5$ used against bacteria and some protozoa esp. in infections of the gastrointestinal tract

fur·bear·er \'fər-,bar-ər, -,ber-\ *n* (1875) **:** an animal that bears fur esp. of a commercially desired quality

fur·be·low \'fər-bə-,lō\ *n* [by folk etymology fr. F dial. *farbella*] (1706)   **1 :** a pleated or gathered piece of material; *esp* **:** a flounce on women's clothing   **2 :** something that suggests a furbelow esp. in being showy or superfluous — **furbelow** *vt*

fur·bish \'fər-bish\ *vt* [ME *furbisshen,* fr. MF *fourbiss-,* stem of *fourbir,* of Gmc origin; akin to OHG *furben* to polish] (14c)   **1 :** to make lustrous **:** POLISH   **2 :** to give a new look to **:** RENOVATE — often used with *up* — **fur·bish·er** *n*

fur·ca·tion \,fər-'kā-shən\ *n* [ML *furcation-, furcatio,* fr. *furcare* to branch, fr. L *furca* fork] (1646)   **1 :** something that is branched **:** FORK   **2 :** the act or process of branching

fur·cu·la \'fər-kyə-lə\ *n, pl* **-lae** \-,lē, -,lī\ [NL, fr. L, forked prop, dim. of *furca*] (1859)   **1 :** a forked process or part: as   **a :** WISHBONE   **b :** the forked leaping appendage arising from the fourth abdominal segment of a springtail

fur·fu·ral \'fər-f(y)ə-,ral\ *n* [L *furfur* bran + ISV ³-*al*] (1879) **:** a liquid aldehyde $C_5H_4O_2$ of penetrating odor that is usu. made from plant materials and used esp. in making furan or phenolic resins and as a solvent

fu·ri·o·so \,fyu̇r-ē-'ō-(,)sō, -(,)zō\ *adv or adj* [It, lit., furious] (ca. 1823) **:** with great force or vigor — used as a direction in music

fu·ri·ous \'fyu̇r-ē-əs\ *adj* [ME, fr. MF *furieus,* fr. L *furiosus,* fr. *furia* madness, fury] (14c)   **1 a (1) :** exhibiting or goaded by anger   **(2) :** indicative of or proceeding from anger   **b :** giving a stormy or turbulent appearance ⟨∼ bursts of flame⟩   **2 :** marked by noise, excitement, activity, or rapidity   **2 :** INTENSE 1a ⟨the ∼ growth of tropical vegetation⟩ — **fu·ri·ous·ly** *adv*

¹furl \'fər(-ə)l\ *vb* [MF *ferler,* fr. ONF *ferlier* to tie tightly, fr. OF *fer,*

ferm tight (fr. L *firmus* firm) + *lier* to tie, fr. L *ligare* — more at LIGATURE] *vt* (1556) : to wrap or roll (as a sail or a flag) close to or around something ~ *vi* : to curl or fold as in being furled
²**furl** *n* (1643) **1** : a furled coil **2** : the act of furling
fur·long \'fər-,lȯŋ\ *n* [ME, fr. OE *furlang*, fr. *furh* furrow + *lang* long] (14c) : a unit of distance equal to 220 yards (about 201 meters)
¹**fur·lough** \'fər-(,)lō\ *n* [D *verlof*, lit., permission, fr. MD, fr. *ver-* for- + *lof* permission; akin to MHG *loube* permission — more at FOR-, LEAVE] (1625) : a leave of absence from duty granted esp. to a soldier; *also* : a document authorizing such a leave of absence
²**furlough** *vt* (1781) **1** : to grant a furlough to **2** : to lay off from work
fur·mi·ty \'fər-mə-tē\ *var of* FRUMENTY
fur·nace \'fər-nəs\ *n* [ME *furnas*, fr. OF *fornaise*, fr. L *fornac-, fornax*; akin to L *formus* warm — more at THERM] (13c) : an enclosed structure in which heat is produced (as for heating a house or for reducing ore)
fur·nish \'fər-nish\ *vt* [ME *furnisshen*, fr. MF *fourniss-*, stem of *fournir* to complete, equip, of Gmc origin; akin to OHG *frummen* to further, *fruma* advantage — more at FOREMOST] (15c) **1** : to provide with what is needed; *esp* : to equip with furniture **2** : SUPPLY, GIVE ⟨~*ed* food and shelter for the refugees⟩ — **fur·nish·er** *n*
syn FURNISH, EQUIP, OUTFIT, APPOINT, ACCOUTRE mean to supply one with what is needed. FURNISH implies the provision of any or all essentials for performing a function ⟨a sparsely *furnished* apartment⟩. EQUIP suggests the provision of something making for efficiency in action or use ⟨a fully *equipped* kitchen⟩. OUTFIT implies provision of a complete list or set of articles as for a journey, an expedition, or a special occupation ⟨*outfitted* the family for a ski trip⟩. APPOINT implies provision of complete and usu. elegant or elaborate equipment or furnishings ⟨a lavishly *appointed* apartment⟩. ACCOUTRE suggests the supplying of personal dress or equipment for a special activity ⟨fully *accoutred* members of a polar expedition⟩.
fur·nish·ing *n* (1594) **1** : an article or accessory of dress — usu. used in pl. **2** : an object that tends to increase comfort or utility; *esp* : an article of furniture for the interior of a building — usu. used in pl.
fur·ni·ture \'fər-ni-chər\ *n* [MF *fourniture*, fr. *fournir*] (1542) : equipment that is necessary, useful, or desirable: as **a** *archaic* : the trappings of a horse **b** : movable articles used in readying an area (as a room or patio) for occupancy or use
furniture beetle *n* (1925) : a widespread deathwatch beetle (*Anobium punctatum*) noted for boring in and damaging furniture and seasoned wood
fu·ror \'fyu̇r-,ȯr, -,ōr, -ər\ *n* [MF & L; MF, fr. L, fr. *furere* to rage] (15c) **1** : an angry or maniacal fit : RAGE **2** : FURY **3** **a** : a fashionable craze : VOGUE **4** **a** : furious or hectic activity : **b** : an outburst of public excitement or indignation : UPROAR
fu·rore \'fyu̇r-,ȯr, -,ȯr, -ər, *esp Brit* fyu̇-'rō-ri\ *n* [It, fr. L *furor*] (1790) **1** : FUROR 4b **2** : FUROR 3
fu·ro·se·mide \fyu̇-'rō-sə-,mīd\ *n* [*furfural* + *-o-* + *sulf-* + *-emide*, prob. alter. of *amide*] (1965) : a powerful diuretic $C_{12}H_{11}ClN_2O_5S$ used esp. to treat edema
furred \'fərd\ *adj* [ME] (14c) **1** : lined, trimmed, or faced with fur **2** : coated as if with fur; *specif* : having a coating consisting chiefly of mucus and dead epithelial cells ⟨a ~ tongue⟩ **3** : bearing or wearing fur **4** : provided with furring ⟨~ wall⟩
fur·ri·er \'fər-ē-ər, 'fə-rē-\ *n* [alter. of ME *furrer*, fr. AF *furrere*, fr. OF *forrer* to fur — more at FUR] (14c) **1** : a fur dealer **2** : one that dresses furs **b** : one that makes, repairs, alters, or cleans fur garments
fur·ri·ery \-ə-rē\ *n* (ca. 1864) **1** : the fur business **2** : fur craftsmanship
fur·rin·er \'fər-ə-nər\ *n* [alter. of *foreigner*] (1849) : FOREIGNER 2 — used to represent a dial. pronunc.
fur·ring \'fər-iŋ\ *n* (14c) **1** : a fur trimming or lining **2** **a** : the application of thin wood, brick, or metal to joists, studs, or walls to form a level surface (as for attaching wallboard) or an air space **b** : the material used in this process
¹**fur·row** \'fər-(,)ō, -ə(-w); 'fə-(,)rō, -rə(-w)\ *n* [ME *furgh, forow*, fr. OE *furh*; akin to OHG *furuh* furrow, L *porca*] (bef. 12c) **1** **a** : a trench in the earth made by a plow **b** : plowed land : FIELD **2** : something that resembles the track of a plow: as **a** : a marked narrow depression : GROOVE **b** : a deep wrinkle ⟨~*s* in his brow⟩
²**furrow** *vt* (15c) **1** : to make furrows, grooves, wrinkles, or lines in ~ *vi* : to make or form furrows, grooves, wrinkles, or lines
fur·ry \'fər-ē\ *adj* **fur·ri·er; -est** (ca. 1674) **1** : consisting of or resembling fur ⟨animals with ~ coats⟩ **2** : covered with fur **3** : thick in quality ⟨spoke with a ~ voice⟩
fur seal *n* (1775) : any of two genera (*Callorhinus* and *Arctocephalus*) of eared seals that have a double coat with a dense soft underfur
¹**fur·ther** \'fər-thər\ *adv* [ME, fr. OE *furthor* (akin to OHG *furthar* further), compar., fr. the base of OE *forth* forth] (bef. 12c) **1** : FARTHER 1 ⟨my ponies are tired, and I have ~ to go —Thomas Hardy⟩ **2** : in addition : MOREOVER **3** : to a greater degree or extent ⟨~ annoyed by a second intrusion⟩ **usage** see FARTHER
²**further** *vt* **fur·thered; fur·ther·ing** \'fərth-riŋ, 'fər-thə-\ (bef. 12c) : to help forward : PROMOTE **syn** see ADVANCE — **fur·ther·er** \'fər-thər-ər\ *n*
³**further** *adj* (13c) **1** : FARTHER 1 ⟨rode . . . across the valley and up the ~ slopes —T. E. Lawrence⟩ **2** : going or extending beyond : ADDITIONAL ⟨~ volumes⟩ ⟨~ education⟩ **usage** see FARTHER
fur·ther·ance \'fərth-rən(t)s, 'fər-thə-\ *n* (15c) : the act of furthering : ADVANCEMENT
further education *n* (1937) *Brit* : ADULT EDUCATION
fur·ther·more \'fər-thə(r)-,mōr, -,mȯr\ *adv* (13c) : in addition to what precedes : BESIDES
fur·ther·most \-thər-,mōst\ *adj* (15c) : most distant : FARTHEST
fur·thest \'fər-thəst\ *adv or adj* (14c) : FARTHEST
fur·tive \'fər-tiv\ *adj* [F or L; F *furtif*, fr. L *furtivus*, fr. *furtum* theft, fr. *fur* thief, fr. or akin to Gk *phōr* thief, *pherein* to carry — more at BEAR] (1612) **1** **a** : done by stealth : SURREPTITIOUS **b** : expressive of stealth : SLY ⟨had a ~ look about him⟩ **2** : obtained underhandedly : STOLEN **syn** see SECRET — **fur·tive·ly** *adv* — **fur·tive·ness** *n*
fu·run·cle \'fyu̇r-,əŋ-kəl\ *n* [L *furunculus* petty thief, boil, dim. of *furon-, furo* ferret, thief, fr. *fur*] (1676) : ²BOIL

fu·run·cu·lo·sis \fyu̇-,rəŋ-kyə-'lō-səs\ *n, pl* **-lo·ses** \-,sēz\ [NL] (1886) **1** : the condition of having or tending to develop multiple furuncles **2** : a highly infectious disease of various salmonoid fishes (as trout) that is caused by a bacterium (*Bacterium salmonicida*) and is esp. virulent in dense fish populations (as in hatcheries)
fu·ry \'fyu̇r-ē\ *n, pl* **furies** [ME *furie*, fr. MF & L; MF, fr. L *furia*, fr. *furere* to rage] (14c) **1** : intense, disordered, and often destructive rage **2** **a** *cap* : any of the avenging deities in Greek mythology who torment criminals and inflict plagues **b** : an avenging spirit **c** : one who resembles an avenging spirit; *esp* : a spiteful woman **3** : extreme fierceness or violence **4** : a state of inspired exaltation : FRENZY **syn** see ANGER
furze \'fərz\ *n* [ME *firse*, fr. OE *fyrs*; akin to Russ *pyreī* quack grass, Gk *pyros* wheat] (bef. 12c) : GORSE — **furzy** \'fər-zē\ *adj*
fus·cous \'fəs-kəs\ *adj* [L *fuscus* — more at DUSK] (1662) : of any of several colors averaging a brownish gray
¹**fuse** \'fyüz\ *vb* **fused; fus·ing** [L *fusus*, pp. of *fundere* to pour, melt — more at FOUND] *vt* (1592) **1** : to reduce to a liquid or plastic state by heat **2** : to blend thoroughly by or as if by melting together : COMBINE ⟨in her richest work she ~*s* comedy and tragedy —T. A. Gullason⟩ **3** : to stitch by applying heat and pressure with or without the use of an adhesive ~ *vi* **1** **a** : to become fluid with heat **b** *Brit* : to fail because of the blowing of a fuse **2** : to become blended or joined by or as if by melting together **syn** see MIX
²**fuse** *n* (1884) : an electrical safety device consisting of or including a wire or strip of fusible metal that melts and interrupts the circuit when the current exceeds a particular amperage
³**fuse** *n* [It *fuso* spindle, fr. L *fusus*, of unknown origin] (1644) **1** : a continuous train of a combustible substance enclosed in a cord or cable for setting off an explosive charge by transmitting fire to it **2** *usu* **fuze** : a mechanical or electrical detonating device for setting off the bursting charge of a projectile, bomb, or torpedo
⁴**fuse** *or* **fuze** \'fyüz\ *vt* **fused** *or* **fuzed; fus·ing** *or* **fuz·ing** (1802) : to equip with a fuse
fused quartz *n* (1925) : QUARTZ GLASS — called also *fused silica*
fu·see \fyü-'zē\ *n* [F *fusée*, lit., spindleful of yarn, fr. OF, fr. *fus* spindle, fr. L *fusus*] (1622) **1** : a conical spirally grooved pulley in a timepiece from which a cord or chain unwinds onto a barrel containing the spring and which by its increasing diameter compensates for the lessening power of the spring **2** : a red signal flare used esp. for protecting stalled trains and trucks
fu·se·lage \'fyü-sə-,läzh, -zə-\ *n* [F, fr. *fuselé* spindle-shaped, fr. MF, fr. *fusel*, dim. of *fus*] (1909) : the central body portion of an aircraft designed to accommodate the crew and the passengers or cargo — see AIRPLANE illustration
fu·sel oil \'fyü-zəl-\ *n* [G *Fusel* bad liquor] (1850) : an acrid oily liquid occurring in insufficiently distilled alcoholic liquors, consisting chiefly of amyl alcohol, and used esp. as a source of alcohols and as a solvent
fus·ible \'fyü-zə-bəl\ *adj* (14c) : capable of being fused and esp. liquefied by heat ⟨~ alloy⟩ — **fus·ibil·i·ty** \,fyü-zə-'bi-lə-tē\ *n*
fu·si·form \'fyü-zə-,fȯrm\ *adj* [L *fusus* spindle] (1746) : tapering toward each end ⟨~ bacteria⟩
¹**fu·sil** \'fyü-zəl\ *or* **fu·sile** \'fyü-zəl, -,zīl\ *adj* [ME, fr. L *fusilis*, fr. *fundere*] (14c) **1** *archaic* **a** : made by melting and pouring into forms : CAST **b** : liquefied by heat **2** *archaic* : FUSIBLE
²**fusil** *n* [F, lit., steel for striking fire, fr. OF *foisil*, fr. (assumed) VL *focilis*, fr. LL *focus* fire — more at FUEL] (1680) : a light flintlock musket
fu·sil·ier *or* **fu·sil·eer** \,fyü-zə-'lir\ *n* [F *fusilier*, fr. *fusil*] (1680) **1** : a soldier armed with a fusil **2** : a member of a British regiment formerly armed with fusils
fu·sil·lade \'fyü-sə-,läd, -,lȧd, ,fyü-sə-', -zə-\ *n* [F, fr. *fusiller* to shoot, fr. *fusil*] (1801) **1** **a** : a number of shots fired simultaneously or in rapid succession **b** : something that gives the effect of a fusillade ⟨a ~ of rocks and bottles⟩ **2** : a spirited outburst esp. of criticism
fu·sil·li \'fyü-'si-lē, -'sē-\ *n* [It, pl. of *fusillo*, fr. It dial. (southern Italy), dim. of *fuso* spindle, fr. L *fusus*] (1948) : spiral-shaped pasta
fu·sion \'fyü-zhən\ *n, often attrib* [L *fusion-, fusio*, fr. *fundere*] (1555) **1** : the act or process of liquefying or rendering plastic by heat **2** **a** : a union or process of if by melting: as **a** : a merging of diverse, distinct, or separate elements into a unified whole **b** : a political partnership : COALITION **c** : popular music combining different styles (as jazz and rock) **3** : the union of atomic nuclei to form heavier nuclei resulting in the release of enormous quantities of energy when certain light elements unite
fu·sion·ist \'fyü-zhᵊn-ist\ *n* (1851) : a person involved in a political fusion or in nuclear or musical fusion
¹**fuss** \'fəs\ *n* [origin unknown] (1701) **1** **a** : needless bustle or excitement : COMMOTION **b** : a show of flattering attention ⟨made a big ~ over his favorite niece⟩ **2** **a** : a state of agitation esp. over a trivial matter **b** : OBJECTION, PROTEST **c** : an often petty controversy or quarrel ⟨ended up having a pretty good ~ with my wife —Mac Hyman⟩
²**fuss** *vi* (1792) **1** **a** : to create or be in a state of restless activity; *esp* : to shower flattering attentions ⟨~*ing* over the grandchildren⟩ **b** : to pay close or undue attention to small details ⟨~*ed* with her hair⟩ **2** **a** : to become upset : WORRY **b** : to express annoyance or pique : COMPLAIN ~ *vt* : AGITATE, UPSET — **fuss·er** *n*
fuss·bud·get \'fəs-,bə-jət\ *n* (ca. 1904) : one who fusses or is fussy esp. about trifles — **fuss·bud·gety** \-jə-tē\ *adj*
fuss·pot \'fəs-,pät\ *n* (1921) : FUSSBUDGET
fussy \'fə-sē\ *adj* **fuss·i·er; -est** (1831) **1** : easily upset : IRRITABLE **2** : overly decorative ⟨a ~ wallpaper pattern⟩ **3** **a** : requiring or giving close attention to details ⟨~ bookkeeping procedures⟩ **b** : revealing a sometimes extreme concern for niceties : FASTIDIOUS, PICKY — **fuss·i·ly** \'fə-sə-lē\ *adv* — **fuss·i·ness** \'fə-sē-nəs\ *n*
fus·tian \'fəs-chən\ *n* [ME, fr. OF *fustaine*, fr. ML *fustaneum*, perh. fr. *fustis* tree trunk, fr. L, club] (13c) **1** **a** : a strong cotton and linen fabric **b** : a class of cotton fabrics usu. having a pile face and twill weave **2** : highflown or affected writing or speech; *broadly* : anything highflown or affected in style — **fustian** *adj*
fus·tic \'fəs-tik\ *n* [ME *fustyk* smoke tree, fr. MF *fustoc*, fr. Ar *fustuq*, fr. Gk *pistakē* pistachio tree — more at PISTACHIO] (15c) : the wood of a tropical American tree (*Chlorophora tinctoria*) of the mulberry family that yields a yellow dye; *also* : any of several similar dyewoods
fus·ti·gate \'fəs-tə-,gāt\ *vt* **-gat·ed; -gat·ing** [LL *fustigatus*, pp. of

fustigare, fr. L *fustis* + *-igare* (as in *fumigare* to fumigate)] (ca. 1661) **1** : CUDGEL **2** : to criticize severely — **fus·ti·ga·tion** \ˌfəs-tə-'gā-shən\ *n*

fus·ty \'fəs-tē\ *adj* **fus·ti·er; -est** [ME, fr. *fust* wine cask, fr. MF, club, cask, fr. L *fustis*] (14c) **1** *Brit* : impaired by age or dampness : MOLDY **2** : saturated with dust and stale odors : MUSTY **3** : rigidly old= fashioned or reactionary *syn* see MALODOROUS — **fus·ti·ly** \-tə-lē\ *adv* — **fus·ti·ness** \-tē-nəs\ *n*

fu·su·li·nid \ˌfyü-zə-'li-nid, -'lē-, -'li-\ *n* [NL *Fusulinidae*, fr. *Fusulina*, a genus, fr. L *fusus* spindle + *-ulus* -ule + NL *-ina*, dim. suffix] (1941) : any of a family (Fusulinidae) of extinct marine foraminifers

fu·thark \'fü-ˌthärk\ *also* **fu·thorc** *or* **fu·thork** \-ˌthórk\ *n* [fr. the first six letters, *f*, *u*, *þ* (*th*), *o* (or a), *r*, *c* (=k)] (1851) : the runic alphabet — see RUNE illustration

fu·tile \'fyü-t'l, 'fyü-ˌtīl\ *adj* [MF or L; MF, fr. L *futilis* brittle, point-less, prob. fr. *fu-* (akin to *fundere* to pour) — more at FOUND] (ca. 1555) **1** : serving no useful purpose : completely ineffective ⟨efforts to con-vince him were ∼⟩ **2** : occupied with trifles : FRIVOLOUS — **fu·tile·ly** \-t'l-(l)ē, -ˌtīl-lē\ *adv* — **fu·tile·ness** \-t'l-nəs, -ˌtīl-nəs\ *n*

syn FUTILE, VAIN, FRUITLESS mean producing no result. FUTILE may connote completeness of failure or unwisdom of undertaking ⟨resis-tance had proved so *futile* that surrender was the only choice left⟩. VAIN usu. implies simple failure to achieve a desired result ⟨a *vain* attempt to get the car started⟩. FRUITLESS comes close to VAIN but often suggests long and arduous effort or severe disappointment ⟨*fruitless* efforts to obtain a lasting peace⟩.

fu·til·i·tar·i·an \fyü-ˌti-lə-'ter-ē-ən, ˌfyü-\ *n* [blend of *futile* and *utilitar-ian*] (1827) : one who believes that human striving is futile — **futili-tarian** *adj* — **fu·til·i·tar·i·an·ism** \-ē-ə-ˌni-zəm\ *n*

fu·til·i·ty \fyü-'ti-lə-tē\ *n, pl* **-ties** (1623) **1** : the quality or state of being futile : USELESSNESS **2** : a useless act or gesture ⟨the *futilities* of debate for its own sake —W. A. White⟩

fu·ton \'fü-ˌtän\ *n, pl* **futons** *also* **futon** [Jp] (1876) : a usu. cotton-filled mattress used on the floor or in a frame as a bed

fut·tock \'fə-tək\ *n* [ME *votek*, *futtek*] (13c) : one of the curved timbers scarfed together to form the lower part of the compound rib of a ship

futtock shroud *n* (1840) : a short iron rod connecting the topmast rigging with the lower mast

¹fu·ture \'fyü-chər\ *adj* [ME, fr. MF & L; MF *futur*, fr. L *futurus* about to be — more at BE] (14c) **1** : that is to be; *specif* : existing after death **2** : of, relating to, or constituting a verb tense expressive of time yet to come **3** : existing or occurring at a later time ⟨met his ∼ wife⟩

²future *n* (15c) **1 a** : time that is to come **b** : what is going to hap-pen **2** : an expectation of advancement or progressive development **3** : something (as a bulk commodity) bought for future acceptance or sold for future delivery — usu. used in pl. ⟨grain ∼s⟩ **4 a** : the future tense of a language **b** : a verb form in the future tense

fu·ture·less \'fyü-chər-ləs\ *adj* (1863) : having no future — **fu·ture·less·ness** *n*

future perfect *adj* (ca. 1898) : of, relating to, or constituting a verb tense that is traditionally formed in English with *will have* and *shall have* and that expresses completion of an action by a specified time that is yet to come — **future perfect** *n*

future shock *n* (1965) : the physical and psychological distress suf-fered by one who is unable to cope with the rapidity of social and tech-nological changes

fu·tur·ism \'fyü-chə-ˌri-zəm\ *n* (1909) **1** : a movement in art, music, and literature begun in Italy about 1909 and marked esp. by an effort to give formal expression to the dynamic energy and movement of mechanical processes **2** : a point of view that finds meaning or fulfill-ment in the future rather than in the past or present

fu·tur·ist \'fyü-chə-rist\ *n* (1911) **1** : one who advocates or practices futurism **2** : one who studies and predicts the future esp. on the basis of current trends — **futurist** *adj*

fu·tur·is·tic \ˌfyü-chə-'ris-tik\ *adj* (1915) : of, relating to, or character-istic of the future, futurism, or futurology; *also* : very modern — **fu·tur·is·ti·cal·ly** \-ti-k(ə-)lē\ *adv*

fu·tur·is·tics \-tiks\ *n pl but sing in constr* (1969) : FUTUROLOGY

fu·tur·i·ty \fyü-'tur-ə-tē, -'tyur-, -'chur-\ *n, pl* **-ties** (1604) **1** : time to come : FUTURE **2** : the quality or state of being future **3** *pl* : future events or prospects **4 a** : a horse race usu. for two-year-olds in which the competitors are nominated at birth or before **b** : a race or compe-tition for which entries are made well in advance of the event

fu·tur·ol·o·gy \ˌfyü-chə-'rä-lə-jē\ *n* (1946) : a study that deals with future possibilities based on current trends — **fu·tur·olog·i·cal** \-rə-'lä-ji-kəl\ *adj* — **fu·tur·olo·gist** \-'rä-lə-jist\ *n*

futz \'fəts\ *vi* [perh. part modif., part trans. of Yiddish *arumfartsn zikh*, lit., to fart around] (1932) *slang* : FOOL AROUND 1 — often used with *around* ⟨∼ around without producing any worthwhile music —John Koegel⟩

fuze, fu·zee *var of* FUSE, FUSEE

¹fuzz \'fəz\ *n* [prob. back-formation fr. *fuzzy*] (1674) **1** : fine light particles or fibers (as of down or fluff) **2** : a blurred effect

²fuzz *vi* (ca. 1702) **1** : to fly off in or become covered with fluffy parti-cles **2** : to become blurred ⟨her frame of reference ∼*ing* at the edges —Jane O'Reilly⟩ ∼ *vt* **1** : to make fuzzy **2** : to envelop in a haze : BLUR

³fuzz *n* [origin unknown] (1927) : POLICE; *also* : a police officer

fuzzy \'fə-zē\ *adj* **fuzz·i·er; -est** [perh. fr. LG *fussig* loose, spongy] (1713) **1** : marked by or giving a suggestion of fuzz ⟨a ∼ covering of felt⟩ **2** : lacking in clarity or definition ⟨moving the camera causes ∼ photos⟩ ⟨∼ thinking⟩ — **fuzz·i·ly** \'fə-zə-lē\ *adv* — **fuzz·i·ness** \'fə-zē-nəs\ *n*

-fy \ˌfī\ *vb suffix* [ME *-fien*, fr. OF *-fier*, fr. L *-ficare*, fr. *-ficus* -fic] **1** : make : form into ⟨dandi*fy*⟩ **2** : invest with the attributes of : make similar to ⟨citi*fy*⟩

fyce \'fis\ *var of* FEIST

fyke \'fik\ *n* [D *fuik*] (1832) : a long bag net kept open by hoops

fyl·fot \'fil-ˌfät\ *n* [ME, device used to fill the lower part of a painted glass window (fr. a conjectural MS reading)] (1842) : SWASTIKA

---

g \'jē\ *n, pl* **g's** *or* **gs** \'jēz\ *often cap, often attrib* (bef. 12c) **1 a** : the 7th letter of the English alphabet **b** : a graphic representation of this letter **c** : a speech counterpart of orthographic g **2** : the 5th tone of a C-major scale **3** : a graphic device for reproducing the letter g **4** : one desig-nated g esp. as the 7th in order or class **5** [*gravity*] : ACCELERATION OF GRAVITY; *also* : a unit of force equal to the force exerted by gravity on a body at rest and used to indicate the force to which a body is subjected when accelerated **6** [*grand*] *slang* : a sum of $1000 **7** : something shaped like the letter G

G *certification mark* — used to certify that a motion picture is of such a nature that persons of all ages may be allowed admission; compare NC-17, PG, PG-13, R

¹gab \'gab\ *vi* **gabbed; gab·bing** [prob. short for *gabble*] (1786) : to talk in a rapid or thoughtless manner : CHATTER — **gab·ber** *n*

²gab *n* (1790) : TALK; *esp* : idle talk

³gab *n* (1939) : GABARDINE 2

gab·ar·dine \'ga-bər-ˌdēn\ *n* [MF *gaverdine*] (1520) **1** : GABERDINE 1 **2 a** : a firm hard-finish durable fabric (as of wool or rayon) twilled with diagonal ribs on the right side **b** : a garment of gabardine

gab·ble \'ga-bəl\ *vb* **gab·bled; gab·bling** \-b(ə-)liŋ\ [prob. of imit. origin] *vi* (1577) **1** : to talk fast or foolishly : JABBER **2** : to utter inarticulate or animal sounds ∼ *vt* : to say with incoherent rapidity : BABBLE — **gabble** *n* — **gab·bler** \-b(ə-)lər\ *n*

gab·bro \'ga-(ˌ)brō\ *n, pl* **gabbros** [It, prob. modif. of L *glaber* smooth — more at GLAD] (ca. 1828) : a granular igneous rock composed essen-tially of calcic plagioclase, a ferromagnesian mineral, and accessory minerals — **gab·bro·ic** \ga-'brō-ik\ *adj*

gab·by \'ga-bē\ *adj* **gab·bi·er; -est** (1719) : TALKATIVE, GARRULOUS

ga·belle \gə-'bel\ *n* [ME, fr. MF, fr. OIt *gabella*, fr. Ar *qabālah*] (15c) : a tax on salt levied in France prior to 1790

gab·er·dine \'ga-bər-ˌdēn\ *n* [MF *gaverdine*] (1520) **1** : a long loose outer garment worn in medieval times and associated esp. with Jews since the 16th century **2** : GABARDINE 2

gab·fest \'gab-ˌfest\ *n* (1897) **1** : an informal gathering for general talk ⟨political ∼s⟩ **2** : an extended conversation

ga·bi·on \'gā-bē-ən, 'ga-\ *n* [MF, fr. OIt *gabbione*, lit., large cage, aug. of *gabbia* cage, fr. L *cavea* — more at CAGE] (1579) : a basket or cage filled with earth or rocks and used esp. in building a support or abut-ment

ga·ble \'gā-bəl\ *n* [ME, fr. MF, of Gmc origin; akin to ON *gafl* gable — more at CEPHALIC] (14c) **1 a** : the vertical trian-gular end of a building from cornice or eaves to ridge **b** : the similar end of a gambrel roof **c** : the end wall of a build-ing **2** : a triangular part or structure — **ga·bled** \-bəld\ *adj*

gable roof *n* (1850) : a double-sloping roof that forms a gable at each end

1 gable 1a

gab·oon \gə-'bün, ga-\ *n* [alter. of ¹*gob* + *-oon* (as in *spittoon*)] (1929) *dial* : SPITTOON

Ga·bri·el \'gā-brē-əl\ *n* [Heb *Gabhrī'ēl*] : one of the four archangels named in Hebrew tradition

ga·by \'gā-bē\ *n, pl* **gabies** [perh. of Scand origin; akin to ON *gapa* to gape — more at GAPE] (ca. 1796) *dial chiefly Eng* : SIMPLETON

¹gad \'gad\ *n* [ME, spike, fr. ON *gaddr*; akin to OE *geard* rod — more at YARD] (1671) **1** : a chisel or pointed iron or steel bar for loosening ore or rock **2** *chiefly dial* : a long stick

²gad *vi* **gad·ded; gad·ding** [ME *gadden*] (15c) : to be on the go with-out a specific aim or purpose — usu. used with *about*

³gad *interj* [euphemism for *God*] (1608) — used as a mild oath

Gad \'gad\ *n* [Heb *Gādh*] : a son of Jacob and the traditional epony-mous ancestor of one of the tribes of Israel — **Gad·ite** \'ga-ˌdīt\ *n*

\ə\ abut \ᵊ\ kitten, F table \ər\ further \a\ ash \ā\ ace \ä\ mop, mar \au̇\ out \ch\ chin \e\ bet \ē\ easy \g\ go \i\ hit \ī\ ice \j\ job \ŋ\ sing \ō\ go \ȯ\ law \ȯi\ boy \th\ thin \t̶h̶\ the \ü\ loot \u̇\ foot \y\ yet \zh\ vision \ä, k̲, ⁿ, œ, œ̄, ᵫ, ᵫ̄, ʸ\ *see* Guide to Pronunciation

gad·about \'ga-də-ˌbaůt\ *n* (1837) : a person who flits about in social activity — **gadabout** *adj*

gad·a·rene \'ga-də-ˌrēn\ *adj, often cap* [fr. the demon-possessed *Gadarene* swine in Mt 8:28 that rushed into the sea] (1922) : HEADLONG, PRECIPITATE ⟨a ~ rush to the cities⟩

gad·fly \'gad-ˌflī\ *n* [¹*gad*] (1626) **1** : any of various flies (as a horsefly, botfly, or warble fly) that bite or annoy livestock **2** : a person who stimulates or annoys esp. by persistent criticism

gad·get \'ga-jət\ *n* [origin unknown] (1886) : an often small mechanical or electronic device with a practical use that bite or annoy livestock as a novelty — **gad·ge·teer** \ˌga-jə-'tir\ *n* — **gad·get·ry** \'ga-jə-trē\ *n* — **gad·gety** \-jə-tē\ *adj*

ga·doid \'gā-ˌdȯid, 'ga-\ *adj* [NL *Gadus*, genus of fishes, fr. Gk *gados*, a fish] (ca. 1842) : resembling or related to the cods — **gadoid** *n*

gad·o·lin·ite \'ga-dᵊl-ə-ˌnīt\ *n* [G *Gadolinit*, fr. Johann *Gadolin* †1852 Finn. chemist] (1802) : a black or brown mineral that is a source of rare earths and consists of a silicate of iron, beryllium, yttrium, cerium, and erbium

gad·o·lin·i·um \ˌga-də-'li-nē-əm\ *n* [NL, fr. J. *Gadolin*] (1886) : a magnetic metallic element of the rare-earth group occurring in combination in gadolinite and several other minerals — see ELEMENT table

ga·droon \gə-'drün\ *n* [F *godron* round plait, gadroon] (ca. 1724) **1** : the ornamental notching or carving of a rounded molding **2** : a short often oval fluting or reeding used in decoration — **gadroon** *vt* — **ga·droon·ing** *n*

gad·wall \'gad-ˌwȯl\ *n, pl* **gadwalls** *or* **gadwall** [origin unknown] (1666) : a grayish brown medium-sized dabbling duck (*Anas strepera*)

gad·zook·ery \gad-'zü-kə-rē, -'zů-\ *n* (1955) *Brit* : the use of archaisms (as in a historical novel)

gad·zooks \gad-'züks, -'zůks\ *interj, often cap* [perh. fr. *God's hooks*, the nails of the Crucifixion] (1694) *archaic* — used as a mild oath

Gaea \'jē-ə\ *n* [Gk *Gaia*] : the Greek earth goddess and mother of the Titans

Gael \'gā(ə)l\ *n* [ScGael *Gàidheal* & Ir *Gaedheal*] (1753) **1** : a Scottish Highlander **2** : a Celtic esp. Gaelic-speaking inhabitant of Ireland, Scotland, or the Isle of Man — **Gael·dom** \-dəm\ *n*

Gael·ic \'gā-lik, 'ga-, 'gä-\ *adj* [ScGael *Gàidheal* Gael] (1741) **1** : of or relating to the Gaels and esp. the Celtic Highlanders of Scotland **2** : of, relating to, or constituting the Goidelic speech of the Celts in Ireland, the Isle of Man, and the Scottish Highlands — **Gaelic** *n*

Gael·tacht \'gā(ə)l-ˌtäkt\ *n* [Ir, fr. *Gael*, spelling var. of *Gaedheal* Irishman, Gael] (1929) : any of the Irish-speaking regions remaining in Ireland

¹gaff \'gaf\ *n* [F *gaffe*, fr. Prov *gaf*] (ca. 1656) **1 a** : a spear or spearhead for taking fish or turtles **b** : a handled hook for holding or lifting heavy fish **c** : a metal spur for a gamecock **d** : a butcher's hook **e** : a climbing iron or its steel point used by a telephone lineman **2** : the spar on which the head of a fore-and-aft sail is extended **3** : GAFFE

²gaff *vt* (1844) **1** : to strike or secure with a gaff **2** : to fit (a gamecock) with a gaff

³gaff *n* [origin unknown] (1812) *Brit* : a cheap theater or music hall

⁴gaff *n* [origin unknown] (1896) **1 a** : something painful or difficult to bear : ORDEAL — usu. used in the phrase *stand the gaff; esp* : persistent raillery or criticism **b** : rough treatment : ABUSE **2 a** : HOAX, FRAUD **b** : GIMMICK, TRICK

⁵gaff *vt* (1933) **1** : DECEIVE, TRICK; *also* : FLEECE **2** : to fix for the purpose of cheating ⟨~ the dice⟩

gaffe \'gaf\ *n* [F, *gaff, gaffe*] (1909) : a social or diplomatic blunder

gaf·fer \'ga-fər\ *n* [alter. of *godfather*] (1575) **1** : an old man — compare GAMMER **2** *Brit* **a** : FOREMAN, OVERSEER **b** : EMPLOYER **3** : a head glassblower **4** : a lighting electrician on a motion-picture or television set

gaff–top·sail \'gaf-'täp-ˌsäl, -səl\ *n* (1794) : a usu. triangular topsail with its foot extended upon the gaff — see SAIL illustration

¹gag \'gag\ *vb* **gagged; gag·ging** [ME *gaggen* to strangle, of imit. origin] *vt* (1509) **1 a** : to restrict use of the mouth of by inserting a gag **b** : to prevent from exercising freedom of speech or expression **c** : to pry or hold open with a gag **2** : to provide or write quips or pranks for ⟨~ a show⟩ **3** : to choke or cause to retch ~ *vi* **1 a** : CHOKE; *also* : to suffer a throat spasm that makes swallowing or breathing difficult **b** : RETCH **2** : to be unable to endure something : BALK **3** : to make quips — **gag·ger** *n*

²gag *n* (1553) **1** : something thrust into the mouth to keep it open or to prevent speech or outcry **2** : an official check or restraint on debate or free speech ⟨a ~ order⟩ ⟨a ~ rule⟩ **3** : a laugh-provoking remark or act **4** : PRANK, TRICK

ga·ga \'gä-(ˌ)gä\ *adj* [F, fr. *gaga* fool, of imit. origin] (1920) **1** : CRAZY, FOOLISH **2** : marked by wild enthusiasm : INFATUATED, DOTING

ga·ga·ku \gä-'gä-(ˌ)kü\ *n* [Jp, fr. *ga* elegance + *gaku* music] (1929) : the ancient court music of Japan

¹gage \'gāj\ *n* [ME, fr. MF, of Gmc origin; akin to OHG *wetti* pledge — more at WED] (14c) **1** : a token of defiance; *specif* : a glove or cap cast on the ground to be taken up by an opponent as a pledge of combat **2** : something deposited as a pledge of performance

²gage *vt* (15c) **1** *archaic* : PLEDGE **2** *archaic* : STAKE, RISK

³gage *var of* GAUGE

⁴gage *n* (1847) : GREENGAGE

gag·gle \'ga-gəl\ *n* [ME *gagyll*, fr. *gagelen* to cackle] (15c) **1** : FLOCK; *esp* : a flock of geese when not in flight — compare SKEIN **2** : AGGREGATION, CLUSTER ⟨a ~ of reporters and photographers⟩

gag·man \'gag-ˌman\ *n* (1928) **1** : a gag writer **2** : COMEDIAN 2

gag·ster \'gag-stər\ *n* (1935) : GAGMAN; *also* : one who plays practical jokes

gahn·ite \'gä-ˌnīt\ *n* [G *Gahnit*, fr. J. G. *Gahn* †1818 Swed. chemist] (ca. 1808) : a usu. dark green mineral consisting of an oxide of zinc and aluminum

gai·ety \'gā-ə-tē\ *n, pl* **-eties** [F *gaieté*] (1634) **1** : MERRYMAKING; *also* : festive activity — often used in pl. **2** : high spirits : MERRIMENT **3** : ELEGANCE, FINERY

gai·jin \'gī-(ˌ)jēn, -(ˌ)jin\ *n, pl* **gaijin** [Jp, fr. *gai-* outer, foreign + *-jin* person] (1964) : a foreigner in Japan

gail·lar·dia \gə-'lär-d(ē-)ə\ *n* [NL, fr. *Gaillard* de Marentonneau, 18th cent. Fr. botanist] (1888) : any of a genus (*Gaillardia*) of chiefly western American composite herbs with showy flower heads

gai·ly \'gā-lē\ *adv* (14c) : in a gay manner : marked by gaiety

¹gain \'gān\ *n* [ME *gayne, gain*, fr. MF *gaigne, gain*, fr. OF *gaaigne, gaaing*, fr. *gaaignier* to till, earn, gain, of Gmc origin; akin to OHG *weidanōn* to hunt for food, OE *wāth* pursuit, hunt] (14c) **1** : resources or advantage acquired or increased : PROFIT ⟨made substantial ~s last year⟩ **2** : the act or process of gaining **3 a** : an increase in amount, magnitude, or degree ⟨a ~ in efficiency⟩ **b** : the increase (as of voltage or signal intensity) caused by an amplifier; *esp* : the ratio of output over input ⟨~ the signal-gathering ability of an antenna

²gain *vt* (14c) **1 a** : to acquire or get possession of usu. by industry, merit, or craft ⟨~ an advantage⟩ ⟨he stood to ~ a fortune⟩ **b** : to win in competition or conflict ⟨the troops ~ed enemy territory⟩ **c** (1) : to arrive at : REACH, ATTAIN ⟨~ed the river that night⟩ (2) : TRAVERSE, COVER ⟨~ed 10 yards on the play⟩ **d** : to get by a natural development or process ⟨~ strength⟩ **e** : to establish a specific relationship with ⟨~ a friend⟩ **2 a** : to make an increase of (a specified amount) ⟨~ed 3% in the past month⟩ **b** : to increase in (a particular quality) ⟨~ momentum⟩ **3** : to win to one's side : PERSUADE ⟨~ adherents to a cause⟩ **4** : to cause to be obtained or given : ATTRACT ⟨~ attention⟩ **5** *of a timepiece* : to run fast by the amount of ⟨the clock ~s a minute a day⟩ ~ *vi* **1** : to get advantage : PROFIT ⟨hoped to ~ by the deal⟩ **2 a** : INCREASE ⟨the day was ~ing in warmth⟩ **b** : to increase in weight **c** : to improve in health or ability **3** *of a timepiece* : to run fast **4** : to get closer to something pursued — usu. used with *on* or *upon* — **gain·er** *n* — **gain ground** : to make progress

gain·ful \'gān-fəl\ *adj* (1555) : productive of gain : PROFITABLE ⟨~ employment⟩ — **gain·ful·ly** \-fə-lē\ *adv* — **gain·ful·ness** *n*

gain·giv·ing \'gān-ˌgi-viŋ, ˌgān-'\ *n* [*gain-* (against) + *giving*] (1602) *archaic* : MISGIVING

gain·say \ˌgān-'sā\ *vt* **-said** \-'sād, -'sed\; **-say·ing** \-'sā-iŋ\; **-says** \-'säz, -'sez\ [ME *gainsayen*, fr. *gain-* against (fr. OE *gēan-*) + *sayen* to say — more at AGAIN] (14c) **1** : to declare to be untrue or invalid **2** : CONTRADICT, OPPOSE *syn* see DENY — **gain·say·er** *n*

¹gait \'gāt\ *n* [ME *gait, gate* gate, way] (1509) **1** : a manner of walking or moving on foot **2** : a sequence of foot movements (as a walk, trot, pace, or canter) by which a horse or a dog moves forward **3** : a manner or rate of movement or progress ⟨the leisurely ~ of summer⟩

²gait *vt* (ca. 1900) **1** : to train (a horse or a dog) to use a particular gait or set of gaits **2** : to lead (a show dog) before a judge to display carriage and movement ~ *vi* : to walk with a particular gait

gait·ed \'gā-təd\ *adj* (1588) : having a particular gait or so many gaits ⟨slow-*gaited*⟩ ⟨a ~ horse⟩

gai·ter \'gā-tər\ *n* [F *guêtre*] (1775) **1** : a cloth or leather leg covering reaching from the instep to above the ankle or to mid-calf or knee **2 a** : an overshoe with fabric upper **b** : an ankle-high shoe with elastic gores in the sides

¹gal \'gal\ *n* [by alter.] (1795) : GIRL, WOMAN

²gal *n* [*Galileo* Galilei] (1914) : a unit of acceleration equivalent to one centimeter per second per second — used esp. for values of gravity

ga·la \'gā-lə, 'ga-, 'gä-\ *n* [It, fr. MF *gale* festivity, pleasure — more at GALLANT] (1777) : a festive celebration; *esp* : a public entertainment marking a special occasion — **gala** *adj*

ga·la·bia *or* **ga·la·bi·eh** *or* **ga·la·bi·ya** \gə-'lä-b(ē-)ə\ *n* [Ar dial. (Egypt) *gallābīyah*] (1725) : DJELLABA

galact- *or* **galacto-** *comb form* [L *galact-*, fr. Gk *galakt-, galakto-*, fr. *galakt-, gala*] **1** : milk ⟨*galactorrhea*⟩ **2** : related to galactose ⟨*galactosemia*⟩

ga·lac·tic \gə-'lak-tik\ *adj* (1839) **1** : of or relating to a galaxy and esp. the Milky Way galaxy **2** : HUGE ⟨a ~ sum of money⟩

ga·lac·tor·rhea \gə-ˌlak-tə-'rē-ə\ *n* (ca. 1860) : a spontaneous flow of milk from the nipple

ga·lac·tos·amine \gə-ˌlak-'tō-sə-ˌmēn, -zə-\ *n* (1900) : an amino derivative $C_6H_{13}O_5N$ of galactose that occurs in cartilage

ga·lac·tose \gə-'lak-ˌtōs, -ˌtōz\ *n* [F, fr. *galact-*] (1869) : a sugar $C_6H_{12}O_6$ less soluble and less sweet than glucose

ga·lac·to·se·mia \gə-ˌlak-tə-'sē-mē-ə\ *n* (1934) : an inherited metabolic disorder in which galactose accumulates in the blood due to deficiency of an enzyme catalyzing its conversion to glucose — **ga·lac·to·se·mic** \-mik\ *adj*

ga·lac·to·si·dase \gə-ˌlak-'tō-sə-ˌdās, -zə-ˌdāz\ *n* (1917) : an enzyme (as lactase) that hydrolyzes a galactoside

ga·lac·to·side \gə-'lak-tə-ˌsīd\ *n* (1862) : a glycoside that yields galactose on hydrolysis

ga·lac·to·syl \gə-'lak-tə-ˌsil\ *n* (1950) : a glycosyl radical $C_6H_{11}O_5$ that is derived from galactose

ga·lact·uron·ic acid \gə-ˌlak-tù-'rä-nik-, -tyù-\ *n* [ISV] (1917) : a crystalline aldehyde-acid $C_6H_{10}O_7$ that occurs esp. in polymerized form in pectin

ga·la·go \gə-'lä-(ˌ)gō, -'lä-\ *n, pl* **-gos** [NL, perh. fr. Wolof *golokh* monkey] (ca. 1848) : any of several small active nocturnal arboreal African primates (*Galago* and related genera) with large eyes, long ears, a long tail, and elongated hind limbs that enable them to leap with great agility — called also *bush baby*

ga·lah \gə-'lä\ *n* [Yuwaalaraay (Australian aboriginal language of northern New South Wales) *gilaa*] (1862) : a showy Australian cockatoo (*Eolophus roseicapillus*) that is a pest in wheat-growing areas and is often kept as a cage bird

Gal·a·had \'ga-lə-ˌhad\ *n* **1** : the knight of the Round Table who successfully seeks the Holy Grail **2** : one who is pure, noble, and unselfish

gal·an·tine \'ga-lən-ˌtēn\ *n* [F, fr. OF *galentine, galatine* fish sauce, fr. ML *galatina*, prob. fr. L *gelatus*, pp. of *gelare* to congeal, freeze — more at COLD] (1725) : a cold dish consisting of boned meat or fish that has been stuffed, poached, and covered with aspic

galago

Gal·a·tea \ˌga-lə-'tē-ə\ n [L, fr. Gk *Galateia*] : a female figure sculpted by Pygmalion and given life by Aphrodite in fulfillment of his prayer

Ga·la·tians \gə-'lā-shənz\ n pl *but sing in constr* : an argumentative letter of St. Paul written to the Christians of Galatia and included as a book in the New Testament — see BIBLE table

gal·a·vant *var of* GALLIVANT

ga·lax \'gā-ˌlaks\ n [NL] (ca. 1753) : an evergreen herb (*Galax urceolata* syn. *G. aphylla* of the order Diapensiales) of the southeastern U.S. that has glossy leaves and is related to the heaths (order Ericales)

gal·axy \'gal-ək-sē\ n, pl **-ax·ies** [ME *galaxie, galaxias*, fr. LL *galaxias*, fr. Gk, fr. *galakt-, gala* milk; akin to L *lac* milk] (14c) **1 a** *often cap* : MILKY WAY GALAXY — used with *the* **b** : any of the very large groups of stars and associated matter that are found throughout the universe **2** : an assemblage of brilliant or notable persons or things ⟨a ~ of artists⟩

gal·ba·num \'gal-bə-nəm, 'gȯl-\ n [ME, fr. L, fr. Gk *chalbanē*, of Sem origin; akin to Heb *helbĕnāh* galbanum] (14c) : a yellowish to green or brown aromatic bitter gum resin derived from several Asian plants (as *Ferula galbaniflua*) and used in incense

gale \'gā(ə)l\ n [origin unknown] (ca. 1547) **1 a** : a strong current of air: (1) : a wind from 32 to 63 miles per hour (about 51 to 101 kilometers per hour) (2) : FRESH GALE — see BEAUFORT SCALE table **b** *archaic* : BREEZE **2** : an emotional outburst ⟨~s of laughter⟩

ga·lea \'gā-lē-ə\ n [NL, fr. L, helmet] (1834) : an anatomical part suggesting a helmet: as **a** : the upper lip of the corolla of a mint **b** : the outer or lateral lobe of the maxilla in mandibulate insects — **ga·le·ate** \-lē-ˌāt\ adj

ga·le·na \gə-'lē-nə\ n [L, lead ore] (1671) : a bluish gray mineral with metallic luster consisting of lead sulfide, showing highly perfect cubic cleavage, and constituting the principal ore of lead

ga·len·i·cal \gə-'le-ni-kəl, gā-\ n [*Galen* + ¹-*ic* + ¹-*al*] (1768) : a medicine prepared by extracting one or more active constituents of a plant

ga·lère \ga-'ler\ n [F, galley, fr. MF, fr. Catal *galera*, fr. MGk *galea*] (1756) : a group of people having an attribute in common

gal Friday n (1958) : GIRL FRIDAY

Gal·i·le·an \ˌga-lə-'lē-ən, -'lā-\ adj (ca. 1751) : of, relating to, or discovered by Galileo Galilei

gal·i·lee \'ga-lə-ˌlē\ n [AF, fr. ML *galilaea*, prob. fr. *Galilaea* Galilee, fr. L] (15c) : a chapel or porch at the entrance of an English church

gal·in·gale \'ga-lən-ˌgāl, -liŋ-\ n [ME, a kind of ginger, fr. MF *galingal*, fr. Ar *khalanjān*] (1578) : an Old World sedge (*Cyperus longus*) that is used for papermaking and basket-weaving and has an aromatic root; *broadly* : any of various other sedges of the same genus

gal·i·ot *var of* GALLIOT

¹gall \'gȯl\ n [ME, fr. OE *gealla*; akin to Gk *cholē, cholos* gall, wrath, OE *geolu* yellow — more at YELLOW] (bef. 12c) **1 a** : BILE *esp* : bile obtained from an animal and used in the arts or medicine **b** : something bitter to endure **c** : bitterness of spirit : RANCOR **2** : brazen boldness coupled with impudent assurance and insolence *syn* see TEMERITY

²gall n [ME *galle*, fr. OE *gealla*, fr. L *galla* gallnut] (bef. 12c) **1 a** : a skin sore caused by chronic irritation **b** : a cause or state of exasperation **2** *archaic* : FLAW

³gall vt (14c) **1** : to fret and wear away by friction : CHAFE ⟨the loose saddle ~ed the horse's back⟩ ⟨the ~ing of a metal bearing⟩ **2** : IRRITATE, VEX ⟨sarcasm ~s her⟩ ~ vi **1** : to become sore or worn by rubbing **2** : SEIZE 2

⁴gall n [ME *galle*, fr. MF, fr. L *galla*] (14c) : a swelling of plant tissue usu. due to fungi or insect parasites and sometimes forming an important source of tannin

Gal·la \'ga-lə\ n, pl **Galla** or **Gallas** (1875) : OROMO

gal·la·mine tri·eth·io·dide \'ga-lə-ˌmēn-ˌtrī-ə-'thī-ə-ˌdīd\ n [*pyrogallol* + *amine* + *triethyl* + *iodide*] (1951) : a substituted ammonium salt $C_{30}H_{60}I_3N_3O_3$ that is used to produce muscle relaxation esp. during anesthesia — called also *gallamine*

¹gal·lant \'ga-lənt, gə-'länt, gə-'lant\ n (14c) **1** : a young man of fashion **2 a** : LADIES' MAN **b** : SUITOR **c** : PARAMOUR

²gal·lant \gə-'länt (*usu in sense 2*); gə-'lant, 'ga-lənt (*usu in sense 3*)\ adj [ME *galaunt*, fr. MF *galant*, fr. prp. of *galer* to have a good time, fr. *gale* pleasure, of Gmc origin; akin to OE *wela* weal — more at WEAL] (15c) **1** : showy in dress or bearing : SMART **2 a** : SPLENDID, STATELY ⟨a ~ ship⟩ **b** : SPIRITED, BRAVE ⟨~ efforts against the enemy⟩ **c** : nobly chivalrous and often self-sacrificing **3** : courteously and elaborately attentive esp. to ladies *syn* see CIVIL — **gal·lant·ly** adv

³gal·lant \gə-'lant, -'länt\ vt (1672) **1** : to pay court to (a lady) : ATTEND ⟨used to ~ her in his youth —Washington Irving⟩ **2** *obs* : to manipulate (a fan) in a modish manner ~ vi : to pay court to ladies

gal·lant·ry \'ga-lən-trē\ n, pl **-ries** (1613) **1** *archaic* : gallant appearance **2 a** : an act of marked courtesy **b** : courteous attention to a lady **c** : amorous attention or pursuit **3** : spirited and conspicuous bravery

gal·late \'ga-ˌlāt, 'gȯ-\ n (1794) : a salt or ester of gallic acid

gall·blad·der \'gȯl-ˌbla-dər\ n (1676) : a membranous muscular sac in which bile from the liver is stored

gal·le·ass \'ga-lē-əs\ n [MF *galeasse*, fr. OF *galie* galley] (1544) : a large fast galley used esp. as a warship by Mediterranean countries in the 16th and 17th centuries and having both sails and oars but usu. propelled chiefly by rowing

gal·le·on \'ga-lē-ən\ n [OSp *galeón*, fr. MF *galion*, fr. OF *galie*] (1529) : a heavy square-rigged sailing ship of the 15th to early 18th centuries used for war or commerce esp. by the Spanish

gal·le·ria \ˌga-lə-'rē-ə\ n [It, gallery, fr. ML *galeria*] (ca. 1901) : a roofed and usu. glass-enclosed promenade or court (as at a mall)

gal·lery \'ga-lə-rē, 'gal-rē\ n, pl **-ler·ies** [ME *galerie*, fr. ML *galeria*, prob. alter. of *galilaea* galilee] (15c) **1 a** : a roofed promenade : COLONNADE **b** : CORRIDOR **2 a** : an outdoor balcony **b** *Southern & Midland* : PORCH, VERANDA **c** : a platform at the quarters or stern of a ship **3 a** : a long and narrow passage, apartment, or corridor **b** : a subterranean passageway in a cave or military mining system; *also* : a working drift or level in mining **c** : an underground passage made by a mole or ant or a passage made in wood by an insect **4 a** : a room or building devoted to the exhibition of works of art **b** : an institution or business exhibiting or dealing in works of art **c** : COLLECTION, AGGREGATION ⟨the rich ~ of characters in this novel —H. S. Canby⟩ **5**

a : a structure projecting from one or more interior walls of an auditorium to accommodate additional people; *esp* : the highest balcony in a theater commonly having the cheapest seats **b** : the part of a theater audience seated in the top gallery **c** : the undiscriminating general public **d** : the spectators at a tennis or golf match **6** : a small ornamental barrier or railing (as along the edge of a table or shelf) **7** : a photographer's studio — **gal·ler·ied** \-rēd\ adj — **gal·lery·ite** \-rē-ˌīt\ n

gallery forest n (1920) : a forest growing along a watercourse in a region otherwise devoid of trees

gal·lery·go·er \'ga-lə-rē-ˌgō(-ə)r, 'gal-rē-\ n (1888) : one who frequently goes to art galleries

gal·le·ta \gä-'ye-tə, gĭ-'e-tə\ n [Sp, hardtack] (1872) : either of two perennial forage grasses (*Hilaria rigida* and *H. jamesii*) used for hay in the southwestern U.S. and in Mexico

gal·ley \'ga-lē\ n, pl **galleys** [ME *galeie*, fr. OF *galie, galee*, ultim. fr. MGk *galea*] (13c) **1** : a ship or boat propelled solely or chiefly by oars: as **a** : a long low ship used for war and trading esp. in the Mediterranean Sea from the Middle Ages to the 19th century; *also* : GALLEASS **b** : a warship of classical antiquity — compare BIREME, TRIREME **c** : a large open boat (as a gig) formerly used in England **2** : the kitchen and cooking apparatus esp. of a ship or airplane **3 a** : an oblong tray to hold esp. a single column of set type **b** : a proof of typeset matter esp. in a single column before being made into pages

gal·ley-west \ˌga-lē-'west\ adv [prob. alter. of E dial. *collywest* (badly askew)] (1875) : into destruction or confusion ⟨was knocked ~⟩

gall·fly \'gȯl-ˌflī\ n (ca. 1834) : an insect (as a gall wasp) that deposits its eggs in plants causing the formation of galls in which the larvae feed

¹gal·liard \'gal-yərd\ adj [ME *gaillard*, fr. MF] (14c) *archaic* : GAY, LIVELY

²galliard n (1533) : a sprightly dance with five steps to a phrase popular in the 16th and 17th centuries

Gal·lic \'ga-lik\ adj [L *Gallicus*, fr. *Gallia* Gaul] (1672) : of or relating to Gaul or France

gal·lic acid \'ga-lik-, 'gȯ-lik-\ n [F *gallique*, fr. *galle* gall] (1791) : a white crystalline acid $C_7H_6O_5$ found widely in plants or combined in tannins and used esp. in dyes and as a photographic developer

Gal·li·can \'ga-li-kən\ adj (1562) **1** : GALLIC 2 *often not cap* : of or relating to Gallicanism — **Gallican** n

Gal·li·can·ism \-kə-ˌni-zəm\ n (1858) : a movement originating in France and advocating administrative independence from papal control for the Roman Catholic Church in each nation

gal·li·cism \'ga-lə-ˌsi-zəm\ n, *often cap* (ca. 1656) **1** : a characteristic French idiom or expression appearing in another language **2** : a French trait

gal·li·cize \-ˌsīz\ vt **-cized; -ciz·ing** *often cap* (1773) : to cause to conform to a French mode or idiom — **gal·li·ci·za·tion** \ˌga-lə-sə-'zā-shən\ n, *often cap*

gal·li·gas·kins \ˌga-li-'gas-kənz\ n pl [prob. modif. of MF *garguesques*, fr. OSp *greguescos*, fr. *griego* Greek, fr. L *Graecus*] (1577) **1 a** : loose wide hose or breeches worn in the 16th and 17th centuries **b** : very loose trousers **2** *dial chiefly Brit* : LEGGINGS

gal·li·mau·fry \ˌga-lə-'mȯ-frē\ n, pl **-fries** [MF *galimafree* stew] (ca. 1556) : HODGEPODGE ⟨a ~ of opinions⟩

gal·li·na·ceous \ˌga-lə-'nā-shəs\ adj [L *gallinaceus* of domestic fowl, fr. *gallina* hen, fr. *gallus* cock] (1783) : of or relating to an order (Galliformes) of heavy-bodied largely terrestrial birds including the pheasants, turkeys, grouse, and the common domestic fowl

gall·ing \'gȯ-liŋ\ adj [³*gall*] (1583) : markedly irritating : VEXING ⟨a most ~ defeat⟩ — **gall·ing·ly** \-liŋ-lē\ adv

gal·li·nip·per \'ga-lə-ˌni-pər\ n [origin unknown] (1709) *chiefly Southern & Midland* : any of various insects (as a large mosquito or crane fly)

gal·li·nule \'ga-lə-ˌnü(ə)l, -ˌnyü(ə)l\ n [NL *Gallinula*, genus of birds, fr. L, pullet, dim. of *gallina*] (1776) : any of several aquatic birds of the rail family with long thin feet and a platelike frontal area on the head; *esp* : one (*Gallinula chloropus*) widespread in the New World, Eurasia, and Africa that has a largely red bill, red frontal area on the head, and a white band on the flanks

gal·li·ot \'ga-lē-ət\ n [ME *galiote*, fr. MF, fr. ML *galeota*, dim. of *galea* galley, fr. MGk] (14c) **1** : a small swift galley formerly used in the Mediterranean **2** [D *galjoot*, fr. MF *galiote*] : a long narrow shallow-draft Dutch merchant sailing ship

gal·li·pot \'ga-li-ˌpät\ n [ME *galy pott*] (15c) **1** : a small usu. ceramic vessel **2** *archaic* : DRUGGIST

gal·li·um \'ga-lē-əm\ n [NL, fr. L *gallus* cock (intended as trans. of surname of Paul *Lecoq* de Boisbaudran †1912 Fr. chemist)] (1875) : a rare bluish white metallic element that is hard and brittle at low temperatures but melts just above room temperature and expands on freezing — see ELEMENT table

gallium arsenide n (ca. 1961) : a synthetic compound GaAs used esp. as a semiconducting material

gal·li·vant \'ga-lə-ˌvant\ vi [perh. alter. of ³*gallant*] (1823) **1** : to go about usu. ostentatiously or indiscreetly with members of the opposite sex **2** : to travel, roam, or move about for pleasure

gall midge n (ca. 1889) : any of numerous minute dipteran flies (family Cecidomyiidae) most of which cause gall formation in plants

gall mite n (1881) : any of various minute 4-legged mites (family Eriophyidae) that form galls on plants

gall·nut \'gȯl-ˌnət\ n [⁴*gall*] (1572) : a gall resembling a nut

gal·lon \'ga-lən\ n [ME *galon*, a liquid measure, fr. ONF, fr. ML *galeta* pail, a liquid measure] (13c) : a unit of liquid capacity equal to 231 cubic inches or four quarts — see WEIGHT table

gal·lon·age \'ga-lə-nij\ n (ca. 1909) : amount in gallons

gal·loon \gə-'lün\ n [F *galon*] (1604) : a narrow trimming (as of lace, embroidery, or braid with metallic threads) having both edges scalloped

---

¹**gal·lop** \'ga-ləp\ *vi* (15c) **1 :** to progress or ride at a gallop **2 :** to run fast ~ *vt* **1 :** to cause to gallop **2 :** to transport at a gallop — **gal·lop·er** *n*

²**gallop** *n* [MF *galop*] (1523) **1 :** a bounding gait of a quadruped; *specif* **:** a fast natural 3-beat gait of the horse — compare ³CANTER, RUN **2 :** a ride or run at a gallop **3 :** a stretch of land suitable for galloping horses **4 :** a rapid or hasty progression or pace

gal·lo·pade \,ga-lə-'pād, -'päd\ *n* (1831) : GALOP

Gal·lo·phile \'ga-lə-ˌfil\ *adj* [L *Gallus* Gaul + E *-phile*] (1923) : FRAN-COPHILE — **Gallophile** *n*

gal·lop·ing *adj* (1642) : progressing, developing, or increasing rapidly ⟨~ inflation⟩ ⟨a ~ farce⟩ ⟨~ alcoholism⟩

Gal·lo·way \'ga-lə-ˌwā\ *n* [*Galloway*, Scotland] (1805) : any of a breed of hardy medium-sized hornless chiefly black beef cattle native to southwestern Scotland

gal·low·glass \'ga-lō-ˌglas\ *n* [alter. of Ir *gallóglach*, fr. *gall* foreigner + *óglach* young man, warrior] (ca. 1515) **1 :** a mercenary or retainer of an Irish chief **2 :** an armed Irish foot soldier

¹**gal·lows** \'ga-lə-(ˌ)lōz, -ləz\ *n, pl* **gallows** *or* **gal·low·es** [ME *galwes*, pl. of *galwe*, fr. OE *gealga*; akin to ON *gelgja* pole, stake, Arm *jalk* twig] (bef. 12c) **1 a :** a frame usu. of two upright posts and a transverse beam from which criminals are hanged — called also *gallows tree* **b :** the punishment of hanging **2 :** a structure consisting of an upright frame with a crosspiece **3 :** SUSPENDER 2a

²**gallows** *adj* (15c) : deserving the gallows

gallows bird *n* (ca. 1785) : a person who deserves hanging

gallows humor *n* (1901) : humor that makes fun of a life-threatening, disastrous, or terrifying situation

gall·stone \'gȯl-ˌstōn\ *n* (1758) : a calculus formed in the gallbladder or biliary passages

gal·lus \'ga-ləs\ *n* [alter. of ¹*gallows*] (1836) : SUSPENDER 2a — usu. used in pl.

gal·lused \'ga-ləst\ *adj* (1927) : wearing galluses

gall wasp *n* (1879) : any of a family (Cynipidae) of hymenopterous gallflies

gal·ly \'ga-lē\ *vt* **gal·lied; gal·ly·ing** [origin unknown] (1605) *chiefly dial* : FRIGHTEN, TERRIFY

Ga·lois theory \(ˌ)gal-'wä-, 'gal-ˌwä-\ *n* [*Évariste Galois*] (1893) : a part of the theory of mathematical groups concerned esp. with the conditions under which a solution to a polynomial equation with coefficients in a given mathematical field can be obtained in the field by the repetition of operations and the extraction of nth roots

ga·loot \gə-'lüt\ *n* [origin unknown] (1866) *slang* : FELLOW; *esp* : one who is strange or foolish

ga·lop \'ga-ləp, gə-'lō\ *n* [F] (1831) : a lively dance in duple measure; *also* : the music of a galop

ga·lore \gə-'lōr, -'lȯr\ *adj* [Ir *go leor* enough] (1628) : ABUNDANT, PLENTIFUL — used postpositively ⟨bargains ~⟩

ga·losh \gə-'läsh\ *n* [ME *galoche*, fr. MF] (14c) **1** *obs* : a shoe with a heavy sole **2 :** a high overshoe worn esp. in snow and slush — **ga·loshed** \-'läsht\ *adj*

ga·lumph \gə-'ləm(p)f\ *vi* [prob. alter. of ¹*gallop*] (1872) : to move with a clumsy heavy tread

gal·van·ic \gal-'va-nik\ *adj* (1797) **1 :** of, relating to, or producing a direct current of electricity ⟨a ~ cell⟩ **2 a :** having an electric effect : intensely exciting ⟨a ~ performance⟩ **b :** produced as if by an electric shock ⟨had a ~ effect on the audience⟩ — **gal·van·i·cal·ly** \-ni-k(ə-)lē\ *adv*

galvanic skin response *n* (1942) : a change in the electrical resistance of the skin that is a physiochemical response to an emotional change

gal·va·nise *Brit var of* GALVANIZE

gal·va·nism \'gal-və-ˌni-zəm\ *n* [F or It; F *galvanisme*, fr. It *galvanismo*, fr. Luigi *Galvani*] (1797) **1 :** a direct current of electricity esp. when produced by chemical action **2 :** the therapeutic use of direct electric current **3 :** vital or forceful activity

gal·va·nize \'gal-və-ˌnīz\ *vb* **-nized; -niz·ing** *vt* (1802) **1 a :** to subject to the action of an electric current esp. for the purpose of stimulating physiologically ⟨~ a muscle⟩ **b :** to stimulate or excite as if by an electric shock ⟨an issue that would ~ public opinion⟩ **2 :** to coat (iron or steel) with zinc; *esp* : to immerse in molten zinc to produce a coating of zinc-iron alloy ~ *vi* : to react as if stimulated by an electric shock ⟨they *galvanized* into action⟩ — **gal·va·ni·za·tion** \ˌgal-və-nə-'zā-shən\ *n* — **gal·va·niz·er** \'gal-və-ˌnī-zər\ *n*

galvano- *comb form* [*galvanic*] : galvanic current ⟨*galvano*meter⟩

gal·va·nom·e·ter \ˌgal-və-'nä-mə-tər\ *n* (1802) : an instrument for detecting or measuring a small electric current by movements of a magnetic needle or of a coil in a magnetic field — **gal·va·no·met·ric** \-nō-'me-trik\ *adj*

gal·va·no·scope \gal-'va-nə-ˌskōp, 'gal-və-nə-\ *n* (1832) : an instrument for detecting the presence and direction of an electric current by the deflection of a magnetic needle

¹**gam** \'gam\ *n* [prob. ultim. fr. Lingua Franca *gamba* leg, fr. It, fr. LL] (1781) *slang* : LEG

²**gam** *n* [perh. short for obs. *gammon* (talk)] (1846) **1 :** a visit or friendly conversation at sea or ashore esp. between whalers **2 :** a school of whales

³**gam** *vb* **gammed; gam·ming** *vi* (1849) : to engage in a gam ~ *vt* **1 :** to have a gam with **2 :** to spend or pass (as time) talking

gam- *or* **gamo-** *comb form* [NL, fr. Gk, marriage, fr. *gamos*, fr. *gamein* to marry] : united : joined ⟨*gamo*petalous⟩

gama grass \'ga-mə-\ *n* [prob. alter. of *grama*] (1833) : a tall coarse American grass (*Tripsacum dactyloides*) valuable for forage

ga·may \ga-'mā, 'ga-ˌmā\ *n, often cap* [F, fr. *Gamay*, village in Burgundy] (ca. 1941) : a light dry red table wine made from the same grape used for French Beaujolais ⟨~ rosé⟩

gam·ba \'gäm-bə, 'gam-\ *n* (1598) : VIOLA DA GAMBA

¹**gam·ba·do** \gam-'bä-(ˌ)dō\ *n, pl* **-does** *also* **-dos** [perh. modif. of It *gambale*, fr. *gamba* leg] (ca. 1656) : a horseman's legging

²**gambado** *n, pl* **-does** *also* **-dos** [modif. of F *gambade* — more at GAMBOL] (1820) **1 :** a spring of a horse **2 :** CAPER, GAMBOL

gam·bier *also* **gam·bir** \'gam-ˌbir\ *n* [Malay *gambir*] (1830) : a yellowish catechu that is obtained from a Malayan woody vine (*Uncaria gambir*) of the madder family and is used for chewing with the betel nut and for tanning and dyeing

gam·bit \'gam-bət\ *n* [It *gambetto*, lit., act of tripping someone, fr. *gamba* leg, fr. LL *gamba, camba*, fr. Gk *kampē* bend; prob. akin to Goth *hamfs* maimed, Lith *kampas* corner] (1656) **1 :** a chess opening in which a player risks one or more minor pieces to gain an advantage in position **2 a** (1) **:** a remark intended to start a conversation or make a telling point (2) **:** TOPIC **b :** a calculated move : STRATAGEM

¹**gam·ble** \'gam-bəl\ *vb* **gam·bled; gam·bling** \-b(ə-)liŋ\ [prob. back-formation fr. *gambler*, prob. alter. of obs. *gamner*, fr. obs. *gamen* (to play)] *vi* (ca. 1775) **1 a :** to play a game for money or property **b :** to bet on an uncertain outcome **2 :** to stake something on a contingency : take a chance ~ *vt* **1 :** to risk by gambling : WAGER **2 :** VENTURE, HAZARD — **gam·bler** \-blər\ *n*

²**gamble** *n* (1823) **1 a :** an act having an element of risk **b :** something chancy **2 :** the playing of a game of chance for stakes

gam·boge \gam-'bōj, -'büzh\ *n* [NL *gambogium*, alter. of *cambugium*, fr. or akin to Pg *Camboja* Cambodia] (1712) **1 :** an orange to brown gum resin from southeast Asian trees (genus *Garcinia*) of the Saint-John's-wort family that is used as a yellow pigment and cathartic **2 :** a strong yellow

¹**gam·bol** \'gam-bəl\ *vi* **-boled** *or* **-bolled; -bol·ing** *or* **-bol·ling** \-bə-liŋ *also* -bliŋ\ (1508) : to skip about in play : FRISK, FROLIC

²**gambol** *n* [modif. of MF *gambade* spring of a horse, gambol, prob. fr. OProv *camba* leg, fr. LL] (ca. 1510) : a skipping or leaping about in play

gam·brel \'gam-brəl\ *n* [ONF *gamberel*, fr. *gambe* leg, fr. LL *gamba*] (1547) : a stick or iron for suspending slaughtered animals

gambrel roof *n* (1765) : a roof with a lower steeper slope and an upper less steep one on each of its two sides — see ROOF illustration

gam·bu·sia \gam-'bü-zh(ē-)ə, -'byü-\ *n* [NL, modif. of AmerSp *gam-busino* gambusia] (ca. 1889) : any of a genus (*Gambusia*) of live-bearers (family Poeciliidae) introduced as exterminators of mosquito larvae in warm fresh waters

¹**game** \'gām\ *n* [ME, fr. OE *gamen*; akin to OHG *gaman* amusement] (bef. 12c) **1 a** (1) **:** activity engaged in for diversion or amusement : PLAY (2) **:** the equipment for a game **b :** often derisive or mocking jesting : FUN, SPORT ⟨make ~ of a nervous player⟩ **2 a :** a procedure or strategy for gaining an end : TACTIC **b :** an illegal or shady scheme or maneuver : RACKET **3 a** (1) **:** a physical or mental competition conducted according to rules with the participants in direct opposition to each other (2) **:** a division of a larger contest (3) **:** the number of points necessary to win (4) **:** points scored in certain card games (as in all fours) by a player whose cards count up the highest (5) **:** the manner of playing in a contest (6) **:** the set of rules governing a game (7) **:** a particular aspect or phase of play in a game or sport ⟨a football team's kicking ~⟩ **b** *pl* **:** organized athletics **c** (1) **:** a field of gainful activity : LINE ⟨the newspaper ~⟩ (2) **:** any activity undertaken or regarded as a contest involving rivalry, strategy, or struggle ⟨the dating ~⟩ ⟨the ~ of politics⟩; *also* : the course or period of such an activity ⟨got into aviation early in the ~⟩ (3) **:** area of expertise : SPECIALTY 3 ⟨comedy is not my ~⟩ **4 a** (1) **:** animals under pursuit or taken in hunting; *esp* : wild animals hunted for sport or food (2) **:** the flesh of game animals **b** *archaic* **:** PLUCK **c :** a target or object esp. of ridicule or attack — often used in the phrase *fair game* **syn** see FUN — **game·like** \-līk\ *adj*

²**game** *vb* **gamed; gam·ing** *vi* (1529) : to play for a stake ~ *vt, archaic* : to lose or squander by gambling

³**game** *adj* (1610) **1 a :** having or showing a resolute unyielding spirit ⟨~ to the end⟩ **b :** willing or ready to proceed ⟨were ~ for anything⟩ **2 :** of or relating to game ⟨~ laws⟩ — **game·ly** *adv* — **game·ness** *n*

⁴**game** *adj* [origin unknown] (ca. 1787) : LAME ⟨a ~ leg⟩

game ball *n* (1966) : a ball (as a football) presented to a player or coach in recognition of an outstanding contribution to a team victory

game bird *n* (1866) : a bird that may be legally hunted according to the laws esp. of a state of the U.S.

game·cock \'gām-ˌkäk\ *n* (1677) : a rooster of the domestic chicken trained for fighting

game fish *n* (1862) **1 :** a fish of a family (Salmonidae) including salmons, trouts, chars, and whitefishes **2 :** SPORT FISH; *also* : a fish made a legal catch by law

game·keep·er \'gām-ˌkē-pər\ *n* (ca. 1671) : a person in charge of the breeding and protection of game animals or birds on a private preserve

gam·elan \'ga-mə-ˌlan\ *n* [Jav] (1817) : an Indonesian orchestra made up esp. of percussion instruments (as gongs, xylophones, and drums)

game of chance *n* (ca. 1925) : a game (as a dice game) in which chance rather than skill determines the outcome

game plan *n* (1941) : a strategy for achieving an objective

game point *n* (ca. 1949) : a situation (as in tennis) in which one player will win the game by winning the next point; *also* : the point itself

gam·er \'gā-mər\ *n* (ca. 1630) : a player who is game; *esp* : an athlete who relishes competition

game show *n* (1958) : a television program on which contestants compete for prizes in a game (as a quiz)

games·man \'gāmz-mən, -ˌman\ *n* (1947) : one who practices gamesmanship; *also* : one who plays games

games·man·ship \'gāmz-mən-ˌship\ *n* (1947) **1 :** the art or practice of winning games by questionable expedients without actually violating the rules **2 :** the use of ethically dubious methods to gain an objective

game·some \'gām-səm\ *adj* [ME] (14c) : MERRY, FROLICSOME — **game·some·ly** *adv* — **game·some·ness** *n*

game·ster \'gām-stər\ *n* (1553) : one who plays games; *esp* : GAMBLER

gamet- *or* **gameto-** *comb form* [NL, fr. *gameta*] : gamete ⟨*gameto*phore⟩

gam·etan·gi·um \ˌga-mə-'tan-jē-əm\ *n, pl* **-gia** \-jē-ə\ [NL, fr. *gamet-* + Gk *angeion* vessel — more at ANGI-] (1886) : a cell or organ in which gametes are developed

gam·ete \'ga-ˌmēt *also* gə-'mēt\ *n* [NL *gameta*, fr. Gk *gametēs* husband, fr. *gamein* to marry] (1886) : a mature male or female germ cell usu. possessing a haploid chromosome set and capable of initiating formation of a new diploid individual by fusion with a gamete of the opposite sex — **ga·met·ic** \gə-'me-tik, -'mē-\ *adj* — **ga·met·i·cal·ly** \-ti-k(ə-)lē\ *adv*

game theory *n* (1949) : the analysis of a situation involving conflicting interests (as in business or military strategy) in terms of gains and losses among opposing players — **game theorist** *n*

ga·me·to·cyte \gə-'mē-tə-ˌsīt\ n [ISV] (1899) : a cell (as of a protozoan causing malaria) that divides to produce gametes
ga·me·to·gen·e·sis \gə-ˌmē-tə-'je-nə-səs, ˌga-mə-tə-\ n [NL] (ca. 1900) : the production of gametes — **ga·me·to·gen·ic** \-'je-nik\ or **gametog·e·nous** \ˌga-mə-'tä-jə-nəs\ adj
ga·me·to·phore \gə-'mē-tə-ˌfōr, -ˌfȯr\ n (1895) : a modified branch (as of a moss) bearing gametangia
ga·me·to·phyte \gə-'mē-tə-ˌfīt\ n [ISV] (ca. 1889) : the individual or generation of a plant exhibiting alternation of generations that bears sex organs — compare SPOROPHYTE — **ga·me·to·phyt·ic** \-ˌmē-tə-'fi-tik\ adj
-gamic adj comb form [ISV, fr. Gk -gamos -gamous] : having (such) reproductive organs ⟨cleistogamic⟩
gam·in \'ga-mən\ n [F] (1840) **1** : a boy who hangs around on the streets : URCHIN **2** : GAMINE
¹ga·mine \ga-'mēn, 'ga-ˌmēn\ n [F, fem. of gamin] (1889) **1** : a girl who hangs around on the streets **2** : a small playfully mischievous girl
²gamine adj (1925) : of, relating to, or suggesting a gamine
gam·ing \'gā-miŋ\ n (1501) **1** : the practice of gambling **2** : the playing of games that simulate actual conditions (as of business or war) esp. for training or testing purposes
¹gam·ma \'ga-mə\ n [ME, fr. LL, fr. Gk, of Sem origin; akin to Heb gīmel gimel] (15c) **1** : the 3d letter of the Greek alphabet — see ALPHABET table **2** : the degree of contrast of a developed photographic image or of a television image **3** : a unit of magnetic flux density equal to one nanotesla **4** : GAMMA RAY — usu. used as the attributive form of gamma ray ⟨∼ counter⟩ **5** : MICROGRAM
²gamma adj (1896) **1** : of, relating to, or being one of three or more closely related chemical substances **2** : third in position in the structure of an organic molecule from a particular group or atom — symbol γ
gam·ma–ami·no·bu·tyr·ic acid \ˌga-mə-ə-ˌmē-(ˌ)nō-byü-'tir-ik-, ˌga-mə-ˌa-mə-(ˌ)nō-\ n (1957) : an amino acid $C_4H_9NO_2$ that is a neurotransmitter in the central nervous system
gamma camera n (1964) : a camera that detects the radiation from a radioactive tracer injected into the body and is used esp. in medical diagnostic scanning
gamma globulin n (1937) **1 a** : a protein fraction of blood rich in antibodies **b** : a sterile solution of gamma globulin from pooled human blood administered esp. for passive immunity against measles, German measles, infectious hepatitis, or poliomyelitis **2** : any of numerous globulins of blood plasma or serum that have less electrophoretic mobility at alkaline pH than serum albumins, alpha globulins, or beta globulins and that include most antibodies — compare ANTIBODY
gamma radiation n (1904) : radiation composed of gamma rays
gamma ray n (1903) : a photon emitted spontaneously by a radioactive substance; also : a high-energy photon — usu. used in plural
gam·mer \'ga-mər\ n [alter. of godmother] (1575) archaic : an old woman — compare GAFFER
¹gam·mon \'ga-mən\ n [ME, fr. ONF gambon ham, fr. gambe leg — more at GAM] (15c) **1** chiefly Brit : HAM **2** **2** chiefly Brit **a** : a side of bacon **b** : the lower end of a side of bacon
²gammon n [perh. alter. of ME gamen game] (ca. 1734) **1** archaic : BACKGAMMON **2** : the winning of a backgammon game before the loser removes any men from the board
³gammon vt (1735) : to beat by scoring a gammon
⁴gammon vi (1789) **1** : to talk gammon **2** : PRETEND, FEIGN ∼ vt : DECEIVE, FOOL
⁵gammon n [obs. gammon (talk)] (1805) : talk intended to deceive : HUMBUG
gam·my \'ga-mē\ adj [perh. fr. ⁴game] (1870) Brit : LAME, GAME
gamo- — see GAM-
gamo·pet·al·ous \ˌga-mə-'pe-tᵊl-əs\ adj (1830) : having the corolla composed of united petals ⟨the morning glory is ∼⟩
-gamous adj comb form [Gk -gamos, fr. gamos marriage, fr. gamein to marry] **1** : characterized by having or practicing (such) a marriage or (such or so many) marriages ⟨exogamous⟩ **2** : -GAMIC ⟨heterogamous⟩
gamp \'gamp\ n [Sarah Gamp, nurse with a large umbrella in Martin Chuzzlewit by Charles Dickens] (1864) Brit : a large umbrella
gam·ut \'ga-mət\ n [ML gamma, lowest note of a medieval scale (fr. LL, 3d letter of the Greek alphabet) + ut ut] (15c) **1** : the whole series of recognized musical notes **2** : an entire range or series ⟨ran the ∼ from praise to contempt⟩ syn see RANGE
gamy or **gam·ey** \'gā-mē\ adj **gam·i·er; -est** (1844) **1** : BRAVE, PLUCKY — used esp. of animals **2 a** : having the flavor of game; esp : having the flavor of game near tainting **b** : SMELLY **3 a** : SORDID, SCANDALOUS ⟨give us all the ∼ details⟩ **b** : CORRUPT, DISREPUTABLE ⟨a ∼ character⟩ **c** : sexually suggestive : RACY ⟨∼ witticisms⟩ — **gam·i·ly** \-mə-lē\ adv — **gam·i·ness** \-mē-nəs\ n
-gamy n comb form [ME -gamie, fr. LL -gamia, fr. Gk, fr. gamein to marry] **1** : marriage ⟨exogamy⟩ **2** : union for propagation or reproduction ⟨allogamy⟩ **3** : possession of (such) reproductive organs or (such) a mode of fertilization ⟨cleistogamy⟩
gan past of GIN
ga·nache \(ˌ)gä-'näsh, gə-\ n [F, lit., jowl, fr. It ganascia, modif. of Gk gnathos jaw — more at -GNATHOUS] (1977) : a sweet creamy chocolate mixture used esp. as a filling or frosting
Gan·da \'gan-də, 'gän-\ n, pl **Ganda** or **Gandas** (1934) **1** : a member of a Bantu-speaking people of Uganda **2** : LUGANDA
¹gan·der \'gan-dər\ n [ME, fr. OE gandra; akin to OE gōs goose] (bef. 12c) **1** : the adult male goose **2** : SIMPLETON
²gander n [prob. fr. ¹gander; fr. the outstretched neck of a person craning to look at something] (ca. 1914) : LOOK, GLANCE ⟨take a ∼⟩
gan·dy dancer \'gan-dē-\ n [origin unknown] (1923) **1** : a laborer in a railroad section gang **2** : an itinerant or seasonal laborer
ga·nef \'gä-nəf\ n [Yiddish, fr. Heb gannābh thief] (1923) slang : THIEF, RASCAL
Ga·ne·lon \ˌga-nᵊl-'ōⁿ\ n [F] : the traitor in the Charlemagne romances who is responsible for the death of Roland
¹gang \'gaŋ\ n [ME, fr. OE gang; akin to Lith žengti to stride] (bef. 12c) Scot : GO
²gang n [ME, walking, journey, fr. OE; akin to OE gangan] (15c) **1 a** (1) : a set of articles : OUTFIT ⟨a ∼ of oars⟩ (2) : a combination of similar implements or devices arranged for convenience to act together

⟨a ∼ of saws⟩ **b** : GROUP: as (1) : a group of persons working together (2) : a group of persons working to unlawful or antisocial ends; esp : a band of antisocial adolescents **2** : a group of persons having informal and usu. close social relations
³gang vt (1856) **1 a** : to assemble or operate simultaneously as a group **b** : to arrange in or produce as a gang **2** : to attack in a gang ∼ vi : to move or act as a gang
gang bang n (1950) **1** : copulation by several persons in succession with the same passive partner — often considered vulgar **2** : GANG RAPE — often considered vulgar — **gang–bang** vb
gang–bang·er \'gaŋ-ˌbaŋ-ər\ n (ca. 1972) : a member of a street gang
gang·bust·er \'gaŋ-ˌbəs-tər\ n (1940) : one engaged in the aggressive breakup of organized criminal gangs — **like gangbusters** : with great or excessive force or aggressiveness ⟨came on like gangbusters⟩; also : with great speed or success ⟨making money like gangbusters — Martha Hume⟩
gangbusters also **gangbuster** adj (1971) : outstandingly excellent or successful ⟨doesn't make her a ∼ ... player —Tim Allis⟩ — **gangbusters** adv
gang·er \'gaŋ-ər\ n (1849) Brit : the foreman of a gang of workers
gang hook n (ca. 1934) : two or three fishhooks with their shanks joined together
gang·land \'gaŋ-ˌland, -lənd\ n, often attrib (1912) : the world of organized crime
gan·gling \'gaŋ-gliŋ, -glən\ adj [perh. alter. of Sc gangrel vagrant, lanky person] (ca. 1825) : loosely and awkwardly built : LANKY
gan·gli·on \'gaŋ-glē-ən\ n, pl **-glia** \-glē-ə\ also **-gli·ons** [LL, fr. Gk] (ca. 1681) **1** : a small cystic tumor connected either with a joint membrane or tendon sheath **2 a** : a mass of nerve tissue containing nerve cells external to the brain or spinal cord; also : NUCLEUS 2b **b** : something likened to a nerve ganglion — **gan·gli·on·at·ed** \'gaŋ-glē-ə-ˌnā-təd\ adj — **gan·gli·on·ic** \ˌgaŋ-glē-'ä-nik\ adj
gan·gli·o·side \'gaŋ-glē-ə-ˌsīd\ n [ISV ganglion + ²-ose + -ide] (1943) : any of a group of glycolipids that yield a hexose sugar on hydrolysis and are found esp. in the plasma membrane of cells of the gray matter
gan·gly \'gaŋ-glē\ adj **gan·gli·er; -est** (1872) : GANGLING
gang·plank \'gaŋ-ˌplaŋk\ n (1846) : a movable bridge used in boarding or leaving a ship at a pier
gang·plow \-ˌplau̇\ n (1850) : a plow designed to turn two or more furrows at one time
gang rape n (1968) : rape of one person by several attackers in succession — **gang–rape** vt
gang·rel \'gaŋ-(ə-)rəl\ n [ME, fr. gangen to go, fr. OE gangan] (14c) Scot : VAGRANT
¹gan·grene \'gaŋ-ˌgrēn, gaŋ-', 'gaŋ-ˌ, gan-'\ n [L gangraena, fr. Gk gangraina; akin to Gk gran to gnaw] (1543) **1** : local death of soft tissues due to loss of blood supply **2** : pervasive decay or corruption : ROT ⟨moral ∼⟩ — **gan·gre·nous** \'gaŋ-grə-nəs\ adj
²gangrene vb **gan·grened; gan·gren·ing** vt (1607) : to make gangrenous ∼ vi : to become gangrenous
gang·ster \'gaŋ-stər\ n (1896) : a member of a gang of criminals : RACKETEER — **gang·ster·dom** \-dəm\ n — **gang·ster·ish** \-stə-rish\ adj — **gang·ster·ism** \-stə-ˌri-zəm\ n
gang–tackle \'gaŋ-ˌta-kəl\ vt (1951) : to bring down (a ballcarrier in football) with several tacklers
gangue \'gaŋ\ n [F, fr. G Gang vein of metal, fr. OHG, act of going] (1809) : the worthless rock or vein matter in which valuable metals or minerals occur
gang up n (1925) **1** : to make a joint assault ⟨ganged up on him and beat him up⟩ **2** : to combine for a specific purpose ⟨ganged up to raise prices⟩ **3** : to exert group pressure ⟨the class ganged up against the teacher⟩
gang·way \'gaŋ-ˌwā\ n (bef. 12c) **1** : PASSAGEWAY; esp : a temporary way of planks **2 a** : either of the sides of the upper deck of a ship **b** : the opening by which a ship is boarded **c** : GANGPLANK **3** Brit : AISLE **4 a** : a cross aisle dividing the front benches from the backbenches in the British House of Commons **b** : an aisle in the British House of Commons that separates government and opposition benches **5** : a clear passage through a crowd — often used as an interjection
gan·is·ter also **gan·nis·ter** \'ga-nə-stər\ n [origin unknown] (1811) : a fine-grained quartzite used in the manufacture of refractory brick
gan·ja \'gän-jə, 'gan-\ n [Hindi gājā, fr. Skt gañjā hemp] (1689) : a potent and selected preparation of marijuana used esp. for smoking; broadly : MARIJUANA
gan·net \'ga-nət\ n, pl **gannets** also **gannet** [ME ganet, fr. OE ganot; akin to OE gōs goose] (bef. 12c) : any of a genus (Morus of the family Sulidae) of large fish-eating seabirds that breed in colonies chiefly on offshore islands
¹gan·oid \'ga-ˌnȯid\ adj [ultim. fr. Gk ganos brightness; akin to Gk gēthein to rejoice — more at JOY] (ca. 1847) : of, having, or being fish scales consisting of bone and an outer shiny layer resembling enamel; also : relating to or being fish with ganoid scales
²ganoid n (ca. 1839) : a fish (as a sturgeon or gar) with ganoid scales
gante·lope or **gant·lope** \'gant-ˌlōp\ n [modif. of Sw gatlopp, fr. OSw gatulop, fr. gata road + lop course] (1646) archaic : ²GAUNTLET
gant·let \'gȯnt-lət, 'gänt-\ n, var of GAUNTLET
gan·try \'gan-trē\ n, pl **gantries** [perh. modif. of ONF gantier, fr. L cantherius trellis] (ca. 1574) **1** : a frame for supporting barrels **2** : a frame structure raised on side supports so as to span over or around something: as **a** : a platform made to carry a traveling crane and supported by towers or side frames running on parallel tracks; also : a movable structure with platforms at different levels used for erecting and servicing rockets before launching **b** : a structure spanning several railroad tracks and displaying signals for each
Gan·y·mede \'ga-ni-ˌmēd\ n [L Ganymedes, fr. Gk Ganymēdēs] : a beautiful youth in classical mythology carried off to Olympus to be the cupbearer of the gods

---

\ə\ abut \ᵊ\ kitten, F table \ər\ further \a\ ash \ā\ ace \ä\ mop, mar
\au̇\ out \ch\ chin \e\ bet \ē\ easy \g\ go \i\ hit \ī\ ice \j\ job
\ŋ\ sing \ō\ go \ȯ\ law \ȯi\ boy \th\ thin \t̲h\ the \ü\ loot \u̇\ foot
\y\ yet \zh\ vision \á, k̲, ⁿ, œ, œ̄, ue, ᵁE, ᴿ\ see Guide to Pronunciation

gaol \'jā(ə)l\, **gaol·er** \'jā-lər\ *chiefly Brit var of* JAIL, JAILER
¹gap \'gap\ *n* [ME, fr. ON, chasm, hole; akin to ON *gapa* to gape] (14c)
1 a : a break in a barrier (as a wall, hedge, or line of military defense)
b : an assailable position **2 a :** a mountain pass **b :** RAVINE **3**
: SPARK GAP **4 a :** a separation in space **b :** an incomplete or deficient area ⟨a ~ in her knowledge⟩ **5 :** a break in continuity : HIATUS
6 : a break in the vascular cylinder of a plant where a vascular trace
departs from the central cylinder **7 :** lack of balance : DISPARITY ⟨the
~ between imports and exports⟩ **8 :** a wide difference in character or
attitude ⟨the generation ~⟩ **9 :** a problem caused by some disparity
⟨a communication ~⟩ ⟨credibility ~⟩ — **gap·py** \'ga-pē\ *adj*
²gap *vb* **gapped; gap·ping** *vt* (1879) **1 :** to make an opening in **2 :** to
adjust the space between the electrodes of (a spark plug) ~ *vi* **:** to fall
or stand open
¹gape \'gāp *sometimes* 'gap\ *vi* **gaped; gap·ing** [ME, fr. ON *gapa;* perh.
akin to L *hiare* to gape, yawn — more at YAWN] (13c) **1 a :** to open
the mouth wide **b :** to open or part widely ⟨holes gaped in the pavement⟩ **2 :** to gaze stupidly or in openmouthed surprise or wonder **3**
: YAWN — **gap·ing·ly** \'gā-piŋ-lē, 'ga-piŋ-\ *adv*
²gape *n* (1535) **1 :** an act of gaping : **a :** YAWN **b :** an openmouthed
stare **2 :** an unfilled space or extent **3 a :** the median margin-to-
margin length of the open mouth **b :** the line along which the mandibles of a bird close **c :** the width of an opening **4** *pl but sing in constr*
a : a disease of birds and esp. young birds in which gapeworms invade
and irritate the trachea **b :** a fit of yawning
gap·er \'gā-pər *sometimes* 'ga-pər\ *n* (ca. 1637) **1 :** one that gapes **2**
: any of several large sluggish burrowing clams (families Myacidae and
Mactridae) including several used for food
gape·worm \'gāp-,wərm *sometimes* 'gap-\ *n* (1873) **:** a nematode worm
(*Syngamus trachea*) that causes gapes in birds
gap·ing \'gā-piŋ\ *adj* (1588) **:** wide open ⟨a ~ hole⟩
gap junction *n* (1967) **:** an area of contact between adjacent cells characterized by modification of the cell membranes for intercellular communication or transfer of low molecular-weight substances
gapped scale *n* (1910) **:** a musical scale derived from a larger system of
tones by omitting certain tones
gap–toothed \'gap-,tütht\ *adj* (1567) **:** having gaps between the teeth
¹gar \'gär\ *interj* [euphemism for *God*] (1598) — used as a mild oath in
the phrase *by gar*
²gar *n* [short for *garfish*] (1765) **:** any of various fishes that have an
elongate body resembling that of a pike and long and narrow jaws: as
a : NEEDLEFISH 1 **b :** any of several predaceous No. American freshwater bony fishes (family Lepisosteidae) with heavy ganoid scales
¹ga·rage \gə-'räzh, -'räj; *chiefly NewEng* -'räzh, -'raj; *Canad also* -'razh,
-'raj; *Brit usu* 'gar-(,)äzh, -(,)äj, -ij\ *n* [F, act of docking, garage, fr.
garer to dock, of Gmc origin; akin to OHG bi*warōn* to protect — more
at WARE] (1902) **:** a shelter or repair shop for automotive vehicles
²garage *vt* **ga·raged; ga·rag·ing** (1905) **:** to keep or put in a garage
ga·rage·man \-,man\ *n* (1919) **:** one who works in a garage
garage sale *n* (1964) **:** a sale of used household or personal articles (as
furniture, tools, or clothing) held on the seller's own premises
ga·ram ma·sa·la \gä-'räm-mə-'sä-lə\ *n* [Hindi *garam masālā,* lit., hot
spices] (1970) **:** a pungent and aromatic mixture of ground spices used
in Indian cooking
Ga·rand rifle \gə-'rand-, 'gar-ənd-\ *n* [John C. *Garand*] (1931) **:** M1
RIFLE
¹garb \'gärb\ *n* [MF or OIt; MF *garbe* graceful contour, grace, fr. OIt
garbo grace] (1599) **1** *pl:* FASHION, MANNER **2 a :** a style of apparel
b : outward form : APPEARANCE
²garb *vt* (1846) **:** to cover with or as if with clothing ⟨~ed in T-shirt
and blue jeans⟩
gar·bage \'gär-bij\ *n* [ME, offal] (15c) **1 a :** food waste **b :** discarded or useless material **2 a :** TRASH 1b **b :** inaccurate or useless
data
gar·bage·man \-,man\ *n* (1888) **:** one who collects and hauls away
garbage
gar·ban·zo \gär-'bän-(,)zō, *also* -'ban-\ *n, pl* **-zos** [Sp] (1759) **:** CHICK-
PEA
garbanzo bean *n* (1944) **:** CHICKPEA
¹gar·ble \'gär-bəl\ *vt* **gar·bled; gar·bling** \-b(ə-)liŋ\ [ME *garbelen,* fr.
OIt *garbellare* to sift, fr. Ar *gharbala,* fr. LL *cribellare,* fr. *cribellum*
sieve; akin to L *cernere* to sift — more at CERTAIN] (15c) **1** *archaic*
: CULL **2 :** to sift impurities from **3 a :** to so alter or distort as to
create a wrong impression or change the meaning ⟨~ a story⟩ **b :** to
introduce textual error into (a message) by inaccurate encipherment,
transmission, or decipherment — **gar·bler** \-b(ə-)lər\ *n*
²garble *n* (1502) **1 :** the impurities removed from spices in sifting **2**
: an act or an instance of garbling
gar·board \'gär-,bōrd, -,bȯrd\ *n* [obs. D *gaarboord*] (1627) **:** the strake
next to a ship's keel
gar·boil \-,bȯil\ *n* [MF *garbouil,* fr. OIt *garbuglio*] (1548) *archaic* **:** a
confused disordered state : TURMOIL
gar·çon \gär-'sōⁿ\ *n, pl* **garçons** \-'sōⁿ(z)\ [F, boy, servant, fr. OF, of
Gmc origin; akin to OHG *hrechjo* fugitive — more at WRETCH] (1788)
: WAITER
garde–man·ger \,gärd-mäⁿ-'zhā\ *n, pl* **garde–mangers** \-'zhā(z)\ [F,
lit., one who keeps food] (1928) **:** a cook who specializes in the preparation of cold foods (as meats, fish, and salads)
¹gar·den \'gär-dᵊn\ *n* [ME *gardin,* fr. ONF, of Gmc origin; akin to
OHG *gart* enclosure — more at YARD] (13c) **1 a :** a plot of ground
where herbs, fruits, flowers, or vegetables are cultivated **b :** a rich
well-cultivated region **c :** a container (as a window box) planted with
usu. a variety of small plants **2 a :** a public recreation area or park
usu. ornamented with plants and trees ⟨a botanical ~⟩ **b :** an open-
air eating or drinking place **c :** a large hall for public entertainment
— **gar·den·ful** \-,fúl\ *n*
²garden *vb* **gar·dened; gar·den·ing** \'gär-dᵊn-iŋ, 'gärd-niŋ\ *vi* (1577)
: to lay out or work in a garden ~ *vt* **:** to make into a garden **2**
: to ornament with gardens — **gar·den·er** \'gär-dᵊn-ər, 'gärd-nər\ *n*
³garden *adj* (1622) **1 :** of, relating to, used in, or frequenting a garden
2 a : of a kind grown in the open as distinguished from one more
delicate ⟨~ plant⟩ **b :** commonly found : GARDEN-VARIETY
garden apartment *n* (1946) **:** a multiple-unit low-rise dwelling having
considerable lawn or garden space

garden city *n* (1898) **:** a planned residential community with park and
planted areas
garden cress *n* (1577) **:** an annual herb (*Lepidium sativum*) of the
mustard family sometimes cultivated for its pungent basal leaves
garden heliotrope *n* (ca. 1902) **:** a tall rhizomatous Old World valerian (*Valeriana officinalis*) widely cultivated for its fragrant tiny flowers
and for its roots which yield the drug valerian
gar·de·nia \gär-'dē-nyə\ *n* [NL, fr. Alexander *Garden* †1791 Scot.
naturalist] (1760) **:** any of a large genus (*Gardenia*) of Old World tropical trees and shrubs of the madder family with showy fragrant white or
yellow flowers
Garden of Eden (1535) **:** EDEN
garden rocket *n* (1832) **:** ARUGULA
garden–variety *adj* (1928) **:** ORDINARY, COMMONPLACE
garde·robe \'gär-,drōb\ *n* [ME, fr. MF; akin to ONF *warderobe* wardrobe] (15c) **1 :** a wardrobe or its contents **2 :** a private room : BED-
ROOM **3 :** PRIVY 1
gar·dy·loo \,gär-dē-'lü\ *interj* [perh. fr. F *garde à l'eau!* look out for the
water!] (1622) — used in Edinburgh as a warning cry when it was
customary to throw slops from the windows into the streets
Gar·eth \'gar-əth\ *n* **:** a knight of the Round Table and nephew of
King Arthur
gar·fish \'gär-,fish\ *n* [ME *garfysshe*] (15c) **:** GAR
Gar·gan·tua \gär-'gan(t)-sh(ə-)wə\ *n* [F] **:** a gigantic king in Rabelais'
Gargantua having a great capacity for food and drink
gar·gan·tuan \-wən\ *adj, often cap* [*Gargantua*] (1596) **:** of tremendous
size or volume : GIGANTIC, COLOSSAL ⟨~ waterfalls⟩
¹gar·gle \'gär-gəl\ *vb* **gar·gled; gar·gling** \-g(ə-)liŋ\ [MF *gargouiller,*
of imit. origin] *vt* (1527) **1 a :** to hold (a liquid) in the mouth or
throat and agitate with air from the lungs **b :** to cleanse or disinfect
(the oral cavity) in this manner **2 :** to utter with a gargling sound ~
vi **1 :** to use a gargle **2 :** to speak or sing as if gargling
²gargle *n* (1657) **1 :** a liquid used in gargling **2 :** a sound of or like
that of gargling
gar·goyle \'gär-,gȯil\ *n* [ME *gargoyl,* fr. MF
gargouille; akin to MF *gargouiller*] (13c) **1 a**
: a spout in the form of a grotesque human or
animal figure projecting from a roof gutter to
throw rainwater clear of a building **b :** a grotesquely carved figure **2 :** a person with an
ugly face — **gar·goyled** \-,gȯild\ *adj*
gar·i·bal·di \,gar-ə-'bȯl-dē\ *n* (1862) **:** a woman's blouse copied from the red shirt worn by
the Italian patriot Garibaldi
ga·rigue \gə-'rēg\ *n* [F] (1896) **:** a low open
scrubland with many evergreen shrubs, low
trees, aromatic herbs, and bunchgrasses found
in poor or dry soil in the Mediterranean region

gargoyle 1a

gar·ish \'gar-ish, 'ger-\ *adj* [origin unknown] (1545) **1 :** clothed in
vivid colors **2 a :** excessively vivid : FLASHY **b :** offensively or distressingly bright : GLARING **3 :** tastelessly showy *syn* see GAUDY —
gar·ish·ly *adv* — **gar·ish·ness** *n*
¹gar·land \'gär-lənd\ *n* [ME, fr. MF *garlande*] (14c) **1 :** WREATH,
CHAPLET **2 :** ANTHOLOGY, COLLECTION
²garland *vt* (15c) **1 :** to form into a garland **2 :** to adorn with or as if
with a garland
gar·lic \'gär-lik\ *n* [ME *garlek,* fr. OE *gārlēac,* fr. *gār* spear + *lēac* leek
— more at GORE] (bef. 12c) **1 :** a European bulbous herb (*Allium
sativum*) of the lily family widely cultivated for its pungent compound
bulbs much used in cookery; *broadly* **:** any plant of the same genus **2**
: a bulb of garlic — **gar·licky** \-li-kē\ *adj*
gar·licked \'gär-likt\ *adj* (1950) **:** containing or prepared with garlic
garlic salt *n* (1927) **:** a seasoning of ground dried garlic and salt
¹gar·ment \'gär-mənt\ *n* [ME, fr. MF *garnement,* fr. OF, fr. *garnir* to
equip — more at GARNISH] (14c) **:** an article of clothing
²garment *vt* (1547) **:** to clothe with or as if with a garment
garment bag *n* (1927) **:** a bag used by travelers that folds in half and
has a center handle for easy carrying
¹gar·ner \'gär-nər\ *n* [ME, fr. OF *gernier, grenier,* fr. L *granarium,* fr.
granum grain — more at CORN] (12c) **1 a :** GRANARY **b :** a grain bin
2 : something that is collected : ACCUMULATION
²garner *vt* **gar·nered; gar·ner·ing** \'gärn-riŋ, 'gär-nə-\ (14c) **1 a**
: to gather into storage **b :** to deposit as if in a granary ⟨volumes in
which he has ~ed the fruits of his lifetime labors —Reinhold Niebuhr⟩
2 a : to acquire by effort : EARN **b :** ACCUMULATE, COLLECT
gar·net \'gär-nət\ *n* [ME *grenat,* fr. MF, fr. *grenat,* adj., red like a
pomegranate, fr. (*pomme*) *grenate* pomegranate] (14c) **1 :** a brittle
and more or less transparent usu. red silicate mineral that has a vitreous luster, occurs mainly in crystals but also in massive form and in
grains, is found commonly in gneiss and mica schist, and is used as a
semiprecious stone and as an abrasive **2 :** a variable color averaging a
dark red — **gar·net·if·er·ous** \,gär-nə-'ti-f(ə-)rəs\ *adj*
garnet paper *n* (ca. 1902) **:** an abrasive paper with crushed garnet as
the abrasive
gar·ni·er·ite \'gär-nē-ə-,rīt\ *n* [Jules *Garnier* †1904 Fr. geologist]
(1875) **:** a soft mineral consisting of hydrous nickel magnesium silicate
and constituting an important ore of nickel
¹gar·nish \'gär-nish\ *vt* [ME, fr. MF *garniss-,* stem of *garnir* to warn,
equip, garnish, of Gmc origin; akin to OHG *warnōn* to take heed —
more at WARN] (14c) **1 a :** DECORATE, EMBELLISH **b :** to add decorative or savory touches to (food or drink) **2 :** to equip with accessories
: FURNISH **3 :** GARNISHEE *syn* see ADORN
²garnish *n* (1596) **1 :** EMBELLISHMENT, ORNAMENT **2 :** something (as
lemon wedges or parsley) used to garnish food or drink **3 a :** an
unauthorized fee formerly extorted from a new inmate of an English
jail **b :** a similar payment required of a new worker
¹gar·nish·ee \,gär-nə-'shē\ *n* (1627) **:** a person who is served with a
legal process of garnishment
²garnishee *vt* **-eed; -ee·ing** (ca. 1876) **1 :** to serve with a garnishment
2 : to take (as a debtor's wages) by legal authority
gar·nish·ment \'gär-nish-mənt\ *n* (1550) **1 :** GARNISH **2 :** a legal
summons or warning concerning the attachment of property to satisfy
a debt **3 :** a stoppage of a specified sum from wages to satisfy a creditor

gar·ni·ture \'gär-ni-chər, -nə-ˌchu̇r\ n [MF, equipment, alter. of OF *garnesture*, fr. *garnir*] (1667) 1 : EMBELLISHMENT, TRIMMING 2 : a set of decorative objects (as vases, urns, or clocks)

gar·pike \'gär-ˌpīk\ n (1776) : GAR b

gar·ret \'gar-ət\ n [ME *garette* watchtower, fr. MF *garite* watchtower, refuge, fr. OF *garir*] (14c) : a room or unfinished part of a house just under the roof

¹gar·ri·son \'gar-ə-sən\ n [ME *garisoun* protection, fr. OF *garison*, fr. *garir* to protect, of Gmc origin; akin to OHG *werien* to defend — more at WEIR] (15c) 1 : a military post; *esp* : a permanent military installation 2 : the troops stationed at a garrison

²garrison vt **gar·ri·soned; gar·ri·son·ing** \'gar-ə-s(ə-)niŋ\ (1569) 1 : to station troops in 2 a : to assign as a garrison b : to occupy with troops

garrison cap n (1944) : a visorless folding cap worn as part of a military uniform — compare SERVICE CAP

Gar·ri·son finish \'gar-ə-sən-\ n [prob. fr. Edward "Snapper" *Garrison*, 19th cent. Am. jockey] (1935) : a finish in which the winner comes from behind at the end

garrison house n (1676) 1 : a house fortified against Indian attack 2 : BLOCKHOUSE 3 : a house having the second story overhanging the first in the front

garrison state n (1937) : a state organized to serve primarily its own need for military security; *also* : a state maintained by military power

gar·ron \'gar-ən, gə-'rȯn\ n [Ir *gearrán* & ScGael *gearran*, gelding] (1540) *Scot & Irish* : a small sturdy workhorse

¹gar·rote or **ga·rotte** \gə-'rät, -'rōt; 'gar-ət\ n [Sp *garrote*] (1622) 1 a : a method of execution by strangulation b : the apparatus used 2 : an implement (as a wire with a handle at each end) for strangulation

²garrote or **garotte** vt **gar·rot·ed** or **ga·rott·ed; gar·rot·ing** or **ga·rott·ing** (1851) : to strangle with or as if with a garrote — **gar·rot·er** n

gar·ru·li·ty \gə-'rü-lə-tē, ga-\ n (1581) : the quality or state of being garrulous

gar·ru·lous \'gar-ə-ləs *also* 'gar-yə-\ adj [L *garrulus*, fr. *garrire* to chatter — more at CARE] (ca. 1611) 1 : given to prosy, rambling, or tedious loquacity : pointlessly or annoyingly talkative : WORDY 1 ⟨~ speeches⟩ *syn* see TALKATIVE — **gar·ru·lous·ly** adv — **gar·ru·lous·ness** n

¹gar·ter \'gär-tər\ n [ME, fr. ONF *gartier*, fr. *garet* bend of the knee, of Celt origin; akin to W *gar* shank] (14c) 1 a : a band worn to hold up a stocking or sock b : a band worn to hold up a shirt sleeve c : a strap hanging from a girdle or corset to support a stocking 2 cap a : the British Order of the Garter; *also* : the blue velvet garter that is its badge b : membership in the order

²garter vt (15c) : to support with or as if with a garter

garter snake n (1769) : any of a genus (*Thamnophis*) of harmless viviparous American snakes with longitudinal stripes on the back

garth \'gärth\ n [ME, fr. ON *garthr* yard; akin to OHG *gart* enclosure — more at YARD] (14c) : a small yard or enclosure : CLOSE

gar·vey \'gär-vē\ n, pl **garveys** [prob. fr. the name *Garvey*] (ca. 1896) : a small scow esp. of the New Jersey coast

¹gas \'gas\ n, pl **gas·es** *also* **gas·ses** [NL, alter. of L *chaos* space, chaos] (1779) 1 : a fluid (as air) that has neither independent shape nor volume but tends to expand indefinitely 2 a : a combustible gas or gaseous mixture for fuel or lighting; *esp* : NATURAL GAS b : a gaseous product of digestion; *also* : discomfort from this c : a gas or gaseous mixture used to produce anesthesia d : a substance that can be used to produce a poisonous, asphyxiating, or irritant atmosphere 3 : empty talk : BOMBAST 4 : GASOLINE; *also* : the accelerator pedal of an automotive vehicle 5 : driving force : ENERGY ⟨I was young, and full of ~ —H. L. Mencken⟩ ⟨ran out of ~ in the seventh inning⟩ 6 *slang* : something that gives pleasure : DELIGHT ⟨the party was a ~⟩

²gas vb **gassed; gas·sing** vi (1852) 1 : to talk idly or garrulously 2 : to give off gas 3 : to fill the tank (as of an automobile) with gasoline — usu. used with *up* ~ vt 1 : to supply with gas or esp. gasoline ⟨~ up the car⟩ 2 a : to treat chemically with gas b : to poison or otherwise affect adversely with gas 3 *slang* : to please greatly

gas·bag \'gas-ˌbag\ n (1827) 1 : a bag for holding gas 2 : an idle or garrulous talker

gas chamber n (1945) : a chamber in which prisoners are executed by poison gas

gas chromatograph n (1958) : an instrument used to separate a sample into components in gas chromatography

gas chromatography n (1952) : chromatography in which the sample mixture is vaporized and injected into a stream of carrier gas (as nitrogen or helium) moving through a column containing a stationary phase composed of a liquid or particulate solid and is separated into its component compounds according to their affinity for the stationary phase — **gas chromatographic** adj

gas·con \'gas-kən\ n (14c) 1 cap a : a native of Gascony b : the Romance speech of Gascony 2 : a boastful swaggering person — **Gascon** adj

gas·co·nade \ˌgas-kə-'nād\ n [F *gasconnade*, fr. *gasconner* to boast, fr. *gascon* gascon, boaster] (1709) : BRAVADO, BOASTING — **gasconade** vi — **gas·con·ad·er** n

gas·eous \'ga-sē-əs, 'ga-shəs\ adj (1799) 1 : having the form of or being gas; *also* : of or relating to gases 2 a : lacking substance or solidity b : GASSY 3 ⟨trick phrases and ~ circumlocutions —Edwin Newman⟩ — **gas·eous·ness** n

gas fitter n (ca. 1858) : a worker who installs or repairs gas pipes and appliances

gas gangrene n (1914) : progressive gangrene marked by impregnation of the dead and dying tissue with gas and caused by one or more toxin-producing clostridia

gas–guz·zler \'gas-ˌgəz-lər, -ˌgə-zə-\ n (1973) : a usu. large automobile that gets relatively poor mileage — **gas–guz·zling** \-liŋ\ adj

¹gash \'gash\ n (1548) 1 : a deep long cut in flesh 2 : a deep narrow depression or cut ⟨cut a ~ through the forest⟩ ⟨a ~ in the hull⟩

²gash vb [alter. of ME *garsen*, fr. ONF *garser*, fr. (assumed) VL *charissare*, fr. Gk *charassein* to scratch, engrave] vt (1570) : to make a gash in ~ vi : to make a gash : CUT

³gash adj [origin unknown] (1706) 1 *chiefly Scot* : KNOWING, WITTY 2 *chiefly Scot* : well-dressed : TRIM

gas·hold·er \'gas-ˌhōl-dər\ n (1802) : a container for gas; *esp* : a huge cylindrical tank for storing fuel gas under pressure

gas·house \-ˌhau̇s\ n (1880) : GASWORKS

gas·i·fi·ca·tion \ˌga-sə-fə-'kā-shən\ n (1812) : conversion into gas; *esp* : conversion of coal into natural gas

gas·i·fy \'ga-sə-ˌfī\ vb **-i·fied; -i·fy·ing** vt (ca. 1828) : to convert into gas ⟨~ coal⟩ ~ vi : to become gaseous — **gas·i·fi·er** \'ga-sə-ˌfī(-ə)r\ n

gas·ket \'gas-kət\ n [perh. modif. of F *garcette*] (ca. 1889) : a material (as rubber) or a member (as an O-ring) used to make a joint fluid-tight

gas·kin \'gas-kən\ n [prob. short for *galligaskins*] (1573) 1 pl, obs : HOSE, BREECHES 2 : a part of the hind leg of a quadruped between the stifle and the hock — see HORSE illustration

gas·light \'gas-ˌlīt, -'līt\ n (1808) 1 : light made by burning illuminating gas 2 : a gas flame or gas lighting fixture

gas–liquid chromatography n (1952) : gas chromatography in which the stationary phase is a liquid — **gas–liquid chromatographic** adj

gas·lit \-ˌlit, -'lit\ adj (1837) : illuminated by gaslight

gas log n (1885) : a hollow perforated imitation log used as a gas burner in a fireplace

gas mask n (1915) : a mask connected to a chemical air filter and used to protect the face and lungs from toxic gases; *broadly* : RESPIRATOR 1

gas·o·gene \'ga-sə-ˌjēn\ n [F *gazogène*, fr. *gaz* gas (fr. NL *gas*) + *-o-* + *-gène* -gen] (ca. 1853) 1 : a portable apparatus for carbonating liquids 2 : an apparatus carried by a vehicle to produce gas for fuel by partial burning of charcoal or wood

gas·o·hol \'ga-sə-ˌhȯl\ n [blend of *gasoline* and *alcohol*] (1977) : a fuel consisting of a blend usu. of 10 percent ethyl alcohol and 90 percent gasoline

gas oil n (1901) : a hydrocarbon oil used as a fuel oil; *esp* : a petroleum distillate intermediate in boiling range and viscosity between kerosene and lubricating oil

gas·olier \ˌga-sə-'lir\ n [alter. of *gaselier*, fr. *gas* + *-elier* (as in *chandelier*)] (1905) : a gaslight chandelier

gas·o·line \ˌga-sə-'lēn, 'ga-sə-ˌlēn, ˌga-sə-' *also* -zə-\ n [¹*gas* + ²*-ol* + ²*-ine* or *-ene*] (1865) : a volatile flammable liquid hydrocarbon mixture used as a fuel esp. for internal combustion engines and usu. blended from several products of natural gas and petroleum — **gas·o·lin·ic** \ˌga-sə-'lē-nik, -'li-\ adj

gas·om·e·ter \ga-'sä-mə-tər\ n [F *gazomètre*, fr. *gaz* + *-o-* + *-mètre* -meter] (1808) 1 : GASHOLDER 2 : a laboratory apparatus for holding and measuring gases

gas–operated adj (1944) *of a firearm* : using part of the force of expanding propellant gases to operate the action

gasp \'gasp\ vb [ME; akin to ON *geispa* to yawn] vi (14c) 1 : to catch the breath convulsively and audibly (as with shock) 2 : to breathe laboriously ~ vt : to utter in a gasping manner — **gasp** n

gasp·er \'gäs-pə(r)\ n (1914) *slang Brit* : CIGARETTE

gas plant n (ca. 1909) : FRAXINELLA

gas ring n (1901) : a ring-shaped portable gas burner for cooking

gassed \'gast\ adj (ca. 1925) : DRUNK 1

gas·ser \'ga-sər\ n (ca. 1944) *slang* : something outstanding

gas station n (1925) : SERVICE STATION 1

gas·sy \'ga-sē\ adj **gas·si·er; -est** (1757) 1 : full of or containing gas 2 : having the characteristics of gas 3 : characterized by many words but little content : emptily verbose — **gas·si·ly** \'ga-sə-lē\ adv — **gas·si·ness** n

gast \'gast\ vt [ME, fr. *gast*, *gost* ghost — more at GHOST] (14c) *obs* : SCARE ⟨~ed by the noise I made, full suddenly he fled —Shak.⟩

Gast·ar·beit·er \'gast-ˌ(y)ār-ˌbī-tər\ n, pl **Gastarbeiter** *also* **Gastarbeiters** [G, fr. *Gast* guest + *Arbeiter* worker] (1970) : a foreign worker esp. in Germany

gas·ter \'gas-tər\ n [Gk *gastēr*] (ca. 1909) : the enlarged part of the abdomen behind the pedicel in hymenopterous insects (as ants)

gas·tight \'gas-'tīt\ adj (1831) : impervious to gas — **gas·tight·ness** n

gast·ness \'gas(t)-nəs\ n (14c) *obs* : FRIGHT, TERROR

gastr- or **gastro-** *also* **gastri-** comb form [Gk, fr. *gastr-*, *gastēr*] 1 : stomach ⟨*gastrectomy*⟩ 2 : gastric and ⟨*gastrointestinal*⟩

gas·trea *also* **gas·traea** \ga-'strē-ə\ n [NL, fr. Gk *gastr-*, *gastēr*] (1879) : a hypothetical metazoan ancestral form corresponding in organization to a simple invaginated gastrula

gas·trec·to·my \ga-'strek-tə-mē\ n, pl **-mies** [ISV] (1886) : surgical removal of all or part of the stomach

gas·tric \'gas-trik\ adj [Gk *gastr-*, *gastēr*, alter. of (assumed) Gk *grastēr*, fr. Gk *gran* to gnaw, eat] (1656) : of or relating to the stomach

gastric gland n (1900) : any of various glands in the walls of the stomach that secrete gastric juice

gastric juice n (ca. 1736) : a thin watery acid digestive fluid secreted by glands in the mucous membrane of the stomach

gastric ulcer n (ca. 1910) : a peptic ulcer situated in the stomach

gas·trin \'gas-trən\ n (1905) : any of various polypeptide hormones that are secreted by the gastric mucosa and induce secretion of gastric juice

gas·tri·tis \ga-'strī-təs\ n (1806) : inflammation esp. of the mucous membrane of the stomach

gas·troc·ne·mi·us \ˌgas-ˌträk-'nē-mē-əs, -trək-\ n, pl **-mii** \-mē-ˌī\ [NL, fr. Gk *gastroknēmē* calf of the leg, fr. *gastr-* + *knēmē* shank — more at HAM] (1676) : the largest and most superficial muscle of the calf of the leg arising by two heads from the condyles of the femur and attaching to a tendon that becomes part of the Achilles tendon

gas·tro·du·o·de·nal \ˌgas-trō-ˌd(y)ü-ə-'dē-n'l, -d(y)ü-'äd-ᵊn-əl\ adj (1854) : of, relating to, or involving the stomach and the duodenum

gas·tro·en·ter·i·tis \ˌgas-trō-ˌen-tə-'rī-təs\ n (ca. 1829) : inflammation of the lining membrane of the stomach and the intestines

gas·tro·en·ter·ol·o·gy \-ˌen-tə-'rä-lə-jē\ n [ISV] (ca. 1904) : a branch of medicine concerned with the structure, functions, diseases, and pathology of the stomach and intestines — **gas·tro·en·ter·o·log·i·cal** \-rə-'lä-ji-kəl\ adj — **gas·tro·en·ter·ol·o·gist** \-ˌen-tə-'rä-lə-jist\ n

\ə\ abut \ᵊ\ kitten, F table \ər\ further \a\ ash \ā\ ace \ä\ mop, mar \au̇\ out \ch\ chin \e\ bet \ē\ easy \g\ go \i\ hit \ī\ ice \j\ job \ŋ\ sing \ō\ go \ȯ\ law \ȯi\ boy \th\ thin \t̲h̲\ the \ü\ loot \u̇\ foot \y\ yet \zh\ vision \ä, k̲, ⁿ, œ, œ̄, ᵫ, ᵾ, ᵍ\ see Guide to Pronunciation

gas·tro·esoph·a·ge·al \'gas-trō-i-ˌsä-fə-'jē-əl\ *adj* (ca. 1909) : of, relating to, or involving the stomach and esophagus
gas·tro·in·tes·ti·nal \ˌgas-trō-in-'tes-tə-n²l, -'tes(t)-nəl\ *adj* (1831) : of, relating to, affecting, or including both stomach and intestine ⟨~ tract⟩
gas·tro·lith \'gas-trə-ˌlith\ *n* (1854) : a stone or pebble ingested by an animal and functioning to grind food in gastric digestion
gas·tro·nome \'gas-trə-ˌnōm\ *n* [F, back-formation fr. *gastronomie*] (1823) : a lover of good food; *esp* : one with a serious interest in gastronomy   *syn* see EPICURE
gas·tro·nom·i·cal·ly \ˌgas-trə-'nä-mi-k(ə-)lē\ *adv* (1875)   **1** : from the standpoint of gastronomy ⟨~ fashionable⟩   **2** : toward gastronomy ⟨~ inclined⟩
gas·tron·o·mist \ga-'strä-nə-mist\ *n* (1825) : GASTRONOME
gas·tron·o·my \-mē\ *n* [F *gastronomie*, fr. Gk *Gastronomia*, title of a 4th cent. B.C. poem, fr. *gastro-* *gastr-* + *-nomia* *-nomy*] (1814)   **1** : the art or science of good eating   **2** : culinary customs or style — **gas·tro·nom·ic** \ˌgas-trə-'nä-mik\ *also* **gas·tro·nom·i·cal** \-mi-kəl\ *adj*
gas·tro·pod \'gas-trə-ˌpäd\ *n* [NL *Gastropoda*, class name] (1826) : any of a large class (Gastropoda) of mollusks (as snails and slugs) usu. with a univalve shell or none and a distinct head bearing sensory organs — **gastropod** *adj*
gas·tro·scope \'gas-trə-ˌskōp\ *n* [ISV] (1888) : an instrument for viewing the interior of the stomach — **gas·tro·scop·ic** \ˌgas-trə-'skä-pik\ *adj* — **gas·tros·co·pist** \ga-'sträs-kə-pist\ *n* — **gas·tros·co·py** \-pē\ *n*
gas·tro·trich \'gas-trə-ˌtrik\ *n* [ultim. fr. Gk *gastr-* + *trich-*, *thrix* hair — more at TRICH-] (1940) : any of a phylum (Gastrotricha) of minute aquatic pseudocoelomate animals that usu. have a spiny or scaly cuticle and cilia on the ventral surface
gas·tro·vas·cu·lar \ˌgas-trō-'vas-kyə-lər\ *adj* [ISV] (1876) : functioning in both digestion and circulation ⟨the ~ cavity of a coelenterate⟩
gas·tru·la \'gas-trə-lə\ *n, pl* **-las** *or* **-lae** \-ˌlē, -ˌlī\ [NL, fr. *gastr-*] (1877) : an early metazoan embryo in which the ectoderm, mesoderm, and endoderm are established either by invagination of the blastula (as in fish and amphibians) to form a multilayered cellular cup with a blastopore opening into the archenteron or by differentiation of the blastodisc (as in reptiles, birds, and mammals) and inward cellular migration — compare BLASTULA, MORULA — **gas·tru·lar** \-lər\ *adj*
gas·tru·la·tion \ˌgas-trə-'lā-shən\ *n* (1879) : the process of becoming or of forming a gastrula — **gas·tru·late** \'gas-trə-ˌlāt\ *vi*
gas turbine *n* (1904) : an internal combustion engine in which expanding gases from the combustion chamber drive the blades of a turbine
gas·works \'gas-ˌwərks\ *n pl but sing or pl in constr* (1819) : a plant for manufacturing gas and esp. illuminating gas
¹gat \'gat\ *archaic past of* GET
²gat *n* [prob. fr. D, lit., hole; akin to OE *geat* gate] (1723) : a natural or artificial channel or passage
³gat *n* [short for *Gatling gun*] (1904) *slang* : HANDGUN
¹gate \'gāt\ *n* [ME, fr. OE *geat*; akin to ON *gat* opening] (bef. 12c)   **1** : an opening in a wall or fence   **2** : a city or castle entrance often with defensive structures (as towers)   **3 a** : the frame or door that closes a gate   **b** : a movable barrier (as at a grade crossing)   **4 a** : a means of entrance or exit   **b** : STARTING GATE   **c** : an area (as at a railroad station or an airport) for departure or arrival   **d** : a space between two markers through which a competitor must pass in the course of a slalom race   **5 a** : a door, valve, or other device for controlling the passage esp. of a fluid   **b** (1) : an electronic switch that allows or prevents the flow of current in a circuit   (2) : an electrode in a field-effect transistor that modulates the current flowing through the transistor according to the voltage applied to the electrode — compare DRAIN, SOURCE   **c** : a device (as in a computer) that outputs a signal when specified input conditions are met ⟨logic ~⟩   **d** : a molecular mechanism controlling the flow of a fluid, ion, or molecule through a channel esp. in a cell membrane   **6** *slang* : DISMISSAL ⟨gave him the ~⟩   **7** : the total admission receipts or the number of spectators (as at a sports event)
²gate *vt* **gat·ed; gat·ing** (1835)   **1** *Brit* : to punish by confinement to a campus or dormitory   **2** : to supply with a gate   **3** : to control by means of a gate
³gate *n* [ME, fr. ON *gata* road; akin to OHG *gazza* road] (13c)   **1** *archaic* : WAY, PATH   **2** *dial* : METHOD, STYLE
-gate \ˌgāt\ *n comb form* [Watergate] : usu. political scandal often involving the concealment of wrongdoing ⟨Irangate⟩
gâ·teau *or* **ga·teau** \(ˌ)gä-'tō\ *n, pl* **gâ·teaux** *or* **ga·teaux** \-'tō(z)\ *also* **gateaus** [F, fr. OF *gastel*, prob. of Gmc origin; akin to OE *wist* sustenance, food] (1845)   **1** : a rich or fancy cake
gate–crash·er \'gāt-ˌkra-shər\ *n* (1921) : a person who enters, attends, or participates without ticket or invitation — **gate–crash** *vb*
gate·fold \-ˌfōld\ *n* (1946) : FOLDOUT; *esp* : one with a single fold that opens out like a gate
gate·house \-ˌhaủs\ *n* (14c) : a building or house connected or associated with a gate
gate·keep·er \-ˌkē-pər\ *n* (1572)   **1** : one that tends or guards a gate   **2** : a person who controls access — **gate·keep·ing** \-piŋ\ *adj*
gate·leg table \'gāt-ˌleg-, -ˌlāg-\ *n* (1926) : a table with drop leaves supported by movable paired legs
gate·post \'gāt-ˌpōst\ *n* (1522) : the post to which a gate is hung or the one against which it closes
gate·way \-ˌwā\ *n* (1707)   **1** : an opening for a gate   **2** : GATE 4a
¹gath·er \'ga-thər *also* 'ge-\ *vb* **gath·ered; gath·er·ing** \'gath-riŋ, 'ga-thə-\ [ME *gaderen*, fr. OE *gaderian;* akin to Skt *gadhya* what one clings to — more at GOOD] *vt* (bef. 12c)   **1** : to bring together : COLLECT ⟨tried to ~ a crowd⟩ ⟨~ed firewood⟩   **2 a** : PICK, HARVEST ⟨~ flowers⟩   **b** : to pick up or accumulate as if by harvesting ⟨~ing ideas for the project⟩   **c** : to assemble (the signatures of a book) in sequence for binding   **3** : to serve as a center of attraction for   **4** : to effect the collection of (as tax)   **5 a** : to summon up ⟨~ed his cour-

gateleg table

age⟩   **b** : to gain by gradual increase : ACCUMULATE ⟨~ speed⟩   **c** : to prepare (as oneself) by mustering strength   **6** : to reach a conclusion often intuitively from hints or through inferences ⟨I ~ that you want to leave⟩   **7 a** : to pull (fabric) along a line of stitching so as to draw into puckers   **b** : to draw about or close to something ⟨~ing her cloak about her⟩   **c** : to bring together the parts of   **d** : to haul in ~ *vi*   **1 a** : to come together in a body   **b** : to cluster around a focus of attraction   **2 a** : to swell and fill with pus   **b** : GROW, INCREASE — **gath·er·er** \-thər-ər\ *n*
syn GATHER, COLLECT, ASSEMBLE, CONGREGATE mean to bring or come together into a group, mass, or unit. GATHER is the most general term for bringing or coming together from a spread-out or scattered state ⟨a crowd quickly *gathered*⟩. COLLECT often implies careful selection or orderly arrangement ⟨*collected* books on gardening⟩. ASSEMBLE implies an ordered union or organization of persons or things often for a definite purpose ⟨experts *assembled* for a conference⟩. CONGREGATE implies a spontaneous flocking together into a crowd or huddle ⟨*congregating* under shelter in a storm⟩.   *syn* see in addition INFER
²gather *n* (1555)   **1** : something gathered: as   **a** : a puckering in cloth made by gathering   **b** : a mass of molten glass collected for use in glassblowing   **2** : an act or instance of gathering
gath·er·ing *n* (bef. 12c)   **1** : ASSEMBLY, MEETING   **2** : a suppurating swelling : ABCESS   **3** : the collecting of food or raw materials from the wild   **4** : COLLECTION, COMPILATION   **5** : a gather in cloth
Gat·ling gun \'gat-liŋ-\ *n* [Richard J. *Gatling* †1903 Am. inventor] (1867) : a machine gun with a revolving cluster of barrels fired once each per revolution
ga·tor \'gā-tər\ *n* (1844) : ALLIGATOR
gauche \'gōsh\ *adj, sometimes* **gauch·er;** *sometimes* **gauch·est** [F, lit., left] (1751)   **1 a** : lacking social experience or grace; *also* : not tactful : CRUDE ⟨it would be ~ to mention the subject⟩   **b** : crudely made or done ⟨a ~ turn of phrase⟩   **2** : not planar ~ conformation of molecules⟩   *syn* see AWKWARD — **gauche·ly** *adv* — **gauche·ness** *n*
gau·che·rie \ˌgō-shə-'rē\ *n* [F] (1826) : a tactless or awkward act
Gau·cher's disease \(ˌ)gō-'shāz-\ *n* [Philippe C. E. *Gaucher* †1918 Fr. physician] (1902) : a rare hereditary disorder of lipid metabolism caused by an enzyme deficiency and characterized by enlargement of the spleen and neurological impairment
gau·cho \'gaủ-(ˌ)chō\ *n, pl* **gauchos** [AmerSp] (1824) : a cowboy of the So. American pampas
gaud \'gȯd, 'gäd\ *n* [ME *gaude*] (15c) : ORNAMENT, TRINKET
gaud·ery \'gȯ-də-rē, 'gä-\ *n* (ca. 1598) : showy ornamentation; *esp* : personal finery
¹gau·dy \'gȯ-dē, 'gä-\ *adj* **gaud·i·er; -est** (1582)   **1** : ostentatiously or tastelessly ornamented   **2** : marked by dazzling brilliance, showiness, or extravagance ⟨~ praise⟩ — **gaud·i·ly** \'gȯ-d²l-ē, 'gä-\ *adv* — **gaud·i·ness** \'gȯ-dē-nəs, 'gä-\ *n*
syn GAUDY, TAWDRY, GARISH, FLASHY, MERETRICIOUS mean vulgarly or cheaply showy. GAUDY implies a tasteless use of overly bright, often clashing colors or excessive ornamentation ⟨circus performers in *gaudy* costumes⟩. TAWDRY applies to what is at once gaudy and cheap and sleazy ⟨*tawdry* saloons⟩. GARISH describes what is distressingly or offensively bright ⟨*garish* neon signs⟩. FLASHY implies an effect of brilliance quickly and easily seen to be shallow or vulgar ⟨a *flashy* nightclub act⟩. MERETRICIOUS stresses falsity and may describe a tawdry show that beckons with a false allure or promise ⟨a *meretricious* wasteland of casinos and bars⟩.
²gaudy *n, pl* **gaudies** [prob. fr. L *gaudium* joy — more at JOY] (1651) : a feast or entertainment esp. in the form of an annual college dinner at a British university
gauf·fer \'gä-fər, 'gȯ-\ *n* *var of* GOFFER
¹gauge \'gāj\ *n* [ME *gauge*, fr. ONF] (15c)   **1 a** : a measurement (as of linear dimension) according to some standard or system: as   (1) : the distance between the rails of a railroad   (2) : the size of a shotgun barrel's inner diameter nominally expressed as the number of lead balls each just fitting that diameter required to make a pound ⟨a 12-*gauge* shotgun⟩   (3) : the thickness of a thin material (as sheet metal or plastic film)   (4) : the diameter of a slender object (as wire or a hypodermic needle)   (5) : the fineness of a knitted fabric expressed by the number of loops per unit width   **b** : DIMENSIONS, SIZE   **c** : MEASURE 1 ⟨surveys are a ~ of public sentiment⟩   **2** : an instrument for a means of measuring or testing: as   **a** : an instrument for measuring a dimension or for testing mechanical accuracy   **b** : an instrument with a graduated scale or dial for measuring or indicating quantity   **3** : relative position of a ship with reference to another ship and the wind   **4** : a function introduced into a field equation to produce a convenient form of the equation but having no observable physical consequences   *syn* see STANDARD
²gauge *vt* **gauged; gaug·ing** (15c)   **1 a** : to measure precisely the size, dimensions, or other measurable quantity of   **b** : to determine the capacity or contents of   **c** : ESTIMATE, JUDGE ⟨hard to ~ his moods⟩   **2 a** : to check for conformity to specifications or limits   **b** : to measure off or set out
gauged \'gājd\ *adj* (1823) *of masonry* : dressed to size
gaug·er \'gā-jər\ *n* (15c)   **1** : one that gauges   **2** *chiefly Brit* : an exciseman who inspects dutiable bulk goods
gauge theory *n* (1925) : any of several theories in physics that explain the transmission of a fundamental force between two interacting particles by the exchange of an elementary particle
Gaul \'gȯl\ *n* (1625)   **1** : a Celt of ancient Gaul   **2** : FRENCHMAN
¹Gaul·ish \'gȯ-lish\ *adj* (1659) : of or relating to the Gauls or their language or land
²Gaulish *n* (1668) : the Celtic language of the ancient Gauls — see INDO-EUROPEAN LANGUAGES table
Gaull·ism \'gō-ˌli-zəm, 'gȯ-\ *n* [Charles de *Gaulle*] (1943)   **1** : a French political movement during World War II led by Charles de Gaulle in opposition to the Vichy regime   **2** : a postwar French political movement led by Charles de Gaulle — **Gaull·ist** \-list\ *adj or n*
gault \'gȯlt\ *n* [prob. of Scand origin; akin to ON *gald* hard-packed snow] (1575) *chiefly Brit* : a heavy thick clay soil
gaum \'gȯm, 'gäm\ *vt* [origin unknown] (1796) *dial* : SMUDGE, SMEAR
gaunt \'gȯnt, 'gänt\ *adj* [ME] (15c)   **1** : excessively thin and angular ⟨a long ~ face⟩   **2** : BARREN, DESOLATE   *syn* see LEAN — **gaunt·ly** *adv* — **gaunt·ness** *n*

¹**gaunt·let** \'gȯnt-lət, 'gänt-\ n [ME, fr. MF gantelet, dim. of gant glove, of Gmc origin; akin to MD want glove, ON vǫttr] (15c) **1** : a glove worn with medieval armor to protect the hand **2** : any of various protective gloves used esp. in industry **3** : an open challenge (as to combat) — used in phrases like throw down the gauntlet **4** : a dress glove extending above the wrist — **gaunt·let·ed** \-lə-təd\ adj

²**gauntlet** n [by folk etymology fr. gantelope] (1661) **1** : a severe trial : ORDEAL ⟨ran the ~ of criticism and censure⟩ **2** a : a double file of men facing each other and armed with clubs or other weapons with which to strike at an individual who is made to run between them — used with run **b** : a long line (as of guards or well-wishers)

gaur \'gaůr\ n [Hindi, fr. Skt gaura; akin to Skt go bull, cow — more at COW] (1806) : a large wild ox (Bos gaurus) of India and southeast Asia with a broad forehead and short thick curved horns

gauss \'gaůs\ n, pl gauss also gauss·es [Karl F. Gauss] (1882) : the centimeter-gram-second unit of magnetic flux density that is equal to 1 × 10⁻⁴ tesla

Gauss·ian \'gaů-sē-ən\ adj [Karl F. Gauss] (1905) : being or having the shape of a Gaussian curve or a Gaussian distribution

Gaussian curve n (1905) : NORMAL CURVE

Gaussian distribution n (1905) : NORMAL DISTRIBUTION

gauze \'gȯz\ n [MF gaze] (1561) **1** a : a thin often transparent fabric used chiefly for clothing or draperies **b** : a loosely woven cotton surgical dressing **c** : a firm woven fabric of metal or plastic filaments **2** : HAZE — **gauze·like** \-ˌlīk\ adj — **gauz·i·ly** \'gȯ-zə-lē\ adv — **gauzy** \-zē\ adj

ga·vage \gə-'väzh, gä-\ n [F, fr. gaver to stuff, force-feed, fr. MF dial. (Picardy) gave gullet, crop] (1889) : introduction of material into the stomach by a tube

gave past of GIVE

¹**gav·el** \'ga-vəl\ n [ME, fr. OE gafol; akin to OE giefan to give] (bef. 12c) : rent or tribute in medieval England

²**gavel** n [origin unknown] (ca. 1859) : a mallet used (as by a presiding officer or auctioneer) for commanding attention or confirming an action (as a vote or sale)

³**gavel** vt -eled or -elled; -el·ing or -el·ling \'gav-liŋ, 'ga-və-\ (1925) : to bring or force by use of a gavel ⟨~ed the audience to silence⟩

gav·el·kind \'ga-vəl-ˌkīnd\ n [ME gavelkynde, fr. ¹gavel + kinde kind] (14c) : a tenure of land existing chiefly in Kent from Anglo-Saxon times until 1925 and providing for division of an intestate's estate equally among the sons of their heirs

gavel–to–gavel adj (1968) : extending from the beginning to the end of a meeting or session ⟨~ television coverage⟩

ga·vi·al \'gä-vē-əl\ n [F, modif. of Bengali ghāriyal or Hindi gharyal, fr. Skt ghanṭika crocodilian] (ca. 1825) : a large long-snouted crocodilian (Gavialis gangeticus) of India

ga·votte \gə-'vät\ n [F, fr. MF, fr. OProv gavoto, fr. gavot Alpine dweller] (1696) **1** : a dance of French peasant origin marked by the raising rather than sliding of the feet **2** : a tune for the gavotte in moderately quick ⁴/₄ time — **gavotte** vi

Ga·wain \gə-'wän, gä-ˌwän, gaů-ən\ n : a knight of the Round Table and nephew of King Arthur

¹**gawk** \'gȯk\ n [prob. fr. E dial. gawk (left-handed)] (1757) : a clumsy stupid person : LOUT

²**gawk** vi [perh. alter. of obs. gaw (to stare)] (1785) : to gape or stare stupidly — **gawk·er** n

gawk·ish \'gȯ-kish\ adj (1876) : GAWKY — **gawk·ish·ly** adv — **gawk·ish·ness** n

gawky \'gȯ-kē\ adj gawk·i·er; -est (1759) : AWKWARD, CLUMSY ⟨a ~ adolescent⟩ — **gawk·i·ly** \-kə-lē\ adv — **gawky** n

gawp \'gȯp, 'gäp\ vi [E dial. gawp to yawn, gape, fr. obs. galp, fr. ME] (1855) chiefly Brit : GAWK — **gawp·er** \'gȯ-pər, 'gä-\ n

¹**gay** \'gā\ adj [ME, fr. MF gai] (14c) **1** a : happily excited : MERRY **b** : keenly alive and exuberant : having or inducing high spirits ⟨abandoned a sober traditional style for one more timely and ~⟩ **2** a : BRIGHT, LIVELY ⟨~ sunny meadows⟩ **b** : brilliant in color **3** : given to social pleasures; also : LICENTIOUS **4** a : HOMOSEXUAL **b** : of, relating to, or used by homosexuals ⟨the ~ rights movement⟩ ⟨a ~ bar⟩ syn see LIVELY — **gay** adv — **gay·ness** n

²**gay** n (1953) : HOMOSEXUAL

gay·e·ty, gay·ly var of GAIETY, GAILY

ga·za·nia \gə-'zä-nē-ə, -nyə\ n [NL, fr. Theodorus Gaza †1478 Greek scholar] (1813) : any of a genus (Gazania) of So. African composite herbs often cultivated for their brightly colored flowers

ga·zar \gə-'zär\ n [origin unknown] (1967) : a silk organza

¹**gaze** \'gāz\ vi gazed; gaz·ing (14c) : to fix the eyes in a steady and intent look and often with eagerness or studious attention — **gaz·er** n

²**gaze** n (1566) : a fixed intent look

ga·ze·bo \gə-'zē-(ˌ)bō also -'zä-\ n, pl -bos [perh. fr. ¹gaze + L -ebo (as in videbo I shall see)] (1752) **1** : BELVEDERE **2** : a freestanding roofed structure usu. open on the sides

gaze·hound \'gāz-ˌhaůnd\ n (1610) : a dog that hunts by sight rather than by scent; esp : GREYHOUND

ga·zelle \gə-'zel\ n, pl gazelles also gazelle [F, fr. MF, fr. Ar ghazāl] (1600) : any of numerous small to medium graceful and swift African and Asian antelopes (Gazella and related genera)

¹**ga·zette** \gə-'zet\ n [F, fr. It gazzetta] (ca. 1598) **1** : NEWSPAPER **2** : an official journal **3** Brit : an announcement in an official gazette

²**gazette** vt ga·zett·ed; ga·zett·ing (1678) **1** chiefly Brit : to announce or publish in a gazette **2** Brit : to announce the appointment or status of in an official gazette

gaz·et·teer \ˌga-zə-'tir\ n (1611) **1** archaic : JOURNALIST, PUBLICIST **2** [The Gazetteer's: or, Newsman's Interpreter, a geographical index edited by Laurence Echard] : a geographical dictionary; also : a book in which a subject is treated esp. in regard to geographic distribution and regional specialization

gaz·o·gene \'ga-zə-ˌjēn\ var of GASOGENE

gaz·pa·cho \gə-'spä-(ˌ)chō, gə-'spä-\ n, pl -chos [Sp] (1845) : a spicy soup that is usu. made from chopped raw vegetables (as tomato, onion, pepper, and cucumber) and that is served cold

GB \ˌjē-'bē\ n [code name] (1961) : SARIN

G clef n (1596) : TREBLE CLEF

ge- or **geo-** comb form [ME geo-, fr. MF & L; MF, fr. L, fr. Gk gē-, geō-, fr. gē] **1** : earth : ground : soil ⟨geanticline⟩ ⟨geophyte⟩ **2** : geographic : geography and ⟨geopolitics⟩

ge·an·ti·cline \jē-ˈan-ti-ˌklīn\ n (1889) : a great upward flexure of the earth's crust — compare GEOSYNCLINE

¹**gear** \'gir\ n [ME gere, fr. ON gervi, gǫrvi; akin to OE gearwe equipment, clothing, gearu ready — more at YARE] (14c) **1** a : CLOTHING, GARMENTS **b** : movable property : GOODS **2** : EQUIPMENT, PARAPHERNALIA ⟨fishing ~⟩ **3** a : the rigging of a ship or boat **b** : the harness esp. of horses **4** dial chiefly Brit : absurd talk : NONSENSE **5** dial chiefly Brit : DOINGS **6** a (1) : a mechanism that performs a specific function in a complete machine ⟨steering ~⟩ (2) : a toothed wheel (3) : working relation, position, order, or adjustment ⟨got her career in ~⟩ **b** : one of two or more adjustments of a transmission (as of a bicycle or motor vehicle) that determine mechanical advantage, relative speed, and direction of travel — **gear·less** \-ləs\ adj

²**gear** vt (1851) **1** a : to provide (as machinery) with gearing **b** : to connect by gearing **2** a : to make ready for effective operation **b** : to adjust so as to match, blend with, or satisfy something ⟨~ing wages to productivity⟩ ~ vi **1** a Brit, of machinery : to be in gear : MESH **b** : SHIFT 1c ⟨~ down⟩ **2** : to become adjusted so as to match, blend, or harmonize

gear·box \'gir-ˌbäks\ n (1887) **1** : GEARING 2 **2** : TRANSMISSION 3

gear–change \-ˌchānj\ n (1927) Brit : GEARSHIFT

gear·ing \'gir-iŋ\ n (1833) **1** : the act or process of providing or fitting with gears **2** : the parts by which motion is transmitted from one portion of machinery to another; esp : a train of gears

gear·shift \'gir-ˌshift\ n (1926) : a mechanism by which the transmission gears in a power-transmission system are engaged and disengaged; also : a lever for controlling such a mechanism

gear up vi (1951) : to get ready ⟨the team is gearing up for the big game⟩

gear·wheel \'gir-ˌhwēl, -ˌwēl\ n (ca. 1874) : GEAR 6a(2)

Geat \'gēt, 'gā-ət, 'yaət\ n [OE Gēat] (bef. 12c) : a member of a Scandinavian people of southern Sweden to which the legendary hero Beowulf belonged — **Geat·ish** \'gē-tish, 'gā-, 'yaə-\ adj

geck·o \'ge-(ˌ)kō\ n, pl geck·os or geck·oes [perh. fr. Malay dial. ge⁷kok] (1774) : any of numerous small harmless chiefly tropical and nocturnal insectivorous lizards (family Gekkonidae)

ge·dank·en·ex·per·i·ment \gə-ˈdäŋ-kən-ik-ˌsper-ə-mənt also -ˌspir-\ n [G, fr. Gedanke thought + Experiment experiment] (1941) : an experiment carried out in thought only

gecko

¹**gee** \'jē\ vb [origin unknown] (1628) vb imper — used as a direction to turn to the right or move ahead; compare ⁵HAW ~ vi geed; gee·ing : to turn to the right side

²**gee** interj [euphemism for Jesus] (1895) — used as an introductory expletive or to express surprise or enthusiasm

³**gee** n (1926) **1** : the letter g **2** [grand]: slang : a thousand dollars

gee·gaw \'jē-(ˌ)gȯ, 'gē-\ var of GEWGAW

geek \'gēk\ n [prob. fr. E dial. geek, geck fool, fr. LG geck, fr. MLG] (1914) **1** : a person often of an intellectual bent who is disapproved of **2** : a carnival performer often billed as a wild man whose act usu. includes biting the head off a live chicken or snake — **geeky** \'gē-kē\ adj

geese pl of GOOSE

gee–whiz \'jē-ˌhwiz, -ˌwiz\ adj (1934) **1** : designed to arouse wonder or excitement or to amplify the merits or significance of something esp. by the use of clever or sensational language ⟨play-by-play specialists who wallow in ~ banality —Jack Gould⟩ **2** : marked by spectacular or astonishing qualities or achievement ⟨~ technology⟩ **3** : characterized by wide-eyed enthusiasm, excitement, and wonder

gee whiz \(ˌ)jē-\ interj (1885) : ²GEE

geez var of JEEZ

Ge·ez \gē-ˈez; 'gē-(ˌ)ez, 'gā-\ n (1790) : a Semitic language formerly spoken in Ethiopia and still used as the liturgical language of the Christian church in Ethiopia

gee·zer \'gē-zər\ n [prob. alter. of Sc guiser (one in disguise)] (1885) : a queer, odd, or eccentric person — used esp. of elderly men

ge·fil·te fish \gə-ˈfil-tə-\ n [Yiddish, lit., stuffed fish] (1892) : balls or cakes of seasoned minced fish usu. simmered in a fish stock or baked in a tomato sauce

ge·gen·schein \'gā-gən-ˌshīn\ n, often cap [G, fr. gegen against, counter- + Schein shine] (1880) : a faint light about 20° across on the celestial sphere opposite the sun probably caused by backscatter of sunlight by solar-system dust

Ge·hen·na \gi-ˈhe-nə\ n [LL, fr. Gk Geenna, fr. Heb Gē' Hinnōm, lit., valley of Hinnom] (1594) **1** : a place or state of misery : HELL 1a(2)

Gei·ger counter \'gī-gər-\ n [Hans Geiger †1945 Ger. physicist] (1924) : an instrument for detecting the presence and intensity of radiations (as cosmic rays or particles from a radioactive substance) by means of the ionizing effect on an enclosed gas which results in a pulse that is amplified and fed to a device giving a visible or audible indication

Gei·ger–Mül·ler counter \-ˈmyü-lər, -ˈmi-, -ˈmə-\ n [W. Müller, 20th cent. Ger. physicist] (1932) : GEIGER COUNTER

gei·sha \'gā-shə, also 'gē-\ n, pl geisha or geishas [Jp, fr. gei art + -sha person] (1887) : a Japanese girl or woman who is trained to provide entertaining and lighthearted company esp. for a man or a group of men

¹**gel** \'jel\ n [gelatin] (1899) **1** : a colloid in a more solid form than a sol; broadly : JELLY **2** : a thin colored transparent sheet used over a stage light to color it **3** : a gelatinous preparation used in styling hair

---

\ə\ abut \ᵊ\ kitten, F table \ər\ further \a\ ash \ā\ ace \ä\ mop, mar
\aů\ out \ch\ chin \e\ bet \ē\ easy \g\ go \i\ hit \ī\ ice \j\ job
\ŋ\ sing \ō\ go \ȯ\ law \ȯi\ boy \th\ thin \t͟h\ the \ü\ loot \ů\ foot
\y\ yet \zh\ vision \ä, k̲, ⁿ, œ, œ̄, ue, ūe, ʸ\ see Guide to Pronunciation

²gel *vi* **gelled; gel·ling** (1917) : to change into or take on the form of a gel — SET — **gel·able** \'je-lə-bəl\ *adj*

gel·a·da baboon \'je-lə-də-, 'ge-; jə-'lä-də-\ *n* [Amharic *č'ällada*] (1878) : a large long-haired primate (*Theropithecus gelada*) of Ethiopia related to the baboon — called also *gelada*

ge·län·de·sprung \gə-'len-də-ˌshprùŋ, -ˌsprùŋ\ *n* [G, fr. *Gelände* open fields + *Sprung* jump] (1931) : a jump usu. over an obstacle in skiing that is made from a low crouch with the aid of both ski poles

gel·ate \'je-ˌlāt\ *vi* **gel·at·ed; gel·at·ing** (1915) : GEL

gel·a·tin *also* **gel·a·tine** \'je-lə-t²n\ *n* [F *gélatine* edible jelly, gelatin, fr. It *gelatina*, fr. *gelato*, pp. of *gelare* to freeze, fr. L — more at COLD] (1800) **1** : glutinous material obtained from animal tissues by boiling; *esp* : a colloidal protein used as a food, in photography, and in medicine **2 a** : any of various substances (as agar) resembling gelatin **b** : an edible jelly made with gelatin **3** : GEL 2

ge·la·ti·ni·za·tion \jə-ˌla-t²n-ə-'zā-shən, je-lə-t²n-\ *n* (1843) : the process of converting into a gelatinous form or into a jelly — **ge·la·ti·nize** \jə-'la-t²n-ˌiz, 'je-lə-t²n-\ *vb*

ge·lat·i·nous \jə-'lat-nəs, -'la-t²n-əs\ *adj* (1766) **1** : resembling gelatin or jelly : VISCOUS ⟨a ~ precipitate⟩ **2** : of, relating to, or containing gelatin — **ge·lat·i·nous·ly** *adv* — **ge·lat·i·nous·ness** *n*

¹ge·la·tion \ji-'lā-shən\ *n* [L *gelation-, gelatio*, fr. *gelare*] (1854) : the action or process of freezing

²gel·ation \je-'lā-shən\ *n* [¹*gel* + *-ation*] (1915) : the formation of a gel from a sol

ge·la·to \je-'lä-(ˌ)tō\ *n, pl* **-ti** \-tē\ *also* **-tos** [It, lit., frozen] (1929) : a soft rich ice cream containing little or no air

¹geld \'geld\ *vt* [ME, fr. ON *gelda*; akin to OE *gelde* sterile] (14c) **1** : CASTRATE **2** : to deprive of a natural or essential part ⟨sick of working men being ~*ed* of their natural expression —*Atlantic*⟩

²geld *n* [OE *gield, geld* service, tribute; akin to OE *gieldan* to pay, yield — more at YIELD] (1610) : the crown tax paid under Anglo-Saxon and Norman kings

geld·ing \'gel-diŋ\ *n* [ME, fr. ON *geldingr*, fr. *gelda*] (14c) **1** : a castrated animal; *specif* : a castrated male horse **2** *archaic* : EUNUCH

ge·lée \zhə-'lā\ *n* [F, jelly, fr. MF — more at JELLY] (1966) : a cosmetic gel

gel electrophoresis *n* (1960) : electrophoresis in which molecules (as proteins and nucleic acids) migrate through a gel and esp. a polyacrylamide gel and separate into bands according to size

gel·id \'je-ləd\ *adj* [L *gelidus*, fr. *gelu* frost, cold — more at COLD] (1599) : extremely cold : ICY ⟨~ water⟩ ⟨a man of ~ reserve —*New Yorker*⟩ — **ge·lid·i·ty** \jə-'li-də-tē, je-\ *n* — **gel·id·ly** \'je-ləd-lē\ *adv*

gel·ig·nite \'je-lig-ˌnīt\ *n* [*gelatin* + L *ignis* fire + E *-ite* — more at IGNEOUS] (1889) : a dynamite in which the adsorbent base is largely potassium nitrate or a similar nitrate usu. with some wood pulp

gel·lant \'je-lənt\ *n* (1956) : a substance used to produce gelling

gel permeation chromatography *n* (1966) : chromatography in which macromolecules (as polymers) in a solution are separated by size on a column packed with a gel (as of polystyrene)

gelt \'gelt\ *n* [D & G *geld* & Yiddish *gelt*; all akin to OE *geld* ²*geld*] (ca. 1529) : MONEY

¹gem \'jem\ *n* [ME *gemme*, fr. MF, fr. L *gemma* bud, gem] (14c) **1 a** : JEWEL **b** : a precious or sometimes semiprecious stone cut and polished for ornament **2 a** : something prized esp. for great beauty or perfection **b** : a highly prized or well-beloved person **3** : MUFFIN

²gem *vt* **gemmed; gem·ming** (1610) : to adorn with or as if with gems

Ge·ma·ra \gə-'mär-ə, -'mòr-\ *n* [Aram *gĕmārā* completion] (1613) : a commentary on the Mishnah forming the second part of the Talmud — **Ge·ma·ric** \-ik\ *adj* — **Ge·ma·rist** \-ist\ *n*

ge·mein·schaft \gə-'mīn-ˌshäft\ *n* [G, community, fr. *gemein* common, general (fr. OHG *gimeini*) + *-schaft* -ship — more at MEAN] (1937) : a spontaneously arising organic social relationship characterized by strong reciprocal bonds of sentiment and kinship within a common tradition; *also* : a community or society characterized by this relationship — compare GESELLSCHAFT

gem·i·nal \'je-mə-n²l\ *adj* [L *geminus* twin] (1967) : relating to or characterized by two usu. similar substituents on the same atom — **gem·i·nal·ly** \-n²l-ē\ *adv*

¹gem·i·nate \'je-mə-nət, -ˌnāt\ *adj* [L *geminatus*, pp. of *geminare* to double, fr. *geminus* twin] (15c) **1** : arranged in pairs : DUPLICATE **2** : being a sequence of identical speech sounds (as in *meanness* or Italian *notte* \'nòt-te\ "night")

²gem·i·nate \-ˌnāt\ *vb* **-nat·ed; -nat·ing** *vt* (1637) : to make geminate ~ *vi* : to be or become geminate — **gem·i·na·tion** \je-mə-'nā-shən\ *n*

Gem·i·ni \'je-mə-(ˌ)nē, -ˌnī; 'ge-mə-ˌnē\ *n pl but sing in constr* [L (gen. *Geminorum*), lit., the twins (Castor and Pollux)] **1** : the 3d zodiacal constellation pictorially represented as the twins Castor and Pollux sitting together and located on the opposite side of the Milky Way from Taurus and Orion **2 a** : the 3d sign of the zodiac in astrology — see ZODIAC table **b** : one born under the sign of Gemini

gem·ma \'je-mə\ *n, pl* **gem·mae** \-ˌmē\ [L] (1830) : BUD; *broadly* : an asexual reproductive body that becomes detached from a parent plant

gem·ma·tion \je-'mā-shən\ *n* (ca. 1839) : reproduction by gemmae

gem·mule \'jem-(ˌ)yü(ə)l\ *n* [F, fr. L *gemmula*, dim. of *gemma*] (ca. 1841) : a small bud: **a** : a theoretical particle proposed in the theory of pangenesis that is shed by a somatic cell and contains all the information necessary to reproduce that cell type (as in an offspring) **b** : a reproductive bud produced by freshwater and some marine sponges that consists of a usu. hardened aggregate of cells

gem·my \'je-mē\ *adj* (15c) : having the characteristics desired in a gemstone : BRIGHT, GLITTERING

gem·ol·o·gist *also* **gem·mol·o·gist** \je-'mä-lə-jist, jə-\ *n* (1931) : a specialist in gems; *specif* : one who appraises gems

gem·ol·o·gy *or* **gem·mol·o·gy** \-jē\ *n* [L *gemma* gem] (1811) : the science of gems — **gem·o·log·i·cal** \ˌje-mə-'lä-ji-kəl\ *adj*

ge·mot *or* **ge·mote** \gə-'mōt, yə-\ *n* [OE *gemōt*, fr. *ge-* (perfective prefix) + *mōt* assembly — more at CO-, MOOT] (bef. 12c) : a judicial or legislative assembly in Anglo-Saxon England

gems·bok \'gemz-ˌbäk\ *n* [Afrik, fr. G *Gemsbock* male chamois, fr. *Gems* chamois + *Bock* male goat] (1777) : a large and strikingly marked oryx (*Oryx gazella*) formerly abundant in southern Africa

gem·stone \'jem-ˌstōn\ *n* (bef. 12c) : a mineral or petrified material that when cut and polished can be used in jewelry

ge·müt·lich \gə-'müet-lik, -'müt-lik\ *adj* [G, fr. MHG *gemüetlich* pleasant, fr. *gemüete* mentality, mind] (1852) : agreeably pleasant : COMFORTABLE

ge·müt·lich·keit \gə-'müet-lik-ˌkit, -'müt-lik-\ *n* [G, fr. *gemütlich* + *-keit*, alter. of *-heit* -hood] (1892) : CORDIALITY, FRIENDLINESS

gen \'jen\ *n* [perh. fr. *general information*] (1940) *chiefly Brit* : INFORMATION 2a

¹gen- *or* **geno-** *comb form* [Gk *genos* birth, race, kind — more at KIN] **1** : race ⟨*genocide*⟩ **2** : genus : kind ⟨*genotype*⟩

²gen- *or* **geno-** *comb form* : gene ⟨*genome*⟩

-gen *also* **-gene** *n comb form* [F *-gène*, fr. Gk *-genēs* born; akin to Gk *genos* birth] **1** : producer ⟨*androgen*⟩ **2** : one that is (so) produced ⟨*cultigen*⟩

gen·darme \'zhän-ˌdärm *also* 'jän-\ *n* [F, fr. MF, back-formation fr. *gensdarmes*, pl. of *gent d'armes*, lit., armed people] (1796) **1** : a member of a body of soldiers esp. in France serving as an armed police force for the maintenance of public order **2** : POLICE OFFICER

gen·dar·me·rie *or* **gen·dar·mery** \zhän-'där-mə-rē, jän-\ *n, pl* **-mer·ies** [F *gendarmerie*, fr. *gendarme*] (ca. 1796) : a body of gendarmes

¹gen·der \'jen-dər\ *n* [ME *gendre*, fr. MF *genre, gendre*, fr. L *gener-, genus* birth, race, kind, gender — more at KIN] (14c) **1 a** : a subclass within a grammatical class (as noun, pronoun, adjective, or verb) of a language that is partly arbitrary but also partly based on distinguishable characteristics (as shape, social rank, manner of existence, or sex) and that determines agreement with and selection of other words or grammatical forms **b** : membership of a word or a grammatical form in such a subclass **c** : an inflectional form showing membership in such a subclass **2 a** : SEX ⟨the feminine ~⟩ **b** : the behavioral, cultural, or psychological traits typically associated with one sex

²gender *vb* **gen·dered; gen·der·ing** \-d(ə-)riŋ\ [ME *gendren*, fr. MF *gendrer*, fr. L *generare* — more at GENERATE] (14c) : ENGENDER

gender bender *n* (1980) : a person who dresses and behaves like a member of the opposite sex — **gender-bending** *adj or n*

gen·dered \'jen-dərd\ *adj* (1972) : reflecting the experience, prejudices, or orientations of one sex more than the other ⟨~ language⟩

gene \'jēn\ *n* [G *Gen*, short for *Pangen*, fr. *pan-* + *-gen*] (1911) : a specific sequence of nucleotides in DNA or RNA that is located in the germ plasm usu. on a chromosome and that is the functional unit of inheritance controlling the transmission and expression of one or more traits by specifying the structure of a particular polypeptide and esp. a protein or controlling the function of other genetic material

ge·ne·al·o·gist \ˌjē-nē-'ä-lə-jist *also* -'a-lə- *also* ˌje-nē-\ *n* (1605) : a person who traces or studies the descent of persons or families

ge·ne·al·o·gy \-jē\ *n, pl* **-gies** [ME *genealogie*, fr. MF, fr. LL *genealogia*, fr. Gk, fr. *genea* race, family + *-logia* -logy; akin to Gk *genos* race] (14c) **1** : an account of the descent of a person, family, or group from an ancestor or from older forms **2** : regular descent of a person, family, or group of organisms from a progenitor or older form : PEDIGREE **3** : the study of family pedigrees — **ge·ne·a·log·i·cal** \ˌjē-nē-ə-'lä-ji-kəl, ˌje-nē-\ *adj* — **ge·ne·a·log·i·cal·ly** \-k(ə-)lē\ *adv*

gene amplification *n* (1968) : replication and esp. massive replication (as in the polymerase chain reaction) of the genetic material in part of a genome

gene conversion *n* (1955) : a genetic process in which a heterozygote with one damaged strand of DNA produces gametes in an aberrant allelic ratio (as 3:1) instead of the normal 1:1 Mendelian ratio due to repair of the damaged strand with genetic material complementary to the other strand

gene flow *n* (1947) : the passage and establishment of genes typical of one breeding population into the gene pool of another by hybridization and backcrossing

gene frequency *n* (1930) : the ratio of the number of a specified allele in a population to the total of all alleles at its genetic locus

gene mutation *n* (1927) : POINT MUTATION

gene pool *n* (1946) : the collection of genes of all the individuals in an interbreeding population

genera *pl of* GENUS

¹gen·er·al \'jen-rəl, 'je-nə-\ *adj* [ME, fr. MF, fr. L *generalis*, fr. *gener-, genus* kind, class — more at KIN] (14c) **1** : involving, applicable to, or affecting the whole **2** : involving, relating to, or applicable to every member of a class, kind, or group ⟨the ~ equation of a straight line⟩ **3** : not confined by specialization or careful limitation **4** : belonging to the common nature of a group of like individuals : GENERIC **5 a** : applicable to or characteristic of the majority of individuals involved : PREVALENT **b** : concerned or dealing with universal rather than particular aspects **6** : relating to, determined by, or concerned with main elements rather than limited details ⟨bearing a ~ resemblance to the original⟩ **7** : holding superior rank or taking precedence over others similarly titled ⟨the ~ manager⟩

²general *n* (14c) **1** : something (as a concept, principle, or statement) that involves or is applicable to the whole **2** : SUPERIOR GENERAL **3** *archaic* : the general public : PEOPLE **4 a** : GENERAL OFFICER **b** : a commissioned officer in the army, air force, or marine corps who ranks above a lieutenant general and whose insignia is four stars — compare ADMIRAL — **in general** : for the most part : GENERALLY

general admission *n* (ca. 1949) : a fee paid for admission to a usu. unreserved seating area (as in an auditorium or stadium)

general agent *n* (1835) **1** : one employed to transact generally all legal business entrusted to him by his principal **2** : an insurance company agent working within a specified area

general assembly *n* (1619) **1** : the highest governing body in a religious denomination (as the United Presbyterian Church) **2** : a legislative assembly; *esp* : a U.S. state legislature **3** *cap* G&A : the supreme deliberative body of the United Nations

general aviation *n* (1966) : the operation of civilian aircraft not under the control of a common carrier; *also* : such aircraft collectively

General Court *n* (1629) : a legislative assembly; *specif* : the state legislature in Massachusetts and New Hampshire

general delivery *n* (1846) : a department of a post office that handles the delivery of mail at a post office window to persons who call for it

general election *n* (1716) : an election usu. held at regular intervals in which candidates are elected in all or most constituencies of a nation or state

...

gen·er·al·isa·tion, gen·er·al·ise, gen·er·al·ised *Brit var of* GENERAL-IZATION, GENERALIZE, GENERALIZED

gen·er·a·lis·si·mo \ˌjen-rə-ˈli-sə-ˌmō, ˌje-nə-\ *n, pl* **-mos** [It, fr. *generale* general] (1621) : the chief commander of an army

gen·er·al·ist \ˈjen-rə-list, ˈje-nə-\ *n* (1611) : one whose skills, interests, or habits are varied or unspecialized

gen·er·al·i·ty \ˌje-nə-ˈra-lə-tē\ *n, pl* **-ties** (15c) **1** : the quality or state of being general **2 a** : GENERALIZATION **2 b** : a vague or inadequate statement **3** : the greatest part : BULK ⟨the ~ of the population⟩

gen·er·al·iza·tion \ˌjen-rə-lə-ˈzā-shən, ˌje-nə-\ *n* (1761) **1** : the act or process of generalizing **2** : a general statement, law, principle, or proposition **3** : the act or process whereby a response is made to a stimulus similar to but not identical with a reference stimulus

gen·er·al·ize \ˈjen-rə-ˌlīz, ˈje-nə-\ *vb* **-ized; -iz·ing** *vt* (ca. 1751) **1** : to give a general form to **2 a** : to derive or induce (a general conception or principle) from particulars **b** : to draw a general conclusion from **3** : to give general applicability to ⟨~ a law⟩; *also* : to make indefinite ~ *vi* **1** : to form generalizations; *also* : to make vague or indefinite statements **2** : to spread or extend throughout the body — **gen·er·al·iz·abil·i·ty** \ˌjen-rə-ˌlī-zə-ˈbi-lə-tē, ˌje-nə-\ *n* — **gen·er·al·iz·able** \-ˌlī-zə-bəl\ *adj* — **gen·er·al·iz·er** *n*

gen·er·al·ized *adj* (ca. 1843) : made general; *esp* : not highly differentiated biologically nor strictly adapted to a particular environment

gen·er·al·ly \ˈjen-rə-lē, ˈje-nə-, ˈje-nər-lē\ *adv* (14c) : in a general manner: as **a** : in disregard of specific instances and with regard to an overall picture ⟨~ speaking⟩ **b** : as a rule : USUALLY

general officer *n* (1681) : any of the officers in the army, air force, or marine corps above colonel — compare COMPANY OFFICER, FIELD OFFICER, FLAG OFFICER

general of the air force (1949) : a general of the highest rank in the air force whose insignia is five stars

general of the army (1945) : a general of the highest rank in the army whose insignia is five stars

general paresis *n* (1874) : insanity caused by syphilitic alteration of the brain that leads to dementia and paralysis — called also *general paralysis of the insane*

general partner *n* (1887) : a partner whose liability for partnership debts and obligations is unlimited

general practitioner *n* (ca. 1885) : a physician or veterinarian whose practice is not limited to a specialty; *broadly* : GENERALIST

general–purpose *adj* (1894) : suitable to be used for two or more basic purposes

general quarters *n pl* (1902) : a condition of maximum readiness for action on a warship for action

general relativity *n* (1916) : RELATIVITY 3b

general semantics *n pl but sing or pl in constr* (1933) : a doctrine and educational discipline intended to improve habits of response of human beings to their environment and one another esp. by training in the more critical use of words and other symbols

gen·er·al·ship \ˈjen-rəl-ˌship, ˈje-nə-\ *n* (1610) **1** : office or tenure of office of a general **2** : LEADERSHIP **3** : military skill in a high commander

general store *n* (1835) : a retail store located usu. in a small or rural community that carries a wide variety of goods including groceries but is not divided into departments

general theory of relativity (1921) : RELATIVITY 3b

general will *n* (ca. 1902) : the collective will of a community that is the embodiment or expression of its common interest

gen·er·ate \ˈje-nə-ˌrāt\ *vt* **-at·ed; -at·ing** [L *generatus*, pp. of *generare*, fr. *gener-, genus* descent, birth — more at KIN] (1509) **1** : to bring into existence: as **a** : PROCREATE, BEGET **b** : to originate by a vital, chemical, or physical process : PRODUCE ⟨~ electricity⟩ **2** : to be the cause of (a situation, action, or state of mind) ⟨these stories . . . ~ a good deal of psychological suspense —*Atlantic*⟩ **3** : to define or originate (as a mathematical or linguistic set or structure) by the application of one or more rules or operations; *esp* : to trace out (as a curve) by a moving point or trace out (as a surface) by a moving curve

gen·er·a·tion \ˌje-nə-ˈrā-shən\ *n* (14c) **1 a** : a body of living beings constituting a single step in the line of descent from an ancestor **b** : a group of individuals born and living contemporaneously **c** : a group of individuals having contemporaneously a status (as that of students in a school) which each one holds only for a limited period **d** : a type or class of objects usu. developed from an earlier type ⟨first of the . . . new ~ of powerful supersonic fighters —Kenneth Koyen⟩ **2 a** : the action or process of producing offspring : PROCREATION **b** : the process of coming or bringing into being ⟨~ of income⟩ **c** : origination by a generating process : PRODUCTION; *esp* : formation of a geometric figure by motion of another **3** : the average span of time between the birth of parents and that of their offspring — **gen·er·a·tion·al** \-shnəl, -shə-nᵊl\ *adj* — **gen·er·a·tion·al·ly** \-shnə-lē, shə-nᵊl-ē\ *adv*

gen·er·a·tive \ˈjen-rə-tiv, ˈje-nə-, -ˌrā-tiv\ *adj* (14c) : having the power or function of generating, originating, producing, or reproducing

generative cell *n* (ca. 1892) : a sexual reproductive cell : GAMETE

generative grammar \usu ˈje-nə-rə-tiv-\ *n* (1959) **1** : a description in the form of an ordered set of rules for producing the grammatical sentences of a language **2** : TRANSFORMATIONAL GRAMMAR

generative nucleus *n* (ca. 1892) : the one of the two nuclei resulting from the first division in the pollen grain of a seed plant that gives rise to sperm nuclei — compare TUBE NUCLEUS

generative semantics \usu ˈje-nə-rə-tiv-\ *n pl but usu sing in constr* (1970) : a description of a language emphasizing a semantic deep structure that is logical in form, that provides syntactic structure, and that is related to surface structure by transformations

gen·er·a·tor \ˈje-nə-ˌrā-tər\ *n* (1646) **1** : one that generates **2** : an apparatus in which vapor or gas is formed **3** : a machine by which mechanical energy is changed into electrical energy **4** : a mathematical entity that when subjected to one or more operations yields another mathematical entity or its elements; *specif* : GENERATRIX

gen·er·a·trix \ˌje-nə-ˈrā-triks\ *n, pl* **-er·a·tri·ces** \-trə-ˌsēz, -ə-rə-ˈtrī-(ˌ)sēz\ (1840) : a point, line, or surface whose motion generates a line, surface, or solid

¹ge·ner·ic \jə-ˈner-ik\ *adj* [F *générique*, fr. L *gener-, genus* birth, kind, class] (1676) **1 a** : relating to or characteristic of a whole group or class : GENERAL **b** : being or having a nonproprietary name **c** : hav-

ing no particularly distinctive quality or application **2** : relating to or having the rank of a biological genus — **ge·ner·i·cal·ly** \-i-k(ə-)lē\ *adv* — **ge·ner·ic·ness** *n*

²generic *n* (1967) : a generic product (as a drug)

gen·er·os·i·ty \ˌje-nə-ˈrä-sə-tē, -ˈräs-tē\ *n, pl* **-ties** (ca. 1616) **1 a** : the quality or fact of being generous **b** : a generous act **2** : ABUNDANCE

gen·er·ous \ˈjen-rəs, ˈje-nə-\ *adj* [MF or L; MF *genereus*, fr. L *generosus*, fr. *gener-, genus*] (1588) **1** *archaic* : HIGHBORN **2 a** : characterized by a noble or forbearing spirit : MAGNANIMOUS, KINDLY **b** : liberal in giving : OPENHANDED **c** : marked by abundance or ample proportions : COPIOUS *syn* see LIBERAL — **gen·er·ous·ly** *adv* — **gen·er·ous·ness** *n*

gen·e·sis \ˈje-nə-səs\ *n, pl* **-e·ses** \-ˌsēz\ [L, fr. Gk, fr. *gignesthai* to be born — more at KIN] (ca. 1604) : the origin or coming into being of something

Genesis *n* [Gk] : the mainly narrative first book of canonical Jewish and Christian Scriptures — see BIBLE table

gene–splic·ing \ˈjēn-ˌsplī-siŋ\ *n* (ca. 1978) : any of various techniques by which recombinant DNA is produced and made to function in an organism

gen·et \ˈje-nət\ *n* [ME *genete*, fr. MF, fr. Ar *jarnayṭ*] (15c) : any of a genus (*Genetta*) of small Old World usu. carnivorous mammals related to the civets and having retractile claws, spotted or striped fur, and a ringed tail

gene therapy *n* (1974) : the insertion of normal or genetically altered genes into cells usu. to replace defective genes esp. in the treatment of genetic disorders

ge·net·ic \jə-ˈne-tik\ *also* **ge·net·i·cal** \-ti-kəl\ *adj* [*genesis*] (1831) **1** : relating to or determined by the origin, development, or causal antecedents of something **2 a** : of, relating to, or involving genetics **b** : GENIC — **ge·net·i·cal·ly** \-ti-k(ə-)lē\ *adv*

-ge·net·ic *adj comb form* : -GENIC 1, 2 ⟨psychogenetic⟩

genetic code *n* (1961) : the biochemical basis of heredity consisting of codons in DNA and RNA that determine the specific amino acid sequence in proteins and appear to be uniform for all known forms of life

genetic counseling *n* (1968) : medical education of affected individuals and the general public concerning inherited disorders

genetic drift *n* (1945) : random changes in gene frequency esp. in small populations when leading to preservation or extinction of particular genes

genetic engineering *n* (1966) : the directed alteration of genetic material by intervention in genetic processes; *esp* : GENE-SPLICING — **genetically engineered** *adj* — **genetic engineer** *n*

genetic map *n* (ca. 1960) : MAP 3

genetic marker *n* (1950) : a usu. dominant gene or trait that serves esp. to identify genes or traits linked with it

ge·net·ics \jə-ˈne-tiks\ *n pl but sing in constr* (1905) **1** : a branch of biology that deals with the heredity and variation of organisms **2** : the genetic makeup and phenomena of an organism, type, group, or condition — **ge·net·i·cist** \-ˈne-tə-sist\ *n*

ge·ne·va \jə-ˈnē-və\ *n* [modif. of obs. D *genever* (now *jenever*), lit., juniper, fr. MD, fr. OF *geneivre*, ultim. fr. L *juniperus*] (1706) : a highly aromatic bitter gin orig. made in the Netherlands

Ge·ne·va bands \jə-ˈnē-və-\ *n pl* [*Geneva*, Switzerland; fr. their use by the Calvinist clergy of Geneva] (1882) : two strips of white cloth suspended from the front of a clerical collar and sometimes used by Protestant clergymen — called also *Geneva tabs*

Geneva convention *n* (1880) : one of a series of agreements concerning the treatment of prisoners of war and of the sick, wounded, and dead in battle first made at Geneva, Switzerland in 1864 and subsequently accepted in later revisions by most nations

Geneva cross *n* [fr. its adoption by the Geneva convention] (ca. 1889) : RED CROSS

Geneva gown *n* [fr. its use by the Calvinist clergy of Geneva] (1820) : a loose large-sleeved black academic gown widely used as a vestment by members of the Protestant clergy

Geneva bands

Ge·ne·van \jə-ˈnē-vən\ *adj* (1573) **1** : of or relating to Geneva, Switzerland **2** : of or relating to Calvinism — **Genevan** *n*

¹ge·nial \ˈjēn-yəl, ˈjē-nē-əl\ *adj* [L *genialis*, fr. *genius*] (1566) **1** *obs* : of or relating to marriage or generation ⟨the ~ bed —John Milton⟩ **2** *obs* : INBORN, NATIVE **3 a** : favorable to growth or comfort : MILD ⟨~ sunshine⟩ **b** : marked by or diffusing sympathy or friendliness ⟨your ~ host⟩ **4** : displaying or marked by genius *syn* see GRACIOUS — **ge·nial·i·ty** \ˌjē-nē-ˈa-lə-tē, jēn-ˈyal-\ *n* — **ge·nial·ly** \ˈjēn-yə-lē\ *adv*

²ge·ni·al \ji-ˈnī(-ə)l\ *adj* [Gk *geneion* chin, fr. *genys* jaw — more at CHIN] (1831) : of or relating to the chin

gen·ic \ˈjē-nik, ˈje-\ *adj* (1918) : of, relating to, or being a gene — **gen·i·cal·ly** \-ni-k(ə-)lē\ *adv*

-gen·ic *adj comb form* [ISV *-gen & -geny + -ic*] **1** : producing : forming ⟨carcinogenic⟩ **2** : produced by : formed from ⟨biogenic⟩ **3** ⟨photogenic⟩ : suitable for production or reproduction by (such) a medium ⟨telegenic⟩

ge·nic·u·late \jə-ˈni-kyə-lət\ *or* **ge·nic·u·lat·ed** \-ˌlā-təd\ *adj* [L *geniculatus*, fr. *geniculum*, dim. of *genu* knee — more at KNEE] (1657) : bent abruptly at an angle like a bent knee

ge·nie \ˈjē-nē\ *n, pl* **ge·nies** *also* **ge·nii** \ˈjē-nē-(ˌ)ī\ [F *génie*, fr. Ar *jinnīy*] (1748) **1** : JINNI **2** : a magic spirit believed to take human form and serve the person who calls it

gen·i·tal \ˈje-nə-tᵊl\ *adj* [ME, fr. L *genitalis*, fr. *genitus*, pp. of *gignere* to beget — more at KIN] (14c) **1** : GENERATIVE **2** : of, relating to, or

\ə\ abut \ᵊ\ kitten, F table \ər\ further \a\ ash \ā\ ace \ä\ mop, mar \au̇\ out \ch\ chin \e\ bet \ē\ easy \g\ go \i\ hit \ī\ ice \j\ job \ŋ\ sing \ō\ go \ȯ\ law \ȯi\ boy \th\ thin \t͟h\ the \ü\ loot \u̇\ foot \y\ yet \zh\ vision \ä, k̟, ⁿ, œ, œ̄, ᴜᴇ, ᵫ, ᵞ\ see Guide to Pronunciation being a sexual organ **3** : of, relating to, or characterized by the stage of psychosexual development in psychoanalytic theory during which oral and anal impulses are subordinated to adaptive interpersonal mechanisms — **gen·i·tal·ly** \-tə-lē\ *adv*

genital herpes *n* (1968) : herpes simplex of the type typically affecting the genitalia

gen·i·ta·lia \ˌje-nə-ˈtāl-yə\ *n pl* [L, fr. neut. pl. of *genitalis*] (1876) : the organs of the reproductive system; *esp* : the external genital organs — **gen·i·ta·lic** \-ˈta-lik, -ˈtā-\ *adj*

gen·i·tals \ˈje-nə-tᵊlz\ *n pl* (14c) : GENITALIA

gen·i·ti·val \ˌje-nə-ˈtī-vəl\ *adj* (1818) : of, relating to, or formed with or from the genitive case — **gen·i·ti·val·ly** \-və-lē\ *adv*

gen·i·tive \ˈje-nə-tiv\ *adj* [ME, fr. L *genitivus*, lit., of generation (erroneous translation of Gk *genikos* genitive), fr. *genitus*] (14c) **1** : of, relating to, or constituting a grammatical case marking typically a relationship of possessor or source — compare POSSESSIVE **2** : expressing a relationship that in some inflected languages is often marked by a genitive case — used esp. of English prepositional phrases introduced by *of* — **genitive** *n*

genito- *comb form* [*genital*] : genital and ⟨*genito*urinary⟩

gen·i·to·uri·nary \ˌje-nə-tō-ˈyùr-ə-ˌner-ē\ *adj* (ca. 1836) : of or relating to the genital and urinary organs or functions

gen·i·ture \ˈje-nə-ˌchùr, -chər, -ˌt(y)ùr\ *n* (15c) : NATIVITY, BIRTH

ge·nius \ˈjēn-yəs, ˈjē-nē-əs\ *n, pl* **ge·nius·es** *or* **ge·nii** \-nē-ˌī\ [L, tutelary spirit, natural inclinations, fr. *gignere* to beget] (1513) **1 a** *pl* **genii** : an attendant spirit of a person or place **b** *pl usu* **genii** : a person who influences another for good or bad **2** : a strong leaning or inclination : PENCHANT **3 a** : a peculiar, distinctive, or identifying character or spirit **b** : the associations and traditions of a place **c** : a personification or embodiment esp. of a quality or condition **4** *pl usu* **genii** : SPIRIT, JINNI **5** *pl usu* **geniuses** **a** : a single strongly marked capacity or aptitude ⟨had a ~ for getting along with boys —Mary Ross⟩ **b** : extraordinary intellectual power esp. as manifested in creative activity **c** : a person endowed with transcendent mental superiority; *esp* : a person with a very high intelligence quotient **syn** see GIFT

genius lo·ci \-ˈlō-ˌsī, -ˌkē\ *n* [L] (1605) **1** : the pervading spirit of a place **2** : a tutelary deity of a place

geno- — see GEN-

gen·oa \ˈje-nə-wə\ *n* [*Genoa*, Italy] (1932) : a large jib that overlaps the mainsail and is used esp. in racing

geno·cide \ˈje-nə-ˌsīd\ *n* (1944) : the deliberate and systematic destruction of a racial, political, or cultural group — **geno·cid·al** \ˌje-nə-ˈsī-dᵊl\ *adj*

ge·noise *or* **gé·noise** \zhā-ˈnwäz\ *n* [F *génoise*, fr. fem. of *génois* of Genoa, Italy] (1931) : a sponge cake containing butter and leavened by stiffly beaten eggs

ge·nome \ˈjē-ˌnōm\ *n* [G *Genom*, fr. *Gen* gene + *-om* (as in *Chromosom* chromosome)] (1930) : one haploid set of chromosomes with the genes they contain; *broadly* : the genetic material of an organism — **ge·no·mic** \ji-ˈnō-mik, -ˈnä-\ *adj*

ge·no·type \ˈjē-nə-ˌtīp, ˈje-\ *n* (1897) **1** [ISV ¹*gen*-] : TYPE SPECIES **2** [ISV ²*gen*-] : all or part of the genetic constitution of an individual or group — compare PHENOTYPE — **ge·no·typ·ic** \ˌjē-nə-ˈti-pik, ˌje-\ *also* **ge·no·typ·i·cal** \-pi-kəl\ *adj* — **ge·no·typ·i·cal·ly** \-pi-k(ə-)lē\ *adv*

-genous *adj comb form* [-*gen* + -*ous*] **1** : producing : yielding ⟨erogenous⟩ **2** : having (such) an origin ⟨terrigenous⟩

genre \ˈzhän-rə, ˈzhä̃-; ˈzhä̃r; ˈjän-rə\ *n* [F, fr. MF, kind, gender — more at GENDER] (1770) **1** : a category of artistic, musical, or literary composition characterized by a particular style, form, or content **2** : KIND, SORT **3** : painting that depicts scenes or events from everyday life usu. realistically

gen·ro \ˈgen-ˈrō\ *n pl, often cap* [Jp *genrō*] (1876) : the elder statesmen of Japan who formerly advised the emperor

gens \ˈjenz, ˈgen(t)s\ *n, pl* **gen·tes** \ˈjen-ˌtēz, ˈgen-ˌtās\ [L *gent-, gens* — more at GENTLE] (1847) **1** : a Roman clan embracing the families of the same stock in the male line with the members having a common name and worshiping a common ancestor **2** : CLAN; *esp* : a patrilineal clan **3** : a distinguishable group of related organisms

¹gent \ˈjent\ *adj* [ME, noble, graceful, fr. OF, fr. L *genitus*, pp. of *gignere* to beget — more at KIN] (13c) *archaic* : PRETTY, GRACEFUL

²gent *n* (1564) : GENTLEMAN

gen·ta·mi·cin \ˌjen-tə-ˈmī-sᵊn\ *n* [alter. of earlier *gentamycin*, fr. *gentian* violet + kan*amycin*; fr. the color of the actinomycete] (1963) : a broad-spectrum antibiotic that is derived from an actinomycete (*Micromonospora purpurea* or *M. echinospora*) and is extensively used as the sulfate in treating infections esp. of the urinary tract

gen·teel \jen-ˈtē(ə)l\ *adj* [MF *gentil* gentle] (1599) **1 a** : having an aristocratic quality or flavor : STYLISH **b** : of or relating to the gentry or upper class **c** : elegant or graceful in manner, appearance, or shape **d** : free from vulgarity or rudeness : POLITE **2 a** : maintaining or striving to maintain the appearance of superior or middle-class social status or respectability **b** (1) : marked by false delicacy, prudery, or affectation (2) : conventionally or insipidly pretty ⟨timid and ~ artistic style⟩ — **gen·teel·ly** \-ˈtē(ə)(l)-lē\ *adv* — **gen·teel·ness** *n*

gen·teel·ism \-ˈtē(ə)(l)-ˌli-zəm\ *n* (1926) : a word believed by its user to be more polite and less vulgar than a common synonym; *also* : the use of genteelisms

gen·tian \ˈjen(t)-shən\ *n* [ME *gencian*, fr. MF *gentiane*, fr. L *gentiana*] (14c) **1** : any of numerous herbs (family Gentianaceae, the gentian family, and esp. genus *Gentiana*) with opposite smooth leaves and showy usu. blue flowers **2** : the rhizome and roots of a yellow-flowered gentian (*Gentiana lutea*) of southern Europe that is used as a tonic, stomachic, and flavoring in vermouth

gentian violet *n, often cap G&V* (1897) : any of several dyes or dye mixtures consisting of one or more methyl derivatives of pararosaniline; *esp* : a dark green or greenish mixture used esp. as a bactericide, fungicide, and anthelmintic

¹gen·tile \ˈjen-ˌtīl\ *n* [ME, fr. LL *gentilis*, fr. L *gent-, gens* nation] (14c) **1** *often cap* : a person of a non-Jewish nation or of non-Jewish faith; *esp* : a Christian as distinguished from a Jew **2** : HEATHEN, PAGAN **3** *often cap* : a non-Mormon

²gentile *adj* (15c) **1** *often cap* **a** : of or relating to the nations at large as distinguished from the Jews; *also* : of or relating to Christians as

distinguished from the Jews **b** : of or relating to non-Mormons **2** : HEATHEN, PAGAN **3** [L *gentilis*] : relating to a tribe or clan

gen·ti·lesse \ˌjen-tᵊl-ˈes\ *n* [ME, fr. MF, fr. *gentil*] (14c) : decorum of conduct befitting a member of the gentry

gen·til·i·ty \jen-ˈti-lə-tē\ *n, pl* -**ties** (14c) **1 a** : the condition of belonging to the gentry **b** : GENTLEFOLK, GENTRY **2 a** (1) : decorum of conduct : COURTESY (2) : attitudes or activity marked by false delicacy, prudery, or affectation **b** : superior social status or prestige evidenced by manners, possessions, or mode of life

¹gen·tle \ˈjen-tᵊl\ *adj* **gen·tler** \ˈjent-lər, -tᵊl-ər\; **gen·tlest** \ˈjent-ləst, -tᵊl-əst\ [ME *gentil*, fr. OF, fr. L *gentilis* of a gens, of one's family, fr. *gent-, gens* gens, nation; akin to L *gignere* to beget — more at KIN] (13c) **1 a** : belonging to a family of high social station **b** *archaic* : CHIVALROUS **c** : HONORABLE, DISTINGUISHED; *specif* : of or relating to a gentleman **d** : KIND, AMIABLE — used esp. in address as a complimentary epithet ⟨~ reader⟩ **e** : suited to a person of high social station **2 a** : TRACTABLE, DOCILE **b** : free from harshness, sternness, or violence **3** : SOFT, DELICATE **4** : MODERATE — **gent·ly** \ˈjent-lē\ *adv*

²gentle *n* (14c) : a person of gentle birth or status

³gentle *vb* **gen·tled; gen·tling** \ˈjent-liŋ, ˈjen-tᵊl-iŋ\ *vt* (14c) **1** : to raise from the commonalty : ENNOBLE **2 a** : to make gentler **b** : to make (an animal) tame and docile **c** : MOLLIFY, PLACATE **d** : to stroke soothingly : PET ~ *vi* : to become gentle ⟨the wind *gentled*⟩

gentle breeze *n* (ca. 1881) : wind having a speed of 8 to 12 miles per hour (about 13 to 19 kilometers per hour) — see BEAUFORT SCALE table

gen·tle·folk \ˈjen-tᵊl-ˌfōk\ *also* **gen·tle·folks** \-ˌfōks\ *n pl* (1594) : persons of gentle or good family and breeding

gen·tle·man \ˈjen-tᵊl-mən, ˈje-nᵊl-, in rapid speech also ˈjen-tə-mən, ˈje-nə-\ *n, often attrib* [ME *gentilman*] (12c) **1 a** : a man of noble or gentle birth **b** : a man belonging to the landed gentry **c** (1) : a man who combines gentle birth or rank with chivalrous qualities (2) : a man whose conduct conforms to a high standard of propriety or correct behavior **d** (1) : a man of independent means who does not engage in any occupation or profession for gain (2) : a man who does not engage in a menial occupation or in manual labor for gain **2** : VALET — often used in the phrase *gentleman's gentleman* **3** : a man of any social class or condition — often used in a courteous reference ⟨show this ~ to a seat⟩ or usu. in the pl. in address ⟨ladies and gentlemen⟩ — **gen·tle·man·like** \-mən-ˌlīk\ *adj* — **gen·tle·man·like·ness** *n*

gentleman–at–arms *n, pl* **gentlemen–at–arms** (1859) : one of a military corps of 40 gentlemen who attend the British sovereign on state occasions

gentleman–commoner *n, pl* **gentlemen–commoners** (1687) : any of a privileged class of commoners formerly required to pay higher fees than ordinary commoners at the universities of Oxford and Cambridge

gentleman farmer *n, pl* **gentlemen farmers** (1749) : a man who farms mainly for pleasure rather than for profit

gen·tle·man·ly \-lē\ *adj* (15c) : characteristic of or having the character of a gentleman — **gen·tle·man·li·ness** *n*

gentleman of fortune (1883) : ADVENTURER

gentleman's agreement *or* **gentlemen's agreement** *n* (1886) : an agreement secured only by the honor of the participants

gen·tle·ness \ˈjen-tᵊl-nəs\ *n* (14c) : the quality or state of being gentle; *esp* : mildness of manners or disposition

gen·tle·per·son \ˈjen-tᵊl-ˌpər-sᵊn\ *n* (1943) : a gentleman or lady

gentle sex *n* (1583) : the female sex : women in general

gen·tle·wom·an \ˈjen-tᵊl-ˌwù-mən\ *n* (13c) **1 a** : a woman of noble or gentle birth **b** : a woman attendant upon a lady of rank **2 a** : a woman of refined manners or good breeding : LADY

Gen·too \ˈjen-(ˌ)tü\ *n, pl* **Gentoos** [Pg *gentio*, lit., gentile, fr. LL *gentilis*] (1638) *archaic* : HINDU

gen·too penguin \ˈjen-(ˌ)tü-\ *n* [perh. fr. *Gentoo*] (1860) : a penguin (*Pygoscelis papua*) of Antarctica and nearby islands with a gray back and throat, white underparts, and white spots above the eyes — called also *gentoo*

gen·trice \ˈjen-trəs\ *n* [ME *gentrise*, fr. OF *genterise*, alter. of *gentelise*, fr. *gentil* gentle] (14c) *archaic* : gentility of birth : RANK

gen·tri·fi·ca·tion \ˌjen-trə-fə-ˈkā-shən\ *n* (1964) : the process of renewal and rebuilding accompanying the influx of middle-class or affluent people into deteriorating areas that often displaces earlier usu. poorer residents

gen·tri·fy \ˈjen-trə-ˌfī\ *vb* -**fied;** -**fy·ing** *vt* (1972) : to attempt or accomplish the gentrification of ~ *vi* : to become gentrified — **gen·tri·fi·er** \-ˌfī(-ə)r\ *n*

gen·try \ˈjen-trē\ *n, pl* **gentries** [ME *gentrie*, alter. of *gentrise*] (14c) **a** *obs* : the qualities appropriate to a person of gentle birth; *esp* : COURTESY **b** : the condition or rank of a gentleman **2 a** : upper or ruling class : ARISTOCRACY **b** : a class whose members are entitled to bear a coat of arms though not of noble rank; *esp* : the landed proprietors having such status **3** : people of a specified class or kind : FOLKS ⟨no real heroes or heroines among the academic ~ —R. G. Hanvey⟩

gents \ˈjen(t)s\ *n, often cap* (1938) *chiefly Brit* : MEN'S ROOM

gen·u·flect \ˈjen-yə-ˌflekt\ *vi* [LL *genuflectere*, fr. L *genu* knee + *flectere* to bend — more at KNEE] (1630) **1 a** : to bend the knee **b** : to touch the knee to the floor or ground esp. in worship **2** : to be servilely obedient or respectful — **gen·u·flec·tion** \ˌjen-yə-ˈflek-shən\ *n*

gen·u·ine \ˈjen-yə-wən, -(ˌ)win, ÷-ˌwīn\ *adj* [L *genuinus* innate, genuine; akin to L *gignere* to beget — more at KIN] (ca. 1639) **1 a** : actually having the reputed or apparent qualities or character ⟨~ vintage wines⟩ **b** : actually produced by or proceeding from the alleged source or author ⟨the signature is ~⟩ **c** : sincerely and honestly felt or experienced ⟨a deep and ~ love⟩ **d** : ACTUAL, TRUE ⟨a ~ improvement⟩ **2** : free from hypocrisy or pretense : SINCERE **syn** see AUTHENTIC — **gen·u·ine·ly** *adv* — **gen·u·ine·ness** \-wən(-nəs\ *n*

usage The objection which some commentators make to the pronunciation \ˈjen-yə-ˌwīn\ is perhaps occasioned by the fact that it is more frequent among those with less schooling. However, this variant is heard in the speech of cultured or highly educated speakers sufficiently frequently for it to be recognized as a widespread pronunciation at all social levels. This variant was recorded as early as 1890 and appears to be simply a long-standing spelling pronunciation.

ge·nus \ˈjē-nəs, ˈje-\ *n, pl* **gen·era** \ˈje-nə-rə\ [L *gener-, genus* birth, race, kind — more at KIN] (1551) **1** : a class, kind, or group marked by common characteristics or by one common characteristic; *specif* : a category of biological classification ranking between the family and the species, comprising structurally or phylogenetically related species or an isolated species exhibiting unusual differentiation, and being designated by a Latin or latinized capitalized singular noun **2** : a class of objects divided into several subordinate species

-geny *n comb form* [Gk *-geneia* act of being born, fr. *-genēs* born — more at -GEN] : generation : production ⟨phylo*geny*⟩

geo- — see GE-

geo·bot·a·ny \ˌjē-ō-'bä-t²n-ē, -'bät-nē\ *n* (1904) : PHYTOGEOGRAPHY — **geo·bo·tan·i·cal** \-bə-'ta-ni-kəl\ *also* **geo·bo·tan·ic** \-nik\ *adj* — **geo·bot·a·nist** \-'bä-t²n-ist, -'bät-nist\ *n*

geo·cen·tric \ˌjē-ō-'sen-trik\ *adj* (1686) **1 a** : relating to, measured from, or as if observed from the earth's center — compare TOPOCENTRIC **b** : having or relating to the earth as center — compare HELIOCENTRIC **2** : taking or based on the earth as the center of perspective and valuation — **geo·cen·tri·cal·ly** \-tri-k(ə-)lē\ *adv*

geo·chem·is·try \ˌjē-ō-'ke-mə-strē\ *n* (1902) **1** : a science that deals with the chemical composition of and chemical changes in the solid matter of the earth or a celestial body (as the moon) **2** : the related chemical and geological properties of a substance — **geo·chem·i·cal** \-'ke-mi-kəl\ *adj* — **geo·chem·i·cal·ly** \-k(ə-)lē\ *adv* — **geo·chem·ist** \-'ke-mist\ *n*

geo·chro·nol·o·gy \ˌjē-ō-krə-'nä-lə-jē\ *n* (1893) **1** : the chronology of the past as indicated by geologic data **2** : the study of geochronology — **geo·chro·no·log·i·cal** \-ˌkrä-n°l-'ä-ji-kəl, -ˌkrō-\ *also* **geo·chro·no·log·ic** \-'ä-jik\ *adj* — **geo·chro·no·log·i·cal·ly** \-ji-k(ə-)lē\ *adv* — **geo·chro·nol·o·gist** \-krə-'nä-lə-jist\ *n*

ge·ode \'jē-ˌōd\ *n* [L *geodes*, a gem, fr. Gk *geōdēs* earthlike, fr. *gē* earth] (ca. 1732) **1** : a nodule of stone having a cavity lined with crystals or mineral matter **2** : the cavity in a geode

¹geo·de·sic \ˌjē-ə-'de-sik, -'dē-, -zik\ *adj* (1821) **1** : GEODETIC **2** : made of light straight structural elements mostly in tension ⟨a ∼ dome⟩

²geodesic *n* (1883) : the shortest line between two points that lies in a given surface

ge·od·e·sy \jē-'ä-də-sē\ *n* [Gk *geōdaisia*, fr. *geō-* ge- + *daiesthai* to divide — more at TIDE] (1570) : a branch of applied mathematics concerned with the determination of the size and shape of the earth and the exact positions of points on its surface and with the description of variations of its gravity field — **ge·od·e·sist** \-də-sist\ *n*

geo·det·ic \ˌjē-ə-'de-tik\ *also* **geo·det·i·cal** \-ti-kəl\ *adj* [*geodesy;* after such pairs as *heresy : heretic*] (ca. 1828) : of, relating to, or determined by geodesy

geodetic survey *n* (1880) : a survey of a large land area in which corrections are made for the curvature of the earth's surface

Geo·dim·e·ter \ˌjē-ə-'di-mə-tər\ *trademark* — used for an electronic optical device that measures distance using the velocity of light

geo·duck \'gü-ˌē-ˌdək\ *n* [Lushootseed (Salishan language of the Puget Sound region) *gʷídəq*] (1883) : a large edible clam (*Panopea abrupta* syn. *P. generosa*) of the Pacific coast that sometimes weighs over five pounds

ge·og·ra·pher \jē-'ä-grə-fər\ *n* (1542) : a specialist in geography

geo·graph·ic \ˌjē-ə-'gra-fik\ *or* **geo·graph·i·cal** \-fi-kəl\ *adj* (1559) **1** : of or relating to geography **2** : belonging to or characteristic of a particular region — **geo·graph·i·cal·ly** \-fi-k(ə-)lē\ *adv*

geographical mile *n* (1823) : NAUTICAL MILE a

ge·og·ra·phy \jē-'ä-grə-fē\ *n, pl* **-phies** [L *geographia*, fr. Gk *geō-graphia*, fr. *geōgraphein* to describe the earth's surface, fr. *geō-* + *graphein* to write — more at CARVE] (15c) **1** : a science that deals with the description, distribution, and interaction of the diverse physical, biological, and cultural features of the earth's surface **2** : the geographic features of an area **3** : a treatise on geography **4** : a delineation or systematic arrangement of constituent elements : CONFIGURATION ⟨the philosophers . . . have tried to construct *geographies* of human reason —*Times Lit. Supp.*⟩

geo·hy·drol·o·gy \ˌjē-ō-hī-'drä-lə-jē\ *n* (ca. 1909) : a science that deals with the character, source, and mode of occurrence of underground water — **geo·hy·dro·log·ic** \-ˌhī-drə-'lä-jik\ *adj* — **geo·hy·drol·o·gist** \-hī-'drä-lə-jist\ *n*

ge·oid \'jē-ˌóid\ *n* [G, fr. Gk *geoeidēs* earthlike, fr. *gē*] (1881) : the surface within or around the earth that is everywhere normal to the direction of gravity and coincides with mean sea level in the oceans — **ge·oi·dal** \jē-'ói-d²l\ *adj*

geo·log·ic \ˌjē-ə-'lä-jik\ *or* **geo·log·i·cal** \-ji-kəl\ *adj* (1791) : of, relating to, or based on geology — **geo·log·i·cal·ly** \-ji-k(ə-)lē\ *adv*

geologic time *n* (1861) : the long period of time occupied by the earth's geologic history

GEOLOGIC TIME

EON	ERA	PERIODS AND SYSTEMS	EPOCHS AND SERIES	BEGINNING OF INTERVAL*	BIOLOGICAL FORMS
Phanerozoic	Cenozoic	Quaternary	Holocene	0.01	
			Pleistocene	1.6	Earliest humans
		Tertiary	Pliocene	5	
			Miocene	24	Earliest hominids
			Oligocene	37	
			Eocene	58	Earliest grasses
			Paleocene	65	Earliest large mammals
	Cretaceous-Tertiary boundary (65 million years ago): extinction of dinosaurs				
	Mesozoic	Cretaceous	Upper	98	
			Lower	144	Earliest flowering plants; dinosaurs in ascendance
		Jurassic		208	Earliest birds & mammals
		Triassic		245	Age of Dinosaurs begins
	Paleozoic	Permian		286	
		Carboniferous			
		Pennsylvanian		320	Earliest reptiles
		Mississippian		360	Earliest winged insects
		Devonian		408	Earliest vascular plants (as ferns & mosses) & amphibians
		Silurian		438	Earliest land plants & insects
		Ordovician		505	Earliest corals
		Cambrian		570	Earliest fish
Proterozoic	Precambrian			2500	Earliest colonial algae & soft-bodied invertebrates
Archean				4000	Life appears: earliest algae & primitive bacteria

*In millions of years before the present

ge·ol·o·gize \jē-'ä-lə-ˌjīz\ *vi* **-gized; -giz·ing** (1831) : to study geology or make geologic investigations

ge·ol·o·gy \jē-'ä-lə-jē\ *n, pl* **-gies** [NL *geologia,* fr. *ge-* + *-logia* -logy] (1735) **1 a :** a science that deals with the history of the earth and its life esp. as recorded in rocks **b :** a study of the solid matter of a celestial body (as the moon) **2 :** geologic features **3 :** a treatise on geology — **ge·ol·o·gist** \-jist\ *n*

geo·mag·net·ic \jē-ō-mag-'ne-tik\ *adj* (1904) : of or relating to terrestrial magnetism — **geo·mag·net·i·cal·ly** \-ti-k(ə-)lē\ *adv* — **geo·mag·ne·tism** \-'mag-nə-ˌti-zəm\ *n*

geomagnetic storm *n* (1941) : MAGNETIC STORM

geo·man·cy \'jē-ə-ˌman(t)-sē\ *n* [ME *geomancie,* fr. MF, fr. ML *geomantia,* fr. LGk *geōmanteia,* fr. Gk *geō-* + *-manteia* -mancy] (14c) : divination by means of figures or lines or geographic features — **geo·man·cer** \-sər\ *n* — **geo·man·tic** \jē-ə-'man-tik\ *adj*

ge·om·e·ter \jē-'ä-mə-tər\ *n* (15c) **1 :** a specialist in geometry **2** : GEOMETRID

geo·met·ric \ˌjē-ə-'me-trik\ *or* **geo·met·ri·cal** \-'me-tri-kəl\ *adj* (14c) **1 a :** of, relating to, or according to the methods or principles of geometry **b :** increasing in a geometric progression ⟨~ population growth⟩ **2** *cap :* of or relating to a style of ancient Greek pottery characterized by geometric decorative motifs **3 a :** utilizing rectilinear or simple curvilinear motifs or outlines in design **b :** of or relating to art based on simple geometric shapes (as straight lines, circles, or squares) ⟨~ abstractions⟩ — **geo·met·ri·cal·ly** \-tri-k(ə-)lē\ *adv*

geo·me·tri·cian \(ˌ)jē-ˌä-mə-'tri-shən, ˌjē-ə-mə-\ *n* (15c) : GEOMETER 1

geometric mean *n* (ca. 1901) : the nth root of the product of *n* numbers; *specif :* a number that is the second term of three consecutive terms of a geometric progression ⟨the *geometric mean* of 9 and 4 is 6⟩

geometric progression *n* (ca. 1856) : a sequence (as 1, ½, ¼) in which the ratio of a term to its predecessor is always the same — called also *geometrical progression, geometric sequence*

geo·met·rics \ˌjē-ə-'me-triks\ *n pl* (1977) : decorative patterns or designs based on geometric shapes

geometric series *n* (ca. 1909) : a series (as $1 + x + x^2 + x^3 + \ldots$) whose terms form a geometric progression

geo·me·trid \jē-'ä-mə-trəd, ˌjē-ə-'me-trəd\ *n* [ultim. fr. Gk *geōmetrēs* geometer, fr. *geōmetrein*] (1876) : any of a family (Geometridae) of usu. medium-sized moths with large wings and larvae that are loopers — **geometrid** *adj*

ge·om·e·trise *Brit var of* GEOMETRIZE

ge·om·e·trize \jē-'ä-mə-ˌtrīz\ *vb* **-trized; -triz·ing** *vi* (1603) : to work by or as if by geometric methods or laws ~ *vt* **1 :** to represent geometrically **2 :** to make conform to geometric principles and laws — **ge·om·e·tri·za·tion** \-ˌä-mə-trə-'zā-shən\ *n*

ge·om·e·try \jē-'ä-mə-trē\ *n, pl* **-tries** [ME *geometrie,* fr. MF, fr. L *geometria,* fr. Gk *geōmetria,* fr. *geōmetrein* to measure the earth, fr. *geō-* + *metron* measure — more at MEASURE] (14c) **1 a :** a branch of mathematics that deals with the measurement, properties, and relationships of points, lines, angles, surfaces, and solids; *broadly :* the study of properties of given elements that remain invariant under specified transformations **b :** a particular type or system of geometry **2 a** : CONFIGURATION **b :** surface shape **3 :** an arrangement of objects or parts that suggests geometric figures

geo·mor·phic \ˌjē-ə-'mȯr-fik\ *adj* (1893) : GEOMORPHOLOGICAL

geo·mor·pho·log·i·cal \-ˌmȯr-fə-'lä-ji-kəl\ *adj* (1896) : of or relating to the form or surface features of the earth or other celestial body (as the moon)

geo·mor·phol·o·gy \-ˌmȯr-'fä-lə-jē\ *n, pl* **-gies** [ISV] (1893) **1 :** a science that deals with the relief features of the earth or of another celestial body (as the moon) and seeks a genetic interpretation of them **2 :** the features dealt with in geomorphology — **geo·mor·phol·o·gist** \-mȯr-'fä-lə-jist\ *n*

ge·oph·a·gy \jē-'ä-fə-jē\ *n* [ISV] (1850) : a practice in rural or preindustrial societies of eating earthy substances (as clay) to augment a scanty or mineral-deficient diet — compare [1]PICA

geo·phone \'jē-ə-ˌfōn\ *n* (1919) : an instrument for detecting vibrations passing through rocks, soil, or ice

geo·phys·ics \ˌjē-ə-'fi-ziks\ *n pl but sing or pl in constr* [ISV] (ca. 1889) : a branch of earth science dealing with the physical processes and phenomena occurring esp. in the earth and in its vicinity — **geo·phys·i·cal** \-zi-kəl\ *adj* — **geo·phys·i·cal·ly** \-zi-k(ə-)lē\ *adv* — **geo·phys·i·cist** \-'fi-zə-sist\ *n*

geo·phyte \'jē-ə-ˌfīt\ *n* (ca. 1900) : a perennial plant that bears its perennating buds below the surface of the soil

geo·pol·i·ti·cian \ˌjē-ō-ˌpä-lə-'ti-shən\ *n* (1941) : a specialist in geopolitics

geo·pol·i·tics \-'pä-lə-ˌtiks\ *n pl but sing in constr* (1904) **1 :** a study of the influence of such factors as geography, economics, and demography on the politics and esp. the foreign policy of a state **2 :** a governmental policy guided by geopolitics **3 :** a combination of political and geographic factors relating to something (as a state or particular resources) — **geo·po·lit·i·cal** \-pə-'li-ti-kəl\ *adj* — **geo·po·lit·i·cal·ly** \-ti-k(ə-)lē\ *adv*

geo·pres·sured \ˌjē-ō-'pre-shərd\ *adj* (1968) : subjected to great pressure from geologic forces ⟨~ methane⟩

Geor·die \'jȯr-dē\ *n* [fr. *Geordie,* dim. of the name *George*] (1866) *chiefly Brit :* an inhabitant of Newcastle upon Tyne or its environs; *also* : the dialect of English spoken by Geordies

George \'jȯrj\ *n* [*St. George*] (1506) **1 :** either of two of the insignia of the British Order of the Garter **2 :** a British coin bearing the image of St. George

geor·gette \jȯr-'jet\ *n* [fr. *Georgette,* a trademark] (1915) : a sheer crepe woven from hard-twisted yarns to produce a dull pebbly surface

[1]Geor·gian \'jȯr-jən\ *n* (15c) **1 :** a native or inhabitant of Georgia in the Caucasus **2 :** the language of the Georgian people

[2]Georgian *adj* (1607) **:** of, relating to, or constituting Georgia in the Caucasus, the Georgians, or Georgian

[3]Georgian *n* (1741) : a native or resident of the state of Georgia

[4]Georgian *adj* (1762) : of, relating to, or characteristic of the state of Georgia or its people

[5]Georgian *adj* (ca. 1855) **1 :** of, relating to, or characteristic of the reigns of the first four Georges of Great Britain **2 :** of, relating to, or characteristic of the reign of George V of Great Britain

[6]Georgian *n* (1901) **1 :** one belonging to either of the Georgian periods; *esp :* a poet of the second decade of the 20th century **2 :** Georgian taste or style esp. in architecture

[1]geor·gic \'jȯr-jik\ *n* [the *Georgics,* poem by Virgil, fr. L *georgicus*] (1513) : a poem dealing with agriculture

[2]georgic *adj* [L *georgicus,* fr. Gk *geōrgikos,* fr. *geōrgos* farmer, fr. *geō-* ge- + *ergon* work — more at WORK] (ca. 1720) : of or relating to agriculture

geo·sci·ence \ˌjē-ō-'sī-ən(t)s\ *n* (1942) **1 :** the sciences (as geology, geophysics, and geochemistry) dealing with the earth **2 :** any of the geosciences — compare EARTH SCIENCE — **geo·sci·en·tist** \-ən-tist\ *n*

geo·sta·tion·ary \-'stā-shə-ˌner-ē\ *adj* (1961) : being or having an equatorial orbit requiring an angular velocity the same as that of the earth so that the position of a satellite in such an orbit is fixed with respect to the earth

geo·strat·e·gy \-'stra-tə-jē\ *n* (1942) **1 :** a branch of geopolitics that deals with strategy **2 :** the combination of geopolitical and strategic factors characterizing a particular geographic region **3 :** the use by a government of strategy based on geopolitics — **geo·stra·te·gic** \-stra-'tē-jik\ *adj* — **geo·strat·e·gist** \-'stra-tə-jist\ *n*

geo·stroph·ic \ˌjē-ə-'strä-fik\ *adj* [ge- + Gk *strophikos* turned, fr. *strophē* turning — more at STROPHE] (1916) : of, relating to, or arising from the Coriolis force — **geo·stroph·i·cal·ly** \-fi-k(ə-)lē\ *adv*

geo·syn·chro·nous \ˌjē-ō-'siŋ-krə-nəs, -'sin-\ *adj* (1968) : GEOSTATIONARY

geo·syn·cline \-'sin-ˌklīn\ *n* (1895) : a great downward flexure of the earth's crust — compare GEANTICLINE — **geo·syn·cli·nal** \-ˌsin-'klī-nəl\ *adj*

geo·tac·tic \ˌjē-ō-'tak-tik\ *adj* (1899) : of or relating to geotaxis

geo·tax·is \-'tak-səs\ *n* [NL] (1899) : a taxis in which the force of gravity is the directive factor

geo·tech·ni·cal \-'tek-ni-kəl\ *adj* (1967) : of or relating to geotechnical engineering

geotechnical engineering *n* (1974) : a science that deals with the application of geology to engineering

geo·tec·ton·ic \-tek-'tä-nik\ *adj* (1882) : of or relating to the form, arrangement, and structure of rock masses of the earth's crust resulting from folding or faulting — **geo·tec·ton·i·cal·ly** \-ni-k(ə-)lē\ *adv*

geo·ther·mal \-'thər-məl\ *adj* [ISV] (1875) : of, relating to, or utilizing the heat of the earth's interior; *also* : produced or permeated by such heat ⟨~ steam⟩ ⟨~ region⟩ — **geo·ther·mal·ly** \-mə-lē\ *adv*

geo·tro·pic \-'trō-pik, -'trä-\ *adj* (1875) : of or relating to geotropism — **geo·tro·pi·cal·ly** \-'trō-pi-k(ə-)lē, -'trä-\ *adv*

ge·ot·ro·pism \jē-'ä-trə-ˌpi-zəm\ *n* [ISV] (1875) : a tropism (as of plant roots) in which gravity is the orienting factor

ge·rah \'gir-ə\ *n* [Heb *gērāh*] (1530) : an ancient Hebrew unit of weight equal to 1/20 shekel

ge·ra·ni·ol \jə-'rā-nē-ˌȯl, -ˌōl\ *n* [ISV, fr. NL *Geranium*] (1871) : a fragrant liquid unsaturated alcohol $C_{10}H_{18}O$ used chiefly in perfumes and soap

ge·ra·ni·um \jə-'rā-nē-əm, -nyəm\ *n* [NL, fr. L *geranium,* fr. Gk *geranion,* fr. dim. of *geranos* crane — more at CRANE] (1548) **1 :** any of a widely distributed genus (*Geranium* of the family Geraniaceae, the geranium family) of plants having regular usu. white, pink, or purple flowers with elongated styles and glands that alternate with the petals **2 :** PELARGONIUM **3 :** a vivid or strong red

ge·rar·dia \jə-'rär-dē-ə\ *n* [NL, fr. John Gerard †1612 Eng. botanist] (1851) : any of a genus (*Agalinis* syn. *Gerardia*) of often root-parasitic herbs of the snapdragon family having pink, purple, or yellow flowers

ger·bera \'gər-bə-rə, 'jər-\ *n* [NL, fr. Traugott *Gerber* †1743 Ger. naturalist] (1889) : any of a genus (*Gerbera*) of Old World composite herbs having basal tufted leaves and showy heads of yellow, pink, or orange flowers with prominent rays

ger·bil *also* **ger·bille** \'jər-bəl\ *n* [F *gerbille,* fr. NL *Gerbillus,* dim. of *gerboa, jerboa* jerboa] (1849) : any of numerous Old World burrowing desert rodents (*Gerbillus* and related genera) with long hind legs adapted for leaping

ge·rent \'jir-ənt\ *n* [L *gerent-, gerens,* prp. of *gerere* to bear, carry on] (1576) : one that rules or manages

ge·re·nuk \'ger-ə-ˌnůk, gə-'re-nək\ *n, pl* **gerenuk** *or* **gerenuks** [Somali *gáránúug*] (1895) : a large-eyed antelope (*Litocranius walleri*) of eastern Africa with a long neck and limbs

ger·fal·con *var of* GYRFALCON

[1]ger·i·at·ric \ˌjer-ē-'a-trik, jir-\ *n* (1909) **1** *pl but sing in constr :* a branch of medicine that deals with the problems and diseases of old age and aging people — compare GERONTOLOGY **2 :** an aged person

[2]geriatric *adj* [Gk *gēras* old age + E *-iatric*] (1926) **1 a :** of or relating to geriatrics or the process of aging **b :** of, relating to, or appropriate for elderly people ⟨the ~ set⟩ **2 a :** OLD, ELDERLY ⟨a ~ dachshund⟩ **b :** being old and outmoded ⟨~ airplanes⟩

ger·i·a·tri·cian \ˌjer-ē-ə-'tri-shən, jir-\ *n* (1926) : a specialist in geriatrics

germ \'jərm\ *n* [F *germe,* fr. L *germin-, germen* to beget — more at KIN] (1644) **1 a :** a small mass of living substance capable of developing into an organism or one of its parts **b** : the embryo with the scutellum of a cereal grain that is usu. separated from the starchy endosperm during milling **2 :** something that initiates development or serves as an origin : RUDIMENTS, BEGINNING **3** : MICROORGANISM; *esp :* a microorganism causing disease

[1]ger·man \'jər-mən\ *adj* [ME *germain,* fr. MF, fr. L *germanus* having the same parents, fr. *germen*] (14c) : having the same parents or the same grandparents on either the maternal or paternal side — usu. used after the noun which it modifies and joined to it by a hyphen ⟨brother≠ german⟩ ⟨cousin-german⟩

[2]german *n* (15c) *obs :* a near relative

[1]Ger·man \'jər-mən\ *n* [ME, fr. ML *Germanus,* fr. L] (14c) **1 :** a member of any of the Germanic peoples inhabiting western Europe in Roman times **2 a :** a native or inhabitant of Germany **b :** a person

gerenuk

of German descent   **c :** one whose native language is German and who is a native of a country other than Germany   **3 a :** the Germanic language spoken mainly in Germany, Austria, and parts of Switzerland   **b :** the literary and official language of Germany   **4** *often not cap*   **a :** a dance consisting of intricate figures that are improvised and intermingled with waltzes   **b** *chiefly Midland* **:** a dancing party; *specif* **:** one at which the german is danced

²German *adj* (1552) **:** of, relating to, or characteristic of Germany, the Germans, or German

German cockroach *n* (1896) **:** a small active winged cockroach (*Blattella germanica*) prob. of African origin that is a common household pest in the U.S. — called also *Croton bug*

ger·man·der \(ˌ)jər-'man-dər\ *n* [ultim. fr. Gk *chamaidrys*, fr. *chamai* on the ground + *drys* tree — more at HUMBLE, TREE] (15c) **:** any of a genus (*Teucrium*) of plants of the mint family with flowers having four exserted stamens, a short corolla tube, and a prominent lower lip

ger·mane \(ˌ)jər-'mān\ *adj* [ME *germain*, lit., having the same parents, fr. MF] (14c) **1** *obs* **:** closely akin   **2 :** being at once relevant and appropriate **:** FITTING ⟨omit details that are not ~ to the discussion⟩ *syn* see RELEVANT — **ger·mane·ly** *adv*

¹Ger·man·ic \(ˌ)jər-'ma-nik\ *adj* (1633)   **1 :** GERMAN   **2 :** of, relating to, or characteristic of the Germanic-speaking peoples   **3 :** of, relating to, or constituting Germanic

²Germanic *n* (1892) **:** a branch of the Indo-European language family containing English, German, Dutch, Afrikaans, Flemish, Frisian, the Scandinavian languages, and Gothic — see INDO-EUROPEAN LANGUAGES table

Ger·man·ism \'jər-mə-ˌni-zəm\ *n* (1611)   **1 :** a characteristic feature of German occurring in another language   **2 :** partiality for Germany or German customs   **3 :** the practices or objectives characteristic of the Germans

Ger·man·ist \-nist\ *n* (1831) **:** a specialist in German or Germanic language, literature, or culture

ger·ma·ni·um \(ˌ)jər-'mā-nē-əm\ *n* [NL, fr. ML *Germania* Germany] (1886) **:** a grayish white hard brittle metalloid element that resembles silicon and is used as a semiconductor — see ELEMENT table

ger·man·ize \'jər-mə-ˌnīz\ *vb* **-ized; -iz·ing** *often cap*, *vt* (1598)   **1** *archaic* **:** to translate into German   **2 :** to cause to acquire German characteristics ~ *vi* **:** to have or acquire German customs or leanings — **ger·man·iza·tion** \ˌjər-mə-nə-'zā-shən\ *n, often cap*

German measles *n pl but sing or pl in constr* (ca. 1875) **:** an acute contagious virus disease that is milder than typical measles but is damaging to the fetus when occurring early in pregnancy

Ger·mano- *comb form* **:** German ⟨*Germanophile*⟩

¹Ger·mano·phile \(ˌ)jər-'ma-nə-ˌfīl\ *adj* (1898) **:** approving or favoring the German people and their institutions and customs

²Germanophile *n* (1911) **:** one that is Germanophile

German shepherd *n* (1926) **:** any of a breed of working dogs of German origin that are intelligent and responsive and are often used in police work and as guide dogs for the blind — called also *Alsatian*

German shorthaired pointer *n* (1931) **:** any of a breed of gundogs of German origin that have a liver or liver and white coat

German silver *n* (1830) **:** a silver-white alloy of copper, zinc, and nickel

German wirehaired pointer *n* (ca. 1964) **:** any of a breed of gundogs of German origin that have a liver or liver and white flat-lying wiry coat

germ cell *n* (ca. 1855) **:** a gamete (as an egg or sperm cell) or one of its antecedent cells

ger·men \'jər-mən\ *n* [L] (1605) *archaic* **:** GERM 1a, 2

germ-free \'jərm-ˌfrē\ *adj* (1926) **:** free of microorganisms **:** AXENIC

ger·mi·cid·al \ˌjər-mə-'sī-dᵊl\ *adj* (ca. 1888) **:** of or relating to a germicide; *also* **:** destroying germs

ger·mi·cide \'jər-mə-ˌsīd\ *n* (1881) **:** an agent that destroys germs

ger·mi·na·bil·i·ty \ˌjər-mə-nə-'bi-lə-tē\ *n* (1896) **:** the capacity to germinate

ger·mi·nal \'jərm-nəl, 'jər-mə-nᵊl\ *adj* [F, fr. L *germin-, germen* — more at GERM] (1808)   **1 a :** being in the earliest stage of development   **b :** CREATIVE, PRODUCTIVE   **2 :** of, relating to, or having the characteristics of a germ cell or early embryo — **ger·mi·nal·ly** *adv*

germinal vesicle *n* (ca. 1856) **:** the enlarged nucleus of the egg before completion of meiosis

ger·mi·nate \'jər-mə-ˌnāt\ *vb* **-nat·ed; -nat·ing** [L *germinatus*, pp. of *germinare* to sprout, fr. *germin-, germen* bud, germ] *vi* (1610) **:** to cause to sprout or develop ~ *vi* **:** to come into being **:** EVOLVE ⟨before Western civilization began to ~ —A. L. Kroeber⟩   **2 :** to begin to grow **:** SPROUT — **ger·mi·na·tion** \ˌjər-mə-'nā-shən\ *n* — **ger·mi·na·tive** \'jər-mə-ˌnā-tiv, -mə-nə-\ *adj*

germ layer *n* (1879) **:** any of the three primary layers of cells differentiated in most embryos during and immediately following gastrulation

germ plasm *n* (1889)   **1 :** germ cells and their precursors serving as the bearers of heredity and being fundamentally independent of other cells   **2 :** the hereditary material of the germ cells **:** GENES

germ-proof \'jərm-ˌprüf\ *adj* (1902) **:** impervious to the penetration or action of germs

germ theory *n* (1871) **:** a theory in medicine: infections, contagious diseases, and various other conditions result from the action of microorganisms

germ warfare *n* (1938) **:** the use of harmful microorganisms (as bacteria) as weapons in war

germy \'jər-mē\ *adj* **germ·i·er; -est** (1912) **:** full of germs

geront- or **geronto-** *comb form* [F *géront-, géronto-*, fr. Gk *geront-, geronto-*, fr. *geront-, gerōn* old man; akin to Gk *gēras* old age, Skt *jarati* he grows old] **:** aged one **:** old age ⟨*gerontology*⟩

ge·ron·tic \jə-'rän-tik\ *adj* (1885) **:** of or relating to decadence or old age

ger·on·toc·ra·cy \ˌjer-ən-'tä-krə-sē\ *n, pl* **-cies** [F *gérontocratie*, fr. *géronto-* geront- + -*cratie* -cracy] (1830) **:** rule by elders; *specif* **:** a form of social organization in which a group of old men or a council of elders dominates or exercises control — **ge·ron·to·crat** \jə-'rän-tə-ˌkrat\ *n* — **ge·ron·to·crat·ic** \-ˌrän-tə-'kra-tik\ *adj*

ger·on·tol·o·gy \ˌjer-ən-'tä-lə-jē\ *n* [ISV] (1903) **:** the comprehensive study of aging and the problems of the aged — compare GERIATRIC 1 —

ge·ron·to·log·i·cal \jə-ˌrän-tᵊl-'ä-ji-kəl\ *also* **ge·ron·to·log·ic** \-jik\ *adj* — **ger·on·tol·o·gist** \ˌjer-ən-'tä-lə-jist\ *n*

ge·ron·to·mor·phic \jə-ˌrän-tə-'mȯr-fik\ *adj* (1939) **:** characterized by physical specialization most fully developed in the aged male of a species ⟨~ traits⟩

¹ger·ry·man·der \'jer-ē-ˌman-dər, *also* 'ger-; *orig* 'ger-\ *n* [Elbridge *Gerry* + sala*mander*; fr. the shape of an election district formed during Gerry's governorship of Mass.] (1812)   **1 :** the act or method of gerrymandering   **2 :** a district or pattern of districts varying greatly in size or population as a result of gerrymandering

²gerrymander *vt* **-dered; -der·ing** \-d(ə-)riŋ\ (1812)   **1 :** to divide (a territorial unit) into election districts to give one political party an electoral majority in a large number of districts while concentrating the voting strength of the opposition in as few districts as possible   **2 :** to divide (an area) into political units to give special advantages to one group ⟨~ a school district⟩

ger·und \'jer-ənd\ *n* [LL *gerundium*, fr. L *gerundus*, gerundive of *gerere* to bear, carry on] (1513)   **1 :** a verbal noun in Latin that expresses generalized or uncompleted action   **2 :** any of several linguistic forms analogous to the Latin gerund in languages other than Latin; *esp* **:** the English verbal noun in -*ing* that has the function of a substantive and at the same time shows the verbal features of tense, voice, and capacity to take adverbial qualifiers and to govern objects

ge·run·dive \jə-'rən-div\ *n* (15c)   **1 :** the Latin future passive participle that functions as the verbal adjective, that expresses the fitness or necessity of the action to be performed, and that has the same suffix as the gerund   **2 :** a verbal adjective in a language other than Latin analogous to the gerundive

ge·sell·schaft \gə-'zel-ˌshäft\ *n* [G, companionship, society] (1887) **:** a rationally developed mechanistic type of social relationship characterized by impersonally contracted associations between persons; *also* **:** a community or society characterized by this relationship — compare GEMEINSCHAFT

ges·ne·ri·ad \ges-'nir-ē-ˌad\ *n* [NL *Gesneria*, genus name, fr. Konrad *Gesner* †1565 Swiss naturalist] (ca. 1925) **:** any of a family (Gesneriaceae) of tropical herbs (as an African violet or gloxinia) with chiefly opposite leaves and highly zygomorphic flowers

ges·so \'je-(ˌ)sō\ *n, pl* **gessoes** [It, lit., gypsum, fr. L *gypsum*] (1596)   **1 :** plaster of paris or gypsum prepared with glue for use in painting or making bas-reliefs   **2 :** a paste prepared by mixing whiting with size or glue and spread upon a surface to fit it for painting or gilding — **ges·soed** \-(ˌ)sōd\ *adj*

gest *or* **geste** \'jest\ *n* [ME *geste* — more at JEST] (13c)   **1 :** a tale of adventures; *esp* **:** a romance in verse   **2 :** ADVENTURE, EXPLOIT

ge·stalt \gə-'stält, -'shtält, -'stȯlt, -'shtȯlt\ *n, pl* **ge·stalt·en** \-'stäl-tᵊn, -'shtäl-, -'stȯl-, -'shtȯl-\ *or* **gestalts** [G, lit., shape, form] (1922) **:** a structure, configuration, or pattern of physical, biological, or psychological phenomena so integrated as to constitute a functional unit with properties not derivable by summation of its parts

ge·stalt·ist \-'stäl-tist, -'shtäl-, -'stȯl-, -'shtȯl-\ *n, often cap* (1931) **:** a specialist in Gestalt psychology

Gestalt psychology *n* (1927) **:** the study of perception and behavior from the standpoint of an individual's response to configurational wholes with stress on the uniformity of psychological and physiological events and rejection of analysis into discrete events of stimulus, percept, and response

ge·sta·po \gə-'stä-(ˌ)pō\ *n, pl* **-pos** [G, fr. *Geheime Staatspolizei*, lit., secret state police] (1934) **:** a secret-police organization employing underhanded and terrorist methods against persons suspected of disloyalty

ges·tate \'jes-ˌtāt\ *vb* **ges·tat·ed; ges·tat·ing** [back-formation fr. *gestation*] *vt* (1866)   **1 :** to carry in the uterus during pregnancy   **2 :** to conceive and gradually develop in the mind ~ *vi* **:** to be in the process of gestation

ges·ta·tion \je-'stä-shən\ *n* [L *gestation-, gestatio*, fr. *gestare* to bear, freq. of *gerere* to bear] (1615)   **1 :** the carrying of young in the uterus **:** PREGNANCY   **2 :** conception and development esp. in the mind — **ges·ta·tion·al** \-shnəl, -shə-nᵊl\ *adj*

geste *also* **gest** \'jest\ *n* [MF *geste*, fr. L *gestus*, fr. *gerere*] (14c)   **1** *archaic* **:** DEPORTMENT   **2** *archaic* **:** GESTURE

ges·tic \'jes-tik\ *adj* (1764) **:** relating to or consisting of bodily movements or gestures

ges·tic·u·lant \je-'sti-kyə-lənt\ *adj* (1877) **:** making gesticulations ⟨the little wiry man ~ and wild —William Faulkner⟩

ges·tic·u·late \je-'sti-kyə-ˌlāt\ *vi* **-lat·ed; -lat·ing** [L *gesticulatus*, pp. of *gesticulari*, fr. (assumed) L *gesticulus*, dim. of L *gestus*] (ca. 1609) **:** to make gestures esp. when speaking — **ges·tic·u·la·tive** \je-'sti-kyə-ˌlā-tiv\ *adj* — **ges·tic·u·la·tor** \-ˌlā-tər\ *n* — **ges·tic·u·la·to·ry** \-lə-ˌtȯr-ē, -ˌtōr-\ *adj*

ges·tic·u·la·tion \je-ˌsti-kyə-'lā-shən\ *n* (15c)   **1 :** the act of making gestures   **2 :** GESTURE; *esp* **:** an expressive gesture made in showing strong feeling or in enforcing an argument

¹ges·ture \'jes-chər, 'jesh-\ *n* [ME, fr. ML *gestura* mode of action, fr. L *gestus*, pp. of *gerere*] (15c)   **1** *archaic* **:** CARRIAGE, BEARING   **2 :** a movement usu. of the body or limbs that expresses or emphasizes an idea, sentiment, or attitude   **3 :** the use of motions of the limbs or body as a means of expression   **4 :** something said or done by way of formality or courtesy, as a symbol or token, or for its effect on the attitudes of others ⟨a political ~ to draw popular support —V. L. Parrington⟩ — **ges·tur·al** \-chə-rəl\ *adj* — **ges·tur·al·ly** \-chə-rə-lē\ *adv*

²gesture *vb* **ges·tured; ges·tur·ing** *vi* (1542) **:** to make a gesture ~ *vt* **:** to express or direct by a gesture

gesture language *n* (1865) **:** communication by gestures; *esp* **:** SIGN LANGUAGE — called also *gestural language*

ge·sund·heit \gə-'zunt-ˌhīt\ *interj* [G, lit., health, fr. *gesund* healthy (fr. OHG *gisunt*) + -*heit* -hood — more at SOUND] (1914) — used to wish good health esp. to one who has just sneezed

---

\ə\ abut \ᵊ\ kitten, F table \ər\ further \a\ ash \ā\ ace \ä\ mop, mar
\aů\ out \ch\ chin \e\ bet \ē\ easy \g\ go \i\ hit \ī\ ice \j\ job
\ŋ\ sing \ō\ go \ȯ\ law \ȯi\ boy \th\ thin \th\ the \ü\ loot \ů\ foot
\y\ yet \zh\ vision \ä, k̟, ⁿ, œ, œ̄, ue, ūe, ᵥ\ see Guide to Pronunciation

¹get \'get, ÷'git\ *vb* **got** \'gät\; **got** *or* **got·ten** \'gä-t²n\; **get·ting** [ME, fr. ON *geta* to get, beget; akin to OE bi*gietan* to beget, L pre*hendere* to seize, grasp, Gk *chandanein* to hold, contain] *vt* (13c) **1 a :** to gain possession of **b :** to receive as a return : EARN ⟨he *got* a bad reputation for carelessness⟩ **2 a :** to obtain by concession or entreaty ⟨~ your mother's permission to go⟩ **b :** to become affected by (a disease or bodily condition) : CATCH ⟨*got* measles from his sister⟩ **3 a :** to seek out and obtain ⟨hoped to ~ dinner at the inn⟩ **b :** to obtain and bring where wanted or needed ⟨~ a pencil from the desk⟩ **4 :** BEGET **5 a :** to cause to come or go ⟨quickly *got* his luggage through customs⟩ **b :** to cause to move ⟨~ it out of the house⟩ **c :** to cause to be in a certain position or condition ⟨*got* his feet wet⟩ **d :** to make ready : PREPARE ⟨~ breakfast⟩ **6 a :** to be subjected to ⟨*got* a bad fall⟩ **b :** to receive by way of punishment **c :** to suffer a specified injury to ⟨*got* my nose broken⟩ **7 a :** to achieve as a result of military activity **b :** to obtain or receive by way of benefit or advantage ⟨he *got* little for his trouble⟩ ⟨~ the better of an enemy⟩ **8 a :** SEIZE **b :** OVERCOME **c :** to have an emotional effect on ⟨the final scene always ~s me⟩ **d :** IRRITATE ⟨the delays were starting to ~ her⟩ **e :** PUZZLE **f :** to take vengeance on; *specif* : KILL **g :** HIT **9 :** to prevail on : CAUSE ⟨finally *got* them to tidy up their room⟩ **10 a :** HAVE — used in the present perfect tense form with present meaning ⟨I've *got* no money⟩ **b :** to have as an obligation or necessity — used in the present perfect tense form with present meaning ⟨you have *got* to come⟩ **11 a :** to find out by calculation ⟨~ the answer to a problem⟩ **b :** MEMORIZE ⟨*got* the verse by heart⟩ **c :** HEAR **d :** UNDERSTAND **12 :** to establish communication with **13 :** to put out in baseball **14 :** DELIVER 6b ⟨the car ~s 20 miles to the gallon⟩ ~ *vi* **1 a :** to succeed in coming or going : to bring or move oneself ⟨~ away to the country⟩ ⟨*got* into the car⟩ **b :** to reach or enter into a certain condition ⟨*got* to sleep after midnight⟩ **c :** to make progress ⟨hasn't *gotten* far with the essay⟩ **2 :** to acquire wealth **3 a :** to be able ⟨never *got* to go to college⟩ **b :** to come to be — often used with following present participle ⟨*got* talking about old times⟩ **4 a :** to succeed in becoming : BECOME ⟨how to ~ clear of all the debts I owe —Shak.⟩ **b :** to become involved ⟨people who ~ into trouble with the law⟩ **5 :** to leave immediately ⟨told them to ~⟩ — **verbal auxiliary** — used with the past participle of transitive verbs as a passive voice auxiliary ⟨they *got* caught in the act⟩ — **get a bead on** : to gain a precise and telling knowledge or understanding of ⟨*got* a bead on his motives⟩ — **get after** : to pursue with exhortation, reprimand, or attack — **get ahead** : to achieve success ⟨determined to *get ahead* in life⟩ — **get a move on** : HURRY — **get at 1** : to reach effectively **2 :** to influence corruptly : BRIBE **3 :** to turn one's attention to **4 :** to try to prove or make clear ⟨what is he *getting* at⟩ — **get away with** : to avoid criticism or punishment for or the consequences of (as a reprehensible act) — **get cracking** : to make a start : get going ⟨ought to *get cracking* on that assignment⟩ — **get even** : to get revenge — **get even with** : to repay in kind — **get going** : to make a start — **get into** : to become strongly involved with or deeply interested in — **get it** : to receive a scolding or punishment — **get it on 1** : to become enthusiastic, energetic, or excited **2 :** to engage in sexual intercourse — **get on** : to produce an unfortunate effect on : UPSET ⟨the noise *got on* my nerves⟩ — **get one's act together 1** : to put one's life, thoughts, or emotions in order : cease to be confused or misdirected **2 :** to begin to function in a skillful or efficient manner ⟨the company finally *got its act together*⟩ — **get one's goat** : to make one angry or annoyed — **get over 1 a :** OVERCOME, SURMOUNT **b :** to recover from **c :** to reconcile oneself to : become accustomed to **2 :** to move or travel across — **get somewhere** : to be successful — **get there** : to be successful — **get through** : to reach the end of : COMPLETE — **get to 1 a :** BEGIN ⟨*gets* to worrying over nothing at all⟩ **b :** to be ready to begin or deal with ⟨I'll *get to* the accounts as soon as I can⟩ **2 :** to have an effect on: as **a :** INFLUENCE **b :** BOTHER — **get together 1** : to bring together : ACCUMULATE **2 :** to come together : ASSEMBLE, MEET **3 :** to reach agreement — **get wind of** : to become aware of — **get with it** : to become alert or aware : show sophisticated consciousness

usage The pronunciation \'git\ has been noted as a feature of some British and American dialects since the 16th century. In the phonetic spelling of his own speech Benjamin Franklin records *git*. However, since at least 1687 some grammarians and teachers have disapproved this pronunciation. It nonetheless remains in widespread and unpredictable use in many dialects, often, but not exclusively, when *get* is a passive auxiliary (as in *get married*) or an imperative (as in *get up!*).

²get \'get\ *n* (14c) **1 a :** something begotten: (1) : OFFSPRING (2) : the entire progeny of a male animal **b :** LINEAGE **2 :** a return of a difficult shot in a game (as tennis)

³get \'get\ *n, pl* **git·tin** \gē-'tēn, 'gi-tin\ [LHeb *gēṭ*] (1892) **1 :** a document of release from obligation in Jewish law; *specif* : a bill of divorce **2 :** a religious divorce by Jewish law

ge·ta \'ge-(ˌ)tä, -tə\ *n, pl* **geta** *or* **getas** [Jp] (1884) **:** a Japanese wooden clog for outdoor wear

get about *vi* (1816) **1 :** to become current : CIRCULATE **2 :** to be up and about : begin to walk ⟨able to *get about* again⟩

get across *vi* (1913) **:** to become clear or convincing ~ *vt* **:** to make clear or convincing ⟨we couldn't *get* our point *across*⟩

get along *vi* (1768) **1 a :** to proceed toward a destination : PROGRESS **b :** to approach an advanced stage : approach old age **2 :** to meet one's needs : MANAGE ⟨we *got along* on a minimum of clothing⟩ **3 :** to be or remain on congenial terms

get around *vt* (1875) **1 :** CIRCUMVENT, EVADE **2 :** to get the better of ~ *vi* **1 a :** to find or take the necessary time or effort — used with *to* **b :** to give attention or consideration — used with *to* **2 :** to go from place to place **3 :** to become known or current ⟨word *got around* that he was resigning⟩

get·at·a·ble \get-'a-tə-bəl\ *adj* (1799) **:** ACCESSIBLE, APPROACHABLE

get·a·way \'ge-tə-ˌwä\ *n* (1890) **1 :** an act or instance of getting away: as **a :** ESCAPE **b :** START **2 :** a place suitable for a vacation **3 :** a vacation esp. of brief duration

get back *vi* (1605) **1 :** to come or go again to a person, place, or condition : RETURN, REVERT ⟨*getting back* to the main topic of the lecture⟩

geta

2 : to gain revenge : RETALIATE — used with *at* ~ *vt* **:** to regain possession of : RECOVER

get by *vi* (1908) **1 :** to succeed with the least possible effort or accomplishment **2 :** to make ends meet : SURVIVE **3 :** to proceed without being discovered, criticized, or punished

get down *vi* (1757) **1 :** to alight esp. from a vehicle : DESCEND **2 :** to give one's attention or consideration — used with *to* ⟨*get down* to business⟩ ~ *vt* **1 :** to be physically, mentally, or emotionally exhausted : DEPRESS ⟨the weather was *getting* her *down*⟩ **2 :** to manage to swallow **3 :** to commit to writing : DESCRIBE

get-go \'git-ˌgō, 'get-\ *n* (1980) **:** the very beginning — used in the phrase *from the get-go* ⟨didn't like me from the ~⟩

Geth·sem·a·ne \geth-'se-mə-nē\ *n* [Gk *Gethsēmanē*] **1 :** the garden outside Jerusalem mentioned in Mk 14 as the scene of the agony and arrest of Jesus **2 :** a place or occasion of great mental or spiritual suffering

get in *vi* (ca. 1533) **1 a :** ENTER **b :** ARRIVE **2 a :** to become friendly **b :** to become involved **3 :** to become accepted for membership or chosen for office ~ *vt* **1 :** to succeed in doing, making, or delivering **2 :** to include in one's schedule **3 :** INVOLVE 2a, b

get off *vi* (1640) **1 :** to avoid the most serious consequences of a dangerous situation or punishment ⟨*get off* with a light sentence⟩ **2 :** START, LEAVE ⟨*got off* on the trip early⟩ **3 :** to leave work with permission or as scheduled **4 :** to get high on a drug **5 :** to experience orgasm **6 :** to experience great pleasure — often used with *on* ~ *vt* **1 :** to secure the release of or procure a modified penalty for ⟨his lawyers *got* him *off*⟩ **2 :** UTTER ⟨*get off* a joke⟩ **b :** to write and send **3 :** to succeed in doing, making, or delivering **4 :** to cause to get off

get on *vi* (1816) **1 :** GET ALONG ⟨was *getting on* in years⟩ ⟨*got on* well with the boss⟩ ⟨*get on* with the game⟩ **2 :** to gain knowledge or understanding ⟨*get on* to the racket⟩

get out *vi* (14c) **1 :** LEAVE, ESCAPE ⟨doubted that he would *get out* alive⟩ **2 :** to become known : leak out ⟨their secret *got out*⟩ ~ *vt* **1 :** to cause to leave or escape **2 :** to bring before the public; *esp* : PUBLISH

get round *vi* (1748) **:** GET AROUND

get·ter \'ge-tər\ *n* (15c) **1 :** one that gets **2 :** a substance introduced into a vacuum tube or electric lamp to remove traces of gas

get through *vi* (1694) **1 :** to reach a destination **2 :** to gain approval or a desired outcome **3 a :** to make something clear **b :** to complete a communications connection

get-to-geth-er \'get-tə-ˌge-thər\ *n* (1911) **:** MEETING; *esp* : an informal social gathering

get·up \'get-ˌəp\ *n* (1847) **1 :** OUTFIT, COSTUME **2 :** general composition or structure

get up *vi* (14c) **1 a :** to arise from bed **b :** to rise to one's feet **c :** CLIMB, ASCEND **2 :** to go ahead or faster — used in the imperative as a command esp. to driven animals ~ *vt* **1 :** to make preparations for : ORGANIZE ⟨*got up* a party for the newcomers⟩ **2 :** to arrange as to external appearance : DRESS **3 :** to acquire a knowledge of **4 :** to create in oneself ⟨cannot *get up* the courage to tell them⟩

get-up-and-go \ˌget-ˌəp-²n-'gō, ˌgit-, -'m-, -²ŋ-\ *n* (1906) **:** ENERGY, DRIVE

ge·um \'jē-əm\ *n* [L] (ca. 1548) **:** AVENS

gew·gaw \'g(y)ü-(ˌ)gó\ *n* [origin unknown] (ca. 1529) **:** a showy trifle : BAUBLE, TRINKET

ge·würz·tra·mi·ner \gə-'vùrt-ˌstra-mə-nər, -'vərt-, -ˌsträ; -strə-'mē-nər\ *n, often cap* [G, variety of grape, fr. *Gewürz* spice + *Traminer*, variety of grape, fr. *Tramin* (Termeno, Italy)] (ca. 1950) **:** a light dry Alsatian white wine with a spicy bouquet; *also* : a similar wine made elsewhere

gey \'gā\ *adv* [alter. of *gay*, adv.] (1796) *chiefly Scot* : VERY, QUITE

gey·ser \'gī-zər, *Brit sometimes* 'gā- *or* 'gē- *for 1 & usu* 'gē-zər *for 2*\ *n* [Icel *Geysir*, hot spring in Iceland, fr. *geysa* to rush forth, fr. ON; akin to OE *gēotan* to pour — more at FOUND] (1780) **1 :** a spring that throws forth intermittent jets of heated water and steam **2** *Brit* : an apparatus for heating water rapidly with a gas flame (as for a bath)

gey·ser·ite \-zə-ˌrīt\ *n* [F *geysérite*, fr. *geyser*, fr. Icel *Geysir*] (ca. 1814) **:** a hydrous silica that constitutes one variety of opal and is deposited around some hot springs and geysers in white or grayish concretions

g–fac·tor \'jē-ˌfak-tər\ *n* (1942) **:** GYROMAGNETIC RATIO

gha·ri·al \'ger-ē-əl\ *n* [Hindi *gharyāl*] (ca. 1809) **:** GAVIAL

ghar·ry \'gar-ē, 'gär-\ *n, pl* **gharries** [Hindi *gāṛī*] (1810) **:** a horse-drawn cab used esp. in India and Egypt

ghast \'gast\ *adj* (1622) *archaic* : GHASTLY

ghast·ful \-fəl\ *adj* (14c) *archaic* : FRIGHTFUL — **ghast·ful·ly** *adv, archaic*

ghast·ly \'gast-lē\ *adj* **ghast·li·er; -est** [ME *gastly*, fr. *gasten* to terrify — more at GAST] (14c) **1 a :** terrifyingly horrible to the senses : FRIGHTENING ⟨a ~ crime⟩ **b :** intensely unpleasant, disagreeable, or objectionable ⟨such a life seems ~ in its emptiness and sterility —Aldous Huxley⟩ **2 :** resembling a ghost **3** *obs* : filled with fear **4 :** very great ⟨~ mistake⟩ — **ghast·li·ness** *n* — **ghastly** *adv*

syn GHASTLY, GRISLY, GRUESOME, MACABRE, LURID mean horrifying and repellent in appearance or aspect. GHASTLY suggests the terrifying aspects of corpses and ghosts ⟨a *ghastly* accident⟩. GRISLY and GRUESOME suggest additionally the results of extreme violence or cruelty ⟨an unusually *grisly* murder⟩ ⟨the *gruesome* history of the Nazi death camps⟩. MACABRE suggests a morbid preoccupation with the physical aspects of death ⟨a *macabre* tale of premature burial⟩. LURID adds to GRUESOME the suggestion of shuddering fascination with violent death and esp. with murder ⟨the *lurid* details of a crime⟩.

ghat \'gòt, 'gät\ *n* [Hindi *ghāṭ*, fr. Skt *ghaṭṭa*] (1783) **:** a broad flight of steps that is situated on an Indian riverbank and that provides access to the water esp. for bathing

ghee *or* **ghi** \'gē\ *n* [Hindi *ghī*, fr. Skt *ghṛta*] (1665) **:** a semifluid clarified butter made esp. in India

gher·kin \'gər-kən\ *n* [D *gurken*, pl. of *gurk* cucumber, ultim. fr. MGk *agouros*] (1661) **1 :** a small prickly fruit used for pickling; *also* : the slender annual vine (*Cucumis anguria*) of the gourd family that bears it **2 :** the immature fruit of the cucumber

¹ghet·to \'ge-(ˌ)tō\ *n, pl* **ghettos** *also* **ghettoes** [It, fr. Venetian dial. *ghèto* island where Jews were forced to live, lit., foundry (located on the island), fr. *ghetàr* to cast, fr. L *jactare* to throw — more at JET] (1611) **1 :** a quarter of a city in which Jews were formerly required to live **2 :** a quarter of a city in which members of a minority group live esp.

because of social, legal, or economic pressure **3 a** : an isolated group ⟨a geriatric ∼⟩ **b** : a situation that resembles a ghetto esp. in conferring inferior status or limiting opportunity ⟨stuck in daytime TV's ∼⟩

²ghetto vt (1936) : GHETTOIZE

ghetto blaster n (1983) : BOOM BOX

ghet·to·ize \'ge-tō-ˌiz\ vt **-ized; -iz·ing** (1939) : to isolate in or as if in a ghetto — **ghet·to·iza·tion** \ˌge-tō-ə-'zā-shən\ n

Ghib·el·line \'gi-bə-ˌlēn, -ˌlin, -lən\ n [It Ghibellino] (1573) : a member of an aristocratic political party in medieval Italy supporting the authority of the German emperors — compare GUELF

ghib·li \'gib-lē\ n [Ar dial. gibliy south wind, fr. Ar qibli southern] (1942) : a hot desert wind of northern Africa

ghil·lie var of GILLIE

¹ghost \'gōst\ n [ME gost, gast, fr. OE gāst; akin to OHG geist spirit, Skt heda anger] (bef. 12c) **1** : the seat of life or intelligence : SOUL ⟨give up the ∼⟩ **2** : a disembodied soul; esp : the soul of a dead person believed to be an inhabitant of the unseen world or to appear to the living in bodily likeness **3** : SPIRIT, DEMON **4 a** : a faint shadowy trace ⟨a ∼ of a smile⟩ **b** : the least bit ⟨not a ∼ of a chance⟩ **5** : a false image in a photographic negative or on a television screen caused esp. by reflection **6** : one who ghostwrites **7** : a red blood cell that has lost its hemoglobin — **ghost·like** \-ˌlik\ adj — **ghosty** \'gō-stē\ adj

²ghost vi (1606) **1** : to haunt like a ghost **2** : GHOSTWRITE ∼ vt **1 a** : to move silently like a ghost **b** : to sail quietly in light winds **2** : GHOSTWRITE

Ghost Dance n (1890) : a group dance of a late 19th century American Indian messianic cult believed to promote the return of the dead and the restoration of traditional ways of life

ghost·ing n (ca. 1957) : a false image on a television screen; also : the formation of such images

ghost·ly \'gōst-lē\ adj **ghost·li·er; -est** (bef. 12c) **1** : of or relating to the soul : SPIRITUAL **2** : of, relating to, or having the characteristics of a ghost : SPECTRAL — **ghost·li·ness** n — **ghostly** adv

ghost story n (1819) **1** : a story about ghosts **2** : a tale based on imagination rather than fact

ghost town n (1931) : a once-flourishing town wholly or nearly deserted usu. as a result of the exhaustion of some natural resource

ghost word n (1886) : a word form never in established usage

ghost·write \'gōs(t)-ˌrit\ vb **-wrote** \-ˌrōt\; **-writ·ten** \-ˌri-t³n\ [back-formation fr. ghostwriter] vi (1927) : to write for and in the name of another ∼ vt : to write (as a speech) for another who is the presumed author — **ghost·writ·er** n

ghoul \'gül\ n [Ar ghūl] (1786) **1** : a legendary evil being that robs graves and feeds on corpses **2** : one suggestive of a ghoul — **ghoul·ish** \'gü-lish\ adj — **ghoul·ish·ly** adv — **ghoul·ish·ness** n

ghou·lie \'gü-lē\ n (1928) : GHOUL 1

¹GI \ˌjē-'i\ adj [galvanized iron; fr. abbr. used in listing such articles as garbage cans, but taken as abbr. for government issue] (ca. 1935) **1** : provided by an official U.S. military supply department ⟨∼ shoes⟩ **2** : of, relating to, or characteristic of U.S. military personnel **3** : conforming to military regulations or customs ⟨a ∼ haircut⟩

²GI n, pl **GIs** or **GI's** \-'iz\ (1943) : a member or former member of the U.S. armed forces; esp : a man enlisted in the army

³GI adv (1949) : in a strictly regulation manner

⁴GI vt **GI'd** \-'id\; **GI'ing** \-'i-iŋ\ (1951) : to clean thoroughly (as floors) in preparation for or as if for a military inspection

¹gi·ant \'ji-ənt\ n [ME giaunt, fr. OF geant, fr. L gigant-, gigas, fr. Gk] (14c) **1** : a legendary humanlike being of great stature and strength **2 a** : a living being of great size **b** : a person of extraordinary powers **3** : something unusually large or powerful — **gi·ant·like** \-ˌlik\ adj

²giant adj (15c) : having extremely large size, proportion, or power

giant anteater n (1940) : a large bushy-tailed anteater (Myrmecophaga tridactyla) of Central and South America

giant cactus n (ca. 1884) : SAGUARO

giant clam n (ca. 1889) : a very large clam (Tridacna gigas) found on the coral reefs of the Indian and Pacific oceans that sometimes weighs more than 500 pounds (227 kilograms)

gi·ant·ess \'ji-ən-təs\ n (14c) : a female giant

gi·ant·ism \'ji-ən-ˌti-zəm\ n (1639) **1** : the quality or state of being a giant ⟨∼ in industry⟩ **2** : GIGANTISM 2

giant panda n (1920) : a large black-and-white mammal (Ailuropoda melanoleuca) of chiefly central China now usu. classified with the bears (family Ursidae) — see PANDA illustration

giant reed n (1851) : a tall European grass (Arundo donax) with woody stems used esp. in making organ reeds, baskets, and shelters

giant schnauzer n (ca. 1934) : any of a breed of powerful heavyset schnauzers that attain a height of 23½ to 27½ inches (60 to 70 centimeters)

giant sequoia n (ca. 1931) : BIG TREE

giant slalom n (1952) : a slalom race for skiers on a longer and steeper course than that used for the regular slalom

giant squid n (ca. 1890) : any of a genus (Architeuthis) of extremely large squids that include the largest mollusks known

giant star n (1912) : a star of great luminosity and of large mass

giant tortoise n (ca. 1909) : any of various large long-lived herbivorous land tortoises (genus Geochelone) formerly common on the islands of the western Indian Ocean and on the Galapagos Islands

giant water bug n (1901) : any of a family (Belostomatidae and esp. genus Lethocerus) of very large predatory bugs capable of inflicting a painful bite

gia·our \'jaů-(-ə)r\ n [F, fr. It dial. (Venetian) giaur, fr. Turk gâvur, fr. Pers gawr] (1564) : one outside the Islamic faith : INFIDEL 2a

giar·di·a·sis \ˌ(ˌ)jē-ˌär-'dī-ə-səs, jē-ər-, jär-\ n, pl **-a·ses** \-ˌsēz\ [NL, fr. Giardia, fr. Alfred M. Giard †1908 Fr. biologist] (1919) : infestation with or disease caused by a flagellate protozoan (genus Giardia and esp. G. lamblia in humans) that is often characterized by diarrhea

¹gib \'gib\ n [ME, fr. Gib, nickname for Gilbert] (1561) : a male cat; specif : a castrated male cat

²gib n [origin unknown] (1795) : a plate of metal or other material machined to hold other parts in place, to afford a bearing surface, or to provide means for overcoming looseness

gib·ber \'ji-bər\ vi **gib·bered; gib·ber·ing** \-b(ə-)riŋ\ [imit.] (1604) : to speak rapidly, inarticulately, and often foolishly — **gibber** n

gib·ber·el·lic acid \ˌji-bə-'re-lik-\ n (1954) : a crystalline acid $C_{19}H_{22}O_6$ that is a gibberellin used esp. in the malting of barley

gib·ber·el·lin \-'re-lən\ n [NL Gibberella fujikoroi, fungus from which it was first isolated] (1939) : any of several growth-regulating plant hormones that promote cell elongation and activity of the cambium, induce parthenocarpy, and stimulate synthesis of nucleic acids and proteins

gib·ber·ish \'ji-b(ə-)rish, 'gi-\ n [prob. fr. gibber] (ca. 1554) : unintelligible or meaningless language: **a** : a technical or esoteric language **b** : pretentious or needlessly obscure language

¹gib·bet \'ji-bət\ n [ME gibet, fr. OF] (13c) **1** : GALLOWS **2** : an upright post with a projecting arm for hanging the bodies of executed criminals as a warning

²gibbet vt (1646) **1 a** : to expose to infamy or public scorn **b** : to hang on a gibbet **2** : to execute by hanging on a gibbet

gib·bon \'gi-bən\ n [F] (1774) : any of a genus (Hylobates) of brachiating tailless apes of southeastern Asia that are the smallest and most arboreal anthropoid apes

gib·bos·i·ty \ji-'bä-sə-tē, gi-\ n, pl **-ties** (14c) : PROTUBERANCE, SWELLING

gib·bous \'ji-bəs, 'gi-\ adj [ME, fr. MF gibbeux, fr. LL gibbosus humpbacked, fr. L gibbus hump] (14c) **1 a** : marked by convexity or swelling **b** of the moon or a planet : seen with more than half but not all of the apparent disk illuminated **2** : having a hump : HUMPBACKED

gibbon

gibe \'jib\ vb **gibed; gib·ing** [perh. fr. MF giber to shake, handle roughly] vi (1567) : to utter taunting words ∼ vt : to deride or tease with taunting words **syn** see SCOFF — **gibe** n — **gib·er** n

gib·lets \'jib-ləts also 'gib-\ n pl [ME gibelet entrails, garbage, fr. MF, stew of wildfowl] (15c) : the edible viscera of a fowl

Gi·bral·tar \jə-'brȯl-tər\ n [Gibraltar, fortress in the Brit. colony of Gibraltar] (1856) : an impregnable stronghold

Gib·son \'gib-sən\ n [fr. the name Gibson] (1948) : a martini garnished with a cocktail onion

Gibson girl adj [Charles D. Gibson] (1936) : of or relating to a style esp. in women's clothing characterized by high necks, full sleeves, and wasp waists

gid \'gid\ n [back-formation fr. giddy] (1601) : a disease esp. of sheep caused by the larva of a tapeworm (Multiceps multiceps) in the brain

gid·dap \gi-'dap, -'dəp\ also **gid·dy·ap** \ˌgi-dē-'ap, -'əp\ vb imper [alter. of get up] (ca. 1897) — a command to a horse to go ahead or go faster

¹gid·dy \'gi-dē\ adj **gid·di·er; -est** [ME gidy mad, foolish, fr. OE gydig possessed, mad; akin to OE god god] (14c) **1 a** : DIZZY ⟨∼ from the unaccustomed exercise⟩ **b** : causing dizziness ⟨a ∼ height⟩ **c** : whirling rapidly **2 a** : lightheartedly silly : FRIVOLOUS **b** : joyfully elated : EUPHORIC — **gid·di·ly** \'gi-də-lē\ adv — **gid·di·ness** \'gi-dē-nəs\ n

²giddy vb **gid·died; gid·dy·ing** vt (1602) : to make giddy ∼ vi : to become giddy

Gid·e·on \'gi-dē-ən\ n [Heb Gidh'ōn] **1** : an early Hebrew hero noted for his defeat of the Midianites **2** : a member of an interdenominational organization whose activities include the placing of Bibles in hotel rooms

gie \'gē\ chiefly Scot var of GIVE

Giem·sa stain \gē-'em-zə-\ n [Gustav Giemsa †1948 Ger. chemotherapist] (ca. 1909) : a stain consisting of eosin and a blue dye and used chiefly in the differential staining of blood films — called also Giemsa, Giemsa's stain

¹gift \'gift\ n [ME, fr. ON, something given, talent; akin to OE giefan to give] (12c) **1** : a notable capacity, talent, or endowment **2** : something voluntarily transferred by one person to another without compensation **3** : the act, right, or power of giving

syn GIFT, FACULTY, APTITUDE, BENT, TALENT, GENIUS, KNACK mean a special ability for doing something. GIFT often implies special favor by God or nature ⟨the gift of singing beautifully⟩. FACULTY applies to an innate or less often acquired ability for a particular accomplishment or function ⟨a faculty for remembering names⟩. APTITUDE implies a natural liking for some activity and the likelihood of success in it ⟨a mechanical aptitude⟩. BENT is nearly equal to APTITUDE but it stresses inclination perhaps more than specific ability ⟨a family with an artistic bent⟩. TALENT suggests a marked natural ability that needs to be developed ⟨has enough talent to succeed⟩. GENIUS suggests impressive inborn creative ability ⟨has no great genius for poetry⟩. KNACK implies a comparatively minor but special ability making for ease and dexterity in performance ⟨the knack of getting along⟩.

²gift vt (ca. 1550) **1** : to endow with some power, quality, or attribute **2** : PRESENT ⟨generously ∼ed us with a copy —Saturday Rev.⟩

gift certificate n (1942) : a certificate entitling the recipient to purchase goods or services in the establishment of the issuer to the amount specified

gift·ed \'gif-təd\ adj (1644) **1** : having great natural ability : TALENTED ⟨∼ children⟩ **2** : revealing a special gift ⟨∼ voices⟩ — **gift·ed·ly** adv — **gift·ed·ness** n

gift of gab (ca. 1890) : the ability to talk glibly and engagingly

gift of tongues [fr. the gifts of the Spirit in 1 Cor 12:1–13] (1560) : the charismatic gift of ecstatic speech

gift·ware \'gift-ˌwar, -ˌwer\ n (1904) : wares or goods suitable for gifts

gift wrap vt (1936) : to wrap (merchandise intended as a gift) decoratively

¹gig \'gig\ n [ME -gyge (in whyrlegyge whirligig), of unknown origin] (1570) **1** : something that whirls or is whirled: as **a** obs : TOP, WHIRLIGIG **b** : a 3-digit selection in a numbers game **2** : a person of odd or

\ə\ abut \ᵊ\ kitten, F table \ər\ further \a\ ash \ā\ ace \ä\ mop, mar \aů\ out \ch\ chin \e\ bet \ē\ easy \g\ go \i\ hit \ī\ ice \j\ job \ŋ\ sing \ō\ go \ȯ\ law \ȯi\ boy \th\ thin \t͟h\ the \ü\ loot \ů\ foot \y\ yet \zh\ vision \á, k̲, ⁿ, œ, œ̄, ɷe, ūe, ᵊ\ see Guide to Pronunciation grotesque appearance **3 a :** a long light ship's boat **b :** a rowboat designed for speed rather than for work **4 :** a light two-wheeled one-horse carriage

²**gig** *vi* **gigged; gig·ging** (1807) **:** to travel in a gig

³**gig** *n* [short for earlier *fizgig, fishgig,* of unknown origin] (1722) **1 :** a pronged spear for catching fish **2 :** an arrangement of hooks to be drawn through a school of fish in order to hook their bodies

⁴**gig** *vb* **gigged; gig·ging** *vt* (1803) **1 :** to spear with a gig **2** *a chiefly West :* SPUR, JAB **b :** GOAD, PROVOKE ~ *vi :* to fish with a gig

⁵**gig** *n* [origin unknown] (1926) **:** a job usu. for a specified time; *esp :* an entertainer's engagement

⁶**gig** *vi* **gigged; gig·ging** (1939) **:** to work as a musician 〈gigged with various bands —*Downbeat*〉

⁷**gig** *n* [origin unknown] (ca. 1941) **:** a military demerit

⁸**gig** *vt* **gigged; gig·ging** (ca. 1941) **:** to give a military gig to

giga- \'ji-gə, 'gi-\ *comb form* [ISV, fr. Gk *gigas* giant] **:** billion 〈giga-hertz〉 〈gigawatt〉

giga·bit \-ˌbit\ *n* (1970) **:** a unit of information equal to one billion bits

giga·byte \-ˌbīt\ *n* (1975) **:** 1,073,741,824 bytes

giga·hertz \-ˌhərts, -ˌherts\ *n* (1964) **:** a unit of frequency equal to one billion hertz

gi·gan·tesque \ˌjī-gan-'tesk, -gən-\ *adj* (1821) **:** of enormous or grotesquely large proportions

gi·gan·tic \jī-'gan-tik, jə-\ *adj* [Gk *gigantikos,* fr. *gigant-, gigas* giant] (1651) **:** exceeding the usual or expected (as in size, force, or prominence) 〈a man of ~ stature〉 〈made a last ~ effort〉 〈~ industrial combines〉 *syn* see ENORMOUS — **gi·gan·ti·cal·ly** \-ti-k(ə-)lē\ *adv*

gi·gan·tism \jī-'gan-ˌti-zəm, jə-; 'jī-gən-\ *n* (ca. 1885) **1 :** GIANTISM 1 **2 :** development to abnormally large size **3 :** excessive vegetative growth often accompanied by the inhibiting of reproduction

gi·gas \'jī-gəs\ *adj* [NL, fr. L, giant, fr. Gk] (1915) *of a polyploid plant* **:** having thicker stem, taller growth, darker thicker leaves, and larger flowers and seeds than a corresponding diploid

giga·watt \'ji-gə-ˌwät, 'gi-\ *n* (ca. 1962) **:** a unit of power equal to one billion watts

¹**gig·gle** \'gi-gəl\ *vb* **gig·gled; gig·gling** \-g(ə-)liŋ\ [imit.] *vi* (1509) **:** to laugh with repeated short catches of the breath ~ *vt :* to utter with a giggle — **gig·gler** \-g(ə-)lər\ *n* — **gig·gling·ly** \-g(ə-)liŋ-lē\ *adv* — **gig·gly** \-g(ə-)lē\ *adj*

²**giggle** *n* (ca. 1677) **1 :** the act of giggling **2** *chiefly Brit :* a source of amusement

gig·o·lo \'ji-gə-ˌlō, 'zhi-\ *n, pl* **-los** [F] (1922) **1 :** a man supported by a woman usu. in return for his attentions **2 :** a professional dancing partner or male escort

gi·got \'ji-gət, zhē-'gō\ *n, pl* **gi·gots** \-gəts, -'gō(z)\ [MF, dim. of *gigue* fiddle; fr. its shape — more at JIG] (1526) **1 :** a leg of meat (as lamb) esp. when cooked **2 :** a leg-of-mutton sleeve

gigue \'zhēg\ *n* [F, fr. E *jig*] (1685) **:** a lively dance movement (as of a suite) having compound triple rhythm and composed in fugal style

Gi·la monster \'hē-lə-\ *n* [*Gila* River, Ariz.] (1877) **:** a large orange and black venomous lizard (*Heloderma suspectum*) of the southwestern U.S.; *also :* a related lizard (*H. horridum*) of Mexico

gil·bert \'gil-bərt\ *n* [William *Gilbert*] (1893) **:** the centimeter-gram-second unit of magnetomotive force equivalent to 10 ÷ 4π ampere-turn

¹**gild** \'gild\ *vt* **gild·ed** \'gil-dəd\ *or* **gilt** \'gilt\; **gild·ing** [ME, fr. OE *gyldan;* akin to OE *gold* gold] (14c) **1 :** to overlay with or as if with a thin covering of gold **2 a :** to give money to **b :** to give an attractive but often deceptive appearance to **c** *archaic :* to make bloody — **gild·er** *n* — **gild the lily :** to add unnecessary ornamentation to something beautiful in its own right

²**gild** *var of* GUILD

Gil·ga·mesh \'gil-gə-ˌmesh\ **:** a legendary Sumerian king and hero of the *Gilgamesh Epic*

¹**gill** \'jil\ *n* [ME *gille,* fr. ML *gillus,* fr. LL *gillo, gello* water pot] (14c) — see WEIGHT table

²**gill** \'gil\ *n* [ME *gile,* of Scand origin; akin to Sw *gäl* gill, ON *gjǫlnar* lips; akin to Gk *chelynē* lip, jawbone] (14c) **1 :** an organ (as of a fish) for obtaining oxygen from water **2 a :** WATTLE 2 **b :** the flesh under or about the chin or jaws — usu. used in pl. **c :** one of the radiating plates forming the undersurface of the cap of a mushroom fungus — **gilled** \'gild\ *adj* — **to the gills :** as full as possible

³**gill** \'gil\ *vt* (1884) **1 :** GILLNET ~ *vi, of fish :* to become entangled in a gill net — **gill·er** *n*

⁴**gill** \'gil\ *n* [ME *gille,* fr. ON *gil;* akin to OHG *gil* hernia] (14c) **1** *Brit :* RAVINE **2** *Brit :* a narrow stream or rivulet

⁵**gill** \'jil\ *n, often cap* [ME, fr. *Gill,* nickname for *Gillian*] (15c) **:** GIRL, SWEETHEART

gill arch *n* (1879) **1 :** any of the bony or cartilaginous arches or curved bars extending dorsoventrally and placed one behind the other on each side of the pharynx and supporting the gills of fishes and amphibians **2 :** any of the rudimentary ridges in the embryos of all higher vertebrates that correspond to the gill arches

gill cleft *n* (ca. 1889) **:** GILL SLIT 1, 2

gill cover *n* (1776) **:** OPERCULUM 1b

¹**gil·lie** \'gi-lē\ *n* [ScGael *gille* & Ir *giolla* youth, gillie] (1705) **1 :** a male attendant on a Scottish Highland chief; *broadly :* ATTENDANT **2** *chiefly Scot & Irish :* a fishing and hunting guide **3 :** a shoe with a low top and decorative lacing

²**gillie** *vi* **gil·lied; gil·ly·ing** (1900) **:** to serve as a gillie

¹**gill·net** \'gil-ˌnet\ *vt* (1949) **:** to catch (fish) with a gill net

²**gill net** *n* (1796) **:** a flat net suspended vertically in the water with meshes that allow the head of a fish to pass but entangle it as it seeks to withdraw

gill·net·ter \-ˌne-tər\ *n* (ca. 1889) **:** a boat equipped for or engaged in fishing with gill nets; *also :* a person who fishes with a gill net

gill raker *n* (1880) **:** any of the bony processes on a gill arch that divert solid substances away from the gills

gill slit *n* (1854) **1 :** any of the openings or clefts between the gill arches in vertebrates that breathe by gills through which water taken in at the mouth passes to the exterior and so bathes the gills **2 :** any of the rudimentary grooves in the neck region of the embryos of air-breathing vertebrates that correspond to the gill slits **3 :** the external opening to the cavity containing the gills when a protective covering of the gills is present

gil·ly·flow·er \'ji-lē-ˌflaù-(-ə)r\ *n* [by folk etymology fr. ME *gilofre* clove, fr. MF *girofle, gilofre,* fr. L *caryophyllum,* fr. Gk *karyophyllon,* fr. *karyon* nut + *phyllon* leaf — more at CAREEN, BLADE] (1551) **:** CARNATION 2

Gil·son·ite \'gil-sə-ˌnīt\ *trademark* — used for uintaite

¹**gilt** \'gilt\ *adj* [ME, fr. pp. of *gilden* to gild] (14c) **:** covered with gold or gilt **:** of the color of gold

²**gilt** *n* (15c) **1 :** gold or something that resembles gold laid on a surface **2** *slang :* MONEY **3 :** superficial brilliance **4 :** a bond issued by the government of the United Kingdom

³**gilt** *n* [ME *gylte,* fr. ON *gyltr;* akin to OE *gelde* sterile — more at GELD] (14c) **:** a young female swine

gilt–edged \'gilt-ˌejd\ *or* **gilt–edge** \-'ej\ *adj* (1818) **1 :** having a gilt edge **2 :** of the best quality or rating 〈~ securities〉

¹**gim·bal** \'gim-bəl, 'jim-\ *n* [alter. of obs. *gemel* (double ring)] (1780) **:** a device that permits a body to incline freely in any direction or suspends it so that it will remain level when its support is tipped — usu. used in pl.; called also *gimbal ring*

²**gimbal** *vt* **-balled** *or* **-baled; -bal·ling** *or* **-bal·ing** (1875) **:** to provide with or support on gimbals

gim·crack \'jim-ˌkrak\ *n* [origin unknown] (1676) **:** a showy object of little use or value **:** GEWGAW — **gimcrack** *adj* — **gim·crack·ery** \-ˌkra-k(ə-)rē\ *n*

gim·el \'gi-məl\ *n* [Heb *gīmel*] (1828) **:** the 3d letter of the Hebrew alphabet — see ALPHABET table

¹**gim·let** \'gim-lət\ *n* [ME, fr. MF *guimbelet,* prob. modif. of MD *wimmelkijn,* fr. *wimmel* wimble] (14c) **:** a small tool with a screw point, grooved shank, and cross handle for boring holes

²**gimlet** *adj* (1752) **:** having a piercing or penetrating quality

³**gimlet** *vt* (1840) **:** to pierce as if with a gimlet

⁴**gimlet** *n* [prob. fr. ¹*gimlet*] (1928) **:** a drink consisting of sweetened lime juice and gin or vodka and sometimes carbonated or plain water

gim·let–eyed \-'īd\ *adj* (1752) **:** SHARP-SIGHTED

gim·mal \'gi-məl, 'ji-\ *n* [alter. of obs. *gemel* (double ring)] (1598) **1 :** joined work (as in a clock) whose parts move within each other **2 :** a pair or series of interlocked rings

¹**gimlet**

gim·me \'gi-mē\ *n, pl* **gimmes** [fr. *gimme,* contr. of *give me*] (1982) **:** something easily achieved or won esp. in a contest

¹**gim·mick** \'gi-mik\ *n* [origin unknown] (ca. 1926) **1 a :** a mechanical device for secretly and dishonestly controlling gambling apparatus **b :** an ingenious or novel mechanical device **:** GADGET **2 a :** an important feature that is not immediately apparent **:** CATCH 〈what's the ~ . . . what's in it for you —Maxwell Griffith〉 **b :** an ingenious and usu. new scheme or angle — **gim·micky** \-mi-kē\ *adj*

²**gimmick** *vt* (1928) **1 :** to alter or influence by means of a gimmick **2 :** to provide with a gimmick — often used with *up*

gim·mick·ry \'gi-mi-krē\ *n, pl* **-ries** (1948) **:** an array or profusion of gimmicks; *also :* use of gimmicks

¹**gimp** \'gimp\ *n* [perh. fr. D] (1664) **:** an ornamental flat braid or round cord used as a trimming

²**gimp** *n* [perh. fr. *gimp* (fish line strengthened with wire)] (1901) **:** SPIRIT, VIM

³**gimp** *n* [origin unknown] (1929) **1 :** CRIPPLE **2 :** LIMP 〈walks with a ~ —Damon Runyon〉 — **gimpy** \'gim-pē\ *adj*

⁴**gimp** *vi* (1948) **:** LIMP, HOBBLE 〈~*ing* up the stairs〉

¹**gin** \'gin\ *vb* **gan** \'gan\; **gin·ning** [ME *ginnen,* short for *beginnen*] (13c) *archaic :* BEGIN

²**gin** \'gin\ *n* [ME *gin,* modif. of OF *engin* — more at ENGINE] (13c) **:** any of various tools or mechanical devices: as **a :** a snare or trap for game **b :** COTTON GIN

³**gin** \'jin\ *vt* **ginned; gin·ning** (ca. 1625) **1 :** SNARE **2 :** to separate (cotton fiber) from seeds and waste material — **gin·ner** *n*

⁴**gin** \'jin\ *conj* [perh. by contr. fr. dial. *gif* if + *an* if] (1580) *dial :* IF

⁵**gin** \'jin\ *n* [by shortening & alter. fr. *geneva*] (1714) **1 :** a colorless alcoholic beverage made from distilled or redistilled neutral grain spirits flavored with juniper berries and aromatics (as anise and caraway seeds) **2 a :** GIN RUMMY **b :** the act of laying down a full hand of matched cards in gin rummy — **gin·ny** \'jin-ē\ *adj*

gin·ger \'jin-jər\ *n* [ME, fr. OE *gingifer,* fr. ML *gingiber,* alter. of L *zingiber,* fr. Gk *zingiberi,* ultim. fr. Pali *singivēra*] (bef. 12c) **1 a** (1) **:** a thickened pungent aromatic rhizome that is used as a spice and sometimes medicinally (2) **:** the spice usu. prepared by drying and grinding ginger **b :** any of a genus (*Zingiber* of the family Zingiberaceae, the ginger family) of herbs with pungent aromatic rhizomes; *esp :* a widely cultivated tropical herb (*Z. officinale*) that supplies most of the ginger of commerce **2 :** high spirit **:** PEP 〈the ~ to care hard and work hard —Willa Cather〉 **3 :** a strong brown — **gin·gery** \'jinj-rē, 'jin-jə-\ *adj*

²**ginger** *vt* **gin·gered; gin·ger·ing** \'jinj-riŋ, 'jin-jə-\ (1849) **:** to make lively **:** pep up 〈~ up the tourist trade —*N.Y. Times*〉

ginger ale *n* (1886) **:** a sweetened carbonated nonalcoholic beverage flavored mainly with ginger extract

ginger beer *n* (1809) **:** a sweetened carbonated nonalcoholic beverage heavily flavored with ginger or capsicum or both

gin·ger·bread \'jin-jər-ˌbred\ *n* (15c) **1 :** a cake whose ingredients include molasses and ginger **2** [fr. the fancy shapes and gilding formerly often applied to gingerbread] **:** lavish or superfluous ornament esp. in architecture — **gingerbread** *adj* — **gin·ger·bread·ed** \-ˌbre-dəd\ *adj* — **gin·ger·bready** \-dē\ *adj*

ginger group *n* (1925) *chiefly Brit :* a group that serves as an energizing force within a larger body (as a political party)

gin·ger·ly \'jin-jər-lē\ *adj* [perh. fr. ¹*ginger*] (1594) **:** very cautious or careful — **gin·ger·li·ness** *n* — **gingerly** *adv*

ginger nut *n* (1842) *Brit :* GINGERSNAP

gin·ger·root \'jin-jər-ˌr)üt, -ˌr)ùt\ *n* (1831) **:** GINGER 1a(1)

gin·ger·snap \-ˌsnap\ *n* (1805) **:** a thin brittle cookie sweetened with molasses and flavored with ginger

ging·ham \'giŋ-əm\ *n* [modif. of Malay *genggang* striped cloth] (1615) **:** a clothing fabric usu. of yarn-dyed cotton in plain weave

gin·gi·va \'jin-jə-və, jin-'jī-\ *n, pl* **-vae** \-,vē\ [L] (ca. 1889) : ¹GUM — **gin·gi·val** \'jin-jə-vəl\ *adj*

gin·gi·vec·to·my \,jin-jə-'vek-tə-mē\ *n, pl* **-mies** (ca. 1927) : the excision of a portion of the gingiva

gin·gi·vi·tis \,jin-jə-'vī-təs\ *n* (1874) : inflammation of the gums

gink \'giŋk\ *n* [origin unknown] (1908) *slang* : PERSON, GUY

gink·go *also* **ging·ko** \'giŋ-(,)kō *also* 'giŋk-(,)gō\ *n, pl* **ginkgoes** *or* **ginkgos** [NL *Ginkgo*, fr. Jp *ginkyō*] (1773) : a gymnospermous tree (*Ginkgo biloba*) of eastern China that is widely grown as an ornamental or shade tree and has fan-shaped leaves and yellow fruit

gin mill *n* (1865) : BAR, SALOON

gin rummy *n* [⁵*gin*] (1941) : a rummy game for two players in which each player is dealt 10 cards and in which a player may win a hand by matching all the cards in it or may end play when the unmatched cards count up to 10 points or less

gin·seng \'jin-,seŋ, -,siŋ\ *n* [Chin (Beijing) *rénshēn*] (1654) **1 a** : a Chinese perennial herb (*Panax schinseng* of the family Araliaceae, the ginseng family) having 5≠foliolate leaves, scarlet berries, and an aromatic root valued esp. locally as a medicine **b** : any of several plants related to ginseng; *esp* : a No. American herb (*P. quinquefolius*) **2** : the root of a ginseng

Gip·sy *chiefly Brit var of* GYPSY

gi·raffe \jə-'raf\ *n, pl* **giraffes** [It *giraffa*, fr. Ar *zirāfah*] (ca. 1600) **1** *or pl* **giraffe** : a large fleet African ruminant mammal (*Giraffa camelopardalis*) that is the tallest of living quadrupeds and has a very long neck and a short coat with dark blotches separated by pale lines **2** *cap* : CAMELOPARDALIS — **gi·raff·ish** \-'ra-fish\ *adj*

ginseng: *1* root, *2* leaves and flowers

gir·an·dole \'jir-ən-,dōl\ *n* [F & It; F, fr. It *girandola*, fr. *girare* to turn, fr. LL *gyrare*, fr. L *gyrus* gyre] (1749) **1** : a radiating and showy composition (as a cluster of skyrockets fired together) **2** : an ornamental branched candlestick **3** : a pendant earring usu. with three ornaments hanging from a central piece

gir·a·sole *also* **gir·a·sol** \'jir-ə-,sōl, -,sōl, -,säl\ *n* [It *girasole* sunflower, fr. *girare* + *sole* sun, fr. L *sol* — more at SOLAR] (ca. 1586) **1** : JERUSALEM ARTICHOKE **2** *usu girasol* : an opal of varying color that gives out fiery reflections in bright light

¹**gird** \'gərd\ *vb* **gird·ed** \'gər-dəd\ *or* **girt** \'gərt\; **gird·ing** [ME, fr. OE *gyrdan;* akin to OE *geard* yard — more at YARD] *vt* (bef. 12c) **1 a** : to encircle or bind with a flexible band (as a belt) **b** : to make fast (as a sword by a belt or clothing with a cord) **c** : SURROUND **2** : PROVIDE, EQUIP; *esp* : to invest with the sword of knighthood **3** : to prepare (oneself) for action ~ *vi* : to prepare for action — **gird one's loins** : to prepare for action : muster up one's resources

²**gird** *vb* [ME, to strike, thrust] *vi* (1546) : GIBE, RAIL ~ *vt* : to sneer at : MOCK

³**gird** *n* (1566) : a sarcastic remark

gird·er \'gər-dər\ *n* [¹*gird*] (1611) : a horizontal main structural member (as in a building or bridge) that supports vertical loads and that consists of a single piece or of more than one piece bound together

¹**gir·dle** \'gər-d²l\ *n* [ME *gurdel*, fr. OE *gyrdel;* akin to OHG *gurtil* girdle, OE *gyrdan* to gird] (bef. 12c) **1** : something that encircles or confines: as **a** : an article of dress encircling the body usu. at the waist **b** : a woman's close-fitting undergarment often boned and usu. elasticized that extends from the waist to below the hips **c** (1) : PECTORAL GIRDLE (2) : PELVIC GIRDLE **2** : the edge of a brilliant that is grasped by the setting — see BRILLIANT illustration

²**girdle** *vt* **gir·dled; gir·dling** (1582) **1** : to encircle with or as if with a girdle **2** : to cut away the bark and cambium in a ring around (a plant) usu. to kill by interrupting the circulation of water and nutrients **3** : to move around : CIRCLE ⟨*girdled* the world⟩

girl \'gər(-ə)l\ *n* [ME *gurle, girle* young person of either sex] (14c) **1 a** : a female child **b** : a young unmarried woman **c** : a single or married woman of any age — sometimes taken to be offensive **2 a** : SWEETHEART **b** : a female servant or employee — sometimes taken to be offensive **c** : DAUGHTER — **girl·hood** \-,hud\ *n*

girl Friday *n* [*girl* + *Friday* (as in *man Friday*)] (1940) : a female assistant (as in an office) entrusted with a wide variety of tasks

girl·friend \'gər(-ə)l-,frend\ *n* (1859) **1** : a female friend **2** : a frequent or regular female companion of a boy or man **3** : MISTRESS 4a

Girl Guide *n* (1909) : a member of a worldwide scouting movement for girls 7 to 18 years of age that is equivalent to the Girl Scouts in the U.S.

girl·ie *also* **girly** \'gər-lē\ *adj* (1942) : featuring scantily clothed women ⟨~ magazines⟩ ⟨~ show⟩

girl·ish \'gər-lish\ *adj* (1565) : of, relating to, or having the characteristics of a girl or girlhood — **girl·ish·ly** *adv* — **girl·ish·ness** *n*

Girl Scout *n* (1909) : a member of any of the scouting programs of the Girl Scouts of the United States of America for girls ages 5 through 17

girn \'gərn\ *vi* [ME, alter. of *grinnen* to grin, snarl] (12c) *chiefly Scot* : SNARL — **girn** *n, chiefly Scot*

gi·ro \'jir-(,)ō, 'zhir-; 'jē-(,)rō, 'zhē-, *esp Brit* 'jī-\ *n* [G, circulation (of currency), fr. It, fr. L *gyrus* gyre] (1890) : a service of many European banks that permits authorized direct transfer of funds among account holders as well as conventional transfers by check

gi·ron *var of* GYRON

Gi·ron·din \jə-'rän-din, zhə-\ *n* [F, fr. *girondin* of Gironde] (1837) : GIRONDIST

Gi·rond·ist \-dist\ *n* [F *girondiste*, fr. *Gironde*, a political party, fr. *Gironde*, department of France represented by its leaders] (1795) : a member of the moderate republican party in the French legislative assembly in 1791

girt \'gərt\ *vb* [ME *girten*, alter. of *girden*] *vt* (15c) **1** : GIRD **2** : to fasten by means of a girth ~ *vi* : to measure in girth

¹**girth** \'gərth\ *n* [ME, fr. ON *gjorth;* akin to OE *gyrdan* to gird] (13c) **1** : a band or strap that encircles the body of an animal to fasten something (as a saddle) on its back **2 a** : a measure around a body ⟨a man of more than average ~⟩ **b** : SIZE, DIMENSIONS

²**girth** *vt* (15c) **1** : ENCIRCLE **2** : to bind or fasten with a girth **3** : to measure the girth of

gi·sarme \gi-'zärm\ *n* [ME, fr. OF] (13c) : a medieval weapon consisting of a blade mounted on a long staff and carried by foot soldiers

gist \'jist\ *n* [AF, it lies, fr. MF, fr. *gesir* to lie, ultim. fr. L *jacēre* — more at ADJACENT] (ca. 1711) **1** : the ground of a legal action **2** : the main point or part : ESSENCE ⟨the ~ of an argument⟩

git \'git\ *n* [var. of *get*, term of abuse, fr. ²*get*] (1943) *Brit* : a foolish or worthless person

git–go \'git-,gō\ *var of* GET-GO

git·tern \'gi-tərn\ *n* [ME *giterne*, fr. MF *guiterne*, modif. of OSp *guitarra* guitar] (14c) : a medieval guitar

¹**give** \'giv\ *vb* **gave** \'gāv\; **giv·en** \'gi-vən\; **giv·ing** [ME, of Scand origin; akin to OSw *giva* to give; akin to OE *giefan, gifan* to give, and perh. to L *habēre* to have, hold] *vt* (13c) **1** : to make a present of ⟨~ a doll to a child⟩ **2 a** : to grant or bestow by formal action ⟨the law ~s citizens the right to vote⟩ **b** : to accord or yield to another ⟨*gave* him her confidence⟩ **3 a** : to put into the possession of another for his use **b** (1) : to administer as a sacrament (2) : to administer as a medicine **c** : to commit to another as a trust or responsibility and usu. for an expressed reason **d** : to transfer from one's authority or custody ⟨the sheriff *gave* the prisoner to the warden⟩ **e** : to execute and deliver ⟨all employees must ~ bond⟩ **f** : to convey to another ⟨~ them my regards⟩ **4 a** : to offer to the action of another : PROFFER ⟨*gave* her his hand⟩ **b** : to yield (oneself) to a man in sexual intercourse **5 a** : to present in public performance ⟨~ a concert⟩ **b** : to present to view or observation ⟨*gave* the signal to start⟩ **6** : to provide by way of entertainment ⟨~ a party⟩ **7** : to propose as a toast **8 a** : to designate as a share or portion : ALLOT ⟨all the earth to thee and to thy race I ~ —John Milton⟩ **b** : to make assignment of (a name) **c** : to set forth as an actual or hypothetical datum ⟨~ the dimensions of the room⟩ **d** : to attribute in thought or utterance : ASCRIBE ⟨*gave* the credit to you⟩ **9 a** : to yield as a product, consequence, or effect : PRODUCE ⟨cows ~ milk⟩ ⟨84 divided by 12 ~s 7⟩ **b** : to bring forth : BEAR **10 a** : to yield possession of by way of exchange : PAY **b** : to dispose of for a price : SELL **11 a** : to deliver by some bodily action ⟨*gave* him a push⟩ **b** : to carry out (as a bodily movement) ⟨*gave* a cynical smile⟩ **c** : to inflict as punishment **d** : to award by formal verdict ⟨judgment was *given* against the plaintiff⟩ **12** : to offer for consideration, acceptance, or use ⟨~s no reason for his absence⟩ **13 a** : to suffer the loss of : SACRIFICE **b** : to offer as appropriate or due esp. to something higher or more worthy ⟨*gave* his spirit to God⟩ **c** : to apply freely or fully : DEVOTE ⟨*gave* themselves to their work⟩ **d** : to offer as a pledge ⟨I ~ you my word⟩ **14 a** : to cause one to have or receive ⟨mountains always *gave* him pleasure⟩ **b** : to cause a person to catch by contagion, infection, or exposure **15 a** : to allow one to have or take ⟨~ me time⟩ **b** : to lead or attempt to lead — used with an infinitive ⟨you *gave* me to understand you'd be late⟩ **16** : to care to the extent of ⟨didn't ~ a hang⟩ ~ *vi* **1** : to make gifts or presents **2 a** : to yield to physical force or strain **b** : to collapse from the application of force or pressure **c** : to undergo or submit to change ⟨for the strike to be settled, something has to ~⟩ **3** : to afford a view or passage : OPEN **4** : to enter wholeheartedly into an activity **5** *slang* : GO ON, HAPPEN ⟨wants to know what ~s⟩ — **give a good account of** : to acquit (oneself) well — **give birth** : to have a baby ⟨*gave birth* last Thursday⟩ — **give birth to 1** : to produce as offspring ⟨*gave birth to* a son⟩ **2** : to be the source of — **give chase** : to set off in pursuit — **give ground** : to withdraw before superior force : RETREAT — **give of** : to make available : provide generously ⟨freely *gave* of their time⟩ — **give or take** : as an estimate accurate within ⟨an amount to be added or subtracted⟩ — **give place to** : to be replaced or succeeded by ⟨optimism *gave place to* worry⟩ — **give rise to** : to be the cause or source of : PRODUCE — **give the gun** : to open the throttle of : speed up — **give the lie to 1** : to accuse of falsehood **2** : to show to be false, inaccurate, or invalid — **give tongue** *of hounds* : to begin barking on the scent — **give way 1 a** : RETREAT **b** : to yield the right of way **2** : to yield oneself without restraint or control **3 a** : to yield to or as if to physical stress **b** : to yield to entreaty or insistence **4** : to yield place **5** : to begin to row

syn GIVE, PRESENT, DONATE, BESTOW, CONFER, AFFORD mean to convey to another as a possession. GIVE, the general term, is applicable to any passing over of anything by any means ⟨*give* alms⟩ ⟨*gave* her a ride on a pony⟩ ⟨*give* my love to your mother⟩. PRESENT carries a note of formality and ceremony ⟨*present* an award⟩. DONATE is likely to imply a publicized giving (as to charity) ⟨*donate* a piano to the orphanage⟩. BESTOW implies the conveying of something as a gift and may suggest condescension on the part of the giver ⟨*bestow* unwanted advice⟩. CONFER implies a gracious giving (as of a favor or honor) ⟨*confer* an honorary degree⟩. AFFORD implies a giving or bestowing usu. as a natural or legitimate consequence of the character of the giver ⟨the trees *afford* shade⟩ ⟨a development that *affords* us some hope⟩.

²**give** *n* (1868) **1** : capacity or tendency to yield to force or strain : FLEXIBILITY **2** : the quality or state of being springy

give–and–go \,giv-ən-'gō\ *n* (1965) : a play (as in basketball or hockey) in which a player passes to a teammate and immediately cuts toward the net or goal to receive a return pass

give–and–take \,giv-ən-'tāk\ *n* (1778) **1** : the practice of making mutual concessions : COMPROMISE **2** : a usu. good-natured exchange (as of ideas or comments)

give·away \'gi-və-,wā\ *n* (1882) **1** : an unintentional revelation or betrayal **2 a** : something given away free; *specif* : PREMIUM 1d **b** : the act of giving something away free ⟨staging a promotional ~⟩ **3** : a radio or television program on which prizes are given away

\ə\ abut \ᵊ\ kitten, F table \ər\ further \a\ ash \ā\ ace \ä\ mop, mar \aú\ out \ch\ chin \e\ bet \ē\ easy \g\ go \i\ hit \ī\ ice \j\ job \ŋ\ sing \ō\ go \ò\ law \òi\ boy \th\ thin \ṯh\ the \ü\ loot \ú\ foot \y\ yet \zh\ vision \á, k̫, ⁿ, œ, œ̄, ᵫ, ūᴇ, ᵛ\ see Guide to Pronunciation

give away vt (14c) **1** : to make a present of **2** : to deliver (a bride) ceremonially to the bridegroom at a wedding **3 a** : BETRAY **b** : DISCLOSE, REVEAL **4** : to give (as weight) by way of a handicap

give-back \'giv-,bak\ n (1978) : a previous gain (as an increase in wages or benefits) given back to management by workers (as in a labor contract)

give back vi (1548) : RETIRE, RETREAT ~ vt : to send in return or reply : RESTORE, RETURN

give in vt (1602) : DELIVER, SUBMIT ⟨gave in his resignation⟩ ~ vi : to yield under insistence or entreaty : SURRENDER

¹**giv·en** \'gi-vən\ adj (14c) **1** : PRONE, DISPOSED ⟨~ to swearing⟩ **2** : presented as a gift : bestowed without compensation **3** : PARTICULAR, SPECIFIED ⟨at a ~ time⟩ **4** of an official document : having been executed : DATED **5** : immediately present in experience

²**given** n (1879) : something given; esp : something taken for granted : a basic condition or assumption

³**given** prep (1904) : in view of : CONSIDERING ⟨~ what she knew about others' lives, how could she complain about her own? —Marilyn French⟩

given name n (1827) : a name that precedes one's surname; esp : FIRST NAME

give off vt (1831) **1** : to send out as a branch **2** : EMIT ⟨gave off an unpleasant smell⟩ ~ vi : to branch off

give out vt (14c) **1 a** : DECLARE, PUBLISH ⟨giving out that the doctor . . . required a few days of complete rest —Charles Dickens⟩ **b** : to read aloud the words of (a hymn or psalm) for congregational singing **2** : EMIT ⟨gave out a constant hum⟩ **3** : ISSUE ⟨gave out new uniforms⟩ ~ vi **1** : BREAK DOWN, FAIL **2** : to become exhausted : COLLAPSE

give over vt (14c) **1** : CEASE **2** : ENTRUST **3 a** : to yield without restraint or control : ABANDON ⟨gave themselves over to laughter⟩ **b** : to set apart for a particular purpose or use **4** archaic : to pronounce incurable ~ vi, Brit : to cease an activity : STOP ⟨told him to give over and let me alone —Brendan Behan⟩

giv·er \'gi-vər\ n (14c) : one that gives : DONOR

give up vt (13c) **1** : to yield control or possession of : SURRENDER ⟨forced to give up his job⟩ **2** : to desist from : ABANDON ⟨refused to give up her efforts⟩ **3** : to declare incurable or insoluble **4 a** : to abandon (oneself) to a particular feeling, influence, or activity ⟨gave himself up to despair⟩ **b** : to devote to a particular purpose or use **5** : to despair of seeing ⟨we'd given you up⟩ **6** : to allow (a hit or run in baseball) while pitching ~ vi **1** : to cease doing or attempting something esp. as an admission of defeat : QUIT — often used with on ⟨don't give up on the project⟩ — **give up the ghost** : to cease to live or function : DIE

giz·mo also **gis·mo** \'giz-(,)mō\ n, pl **gizmos** also **gismos** [origin unknown] (1943) : GADGET

giz·zard \'gi-zərd\ n [alter. of ME giser, fr. OF guisier, giser, fr. L gigeria (pl.) giblets] (1565) **1 a** : the muscular enlargement of the alimentary canal of birds that has usu. thick muscular walls and a tough horny lining for grinding the food and when the crop is present follows it and the proventriculus **b** : a thickened part of the alimentary canal in some animals (as an insect or an earthworm) that is similar in function to the crop of a bird **2** : INNARDS

gla·bel·la \glə-'be-lə\ n, pl **-bel·lae** \-'be-(,)lē, -,lī\ [NL, fr. L, fem. of glabellus hairless, dim. of glaber] (ca. 1823) : the smooth prominence between the eyebrows — **gla·bel·lar** \-'be-lər\ adj

gla·bres·cent \glə-'bre-sºnt\ adj (1857) **1** : somewhat glabrous **2** : tending to become glabrous

gla·brous \'glā-brəs\ adj [L glabr-, glaber smooth, bald — more at GLAD] (1640) : SMOOTH; esp : having a surface without hairs or projections ⟨~ skin⟩ ⟨~ leaves⟩

gla·cé \gla-'sā\ adj [F, fr. pp. of glacer to freeze, ice, glaze, fr. L glaciare, fr. glacies] (1847) **1** : made or finished so as to have a smooth glossy surface ⟨~ silk⟩ **2** also **gla·céed** \-'sād\ : coated with a glaze : CANDIED ⟨~ cherries⟩

gla·cial \'glā-shəl\ adj [L glacialis, fr. glacies] (1656) **1 a** : extremely cold : FRIGID ⟨a ~ wind⟩ **b** : devoid of warmth and cordiality ⟨a ~ handshake⟩ **c** : coldly imperturbable ⟨maintained a ~ calm⟩ **2** : resembling ice in appearance ⟨~ acetic acid⟩ **3 a** (1) : of, relating to, or being any of those parts of geologic time from Precambrian onward when a much larger portion of the earth was covered by glaciers than at present (2) cap : PLEISTOCENE **b** : of, relating to, or produced by glaciers **c** : suggestive of the very slow movement of glaciers ⟨progress on the bill has been ~⟩ — **gla·cial·ly** \-shə-lē\ adv

gla·ci·ate \'glā-shē-,āt, -sē-\ vt **-at·ed; -at·ing** (ca. 1623) **1** : FREEZE **2 a** : to subject to glacial action; also : to produce glacial effects in or on **b** : to cover with a glacier — **gla·ci·a·tion** \,glā-shē-'ā-shən, -sē-\ n

gla·cier \'glā-shər also -zhər, esp Brit 'gla-sē-ər or gla-sē-\ n [F dial., fr. MF dial., fr. MF glace ice, fr. L glacies; akin to L gelu frost — more at COLD] (1744) : a large body of ice moving slowly down a slope or valley or spreading outward on a land surface

gla·ci·ol·o·gy \,glā-shē-'ä-lə-jē, -sē-\ n [L glacies + ISV -logy] (1889) : any of the branches of science dealing with snow or ice accumulation, glaciation, or glacial epochs — **gla·ci·o·log·i·cal** \-ə-'lä-ji-kəl\ adj — **gla·ci·ol·o·gist** \-'ä-lə-jist\ n

gla·cis \gla-'sē, 'gla-sē\ n, pl **glacis** \-'sēz, -sēz\ [F, fr. glacer to freeze, slide] (1672) **1 a** : a gentle slope : INCLINE **b** : a slope that runs downward from a fortification : BUFFER STATE; also : BUFFER ZONE

¹**glad** \'glad\ adj **glad·der; glad·dest** [ME, shining, glad, fr. OE glæd; akin to OHG glat shining, smooth, L glaber smooth, bald] (bef. 12c) **1** archaic : having a cheerful or happy disposition by nature **2 a** : experiencing pleasure, joy, or delight : made happy **b** : made pleased, satisfied, or grateful — often used with of ⟨was ~ of their help⟩ **c** : very willing ⟨~ to do it⟩ **3 a** : marked by, expressive of, or caused by happiness and joy ⟨~ a shout⟩ **b** : causing happiness and joy : PLEASANT ⟨~ tidings⟩ **4** : full of brightness and cheerfulness ⟨a ~ spring morning⟩ — **glad·ly** adv — **glad·ness** n

²**glad** vb **glad·ded; glad·ding** (bef. 12c) archaic : GLADDEN

³**glad** n (1923) : GLADIOLUS 1

glad·den \'gla-dºn\ vb **glad·dened; glad·den·ing** \'gla-dºn-iŋ\ (13c) archaic : to be glad ~ vt : to make glad

glade \'glād\ n [perh. fr. ¹glad] (1529) : an open space surrounded by woods — **glady** \'glā-dē\ adj

glad–hand \'glad-,hand\ vt (1903) : to extend a glad hand to ⟨candidates ~ing everyone they meet⟩ ~ vi : to extend a glad hand ⟨~ing as if he were running for mayor⟩ — **glad–hand·er** \'glad-,han-dər\ n

glad hand n (ca. 1895) : a warm welcome or greeting often prompted by ulterior reasons

glad·i·a·tor \'gla-dē-,ā-tər\ n [L, fr. gladius sword, of Celt origin; akin to W cleddyf sword] (15c) **1** : a person engaged in a fight to the death as public entertainment for ancient Romans **2** : a person engaged in a public fight or controversy **3** : a trained fighter; esp : a professional boxer — **glad·i·a·to·ri·al** \,gla-dē-ə-'tōr-ē-əl, -'tȯr-\ adj

glad·i·o·la \,gla-dē-'ō-lə\ n [back-formation fr. gladiolus, taken as a pl.] (1926) : GLADIOLUS 1

glad·i·o·lus \,gla-dē-'ō-ləs\ n, pl **-li** \-(,)lē, -,lī\ [NL, fr. L, gladiolus, fr. dim. of gladius] (15c) **1** or pl **gladiolus** also **glad·i·o·lus·es** : any of a genus (Gladiolus) of chiefly African plants of the iris family with erect sword-shaped leaves and spikes of brilliantly colored irregular flowers arising from corms **2** : the large middle portion of the sternum

glad rags n pl (1896) : dressy clothes

glad·some \'glad-səm\ adj (14c) : giving or showing joy : CHEERFUL — **glad·some·ly** adv — **glad·some·ness** n

glad·stone \'glad-,stōn, chiefly Brit -stən\ n, often cap [W. E. Gladstone] (1889) : a suitcase with flexible sides on a rigid frame that opens flat into two equal compartments — called also gladstone bag

glai·kit or **glai·ket** \'glā-kət\ adj [ME (Sc) glaikit] (15c) chiefly Scot : FOOLISH, GIDDY

glair or **glaire** \'glar, 'gler\ n [ME gleyre egg white, fr. MF glaire, modif. of (assumed) VL claria, fr. L clarus clear — more at CLEAR] (13c) **1** : a sizing liquid made from egg white **2** : a viscid substance suggestive of an egg white

glairy \-ē\ adj **glair·i·er; -est** (1662) : having the characteristics of or overlaid with glair

glaive \'glāv\ n [ME, fr. MF, javelin, sword, modif. of L gladius sword] (15c) archaic : SWORD; esp : BROADSWORD

glam·o·rise Brit var of GLAMORIZE

glam·or·ize also **glam·our·ize** \'gla-mə-,rīz\ vt **-ized; -iz·ing** (1936) **1** : to look upon or depict as glamorous : ROMANTICIZE ⟨the novel ~s war⟩ **2** : to make glamorous ⟨~ the living room⟩ — **glam·or·iza·tion** \,gla-mə-rə-'zā-shən\ n — **glam·or·iz·er** \'gla-mə-,rī-zər\ n

glam·or·ous also **glam·our·ous** \'glam-rəs, (,)la-mə-\ adj (1882) : full of glamour — **glam·or·ous·ly** adv — **glam·or·ous·ness** n

glam·our or **glam·or** \'gla-mər\ n [Sc glamour, alter. of E grammar; fr. the popular association of erudition with occult practices] (1715) **1** : a magic spell ⟨the girls appeared to be under a ~ —Llewelyn Powys⟩ **2** : an exciting and often illusory and romantic attractiveness; esp : alluring or fascinating personal attraction — often used attributively ⟨~ stock⟩ ⟨~ boy⟩ ⟨~ girl⟩ — **glamour** vt — **glam·our·less** \-ləs\ adj

glam·our–puss \-,pus\ n (1941) : a glamorously attractive person

¹**glance** \'glan(t)s\ vb **glanced; glanc·ing** [ME glencen, glenchen] vi (15c) **1** : to strike a surface obliquely so as to go off at an angle ⟨the bullet glanced off the wall⟩ **2 a** : to make sudden quick movements ⟨dragonflies glancing over the pond⟩ **b** : to flash or gleam with quick intermittent rays of light ⟨brooks glancing in the sun⟩ **3** : to touch on a subject or refer to it briefly or indirectly ⟨the work ~s at the customs of ancient cultures⟩ **4 a** of the eyes : to move swiftly from one thing to another **b** : to take a quick look at something ⟨glanced at his watch⟩ ~ vt **1** archaic : to take a quick look at **b** : to catch a glimpse of **2** : to give an oblique path of direction to: **a** : to throw or shoot so that the object glances from a surface **b** archaic : to aim (as an innuendo) indirectly : INSINUATE — **glanc·er** n

²**glance** n (1503) **1 a** : a quick intermittent flash or gleam **b** archaic : a sudden quick movement **2** archaic : a rapid oblique movement **b** : a deflected impact or blow **3 a** : a swift movement of the eyes **b** : a quick or cursory look **4** archaic **a** : a brief satirical reference to something : GIBE **b** : ALLUSION — **at first glance** : on first consideration ⟨at first glance the subject seems harmless enough⟩

glanc·ing \'glan(t)-siŋ\ adj (ca. 1541) **1** : hitting so as to glance off ⟨a ~ blow⟩ **2** : INCIDENTAL, INDIRECT ⟨made ~ allusions to her past⟩ — **glanc·ing·ly** \-siŋ-lē\ adv

¹**gland** \'gland\ n [F glande, fr. OF, glandular swelling on the neck, gland, ultim. fr. L gland-, glans acorn; akin to Gk balanos acorn] (1692) **1 a** : a cell, group of cells, or organ of endothelial origin that selectively removes materials from the blood, concentrates or alters them, and secretes them for further use in the body or for elimination from the body **b** : any of various animal structures suggestive of glands though not secretory in function **2** : any of various secreting organs (as a nectary) of plants — **gland·less** \'gland-ləs\ adj

²**gland** n [origin unknown] (1839) **1** : a device for preventing leakage of fluid past a joint in machinery **2** : the movable part of a stuffing box by which the packing is compressed

glan·dered \'glan-dərd\ adj (1667) : affected with glanders

glan·ders \-dərz\ n pl but sing or pl in constr [MF glandre glandular swelling on the neck, fr. L glandulae, fr. pl. of glandula, dim. of gland-, glans] (1523) : a contagious and destructive disease esp. of horses caused by a bacterium (Pseudomonas mallei syn. Actinobacillus mallei) and characterized by caseating nodular lesions esp. on the respiratory mucosae and lungs that tend to break down and form ulcers

glan·du·lar \'glan-jə-lər\ adj (ca. 1740) **1 a** : of, relating to, or involving glands, gland cells, or their products **b** : having the characteristics or function of a gland **2 a** : INNATE, INHERENT ⟨the almost ~ . . . instinct for adventure and romance —Newsweek⟩ **b** : PHYSICAL, SEXUAL — **glan·du·lar·ly** adv

glandular fever n (1902) : INFECTIOUS MONONUCLEOSIS

glans \'glanz\ n, pl **glan·des** \'glan-,dēz\ [L gland-, glans, lit., acorn] (1650) **1** : a conical vascular body forming the extremity of the penis — called also glans penis **2** : a structure of the clitoris similar to the glans penis — called also glans clito·ri·dis \-klə-'tȯr-ə-dəs\

¹**glare** \'glar, 'gler\ vb **glared; glar·ing** [ME glaren; akin to OE glæs glass] vi (13c) **1 a** : to shine with a harsh uncomfortably brilliant light **b** : STAND OUT, OBTRUDE **2** : to stare angrily or fiercely ~ vt **1** : to express (as hostility) by staring angrily **2** archaic : to cause to be sharply reflected

²**glare** n (15c) **1 a** : a harsh uncomfortably bright light ⟨the ~ of a neon sign⟩ ⟨the ~ of publicity⟩; esp : painfully bright sunlight **b**

: cheap showy brilliance : GARISHNESS **2** : an angry or fierce stare **3** : a surface or sheet of smooth and slippery ice

glar·ing \'glar-iŋ, 'gler-\ adj (14c) **1** : having a fixed look of hostility, fierceness, or anger **2 a** : shining with or reflecting an uncomfortable bright light **b** (1) : GARISH (2) : vulgarly ostentatious **3** : obtrusively and often painfully obvious ⟨a ~ error⟩ *syn* see FLAGRANT — **glar·ing·ly** \-iŋ-lē\ adv — **glar·ing·ness** n

glary \'glar-ē, 'gler-\ adj **glar·i·er; -est** (1632) : having a dazzling brightness : GLARING

glas·nost \'glaz-(,)nöst, 'glas-, 'gläz-, 'gläs-\ n [Russ *glasnost'*, lit., publicity, fr. *glas* voice, fr. OCS *glasŭ* — more at CALL] (1986) : a Soviet policy permitting open discussion of political and social issues and freer dissemination of news and information

¹glass \'glas, 'gläs\ n, often attrib [ME glas, fr. OE glæs; akin to OE geolu yellow — more at YELLOW] (bef. 12c) **1** : any of various amorphous materials formed from a melt by cooling to rigidity without crystallization: as **a** : a usu. transparent or translucent material consisting esp. of a mixture of silicates **b** : a material (as obsidian) produced by fast cooling of magma **2 a** : something made of glass: as (1) : TUMBLER; *also* : GLASSWARE (2) : MIRROR (3) : BAROMETER (4) : HOURGLASS (5) : BACKBOARD **b** (1) : an optical instrument or device that has one or more lenses and is designed to aid in the viewing of objects not readily seen (2) : FIELD GLASSES, BINOCULARS — usu. used in pl. **c** pl : a device used to correct defects of vision or to protect the eyes that consists typically of a pair of glass or plastic lenses and the frame by which they are held in place — called also *eyeglasses, spectacles* **3** : the quantity held by a glass container **4** : FIBERGLASS — **glass·ful** \'glas-,fůl\ n — **glass·less** \-ləs\ adj

²glass vt (14c) **1 a** : to provide with glass : GLAZE 1 **b** : to enclose, case, or wall with glass ⟨the sunroom was ~ed in⟩ **2** : to make glassy **3 a** : REFLECT **b** : to see mirrored **4** : to look at through an optical instrument (as binoculars) ~ vi : ¹GLAZE 1

glass·blow·ing \-,blō-iŋ\ n (ca. 1829) : the art of shaping a mass of glass that has been softened by heat by blowing air into it through a tube — **glass·blow·er** \-,blō(-ə)r\ n

glass ceiling n (1986) : an intangible barrier within the hierarchy of a company that prevents women or minorities from obtaining upper-level positions

glass eye n (1687) **1** : an artificial eye made of glass **2** : an eye having a pale, whitish, or colorless iris — **glass-eyed** \-,īd\ adj

glass fiber n (1882) : FIBERGLASS

glass harmonica n (ca. 1909) : a musical instrument consisting of a series of rotating glass bowls of differing sizes played by touching the dampened edges with a finger

glass·house \'glas-,haůs\ n (14c) **1** : a place where glass is made **2** chiefly Brit : GREENHOUSE **3** Brit : a military prison

glass·ie \'gla-sē\ or glassy n, pl **glass·ies** (1887) : a playing marble made of glass

glass·ine \gla-'sēn\ n (1916) : a thin dense transparent or semitransparent paper highly resistant to the passage of air and grease

glass jaw n (1940) : vulnerability (as of a boxer) to knockout punches

glass·mak·er \'glas-,mā-kər\ n (1576) : one that makes glass — **glass·mak·ing** \-kiŋ\ n

glass·pa·per \'gläs-,pā-pər\ n (1815) Brit : abrasive paper coated with pulverized glass and used like sandpaper — **glasspaper** vb

glass snake n (1709) : any of a genus (*Ophisaurus*) of limbless snakelike lizards of the southern U.S., Eurasia, and Africa with a fragile tail that readily breaks into pieces

glass sponge n (1875) : any of a class (Hexactinellida syn. Hyalospongiae) of chiefly deep-water siliceous sponges with 6-rayed spicules and a skeleton often resembling blown glass when dried

glass·ware \'glas-,war, -,wer\ n (1745) : articles made of glass

glass wool n (1879) : glass fibers in a mass resembling wool and being used esp. for thermal insulation and air filters

glass·work \'glas-,wərk\ n (1611) **1 a** : the manufacture of glass or glassware; *also* : glaziers' work **b** pl : GLASSHOUSE 1 **2** : GLASSWARE — **glass·work·er** \-,wər-kər\ n

glass·wort \-,wərt, -,wórt\ n [fr. its former use in the manufacture of glass] (1597) : any of a genus (*Salicornia*) of woody jointed succulent herbs of the goosefoot family with leaves reduced to fleshy sheaths

glassy \'gla-sē\ adj **glass·i·er; -est** (14c) **1** : resembling or made of glass **2** : having little animation : DULL, LIFELESS ⟨~ eyes⟩ — **glass·i·ly** \'gla-sə-lē\ adv — **glass·i·ness** \'gla-sē-nəs\ n

glassy-eyed \-,īd\ adj (1895) : marked by or having glassy eyes

Glau·ber's salt \'glaů-bər(z)-\ n [Johann R. Glauber †1668 Ger. chemist] (1736) : a colorless crystalline sulfate of sodium Na₂SO₄·10H₂O used esp. in dyeing, as a cathartic, and in solar energy systems — called also *Glauber salt*; sometimes used in pl.

glau·co·ma \glaů-'kō-mə, gló-\ n [L, cataract, fr. Gk *glaukōma*, fr. *glaukoun* to have a cataract, fr. *glaukos*] (1885) : a disease of the eye marked by increased pressure within the eyeball that can result in damage to the optic disk and gradual loss of vision

glau·co·nite \'glô-kə-,nīt\ n [G Glaukonit, irreg. fr. Gk *glaukos*] (1836) : a mineral consisting of a dull green earthy iron potassium silicate occurring in greensand — **glau·co·nit·ic** \,glô-kə-'ni-tik\ adj

glau·cous \'glô-kəs\ adj [L glaucus, fr. Gk glaukos gleaming, gray] (1671) **1 a** : of a pale yellow-green color **b** : of a light bluish gray or bluish white color **2** : having a powdery or waxy coating that gives a frosted appearance and tends to rub off — **glau·cous·ness** n

¹glaze \'glāz\ vb **glazed; glaz·ing** [ME glasen, fr. glas glass] vt (14c) **1** : to furnish or fit with glass **2 a** : to coat with or as if with a glaze ⟨the storm glazed trees with ice⟩ **b** : to apply a glaze to ⟨~ doughnuts⟩ **3** : to give a smooth glossy surface to ~ vi **1** : to become glazed or glassy ⟨my eyes glazed over⟩ **2** : to form a glaze — **glaz·er** n

²glaze n (1752) **1** : a smooth slippery coating of thin ice **2 a** (1) : a liquid preparation applied to food on which it forms a firm glossy coating (2) : a mixture mostly of oxides (as silica and alumina) applied to the surface of ceramic wares to form a moisture-impervious and often lustrous or ornamental coating **b** : a transparent or translucent color applied to modify the effect of a painted surface **c** : a smooth glossy or lustrous surface or finish **3** : a glassy film

³glaze vi **glazed; glaz·ing** [prob. blend of glare and gaze] (1601) archaic : STARE

glazed \'glāzd\ adj (15c) **1** : covered with or as if with a glassy film ⟨~ eyes⟩ **2** : marked by lack of expression

gla·zier \'glā-zhər, -zē-ər\ n (14c) : one who sets glass — **gla·ziery** \'glā-zh(ə-)rē, 'glā-zē-ə-rē\ n

glaz·ing \'glā-ziŋ\ n (1677) **1** : the action, process, or trade of fitting windows with glass **2 a** : GLASSWORK **b** : GLAZE **3** : transparent material (as glass) used for windows

¹gleam \'glēm\ n [ME gleem, fr. OE glǣm; akin to OE geolu yellow — more at YELLOW] (15c) **1 a** : a transient appearance of subdued or partly obscured light ⟨the ~ of dawn in the east⟩ **b** (1) : a small bright light ⟨the ~ of a match⟩ (2) : GLINT ⟨a ~ in his eyes⟩ **2 a** : brief or faint appearance ⟨a ~ of hope⟩ — **gleamy** \'glē-mē\ adj

²gleam vi (1508) **1** : to shine with or as if with subdued steady light or moderate brightness **2** : to appear briefly or faintly ⟨a light ~ed in the distance⟩ ~ vt : to cause to gleam *syn* see FLASH

glean \'glēn\ vb [ME glenen, fr. MF glener, fr. LL glennare, of Celtic origin; akin to OIr doglenn he selects] vi (14c) **1** : to gather grain or other produce left by reapers **2** : to gather information or material bit by bit ~ vt **1 a** : to pick up after a reaper **b** : to strip (as a field) of the leavings of reapers **2 a** : to gather (as information) bit by bit **b** : to pick over in search of relevant material ⟨~ing old files for information⟩ **3** : FIND OUT — **glean·able** \'glē-nə-bəl\ adj — **glean·er** n

glean·ings \'glē-niŋz\ n pl (15c) : things acquired by gleaning

glebe \'glēb\ n [L gleba clod, sand] (14c) **1** archaic : LAND; *specif* : a plot of cultivated land **2** : land belonging or yielding revenue to a parish church or ecclesiastical benefice

glede \'glēd\ n [ME, fr. OE glida; akin to OE glīdan to glide] (bef. 12c) : any of several birds of prey (as a kite of Europe)

glee \'glē\ n [ME, fr. OE glēo entertainment, music; akin to ON glȳ joy, and perh. to Gk chleuē joke] (bef. 12c) **1** : exultant high-spirited joy : MERRIMENT **2** : a part-song for usu. male voices

glee club n (1844) : a chorus organized for singing usu. short pieces

gleed \'glēd\ n [ME, fr. OE glēd; akin to OE glōwan to glow] (bef. 12c) archaic : a glowing coal

glee·ful \'glē-fəl\ adj (1586) : full of glee : MERRY — **glee·ful·ly** \-fə-lē\ adv — **glee·ful·ness** n

gleek \'glēk\ vi [origin unknown] (1590) archaic : GIBE, JOKE

glee·man \'glē-mən\ n [ME gleman, fr. OE glēoman, fr. glēo + man man] (bef. 12c) : JONGLEUR

glee·some \'glē-səm\ adj (1603) archaic : GLEEFUL

gleet \'glēt\ n [ME glet slimy or mucous matter, fr. MF glete, fr. L glittus viscous; akin to L gluten glue — more at CLAY] (14c) : a chronic inflammation (as gonorrhea) of a bodily orifice usu. accompanied by an abnormal discharge; *also* : the discharge itself

gleg \'gleg\ adj [ME, fr. ON gloggr clear-sighted] (14c) Scot : marked by quickness of perception or movement

glei·za·tion \glā-'zā-shən\ n (1938) : development of or conversion into gley

glen \'glen\ n [ME (Sc), valley, fr. (assumed) ScGael glenn; akin to MIr glend valley] (15c) : a secluded narrow valley

glen·gar·ry \glen-'gar-ē\ n, pl **-ries** often cap [Glengarry, valley in Scotland] (1845) : a woolen cap of Scottish origin — called also *glengarry bonnet*

glen plaid \'glen-\ n [short for glenurquhart plaid, fr. Glen Urquhart, valley in Invernesshire, Scotland] (1926) : a twill pattern of broken checks; *also* : a fabric woven in this pattern — called also *glen check*

gley \'glā\ n, often attrib [Ukrainian gleĭ clayey earth; akin to OE clǣg clay — more at CLAY] (1927) : a sticky clay soil or soil layer formed under the surface of some waterlogged soils — **gleyed** adj

gley·ing \'glā-iŋ\ n (1949) : GLEIZATION

glia \'glē-ə, 'glī-ə\ n [NL, fr. MGk, glue — more at CLAY] (1891) : NEUROGLIA — **gli·al** \-əl\ adj

gli·a·din \'glī-ə-dən\ n [It gliadina, fr. MGk glia] (ca. 1828) : PROLAMIN; *esp* : one obtained by alcoholic extraction of gluten from wheat and rye

glib \'glib\ adj **glib·ber; glib·best** [prob. modif. of LG glibberig slippery] (1593) **1 a** : marked by ease and informality : NONCHALANT **b** : showing little forethought or preparation : OFFHAND ⟨~ answers⟩ **c** : lacking depth and substance : SUPERFICIAL ⟨~ solutions to knotty problems⟩ **2** archaic : SMOOTH, SLIPPERY **3** : marked by ease and fluency in speaking or writing often to the point of being insincere or deceitful ⟨a ~ politician⟩ — **glib·ly** adv — **glib·ness** n

¹glide \'glīd\ vb **glid·ed; glid·ing** [ME, fr. OE glīdan; akin to OHG glītan to glide] vi (bef. 12c) **1** : to move smoothly, continuously, and effortlessly ⟨swans gliding over the lake⟩ **2** : to go or pass imperceptibly ⟨hours glided by⟩ **3** of an airplane : to descend gradually in controlled flight **b** : to fly in a glider **4** : to produce a glide (as in music or speech) ~ vt : to cause to glide

²glide n (1596) **1** : the act or action of gliding **2** : a calm stretch of shallow water flowing smoothly **3** : PORTAMENTO **4 a** : a less prominent vowel sound produced by the passing of the vocal organs to or from the articulatory position of a speech sound — compare DIPHTHONG **b** : SEMIVOWEL **5** : a device for facilitating movement of something; *esp* : a circular usu. metal button attached to the bottom of furniture legs to provide a smooth surface

glide path n (1936) : GLIDE SLOPE

glid·er \'glī-dər\ n (15c) **1** : one that glides: as **a** : an aircraft similar to an airplane but without an engine **b** : a porch seat suspended from an upright framework **2** : something that aids gliding

glide slope n (ca. 1949) **1** : the proper path of descent for an aircraft preparing to land; *esp* : such a path indicated by a radio beam **2** : the radio beam that marks a glide slope

glengarry

\ə\ abut \ᵊ\ kitten, F table \ər\ further \a\ ash \ā\ ace \ä\ mop, mar \aů\ out \ch\ chin \e\ bet \ē\ easy \g\ go \i\ hit \ī\ ice \j\ job \ŋ\ sing \ō\ go \ò\ law \òi\ boy \th\ thin \t̲h̲\ the \ü\ loot \ů\ foot \y\ yet \zh\ vision \à, k, ⁿ, œ, œ̄, ǣ, ūe, ᵊ\ see Guide to Pronunciation

glim \'glim\ *n* [perh. short for ²*glimmer*] (ca. 1700) : something that furnishes light (as a lantern or candle); *also* : illumination given off by such a source

¹**glim·mer** \'gli-mər\ *vi* **glim·mered; glim·mer·ing** \'glim-riŋ, 'gli-mə-\ [ME *glimeren;* akin to OE *glǣm* gleam] (15c) **1 a** : to shine faintly or unsteadily **b** : to give off a subdued unsteady reflection **2** : to appear indistinctly with a faintly luminous quality   *syn* see FLASH

²**glimmer** *n* (1590) **1 a** : a feeble or intermittent light **b** : a subdued unsteady shining or sparkle **2 a** : a dim perception or faint idea : IN-KLING **b** : HINT, SPARK 〈a ~ of intelligence〉

glim·mer·ing *n* (15c) : GLIMMER

¹**glimpse** \'glim(p)s\ *vb* **glimpsed; glimps·ing** [ME *glimsen;* akin to MHG *glimsen* to glimmer, OE *glǣm* gleam] *vi* (14c) **1** *archaic* : GLIM-MER **2** : to look briefly ~ *vt* : to get a brief look at — **glimps·er** *n*

²**glimpse** *n* (ca. 1540) **1** *archaic* : GLIMMER **2** : a fleeting view or look

¹**glint** \'glint\ *vb* [ME, to dart obliquely, glint, alter. of *glenten*, of Scand origin; akin to Sw dial. *glänta* to clear up; akin to OHG *glanz* bright, OE *geolu* yellow — more at YELLOW] *vi* (14c) **1 a** *archaic* : to glance off an object **b** : of rays of light : to be reflected at an angle from a surface **2** : to give off reflection in brilliant flashes; *also* : GLEAM **3** : to look quickly or briefly ~ *vt* **4** : to appear briefly or faintly ~ *vt* : to cause to glint   *syn* see FLASH

²**glint** *n* (14c) **1** : a tiny bright flash of light **2** : a brief or faint manifestation : GLIMMER 〈a ~ of recognition〉; *also* : a trace of emotion expressed through the eyes 〈a steely ~ in his eye〉

glio·blas·to·ma \ˌglī-ō-ˌbla-'stō-mə\ *n, pl* **-mas** *or* **-ma·ta** \-mə-tə\ [NL, fr. *glia* neuroglia + *blast-* + *-oma*] (ca. 1923) : a malignant tumor of the central nervous system and usu. of a cerebral hemisphere

gli·o·ma \glē-'ō-mə, glī-\ *n, pl* **-mas** *or* **-ma·ta** \-mə-tə\ [NL, fr. *glia*] (1870) : a tumor arising from neuroglia

¹**glis·sade** \gli-'säd, -'säd\ *vi* **glis·sad·ed; glis·sad·ing** [F, n., slide, glissade, fr. *glisser* to slide, fr. OF *glicier*, alter. of *glier*, of Gmc origin; akin to OHG *glītan* to glide] (1837) **1** : to perform a ballet glissade **2** : to slide in a standing or squatting position down a snow-covered slope without the aid of skis — **glis·sad·er** *n*

²**glissade** *n* (1843) **1** : a gliding step in ballet **2** : the action of glissading

glis·san·do \gli-'sän-(ˌ)dō\ *n, pl* **-di** \-(ˌ)dē\ *or* **-dos** [prob. modif. of F *glissade*] (ca. 1854) : a rapid sliding up or down the musical scale

¹**glis·ten** \'gli-sᵊn\ *vi* **glis·tened; glis·ten·ing** \'gli-sᵊn-iŋ\ [ME *glistnen*, fr. OE *glisnian;* akin to OE *glisian* to glitter, *geolu* yellow — more at YELLOW] (bef. 12c) : to give off a sparkling or lustrous reflection of or as if of a moist or polished surface   *syn* see FLASH

²**glisten** *n* (1840) : GLITTER, SPARKLE

glis·ter \'gli-stər\ *vi* **glis·tered; glis·ter·ing** \-t(ə-)riŋ\ [ME *glistren;* akin to OE *glisian*] (14c) : GLITTER — **glister** *n*

glitch \'glich\ *n* [perh. fr. Yiddish *glitsh* slippery place, fr. *glitshn* (*zikh*) to slide, glide; akin to OHG *glītan* to glide — more at GLIDE] (1962) **1 a** : a usu. minor malfunction 〈a ~ in a spacecraft's fuel cell〉; *also* : ²BUG 2 **b** : a minor problem that causes a temporary setback : SNAG **2** : a false or spurious electronic signal

¹**glit·ter** \'gli-tər\ *vi* [ME *gliteren*, fr. ON *glitra;* akin to OE *geolu* yellow] (14c) **1 a** : to shine by reflection with many small flashes of brilliant light : SPARKLE 〈sequins ~*ed* in the spotlight〉 **b** : to shine with strong emotion : FLASH 〈eyes ~*ing* in anger〉 **2** : to be brilliantly attractive, lavish, or spectacular; *also* : to be superficially attractive or exciting   *syn* see FLASH — **glit·ter·ing·ly** \-tə-riŋ-lē\ *adv*

²**glitter** *n* (1602) **1 a** : sparkling brilliance of something that glitters **b** : a bright usu. superficial attractiveness **c** : the quality of being spectacular **2** : small glittering objects used for ornamentation — **glit·tery** \'gli-tə-rē\ *adj*

glit·te·ra·ti \ˌgli-tə-'rä-tē\ *n pl* [blend of ²*glitter* and *literati*] (1940) : CELEBRITIES, BEAUTIFUL PEOPLE

glitter rock *n* (1973) : rock music characterized by performers wearing glittering costumes and bizarre often grotesque makeup

glitz \'glits\ *n* [perh. modif. of G *glitzern* to glitter, fr. MHG *glitzen;* akin to ON *glitra* to glitter] (1971) : extravagant showiness : GLITTER, OSTENTATION — **glitzy** \'glit-sē\ *adj*

gloam \'glōm\ *n* [Sc *gloam* to become twilight, back-formation fr. *gloaming*] (ca. 1821) *archaic* : TWILIGHT

gloam·ing \'glō-miŋ\ *n* [ME (Sc) *gloming*, fr. OE *glōming*, fr. *glōm* twilight; akin to OE *glōwan* to glow] (bef. 12c) : TWILIGHT, DUSK

¹**gloat** \'glōt\ *vi* [prob. of Scand origin; akin to ON *glotta* to grin scornfully] (1676) **1** *obs* : to look or glance admiringly or amorously **2** : to observe or think about something with triumphant and often malicious satisfaction, gratification, or delight 〈~ over an enemy's misfortune〉 — **gloat·er** *n* — **gloat·ing·ly** *adv*

²**gloat** *n* (1899) : the act or feeling of one who gloats

glob \'gläb\ *n* [perh. blend of *globe* and *blob*] (1900) **1** : a small drop : BLOB **2** : a usu. large and rounded mass — **glob·by** \'glä-bē\ *adj*

glob·al \'glō-bəl\ *adj* (1676) **1** : SPHERICAL **2** : of, relating to, or involving the entire world : WORLDWIDE 〈~ warfare〉 〈a ~ system of communication〉; *also* : of or relating to a celestial body (as the moon) **3** : of, relating to, or applying to a whole (as a mathematical function or a computer program) 〈a ~ search of a file〉 — **glob·al·ly** \-glō-bə-lē\ *adv*

glob·al·ise *Brit var of* GLOBALIZE

glob·al·ism \'glō-bə-ˌli-zəm\ *n* (1943) : a national policy of treating the whole world as a proper sphere for political influence — compare IMPERIALISM, INTERNATIONALISM — **glob·al·ist** \-list\ *n*

glob·al·ize \'glō-bə-ˌlīz\ *vt* **-ized; -iz·ing** (1944) : to make global; *esp* : to make worldwide in scope or application — **glob·al·iza·tion** \ˌglō-bə-lə-'zā-shən\ *n*

global village *n* (1960) : the world viewed as a community in which distance and isolation have been dramatically reduced by electronic media (as television)

¹**globe** \'glōb\ *n* [MF, fr. L *globus*] (15c) : something spherical or rounded: as **a** : a spherical representation of the earth, a celestial body, or the heavens **b** : EARTH 4 **c** : ORB 5

²**globe** *vt* **globed; glob·ing** (1641) *archaic* : to form into a globe

globe artichoke *n* (ca. 1858) : ARTICHOKE 1

globe·fish \-ˌfish\ *n* (1668) : PUFFER 2a

globe·flow·er \-ˌflau̇(-ə)r\ *n* (1597) : any of a genus (*Trollius*) of plants of the buttercup family with globose yellow flowers

globe thistle *n* (1597) : any of a genus (*Echinops*) of widely-cultivated Asian and Mediterranean composite herbs with spiky globose blue or white flowers

globe–trot·ter \-ˌträ-tər\ *n* (1875) : a person who travels widely — **globe–trot·ting** \-ˌträ-tiŋ\ *n or adj*

glo·bin \'glō-bən\ *n* [ISV, fr. *hemoglobin*] (1877) : a colorless protein obtained by removal of heme from a conjugated protein and esp. hemoglobin

glo·boid \'glō-ˌbȯid\ *adj* (1887) : shaped like a sphere

glo·bose \'glō-ˌbōs\ *adj* (15c) : GLOBULAR 1a(1) 〈~ pollen〉

glob·u·lar \'glä-byə-lər, 1b is also 'glō-\ *adj* [partly fr. L *globus* + E *-ular;* partly fr. L *globulus* + E *-ar*] (1654) **1 a** (1) : having the shape of a globe or globule (2) : having a compact folded molecular structure 〈~ proteins〉 **b** : GLOBAL 2 **c** : having or consisting of globules

globular cluster *n* (1859) : any of various approximately spherical clusters of gravitationally associated stars that typically populate galactic halos

glob·ule \'glä-(ˌ)byü(ə)l\ *n* [F, fr. L *globulus*, dim. of *globus*] (1661) : a tiny globe or ball esp. of a liquid 〈~s of mercury〉

glob·u·lin \'glä-byə-lən\ *n* (1845) : any of a class of simple proteins (as myosin) that are insoluble in pure water but are soluble in dilute salt solutions and that occur widely in plant and animal tissues — compare ALPHA GLOBULIN, BETA GLOBULIN, GAMMA GLOBULIN

glo·chid·i·um \glō-'ki-dē-əm\ *n, pl* **-ia** \-dē-ə\ [NL, fr. Gk *glōchis* projecting point + NL *-idium*] (1882) : the larva of a freshwater mussel (family Unionidae) that develops as an external parasite on fish

glock·en·spiel \'glä-kən-ˌspēl, -ˌshpēl\ *n* [G, fr. *Glocke* bell + *Spiel* play] (ca. 1834) : a percussion instrument consisting of a series of graduated metal bars tuned to the chromatic scale and played with two hammers

glogg *or* **glögg** \'glu̇g, 'glüg\ *n* [Sw *glögg*, fr. *glödga* to burn, mull, fr. *glöd* glowing coal, fr. ON *glōth;* akin to OE *glēd* glowing coal — more at GLEED] (1927) : a hot spiced wine and liquor punch served in Scandinavian countries as a Christmas drink

glockenspiel

glom \'gläm\ *vt* **glommed; glom·ming** [alter. of E dial. *glaum* to grab] (1907) **1** : TAKE, STEAL **2** : SEIZE, CATCH — **glom on to** : to grab hold of : appropriate to oneself

glo·mer·u·lar \glə-'mer-(y)ə-lər, glō-\ *adj* (1885) : of, relating to, or produced by a glomerulus 〈~ nephritis〉 〈~ capillaries〉

glom·er·ule \'glä-mə-ˌrül, -mər-, ˌyü(ə)l\ *n* [NL *glomerulus*] (1793) : a compacted cyme of almost sessile and usu. small flowers

glo·mer·u·lo·ne·phri·tis \glə-ˌmer-(y)ə-lō-ni-'frī-təs\ *n, pl* **-phrit·i·des** \-'fri-tə-ˌdēz\ (ca. 1886) : nephritis marked by inflammation of the capillaries of the renal glomeruli

glo·mer·u·lus \glə-'mer-(y)ə-ləs, glō-\ *n, pl* **-li** \-ˌlī, -ˌlē\ [NL, glomerulus, glomerule, dim. of L *glomer-, glomus* ball; akin to L *globus* globe] (1856) : a small convoluted or intertwined mass; *esp* : a tuft of capillaries at the point of origin of each vertebrate nephron that passes a protein-free filtrate to the surrounding Bowman's capsule

glo·mus \'glō-məs\ *n, pl* **glo·mera** \'glä-mə-rə, 'glō-\ [NL, fr. L *glomer-, glomus*] (1903) : a small arteriovenous anastomosis together with its supporting structures

¹**gloom** \'glüm\ *vb* [ME *gloumen*] *vi* (14c) **1** : to look, feel, or act sullen or despondent **2** : to be or become overcast **3** : to loom up dimly ~ *vt* : to make dark, murky, or somber : make gloomy

²**gloom** *n* (1629) **1 a** : partial or total darkness **b** : a dark or shadowy place **2 a** : lowness of spirits : DEJECTION **b** : an atmosphere of despondency 〈a ~ fell over the household〉

gloomy \'glü-mē\ *adj* **gloom·i·er; -est** (1588) **1 a** : partially or totally dark; *esp* : dismally and depressingly dark 〈~ weather〉 **b** : having a frowning or scowling appearance : FORBIDDING 〈a ~ countenance〉 **c** : low in spirits : MELANCHOLY **2 a** : causing gloom : DEPRESSING 〈a ~ story〉 〈a ~ landscape〉 **b** : lacking in promise or hopefulness : PESSIMISTIC 〈~ prophecies〉 〈a ~ future〉   *syn* see SULLEN — **gloom·i·ly** \-mə-lē\ *adv* — **gloom·i·ness** \-mē-nəs\ *n*

glop \'gläp\ *n* [origin unknown] (ca. 1944) **1** : a thick semiliquid substance (as food) that is usu. unattractive in appearance **2** : tasteless or worthless material — **glop·py** \'glä-pē\ *adj*

Glo·ria \'glōr-ē-ə, 'glȯr-\ *n* [L, glory] (13c) **1** : GLORIA IN EXCELSIS **2** : GLORIA PATRI

Gloria in Ex·cel·sis \-ˌin-eks-'chel-səs, -ek-'shel-\ [LL, glory (be to God) on high] (14c) : a Christian liturgical hymn having the verse form of the Psalms

Gloria Pa·tri \-'pä-(ˌ)trē\ *n* [LL, glory (be) to the Father] (13c) : a 2-verse doxology to the Trinity

glo·ri·fy \'glōr-ə-ˌfī, 'glȯr-\ *vt* **-fied; -fy·ing** [ME *glorifien*, fr. MF *glorifier*, fr. LL *glorificare*, fr. L *gloria*] (14c) **1 a** : to make glorious by bestowing honor, praise, or admiration **b** : to elevate to celestial glory **2** : to light up brilliantly 〈a large chandelier *glorifies* the whole room〉 **3 a** : to represent as glorious : EXTOL 〈a song ~*ing* romantic love〉 **b** : to cause to be or seem to be better than the actual condition 〈her new position is just a *glorified* version of the old stockroom job〉 **4** : to give glory to (as in worship) — **glo·ri·fi·ca·tion** \ˌglōr-ə-fə-'kā-shən, ˌglȯr-\ *n* — **glo·ri·fi·er** \'glōr-ə-ˌfi(-ə)r, 'glȯr-\ *n*

glo·ri·ous \'glōr-ē-əs, 'glȯr-\ *adj* [ME, fr. OF & L; OF *glorieus, glorios*, fr. L *gloriosus* glorious, vainglorious, fr. *gloria*] (13c) **1 a** : possessing or deserving glory : ILLUSTRIOUS **b** : entitling one to glory 〈a ~ victory〉 **2** : marked by great beauty or splendor : MAGNIFICENT **3** : DELIGHTFUL, WONDERFUL 〈had a ~ weekend〉   *syn* see SPLENDID — **glo·ri·ous·ly** *adv* — **glo·ri·ous·ness** *n*

¹**glo·ry** \'glōr-ē, 'glȯr-\ *n, pl* **glories** [ME *glorie*, fr. MF & L; MF, fr. L *gloria*] (14c) **1 a** : praise, honor, or distinction extended by common consent : RENOWN **b** : worshipful praise, honor, and thanksgiving 〈giving ~ to God〉 **2 a** : something that secures praise or renown 〈the ~ of a brilliant career〉 **b** : a distinguished quality or asset **3** (1) : great beauty and splendor : MAGNIFICENCE 〈the ~ that was Greece and the grandeur that was Rome — E. A. Poe〉 (2) : something marked by beauty or resplendence 〈a perfect ~ of a day〉 **b** : the splendor and beatific happiness of heaven; *broadly* : ETERNITY **4 a** : a state of great gratification or exaltation 〈when she's acting she's in her

~⟩ **b** : a height of prosperity or achievement **5** : a ring or spot of light: as **a** : AUREOLE **b** : CORONA 2a, b

²**glory** *vi* **glo·ried; glo·ry·ing** (14c) : to rejoice proudly — used with *in*

³**glory** *or* **glory be** *interj* (1816) — used to express surprise or delight

glory–of–the–snow *n* (ca. 1890) : any of a genus (*Chionodoxa*) of hardy spring-flowering bulbous herbs of the lily family with narrow basal leaves and terminal racemes of blue, white, or pink flowers

¹**gloss** \'gläs, 'glȯs\ *n* [prob. of Scand origin; akin to Icel *glossa* to glow; akin to OE *geolu* yellow] (1538) **1** : a surface luster or brightness : SHINE **2 a** : a deceptively attractive appearance ⟨selfishness that had a ~ of humanitarianism about it⟩ **b** : bright often superficial attractiveness ⟨show-biz ~⟩ **3** : a transparent cosmetic preparation for adding shine and usu. color to the lips

²**gloss** *vt* (1656) **1 a** : to mask the true nature of : give a deceptively attractive appearance to — used with *over* ⟨the misery was general, where not ~ed over by liberal application of alcohol —Marston Bates⟩ **b** : to deal with (a subject or problem) too lightly or not at all — used with *over* ⟨~es over scholarly controversies rather than confronting them head-on —John Israel⟩ **2** : to give a gloss to

³**gloss** *n* [alter. of *gloze*, fr. ME *glose*, fr. MF, fr. ML *glosa, glossa*, fr. Gk *glōssa, glōtta* tongue, language, obscure word; akin to Gk *glōchis* projecting point] (1548) **1 a** : a brief explanation (as in the margin or between the lines of a text) of a difficult or obscure word or expression **b** : a false and often willfully misleading interpretation (as of a text) **2 a** : GLOSSARY **b** : an interlinear translation **c** : a continuous commentary accompanying a text **3** : COMMENTARY, INTERPRETATION

⁴**gloss** *vt* (1603) **1 a** : to provide a gloss for : EXPLAIN, DEFINE **b** : INTERPRET **2** : to dispose of by false or perverse interpretation ⟨trying to ~ away the irrationalities of the universe —Irwin Edman⟩

gloss- *or* **glosso-** *comb form* [L, fr. Gk *glōss-, glōsso-*, fr. *glōssa*] **1** : tongue ⟨*glossitis*⟩ **2** : language ⟨*glossolalia*⟩

glos·sa \'glä-sə, 'glȯ-\ *n, pl* **glos·sae** \-,sē, -,sī\ *also* **glossas** [NL, fr. Gk *glōssa*] (ca. 1852) : a tongue or lingual structure esp. in an insect; *esp* : the median distal lobe of the labium of an insect

glos·sa·rist \'glä-sə-rist, 'glȯ-\ *n* (1774) : GLOSSATOR

glos·sa·ry \-sə-rē\ *n, pl* **-ries** (14c) : a collection of textual glosses or of specialized terms with their meanings — **glos·sar·i·al** \glä-'sar-ē-əl, glȯ-, -'ser-\ *adj*

glos·sa·tor \'glä-,sā-tər, 'glȯ-\ *n* (14c) **1** : one that makes textual glosses **2** : a compiler of a glossary

glos·si·tis \glä-'sī-təs, 'glȯ-\ *n* (ca. 1834) : inflammation of the tongue

glos·sog·ra·pher \glä-'sä-grə-fər, glȯ-\ *n* [Gk *glōssographos*, fr. *glōssa* + *graphein* to write — more at CARVE] (1607) : GLOSSATOR

glos·so·la·lia \,glä-sə-'lä-lē-ə, ,glȯ-\ *n* [NL] (1879) : TONGUE 4c — **glos·so·la·list** \-'lä-list\ *n*

glos·so·pha·ryn·geal nerve \,glä-sō-,far-ən-'jē-əl-, ,glȯ-, -fə-'rin-j(ē-)əl-\ *n* (ca. 1823) : either of the 9th pair of cranial nerves that are mixed nerves and supply chiefly the pharynx, posterior tongue, and parotid gland — called also *glossopharyngeal*

¹**glossy** \'glä-sē, 'glȯ-\ *adj* **gloss·i·er; -est** (1556) **1** : having a surface luster or brightness ⟨rich ~ leather⟩ ⟨~ paper⟩ **2** : attractive in an artificially opulent, sophisticated, or smoothly captivating manner : SLICK ⟨lots of ~ and phony chatter⟩ *syn* see SLEEK — **gloss·i·ly** \-sə-lē\ *adv* — **gloss·i·ness** \-sē-nəs\ *n*

²**glossy** *n, pl* **gloss·ies** (1928) **1** : a photograph printed on smooth shiny paper **2** *chiefly Brit* : SLICK 3

glott- *or* **glotto-** *comb form* [Gk *glōtt-, glōtto-* tongue, fr. *glōssa, glōtta*] : language ⟨*glottochronology*⟩

glot·tal \'glä-t²l\ *adj* (ca. 1846) : of, relating to, or produced in or by the glottis ⟨~ constriction⟩

glottal stop *n* (1888) : the interruption of the breath stream during speech by closure of the glottis

glot·tis \'glä-təs\ *n, pl* **glot·tis·es** *or* **glot·ti·des** \-tə-,dēz\ [Gk *glōttid-, glōttis*, fr. *glōtta* tongue — more at GLOSS] (1578) : the elongated space between the vocal cords; *also* : the structures that surround this space — compare EPIGLOTTIS

glot·to·chro·nol·o·gy \,glä-tō-krə-'nä-lə-jē\ *n* (1953) : a linguistic method that uses the rate of vocabulary replacement to estimate the date of divergence for distinct but genetically related languages — **glot·to·chro·no·log·i·cal** \-krä-n²l-'ä-ji-kəl, -,krō-\ *adj*

glout \'glüt, 'glaȯt\ *vi* [ME, prob. of Scand origin; akin to ON *glotta* to grin scornfully] (14c) *archaic* : FROWN, SCOWL

¹**glove** \'gləv\ *n* [ME, fr. OE *glōf;* akin to ON *glōfi* glove] (bef. 12c) **1 a** : a covering for the hand having separate sections for each of the fingers and the thumb and often extending part way up the arm **b** : ¹GAUNTLET 1, 3 **2 a** (1) : a padded leather covering for the hand used in baseball to catch a thrown or batted ball; *specif* : one having individual thumb and finger sections usu. connected with a lacing or webbing — compare MITT ⟨fielding ability ⟨he's got a good ~ at three positions and can pinch-hit —Casey Stengel⟩ **b** : BOXING GLOVE

²**glove** *vt* **gloved; glov·ing** (15c) **1 a** : to cover with or as if with a glove **b** : to furnish with gloves **2** : to catch (a baseball) in one's gloved hand

glove box *n* (1946) **1** : GLOVE COMPARTMENT **2** : a sealed protectively lined compartment having holes to which are attached gloves for use in handling dangerous materials inside the compartment

glove compartment *n* (1939) : a small storage cabinet in the dashboard of an automobile

glove leather *n* (1721) : a soft lightweight leather

glov·er \'glə-vər\ *n* (14c) : one that makes or sells gloves

¹**glow** \'glō\ *vi* [ME, fr. OE *glōwan;* akin to OE *geolu* yellow — more at YELLOW] (bef. 12c) **1 a** : to shine with or as if with an intense heat ⟨embers ~ing in the darkness⟩ **b** (1) : to have a rich warm typically ruddy color ⟨cheeks ~ing with health⟩ (2) : FLUSH, BLUSH ⟨the children ~ed with excitement⟩ **2 a** : to experience a sensation of or as if of heat ⟨~ing with rage⟩ **b** : to show exuberance or elation ⟨~ with pride⟩ — **glow·ing·ly** \-iŋ-lē\ *adv*

²**glow** *n* (1600) **1** : brightness or warmth of color; *esp* : REDNESS **2 a** : warmth of feeling or emotion **b** : a sensation of warmth ⟨the drug produces a sustained ~⟩ **3 a** : the state of glowing with heat and light **b** : light such as is emitted by a solid body heated to luminosity : INCANDESCENCE

glow discharge *n* (1844) : a luminous electrical discharge without sparks through a gas

¹**glow·er** \'glaȯ(-ə)r, ÷'glō(-ə)r\ *vi* [ME (Sc) *glowren;* perh. of Scand origin; akin to Norw dial. *glȳra* to look askance, Icel *glossa* to glow — more at GLOSS] (15c) : to look or stare with sullen annoyance or anger

²**glower** *n* (1715) : a sullen brooding look of annoyance or anger

glow lamp *n* (1884) : a gas-discharge electric lamp in which most of the light proceeds from the glow of the gas near the cathode

glow plug *n* (ca. 1941) : a heating element in a diesel-engine cylinder to preheat the air and to facilitate starting; *also* : a similar element for ignition in other internal-combustion engines

glow-worm \'glō-,wərm\ *n* [ME] (14c) : any of various luminous insect larvae or adults with wings rudimentary or lacking; *esp* : a larva or wingless female of a firefly (family Lampyridae) that emits light from the abdomen

glox·in·ia \gläk-'si-nē-ə\ *n* [NL, fr. B. P. *Gloxin* 18th cent. Ger. botanist] (ca. 1820) : any of a genus (*Sinningia*) of Brazilian tuberous herbaceous gesneriads; *esp* : a plant (*S. speciosa*) widely cultivated for its showy bell-shaped or slipper-shaped flowers

¹**gloze** \'glōz\ *vt* **glozed; gloz·ing** [ME *glosen* to gloss, flatter, fr. *glose* gloss] (14c) *archaic* : ⁴GLOSS 1

²**gloze** *vt* **glozed; gloz·ing** (14c) : ²GLOSS 1 — often used with *over*

gloxinia

gluc- *or* **gluco-** *comb form* [ISV] **1** : glucose ⟨*glucokinase*⟩ **2** : related to or containing glucose ⟨*glucosamine*⟩

glu·ca·gon \'glü-kə-,gän\ *n* [*gluc-* + *-agon* (perh. fr. Gk *agōn*, prp. of *agein* to lead, drive) — more at AGENT] (1923) : a protein hormone that is produced esp. by the islets of Langerhans and that promotes an increase in the sugar content of the blood by increasing the rate of glycogen breakdown in the liver

glu·can \'glü-,kan, -kən\ *n* (1941) : a polysaccharide (as glycogen or cellulose) that is a polymer of glucose

glu·co·cor·ti·coid \,glü-kō-'kȯr-ti-,kȯid\ *n* (1950) : any of a group of corticoids (as hydrocortisone) that are involved esp. in carbohydrate, protein, and fat metabolism, that are anti-inflammatory and immunosuppressive, and that are used widely in medicine (as in the alleviation of the symptoms of rheumatoid arthritis) — compare MINERALOCORTICOID

glu·co·ki·nase \-'kī-,nās, -,nāz\ *n* (1950) : a hexokinase found esp. in the liver that catalyzes the phosphorylation of glucose

glu·co·nate \'glü-kə-,nāt\ *n* (1884) : a salt or ester of gluconic acid

glu·co·neo·gen·e·sis \,glü-kə-,nē-ə-'je-nə-səs\ *n* [NL] (1912) : formation of glucose within the animal body esp. by the liver from substances (as fats and proteins) other than carbohydrates

glu·con·ic acid \(,)glü-'kä-nik-\ *n* [ISV, irreg. fr. *glucose* + *-ic*] (1871) : a crystalline acid $C_6H_{12}O_7$ obtained by oxidation of glucose and used chiefly in cleaning metals

glu·cos·amine \glü-'kō-sə-,mēn, -zə-\ *n* (1884) : an amino derivative $C_6H_{13}NO_5$ of glucose that occurs esp. as a constituent of polysaccharides in animal supporting structures and some plant cell walls

glu·cose \'glü-,kōs, -,kōz\ *n* [F, modif. of Gk *gleukos* must, sweet wine; akin to Gk *glykys* sweet — more at DULCET] (1840) **1** : an optically active sugar $C_6H_{12}O_6$ that has an aldehydic carbonyl group; *esp* : the sweet colorless soluble dextrorotatory form that occurs widely in nature and is the usual form in which carbohydrate is assimilated by animals **2** : a light-colored syrup made from cornstarch

glucose–1–phosphate *n* [fr. the position at which the phosphate group is attached] (1938) : an ester $C_6H_{13}O_9P$ that reacts in the presence of a phosphorylase with aldoses and ketoses to yield disaccharides or with itself in liver and muscle to yield glycogen and phosphoric acid

glucose phosphate *n* (1912) : a phosphate ester of glucose: as **a** : GLUCOSE-1-PHOSPHATE **b** : GLUCOSE-6-PHOSPHATE

glucose–6–phosphate *n* [fr. the position at which the phosphate group is attached] (1954) : an ester $C_6H_{13}O_9P$ that is formed from glucose and ATP in the presence of a glucokinase and that is an essential early stage in glucose metabolism

glucose–6–phosphate dehydrogenase *n* (1954) : an enzyme found esp. in red blood cells that dehydrogenates glucose-6-phosphate in a glucose degradation pathway alternative to the Krebs cycle

glu·co·si·dase \glü-'kō-sə-,dās, -zə-,dāz\ *n* (ca. 1926) : an enzyme (as maltase) that hydrolyzes a glucoside

glu·co·side \'glü-kə-,sīd\ *n* (1855) : GLYCOSIDE; *esp* : a glycoside that yields glucose on hydrolysis — **glu·co·sid·ic** \,glü-kə-'si-dik\ *adj*

glu·cu·ron·ic acid \,glü-kyə-'rä-nik-\ *n* (1911) : a compound $C_6H_{10}O_7$ that occurs esp. as a constituent of mucopolysaccharides (as hyaluronic acid) and combined as a glucuronide

glu·cu·ron·i·dase \-'rä-nə-,dās, -,dāz\ *n* (1945) : an enzyme that hydrolyzes a glucuronide; *esp* : one that occurs widely (as in liver and spleen) and hydrolyzes the beta form of a glucuronide

glu·cu·ro·nide \glü-'kyùr-ə-,nīd\ *n* (1934) : any of various derivatives of glucuronic acid that are formed esp. as combinations with often toxic aromatic hydroxyl compounds and are excreted in the urine

¹**glue** \'glü\ *n* [ME *glu*, fr. MF, fr. LL *glut-, glus;* akin to L *gluten* glue — more at CLAY] (14c) **1 a** : any of various strong adhesive substances; *esp* : a hard protein chiefly gelatinous substance that absorbs water to form a viscous solution with strong adhesive properties and that is obtained by cooking down collagenous materials (as hides or bones) **b** : a solution of glue used for sticking things together **2** : something that binds together ⟨enough social ~ . . . to satisfy the human desire for community —E. D. Hirsch, Jr.⟩ — **glu·ey** \'glü-ē\ *adj* — **glu·i·ly** \'glü-ə-lē\ *adv*

²**glue** *vt* **glued; glu·ing** *also* **glue·ing** (14c) **1** : to cause to stick tightly with or as if with glue ⟨*gluing* the wings onto the model airplane⟩ ⟨used that war to ~ together a frail story —Gloria Emerson⟩ **2** : to fix (as

---

\ə\ abut \²\ kitten, F table \ər\ further \a\ ash \ā\ ace \ä\ mop, mar
\aù\ out \ch\ chin \e\ bet \ē\ easy \g\ go \i\ hit \ī\ ice \j\ job
\ŋ\ sing \ō\ go \ȯ\ law \ȯi\ boy \th\ thin \t̲h̲\ the \ü\ loot \ù\ foot
\y\ yet \zh\ vision \ä, k̲, ⁿ, œ, œ̄, ue, uē, ᵛ\ *see* Guide to Pronunciation

the eyes) on an object steadily or with deep concentration ⟨kept his eyes *glued* to the TV screen⟩

glum \'gləm\ *adj* **glum·mer; glum·mest** [akin to ME *gloumen* to gloom] (1547) **1**: broodingly morose ⟨became ~ when they heard the news⟩ **2**: DREARY, GLOOMY ⟨a ~ countenance⟩ *syn* see SULLEN — **glum·ly** *adv* — **glum·ness** *n*

glume \'glüm\ *n* [NL *gluma*, fr. L, hull, husk; akin to L *glubere* to peel — more at CLEAVE] (1789) : a chaffy bract; *specif* : either of two empty bracts at the base of the spikelet in grasses

glu·on \'glü-,än\ *n* [¹*glue* + ²-*on*] (1971) : a hypothetical neutral massless particle held to bind together quarks to form hadrons

¹**glut** \'glət\ *vb* **glut·ted; glut·ting** [ME *glouten*, prob. fr. MF *gloutir* to swallow, fr. L *gluttire* — more at GLUTTON] *vt* (14c) **1**: to fill esp. with food to satiety **2**: to flood (the market) with goods so that supply exceeds demand ~ *vi*: to eat gluttonously *syn* see SATIATE

²**glut** *n* (ca. 1546) **1**: an excessive quantity : OVERSUPPLY **2** *archaic* : the act or process of glutting

³**glut** *vt* **glut·ted; glut·ting** [prob. fr. obs. *glut*, n., swallow] (1600) *archaic* : to swallow greedily

glu·ta·mate \'glü-tə-,māt\ *n* (1876) : a salt or ester of glutamic acid — compare MONOSODIUM GLUTAMATE

glu·tam·ic acid \(,)glü-'ta-mik-\ *n* [ISV *gluten* + *amino* + -*ic*] (1871) : a crystalline amino acid $C_5H_9NO_4$ widely distributed in plant and animal proteins

glu·ta·min·ase \'glü-tə-mə-,nās, glü-'ta-mə-, -,nāz\ *n* (1938) : an enzyme that hydrolyzes glutamine to glutamic acid and ammonia

glu·ta·mine \'glü-tə-,mēn\ *n* [ISV *gluten* + *amine*] (ca. 1885) : a crystalline amino acid $C_5H_{10}N_2O_3$ that is found both free and in proteins in plants and animals and that yields glutamic acid and ammonia on hydrolysis

glu·tar·al·de·hyde \,glü-tə-'ral-də-,hīd\ *n* [*glutaric* acid + *aldehyde*] (1951) : a compound $C_5H_8O_2$ that contains two aldehyde groups and is used esp. in tanning leather and in the fixation of biological tissues

glu·tar·ic acid \glü-'tar-ik-\ *n* [prob. fr. *gluten* + -*aric* (as in *tartaric acid*)] (ca. 1885) : a crystalline acid $C_5H_8O_4$ used esp. in organic synthesis

glu·ta·thi·one \,glü-tə-'thī-,ōn\ *n* [ISV *gluta-* (fr. *glutamic acid*) + *thi-* + -*one*] (1921) : a peptide $C_{10}H_{17}N_3O_6S$ that contains one amino-acid residue each of glutamic acid, cysteine, and glycine, that occurs widely in plant and animal tissues, and that plays an important role in biological oxidation-reduction processes and as a coenzyme

glu·te·al \'glü-tē-əl, glü-'tē-\ *adj* (1804) : of or relating to the gluteus muscles

glu·ten \'glü-t⁹n\ *n* [L *glutin-, gluten* glue — more at CLAY] (1803) : a tenacious elastic protein substance esp. of wheat flour that gives cohesiveness to dough — **glu·ten·ous** \'glüt-nəs, 'glü-t⁹n-əs\ *adj*

glu·teth·i·mide \glü-'te-thə-,mīd, -məd\ *n* [*gluten* + *eth-* + *imide*] (1955) : a sedative-hypnotic drug $C_{13}H_{15}NO_2$ that induces sleep with less depression of respiration than occurs with comparable doses of barbiturates

glu·te·us \'glü-tē-əs, glü-'tē-\ *n, pl* **glu·tei** \'glü-tē-,ī, -tē-,ē\ [NL *glutaeus, gluteus*, fr. Gk *gloutos* buttock — more at CLOUD] (ca. 1681) : any of the large muscles of the buttocks; *esp* : GLUTEUS MAXIMUS

glu·te·us max·i·mus \-'mak-sə-məs\ *n, pl* **glu·tei max·i·mi** \-'mak-sə-,mī\ [NL, lit., largest gluteus] (1886) : the outermost muscle of the three glutei found in each of the human buttocks

glu·ti·nous \'glüt-nəs, 'glü-t⁹n-əs\ *adj* [MF or L; MF *glutineux*, fr. L *glutinosus*, fr. *glutin-, gluten*] (15c) : having the quality of glue : GUMMY — **glu·ti·nous·ly** *adv*

glut·ton \'glə-t⁹n\ *n* [ME *glotoun*, fr. OF *gloton*, fr. L *glutton-, glutto*; akin to L *gluttire* to swallow, *gula* throat, OE *ceole*] (13c) **1 a**: one given habitually to greedy and voracious eating and drinking **b**: one that has a great capacity for accepting or enduring something ⟨a ~ for punishment⟩ **2**: WOLVERINE 1a

glut·ton·ous \'glət-nəs, 'glə-t⁹n-əs\ *adj* (14c) : marked by or given to gluttony *syn* see VORACIOUS — **glut·ton·ous·ly** *adv* — **glut·ton·ous·ness** *n*

glut·tony \'glət-nē, 'glə-t⁹n-ē\ *n, pl* **-ton·ies** (13c) **1**: excess in eating or drinking **2**: greedy or excessive indulgence

glyc- or **glyco-** *comb form* [ISV, fr. Gk *glyk-* sweet, fr. *glykys*] **1**: carbohydrate and esp. sugar ⟨*glycoprotein*⟩ **2**: glycine ⟨*glycyl*⟩

gly·can \'glī-,kan\ *n* (1953) : POLYSACCHARIDE

glyc·er·al·de·hyde \,gli-sə-'ral-də-,hīd\ *n* [*glyceric* acid + *aldehyde*] (1882) : a sweet crystalline compound $C_3H_6O_3$ that is formed as an intermediate in carbohydrate metabolism by the breakdown of sugars and that yields glycerol on reduction

gly·cer·ic acid \gli-'ser-ik-\ *n* [ISV, fr. *glycerin*] (ca. 1864) : a syrupy acid $C_3H_6O_4$ obtainable by oxidation of glycerol or glyceraldehyde

glyc·er·ide \'gli-sə-,rīd\ *n* (ca. 1864) : an ester of glycerol esp. with fatty acids — **glyc·er·id·ic** \,gli-sə-'ri-dik\ *adj*

glyc·er·in or **glyc·er·ine** \'glis-rən, 'gli-sə-\ *n* [F *glycérine*, fr. Gk *glykeros* sweet; akin to Gk *glykys*] (1838) : GLYCEROL

glyc·er·in·ate \'glis-rə-,nāt, 'gli-sə-\ *vt* -**at·ed; -at·ing** (1897) : to treat with or preserve in glycerin

glyc·er·ol \'gli-sə-,ról, -,rōl\ *n* [*glycerin* + -*ol*] (1884) : a sweet syrupy hygroscopic trihydroxy alcohol $C_3H_8O_3$ usu. obtained by the saponification of fats and used esp. as a solvent and plasticizer

glyc·er·yl \'glis-rəl, 'gli-sə-\ *n* (1845) : a radical derived from glycerol by removal of hydroxide; *esp* : a trivalent radical CH_2CHCH_2

gly·cine \'glī-,sēn, 'gli-s⁹n\ *n* (1851) : a sweet crystalline amino acid $C_2H_5NO_2$ obtained esp. by hydrolysis of proteins

gly·co·gen \'glī-kə-jən\ *n* (ca. 1864) : a white amorphous tasteless polysaccharide $(C_6H_{10}O_5)_x$ that is the principal form in which carbohydrate is stored in animal tissues and esp. muscle and liver tissue

gly·co·gen·e·sis \,glī-kə-'je-nə-səs\ *n* [NL] (ca. 1886) : the formation and storage of glycogen

gly·co·gen·ol·y·sis \,glī-kə-jə-'nä-lə-səs\ *n, pl* -**y·ses** \-,sēz\ [NL] (1909) : the breakdown of glycogen esp. to glucose in the animal body — **gly·co·gen·o·lyt·ic** \-jə-n⁹l-'i-tik, -je-\ *adj*

gly·col \'glī-,kól, -,kōl\ *n* [ISV *glyc-* + -*ol*] (1858) : DIOL; *esp* : ETHYLENE GLYCOL

gly·col·ic acid or **gly·col·lic acid** \(,)glī-'kä-lik-\ *n* [ISV *glycol* + ¹-*ic*] (1852) : a translucent crystalline compound $C_2H_4O_3$ found esp. in

unripe grapes and sugar beets and used esp. in textile and leather processing

gly·co·lip·id \,glī-kō-'li-pəd\ *n* (1936) : a lipid (as a ganglioside or a cerebroside) that contains a carbohydrate radical

gly·col·y·sis \glī-'kä-lə-səs\ *n* [NL] (1892) : the enzymatic breakdown of a carbohydrate (as glucose) by way of phosphate derivatives with the production of pyruvic or lactic acid and energy stored in high-energy phosphate bonds of ATP — **gly·co·lyt·ic** \,glī-kə-'li-tik\ *adj*

gly·co·pep·tide \,glī-kō-'pep-,tīd\ *n* (1959) : GLYCOPROTEIN

gly·co·pro·tein \-'prō-,tēn, -'prō-tē-ən\ *n* (ca. 1908) : a conjugated protein in which the nonprotein group is a carbohydrate

gly·co·s·ami·no·gly·can \,glī-kō-sə-,mē-nō-'glī-,kan, -kō-,sa-mə-nō-\ *n* [*glyc-* + *hexosamine* (amine derived from a hexose) + -*o-* + *glycan*] (1962) : any of various polysaccharides derived from an amino hexose that are constituents of mucoproteins, glycoproteins, and blood-group substances — called also *mucopolysaccharide*

gly·co·si·dase \glī-'kō-sə-,dās, -'kä-, -,dāz\ *n* (1944) : an enzyme that catalyzes the hydrolysis of a bond joining a sugar of a glycoside to an alcohol or another sugar unit

gly·co·side \'glī-kə-,sīd\ *n* [alter. of *glucoside*] (ca. 1889) : any of numerous sugar derivatives that contain a nonsugar group bonded to an oxygen or nitrogen atom and that on hydrolysis yield a sugar (as glucose) — **gly·co·sid·ic** \,glī-kə-'si-dik\ *adj* — **gly·co·sid·i·cal·ly** \-di-k(ə-)lē\ *adv*

gly·co·suria \,glī-kō-'shúr-ē-ə, ,glī-kəs-'yùr-\ *n* [NL, fr. ISV *glycose* glucose + NL -*uria*] (1860) : the presence in the urine of abnormal amounts of sugar

gly·co·syl \'glī-kə-,sil\ *n* [ISV *glycose* glucose] (1945) : a univalent radical derived from a cyclic form of glucose by removal of the hemiacetal hydroxyl group

gly·co·syl·a·tion \,glī-kō-sə-'lā-shən\ *n* (1946) : the process of adding glycosyl groups to a protein to form a glycoprotein — **gly·co·sy·late** \,glī-kō-'sī-,lāt\ *vt*

gly·cyl \'glī-səl\ *n* (1901) : the univalent acyl radical NH_2CH_2CO- of glycine

glyph \'glif\ *n* [Gk *glyphē* carved work, fr. *glyphein* to carve — more at CLEAVE] (1775) **1**: an ornamental vertical groove esp. in a Doric frieze **2**: a symbolic figure or a character (as in the Mayan system of writing) usu. incised or carved in relief **3**: a symbol (as a curved arrow on a road sign) that conveys information nonverbally — **glyph·ic** \'gli-fik\ *adj*

Glyp·tal \'glip-t⁹l\ *trademark* — used for an alkyd

glyp·tic \'glip-tik\ *n* [prob. fr. F *glyptique*, fr. Gk *glyptikē*, fr. *glyphein*] (ca. 1818) : the art or process of carving or engraving esp. on gems

G–man \'jē-,man\ *n* [prob. fr. *government man*] (1928) : a special agent of the Federal Bureau of Investigation

gnar or **gnarr** \'när\ *vi* **gnarred; gnar·ring** [imit.] (15c) : SNARL, GROWL

¹**gnarl** \'när(-ə)l\ *vi* [prob. freq. of *gnar*] (1593) : SNARL, GROWL

²**gnarl** *vt* [back-formation fr. *gnarled*] (1814) : to twist into a state of deformity

³**gnarl** *n* (1824) : a hard protuberance with twisted grain on a tree

gnarled \'när(-ə)ld\ *adj* [prob. alter. of *knurled*] (1603) **1**: full of knots or gnarls : KNOTTY ⟨~ hands⟩ **2**: crabbed in disposition, aspect, or character

gnarly \'när-lē\ *adj* (1829) **1**: GNARLED **2** *slang* — used as a generalized term of approval or disparagement

gnash \'nash\ *vt* [alter. of ME *gnasten*] (15c) : to strike or grind (as the teeth) together — **gnash** *n*

gnat \'nat\ *n* [ME, fr. OE *gnætt;* akin to OE *gnagan* to gnaw] (bef. 12c) : any of various small usu. biting dipteran flies — **gnat·ty** \-ē\ *adj*

gnat·catch·er \'nat-,ka-chər, -,ke-\ *n* (1839) : any of a genus (*Polioptila*) of several small No. and So. American insectivorous oscine birds

gnath·ic \'na-thik\ or **gna·thal** \'nā-thəl, 'na-\ *adj* [Gk *gnathos* jaw] (1882) : of or relating to the jaw

-gnathous *adj comb form* [NL -*gnathus*, fr. Gk *gnathos;* akin to Gk *genys* jaw — more at CHIN] : having (such) a jaw ⟨*prognathous*⟩

gnaw \'nó\ *vb* [ME *gnawen*, fr. OE *gnagan;* akin to OHG *gnagan* to gnaw] *vt* (bef. 12c) **1 a**: to bite or chew on with the teeth; *esp* : to wear away by persistent biting or nibbling ⟨a dog ~*ing* a bone⟩ **b**: to make by gnawing ⟨rats ~*ed* a hole⟩ **2 a**: to be a source of vexation to : PLAGUE ⟨anxiety always ~*ing* him⟩ **b**: to affect like gnawing ⟨hunger ~*ing* her vitals⟩ **3**: ERODE, CORRODE ~ *vi* **1**: to bite or nibble persistently ⟨~*ing* at his underlip⟩ **2**: to produce an effect of or as if of gnawing ⟨waves ~*ing* away at the cliffs⟩ — **gnaw·er** \'nó(-ə)r\ *n*

gneiss \'nīs\ *n* [G *Gneis*, alter. of MHG *gneiste* spark, fr. OHG *gneisto;* akin to OE *fȳrgnāst* spark] (1757) : a foliated metamorphic rock corresponding in composition to a feldspathic plutonic rock (as granite) — **gneiss·ic** \'nī-sik\ *adj* — **gneiss·oid** \-,sóid\ *adj* — **gneiss·ose** \-,sōs\ *adj*

gnoc·chi \'nò-kē, 'nyó-, 'nä-\ *n pl* [It, pl. of *gnocco*, fr. It dial. (Veneto), prob. of Gmc origin; akin to MHG *knöchel* knuckle, *knoche* bone — more at KNUCKLE] (1891) : dumplings usu. made with potato or semolina and served with sauce

¹**gnome** \'nōm\ *n* [Gk *gnōmē*, fr. *gignōskein* to know — more at KNOW] (1577) : MAXIM, APHORISM

²**gnome** *n* [F, fr. NL *gnomus*] (1712) **1**: an ageless and often deformed dwarf of folklore who lives in the earth and usu. guards treasure **2**: an elemental being in the theory of Paracelsus that inhabits earth — **gnome·like** \-,līk\ *adj* — **gnom·ish** \'nō-mish\ *adj*

gno·mic \'nō-mik\ *adj* (1815) **1**: characterized by aphorism ⟨~ utterances⟩ **2**: given to the composition of gnomic writing ⟨a ~ poet⟩

gno·mon \'nō-,män, -,mən\ *n* [L, fr. Gk *gnōmōn* interpreter, pointer on a sundial, fr. *gignōskein*] (1546) **1**: an object that by the position or length of its shadow serves as an indicator esp. of the hour of the day: as **a**: the pin of a sundial **b**: a column or shaft erected perpendicular to the horizon **2**: the remainder of a parallelogram after the removal of a similar

bcdefg gnomon 2

parallelogram containing one of its corners

gno·sis \'nō-səs\ n [Gk gnōsis, lit., knowledge, fr. gignōskein] (1703) : esoteric knowledge of spiritual truth held by the ancient Gnostics to be essential to salvation

gnos·tic \'näs-tik\ n, often cap [LL gnosticus, fr. Gk gnōstikos of knowledge, fr. gignōskein] (ca. 1587) : an adherent of gnosticism — **gnostic** adj, often cap

gnos·ti·cism \'näs-tə-,si-zəm\ n, often cap (1664) : the thought and practice esp. of various cults of late pre-Christian and early Christian centuries distinguished by the conviction that matter is evil and that emancipation comes through gnosis

gno·to·bi·ot·ic \,nō-tō-bī-'ä-tik, -bē-\ adj [Gk gnōtos known (fr. gignōskein to know) + biotē life, way of life — more at KNOW, BIOTA] (1949) : of, relating to, living in, or being a controlled environment containing one or a few kinds of organisms; also : AXENIC — **gno·to·bi·ot·i·cal·ly** \-ti-k(ə-)lē\ adv

gnu \'nü also 'nyü\ n, pl gnu or gnus [Khoikhoi t'gnu] (1777) : either of two large African antelopes (Connochaetes gnou and C. taurinus) with a head like that of an ox, short mane, long tail, and horns in both sexes that curve downward and outward

¹go \'gō\ vb **went** \'went\; **gone** \'gȯn also 'gän\; **go·ing** \'gō-iŋ, 'gȯ(-)iŋ; "going to" in sense 13 is often 'gō-nə or 'gȯ-nə or 'gȯ-nə\; **goes** \'gōz\ [ME gon, fr. OE gān; akin to OHG gān to go, Gk kichanein to reach, attain] vi (bef. 12c) **1** : to move on a course : PROCEED ⟨~ slow⟩ ⟨went by train⟩ — compare STOP **2** : to move out of or away from a place expressed or implied : LEAVE, DEPART ⟨went from school to the party⟩ ⟨~ing away for vacation⟩ **3** a : to take a certain course or follow a certain procedure ⟨reports ~ through channels to the president⟩ b : to pass by means of a process like journeying ⟨the message went by wire⟩ c : to proceed without delay and often in a thoughtless or reckless manner — used esp. to intensify a complementary verb ⟨why did you ~ and spoil it⟩ ⟨~ jump in a lake⟩ d (1) : to extend from point to point or in a certain direction ⟨the road ~es to the lake⟩ (2) : to give access : LEAD ⟨that door ~es to the cellar⟩ **4** obs : WALK **5** : to be habitually in a certain state or condition ⟨~ bareheaded⟩ **6** a : to become lost, consumed, or spent ⟨our time has gone⟩ b : DIE c : to slip away : ELAPSE ⟨the evening went quickly⟩ d : to come to be given up or discarded ⟨these slums have to ~⟩ e : to pass by sale ⟨went for a good price⟩ f : to become impaired or weakened ⟨his hearing started to ~⟩ g : to give way esp. under great force or pressure : BREAK ⟨the roof went⟩ **7** a : to move along in a specified manner : FARE ⟨everything was ~ing well⟩ b : to be in general or on an average ⟨cheap, as yachts ~⟩ c : to be or become esp. as the result of a contest ⟨the election went in her favor⟩ d : to turn out well : SUCCEED ⟨worked hard to make the party ~⟩ **8** a : to apply oneself ⟨went to work⟩ b : to put or subject oneself ⟨went to unnecessary expense⟩ c chiefly Southern & Midland : INTEND ⟨I didn't ~ to do it⟩ **9** : to have recourse to another for corroboration, vindication, or decision : RESORT ⟨~ to court to recover damages⟩ **10** a : to begin an action or motion ⟨here ~es⟩ b : to maintain or perform a certain action or motion ⟨still ~ing strong⟩ c : to function in the proper or expected manner : RUN ⟨the motor won't ~⟩ **11** : to be known ⟨~es by an alias⟩ **12** a : to act in accordance or harmony ⟨a good rule to ~ by⟩ b : to come to be determined ⟨dreams ~ by contraries⟩ c : to come to be applied or appropriated ⟨all proceeds ~ to charity⟩ d : to pass by award, assignment, or lot ⟨the prize went to a sophomore⟩ e (1) : to contribute to an end or result ⟨qualities that ~ to make a hero⟩ (2) : to be of advantage ⟨has a lot ~ing for her⟩ **13** : to be about, intending, or expecting something — used in a progressive tense before an infinitive ⟨is ~ing to leave town⟩ **14** a : EXTEND ⟨his knowledge fails to ~ very deep⟩ b : to come or arrive at a certain state or condition ⟨~ to sleep⟩ c : to come to be : BECOME ⟨the tire went flat⟩ — often used to express conversion to specified values or a specified state ⟨gone Hollywood⟩ ⟨~ condo⟩ d : to undergo a change ⟨leaves ~ from green to red⟩ **15** a : to be in phrasing or expression : READ ⟨as the story ~es⟩ b : to be capable of being sung or played ⟨the tune ~es like this⟩ **16** : to be compatible, suitable, or becoming : HARMONIZE ⟨the tie ~es with his suit⟩ **17** a : to be capable of passing, extending, or being contained or inserted ⟨will these clothes ~ in your suitcase⟩ b : to have a usual or proper place or position : BELONG ⟨these books ~ on the top shelf⟩ **18** : to have a tendency : CONDUCE ⟨~es to show⟩ **19** a (1) : to carry authority ⟨what she said went⟩ (2) : to be acceptable, satisfactory, or adequate ⟨anything ~es here⟩ b : to hold true : be valid ⟨the rule ~es for you, too⟩ **20** : to empty the bladder or bowels ~ vt **1** : to proceed along or according to : FOLLOW ⟨if I were ~ing his way⟩ ⟨went the conventional route⟩ **2** : to travel through or along : TRAVERSE ⟨went the length of the street⟩ **3** a : to make a wager of : BET ⟨~ a dollar on the outcome⟩ b : to make an offer of : BID ⟨willing to ~ $50 for the clock⟩ **4** a : to assume the function or obligation of ⟨promised to ~ bail for his friend⟩ b : to participate to the extent of ⟨decided to ~ halves on the winnings⟩ **5** : YIELD, WEIGH ⟨this fish ~es ten pounds⟩ **6** a : to put up with : TOLERATE ⟨couldn't ~ the noise⟩ b : AFFORD ⟨can't ~ the price⟩ c : ENJOY ⟨I could ~ a soda⟩ **7** a : to cause (a characteristic sound) to occur ⟨the gun went bang⟩ b : SAY — used chiefly in oral narration of speech **8** : to engage in ⟨don't ~ telling everyone⟩ **9** of a sports team or player : to have a record of ⟨went 11-0 last season⟩ — **go·er** \'gō(-ə)r\ n — **go about 1** : to set about — **go after** : to try to get : SEEK — **go all the way 1** : to enter into complete agreement **2** : to engage in sexual intercourse — **go at 1** a : to make an attack on b : to make an approach to **2** : UNDERTAKE — **go back on 1** : ABANDON **2** : BETRAY **3** : FAIL — **go begging** : to be in little demand — **go by the board 1** : to be carried over a ship's side **2** : to be discarded — **go down the line** : to give wholehearted support — **go easy 1** : to be sparing ⟨go easy with the sugar⟩ ⟨go easy on the kid⟩ — **go fly a kite 1** : to stop being an annoyance or disturbance ⟨told him to go fly a kite⟩ — **go for 1** : to pass for or serve as **2** : to try to secure or attain (as a goal) ⟨go for the prize⟩ **3** a : FAVOR, ACCEPT ⟨cannot go for your suds⟩ b : to have an interest in or liking for ⟨she went for him in a big way⟩ —Chandler Brossard⟩ **4** : ATTACK, ASSAIL ⟨my dog went for the intruder⟩ — **go for broke** : to put forth all one's strength or resources — **go great guns** : to achieve great success — **go hang** : to cease to be of interest or concern — **go into** : to be contained in ⟨5 goes into 60 12 times⟩ — **go it 1** : to behave in a reckless, excited, or impromptu

manner **2** : to proceed in a rapid or furious manner **3** : to conduct one's affairs : ACT ⟨insists on going it alone⟩ — **go missing** chiefly Brit : to become lost : DISAPPEAR — **go one better** : OUTDO, SURPASS — **go over 1** : EXAMINE **2** a : REPEAT b : STUDY, REVIEW — **go places** : to be on the way to success — **go public 1** of a close corporation : to offer shares for sale to the general public **2** : to make a public disclosure — **go steady** : to date one person exclusively and frequently — **go the vole** : to risk all for great gains — **go through 1** : to subject to thorough examination, consideration, or study **2** : EXPERIENCE, UNDERGO **3** : CARRY OUT, PERFORM ⟨went through his work in a daze⟩ — **go to bat for** : to give active support or assistance to : DEFEND, CHAMPION — **go to bed with** : to have sexual intercourse with — **go to one's head 1** : to cause one to become confused, excited, or dizzy **2** : to cause one to become conceited or overconfident — **go to pieces** : to become shattered (as in nerves or health) — **go to the mat** : to make an all-out combative effort (as in support of a position) — **go to town 1** : to work or act rapidly or efficiently **2** : to be markedly successful **3** : to indulge oneself excessively — **go with 1** : DATE **2** : CHOOSE 2 ⟨went with an iron off the tee⟩ — **go without saying** : to be self-evident — **go with the flow** : CONFORM 2b — **to go 1** : still remaining ⟨ten minutes to go⟩ **2** of prepared food : sold for consumption off the premises

²go \'gō\ n, pl **goes** (1727) **1** : the act or manner of going **2** : the height of fashion : RAGE ⟨elegant shawls labeled . . . "quite the ~" — R. S. Surtees⟩ **3** : an often unexpected turn of affairs : OCCURRENCE **4** : the quantity used or furnished at one time ⟨you can obtain a ~ of brandy for sixpence —C. B. Fairbanks⟩ **5** : ENERGY, VIGOR **6** a : a turn in an activity (as a game) ⟨it's your ~⟩ b : ATTEMPT, TRY ⟨have a ~ at painting⟩ **7** a : a spell of activity ⟨finished the job at one ~⟩ **8** : SUCCESS ⟨made a ~ of the business⟩ **9** : permission to proceed : GO-AHEAD ⟨gave the astronauts a ~ for another orbit⟩ — **no go** : to no avail : USELESS — **on the go** : constantly or restlessly active

³go adj (1961) : functioning properly : being in good and ready condition ⟨declared all systems ~⟩

⁴go n, often cap [Jp] (1890) : a Japanese game played between two players who alternately place black and white stones on a board checkered by 19 vertical lines and 19 horizontal lines in an attempt to enclose the larger area on the board

¹goad \'gōd\ n [ME gode, fr. OE gād spear, goad; akin to Langobardic gaida spear, and perh. to Skt hinoti he urges on] (bef. 12c) **1** a : something that pricks like a goad : THORN b : something that urges or stimulates into action : SPUR **2** : a pointed rod used to urge on an animal syn see MOTIVE

²goad vt (1579) **1** : to incite or rouse as if with a goad **2** : to drive (as cattle) with a goad

¹go-ahead \'gō-ə-,hed\ adj (1834) **1** : marked by energy and enterprise : PROGRESSIVE ⟨a vigorous ~ company⟩ **2** : indicating that one may proceed ⟨~ signal⟩ **3** : being a score that gives a team the lead in a game ⟨drove in the ~ run⟩

²go-ahead n (1840) **1** a : ENERGY, SPIRIT ⟨had a great deal of courage and ~⟩ b : one possessing go-ahead **2** : a sign, signal, or authority to proceed : GREEN LIGHT

goal \'gōl, chiefly Northern esp in 1b & 3a also 'gül\ n [ME gol boundary, limit] (1531) **1** a : the terminal point of a race b : an area to be reached safely in children's games **2** : the end toward which effort is directed : AIM **3** a : an area or object toward which players in various games attempt to advance a ball or puck and usu. through or into which it must go to score points b : the act or action of causing a ball or puck to go through or into such a goal c : the score resulting from such an act syn see INTENTION — **goal** vi — **goal·less** \'gō(l)-ləs\ adj

goal·ie \'gō-lē\ n (1921) : GOALKEEPER

goal·keep·er \'gōl-,kē-pər\ n (1658) : a player who defends the goal in any of various games (as hockey, lacrosse, or soccer)

goal kick n (1891) : a free kick in soccer awarded to a defensive player when the ball is driven out of bounds over the end line by an opposing player

goal line n (1867) : a line at either end and usu. running the width of a playing area on which a goal or goalpost is situated

goal·mouth \'gōl-,maúth\ n (1882) : the area directly in front of the goal (as in soccer or hockey)

go along vi (1602) **1** : to move along : PROCEED **2** : to go or travel as a companion **3** : to act in cooperation or express agreement ⟨go along with the crowd⟩

goal·post \'gōl-,pōst\ n (1857) : one of usu. two vertical posts that with or without a crossbar constitute the goal in various games

goal·tend·er \'gōl-,ten-dər\ n (ca. 1909) : GOALKEEPER

goal·tend·ing \-,diŋ\ n (1968) **1** : the act of guarding a goal (as in hockey) **2** : a violation in basketball that involves touching or deflecting a ball that is on its downward path toward the basket or on or within the rim of the basket

goal·ward \'gōl-wərd\ adv or adj (1949) : toward a goal

go·an·na \gō-'a-nə\ n [alter. of iguana] (1831) : any of several large Australian monitor lizards (genus Varanus of the family Varanidae)

go-around \'gō-ə-,raúnd\ n (ca. 1929) **1** : RUNAROUND ⟨gave me the ~⟩ **2** a : ROUND ⟨reached an agreement during the first ~⟩ b : a heated argument or struggle ⟨had a real ~ with her about it⟩ **3** : an act or instance of going around (as in an air traffic pattern)

go around vi (ca. 1520) **1** a : to pass from place to place b : to have currency : CIRCULATE ⟨an amusing story is going around⟩ **2** : to satisfy demand : fill the need ⟨not enough jobs to go around⟩

goat \'gōt\ n, pl **goats** [ME gote, fr. OE gāt; akin to OHG geiz goat, ON geit, L haedus kid] (bef. 12c) **1** a or pl **goat** : any of various hollow-horned ruminant mammals (esp. of the genus Capra) related to the sheep but of lighter build and with backwardly arching horns, a short tail, and usu. straight hair b cap : CAPRICORN **2** : a licentious

\ə\ abut \ᵊ\ kitten, F table \ər\ further \a\ ash \ā\ ace \ä\ mop, mar \aú\ out \ch\ chin \e\ bet \ē\ easy \g\ go \i\ hit \ī\ ice \j\ job \ŋ\ sing \ō\ go \ȯ\ law \ȯi\ boy \th\ thin \th̷\ the \ü\ loot \ú\ foot \y\ yet \zh\ vision \à, k, ⁿ, œ, œ̄, ᵫ, ᵫ̄, ᵊ\ see Guide to Pronunciation man : LECHER **3** : SCAPEGOAT 2 — **goat·ish** \'gō-tish\ adj — **goat-like** \-ˌlīk\ adj

goat cheese n (1893) : any of various cheeses made from goat's milk

goa·tee \gō-'tē\ n [fr. its resemblance to the beard of a he-goat] (1844) : a small pointed or tufted beard on a man's chin — **goa·teed** \-'tēd\ adj

goat·fish \'gōt-ˌfish\ n (ca. 1639) : any of a family (Mullidae) of moderate-sized usu. red or golden fishes with two barbels on the chin — called also *red mullet*

goat·herd \-ˌhərd\ n [ME *goteherd*, fr. OE *gāthyrd*] (bef. 12c) : a person who tends goats

goat·skin \-ˌskin\ n (14c) **1** : the skin of a goat **2** : leather made from goatskin

goat·suck·er \-ˌsə-kər\ n (1611) : NIGHTJAR

¹**gob** \'gäb\ n [ME *gobbe*, fr. MF *gobe* large piece of food, backformation fr. *gobet*] (14c) **1** : LUMP **2** : a large amount — usu. used in pl. ⟨~s of money⟩

²**gob** \'gäb, 'gäb\ n [prob. fr. ScGael, mouth & Ir, beak, pursed mouth] (ca. 1550) *chiefly Brit* : MOUTH

³**gob** \'gäb, 'gäb\ n [origin unknown] (1915) : SAILOR

gob·bet \'gä-bət\ n [ME *gobet*, fr. MF, mouthful, piece] (14c) **1** : a piece or portion (as of meat) **2** : LUMP, MASS **3** : a small fragment or extract ⟨a ~ of information⟩ **4** : a small quantity of liquid : DROP

¹**gob·ble** \'gä-bəl\ vt **gob·bled; gob·bling** \-b(ə-)liŋ\ [prob. irreg. fr. ¹*gob*] (1601) **1** : to swallow or eat greedily **2** : to take eagerly : GRAB — usu. used with *up* **3** : to read rapidly or greedily — usu. used with *up*

²**gobble** vi **gob·bled; gob·bling** \-b(ə-)liŋ\ [imit.] (1680) **1** : to make the natural guttural noise of a male turkey **2** : to make a sound resembling the gobble of a turkey — **gobble** n

gob·ble·dy·gook also **gob·ble·de·gook** \'gä-bəl-dē-ˌgùk, -ˌgük\ n [irreg. fr. gobble, n.] (1944) : wordy and generally unintelligible jargon

¹**gob·bler** \'gä-blər\ n (ca. 1737) : a male turkey

²**gobbler** n (ca. 1755) : one that gobbles

Go·be·lin \'gō-bə-lən, ˌgō-bə-'laⁿ\ adj [*Gobelin* dye and tapestry works, Paris, France] (1788) : of, relating to, or characteristic of tapestry produced at the Gobelin works in Paris — **Gobelin** n

go·be·tween \'gō-bə-ˌtwēn\ n (1598) : an intermediate agent : BROKER

gob·let \'gäb-lət\ n [ME *gobelet*, fr. MF] (14c) **1** *archaic* : a bowl-shaped drinking vessel without handles **2** : a drinking vessel (as of glass) with a foot and stem — compare TUMBLER

goblet cell n [fr. its shape] (1878) : a mucus-secreting epithelial cell (as of intestinal columnar epithelium) that is distended at the free end

gob·lin \'gäb-lən\ n [ME *gobelin*, fr. MF, fr. ML *gobelinus*, ultim. fr. Gk *kobalos* rogue] (14c) : an ugly or grotesque sprite that is mischievous and sometimes evil and malicious

go·bo \'gō-(ˌ)bō\ n, pl **gobos** also **goboes** [origin unknown] (ca. 1930) **1** : a dark strip (as of wallboard) to shield a motion-picture or television camera from light **2** : a device to shield a microphone from sound

go·by \'gō-bē\ n, pl **gobies** also **goby** [L *gobius* gudgeon, fr. Gk *kōbios*] (1769) : any of numerous spiny-finned fishes (family Gobiidae) that usu. have the pelvic fins united to form a ventral sucking disk

go by vi (1508) : PASS 3b ⟨as time *goes by*⟩

go-cart \'gō-ˌkärt\ n (1689) **1 a** : WALKER **b** : STROLLER **2** : HANDCART **3** : a light open carriage

¹**god** \'gäd *also* 'gòd\ n [ME, fr. OE; akin to OHG *got* god] (bef. 12c) **1** *cap* : the supreme or ultimate reality: as **a** : the Being perfect in power, wisdom, and goodness who is worshipped as creator and ruler of the universe **b** *Christian Science* : the incorporeal divine Principle ruling over all as eternal Spirit : infinite Mind **2** : a being or object believed to have more than natural attributes and powers and to require human worship; *specif* : one controlling a particular aspect or part of reality **3** : a person or thing of supreme value **4** : a powerful ruler

²**god** vt **god·ded; god·ding** (1595) : to treat as a god : IDOLIZE, DEIFY

god-aw·ful \ˌgä-'dò-fəl\ adj [*god* damned + *awful*] (1878) : extremely unpleasant or disagreeable : ABOMINABLE ⟨~ weather⟩

god·child \'gäd-ˌchīld *also* 'gòd-\ n (13c) : a person for whom another person becomes sponsor at baptism

¹**god·damn** *or* **god·dam** \'gä(d)-'dam\ n, often cap (1640) : DAMN ⟨they were in no mood to give a good ~ about anything —Robert Lowry⟩

²**goddamn** *or* **goddam** vb, often cap (1928) : DAMN

god·damned \ˌgä(d)-ˈdamd\ *or* **god·damn** *or* **god·dam** \-ˌdam\ adj or adv (1918) : DAMNED

god·daugh·ter \'gäd-ˌdò-tər *also* 'gòd-\ n (bef. 12c) : a female godchild

god·dess \'gä-dəs *also* 'gò-\ n (14c) **1** : a female god **2** : a woman whose great charm or beauty arouses adoration

Go·del's theorem \'gō-dəlz-, 'gər-, 'gœ-\ n [Kurt Gödel †1978 Am. mathematician] (1933) : a theorem in advanced logic: in any logical system as complex as or more complex than the arithmetic of the integers there can always be found either a statement which can be shown to be both true and false or a statement whose truth or falsity cannot be deduced from other statements in the system — called also *Godel's incompleteness theorem*

go·det \gō-'det, 'gō-ˌdā\ n, *often attrib* [F, fr. *goder* to form creases, prob. fr. *goderon* rounded pleat on a ruffle, gadroon] (1872) : an inset of cloth placed in a seam to give fullness (as at the bottom of a skirt)

go-dev·il \'gō-ˌde-vəl\ n (1852) : any of various devices: as **a** : a cultivator with wooden runners **b** : a weight formerly dropped in a bored hole (as of an oil well) to set off an explosive **c** : a cleaning scraper propelled through a pipeline **d** : a handcar or small gasoline car used on a railroad **e** : a child's sled

¹**god·fa·ther** \'gäd-ˌfä-thər, 'fä-, *also* 'gòd-\ n (bef. 12c) **1** : a man who sponsors a person at baptism **2** : one having a relation to someone or something analogous to that of a male sponsor to his godchild: as **a** : one that founds, supports, or inspires ⟨made him the ~ of a whole generation of rebels —*Times Lit. Supp.*⟩ **b** : the leader of an organized crime syndicate

²**godfather** vt (1780) : to act as godfather to

God-fear·ing \-ˌfir-iŋ\ adj (1835) : having a reverent feeling toward God : DEVOUT

god-for·sak·en \-fər-ˌsā-kən\ adj (1860) **1** : REMOTE, DESOLATE **2** : neglected and miserable in appearance or circumstances

god·head \-ˌhed\ n [ME *godhed*, fr. *god* + *-hed* -hood; akin to ME *-hod* -hood] (13c) **1** : divine nature or essence : DIVINITY **2** *cap* : GOD 1 **b** : the nature of God esp. as existing in three persons — used with *the*

god·hood \-ˌhùd\ n [ME *godhod*, fr. OE *godhād*, fr. *god* + *-hād* -hood] (1563) : DIVINITY

Go·di·va \gə-'dī-və\ n : an English earl's wife who in legend rode naked through Coventry to save its citizens from a tax

god·less \'gäd-ləs *also* 'gòd-\ adj (1528) : not acknowledging a deity or divine law — **god·less·ness** n

god·like \-ˌlīk\ adj (bef. 12c) : resembling or having the qualities of God or a god : DIVINE — **god·like·ness** n

god·ling \-liŋ\ n (ca. 1500) : an inferior or local god

god·ly \-lē\ adj **god·li·er; -est** (14c) **1** : DIVINE **2** : PIOUS, DEVOUT — **god·li·ness** n — **godly** adv, archaic

god·moth·er \-ˌmə-thər\ n (bef. 12c) : a woman who sponsors a person at baptism

go·down \'gō-ˌdaùn\ n [by folk etymology fr. Malay *gudang*] (1552) : a warehouse in an oriental country

go down vi (14c) **1 a** : to go below the horizon : SET ⟨the sun *went down*⟩ **b** : to fall to or as if to the ground ⟨the plane *went down* in flames⟩ **c** : to become submerged : SINK ⟨the ship *went down* with all hands⟩ **2** : to admit of being swallowed ⟨the medicine *went down* easily⟩ **3 a** : to find acceptance ⟨will the plan *go down* with the farmers⟩ **b** : to come to be remembered esp. in posterity ⟨will he *go down* in history as a great president⟩ **4** *Brit* : to leave a university **5 a** : to undergo defeat or failure **b** *chiefly Brit* : to become incapacitated ⟨*went down* with . . . acute tonsillitis —Helen Cathcart⟩ **6** *slang* : to take place : HAPPEN — **go down on** : to perform fellatio or cunnilingus on

god·par·ent \'gäd-ˌpar-ənt, -ˌper- *also* 'gòd-\ n (1865) : a sponsor at baptism

God's acre n (1617) : CHURCHYARD

god·send \'gäd-ˌsend *also* 'gòd-\ n [back-formation fr. *god-sent*] (1820) : a desirable or needed thing or event that comes unexpectedly

god·son \-ˌsən\ n (bef. 12c) : a male godchild

God-speed \-'spēd\ n [ME *god speid*, fr. the phrase *God spede you* God prosper you] (15c) : a prosperous journey : SUCCESS ⟨bade him ~⟩

god·wit \'gäd-ˌwit\ n [origin unknown] (1552) : any of a genus (*Limosa*) of wading birds that are related to the curlews and sandpipers and have a long slender slightly upturned or straight bill

goes pres 3d sing of GO, pl of GO

goe·thite \'gə(r)-ˌtīt\ n [G *Göthit*, fr. J. W. von Goethe] (ca. 1823) : a mineral that consists of an iron hydrogen oxide and is the commonest constituent of many forms of natural rust

go·fer \'gō-fər\ n [alter. of *go for*] (1967) : an employee whose duties include running errands

gof·fer \'gä-fər, 'gò-\ vt [F *gaufrer*, fr. *gaufre* honeycomb, waffle, fr. OF, of Gmc origin; akin to MD *wafel* waffle] (1706) : to crimp, plait, or flute (as linen or lace) esp. with a heated iron — **goffer** n

go-get·ter \'gō-ˈge-tər, -ˌge-\ n (1921) : an aggressively enterprising person — **go-get·ting** \-ˌge-tiŋ\ adj or n

¹**gog·gle** \'gä-gəl\ vi **gog·gled; gog·gling** [ME *gogelen* to squint] (1616) : to stare with wide or protuberant eyes — **gog·gler** \'gä-g²-lər\ n

²**goggle** adj (1540) : PROTUBERANT, STARING ⟨~ eyes⟩ — **gog·gly** \'gä-g²-lē\ adj

gog·gle-eye \'gä-g²l-ˌī\ n (1840) **1** : ROCK BASS **2** : WARMOUTH

gog·gle-eyed \-ˌīd\ adj (1711) : having bulging or rolling eyes

gog·gles \'gä-g²lz\ n pl (1715) : protective glasses set in a flexible frame (as of rubber or plastic) that fits snugly against the face — **gog·gled** \-g²ld\ adj

go-go \'gō-(ˌ)gō\ adj [partly fr. *a-go-go*, partly fr. redupl. of ¹*go*] (1965) **1 a** : employed to entertain in a disco ⟨~ dancers⟩ **b** : of, relating to, or being a disco or the music or dances performed there **2** : marked by spirited or aggressive action ⟨~ baseball⟩ **3 a** : relating to or dealing in popular often speculative investment expected to yield high returns ⟨~ mutual funds⟩ **b** : relating to, involved in, or marked by business growth and prosperity and aggressive efforts to turn a quick profit ⟨~ bankers and entrepreneurs . . . who put together the megabuck deals —Ken Auletta⟩

¹**Goi·del·ic** \gòi-'de-lik\ adj [MIr *Goídel* Gael, Irishman] (1896) **1** : of, relating to, or characteristic of the Gaels **2** : of, relating to, or constituting Goidelic

²**Goidelic** n (1882) : the branch of the Celtic languages that includes Irish, Scottish Gaelic, and Manx — see INDO-EUROPEAN LANGUAGES table

go in vi (1812) **1** : to make an approach (as in attacking) **2 a** : to take part in a game or contest **b** : to call the opening bet in poker : STAY **3** *of a celestial body* : to become obscured by a cloud **4** : to form a union or alliance : JOIN — used with *with* ⟨asked the rest of us to *go in* with them⟩ — **go in for** **1** : to give support to : ADVOCATE **2** : to have or show an interest in or a liking for **3** : to engage in : take part in

¹**go·ing** \'gō-iŋ, 'gò(-)iŋ\ n (14c) **1** : an act or instance of going **2** pl : BEHAVIOR, ACTIONS ⟨for his eyes are upon the ways of man, and he seeth all his ~s —Job 34:21 (AV)⟩ **3** : the condition of the ground (as for walking) **4** : advance toward an objective ⟨when the ~ gets tough⟩

²**going** adj (14c) **1 a** : that goes — often used in combination ⟨easygoing⟩ ⟨outgoing⟩ **b** : WORKING, MOVING ⟨everything was in ~ order⟩ **2** : LIVING, EXISTING ⟨the best novelist ~⟩ **3** : CURRENT, PREVAILING ⟨~ price⟩ **4** : conducting business with the expectation of indefinite continuance ⟨~ concern⟩ — **going on** : drawing near to : APPROACHING ⟨is six years old *going on* seven⟩

go·ing-over \ˌgō-iŋ-'ō-vər, ˌgò(-)iŋ-\ n, pl **go·ings-over** (1872) **1 a** : a severe scolding **b** : BEATING **2** : a thorough examination or investigation

go·ings-on \ˌgō-iŋ-'zòn, ˌgò(-)iŋ-, -'zän\ n pl (1775) **1** : ACTIONS, EVENTS **2** : irregular or reprehensible happenings or conduct ⟨titillating stories about the ~ of the carefree millionaires —Eleanor Early⟩

goby

goi·ter \'gȯi-tər\ *n* [F *goitre*, fr. MF, back-formation fr. *goitron* throat, fr. (assumed) VL *guttrion-, guttrio*, fr. L *guttur*] (1625) : an enlargement of the thyroid gland visible as a swelling of the front of the neck — compare HYPERTHYROIDISM, HYPOTHYROIDISM — **goi·trous** \'gȯi-trəs, 'gȯi-tə-rəs\ *adj*

goi·tre *chiefly Brit var of* GOITER

goi·tro·gen \'gȯi-trə-jən\ *n* [*goiter* + *-o-* + *-gen*] (1946) : a substance (as thiourea or thiouracil) that induces goiter formation

goi·tro·gen·ic \,gȯi-trə-'je-nik\ *adj* (1929) : producing or tending to produce goiter — **goi·tro·ge·nic·i·ty** \,gȯi-trə-jə-'ni-sə-tē\ *n*

Gol·con·da \gäl-'kän-də\ *n* [*Golconda*, India, famous for its diamonds] (1884) : a rich mine; *broadly* : a source of great wealth

gold \'gōld\ *n, often attrib* [ME, fr. OE; akin to OHG *gold* gold, OE *geolu* yellow — more at YELLOW] (bef. 12c) **1 a** : a malleable ductile yellow metallic element that occurs chiefly free or in a few minerals and is used esp. in coins, jewelry, and dentures — see ELEMENT table **2 a** (1) : gold coins (2) : a gold piece **b** : MONEY **c** : GOLD STANDARD **3** : a variable color averaging deep yellow **4** : something resembling gold; *esp* : something valued as the finest of its kind ⟨a heart of ~⟩ **5** : a medal awarded as the top prize in a competition : a gold medal

¹gold·brick \'gōl(d)-,brik\ *n* (1881) **1 a** : a worthless brick that appears to be of gold **b** : something that appears to be valuable but is actually worthless **2** : a person who shirks assigned work

²goldbrick *vt* (1902) : SWINDLE ~ *vi* : to shirk duty or responsibility

gold·bug \-,bəg\ *n* (1878) **1** : a supporter of the gold standard **2** : a person who invests in or hoards gold

gold coast *n, often cap G&C* (1877) : an exclusive residential district

gold digger *n* (1830) **1** : one who digs for gold **2** : a person who uses charm to extract money or gifts from others

gold·en \'gōl-dən\ *adj* [ME] (13c) **1** : consisting of, relating to, or containing gold **2 a** : being or having the color gold or the color of gold **b** : BLOND 1a **3** : LUSTROUS, SHINING **4** : of a high degree of excellence : SUPERB **5** : PROSPEROUS, FLOURISHING ⟨~ days⟩ **6 a** : radiantly youthful and vigorous **b** : possessing talents that promise worldly success — often used with *boy* **c** : highly favored : POPULAR **7** : FAVORABLE, ADVANTAGEOUS ⟨a ~ opportunity⟩ **8** : of, relating to, or being a 50th anniversary or its celebration **9** : MELLOW, RESONANT ⟨a smooth ~ tenor⟩ — **gold·en·ly** *adv* — **gold·en·ness** \-də(n)-nəs\ *n*

golden age *n* (1555) : a period of great happiness, prosperity, and achievement

gold·en-ag·er \'gōl-dən-'ā-jər\ *n* (1961) : an elderly and often retired person usu. engaging in club activities

golden al·ex·an·ders \-,a-lig-'zan-dərz, -,e-lig-\ *n pl but sing or pl in constr, often cap A* [ML *alexandrum*] (ca. 1923) : a No. American yellow-flowered perennial herb (*Zizia aurea*) of the carrot family occurring in moist woods and meadows; *also* : any of several related herbs

golden–brown alga *n* (ca. 1957) : any of a division (Chrysophyta) of marine and freshwater algae (as diatoms) containing yellowish green to golden brown pigments that obscure the chlorophyll — called also *chrysophyte, golden alga*

golden club *n* (1837) : an American aquatic plant (*Orontium aquaticum*) of the arum family with a spadix of tiny yellow flowers

golden eagle *n* (1839) : a brown eagle (*Aquila chrysaetos*) of the northern hemisphere with gold-colored feathers on the back of the head and neck

gold·en·eye \'gōl-dən-,ī\ *n* (ca. 1678) **1** : either of two diving ducks (genus *Bucephala*); *esp* : a large-headed swift-flying Holarctic diving duck (*B. clangula*) with the male having a green head and striking black and white markings **2** : a lacewing (family Chrysopidae) with yellow eyes

Golden Fleece *n* (14c) : a fleece of gold placed by the king of Colchis in a dragon-guarded grove and recovered by the Argonauts

golden glow *n* (1902) : a tall branching composite herb (*Rudbeckia laciniata hortensia*) with showy yellow flower heads

golden hamster *n* (1939) : a small tawny hamster (*Mesocricetus auratus*) native to Asia Minor — called also *Syrian hamster*

golden handshake *n* (1960) : a generous severance agreement given esp. as an inducement to early retirement

Golden Horde *n* (1863) : a body of Mongols that overran eastern Europe in the 13th century and dominated Russia until 1486

golden lion tamarin *n* (1975) : a marmoset (*Leontopithecus rosalia rosalia*) with a reddish gold coat and long mane that occurs in remnants of tropical forest in southeastern Brazil

golden hamster

golden mean *n* (1587) : the medium between extremes : MODERATION

golden nematode *n* (1946) : a small yellowish Old World nematode worm (*Globodera rostochiensis* syn. *Heterodera rostochiensis*) established locally as a pest of potatoes in eastern No. America

golden oldie *n* (1970) : one that was a hit or favorite in the past

golden parachute *n* (1981) : a generous severance agreement for an executive in the event of a sudden dismissal (as because of a merger)

golden plover *n* (1785) : either of two gregarious plovers (genus *Pluvialis*); *esp* : one (*P. dominica*) that breeds in arctic America and Siberia and winters in Hawaii and the southern hemisphere

gold·en-rain tree \'gōl-dən-,rān-\ *n* (1923) : an Asian tree (*Koelreuteria paniculata* of the family Sapindaceae) that has a rounded crown with very long showy clusters of yellow flowers

golden retriever *n* (1919) : any of a breed of medium-sized retrievers having a flat moderately long golden coat

gold·en·rod \'gōl-dən-,räd\ *n* (1568) : any of numerous chiefly No. American composite biennial or perennial plants (esp. of the genus *Solidago*) with alternate leaves and heads of small yellow or sometimes white flowers often clustered in panicles

golden rule *n* (1861) **1** : a guiding principle **2** *cap G&R* : a rule of ethical conduct referring to Mt 7:12 and Lk 6:31: do to others as you would have them do to you

gold·en·seal \'gōl-dən-,sēl\ *n* (1839) : a perennial American herb (*Hydrastis canadensis*) of the buttercup family with large rounded leaves and a thick knotted yellow rootstock sometimes used in pharmacy

golden section *n* (1875) : a proportion (as one involving a line divided into two segments or the length and width of a rectangle and their sum) in which the ratio of the whole to the larger part is the same as the ratio of the larger part to the smaller

golden shiner *n* (ca. 1889) : a common cyprinid fish (*Notemigonus crysoleucas*) of eastern No. America having silvery sides with bright golden reflections

golden syrup *n* (1860) *chiefly Brit* : TREACLE 2b

gold·field \'gōl(d)-,fēld\ *n* (1851) : a gold-mining district

gold–filled \-'fild\ *adj* (ca. 1903) : consisting of a base metal covered with a layer of gold ⟨a ~ bracelet⟩

gold·finch \-,finch\ *n* (bef. 12c) **1** : a small Palearctic finch (*Carduelis carduelis*) with a red, white, and black head and yellow and black wings **2** : any of three small American finches (genus *Carduelis* esp. *C. tristis*) having the breeding plumage of the male variably yellow with black markings on the wings, tail, and crown

gold·fish \-,fish\ *n* (1791) : a small usu. golden yellow or orange cyprinid fish (*Carassius auratus*) often kept as an aquarium and pond fish

goldfish bowl *n* (1935) : a place or situation offering no privacy

gold leaf *n* (ca. 1741) : an extremely thin sheet of gold that is used esp. for gilding

gold mine *n* (1833) : a rich source of something desired

gold of pleasure *n* (1597) : a European herb (*Camelina sativa*) of the mustard family that is cultivated for its oil-rich seeds

gold rush *n* (1876) **1** : a rush to newly discovered goldfields in pursuit of riches **2** : the headlong pursuit of sudden wealth in a new or lucrative field — **gold rush·er** \-'rə-shər\ *n*

gold·smith \'gōl(d)-,smith\ *n* (bef. 12c) : one who makes or deals in articles of gold

gold standard *n* (1831) : a monetary standard under which the basic unit of currency is defined by a stated quantity of gold and which is usu. characterized by the coinage and circulation of gold, unrestricted convertibility of other money into gold, and the free export and import of gold for the settlement of international obligations

gold·stone \'gōl(d)-,stōn\ *n* (ca. 1889) : aventurine glass spangled close and fine with particles of gold-colored material

go·lem \'gō-ləm, 'gȯi-, 'gā-\ *n* [Yiddish *goylem*, fr. Heb *gōlem* shapeless mass] (1897) **1** : an artificial human being in Hebrew folklore endowed with life **2** : something or someone resembling a golem: as **a** : AUTOMATON **b** : BLOCKHEAD

golf \'gälf, 'gȯlf, 'gäf, 'gȯf *sometimes* 'gȯlf\ *n, often attrib* [ME (Sc)] (15c) : a game in which a player using special clubs attempts to sink a ball with as few strokes as possible into each of the 9 or 18 successive holes on a course — **golf** *vi* — **golf·er** *n*

Golf (1952) — a communications code word for the letter g

golf ball *n* (1545) **1** : a small hard dimpled ball used in golf **2** : the spherical printing element of an electric typewriter or printer

golf cart *n* (1899) **1** : a small cart for wheeling a golf bag around a golf course **2** : a motorized cart for carrying golfers and their equipment over a golf course — called also *golf car*

golf course *n* (1890) : an area of land laid out for golf with a series of 9 or 18 holes each including tee, fairway, and putting green and often one or more natural or artificial hazards — called also *golf links*

Gol·gi \'gȯl-(,)jē\ *adj* (1891) : of or relating to the Golgi apparatus, Golgi bodies, or a method of staining nerve tissue ⟨~ vesicles⟩

Golgi apparatus *n* [Camillo *Golgi*] (1916) : a cytoplasmic organelle that consists of a stack of smooth membranous saccules and associated vesicles and that is active in the modification and transport of proteins — called also *Golgi complex*; see CELL illustration

Golgi body *n* (1925) : GOLGI APPARATUS; *also* : DICTYOSOME

go·liard \'gōl-yərd, -,yärd\ *n* [ME, fr. MF, goliard, glutton, fr. *gole* throat, fr. L *gula* — more at GLUTTON] (15c) : a wandering student of the 12th or 13th century given to the writing of satiric Latin verse and to convivial living and minstrelsy — **go·liar·dic** \gōl-'yär-dik\ *adj*

Go·li·ath \gə-'lī-əth\ *n* [Heb *Golyath*] **1** : a Philistine champion who in I Samuel 17 is killed by David **2** : GIANT

gol·li·wog *also* **gol·ly·wog** *or* **gol·li·wogg** \'gä-lē-,wäg\ *n* [Golliwogg, an animated doll in children's fiction by Bertha Upton †1912 Am. writer] (1895) **1** : a grotesque black doll **2** : a person resembling a golliwog

gol·ly \'gä-lē\ *interj* [euphemism for *God*] (1775) — used as a mild oath or to express surprise

Go·mor·rah \gə-'mȯr-ə\ *n* [fr. *Gomorrah*, ancient city destroyed by God for its wickedness in Gen 19] (1907) : a place notorious for vice and corruption

gon- *or* **gono-** *comb form* [Gk, fr. *gonos* procreation, seed, fr. *gignesthai* to be born — more at KIN] : sexual : generative : semen : seed ⟨*gonocyte*⟩

-gon *n comb form* [NL *-gonum*, fr. Gk *-gōnon*, fr. *gōnia* angle; akin to Gk *gony* knee — more at KNEE] : figure having (so many) angles ⟨*decagon*⟩

go·nad \'gō-,nad\ *n* [NL *gonad-, gonas*, fr. Gk *gonos*] (1880) : a reproductive gland (as an ovary or testis) that produces gametes — **go·nad·al** \gō-'na-d⁰l\ *adj*

go·nad·ec·to·my \,gō-nə-'dek-tə-mē\ *n, pl* **-mies** (1915) : surgical removal of an ovary or testis — **go·nad·ec·to·mized** \-,mīzd\ *adj*

go·nad·o·trop·ic \gō-,na-də-'trä-pik\ *also* **go·nad·o·tro·phic** \-'trō-fik, -'trä-\ *adj* (ca. 1923) : acting on or stimulating the gonads

go·nad·o·tro·pin \-'trō-pən\ *also* **go·nad·o·tro·phin** \-fən\ *n* (1931) : a gonadotropic hormone (as follicle-stimulating hormone)

Gond \'gänd\ *n* (1801) : a member of a Dravidian or pre-Dravidian people of central India

Gondi \'gän-dē\ *n* (1855) : the Dravidian language of the Gonds

gon·do·la \'gän-də-lə (*usual for sense 1*), gän-'dō-\ *n* [It dial. (Venetian),

---

\ə\ abut \'ə\ kitten, F table \ər\ further \a\ ash \ā\ ace \ä\ mop, mar \au̇\ out \ch\ chin \e\ bet \ē\ easy \g\ go \i\ hit \ī\ ice \j\ job \ŋ\ sing \ō\ go \ȯ\ law \ȯi\ boy \th\ thin \th̠\ the \ü\ loot \u̇\ foot \y\ yet \zh\ vision \à, ḵ, ⁿ, œ, œ̄, ᵫ, ᵫ̄, ᵊ\ *see* Guide to Pronunciation prob. fr. MGk *kontoura* small vessel] (1549) **1** **a** : a long narrow flat-bottomed boat with a high prow and stern used on the canals of Venice **2** : a heavy flat-bottomed boat used on New England rivers and on the Ohio and Mississippi rivers **3** : a railroad car with no top, a flat bottom, and fixed sides that is used chiefly for hauling heavy bulk commodities **4** **a** : an

gondola 1

elongated car attached to the underside of an airship **b** : an often spherical airtight enclosure suspended from a balloon for carrying passengers or instruments **c** : an enclosed car suspended from a cable and used for transporting passengers; *esp* : one used as a ski lift
gon·do·lier \ˌgän-də-ˈlir\ *n* (1603) : one who propels a gondola
gone \ˈgȯn *also* ˈgän\ *adj* [fr. pp. of *go*] (1598) **1** **a** : DEAD **b** : LOST, RUINED 〈lost looks and ~ faculties —Penelope Gilliatt〉 **c** : characterized by sinking or dropping 〈the empty or ~ feeling in the abdomen so common in elevators —H. G. Armstrong〉 **2** **a** : INVOLVED, ABSORBED 〈far ~ in hysteria〉 **b** : possessed with a strong attachment or a foolish or unreasoning love or desire : INFATUATED — often used with *on* 〈was real ~ on that man —Pete Martin〉 **c** : PREGNANT 〈she's six months ~〉 **3** PAST 〈memories of ~ summers —John Cheever〉 **4** *slang* : GREAT 〈a real ~ fashion reporter —Inez Robb〉
G₁ phase \ˌjē-ˈwən-\ *n* [*growth*] (1966) : the period in the cell cycle from the end of cell division to the beginning of DNA replication — compare G₂ PHASE, M PHASE, S PHASE
gon·er \ˈgȯ-nər *also* ˈgä-nər\ *n* (1854) : one whose case is hopeless
gon·fa·lon \ˈgän-fə-ˌlän, -lən\ *n* [It *gonfalone*] (1595) **1** : the ensign of certain princes or states (as the medieval republics of Italy) **2** : a flag that hangs from a crosspiece or frame
gong \ˈgäŋ, ˈgȯŋ\ *n* [Malay & Jav, of imit. origin] (ca. 1590) **1** : a disk-shaped percussion instrument that produces a resounding tone when struck with a usu. padded hammer **2** **a** : a saucer-shaped bell (as in a fire alarm) that is struck by a mechanical hammer **b** : a wire rod wound in a flat spiral for sounding the time or chime or alarm (as in a clock) **3** *Brit* : MEDAL — **gong** *vi*
Gon·go·rism \ˈgäŋ-gə-ˌri-zəm\ *n* [Sp *gongorismo*, fr. Luis de Góngora y Argote †1627 Span. poet] (1813) : a literary style characterized by studied obscurity and by the use of various ornate devices — **gon·go·ris·tic** \ˌgäŋ-gə-ˈris-tik\ *adj*
go·nid·i·um \gō-ˈni-dē-əm\ *n, pl* **-ia** \-dē-ə\ [NL, fr. Gk *gon-* + *-idium*] (1882) : an asexual reproductive cell or group of cells esp. in algae (as volvox)
gon·if, gon·iff \ˈgä-nəf\ *var of* GANEF
go·ni·om·e·ter \ˌgō-nē-ˈä-mə-tər\ *n* [Gk *gōnia* angle] (1766) **1** : an instrument for measuring angles **2** : DIRECTION FINDER — **go·nio·met·ric** \-nē-ə-ˈme-trik\ *adj* — **go·ni·om·e·try** \-nē-ˈä-mə-trē\ *n*
-gonium *comb form* [NL, fr. Gk *gonos*] **1** : germ cell 〈spermatogonium〉 **2** : reproductive structure of a plant or fungus 〈oogonium〉
gon·o·coc·cus \ˌgä-nə-ˈkä-kəs\ *n, pl* **-coc·ci** \-ˈkäk-ˌsī, -(ˌ)sē; -ˈkä-ˌkī, -(ˌ)kē\ [NL] (1889) : a pus-producing bacterium (*Neisseria gonorrhoeae*) that causes gonorrhea — **gon·o·coc·cal** \-ˈkä-kəl\ *adj*
gon·o·cyte \ˈgä-nə-ˌsīt\ *n* [ISV] (1900) : a cell that produces gametes; *esp* : GAMETOCYTE
go-no-go \ˈgō-ˈnō-ˌgō\ *adj* (ca. 1945) **1** : being or relating to a required decision to continue or stop a course of action **2** : being or relating to a point at which a go-no-go decision must be made
gon·o·phore \ˈgä-nə-ˌfōr, -ˌfȯr\ *n* [ISV] (1859) : an attached reproductive zooid of a hydroid colony
gon·o·pore \ˈgä-nə-ˌpōr, -ˌpȯr\ *n* (1897) : a genital pore in some invertebrates and esp. some insects
gon·or·rhea \ˌgä-nə-ˈrē-ə\ *n* [NL, fr. LL, morbid loss of semen, fr. Gk *gonorrhoia*, fr. *gon-* + *-rrhoia* -rrhea] (ca. 1526) : a contagious inflammation of the genital mucous membrane caused by the gonococcus — called also *clap* — **gon·or·rhe·al** \-ˈrē-əl\ *adj*
-gony *n comb form* [L *-gonia*, fr. Gk, fr. *gonos*] : generation : reproduction : manner of coming into being 〈isogony〉
gon·zo \ˈgän-(ˌ)zō\ *adj* [origin unknown] (1971) : idiosyncratically subjective but engagé 〈~ journalism〉; *also* : BIZARRE
goo \ˈgü\ *n* [perh. short for *burgoo*] (1900) **1** : a viscid or sticky substance **2** : sentimental tripe — **goo·ey** \-ē\ *adj* — **goo·ey·ness** \-nəs\ *n*
goo·ber \ˈgü-bər, ˈgu̇-\ *n* [of Bantu origin; akin to Kimbundu *nguba* peanut] (1833) *Southern & Midland* : PEANUT
¹good \ˈgu̇d\ *adj* **bet·ter** \ˈbe-tər\; **best** \ˈbest\ [ME, fr. OE *gōd*; akin to OHG *guot* good, Skt *gadhya* what one clings to] (bef. 12c) **1** **a** (1) : of a favorable character or tendency 〈~ news〉 (2) : BOUNTIFUL, FERTILE 〈~ land〉 (3) : HANDSOME, ATTRACTIVE 〈~ looks〉 **b** (1) : SUITABLE, FIT 〈~ to eat〉 (2) : free from injury or disease 〈one ~ arm〉 (3) : not depreciated 〈bad money drives out ~〉 (4) : commercially sound 〈a ~ risk〉 (5) : that can be relied on 〈~ for another year〉 〈~ for a hundred dollars〉 〈always ~ for a laugh〉 **c** (1) : PROFITABLE, ADVANTAGEOUS 〈made a very ~ deal〉 **c** (1) : AGREEABLE, PLEASANT 〈had a ~ time〉 (2) : SALUTARY, WHOLESOME 〈~ for a cold〉 (3) : AMUSING, CLEVER 〈a ~ joke〉 **d** (1) : of a noticeably large size or quantity : CONSIDERABLE 〈won by a ~ margin〉 〈a ~ bit of the time〉 (2) : FULL 〈waited a ~ hour〉 (3) — used as an intensive 〈a ~ many of us〉 **e** (1) : WELL-FOUNDED, COGENT 〈~ reasons〉 (2) : TRUE 〈holds ~ for society at large〉 (3) : deserving of respect : HONORABLE 〈in ~ standing〉 (4) : legally valid or effectual 〈~ title〉 **f** (1) : ADEQUATE, SATISFACTORY 〈~ care〉 — often used in faint praise 〈his serve is only ~ —Frank Deford〉 (2) : conforming to a standard 〈~ English〉 (3) : CHOICE, DISCRIMINATING 〈~ taste〉 (4) : containing less fat and being less tender than higher grades — used of meat and esp. of beef **2** **a** (1) : VIRTUOUS, RIGHT, COMMENDABLE 〈a ~ person〉 〈~ conduct〉 (2) : KIND, BENEVOLENT 〈~ intentions〉 **b** : UPPER-CLASS 〈a ~ family〉 **c** : COMPETENT, SKILLFUL 〈a ~ doctor〉 **d** (1) : LOYAL 〈a ~ party man〉 〈a ~ Catholic〉 (2) : CLOSE 〈a ~ friend〉 **e** : free from infirmity or sorrow 〈I feel ~〉 — **good·ish** \ˈgu̇-dish\ *adj* — **as good as** : in effect : VIRTUALLY 〈as good as dead〉 — **as good as gold** **1** : of the highest worth or reliability 〈his promise is *as good as gold*〉 **2** : well-behaved

〈the child was *as good as gold*〉 — **good and** \ˌgu̇d-²n\ : VERY, ENTIRELY 〈was *good and* mad〉
usage An old notion that it is wrong to say "I feel good" in reference to health still occas. appears in print. The origins of this notion, which goes back to the turn of the century, are obscure, but they seem to combine someone's idea that *good* should be reserved to describe virtue and uncertainty about whether an adverb or an adjective should follow *feel*. Today nearly everyone agrees that both *good* and *well* can be predicate adjectives after *feel*. Both are used to express good health, but *good* may connote good spirits in addition to good health.
²good *n* (bef. 12c) **1** **a** : something that is good **b** (1) : something conforming to the moral order of the universe (2) : praiseworthy character : GOODNESS **c** : a good element or portion **2** **a** : advancement of prosperity or well-being 〈the ~ of the community〉 〈it's for your own ~〉 **b** : something useful or beneficial 〈it's no ~ trying〉 **3** **a** : something that has economic utility or satisfies an economic want **b** *pl* : personal property having intrinsic value but usu. excluding money, securities, and negotiable instruments **c** *pl* : CLOTH **d** *pl* : something manufactured or produced for sale : WARES, MERCHANDISE 〈canned ~s〉 **e** *pl, Brit* : FREIGHT **4** : good persons — used with *the* **5** *pl* **a** : the qualities required to achieve an end **b** : proof of wrongdoing 〈didn't have the ~s on him —T. G. Cooke〉 — **for good** *also* **for good and all** : FOREVER, PERMANENTLY — **in good with** : in a favored position with — **to the good** **1** : for the best : BENEFICIAL 〈efforts to restrict credit were all *to the good* —*Time*〉 **2** : in a position of net gain or profit 〈wound up $10 *to the good*〉
³good *adv* (13c) **1** : WELL 〈he showed me how ~ I was doing —Herbert Gold〉 **2** — used as an intensive 〈a ~ 200 pounds〉 〈a ~ long time〉
usage Adverbial *good* has been under attack from the schoolroom since the 19th century. Insistence on *well* rather than *good* has resulted in a split in connotation: *well* is standard, neutral, and colorless, while *good* is emotionally charged and emphatic. This makes *good* the adverb of choice in sports 〈"I'm seeing the ball real *good*" is what you hear —Roger Angell〉. In such contexts as 〈listen up. And listen *good* —Alex Karras〉 〈lets fly with his tomatoes before they can flee. He gets Clarence *good* —Charles Dickinson〉 *good* cannot be adequately replaced by *well*. Adverbial *good* is primarily a spoken form; in writing it occurs in reported and fictional speech and in generally familiar or informal contexts.
good book *n, often cap* G&B (1860) : BIBLE
good-bye *or* **good-by** \gu̇d-ˈbī, gə(d)-\ *n* [alter. of *God be with you*] (ca. 1580) **1** : a concluding remark or gesture at parting — often used interjectionally **2** : a taking of leave 〈a tearful ~〉
good deal *n* (1881) : a considerable quantity or extent : LOT 〈knows a *good deal* about disease〉 〈a *good deal* faster〉
good faith *n* (1893) : honesty or lawfulness of purpose
good fellow *n* (13c) : an affable companionable person — **good-fellow·ship** \ˌgu̇d-ˈfe-lō-ˌship, -ˈfe-lə-\ *n*
good-for-noth·ing \ˈgu̇d-fər-ˌnə-thiŋ\ *adj* (1533) : of no use or value — **good-for-nothing** *n*
Good Friday *n* [fr. its special sanctity] (13c) : the Friday before Easter observed in churches as the anniversary of the crucifixion of Christ and in some states of the U.S. as a legal holiday
good-heart·ed \ˈgu̇d-ˈhär-təd\ *adj* (1552) : having a kindly generous disposition — **good-heart·ed·ly** *adv* — **good-heart·ed·ness** *n*
good-hu·mored \-ˈ(h)yü-mərd\ *adj* (1662) : GOOD-NATURED, CHEERFUL — **good-hu·mored·ly** *adv* — **good-hu·mored·ness** *n*
good life *n* (1946) : a life marked by a high standard of living
good-look·ing \ˈgu̇d-ˈlu̇-kiŋ\ *adj* (1780) : having a pleasing or attractive appearance — **good-look·er** \-ˈlu̇-kər\ *n*
good·ly \ˈgu̇d-lē\ *adj* **good·li·er; -est** (bef. 12c) **1** : pleasantly attractive **2** : significantly large : CONSIDERABLE 〈a ~ number〉
good·man \ˈgu̇d-mən\ *n* (13c) **1** *archaic* : the master of a household **2** *archaic* : MR.
good-na·tured \-ˈnā-chərd\ *adj* (1577) : of a pleasant cheerful cooperative disposition **syn** see AMIABLE — **good-na·tured·ly** *adv* — **good-na·tured·ness** *n*
good-neighbor *adj* (1936) : marked by principles of friendship, cooperation, and noninterference in the internal affairs of another country 〈a ~ policy〉
good·ness \ˈgu̇d-nəs\ *n* (bef. 12c) **1** : the quality or state of being good **2** — used interjectionally or in phrases esp. to express mild surprise or shock 〈oh, my ~ !〉 〈~ knows〉 **3** : the nutritious, flavorful, or beneficial part of something
goodness of fit (ca. 1939) : the conformity between an experimental result and theoretical expectation or between data and an approximating curve
good offices *n pl* (1904) : services as a mediator
good old boy *or* **good ol' boy** *or* **good ole boy** \ˈgu̇-ˌdōl(-)-ˌbȯi\ *n* (ca. 1967) : a usu. white Southerner who conforms to the social behavior of his peers
Good Samaritan *n* (1846) : SAMARITAN 2
good-tem·pered \ˈgu̇d-ˈtem-pərd\ *adj* (1768) : not easily vexed — **good-tem·pered·ly** *adv* — **good-tem·pered·ness** *n*
good·wife \ˈgu̇d-ˌwif\ *n* (13c) **1** *archaic* : the mistress of a household **2** *archaic* : MRS.
good·will \ˌgu̇d-ˈwil\ *n* (bef. 12c) **1** **a** : a kindly feeling of approval and support : benevolent interest or concern **b** (1) : the favor or prestige that a business has acquired beyond the mere value of what it sells (2) : the value of projected earnings increases of a business esp. as part of its purchase price (3) : the value of other intangible assets (as tax credits) of a business esp. as part of its purchase price **2** **a** : cheerful consent **b** : willing effort — **good-willed** \-ˈwild\ *adj*
¹goody \ˈgu̇-dē\ *n* [alter. of *goodwife*] (1559) *archaic* : a usu. married woman of lowly station — used as a title preceding a surname
²goody *or* **good·ie** \n, pl* **good·ies** (1756) **1** : something that is particularly attractive, pleasurable, good, or desirable **2** *chiefly Brit* : one that is good; *esp* : an exponent of the villain (as in a motion picture)
goody-goody \ˌgu̇-dē-ˈgu̇-dē\ *adj* (1871) : affectedly or ingratiatingly good or proper — **goody-goody** *n*
Goody Two-shoes \ˈgu̇-dē-ˈtü-ˌshüz\ *n, often cap* S [fr. *Goody Two-Shoes*, heroine of a children's story perh. by Oliver Goldsmith] (1934)

: a person who is goody-goody; *also* : a person who is uncommonly good — **goody–two–shoes** *adj*

¹goof \'güf\ *n* [prob. alter. of E dial. *goff* (simpleton)] (1915) **1** : a silly or stupid person **2** : BLUNDER

²goof *vi* (1932) **1 a** : to spend time idly or foolishly — usu. used with *off* **b** : to engage in playful activity — usu. used with *around* **2** : to make a usu. foolish or careless mistake : BLUNDER — often used with *up* ~ *vt* **1** : to make a mess of : BUNGLE — usu. used with *up* — **goof on** *slang* : to make fun of : KID, PUT ON ⟨you're *goofing on* me, right?⟩

goof·ball \'güf-,bȯl\ *n* (1950) **1** *slang* : a barbiturate sleeping pill **2** : a goofy person

go off *vi* (1579) **1** : EXPLODE **2** : to burst forth or break out suddenly or noisily **3** : to go forth, out, or away : LEAVE **4** : to undergo decline or deterioration **5** : to follow the expected or desired course : PROCEED ⟨the party *went off* well⟩ **6** : to make a characteristic noise : SOUND — **go off the deep end 1** : to enter recklessly on a course **2** : to become very much excited

goof–off \'güf-,ȯf\ *n* (1953) : one who evades work or responsibility

goofy \'gü-fē\ *adj* **goof·i·er; -est** (1921) : being crazy, ridiculous, or mildly ludicrous : SILLY — **goof·i·ly** \-fə-lē\ *adv* — **goof·i·ness** \-fē-nəs\ *n*

goo·gly–eyed \'gü-glē-,īd\ *adj* [by alter.] (1926) : GOGGLE-EYED

goo·gol \'gü-,gȯl\ *n* [coined by Milton Sirotta *b ab* 1929 nephew of Edward Kasner †1955 Am. mathematician] (1938) : the figure 1 followed by 100 zeroes equal to 10¹⁰⁰

goo·gol·plex \-,pleks\ *n* (1938) : the figure 1 followed by a googol of zeroes equal to

$$10^{googol} \text{ or } 10^{10^{100}}$$

¹goo–goo \'gü-,gü\ *adj* [perh. alter. of ²*goggle*] (1900) : LOVING, ENTICING — used chiefly in the phrase *goo-goo eyes*

²goo–goo *n, pl* **goo–goos** [fr. *good government*] (1912) : a member or advocate of a political reform movement

¹gook \'gük\ *n* [origin unknown] (1935) : a nonwhite or non-American person; *specif* : ASIAN — usu. used disparagingly

²gook \'gȯk, 'gük\ *var of* GUCK

goon \'gün\ *n* [prob. short for E dial. *gooney* (simpleton)] (1921) **1** : a stupid person **2** : a man hired to terrorize or eliminate opponents

go on *vi* (15c) **1 a** : to continue on or as if on a journey ⟨life *goes on*⟩ ⟨*went on* to greater things⟩ **b** : to keep on : CONTINUE ⟨*went on* smoking⟩ **c** : PROCEED ⟨*went on* to win the election⟩ **2** : to take place : HAPPEN ⟨what's *going on*⟩ **3** : to talk esp. in an effusive manner ⟨the way people *go on* about their ancestors —Hamilton Basso⟩

goo·ney *or* **goo·ny** \'gü-nē\ *n, pl* **gooneys** *or* **goonies** [prob. fr. E dial. *gooney* (simpleton)] (1895) : BLACK-FOOTED ALBATROSS; *broadly* : ALBATROSS

goop \'güp\ *n* [prob. alter. of *goo*] (ca. 1958) : GOO, GUNK

goo·san·der \gü-'san-dər\ *n* [origin unknown] (1766) : the common merganser (*Mergus merganser*) of the northern hemisphere

¹goose \'güs\ *n, pl* **geese** \'gēs\ [ME *gos*, fr. OE *gōs*; akin to OHG *gans* goose, L *anser*, Gk *chēn*] (bef. 12c) **1 a** : any of numerous large waterfowl (family Anatidae) that are intermediate between the swans and ducks and have long necks, feathered lores, and reticulate tarsi **b** : a female goose as distinguished from a gander : SIMPLETON, DOLT **3** *pl* **goos·es** : a tailor's smoothing iron with a gooseneck handle **4** *pl* **goos·es** : a poke between the buttocks

²goose *vt* **goosed; goos·ing** (ca. 1880) **1** : to poke between the buttocks with an upward thrust **2** : to increase the activity, speed, power, intensity, or amount of : SPUR ⟨an effort to ~ newsstand sales⟩

goose·ber·ry \'güs-,ber-ē, 'güz-, -b(ə-)rē, *chiefly Brit* 'gúz-\ *n* (1573) **1** : the acid usu. prickly fruit of any of several shrubs (genus *Ribes*) of the saxifrage family **2** : a shrub bearing gooseberries **2** : CURRANT 2

goose bumps *n pl* (1933) : a roughness of the skin produced by erection of its papillae esp. from cold, fear, or a sudden feeling of excitement

goose egg *n* (1866) : ZERO, NOTHING; *esp* : a score of zero in a game or contest

goose·fish \'güs-,fish\ *n* (1807) : any of a family (Lophiidae) of pediculate fishes with a large flattened head, a fringe of flaps along each side of the lower jaw, head, and body, and a long stalk on the head with a flap of flesh at the tip for attracting prey; *esp* : MONKFISH

gooseberry: leaves and fruit

goose·flesh \'güs-,flesh\ *n* (ca. 1810) : GOOSE BUMPS

goose·foot \-,fút\ *n, pl* **goose·foots** (1548) : any of a genus (*Chenopodium*) or family (Chenopodiaceae, the goosefoot family) of glabrous herbs with utricular fruit

goose·grass \-,gras\ *n* (1530) **1** : CLEAVERS **2** : YARD GRASS

goose·neck \'güs-,nek\ *n, often attrib* (1688) **1** : something (as a flexible jointed metal pipe) curved like the neck of a goose or U-shaped **2** : a truck trailer (as for transporting livestock) with a projecting front end designed to attach to the bed of a pickup truck — **goose·necked** \-,nekt\ *adj*

goose pimples *n pl* (ca. 1889) : GOOSE BUMPS

goose–step \'güs-,step\ *vi* (1879) **1** : to march in a goose step **2** : to practice an unthinking conformity

goose step *n* (1806) : a straight-legged stiff-kneed step used by troops of some armies when passing in review

goos·ey \'gü-sē\ *adj* **goos·i·er; -est** (1811) **1** : resembling a goose **2 a** : affected with goose bumps : SCARED **b** : very nervous **c** : reacting strongly when goosed or startled

go out *vi* (bef. 12c) **1 a** : to go forth, abroad, or outdoors; *specif* : to leave one's house **b** (1) : to take the field as a soldier (2) : to participate as a principal in a duel **c** : to travel as or as if a colonist or immigrant **d** : to work away from home **2 a** : to come to an end **b** : to give up office : RESIGN **c** : to become obsolete or unfashionable **d** (1) : to play the last card of one's hand (2) : to reach or exceed the total number of points required for game in cards **3** : to take part in social activities **4** : to go on strike **5** : BREAK, COLLAPSE **6** : to become a candidate ⟨*went out* for the football team⟩

go over *vi* (1645) **1** : to go on a journey **2** : to become converted **3** : to receive approval : SUCCEED ⟨his plan *went over* well⟩

¹go·pher \'gō-fər\ *n* [origin unknown] (1791) **1 a** : a burrowing land tortoise (*Gopherus polyphemus*) of the southern U.S.; *broadly* : any of several related land tortoises — called also *gopher tortoise* **b** : any of a family (Geomyidae) of burrowing rodents of western No. America, Central America, and the southern U.S. that are the size of a large rat and have large cheek pouches opening beside the mouth — called also *pocket gopher* **b** : any of several small ground squirrels (genus *Citellus*) of the prairie region of No. America closely related to the chipmunks **3** : GOPHER BALL

²gopher *var of* GOFER

gopher ball *n* (ca. 1949) : a pitched baseball hit for a home run

gopher snake *n* (1837) **1** : INDIGO SNAKE **2** : BULL SNAKE

Gor·di·an knot \'gȯr-dē-ən-\ *n* **1** : an intricate problem; *esp* : a problem insoluble in its own terms — usu. used in the phrase *cut the Gordian knot* **2** : a knot tied by Gordius, king of Phrygia, held to be capable of being untied only by the future ruler of Asia, and cut by Alexander the Great with his sword

Gor·don setter \'gȯr-d⁽ᵊ⁾n-\ *n* [Alexander, 4th Duke of *Gordon* †1827 Scot. sportsman] (1865) : any of a breed of large bird dogs that have a long flat black-and-tan coat

¹gore \'gōr, 'gȯr\ *n* [ME, fr. OE *gāra*; akin to OE *gār* spear, and perh. to Gk *chaion* shepherd's staff] (bef. 12c) **1** : a small usu. triangular piece of land **2 a** : a tapering or triangular piece (as of cloth in a skirt) **b** : an elastic gusset for providing a snug fit in a shoe

²gore *vt* **gored; gor·ing** (1548) **1** : to cut into a tapering triangular form **2** : to provide with a gore

³gore *vt* **gored; gor·ing** [ME] (15c) : to pierce or wound with something pointed (as a horn or knife) ⟨*gored* by a bull⟩

⁴gore *n* [ME, filth, fr. OE *gor*] (1563) : BLOOD; *esp* : clotted blood

¹gorge \'gȯrj\ *n* [ME, fr. MF, fr. LL *gurga*, alter. of *gurges*, fr. L, whirlpool — more at VORACIOUS] (14c) **1** : THROAT — often used with *rise* to indicate revulsion accompanied by a sensation of constriction ⟨my ~ rises at the sight of blood⟩ **2 a** : a hawk's crop **3** : STOMACH, BELLY **3** : the entrance into an outwork (as a bastion) of a fort **4** : a narrow passage through land; *esp* : a narrow steep-walled canyon or part of a canyon **5** : a primitive device used instead of a fishhook that consists of an object (as a piece of bone attached in the middle of a line) easy to swallow but difficult to eject **6** : a mass choking a passage ⟨a river dammed by an ice ~⟩ **7** : the line on the front of a coat or jacket formed by the crease of the lapel and collar

²gorge *vb* **gorged; gorg·ing** *vi* (14c) : to eat greedily or to repletion ~ *vt* **1 a** : to stuff to capacity : GLUT **b** : to fill completely or to the point of distension ⟨veins *gorged* with blood⟩ **2** : to consume greedily *syn* see SATIATE — **gorg·er** *n*

³gorge *n* (1854) : the act or an instance of gorging

gor·geous \'gȯr-jəs\ *adj* [ME *gorgayse*, fr. MF *gorgias* elegant, fr. *gorgias* wimple, fr. *gorge* (gorget)] (15c) : splendidly or showily brilliant or magnificent *syn* see SPLENDID — **gor·geous·ly** *adv* — **gor·geous·ness** *n*

gor·get \'gȯr-jət\ *n* [ME, fr. MF, fr. *gorge*] (15c) **1** : a piece of armor protecting the throat — see ARMOR illustration **2 a** : an ornamental collar **b** : a part of a wimple covering the throat and shoulders

gor·gon \'gȯr-gən\ *n* [L *Gorgon-, Gorgo*, fr. Gk *Gorgōn*] **1** *cap* : any of three snake-haired sisters in Greek mythology whose appearance turns the beholder to stone **2** : an ugly or repulsive woman — **Gor·go·ni·an** \gȯr-'gō-nē-ən\ *adj*

gor·go·ni·an \gȯr-'gō-nē-ən\ *n* [NL *Gorgonia*, a coral genus, fr. L, coral, fr. *Gorgon-, Gorgo*] (1835) : any of an order (Gorgonacea) of colonial anthozoans with a usu. horny and branching axial skeleton — **gorgonian** *adj*

gor·gon·ize \'gȯr-gə-,nīz\ *vt* **-ized; -iz·ing** (1609) : to have a paralyzing or mesmerizing effect on : STUPEFY, PETRIFY

Gor·gon·zo·la \,gȯr-gən-'zō-lə\ *n* [It, fr. *Gorgonzola*, Italy] (1878) : a pungent blue cheese of Italian origin

go·ril·la \gə-'ri-lə\ *n* [NL, fr. Gk *Gorillai*, pl., a tribe of hairy women mentioned in an account of a voyage around Africa] (1847) **1 a** : an anthropoid ape (*Gorilla gorilla*) of western equatorial Africa related to the chimpanzee but less erect and much larger **2 a** : an ugly or brutal man **b** : THUG, GOON

gor·man·dise *chiefly Brit var of* GORMANDIZE

gor·man·dize \'gȯr-mən-,dīz\ *vb* **-dized; -diz·ing** [*gormand*, alter. of *gourmand*] *vi* (1548) : to eat gluttonously or ravenously ~ *vt* : to eat greedily : DEVOUR — **gor·man·diz·er** *n*

gorm·less \'gȯrm-ləs\ *adj* [alter. of E dial. *gaumless*, fr. *gaum* attention, understanding, fr. ME *gome*, fr. ON *gaum, gaumr*) + *-less*] (1883) *chiefly Brit* : lacking intelligence : STUPID

go–round \'gō-,raúnd\ *n* (1891) : GO-AROUND

gorp \'gȯrp\ *n* [origin unknown] (1968) : a snack consisting of high-energy food (as raisins and nuts)

gorse \'gȯrs\ *n* [ME *gorst*, fr. OE; akin to OHG *gersta* barley, L *hordeum*] (bef. 12c) : a spiny yellow-flowered European shrub (*Ulex europaeus*) of the legume family; *broadly* : any of several related plants (genera *Ulex* and *Genista*) — **gorsy** \'gȯr-sē\ *adj*

gory \'gōr-ē, 'gȯr-\ *adj* **gor·i·er; -est** (15c) **1** : covered with gore : BLOODSTAINED **2** : BLOODCURDLING, SENSATIONAL ⟨wanted to hear the ~ details⟩ *syn* see BLOODY

gosh \'gäsh, 'gȯsh\ *interj* [euphemism for *God*] (1757) — used as a mild oath or to express surprise

gos·hawk \'gäs-,hȯk\ *n* [ME *goshawke*, fr. OE *gōshafoc*, fr. *gōs* goose + *hafoc* hawk] (bef. 12c) : any of several long-tailed accipitrine hawks with short rounded wings; *esp* : a hawk (*Accipiter gentilis*) of the northern parts of both the Old and the New World that is larger than a crow and has a white stripe above and behind the eye

gos·ling \'gäz-liŋ, 'gȯz-, -lən\ *n* [ME, fr. *gos* goose] (14c) **1** : a young goose **2** : a foolish or callow person

\ə\ abut \ᵊ\ kitten, F table \ər\ further \a\ ash \ā\ ace \ä\ mop, mar \aú\ out \ch\ chin \e\ bet \ē\ easy \g\ go \i\ hit \ī\ ice \j\ job \ŋ\ sing \ō\ go \ȯ\ law \ȯi\ boy \th\ thin \t͟h\ the \ü\ loot \ú\ foot \y\ yet \zh\ vision \ä, k̲, ⁿ, œ, œ̄, ᵫ, ᵫ̄, ᶦ\ *see* Guide to Pronunciation

go-slow \ˌgō-ˈslō\ n (1926) Brit : SLOWDOWN

¹gos·pel \ˈgäs-pəl\ n [ME, fr. OE gōdspel (trans. of LL evangelium), fr. gōd good + spell tale — more at SPELL] (bef. 12c) **1** a often cap : the message concerning Christ, the kingdom of God, and salvation **b** cap : one of the first four New Testament books telling of the life, death, and resurrection of Jesus Christ; also : a similar apocryphal book **c** : an interpretation of the Christian message ⟨the social ∼⟩ **2** cap : a lection from one of the New Testament Gospels **3** : the message or teachings of a religious teacher **4** : something accepted as infallible truth or as a guiding principle ⟨the ∼ of conservation —R. M. Hodesh⟩ **5** : gospel music

²gospel adj (bef. 12c) **1** a : having a basis in or being in accordance with the gospel : EVANGELICAL ⟨ordained to the ∼ ministry —Christian Century⟩ **b** : marked by special or fervid emphasis on the gospel ⟨a ∼ meeting⟩ **2** : of, relating to, or being religious songs of American origin associated with evangelism and popular devotion and marked by simple melody and harmony and elements of folk songs and blues

gos·pel·er or **gos·pel·ler** \ˈgäs-p(ə-)lər\ n (1506) **1** : one who reads or sings the liturgical Gospel **2** : one who preaches or propounds a gospel

gospel side n, often cap G [fr. the custom of reading the Gospel from this side] (1891) : the left side of an altar or chancel as one faces it

¹gos·sa·mer \ˈgä-sə-mər also ˈgäz-mər, ˈgä-zə-\ n [ME gossomer, fr. gos goose + somer summer] (14c) **1** : a film of cobwebs floating in air in calm clear weather **2** : something light, delicate, or insubstantial ⟨the ∼ of youth's dreams —Andrea Parke⟩ — **gos·sa·mery** \-mə-rē\ adj

²gossamer adj (ca. 1807) : extremely light, delicate, or tenuous

gos·san \ˈgä-sᵊn\ n [Corn gossen, fr. gōs blood] (1776) : decomposed rock or vein material of reddish or rusty color that results from oxidized pyrites

¹gos·sip \ˈgä-səp\ n [ME gossib, fr. OE godsibb, fr. god god + sibb kinsman, fr. sibb related — more at SIB] (bef. 12c) **1** a dial Brit : GODPARENT **b** : COMPANION, CRONY **c** : a person who habitually reveals personal or sensational facts about others **2** a : rumor or report of an intimate nature **b** : a chatty talk **c** : the subject matter of gossip — **gos·sip·ry** \-sə-prē\ n

²gossip vi (1627) : to relate gossip — **gos·sip·er** n

gos·sip·mon·ger \ˈgä-səp-ˌmən-gər, -ˌmäŋ-\ n (1836) : a person who starts or spreads gossip

gos·sipy \ˈgä-sə-pē\ adj (1818) : characterized by, full of, or given to gossip ⟨a ∼ letter⟩ ⟨∼ neighbors⟩

gos·sy·pol \ˈgä-sə-ˌpȯl, -ˌpōl\ n [ISV, ultim. fr. L gossypion cotton] (1899) : a toxic phenolic pigment $C_{30}H_{30}O_8$ in cottonseed

got past and past part of GET

Goth \ˈgäth\ n [ME Gothes, Gotes (pl.), partly fr. OE Gotan (pl.); partly fr. LL Gothi (pl.)] (14c) : a member of a Germanic people that overran the Roman Empire in the early centuries of the Christian era

¹Goth·ic \ˈgä-thik\ adj (1591) **1** a : of, relating to, or resembling the Goths, their civilization, or their language **b** : TEUTONIC, GERMANIC **c** : MEDIEVAL **d** : UNCOUTH, BARBAROUS **2** a : of, relating to, or having the characteristics of a style of architecture developed in northern France and spreading through western Europe from the middle of the 12th century to the early 16th century that is characterized by the converging of weights and strains at isolated points upon slender vertical piers and counterbalancing buttresses and by pointed arches and vaulting **b** : of or relating to an architectural style reflecting the influence of the medieval Gothic **3** often not cap : of or relating to a style of fiction characterized by the use of desolate or remote settings and macabre, mysterious, or violent incidents — **goth·i·cal·ly** \-thi-k(ə-)lē\ adv — **Goth·ic·ness** \-thik-nəs\ n

²Gothic n (1691) **1** a : BLACK LETTER **b** : SANS SERIF **2** : Gothic art style or decoration; specif : the Gothic architectural style **3** : the East Germanic language of the Goths — see INDO-EUROPEAN LANGUAGES table **4** often not cap : a work of fiction in the gothic style

Gothic arch n (1739) : a pointed arch; esp : one with a joint instead of a keystone at its apex

Goth·i·cism \ˈgä-thə-ˌsi-zəm\ n (1710) **1** : barbarous lack of taste or elegance **2** : conformity to or practice of Gothic style — **Goth·i·cist** \-sist\ n

goth·i·cize \-ˌsīz\ vt **-cized; -ciz·ing** often cap (1712) : to make Gothic

Goth·ick chiefly Brit var of GOTHIC

Gothic Revival n (1869) : an artistic style or movement of the 18th and 19th centuries inspired by and imitative of the Gothic style esp. in architecture

go through vi (1513) **1** : to continue firmly or obstinately to the end ⟨I was going through with it if it killed me —A. W. Long⟩ **2** a : to receive approval or sanction : PASS **b** : to come to a desired or satisfactory conclusion

go to vi (15c) **1** archaic — used interjectionally as an exhortation ⟨and they said one to another, go to, let us make brick —Gen 11:3 (AV)⟩ **2** archaic — used interjectionally to express disapproval or disbelief ⟨go to, go to; you have known what you should not —Shak.⟩

gotten past part of GET

Göt·ter·däm·mer·ung \ˌgə(r)-tər-ˈde-mə-ˌrủŋ, -ˈda-\ n [G, lit., twilight of the gods, fr. Götter (pl. of Gott god) + Dämmerung twilight] (1909) : a collapse (as of a society or regime) marked by catastrophic violence and disorder

gouache \ˈgwäsh\ n [F, fr. It guazzo, lit., puddle, prob. fr. L aquatio watering place, fr. aquari to fetch water, fr. aqua water — more at ISLAND] (1882) **1** : a method of painting with opaque watercolors **2** a : a picture painted by gouache **b** : the pigment used in gouache

Gou·da \ˈgü-də\ n [Gouda, Netherlands] (1885) : a mild cheese of Dutch origin that is similar to Edam but contains more fat

¹gouge \ˈgaủj\ n [ME gowge, fr. MF gouge, fr. LL gulbia, of Celt origin; akin to OIr gulban beak, sting] (14c) **1** : a chisel with a concavo-convex cross section **2** a : the act of gouging **b** : a groove or cavity scooped out **3** : an excessive or improper exaction : EXTORTION

²gouge vt gouged; goug·ing (1570) **1** : to scoop out with or as if with a gouge **2** a : to force out (an eye) with the thumb **b** : to thrust the thumb into the eye of **3** : to subject to extortion or undue exaction : OVERCHARGE — **goug·er** n

gou·lash \ˈgü-ˌläsh, -ˌlash\ n [Hung gulyás, short for gulyáshús, lit., herdsman's meat] (1866) **1** : a stew made with meat (as beef), as-

sorted vegetables, and paprika **2** : a round in bridge played with hands produced by a redistribution of previously dealt cards **3** : a mixture of heterogeneous elements : JUMBLE

go under vi (1848) : to be overwhelmed, destroyed, or defeated : FAIL

go up vi (15c) **1** chiefly Brit : to attend a university **2** of an actor : to become confused — **go up in flames** : BURN — **go up in smoke** : to be destroyed by or as if by burning

gou·ra·mi \gü-ˈrä-mē\ n, pl **-mi** or **-mis** also **-mies** [Malay dial. (Java), fr. Jav graméh] (1878) : any of numerous African and Asian tropical freshwater fishes (order Perciformes): as **a** : a large Asian food fish (Osphronemus goramy, family Osphronemidae) **b** : any of various small fishes (families Belontiidae and Helostomatidae) often kept in aquariums

gourd \ˈgȯrd, ˈgȯrd, ˈgủrd\ n [ME gourde, fr. MF, fr. L cucurbita] (14c) **1** : any of a family (Cucurbitaceae, the gourd family) of chiefly herbaceous tendril-bearing vines including the cucumber, melon, squash, and pumpkin **2** : the fruit of a gourd : PEPO; esp : any of various hard-rinded inedible fruits of plants of two genera (Lagenaria and Cucurbita) often used for ornament or for vessels and utensils — **out of one's gourd** also **off one's gourd** : CRAZY

gourde \ˈgủrd\ n [AmerF] (ca. 1858) — see MONEY table

gour·mand \ˈgủr-ˌmänd, -mənd\ n [ME, fr. MF gourmant] (15c) **1** : one who is excessively fond of eating and drinking **2** : one who is heartily interested in good food and drink syn see EPICURE — **gour·mand·ism** \ˈgủr-ˌmän-ˌdi-zəm, -mən-\ n — **gour·man·dize** \-ˌdīz\ vi

gour·man·dise \ˌgủr-män-ˈdēz\ n [F, fr. MF, fr. gourmand] (15c) : appreciation of or interest in good food and drink : GOURMANDISM

gour·met \ˈgủr-ˌmā, gủr-ˈ\ n [F, fr. MF, alter. of gromet boy servant, vintner's assistant, prob. ultim. fr. ME grom groom] (1820) : a connoisseur of food and drink; broadly : CONNOISSEUR 2 ⟨a film ∼⟩ syn see EPICURE — **gourmet** adj

gout \ˈgaủt\ n [ME goute, fr. OF, gout, drop, fr. L gutta drop] (13c) **1** : a metabolic disease marked by a painful inflammation of the joints, deposits of urates in and around the joints, and usu. an excessive amount of uric acid in the blood **2** : a mass or aggregate esp. of something fluid often gushing or bursting forth — **gouty** \-ē\ adj

gov·ern \ˈgə-vərn\ vb [ME, fr. OF governer, fr. L gubernare to steer, govern, fr. Gk kybernan] vt (14c) **1** a : to exercise continuous sovereign authority over; esp : to control and direct the making and administration of policy in **b** : to rule without sovereign power and usu. without having the authority to determine basic policy **2** a archaic : MANIPULATE **b** : to control the speed of (as a machine) esp. by automatic means **3** a : to control, direct, or strongly influence the actions and conduct of **b** : to exert a determining or guiding influence in or over ⟨income must ∼ expenditure⟩ **c** : to hold in check : RESTRAIN **4** : to require (a word) to be in a certain case **5** : to serve as a precedent or deciding principle for ⟨customs that ∼ human decisions⟩ ∼ vi **1** : to prevail or have decisive influence : CONTROL **2** : to exercise authority — **gov·ern·able** \-vər-nə-bəl\ adj

gov·er·nance \ˈgə-vər-nən(t)s\ n (14c) : GOVERNMENT

gov·ern·ess \ˈgə-vər-nəs\ n (15c) **1** : a woman who governs **2** : a woman entrusted with the care and supervision of a child esp. in a private household

gov·ern·essy \ˈgə-vər-ni-sē\ adj (1872) : characteristic of or resembling a governess (as in primness)

gov·ern·ment \ˈgə-vər(n)-mənt, -və-mənt; ˈgə-bᵊm-ənt, -vᵊm-\ n, often attrib (14c) **1** : the act or process of governing; specif : authoritative direction or control **2** obs : moral conduct or behavior : DISCRETION **3** a : the office, authority, or function of governing **b** obs : the term during which a governing official holds office **4** : the continuous exercise of authority over and the performance of functions for a political unit : RULE **5** a : the organization, machinery, or agency through which a political unit exercises authority and performs functions and which is usu. classified according to the distribution of power within it **b** : the complex of political institutions, laws, and customs through which the function of governing is carried out **6** : the body of persons that constitutes the governing authority of a political unit or organization: as **a** : the officials comprising the governing body of a political unit and constituting the organization as an active agency **b** cap : the executive branch of the U.S. federal government **c** cap : a small group of persons holding simultaneously the principal political executive offices of a nation or other political unit and being responsible for the direction and supervision of public affairs: (1) : such a group in a parliamentary system constituted by the cabinet or by the ministry (2) : ADMINISTRATION 4b **7** : POLITICAL SCIENCE — **gov·ern·men·tal** \ˌgə-vər(n)-ˈmen-tᵊl\ adj — **gov·ern·men·tal·ize** \-ˈt-ᵊl-ˌīz\ vt — **gov·ern·men·tal·ly** \-ˈt-ᵊl-ē\ adv

gov·ern·men·tal·ism \ˌgə-vər(n)-ˈmen-tᵊl-i-zəm\ n (1848) **1** : a theory advocating extension of the sphere and degree of government activity **2** : the tendency toward extension of the role of government — **gov·ern·men·tal·ist** \-ᵊl-ist\ n

gov·ern·men·tese \ˌgə-vər-mən-ˈtēz\ n (1944) : jargon held to be characteristic of government officials

gov·er·nor \ˈgə-vᵊn-ər also ˈgə-vər-nər\ n (14c) **1** : one that governs: as **a** : one that exercises authority esp. over an area or group **b** : an official elected or appointed to act as ruler, chief executive, or nominal head of a political unit **c** : COMMANDING OFFICER **d** : the managing director and usu. the principal officer of an institution or organization **e** : a member of a group that directs or controls an institution or society **2** : TUTOR **3** a slang : one looked upon as governing **b** : MISTER, SIR — usu. used as a term of address **4** a : an attachment to a machine (as a gasoline engine) for automatic control or limitation of speed **b** : a device giving automatic control (as of pressure or temperature) — **gov·er·nor·ate** \-ət, -ˌāt\ n

governor–general n, pl **governors–general** or **governor–generals** (1586) : a governor of high rank; esp : one who governs a large territory or has deputy governors under him

gov·er·nor·ship \ˈgə-vᵊn-ər-ˌship also ˈgə-vər-nər-\ n (1658) **1** : the office of governor **2** : the period of incumbency of a governor

gow·an \ˈgaủ-ən\ n [prob. alter. of ME gollan] (1570) chiefly Scot : DAISY 1; broadly : a white or yellow field flower — **gow·any** \-ə-nē\ adj, chiefly Scot

gown \ˈgaủn\ n [ME, fr. MF goune, fr. LL gunna, a fur or leather garment] (14c) **1** a : a loose flowing outer garment formerly worn by men   **b** : a distinctive robe worn by a professional or academic person   **c** : a woman's dress   **d** (1) : DRESSING GOWN (2) : NIGHTGOWN   **e** : a coverall worn in an operating room   **2** : the body of students and faculty of a college or university ⟨rivalry between town and ~⟩ — **gown** vt

gowns·man \'gaúnz-mən\ n (1627) : a professional or academic person

goy \'gói\ n, pl **goy·im** \'gói-əm\ also **goys** [Yiddish, fr. Heb gōy people, nation] (1841) : GENTILE 1 — sometimes used disparagingly — **goy·ish** \'gói-ish\ adj

graaf·ian follicle \.grä-fē-ən-, .gra-\ n, often cap G [Regnier de Graaf †1673 Du. anatomist] (1883) : a liquid-filled cavity in a mammalian ovary containing a mature egg before ovulation

¹grab \'grab\ vb **grabbed; grab·bing** [obs. D or LG grabben] vt (ca. 1581)   **1** : to take or seize by or as if by a sudden motion or grasp ⟨~ up an ax⟩ ⟨grabbed the opportunity⟩ ⟨~ attention⟩   **2** : to obtain unscrupulously ⟨~ public lands⟩   **3** : to take hastily ⟨~ a bite to eat⟩ ⟨~ a cab⟩   **4** a : to seize the attention of ⟨the technique of grabbing an audience —Pauline Kael⟩   **b** : to impress favorably and deeply ~ vi : to make a grab   syn see TAKE — **grab·ber** n

²grab adj (1608)   **1** : intended to be grabbed ⟨a ~ rail⟩   **2** : taken at random ⟨~ samples of rocks⟩

³grab n (1777)   **1** a : something grabbed   **b** : a sudden snatch   **c** : an unlawful or unscrupulous seizure   **2** chiefly Brit   a : a device for clutching an object   **b** : CLAMSHELL — **up for grabs** : available for anyone to take, win, or settle

grab bag n (1855)   **1** : a receptacle (as a bag) containing small articles which are to be drawn (as at a party or fair) without being seen   **2** : a miscellaneous collection : POTPOURRI

grab·ble \'gra-bəl\ vi **grab·bled; grab·bling** \-b(ə-)liŋ\ [D grabbelen, fr. MD, freq. of grabben] (ca. 1580)   **1** : to search with the hand : GROPE   **2** : to lie or fall prostrate — **grab·bler** \-b(ə-)lər\ n

grab·by \'gra-bē\ adj **grab·bi·er; -est** (1910)   **1** : tending to grab : GRASPING, GREEDY   **2** : having the power to grab the attention ⟨~ previews⟩

gra·ben \'grä-bən\ n [G, ditch, fr. OHG grabo, fr. graban to dig — more at GRAVE] (1896) : a depressed segment of the crust of the earth or a celestial body (as the moon) bounded on at least two sides by faults

¹grace \'grās\ n [ME, fr. OF, fr. L gratia favor, charm, thanks, fr. gratus pleasing, grateful; akin to Skt gṛṇāti he praises] (12c)   **1** a : unmerited divine assistance given humans for their regeneration or sanctification   **b** : a virtue coming from God   **c** : a state of sanctification enjoyed through divine grace   **2** a : APPROVAL, FAVOR ⟨stayed in his good ~s⟩   **b** archaic : MERCY, PARDON   **c** : a special favor : PRIVILEGE ⟨each in his place, by right, not ~, shall rule his heritage —Rudyard Kipling⟩   **d** : disposition to or an act or instance of kindness, courtesy, or clemency   **e** : a temporary exemption : REPRIEVE   **3** a : a charming or attractive trait or characteristic   **b** : a pleasingly graceful appearance or effect : CHARM   **c** : ease and suppleness of movement or bearing   **4** — used as a title of address or reference for a duke, a duchess, or an archbishop   **5** : a short prayer at a meal asking a blessing or giving thanks   **6** pl, cap : three sister goddesses in Greek mythology who are the givers of charm and beauty   **7** : a musical trill, turn, or appoggiatura   **8** a : sense of propriety or right ⟨had the ~ not to run for elective office —Calvin Trillin⟩   **b** : the quality or state of being considerate or thoughtful   syn see MERCY

²grace vt **graced; grac·ing** (1585)   **1** : to confer dignity or honor on   **2** : ADORN, EMBELLISH ⟨graveled walks graced with statues —J. A. Michener⟩

grace·ful \'grās-fəl\ adj (ca. 1586) : displaying grace in form or action : pleasing or attractive in line, proportion, or movement — **grace·ful·ly** \-fə-lē\ adv — **grace·ful·ness** n

grace·less \'grā-sləs\ adj (14c)   **1** : lacking in divine grace : IMMORAL, UNREGENERATE   **2** a : lacking a sense of propriety   **b** : devoid of attractive qualities   **3** : artistically inept or unbeautiful — **grace·less·ly** adv — **grace·less·ness** n

grace note n (ca. 1823)   **1** : a musical note added as an ornament : esp : APPOGGIATURA   **2** : a small addition or embellishment

grace period n (1945) : a period of time beyond a due date during which a financial obligation may be met without penalty or cancellation

grac·ile \'gra-səl, -,sil\ adj [L gracilis] (1623)   **1** : SLENDER, SLIGHT   **2** : GRACEFUL   **3** : relating to, resembling, or being any of the primitive relatively small slender hominids (genus Australopithecus) characterized esp. by molars and incisors of similar size that are adapted to an omnivorous diet — compare ROBUST — **gra·cile·ness** n — **gra·cil·i·ty** \gra-'si-lə-tē\ n

gra·ci·o·so \.grä-sē-'ō-(,)sō, -(,)zō\ n, pl **-sos** [Sp, fr. gracioso, adj., agreeable, amusing, fr. L gratiosus] (1749) : a buffoon in Spanish comedy

gra·cious \'grā-shəs\ adj [ME, fr. MF gracieus, fr. L gratiosus enjoying favor, agreeable, fr. gratia] (14c)   **1** a obs : GODLY   **b** archaic : PLEASING, ACCEPTABLE   **2** a : marked by kindness and courtesy   **b** : GRACEFUL   **c** : marked by tact and delicacy : URBANE   **3** : characterized by charm, good taste, generosity of spirit, and the tasteful leisure of wealth and good breeding ⟨~ living⟩   **3** : MERCIFUL, COMPASSIONATE — used conventionally of royalty and high nobility — **gra·cious·ly** adv — **gra·cious·ness** n

syn GRACIOUS, CORDIAL, AFFABLE, GENIAL, SOCIABLE mean markedly pleasant and easy in social intercourse. GRACIOUS implies courtesy and kindly consideration ⟨the gracious award winner thanked her colleagues⟩. CORDIAL stresses warmth and heartiness ⟨our host was cordial as he greeted us⟩. AFFABLE implies easy approachability and readiness to respond pleasantly to conversation or requests or proposals ⟨though wealthy, she was affable to all⟩. GENIAL stresses cheerfulness and even joviality ⟨a genial companion with a ready quip⟩. SOCIABLE suggests a genuine liking for the companionship of others ⟨sociable people who enjoy entertaining⟩.

grack·le \'gra-kəl\ n [NL Gracula, genus name, alter. of L graculus jackdaw] (1772)   **1** : any of a genus (Quiscalus of the family Icteridae) of large American blackbirds having iridescent black plumage   **2** : any of various Asian starlings (as the hill mynahs)

¹grad \'grad\ n or adj [by shortening] (ca. 1871) : GRADUATE

²grad n [F grade degree, fr. L gradus] (1898) : one hundredth of a right angle

gra·da·tion \grā-'dā-shən, grə-\ n (1549)   **1** a : a series forming successive stages   **b** : a step or place in an ordered scale   **2** : an advance by regular degrees   **3** : a gradual passing from one tint or shade to another   **4** : the act or process of grading   **5** : ABLAUT — **gra·da·tion·al** \-shnəl, -shə-n²l\ adj — **gra·da·tion·al·ly** adv

¹grade \'grād\ n [F, fr. L gradus degree, step, fr. L gradi to step, go; akin to Lith gridyti to go, wander] (1796)   **1** a (1) : a stage in a process   (2) : a position in a scale of ranks or qualities   **b** : a degree of severity in illness ⟨~ III carcinoma⟩   **c** : a class organized for the work of a particular year of a school course   **d** : a military or naval rank   **2** a : a class of things of the same stage or degree   **b** : a mark indicating a degree of accomplishment in school   **c** : a standard of food quality   **3** a : the degree of inclination of a road or slope; also : a sloping road   **b** : a datum or reference level; esp : ground level   **4** a : a domestic animal with one parent purebred and the other of inferior breeding   **5** pl : the elementary school system — **grade·less** \-ləs\ adj

²grade vb **grad·ed; grad·ing** (1659)   **1** a : to arrange in grades : SORT   **b** : to arrange in a scale or series   **c** : to assign to a grade or assign a grade to   **2** : to level off to a smooth horizontal or sloping surface ~ vi   **1** a : to form a series   **b** : BLEND   **2** : to be of a particular grade — **grad·able** \'grā-də-bəl\ adj

³grade adj (1852) : being, involving, or yielding domestic animals of improved but not pure stock ⟨~ ewes⟩ ⟨~ breeding⟩

-grade \.grād\ adj comb form [F, fr. L -gradus, fr. gradi] : walking ⟨plantigrade⟩

grade crossing n (ca. 1890) : a crossing of highways, railroad tracks, or pedestrian walks or combinations of these on the same level

grade point n (1951) : one of the points assigned to each course credit (as in a college) in accordance with the letter grade earned in the course — called also quality point

grade point average n (1966) : the average obtained by dividing the total number of grade points earned by the total number of credits attempted — called also quality point average

grad·er \'grā-dər\ n (1832)   **1** : one that grades   **2** : a machine for leveling earth   **3** : a pupil in a school grade ⟨a fifth ~⟩

grade school n (1869) : ELEMENTARY SCHOOL — **grade–school·er** \'grād-,skü-lər\ n

grade separation n (ca. 1949) : a highway or railroad crossing using an underpass or overpass

grade up vt (1903) : to improve by breeding females to purebred males

gra·di·ent \'grā-dē-ənt\ n [L gradient-, gradiens, prp. of gradi] (1835)   **1** a : the rate of regular or graded ascent or descent : INCLINATION   **b** : a part sloping upward or downward   **2** : change in the value of a quantity (as temperature, pressure, or concentration) with change in a given variable and esp. per unit distance in a specified direction   **3** : the vector sum of the partial derivatives with respect to the three coordinate variables x, y, and z of a scalar quantity whose value varies from point to point   **4** : a graded difference in physiological activity along an axis (as of the body or an embryonic field)   **5** : change in response with distance from the stimulus

gra·di·om·e·ter \.grā-dē-'ä-mə-tər\ n [gradient + -o- + -meter] (1899) : an instrument for measuring the gradient of a physical quantity (as the earth's magnetic field)

¹grad·u·al \'gra-jə-wəl, -jəl, 'graj-wəl\ n, often cap [ME, fr. ML graduale, fr. L gradus step, fr. its being sung on the steps of the altar] (15c)   **1** : a book containing the choral parts of the Mass   **2** : a pair of verses (as from the Psalms) proper after the Epistle in the Mass

²gradual adj [ML gradualis, fr. L gradus] (1692)   **1** : proceeding by steps or degrees   **2** : moving, changing, or developing by fine or often imperceptible degrees — **grad·u·al·ly** adv — **grad·u·al·ness** n

grad·u·al·ism \-jə-wə-,li-zəm, -jə-,li-\ n (1835)   **1** : the policy of approaching a desired end by gradual stages   **2** : the evolution of new species by gradual accumulation of small genetic changes over long periods of time; also : a theory or model of evolution emphasizing this — compare PUNCTUATED EQUILIBRIUM — **grad·u·al·ist** \-list\ n or adj

grad·u·and \.gra-jə-'wand\ n [ML graduandus, gerundive of graduare] (1882) Brit : one about to graduate : a candidate for a degree

¹grad·u·ate \'gra-jə-wət, -,wāt, 'graj-wət\ n (15c)   **1** : a holder of an academic degree or diploma   **2** : a graduated cup, cylinder, or flask

²graduate adj (15c)   **1** : holding an academic degree or diploma   **2** : of, relating to, or engaged in studies beyond the first or bachelor's degree ⟨~ school⟩ ⟨a ~ student⟩

³grad·u·ate \'gra-jə-,wāt\ vb **-at·ed; -at·ing** [ML graduare, fr. L gradus step, degree] vt (15c)   **1** a : to grant an academic degree or diploma to   **b** : to be graduated from   **2** a : to mark with degrees of measurement   **b** : to divide into grades or intervals   **3** : to admit to a particular standing or grade ~ vi   **1** : to receive an academic degree or diploma   **2** : to pass from one stage of experience, proficiency, or prestige to a usu. higher one   **3** : to change gradually — **grad·u·a·tor** \-,wā-tər\ n

usage In the 19th century the transitive sense (1a) was prescribed; the intransitive (I graduated from college) was condemned. The intransitive prevailed nonetheless, and today it is the sense likely to be prescribed and the newer transitive (sense 1b) the one condemned. All three are standard. The intransitive is currently the most common, the new transitive the least common.

grad·u·at·ed adj (1861) of a tax : increasing in rate with increase in taxable base : PROGRESSIVE ⟨~ income tax⟩

graduated cylinder n (1948) : a tall narrow container with a volume scale used esp. for measuring liquids

grad·u·a·tion \.gra-jə-'wā-shən\ n (1594)   **1** : a mark on an instrument or vessel indicating degrees or quantity; also : these marks   **2** a : the award or acceptance of an academic degree or diploma   **b** : COMMENCEMENT   **3** : arrangement in degrees or ranks

Graeco- — see GRECO-

\ə\ abut   \²\ kitten, F table   \ər\ further   \a\ ash   \ā\ ace   \ä\ mop, mar \aú\ out   \ch\ chin   \e\ bet   \ē\ easy   \g\ go   \i\ hit   \ī\ ice   \j\ job \ŋ\ sing   \ō\ go   \ó\ law   \ói\ boy   \th\ thin   \th̲\ the   \ü\ loot   \ù\ foot \y\ yet   \zh\ vision   \à, k̲, ⁿ, œ, œ̄, ue, ūe, ʸ\ see Guide to Pronunciation

graf·fi·to \grə-'fē-(ˌ)tō, gra-, grä-\ *n, pl* **-ti** \-(ˌ)tē\ [It, incised inscription, fr. *graffiare* to scratch, prob. fr. *grafio* stylus, fr. L *graphium*] (1851) : an inscription or drawing made on some public surface (as a rock or wall); *also* : a message or slogan written as or as if as a graffito — **graf·fi·tist** \-'fē-tist\ *n*

usage The plural *graffiti* is sometimes used with a singular verb as a mass noun ⟨the *graffiti* is being covered with fresh paint —*Springfield (Mass.) Union*⟩ ⟨*graffiti* comes in various styles —S. K. Oberbeck⟩ but this use is not yet as well established as the mass-noun use of *data*. Use of *graffiti* as a singular count noun is still quite rare and is not standard.

¹**graft** \'graft\ *n* [ME *graffe, grafte*, fr. MF *grafe*, fr. ML *graphium*, fr. L, stylus, fr. Gk *grapheion*, fr. *graphein* to write — more at CARVE] (14c) **1 a** : a grafted plant **b** : SCION 1 **c** : the point of insertion of a scion upon a stock **2 a** : the act of grafting **b** : something grafted; *specif* : living tissue used in grafting

²**graft** *vt* (14c) **1 a** : to cause (a scion) to unite with a stock; *also* : to unite (plants or scion and stock) to form a graft **b** : to propagate (a plant) by grafting **2 a** : to join or unite as if by grafting **b** : to attach (a chemical unit) to a main molecular chain **3** : to implant (living tissue) surgically ~ *vi* **1** : to become grafted **2** : to perform grafting — **graft·er** *n*

³**graft** *n* [E dial. *graft*, vb., to work, perh. alter. of ¹*grave* (to dig)] (1853) *chiefly Brit* : WORK, LABOR

⁴**graft** [origin unknown] *vt* (1859) **1** : to get (illicit gain) by graft ~ *vi* : to practice graft

⁵**graft** *n* (1865) : the acquisition of gain (as money) in dishonest or questionable ways; *also* : illegal or unfair gain

graft·age \'graf-tij\ *n* (ca. 1895) : the principles and practice of grafting

graft–versus–host *adj* (1972) : relating to or being the bodily condition that results when cells from a tissue or organ transplant mount an immunological attack against the cells or tissues of the host

gra·ham cracker \'gram-, 'grä-əm-\ *n* [*graham flour*] (1882) : a slightly sweet cracker made of whole wheat flour

graham flour *n* [Sylvester *Graham* †1851 Am. dietary reformer] (1834) : whole wheat flour

grail \'grā(ə)l\ *n* [ME *graal*, fr. MF, bowl, grail, fr. ML *gradalis*] **1** *cap* : the cup or platter used according to medieval legend by Christ at the Last Supper and thereafter the object of knightly quests **2** : the object of an extended or difficult quest

¹**grain** \'grān\ *n* [ME, fr. MF, grain cereal grain, fr. L *granum*; partly fr. MF *graine* seed, kermes, fr. L *grana*, pl. of *granum* — more at CORN] (14c) **1 a** (1) *obs* : a single small hard seed (2) : a seed or fruit of a cereal grass : CARYOPSIS **b** : the seeds or fruits of various food plants including the cereal grasses and in commercial and statutory usage other plants (as the soybean) **c** : plants producing grain **2 a** (1) : a small hard particle or crystal (2) : any of the particles produced in a photographic material by its development; *also* : the size of such grains in the aggregate (3) : an individual crystal in a metal **b** : a minute portion or particle **c** : the least amount possible ⟨a ~ of truth⟩ **3 a** : kermes or a scarlet dye made from it **b** : cochineal or a brilliant scarlet dye made from it **c** : a fast dye **d** *archaic* : COLOR, TINT **4 a** : a granulated surface or appearance **b** : the outer or hair side of a skin or hide **5** : a unit of weight based on the weight of a grain of wheat taken as an average of the weight of grains from the middle of the ear — see WEIGHT table **6 a** : the stratification of the wood fibers in a piece of wood **b** : a texture due to constituent particles or fibers ⟨the ~ of a rock⟩ **c** : the direction of threads in cloth **7** : tactile quality **8 a** : natural disposition : TEMPER ⟨against my ~⟩ **b** : a basic or characteristic quality ⟨doctrines . . . very much in the American ~ —R. W. Noland⟩ — **grained** \'grānd\ *adj*

²**grain** *vt* (1530) **1** : INGRAIN **2** : to form into grains : GRANULATE **3** : to paint in imitation of the grain of wood or stone **4** : to feed with grain ~ *vi* : to become granular : GRANULATE — **grain·er** *n*

grain alcohol *n* (1889) : ETHANOL

grain elevator *n* (1852) : a building for elevating, storing, discharging, and sometimes processing grain

grain-field \'grān-ˌfēld\ *n* (ca. 1818) : a field where grain is grown

grain of salt (1647) : a skeptical attitude

grains of paradise (15c) : the pungent seeds of a West African plant (*Aframomum melegueta*) of the ginger family that are used as a spice

grain sorghum *n* (1920) : any of several sorghums cultivated primarily for grain — compare SORGO

grainy \'grā-nē\ *adj* **grain·i·er; -est** (15c) **1** : resembling or having some characteristic of grain : not smooth or fine **2** *of a photograph* : appearing to be composed of grain-like particles — **grain·i·ness** *n*

¹**gram** \'gram\ *n* [obs. Pg (now spelled *grão*), grain, fr. L *granum*] (1702) : any of several leguminous plants (as a chickpea) grown esp. for their seed; *also* : their seeds

²**gram** \'gram\ *n* [F *gramme*, fr. LL *gramma*, a small weight, fr. Gk *grammat-, gramma* letter, writing, a small weight, fr. *graphein* to write — more at CARVE] (1810) **1** : a metric unit of mass equal to ¹/₁₀₀₀ kilogram and nearly equal to the mass of one cubic centimeter of water at its maximum density — see METRIC SYSTEM table **2** : the weight of a gram under standard gravity

³**gram** *n* [by shortening & alter.] (ca. 1934) : GRANDMOTHER

-gram \ˌgram\ *n comb form* [L *-gramma*, fr. Gk, fr. *gramma*] : drawing : writing : record ⟨chronogram⟩ ⟨telegram⟩

grama \'gra-mə\ *n* [Sp, fr. L *gramina*, pl. of *gramen* grass] (1828) : any of several pasture grasses (genus *Bouteloua*) of the western U.S.

gram–atomic weight *n* (1927) : the mass of one mole of an element equal in grams to the atomic weight — called also *gram-atom*

gram calorie *n* (1902) : CALORIE 1a

gram equivalent *n* (ca. 1897) : the quantity of an element, group, or compound that has a mass in grams equal to the equivalent weight

gra·mer·cy \grə-'mər-sē\ *interj* [ME *grand mercy*, fr. MF *grand merci* great thanks] (14c) *archaic* — used to express gratitude or surprise

gram·i·ci·din \ˌgra-mə-'sī-dᵊn\ *n* [*gram*-positive + *-i-* + *-cide* + *-in*] (1940) : any of several toxic polypeptide antibiotics produced by a soil bacterium (*Bacillus brevis*) and used against gram-positive bacteria in local infections

gra·min·e·ous \grə-'mi-nē-əs\ *adj* [L *gramineus*, fr. *gramin-, gramen* grass] (ca. 1658) : of or relating to a grass

gram·i·niv·o·rous \ˌgra-mə-'ni-v(ə-)rəs\ *adj* [L *gramin-, gramen*] (1739) : feeding on grass or the seeds of grass ⟨~ locusts⟩ ⟨~ birds⟩

gram·mar \'gra-mər\ *n* [ME *gramere*, fr. MF *gramaire*, modif. of L *grammatica*, fr. Gk *grammatikē*, fr. fem. of *grammatikos* of letters, fr. *grammat-, gramma* — more at GRAM] (14c) **1 a** : the study of the classes of words, their inflections, and their functions and relations in the sentence **b** : a study of what is to be preferred and what avoided in inflection and syntax **2 a** : the characteristic system of inflections and syntax of a language **b** : a system of rules that defines the grammatical structure of a language **3 a** : a grammar textbook **b** : speech or writing evaluated according to its conformity to grammatical rules **4** : the principles or rules of an art, science, or technique ⟨a ~ of the theater⟩ — **gram·mar·i·an** \grə-'mer-ē-ən, -'mar-\ *n*

grammar school *n* (14c) **1 a** : a secondary school emphasizing Latin and Greek in preparation for college **b** : a British college preparatory school **2** : a school intermediate between primary school and high school **3** : ELEMENTARY SCHOOL

gram·mat·i·cal \grə-'ma-ti-kəl\ *adj* (1530) **1** : of or relating to grammar **2** : conforming to the rules of grammar — **gram·mat·i·cal·i·ty** \-ˌma-tə-'ka-lə-tē\ *n* — **gram·mat·i·cal·ly** \-'ma-ti-k(ə-)lē\ *adv* — **gram·mat·i·cal·ness** \-kəl-nəs\ *n*

grammatical meaning *n* (1769) : the part of meaning that varies from one inflectional form to another (as from *plays* to *played* to *playing*) — compare LEXICAL MEANING

gramme *chiefly Brit var of* ²GRAM

gram molecular weight *n* (ca. 1902) : the mass of one mole of a compound equal in grams to the molecular weight — called also *gram-molecule*

Gram·my \'gra-mē\ *service mark* — used for the annual presentation of a statuette for notable achievement in the recording industry

gram–neg·a·tive \'gram-'ne-gə-tiv\ *adj* (1907) : not holding the purple dye when stained by Gram's stain — used chiefly of bacteria

gram·o·phone \'gra-mə-ˌfōn\ *n* [fr. *Gramophone*, a trademark] (1887) : PHONOGRAPH

gramp \'gramp\ *or* **gramps** \'gram(p)s\ *n, pl* **gramps** [by shortening & alter.] (ca. 1900) : GRANDFATHER

gram–pos·i·tive \'gram-'pä-zə-tiv, -'päz-tiv\ *adj* (1907) : holding the purple dye when stained by Gram's stain — used chiefly of bacteria

gram·pus \'gram-pəs\ *n* [alter. of ME *graspey, grapay*, fr. MF *graspeis*, fr. *gras* fat (fr. L *crassus*) + *peis* fish, fr. L *piscis* — more at CRASS, FISH] (ca. 1529) **1** : a dolphin (*Grampus griseus*) of temperate and tropical seas; *also* : any of various small cetaceans **2** : the giant whip scorpion (*Mastigoproctus giganteus*) of the southern U.S.

Gram's stain \'gramz-\ *or* **Gram stain** \'gram-\ *n* [Hans C. J. *Gram* †1938 Dan. physician] (1903) **1** : a method for the differential staining of bacteria by treatment with a watery solution of iodine and the iodide of potassium after staining with a triphenylmethane dye (as crystal violet) — called also *Gram's method* **2** : the chemicals used in Gram's stain

gram–vari·able \'gram-'ver-ē-ə-bəl, -'var-\ *adj* (1956) : staining irregularly or inconsistently by Gram's stain

grana *pl of* GRANUM

gran·a·dil·la \ˌgran-ə-'di-lə, -'dē-(y)ə\ *n* [Sp, dim. of *granada* pomegranate, fr. LL *granata* — more at GRENADE] (1613) : the oblong fruit of various passionflowers (esp. *Passiflora quadrangularis* of tropical America) used as a dessert; *also* : a plant that produces granadillas

gra·na·ry \'grā-nə-rē, 'gra-\ *n, pl* **-ries** [L *granarium*, fr. *granum* grain] (1530) **1 a** : a storehouse for threshed grain **b** : a region producing grain in abundance **2** : a chief source or storehouse

¹**grand** \'grand\ *adj* [MF, large, great, grand, fr. L *grandis*] (1584) **1 a** : having more importance than others : FOREMOST **b** : having higher rank than others bearing the same general designation ⟨the ~ champion⟩ **2 a** : INCLUSIVE, COMPREHENSIVE ⟨the ~ total of all money paid out⟩ **b** : DEFINITIVE, INCONTROVERTIBLE ⟨~ example⟩ **3** : CHIEF, PRINCIPAL **4** : large and striking in size, scope, extent, or conception ⟨~ design⟩ **5 a** : LAVISH, SUMPTUOUS ⟨a ~ celebration⟩ **b** : marked by a regal form and dignity **c** : fine or imposing in appearance or impression **d** : LOFTY, SUBLIME ⟨writing in the ~ style⟩ **6 a** : pretending to social superiority : SUPERCILIOUS **b** : intended to impress ⟨a person of ~ gestures⟩ **7** : very good : WONDERFUL ⟨a ~ time⟩ — **grand·ly** \'gran-(d)lē\ *adv* — **grand·ness** \'gran(d)-nəs\ *n*

syn GRAND, MAGNIFICENT, IMPOSING, STATELY, MAJESTIC, GRANDIOSE mean large and impressive. GRAND adds to greatness of size the implications of handsomeness and dignity ⟨a *grand* staircase⟩. MAGNIFICENT implies an impressive largeness proportionate to scale without sacrifice of dignity or good taste ⟨*magnificent* paintings⟩. IMPOSING implies great size and dignity but esp. stresses impressiveness ⟨an *imposing* edifice⟩. STATELY may suggest poised dignity, erectness of bearing, handsomeness of proportions, ceremonious deliberation of movement ⟨the *stately* procession⟩. MAJESTIC combines the implications of IMPOSING and STATELY and usu. adds a suggestion of solemn grandeur ⟨a *majestic* waterfall⟩. GRANDIOSE implies a size or scope exceeding ordinary experience ⟨*grandiose* hydroelectric projects⟩ but is most commonly applied derogatorily to inflated pretension or absurd exaggeration ⟨*grandiose* schemes⟩.

²**grand** *n* (1840) **1** : GRAND PIANO **2** *slang* : a thousand dollars

gran–dam \'gran-ˌdam, -dəm\ *n* [ME *graundam*, fr. AF *graund dame*, lit., great lady] (13c) *or* **gran–dame** \-ˌdām\ **1 a** : GRANDMOTHER **b** : an old woman **2** *or* **grand–dam** \-ˌdam, -dəm\ : a dam's or sire's dam — used of an animal

grand·aunt \'gran-ˌdant, -ˌdänt\ *n* (1826) : the aunt of one's father or mother — called also *great-aunt*

grand·ba·by \'gran-ˌdā-bē\ *n* (1916) : an infant grandchild

grand·child \-ˌchīld\ *n* (1587) : the child of one's son or daughter

grand·dad *or* **gran·dad** \'gran-ˌdad\ *n* (1782) : GRANDFATHER

grand·dad·dy \-ˌda-dē\ *also* **gran·dad·dy** \-ˌda-dē\ *n* (1769) **1** : GRANDFATHER **2** : one that is the first, earliest, or most venerable of its kind

grand·daugh·ter \-ˌdȯ-tər\ *n* (1611) : the daughter of one's son or daughter

grand duchess *n* (ca. 1757) **1** : a woman who rules a grand duchy in her own right **2** : the wife or widow of a grand duke
grand duchy *n* (1835) : the territory or dominion of a grand duke or grand duchess
grand duke *n* (ca. 1693) **1** : the sovereign duke of any of various European states **2** : a male descendant of a Russian czar in the male line
grande dame \'grän-'däm, grä°d-dám\ *n*, *pl* **grandes dames** \-'däm(z), -dám(z)\ *also* **grande dames** *same*\ [F, lit., great lady] (1775) : a usu. elderly woman of great prestige or ability
gran·dee \gran-'dē\ *n* [Sp *grande*, fr. *grande*, adj., large, great, fr. L *grandis*] (1598) : a man of elevated rank or station; *esp* : a Spanish or Portuguese nobleman of the first rank
gran·deur \'gran-jər, -ju̇r, -,d(y)u̇r, -d(y)ər\ *n* [ME, fr. MF, fr. *grand*] (1600) **1** : the quality or state of being grand : MAGNIFICENCE ⟨the glory that was Greece and the ~ that was Rome —E. A. Poe⟩ **2** : an instance or example of grandeur
¹grand·fa·ther \'grand(d)-,fä-t͟hər, -'fä-\ *n* (15c) : the father of one's father or mother; *also* : ANCESTOR 1a — **grand·fa·ther·ly** \-lē\ *adj*
²grandfather *vt* (1972) : to permit to continue under a grandfather clause
grandfather clause *n* (1900) : a clause creating an exemption based on circumstances previously existing; *esp* : a provision in several southern state constitutions designed to enfranchise poor whites and disfranchise Negroes by waiving high voting requirements for descendants of men voting before 1867
grandfather clock *n* [fr. the song *My Grandfather's Clock* (1876) by Henry C. Work †1884 Am. songwriter] (1909) : a tall pendulum clock that stands on the floor — called also *grandfather, grandfather's clock*
grand finale *n* (1800) : a climactic finale (as of an opera)
grand fir *n* (1897) : a lofty fir tree (*Abies grandis*) of the northwestern Pacific coastal region of No. America with cylindrical greenish cones and soft wood
Grand Gui·gnol \,grä°-gēn-'yȯl, -'yȯl\ *n* [*Le Grand Guignol*, small theater in Montmartre, Paris, specializing in such performances] (1908) : dramatic entertainment featuring the gruesome or horrible — **Grand Guignol** *adj*
gran·di·flo·ra \,gran-də-'flȯr-ə, -'flȯr-\ *n* [NL, fr. L *grandis* great + *flor-, flos* flower — more at BLOW] (1944) : a bush rose derived from crosses of floribunda and hybrid tea roses and characterized by production of blooms both singly and in clusters on the same plant
gran·dil·o·quence \gran-'di-lə-kwən(t)s\ *n* [prob. fr. MF, fr. L *grandiloquus* using lofty language, fr. *grandis* + *loqui* to speak] (1589) : a lofty, extravagantly colorful, pompous, or bombastic style, manner, or quality esp. in language — **gran·dil·o·quent** \-kwənt\ *adj* — **gran·dil·o·quent·ly** *adv*
gran·di·ose \'gran-dē-,ōs, ,gran-dē-'\ *adj* [F, fr. It *grandioso*, fr. *grande* great, fr. L *grandis*] (1840) **1** : characterized by affectation of grandeur or splendor or by absurd exaggeration **2** : impressive because of uncommon largeness, scope, effect, or grandeur *syn* see GRAND — **gran·di·ose·ly** *adv* — **gran·di·ose·ness** *n* — **gran·di·os·i·ty** \,gran-dē-'ä-sə-tē\ *n*
gran·di·o·so \,grän-dē-'ō-(,)sō, ,gran-, -(,)zō\ *adv or adj* [It] (ca. 1859) : in a broad and noble style — used as a direction in music
grand jury *n* (15c) : a jury that examines accusations against persons charged with crime and if the evidence warrants makes formal charges on which the accused persons are later tried — **grand juror** *n*
grand·kid \'gran(d)-,kid\ *n* (1927) : GRANDCHILD
Grand Lama *n* (1807) : DALAI LAMA
grand larceny *n* (1828) : larceny of property of a value greater than that fixed as constituting petit larceny
grand·ma \'gran(d)-,mä, -,mȯ; 'gra-,mä, -,mȯ\ *n* (1867) : GRANDMOTHER
grand mal \'grän(d)-,mäl, 'grä°-,mäl, -,mal; 'gran(d)-,mal\ *n* [F, lit., great illness] (1897) : severe epilepsy
grand manner *n* (1775) : an elevated or grand style (as in music or literature)
grand march *n* (1898) : an opening ceremony at a ball that consists of a march participated in by all the guests
grand marshal *n* (1951) : a person honored as the ceremonial marshal of a parade
grand master *n* (1724) **1** : the chief officer of a principal lodge in various fraternal orders (as Freemasonry) **2** : an expert player (as of chess) who has consistently scored high in international competition
grand·moth·er \'gran(d)-,mə-t͟hər\ *n* (15c) : the mother of one's father or mother; *also* : a female ancestor — **grand·moth·er·ly** \-lē\ *adj*
grand·neph·ew \'gran(d)-'nef-(,)yü, *chiefly Brit* -'nev-\ *n* (ca. 1639) : a grandson of one's brother or sister
grand·niece \-'nēs\ *n* (ca. 1830) : a granddaughter of one's brother or sister
grand old man *n* (1860) : a venerated practitioner or former practitioner of an art, profession, or sport ⟨the *grand old man* of jazz⟩
grand opera *n* (1803) : opera in which the plot is serious or tragic and the entire text is set to music
grand·pa \'gran(d)-,pä, -,pȯ; 'gram-,pä, -,pȯ\ *n* (ca. 1889) : GRANDFATHER
grand·par·ent \'gran(d)-,par-ənt, -,per-\ *n* (1830) : a parent of one's father or mother — **grand·pa·ren·tal** \,gran(d)-pə-'ren-t°l\ *adj* — **grand·par·ent·hood** \'gran(d)-'par-ent-,hu̇d, -'per-\ *n*
grand piano *n* (1834) : a piano with horizontal frame and strings — compare UPRIGHT PIANO
grand prix \'grä°-'prē\ *n*, *pl* **grand prix** *also* **grands prix** \-'prē(z)\ *often cap* G&P [F *Grand Prix de Paris*, an international horse race established 1863, lit., grand prize of Paris] (1863) **1** : the highest level of international equestrian competition; *also* : a contest at this level **2** : one of a series of international formula car races
grand·sire \'gran(d)-,sīr\ *n* [ME] (14c) **1 or grand·sir** \'gran(t)-sər\ *dial* : GRANDFATHER **2** *archaic* : FOREFATHER **3** *archaic* : an aged man **4** : a dam's or sire's sire — used of animal
grand slam *n* (1814) **1** : the winning of all the tricks in one hand of a card game (as bridge) **2** : a clean sweep or total success; *specif* : the winning of all the major or specified tournaments on a tour ⟨twice won the tennis *grand slam*⟩ **3** : a home run made with the bases loaded — **grand·slam** *adj*
grand·son \'gran(d)-,sən\ *n* (1586) : the son of one's son or daughter

¹grand·stand \-,stand\ *n* (1834) **1** : a usu. roofed stand for spectators at a racecourse or stadium **2** : AUDIENCE
²grandstand *adj* (1893) : done for show or to impress onlookers ⟨a ~ play⟩
³grandstand *vi* (ca. 1917) : to play or act so as to impress onlookers — **grand·stand·er** *n*
grand theft *n* (ca. 1930) : GRAND LARCENY
grand tour *n* (1670) **1** : an extended tour of the Continent that was formerly a usual part of the education of young British gentlemen **2** : an extensive and usu. educational tour
grand touring car *n* (1970) : a usu. 2-passenger coupe
grand·un·cle \'gran-'dən-kəl\ *n* (15c) : an uncle of one's father or mother
grand unified theory *n* (1978) : any of several theories that seek to unite in a single mathematical framework the electromagnetic and weak forces with the strong force or with the strong force and gravity — called also *grand unification theory*

grand touring car

grange \'grānj\ *n* [ME, fr. MF, fr. ML *granica*, fr. L *granum* grain] (14c) **1** *archaic* : GRANARY, BARN **2** : FARM; *esp* : a farmhouse with outbuildings **3** *cap* : one of the lodges of a national fraternal association orig. made up of farmers; *also* : the association itself
grang·er \'grān-jər\ *n* (1873) **1** *cap* : a member of a Grange **2** *chiefly West* : FARMER, HOMESTEADER
grang·er·ism \'grān-jə-,ri-zəm\ *n* (1875) : the policy or methods of the grangers
gra·ni·ta \grə-'nē-tə\ *n* [It, fr. fem. of *granito*, pp. of *granire*] (1869) : a coarse-textured ice confection typically made from fruit
gran·ite \'gra-nət\ *n* [It *granito*, fr. pp. of *granire* to granulate, fr. *grano* grain, fr. L *granum*] (1646) **1** : a very hard natural igneous rock formation of visibly crystalline texture formed essentially of quartz and orthoclase or microcline and used esp. for building and for monuments **2** : unyielding firmness or endurance ⟨the cold ~ of Puritan formalism —V. L. Parrington⟩ — **gra·nit·ic** \-'ni-tik\ *adj* — **gran·it·oid** \'gra-nə-,tȯid\ *adj*
gran·ite·ware \'gra-nət-,war, -,wer\ *n* (1878) : ironware with grayish or bluish mottled enamel
gra·niv·o·rous \grə-'niv-ə-rəs, grā-, -'ni-və-\ *adj* [L *granum* grain] (1646) : feeding on seeds or grain ⟨~ rodents⟩
gran·ny *or* **gran·nie** \'gra-nē\ *n*, *pl* **grannies** [by shortening & alter.] (1663) **1 a** : GRANDMOTHER **b** : a fussy person **2** *chiefly Southern & south Midland* : MIDWIFE
granny dress *n* (1909) : a long loose-fitting dress usu. with high neck and long sleeves
granny glasses *n pl* (1966) : spectacles with usu. small oval, round, or square lenses and metal frames
granny knot *n* (1853) : an insecure knot often made instead of a square knot — see KNOT illustration
Granny Smith \-'smith\ *n* [Maria Ann *Smith* †1870 who cultivated it near Sydney, Australia] (1895) : a tart green apple of Australian origin
grano- *comb form* [G, fr. granit, fr. It *granito*] : granite : granitic ⟨*granodiorite*⟩
grano·di·o·rite \,gra-nō-'dī-ə-,rīt\ *n* (1893) : a granular intrusive quartzose igneous rock intermediate between granite and quartz-containing diorite with plagioclase predominant over orthoclase — **grano·di·o·rit·ic** \-,dī-ə-'ri-tik\ *adj*
gra·no·la \grə-'nō-lə\ *n* [fr. *Granola*, a trademark] (1970) : a mixture typically of rolled oats and various added ingredients (as brown sugar, raisins, coconut, and nuts) that is eaten esp. for breakfast or as a snack
grano·lith·ic \,gra-nə-'li-thik\ *adj* (1881) : relating to or composed of a mixture of crushed granite and cement
grano·phyre \'gran-ə-,fī(-ə)r\ *n* [ISV, fr. *grano-* + F *-phyre* (as in *porphyre* porphyry)] (1882) : a porphyritic igneous rock chiefly of feldspar and quartz with granular groundmass — **grano·phyr·ic** \,gran-ə-'fir-ik\ *adj*
¹grant \'grant\ *vt* [ME, fr. OF *creanter, graanter*, fr. (assumed) VL *credentare*, fr. L *credent-, credens*, prp. of *credere* to believe — more at CREED] (13c) **1 a** : to consent to carry out for a person : allow fulfillment of ⟨~ a request⟩ **b** : to permit as a right, privilege, or favor ⟨luggage allowances ~ed to passengers⟩ **2** : to bestow or transfer formally ⟨~ a scholarship to a student⟩; *specif* : to give the possession or title of by a deed **3 a** : to be willing to concede **b** : to assume to be true ⟨~ing that you are correct, you may find it hard to prove your point⟩ — **grant·able** \'gran-tə-bəl\ *adj* — **grant·er** \-tər\ *n* — **grant·or** \'gran-tər, -,tȯr; gran-'tȯr\ *n*
syn GRANT, CONCEDE, VOUCHSAFE, ACCORD, AWARD mean to give as a favor or a right. GRANT implies giving to a claimant or petitioner something that could be withheld ⟨*granted* them a new hearing⟩. CONCEDE implies yielding something reluctantly in response to a rightful or compelling claim (even her critics *concede* she can be charming). VOUCHSAFE implies granting something as a courtesy or an act of gracious condescension ⟨*vouchsafed* the secret to only a few chosen disciples⟩. ACCORD implies giving to another what is due or proper ⟨*accorded* all the honors befitting a head of state⟩. AWARD implies giving what is deserved or merited usu. after a careful weighing of pertinent factors ⟨*awarded* the company a huge defense contract⟩.
²grant *n* (13c) **1** : the act of granting **2** : something granted; *esp* : a gift (as of land or money) for a particular purpose **3 a** : a transfer of property by deed or writing **b** : the instrument by which such a transfer is made; *also* : the property so transferred **4** : a minor territorial division of Maine, New Hampshire, or Vermont orig. granted by the state to an individual or institution
grant·ee \gran-'tē\ *n* (15c) : one to whom a grant is made

\ə\ abut \°\ kitten, F table \ər\ further \a\ ash \ā\ ace \ä\ mop, mar \au̇\ out \ch\ chin \e\ bet \ē\ easy \g\ go \i\ hit \ī\ ice \j\ job \ŋ\ sing \ō\ go \ȯ\ law \ȯi\ boy \th\ thin \t͟h\ the \ü\ loot \u̇\ foot \y\ yet \zh\ vision \á, k̲, ⁿ, œ, œ̄, ư, ư̄, ᵞ\ see Guide to Pronunciation

grant–in–aid \‚gran-t⁽ə⁾n-'ād\ *n, pl* **grants–in–aid** \‚gran(t)-s⁽ə⁾n-'ād\ (1851) **1** : a grant or subsidy for public funds paid by a central to a local government in aid of a public undertaking **2** : a grant or subsidy to a school or individual for an educational or artistic project
grants-man \'grant⁽s⁾-smən\ *n* (1966) : a specialist in grantsmanship
grants-man-ship \-‚ship\ *n* [*grants* + *-manship*] (1961) : the art of obtaining grants (as for research)
granul- *or* **granuli-** *or* **granulo-** *comb form* [LL *granulum*] : granule ⟨*granulocyte*⟩
gran-u-lar \'gran-yə-lər\ *adj* (1794) : consisting of or appearing to consist of granules : GRAINY — **gran-u-lar-i-ty** \‚gran-yə-'lar-ə-tē\ *n*
gran-u-late \'gran-yə-‚lāt\ *vb* **-lat-ed; -lat-ing** *vt* (1666) : to form or crystallize into grains or granules ∼ *vi* : to form granulations ⟨an open *granulating* wound⟩ — **gran-u-la-tor** \-‚lā-tər\ *n*
gran-u-la-tion \‚gran-yə-'lā-shən\ *n* (1612) **1** : the act or process of granulating : the condition of being granulated **2** : one of the minute red granules of new capillaries formed on the surface of a wound in healing **3** : GRANULE 2
granulation tissue *n* (1873) : tissue made up of granulations that temporarily replaces lost tissue in a wound
gran-ule \'gran-(‚)yü(ə)l\ *n* [LL *granulum*, dim. of L *granum* grain] (1652) **1** : a small particle; *esp* : one of numerous particles forming a larger unit **2** : any of the small short-lived brilliant spots on the sun's photosphere
gran-u-lite \'gran-yə-‚līt\ *n* (1849) : a granular metamorphic rock consisting mainly of feldspar and quartz — **gran-u-lit-ic** \‚gran-yə-'li-tik\ *adj*
gran-u-lo-cyte \'gran-yə-lō-‚sīt\ *n* [ISV] (1906) : a polymorphonuclear white blood cell with granule-containing cytoplasm — **gran-u-lo-cyt-ic** \‚gran-yə-lō-'si-tik\ *adj*
gran-u-lo-cy-to-poi-e-sis \'gran-yə-lō-‚sī-tə-pȯi-'ē-səs\ *n* [NL] (1944) : the formation of blood granulocytes typically in the bone marrow
gran-u-lo-ma \‚gran-yə-'lō-mə\ *n, pl* **-mas** *or* **-ma-ta** \-mə-tə\ (1861) : a mass or nodule of chronically inflamed tissue with granulations that is usu. associated with an infective process — **gran-u-lo-ma-tous** \-mə-təs\ *adj*
granuloma in-gui-na-le \-‚iŋ-gwə-'na-lē, -'nä-, -'nā-\ *n* [NL, lit., inguinal granuloma] (1918) : a sexually transmitted disease characterized by ulceration and formation of granulations on the genitalia and in the groin area and caused by a bacterium (*Calymmatobacterium granulomatis,* syn. *Donovania granulomatis*)
gran-u-lo-sa cell \‚gran-yə-'lō-sə-\ *n* [NL *granulosa,* fr. fem. of *granulosus* granulose] (1936) : one of the estrogen-secreting cells of the epithelial lining of a graafian follicle or its follicular precursor
gran-u-lose \'gran-yə-‚lōs\ *adj* (1852) : GRANULAR; *esp* : having the surface roughened with granules
gran-u-lo-sis \‚gran-yə-'lō-səs\ *n, pl* **-lo-ses** \-‚sēz\ [NL] (1949) : a virus disease of insect larvae distinguished by the presence of minute granular inclusions in infected cells
gra-num \'grā-nəm\ *n, pl* **gra-na** \-nə\ [NL, fr. L, grain — more at CORN] (1894) : one of the lamellar stacks of chlorophyll-containing thylakoids found in plant chloroplasts
grape \'grāp\ *n, often attrib* [ME, fr. OF *crape, grape* hook, grape stalk, bunch of grapes, grape, of Gmc origin; akin to OHG *krāpfo* hook] (14c) **1** : a smooth-skinned juicy greenish white to deep red or purple berry eaten dried or fresh as a fruit or fermented to produce wine **2** : any of numerous woody vines (genus *Vitis* of the family Vitaceae, the grape family) that usu. climb by tendrils, produce clustered fruits that are grapes, and are nearly cosmopolitan in cultivation **3** : GRAPESHOT — **grape-like** \-‚līk\ *adj*
grape-fruit \'grāp-‚früt\ *n* (1814) **1** *pl* **grapefruit** *or* **grapefruits** : a large citrus fruit with a bitter yellow rind and inner skin and a highly flavored somewhat acid juicy pulp **2** : a small roundheaded tree (*Citrus paradisi*) that produces grapefruit
grape hyacinth *n* (1733) : any of several small bulbous spring-flowering herbs (genus *Muscari*) of the lily family with racemes of usu. blue flowers
grape-shot \'grāp-‚shät\ *n* (1747) : an antipersonnel weapon consisting of a cluster of small iron balls shot from a cannon
grape sugar *n* (1831) : DEXTROSE
grape-vine \'grāp-‚vīn\ *n* (ca. 1736) **1** : GRAPE 2 **2 a** : an informal person-to-person means of circulating information or gossip ⟨heard about the meeting through the ∼⟩ **b** : a secret source of information
¹graph \'graf\ *n* [short for *graphic formula*] (1886) **1** : the collection of all points whose coordinates satisfy a given relation (as a function) **2** : a diagram (as a series of one or more points, lines, line segments, curves, or areas) that represents the variation of a variable in comparison with that of one or more other variables
²graph *vt* (1898) **1** : to represent by a graph **2** : to plot on a graph
³graph *n* [prob. fr. *-graph*] (1933) **1** : a written or printed representation of a basic unit of speech (as a phoneme or syllable); *esp* : GRAPHEME 2 **2** : a single occurrence of a letter of an alphabet in any of its various shapes
-graph \‚graf\ *n comb form* [MF *-graphe,* fr. L *-graphum,* fr. Gk *-graphon,* fr. neut. of *-graphos* written, fr. *graphein* to write — more at CARVE] **1** : something written or drawn ⟨monograph⟩ **2** [F *-graphe,* fr. LL *-graphus*] : instrument for making or transmitting records or images ⟨chronograph⟩
graph-eme \'gra-‚fēm\ *n* (1935) **1** : the set of units of a writing system (as letters and letter combinations) that represent a phoneme **2** : a unit (as a letter) of a writing system — **gra-phe-mic** \gra-'fē-mik\ *adj* — **gra-phe-mi-cal-ly** \-mi-k(ə-)lē\ *adv*
gra-phe-mics \gra-'fē-miks\ *n but sing or pl in constr* (1951) : the study and analysis of a writing system in terms of graphemes
¹graph-ic \'gra-fik\ *also* **graph-i-cal** \-fi-kəl\ *adj* [L *graphicus,* fr. Gk *graphikos,* fr. *graphein*] (1637) **1** : formed by writing, drawing, or engraving **2** *usu* **graphic a** : marked by clear lifelike or vividly realistic description **b** : vividly or plainly shown or described **3 a** : of or relating to the pictorial arts; *also* : PICTORIAL **b** : of, relating to, or involving such reproductive methods as those of engraving, etching, lithography, photography, serigraphy, and woodcut **c** : of or relating to the art of printing **d** : relating or according to graphics **4** *usu* **graphical** : of, relating to, or represented by a graph **5** : of or relating to the written or printed word or the symbols or devices used in writing

or printing to represent sound or convey meaning — **graph-i-cal-ly** \-fi-k(ə-)lē\ *adv* — **graph-ic-ness** \-fik-nəs\ *n*
syn GRAPHIC, VIVID, PICTURESQUE mean giving a clear visual impression in words. GRAPHIC stresses the evoking of a clear lifelike picture ⟨a *graphic* account of combat⟩. VIVID suggests an impressing on the mind of the vigorous aliveness of something ⟨a *vivid* re-creation of an exciting event⟩. PICTURESQUE suggests the presentation of a striking or effective picture composed of features notable for their distinctness and charm ⟨a *picturesque* account of his travels⟩.
²graphic *n* (1944) **1 a** : a product of graphic art **b** *pl* : the graphic media **2 a** : a graphic representation (as a picture, map, or graph) used esp. for illustration **b** *pl but sing or pl in constr* : the art or science of drawing a representation of an object on a two-dimensional surface according to mathematical rules of projection **3** *pl but sing or pl in constr* : the process whereby a computer displays graphics on a CRT and an operator can manipulate them (as with a light pen) **4** : a printed message superimposed on a television picture
-graphic *or* **-graphical** *adj comb form* [LL *-graphicus,* fr. Gk *-graphikos,* fr. *graphikos*] : written or transmitted in a (specified) way ⟨stylographic⟩
graphic arts *n pl* (1882) : the fine and applied arts of representation, decoration, and writing or printing on flat surfaces together with the techniques and crafts associated with them
graphic design *n* (1956) : the art or profession of using design elements (as typography and images) to convey information or create an effect; *also* : a product of this art — **graphic designer** *n*
graphic equalizer *n* (1969) : an electronic device for adjusting the frequency response of an audio system by means of a number of slides each of which controls the response for a band centered on a particular frequency
graphic novel *n* (1978) : a fictional story for adults that is presented in comic-strip format and published as a book
graphics tablet *n* (1980) : a device by which pictorial information is entered into a computer in a manner similar to drawing
graph-ite \'gra-‚fīt\ *n* [G *Graphit,* fr. Gk *graphein* to write] (1796) **1** : a soft black lustrous form of carbon that conducts electricity and is used in lead pencils and electrolytic anodes, as a lubricant, and as a moderator in nuclear reactors **2** : a composite material in which carbon fibers are the reinforcing material — **gra-phit-ic** \gra-'fi-tik\ *adj*
graph-i-tize \'gra-fə-‚tīz, -‚fit-īz\ *vt* **-tized; -tiz-ing** (1899) : to convert into graphite — **graph-i-tiz-able** \-‚tī-zə-bəl, -‚fit-īz-\ *adj* — **graph-i-ti-za-tion** \‚gra-fə-tə-'zā-shən, -‚fī-\ *n*
grapho- *comb form* [F, fr. MF, fr. Gk, fr. *graphē,* fr. *graphein* to write] : writing ⟨grapholect⟩
graph-o-lect \'gra-fə-‚lekt\ *n* [*grapho-* + *-lect* (as in *dialect*)] (1977) : a standard written language
gra-phol-o-gist \gra-'fä-lə-jist\ *n* (1885) : a specialist in graphology
gra-phol-o-gy \-jē\ *n* [F *graphologie,* fr. *grapho-* + *-logie* *-logy*] (1886) : the study of handwriting esp. for the purpose of character analysis — **graph-o-log-i-cal** \‚gra-fə-'lä-ji-kəl\ *adj*
graph paper *n* (1927) : paper ruled for drawing graphs
-graphy *n comb form* [L *-graphia,* fr. Gk, fr. *graphein*] **1** : writing or representation in a (specified) manner or by a (specified) means or of a (specified) object ⟨stenography⟩ ⟨photography⟩ **2** : writing on a (specified) subject or in a (specified) field ⟨hagiography⟩
grap-nel \'grap-n⁽ə⁾l\ *n* [ME *grapenel,* fr. (assumed) MF *grapinel,* dim. of *grapin,* dim. of *grape* hook — more at GRAPE] (14c) : a small anchor with usu. four or five flukes used in dragging or grappling operations and for anchoring a dory or skiff — see ANCHOR illustration
grap-pa \'grä-pə\ *n* [It, fr. It dial., grape stalk, of Gmc origin; akin to OHG *krāpfo* hook] (ca. 1893) : a dry colorless brandy distilled from fermented grape pomace
¹grap-ple \'gra-pəl\ *n* [OF *grappelle,* dim. of *grape* hook — more at GRAPE] (1601) **1 a** : the act or an instance of grappling **b** : a hand-to-hand struggle **c** : a contest for superiority or mastery **2 a** : a bucket similar to a clamshell but usu. having more jaws
²grapple *vb* **grap-pled; grap-pling** \'gra-p(ə-)liŋ\ *vt* (1530) **1** : to seize with or as if with a grapple **2** : to come to grips with : WRESTLE **3** : to bind closely ∼ *vi* **1** : to make a ship fast with a grappling iron **2** : to come to grips **3** : to use a grapple — **grap-pler** \-p(ə-)lər\ *n*
grap-pling *n* (1582) **1** : GRAPNEL **2** : GRAPPLING IRON
grappling iron *n* (1538) : a hooked iron for anchoring a boat, grappling ships to each other, or recovering sunken objects — called also **grappling hook**
grap-to-lite \'grap-tə-‚līt\ *n* [Gk *graptos* painted (fr. *graphein* to write, paint) + E *-lite* — more at CARVE] (1841) : any of numerous extinct fossil colonial Paleozoic animals (group Graptolitoidea) with zooids in cups along a chitinous support
grapy *or* **grap-ey** \'grā-pē\ *adj* **grap-i-er; -est** (1594) : of or relating to grapes; *esp,* of *wine* : having the taste or aroma of fresh grapes — **grap-i-ness** \-nəs\ *n*
¹grasp \'grasp\ *vb* [ME *graspen*] *vi* (14c) : to make the motion of seizing : CLUTCH ∼ *vt* **1** : to take or seize eagerly **2** : to clasp or embrace esp. with the fingers or arms **3** : to lay hold of with the mind : COMPREHEND *syn* see TAKE — **grasp-able** \'gras-pə-bəl\ *adj* — **grasp-er** *n* — **grasp at straws** : to reach for or try anything in desperation — **grasp the nettle** : to act boldly
²grasp *n* (1561) **1 a** : HANDLE **b** : EMBRACE **2** : HOLD, CONTROL **3 a** : the reach of the arms **b** : the power of seizing and holding or attaining **4** : mental hold or comprehension esp. when broad
grasp-ing *adj* (1748) : desiring material possessions urgently and excessively and often to the point of ruthlessness *syn* see COVETOUS — **grasp-ing-ly** \-gras-piŋ-lē\ *adv* — **grasp-ing-ness** *n*
¹grass \'gras\ *n, often attrib* [ME *gras,* fr. OE *græs;* akin to OHG *gras* grass, OE *grōwan* to grow] (bef. 12c) **1** : herbage suitable or used for grazing animals **2** : any of a large family (Gramineae) of monocotyledonous mostly herbaceous plants with jointed stems, slender sheathing leaves, and flowers borne in spikelets of bracts **3** : land (as a lawn or a turf racetrack) covered with growing grass ⟨keep off the ∼⟩ ⟨the horse had never won on ∼⟩ **4** *pl* : leaves or plants of grass **5** : a state or place of retirement ⟨put out to ∼⟩ **6** [short for *grasshopper,* rhyming slang for *copper*]: *slang Brit* : a police informer **7** : electronic noise on a radarscope that takes the form of vertical lines resembling lawn grass **8** : MARIJUANA — **grass-less** \-ləs\ *adj* — **grass-like** \-‚līk\ *adj*

²grass *vt* (ca. 1500) **1** : to feed (livestock) on grass sometimes without grain or other concentrates **2** : to cover with grass; *esp* : to seed to grass ~ *vi* **1** : to produce grass **2** *slang Brit* : INFORM **2** — often used with *on*

grass carp *n* (1885) : an herbivorous cyprinid fish (*Ctenopharyngodon idella*) of Russia and mainland China that has been introduced elsewhere to control aquatic weeds — called also *white amur*

grass cloth *n* (1857) : a lustrous plain textile of usu. loosely woven fibers

grass court *n* (1883) : a tennis court with a grass surface

grass·hop·per \'gras-ˌhä-pər\ *n* (14c) **1** : any of numerous plant-eating orthopterous insects (Acrididae, Tettigoniidae, and some related families) having the hind legs adapted for leaping and sometimes engaging in migratory flights in which whole regions may be stripped of vegetation **2** : a cocktail made with crème de menthe, crème de cacao, and light cream

grass·land \-ˌland\ *n* (1682) **1** : farmland occupied chiefly by forage plants and esp. grasses **2 a** : land on which the natural dominant plant forms are grasses and forbs **b** : an ecological community in which the characteristic plants are grasses

grass·roots \'gras-ˌrüts, -ˌrüts\ *also* **grass-root** \-ˌrüt, -ˌrüt\ *adj* (1907) **1** : BASIC, FUNDAMENTAL ⟨the ~ factor in deciding to buy a house⟩ **2** : being, originating, or operating in or at the grass roots ⟨a ~ organization⟩ ⟨~ political support⟩ **3** : not adapted from or added to an existing facility or operation : totally new ⟨a ~ refinery⟩

grass roots *n pl but sing or pl in constr, often attrib* (1901) **1** : the very foundation or source **2** : the basic level of society or of an organization esp. as viewed from higher or more centralized positions of power

grass tree *n* (1802) : any of a genus (*Xanthorrhoea*) of Australian plants of the lily family with a thick woody trunk bearing a cluster of stiff linear leaves and a terminal spike of small flowers

grass widow *n* (1528) **1** *chiefly dial* **a** : a discarded mistress **b** : a woman who has had an illegitimate child **2 a** : a woman whose husband is temporarily away from her **b** : a woman divorced or separated from her husband

grass widower *n* (1862) **1** : a man divorced or separated from his wife **2** : a man whose wife is temporarily away from him

grassy \'gra-sē\ *adj* **grass·i·er; -est** (15c) **1 a** : covered or abounding with grass ⟨~ lawns⟩ **b** : having a flavor or odor of grass ⟨~ tea⟩ ⟨wine with a ~ bouquet⟩ **2** : resembling grass esp. in color

grat *past of* GREET

¹grate \'grāt\ *vb* **grat·ed; grat·ing** [ME, fr. MF *grater* to scratch, of Gmc origin; akin to OHG *krazzōn* to scratch] *vt* (14c) **1** *archaic* : ABRADE **2** : to reduce into small particles by rubbing on something rough ⟨~ cheese⟩ **3** : FRET, IRRITATE **4 a** : to gnash or grind noisily **b** : to cause to make a rasping sound **c** : to utter in a harsh voice ~ *vi* **1** : to rub or rasp noisily **2** : to cause irritation : JAR ⟨dry, cerebral talk that tends to ~ on the nerves —Hollis Alpert⟩ — **grat·er** *n* — **grat·ing·ly** \'grā-tiŋ-lē\ *adv*

²grate *n* [ME, fr. ML *crata, grata* hurdle, alter. of L *cratis* — more at HURDLE] (14c) **1 a** : a barred frame for cooking over a fire **b** : a frame or bed of iron bars to hold a stove or furnace fire **c** : FIREPLACE **2** : GRATING **3** *obs* : CAGE, PRISON

³grate *vt* **grat·ed; grat·ing** (1547) : to furnish with a grate

grate·ful \'grāt-fəl\ *adj* [obs. *grate* pleasing, thankful, fr. L *gratus* — more at GRACE] (1552) **1 a** : appreciative of benefits received **b** : expressing gratitude **2 a** : affording pleasure or contentment : PLEASING **b** : pleasing by reason of comfort supplied or discomfort alleviated — **grate·ful·ly** \-fə-lē\ *adv* — **grate·ful·ness** *n*

grat·i·cule \'gra-tə-ˌkyü(ə)l\ *n* [F, fr. L *craticula* fine latticework, dim. of *cratis* wickerwork, hurdle] (1914) **1** : RETICLE **2** : the network of lines of latitude and longitude upon which a map is drawn

grat·i·fi·ca·tion \ˌgra-tə-fə-'kā-shən\ *n* (1576) **1** : REWARD, RECOMPENSE; *esp* : GRATUITY **2** : the act of gratifying : the state of being gratified **3** : a source of satisfaction or pleasure

grat·i·fy \'gra-tə-ˌfī\ *vt* **-fied; -fy·ing** [MF *gratifier*, fr. L *gratificari* to show kindness to, fr. *gratus* + *-ificari*, pass. of *-ificare* -ify] (1539) **1** *archaic* : REMUNERATE, REWARD **2** : to be a source of or give pleasure or satisfaction to ⟨it *gratified* him to have his wife wear jewels —Willa Cather⟩ **3** : to give in to : INDULGE, SATISFY ⟨~ a whim⟩

grat·i·fy·ing *adj* (ca. 1611) : giving pleasure or satisfaction : PLEASING — **grat·i·fy·ing·ly** \-ˌfī-iŋ-lē\ *adv*

gra·tin \'gra-tᵊn, 'grä-\ *n* [F, fr. MF, fr. *grater* to scratch] (1806) : a brown crust formed on food that has been cooked au gratin; *also* : a dish so cooked **2** : UPPER CRUST ⟨the ~ of London society⟩

gra·ti·né *or* **gra·ti·née** \ˌgra-tᵊn-'ā, ˌgrä-\ *adj* [F, pp. of *gratiner* to cook au gratin, fr. *gratin*] (1931) : AU GRATIN

gra·ti·née *or* **gra·ti·nee** \ˌgra-tᵊn-'ā, ˌgrä-\ *vt, past & past part* **gra·ti·néed** *or* **gra·ti·need** (1974) : to cook au gratin

grat·ing \'grā-tiŋ\ *n* (1626) **1** : a wooden or metal lattice used to close or floor any of various openings **2** : a partition, covering, or frame of parallel bars or crossbars **3** : a system of close equidistant and parallel lines or bars ruled on a polished surface to produce spectra by diffraction

gra·tis \'gra-təs, 'grä-\ *adv or adj* [ME, fr. L *gratiis, gratis*, fr. abl. pl. of *gratia* favor — more at GRACE] (15c) : without charge or recompense : FREE

grat·i·tude \'gra-tə-ˌtüd, -ˌtyüd\ *n* [ME, fr. MF or ML; MF, fr. ML *gratitudo*, fr. L *gratus* grateful] (1565) : the state of being grateful : THANKFULNESS

gra·tu·itous \grə-'tü-ə-təs, -'tyü-\ *adj* [L *gratuitus*, fr. *gratus*] (1656) **1 a** : given unearned or without recompense **b** : not involving a return benefit, compensation, or consideration **c** : costing nothing : FREE **2** : not called for by the circumstances : UNWARRANTED ⟨~ insolence⟩ ⟨~ assumption⟩ — **gra·tu·itous·ly** *adv* — **gra·tu·itous·ness** *n*

gra·tu·ity \grə-'tü-ə-tē, -'tyü-\ *n, pl* **-ities** (1540) : something given voluntarily or beyond obligation usu. for some service; *esp* : TIP

grat·u·late \'gra-chə-ˌlāt\ *vt* [L *gratulatus*, pp. of *gratulari* — more at CONGRATULATE] (1584) *archaic* : CONGRATULATE — **grat·u·la·tion** \ˌgra-chə-'lā-shən\ *n* — **grat·u·la·to·ry** \'gra-chə-lə-ˌtȯr-ē, -ˌtȯr-\ *adj*

grau·pel \'graù-pəl\ *n* [G] (1889) : granular snow pellets — called also *soft hail*

Grau·stark \'graù-ˌstärk, 'grȯ-\ *n* [*Graustark*, imaginary country in the novel *Graustark* (1901) by George B. McCutcheon †1928 Am. novelist]

(1941) : an imaginary land of high romance; *also* : a highly romantic piece of writing — **Grau·stark·i·an** \graù-'stär-kē-ən, grȯ-\ *adj*

gra·va·men \grə-'vā-mən\ *n, pl* **-va·mens** *or* **-vam·i·na** \-'va-mə-nə\ [LL, burden, fr. L *gravare* to burden, fr. *gravis*] (1647) : the material or significant part of a grievance or complaint

¹grave \'grāv\ *vt* **graved; grav·en** \'grā-vən\ *or* **graved; grav·ing** [ME, fr. OE *grafan*; akin to OHG *graban* to dig, OCS *pogreti* to bury] (bef. 12c) **1** *archaic* : DIG, EXCAVATE **2 a** : to carve or shape with a chisel : SCULPTURE **b** : to carve or cut (as letters or figures) into a hard surface : ENGRAVE **3 a** : to impress or fix (as a thought) deeply

²grave *n* [ME, fr. OE *græf*; akin to OHG *grab* grave, OE *grafan* to dig] (bef. 12c) **1** : an excavation for burial of a body; *broadly* : a burial place **2** : DEATH 1, 4

³grave *vt* **graved; grav·ing** [ME *graven*] (15c) : to clean and pay with pitch ⟨~ a ship's bottom⟩

⁴grave \'grāv, *in sense 5 often* 'gräv\ *adj* **grav·er; grav·est** [MF, fr. L *gravis* heavy, grave — more at GRIEVE] (1539) **1 a** *obs* : AUTHORITATIVE, WEIGHTY **b** : meriting serious consideration : IMPORTANT ⟨~ problems⟩ **c** : likely to produce great harm or danger ⟨a ~ mistake⟩ **d** : significantly serious : CONSIDERABLE, GREAT ⟨~ importance⟩ **2** : having a serious and dignified quality or demeanor ⟨a ~ and thoughtful look⟩ **3** : drab in color : SOMBER **4** : low-pitched in sound **5 a** *of an accent mark* : having the form ` **b** : marked with a grave accent ` **c** : of the variety indicated by a grave accent *syn* see SERIOUS — **grave·ly** *adv* — **grave·ness** *n*

⁵grave \'grāv, 'grav\ *n* (1609) : a grave accent ` used to show that a vowel is pronounced with a fall of pitch (as in ancient Greek), that a vowel has a certain quality (as è in French), that a final e is stressed and close and that a final o is stressed and low (as in Italian), that a syllable has a degree of stress between maximum and minimum (as in phonetic transcription), or that the e of the English ending -ed is to be pronounced (as in "this cursèd day")

⁶gra·ve \'grä-(ˌ)vā\ *adv or adj* [It, lit., grave, fr. L *gravis*] (1683) : slowly and solemnly — used as a direction in music

¹grav·el \'gra-vəl\ *n* [ME, fr. OF *gravele*, dim. of *grave, greve* pebbly ground, beach] (13c) **1** *obs* : SAND **2 a** : loose rounded fragments of rock **b** : a stratum or deposit of gravel; *also* : a surface covered with gravel ⟨a ~ road⟩ **3** : a deposit of small calculous concretions in the kidneys and urinary bladder

²gravel *vt* **-eled** *or* **-elled; -el·ing** *or* **-el·ling** \'grav-liŋ, 'gra-və-\ (1543) **1** : to cover or spread with gravel **2 a** : PERPLEX, CONFOUND **b** : IRRITATE, NETTLE

³gravel *adj* (1939) : GRAVELLY 2 — used of the human voice

grav·el–blind \'gra-vəl-ˌblīnd\ *adj* [suggested by *sand-blind*] (1596) : having very weak vision

grave·less \'grāv-ləs\ *adj* (1606) **1** : not buried ⟨these ~ bones⟩ **2** : not requiring graves : DEATHLESS ⟨the ~ home of the blessed⟩

grav·el·ly \'grav-lē, 'gra-və-\ *adj* (14c) **1** : of, containing, or covered with gravel **2** : having a rough or grating sound ⟨a ~ voice⟩

graven image *n* [*graven*, pp. of ¹*grave*] (14c) : an object of worship carved usu. from wood or stone : IDOL

grav·er \'grā-vər\ *n* [ME] (13c) **1** : SCULPTOR, ENGRAVER **2** : any of various cutting or shaving tools used in graving or in hand metalturning

Graves' disease \'grāvz-\ *n* [Robert J. *Graves* †1853 Irish physician] (1868) : a common form of hyperthyroidism characterized by goiter and often a slight protrusion of the eyeballs

grave·side \'grāv-ˌsīd\ *n* (1838) : the area beside a grave ⟨mourners at ~⟩

grave·stone \'grāv-ˌstōn\ *n* (14c) : a burial monument

grave·yard \-ˌyärd\ *n* (1773) **1** : CEMETERY **2** : something resembling a graveyard ⟨an automobile ~⟩

graveyard shift *n* (1908) : a work shift beginning late at night (as 11 o'clock); *also* : the workers on such a shift

gravi- *comb form* [MF, fr. L, fr. *gravis*] : weight ⟨*gravi*metric⟩

grav·id \'gra-vəd\ *adj* [L *gravidus*, fr. *gravis* heavy] (1597) **1** : PREGNANT **2** : distended with or full of eggs — **gra·vid·i·ty** \gra-'vi-də-tē\ *n*

grav·i·da \'gra-və-də\ *n, pl* **-i·das** *or* **-i·dae** \-və-ˌdē\ [L, fr. fem. of *gravidus*] (1926) : a pregnant woman — often used with a number to indicate the number of pregnancies a woman has had ⟨a 4-*gravida*⟩

gra·vim·e·ter \gra-'vi-mə-tər, 'gra-və-ˌmē-\ *n* [F *gravimètre*, fr. *gravi-* + *-mètre* -meter] (1932) : a sensitive weighing instrument for measuring variations in the gravitational field of the earth or moon

gravi·met·ric \ˌgra-və-'me-trik\ *adj* (1873) **1** : of or relating to measurement by weight **2** : of or relating to variations in the gravitational field determined by means of a gravimeter — **gravi·met·ri·cal·ly** \-tri-k(ə-)lē\ *adv*

gra·vim·e·try \gra-'vi-mə-trē\ *n* (1858) : the measurement of weight, a gravitational field, or density

graving dock *n* (1840) : DRY DOCK

grav·i·tas \'gra-və-ˌtäs, -ˌtas\ *n* [L] (1924) : high seriousness (as in a person's bearing or in the treatment of a subject)

grav·i·tate \'gra-və-ˌtāt\ *vi* **-tat·ed; -tat·ing** (1692) **1** : to move under the influence of gravitation **2 a** : to move toward something **b** : to be drawn or attracted esp. by natural inclination ⟨youngsters . . . ~ toward a strong leader —Rose Friedman⟩

grav·i·ta·tion \ˌgra-və-'tā-shən\ *n* (ca. 1645) **1** : a force manifested by acceleration toward each other of two free material particles or bodies or of radiant-energy quanta : GRAVITY 3a(2) **2** : the action or process of gravitating — **grav·i·ta·tion·al** \-shnəl, -shə-nᵊl\ *adj* — **grav·i·ta·tion·al·ly** *adv* — **grav·i·ta·tive** \'gra-və-ˌtā-tiv\ *adj*

gravitational lens *n* (1950) : a massive celestial object (as a galaxy) that bends and focuses the light of another more distant object (as a quasar) by gravity and that is usu. detected by the multiple images it forms of the second object

\ə\ abut \ᵊ\ kitten, F table \ər\ further \a\ ash \ā\ ace \ä\ mop, mar \aù\ out \ch\ chin \e\ bet \ē\ easy \g\ go \i\ hit \ī\ ice \j\ job \ŋ\ sing \ō\ go \ȯ\ law \ȯi\ boy \th\ thin \t̲h̲\ the \ü\ loot \ù\ foot \y\ yet \zh\ vision \ä, k̲, ⁿ, œ, œ̄, ɶ, ᵫ, ᵞ\ *see* Guide to Pronunciation

gravitational wave *n* (1906) : a hypothetical wave held to travel at the speed of light and to propagate the gravitational field — called also *gravity wave*

grav·i·ton \'gra-və-,tän\ *n* [ISV *gravity* + *²-on*] (1942) : a hypothetical particle with zero charge and rest mass that is held to be the quantum of the gravitational field

grav·i·ty \'gra-və-tē\ *n, pl* **-ties** *often attrib* [MF or L; MF *gravité*, fr. L *gravitat-, gravitas*, fr. *gravis*] (1509) **1 a** : dignity or sobriety of bearing **b** : IMPORTANCE, SIGNIFICANCE; *esp* : SERIOUSNESS **c** : a serious situation or problem **2** : WEIGHT **3 a** (1) : the gravitational attraction of the mass of the earth, the moon, or a planet for bodies at or near its surface (2) : a fundamental physical force that is responsible for interactions which occur because of mass between particles, between aggregations of matter (as stars and planets), and between particles (as photons) and aggregations of matter, that is 10^{39} times weaker than the strong force, and that extends over infinite distances but is dominant over macroscopic distances esp. between aggregations of matter — called also *gravitation, gravitational force;* compare ELECTROMAGNETISM 2a, STRONG FORCE, WEAK FORCE **b** : ACCELERATION OF GRAVITY **c** : SPECIFIC GRAVITY

grav·lax *or* **grav·laks** \'gräv-,läks\ *n* [Sw *gravlax* or Norw *gravlaks*, fr. *grav* buried + Sw *lax*, Norw *laks* salmon — more at LOX] (1977) : salmon usu. cured with salt, pepper, dill, and aquavit

gra·vure \grə-'vyu̇r, grā-\ *n* [F, fr. *graver* to grave, of Gmc origin; akin to OHG *graban* to dig, engrave — more at GRAVE] (1893) : PHOTOGRAVURE

gra·vy \'grā-vē\ *n, pl* **gravies** [ME *gravey*, fr. MF *gravé*] (14c) **1** : a sauce made from the thickened and seasoned juices of cooked meat **2 a** : something additional or unexpected that is pleasing or valuable ⟨with expenses now paid, future money is pure ~ —K. Crossen⟩ **b** : unearned or illicit gain : *⁵*GRAFT

gravy train *n* (ca. 1927) : a much exploited source of easy money; *also* : GRAVY 2a

¹gray \'grā\ *adj* [ME, fr. OE *grǣg;* akin to OHG *gris, grāo* gray] (bef. 12c) **1 a** : of the color gray **b** : tending toward gray ⟨blue-*gray* eyes⟩ **c** : dull in color **2** : having the hair gray : HOARY **3** : clothed in gray **4 a** : lacking cheer or brightness in mood, outlook, style, or flavor; *also* : DISMAL, GLOOMY ⟨a ~ day⟩ **b** : prosaically ordinary : DULL, UNINTERESTING **5** : having an intermediate and often vaguely defined position, condition, or character ⟨an ethically ~ area⟩ — **gray·ly** *adv* — **gray·ness** *n*

²gray *n* (13c) **1** : something (as an animal, garment, cloth, or spot) of a gray color **2** : any of a series of neutral colors ranging between black and white **3** : one who wears a gray uniform: as **a** : a soldier in the Confederate army during the American Civil War **b** : the Confederate army

³gray *vt* (14c) : to make gray ~ *vi* **1** : to become gray ⟨*~ing* hair⟩ **2** : AGE; *also* : to contain an increasing percentage of older people

gray·beard \'grā-,bird\ *n* (ca. 1580) : an old man

gray birch *n* (1851) **1** : a small birch (*Betula populifolia*) of northeastern No. America that has many lateral branches, grayish white bark, triangular leaves, and soft weak wood and that occurs esp. in old fields reverting to woodland **2** : YELLOW BIRCH

gray eminence *n* [trans. of F *Éminence grise*, nickname of Père Joseph (François Joseph du Tremblay) †1638 Fr. monk and diplomat who was confidant of Cardinal Richelieu, styled *Éminence rouge* (red eminence); fr. the colors of their respective habits] (1941) : a person who exercises power behind the scenes

gray·fish \'grā-,fish\ *n* (1917) : DOGFISH

gray fox *n* (ca. 1679) : a fox (*Urocyon cinereoargenteus*) with coarse gray hair and white underparts that occurs from southern Canada to northern So. America

gray·ish \'grā-ish\ *adj* (1562) **1** : somewhat gray **2** *of a color* : low in saturation

gray·ling \'grā-liŋ\ *n, pl* **grayling** *also* **graylings** (15c) : any of several freshwater salmonoid fishes (genus *Thymallus*) valued as food and sport fishes

gray market *n* (1946) : a market employing irregular but not illegal methods; *esp* : a market that legally circumvents authorized channels of distribution to sell goods at prices lower than those intended by the manufacturer

gray matter *n* (1840) **1** : neural tissue esp. of the brain and spinal cord that contains nerve-cell bodies as well as nerve fibers and has a brownish gray color **2** : BRAINS, INTELLECT

gray squirrel *n* (1674) : a common light gray to black squirrel (*Sciurus carolinensis*) that is native to eastern No. America and has been introduced into England

gray·wacke \'grā-,wak, -,wa-kə\ *n* [partial trans. of G *Grauwacke*] (1811) : a coarse usu. dark gray sandstone or fine-grained conglomerate composed of firmly cemented fragments (as of quartz or feldspar)

gray whale *n* (1860) : a large baleen whale (*Eschrichtius robustus*) of the northern Pacific having short jaws and no dorsal fin

gray wolf *n* (1814) : a large usu. gray Holarctic wolf (*Canis lupus*) now restricted to northern No. America and Asia — called also *timber wolf*

¹graze \'grāz\ *vb* **grazed; graz·ing** [ME *grasen*, fr. OE *grasian*, fr. *græs* grass] *vi* (bef. 12c) **1** : to feed on growing herbage, attached algae, or phytoplankton **2** : to eat small amounts of various foods several times a day ~ *vt* **1 a** : to crop and eat in the field **b** : to feed on the herbage of **2** : to put to graze ⟨*grazed* the cows on the meadow⟩ **b** : to put cattle to graze on **3** : to supply herbage for the grazing of — **graze·able** *or* **graz·able** \'grā-zə-bəl\ *adj* — **graz·er** *n*

²graze *n* (1692) **1** : an act of grazing **2** : herbage for grazing

³graze *vb* **grazed; graz·ing** [perh. fr. *¹graze*] *vt* (1604) **1** : to touch lightly in passing **2** : ABRADE, SCRATCH ⟨*grazed* her knee when she fell⟩ ~ *vi* : to touch or rub against something in passing

⁴graze *n* (1847) : a scraping along a surface or an abrasion made by it; *esp* : a superficial abrasion of the skin

gra·zier \'grā-zhər\ *n* (15c) **1** : a person who grazes cattle; *broadly* : RANCHER **2** *Austral* : a sheep raiser

grazing *n* (1517) : herbage or land for grazing

¹grease \'grēs\ *n* [ME *grese*, fr. OF *craisse, graisse*, fr. (assumed) VL *crassia*, fr. L *crassus* fat] (13c) **1 a** : rendered animal fat **b** : oily matter **c** : a thick lubricant **2** : wool as it comes from the sheep retaining the natural oils or fats — **grease·less** \'grēs-ləs\ *adj* —

grease-proof \'grēs-'prüf\ *adj* — **in the grease** *of wool or fur* : in the natural uncleaned condition

²grease \'grēs, 'grēz\ *vt* **greased; greas·ing** (14c) **1** : to smear or daub with grease **2** : to lubricate with grease **3** : to soil with grease **4** : to hasten the process or progress of; *also* : FACILITATE — **grease the hand of** *or* **grease the palm of** : BRIBE

grease·ball \'grēs-,bȯl\ *n* (ca. 1922) : a person of Hispanic or Mediterranean descent — usu. used disparagingly

grease monkey *n* (1928) : MECHANIC

grease·paint \'grēs-,pānt\ *n* (1886) **1** : a melted tallow or grease used in theater makeup **2** : theater makeup

grease pencil *n* (1944) : a pencil in which the marking substance is pigment and grease

greaseproof paper *n* (1900) *Brit* : a heavy stiff waxed paper — called also *greaseproof*

greas·er \'grē-zər, -sər\ *n* [*¹grease*] (1641) **1** : one that greases **2 a** : a native or inhabitant of Latin America or a Mediterranean land; *esp* : MEXICAN — usu. used disparagingly **3** : an aggressive swaggering young white male usu. of working-class background

grease·wood \'grēs-,wu̇d\ *n* (1838) : a low stiff shrub (*Sarcobatus vermiculatus*) of the goosefoot family common in alkaline soils in the western U.S.; *also* : any of various related or similar shrubs

greasy \'grē-sē, -zē\ *adj* **greas·i·er; -est** (1514) **1 a** : smeared or soiled with grease ⟨~ clothes⟩ **b** : oily in appearance, texture, or manner ⟨his ~ smile —Jack London⟩ **c** : SLIPPERY **2** : containing an unusual amount of grease ⟨~ food⟩ — **greas·i·ly** \-sə-lē, -zə-\ *adv* — **greas·i·ness** \-sē-nəs, -zē-\ *n*

greasy spoon *n* (ca. 1925) : a dingy small cheap restaurant

¹great \'grāt, *Southern also* 'gre(ə)t\ *adj* [ME *grete*, fr. OE *grēat;* akin to OHG *grōz* large] (bef. 12c) **1 a** : notably large in size : HUGE **b** : of a kind characterized by relative largeness — used in plant and animal names **c** : ELABORATE, AMPLE ⟨~ detail⟩ **2 a** : large in number or measure : NUMEROUS ⟨~ multitudes⟩ **b** : PREDOMINANT ⟨the ~ majority⟩ **3** : remarkable in magnitude, degree, or effectiveness ⟨~ bloodshed⟩ **4** : full of emotion ⟨~ with anger⟩ **5 a** : EMINENT, DISTINGUISHED ⟨a ~ poet⟩ **b** : chief or preeminent over others — often used in titles ⟨Lord *Great* Chamberlain⟩ **c** : ARISTOCRATIC, GRAND ⟨~ ladies⟩ **6** : long continued ⟨a ~ while⟩ **7** : PRINCIPAL, MAIN ⟨a reception in the ~ hall⟩ **8** : more remote in a family relationship by a single generation than a specified relative ⟨*great*-grandfather⟩ **9** : markedly superior in character or quality; *esp* : NOBLE ⟨~ of soul⟩ **10 a** : remarkably skilled ⟨~ at tennis⟩ **b** : marked by enthusiasm : KEEN ⟨~ on science fiction⟩ **11** — used as a generalized term of approval ⟨had a ~ time⟩ ⟨it was just ~⟩ — **great·ness** *n*

²great *adv* (13c) : in a great manner : SUCCESSFULLY, WELL ⟨things are going ~⟩

³great *n, pl* **great** *or* **greats** (13c) : an outstandingly superior or skillful person

great ape *n* (1949) : any of a family (Pongidae) of primates including the gorilla, orangutan, and chimpanzees — called also *pongid*

great auk *n* (ca. 1828) : an extinct large flightless auk (*Pinguinus impennis*) formerly abundant along No. Atlantic coasts

great–aunt *n* (1656) : GRANDAUNT

Great Bear *n* : URSA MAJOR

great blue heron *n* (1835) : a large slaty-blue American heron (*Ardea herodias*) with a crested head

great circle *n* (1594) : a circle formed on the surface of a sphere by the intersection of a plane that passes through the center of the sphere; *specif* : such a circle on the surface of the earth an arc of which connecting two terrestrial points constitutes the shortest distance on the earth's surface between them

great·coat \'grāt-,kōt\ *n* (ca. 1685) : a heavy overcoat

Great Dane *n* (1774) : any of a breed of tall massive powerful smooth-coated dogs

great divide *n* [the *Great Divide*, No. Am. watershed] (1868) : a significant point of division; *esp* : DEATH

great·en \'grā-tᵊn\ *vb* **great·ened; great·en·ing** \'grā-tᵊn-iŋ\ *vt* (1614) : to make greater ~ *vi* : to become greater

great·er *adj, often cap* [compar. of *great*] (1882) : consisting of a central city together with adjacent areas that are naturally or administratively connected with it ⟨*Greater* London⟩

greater yellowlegs *n pl but sing or pl in constr* (ca. 1909) : a common No. American marsh and shorebird (*Tringa melanoleuca*) that is largely gray above and white below with black or dark gray flecks and yellow legs — compare LESSER YELLOWLEGS

greatest common divisor *n* (ca. 1924) : the largest integer or the polynomial of highest degree that is an exact divisor of each of two or more integers or polynomials — called also *greatest common factor*

great group *n* (1960) : a group of soils that is characterized by common characteristics usu. developed under the influence of environmental factors (as vegetation and climate) active over a considerable geographic range and that comprises one or more families of soil — called also *great soil group*

great·heart·ed \'grāt-,här-təd\ *adj* (14c) **1** : characterized by bravery : COURAGEOUS **2** : GENEROUS, MAGNANIMOUS — **great·heart·ed·ly** *adv* — **great·heart·ed·ness** *n*

great horned owl *n* (1812) : a large American owl (*Bubo virginianus*) with conspicuous ear tufts

great laurel *n* (1784) : a large-leaved evergreen rhododendron (*Rhododendron maximum*) of eastern No. America with rosy bell-shaped flowers more or less speckled with green — called also *rosebay rhododendron*

great·ly \'grāt-lē\ *adv* (13c) **1** : to a great extent or degree : very much ⟨contributed ~ to improved relations⟩ ⟨not ~ bothered⟩ **2** : in a great manner : NOBLY, MAGNANIMOUSLY ⟨a man may live ~ in the law —O. W. Holmes †1935⟩

Great Mogul *n* (1588) : the sovereign of the empire founded in India by the Moguls in the 16th century

great–nephew *n* (1581) : GRANDNEPHEW

great–niece *n* (1884) : GRANDNIECE

great octave *n* (ca. 1854) : the musical octave that begins on the second C below middle C — see PITCH illustration

great power *n, often cap G&P* (ca. 1890) : one of the nations that figure most decisively in international affairs : SUPERPOWER

Great Pyr·e·nees \-'pir-ə-ˌnēz\ *n, pl* **Great Pyrenees** (1938) : any of a breed of large heavy-coated white dogs often used to guard livestock
great room *n* (1700) : a large room usu. combining several functions (as of a dining room, living room, and family room)
Great Russian *n* (1854) : RUSSIAN 1b — **Great Russian** *adj*
great seal *n* (15c) : a large seal that constitutes an emblem of sovereignty and is used esp. for the authentication of important documents
great skua *n* (ca. 1954) : a large seabird (*Catharacta skua*) that is related to the jaeger, has dusky plumage and broad rounded wings, breeds chiefly along arctic and antarctic shores, and forages over most cold and temperate seas
great–uncle *n* (1656) : GRANDUNCLE
great vowel shift *n, often cap G&V&S* (1909) : a change in pronunciation of the long vowels of Middle English that began in the 15th century and continued into the 16th century in which the high vowels were diphthongized and the other vowels were raised
great white shark *n* (ca. 1931) : a large mackerel shark (*Carcharodon carcharias*) of warm seas that is bluish when young but becomes whitish with age and is a man-eater — called also *white shark*; see SHARK illustration
great year *n* (ca. 1741) : the period of about 25,800 years required for one complete cycle of the equinoxes around the ecliptic
greave \'grēv\ *n* [ME *greve*, fr. MF] (14c) : armor for the leg below the knee
grebe \'grēb\ *n* [F *grèbe*] (1766) : any of a family (Podicipedidae) of swimming and diving birds closely related to the loons but having lobate toes — compare DABCHICK
Gre·cian \'grē-shən\ *adj* [ME *greciane*, fr. L *Graecia* Greece] (15c) : GREEK — **Grecian** *n* — **gre·cian·ize** \-shə-ˌnīz\ *vt, often cap*
Gre·cism \'grē-ˌsi-zəm\ *n* (1570) 1 : a Greek idiom 2 : a quality or style imitative of Greek art or culture
gre·cize \-ˌsīz\ *vt* **gre·cized; gre·ciz·ing** *often cap* (1692) : to make Greek or Hellenistic in character
Gre·co- \'gre-kō, 'grē-\ *or* **Grae·co-** \'gre-kō\ *comb form* [L *Graeco-*, fr. *Graecus*] 1 : Greece : Greeks ⟨*Grecophile*⟩ 2 : Greek and ⟨*Graeco-Roman*⟩
¹gree \'grē\ *n* [ME, fr. MF *grē* step, degree, fr. L *gradus* — more at GRADE] (14c) *Scot* : MASTERY, SUPERIORITY
²gree *vb* **greed; gree·ing** [ME *green*, short for *agreen*] (14c) *dial* : AGREE
greed \'grēd\ *n* [back-formation fr. *greedy*] (1609) : excessive or reprehensible acquisitiveness : AVARICE
greedy \'grē-dē\ *adj* **greed·i·er; -est** [ME *gredy*, fr. OE *grǣdig*; akin to OHG *grātac* greedy] (bef. 12c) 1 : having a strong desire for food or drink 2 : marked by greed 3 : EAGER, KEEN ⟨elated and ~ for the future —Frances G. Patton⟩ *syn* see COVETOUS — **greed·i·ly** \'grē-dᵊl-ē\ *adv* — **greed·i·ness** \'grē-dē-nəs\ *n*
¹Greek \'grēk\ *n* [ME *Greke*, fr. OE *Grēca*, fr. L *Graecus*, fr. Gk *Graikos*] (bef. 12c) 1 **a** : a native or inhabitant of ancient or modern Greece **b** : a person of Greek descent 2 **a** : the language used by the Greeks from prehistoric times to the present constituting a branch of Indo-European — see INDO-EUROPEAN LANGUAGES table **b** : ancient Greek as used from the time of the earliest records to the end of the 2d century A.D. — see INDO-EUROPEAN LANGUAGES table **c** *often not cap* [trans. of L *Graecum* (in the medieval phrase *Graecum est; non potest legi* It is Greek; it cannot be read)] : something unintelligible (it's ~ to me⟩ 3 : a member of a Greek-letter fraternity or sorority
²Greek *adj* (14c) 1 : of, relating to, or characteristic of Greece, the Greeks, or Greek ⟨~ architecture⟩ 2 **a** : EASTERN ORTHODOX **b** : of or relating to an Eastern church using the Byzantine rite in Greek **c** : of or relating to the established Orthodox church of Greece
Greek Catholic *n* (1909) 1 : a member of an Eastern church 2 : a member of an Eastern rite of the Roman Catholic Church
Greek cross *n* (1725) : a cross having an upright and a transverse shaft equal in length and intersecting at their middles — see CROSS illustration
Greek fire *n* (ca. 1823) : an incendiary composition used in warfare by the Byzantine Greeks that is said to have burst into flame on wetting
Greek·less \'grēk-ləs\ *adj* (1891) : not proficient in Greek
Greek Orthodox *adj* (ca. 1900) : EASTERN ORTHODOX; *specif* : GREEK 2c
Greek Revival *n* (1918) 1 : a style of architecture in the first half of the 19th century marked by the use or imitation of Greek orders 2 : a style of decoration (as of furniture) using or imitating the decorative motifs of ancient Greece
¹green \'grēn\ *adj* [ME *grene*, fr. OE *grēne*; akin to OE *grōwan* to grow] (bef. 12c) 1 : of the color green 2 **a** : covered by green growth or foliage ⟨~ fields⟩ **b** *of winter* : MILD, CLEMENT **c** : consisting of green plants and usu. edible herbage ⟨a ~ salad⟩ 3 : pleasantly alluring 4 : YOUTHFUL, VIGOROUS 5 : not ripened or matured : IMMATURE ⟨~ apples⟩ ⟨tender ~ grasses⟩ 6 : FRESH, NEW 7 **a** : marked by a pale, sickly, or nauseated appearance **b** : ENVIOUS 1 — used esp. in the phrase *green with envy* 8 **a** : not fully processed or treated: as (1) : not aged ⟨~ liquor⟩ (2) : not dressed or tanned ⟨~ hides⟩ (3) : freshly sawed : UNSEASONED **b** : not in condition for a particular use 9 **a** : deficient in training, knowledge, or experience **b** : deficient in sophistication and savoir faire : NAIVE **c** : not fully qualified for or experienced in a particular function ⟨~ horse⟩ 10 **a** *often cap* : relating to or being an environmentalist political movement **b** : concerned with or supporting environmentalism — **green·ish** \'grē-nish\ *adj* — **green·ish·ness** *n* — **green·ly** *adv* — **green·ness** \'grē(n)-nəs\ *n* — **green around the gills** : pale or sickly in appearance
²green *vi* (bef. 12c) : to become green ~ *vt* 1 : to make green 2 : REJUVENATE, REVITALIZE
³green *n* (13c) 1 : a color whose hue is somewhat less yellow than that of growing fresh grass or of the emerald or is that of the part of the spectrum lying between blue and yellow 2 : something of a green color 3 : green vegetation: as **a** *pl* : leafy parts of plants for use as decoration **b** *pl* (1) : leafy herbs (as spinach, dandelions, Swiss chard) that are cooked as a vegetable : POTHERBS (2) : GREEN VEGETABLES 4 : a grassy plain or plot: as **a** : a common or park in the center of a town or village **b** : PUTTING GREEN 5 : MONEY; *esp* : GREENBACKS 6 *often cap* : ENVIRONMENTALIST; *esp* : a member of an environmentalist political party — **greeny** \'grē-nē\ *adj*

green alga *n* (1903) : any of a division (Chlorophyta) of green-colored algae that have chloroplasts and occur esp. in freshwater
green·back \'grēn-ˌbak\ *n* (1862) : a legal-tender note issued by the U.S. government
green·back·er \-ˌba-kər\ *n* (1876) 1 *cap* : a member of a post-Civil War American political party opposing reduction in the amount of paper money in circulation 2 : one who advocates a paper currency backed only by the U.S. government — **green·back·ism** \-ˌki-zəm\ *n*
green bean *n* (1847) : a kidney bean that is used as a snap bean when the pods are colored green
green·belt \'grēn-ˌbelt\ *n* (1932) : a belt of parkways, parks, or farmlands that encircles a community
Green Beret *n* [fr. the beret worn by Special Forces soldiers] (1962) : a member of the U.S. Army Special Forces
green·bri·er \-ˌbrī(-ə)r\ *n* (ca. 1785) : any of a genus (*Smilax*) of woody or herbaceous vines of the lily family; *esp* : a prickly vine (*S. rotundifolia*) of the eastern U.S. with umbels of small greenish flowers
green·bug \-ˌbəg\ *n* (1712) : a green aphid (*Schizaphis graminum*) very destructive to small grains
green card *n* [fr. the fact that it was formerly colored green] (1969) : an identity card attesting the permanent resident status of an alien in the U.S. — **green–carder** *n*
green corn *n* (1645) : the young tender ears of Indian corn
green dragon *n* (ca. 1818) : an American arum (*Arisaema dracontium*) with digitate leaves, slender green spathe, and elongated spadix
green·ery \'grēn-rē, 'grē-nər-ē\ *n, pl* **-er·ies** (1797) 1 : green foliage or plants 2 : GREEN 3a
green–eyed \'grē-ˌnīd\ *adj* (1596) : JEALOUS
green–eyed monster *n* (1604) : JEALOUSY
green·finch \'grēn-ˌfinch\ *n* (15c) : a very common European finch (*Carduelis chloris*) having olive-green and yellow plumage
green fingers *n pl* (1934) : GREEN THUMB
green flash *n* (1912) : a momentary green appearance of the uppermost part of the sun's disk at sunrise or sunset that results from atmospheric refraction
green·fly \'grēn-ˌflī\ *n* (ca. 1750) *Brit* : APHID; *esp* : GREEN PEACH APHID
green·gage \-ˌgāj\ *n* [*green* + Sir William *Gage* †1820 Eng. botanist] (1724) : any of several rather small rounded greenish or greenish yellow cultivated plums
green gland *n* (ca. 1890) : one of a pair of large green glands in some crustaceans (as crayfishes) that have an excretory function and open at the bases of the larger antennae
green·gro·cer \'grēn-ˌgrō-sər, -shər\ *n* (1723) *chiefly Brit* : a retailer of fresh vegetables and fruit — **green·gro·cery** \-ˌgrō-sə-rē, -ˌgrōsh-rē\ *n*
green·head \'grēn-ˌhed\ *n* (1837) : any of several green-eyed horseflies (as *Tabanus nigrovittatus*)
green·heart \-ˌhärt\ *n* (1756) : a tropical So. American evergreen tree (*Ocotea rodiaei* syn. *Nectandra rodiaei*) of the laurel family with a hard greenish wood; *also* : its wood
green·horn \-ˌhȯrn\ *n* [obs. *greenhorn* (animal with young horns)] (1682) 1 : an inexperienced or unsophisticated person 2 : a newcomer (as to a country) unacquainted with local manners and customs
¹green·house \-ˌhau̇s\ *n* (1664) 1 : a structure enclosed (as by glass) and used for the cultivation or protection of tender plants 2 : a clear plastic shell (as a canopy) covering a section of an airplane; *also* : a compartment (as for a bombardier) enclosed by such a shell
²greenhouse *adj* (1969) : of, relating to, or caused by the greenhouse effect ⟨~ warming⟩ ⟨~ gas⟩
greenhouse effect *n* (1937) : warming of the surface and lower atmosphere of a planet (as the earth or Venus) that is caused by conversion of solar radiation into heat in a process involving selective transmission of short wave solar radiation by the atmosphere, its absorption by the planet's surface, and reradiation as infrared which is absorbed and partly reradiated back to the surface by atmospheric gases
green·ing \'grē-niŋ\ *n* (ca. 1660) : any of several green-skinned apples
green·keep·er \'grēn-ˌkē-pər\ *or* **greens·keep·er** \'grēnz-\ *n* (ca. 1730) : a person responsible for the care and upkeep of a golf course
green·let \'grēn-lət\ *n* (1831) : VIREO
green light *n* [fr. the green traffic light which signals permission to proceed] (1937) : authority or permission to proceed
green·ling \'grēn-liŋ\ *n* (ca. 1898) : any of several food fishes (family Hexagrammidae) of the rocky coasts of the northern Pacific; *esp* : a common food and sport fish (*Hexagrammos decagrammus*)
green·mail \'grēn-ˌmā(ə)l\ *n* (1983) : the practice of buying enough of a company's stock to threaten a hostile takeover and reselling it to the company at a price above market value; *also* : the money paid for such stock — **greenmail** *vt* — **green·mail·er** \-ˌmā-lər\ *n*
green manure *n* (1842) : an herbaceous crop (as clover) plowed under while green to enrich the soil — **green–manure** *vt*
green mold *n* (1919) : a green or green-spored mold (as of the genera *Penicillium* or *Aspergillus*)
green monkey *n* (1840) : a long-tailed monkey of any of several African races of a guenon (*Cercopithecus aethiops*) having greenish-appearing hair and often used in medical research
gree·nock·ite \'grē-nə-ˌkīt\ *n* [Charles M. Cathcart, Lord *Greenock* †1859 Eng. soldier] (1844) : a mineral consisting of native cadmium sulfide occurring in yellow translucent hexagonal crystals or as an earthy incrustation
green onion *n* (1847) : a young onion pulled before the bulb has enlarged and used esp. in salads
green paper *n, often cap G&P* (1967) *Brit* : a government document that proposes and invites discussion on approaches to a problem
green peach aphid *n* (1922) : a nearly cosmopolitan yellowish green aphid (*Myzus persicae*) that is frequently a vector of plant virus diseases
green pepper *n* (1700) : a sweet pepper before it turns red at maturity

---

\ə\ abut \ᵊ\ kitten, F table \ər\ further \a\ ash \ā\ ace \ä\ mop, mar
\au̇\ out \ch\ chin \e\ bet \ē\ easy \g\ go \i\ hit \ī\ ice \j\ job
\ŋ\ sing \ō\ go \ȯ\ law \ȯi\ boy \th\ thin \t̲h̲\ the \ü\ loot \u̇\ foot
\y\ yet \zh\ vision \ȧ, k̲, ⁿ, œ, œ̄, ue, ūe, ᵊ\ see Guide to Pronunciation

green revolution *n* (1968) : the great increase in production of food grains (as rice and wheat) due to the introduction of high-yielding varieties, to the use of pesticides, and to better management techniques

green·room \'grēn-ˌrüm, -ˌrum\ *n* (1701) : a room in a theater or concert hall where performers can relax before or after appearances

green·sand \-ˌsand\ *n* (1796) : a sedimentary deposit that consists largely of dark greenish grains of glauconite often mingled with clay or sand

greens fee \'grēnz-\ *n* (1909) : a fee paid for the privilege of playing on a golf course — called also *green fee*

green·shank \'grēn-ˌshaŋk\ *n* (1766) : an Old World sandpiper (*Tringa nebularia*) with greenish legs and a slightly upturned bill

green·sick·ness \-ˌsik-nəs\ *n* (1583) : CHLOROSIS — **green·sick** *adj*

green snake *n* (1709) : either of two bright green harmless largely insectivorous No. American colubrid snakes (*Opheodrys vernalis* and *O. aestivus*)

green soap *n* (ca. 1840) : a soft soap made from vegetable oils and used esp. in the treatment of skin diseases

green·stick fracture \'grēn-ˌstik-\ *n* (ca. 1885) : a bone fracture in a young individual in which the bone is partly broken and partly bent

green·stone \'grēn-ˌstōn\ *n* (ca. 1784) 1 : NEPHRITE 2 : any of numerous usu. altered dark green compact rocks (as diorite)

green·stuff \-ˌstəf\ *n* (1851) : green vegetation used as foodstuff

green sunfish *n* (ca. 1896) : a sunfish (*Lepomis cyanellus*) of the Great Lakes region and southwestward to the Rio Grande that is largely greenish above with a blue spot on each scale

green·sward \-ˌswȯrd\ *n* (1600) : turf green with growing grass

green tea *n* (1704) : tea that is light in color from incomplete fermentation of the leaf before firing

green thumb *n* (1943) : an unusual ability to make plants grow — **green·thumbed** \'grēn-ˌthəmd\ *adj*

green turtle *n* (1657) : a large usu. herbivorous sea turtle (*Chelonia mydas*) of warm waters with a smooth greenish or olive-colored shell

green vegetable *n* (1826) : a vegetable whose foliage or foliage-bearing stalks are the chief edible part

green·way \'grēn-ˌwā\ *n* (1966) : a corridor of undeveloped land in or near a city that is designed for recreational use

Green·wich mean time \'gri-nij, 'gre-, -nich\ *n, often cap M&T* [*Greenwich*, England] (1938) : the mean solar time of the meridian of Greenwich used as the prime basis of standard time throughout the world — called also *Greenwich time*

green·wing \'grēn-ˌwiŋ\ *n* (ca. 1889) : GREEN-WINGED TEAL

green–winged teal \'grēn-ˌwiŋ(d)-\ *n* (1792) : a small dabbling duck (*Anas crecca*) the male of which has a chestnut head with a green eye patch and a metallic green area on the wing speculum

green·wood \'grēn-ˌwud\ *n* (14c) : a forest green with foliage

¹greet \'grēt\ *vt* [ME *greten*, fr. OE *grētan*; akin to OE *grǣtan* to weep] (bef. 12c) 1 : to address with expression of kind wishes : HAIL 2 a : to meet or react to in a specified manner ⟨~ed him with boos⟩ b : to occur as a response to ⟨apathy ~ed the plan⟩ 3 : to appear to the perception of ⟨a surprising sight ~ed her eyes⟩ — **greet·er** *n*

²greet *vi* **grat** \'grat\; **grut·ten** \'grə-t²n\ [ME *greten*, fr. OE *grǣtan*; akin to ON *grāta* to weep] (bef. 12c) *Scot* : WEEP, LAMENT

greet·ing *n* (bef. 12c) 1 : a salutation at meeting 2 : an expression of good wishes : REGARDS — usu. used in plural ⟨holiday ~s⟩

greeting card *n* (1898) : a piece of paper or thin paperboard having any of a variety of shapes and formats and bearing a greeting or message of sentiment

greg·a·rine \'gre-gə-ˌrēn\ *n* [ultim. fr. L *gregarius*] (1867) : any of a subclass (Gregarinia) of parasitic vermiform sporozoan protozoans that occur esp. in insects and other invertebrates — **gregarine** *adj*

gre·gar·i·ous \gri-'gar-ē-əs, -'ger-\ *adj* [L *gregarius* of a flock or herd, fr. *greg-, grex* flock, herd] (1668) 1 a : tending to associate with others of one's kind : SOCIAL b : marked by or indicating a liking for companionship : SOCIABLE c : of or relating to a social group 2 a *of a plant* : growing in a cluster or a colony b : living in contiguous nests but not forming a true colony — used esp. of wasps and bees — **gre·gar·i·ous·ly** *adv* — **gre·gar·i·ous·ness** *n*

¹Gre·go·ri·an \gri-'gȯr-ē-ən, -'gȯr-\ *adj* (1642) : of or relating to Pope Gregory XIII or the Gregorian calendar

²Gregorian *adj* (1653) 1 : of or relating to Pope Gregory I 2 : of, relating to, or having the characteristics of Gregorian chant

³Gregorian *adj* [St. *Gregory* the Illuminator †332, apostle of Armenia] (1955) : of or relating to the Armenian national church

Gregorian calendar *n* (ca. 1771) : a calendar in general use introduced in 1582 by Pope Gregory XIII as a revision of the Julian calendar, adopted in Great Britain and the American colonies in 1752, marked by the suppression of 10 days or after 1700 11 days, and having leap years in every year divisible by four with the restriction that centesimal years are leap years only when divisible by 400 — see MONTH table

Gregorian chant *n* (1751) : a monodic and rhythmically free liturgical chant of the Roman Catholic Church

greige \'grā(zh)\ *adj* [F *grège* raw (of silk), fr. It *greggio*] (1926) : being in an unbleached undyed state as taken from a loom — used of textiles

grei·sen \'grī-z²n\ *n* [G] (1878) : a crystalline rock consisting of quartz and mica that is common in Cornwall and Saxony

grem·lin \'grem-lən\ *n* [origin unknown] (1941) : a cause of error or equipment malfunction (as in aircraft) conceived of as a small mischievous gnome

gre·nade \grə-'nād\ *n* [MF, pomegranate, fr. LL *granata*, fr. L, fem. of *granatus* seedy, fr. *granum* grain — more at CORN] (1591) : a small missile that contains an explosive or a chemical agent (as tear gas, a flame producer, or a smoke producer) and that is thrown by hand or projected (as by a rifle or special launcher)

gren·a·dier \ˌgren-ə-'dir\ *n* [F, fr. *grenade* grenade] (1676) 1 a : a soldier who carries and throws grenades b : a member of a special regiment or corps formerly armed with grenades 2 : any of various deep-sea fishes (family Macruridae) that are related to the cods and have an elongate tapering body and compressed pointed tail

gren·a·dine \ˌgren-ə-'dēn, 'gren-ə-ˌ\ *n* [F, fr. *grenade* coarse silk fabric, pomegranate] (1852) 1 : an open-weave fabric of various fibers 2 : a moderate reddish orange 3 : a syrup flavored with pomegranates and used in mixed drinks

Gren·del \'gren-d²l\ *n* [OE] : a monstrous man-eating descendant of Cain slain by Beowulf in the Old English poem *Beowulf*

Gresh·am's law \'gre-shəmz-\ *n* [Sir Thomas *Gresham*] (1858) : an observation in economics: when two coins are equal in debt-paying value but unequal in intrinsic value, the one having the lesser intrinsic value tends to remain in circulation and the other to be hoarded or exported as bullion; *broadly* : any process by which inferior products or practices drive out superior ones

Gret·na Green \ˌgret-nə-'grēn\ *n* [*Gretna Green*, village in Scotland] (1813) : a place where many eloping couples are married

Gre·vy's zebra \(ˌ)grā-'vēz-\ *n* [Jules *Grévy* (1891) : a zebra (*Equus grevyi*) of eastern Africa with narrow stripes and a white belly

grew *past of* GROW

grew·some *var of* GRUESOME

grey *var of* GRAY

grey friar *n, often cap G&F* (14c) : a Franciscan friar

grey·hound \'grā-ˌhaund\ *n* [ME *grehound*, fr. OE *grīghund*, fr. *grīg-* (akin to ON *grey* bitch) + *hund* hound] (bef. 12c) : any of a breed of tall slender graceful smooth-coated dogs characterized by swiftness and keen sight and used for coursing game and racing; *also* : any of several related dogs

grey·lag \-ˌlag\ *n* [perh. fr. *gray* + *lag* (last)] (ca. 1713) : the common gray wild goose (*Anser anser*) of Europe — called also *greylag goose*

grib·ble \'gri-bəl\ *n* [perh. alter. of ²*grub*] (1838) : either of two small marine isopods (*Limnoria lignorum* and *L. tripunctata*) that destroy submerged timber

grid \'grid\ *n* [back-formation fr. *gridiron*] (1839) 1 : GRATING 2 a (1) : a perforated or ridged metal plate used as a conductor in a storage battery (2) : an electrode consisting of a mesh or a spiral of fine wire in an electron tube (3) : a network of conductors for distribution of electric power; *also* : a network of radio or television stations b : a network of uniformly spaced horizontal and perpendicular lines (as for locating points on a map); *also* : something resembling such a network ⟨a road ~⟩ c : GRIDIRON 3; *broadly* : FOOTBALL 3 : the starting positions of cars on a racecourse 4 : a device in a photocomposer on which are located the characters to be exposed as the text is composed

grid·der \'gri-dər\ *n* (1928) : a football player

grid·dle \'gri-d²l\ *n* [ME *gredil* gridiron, fr. ONF, fr. L *craticulum*, dim. of *cratis* wickerwork — more at HURDLE] (14c) : a flat metal surface or pan on which food is cooked by dry heat

griddle cake *n* (1783) : PANCAKE

grid·iron \'grid-ˌī(-ə)rn\ *n* [ME *gredire*] (14c) 1 : a grate for broiling food 2 : something consisting of or covered with a network 3 : a football field

grid·lock \-ˌläk\ *n* (1980) 1 : a traffic jam in which a grid of intersecting streets is so completely congested that no vehicular movement is possible 2 : a situation resembling a gridlock — **gridlock** *vt*

grief \'grēf\ *n* [ME *gref*, fr. MF, heavy, grave, fr. (assumed) VL *grevis*, alter. of L *gravis*] (15c) 1 *obs* : GRIEVANCE 3 2 a : deep and poignant distress caused by or as if by bereavement b : a cause of such suffering 3 a : an unfortunate outcome : DISASTER — used chiefly in the phrase *come to grief* b : MISHAP, MISADVENTURE c : TROUBLE, ANNOYANCE ⟨enough ~ for one day⟩ *syn* see SORROW

griev·ance \'grē-vən(t)s\ *n* (14c) 1 *obs* : SUFFERING, DISTRESS 2 : a cause of distress (as an unsatisfactory working condition) felt to afford reason for complaint or resistance 3 : the formal expression of a grievance : COMPLAINT *syn* see INJUSTICE

grievance committee *n* (1927) : a committee formed by a labor union or by employer and employees jointly to discuss and where possible to eliminate grievances

griev·ant \-vənt\ *n* (1958) : one who submits a grievance for arbitration

grieve \'grēv\ *vb* **grieved; griev·ing** [ME *greven*, fr. OF *grever*, fr. L *gravare* to burden, fr. *gravis* heavy, grave; akin to Gk *barys* heavy, Skt *guru*] *vt* (13c) : to cause to suffer : DISTRESS ~ *vi* : to feel grief : SORROW — **griev·er** *n*

griev·ous \'grē-vəs\ *adj* (13c) 1 : causing or characterized by severe pain, suffering, or sorrow ⟨a ~ wound⟩ ⟨a ~ loss⟩ 2 : OPPRESSIVE, ONEROUS ⟨~ costs of war⟩ 3 : SERIOUS, GRAVE ⟨~ fault⟩ — **griev·ous·ly** *adv* — **griev·ous·ness** *n*

grif·fin *or* **grif·fon** \'gri-fən\ *n* [ME *griffon*, fr. MF *grifon*, fr. *grif*, fr. L *gryphus*, fr. Gk *gryp-, gryps*] (14c) : a mythical animal typically having the head, forepart, and wings of an eagle and the body, hind legs, and tail of a lion

grif·fon \'gri-fən\ *n* [F, lit., griffin] (1882) 1 : BRUSSELS GRIFFON 2 : WIREHAIRED POINTING GRIFFON

griffin

grift \'grift\ *vt* [*grift*, n., perh. alter. of *graft*] (1915) *slang* : to obtain (money) illicitly (as in a confidence game) — **grift** *n, slang* — **grift·er** *n, slang*

grig \'grig\ *n* [ME *grege*] (1566) : a lively light-hearted usu. young or young person

gri·gri *var of* GRIS-GRIS

¹grill \'gril\ *vt* (1668) 1 : to broil on a grill; *also* : to fry or toast on a griddle 2 a : to torment as if by broiling b : to question intensely ⟨the police ~ed the suspect⟩ — **grill·er** *n*

²grill *n* [F *gril*, fr. L *craticulum* — more at GRIDDLE] (1685) 1 : a cooking utensil of parallel bars on which food is exposed to heat (as from charcoal or electricity) 2 : food that is broiled esp. on a grill — compare MIXED GRILL 3 : a usu. informal restaurant or dining room

grill·age \'gri-lij\ *n* [F, fr. *griller* to supply with grillwork, fr. *gril*] (1776) 1 : a framework of timber or steel for support in marshy or treacherous soil 2 : a framework for supporting a load (as a column)

grille *or* **grill** \'gril\ *n* [F *grille*, alter. of OF *greille*, fr. L *craticula*, dim. of *cratis* wickerwork — more at HURDLE] (1686) 1 : a grating forming a barrier or screen; *esp* : an ornamental one at the front end of an automobile 2 : an opening covered with a grille

grill·room \'gril-ˌrüm, -ˌrum\ *n* (1883) : GRILL 3

grill·work \'gril-ˌwərk\ *n* (1896) : work constituting or resembling a grille

grilse \'grils\ *n, pl* **grilse** [ME *grills*] (15c) : a young Atlantic salmon returning to its native river to spawn for the first time after one winter at sea; *broadly* : any of various salmon at such a stage of development

grim \'grim\ *adj* **grim·mer; grim·mest** [ME, fr. OE *grimm;* akin to OHG *grimm* fierce, Gk *chremetizein* to neigh] (bef. 12c) **1 :** fierce in disposition or action : SAVAGE **2 a :** stern or forbidding in action or appearance ⟨a ~ taskmaster⟩ **b :** SOMBER, GLOOMY **3 :** ghastly, repellent, or sinister in character ⟨a ~ tale⟩ **4 :** UNFLINCHING, UNYIELDING ⟨~ determination⟩ — **grim·ly** *adv* — **grim·ness** *n*

gri·mace \'gri-məs, gri-'mās\ *n* [F, fr. MF, alter. of *grimache,* of Gmc origin; akin to OE *grima* mask] : a facial expression usu. of disgust or disapproval — **grimace** *vi* — **gri·mac·er** *n*

gri·mal·kin \gri-'mȯl)kən, -'mal-\ *n* [*gray* + *malkin*] (1630) **1 :** a domestic cat; *esp* : an old female cat

grime \'grīm\ *n* [MD *grime* soot, mask; akin to OE *grīma* mask] (14c) : soot, smut, or dirt adhering to or embedded in a surface; *broadly* : accumulated dirtiness and disorder — **grime** *vt*

Grimm's law \'grimz-\ *n* [Jacob *Grimm*] (1838) : a statement in historical linguistics: Proto-Indo-European voiceless stops became Proto-Germanic voiceless fricatives (as in Greek *pyr, treis, kardia* compared with English *fire, three, heart*), Proto-Indo-European voiced stops became Proto-Germanic voiceless stops (as in Latin *duo, genus* compared with English *two, kin*), and Proto-Indo-European voiced aspirated stops became Proto-Germanic voiced fricatives (as in Sanskrit *nābhi, madhya,* "mid" compared with English *navel,* Old Norse *mithr* "mid")

grim reaper *n, often cap G&R* (ca. 1927) : death esp. when personified as a man or skeleton with a scythe

grimy \'grī-mē\ *adj* **grim·i·er; -est** (1612) : full of or covered with grime : DIRTY — **grim·i·ness** *n*

grin \'grin\ *vi* **grinned; grin·ning** [ME *grennen,* fr. OE *grennian;* akin to OHG *grennen* to snarl] (bef. 12c) : to draw back the lips so as to show the teeth esp. in amusement or laughter; *broadly* : SMILE — **grin** *n* — **grin·ner** *n* — **grin·ning·ly** \'gri-niŋ-lē\ *adv*

grinch \'grinch\ *n* [fr. the *Grinch,* character in the children's story *How the Grinch Stole Christmas* (1957) by Dr. Seuss] (1979) : KILLJOY, SPOILSPORT

1grind \'grīnd\ *vb* **ground** \'grau̇nd\; **grind·ing** [ME, fr. OE *grindan;* akin to L *frendere* to crush, grind] *vt* (bef. 12c) **1 :** to reduce to powder or small fragments by friction (as in a mill or with the teeth) **2 :** to wear down, polish, or sharpen by friction ⟨~ an ax⟩ **3 a :** OPPRESS, HARASS **b :** to weaken or destroy gradually — usu. used with *down* ⟨poverty *ground* her spirit down⟩ **4 a :** to press together with a rotating motion ⟨~ the teeth⟩ **b :** to rub or press harshly ⟨*ground* the cigarette out⟩ **5 :** to operate or produce by turning a crank ⟨~ a hand organ⟩ ~ *vi* **1 :** to perform the operation of grinding **2 :** to become pulverized, polished, or sharpened by friction **3 :** to move with difficulty or friction esp. so as to make a grating noise ⟨gears ~*ing*⟩ **4 :** DRUDGE; *esp* : to study hard ⟨~ for an exam⟩ **5 :** to rotate the hips in an erotic manner (as in a burlesque striptease) — **grind·ing·ly** \'grin-diŋ-lē\ *adv*

2grind *n* (13c) **1 a :** an act of grinding **b :** the sound of grinding **2 a :** dreary, monotonous, or difficult labor, study, or routine **b :** one who works or studies excessively **3 :** the result of grinding; *also* : material ground to a particular degree of fineness ⟨a drip ~ of coffee⟩ **4 :** the act of rotating the hips in an erotic manner *syn* see WORK

grind·er \'grīn-dər\ *n* (14c) **1 a :** MOLAR **b** *pl* : TEETH **2 :** one that grinds **3 :** a machine or device for grinding **4 :** SUBMARINE 2

grind house *n* (1927) : an often shabby movie theater having continuous showings esp. of pornographic or violent films

grind out *vt* (1868) : to produce in a mechanical way

grind·stone \'grin-ˌstōn\ *n* (13c) **1 :** MILLSTONE 1 **2 :** a flat circular stone of natural sandstone that revolves on an axle and is used for grinding, shaping, or smoothing

grin·go \'griŋ-(ˌ)gō\ *n, pl* **gringos** [Sp, alter. of *griego* Greek, stranger, fr. L *Graecus* Greek] (1849) : a foreigner in Spain or Latin America esp. when of English or American origin; *broadly* : a non-Hispanic person — often used disparagingly

gri·ot \'grē-ˌō\ *n* [F] (1906) : any of a class of musician-entertainers of western Africa whose performances include tribal histories and genealogies

1grip \'grip\ *vt* **gripped; grip·ping** [ME *grippen,* fr. OE *grippan;* akin to OE *gripan*] (bef. 12c) **1 :** to seize or hold firmly **2 :** to hold the interest of strongly ⟨a story that ~s the reader⟩ — **grip·per** *n* — **grip·ping·ly** \'gri-piŋ-lē\ *adv*

2grip *n* (bef. 12c) **1 a :** a strong or tenacious grasp **b :** strength in gripping **c :** manner or style of gripping **2 a :** a firm tenacious hold typically giving control, mastery, or understanding **b :** mental grasp **3 :** a part or device for gripping **4 :** a part by which something is grasped; *esp* : HANDLE **5 :** SUITCASE **6 :** STAGEHAND

1gripe \'grīp\ *vb* **griped; grip·ing** [ME *gripen,* fr. OE *gripan;* akin to OHG *grifan* to grasp, Lith *griebti*] *vt* (bef. 12c) **1** *archaic* : SEIZE, GRASP **2 a :** AFFLICT, DISTRESS **b :** IRRITATE, VEX **3 :** to cause pinching and spasmodic pain in the bowels of ~ *vi* **1 :** to experience gripes **2 :** to complain with grumbling — **grip·er** *n*

2gripe *n* (13c) **1** *archaic* : CLUTCH, GRASP; *broadly* : CONTROL, MASTERY **2 :** a pinching spasmodic intestinal pain — usu. used in pl. **3 :** GRIEVANCE, COMPLAINT

grip·man \'grip-mən, -ˌman\ *n* (1886) : a cable car operator

grippe \'grip\ *n* [F, lit., seizure] (1776) : an acute febrile contagious virus disease; *esp* : INFLUENZA 1 — **grippy** \'gri-pē\ *adj*

grip·sack \'grip-ˌsak\ *n* (1877) : SUITCASE

gri·saille \gri-'zī, -'zā(ə)l\ *n* [F, fr. *gris* gray, fr. MF — more at GRIZZLE] (1848) : decoration in tones of a single color and esp. gray designed to produce a three-dimensional effect

Gri·sel·da \gri-'zel-də\ *n* [ME, fr. It] : a woman of humble origins in medieval legend who endures tests of wifely patience laid on her by her wellborn husband

gris·eo·ful·vin \ˌgri-zē-ō-'fu̇l-vən, ˌgri-sē-, -'fəl-\ *n* [NL *griseofulvum,* specific epithet of *Penicillium griseofulvum,* mold from which it is obtained] (1939) : an antibiotic $C_{17}H_{17}ClO_6$ used systematically in treating superficial fungal infections

gri·sette \gri-'zet\ *n* [F, grisette, cheap unbleached cloth, fr. *gris*] (1723) **1 :** a young French working-class woman **2 :** a young woman combining part-time prostitution with some other occupation

gris–gris \'grē-(ˌ)grē\ *n, pl* **gris–gris** \-(ˌ)grēz\ [F] (1698) : an amulet or incantation used chiefly by people of black African ancestry

gris·ly \'griz-lē\ *adj* **gris·li·er; -est** [ME, fr. OE *grislic,* fr. *gris-* (akin to OE *āgrisan* to fear); akin to OHG *grisenlih* terrible] (12c) **1 :** inspiring horror or intense fear ⟨houses that were dark and ~ under the blank, cold sky —D. H. Lawrence⟩ **2 :** inspiring disgust or distaste ⟨a ~ account of the fire⟩ *syn* see GHASTLY — **gris·li·ness** *n*

grist \'grist\ *n* [ME, fr. OE *grīst;* akin to OE *grindan* to grind] (bef. 12c) **1 a :** grain or a batch of grain for grinding **b :** the product obtained from a grist of grain including the flour or meal and the grain offals **2 :** a required or usual amount **3 :** matter of interest or value forming the basis of a story or analysis **4 :** something turned to advantage or use — used esp. in the phrase *grist for one's mill*

gris·tle \'gri-səl, -zəl\ *n* [ME *gristil,* fr. OE *gristle;* akin to MLG *gristel* gristle] (bef. 12c) : CARTILAGE; *broadly* : tough cartilaginous, tendinous, or fibrous matter esp. in table meats

gris·tly \'gri-sə-lē, 'gris-lē, 'griz-\ *adj* **gris·tli·er; -est** (14c) : consisting of or containing gristle ⟨~ steak⟩ — **gris·tli·ness** *n*

grist·mill \'grist-ˌmil\ *n* (1602) : a mill for grinding grain

1grit \'grit\ *n* [ME *grete,* fr. OE *grēot;* akin to OHG *grioz* sand] (bef. 12c) **1 a :** SAND, GRAVEL **b :** a hard sharp granule (as of sand); *also* : material (as many abrasives) composed of such granules **2 :** any of several sandstones **3 a :** the structure of a stone that adapts it to grinding **b :** the size of abrasive particles usu. expressed as their mesh **4 :** firmness of mind or spirit : unyielding courage in the face of hardship or danger **5** *cap* : a Liberal in Canadian politics

2grit *vb* **grit·ted; grit·ting** *vi* (1762) : to give forth a grating sound ~ *vt* **1 :** to cause (as one's teeth) to grind or grate **2 :** to cover or spread with grit; *esp* : to smooth (as marble) with a coarse abrasive

grith \'grith\ *n* [ME, fr. OE, fr. ON, security] (bef. 12c) : peace, security, or sanctuary imposed or guaranteed in early medieval England under various special conditions

grits \'grits\ *n pl but sing or pl in constr* [perh. partly fr. 1grit, partly fr. dial. grit coarse meal, fr. OE *grytt;* akin to OE *grēot*] (1579) : coarsely ground hulled grain; *esp* : ground hominy with the germ removed

grit·ty \'gri-tē\ *adj* **grit·ti·er; -est** (1598) **1 :** containing or resembling grit **2 :** courageously persistent : PLUCKY **3 :** having strong qualities of tough uncompromising realism ⟨a ~ novel⟩ — **grit·ti·ly** \'gri-tᵊl-ē\ *adv* — **grit·ti·ness** \'gri-tē-nəs\ *n*

1griz·zle \'gri-zəl\ *n* [ME *grisel,* gray, fr. MF, fr. *gris,* of Gmc origin; akin to OHG *grīs* gray] (1601) **1** *archaic* : gray hair **2 a :** a roan coat pattern or color **b :** a gray or roan animal

2grizzle *vb* **griz·zled; griz·zling** \'griz-liŋ, 'gri-zə-\ *vt* (1740) : to make grayish ~ *vi* **1 :** GRIPE, GRUMBLE **2 :** to become grayish

griz·zled \'gri-zəld\ *adj* (15c) : sprinkled or streaked with gray : GRAYING ⟨a ~ beard⟩

1griz·zly \'griz-lē\ *adj* **griz·zli·er; -est** (1594) : GRIZZLED

2grizzly *var of* GRISLY

grizzly bear *n* (1791) : a very large brown bear (*Ursus arctos horribilis*) of the uplands of western No. America — called also *grizzly*

groan \'grōn\ *vb* [ME *gronen,* fr. OE *grānian;* akin to OHG *grīnan* to growl] *vi* (bef. 12c) **1 :** to utter a deep moan indicative of pain, grief, or annoyance **2 :** to make a harsh sound (as of creaking) under sudden or prolonged strain ~ *vt* : to utter or express with groaning — **groan** *n*

groan·er \'grō-nər\ *n* (1795) **1 :** one that groans **2 :** a stale or corny joke, observation, or story

1groat \'grōt\ *n* [ME *grotes,* pl., fr. OE *grotan,* pl. of *grot;* akin to OE *grēot* grit] (12c) **1** *usu pl but sing or pl in constr* : hulled grain broken into fragments larger than grits **2 :** a grain (as of oats) exclusive of the hull

2groat *n* [ME *groot,* fr. MD] (14c) : an old British coin worth four pennies

gro·cer \'grō-sər, -shər\ *n* [ME, fr. MF *grossier* wholesaler, fr. *gros* coarse, wholesale — more at GROSS] (15c) : a dealer in staple foodstuffs, meats, produce, and dairy products and usu. household supplies

gro·cery \'grōs-rē, 'grō-sə-; 'grōsh-rē\ *n, pl* **-cer·ies** (15c) **1** *pl* : commodities sold by a grocer — usu. sing. in Brit. usage **2 :** a grocer's store

grog \'gräg\ *n* [*Old Grog,* nickname of Edward Vernon †1757 Eng. admiral responsible for diluting the sailors' rum] (1770) **1 :** alcoholic liquor; *esp* : liquor (as rum) cut with water and now often served hot with lemon juice and sugar sometimes added **2 :** refractory materials (as crushed pottery and firebricks) used in the manufacture of refractory products (as crucibles) to reduce shrinkage in drying and firing

grog·gy \'grä-gē\ *adj* **grog·gi·er; -est** [*grog*] (1832) : weak and unsteady on the feet or in action — **grog·gi·ly** \'grä-gə-lē\ *adv* — **grog·gi·ness** \'grä-gē-nəs\ *n*

gro·gram \'grä-grəm, 'grō-\ *n* [MF *gros grain* coarse texture] (1562) : a coarse loosely woven fabric of silk, silk and mohair, or silk and wool — compare GROSGRAIN

grog·shop \'gräg-ˌshäp\ *n* (1790) *chiefly Brit* : a usu. low-class barroom

1groin \'grȯin\ *n* [alter. of ME *grynde,* fr. OE, abyss; akin to OE *grund* ground] (ca. 1532) **1 :** the fold or depression marking the juncture of the lower abdomen and the inner part of the thigh; *also* : the region of this line **2 a :** the projecting curved line along which two intersecting vaults meet **b :** a rib that covers this edge **3 :** a rigid structure

groin 2a

\ə\ abut \ᵊ\ kitten, F table \ər\ further \a\ ash \ā\ ace \ä\ mop, mar \au̇\ out \ch\ chin \e\ bet \ē\ easy \g\ go \i\ hit \ī\ ice \j\ job \ŋ\ sing \ō\ go \ȯ\ law \ȯi\ boy \th\ thin \t͟h\ the \ü\ loot \u̇\ foot \y\ yet \zh\ vision \ȧ, ḵ, ⁿ, œ, œ̄, ᵫ, ᵫ̄, ᷱ\ *see* Guide to Pronunciation built out from a shore to protect the shore from erosion, to trap sand, or to direct a current for scouring a channel

²**groin** *vt* (ca. 1816) : to build or equip with groins

grom·met \'grä-mət, 'grə-\ *n* [obs. F *gormette* curb of a bridle] (1626) **1** : a flexible loop that serves as a fastening, support, or reinforcement **2** : an eyelet of firm material to strengthen or protect an opening or to insulate or protect something passed through it

grom·well \'gräm-,wel, -wəl\ *n* [ME *gromil*, fr. MF] (14c) : any of a genus (*Lithospermum*) of plants of the borage family having polished white stony nutlets

¹**groom** \'grüm, 'grùm\ *n* [ME *grom*] (14c) **1** *archaic* : MAN, FELLOW **2 a** (1) *archaic* : MANSERVANT (2) : one of several officers of the English royal household   **b** : a person responsible for the feeding, exercising, and stabling of horses   **3** : BRIDEGROOM

²**groom** *vt* (1809) **1** : to clean and condition (as a horse or dog)   **2** : to make neat or attractive ⟨an impeccably *~ed* woman⟩   **3** : to get into readiness for a specific objective : PREPARE ⟨was being *~ed* as a presidential candidate⟩ *~ vi* : to groom oneself

groom·er \'grü-mər\ *n* (ca. 1890) : one who grooms (as dogs)

grooms·man \'grümz-mən, 'grùmz-\ *n* (1698) : a male friend who attends a bridegroom at his wedding

¹**groove** \'grüv\ *n* [ME *groof*; akin to OE *grafan* to dig — more at GRAVE] (1659) **1 a** : a long narrow channel or depression   **b** : a fixed routine : RUT   **c** : a situation suited to one's abilities or interests : NICHE   **3** : top form ⟨a great talker when he is in the *~*⟩   **4** : the middle of the strike zone in baseball where a pitch is most easily hit ⟨a fastball right in the *~*⟩   **5** : an enjoyable or exciting experience   **6** : a pronounced enjoyable rhythm

²**groove** *vb* **grooved; groov·ing** *vt* (1686) **1 a** : to make a groove in   **b** : to join by a groove   **2** : to perfect by repeated practice ⟨*grooved* her golf swing⟩   **3** : to throw (a pitch) in the groove   *~ vi* **1** : to become joined or fitted by a groove   **2** : to form a groove   **3** : to enjoy oneself intensely   **4** : to interact harmoniously ⟨contemporary minds and rock *~* together —Contemporary Authors⟩ — **groov·er** *n*

groovy \'grü-vē\ *adj* **groov·i·er; -est** (ca. 1937) **1** : MARVELOUS, WONDERFUL, EXCELLENT ⟨felt that this poetry was . . . enjoyable, not to mention *~* —R. M. Muccigrosso⟩   **2** : HIP ⟨a younger and *groovier* audience —Robert MacKenzie⟩

grope \'grōp\ *vb* **groped; grop·ing** [ME, fr. OE *grāpian*; akin to OE *gripan* to seize] *vi* (bef. 12c) **1** : to feel about blindly or uncertainly in search ⟨*~* for the light switch⟩   **2** : to look for something blindly or uncertainly ⟨*~* for the right words⟩   **3** : to feel one's way *~ vt* **1** : FEEL UP   **2** : to find (as one's way) by groping — **grope** *n* — **grop·er** *n*

gros·beak \'grōs-,bēk\ *n* [part trans. of F *grosbec*, fr. *gros* thick + *bec* beak] (ca. 1678) : any of several finches of Europe or America having large stout conical bills

gro·schen \'grō-shən, 'grò-\ *n, pl* **groschen** [G] (1946) — see *schilling* at MONEY table

gros·grain \'grō-,grān\ *n* [F *gros grain* coarse texture] (1869) : a strong close-woven corded fabric usu. of silk or rayon and often with cotton filler — compare GROGRAM

¹**gross** \'grōs\ *adj* [ME, fr. MF *gros* thick, coarse, fr. L *grossus*] (14c) **1 a** *archaic* : immediately obvious   **b** (1) : glaringly noticeable usu. because of inexcusable badness or objectionableness ⟨*~* error⟩ (2) : OUT-AND-OUT, UTTER ⟨*~* injustice⟩   **c** : visible without the aid of a microscope   **2 a** : BIG, BULKY; *esp* : excessively fat   **b** : growing or spreading with excessive luxuriance   **3 a** : of, relating to, or dealing with general aspects or broad distinctions   **b** : consisting of an overall total exclusive of deductions ⟨*~* income⟩ — compare NET   **4** : made up of material or perceptible elements   **5** *archaic* : not fastidious in taste : UNDISCRIMINATING   **6 a** : coarse in nature or behavior : UNREFINED   **b** : gravely deficient in civility or decency : crudely vulgar ⟨merely *~*, a scatological rather than a pornographic impropriety —Aldous Huxley⟩   **c** *slang* : inspiring disgust or distaste ⟨that sandwich looks *~*⟩   **7** : deficient in knowledge : IGNORANT, UNTUTORED   *syn* see COARSE, FLAGRANT — **gross·ly** *adv* — **gross·ness** *n*

²**gross** *n* (1579) **1** *obs* : AMOUNT, SUM   **2** : overall total exclusive of deductions

³**gross** *vt* (1884) : to earn or bring in (an overall total) exclusive of deductions (as for taxes or expenses) — **gross·er** *n*

⁴**gross** *n, pl* **gross** [ME *groce*, fr. MF *grosse*, fr. fem. of *gros*] (14c) : an aggregate of 12 dozen things ⟨a *~* of pencils⟩

gross anatomy *n* (1888) : a branch of anatomy that deals with the macroscopic structure of tissues and organs

gross national product *n* (1947) : the total value of the goods and services produced by the residents of a nation during a specified period (as a year)

gross–out \'grō,saút\ *n, often attrib* (1973) : something inspiring disgust or distaste

gross out *vt* (1968) : to offend, insult, or disgust by something gross

gros·su·lar \'gräs-yə-lər\ *n* [NL *Grossularia*, genus name of the gooseberry] (1819) : a variety of garnet that is most commonly green and consists of calcium aluminum silicate

gros·su·la·rite \-lə-,rīt\ *n* [G *Grossularit*, fr. NL *Grossularia*] (ca. 1847) : GROSSULAR

gro·szy \'grò-shē\ *also* **grosz** *or* **grosze** \'grōsh\ *n, pl* **groszy** [Pol] (1916) — see *zloty* at MONEY table

grot \'grät\ *n* [MF *grotte*, fr. It *grotta*] (1506) : GROTTO

¹**gro·tesque** \grō-'tesk\ *n* [MF & OIt; MF, fr. OIt (*pittura*) *grottesca*, lit., cave painting, fem. of *grottesco* of a cave, fr. *grotta*] (1561) **1 a** : a style of decorative art characterized by fanciful or fantastic human and animal forms often interwoven with foliage or similar figures that may distort the natural into absurdity, ugliness, or caricature   **b** : a piece of work in this style   **2** : one that is grotesque   **3** : SANS SERIF

²**grotesque** *adj* (1603) : of, relating to, or having the characteristics of the grotesque: as   **a** : FANCIFUL, BIZARRE   **b** : absurdly incongruous   **c** : departing markedly from the natural, the expected, or the typical   *syn* see FANTASTIC — **gro·tesque·ly** *adv* — **gro·tesque·ness** *n*

gro·tes·que·rie *also* **gro·tes·que·ry** \grō-'tes-kə-rē\ *n, pl* **-ries** [*grotesque* + F *-erie* -ery] (ca. 1666) **1** : something that is grotesque   **2** : the quality or state of being grotesque : GROTESQUENESS

grot·to \'grä-(,)tō\ *n, pl* **grottoes** *also* **grottos** [It *grotta*, *grotto*, fr. L *crypta* cavern, crypt] (1617) **1** : CAVE   **2** : an artificial recess or structure made to resemble a natural cave

grot·ty \'grä-tē\ *adj* **grot·ti·er; -est** [origin unknown] (1964) *chiefly Brit* : wretchedly shabby : of poor quality

grouch \'graúch\ *n* [prob. alter. of *grutch* (grudge)] (ca. 1895) **1 a** : a fit of bad temper   **b** : GRUDGE, COMPLAINT   **2** : a habitually irritable or complaining person : GRUMBLER — **grouch** *vi*

grouchy \'graú-chē\ *adj* **grouch·i·er; -est** (ca. 1895) : given to grumbling : PEEVISH — **grouch·i·ly** \-chə-lē\ *adv* — **grouch·i·ness** \-chē-nəs\ *n*

¹**ground** \'graúnd\ *n, often attrib* [ME, fr. OE *grund*; akin to OHG *grunt* ground] (bef. 12c) **1 a** : the bottom of a body of water   **b** *pl* (1) : SEDIMENT 1 (2) : ground coffee beans after brewing   **2 a** : a basis for belief, action, or argument ⟨*~* for complaint⟩ — often used in pl.   **b** (1) : a fundamental logical condition (2) : a basic metaphysical cause   **3 a** : a surrounding area : BACKGROUND   **b** : material that serves as a substratum   **4 a** : the surface of the earth   **b** : an area used for a particular purpose ⟨parade *~*⟩ ⟨fishing *~s*⟩   **c** *pl* : the area around and belonging to a house or other building   **d** : an area to be won or defended in or as if in battle   **e** : an area of knowledge or special interest ⟨covered a lot of *~* in his lecture⟩   **5 a** : SOIL, EARTH   **b** : a special soil   **6 a** : an object that makes an electrical connection with the earth   **b** : a large conducting body (as the earth) used as a common return for an electric circuit and as an arbitrary zero of potential   **c** : electric connection with a ground   **7** : a football offense utilizing primarily running plays — **from the ground up** **1** : entirely new or afresh   **2** : from top to bottom : THOROUGHLY — **into the ground** : beyond what is necessary or tolerable : to exhaustion ⟨labored an issue *into the ground* —Newsweek⟩ — **off the ground** : in or as if in flight : off to a good start ⟨the program never got *off the ground*⟩ — **on the ground** : at the scene of action — **to ground** **1** : into a burrow ⟨the fox went *to ground*⟩   **2** : into hiding ⟨might need to make a run for it and go *to ground* someplace —Edward Hoagland⟩

²**ground** *vt* (13c) **1 a** : to bring to or place on the ground   **b** : to cause to run aground   **2 a** : to provide a reason or justification for ⟨our fears about technological change may be well *~ed* —L. K. Williams⟩   **b** : to furnish with a foundation of knowledge : BASE ⟨an understanding . . . that is *~ed* in fact —Michael Kimmelman⟩   **3** : to connect electrically with a ground   **4 a** : to restrict to the ground ⟨*~* a pilot⟩   **b** : to prohibit from taking part in some usual activities ⟨*~ed* her for a week⟩   **5** : to throw (a football) intentionally to the ground to avoid being tackled for a loss   *~ vi* **1** : to have a ground or basis : RELY   **2** : to run aground   **3** : to hit a grounder

³**ground** *past and past part of* GRIND

ground ball *n* (1857) : a batted baseball that bounds or rolls along the ground

ground bass *n* (1699) : a short bass passage continually repeated below constantly changing melody and harmony

ground beetle *n* (1848) : any of a large cosmopolitan family (Carabidae) of soil-inhabiting usu. carnivorous often shiny black or metallic beetles commonly having fused elytra

ground·break·er \'graún(d)-,brā-kər\ *n* (1940) : one that innovates : PIONEER

ground·break·ing \-,brā-kiŋ\ *adj* (1907) : markedly innovative ⟨has written a *~* work⟩

ground·burst \-,bərst\ *n* (ca. 1951) : the detonation of a nuclear warhead at ground level

ground–cher·ry \'graún(d)-'cher-ē\ *n* (1807) : any of numerous chiefly New World plants (genus *Physalis*) of the nightshade family with pulpy fruits in papery husks; *also* : the fruit of the ground-cherry

ground cloth *n* (1931) : a waterproof sheet placed on the ground for protection (as of a sleeping bag) against soil moisture

ground cover *n* (1900) **1** : the small plants on a forest floor except young trees   **2 a** : a planting of low plants (as ivy) that covers the ground in place of turf   **b** : a plant adapted for use as ground cover

ground crew *n* (1934) : the mechanics and technicians who maintain and service an airplane

ground–effect machine *n* [fr. the lift provided by compression of air between the vehicle and the ground] (1962) : HOVERCRAFT

ground·er \'graún-dər\ *n* (ca. 1867) : GROUND BALL

ground·fish \'graún(d)-,fish\ *n* (1856) : a bottom fish; *esp* : a marine fish (as a cod, haddock, pollack, or flounder) of commercial importance

ground floor *n* (1601) **1** : the floor of a house most nearly on a level with the ground — compare FIRST FLOOR   **2** : a favorable position or privileged opportunity usu. obtained by early participants — used esp. in the phrase *in on the ground floor*

ground glass *n* (1848) : glass with a light-diffusing surface produced by etching or abrading

ground·hog \'graún(d)-,hóg, -,häg\ *n* (1742) : WOODCHUCK

Groundhog Day *n* [fr. the legend that a groundhog emerging from its burrow returns to hibernate if it sees its shadow on this day] (1871) : February 2 that traditionally indicates six more weeks of winter if sunny or an early spring if cloudy

ground·ing \'graún-diŋ\ *n* (1644) : training or instruction in the fundamentals of a field of knowledge

ground ivy *n* (14c) : a trailing mint (*Glechoma hederacea*) with rounded leaves and blue-purple flowers

ground·less \'graún(d)-ləs\ *adj* (1620) : having no ground or foundation ⟨*~* fears⟩ — **ground·less·ly** *adv* — **ground·less·ness** *n*

ground·ling \'graún(d)-liŋ\ *n* (1602) **1 a** : a spectator who stood in the pit of an Elizabethan theater   **b** : a person of unsophisticated taste   **2** : one that lives or works on or near the ground

ground loop *n* (1928) : a sharp uncontrollable turn made by an aircraft on the ground and usu. caused by an unbalanced drag (as from a wingtip touching the ground)

ground·mass \'graún(d)-,mas\ *n* (1879) : the fine-grained or glassy base of a porphyry in which the larger distinct crystals are embedded

ground meristem *n* (1938) : the part of a primary apical meristem remaining after differentiation of protoderm and procambium

ground·nut \'graún(d)-,nət\ *n* (1602) **1 a** : any of several plants having edible tuberous roots; *esp* : a No. American leguminous vine

(*Apios americana*) with pinnate leaves and clusters of brownish purple fragrant flowers **b** : the root of a groundnut **2** *chiefly Brit* : PEANUT

ground·out \'graùn-,daùt\ *n* (1965) : a play in baseball in which a batter is put out after hitting a grounder to an infielder

ground pine *n* (1551) **1** : a European bugle (*Ajuga chamaepitys*) with a resinous odor **2** : any of several club mosses (esp. *Lycopodium clavatum* and *L. complanatum*) with long creeping stems and erect branches

ground plan *n* (1731) **1** : a plan of a floor of a building as distinguished from an elevation **2** : a first or basic plan

ground rent *n* (1667) : the rent paid by a lessee for the use of land esp. for building

ground rule *n* (1890) **1** : a sports rule adopted to modify play on a particular field, court, or course **2** : a rule of procedure ⟨*ground rules* for selecting a superintendent —*Amer. School Board Jour.*⟩

¹ground·sel \'graùn(d)-səl\ *n* [ME *groundeswele*, fr. OE *grundeswelge*, fr. *grund* ground + *swelgan* to swallow — more at SWALLOW] (bef. 12c) : any of various senecios (as the nearly cosmopolitan weed *Senecio vulgaris*)

²groundsel *n* [ME *ground sille*, fr. *ground* + *sille* sill] (15c) : a foundation timber

ground·sheet \'graùn(d)-,shēt\ *n* (1907) : GROUND CLOTH

grounds·keep·er \'graùn(d)z-,kē-pər\ *n* (1903) : a person who cares for the grounds of a usu. large property (as a sports field)

ground sloth *n* (1860) : any of various often huge extinct American edentates related to the recent sloths

grounds·man \'graùn(d)z-mən\ *n* (1886) *chiefly Brit* : GROUNDSKEEPER

ground speed *n* (1917) : the speed (as of an airplane) with relation to the ground — compare AIRSPEED

ground squirrel *n* (1688) : any of various burrowing rodents (esp. genus *Spermophilus*) of No. America and Eurasia that are related to the squirrels and often live in colonies esp. in open areas — called also *spermophile*

ground state *n* (1926) : the state of a physical system (as of an atomic nucleus or an atom) having the least energy of all the possible states — called also *ground level*

ground stroke *n* (1895) : a stroke made (as in tennis) by hitting a ball that has rebounded from the ground — compare VOLLEY

ground substance *n* (1882) : a more or less homogeneous matrix in which the specific differentiated elements of a system are suspended: **a** : the intercellular substance of tissues **b** : CYTOSOL

ground·swell \'graùnd-,swel\ *n* (1818) **1** *usu* **ground swell** : a broad deep undulation of the ocean caused by an often distant gale or seismic disturbance **2** : a rapid spontaneous growth (as of political opinion) ⟨a ~ of support⟩

ground·wa·ter \-,wȯ-tər, -,wä-\ *n* (ca. 1889) : water within the earth that supplies wells and springs

ground wave *n* (1925) : a radio wave that is propagated along the surface of the earth

ground·wood \'graùnd-,wùd\ *n* [³*ground*] (1885) : wood ground up and used to make pulp for paper

ground·work \'graùnd-,wərk\ *n* (15c) : FOUNDATION, BASIS ⟨laid the ~ for a new program⟩; *also* : preparation made beforehand ⟨the ~ was done before the winter tour —Susan Reiter⟩

ground zero *n* (1946) **1** : the point directly above, below, or at which a nuclear explosion occurs **2** : the center or origin of rapid, intense, or violent activity or change **3** : the very beginning : SQUARE ONE

¹group \'grüp\ *n, often attrib* [F *groupe*, fr. It *gruppo*, of Gmc origin; akin to OHG *kropf* craw — more at CROP] (1686) **1** : two or more figures forming a complete unit in a composition **2 a** : a number of individuals assembled together or having some unifying relationship **b** : an assemblage of objects regarded as a unit **c** (1) : a military unit consisting of a headquarters and attached battalions (2) : a unit of the U.S. Air Force higher than a squadron and lower than a wing **3 a** : an assemblage of related organisms — often used to avoid taxonomic connotations when the kind or degree of relationship is not clearly defined **b** (1) : two or more atoms joined together or sometimes a single atom forming part of a molecule; *esp* : FUNCTIONAL GROUP ⟨a methyl ~⟩ (2) : an assemblage of elements forming one of the vertical columns of the periodic table **c** : a stratigraphic division comprising rocks deposited during an era **4** : a mathematical set that is closed under a binary associative operation, contains an identity element, and has an inverse for every element

²group *vt* (1718) **1** : to combine in a group **2** : to assign to a group : CLASSIFY ~ *vi* **1** : to form a group **2** : to belong to a group **3** : to make groups of closely spaced hits on a target ⟨the gun ~ed beautifully —R. C. Ruark⟩ — **group·able** \'grü-pə-bəl\ *adj*

group captain *n* (1919) : a commissioned officer in the British air force who ranks with a colonel in the army

group dynamics *n pl but sing or pl in constr* (1939) : the interacting forces within a small human group; *also* : the sociological study of these forces

grou·per \'grü-pər\ *n, pl* **groupers** *also* **grouper** [Pg *garoupa*] (1671) : any of numerous fishes (family Serranidae and esp. genera *Epinephelus* and *Mycteroperca*) that are typically large solitary bottom≈ dwelling fishes of warm seas

group·ie \'grü-pē\ *n* (1967) **1** : a fan of a rock group who usu. follows the group around on concert tours **2** : an admirer of a celebrity who attends as many of his or her public appearances as possible **3** : ENTHUSIAST, AFICIONADO ⟨a political ~⟩ ⟨golf ~s⟩

group·ing \'grü-piŋ\ *n* (1748) **1** : the act or process of combining in groups **2** : a set of objects combined in a group ⟨a furniture ~⟩

group practice *n* (1942) : medicine practiced by a group of associated physicians or dentists (as specialists in different fields) working as partners or as partners and employees

group theory *n* (1898) : a branch of mathematics concerned with finding all mathematical groups and determining their properties

group therapy *n* (1943) : therapy in the presence of a therapist in which several patients discuss and share their personal problems — called also *group psychotherapy* — **group therapist** *n*

group·think \'grüp-,thiŋk\ *n* [¹*group* + -*think* (as in *doublethink*)] (1952) : a pattern of thought characterized by self-deception, forced manufacture of consent, and conformity to group values and ethics

grou·pus·cule \grü-'pəs-,kyül\ *n* [F, fr. *groupe* group + -*uscule* (as in *corpuscule* corpuscle)] (1969) : a small group of political activists

¹grouse \'graùs\ *n, pl* **grouse** *or* **grouses** [origin unknown] (1531) : any of numerous chiefly ground-dwelling birds (family Tetraonidae) that are usu. of reddish brown or other protective color and have feathered legs and that include many important game birds

²grouse *vi* **groused; grous·ing** [origin unknown] (1887) : COMPLAIN, GRUMBLE — **grous·er** *n*

³grouse *n* (1918) : COMPLAINT

¹grout \'graùt\ *n* [ME, coarse meal, fr. OE *grūt*; akin to OE *grēot* grit] (1638) **1 a** : thin mortar used for filling spaces (as the joints in masonry); *also* : any of various other materials (as a mixture of cement and water or chemicals that solidify) used for a similar purpose **b** : PLASTER **2** : LEES

²grout *vt* (1838) **1** : to fill up or finish with grout **2** : to fix in place by means of grout ⟨~ a bolt into a wall⟩ — **grout·er** *n*

grove \'grōv\ *n* [ME, fr. OE *grāf*] (bef. 12c) **1** : a small wood without underbrush ⟨a picnic ~⟩ **2** : a planting of fruit or nut trees

grov·el \'grä-v³l, 'grə-\ *vi* -**eled** *or* -**elled**; -**el·ing** *or* -**el·ling** [back≈ formation fr. *groveling* prone, fr. *groveling*, adv., fr. ME, fr. *gruf*, adv., on the face (fr. ON *ā grūfu*) + -*ling*] (1593) **1** : to creep with the face to the ground : CRAWL **2 a** : to lie or creep with the body prostrate in token of subservience or abasement **b** : to abase oneself **3** : to give oneself over to what is base or unworthy : WALLOW ⟨~ing in self-pity⟩ — **grov·el·er** \-v³l-ər\ *n* — **grov·el·ing·ly** \-v³l-iŋ-lē\ *adv*

groves of academe *often cap A* (1849) : the academic world

grow \'grō\ *vb* **grew** \'grü\; **grown** \'grōn\; **grow·ing** [ME, fr. OE *grōwan*; akin to OHG *gruoan* to grow] *vi* (bef. 12c) **1 a** : to spring up and develop to maturity **b** : to be able to grow in some place or situation ⟨trees that ~ in the tropics⟩ **c** : to assume some relation through or as if through a process of natural growth ⟨ferns ~*ing* from the rocks⟩ **2 a** : to increase in size by assimilation of material into the living organism or by accretion of material in a nonbiological process (as crystallization) **b** : INCREASE, EXPAND ⟨~s in wisdom⟩ **3** : to develop from a parent source ⟨the book *grew* out of a series of lectures⟩ **4 a** : to pass into a condition : BECOME ⟨*grew* pale⟩ **b** : to have an increasing influence ⟨habit ~s on a person⟩ **c** : to become increasingly acceptable or attractive ⟨didn't like it at first, but it *grew* on him⟩ ~ *vt* **1** : to cause to grow ⟨~ wheat⟩ **2** : DEVELOP **5** — **grow·er** \'grō-(ə)r\ *n* — **grow·ing·ly** \'grō-iŋ-lē\ *adv*

growing pains *n pl* (1810) **1** : pains in the legs of growing children having no demonstrable relation to growth **2** : the stresses and strains attending a new project or development

growing point *n* (1835) : the undifferentiated end of a plant shoot from which additional shoot tissues differentiate

¹growl \'graù(ə)l\ *vb* [ME *groulen, grollen*] *vi* (14c) **1 a** : RUMBLE ⟨his stomach ~ed⟩ **b** : to utter a growl ⟨the dog ~ed at the stranger⟩ **2** : to complain angrily ~ *vt* : to utter with a growl : utter angrily

²growl *n* (1727) : a deep guttural inarticulate sound

growl·er \'graù-lər\ *n* (1753) **1** : one that growls **2** : a container (as a can or pitcher) for beer bought by the measure **3** : a small iceberg

growl·ing \'graù-liŋ\ *adj* (1752) : marked by a growl ⟨a low ~ voice⟩ ⟨listened to the ~ thunder⟩ — **growl·ing·ly** \-liŋ-lē\ *adv*

growly \'graù-lē\ *adj* **growl·i·er; -est** (1920) : resembling a growl ⟨a ~ voice⟩ — **growl·i·ness** *n*

grown \'grōn\ *adj* (1645) **1** : fully grown : MATURE ⟨~ men and women⟩ **2** : covered or surrounded with vegetation ⟨land well ~ with trees⟩ **3 a** : cultivated or produced in a specified way or locality — used in combination ⟨shade-*grown* tobacco⟩ **b** : overgrown with — used in combination ⟨a weed-*grown* patio⟩

¹grown–up \'grō-,nəp\ *adj* (1633) : not childish or immature : ADULT

²grown–up *n* (1813) : ADULT

growth \'grōth\ *n* (1557) **1 a** (1) : a stage in the process of growing : SIZE (2) : full growth **b** : the process of growing **c** : progressive development : EVOLUTION **d** : INCREASE, EXPANSION ⟨the ~ of the oil industry⟩ **2 a** : something that grows or has grown **b** : an abnormal proliferation of tissue (as a tumor) **c** : OUTGROWTH **d** : the result of growth : PRODUCT **3** : a producing esp. by growing ⟨fruits of his own ~⟩

growth company *n* (1959) : a company that grows at a greater rate than the economy as a whole and that usu. directs a relatively high proportion of income back into the business

growth factor *n* (1926) : a substance (as a vitamin B_{12} or an interleukin) that promotes growth and esp. cellular growth

growth hormone *n* (1924) **1** : a vertebrate polypeptide hormone that is secreted by the anterior lobe of the pituitary gland and regulates growth — called also *somatotropin* **2** : GROWTH REGULATOR

growth regulator *n* (1936) : any of various synthetic or naturally occurring plant substances (as an auxin or gibberellin) that regulate growth

growth ring *n* (1907) : a layer of wood (as an annual ring) produced during a single period of growth

growthy \'grō-thē\ *adj* **growth·i·er; -est** (1884) *of livestock* : exceptionally fast in growing and gaining weight — **growth·i·ness** \-nəs\ *n*

grow up *vi* (1535) : to grow toward or arrive at full stature or physical or mental maturity ⟨*growing up* intellectually, socially, and physically⟩

groyne \'grȯin\ *n* [by alter.] (1582) : GROIN 3

¹grub \'grəb\ *vb* **grubbed; grub·bing** [ME *grubben*; akin to OE *grafan* to dig — more at GRAVE] *vt* (14c) **1** : to clear by digging up roots and stumps **2** : to dig up by or as if by the roots ~ *vi* **1 a** : to dig in the ground esp. for something that is difficult to find or extract **b** : to search about ⟨*grubbed* in the countryside for food —*Lamp*⟩ **2** : TOIL, DRUDGE ⟨folks who ~ for money —James Street⟩ — **grub·ber** *n*

²grub *n* [ME *grubbe*, fr. *grubben*] (15c) **1** : a soft thick wormlike larva of an insect **2** : one who does menial work : DRUDGE **b** : a slovenly person **3** : FOOD

grub·by \'grə-bē\ *adj* **grub·bi·er; -est** (1725) **1** : infested with fly

\a\ abut \ᵊ\ kitten, F table \ər\ further \a\ ash \ā\ ace \ä\ mop, mar \aù\ out \ch\ chin \e\ bet \ē\ easy \g\ go \i\ hit \ī\ ice \j\ job \ŋ\ sing \ō\ go \ȯ\ law \ȯi\ boy \th\ thin \t͟h\ the \ü\ loot \ù\ foot \y\ yet \zh\ vision \ä, k̲, ⁿ, œ, œ̄, ue, u̅e, ᵊ\ *see* Guide to Pronunciation maggots **2 a** : DIRTY, GRIMY ⟨~ hands⟩ **b** : SLOVENLY, SLOPPY **3** : worthy of contempt : BASE ⟨~ political motives⟩ — **grub·bi·ly** \ˈgrə-bə-lē\ adv — **grub·bi·ness** \-bē-nəs\ n

¹**grub·stake** \ˈgrəb-ˌstāk\ n (1863) **1** : supplies or funds furnished a mining prospector on promise of a share in his discoveries **2** : material assistance (as a loan) provided for launching an enterprise or for a person in difficult circumstances

²**grubstake** vt (1879) : to provide with a grubstake — **grub·stak·er** n

Grub Street \ˈgrəb-\ n [Grub Street, London, formerly inhabited by literary hacks] (1630) : the world or category of needy literary hacks

¹**grudge** \ˈgrəj\ vt **grudged; grudg·ing** [ME grucchen, grudgen to grumble, complain, fr. MF groucier, of Gmc origin; akin to MHG grogezen to howl] (14c) **1** : to be unwilling to give or admit : give or allow reluctantly or resentfully ⟨didn't ~ the time⟩ — **grudg·er** n

²**grudge** n (15c) : a feeling of deep-seated resentment or ill will syn see MALICE

grudg·ing \ˈgrə-jiŋ\ adj (ca. 1533) **1** : UNWILLING, RELUCTANT **2** : done, given, or allowed unwillingly, reluctantly, or sparingly ⟨~ compliance⟩ — **grudg·ing·ly** \-jiŋ-lē\ adv

gru·el \ˈgrü-əl\ n [ME grewel, fr. MF gruel, of Gmc origin; akin to OE grūt grout] (14c) **1** : a thin porridge **2** chiefly Brit : PUNISHMENT

gru·el·ing or **gru·el·ling** \ˈgrü-ə-liŋ\ adj [fr. prp. of obs. gruel (to exhaust)] (1852) : trying or taxing to the point of exhaustion : PUNISHING ⟨a ~ race⟩ — **gru·el·ing·ly** \-liŋ-lē\ adv

grue·some \ˈgrü-səm\ adj [alter. of earlier growsome, fr. E dial. grow, grue to shiver, fr. ME gruen, prob. fr. MD grūwen; akin to OHG ingrüen to shiver] (1816) : inspiring horror or repulsion : GRISLY syn see GHASTLY — **grue·some·ly** adv — **grue·some·ness** n

¹**gruff** \ˈgrəf\ adj [D grof; akin to OHG grob coarse, hruf scurf — more at DANDRUFF] (1706) **1** : rough, brusque, or stern in manner, speech, or aspect ⟨a ~ reply⟩ **2** : being deep and harsh : HOARSE ⟨a ~ voice⟩ syn see BLUFF — **gruff·ly** adv — **gruff·ness** n

²**gruff** vt (1706) : to utter in a gruff voice or manner

grum·ble \ˈgrəm-bəl\ vb **grum·bled; grum·bling** \-b(ə-)liŋ\ [prob. fr. MF grommeler, ultim. fr. MD grommen; akin to OHG grimm grim] vi (ca. 1586) **1** : to mutter in discontent **2** : GROWL, RUMBLE ~ vt : to express with grumbling — **grumble** n — **grum·bler** \-b(ə-)lər\ n — **grum·bling·ly** \-b(ə-)liŋ-lē\ adv — **grum·bly** \-b(ə-)lē\ adj

grum·met \ˈgrə-mət\ var of GROMMET

¹**grump** \ˈgrəmp\ n [obs. E grumps (snubs, slights)] (1844) **1** : a fit of ill humor or sulkiness — usu. used in pl. **2** : a person given to complaining

²**grump** vi (1875) **1** : SULK **2** : GRUMBLE, COMPLAIN ~ vt : to utter in a grumpy manner

grumpy \ˈgrəm-pē\ adj **grump·i·er; -est** (1778) : moodily cross : SURLY — **grump·i·ly** \-pə-lē\ adv — **grump·i·ness** \-pē-nəs\ n

grunge \ˈgrənj\ n [back-formation fr. grungy] (1965) **1** : one that is grungy **2** : rock music incorporating elements of punk rock and heavy metal; also : the untidy working-class fashions typical of fans of grunge

grun·gy \ˈgrən-jē\ adj **grun·gi·er; -est** [origin unknown] (1965) : shabby or dirty in character or condition

grun·ion \ˈgrən-yən\ n [prob. fr. Sp gruñón grunter] (1917) : a silversides (Leuresthes tenuis) of the California coast notable for the regularity with which it comes inshore to spawn at nearly full moon

¹**grunt** \ˈgrənt\ vb [ME grunten, fr. OE grunnettan, freq. of grunian, of imit. origin] vi (bef. 12c) : to utter a grunt ~ vt : to utter with a grunt — **grunt·er** n

²**grunt** n (1553) **1 a** : the deep short sound characteristic of a hog **b** : a similar sound **2** [fr. the noise it makes when taken from the water] : any of a family (Haemulidae syn. Pomadasyidae) of chiefly tropical marine bony fishes **3** : a dessert made by dropping biscuit dough on top of boiling berries and steaming ⟨blueberry ~⟩ **4** : a U.S. army or marine foot soldier esp. in the Vietnam war **5** : one who does routine unglamorous work — often used attributively ⟨~ work⟩

grunt 2

grun·tle \ˈgrən-tᵊl\ vt **grun·tled; grun·tling** \ˈgrənt-liŋ, ˈgrən-tᵊl-iŋ\ [back-formation fr. disgruntle] (1926) : to put in a good humor ⟨were gruntled with a good meal and good conversation —W. P. Webb⟩

grutch \ˈgrəch\ vt [ME grucchen] (14c) obs : BEGRUDGE

grutten past part of GREET

Gru·yère \grü-ˈyer, grē-\ n [Gruyère, district in Switzerland] (1802) **1** : a firm cheese with small holes and a nutty flavor that is of Swiss origin **2** : a process cheese made from natural Gruyère

gryph·on var of GRIFFIN

G–string \ˈjē-ˌstriŋ\ n [origin unknown] (1878) : a strip of cloth passed between the legs and supported by a waist cord that is worn esp. by striptease dancers

G suit n [gravity suit] (1944) : a suit designed to counteract the physiological effects of acceleration on an aviator or astronaut

GT \ˌjē-ˈtē\ n [It Gran Turismo] (1966) : GRAND TOURING CAR

GTP \ˌjē-(ˌ)tē-ˈpē\ n [guanosine triphosphate] (1961) : an energy-rich nucleotide analogous to ATP that is composed of guanine, ribose, and three phosphate groups and is necessary for peptide-bond formation during protein synthesis — called also guanosine triphosphate

G₂ phase \ˌjē-ˈtü-\ n [growth] (1968) : the period in the cell cycle from the completion of DNA replication to the beginning of cell division — compare G₁ PHASE, M PHASE, S PHASE

gua·ca·mo·le \ˌgwä-kə-ˈmō-lē\ n [MexSp, fr. Nahuatl āhuacamōlli, fr. āhuacatl avocado + mōlli sauce] (1920) : pureed or mashed avocado seasoned with condiments

gua·cha·ro \ˈgwä-chə-ˌrō\ n, pl **-ros** or **-roes** [AmerSp guácharo] (1830) : OILBIRD

guai·ac \ˈgwī-ˌak, ˈgī-\ n [NL Guaiacum] (ca. 1751) : GUAIACUM 2

guai·a·cum \ˈgwī-ə-kəm, ˈgī-\ n [NL, fr. Sp guayaco, fr. Taino guayacan] (1553) **1** : any of a genus (Guaiacum) of the caltrop family of tropical American evergreen trees and shrubs having pinnate leaves,

usu. blue flowers, and capsular fruit **2 a** : the hard greenish brown wood of a guaiacum (esp. Guaiacum officinale) **b** : a resin with a faint balsamic odor that is obtained from the trunk of two guaiacums (G. officinale and G. sanctum) and often used as a clinical reagent

guan \ˈgwän\ n [alter. of earlier quam, prob. fr. Cuna (Chibchan language of Panama) kwama] (1743) : any of various large tropical American lowland-forest birds (family Cracidae) that somewhat resemble turkeys

gua·na·co \gwə-ˈnä-(ˌ)kō\ n, pl **-cos** also **-co** [Sp, fr. Quechua wanaku] (1604) : a So. American mammal (Lama guanicoe) of dry open country that has a soft thick fawn-colored coat and is related to the camel but lacks a dorsal hump

gua·neth·i·dine \gwä-ˈne-thə-ˌdēn\ n [guanidine + eth-] (1959) : a drug C₁₀H₂₂N₄ used esp. as the sulfate in treating severe high blood pressure

gua·ni·dine \ˈgwä-nə-ˌdēn\ n [ISV, fr. guanine] (ca. 1864) : a base CH₅N₃ derived from guanine, found esp. in young tissues, and used in organic synthesis and as a parasympathetic stimulant in medicine esp. as the hydrochloride salt

gua·nine \ˈgwä-ˌnēn\ n [guano + -ine; fr. its being found esp. in guano] (1850) : a purine base C₅H₅N₅O that codes genetic information in the polynucleotide chain of DNA or RNA — compare ADENINE, CYTOSINE, THYMINE, URACIL

gua·no \ˈgwä-(ˌ)nō\ n [Sp, fr. Quechua wanu fertilizer, dung] (1604) : a substance composed chiefly of the excrement of seafowl and used as a fertilizer; also : a similar substance (as bat excrement or cannery waste) esp. when used for fertilizer

gua·no·sine \ˈgwä-nə-ˌsēn\ n [guan- (as in guanine) + ribose + -ine] (1909) : a nucleoside C₁₀H₁₃N₅O₅ composed of guanine and ribose

guanosine triphosphate n (ca. 1962) : GTP

guar \ˈgwär\ n [Hindi guār] (1882) : a drought-tolerant legume (Cyamopsis tetragonoloba) cultivated in warm regions as a vegetable, for forage, and for its seeds which produce guar gum

gua·ra·ni \ˌgwär-ə-ˈnē\ n [Sp guaraní] (1797) **1** cap a pl **guarani** or **guaranis** : a member of a Tupi-Guaranian people of Bolivia, Paraguay, and southern Brazil **b** : the language of the Guarani **2** pl **guaranies** also **guaranis** — see MONEY table

¹**guar·an·tee** \ˌgar-ən-ˈtē, ˌgär- also ˈgar-ən-, or ˈgär-ən-,\ n [prob. alter. of ¹guaranty] (1710) **1** : GUARANTOR **2** : GUARANTY 1 **3** : an assurance for the fulfillment of a condition: as **a** : an agreement by which one person undertakes to secure another in the possession or enjoyment of something **b** : an assurance of the quality of or of the length of use to be expected from a product offered for sale often with a promise of reimbursement **4** : GUARANTY 4

²**guarantee** vt **-teed; -tee·ing** (1791) **1** : to undertake to answer for the debt, default, or miscarriage of **2** : to engage for the existence, permanence, or nature of : undertake to do or secure ⟨~ the winning of three tricks⟩ **3** : to give security to **4** : to assert confidently

guar·an·tor \ˌgar-ən-ˈtor, ˈgar-ən-tor, ˌgär-, ˈgär-\ n (ca. 1828) **1** : one that makes or gives a guaranty **2** : one that guarantees

¹**guar·an·ty** \ˈgar-ən-tē, ˈgär-\ n, pl **-ties** [MF garantie, fr. OF, fr. garantir to guarantee, fr. garant warrant, of Gmc origin; akin to OHG werēnto guarantor — more at WARRANT] (1592) **1** : an undertaking to answer for the payment of a debt or the performance of a duty of another in case of the other's default or miscarriage **2** : GUARANTEE 3 **3** : GUARANTOR **4** : something given as security : PLEDGE **5** : the protection of a right afforded by legal provision (as in a constitution)

²**guaranty** vt **-tied; -ty·ing** (1753) : GUARANTEE

¹**guard** \ˈgärd\ n [ME garde, fr. MF, fr. OF, fr. garder to guard, defend, of Gmc origin; akin to OHG wartēn to watch, take care — more at WARD] (15c) **1** : one assigned to protect or oversee another: as **a** : a person or a body of persons on sentinel duty **b** pl : troops attached to the person of the sovereign ⟨a Brit : CONDUCTOR **2 a** : a defensive state or attitude ⟨asked him out when his ~ was down⟩ **b** : a defensive position (as in boxing) **3 a** : the act or duty of protecting or defending **b** : the state of being protected : PROTECTION **4** : a protective or safety device; specif : a device for protecting a machine part or the operator of a machine **5** archaic : PRECAUTION **6 a** : a position or player next to the center in a football line **b** : a player stationed in the backcourt in basketball — **off guard** : in an unprepared or unsuspecting state — **on guard** : defensively watchful : ALERT

²**guard** vt (1500) **1** : to protect an edge of with an ornamental border **2 a** : to protect from danger esp. by watchful attention : make secure ⟨police ~ing our cities⟩ **b** : to stand at the entrance of as if on guard or as a barrier **c** : to tend to carefully : PRESERVE, PROTECT ⟨~ed their privacy⟩ **3** archaic : ESCORT **4 a** : to watch over so as to prevent escape, disclosure, or indiscretion **b** : to attempt to prevent (an opponent) from playing effectively or scoring ~ vi : to watch by way of caution or defense : stand guard syn see DEFEND — **guard·er** n

¹**guar·dant** \ˈgär-dᵊnt\ adj [MF gardant, prp. of garder to guard, look at] (1572) : having the head turned toward the spectator — used of a heraldic animal whose body is seen from the side ⟨a lion passant ~⟩

²**guardant** n (1591) obs : GUARDIAN

guard cell n (1875) : one of the two crescent-shaped epidermal cells that border and open and close a plant stoma

guard·ed \ˈgär-dəd\ adj (1709) **1** : CAUTIOUS, CIRCUMSPECT — **guard·ed·ly** adv — **guard·ed·ness** n

guard hair n (1913) : one of the long coarse hairs forming a protective coating over the undercoat of a mammal

guard·house \ˈgärd-ˌhaůs\ n (1592) **1** : a building occupied by a guard or used as a headquarters by soldiers on guard duty **2** : a military jail

guard·ian \ˈgär-dē-ən\ n (15c) **1** : one that guards : CUSTODIAN **2** : a superior of a Franciscan monastery **3** : one who has the care of the person or property of another — **guard·ian·ship** \-ˌship\ n

guardian angel n (ca. 1631) : an angel believed to have special care of a particular individual; broadly : SAVIOR 1, PROTECTOR

guard of honor (1887) : HONOR GUARD

guard·rail \ˈgär-ˌdrāl\ n (1860) : a railing for guarding against danger or trespass; esp : a barrier (as of steel cables) placed along the edge of a highway at dangerous points

guard·room \ˈgär-ˌdrüm, -ˌdrům\ n (1762) **1** : a room occupied by a military guard during its term of duty **2** : a room where military prisoners are confined

guards·man \'gärdz-mən\ n (1817) : a member of a military body called *guard* or *guards*

guar gum n (1950) : a gum that consists of the ground endosperm of guar seeds and is used esp. as a thickening agent and as a sizing material for paper and textiles

Guar·ne·ri·us \gwär-'nir-ē-əs, -'ner-\ n [NL, fr. It *Guarneri*] (1866) : a violin made by one of the Italian Guarneri family in the 17th and 18th centuries

gua·va \'gwä-və\ n [Sp *guaba, guayaba*, perh. fr. Taino] (1604) **1** : any of several tropical American shrubs or small trees (genus *Psidium*) of the myrtle family; *esp* : a shrubby tree (*P. guajava*) widely cultivated for its sweet acid yellow or pink fruit **2** : the globose to pear-shaped fruit of a guava

gua·ya·be·ra \gwi-ə-'ber-ə\ n [AmerSp] (1947) : a usu. short-sleeved lightweight sport shirt designed to be worn untucked

gua·yu·le \gwi-'ü-lē, wī-\ n [AmerSp, fr. Nahuatl *cuauholli* or *huauholli*] (1906) : a much-branched composite shrub (*Parthenium argentatum*) of Mexico and the southwestern U.S. cultivated as a source of rubber

gu·ber·na·to·ri·al \gü-bə(r)-nə-'tōr-ē-əl, gyü-, gü-, -'tòr-\ adj [L *gubernator* governor, steersman, fr. *gubernare* to govern — more at GOVERN] (1734) : of or relating to a governor

guck \'gək\ n [perh. alter. of goo] (1949) : oozy sloppy dirt or debris; *broadly* : GOO, GUNK

¹gud·geon \'gə-jən\ n [ME *gudyon*, fr. MF *goujon*] (15c) **1** : PIVOT 1, JOURNAL **2** : a socket for a rudder pintle

²gudgeon n [ME *gojune*, fr. MF *gouion, gougon*, fr. L *gobion-, gobio*, alter. of *gobius* — more at GOBY] (15c) : a small European freshwater fish (*Gobio gobio*) related to the carps and often used for food or bait

gudgeon pin n (1891) : WRIST PIN

Gud·run \'gud-,rün\ n [ON *Guthrūn*] : the wife of Sigurd and later of Atli in Norse mythology

guel·der rose \'gel-də(r)-\ n [*Guelderland, Gelderland*, Netherlands] (1597) : a bush of a cultivated variety of the cranberry bush with large globose heads of sterile flowers

Guelf or **Guelph** \'gwelf\ n [It *Guelfo*] (1579) : a member of a papal and popular political party in medieval Italy that opposed the authority of the German emperors in Italy — compare GHIBELLINE

gue·non \'gwe-nən; gə-nōⁿ\ n [F] (1838) : any of various long-tailed chiefly arboreal African monkeys (genera *Cercopithecus* and *Erythrocebus*)

guer·don \'gər-d⁹n\ n [ME, fr. MF, fr. OF, of Gmc origin; akin to OHG *widarlōn* reward] (14c) : REWARD, RECOMPENSE — **guerdon** vt

gue·ri·don \gā-rē-dō⁹\ n [F *guéridon*, fr. *Gueridon*, character in 17th= cent. farces and popular songs] (1853) : a small usu. ornately carved and embellished stand or table

guern·sey \'gərn-zē\ n, pl **guernseys** often cap [*Guernsey*, Channel islands] (1834) : any of a breed of fawn and white dairy cattle that are larger than the jersey and produce rich yellowish milk

¹guer·ril·la or **gue·ril·la** \gə-'ri-lə, ge-, g(y)i-\ n [Sp *guerrilla*, fr. dim. of *guerra* war, of Gmc origin; akin to OHG *werra* strife — more at WAR] (1809) : a person who engages in irregular warfare esp. as a member of an independent unit carrying out harassment and sabotage

²guerrilla adj (1811) : of, relating to, or characteristic of guerrillas esp. in being aggressive, radical, or unconventional

guerrilla theater n (1968) : STREET THEATER

¹guess \'ges\ vb [ME *gessen*, prob. of Scand origin; akin to ON *geta* to get, guess — more at GET] vt (14c) **1** : to form an opinion of from little or no evidence **2** : BELIEVE, SUPPOSE ⟨I ~ you're right⟩ **3** : to arrive at a correct conclusion about by conjecture, chance, or intuition ⟨~ the answer⟩ ~ vi : to make a guess — **guess·able** \'ge-sə-bəl\ adj — **guess·er** n

²guess n (14c) : CONJECTURE, SURMISE

guess·ti·mate \'ges-tə-mət\ n [blend of *guess* and *estimate*] (1923) : an estimate usu. made without adequate information — **guess·ti·mate** \-,māt\ vt

guess·work \'ges-,wərk\ n (1725) : work performed or results obtained by guess : CONJECTURE

¹guest \'gest\ n [ME *gest*, fr. ON *gestr*; akin to OE *giest* guest, stranger, L *hostis* stranger, enemy] (13c) **1 a** : a person entertained in one's house **b** : a person to whom hospitality is extended **c** : a person who pays for the services of an establishment (as a hotel or restaurant) **2** : an organism (as an insect) sharing the dwelling of another; *esp* : INQUILINE **3** : a substance that is incorporated in a host substance **4** : a usu. prominent person not a regular member of a cast or organization who appears in a program or performance

²guest vi (14c) : to receive as a guest ~ vi : to appear as a guest

guest worker n (1967) : a foreign laborer working temporarily in an industrialized usu. European country

guff \'gəf\ n [prob. imit.] (1888) : NONSENSE, HUMBUG

guf·faw \(,)gə-'fò, 'gə-,fò\ n [imit.] (1720) : a loud or boisterous burst of laughter — **guf·faw** \(,)gə-'fò\ vi

gug·gle \'gə-gəl\ vi **gug·gled**; **gug·gling** \-g(ə-)liŋ\ [imit.] (1611) : GURGLE — **guggle** n

guid·able \'gī-də-bəl\ adj (1676) : capable of being guided

guid·ance \'gī-d⁹n(t)s\ n (1590) **1** : the act or process of guiding **2 a** : the direction provided by a guide **b** : advice on vocational or educational problems given to students **3** : the process of controlling the course of a projectile by a built-in mechanism

¹guide \'gīd\ n [ME, fr. MF, fr. OProv *guida*, of Gmc origin; akin to OE *wītan* to look after, *witan* to know — more at WIT] (14c) **1 a** : one that leads or directs another's way **b** : a person who exhibits and explains points of interest **c** : something that provides a person with guiding information **d** : SIGNPOST 1 **e** : a person who directs another's conduct or course of life **2 a** : a device for steadying or directing the motion of something **b** : a ring or loop for holding the line of a fishing rod in position **c** : a sheet or a card with projecting tab for labeling inserted in a card index to facilitate reference **3** : a member of a unit on whom the movements or alignments of a military command are regulated — used esp. in commands ⟨~ right⟩

²guide vb **guid·ed**; **guid·ing** vt (14c) **1** : to act as a guide to : direct in a way or course **2 a** : to direct, supervise, or influence usu. to a particular end **b** : to superintend the training or instruction of ~ vi : to act or work as a guide — **guid·er** n

syn GUIDE, LEAD, STEER, PILOT, ENGINEER mean to direct in a course or show the way to be followed. GUIDE implies intimate knowledge of the way and of all its difficulties and dangers ⟨*guided* the scouts through the cave⟩. LEAD implies showing the way and often keeping those that follow under control and in order ⟨*led* his team to victory⟩. STEER implies an ability to keep to a chosen course and stresses the capacity of maneuvering correctly ⟨*steered* the ship through a narrow channel⟩. PILOT suggests guidance over a dangerous, intricate, or complicated course ⟨*piloted* the bill through the Senate⟩. ENGINEER implies guidance by one who finds ways to avoid or overcome difficulties in achieving an end or carrying out a plan ⟨*engineered* his son's election to the governorship⟩.

guide·book \'gīd-,buk\ n (1814) : HANDBOOK 1; *esp* : a book of information for travelers

guided missile n (1945) : a missile whose course may be altered during flight (as by a target-seeking radar device)

guide dog n (1932) : a dog trained to lead the blind

guide·line \'gīd-,līn\ n (1785) : a line by which one is guided: as **a** : a cord or rope to aid a passer over a difficult point or to permit retracing a course **b** : an indication or outline of policy or conduct

guide·post \-,pōst\ n (1761) **1** : INDICATION, SIGN **2** : GUIDELINE b

guide·way \-,wā\ n (1876) : a channel or track for controlling the line of motion of something

guide word n (ca. 1928) : either of the terms at the head of a page of an alphabetical reference work (as a dictionary) indicating the alphabetically first and last words on the page

gui·don \'gī-,dän, -d⁹n\ n [MF, fr. *guide*] (1548) **1** : a small flag; *esp* : one borne by a military unit as a unit marker **2** : one who carries a guidon

guid·will·ie \gōed-'wi-lē, gid-\ adj [Sc *guidwill* goodwill] (1788) *Scot* : CORDIAL, CHEERING

guild \'gild\ n [ME *gilde*, fr. ON *gildi* payment, guild; akin to OE *gield* tribute, guild — more at GELD] (14c) : an association of people with similar interests or pursuits; *esp* : a medieval association of merchants or craftsmen — **guild·ship** \'gil(d)-,ship\ n

guil·der \'gil-dər\ n [ME *gylder, gyldren*, modif. of MD *gulden*] (15c) : GULDEN

guild·hall \'gild-,hòl\ n (14c) : a hall where a guild or corporation usu. assembles

guilds·man \'gil(d)z-mən\ n (1873) **1** : a guild member **2** : an advocate of guild socialism

guild socialism n (1912) : an early 20th century English socialist theory advocating state ownership of industry with control and management by guilds of workers

guile \'gī(ə)l\ n [ME, fr. OF, prob. of Gmc origin; akin to OE *wigle* divination — more at WITCH] (13c) **1** : deceitful cunning : DUPLICITY **2** *obs* : STRATAGEM, TRICK — **guile·ful** \-fəl\ adj — **guile·ful·ly** \-fə-lē\ adv — **guile·ful·ness** n

guile·less \'gī(ə)l-ləs\ adj (1728) : INNOCENT, NAIVE — **guile·less·ly** adv — **guile·less·ness** n

Guil·lain–Bar·ré syndrome \,gē-,lan-,bä-'rä-, ,gē-yan⁻-\ n [Georges *Guillain* †1961 Fr. physician and Jean A. *Barré* b1880 Fr. neurologist] (1940) : a polyneuritis of unknown cause characterized esp. by muscle weakness and paralysis

guil·le·met \,gē-(y)ə-'mā, ,gi-lə-'met\ n [F, fr. dim. of *Guillaume* William (perh. a printer's name)] (ca. 1905) : either of the marks « or » used as quotation marks in French writing

guil·le·mot \'gi-lə-,mät\ n [F, fr. MF, dim. of *Guillaume* William] (1678) **1** *Brit* : a common murre (*Uria aalge*) **2** : any of a genus (*Cepphus*) of narrow-billed auks of northern seas

guil·loche \gi-'lōsh, gē-'(y)ōsh\ n [F *guillochis*] (ca. 1842) **1** : an architectural ornament formed of two or more interlaced bands with openings containing round devices **2** : a pattern (as on metalwork) made by interlacing curved lines

guil·lo·tine \'gi-lə-,tēn; ,gē-(y)ə-', 'gē-(y)ə-,\ n [F, fr. Joseph *Guillotin* †1814 Fr. physician] (1793) **1** : a machine for beheading by means of a heavy blade that slides down in vertical guides **2** : a shearing machine or instrument (as a paper cutter) that in action resembles a guillotine **3** *chiefly Brit* : closure by the imposition of a predetermined time limit on the consideration of specific sections of a bill or portions of other legislative business — **guillotine** vt

guilt \'gilt\ n [ME, delinquency, guilt, fr. OE *gylt* delinquency] (bef. 12c) **1** : the fact of having committed a breach of conduct esp. violating law and involving a penalty; *broadly* : guilty conduct **2 a** : the state of one who has committed an offense esp. consciously **b** : feelings of culpability esp. for imagined offenses or from a sense of inadequacy : SELF-REPROACH **3** : a feeling of culpability for offenses

guilt·less \'gilt-ləs\ adj (13c) : INNOCENT — **guilt·less·ly** adv — **guilt·less·ness** n

guilty \'gil-tē\ adj **guilt·i·er; -est** (bef. 12c) **1** : justly chargeable with or responsible for a usu. grave breach of conduct or a crime **2** *obs* : justly liable to or deserving of a penalty **3 a** : suggesting or involving guilt ⟨~ looks⟩ **b** : aware of or suffering from guilt ⟨~ consciences⟩ *syn* see BLAMEWORTHY — **guilt·i·ly** \-tə-lē\ adv — **guilt·i·ness** \-tē-nəs\ n

guimpe \'gamp, 'gimp\ n [F, fr. OF *guimple*, of Gmc origin; akin to OE *wimpel* wimple] (1850) **1** : a blouse worn under a jumper or pinafore **2** : a wide cloth used by some nuns to cover the neck and shoulders **3** [by alter.] : ¹GIMP

guin·ea \'gi-nē\ n [*Guinea*, Africa, supposed source of the gold from which it was made] (1664) **1** : an English gold coin issued from 1663 to 1813 and fixed in 1717 at 21 shillings **2** : a unit of value equal to one pound and one shilling

guinea fowl n (1788) : an African bird (*Numida meleagris*) related to the pheasants, raised for food in many parts of the world, and marked by a bare neck and head and slaty plumage speckled with white;

\ə\ abut \ᵊ\ kitten, F table \ər\ further \a\ ash \ā\ ace \ä\ mop, mar \aú\ out \ch\ chin \e\ bet \ē\ easy \g\ go \i\ hit \ī\ ice \j\ job \ŋ\ sing \ō\ go \ò\ law \òi\ boy \th\ thin \t̶h̶\ the \ü\ loot \ù\ foot \y\ yet \zh\ vision \ä, ḵ, ⁿ, œ, œ̄, ue, ūe, ᵞ\ see Guide to Pronunciation

broadly : any of several related birds

guinea grass n (1785) : a tall African forage grass (*Panicum maximum*) introduced into tropical America and the southern U.S.

guinea hen n (1599) : a female guinea fowl; *broadly* : GUINEA FOWL

guinea pepper n (1597) : GRAINS OF PARADISE

guinea pig n (1664) **1 a** : a small stout-bodied short-eared tailless domesticated rodent (*Cavia porcellus*) often kept as a pet and widely used in biological research — called also *cavy* **2** : a subject of research, experimentation, or testing

guinea fowl

guinea worm n (1699) : a slender nematode worm (*Dracunculus medinensis*) of tropical regions parasitic in mammals including humans and having an adult female that infests subcutaneous tissues and may attain a length of several feet

Guin·e·vere \'gwi-nə-ˌvir, *Brit also* 'gi-\ n : the wife of King Arthur and mistress of Lancelot

gui·pure \gi-'pyùr, -'pùr\ n [F] (1843) : a heavy large-patterned decorative lace

gui·ro \'wē-(ˌ)rō, 'gwir-(ˌ)ō\ n [AmerSp *güiro*, lit., calabash] (1898) : a percussion instrument of Latin-American origin made of a serrated gourd and played by scraping a stick along its surface

gui·sard \'gī-zərd\ n [obs. Sc *gyze* to disguise, fr. ME *gyzen* to dress, fr. *guise, gyze* guise] (1626) *chiefly Scot* : MASKER, MUMMER

guise \'gīz\ n [ME, fr. OF, of Gmc origin; akin to OHG *wīsa* manner — more at WISE] (13c) **1** : a form or style of dress : COSTUME **2 a** *obs* : MANNER, FASHION **b** *archaic* : a customary way of speaking or behaving **3 a** : external appearance : SEMBLANCE **b** : PRETEXT

gui·tar \gə-'tär, gi-, *esp Southern & Midland also* 'gi-ˌtär\ n [F *guitare*, fr. Sp *guitarra*, fr. Ar *qītār*, fr. Gk *kithara* cithara] (1621) : a flat-bodied stringed instrument with a long fretted neck and usu. six strings plucked with a pick or with the fingers — **gui·tar·ist** \-ist\ n

gui·tar·fish \-ˌfish\ n (ca. 1900) : any of several viviparous rays (family Rhinobatidae) somewhat like a guitar in shape viewed from above

Gu·ja·ra·ti \ˌgü-jə-'rä-tē, ˌgù-\ n [Hindi *gujarāti*, fr. *Gujarāt* Gujarat] (1808) **1** *or* **Gu·je·ra·ti** *same*\ : the Indo-Aryan language of Gujarat and neighboring regions in northwestern India **2** *or* **Guj·ra·ti** \'güj-ˌrä-, gùj-'rä-\ : a member of a people chiefly of Gujarat speaking the Gujarati language

gul \'gül\ n [Per] (1813) *archaic* : ROSE 1

gu·lag \'gü-ˌläg\ n, *often cap* [Russ, fr. *Glavnoe upravlenie ispravitel'no-trudovykh lagerei* chief administration of corrective labor camps] (1974) : the penal system of the U.S.S.R. consisting of a network of labor camps; *also* : LABOR CAMP 1

gu·lar \'g(y)ü-lər\ adj [L *gula* throat — more at GLUTTON] (1828) : of, relating to, or situated on the throat

gulch \'gəlch\ n [perh. fr. E dial. *gulch* to gulp, fr. ME *gulchen*] (1832) : a deep or precipitous cleft : RAVINE; *esp* : one occupied by a torrent

gul·den \'gül-dən, 'gùl-\ n, pl **guldens** *or* **gulden** [ME (Sc), fr. MD *gulden florijn* golden florin] (15c) — see MONEY table

gules \'gyü(ə)lz\ n, pl **gules** [ME *goules*, fr. MF] (14c) : the heraldic color red

¹gulf \'gəlf\ n [ME *goulf*, fr. MF *golfe*, fr. It *golfo*, fr. LL *colpus*, fr. Gk *kolpos* bosom, gulf; akin to OE *hwealf* vault, OHG *walbo*] (15c) **1** : a part of an ocean or sea extending into the land **2** : a deep chasm : ABYSS **3** : WHIRLPOOL **4** : a wide gap ⟨the ~ between generations⟩

²gulf vt (1807) : ENGULF

gulf·weed \'gəlf-ˌwēd\ n [*Gulf* of Mexico] (1674) : any of several sargassums; *esp* : a branching olive-brown seaweed (*Sargassum baciferum*) of tropical American seas with numerous berrylike air vesicles

¹gull \'gəl\ n [ME, of Celt origin; akin to W *gwylan* gull] (15c) : any of numerous long-winged web-footed aquatic birds (subfamily Larinae of the family Laridae); *esp* : a usu. gray and white bird (as of the genus *Larus*) differing from a tern in usu. larger size, stouter build, thicker somewhat hooked bill, less pointed wings, and short unforked tail

²gull vt [obs. *gull* gullet, fr. ME *golle*, fr. MF *goule*] (ca. 1550) : to take advantage of (one who is foolish or unwary) : DECEIVE **syn** see DUPE

³gull n (1594) : a person who is easily deceived or cheated : DUPE

Gul·lah \'gə-lə\ n (1822) **1** : a member of a group of blacks inhabiting the sea islands and coastal districts of So. Carolina, Georgia, and northeastern Florida **2** : an English-based creole spoken by the Gullahs that is marked by vocabulary and grammatical elements from various African languages

gul·let \'gə-lət\ n [ME *golet*, fr. MF *goulet*, dim. of *goule* throat, fr. L *gula* — more at GLUTTON] (14c) **1** : ESOPHAGUS; *broadly* : THROAT **2** : an invagination of the protoplasm in various protozoans (as a paramecium) that sometimes functions in the intake of food **3** : the space between the tips of adjacent saw teeth

gull·ible *also* **gull·able** \'gə-lə-bəl\ adj (1818) : easily duped or cheated — **gull·ibil·i·ty** \ˌgə-lə-'bi-lə-tē\ n — **gull·ibly** \'gə-lə-blē\ adv

Gul·li·ver \'gə-lə-vər\ n : an Englishman in Jonathan Swift's satire *Gulliver's Travels* who makes voyages to the imaginary lands of the Lilliputians, Brobdingnagians, Laputans, and Houyhnhnms

¹gul·ly *also* **gul·ley** \'gə-lē, 'gə-\ n, pl **gullies** [short for E dial. *gully knife*] (1582) *dial Brit* : a large knife

²gul·ly *also* **gul·ley** \'gə-lē\ n, pl **gullies** [obs. E *gully* (gullet)] (1637) **1** : a trench which was orig. worn in the earth by running water and through which water often runs after rains **2** : a small valley or gulch

³gul·ly \'gə-lē\ vb **gul·lied; gul·ly·ing** vt (1754) : to make gullies in ~ vi : to undergo erosion : form gullies

gully erosion n (1928) : soil erosion produced by running water

gu·los·i·ty \g(y)ü-'lä-sə-tē\ n [ME *gulosite*, fr. LL *gulositas*, fr. L *gulosus* gluttonous, fr. *gula* gullet] (15c) : excessive appetite : GREEDINESS

gulp \'gəlp\ vb [ME, fr. a MD or MLG word akin to D & Fris *gulpen* to bubble forth, drink deep; akin to OE *gielpan* to boast — more at YELP] vt (14c) **1** : to swallow hurriedly or greedily or in one swallow **2** : to keep back as if by swallowing ⟨~ down a sob⟩ **3** : to take in readily as if by swallowing ⟨~ down knowledge⟩ ~ vi : to catch the breath as if in taking a long drink — **gulp** n — **gulp·er** n

¹gum \'gəm\ n [ME *gome*, fr. OE *gōma* palate; akin to OHG *guomo* palate, and perh. to Gk *chaos* abyss] (bef. 12c) : the tissue that surrounds the necks of teeth and covers the alveolar parts of the jaws; *broadly* : the alveolar portion of a jaw with its enveloping soft tissues

²gum vt **gummed; gum·ming** (1777) **1** : to enlarge gullets of (a saw) **2** : to chew with the gums

³gum n [ME *gomme*, fr. MF, fr. L *cummi, gummi*, fr. Gk *kommi*, fr. Egypt *qmyt*] (14c) **1 a** : any of numerous colloidal polysaccharide substances of plant origin that are gelatinous when moist but harden on drying and are salts of complex organic acids — compare MUCILAGE **1 b** : any of various plant exudates (as an oleoresin or gum resin) **2** : a substance or deposit resembling a plant gum (as in sticky or adhesive quality) **3 a** : a tree (as a black gum) that yields gum **b** *Austral* : EUCALYPTUS **4** : the wood or lumber of a gum; *esp* : that of the sweet gum **5** : CHEWING GUM

⁴gum vb **gummed; gum·ming** vt (1597) : to clog, impede, or damage with or as if with gum ⟨~ up the works⟩ ~ vi **1** : to exude or form gum **2** : to become gummy — **gum·mer** n

gum arabic n (14c) : a water-soluble gum obtained from several acacias (esp. *Acacia senegal*) and used esp. in the manufacture of inks, adhesives, pharmaceuticals, and confections

¹gum·bo \'gəm-(ˌ)bō\ n, pl **gumbos** [AmerF *gombo*, of Bantu origin; akin to Umbundu *ochinggômbo* okra] (1805) **1** : a soup thickened with okra pods or filé and containing meat or seafoods and usu. vegetables **2** : OKRA 1 **3** : any of various fine-grained silty soils esp. of the central U.S. that when wet become impervious and soapy or waxy and very sticky **4** : a heavy sticky mud **4** : MIXTURE, MÉLANGE — **gumbo** adj

²gumbo n, *often cap* [AmerF *gombo*, perh. fr. Kongo *nkômbô* runaway slave] (1838) : CREOLE 4a

gum·boil \'gəm-ˌbòil\ n (1753) : an abscess in the gum

gum·bo·lim·bo \ˌgəm-bō-'lim-(ˌ)bō\ n [origin unknown] (1837) : a tree (*Bursera simaruba* of the family Burseraceae) of southern Florida and the American tropics that has a smooth coppery bark and supplies a reddish resin used locally in cements and varnishes

gum boot n (1850) : a rubber boot

gum·drop \'gəm-ˌdräp\ n (1860) : a sugar-coated candy made usu. from corn syrup with gelatin or gum arabic

gum·ma \'gə-mə\ n, pl **gummas** *also* **gum·ma·ta** \'gə-mə-tə\ [NL *gummat-, gumma*, fr. LL, gum, alter. of L *gummi* gum] (ca. 1722) : a tumor of gummy or rubbery consistency that is characteristic of the tertiary stage of syphilis — **gum·ma·tous** \-mə-təs\ adj

gum·mite \'gə-ˌmīt\ n (1868) : a yellow to reddish brown mixture of hydrous oxides of uranium, thorium, and lead

gum·mo·sis \ˌgə-'mō-səs\ n [NL] (1882) : a pathological production of gummy exudate in a plant; *also* : a plant disease marked by gummosis

gum·mous \'gə-məs\ adj (1669) : resembling or composed of gum

gum·my \'gə-mē\ adj **gum·mi·er; -est** (14c) **1** : VISCOUS, STICKY **2 a** : consisting of or containing gum **b** : covered with gum — **gum·mi·ness** n

gump·tion \'gəm(p)-shən\ n [origin unknown] (1719) **1** *chiefly dial* : COMMON SENSE, HORSE SENSE **2** : ENTERPRISE, INITIATIVE ⟨lacked the ~ to try⟩

gum resin n (1712) : a product consisting essentially of a mixture of gum and resin usu. obtained by making an incision in a plant and allowing the juice which exudes to solidify

¹gum·shoe \'gəm-ˌshü\ n (1906) : DETECTIVE

²gumshoe vi **gum·shoed; gum·shoe·ing** (1930) : to engage in detective work

gum tragacanth n (1573) : TRAGACANTH

gum tree n (1676) : ³GUM 3

gum turpentine n (1926) : TURPENTINE 2a

gum·wood \'gəm-ˌwúd\ n (1709) : ³GUM 4

¹gun \'gən\ n [ME *gonne, gunne*] (14c) **1 a** : a piece of ordnance usu. with high muzzle velocity and comparatively flat trajectory **b** : a portable firearm (as a rifle or handgun) **c** : a device that throws a projectile **2 a** : a discharge of a gun esp. as a salute or signal **b** : a signal marking a beginning or ending **3 a** : HUNTER **b** : GUNMAN **4** : something suggesting a gun in shape or function **5** : THROTTLE — **gunned** \'gənd\ adj — **under the gun** : under pressure or attack

²gun vb **gunned; gun·ning** vt (1622) **1** : to hunt with a gun ~ vt **1 a** : to fire on **b** : SHOOT ⟨*gunned* down by a hit man⟩ **2 a** : to open up the throttle of so as to increase speed ⟨~ the engine⟩ **b** : FIRE 3b ⟨*gunned* the ball to first base⟩ — **gun for** : to aim at or go after with determination or effort

gun·boat \'gən-ˌbōt\ n (1777) : an armed ship of shallow draft

gunboat diplomacy n (1927) : diplomacy backed by the use or threat of military force

gun control n (1969) : regulation of the selling, owning, and use of guns

gun·cot·ton \-ˌkä-tᵊn\ n (1846) : NITROCELLULOSE; *esp* : an explosive highly nitrated product used chiefly in smokeless powder

gun·dog \-ˌdòg\ n (1744) : a dog trained to work with hunters by locating and retrieving game

gun·fight \-ˌfīt\ n (1659) : a hostile encounter in which antagonists fire upon each other — **gun·fight·er** \-ˌfī-tər\ n

gun·fire \-ˌfī(-ə)r\ n (1801) : the firing of guns

gun·flint \-ˌflint\ n (1731) : a small sharp flint fashioned to ignite the priming in a flintlock

gung ho \'gəŋ-'hō\ adj [*Gung ho!*, motto (interpreted as meaning "work together") adopted by certain U.S. marines, fr. Chin (Beijing) *gōnghé*, short for *Zhōngguó Gōngyè Hézuò Shè* Chinese Industrial Cooperative Society] (1942) : extremely or overly zealous or enthusiastic

gun·ite \'gə-ˌnīt\ n (1914) : a building material consisting of a mixture of cement, sand, and water that is sprayed onto a mold

gunk \'gəŋk\ n [fr. *Gunk*, trademark for a cleaning solvent] (1943) : filthy, sticky, or greasy matter — **gunky** \'gəŋ-kē\ adj

gun lap n (ca. 1949) : the final lap of a race in track signaled by the firing of a gun as the leader begins the lap

gun·man \-mən\ n (1624) **1** : a man armed with a gun; *esp* : a professional killer **2** : a man noted for speed or skill in handling a gun

gun·met·al \'gən-ˌme-tᵊl\ n (1541) **1** : a metal used for guns; *specif* : a bronze formerly much used as a material for cannon **2** : an alloy or metal treated to imitate nearly black tarnished copper-alloy gunmetal **3** : a bluish gray color

gun moll \-₁mäl, -₁mȯl\ *n* [slang *gun* thief, rascal, by shortening & alter. fr. *gonoph, ganef* thief — more at GANEF] (ca. 1908) *slang* : MOLL 2b

Gun·nar \'gú-₁när, 'gü-, -nər\ *n* [ON *Gunnarr*] : the king of the Nibelungs and husband of Brynhild in Norse mythology

¹**gun·nel** \'gə-n²l\ *var of* GUNWALE

²**gunnel** *n* [origin unknown] (1740) : a small slimy elongate north Atlantic blenny (*Pholis gunnellus*); *broadly* : any fish of the family (Pholidae) to which the gunnel belongs

gun·ner \'gə-nər\ *n* (14c) **1** : a soldier or airman who operates or aims a gun **2** : one who hunts with a gun **3** : a warrant officer who supervises ordnance and ordnance stores

gun·nery \'gən-rē, 'gə-nə-\ *n* (1605) : the use of guns; *esp* : the science of the flight of projectiles and of the effective use of guns

gunnery sergeant *n* (ca. 1961) : a noncommissioned officer in the marine corps ranking above a staff sergeant and below a master sergeant or first sergeant

gun·ny·sack \'gə-nē-₁sak\ *n* [*gunny* coarse fabric, of Indo-Aryan origin; akin to Hindi *gon* sack, Punjabi *gūṇī*] (1862) : a sack made of a coarse heavy fabric (as burlap)

gun·play \'gən-₁plā\ *n* (1881) : the shooting of small arms with intent to scare or kill

gun·point \-₁pȯint\ *n* (1951) : the muzzle of a gun — **at gunpoint** : under a threat of death by being shot

gun·pow·der \-₁pau̇-dər\ *n* (15c) : an explosive mixture of potassium nitrate, charcoal, and sulfur used in gunnery and blasting; *broadly* : any of various powders used in guns as propelling charges

gun room *n* (1626) : quarters on a British warship orig. used by the gunner and his mates but now by midshipmen and junior officers

gun·run·ner \'gən-₁rə-nər\ *n* (1899) : one that traffics in contraband arms and ammunition — **gun·run·ning** \-₁rə-niŋ\ *n*

gun·sel \'gən(t)-səl\ *n* [slang *gunsel* catamite, perh. modif. of Yiddish *gendzl* gosling] (1944) *slang* : GUNMAN

gun·ship \'gən-₁ship\ *n* (1966) : a helicopter or cargo aircraft armed with rockets and machine guns

gun·shot \'gən-₁shät\ *n* (15c) **1** : shot or a projectile fired from a gun **2** : the range of a gun **3** : the firing of a gun

gun–shy \-₁shī\ *adj* (1884) **1** : afraid of loud noise (as that of a gun) **2** : markedly distrustful, afraid, or cautious

gun·sling·er \-₁sliŋ-ər\ *n* (1928) : a person noted for speed and skill in handling and shooting a gun esp. in the American West

gun·sling·ing \-₁sliŋ-iŋ\ *n* (ca. 1944) : the shooting of a gun esp. in a gunfight

gun·smith \-₁smith\ *n* (1588) : one who designs, makes, or repairs small firearms — **gun·smith·ing** \-₁smi-thiŋ\ *n*

Gun·ter's chain \'gən-tərz-\ *n* [Edmund *Gunter*] (ca. 1679) : a chain 66 feet (20.1 meters) long that is the unit of length for surveys of U.S. public lands

Gun·ther \'gùn-tər\ *n* [G] : a Burgundian king and husband of Brunhild in Germanic legend

gun·wale *also* **gun·nel** \'gə-n²l\ *n* [ME *gonne-wale*, fr. *gonne* gun + ¹*wale*; fr. its former use as a support for guns] (15c) : the upper edge of a ship's or boat's side — **to the gunwales** : as full as possible

gup·py \'gə-pē\ *n, pl* **guppies** [R.J.L. *Guppy* †1916 Trinidadian naturalist] (1925) : a small live-bearer (*Poecilia reticulata* of the family Poeciliidae) of Barbados, Trinidad, and Venezuela often kept as an aquarium fish

gur·gle \'gər-gəl\ *vi* **gur·gled; gur·gling** \-g(ə-)liŋ\ [prob. imit.] (1713) **1** : to flow in a broken irregular current ⟨the brook *gurgling* over the rocks⟩ **2** : to make a sound like that of a gurgling liquid ⟨the baby *gurgling* in his crib⟩ — **gurgle** *n*

Gur·kha \'gùr-kə, 'gər-\ *n* [*Ghurka*, member of a Rajput clan who dominated Nepal in the 18th cent.] (1811) : a soldier from Nepal in the British or Indian army

gur·nard \'gər-nərd\ *n, pl* **gurnard** *or* **gurnards** [ME, fr. MF *gornart*, irreg. fr. *grognier* to grunt, fr. L *grunnire*, of imit. origin] (14c) : SEA ROBIN — compare FLYING GURNARD

gur·ney \'gər-nē\ *n, pl* **gurneys** [prob. fr. the name *Gurney*] (1939) : a wheeled cot or stretcher

gur·ry \'gər-ē, 'gə-rē\ *n* [origin unknown] (1850) : fishing offal

gu·ru \'gür-(₁)ü *also* gə-'rü\ *n, pl* **gurus** [Hindi *gurū*, fr. Skt *guru*, fr. *guru*, adj., heavy, venerable — more at GRIEVE] (1613) **1** : a personal religious teacher and spiritual guide in Hinduism **2 a** : a teacher and esp. intellectual guide in matters of fundamental concern **b** : one who is an acknowledged leader or chief proponent **c** : a person with knowledge or expertise : EXPERT

¹**gush** \'gəsh\ *vb* [ME *guschen*] *vi* (15c) **1** : to issue copiously or violently **2** : to emit a sudden copious flow **3** : to make an effusive display of affection or enthusiasm ⟨an aunt ~*ing* over the baby⟩ ~ *vt* **1** : to emit in a copious free flow **2** : to say or write effusively — **gush·ing·ly** \'gə-shiŋ-lē\ *adv*

²**gush** *n* (ca. 1682) **1 a** : a sudden outpouring **b** : something emitted in a gushing form **2** : an effusive display or outpouring

gush·er \'gə-shər\ *n* (1864) : one that gushes; *specif* : an oil well with a copious natural flow

gushy \'gə-shē\ *adj* **gush·i·er; -est** (1845) : marked by effusive sentimentality — **gush·i·ly** \'gə-shə-lē\ *adv* — **gush·i·ness** \'gə-shē-nəs\ *n*

gus·set \'gə-sət\ *n* [ME, piece of armor covering the joints in a suit of armor, fr. MF *gousset*] (ca. 1570) **1 a** : a usu. diamond-shaped or triangular insert in a seam (as of a sleeve, pocketbook, or shoe upper) to provide expansion or reinforcement **2** : a plate or bracket for strengthening an angle in framework (as in a building or bridge) — **gusset** *vt*

gus·sy up \'gə-sē-'əp\ *vt* **gus·sied up; gus·sy·ing up** [origin unknown] (1952) : DRESS UP, EMBELLISH

¹**gust** \'gəst\ *n* [ME *guste*, fr. L *gustus*; akin to L *gustare* to taste — more at CHOOSE] (15c) **1** *obs* **a** : the sensation of taste **b** : INCLINATION, LIKING **2** : keen delight

²**gust** *n* [prob. fr. ON *gustr*; akin to OHG *gussa* flood, and perh. to OE *gēotan* to pour — more at FOUND] (1588) **1** : a sudden brief rush of wind **2** : a sudden outburst : SURGE ⟨a ~ of emotion⟩ — **gust·i·ly** \'gəs-tə-lē\ *adv* — **gust·i·ness** \-tē-nəs\ *n* — **gusty** \-tē\ *adj*

³**gust** *vi* (1813) : to blow in gusts ⟨winds ~*ing* up to 40 mph⟩

gus·ta·tion \₁gəs-'tā-shən\ *n* [L *gustation-, gustatio*, fr. *gustare*] (1599) : the act or sensation of tasting

gus·ta·to·ry \'gəs-tə-₁tōr-ē, -₁tȯr-\ *adj* (1684) : relating to or associated with eating or the sense of taste — **gus·ta·to·ri·ly** \₁gəs-tə-'tōr-ə-lē, -'tȯr-\ *adv*

gus·to \'gəs-(₁)tō\ *n, pl* **gustoes** [It, fr. L *gustus*, pp.] (1620) **1 a** : an individual or special taste ⟨different ~*es*⟩ **b** : enthusiastic and vigorous enjoyment or appreciation **c** : vitality marked by an abundance of vigor and enthusiasm **2** *archaic* **c** : artistic style

¹**gut** \'gət\ *n* [ME, fr. OE *guttas*, pl.; prob. akin to OE *gēotan* to pour] (bef. 12c) **1 a** (1) : BOWELS, ENTRAILS — usu. used in pl. (2) : the basic visceral or emotional part of a person **b** : the alimentary canal or part of it (as the intestine or stomach) **c** : BELLY, ABDOMEN **d** : CATGUT **2** *pl* : the inner essential parts ⟨the ~s of a car⟩ **3** : a narrow passage; *also* : a narrow waterway or small creek **4** : the sac of silk taken from a silkworm ready to spin its cocoon and drawn out into a thread for use as a snell **5** *pl* : fortitude and stamina in coping with what alarms, repels, or discourages : COURAGE, PLUCK **6** : GUT COURSE

²**gut** *vt* **gut·ted; gut·ting** (14c) **1 a** : EVISCERATE **b** : to extract all the essential passages or portions from **2 a** : to destroy the inside of ⟨fire *gutted* the building⟩ **b** : to destroy the essential power or effectiveness of ⟨inflation *gutting* the economy⟩ — **gut it out** : PERSEVERE

³**gut** *adj* (1964) **1** : arising from one's inmost self : VISCERAL ⟨a ~ reaction⟩ **2** : having strong impact or immediate relevance ⟨~ issues⟩

gut·buck·et \'gət-₁bə-kət\ *n* (1929) **1** : BARRELHOUSE 2 **2** : a homemade bass fiddle consisting of a stick attached to an inverted washtub and having a single string

gut course *n* (1948) : a course (as in college) that is easily passed

gut·less \'gət-ləs\ *adj* (1900) **1** : lacking courage : COWARDLY **2** : lacking significance or vitality — **gut·less·ness** *n*

gutsy \'gət-sē\ *adj* **guts·i·er; -est** (ca. 1893) **1** : marked by courage, pluck, or determination ⟨a ~ little fighter⟩ ⟨a ~ decision⟩ **2 a** : expressing or characterized by basic physical senses or passions ⟨~ macho talk⟩ ⟨~ country blues⟩ **b** : rough or plain in style : not bland or sophisticated ⟨a ~ soup⟩ — **guts·i·ly** \-sə-lē\ *adv* — **guts·i·ness** *n*

gut·ta \'gə-tə, 'gù-tə\ *n, pl* **gut·tae** \-tə-₁tē, 'gù-, -₁tī\ [L, lit., drop] (1563) : one of a series of ornaments in the Doric entablature that is usu. in the form of a frustum of a cone

gut·ta–per·cha \₁gə-tə-'pər-chə\ *n* [Malay *gětah-pěrcha*, fr. *gětah* sap, latex + *pěrcha* scrap, rag] (1845) : a tough plastic substance from the latex of several Malaysian trees (genera *Payena* and *Palaquium*) of the sapodilla family that resembles rubber but contains more resin and is used esp. as insulation and in dentistry

gut·ta·tion \₁gə-'tā-shən\ *n* [L *gutta* drop] (ca. 1889) : the exudation of liquid water from the uninjured surface of a plant leaf

¹**gut·ter** \'gə-tər\ *n* [ME *goter*, fr. MF *goutiere*, fr. *goute* drop, fr. L *gutta*] (14c) **1 a** : a trough along the eaves to catch and carry off rainwater **b** : a low area (as at the edge of a street) to carry off surface water (as to a sewer) **c** : a trough or groove to catch and direct something ⟨the ~s of a bowling alley⟩ **2** : a white space formed by the adjoining inside margins of two facing pages (as of a book) **3** : the lowest or most vulgar level or condition of human life

²**gutter** *vt* (14c) **1** : to cut or wear gutters in **2** : to provide with a gutter ~ *vi* **1 a** : to flow in rivulets **b** *of a candle* : to melt away through a channel out of the side of the cup hollowed out by the burning wick **2** : to incline downward in a draft ⟨the candle flame ~*ing*⟩

³**gutter** *adj* (15c) : of, relating to, or characteristic of the gutter; *esp* : marked by extreme vulgarity, cheapness, or indecency ⟨~ politics⟩

gut·ter·ing \-iŋ\ *n* (1703) **1** : material for gutters : GUTTER 1a

gutter out *vi* (1875) **1** : to become gradually weaker and then go out ⟨the candle *guttered out*⟩ **2** : to end feebly or undramatically ⟨his screen career had slowly *guttered out*⟩

gut·ter·snipe \'gə-tər-₁snīp\ *n* (ca. 1869) **1** : STREET ARAB **2** : a person of the lowest moral or economic station — **gut·ter·snip·ish** \-₁snī-pish\ *adj*

gut·tur·al \'gə-tə-rəl, 'gə-trəl\ *adj* [MF, prob. fr. ML *gutturalis*, fr. L *guttur* throat] (1594) **1** : articulated in the throat ⟨~ sounds⟩ **2** : VELAR **3** : being or marked by utterance that is strange, unpleasant, or disagreeable — **guttural** *n* — **gut·tur·al·ism** \'gə-tə-rə-₁li-zəm, 'gə-trə-\ *n*

gut·ty \'gə-tē\ *adj* **gut·ti·er; -est** (1947) **1** : GUTSY 1 ⟨a ~ quarterback⟩ **2** : having a vigorous challenging quality ⟨~ realism⟩

gut–wrench·ing \'gət-₁ren-chiŋ\ *adj* (1974) : causing mental or emotional anguish

¹**guy** \'gī\ *n* [prob. fr. D *gei* brail] (1623) : a rope, chain, rod, or wire attached to something as a brace or guide — called also *guyline*

²**guy** *vt* (1712) : to steady or reinforce with a guy

³**guy** *n* [*Guy Fawkes*] (1806) **1** *often cap* : a grotesque effigy of Guy Fawkes traditionally displayed and burned in England on Guy Fawkes Day **2** *chiefly Brit* : a person of grotesque appearance **3 a** : MAN, FELLOW **b** : PERSON — used in pl. to refer to the members of a group regardless of sex ⟨saw her and the rest of the ~s⟩

⁴**guy** *vt* (1854) : to make fun of : RIDICULE

Guy Fawkes Day \'gī-'fȯks-\ *n* (1825) : November 5 observed in England in commemoration of the seizure of Guy Fawkes in 1605 for an attempt to blow up the houses of parliament

guy·ot \'gē-(₁)ō\ *n* [Arnold H. *Guyot* †1884 Am. geographer & geologist] (1946) : a flat-topped seamount

guz·zle \'gə-zəl\ *vb* **guz·zled; guz·zling** \'gəz-liŋ, 'gə-zə-\ [origin unknown] *vi* (1583) : to drink esp. liquor greedily, continually, or habitually ~ *vt* : to drink greedily or habitually ⟨~ beer⟩ — **guz·zler** \'gəz-lər, 'gə-zə-\ *n*

gwe·duc \'gü-ē-₁dək\ *var of* GEODUCK

gybe \'jīb\ *var of* JIBE

gym \'jim\ *n* (ca. 1871) **1** : GYMNASIUM **2** : PHYSICAL EDUCATION **3** : a usu. metal frame supporting an assortment of outdoor play equipment (as a swing, seesaw, and rings)

gym·kha·na \jim-'kä-nə, -'ka-\ *n* [prob. modif. of Hindi *gēdkhāna*, lit., ball court] (1877) : a meet featuring sports contests or athletic skills: as

\ə\ abut \ᵊ\ kitten, F table \ər\ further \a\ ash \ā\ ace \ä\ mop, mar \au̇\ out \ch\ chin \e\ bet \ē\ easy \g\ go \i\ hit \ī\ ice \j\ job \ŋ\ sing \ō\ go \ȯ\ law \ȯi\ boy \th\ thin \ṯẖ\ the \ü\ loot \u̇\ foot \y\ yet \zh\ vision \à, ḵ, ⁿ, œ, œ̄, ᵫ, ᵫ̄, ʸ\ *see* Guide to Pronunciation

a : competitive games on horseback   **b** : a timed contest for automobiles featuring a series of events designed to test driving skill

gym·na·si·um \sense 1 jim-'nā-zē-əm, -zhəm; sense 2 usu gim-'nä-zē-əm\ *n, pl* **-na·si·ums** *or* **-na·sia** \-'nä-zē-ə, -'nä-zhə; -'nä-zē-ə\ [L, exercise ground, school, fr. Gk *gymnasion*, fr. *gymnazein* to exercise naked, fr. *gymnos* naked — more at NAKED] (1598)   **1   a** : a large room used for various indoor sports (as basketball or boxing) and usu. equipped with gymnastic apparatus   **b** : a building (as on a college campus) containing space and equipment for various indoor sports activities and usu. including spectator accommodations, locker and shower rooms, offices, classrooms, and a swimming pool   **2** [G, fr. L, school] : a European secondary school that prepares students for the university

gym·nast \'jim-,nast, -nəst\ *n* [MF *gymnaste*, fr. Gk *gymnastēs* trainer, fr. *gymnazein*] (1594) : one trained in gymnastics

¹gym·nas·tic \jim-'nas-tik\ *adj* (1574) : of or relating to gymnastics : ATHLETIC — **gym·nas·ti·cal·ly** \-ti-k(ə-)lē\ *adv*

²gymnastic *n* (1652)   **1** *pl but sing in constr*   **a** : physical exercises designed to develop strength and coordination   **b** : a competitive sport in which individuals perform optional and prescribed acrobatic feats mostly on special apparatus in order to demonstrate strength, balance, and body control   **2** : an exercise in intellectual or artistic dexterity ⟨my earlier philosophic study had been an intellectual ∼ —John Dewey⟩ ⟨mental ∼s⟩   **3** : a physical feat or contortion ⟨the ∼s necessary for the killer to have swung from the fire escape —E. D. Radin⟩

gym·nos·o·phist \jim-'nä-sə-fist\ *n* [L *gymnosophista*, fr. Gk *gymnosophistēs*, fr. *gymnos + sophistēs* wise man, sophist] (15c) : any of a sect of ascetics in ancient India who went naked and practiced meditation

gym·no·sperm \'jim-nə-,spərm\ *n* [ultim. fr. Gk *gymnos + sperma* seed — more at SPERM] (ca. 1838) : any of a class (Gymnospermae) of woody vascular seed plants (as conifers) that produce naked seeds not enclosed in an ovary and that in some instances have motile spermatozoids — **gym·no·sper·mous** \,jim-nə-'spər-məs\ *adj* — **gym·no·sper·my** \'jim-nə-,spər-mē\ *n*

gyn- *or* **gyno-** *comb form* [Gk *gyn-*, fr. *gynē* woman — more at QUEEN] : female reproductive organ : ovary ⟨gynophore⟩

gy·nae·col·o·gy *chiefly Brit var of* GYNECOLOGY

gyn·an·dro·morph \,gin-'an-drə-,mórf, ,jin-\ *n* [ISV, fr. Gk *gynandros + -morph*] (ca. 1890) : an abnormal individual exhibiting characters of both sexes in various parts of the body : a sexual mosaic — **gyn·an·dro·mor·phic** \-(,)gin-,an-drə-'mór-fik, -(,)jin-\ *adj* — **gyn·an·dro·mor·phism** \-,fi-zəm\ *n* — **gyn·an·dro·mor·phy** \,gin-'an-drə-,mór-fē, ,jin-\ *n*

gyn·an·drous \,gin-'an-drəs, ,jin-\ *adj* [Gk *gynandros* of doubtful sex, fr. *gynē* woman + *andr-, anēr* man — more at ANDR-] (1807) : having the androecium and gynoecium united in a column

-gyne *n comb form* [Gk *gynē*] : female reproductive organ ⟨trichogyne⟩

gynec- *or* **gyneco-** *also* **gynaec-** *or* **gynaeco-** *comb form* [Gk *gynaik-, gynaiko-*, fr. *gynaik-, gynē* woman — more at QUEEN] : woman ⟨gynecology⟩

gy·ne·coc·ra·cy \,gī-ni-'kä-krə-sē, ,ji-\ *n, pl* **-cies** [Gk *gynaikokratia*, fr. *gynaik- + -kratia* -cracy] (1612) : political supremacy of women — **gy·ne·co·crat·ic** \,gī-ni-kō-'kra-tik, ,ji-\ *adj*

gy·ne·coid \'gī-ni-,kóid, 'ji-\ *adj* (1907) : typical or characteristic of the human female ⟨∼ pelvis⟩

gy·ne·col·o·gy \,gī-nə-'kä-lə-jē, ,ji-\ *n* [ISV] (ca. 1847) : a branch of medicine that deals with the diseases and routine physical care of the reproductive system of women — **gy·ne·co·log·ic** \,gī-ni-kə-'lä-jik, ,ji-\ *or* **gy·ne·co·log·i·cal** \-ji-kəl\ *adj* — **gy·ne·col·o·gist** \,gī-nə-'kä-lə-jist, ,ji-\ *n*

gy·neco·mas·tia \,gī-nə-kō-'mas-tē-ə\ *n* [NL, fr. *gynec- +* Gk *mastos* breast + NL *-ia*] (1881) : excessive development of the breast in the male

gy·noe·ci·um \jī-'nē-shē-əm, gī-, -sē-\ *n, pl* **-cia** \-shē-ə, -sē-\ [NL, alter. of L *gynaeceum* women's apartments, fr. Gk *gynaikeion*, fr. *gynaik-, gynē*] (1832) : the aggregate of carpels or pistils in a flower

gy·no·gen·e·sis \,gī-nə-'je-nə-səs\ *n* [NL] (1925) : development in which the embryo contains only maternal chromosomes due to activation of an egg by a sperm that degenerates without fusing with the egg nucleus — **gy·no·ge·net·ic** \-jə-'ne-tik\ *adj*

gy·no·phore \'gī-nə-,fōr, 'ji-, -,fór\ *n* (1821) : a prolongation of the receptacle (as in a caper flower) with the gynoecium at its apex

-gynous *adj comb form* [NL *-gynus*, fr. Gk *-gynos*, fr. *gynē* woman — more at QUEEN]   **1** : of, relating to, or having (such or so many) wives ⟨monogynous⟩   **2** : situated (in a specified place) in relation to a female organ of a plant ⟨hypogynous⟩

-gyny *n comb form*   **1** : existence of or condition of having (such or so many) wives ⟨polygyny⟩   **2** : condition of being situated (in a specified place) in relation to a female organ of a plant ⟨epigyny⟩

¹gyp \'jip\ *n* [prob. short for *gypsy*] (1750)   **1** *Brit* : a college servant   **2   a** : CHEAT, SWINDLER   **b** : FRAUD, SWINDLE

²gyp *vb* **gypped; gyp·ping** (1880) : CHEAT

gyp·se·ous \'jip-sē-əs\ *adj* (1661) : resembling, containing, or consisting of gypsum ⟨∼ clay loam⟩

gyp·sif·er·ous \jip-'si-f(ə-)rəs\ *adj* (ca. 1847) : containing gypsum

gyp·soph·i·la \jip-'sä-fə-lə\ *n* [NL, fr. L *gypsum* + NL *-phila* -phil] (1771) : any of a large genus (*Gypsophila*) of Old World herbs of the pink family having small delicate usu. paniculate flowers

gyp·sum \'jip-səm\ *n* [L, fr. Gk *gypsos*] (14c)   **1** : a widely distributed mineral consisting of hydrous calcium sulfate that is used esp. as a soil amendment and in making plaster of paris   **2** : PLASTERBOARD

gyp·sy \'jip-sē\ *vi* **gyp·sied; gyp·sy·ing** (ca. 1627) : to live or roam like a Gypsy

Gyp·sy \'jip-sē\ *n, pl* **Gypsies** [by shortening & alter. fr. *Egyptian*] (1537)   **1** : a member of a traditionally itinerant people who originated in northern India and now live chiefly in south and southwest Asia, Europe, and No. America   **2** : ROMANY 2   **3** *not cap* : one that resembles a Gypsy; *esp* : WANDERER

gypsy cab *n* (1964) : a taxicab licensed only to answer calls; *esp* : such a cab that cruises in search of passengers

gypsy moth *n* (1819) : an Old World tussock moth (*Lymantria dispar*) that was introduced about 1869 into the U.S. and has a grayish brown mottled hairy caterpillar which is a destructive defoliator of many trees

gyr- *or* **gyro-** *comb form* [prob. fr. MF, fr. L, fr. Gk, fr. *gyros* rounded]   **1** : ring : circle : spiral ⟨gyromagnetic⟩   **2** : gyroscope ⟨gyrocompass⟩

gyr·ase \'jī-,rās\ *n* [*gyr- + -ase*] (1976) : an enzyme that catalyzes the breaking and rejoining of bonds linking adjacent nucleotides in DNA to generate supercoiled DNA helices

¹gy·rate \'jī-,rāt\ *adj* (1830) : winding or coiled around : CONVOLUTED ⟨∼ branches of a tree⟩

²gyrate *vi* **gy·rat·ed; gy·rat·ing** (1830)   **1** : to revolve around a point or axis   **2** : to oscillate with or as if with a circular or spiral motion — **gy·ra·tor** \-,rā-tər\ *n* — **gy·ra·to·ry** \'jī-rə-,tōr-ē, -,tór-\ *adj*

gy·ra·tion \jī-'rā-shən\ *n* (1615)   **1** : an act or instance of gyrating   **2** : something (as a coil of a shell) that is gyrate — **gy·ra·tion·al** \-shnəl, -shə-n°l\ *adj*

¹gyre \'jī(-ə)r\ *n* [L *gyrus*, fr. Gk *gyros*] (1566) : a circular or spiral motion or form; *esp* : a giant circular oceanic surface current — **gy·ral** \'jī-rəl\ *adj*

²gyre *vi* **gyred; gyr·ing** [LL *gyrare*, fr. L *gyrus*] (1593) : to move in a circle or spiral

gy·rene \jī-'rēn\ *n* [prob. alter. of *marine*] (1944) *slang* : a U.S. marine

gyr·fal·con \'jər-,fal-kən, -,fól- *also* -,fó-kən\ *n* [ME *gerfaucon*, fr. OF *girfaucon*, prob. fr. *gir* vulture (fr. OHG *gīr*) + *faucon* falcon] (14c) : an arctic falcon (*Falco rusticolus*) that occurs in several color forms and is the largest of all falcons

gyrfalcon

¹gy·ro \'jī-(,)rō\ *n, pl* **gyros** (1910)   **1** : GYROCOMPASS   **2** : GYROSCOPE

²gy·ro \'yē-,rō, 'zhir-ō\ *n, pl* **gyros** [NGk *gyros* turn, fr. Gk; fr. the rotation of the meat on a spit] (1971) : a sandwich esp. of lamb and beef, tomato, and onion on pita bread

Gy·ro \'jī-(,)rō\ *n, pl* **Gyros** [*Gyro* International (association)] (1971) : a member of a major international service club

gy·ro·com·pass \'jī-rō-,kəm-pəs *also* -,käm-\ *n* (1910) : a compass consisting of a continuously driven gyroscope whose spinning axis is confined to a horizontal plane so that the earth's rotation causes it to assume a position parallel to the earth's axis and thus point to the true north

gy·ro·fre·quen·cy \-,frē-kwən(t)-sē\ *n* (1938) : the frequency with which a charged particle (as an electron) executes spiral gyrations in moving obliquely across a magnetic field

gyro horizon *n* (1938) : ARTIFICIAL HORIZON

gy·ro·mag·net·ic \,jī-rō-mag-'ne-tik\ *adj* (1922) : of or relating to the magnetic properties of a rotating electrical particle

gyromagnetic ratio *n* (1922) : the ratio of the magnetic moment of a spinning charged particle to its angular momentum

gy·ron \'jī-rən\ *n* [MF *giron* gore, of Gmc origin; akin to OHG *gēra* wedge-shaped object, OE *gār* spear — more at GORE] (1572) : a heraldic charge of triangular form having one side at the edge of the field and the opposite angle at the fess point

gy·ro·plane \'jī-rə-,plān\ *n* [ISV] (1907) : an airplane balanced and supported by the aerodynamic forces acting on rapidly rotating horizontal or slightly inclined airfoils

gy·ro·scope \'jī-rə-,skōp, *Brit also* 'gī-\ *n* [F] (1856) : a wheel or disk mounted to spin rapidly about an axis and also free to rotate about one or both of two axes perpendicular to each other and to the axis of spin so that a rotation of one of the two mutually perpendicular axes results from application of torque to the other when the wheel is spinning and so that the entire apparatus offers considerable opposition depending on the angular momentum to any torque that would change the direction of the axis of spin — **gy·ro·scop·ic** \,jī-rə-'skä-pik\ *adj* — **gy·ro·scop·i·cal·ly** \-pi-k(ə-)lē\ *adv*

gy·ro·sta·bi·liz·er \,jī-rō-'stā-bə-,lī-zər\ *n* (1921) : a stabilizing device (as for a ship or airplane) that consists of a continuously driven gyro spinning about a vertical axis and pivoted so that its axis of spin may be tipped fore-and-aft in the vertical plane and that serves to oppose sideways motion — called also *gyrostat* \'jī-rə-,stat\

gy·rus \'jī-rəs\ *n, pl* **gy·ri** \'jī-,rī\ [NL, fr. L, circle — more at GYRE] (ca. 1842) : a convoluted ridge (as a convolution of the brain) between anatomical grooves

gyve \'jīv, 'gīv\ *n* [ME] (13c) : FETTER, SHACKLE — **gyve** *vt*

H

h \'āch\ *n, pl* **h's** *or* **hs** \'ā-chəz\ *often cap, often attrib* (bef. 12c) **1 a** : the 8th letter of the English alphabet **b** : a graphic representation of this letter **c** : a speech counterpart of orthographic *h* **2** : a graphic device for reproducing the letter *h* **3** : one designated *h* esp. as the 8th in order or class **4** : something shaped like the letter H

ha \'hä\ *interj* [ME, fr. OE] (bef. 12c) — used esp. to express surprise or joy

Ha·ba·cuc \'ha-bə-ˌkək, hə-'ba-kək\ *n* [LL, fr. Heb *Ḥăbaqqūq*] : HABAKKUK

Ha·bak·kuk \'ha-bə-ˌkək, hə-'ba-kək\ *n* [Heb *Ḥăbhaqqūq*] **1** : a Hebrew prophet of 7th century B.C. Judah who prophesied an imminent Chaldean invasion **2** : a prophetic book of canonical Jewish and Christian Scripture — see BIBLE table

ha·ba·ne·ra \ˌ(h)ä-bə-'ner-ə\ *n* [Sp (*danza*) *habanera*, lit., Havanan dance] (1878) **1** : a Cuban dance in slow duple time **2** : the music for the habanera

hab·da·lah \ˌhäv-də-'lä, häv-'dò-lə\ *n, often cap* [Heb *habhdālāh* separation] (1733) : a Jewish ceremony marking the close of a Sabbath or holy day

ha·be·as cor·pus \'hā-bē-əs-'kòr-pəs\ *n* [ME, fr. ML, lit., you should have the body (the opening words of the writ)] (15c) **1** : any of several common-law writs issued to bring a party before a court or judge; *esp* : HABEAS CORPUS AD SUBJICIENDUM **2** : the right of a citizen to obtain a writ of habeas corpus as a protection against illegal imprisonment

habeas corpus ad sub·ji·ci·en·dum \-ˌad-səb-ˌyi-kē-'en-dəm\ *n* [NL, lit., you should have the body for submitting] (1768) : a writ for inquiring into the lawfulness of the restraint of a person who is imprisoned or detained in another's custody

hab·er·dash·er \'ha-bə(r)-ˌda-shər\ *n* [ME *haberdassher*, fr. modif. of AF *hapertas* petty merchandise] (14c) **1** *Brit* : a dealer in notions **2** : a dealer in men's clothing and accessories

hab·er·dash·ery \-ˌda-sh(ə-)rē\ *n, pl* **-er·ies** (1593) **1** : goods sold by a haberdasher **2** : a haberdasher's shop

ha·ber·geon \'ha-bər-jən, hə-'bər-jē-ən, -jən\ *n* [ME *haubergeoun*, fr. MF *haubergeon*, dim. of *hauberc* hauberk] (14c) **1** : a medieval jacket of mail shorter than a hauberk **2** : HAUBERK

Ha·ber process \'hä-bər-\ *n* [Fritz *Haber* †1934 Ger. chemist] (1916) : a catalytic process for synthesizing ammonia from nitrogen and hydrogen

hab·ile \'ha-bəl, -ˌbīl\ *adj* [F, fr. L *habilis* — more at ABLE] (15c) : having general skill : ABLE, SKILLFUL

ha·bil·i·ment \hə-'bi-lə-mənt\ *n* [MF *habillement*, fr. *habiller* to dress, prepare, fr. OF *abiller*, fr. *bille* log — more at BILLET] (15c) **1** *pl* : characteristic apparatus : FITTINGS ⟨the ~s of civilization —W. P. Webb⟩ **2 a** : the dress characteristic of an occupation or occasion — usu. used in pl. **b** : CLOTHES — usu. used in pl.

ha·bil·i·tate \hə-'bi-lə-ˌtāt\ *vb* **-tat·ed; -tat·ing** [LL *habilitatus*, pp. of *habilitare*, fr. L *habilitas* ability — more at ABILITY] *vt* (1604) **1** : to make fit or capable (as for functioning in society) **2** : CLOTHE, DRESS ~ *vi* : to qualify oneself — **ha·bil·i·ta·tion** \hə-ˌbi-lə-'tā-shən\ *n*

¹hab·it \'ha-bət\ *n* [ME, fr. OF, fr. L *habitus* condition, character, fr. *habēre* to have, hold — more at GIVE] (13c) **1** *archaic* : CLOTHING **2 a** : a costume characteristic of a calling, rank, or function ⟨a nun's ~⟩ **b** : a costume worn for horseback riding **3** : manner of conducting oneself : BEARING **4** : bodily appearance or makeup ⟨a man of fleshy ~⟩ **5** : the prevailing disposition or character of a person's thoughts and feelings : mental makeup **6** : a settled tendency or usual manner of behavior **7 a** : a behavior pattern acquired by frequent repetition or physiologic exposure that shows itself in regularity or increased facility of performance **b** : an acquired mode of behavior that has become nearly or completely involuntary **c** : ADDICTION **8** : characteristic mode of growth or occurrence ⟨a grass similar to Indian corn in ~⟩ **9** *of a crystal* : characteristic assemblage of forms at crystallization leading to a usual appearance

syn HABIT, PRACTICE, USAGE, CUSTOM, WONT mean a way of acting fixed through repetition. HABIT implies a doing unconsciously and often compulsively ⟨had a *habit* of tapping his fingers⟩. PRACTICE suggests an act or method followed with regularity and usu. through choice ⟨our *practice* is to honor all major credit cards⟩. USAGE suggests a customary action so generally followed that it has become a social norm ⟨western-style dress is now common *usage* in international business⟩. CUSTOM applies to a practice or usage so steadily associated with an individual or group as to have almost the force of unwritten law ⟨the *custom* of wearing black at funerals⟩. WONT usu. applies to an habitual manner, method, or practice of an individual or group ⟨as was her *wont*, she slept until noon⟩.

²habit *vt* (1594) : CLOTHE, DRESS

hab·it·able \'ha-bə-tə-bəl *also* hə-'bi-tə-\ *adj* (14c) : capable of being lived in : suitable for habitation — **hab·it·abil·i·ty** \ˌha-bə-tə-'bi-lə-tē\ *n* — **hab·it·able·ness** \'ha-bə-tə-bəl-nes\ *n* — **hab·it·ably** \-blē\ *adv*

hab·i·tant *n* (15c) **1** \'ha-bə-tənt\ : INHABITANT, RESIDENT **2** \ˌ(h)a-bi-'täⁿ\ *also* **ha·bi·tan** \-'täⁿ\ : a settler or descendant of a settler of French origin working as a farmer in Canada

hab·i·tat \'ha-bə-ˌtat\ *n* [L, it inhabits, fr. *habitare*] (1796) **1 a** : the place or environment where a plant or animal naturally or normally lives and grows **b** : the typical place of residence of a person or a group **c** : a housing for a controlled physical environment in which people can live surrounding inhospitable conditions (as under the sea) **2** : the place where something is commonly found

hab·i·ta·tion \ˌha-bə-'tā-shən\ *n* [ME *habitacioun*, fr. MF *habitation*, fr. L *habitation-, habitatio*, fr. *habitare* to inhabit, freq. of *habēre*] (14c) **1** : the act of inhabiting : OCCUPANCY **2** : a dwelling place : RESIDENCE **3** : SETTLEMENT, COLONY

hab·it–form·ing \'ha-bət-ˌfòr-miŋ\ *adj* (1913) : inducing the formation of an addiction

ha·bit·u·al \hə-'bi-ch(ə-)wəl, ha-, -'bi-chəl\ *adj* (1611) **1** : having the nature of a habit : being in accordance with habit : CUSTOMARY ⟨~ smoking⟩ **2** : doing, practicing, or acting in some manner by force of habit ⟨~ drunkard⟩ **3** : resorted to on a regular basis ⟨our ~ diet⟩ **4** : inherent in an individual ⟨~ grace⟩ *syn* see USUAL — **ha·bit·u·al·ly** *adv* — **ha·bit·u·al·ness** *n*

ha·bit·u·ate \hə-'bi-chə-ˌwāt, ha-\ *vb* **-at·ed; -at·ing** *vt* (15c) **1** : to make used to something : ACCUSTOM **2** : FREQUENT 1 ~ *vi* **1** : to cause habituation **2** : to undergo habituation ⟨~ to a stimulus⟩

ha·bit·u·a·tion \-ˌbi-chə-'wā-shən\ *n* (15c) **1** : the process of habituating : the state of being habituated **2 a** : tolerance to the effects of a drug acquired through continued use **b** : psychological dependence on a drug after a period of use — compare ADDICTION **3** : decrease in responsiveness upon repeated exposure to a stimulus

hab·i·tude \'ha-bə-ˌtüd, ˌtyüd\ *n* (14c) **1** *archaic* : native or essential character **2** *obs* : habitual association **3 a** : habitual disposition or mode of behavior or procedure **b** : CUSTOM

ha·bi·tué *also* **ha·bi·tue** \hə-'bi-chə-ˌwā, ha-, -ˌbi-chə-'\ *n* [F, fr. pp. of *habituer* to frequent, fr. L *habituare* to habituate, fr. L *habitus*] (1818) **1** : one who may be regularly found in or at a particular place or kind of place ⟨café ~s⟩ **2** : DEVOTEE ⟨an ~ of science-fiction movies⟩

hab·i·tus \'ha-bə-təs\ *n, pl* **habitus** \-təs, -ˌtüs\ [NL, fr. L] (1886) : HABIT; *specif* : body build and constitution esp. as related to predisposition to disease

ha·boob \hə-'büb\ *n* [Ar *habūb* violent storm] (1897) : a violent dust storm or sandstorm esp. of Sudan

Habs·burg \'haps-, 'häps-\ *var of* HAPSBURG

ha·ček \'hä-ˌchek\ *n* [Czech *háček*, lit., little hook] (1953) : a diacritic ˇ placed over a letter (as in *č*) to modify it : an inverted circumflex

ha·cen·da·do \ˌ(h)ä-sᵊn-'dä-(ˌ)dō *also* **ha·ci·en·da·do** \ˌhä-sē-en-\ *n, pl* **-dos** [Sp, fr. *hacienda*] (1840) : the owner or proprietor of a hacienda

¹ha·chure \ha-'shùr\ *n* [F, fr. *hacher* to chop up, hash] (1858) : a short line used for shading and denoting surfaces in relief (as in map drawing) and drawn in the direction of slope

²hachure *vt* **ha·chured; ha·chur·ing** (ca. 1859) : to shade with or show by hachures

ha·ci·en·da \ˌ(h)ä-sē-'en-də\ *n* [Sp, fr. OSp *facienda*, fr. L, lit., things to be done, neut. pl. of *faciendus*, gerundive of *facere* to do — more at DO] (ca. 1772) **1** : a large estate esp. in a Spanish-speaking country : PLANTATION **2** : the main dwelling of a hacienda

¹hack \'hak\ *vb* [ME *hakken*, fr. OE *-haccian*; akin to OHG *hacchōn* to hack, OE *hōc* hook] *vt* (13c) **1 a** : to cut or sever with repeated irregular or unskillful blows **b** : to cut or shape by or as if by crude or ruthless strokes ⟨~ing out new election districts⟩ **c** : ANNOY, VEX — often used with *off* **2** : to clear or make by or as if by cutting away vegetation ⟨~ed his way through the brush⟩ **3 a** : to manage successfully ⟨just couldn't ~ the new job⟩ **b** : TOLERATE ⟨I can't ~ all this noise⟩ ~ *vi* **1 a** : to make chopping strokes or blows ⟨~ed at the weeds⟩; *also* : to make cuts as if by chopping ⟨~ing away at the work force⟩ **b** : to play inexpert golf **2** : to cough in a short dry manner **3** : LOAF — usu. used with *around* **4 a** : to write computer programs for enjoyment **b** : to gain access to a computer illegally

²hack *n* (14c) **1** : an implement for hacking **2** : NICK, NOTCH **3** : a short dry cough **4** : a hacking stroke or blow **5** : restriction to quarters as punishment for naval officers — usu. used in the phrase *under hack*

³hack *n* [short for *hackney*] (ca. 1721) **1 a** (1) : a horse let out for common hire (2) : a horse used in all kinds of work **b** : a horse worn out in service : JADE **c** : a light easy saddle horse; *esp* : a three-gaited saddle horse **d** : a ride on a horse **2 a** : HACKNEY **b** (1) : TAXICAB (2) : CABDRIVER **3 a** : a person who works solely for mercenary reasons : HIRELING ⟨party ~s⟩ **b** : a writer who works on order; *also* : a writer who aims solely for commercial success

⁴hack *adj* (ca. 1734) **1** : working for hire esp. with mediocre professional standards **2** : performed by, suited to, or characteristic of a hack ⟨~ writing⟩ **3** : HACKNEYED, TRITE

⁵hack *vi* (ca. 1888) **1** : to ride or drive at an ordinary pace or over the roads esp. as distinguished from racing or hunting **2** : to operate a taxicab ~ *vt* : to ride (a horse) at an ordinary pace

⁶hack *n* [origin unknown] (ca. 1914) *slang* : a guard esp. at a prison

hack·a·more \'ha-kə-ˌmòr, -ˌmór\ *n* [by folk etymology fr. Sp *jáquima* bridle] (1850) : a bridle with a loop capable of being tightened about the nose in place of a bit or with a slip noose passed under the lower jaw

hack·ber·ry \'hak-ˌber-ē\ *n* [alter. of *hagberry* (a cherry resembling the chokecherry)] (1779) : any of a genus (*Celtis*) of trees and shrubs of the elm family with small often edible berries; *also* : its wood

hack·er \'ha-kər\ *n* (14c) **1** : one that hacks **2** : a person who is inexperienced or unskilled at a particular activity ⟨a tennis ~⟩ **3** : an expert at programming and solving problems with a computer **4** : a person who illegally gains access to and sometimes tampers with information in a computer system

hack·ie \'ha-kē\ *n* (ca. 1926) : CABDRIVER

¹hack·le \'ha-kəl\ *n* [ME *hakell*; akin to OHG *hāko* hook — more at HOOK] (15c) **1 a** : one of the long narrow feathers on the neck or saddle of a bird **b** : the neck plumage of the domestic fowl **2 a** : a comb or board with long metal teeth for dressing flax, hemp, or jute **3** *pl* **a** : erectile hairs along the neck and back esp. of a dog **b** : TEMPER, DANDER **4 a** : an artificial fishing fly made chiefly of the filaments of a cock's neck feathers **b** : filaments of cock feather projecting from the head of an artificial fly

²hackle *vt* **hack·led; hack·ling** (1616) : to comb out with a hackle — **hack·ler** \-k-(ə-)lər\ *n*

hack·ly \'ha-k(ə-)lē\ *adj* (1796) : having the appearance of something hacked : JAGGED

hack·man \'hak-mən\ *n* (1796) : CABDRIVER

hack·ma·tack \'hak-mə-ˌtak\ *n* [earlier *hakmantak*, prob. fr. Western Abenaki (Algonquian language of New Hampshire and Vermont)] (1792) : TAMARACK

¹hack·ney \'hak-nē\ *n, pl* **hack·neys** [ME *hakeney*] (14c) **1 a** : a horse suitable for ordinary riding or driving **b** : a trotting horse used chiefly for driving **c** *often cap* : any of an English breed of rather compact usu. chestnut, bay, or brown high-stepping horses **2** *obs* : one that works for hire **3** : a carriage or automobile kept for hire

---

\ə\ abut \ᵊ\ kitten, F table \ər\ further \a\ ash \ā\ ace \ä\ mop, mar \aù\ out \ch\ chin \e\ bet \ē\ easy \g\ go \i\ hit \ī\ ice \j\ job \ŋ\ sing \ō\ go \ò\ law \òi\ boy \th\ thin \ṯẖ\ the \ü\ loot \ù\ foot \y\ yet \zh\ vision \å, k̲, ⁿ, œ, œ̄, ᵫ, ᵫ̄, ᵊ\ *see* Guide to Pronunciation

²**hackney** *adj* (1589) **1** : kept for public hire **2** : HACKNEYED **3** *archaic* : done or suitable for doing by a drudge
³**hackney** *vt* **hack·ney·ed; hack·ney·ing** (1596) **1 a** : to make common or frequent use of **b** : to make trite, vulgar, or commonplace **2** *archaic* : to make sophisticated or jaded
hackney coach *n* (1635) : a coach kept for hire; *esp* : a four-wheeled carriage drawn by two horses and having seats for six persons
hack·neyed \'hak-nēd\ *adj* (1749) : lacking in freshness or originality
syn see TRITE
hack·saw \'hak-.sò\ *n* (1654) : a fine-tooth saw with a blade under tension in a frame that is used for cutting hard materials (as metal)
hack·work \-.work\ *n* (1851) : literary, artistic, or professional work done on order usu. according to formula and in conformity with commercial standards
had *past and past part of* HAVE
ha·dal \'hā-d³l\ *adj* [F, fr. *Hadès* Hades] (1959) : of, relating to, or being the parts of the ocean below 6000 meters
had·dock \'ha-dək\ *n, pl* **haddock** *also* **haddocks** [ME *haddok*] (14c) : an important food fish (*Melanogrammus aeglefinus*) that is usu. smaller than the related cod and that occurs on both sides of the No. Atlantic
Ha·des \'hā-(.)dēz\ *n* [Gk *Haidēs*] **1** : PLUTO **2** : the underground abode of the dead in Greek mythology **3** : SHEOL **4** *often not cap* : HELL
ha·dith \hə-'dēth\ *n, pl* **hadith** *or* **hadiths** *often cap* [Ar *ḥadīth*, lit., speech, report] (ca. 1817) **1** : a narrative record of the sayings or customs of Muhammad and his companions **2** : the collective body of traditions relating to Muhammad and his companions
hadj, hadji *var of* HAJJ, HAJJI
Had·ley cell \'had-lē-\ *n* [George *Hadley* †1768 Eng. scientific writer] (1969) : a pattern of atmospheric circulation in which warm air rises near the equator, cools as it travels poleward at high altitude, sinks as cold air, and warms as it travels equatorward; *also* : a similar atmospheric circulation pattern on another planet (as Mars)
hadn't \'ha-d³nt, -d³n, *dial also* 'ha-t³n(t) *or* 'hant\ (1695) : had not
had·ron \'ha-.drän\ *n* [ISV *hadr-* thick, heavy (fr. Gk. *hadros* thick) + ²-*on*] (1962) : any of the subatomic particles that are made up of quarks and are subject to the strong force — **ha·dron·ic** \ha-'drä-nik\ *adj*
had·ro·saur \'ha-drə-.sòr\ *n* [NL *Hadrosaurus*, genus name, fr. Gk *hadros* thick, bulky + *sauros* lizard] (1877) : any of a family (Hadrosauridae) of medium-sized bipedal herbivorous dinosaurs of the Upper Cretaceous with long flat snouts and an often crested skull
hadst \'hadst, hədst, *or* t *for* d\ *archaic past 2d sing of* HAVE
hae \'hā\ *chiefly Scot var of* HAVE
haem *chiefly Brit var of* HEME
haem- *or* **haemo-** *chiefly Brit var of* HEM-
haema- *chiefly Brit var of* HEMA-
haemat- *or* **haemato-** *chiefly Brit var of* HEMAT-
hae·ma·tite *Brit var of* HEMATITE
-haemia *chiefly Brit var of* -EMIA
haet \'hāt\ *n* [contr. of Sc *hae it* (as in *Deil hae it!* Devil take it!)] (1603) *chiefly Scot* : a small quantity : WHIT, BIT
haf·fet \'ha-fət\ *n* [ME (Sc) *halfheid*, fr. ME *half* half + *hed* head] (1513) *Scot* : CHEEK, TEMPLE
haf·ni·um \'haf-nē-əm\ *n* [NL, fr. *Hafnia* (Copenhagen), Denmark] (1923) : a metallic element that resembles zirconium in its chemical properties and occurs in zirconium minerals and that readily absorbs neutrons — see ELEMENT table
¹**haft** \'haft\ *n* [ME, fr. OE *hæft;* akin to OE *hebban* to lift — more at HEAVE] (bef. 12c) : the handle of a weapon or tool
²**haft** *vt* (15c) : to set in or furnish with a haft
haf·ta·rah *or* **haf·to·rah** \häf-'tòr-ə, .häf-tə-'rä\ *n* [Heb *haphṭārāh* conclusion] (1723) : one of the biblical selections from the Books of the Prophets read after the parashah in the Jewish synagogue service
¹**hag** \'hag\ *n* [ME *hagge* demon, old woman] (14c) **1** : an ugly, slatternly, or evil-looking old woman **2** *archaic* **a** : a female demon **b** : an evil or frightening spirit : HOBGOBLIN **3** : WITCH — **hag·gish** \'ha-gish\ *adj*
²**hag** *n* [Sc, break in a moor, fr. ON *hǫgg* cut, cleft; akin to OE *hēawan* to hew] (1662) **1** *Brit* : QUAGMIRE, BOG **2** *Brit* : a firm spot in a bog
Ha·gar \'hā-.gär, -gər\ *n* [Heb *Hāghār*] : a concubine of Abraham driven into the desert with her son Ishmael because of Sarah's jealousy according to the account in Genesis
hag·fish \'hag-.fish\ *n* (1611) : any of a family (Myxinidae) of marine cyclostomes that are related to the lampreys and in general resemble eels but have a round mouth surrounded by barbels and that feed upon other fishes and invertebrates by boring into their bodies
Hag·ga·dah \hə-'gä-də, hä-, -'gò-\ *n, pl* **Hag·ga·doth** \-'gä-.dōt, -'gò-, -.dōth\ [Heb *haggādhāh*] (1856) **1** : ancient Jewish lore forming esp. the nonlegal part of the Talmud **2** : the prayer book containing the seder ritual — **hag·ga·dic** \-'gä-dik, -'gò-\ *adj, often cap*
hag·ga·dist \-'gä-dist, -'gò-\ *n, often cap* (1886) **1** : a haggadic writer **2** : a student of the Haggadah — **hag·ga·dis·tic** \.ha-gə-'dis-tik, .hä-\ *adj, often cap*
Hag·gai \'ha-gē-.ī, 'ha-.gī\ *n* [Heb *Ḥaggai*] **1** : a Hebrew prophet who flourished about 500 B.C. and who advocated that the Temple in Jerusalem be rebuilt **2** : a prophetic book of canonical Jewish and Christian Scriptures — see BIBLE table
¹**hag·gard** \'ha-gərd\ *adj* [MF *hagard*] (1567) **1** *of a hawk* : not tamed **2 a** : wild in appearance **b** : having a worn or emaciated appearance : GAUNT ⟨~ faces looked up sadly from out of the straw —W. M. Thackeray⟩ — **hag·gard·ly** *adv* — **hag·gard·ness** *n*
²**haggard** *n* (1567) **1** : an adult hawk caught wild **2** *obs* : an intractable person
hag·gis \'ha-gəs\ *n* [ME *hagese*] (15c) : a traditionally Scottish dish that consists of the heart, liver, and lungs of a sheep or a calf minced with suet, onions, oatmeal, and seasonings boiled in the stomach of the animal
¹**hag·gle** \'ha-gəl\ *vb* **hag·gled; hag·gling** \-g(ə-)liŋ\ [freq. of *hag* (to hew)] *vt* (1599) **1** : to cut roughly or clumsily : HACK **2** *archaic* : to annoy or exhaust with wrangling ~ *vi* : BARGAIN, WRANGLE — **hag·gler** \-g(ə-)lər\ *n*
²**haggle** *n* (1858) : an act or instance of haggling

hagi- *or* **hagio-** *comb form* [LL, fr. Gk, fr. *hagios*] **1** : holy ⟨*hagio*scope⟩ **2** : saints ⟨*hagio*graphy⟩
Ha·gi·og·ra·pha \.ha-gē-'ä-grə-fə, .hā-, -.jē-\ *n pl but sing or pl in constr* [LL, fr. LGk, fr. *hagio-* + *graphein* to write — more at CARVE] (1583) : the third part of the Jewish scriptures — see BIBLE table
ha·gi·og·ra·pher \-fər\ *n* (1849) : a writer of hagiography
ha·gio·graph·ic \.ha-gē-ə-'gra-fik, .hā-, -.jē-\ *also* **ha·gio·graph·i·cal** \-fi-kəl\ *adj* (1819) **1** : of or relating to hagiography **2** : of or relating to the Hagiographa
ha·gi·og·ra·phy \-gē-'ä-grə-fē, -.jē-\ *n* (1821) **1** : biography of saints or venerated persons **2** : idealizing or idolizing biography
ha·gi·ol·o·gy \-gē-'ä-lə-jē, -.jē-\ *n* (1807) **1** : literature dealing with venerated persons or writings **2** : a list of venerated figures — **ha·gi·o·log·ic** \-gē-ə-'lä-jik, -.jē-\ *or* **ha·gi·o·log·i·cal** \-ji-kəl\ *adj*
ha·gio·scope \'ha-gē-ə-.skōp, 'hā-jē-\ *n* (ca. 1840) : an opening in the interior walls of a cruciform church so placed as to afford a view of the altar to those in the transept — **ha·gio·scop·ic** \.ha-gē-ə-'skä-pik, .hā-, -jē-\ *adj*
hag·ride \'hag-.rīd\ *vt* **-rode** \-.rōd\; **-rid·den** \-.ri-d³n\ (1702) : HARASS, TORMENT
hah *var of* HA
¹**ha–ha** \(')hä-'hä\ *interj* [ME, fr. OE *ha ha*] (bef. 12c) — used to express amusement or derision
²**ha–ha** \'hä-.hä\ *n* [F *haha*] (1749) : SUNK FENCE
hahn·ium \'hä-nē-əm\ *n* [NL, fr. Otto *Hahn*] (1970) : UNNILPENTIUM
Hai·da \'hī-də\ *n, pl* **Haida** *or* **Haidas** (1841) **1** : a member of an American Indian people of the Queen Charlotte islands, British Columbia, and Prince of Wales island, Alaska **2** : the language of the Haida people
haik \'hīk\ *n* [Ar *ḥā'ik*] (1713) : a voluminous piece of usu. white cloth worn as an outer garment in northern Africa
hai·ku \'hī-(.)kü\ *n, pl* **haiku** [Jp] (1902) : an unrhymed verse form of Japanese origin having three lines containing usu. 5, 7, and 5 syllables respectively; *also* : a poem in this form usu. having a seasonal reference — compare TANKA
¹**hail** \'hā(ə)l\ *n* [ME, fr. OE *hægl;* akin to OHG *hagal* hail] (bef. 12c) **1** : precipitation in the form of small balls or lumps usu. consisting of concentric layers of clear ice and compact snow **2** : something that gives the effect of a shower of hail ⟨a ~ of rifle fire⟩
²**hail** *vi* (bef. 12c) **1** : to precipitate hail ⟨it was ~*ing* hard⟩ **2** : to pour down or strike like hail
³**hail** *interj* [ME, fr. ON *heill,* fr. *heill* healthy — more at WHOLE] (13c) **1** *archaic* — used as a salutation **2** — used to express acclamation ⟨~ to the chief —Sir Walter Scott⟩
⁴**hail** *vt* (13c) **1 a** : SALUTE, GREET **b** : to greet with enthusiastic approval : ACCLAIM **2** : to greet or summon by calling ⟨~ a taxi⟩ ~ *vi* : to call out; *esp* : to call a greeting to a passing ship — **hail·er** \'hā-lər\ *n* — **hail from** : to be or have been native to or a resident of
⁵**hail** *n* (1500) **1** : an exclamation of greeting or acclamation **2** : a calling to attract attention **3** : hearing distance ⟨stayed within ~⟩
hail–fel·low \'hāl-.fe-(.)lō\ *adj* (1580) : HAIL-FELLOW-WELL-MET — **hail–fellow** *n*
hail–fel·low–well–met \-lō-.wel-'met, -lə-.wel\ *adj* [fr. the archaic salutation "Hail, fellow! Well met!"] (1581) : heartily informal : COMRADELY — **hail–fellow–well–met** *n*
Hail Mary *n* [trans. of ML *Ave, Maria,* fr. the opening words] (15c) : a Roman Catholic prayer to the Virgin Mary that consists of salutations and a plea for her intercession
hail·stone \'hā(ə)l-.stōn\ *n* (bef. 12c) : a pellet of hail
hail·storm \-.stòrm\ *n* (15c) : a storm accompanied by hail
hair \'har, 'her\ *n, often attrib* [ME, fr. OE *hær;* akin to OHG *hār* hair] (bef. 12c) **1 a** : a slender threadlike outgrowth of the epidermis of an animal; *esp* : one of the usu. pigmented filaments that form the characteristic coat of a mammal **b** : the hairy covering of an animal or a body part; *esp* : the coating of hairs on a human head **2** : HAIR-CLOTH **3 a** : a minute distance or amount ⟨won by a ~⟩ **b** : a precise degree ⟨aligned to a ~⟩ **4** *obs* : NATURE, CHARACTER **5** : a filamentous structure that resembles hair ⟨leaf ~⟩ — **hair·less** *adj* — **hair·less·ness** *n* — **hair·like** \-.līk\ *adj*

hair 1a: *1* shaft, *2* sebaceous gland, *3* epidermis, *4* dermis, *5* hair follicle, *6* bulb, *7* papilla

hair ball *n* (1712) : a compact mass of hair formed in the stomach esp. of a shedding animal (as a cat) that cleanses its coat by licking
¹**hair·breadth** \'har-.bretth, 'her-, -.breth, -.bredth\ *or* **hairs·breadth** \'harz-, 'herz-\ *n* (1561) : a very small distance or margin
²**hairbreadth** *adj* (1604) : very narrow ⟨CLOSE ⟨a ~ escape⟩
hair·brush \'har-.brəsh, 'her-\ *n* (1599) : a brush for the hair
hair cell *n* (ca. 1890) : a cell with hairlike processes; *esp* : one of the sensory cells in the auditory epithelium of the organ of Corti
hair·cloth \'har-.klòth, 'her-\ *n* (1500) : any of various stiff wiry fabrics esp. of horsehair or camel hair used for upholstery or for stiffening in garments
hair·cut \-.kət\ *n* (1899) : the act, process, or result of cutting and shaping the hair — **hair·cut·ter** \-.kə-tər\ *n* — **hair·cut·ting** \-.kə-tiŋ\ *n*
hair·do \-.dü\ *n, pl* **hairdos** (1932) : a way of wearing the hair : COIFFURE
hair·dress·er \-.dre-sər\ *n* (1770) **1** : one whose occupation is the dressing or cutting of hair **2** *Brit* : BARBER
hair·dress·ing \-.dre-siŋ\ *n* (1771) **1 a** : the action or process of washing, cutting, curling, or arranging the hair **b** : the occupation of a hairdresser **2** : a preparation for grooming and styling the hair
haired \'hard, 'herd\ *adj* (14c) : having hair esp. of a specified kind — usu. used in combination ⟨dark-*haired*⟩

hair follicle n (1838) : the tubular epithelial sheath that surrounds the lower part of the hair shaft and encloses at the bottom a vascular papilla supplying the growing basal part of the hair with nourishment

hair·line \-'līn\ n (1846) **1 : a** very slender line: as   **a :** a tiny line or crack on a surface ⟨a ~ bone fracture⟩   **b :** a fine line connecting thicker strokes in a printed letter   **2 :** HAIRBREADTH   **3 a :** a textile design consisting of lengthwise or crosswise lines usu. one thread wide   **b :** a fabric with such a design   **4 a :** the outline of scalp hair esp. on the forehead   **b :** the way the hair frames the face — **hairline** adj

hair·piece \-,pēs\ n (1926) **1 :** supplementary hair (as a switch) used in some feminine coiffures   **2 :** TOUPEE 2

¹hair·pin \-,pin\ n (1779) **1 :** a pin to hold the hair in place; specif : a long U-shaped pin   **2 :** something shaped like a hairpin; specif : a sharp U-shaped turn in a road

²hairpin adj (1887) : having the shape of a hairpin ⟨a ~ turn⟩; also : having hairpin turns ⟨a steep ~ road⟩

hair–rais·er \'har-,rā-zər, 'her-\ n (1897) : THRILLER

hair–rais·ing \-,rā-ziŋ\ adj (1900) : causing terror, excitement, or astonishment — **hair–rais·ing·ly** \-ziŋ-lē\ adv

hair seal n (1865) : any of a family (Phocidae) of seals having a coarse hairy coat, the hind limbs reduced to swimming flippers, and no external ears — called also true seal; compare EARED SEAL

hair shirt n (14c) **1 :** a shirt made of rough animal hair worn next to the skin as a penance   **2 :** one that irritates like a hair shirt

hair·split·ter \'har-,spli-tər, 'her-\ n (1849) : one that makes excessively fine distinctions in reasoning : QUIBBLER — **hair·split·ting** \-,spli-tiŋ\ adj or n

hair·spring \-,spriŋ\ n (1830) : a slender spiraled recoil spring that regulates the motion of the balance wheel of a timepiece

hair·streak \-,strēk\ n (1816) : any of a subfamily (Theclinae of the family Lycaenidae) of small butterflies usu. having striped markings on the underside of the wings and thin filamentous projections from the hind wings

hair·style \'har-,stīl\ n (1913) : HAIRDO

hair·styl·ing \-,stī-liŋ\ n (1936) : the work of a hairstylist

hair·styl·ist \-,stī-list\ n (1935) : HAIRDRESSER; esp : one who does creative styling of coiffures

hair–trigger adj (1834) **1 :** immediately responsive to the slightest stimulus ⟨a ~ temper⟩   **2 :** delicately adjusted or easily disrupted

hair trigger n (1806) : a gun trigger so adjusted as to permit the firearm to be fired by a very slight pressure

hair·worm \'har-,wərm, 'her-\ n (1658) **1 :** any of a phylum (Nematomorpha) of elongated worms that have separate sexes, are parasitic in arthropods as larvae, and are free-living in water as adults — called also horsehair worm   **2 :** any of a genus (Capillaria) of nematode worms that include serious parasites of the alimentary tract of fowls and tissue and organ parasites of mammals

hairy \'har-ē, 'her-\ adj **hair·i·er; -est** (14c) **1 a :** covered with hair or hairlike material   **b :** having a downy fuzz on the stems and leaves   **2 :** made of or resembling hair   **3 a :** tending to cause nervous tension (as from danger) ⟨a ~ adventure⟩   **b :** difficult to deal with or comprehend ⟨a ~ math problem⟩ — **hair·i·ness** \'har-ē-nəs, 'her-\ n

hairy cell leukemia n (1979) : a lymphocytic leukemia that is usu. of B cell origin and is characterized by malignant cells with a ciliated appearance

hairy–chest·ed \-,ches-təd\ adj (ca. 1937) : characterized by esp. exaggerated or stereotypical manliness

hairy vetch n (1901) : a Eurasian vetch (Vicia villosa) extensively cultivated as a cover and early forage crop

hairy woodpecker n (ca. 1728) : a common No. American woodpecker (Picoides villosus) closely resembling the downy woodpecker but larger with a longer bill

Hai·tian \'hā-shən also 'hā-tē-ən\ n (1805) **1 :** a native or inhabitant of Haiti   **2 :** HAITIAN CREOLE — **Haitian** adj

Haitian Creole n (ca. 1938) : a French-based creole spoken by Haitians

hajj \'haj\ n [Ar ḥajj] (1673) : the pilgrimage to Mecca prescribed as a religious duty for Muslims

hajji \'ha-jē\ n [Ar ḥajjī, fr. ḥajj] (1609) : one who has made a pilgrimage to Mecca — often used as a title

hake \'hāk\ n [ME] (14c) : any of several marine food fishes (as of the genera Merluccius and Urophycis) that are related to the common Atlantic cod

¹ha·kim \hä-kēm\ n [Ar ḥākim] (1611) : an administrator in a Muslim country

²ha·kim \hə-'kēm\ n [Ar ḥakīm, lit., wise one] (1638) : a physician in a Muslim country

hal- or **halo-** comb form [F, fr. Gk, fr. hals — more at SALT] **1 :** salt ⟨halophyte⟩ **2** [ISV, fr. halogen] : halogen ⟨halide⟩

ha·la·kah or **ha·la·cha** \hä-'lä-kə, ,hä-lə-'kä\ n, often cap [Heb halākhāh, lit., way] (1856) : the body of Jewish law supplementing the scriptural law and forming esp. the legal part of the Talmud — **ha·lak·ic** \hä-'lä-kik, hä-'lä-\ adj, often cap

ha·la·la \hə-'lä-lə\ n, pl **halala** or **halalas** [Ar] (1970) — see riyal at MONEY table

ha·la·tion \hā-'lā-shən\ n [halo + -ation] (1859) **1 :** the spreading of light beyond its proper boundaries in a developed photographic image   **2 :** a bright ring that sometimes surrounds a bright object on a television screen

hal·berd \'hal-bərd, 'hȯl-\ also **hal·bert** \-bərt\ n [ME, fr. MF hallebarde, fr. MHG helmbarte, fr. helm handle (fr. OHG helmo) + barte ax, fr. OHG barta; akin to OHG bart beard — more at HELM, BEARD] (15c) : a weapon esp. of the 15th and 16th centuries consisting typically of a battle-ax and pike mounted on a handle about six feet long

¹hal·cy·on \'hal-sē-ən\ n [ME alceon, fr. L halcyon, fr. Gk alkyōn, halkyōn] (14c) **1 :** a bird identified with the kingfisher and held in ancient legend to nest at sea about the time of the winter solstice and to calm the waves during incubation   **2 :** KINGFISHER

²halcyon adj (1540) **1 :** of or relating to the halcyon or its nesting period   **2 a :** CALM, PEACEFUL   **b :** HAPPY, GOLDEN   **c :** PROSPEROUS, AFFLUENT

¹hale \'hā(ə)l\ adj [partly fr. ME (northern) hale, fr. OE hāl; partly fr. ME hail, fr. ON heill — more at WHOLE] (bef. 12c) : free from defect,

disease, or infirmity : SOUND; also : retaining exceptional health and vigor ⟨a ~ and hearty old man⟩   **syn** see HEALTHY

²hale vt **haled; hal·ing** [ME halen, fr. OF haler — more at HAUL] (13c) **1 :** HAUL, PULL   **2 :** to compel to go

ha·ler \'hä-lər, -,ler\ n, pl **ha·le·ru** \'hä-lə-,rü\ [Czech haléř, gen. pl. haléřů] (ca. 1934) — see koruna at MONEY table

¹half \'haf, 'håf\ n, pl **halves** \'havz, 'håvz\ [ME, fr. OE healf; akin to OHG halb half] (bef. 12c) **1 :** either of two equal parts into which a thing is divisible; also : a part of a thing approximately equal to the remainder — often used without of ⟨~ the distance⟩   **b :** half an hour — used in designation of time   **2 :** one of a pair: as   **a :** PARTNER   **b :** SEMESTER, TERM   **c :** either of the two equal periods that together make up the playing time of some games (as football); also : the midpoint in playing time (the score was tied at the ~)   **3 :** HALF-DOLLAR   **4 :** HALFBACK — **by half :** by a great deal — **by halves :** in part : HALFHEARTEDLY — **half again as :** one-and-a-half times as ⟨half again as many⟩ — **in half :** into two equal or nearly equal parts

²half adj (bef. 12c) **1 a :** being one of two equal parts ⟨a ~ share⟩ ⟨a ~ sheet of paper⟩   **b** (1) : amounting to approximately half ⟨a ~ mile⟩ ⟨a ~ million⟩   (2) : falling short of the full or complete thing : PARTIAL ⟨~ measures⟩ ⟨a ~ smile⟩   **2 :** extending over or covering only half ⟨a ~ window⟩ ⟨a ~ mask⟩ — **half·ness** n

³half adv (12c) **1 a :** in an equal part or degree ⟨the crowd was ~ jeering, ~ respectful⟩   **b :** not completely : PARTIALLY ⟨~ persuaded⟩   **2 :** by any means : AT ALL ⟨her singing isn't ~ bad⟩

half–and–half \,haf-°n-'haf, ,håf-°n-'håf\ n (1756) : something that is approximately half one thing and half another: as   **a :** a mixture of two malt beverages (as dark and light beer)   **b :** a mixture of cream and whole milk — **half–and–half** adj or adv

half–assed \'haf-'ast, 'håf-'åst\ adj (ca. 1932) **1 :** lacking significance, adequacy, or completeness — often considered vulgar   **2 :** lacking intelligence, character, or effectiveness — often considered vulgar — **half–assed** adv

half·back \'haf-,bak, 'håf-\ n (1882) **1 :** one of the backs stationed near either flank in football   **2 :** a player stationed immediately behind the forward line (as in field hockey, soccer, or rugby)

half–baked \-'bākt\ adj (1621) **1 a :** lacking adequate planning or forethought ⟨a ~ scheme for getting rich⟩   **b :** lacking in judgment, intelligence, or common sense   **2 :** imperfectly baked : UNDERDONE

half–beak \-,bēk\ n (1880) : any of various narrow-bodied fishes of warm waters that have an elongated lower jaw and are grouped with the flying fishes (family Exocoetidae) or placed in their own family (Hemiramphidae)

half–blood \-'bləd\ or **half–blood·ed** \-'blə-dəd\ adj (1605) : having half blood or being a half blood

half blood n (1553) **1 a :** the relation between persons having only one parent in common   **b :** a person so related to another   **2 :** HALF-BREED   **3 :** GRADE 4

half boot n (1787) : a boot with a top reaching above the ankle and ending below the knee

half–bound \'haf-,baúnd, 'håf-\ adj (1775) of a book : bound in material of two qualities with the material of better quality on the spine and corners — **half binding** n

half–bred \-,bred\ adj (1701) : having one purebred parent — **half–bred** n

half–breed \-,brēd\ n (1760) : the offspring of parents of different races; esp : the offspring of an American Indian and a white person — often used disparagingly — **half–breed** adj

half brother n (14c) : a brother related through one parent only

half–caste \'haf-,kast, 'håf-\ n (1789) : one of mixed racial descent : HALF-BREED — **half–caste** adj

half cock n (1745) **1 :** the position of the hammer of a firearm when about half retracted and held by the sear so that it cannot be operated by a pull on the trigger   **2** chiefly Brit : a state of inadequate preparation or mental confusion ⟨go off at half cock⟩

half–cocked \'haf-'käkt, 'håf-\ adj (1809) **1 :** being at half cock   **2 :** lacking adequate preparation or forethought ⟨go off ~⟩

half–court \'haf-'kȯrt, -'kȯrt, 'håf-\ n (1888) : a dividing line that separates a playing court into equal halves (as in basketball); also : the area comprising each half

half crown n (1542) : a British coin worth two shillings and sixpence used as legal tender until 1970

half dime n (1792) : a silver 5-cent coin struck by the U.S. mint in 1792 and from 1794 to 1873

half disme n (1792) : a half dime struck in 1792

half–dol·lar \'haf-'dä-lər, 'håf-\ n (1786) **1 :** a coin representing one half of a dollar   **2 :** the sum of 50 cents

half duplex n (1950) : a mode of communication esp. with a computer via telephone line in which information can be sent in only one direction at a time — compare DUPLEX

half eagle n (1786) : a 5-dollar gold piece issued by the U.S. from 1795 to 1916 and in 1929

half–hardy adj (1824) of a plant : able to withstand a moderately low temperature but injured by severe freezing and surviving the winter in cold climates only if properly protected

half–heart·ed \'haf-'här-təd, 'håf-\ adj (15c) : lacking heart, spirit, or interest — **half–heart·ed·ly** adv — **half–heart·ed·ness** n

half hitch n (1769) : a simple knot tied by passing the end of a line around an object, across the main part of the line, and then through the resulting loop — see KNOT illustration

half hour n (15c) **1 :** thirty minutes   **2 :** the middle point of an hour — **half–hour·ly** \'haf-'aú(-ə)r-lē, 'håf-\ adv or adj

half–knot \'haf-,nät, 'håf-\ n (1933) : a knot intertwining the ends of two cords and used in tying other knots

half–length \'haf-'leŋ(k)th, 'håf-\ n (1699) : something (as a portrait) that is or represents only half the complete length

half–life \-,līf\ n (1907) **1 :** the time required for half of something to

\ə\ abut   \ᵊ\ kitten, F table   \ər\ further   \a\ ash   \ā\ ace   \ä\ mop, mar
\aú\ out   \ch\ chin   \e\ bet   \ē\ easy   \g\ go   \i\ hit   \ī\ ice   \j\ job
\ŋ\ sing   \ō\ go   \ȯ\ law   \ȯi\ boy   \th\ thin   \t̲h̲\ the   \ü\ loot   \ú\ foot
\y\ yet   \zh\ vision   \á, k̲, ⁿ, œ, œ̄, ᵫ, ᵫ̄, ᵊ\ see Guide to Pronunciation

undergo a process: as **a** : the time required for half of the atoms of a radioactive substance to become disintegrated **b** : the time required for half the amount of a substance (as a drug or radioactive tracer) in or introduced into a living system or ecosystem to be eliminated or disintegrated by natural processes **2** : a period of usefulness or popularity preceding decline or obsolescence ⟨slang usually has a short ~⟩
half-light \-₁līt\ n (1625) : dim grayish light
half line n (ca. 1914) : a straight line extending from a point indefinitely in one direction only
¹half–mast \-'mast\ n (1627) : a point some distance but not necessarily halfway down below the top of a mast or staff or the peak of a gaff
²half–mast vt (1891) : to cause to hang at half-mast ⟨~ a flag⟩
half–moon \'haf-₁mün, 'haf-\ n (15c) **1** : the moon when half its disk appears illuminated **2** : something shaped like a crescent **3** : the lunule of a fingernail — **half–moon** adj
half nelson n (1889) : a wrestling hold in which one arm is thrust under the corresponding arm of an opponent and the hand placed on the back of the opponent's neck — compare FULL NELSON
half note n (1597) : a musical note with the time value of ½ of a whole note — see NOTE illustration
half–pen·ny \'hāp-nē, 'hā-pə-, US also 'haf-₁pe-nē, 'haf-\ n (13c) **1** pl **halfpence** \'hā-pən(t)s, US also 'haf-₁pen(t)s, 'haf-\ or **halfpennies** : a former British coin representing one half of a penny **2** : the sum of half a penny **3** : a small amount — **halfpenny** adj
¹half–pint \'haf-₁pint, 'haf-\ n (1611) **1** : half a pint **2** : a short, small, or inconsequential person
²half–pint adj (ca. 1926) : of less than average size : DIMINUTIVE
half plane n (1891) : the part of a plane on one side of an indefinitely extended straight line drawn in the plane
half rest n (ca. 1899) : a musical rest corresponding in time value to a half note — see REST illustration
half shell n (1860) : either of the valves of a bivalve — **on the half shell** : served in a half shell ⟨oysters on the half shell⟩
half sister n (13c) : a sister related through one parent only
half–slip \'haf-₁slip, 'haf-\ n (ca. 1948) : a topless slip with an elasticized waistband
half–sole vt (1795) : to put half soles on
half sole n (1865) : a shoe sole extending from the shank forward
half sovereign n (ca. 1504) : a British gold coin worth 10 shillings
half–space \'haf-₁spās, 'haf-\ n (1962) : the part of three-dimensional euclidean space lying on one side of a plane
half–staff \-'staf\ n (1708) : HALF-MAST
half step n (1904) **1** : a walking step of 15 inches or in double time of 18 inches **2** : a musical interval (as E-F or B-C) equivalent to one twelfth of an octave — called also semitone
half–timber or **half–tim·bered** \'haf-'tim-bərd, 'haf-\ adj (ca. 1876) of a building : constructed of wood framing with spaces filled with masonry — **half–tim·ber·ing** \-b(ə-)riŋ\ n
half–time \-₁tīm\ n (1871) : an intermission between halves of a game or contest (as in football or basketball)
half–time adj (1961) : involving or working half the standard hours — **half–time** adv
half title n (1879) : the title of a book appearing alone on a right-hand page immediately preceding the title page; also : the page itself
half–tone \'haf-₁tōn, 'haf-\ n (1651) **1** : HALF STEP 2 **2 a** : any of the shades of gray between the darkest and the lightest parts of a photographic image **b** : a photoengraving made from an image photographed through a screen and then etched so that the details of the image are reproduced in dots — **halftone** adj
half–track \-₁trak\ n (1935) **1** : an endless chain-track drive system that propels a vehicle supported in front by a pair of wheels **2** : a motor vehicle propelled by half-tracks; specif : one lightly armored for military use — **half–track** or **half–tracked** \-₁trakt\ adj
half–truth \-₁trüth\ n (1658) **1** : a statement that is only partially true **2** : a statement that mingles truth and falsehood with deliberate intent to deceive
half volley n (1843) : a stroke of a ball (as in tennis) at the instant it rebounds from the ground — **half–volley** vb
half·way \'haf-₁wā, 'haf-\ adj (1694) **1** : midway between two points **2** : PARTIAL — **halfway** adv
halfway house n (1694) **1 a** : a place to stop midway on a journey **b** : a halfway place in a progression **2** : a residence for formerly institutionalized individuals (as mental patients, drug addicts, or convicts) that is designed to facilitate their readjustment to private life
half–wit \'haf-₁wit, 'haf-\ n (1640) : a foolish or imbecilic person — **half–wit·ted** \-'wi-təd\ adj — **half–wit·ted·ness** n
half–world \-₁wərld\ n (1870) : DEMIMONDE
hal·i·but \'ha-lə-bət also 'hä-\ n, pl **halibut** also **halibuts** [ME halybutte, fr. haly, holy holy + butte flatfish, fr. MD or MLG but; fr. its being eaten on holy days] (14c) : any of several marine flatfishes (esp. Hippoglossus hippoglossus of the Atlantic and H. stenolepis of the Pacific) that are widely used for food and include some of the largest bony fishes
ha·lide \'ha-₁līd, 'hā-\ n (1876) : a binary compound of a halogen with a more electropositive element or radical
hal·i·dom \'ha-lə-dəm\ or **hal·i·dome** \-₁dōm\ n [ME, fr. OE hāligdōm, fr. hālig holy + -dōm -dom] (bef. 12c) archaic : something held sacred
ha·lite \'ha-₁līt, 'hā-\ n (1868) : ROCK SALT
hal·i·to·sis \₁ha-lə-'tō-səs\ n [NL, fr. L halitus breath, fr. halare to breathe — more at EXHALE] (1874) : a condition of having fetid breath
hall \'hol\ n [ME halle, fr. OE heall; akin to L cella small room, celare to conceal — more at HELL] (bef. 12c) **1 a** : the castle or house of a medieval king or noble **b** : the chief living room in such a structure **2** : the manor house of a landed proprietor **3** : a large usu. imposing building for public or semipublic purposes **4 a** (1) : a building used by a college or university for some special purpose (2) : DORMITORY **b** : a college or a division of a college at some universities **c** (1) : the common dining room of an English college (2) : a meal served there **5 a** : the entrance room of a building : LOBBY **b** : a corridor or passage in a building **6** : a large room for assembly : AUDITORIUM **7** : a place used for public entertainment
hal·lah \'kä-lə, 'hä-\ var of CHALLAH
Hall effect \'hol-\ n [Edwin H. Hall †1938 Am. physicist] (ca. 1889)

: a potential difference observed between the edges of a conducting strip carrying a longitudinal current when placed in a magnetic field perpendicular to the plane of the strip
Hal·lel \hä-'lā(ə)l\ n [Heb hallēl praise] (1702) : a selection comprising Psalms 113–118 chanted during Jewish feasts (as the Passover)
¹hal·le·lu·jah \₁ha-lə-'lü-yə\ interj [Heb hallēlūyāh praise (ye) the Lord] (1535) — used to express praise, joy, or thanks
²hallelujah n (1625) : a shout or song of praise or thanksgiving
hal·liard var of HALYARD
¹hall·mark \'hol-₁märk\ n [Goldsmiths' Hall, London, England, where gold and silver articles were assayed and stamped] (1721) **1 a** : an official mark stamped on gold and silver articles in England to attest their purity **b** : a mark or device placed or stamped on an article of trade to indicate origin, purity, or genuineness **2** : a distinguishing characteristic, trait, or feature ⟨the dramatic flourishes which are the ~ of the trial lawyer —Marion K. Sanders⟩
²hallmark vt (1773) : to stamp with a hallmark
hal·lo \hə-'lō, ha-\ or **hal·loo** \-'lü\ var of HOLLO
Hall of Fame n (ca. 1909) **1** : a structure housing memorials to famous or illustrious individuals usu. chosen by a group of electors **2** : a group of individuals in a particular category (as a sport) who have been selected as particularly illustrious — **Hall of Fam·er** \-'fā-mər\
hal·low \'ha-(₁)lō\ vt [ME halowen, fr. OE hālgian, fr. hālig holy — more at HOLY] (bef. 12c) **1** : to make holy or set apart for holy use **2** : to respect greatly : VENERATE syn see DEVOTE
hal·lowed \'ha-(₁)lōd, 'ha-ləd, in the Lord's Prayer often 'ha-lə-wəd\ adj (bef. 12c) **1** : HOLY, CONSECRATED **2** : SACRED, REVERED ⟨~ customs⟩
Hal·low·een also **Hal·low·e'en** \₁ha-lə-'wēn, ₁hä-\ n [short for All Hallow Even (All Saints' Eve)] (ca. 1700) : October 31 observed esp. with dressing up in disguise, trick-or-treating, and displaying jack-o'-lanterns during the evening
Hal·low·mas \'ha-lō-₁mas, 'ha-lə-, -məs\ n [short for ME Alholowmesse, fr. OE ealra halgena mæsse, lit., all saints' mass] (14c) : ALL SAINTS' DAY
halls of ivy [fr. the traditional training of ivy on the walls of older college buildings] (1965) : UNIVERSITY, COLLEGE
Hall·statt also **Hall·stadt** \'hol-₁stat; 'häl-₁shtät, -₁stät\ adj [Hallstatt, Austria] (1899) : of or relating to the earlier period of the Iron Age in Europe
hal·lu·ci·nate \hə-'lü-sⁿ-₁āt\ vb **-nat·ed; -nat·ing** [L hallucinatus, pp. of hallucinari, allucinari to prate, dream, modif. of Gk alyein to be distressed, to wander] vt (ca. 1834) **1** : to affect with visions or imaginary perceptions **2** : to perceive or experience as an hallucination ~ vi : to have hallucinations — **hal·lu·ci·na·tor** \-₁ā-tər\ n
hal·lu·ci·na·tion \hə-₁lü-sⁿ-'ā-shən\ n (1629) **1 a** : perception of objects with no reality usu. arising from disorder of the nervous system or in response to drugs (as LSD) **b** : the object so perceived **2** : an unfounded or mistaken impression or notion : DELUSION
hal·lu·ci·na·to·ry \hə-'lü-sⁿ-ə-₁tōr-ē, -₁lüs-nə-, -₁tōr-\ adj (1830) **1** : tending to produce hallucination ⟨~ drugs⟩ **2** : resembling, involving, or being an hallucination ⟨~ dreams⟩ ⟨an ~ figure⟩
hal·lu·ci·no·gen \hə-'lü-sⁿ-ə-jən\ n [hallucination + -o- + -gen] (1954) : a substance that induces hallucinations — **hal·lu·ci·no·gen·ic** \-₁lü-sⁿ-ə-'je-nik\ adj or n
hal·lu·ci·no·sis \hə-₁lü-sⁿ-'ō-səs\ n [NL] (1905) : a pathological mental state characterized by hallucinations
hal·lux \'ha-ləks\ n, pl **hal·lu·ces** \'ha-lə-₁sēz, 'hal-yə-\ [NL, fr. L hallus, hallux] (1831) : the innermost digit (as the big toe) of a hind or lower limb
hall·way \'hol-₁wā\ n (1876) **1** : an entrance hall **2** : CORRIDOR
hal·ma \'hal-mə\ n [Gk halma leap, fr. hallesthai to leap — more at SALLY] (1889) : a game played on a square board and having rules similar to those of Chinese checkers
¹ha·lo \'hā-(₁)lō\ n, pl **halos** or **haloes** [L halos, fr. Gk halōs threshing floor, disk, halo] (1603) **1** : a circle of light appearing to surround the sun or moon and resulting from refraction or reflection of light by ice particles in the atmosphere **2** : something resembling a halo: as **a** : NIMBUS **b** : a region of space surrounding a galaxy that is sparsely populated with luminous objects (as globular clusters) but is believed to contain a great deal of dark matter **c** : a differentiated zone surrounding a central zone or object **3** : the aura of glory, veneration, or sentiment surrounding an idealized person or thing
²halo vt (1801) : to form into or surround with a halo ⟨rainbows ~ed the waterfalls —Michael Crawford⟩
halo- — see HAL-
hal·o·car·bon \'ha-lə-₁kär-bən\ n (1950) : any of various compounds (as fluorocarbon) of carbon and one or more halogens
hal·o·cline \'ha-lə-₁klīn\ n (1960) : a usu. vertical gradient in salinity (as of the ocean)
halo effect n (ca. 1928) : generalization from the perception of one outstanding personality trait to an overly favorable evaluation of the whole personality
hal·o·gen \'ha-lə-jən\ n [Sw, fr. hal- + -gen] (1842) : any of the five elements fluorine, chlorine, bromine, iodine, and astatine that form part of group VII A of the periodic table and exist in the free state normally as diatomic molecules — **ha·log·e·nous** \ha-'lä-jə-nəs\ adj
ha·lo·ge·nate \'ha-lə-jə-₁nāt, ha-'lä-jə-\ vt **-nat·ed; -nat·ing** (1882) : to treat or cause to combine with a halogen — **ha·lo·ge·na·tion** \₁ha-lə-jə-'nā-shən, ha-₁lä-jə-\ n
hal·o·ge·ton \₁ha-lə-'jē-₁tän\ n [NL, fr. hal- + Gk geitōn neighbor] (1943) : a coarse annual herb (Halogeton glomeratus) of the goosefoot family that is a noxious weed in western American ranges
hal·o·mor·phic \₁ha-lə-'mor-fik\ adj (ca. 1938) of a soil : developed in the presence of neutral or alkali salts or both
hal·o·per·i·dol \₁ha-lō-'per-ə-₁dol, -₁dōl\ n [hal- + piperidine + ¹-ol] (1960) : a depressant $C_{21}H_{23}ClFNO_2$ of the central nervous system used esp. as an antipsychotic drug
hal·o·phile \'ha-lə-₁fīl\ n [ISV] (1923) : an organism that flourishes in a salty environment — **hal·o·phil·ic** \₁ha-lə-'fi-lik\ adj
hal·o·phyte \'ha-lə-₁fīt\ n [ISV] (ca. 1886) : a plant (as saltbush or sea lavender) that grows in salty soil and usu. has a physiological resemblance to a true xerophyte — **hal·o·phyt·ic** \₁ha-lə-'fi-tik\ adj
hal·o·thane \'ha-lə-₁thān\ n [halo- + ethane] (1957) : a nonexplosive inhalational anesthetic $C_2HBrClF_3$

¹halt \'hȯlt\ *adj* [ME, fr. OE *healt;* akin to OHG *halz* lame] (bef. 12c)
: LAME

²halt *vi* (bef. 12c) **1 :** to walk or proceed lamely : LIMP **2 :** to stand in perplexity or doubt between alternate courses : WAVER **3 :** to display weakness or imperfection : FALTER

³halt *n* [G, fr. MHG, fr. *halt,* imper. of *halten* to hold, fr. OHG *haltan* — more at HOLD] (ca. 1598) : STOP

⁴halt *vi* (1656) **1 :** to cease marching or journeying **2 :** DISCONTINUE, TERMINATE ⟨the project ∼ed for lack of funds⟩ ∼ *vt* **1 :** to bring to a stop ⟨the strike ∼ed subways and buses⟩ **2 :** to cause the discontinuance of : END

¹hal·ter \'hȯl-tǝr\ *n* [ME, fr. OE *hælftre;* akin to OHG *halftra* halter, OE *hielfe* helve] (bef. 12c) **1 a :** a rope or strap for leading or tying an animal **b :** a headstall usu. with noseband and throatlatch to which a lead may be attached **2 :** a rope for hanging criminals : NOOSE; *also* : death by hanging **3** : a woman's blouse that leaves the back, arms, and midriff bare and that is typically held in place by straps around the neck and across the back

²halter *vt* **hal·tered; hal·ter·ing** \-t(ǝ-)riŋ\ (14c) **1 a :** to catch with or as if with a halter; *also* : to put a halter on **b :** HANG **2** : to put restraint upon : HAMPER

hal·ter·break \'hȯl-tǝr-ˌbrāk\ *vt* **-broke** \-ˌbrōk\; **-bro·ken** \-ˌbrō-kǝn\; **-break·ing** (1837) : to break (as a colt) to a halter

hal·tere \'hȯl-ˌtir, 'hal-\ *n, pl* **hal·teres** \'hȯl-ˌtirz, 'hal-; hȯl-'tir-ēz, hal-\ [NL *halter,* fr. L. jumping weight, fr. Gk *haltēr,* fr. *hallesthai* to leap — more at SALLY] (1823) : one of a pair of club-shaped organs in a dipteran insect that are the modified second pair of wings and function as sensory flight stabilizers

halt·ing \'hȯl-tiŋ\ *adj* (1585) : marked by a lack of sureness or effectiveness ⟨spoke in a ∼ manner⟩ — **halt·ing·ly** \-tiŋ-lē\ *adv*

hal·vah *or* **hal·va** \häl-'vä; 'häl-(ˌ)vä, -vǝ\ *n* [Yiddish *halva,* fr. Rom, fr. Turk *helva,* fr. Ar *ḥalwā* sweetmeat] (1846) : a flaky confection of crushed sesame seeds in a base of syrup (as of honey)

halve \'hav, 'hȧv\ *vt* **halved; halv·ing** [ME, fr. *half* half] (13c) **1 a** : to divide into two equal parts **b :** to reduce to one half ⟨*halving* the present cost⟩ **c :** to share equally **2 :** to play (as a hole in golf) in the same number of strokes as one's opponent

halv·ers \'ha-vǝrz, 'hȧ-\ *n pl* (1517) : half shares : HALVES

halves *pl of* HALF

hal·yard \'hal-yǝrd\ *n* [ME *halier,* fr. *halen* to pull — more at HALE] (14c) : a rope or tackle for hoisting and lowering something (as sails)

¹ham \'ham\ *n* [ME *hamme,* fr. OE *hamm;* akin to OHG *hamma* ham, Gk *knēmē* shinbone, OIr *cnáim* bone] (bef. 12c) **1 a :** the hollow of the knee **b :** a buttock with its associated thigh — usu. used in pl. **2** : a cut of meat consisting of a thigh; *esp* : one from a hog **3** [short for *hamfatter,* fr. "The *Ham-fat* Man," minstrel song] **a :** a showy performer; *esp* : an actor performing in an exaggerated theatrical style **b** : a licensed operator of an amateur radio station **4 :** a cushion used esp. by tailors for pressing curved areas of garments — **ham** *adj*

²ham *vb* **hammed; ham·ming** (1933) : to execute with exaggerated speech or gestures : OVERACT ∼ *vt* : to overplay a part

Ham \'ham\ *n* [Heb] : a son of Noah held to be the progenitor of the Egyptians, Nubians, and Canaanites

hama·dry·ad \ˌha-mǝ-'drī-ǝd, -ǝd\ *n* [L *hamadryad-, hamadryas,* fr. Gk, fr. *hama* together with + *dryad-, dryas* dryad — more at SAME] (14c) **1 :** WOOD NYMPH **2 :** KING COBRA

hama·dry·as baboon \ˌha-mǝ-'drī-ǝs-\ *n* [NL *hamadryas,* fr. L] (ca. 1890) : a baboon (*Papio hamadryas*) that has a reddish pink muzzle and a large bare patch of pink skin on each buttock and that was venerated by the ancient Egyptians — called also *sacred baboon*

ha·mal *also* **ham·mal** \hä-'mäl\ *n* [Ar *ḥammāl* porter] (ca. 1760) : a porter in eastern countries (as Turkey)

Ha·man \'hä-mǝn\ *n* [Heb *Hāmān*] : an enemy of the Jews hanged according to the book of Esther for plotting their destruction

ha·man·tasch \'hä-mǝn-ˌtäsh, 'hȯ-, -ˌtȯsh\ *n, pl* **-tasch·en** \-ˌtä-shǝn, -ˌtȯ-\ [Yiddish *homentash,* fr. *Homen* Haman + *tash* pocket, bag] (1927) : a three-cornered pastry with a filling (as of poppy seeds or prunes) traditionally eaten during the Jewish holiday Purim

ha·mar·tia \ˌhä-ˌmär-'tē-ǝ\ *n* [Gk, fr. *hamartanein* to miss the mark, err] (1927) : TRAGIC FLAW

ha·mate \'hä-ˌmāt\ *n* [L *hamatus* hooked, fr. *hamus* hook] (1924) : a bone on the inner side of the second row of the carpus in mammals

ham·burg·er \'ham-ˌbǝr-gǝr\ *or* **ham·burg** \-ˌbǝrg\ *n* [G *Hamburger* of Hamburg, Germany] (1884) **1 a :** ground beef **b :** a patty of ground beef **2 :** a sandwich consisting of a patty of hamburger in a split round bun

¹hame \'hām\ *n* [ME] (14c) : one of two curved supports attached to the collar of a draft horse to which the traces are fastened

²hame *Scot var of* HOME

ham–fist·ed \'ham-ˌfis-tǝd\ *adj* (1928) : HAM-HANDED

ham–hand·ed \-ˌhan-dǝd\ *adj* (1918) : lacking dexterity or grace : HEAVY-HANDED — **ham–hand·ed·ly** \-lē\ *adv* — **ham–hand·ed·ness** \-dǝd-nǝs\ *n*

Ham·il·to·ni·an \ˌha-mǝl-'tō-nē-ǝn\ *n* [Sir William *Hamilton* †1865 Irish mathematician] (1933) : a function that is used to describe a dynamic system (as the motion of a particle) in terms of components of momentum and coordinates of space and time and that is equal to the total energy of the system when time is not explicitly part of the function — compare LAGRANGIAN

Ham·il·to·ni·an·ism \-nē-ǝ-ˌni-zǝm\ *n* (1901) : the political principles and ideas held by or associated with Alexander Hamilton that center around a belief in a strong central government, broad interpretation of the federal constitution, encouragement of an industrial and commercial economy, and a general distrust of the political capacity or wisdom of the common man — **Hamiltonian** \-'tō-nē-ǝn\ *adj*

Ham·ite \'ha-ˌmīt\ *n* [*Ham*] (1854) : a member of a Hamitic-speaking people

¹Ham·it·ic \ha-'mi-tik, hǝ-\ *adj* (1844) : of, relating to, or characteristic of the Hamites or one of the Hamitic languages

²Hamitic *n* (ca. 1890) : HAMITIC LANGUAGES

Hamitic languages *n pl* (ca. 1890) : any of various groupings of non-Semitic Afro-Asiatic languages (as Berber, Egyptian, and Cushitic) that were formerly thought to comprise a single branch of the Afro-Asiatic family

Ham·i·to–Se·mit·ic \ˌha-mǝ-(ˌ)tō-sǝ-'mi-tik, -'mi-tō-\ *adj* (1901) : of, relating to, or constituting the Afro-Asiatic languages — **Hamito–Semitic** *n*

ham·let \'ham-lǝt\ *n* [ME, fr. MF *hamelet,* dim. of *ham* village, of Gmc origin; akin to OE *hām* village, home] (bef. 12c) : a small village

Ham·let \'ham-lǝt\ *n* : a legendary Danish prince and hero of Shakespeare's play *Hamlet*

¹ham·mer \'ha-mǝr\ *n* [ME *hamer,* fr. OE *hamor;* akin to OHG *hamar* hammer, and perh. to OCS *kamen-, kamy* stone, Gk *akmē* point, edge — more at EDGE] (bef. 12c) **1 a :** a hand tool consisting of a solid head set crosswise on a handle and used for pounding **b :** a power tool that often substitutes a metal block or a drill for the hammerhead **2 :** something that resembles a hammer in form or action: as **a :** a lever with a striking head for ringing a bell or striking a gong **b** (1) : an arm that strikes the cap in a percussion lock to ignite the propelling charge (2) : a part of the action of a modern gun that strikes the primer of the cartridge in firing or that strikes the firing pin to ignite the cartridge **c :** MALLEUS **d :** GAVEL **e** (1) : a padded mallet in a piano action for striking a string (2) : a hand mallet for playing on various percussion instruments (as a xylophone) **3 :** a metal sphere thrown for distance in the hammer throw **4 :** ACCELERATOR **b — under the hammer :** for sale at auction

²hammer *vb* **ham·mered; ham·mer·ing** \'ha-mǝr-iŋ, 'ham-riŋ\ *vi* (14c) **1 :** to strike blows esp. repeatedly with or as if with a hammer : POUND **2 :** to make repeated efforts; *esp* : to reiterate an opinion or attitude ⟨the lectures all ∼ed away at the same points⟩ ∼ *vt* **1 a :** to beat, drive, or shape with repeated blows of a hammer **b :** to fasten or build with a hammer **2 :** to strike or drive with a force suggesting a hammer blow or repeated blows ⟨∼ed the ball over the fence⟩ ⟨tried to ∼ me into submission⟩ — **ham·mer·er** \'ha-mǝr-ǝr\ *n*

hammer and sickle *n* (1921) : an emblem consisting of a crossed hammer and sickle used esp. as a symbol of Soviet Communism

hammer and tongs *adv* (ca. 1780) : with great force, vigor, or violence ⟨went at it *hammer and tongs*⟩ — **hammer–and–tongs** *adj*

hammer dulcimer *n* (1953) : DULCIMER 1 — called also *hammered dulcimer*

hammered *adj* (1522) : having surface indentations produced or appearing to have been produced by hammering ⟨∼ copper⟩

ham·mer·head \'ha-mǝr-ˌhed\ *n* (1562) **1 :** the striking part of a hammer **2 :** BLOCKHEAD **3 :** any of a family (Sphyrnidae) of active voracious medium-sized sharks that have the eyes at the ends of lateral extensions of the flattened head — see SHARK illustration

ham·mer·less \-lǝs\ *adj* (1875) : having the hammer concealed ⟨a ∼ revolver⟩

ham·mer·lock \-ˌläk\ *n* (1897) : a wrestling hold in which an opponent's arm is held bent behind his back; *broadly* : a strong hold

hammer mill *n* (1610) : a grinder or crusher in which materials esp. broken up by hammers

hammer out *vt* (ca. 1632) : to produce or bring about as if by repeated blows ⟨*hammered out* an agreement⟩

hammer throw *n* (1898) : a field event in which a usu. 16-pound metal sphere attached to a flexible handle is thrown for distance

ham·mer·toe \'ha-mǝr-ˌtō\ *n* (ca. 1885) : a deformed claw-shaped toe and esp. the second that results from permanent angular flexion between one or both phalangeal joints

¹ham·mock \'ha-mǝk\ *n* [Sp *hamaca,* fr. Taino] (1555) : a swinging couch or bed usu. made of netting or canvas and slung by cords from supports at each end

²hammock *n* [origin unknown] (1555) **1 :** HUMMOCK 2 **:** a fertile area in the southern U.S. and esp. Florida that is usu. higher than its surroundings and that is characterized by hardwood vegetation and deep humus-rich soil

ham·my \'ha-mē\ *adj* **ham·mi·er; -est** (1929) : marked by exaggerated and usu. self-conscious theatricality — **ham·mi·ly** \'ha-mǝ-lē\ *adv* — **ham·mi·ness** \'ha-mē-nǝs\ *n*

¹ham·per \'ham-pǝr\ *vt* **ham·pered; ham·per·ing** \-p(ǝ-)riŋ\ [ME] (14c) **1 a :** to restrict the movement of by bonds or obstacles : IMPEDE **b :** to interfere with the operation of : DISRUPT **2 a :** CURB, RESTRAIN **b :** to interfere with : ENCUMBER

syn HAMPER, TRAMMEL, CLOG, FETTER, SHACKLE, MANACLE mean to hinder or impede in moving, progressing, or acting. HAMPER may imply the effect of any impeding or restraining influence ⟨*hampered* the investigation by refusing to cooperate⟩. TRAMMEL suggests entangling by or confining within a net ⟨rules that *trammel* the artist's creativity⟩. CLOG usu. implies a slowing by something extraneous or encumbering ⟨a court system *clogged* by frivolous suits⟩. FETTER suggests a restraining so severe that freedom to move or progress is almost lost ⟨a nation *fettered* by an antiquated class system⟩. SHACKLE and MANACLE are stronger than FETTER and suggest total loss of freedom ⟨a mind *shackled* by stubborn prejudice⟩ ⟨a people *manacled* by tyranny⟩.

²hamper *n* [ME *hampere,* alter. of *hanaper,* lit., case to hold goblets, fr. MF *hanapier,* fr. *hanap* goblet, of Gmc origin; akin to OE *hnæpp* bowl] (14c) : a large basket usu. with a cover for packing, storing, or transporting articles (as food or laundry)

Hamp·shire \'ham(p)-ˌshir, -shǝr\ *n* [*Hampshire,* England] (1918) **1** : any of a British breed of large hornless black-faced mutton-producing sheep — called also *Hampshire Down* **2 :** any of an American breed of black white-belted swine

ham·ster \'ham(p)-stǝr\ *n* [G, fr. OHG *hamustro,* of Slavic origin; akin to ORuss *choměstorŭ* hamster, of Iranian origin; akin to Av *hamaēstar-*

halter 1b

\ǝ\ abut \ᵊ\ kitten, F table \ǝr\ further \a\ ash \ā\ ace \ä\ mop, mar \aů\ out \ch\ chin \e\ bet \ē\ easy \g\ go \i\ hit \ī\ ice \j\ job \ŋ\ sing \ō\ go \ȯ\ law \ȯi\ boy \th\ thin \ṯh\ the \ü\ loot \ů\ foot \y\ yet \zh\ vision \ȧ, ̲k, ⁿ, œ, œ̄, ᵫ, ᵫᵉ, ʸ\ *see* Guide to Pronunciation oppressor] (1607) : any of a subfamily (Cricetinae) of small Old World rodents having very large cheek pouches

¹ham·string \'ham-ˌstriŋ\ *n* (1565) **1 a** : either of two groups of tendons at the back of the human knee **b** : HAMSTRING MUSCLE **2** : a large tendon above and behind the hock of a quadruped

²hamstring *vt* **-strung** \-ˌstrəŋ\; **-string·ing** \-ˌstriŋ-iŋ\ (1641) **1** : to make ineffective or powerless : CRIPPLE ⟨hamstrung by guilt⟩ **2** : to cripple by cutting the leg tendons

hamstring muscle *n* (ca. 1888) : any of three muscles at the back of the thigh that function to flex and rotate the leg and extend the thigh

ham·u·lus \'ham-yə-ləs\ *n, pl* **-u·li** \-ˌlī, -ˌlē\ [NL, fr. L, dim. of *hamus* hook] (ca. 1751) : a hook or hooked process (as of a bone)

ham·za *or* **ham·zah** \'ham-zə, 'häm-\ *n* [Ar *hamzah*, lit., compression] (1938) : the sign for a glottal stop in Arabic orthography usu. represented in English by an apostrophe

Han \'hän\ *n* [Chin (Beijing) *Hàn*] (1736) **1** : a Chinese dynasty dated 207B.C.–A.D.220 and marked by centralized control through an appointive bureaucracy, a revival of learning, and the penetration of Buddhism **2** : the Chinese peoples esp. as distinguished from non-Chinese (as Mongolian) elements in the population

¹hand \'hand\ *n, often attrib* [ME, fr. OE; akin to OHG *hant* hand] (bef. 12c) **1 a** (1) : the terminal part of the vertebrate forelimb when modified (as in humans) as a grasping organ (2) : the forelimb segment (as the terminal section of a bird's wing) of a vertebrate higher than the fishes that corresponds to the hand irrespective of its form or functional specialization **b** : a part serving the function of or resembling a hand: as (1) : the hind foot of an ape (2) : the chela of a crustacean **c** : something resembling a hand: as (1) : an indicator or pointer on a dial ⟨the ∼s of a clock⟩ (2) : INDEX 5 (3) : a cluster of bananas developed from a single flower group (4) : a branched rootstock of ginger (5) : a bunch of large leaves (as of tobacco) tied together usu. with another leaf **2 a** : personal possession — usu. used in pl. ⟨the documents fell into the ∼s of the enemy⟩ **b** : CONTROL, SUPERVISION — usu. used in pl. ⟨left the matter in her ∼s⟩ **3 a** : SIDE, DIRECTION ⟨men fighting on either ∼⟩ **b** : one of two sides or aspects of an issue or argument ⟨on the one ∼ we can appeal for peace, and on the other, declare war⟩ **4** : a pledge esp. of betrothal or bestowal in marriage **5 a** : style of penmanship : HANDWRITING ⟨wrote in a fancy ∼⟩ **b** : SIGNATURE **6 a** : SKILL, ABILITY ⟨tried her ∼ at sailing⟩ **b** : an instrumental part ⟨had a ∼ in the victory⟩ **7** : a unit of measure equal to 4 inches (10.2 centimeters) used esp. for the height of horses **8 a** : assistance or aid esp. involving physical effort ⟨lend a ∼⟩ **b** : PARTICIPATION, INTEREST ⟨a ∼ in the business⟩ **9 a** (1) : a round of applause ⟨big ∼⟩ **b** : a player in a card game or board game (2) : the cards or pieces held by a player **b** : a single round in a game **c** : the force or solidity of one's position ⟨as in negotiations⟩ **10 a** : a person who performs or executes a particular work ⟨two portraits by the same ∼⟩ **b** (1) : a person employed at manual labor or general tasks ⟨a ranch ∼⟩ (2) : WORKER, EMPLOYEE ⟨employed over a hundred ∼s⟩ **c** : a member of a ship's crew ⟨all ∼s on deck⟩ **d** : a person skilled in a particular action or pursuit ⟨a specialist or veteran in a usu. designated activity or region ⟨a China ∼⟩ **11 a** : HANDIWORK, DOINGS **b** : style of execution : WORKMANSHIP ⟨the ∼ of a master⟩ **c** : the feel of or tactile reaction to something (as silk or leather) **12** : a punch made with a specified hand ⟨knocked him out with a good right ∼⟩ — **at hand 1** : near in time or place : within reach ⟨use whatever ingredients are at hand⟩ **2** : currently receiving or deserving attention ⟨the business at hand⟩ — **at the hands of** *also* **at the hand of** : by or through the action of — **by hand 1** : with the hands or a hand-worked implement (as a tool or pen) rather than with a machine **2** : from one individual directly to another ⟨deliver the document by hand⟩ — **in hand 1** : in one's possession or control **2** : in preparation **3** : under consideration — **on all hands** *or* **on every hand** : EVERYWHERE — **on hand 1** : in present possession or readily available **2** : about to appear : PENDING **3** : in attendance : PRESENT — **on one's hands** : in one's possession or care ⟨too much time on my hands⟩ — **out of hand 1** : without delay or deliberation; *also* : in a summary or peremptory manner **2** : done with : FINISHED **3** : out of control **4** : with the hands ⟨fruit eaten out of hand⟩ — **to hand 1** : into possession **2** : within reach

²hand *adv* (bef. 12c) : with the hands rather than by machine

³hand *vt* (15c) **1 a** *obs* : to touch or manage with the hands; *also* : to deal with **b** : FURL **2** : to lead, guide, or assist with the hand ⟨∼ a lady into a bus⟩ **3 a** : to give, pass, or transmit with the hand ⟨∼ a letter to her⟩ **b** : to present or provide with ⟨∼ed him a surprise⟩ — **hand it to** : to give credit to : concede the excellence of

hand and foot *adv* (bef. 12c) : TOTALLY, ASSIDUOUSLY

hand ax *n* (13c) **1** : a short-handled ax intended for use with one hand **2** : a prehistoric stone tool having one end pointed for cutting and the other end rounded for holding in the hand

hand·bag \'han(d)-ˌbag\ *n* (1862) **1** : SUITCASE **2** : a bag held in the hand or hung from a shoulder strap and used for carrying small personal articles and money

hand·ball \-ˌbȯl\ *n* (1886) **1** : a game played in a walled court or against a single wall or board by two or four players who use their hands to strike the ball **2** : a small rubber ball used in handball

hand·bar·row \-ˌbar-(ˌ)ō\ *n* (15c) : a flat rectangular frame with handles at both ends that is carried by two persons

hand·bas·ket \-ˌbas-kət\ *n* (15c) : a small portable basket — usu. used in the phrase *to hell in a handbasket* denoting rapid and utter ruination

hand·bell \-ˌbel\ *n* (bef. 12c) : a small bell with a handle; *esp* : one of a set tuned in a scale for musical performance

hand·bill \-ˌbil\ *n* (1753) : a small printed sheet to be distributed (as for advertising) by hand

hand·blown \-'blōn\ *adj* (1925) : made by glassblowing and molded by hand

hand·book \-ˌbük\ *n* (bef. 12c) **1 a** : a book capable of being conveniently carried as a ready reference : MANUAL **b** : a concise reference book covering a particular subject **2 a** : a bookmaker's book of bets **b** : a place where bookmaking is carried on

hand·breadth \-ˌbretth, -ˌbreth, -ˌbredth\ *n* (bef. 12c) : any of various units of length varying from about 2½ to 4 inches based on the breadth of a hand

hand·car \'han(d)-ˌkär\ *n* (1850) : a small four-wheeled railroad car propelled by a hand-operated mechanism or by a small motor

hand·cart \-ˌkärt\ *n* (1640) : a cart drawn or pushed by hand

hand cheese *n* (1890) : a soft cheese with a sharp pungent odor and flavor that was orig. molded by hand

hand·clasp \'han(d)-ˌklasp\ *n* (1583) : HANDSHAKE

¹hand·craft \-ˌkraft\ *n* (bef. 12c) : HANDICRAFT

²handcraft *vt* (1947) : to fashion by handicraft

hand·crafts·man \-ˌkraf(t)-smən\ *n* (15c) : a person who is skilled in handicraft — **hand·crafts·man·ship** \-ˌship\ *n*

¹hand·cuff \-ˌkəf\ *n* (1695) : a metal fastening that can be locked around a wrist and is usu. connected by a chain or bar with another such fastening — usu. used in pl.

²handcuff *vt* (1720) **1** : to apply handcuffs to : MANACLE **2** : to hold in check : make ineffective or powerless

hand down *vt* (1692) **1** : to transmit in succession (as from father to son) **2** : to make official formulation of and express (the opinion of a court)

hand·ed \'han-dəd\ *adj* (15c) **1** : having a hand or hands esp. of a specified kind or number — usu. used in combination ⟨a large-*handed* man⟩ **2** : using a specified hand or number of hands — used in combination ⟨right-*handed*⟩ ⟨a one-*handed* catch⟩

hand·ed·ness \-nəs\ *n* (1915) **1** : a tendency to use one hand rather than the other **2 a** : the property of an object (as a molecule) of not being identical with its mirror image **b** : either of the two configurations of an object that may exist in forms which are nonidentical mirror images

hand·fast \'han-ˌfast\ *n* [ME, fr. OE *handfæst*] (1611) *archaic* : a contract or covenant esp. of betrothal or marriage

hand–feed \'han(d)-ˈfēd\ *vt* **-fed** \-ˈfed\; **-feed·ing** (1805) : to feed (as animals) by hand

hand·ful \'han(d)-ˌfül\ *n, pl* **handfuls** \-ˌfülz\ *also* **hands·ful** \'han(d)z-ˌfül\ (bef. 12c) **1** : as much or as many as the hand will grasp **2** : a small quantity or number **3** : as much as one can manage

hand glass *n* (1882) : a small mirror with a handle

hand·grip \'han(d)-ˌgrip\ *n* (bef. 12c) **1** : a grasping with the hand **2** : HANDLE **3** *pl* : hand-to-hand combat

hand·gun \-ˌgən\ *n* (15c) : a firearm (as a revolver or pistol) designed to be held and fired with one hand

hand·held \-ˌheld, -ˈheld\ *adj* (1923) : held in the hand; *esp* : designed to be operated while being held in the hand ⟨∼ computers⟩ — **hand·held** \-ˌheld\ *n*

hand·hold \'han(d)-ˌhōld\ *n* (1643) **1** : HOLD, GRIP **2** : something to hold on to (as in mountain climbing)

hand–hold·ing \-ˌhōl-diŋ\ *n* (1967) : solicitous attention, support, or instruction (as in the use of new technology)

¹hand·i·cap \'han-di-ˌkap, -dē-\ *n* [obs. E *handicap* (a game in which forfeit money was held in a cap), fr. *hand in cap*] (1754) **1 a** : a race or contest in which an artificial advantage is given or disadvantage imposed on a contestant to equalize chances of winning **b** : an advantage given or disadvantage imposed usu. in the form of points, strokes, weight to be carried, or distance from the target or goal **2 a** : a disadvantage that makes achievement unusually difficult **b** : a physical disability

²handicap *vt* **-capped; -cap·ping** (1852) **1 a** : to give a handicap to **b** : to assess the relative winning chances of (contestants) or the likely winner of (a contest) **2** : to put at a disadvantage

hand·i·capped *adj* (1915) : having a physical or mental disability that substantially limits activity esp. in relation to employment or education; *also* : of or reserved for handicapped persons ⟨∼ parking spaces⟩

hand·i·cap·per \-ˌka-pər\ *n* (1754) **1** : a person who assigns handicaps **2** : a person who predicts the winners in a race (as a horse race) **3** : a person who competes with a (specified) handicap (as in golf) — usu. used in combination ⟨a 5-*handicapper*⟩

hand·i·craft \'han-di-ˌkraft, -dē-\ *n* [ME *handi-crafte*, alter. of *hand-craft*] (13c) **1 a** : manual skill **b** : an occupation requiring skill with the hands **2** : the articles fashioned by those engaged in handicraft — **hand·i·craft·er** \-ˌkraf-tər\ *n*

hand·i·crafts·man \-ˌkraf(t)-smən\ *n* (1551) : a person who engages in a handicraft : ARTISAN

Hand·ie–Talk·ie \ˌhan-dē-ˈtȯ-kē\ *trademark* — used for a small portable radio transmitter-receiver

hand·i·ly \'han-də-lē\ *adv* (1719) **1** : in a dexterous manner **2** : EASILY ⟨defeated the other candidate ∼⟩ **3** : conveniently nearby

hand in *vt* (1837): SUBMIT 2 ⟨hand in your homework⟩

hand in glove *or* **hand and glove** *adv* (1680) : in extremely close relationship or agreement ⟨working *hand in glove* with the police⟩

hand in hand *adv* (15c) **1** : with hands clasped (as in intimacy or affection) **2** : in close association : TOGETHER

hand·i·work \'han-di-ˌwork, -dē-\ *n* [ME *handiwerk*, fr. OE *handgeweorc*, fr. *hand* + *geweorc*, fr. ge- (collective prefix) + *weorc* work — more at CO-] (bef. 12c) **1 a** : work done by the hands **b** : work done personally **2** : the product of handiwork

hand·ker·chief \'han-kər-chəf, -(ˌ)chif, -(ˌ)chif, -ˌchēf\ *n, pl* **-chiefs** *also* **-chieves** \-chəfs, -(ˌ)chifs, -ˌchefs, -ˌchēfs, -chəvz, -(ˌ)chivz\ (1530) **1** : a small usu. square piece of cloth used for usu. personal purposes (as blowing the nose) or as a clothing accessory **2** : KERCHIEF 1

¹han·dle \'han-d²l\ *n* [ME *handel*, fr. OE *handle*, akin to OE *hand*] (bef. 12c) **1** : a part that is designed esp. to be grasped by the hand **2** : something that resembles a handle **3 a** : TITLE 8 **b** : NAME; *also* : NICKNAME **4** : HAND 11c **5** : the total amount of money bet on a race, game, or event **6** : a means of understanding or controlling ⟨can't quite get a ∼ on things⟩ — **han·dled** \-d²ld\ *adj* — **han·dle·less** \-d²l-(l)əs, -d²ləs\ *adj* — **off the handle** : into a state of sudden and violent anger — usu. used with *fly*

²handle *vb* **han·dled; han·dling** \'han-d²liŋ, 'han-d²l-iŋ\ *vt* (bef. 12c) **1 a** : to try or examine (as by touching, feeling, or moving) with the hand ⟨∼ silk to judge its weight⟩ **b** : to manage with the hands ⟨∼ a horse⟩ **2 a** : to deal with in writing or speaking or in the plastic arts **b** : to have overall responsibility for supervising or directing : MANAGE ⟨a lawyer ∼s all my affairs⟩ **c** : to train and act as second for (a boxer) **d** : to put up with : STAND ⟨can't ∼ the heat⟩ **3** : to act on or perform a required function with regard to ⟨∼ the day's mail⟩ **4** : to engage in the buying, selling, or distributing of (a commodity) ∼ *vi* : to act, behave, or feel in a certain way when handled or directed ⟨a car that ∼s well⟩ — **han·dle·able** \-d²l-ə-bəl\ *adj*

han·dle·bar \'han-d⁰l-₁bär\ *n* (1886) : a straight or bent bar with a handle at each end; *specif* : one used to steer a bicycle or similar vehicle — usu. used in pl.

handlebar mustache *n* (1933) : a heavy mustache with long sections that curve upward at each end

hand lens *n* (1930) : a magnifying glass to be held in the hand

han·dler \'han(d)-lər, 'han-d⁰l-ər\ *n* (14c) **1** : one that handles something **2 a** : a person in immediate physical charge of an animal; *esp* : a person who exhibits dogs at shows or field trials **b** : a person who trains or acts as second for a boxer **c** : a manager of a political figure or campaign

hand·less \'han(d)-ləs\ *adj* (15c) **1** : having no hands **2** : inefficient in manual tasks : CLUMSY

han·dling \'han(d)-liŋ, 'han-d⁰l-iŋ\ *n* (bef. 12c) **1 a** : the action of one that handles something **b** : a process by which something is handled in a commercial transaction; *esp* : the packaging and shipping of an object or material (as to a consumer) **2** : the manner in which something is treated (as in a musical, literary, or art work)

hand·list \'han(d)-₁list\ *n* (1859) : a list (as of books) for purposes of reference or checking

hand·made \'han(d)-'mād\ *adj* (1613) : made by hand or by a hand process

hand·maid·en \-₁mā-d⁰n\ *also* **hand·maid** \-₁mād\ *n* (13c) **1** : a personal maid or female servant **2** : something whose essential function is to serve or assist (criticism is not the enemy of art but rather its ∼ —Gary Michael)

hand-me-down \'han(d)-mē-₁daun\ *adj* (1827) **1** : put in use by one person or group after being used, discarded, or handed down by another (∼ clothes) (∼ anecdotes) **2** : ready-made and usu. cheap and shoddy — **hand-me-down** *n*

hand off *vt* (1949) : to hand (a football) to a nearby teammate on a play ∼ *vi* : to hand off a football — **hand-off** \'han-₁dof\ *n*

hand on *vt* (1865) : HAND DOWN

hand organ *n* (1796) : a barrel organ operated by a hand crank

hand·out \'han-₁daut\ *n* (1882) **1** : a portion of food, clothing, or money given to or as if to a beggar **2** : a folder or circular of information for free distribution **3** : a prepared statement released to the news media

hand out *vt* (1877) **1 a** : to give without charge **b** : to give freely **2** : ADMINISTER (handed out a severe punishment)

hand over *vt* (1816) : to yield control of — **hand-over** \'han-₁dō-vər\ *n*

hand over fist *adv* (1825) : quickly and in large amounts

hand-pick \'han(d)-'pik\ *vt* (1831) **1** : to pick by hand as opposed to a machine process **2** : to select personally or for personal ends

hand-press \-₁pres\ *n* (1679) : a hand-operated press

hand-print \-₁print\ *n* (1886) : an impression of a hand on a surface

hand puppet *n* (1947) : PUPPET 1a

hand·rail \'han(d)-₁rāl\ *n* (1793) : a narrow rail for grasping with the hand as a support

hand running *adv* (1828) *dial* : in unbroken succession

hand·saw \'han(d)-₁so\ *n* (14c) : a saw designed to be used with one hand

hands·breadth \'han(d)z-₁bredth, -₁bretth\ *var of* HANDBREADTH

hands down \'han(d)z-'daun\ *adv* (1867) **1** : without much effort : EASILY **2** : without question — **hands-down** \'han(d)z-₁daun\ *adj*

¹hand·sel \'han(t)-səl\ *n* [ME *hansell*] (14c) **1** : a gift made as a token of good wishes or luck esp. at the beginning of a new year **2** : something received first (as in a day of trading) and taken to be a token of good luck **3 a** : a first installment : earnest money **b** : EARNEST, FORETASTE

²handsel *vt* -seled *or* -selled; -sel·ing *or* -sel·ling \-s(ə-)liŋ\ (15c) **1** : to give a handsel to **2** : to inaugurate with a token or gesture of luck or pleasure **3** : to use or do for the first time

hand·set \'han(d)-₁set\ *n* (ca. 1919) : a combined telephone transmitter and receiver mounted on a handle

hand·shake \-₁shāk\ *n* (1873) : a clasping usu. of right hands by two people (as in greeting or farewell)

hands–off \'han(d)-'zof\ *adj* (1902) : characterized by noninterference (a ∼ policy toward the internal affairs of other nations)

hand·some \'han(t)-səm\ *adj* **hand·som·er**; -est [ME *handsom* easy to manipulate] (1530) **1** *chiefly dial* : APPROPRIATE, SUITABLE **2** : moderately large : SIZABLE (a painting that commanded a ∼ price) **3** : marked by skill or cleverness : ADROIT **4** : marked by graciousness or generosity : LIBERAL (∼ contributions to charity) **5** : having a pleasing and usu. impressive or dignified appearance *syn* see BEAUTIFUL — **hand·some·ly** *adv* — **hand·some·ness** *n*

hands–on \'han(d)-'zon, -'zän\ *adj* (1969) **1** : relating to, being, or providing direct practical experience in the operation or functioning of something (∼ training); *also* : involving or allowing use of or touching with the hands (a ∼ museum display) **2** : characterized by active personal involvement (a ∼ manager)

hand·spike \'han(d)-₁spīk\ *n* [by folk etymology fr. D *handspaak*, fr. *hand* hand + *spaak* pole; akin to OE *spāca* spoke] (1615) : a bar used as a lever

hand·spring \-₁spriŋ\ *n* (1875) : an acrobatic feat in which the body turns forward or backward in a full circle from a standing position and lands first on the hands and then on the feet

hand·stand \-₁stand\ *n* (1899) : an act of supporting the body on the hands with the trunk and legs balanced in the air

hand–to–hand \'han-tə-'hand, -də-\ *adj* (1836) : involving physical contact or close enough range for physical contact (∼ fighting)

hand to hand *adv* (ca. 1533) : at very close range

hand–to–mouth \-'mauth\ *adj* (1748) : having or providing nothing to spare beyond basic necessities (a ∼ existence)

hand truck *n* (1920) : a small hand-propelled truck; *esp* : TRUCK 3b

hand up *vt* (1970) *of a jury* : to deliver (an indictment) to a judge or higher judicial authority

hand·wheel \'han(d)-₁(h)wēl\ *n* (ca. 1889) : a wheel worked by hand

hand·work \'hand-₁wərk\ *n* (bef. 12c) : work done with the hands and not by machines : HANDIWORK — **hand·work·er** \-₁wər-kər\ *n*

hand·wo·ven \-'wō-vən\ *adj* (1880) **1** : produced on a hand-operated loom **2** : woven by hand (∼ baskets)

hand–wring·ing \-₁riŋ-iŋ\ *n* (1922) : an overwrought expression of concern or guilt — **hand·wring·er** *n*

hand-write \-₁rīt\ *vt* -wrote \-₁rōt\; -writ·ten \-₁ri-t⁰n\; -writ·ing \-₁rī-tiŋ\ [back-formation fr. *handwriting*] (ca. 1853) : to write by hand

hand·writ·ing \'hand-₁ri-tiŋ\ *n* (15c) **1** : writing done by hand; *esp* : the form of writing peculiar to a particular person **2** : something written by hand — **handwriting on the wall** : an omen of one's unpleasant fate

hand-wrought \'hand-'rot\ *adj* (1876) : fashioned by hand or chiefly by hand processes (∼ silver)

handy \'han-dē\ *adj* **hand·i·er**; -est (1650) **1 a** : conveniently near **b** : convenient for use **c** *of a ship* : easily handled **2** : clever in using the hands esp. in a variety of useful ways (∼ with a hammer as well as with a paintbrush) — **hand·i·ness** *n*

handy·man \-dē-₁man\ *n* (1872) **1** : one who does odd jobs **2** : one competent in a variety of small skills or inventive or ingenious in repair or maintenance work — called also *handyperson*

¹hang \'haŋ\ *vb* **hung** \'həŋ\ *also* **hanged** \'haŋd\; **hang·ing** \'haŋ-iŋ\ [partly fr. ME *hon*, fr. OE *hōn*, v.t.; partly fr. ME *hangen*, fr. OE *hangian*, v.i. & v.t.; both akin to OHG *hāhan*, v.t., to hang, *hangēn*, v.i. — more at CUNCTATION] *vt* (bef. 12c) **1 a** : to fasten to some elevated point without support from below : to suspend by the neck until dead — often *hanged* in the past; often used as a mild oath (I'll be ∼ed) **c** : to fasten so as to allow free motion within given limits upon a point of suspension (∼ a door) **d** : to adjust the hem of (a skirt) so as to hang evenly and at a proper height **2** : to furnish with hanging decorations (as flags or bunting) **3** : to hold or bear in a suspended or inclined manner (*hung* his head in shame) **4** : to apply to a wall (∼ wallpaper) **5** : to display (pictures) in a gallery **6** : to throw (as a curveball) so that it fails to break properly **7** : to make (a turn) esp. while driving (∼ a right) (*hung* a quick U-turn —Tom Clancy) ∼ *vi* **1 a** : to remain suspended or fastened to some point above without support from below : DANGLE **b** : to die by hanging — often *hanged* in the past (he ∼ed for his crimes) **2** : to remain poised or stationary in the air (clouds ∼ing low overhead) **3** : LINGER, PERSIST **4** : to be imminent : IMPEND (doom *hung* over the nation) **5** : to fall or droop from a usu. tense or taut position **6** : DEPEND (election ∼s on one vote) **7 a** (1) : to take hold for support : CLING (she *hung* on his arm) (2) : to keep persistent contact (dogs *hung* to the trail) **b** : to be burdensome or oppressive (time ∼s on his hands) **8** : to be uncertain or in suspense (the decision is still ∼ing) **9** : to lean, incline, or jut over or downward **10** : to be in a state of rapt attention (*hung* on her every word) **11** : to fit or fall from the figure in easy lines (the coat ∼s loosely) **12** *of a thrown ball* : to fail to break or drop as intended — **hang·able** \'haŋ-ə-bəl\ *adj* — **hang fire 1** : to be slow in the explosion of a charge after its primer has been discharged **2** : DELAY, HESITATE **3** : to remain unsettled or unresolved — **hang it up** : to cease an activity or effort — **hang loose** : to remain calm or relaxed — **hang one on 1** : to inflict a blow on **2** *slang* : to get very drunk — **hang one's hat** : to situate oneself in (as a residence or place of employment) — **hang tough** : to remain resolute in the face of adversity : HANG IN

usage For both transitive and intransitive senses 1b the past and past participle *hung*, as well as *hanged*, is standard. *Hanged* is most appropriate for official executions (he was to be *hanged*, cut down whilst still alive . . . and his bowels torn out —Louis Allen) but *hung* is also used (gave orders that she should be *hung* —Peter Quennell). *Hung* is more appropriate for less formal hangings (by morning I'll be *hung* in effigy —Ronald Reagan).

²hang *n* (ca. 1797) **1** : the manner in which a thing hangs **2** : DECLIVITY, SLOPE; *also* : DROOP **3** : facility with or an understanding of something (can't get the ∼ of this) **4** : a hesitation or slackening in motion or in a course — **give a hang** *or* **care a hang** : to be the least bit concerned or worried

hang about *vi* (1849) *Brit* : HANG AROUND

¹han·gar \'haŋ-ər, 'haŋ-gər\ *n* [F] (1852) : SHELTER, SHED; *esp* : a covered and usu. enclosed area for housing and repairing aircraft

²hangar *vt* (1943) : to place or store in a hangar

hang around *vi* (1830) **1** : to pass time or stay aimlessly : loiter idly **2** : to spend one's time in company ∼ *vt* : to pass time or stay aimlessly in or at (*hang around* the house all day)

hang back *vi* (1581) **1** : to drag behind others **2** : to be reluctant

¹hang·dog \'haŋ-₁dog\ *adj* (1677) **1** : SAD, DEJECTED **2** : SHEEPISH

²hangdog *n* (1687) : a despicable or miserable person

hang·er \'haŋ-ər\ *n* (15c) **1** : one that hangs or causes to be hung or hanged **2** : something that hangs, overhangs, or is suspended: as **a** : a decorative strip of cloth **b** : a small sword formerly used by seamen **c** *chiefly Brit* : a small wood on steeply sloping land **3** : a device by which or to which something is hung or hangs: as **a** : a strap on a sword belt by which a sword or dagger can be suspended **b** : a loop by which a garment is hung up **c** : a device that fits inside or around a garment for hanging from a hook or rod

hang·er–on \-₁on, -₁än\ *n*, *pl* **hang·ers–on** (1542) : one that hangs around a person, place, or institution esp. for personal gain

hang glider *n* (1930) : a kitelike glider from which a harnessed rider hangs while gliding down from a cliff or hill — **hang glid·ing** *n*

hang in *vi* (1966) : to refuse to be discouraged or intimidated : show pluck (*hang in* there)

¹hang·ing \'haŋ-iŋ\ *adj* (12c) **1** : situated or lying on steeply sloping ground **2 a** : jutting out : OVERHANGING (a ∼ rock) **b**

hang glider

\ə\ abut \ᵊ\ kitten, F table \ər\ further \a\ ash \ā\ ace \ä\ mop, mar \au\ out \ch\ chin \e\ bet \ē\ easy \g\ go \i\ hit \ī\ ice \j\ job \ŋ\ sing \ō\ go \o\ law \oi\ boy \th\ thin \t͟h\ the \ü\ loot \u̇\ foot \y\ yet \zh\ vision \å, ᵏ, ⁿ, œ, œ̄, ᵫ, ᵫ̄, ᵞ\ *see* Guide to Pronunciation

: supported only by the wall on one side ⟨a ∼ staircase⟩ **3** *archaic* : downcast in appearance **4** : adapted for sustaining a hanging object **5** : deserving, likely to cause, or prone to inflict death by hanging
²**hanging** *n* (14c) **1** : an execution by strangling or breaking the neck by a suspended noose **2** : something hung: as **a** : CURTAIN **b** : a covering (as a tapestry) for a wall **3** : a downward slope : DECLIVITY
hanging indention *n* (1904) : indention of all the lines of a paragraph except the first
hang·man \'haŋ-mən\ *n* (14c) : one who hangs a condemned person; *also* : public executioner
hang·nail \-ˌnāl\ *n* [by folk etymology fr. *agnail* (inflammation about the nail), fr. ME, corn on the foot or toe, fr. OE *angnægl*, fr. *ang-* (akin to *enge* tight, painful) + *nægl* nail — more at ANGER] (1678) : a bit of skin hanging loose at the side or root of a fingernail
hang off *vi* (1641) : HANG BACK
hang on *vi* (ca. 1719) **1** : to keep hold : hold onto something **2** : to persist tenaciously ⟨a cold that *hung on* all spring⟩ **3** : HOLD ON **2** ⟨*hang on* a second while I look it up⟩ — **hang on to** : to hold, grip, or keep tenaciously ⟨*hang on to* your money⟩
hang·out \'haŋ-ˌaút\ *n* (ca. 1893) : a favorite place for spending time; *also* : a place frequented for entertainment or for socializing
hang out *vi* (14c) **1** : to protrude and droop **2 a** *slang* : LIVE, RESIDE **b** : HANG AROUND ∼ *vt* : to display outside as an announcement to the public — used chiefly in the phrase *hang out one's shingle*
hang·over \'haŋ-ˌō-vər\ *n* (1894) **1** : something (as a surviving custom) that remains from what is past **2 a** : disagreeable physical effects following heavy consumption of alcohol or the use of drugs **b** : a letdown following great excitement or excess
hang·tag \'haŋ-ˌtag\ *n* (1952) : a tag attached to an article of merchandise giving information about its material and proper care
hang time *n* (1976) : the amount of time a kicked football remains in the air; *also* : the length of time a leaping athlete is in the air
hang together *vi* (1551) **1** : to remain united : stand by one another **2** : to have unity : form a consistent or coherent whole
Hang·town fry \'haŋ-ˌtaún-\ *n, often cap F* [*Hangtown*, nickname for Placerville, Calif.] (1949) : an omelet or scrambled eggs containing oysters
han·gul \'hän-ˌgül\ *n, often cap* [Korean *hangŭl*] (1946) : the alphabetic script in which Korean is written
hang-up \'haŋ-ˌəp\ *n* (1959) : a source of mental or emotional difficulty; *broadly* : PROBLEM
hang up *vt* (12c) **1 a** : to place on a hook or hanger designed for the purpose ⟨*hang up* your coat⟩ **b** : to replace (a telephone receiver) on the cradle so that the connection is broken **2** : to keep delayed, suspended, or held up **3** : to cause to stick or snag immovably ⟨the ship was *hung up* on a sandbar⟩ ∼ *vi* **1** : to break a telephone connection **2** : to become stuck or snagged so as to be immovable
ha·ni·wa \'hä-nə-ˌwä\ *n pl, often cap* [Jp] (1931) : large hollow baked clay sculptures placed on ancient Japanese burial mounds
hank \'haŋk\ *n* [ME, of Scand origin; akin to ON *hǫnk* hank; akin to OE *hangian* to hang] (14c) **1** : COIL, LOOP; *specif* : a coiled or looped bundle (as of yarn or rope) usu. containing a definite yardage **2** : any of a series of rings or clips by which a jib or staysail is attached to a stay
han·ker \'haŋ-kər\ *vi* **han·kered; han·ker·ing** \-k(ə-)riŋ\ [prob. fr. Flem *hankeren*, freq. of *hangen* to hang; akin to OE *hangian*] (1642) : to have a strong or persistent desire : YEARN — often used with *for* or *after* *syn* see LONG — **han·ker·er** \-kər-ər\ *n*
han·kie *or* **han·ky** \'haŋ-kē\ *n, pl* **hankies** [*hand*kerchief + *-ie*] (1895) : HANDKERCHIEF
han·ky-pan·ky \ˌhaŋ-kē-'paŋ-kē\ *n* [origin unknown] (1841) **1** : questionable or underhanded activity **2** : sexual dalliance
¹**Han·o·ve·ri·an** \ˌha-nə-'vir-ē-ən, -'ver-\ *adj* [*Hanover*, Germany] (ca. 1775) **1** : of, relating to, or supporting the German ducal house of Hanover **2** : of or relating to the British royal house that ruled from 1714 to 1901
²**Hanoverian** *n* (1827) : a member or supporter of the ducal or of the British royal Hanoverian house
Han·sa \'han(t)-sə, 'hän-(ˌ)zä\ *or* **Hanse** \'han(t)s, 'hän-zə\ *n* [*Hansa* fr. ML, fr. MLG *hanse*; *Hanse* fr. ME *Hanze*, fr. MF *hanse*, fr. MLG] (15c) **1** : a league orig. constituted of merchants of various free German cities dealing abroad in the medieval period and later of the cities themselves and organized to secure greater safety and privileges in trading **2** : a medieval merchant guild or trading association — **Han·se·at·ic** \ˌhan(t)-sē-'a-tik\ *n or adj*
Han·sard \'han(t)-sərd, 'han-ˌsärd\ *n* [Luke *Hansard*] (ca. 1859) : the official published report of debates in a Commonwealth parliament
han·sel *var of* HANDSEL
Han·sen's disease \'han(t)-sənz-\ *n* [Armauer *Hansen* †1912 Norw. physician] (1938) : LEPROSY
han·som \'han(t)-səm\ *n* [Joseph A. *Hansom* †1882 Eng. architect] (1847) : a light 2-wheeled covered carriage with the driver's seat elevated behind — called also *hansom cab*
hant \'hant\ *dial var of* HAUNT
Ha·nuk·kah \'hä-nə-kə, 'kä-\ *n* [Heb *ḥănukkāh* dedication] (1891) : an 8-day Jewish holiday beginning on the 25th of Kislev and commemorating the rededication of the Temple of Jerusalem after its defilement by Antiochus of Syria
hao \'haú\ *n, pl* **hao** [Vietnamese *hào*] (1948) : a monetary unit of Vietnam equal to ¹/₁₀ dong
hao·le \'haú-lē, -ˌ(ˌ)lä\ *n* [Hawaiian] (1834) : one who is not descended from the aboriginal Polynesian inhabitants of Hawaii; *esp* : WHITE — sometimes used disparagingly
¹**hap** \'hap\ *n* [ME, fr. ON *happ* good luck; akin to OE *gehæp* suitable, OCS *kobĭ* lot, fate] (13c) **1** : HAPPENING 1 **2** : CHANCE, FORTUNE
²**hap** *vi* **happed; hap·ping** (14c) : HAPPEN
³**hap** *vt* **happed; hap·ping** [ME *happen*] (14c) *dial* : CLOTHE, COVER

hansom

⁴**hap** *n* (1724) *dial* : something (as a bed quilt or cloak) that serves as a covering or wrap
ha·pa hao·le \ˌhä-pə-'haú-lē, -ˌ(ˌ)lä\ *adj* [Hawaiian, fr. *hapa* half (fr. E *half*) + *haole*] (1919) : of part-white ancestry or origin; *esp* : of white and Hawaiian ancestry
ha·pax le·go·me·non \ˌha-ˌpaks-li-'gä-mə-ˌnän, ˌhä-ˌpäks-, -nən\ *n, pl* **hapax le·go·me·na** \-nə\ [Gk, something said only once] (1882) : a word or form occurring only once in a document or corpus
ha'·pen·ny \'häp-nē, 'hā-pə-\ *n* [by contr.] (ca. 1550) : HALFPENNY
¹**hap·haz·ard** \(ˌ)hap-'ha-zərd\ *n* [¹*hap* + *hazard*] (1576) : CHANCE
²**haphazard** *adj* (1671) : marked by lack of plan, order, or direction *syn* see RANDOM — **haphazard** *adv* — **hap·haz·ard·ly** *adv* — **hap·haz·ard·ness** *n*
hapl- *or* **haplo-** *comb form* [NL, fr. Gk, fr. *haploos*, fr. *ha-* one (akin to *homos* same) + *-ploos* multiplied; akin to L *-plex* -fold — more at SAME, -FOLD] **1** : single ⟨*haplology*⟩ **2** : haploid ⟨*haplont*⟩
hap·less \'ha-pləs\ *adj* (14c) : having no luck : UNFORTUNATE — **hap·less·ly** *adv* — **hap·less·ness** *n*
hap·loid \'ha-ˌplóid\ *adj* [ISV, fr. Gk *haploeidēs* single, fr. *haploos*] (1908) : having the gametic number of chromosomes or half the number characteristic of somatic cells — compare DIPLOID — **haploid** *n* — **hap·loi·dy** \-ˌplói-dē\ *n*
hap·lol·o·gy \ha-'plä-lə-jē\ *n* (1895) : contraction of a word by omission of one or more similar sounds or syllables (as in *mineralogy* for *mineralology* or \'prä-blē\ for *probably*)
hap·lont \'ha-ˌplänt\ *n* [ISV] (1920) : an organism (as some primitive algae) having a diploid zygote that undergoes meiosis to produce haploid cells — compare DIPLONT — **hap·lon·tic** \ha-'plän-tik\ *adj*
hap·lo·type \'ha-plō-ˌtīp\ *n* (1969) : a set of genes that determine different antigens but are closely enough linked to be inherited as a unit; *also* : the antigenic phenotype determined by a haplotype
hap·ly \'ha-plē\ *adv* (14c) : by chance, luck, or accident
hap·pen \'ha-pən, -p³m\ *vi* **hap·pened; hap·pen·ing** \'hap-niŋ, 'ha-pə-\ [ME, fr. *hap*] (14c) **1** : to occur by chance — often used with *it* ⟨it so ∼s I'm going your way⟩ **2** : to come into being or occur as an event, process, or result ⟨mistakes will ∼⟩ ⟨what good things ∼*ed* to you?⟩ **3** : to do, encounter, or attain something by or as if by chance ⟨∼*ed* upon the plotters⟩ **4 a** : to meet or discover something by chance ⟨∼*ed* upon a system that worked —Richard Corbin⟩ **b** : to come or go casually : make a chance appearance ⟨he ∼*ed* into the room just then⟩ **5** : to come esp. by way of injury or harm ⟨I promise nothing will ∼ to you⟩
hap·pen·chance \'ha-pən-ˌchan(t)s, 'ha-p³m-\ *n* (1876) : HAPPENSTANCE
hap·pen·ing *n* (1551) **1** : something that happens : OCCURRENCE **2** : an event or series of events designed to evoke a spontaneous reaction to sensory, emotional, or spiritual stimuli **3** : something (as an event) that is particularly interesting, entertaining, or important
hap·pen·stance \'ha-pən-ˌstan(t)s, 'ha-p³m-\ *n* [*happen* + circumstance] (1897) : a circumstance esp. that is due to chance — **hap·pen·stance** *adj*
hap·pi·ly \'ha-pə-lē\ *adv* (14c) **1 a** : in a fortunate manner **b** : fortunately happens ⟨∼, some boyhood pleasures don't change —P. A. Witteman⟩ **2** *archaic* : by chance **3** : in a happy manner or state ⟨lived ∼ ever after⟩ **4** : in an adequate or fitting manner : SUCCESSFULLY
hap·pi·ness \'ha-pi-nəs\ *n* (15c) **1** *obs* : good fortune : PROSPERITY **2 a** : a state of well-being and contentment : JOY **b** : a pleasurable or satisfying experience **3** : FELICITY, APTNESS
hap·py \'ha-pē\ *adj* **hap·pi·er; -est** [ME, fr. *hap*] (14c) **1** : favored by luck or fortune : FORTUNATE **2** : notably fitting, effective, or well adapted : FELICITOUS ⟨a ∼ choice⟩ **3 a** : enjoying or characterized by well-being and contentment : JOYOUS **b** : expressing or suggestive of happiness : PLEASANT **c** : GLAD, PLEASED **d** : having or marked by an atmosphere of good fellowship : FRIENDLY **4 a** : characterized by a dazed irresponsible state ⟨a punch-*happy* boxer⟩ **b** : impulsively or obsessively quick to use or do something ⟨trigger-*happy*⟩ **c** : enthusiastic about something to the point of obsession : OBSESSED ⟨education-conscious and statistic-*happy* —Helen Rowen⟩ *syn* see LUCKY, FIT
hap·py-go-lucky \ˌha-pē-gō-'lə-kē\ *adj* (1856) : blithely unconcerned : CAREFREE
happy hour *n* (1961) : a period of time during which the price of drinks (as at a bar) is reduced or hors d'oeuvres are served free
happy hunting ground *n* (1837) **1** : the paradise of some American Indian tribes to which the souls of warriors and hunters pass after death to spend a happy hereafter in hunting and feasting **2** : a choice or profitable area of activity or exploitation
happy talk *n* (1973) : informal talk among the participants in a television news broadcast; *also* : a broadcast format featuring such talk
Haps·burg \'haps-ˌbərg, 'häps-ˌbùrg\ *adj* [*Habsburg*, Aargau, Switzerland] (ca. 1895) : of or relating to the German royal house to which belong the rulers of Austria from 1278 to 1918, the rulers of Spain from 1516 to 1700, and many of the Holy Roman emperors — **Hapsburg** *n*
hap·ten \'hap-ˌten\ *n* [G, fr. Gk *haptein* to fasten] (1921) : a small separable part of an antigen that reacts specif. with an antibody but is incapable of stimulating antibody production except in combination with a carrier protein molecule — **hap·ten·ic** \hap-'te-nik\ *adj*
hap·tic \'hap-tik\ *adj* [ISV, fr. Gk *haptesthai* to touch] (ca. 1890) **1** : relating to or based on the sense of touch **2** : characterized by a predilection for the sense of touch ⟨a ∼ person⟩
hap·to·glo·bin \'hap-tə-ˌglō-bən\ *n* [ISV, fr. Gk *haptein* + ISV *hemoglobin*] (1941) : any of several carbohydrate-containing serum alpha globulins that can combine with free hemoglobin in the plasma
hara—kiri \ˌhar-i-'kir-ē, -'kar-ē\ *n* [Jp *harakiri*, fr. *hara* belly + *kiri* cutting] (1840) **1** : ritual suicide by disembowelment practiced by the Japanese samurai or formerly decreed by a court in lieu of the death penalty **2** : SUICIDE 1b
¹**ha·rangue** \hə-'raŋ\ *n* [ME *arang*, fr. MF *arenge*, fr. OIt *aringa*, fr. *aringare* to speak in public, fr. *aringo* public assembly, of Gmc origin; akin to OHG *hring* ring] (15c) **1** : a speech addressed to a public assembly **2** : a ranting speech or writing **3** : LECTURE
²**harangue** *vb* **ha·rangued; ha·rang·ing** *vi* (1660) : to make a harangue : DECLAIM ∼ *vt* : to address in a harangue ⟨*haranguing* me ... on the folly of my ways —Jay Jacobs⟩ — **ha·rang·uer** *n*

ha·rass \hə-'ras, 'har-əs\ *vt* [F *harasser*, fr. MF, fr. *harer* to set a dog on, fr. OF *hare*, interj. used to incite dogs, of Gmc origin; akin to OHG *hier* here — more at HERE] (1617) **1 a :** EXHAUST, FATIGUE **b :** to annoy persistently **2 :** to worry and impede by repeated raids ⟨~ed the enemy⟩ *syn* see WORRY — **ha·rass·er** *n* — **ha·rass·ment** \-mənt\ *n*

¹har·bin·ger \'här-bən-jər\ *n* [ME *herbergere*, fr. MF, host, fr. *herberge* hostelry, of Gmc origin; akin to OHG *heriberga*] (14c) **1** *archaic* **:** a person sent ahead to provide lodgings **2 a :** one that pioneers in or initiates a major change : PRECURSOR **b :** one that presages or foreshadows what is to come *syn* see FORERUNNER

²harbinger *vt* (1646) **:** to be a harbinger of : PRESAGE

¹har·bor \'här-bər\ *n* [ME *herberge, herberwe,* fr. OE *hereborg* military quarters, fr. *here* army (akin to OHG *heri*) + *beorg* refuge; akin to OE *burg* fortified town — more at HARRY, BOROUGH] (12c) **1 :** a place of security and comfort : REFUGE **2 :** a part of a body of water protected and deep enough to furnish anchorage; *esp* : one with port facilities — **har·bor·ful** \-,fu̇l\ *n* — **har·bor·less** \-ləs\ *adj*

²harbor *vb* **har·bored; har·bor·ing** \-b(ə-)riŋ\ *vt* (12c) **1 a :** to give shelter or refuge to **b :** to be the home or habitat of ⟨the ledges still ~ rattlesnakes⟩; *broadly* : CONTAIN **2 :** to hold esp. persistently in the mind : CHERISH ⟨~ed a grudge⟩ ~ *vi* **1 :** to take shelter in or as if in a harbor **2 :** LIVE — **har·bor·er** \-bər-ər\ *n*

har·bor·age \-bə-rij\ *n* (15c) **:** SHELTER, HARBOR

har·bor·mas·ter \'här-bər-,mas-tər\ *n* (1769) **:** an officer who executes the regulations respecting the use of a harbor

harbor seal *n* (1766) **:** a small seal (*Phoca vitulina*) that occurs along oceanic coasts of the northern hemisphere and often ascends rivers

har·bor·side \'här-bər-,sīd\ *adj* (1924) **:** located next to a harbor

har·bour *chiefly Brit var of* HARBOR

¹hard \'härd\ *adj* [ME, fr. OE *heard;* akin to OHG *hart* hard, Gk *kratos* strength] (bef. 12c) **1 a :** not easily penetrated : not easily yielding to pressure ⟨a ~ bed⟩ *of cheese* : not capable of being spread : very firm **2 a** *of liquor* (1) **:** having a harsh or acid taste (2) **:** strongly alcoholic **b :** characterized by the presence of salts (as of calcium or magnesium) that prevent lathering with soap ⟨~ water⟩ **3 a :** of or relating to radiation of relatively high penetrating power ⟨~ X rays⟩ **b :** having or producing relatively great photographic contrast ⟨a ~ negative⟩ **4 a :** metallic as distinct from paper ⟨~ money⟩ **b** *of currency* : convertible into gold : stable in value **c :** usable as currency ⟨paid in ~ cash⟩ **d** *of currency* : readily acceptable in international trade **e :** being high and firm ⟨~ prices⟩ **5 a :** firmly and closely twisted ⟨~ yarns⟩ **b :** having a smooth close napless finish ⟨a ~ worsted⟩ **6 a :** physically fit ⟨in good ~ condition⟩ **b :** resistant to stress (as disease) **c :** free of weakness or defects **7 a** (1) **:** FIRM, DEFINITE ⟨reached a ~ agreement⟩ (2) **:** not speculative or conjectural : FACTUAL ⟨~ evidence⟩ (3) **:** important or informative rather than sensational or entertaining ⟨~ news⟩ **b** (1) **:** CLOSE, SEARCHING ⟨gave a ~ look⟩ **c :** free from sentimentality or illusion : REALISTIC ⟨good ~ sense⟩ **8 a** (1) **:** difficult to bear or endure ⟨~ luck⟩ ⟨~ times⟩ (2) **:** OPPRESSIVE, INEQUITABLE ⟨sales taxes are ~ on the poor⟩ ⟨a ~ restriction⟩ **b** (1) **:** lacking consideration, compassion, or gentleness : CALLOUS ⟨a ~ greedy landlord⟩ (2) **:** INCORRIGIBLE, TOUGH ⟨a ~ gang⟩ **c** (1) **:** harsh, severe, or offensive in tendency or effect ⟨said some ~ things⟩ (2) **:** RESENTFUL ⟨~ feelings⟩ (3) **:** STRICT, UNRELENTING ⟨drives a ~ bargain⟩ **d :** INCLEMENT ⟨~ winter⟩ **e** (1) **:** intense in force, manner, or degree ⟨~ blows⟩ (2) **:** demanding the exertion of energy : calling for stamina and endurance ⟨~ work⟩ (3) **:** performing or carrying on with great energy, intensity, or persistence ⟨a ~ worker⟩ **f :** EXTREME **4a** ⟨the political right⟩ **9 a :** characterized by sharp or harsh outline, rigid execution, and stiff drawing **b :** sharply defined : STARK ⟨~ shadows⟩ **c :** lacking in shading, delicacy, or resonance ⟨~ singing tones⟩ **d :** sounding as in *arcing* and *geese* respectively — used of *c* and *g* **e :** suggestive of toughness or insensitivity ⟨~ eyes⟩ **10 a** (1) **:** difficult to accomplish or resolve : TROUBLESOME ⟨~ problems⟩ ⟨the true story was ~ to come by⟩ (2) **:** difficult to comprehend or explain ⟨a ~ concept⟩ **b :** having difficulty in doing something ⟨~ of hearing⟩ **c :** difficult to magnetize or demagnetize **11 :** being at once addictive and gravely detrimental to health ⟨such ~ drugs as heroin⟩ **12 :** resistant to biodegradation ⟨~ detergents⟩ ⟨~ pesticides like DDT⟩ **13 :** being, schooled in, or using the methods of the natural sciences and esp. of the physical sciences ⟨a ~ scientist⟩

syn HARD, DIFFICULT, ARDUOUS mean demanding great exertion or effort. HARD implies the opposite of all that is easy ⟨farming is *hard* work⟩. DIFFICULT implies the presence of obstacles to be surmounted or puzzles to be resolved and suggests the need of skill, patience, or courage ⟨the *difficult* ascent of the main face of the mountain⟩. ARDUOUS stresses the need of laborious and persevering exertion ⟨the *arduous* task of rebuilding⟩.

²hard *adv* (bef. 12c) **1 a :** with great or utmost effort or energy : STRENUOUSLY ⟨were ~ at work⟩ ⟨the children played ~⟩ **b :** in a violent manner : FIERCELY **c :** to the full extent — usu. used in nautical directions ⟨steer ~ aport⟩ **d :** to an immoderate degree ⟨hitting the bottle ~⟩ **e :** in a searching, close, or concentrated manner ⟨stared ~ at me⟩ **2 a :** in such a manner as to cause hardship, difficulty, or pain **b :** with rancor, bitterness, or grief ⟨took the defeat ~⟩ **3 :** in a firm manner : TIGHTLY **4 :** to the point of hardness ⟨frozen ~⟩ **5 :** close in time or space ⟨stands ~ by the river⟩

hard–and–fast \,här-d°n-'fast\ *adj* (1867) **:** not to be modified or evaded : STRICT ⟨a ~ rule⟩

hard–ass \'här-,das\ *n* (1972) **:** a tough, demanding, or uncompromising person — often considered vulgar — **hard–assed** \-,dast\ *adj*

hard–back \'härd-,bak\ *n* (1952) **:** a book bound in hard covers

hard·ball \-,bȯl\ *n* (ca. 1883) **1 :** BASEBALL **2 :** forceful uncompromising methods employed to gain an end ⟨played political ~⟩

hard–bit·ten \-'bi-t°n\ *adj* (1784) **1 :** inclined to bite hard **2 :** seasoned or steeled by difficult experience : TOUGH

hard·board \'härd-,bȯrd, -,bȯrd\ *n* (1925) **:** a very dense fiberboard usu. having one smooth face

hard–boil \-'bȯi(ə)l\ *vt* [back-formation fr. *hard-boiled*] (1895) **:** to cook (an egg) in the shell until both white and yolk have solidified

hard–boiled \-'bȯi(ə)ld\ *adj* (1886) **1 a :** devoid of sentimentality : TOUGH ⟨a ~ drill sergeant⟩ **b :** of, relating to, or being a detective

story featuring a tough unsentimental protagonist and a matter-of-fact attitude towards violence **2 :** HARDHEADED, PRACTICAL ⟨handle aid programs on a friendly but ~ business basis —*N.Y. Times*⟩

hard–boot \-,bu̇t\ *n* (1922) **:** an esp. small-time horseman

hard–bound \-,bau̇nd\ *adj* (1926) **:** HARDCOVER

hard candy *n* (1925) **:** a candy made of sugar and corn syrup boiled without crystallizing

hard–case \'härd-'kās\ *adj* (1896) **:** HARD-BITTEN, TOUGH

hard case \-,kās\ *n* (1836) **:** a tough or hardened person

hard cheese *n* (1861) *chiefly Brit* : tough luck — often used interjectionally

hard cider *n* (1789) **:** fermented apple juice

hard clam *n* (1846) **:** a clam with a thick hard shell; *specif* : QUAHOG

hard coal *n* (1846) **:** ANTHRACITE

hard–coat·ed \'härd-'kō-təd\ *adj* (ca. 1898) *of a dog* : having a crisp harsh-textured coat

hard copy *n* (1954) **:** a copy of textual or graphic information (as from microfilm or computer storage) produced on paper in normal size

hard–core \-'kȯr, -'kȯr\ *adj* (1940) **1 a :** of, relating to, or being part of a hard core ⟨~ poverty⟩ ⟨the ~ unemployed⟩ **b :** CONFIRMED, DIEHARD ⟨~ rock fans⟩ ⟨a ~ liberal⟩ **2** *of pornography* : containing explicit descriptions of sex acts or scenes of actual sex acts — compare SOFT-CORE **3 :** characterized by or being the purest or most basic form of something : FUNDAMENTAL ⟨a room gussied up in ~ French provincial style —John Canaday⟩

hard core *n* (1936) **1 :** a central or fundamental and usu. enduring group or part: as **a :** a relatively small enduring core of society marked by apparent resistance to change or inability to escape a persistent wretched condition (as poverty or chronic unemployment) **b :** a militant or fiercely loyal faction **2** *usu* **hard-core** \-,kȯr, -,kȯr\ *chiefly Brit* : hard material in pieces (as broken bricks or stone) used as a bottom (as in making roads and in foundations)

hard–cov·er \'härd-'kə-vər\ *adj* (1949) **1 :** having rigid boards on the sides covered in cloth or paper ⟨~ books⟩ **2 :** of or relating to hardcover books ⟨~ sales⟩ — **hardcover** *n*

hard disk *n* (1978) **:** a rigid metal disk that is sealed against dust and is used as a high-capacity storage device for a microcomputer

hard drive *n* (1983) **:** a disk drive containing one or more hard disks

hard–edge \'härd-'ej\ *adj* (1961) **:** of or relating to abstract painting characterized by geometric forms with clearly defined boundaries

hard–edged \-'ejd\ *adj* (1954) **:** having a tough, driving, or sharp quality ⟨~ stories about life in the city⟩

hard·en \'här-d°n\ *vb* **hard·ened; hard·en·ing** \'härd-niŋ, 'här-d°n-iŋ\ *vt* (13c) **1 :** to make hard or harder **2 :** to confirm in disposition, feelings, or action; *esp* : to make callous ⟨~ed his heart⟩ **3 a :** INURE, TOUGHEN ⟨~ troops⟩ **b :** to inure to unfavorable environmental conditions (as cold) — often used with *off* ⟨~ off plants⟩ **4 :** to protect from blast, heat, or radiation (as by a thick barrier or placement underground) ~ *vi* **1 :** to become hard or harder **2 a :** to become firm, stable, or settled **b :** to assume an appearance of harshness or severity ⟨her face ~ed at the word⟩

hard·en·er \'härd-nər, 'här-d°n-ər\ *n* (1611) **:** one that hardens; *esp* : a substance added (as to a paint or varnish) to harden the film

hard·en·ing *n* (1953) **:** SCLEROSIS ⟨~ of the arteries⟩

hard–fist·ed \'härd-'fis-təd\ *adj* (ca. 1656) **1 :** STINGY, CLOSEFISTED **2 :** HARDHANDED 2

hard goods *n pl* (1934) **:** DURABLES

hard·hack \'härd-,hak\ *n* (1814) **:** a shrubby American spirea (*Spiraea tomentosa*) with dense terminal panicles of pink or occas. white flowers and leaves having a hairy and yellow to rust-colored underside

hard·hand·ed \-'han-dəd\ *adj* (1590) **1 :** having hands made hard by labor **2 :** STRICT, OPPRESSIVE — **hard·hand·ed·ness** *n*

hard hat \usu -'hat *for 1 and* -,hat *for 2 & 3*\ *n* (1926) **1 a :** a protective hat made of rigid material (as metal or fiberglass) and worn esp. by construction workers **b :** a construction worker **2 :** a conservative who is intolerant of opposing views

hard·head \'härd-,hed\ *n* (15c) **1 a :** a hardheaded person **b :** BLOCKHEAD **2** *pl* **hardheads** *also* **hardhead** : any of several fishes esp. with a spiny or bony head; *esp* : ATLANTIC CROAKER

hard·head·ed \-'he-dəd\ *adj* (1583) **1 :** STUBBORN, WILLFUL **2 :** concerned with or involving practical considerations : SOBER, REALISTIC ⟨some ~ advice⟩ ⟨a ~ appraisal of winds and tides⟩ — **hard·head·ed·ly** *adv* — **hard·head·ed·ness** *n*

hard–heart·ed \-'här-təd\ *adj* (13c) **:** lacking in sympathetic understanding : UNFEELING, PITILESS — **hard–heart·ed·ly** *adv* — **hard–heart·ed·ness** *n*

hard–hit·ting \-'hi-tiŋ\ *adj* (1926) **:** strikingly effective in force or result ⟨a ~ exposé⟩ ⟨plain ~ English⟩

har·di·hood \'här-dē-,hu̇d\ *n* (1570) **1 a :** resolute courage and fortitude **b :** resolute and self-assured audacity often carried to the point of impudent insolence **2 :** VIGOR, ROBUSTNESS *syn* see TEMERITY

har·di·ment \-mənt\ *n* [ME, fr. MF, fr. OF, fr. *hardi* bold, hardy] (14c) **1** *archaic* : HARDIHOOD **2** *obs* : a bold deed

har·ding·grass \'här-diŋ-,gras\ *n, often cap* [R. R. *Harding* fl ab 1900 Australian botanist] (1917) **:** a perennial grass (*Phalaris tuberosa* var. *stenoptera*) widely used as a forage grass

hard knocks *n pl* (1913) **:** rough unsparing treatment (as in use or in life) — often used in the phrase *school of hard knocks*

hard labor *n* (1841) **:** compulsory labor of imprisoned criminals as a part of the prison discipline

hard–line \'härd-'līn\ *adj* (1962) **:** advocating or involving a rigidly uncompromising course of action — **hard–lin·er** \-'lī-nər\ *n*

hard lines *n pl* (1824) *chiefly Brit* : hard luck — often used interjectionally

hard·ly \'härd-lē\ *adv* (bef. 12c) **1 :** with force : VIGOROUSLY **2 :** in a severe manner : HARSHLY **3 :** with difficulty : PAINFULLY **4 a :** used to emphasize a minimal amount ⟨I ~ knew her⟩ ⟨almost new — ~ a

\ə\ abut \³\ kitten, F table \ər\ further \a\ ash \ā\ ace \ä\ mop, mar \au̇\ out \ch\ chin \e\ bet \ē\ easy \g\ go \i\ hit \ī\ ice \j\ job \ŋ\ sing \ō\ go \ȯ\ law \ȯi\ boy \th\ thin \th\ the \ü\ loot \u̇\ foot \y\ yet \zh\ vision \ä, k̯, ⁿ, œ, œ̄, ue, ūe, ᵜ\ see Guide to Pronunciation scratch on it⟩ **b** — used to soften a negative ⟨you can't ~ tell who anyone is —G. B. Shaw⟩ **5** : certainly not ⟨that news is ~ surprising⟩ *usage Hardly* in sense 5 is used sometimes with *not* for emphasis ⟨just another day at the office? Not *hardly*⟩. In sense 4b with a negative verb (as *can't, wouldn't, didn't*) it does not make a double negative but softens the negative. In "you can't hardly find a red one," the sense is that you can find a red one, but only with difficulty; in "you can't find a red one," the sense is that red ones are simply not available. Use of *hardly* with a negative verb is a speech form; it is most commonly heard in Southern and Midland speech areas. In other speech areas and in all discursive prose, *hardly* is normally used with a positive ⟨you can *hardly* find a red one⟩.

hard maple *n* (1790) : SUGAR MAPLE

hard-mouthed \'härd-'mau̇thd, -'mau̇tht\ *adj* (1617) **1** *of a horse* : not sensitive to the bit **2** : OBSTINATE, STUBBORN

hard-ness \-nəs\ *n* (bef. 12c) **1** : the quality or state of being hard **2 a** : the cohesion of the particles on the surface of a mineral as determined by its capacity to scratch another or be itself scratched — compare MOHS' SCALE **b** : resistance of metal to indentation under a static load or to scratching

hard-nose \'härd-ˌnōz\ *n* (ca. 1960) : a hard-nosed person

hard-nosed \'härd-'nōzd\ *adj* (ca. 1927) **1** : being tough, stubborn, or uncompromising **2** : HARDHEADED 2, TOUGH-MINDED

hard-of-hear-ing \ˌhärd-əv(v)-'hir-iŋ\ *adj* (1564) : of or relating to a defective but functional sense of hearing

hard-on \'här-ˌdȯn, -ˌdän\ *n, pl* **hard-ons** (ca. 1893) : an erection of the penis — sometimes considered vulgar

hard palate *n* (ca. 1847) : the bony anterior part of the palate forming the roof of the mouth

hard-pan \'härd-ˌpan\ *n* (1817) **1** : a cemented or compacted and often clayey layer in soil that is impenetrable by roots **2** : a fundamental part : BEDROCK

hard pine *n* (1884) **1** : a pine (as longleaf pine or pitch pine) that has hard wood and leaves usu. in groups of two or three; *also* : the wood of a hard pine

hard-pressed \'härd-'prest\ *adj* (1825) : HARD PUT; *also* : being under financial strain

hard put *adj* (1893) : barely able : faced with difficulty or perplexity ⟨was *hard put* to find an explanation⟩

hard rock *n* (1967) : rock music marked by a heavy regular beat, high amplification, and usu. frenzied performances

hard rubber *n* (1860) : a firm rubber or rubber product; *esp* : a normally black horny substance made by vulcanizing natural rubber with high percentages of sulfur

hard sauce *n* (1880) : a creamed mixture of butter and powdered sugar often with added cream and flavoring (as vanilla or rum)

hard-scrab-ble \'härd-ˌskra-bəl\ *adj* (1804) **1** : being or relating to a place of barren or barely arable soil ⟨a ~ farm⟩ ⟨~ prairies⟩ **b** : getting a meager living from poor soil ⟨a ~ farmer⟩ **2** : marked by poverty ⟨a ~ cotton town⟩ ⟨a ~ childhood⟩

hard sell *n* (1952) : aggressive high-pressure salesmanship — compare SOFT SELL

hard-set \'härd-'set\ *adj* (1813) : RIGID, FIXED

hard-shell \-ˌshel\ *or* **hard-shelled** \-ˌsheld\ *adj* (1838) : FUNDAMENTAL 2b, FUNDAMENTALIST ⟨a ~ preacher⟩ ⟨~ Baptists⟩; *also* : UNCOMPROMISING, HIDEBOUND ⟨a ~ conservative⟩

hard-shell clam *n* (1799) : QUAHOG — called also *hard-shelled clam*

hard-shell crab *n* (1902) : a crab that has not recently shed its shell — called also *hard-shelled crab*

hard-ship \'härd-ˌship\ *n* (13c) **1** : PRIVATION, SUFFERING **2** : something that causes or entails suffering or privation

hard-stand \-ˌstand\ *n* (1944) : a paved area for parking an airplane

hard-stand-ing \-ˌstan-diŋ\ *n* (1944) *chiefly Brit* : HARDSTAND; *also* : PARKING LOT

hard stone *n* (1931) : an opaque usu. semiprecious stone that can be shaped or carved (as for jewelery or mosaics)

hard-tack \-ˌtak\ *n, pl* **hardtack** *or* **hardtacks** (1836) **1** : a saltless hard biscuit, bread, or cracker **2** : any of several mountain mahoganies (esp. *Cercocarpus betuloides*)

hard-times token *n* (1922) : any of the tokens issued during the controversy between the Jackson administration and the bank of the U.S.

hard-top \'härd-ˌtäp\ *n* (1950) : an automobile or a motorboat having a permanent rigid top; *also* : such an automobile styled to resemble a convertible

hard up *adj* (1821) **1** : short of money **2** : poorly provided ⟨*hard up* for friends⟩

hard-ware \'härd-ˌwar, -ˌwer\ *n* (ca. 1515) **1** : ware (as fittings, cutlery, tools, utensils, or parts of machines) made of metal **2** : major items of equipment or their components used for a particular purpose ⟨educational ~⟩: as **a** : military equipment **b** : the physical components (as electronic and electrical devices) of a vehicle (as a spacecraft) or an apparatus (as a computer)

hardware cloth *n* (ca. 1914) : rugged galvanized screening

hard wheat *n* (1812) : a wheat with hard flinty kernels that are high in gluten and that yield a flour esp. suitable for bread and macaroni

hard-wired \'härd-ˌwird\ *adj* (1968) : implemented in the form of permanent electronic circuits; *also* : having permanent electrical connections ⟨~ phone⟩

hard-won \-'wən\ *adj* (ca. 1843) : gained by great effort

¹hard-wood \'härd-ˌwu̇d\ *n* (1568) **1** : the wood of an angiospermous tree as distinguished from that of a coniferous tree **2** : a tree that yields hardwood

²hardwood *adj* (ca. 1817) **1** : having or made of hardwood ⟨~ floors⟩ **2** : consisting of mature woody tissue ⟨~ cuttings⟩

hard-work-ing \'härd-ˌwər-kiŋ\ *adj* (1774) : INDUSTRIOUS

har-dy \'här-dē\ *adj* **har-di-er; -est** [ME *hardi*, fr. OF, fr. (assumed) OF *hardir* to make hard, of Gmc origin; akin to OE *heard* hard] (13c) **1** : BOLD, BRAVE **2** : AUDACIOUS, BRAZEN **3 a** : inured to fatigue or hardships : ROBUST **b** : capable of withstanding adverse conditions ⟨~ outdoor furniture⟩ ⟨~ plants⟩ ⟨~ cattle⟩ — **har-di-ly** \'här-dᵊl-ē\ *adv* — **har-di-ness** \'här-dē-nəs\ *n*

Har-dy–Wein-berg law \ˌhär-dē-'wīn-ˌbərg-\ *n* [G. H. *Hardy* †1947 Eng. mathematician and W. *Weinberg*, 20th cent. Ger. scientist] (1950) : a fundamental principle of population genetics: population gene frequencies and genotype frequencies remain constant from generation to generation if mating is random and if mutation, selection, immigration, and emigration do not occur — called also *Hardy-Weinberg principle*

¹hare \'har, 'her\ *n, pl* **hare** *or* **hares** [ME, fr. OE *hara*; akin to OHG *haso* hare, Skt *śaśa*, OE *hasu* gray] (bef. 12c) : any of various swift long-eared lagomorph mammals (family Leporidae and esp. genus *Lepus*) that are usu. solitary or sometimes live in pairs and have the young open-eyed and furred at birth — compare RABBIT 1A

²hare *vi* **hared; har-ing** (1719) : to go swiftly : ³TEAR

hare and hounds *n* (ca. 1845) : a game in which some of the players leave a trail and others try to follow the trail to find and catch them

hare-bell \'har-ˌbel, 'her-\ *n* (1765) : a slender blue-flowered herb (*Campanula rotundifolia*) with linear leaves on the stem

hare-brained \-'brānd\ *adj* (1534) : FOOLISH 1, 2a

Ha-re Krish-na \ˌhär-ē-'krish-nə, ˌhar-\ *n, pl* **Hare Krishna** *or* **Hare Krishnas** [fr. *Hare Krishna*, phrase in a chant, fr. Hindi *hare Kṛṣṇa* O Krishna!] (1969) : a member of a religious group dedicated to the worship of the Hindu god Krishna

hare-lip \'har-'lip, 'her-\ *n* (1567) : a congenital deformity characterized by a cleft upper lip resulting from failure of the embryonic parts of the lip to unite

har-em \'har-əm, 'her-\ *n* [Ar *harīm*, lit., something forbidden & *haram*, lit., sanctuary] (1623) **1 a** : a usu. secluded house or part of a house allotted to women in a Muslim household **b** : the wives, concubines, female relatives, and servants occupying a harem **2** : a group of women associated with one man **3** : a group of females associated with one male — used of polygamous animals

harem pants *n* [fr. their oriental appearance] (1952) : women's loose trousers that fit closely at the ankle

har-i-cot \'(h)ar-i-ˌkō\ *n* [F] (1653) : the ripe seed or the unripe pod of any of several beans (genus *Phaseolus* and esp. *P. vulgaris*)

ha-ri-jan \ˌhär-i-'jän\ *n, often cap* [Skt *harijana* one belonging to the god Vishnu, fr. *Hari* Vishnu + *jana* person] (1931) : a member of the outcaste group in India : UNTOUCHABLE

hari-kari \ˌhar-i-'kar-ē, -'kir-\ *var of* HARA-KIRI

hark \'härk\ *vi* [ME *herkien*; akin to OHG *hōrechen* to listen, OE *hīeran* to hear] (14c) : to pay close attention : LISTEN

hark back *vi* (1829) **1** : to turn back to an earlier topic or circumstance **2** : to go back to something as an origin or source

harken *vi* (bef. 12c) **1** : HEARKEN **2** : HARK BACK — usu. used with *back*

har-le-quin \'här-li-k(w)ən\ *n* [ultim. fr. It *arlecchino*, fr. MF *Helquin*, a demon] (1590) **1 a** *cap* : a character in comedy and pantomime with a shaved head, masked face, variegated tights, and wooden sword **b** : BUFFOON **2 a** : a variegated pattern (as of a textile) **b** : a combination of patches on a solid ground of contrasting color (as in the coats of some dogs)

har-le-quin-ade \ˌhär-li-k(w)ə-'nād\ *n* (1790) : a play or pantomime in which Harlequin has a leading role

har-lot \'här-lət\ *n* [ME, fr. OF *herlot* rogue] (15c) : PROSTITUTE

har-lot-ry \-lə-trē\ *n, pl* **-ries** (14c) **1** : sexual profligacy : PROSTITUTION **2** : an unprincipled or immoral woman ⟨he sups tonight with a ~ —Shak.⟩

¹harm \'härm\ *n* [ME, fr. OE *hearm*; akin to OHG *harm* injury, OCS *sramŭ* shame] (bef. 12c) **1** : physical or mental damage : INJURY **2** : MISCHIEF, HURT

²harm *vt* (bef. 12c) : to cause harm to **syn** see INJURE — **harm-er** *n*

har-mat-tan \ˌhär-mə-'tan, här-'ma-tᵊn\ *n, often cap* [Twi *haramata*] (1671) : a dust-laden wind on the Atlantic coast of Africa in some seasons

harm-ful \'härm-fəl\ *adj* (14c) : of a kind likely to be damaging : INJURIOUS — **harm-ful-ly** \-fə-lē\ *adv* — **harm-ful-ness** *n*

harm-less \'härm-ləs\ *adj* (14c) **1** : free from harm, liability, or loss **2** : lacking capacity or intent to injure : INNOCUOUS — **harm-less-ly** *adv* — **harm-less-ness** *n*

¹har-mon-ic \här-'mä-nik\ *adj* (1570) **1** : MUSICAL **2** : of or relating to musical harmony or a harmonic **3** : pleasing to the ear : HARMONIOUS **4** : of an integrated nature : CONGRUOUS — **har-mon-i-cal-ly** \-ni-k(ə-)lē\ *adv*

²harmonic *n* (1777) **1 a** : OVERTONE; *esp* : one whose vibration frequency is an integral multiple of that of the fundamental **b** : a flutelike tone produced on a stringed instrument by touching a vibrating string at a nodal point **2** : a component frequency of a complex wave (as of electromagnetic energy) that is an integral multiple of the fundamental frequency

har-mon-i-ca \här-'mä-ni-kə\ *n* [It *armonica*, fem. of *armonico* harmonious] (1762) **1** : GLASS HARMONICA **2** : a small rectangular wind instrument with free reeds recessed in air slots from which tones are sounded by exhaling and inhaling — **har-mon-i-cist** \-nə-sist\ *n*

harmonic analysis *n* (1867) : the expression of a periodic function as a sum of sines and cosines and specif. by a Fourier series

harmonic mean *n* (1856) : the reciprocal of the arithmetic mean of the reciprocals of a finite set of numbers

harmonic motion *n* (1867) : a periodic motion (as of a sounding violin string or swinging pendulum) that has a single frequency or amplitude or a periodic motion that is composed of two or more such simple periodic motions

harmonic progression *n* (1856) : a sequence of numbers whose reciprocals form an arithmetic progression

harmonic series *n* (1866) : a series of the form

$$1 + \frac{1}{2^\alpha} + \frac{1}{3^\alpha} + \frac{1}{4^\alpha} \cdots$$

which diverges for $0 \leq \alpha \leq 1$ and converges for $\alpha > 1$

har-mo-ni-ous \här-'mō-nē-əs\ *adj* (1530) **1** : musically concordant **2** : having the parts agreeably related : CONGRUOUS ⟨blended into a ~ whole⟩ **3** : marked by accord in sentiment or action — **har-mo-ni-ous-ly** *adv* — **har-mo-ni-ous-ness** *n*

Harlequin

har·mo·nise *Brit var of* HARMONIZE

har·mo·ni·um \här-'mō-nē-əm\ *n* [F, fr. MF *harmonie, armonie*] (1847) : REED ORGAN

har·mo·nize \'här-mə-ˌnīz\ *vb* -**nized; -niz·ing** *vi* (15c) **1** : to play or sing in harmony **2** : to be in harmony ～ *vt* **1** : to bring into consonance or accord **2** : to provide or accompany with harmony — **har·mo·ni·za·tion** \ˌhär-mə-nə-'zā-shən\ *n* — **har·mo·niz·er** \'här-mə-ˌnī-zər\ *n*

har·mo·ny \'här-mə-nē\ *n, pl* -**nies** [ME *armony*, fr. MF *armonie*, fr. L *harmonia*, fr. Gk, joint, harmony, fr. *harmos* joint — more at ARM] (14c) **1** *archaic* : tuneful sound : MELODY **2 a** : the combination of simultaneous musical notes in a chord **b** : the structure of music with respect to the composition and progression of chords **c** : the science of the structure, relation, and progression of chords **3** : pleasing or congruent arrangement of parts ⟨a painting exhibiting ～ of color and line⟩ **b** : CORRESPONDENCE, ACCORD ⟨lives in ～ with her neighbors⟩ **c** : internal calm : TRANQUILLITY **4 a** : an interweaving of different accounts into a single narrative **b** : a systematic arrangement of parallel literary passages (as of the Gospels) for the purpose of showing agreement or harmony

harm's way *n* (ca. 1661) : a dangerous place or situation ⟨was placed in *harm's way*⟩ ⟨got them out of *harm's way*⟩

¹har·ness \'här-nəs\ *n* [ME *herneis* baggage, gear, fr. OF] (14c) **1 a** : the gear other than a yoke of a draft animal **b** : GEAR, EQUIPMENT; *esp* : military equipment for a horse or man **2 a** : occupational surroundings or routine ⟨get back into ～ after a vacation⟩ **b** : close association ⟨ability to work in ～ with others —R. P. Brooks⟩ **3 a** : something that resembles a harness (as in holding or fastening something) ⟨a parachute ～⟩ **b** : prefabricated wiring with insulation and terminals ready to be attached **4** : a part of a loom which holds and controls the heddles

²harness *vt* (14c) **1 a** : to put a harness on **b** : to attach by means of a harness **2** : to tie together : YOKE **3** : UTILIZE ⟨～ the computer's potential⟩

harness horse *n* (1861) : a horse for racing or working in harness

harness racing *n* (1901) : the sport of racing standardbred horses harnessed to 2-wheeled sulkies

¹harp \'härp\ *n* [ME, fr. OE *hearpe*; akin to OHG *harpha* harp] (bef. 12c) **1** : a plucked stringed instrument consisting of a resonator, an arched or angled neck that may be supported by a post, and strings of graded length that are perpendicular to the soundboard **2** : something that resembles a harp **3** : HARMONICA 2 — **harp·ist** \'här-pist\ *n*

²harp *vi* (bef. 12c) **1** : to play on a harp **2** : to dwell on or recur to a subject tiresomely or monotonously — usu. used with *on*

harp·er \'här-pər\ *n* (bef. 12c) **1** : a harp player **2** : one that harps

har·poon \här-'pün\ *n* [prob. fr. OF *harpon* brooch, fr. *harper* to grapple] (1625) : a barbed spear or javelin used esp. in hunting large fish or whales — **harpoon** *vt* — **har·poon·er** *n*

harp seal *n* [fr. the shape of its markings] (1766) : a dark-faced seal (*Phoca groenlandicus*) of the No. Atlantic that is a variable light gray with the male usu. having a dark crescent on its back and sides

harp·si·chord \'härp-si-ˌkȯrd\ *n* [modif. of It *arpicordo*, fr. *arpa* harp + *corda* string] (1611) : a stringed instrument resembling a grand piano but usu. having two keyboards and two or more strings for each note and producing tones by the plucking of strings with plectra — **harp·si·chord·ist** \-ˌkȯr-dist\ *n*

har·py \'här-pē\ *n, pl* **harpies** [L *Harpyia*, fr. Gk] (1513) **1** *cap* : a foul malign creature in Greek mythology that is part woman and part bird **2 a** : a predatory person : LEECH **b** : a shrewish woman

harpy eagle *n* (1830) : a large powerful crested eagle (*Harpia harpyja*) of Central and So. America

har·que·bus \'här-kwi-(ˌ)bəs, -kə-bəs\ *n* [MF *harquebuse, arquebuse*, modif. of MD *hakebusse*, fr. *hake* hook + *busse* tube, box, gun, fr. LL *buxis* box] (1532) : a matchlock gun invented in the 15th century which was portable but heavy and was usu. fired from a support — **har·que·bus·ier** \ˌhär-kwi-(ˌ)bə-'sir, -kə-bə-\ *n*

har·ri·dan \'har-ə-dᵊn\ *n* [perh. modif. of F *haridelle* old horse, gaunt woman] (ca. 1700) : SHREW 2

¹har·ried \'har-ēd\ *adj* (ca. 1915) : beset by problems : HARASSED

¹har·ri·er \'har-ē-ər\ *n* [irreg. fr. ¹hare] (1542) **1** : any of a breed of hunting dogs resembling a small foxhound and orig. bred for hunting rabbits **2** : a runner on a cross-country team

²harrier *n* [alter. of *harrower*, fr. ¹harrow] (1556) : any of a genus (*Circus*) of slender hawks having long angled wings and long legs and feeding chiefly on small mammals, reptiles, and insects

³harrier *n* (1906) : one that harries

¹har·row \'har-(ˌ)ō\ *vt* [ME *harwen*, fr. OE *hergian*] (bef. 12c) *archaic* : PILLAGE, PLUNDER

²harrow *n* [ME *harwe*, prob. of Scand origin; akin to ON *hervi* harrow] (14c) : a cultivating implement set with spikes, spring teeth, or disks and used primarily for pulverizing and smoothing the soil

³harrow *vt* (14c) **1** : to cultivate with a harrow **2** : TORMENT, VEX — **har·row·er** \'har-ə-wər\ *n*

har·rumph \hə-'rəm(p)f\ *vi* [imit.] (1942) **1** : to clear the throat in a pompous way **2** : to comment disapprovingly

har·ry \'har-ē\ *vt* **har·ried; har·ry·ing** [ME *harien*, fr. OE *hergian*; akin to OHG *heriōn* to lay waste, *heri* army, Gk *koiranos* ruler] (bef. 12c) **1** : to make a pillaging or destructive raid on : ASSAULT **2** : to force to move along by harassing ⟨～ing the terrified horses down out of the mountains —R. A. Sokolov⟩ **3** : to torment by or as if by constant attack *syn* see WORRY

harsh \'härsh\ *adj* [ME *harsk*, of Scand origin; akin to Norw *harsk* harsh] (14c) **1** : having a coarse uneven surface that is rough or unpleasant to the touch **2 a** : causing a disagreeable or painful sensory reaction : IRRITATING **b** : physically discomforting : PAINFUL **3** : unduly exacting : SEVERE **4** : lacking in aesthetic appeal or refinement : CRUDE *syn* see ROUGH — **harsh·ly** *adv* — **harsh·ness** *n*

harsh·en \'här-shən\ *vb* **harsh·ened; harsh·en·ing** \-sh(ə-)niŋ\ *vt* (1824) : to make (as a voice) harsh ～ *vi* : to become harsh ⟨saw the grain of his skin ～ing over face bones —Elizabeth Bowen⟩

hart \'härt\ *n* [ME *hert*, fr. OE *heort*; akin to L *cervus* hart, Gk *keras* horn — more at HORN] (bef. 12c) *chiefly Brit* : the male of the red deer esp. when over five years old : STAG — compare HIND

harte·beest \'härt-ə-ˌbēst\ *n* [obs. Afrik (now *hartbees*), fr. D, fr. *hart* deer + *beest* beast] (1786) : either of two large African antelopes (*Alcelaphus buselaphus* and *Sigmoceros lichtensteini*) with long faces and short annulate divergent horns; *also* : a smaller antelope (*Damaliscus hunteri* syn. *Beatragus hunteri*) of eastern Africa having a horizontal white line between the eyes

harts·horn \'härts-ˌhȯrn\ *n* [fr. the earlier use of hart's horns as the chief source of ammonia] (1685) : a preparation of ammonia used as smelling salts

har·um–scar·um \ˌhar-əm-'skar-əm, ˌher-əm-'sker-\ *adj* [perh. fr. archaic *hare* (to harass) + *scare*] (1751) : RECKLESS, IRRESPONSIBLE — **harum–scarum** *adv*

ha·rus·pex \hə-'rəs-ˌpeks, 'har-əs-\ *n, pl* **ha·rus·pi·ces** \hə-'rəs-pə-ˌsēz\ [L, fr. *haru-* (akin to *chordē* gut, cord) + *-spex*, fr. *specere* to look — more at YARN, SPY] (1584) : a diviner in ancient Rome basing his predictions on inspection of the entrails of sacrificial animals

ha·rus·pi·ca·tion \hə-ˌrəs-pə-'kā-shən\ *n* (1871) *chiefly Brit* : an act or instance of foretelling something

¹har·vest \'här-vəst\ *n, often attrib* [ME *hervest*, fr. OE *hærfest*; akin to L *carpere* to pluck, gather, Gk *karpos* fruit] (bef. 12c) **1** : the season for gathering in agricultural crops **2** : the act or process of gathering in a crop **3 a** : a mature crop (as of grain or fruit) : YIELD **b** : the quantity of a natural product gathered in a single season ⟨deer ～⟩ ⟨ice ～⟩ **4** : an accumulated store or productive result ⟨a fantastic revenue ～ from lower tax rates —Peter Passell⟩

²harvest *vt* (15c) **1 a** : to gather in (a crop) : REAP **b** : to gather, catch, hunt, or kill (as salmon, oysters, or deer) for human use, sport, or population control **c** : to remove or extract (as living cells, tissues, or organs) from culture or a living or recently deceased body esp. for transplanting **2 a** : to accumulate a store of ⟨has now ～ed this new generation's scholarly labors —M. J. Wiener⟩ **b** : to win by achievement ⟨the team ～ed several awards⟩ ～ *vi* : to gather in a crop esp. for food — **har·vest·able** \-və-stə-bəl\ *adj* — **har·vest·er** *n*

harvest fly *n* (ca. 1753) : CICADA

harvest home *n* (1596) **1** : the gathering or the time of harvest **2** : a feast at the close of harvest **3** : a song sung by the reapers at the close of the harvest

har·vest·man \'här-vəs(t)-mən\ *n* (1830) : an arachnid (order Phalangida) that superficially resembles a true spider but has a small rounded body and very long slender legs — called also *daddy longlegs*

harvest mite *n* (1873) : CHIGGER 2

harvest moon *n* (1706) : the full moon nearest the time of the September equinox

har·vest·time \'här-vəs(t)-ˌtīm\ *n* (14c) : the time during which an annual crop (as wheat) is harvested

has *pres 3d sing of* HAVE

has–been \'haz-ˌbin, *chiefly Brit* -ˌbēn\ *n* (1606) : one that has passed the peak of effectiveness or popularity

ha·sen·pfef·fer \'hä-zᵊn-ˌ(p)fe-fər, 'hä-sᵊn-\ *n* [G, fr. *Hase* hare + *Pfeffer* pepper] (1892) : a highly seasoned stew made of marinated rabbit meat

¹hash \'hash\ *vt* [F *hacher*, fr. OF *hachier*, fr. *hache* battle-ax, of Gmc origin; akin to OHG *happa* sickle; akin to Gk *koptein* to cut — more at CAPON] (1590) **1 a** : to chop (as meat and potatoes) into small pieces **b** : CONFUSE, MUDDLE **2** : to talk about : REVIEW — often used with *over* or *out*

²hash *n* (ca. 1663) **1** : chopped food; *specif* : chopped meat mixed with potatoes and browned **2** : a restatement of something that is already known **3** : HODGEPODGE, JUMBLE **b** : a confused muddle ⟨made a ～ of the whole project⟩

³hash *n* (1959) : HASHISH

hash browns *n pl* (1951) : boiled potatoes that have been diced, mixed with chopped onions and shortening, and fried usu. until they form a browned cake — called also *hash brown potatoes, hashed brown potatoes, hashed browns*

Hash·em·ite *or* **Hash·im·ite** \'ha-shə-ˌmīt\ *n* [*Hashim*, greatʐ grandfather of Muhammad] (1697) : a member of an Arab family having common ancestry with Muhammad and founding dynasties in countries of the eastern Mediterranean

hash house *n* (1869) : an inexpensive eating place

hash·ish \'ha-ˌshēsh, ha-'shēsh\ *n* [Ar *hashīsh*] (1598) : the concentrated resin from the flowering tops of the female hemp plant (*Cannabis sativa*) that is smoked, chewed, or drunk for its intoxicating effect — called also *charas*; compare BHANG, MARIJUANA

hash mark *n* (1907) **1** : SERVICE STRIPE **2** : INBOUNDS LINE

Ha·sid \'kä-səd, 'kä-\ *n, pl* **Ha·si·dim** \'ha-sə-dəm, kä-'sē-\ [Heb *hāsidh* pious] (1812) **1** : a member of a Jewish sect of the second century B.C. opposed to Hellenism and devoted to the strict observance of the ritual law **2** *also* **Has·sid** : a member of a Jewish mystical sect founded in Poland about 1750 in opposition to rationalism and ritual laxity — **Ha·sid·ic** *also* **Has·sid·ic** \ha-'si-dik, hä-, kä-\ *adj*

Ha·si·dism \'ha-sə-ˌdi-zəm, 'hä-, 'kä-\ *n* (1893) : the practices and beliefs of the Hasidim **2** : the Hasidic movement

Has·mo·nae·an *or* **Has·mo·ne·an** \ˌhaz-mə-'nē-ən\ *n* [LL *Asmonaeus* Hasmon, ancestor of the Maccabees, fr. Gk *Asamōnaios*] (1620) : a member of the Maccabees — **Hasmonaean** *or* **Hasmonean** *adj*

hasn't \'ha-zᵊnt, -zᵊn\ (1746) : has not

hasp \'hasp\ *n* [ME, alter. fr. OE *hæpse*; akin to MHG *haspe* hasp] (bef. 12c) : any of several devices for fastening; *esp* : a fastener esp. for a door or lid consisting of a hinged metal strap that fits over a staple and is secured by a pin or padlock — **hasp** *vt*

hasp

¹has·sle \'ha-səl\ *n* (1945) **1** : a heated often protracted argument : WRANGLE

\ə\ abut \ᵊ\ kitten, F table \ər\ further \a\ ash \ā\ ace \ä\ mop, mar \au̇\ out \ch\ chin \e\ bet \ē\ easy \g\ go \i\ hit \ī\ ice \j\ job \ŋ\ sing \ō\ go \ȯ\ law \ȯi\ boy \th\ thin \t͟h\ the \ü\ loot \u̇\ foot \y\ yet \zh\ vision \ä, k̇, ⁿ, œ, œ̄, ᵫ, ᵫ̄, ᵊ\ *see* Guide to Pronunciation

2 : a violent skirmish : FIGHT **3 a** : a state of confusion : TURMOIL **b** : an annoying or troublesome concern

²**hassle** vb **has·sled; has·sling** \-s(ə-)liŋ\ [perh. blend of *harass* and *hustle*] vi (1951) : ARGUE, FIGHT ⟨*hassled* with the umpire⟩ ~ vt : to annoy persistently or acutely : HARASS ⟨he gets *hassled* in the street because he dresses funny —William Kloman⟩

has·sock \'has-sək\ n [ME, sedge, fr. OE *hassuc*] (bef. 12c) **1** : TUSSOCK **2 a** : a cushion for kneeling (a church ~) **b** : a padded cushion or low stool that serves as a seat or leg rest

hast \'hast, (h)əst\ *archaic pres 2d sing of* HAVE

has·tate \'has-ˌtāt\ adj [NL *hastatus*, fr. L *hasta* spear — more at YARD] (1788) **1** : triangular with sharp basal lobes spreading away from the base of the petiole ⟨~ leaves⟩ — see LEAF illustration **2** : shaped like a spear or the head of a spear ⟨a ~ spot of a bird⟩

¹**haste** \'hāst\ n [ME, fr. MF, of Gmc origin; akin to OE *hǣst* violence] (14c) **1** : rapidity of motion : SWIFTNESS **2** : rash or headlong action : PRECIPITATENESS ⟨the beauty of speed uncontaminated by ~ —Harper's⟩ **3** : undue eagerness to act

syn HASTE, HURRY, SPEED, EXPEDITION, DISPATCH mean quickness in movement or action. HASTE applies to personal action and implies urgency and precipitancy and often rashness ⟨marry in *haste*⟩. HURRY often has a strong suggestion of agitated bustle or confusion ⟨in the *hurry* of departure she forgot her toothbrush⟩. SPEED suggests swift efficiency in movement or action ⟨exercises to increase your reading *speed*⟩. EXPEDITION and DISPATCH both imply speed and efficiency in handling affairs but EXPEDITION stresses ease or efficiency of performance and DISPATCH stresses promptness in concluding matters ⟨the case came to trial with *expedition*⟩ ⟨paid bills with *dispatch*⟩.

²**haste** vb **hast·ed; hast·ing** vt (14c) *archaic* : to urge on : HASTEN ~ vi : to move or act swiftly

has·ten \'hā-sᵊn\ vb **has·tened; has·ten·ing** \'hās-niŋ, 'hā-sᵊn-iŋ\ vi (1568) **1** : to move or act quickly ~ vt **1** : to urge on ⟨~ed her to the door —A. J. Cronin⟩ **2** : ACCELERATE ⟨~ the coming of a new order —D. W. Brogan⟩ — **has·ten·er** \'hās-nər, 'hā-sᵊn-ər\ n

hast·i·ly \'hā-stə-lē\ adv (14c) : in haste : HURRIEDLY

hasty \'hā-stē\ adj **hast·i·er; -est** (14c) **1 a** *archaic* : rapid in action or movement : SPEEDY **b** : done or made in a hurry ⟨~ fast and typically superficial ⟨made a ~ examination of the wound⟩ **2** : EAGER, IMPATIENT **3** : PRECIPITATE, RASH **4** : prone to anger : IRRITABLE *syn* see FAST — **hast·i·ness** n

hasty pudding n (1599) **1** *Brit* : a porridge of oatmeal or flour boiled in water **2** *NewEng* **a** : cornmeal mush **b** : INDIAN PUDDING

¹**hat** \'hat\ n [ME, fr. OE *hæt*; akin to OHG *huot* head covering — more at HOOD] (bef. 12c) **1** : a covering for the head usu. having a shaped crown and brim **2 a** : a distinctive head covering worn as a symbol of office **b** : an office, position, or role assumed by or as if by the wearing of a special hat — **hat·less** \-ləs\ adj

²**hat** vb **hat·ted; hat·ting** vt (15c) : to furnish or provide with a hat ~ vi : to make or supply hats

hat·band \'hat-ˌband\ n (15c) : a band (as of fabric, leather, or cord) around the crown of a hat just above the brim

hat-box \-ˌbäks\ n (1794) **1** : a box for holding or storing a hat **2** : a usu. round piece of luggage designed esp. for carrying hats

¹**hatch** \'hach\ n [ME *hache*, fr. OE *hæc*; akin to MD *hecke* trapdoor] (bef. 12c) **1** : a small door or opening (as in an airplane or spaceship) ⟨an escape ~⟩ **2 a** : an opening in the deck of a ship or in the floor or roof of a building **b** : the covering for such an opening **c** : HATCHWAY **d** : COMPARTMENT **3** : FLOODGATE

²**hatch** vb [ME *hacchen*; akin to MHG *hecken* to mate] vi (13c) **1** : to produce young by incubation **2 a** : to emerge from an egg, chrysalis, or pupa **b** : to give forth young or imagoes **3** : to incubate eggs : BROOD ~ vt **1** : to produce (young) from an egg by applying natural or artificial heat : INCUBATE **1 2** : to bring into being : ORIGINATE; *esp* : to concoct in secret — **hatch·abil·i·ty** \ˌha-chə-'bi-lə-tē\ n — **hatch·able** \'ha-chə-bəl\ adj — **hatch·er** n

³**hatch** n (1601) **1** : an act or instance of hatching **2** : a brood of hatched young

⁴**hatch** vt [ME *hachen*, fr. MF *hacher* to inlay, chop up, fr. OF *hachier* — more at HASH] (15c) **1** : to inlay with narrow bands of distinguishable material ⟨a silver handle ~ed with gold⟩ **2** : to mark (as a drawing or engraving) with fine closely spaced lines

⁵**hatch** n (1658) : LINE; *esp* : one used to give the effect of shading

hatch·back \'hach-ˌbak\ n (1970) : an automobile the back of which consists of a hatch that opens upward; *also* : the back itself

hat-check \'hat-ˌchek\ adj (1917) : employed in checking hats and articles of outdoor clothing ⟨a ~ girl⟩

hatch·ery \'ha-chə-rē\ n, pl **-er·ies** (1880) : a place for hatching eggs (as of poultry or fish)

hatch·et \'ha-chət\ n [ME *hachet*, fr. MF *hachette*, dim. of *hache* battle-ax — more at HASH] (14c) **1** : a short-handled ax often with a hammerhead to be used with one hand **2** : TOMAHAWK

hatchet face n (ca. 1666) : a thin sharp face — **hatch·et-faced** \'ha-chət-ˌfāst\ adj

hatchet job n (1944) : a forceful or malicious verbal attack

hatchet man n (1880) **1** : one hired for murder, coercion, or attack **2 a** : a writer specializing in invective **b** : a person hired to perform underhanded or unscrupulous tasks (as ruin reputations)

hatchet work n (1944) : the work of a hatchet man

hatch·ing n (1662) : the engraving or drawing of fine lines in close proximity esp. to give an effect of shading; *also* : the pattern so made

hatch·ling \'hach-liŋ\ n (1899) : a recently hatched animal

hatch·ment \'hach-mənt\ n [perh. alter. of *achievement*] (1548) : a panel on which a coat of arms of a deceased person is temporarily displayed

hatch·way \'hach-ˌwā\ n (1626) : a passage giving access usu. by a ladder or stairs to an enclosed space (as a cellar); *also* : HATCH 2a

¹**hate** \'hāt\ n, *often attrib* [ME, fr. OE *hete*; akin to OHG *haz* hate, Gk *kēdos* care] (bef. 12c) **1 a** : intense hostility and aversion usu. deriving from fear, anger, or sense of injury **b** : extreme dislike or antipathy : LOATHING ⟨had a great ~ of hard work⟩ **2** : an object of hatred ⟨a generation whose finest ~ had been big business —F. L. Paxson⟩

²**hate** vb **hat·ed; hat·ing** vt (bef. 12c) **1** : to feel extreme enmity toward ⟨~s his country's enemies⟩ **2** : to have a strong aversion to : find very distasteful ⟨*hated* to have to meet strangers⟩ ⟨~ hypocrisy⟩

~ vi : to express or feel extreme enmity or active hostility — **hat·er** n — **hate one's guts** : to hate someone with great intensity

syn HATE, DETEST, ABHOR, ABOMINATE, LOATHE mean to feel strong aversion or intense dislike for. HATE implies an emotional aversion often coupled with enmity or malice ⟨*hated* the enemy with a passion⟩. DETEST suggests violent antipathy ⟨*detests* cowards⟩. ABHOR implies a deep often shuddering repugnance ⟨a crime *abhorred* by all⟩. ABOMINATE suggests strong detestation and often moral condemnation ⟨every society *abominates* incest⟩. LOATHE implies utter disgust and intolerance ⟨*loathed* self-appointed moral guardians⟩.

hate crime n (1989) : any of various crimes (as assault or defacement of property) when motivated by hostility to the victim as a member of a group (as one based on color, creed, gender, or sexual orientation)

hate·ful \'hāt-fəl\ adj (14c) **1** : full of hate : MALICIOUS **2** : deserving of or arousing hate — **hate·ful·ly** \-fə-lē\ adv — **hate·ful·ness** n

hath \'hath, (h)əth\ *archaic pres 3d sing of* HAVE

hatha yoga \'hə-tə-'yō-gə, 'hä-\ n [Skt *haṭha* force + *yoga* yoga] (1890) : a system of physical exercises for the control and perfection of the body that constitutes one of the four chief Hindu disciplines

hat in hand adv (1851) : in an attitude of respectful humility ⟨have to go *hat in hand* to apologize⟩

hat·mak·er \'hat-ˌmā-kər\ n (15c) : one who makes hats

ha·tred \'hā-trəd\ n [ME, fr. *hate* + OE *rǣden* condition — more at KINDRED] (12c) **1** : HATE **2** : prejudiced hostility or animosity ⟨racial prejudices and national ~s —Peter Thomson⟩

hat·ter \'ha-tər\ n (14c) : one that makes, sells, or cleans and repairs hats

hat trick n [prob. fr. the former practice of rewarding the feat with the gift of a hat] (1877) **1** : the retiring of three batsmen with three consecutive balls by a bowler in cricket **2** : the scoring of three goals in one game (as of hockey or soccer) by a single player **3** : a succession of three victories, successes, or related accomplishments ⟨scored a *hat trick* when her three best steers corralled top honors —People⟩

hau·berk \'hó-(ˌ)bərk\ n [ME, fr. OF *hauberc*, of Gmc origin; akin to OE *healsbeorg* neck armor] (14c) : a tunic of chain mail worn as defensive armor from the 12th to the 14th century

haugh \'hó(k)\ n [ME (Sc) *halch*, fr. OE *healh* corner of land; akin to OE *holh* hole] (bef. 12c) *Scot* : a low-lying meadow by the side of a river

haugh·ty \'hó-tē, 'hä-\ adj **haugh·ti·er; -est** [obs. *haught*, fr. ME *haute*, fr. MF *haut*, lit., high, fr. L *altus* — more at OLD] (15c) : blatantly and disdainfully proud *syn* see PROUD — **haugh·ti·ly** \'hó-tᵊl-ē, 'hä-\ adv — **haugh·ti·ness** \'hó-tē-nəs, 'hä-\ n

¹**haul** \'hól\ vb [ME *halen* to pull, fr. OF *haler*, of Gmc origin; akin to MD *halen* to pull; akin to OE *geholian* to obtain] vt (13c) **1 a** : to exert traction on : DRAW ⟨~ a wagon⟩ **b** : to obtain or move by or as if by hauling ⟨was ~ed to parties night after night by his wife⟩ **c** : to transport in a vehicle : CART **2** : to change the course of (a ship) esp. so as to sail closer to the wind **3** : to bring before an authority for interrogation or judgment : HALE ⟨~ traffic violators into court⟩ ~ vi **1** : to exert traction : PULL **2** : to move along : PROCEED **3** : to furnish transportation **4** *of the wind* : SHIFT — **haul ass** : to move quickly — often considered vulgar

²**haul** n (1670) **1 a** : the act or process of hauling : PULL **b** : a device for hauling **2 a** : the result of an effort to obtain, collect, or win ⟨the burglar's ~⟩ **b** : the fish taken in a single draft of a net **3 a** : transportation by hauling **b** : the length or course of a transportation route ⟨a long ~⟩ **c** : a quantity transported : LOAD

haul·age \'hó-lij\ n (1826) **1** : the act or process of hauling **2** : a charge made for hauling

haul·er \'hó-lər\ n (1674) : one that hauls: as **a** : a commercial establishment or worker whose business is hauling **b** : an automotive vehicle for hauling goods or material

haul·ier \'hól-yər\ *Brit var of* HAULER

haulm \'hóm\ n [ME *halm*, fr. OE *healm*; akin to OHG *halm* stem, L *culmus* stalk, Gk *kalamos* reed] (bef. 12c) : the stems or tops of crop plants (as peas or potatoes) esp. after the crop has been gathered

haul off vi (1870) : to get ready — used with *and* and a following verb describing a usu. sudden and violent act ⟨I *hauled off* and hit him⟩

haunch \'hónch, 'hänch\ n [ME *haunche*, fr. OF *hanche*, of Gmc origin; akin to MD *hanke* haunch] (13c) **1 a** : HIP 1a **b** : HINDQUARTER **2** — usu. used in pl. **2** : HINDQUARTER 1 **3** : either side of an arch between the springing and the crown — **on one's haunches** : in a squatting position

¹**haunt** \'hónt, 'hänt\ vb [ME, fr. OF *hanter*, prob. fr. ON *heimta* to lead home, pull, claim, fr. *heimr* home] vt (14c) **1 a** : to visit often : FREQUENT **b** : to continually seek the company of **2 a** : to have a disquieting or harmful effect on : TROUBLE ⟨problems we ignore now will come back to ~ us⟩ **b** : to recur constantly and spontaneously to ⟨the tune ~ed her⟩ **c** : to reappear continually in ⟨a sense of tension that ~s his writing⟩ **3** : to visit or inhabit as a ghost ~ vi **1** : to stay around or persist : LINGER **2** : to appear habitually as a ghost — **haunt·er** n — **haunt·ing·ly** \'hón-tin-lē, 'hän-\ adv

²**haunt** \'hónt, 'hänt, 2 is usu 'hant\ n (14c) : a place habitually frequented **2** *chiefly dial* : GHOST

Hau·sa \'haù-sə, -zə\ n, pl **Hausa** or **Hausas** (1853) **1** : the Chadic language of the Hausa people widely used in western Africa as a trade language **2** : a member of a black people of northern Nigeria and southern Niger

haus·frau \'haus-ˌfraù\ n [G, fr. *Haus* house + *Frau* woman, wife] (1798) : HOUSEWIFE

haus·tel·lum \hó-'ste-ləm\ n, pl **-la** \-lə\ [NL, dim. of L *haustrum* scoop on a waterwheel, fr. *haurire* to drink, draw — more at EXHAUST] (1816) : a proboscis (as of an insect) adapted to suck blood or juices of plants

haus·to·ri·al \hó-'stōr-ē-əl, -'stór-\ adj (1894) : of, relating to, or having a haustorium

haus·to·ri·um \-ē-əm\ n, pl **-ria** \-ē-ə\ [NL, fr. L *haurire*] (1875) : a food-absorbing outgrowth of a plant organ (as a hypha or stem)

1 hauberk

haut·bois or **haut·boy** \'(h)ō-,bòi\ n, pl **hautbois** \-,bòiz\ or **haut-boys** [MF hautbois, fr. haut high + bois wood] (1575) : OBOE
haute \'ōt\ also **haut** \'ōt, 'ō\ adj [F] (1787) : FASHIONABLE, HIGH-CLASS 〈~ interior decorators〉 〈a store filled with ~ kitsch〉
haute cou·ture \,ōt-kú-'túr\ n [F, lit., high sewing] (1908) : the houses or designers that create exclusive and often trend-setting fashions for women; also : the fashions created
haute cui·sine \-kwi-'zēn\ n [F, lit., high cooking] (1928) : artful or elaborate cuisine; esp : traditionally elaborate French cuisine
haute école \-ā-'kòl, -'kəl\ n [F, lit., high school] (1858) : a highly stylized form of classical riding : advanced dressage
hau·teur \hò-'tər, (h)ō-\ n [F, fr. haut high — more at HAUGHTY] (ca. 1628) : ARROGANCE, HAUGHTINESS
haut monde \ō-'mänd, ō-mōⁿd\ also **haute monde** \ōt-\ n [F, lit., high world] (1864) : high society
Ha·va·na \hə-'va-nə\ n [prob. fr. Sp habano, fr. habano of Havana, fr. La Habana (Havana), Cuba] (1826) 1 : a cigar made from Cuban tobacco 2 : a tobacco orig. grown in Cuba
Ha·var·ti \hə-'vär-tē\ n [Havarti, locale in Denmark] (1957) : a semi-soft Danish cheese having a porous texture and a mild flavor
havdalah var of HABDALAH
¹**have** \'hav, (h)əv, v; in "have to" meaning "must" usu 'haf\ vb **had** \'had, (h)əd, d\; **hav·ing** \'ha-viŋ\; **has** \'haz, (h)əz, z, s; in "has to" meaning "must" usu 'has\ [ME, fr. OE habban; akin to OHG habēn to have, and perh. to hevan to lift — more at HEAVE] vt (bef. 12c) 1 **a** : to hold or maintain as a possession, privilege, or entitlement 〈they ~ a new car〉 〈I ~ my rights〉 **b** : to hold in one's use, service, regard, or at one's disposal 〈the group will ~ enough tickets for everyone〉 〈we don't ~ time to stay〉 **c** : to hold, include, or contain as a part or whole 〈the car has power brakes〉 〈April has 30 days〉 2 **a** : to feel obligation in regard to — usu. used with an infinitive with to 〈we ~ things to do〉 〈~ a deadline to meet〉 **b** : to stand in a certain relationship to 〈has three fine children〉 〈we will ~ the wind at our backs〉 4 **a** : to acquire or get possession of : OBTAIN 〈these shoes are the best to be had〉 **b** : RECEIVE 〈had news〉 **c** : ACCEPT; specif : to accept in marriage **d** : to copulate with 5 **a** : to be marked or characterized by 〈a quality, attribute, or faculty〉 〈both ~ red hair〉 〈has a way with words〉 **b** : EXHIBIT, SHOW 〈had the gall to refuse〉 **c** : USE, EXERCISE 〈~ mercy on us〉 6 **a** : to experience esp. by submitting to, undergoing, or suffering 〈I ~ a cold〉 **b** : to make the effort to perform (an action) or engage in (an activity) 〈~ a look at that cut〉 **c** : to entertain in the mind 〈~ an opinion〉 7 **a** : to cause or command to do something — used with the infinitive without to 〈~ the children stay〉 **b** : to cause to be in a certain place or state 〈has people around at all times〉 8 : ALLOW 〈we'll ~ no more of that〉 9 : to be competent in 〈has only a little French〉 10 **a** : to hold in a position of disadvantage or certain defeat 〈we ~ him now〉 **b** : to take advantage of : TRICK, FOOL 〈been had by a partner〉 11 : BEGET, BEAR 〈~ a baby〉 12 : to partake of 〈~ dinner〉 〈~ a smoke〉 13 : BRIBE, SUBORN 〈can be had for a price〉 ~ verbal auxiliary 1 — used with the past participle to form the present perfect, past perfect, or future perfect 〈has gone home〉 〈had already eaten〉 〈will ~ finished dinner by then〉 2 : to be compelled, obliged, or required — used with an infinitive with to or to alone 〈we had to go〉 〈do what you have to〉 〈it has to be said〉 — **had better** or **had best** : would be wise to — **have at** : to go at or deal with : ATTACK — **have coming** : to deserve or merit what one gets, benefits by, or suffers 〈he had that coming〉 — **have done** : FINISH, STOP — **have done with** : to bring to an end : have no further concern with 〈let us have done with name-calling〉 — **have had it** 1 : to have had or have done all one is going to be allowed to 2 : to have experienced, endured, or suffered all one can — **have it** : ASSERT, CLAIM 〈rumor has it that he was drunk〉 — **have it in for** : to intend to do harm to — **have it out** : to settle a matter of contention by discussion or a fight — **have none of** : to refuse to have anything to do with — **have one's eye on** 1 **a** : to look at **b** : to watch constantly and attentively 〈I have as an objective〉 — **have to do with** 1 : to deal with 〈the story has to do with real people〉 —Alice M. Jordan 2 : to have a specified relationship with or effect on 〈the size of the brain has nothing to do with intelligence〉 —Ruth Benedict〉
²**have** \'hav\ n (1836) : one that is well-endowed esp. in material wealth
have·lock \'hav-,läk, -lək\ n [Sir Henry Havelock] (1861) : a covering attached to a cap to protect the neck from the sun or bad weather
ha·ven \'hā-vən\ n [ME, fr. OE hæfen; akin to MHG habene harbor] (bef. 12c) 1 : HARBOR, PORT 2 : a place of safety : ASYLUM 3 : a place offering favorable opportunities or conditions 〈a tourist's ~〉 — **haven** vt
have–not \'hav-,nät, -'nät\ n (1836) : one that is poor esp. in material wealth
haven't \'ha-vənt, 'ha-bᵊm(t)\ (1777) : have not
have on vt (bef. 12c) 1 : WEAR 〈has on a new suit〉 2 chiefly Brit : to trick or deceive intentionally : PUT ON 5 3 : to have plans for 〈what do you have on for tomorrow〉
ha·ver \'hā-vər\ vi [origin unknown] (1866) chiefly Brit : to hem and haw
hav·er·sack \'ha-vər-,sak\ n [F havresac, fr. G Habersack bag for oats, fr. Haber oats + Sack bag] (1749) : a bag similar to a knapsack but worn over one shoulder
ha·ver·sian canal \hə-'vər-zhən-\ n, often cap H [Clopton Havers †1702 Eng. physician & anatomist] (1842) : any of the small canals through which the blood vessels ramify in bone
haversian system n, often cap H (ca. 1846) : a haversian canal with the concentrically arranged laminae of bone that surround it
¹**hav·oc** \'ha-vək, -vik\ n [ME havok, fr. AF, modif. of OF havot plunder] (15c) 1 : wide and general destruction : DEVASTATION 2 : great confusion and disorder 〈children can create ~ in a house〉
²**havoc** vt **hav·ocked; hav·ock·ing** (1577) : to lay waste : DESTROY
¹**haw** \'hò\ n [ME hawe, fr. OE haga — more at HEDGE] (bef. 12c) 1 : a hawthorn berry 2 : HAWTHORN
²**haw** n [origin unknown] (15c) : NICTITATING MEMBRANE; esp : an inflamed nictitating membrane of a domesticated mammal
³**haw** \'hò\ vb [imit.] (1632) 1 : to utter the sound represented by haw 〈hemmed and ~ed before answering〉 2 : EQUIVOCATE 〈the administration hemmed and ~ed over the students' demands〉

⁴**haw** interj (1679) — often used to indicate a vocalized pause in speaking
⁵**haw** \'hò\ vb [origin unknown] (1777) vb imper — used as a direction to turn to the left; compare GEE ~ vi : to turn to the near or left side
Hawaii–Aleutian time n (1983) : the time of the 10th time zone west of Greenwich that includes the Hawaiian islands and the Aleutians west of the Fox group
Ha·wai·ian \hə-'wä-yən, -'wī-(y)ən, -'wò-yən\ n (ca. 1864) 1 : a native or resident of Hawaii; esp : one of Polynesian ancestry 2 : the Polynesian language of the Hawaiians — **Hawaiian** adj
Hawaiian goose n (ca. 1909) : NENE
Hawaiian guitar n (1928) : a usu. electric stringed instrument having a long fretted neck and six to eight steel strings that are plucked while being pressed with a movable steel bar for a glissando effect
Hawaiian shirt n (1962) : a usu. short-sleeved sport shirt with a colorful pattern
haw·finch \'hò-,finch\ n [¹haw] (ca. 1674) : an Old World finch (Coccothraustes coccothraustes) with a large heavy bill and short thick neck and the male marked with black, white, and brown
¹**hawk** \'hòk\ n [ME hauk, fr. OE hafoc; akin to OHG habuh hawk, Russ kobets a falcon] (bef. 12c) 1 : any of numerous diurnal birds of prey belonging to a suborder (Falcones of the order Falconiformes) and including all the smaller members of this group; esp : ACCIPITER — compare OWL 2 : a small board or metal sheet with a handle on the underside used to hold mortar 3 : one who takes a militant attitude and advocates vigorous immediate action; esp : a supporter of a war or warlike policy — compare DOVE — **hawk·ish** \'hò-kish\ adj — **hawk·ish·ly** adv — **hawk·ish·ness** n
²**hawk** vi (14c) 1 : to hunt birds by means of a trained hawk 2 : to soar and strike like a hawk ~ vt : to hunt on the wing like a hawk
³**hawk** vb [imit.] (1581) vt : to raise by trying to clear the throat 〈~ up phlegm〉 ~ vi : to utter a harsh guttural sound in or as if in hawking
⁴**hawk** n (1604) : an audible effort to force up phlegm from the throat
⁵**hawk** vt [back-formation fr. ²hawker] (1713) : to offer for sale by calling out in the street 〈~ing newspapers〉; broadly : SELL
¹**hawk·er** \'hò-kər\ n [ME, fr. OE hafocere, fr. hafoc] (bef. 12c) : FALCONER
²**hawker** n [by folk etymology fr. LG höker, fr. MLG höker, fr. höken to peddle] (1512) : one that hawks wares
Hawk·eye \'hò-,kī\ n (1823) : a native or resident of Iowa — used as a nickname
hawk·eyed \'hò-,kīd\ adj (ca. 1818) : having keen sight
hawk·moth \'hòk-,mòth\ n (1785) : any of a family (Sphingidae) of stout-bodied moths with a long proboscis, long narrow more or less pointed forewings, and small hind wings — called also sphinx
hawks·bill \'hòks-,bil\ n (1712) : a small brown or brown and yellow sea turtle (Eretmochelys imbricata) of warm waters that has a carapace of overlapping plates — compare TORTOISESHELL 1
hawk·shaw \'hòk-,shò\ n [fr. Hawkshaw, detective in the play The Ticket of Leave Man (1863) by Tom Taylor] (1888) : DETECTIVE
hawk·weed \'hòk-,wēd\ n (1562) : any of a genus (Hieracium) of composite plants usu. having flower heads with red or orange rays — compare ORANGE HAWKWEED

hawksbill

hawse \'hòz\ n [alter. of ME halse, fr. ON hals neck, hawse — more at COLLAR] (14c) 1 **a** : the part of a ship's bow that contains the hawse-holes **b** : HAWSEHOLE 2 : the distance between a ship's bow and her anchor
hawse·hole \-,hōl\ n (1664) : a hole in the bow of a ship through which a cable passes
haw·ser \'hò-zər\ n [ME, fr. AF hauceour, fr. MF haucier to hoist, fr. (assumed) VL altiare, fr. L altus high — more at OLD] (13c) : a large rope for towing, mooring, or securing a ship
haw·ser–laid \'hò-zər-,lād\ adj (1769) : composed of three ropes laid together right-handed with each containing three strands twisted together
haw·thorn \'hò-,thòrn\ n [ME hawethorn, fr. OE hagathorn, fr. haga hawthorn + thorn — more at HEDGE] (bef. 12c) : any of a genus (Crataegus) of spring-flowering spiny shrubs of the rose family with glossy and often lobed leaves, white or pink fragrant flowers, and small red fruits
Haw·thorne effect \'hò-,thòrn-\ n [fr. the Hawthorne Works of the Western Electric Co., Cicero, Ill., where its existence was established by experiment] (1962) : the stimulation to output or accomplishment that results from the mere fact of being under observation; also : such an increase in output or accomplishment
¹**hay** \'hā\ n [ME hey, fr. OE hieg; akin to OHG hewi hay, OE hēawan to hew] (bef. 12c) 1 : herbage and esp. grass mowed and cured for fodder 2 : REWARD 3 slang : BED 4 : a small sum of money 〈a saving of . . . $14 million is not ~ —H. C. Schonberg〉
²**hay** vi (1556) : to cut, cure, and store hay ~ vt : to feed with hay
hay·cock \'hā-,käk\ n (13c) : a somewhat rounded conical pile of hay
hay fever n (1829) : an acute allergic rhinitis and conjunctivitis; esp : POLLINOSIS
hay·lage \'hā-lij\ n [hay + silage] (ca. 1958) : a stored forage that is essentially a grass silage wilted to 35 to 50 percent moisture
hay·loft \'hā-,lòft\ n (1573) : a loft esp. for storing hay
hay·mak·er \-,mā-kər\ n (1912) : a powerful blow
hay·mow \-,maù\ n (15c) : a mow esp. of or for hay
hay·rack \-,rak\ n (1825) 1 : a feeding rack that holds hay for livestock 2 : a frame mounted on the running gear of a wagon and used esp. in hauling hay or straw; also : a wagon equipped with a hayrack

\ə\ abut \ᵊ\ kitten, F table \ər\ further \a\ ash \ā\ ace \ä\ mop, mar
\aù\ out \ch\ chin \e\ bet \ē\ easy \g\ go \i\ hit \ī\ ice \j\ job
\ŋ\ sing \ō\ go \ò\ law \òi\ boy \th\ thin \t̲h̲\ the \ü\ loot \ù\ foot
\y\ yet \zh\ vision \à, k̲, ⁿ, œ, œ̄, ᵫ, ᵬ, ᵊ\ see Guide to Pronunciation

hay·rick \-ˌrik\ *n* (15c) : a relatively large sometimes thatched outdoor pile of hay : HAYSTACK

hay·ride \-ˌrīd\ *n* (1896) : a pleasure ride usu. at night by a group in a wagon, sleigh, or open truck partly filled with straw or hay

hay–scent·ed fern \ˈhā-ˌsen-təd-\ *n* (1915) : a common fern (*Dennstaedtia punctilobula*) of eastern No. America with fragrant finely divided pale green fronds

hay·seed \ˈhā-ˌsēd\ *n, pl* **hayseed** *or* **hayseeds** (1577) , 1 a : seed shattered from hay b : clinging bits of straw or chaff from hay 2 *pl* **hayseeds** : BUMPKIN, YOKEL

hay·stack \-ˌstak\ *n* (15c) 1 : a stack of hay 2 : a vertical standing wave in turbulent river waters

hay·wire \-ˌwīr\ *adv or adj* [fr. the use of baling wire for makeshift repairs] (1929) 1 : being out of order or having gone wrong ⟨the radio went ∼⟩ 2 : emotionally or mentally upset or out of control ⟨she ⟨is going ∼ with grief⟩

ha·zan \kə-ˈzän, ˈkä-z°n\ *n, pl* **ha·za·nim** \kə-ˈzä-nəm\ [LHeb *ḥazzān*] (1650) 1 : an official of a Jewish synagogue or community of the period when the Talmud was compiled 2 : CANTOR 2

¹haz·ard \ˈha-zərd\ *n* [ME, fr. MF *hasard*, fr. Ar *az-zahr* the die] (14c) 1 : a game of chance like craps played with two dice 2 : a source of danger 3 a : CHANCE, RISK b : a chance event : ACCIDENT 4 *obs* : STAKE 3a 5 : a golf-course obstacle — **at hazard** : at stake

²hazard *vt* (1530) : VENTURE, RISK ⟨∼ a guess as to the outcome⟩

haz·ard·ous \ˈha-zər-dəs\ *adj* (1585) 1 : depending on hazard or chance 2 : involving or exposing one to risk (as of loss or harm) ⟨a ∼ occupation⟩ ⟨disposing of ∼ waste⟩ *syn* see DANGEROUS — **haz·ard·ous·ly** *adv* — **haz·ard·ous·ness** *n*

¹haze \ˈhāz\ *n* [prob. back-formation fr. *hazy*] (1706) 1 a : fine dust, smoke, or light vapor causing lack of transparency of the air b : a cloudy appearance in a transparent liquid or solid; *also* : a dullness of finish (as on furniture) 2 : something suggesting atmospheric haze; *esp* : vagueness of mind or mental perception

²haze *vb* **hazed; haz·ing** *vt* (1801) : to make hazy, dull, or cloudy ∼ *vi* : to become hazy or cloudy

³haze *vt* **hazed; haz·ing** [origin unknown] (1840) 1 a : to harass by exacting unnecessary or disagreeable work b : to harass by banter, ridicule, or criticism 2 : to haze by way of initiation ⟨∼ the fraternity pledges⟩ 3 *West* : to drive (as cattle or horses) from horseback — **haz·er** *n*

¹ha·zel \ˈhā-zəl\ *n* [ME *hasel*, fr. OE *hæsel*; akin to OHG *hasal* hazel, L *corulus*] (bef. 12c) 1 : any of a genus (*Corylus* and esp. the American *C. americana* and the European *C. avellana*) of shrubs or small trees of the birch family bearing nuts enclosed in a leafy involucre 2 : a light brown to strong yellowish brown

²hazel *adj* (14c) 1 : consisting of hazels or of the wood of the hazel 2 : of the color hazel

hazel hen *n* (1661) : a European woodland grouse (*Bonasa bonasia*) related to the ruffed grouse — called also *hazel grouse*

ha·zel·nut \ˈhā-zəl-ˌnət\ *n* (bef. 12c) : the nut of a hazel

haz·ing \ˈhā-ziŋ\ *n* (ca. 1855) : the action of hazing; *esp* : an initiation process involving harassment

hazy \ˈhā-zē\ *adj* **haz·i·er; -est** [origin unknown] (1625) 1 : obscured or made dim or cloudy by or as if by haze 2 : VAGUE, INDEFINITE ⟨has only a ∼ recollection⟩; *also* : UNCERTAIN ⟨I'm ∼ on that point⟩ — **haz·i·ly** \-zə-lē\ *adv* — **haz·i·ness** \-zē-nəs\ *n*

H–bomb \ˈāch-ˌbäm\ *n* (1950) : HYDROGEN BOMB

HDL \ˌāch-(ˌ)dē-ˈel\ *n* [high-density lipoprotein] (ca. 1965) : a cholesterol-poor protein-rich lipoprotein of blood plasma correlated with reduced risk of atherosclerosis — compare LDL

¹he \ˈhē, ē\ *pron* [ME, fr. OE; akin to OE *hēo* she, *hit* it, OHG *hē* he, L *cis, citra* on this side, Gk *ekeinos* that person] (bef. 12c) 1 : that male one who is neither speaker nor hearer ⟨∼ is my father⟩ — compare HIM, HIS, IT, SHE, THEY 2 — used in a generic sense or when the sex of the person is unspecified ⟨∼ that hath ears to hear, let him hear — Mt 11:15 (AV)⟩ ⟨one should do the best ∼ can⟩

²he \ˈhē\ *n* (bef. 12c) 1 : a male person or animal 2 : one that is strongly masculine or has strong masculine appeal — usu. used in combination ⟨that's what I call *he*-literature —Sinclair Lewis⟩

³he \ˈhā\ *n* [Heb *hē*] (1639) : the 5th letter of the Hebrew alphabet — see ALPHABET table

¹head \ˈhed\ *n* [ME *hed*, fr. OE *hēafod*; akin to OHG *houbit* head, L *caput*] (bef. 12c) 1 : the upper or anterior division of the animal body that contains the brain, the chief sense organs, and the mouth 2 a : the seat of the intellect : MIND ⟨two ∼s are better than one⟩ b : a person with respect to mental qualities ⟨let wiser ∼s prevail⟩ c : natural aptitude or talent ⟨a good ∼ for figures⟩ d : mental or emotional control : POISE ⟨a level ∼⟩ e : HEADACHE 3 : the obverse of a coin — usu. used in pl. ⟨∼s, I win⟩ 4 a : PERSON, INDIVIDUAL ⟨count ∼s⟩ b *pl* **head** : one of a number (as of domestic animals) 5 a : the end that is upper or higher or opposite the foot ⟨the ∼ of the table⟩ ⟨∼ of a sail⟩ b : the source of a stream c : either end of something (as a drum) whose two ends need not be distinguished 6 : DIRECTOR, LEADER: as a : HEADMASTER b : one in charge of a division or department in an office or institution ⟨the ∼ of the English department⟩ 7 a : CAPITULUM 2 b : the foliaged part of a plant esp. when consisting of a compact mass of leaves or close fructification 8 a : the leading element of a military column or a procession b : HEADWAY 9 a : the uppermost extremity or projecting part of an object : TOP b : the striking part of a weapon, tool, or implement c : the rounded proximal end of a long bone (as the humerus) : the end of a muscle nearest the origin — compare ORIGIN e : the oval part of a printed musical note 10 a : a body of water kept in reserve at a height; *also* : the containing bank, dam, or wall b : a mass of water in motion 11 a : the difference in elevation between two points in a body of fluid b : the resulting pressure of the fluid at the lower point expressible as this height; *broadly* : pressure of a fluid 12 a : the bow and adjacent parts of a ship b : a ship's toilet; *broadly* : TOILET 13 : the approximate length of the head of a horse ⟨won by a ∼⟩ 14 : the place of leadership, honor, or command ⟨at the ∼ of her class⟩ 15 a (1) : a word or series of words often in larger letters placed at the beginning of a passage or at the top of a page in order to introduce or categorize (2) : a separate part or topic b : a portion of a page or sheet that is above the first line of printing 16 : the foam or scum that rises on a fermenting or effervescing liquid (as beer) 17 a : the part of a boil, pimple, or abscess at which it is likely to break b : culminating point of action : CRISIS ⟨events came to a ∼⟩ 18 a : a part or attachment of a machine or machine tool containing a device (as a cutter or drill); *also* : the part of an apparatus that performs the chief function or a particular function b : an electromagnet used as a transducer in magnetic recording for recording on, reading, or erasing a magnetic medium (as tape) 19 : an immediate constituent of a construction that can have the same grammatical function as the whole (as *man* in "an old man", "a very old man", or "the man in the street") 20 a : one who uses a drug b : DEVOTEE ⟨chili ∼s⟩ 21 : FELLATIO, CUNNILINGUS — usu. used with *give*; often considered vulgar — **by the head** : drawing the greater depth of water forward — **off one's head** : CRAZY, DISTRACTED — **out of one's head** : DELIRIOUS — **over one's head** 1 : beyond one's comprehension or competence ⟨the most awful intellectual detail, all of it *over my head* —E. B. White⟩ 2 : so as to pass over one's superior standing or authority ⟨went *over my head* to complain⟩

²head *adj* (bef. 12c) 1 : of, relating to, or intended for the head 2 : PRINCIPAL, CHIEF ⟨∼ cook⟩ 3 : situated at the head 4 : coming from in front ⟨∼ sea⟩

³head *vt* (14c) 1 : BEHEAD 2 a : to put a head on : fit a head to ⟨∼ an arrow⟩ b : to form the head or top of ⟨tower ∼*ed* by a spire⟩ 3 : to act as leader or head to ⟨∼ a revolt⟩ 4 a : to get in front of so as to hinder, stop, or turn back b : to take a lead over (as a racehorse) : SURPASS c : to pass (a stream) by going round above the source 5 a : to put something at the head of (as a list) b : to stand as the first or leading member of ⟨∼s the list of heroes⟩ 6 : to set the course of ⟨∼ a ship northward⟩ 7 : to drive (as a soccer ball) with the head ∼ *vi* 1 : to form a head ⟨this cabbage ∼s early⟩ 2 : to point or proceed in a certain direction ⟨the fleet was ∼*ing* out⟩ 3 : to have a source : ORIGINATE

head·ache \ˈhe-ˌdāk\ *n* (bef. 12c) 1 : pain in the head 2 : a vexatious or baffling situation or problem — **head·achy** \-ˌdā-kē\ *adj*

head and shoulders *adv* (ca. 1864) : beyond comparison : by far ⟨*head and shoulders* above the competition⟩

head·band \ˈhed-ˌband\ *n* (1535) 1 : a band worn on or around the head 2 : a narrow strip of cloth sewn or glued by hand to a book at the extreme ends of the backbone

head·board \-ˌbōrd, -ˌbord\ *n* (1730) : a board forming the head (as of a bed)

head·cheese \-ˌchēz\ *n* (1841) : a jellied loaf or sausage made from edible parts of the head, feet, and sometimes the tongue and heart esp. of a pig

head cold *n* (1937) : a common cold centered in the nasal passages and adjacent mucous tissues

head·dress \ˈhed-ˌdres\ *n* (1703) : an often elaborate covering for the head

head·ed \ˈhe-dəd\ *adj* (13c) 1 : having a head or a heading 2 : having a head or heads of a specified kind or number — used in combination ⟨became light-*headed* from the fever⟩ ⟨a round*headed* screw⟩

head·er \ˈhe-dər\ *n* (15c) 1 : one that removes heads; *esp* : a grain-harvesting machine that cuts off the grain heads and elevates them to a wagon 2 a : a brick or stone laid in a wall with its end toward the face of the wall b : a beam fitted at one side of an opening to support free ends of floor joists, studs, or rafters c : a horizontal structural or finish piece over an opening : LINTEL d : a conduit (as an exhaust pipe for a many-cylindered engine) into which a number of smaller conduits open e : a mounting plate through which electrical terminals pass from a sealed device (as a transistor) 3 : a fall or dive headfirst 4 : a shot or pass in soccer made by heading the ball 5 : HEAD 15a(1)

head·first \ˈhed-ˈfərst\ *adv* (ca. 1828) : with the head foremost : HEADLONG ⟨dove ∼ into the waves⟩ — **headfirst** *adj*

head·fore·most \-ˈfōr-ˌmōst, -ˈfor-\ *adv* (1697) : HEADFIRST

head·gate \ˈhed-ˌgāt\ *n* (1832) : a gate for controlling the water flowing into a channel (as an irrigation ditch)

head·gear \-ˌgir\ *n* (15c) 1 : a covering or protective device for the head 2 : a harness for a horse's head

head·hunt·er \-ˌhən-tər\ *n* (1853) 1 : one that engages in headhunting 2 : a recruiter of personnel esp. at the executive level

head–hunt·ing \-ˌhən-tiŋ\ *n* (1853) 1 : the act or custom of seeking out, decapitating, and preserving the heads of enemies as trophies 2 : a seeking to deprive usu. political enemies of position or influence

head·ing \ˈhe-diŋ\ *n* (1676) 1 a : something that forms or serves as a head; *esp* : an inscription, headline, or title standing at the top or beginning (as of a letter or chapter) b : the address and date at the beginning of a letter showing its place and time of origin 2 : the compass direction in which the longitudinal axis of a ship or aircraft points; *broadly* : DIRECTION 3 : DRIFT 6

head·lamp \-ˌlamp\ *n* (1885) : HEADLIGHT

head·land \ˈhed-lənd, -ˌland\ *n* (bef. 12c) 1 : unplowed land at the ends of furrows or near a fence 2 : a point of usu. high land jutting out into a body of water : PROMONTORY

head·less \-ləs\ *adj* (bef. 12c) 1 a : having no head b : having the head cut off : BEHEADED 2 : having no chief 3 : lacking good sense or prudence : FOOLISH — **head·less·ness** *n*

head·light \-ˌlīt\ *n* (1861) 1 : a light with a reflector and special lens mounted on the front of a vehicle to illuminate the road ahead; *also* : the beam cast by a headlight 2 : a light worn on the forehead (as of a miner or physician)

¹head·line \-ˌlīn\ *n* (1824) 1 : words set at the head of a passage or page to introduce or categorize 2 a : a head of a newspaper story or article usu. printed in large type and giving the gist of the story or article that follows b *pl* : front-page news ⟨the scandal made ∼s⟩

²headline *vt* (1891) 1 : to provide with a headline 2 : to publicize highly 3 : to be engaged as a leading performer in (a show)

head·lin·er \ˈhed-ˌlī-nər\ *n* (1896) 1 : the principal performer in a show : STAR; *broadly* : PERSONALITY 4b 2 : fabric covering the inside of the roof of an automobile

head linesman *n* (ca. 1949) : a football linesman

head·lock \ˈhed-ˌläk\ *n* (1905) : a hold in which a wrestler encircles his opponent's head with one arm

¹head·long \-ˈloŋ\ *adv* [ME *hedlong*, alter. of *hedling*, fr. *hed* head] (14c) 1 : HEADFIRST 2 : without deliberation : RECKLESSLY 3 : without pause or delay

²**head·long** \-,lȯn\ *adj* (ca. 1550) **1** *archaic* : STEEP, PRECIPITOUS **2** : lacking in calmness or restraint : PRECIPITATE ⟨a ~ torrent of emotion⟩ **3** : plunging headforemost *syn* see PRECIPITATE

head louse *n* (1547) : one of a variety (*Pediculus humanus capitis*) of the common louse that lives on the human scalp

head·man *n* (bef. 12c) **1 a** \'hed-'man\ : FOREMAN, OVERSEER **b** \-'man, -,man\ : a lesser chief of a primitive community **2** \-mən\ : HEADSMAN

head·mas·ter \'hed-,mas-tər, -'mas-\ *n* (1576) : a man heading the staff of a private school : PRINCIPAL — **head·mas·ter·ship** \-,ship\ *n*

head·mis·tress \-,mis-trəs, -'mis-\ *n* (1872) : a woman heading the staff of a private school

head·most \'hed-,mōst\ *adj* (1628) : most advanced : LEADING

head·note \-,nōt\ *n* (1855) **1** : a prefixed note of comment or explanation **2** : a note prefixed to the report of a decided legal case

head off *vt* (1841) : to turn back or turn aside : BLOCK, PREVENT ⟨*head* them *off* at the pass⟩ ⟨attempts to *head off* the imminent crisis⟩

¹**head–on** \'hed-'ȯn, -'än\ *adv* (1840) **1** : with the head or front making the initial contact ⟨the cars collided ~⟩ **2** : in direct opposition, confrontation, or contradiction ⟨met the problem ~⟩

²**head–on** *adj* (1903) **1** : having the front facing in the direction of initial contact or line of sight ⟨a ~ collision⟩ **2** : FRONTAL

head over heels *adv* (1771) **1 a** : in or as if in a somersault : HELTER-SKELTER **b** : UPSIDE DOWN **2** : very much : DEEPLY ⟨*head over heels* in love⟩

head·phone \'hed-,fōn\ *n* (1914) : an earphone held over the ear by a band worn on the head — usu. used in pl.

head·piece \-,pēs\ *n* (1535) **1 a** : a protective or defensive covering for the head **b** : an ornamental, ceremonial, or traditional covering for the head **2** : BRAINS, INTELLIGENCE **3** : an ornament esp. at the beginning of a chapter

head·pin \-,pin\ *n* (1927) : a bowling pin that stands foremost in the arrangement of pins

head·quar·ter \'hed-,kwȯ(r)-tər, -,kȯr-, (')hed-'\ *vt* (1903) : to place in headquarters ~ *vi* : to make one's headquarters

head·quar·ters \-,tərz\ *n pl but sing or pl in constr* (1647) **1** : a place from which a commander performs the functions of command **2** : the administrative center of an enterprise

head·rest \-,rest\ *n* (1853) **1** : a support for the head **2** : HEAD RESTRAINT

head restraint *n* (1967) : a resilient pad at the top of the back of an automobile seat esp. for preventing whiplash injury

head rhyme *n* (ca. 1943) : ALLITERATION

head·room \'hed-,rüm, -,rum\ *n* (1851) : vertical space in which to stand, sit, or move

head·sail \-,sāl, -səl\ *n* (1627) : a sail set forward of the foremast

head·set \-,set\ *n* (1921) **1** : an attachment for holding an earphone and transmitter at one's head **2** : a pair of headphones

head·ship \-,ship\ *n* (1582) : the position, office, or dignity of a head

head shop *n* (1968) : a shop specializing in articles (as hashish pipes and roach clips) of interest to drug users

head·shrink·er \-,shriṇ-kər, *esp Southern* -,sriṇ-\ *n* (1950) : SHRINK 3

heads·man \'hedz-mən\ *n* (1601) : one that beheads : EXECUTIONER

head·space \'hed-,spās\ *n* (1936) : the volume above a liquid or solid in a closed container

head·spring \'hed-,sprin\ *n* (14c) : FOUNTAINHEAD, SOURCE

head·stall \-,stȯl\ *n* (14c) : a part of a bridle or halter that encircles the head

head·stand \-,stand\ *n* (ca. 1934) : the gymnastic feat of standing on one's head usu. with support from the hands

head start *n* (1886) **1** : an advantage granted or achieved at the beginning of a race, a chase, or a competition ⟨a 10-minute *head start*⟩ **2** : a favorable or promising beginning

head·stock \'hed-,stäk\ *n* (1731) : a bearing or pedestal for a revolving or moving part; *specif* : a part of a lathe that holds the revolving spindle and its attachments

head·stone \-,stōn\ *n* (1775) : a memorial stone at the head of a grave

head·stream \-,strēm\ *n* (14c) : a stream that is the source of a river

head·strong \-,strȯn\ *adj* (14c) **1** : not easily restrained : impatient of control, advice, or suggestions **2** : directed by ungovernable will ⟨violent ~ actions⟩ *syn* see UNRULY

heads–up \'hed-'zəp\ *adj* (1947) : ALERT, RESOURCEFUL ⟨~ football⟩

heads up *interj* (ca. 1941) — used as a warning to look out for danger esp. overhead or to clear a passageway

head–to–head *adv or adj* (ca. 1728) : in a direct confrontation or encounter usu. between individuals

head·wait·er \'hed-'wā-tər\ *n* (1805) : the head of the dining-room staff of a restaurant or hotel

head·wa·ter \-,wȯ-tər, -,wä-\ *n* (1802) : the source of a stream — usu. used in pl.

head·way \-,wā\ *n* (1748) **1 a** : motion or rate of motion in a forward direction **b** : ADVANCE, PROGRESS **2** : headroom (as under an arch) sufficient to allow passage **3** : the time interval between two vehicles traveling in the same direction on the same route

head·word \'hed-,wərd\ *n* (ca. 1823) **1** : a word or term placed at the beginning (as of a chapter or an entry in an encyclopedia) **2** : HEAD 19

head·work \-,wərk\ *n* (1837) : mental labor; *esp* : clever thinking

heady \'he-dē\ *adj* **head·i·er; -est** (14c) **1 a** : WILLFUL, RASH ⟨~ opinions⟩ **b** : VIOLENT, IMPETUOUS **2 a** : tending to intoxicate or make giddy or elated ⟨~ wine⟩ ⟨being in such distinguished company was a ~ experience⟩ **b** : GIDDY, EXHILARATED ⟨~ with his success⟩ **c** : RICH ⟨a ~ sauce⟩ ⟨a ~ variety⟩ **d** : IMPRESSIVE ⟨a man of ~ accomplishments⟩ **3** : marked by or showing good judgment : SHREWD, INTELLIGENT **b** : intellectually stimulating or demanding — **head·i·ly** \'he-dᵊl-ē\ *adv* — **head·i·ness** \'he-dē-nəs\ *n*

heal \'hē(ə)l\ *vb* [ME *helen*, fr. OE *hǣlan*; akin to OHG *heilen* to heal, OE *hāl* whole — more at WHOLE] *vt* (bef. 12c) **1 a** : to make sound or whole ⟨~ a wound⟩ **b** : to restore to health **2 a** : to cause (an undesirable condition) to be overcome : MEND ⟨the troubles . . . had not been forgotten, but they had been ~ed —William Power⟩ **b** : to patch up (a breach or division) ⟨~ a breach between friends⟩ **3** : to restore to original purity or integrity ⟨~ed of sin⟩ ~ *vi* : to return to a sound state

heal·er \'hē-lər\ *n* (12c) **1** : one that heals **2** : a Christian Science practitioner

health \'helth *also* 'helth\ *n*, *often attrib* [ME *helthe*, fr. OE *hǣlth*, fr. *hāl*] (bef. 12c) **1 a** : the condition of being sound in body, mind, or spirit; *esp* : freedom from physical disease or pain **b** : the general condition of the body ⟨in poor ~⟩ ⟨enjoys good ~⟩ **2 a** : flourishing condition : WELL-BEING ⟨defending the ~ of the beloved oceans —Peter Wilkinson⟩ **b** : general condition or state ⟨poor economic ~⟩ **3** : a toast to someone's health or prosperity

health food *n* (1882) : a food promoted as highly conducive to health

health·ful \'helth-fəl *also* 'helth-\ *adj* (14c) **1** : beneficial to health of body or mind **2** : HEALTHY ⟨he felt incapable of looking into the girl's pretty, ~ face —Saul Bellow⟩ — **health·ful·ness** *n*
  syn HEALTHFUL, WHOLESOME, SALUBRIOUS, SALUTARY mean favorable to the health of mind or body. HEALTHFUL implies a positive contribution to a healthy condition ⟨a *healthful* diet⟩. WHOLESOME applies to what benefits, builds up, or sustains physically, mentally, or spiritually ⟨*wholesome* foods⟩ ⟨the movie is *wholesome* family entertainment⟩. SALUBRIOUS applies chiefly to the helpful effects of climate or air ⟨cool and *salubrious* weather⟩. SALUTARY describes something corrective or beneficially effective, even though it may in itself be unpleasant ⟨a *salutary* warning that resulted in increased production⟩.

health insurance *n* (1901) : insurance against loss through illness of the insured; *esp* : insurance providing compensation for medical expenses

health maintenance organization *n* (1973) : HMO

health spa *n* (1960) : a commercial establishment (as a resort) providing facilities devoted to health and fitness

healthy \'hel-thē *also* 'helt-\ *adj* **health·i·er; -est** (1552) **1** : enjoying health and vigor of body, mind, or spirit : WELL **2** : evincing health ⟨a ~ complexion⟩ **3** : conducive to health ⟨walk three miles every day . . . a beastly bore, but ~ —G. S. Patton⟩ **4 a** : PROSPEROUS, FLOURISHING **b** : not small or feeble : CONSIDERABLE — **health·i·ly** \-thə-lē\ *adv* — **health·i·ness** \-thē-nəs\ *n*
  syn HEALTHY, SOUND, WHOLESOME, ROBUST, HALE, WELL mean enjoying or indicative of good health. HEALTHY implies full strength and vigor as well as freedom from signs of disease ⟨a *healthy* family⟩. SOUND emphasizes the absence of disease, weakness, or malfunction ⟨a *sound* heart⟩. WHOLESOME implies appearance and behavior indicating soundness and balance ⟨a face with a *wholesome* glow⟩. ROBUST implies the opposite of all that is delicate or sickly ⟨a lively, *robust* little boy⟩. HALE applies particularly to robustness in old age ⟨still *hale* at the age of eighty⟩. WELL implies merely freedom from disease or illness ⟨she has never been a *well* person⟩.

¹**heap** \'hēp\ *n* [ME *heep*, fr. OE *hēap*; akin to OHG *houf* heap] (bef. 12c) **1** : a collection of things thrown one on another : PILE **2** : a great number or large quantity : LOT

²**heap** *vt* (bef. 12c) **1 a** : to throw or lay in a heap : pile or collect in great quantity ⟨his sole object was to ~ up riches⟩ **b** : to form or round into a heap ⟨~ed the dirt into a mound⟩ **c** : to form a heap on : load heavily ⟨~ the plates with food⟩ **2** : to accord or bestow lavishly or in large quantities ⟨~ed honors upon them⟩

hear \'hir\ *vb* **heard** \'hərd\; **hear·ing** \'hir-in\ [ME *heren*, fr. OE *hieran*; akin to OHG *hōren* to hear, and prob. to L *cavēre* to be on guard, Gk *akouein* to hear] *vt* (bef. 12c) **1** : to perceive or apprehend by the ear **2** : to gain knowledge of by hearing **3 a** : to listen to with attention : HEED **b** : ATTEND ⟨~ mass⟩ **4 a** : to give a legal hearing to **b** : to take testimony from ⟨~ witnesses⟩ ~ *vi* **1** : to have the capacity of apprehending sound **2 a** : to gain information : LEARN **b** : to receive communication ⟨haven't *heard* from her lately⟩ **3** : to entertain the idea — used in the negative ⟨wouldn't ~ of it⟩ **4** — often used in the expression *Hear! Hear!* to express approval (as during a speech) — **hear·er** \'hir-ər\ *n*

hear·ing *n* (13c) **1 a** : the process, function, or power of perceiving sound; *specif* : the special sense by which noises and tones are received as stimuli **b** : EARSHOT **2 a** : opportunity to be heard, to present one's side of a case, or to be generally known or appreciated **b** (1) : a listening to arguments (2) : a preliminary examination in criminal procedure **c** : a session (as of a legislative committee) in which testimony is taken from witnesses **3** *chiefly dial* : a piece of news

hearing aid *n* (1922) : an electronic device usu. worn by a person for amplifying sound before it reaches the receptor organs

hearing dog *n* (1952) : a dog trained to alert its deaf or hearing-impaired owner to sounds (as of a doorbell, alarm, or telephone) — called also *hearing ear dog*

hear·ken \'här-kən\ *vb* **hear·kened; hear·ken·ing** \'härk-nin, 'här-kə-\ [ME *herknen*, fr. OE *heorcnian*; akin to OHG *hōrechen* to listen, OE *hieran* to hear] *vi* (bef. 12c) **1** : LISTEN **2** : to give respectful attention ~ *vt*, *archaic* : to give heed to : HEAR

hearken back *vi* (1933) : HARK BACK

hear·say \'hir-,sā\ *n* (ca. 1532) : RUMOR

hearsay evidence *n* (1753) : evidence based not on a witness's personal knowledge but on another's statement not made under oath

¹**hearse** \'hərs\ *n* [ME *herse*, fr. MF *herce* harrow, frame for holding candles, fr. L *hirpic-, hirpex* harrow] (14c) **1 a** : an elaborate framework erected over a coffin or tomb to which memorial verses or epitaphs are attached **b** : a triangular candelabrum for 15 candles used esp. at Tenebrae **2 a** *archaic* : COFFIN **b** *obs* : BIER **2 3** : a vehicle for conveying the dead to the grave

²**hearse** *vt* **hearsed; hears·ing** (1592) **1 a** *archaic* : to place on or in a hearse **b** : to convey in a hearse **2** : BURY

¹**heart** \'härt\ *n* [ME *hert*, fr. OE *heorte*; akin to OHG *herza* heart, L *cord-, cor*, Gk *kardia*] (bef. 12c) **1 a** : a hollow muscular organ of vertebrate animals that by its rhythmic contraction acts as a force pump maintaining the circulation of the blood **b** : a structure in an invertebrate animal functionally analogous to the vertebrate heart **c** : BREAST, BOSOM **d** : something resembling a heart in shape; *specif* : a

\ə\ abut \ᵊ\ kitten, F table \ər\ further \a\ ash \ā\ ace \ä\ mop, mar \aů\ out \ch\ chin \e\ bet \ē\ easy \g\ go \i\ hit \ī\ ice \j\ job \ŋ\ sing \ō\ go \ȯ\ law \ȯi\ boy \th\ thin \t͟h\ the \ü\ loot \ů\ foot \y\ yet \zh\ vision \ȧ, k̲, ⁿ, œ, œ̄, ue, ūe, ᵊ\ see Guide to Pronunciation stylized representation of a heart **2 a** : a playing card marked with a stylized figure of a red heart **b** *pl* : the suit comprising cards marked with hearts **c** *pl but sing or pl in constr* : a game in which the object is to avoid taking tricks containing hearts **3 a** : PERSONALITY, DISPOSITION ⟨a cold ∼⟩ **b** *obs* : INTELLECT **4** : the emotional or moral as distinguished from the intellectual nature: as **a** : generous disposition : COMPASSION ⟨a leader with ∼⟩ **b** : LOVE, AFFECTIONS ⟨won her ∼⟩ **c** : COURAGE, ARDOR ⟨never lost ∼⟩ **5** : one's innermost character, feelings, or inclinations ⟨knew it in his ∼⟩ ⟨a man after my own ∼⟩ **6 a** : the central or innermost part : CENTER **b** : the essential or most vital part of something **c** : the younger central compact part of a leafy rosette (as a head of lettuce) — **at heart** : in essence : BASICALLY, ESSENTIALLY — **by heart** : by rote or from memory — **to heart** : with deep concern

heart 1a: *1* aorta, *2* pulmonary artery, *3* left atrium, *4* left ventricle, *5* right ventricle, *6* right atrium

²heart *vt* (bef. 12c) **1** *archaic* : HEARTEN **2** *archaic* : to fix in the heart
heart·ache \'härt-ˌāk\ *n* (1602) : anguish of mind : SORROW
heart attack *n* (1928) : an acute episode of heart disease (as myocardial infarction) due to insufficient blood supply to the heart muscle esp. when caused by a coronary thrombosis or a coronary occlusion
heart·beat \'härt-ˌbēt\ *n* (1850) **1** : one complete pulsation of the heart **2** : the vital center or driving impulse
heart block *n* (1903) : incoordination of the heartbeat in which the atria and ventricles beat independently and which is marked by decreased cardiac output
heart·break \'härt-ˌbrāk\ *n* (14c) : crushing grief
heart·break·er \-ˌbrā-kər\ *n* (1863) : one that causes heartbreak
heart·break·ing \-ˌbrā-kiŋ\ *adj* (1591) **1 a** : causing intense sorrow or distress **b** : extremely trying or difficult **2** : producing an intense emotional reaction or response ⟨∼ beauty⟩ — **heart·break·ing·ly** \-kiŋ-lē\ *adv*
heart·bro·ken \-ˌbrō-kən\ *adj* (ca. 1586) : overcome by sorrow
heart·burn \-ˌbərn\ *n* (1597) : a burning discomfort behind the lower part of the sternum usu. related to spasm of the lower end of the esophagus or of the upper part of the stomach
heart·burn·ing \-ˌbər-niŋ\ *n* (1513) : intense or rancorous jealousy or resentment
heart disease *n* (1864) : an abnormal organic condition of the heart or of the heart and circulation
heart·ed \'här-təd\ *adj* (13c) **1** : having a heart esp. of a specified kind — usu. used in combination ⟨a faint*hearted* leader⟩ ⟨a light*hearted* wanderer⟩ **2** : seated in the heart
heart·en \'här-t⁰n\ *vt* **heart·ened; heart·en·ing** \'härt-niŋ, 'här-t⁰n-iŋ\ (1526) : to give heart to : CHEER *syn* see ENCOURAGE — **heart·en·ing·ly** \-niŋ-lē, -t⁰n-iŋ-\ *adv*
heart failure *n* (1894) **1** : a condition in which the heart is unable to pump blood at an adequate rate or in adequate volume **2** : cessation of heartbeat : DEATH
heart·felt \'härt-ˌfelt\ *adj* (1734) : deeply felt : EARNEST *syn* see SINCERE
heart—free \-ˌfrē\ *adj* (1748) : not in love
hearth \'härth\ *n* [ME *herth*, fr. OE *heorth*; akin to OHG *herd* hearth, and prob. to Skt *kūdayāti* he scorches] (bef. 12c) **1 a** : a brick, stone, or cement area in front of a fireplace **b** : the floor of a fireplace; *also* : FIREPLACE **c** : the lowest section of a furnace; *esp* : the section of a furnace on which the ore or metal is exposed to the flame or heat **2** : HOME **3** : a vital or creative center ⟨the central ∼ of occidental civilization —A. L. Kroeber⟩
hearth·stone \-ˌstōn\ *n* (14c) **1** : stone forming a hearth **2** : HOME
heart·i·ly \'härt-⁰l-ē\ *adv* (14c) **1** : in a hearty manner **2 a** : with all sincerity : WHOLEHEARTEDLY **b** : with zest or gusto **3** : WHOLLY, THOROUGHLY ⟨∼ sick of all this talk⟩
heart·land \'härt-ˌland\ *n* (1904) : a central area: as **a** : a central land area (as northern Eurasia) having strategic advantages **b** : a central geographical region esp. of the U.S. in which mainstream or traditional values predominate
heart·less \-ləs\ *adj* (14c) **1** *archaic* : SPIRITLESS **2** : lacking feeling : CRUEL — **heart·less·ly** *adv* — **heart·less·ness** *n*
heart–lung machine *n* (1953) : a mechanical pump that maintains circulation during heart surgery by shunting blood away from the heart, oxygenating it, and returning it to the body
heart·rend·ing \'härt-ˌren-diŋ\ *adj* (1594) : HEARTBREAKING 1a — **heart·rend·ing·ly** \-diŋ-lē\ *adv*
hearts·ease \'härts-ˌēz\ *n* (15c) **1** : peace of mind : TRANQUILLITY **2** : any of various violas; *esp* : JOHNNY-JUMP-UP
heart·sick \'härt-ˌsik\ *adj* (1526) : very despondent : DEPRESSED — **heart·sick·ness** *n*
heart·some \'hert-səm\ *adj* (1596) *chiefly Scot* : giving spirit or vigor : ANIMATING, ENLIVENING — **heart·some·ly** *adv, chiefly Scot*
heart·sore \'härt-ˌsōr, -ˌsór\ *adj* (1591) : HEARTSICK
heart·string \-ˌstriŋ\ *n* (15c) **1** *obs* : a nerve once believed to sustain the heart **2** : the deepest emotions or affections ⟨pulled at his ∼s⟩
heart·throb \-ˌthräb\ *n* (1839) **1** : the throb of a heart **2 a** : sentimental emotion : PASSION **b** : SWEETHEART
¹heart—to—heart \'härt-tə-'härt\ *adj* (1867) : SINCERE, FRANK ⟨a ∼ talk⟩
²heart—to—heart *n* (1910) : a frank, serious, and often intimate conversation
heart·warm·ing \'härt-ˌwor-miŋ\ *adj* (1899) : inspiring sympathetic feeling : CHEERING — **heart·warm·er** *n*
heart—whole \-ˌhōl\ *adj* (1600) **1** : HEART-FREE **2** : SINCERE, GENUINE
heart·wood \-ˌwud\ *n* (1810) : the older harder nonliving central wood of trees that is usu. darker, denser, less permeable, and more durable than the surrounding sapwood

heart·worm \-ˌwərm\ *n* (1888) : a filarial worm (*Dirofilaria immitis*) that is a parasite esp. in the right heart of dogs and is transmitted by mosquitoes; *also* : infestation or disease caused by the heartworm
¹hearty \'här-tē\ *adj* **heart·i·er; -est** (14c) **1 a** : giving unqualified support ⟨a ∼ endorsement⟩ **b** : enthusiastically or exuberantly cordial : JOVIAL **c** : expressed unrestrainedly **2 a** : exhibiting vigorous good health **b** (1) : having a good appetite (2) : abundant, rich, or flavorful enough to satisfy the appetite **3** : VIGOROUS, VEHEMENT ⟨a ∼ pull⟩ *syn* see SINCERE — **heart·i·ness** *n*
²hearty *n, pl* **heart·ies** (1803) : a hearty fellow; *also* : SAILOR
¹heat \'hēt\ *vb* [ME *heten*, fr. OE *hætan*; akin to OE *hāt* hot] *vi* (bef. 12c) **1** : to become warm or hot **2** : to start to spoil from heat — ∼ *vt* **1** : to make warm or hot **2** : EXCITE — **heat·able** \'hē-tə-bəl\ *adj*
²heat *n* [ME *hete*, fr. OE *hǣte, hǣtu*; akin to OE *hāt* hot] (bef. 12c) **1 a** (1) : a condition of being hot : WARMTH (2) : a marked or notable degree of hotness **b** : pathological excessive bodily temperature **c** : a hot place or situation **d** (1) : a period of heat (2) : a single complete operation of heating; *also* : the quantity of material so heated **e** (1) : added energy that causes substances to rise in temperature, fuse, evaporate, expand, or undergo any of various other related changes, that flows to a body by contact with or radiation from bodies at higher temperatures, and that can be produced in a body (as by compression) (2) : the energy associated with the random motions of the molecules, atoms, or smaller structural units of which matter is composed **f** : appearance, condition, or color of a body as indicating its temperature **2 a** : intensity of feeling or reaction : PASSION **b** : the height or stress of an action or condition ⟨in the ∼ of battle⟩ **c** : sexual excitement esp. in a female mammal; *specif* : ESTRUS **3** : a single continuous effort: as **a** : a single round of a contest (as a race) having two or more rounds for each contestant **b** : one of several preliminary contests held to eliminate less competent contenders **4** : pungency of flavor **5** *slang* (1) : the intensification of law-enforcement activity or investigation (2) : POLICE **b** : PRESSURE, COERCION **c** : ABUSE, CRITICISM ⟨took a lot of ∼⟩ **6** : SMOKE **8** — **heat·less** \'hēt-ləs\ *adj* — **heat·proof** \-'prüf\ *adj*
heat cramps *n pl* (1938) : a condition that is marked by sudden development of cramps in skeletal muscles and that results from prolonged work in high temperatures accompanied by profuse perspiration with loss of sodium chloride from the body
heat·ed \'hē-təd\ *adj* (1886) : marked by anger ⟨a ∼ argument⟩ — **heat·ed·ly** *adv*
heat engine *n* (ca. 1895) : a mechanism (as an internal-combustion engine) for converting heat energy into mechanical or electrical energy
heat·er \'hē-tər\ *n* (15c) **1** : one that heats; *esp* : a device that imparts heat or holds something to be heated **2** : FASTBALL
heat exchanger *n* (1902) : a device (as an automobile radiator) for transferring heat from one fluid to another without allowing them to mix
heat exhaustion *n* (1939) : a condition marked by weakness, nausea, dizziness, and profuse sweating that results from physical exertion in a hot environment — called also *heat prostration*; compare HEATSTROKE
heath \'hēth\ *n* [ME *heth*, fr. OE *hǣth*; akin to OHG *heida* heather, OW *coit* forest] (bef. 12c) **1 a** : a tract of wasteland **b** : an extensive area of rather level open uncultivated land usu. with poor coarse soil, inferior drainage, and a surface rich in peat or peaty humus **2 a** : any of a family (Ericaceae, the heath family) of shrubby dicotyledonous and often evergreen plants that thrive on open barren usu. acid and ill-drained soil; *esp* : an evergreen subshrub of either of two genera (*Erica* and *Calluna*) with whorls of needlelike leaves and clusters of small flowers **b** : any of various plants that resemble true heaths — **heath·less** \-ləs\ *adj* — **heath·like** \-ˌlīk\ *adj* — **heathy** \'hē-thē\ *adj*
¹hea·then \'hē-thən\ *adj* [ME *hethen*, fr. OE *hǣthen*; akin to OHG *heidan* heathen, and prob. to OE *hǣth* heath] (bef. 12c) **1** : of or relating to heathens, their religions, or their customs **2** : STRANGE, UNCIVILIZED
²heathen *n, pl* **heathens** or **heathen** (bef. 12c) **1** : an unconverted member of a people or nation that does not acknowledge the God of the Bible **2** : an uncivilized or irreligious person — **hea·then·dom** \-dəm\ *n* — **hea·then·ism** \-thə-ˌni-zəm\ *n* — **hea·then·ize** \-thə-ˌnīz\ *vt*
hea·then·ish \'hē-thə-nish\ *adj* (1593) : resembling or characteristic of heathens — **hea·then·ish·ly** *adv*
¹heath·er \'he-thər\ *n* [ME (northern) *hather*] (14c) : HEATH 2a; *esp* : a common Eurasian heath (*Calluna vulgaris*) of northern and alpine regions that has small crowded sessile leaves and racemes of tiny usu. purplish pink flowers and is naturalized in the northeastern U.S.
²heather *adj* (1615) : HEATHERY
heath·ery \'heth-rē, 'he-thə-\ *adj* (1535) **1** : of, relating to, or resembling heather **2** : having flecks of various colors ⟨a soft ∼ tweed⟩
heath hen *n* (1644) : a now extinct grouse (*Tympanuchus cupido cupido*) of the northeastern U.S. — compare PRAIRIE CHICKEN
heath·land \'hēth-ˌland\ *n* (1819) : HEATH 1
heat lightning *n* (1834) : vivid and extensive flashes of electric light without thunder seen near the horizon esp. at the close of a hot day and ascribed to far-off lightning reflected by high clouds
heat prostration *n* (1938) : HEAT EXHAUSTION
heat pump *n* (1894) : an apparatus for heating or cooling a building by transferring heat by mechanical means from or to a reservoir (as the ground, water, or air) outside the building
heat rash *n* (1887) : PRICKLY HEAT
heat shield *n* (1962) : a barrier of ablative material to protect a space capsule from heat on its entry into an atmosphere
heat sink *n* (1936) : a substance or device for the absorption or dissipation of unwanted heat (as from a process or an electronic device)
heat·stroke \'hēt-ˌstrōk\ *n* (1874) : a condition marked esp. by cessation of sweating, extremely high body temperature, and collapse that results from prolonged exposure to high temperature — compare HEAT EXHAUSTION
heat—treat \'hēt-ˌtrēt\ *vt* (1907) : to subject to heat; *esp* : to treat (as metals) by heating and cooling in a way that will produce desired properties — **heat treater** *n* — **heat treatment** *n*
heat wave *n* (1893) : a period of unusually hot weather
¹heave \'hēv\ *vb* **heaved** or **hove** \'hōv\; **heav·ing** [ME *heven*, fr. OE *hebban*; akin to OHG *hevan* to lift, L *capere* to take] *vt* (bef. 12c) **1** *obs*

: ELEVATE 2 : LIFT, RAISE 3 : THROW, CAST 4 a : to cause to swell or rise b : to displace (as a rock stratum) esp. by a fault 5 : to utter with obvious effort or with a deep breath 6 : HAUL, DRAW ~ vi 1 : LABOR, STRUGGLE 2 : RETCH 3 a : to rise and fall rhythmically b : PANT 4 a : PULL, PUSH b : to move a ship in a specified direction or manner c *past usu hove* : to move in an indicated way — used of a ship 5 : to rise or become thrown or raised up *syn* see LIFT — **heaver** *n* — **heave to** : to bring a ship to a stop

²**heave** *n* (ca. 1571) 1 a : an effort to heave or raise b : HURL, CAST 2 : an upward motion : RISING; *esp* : a rhythmical rising 3 : horizontal displacement esp. by the faulting of a rock 4 *pl but sing or pl in constr* : chronic pulmonary emphysema of the horse resulting in difficult expiration, heaving of the flanks, and a persistent cough

heave–ho \'hēv-'hō\ *n* [fr. *heave ho!,* interjection used when heaving on a rope] (1947) : DISMISSAL ⟨gave him the old ~⟩

heav·en \'he-vən\ *n* [ME *heven,* fr. OE *heofon*; akin to OHG *himil* heaven] (bef. 12c) 1 : the expanse of space that seems to be over the earth like a dome : FIRMAMENT — usu. used in pl. 2 *often cap* : the dwelling place of the Deity and the joyful abode of the blessed dead b : a spiritual state of everlasting communion with God 3 *cap* : GOD 1 4 : a place or condition of utmost happiness 5 *Christian Science* : a state of thought in which sin is absent and the harmony of divine Mind is manifest

heav·en·ly \-lē\ *adj* (bef. 12c) 1 : of or relating to heaven or the heavens : CELESTIAL ⟨the ~ choirs⟩ ⟨use a telescope to study the ~ bodies⟩ 2 a : suggesting the blessed state of heaven : BEATIFIC ⟨~ peace⟩ b : DELIGHTFUL — **heav·en·li·ness** *n*

heav·en–sent \-ˌsent\ *adj* (ca. 1649) : PROVIDENTIAL

heav·en·ward \-wərd\ *adv or adj* (13c) : toward heaven

heav·en·wards \-wərdz\ *adv* (1650) : HEAVENWARD

heavier–than–air *adj* (1903) : of greater weight than the air displaced

heavi·ly \'he-və-lē\ *adv* (bef. 12c) 1 : to a great degree : SEVERELY 2 : slowly and laboriously : DULLY 3 *archaic* : with sorrow : GRIEVOUSLY 4 : in a heavy manner

Heav·i·side layer \'he-vē-ˌsīd-\ *n* [Oliver *Heaviside*] (1912) : IONOSPHERE

¹**heavy** \'he-vē\ *adj* **heavi·er**; **-est** [ME *hevy,* fr. OE *hefig*; akin to OHG *hebic* heavy, OE *hebban* to lift — more at HEAVE] (bef. 12c) 1 a : having great weight; *also* : characterized by mass or weight ⟨how ~ is it?⟩ b : having a high specific gravity : having great weight in proportion to bulk c (1) *of an isotope* : having or being atoms of greater than normal mass for that element (2) *of a compound* : containing heavy isotopes 2 : hard to bear; *specif* : GRIEVOUS, AFFLICTIVE ⟨a ~ sorrow⟩ 3 : of weighty import : SERIOUS 4 : DEEP, PROFOUND 5 a : borne down by something oppressive : BURDENED b : PREGNANT; *esp* : approaching parturition 6 a : slow or dull from loss of vitality or resiliency : SLUGGISH b : lacking sparkle or vivacity : DRAB c : lacking mirth or gaiety : DOLEFUL d : characterized by declining prices 7 : dulled with weariness : DROWSY 8 : greater in quantity or quality than the average of its kind or class: as a : of unusually large size or amount ⟨a ~ turnout⟩ ⟨~ traffic⟩ b : of great force ⟨~ seas⟩ c : threatening to rain or snow d (1) : impeding motion (2) : full of clay and inclined to hold water e : coming as if from a depth : LOUD ⟨~ breathing⟩ f : THICK, COARSE g : OPPRESSIVE ⟨~ odor⟩ h : STEEP, ACUTE i : LABORIOUS, DIFFICULT ⟨~ going⟩ j : IMMODERATE ⟨a ~ smoker⟩ k : more powerful than usual for its kind ⟨~ cavalry⟩ ⟨~ cruiser⟩ l : of large capacity or output 9 a : very rich and hard to digest ⟨~ desserts⟩ b : not properly raised or leavened ⟨~ bread⟩ 10 : producing goods (as coal, steel, or chemicals) used in the production of other goods ⟨~ industry⟩ 11 a : having stress ⟨~ rhythm⟩ — used esp. of syllables in accentual verse b : being the strongest degree of stress in speech 12 : relating to theatrical parts of a grave or somber nature 13 : LONG 9 ⟨~ on ideas⟩ 14 : IMPORTANT, PROMINENT ⟨a ~ politician⟩ — **heavi·ness** *n*
syn HEAVY, WEIGHTY, PONDEROUS, CUMBROUS, CUMBERSOME mean having great weight. HEAVY implies that something has greater density or thickness than the average of its kind or class ⟨a *heavy* child for his age⟩. WEIGHTY suggests having actual and not just relative weight ⟨a load of *weighty* boxes⟩. PONDEROUS implies having great weight because of size and massiveness with resulting great inertia ⟨*ponderous* elephants in a circus parade⟩. CUMBROUS and CUMBERSOME imply heaviness and bulkiness that make for difficulty in grasping, moving, carrying, or manipulating ⟨wrestled with the *cumbrous* furniture⟩ ⟨early cameras were *cumbersome* and inconvenient⟩.

²**heavy** *adv* (bef. 12c) : in a heavy manner : HEAVILY

³**heavy** *n, pl* **heav·ies** (1897) 1 : HEAVYWEIGHT 2 2 a : a theatrical role of a dignified or somber character; *also* : an actor playing such a role b : VILLAIN 4 c : someone or something influential, serious, or important

heavy chain *n* (1964) : either of the two larger of the four polypeptide chains comprising antibodies — compare LIGHT CHAIN

heavy cream *n* (1930) : a cream that is markedly thick; *esp* : cream that by law contains not less than 36 percent butterfat

heavy–du·ty \'he-vē-'dü-tē, -'dyü-\ *adj* (1914) 1 : able or designed to withstand unusual strain 2 : INTENSIVE ⟨~ bargaining⟩

heavy–foot·ed \-'fu̇-təd\ *adj* (1625) : heavy and slow in movement

heavy–hand·ed \-'han-dəd\ *adj* (1647) 1 : CLUMSY 2 : OPPRESSIVE, HARSH — **heavy–hand·ed·ly** *adv* — **heavy–hand·ed·ness** *n*

heavy–heart·ed \-'här-təd\ *adj* (14c) : DESPONDENT, SADDENED — **heavy–heart·ed·ly** *adv* — **heavy–heart·ed·ness** *n*

heavy hitter *n* (1976) : BIG SHOT, HEAVY

heavy hydrogen *n* (1933) : DEUTERIUM

heavy metal *n* (1974) : energetic and highly amplified electronic rock music having a hard beat

heavy–set \ˌhe-vē-'set\ *adj* (1922) : stocky and compact and sometimes tending to stoutness in build

heavy water *n* (1933) 1 : the compound D_2O composed of deuterium and oxygen — called also *deuterium oxide* 2 : water enriched in deuterium

heavy·weight \'he-vē-ˌwāt\ *n* (1857) 1 : one that is above average in weight 2 : one in the usu. heaviest class of contestants: as a : a boxer in an unlimited weight division — compare LIGHT HEAVYWEIGHT b : a weight lifter weighing more than 198 pounds 3 : BIG SHOT, HEAVY

heb·do·mad \'heb-də-ˌmad\ *n* [L *hebdomad-, hebdomas,* fr. Gk, fr. *hebdomos* seventh, fr. *hepta* seven — more at SEVEN] (1545) 1 : a group of seven 2 : a period of seven days : WEEK

heb·dom·a·dal \heb-'dä-mə-d²l\ *adj* (1711) : WEEKLY — **heb·dom·a·dal·ly** \-d²l-ē\ *adv*

hebe \'hēb\ *n, often cap* [short for *Hebrew*] (1932) : JEW — usu. taken to be offensive

He·be \'hē-bē\ *n* [L, fr. Gk *Hēbē*] : the Greek goddess of youth and a cupbearer to the gods

he·be·phre·nia \ˌhē-bə-'frē-nē-ə, -'fre-nē-\ *n* [NL, irreg. fr. Gk *hēbētēs* young adult (fr. *hēbē* youth) + E *-phrenia*; fr. the childish behavior which is often found with it] (1883) : a form of schizophrenia characterized esp. by incoherence, delusions lacking an underlying theme, and affect that is flat, inappropriate, or silly — **he·be·phre·nic** \-'fre-nik, -'frē-nik\ *adj or n*

heb·e·tate \'he-bə-ˌtāt\ *vt* **-tat·ed; -tat·ing** [L *hebetatus,* pp. of *hebetare,* fr. *hebet-, hebes* dull] (1574) : to make dull or obtuse — **heb·e·ta·tion** \ˌhe-bə-'tā-shən\ *n*

heb·e·tude \'he-bə-ˌtüd, -ˌtyüd\ *n* [LL *hebetudo,* fr. *hebēre* to be dull; akin to L *hebes* dull] (ca. 1621) : LETHARGY, DULLNESS — **heb·e·tu·di·nous** \ˌhe-bə-'tü-d²n-əs, -'tyü-\ *adj*

He·bra·ic \hi-'brā-ik\ *adj* [ME *Ebrayke,* fr. LL *Hebraicus,* fr. Gk *Hebraikos,* fr. *Hebraios*] (14c) : of, relating to, or characteristic of the Hebrews or their language or culture — **He·bra·i·cal·ly** \-'brā-ə-k(ə-)lē\ *adv*

He·bra·ism \'hē-(ˌ)brā-ˌi-zəm\ *n* (1570) 1 : a characteristic feature of Hebrew occurring in another language 2 : the thought, spirit, or practice characteristic of the Hebrews 3 : a moral theory or emphasis attributed to the Hebrews

He·bra·ist \-ˌbrā-ist\ *n* (ca. 1755) : a specialist in Hebrew and Hebraic studies

He·bra·is·tic \ˌhē-brā-'is-tik\ *adj* (1690) 1 : marked by Hebraisms 2 : HEBRAIC

he·bra·ize \'hē-brā-ˌīz\ *vb* **-ized; -iz·ing** *often cap, vi* (1645) : to use Hebraisms ~ *vt* : to make Hebraic in character or form — **he·bra·iza·tion** \ˌhē-ˌbrā-ə-'zā-shən\ *n, often cap*

He·brew \'hē-(ˌ)brü\ *n* [ME *Ebreu,* fr. OF, fr. LL *Hebraeus,* fr. L, adj., fr. Gk *Hebraios,* fr. Aram *'Ebrai*] (13c) 1 a : the Semitic language of the ancient Hebrews b : any of various later forms of this language 2 : a member of or descendant from one of a group of northern Semitic peoples including the Israelites; *esp* : ISRAELITE — **Hebrew** *adj*

He·brews \'hē-(ˌ)brüz\ *n pl but sing in constr* : a theological treatise addressed to early Christians and included as a book in the New Testament — see BIBLE table

Hec·ate \'he-kə-tē, 'he-kət\ *n* [L, fr. Gk *Hekatē*] : a Greek goddess associated esp. with the underworld, night, and witchcraft

hec·a·tomb \'he-kə-ˌtōm\ *n* [L *hecatombe,* fr. Gk *hekatombē,* fr. *hekaton* hundred + *-bē*; akin to Gk *bous* cow — more at HUNDRED, COW] (ca. 1592) 1 : an ancient Greek and Roman sacrifice of 100 oxen or cattle 2 : the sacrifice or slaughter of many victims

heck \'hek\ *n* [euphemism] (1887) : HELL ⟨a ~ of a lot of money⟩

heck·le \'he-kəl\ *vt* **heck·led; heck·ling** \-k(ə-)liŋ\ [ME *hekelen* to dress flax, scratch, fr. *heckele* hackle; akin to OHG *hāko* hook — more at HOOK] (ca. 1825) : to harass and try to disconcert with questions, challenges, or gibes : BADGER ~ *vi* : to heckle a speaker — **heck·ler** \-k(ə-)lər\ *n*

hect- or **hecto-** *comb form* [F, irreg. fr. Gk *hekaton*] : hundred ⟨*hectare*⟩

hect·are \'hek-ˌtar, -ˌter, -ˌtär\ *n* [F, fr. *hect-* + *are* ²are] (1810) — see METRIC SYSTEM table

hec·tic \'hek-tik\ *adj* [ME *etyk,* fr. MF *etique,* fr. LL *hecticus,* fr. Gk *hektikos* habitual, consumptive, fr. *echein* to have — more at SCHEME] (14c) 1 : of, relating to, or being a fluctuating but persistent fever (as in tuberculosis) 2 : having a hectic fever 3 : RED, FLUSHED 4 : characterized by activity, excitement, or confusion ⟨the ~ days before Christmas⟩ — **hec·ti·cal·ly** \-ti-k(ə-)lē\ *adv*

hec·to·gram \'hek-tə-ˌgram\ *n* [F *hectogramme,* fr. *hect-* + *gramme* gram] (1810) — see METRIC SYSTEM table

hec·to·graph \-ˌgraf\ *n* [G *Hektograph,* fr. *hekto-* hect- + *-graph* -graph] (1880) : a machine for making copies of a writing or drawing produced on a gelatin surface — **hectograph** *vt*

hec·to·li·tre \'hek-tə-ˌlē-tər\ *n* [F *hectolitre,* fr. *hect-* + *litre* liter] (1810) — see METRIC SYSTEM table

hec·to·me·ter \'hek-tə-ˌmē-tər, hek-'tä-mə-tər\ *n* [F *hectomètre,* fr. *hect-* + *mètre* meter] (1810) — see METRIC SYSTEM table

¹**hec·tor** \'hek-tər\ *n* [L, fr. Gk *Hektōr*] 1 *cap* : a son of Priam, husband of Andromache, and Trojan champion slain by Achilles 2 : BULLY, BRAGGART

²**hector** *vb* **hec·tored; hec·tor·ing** \-t(ə-)riŋ\ *vi* (1660) 1 : to play the bully : SWAGGER ~ *vt* : to intimidate or harass by bluster or personal pressure *syn* see BAIT — **hec·tor·ing·ly** \-t(ə-)riŋ-lē\ *adv*

Hec·u·ba \'he-kyə-bə\ *n* [L, fr. Gk *Hekabē*] : the wife of Priam in Homer's *Iliad*

he'd \'hēd, ēd\ (ca. 1600) : he had : he would

hed·dle \'he-d²l\ *n* [prob. alter. of ME *helde,* fr. OE *hefeld*; akin to ON *hafald* heddle, OE *hebban* to lift — more at HEAVE] (1513) : one of the sets of parallel cords or wires that with their mounting compose the harness used to guide warp threads in a loom

he·der \'kä-dər, 'ke-\ *n* [Yiddish *kheyder,* fr. Heb *ḥedher* room] (1882) : an elementary Jewish school in which children are taught to read the Torah and other books in Hebrew

¹**hedge** \'hej\ *n* [ME *hegge,* fr. OE *hecg*; akin to OE *haga* hedge, hawthorn] (bef. 12c) 1 a : a fence or boundary formed by a dense row of shrubs or low trees b : BARRIER, LIMIT 2 : a means of protection or defense (as against financial loss) 3 : a calculatedly noncommittal or evasive statement

²**hedge** *vb* **hedged; hedg·ing** *vt* (14c) 1 : to enclose or protect with or as if with a hedge : ENCIRCLE 2 : to hem in or obstruct with or as if

\ə\ abut \ᵊ\ kitten, F table \ər\ further \a\ ash \ā\ ace \ä\ mop, mar \au̇\ out \ch\ chin \e\ bet \ē\ easy \g\ go \i\ hit \ī\ ice \j\ job \ŋ\ sing \ō\ go \ȯ\ law \ȯi\ boy \th\ thin \t̲h̲\ the \ü\ loot \u̇\ foot \y\ yet \zh\ vision \å, ḵ, ⁿ, œ, œ̄, ᵫ, ᵬ, ᵎ\ see Guide to Pronunciation

with a barrier : HINDER ⟨*hedged* about by special regulations and statutes —Sandi Rosenbloom⟩ **3** : to protect oneself from losing or failing by a counterbalancing action ⟨~ a bet⟩ ~ *vi* **1** : to plant, form, or trim a hedge **2** : to evade the risk of commitment esp. by leaving open a way of retreat : TRIM **3** : to protect oneself financially: as **a** : to buy or sell commodity futures as a protection against loss due to price fluctuation **b** : to minimize the risk of a bet — **hedg·er** *n* — **hedg·ing·ly** \'he-jiŋ-lē\ *adv*
³**hedge** *adj* (14c) **1** : of, relating to, or designed for a hedge **2** : born, living, or made near or as if near hedges : ROADSIDE **3** : INFERIOR 3
hedge fund *n* (1967) : an investing group usu. in the form of a limited partnership that employs speculative techniques in the hope of obtaining large capital gains
hedge·hog \'hej-,hȯg, -,häg\ *n* (15c) **1 a** : any of a subfamily (Erinaceinae) of Old World nocturnal insectivores that have both hair and spines which they present outwardly by rolling themselves up when threatened **b** : any of several spiny mammals (as a porcupine) **2 a** : a military defensive obstacle (as of barbed wire) **b** : a well-fortified military stronghold

hedgehog 1a

hedge·hop \-,häp\ *vi* [back-formation fr. *hedgehopper*] (1926) : to fly an airplane close to the ground and rise over obstacles as they appear — **hedge·hop·per** *n*
hedge·pig \-,pig\ *n* (1605) : HEDGEHOG
hedge·row \-,rō\ *n* (bef. 12c) : a row of shrubs or trees enclosing or separating fields
he·don·ic \hi-'dä-nik\ *adj* (1656) **1** : of, relating to, or characterized by pleasure **2** : of, relating to, or characterized by hedonism — **he·don·i·cal·ly** \-ni-k(ə-)lē\ *adv*
he·do·nism \'hē-d²n-,i-zəm\ *n* [Gk *hēdonē* pleasure; akin to Gk *hēdys* sweet — more at SWEET] (1856) **1** : the doctrine that pleasure or happiness is the sole or chief good in life **2** : a way of life based on or suggesting the principles of hedonism — **he·do·nist** \-d²n-ist\ *n* — **he·do·nis·tic** \,hē-d²n-'is-tik\ *adj* — **he·do·nis·ti·cal·ly** \-ti-k(ə-)lē\ *adv*
-he·dral \'hē-drəl\ *adj comb form* [NL *-hedron*] : having (such) a surface or (such or so many) surfaces ⟨di*hedral*⟩
-he·dron \'hē-drən\ *n comb form, pl* **-hedrons** *or* **-he·dra** \-drə\ [NL, fr. Gk *-edron*, fr. *hedra* seat — more at SIT] : crystal or geometrical figure having a (specified) form or number of surfaces ⟨penta*hedron*⟩ ⟨trapezo*hedron*⟩
hee·bie-jee·bies \,hē-bē-'jē-bēz\ *n pl* [coined by Billy DeBeck †1942 Am. cartoonist] (1923) : JITTERS, CREEPS
¹**heed** \'hēd\ *vb* [ME, fr. OE *hēdan*; akin to OHG *huota* guard, OE *hōd* hood] *vi* (bef. 12c) : to pay attention ~ *vt* : to give consideration or attention to : MIND ⟨~ what he says⟩ ⟨~ the call⟩
²**heed** *n* (14c) : ATTENTION, NOTICE
heed·ful \'hēd-fəl\ *adj* (1548) : taking heed : ATTENTIVE ⟨~ of what they were doing⟩ — **heed·ful·ly** \-fə-lē\ *adv* — **heed·ful·ness** *n*
heed·less \-ləs\ *adj* (1579) : not taking heed : INCONSIDERATE, THOUGHTLESS ⟨~ follies of unbridled youth —John DeBruyn⟩ — **heed·less·ly** *adv* — **heed·less·ness** *n*
hee–haw \'hē-,hȯ, -'hȯ\ *n* [imit.] (1815) **1** : the bray of a donkey **2** : a loud rude laugh : GUFFAW — **hee–haw** *vi*
¹**heel** \'hē(ə)l\ *n* [ME, fr. OE *hēla*; akin to ON *hæll* heel, OE *hōh* — more at HOCK] (bef. 12c) **1 a** : the back of the human foot below the ankle and behind the arch **b** : the part of the hind limb of other vertebrates that is homologous with the human heel **2** : an anatomical structure suggestive of the human heel; *esp* : the part of the palm of the hand nearest the wrist **3** : one of the crusty ends of a loaf of bread **4 a** : the part (as of a shoe) that covers the human heel **b** : a solid attachment of a shoe or boot forming the back of the sole under the heel of the foot **5** : a rear, low, or bottom part: as **a** : the after end of a ship's keel or the lower end of a mast **b** : the base of a tuber or cutting of a plant used for propagation **c** : the base of a ladder **6** : a contemptible person — **heel·less** \'hē(ə)l-ləs\ *adj* — **by the heels** : in a tight grip — **down at heel** *or* **down at the heel** : in or into a rundown or shabby condition — **on the heels of** : immediately following — **to heel 1** : close behind **2** : into agreement or line — **under heel** : under control or subjection
²**heel** *vt* (1605) **1 a** : to furnish with a heel **b** : to supply esp. with money **2 a** : to exert pressure on, propel, or strike with the heel ⟨~*ed* her horse⟩ **b** : to urge (as a lagging animal) by following closely or by nipping at the heels ⟨dogs ~*ing* cattle⟩ ~ *vi* : to move along at someone's heels
³**heel** *vb* [alter. of ME *heelden*, fr. OE *hieldan*; akin to OHG *hald* inclined, Lith *šalis* side, region] *vi* (1575) : to lean to one side : TIP; *esp, of a boat or ship* : to lean temporarily (as from the action of wind or waves) — compare LIST ~ *vt* : to cause (a boat) to heel
⁴**heel** *n* (1760) : a tilt (as of a boat) to one side; *also* : the extent of such a tilt
heel–and–toe \,hē-lən-'tō\ *adj* (1827) : marked by a stride in which the heel of one foot touches the ground before the toe of the other foot leaves it ⟨~ walking⟩
heel·ball \'hē(ə)l-,bȯl\ *n* (1822) : a composition of wax and lampblack used by shoemakers for polishing and by antiquarians for making rubbings of inscriptions
heel·er \'hē-lər\ *n* (1665) **1 a** : one that heels **b** : AUSTRALIAN CATTLE DOG **2 a** : a henchman of a local political boss **b** : a worker for a local party organization; *esp* : WARD HEELER
heel fly *n* (1878) : CATTLE GRUB
heel·piece \'hē(ə)l-,pēs\ *n* (1709) : a piece designed for or forming the heel (as of a shoe)
heel·tap \-,tap\ *n* (1780) : a small quantity of alcoholic beverage remaining (as in a glass after drinking)
¹**heft** \'heft\ *n* [fr. *heave*, after such pairs as *weave* : *weft*] (15c) **1 a** : WEIGHT, HEAVINESS **b** : IMPORTANCE, INFLUENCE **2** *archaic* : the greater part of something : BULK
²**heft** *vt* (1661) **1** : to heave up : HOIST **2** : to test the weight of by lifting ⟨~*ing* the rod ... to get the feel of it —*Consumer Reports*⟩

hefty \'hef-tē\ *adj* **heft·i·er; -est** (1867) **1** : quite heavy **2** : marked by bigness, bulk, and usu. strength ⟨a ~ football player⟩ **b** : POWERFUL, MIGHTY **c** : impressively large : SUBSTANTIAL ⟨~ portions⟩ — **heft·i·ly** \-tə-lē\ *adv* — **heft·i·ness** \-tē-nəs\ *n*
he·gari \hi-'gar-ē, -'gar-ə, -'ger-; 'hī-,gir\ *n* [Ar dial. (Sudan) *hegirī*] (1919) : any of several Sudanese grain sorghums having chalky white seeds including one grown in the southwestern U.S.
¹**He·ge·li·an** \hā-'gā-lē-ən, hi-\ *adj* (1838) : of, relating to, or characteristic of Hegel, his philosophy, or his dialectic method
²**Hegelian** *n* (1843) : a follower of Hegel : an adherent of Hegelianism
He·ge·li·an·ism \-lē-ə-,ni-zəm\ *n* (1846) : the philosophy of Hegel that places ultimate reality in ideas rather than in things and that uses dialectic to comprehend an absolute idea behind phenomena
he·ge·mo·ny \hi-'je-mə-nē, -'ge-; 'he-jə-,mō-nē\ *n* [Gk *hēgemonia*, fr. *hēgemōn* leader, fr. *hēgeisthai* to lead — more at SEEK] (1567) : preponderant influence or authority over others : DOMINATION — **heg·e·mon·ic** \,he-jə-'mä-nik, ,he-gə-\ *adj*
he·gi·ra *also* **he·ji·ra** \hi-'jī-rə, 'he-jə-rə\ *n* [the *Hegira*, flight of Muhammad from Mecca in A.D. 622, fr. ML, fr. Ar *hijrah*, lit., flight] (1753) : a journey esp. when undertaken to escape from a dangerous or undesirable situation : EXODUS
Hei·del·berg man \'hī-d²l-,bərg-, -,berg-\ *n* [*Heidelberg*, Germany] (1920) : an early Pleistocene man known from a massive fossilized jaw with distinctly human dentition and now classified with the pithecanthropines
heif·er \'he-fər\ *n* [ME *hayfare*, fr. OE *hēahfore*] (bef. 12c) : a young cow; *esp* : one that has not had a calf
heigh–ho \'hī-'hō, 'hā-\ *interj* (ca. 1553) — used typically to express boredom, weariness, or sadness or sometimes as a cry of encouragement
height \'hīt, ÷'hītth\ *n* [ME *heighthe*, fr. OE *hiehthu*; akin to OHG *hōhida* height, OE *hēah* high] (bef. 12c) **1 a** : the highest part : SUMMIT **b** : highest or most advanced point : ZENITH ⟨at the ~ of his powers⟩ **2 a** : the distance from the bottom to the top of something standing upright **b** : the extent of elevation above a level **3** : the condition of being tall or high **4 a** : an extent of land rising to a considerable degree above the surrounding country **b** : a high point or position **5** *obs* : an advanced social rank
syn HEIGHT, ALTITUDE, ELEVATION mean vertical distance either between the top and bottom of something or between a base and something above it. HEIGHT refers to something measured vertically whether high or low ⟨a wall two meters in *height*⟩. ALTITUDE and ELEVATION apply to height as measured by angular measurement or atmospheric pressure; ALTITUDE is preferable when referring to vertical distance above the surface of the earth or above sea level; ELEVATION is used esp. in reference to vertical height on land ⟨fly at an *altitude* of 10,000 meters⟩ ⟨Denver is a city with a high *elevation*⟩.
height·en \'hī-t²n\ *vb* **height·ened; height·en·ing** \'hīt-niŋ, 'hī-t²n-iŋ\ *vt* (1523) **1 a** : to increase the amount or degree of : AUGMENT **b** : to make brighter or more intense : DEEPEN **c** : to bring out more strongly : point up **d** : to make more acute : SHARPEN **2 a** : to raise high or higher : ELEVATE **b** : to raise above the ordinary or trite **3** *obs* : ELATE ~ *vi* **1** *archaic* : GROW, RISE **2 a** : to become great or greater in amount, degree, or extent **b** : to become brighter or more intense
height to paper (1771) : the height of printing type standardized at 0.9186 inch (2.333 centimeters) in English-speaking countries
Heim·lich maneuver \'hīm-lik-\ *n* [Henry J. *Heimlich* b1920 Am. surgeon] (1974) : the manual application of sudden upward pressure on the upper abdomen of a choking victim to force a foreign object from the windpipe
hei·nie \'hī-nē\ *n* [alter. of ²*hinder*] (1940) *slang* : BUTTOCKS
hei·nous \'hā-nəs\ *adj* [ME, fr. MF *haineus*, fr. *haine* hate, fr. *hair* to hate, of Gmc origin; akin to OHG *haz* hate — more at HATE] (14c) : hatefully or shockingly evil : ABOMINABLE — **hei·nous·ly** *adv* — **hei·nous·ness** *n*
¹**heir** \'ar, 'er\ *n* [ME, fr. OF, fr. L *hered-*, *heres*; akin to Gk *chēros* bereaved] (13c) **1** : one who inherits or is entitled to inherit property **2** : one who inherits or is entitled to succeed to a hereditary rank, title, or office ⟨~ to the throne⟩ **3** : one who receives or is entitled to receive some endowment or quality from a parent or predecessor — **heir·less** \-ləs\ *adj* — **heir·ship** \-,ship\ *n*
²**heir** *vt* (14c) *chiefly dial* : INHERIT
heir apparent *n, pl* **heirs apparent** (14c) **1** : an heir whose right to an inheritance is indefeasible in law if he survives the legal ancestor **2** : HEIR PRESUMPTIVE **3** : one whose succession esp. to a position or role appears certain under existing circumstances
heir at law (1729) : an heir in whom an intestate's real property is vested by operation of law
heir·ess \'ar-əs, 'er-\ *n* (1607) : a female heir; *esp* : a female heir to great wealth
heir·loom \'ar-,lüm, 'er-\ *n* [ME *heirlome*, fr. *heir* + *lome* implement — more at LOOM] (15c) **1** : a piece of property that descends to the heir as an inseparable part of an inheritance of real property **2** : something of special value handed on from one generation to another
heir presumptive *n, pl* **heirs presumptive** (ca. 1737) : an heir whose legal right to an inheritance may be defeated (as by the birth of a nearer relative)
Hei·sen·berg uncertainty principle \'hī-z²n-,bərg-, -,bərk-\ *n* [Werner *Heisenberg*] (1939) : UNCERTAINTY PRINCIPLE — called also *Heisenberg's uncertainty principle*
¹**heist** \'hīst\ *vt* [var. of ¹*hoist*] (1865) **1** *chiefly dial* : HOIST **2** *slang* **a** : to commit armed robbery on **b** : STEAL 1a
²**heist** *n* (1930) *slang* : armed robbery : HOLDUP; *also* : THEFT
Hel \'hel\ *n* [ON] : the Norse goddess of the dead and queen of the underworld
hela cell \'he-lə-\ *n, often cap H&1stL* [*H*enrietta *L*acks †1951 patient from whom the cells were taken] (1953) : a cell of a continuously cultured strain isolated from a human uterine cervical carcinoma in 1951 and used in biomedical research esp. to culture viruses
held *past and past part of* HOLD
hel·den·te·nor \'hel-dən-,tā-,nȯr, -,nōr, -,te-nər\ *n, often cap* [G, fr. *Held* hero + *Tenor* tenor] (ca. 1903) : a tenor with a powerful dramatic voice well suited to heroic (as Wagnerian) roles

Helen of Troy \ˌhe-lə-nəv-ˈtrȯi\ : the wife of Menelaus whose abduction by Paris brings about the Trojan War

¹**heli-** or **helio-** comb form [L, fr. Gk hēli-, hēlio-, fr. hēlios — more at SOLAR] : sun ⟨heliocentric⟩

²**heli-** comb form [by shortening] : helicopter ⟨heliport⟩

he·li·a·cal \hi-ˈlī-ə-kəl\ adj [LL heliacus, fr. Gk hēliakos, fr. hēlios] (1545) : relating to or near the sun — used esp. of the last setting of a star before and its first rising after invisibility due to conjunction with the sun — **he·li·a·cal·ly** \-k(ə-)lē\ adv

helic- or **helico-** comb form [Gk helik-, heliko-, fr. helik-, helix spiral — more at HELIX] : helix : spiral ⟨helical⟩

he·li·cal \ˈhe-li-kəl, ˈhē-\ adj (1591) : of, relating to, or having the form of a helix; broadly : SPIRAL 1a — **he·li·cal·ly** \-k(ə-)lē\ adv

he·li·coid \ˈhe-lə-ˌkȯid, ˈhē-\ or **he·li·coi·dal** \ˌhe-lə-ˈkȯi-dᵊl, ˌhē-\ adj (1704) 1 : forming or arranged in a spiral 2 : having the form of a flat coil or flattened spiral ⟨~ snail shell⟩

hel·i·con \ˈhe-lə-ˌkän, -i-kən\ n [prob. fr. Gk helik-, helix + E -on (as in bombardon); from its tube's forming a spiral encircling the player's body] (1875) : a large circular tuba similar to a sousaphone but lacking an adjustable bell

¹**he·li·cop·ter** \ˈhe-lə-ˌkäp-tər, ˈhē-\ n [F hélicoptère, fr. Gk heliko- + pteron wing — more at FEATHER] (1887) : an aircraft whose lift is derived from the aerodynamic forces acting on one or more powered rotors turning about substantially vertical axes

²**helicopter** vi (1952) : to travel by helicopter ~ vt : to transport by helicopter

he·lio·cen·tric \ˌhē-lē-ō-ˈsen-trik\ adj (1685) 1 : referred to or measured from the sun's center or appearing as if seen from it 2 : having or relating to the sun as center — compare GEOCENTRIC

he·lio·graph \-ˌgraf\ n [ISV] (1877) : an apparatus for telegraphing by means of the sun's rays flashed from a mirror — **heliograph** vt

he·lio·graph·ic \ˌhē-lē-ō-ˈgra-fik\ adj (1706) : measured on the sun's disk ⟨~ latitude⟩

he·li·ol·a·try \ˌhē-lē-ˈä-lə-trē\ n (ca. 1828) : sun worship — **he·li·ol·a·trous** \-trəs\ adj

he·li·om·e·ter \ˌhē-lē-ˈä-mə-tər\ n [F héliomètre, fr. hélio- ¹heli- + -mètre -meter] (1753) : a visual telescope that has a divided objective designed for measuring the apparent diameter of the sun but also used for measuring angles between celestial bodies or between points on the moon — **he·lio·met·ric** \ˌhē-lē-ō-ˈme-trik\ adj — **he·lio·met·ri·cal·ly** \-tri-k(ə-)lē\ adv

He·li·os \ˈhē-lē-əs, -(ˌ)ōs\ n [Gk Hēlios] : the god of the sun in Greek mythology — compare SOL

he·lio·stat \ˈhē-lē-ə-ˌstat\ n [NL heliostata, fr. ¹heli- + Gk -statēs -stat] (1747) : an instrument consisting of a mirror mounted on an axis moved by clockwork by which a sunbeam is steadily reflected in one direction

he·lio·trope \ˈhē-lē-ə-ˌtrōp, ˈhēl-yə-, Brit also ˈhel-yə-\ n [L heliotropium, fr. Gk hēliotropion, fr. hēlio- ¹heli- + tropos turn; fr. its flowers' turning toward the sun — more at TROPE] (ca. 1626) 1 : any of a genus (Heliotropium) of herbs or shrubs of the borage family — compare GARDEN HELIOTROPE 2 : BLOODSTONE 3 : a variable color averaging a moderate to reddish purple

he·lio·tro·pism \ˌhē-lē-ˈä-trə-ˌpi-zəm\ n (ca. 1854) : phototropism in which sunlight is the orienting stimulus — **he·lio·tro·pic** \-lē-ə-ˈtrō-pik, -ˈträ-\ adj

he·lio·zo·an \ˌhē-lē-ə-ˈzō-ən\ n [NL Heliozoa, fr. ¹heli- + -zoa] (ca. 1889) : any of a class (Heliozoa) of free-living holozoic usu. freshwater rhizopod protozoans that reproduce by binary fission or budding

he·li·pad \ˈhe-lə-ˌpad, ˈhē-\ n (1960) : HELIPORT

he·li·port \-ˌpȯrt, -ˌpȯrt\ n (1948) : a landing and takeoff place for a helicopter

he·li·ski·ing \-ˌskē-iŋ\ n (1976) : downhill skiing on remote mountains reached by helicopter

he·li·um \ˈhē-lē-əm, ˈhēl-yəm\ n [NL, fr. Gk hēlios] (1872) : a light colorless nonflammable gaseous element found esp. in natural gases and used chiefly for inflating airships and balloons, for filling incandescent lamps, and for cryogenic research — see ELEMENT table

he·lix \ˈhē-liks\ n, pl **he·li·ces** \ˈhe-lə-ˌsēz, ˈhē-\ also **he·lix·es** \ˈhē-lik-səz\ [L, fr. Gk; akin to Gk eilyein to roll, wrap — more at VOLUBLE] (1563) 1 : something spiral in form: as a : an ornamental volute b : a coil formed by winding wire around a uniform tube 2 : the incurved rim of the external ear 3 : a curve traced on a cylinder or cone by the rotation of a point crossing its right sections at a constant oblique angle; broadly : SPIRAL 1b

hell \ˈhel\ n [ME, fr. OE; akin to OE helan to conceal, OHG helan, L celare, Gk kalyptein] (bef. 12c) 1 a (1) : a nether world in which the dead continue to exist : HADES (2) : the nether realm of the devil and the demons in which the damned suffer everlasting punishment — often used in curses ⟨go to ~⟩ or as a generalized term of abuse ⟨the ~ with it⟩ b Christian Science : ERROR 2b, SIN 2 a : a place or state of misery, torment, or wickedness ⟨war is ~ —W. T. Sherman⟩ b : a place or state of turmoil or destruction ⟨all ~ broke loose⟩ c : a severe scolding ⟨got ~ for coming in late⟩ d : unrestrained fun or sportiveness ⟨the kids were full of ~⟩ — often used in the phrase for the hell of it esp. to suggest action on impulse or without a serious motive ⟨decided to go for the ~ of it⟩ 3 archaic : a tailor's receptacle 4 — used as an interjection ⟨~, I don't know!⟩ or as an intensive ⟨hurts like ~⟩ ⟨funny as ~⟩; often used in the phrase hell of a ⟨it was one ~ of a good fight⟩ or hell out of ⟨scared the ~ out of him⟩ or with the or in ⟨moved way the ~ up north⟩ ⟨what in ~ is wrong, now?⟩ — **from hell** : being the worst or most dreadful of its kind — **hell on** : very hard on or destructive to ⟨the constant traveling is hell on your digestive system⟩ — **hell or high water** : difficulties of whatever kind or size ⟨will stand by her convictions come hell or high water⟩ — **hell to pay** : dire consequences ⟨if he's late there'll be hell to pay⟩

he'll \ˈhē(ə)l, ˈhil, ēl, il\ (1588) : he will : he shall

hel·la·cious \he-ˈlā-shəs\ adj [hell + -acious (as in audacious)] (1943) 1 : exceptionally powerful or violent 2 : remarkably good 3 : extremely difficult 4 : extraordinarily large — **hel·la·cious·ly** adv

hell·ben·der \ˈhel-ˌben-dər\ n (1812) : a large aquatic usu. gray salamander (Cryptobranchus alleganiensis) of the Ohio valley region

hell·bent \-ˌbent\ adj (1835) : stubbornly and often recklessly determined or intent ⟨~ on winning⟩ — **hell·bent** adv

hell·broth \-ˌbrȯth\ n (1605) : a brew for working black magic

hell·cat \-ˌkat\ n (ca. 1605) 1 : WITCH 2 2 : a violently temperamental person; esp : an ill-tempered woman

hel·le·bore \ˈhe-lə-ˌbȯr, -ˌbȯr\ n [ME elebre, fr. L elleborus, helleborus, fr. Gk helleboros] (15c) 1 : any of a genus (Helleborus) of poisonous herbs of the buttercup family having showy flowers with petaloid sepals; also : the dried rhizome or an extract or powder of this formerly used in medicine 2 : a poisonous herb (genus Veratrum) of the lily family; also : the dried rhizome of a hellebore (Veratrum album or V. viride) or a powder or extract of this containing alkaloids used as a cardiac and respiratory depressant and as an insecticide

hellbender

Hel·lene \ˈhe-ˌlēn\ n [Gk Hellēn] (1662) : GREEK 1a

¹**Hel·len·ic** \he-ˈle-nik, hə-\ adj (1644) : of or relating to Greece, its people, or its language; specif : of or relating to ancient Greek history, culture, or art before the Hellenistic period

²**Hellenic** n (1847) : GREEK 2a

Hel·le·nism \ˈhe-lə-ˌni-zəm\ n (1609) 1 : GRECISM 1 2 : devotion to or imitation of ancient Greek thought, customs, or styles 3 : Greek civilization esp. as modified in the Hellenistic period by oriental influences 4 : a body of humanistic and classical ideals associated with ancient Greece and including reason, the pursuit of knowledge and the arts, moderation, civic responsibility, and bodily development

Hel·le·nist \-nist\ n (1613) 1 : a person living in Hellenistic times who was Greek in language, outlook, and way of life but was not Greek in ancestry; esp : a hellenized Jew 2 : a specialist in the language or culture of ancient Greece

Hel·le·nis·tic \ˌhe-lə-ˈnis-tik\ adj (ca. 1706) 1 : of or relating to Greek history, culture, or art after Alexander the Great 2 : of or relating to the Hellenists — **Hel·le·nis·ti·cal·ly** \-ti-k(ə-)lē\ adv

hel·le·nize \ˈhe-lə-ˌnīz\ vb -nized; -niz·ing often cap, vi (1613) : to become Greek or Hellenistic ~ vt : to make Greek or Hellenistic in form or culture — **hel·le·ni·za·tion** \ˌhe-lə-nə-ˈzā-shən\ n, often cap

hell·er \ˈhe-lər\ n (ca. 1895) : HELLION

hel·leri \ˈhe-lə-ˌrī, -(ˌ)rē\ n, pl **-ler·ies** [NL (specific epithet of Xiphophorus helleri), fr. C. Heller, 20th cent. tropical fish collector] (1931) 1 : SWORDTAIL 2 : any of various brightly colored aquarium fishes developed by hybridization of swordtails and platys

hell·fire \ˈhel-ˌfīr\ n (bef. 12c) : the eternal fire of hell that tortures sinners — **hellfire** adj

¹**hell–for–leather** adv (1889) : in a hell-for-leather manner : at full speed ⟨rode ~ down the trail⟩

²**hell–for–leather** adj (1920) : marked by determined recklessness, great speed, or lack of restraint ⟨a cocky, ~ fighting man —H. H. Martin⟩

hell·gram·mite \ˈhel-grə-ˌmīt\ n [origin unknown] (1866) : a carnivorous aquatic No. American insect larva that is the young form of a dobsonfly (esp. Corydalis cornutus) and is used for fish bait

hell·hole \ˈhel-ˌhōl\ n (1866) : a place of extreme misery or squalor

hell·hound \-ˌhau̇nd\ n (bef. 12c) 1 : a dog represented in mythology as a guardian of the underworld 2 : a fiendish person

hel·lion \ˈhel-yən\ n [prob. alter. (influenced by hell) of hallion (scamp)] (1787) : a troublesome or mischievous person

hell·ish \ˈhe-lish\ adj (ca. 1530) : of, resembling, or befitting hell; broadly : TERRIBLE — **hell·ish·ly** adv — **hell·ish·ness** n

hel·lo \hə-ˈlō, he-\ n, pl **hellos** [alter. of hollo] (1889) : an expression or gesture of greeting — used interjectionally in greeting, in answering the telephone, or to express surprise

hell–rais·er \ˈhel-ˌrā-zər\ n (1914) : one given to wild, boisterous, or intemperate behavior — **hell–rais·ing** \-ˌrā-ziŋ\ n or adj

¹**helm** \ˈhelm\ n [ME, fr. OE] (bef. 12c) : HELMET 1

²**helm** vt (bef. 12c) : to cover or furnish with a helmet

³**helm** n [ME helme, fr. OE helma; akin to OHG helmo tiller] (bef. 12c) 1 a : a lever or wheel controlling the rudder of a ship for steering; broadly : the entire apparatus for steering a ship b : position of the helm with respect to the amidships position ⟨turn the ~ hard alee⟩ 2 : a position of control : HEAD ⟨a new dean is at the ~ of the medical school⟩

⁴**helm** vt (1603) : to direct with or as if with a helm : STEER

hel·met \ˈhel-mət\ n [MF, dim. of helme helmet, of Gmc origin; akin to OE helm helmet, OHG helan to conceal — more at HELL] (15c) 1 : a covering or enclosing headpiece of ancient or medieval armor — see ARMOR illustration 2 : any of various protective head coverings usu. made of a hard material to resist impact 3 : something resembling a helmet — **hel·met·ed** \-mə-təd\ adj — **hel·met·like** \-mət-ˌlīk\ adj

hel·minth \ˈhel-ˌmin(t)th\ n [Gk helminth-, helmis] (1852) : a parasitic worm (as a tapeworm, liver fluke, ascarid, or leech); esp : an intestinal worm — **hel·min·thic** \hel-ˈmin(t)-thik\ adj

hel·min·thi·a·sis \ˌhel-mən-ˈthī-ə-səs\ n, pl **-a·ses** \-ə-ˌsēz\ [NL] (ca. 1811) : infestation with or disease caused by parasitic worms

hel·min·thol·o·gy \ˌhel-mən-ˈthä-lə-jē\ n (1819) : a branch of zoology concerned with helminths; esp : the study of parasitic worms

helms·man \ˈhelmz-mən\ n (1627) : the person at the helm : STEERSMAN — **helms·man·ship** \-ˌship\ n

he·lo \ˈhe-(ˌ)lō\ n, pl **helos** [by shortening & alter.] (1968) : HELICOPTER

hel·ot \ˈhe-lət\ n [L Helotes, pl., fr. Gk Heilōtes] (1579) 1 cap : a member of a class of serfs in ancient Sparta 2 : SERF, SLAVE — **hel·ot·ry** \ˈhe-lə-trē\ n

\ə\ abut \ᵊ\ kitten, F table \ər\ further \a\ ash \ā\ ace \ä\ mop, mar \au̇\ out \ch\ chin \e\ bet \ē\ easy \g\ go \i\ hit \ī\ ice \j\ job \ŋ\ sing \ō\ go \ȯ\ law \ȯi\ boy \th\ thin \t͟h\ the \ü\ loot \u̇\ foot \y\ yet \zh\ vision \á, k̵, ⁱ, œ, œ̄, ᵫ, ᵫ̄, ᵊ\ see Guide to Pronunciation

hel·ot·ism \'he-lə-‚ti-zəm\ n (ca. 1900) : the physiological relation existing in a lichen where a fungus appears to control an alga

¹help \'help; *Southern often* 'hep *also* 'heəp\ vb [ME, fr. OE *helpan;* akin to OHG *helfan* to help, and perh. to Lith *šelpti*] vt (bef. 12c) **1 a :** to give assistance or support to ⟨~ a child with homework⟩ **2 a :** to make more pleasant or bearable : IMPROVE, RELIEVE ⟨bright curtains will ~ the room⟩ ⟨took an aspirin to ~ her headache⟩ **b** *archaic* : RESCUE, SAVE **3 a :** to be of use to : BENEFIT **b :** to further the advancement of : PROMOTE **4 a :** to change for the better **b :** to refrain from : AVOID **c :** to keep from occurring : PREVENT ⟨they couldn't ~ the accident⟩ **d :** to restrain (oneself) from doing something ⟨knew they shouldn't go but couldn't ~ themselves⟩ **5 :** to serve with food or drink esp. at a meal ⟨told the guests to ~ themselves⟩ **6 :** to appropriate something for (oneself) ⟨~ed himself to the car keys⟩ ~ vi **1 :** give assistance or support — often used with *out* **2 :** to be of use or benefit *syn* see IMPROVE — **so help me :** upon my word : believe it or not

²help n (bef. 12c) **1 :** AID, ASSISTANCE **2 :** a source of aid ⟨printed ~s to the memory —C. S. Braden⟩ **3 :** REMEDY, RELIEF ⟨there was no ~ for it⟩ **4 a :** one who serves or assists another (as in housework) : HELPER **b :** EMPLOYEE ⟨~ wanted⟩ — often used collectively ⟨the hired ~⟩

help·er n (13c) : one that helps; *esp* : a relatively unskilled worker who assists a skilled worker usu. by manual labor

helper T cell n (1976) : a T cell that participates in an immune response by recognizing a foreign antigen and secreting lymphokines to activate T cell and B cell proliferation, that usu. carries CD4 molecular markers on its cell surface, and that is reduced to 20 percent or less of normal numbers in AIDS — called also *helper cell, T-helper cell*

help·ful \'help-fəl; *Southern often* 'hep- *also* 'heəp-\ adj (14c) : of service or assistance : USEFUL — **help·ful·ly** \-fə-lē\ adv — **help·ful·ness** n

help·ing n (1883) : a portion of food : SERVING

helping hand n (15c) : HAND 8a

helping verb n (1711) : an auxiliary verb

help·less \'hel-pləs; *Southern often* 'hep-ləs *also* 'heəp-\ adj (bef. 12c) **1 :** lacking protection or support : DEFENSELESS **2 a :** marked by an inability to act or react ⟨the crowd looked on in ~ horror —*Current Biog.*⟩ **b :** not able to be controlled or restrained ⟨~ laughter⟩ — **help·less·ly** adv — **help·less·ness** n

help·mate \'help-‚māt; *Southern often* 'hep- *also* 'heəp-\ n [by folk etymology fr. *helpmeet*] (ca. 1714) : one who is a companion and helper; *esp* : WIFE

help·meet \-‚mēt\ n [²*help* + *meet*, adj.] (1673) : HELPMATE

¹hel·ter–skel·ter \‚hel-tər-'skel-tər\ adv [perh. fr. ME *skelten* to come, go] (1593) **1 :** in undue haste, confusion, or disorder ⟨ran ~, getting in each other's way —F. V. W. Mason⟩ **2 :** in a haphazard manner

²helter–skelter n (1713) **1 :** a disorderly confusion : TURMOIL **2** *Brit* : a spiral slide around a tower at an amusement park

³helter–skelter adj (1785) **1 :** confusedly hurried : PRECIPITATE **2 :** marked by a lack of order or plan : HAPHAZARD ⟨the ~ arrangement of the papers, all mussed and frayed —Jean Stafford⟩

helve \'helv\ n [ME, fr. OE *hielfe;* prob. akin to OE *helma* helm] (bef. 12c) : a handle of a tool or weapon : HAFT

Hel·ve·tii \hel-'vē-shē-‚ī\ n pl [L] (1889) : an early Celtic people in the area of western Switzerland at the time of Julius Caesar

¹hem \'hem\ n [ME, fr. OE; akin to MHG *hemmen* to hem in, Arm *kamel* to press] (bef. 12c) **1 :** a border of a cloth article doubled back and stitched down **2 :** RIM, MARGIN ⟨bright green ~ of reeds about the ponds —R. M. Lockley⟩

²hem vb **hemmed; hem·ming** vt (14c) **1 a :** to finish with a hem **b :** BORDER, EDGE **2 :** to surround in a restrictive manner : CONFINE — usu. used with *in* ⟨hemmed in by enemy troops⟩ ~ vi **1 :** to make a hem in sewing — **hem·mer** n

³hem \'hem\ vi **hemmed; hem·ming** (15c) **1 :** to utter the sound represented by *hem* ⟨hemmed and hawed before answering⟩ **2 :** EQUIVOCATE ⟨the administration hemmed and hawed over the students' demands⟩

⁴hem *usu read as* 'hem\ interj [imit.] — often used to indicate a vocalized pause in speaking

hem- *or* **hemo-** *comb form* [MF *hemo-*, fr. L *haem-, haemo-*, fr. Gk *haim-, haimo-*, fr. *haima*] : blood ⟨hemagglutination⟩ ⟨hemoflagellate⟩

hema- *comb form* [NL, fr. Gk *haima*] : HEM- ⟨hemacytometer⟩

he·ma·cy·tom·e·ter \‚hē-mə-sī-'tä-mə-tər\ n (1877) : an instrument for counting blood cells

hem·ag·glu·ti·na·tion \‚hē-mə-‚glü-tᵊn-'ā-shən\ n (1907) : agglutination of red blood cells — **hem·ag·glu·ti·nate** \-'glü-tᵊn-‚āt\ vt

hem·ag·glu·ti·nin \-'glü-tᵊn-ən\ n [ISV] (ca. 1903) : an agglutinin (as an antibody or viral capsid protein) that causes hemagglutination

he–man \'hē-‚man\ n (1832) : a strong virile man

hem·an·gi·o·ma \hi-‚man-jē-'ō-mə\ n [NL, fr. *hem-* + *angioma*] (ca. 1890) : a usu. benign tumor made up of blood vessels that typically occurs as a purplish or reddish slightly elevated area of skin

hemat- *or* **hemato-** *comb form* [L *haemat-, haemato-*, fr. Gk *haimat-, haimato-*, fr. *haimat-, haima*] : HEM- ⟨hematogenous⟩

he·ma·tin \'hē-mə-tən\ n (1845) : a brownish black or bluish black derivative $C_{34}H_{33}NO_5Fe$ of oxidized heme; *also* : any of several similar compounds

he·ma·tin·ic \‚hē-mə-'ti-nik\ n (1855) : an agent that tends to stimulate blood cell formation or to increase the hemoglobin in the blood — **hematinic** adj

he·ma·tite \'hē-mə-‚tīt\ n (1540) : a mineral constituting an important iron ore and occurring in crystals or in a red earthy form — **he·ma·ti·tic** \‚hē-mə-'ti-tik\ adj

he·mat·o·crit \hi-'ma-tə-krət, -‚krit\ n [ISV *hemat-* + Gk *kritēs* judge, fr. *krinein* to judge — more at CERTAIN] (ca. 1903) **1 :** an instrument for determining usu. by centrifugation the relative amounts of plasma and corpuscles in blood **2 :** the ratio of the volume of packed red blood cells to the volume of whole blood as determined by a hematocrit

he·ma·tog·e·nous \‚hē-mə-'tä-jə-nəs\ adj (1886) **1 :** producing blood **2 :** involving, spread by, or arising in the blood ⟨~ spread of infection⟩

he·ma·to·log·ic \‚hē-mə-tᵊl-'ä-jik\ *also* **he·ma·to·log·i·cal** \-ji-kəl\ adj (1854) : of or relating to blood or to hematology

he·ma·tol·o·gy \‚hē-mə-'tä-lə-jē\ n (ca. 1811) : a medical science that deals with the blood and blood-forming organs — **he·ma·tol·o·gist** \-jist\ n

he·ma·to·ma \-'tō-mə\ n, pl **-mas** or **-ma·ta** \-mə-tə\ [NL] (ca. 1849) : a mass of usu. clotted blood that forms in a tissue, organ, or space as a result of a broken blood vessel

he·ma·toph·a·gous \-'tä-fə-gəs\ adj [ISV] (ca. 1854) : feeding on blood

he·ma·to·poi·e·sis \hi-‚ma-tə-pȯi-'ē-səs, ‚hē-mə-tō-\ n [NL] (ca. 1854) : the formation of blood or of blood cells in the living body — **he·ma·to·poi·et·ic** \-'e-tik\ adj

he·ma·to·por·phy·rin \-'pȯr-fə-rən\ n [ISV] (1885) : any of several isomeric porphyrins $C_{34}H_{38}O_6N_4$ that are hydrated derivatives of protoporphyrins; *esp* : the deep red crystalline pigment obtained by treating hematin or heme with acid

he·ma·tox·y·lin \‚hē-mə-'täk-sə-lən\ n [ISV, fr. NL *Haematoxylon,* genus of plants] (ca. 1847) : a crystalline phenolic compound $C_{16}H_{14}O_6$ found in logwood and used chiefly as a biological stain

he·ma·tu·ria \-'tür-ē-ə, -'tyür-\ n [NL] (ca. 1811) : the presence of blood or blood cells in the urine

heme \'hēm\ n [ISV, fr. *hematin*] (1925) : the deep red iron-containing prosthetic group $C_{34}H_{32}N_4O_4Fe$ of hemoglobin and myoglobin

hem·el·y·tron \he-'me-lə-‚trän\ n, pl **-tra** \-trə\ [NL, fr. *hemi-* + *elytron*] (ca. 1889) : one of the basally thickened anterior wings of various insects (as true bugs)

hem·ero·cal·lis \‚he-mə-rō-'ka-ləs\ n [NL, fr. Gk *hēmerokalles,* fr. *hēmera* day + *kallos* beauty] (1625) : DAYLILY

hem·er·y·thrin \‚hē-'mer-ə-thrən\ n [*hem-* + *erythr-* + ¹*-in*] (1903) : an iron-containing respiratory pigment in the blood of various invertebrates (as some annelids)

hemi- *prefix* [ME, fr. L, fr. Gk *hēmi-* — more at SEMI-] : half ⟨hemihedral⟩

-hemia — see -EMIA

hemi·ac·e·tal \‚he-mē-'a-sə-‚tal\ n (1893) : any of a class of compounds characterized by the grouping C(OH)(OR) where R is an alkyl group and usu. formed as intermediates in the preparation of acetals from aldehydes or ketones

he·mic \'hē-mik\ adj (1857) : of, relating to, or produced by the blood or the circulation of blood ⟨a ~ murmur⟩

hemi·cel·lu·lose \‚he-mi-'sel-yə-‚lōs, -‚lōz\ n [ISV] (1891) : any of various plant polysaccharides less complex than cellulose and easily hydrolyzable to simple sugars and other products

hemi·chor·date \-'kȯr-dət, -‚kȯr-‚dāt\ n [NL *Hemichordata,* fr. *hemi-* + *Chordata* chordates] (1885) : any of a phylum (Hemichordata) of wormlike marine animals (as an acorn worm) that have in the proboscis an outgrowth of the pharyngeal wall which superficially resembles the notochord of chordates

hemi·cy·cle \'he-mi-‚sī-kəl\ n [F *hémicycle,* fr. L *hemicyclium,* fr. Gk *hēmikyklion,* fr. *hēmi-* + *kyklos* circle — more at CYCLE] (15c) : a curved or semicircular structure or arrangement

hemi·demi·semi·qua·ver \‚he-mi-‚de-mi-'se-mi-‚kwä-vər\ n (1853) : SIXTY-FOURTH NOTE

hemi·he·dral \‚he-mi-'hē-drəl\ adj [*hemi-* + *-hedron*] (1837) *of a crystal* : having half the faces required by complete symmetry — compare HOLOHEDRAL, TETARTOHEDRAL

hemi·hy·drate \-'hī-‚drāt\ n (ca. 1901) : a hydrate (as plaster of paris) containing half a mole of water to one mole of the compound forming the hydrate — **hemi·hy·drat·ed** \-‚drā-təd\ adj

hemi·me·tab·o·lous \‚he-mi-mə-'ta-bə-ləs\ adj (1870) : characterized by incomplete metamorphosis ⟨~ insects⟩ — compare HOLOMETABOLOUS

hemi·mor·phic \‚he-mi-'mȯr-fik\ adj [ISV] (ca. 1859) *of a crystal* : having different crystalline forms at each end of a crystallographic axis — **hemi·mor·phism** \-‚fi-zəm\ n

he·min \'hē-mən\ n [ISV] (1857) : a red-brown to blue-black crystalline salt $C_{34}H_{32}N_4O_4FeCl$ derived from oxidized heme but usu. obtained in a characteristic crystalline form from hemoglobin

hemi·o·la \‚he-mē-'ō-lə\ n [LL *hemiolia,* fr. Gk *hēmiolia* ratio of one and a half to one, fr. *hēmi-* + *holos* whole — more at SAFE] (ca. 1934) : a musical rhythmic alteration in which six equal notes may be heard as two groups of three or three groups of two

hemi·ple·gia \‚he-mi-'plē-j(ē-)ə\ n [NL, fr. MGk *hēmiplēgia* paralysis, fr. Gk *hēmi-* + *-plēgia* -plegia] (1600) : total or partial paralysis of one side of the body that results from disease of or injury to the motor centers of the brain — **hemi·ple·gic** \-jik\ adj *or* n

he·mip·ter·an \hi-'mip-tə-rən\ n [ultim. fr. Gk *hēmi-* + *pteron* wing — more at FEATHER] (ca. 1864) : any of a large order (Hemiptera) of hemimetabolous insects (as the true bugs) that have hemelytra and mouthparts adapted to piercing and sucking — **he·mip·ter·ous** \-rəs\ adj

hemi·sphere \'he-mə-‚sfir\ n [ME *hemispere,* fr. L *hemisphaerium,* fr. Gk *hēmisphairion,* fr. *hēmi-* + *sphairion,* dim. of *sphaira* sphere] (14c) **1 a :** a half of the celestial sphere divided into two halves by the horizon, the celestial equator, or the ecliptic **b :** half of a spherical or roughly spherical body (as a planet); *specif* : the northern or southern half of the earth divided by the equator or the eastern or western half divided by a meridian **c :** the inhabitants of a terrestrial hemisphere **2 :** REALM, PROVINCE **3 :** one of two half spheres formed by a plane through the sphere's center **4 :** a map or projection of a celestial or terrestrial hemisphere **5 :** CEREBRAL HEMISPHERE — **hemi·spher·ic** \‚he-mə-'sfir-ik, -'sfer-\ *or* **hemi·spher·i·cal** \'sfir-i-kəl, -'sfer-\ adj

hemi·stich \'he-mi-‚stik\ n [L *hemistichium,* fr. Gk *hēmistichion,* fr. *hēmi-* + *stichos* line, verse; akin to Gk *steichein* to go — more at STAIR] (1575) : half a poetic line of verse usu. divided by a caesura

hemi·zy·gous \‚he-mi-'zī-gəs\ adj (ca. 1921) : having or characterized by one or more genes (as in a genetic deficiency or in an X chromosome paired with a Y chromosome) that have no allelic counterparts

hem·line \'hem-‚līn\ n (1923) : the line formed by the lower edge of a dress, skirt, or coat

hem·lock \'hem-‚läk\ n [ME *hemlok,* fr. OE *hemlic*] (bef. 12c) **1 a :** any of several poisonous herbs (as a poison hemlock or a water hemlock) of the carrot family having finely cut leaves and small white flowers **b :** a drug or lethal drink prepared from the poison hemlock (*Conium maculatum*) **2 a :** any of a genus (*Tsuga*) of evergreen coniferous

trees of the pine family; *also* : the soft light splintery wood of a hemlock
hemo- — see HEM-
he·mo·chro·ma·to·sis \,hē-mə-,krō-mə-'tō-səs\ *n* [NL, fr. *hem-* + *chromat-* + *-osis*] (1899) : a metabolic disorder involving the deposition of iron-containing pigments in the tissues and characterized by bronzing of the skin, diabetes, and weakness
he·mo·coel \'hē-mə-,sēl\ *n* (1839) : a body cavity (as in arthropods or some mollusks) that contains blood or hemolymph and functions as part of the circulatory system
he·mo·cy·a·nin \,hē-mō-'sī-ə-nən\ *n* [ISV *hem-* + *cyan-* + [1]-*in*] (1885) : a colorless copper-containing respiratory pigment in the circulatory fluid of various arthropods and mollusks
he·mo·cyte \'hē-mə-,sīt\ *n* [ISV] (ca. 1903) : a blood cell esp. of an invertebrate animal
he·mo·cy·tom·e·ter \,hē-mə-sī-'tä-mə-tər\ *n* [ISV] (1877) : HEMACYTOMETER
he·mo·di·al·y·sis \,hē-mō-dī-'a-lə-səs\ *n* (1947) : the process of removing blood from an artery (as of a kidney patient), purifying it by dialysis, adding vital substances, and returning it to a vein
he·mo·di·lu·tion \-dī-'lü-shən, -də-\ *n* (1939) : decreased concentration of cells and solids in the blood resulting from gain of fluid
he·mo·dy·nam·ic \-dī-'na-mik, -də-\ *adj* (1907) **1** : of, relating to, or involving hemodynamics **2** : relating to or functioning in the mechanics of blood circulation — **he·mo·dy·nam·i·cal·ly** \-mi-k(ə-)lē\ *adv*
he·mo·dy·nam·ics \-miks\ *n pl but sing or pl in constr* (ca. 1857) **1** : a branch of physiology that deals with the circulation of the blood **2** : the forces or mechanisms involved in circulation
he·mo·fla·gel·late \,hē-mō-'fla-jə-lət, -,lāt; -flə-'je-lət\ *n* (1909) : a flagellate (as a trypanosome) that is a blood parasite
he·mo·glo·bin \'hē-mə-,glō-bən\ *n* [ISV, short for earlier *hematoglobulin*] (1869) **1** : an iron-containing respiratory pigment of vertebrate red blood cells that consists of a globin composed of four subunits each of which is linked to a heme molecule, that functions in oxygen transport to the tissues after conversion to oxygenated form in the gills or lungs, and that assists in carbon dioxide transport back to the gills or lungs after surrender of its oxygen **2** : any of numerous iron-containing respiratory pigments of invertebrates and some plants (as yeasts)
he·mo·glo·bin·op·a·thy \,hē-mə-,glō-bə-'nä-pə-thē\ *n, pl* **-thies** (1957) : a blood disorder (as sickle-cell anemia) caused by a genetically determined change in the molecular structure of hemoglobin
hemoglobin S *n* (1954) : an abnormal hemoglobin that occurs in the red blood cells in sickle-cell anemia and sickle-cell trait
he·mo·glo·bin·uria \,hē-mə-,glō-bə-'nur-ē-ə, -'nyur-\ *n* [NL] (1866) : the presence of free hemoglobin in the urine — **he·mo·glo·bin·uric** \-'nur-ik, -'nyur-\ *adj*
he·mo·lymph \'hē-mə-,lim(p)f\ *n* (1885) : the circulatory fluid of various invertebrate animals that is functionally comparable to the blood and lymph of vertebrates
he·mo·ly·sin \,hē-mə-'li-s²n\ *n* [ISV] (1900) : a substance that causes the dissolution of red blood cells
he·mo·ly·sis \hi-'mä-lə-səs, ,hē-mə-'lī-səs\ *n* [NL] (1890) : lysis of red blood cells with liberation of hemoglobin — **he·mo·lyt·ic** \,hē-mə-'li-tik\ *adj*
hemolytic anemia *n* (1938) : anemia caused by excessive destruction (as in chemical poisoning, infection, or sickle-cell anemia) of red blood cells
hemolytic disease of the newborn (1948) : ERYTHROBLASTOSIS FETALIS
he·mo·lyze \'hē-mə-,līz\ *vb* **-lyzed; -lyz·ing** [irreg. fr. *hemolysis*] *vt* (1902) : to cause hemolysis of ~ *vi* : to undergo hemolysis
he·mo·phil·ia \,hē-mə-'fi-lē-ə\ *n* [NL] (1872) : a sex-linked hereditary blood defect that occurs almost exclusively in males and is characterized by delayed clotting of the blood and consequent difficulty in controlling hemorrhage even after minor injuries
[1]he·mo·phil·i·ac \-'fi-lē-,ak\ *adj* (1896) : of, resembling, or affected with hemophilia
[2]hemophiliac *n* (1897) : one affected with hemophilia — called also *bleeder*
he·mo·phil·ic \-'fi-lik\ *n or adj* (1864) : HEMOPHILIAC
he·mo·poi·e·sis \,hē-mə-pòi-'ē-səs\ *n* [NL] (ca. 1900) : HEMATOPOIESIS — **he·mo·poi·et·ic** \-'e-tik\ *adj*
he·mo·pro·tein \-'prō-,tēn, -'prō-tē-ən\ *n* (1948) : a conjugated protein (as hemoglobin or cytochrome) whose prosthetic group is a porphyrin combined with iron
he·mop·ty·sis \hi-'mäp-tə-səs\ *n* [NL, fr. *hem-* + Gk *ptysis* act of spitting, fr. *ptyein* to spit — more at SPEW] (1646) : expectoration of blood from some part of the respiratory tract
[1]hem·or·rhage \'hem-rij, 'he-mə-\ *n* [L *haemorrhagia*, fr. Gk *haimorrhagia*, fr. *haimo-* hem- + -*rrhagia*] (1671) : a copious discharge of blood from the blood vessels — **hem·or·rhag·ic** \,he-mə-'ra-jik\ *adj*
[2]hemorrhage *vb* **-rhaged; -rhag·ing** *vi* (1928) : to undergo heavy or uncontrollable bleeding ~ *vt* : to lose rapidly and uncontrollably ⟨~ money⟩
hemorrhagic fever *n* (1948) : any of a diverse group of arthropod-borne virus diseases characterized by a sudden onset, fever, aching, bleeding in the internal organs, petechiae, and shock
hem·or·rhoid \'hem-,ròid, 'he-mə-\ *n* [ME *emeroides*, pl., fr. MF *hemorrhoides*, fr. L *haemorrhoidae*, fr. Gk *haimorrhoides*, fr. *haimorrhoos* flowing with blood, fr. *haimo-* hem- + *rhein* to flow — more at STREAM] (14c) : a mass of dilated veins in swollen tissue at the margin of the anus or nearby within the rectum — usu. used in pl.; called also *piles*
[1]hem·or·rhoid·al \,hem-'ròi-d²l, ,he-mə-\ *n* (15c) : a hemorrhoidal part (as an artery or vein)
[2]hemorrhoidal *adj* (1651) **1** : of, relating to, or involving hemorrhoids **2** : RECTAL
he·mo·sid·er·in \,hē-mō-'si-də-rən\ *n* [ISV *hem-* + *sider-* + [1]-*in*] (ca. 1885) : a yellowish brown granular pigment that is formed in some phagocytic cells by the breakdown of hemoglobin and is probably essentially a denatured form of ferritin
he·mo·sta·sis \,hē-mə-'stā-səs\ *n* [NL, fr. Gk *haimostasis* styptic, fr. *haimo-* hem- + *-stasis*] (1843) : arrest of bleeding

he·mo·stat \'hē-mə-,stat\ *n* (ca. 1900) : HEMOSTATIC; *esp* : an instrument for compressing a bleeding vessel
[1]he·mo·stat·ic \,hē-mə-'sta-tik\ *n* (ca. 1706) : a hemostatic agent
[2]hemostatic *adj* (1834) **1** : of or caused by hemostasis **2** : serving to check bleeding
hemp \'hemp\ *n* [ME, fr. OE *hænep; akin to OHG *hanaf* hemp, Gk *kannabis*] (bef. 12c) **1 a** : a tall widely cultivated Asian herb (*Cannabis sativa*) of the mulberry family with tough bast fiber used esp. for cordage **b** : the fiber of hemp **c** : a psychoactive drug (as marijuana or hashish) from hemp **2** : a fiber (as jute) from a plant other than the true hemp; *also* : a plant yielding such fiber
hemp·en \'hem-pən\ *adj* (14c) : composed of hemp
hemp nettle (1801) : any of a genus (*Galeopsis*) of coarse Old World herbs of the mint family; *esp* : a bristly Eurasian herb (*G. tetrahit*) naturalized in the U.S. as a weed
[1]hem·stitch \'hem-,stich\ *vt* (1839) : to decorate (as a border) with hemstitch — **hem·stitch·er** *n*
[2]hemstitch *n* (1853) **1** : decorative needlework similar to drawnwork that is used esp. on or next to the stitching line of hems **2** : a stitch used in hemstitching

hemstitch

hen \'hen\ *n* [ME, fr. OE *henn; akin to OE *hana* rooster — more at CHANT] (bef. 12c) **1 a** : a female chicken esp. over a year old; *broadly* : a female bird **b** : the female of various mostly aquatic animals (as lobsters or fish) **2** : WOMAN; *esp* : a fussy middle-aged woman
hen and chickens *n* (1884) : any of several plants having offsets, runners, or flowers that send out shoots; *esp* : HOUSELEEK
hen·bane \'hen-,bān\ *n* (14c) : a poisonous fetid Old World herb (*Hyoscyamus niger*) of the nightshade family having sticky hairy dentate leaves and yellowish brown flowers and yielding hyoscyamine and scopolamine
hen·bit \'hen-,bit\ *n* (1597) : a Eurasian herb (*Lamium amplexicaule*) of the mint family that has scalloped reniform leaves and purplish flowers and is naturalized in No. America
hence \'hen(t)s\ *adv* [ME *hennes, henne*, fr. OE *heonan; akin to OHG *hinnan* away, OE *hēr* here] (13c) **1** : from this place : AWAY **2 a** *archaic* : HENCEFORTH **b** : from this time **3** : because of a preceding fact or premise : THEREFORE **4** : from this source or origin — **from hence** *archaic* : from this place : from this time
hence·forth \'hen(t)s-,fòrth, -,fòrth, hen(t)s-'\ *adv* (14c) : from this point on
hence·for·ward \hen(t)s-'fòr-wərd\ *adv* (14c) : HENCEFORWARD
hench·man \'hench-mən\ *n* [ME *henshman, hengestman* groom, fr. *hengest* stallion (fr. OE) + *man; akin to OHG *hengist* gelding] (15c) **1** *obs* : a squire or page to a person of high rank **2 a** : a trusted follower **b** : a political follower whose support is chiefly for personal advantage **c** : a member of a gang
hen·deca·syl·lab·ic \(,)hen-,de-kə-sə-'la-bik\ *adj* [L *hendecasyllabus*, fr. Gk *hendeka* eleven (fr. *hen-, heis* one + *deka* ten) + *syllabē* syllable — more at SAME, TEN] (ca. 1751) : consisting of 11 syllables or composed of verses of 11 syllables — **hendecasyllabic** *n* — **hen·deca·syl·la·ble** \hen-'de-kə-si-lə-bəl, (,)hen-,de-kə-'\ *n*
hen·di·a·dys \hen-'dī-ə-dəs\ *n* [LL *hendiadys, hendiadyoin*, modif. of Gk *hen dia dyoin*, lit., one through two] (ca. 1577) : the expression of an idea by the use of usu. two independent words connected by *and* (as *nice* and *warm*) instead of the usual combination of independent word and its modifier (as *nicely warm*)
hen·e·quen \'he-ni-kən, ,he-ni-'ken\ *n* [Sp *henequén*] (1880) : a strong yellowish or reddish hard fiber obtained from the leaves of a tropical American agave chiefly in Yucatán and used esp. for binder twine; *also* : a plant (*Agave fourcroydes*) that yields henequen
hen·house \'hen-,haùs\ *n* (ca. 1513) : a house or shelter for fowl
Hen·le's loop \'hen-lēz-\ *n* (ca. 1890) : LOOP OF HENLE
[1]hen·na \'he-nə\ *n* [Ar *hinnā'*] (1600) **1** : a reddish brown dye obtained from leaves of the henna plant and used esp. on hair **2** : an Old World tropical shrub or small tree (*Lawsonia inermis*) of the loosestrife family with small opposite leaves and axillary panicles of fragrant white flowers
[2]henna *vt* (1919) : to dye (as hair) with henna
hen·nery \'he-nə-rē\ *n, pl* **-ner·ies** (1850) : a poultry farm; *also* : an enclosure for poultry
heno·the·ism \'he-nə-(,)thē-i-zəm\ *n* [G *Henotheismus*, fr. Gk *hen-, heis* one + *theos* god — more at SAME] (1860) : the worship of one god without denying the existence of other gods — **heno·the·ist** \-,thē-ist\ *n* — **heno·the·is·tic** \,he-nə-thē-'is-tik\ *adj*
hen party *n* (ca. 1885) : a party for women only
hen·peck \'hen-,pek\ *vt* (1688) : to subject (one's husband) to persistent nagging and domination
hen·ry \'hen-rē\ *n, pl* **henrys** or **henries** [Joseph Henry] (ca. 1890) : the practical meter-kilogram-second unit of inductance equal to the self-inductance of a circuit or the mutual inductance of two circuits in which the variation of one ampere per second results in an induced electromotive force of one volt
hent \'hent\ *vt* [ME, fr. OE *hentan* — more at HUNT] (bef. 12c) *archaic* : SEIZE
hen track *n* (1907) : an illegible or scarcely legible mark intended as handwriting — called also *hen scratch*
[1]hep \'hep, 'həp, 'hət\ *interj* [origin unknown] (1862) — used to mark a marching cadence
[2]hep \'hep\ *adj* [origin unknown] (1904) : [4]HIP
hep·a·rin \'he-pə-rən\ *n* [ISV, fr. Gk *hēpar* liver] (1918) : a mucopolysaccharide sulfuric acid ester that is found esp. in liver, that prolongs

\ə\ abut \²\ kitten, F table \ər\ further \a\ ash \ā\ ace \ä\ mop, mar \aù\ out \ch\ chin \e\ bet \ē\ easy \g\ go \i\ hit \ī\ ice \j\ job \ŋ\ sing \ō\ go \ò\ law \òi\ boy \th\ thin \th\ the \ü\ loot \ù\ foot \y\ yet \zh\ vision \à, k̲, ⁿ, œ, œ̄, ᵫ, ūe, ᵚ\ *see* Guide to Pronunciation the clotting time of blood, and that is used medically — **hep·a·rin·ized** \-rə-ˌnīzd\ *adj*

hepat- *or* **hepato-** *comb form* [L, fr. Gk hēpat-, hēpato-, fr. hēpat-, hēpar; akin to L jecur liver] **1** : liver ⟨*hepat*ectomy⟩ ⟨*hepato*toxic⟩ **2** : hepatic and ⟨*hepato*cellular⟩

hep·a·tec·to·my \ˌhe-pə-'tek-tə-mē\ *n, pl* **-mies** (ca. 1890) : excision of the liver or of part of the liver — **hep·a·tec·to·mized** \-ˌmīzd\ *adj*

¹he·pat·ic \hi-'pa-tik\ *adj* [L hepaticus, fr. Gk hēpatikos, fr. hēpat-, hēpar] (1599) : of, relating to, affecting, associated with, supplying, or draining the liver ⟨a ~ complaint⟩ ⟨~ arteries⟩

²hepatic *n* (1900) : LIVERWORT

he·pat·i·ca \hi-'pa-ti-kə\ *n* [NL, fr. ML, liverwort, fr. L, fem. of hepaticus] (1578) : any of a genus (*Hepatica*) of herbs of the buttercup family with lobed leaves and delicate flowers

hep·a·ti·tis \ˌhe-pə-'tī-təs\ *n, pl* **-tit·i·des** \-'ti-tə-ˌdēz\ [NL] (ca. 1751) **1** : inflammation of the liver **2** : a disease or condition (as hepatitis A or hepatitis B) marked by inflammation of the liver

hepatitis A *n* (1972) : an acute usu. benign hepatitis caused by an RNA virus that does not persist in the blood serum and is transmitted esp. in food and water contaminated with infected fecal matter — called also *infectious hepatitis*

hepatitis B *n* (1972) : a sometimes fatal hepatitis caused by a double-stranded DNA virus that tends to persist in the blood serum and is transmitted esp. by contact with infected blood (as by transfusion) or blood products — called also *serum hepatitis*

he·pa·to·cel·lu·lar \ˌhe-pə-tō-'sel-yə-lər, hi-ˌpa-tə-'sel-\ *adj* (1940) : of or involving hepatocytes ⟨~ carcinoma⟩

he·pa·to·cyte \hi-'pa-tə-ˌsīt, 'he-pə-tə-\ *n* (1965) : an epithelial parenchymatous cell of the liver

hep·a·to·ma \ˌhe-pə-'tō-mə\ *n, pl* **-mas** *or* **-ma·ta** \-mə-tə\ [NL] (ca. 1923) : a usu. malignant tumor of the liver

he·pa·to·meg·a·ly \ˌhe-pə-tō-'me-gə-lē, hi-ˌpa-tə-'me-\ *n, pl* **-lies** (ca. 1901) : enlargement of the liver

he·pa·to·pan·cre·as \ˌhe-pə-tō-'paŋ-krē-əs, -'pan-\ *n* (1884) : a glandular structure (as of a crustacean) that combines the digestive functions of the vertebrate liver and pancreas

hep·a·to·tox·ic \-'täk-sik\ *adj* (1926) : relating to or causing injury to the liver ⟨~ drugs⟩

hep·a·to·tox·ic·i·ty \-täk-'si-sə-tē\ *n* (1952) **1** : a state of toxic damage to the liver **2** : a tendency or capacity to cause hepatotoxicity

hep·cat \'hep-ˌkat\ *n* (1938) : HIPSTER

He·phaes·tus \hi-'fes-təs, -'fēs-\ *n* [L, fr. Gk Hēphaistos] : the Greek god of fire and metalworking — compare VULCAN

hepped up *adj* (1947) : ENTHUSIASTIC

Hep·ple·white \'he-pəl-ˌhwīt, -ˌwīt\ *adj* [George Hepplewhite] (1897) : of, relating to, or imitating a style of furniture originating in late 18th century England

hepta- *or* **hept-** *comb form* [Gk, fr. hepta — more at SEVEN] **1** : seven ⟨*hepta*meter⟩ **2** : containing seven atoms, groups, or equivalents ⟨*hept*ane⟩

hep·ta·chlor \'hep-tə-ˌklōr, -ˌklȯr\ *n* [hepta- + chlorine] (1949) : a cyclodiene chlorinated hydrocarbon pesticide $C_{10}H_5Cl_7$ that causes liver disease in animals and is a suspected human carcinogen

hep·tad \'hep-ˌtad\ *n* [Gk heptad-, heptas, fr. hepta] (1660) : a group of seven

hep·ta·gon \'hep-tə-ˌgän\ *n* [Gk heptagōnon, fr. hepta + gōnia angle — more at -GON] (1570) : a polygon of seven angles and seven sides — **hep·tag·o·nal** \hep-'ta-gə-nᵊl\ *adj*

hep·tam·e·ter \hep-'ta-mə-tər\ *n* (ca. 1898) : a line of verse consisting of seven metrical feet

hep·tane \'hep-ˌtān\ *n* (1877) : any of several isomeric alkanes C_7H_{16} ; *esp* : the liquid normal isomer occurring in petroleum and used esp. as a solvent and in determining octane numbers

hep·tar·chy \'hep-ˌtär-kē\ *n* (1576) : a hypothetical confederacy of seven Anglo-Saxon kingdoms of the 7th and 8th centuries

Hep·ta·teuch \'hep-tə-ˌtük, -ˌtyük\ *n* [LL heptateuchos, fr. Gk, fr. hepta + teuchos book — more at PENTATEUCH] (1678) : the first seven books of the canonical Jewish and Christian Scriptures

hep·tose \'hep-ˌtōs, -ˌtōz\ *n* (1890) : any of various monosaccharides $C_7H_{14}O_7$ containing seven carbon atoms in a molecule

¹her \(h)ər, ˈhər\ *adj* [ME hire, fr. OE hiere, gen. of hēo she — more at HE] (bef. 12c) : of or relating to her or herself esp. as possessor, agent, or object of an action ⟨~ house⟩ ⟨~ research⟩ ⟨~ rescue⟩ — compare ¹SHE

²her *pron* objective case of SHE

He·ra \'hir-ə, 'hē-rə, 'her-ə\ *n* [Gk Hēra, Hērē] : the sister and consort of Zeus — compare JUNO

Her·a·cles \'her-ə-ˌklēz\ *n* [Gk Hēraklēs] : HERCULES

¹her·ald \'her-əld\ *n* [ME, fr. MF hiraut, fr. an (assumed) Gmc compound whose first component is akin to OHG heri army, and whose second is akin to OHG waltan to rule — more at HARRY, WIELD] (14c) **1 a** : an official at a tournament of arms with duties including the making of announcements and the marshaling of combatants **b** : an officer with the status of ambassador acting as official messenger between leaders esp. in war **c** (1) : OFFICER OF ARMS (2) : an officer of arms ranking above a pursuivant and below a king of arms **2** : an official crier or messenger **3 a** : one that precedes or foreshadows **b** : one that conveys news or proclaims : ANNOUNCER ⟨it was the lark, the ~ of the morn —Shak.⟩ **c** : one who actively promotes or advocates : EXPONENT *syn* see FORERUNNER

²herald *vt* (14c) **1** : to give notice of : ANNOUNCE **2 a** : to greet esp. with enthusiasm : HAIL **b** : PUBLICIZE **3** : to signal the approach of : FORESHADOW

he·ral·dic \he-'ral-dik, hə-\ *adj* (1772) : of or relating to heralds or heraldry — **he·ral·di·cal·ly** \-di-k(ə-)lē\ *adv*

her·ald·ry \'her-əl-drē\ *n, pl* **-ries** (1572) **1** : the practice of devising, blazoning, and granting armorial insignia and of tracing and recording genealogies **2** : an armorial ensign; *broadly* : INSIGNIA **3** : PAGEANTRY

herb \'ərb, *US also* & *Brit usu* 'hərb\ *n, often attrib* [ME herbe, fr. OF, fr. L herba] (14c) **1** : a seed-producing annual, biennial, or perennial that does not develop persistent woody tissue but dies down at the end of a growing season **2** : a plant or plant part valued for its medicinal, savory, or aromatic qualities **3** *slang* : MARIJUANA **2** — **herb·like** \'(h)ər-ˌblik\ *adj* — **herby** \'(h)ər-bē\ *adj*

her·ba·ceous \ˌ(h)ər-'bā-shəs\ *adj* (1646) **1 a** : of, relating to, or having the characteristics of an herb **b** *of a stem* : having little or no woody tissue and persisting usu. for a single growing season **2** : having the texture, color, or appearance of a leaf

herb·age \'(h)ər-bij\ *n* (14c) **1** : herbaceous vegetation (as grass) esp. when used for grazing **2** : the succulent parts of herbaceous plants

¹herb·al \'(h)ər-bəl\ *n* (1516) **1** : a book about plants esp. with reference to their medicinal properties **2** *archaic* : HERBARIUM 1

²herbal *adj* (1612) : of, relating to, or made of herbs

herb·al·ist \'(h)ər-bə-list\ *n* (1589) **1** : one who practices healing by the use of herbs **2** : one who collects or grows herbs

her·bar·i·um \ˌ(h)ər-'bar-ē-əm, -'ber-\ *n, pl* **-ia** \-ē-ə\ (1776) **1** : a collection of dried plant specimens usu. mounted and systematically arranged for reference **2** : a place that houses an herbarium

herb doctor *n* (1828) : HERBALIST 1

herbed \'(h)ərbd\ *adj* (1950) : seasoned with herbs

her·bi·cide \'(h)ər-bə-ˌsīd\ *n* [L herba + ISV -cide] (1899) : an agent used to destroy or inhibit plant growth — **her·bi·cid·al** \ˌ(h)ər-bə-'sī-dᵊl\ *adj* — **her·bi·cid·al·ly** \-'dᵊl-ē\ *adv*

her·bi·vore \'(h)ər-bə-ˌvōr, -ˌvȯr\ *n* [NL Herbivora, group of mammals, fr. neut. pl. of herbivorus] (1854) : a plant-eating animal

her·biv·o·rous \ˌ(h)ər-'biv-rəs, -'bi-və-\ *adj* [NL herbivorus, fr. L herba grass + -vorus -vorous] (1661) : feeding on plants — **her·biv·o·ry** \-'bi-və-rē\ *n*

herb Robert \'(h)ərb-'rä-bərt\ *n* [ML herba Roberti, prob. fr. Robertus (St. Robert) †1067 Fr. ecclesiastic] (13c) : a sticky low geranium (*Geranium robertianum*) with small reddish purple flowers

Her·cu·le·an \ˌhər-kyə-'lē-ən, ˌhər-'kyü-lē-\ *adj* (1593) **1** : of, relating to, or characteristic of Hercules **2** *often not cap* : of extraordinary power, extent, intensity, or difficulty

Her·cu·les \'hər-kyə-ˌlēz\ *n* [L, fr. Gk Hēraklēs] **1** : a mythical Greek hero renowned for his great strength and esp. for performing 12 labors imposed on him by Hera **2** [L (gen. Herculis)]: a northern constellation between Corona Borealis and Lyra

Her·cu·les'–club \'hər-kyə-ˌlēz-kləb\ *n* (1847) **1** : a small prickly eastern U.S. tree (*Aralia spinosa*) of the ginseng family — called also *angelica tree* **2** : a small prickly southern U.S. tree (*Zanthoxylum clava-herculis*) of the rue family

¹herd \'hərd\ *n* [ME, fr. OE heord; akin to OHG herta herd, MW cordd troop, Lith kerdžius shepherd] (bef. 12c) **1 a** : a number of animals of one kind kept together under human control **b** : a congregation of gregarious wild animals **2 a** (1) : a group of people usu. having a common bond (2) : a large assemblage of like things **b** : the undistinguished masses : CROWD ⟨isolate the individual prophets from the ~ —Norman Cousins⟩ — **herd·like** \-ˌlīk\ *adj*

²herd *vt* (13c) **1 a** : to gather, lead, or drive as if in a herd ⟨seventy-five boys and girls were ~ed by six or eight teachers —W. A. White⟩ **b** : to keep or move (animals) together **2** : to place in a group ~ *vi* **1** : to assemble or move in a herd **2** : to place oneself in a group : ASSOCIATE

herd·er \'hər-dər\ *n* (1635) : one that herds; *specif* : HERDSMAN 1

herds·man \'hərdz-mən\ *n* (1603) **1** : a manager, breeder, or tender of livestock **2** *cap* : BOÖTES

¹here \'hir\ *adv* [ME, fr. OE hēr; akin to OHG hier here, OE hē he] (bef. 12c) **1 a** : in or at this place ⟨turn ~⟩ — often used interjectionally esp. in answering a roll call **b** : NOW ⟨~ it's morning already⟩ **c** : in an arbitrary location ⟨a book ~, a paper there⟩ **2** : at or in this point, particular, or case ⟨~ we agree⟩ **3** : in the present life or state **4** : HITHER ⟨come ~⟩ **5** — used interjectionally in rebuke or encouragement — **here goes** — used interjectionally to express resolution or resignation esp. at the beginning of a difficult or unpleasant undertaking — **neither here nor there** : having no interest or relevance : of no consequence ⟨comfort is *neither here nor there* to a real sailor⟩

²here *adj* (15c) **1** — used for emphasis esp. after a demonstrative pronoun or after a noun modified by a demonstrative adjective ⟨this book ~⟩ **2** *nonstand* — used for emphasis after a demonstrative adjective but before the noun modified ⟨this ~ book⟩

³here *n* (1605) : this place

here·abouts \'hir-ə-ˌbaúts\ *or* **here·about** \-ˌbaút\ *adv* (13c) : in this vicinity

¹here·af·ter \hir-'af-tər\ *adv* (bef. 12c) **1** : after this in sequence or in time **2** : in some future time or state

²hereafter *n, often cap* (1546) **1** : FUTURE **2** : an existence beyond earthly life

³hereafter *adj* (1591) *archaic* : FUTURE

here and now *n* (1829) : the present time — used with *the* ⟨man's obligation is in the *here and now* —W. H. Whyte⟩

here and there *adv* (14c) **1** : in one place and another **2** : from time to time

here·away \'hir-ə-ˌwä\ *or* **here·aways** \-ˌwäz\ *adv* (14c) *dial* : HEREABOUTS

here·by \hir-'bī, 'hir-ˌ\ *adv* (13c) : by this means

her·e·dit·a·ment \ˌher-ə-'di-tə-mənt\ *n* [ML hereditamentum, fr. LL hereditare to inherit, fr. L hered-, heres] (15c) : heritable property

he·red·i·tar·i·an \hə-ˌre-də-'ter-ē-ən\ *n* (1881) : an advocate of the theory that individual differences in human beings can be accounted for primarily on the basis of genetics — **hereditarian** *adj*

he·red·i·tary \hə-'re-də-ˌter-ē\ *adj* [L hereditarius, fr. hereditas] (15c) **1 a** : genetically transmitted or transmittable from parent to offspring **b** : characteristic of or fostered by one's predecessors **2 a** : received or passing by inheritance or required to pass by inheritance or by reason of birth **b** : having title or possession through inheritance or by reason of birth **3** : of a kind established by tradition ⟨~ enemies⟩ **4** : of or relating to inheritance or heredity *syn* see INNATE — **he·red·i·tar·i·ly** \-ˌre-də-'ter-ə-lē\ *adv*

he·red·i·ty \hə-'re-də-tē\ *n* [MF heredité, fr. L hereditat-, hereditas, fr. hered-, heres heir — more at HEIR] (ca. 1540) **1 a** : INHERITANCE **b** : TRADITION **2 a** : the sum of the qualities and potentialities genetically derived from one's ancestors **b** : the transmission of such qualities from ancestor to descendant through the genes

Her·e·ford \'hər-fərd *sometimes* 'her-ə-\ *n* [*Hereford* former county in England] (1805) : any of a breed of hardy red-coated beef cattle of English origin with white faces and markings

here·in \hir-'in\ *adv* (bef. 12c) : in this

here·in·above \(,)hir-,in-ə-'bəv\ *adv* (ca. 1812) : at a prior point in this writing or document

here·in·af·ter \,hir-ə-'naf-tər\ *adv* (1590) : in the following part of this writing or document

here·in·be·fore \(,)hir-,in-bi-'fōr, -'fȯr\ *adv* (1687) : in the preceding part of this writing or document

here·in·be·low \-bi-'lō\ *adv* (1946) : at a subsequent point in this writing or document

here·of \hir-'əv, -'äv\ *adv* (bef. 12c) : of this

here·on \-'ȯn, -'än\ *adv* (12c) : on this

He·re·ro \hə-'rer-(,)ō, 'her-ə-,rō\ *n, pl* **Herero** *or* **Hereros** (1880) : a member of a Bantu people of central Namibia

he·re·si·arch \hə-'rē-zē-,ärk, 'her-ə-sē-\ *n* [LL *haeresiarcha,* fr. LGk *hairesiarchēs,* fr. *hairesis* + Gk *-archēs* -arch] (1624) : an originator or chief advocate of a heresy

her·e·sy \'her-ə-sē\ *n, pl* **-sies** [ME *heresie,* fr. OF, fr. LL *haeresis,* fr. LGk *hairesis,* fr. Gk, action of taking, choice, sect, fr. *hairein* to take] (13c) 1 a : adherence to a religious opinion contrary to church dogma b : denial of a revealed truth by a baptized member of the Roman Catholic Church c : an opinion or doctrine contrary to church dogma 2 a : dissent or deviation from a dominant theory, opinion, or practice b : an opinion, doctrine, or practice contrary to the truth or to generally accepted beliefs or standards

her·e·tic \'her-ə-,tik\ *n* (14c) 1 : a dissenter from established church dogma; *esp* : a baptized member of the Roman Catholic Church who disavows a revealed truth 2 : one who dissents from an accepted belief or doctrine : NONCONFORMIST

he·ret·i·cal \hə-'re-ti-kəl\ *also* **he·re·tic** \'her-ə-,tik\ *adj* (15c) 1 : of, relating to, or characterized by heresy 2 : of, relating to, or characterized by departure from accepted beliefs or standards : UNORTHODOX — **he·ret·i·cal·ly** \hə-'re-ti-k(ə-)lē\ *adv*

here·to \hir-'tü\ *adv* (12c) : to this writing or document

here·to·fore \'hir-tə-,fōr, -,fȯr, ,hir-tə-'\ *adv* (13c) : up to this time : HITHERTO

here·un·der \hir-'ən-dər\ *adv* (15c) : under or in accordance with this writing or document

here·un·to \hir-ən-(,)tü, ,hir-(,)ən-'tü\ *adv* (1509) : to this

here·up·on \'hir-ə-,pȯn, -,pän, ,hir-ə-'\ *adv* (12c) : on this : immediately after this

here·with \hir-'with, -'with\ *adv* (bef. 12c) 1 : with this communication : enclosed in this 2 : HEREBY

He·rez \hə-'rez\ *or* **He·riz** \-'riz\ *n* [*Herez, Heriz,* town in Iran] (ca. 1922) : a Persian rug characterized by a large central geometric medallion and by angular floral designs

her·i·ot \'her-ē-ət\ *n* [ME, fr. OE *heregeatwe,* pl., military equipment, fr. *here* army (akin to OHG *heri* army) + *geatwe* equipment — more at HARRY] (bef. 12c) : a feudal duty or tribute due under English law to a lord on the death of a tenant

her·i·ta·bil·i·ty \,her-ə-tə-'bi-lə-tē\ *n* (1832) 1 : the quality or state of being heritable 2 : the proportion of observed variation in a particular trait (as intelligence) that can be attributed to inherited genetic factors in contrast to environmental ones

her·i·ta·ble \'her-ə-tə-bəl\ *adj* (14c) 1 : capable of being inherited or of passing by inheritance 2 : HEREDITARY

her·i·tage \'her-ə-tij\ *n* [ME, fr. MF, fr. *heriter* to inherit, fr. LL *hereditare,* fr. L *hered-, heres* heir — more at HEIR] (13c) 1 : property that descends to an heir 2 a : something transmitted by or acquired from a predecessor : LEGACY, INHERITANCE b : TRADITION 3 : something possessed as a result of one's natural situation or birth : BIRTHRIGHT ⟨the nation's ~ of tolerance⟩

her·i·tor \'her-ə-tər\ *n* (15c) : one that inherits : INHERITOR

herky-jerky \'hər-kē-'jər-kē\ *adj* [redupl. of *jerky*] (1957) : characterized by sudden, irregular, or unpredictable movement or style

herm \'hərm\ *n* [L *hermes,* fr. Gk *hermēs* statue of Hermes, herm, fr. *Hermēs*] (ca. 1580) : a statue in the form of a square stone pillar surmounted by a bust or head esp. of Hermes

her·ma \'hər-mə\ *n, pl* **her·mae** \-,mē, -,mī\ *or* **her·mai** \-,mī\ (1638) : HERM

her·maph·ro·dite \(,)hər-'ma-frə-,dīt\ *n* [ME *hermofrodite,* fr. L *hermaphroditus,* fr. Gk *hermaphroditos,* fr. *Hermaphroditos*] (14c) 1 : an animal or plant having both male and female reproductive organs 2 : something that is a combination of diverse elements — **hermaphrodite** *adj* — **her·maph·ro·dit·ic** \(,)hər-,ma-frə-'di-tik\ *adj* — **her·maph·ro·dit·ism** \-'ma-frə-,dī-,ti-zəm\ *n*

Her·maph·ro·di·tus \(,)hər-,ma-frə-'dī-təs\ *n* [L, fr. Gk *Hermaphroditos,* fr. *Hermēs* + *Aphroditē* Aphrodite] : a son of Hermes and Aphrodite who becomes joined in one body with a nymph while bathing

her·ma·typ·ic \,hər-mə-'ti-pik\ *adj* [Gk *herma* prop, reef + *typtein* to strike, coin + E *-ic* — more at TYPE] (1950) : building reefs ⟨~ corals⟩

her·me·neu·ti·cal \,hər-mə-'nü-ti-kəl, -'nyü-\ *or* **her·me·neu·tic** \-tik\ *adj* [Gk *hermēneutikos,* fr. *hermēneuein* to interpret, fr. *hermēneus* interpreter] (1678) : of or relating to hermeneutics : INTERPRETATIVE — **her·me·neu·ti·cal·ly** \-ti-k(ə-)lē\ *adv*

her·me·neu·tics \-tiks\ *n pl but sing or pl in constr* (1737) : the study of the methodological principles of interpretation (as of the Bible)

Her·mes \'hər-(,)mēz\ *n* [L, fr. Gk *Hermēs*] : a Greek god of commerce, eloquence, invention, travel, and theft who serves as herald and messenger of the other gods — compare MERCURY

Hermes Tris·me·gis·tus \-,tris-mə-'jis-təs\ *n* [ML, fr. Gk *Hermēs trismegistos,* lit., Hermes thrice greatest] : a legendary author of works embodying magical, astrological, and alchemical doctrines

her·met·ic \(,)hər-'me-tik\ *also* **her·met·i·cal** \-ti-kəl\ *adj* [NL *hermeticus,* fr. *Hermet-, Hermes Trismegistus*] (1605) 1 *often cap* a : of or relating to the Gnostic writings or teachings arising in the first three centuries A.D. and attributed to Hermes Trismegistus b : relating to or characterized by occultism or abstruseness : RECONDITE 2 [fr. the belief that Hermes Trismegistus invented a magic seal to keep vessels airtight] a : AIRTIGHT ⟨~ seal⟩ b : impervious to external influence

⟨trapped inside the ~ military machine —Jack Newfield⟩ c : RECLUSE, SOLITARY ⟨leads a ~ life⟩ — **her·met·i·cal·ly** \-ti-k(ə-)lē\ *adv*

her·met·i·cism \-'me-tə-,si-zəm\ *n, often cap* (1897) : HERMETISM

her·me·tism \'hər-mə-,ti-zəm\ *n, often cap* (1897) 1 a : a system of ideas based on hermetic teachings b : adherence to or practice of hermetic doctrine 2 : the practice of being hermetically mysterious ⟨it is not . . . willful ~, if the message of their art is veiled and indirect — R. J. Goldwater⟩ — **her·me·tist** \-mə-tist\ *n*

her·mit \'hər-mət\ *n* [ME *eremite,* fr. OF, fr. LL *eremita,* fr. LGk *erēmitēs,* fr. Gk, adj., living in the desert, fr. *erēmia* desert, fr. *erēmos* desolate] (12c) 1 a : one that retires from society and lives in solitude esp. for religious reasons : RECLUSE b *obs* : BEADSMAN 2 : a spiced molasses cookie — **her·mit·ism** \'hər-mə-,ti-zəm\ *n*

her·mit·age \'hər-mə-tij\ *n* (14c) 1 a : the habitation of a hermit b : a secluded residence or private retreat : HIDEAWAY c : MONASTERY 2 : the life or condition of a hermit

Her·mi·tage \,her-mi-'täzh\ *n* [Tain-l'*Ermitage,* commune in France] (1680) : a red or white Rhone valley wine

hermit crab *n* (1735) : any of numerous chiefly marine decapod crustaceans (esp. families Diogenidae, Paguridae, and Parapaguridae) having soft asymmetrical abdomens and occupying the empty shells of gastropods

Her·mi·tian matrix \er-'mē-shən-, ,hər-'mi-shən-\ *n* [Charles *Hermite* †1901 Fr. mathematician] (1935) : a square matrix having the property that each pair of elements in the *i*th row and *j*th column and in the *j*th row and *i*th column are conjugate complex numbers

hermit crab

hern \'hern, 'hərn\ *dial var of* HERON

her·nia \'hər-nē-ə\ *n, pl* **-ni·as** *or* **-ni·ae** \-nē-,ē, -nē-,ī\ [L — more at YARN] (14c) : a protrusion of an organ or part through connective tissue or through a wall of the cavity in which it is normally enclosed — called also *rupture* — **her·ni·al** \-nē-əl\ *adj*

her·ni·ate \'hər-nē-,āt\ *vi* **-at·ed; -at·ing** (ca. 1922) : to protrude through an abnormal body opening : RUPTURE — **her·ni·a·tion** \,hər-nē-'ā-shən\ *n*

he·ro \'hir-(,)ō, 'hē-(,)rō\ *n, pl* **heroes** [L *heros,* fr. Gk *hērōs*] (14c) 1 a : a mythological or legendary figure often of divine descent endowed with great strength or ability b : an illustrious warrior c : a man admired for his achievements and noble qualities d : one that shows great courage 2 a : the principal male character in a literary or dramatic work b : the central figure in an event, period, or movement 3 *pl usu* **heros** : SUBMARINE 2 4 : an object of extreme admiration and devotion : IDOL

Hero *n* [L, fr. Gk *Hērō*] : a legendary priestess of Aphrodite loved by Leander

¹**he·ro·ic** \hi-'rō-ik *also* her-'ō- *or* hē-'rō-\ *also* **he·ro·i·cal** \-i-kəl\ *adj* (1549) 1 : of, relating to, or resembling heroes esp. of antiquity 2 a : exhibiting or marked by courage and daring b : supremely noble or self-sacrificing 3 a : of impressive size, power, extent, or effect : POTENT ⟨~ doses⟩ ⟨a ~ voice⟩ b (1) : of great intensity : EXTREME, DRASTIC ⟨~ effort⟩ (2) : of a kind that is likely only to be undertaken to save a life ⟨~ surgery⟩ 4 : of, relating to, or constituting drama written during the Restoration in heroic couplets and concerned with a conflict between love and honor — **he·ro·i·cal·ly** \-i-k(ə-)lē\ *adv*

²**heroic** *n* (1596) 1 : a heroic verse or poem 2 *pl* a : flamboyantly heroic language or action b : heroic action or behavior c : determined effort esp. in the face of difficulty

heroic couplet *n* (1889) : a rhyming couplet in iambic pentameter

he·roi·com·ic \hi-,rō-i-'kä-mik\ *or* **he·roi·com·i·cal** \-'kä-mi-kəl\ *adj* [F *héroïcomique,* fr. *héroïque* heroic + *comique* comic] (1756) : comic by being ludicrously noble, bold, or elevated

heroic poem *n* (1693) : an epic or a poem in epic style

heroic stanza *n* (ca. 1922) : a rhymed quatrain in heroic verse with a rhyme scheme of *abab* — called also *heroic quatrain*

heroic verse *n* (1586) 1 : dactylic hexameter esp. of epic verse of classical times — called also *heroic meter* 2 : the iambic pentameter used esp. in English epic poetry during the 17th and 18th centuries — called also *heroic line, heroic meter*

her·o·in \'her-ə-wən\ *n* [fr. *Heroin,* a trademark] (1898) : a strongly physiologically addictive narcotic $C_{21}H_{23}NO_5$ that is made by acetylation of but is more potent than morphine and that is prohibited for medical use in the U.S. but is used illicitly for its euphoric effects — **her·o·in·ism** \-wə-,ni-zəm\ *n*

her·o·ine \'her-ə-wən, 'hir-\ *n* [L *heroina,* fr. Gk *hērōinē,* fem. of *hērōs*] (1609) 1 a : a mythological or legendary woman having the qualities of a hero b : a woman admired and emulated for her achievements and qualities 2 a : the principal female character in a literary or dramatic work b : the central female figure in an event or period

her·o·ism \'her-ə-,wi-zəm *also* 'hir-\ *n* (1717) 1 : heroic conduct esp. as exhibited in fulfilling a high purpose or attaining a noble end 2 : the qualities of a hero

he·ro·ize \'hē-(,)rō-,īz, 'hir-(,)ō-; 'her-ə-,wīz\ *vt* **-ized; -iz·ing** (1738) : to make heroic

her·on \'her-ən\ *n, pl* **herons** *also* **heron** [ME *heiroun,* fr. MF *hairon,* of Gmc origin; akin to OHG *heigaro* heron] (14c) : any of various long-necked wading birds (family Ardeidae) with a long tapering bill, large wings, and soft plumage

her·on·ry \-ən-rē\ *n, pl* **-ries** (1616) : a heron rookery

hero-worship *vt* (1884) : to feel or express hero worship for — **hero-worshiper** *n*

hero worship *n* (1774) 1 : veneration of a hero 2 : foolish or excessive adulation for an individual

\ə\ abut \ᵊ\ kitten, F table \ər\ further \a\ ash \ā\ ace \ä\ mop, mar
\aù\ out \ch\ chin \e\ bet \ē\ easy \g\ go \i\ hit \ī\ ice \j\ job
\ŋ\ sing \ō\ go \ȯ\ law \ȯi\ boy \th\ thin \t͟h\ the \ü\ loot \ù\ foot
\y\ yet \zh\ vision \ȧ, k̟, ⁿ, œ, œ̄, ᴜᴇ, ū̄ᴇ, ʸ\ *see* Guide to Pronunciation

her·pes \'hər-(ˌ)pēz\ *n* [L, fr. Gk *herpēs*, fr. *herpein* to creep — more at SERPENT] (14c) : any of several inflammatory virus diseases of the skin characterized by clusters of vesicles; *esp* : HERPES SIMPLEX — **her·pet·ic** \(ˌ)hər-'pe-tik\ *adj*

her·pes sim·plex \-'sim-ˌpleks\ *n* [NL, lit., simple herpes] (1907) : either of two virus diseases marked in one case by groups of watery blisters on the skin or mucous membranes (as of the mouth and lips) above the waist and in the other by such blisters on the genitals

her·pes·vi·rus \-'vī-rəs\ *n* (1925) : any of a group of DNA-containing viruses that replicate in cell nuclei and produce herpes

herpes zos·ter \-'zäs-tər\ *n* [NL, lit., girdle herpes] (1807) : an acute viral inflammation of the sensory ganglia of spinal and cranial nerves associated with a vesicular eruption and neuralgic pains and caused by reactivation of the poxvirus causing chicken pox — called also *shingles*

her·pe·tol·o·gy \ˌhər-pə-'tä-lə-jē\ *n* [Gk *herpeton* quadruped, reptile, fr. neut. of *herpetos* crawling, fr. *herpein*] (1824) : a branch of zoology dealing with reptiles and amphibians — **her·pe·to·log·i·cal** \-tə-'lä-ji-kəl\ *adj* — **her·pe·tol·o·gist** \ˌhər-pə-'tä-lə-jist\ *n*

Herr \(ˌ)her\ *n, pl* **Her·ren** \ˌher-ən, (ˌ)hern\ [G] (1653) — used among German-speaking people as a title equivalent to *Mr.*

her·ren·volk \'her-ən-ˌfōk, -ˌfȯlk\ *n, often cap* [G] (1940) : MASTER RACE

her·ring \'her-iŋ\ *n, pl* **herring** *or* **herrings** [ME *hering*, fr. OE *hǣring*; akin to OHG *hāring* herring] (bef. 12c) **1** : either of two clupeid food fishes (genus *Clupeus*) **a** : one (*C. harengus*) that is abundant in the temperate and colder parts of the No. Atlantic and that in the adult state is preserved by smoking or salting and in the young state is extensively canned and sold as sardines **b** : one (*C. pallasi* syn. *C. h. pallasi*) of the No. Pacific harvested esp. for its roe **2** : CLUPEID

¹her·ring·bone \'her-iŋ-ˌbōn\ *n, often attrib* (1659) **1** : a pattern made up of rows of parallel lines which in any two adjacent rows slope in opposite directions **2 a** : a twilled fabric with a herringbone pattern; *also* : a suit made of this fabric **b** : a herringbone arrangement (as of materials or parts) **3** : a method in skiing of ascending a slope by herringboning

²herringbone *vt* (1787) **1** : to produce a herringbone pattern on **2** : to arrange in a herringbone pattern ~ *vi* **1** : to produce a herringbone pattern **2** : to ascend a slope by toeing out on skis and placing the weight on the inner side

herringbone 1

herring gull *n* (1857) : a common large gull (*Larus argentatus*) of the northern hemisphere that as an adult is largely white with a gray mantle, dark wing tips, pink feet, and yellow bill

hers \'hərz\ *pron, sing or pl in constr* : that which belongs to her — used without a following noun as a pronoun equivalent in meaning to the adjective *her*

her·self \(h)ər-'self, *Southern also* -'sef\ *pron* (bef. 12c) **1** : that identical female one — compare ¹SHE; used reflexively, for emphasis, in absolute constructions, or in place of *her* esp. when joined to another object ⟨she considers ~ lucky⟩ ⟨she ~ did it⟩ ⟨~ an orphan, she understood the situation⟩ ⟨accepted the award for her colleagues and ~⟩ **2** : her normal, healthy, or sane condition or self **3** *chiefly Irish & Scot* : a woman of consequence; *esp* : the mistress of the house

her·sto·ry \'hər-st(ə-)rē\ *n, pl* **-ries** [blend of *her* and *history*] (1971) : HISTORY; *specif* : history considered or presented from a feminist viewpoint or with special attention to the experience of women

hertz \'hərts, 'herts\ *n, pl* **hertz** [Heinrich R. *Hertz*] (ca. 1928) : a unit of frequency equal to one cycle per second — abbr. *Hz*

he's \'hēz, ēz\ (1588) : he is : he has

he/she \'hē-shē, 'hē-ər-; 'hē-'slash-\ *pron* (1974) : he or she — used in writing as a pronoun of common gender

Hesh·van \'kesh-vən\ *n* [Heb *Ḥeshwān*] (ca. 1769) : the 2d month of the civil year or the 8th month of the ecclesiastical year in the Jewish calendar — see MONTH table

hes·i·tance \'he-zə-tən(t)s\ *n* (1601) : HESITANCY

hes·i·tan·cy \-tən(t)-sē\ *n, pl* **-cies** (1617) **1** : the quality or state of being hesitant: as **a** : INDECISION **b** : RELUCTANCE ⟨took that drastic step only with the greatest ~⟩ **2** : HESITATION 1

hes·i·tant \'he-zə-tənt\ *adj* (1647) : tending to hesitate **syn** see DISINCLINED — **hes·i·tant·ly** *adv*

hes·i·tate \'he-zə-ˌtāt\ *vb* **-tat·ed; -tat·ing** [L *haesitatus*, pp. of *haesitare* to stick fast, hesitate, freq. of *haerēre* to stick] *vi* (ca. 1623) **1** : to hold back in doubt or indecision **2** : to delay momentarily : PAUSE **3** : STAMMER ~ *vt* : to hold back from in doubt or uncertainty ⟨wouldn't ~ to commit herself⟩ — **hes·i·tat·er** *n* — **hes·i·tat·ing·ly** \-ˌtā-tiŋ-lē\ *adv*

syn HESITATE, WAVER, VACILLATE, FALTER mean to show irresolution or uncertainty. HESITATE implies a pause before deciding or acting or choosing ⟨*hesitated* before answering the question⟩. WAVER implies hesitation after seeming to decide and so connotes weakness or a retreat ⟨*wavered* in his support of the rebels⟩. VACILLATE implies prolonged hesitation from inability to reach a firm decision ⟨*vacillated* until events were out of control⟩. FALTER implies a wavering or stumbling and often connotes nervousness, lack of courage, or outright fear ⟨never once *faltered* during her testimony⟩.

hes·i·ta·tion \ˌhe-zə-'tā-shən\ *n* (14c) **1** : an act or instance of hesitating **2** : a pausing or faltering in speech

Hes·pe·ri·an \he-'spir-ē-ən\ *adj* [L *Hesperia*, the west, fr. Gk, fr. fem. of *hesperios* of the evening, western, fr. *hesperos* evening — more at WEST] (15c) : WESTERN, OCCIDENTAL

Hes·per·i·des \he-'sper-ə-ˌdēz\ *n pl* [L, fr. Gk] **1** : the nymphs in classical mythology who guard with the aid of a dragon a garden in which golden apples grow **2** : a legendary garden at the western extremity of the world producing golden apples

hes·per·i·din \he-'sper-ə-dⁿn\ *n* [NL *hesperidium* orange, fr. L *Hesperides*] (1838) : a crystalline glycoside $C_{28}H_{34}O_{15}$ found in most citrus fruits and esp. in orange peel

hes·per·id·i·um \ˌhes-pə-'ri-dē-əm\ *n, pl* **-id·ia** \-dē-ə\ [NL] (ca. 1866) : a berry (as an orange or lime) having a leathery rind

Hes·per·us \'hes-p(ə-)rəs\ *n* [ME, fr. L, fr. Gk *Hesperos*] (14c) : EVENING STAR 1

hes·sian \'he-shən\ *n* (1729) **1** *cap* **a** : a native of Hesse **b** : a German mercenary serving in the British forces during the American Revolution; *broadly* : a mercenary soldier **2** *chiefly Brit* : BURLAP

Hessian boot *n* (1809) : a high boot that extends to just below the knee and is commonly ornamented with a tassel and that was introduced into England by the Hessians early in the 19th century

Hessian fly *n* (1786) : a small dipteran fly (*Mayetiola destructor*) that is destructive to wheat in the U.S.

hess·ite \'he-ˌsīt\ *n* [G *Hessit*, fr. Henry *Hess* †1850 Swiss chemist] (1849) : a mineral consisting of a lead-gray sectile silver telluride

hes·so·nite \'he-sⁿn-ˌīt\ *var of* ESSONITE

hest \'hest\ *n* [ME *hest, hes*, fr. OE *hǣs*; akin to OE *hātan* to command — more at HIGHT] (bef. 12c) *archaic* : COMMAND, PRECEPT

Hes·tia \'hes-tē-ə; 'hes-chə, 'hesh-\ *n* [Gk] : the Greek goddess of the hearth and childbirth or domestic activity — compare VESTA

he·tae·ra \hi-'tir-ə\ *or* **he·tai·ra** \-'tī-rə\ *n, pl* **he·tae·rae** \-'tir-(ˌ)ē\ *or* **hetaeras** *or* **hetairas** *or* **he·tai·rai** \-'tī-ˌrī\ [Gk *hetaira*, lit., companion, fem. of *hetairos*] (1820) **1** : one of a class of highly cultivated courtesans in ancient Greece **2** : DEMIMONDAINE

heter- *or* **hetero-** *comb form* [MF or LL; MF, fr. LL, fr. Gk, fr. *heteros*; akin to Gk *heis* one — more at SAME] **1** : other than usual : other : different ⟨*hetero*phyllous⟩ **2** : containing atoms of different kinds ⟨*hetero*cyclic⟩

het·ero \'he-tə-ˌrō\ *n, pl* **-er·os** (1933) : HETEROSEXUAL — **hetero** *adj*

het·ero·at·om \'he-tə-rō-ˌa-təm\ *n* (1900) : an atom other than carbon in the ring of a heterocyclic compound

het·ero·aux·in \ˌhe-tə-rō-'ȯk-sən\ *n* (1935) : INDOLEACETIC ACID

het·ero·cer·cal \-'sər-kəl\ *adj* (1838) **1** *of a fish tail fin* : having the upper lobe larger than the lower with the vertebral column extending into the upper lobe **2** : having or relating to a heterocercal tail fin

het·ero·chro·ma·tin \-'krō-mə-tən\ *n* [G] (1932) : densely staining chromatin that appears as nodules in or along chromosomes and contains relatively few genes — **het·ero·chro·mat·ic** \-krə-'ma-tik\ *adj*

¹het·ero·clite \'he-tə-rə-ˌklīt\ *n* (1580) **1** : a word irregular in inflection; *esp* : a noun irregular in declension **2** : one that deviates from common rules or forms

²heteroclite *adj* [MF or LL; MF, fr. LL *heteroclitus*, fr. Gk *heteroklitos*, fr. *heter-* + *klinein* to lean, inflect — more at LEAN] (1598) : deviating from common forms or rules

het·ero·cy·clic \ˌhe-tə-rō-'sī-klik, -'si-\ *adj* [ISV] (1899) : relating to, characterized by, or being a ring composed of atoms of more than one kind — **het·ero·cy·cle** \'he-tə-rō-ˌsī-kəl\ *n* — **heterocyclic** *n*

het·ero·cyst \'he-tə-rō-ˌsist\ *n* (1872) : a large transparent thick-walled cell that is found in the filaments of some blue-green algae and is the site of nitrogen fixation — **het·ero·cys·tous** \ˌhe-tə-rō-'sis-təs\ *adj*

het·ero·dox \'he-tə-rə-ˌdäks, 'he-trə-\ *adj* [LL *heterodoxus*, fr. Gk *heterodoxos*, fr. *heter-* + *doxa* opinion — more at DOXOLOGY] (ca. 1650) **1** : contrary to or different from an acknowledged standard, a traditional form, or an established religion : UNORTHODOX, UNCONVENTIONAL ⟨a ~ book⟩ ⟨~ ideas⟩ **2** : holding unorthodox opinions or doctrines

het·ero·doxy \-ˌdäk-sē\ *n, pl* **-dox·ies** (1659) **1** : the quality or state of being heterodox **2** : a heterodox opinion or doctrine

het·ero·du·plex \ˌhe-tə-rō-'dü-ˌpleks, -'dyü-\ *n* (1962) : a nucleic-acid molecule composed of two chains with each derived from a different parent molecule — **heteroduplex** *adj*

¹het·ero·dyne \'he-tə-rə-ˌdīn, 'he-trə-\ *adj* [*heter-* + *-dyne*, modif. of Gk *dynamis* power — more at DYNAMIC] (1908) : of or relating to the production of an electrical beat between two radio frequencies of which one usu. is that of a received signal-carrying current and the other that of an uninterrupted current introduced into the apparatus; *also* : of or relating to the production of a beat between two optical frequencies

²heterodyne *vt* **-dyned; -dyn·ing** (1923) : to combine (as a radio frequency) with a different frequency so that a beat is produced

het·er·oe·cious \ˌhe-tə-'rē-shəs\ *adj* [*heter-* + Gk *oikia* house — more at VICINITY] (1882) : passing through the different stages in the life cycle on alternate and often unrelated hosts ⟨~ insects⟩ — **het·er·oe·cism** \-'rē-ˌsi-zəm\ *n*

het·ero·ga·mete \ˌhe-tə-rō-'ga-ˌmēt *also* -gə-'mēt\ *n* [ISV] (1897) : either of a pair of gametes that differ in form, size, or behavior and occur typically as large nonmotile oogametes and small motile sperms

het·ero·ga·met·ic \-gə-'me-tik\ *adj* (1910) : forming two kinds of gametes of which one produces male offspring and the other female offspring ⟨the human male is ~⟩ — **het·ero·gam·e·ty** \-'gam-ə-tē\ *n*

het·er·og·a·mous \ˌhe-tə-'rä-gə-məs\ *adj* (1839) : having or characterized by fusion of unlike gametes — compare ANISOGAMOUS, ISOGAMOUS

het·er·og·a·my \-mē\ *n* (ca. 1894) **1** : sexual reproduction involving fusion of unlike gametes often differing in size, structure, and physiology **2** : the condition of reproducing by heterogamy

het·er·o·ge·ne·ity \ˌhe-tə-rō-jə-'nē-ə-tē, ˌhe-trō-\ *n* (1641) : the quality or state of being heterogeneous

het·er·o·ge·neous \ˌhe-tə-rō-'jē-nē-əs, ˌhe-trə-, -nyəs\ *adj* [ML *heterogeneus*, fr. Gk *heterogenēs*, fr. *heter-* + *genos* kind — more at KIN] (1630) : consisting of dissimilar or diverse ingredients or constituents : MIXED — **het·er·o·ge·neous·ly** *adv* — **het·er·o·ge·neous·ness** *n*

het·er·og·e·nous \ˌhe-tə-'rä-jə-nəs\ *adj* (1695) : HETEROGENEOUS

het·er·og·e·ny \-nē\ *n* (1838) : a heterogeneous collection or group

het·er·og·o·ny \ˌhe-tə-'rä-gə-nē\ *n* (ca. 1887) **1** : ALTERNATION OF GENERATIONS; *esp* : alternation of a dioecious with a parthenogenetic generation **2** : ALLOMETRY — **het·ero·gon·ic** \ˌhe-tə-rə-'gä-nik\ *adj*

het·ero·graft \'he-tə-rō-ˌgraft\ *n* (1923) : a graft of tissue taken from a donor of one species and grafted into a recipient of another species — called also *xenograft;* compare HOMOGRAFT

het·ero·kary·on \ˌhe-tə-rō-'kar-ē-ˌän, -ən\ *n* [NL, fr. *heter-* + *karyon,* caryon* nucleus, fr. Gk *karyon* nut, kernel] (1941) : a cell (as in the mycelium of a fungus) that contains two or more genetically unlike nuclei

het·ero·kary·o·sis \ˌhe-tə-rō-ˌkar-ē-'ō-səs\ *n* [NL] (1916) : the condition of having cells that are heterokaryons — **het·ero·kary·ot·ic** \-ē-'ä-tik\ *adj*

het·er·ol·o·gous \-'rä-lə-gəs\ *adj* [*heter-* + *-logous* (as in *homologous*)] (1893) : derived from a different species ⟨~ DNAs⟩ ⟨~ transplants⟩ — **het·er·ol·o·gous·ly** *adv*

het·ero·ly·sis \,he-tə-'rä-lə-səs, -ə-rə-'lī-səs\ *n* [NL] (1938) : decomposition of a compound into two oppositely charged particles or ions — **het·ero·lyt·ic** \-ə-rə-'li-tik\ *adj*

het·ero·mor·phic \,he-tə-rə-'môr-fik\ *adj* [ISV] (ca. 1859) 1 : deviating from the usual form 2 : exhibiting diversity of form or forms ⟨~ pairs of chromosomes⟩ — **het·ero·mor·phism** \-,fi-zəm\ *n*

het·er·on·o·mous \,he-tə-'rä-nə-məs\ *adj* (ca. 1871) : subject to external controls and impositions

het·er·on·o·my \-mē\ *n* [*heter-* + *-nomy* (as in *autonomy*)] (1798) : subjection to something else; *esp* : a lack of moral freedom or self-determination

het·ero·nym \'he-tə-rə-,nim\ *n* (ca. 1889) : one of two or more homographs (as a *bass* voice and *bass*, a fish) that differ in pronunciation and meaning

het·ero·phile \'he-tə-rə-,fīl\ *or* **het·ero·phil** \-,fil\ *adj* (1920) : relating to or being any of a group of antigens in organisms of different species that induce the formation of antibodies that will cross-react with the other antigens of the group; *also* : being or relating to any of these antibodies

het·er·oph·o·ny \,he-tə-'rä-fə-nē\ *n, pl* **-nies** [Gk *heterophōnia* diversity of note, fr. *heter-* + *-phōnia* -phony] (1919) : independent variation on a single melody by two or more voices

het·ero·phyl·lous \,he-tə-rō-'fi-ləs\ *adj* (ca. 1828) : having the foliage leaves of more than one form on the same plant or stem — **het·ero·phyl·ly** \'he-tə-rō-,fi-lē\ *n*

het·ero·ploid \'he-tə-rə-,ploid\ *adj* [ISV] (1926) : having a chromosome number that deviates from and is not an integral multiple of the number characteristic of a given species — **heteroploid** *n* — **het·ero·ploi·dy** \-,ploi-dē\ *n*

het·er·op·ter·ous \,he-tə-'räp-tə-rəs\ *adj* [ultim. fr. Gk *heter-* + *pteron* wing — more at FEATHER] (1895) : of or relating to an insect order or suborder (Heteroptera) comprising the true bugs

¹**het·ero·sex·u·al** \,he-tə-rō-'sek-sh(ə-)wəl, -'sek-shəl\ *adj* [ISV] (1892) 1 a : of, relating to, or characterized by a tendency to direct sexual desire toward the opposite sex b : of, relating to, or involving sexual intercourse between individuals of opposite sex 2 : of or relating to different sexes — **het·ero·sex·u·al·i·ty** \-,sek-shə-'wa-lə-tē\ *n* — **het·ero·sex·u·al·ly** \-'sek-sh(ə-)wə-lē, -'sek-shə-lē\ *adv*

²**heterosexual** *n* (1920) : a heterosexual person

het·er·o·sis \,he-tə-'rō-səs\ *n* [NL] (1914) : the marked vigor or capacity for growth often exhibited by crossbred animals or plants — called also *hybrid vigor* — **het·er·ot·ic** \-'rä-tik\ *adj*

het·ero·spo·ry \'he-tə-rə-,spōr-ē, -,spor-; ,he-tə-'räs-pə-rē\ *n* (1898) : the production of microspores and megaspores (as in seed plants and some ferns) — **het·ero·spo·rous** \,he-tə-rə-'spōr-əs, -'spor-; -'räs-pə-rəs\ *adj*

het·ero·thal·lic \,he-tə-rō-'tha-lik\ *adj* [*heter-* + *thallus* + *-ic*] (1904) 1 : having two or more morphologically similar haploid phases or types of which individuals from the same type are mutually sterile but individuals from different types are cross-fertile ⟨~ fungi⟩ ⟨~ spores⟩ 2 : DIOECIOUS — **het·ero·thal·lism** \-'tha-,li-zəm\ *n*

het·ero·top·ic \,he-tə-rō-'tä-pik\ *adj* [*heter-* + Gk *topos* place] (1878) : occurring in an abnormal place ⟨~ bone formation⟩ ⟨~ liver transplantation⟩

het·ero·troph \'he-tə-rə-,trōf, -,träf\ *n* (ca. 1900) : a heterotrophic individual

het·ero·tro·phic \,he-tə-rə-'trō-fik\ *adj* (1893) : requiring complex organic compounds of nitrogen and carbon for metabolic synthesis — **het·ero·tro·phi·cal·ly** \-fi-k(ə-)lē\ *adv* — **het·ero·tro·phy** \,he-tə-'rä-trə-fē, 'he-tə-rə-,trō-\ *n*

het·ero·typ·ic \,he-tə-rō-'ti-pik\ *adj* (1889) : different in kind, arrangement, or form

het·ero·zy·go·sis \-(,)zī-'gō-səs\ *n* [NL] (1902) : HETEROZYGOSITY

het·ero·zy·gos·i·ty \-'gä-sə-tē\ *n* (1912) : the state of being heterozygous

het·ero·zy·gote \-'zī-,gōt\ *n* (1902) : a heterozygous individual

het·ero·zy·gous \-gəs\ *adj* (1902) : having the two alleles at corresponding loci on homologous chromosomes different for one or more loci

heth \'kät, 'käth, 'ket, 'keth\ *n* [Heb *ḥēth*] (1823) : the 8th letter of the Hebrew alphabet — see ALPHABET table

het·man \'het-mən\ *n, pl* **hetmans** [Ukrainian *het'man*] (1710) : a cossack leader

het up \'het-'əp\ *adj* [*het*, dial. past of *heat*] (1909) : highly excited : UPSET

heu·land·ite \'hyü-lən-,dīt\ *n* [Henry *Heuland*, 19th cent. Eng. mineral collector] (1822) : a zeolite consisting of a hydrous aluminosilicate of sodium and calcium

¹**heu·ris·tic** \hyü-'ris-tik\ *adj* [G *heuristisch*, fr. NL *heuristicus*, fr. Gk *heuriskein* to discover; akin to OIr fo-*fúair* he found] (1821) : involving or serving as an aid to learning, discovery, or problem-solving by experimental and esp. trial-and-error methods ⟨~ techniques⟩ ⟨a ~ assumption⟩; *also* : of or relating to exploratory problem-solving techniques that utilize self-educating techniques (as the evaluation of feedback) to improve performance ⟨a ~ computer program⟩ — **heu·ris·ti·cal·ly** \-ti-k(ə-)lē\ *adv*

²**heuristic** *n* (1860) 1 : the study or practice of heuristic procedure 2 : heuristic argument 3 : a heuristic method or procedure

hew \'hyü\ *vb* **hewed; hewed** *or* **hewn** \'hyün\; **hew·ing** [ME, fr. OE *hēawan*; akin to OHG *houwan* to hew, Lith *kauti* to forge, L *cudere* to beat] *vt* (bef. 12c) 1 : to cut with blows of a heavy cutting instrument 2 : to fell by blows of an ax ⟨~ a tree⟩ 3 : to give form or shape to with or as if with heavy cutting blows ⟨~ed their farms from the wilderness —J. T. Shotwell⟩ ~ *vi* 1 : to make cutting blows 2 : CONFORM, ADHERE — often used in the phrase *hew to the line* ⟨no pressure . . . on newspapers to ~ to the official line —*N.Y. Times Mag.*⟩ — **hew·er** *n*

¹**hex** \'heks\ *vb* [PaG *hexe*, fr. G *hexen*, fr. *Hexe* witch, fr. OHG *hagzissa*; akin to ME *hagge* hag] *vi* (1830) : to practice witchcraft ~ *vt* 1 : to put a hex on 2 : to affect as if by an evil spell : JINX ⟨giving in to an unscientific fear of ~*ing* the whole project —Daniel Lang⟩ — **hex·er** *n*

²**hex** *n* (1856) 1 : a person who practices witchcraft : WITCH 2 : SPELL, JINX

³**hex** *adj* (1924) : HEXAGONAL ⟨a bolt with a ~ head⟩

⁴**hex** *adj or n* (1970) : HEXADECIMAL

hexa- *or* **hex-** *comb form* [Gk, fr. *hex* six — more at SIX] 1 : six ⟨*hexa*ploid⟩ 2 : containing six atoms, groups, or equivalents ⟨*hexa*ne⟩

hexa·chlo·ro·eth·ane \,hek-sə-,klōr-'ō-,e-,thän, -,klōr-\ *or* **hexa·chlor·eth·ane** \-,klōr-'e-, -,klor-\ *n* [ISV] (1898) : a toxic crystalline compound C_2Cl_6 used esp. in smoke bombs and in the control of liver flukes in ruminants

hexa·chlo·ro·phene \-'klōr-ə-,fēn, -'klor-\ *n* [*hexa-* + *chlor-* + *phenol*] (1948) : a powdered phenolic bacteria-inhibiting agent $C_{13}Cl_6H_6O_2$

hexa·chord \'hek-sə-,kord\ *n* [*hexa-* + Gk *chordē* string — more at YARN] (1730) : a diatonic series of six tones having a semitone between the third and fourth tones

hexa·dec·i·mal \,hek-sə-'des-məl, -'de-sə-\ *adj* (1954) : of, relating to, or being a number system with a base of 16 — **hexadecimal** *n*

hexa·gon \'hek-sə-,gän\ *n* [Gk *hexagōnon*, neut. of *hexagōnos* hexagonal, fr. *hexa-* + *gōnia* angle — more at -GON] (1570) : a polygon of six angles and six sides

hex·ag·o·nal \hek-'sa-gə-n°l\ *adj* (1571) 1 : having six angles and six sides 2 : having a hexagon as section or base 3 : relating to or being a crystal system characterized by three equal lateral axes intersecting at angles of 60 degrees and a vertical axis of variable length at right angles — **hex·ag·o·nal·ly** \-n°l-ē\ *adv*

hexa·gram \'hek-sə-,gram\ *n* [ISV] (1871) : a plane figure that has the shape of a 6-pointed star, that consists of two intersecting congruent equilateral triangles having the same point as center and their sides parallel, and that can be formed by constructing external equilateral triangles on the sides of a regular hexagon — compare SOLOMON'S SEAL 2

hexagram

hexa·he·dron \,hek-sə-'hē-drən\ *n, pl* **-drons** *also* **-dra** \-drə\ [LL, fr. Gk *hexaedron*, fr. neut. of *hexaedros* of six surfaces, fr. *hexa-* + *hedra* seat — more at SIT] (1571) : a polyhedron of six faces (as a cube)

hexa·hy·drate \-'hī-,drāt\ *n* (1908) : a chemical compound with six molecules of water

hex·am·e·ter \hek-'sa-mə-tər\ *n* [L, fr. Gk *hexametron*, fr. neut. of *hexametros* having six measures, fr. *hexa-* + *metron* measure — more at MEASURE] (1546) : a line of verse consisting of six metrical feet

hexa·me·tho·ni·um \,hek-sə-mə-'thō-nē-əm\ *n* [*hexa-* + *meth-* + *-onium*] (1949) : either of two compounds $C_{12}H_{30}Br_2N_2$ or $C_{12}H_{30}Cl_2N_2$ used as ganglionic blocking agents in the treatment of hypertension

hexa·meth·y·lene·tet·ra·mine \,hek-sə-'me-thə-,lēn-'te-trə-,mēn\ *n* [ISV *hexa-* + *methylene* + *tetra-* + *amine*] (1888) : a crystalline compound $C_6H_{12}N_4$ used esp. as an accelerator in vulcanizing rubber and as a urinary antiseptic — compare METHENAMINE

hex·ane \'hek-,sān\ *n* [ISV] (1887) : any of several isomeric volatile liquid alkanes C_6H_{14} found in petroleum

hex·a·no·ic acid \,hek-sə-'nō-ik-\ *n* [ISV *hexane* + *-oic*] (1926) : CAPROIC ACID

hexa·ploid \'hek-sə-,ploid\ *adj* [ISV] (1912) : having or being six times the monoploid chromosome number — **hexaploid** *n* — **hexa·ploi·dy** \-,ploi-dē\ *n*

¹**hexa·pod** \'hek-sə-,päd\ *n* [Gk *hexapod-, hexapous* having six feet, fr. *hexa-* + *pod-, pous* foot — more at FOOT] (1668) : INSECT 1b

²**hexapod** *adj* (ca. 1847) 1 : six-footed 2 : of or relating to insects

Hexa·teuch \'hek-sə-,tük, -,tyük\ *n* [*hexa-* + Gk *teuchos* book — more at PENTATEUCH] (1878) : the first six books of the Bible

hex·e·rei \,hek-sə-'rī\ *n* [PaG, fr. G, fr. *Hexe* witch] (1898) : WITCHCRAFT

hexo·bar·bi·tal \,hek-sə-'bär-bə-,tól\ *n* [*hexo-* (fr. *hexa-*) + *barbital*] (1941) : a barbiturate $C_{12}H_{16}N_2O_3$ used as a sedative and hypnotic and in the form of its soluble sodium salt as an intravenous anesthetic of short duration

hexo·ki·nase \,hek-sə-'kī-,nās, -,nāz\ *n* [*hexose* + *kinase*] (1930) : any of a group of enzymes that accelerate the phosphorylation of hexoses (as in the formation of glucose-6-phosphate from glucose and ATP) in carbohydrate metabolism

hex·os·a·min·i·dase \,hek-sä-sə-'mi-nə-,dās, -,dāz\ *n* [*hexose* + *amino* + *-ide* + *-ase*] (1969) : either of two hydrolytic enzymes that catalyze the splitting off of a hexose from a ganglioside and are deficient in some metabolic diseases (as a variant of Tay-Sachs disease)

hex·o·san \'hek-sə-,san\ *n* (1894) : a polysaccharide yielding only hexoses on hydrolysis

hex·ose \'hek-,sōs, -,sōz\ *n* [ISV] (1892) : a monosaccharide (as glucose) containing six carbon atoms in the molecule

hex·yl \'hek-səl\ *n* [ISV] (1869) : an alkyl radical C_6H_{13}— derived from a hexane

hex·yl·res·or·cin·ol \,hek-səl-rə-'zór-s°n-,ól, -,ōl\ *n* (1924) : a crystalline phenol $C_{12}H_{18}O_2$ used as an antiseptic and anthelmintic

hey \'hā\ *interj* [ME] (13c) — used esp. to call attention to or to express interrogation, surprise, or exultation

¹**hey·day** \'hā-,dā\ *interj* [irreg. fr. *hey*] (1672) *archaic* — used to express elation or wonder

²**heyday** *n* (1590) 1 *archaic* : high spirits 2 : the period of one's greatest strength, vigor, or prosperity

hey presto \'hā-'pres-(,)tō\ *interj* (1731) *Brit* : suddenly as if by magic

Hez·e·ki·ah \,he-zə-'kī-ə\ *n* [Heb *Ḥizqīyāh*] : a king of Judah under whom the kingdom underwent a ruinous Assyrian invasion at the end of the 8th century B.C.

hi \'hī(-ē)\ *interj* [ME *hy*] (15c) — used esp. as a greeting

\ə\ abut \ᵊ\ kitten, F table \ər\ further \a\ ash \ā\ ace \ä\ mop, mar \aů\ out \ch\ chin \e\ bet \ē\ easy \g\ go \i\ hit \ī\ ice \j\ job \ŋ\ sing \ō\ go \ó\ law \ói\ boy \th\ thin \th\ the \ü\ loot \ů\ foot \y\ yet \zh\ vision \à, k̲, ⁿ, œ, œ̄, ᵫ, ᵫ̄, ᵜ\ see Guide to Pronunciation

hi·a·tal \hī-'ā-t³l\ *adj* (1909) : of, relating to, or involving a hiatus

hiatal hernia *n* (ca. 1944) : a hernia in which an anatomical part (as the stomach) protrudes through the esophageal hiatus of the diaphragm — called also *hiatus hernia*

hi·a·tus \hī-'ā-təs\ *n* [L, fr. *hiare* to yawn — more at YAWN] (1563) **1 a** : a break in or as if in a material object — GAP ⟨the ~ between the theory and the practice of the party —J. G. Colton⟩ **b** : a gap or passage in an anatomical part or organ **2 a** : an interruption in time or continuity : BREAK **b** : the occurrence of two vowel sounds without pause or intervening consonantal sound

Hi·a·wa·tha \,hī-ə-'wȯ-thə, ,hē-ə-, -'wä-\ *n* : the Indian hero of Longfellow's poem *The Song of Hiawatha*

hi·ba·chi \hi-'bä-chē\ *n* [Jp] (1863) : a charcoal brazier

hi·ber·nac·u·lum \,hī-bər-'na-kyə-ləm\ *n, pl* **-la** \-lə\ [NL, fr. L, winter residence, fr. *hibernare*] (1789) : a shelter occupied during the winter by a dormant animal (as an insect or reptile)

hi·ber·nal \hī-'bər-n³l\ *adj* (1646) : of, relating to, or occurring in winter

hi·ber·nate \'hī-bər-,nāt\ *vi* **-nat·ed; -nat·ing** [L *hibernatus,* pp. of *hibernare* to pass the winter, fr. *hibernus* of winter; akin to L *hiems* winter, Gk *cheimōn*] (ca. 1802) **1** : to pass the winter in a torpid or resting state **2** : to be or become inactive or dormant — **hi·ber·na·tion** \,hī-bər-'nā-shən\ *n* — **hi·ber·na·tor** \'hī-bər-,nā-tər\ *n*

¹Hi·ber·ni·an \hī-'bər-nē-ən\ *adj* [L *Hibernia* Ireland] (1632) : of, relating to, or characteristic of Ireland or the Irish

²Hibernian *n* (1709) : a native or inhabitant of Ireland

Hi·ber·no- *comb form* [L *Hibernia*] **1** : Irish and ⟨*Hiberno*-British⟩ **2** : Irish ⟨*Hiberno*-English⟩

Hiberno–English *n* (1985) : the English language spoken in Ireland

hi·bis·cus \hī-'bis-kəs, hə-\ *n* [NL, fr. L, marshmallow] (1706) : any of a large genus (*Hibiscus*) of herbs, shrubs, or small trees of the mallow family with large showy flowers and usu. dentate leaves

¹hic·cup *also* **hic·cough** \'hi-(,)kəp\ *n* [imit.] (ca. 1580) **1** : a spasmodic inhalation with closure of the glottis accompanied by a peculiar sound **2** : an attack of hiccuping — usu. used in pl. but sing or pl. in constr.

²hiccup *also* **hiccough** *vi* **hic·cuped** *also* **hic·cupped; hic·cup·ing** *also* **hic·cup·ping** (ca. 1580) : to make a hiccup; *also* : to be affected with hiccups

hic ja·cet \'hik-'jā-sət, 'hēk-'yä-kət\ *n* [L, lit., here lies] (1654) : EPITAPH

¹hick \'hik\ *n* [*Hick,* nickname for *Richard*] (ca. 1690) : an unsophisticated provincial person — **hick·ish** \'hi-kish\ *adj*

²hick *adj* (1920) : UNSOPHISTICATED, PROVINCIAL ⟨a ~ town⟩

¹hick·ey \'hi-kē\ *n, pl* **hickeys** [origin unknown] (1913) : DEVICE, GADGET

²hickey *n, pl* **hickeys** [origin unknown] (ca. 1915) **1 a** : PIMPLE **b** : a temporary red mark on the skin (as one produced by biting and sucking) **2** *pl also* **hick·ies** : a small imperfection in printing

hick·o·ry \'hi-k(ə-)rē\ *n, pl* **-ries** [short for obs. *pokahickory,* fr. Virginia Algonquian *pawcohiccora* food prepared from pounded nuts] (1670) **1 a** : any of a genus (*Carya*) of No. American hardwood trees of the walnut family that often have sweet edible nuts **b** : the usu. tough wood of a hickory **2** : a switch or cane (as of hickory wood) used esp. for punishing a child — **hickory** *adj*

hid \'hid\ *adj* (12c) : HIDDEN

hi·dal·go \hi-'dal-(,)gō, ē-'thäl-\ *n, pl* **-gos** *often cap* [Sp, fr. OSp *fijo dalgo,* lit., son of something] (1594) : a member of the lower nobility of Spain

Hi·dat·sa \hi-'dät-sə\ *n, pl* **Hidatsa** *also* **Hidatsas** (1873) **1** : a member of an American Indian people of the Missouri River valley in No. Dakota **2** : the Siouan language of the Hidatsa

hid·den \'hi-d³n\ *adj* (13c) **1** : being out of sight or not readily apparent : CONCEALED **2** : OBSCURE, UNEXPLAINED, UNDISCLOSED — **hid·den·ness** \-nəs\ *n*

hidden agenda *n* (1971) : an ulterior motive

hid·den·ite \'hi-d³n-,īt\ *n* [William E. *Hidden* †1918 Am. mineralogist] (1881) : a transparent yellow to green spodumene valued as a gem

hidden tax *n* (1936) **1** : a tax that is ultimately paid by someone other than the person on whom it is levied **2** : an economic inequity that reduces one's real income or buying power

¹hide \'hīd\ *n* [ME, fr. OE *hīgid, hīd*] (bef. 12c) : any of various old English units of land area; *esp* : a unit of 120 acres

²hide *vb* **hid** \'hid\; **hid·den** \'hi-d³n\ *or* **hid; hid·ing** \'hī-diŋ\ [ME *hiden,* fr. OE *hȳdan;* akin to Gk *keuthein* to conceal] *vt* (bef. 12c) **1 a** : to put out of sight : SECRETE **b** : to conceal for shelter or protection : SHIELD **2** : to keep secret **3** : to screen from or as if from view : OBSCURE **4** : to turn (the eyes or face) away in shame or anger ~ *vi* **1** : to remain out of sight — often used with *out* **2** : to seek protection or evade responsibility — **hid·er** \'hī-dər\ *n*

syn HIDE, CONCEAL, SCREEN, SECRETE, BURY mean to withhold or withdraw from sight. HIDE may or may not suggest intent ⟨*hide* in the closet⟩ ⟨a house *hidden* in the woods⟩. CONCEAL usu. does imply intent and often specif. implies a refusal to divulge ⟨*concealed* the weapon⟩. SCREEN implies an interposing of something that prevents discovery ⟨a house *screened* by trees⟩. SECRETE suggests a depositing in a place unknown to others ⟨*secreted* the amulet inside his shirt⟩. BURY implies covering up so as to hide completely ⟨*buried* the treasure⟩.

³hide *n* (14c) *chiefly Brit* : BLIND 2

⁴hide *n* [ME, fr. OE *hȳd;* akin to OHG *hūt* hide, L *cutis* skin, Gk *kytos* hollow vessel] (bef. 12c) **1** : the skin of an animal whether raw or dressed — used esp. of large heavy skins **2** : the life or physical well= being of a person ⟨betrayed his friend to save his own ~⟩ — **hide or hair** *or* **hide nor hair** : a vestige or trace of someone or something ⟨a wife he hasn't seen *hide or hair* of in over 20 years —H. L. Davis⟩

⁵hide *vt* **hid·ed; hid·ing** (ca. 1825) : to give a beating to : FLOG

hide–and–seek \,hī-d³n-'sēk\ *n* (ca. 1727) : a children's game in which one player does not look while others hide and then goes to find them

hide·away \'hī-də-,wā\ *n* (1926) : RETREAT, HIDEOUT

hide·bound \'hīd-,baùnd\ *adj* (1559) **1** *of a domestic animal* : having a dry skin lacking in pliancy and adhering closely to the underlying flesh **2** : having an inflexible or ultraconservative character

hid·eous \'hi-dē-əs\ *adj* [alter. of ME *hidous,* fr. MF, fr. *hisde, hide* terror] (14c) **1** : offensive to the senses and esp. to sight : exceedingly

ugly **2** : morally offensive : SHOCKING — **hid·eos·i·ty** \,hi-dē-'ä-sə-tē\ *n* — **hid·eous·ly** *adv* — **hid·eous·ness** *n*

hide-out \'hī-,daùt\ *n* (1904) : a place of refuge, retreat, or concealment

hid·ey–hole *or* **hidy–hole** \'hī-dē-,hōl\ *n* [alter. of earlier *hiding-hole*] (1817) : HIDEAWAY

hie \'hī\ *vb* **hied; hy·ing** *or* **hie·ing** [ME, fr. OE *hīgian* to strive, hasten] *vi* (12c) : to go quickly : HASTEN ~ *vt* : to cause (oneself) to go quickly

hi·er·arch \'hī-(ə-),rärk\ *n* [ME *ierarchis,* pl., fr. MF or ML; MF *hierarche,* fr. ML *hierarcha,* fr. Gk *hierarchēs,* fr. *hieros* sacred + *-archēs* -arch] (15c) **1** : a religious leader in a position of authority **2** : a person high in a hierarchy — **hi·er·ar·chal** \,hī-(ə-)'rär-kəl\ *adj*

hi·er·ar·chi·cal \,hī-(ə-)'rär-ki-kəl *also* hir-'är-\ *or* **hi·er·ar·chic** \-kik\ *adj* (1561) : of, relating to, or arranged in a hierarchy — **hi·er·ar·chi·cal·ly** \-ki-k(ə-)lē\ *adv*

hi·er·ar·chize \'hī-(ə-),rär-,kīz\ *vt* **-chized; -chiz·ing** (1884) : to arrange in a hierarchy

hi·er·ar·chy \'hī-(ə-),rär-kē *also* 'hī-(ə-)r,är-\ *n, pl* **-chies** (14c) **1** : a division of angels **2 a** : a ruling body of clergy organized into orders or ranks each subordinate to the one above it; *esp* : the bishops of a province or nation **b** : church government by a hierarchy **3** : a body of persons in authority **4** : the classification of a group of people according to ability or to economic, social, or professional standing; *also* : the group so classified **5** : a graded or ranked series ⟨Christian ~ of values⟩ ⟨a machine's ~ of responses⟩

hi·er·at·ic \,hī-(ə-)'ra-tik\ *adj* [L *hieraticus* sacerdotal, fr. Gk *hieratikos,* fr. *hierasthai* to perform priestly functions, fr. *hieros* sacred; prob. akin to Skt *isara* vigorous] (1669) **1** : constituting or belonging to a cursive form of ancient Egyptian writing simpler than the hieroglyphic **2** : SACERDOTAL **3** : highly stylized or formal ⟨~ poses⟩ — **hi·er·at·i·cal·ly** \-ti-k(ə-)lē\ *adv*

hi·ero·dule \'hī-(ə-)rō-,dü(ə)l, hī-'er-ə-, -,dyü(ə)l\ *n* [LL *hierodulus,* fr. Gk *hierodoulos,* fr. *hieron* temple + *doulos* slave] (1835) : a slave or prostitute in the service of a temple (as in ancient Greece)

hi·ero·glyph \'hī-(ə-)rə-,glif\ *n* [F *hiéroglyphe,* fr. MF, back-formation fr. *hiéroglyphique*] (1598) **1** : a character used in a system of hieroglyphic writing **2** : something that resembles a hieroglyph

¹hi·ero·glyph·ic \,hī-(ə-)rə-'gli-fik\ *also* **hi·ero·glyph·i·cal** \-fi-kəl\ *adj* [MF *hieroglyphique,* fr. LL *hieroglyphicus,* fr. Gk *hieroglyphikos,* fr. *hieros* + *glyphein* to carve — more at CLEAVE] (1585) **1** : written in, constituting, or belonging to a system of writing mainly in pictorial characters **2** : inscribed with hieroglyphic **3** : resembling hieroglyphic in difficulty of decipherment — **hi·ero·glyph·i·cal·ly** \-fi-k(ə-)lē\ *adv*

²hieroglyphic *n* (1586) **1** : HIEROGLYPH **2** : a system of hieroglyphic writing; *specif* : the picture script of the ancient Egyptian priesthood — often used in pl. but sing. or pl. in constr. **3** : something that resembles a hieroglyph esp. in difficulty of decipherment

hieroglyphic 2

hi·ero·phant \'hī-(ə-)rə-,fant, hī-'er-ə-fənt\ *n* [LL *hierophanta,* fr. Gk *hierophantēs,* fr. *hieros* + *phainein* to show — more at FANCY] (1677) **1** : a priest in ancient Greece; *specif* : the chief priest of the Eleusinian mysteries **2 a** : EXPOSITOR **b** : ADVOCATE — **hi·ero·phan·tic** \,hī-(ə-)rə-'fan-tik, (,)hī-,er-ə-\ *adj*

hi·fa·lu·tin *var of* HIGHFALUTIN

hi–fi \'hī-'fī\ *n* (1950) **1** : HIGH FIDELITY **2** : equipment for reproduction of sound with high fidelity

hig·gle \'hi-gəl\ *vi* **hig·gled; hig·gling** \-g(ə-)liŋ\ [prob. alter. of *haggle*] (1633) : HAGGLE — **hig·gler** \-g(ə-)lər\ *n*

hig·gle·dy–pig·gle·dy \,hi-gəl-dē-'pi-gəl-dē\ *adv* [origin unknown] (ca. 1598) : in a confused, disordered, or random manner ⟨tiny hovels piled ~ against each other —Edward Behr⟩ — **higgledy–piggledy** *adj*

¹high \'hī\ *adj* [ME, fr. OE *hēah;* akin to OHG *hōh* high, Lith *kaukaras* hill] (bef. 12c) **1 a** : having large extension upward : taller than average, usual, or expected ⟨a ~ wall⟩ **b** : having a specified elevation : TALL ⟨six feet ~⟩ — often used in combinations ⟨sky-*high*⟩ ⟨waist-*high*⟩ **2 a** (1) : advanced toward the acme or culmination ⟨~ summer⟩ (2) : advanced toward the most active or culminating period ⟨on the Riviera during ~ season⟩ (3) : constituting the late, most fully developed, or most creative stage or period ⟨~ Gothic⟩ (4) : advanced in complexity, development, or elaboration ⟨the ~*er* apes⟩ ⟨~*er* mathematics⟩ **b** : verging on lateness — usu. used in the phrase *high time* **c** : long past : REMOTE ⟨~ antiquity⟩ **3** : elevated in pitch ⟨a ~ note⟩ **4** : relatively far from the equator ⟨~ latitude⟩ **5** : rich in quality : LUXURIOUS ⟨~ living⟩ **6** : slightly tainted ⟨~ game⟩ : MALODOROUS ⟨smelled rather ~⟩ **7** : exalted in character : NOBLE ⟨~ purposes⟩ **8** : of greater degree, amount, cost, value, or content than average, usual, or expected ⟨~ prices⟩ ⟨food ~ in iron⟩ ⟨the ~ bid⟩ **9** : of relatively great importance: as **a** : foremost in rank, dignity, or standing ⟨~ officials⟩ **b** : SERIOUS, GRAVE ⟨~ crimes⟩ **c** : observed with the utmost solemnity ⟨~ religious observances⟩ **d** : CRITICAL, CLIMACTIC ⟨the ~ point of the novel⟩ **e** : intellectually or artistically of the first order ⟨~ culture⟩ **f** : marked by sublime, heroic, or stirring events or subject matter ⟨~ tragedy⟩ ⟨~ adventure⟩ **10** : FORCIBLE, STRONG ⟨~ winds⟩ **11** : stressing matters of doctrine and ceremony; *specif* : HIGH CHURCH **12 a** : filled with or expressing great joy or excitement ⟨~ spirits⟩ **b** : INTOXICATED; *also* : excited or stupefied by or as if by a drug **13** : articulated with some part of the tongue close to the palate ⟨a ~ vowel⟩ — **high on** : enthusiastically in favor or support of

syn HIGH, TALL, LOFTY mean above the average in height. HIGH implies marked extension upward and is applied chiefly to things which rise from a base or foundation or are placed at a conspicuous height above a lower level ⟨a *high* hill⟩ ⟨a *high* ceiling⟩. TALL applies to what grows or rises high by comparison with others of its kind and usu. implies relative narrowness ⟨a *tall* thin man⟩. LOFTY suggests great or imposing altitude ⟨*lofty* mountain peaks⟩.

²high *adv* (bef. 12c) **1** : at or to a high place, altitude, level, or degree ⟨climbed ~*er*⟩ ⟨passions ran ~⟩ **2** : WELL, LUXURIOUSLY — often used in the phrases *high off the hog* and *high on the hog*

³high *n* (13c) **1** : an elevated place or region: as **a** : HILL, KNOLL **b**

: the space overhead : SKY — usu. used with *on*   **c** : HEAVEN — usu. used with *on*   **2** : a region of high barometric pressure — called also *anticyclone*   **3 a** : a high point or level : HEIGHT 〈sales reached a new ~〉   **b** : the transmission gear of a vehicle (as an automobile) giving the highest speed of travel   **4 a** : an excited, euphoric, or stupefied state produced by or as if by a drug   **b** : a state of elation or high spirits

high altar *n* (bef. 12c) : the principal altar in a church

high analysis *n* (1949) *of a fertilizer* : containing more than 20 percent of total plant nutrients

high and dry *adj* (1822)   **1** : being out of reach of the current or tide or out of the water   **2** : being in a helpless or abandoned position

high and low *adv* (14c) : EVERYWHERE

high-and-mighty *adj* (1654) : characterized by arrogance : IMPERIOUS

¹high-ball \'hī-,bȯl\ *n* (1897)   **1** : a railroad signal for a train to proceed at full speed   **2** : an iced drink containing liquor (as whiskey) and water or a carbonated beverage and served in a tall glass

²highball *vi* (1912) : to go at full or high speed 〈a ~*ing* express train〉

high beam *n* (1939) : the long-range focus of a vehicle headlight

high-bind-er \'hī-,bīn-dər\ *n* [the *Highbinders*, gang of ruffians in New York City *ab*1806] (1876)   **1** : a professional killer operating in the Chinese quarter of an American city   **2** : a corrupt politician

high blood pressure *n* (1916) : HYPERTENSION

high-born \'hī-'bȯrn\ *adj* (13c) : of noble birth

high-boy \-,bȯi\ *n* (1891) : a tall chest of drawers with a legged base

high-bred \-'bred\ *adj* (1674) : coming from superior stock

high-brow \-,braù\ *n* (ca. 1903) : a person who possesses or has pretensions to superior learning or culture — **highbrow** *adj* — **high-browed** \-,braùd\ *adj* — **high-brow-ism** \-,braù-i-zəm\ *n*

high-bush \-'bùsh\ *adj* (1805) : forming a notably tall or erect bush; *also* : borne on a highbush plant

highbush blueberry *n* (1913) : a variable moisture-loving No. American shrub (*Vaccinium corymbosum*) that is the source of most cultivated blueberries; *also* : its fruit

high chair *n* (1848) : a child's chair with long legs, a footrest, and usu. a feeding tray

High Church *adj* (1687) : favoring esp. in Anglican worship the sacerdotal, liturgical, ceremonial, and traditional elements in worship

High Churchman *n* (1687) : an Anglican who adheres to High Church elements in worship

high-class \'hī-'klas\ *adj* (1864) : of superior quality or status

high comedy *n* (1895) : comedy employing subtle characterizations and witty dialogue — compare LOW COMEDY

high command *n* (1917)   **1** : the supreme headquarters of a military force   **2** : the highest leaders in an organization

high commissioner *n* (1881) : a principal or a high-ranking commissioner; *esp* : an ambassadorial representative of the government of one country stationed in another

high-con-cept \'hī-'kän-,sept\ *adj* (1985) : having or exploiting elements (as fast action, glamour, or suspense) that appeal to a wide audience 〈~ movies〉

high-count \'hī-'kaùnt\ *adj* (1926) : having a large number of warp and weft yarns to the square inch 〈~ percale sheeting〉

high court *n* (14c) : SUPREME COURT

high-density lipoprotein *n* (1960) : HDL

high-end \'hī-'end\ *adj* (1980) : UPSCALE 〈~ boutiques〉

high-energy *adj* (1934)   **1 a** : having such speed and kinetic energy as to exhibit relativistic departure from classical laws of motion — used esp. of elementary particles whose velocity has been imparted by an accelerator   **b** : of or relating to high-energy particles 〈a ~ reaction〉   **2** : yielding a relatively large amount of energy when undergoing hydrolysis 〈~ phosphate bonds in ATP〉

high-energy physics *n* (1964) : PARTICLE PHYSICS

higher criticism *n* (1836) : study of biblical writings to determine their literary history and the purpose and meaning of the authors — compare LOWER CRITICISM — **higher critic** *n*

higher education *n* (1866) : education beyond the secondary level; *esp* : education provided by a college or university

higher law *n* (1844) : a principle of divine or moral law that is considered to be superior to constitutions and enacted legislation

higher learning *n* (1926) : education, learning, or scholarship on the collegiate or university level

high-er-up \,hī-ə-'rəp, 'hī-ə-,\ *n* (1911) : a superior officer or official

high explosive *n* (1877) : an explosive (as TNT) that generates gas with extreme rapidity and has a shattering effect

high-fa-lu-tin \,hī-fə-'lü-tⁿn\ *adj* [perh. fr. ²*high* + alter. of *fluting*, prp. of *flute*] (1839)   **1** : PRETENTIOUS   **2** : expressed in or marked by the use of high-flown bombastic language : POMPOUS

high fashion *n* (1945)   **1** : HIGH STYLE   **2** : HAUTE COUTURE

high fidelity *n* (1934) : the reproduction of an effect (as sound or an image) with a high degree of faithfulness to the original — **high-fidelity** *adj*

high five *n* (1981) : a slapping of upraised right hands by two people (as in celebration) — **high-five** *vb*

high-fli-er *or* **high-fly-er** \'hī-'flī(-ə)r\ *n* (ca. 1961)   **1** : a stock whose price rises much more rapidly than the market average   **2** : a company whose stock is a highflier   **3** : an ambitiously competitive person with high aspirations

high-flown \'hī-'flōn\ *adj* (1647)   **1** : exceedingly or excessively high or favorable   **2** : having an excessively embellished or inflated character : PRETENTIOUS 〈inflated rhetoric and ~ vocabulary —James Yaffe〉

high-fly-ing \-'flī-iŋ\ *adj* (1581)   **1** : marked by extravagance, pretension, or excessive ambition   **2** : rising to considerable height

high frequency *n* (1892) : a radio frequency between very high frequency and medium frequency — see RADIO FREQUENCY table

high gear *n* (1896)   **1** : HIGH 3b   **2** : a state of intense or maximum activity — usu. used with *in*

High German *n* (1673)   **1** : German as natively used in southern and central Germany   **2** : GERMAN 3b

high-grade *adj* (1878)   **1** : of superior grade or quality 〈~ bonds〉   **2** : being near the upper or most favorable extreme of a specified range

high ground *n* (1944) : a position of advantage or preeminence

high-hand-ed \-'han-dəd\ *adj* (1631) : having or showing no regard for the rights, concerns, or feelings of others : ARBITRARY, OVERBEARING — **high-hand-ed-ly** *adv* — **high-hand-ed-ness** *n*

high-hat \'hī-'hat\ *adj* (1924) : SUPERCILIOUS, SNOBBISH — **high-hat** *vt*

high hat *n* (1889)   **1** : ¹BEAVER 2   **2** *or* **hi-hat** : a pair of cymbals operated by a foot pedal

high heels *n pl* (1671) : shoes with high heels

High Holiday *n* (1946) : either of two important Jewish holidays: **a** : ROSH HASHANAH   **b** : YOM KIPPUR

high horse *n* (1721) : an arrogant and unyielding mood or attitude

high-jack \'hī-,jak\ *var of* HIJACK

high jinks *n pl* (1825) : boisterous or rambunctious carryings-on : carefree antics or horseplay

high jump *n* (1895) : a jump for height over a horizontal bar in a track-and-field contest — **high jumper** *n*

¹high-land \'hī-lənd\ *n* (bef. 12c) : elevated or mountainous land

²highland *adj* (15c)   **1** : of or relating to a highland   **2** *cap* : of or relating to the Highlands of Scotland

high-land-er \-lən-dər\ *n* (1610)   **1** : an inhabitant of a highland   **2** *cap* : an inhabitant of the Highlands of Scotland

Highland fling *n* (1804) : a lively Scottish folk dance

high-lev-el \'hī-'le-vəl\ *adj* (1876)   **1** : occurring, done, or placed at a high level   **2** : being of high importance or rank 〈~ diplomats〉   **3** : of, relating to, or being a computer programming language (as BASIC or Pascal) which is similar to a natural language (as English) and in which each statement is translated by a compiler usu. into several machine language instructions

¹high-light \'hī-,līt\ *n* (ca. 1889)   **1** : the lightest spot or area (as in a painting) : any of several spots in a modeled drawing or painting that receives the greatest amount of illumination   **2** : something (as an event or detail) that is of major significance or special interest

²highlight *vt* **-light-ed; -light-ing** (1927)   **1** : to throw a strong light on   **2 a** : to center attention on   **b** : to constitute a highlight of

high-low-jack \,hī-,lō-'jak\ *n* (1818) : an all-fours game in which scores are made by winning the highest trump, the lowest trump, the jack of trumps, and either the ten of trumps or the most points

high-ly \'hī-lē\ *adv* (bef. 12c)   **1** : in or to a high place, level, or rank   **2** : in or to a high degree or amount   **3** : with approval : FAVORABLY

high mass *n*, *often cap H&M* (12c) : a mass marked by the singing of prescribed parts by the celebrant and the choir or congregation

high-mind-ed \'hī-'mīn-dəd\ *adj* (1556) : marked by elevated principles and feelings; *also* : PRETENTIOUS 〈too ~ to read any fiction —Alfred Kazin〉 — **high-mind-ed-ly** *adv* — **high-mind-ed-ness** *n*

high-muck-a-muck \,hī-'mə-ki-,mək\ *or* **high-muck-e-ty-muck** \,hī-'mə-kə-tē-,mək\ *n* [by folk etymology fr. Chinook Jargon *hayo makamak* plenty to eat] (1856) : an important and often arrogant person

high-ness \'hī-nəs\ *n* (bef. 12c)   **1** : the quality or state of being high   **2** — used as a title for a person of exalted rank (as a king or prince)

high noon *n* (1523)   **1** : precisely noon   **2** : the most advanced, flourishing, or creative stage or period 〈the *high noon* of her career〉

high-octane *adj* (1932)   **1** : having a high octane number and hence good antiknock properties 〈~ gasoline〉   **2** : HIGH-POWERED

high-pitched \'hī-'picht\ *adj* (1748)   **1** : having a high pitch 〈a ~ voice〉   **2** : marked by or exhibiting strong feeling : AGITATED 〈a ~, almost frantic campaign —Geoffrey Rice〉

high place *n* (14c) : a temple or altar used by the ancient Semites and built usu. on a hill or elevation

high polymer *n* (1942) : a substance (as polystyrene) consisting of molecules that are large multiples of units of low molecular weight

high-pow-ered \'hī-'paù(-ə)rd\ *also* **high-pow-er** \-'paù(-ə)r\ *adj* (1893)   **1** : having great drive, energy, or capacity : DYNAMIC 〈a ~ executive〉   **2** : having or conferring great influence 〈a ~ job〉

¹high-pressure *adj* (1824)   **1 a** : having or involving a high or comparatively high pressure esp. greatly exceeding that of the atmosphere   **b** : having a high barometric pressure   **2 a** : using or involving aggressive and insistent sales techniques   **b** : imposing or involving severe strain or tension 〈~ occupations〉

²high-pressure *vt* (1926) : to sell or influence by high-pressure tactics

high priest *n* (14c)   **1** : a chief priest esp. of the ancient Jewish Levitical priesthood traditionally traced from Aaron   **2** : a priest of the Melchizedek priesthood in the Mormon Church   **3** : the head of a movement or chief exponent of a doctrine or an art — **high priest-hood** *n*

high priestess *n* (1645) : a chief priestess

high relief *n* (ca. 1828) : sculptural relief in which at least half of the circumference of the modeled form projects

high-rise \'hī-'rīz\ *adj* (1954)   **1** : being multistory and equipped with elevators 〈~ apartments〉   **2** : of, relating to, or characterized by high-rise buildings — **high-rise** \-,\ *n*

high road *n* (1709)   **1** : HIGHWAY   **2** : the easiest course   **3** : an ethical course

high roller *n* (1881)   **1** : a person who spends freely in luxurious living   **2** : a person who gambles recklessly or for high stakes — **high-rolling** *adj*

¹high school *n* (1824) : a school esp. in the U.S. usu. including grades 9–12 or 10–12 — **high school-er** \-'skü-lər\ *n*

²high school *n* [trans. of F *haute école*] (1884) : a system of advanced exercises in horsemanship

high sea *n* (bef. 12c) : the open part of a sea or ocean esp. outside territorial waters — usu. used in pl.

high sign *n* (1902) : a gesture used as a signal (as of approval or warning) — usu. used in the phrase *give the high sign*

high-sound-ing \'hī-'saùn-diŋ\ *adj* (1784) : POMPOUS, IMPOSING

highboy

\ə\ abut   \ᵊ\ kitten, F table   \ər\ further   \a\ ash   \ā\ ace   \ä\ mop, mar
\aù\ out   \ch\ chin   \e\ bet   \ē\ easy   \g\ go   \i\ hit   \ī\ ice   \j\ job
\ŋ\ sing   \ō\ go   \ȯ\ law   \ȯi\ boy   \th\ thin   \t̲h̲\ the   \ü\ loot   \ù\ foot
\y\ yet   \zh\ vision   \ä, k̲, ⁿ, œ, œ̄, ue, ūe, ᵞ\ see Guide to Pronunciation

high–speed \'hī-'spēd\ adj (1873)　**1** : operated or adapted for operation at high speed　**2** : relating to the production of short-exposure photographs of rapidly moving objects or events of short duration

high–spir·it·ed \-'spir-ə-təd\ adj (ca. 1631) : characterized by a bold or energetic spirit — **high–spir·it·ed·ly** adv — **high–spir·it·ed·ness** n

high–spot \'hī-,spät\ n (1910) : HIGHLIGHT 2

high–stick·ing \-,sti-kiŋ\ n (1947) : the act of carrying the blade of the stick at an illegal height in ice hockey

high street n (bef. 12c) Brit : a main or principal street

high–strung \'hī-'strəŋ\ adj (1748) : having an extremely nervous or sensitive temperament

high style n (1939) : the newest style in fashion or design usu. adopted by a limited number of people

hight \'hīt\ adj [ME, pp. (earlier past) of hoten to command, call, be called, fr. OE hātan; akin to OHG heizzan to command, call] (15c) archaic : being called : NAMED

high table n (1711) : an elevated table in the dining room of a British college for use by the master and fellows and distinguished guests

high–tail \'hī-,tāl\ vi (1925) : to move at full speed or rapidly often in making a retreat — usu. used with it

high tea n (1831) : a fairly substantial late afternoon or early evening meal at which tea is served

high tech \-'tek\ n (1973)　**1** : HIGH TECHNOLOGY　**2** : a style of interior design featuring industrial products, materials, or designs — **high–tech** adj

high technology n (1968) : scientific technology involving the production or use of advanced or sophisticated devices esp. in the fields of electronics and computers

high–tension adj (1905) : having or using a high voltage

high–test adj (1923) : meeting a high standard; also : HIGH-OCTANE

high tide n (1745)　**1** : the tide when the water is at its greatest elevation　**2** : culminating point : CLIMAX

high–toned \'hī-'tōnd\ adj (1807)　**1** : high in social, moral, or intellectual quality　**2** : PRETENTIOUS, POMPOUS

high–top \'hī-,täp\ adj (1966) : extending up over the ankle ⟨~ sneakers⟩ — **high–tops** n pl

high treason n (15c) : TREASON 2

high–volt·age \'hī-'vōl-tij\ adj (1948) : marked by great energy : ELECTRIC, DYNAMIC ⟨a ~ performance⟩

high–water adj (1856) : unusually short ⟨~ pants⟩

high water n (15c) : a high stage of the water in a river or lake; also : HIGH TIDE

high–water mark n (1814) : highest point : PEAK

high·way \'hī-,wā\ n (bef. 12c) : a public way; esp : a main direct road

high·way·man \-mən\ n (1649) : a person who robs travelers on a road

highway robbery n (1778)　**1** : robbery committed on or near a public highway usu. against travelers　**2** : excessive profit or advantage derived from a business transaction

high–wire \'hī-,wī(-ə)r\ adj (1956)　**1** : involving great risk ⟨a financial ~ act⟩　**2** : DARING ⟨~ prose⟩

high–wrought \'hī-'rȯt\ adj (1604) : extremely agitated

high yellow n (1923) : a black person of light complexion — called also high yal·ler \-'ya-lər\; often taken to be offensive

hi–hat var of HIGH HAT 2

hi·jack \'hī-,jak\ vt [origin unknown] (1923)　**1 a** : to steal by stopping a vehicle on the highway　**b** : to commandeer (a flying airplane) esp. by coercing the pilot at gunpoint　**c** : to stop and steal from (a vehicle in transit)　**d** : KIDNAP　**2 a** : to steal or rob as if by hijacking　**b** : to subject to extortion or swindling — **hijack** n — **hi·jack·er** n

hi–jinks \'hī-,jiŋks\ var of HIGH JINKS

¹**hike** \'hīk\ vb **hiked; hik·ing** [perh. akin to ¹hitch] vi (1804)　**1 a** : to go on a hike　**b** : to travel by any means　**2** : to rise up; esp : to work upward out of place ⟨skirt had hiked up in back⟩ ~ vt　**1 a** : to move, pull, or raise with a sudden motion ⟨hiked himself onto the top bunk⟩　**b** : SNAP 6b　**c** : to raise in amount sharply or suddenly ⟨~ rents⟩　**2** : to take on a hike — **hik·er** n

²**hike** n (1865)　**1** : a long walk esp. for pleasure or exercise　**2** : an increase esp. in quantity or amount ⟨a new wage ~⟩　**3** : SNAP 11

hi·lar \'hī-lər\ adj (ca. 1859) : of, relating to, or located near a hilum

hi·lar·i·ous \hi-'lar-ē-əs, hī-, -'ler-\ adj [irreg. fr. L hilarus, hilaris cheerful, fr. Gk hilaros] (ca. 1840) : marked by or affording hilarity — **hi·lar·i·ous·ly** adv — **hi·lar·i·ous·ness** n

hi·lar·i·ty \-ə-tē\ n (15c) : high spirits that may be carried to the point of boisterous conviviality or merriment

Hil·bert space \'hil-bərt-\ n [David Hilbert] (1939) : a vector space for which a scalar product is defined and in which every Cauchy sequence composed of elements in the space converges to a limit in the space

hil·ding \'hil-diŋ\ n [hilding, adj. (base)] (1592) archaic : a base contemptible person

¹**hill** \'hil\ n [ME, fr. OE hyll; akin to L collis hill, culmen top] (bef. 12c)　**1** : a usu. rounded natural elevation of land lower than a mountain　**2** : an artificial heap or mound (as of earth)　**3** : several seeds or plants planted in a group rather than a row　**4** : SLOPE, INCLINE

²**hill** vt (1581)　**1** : to form into a heap　**2** : to draw earth around the roots or base of — **hill·er** n

hill·bil·ly \'hil-,bi-lē\ n, pl **-lies** [¹hill + Billy, nickname for William] (1900) : a person from a backwoods area

hillbilly music n (1943) : COUNTRY MUSIC

hill climb n (1905) : a road race for automobiles or motorcycles in which competitors are individually timed up a hill

hill-crest \'hil-,krest\ n (ca. 1898) : the top line of a hill

hill mynah n (ca. 1890) : a largely black Asian mynah (Gracula religiosa) often tamed and taught to pronounce words

hill·ock \'hi-lək\ n (14c) : a small hill — **hill·ocky** \-lə-kē\ adj

Hill reaction \'hil-\ n [Robert Hill †1991 Brit. biochemist] (1950) : the light-dependent transfer of electrons by chloroplasts in photosynthesis that results in the cleavage of water molecules and liberation of oxygen

hill-side \-,sīd\ n (14c) : a part of a hill between the top and the foot

hill-top \'hil-,täp\ n (15c) : the highest part of a hill

hilly \'hi-lē\ adj **hill·i·er; -est** (14c) : abounding in hills

hilt \'hilt\ n [ME, fr. OE; akin to OHG helza hilt] (bef. 12c) : a handle esp. of a sword or dagger — **to the hilt** : to the very limit : COMPLETELY

hi·lum \'hī-ləm\ n, pl **hi·la** \-lə\ [NL, fr. L, trifle] (ca. 1753)　**1** : a scar on a seed (as a bean) marking the point of attachment of the ovule　**2** : a notch in or opening from a bodily part suggesting the hilum of a bean

him \im, 'him\ pron objective case of HE

Hi·ma·la·yan \,hi-mə-'lā-ən, hi-'mäl-yən, -'mä-lē-ən\ n [Himalaya Mountains] (1949) : any of a breed of domestic cats developed by crossing the Persian and the Siamese and having the stocky build and long thick coat of the former and the blue eyes and coat patterns of the latter

hi·mat·i·on \hi-'ma-tē-,än, -ən\ n [Gk, dim. of heimat-, heima garment; akin to Gk hennynai to clothe — more at WEAR] (1850) : a rectangular cloth draped over the left shoulder and about the body and worn as a garment in ancient Greece

him/her \'him-'hər, 'hi-mər-, 'him-'slash-\ pron, objective case of HE/SHE

him·self \(h)im-'self, Southern also -'sef\ pron (bef. 12c)　**1 a** : that identical male one — compare ¹HE; used reflexively, for emphasis, in absolute constructions, and in place of him esp. when joined to another object ⟨considers ~ lucky⟩ ⟨he ~ did it⟩ ⟨~ unhappy, he understood the situation⟩ ⟨a gift to his wife and ~⟩　**b** — used reflexively when the sex of the antecedent is unspecified ⟨everyone must fend for ~⟩　**2** : his normal, healthy, or sane condition or self　**3** chiefly Irish & Scot : a man of consequence; esp : the master of the house

hin \'hin\ n [Heb hin, fr. Egypt hnw] (14c) : an ancient Hebrew unit of liquid measure equal to about 1.5 gallons (5.7 liters)

Hi·na·ya·na \,hi-nə-'yä-nə, ,hē-\ n [Skt hīnayāna lesser vehicle] (1868) : THERAVADA — **Hi·na·ya·nist** \-'yä-nist\ n — **Hi·na·ya·nis·tic** \-yä-'nis-tik\ adj

¹**hind** \'hind\ n, pl **hinds** also **hind** [ME, fr. OE; akin to OHG hinta hind, Gk kemas young deer] (bef. 12c)　**1** : the female of the red deer — compare HART　**2** : any of various spotted groupers (esp. genus Epinephelus)

²**hind** n [ME hine servant, farmhand, fr. OE hīna, gen. of hīwan, pl., members of a household; akin to OHG hīwo spouse, L civis fellow citizen, and prob. to OIr cóim dear, Lith šeima family] (1520)　**1** : a British farm assistant　**2** archaic : RUSTIC

³**hind** adj [ME, prob. back-formation fr. OE hinder, adv., behind; akin to OHG hintar, prep., behind] (14c) : of or forming the part that follows or is behind : REAR

hind·brain \'hin(d)-,brān\ n (1888)　**1** : the posterior of the three primary divisions of the developing vertebrate brain or the corresponding part of the adult brain that includes the cerebellum, the medulla oblongata, and in mammals the pons and that controls autonomic functions and equilibrium — called also rhombencephalon; compare METENCEPHALON, MYELENCEPHALON　**2** : the posterior segment of the brain of an invertebrate

¹**hin·der** \'hin-dər\ vb **hin·dered; hin·der·ing** \-d(ə-)riŋ\ [ME hindren, fr. OE hindrian; akin to OE hinder behind] vt (bef. 12c)　**1** : to make slow or difficult the progress of : HAMPER　**2** : to hold back : CHECK ~ vi : to delay, impede, or prevent action — **hin·der·er** \-dər-ər\ n

syn HINDER, IMPEDE, OBSTRUCT, BLOCK mean to interfere with the activity or progress of. HINDER stresses causing harmful or annoying delay or interference with progress ⟨rain hindered the climb⟩. IMPEDE implies making forward progress difficult by clogging, hampering, or fettering ⟨tight clothing that impedes movement⟩. OBSTRUCT implies interfering with something in motion or in progress by the sometimes intentional placing of obstacles in the way ⟨the view was obstructed by billboards⟩. BLOCK implies complete obstruction to passage or progress ⟨a landslide blocked the road⟩.

²**hind·er** \'hin-dər\ adj [ME, fr. OE hinder, adv.] (13c) : situated behind or in the rear : POSTERIOR

hind·gut \'hin(d)-,gət\ n (1878) : the posterior part of the alimentary canal

Hin·di \'hin-(,)dē\ n [Hindi hindī, fr. Hind India, fr. Per] (1801)　**1** : a literary and official language of northern India　**2** : a complex of Indo-Aryan languages and dialects of northern India for which Hindi is the usual literary language — **Hindi** adj

hind·most \'hīn(d)-,mōst\ adj (14c) : farthest to the rear : LAST

hind·quar·ter \-'kwȯ(r)-tər, -,kȯ(r)-\ n (1881)　**1** : one side of the back half of the carcass of a quadruped including a leg and usu. one or more ribs　**2** pl : the hind pair of legs of a quadruped; broadly : all the structures of a quadruped that lie posterior to the attachment of the hind legs to the trunk

hin·drance \'hin-drən(t)s\ n (1526)　**1** : the state of being hindered　**2** : IMPEDIMENT　**3** : the action of hindering

hind·sight \'hīn(d)-,sīt\ n (1866) : perception of the nature of an event after it has happened

¹**Hin·du** also **Hin·doo** \'hin-(,)dü\ n [Per Hindū inhabitant of India, fr. Hind India] (1662)　**1** : an adherent of Hinduism　**2** : a native or inhabitant of India

²**Hindu** also **Hindoo** adj (1698) : of, relating to, or characteristic of the Hindus or Hinduism

Hindu–Arabic adj (1925) : relating to, being, or composed of Arabic numerals ⟨~ numeration system⟩

Hindu calendar n (ca. 1909) : a lunar calendar usu. dating from 3101 B.C. and used esp. in India

Hin·du·ism \'hin-(,)dü-,i-zəm\ n (1809) : the dominant religion of India that emphasizes dharma with its resulting ritual and social observances and often mystical contemplation and ascetic practices

¹**Hin·du·sta·ni** \,hin-dù-'sta-nē, -'stä-nē\ n [Hindi Hindūstānī, fr. Per Hindūstān India] (1808) : a group of Indo-Aryan dialects of northern India of which literary Hindi and Urdu are considered diverse written forms

²**Hindustani** also **Hindostani** adj (1800) : of or relating to Hindustan or its people or Hindustani

hind wing n (1899) : either of the posterior wings of a 4-winged insect

¹**hinge** \'hinj\ n [ME heng; akin to MD henge hook, OE hangian to hang] (14c)　**1 a** : a jointed or flexible device on which a door, lid, or other swinging part turns　**b** : a flexible ligamentous joint　**c** : a small

piece of thin gummed paper used in fastening a postage stamp in an album 2 : a determining factor : TURNING POINT

²hinge vb hinged; hing·ing vi (1719) : to be contingent on a single consideration or point — used with on or upon ~ vt : to attach by or furnish with hinges

hinge joint n (1802) : a joint between bones (as at the elbow) that permits motion in only one plane

hin·ny \'hi-nē\ n, pl hinnies [L hinnus, fr. Gk innos] (1688) : a hybrid between a stallion and a female donkey — compare MULE

¹hint \'hint\ n [prob. alter. of obs. hent act of seizing, fr. hent vb.] (1604) 1 archaic : OPPORTUNITY, TURN 2 a : a statement conveying by implication what it is preferred not to say explicitly b : an indirect or summary suggestion ⟨helpful ~s⟩ 3 : a slight indication of the existence, approach, or nature of something : CLUE 4 : a very small amount : SUGGESTION

²hint vt (1648) : to convey indirectly and by allusion rather than explicitly ⟨a suspicion that she scarcely dared to ~⟩ ~ vi : to give a hint — usu. used with at syn see SUGGEST — hint·er n

hin·ter·land \'hin-tər-,land, -lənd\ n [G, fr. hinter hinder + Land] (1890) 1 : a region lying inland from a coast 2 a : a region remote from urban areas b : a region lying beyond major metropolitan or cultural centers

¹hip \'hip\ n [ME hipe, fr. OE hēope; akin to OHG hiafo hip] (bef. 12c) : ROSE HIP

²hip n [ME, fr. OE hype; akin to OHG huf hip] (bef. 12c) 1 a : the laterally projecting region of each side of the lower or posterior part of the mammalian trunk formed by the lateral parts of the pelvis and upper part of the femur together with the fleshy parts covering them b : HIP JOINT 2 : the external angle formed by the meeting of two sloping sides of a roof that have their wall plates running in different directions

³hip interj [origin unknown] (1827) — used in a cheer ⟨~ ~ hooray⟩

⁴hip adj hip·per; hip·pest [alter. of ²hep] (1904) : characterized by a keen informed awareness of or involvement in the newest developments or styles

⁵hip vt hipped; hip·ping (ca. 1932) : to make aware : TELL, INFORM

⁶hip n (1952) : HIPNESS

hip and thigh adv (1560) : in a fierce or ruthless manner : UNSPARINGLY

hip·bone \'hip-'bōn, -,bōn\ n (12c) : INNOMINATE BONE

hip boot n (1893) : a waterproof boot reaching to the hips

hip–hop \'hip-,häp\ n, often attrib [perh. fr. ⁴hip + ¹hop] (1983) : a subculture esp. of inner-city youths whose amusements include rap music, graffiti, and break dancing; also : an element or art form prevalent within this subculture

hip joint n (1794) : the articulation between the femur and the innominate bone

hip-line \'hip-,līn\ n (1907) 1 : an arbitrary line encircling the fullest part of the hips 2 : body circumference at the hips

hip·ness \'hip-nəs\ n (1946) : the quality or state of being hip

¹hipped \'hipt\ adj (1508) 1 : having hips esp. of a specified kind — often used in combination ⟨a broad-hipped person⟩ 2 : constructed with hips ⟨a ~ roof⟩

²hipped adj [hip (hypochondria)] (ca. 1710) : DEPRESSED

³hipped adj [⁵hip] (1920) : extremely absorbed or interested ⟨~ on astrology⟩

hip·pie or hip·py \'hi-pē\ n, pl hippies [⁴hip + -ie] (1965) : a usu. young person who rejects the mores of established society (as by dressing unconventionally or favoring communal living) and advocates a nonviolent ethic; broadly : a long-haired unconventionally dressed young person — hip·pie·dom \-pē-dəm\ n — hip·pie·ness or hip·pi·ness \-pē-nəs\ n

hip·po \'hi-(,)pō\ n, pl hippos (1872) : HIPPOPOTAMUS

hip·po·cam·pus \,hi-pə-'kam-pəs\ n, pl -pi \-,pī, -(,)pē\ [NL, fr. Gk hippokampos sea horse, fr. hippos horse + kampos sea monster — more at EQUINE] (1706) : a curved elongated ridge that extends over the floor of the descending horn of each lateral ventricle of the brain and consists of gray matter covered on the ventricular surface with white matter — hip·po·cam·pal \-pəl\ adj

hip·po·cras \'hi-pə-,kras\ n [ME ypocras, fr. Ypocras Hippocrates, to whom its invention was ascribed] (14c) : a mulled wine popular in medieval Europe

Hip·po·crat·ic \,hi-pə-'kra-tik\ adj (ca. 1620) : of or relating to Hippocrates or to the school of medicine that took his name

Hippocratic oath n (1747) : an oath embodying a code of medical ethics usu. taken by those about to begin medical practice

Hip·po·crene \'hi-pə-,krēn, ,hi-pə-'krē-nē\ n [L, fr. Gk Hippokrēnē] (1605) : a fountain on Mount Helicon sacred to the Muses and believed to be a source of poetic inspiration

hip·po·drome \'hi-pə-,drōm\ n [MF, fr. L hippodromos, fr. Gk, fr. hippos + dromos racecourse — more at DROMEDARY] (1585) 1 : an oval stadium for horse and chariot races in ancient Greece 2 : an arena for equestrian performances

hip·po·griff \-,grif\ n [F hippogriffe, fr. It ippogrifo, fr. ippo- (fr. Gk hippos horse) + grifo griffin, fr. L gryphus] (ca. 1656) : a legendary animal having the foreparts of a griffin and the body of a horse

Hip·pol·y·ta \hi-'pä-lə-tə\ n [L, fr. Gk Hippolytē] : a queen of the Amazons given in marriage to Theseus by Hercules

Hip·pol·y·tus \-ə-təs\ n [L, fr. Gk Hippolytos] : a son of Theseus falsely accused of amorous advances by his stepmother and killed by his father through the agency of Poseidon

Hip·pom·e·nes \hi-'pä-mə-nēz\ n [L, fr. Gk Hippomenēs] : the successful suitor of Atalanta in Greek mythology

hip·po·pot·a·mus \,hi-pə-'pä-tə-məs\ n, pl -mus·es or -mi \-,mī, -(,)mē\ [L, fr. Gk hippopotamos, alter. of hippos potamios, lit., riverine horse] (1563) : a very large herbivorous 4-toed chiefly aquatic artiodactyl mammal (Hippopotamus amphibius) of sub-Saharan Africa with an extremely large head and mouth, bare and very thick grayish

hippopotamus

skin, and short legs; also : a smaller closely related mammal (Choeropsis liberiensis) of western Africa

hip·py \'hi-pē\ adj (1919) : having large hips

hip roof n (ca. 1741) : a roof having sloping ends and sloping sides — see ROOF illustration

hip–shoot·ing \'hip-,shü-tiŋ\ n (1951) : action or reaction that is quick and often reckless — hip shooter n

hip·ster \'hip-stər\ n [⁴hip] (ca. 1941) : a person who is unusually aware of and interested in new and unconventional patterns (as in jazz or the use of stimulants)

hip·ster·ism \-stə-,ri-zəm\ n (1958) 1 : HIPNESS 2 : the way of life characteristic of hipsters

hi·ra·ga·na \,hir-ə-'gä-nə\ n [Jp, fr. hira- ordinary + kana syllabary] (1859) : the cursive script that is one of two sets of symbols of Japanese syllabic writing — compare KATAKANA

¹hire \'hī(-ə)r\ n [ME, fr. OE hȳr; akin to OS hūria hire] (bef. 12c) 1 a : payment for the temporary use of something b : payment for labor or personal services : WAGES 2 a : the act or an instance of hiring b : the state of being hired : EMPLOYMENT 3 Brit : RENTAL — often used attributively 4 : one who is hired ⟨starting wage for the new ~s⟩ — for hire also on hire : available for use or service in return for payment

²hire vb hired; hir·ing vt (bef. 12c) 1 a : to engage the personal services of a set sum ⟨a crew⟩ b : to engage the temporary use of for a fixed sum ⟨~ a hall⟩ 2 : to grant the personal services of or temporary use of for a fixed sum ⟨~ themselves out⟩ 3 : to get done for pay ⟨~ the mowing done⟩ ~ vi : to take employment ⟨~ out as a guide during the tourist season⟩ — hir·er n
syn HIRE, LET, LEASE, RENT, CHARTER mean to engage or grant for use at a price. HIRE and LET, strictly speaking, are complementary terms, HIRE implying the act of engaging or taking for use and LET the granting of use ⟨we hired a car for the summer⟩ ⟨decided to let the cottage to a young couple⟩. LEASE strictly implies a letting under the terms of a contract but is often applied to hiring on a lease ⟨the diplomat leased an apartment for a year⟩. RENT stresses the payment of money for the full use of property and may imply either hiring or letting ⟨instead of buying a house, they decided to rent⟩ ⟨will not rent to families with children⟩. CHARTER applies to the hiring or letting of a vehicle usu. for exclusive use ⟨charter a bus to go to the game⟩.

hired gun n (1971) : an expert hired to do a specific job; esp : HIRELING — often used disparagingly

hire·ling \'hī(-ə)r-liŋ\ n (bef. 12c) : a person who serves for hire esp. for purely mercenary motives

hire purchase n (1895) chiefly Brit : purchase on the installment plan

hiring hall n (1934) : a union-operated placement office where registered applicants are referred in rotation to jobs

hir·sute \'hər-,süt, 'hir-, ,hər-', hir-'\ adj [L hirsutus; akin to L horrēre to bristle — more at HORROR] (1621) 1 : HAIRY 1; esp : covered with coarse stiff hairs ⟨~ leaf⟩ — hir·sute·ness n

hir·sut·ism \'hər-sə-,ti-zəm, 'hir-\ n (1927) : excessive growth of hair of normal or abnormal distribution

hi·ru·din \hi-'rü-d²n, 'hir-(y)ə-\ n [fr. Hirudin, a trademark] (1905) : an anticoagulant extracted from the buccal glands of a leech

¹his \(h)iz, ,hiz\ adj [ME, fr. OE, gen. of hē he] (bef. 12c) : of or relating to him or himself esp. as possessor, agent, or object of an action ⟨~ house⟩ ⟨~ writings⟩ ⟨~ confirmation⟩ — compare ¹HE

²his \'hiz\ pron, sing or pl in constr (bef. 12c) : that which belongs to him — used without a following noun as a pronoun equivalent in meaning to the adjective his

his/her \'hiz-'hər, 'hi-zər-'hər, 'hiz-'slash-\ adj (1952) : his or her — used in writing as an adjective of common gender

His·pan·ic \hi-'spa-nik\ adj [L hispanicus, fr. Hispania Iberian Peninsula, Spain] (ca. 1889) : of, relating to, or being a person of Latin American descent living in the U.S.; esp : one of Cuban, Mexican, or Puerto Rican origin — Hispanic n — His·pan·i·cism \-'spa-nə-,si-zəm\ n — His·pan·i·cist \-sist\ n — His·pan·i·cize \-,sīz\ vt

his·pa·ni·dad \,is-,pa-ni-'thä(th)\ n (1941) : HISPANISM 1

his·pa·nism \'his-pə-,ni-zəm\ n, often cap (1940) 1 : a movement to reassert the cultural unity of Spain and Latin America 2 : a characteristic feature of Spanish occurring in another language

His·pa·nist \-nist\ n (1786) : a scholar specially informed in Spanish or Portuguese language, literature, linguistics, or civilization

His·pa·no \hi-'spa-(,)nō, 'his-pə-,nō\ n, pl -nos [AmerSp hispano, prob. short for hispanoamericano, lit., Spanish-American] (1946) : a native or resident of the southwestern U.S. descended from Spaniards settled there before annexation; also : MEXICAN 1

his·pid \'his-pəd\ adj [L hispidus; akin to L horrēre] (1646) : rough or covered with bristles, stiff hairs, or minute spines ⟨~ leaf⟩

hiss \'his\ vb [ME, of imit. origin] vi (14c) : to make a sharp sibilant sound ⟨the crowd ~ed in disapproval⟩ ⟨~ing steam⟩ ~ vt 1 : to express disapproval of by hissing 2 : to utter or whisper angrily or threateningly and with a hiss — hiss n — hiss·er n

his·self \(h)i-'self, -'sef\ pron (12c) chiefly dial : HIMSELF 1

hissy \'hi-sē\ n [perh. by shortening & alter. fr. hysterical] (ca. 1934) chiefly Southern & southern Midland : TANTRUM — called also hissy fit

¹hist \s often prolonged and usu with p preceding and t following; often read as 'hist\ interj [origin unknown] (1592) — used to attract attention

²hist \'hist\ dial var of HOIST

hist- or histo- comb form [F, fr. Gk histos mast, loom beam, web, fr. histanai to cause to stand — more at STAND] : tissue ⟨histophysiology⟩

his·ta·mi·nase \hi-'sta-mə-,nās, 'his-tə-mə-, -,nāz\ n [ISV] (1930) : a widely occurring flavoprotein enzyme that oxidizes histamine and various diamines

his·ta·mine \'his-tə-,mēn, -mən\ n [ISV hist- + amine] (ca. 1913) : a compound $C_5H_9N_3$ esp. of mammalian tissues that causes dilatation of capillaries, contraction of smooth muscle, and stimulation of gastric

\ə\ abut \³\ kitten, F table \ər\ further \a\ ash \ā\ ace \ä\ mop, mar \aú\ out \ch\ chin \e\ bet \ē\ easy \g\ go \i\ hit \ī\ ice \j\ job \ŋ\ sing \ō\ go \ó\ law \ói\ boy \th\ thin \th\ the \ü\ loot \ú\ foot \y\ yet \zh\ vision \á, k̶, ⁿ, œ, œ̄, ᴜ, ᵫ, ᵋ\ see Guide to Pronunciation acid secretion, that is released during allergic reactions, and that is formed by decarboxylation of histidine

his·ta·min·er·gic \ˌhis-tə-mə-'nər-jik\ adj [ISV] (1936) of autonomic nerve fibers : liberating or activated by histamine ⟨~ receptors⟩

his·ti·dine \'his-tə-ˌdēn\ n [ISV hist- + -idine] (1896) : a crystalline essential amino acid $C_6H_9N_3O_2$ formed by the hydrolysis of most proteins

his·tio·cyte \'his-tē-ə-ˌsīt\ n [Gk histion web (dim. of histos) + ISV -cyte] (1924) : a nonmotile macrophage of extravascular tissues and esp. connective tissue — **his·tio·cyt·ic** \ˌhis-tē-ə-'si-tik\ adj

his·to·chem·is·try \ˌhis-tō-'ke-mə-strē\ n [ISV] (ca. 1860) : a science that combines the techniques of biochemistry and histology in the study of the chemical constitution of cells and tissues — **his·to·chem·i·cal** \-'ke-mi-kəl\ adj — **his·to·chem·i·cal·ly** \-k(ə-)lē\ adv

his·to·com·pat·i·bil·i·ty \'his-(ˌ)tō-kəm-ˌpa-tə-'bi-lə-tē\ n (1948) : a state of mutual tolerance that allows some tissues to be grafted effectively to others

his·to·gen·e·sis \ˌhis-tə-'je-nə-səs\ n [NL] (ca. 1854) : the formation and differentiation of tissues — **his·to·ge·net·ic** \-jə-'ne-tik\ adj

his·to·gram \'his-tə-ˌgram\ n [Gk histos mast, web + E -gram] (1891) : a representation of a frequency distribution by means of rectangles whose widths represent class intervals and whose areas are proportional to the corresponding frequencies

his·tol·o·gy \his-'tä-lə-jē\ n, pl -gies [F histologie, fr. hist- + -logie -logy] (ca. 1847) 1 : a branch of anatomy that deals with the minute structure of animal and plant tissues as discernible with the microscope 2 : a treatise on histology 3 : tissue structure or organization — **his·to·log·i·cal** \ˌhis-tə-'lä-ji-kəl\ or **his·to·log·ic** \-'lä-jik\ adj — **his·to·log·i·cal·ly** \-ji-k(ə-)lē\ adv — **his·tol·o·gist** \his-'tä-lə-jist\ n

his·tol·y·sis \his-'tä-lə-səs\ n [NL] (ca. 1857) : the breakdown of bodily tissues

his·tone \'his-ˌtōn\ n [G Histon] (1885) : any of various simple water-soluble proteins that are rich in the basic amino acids lysine and arginine and are complexed with DNA in the nucleosomes of eukaryotic chromatin

his·to·pa·thol·o·gy \ˌhis-tō-pə-'thä-lə-jē, -pa-\ n [ISV] (1896) 1 : a branch of pathology concerned with the tissue changes characteristic of disease 2 : the tissue changes that affect a part or accompany a disease — **his·to·path·o·log·ic** \-ˌpa-thə-'lä-jik\ or **his·to·path·o·log·i·cal** \-ji-kəl\ adj — **his·to·path·o·log·i·cal·ly** \-ji-k(ə-)lē\ adv — **his·to·pa·thol·o·gist** \-pə-'thä-lə-jist, -pa-\ n

his·to·phys·i·ol·o·gy \-ˌfi-zē-'ä-lə-jē\ n (ca. 1886) 1 : a branch of physiology concerned with the function and activities of tissues 2 : structural and functional tissue organization — **his·to·phys·i·o·log·i·cal** \-ē-ə-'lä-ji-kəl\ or **his·to·phys·i·o·log·ic** \-jik\ adj

his·to·plas·mo·sis \ˌhis-tə-plaz-'mō-səs\ n [NL, fr. Histoplasma, genus of fungi] (1907) : a respiratory disease with symptoms like those of influenza that is caused by a fungus (Histoplasma capsulatum) and is marked by benign involvement of lymph nodes of the trachea and bronchi or by severe progressive generalized involvement of the lymph nodes and the reticuloendothelial system

his·to·ri·an \hi-'stōr-ē-ən, -'stor-, -'stär-\ n (15c) 1 : a student or writer of history; esp : one that produces a scholarly synthesis 2 : a writer or compiler of a chronicle

his·tor·ic \hi-'stor-ik, -'stär-\ adj (1607) 1 : HISTORICAL: as a : famous or important in history ⟨~ battlefields⟩ b : having great and lasting importance ⟨an ~ occasion⟩ c : known or established in the past ⟨~ interest rates⟩ d : dating from or preserved from a past time or culture ⟨~ buildings⟩ ⟨~ artifacts⟩

his·tor·i·cal \-i-kəl\ adj (15c) 1 a : of, relating to, or having the character of history b : based on history c : used in the past and reproduced in historical presentations 2 : famous in history : HISTORIC 3 a : SECONDARY 1c b : DIACHRONIC ⟨~ grammar⟩ — **his·tor·i·cal·ness** \-i-kəl-nəs\ n

his·tor·i·cal·ly \-i-k(ə-)lē\ adv (1550) 1 : in accordance with or with respect to history ⟨an ~ accurate account⟩ 2 : in the past ⟨~, stagnant cities seldom have recovered —Jane Jacobs⟩

historical materialism n (1925) : the Marxist theory of history and society that holds that ideas and social institutions develop only as the superstructure of a material economic base — compare DIALECTICAL MATERIALISM

historical present n (1867) : the present tense used in relating past events

his·tor·i·cism \hi-'stor-ə-ˌsi-zəm, -'stär-\ n (1895) : a theory, doctrine, or style that emphasizes the importance of history: as a : a theory in which history is seen as a standard of value or as a determinant of events b : a style (as in architecture) characterized by the use of traditional forms and elements — **his·tor·i·cist** \-sist\ adj or n

his·tor·ic·i·ty \ˌhis-tə-'ri-sə-tē\ n (1880) : historical actuality

his·tor·i·cize \hi-'stor-ə-ˌsīz, -'stär-\ vb -cized; -ciz·ing vt (1846) : to make historical ~ vi : to use historical material

his·to·ri·og·ra·pher \hi-ˌstor-ē-'ä-grə-fər, -ˌstor-\ n [MF historiographeur, fr. LL historiographus, fr. Gk historiographos, fr. historia + graphein to write — more at CARVE] (15c) : HISTORIAN

his·to·ri·og·ra·phy \-fē\ n (1569) 1 a : the writing of history; esp : the writing of history based on the critical examination of sources, the selection of particulars from the authentic materials, and the synthesis of particulars into a narrative that will stand the test of critical methods b : the principles, theory, and history of historical writing ⟨a course in ~⟩ 2 : the product of historical writing : a body of historical literature — **his·to·rio·graph·i·cal** \-ē-ə-'gra-fi-kəl\ also **his·to·rio·graph·ic** \-fik\ adj — **his·to·rio·graph·i·cal·ly** \-ē-ə-'gra-fi-k(ə-)lē\ adv

his·to·ry \'his-t(ə-)rē\ n, pl -ries [L historia, fr. Gk, inquiry, history, fr. histōr, istōr knowing, learned; akin to Gk eidenai to know — more at WIT] (14c) 1 : TALE, STORY 2 a : a chronological record of significant events (as affecting a nation or institution) often including an explanation of their causes b : a treatise presenting systematically related natural phenomena c : an account of a patient's medical background d : an established record ⟨a prisoner with a ~ of violence⟩ 3 : a branch of knowledge that records and explains past events ⟨medieval ~⟩ 4 : events that form the subject matter of a history b : events of the past c : one that is finished or done for ⟨the winning

streak was ~⟩ ⟨you're ~⟩ d : previous treatment, handling, or experience (as of a metal)

his·tri·on·ic \ˌhis-trē-'ä-nik\ adj [LL histrionicus, fr. L histrion-, histrio actor] (1648) 1 : deliberately affected : THEATRICAL 2 : of or relating to actors, acting, or the theater syn see DRAMATIC — **his·tri·on·i·cal·ly** \-ni-k(ə-)lē\ adv

his·tri·on·ics \-niks\ n pl but sing or pl in constr (1864) 1 : theatrical performances 2 : deliberate display of emotion for effect

¹**hit** \'hit\ vb hit; hit·ting [ME, fr. OE hittan, fr. ON hitta to meet with, hit] vt (bef. 12c) 1 a : to reach with or as if with a blow b : to come in contact with ⟨the ball ~ the window⟩ 2 a : to cause to come into contact b : to deliver (as a blow) by action c : to apply forcefully or suddenly ⟨~ the brakes⟩ 3 : to affect esp. detrimentally ⟨farmers ~ by drought⟩ 4 : to make a request of ⟨~ his friend for 10 dollars⟩ — often used with up 5 : to discover or meet esp. by chance 6 a : to accord with : SUIT b : REACH, ATTAIN ⟨prices ~ a new high⟩ c : to arrive or appear at, in, or on ⟨~ town⟩ ⟨the best time to ~ the stores⟩ d of fish : to bite at or on e : to reflect accurately ⟨~ the right note⟩ f : to reach or strike (as a target) esp. for a score in a game or contest ⟨couldn't seem to ~ the basket⟩ g : BAT 2b 7 : to indulge in excessively ⟨~ the bottle⟩ ~ vi 1 a : to strike a blow b : to arrive with a forceful effect like that of a blow ⟨the storm ~⟩ 2 a : to come into contact with something b : ATTACK c of a fish : STRIKE 11b d : BAT 1 3 : to succeed in attaining or coming up with something — often used with on or upon ⟨~ on a solution⟩ 4 obs : to be in agreement : SUIT 5 of an internal-combustion engine : to fire the charge in the cylinders — **hit·ter** n — **hit it big** : to achieve great success — **hit it off** : to get along well : become friends ⟨they hit it off immediately⟩ — **hit on** : to make esp. sexual overtures to — **hit one's stride** : to reach one's best speed or highest potential — **hit the books** : to study esp. with intensity — **hit the fan** : to have a major usu. undesirable impact — **hit the hay** or **hit the sack** : to go to bed — **hit the high points** or **hit the high spots** : to touch on or at the most important points or places — **hit the jackpot** : to become notably and unexpectedly successful — **hit the nail on the head** : to be exactly right — **hit the road** : LEAVE, TRAVEL; also : to set out — **hit the roof** or **hit the ceiling** : to give vent to a burst of anger or angry protest — **hit the spot** : to give complete or special satisfaction — used esp. of food or drink

²**hit** n (15c) 1 : an act or instance of hitting or being hit ⟨more ~s than misses⟩ ⟨took a financial ~⟩ 2 a : a stroke of luck b : a great success 3 : a telling or critical remark 4 : BASE HIT 5 : a quantity of a narcotic drug ingested at one time 6 : a premeditated murder committed esp. by a member of a crime syndicate — **hit·less** \'hit-ləs\ adj

hit-and-miss \ˌhi-tᵊn-'mis\ adj (1897) : sometimes successful and sometimes not : not reliably good or successful

¹**hit-and-run** \-'rən\ adj (1899) 1 : being or relating to a hit-and-run in baseball 2 : being or involving a motor-vehicle driver who does not stop after being involved in an accident 3 : involving or intended for quick specific action or results

²**hit-and-run** n (1904) : a baseball play calling for a runner on first to begin running as a pitch is delivered and for the batter to attempt to hit the pitch

³**hit-and-run** vi (1966) : to execute a hit-and-run play in baseball

¹**hitch** \'hich\ vb [ME hytchen] vt (14c) 1 : to move by jerks or with a tug 2 a : to catch or fasten by or as if by a hook or knot ⟨~ed his horse to the fence post⟩ b (1) : to connect (a vehicle or implement) with a source of motive power ⟨~ a rake to a tractor⟩ (2) : to attach (a source of motive power) to a vehicle or instrument ⟨~ the horses to the wagon⟩ c : to join in marriage ⟨got ~ed⟩ 3 : HITCHHIKE ~ vi 1 : to move with halts and jerks : HOBBLE 2 a : to become entangled, made fast, or linked b : to become joined in marriage 3 : HITCHHIKE — **hitch·er** n

²**hitch** n (1664) 1 : LIMP 2 : a sudden movement or pull : JERK ⟨gave his trousers a ~⟩ 3 a : a sudden halt : STOPPAGE b : a usu. unforeseen difficulty or obstacle ⟨the plan went off without a ~⟩ 4 : the act or fact of catching hold 5 : a connection between a vehicle or implement and a detachable source of power (as a tractor or horse) 6 : a delimited period esp. of military service 7 : any of various knots used to form a temporary noose in a line or to secure a line temporarily to an object 8 : LIFT 5b

hitch·hike \'hich-ˌhīk\ vi (1926) 1 : to travel by securing free rides from passing vehicles 2 : to be carried or transported by chance or unintentionally ⟨destructive insects hitchhiking on ships⟩ ~ vt : to solicit and obtain (a free ride) esp. in a passing vehicle — **hitch·hik·er** n

hitch up vt (1817) : to hitch a draft animal or team to a vehicle

hi-tech var of HIGH-TECH

¹**hith·er** \'hi-thər\ adv [ME hider, hither, fr. OE hider; akin to Goth hidre hither, L citra on this side — more at HE] (bef. 12c) : to this place

²**hither** adj (14c) : being on the near or adjacent side

hith·er·most \-ˌmōst\ adj (1563) : nearest on this side

hith·er·to \-ˌtü, hi-thər-'tü\ adv (13c) : up to this or that time

hith·er·ward \-thər(-)wərd\ adv (bef. 12c) : HITHER

Hit·ler·ism \'hit-lə-ˌri-zəm\ n (1930) : the principles and policies associated with Hitler — **Hit·ler·ite** \-ˌrīt\ n or adj

hit list n (1972) : a list of persons or programs to be opposed or eliminated; broadly : a list of those targeted for special attention or treatment

hit man n (1968) 1 : a professional assassin who works for a crime syndicate 2 : HATCHET MAN

hit-or-miss \ˌhit-ər-'mis\ adj (1848) : marked by a lack of care, forethought, system, or plan; also : HIT-AND-MISS

hit or miss adv (1606) : in a hit-or-miss manner : HAPHAZARDLY

hit parade n (1929) : a group or listing of the most popular or noteworthy items of a particular kind (as popular songs)

Hit·tite \'hi-ˌtīt\ n [Heb Ḥitti, fr. Hitt ḥatti] (1608) 1 : a member of a conquering people in Asia Minor and Syria with an empire in the 2d millennium B.C. 2 : the extinct Indo-European language of the Hittites — see INDO-EUROPEAN LANGUAGES table — **Hittite** adj

HIV \ˌāch-ˌī-'vē\ n (1986) : any of a group of retroviruses and esp. HIV-1 that infect and destroy helper T cells of the immune system causing the marked reduction in their numbers that is diagnostic of AIDS — called also AIDS virus, human immunodeficiency virus

¹**hive** \'hīv\ *n* [ME, fr. OE *hȳf;* perh. akin to ON *hūfr* ship's hull, L *cūpa* tub, Skt *kūpa* cave] (bef. 12c) **1 :** a container for housing honeybees **2 :** a colony of bees **3 :** a place swarming with activity — **hive·less** \-ləs\ *adj*
²**hive** *vb* **hived; hiv·ing** *vi* (14c) **1** *of bees* **:** to enter and take possession of a hive **2 :** to reside in close association ~ *vt* **1 :** to collect into a hive **2 :** to store up in or as if in a hive
hive off *vi* (ca. 1856) *chiefly Brit* **:** to break away from or as if from a group **:** become separate ~ *vt, chiefly Brit* **:** to make separate: as **a :** to remove from a group ⟨*hive off* the youngest campers into another room⟩ **b :** to assign (as assets or responsibilities) to another **c :** SPIN OFF
hives \'hīvz\ *n pl but sing or pl in constr* [origin unknown] (ca. 1500) **:** URTICARIA
HIV-1 \-'wən\ *n* (1986) **:** a retrovirus that is the most common HIV
hiz·zon·er \hi-'zä-nər\ *n, often cap* [alter. of *his honor*] (ca. 1924) — used as a title for a man holding the office of mayor
HLA \ˌāch-(ˌ)el-'ā\ *n* [*human* *l*eukocyte *a*ntigen] (1968) **1 :** the major histocompatibility complex in humans **2 :** a genetic locus, gene, or antigen of HLA — often used with one or more letters to designate a locus or with letters and a number to designate an allele at the locus or the antigen corresponding to the locus and allele
HMO \ˌāch-(ˌ)em-'ō\ *n* (1972) **:** an organization that provides comprehensive health care to voluntarily enrolled individuals and families in a particular geographic area by member physicians with limited referral to outside specialists and that is financed by fixed periodic payments determined in advance — called also *health maintenance organization*
ho \'hō\ *interj* [ME] (15c) — used esp. to attract attention to something specified ⟨land ~⟩
hoa·gie *also* **hoa·gy** \'hō-gē\ *n, pl* **hoagies** [origin unknown] (1955) **:** SUBMARINE 2
¹**hoar** \'hōr, 'hȯr\ *adj* [ME *hor,* fr. OE *hār;* akin to OHG *hēr* hoary] (bef. 12c) **:** HOARY
²**hoar** *n* [ME *hor* hoariness, fr. *hor,* adj.] (1567) **:** FROST 1c
¹**hoard** \'hōrd, 'hȯrd\ *n* [ME *hord,* fr. OE; akin to Goth *huzd* treasure, OE *hȳdan* to hide] (bef. 12c) **:** a supply or fund stored up and often hidden away
²**hoard** *vt* (bef. 12c) **1 :** to lay up a hoard of **2 :** to keep (as one's thoughts) to oneself ~ *vi* **:** to lay up a hoard — **hoard·er** *n*
hoard·ing \'hȯr-diŋ, 'hȯr-\ *n* [*hoard, hoard* (hoarding)] (ca. 1823) **1 :** a temporary board fence put about a building being erected or repaired — called also *hoard* **2** *Brit* **:** BILLBOARD
hoar·frost \'hōr-ˌfrȯst, 'hȯr-\ *n* (14c) **:** FROST 1c
hoarse \'hōrs, 'hȯrs\ *adj* **hoars·er; hoars·est** [ME *hos, hors,* prob. fr. (assumed) ON *hārs;* akin to OE *hās* hoarse, OHG *heis*] (bef. 12c) **1 :** rough or harsh in sound **:** GRATING ⟨a ~ voice⟩ **2 :** having a hoarse voice ⟨shouted himself ~⟩ — **hoarse·ly** *adv* — **hoarse·ness** *n*
hoars·en \'hȯr-s⁰n, 'hȯr-\ *vb* **hoars·ened; hoars·en·ing** \'hȯrs-niŋ, 'hȯrs-, 'hȯr-sə-, 'hȯr-\ *vt* (1748) **:** to make hoarse ~ *vi* **:** to become hoarse
hoary \'hōr-ē, 'hȯr-\ *adj* **hoar·i·er; -est** (1530) **1 :** gray or white with or as if with age **2 :** extremely old **:** ANCIENT ⟨~ legends⟩ — **hoar·i·ness** *n*
hoa·tzin \wä(t)-'sēn\ *n* [Nahuatl *huāctzin* the laughing falcon (*Herpetotheres cachinnans*)] (1661) **:** a crested large So. American bird (*Opisthocomos hoazin* syn. *O. hoatzin*) with blue facial skin, red eyes, brown plumage marked with white above, and claws on the first and second digits of the wing when young
¹**hoax** \'hōks\ *vt* [prob. contr. of *hocus*] (ca. 1796) **:** to trick into believing or accepting as genuine something false and often preposterous *syn* see DUPE — **hoax·er** *n*
²**hoax** *n* (1808) **1 :** an act intended to trick or dupe **:** IMPOSTURE **2 :** something accepted or established by fraud or fabrication
¹**hob** \'häb\ *n* [ME *hobbe,* fr. *Hobbe,* nickname for Robert] (15c) **1** *dial Eng* **:** HOBGOBLIN, ELF **2 :** MISCHIEF, TROUBLE — used with *play* and *raise* ⟨always raising ~⟩
²**hob** *n* [origin unknown] (1511) **1 :** a projection at the back or side of a fireplace on which something may be kept warm **2 :** a cutting tool used for cutting the teeth of worm wheels or gears
³**hob** *vt* **hobbed; hob·bing** (1799) **1 :** to cut with a hob **2 :** to furnish with hobnails
Hobbes·ian \'häb-zē-ən\ *adj* (1776) **:** of or relating to the English philosopher Thomas Hobbes or Hobbism
Hob·bism \'hä-ˌbi-zəm\ *n* (1691) **:** the philosophical system of Thomas Hobbes; *esp* **:** the Hobbesian theory that people have a fundamental right to self-preservation and to pursue selfish aims but will relinquish these rights to an absolute monarch in the interest of common safety and happiness — **Hob·bist** \'hä-bist\ *n or adj*
hob·bit \'hä-bət\ *n* [coined by J.R.R. Tolkien] (1937) **:** a member of a fictitious peaceful and genial race of small humanlike creatures that dwell underground
¹**hob·ble** \'hä-bəl\ *vb* **hob·bled; hob·bling** \-b(ə-)liŋ\ [ME *hoblen;* akin to MD *hobbelen* to turn, roll] *vi* (14c) **:** to move along unsteadily or with difficulty; *esp* **:** to limp along ~ *vt* **1 :** to cause to limp **:** make lame **:** CRIPPLE **2** [prob. alter. of *hopple* (to hobble)] **a :** to fasten together the legs of (as a horse) to prevent straying **:** FETTER **b :** to place under handicap **:** HAMPER, IMPEDE — **hob·bler** \-b(ə-)lər\ *n*
²**hobble** *n* (1726) **1 :** a hobbling movement **2** *archaic* **:** an awkward situation **3 :** something used to hobble an animal
hob·ble·bush \'hä-bəl-ˌbush\ *n* (ca. 1818) **:** a white-flowered shrubby viburnum (*Viburnum alnifolium*) of northeastern No. America having serrate rounded leaves and red berries
hob·ble·de·hoy \'hä-bəl-di-ˌhȯi\ *n* [origin unknown] (1540) **:** an awkward gawky youth
hobble skirt *n* (1911) **:** a skirt constricted at the bottom
¹**hob·by** \'hä-bē\ *n, pl* **hobbies** [ME *hoby,* fr. MF *hobé*] (15c) **:** a small Old World falcon (*Falco subbuteo*) formerly trained to catch small birds (as larks)
²**hobby** *n, pl* **hobbies** [short for *hobbyhorse*] (1816) **:** a pursuit outside one's regular occupation engaged in esp. for relaxation — **hob·by·ist** \-bē-ist\ *n*
hob·by·horse \'hä-bē-ˌhȯrs\ *n* [*hobby* (small light horse)] (1557) **1 a :** a figure of a horse fastened about the waist in the morris dance **b :** a dancer wearing this figure **2** *obs* **:** BUFFOON **3 a :** a stick having an

imitation horse's head at one end that a child pretends to ride **b :** ROCKING HORSE **c :** a toy horse suspended by springs from a frame **4 a :** a topic to which one constantly reverts **b :** ²HOBBY
hob·gob·lin \'häb-ˌgäb-lən\ *n* (1530) **1 a :** a mischievous goblin **2 :** BOGEY 2, BUGABOO
hob·nail \-ˌnāl\ *n* [²*hob*] (1592) **:** a short large-headed nail for studding shoe soles — **hob·nailed** \-ˌnāld\ *adj*
hob·nob \-ˌnäb\ *vi* **hob·nobbed; hob·nob·bing** [fr. the obs. phrase *drink hobnob* (to drink alternately to one another)] (1763) **1** *archaic* **:** to drink sociably **2 :** to associate familiarly — **hob·nob·ber** *n*
¹**ho·bo** \'hō-(ˌ)bō\ *n, pl* **hoboes** *also* **hobos** [origin unknown] (1889) **1 :** a migratory worker **2 :** a homeless and usu. penniless person who wanders from place to place
²**hobo** *vi* (1906) **:** to live or travel in the manner of a hobo
Hob·son's choice \'häb-sənz-\ *n* [Thomas *Hobson* †1631 Eng. liveryman, who required every customer to take the horse nearest the door] (1649) **:** an apparently free choice when there is no real alternative
¹**hock** \'häk\ *n* [ME *hoch, hough,* fr. OE *hōh* heel; akin to ON *hāsin* hock] (1540) **1 a :** the tarsal joint or region in the hind limb of a digitigrade quadruped (as the horse) corresponding to the human ankle but elevated and bending backward — see HORSE illustration **b :** a joint of a fowl's leg that corresponds to the hock of a quadruped **2 :** a small cut of meat from either the front or hind leg just above the foot ⟨ham ~⟩
²**hock** *n, often cap* [modif. of G *Hochheimer,* fr. *Hochheim,* Germany] (ca. 1625) *chiefly Brit* **:** RHINE WINE 1
³**hock** *vt* (1878) **:** PAWN — **hock·er** *n*
⁴**hock** *n* [D *hok* pen, prison] (1883) **1 a :** ²PAWN 2 ⟨got his watch out of ~⟩ **b :** DEBT 3 ⟨in ~ to the bank⟩ **2 :** PRISON
hock·ey \'hä-kē\ *n* [perh. fr. MF *hoquet* shepherd's crook, dim. of *hoc* hook, of Gmc origin; akin to OE *hōc* hook] (1527) **1 :** FIELD HOCKEY **2 :** ICE HOCKEY
hock·shop \'häk-ˌshäp\ *n* (1871) **:** PAWNSHOP
ho·cus \'hō-kəs\ *vt* **ho·cussed** *or* **ho·cused; ho·cus·sing** *or* **ho·cus·ing** [obs. *hocus,* n., short for *hocus-pocus*] (1675) **1 :** to perpetrate a trick or hoax on **:** DECEIVE **2 :** to befuddle often with drugged liquor; *also* **:** DOPE, DRUG ⟨*hocussed* the favorite before the race⟩
¹**ho·cus-po·cus** \ˌhō-kəs-'pō-kəs\ *n* [prob. fr. *hocus pocus,* imitation Latin phrase used by jugglers] (1647) **1 :** SLEIGHT OF HAND **2 :** nonsense or sham used esp. to cloak deception
²**hocus-pocus** *vt* **-cussed** *or* **-cused; -cus·sing** *or* **-cus·ing** (1774) **:** to play tricks on
hod \'häd\ *n* [prob. fr. MD *hodde;* akin to MHG *hotte* cradle] (1573) **1 :** a tray or trough that has a pole handle and that is borne on the shoulder for carrying loads (as of mortar or brick) **2 :** a coal scuttle
hod carrier *n* (1771) **:** a laborer employed in carrying supplies to bricklayers, stonemasons, cement finishers, or plasterers on the job
hodge·podge \'häj-ˌpäj\ *n* [alter. of *hotchpotch*] (15c) **:** a heterogeneous mixture **:** JUMBLE
Hodg·kin's disease \'häj-kinz-\ *n* [Thomas *Hodgkin* †1866 Eng. physician] (1865) **:** a neoplastic disease that is characterized by progressive enlargement of lymph nodes, spleen, and liver and by progressive anemia
ho·do·scope \'hä-də-ˌskōp, 'hō-\ *n* [Gk *hodos* road, path + E *-scope*] (ca. 1933) **:** an instrument for tracing the paths of ionizing particles by means of ion counters in close array

hod 1

¹**hoe** \'hō\ *n* [ME *howe,* fr. MF *houe,* of Gmc origin; akin to OHG *houwa* mattock, *houwan* to hew — more at HEW] (14c) **1 :** any of various implements for tilling, mixing, or raking; *esp* **:** an implement with a thin flat blade on a long handle used esp. for cultivating, weeding, or loosening the earth around plants **2 :** BACKHOE
²**hoe** *vb* **hoed; hoe·ing** *vi* (15c) **:** to use a hoe **:** work with a hoe ~ *vt* **1 :** to weed, cultivate, or thin (a crop) with a hoe **2 :** to remove (weeds) by hoeing **3 :** to dress or cultivate (land) by hoeing — **ho·er** \'hō-(ə)r\ *n*
hoe·cake \'hō-ˌkāk\ *n* (1745) **:** a small cake made of cornmeal
hoe·down \-ˌdaun\ *n* (1841) **1 :** SQUARE DANCE **2 :** a gathering featuring hoedowns
¹**hog** \'hȯg, 'häg\ *n, pl* **hogs** *also* **hog** [ME *hogge,* fr. OE *hogg*] (14c) **1 :** a domestic swine esp. when weighing more than 120 pounds; *broadly* **:** any of various wild and domestic swine **2** *usu* **hogg** *Brit* **:** a young unshorn sheep; *also* **:** wool from such a sheep **3 a :** a selfish, gluttonous, or filthy person **b :** one that uses something to excess ⟨old cars that are gas ~s⟩
²**hog** *vb* **hogged; hog·ging** *vt* (1769) **1 :** to cut (a horse's mane) short **:** ROACH **2 :** to cause to arch **3 :** to take in excess of one's due ⟨~ the credit⟩ **4 :** to tear up or shred (as waste wood) into bits by machine ~ *vi* **:** to become curved upward in the middle — used of a ship's bottom or keel
ho·gan \'hō-ˌgän\ *n* [Navajo *hooghan*] (1871) **:** a Navajo Indian dwelling usu. made of logs and mud with a door traditionally facing east
hog·back \'hȯg-ˌbak, 'häg-\ *n* (1840) **:** a ridge of land formed by the outcropping edges of tilted strata; *broadly* **:** a ridge with a sharp summit and steeply sloping sides
hog cholera *n* (1859) **:** a highly infectious often fatal virus disease of swine characterized by fever, loss of appetite, weakness, erythematous lesions esp. in light-skinned animals, and severe leukopenia
hog·fish \'hȯg-ˌfish, 'häg-\ *n* (1734) **:** a large West Indian and Florida wrasse (*Lachnolaimus maximus*) often used for food
hog·get \'hä-gət, 'hȯ-\ *n* [ME, fr. ¹*hog* + *-et*] (15c) *chiefly Brit* **:** HOG 2
hog·gish \'hȯ-gish, 'hä-\ *adj* (15c) **:** grossly selfish, gluttonous, or filthy — **hog·gish·ly** *adv* — **hog·gish·ness** *n*

\ə\ abut \ᵊ\ kitten, F table \ər\ further \a\ ash \ā\ ace \ä\ mop, mar \au\ out \ch\ chin \e\ bet \ē\ easy \g\ go \i\ hit \ī\ ice \j\ job \ŋ\ sing \ō\ go \ȯ\ law \ȯi\ boy \th\ thin \t͟h\ the \ü\ loot \u̇\ foot \y\ yet \zh\ vision \ä, k̟, ⁿ, œ, œ̄, ᴜᴇ, ᴜ̄ᴇ, ᵞ\ *see* Guide to Pronunciation

hog heaven *n* (1945) : an extremely satisfying state or situation
Hog·ma·nay \ˌhäg-mə-'nā, 'häg-mə-ˌ\ *n* [origin unknown] (ca. 1680) **1** *Scot* : the eve of New Year's Day **2** *Scot* : a gift solicited or given at Hogmanay
hog-nose snake \'hȯg-ˌnōz-, 'häg-\ *n* (1736) : any of a genus (*Heterodon*) of rather small harmless stout-bodied No. American colubrid snakes with keeled scales and an upturned snout that seldom bite but hiss wildly and often play dead when disturbed — called also *hog-nosed snake, puff adder*
hog score *n* [*hog* (curling stone that fails to reach the score)] (1685) : a line which is marked across a curling rink seven yards from the tee and beyond which a stone must pass or be removed from the ice — called also *hog line*
hogs·head \'hȯgz-ˌhed, 'hägz-\ *n* (14c) **1** : a large cask or barrel **2** : any of various units of capacity; *esp* : a U.S. unit equal to 63 gallons (238 liters)
hog sucker *n* (1877) : a No. American sucker (*Hypentelium nigricans*) that is brassy olive marked with brown and is sometimes used for food
hog-tie \'hȯg-ˌtī, 'häg-\ *vt* (1894) **1** : to tie together the feet of **2** : to make helpless
hog-wash \-ˌwȯsh, -ˌwäsh\ *n* (15c) **1** : SWILL 2a, SLOP **2** : NONSENSE, BALDERDASH
hog-wild \-'wī(ə)ld\ *adj* (1904) : lacking in restraint of judgment or temper 〈~ enthusiasm〉〈would go ~ if unconfined by constitutional limitations —Leo Egan〉
[1]Ho·hen·stau·fen \hō-ən-ˌshtau̇-fən, -ˌstau̇-\ *n* (ca. 1895) : a member of the Hohenstaufen family; *esp* : a Hohenstaufen monarch
[2]Hohenstaufen *adj* (1921) : of or relating to a princely German family that reigned over the Holy Roman Empire from 1138–1254 and over Sicily from 1194–1266
[1]Ho·hen·zol·lern \ˌhō-ən-'zä-lərn, -'zȯ-\ *n* (ca. 1895) : a member of the Hohenzollern family; *esp* : a Hohenzollern monarch
[2]Hohenzollern *adj* (1924) : of or relating to a princely German family that reigned in Prussia from 1701–1918 and in Germany from 1871–1918
Ho·ho·kam \hō-hō-'käm\ *n, pl* **Hohokam** [O'odham (Uto-Aztecan language of southern Arizona) *huhugam*, lit., those who have gone] (1884) : a member of a prehistoric desert culture of the southwestern U.S. centering in the Gila Valley of Arizona and characterized esp. by irrigated agriculture — **Hohokam** *adj*
ho–hum \'hō-'həm\ *adj* (1969) **1** : ROUTINE, DULL 〈a ~ existence〉 **2** : BORED, INDIFFERENT 〈a ~ reaction〉
ho hum *interj* [imit.] (1924) — used to express weariness, boredom, or disdain
hoick \'hȯik\ *vt* [prob. alter. of [1]*hike*] (1898) : to move or pull abruptly : YANK 〈was ~ed out of my job —Vincent Sheean〉
hoi pol·loi \ˌhȯi-pə-'lȯi\ *n pl* [Gk, the many] (1837) : the general populace : MASSES
hoise \'hȯiz\ *vt* **hoised** \'hȯizd\ *or* **hoist** \'hȯist\; **hois·ing** \'hȯi-ziŋ\ [alter. of *hysse* to hoist, perh. fr. LG *hissen*] (1509) : HOIST — **hoist with one's own petard** : victimized or hurt by one's own scheme
[1]hoist \'hȯist, *chiefly dial* 'hīst\ *vb* [alter. of *hoise*] *vt* (15c) **1** : LIFT, RAISE; *esp* : to raise into position by or as if by means of tackle **2** : DRINK 1 〈~ a few beers〉 ~ *vi* : to become hoisted : RISE *syn* see LIFT — **hoist·er** *n*
[2]hoist *n* (1654) **1** : an act of hoisting : LIFT **2** : an apparatus for hoisting **3** : the height of a flag when viewed flying
[1]hoi·ty–toi·ty \ˌhȯi-tē-'tȯi-tē, ˌhī-tē-'tī-tē\ *n* [rhyming compound fr. E dial. *hoit* to play the fool] (1668) : thoughtless giddy behavior
[2]hoity–toity *adj* (1690) **1** : thoughtlessly silly or frivolous : FLIGHTY **2** : marked by an air of assumed importance : HIGHFALUTIN
hoke \'hōk\ *vt* **hoked; hok·ing** [*hokum*] (1925) : to give an impressive but false value or quality to : FAKE — usu. used with *up* 〈used parts of B-grade movies to ~ up a film —Robert Sherrill〉
hok·ey \'hō-kē\ *adj* **hok·i·er; -est** (1927) **1** : [1]CORNY 3 〈the usual ~ melodrama〉 **2** : obviously contrived : PHONY 〈the plots are tricky but not ~ —Cleveland Amory〉 — **hok·ey·ness** *or* **hok·i·ness** \'hō-kē-nəs\ *n* — **hok·i·ly** \-kə-lē\ *adv*
ho·key–po·key \ˌhō-kē-'pō-kē\ *n* (ca. 1878) **1** : HOCUS-POCUS **2** : ice cream sold by street vendors
hok·ku \'hȯ-(ˌ)kü\ *n, pl* **hokku** [Jp] (1898) : HAIKU
ho·kum \'hō-kəm\ *n* [prob. blend of *hocus-pocus* and *bunkum*] (1917) **1** : a device used (as by showmen) to evoke a desired audience response **2** : pretentious nonsense : BUNKUM
hol- *or* **holo-** *comb form* [ME, fr. OF, fr. L, fr. Gk, fr. *holos* whole — more at SAFE] **1** : complete : total 〈*holohedral*〉 **2** : completely : totally 〈*holandric*〉
hol·an·dric \hō-'lan-drik, hä-\ *adj* [ISV, fr. *hol-* + *andr-* + *-ic*] (1930) : transmitted by a gene in the nonhomologous portion of the Y chromosome
Hol·arc·tic \hō-'lärk-tik, hä-, -'lär-tik\ *adj* (1883) : of, relating to, or being the biogeographic region including the northern parts of the Old and the New Worlds and comprising the Nearctic and Palearctic regions or subregions
[1]hold \'hōld\ *vb* **held** \'held\; **hold·ing** [ME, fr. OE *healdan;* akin to OHG *haltan* to hold, and perh. to L *celer* rapid, Gk *klonos* agitation] *vt* (bef. 12c) **1 a** : to have possession or ownership of or have at one's disposal 〈~s property worth millions〉〈the bank ~s the title to the car〉 **b** : to have as a privilege or position of responsibility 〈a professorship〉 **c** : to have as a mark of distinction 〈~s the record for the 100-yard dash〉〈~s a PhD〉 **2** : to keep under restraint 〈~ price increases to a minimum〉: as **a** : to prevent free expression of 〈~ your temper〉 **b** : to prevent from some action 〈ordered the troops to ~ fire〉〈the only restraining motive which may ~ the hand of a tyrant —Thomas Jefferson〉 **c** : to keep back from use 〈ask them to ~ a room for us〉 **d** : to delay temporarily the handling of 〈please ~ all my calls〉 **3** : to make liable or accountable or bound to an obligation 〈I'll ~ you to your promise〉 **4 a** : to have or maintain in the grasp 〈~ my hand〉 〈this is how you ~ the racket〉; *also* : AIM, POINT 〈*held* a gun on them〉 **b** : to support in a particular position or keep from falling or moving 〈~ me up so I can see〉〈~ the ladder steady〉〈a clamp ~s the whole thing together〉〈~ your head up〉 **c** : to bear the pressure of : SUPPORT 〈can the roof ~ all of that weight〉 **5** : to prevent from leaving or getting away 〈~ the train〉: as

a : to avoid emitting or letting out 〈how long can you ~ your breath〉 **b** : to restrain as or as if a captive 〈the suspect was *held* without bail〉 〈*held* them at gunpoint〉; *also* : to have strong appeal to 〈the book *held* my interest throughout〉 **6 a** : to enclose and keep in a container or within bounds : CONTAIN 〈the jug ~s one gallon〉〈this corral will not ~ all of the horses〉 **b** : to be able to consume easily or without undue effect 〈can't ~ any more pie〉; *esp* : to be able to drink (alcoholic beverages) without becoming noticeably drunk 〈can't ~ your liquor〉 **c** : ACCOMMODATE 〈the restaurant ~s 400 diners〉 **7 a** : to have as a principal or essential feature or attribute 〈the book ~s a number of surprises〉; *also* : to have in store 〈no one knows what the future ~s〉 **b** : to have in the mind or express as a judgment, opinion, or belief 〈I ~ the view that this is wrong〉〈~ a grudge〉〈~*ing* that it is nobody's business but his —Jack Olsen〉 — often used with *against* 〈in America they ~ everything you say against you —Paul McCartney〉 **b** : to think of in a particular way : REGARD 〈were *held* in high esteem〉 **8 a** : to assemble for and carry on the activity of 〈*held* a convention〉 **b** : to cause to be carried on : CONDUCT 〈will ~ a seminar〉 **c** : to produce or sponsor esp. as a public exhibition 〈will ~ an art show〉 **9 a** : to maintain occupation, control, or defense of 〈the troops *held* the ridge〉; *also* : to resist the offensive efforts or advance of 〈*held* the opposing team to just two points〉 **b** : to maintain (a certain condition, situation, or course of action) without change 〈~ a course due east〉 **10** : to cover (a part of the body) esp. for protection 〈had to ~ their ears because of the cold〉 ~ *vi* **1 a** : to maintain position : refuse to give ground 〈the defensive line is ~*ing*〉 **b** : to continue in the same way or to the same degree : LAST 〈hopes the weather will ~〉 — often used with *up* **2** : to derive right or title — often used with *of* or *from* **3** : to be or remain valid : APPLY 〈the rule ~s in most cases〉 — often used in the phrase **hold true** **4** : to maintain a grasp on something : remain fastened to something 〈the anchor *held* in the rough sea〉 **5** : to go ahead as one has been going 〈*held* south for several miles〉 **6** : to bear or carry oneself 〈asked him to ~ still〉 **7** : to forbear an intended or threatened action : HALT, PAUSE — often used as a command **8** : to stop counting during a countdown **9** *slang* : to have illicit drug material in one's possession *syn* see CONTAIN — **hold a candle to** : to qualify for comparison with — **hold court** : to be the center of attention among friends or admirers — **hold forth** : to speak at length : EXPATIATE — **hold hands** : to engage one's hand with another's esp. as an expression of affection — **hold one's horses** : to slow down or stop for a moment — usu. used in the imperative — **hold one's own** : to do well in the face of difficulty or opposition — **hold one's tongue** : to keep silent — **hold sway** : to have a dominant influence : RULE — **hold the bag 1** : to be left empty-handed **2** : to bear alone a responsibility that should have been shared by others — **hold the fort 1** : to maintain a firm position **2** : to take care of usual affairs 〈is *holding* the fort until the manager returns〉 — **hold the line** : to maintain the current position or situation 〈*hold* the line on prices〉 — **hold to** : to give firm assent to : adhere to strongly 〈*holds* to his promise〉 — **hold to account** : to hold responsible — **hold water** : to stand up under criticism or analysis — **hold with** : to agree with or approve of
[2]hold *n* (14c) **1** : STRONGHOLD 1 **2 a** : CONFINEMENT, CUSTODY **b** : PRISON **3 a** (1) : the act or the manner of holding or grasping : GRIP 〈released his ~ on the handle〉 (2) : a manner of grasping an opponent in wrestling **b** : a nonphysical bond that attaches, restrains, or constrains or by which something is affected, controlled, or dominated 〈has lost its ~ on the broad public —Oscar Cargill〉 **c** : full comprehension 〈get ~ of exactly what is happening —J. P. Lyford〉 **d** : full or immediate control : POSSESSION 〈get ~ of yourself〉〈wants to get ~ of a road map〉 **e** : TOUCH 14 — used with *of* 〈tried to get ~ of me〉 **4** : something that may be grasped as a support **5 a** : FERMATA **b** : the time between the onset and the release of a vocal articulation **6** : a sudden motionless posture at the end of a dance **7 a** : an order or indication that something is to be reserved or delayed **b** : a delay in a countdown (as in launching a spacecraft) — **on hold 1** : into a state of interruption during a telephone call when one party switches to another line without totally disconnecting the other party **2** : into a state or period of indefinite suspension 〈put our plans on *hold*〉
[3]hold *n* [alter. of *hole*] (1591) **1** : the interior of a ship below decks; *esp* : the cargo deck of a ship **2** : the cargo compartment of a plane
hold-all \'hōl-ˌdȯl\ *n* (1851) *chiefly Brit* : an often cloth traveling case or bag
hold-back \'hōl(d)-ˌbak\ *n* (1581) **1** : something that retains or restrains **2 a** : the act of holding back **b** : something held back
hold back *vt* (1535) **1** : to hinder the progress or achievement of : RESTRAIN **2** : to refrain from revealing or parting with ~ *vi* **1** : to keep oneself in check **2** : to refrain from revealing or parting with something
hold–down \'hōl-ˌdau̇n\ *n* (1888) **1** : something used to fasten an object in place **2 a** : an act of holding down **b** : LIMIT 〈agreed to wage-rate ~s〉
hold down *vt* (1533) **1** : to keep within limits 〈holding the noise *down*〉 **2** : to assume the responsibility for 〈*holding down* two jobs〉
hold·en \'hōl-dən\ *archaic past part* of HOLD
hold·er \'hōl-dər\ *n* (14c) **1** : a person that holds: as **a** (1) : OWNER (2) : TENANT **b** : a person in possession of and legally entitled to receive payment of a bill, note, or check **2** : a device that holds 〈cigarette ~〉
holder in due course (1882) : one other than the original recipient who holds a legally effective negotiable instrument (as a promissory note) and who has a right to collect from and no responsibility toward the issuer
hold-fast \'hōl(d)-ˌfast\ *n* (1566) **1** : something to which something else may be firmly secured **2 a** : a part by which a plant clings to a flat surface **b** : an organ by which a parasitic animal attaches itself to its host
[1]hold·ing \'hōl-diŋ\ *n* (15c) **1 a** : land held esp. by a vassal or tenant **b** : property (as land or securities) owned — usu. used in pl. **2 a** : a ruling of a court esp. on an issue of law raised in a case — compare DICTUM **3** : something that holds
[2]holding *adj* (1568) **1** : having the effect of holding back or delaying something 〈the [war] represented a ~ action against the spread of

world Communism —Sidney Offit⟩ **2** : intended for usu. temporary storage or retention ⟨a ~ tank⟩

holding company n (1906) : a company whose primary business is holding a controlling interest in the securities of other companies — compare INVESTMENT COMPANY

holding pattern n (ca. 1952) **1** : the usu. oval course flown (as over an airport) by aircraft awaiting clearance esp. to land **2** : a state of waiting or suspended activity or progress

hold off vt (15c) **1** : to block from an objective : DELAY **2** : to defer action on : POSTPONE **3** : to fight to a standoff : WITHSTAND ~ vi : to defer or temporarily stop doing something

hold on vi (13c) **1 a** : to maintain a condition or position : PERSIST **b** : to maintain a grasp on something : HANG ON **2** : to await something (as a telephone connection) desired or requested; *broadly* : WAIT — **hold on to** : to maintain possession of or adherence to

hold-out \'hōl-ˌdaut\ n (1945) : one that holds out (as in negotiations); *also* : an instance of holding out

hold out vi (1585) **1** : to remain unsubdued or operative : continue to cope or function **2** : to refuse to go along with others in a concerted action or to come to an agreement ⟨*holding out* for a shorter workweek⟩ ~ vt **1** : to present as something realizable : PROFFER **2** : to represent to be — **hold out on** : to withhold something (as information) from

hold-over \'hōl-ˌdō-vər\ n (1893) : one that is held over

hold over vi (1647) **1** : to continue (as in office) for a prolonged period ~ vt **1 a** : POSTPONE, DEFER **b** : to retain in a condition or position from an earlier period **2** : to prolong the engagement of ⟨the film was *held over* another week⟩

hold-up \'hōl-ˌdəp\ n (1837) **1** : DELAY **2** : a robbery carried out at gunpoint

hold up vt (1851) **1** : to rob at gunpoint **2** : DELAY, IMPEDE **3** : to call attention to : single out ⟨his work was *held up* to ridicule⟩ ⟨*hold* this *up* as perfection —*Times Lit. Supp.*⟩ ~ vi : to continue in the same condition without failing or losing effectiveness or force ⟨you seem to be *holding up* under the strain⟩

¹hole \'hōl\ n [ME, fr. OE *hol* (fr. neut. of *hol*, adj., hollow) & *holh*; akin to OHG *hol*, adj., hollow; perh. akin to OE *helan* to conceal — more at HELL] (bef. 12c) **1 a** : an opening through something : PERFORATION ⟨have a ~ in my coat⟩ **b** : an area where something is missing : GAP: as **(1)** : a serious discrepancy : FLAW, WEAKNESS ⟨there are ~s in your logic⟩ **(2)** : an opening in a defensive formation; *esp* : the area of a baseball field between the positions of shortstop and third baseman **(3)** : a defect in a crystal (as of a semiconductor) that is due to an electron's having left its normal position in one of the crystal bonds and that is equivalent in many respects to a positively charged particle **2** : a hollowed-out place: as **a** : a cave, pit, or well in the ground **b** : BURROW **c** : an unusually deep place in a body of water **3** : a wretched or dreary place **4 a** : a shallow cylindrical hole in the putting green of a golf course into which the ball is played **b** : a part of the golf course from tee to putting green ⟨just beginning play on the third ~⟩; *also* : the play on such a hole as a unit of scoring ⟨won the ~ by two strokes⟩ **5** : an awkward position or circumstance : FIX ⟨got the rebels out of a ~ at the battle —Kenneth Roberts⟩ **b** : a position of owing or losing money ⟨$10 million in the ~⟩ ⟨raising money to get out of the ~⟩ — **in the hole** **1** : having a score below zero **2** : at a disadvantage

²hole vb **holed; hol·ing** vt (bef. 12c) **1** : to make a hole in **2** : to drive or hit into a hole ~ vi : to make a hole in something

hole-and-corner adj (1835) **1** : being or carried on in a place away from public view : CLANDESTINE **2** : INSIGNIFICANT

hole card n (1908) : a card in stud poker that is properly dealt facedown and that the holder need not expose before the showdown

hole in one n (1925) : ACE 4

hole-in-the-wall n, pl **holes-in-the-wall** (1856) : a small and often unpretentious out-of-the-way place (as a restaurant)

hole out vi (1857) : to play one's ball into the hole in golf

hole up vi (1875) : to take refuge or shelter in or as if in a hole or cave ~ vt : to place in or as if in a refuge or hiding place

hol·ey \'hō-lē\ adj (13c) : having holes

¹hol·i·day \'hä-lə-ˌdā, *Brit* usu 'hä-lə-dē\ n [ME, fr. OE *hāligdæg*, fr. *hālig* holy + *dæg* day] (bef. 12c) **1** : HOLY DAY **2** : a day on which one is exempt from work; *specif* : a day marked by a general suspension of work in commemoration of an event **3** *chiefly Brit* : a period of relaxation : VACATION — often used in the phrase *on holiday*; often used in pl.

²holiday vi (1869) : to take or spend a holiday esp. in travel or at a resort — **hol·i·day·er** n

hol·i·day·mak·er \'hä-lə-dē-ˌmā-kər, 'hä-lə-ˌdā-\ n (1836) *chiefly Brit* : VACATIONER

hol·i·days \-lə-ˌdāz, *Brit* usu -lə-dēz\ adv (ca. 1961) : on holidays repeatedly : on any holiday

ho·li·er-than-thou \ˌhō-lē-ər-thən-'thau\ adj (1859) : marked by an air of superior piety or morality

¹ho·li·ness \'hō-lē-nəs\ n (bef. 12c) **1** : the quality or state of being holy — used as a title for various high religious dignitaries ⟨his *holiness* the pope⟩ **2** : SANCTIFICATION 2

²holiness adj, often cap (1888) : emphasizing the doctrine of the second blessing; *specif* : of or relating to a perfectionist movement arising in U.S. Protestantism in the late 19th century

ho·lism \'hō-ˌli-zəm\ n [hol- + -ism] (1926) **1** : a theory that the universe and esp. living nature is correctly seen in terms of interacting wholes (as of living organisms) that are more than the mere sum of elementary particles **2** : a holistic study or method of treatment — **hol·ist** \'hō-list\ n

ho·lis·tic \hō-'lis-tik\ adj (1926) **1** : of or relating to holism **2** : relating to or concerned with wholes or with complete systems rather than with the analysis of, treatment of, or dissection into parts ⟨~ medicine attempts to treat both the mind and the body⟩ ⟨~ ecology views man and the environment as a single system⟩ — **ho·lis·ti·cal·ly** \-ti-k(ə-)lē\ adv

hol·land \'hä-lənd\ n, often cap [ME *holand*, fr. *Holand*, county in the Netherlands, fr. MD *Holland*] (14c) : a cotton or linen fabric in plain weave usu. heavily sized or glazed and used for window shades, bookbinding, and clothing

hol·lan·daise \ˌhä-lən-'dāz\ n [F *sauce hollandaise*, lit., Dutch sauce] (1907) : a rich sauce made basically of butter, egg yolks, and lemon juice or vinegar

Hol·lands \'hä-lən(d)z\ n [D *hollandsch*, fr. *hollandsch genever* Dutch gin] (1788) : gin made in the Netherlands — called also *Holland gin*

¹hol·ler \'hä-lər\ vb **hol·lered; hol·ler·ing** \'häl-riŋ, 'hä-lə-\ [alter. of *hollo*] vi (1699) **1** : to cry out (as to attract attention or in pain) : SHOUT **2** : GRIPE, COMPLAIN ~ vt : to call out (a word or phrase)

²holler n (1825) **1** : SHOUT, CRY **2** : COMPLAINT **3** : a freely improvised work song of black Americans ⟨field ~s⟩

³holler *chiefly dial var of* HOLLOW

Hol·ler·ith card \'hä-lə-rith-\ n [Herman *Hollerith* †1929 Am. engineer] (1946) : PUNCHED CARD

Hollerith code n (1962) : a system for encoding alphanumeric information on punched cards

¹hol·lo *also* **hol·loa** \'hä-(ˌ)lō *or* **hol·la** \'hä-lə\ vi (14c) : to cry hollo : HOLLER ~ vt **1** : to call or cry hollo to **2** : to utter loudly : HOLLER

²hollo *also* **holloa** *or* **holla** n, pl **hollos** *also* **holloas** *or* **hollas** (15c) : an exclamation or call of hollo

³hol·lo \'hä-ˌlō, hə-\ *also* **hol·loa** \'hä-ˌlō, hə-\ *or* **hol·la** \hə-'lä, 'hä-(ˌ)\ *interj* [origin unknown] (1588) **1** — used to attract attention (as when a fox is spied during a fox hunt) **2** — used as a call of encouragement or jubilation

¹hollow n (bef. 12c) **1** : an unfilled space : CAVITY, HOLE **2** : a depressed or low part of a surface; *esp* : a small valley or basin

²hol·low \'hä-(ˌ)lō\ adj **hol·low·er** \'hä-lə-wər\; **hol·low·est** \-lə-wəst\ [ME *holw, holh*, fr. *holh* hole, den, fr. OE *holh* hole, hollow — more at HOLE] (13c) **1** : having an indentation or inward curve : CONCAVE, SUNKEN **2** : having a cavity within ⟨~ tree⟩ **3** : lacking in real value, sincerity, or substance : FALSE, MEANINGLESS ⟨~ promises⟩ ⟨a victory over a weakling is ~ and without triumph —Ernest Beaglehole⟩ **4** : reverberating like a sound made in or by beating on a large empty enclosure : MUFFLED *syn* see VAIN — **hol·low·ly** \'hä-lō-lē, -lə-lē\ adv — **hol·low·ness** n

³hollow vt (15c) **1** : to make hollow **2** : to form by a hollowing action — usu. used with *out* ⟨rain barrels ~ed out from trees —Robert Shaplen⟩ ~ vi : to become hollow

⁴hollow adv (1601) **1** : so as to have a hollow sound **2** : COMPLETELY, THOROUGHLY ⟨an ongoing story that has the old cowboy-and-Indians genre beat ~ —Barbara Bannon⟩ — often used with *all*

hol·low·ware *or* **hol·o·ware** \'hä-(ˌ)lō-ˌwar, -ˌwer\ n (1682) : vessels (as bowls, cups, or vases) usu. of pottery, glass, or metal that have a significant depth and volume — compare FLATWARE

hol·ly \'hä-lē\ n, pl **hollies** [ME *holin, holly*, fr. OE *holen*; akin to OHG *hulis* holly, MIr *cuilenn*] (bef. 12c) **1** : any of a genus (*Ilex* of the family Aquifoliaceae, the holly family) of trees and shrubs; *esp* : either of two (*I. opaca* of the eastern U.S. and *I. aquifolium* of Eurasia) with spiny-margined evergreen leaves and usu. red berries often used for Christmas decorations **2** : the foliage or branches of the holly

hol·ly·hock \'hä-lē-ˌhäk, -ˌhók\ n [ME *holihoc* marshmallow, fr. *holi* holy + *hoc* mallow, fr. OE] (1548) : a tall widely cultivated perennial Chinese herb (*Alcea rosea* syn. *Althaea rosea*) of the mallow family with large coarse rounded leaves and tall spikes of showy flowers

¹Hol·ly·wood \'hä-lē-ˌwud\ n [*Hollywood*, district of Los Angeles, Calif.] (1923) : the American motion-picture industry — **Hol·ly·wood·ish** \-ˌwu-dish\ adj

²Hollywood adj (1935) : of or characteristic of people in the American motion-picture industry ⟨~ lifestyle⟩

Hollywood bed n (1947) : a mattress on a box spring supported by low legs and often having an upholstered headboard

hollyhock

holm \'hō(l)m\ n [ME, fr. OE, fr. ON *hōlmr*; akin to OE *hyll* hill] (bef. 12c) *Brit* : a small inland or inshore island; *also* : BOTTOMS

Holmes·ian \'hōm-zē-ən *also* 'hōlm-\ adj [Sherlock *Holmes*, detective in stories by Sir Arthur Conan Doyle] (1929) : of, characteristic of, or suggestive of the detective Sherlock Holmes

hol·mi·um \'hō(l)-mē-əm\ n [NL, fr. *Holmia* Stockholm, Sweden] (1879) : a metallic element of the rare-earth group that occurs with yttrium and forms highly magnetic compounds — see ELEMENT table

holm oak n (1597) : a southern European evergreen oak (*Quercus ilex*)

holo- — see HOL-

ho·lo·blas·tic \ˌhō-lə-'blas-tik, ˌhä-\ adj [ISV] (1872) : characterized by cleavage planes that divide the whole egg into distinct and separate though coherent blastomeres — compare MEROBLASTIC

ho·lo·caust \'hō-lə-ˌkóst, 'hä- *also* -ˌkäst *or* 'hó-lə-ˌkóst\ n [ME, fr. OF *holocauste*, fr. LL *holocaustum*, fr. Gk *holokauston*, fr. neut. of *holokaustos* burnt whole, fr. *hol-* + *kaustos* burnt, fr. *kaiein* to burn — more at CAUSTIC] (13c) **1** : a sacrifice consumed by fire **2** : a thorough destruction involving extensive loss of life esp. through fire ⟨a nuclear ~⟩ **3** *often cap* : the mass slaughter of European civilians and esp. Jews by the Nazis during World War II — usu. used with *the* **b** : a mass slaughter of people; *esp* : GENOCIDE

Ho·lo·cene \'hō-lə-ˌsēn, 'hä-\ adj [ISV] (1897) : of, relating to, or being the present or post-Pleistocene geologic epoch — see GEOLOGIC TIME table — **Holocene** n

ho·lo·crine \-krən, -ˌkrīn, -ˌkrēn\ adj [ISV *hol-* + Gk *krinein* to separate — more at CERTAIN] (ca. 1905) : producing or being a secretion resulting from lysis of secretory cells ⟨~ gland⟩

ho·lo·en·zyme \ˌhō-lō-'en-ˌzīm\ n [ISV] (1943) : a catalytically active enzyme consisting of an apoenzyme combined with its cofactor

\a\ abut \ᵊ\ kitten, F table \ər\ further \a\ ash \ā\ ace \ä\ mop, mar \au\ out \ch\ chin \e\ bet \ē\ easy \g\ go \i\ hit \ī\ ice \j\ job \ŋ\ sing \ō\ go \o\ law \oi\ boy \th\ thin \th\ the \ü\ loot \u\ foot \y\ yet \zh\ vision \à, k, ⁿ, œ, œ̄, ᵫ, ūē, ᵛ\ see Guide to Pronunciation

Ho·lo·fer·nes \,hä-lə-'fər-(,)nēz, ,hō-\ n [LL, fr. Gk *Holophernēs*] : a general of Nebuchadnezzar's who led an Assyrian army against Israel and was beheaded in his sleep by Judith

ho·lo·gram \'hō-lə-,gram, 'hä-\ n (1949) : a three-dimensional image reproduced from a pattern of interference produced by a split coherent beam of radiation (as a laser); *also* : the pattern of interference itself

ho·lo·graph \'hō-lə-,graf, 'hä-\ n [LL *holographus*, fr. LGk *holographos*, fr. Gk *hol-* + *graphein* to write — more at CARVE] (ca. 1623) : a document wholly in the handwriting of its author; *also* : the handwriting itself (a letter in the president's ∼) — **holograph** *or* **ho·lo·graph·ic** \,hō-lə-'gra-fik, ,hä-\ *adj*

ho·log·ra·phy \hō-'lä-grə-fē\ n (1964) : the art or process of making or using a hologram — **ho·lo·graph** \'hō-lə-,graf, 'hä-\ *vt* — **ho·log·ra·pher** \hō-'lä-grə-fər\ n — **ho·lo·graph·ic** \,hō-lə-'gra-fik, ,hä-\ *adj* — **ho·lo·graph·i·cal·ly** \-fi-k(ə-)lē\ *adv*

ho·lo·he·dral \,hō-lə-'hē-drəl, ,hä-\ *adj* (1837) *of a crystal* : having all the faces required by complete symmetry — compare HEMIHEDRAL, TETARTOHEDRAL

ho·lo·me·tab·o·lous \,hō-lō-mə-'ta-bə-ləs, ,hä-\ *adj* (1870) : characterized by complete metamorphosis (∼ insects) — compare HEMIMETABOLOUS — **ho·lo·me·tab·o·lism** \-,li-zəm\ n

ho·lo·phras·tic \,hō-lə-'fras-tik, ,hä-\ *adj* [ISV *hol-* + *-phrastic* (fr. Gk *phrazein* to point out, declare)] (1860) : expressing a complex of ideas in a single word or in a fixed phrase

ho·lo·phyt·ic \-'fi-tik\ *adj* (1885) : obtaining food after the manner of a green plant by photosynthetic activity

ho·lo·thu·ri·an \-'thur̄-ē-ən, -'thyúr-\ n [ultim. fr. Gk *holothourion* water polyp] (ca. 1842) : SEA CUCUMBER — **holothurian** *adj*

ho·lo·type \'hō-lə-,tip, 'hä-\ n (1897) 1 : the single specimen designated by an author as the type of a species or lesser taxon at the time of establishing the group 2 : the type of a species or lesser taxon designated at a date later than that of establishing a group or by another person than the author of the taxon — **ho·lo·typ·ic** \,hō-lə-'ti-pik, ,hä-\ *adj*

ho·lo·zo·ic \,hō-lə-'zō-ik, ,hä-\ *adj* (1885) : characterized by food procurement after the manner of most animals by the ingestion of complex organic matter : HETEROTROPHIC (∼ nutrition)

holp \'hō(l)p\ *chiefly dial past of* HELP

hol·pen \'hō(l)-pən\ *chiefly dial past part of* HELP

hols \'hälz\ n pl [short for *holidays*] (1905) *Brit* : VACATION 2

Hol·stein \'hōl-,stēn, -,stīn\ n [short for *Holstein-Friesian*] (1865) : any of a breed of large usu. black-and-white dairy cattle orig. from northern Holland and Friesland that produce large quantities of comparatively low-fat milk

Hol·stein–Frie·sian \-'frē-zhən\ n [*Holstein*, Germany, its later locality + *Friesian* (var. of *Frisian*)] (1889) : HOLSTEIN

hol·ster \'hōl-stər\ n [D; akin to OE *heolstor* cover, *helan* to conceal — more at HELL] (1663) : a leather or fabric case for carrying a firearm on the person (as on the hip or chest), on a saddle, or in a vehicle

holt \'hōlt\ n [ME, fr. OE; akin to OHG *holz* wood, Gk *klados* twig] (bef. 12c) *archaic* : a small woods : COPPICE

ho·lus–bo·lus \,hō-ləs-'bō-ləs\ *adv* [prob. redupl. of *bolus*] (1857) : all at once

ho·ly \'hō-lē\ *adj* **ho·li·er; -est** [ME, fr. OE *hālig*; akin to OE *hāl* whole — more at WHOLE] (bef. 12c) 1 : exalted or worthy of complete devotion as one perfect in goodness and righteousness 2 : DIVINE (for the Lord our God is ∼ —Ps 99:9 (AV)) 3 : devoted entirely to the deity or the work of the deity (a ∼ temple) (∼ prophets) 4 a : having a divine quality (∼ love) b : venerated as or as if sacred (∼ scripture) (a ∼ relic) (lampooning the ∼ conventions of playwriting — William Zinsser) 5 — used as an intensive (this is a ∼ mess) (he was a ∼ terror when he drank —Thomas Wolfe); often used in combination as a mild oath (∼ smoke) — **ho·li·ly** \-lə-lē\ *adv*

holy city n (14c) : a city that is the center of religious worship and traditions

Holy Communion n (1548) : COMMUNION 2a

holy day n (bef. 12c) : a day set aside for special religious observance

holy day of obligation (1909) : a feast on which Roman Catholics are duty-bound to attend mass

Holy Father n (15c) : POPE 1

Holy Ghost n (bef. 12c) : the third person of the Trinity : HOLY SPIRIT

Holy Grail n (1590) : GRAIL

Holy Joe \'hō-lē-'jō\ n (ca. 1874) *slang* : PARSON, CHAPLAIN

Holy Office n (ca. 1741) : a congregation of the curia charged with protecting faith and morals

holy of holies [trans. of LL *sanctum sanctorum*, trans. of Heb *qōdhesh haq-qōdhāshīm*] (1641) : the innermost and most sacred chamber of the Jewish tabernacle and temple

holy oil n (14c) : olive oil blessed by a bishop for use in a sacrament or sacramental

holy order n, *often cap H&O* (14c) 1 a : MAJOR ORDER — usu. used in pl. b : one of the orders of the ministry in the Anglican or Episcopal church 2 : the rite or sacrament of ordination — usu. used in pl.

Holy Roller n (1842) : a member of one of the Protestant sects whose worship meetings are characterized by spontaneous expressions of emotional excitement — often taken to be offensive

Holy Roman Empire n (1728) : an empire consisting primarily of a loose confederation of German and Italian territories under the suzerainty of an emperor and existing from the 9th or 10th century to 1806

Holy Saturday n (14c) : the Saturday before Easter

Holy See n (1765) : the see of the pope

Holy Spirit n (14c) : the third person of the Christian Trinity

ho·ly·stone \'hō-lē-,stōn\ n (ca. 1823) : a soft sandstone used to scrub a ship's decks — **holystone** *vt*

Holy Synod n (1768) : the governing body of a national Eastern church

Holy Thursday n (13c) 1 : ASCENSION DAY 2 : MAUNDY THURSDAY

holy war n (1691) : a war waged by religious partisans to propagate or defend their faith

holy water n (bef. 12c) : water blessed by a priest and used as a purifying sacramental

Holy Week n (1710) : the week before Easter during which the last days of Christ's life are commemorated

holy writ n, *often cap H&W* (bef. 12c) 1 : BIBLE 1 2 : a writing or utterance having unquestionable authority (its financial precepts were not necessarily *Holy Writ* —Herbert Stein)

Holy Year n (1900) : a Roman Catholic jubilee year

hom- *or* **homo-** *comb form* [L, fr. Gk, fr. *homos* — more at SAME] 1 : one and the same : similar : alike (*homograph*) (*homo*sporous) 2 : homosexual (*homo*phobia)

hom·age \'ä-mij, 'hä-\ n [ME, fr. OF *hommage*, fr. *homme* man, vassal, fr. L *homin-*, *homo* human being; akin to OE *guma* human being, L *humus* earth — more at HUMBLE] (14c) 1 a : a feudal ceremony by which a man acknowledges himself the vassal of a lord b : the relationship between a feudal lord and his vassal c : an act done or payment made in meeting the obligations of vassalage 2 a : expression of high regard : RESPECT — often used with *pay* b : something that shows respect or attests to the worth or influence of another : TRIBUTE (his long life filled with international ∼s to his unique musical talent —*People*) **syn** see HONOR

hom·ag·er \'ä-mi-jər, 'hä-\ n (15c) : VASSAL

hom·bre \'äm-brā, 'əm-, 'ōm-, -,brē\ n [Sp, man, fr. L *homin-*, *homo*] (1846) : GUY, FELLOW

hom·burg \'häm-,bərg\ n [*Bad Homburg*, Germany] (1894) : a man's felt hat with a stiff curled brim and a high crown creased lengthwise

¹home \'hōm\ n [ME *hom*, fr. OE *hām* village, home; akin to OHG *heim* home] (bef. 12c) 1 a : one's place of residence : DOMICILE b : HOUSE 2 : the social unit formed by a family living together 3 a : a familiar or usual setting : congenial environment; *also* : the focus of one's domestic attention (∼ is where the heart is) b : HABITAT 4 a : a place of origin (salmon returning to their ∼ to spawn); *also* : one's own country (having troubles at ∼ and abroad) b : HEADQUARTERS 2 (∼ of the dance company) 5 : an establishment providing residence and care for people with special needs (∼s for the elderly) (a ∼ for unwed mothers) 6 : the objective in various games; *esp* : HOME PLATE — **at home** 1 : relaxed and comfortable : at ease (felt completely *at home* on the stage) 2 : in harmony with the surroundings 3 : on familiar ground : KNOWLEDGEABLE (teachers *at home* in their subject fields)

²home *adv* (bef. 12c) 1 : to, from, or at one's home (go ∼) (left ∼ at the age of 12) 2 a : to a final, closed, or ultimate position (drive a nail ∼) b : to or at an ultimate objective (as a goal or finish line) 3 : to a vital sensitive core (the truth struck ∼) — **home free** : out of jeopardy : in a comfortable position with respect to some objective

³home *adj* (1552) 1 : of, relating to, or being a home, place of origin, or base of operations (∼ office) (checkers in position on their ∼ squares) 2 : prepared, done, or designed for use in a home (∼ remedies) (∼ cooking) (a ∼ videotape system) 3 : operating or occurring in a home area (the ∼ team) (∼ games)

⁴home *vb* **homed; hom·ing** *vi* (1765) 1 : to go or return home 2 *of an animal* : to return accurately to one's home or natal area from a distance 3 : to proceed to or toward a source of radiated energy used as a guide (missiles ∼ in on radar) 4 : to proceed or direct attention toward an objective (science is *homing* in on the mysterious human process —Sam Glucksberg) ∼ *vt* : to send to or provide with a home

home·body \'hōm-,bä-dē\ n (1821) : one whose life centers in the home

¹home·bound \'hōm-,baùnd\ *adj* [*home* + ¹*bound*] (ca. 1625) : going homeward : bound for home (∼ travelers)

²homebound *adj* [*home* + ⁵*bound*] (1882) : confined to the home

home·boy \'hōm-,bói\ n (1927) 1 : a boy or man from one's neighborhood, hometown, or region 2 : a fellow member of a youth gang

home·bred \'hōm-'bred\ *adj* (1587) : produced at home : INDIGENOUS

home brew n (1853) : an alcoholic beverage (as beer) made at home

home·built \'hōm-'bilt\ *adj* (1676) : HOMEMADE 1

home·com·ing \'hōm-,kə-miŋ\ n (14c) 1 : a return home 2 : the return of a group of people usu. on a special occasion to a place formerly frequented or regarded as home; *esp* : an annual celebration for alumni at a college or university

home computer n (1976) : a small inexpensive microcomputer

home economics n pl but sing or pl in constr (1899) : the theory and practice of homemaking — called also *home ec* \-'ek\— **home economist** n

home fries n pl (1951) : potatoes that have usu. been parboiled, sliced, and then fried — called also *home fried potatoes*

home front n (1919) : the sphere of civilian activity in war

home·grown \'hōm-'grōn\ *adj* (1827) 1 : grown or produced at home or in a particular local area (∼ vegetables) (∼ films) 2 : native to or characteristic of a particular area (the festival will feature ∼ artists)

home·land \-,land *also* -lənd\ n (1670) 1 : native land : FATHERLAND 2 : a state or area set aside to be a state for a people of a particular national, cultural, or racial origin; *esp* : BANTUSTAN

home·less \-ləs\ *adj* (1615) : having no home or permanent place of residence — **home·less·ness** n

home·like \'hōm-,līk\ *adj* (1817) : characteristic of a home

home·ly \'hōm-lē\ *adj* **home·li·er; -est** (14c) 1 : suggestive or characteristic of a home 2 : being something familiar with which one is at home (satisfy themselves with houses, furniture, books and clothes that were worn and ∼ and friendly to the touch —Brendan Gill) 3 a : unaffectedly natural : SIMPLE b : not elaborate or complex (∼ virtues) 4 : plain or unattractive in appearance — **home·li·ness** n

home·made \'hō(m)-'mād\ *adj* (ca. 1659) 1 : made in the home, on the premises, or by one's own efforts 2 : of domestic manufacture

home·mak·er \'hōm-,mā-kər\ n (1876) : one who manages a household esp. as a wife and mother — **home·mak·ing** \-,kiŋ\ n or adj

homeo- *or* **homoeo-** *or* **homoio-** *also* **homoio-** *comb form* [L & Gk; L *homoeo-*, fr. Gk *homoi-*, *homoio-*, fr. *homoios*, fr. *homos* same — more at SAME] 1 : like : similar (*homeo*stasis) (*homeo*thermic) 2 : homeotic (*homeo*box)

ho·meo·box \'hō-mē-ə-,bäks\ n (1984) : a short usu. highly conserved DNA sequence in various eukaryotic genes (as many homeotic genes) that codes for a peptide which may be a DNA-binding protein

ho·meo·mor·phism \,hō-mē-ə-'mór-,fi-zəm\ n [ISV] (1854) : a function that is a one-to-one mapping between sets such that both the function and its inverse are continuous and that in topology exists for geometric figures which can be transformed one into the other by an elastic deformation — **ho·meo·mor·phic** \-'mór-fik\ *adj*

ho·meo·path·ic \ˌhō-mē-ə-'pa-thik\ adj (1830) **1** : of or relating to homeopathy **2** : of a diluted or insipid nature ⟨a ~ abolitionist —W. A. White⟩ — **ho·meo·path·i·cal·ly** \-thi-k(ə-)lē\ adv

ho·me·op·a·thy \ˌhō-mē-'ä-pə-thē, ˌhä-\ n [G Homöopathie, fr. homöo- homeo- + -pathie -pathy] (1826) : a system of medical practice that treats a disease esp. by the administration of minute doses of a remedy that would in healthy persons produce symptoms similar to those of the disease — **ho·meo·path** \'hō-mē-ə-ˌpath\ n

ho·meo·sta·sis \ˌhō-mē-ō-'stā-səs\ n [NL] (1926) : a relatively stable state of equilibrium or a tendency toward such a state between the different but interdependent elements or groups of elements of an organism, population, or group — **ho·meo·stat·ic** \-'sta-tik\ adj

ho·meo·ther·mic \-'thər-mik\ adj (1870) : WARM-BLOODED 1 — **homeotherm** n — **homeothermy** n

ho·me·o·tic \ˌhō-mē-'ä-tik, ˌhä-\ adj [fr. homeosis, homoeosis a shift in structural development, fr. Gk homoiōsis assimilation, resemblance, fr. homoioun to make like, fr. homoios] (ca. 1903) : relating to or being a gene producing a usu. major shift in structural development

home plate n (1875) : a 5-sided rubber slab at one corner of a baseball diamond at which a batter stands when batting and which must be touched by a base runner in order to score

home·port \'hōm-ˌpōrt, -ˌpòrt\ vt (1957) : to provide with or assign to a home port

home port n (ca. 1891) : the port from which a ship hails or from which it is documented

¹ho·mer \'hō-mər\ n [Heb hōmer] (1535) : an ancient Hebrew unit of capacity equal to about 11½ or later 11½ bushels or 100 gallons (378 liters)

²hom·er \'hō-mər\ n [¹home] (1868) **1** : HOME RUN **2** : HOMING PIGEON

³hom·er vi (1940) : to hit a home run

home range n (1884) : the area to which an animal usu. confines its daily activities

Ho·mer·ic \hō-'mer-ik\ adj (ca. 1771) **1** : of, relating to, or characteristic of the Greek poet Homer, his age, or his writings **2** : of epic proportions : HEROIC ⟨~ feats of reporting —Stanley Walker⟩ — **Ho·mer·i·cal·ly** \-i-k(ə-)lē\ adv

home·room \'hōm-ˌrüm, -ˌrùm\ n (1915) : a classroom where pupils report esp. at the beginning of each school day

home rule n (1860) : self-government or limited autonomy in internal affairs by a dependent political unit (as a territory or municipality)

home run n (1856) : a hit in baseball that enables the batter to make a complete circuit of the bases and score a run

home·school \'hōm-ˌskül\ vi (1980) : to teach school subjects to one's children at home ~ vt : to teach (one's children) at home — **home·school·er** \-ˌskü-lər\ n

home screen n (1968) : TELEVISION 2

home·sick \'hōm-ˌsik\ adj (1756) : longing for home and family while absent from them — **home·sick·ness** n

home·site \-ˌsīt\ n (1911) : a location of or suitable for a home

¹home·spun \-ˌspən\ adj (1591) **1** a : spun or made at home b : made of homespun **2** : SIMPLE, HOMELY ⟨~ philosophy⟩

²homespun n (1607) : a loosely woven usu. woolen or linen fabric orig. made from homespun yarn

home stand n (1965) : a series of baseball games played at a team's home field

home·stay \'hōm-ˌstā\ n (1956) : a period during which a visitor in a foreign country lives with a local family

¹home·stead \'hōm-ˌsted, -stid\ n (bef. 12c) **1** a : the home and adjoining land occupied by a family b : an ancestral home c : HOUSE 2 **2** : a tract of land acquired from U.S. public lands by filing a record and living on and cultivating the land

²home·stead \-ˌsted\ vt (1872) : to acquire or occupy as a homestead ~ vi : to acquire or settle on land under a homestead law — **home·stead·er** \-ˌste-dər\ n

homestead law n (1850) **1** : a law exempting a homestead from attachment or sale under execution for general debts **2** : any of several legislative acts authorizing the sale of public lands in homesteads

home·stretch \'hōm-'strech\ n (1841) **1** : the part of a racecourse between the last turn and the winning post **2** : a final stage (as of a project)

home·town \-'taùn\ n, often attrib (1912) : the city or town where one was born or grew up; also : the place of one's principal residence

home truth n (1711) **1** : an unpleasant fact that jars the sensibilities **2** : a statement of undisputed fact

¹home·ward \'hōm-wərd\ or **home·wards** \-wərdz\ adv (bef. 12c) : toward home ⟨look ~, angel —John Milton⟩

²homeward adj (1566) : being or going in the direction of home

home·work \'hōm-ˌwərk\ n (ca. 1683) **1** : piecework done at home for pay **2** : an assignment given to a student to be completed outside the regular class period **3** : preparatory reading or research (as for a discussion or a debate)

hom·ey \'hō-mē\ adj **hom·i·er; -est** (1856) : HOMELIKE ⟨a restaurant with a ~ atmosphere⟩ — **hom·ey·ness** or **hom·i·ness** n

ho·mi·cid·al \ˌhä-mə-'sī-d²l, ˌhō-\ adj (1725) : of, relating to, or tending toward homicide — **ho·mi·cid·al·ly** \-d²l-ē\ adv

ho·mi·cide \'hä-mə-ˌsīd, 'hō-\ n [in sense 1, fr. ME, fr. MF, fr. L homicida, fr. homo human being + -cida -cide; in sense 2, fr. ME, fr. MF, fr. L homicidium, fr. homo + -cidium -cide] (14c) **1** : a person who kills another **2** : a killing of one human being by another

hom·i·let·ic \ˌhä-mə-'le-tik\ or **hom·i·let·i·cal** \-ti-kəl\ adj [LL homileticus, fr. Gk homilētikos of conversation, fr. homilein] (1644) **1** : of, relating to, or resembling a homily **2** : of or relating to homiletics; also : PREACHY

hom·i·let·ics \-tiks\ n pl but sing in constr (1830) : the art of preaching

hom·i·ly \'hä-mə-lē\ n, pl **-lies** [ME omelie, fr. MF, fr. LL homilia, LGk, fr. Gk, conversation, discourse, fr. homilein to consort with, address, fr. homilos crowd, assembly; akin to Gk homos same — more at SAME] (14c) **1** : a usu. short sermon **2** : a lecture or discourse on or of a moral theme **3** : an inspirational catchphrase; also : PLATITUDE

homing pigeon n (1886) : a racing pigeon trained to return home

hom·i·nid \'hä-mə-nəd, -ˌnid\ n [NL Hominidae, fr. Homin-, Homo + -idae] (ca. 1889) : any of a family (Hominidae) of erect bipedal primate mammals comprising recent humans together with extinct ancestral and related forms — **hominid** adj

hom·i·ni·za·tion \ˌhä-mə-nə-'zā-shən\ n [L homin-, homo + E -ization] (1952) : the evolutionary development of human characteristics that differentiate hominids from their primate ancestors

hom·i·noid \'hä-mə-ˌnòid\ n [NL Hominoidea, fr. Homin-, Homo + -oidea, suffix of higher taxa, fr. L -oides ²-oid] (1949) : any of a superfamily (Hominoidea) of primates including recent hominids, gibbons, and pongids together with extinct ancestral and related forms (as of the genera Proconsul and Dryopithecus) — **hominoid** adj

hom·i·ny \'hä-mə-nē\ n [Virginia Algonquian -homen, lit., that treated (in the way specified)] (1629) : kernels of corn that have been soaked in a caustic solution (as of lye) and then washed to remove the hulls

hominy grits n pl but sing or pl in constr (1879) : GRITS

¹ho·mo \'hō-(ˌ)mō\ n, pl **homos** [NL Homin-, Homo, fr. L, human being — more at HOMAGE] (1596) : any of a genus (Homo) of primate mammals that includes modern humans (H. sapiens) and several extinct related species

²homo n, pl **homos** [by shortening] (1929) : HOMOSEXUAL — often used disparagingly

homo- — see HOM-

ho·mo·cer·cal \ˌhō-mə-'sər-kəl, ˌhä-\ adj (1838) **1** of a fish tail fin : having the upper and lower lobes approximately symmetrical and the vertebral column ending at or near the middle of the base **2** : having or relating to a homocercal tail fin

homoe- — see HOMEO-

ho·mo·erot·ic \ˌhō-mō-i-'rä-tik\ adj (1916) : HOMOSEXUAL — **ho·mo·erot·i·cism** \-'rä-tə-ˌsi-zəm\ n

ho·mo·ga·met·ic \ˌhō-mō-gə-'me-tik, ˌhä-\ adj (1910) : forming gametes which all have the same type of sex chromosome

ho·mog·a·my \hō-'mä-gə-mē\ n [G Homogamie, fr. hom- + -gamie -gamy] (1897) : the mating of like with like — **ho·mog·a·mous** \-məs\ adj

ho·mog·e·nate \hō-'mä-jə-ˌnāt, hə-\ n (1941) : a product of homogenizing

ho·mo·ge·ne·i·ty \ˌhō-mə-jə-'nē-ə-tē, -'nä- also ÷-'nī-; esp Brit ˌhä-\ n (1625) **1** : the quality or state of being homogeneous **2** : the state of having identical distribution functions or values (~ of variances)

ho·mo·ge·neous \-'jē-nē-əs, -nyəs\ adj [ML homogeneus, homogenus, fr. Gk homogenēs, fr. hom- + genos kind — more at KIN] (1641) **1** : of the same or a similar kind or nature **2** : of uniform structure or composition throughout ⟨a culturally ~ neighborhood⟩ **3** : having the property that if each variable is replaced by a constant times that variable the constant can be factored out : having each term of the same degree if all variables are considered ⟨a ~ equation⟩ — **ho·mo·ge·neous·ly** adv — **ho·mo·ge·neous·ness** n

ho·mog·e·ni·sa·tion, ho·mog·e·nise Brit var of HOMOGENIZATION, HOMOGENIZE

ho·mog·e·ni·za·tion \hō-ˌmä-jə-nə-'zā-shən, hə-\ n (1908) **1** : the act or process of homogenizing **2** : the quality or state of being homogenized

ho·mog·e·nize \hō-'mä-jə-ˌnīz, hə-\ vb **-nized; -niz·ing** vt (1886) **1** a : to blend (diverse elements) into a uniform mixture b : to make homogeneous **2** a : to reduce to small particles of uniform size and distribute evenly usu. in a liquid b : to reduce the particles of so that they are uniformly small and evenly distributed; specif : to break up the fat globules of (milk) into very fine particles ~ vi : to become homogenized — **ho·mog·e·niz·er** n

ho·mog·e·nous \-nəs\ adj (1919) **1** : HOMOPLASTIC 2 **2** : HOMOGENEOUS

ho·mo·graft \'hō-mə-ˌgraft, 'hä-\ n (1923) : a graft of tissue taken from a donor of the same species as the recipient — compare HETEROGRAFT

ho·mo·graph \'hä-mə-ˌgraf, 'hō-\ n (1873) : one of two or more words spelled alike but different in meaning or derivation or pronunciation (as the bow of a ship, a bow and arrow) — **ho·mo·graph·ic** \ˌhä-mə-'gra-fik, ˌhō-\ adj

homoio- — see HOMEO-

ho·moio·therm, ho·moio·ther·mic var of HOMEOTHERM, HOMEOTHERMIC

ho·moi·ou·si·an \ˌhō-ˌmòi-'ü-zē-ən, ˌhä-, -'ü-sē-\ n [LGk homoiousios of like substance, fr. Gk homoi- homeo- + ousia essence, substance, fr. ont-, ōn, prp. of einai to be — more at IS] (1732) : an adherent of an ecclesiastical party of the 4th century holding that the Son is essentially like the Father but not of the same substance

ho·mol·o·gate \hō-'mä-lə-ˌgāt, hə-\ vt **-gat·ed; -gat·ing** [ML homologatus, pp. of homologare to agree, fr. Gk homologein, fr. homologos] (1593) : SANCTION, ALLOW; esp : to approve or confirm officially — **ho·mol·o·ga·tion** \-ˌmä-lə-'gä-shən\ n

ho·mo·log·i·cal \ˌhō-mə-'lä-ji-kəl, ˌhä-\ adj (ca. 1847) **1** : HOMOLOGOUS 2 **2** : of or relating to topological homology theory ⟨~ algebra⟩ — **ho·mo·log·i·cal·ly** \-ji-k(ə-)lē\ adv

ho·mol·o·gize \hō-'mä-lə-ˌjīz, hə-\ vt **-gized; -giz·ing** (1811) **1** : to make homologous **2** : to demonstrate the homology of — **ho·mol·o·giz·er** n

ho·mol·o·gous \hō-'mä-lə-gəs, hə-\ adj [Gk homologos agreeing, fr. hom- + legein to say — more at LEGEND] (1660) **1** a : having the same relative position, value, or structure: as (1) : exhibiting biological homology (2) : having the same or allelic genes with genetic loci usu. arranged in the same order ⟨~ chromosomes⟩ b : belonging to or consisting of a chemical series whose successive members have a regular difference in composition esp. of one methylene group **2** : derived from or developed in response to organisms of the same species

ho·mo·logue or **ho·mo·log** \'hō-mə-ˌlòg, 'hä-, -ˌläg\ n (1848) : something (as a chemical compound or a chromosome) homologous

ho·mol·o·gy \hō-'mä-lə-jē, hə-\ n, pl **-gies** (ca. 1656) **1** : a similarity often attributable to common origin **2** a : likeness in structure between parts of different organisms due to evolutionary differentiation from the same or a corresponding part of a remote ancestor — compare ANALOGY b : correspondence in structure between different parts

---

\ə\ abut \²\ kitten, F table \ər\ further \a\ ash \ā\ ace \ä\ mop, mar \aù\ out \ch\ chin \e\ bet \ē\ easy \g\ go \i\ hit \ī\ ice \j\ job \ŋ\ sing \ō\ go \ò\ law \òi\ boy \th\ thin \t̲h̲\ the \ü\ loot \ù\ foot \y\ yet \zh\ vision \à, k̲, ⁿ, œ, œ̄, ᵫ, ūe, ᵛ\ see Guide to Pronunciation of the same individual **3** : similarity of nucleotide or amino-acid sequence in nucleic acids, peptides, or proteins **4** : a branch of the theory of topology concerned with partitioning space into geometric components (as points, lines, and triangles) and with the study of the number and interrelationships of these components esp. by the use of group theory — called also *homology theory*; compare COHOMOLOGY

ho·mo·lyt·ic \ˌhō-mə-'li-tik, ˌhä-\ *adj* (1941) *of a chemical compound* : decomposing into two uncharged atoms or radicals — **ho·mol·y·sis** \hō-'mä-lə-səs\ *n*

ho·mo·mor·phism \ˌhō-mə-'mȯr-ˌfi-zəm, ˌhä-\ *n* [ISV] (1935) : a mapping of a mathematical set (as a group, ring, or vector space) into or onto another set or itself in such a way that the result obtained by applying the operations to elements of the first set is mapped onto the result obtained by applying the corresponding operations to their respective images in the second set — **ho·mo·mor·phic** \-fik\ *adj*

ho·mo·nu·cle·ar \ˌhō-mə-'nü-klē-ər, ˌhä-, -'nyü-, ÷-kyə-lər\ *adj* (1930) : of or relating to a molecule composed of identical nuclei

hom·onym \'hä-mə-ˌnim, 'hō-\ *n* [L *homonymum*, fr. Gk *homōnymon*, fr. neut. of *homōnymos*] (1697) **1 a** : HOMOPHONE **b** : HOMOGRAPH **c** : one of two or more words spelled and pronounced alike but different in meaning (as the noun *quail* and the verb *quail*) **2** : NAMESAKE **3** : a taxonomic designation rejected as invalid because the identical term has been used to designate another group of the same rank — compare SYNONYM — **hom·onym·ic** \ˌhä-mə-'ni-mik, ˌhō-\ *adj*

hom·on·y·mous \hō-'mä-nə-məs\ *adj* [L *homonymus* having the same name, fr. Gk *homōnymos*, fr. *hom-* + *onyma*, *onoma* name — more at NAME] (1621) **1** : AMBIGUOUS **2** : having the same designation **3** : of, relating to, or being homonyms : HOMONYMIC — **hom·on·y·mous·ly** *adv*

hom·on·y·my \-mē\ *n* (1597) : the quality or state of being homonymous

ho·mo·ou·si·an \ˌhō-mō-'ü-zē-ən, hä-, -'ü-sē-\ *n* [LGk *homoousios* of the same substance, fr. Gk *hom-* + *ousia* substance — more at HOMOIOUSIAN] (1565) : an adherent of an ecclesiastical party of the 4th century holding to the doctrine of the Nicene Creed that the Son is of the same substance with the Father

ho·mo·phile \'hō-mə-ˌfīl\ *adj* [*hom-* + ²-*phil*] (1960) : GAY 4b

ho·mo·phobe \-ˌfōb\ *n* (1975) : a person characterized by homophobia

ho·mo·pho·bia \ˌhō-mə-'fō-bē-ə\ *n* (1969) : irrational fear of, aversion to, or discrimination against homosexuality or homosexuals — **ho·mo·pho·bic** \-'fō-bik\ *adj*

ho·mo·phone \'hä-mə-ˌfōn, 'hō-\ *n* [ISV] (1843) **1** : one of two or more words pronounced alike but different in meaning or derivation or spelling (as the words *to*, *too*, and *two*) **2** : a character or group of characters pronounced the same as another character or group — **ho·moph·o·nous** \hō-'mä-fə-nəs\ *adj*

ho·mo·pho·nic \ˌhä-mə-'fä-nik, ˌhō-, -'fō-\ *adj* [Gk *homophōnos* being in unison, fr. *hom-* + *phōnē* sound — more at BAN] (ca. 1879) **1** : CHORDAL **2** : of or relating to homophones — **ho·moph·o·ny** \hō-'mä-fə-nē\ *n*

ho·mo·plas·tic \ˌhō-mə-'plas-tik, ˌhä-\ *adj* (1870) **1** : of or relating to homoplasy **2** : of, relating to, or derived from another individual of the same species ⟨~ grafts⟩

ho·mo·pla·sy \'hō-mə-ˌplā-sē, 'hä-, -ˌpla-; hō-'mä-plə-sē\ *n* (1870) : correspondence between parts or organs acquired as the result of parallel evolution or convergence

ho·mo·po·lar \ˌhō-mə-'pō-lər, ˌhä-\ *adj* (1896) **1** *of a motor or generator* : using or producing direct current without the use of commutators **2** : of or relating to a union of atoms of like polarity : NONIONIC

ho·mo·pol·y·mer \-'pä-lə-mər\ *n* (1946) : a polymer (as polyethylene) consisting of identical monomer units — **ho·mo·pol·y·mer·ic** \-ˌpä-lə-'mer-ik\ *adj*

ho·mop·ter·an \hō-'mäp-tə-rən\ *n* [ultim. fr. Gk *hom-* + *pteron* wing — more at FEATHER] (ca. 1842) : any of a large order or suborder (Homoptera) of insects (as cicadas, aphids, and scale insects) that have sucking mouthparts — **homopteran** *adj* — **ho·mop·ter·ous** \-rəs\ *adj*

homos *pl of* HOMO

Ho·mo sa·pi·ens \ˌhō-(ˌ)mō-'sā-pē-ˌenz, -ənz, *esp Brit* -'sä-pē-ənz\ *n* [NL, species name, fr. *Homo*, genus name + *sapiens*, specific epithet, fr. L, wise, intelligent — more at HOMO, SAPIENT] (1802) : HUMANKIND

ho·mo·sce·das·tic·i·ty \ˌhō-mō-si-ˌdas-'ti-sə-tē, ˌhä-\ *n* [*hom-* + Gk *skedastikos* able to disperse, fr. *skedannynai* to disperse] (1905) : the property of having equal statistical variances — **ho·mo·sce·das·tic** \-'das-tik\ *adj*

¹ho·mo·sex·u·al \ˌhō-mə-'sek-sh(ə-)wəl, -'sek-shəl\ *adj* (1892) **1** : of, relating to, or characterized by a tendency to direct sexual desire toward another of the same sex **2** : of, relating to, or involving sexual intercourse between persons of the same sex — **ho·mo·sex·u·al·ly** *adv*

²homosexual *n* (1902) : a homosexual person and esp. a male

ho·mo·sex·u·al·i·ty \ˌhō-mə-ˌsek-shə-'wa-lə-tē\ *n* (1892) **1** : the quality or state of being homosexual **2** : erotic activity with another of the same sex

ho·mo·spo·rous \ˌhō-mə-'spȯr-əs, ˌhä-, -'spȯr-; hō-'mäs-pə-rəs\ *adj* (1887) : producing asexual spores of one kind only

ho·mo·spo·ry \'hō-mə-ˌspȯr-ē, ˌhä-, -ˌspȯr-; hō-'mäs-pə-rē\ *n* (1903) : the production by various plants (as the club mosses and horsetails) of asexual spores of only one kind

ho·mo·thal·lic \ˌhō-mō-'tha-lik\ *adj* [*hom-* + Gk *thallein* to sprout, grow — more at THALLUS] (1904) **1** : having a haploid phase that produces two kinds of gametes capable of fusing to form a zygote — used esp. of algae and fungi **2** : MONOECIOUS — **ho·mo·thal·lism** \-'tha-ˌli-zəm\ *n*

ho·mo·trans·plant \ˌhō-mō-'tran(t)s-ˌplant, ˌhä-\ *n* (1927) : HOMOGRAFT — **ho·mo·trans·plan·ta·tion** \-ˌtran(t)s-ˌplan-'tā-shən\ *n*

ho·mo·zy·go·sis \ˌhō-mə-zi-'gō-səs, ˌhä-\ *n* [NL] (1905) : HOMOZYGOSITY

ho·mo·zy·gos·i·ty \-'gä-sə-tē\ *n* (1916) : the state of being homozygous

ho·mo·zy·gote \-'zī-ˌgōt\ *n* [ISV] (1902) : a homozygous individual

ho·mo·zy·gous \-'zī-gəs\ *adj* (1902) : having the two genes at corresponding loci on homologous chromosomes identical for one or more loci — **ho·mo·zy·gous·ly** *adv*

ho·mun·cu·lus \hō-'məŋ-kyə-ləs\ *n, pl* -**li** \-ˌlī, -ˌlē\ [L, dim. of *homin-*,

homo human being — more at HOMAGE] (1656) **1** : a little man : MANIKIN **2** : a miniature adult that in the theory of preformation is held to inhabit the germ cell and to produce a mature individual merely by an increase in size

homy *var of* HOMEY

hon \'hən\ *n* (ca. 1906) : HONEY 2a

hon·cho \'hän-(ˌ)chō\ *n, pl* **honchos** [Jp *hanchō* squad leader, fr. *han* squad + *chō* head, chief] (1947) : BOSS, BIG SHOT; *also* : HOTSHOT

¹hone \'hōn\ *n* [ME, fr. OE *hān* stone; akin to ON *hein* whetstone, L *cot-*, *cos*, Skt *śiśāti* he whets] (14c) : WHETSTONE

²hone *vt* **honed; hon·ing** (1826) **1** : to sharpen or smooth with a whetstone **2** : to make more acute, intense, or effective : WHET ⟨helped her ~ her comic timing —Patricia Bosworth⟩ — **hon·er** *n*

³hone *vi* **honed; hon·ing** [MF *hoigner* to grumble] (1600) **1** *dial* : YEARN — often used with *for* or *after* **2** *dial* : GRUMBLE, MOAN

hone in *vi* [alter. of *home in*] (1965) : to move toward or focus attention on an objective ⟨looking back for the ball *honing in* —George Plimpton⟩ ⟨a missile *honing* in on its target —Bob Greene⟩ ⟨*hones* in on the plights and victories of the common man —Lisa Russell⟩

usage The few commentators who have noticed *hone in* consider it to be a mistake for *home in*. It may have arisen from *home in* by the weakening of the \n\ sound to \n\ or may perhaps simply be due to the influence of *hone*. Even though it seems to have established itself in American English (and its mention in a British usage book suggests it is used in British English too), your use of it esp. in writing is likely to be called a mistake. *Home in* or in figurative use *zero in* is an easy alternative.

¹hon·est \'ä-nəst\ *adj* [ME, fr. MF *honeste*, fr. L *honestus* honorable, fr. *honos, honor* honor] (14c) **1 a** : free from fraud or deception : LEGITIMATE, TRUTHFUL ⟨an ~ plea⟩ **b** : GENUINE, REAL ⟨making ~ stops at stop signs —*Christian Science Monitor*⟩ **c** : HUMBLE, PLAIN ⟨good ~ food⟩ **2 a** : REPUTABLE, RESPECTABLE ⟨~ decent people⟩ **b** *chiefly Brit* : GOOD, WORTHY **3** : CREDITABLE, PRAISEWORTHY ⟨an ~ day's work⟩ **4 a** : marked by integrity **b** : marked by free, forthright, and sincere expression : FRANK ⟨an ~ appraisal⟩ **c** : INNOCENT, SIMPLE *syn* see UPRIGHT

²honest *adv* (1596) **1** : in an honest manner : HONESTLY ⟨I have ever found thee ~ true —Shak.⟩ **2** : with all sincerity ⟨I didn't do it, ~⟩

honest broker *n* (ca. 1884) : a neutral mediator

hon·est·ly \'ä-nəst-lē\ *adv* (14c) **1** : in an honest manner: as **a** : without cheating ⟨counted the ballots ~⟩ **b** : REALLY, GENUINELY ⟨was ~ scared⟩ **c** : without frills ⟨food ~ prepared⟩ **2** : to be honest : to tell the truth ⟨~, I don't know⟩

hon·es·ty \'ä-nəs-tē\ *n, pl* -**ties** (14c) **1** *obs* : CHASTITY **2 a** : fairness and straightforwardness of conduct **b** : adherence to the facts : SINCERITY **3** : any of a genus (*Lunaria*) of European herbs of the mustard family with toothed leaves and flat disk-shaped siliques

syn HONESTY, HONOR, INTEGRITY, PROBITY mean uprightness of character or action. HONESTY implies a refusal to lie, steal, or deceive in any way. HONOR suggests an active or anxious regard for the standards of one's profession, calling, or position. INTEGRITY implies trustworthiness and incorruptibility to a degree that one is incapable of being false to a trust, responsibility, or pledge. PROBITY implies tried and proven honesty or integrity.

¹hon·ey \'hə-nē\ *n, pl* **honeys** [ME *hony*, fr. OE *hunig*; akin to OHG *honag* honey, L *canicae* bran] (bef. 12c) **1 a** : a sweet viscid material elaborated out of the nectar of flowers in the honey sac of various bees **b** : a sweet fluid resembling honey that is collected or elaborated by various insects **2 a** : a loved one : SWEETHEART, DEAR **b** : a superlative example **3** : the quality or state of being sweet : SWEETNESS

²honey *vb* **hon·eyed** *also* **hon·ied** \'hə-nēd\; **hon·ey·ing** *vt* (14c) **1** : to sweeten with or as if with honey **2** : to speak ingratiatingly to : FLATTER ~ *vi* : to use blandishments or cajolery

³honey *adj* (14c) **1** : of, relating to, or resembling honey **2** : much loved : DEAR

hon·ey·bee \'hə-nē-ˌbē\ *n* (15c) : a honey-producing bee (*Apis* and related genera; *esp* : a European bee (*A. mellifera*) introduced worldwide and kept in hives for the honey it produces

¹hon·ey·comb \-ˌkōm\ *n* (bef. 12c) **1** : a mass of hexagonal wax cells built by honeybees in their nest to contain their brood and stores of honey **2** : something that resembles a honeycomb in structure or appearance; *esp* : a strong lightweight cellular structural material

²honeycomb *vt* (1774) **1 a** : to cause to be full of cavities like a honeycomb **b** : to make into a checkered pattern : FRET **2 a** : to penetrate into every part : FILL **b** : SUBVERT, WEAKEN ~ *vi* : to become pitted, checked, or cellular

hon·ey·creep·er \'hə-nē-ˌkrē-pər\ *n* (1872) **1** : any of numerous small bright-colored oscine birds (esp. genera *Cyanerpes* and *Chlorophanes* of the family Coerebidae) of tropical America **2** : any of a family (Drepanididae) of oscine birds that are found only in Hawaii

hon·ey·dew \-ˌdü, -ˌdyü\ *n* (1577) : a saccharine deposit secreted on the leaves of plants usu. by aphids or scale insects or sometimes by a fungus

honeydew melon *n* (1916) : a pale smooth-skinned winter melon with sweet greenish flesh

hon·ey·eat·er \-ˌē-tər\ *n* (1822) : any of a family (Meliphagidae) of oscine birds chiefly of the So. Pacific that have a long protrusible tongue adapted for extracting nectar and small insects from flowers

hon·ey·guide \-ˌgīd\ *n* (1777) : any of a family (Indicatoridae) of small plainly colored nonpasserine birds that inhabit Africa, the Himalayas, and the East Indies and that include some which lead people or animals to the nests of bees

honey locust *n* (1743) : a tall usu. spiny No. American leguminous tree (*Gleditsia triacanthos*) with very hard wood and long twisted pods containing a sweet edible pulp and seeds that resemble beans

hon·ey·moon \'hə-nē-ˌmün\ *n* [fr. the idea that the first month of marriage is the sweetest] (1546) **1** : a period of harmony immediately following marriage **2** : a period of unusual harmony esp. following the establishment of a new relationship **3** : a trip or vacation taken by a newly married couple — **honeymoon** *vi* — **hon·ey·moon·er** *n*

honey sac *n* (ca. 1909) : a distension of the esophagus of a bee in which honey is elaborated — called also *honey stomach*

hon·ey·suck·le \'hə-nē-ˌsə-kəl\ *n* [ME *honysoukel* clover, alter. of *honysouke*, fr. OE *hunisūce*, fr. *hunig* honey + *sūcan* to suck] (1548)

: any of a genus (*Lonicera* of the family Caprifoliaceae, the honeysuckle family) of shrubs with opposite leaves and often showy flowers rich in nectar; *broadly* : any of various plants (as a columbine or azalea) with tubular flowers rich in nectar
hong \'häŋ, 'hȯŋ\ *n* [Chin (Guangdong) *hòhng*, lit., row] (1726) : a commercial establishment or house of foreign trade in China

honeysuckle

¹**honk** \'häŋk, 'hȯŋk\ *vb* [imit.] *vi* (ca. 1835) **1** : to make the characteristic cry of a goose **2** : to make a sound resembling the cry of a goose ~ *vt* : to cause (as a horn) to honk — **honker** *n*

²**honk** *n* (1854) : the characteristic cry of a goose; *also* : a similar sound
hon·ky *or* **hon·kie** *also* **hon·key** \'hȯŋ-kē, 'häŋ-\ *n, pl* **honkies** *also* **honkeys** [prob. alter. of *Hunky*] (1967) : a white person — usu. used disparagingly

¹**hon·ky–tonk** \'häŋ-kē-ˌtäŋk, 'hȯŋ-kē-ˌtȯŋk\ *n* [origin unknown] (ca. 1909) **1** : a usu. tawdry nightclub or dance hall; *esp* : one that features country music **2** : a district marked by places of cheap entertainment

²**honky–tonk** *adj* (ca. 1920) **1** : of, used in, or being a form of ragtime piano playing performed typically on an upright piano **2** : marked by or characteristic of honky-tonks

¹**hon·or** \'ä-nər\ *n* [ME, fr. OF *honor*, fr. L *honos, honor*] (13c) **1 a** : good name or public esteem : REPUTATION **b** : a showing of usu. merited respect : RECOGNITION ⟨pay ~ to our founder⟩ **2** : PRIVILEGE **3** : a person of superior standing — now used esp. as a title for a holder of high office ⟨if *Your Honor* please⟩ **4** : one whose worth brings respect or fame : CREDIT ⟨an ~ to the profession⟩ **5** : the center point of the upper half of an armorial escutcheon **6** : an evidence or symbol of distinction: as **a** : an exalted title or rank **b** (1) : BADGE, DECORATION (2) : a ceremonial rite or observance ⟨buried with full military ~s⟩ **c** : an award in a contest or field of competition **d** *archaic* : a gesture of deference : BOW **e** *pl* (1) : an academic distinction conferred on a superior student (2) : a course of study for superior students supplementing or replacing a regular course **7** : CHASTITY, PURITY ⟨fought fiercely for her ~ and her life —Barton Black⟩ **8 a** : a keen sense of ethical conduct : INTEGRITY **b** : one's word given as a guarantee of performance **9** *pl* : social courtesies or civilities extended by a host ⟨did the ~s at the table⟩ **10 a** (1) : an ace, king, queen, jack, or ten esp. of the trump suit in bridge (2) : the scoring value of honors held in bridge — usu. used in pl. **b** : the privilege of playing first from the tee in golf
syn HONOR, HOMAGE, REVERENCE, DEFERENCE mean respect and esteem shown to another. HONOR may apply to the recognition of one's right to great respect or to any expression of such recognition ⟨the nomination is an *honor*⟩. HOMAGE adds the implication of accompanying praise ⟨paying *homage* to Shakespeare⟩. REVERENCE implies profound respect mingled with love, devotion, or awe ⟨great *reverence* for my father⟩. DEFERENCE implies a yielding or submitting to another's judgment or preference out of respect or reverence ⟨showed no *deference* to their elders⟩. *syn* see in addition HONESTY

²**honor** *vt* **hon·ored; hon·or·ing** \'ä-nə-riŋ, 'än-riŋ\ (13c) **1 a** : to regard or treat with honor or respect **b** : to confer honor on **2 a** : to live up to or fulfill the terms of ⟨~ a commitment⟩ **b** : to accept as payment ⟨~ a credit card⟩ **3** : to salute with a bow in square dancing — **hon·or·ee** \ˌä-nə-'rē\ *n* — **hon·or·er** \'ä-nər-ər\ *n*
hon·or·able \'ä-nər-(ə-)bəl, 'än-rə-\ *adj* (14c) **1** : deserving of honor **2 a** : of great renown : ILLUSTRIOUS **b** : entitled to honor — used as a title for the children of certain British noblemen and for various government officials **3** : performed or accompanied with marks of honor or respect **4 a** : attesting to creditable conduct **b** : consistent with an untarnished reputation ⟨an ~ withdrawal⟩ **5** : characterized by integrity : guided by a high sense of honor and duty *syn* see UPRIGHT — **hon·or·able·ness** \ˌän-rə-bəl-nəs, ˈä-nə-\ *n* — **hon·or·ably** \-blē\ *adv*
honorable mention *n* (1866) : a distinction conferred (as in a contest or exhibition) on works or persons of exceptional merit but not deserving of top honors
hon·o·rar·i·um \ˌä-nə-'rer-ē-əm\ *n, pl* **-ia** \-ē-ə\ *also* **-i·ums** [L, fr. neut. of *honorarius*] (1658) : a payment for a service (as making a speech) on which custom or propriety forbids a price to be set
hon·or·ary \'ä-nə-ˌrer-ē\ *adj* [L *honorarius*, fr. *honor*] (1614) **1 a** : having or conferring distinction **b** : COMMEMORATIVE **2** : dependent on honor for fulfillment **3 a** : conferred or elected in recognition of achievement or service without the usual prerequisites or obligations ⟨an ~ degree⟩ ⟨an ~ member⟩ **b** : UNPAID, VOLUNTARY ⟨an ~ chairman⟩ — **hon·or·ari·ly** \ˌä-nə-'rer-ə-lē\ *adv* — **honorary** *n*
honor guard *n* (1925) : a guard assigned to a ceremonial duty (as to accompany a casket at a military funeral)
hon·or·if·ic \ˌä-nə-'ri-fik\ *adj* (1650) **1** : conferring or conveying honor ⟨~ titles⟩ **2** : belonging to or constituting a class of grammatical forms used in speaking to or about a social superior — **honorific** *n* — **hon·or·if·i·cal·ly** \-fi-k(ə-)lē\ *adv*
honor roll *n* (1909) : a roster of names of persons deserving honor; *esp* : a list of students achieving academic distinction
honor society *n* (1927) : a society for the recognition of scholarly achievement esp. of undergraduates
honor system *n* (1904) : a system (as at a college or prison) whereby persons are trusted to abide by the regulations (as for a code of conduct) without supervision or surveillance
hon·our, hon·our·able *chiefly Brit var of* HONOR, HONORABLE
¹**hooch** \'hüch\ *n* [short for *hoochinoo*, a distilled liquor made by the Hoochinoo (Hutsnuwu) Indians, a Tlingit tribe] (1897) *slang* : alcoholic liquor esp. when inferior or illicitly made or obtained
²**hooch** *or* **hootch** \'hüch\ *n* [modif. of Jp *uchi* house] (1960) *slang* : a usu. thatched hut; *broadly* : DWELLING
¹**hood** \'hu̇d\ *n* [ME, fr. OE *hōd;* akin to OHG *huot* head covering, *huota* guard] (bef. 12c) **1 a** (1) : a flexible covering for the head and neck (2) : a protective covering for the head and face **b** : a covering for a hawk's head and eyes **c** : a covering for a horse's head; *also*

: BLINDER **2 a** : an ornamental scarf worn over an academic gown that indicates by its color the wearer's college or university **b** : a color marking or crest on the head of an animal or an expansion of the head that suggests a hood **3 a** : something resembling a hood in form or use **b** : a cover for parts of mechanisms; *specif* : the movable metal covering over the engine of an automobile **c** *chiefly Brit* : a top cover over the passenger section of a vehicle usu. designed to be folded back **d** : an enclosure or canopy provided with a draft for carrying off disagreeable or noxious fumes, sprays, smokes, or dusts **e** : a covering for an opening (as a companion hatch) on a boat — **hood** *vt* — **hood·like** \-ˌlīk\ *adj*
²**hood** \'hu̇d, 'hüd\ *n* (1930) : HOODLUM — **hoody** \'hu̇-dē, 'hü-\ *adj*
³**hood** \'hu̇d\ *n* [by shortening] (1967) : NEIGHBORHOOD 4
-hood \ˌhu̇d\ *n suffix* [ME *-hod*, fr. OE *-hād;* akin to OHG *-heit* state, Goth *haidus* way, manner] **1** : state : condition : quality : character ⟨widower*hood*⟩ ⟨hardi*hood*⟩ **2** : time : period ⟨child*hood*⟩ **3** : instance of a (specified) state or quality ⟨false*hood*⟩ **4** : individuals sharing a (specified) state or character ⟨brother*hood*⟩
hood·ed \'hu̇-dəd\ *adj* (15c) **1** : having a hood **2** : shaped like a hood ⟨~ spathes⟩ **3 a** : having the head conspicuously different in color from the rest of the body ⟨~ bird⟩ **b** : having a crest on the head that suggests a hood ⟨~ seals⟩ **c** : having the skin at each side of the neck capable of expansion by movements of the ribs ⟨~ cobra⟩ **4** : half-closed ⟨~ eyes⟩ — **hood·ed·ness** *n*
hood·lum \'hüd-ləm, 'hu̇d-\ *n* [perh. fr. G dial. (Swabia) *hudelum* disorderly] (1871) **1** : THUG; *esp* : one who commits acts of violence **2** : a young ruffian — **hood·lum·ish** \-lə-mish\ *adj* — **hood·lum·ism** \-ˌmi-zəm\ *n*
hood·man–blind \ˌhu̇d-mən-'blīnd\ *n* (1565) *archaic* : BLINDMAN'S BUFF
¹**hoo·doo** \'hü-(ˌ)dü\ *n, pl* **hoodoos** [of African origin; akin to Hausa *hu³ du³ba¹* to arouse resentment] (1875) **1** : a body of practices of sympathetic magic traditional esp. among blacks in the southern U.S. **2** : a natural column of rock in western No. America often in fantastic form **3** : something that brings bad luck — **hoo·doo·ism** \-ˌi-zəm\ *n*
²**hoodoo** *vt* (1886) : to cast a spell on; *broadly* : to be a source of misfortune to
hood·wink \'hu̇d-ˌwiŋk\ *vt* [¹*hood* + *wink*] (1562) **1** *archaic* : BLINDFOLD **2** *obs* : HIDE **3** : to deceive by false appearance : DUPE — **hood·wink·er** *n*
hoo·ey \'hü-ē\ *n* [origin unknown] (1924) : NONSENSE
¹**hoof** \'hu̇f, 'hüf\ *n, pl* **hooves** \'hu̇vz, 'hüvz\ *also* **hoofs** [ME, fr. OE *hōf;* akin to OHG *huof* hoof, Skt *śapha*] (bef. 12c) **1** : a curved covering of horn that protects the front of or encloses the ends of the digits of an ungulate mammal and that corresponds to a nail or claw **2** : a hoofed foot esp. of a horse — **on the hoof** *of a meat animal* : before butchering : LIVING ⟨90¢ a pound *on the hoof*⟩
²**hoof** *vt* (1641) **1** : WALK ⟨~ed it to the lecture hall⟩ **2** : KICK, TRAMPLE ~ *vi* : to move on the feet; *esp* : DANCE
hoof–and–mouth disease *n* (1884) : FOOT-AND-MOUTH DISEASE
hoof·beat \'hu̇f-ˌbēt, 'hüf-\ *n* (1847) : the sound of a hoof striking a hard surface (as the ground)
hoofed \'hu̇ft, 'hüft, 'hu̇vd, 'hüvd\ *or* **hooved** \'hu̇vd, 'hüvd\ *adj* (1513) : furnished with hooves : UNGULATE
hoof·er \'hu̇-fər, 'hü-\ *n* (ca. 1918) : a professional dancer
hoof·print \'hu̇f-ˌprint, 'hüf-\ *n* (1804) : an impression or hollow made by a hoof
hoo–ha \'hü-ˌhä\ *n* [prob. fr. Yiddish *hu-ha* uproar, exclamation of surprise] (1931) : UPROAR
¹**hook** \'hu̇k\ *n* [ME, fr. OE *hōc;* akin to MD *hoec* fishhook, corner, Lith *kengė* hook] (bef. 12c) **1 a** : a curved or bent device for catching, holding, or pulling **b** : something intended to attract and ensnare **2** : something curved or bent like a hook; *esp, pl* : FINGERS **3 a** : a flight or course of a ball that deviates from straight in a direction opposite to the dominant hand of the player propelling it; *also* : a ball following such a course — compare SLICE **4** : a short blow delivered with a circular motion by a boxer while the elbow remains bent and rigid **5** : HOOK SHOT **6** : BUTTONHOOK **7** : quick or summary removal — used with *get* or *give* ⟨the pitcher got the ~ after giving up three runs⟩ **8** : a device esp. in music or writing that catches the attention **9** : a selling point or marketing scheme — **by hook or by crook** : by any means — **off the hook** **1** : out of trouble **2** : free of responsibility or accountability — **on one's own hook** : by oneself : INDEPENDENTLY
²**hook** *vt* (13c) **1** : to form into a hook : CROOK **2 a** : to seize or make fast by or as if by a hook **b** : to connect by or as if by a hook — often used with *up* **3** : STEAL, PILFER **4** : to make (as a rug) by drawing loops of yarn, thread, or cloth through a coarse fabric with a hook **5** : to hit or throw (a ball) so that a hook results ~ *vi* **1** : to form a hook : CURVE **2** : to become hooked **3** : to work as a prostitute
hoo·kah \'hu̇-kə, 'hü-\ *n* [Ar *ḥuqqah* bottle of a water pipe] (1763) : WATER PIPE 2
hook and eye *n* (ca. 1626) : a 2-part fastening device (as on a garment or a door) consisting of a metal hook that catches over a bar or into a loop
hook and ladder truck *n* (1865) : a piece of mobile fire apparatus carrying ladders and usu. other fire-fighting and rescue equipment — called also *hook and ladder*, *ladder truck*

hoof 2: *1, 2, 3, 4* parts of wall (*1* toe, *2* side walls, *3* quarters, *4* buttresses), *5* bulbs, *6* sole, *7* white line, *8* frog

---

\ə\ abut \ᵊ\ kitten, F table \ər\ further \a\ ash \ā\ ace \ä\ mop, mar
\au̇\ out \ch\ chin \e\ bet \ē\ easy \g\ go \i\ hit \ī\ ice \j\ job
\ŋ\ sing \ō\ go \ȯ\ law \ȯi\ boy \th\ thin \t̲h̲\ the \ü\ loot \u̇\ foot
\y\ yet \zh\ vision \ä, k̲, ⁿ, œ, œ̄, ᵫ, ᵫ̄, ᵊ\ *see* Guide to Pronunciation

hook check *n* (ca. 1939) : an act or instance of attempting to knock the puck away from an opponent in ice hockey by hooking it with the stick

hooked \'hùkt, *1 is also* 'hù-kəd\ *adj* (bef. 12c) **1** : having the form of a hook **2** : provided with a hook **3** : made by hooking ⟨a ~ rug⟩ **4 a** : addicted to narcotics **b** : fascinated by or devoted to something ⟨~ on skiing⟩

¹**hook·er** \'hù-kər\ *n* (1567) **1** : one that hooks **2** : DRINK ⟨a ~ of Scotch⟩ **3** : PROSTITUTE

²**hooker** *n* [D *hoeker*, alter. of MD *hoecboot*, fr. *hoec* fishhook + *boot* boat] (1801) : a one-masted fishing boat used on the English and Irish coasts; *also* : a small clumsy boat

Hooke's law \'hùks-\ *n* [Robert *Hooke*] (1853) : a statement in physics: the stress within an elastic solid is proportional to the strain responsible for it

hook·let \'hùk-lət\ *n* (ca. 1839) : a small hook

hook, line and sinker *adv* [fr. analogy with a well-hooked fish] (1838) : without hesitation or reservation : COMPLETELY ⟨fell for the story *hook, line and sinker*⟩

hook shot *n* (ca. 1932) : a shot in basketball made usu. while standing sideways to the basket by swinging the ball up in an arc with the far hand

hook·up \'hùk-ˌəp\ *n* (1903) **1** : a state of cooperation or alliance **2** : an assemblage (as of circuits) used for a specific purpose (as radio transmission); *also* : the plan of such an assemblage **3** : an arrangement of mechanical parts; *also* : CONNECTION ⟨a campsite with electric, water, and sewer ~s⟩

hook up *vi* (1925) : to become associated esp. in a working or social relationship

hook·worm \'hùk-ˌwərm\ *n* (1902) **1** : any of various parasitic nematode worms (family Ancylostomatidae) that have strong buccal hooks or plates for attaching to the host's intestinal lining and that include serious bloodsucking pests **2** : ANCYLOSTOMIASIS

hooky *or* **hook·ey** \'hù-kē\ *n, pl* **hook·ies** *or* **hookeys** [prob. fr. slang *hook, hook it* (to make off)] (ca. 1848) : TRUANT — used chiefly in the phrase *play hooky*

hoo·li·gan \'hü-li-gən\ *n* [perh. fr. Patrick *Hooligan* *fl*1898 Irish hoodlum in Southwark, London] (1898) : RUFFIAN, HOODLUM — **hoo·li·gan·ism** \-gə-ˌni-zəm\ *n*

¹**hoop** \'hüp *also* 'hùp\ *n, often attrib* [ME, fr. OE *hōp*; akin to MD *hoep* ring, hoop] (12c) **1** : a circular strip used esp. for holding together the staves of containers or as a plaything **2 a** : a circular figure or object : RING **b** : the rim of a basketball goal; *broadly* : the entire goal **3** : a circle or series of circles of flexible material used to expand a woman's skirt **4** : BASKETBALL — usu. used in pl. — **hoop·like** \-ˌlīk\ *adj*

²**hoop** *vt* (15c) : to bind or fasten with or as if with a hoop — **hoop·er** *n*

hoop·la \'hü-ˌplä, 'hù-\ *n* [F *houp-là*, interj.] (1877) : excited commotion : TO-DO; *also* : BALLYHOO

hoo·poe \'hü-(ˌ)pü, -(ˌ)pō\ *n* [alter. of obs. *hoop*, fr. MF *huppe*, fr. L *upupa*, of imit. origin] (1668) : a crested Old World nonpasserine bird (*Upupa epops* of the family Upupidae) having a slender decurved bill and barred black-and-white wings and tail

hoop·skirt \'hüp-ˌskərt *also* 'hùp-\ *n* (1857) : a skirt stiffened with or as if with hoops

hoo·rah \hù-'rä, -'rȯ\, **hoo·ray** \-'rä\ *var of* HURRAH

hoose·gow \'hüs-ˌgaù\ *n* [Sp *juzgado* panel of judges, courtroom, fr. pp. of *juzgar* to judge, fr. L *judicare* — more at JUDGE] (1909) : JAIL

Hoo·sier \'hü-zhər\ *n* [perh. alter. of E dial. *hoozer* anything large of its kind] (1826) : a native or resident of Indiana — used as a nickname — **Hoosier** *adj*

¹**hoot** \'hüt\ *vb* [ME *houten*, of imit. origin] *vi* (13c) **1** : to shout or laugh usu. derisively **2** : to make the natural throat noise of an owl or a similar cry **3** : to make a loud clamorous mechanical sound ~ *vt* **1** : to assail or drive out by hooting ⟨~ed down the speaker⟩ **2** : to express or utter with hoots ⟨~ed their disapproval⟩ — **hoot·er** *n*

²**hoot** *n* (15c) **1** : a sound of hooting; *esp* : the cry of an owl **2** : a minimum amount or degree : the least bit ⟨don't give a ~⟩ **3** : something or someone amusing ⟨the play is a real ~⟩ — **hooty** \'hü-tē\ *adj*

³**hoot** \'hüt\ *or* **hoots** \'hüts\ *interj* [origin unknown] (1540) *chiefly Scot* — used to express impatience, dissatisfaction, or objection

hoo·te·nan·ny \'hü-tᵊn-ˌa-nē\ *n, pl* **-nies** [origin unknown] (1925) **1** *chiefly dial* : GADGET **2** : a gathering at which folksingers entertain often with the audience joining in

Hoo·ver·ville \'hü-vər-ˌvil\ *n* [Herbert *Hoover* + -*ville*] (1933) : a shantytown of temporary dwellings during the depression years in the U.S.; *broadly* : any similar area of temporary dwellings

¹**hop** \'häp\ *vb* **hopped; hop·ping** [ME *hoppen*, fr. OE *hoppian*; prob. akin to OE *hype* hip] *vi* (bef. 12c) **1** : to move by a quick springy leap or in a series of leaps; *also* : to move as if by hopping ⟨~ in the car⟩ **2** : to make a quick trip esp. by air ~ *vt* **1** : to jump over ⟨~ a fence⟩ **2** : to ride on ⟨*hopped* a flight⟩; *also* : to ride surreptitiously and without authorization ⟨~ a freight train⟩

²**hop** *n* (1508) **1 a** : a short brisk leap esp. on one leg **b** : BOUNCE, REBOUND ⟨shortstop scooped it up on the first ~⟩ **2** : DANCE **3 a** : a flight in an aircraft **b** : a short trip

³**hop** *n* [ME *hoppe*, fr. MD; akin to OHG *hopfo* hop] (15c) **1** *pl* : the ripe dried pistillate catkins of a hop used esp. to impart a bitter flavor to malt liquors **2** : a twining vine (*Humulus lupulus*) of the mulberry family with 3-lobed or 5-lobed leaves and inconspicuous flowers of which the pistillate ones are in glandular cone-shaped catkins

⁴**hop** *vt* **hopped; hop·ping** (1572) : to impregnate with hops

¹**hope** \'hōp\ *vb* **hoped; hop·ing** [ME, fr. OE *hopian*; akin to MHG *hoffen* to hope] *vi* (bef. 12c) **1** : to cherish a desire with anticipation ⟨~s for a promotion⟩ **2** *archaic* : TRUST ~ *vt* **1** : to desire with expectation of obtainment **2** : to expect with confidence : TRUST *syn* see EXPECT — **hop·er** *n* — **hope against hope** : to hope without any basis for expecting fulfillment

²**hope** *n* (bef. 12c) **1** *archaic* : TRUST, RELIANCE **2 a** : desire accompanied by expectation of or belief in fulfillment ⟨came in ~s of seeing you⟩; *also* : expectation of fulfillment or success ⟨no ~ of a cure⟩ **b** : someone or something on which hopes are centered ⟨our only ~ for victory⟩ **c** : something hoped for

hope chest *n* (1911) : a young woman's accumulation of clothes and domestic furnishings (as silver and linen) kept in anticipation of her marriage; *also* : a chest for such an accumulation

¹**hope·ful** \'hōp-fəl\ *adj* (1568) **1** : having qualities which inspire hope ⟨~ signs of economic recovery⟩ **2** : full of hope : inclined to hope — **hope·ful·ness** *n*

²**hopeful** *n* (1720) : ASPIRANT ⟨Olympic ~s⟩

hope·ful·ly \'hōp-fə-lē\ *adv* (ca. 1639) **1** : in a hopeful manner **2** : it is hoped : I hope : we hope

usage In the early 1960s the second sense of *hopefully*, which had been in sporadic use since around 1932, underwent a surge of popular use. A surge of popular criticism followed in reaction, but the criticism took no account of the grammar of adverbs. *Hopefully* in its second sense is a member of a class of adverbs known as disjuncts. Disjuncts serve as a means by which the author or speaker can comment directly to the reader or hearer usu. on the content of the sentence to which they are attached. Many other adverbs (as *interestingly, frankly, clearly, luckily, unfortunately*) are similarly used; most are so ordinary as to excite no comment or interest whatsoever. The second sense of *hopefully* is entirely standard.

hope·less \'hō-pləs\ *adj* (1534) **1 a** : having no expectation of good or success : DESPAIRING **b** : not susceptible to remedy or cure **c** : incapable of redemption or improvement **2 a** : giving no ground for hope : DESPERATE **b** : incapable of solution, management, or accomplishment : IMPOSSIBLE *syn* see DESPONDENT — **hope·less·ness** *n*

hope·less·ly \-lē\ *adv* (1616) : in a hopeless manner — used esp. as an intensifier ⟨the formerly despised and ~ middle-class game of golf — Ejner Jensen⟩

hop·head \'häp-ˌhed\ *n* (1911) *slang* : a drug addict

hop hornbeam *n* (1785) : a chiefly eastern U.S. tree (*Ostrya virginiana*) of the birch family with fruiting clusters resembling hops

Ho·pi \'hō-(ˌ)pē\ *n, pl* **Hopi** *or* **Hopis** [Hopi *hópi*, lit., good, peaceful] (1877) **1** : a member of an American Indian people of northeastern Arizona **2** : the Uto-Aztecan language of the Hopi people

hop·lite \'häp-ˌlīt\ *n* [Gk *hoplitēs*, fr. *hoplon* tool, weapon, fr. *hepein* to care for, work at — more at SEPULCHRE] (ca. 1741) : a heavily armed infantry soldier of ancient Greece

hop-o'-my-thumb \ˌhä-pə-mə-'thəm\ *n* [earlier *hop on my thumb*, imperative issued to one supposedly small enough to be held in the hand] (1530) : a very small person

hopped–up \'häpt-'əp, -ˌəp\ *adj* (ca. 1924) **1 a** : being under the influence of a narcotic **b** : full of enthusiasm or excitement; *also* : overly excited **c** : more exciting or attractive than normal or usual **2** : having more than usual power : being souped up

hop·per \'hä-pər\ *n* (13c) **1 a** : one that hops **b** : a leaping insect; *specif* : an immature hopping form of an insect (as a grasshopper or locust) **2** [fr. the shaking motion of hoppers used to feed grain into a mill] **a** : a usu. funnel-shaped receptacle for delivering material (as grain or coal); *also* : any of various other receptacles for the temporary storage of material **b** : a freight car with a floor sloping to one or more hinged doors for discharging bulk materials — called also *hopper car* **c** : a box in which a bill is to be considered by a legislative body is dropped **d** : a tank holding liquid and having a device for releasing its contents through a pipe

¹**hop·ping** \'hä-piŋ\ *adv* (1675) : EXTREMELY, VIOLENTLY — used in the phrase *hopping mad*

²**hopping** *adj* (1785) **1** : intensely active : BUSY ⟨they kept us ~⟩ **2** : extremely angry

³**hopping** *n* (1879) : a going from one place to another of the same kind — usu. used in combination ⟨gallery-*hopping*⟩

hopping John \ˌhä-pən-'jän, -piŋ-\ *or* **hop·pin' John** \ˌhä-pən-\ *n, often cap H* (1838) : a dish made essentially of cowpeas, rice, and salt pork or bacon

hop·py \'hä-pē\ *adj* **hop·pi·er; -est** (ca. 1889) : having the taste or aroma of hops — used esp. of ale or beer

hop·sack \'häp-ˌsak\ *also* **hop·sack·ing** \-ˌsa-kiŋ\ *n* [ME *hopsak* sack for hops, fr. *hoppe* hop + *sak* sack] (1888) : a rough-surfaced loosely woven clothing fabric

¹**hop·scotch** \'häp-ˌskäch\ *n* [¹*hop* + *scotch* (line)] (1801) : a child's game in which a player tosses an object (as a stone) into areas of a figure outlined on the ground and hops through the figure and back to regain the object

²**hopscotch** *vi* (1918) : to move as if by hopping ⟨~ed across Europe⟩

hop, skip, and jump *n* (1760) : a short distance

hop, step, and jump *n* (ca. 1719) : TRIPLE JUMP

ho·ra *also* **ho·rah** \'hȯr-ə, 'hȯr-ə\ *n* [NHeb *hōrāh*, fr. Rom *horă*] (1878) : a circle dance of Romania and Israel

Ho·rae \'hȯr-ē, 'hȯr-, -ˌī\ *n pl* [L, fr. Gk *Hōrai*] : the Greek goddesses of the seasons

ho·ra·ry \'hȯr-ər-ē, 'hȯr-, 'här-\ *adj* [ML *horarius*, fr. L *hora* hour — more at HOUR] (1632) : of or relating to an hour; *also* : HOURLY

Ho·ra·tio Al·ger \hə-'rā-shō-'al-jər\ *adj* (1925) : of, relating to, or resembling the fiction of Horatio Alger in which success is achieved through self-reliance and hard work

Ho·ra·tius \hə-'rā-sh(ē-)əs\ *n* [L] : a hero in Roman legend noted for his defense of a bridge over the Tiber against the Etruscans

horde \'hȯrd, 'hȯrd\ *n* [MF, G, & Pol; MF & G, fr. Pol *horda*, fr. Ukrainian dial. *gorda*, alter. of Ukrainian *orda*, fr. ORuss, fr. Turkic *orda, ordu* khan's residence] (1555) **1 a** : a political subdivision of central Asian nomads **b** : a people or tribe of nomadic life **2 a** : a teeming crowd or throng : SWARM *syn* see CROWD

hore·hound \'hȯr-ˌhaùnd, 'hȯr-\ *n* [ME *horhoune*, fr. OE *hārhūne*, fr. *hār* hoary + *hūne* horehound — more at HOAR] (bef. 12c) **1 a** : a bitter mint (*Marrubium vulgare*) with downy leaves **b** : an extract or confection made from this plant **2** : any of several mints resembling the horehound

ho·ri·zon \hə-'rī-zᵊn\ *n* [ME *orizon*, fr. LL *horizont-, horizon*, fr. Gk *horizont-, horizōn*, fr. prp. of *horizein* to bound, define, fr. *horos* boundary; perh. akin to L *urvum* curved part of a plow] (14c) **1 a** : the apparent junction of earth and sky **b** : the great circle on the celestial sphere formed by the intersection of a plane tangent to the earth's surface at an observer's position with the celestial sphere **c** : range of perception or experience **d** : something that might be attained ⟨new ~s⟩ **2 a** : the geological deposit of a particular time usu. identified by distinctive fossils **b** : any of the reasonably distinct layers of soil or its underlying material in a vertical section of land **c** : a cultural area or level of development indicated by separated groups of artifacts — **ho·ri·zon·al** \-'rī-z°n-əl\ *adj*

ho·ri·zon·less \-ləs\ *adj* (ca. 1839) **1 a** : having no horizon **b** : ENDLESS 1 **2** : HOPELESS

hor·i·zon·tal \,hŏr-ə-'zän-t°l, ,här-\ *adj* (1555) **1 a** : of, relating to, or situated near the horizon **b** : parallel to, in the plane of, or operating in a plane parallel to the horizon or to a base line : LEVEL 〈~ distance〉 〈~ engine〉 **2** : relating to, directed toward, or consisting of individuals or entities of similar status or on the same level 〈~ mergers〉 〈~ hostility〉 — **horizontal** *n* — **hor·i·zon·tal·i·ty** \-,zän-'ta-lə-tē\ *n* — **hor·i·zon·tal·ly** \-'zän-t°l-ē\ *adv*

horizontal bar *n* (1827) **1** : a steel bar supported in a horizontal position approximately eight feet above the floor and used for swinging feats in gymnastics **2** : an event in gymnastics competition in which the horizontal bar is used

hor·mo·go·ni·um \,hŏr-mə-'gō-nē-əm\ *n, pl* **-nia** \-nē-ə\ [NL, fr. Gk *hormos* chain, necklace + NL -*gonium* — more at SERIES] (1880) : a portion of a filament in many blue-green algae that becomes detached as a reproductive body

hor·mon·al \hŏr-'mō-n°l\ *adj* (1926) : of, relating to, or effected by hormones — **hor·mon·al·ly** \-n°l-ē\ *adv*

hor·mone \'hŏr-,mōn\ *n* [Gk *hormōn*, prp. of *horman* to stir up, fr. *hormē* impulse, assault; akin to Gk *ornynai* to rouse — more at RISE] (1905) **1** : a product of living cells that circulates in body fluids or sap and produces a specific effect on the activity of cells remote from its point of origin; *esp* : one exerting a stimulatory effect on a cellular activity **2** : a synthetic substance that acts like a hormone — **hormone·like** \-,līk\ *adj*

horn \'hŏrn\ *n* [ME, fr. OE; akin to OHG *horn*, L *cornu*, Gk *keras*] (bef. 12c) **1 a** : one of the usu. paired bony processes that arise from the head of many ungulates and that are found in some extinct mammals and reptiles: as **(1)** : one of the permanent paired hollow sheaths of keratin usu. present in both sexes of cattle and their relatives that function chiefly for defense and arise from a bony core anchored to the skull — see COW illustration **(2)** : ANTLER **(3)** : a permanent solid horn of keratin that is attached to the nasal bone of a rhinoceros **(4)** : one of a pair of permanent bone protuberances from the skull of a giraffe or okapi that are covered with hairy skin **b** : a part like an animal's horn attributed esp. to the devil **c** : a natural projection or excrescence from an animal resembling or suggestive of a horn **d (1)** : the tough fibrous material consisting chiefly of keratin that covers or forms the horns of cattle and related animals, hooves, or other horny parts (as claws or nails) **(2)** : a manufactured product (as a plastic) resembling horn **e** : a hollow horn used to hold something **2** : something resembling or suggestive of a horn: as **a** : one of the curved ends of a crescent **b** : a sharp mountain peak **c** : a body of land or water shaped like a horn **d** : a beak-shaped part of an anvil **e** : a high pommel of a saddle **f** : CORNU **3 a** : an animal's horn used as a wind instrument **b** : a brass wind instrument: as **(1)** : HUNTING HORN **(2)** : FRENCH HORN **c** : a wind instrument used in a jazz band; *esp* : TRUMPET **d** : a usu. electrical device that makes a noise like that of a horn **4** : a source of strength **5** : one of the equally disadvantageous alternatives presented by a dilemma **6** *slang* : TELEPHONE — **horn** *adj* — **horned** \'hŏrnd *also* 'hŏr-nəd\ *adj* — **horned·ness** \'hŏr-nəd-nəs, 'hŏrn(d)-nəs\ *n* — **horn·less** \'hŏrn-ləs\ *adj* — **horn·less·ness** *n* — **horn·like** \-,līk\ *adj*

horn·beam \'hŏrn-,bēm\ *n* (14c) : any of a genus (*Carpinus*) of trees of the birch family having smooth gray bark and hard white wood

horn·bill \-,bil\ *n* (1773) : any of a family (Bucerotidae) of large nonpasserine Old World birds having enormous bills

horn·blende \-,blend\ *n* [G] (1770) : a mineral that is the common dark variety of aluminous amphibole; *broadly* : AMPHIBOLE 2 — **horn·blend·ic** \hŏrn-'blen-dik\ *adj*

horn·book \-,bŏk\ *n* (ca. 1595) **1** : a child's primer consisting of a sheet of parchment or paper protected by a sheet of transparent horn **2** : a rudimentary treatise

horned lizard *n* (1806) : HORNED TOAD

horned owl *n* (14c) : any of various owls having conspicuous tufts of feathers on the head

horned pout *n* (1837) : a bullhead (genus *Ameiurus*); *esp* : a common bullhead (*A. nebulosus*) of the eastern U.S. that has been introduced into streams of the Pacific coast

horned toad \'hŏrnd-; 'hŏr-nəd-, -,nət-\ *n* (1806) : any of several small harmless insectivorous lizards (genus *Phrynosoma*) of the western U.S. and Mexico having hornlike spines

horned viper *n* (1767) : CERASTES

hor·net \'hŏr-nət\ *n* [ME *hernet*, fr. OE *hyrnet;* akin to OHG *hornaz* hornet, L *crabro*] (bef. 12c) : any of the larger social wasps (family Vespidae) — compare YELLOW JACKET

hornet's nest *n* (ca. 1740) **1** : a troublesome or hazardous situation **2** : an angry reaction 〈must have known that his frank comments . . . would stir up a *hornet's nest* —*U.S. Investor*〉

horn·fels \'hŏrn-,felz\ *n* [G, fr. *Horn* horn + *Fels* cliff, rock] (1854) : a fine-grained silicate rock produced by metamorphism esp. of slate

horn fly *n* (1708) : a small black European fly (*Haematobia irritans*) that has been introduced into No. America where it is a blood-sucking pest of cattle

horn in *vi* (1911) : to participate without invitation or consent : INTRUDE

horn·ist \'hŏr-nist\ *n* (1836) : one who plays a French horn

horn—mad \'hŏrn-'mad\ *adj* (1579) : furiously enraged

horn of plenty (ca. 1586) : CORNUCOPIA

horn·pipe \'hŏrn-,pīp\ *n* (15c) **1** : a single-reed wind instrument consisting of a wooden or bone pipe with finger holes, a bell, and mouthpiece usu. of horn **2** : a lively folk dance of the British Isles orig. accompanied by hornpipe playing

horn—rims \-,rimz\ *n pl* (1927) : glasses with horn rims

horn·stone \'hŏrn-,stōn\ *n* (1728) : a mineral that is a variety of quartz much like flint but more brittle

horn·swog·gle \-,swä-gəl\ *vt* **-swog·gled; -swog·gling** \-g(ə-)liŋ\ [origin unknown] (ca. 1829) *slang* : BAMBOOZLE, HOAX

horn·tail \-,tāl\ *n* (1884) : any of various hymenopterous insects (fam-

ily Siricidae) related to the typical sawflies but having larvae that burrow in woody plants and on the females a stout hornlike ovipositor for depositing the egg

horn·worm \-,wərm\ *n* (1676) : a hawkmoth caterpillar having a hornlike tail process — compare TOMATO HORNWORM

horn·wort \-,wŏrt, -,wŏrt\ *n* (ca. 1805) : any of a genus (*Ceratophyllum*) of rootless thin-stemmed aquatic herbs that have flowers with a sepaloid perianth and a single carpel

horny \'hŏr-nē\ *adj* **horn·i·er; -est** (14c) **1 a** : of or made of horn **b** : HARD, CALLOUS 〈*horny*-handed〉 **c** : compact and homogeneous with a dull luster — used of a mineral **2** : having horns **3** [*horn* erect penis + 1-*y*] **a** : desiring sexual gratification **b** : excited sexually — **horn·i·ness** *n*

hor·o·loge \'hŏr-ə-,lōj, 'här-\ *n* [ME, fr. MF, fr. L *horologium,* fr. Gk *hōrologion,* fr. *hōra* hour + *legein* to gather — more at YEAR, LEGEND] (14c) : a timekeeping device

hor·o·log·i·cal \,hŏr-ə-'lä-ji-kəl\ *adj* (15c) : of or relating to a horologe or horology

ho·rol·o·gist \hə-'rä-lə-jist\ *n* (1798) **1** : a person skilled in the practice or theory of horology **2** : a maker of clocks or watches

ho·rol·o·gy \-jē\ *n* [Gk *hōra* + E -*logy*] (1819) **1** : the science of measuring time **2** : the art of making instruments for indicating time

horo·scope \'hŏr-ə-,skōp, 'här-\ *n* [ME *oruscope,* fr. MF *horoscope,* fr. L *horoscopus,* fr. Gk *hōroskopos,* fr. *hōra* + *skopos* watcher; akin to Gk *skopein* to look at — more at SPY] (14c) **1** : a diagram of the relative positions of planets and signs of the zodiac at a specific time (as at one's birth) for use by astrologers in inferring individual character and personality traits and in foretelling events of a person's life **2** : an astrological forecast

hor·ren·dous \hŏ-'ren-dəs, hä-, hə-\ *adj* [L *horrendus,* fr. gerundive of *horrēre*] (1659) : perfectly horrid : DREADFUL 〈the tax rate was ~〉 — **hor·ren·dous·ly** *adv*

hor·rent \'hŏr-ənt, 'här-\ *adj* [L *horrent-, horrens,* prp. of *horrēre*] (1667) **1** *archaic* : covered with bristling points : BRISTLED **2** *archaic* : standing up like bristles : BRISTLING

hor·ri·ble \'hŏr-ə-bəl, 'här-\ *adj* [ME *orrible, horrible,* fr. MF, fr. L *horribilis,* fr. *horrēre*] (14c) **1** : marked by or conducive to horror **2** : extremely unpleasant or disagreeable — **horrible** *n* — **hor·ri·ble·ness** *n* — **hor·ri·bly** \-blē\ *adv*

hor·rid \'hŏr-əd, 'här-\ *adj* [L *horridus,* fr. *horrēre*] (1590) **1** *archaic* : ROUGH, BRISTLING **2** *archaic* : innately horrible or repulsive : *a* : inspiring horror : SHOCKING **b** : inspiring disgust or loathing : NASTY — **hor·rid·ly** *adv* — **hor·rid·ness** *n*

hor·rif·ic \hŏ-'ri-fik, hä-\ *adj* (1653) : having the power to horrify 〈a ~ account of the tragedy〉 — **hor·rif·i·cal·ly** \-fi-k(ə-)lē\ *adv*

hor·ri·fy \'hŏr-ə-,fī, 'här-\ *vt* **-fied; -fy·ing** (1791) **1** : to cause to feel horror **2** : to fill with distaste : SHOCK *syn* see DISMAY — **hor·ri·fy·ing·ly** \-,fī-iŋ-lē\ *adv*

1hor·ror \'hŏr-ər, 'här-\ *n* [ME *horrour,* fr. MF *horror,* fr. L, action of bristling, fr. *horrēre* to bristle, shiver; akin to Skt *harṣate* he is excited] (14c) **1 a** : painful and intense fear, dread, or dismay 〈astonishment giving place to ~ on the faces of the people about me —H. G. Wells〉 **b** : intense aversion or repugnance **2 a** : the quality of inspiring horror : repulsive, horrible, or dismal quality or character 〈contemplating the ~ of their lives —Liam O'Flaherty〉 **b** : something that inspires horror **3** *pl* : a state of extreme depression or apprehension

2horror *adj* (1797) : calculated to inspire feelings of dread or horror : BLOODCURDLING 〈a ~ story〉

hor·ror—struck \-,strək\ *adj* (1814) : struck with horror 〈stood ~ as they watched . . . their own city destroyed —*Nashville Tennessean*〉

hors de com·bat \,ŏr-də-kōⁿ-'bä\ *adv or adj* [F] (1757) : out of combat : DISABLED

hors d'oeuvre \ŏr-'dərv\ *n, pl* **hors d'oeuvres** *also* **hors d'oeuvre** \-'dərv(z)\ [F *hors-d'œuvre,* lit., outside of the work] (1714) : any of various savory foods usu. served as appetizers

1horse \'hŏrs\ *n, pl* **hors·es** *also* **horse** [ME *hors,* fr. OE; akin to OHG

horse 1a(1): *1* forehead, *2* forelock, *3* poll, *4* mane, *5* withers, *6* back, *7* flank, *8* loin, *9* haunch, *10* croup, *11* point of hip, *12* tail, *13* hock, *14* cannon, *15* gaskin, *16* thigh, *17* stifle, *18* barrel, *19* chestnut, *20* fetlock, *21* pastern, *22* hoof, *23* coronet, *24* knee, *25* forearm, *26* chest, *27* shoulder, *28* neck, *29* throatlatch, *30* cheek

\ə\ abut \ⁿ\ kitten, F table \ər\ further \a\ ash \ā\ ace \ä\ mop, mar \aú\ out \ch\ chin \e\ bet \ē\ easy \g\ go \i\ hit \ī\ ice \j\ job \ŋ\ sing \ō\ go \ò\ law \òi\ boy \th\ thin \t͟h\ the \ü\ loot \ú\ foot \y\ yet \zh\ vision \ä, k̲, ⁿ, œ, œ̄, ɥ, ɯ̄, ᵊ\ *see* Guide to Pronunciation ʰros horse\ (bef. 12c) **1 a** (1) : a large solid-hoofed herbivorous mammal (*Equus caballus*, family Equidae, the horse family) domesticated since a prehistoric period and used as a beast of burden, a draft animal, or for riding (2) : RACEHORSE ⟨play the ~s⟩ **b** : a male horse; *esp* : STALLION **c** : a recent or extinct animal (as a zebra, ass, or onager) of the horse family **2 a** : JACKSTAY **b** : a frame usu. with legs used for supporting something (as planks or staging) **c** (1) : POMMEL HORSE (2) : VAULTING HORSE **3** *horse pl* : CAVALRY **4** : a mass of the same geological character as the wall rock occurring within a vein **5** : HORSEPOWER **6** *slang* : HEROIN **7** : an athlete whose performance is consistently strong and reliable ⟨a team with the ~s to win the pennant⟩ — **horse·less** \'hȯr-sləs\ *adj* — **horse·like** \'hȯrs-ˌlīk\ *adj* — **from the horse's mouth** : from the original source

²**horse** *vb* **horsed; hors·ing** *vt* (bef. 12c) **1** : to provide with a horse **2** : to move by brute force ~ *vi, of a mare* : to be in heat

³**horse** *adj* (15c) **1 a** : of or relating to a horse **b** : hauled or powered by a horse ⟨a ~ barge⟩ **2** : large or coarse of its kind **3** : mounted on horses ⟨~ guards⟩

horse–and–buggy *adj* (ca. 1926) **1** : of or relating to the era before the advent of certain socially revolutionizing inventions (as the automobile) **2** : clinging to outdated attitudes or ideas : OLD-FASHIONED

horse around *vi* (ca. 1928) : to engage in horseplay ⟨*horse around* together, joking and laughing and pushing each other —D. K. Shipler⟩; *also* : FOOL AROUND 1

¹**horse·back** \'hȯrs-ˌbak\ *n* (14c) : the back of a horse

²**horseback** *adv* (1727) : on horseback

³**horseback** *adj* (1879) : given without thorough consideration ⟨a ~ opinion⟩

horse·bean \'hȯrs-ˌbēn\ *n* (1684) **1** : BROAD BEAN **2** : JERUSALEM THORN

horse·car \-ˌkär\ *n* (1833) **1** : a streetcar drawn by horses **2** : a car fitted for transporting horses

horse chestnut *n* (1597) **1** : a large Asian tree (*Aesculus hippocastanum* of the family Hippocastanaceae, the horse-chestnut family) that has palmate leaves and erect conical clusters of showy flowers and is widely cultivated as an ornamental and shade tree and naturalized as an escape; *also* : BUCKEYE **2** : the large glossy brown seed of a horse chestnut

horse coper *n* (1614) *Brit* : COPER

horse-feath·ers \'hȯrs-ˌfe-thərz\ *n pl* (1928) *slang* : NONSENSE, BALDERDASH

horse-flesh \-ˌflesh\ *n* (15c) : horses considered esp. with reference to riding, driving, or racing

horse-fly \-ˌflī\ *n* (14c) : any of a family (Tabanidae) of swift usu. large two-winged flies with bloodsucking females

horse gentian *n* (1837) : FEVERWORT

horse-hair \'hȯrs-ˌhar, -ˌher\ *n* (14c) **1** : the hair of a horse esp. from the mane or tail **2** : cloth made from horsehair

horsehair worm *n* (ca. 1753) : HAIRWORM 1 — called also *horsehair snake*

horse-hide \'hȯrs-ˌhīd\ *n* (14c) **1** : the dressed or raw hide of a horse **2** : the ball used in the game of baseball

horse latitudes *n pl* (1777) : either of two belts or regions in the neighborhood of 30° N and 30° S latitude characterized by high pressure, calms, and light variable winds

horse·laugh \'hȯrs-ˌlaf, -ˌláf\ *n* (1713) : a loud boisterous laugh : GUFFAW

horseless carriage *n* (1895) : AUTOMOBILE

horse mackerel *n* (ca. 1705) **1** : any of various large carangid food fishes; *esp* : JACK MACKEREL **2** : BLUEFIN TUNA

horse·man \'hȯr-smən\ *n* (14c) **1** : a rider or driver of horses; *esp* : one whose skill is exceptional **2** : a person skilled in caring for or managing horses **3** : a person who breeds or raises horses — **horse·man·ship** \-ˌship\ *n*

horse·mint \'hȯrs-ˌmint\ *n* (bef. 12c) : any of various coarse mints; *esp* : MONARDA

horse nettle *n* (ca. 1818) : a coarse prickly weed (*Solanum carolinense* of the nightshade family with bright yellow fruit resembling berries

horse opera *n* (1927) : WESTERN 2

horse·play \'hȯrs-ˌplā\ *n* (1589) : rough or boisterous play

horse·play·er \-ˌər\ *n* (1947) : one who habitually bets on horse races

horse·pow·er \'hȯrs-ˌpaủ(-ə)r\ *n* (1806) **1** : the power that a horse exerts in pulling **2** : a unit of power equal in the U.S. to 746 watts and nearly equivalent to the English gravitational unit of the same name that equals 550 foot-pounds of work per second **3** : effective power ⟨intellectual ~⟩ ⟨computing ~⟩

horse race *n* (1954) : a close contest (as in politics)

horse-rad·ish \'hȯrs-ˌra-dish, -ˌre-\ *n* (1597) **1** : a tall coarse white-flowered herb (*Armoracia lapathifolia*) of the mustard family **2** : a condiment made from ground-up horseradish root

horse's ass \'hȯr-səz-\ *n* (ca. 1942) : a stupid or incompetent person : BLOCKHEAD — often considered vulgar

horse sense *n* (1832) : COMMON SENSE

horse·shit \'hȯrs-ˌshit, 'hȯrsh-\ *n* (1946) : NONSENSE, BUNK — usu. considered vulgar

horse·shoe \'hȯrs-ˌshü, 'hȯrsh-\ *n* (14c) **1** : a usu. U-shaped band of iron fitted and nailed to the rim of a horse's hoof to protect it **2** : something (as a valley) shaped like a horseshoe **3** *pl* : a game like quoits played with horseshoes or with horseshoe-shaped pieces of metal — **horseshoe** *vt* — **horse·sho·er** \-ˌshü-ər\ *n*

horseshoe arch *n* (ca. 1816) : an arch having an intrados that widens above the springing before narrowing to a rounded or pointed crown — see ARCH illustration

horseshoe crab *n* (1797) : any of several closely related marine arthropods (order Xiphosura and class Merostomata) with a broad crescentic cephalothorax — called also *king crab*

horse show *n* (1856) : an exhibition of horses that usu. includes competition in riding, driving, and jumping

horse·tail \'hȯrs-ˌtāl\ *n* (15c) : EQUISETUM

horse trade *n* (1846) : negotiation accompanied by shrewd bargaining and reciprocal concessions ⟨a political *horse trade*⟩ — **horse–trade** *vi* — **horse trader** *n*

horse·weed \'hȯrs-ˌwēd\ *n* (1790) **1** : a common No. American fleabane (*Conyza canadensis* syn. *Erigeron canadensis*) with linear leaves

and small discoid heads of yellowish flowers **2** : a coarse annual ragweed (*Ambrosia trifida*)

horse·whip \'hȯrs-ˌwip, 'hȯrs-ˌhwip\ *vt* (1768) : to flog with or as if with a whip made to be used on a horse — **horse·whip·per** *n*

horse·wom·an \'hȯrs-ˌwủm-ən\ *n* (ca. 1578) **1** : a woman rider or driver of horses; *esp* : one whose skill is exceptional **2** : a woman skilled in caring for or managing horses **3** : a woman who breeds or raises horses

hors·ey or **horsy** \'hȯr-sē\ *adj* **hors·i·er; -est** (1591) **1** : of, relating to, or resembling a horse **2** : having to do with horses or horse racing **3** : characteristic of the manners, dress, or tastes of horsemen or horsewomen — **hors·i·ly** \-sə-lē\ *adv* — **hors·i·ness** \-sē-nəs\ *n*

horst \'hȯrst\ *n* [G, lit., thicket] (1893) : a block of the earth's crust separated by faults from adjacent relatively depressed blocks

hor·ta·tive \'hȯr-tə-tiv\ *adj* [L *hortativus*, fr. L *hortatus*, pp. of *hortari* to urge — more at YEARN] (1623) : giving exhortation : ADVISORY — **hor·ta·tive·ly** *adv*

hor·ta·to·ry \'hȯr-tə-ˌtȯr-ē, -ˌtȯr-\ *adj* (1586) : HORTATIVE, EXHORTATORY

hor·ti·cul·ture \'hȯr-tə-ˌkəl-chər\ *n* [L *hortus* garden + E -*i*- + *culture* — more at YARD] (1678) : the science and art of growing fruits, vegetables, flowers, or ornamental plants — **hor·ti·cul·tur·al** \ˌhȯr-tə-ˈkəl-chə-rəl\ *adj* — **hor·ti·cul·tur·al·ly** \-rə-lē\ *adv* — **hor·ti·cul·tur·ist** \-rist\ *n*

Ho·rus \'hȯr-əs, 'hȯr-\ *n* [LL, fr. Gk *Hōros*, fr. Egypt *Ḥr*] : the Egyptian god of light and the son of Osiris and Isis

ho·san·na *also* **ho·san·nah** \hō-'za-nə *also* -'zä-\ *interj* [ME *osanna*, fr. OE, fr. LL, fr. Gk *hōsanna*, fr. Heb *hōshī'āh-nnā* pray, save (us)!] (bef. 12c) — used as a cry of acclamation and adoration — **hosanna** *n*

HO scale \'(ˌ)ā-'(ˌ)ō-\ *n* [*half* + *O* (*gauge*)] (1939) : a scale of 3.5 millimeters to one foot used esp. for model toys (as automobiles or trains)

¹**hose** \'hōz\ *n, pl* **hose** or **hos·es** [ME, fr. OE *hosa* stocking, husk; akin to OHG *hosa* leg covering] (bef. 12c) **1** *pl* **hose** **a** (1) : a cloth leg covering that sometimes covers the foot (2) : STOCKING, SOCK **b** (1) : a close-fitting garment covering the legs and waist that is usu. attached to a doublet by points (2) : short breeches reaching to the knee **2** : a flexible tube for conveying fluids (as from a faucet or hydrant)

²**hose** *vt* **hosed; hos·ing** (1889) **1** : to spray, water, or wash with a hose — often used with *down* ⟨~ down a stable floor⟩ **2** *slang* **a** : to deprive of something due or expected : TRICK, CHEAT **b** : to shoot with automatic weapons fire

Ho·sea \hō-'zā-ə, -'zē-\ *n* [Heb *Hōshēa'*] **1** : a Hebrew prophet of the 8th century B.C. **2** : a prophetic book of canonical Jewish and Christian Scripture — see BIBLE table

ho·sel \'hō-zəl\ *n* [dim. of ¹*hose*] (1899) : a socket in the head of a golf club into which the shaft is inserted

hose·pipe \'hōz-ˌpīp\ *n* (1835) *chiefly Brit* : HOSE 2

ho·siery \'hōzh-rē, 'hōz-; 'hō-zhə-rē, -zə-\ *n* (1796) **1** : HOSE 1a **2** *chiefly Brit* : KNITWEAR

hos·pice \'häs-pəs\ *n* [F, fr. L *hospitium*, fr. *hospit-, hospes* host — more at HOST] (1818) **1** : a lodging for travelers, young persons, or the underprivileged esp. when maintained by a religious order **2** : a facility or program designed to provide a caring environment for supplying the physical and emotional needs of the terminally ill

hos·pi·ta·ble \hä-'spi-tə-bəl, 'häs-(ˌ)pi-\ *adj* (ca. 1570) **1 a** : given to generous and cordial reception of guests **b** : promising or suggesting generous and cordial welcome **c** : offering a pleasant or sustaining environment **2** : readily receptive : OPEN ⟨~ to new ideas⟩ — **hos·pi·ta·bly** \-blē\ *adv*

hos·pi·tal \'häs-(ˌ)pi-t^əl\ *n, often attrib* [ME, fr. MF, fr. ML *hospitale* hospice, guest house, fr. neut. of L *hospitalis* of a guest, fr. *hospit-, hospes*] (14c) **1** : a charitable institution for the needy, aged, infirm, or young **2** : an institution where the sick or injured are given medical or surgical care — usu. used in British English without an article after a preposition **3** : a repair shop for specified small objects ⟨clock ~⟩

hos·pi·tal·ise *Brit var of* HOSPITALIZE

hos·pi·tal·i·ty \ˌhäs-pə-'ta-lə-tē\ *n, pl* **-ties** (14c) : hospitable treatment, reception, or disposition

hospitality suite *n* (1963) : a room or suite esp. in a hotel set aside as a place for socializing esp. for business purposes

hos·pi·tal·ize \'häs-ˌpi-t^əl-ˌiz\ *vt* **-ized; -iz·ing** (ca. 1899) : to place in a hospital as a patient — **hos·pi·tal·iza·tion** \ˌhäs-ˌpi-t^əl-ə-'zā-shən\ *n*

Hos·pi·tal·ler or **Hos·pi·tal·er** \-t^əl-ər\ *n* [ME *hospitalier*, fr. MF, fr. ML *hospitalarius*, fr. LL *hospitale*] (14c) : a member of a religious military order established in Jerusalem in the 12th century

¹**host** \'hōst\ *n* [ME, fr. OF, fr. LL *hostis*, fr. L, stranger, enemy — more at GUEST] (14c) **1** : ARMY **2** : a very large number : MULTITUDE

²**host** *vi* (15c) : to assemble in a host usu. for a hostile purpose

³**host** *n* [ME *hoste* host, guest, fr. OF, fr. L *hospit-, hospes*, prob. fr. *hostis*] (14c) **1 a** : one that receives or entertains guests socially, commercially, or officially **b** : one that provides facilities for an event or function ⟨our college served as ~ for the basketball tournament⟩ **2 a** : a living animal or plant affording subsistence or lodgment to a parasite **b** : the larger, stronger, or dominant member of a commensal or symbiotic pair **c** : an individual into which a tissue, part, or embryo is transplanted from another **3** : a mineral or rock that is older than the minerals or rocks in it; *also* : a substance that contains a usu. small amount of another substance incorporated in its structure **4** : a radio or television emcee **5** : a computer that controls communications in a network that administers a database

⁴**host** *vt* (15c) **1** : to serve as host to, at, or for ⟨~ friends⟩ ⟨~ a dinner⟩ **2** : EMCEE ⟨~ed a series of TV programs⟩

⁵**host** *n, often cap* [ME *hoste, oste*, fr. MF *hoiste*, fr. LL & L; LL *hostia* Eucharist, fr. L, sacrifice] (14c) : the eucharistic bread

hos·ta \'hō-stə\ *n* [NL, fr. Nicolaus *Host* †1834 Austrian botanist] (1828) : PLANTAIN LILY

hos·tage \'häs-tij\ *n* [ME, fr. OF, fr. *hoste*] (13c) **1 a** : a person held by one party in a conflict as a pledge that promises will be kept or terms met by the other party **b** : a person taken by force to secure the taker's demands **2** : one that is involuntarily controlled by an outside influence

¹**hos·tel** \'häs-t³l\ *n* [ME, fr. OF, fr. ML *hospitale* hospice] (14c) **1** : INN **2 a** *chiefly Brit* : a supervised institutional residence **b** : a supervised lodging for usu. young travelers — called also *youth hostel*

²**hostel** *vi* -teled *or* -telled; -tel·ing *or* -tel·ling (14c) : to stay at hostels overnight in the course of traveling

hos·tel·er *or* **hos·tel·ler** \'häs-tə-lər\ *n* (14c) **1** : one that lodges guests or strangers **2** : a traveler who stops at hostels overnight

hos·tel·ry \'häs-t³l-rē\ *n, pl* -ries (14c) : INN, HOTEL

¹**host·ess** \'hōs-təs\ *n* (14c) **1** : a woman who entertains socially **2 a** : a woman in charge of a public dining room who seats diners **b** : a female employee on a public conveyance (as an airplane) who manages the provisioning of food and attends passengers **c** : a woman who acts as a dancing partner or companion to male patrons in a dance hall or bar

²**hostess** *vi* (1927) : to act as hostess ~ *vt* : to serve as hostess to

hos·tile \'häs-t³l, -,tīl\ *adj* [MF or L; MF, fr. L *hostilis*, fr. *hostis*] (1580) **1 a** : of or relating to an enemy (~ fire) **b** : marked by malevolence (a ~ act) **c** : openly opposed or resisting (a ~ critic) (~ to new ideas) **d** : not hospitable (a ~ environment) **2 a** : of or relating to the opposing party in a legal controversy (a ~ witness) **b** : adverse to the interests of a property owner or corporation management (a ~ takeover) — **hostile** *n* — **hos·tile·ly** \-t³l-(l)ē, -,tīl-lē\ *adv*

hos·til·i·ty \hä-'sti-lə-tē\ *n, pl* -ties (15c) **1 a** : deep-seated usu. mutual ill will **b** (1) : hostile action (2) *pl* : overt acts of warfare : WAR **2** : conflict, opposition, or resistance in thought or principle *syn* see ENMITY

hos·tler \'häs-lər, 'äs-\ *n* [ME, innkeeper, hostler, fr. *hostel*] (14c) **1** : one who takes care of horses or mules **2** : one who moves locomotives in and out of a roundhouse; *also* : one who services locomotives

host·ly \'hōst-lē\ *adj* (1893) : of or appropriate to a host

¹**hot** \'hät\ *adj* **hot·ter; hot·test** [ME, fr. OE *hāt*; akin to OHG *heiz* hot, Lith *kaisti* to get hot] (bef. 12c) **1 a** : having a relatively high temperature **b** : capable of giving a sensation of heat or of burning, searing, or scalding **c** : having heat in a degree exceeding normal body heat **2 a** : VIOLENT, STORMY (a ~ temper) (a ~ battle); *also* : ANGRY (got ~ about the remark) **b** : sexually excited or receptive; *also* : SEXY **c** : EAGER, ZEALOUS (~ for reform) **d** *of jazz* : emotionally exciting and marked by strong rhythms and free melodic improvisations **3** : having or causing the sensation of an uncomfortable degree of body heat (~ and tired) (it's ~ in here) **4 a** : newly made : FRESH (a ~ scent) (~ off the press) **b** : close to something sought (~ on the trail) **5 a** : suggestive of heat or of burning or glowing objects (~ colors) **b** : PUNGENT, PEPPERY **6 a** : of intense and immediate interest (some ~ gossip) **b** : unusually lucky or favorable (on a ~ streak) **c** : temporarily capable of unusual performance (as in a sport) **d** : currently popular or in demand (a ~ commodity) **e** : very good (a ~ idea) (not feeling too ~) **f** : ABSURD, UNBELIEVABLE (wants to fight the champ? that's a ~ one) **7 a** : electrically energized esp. with high voltage **b** : RADIOACTIVE; *also* : dealing with radioactive material **c** *of an atom or molecule* : being in an excited state **8 a** : recently and illegally obtained (~ jewels) **b** : wanted by the police; *also* : unsafe for a fugitive **9** : FAST (a ~ new fighter plane) (a ~ lap around the track) — **hot·ness** *n* — **hot·tish** \'hä-tish\ *adj* — **hot under the collar** : extremely exasperated or angry

²**hot** *adv* (bef. 12c) **1** : HOTLY **2** : FAST, QUICKLY

³**hot** *n* (13c) **1** : HEAT 1d(1) (the ~ of the day) **2** : one that is hot (as a hot meal or a horse just after a workout) **3** *pl* : strong sexual desire — used with *the*

⁴**hot** *vt* **hot·ted; hot·ting** (1561) *chiefly Southern, southern Midland, & Brit* : HEAT, WARM — usu. used with *up*

hot air *n* (1873) : empty talk

hot·bed \'hät-,bed\ *n* (1626) **1** : a bed of soil enclosed in glass, heated esp. by fermenting manure, and used for forcing or for raising seedlings **2** : an environment that favors rapid growth or development (a ~ of activity)

hot-blood·ed \-,bləd\ *n* (1798) **1** : one that is hot-blooded; *esp* : one having strong passions or a quick temper **2** : THOROUGHBRED 1

hot–blood·ed \-'blə-dəd\ *adj* (1598) **1** : easily excited : PASSIONATE **2** *of a horse* : having Arab or Thoroughbred ancestors — **hot–blood·ed·ness** *n*

hot·box \-,bäks\ *n* (1848) : a journal bearing (as of a railroad car) overheated by friction

hot button *n* (1975) : an emotional and usu. controversial issue or concern that triggers immediate intense reaction — **hot–button** *adj*

hot·cake \-,kāk\ *n* (1683) : PANCAKE — **like hotcakes** : at a rapid rate (selling *like hotcakes*)

hotch \'häch\ *vi* [ME, prob. fr. MF *hocher* to shake, fr. OF *hochier*] (15c) **1** *Scot* : WIGGLE, FIDGET **2** *chiefly Scot* : SWARM

hotch·pot \'häch-,pät\ *n* [AF *hochepot*, fr. OF, hotchpotch] (1552) : the combining of properties into a common lot to ensure equality of division among heirs

hotch·potch \'häch-,päch\ *n* [ME *hochepot*, fr. MF, fr. OF, fr. *hochier* to shake + *pot*] (1583) **1 a** : a thick soup or stew of vegetables, potatoes, and usu. meat **b** : HODGEPODGE 2 : HOTCHPOT

hot comb *n* (1970) : a metal comb usu. electrically heated for straightening or styling the hair — **hot–comb** *vt*

hot corner *n* (1903) : the fielding position of the third baseman in baseball

hot·dog \'hät-,dòg\ *vi* [²*hot dog*] (1962) : to perform in a conspicuous or often ostentatious manner; *esp* : to perform fancy stunts and maneuvers (as while surfing or skiing) — **hot·dog·ger** \-,dò-gər\ *n*

¹**hot dog** \'hät-,dòg\ *n* (ca. 1900) **1** : FRANKFURTER; *esp* : a frankfurter heated and served in a long split roll **2** [perh. fr. ²*hot dog*]: one that hotdogs; *also* : SHOW-OFF

²**hot dog** \'hät-'dòg\ *interj* (ca. 1906) — used to express approval or gratification

ho·tel \hō-'tel, 'hō-,\ *n* [F *hôtel*, fr. OF *hostel* hostel] (1765) : an establishment that provides lodging and usu. meals, entertainment, and various personal services for the public : INN — **ho·tel·dom** \-dəm\ *n*

Hotel (1952) — a communications code word for the letter *h*

ho·te·lier \hō-'tel-yər; hō-t³l-'yā, ,ō-\ *n* [F *hôtelier*, fr. OF *hostelier*, fr. *hostel*] (1905) : a proprietor or manager of a hotel

ho·tel·man \hō-'tel-,man, -mən\ *n* (1920) : one who is engaged in the hotel business esp. in a supervisory or managerial capacity

hot flash *n* (1910) : a sudden brief flushing and sensation of heat caused by dilation of skin capillaries usu. associated with menopausal endocrine imbalance — called also *hot flush*

¹**hot·foot** \'hät-,fút\ *adv* (14c) : in haste

²**hotfoot** *vi* (1896) : to go hotfoot : HURRY — usu. used with *it*

³**hotfoot** *n, pl* **hotfoots** (1934) : a practical joke in which a match is surreptitiously inserted between the upper and the sole of a victim's shoe and lighted

hot·head \'hät-,hed\ *n* (1660) : a hotheaded person

hot·head·ed \-'he-dəd\ *adj* (1641) : FIERY, IMPETUOUS — **hot·head·ed·ly** *adv* — **hot·head·ed·ness** *n*

¹**hot·house** \-,hau̇s\ *n* (1511) **1** *obs* : BORDELLO **2** : a greenhouse maintained at a high temperature esp. for the culture of tropical plants **3** : HOTBED 2

²**hothouse** *adj* (1838) **1** : grown in a hothouse **2** : suggestive of growth and development in a hothouse (a ~ existence); *also* : suggesting a hothouse (a ~ atmosphere)

hot line *n* (1955) **1** : a direct telephone line in constant operational readiness so as to facilitate immediate communication **2** : a usu. toll-free telephone service available to the public for some specific purpose (a consumer *hot line*)

hot·ly \'hät-lē\ *adv* (15c) : in a hot manner (a ~ contested series)

hot–melt \'hät-,melt\ *n* (1939) : a fast-drying nonvolatile adhesive applied hot in the molten state

hot metal *n* (1960) : composition in which the type is cast from molten metal

hot money *n* (1936) : investment funds intended for the highest short-term rate of return

hot pepper *n* (1945) : any of various small and usu. thin-walled capsicum fruits of marked pungency; *also* : a plant bearing hot peppers

hot plate *n* (1845) **1** : a heated iron plate for cooking **2** : a simple portable appliance for heating or for cooking in limited spaces

hot pot *n* (1851) **1** : a stew of meat and vegetables **2** : FIREPOT 2

hot potato *n* (1846) : a controversial question or issue that involves unpleasant or dangerous consequences for anyone dealing with it

hot pursuit *n* (ca. 1922) : close continuous pursuit of a fleeing suspected lawbreaker or hostile military force esp. across territorial lines

hot rod *n* (1945) : an automobile rebuilt or modified for high speed and fast acceleration — **hot–rod** \'hät-'räd\ *vb* — **hot–rod·der** \'hät-,rä-dər\ *n*

hot seat *n* (1925) **1** *slang* : ELECTRIC CHAIR **2** : a position of uneasiness, embarrassment, or anxiety

hot·shot \'hät-,shät\ *n, often attrib* (ca. 1925) **1** : a fast freight **2** : a person who is conspicuously talented or successful

hot spot *n* (1929) **1** : a place of more than usual interest, activity, or action **2** : a place in the upper mantle of the earth at which hot magma from the lower mantle upwells to melt through the crust usu. in the interior of a tectonic plate to form a volcanic feature; *also* : a place in the crust overlying a hot spot

hot spring *n* (1669) : a spring whose water issues at a temperature higher than that of its surroundings

hot stuff *n* (1889) : someone or something unusually good

Hot·ten·tot \'hä-t³n-,tät\ *n* [Afrik] (1677) **1** : a member of any of a group of Khoisan-speaking pastoral peoples of southern Africa **2** : the group of Khoisan languages spoken by the Hottentots

hot ticket *n* (1972) : someone or something very popular : RAGE

hot tub *n* (1975) : a large usu. wooden tub of hot water in which bathers soak and usu. socialize

hot up *vi* (1878) *chiefly Brit* : to increase in intensity, pace, or excitement (air raids began to *hot up* about the beginning of February —George Orwell) ~ *vt, chiefly Brit* : to make livelier, speedier, or more intense

hot war *n* (1947) : a conflict involving actual fighting — compare COLD WAR

hot water *n* (1537) : TROUBLE 4, DIFFICULTY (was in *hot water* with the authorities)

hot–wire \'hät-,wī(-ə)r\ *vt* (1954) : to start (as an automobile) by short-circuiting the ignition system

¹**hound** \'hau̇nd\ *n* [ME, fr. OE *hund*; akin to OHG *hunt* dog, L *canis*, Gk *kyōn*] (bef. 12c) **1 a** : DOG **b** : a dog of any of various hunting breeds typically having large drooping ears and a deep voice and following their prey by scent **2** : a mean or despicable person **3** : DOGFISH **4** : a person who pursues like a hound; *esp* : one who avidly seeks or collects something (autograph ~s)

²**hound** *vt* (1528) **1** : to pursue with or as if with hounds **2** : to drive or affect by persistent harassing *syn* see BAIT — **hound·er** *n*

hounds \'hau̇n(d)z\ *n pl* [ME *houne*, fr. ON *hūnn* knob at the top of a masthead] (15c) : the framing at the masthead of a ship that supports the heel of the topmast and the upper parts of the lower rigging

hound's-tongue \'hau̇n(d)z-,təŋ\ *n* (bef. 12c) : any of various coarse plants (genus *Cynoglossum*, esp. *C. officinale*) of the borage family having tongue-shaped leaves and reddish flowers

hounds·tooth check *or* **hound's–tooth check** \'hau̇n(d)z-,tüth-\ *n* (1937) : a usu. small broken-check textile pattern

hour \'au̇(-ə)r\ *n* [ME, fr. OF *heure*, fr. LL & L; LL *hora* canonical hour, fr. L, hour of the day, fr. Gk *hōra* — more at YEAR] (13c) **1 a** : a time or office for daily liturgical devotion; *esp* : CANONICAL HOUR **2** : the 24th part of a day : 60 minutes **3 a** : the time of day reckoned in two 12-hour periods **b** *pl* : the time reckoned in one 24-hour period from midnight to midnight using a 4-digit number of which the first two digits indicate the hour and the last two digits indicate the minute (in the military 4:30 p.m. is called 1630 ~s) **4 a** : a custom-

houndstooth check

\ə\ abut \³\ kitten, F table \ər\ further \a\ ash \ā\ ace \ä\ mop, mar \au̇\ out \ch\ chin \e\ bet \ē\ easy \g\ go \i\ hit \ī\ ice \j\ job \ŋ\ sing \ō\ go \o\̇ law \oi̇\ boy \th\ thin \t͟h\ the \ü\ loot \u̇\ foot \y\ yet \zh\ vision \à, k, ⁿ, œ, œ̄, ᴜε, ᵫ, ᵍ\ *see* Guide to Pronunciation ary or particular time ⟨lunch ~⟩ ⟨in our ~ of need⟩ **b** *pl* : time of going to bed ⟨keeps late ~s⟩; *also* : time of working ⟨banker's ~s⟩ **5** : an angular unit of right ascension equal to 15 degrees measured along the celestial equator **6** : the work done or distance traveled at normal rate in an hour ⟨the city was two ~s away⟩ **7 a** : a class session **b** : CREDIT HOUR, SEMESTER HOUR — **after hours** : after the regular quitting or closing time

hour angle *n* (ca. 1837) : the angle between the celestial meridian of an observer and the hour circle of a celestial object measured westward from the meridian

hour circle *n* (1690) : a circle on the celestial sphere that passes through both celestial poles

¹hour·glass \'aú(-ə)r-ˌglas\ *n* (ca. 1515) : an instrument for measuring time consisting of a glass vessel having two compartments from the uppermost of which a quantity of sand, water, or mercury runs in an hour into the lower one

²hourglass *adj* (ca. 1834) : shaped like an hourglass ⟨an ~ figure⟩

hour hand *n* (1669) : the short hand that marks the hours on the face of a watch or clock

hou·ri \'hùr-ē, 'hü-rē\ *n* [F, fr. Per *hūri*, fr. Ar *hūriyah*] (1737) **1** : one of the beautiful maidens that in Muslim belief live with the blessed in paradise **2** : a voluptuously beautiful young woman

hour–long \'aú(-ə)r-ˌlóŋ\ *adj* (1803) : lasting an hour

¹hour·ly \'aú(-ə)r-lē\ *adv* (15c) : at or during every hour; *also* : FREQUENTLY, CONTINUALLY

²hourly *adj* (ca. 1530) **1 a** : occurring hour by hour ⟨~ bus service⟩ **b** : FREQUENT, CONTINUAL ⟨in ~ expectation of the rain's stopping⟩ **2** : computed in terms of an hour ⟨an ~ wage⟩ **3** : paid by the hour ⟨~ workers⟩

¹house \'haús\ *n, pl* **hous·es** \'haú-zəz *also* -səz\ *often attrib* [ME *hous*, fr. OE *hūs*; akin to OHG *hūs* house] (bef. 12c) **1** : a building that serves as living quarters for one or a few families : HOME **2 a** (1) : a shelter or refuge (as a nest or den) of a wild animal (2) : a natural covering (as a test or shell) that encloses and protects an animal or a colony of zooids **b** : a building in which something is housed ⟨a carriage ~⟩ **3 a** : one of the 12 equal sectors in which the celestial sphere is divided in astrology **b** : a zodiacal sign that is the seat of a planet's greatest influence **4** : HOUSEHOLD **b** : a family including ancestors, descendants, and kindred ⟨the ~ of Tudor⟩ **5 a** : a residence for a religious community or for students **b** : the community or students in residence **6 a** : a legislative, deliberative, or consultative assembly; *esp* : one constituting a division of a bicameral body **b** : the building or chamber where such an assembly meets **c** : a quorum of such an assembly **7 a** : a place of business or entertainment **b** (1) : a business organization ⟨a publishing ~⟩ (2) : a gambling establishment **c** : the audience in a theater or concert hall ⟨a full ~ on opening night⟩ **8** : the circular area 12 feet in diameter surrounding the tee and within which a curling stone must rest in order to count **9** : a type of dance music mixed by a disc jockey that features overdubbing with a heavy repetitive drumbeat and repeated electronic melody lines — **house·ful** \'haús-ˌfúl\ *n* — **house·less** \'haú-sləs\ *adj* — **house·less·ness** *n* — **on the house** : without charge : FREE

²house \'haúz\ *vb* **housed; hous·ing** *vt* (bef. 12c) **1 a** : to provide with living quarters or shelter **2** : to store in a house **3** : to encase, enclose, or shelter as if by putting in a house **3** : to serve as shelter for : CONTAIN ~ *vi* : to take shelter : LODGE

house arrest *n* (1936) : confinement often under guard to one's house or quarters instead of in prison

house·boat \'haús-ˌbōt\ *n* (1790) : a boat fitted for use as a dwelling; *esp* : a pleasure craft with a broad beam, a usu. shallow draft, and a large superstructure resembling a house — **house·boat·er** \-ˌbō-tər\ *n*

house·bound \'haús-ˌbaúnd\ *adj* (1878) : confined to the house

house·boy \-ˌbói\ *n* (ca. 1898) : HOUSEMAN

house·break \-ˌbrāk\ *vt* **-broke** \-ˌbrōk\; **-bro·ken** \-ˌbrō-kən\; **-break·ing** [back-formation fr. *housebroken*] (1944) **1** : to make housebroken **2 a** : to teach acceptable social manners to **b** : TAME, SUBDUE

house·break·ing \'haús-ˌbrā-kiŋ\ *n* (1617) : an act of breaking open and entering the dwelling house of another with a felonious purpose — **house·break·er** \-ˌbrā-kər\ *n*

house·bro·ken \-ˌbrō-kən\ *adj* (1900) **1** : trained to excretory habits acceptable in indoor living — used of a household pet **2** : made tractable or polite

house call *n* (1960) : a visit (as by a doctor or a repair person) to a home to provide a requested service

house·carl \-ˌkär(-ə)l\ *n* [OE *hūscarl*, fr. ON *hūskarl*, fr. *hūs* house + *karl* man; akin to OE *ceorl* churl] (bef. 12c) : a member of the bodyguard of a Danish or early English king or noble

house cat *n* (1607) : CAT 1a

house·clean \'haús-ˌklēn\ *vb* [back-formation fr. *housecleaning*] *vi* (1863) **1** : to clean a house and its furniture **2** : to get rid of unwanted or undesirable items or people ~ *vt* **1** : to clean the surfaces and furnishings of **2** : to improve or reform by ridding of undesirable people or practices — **house·clean·ing** *n*

house·coat \'haús-ˌkōt\ *n* (1913) : a woman's often long-skirted informal garment for wear around the house

house cricket *n* (1774) : a widely distributed cricket (*Acheta domesticus*) usu. living in or about dwellings

house detective *n* (1898) : a person who is employed (as by a hotel) to prevent disorderly or improper conduct of patrons

house·dress \'haús-ˌdres\ *n* (1897) : a dress with simple lines that is suitable for housework and is made usu. of a washable fabric

house·fa·ther \-ˌfä-thər, -ˌfä-\ *n* (1901) : a man in charge of a dormitory, hall, or hostel

house finch *n* (1869) : a small finch (*Carpodacus mexicanus*) that has a male with a red head, breast, and rump and that is native to Mexico and the western U.S. and has been introduced in the eastern U.S.

house·fly \'haús-ˌflī\ *n* (15c) : a cosmopolitan dipteran fly (*Musca domestica*) that is often about human habitations and may act as a mechanical vector of diseases (as typhoid fever); *also* : any of various flies of similar appearance or habitat

house·front \-ˌfrənt\ *n* (1838) : the facade of a house

house girl *n* (1835) : HOUSEMAID

house·guest \'haús-ˌgest\ *n* (1917) : GUEST 1a

¹house·hold \'haús-ˌhōld, 'haú-ˌsōld\ *n* (14c) : those who dwell under the same roof and compose a family; *also* : a social unit comprised of those living together in the same dwelling

²household *adj* (14c) **1** : of or relating to a household : DOMESTIC ⟨cooking and other ~ arts⟩ **2** : FAMILIAR, COMMON ⟨a ~ name⟩

house·hold·er \'haús-ˌhōl-dər, 'haú-ˌsōl-\ *n* (14c) : a person who occupies a house or tenement alone or as the head of a household

household troops *n pl* (1711) : troops appointed to attend and guard a sovereign or the residence of a sovereign

house·hus·band \'haús-ˌhəz-bənd\ *n* (1955) : a husband who does housekeeping usu. while his wife earns the family income

house·keep \'haús-ˌkēp\ *vi* **-kept** \-ˌkept\; **-keep·ing** [back-formation fr. *housekeeper*] (1842) : to perform the routine duties (as cooking and cleaning) of managing a house

house·keep·er \-ˌkē-pər\ *n* (1607) **1** : a woman employed to keep house **2** : HOUSEWIFE 1

house·keep·ing \-piŋ\ *n* (1550) **1** : the management of a house and home affairs **2** : the care and management of property and the provision of equipment and services (as for an industrial organization) **3** : the routine tasks that must be done in order for a system to function or to function efficiently

¹hou·sel \'haú-zəl\ *n* [ME, fr. OE *hūsel* sacrifice, Eucharist; akin to Goth *hunsl* sacrifice] (bef. 12c) *archaic* : the Eucharist or the act of administering or receiving it

²housel *vt* (bef. 12c) *archaic* : to administer communion to

house·leek \'haús-ˌlēk\ *n* (14c) : a pink-flowered thick-leaved European plant (*Sempervivum tectorum*) of the orpine family that tends to form clusters of rosettes and is often grown in rock gardens; *broadly* : SEMPERVIVUM

house·lights \'haús-ˌlīts\ *n pl* (1920) : the lights that illuminate the auditorium of a theater

house·maid \'haús-ˌmād\ *n* (ca. 1694) : a female servant employed to do housework

housemaid's knee *n* [so called fr. its occurrence among women who work a great deal on their knees] (1831) : a swelling over the knee due to an enlargement of the bursa in the front of the patella

house·man \'haús-mən, -ˌman\ *n* (1920) : a person who performs general work about a house or hotel

house·mas·ter \-ˌmas-tər\ *n* (1884) : a master in charge of a house in a boy's boarding school

house·mate \'haús-ˌmāt\ *n* (ca. 1810) : a person who lives in the same house with another

house·moth·er \'haús-ˌmə-thər\ *n* (1882) : a woman acting as hostess, chaperon, and often housekeeper in a group residence

house mouse *n* (1835) : a common nearly cosmopolitan grayish-brown mouse (*Mus musculus*) that usu. lives and breeds about buildings, may act as a vector of diseases, and is an important laboratory animal

house of assembly (1653) : a legislative body or the lower house of a legislature (as in various British colonies, protectorates, and countries of the Commonwealth)

House of Burgesses (1658) : the colonial representative assembly of Virginia

house of cards (1903) : a structure, situation, or institution that is insubstantial, shaky, or in constant danger of collapse

House of Commons (1621) : the lower house of the British and Canadian parliaments

house of correction (ca. 1576) : an institution where persons who have committed a minor offense and are considered capable of reformation are confined

house of delegates (1783) : HOUSE 6a; *esp* : the lower house of the state legislature in Maryland, Virginia, and West Virginia

House of Lords (1818) : the upper house of the British Parliament composed of the lords temporal and spiritual

house of representatives (1716) : the lower house of a legislative body (as the U.S. Congress)

house of studies (1929) : an educational institution serving scholars of a religious order — called also *house of study*

house organ *n* (1907) : a periodical distributed by a business concern among its employees, sales personnel, or customers

house·paint·er \'haús-ˌpān-tər\ *n* (1689) : one whose business or occupation is painting houses

house·par·ent \-ˌpar-ənt, -ˌper-\ *n* : an adult in charge of a dormitory, hall, hostel, or group residence

house party *n* (1876) : a party lasting over one or more nights at a residence (as a home or fraternity house)

house·per·son \'haús-ˌpər-sᵊn\ *n* (1974) : a person who does housekeeping

house·plant \'haús-ˌplant\ *n* (1871) : a plant grown or kept indoors

house·proud \'haús-ˌpraúd\ *adj* (1849) *chiefly Brit* : proud of one's house or housekeeping

hous·er \'haú-zər\ *n* (1940) : one that promotes or administers housing projects

house·rais·ing \'haús-ˌrā-ziŋ\ *n* (1704) : the joint erection of a house or its framework by a gathering of neighbors

house·room \-ˌrüm, -ˌrúm\ *n* (1582) : space for accommodation in or as if in a house ⟨given ~ by a family all too eager to have a celebrity in their midst —Walter Kerr⟩

house rule *n* (1947) : a rule (as in a game) that applies only among a certain group or in a certain place

house seat *n* (1948) : a theater seat reserved by the management for a special guest

house sitter *n* (1971) : a person who occupies a dwelling to provide security and maintenance while the tenant is away — **house–sit** \'haú(s)-ˌsit\ *vi* — **house–sit·ting** \-ˌsi-tiŋ\ *n*

house sparrow *n* (1674) : a sparrow (*Passer domesticus*) native to Eurasia that has been introduced worldwide and is found esp. in urban and agricultural areas — called also *English sparrow*

house-to-house \ˌhaús-tə-'haús\ *adj* (1859) : going or done by going from one building to the next ⟨~ fighting⟩

house·top \'haús-ˌtäp\ *n* (1526) : ROOF; *esp* : the level surface of a flat roof — **from the housetops** : for all to hear : OPENLY ⟨shouting their grievances *from the housetops*⟩

house trailer *n* (1937) : MOBILE HOME

house-train \'haus-,trān\ vt (1924) chiefly Brit : HOUSEBREAK
house-wares \'haus-,warz, -,werz\ n pl (1921) : furnishings for a house; esp : small articles of household equipment (as cooking utensils or small appliances)
house-warm-ing \'haus-,wor-miŋ\ n (1577) : a party to celebrate the taking possession of a house or premises
house-wife \'haus-,wif; esp 2 & in early poetry 'hə-zəf or -səf\ n, pl **house-wives** \'haus-,wīvz also 'hauz-,wivz; 'hə-zəfs, -zəvz, -səfs, -səvz\ (13c) 1 : a married woman in charge of a household 2 : a pocket-size container for small articles (as thread) — **house-wife-li-ness** \-lē-nəs\ n — **house-wife-ly** \-lē\ adj — **house-wif-ery** \-,wī-f(ə-)rē; Brit -(,)wī-f(ə-)rē also 'hə-zə-frē\ n — **house-wif-ey** \'haus-,wi-fē\ adj
house-work \'haus-,wərk\ n (1841) : the work of housekeeping
1hous-ing \'hau-ziŋ\ n (14c) 1 a : SHELTER, LODGING b : dwellings provided for people 2 a : a niche for a sculpture b : the space taken out of a structural member (as a timber) to admit the insertion of part of another 3 : something that covers or protects: as a : a case or enclosure (as for a mechanical part or an instrument) b : a casing (as an enclosed bearing) in which a shaft revolves c : a support (as a frame) for mechanical parts
2housing n [ME, fr. house housing (fr. MF houce, of Gmc origin) + -ing; akin to MHG hult covering] (15c) : CAPARISON 1
housing development n (1951) : a group of individual dwellings or apartment houses typically of similar design that are usu. built and sold or leased by one management
housing estate n (1920) Brit : HOUSING DEVELOPMENT
housing project n (ca. 1937) : a publicly supported and administered housing development planned usu. for low-income families
Hou-yhn-hnm \'hwi-nəm, hü-'i-nəm\ n : a member of a race of horses endowed with reason in Swift's Gulliver's Travels
hove past and past part of HEAVE
hov-el \'hə-vəl, 'hä-\ n [ME] (15c) 1 : an open shed or shelter 2 : TABERNACLE 3 : a small, wretched, and often dirty house : HUT
hov-er \'hə-vər, 'hä-\ vi hov-ered; hov-er-ing \-v(ə-)riŋ\ [ME hoveren, freq. of hoven to hover] (15c) 1 a : to hang fluttering in the air or on the wing b : to remain suspended over a place or object 2 a : to move to and fro near a place : fluctuate around a given point (unemployment ~ed around 10%) b : to be in a state of uncertainty, irresolution, or suspense — **hov-er** n — **hov-er-er** \-vər-ər\ n
hov-er-craft \-vər-,kraft\ n (1959) : a vehicle that is supported above the surface of land or water by a cushion of air produced by downwardly directed fans
1how \'hau\ adv [ME, fr. OE hū; akin to OHG hwuo how, OE hwā who — more at WHO] (bef. 12c) 1 a : in what manner or way b : for what reason (~ c : with what meaning : to what effect d : by what name or title (~ art thou called —Shak.) 2 : to what degree or extent 3 : in what state or condition (~ are you) 4 : at what price (~ a score of ewes now —Shak.) — **how about** : what do you say to or think of (how about it, are you going?) — **how come** : how does it happen that : WHY
2how conj (bef. 12c) 1 a : the way or manner in which (remember ~ they fought); also : the state or condition in which b : THAT (told them ~ he had a situation —Charles Dickens) 2 : HOWEVER, AS (a reader can shift his attention ~ he likes —William Empson)
3how \'hau\ n (1533) 1 : a question about manner or method 2 : MANNER, METHOD
1how-be-it \hau-'bē-ət\ conj (14c) : ALTHOUGH
2howbeit adv (15c) : NEVERTHELESS
how-dah \'hau-də\ n [Hindi hauda, fr. Ar hawdaj] (1774) : a seat or covered pavilion on the back of an elephant or camel
how-dy \'hau-dē\ interj [alter. of how do ye] (1712) — used to express greeting — **howdy** vb
howe \'hau, 'hō\ n [ME (northern) holl hollow place, fr. OE hol, fr. hol, adj., hollow — more at HOLE] (12c) Scot : HOLLOW, VALLEY
1how-ev-er \hau-'e-vər\ conj (14c) 1 : in whatever manner or way that (will help ~ I can) 2 archaic : ALTHOUGH
2however adv (14c) 1 a : in whatever manner or way (shall serve you, sir, truly, ~ else —Shak.) b : to whatever degree or extent (has done this for ~ many thousands of years —Emma Hawkridge) 2 : in spite of that : on the other hand (still seems possible, ~, that conditions will improve) (would like to go; ~, I think I'd better not) 3 : how in the world (~ did you manage to do it)
howff or **howf** \'hauf, 'hōf\ n [D hof enclosure; akin to OE hof enclosure, and perh. to hufil hill] (1711) Scot : HAUNT, RESORT
how-it-zer \'hau-ət-sər\ n [D houwitser, ultim. fr. Czech houfnice ballista] (1695) : a short cannon used to fire projectiles at medium muzzle velocities and with relatively high trajectories
howl \'hau(ə)l\ vb [ME houlen; akin to MHG hiulen to howl] (14c) 1 : to emit a loud sustained doleful sound characteristic of members of the dog family 2 : to cry out loudly and without restraint under strong impulse (as pain, grief, or amusement) 3 : to go on a spree or rampage ~ vt 1 : to utter with unrestrained outcry 2 : to drown out or cause to fail by adverse outcry — used esp. with down (~ed down the speaker) — **howl** n
howl-er \'hau-lər\ n (1800) 1 a : one that howls b : HOWLER MONKEY 2 : a humorous and ridiculous blunder
howler monkey n (1932) : any of a genus (Alouatta) of So. and Central American monkeys that have a long prehensile tail and enlargement of the hyoid and laryngeal apparatus enabling them to make loud howling noises
howl-ing \'hau-liŋ\ adj (1599) 1 : producing or marked by a sound resembling a sustained howl (a ~ storm) 2 : DESOLATE, WILD (a ~ wilderness) 3 : very great : PRONOUNCED (a ~ success) — **howl-ing-ly** adv
how-so-ev-er \,hau-sə-'we-vər\ adv (14c) 1 : in whatever manner 2 : to whatever degree or extent
1how-to \'hau-tü\ adj (1926) : giving practical instruction and advice (as on a craft) (~ books on all sorts of hobbies —Harry Milt)

howdah

2how-to n (1954) : a practical method or instruction (the ~s of balancing a checkbook)
1hoy \'hoi\ interj [ME] (14c) — used in attracting attention or in driving animals
2hoy n [ME, fr. MD hoei] (15c) 1 : a small usu. sloop-rigged coasting ship 2 : a heavy barge for bulky cargo
hoya \'hoi-(y)ə\ n [NL, fr. Thomas Hoy †1821 Eng. gardener] (1851) : any of a genus (Hoya) of climbing Asian and Australian evergreen shrubs of the milkweed family
hoy-den \'hoi-dᵊn\ n [perh. fr. obs D heiden country lout, fr. MD, heathen; akin to OE hǣthen heathen] (1676) : a girl or woman of saucy, boisterous, or carefree behavior — **hoy-den-ish** \-ish\ adj
hoyle \'hoi(ə)l\ n, often cap [Edmond Hoyle †1769 Eng. writer on games] (1906) : an encyclopedia of the rules of indoor games and esp. card games
Hsia \shē-'ä\ n [Chin (Beijing) Xià] (ca. 1909) : the legendary first dynasty of Chinese history traditionally dated from about 2200–1766 B.C.
HTLV \,āch-(,)tē-(,)el-'vē\ n [human T-cell lymphotropic virus] (1980) : any of several retroviruses — often used with a number or Roman numeral to indicate type
HTLV-III \-(,)vē-'thrē\ n (1984) : HIV-1
hua-ra-che \wə-'rä-chē, hə-\ n [MexSp, fr. Tarascan kʷaráčī] (1892) : a low-heeled sandal having an upper made of interwoven leather strips
hub \'həb\ n [prob. alter. of 2hob] (1649) 1 : the central part of a circular object (as a wheel or propeller) 2 a : a center of activity : FOCAL POINT b : an airport or city through which an airline routes most of its traffic 3 : a steel punch from which a working die for a coin or medal is made
hub-and-spoke adj (1980) : being or relating to a system of routing air traffic in which a major airport serves as a central point for coordinating flights to and from other airports
Hub-bard squash \'hə-bərd-\ n [prob. fr. the name Hubbard] (1868) : any of various often large variably green winter squashes — called also Hubbard
hub-ble-bub-ble \'hə-bəl-,bə-bəl\ n [redupl. of bubble] (1634) 1 : WATER PIPE 2 : a flurry of sound or activity : COMMOTION
hub-bub \'hə-,bəb\ n [perh. of Ir origin; akin to ScGael ub ub, interj. of contempt] (1555) 1 : NOISE, UPROAR 2 : CONFUSION, TURMOIL
hub-by \'hə-bē\ n, pl **hubbies** [by alter.] (1688) : HUSBAND
hub-cap \'həb-,kap\ n (1903) : a removable usu. metal cap over the end of an axle; esp : one used on the wheel of a motor vehicle
hu-bris \'hyü-brəs\ n [Gk hybris] (1884) : exaggerated pride or self-confidence — **hu-bris-tic** \hyü-'bris-tik\ adj
huck \'hək\ n (1851) : HUCKABACK
huck-a-back \'hə-kə-,bak\ n [origin unknown] (1690) : an absorbent durable fabric of cotton, linen, or both used chiefly for towels
huck-le-ber-ry \'hə-kəl-,ber-ē\ n [perh. alter. of hurtleberry (huckleberry)] (1670) 1 : any of a genus (Gaylussacia) of American shrubs of the heath family; also : the edible dark blue to black usu. acid berry (esp. of G. baccata) with 10 nutlets 2 : BLUEBERRY
1huck-ster \'hək-stər\ n [ME hukster, fr. MD hokester, fr. hoeken to peddle] (13c) 1 : HAWKER, PEDDLER 2 : one who produces promotional material for commercial clients esp. for radio or television — **huck-ster-ism** \-stə-,ri-zəm\ n
2huckster vb **huck-stered; huck-ster-ing** \-st(ə-)riŋ\ vi (1592) : HAGGLE ~ vt 1 : to deal in or bargain over 2 : to promote by showmanship
hud-dle \'hə-dᵊl\ vb hud-dled; hud-dling \'həd-liŋ, 'hə-dᵊl-iŋ\ [prob. fr. or akin to ME hoderen to huddle] vt (1579) 1 Brit : to arrange carelessly or hurriedly 2 a : to crowd together b : to draw (oneself) together : CROUCH 3 : to wrap closely in (as clothes) ~ vi 1 a : to gather in a close-packed group b : to curl up : CROUCH 2 a : to hold a consultation b : to gather in a huddle in football — **hud-dler** \'həd-lər, 'hə-dᵊl-ər\ n
2huddle n (1586) 1 : a close-packed group : BUNCH (~s of children) (a ~ of cottages) 2 a : MEETING, CONFERENCE (secret ~s were held by five leading Republicans —Newsweek) b : a brief gathering of football players away from the line of scrimmage to receive instructions (as from the quarterback) for the next down
Hu-di-bras-tic \,hyü-də-'bras-tik\ adj [irreg. fr. Hudibras, satirical poem by Samuel Butler †1680] (1712) 1 : written in humorous octosyllabic couplets 2 : MOCK-HEROIC — **Hudibrastic** n
hue \'hyü\ n [ME hewe, fr. OE hīw; akin to ON hȳ plant down, Goth hiwi form] (bef. 12c) 1 : COMPLEXION, ASPECT (political parties of every ~ —Louis Wasserman) 2 a : COLOR b : gradation of color c : the attribute of colors that permits them to be classed as red, yellow, green, blue, or an intermediate between any contiguous pair of these colors — compare BRIGHTNESS 2, LIGHTNESS 2, SATURATION 4
hue and cry n [hue (outcry)] (15c) 1 a : a loud outcry formerly used in the pursuit of one who is suspected of a crime b : the pursuit of a suspect or a written proclamation for the capture of a suspect 2 : a clamor of alarm or protest 3 : HUBBUB
hued \'hyüd\ adj (bef. 12c) : COLORED — usu. used in combination (green-hued)
1huff \'həf\ vb [imit.] vi (1583) 1 : to emit puffs (as of breath or steam) 2 a : to make empty threats : BLUSTER b : to react or behave indignantly (~ed off in anger) ~ vt 1 : to puff up : INFLATE 2 archaic : to treat with contempt : BULLY 3 : to make angry 4 : to utter with indignation or scorn
2huff n (1599) : a usu. peevish and transitory spell of anger or resentment (quit in a ~) syn see OFFENSE
huff-ish \'hə-fish\ adj (ca. 1755) : ARROGANT, SULKY
huffy \'hə-fē\ adj **huff-i-er; -est** (1677) 1 : HAUGHTY, ARROGANT 2 a : roused to indignation : IRRITATED b : easily offended : TOUCHY — **huff-i-ly** \'hə-fə-lē\ adv — **huff-i-ness** \-fē-nəs\ n
hug \'həg\ vt hugged; hug-ging [perh. of Scand origin; akin to ON

\ə\ abut \ᵊ\ kitten, F table \ər\ further \a\ ash \ā\ ace \ä\ mop, mar
\au̇\ out \ch\ chin \e\ bet \ē\ easy \g\ go \i\ hit \ī\ ice \j\ job
\ŋ\ sing \ō\ go \ȯ\ law \ȯi\ boy \th\ thin \t͟h\ the \ü\ loot \u̇\ foot
\y\ yet \zh\ vision \á, k̲, ⁿ, œ, œ̄, ᵫ, ᵫ̄, ᵊ\ see Guide to Pronunciation

hugga to soothe] (1567)   **1** : to press tightly esp. in the arms   **2 a** : CONGRATULATE   **b** : to hold fast : CHERISH ⟨*hugged* his miseries like a sulky child —John Buchan⟩   **3** : to stay close to ⟨the road ~s the river⟩ — **hug** *n* — **hug·ga·ble** \'hə-gə-bəl\ *adj*

huge \'hyüj, 'yüj\ *adj* **hug·er; hug·est** [ME, fr. OF *ahuge*] (12c) : very large or extensive: as   **a** : of great size or area   **b** : great in scale or degree ⟨a ~ deficit⟩   **c** : great in scope or character ⟨a man of ~ talent⟩   *syn* see ENORMOUS — **huge·ly** *adv* — **huge·ness** *n*

huge·ous \'hyü-jəs, 'yü-\ *adj* (1519) : HUGE — **huge·ous·ly** *adv*

¹hug·ger–mug·ger \'hə-gər-,mə-gər\ *n* [origin unknown] (1529)   **1** : SECRECY   **2** : CONFUSION, MUDDLE

²hugger–mugger (1692)   **1** : SECRET   **2** : of a confused or disorderly nature : JUMBLED — **hugger–mugger** *adv*

hug—me—tight \'həg-mē-,tīt\ *n* (1860) : a woman's short usu. knitted sleeveless close-fitting jacket

Hu·gue·not \'hyü-gə-,nät\ *n* [MF, alter. of MF dial. *eyguenot*, adherent of a Swiss political movement, fr. G dial. *Eidgnosse* confederate] (1565) : a member of the French Reformed communion esp. of the 16th and 17th centuries — **Hu·gue·not·ic** \,hyü-gə-'nä-tik\ *adj* — **Hu·gue·not·ism** \'hyü-gə-,nä-,ti-zəm\ *n*

huh \a *grunt articulated as a syllabic* m *or* n *with a voiceless onset, or as the syllable* 'hə *or* 'hə^n, *often ending in a glottal stop, and uttered with a range of intonations; often read as* 'hə\ *interj* [imit. of a grunt] (1608) — used to express surprise, disbelief, or confusion, or as an inquiry inviting affirmative reply

Hui·chol \wē-'chōl\ *n, pl* **Huichol** *or* **Hui·cho·les** [MexSp] (1900)   **1** : a member of an American Indian people of the mountains between Zacatecas and Nayarit, Mexico   **2** : the Uto-Aztecan language of the Huichol people — **Huichol** *adj*

hui·sa·che \wē-'sä-chē\ *n* [MexSp, fr. Nahuatl *huixachi*, fr. *huitzli* thorn + *ixachi* a great amount, many] (1838) : a widely cultivated thorny shrubby acacia (*Acacia farnesiana*) of the southern U.S. and tropical America

hu·la \'hü-lə\ *also* **hu·la–hu·la** \,hü-lə-'hü-lə\ *n* [Hawaiian] (1825) : a sinuous Polynesian dance characterized by rhythmic movement of the hips and mimetic gestures with the hands and often accompanied by chants and rhythmic drumming

hula hoop *n* (1958) : a plastic hoop that is twirled around the body

¹hulk \'həlk\ *n* [ME *hulke*, fr. OE *hulc*, prob. fr. ML *holcas*, fr. Gk *holkas*, fr. *helkein* to pull — more at SULCUS] (bef. 12c)   **1 a** : a heavy clumsy ship   **b** (1) : the body of an old ship unfit for service   (2) : a ship used as a prison — usu. used in pl. ⟨every prisoner sent to the ~s —Kenneth Roberts⟩   **2** : an abandoned wreck or shell (as of a building or automobile)   **3** : one that is bulky or unwieldy ⟨a big ~ of a man⟩

²hulk *vi* (ca. 1825)   **1** *dial Eng* : to move ponderously   **2** : to appear impressively large or massive : LOOM

hulk·ing \'həl-kiŋ\ *adj* (1698) : PONDEROUS, MASSIVE

¹hull \'həl\ *n* [ME, fr. OE *hulu*; akin to OHG *hala* hull, OE *helan* to conceal — more at HELL] (bef. 12c)   **1 a** : the outer covering of a fruit or seed   **b** : the persistent calyx or involucre that subtends some fruits   **2 a** : the frame or body of a ship or boat exclusive of masts, yards, sails, and rigging   **b** : the main body of a usu. large or heavy craft or vehicle (as an airship or tank)   **3** : COVERING, CASING — **hull–less** \'həl-ləs\ *adj*

²hull *vt* (14c) : to remove the hulls of : SHUCK — **hull·er** *n*

hul·la·ba·loo \'hə-lə-bə-,lü\ *n, pl* **-loos** [perh. fr. *hallo* + Sc *balloo*, interj. used to hush children] (1762) : DIN; *also* : UPROAR

hull down *adv or adj* (1775) *of a ship* : at such a distance that only the superstructure is visible

hulled corn *n* (1788) : whole grain corn from which the hulls have been removed by soaking or boiling in lye water

hul·lo \(,)hə-'lō\ *chiefly Brit var of* HELLO

¹hum \'həm\ *vb* **hummed; hum·ming** [ME *hummen;* akin to MHG *hummen* to hum, MD *hommel* bumblebee] *vi* (14c)   **1 a** : to utter a sound like that of the speech sound \m\ prolonged   **b** : to make the natural noise of an insect in motion or a similar sound : DRONE   **c** : to give forth a low continuous blend of sound   **2 a** : to be busily active ⟨the museum *hummed* with visitors⟩   **b** : to run smoothly ⟨the business started to ~⟩ ~ *vt*   **1** : to sing with the lips closed and without articulation ⟨*hummed* his displeasure⟩   **2** : to affect or express by humming ⟨*hummed* his displeasure⟩ — **hum** *n* — **hum·ma·ble** \'hə-mə-bəl\ *adj*

²hum *chiefly Brit var of* HEM

¹hu·man \'hyü-mən, 'yü-\ *adj* [ME *humain*, fr. MF, fr. L *humanus;* akin to L *homo* human being — more at HOMAGE] (14c)   **1** : of, relating to, or characteristic of humans   **2** : consisting of humans   **3 a** : having human form or attributes   **b** : susceptible to or representative of the sympathies and frailties of human nature ⟨such an inconsistency is very —P. E. More⟩ — **hu·man·ness** \-mən-nəs\ *n*

²human *n* (ca. 1533) : a bipedal primate mammal (*Homo sapiens*) : MAN; *broadly* : any living or extinct member of the family (Hominidae) to which the primate belongs — **hu·man·like** \-mən-,līk\ *adj*

human being *n* (1800) : HUMAN

hu·mane \hyü-'mān, yü-\ *adj* [ME *humain*] (ca. 1500)   **1** : marked by compassion, sympathy, or consideration for humans or animals   **2** : characterized by or tending to broad humanistic culture : HUMANISTIC ⟨~ studies⟩ — **hu·mane·ly** *adv* — **hu·mane·ness** \-'mān-nəs\ *n*

human ecology *n* (1907)   **1** : a branch of sociology dealing esp. with the spatial and temporal interrelationships between humans and their economic, social, and political organization   **2** : the ecology of human communities and populations esp. as concerned with preservation of environmental quality (as of air or water) through proper application of conservation and civil engineering practices

human engineering *n* (1920)   **1** : management of humans and their affairs esp. in industry   **2** : ERGONOMICS

human immunodeficiency virus *n* (1986) : HIV

hu·man·ism \'hyü-mə-,ni-zəm, 'yü-\ *n* (1832)   **1 a** : devotion to the humanities : literary culture   **b** : the revival of classical letters, individualistic and critical spirit, and emphasis on secular concerns characteristic of the Renaissance   **2** : HUMANITARIANISM   **3** : a doctrine, attitude, or way of life centered on human interests or values; *esp* : a philosophy that usu. rejects supernaturalism and stresses an individual's dignity and worth and capacity for self-realization through reason

— **hu·man·ist** \-nist\ *n or adj* — **hu·man·is·tic** \,hyü-mə-'nis-tik, ,yü-\ *adj* — **hu·man·is·ti·cal·ly** \-ti-k(ə-)lē\ *adv*

hu·man·i·tar·i·an \hyü-,ma-nə-'ter-ē-ən, yü-\ *n* (1844) : a person promoting human welfare and social reform : PHILANTHROPIST — **humanitarian** *adj* — **hu·man·i·tar·i·an·ism** \-ē-ə-,ni-zəm\ *n*

hu·man·i·ty \hyü-'ma-nə-tē, yü-\ *n, pl* **-ties** (14c)   **1** : the quality or state of being humane   **2 a** : the quality or state of being human   **b** *pl* : human attributes or qualities ⟨his work has the ripeness of the 18th century, and its rough *humanities* —Pamela H. Johnson⟩   **3** *pl* : the branches of learning (as philosophy or languages) that investigate human constructs and concerns as opposed to natural processes (as in physics or chemistry)   **4** : MANKIND 1

hu·man·ize \'hyü-mə-,nīz, 'yü-\ *vt* **-ized; -iz·ing** (1603)   **1 a** : to represent as human : attribute human qualities to   **b** : to adapt to human nature or use   **2** : to make humane — **hu·man·iza·tion** \,hyü-mə-nə-'zā-shən, ,yü-\ *n* — **hu·man·iz·er** *n*

hu·man·kind \'hyü-mən-,kīnd, 'yü-\ *n sing but sing or pl in constr* (ca. 1645) : the human race

hu·man·ly \'hyü-mən-lē, 'yü-\ *adv* (15c)   **1 a** : with regard to human needs and emotions ⟨provide ~ for those who are not needed in the economy —E. F. Bacon⟩   **b** : with regard to or in keeping with human proneness to error or weakness ⟨~ inaccurate⟩   **2 a** : from a human viewpoint ⟨~ speaking, the process works . . . like this —Elizabeth Janeway⟩   **b** : within the range of human capacity ⟨did everything ~ possible⟩   **c** : by humans ⟨~ made⟩

human nature *n* (1668) : the nature of humans; *esp* : the fundamental dispositions and traits of humans

hu·man·oid \'hyü-mə-,nȯid, 'yü-\ *adj* (1918) : having human form or characteristics ⟨~ dentition⟩ ⟨~ robots⟩ — **humanoid** *n*

human relations *n pl but usu sing in constr* (1946)   **1** : a study of human problems arising from organizational and interpersonal relations (as in industry)   **2** : a course, study, or program designed to develop better interpersonal and intergroup adjustments

human resources *n pl* (1975) : PERSONNEL 1a, 2 ⟨director of *human resources*⟩

human rights *n pl* (1791) : rights (as freedom from unlawful imprisonment, torture, and execution) regarded as belonging fundamentally to all persons

hu·mate \'hyü-,māt, 'yü-\ *n* (1844) : a salt or ester of a humic acid

¹hum·ble \'həm-bəl *also chiefly Southern* 'əm-\ *adj* **hum·bler** \-b(ə-)lər\; **hum·blest** \-b(ə-)ləst\ [ME, fr. OF, fr. L *humilis* low, humble, fr. *humus* earth; akin to Gk *chthōn* earth, *chamai* on the ground] (13c)   **1** : not proud or haughty : not arrogant or assertive   **2** : reflecting, expressing, or offered in a spirit of deference or submission ⟨a ~ apology⟩   **3 a** : ranking low in a hierarchy or scale : INSIGNIFICANT, UNPRETENTIOUS   **b** : not costly or luxurious ⟨a ~ contraption⟩ — **hum·ble·ness** \-bəl-nəs\ *n* — **hum·bly** \-blē\ *adv*

²humble *vt* **hum·bled; hum·bling** \-b(ə-)liŋ\ (14c)   **1** : to make humble in spirit or manner   **2** : to destroy the power, independence, or prestige of — **hum·bler** \-b(ə-)lər\ *n* — **hum·bling·ly** \-b(ə-)liŋ-lē\ *adv*

hum·ble–bee \'həm-bəl-,bē\ *n* [ME *humbylbee*, fr. *humbyl-* (akin to MD *hommel* bumblebee) + *bee* — more at HUM] (15c) : BUMBLEBEE

humble pie *n* (1830) : a figurative serving of humiliation usu. in the form of a forced submission, apology, or retraction — often used in the phrase *eat humble pie*

¹hum·bug \'həm-,bəg\ *n* [origin unknown] (1751)   **1 a** : something designed to deceive and mislead   **b** : a willfully false, deceptive, or insincere person   **2** : an attitude or spirit of pretense and deception   **3** : NONSENSE, DRIVEL   **4** *Brit* : a hard usu. mint-flavored candy   *syn* see IMPOSTURE — **hum·bug·gery** \-,bə-g(ə-)rē\ *n*

²humbug *vb* **hum·bugged; hum·bug·ging** *vt* (1751) : DECEIVE, HOAX ~ *vi* : to engage in a hoax or deception

hum·ding·er \'həm-'diŋ-ər\ *n* [prob. alter. of *hummer*] (ca. 1904) : a striking or extraordinary person or thing

hum·drum \'həm-,drəm\ *adj* [redupl. of *hum*] (1553) : MONOTONOUS, DULL — **humdrum** *n*

hu·mec·tant \hyü-'mek-tənt\ *n* [L *humectant-, humectans*, prp. of *humectare* to moisten, fr. *humectus* moist, fr. *humēre* to be moist — more at HUMOR] (ca. 1857) : a substance that promotes retention of moisture — **humectant** *adj*

hu·mer·al \'hyü-mə-rəl\ *adj* (1615)   **1** : of, relating to, or situated in the region of the humerus or shoulder   **2** : of, relating to, or being a body part analogous to the humerus or shoulder — **humeral** *n*

humeral veil *n* (1853) : an oblong vestment worn around the shoulders and over the hands by a priest holding a sacred vessel

hu·mer·us \'hyü-mə-rəs\ *n, pl* **hu·meri** \-,rī, -,rē\ [ME, fr. L *humerus, umerus* upper arm, shoulder; akin to Goth *ams* shoulder, Gk *ōmos*] (15c) : the long bone of the upper arm or forelimb extending from the shoulder to the elbow

hu·mic \'hyü-mik, 'yü-\ *adj* (1844) : of, relating to, or derived at least in part from humus

humic acid *n* (1844) : any of various organic acids obtained from humus

hu·mid \'hyü-məd, 'yü-\ *adj* [F or L; F *humide*, fr. L *humidus*, fr. *humēre*] (15c) : containing or characterized by perceptible moisture esp. to the point of being oppressive   *syn* see WET — **hu·mid·ly** *adv*

hu·mid·i·fi·er \hyü-'mi-də-,fī(-ə)r, yü-\ *n* (1884) : a device for supplying or maintaining humidity

hu·mid·i·fy \-,fī\ *vt* **-fied; -fy·ing** (1885) : to make humid — **hu·mid·i·fi·ca·tion** \-,mi-də-fə-'kā-shən\ *n*

hu·mid·i·stat \hyü-'mi-də-,stat, yü-\ *n* (ca. 1904) : an instrument for regulating or maintaining the degree of humidity

hu·mid·i·ty \hyü-'mi-də-tē, yü-\ *n, pl* **-ties** (15c) : a moderate degree of wetness esp. of the atmosphere — compare RELATIVE HUMIDITY

hu·mi·dor \'hyü-mə-,dȯr, 'yü-\ *n* [*humid* + *-or* (as in *cuspidor*)] (1903) : a case or enclosure (as for storing cigars) in which the air is kept properly humidified

hu·mi·fi·ca·tion \,hyü-mə-fə-'kā-shən, ,yü-\ *n* (1897) : formation or conversion into humus

hu·mi·fied \'hyü-mə-,fīd, 'yü-\ *adj* (1906) : converted into humus

hu·mil·i·ate \hyü-'mi-lē-,āt, yü-\ *vt* **-at·ed; -at·ing** [LL *humiliatus*, pp. of *humiliare*, fr. L *humilis* low — more at HUMBLE] (ca. 1534) : to re-

duce to a lower position in one's own eyes or others' eyes : MORTIFY —
hu·mil·i·a·tion \-ˌmi-lē-'ā-shən\ n
hu·mil·i·at·ing \'hyü-'mi-lē-ˌā-tiŋ, yü-\ adj (1757) : extremely destructive to one's self-respect or dignity : HUMBLING — **hu·mil·i·at·ing·ly** \-tiŋ-lē\ adv
hu·mil·i·ty \hyü-'mi-lə-tē, yü-\ n (14c) : the quality or state of being humble
hum·mer \'hə-mər\ n (1605)   1 : one that hums   2 : HUMMINGBIRD   3 : HUMDINGER   4 : FASTBALL
hum·ming·bird \'hə-miŋ-ˌbərd\ n (1637) : any of a family (Trochilidae) of tiny brightly colored nonpasserine New World birds related to the swifts and like them having narrow wings with long primaries, a slender bill, and a very extensile tongue
hum·mock \'hə-mək\ n [alter. of ²hammock] (1555)   1 : a rounded knoll or hillock   2 : a ridge of ice   3 : ²HAMMOCK 2 — **hummock** vb — **hum·mocky** \-mə-kē\ adj
hum·mus \'hə-məs, 'hu̇-\ n [Ar ḥummuṣ chickpeas] (1950) : a paste of pureed chickpeas usu. mixed with sesame oil or sesame paste and eaten as a dip or sandwich spread
hu·mon·gous \hyü-'məŋ-gəs, yü-, -'mäŋ-\ also **hu·mun·gous** \-'məŋ-gəs\ adj [perh. alter. of huge + monstrous] (ca. 1967) : extremely large : HUGE
¹**hu·mor** \'hyü-mər, 'yü-\ n [ME humour, fr. MF humeur, fr. ML & L; ML humor, fr. L humor, umor moisture; akin to ON vǫkr damp, L humēre to be moist, and perh. to Gk hygros wet] (14c)   1 a : a normal functioning bodily semifluid or fluid (as the blood or lymph)   b : a secretion (as a hormone) that is an excitant of activity   2 a in medieval physiology : a fluid or juice of an animal or plant; specif : one of the four fluids entering into the constitution of the body and determining by their relative proportions a person's health and temperament   b : characteristic or habitual disposition or bent : TEMPERAMENT ⟨of cheerful ∼⟩   c : an often temporary state of mind imposed esp. by circumstances ⟨was in no ∼ to listen⟩   d : a sudden, unpredictable, or unreasoning inclination : WHIM ⟨the uncertain ∼s of nature⟩   3 a : that quality which appeals to a sense of the ludicrous or absurdly incongruous   b : the mental faculty of discovering, expressing, or appreciating the ludicrous or absurdly incongruous   c : something that is or is designed to be comical or amusing syn see WIT — out of humor : out of sorts
²**humor** vt **hu·mored; hu·mor·ing** \'hyüm-riŋ, 'yüm-, 'hyü-mə-, 'yü-\ (1588)   1 : to soothe or content by indulgence   2 : to adapt oneself to syn see INDULGE
hu·mor·al \'hyü-mə-rəl, 'yü-\ adj (15c)   1 : of, relating to, proceeding from, or involving a bodily humor (as a hormone)   2 : relating to or being the part of immunity or the immune response that involves antibodies secreted by B cells and circulating in bodily fluids
hu·mor·esque \ˌhyü-mə-'resk, ˌyü-\ n [G Humoreske, fr. Humor, fr. ML] (1889) : a typically whimsical or fanciful musical composition
hu·mor·ist \'hyü-mə-rist, 'yü-\ n (1589)   1 archaic : a person subject to whims   2 : a person specializing in or noted for humor
hu·mor·is·tic \ˌhyü-mə-'ris-tik, ˌyü-\ adj (1818) : HUMOROUS
hu·mor·less \'hyü-mər-ləs\ adj (ca. 1847)   1 : lacking a sense of humor   2 : lacking humorous characteristics — **hu·mor·less·ly** \-lē\ adv — **hu·mor·less·ness** n
hu·mor·ous \'hyüm-rəs, 'yüm-, 'hyü-mə-, 'yü-\ adj (15c)   1 obs : HUMID   2 a : full of or characterized by humor : JOCULAR   b : indicating or expressive of a sense of humor syn see WITTY — **hu·mor·ous·ly** adv — **hu·mor·ous·ness** n
hu·mour chiefly Brit var of HUMOR
¹**hump** \'həmp\ n [akin to MLG hump bump] (1709)   1 : a rounded protuberance: as   a : HUMPBACK 1   b : a fleshy protuberance on the back of an animal (as a camel, bison, or whale)   c (1) : MOUND, HUMMOCK   (2) : MOUNTAIN, RANGE ⟨the Himalayan ∼⟩   2 Brit : a fit of depression or sulking   3 : a difficult, trying, or critical phase or obstacle — often used in the phrase over the hump — **humped** adj
²**hump** vt (1835)   1 : to copulate with — often considered vulgar   2 : to exert (oneself) vigorously   3 : to make humpbacked : HUNCH   4 chiefly Brit : to put or carry on the back : LUG; also : TRANSPORT ∼ vi   1 : to exert oneself : HUSTLE   2 : to move swiftly : RACE
hump·back \-ˌbak, for 1 also -'bak\ n (1697)   1 : a humped or crooked back; also : KYPHOSIS   2 : HUNCHBACK 1   3 : HUMPBACK WHALE   4 : PINK SALMON
hump·backed \-'bakt\ adj (1681)   1 : having a humped back   2 : convexly curved ⟨a ∼ bridge⟩
humpback whale n (1725) : a large baleen whale (Megaptera novaeangliae) that is black above and white below and has very long flippers, and fleshy tubercles along the snout

humpback whale

¹**humph** \'həm(p)f\ vi (1814) : to utter a humph ∼ vt : to utter (as a remark) in a tone suggestive of a humph
²**humph** \a snort articulated as a syllabic m or n with a voiceless onset and ending in a nasal h or a glottal stop; often read as 'həm(p)f\ interj [imit. of a grunt] (1815) — used to express doubt or contempt
hump·ty–dump·ty \ˌhəm(p)-tē-'dəm(p)-tē\ n, pl **-dumpties** often cap H&D [Humpty-Dumpty, egg-shaped nursery-rhyme character who fell from a wall and broke into bits] (1883) : something that once broken is impossible or almost impossible to put back together

humpy \'həm-pē\ adj **hump·i·er; -est** (1708)   1 : full of humps   2 : covered with humps
hu·mus \'hyü-məs, 'yü-\ n [NL, fr. L, earth — more at HUMBLE] (1796) : a brown or black complex variable material resulting from partial decomposition of plant or animal matter and forming the organic portion of soil
hum·vee \ˌhəm-'vē, 'həm-ˌ\ n [fr. HMMWV (High Mobility Multipurpose Wheeled Vehicle)] (1982) often cap : a diesel-powered multipurpose U.S. military vehicle that replaced the jeep
Hun \'hən\ n [ME, fr. OE Hunas, pl., fr. LL Hunni, pl.] (bef. 12c)   1 : a member of a nomadic central Asian people gaining control of a large part of central and eastern Europe under Attila about A.D. 450   2 a often not cap : a person who is wantonly destructive : VANDAL   b : GERMAN; esp : a German soldier — usu. used disparagingly
Hu·nan \'hü-'nän\ or **Hu·na·nese** \ˌhü-nə-'nēz, -'nēs\ adj [Hunan, China] (1970) : of, relating to, or being a hot and spicy style of Chinese cooking
¹**hunch** \'hənch\ vb [origin unknown] vt (1581)   1 : JOSTLE, SHOVE   2 : to thrust or bend over into a humped or crooked position ∼ vi   1 : to thrust oneself forward   2 a : to assume a bent or crooked posture   b : to draw oneself into a ball : curl up   c : HUDDLE, SQUAT
²**hunch** n (1630)   1 : an act or instance of hunching : PUSH   2 a : a thick piece : LUMP   b : HUMP   3 : a strong intuitive feeling concerning esp. a future event or result
hunch·back \'hənch-ˌbak\ n (1712)   1 : a person with a humpback   2 : HUMPBACK 1 — **hunch·backed** \-ˌbakt\ adj
hun·dred \'hən-drəd, -dərd\ n, pl **hundreds** or **hundred** [ME, fr. OE, fr. hund hundred + -red (akin to Goth rathjo account, number); akin to L centum hundred, Gk hekaton, OE tien ten — more at TEN, REASON] (bef. 12c)   1 — see NUMBER table   2 hundreds pl a : the numbers 100 to 999   b : a great number ⟨∼s of times⟩   3 : a 100-dollar bill   4 : a subdivision of some English and American counties — **hundred** adj — **hun·dred·fold** \-ˌfōld\ adj or adv — **hun·dredth** \-drədth, -drətth\ adj or n
hun·dred–per·cent·er \-pər-'sen-tər\ n [hundred-percent (American)] (1921) : a thoroughgoing nationalist — **hun·dred–per·cent·ism** \-'sen-ˌti-zəm\ n
hundreds place n (1937) : the place three to the left of the decimal point in a number expressed in the Arabic system of notation
hun·dred·weight \'hən-drəd-ˌwāt, -dərd-ˌwāt\ n, pl **hundredweight** or **hundredweights** (1577)   1 : a unit of weight equal to 100 pounds — called also short hundredweight; see WEIGHT table   2 Brit : a unit of weight equal to 112 pounds — called also long hundredweight
¹**hung** past and past part of HANG
²**hung** adj (1848) : unable to reach a decision or verdict ⟨a ∼ jury⟩; also, Brit : not having a political party with an overall majority ⟨a ∼ parliament⟩
Hun·gar·i·an \ˌhəŋ-'ger-ē-ən, -'gar-\ n (1553)   1 a : a native or inhabitant of Hungary : MAGYAR   b : a person of Hungarian descent   2 : the Finno-Ugric language of the Hungarians — **Hungarian** adj
¹**hun·ger** \'həŋ-gər\ n [ME, fr. OE hungor; akin to OHG hungar hunger, Lith kanka torture] (bef. 12c)   1 a : a craving or urgent need for food or a specific nutrient   b : an uneasy sensation occasioned by the lack of food   c : a weakened condition brought about by prolonged lack of food   2 : a strong desire : CRAVING — **from hunger** : very bad or inept ⟨the jokes were from hunger —Mordecai Richler⟩
²**hunger** vb **hun·gered; hun·ger·ing** \-g(ə-)riŋ\ vi (bef. 12c)   1 : to feel or suffer hunger   2 : to have an eager desire ∼ vt : to make hungry syn see LONG
hunger strike n (1889) : refusal (as by a prisoner) to eat enough to sustain life — **hunger striker** n
hung·over \'həŋ-'ō-vər\ adj (1941) : suffering from a hangover
hun·gry \'həŋ-grē\ adj **hun·gri·er; -est** [ME, fr. OE hungrig; akin to OE hungor] (bef. 12c)   1 a : feeling hunger   b : characterized by or characteristic of hunger or appetite   2 a : EAGER, AVID ⟨∼ for affection⟩   b : strongly motivated (as by ambition)   3 : not rich or fertile : BARREN — **hun·gri·ly** \-grə-lē\ adv — **hun·gri·ness** \-grē-nəs\ n
hung up (1948)   1 : delayed or detained for a time   2 : anxiously nervous   3 : being much involved with: as   a : being infatuated   b : ENTHUSIASTIC   c : PREOCCUPIED
hunk \'həŋk\ n [Flem hunke] (ca. 1813)   1 : a large lump, piece, or portion ⟨a ∼ of bread⟩   2 : an attractive well-built man
hun·ker \'hən-kər\ vi **hun·kered; hun·ker·ing** \-k(ə-)riŋ\ [perh. of Scand origin; akin to ON hūka to squat; akin to MLG hōken to squat, peddle — more at HAWKER] (1720)   1 : CROUCH, SQUAT — usu. used with down ⟨∼ to settle in or dig in for a sustained period — used with down ⟨∼ down for a good long wait —New Yorker⟩
hun·kers \'hən-kərz\ n pl (1756) : HAUNCHES
hunks \'həŋ(k)s\ n pl but sing in constr [origin unknown] (1602) : a surly ill-natured person; esp : MISER
hunky \'həŋ-kē\ adj **hunk·i·er; -est** (1911) : muscular and usu. attractive ⟨∼ men⟩
Hun·ky also **Hun·kie** \'həŋ-kē\ n, pl **Hunkies** [alter. of Hungarian] (ca. 1896) : a person of central or east European birth or descent — usu. used disparagingly
hun·ky–do·ry \ˌhəŋ-kē-'dōr-ē, -'dor-\ adj [obs. E dial. hunk (home base) + -dory (origin unknown)] (1866) : quite satisfactory : FINE
Hun·nish \'hə-nish\ adj (1820) : relating to or resembling the Huns
¹**hunt** \'hənt\ vb [ME, fr. OE huntian; akin to OE hentan to seize] vt (bef. 12c)   1 a : to pursue for food or in sport ⟨∼ buffalo⟩   b : to manage in the search for game ⟨∼s a pack of dogs⟩   2 a : to pursue with intent to capture ⟨∼ed the escapees⟩   b : to search out : SEEK   3 : to drive or chase esp. by harrying ⟨members . . . were ∼ed from their homes —J. T. Adams⟩   4 : to traverse in search of prey ⟨∼s the woods⟩ ∼ vi   1 : to take part in a hunt   2 : to attempt to find something   3 : to oscillate alternately to each side (as of a neutral point) or to run alternately faster and slower — used esp. of a device or machine

\ə\ abut \ᵊ\ kitten, F table \ər\ further \a\ ash \ā\ ace \ä\ mop, mar
\au̇\ out \ch\ chin \e\ bet \ē\ easy \g\ go \i\ hit \ī\ ice \j\ job
\ŋ\ sing \ō\ go \ȯ\ law \ȯi\ boy \th\ thin \t̶h\ the \ü\ loot \u̇\ foot
\y\ yet \zh\ vision \ə, k̲, ⁿ, œ, œ̄, ue, ūe, ʸ\ see Guide to Pronunciation

²**hunt** n (14c) **1** : the act, the practice, or an instance of hunting **2** : a group of mounted hunters and their hunting dogs

hunt–and–peck \ˌhənt-ʔn-'pek\ n (1939) : a method of typing in which one looks at the keyboard and types using usu. the forefingers

hunt·er \'hən-tər\ n (13c) **1 a** : a person who hunts game **b** : a dog used or trained for hunting **c** : a horse used or adapted for use in hunting with hounds; *esp* : a fast strong horse trained for cross-country work and jumping **2** : one that searches for something **3** : a pocket watch with a hinged protective cover

hunt·er–gath·er·er \'hən-tər-'ga-thər-ər\ n (1977) : a member of a culture in which food is obtained by hunting, fishing, and foraging rather than by agriculture or animal husbandry

hunter green n (ca. 1930) : a dark yellowish green

hunt·ing n (bef. 12c) **1** : the act of one that hunts; *specif* : the pursuit of game **2** : the process of hunting **3 a** : a periodic variation in speed of a synchronous electrical machine **b** : a self-induced and undesirable oscillation of a variable above and below the desired value in an automatic control system **c** : a continuous attempt by an automatically controlled system to find a desired equilibrium condition

hunting horn n (1694) : a signal horn used in the chase; *specif* : a coiled circular horn with a flared bell and a cup-shaped mouthpiece

Hun·ting·ton's chorea \'hən-tiŋ-tənz-\ n [George *Huntington* †1916 Am. physician] (1889) : hereditary chorea usu. developing in adult life and progressing to dementia — called also *Huntington's disease*

hunt·ress \'hən-trəs\ n (14c) : a woman who hunts game; *also* : a female animal that hunts prey

hunts·man \'hən(t)-smən\ n (1567) **1** : HUNTER 1a **2** : a person who manages a hunt and looks after the hounds

hup \'həp, 'hət\ *interj* [prob. alter. of ¹*hep*] (1951) — used to mark a marching cadence

hur·dies \'hər-dēz\ n pl [origin unknown] (14c) *dial Brit* : RUMP

¹**hur·dle** \'hər-dʔl\ n [ME *hurdel*, fr. OE *hyrdel*; akin to OHG *hurt* hurdle, L *cratis* wickerwork, hurdle] (bef. 12c) **1 a** : a portable panel usu. of wattled withes and stakes used esp. for enclosing land or livestock **b** : a frame or sled formerly used in England for dragging traitors to execution **2 a** : an artificial barrier over which racers must leap **b** pl : any of various track events in which a series of hurdles must be surmounted **3** : BARRIER, OBSTACLE

²**hurdle** vt **hur·dled; hur·dling** \'hərd-liŋ, 'hər-dʔl-iŋ\ (1896) **1** : to leap over esp. while running (as in a sporting competition) **2** : OVERCOME, SURMOUNT — **hur·dler** \'hərd-lər, 'hər-dʔl-ər\ n

hur·dy–gur·dy \'hər-dē-'gər-dē, 'hər-dē-,\ n, pl **-gurdies** [prob. imit.] (1749) **1** : a stringed instrument in which sound is produced by the friction of a rosined wheel turned by a crank against the strings and the pitches are varied by keys **2** : any of various mechanical musical instruments (as the barrel organ)

hurl \'hər(-ə)l\ vb **hurled; hurl·ing** \'hər-liŋ\ [ME] vi (13c) **1** : RUSH, HURTLE **2** : PITCH 5a, b ~ vt **1** : to send or thrust with great vigor ⟨the forces that were to be ~ed against the Turks —N. T. Gilroy⟩ **2** : to throw down with violence **3 a** : to throw forcefully : FLING ⟨~ed the manuscript into the fire⟩ ⟨~ed myself over the fence⟩ **b** : PITCH 2a **4** : to utter with vehemence ⟨~ed insults at the police⟩ *syn* see THROW — **hurl** n — **hurl·er** n

hurl·ing \'hər-liŋ\ n (ca. 1600) : an Irish game resembling field hockey played between two teams of 15 players each

hur·ly \'hər-lē\ n [prob. short for *hurly-burly*] (1594) : UPROAR, TUMULT

hur·ly–bur·ly \ˌhər-lē-'bər-lē\ n [prob. alter. & redupl. of *hurling*, gerund of *hurl*] (1539) : UPROAR, TUMULT — **hurly–burly** adj

Hu·ron \'hyūr-ən, -ˌän\ n, pl **Hurons** or **Huron** [F, lit., boor] (1658) : a member of a confederacy of American Indian peoples formerly occupying the country between Georgian Bay and Lake Ontario

¹**hur·rah** \hu-'rȯ, -'rä, 'hü-,\ n (1686) **1 a** : EXCITEMENT, FANFARE **b** : CHEER 7 **2** : FUSS

²**hur·rah** \hu-'rȯ, -'rä\ also **hur·ray** \hu-'rā\ *interj* [perh. fr. G *hurra*] (1716) — used to express joy, approbation, or encouragement

Hur·ri·an \'hur-ē-ən\ n (1911) **1** : a member of an ancient non-Semitic people of northern Mesopotamia, Syria, and eastern Asia Minor about 1500 B.C. **2** : the language of the Hurrian people

¹**hur·ri·cane** \'hər-ə-ˌkān, -i-kən, 'hə-rə-, 'hə-ri-\ n [Sp *huracán*, fr. Taino *hurakán*] (1555) **1 a** : a tropical cyclone with winds of 74 miles (118 kilometers) per hour or greater that occurs esp. in the western Atlantic, that is usu. accompanied by rain, thunder, and lightning, and that sometimes moves into temperate latitudes — see BEAUFORT SCALE table **2** : something resembling a hurricane esp. in its turmoil

²**hurricane** adj (1894) : having or being a glass chimney providing protection from wind ⟨a ~ lamp⟩

hur·ried \'hər-ēd, 'hə-rēd\ adj (1667) **1** : going or working at speed **2** : done in a hurry : HASTY — **hur·ried·ly** \'hər-əd-lē, 'hə-rəd-\ adv — **hur·ried·ness** \'hər-ēd-nəs, 'hə-rēd-\ n

¹**hur·ry** \'hər-ē, 'hə-rē\ vb **hur·ried; hur·ry·ing** [perh. fr. ME *horyen*] vt (1592) **1 a** : to carry or cause to go with haste ⟨~ them to the hospital⟩ **b** : to impel to rash or precipitate action **2 a** : to impel to greater speed : PROD ⟨used spurs to ~ the horse⟩ **b** : EXPEDITE **3** : to perform with undue haste ⟨~ a minuet⟩ ~ vi : to move or act with haste ⟨please ~ up⟩ — **hur·ri·er** n

²**hurry** n (1600) **1** : disturbed or disorderly activity : COMMOTION **2 a** : agitated and often bustling or disorderly haste **b** : a state of eagerness or urgency : RUSH *syn* see HASTE — **in a hurry 1** : without delay : as rapidly as possible ⟨the police got there *in a hurry*⟩

hur·ry–scur·ry or **hur·ry–skur·ry** \ˌhər-ē-'skər-ē, ˌhə-rē-'skə-rē\ n [redupl. of ²*hurry*] (1754) : a confused rush : TURMOIL — **hurry–scurry** adj or adv

hur·ry–up \'hər-ē-ˌəp, 'hə-rē-\ adj (1902) : speeded up : completed in a hurry ⟨a ~ dinner⟩

¹**hurt** \'hərt\ vb **hurt; hurt·ing** [ME, prob. fr. OF *hurter* to collide with, prob. of Gmc origin; akin to ON *hrūtr* male sheep] vt (13c) **1 a** : to inflict with physical pain : WOUND **b** : to do substantial or material harm to : DAMAGE ⟨the dry summer has ~ the land⟩ **2 a** : to cause emotional pain or anguish to : OFFEND **b** : to be detrimental to

: HAMPER ⟨charges of graft ~ my chances of being elected⟩ ~ vi **1 a** : to suffer pain or grief **b** : to be in need — usu. used with *for* ⟨~ing for money⟩ **2** : to cause damage or distress ⟨hit where it ~s⟩ *syn* see INJURE — **hurt** adj — **hurt·er** n

²**hurt** n (13c) **1** : a cause of injury or damage : BLOW **2 a** : a bodily injury or wound **b** : mental distress or anguish : SUFFERING **3** : WRONG, HARM

hurt·ful \'hərt-fəl\ adj (1526) : causing injury, detriment, or suffering : DAMAGING — **hurt·ful·ly** \-fə-lē\ adv — **hurt·ful·ness** n

hur·tle \'hər-tʔl\ vb **hur·tled; hur·tling** \'hərt-liŋ, 'hər-tʔl-iŋ\ [ME *hurtlen* to collide, freq. of *hurten* to cause to strike, hurt] vi (14c) **1** : to move rapidly or forcefully ~ vt : HURL, FLING — **hurtle** n

hurt·less \'hərt-ləs\ adj (1549) : causing no pain or injury : HARMLESS

¹**hus·band** \'həz-bənd\ n [ME *husbonde*, fr. OE *hūsbonda* master of a house, fr. ON *hūsbōndi*, fr. *hūs* house + *bōndi* householder; akin to ON *būa* to inhabit; akin to OE *būan* to dwell — more at BOWER] (13c) **1** : a male partner in a marriage **2** Brit : MANAGER, STEWARD **3** : a frugal manager — **hus·band·ly** adj

²**husband** vt (15c) **1 a** : to manage prudently and economically **b** : to use sparingly : CONSERVE **2** archaic : to find a husband for : MATE — **hus·band·er** n

hus·band·man \'həz-bən(d)-mən\ n (14c) **1** : one that plows and cultivates land : FARMER **2** : a specialist in a branch of farm husbandry

hus·band·ry \'həz-bən-drē\ n (14c) **1** archaic : the care of a household **2** : the control or judicious use of resources : CONSERVATION **3 a** : the cultivation or production of plants and animals : AGRICULTURE **b** : the scientific control and management of a branch of farming and esp. of domestic animals

¹**hush** \'həsh\ vb [back-formation fr. *husht* (hushed), fr. ME *hussht*, fr. *huissht*, interj. used to enjoin silence] vt (1546) **1** : CALM, QUIET ⟨~ed the children as they entered the library⟩ **2** : to put at rest : MOLLIFY **3** : to keep from public knowledge : SUPPRESS ⟨~ the story up⟩ ~ vi : to become quiet

²**hush** adj (1602) **1** archaic : SILENT, STILL **2** : intended to prevent the dissemination of certain information ⟨~ money⟩

³**hush** n (1689) : a silence or calm esp. following noise : QUIET

hush–hush \'həsh-,həsh\ adj (1916) : SECRET, CONFIDENTIAL

hush puppy n [fr. its occasional use as food for dogs] (ca. 1918) chiefly *Southern & southern Midland* : cornmeal dough shaped into small balls and fried in deep fat — usu. used in pl.

¹**husk** \'həsk\ n [ME] (14c) **1 a** : a usu. dry or membranous outer covering (as a pod or hull or one composed of bracts) of various seeds and fruits; *also* : one of the constituent parts **b** : a carob pod **2 a** : an outer layer : SHELL **b** : an emptied shell : REMNANT **c** : a supporting framework

²**husk** vt (1562) : to strip the husk from — **husk·er** n

husk·ing n (1692) : CORNHUSKING — called also *husking bee*

husk–tomato n (1895) : GROUND-CHERRY

¹**husky** \'həs-kē\ adj **husk·i·er; -est** (1552) : resembling, containing, or full of husks

²**hus·ky** \'həs-kē\ adj **hus·ki·er; -est** [prob. fr. *husk* (huskiness), fr. obs. *husk* (to have a dry cough)] (ca. 1722) : hoarse with or as if with emotion — **hus·ki·ly** \-kə-lē\ adv — **hus·ki·ness** \-kē-nəs\ n

³**hus·ky** n, pl **huskies** [shortening of *Huskemaw, Uskemaw* Eskimo, fr. Cree *aškimew*; akin to Montagnais (Algonquian language of eastern Canada) *aiachkimeθ* Micmac, Eskimo — more at ESKIMO] (1852) **1** : a heavy-coated working dog of the New World arctic region **2** : SIBERIAN HUSKY

⁴**hus·ky** n, pl **huskies** (1864) : one that is husky

⁵**hus·ky** adj **hus·ki·er; -est** [prob. fr. ¹*husk*] (1869) **1** : BURLY, ROBUST **2** : LARGE

hus·sar \(ˌ)hə-'zär, -'sär\ n [Hung *huszár* hussar, (obs.) highway robber, fr. Serbo-Croatian *husar* pirate, fr. ML *cursarius* — more at CORSAIR] (1532) : a member of any of various European units orig. modeled on the Hungarian light cavalry of the 15th century

Huss·ite \'hə-ˌsīt, 'hú-\ n [NL *Hussita*, fr. John *Huss*] (1532) : a member of the Bohemian religious and nationalist movement originating with John Huss — **Hussite** adj — **Huss·it·ism** \-ˌsī-ˌti-zəm\ n

hus·sy \'hə-sē, -zē\ n, pl **hussies** [alter. of ME *huswif* housewife, fr. *hus* house + *wif* wife, woman] (1505) **1** : a lewd or brazen woman **2** : a saucy or mischievous girl

hus·tings \'həs-tiŋz\ n pl but sing or pl in constr [ME, fr. OE *hūsting*, fr. ON *hūsthing*, fr. *hūs* house + *thing* assembly] (bef. 12c) **1 a** : a local court formerly held in various English municipalities and still held infrequently in London **b** : a local court in some cities in Virginia **2 a** : a raised platform used until 1872 for the nomination of candidates for the British Parliament and for election speeches **b** : an election platform : STUMP **c** : the proceedings or locale of an election campaign

hus·tle \'hə-səl\ vb **hus·tled; hus·tling** \'hə-s(ə-)liŋ\ [D *husselen* to shake, fr. MD *hutselen*, freq. of *hutsen*] vt (1751) **1 a** : JOSTLE, SHOVE **b** : to convey forcibly or hurriedly **c** : to urge forward precipitately **2 a** : to obtain by energetic activity ⟨~ up new customers⟩ **b** : to sell something to or obtain something from by energetic and esp. underhanded activity ⟨~ing the suckers⟩ **c** : to sell or promote energetically and aggressively ⟨~ing a new product⟩ **d** : to lure less skillful players into competing against oneself at (a gambling game) ⟨~ pool⟩ ~ vi **1** : SHOVE, PRESS **2** : HASTEN, HURRY **3 a** : to make strenuous efforts to obtain esp. money or business **b** : to obtain money by fraud or deception **c** : to engage in prostitution **4** : to play a game or sport in an alert aggressive manner — **hustle** n — **hus·tler** \'hə-slər\ n

¹**hut** \'hət\ n [MF *hutte*, of Gmc origin; akin to OHG *hutta* hut; prob. akin to OE *hȳd* skin, hide] (1658) **1** : an often small and temporary dwelling of simple construction : SHACK **2** : a simple shelter from the elements — **hut** vb

²**hut** \'hət, 'həp\ *interj* [prob. alter. of ¹*hep*] (1948) — used to mark a marching cadence

hutch \'həch\ n [ME *huche*, fr. OF] (13c) **1 a** : a chest or compartment for storage **b** : a cupboard usu. surmounted by open shelves **2** : a pen or coop for an animal **3** : SHACK, SHANTY

hut·ment \'hət-mənt\ n (1889) **1** : a collection of huts : ENCAMPMENT **2** : HUT

Hut·ter·ite \'hə-tə-ˌrīt, 'hü-\ n [Jakob *Hutter* †1536 Moravian Anabaptist] (1910) : a member of a Mennonite sect of northwestern U.S. and

Canada living communally and holding property in common — **Hut-te·ri·an** \hə-'tir-ē-ən, hü-\ *adj*
Hu·tu \'hü-(,)tü\ *n, pl* **Hutu** *or* **Hutus** (1952) : a member of a Bantu≈ speaking people of Rwanda and Burundi
hutz·pah *or* **hutz·pa** *var of* CHUTZPAH
huz·zah *or* **huz·za** \(,)hə-'zä\ *n* [origin unknown] (1573) : an expression or shout of acclaim — often used interjectionally to express joy or approbation
hy·a·cinth \'hī-ə-(,)sin(t)th, -sən(t)th\ *n* [L *hyacinthus*, a precious stone, a flowering plant, fr. Gk *hyakinthos*] (1553) **1 a** : a precious stone of the ancients sometimes held to be the sapphire **b** : a gem zircon or essonite **2 a** : a plant of the ancients held to be a lily, iris, larkspur, or gladiolus **b** : a bulbous herb (*Hyacinthus orientalis*) of the lily family that is native to the Mediterranean region but is widely grown for its dense spikes of fragrant flowers — compare GRAPE HYA-CINTH, WATER HYACINTH **3** : a light violet to moderate purple — **hy·a·cin·thine** \,hī-ə-'sin(t)-thən\ *adj*
Hy·a·cin·thus \,hī-ə-'sin(t)-thəs\ *n* [L, fr. Gk *Hyakinthos*] : a youth loved and accidentally killed by Apollo who memorializes him with a hyacinth growing from the youth's blood
Hy·a·des \'hī-ə-,dēz\ *n pl* [L, fr. Gk] (14c) : a V-shaped cluster of stars in the head of the constellation Taurus held by the ancients to indicate rainy weather when they rise with the sun
hy·ae·na *var of* HYENA
hyal- *or* **hyalo-** *comb form* [LL, glass, fr. Gk, fr. *hyalos*] : glass : glassy : hyaline ⟨*hyal*uronic acid⟩
¹hy·a·line \'hī-ə-lən, -,līn\ *adj* [LL *hyalinus*, fr. Gk *hyalinos*, fr. *hyalos*] (ca. 1661) : transparent or nearly so and usu. homogeneous
²hy·a·line \'hī-ə-lən, -,līn, *in sense 2* -lən *or* -,lēn\ *n* (1667) **1** : something (as the clear atmosphere) that is transparent **2** *or* **hy·a·lin** \-lən\ : any of several translucent nitrogenous substances related to chitin, found esp. around cells, and readily stained by eosin
hyaline cartilage *n* (1855) : translucent bluish white cartilage with the cells embedded in an apparently homogeneous matrix present in joints and respiratory passages and forming most of the fetal skeleton
hy·a·lite \'hī-ə-,līt\ *n* [G *Hyalit*, fr. Gk *hyalos*] (1794) : a colorless opal that is clear as glass or sometimes translucent or whitish
hy·a·loid \-,lȯid\ *adj* [Gk *hyaloeidēs*, fr. *hyalos*] (1835) : GLASSY, TRANS-PARENT
hy·a·lo·plasm \hī-'a-lə-,pla-zəm, 'hī-ə-lō-\ *n* [prob. fr. G *Hyaloplasma*, fr. *hyal-* + *-plasma* -plasm] (1886) : CYTOSOL
hy·al·uron·ic acid \,hī-yü-'rä-nik-, ,hī-əl-yù-\ *n* [ISV] (1934) : a viscous mucopolysaccharide acid that occurs esp. in the vitreous humor, the umbilical cord, and synovial fluid and as a cementing substance in the subcutaneous tissue
hy·al·uron·i·dase \-'rä-nə-,dās, -,dāz\ *n* [ISV, fr. *hyaluronic* (*acid*) + *-idase* (as in *glucosidase*)] (1940) : a mucolytic enzyme that facilitates the spread of fluids through tissues by lowering the viscosity of hyaluronic acid
hy·brid \'hī-brəd\ *n* [L *hybrida*] (1601) **1** : an offspring of two animals or plants of different races, breeds, varieties, species, or genera **2** : a person whose background is a blend of two diverse cultures or traditions **3 a** : something heterogeneous in origin or composition : COMPOSITE ⟨artificial ~*s* of DNA and RNA⟩ ⟨a ~ of medieval and Renaissance styles⟩ **b** : something (as a power plant, vehicle, or electronic circuit) that has two different types of components performing essentially the same function — **hybrid** *adj* — **hy·brid·ism** \-brə-,di-zəm\ *n* — **hy·brid·i·ty** \hī-'bri-də-tē\ *n*
hybrid computer *n* (1968) : a computer system consisting of a combination of analog and digital computer systems
hy·brid·ize \'hī-brə-,dīz\ *vb* **-ized; -iz·ing** *vt* (1845) : to cause to produce hybrids : INTERBREED ~ *vi* : to produce hybrids — **hy·brid·iza·tion** \,hī-brə-də-'zā-shən\ *n* — **hy·brid·iz·er** *n*
hy·brid·oma \,hī-brə-'dō-mə\ *n* (1978) : a hybrid cell produced by the fusion of an antibody-producing lymphocyte with a tumor cell and used to culture continuously a specific monoclonal antibody
hybrid tea rose *n* (1926) : any of numerous moderately hardy cultivated hybrid bush roses grown esp. for their strongly recurrent bloom of large usu. scentless flowers — called also *hybrid tea*
hybrid vigor *n* (1918) : HETEROSIS
hy·bris \'hī-brəs, 'hē-\ *var of* HUBRIS
hy·da·thode \'hī-də-,thōd\ *n* [ISV, fr. Gk *hydat-, hydōr* water + *hodos* road] (1895) : a specialized pore on the leaves of higher plants that functions in the exudation of water
hy·da·tid \'hī-də-təd, -,tid\ *n* [Gk *hydatid-, hydatis* watery cyst, fr. *hydat-, hydōr*] (1683) : the larval cyst of a tapeworm (genus *Echinococcus*) occurring as a fluid-filled sac containing daughter cysts in which scolices develop
hydr- *or* **hydro-** *comb form* [ME *ydr-, ydro-*, fr. OF, fr. L *hydr-, hydro-*, fr. Gk, fr. *hydōr* — more at WATER] **1 a** : water ⟨*hydro*us⟩ ⟨*hydro*electric⟩ **b** : liquid ⟨*hydro*kinetic⟩ **2** : hydrogen : containing or combined with hydrogen ⟨*hydro*carbon⟩ ⟨*hydro*xyl⟩ **3** : hydroid ⟨*hy·dro*medusa⟩
Hy·dra \'hī-drə\ *n* [ME *Ydra*, fr. L *Hydra*, fr. Gk] **1** : a many-headed serpent or monster in Greek mythology that was slain by Hercules and each head of which when cut off was replaced by two others **2** *not cap* : a multifarious evil not to be overcome by a single effort **3** [L (gen. *Hydrae*), fr. Gk] : a southern constellation of great length that lies south of Cancer, Sextans, Corvus, and Virgo and is represented on old maps by a serpent **4** *not cap* [NL, fr. L, Hydra] : any of numerous small tubular freshwater hydrozoan polyps (*Hydra* and related genera) having at one end a mouth surrounded by tentacles
hy·dra—head·ed \,hī-drə-'he-dəd\ *adj* (1599) : having many centers or branches ⟨a ~ organization⟩
hy·dral·a·zine \hī-'dra-lə-,zēn\ *n* [*hydr-* + *phthal*ic (acid) + *azine*] (1952) : a vasodilator $C_8H_8N_4$ used in the treatment of hypertension
hy·dran·gea \hī-'drän-jə\ *n* [NL, fr. *hydr-* + Gk *angeion* vessel — more at ANGI-] (ca. 1753) : any of a genus (*Hydrangea*) of shrubs and one woody vine of the saxifrage family with opposite leaves and showy clusters of usu. sterile white or tinted flowers
hy·drant \'hī-drənt\ *n* (1806) **1** : a discharge pipe with a valve and spout at which water may be drawn from a water main (as for fighting fires) — called also *fireplug* **2** : FAUCET

hy·dranth \'hī-,dran(t)th\ *n* [ISV *hydr-* + Gk *anthos* flower — more at ANTHOLOGY] (1874) : one of the nutritive zooids of a hydroid colony
hy·drase \'hī-drās, -,drāz\ *n* (1943) : an enzyme that promotes the addition or removal of water to or from its substrate
¹hy·drate \'hī-,drāt\ *n* (1802) : a compound formed by the union of water with some other substance
²hydrate *vb* **hy·drat·ed; hy·drat·ing** *vt* (1850) : to cause to take up or combine with water or the elements of water ~ *vi* : to become a hydrate — **hy·dra·tion** \hī-'drā-shən\ *n* — **hy·dra·tor** \'hī-,drā-tər\ *n*
hy·drau·lic \hī-'drȯ-lik\ *adj* [L *hydraulicus*, fr. Gk *hydraulikos*, fr. *hydraulis* hydraulic organ, fr. *hydr-* + *aulos* reed instrument — more at ALVEOLUS] (1661) **1** : operated, moved, or effected by means of water **2 a** : of or relating to hydraulics ⟨~ engineer⟩ **b** : of or relating to water or other liquid in motion ⟨~ erosion⟩ **3** : operated by the resistance offered or the pressure transmitted when a quantity of liquid (as water or oil) is forced through a comparatively small orifice or through a tube ⟨~ brakes⟩ **4** : hardening or setting under water ⟨~ cement⟩ — **hy·drau·li·cal·ly** \-li-k(ə-)lē\ *adv*
hy·drau·lics \hī-'drȯ-liks\ *n pl but sing in constr* (1671) : a branch of science that deals with practical applications (as the transmission of energy or the effects of flow) of liquid (as water) in motion
hy·dra·zide \'hī-drə-,zīd\ *n* (1888) : any of a class of compounds resulting from the replacement of hydrogen by an acid group in hydrazine or in one of its derivatives
hy·dra·zine \'hī-drə-,zēn\ *n* [ISV] (1887) : a colorless fuming corrosive strongly reducing liquid base N_2H_4 used esp. in fuels for rocket and jet engines; *also* : an organic base derived from this compound
hy·dra·zo·ic acid \,hī-drə-'zō-ik-\ *n* [*hydr-* + *azo-* + ¹-*ic*] (1894) : a colorless volatile poisonous explosive liquid HN_3 that has a foul odor and yields explosive salts of heavy metals
hy·dric \'hī-drik\ *adj* (1926) : characterized by, relating to, or requiring an abundance of moisture ⟨a ~ habitat⟩ ⟨a ~ plant⟩ — compare MESIC, XERIC
-hydric *adj suffix* : containing acid hydrogen ⟨mono*hydric*⟩
hy·dride \'hī-,drīd\ *n* (1869) : a compound of hydrogen with a more electropositive element or group
hy·dri·od·ic acid \,hī-drē-'ä-dik-\ *n* [ISV] (1819) : an aqueous solution of hydrogen iodide HI that is a strong acid resembling hydrochloric acid chemically and that is also a strong reducing agent
¹hy·dro \'hī-(,)drō\ *n, pl* **hydros** [short for *hydropathic establishment*] (1882) *Brit* : an establishment offering hydropathic treatment (as for weight loss) : HEALTH SPA
²hydro *n, often attrib* [short for *hydropower*] (1916) : hydroelectric power
hy·dro·bi·ol·o·gy \,hī-drō-bī-'ä-lə-jē\ *n* (1926) : the biology of bodies or units of water; *esp* : LIMNOLOGY — **hy·dro·bi·o·log·i·cal** \-,bī-ə-'lä-ji-kəl\ *adj* — **hy·dro·bi·ol·o·gist** \-bī-'ä-lə-jist\ *n*
hy·dro·bro·mic acid \,hī-drə-'brō-mik-\ *n* [ISV] (1836) : an aqueous solution of hydrogen bromide HBr that is a strong acid resembling hydrochloric acid chemically, that is a weak reducing agent, and that is used esp. to make bromides
hy·dro·car·bon \'hī-drō-,kär-bən\ *n* (1826) : an organic compound (as acetylene or butane) containing only carbon and hydrogen and often occurring in petroleum, natural gas, coal, and bitumens
hy·dro·cele \'hī-drə-,sēl\ *n* [L, fr. Gk *hydrokēlē*, fr. *hydr-* + *kēlē* tumor — more at -CELE] (1597) : an accumulation of serous fluid in a sacculated cavity (as the scrotum)
hy·dro·ce·phal·ic \,hī-drō-sə-'fa-lik\ *adj* (1815) : relating to, characterized by, or affected with hydrocephalus — **hydrocephalic** *n*
hy·dro·ceph·a·lus \-'se-fə-ləs\ *also* **hy·dro·ceph·a·ly** \-lē\ *n* [NL *hydrocephalus*, fr. LL, hydrocephalic, adj., fr. Gk *hydrokephalos*, fr. *hydr-* + *kephalē* head — more at CEPHALIC] (1670) : an abnormal increase in the amount of cerebrospinal fluid within the cranial cavity that is accompanied by expansion of the cerebral ventricles, enlargement of the skull and esp. the forehead, and atrophy of the brain
hy·dro·chlo·ric acid \,hī-drə-'klōr-ik-, -'klȯr-\ *n* [ISV] (ca. 1828) : an aqueous solution of hydrogen chloride HCl that is a strong corrosive irritating acid, is normally present in dilute form in gastric juice, and is widely used in industry and in the laboratory
hy·dro·chlo·ride \-'klōr-,īd, -'klȯr-\ *n* (1826) : a chemical complex composed of an organic base (as an alkaloid) in association with hydrogen chloride
hy·dro·chlo·ro·thi·a·zide \-,klōr-ə-'thī-ə-,zīd, -,klȯr-\ *n* [*hydr-* + *chlor-* + *thiaz*ine + *-ide*] (1958) : a diuretic and antihypertensive drug $C_7H_8ClN_3O_4S_2$
hy·dro·col·loid \,hī-drə-'kä-,lȯid\ *n* (1916) : a substance that yields a gel with water — **hy·dro·col·loi·dal** \-kə-'lȯi-d²l, -kä-\ *adj*
hy·dro·cor·ti·sone \-'kȯr-tə-,sōn, -,zōn\ *n* (1951) : a glucocorticoid $C_{21}H_{30}O_5$ of the adrenal cortex that is a derivative of cortisone and is used in the treatment of rheumatoid arthritis — called also *cortisol*
hy·dro·crack·ing \'hī-drə-,kra-kiŋ\ *n* (1940) : the cracking of hydrocarbons in the presence of hydrogen — **hy·dro·crack** \-,krak\ *vt* — **hy·dro·crack·er** *n*
hy·dro·cy·an·ic acid \,hī-drō-sī-'a-nik-\ *n* [ISV] (1819) : an aqueous solution of hydrogen cyanide HCN that is a poisonous weak acid and is used chiefly in fumigating and in organic synthesis
hy·dro·dy·nam·ic \-dī-'na-mik\ *also* **hy·dro·dy·nam·i·cal** \-mi-kəl\ *adj* [NL *hydrodynamicus*, fr. *hydr-* + *dynamicus* dynamic] (ca. 1828) : of, relating to, or involving principles of hydrodynamics — **hy·dro·dy·nam·i·cal·ly** \-mi-k(ə-)lē\ *adv*
hy·dro·dy·nam·ics \-miks\ *n pl but sing in constr* (1779) : a branch of physics that deals with the motion of fluids and the forces acting on solid bodies immersed in fluids and in motion relative to them — compare HYDROSTATICS — **hy·dro·dy·nam·i·cist** \-'na-mə-sist\ *n*
hy·dro·elec·tric \,hī-drō-i-'lek-trik\ *adj* [ISV] (1884) : of or relating to production of electricity by waterpower ⟨constructed a ~ power plant

---

\ə\ **abut** \ᵊ\ **kitten, F table** \ər\ **further** \a\ **ash** \ā\ **ace** \ä\ **mop, mar** \au̇\ **out** \ch\ **chin** \e\ **bet** \ē\ **easy** \g\ **go** \i\ **hit** \ī\ **ice** \j\ **job** \ŋ\ **sing** \ō\ **go** \ȯ\ **law** \ȯi\ **boy** \th\ **thin** \t̲h̲\ **the** \ü\ **loot** \u̇\ **foot** \y\ **yet** \zh\ **vision** \ȧ, k̲, ⁿ, œ, œ̄, ᵫ, ūe, ᵊ̄\ *see* Guide to Pronunciation at the dam site⟩ — **hy·dro·elec·tri·cal·ly** \-tri-k(ə-)lē\ *adv* — **hy·dro·elec·tric·i·ty** \-,lek-'tri-sə-tē, -'tris-tē\ *n*

hy·dro·flu·or·ic acid \,hī-drō-'flōr-ik, -'flu̇r-\ *n* [ISV] (ca. 1872) : an aqueous solution of hydrogen fluoride HF that is a weak poisonous acid, that resembles hydrochloric acid chemically but attacks silica and silicates, and that is used esp. in finishing and etching glass

hy·dro·foil \'hī-drə-,fȯil\ *n* (1919) **1** : a body similar to an airfoil but designed for action in or on water   **2** : a motorboat that has metal plates or fins attached by struts fore and aft for lifting the hull clear of the water as speed is attained

hy·dro·gen \'hī-drə-jən, -dər-\ *n* [F *hydrogène*, fr. *hydr-* + *-gène* -gen; fr. the fact that water is generated by its combustion] (1791) : a nonmetallic element that is the simplest and lightest of the elements, is normally a colorless odorless highly flammable diatomic gas, and is used esp. in synthesis — compare DEUTERIUM, TRITIUM; see ELEMENT table — **hy·drog·e·nous** \hī-'drä-jə-nəs\ *adj*

hy·dro·ge·nase \hī-'drä-jə-,nās, -,nāz\ *n* (1900) : an enzyme of various microorganisms that promotes the formation and utilization of gaseous hydrogen

hy·dro·ge·nate \hī-'drä-jə-,nāt, 'hī-drə-\ *vt* **-nat·ed; -nat·ing** (1809) : to combine or treat with or expose to hydrogen; *esp* : to add hydrogen to the molecule of (an unsaturated organic compound) — **hy·dro·ge·na·tion** \hī-,drä-jə-'nā-shən, ,hī-drə-\ *n*

hydrogen bomb *n* (1947) : a bomb whose violent explosive power is due to the sudden release of atomic energy resulting from the fusion of light nuclei (as of hydrogen atoms) at very high temperature and pressure to form helium nuclei

hydrogen bond *n* (1923) : an electrostatic attraction between a hydrogen atom in one polar molecule (as of water) and a small electronegative atom (as of oxygen, nitrogen, or fluorine) in usu. another molecule of the same or a different polar substance — **hydrogen bonding** *n*

hydrogen bromide *n* (1885) : a colorless irritating gas HBr that fumes in moist air and yields hydrobromic acid when dissolved in water

hydrogen chloride *n* (1869) : a colorless pungent poisonous gas HCl that fumes in moist air and yields hydrochloric acid when dissolved in water

hydrogen cyanide *n* (1882) **1** : a poisonous usu. gaseous compound HCN that has the odor of bitter almonds   **2** : HYDROCYANIC ACID

hydrogen fluoride *n* (1885) : a colorless corrosive fuming usu. gaseous compound HF that yields hydrofluoric acid when dissolved in water

hydrogen iodide *n* (1885) : an acrid colorless gas HI that fumes in moist air and yields hydriodic acid when dissolved in water

hydrogen ion *n* (1896) **1** : the cation H+ of acids consisting of a hydrogen atom whose electron has been transferred to the anion of the acid   **2** : HYDRONIUM

hydrogen peroxide *n* (1872) : an unstable compound H_2O_2 used esp. as an oxidizing and bleaching agent, an antiseptic, and a propellant

hydrogen sulfide *n* (1873) : a flammable poisonous gas H_2S that has an odor suggestive of rotten eggs and is found esp. in many mineral waters and in putrefying matter

hy·dro·graph·ic \,hī-drə-'gra-fik\ *adj* [F *hydrographique*, fr. MF, fr. *hydr-* + *-graphique* -graphic] (1665) **1** : of or relating to the characteristic features (as flow or depth) of bodies of water   **2** : relating to the charting of bodies of water — **hy·drog·ra·pher** \hī-'drä-grə-fər\ *n* — **hy·drog·ra·phy** \-grə-fē\ *n*

¹hy·droid \'hī-,drȯid\ *adj* [ultim. fr. NL *Hydra*] (ca. 1864) : of or relating to a hydrozoan; *esp* : resembling a typical hydra

²hydroid *n* (1865) : HYDROZOAN; *esp* : a hydrozoan polyp as distinguished from a medusa

hy·dro·ki·net·ic \,hī-drō-kə-'ne-tik, -(,)kī-\ *adj* (1876) : of or relating to the motions of fluids or the forces which produce or affect such motions — compare HYDROSTATIC

hy·dro·lase \'hī-drə-,lās, -,lāz\ *n* [ISV, fr. NL *hydrolysis* + ISV *-ase*] (1910) : a hydrolytic enzyme

hydrologic cycle *n* (1936) : the sequence of conditions through which water passes from vapor in the atmosphere through precipitation upon land or water surfaces and ultimately back into the atmosphere as a result of evaporation and transpiration — called also *hydrological cycle*

hy·drol·o·gy \hī-'drä-lə-jē\ *n* [NL *hydrologia*, fr. L *hydr-* + *-logia* -logy] (1762) : a science dealing with the properties, distribution, and circulation of water on and below the earth's surface and in the atmosphere — **hy·dro·log·ic** \,hī-drə-'lä-jik\ *or* **hy·dro·log·i·cal** \-ji-kəl\ *adj* — **hy·dro·log·i·cal·ly** \-ji-k(ə-)lē\ *adv* — **hy·drol·o·gist** \hī-'drä-lə-jist\ *n*

hy·dro·ly·sate \hī-'drä-lə-,sāt\ *also* **hy·dro·ly·zate** \-,zāt\ *n* (1915) : a product of hydrolysis

hy·dro·ly·sis \hī-'drä-lə-səs\ *n* [NL] (1880) : a chemical process of decomposition involving the splitting of a bond and the addition of the hydrogen cation and the hydroxide anion of water — **hy·dro·lyt·ic** \,hī-drə-'li-tik\ *adj* — **hy·dro·lyt·i·cal·ly** \-ti-k(ə-)lē\ *adv*

hy·dro·lyze \'hī-drə-,līz\ *vb* **-lyzed; -lyz·ing** [ISV, fr. NL *hydrolysis*] *vt* (1880) : to subject to hydrolysis ∼ *vi* : to undergo hydrolysis — **hy·dro·lyz·able** \-,lī-zə-bəl\ *adj*

hy·dro·mag·net·ic \,hī-drō-mag-'ne-tik\ *adj* (1943) : MAGNETOHYDRODYNAMIC

hy·dro·man·cy \'hī-drə-,man(t)-sē\ *n* [ME *ydromancie*, fr. MF, fr. L *hydromantia*, fr. *hydr-* + *-mantia* -mancy] (14c) : divination by the appearance or motion of liquids (as water)

hy·dro·me·chan·i·cal \,hī-drō-mi-'ka-ni-kəl\ *adj* (1825) : relating to a branch of mechanics that deals with the equilibrium and motion of fluids and of solid bodies immersed in them — **hy·dro·me·chan·ics** \-'ka-niks\ *n pl but sing in constr*

hy·dro·me·du·sa \,hī-drō-mi-'dü-sə, -'dyü-, -zə\ *n, pl* **-sae** \-,sē, -,zē\ [NL] (ca. 1889) : a medusa (as of the orders Anthomedusae and Leptomedusae) produced as a bud from a hydroid

hy·dro·met·al·lur·gy \,hī-drō-'me-tᵊl-,ər-jē\ *n* [ISV] (ca. 1859) : the treatment of ores by wet processes (as leaching) — **hy·dro·met·al·lur·gi·cal** \-,me-tᵊl-'ər-ji-kəl\ *adj* — **hy·dro·met·al·lur·gist** \-'me-tᵊl-,ər-jist\ *n*

hy·dro·me·te·or \,hī-drō-'mē-tē-ər, -tē-,ȯr\ *n* [ISV] (1857) : a product (as fog, rain, or hail) formed by the condensation of atmospheric water vapor

hy·dro·me·te·o·rol·o·gy \-,mē-tē-ə-'rä-lə-jē\ *n* (ca. 1859) : a branch of

meteorology that deals with water in the atmosphere esp. as precipitation — **hy·dro·me·te·o·ro·log·i·cal** \-tē-,ȯr-ə-'lä-ji-kəl, -,är-ə-, -ə-rə-\ *adj* — **hy·dro·me·te·o·rol·o·gist** \-tē-ə-'rä-lə-jist\ *n*

hy·drom·e·ter \hī-'drä-mə-tər\ *n* (1675) : an instrument for determining the specific gravity of a liquid (as battery acid or an alcohol solution) and hence its strength — **hy·dro·met·ric** \,hī-drə-'me-trik\ *adj*

hy·dro·mor·phic \,hī-drə-'mȯr-fik\ *adj* (1938) *of a soil* : developed in the presence of an excess of moisture which tends to suppress aerobic factors in soil-building

hy·dron·ic \hī-'drä-nik\ *adj* [*hydr-* + *-onic* (as in *electronic*)] (1946) : of, relating to, or being a system of heating or cooling that involves transfer of heat by a circulating fluid (as water or vapor) in a closed system of pipes — **hy·dron·i·cal·ly** \-ni-k(ə-)lē\ *adv*

hy·dro·ni·um \hī-'drō-nē-əm\ *n* [ISV *hydr-* + *-onium*] (1908) : a hydrated hydrogen ion H_3O^+

hy·drop·a·thy \hī-'drä-pə-thē\ *n* [ISV] (1843) : the empirical use of water in the treatment of disease — compare HYDROTHERAPY — **hy·dro·path·ic** \,hī-drə-'pa-thik\ *adj*

hy·dro·per·ox·ide \,hī-drō-pə-'räk-,sīd\ *n* (1937) : a compound containing an O_2H group

hy·dro·phane \'hī-drə-,fān\ *n* (1784) : a semitranslucent opal that becomes translucent or transparent on immersion in water

hy·dro·phil·ic \,hī-drə-'fi-lik\ *adj* [NL *hydrophilus*, fr. Gk *hydr-* + *-philos* -philous] (1916) : of, relating to, or having a strong affinity for water (∼ *proteins*) — **hy·dro·phi·lic·i·ty** \,hī-drə-fi-'li-sə-tē\ *n*

hy·dro·pho·bia \,hī-drə-'fō-bē-ə\ *n* [LL, fr. Gk, fr. *hydr-* + *-phobia* -phobia] (1547) **1** : RABIES   **2** : a morbid dread of water

hy·dro·pho·bic \-'fō-bik\ *adj* (1807) **1** : of, relating to, or suffering from hydrophobia   **2** : lacking affinity for water — **hy·dro·pho·bic·i·ty** \-fō-'bi-sə-tē\ *n*

hy·dro·phone \'hī-drə-,fōn\ *n* (1860) : an instrument for listening to sound transmitted through water

hy·dro·phyte \-,fīt\ *n* [ISV] (1832) **1** : a perennial vascular aquatic plant having its overwintering buds under water   **2** : a plant growing in water or in soil too waterlogged for most plants to survive — **hy·dro·phyt·ic** \,hī-drə-'fi-tik\ *adj*

¹hy·dro·plane \'hī-drə-,plān\ *n* (1904) **1** : a powerboat designed for racing that skims the surface of the water   **2** : SEAPLANE

²hydroplane *vi* (1962) : to skim on water; *esp, of a vehicle* : to skid on a wet surface (as pavement) because a film of water on the surface causes the tires to lose contact with it

hy·dro·pon·ics \,hī-drə-'pä-niks\ *n pl but sing in constr* [*hydr-* + *-ponics* (as in *geoponics* agriculture)] (1937) : the growing of plants in nutrient solutions with or without an inert medium to provide mechanical support — **hy·dro·pon·ic** \-nik\ *adj* — **hy·dro·pon·i·cal·ly** \-ni-k(ə-)lē\ *adv*

hy·dro·pow·er \'hī-drə-,pau̇(-ə)r\ *n* (1933) : hydroelectric power

hy·dro·qui·none \,hī-drō-kwi-'nōn, -'kwi-,nōn\ *n* [ISV] (ca. 1872) : a white crystalline strongly reducing phenol $C_6H_6O_2$ used esp. as a photographic developer and as an antioxidant and stabilizer

hy·dro·sere \'hī-drə-,sir\ *n* (1920) : an ecological sere originating in an aquatic habitat

hy·dro·sol \'hī-drə-,säl, -,sȯl\ *n* [*hydr-* + *-sol* (fr. *solution*)] (1864) : a sol in which the liquid is water — **hy·dro·sol·ic** \,hī-drə-'säl-ik\ *adj*

hy·dro·space \-,spās\ *n* (1963) : the regions beneath the surface of the ocean

hy·dro·sphere \-,sfir\ *n* [ISV] (1887) : the aqueous vapor of the atmosphere; *broadly* : the aqueous envelope of the earth including bodies of water and aqueous vapor in the atmosphere — **hy·dro·spher·ic** \,hī-drə-'sfir-ik, -'sfer-\ *adj*

hy·dro·stat·ic \,hī-drə-'sta-tik\ *adj* [prob. fr. NL *hydrostaticus*, fr. *hydr-* + *staticus* static] (1666) : of or relating to fluids at rest or to the pressures they exert or transmit — compare HYDROKINETIC — **hy·dro·stat·i·cal·ly** \-ti-k(ə-)lē\ *adv*

hy·dro·stat·ics \-tiks\ *n pl but sing in constr* (1660) : a branch of physics that deals with the characteristics of fluids at rest and esp. with the pressure in a fluid or exerted by a fluid on an immersed body — compare HYDRODYNAMICS

hy·dro·ther·a·py \,hī-drə-'ther-ə-pē\ *n* [ISV] (1876) : the use of water esp. externally in the treatment of disease or disability

hy·dro·ther·mal \,hī-drə-'thər-məl\ *adj* [ISV] (1849) : of or relating to hot water — used esp. of the formation of minerals by hot solutions rising from a cooling magma — **hy·dro·ther·mal·ly** \-mə-lē\ *adv*

hy·dro·tho·rax \-'thȯr-,aks, -'thōr-\ *n* [NL] (1793) : an excess of serous fluid in the pleural cavity; *esp* : an effusion resulting from failing circulation (as in heart disease or from lung infection)

hy·dro·trop·ism \hī-'drä-trə-,pi-zəm\ *n* [ISV] (ca. 1882) : a tropism (as in plant roots) in which water or water vapor is the orienting factor — **hy·dro·tro·pic** \,hī-drə-'trō-pik, -'trä-\ *adj*

hy·drous \'hī-drəs\ *adj* (1826) : containing water usu. in chemical association (as in hydrates)

hy·drox·ide \hī-'dräk-,sīd\ *n* [ISV] (1851) **1** : the univalent anion OH⁻ consisting of one atom of hydrogen and one of oxygen — called also *hydroxide ion*   **2** : an ionic compound of hydroxide with an element or group

hy·droxy \hī-'dräk-sē\ *adj* [ISV, fr. *hydroxyl*] (1812) : being or containing hydroxyl; *esp* : containing hydroxyl esp. in place of hydrogen — usu. used in combination ⟨*hydroxy*acetic acid⟩

hy·droxy·ap·a·tite \hī-,dräk-sē-'a-pə-,tīt\ *or* **hy·drox·yl·ap·a·tite** \-sə-'la-pə-,tīt\ *n* (1912) : a complex phosphate of calcium $Ca_5(PO_4)_3$-OH that occurs as a mineral and is the chief structural element of vertebrate bone

hy·droxy·bu·tyr·ic acid \hī-,dräk-sē-byü-'tir-ik\ *n* (1879) : a hydroxy derivative $C_4H_8O_3$ of butyric acid that is excreted in increased quantities in the urine in diabetes

hy·drox·yl \hī-'dräk-səl\ *n* [*hydr-* + *ox-* + *-yl*] (1869) **1** : the chemical group or ion OH that consists of one atom of hydrogen and one of oxygen and is neutral or positively charged   **2** : HYDROXIDE 1 — **hy·drox·yl·ic** \,hī-,dräk-'si-lik\ *adj*

hy·drox·yl·amine \hī-,dräk-sə-lə-,mēn, ,hī-,dräk-'si-lə-,mēn\ *n* [ISV] (1869) : a colorless odorless nitrogenous base NH_3O that resembles ammonia in its reactions but is less basic and that is used esp. as a reducing agent

hy·drox·y·lase \hī-'dräk-sə-,lās, -,lāz\ *n* (1953) : any of a group of enzymes that catalyze oxidation reactions in which one of the two atoms of molecular oxygen is incorporated into the substrate and the other is used to oxidize NADH or NADPH

hy·drox·yl·ate \hī-'dräk-sə-ˌlāt\ *vt* **-at·ed; -at·ing** (ca. 1909) : to introduce hydroxyl into — **hy·drox·yl·ation** \-ˌdräk-sə-'lā-shən\ *n*

hy·droxy·pro·line \hī-ˌdräk-sē-'prō-ˌlēn\ *n* (1905) : an amino acid C₅H₉NO₃ that occurs naturally as a constituent of collagen

hy·droxy·tryp·ta·mine \-'trip-tə-ˌmēn\ *n* (1949) : SEROTONIN

hy·droxy·urea \-yu̇-'rē-ə\ *n* (1949) : a compound CH₄N₂O₂ used to treat some forms of leukemia

hy·droxy·zine \hī-'dräk-sə-ˌzēn\ *n* [*hydroxy-* + piperaz*ine*] (1956) : a compound C₂₁H₂₇ClN₂O₂ used as an antihistaminic and tranquilizer

hy·dro·zo·an \ˌhī-drə-'zō-ən\ *n* [ultim. fr. Gk *hydr-* + *zōion* animal — more at ZO-] (1877) : any of a class (Hydrozoa) of coelenterates that includes simple and compound polyps and jellyfishes having no stomodeum or gastric tentacles — **hydrozoan** *adj*

hy·e·na \hī-'ē-nə\ *n, pl* **hyenas** *also* **hyena** [ME *hyene*, fr. L *hyaena*, fr. Gk *hyaina*, fr. *hys* hog — more at SOW] (14c) : any of several large strong nocturnal carnivorous Old World mammals (family Hyaenidae) that usu. feed as scavengers — **hy·en·ic** \-'ē-nik, -'e-nik\ *adj*

Hy·ge·ia \hī-'jē-ə\ *n* [L, fr. Gk *Hygieia*] : the goddess of health in Greek mythology

hy·giene \'hī-ˌjēn *also* hī-'\ *n* [F *hygiène* & NL *hygieia*, fr. Gk, neut. pl. of *hygieinos* healthful, fr. *hygiēs* healthy; akin to Skt *su* well and to L *vivus* living — more at QUICK] (1671) **1 :** a science of the establishment and maintenance of health **2 :** conditions or practices (as of cleanliness) conducive to health — **hy·gien·ic** \ˌhī-jē-nik, -'je- *also* -jē-'e-nik\ *adj* — **hy·gien·i·cal·ly** \-ni-k(ə-)lē\ *adv* — **hy·gien·ist** \hī-'jē-nist, 'hī-jē-, hī-'je-\ *n*

hy·gien·ics \ˌhī-jē-niks, -'je- *also* -jē-'e-niks\ *n pl but sing in constr* (1855) : HYGIENE 1

hygr- *also* **hygro-** *comb form* [Gk, fr. *hygros* wet — more at HUMOR] **:** humidity : moisture (*hygro*phyte)

hy·gro·graph \'hī-grə-ˌgraf\ *n* [ISV] (ca. 1864) : an instrument for recording automatically variations in atmospheric humidity

hy·grom·e·ter \hī-'grä-mə-tər\ *n* [prob. fr. F *hygromètre*, fr. *hygr-* + *-mètre* -meter] (1670) : any of several instruments for measuring the humidity of the atmosphere — **hy·gro·met·ric** \ˌhī-grə-'me-trik\ *adj*

hy·groph·i·lous \hī-'grä-fə-ləs\ *adj* (1863) : living or growing in moist places

hy·gro·phyte \'hī-grə-ˌfīt\ *n* [ISV] (1903) : HYDROPHYTE — **hy·gro·phyt·ic** \ˌhī-grə-'fi-tik\ *adj*

hy·gro·scop·ic \ˌhī-grə-'skä-pik\ *adj* [*hygroscope*, an instrument showing changes in humidity + ¹-*ic*; fr. the use of such materials in the hygroscope] (1790) **1 :** readily taking up and retaining moisture **2 :** taken up and retained under some conditions of humidity and temperature (~ water in clay) — **hy·gro·scop·ic·i·ty** \-(ˌ)skä-'pi-sə-tē\ *n*

hying *pres part of* HIE

Hyk·sos \'hik-ˌsäs, -ˌsōs\ *adj* [Gk *Hyksōs*, dynasty ruling Egypt, perh. fr. Egypt *ḥq̓* ruler + *ḥ̓śt* foreign land] (1602) : of or relating to a Semite dynasty that ruled Egypt from about the 18th to the 16th century B.C.

hy·la \'hī-lə\ *n* [NL, fr. L *Hylas*, a companion of Hercules] (1842) : any of a genus (*Hyla*) of tree frogs

hy·lo·zo·ism \ˌhī-lə-'zō-ˌi-zəm\ *n* [Gk *hylē* matter, lit., wood + *zōos* alive, living; akin to Gk *zōē* life — more at QUICK] (1678) : a doctrine held esp. by early Greek philosophers that all matter has life — **hy·lo·zo·ist** \-'zō-ist\ *n* — **hy·lo·zo·is·tic** \-zō-'is-tik\ *adj*

hy·men \'hī-mən\ *n* [LL, fr. Gk *hymēn* membrane] (1615) : a fold of mucous membrane partly closing the orifice of the vagina — **hy·men·al** \-mə-nᵊl\ *adj*

Hymen *n* [L, fr. Gk *Hymēn*] : the Greek god of marriage

¹hy·me·ne·al \ˌhī-mə-'nē-əl\ *adj* [L *hymenaeus* wedding song, wedding, fr. Gk *hymenaios*, fr. *Hymēn*] (1602) : NUPTIAL — **hy·me·ne·al·ly** \-'nē-ə-lē\ *adv*

²hymeneal *n* (1655) **1** *pl, archaic* : NUPTIALS **2** *archaic* : a wedding hymn

hy·me·ni·um \hī-'mē-nē-əm\ *n, pl* **-nia** \-nē-ə\ *or* **-niums** [NL, fr. Gk *hymēn*] (1830) : a spore-bearing layer in fungi consisting of a group of asci or basidia often interspersed with sterile structures

hy·me·nop·ter·an \ˌhī-mə-'näp-tə-rən\ *n* [NL *Hymenoptera*, fr. Gk, neut. pl. of *hymenopteros* membrane-winged, fr. *hymēn* + *pteron* wing — more at FEATHER] (ca. 1842) : any of an order (Hymenoptera) of highly specialized insects with complete metamorphosis that include the bees, wasps, ants, ichneumon flies, sawflies, gall wasps, and related forms, often associate in large colonies with complex social organization, and have usu. four membranous wings and the abdomen generally borne on a slender pedicel — **hymenopteran** *adj* — **hy·me·nop·ter·ous** \-rəs\ *adj*

hy·me·nop·ter·on \-tə-ˌrän, -rən\ *n, pl* **-tera** \-tə-rə\ *also* **-terons** [NL, fr. Gk, neut. of *hymenopteros*] (1877) : HYMENOPTERAN

¹hymn \'him\ *n* [ME *ymne*, fr. OE *ymen*, fr. L *hymnus* song of praise, fr. Gk *hymnos*] (bef. 12c) **1 :** a song of praise to God **b :** a metrical composition adapted for singing in a religious service **2 :** a song of praise or joy **3 :** something resembling a hymn : PAEAN

²hymn *vb* **hymned** \'himd\; **hymn·ing** \'hi-miŋ\ *vt* (1667) : to praise or worship in or as if in hymns — *vi* : to sing a hymn

hym·nal \'him-nəl\ *n* [ME *hymnale*, fr. ML, fr. L *hymnus*] (15c) : a collection of church hymns

hym·na·ry \'him-nə-rē\ *n, pl* **-ries** (1888) : HYMNAL

hymn·book \'him-ˌbuk\ *n* (bef. 12c) : HYMNAL

hym·no·dy \'him-nə-dē\ *n* [LL *hymnodia*, fr. Gk *hymnōidia*, fr. *hymnos* + *aeidein* to sing — more at ODE] (1711) **1 :** hymn singing **2 :** hymn writing **3 :** the hymns of a time, place, or church

hym·nol·o·gy \him-'nä-lə-jē\ *n* [Gk *hymnologia* singing of hymns, fr. *hymnos* + *-logia* -logy] (ca. 1638) **1 :** HYMNODY **2 :** the study of hymns

hy·oid \'hī-ˌoid\ *adj* [NL *hyoides* hyoid bone] (1842) : of or relating to the hyoid bone

hyoid bone *n* [NL *hyoides*, fr. Gk *hyoeidēs* shaped like the letter upsilon (Υ, υ), being the hyoid bone, fr. *y, hy* upsilon] (ca. 1811) : a bone or complex of bones situated at the base of the tongue and supporting the tongue and its muscles

hy·o·scine \'hī-ə-ˌsēn\ *n* [ISV *hyoscyamine* + *-ine*] (1872) : SCOPOLAMINE; *esp* : the levorotatory form of scopolamine

hy·o·scy·a·mine \ˌhī-ə-'sī-ə-ˌmēn\ *n* [G *Hyoscyamin*, fr. NL *Hyoscyamus*, genus of herbs, fr. L, henbane, fr. Gk *hyoskyamos*, lit., swine's bean, fr. *hyos* (gen. of *hys* swine) + *kyamos* bean — more at SOW] (1858) : a poisonous crystalline alkaloid C₁₇H₂₃NO₃ of which atropine is a racemic mixture; *esp* : its levorotatory form found esp. in the plants belladonna and henbane and used similarly to atropine

hyp- — see HYPO-

hyp·abys·sal \ˌhī-pə-'bi-səl, ˌhī-\ *adj* [ISV] (1895) : of or relating to a fine-grained igneous rock usu. formed at a moderate distance below the surface — **hyp·abys·sal·ly** \-sə-lē\ *adv*

hy·pae·thral \hī-'pē-thrəl\ *adj* [L *hypaethrus* exposed to the open air, fr. Gk *hypaithros*, fr. *hypo-* + *aithēr* ether, air — more at ETHER] (1794) **1 :** having a roofless central space (~ temple) **2 :** open to the sky

hy·pal·la·ge \hī-'pa-lə-jē, hi-\ *n* [L, fr. Gk *hypallagē*, lit., interchange, fr. *hypallassein* to interchange, fr. *hypo-* + *allassein* to change, fr. *allos* other — more at ELSE] (1586) : an interchange of two elements in a phrase or sentence from a more logical to a less logical relationship (as in "a mind is a terrible thing to waste" for "to waste a mind is a terrible thing")

hy·pan·thi·um \hī-'pan(t)-thē-əm\ *n, pl* **-thia** \-thē-ə\ [NL, fr. *hypo-* + *anth-* + *-ium*] (ca. 1855) : an enlargement of the floral receptacle bearing on its rim the stamens, petals, and sepals and often enlarging and surrounding the fruits (as in the rose hip)

¹hype \'hīp\ *n* [by shortening & alter.] (1924) **1** *slang* : a narcotics addict **2** *slang* : HYPODERMIC

²hype *vt* **hyped; hyping** (1938) **1 :** STIMULATE, ENLIVEN — usu. used with *up* **2 :** INCREASE — **hyped–up** \'hīp-'dəp\ *adj*

³hype *vt* **hyped; hyp·ing** [origin unknown] (ca. 1931) **1 :** PUT ON, DECEIVE **2 :** to promote or publicize extravagantly

⁴hype *n* (1955) **1 :** DECEPTION, PUT-ON **2 :** PUBLICITY; *esp* : promotional publicity of an extravagant or contrived kind

hy·per \'hī-pər\ *adj* [short for *hyperactive*] (1971) **1 :** HIGH-STRUNG, EXCITABLE; *also* : highly excited **2 :** extremely active

hyper- *prefix* [ME *iper-*, fr. L *hyper-*, fr. Gk, fr. *hyper* — more at OVER] **1 :** above : beyond : SUPER- (*hyper*market) **2 a :** excessively (*hyper*sensitive) **b :** excessive (*hyper*emia) **3 :** that is or exists in a space of more than three dimensions (*hyper*space)

hy·per·acu·ity	hy·per·ex·cre·tion
hy·per·acute	hy·per·fas·tid·i·ous
hy·per·aes·thet·ic	hy·per·func·tion
hy·per·ag·gres·sive	hy·per·func·tion·al
hy·per·alert	hy·per·func·tion·ing
hy·per·arid	hy·per·im·mune
hy·per·arous·al	hy·per·im·mu·ni·za·tion
hy·per·aware	hy·per·im·mu·nize
hy·per·aware·ness	hy·per·in·flat·ed
hy·per·ca·tab·o·lism	hy·per·in·ner·va·tion
hy·per·cau·tious	hy·per·in·tel·lec·tu·al
hy·per·charged	hy·per·in·tel·li·gent
hy·per·civ·i·lized	hy·per·in·tense
hy·per·co·ag·u·la·bil·i·ty	hy·per·in·vo·lu·tion
hy·per·co·ag·u·la·ble	hy·per·ma·nia
hy·per·com·pet·i·tive	hy·per·man·ic
hy·per·con·cen·tra·tion	hy·per·mas·cu·line
hy·per·con·scious	hy·per·met·a·bol·ic
hy·per·con·scious·ness	hy·per·me·tab·o·lism
hy·per·de·vel·op·ment	hy·per·mo·bil·i·ty
hy·per·ef·fi·cient	hy·per·mod·ern
hy·per·emo·tion·al	hy·per·mod·ern·ist
hy·per·emo·tion·al·i·ty	hy·per·mu·ta·bil·i·ty
hy·per·en·dem·ic	hy·per·mu·ta·ble
hy·per·en·er·get·ic	hy·per·na·tion·al·is·tic
hy·per·ex·cit·abil·i·ty	hy·per·phys·i·cal
hy·per·ex·cit·able	hy·per·pig·men·ta·tion
hy·per·ex·cit·ed	hy·per·pig·ment·ed
hy·per·ex·cite·ment	

hy·per·pro·duc·er
hy·per·pro·duc·tion
hy·per·pure
hy·per·ra·tio·nal
hy·per·ra·tio·nal·i·ty
hy·per·re·ac·tive
hy·per·re·ac·tiv·i·ty
hy·per·re·ac·tor
hy·per·re·spon·sive
hy·per·ro·man·tic
hy·per·sa·line
hy·per·sal·in·i·ty
hy·per·sal·i·va·tion
hy·per·se·cre·tion
hy·per·sen·si·ti·za·tion
hy·per·sen·si·tize
hy·per·som·no·lence
hy·per·stat·ic
hy·per·stim·u·late
hy·per·stim·u·la·tion
hy·per·sus·cep·ti·bil·i·ty
hy·per·sus·cep·ti·ble
hy·per·tense
hy·per·typ·i·cal
hy·per·vig·i·lance
hy·per·vig·i·lant
hy·per·vir·u·lent
hy·per·vis·cos·i·ty

hy·per·acid·i·ty \ˌhī-pər-ə-'si-də-tē\ *n* (ca. 1890) : the condition of containing more than the normal amount of acid — **hy·per·ac·id** \ˌhī-pər-'a-səd\ *adj*

hy·per·ac·tive \ˌhī-pər-'ak-tiv\ *adj* (1867) : affected with or exhibiting hyperactivity; *broadly* : more active than is usual or desirable — **hyperactive** *n*

hy·per·ac·tiv·i·ty \-ˌak-'ti-və-tē\ *n* (1888) : the state or condition of being excessively or pathologically active; *esp* : ATTENTION DEFICIT DISORDER

hy·per·aes·the·sia *var of* HYPERESTHESIA

hy·per·al·i·men·ta·tion \ˌhī-pər-ˌa-lə-mən-'tā-shən\ *n* (1967) : the administration of nutrients by intravenous feeding esp. to patients who cannot ingest food through the alimentary tract

hy·per·bar·ic \ˌhī-pər-'bar-ik\ *adj* [*hyper-* + *bar-* + ¹-*ic*] (1962) : of, relating to, or utilizing greater than normal pressure (as of oxygen) (~ chamber) (~ medicine) — **hy·per·bar·i·cal·ly** \-i-k(ə-)lē\ *adv*

hy·per·bo·la \hī-'pər-bə-lə\ *n, pl* **-las** *or* **-lae** \-ˌlē\ [NL, fr. Gk *hyperbolē*] (1668) : a plane curve generated by a point so moving that the difference of the distances from two fixed points is a constant : a curve formed by the intersection of a dou-

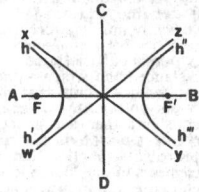

hyperbola: *AB, CD* axes; *F, F'* foci; *xy, zw* asymptotes; *h, h', h'', h'''* hyperbola

\ə\ abut \ᵊ\ kitten, F table \ər\ further \a\ ash \ā\ ace \ä\ mop, mar \aù\ out \ch\ chin \e\ bet \ē\ easy \g\ go \i\ hit \ī\ ice \j\ job \ŋ\ sing \ō\ go \ò\ law \òi\ boy \th\ thin \t̲h̲\ the \ü\ loot \ù\ foot \y\ yet \zh\ vision \à, k̲, ⁿ, œ, œ̄, ᵫ, ᵬ, ᶣ\ *see* Guide to Pronunciation

ble right circular cone with a plane that cuts both halves of the cone
hy·per·bo·le \hī-'pər-bə-(,)lē\ *n* [L, fr. Gk *hyperbolē* excess, hyperbole, hyperbola, fr. *hyperballein* to exceed, fr. *hyper-* + *ballein* to throw — more at DEVIL] (15c) : extravagant exaggeration (as "mile-high ice≠cream cones") — **hy·per·bo·list** \-list\ *n*

¹**hy·per·bol·ic** \,hī-pər-'bä-lik\ *also* **hy·per·bol·i·cal** \-li-kəl\ *adj* (15c) : of, relating to, or marked by hyperbole — **hy·per·bol·i·cal·ly** \-li-k(ə-)lē\ *adv*

²**hyperbolic** *adj* (1646) **1** : of, relating to, or being analogous to a hyperbola **2** : of, relating to, or being a space in which more than one line parallel to a given line passes through a point 〈~ geometry〉
hyperbolic function *n* (ca. 1890) : any of a set of six functions analogous to the trigonometric functions but related to the hyperbola in a way similar to that in which the trigonometric functions are related to a circle
hyperbolic paraboloid *n* (1842) : a saddle-shaped quadric surface whose sections by planes parallel to one coordinate plane are hyperbolas while those sections by planes parallel to the other two are parabolas if proper orientation of the coordinate axes is assumed
hy·per·bo·lize \hī-'pər-bə-,līz\ *vb* **-lized; -liz·ing** *vi* (1599) : to indulge in hyperbole ~ *vt* : to exaggerate to a hyperbolic degree
hy·per·bo·loid \-,lóid\ *n* (1743) : a quadric surface whose sections by planes parallel to one coordinate plane are hyperbolas while those sections by planes parallel to the other two are hyperbolas if proper orientation of the axes is assumed — **hy·per·bo·loi·dal** \(,)hī-,pər-bə-'lói-d°l\ *adj*

¹**hy·per·bo·re·an** \,hī-pər-'bōr-ē-ən, -'bór-; -(,)pər-bə-'rē-ən\ *n* [L *Hyperborei* (pl.), fr. Gk *Hyperboreoi*, fr. *hyper-* + *Boreas*] (15c) **1** *often cap* : a member of a people held by the ancient Greeks to live beyond the north wind in a region of perpetual sunshine **2** : an inhabitant of a cool northern climate

²**hyperborean** *adj* (1591) **1** : of or relating to an extreme northern region : FROZEN **2** : of or relating to any of the arctic peoples
hy·per·cal·ce·mia \,hī-pər-,kal-'sē-mē-ə\ *n* [NL] (1925) : an excess of calcium in the blood — **hy·per·cal·ce·mic** \-'sē-mik\ *adj*
hy·per·cap·nia \-'kap-nē-ə\ *n* [NL, fr. *hyper-* + Gk *kapnos* smoke; prob. akin to Lith *kvapas* breath] (1908) : the presence of excessive amounts of carbon dioxide in the blood — **hy·per·cap·nic** \-nik\ *adj*
hy·per·cat·a·lex·is \-,ka-tə-'lek-səs\ *n, pl* **-lex·es** \-'lek-,sēz\ [NL] (ca. 1890) : the occurrence of an additional syllable after the final complete foot or dipody in a line of verse — **hy·per·cat·a·lec·tic** \-'lek-tik\ *adj*
hy·per·charge \'hī-pər-,chärj\ *n* [short for *hyperonic charge*, fr. *hyperon*] (1956) : a quantum characteristic of a group of subatomic particles governed by the strong force that is related to strangeness and is represented by a number equal to twice the average value of the electric charge of the group
hy·per·cho·les·ter·ol·emia \,hī-pər-kə-,les-tə-rə-'lē-mē-ə\ *n* [NL] (ca. 1894) : the presence of excess cholesterol in the blood — **hy·per·cho·les·ter·ol·emic** \-mik\ *adj*
hy·per·com·plex \,hī-pər-'käm-,pleks\ *adj* (ca. 1889) : of, relating to, or being the most general form of number that extends the complex number to an expression of the same type (as a quaternion) involving a finite number of units or components in which addition is by components and multiplication does not have all of the properties of real or complex numbers
hy·per·cor·rect \,hī-pər-kə-'rekt\ *adj* (1922) : of, relating to, or characterized by the production of a nonstandard linguistic form or construction on the basis of a false analogy (as "badly" in "my eyes have gone badly" and "widely" in "open widely") — **hy·per·cor·rec·tion** \-'rek-shən\ *n* — **hy·per·cor·rect·ly** \-'rek-(t)lē\ *adv* — **hy·per·cor·rect·ness** \-'rek(t)-nəs\ *n*
hy·per·crit·ic \,hī-pər-'kri-tik\ *n* [NL *hypercriticus*, fr. *hyper-* + L *criticus* critic] (1633) : a carping or unduly censorious critic — **hy·per·crit·i·cism** \-'kri-tə-,si-zəm\ *n*
hy·per·crit·i·cal \-'kri-ti-kəl\ *adj* (1605) : meticulously or excessively critical **syn** see CRITICAL — **hy·per·crit·i·cal·ly** \-k(ə-)lē\ *adv*
hy·per·cube \'hī-pər-,kyüb\ *n* (1909) **1** : a geometric figure (as a tesseract) in Euclidean space of *n* dimensions that is analogous to a cube in three dimensions **2** : a computer architecture in which each processor is connected to *n* others based on analogy to a hypercube of *n* dimensions
hy·per·emia \,hī-pər-'ē-mē-ə\ *n* [NL] (ca. 1839) : excess of blood in a body part : CONGESTION — **hy·per·emic** \-mik\ *adj*
hy·per·es·the·sia \,hī-pər-es-'thē-zh(ē-)ə\ *n* [NL, fr. *hyper-* + *-esthesia* (as in *anesthesia*)] (ca. 1852) : unusual or pathological sensitivity of the skin or of a particular sense — **hy·per·es·thet·ic** \-'the-tik\ *adj*
hy·per·eu·tec·tic \,hī-pər-yü-'tek-tik\ *adj* (1902) : HYPEREUTECTOID
hy·per·eu·tec·toid \-,tóid\ *adj* (1908) : containing the minor component in excess of that contained in the eutectoid
hy·per·ex·tend \,hī-pər-ik-'stend\ *vt* (1883) : to extend so that the angle between bones of a joint is greater than normal 〈a ~ed elbow〉 — **hy·per·ex·ten·sion** \-'sten(t)-shən\ *n*
hy·per·fine \'hī-pər-,fīn\ *adj* (1926) : being or relating to a fine≠structure multiplet occurring in an atomic spectrum that is due to interaction between electrons and nuclear spin
hy·per·fo·cal distance \,hi-pər-'fō-kəl-\ *n* [ISV] (1905) : the nearest distance upon which a photographic lens may be focused to produce satisfactory definition at infinity
hy·per·ga·my \hī-'pər-gə-mē\ *n, pl* **-mies** (1883) : marriage into an equal or higher caste or social group
hy·per·geo·met·ric distribution \,hī-pər-,jē-ə-'me-trik-\ *n* (1950) : a probability function that gives the probability of obtaining exactly *x* elements of one kind and *n* − *x* elements of another if *n* elements are chosen at random without replacement from a finite population containing *N* elements of which *M* are of the first kind and *N* − *M* are of the second kind and has the form

$$f(x) = \frac{\binom{M}{x}\binom{N-M}{n-x}}{\binom{N}{n}} \text{ where } \binom{M}{x} = \frac{M!}{x!(M-x)!}$$

hy·per·gly·ce·mia \,hī-pər-glī-'sē-mē-ə\ *n* [NL] (1894) : excess of sugar in the blood — **hy·per·gly·ce·mic** \-mik\ *adj*
hy·per·gol·ic \,hī-pər-'gä-lik\ *adj* [G *Hypergol* a hypergolic fuel, prob. fr. *hyper-* + *erg-* + *-ol* (hydrocarbon)] (1947) **1** : igniting upon con-

tact of components without external aid (as a spark) **2** : of, relating to, or using hypergolic fuel — **hy·per·gol·i·cal·ly** \-li-k(ə-)lē\ *adv*
hy·per·hi·dro·sis \,hī-pər-hī-'drō-səs\ *n* [NL *hidrosis* perspiration, fr. Gk *hidrōsis*, fr. *hidroun* to sweat, fr. *hidrōs* sweat — more at SWEAT] (ca. 1860) : generalized or local excessive sweating
hy·per·in·fla·tion \,hī-pər-in-'flā-shən\ *n* (1930) : inflation growing at a very high rate in a very short time; *also* : a period of hyperinflation — **hy·per·in·fla·tion·ary** \-shə-,ner-ē\ *adj*
hy·per·in·su·lin·ism \,hī-pə-'rin(t)-s(ə-)lə-,ni-zəm\ *n* [ISV] (1924) : the presence of excess insulin in the body resulting in hypoglycemia
Hy·pe·ri·on \hī-'pir-ē-ən\ *n* [L, fr. Gk *Hyperiōn*] : a Titan and the father of Aurora, Selene, and Helios
hy·per·ir·ri·ta·bil·i·ty \,hī-pər-,ir-ə-tə-'bi-lə-tē\ *n* (1913) : abnormally great or uninhibited response to stimuli — **hy·per·ir·ri·ta·ble** \-'ir-ə-tə-bəl\ *adj*
hy·per·ker·a·to·sis \,hī-pər-,ker-ə-'tō-səs\ *n, pl* **-to·ses** \-'tō-,sēz\ [NL] (1841) : hypertrophy of the corneous layer of the skin — **hy·per·ker·a·tot·ic** \-'tä-tik\ *adj*
hy·per·ki·ne·sia \-kə-'nē-zh(ē-)ə, -kī-\ *n* [NL, fr. *hyperkinesis*] (ca. 1848) : HYPERKINESIS
hy·per·ki·ne·sis \-'nē-səs\ *n* [NL] (ca. 1855) **1** : abnormally increased and sometimes uncontrollable activity or muscular movements **2** : a condition esp. of childhood characterized by hyperactivity
hy·per·ki·net·ic \-'ne-tik\ *adj* (1888) : of, relating to, or affected with hyperkinesis or hyperactivity 〈the ~ child〉; *also* : characterized by fast-paced or frenetic activity
hy·per·li·pe·mia \,hī-pər-lī-'pē-mē-ə\ *n* [NL] (ca. 1894) : the presence of excess fat or lipids in the blood — **hy·per·li·pe·mic** \-mik\ *adj*
hy·per·lip·id·emia \-,li-pə-'dē-mē-ə-\ *n* [NL] (1961) : HYPERLIPEMIA
hy·per·mar·ket \'hī-pər-,mär-kət\ *n* (1970) : a very large store that carries products found in a supermarket as well as merchandise commonly found in department stores
hy·per·me·ter \hī-'pər-mə-tər\ *n* [LL *hypermetrus* hypercatalectic, fr. Gk *hypermetros* beyond measure, beyond the meter, fr. *hyper-* + *metron* measure, meter] (ca. 1656) **1** : a verse marked by hypercatalexis **2** : a period comprising more than two or three cola — **hy·per·met·ric** \,hī-pər-'me-trik\ *or* **hy·per·met·ri·cal** \-tri-kəl\ *adj*
hy·per·me·tro·pia \,hī-pər-mi-'trō-pē-ə\ *n* [NL, fr. Gk *hypermetros* + NL *-opia*] (1868) : HYPEROPIA — **hy·per·me·tro·pic** \-'trō-pik, -'trä-\ *adj*
hy·perm·ne·sia \,hī-(,)pərm-'nē-zh(ē-)ə\ *n* [NL, fr. *hyper-* + *-mnesia* (as in *amnesia*)] (1882) : abnormally vivid or complete memory or recall of the past — **hy·perm·ne·sic** \-'nē-zik, -sik\ *adj*
hy·per·on \'hī-pə-,rän\ *n* [prob. fr. *hyper-* + ²*-on*] (1953) : a fundamental particle of the baryon group that is greater in mass than a proton or neutron
hy·per·opia \,hī-pə-'rō-pē-ə\ *n* [NL] (1884) : a condition in which visual images come to a focus behind the retina of the eye and vision is better for distant than for near objects — called also *farsightedness* — **hy·per·opic** \-'rä-pik, -'rä-\ *adj*
hy·per·os·to·sis \,hī-pər-,äs-'tō-səs\ *n, pl* **-to·ses** \-'tō-,sēz\ [NL] (ca. 1836) : excessive growth or thickening of bone tissue — **hy·per·os·tot·ic** \-'tä-tik\ *adj*
hy·per·par·a·site \,hī-pər-'par-ə-,sīt\ *n* (ca. 1889) : a parasite that is parasitic upon another parasite — **hy·per·par·a·sit·ic** \-,par-ə-'si-tik\ *adj* — **hy·per·par·a·sit·ism** \-'par-ə-,sī-,ti-zəm, -'par-ə-sə-\ *n*
hy·per·para·thy·roid·ism \-,par-ə-'thī-,rói-,di-zəm\ *n* (1917) : the presence of excess parathyroid hormone in the body resulting in disturbance of calcium metabolism with increase in serum calcium and decrease in inorganic phosphorus, loss of calcium from bone, and renal damage with frequent kidney-stone formation
hy·per·pha·gia \-'fā-j(ē-)ə\ *n* [NL] (1941) : abnormally increased appetite for consumption of food frequently associated with injury to the hypothalamus — **hy·per·phag·ic** \-'fa-jik\ *adj*
hy·per·pi·tu·ita·rism \-pə-'tü-ə-tə-,ri-zəm, -'tü-ə-,tri-, -'tyü-\ *n* [ISV] (1909) : excessive production of growth hormones by the pituitary gland — **hy·per·pi·tu·itary** \-'tü-ə-,ter-ē, -'tyü-\ *adj*
hy·per·plane \'hī-pər-,plān\ *n* (1903) : a figure in hyperspace corresponding to a plane in ordinary space
hy·per·pla·sia \,hī-pər-'plā-zh(ē-)ə\ *n* [NL] (1861) : an abnormal or unusual increase in the elements composing a part (as cells composing a tissue) — **hy·per·plas·tic** \-'plas-tik\ *adj*
hy·per·ploid \'hī-pər-,plóid\ *adj* [ISV] (1930) : having a chromosome number slightly greater than an exact multiple of the monoploid number — **hyperploid** *n* — **hy·per·ploi·dy** \-,plói-dē\ *n*
hy·per·pnea \,hī-pər-'nē-ə, -,pərp-'nē-\ *n* [NL, fr. Gk *hyper-* (ca. 1860) : abnormally rapid or deep breathing — **hy·per·pne·ic** \-'nē-ik\ *adj*
hy·per·po·lar·ize \,hī-pər-'pō-lə-,rīz\ *vt* (1950) : to produce an increase in potential difference across (a biological membrane) 〈a *hyperpolarized* nerve cell〉 ~ *vi* : to undergo or produce an increase in potential difference across something — **hy·per·po·lar·iza·tion** \-,pō-lə-rə-'zā-shən\ *n*
hy·per·py·rex·ia \-,pī-'rek-sē-ə\ *n* [NL] (1875) : exceptionally high fever (as in a particular disease)
hy·per·re·al·ism \,hī-pər-'rē-ə-,li-zəm, -'ri-ə-\ *n* (1937) : realism in painting characterized by depiction of real life in an unusual or striking manner — compare PHOTO-REALISM — **hy·per·re·al·ist** \-list\ *adj* — **hy·per·re·al·is·tic** \-,rē-ə-'lis-tik, -,ri-\ *adj*
hy·per·sen·si·tive \,hī-pər-'sen(t)-s(ə-)tiv\ *adj* (1871) **1** : excessively or abnormally sensitive **2** : abnormally susceptible physiologically to a specific agent (as a drug or antigen) — **hy·per·sen·si·tive·ness** — **hy·per·sen·si·tiv·i·ty** \-,sen(t)-sə-'ti-və-tē\ *n*
hy·per·sex·u·al \-'sek-sh(ə-)wəl, -'sek-shəl\ *adj* (1942) : exhibiting unusual or excessive concern with or indulgence in sexual activity — **hy·per·sex·u·al·i·ty** \-,sek-shə-'wa-lə-tē\ *n*
hy·per·son·ic \-'sä-nik\ *adj* [ISV] (1946) **1** : of or relating to speed five or more times that of sound in air — compare SONIC **2** : moving, capable of moving, or utilizing air currents that move at hypersonic speed 〈~ wind tunnel〉 — **hy·per·son·i·cal·ly** \-ni-k(ə-)lē\ *adv*
hy·per·space \'hī-pər-,spās\ *n* (1867) **1** : space of more than three dimensions **2** : a fictional space held to support extraordinary events (as travel faster than the speed of light)

hy·per·sthene \'hī-pərs-,thēn\ *n* [F *hypersthène*, fr. Gk *hyper-* + *sthenos* strength] (ca. 1808) : an orthorhombic grayish or greenish black or dark brown pyroxene — **hy·per·sthe·nic** \,hī-pərs-'the-nik, -'thē-\ *adj*

hy·per·sur·face \'hī-pər-,sər-fəs\ *n* (ca. 1909) : a figure that is the analogue in hyperspace of a surface in three-dimensional space

hy·per·ten·sion \,hī-pər-'ten(t)-shən\ *n* [ISV] (1893) : abnormally high blood pressure and esp. arterial blood pressure; *also* : the systemic condition accompanying high blood pressure — **hy·per·ten·sive** \,hī-pər-'ten(t)-siv\ *adj or n*

hy·per·text \'hī-pər-,tekst\ *n* (1986) : a database format in which information related to that on a display can be accessed directly from the display

hy·per·ther·mia \,hī-pər-'thər-mē-ə\ *n* [NL, fr. *hyper-* + *therm-* + *-ia*] (1887) : exceptionally high fever esp. when induced artificially for therapeutic purposes — **hy·per·ther·mic** \-mik\ *adj*

hy·per·thy·roid \-'thī-,róid\ *adj* [back-formation fr. *hyperthyroidism*] (1916) : of, relating to, or affected with hyperthyroidism

hy·per·thy·roid·ism \-,rói-,di-zəm\ *n* [ISV] (ca. 1900) : excessive functional activity of the thyroid gland; *also* : the resulting condition marked esp. by increased metabolic rate, enlargement of the thyroid gland, rapid heart rate, and high blood pressure

hy·per·to·nia \,hī-pər-'tō-nē-ə\ *n* (ca. 1842) : HYPERTONICITY

hy·per·ton·ic \-'tä-nik\ *adj* [ISV] (1855) **1** : exhibiting excessive tone or tension ⟨a ~ baby⟩ ⟨a ~ bladder⟩ **2** : having a higher osmotic pressure than a surrounding medium or a fluid under comparison

hy·per·to·nic·i·ty \-tə-'ni-sə-tē\ *n* (1886) : the quality or state of being hypertonic

¹hy·per·tro·phy \hī-'pər-trə-fē\ *n, pl* **-phies** [prob. fr. NL *hypertrophia*, fr. *hyper-* + *-trophia* -trophy] (1834) **1** : excessive development of an organ or part; *specif* : increase in bulk (as by thickening of muscle fibers) without multiplication of parts **2** : exaggerated growth or complexity — **hy·per·tro·phic** \,hī-pər-'trō-fik\ *adj*

²hypertrophy *vi* **-phied; -phy·ing** (1883) : to undergo hypertrophy

hy·per·ur·ban·ism \,hī-pər-'ər-bə-,ni-zəm\ *n* (1925) : use of hypercorrect forms in language; *also* : such a form

hy·per·uri·ce·mia \,hī-pər-,yùr-ə-'sē-mē-ə\ *n* [NL] (ca. 1894) : excess uric acid in the blood

hy·per·ve·loc·i·ty \-və-'lä-sə-tē, -'läs-tē\ *n* (1949) : a high or relatively high velocity; *esp* : one greater than 10,000 feet (3048 meters) per second

hy·per·ven·ti·late \,hī-pər-'ven-t⁰l-,āt\ *vi* (1931) : to breathe rapidly and deeply : undergo hyperventilation

hy·per·ven·ti·la·tion \-,ven-t⁰l-'ā-shən\ *n* (1928) : excessive rate and depth of respiration leading to abnormal loss of carbon dioxide from the blood

hy·per·vi·ta·min·osis \-,vī-tə-mə-'nō-səs\ *n, pl* **-oses** \-'nō-,sēz\ [NL] (1928) : an abnormal state resulting from excessive intake of one or more vitamins

hy·pha \'hī-fə\ *n, pl* **hy·phae** \-(,)fē\ [NL, fr. Gk *hyphē* web; akin to Gk *hyphos* web — more at WEAVE] (1866) : one of the threads that make up the mycelium of a fungus, increase by apical growth, and are coenocytic or transversely septate — **hy·phal** \-fəl\ *adj*

¹hy·phen \'hī-fən\ *n* [LL & Gk; LL, fr. Gk, fr. *hyph' hen* under one, fr. *hypo* under + *hen*, neut. of *heis* one — more at UP, SAME] (ca. 1620) : a punctuation mark - used esp. to divide or to compound words, word elements, or numbers — **hy·phen·less** \-ləs\ *adj*

²hyphen *vt* (1814) : HYPHENATE

¹hy·phen·ate \'hī-fə-,nāt\ *vt* **-at·ed; -at·ing** (ca. 1889) : to connect (as two words) or divide (as a word at the end of a line of print) with a hyphen — **hy·phen·ation** \,hī-fə-'nā-shən\ *n*

²hyphenate *n* [fr. the hyphens in the titles of such people, as *producer-director*] (1974) : a person who performs more than one function (as on a filmmaking project)

hyphenated *adj* [fr. the use of hyphenated words (as German-American) to designate foreign-born citizens of the U.S.] (ca. 1893) : of, relating to, or being an individual or unit of mixed or diverse background or composition ⟨~ Americans⟩

hypn- *or* **hypno-** *comb form* [F, fr. LL, fr. Gk, fr. *hypnos* — more at SOMNOLENT] **1** : sleep ⟨*hypno*pompic⟩ **2** : hypnotism ⟨*hypno*therapy⟩

hyp·na·go·gic *also* **hyp·no·go·gic** \,hip-nə-'gä-jik, -,gō-\ *adj* [F *hypnagogique*, fr. Gk *hypn-* + *-agōgos* leading, inducing, fr. *agein* to lead — more at AGENT] (1886) : of, relating to, or associated with the drowsiness preceding sleep

hyp·noid \'hip-,nóid\ *or* **hyp·noi·dal** \hip-'nói-d⁰l\ *adj* (1898) : of or relating to sleep or hypnosis

hyp·no·pom·pic \,hip-nə-'päm-pik\ *adj* [*hypn-* + Gk *pompē* act of sending — more at POMP] (ca. 1901) : associated with the semiconsciousness preceding waking ⟨~ illusions⟩

Hyp·nos \'hip-nəs, -,nōs\ *n* [Gk] : the Greek god of sleep

hyp·no·sis \hip-'nō-səs\ *n, pl* **-no·ses** \-,sēz\ [NL] (1876) **1** : a state that resembles sleep but is induced by a person whose suggestions are readily accepted by the subject **2** : any of various conditions that resemble sleep **3** : HYPNOTISM 1

hyp·no·ther·a·py \,hip-nō-'ther-ə-pē\ *n* (1897) **1** : the treatment of disease by hypnotism **2** : psychotherapy that facilitates suggestion, reeducation, or analysis by means of hypnosis — **hyp·no·ther·a·pist** \-pist\ *n*

¹hyp·not·ic \hip-'nä-tik\ *adj* [F or LL; F *hypnotique*, fr. LL *hypnoticus*, fr. Gk *hypnōtikos*, fr. *hypnoun* to put to sleep, fr. *hypnos*] (1625) **1** : tending to produce sleep : SOPORIFIC **2 a** : of or relating to hypnosis or hypnotism **b** : readily holding the attention ⟨a ~ personality⟩ ⟨a simple ~ beat⟩ — **hyp·not·i·cal·ly** \-ti-k(ə-)lē\ *adv*

²hypnotic *n* (1681) **1** : a sleep-inducing agent : SOPORIFIC **2** : one that is or can be hypnotized

hyp·no·tism \'hip-nə-,ti-zəm\ *n* (1842) **1** : the study or act of inducing hypnosis — compare MESMERISM **2** : HYPNOSIS 1 — **hyp·no·tist** \-tist\ *n*

hyp·no·tize \-,tīz\ *vt* **-tized; -tiz·ing** (1843) **1** : to induce hypnosis in **2** : to dazzle or overcome by or as if by suggestion ⟨a voice that ~s its hearers⟩ ⟨drivers *hypnotized* by speed⟩ — **hyp·no·tiz·abil·i·ty** \,hip-nə-,tī-zə-'bi-lə-tē\ *n* — **hyp·no·tiz·able** \'hip-nə-,tī-zə-bəl\ *adj*

¹hy·po \'hī-(,)pō\ *n, pl* **hypos** (1711) : HYPOCHONDRIA

²hypo *n, pl* **hypos** [short for *hyposulfite* thiosulfate] (1855) : SODIUM THIOSULFATE

³hypo *n, pl* **hypos** (1925) **1** : HYPODERMIC SYRINGE **2** : HYPODERMIC INJECTION **3** : STIMULUS

⁴hypo *vt* (1942) : STIMULATE ⟨do everything possible to ~ the economy —Clem Morgello⟩

hypo- *or* **hyp-** *prefix* [ME *ypo-*, fr. OF, fr. LL *hypo-*, *hyp-*, fr. Gk, fr. *hypo* — more at UP] **1** : under : beneath : down ⟨*hypo*blast⟩ ⟨*hypo*dermic⟩ **2** : less than normal or normally ⟨*hyp*esthesia⟩ ⟨*hypo*tension⟩ **3** : in a lower state of oxidation : in a low and usu. the lowest position in a series of compounds ⟨*hypo*chlorous acid⟩ ⟨*hypo*xanthine⟩

hy·po·al·ler·gen·ic \,hī-pō-,a-lər-'je-nik\ *adj* (1940) : having little likelihood of causing an allergic response ⟨~ cosmetics⟩ ⟨~ foods⟩

hy·po·blast \'hī-pə-,blast\ *n* (1875) : the endoderm of an embryo

hy·po·cal·ce·mia \,hī-pō-,kal-'sē-mē-ə\ *n* [NL] (1925) : a deficiency of calcium in the blood — **hy·po·cal·ce·mic** \-mik\ *adj*

hy·po·caust \'hī-pə-,kóst\ *n* [L *hypocaustum*, fr. Gk *hypokauston*, fr. *hypokaiein* to light a fire under, fr. *hypo-* + *kaiein* to burn] (1678) : an ancient Roman central heating system with underground furnace and tile flues to distribute the heat

hy·po·cen·ter \'hī-pə-,sen-tər\ *n* (1905) **1** : the focus of an earthquake — compare EPICENTER 1 **2** : the point on the earth's surface directly below the center of a nuclear bomb explosion — **hy·po·cen·tral** \,hī-pə-'sen-trəl\ *adj*

hy·po·chlo·rite \,hī-pə-'klōr-,īt, -'klòr-\ *n* (ca. 1849) : a salt or ester of hypochlorous acid

hy·po·chlo·rous acid \,hī-pə-'klōr-əs-, -'klòr-\ *n* [ISV] (1841) : an unstable strongly oxidizing but weak acid HClO obtained in solution along with hydrochloric acid by reaction of chlorine with water and used esp. in the form of salts as an oxidizing agent, bleaching agent, disinfectant, and chlorinating agent

hy·po·chon·dria \,hī-pə-'kän-drē-ə\ *n* [NL, fr. LL, pl., upper abdomen (formerly regarded as the seat of hypochondria), fr. Gk, lit., the parts under the cartilage (of the breastbone), fr. *hypo-* + *chondros* cartilage] (1668) : extreme depression of mind or spirits often centered on imaginary physical ailments; *specif* : HYPOCHONDRIASIS

¹hy·po·chon·dri·ac \-drē-,ak\ *adj* [F *hypochondriaque*, fr. Gk *hypochondriakos*, fr. *hypochondria*] (1599) **1** : HYPOCHONDRIACAL **2** : of, relating to, or being the two regions of the abdomen lying on either side of the epigastric region and above the lumbar regions

²hypochondriac *n* (1639) : one affected by hypochondria

hy·po·chon·dri·a·cal \-kən-'drī-ə-kəl, -,kän-\ *adj* (1621) : affected or produced by hypochondria — **hy·po·chon·dri·a·cal·ly** \-k(ə-)lē\ *adv*

hy·po·chon·dri·a·sis \-'drī-ə-səs\ *n, pl* **-a·ses** \-,sēz\ [NL] (1766) : morbid concern about one's health esp. when accompanied by delusions of physical disease

hy·po·chro·mic anemia \,hī-pə-'krō-mik-\ *n* (1934) : an anemia marked by deficient hemoglobin and usu. microcytic red blood cells

hy·po·co·rism \hī-'pä-kə-,ri-zəm; ,hī-pə-'kòr-,i-, -'kòr-\ *n* [LL *hypocorisma*, fr. Gk *hypokorisma*, fr. *hypokorizesthai* to call by pet names, fr. *hypo-* + *korizesthai* to caress, fr. *koros* boy, *korē* girl] (1850) **1** : a pet name **2** : the use of pet names — **hy·po·co·ris·tic** \,hī-pə-kə-'ris-tik\ *or* **hy·po·co·ris·ti·cal** \-ti-kəl\ *adj* — **hy·po·co·ris·ti·cal·ly** \-ti-k(ə-)lē\ *adv*

hy·po·cot·yl \'hī-pə-,kä-t⁰l\ *n* [ISV *hypo-* + *cotyl*edon] (1880) : the part of the axis of a plant embryo or seedling below the cotyledon — see PLUMULE illustration

hy·poc·ri·sy \hi-'pä-krə-sē *also* hī-\ *n, pl* **-sies** [ME *ypocrisie*, fr. OF, fr. LL *hypocrisis*, fr. Gk *hypokrisis* act of playing a part on the stage, hypocrisy, fr. *hypokrinesthai* to answer, act on the stage, fr. *hypo-* + *krinein* to decide — more at CERTAIN] (13c) **1** : a feigning to be what one is not or to believe what one does not; *esp* : the false assumption of an appearance of virtue or religion **2** : an act or instance of hypocrisy

hyp·o·crite \'hi-pə-,krit\ *n* [ME *ypocrite*, fr. OF, fr. LL *hypocrita*, fr. Gk *hypokritēs* actor, hypocrite, fr. *hypokrinesthai*] (13c) : a person who puts on a false appearance of virtue or religion — **hypocrite** *adj*

hyp·o·crit·i·cal \,hi-pə-'kri-ti-kəl\ *adj* (1561) : characterized by hypocrisy; *also* : being a hypocrite — **hyp·o·crit·i·cal·ly** \-k(ə-)lē\ *adv*

hy·po·cy·cloid \,hī-pō-'sī-,klòid\ *n* (1843) : a curve traced by a point on the circumference of a circle rolling internally on the circumference of a fixed circle

hy·po·der·mal \,hī-pə-'dər-məl\ *adj* (1854) **1** : of or relating to a hypodermis **2** : lying beneath an outer skin or epidermis

¹hy·po·der·mic \-mik\ *adj* [ISV] (1863) **1** : adapted for use in or administered by injection beneath the skin **2** : of or relating to the parts beneath the skin **3** : resembling a hypodermic injection in effect : STIMULATING — **hy·po·der·mi·cal·ly** \-mi-k(ə-)lē\ *adv*

²hypodermic *n* (ca. 1889) **1** : HYPODERMIC INJECTION **2** : HYPODERMIC SYRINGE

hypodermic injection *n* (1868) : an injection made into the subcutaneous tissues

hypodermic needle *n* (ca. 1909) **1** : NEEDLE 1c(1) **2** : a hypodermic syringe complete with needle

hypodermic syringe *n* (1893) : a small syringe used with a hollow needle for injection of material into or beneath the skin

hy·po·der·mis \,hī-pə-'dər-məs\ *n* [NL] (ca. 1866) **1** : the tissue immediately beneath the epidermis of a plant esp. when modified to serve as a supporting and protecting layer **2** : the cellular layer that underlies and secretes the chitinous cuticle (as of an arthropod) **3** : SUPERFICIAL FASCIA

hy·po·dip·loid \,hī-pō-'di-,plóid\ *adj* (1962) : having slightly fewer than the diploid number of chromosomes — **hy·po·dip·loi·dy** \-,plói-dē\ *n*

hy·po·eu·tec·toid \,hī-pō-yù-'tek-,tòid\ *adj* (1911) : containing less of the minor component than is contained in the eutectoid

hy·po·gas·tric \,hī-pə-'gas-trik\ *adj* [F *hypogastrique*, fr. *hypogastre* hypogastric region, fr. Gk *hypogastrion*, fr. *hypo-* + *gastr-*, *gastēr* belly — more at GASTRIC] (1656) : of or relating to the lower median region of the abdomen

---

\ə\ abut \'ə\ kitten, F table \ər\ further \a\ ash \ā\ ace \ä\ mop, mar
\au̇\ out \ch\ chin \e\ bet \ē\ easy \g\ go \i\ hit \ī\ ice \j\ job
\ŋ\ sing \ō\ go \ȯ\ law \ȯi\ boy \th\ thin \t͟h\ the \ü\ loot \u̇\ foot
\y\ yet \zh\ vision \a̅, k̲, ⁿ, œ, œ̄, ue, ūe, ᵊ\ see Guide to Pronunciation

hy·po·ge·al \,hī-pə-'jē-əl\ *or* **hy·po·ge·an** \-'jē-ən\ *or* **hy·po·ge·ous** \-'jē-əs\ *adj* [LL *hypogeus* subterranean, fr. Gk *hypogaios*, fr. *hypo-* + *gaia* earth] (1686) **1** : growing or living below the surface of the ground **2** *of a cotyledon* : remaining below the ground while the epicotyl elongates

hy·po·gene \'hī-pə-,jēn\ *adj* [*hypo-* + Gk *-genēs* born, produced — more at -GEN] (1831) : formed, crystallized, or lying at depths below the earth's surface : PLUTONIC — used of various rocks

hy·po·ge·um \,hī-pə-'jē-əm\ *n, pl* **-gea** \-'jē-ə\ [L, fr. Gk *hypogaion*, fr. neut. of *hypogaios*] (1706) : the subterranean part of an ancient building; *also* : an ancient underground burial chamber

hy·po·glos·sal \,hī-pə-'glä-səl\ *adj* (1831) : of or relating to the hypoglossal nerves

hypoglossal nerve *n* (1848) : either of the 12th and final pair of cranial nerves which are motor nerves arising from the medulla oblongata and supplying muscles of the tongue in higher vertebrates — called also *hypoglossal*

hy·po·gly·ce·mia \,hī-pō-glī-'sē-mē-ə\ *n* [NL] (ca. 1894) : abnormal decrease of sugar in the blood — **hy·po·gly·ce·mic** \-mik\ *adj or n*

hy·pog·y·nous \hī-'pä-jə-nəs\ *adj* (1821) **1** *of a floral organ* : inserted upon the receptacle or axis below the gynoecium and free from it **2** : having hypogynous floral organs — **hy·pog·y·ny** \-nē\ *n*

hy·po·ka·le·mia \,hī-pō-,kā-'lē-mē-ə\ *n* [NL, fr. *hypo-* + *kalium* potassium (fr. *kali* alkali, fr. Ar *qily* saltwort) + *-emia*] (1949) : a deficiency of potassium in the blood — **hy·po·ka·le·mic** \-mik\ *adj*

hy·po·lim·ni·on \,hī-pō-'lim-nē-,än, -nē-ən\ *n, pl* **-nia** \-nē-ə\ [NL, fr. *hypo-* + Gk *limnion*, dim. of *limnē* lake — more at LIMNETIC] (1928) : the part of a lake below the thermocline made up of water that is stagnant and of essentially uniform temperature except during the period of overturn

hy·po·mag·ne·se·mia \,hī-pə-,mag-nə-'sē-mē-ə\ *n* [NL, fr. *hypo-* + *magnesium* + *-emia*] (1933) : deficiency of magnesium in the blood esp. of cattle

hy·po·ma·nia \,hī-pə-'mā-nē-ə, -nyə\ *n* [NL] (1882) : a mild mania esp. when part of a manic-depressive cycle — **hy·po·man·ic** \-'ma-nik\ *adj*

hy·po·morph \'hī-pə-,morf\ *n* (1926) : a mutant gene having a similar but weaker effect than the corresponding wild-type gene — **hy·po·mor·phic** \,hī-pə-'mor-fik\ *adj*

hy·po·para·thy·roid·ism \'hī-pō-,par-ə-'thī-,roi-,di-zəm\ *n* (1910) : deficiency of parathyroid hormone in the body; *also* : the resultant abnormal state marked by low serum calcium and a tendency to chronic tetany

hy·po·phar·ynx \'far-in(k)s, -'fer-\ *n* [NL] (1826) **1** : an appendage or thickened fold on the floor of the mouth of many insects that resembles a tongue **2** : the laryngeal part of the pharynx extending from the hyoid bone to the lower margin of the cricoid cartilage

hy·po·phy·se·al *also* **hy·po·phy·si·al** \(,)hī-,pä-fə-'sē-əl, ,hī-pə-, -'zē-; ,hī-pä-'fi-zē-əl\ *adj* [irreg. fr. NL *hypophysis*] (1882) : of or relating to the hypophysis

hy·poph·y·sec·to·mize \(,)hī-,pä-fə-'sek-tə-,mīz\ *vt* **-mized; -miz·ing** (1910) : to remove the pituitary gland from

hy·poph·y·sec·to·my \-mē\ *n, pl* **-mies** (1909) : surgical removal of the pituitary gland

hy·poph·y·sis \hī-'pä-fə-səs\ *n, pl* **-y·ses** \-,sēz\ [NL, fr. Gk, attachment underneath, fr. *hypophyein* to grow beneath, fr. *hypo-* + *phyein* to grow, produce — more at BE] (1825) : PITUITARY GLAND

hy·po·pi·tu·ita·rism \,hī-pō-pə-'tü-ə-tə-,ri-zəm, -'tü-ə-,tri-, -'tyü-\ *n* [ISV] (1909) : deficient production of growth hormones by the pituitary gland — **hy·po·pi·tu·itary** \-'tü-ə-,ter-ē, -'tyü-\ *adj*

hy·po·pla·sia \-'plā-zh(ē-)ə\ *n* [NL] (1889) : a condition of arrested development in which an organ or part remains below the normal size or in an immature state — **hy·po·plas·tic** \-'plas-tik\ *adj*

hy·po·ploid \'hī-pō-,ploid\ *adj* (1930) : having a chromosome number slightly less than an exact multiple of the monoploid number — **hypo·ploid** *n*

hy·po·sen·si·ti·za·tion \,hī-pō-,sen(t)-sə-tə-'zā-shən, -,sen(t)-stə-'zā-\ *n* (1922) : the state or process of being reduced in sensitivity esp. to an allergen : DESENSITIZATION — **hy·po·sen·si·tize** \-'sen(t)-sə-,tīz\ *vt*

hy·po·spa·di·as \,hī-pə-'spā-dē-əs\ *n* [NL, fr. Gk, man with hypospadias, fr. *hypo-* + *-spadias*, fr. *-spad-*, *-spas* something torn, fr. *span* to tear, pluck off] (ca. 1855) : an abnormality of the penis in which the urethra opens on the undersurface

hy·pos·ta·sis \hī-'päs-tə-səs\ *n, pl* **-ta·ses** \-,sēz\ [LL, substance, sediment, fr. Gk, support, foundation, substance, sediment, fr. *hyphistasthai* to stand under, support, fr. *hypo-* + *histasthai* to be standing — more at STAND] (1590) **1 a** : something that settles at the bottom of a fluid **b** : the settling of blood in the dependent parts of an organ or body **2** : PERSON 3 **3 a** : the substance or essential nature of an individual **b** : something that is hypostatized **4** [NL, fr. LL] : failure of a gene to produce its usual effect when coupled with another gene that is epistatic toward it — **hy·po·stat·ic** \,hī-pə-'sta-tik\ *adj* — **hy·po·stat·i·cal·ly** \-ti-k(ə-)lē\ *adv*

hy·pos·ta·tize \hī-'päs-tə-,tīz\ *vt* **-tized; -tiz·ing** [Gk *hypostatos* substantially existing, fr. *hyphistasthai*] (1829) : to attribute real identity to (a concept) — **hy·pos·ta·ti·za·tion** \-,päs-tə-tə-'zā-shən\ *n*

hy·po·stome \'hī-pə-,stōm\ *n* [ISV *hypo-* + *-stome* (fr. Gk *stoma* mouth)] — more at STOMACH] (ca. 1862) : any of several structures associated with the mouth: as **a** : the manubrium of a hydrozoan **b** : a rodlike organ that arises at the base of the beak in various mites and ticks

hy·po·style \'hī-pə-,stīl\ *adj* [Gk *hypostylos*, fr. *hypo-* + *stylos* pillar — more at STEER] (1831) : having the roof resting on rows of columns — **hypostyle** *n*

hy·po·tac·tic \,hī-pə-'tak-tik\ *adj* [Gk *hypotaktikos*, fr. *hypotassein*] (1896) : of or relating to hypotaxis

hy·po·tax·is \-'tak-səs\ *n* [NL, fr. Gk, subjection, fr. *hypotassein* to arrange under, fr. *hypo-* + *tassein* to arrange] (1883) : syntactic subordination (as by a conjunction)

hy·po·ten·sion \,hī-pō-'ten(t)-shən\ *n* [ISV] (1893) : abnormally low blood pressure

¹hy·po·ten·sive \,hī-pō-'ten(t)-siv\ *adj* (1904) **1** : characterized by or due to hypotension **2** : causing low blood pressure or a lowering of blood pressure ⟨~ drugs⟩

²hypotensive *n* (1941) : a person with hypotension

hy·pot·e·nuse \hī-'pä-t²n-,üs, -,yüz\ *also* **hy·poth·e·nuse** \-'pä-thən-\ *n* [L *hypotenusa*, fr. Gk *hypoteinousa*, fr. fem. of *hypoteinōn*, prp. of *hypoteinein* to subtend, fr. *hypo-* + *teinein* to stretch — more at THIN] (1594) **1** : the side of a right-angled triangle that is opposite the right angle **2** : the length of a hypotenuse

ac hypotenuse

hy·po·tha·lam·ic \,hī-pō-thə-'la-mik\ *adj* (1899) : of or relating to the hypothalamus

hy·po·thal·a·mus \-'tha-lə-məs\ *n* [NL] (1896) : a basal part of the diencephalon that lies beneath the thalamus on each side, forms the floor of the third ventricle, and includes vital autonomic regulatory centers

¹hy·poth·e·cate \hi-'pä-thə-,kāt, hī-\ *vt* **-cat·ed; -cat·ing** [ML *hypothecare* to pledge, fr. LL *hypotheca* pledge, fr. Gk *hypothēkē*, fr. *hypotithenai* to put under, deposit as a pledge] (1681) : to pledge as security without delivery of title or possession — **hy·poth·e·ca·tion** \-,pä-thə-'kā-shən\ *n* — **hy·poth·e·ca·tor** \-'pä-thə-,kā-tər\ *n*

²hy·poth·e·cate \hī-'pä-thə-,kāt\ *vt* **-cat·ed; -cat·ing** [Gk *hypothēkē* suggestion, fr. *hypotithenai*] (1906) : HYPOTHESIZE

hy·po·ther·mal \,hī-pō-'thər-məl\ *adj* (1944) : of or relating to a hydrothermal metalliferous ore vein deposited at high temperature

hy·po·ther·mia \-'thər-mē-ə\ *n* [NL] (ca. 1886) : subnormal temperature of the body — **hy·po·ther·mic** \-mik\ *adj*

hy·poth·e·sis \hī-'pä-thə-səs\ *n, pl* **-e·ses** \-,sēz\ [Gk, fr. *hypotithenai* to put under, suppose, fr. *hypo-* + *tithenai* to put — more at DO] (ca. 1656) **1 a** : an assumption or concession made for the sake of argument **b** : an interpretation of a practical situation or condition taken as the ground for action **2** : a tentative assumption made in order to draw out and test its logical or empirical consequences **3** : the antecedent clause of a conditional statement

syn HYPOTHESIS, THEORY, LAW mean a formula derived by inference from scientific data that explains a principle operating in nature. HYPOTHESIS implies insufficient evidence to provide more than a tentative explanation ⟨a *hypothesis* explaining the extinction of the dinosaurs⟩. THEORY implies a greater range of evidence and greater likelihood of truth ⟨the *theory* of evolution⟩. LAW implies a statement of order and relation in nature that has been found to be invariable under the same conditions ⟨the *law* of gravitation⟩.

hy·poth·e·size \-,sīz\ *vb* **-sized; -siz·ing** *vi* (1738) : to make a hypothesis ~ *vt* : to adopt as a hypothesis

hy·po·thet·i·cal \,hī-pə-'the-ti-kəl\ *adj* (1588) : being or involving a hypothesis : CONJECTURAL ⟨~ arguments⟩ ⟨a ~ situation⟩ — **hy·po·thet·i·cal·ly** \-ti-k(ə-)lē\ *adv*

hy·po·thet·i·co–de·duc·tive \,hī-pə-'the-ti-,kō-di-'dək-tiv\ *adj* (1912) : relating to, being, or making use of the method of proposing hypotheses and testing their acceptability or falsity by determining whether their logical consequences are consistent with observed data

hy·po·thy·roid \,hī-pō-'thī-,roid\ *adj* (1909) : of, relating to, or affected with hypothyroidism

hy·po·thy·roid·ism \-,roi-,di-zəm\ *n* [ISV] (1905) : deficient activity of the thyroid gland; *also* : a resultant bodily condition characterized by lowered metabolic rate and general loss of vigor

hy·po·to·nia \,hī-pə-'tō-nē-ə, -pō-\ *n* [NL] (ca. 1886) : the state of having hypotonic muscle tone

hy·po·ton·ic \,hī-pə-'tä-nik, -pō-\ *adj* [ISV] (1895) **1** : having deficient tone or tension ⟨~ children⟩ **2** : having a lower osmotic pressure than a surrounding medium or a fluid under comparison ⟨~ organisms⟩ — **hy·po·to·nic·i·ty** \-tə-'ni-sə-tē\ *n*

hy·po·xan·thine \,hī-pō-'zan-,thēn\ *n* [ISV] (ca. 1857) : a purine base $C_5H_4N_4O$ found in plant and animal tissues that yields xanthine on oxidation

hyp·ox·emia \,hi-,päk-'sē-mē-ə, ,hī-\ *n* [NL] (ca. 1886) : deficient oxygenation of the blood — **hyp·ox·emic** \-mik\ *adj*

hyp·ox·ia \hi-'päk-sē-ə, hī-\ *n* [NL] (1941) : a deficiency of oxygen reaching the tissues of the body — **hyp·ox·ic** \-sik\ *adj*

hyp·som·e·ter \hip-'sä-mə-tər\ *n* [ISV, fr. Gk *hypsos* height (akin to OE *ūp* up) + ISV *-meter* — more at UP] (1927) : any of various instruments for determining the height of trees by triangulation

hyp·so·met·ric \,hip-sə-'me-trik\ *adj* [Gk *hypsos*] (1845) : of, relating to, or indicating elevation (as on a map) ⟨~ curve⟩

hy·rax \'hī-,raks\ *n, pl* **hy·rax·es** \-,rak-səz\ *also* **hy·ra·ces** \-rə-,sēz\ [Gk *hyrak-*, *hyrax* shrew] (1832) : any of a family (Procaviidae) of small ungulate mammals of Africa and the Middle East characterized by thickset body with short legs and ears and rudimentary tail, feet with soft pads and broad nails, and teeth of which the molars resemble those of the rhinoceros and the incisors those of rodents — called also *coney, dassie*

hy·son \'hī-s²n\ *n* [Chin (Guangdong) *héichēun*, lit., bright spring] (1740) : a Chinese green tea made from thinly rolled and twisted leaves

hys·sop \'hi-səp\ *n* [ME *ysop*, fr. OE *ysope*, fr. L *hyssopus*, fr. Gk *hyssōpos*, of Sem origin; akin to Heb *ēzōbh* hyssop] (bef. 12c) **1** : a plant used in purificatory sprinkling rites by the ancient Hebrews **2** : a European mint (*Hyssopus officinalis*) that has highly aromatic and pungent leaves and is sometimes used as a potherb

hyster- *or* **hystero-** *comb form* [F or L; F *hystér-*, fr. L *hyster-*, fr. Gk, fr. *hystera*] : womb ⟨*hysterectomy*⟩

hys·ter·ec·to·my \,his-tə-'rek-tə-mē\ *n, pl* **-mies** (ca. 1886) : surgical removal of the uterus — **hys·ter·ec·to·mized** \-tə-,mīzd\ *adj*

hys·ter·e·sis \,his-tə-'rē-səs\ *n, pl* **-e·ses** \-,sēz\ [NL, fr. Gk *hysterēsis* shortcoming, fr. *hysterein* to be late, fall short, fr. *hysteros* later — more at OUT] (1881) : a retardation of an effect when the forces acting upon a body are changed (as if from viscosity or internal friction); *esp* : a lagging in the values of resulting magnetization in a magnetic material (as iron) due to a changing magnetizing force — **hys·ter·et·ic** \-'re-tik\ *adj*

hys·te·ria \his-'ter-ē-ə, -'tir-\ *n* [NL, fr. E *hysteric*, adj., fr. L *hystericus*, fr. Gk *hysterikos*, fr. *hystera* womb; fr. the Greek notion that hysteria was peculiar to women and caused by disturbances of the uterus] (1801) **1** : a psychoneurosis marked by emotional excitability and disturbances of the psychic, sensory, vasomotor, and visceral functions **2** : behavior exhibiting overwhelming or unmanageable fear or emo-

tional excess ⟨political ~⟩ — **hys·ter·ic** \-'ter-ik\ *n* — **hys·ter·i·cal** \-'ter-i-kəl\ *also* **hysteric** *adj* — **hys·ter·i·cal·ly** \-i-k(ə-)lē\ *adv*
hys·ter·ics \-'ter-iks\ *n pl but sing or pl in constr* (1721) : a fit of uncontrollable laughter or crying
hys·ter·oid \'his-tə-,ròid\ *adj* (ca. 1855) : resembling or tending toward hysteria
hys·ter·on prot·er·on \,his-tə-,rän-'prä-tə-,rän, -tə-rən-'prä-tə-rən,

-'prò-\ *n* [LL, fr. Gk, lit., (the) later earlier, (the) latter first] (1565) : a figure of speech consisting of the reversal of a natural or rational order (as in "then came the thunder and the lightning")
hys·ter·ot·o·my \,his-tə-'rä-tə-mē\ *n, pl* **-mies** [NL *hysterotomia*, fr. *hyster-* + *-tomia* -tomy] (1801) : surgical incision of the uterus; *esp* : CESAREAN SECTION

I

i \'ī\ *n, pl* **i's** *or* **is** \'īz\ *often cap, often attrib* (bef. 12c) **1 a :** the 9th letter of the English alphabet **b :** a graphic representation of this letter **c :** a speech counterpart of orthographic *i* **2 :** ONE — see NUMBER table **3 :** a graphic device for reproducing the letter I **4 :** one designated *i* esp. as the 9th in order or class **5 :** something shaped like the letter I **6 :** a unit vector parallel to the x-axis **7** [abbr. for *incomplete*] **a :** a grade rating a student's work as incomplete **b :** one graded or rated with an I **8 :** I FORMATION
¹I \'ī, ə\ *pron* [ME, fr. OE *ic;* akin to OHG *ih* I, L *ego*, Gk *egō*] (bef. 12c) : the one who is speaking or writing ⟨~ feel fine⟩ — compare ME, MINE, MY, WE   *usage* see ME
²I \'ī\ *n, pl* **I's** *or* **Is** \'īz\ (1539) : someone aware of possessing a personal individuality : SELF
-i- [ME, fr. OF, fr. L, thematic vowel of most nouns and adjectives in combination] — used as a connective vowel to join word elements esp. of Latin origin ⟨matri*lineal*⟩ ⟨rati*cide*⟩
¹-ia *n suffix* [NL, fr. L & Gk, suffix forming feminine nouns] **1 :** pathological condition ⟨hyster*ia*⟩ **2 :** genus of plants or animals ⟨Fuchs*ia*⟩ **3 :** territory : world : society ⟨suburb*ia*⟩
²-ia *n pl suffix* [NL, fr. L (neut. pl. of *-ius*, adj. ending) & Gk, neut. pl. of *-ios*, adj. ending] **1 :** higher taxon (as class or order) consisting of ⟨such plants or animals⟩ ⟨Saur*ia*⟩ **2 :** things derived from or relating to ⟨something specified⟩ ⟨milit*aria*⟩
³-ia *pl of* -IUM
Ia·go \ē-'ä-(,)gō\ *n* : the villain of Shakespeare's tragedy *Othello*
-ial *adj suffix* [ME, fr. MF, fr. L *-ialis*, fr. *-i-* + *-alis* -al] : ¹-AL ⟨manor*ial*⟩
iamb \'ī-,am(b)\ *or* **iam·bus** \ī-'am-bəs\ *n, pl* **iambs** \'ī-,amz\ *or* **iam·bus·es** [L *iambus*, fr. Gk *iambos*] (1586) : a metrical foot consisting of one short syllable followed by one long syllable or of one unstressed syllable followed by one stressed syllable (as in *above*) — **iam·bic** \ī-'am-bik\ *adj or n*
-ian — see -AN
-iana — see -ANA
-iasis *n suffix, pl* **-iases** [NL, fr. L, fr. Gk, suffix of action, fr. denominative verbs in *-ian*, *-iazein*] : disease having characteristics of or produced by ⟨something specified⟩ ⟨onchocerc*iasis*⟩ ⟨ancylostom*iasis*⟩
-iatric *also* **-iatrical** *adj comb form* [NL *-iatria*] : of or relating to ⟨such⟩ medical treatment or healing ⟨pedi*atric*⟩
-iatrics *n pl comb form but sing or pl in constr* : medical treatment ⟨pedi*atrics*⟩
iat·ro·gen·ic \(,)ī-,a-trō-'je-nik\ *adj* [Gk *iatros* physician + E *-genic*] (1924) : induced inadvertently by a physician or surgeon or by medical treatment or diagnostic procedures ⟨an ~ rash⟩ — **iat·ro·gen·i·cal·ly** \-'je-ni-k(ə-)lē\ *adv*
-iatry *n comb form* [F *-iatrie*, fr. NL *-iatria*, fr. Gk *iatreia* art of healing, fr. *iatros* healer, fr. *iasthai* to heal] : medical treatment : healing ⟨po*diatry*⟩
I band \'ī-\ *n* (1948) : an isotropic band of a striated muscle fiber
I beam *n* (ca. 1889) : an iron or steel beam that is I-shaped in cross section
¹Ibe·ri·an \ī-'bir-ē-ən\ *n* [*Iberia*, ancient region of the Caucasus] (1601) : a member of one or more peoples anciently inhabiting the Caucasus in Asia between the Black and Caspian seas — **Iberian** *adj*
²Iberian *n* [*Iberia*, peninsula in Europe] (1611) **1 a :** a member of one or more peoples anciently inhabiting parts of the peninsula comprising Spain and Portugal **b :** a native or inhabitant of Spain or Portugal or the Basque region **2 :** one or more of the languages of the ancient Iberians — **Iberian** *adj*
ibex \'ī-,beks\ *n, pl* **ibex** *or* **ibex·es** [L] (1607) : any of several wild goats (genus *Capra*, esp. *C. ibex*) living chiefly in high mountain areas of the Old World and having large recurved horns transversely ridged in front
ibi·dem \'i-bə-,dem; i-'bī-dəm, -'bē-\ *adv* [L] (ca. 1771) : in the same place
-ibility — see -ABILITY
ibis \'ī-bəs\ *n, pl* **ibis** *or* **ibis·es** [ME, fr. L, fr. Gk, fr. Egypt *hb*] (14c) : any of various wading birds (family Threskiornithidae) related to the herons but distinguished by a long slender downwardly curved bill
Ibi·zan hound \i-'bē-zən-\ *n* [*Ibiza* Island] (1960) : any of a breed of slender agile medium-sized hunting dogs

ibis

developed in the Balearic Islands with a short and smooth or a wire-haired coat
-ible — see -ABLE
Ibo \'ē-(,)bō\ *n, pl* **Ibo** *or* **Ibos** (1732) **1 :** a member of a people of the area around the lower Niger in Africa **2 :** the language of the Ibo people
Ib·sen·ism \'ib-sə-,ni-zəm, 'ip-\ *n* (1890) **1 :** dramatic invention or construction characteristic of Ibsen **2 :** championship of Ibsen's plays and ideas — **Ib·sen·ite** \-,nīt\ *n or adj*
ibu·pro·fen \,ī-byù-'prō-fən *also* ī-'byù-prə-fən\ *n* [*is-* + *butyl* + *pro*pionic acid + *-fen* (alter. of *phenyl*)] (1969) : a nonsteroidal anti-inflammatory drug $C_{13}H_{18}O_2$ used to relieve pain and fever
¹IC \,ī-'sē\ *n* (1947) : IMMEDIATE CONSTITUENT
²IC *n* (1966) : INTEGRATED CIRCUIT
¹-ic *adj suffix* [ME, fr. OF & L; OF *-ique*, fr. L *-icus* — more at -Y] **1 :** having the character or form of : being ⟨panoram*ic*⟩ : consisting of ⟨run*ic*⟩ **2 a :** of or relating to ⟨alderman*ic*⟩ **b :** related to, derived from, or containing ⟨alcohol*ic*⟩ **3 :** in the manner of : like that of : characteristic of ⟨Byron*ic*⟩ **4 :** associated or dealing with ⟨Ved*ic*⟩ : utilizing ⟨electron*ic*⟩ **5 :** characterized by ; exhibiting ⟨nostalg*ic*⟩ : affected with ⟨allerg*ic*⟩ **6 :** caused by ⟨amoeb*ic*⟩ **7 :** tending to produce ⟨analges*ic*⟩ **8 :** having a valence relatively higher than in compounds or ions named with an adjective ending in *-ous* ⟨ferric iron⟩
²-ic *n suffix* : one having the character or nature of : one belonging to or associated with : one exhibiting or affected by : one that produces
-ical *adj suffix* [ME, fr. LL *-icalis* (as in *clericalis* clerical, *radicalis* radical)] : -IC ⟨symmetr*ical*⟩ ⟨geolog*ical*⟩ — sometimes differing from *-ic* in that adjectives formed with *-ical* have a wider or more transferred semantic range than corresponding adjectives in *-ic*
Ic·a·rus \'i-kə-rəs\ *n* [L, fr. Gk *Ikaros*] : the son of Daedalus who to escape imprisonment flies by means of artificial wings but falls into the sea and drowns when the wax of his wings melts as he flies too near the sun
ICBM \,ī-,sē-(,)bē-'em\ *n, pl* **ICBM's** *or* **ICBMs** \-'emz\ (1955) : an intercontinental ballistic missile
¹ice \'īs\ *n, often attrib* [ME *is*, fr. OE *īs;* akin to OHG *īs* ice, Av *isu-* icy] (bef. 12c) **1 a :** frozen water **b :** a sheet or stretch of ice **2 :** a substance resembling ice; *esp* : the solid state of a substance usu. found as a gas or liquid ⟨ammonia ~ in the rings of Saturn⟩ **3 :** a state of coldness (as from formality or reserve) **4 a :** a frozen dessert containing a flavoring (as fruit juice); *esp* : one containing no milk or cream **b** *Brit* : a serving of ice cream **5** *slang* : DIAMONDS; *broadly* : JEWELRY **6 :** an undercover premium paid to a theater employee for choice theater tickets — **ice·less** \'ī-sləs\ *adj* — **on ice 1 :** with every likelihood of being won or accomplished **2 :** in reserve or safekeeping
²ice *vb* **iced; ic·ing** *vt* (15c) **1 a :** to coat with or convert into ice **b :** to chill with ice **c :** to supply with ice **2 :** to cover with or as if with icing **3 :** to put on ice **4 :** SECURE 1b ⟨made two free throws . . . to ~ the win —Jack McCallum⟩ **5 :** to shoot (an ice hockey puck) the length of the rink and beyond the opponents' goal line **6** *slang* : KILL 1a **~** *vi* **1 :** to become ice-cold **2 a :** to become covered with ice — often used with *up* or *over* **b :** to have ice form inside ⟨the carburetor *iced* up⟩
ice age *n* (1873) **1 :** a time of widespread glaciation **2** *cap I&A* : the Pleistocene glacial epoch
ice ax *n* (1820) : a combination pick and adze with a spiked handle that is used in mountain climbing
ice bag *n* (1883) : a waterproof bag to hold ice for local application of cold to the body
ice·berg \'īs-,bərg\ *n* [prob. part trans. of Dan or Norw *isberg*, fr. *is* ice + *berg* mountain] (1820) **1 :** a large floating mass of ice detached from a glacier **2 :** an emotionally cold person **3 :** ICEBERG LETTUCE
iceberg lettuce *n* (1893) : any of various crisp light green lettuces that when mature have the leaves arranged in a compact head
ice·blink \-,blink\ *n* (1817) : a glare in the sky over an ice field
ice·boat \-,bōt\ *n* (ca. 1819) : a skeleton boat or frame on runners propelled on ice usu. by sails
ice·boat·ing \-,bō-tiŋ\ *n* (1885) : the sport of sailing in iceboats — **ice·boat·er** \-,bō-tər\ *n*

ice ax

\ə\ abut \'\ kitten, F table \ər\ further \a\ ash \ā\ ace \ä\ mop, mar
\aù\ out \ch\ chin \e\ bet \ē\ easy \g\ go \i\ hit \ī\ ice \j\ job
\ŋ\ sing \ō\ go \ò\ law \òi\ boy \th\ thin \th\ the \ü\ loot \ù\ foot
\y\ yet \zh\ vision \à, ḵ, ⁿ, œ, œ̄, ue, ūe, ᵞ\ *see* Guide to Pronunciation

ice·bound \-,baůnd\ *adj* (1641) : surrounded, obstructed, or covered by ice

ice·box \-,bäks\ *n* (1846) : REFRIGERATOR

ice·break·er \-,brā-kər\ *n* (1875)   **1** : a ship equipped to make and maintain a channel through ice   **2** : something that breaks the ice on a project or occasion; *esp* : MIXER 1c

ice cap *n* (ca. 1860)   **1** : an ice bag shaped to the head   **2** : a cover of perennial ice and snow; *specif* : a glacier forming on an extensive area of relatively level land and flowing outward from its center

ice–cold \'īs-'kōld\ *adj* (bef. !2c) : extremely cold

ice–cream *adj* (1890) : of a color similar to that of vanilla ice cream

ice cream \'īs-'krēm, 'īs-\ *n* (1744) : a sweet flavored frozen food containing cream or butterfat and usu. eggs

ice–cream chair *n* [fr. its use in ice cream parlors] (1949) : a small armless chair with a circular seat for use at a table (as at a café)

ice–cream cone *n* (1909) : a thin crisp edible cone for holding ice cream; *also* : one filled with ice cream

ice dancing *n* (1925) : a sport in which ice-skating pairs perform to music routines similar to ballroom dances

ice·fall \'īs-,fȯl\ *n* (1817)   **1** : a frozen waterfall   **2** : the mass of usu. jagged blocks into which a glacier may break when it moves down a steep declivity

ice field *n* (1694)   **1** : an extensive sheet of sea ice   **2** : ICE CAP 2

ice floe *n* (1819) : a usu. large flat free mass of floating sea ice

ice fog *n* (1856) : a fog composed of ice particles

ice hockey *n* (1883) : a game played on an ice rink by two teams of six players on skates whose object is to drive a puck into the opponents' goal with a hockey stick

ice·house \'īs-,haůs, 'ī-,saůs\ *n* (1687) : a building in which ice is made or stored

¹Ice·lan·dic \ī-'slan-dik\ *adj* (1674) : of, relating to, or characteristic of Iceland, the Icelanders, or Icelandic

²Icelandic *n* (ca. 1824) : the North Germanic language of Iceland

Ice·land moss \'ī-slən(d)-, -,slan(d)-\ *n* (1805) : a lichen (*Cetraria islandica*) of mountainous and arctic regions sometimes used in medicine or as food

Iceland poppy *n* (1884) : a poppy (*Papaver nudicaule*) of holarctic regions often cultivated for its usu. single showy flowers

Iceland spar *n* (1771) : a doubly refracting transparent calcite

ice·man \'īs-,man\ *n* (1833)   **1** : one who sells or delivers ice   **2** : a man skilled in traveling on ice

ice milk *n* (1947) : a sweetened frozen food made of skim milk

Ice·ni \ī-'sē-,nī\ *n pl* [L] (ca. 1891) : an ancient British people that under their queen Boudicca revolted against the Romans in A.D. 60 — **Ice·ni·an** \ī-'sē-nē-ən\ *or* **Ice·nic** \-'sē-nik, -'se-\ *adj*

ice–out \'īs-,aůt\ *n* (1951) : the disappearance of ice from the surface of a body of water (as a lake) as a result of thawing

ice pack *n* (1853) : an expanse of pack ice

ice pick *n* (ca. 1877) : a hand tool ending in a spike for chipping ice

ice plant *n* (1753) : an Old World annual herb (*Mesembryanthemum crystallinum*) of the carpetweed family that has fleshy foliage covered with glistening papillate dots or vesicles and is widely naturalized in warm regions; *broadly* : FIG MARIGOLD

ice point *n* (1903) : the freezing point of water of 0° Celsius or 273.15 Kelvin at standard atmospheric pressure

ice sheet *n* (1873) : ICE CAP 2

ice show *n* (1948) : an entertainment consisting of various exhibitions by ice-skaters usu. with musical accompaniment

ice–skate \'ī(s-),skāt\ *vi* (ca. 1948) : to skate on ice — **ice–skat·er** \-,skā-tər\ *n*

ice skate *n* (1897) : a shoe with a metal runner attached for ice-skating

ice storm *n* (1876) : a storm in which falling rain freezes on contact

ice water *n* (1722) : chilled or iced water esp. served as a beverage

ich·neu·mon \ik-'nü-mən, -'nyü-\ *n* [ME, fr. L, fr. Gk *ichneumōn*, lit., tracker, fr. *ichneuein* to track, fr. *ichnos* footprint] (15c)   **1** : a mongoose (*Herpestes ichneumon*) of Africa, southern Europe, and southwestern Asia   **2** : ICHNEUMON FLY

ichneumon fly *n* (1713) : any of a large superfamily (Ichneumonoidea) of hymenopterous insects whose larvae are usu. internal parasites of other insect larvae and esp. of caterpillars

ichor \'ī-,kȯr, -kər\ *n* [Gk *ichōr*] (15c)   **1** : a thin watery or blood-tinged discharge   **2** : an ethereal fluid taking the place of blood in the veins of the ancient Greek gods — **ichor·ous** \-kə-rəs\ *adj*

ichthy- *or* **ichthyo-** *comb form* [L, fr. Gk, fr. *ichthys*; akin to Arm *jukn* fish, Lith *žuvìs*] : fish ⟨*ichthyology*⟩

ich·thyo·fau·na \,ik-thē-ō-'fȯ-nə, -'fä-\ *n* [NL] (1883) : the fish life of a region — **ich·thyo·fau·nal** \-'fȯ-n³l, -'fä-\ *adj*

ich·thy·ol·o·gy \,ik-thē-'ä-lə-jē\ *n* (1646) : a branch of zoology that deals with fishes — **ich·thy·o·log·i·cal** \-thē-ə-'lä-ji-kəl\ *adj* — **ich·thy·o·log·i·cal·ly** \-k(ə-)lē\ *adv* — **ich·thy·ol·o·gist** \-thē-'ä-lə-jist\ *n*

ich·thyo·oph·a·gous \ik-thē-'ä-fə-gəs\ *adj* [Gk *ichthyophagos*, fr. *ichthy-* + *-phagos* -phagous] (ca. 1828) : eating or subsisting on fish

ich·thyo·saur \'ik-thē-ə-,sȯr\ *n* [ultim. fr. Gk *ichthy-* + *sauros* lizard] (1830) : any of an order (Ichthyosauria) of extinct marine reptiles of the Mesozoic specialized for aquatic life by a streamlined body with a long snout, limbs reduced to small fins for steering, and a large lunate caudal fin — **ich·thyo·sau·ri·an** \,ik-thē-ə-'sȯr-ē-ən\ *adj or n*

-ician *n suffix* [ME, fr. OF *-icien*, fr. L *-ica* (as in *rhetorica* rhetoric) + OF *-ien* -ian] : specialist : practitioner ⟨*beautician*⟩

ici·cle \'ī-si-kəl\ *n* [ME *isikel*, fr. *is* ice + *ikel* icicle, fr. OE *gicel;* akin to OHG *ihilla* icicle, MIr *aig* ice] (14c)   **1** : a pendent mass of ice formed by the freezing of dripping water   **2** : an emotionally cold person   **3** : a long narrow strip (as of foil) used to decorate a Christmas tree

¹ic·ing \'ī-siŋ\ *n* (1769)   **1** : a sweet flavored usu. creamy mixture used to coat baked goods (as cupcakes) — called also *frosting*   **2** : something that adds to the interest, value, or appeal of an item or event — often used in the phrase *icing on the cake*

²icing *n* (1948) : an act by an ice-hockey player of shooting a puck from within the defensive zone or defensive half of the rink beyond the opponents' goal line but not into the goal

ick·er \'ī-kər\ *n* [(assumed) ME (Sc dial.), fr. OE *ēar, eher* — more at EAR] (1513) *Scot* : a head of grain

icky \'i-kē\ *adj* **ick·i·er; -est** [perh. baby talk alter. of *sticky*] (1929) : offensive to the senses or sensibilities : DISTASTEFUL ⟨put off by her ~ triteness —Renata Adler⟩ — **ick·i·ness** \-nəs\ *n*

icon \'ī-,kän\ *n* [L, fr. Gk *eikōn*, fr. *eikenai* to resemble] (1572)   **1** : a usu. pictorial representation : IMAGE   **2** [LGk *eikōn*, fr. Gk] : a conventional religious image typically painted on a small wooden panel and used in the devotions of Eastern Christians   **3** : an object of uncritical devotion : IDOL   **4** : EMBLEM, SYMBOL ⟨the house became an ~ of 1860's residential architecture —Paul Goldberger⟩   **5   a** : a sign (as a word or graphic symbol) whose form suggests its meaning   **b** : a graphic symbol on a computer display screen that suggests the purpose of an available function — **icon·ic** \ī-'kä-nik\ *adj* — **icon·i·cal·ly** \-ni-k(ə-)lē\ *adv*

icon- *or* **icono-** *comb form* [Gk *eikon-, eikono-*, fr. *eikon-, eikōn*] : image ⟨*iconolatry*⟩

ico·nic·i·ty \,ī-kə-'ni-sə-tē\ *n* (1946) : correspondence between form and meaning ⟨the ~ of the Roman numeral III⟩

icon·o·clasm \ī-'kä-nə-,kla-zəm\ *n* (1797) : the doctrine, practice, or attitude of an iconoclast

icon·o·clast \-,klast\ *n* [ML *iconoclastes*, fr. MGk *eikonoklastēs*, lit., image destroyer, fr. Gk *eikono-* + *klan* to break — more at CLAST] (1641)   **1** : one who destroys religious images or opposes their veneration   **2** : one who attacks settled beliefs or institutions — **icon·o·clas·tic** \(,)ī-,kä-nə-'klas-tik\ *adj* — **icon·o·clas·ti·cal·ly** \-ti-k(ə-)lē\ *adv*

ico·nog·ra·pher \,ī-kə-'nä-grə-fər\ *n* (1888)   **1** : a maker of figures or drawings esp. of a conventional type   **2** : a student of iconography

icon·o·graph·ic \(,)ī-,kä-nə-'gra-fik\ *or* **icon·o·graph·i·cal** \-fi-kəl\ *adj* (ca. 1855)   **1** : of or relating to iconography   **2** : representing something by pictures or diagrams — **icon·o·graph·i·cal·ly** \-fi-k(ə-)lē\ *adv*

ico·nog·ra·phy \,ī-kə-'nä-grə-fē\ *n, pl* **-phies** [ML *iconographia*, fr. Gk *eikonographia* sketch, description, fr. *eikonographein* to describe, fr. *eikon-* + *graphein* to write — more at CARVE] (1678)   **1** : pictorial material relating to or illustrating a subject   **2** : the traditional or conventional images or symbols associated with a subject and esp. a religious or legendary subject   **3** : the imagery or symbolism of a work of art, an artist, or a body of art   **4** : ICONOLOGY

ico·nol·a·try \-'nä-lə-trē\ *n* (1624) : the worship of images or icons

ico·nol·o·gy \-'nä-lə-jē\ *n* [F *iconologie*, fr. *icono-* icon- + *-logie* -logy] (ca. 1736) : the study of icons or artistic symbolism — **icon·o·log·i·cal** \(,)ī-,kä-n³l-'ä-ji-kəl\ *adj*

icon·o·scope \ī-'kä-nə-,skōp\ *n* [fr. *Iconoscope*, a trademark] (1932) : a camera tube containing an electron gun and a photoemissive mosaic screen of which each cell produces a charge proportional to the varying light intensity of the image focused on the screen

ico·nos·ta·sis \,ī-kə-'näs-tə-səs, ,ī-kä-'kä-nə-,stä-səs\ *n, pl* **-ta·ses** \-,sēz\ [modif. of MGk *eikonostasion*, fr. LGk, shrine, fr. Gk *eikono-* + *-stasion* (fr. *histanai* to stand) — more at STAND] (1833) : a screen or partition with doors and tiers of icons that separates the bema from the nave in Eastern churches

ico·sa·he·dral \,ī-,kō-sə-'hē-drəl, -,kä-\ *adj* (ca. 1828) : of or having the form of an icosahedron

ico·sa·he·dron \-drən\ *n, pl* **-drons** *or* **-dra** \-drə\ [Gk *eikosaedron*, fr. *eikosi* twenty + *-edron* -hedron — more at VIGESIMAL] (1570) : a polyhedron having 20 faces

-ics *n pl suffix but sing or pl in constr* [¹*-ic* + ²*-s;* trans. of Gk *-ika*, fr. neut. pl. of *-ikos* -ic]   **1** : study : knowledge : skill : practice ⟨linguistics⟩ ⟨electronics⟩   **2** : characteristic actions or activities ⟨acrobatics⟩   **3** : characteristic qualities, operations, or phenomena ⟨mechanics⟩

ic·ter·ic \ik-'ter-ik\ *adj* (ca. 1600) : of, relating to, or affected with jaundice

ic·ter·us \'ik-tə-rəs\ *n* [NL, fr. Gk *ikteros*] (ca. 1706) : JAUNDICE

ic·tus \'ik-təs\ *n* [L, lit., blow, fr. *icere* to strike] (1752) : the recurring stress or beat in a rhythmic or metrical series of sounds

icy \'ī-sē\ *adj* **ic·i·er; -est** (bef. 12c)   **1** : covered with, abounding in, or consisting of ice   **b** : intensely cold   **2** : characterized by coldness : FRIGID ⟨an ~ stare⟩; *also* : STEELY ⟨~ nerves⟩ — **ic·i·ly** \-sə-lē\ *adv* — **ic·i·ness** \-sē-nəs\ *n*

id \'id\ *n* [NL, fr. L, it] (1924) : the one of the three divisions of the psyche in psychoanalytic theory that is completely unconscious and is the source of psychic energy derived from instinctual needs and drives — compare EGO, SUPEREGO

¹-id *n suffix* [in sense 1, fr. L *-ides*, masc. patronymic suffix, fr. Gk *-idēs*; in sense 2, fr. It *-ide*, fr. L *-id-, -is*, fem. patronymic suffix, fr. Gk]   **1** : one belonging to a (specified) dynastic line ⟨Abbasid⟩   **2** : meteor associated with or radiating from a (specified) constellation or comet ⟨Perseid⟩

²-id *n suffix* [prob. fr. L *-id-, -is*, fem. patronymic suffix, fr. Gk] : body : particle ⟨chromatid⟩

I'd \'īd\ (ca. 1592) : I would : I had : I should

-idae *n pl suffix* [NL, fr. L, fr. Gk *-idai*, pl. of *-idēs*] : members of the family of — in names of zoological families ⟨*Felidae*⟩

Ida·ho \'ī-də-,hȯ\ *n, pl* **Idahos** *or* **Idahoes** (1934) : an elongated baking potato grown esp. in the state of Idaho

ID card \'ī-dē-\ *n* (ca. 1945) : a card bearing identifying data (as age or organizational membership) about the individual whose name appears thereon — called also *identification card, identity card*

-ide *also* **-id** *n suffix* [G & F; G *-id*, fr. F *-ide* (as in *oxide*)]   **1** : binary chemical compound — added to the contracted name of the nonmetallic or more electronegative element ⟨hydrogen sulfide⟩ or group ⟨cyanide⟩   **2** : chemical compound derived from or related to another (usu. specified) compound ⟨anhydride⟩ ⟨glucoside⟩

idea \ī-'dē-ə *also* 'ī-(,)dē-ə *or* 'ī-dē\ *n* [ME, fr. L, fr. Gk, fr. *idein* to see — more at WIT] (14c)   **1   a** : a transcendent entity that is a real pattern of which existing things are imperfect representations   **b** : a standard of perfection : IDEAL   **c** : a plan for action : DESIGN   **2** *archaic* : a visible representation of a conception : a replica of a pattern   **3   a** *obs* : an image recalled by memory   **b** : an indefinite or unformed conception   **c** : an entity (as a thought, concept, sensation, or image) actually or potentially present to consciousness   **4** : a formulated thought or opinion   **5** : whatever is known or supposed about something ⟨a child's ~ of time⟩   **6** : the central meaning or chief end of a particular action or situation   **7** *Christian Science* : an image in Mind — **idea·less** \ī-'dē-ə-ləs\ *adj*

syn IDEA, CONCEPT, CONCEPTION, THOUGHT, NOTION, IMPRESSION mean what exists in the mind as a representation (as of something comprehended) or as a formulation (as of a plan). IDEA may apply to a mental image or formulation of something seen or known or imagined, to a pure abstraction, or to something assumed or vaguely sensed ⟨innovative *ideas*⟩ ⟨my *idea* of paradise⟩. CONCEPT may apply to the idea formed by consideration of instances of a species or genus or, more broadly, to any idea of what a thing ought to be ⟨a society with no *concept* of private property⟩. CONCEPTION is often interchangeable with CONCEPT; it may stress the process of imagining or formulating rather than the result ⟨our changing *conception* of what constitutes art⟩. THOUGHT is likely to suggest the result of reflecting, reasoning, or meditating rather than of imagining ⟨commit your *thoughts* to paper⟩. NOTION suggests an idea not much resolved by analysis or reflection and may suggest the capricious or accidental ⟨you have the oddest *notions*⟩. IMPRESSION applies to an idea or notion resulting immediately from some stimulation of the senses ⟨the first *impression* is of soaring height⟩.

¹**ide·al** \ī-'dē(-ə)l, 'ī-,\ *adj* [ME *ydeall*, fr. LL *idealis*, fr. L *idea*] (15c) **1** : existing as an archetypal idea **2 a** : existing as a mental image or in fancy or imagination only; *broadly* : lacking practicality **b** : relating to or constituting mental images, ideas, or conceptions **3 a** : of, relating to, or embodying an ideal **b** : conforming exactly to an ideal, law, or standard : PERFECT ⟨an ~ gas⟩ — compare REAL 2b(3) **4** : of or relating to philosophical idealism

²**ideal** *n* (15c) **1** : a standard of perfection, beauty, or excellence **2** : one regarded as exemplifying an ideal and often taken as a model for imitation **3** : an ultimate object or aim of endeavor : GOAL **4** : a subset of a mathematical ring that is closed under addition and subtraction and contains the products of any given element of the subset with each element of the ring **syn** see MODEL — **ide·al·less** \ī-'dē(-ə)l-ləs\ *adj*

ide·al·ise *Brit var of* IDEALIZE

ide·al·ism \ī-'dē-(ə-),liz-əm, 'ī-(,)dē-\ *n* (1796) **1 a** (1) : a theory that ultimate reality lies in a realm transcending phenomena (2) : a theory that the essential nature of reality lies in consciousness or reason **b** (1) : a theory that only the perceptible is real (2) : a theory that only mental states or entities are knowable **2 a** : the practice of forming ideals or living under their influence **b** : something that is idealized **3** : literary or artistic theory or practice that affirms the preeminent value of imagination as compared with faithful copying of nature — compare REALISM

¹**ide·al·ist** \-(ə-)list\ *n* (1701) **1 a** : an adherent of a philosophical theory of idealism **b** : an artist or author who advocates or practices idealism in art or writing **2** : one guided by ideals; *esp* : one that places ideals before practical considerations

²**idealist** *adj* (1875) : IDEALISTIC

ide·al·is·tic \(,)ī,-dē-(ə-)'lis-tik, ,ī-dē-\ *adj* (1829) : of or relating to idealists or idealism — **ide·al·is·ti·cal·ly** \-ti-k(ə-)lē\ *adv*

ide·al·i·ty \,ī-dē-'a-lə-tē\ *n, pl* **-ties** (1817) **1 a** : the quality or state of being ideal **b** : existence only in idea **2** : something imaginary or idealized

ide·al·ize \ī-'dē-(ə-),līz\ *vb* **-ized; -iz·ing** *vi* (1786) **1** : to form ideals **2** : to work idealistically ~ *vt* **1 a** : to give an ideal form or value to **b** : to attribute ideal characteristics to **2** : to treat idealistically — **ide·al·i·za·tion** \-,dē-(ə-)lə-'zā-shən\ *n* — **ide·al·iz·er** \-'dē-(ə-),lī-zər\ *n*

ide·al·ly \ī-'dē-ə-lē, -'dē(-ə)l-lē\ *adv* (1598) **1** : in idea or imagination : MENTALLY **2** : in relation to an exemplar **3 a** : conformably to or in respect to an ideal : PERFECTLY **b** : for best results ⟨~, the counselor should vary his techniques for each applicant —T. M. Martinez⟩ **c** : in accordance with an ideal or typical standard : CLASSICALLY

ideal point *n* (1879) : a point added to the plane or to space to eliminate special cases; *specif* : the point at infinity added in projective geometry as the assumed intersection of two parallel lines

ide·ate \'ī-dē-,āt\ *vb* **-at·ed; -at·ing** *vt* (1610) : to form an idea or conception of ~ *vi* : to form an idea

ide·a·tion \,ī-dē-'ā-shən\ *n* (1818) : the forming of ideas (as of things not present to the senses)

ide·a·tion·al \-shnəl, -shə-nᵊl\ *adj* (1853) : of, relating to, or produced by ideation; *broadly* : of or relating to ideas — **ide·a·tion·al·ly** *adv*

idée fixe \(,)ē-,dā-'fēks\ *n, pl* **idées fixes** *same*\ [F, lit., fixed idea] (1836) : an idea that dominates one's mind esp. for a prolonged period : OBSESSION

idem \'ī-,dem, 'ē-, 'i-\ *pron* [ME, fr. L, same — more at IDENTITY] (14c) : something previously mentioned : SAME

idem·po·tent \'ī-dəm-,pō-tᵊnt\ *adj* [L *idem* same + *potent-, potens* having power — more at POTENT] (1870) : relating to or being a mathematical quantity which when applied to itself under a given binary operation (as multiplication) equals itself; *also* : relating to or being an operation under which a mathematical quantity is idempotent — **idempotent** *n*

iden·tic \ī-'den-tik, ə-\ *adj* (1649) : IDENTICAL: as **a** : constituting a diplomatic action or expression in which two or more governments follow precisely the same course or employ an identical form **b** : constituting an action or expression in which a government follows precisely the same course or employs identical forms with reference to two or more other governments

iden·ti·cal \ī-'den-ti-kəl, ə-\ *adj* [prob. fr. ML *identicus*, fr. LL *identitas*] (1599) **1** : being the same : SELFSAME ⟨the ~ place we stopped before⟩ **2** : having such close resemblance as to be essentially the same ⟨~ hats⟩ — often used with *to* or *with* **3 a** : having the same cause or origin ⟨~ infections⟩ **b** : EQUAL **syn** see SAME — **iden·ti·cal·ly** \-k(ə-)lē\ *adv* — **iden·ti·cal·ness** \-kəl-nəs\ *n*

iden·ti·fi·ca·tion \ī-,den-tə-fə-'kā-shən, ə-\ *n* (1644) **1 a** : an act of identifying : the state of being identified **b** : evidence of identity **2 a** : psychological orientation of the self in regard to something (as a person or group) with a resulting feeling of close emotional association **b** : a largely unconscious process whereby an individual models thoughts, feelings, and actions after those attributed to an object that has been incorporated as a mental image

identification card *n* (1908) : ID CARD

iden·ti·fi·er \ī-'den-tə-,fī(-ə)r, ə-\ *n* (1889) : one that identifies

iden·ti·fy \ī-'den-tə-,fī, ə-\ *vb* **-fied; -fy·ing** *vt* (1644) **1 a** : to cause to be or become identical **b** : to conceive as united (as in spirit, outlook, or principle) ⟨groups that are *identified* with conservation⟩ **2 a** : to establish the identity of **b** : to determine the taxonomic position of (a biological specimen) ~ *vi* **1** : to be or become the same **2** : to practice psychological identification ⟨~ with the hero of a novel⟩ — **iden·ti·fi·able** \-,den-tə-'fī-ə-bəl\ *adj* — **iden·ti·fi·ably** \-blē\ *adv*

iden·ti·ty \ī-'den-tə-tē, ə-, -'de-nə-\ *n, pl* **-ties** [MF *identité*, fr. LL *identitat-, identitas*, prob. fr. L *identidem* repeatedly, contr. of *idem et idem*, lit., same and same] (1570) **1 a** : sameness of essential or generic character in different instances **b** : sameness in all that constitutes the objective reality of a thing : ONENESS **2 a** : the distinguishing character or personality of an individual : INDIVIDUALITY **b** : the relation established by psychological identification **3** : the condition of being the same with something described or asserted ⟨establish the ~ of stolen goods⟩ **4** : an equation that is satisfied for all values of the symbols **5** : IDENTITY ELEMENT

identity card *n* (1900) : ID CARD

identity crisis *n* (1954) **1** : personal psychosocial conflict esp. in adolescence that involves confusion about one's social role and often a sense of loss of continuity to one's personality **2** : a state of confusion in an institution or organization regarding its nature or direction

identity element *n* (1902) : an element (as 0 in the set of all integers under addition or 1 in the set of positive integers under multiplication) that leaves any element of the set to which it belongs unchanged when combined with it by a specified operation

identity matrix *n* (ca. 1929) : a square matrix that has numeral 1's along the principal diagonal and 0's elsewhere

ideo- *comb form* [F *idéo-*, fr. Gk *idea*] : idea ⟨ideogram⟩

ideo·gram \'ī-dē-ə-,gram, 'ī-\ *n* (ca. 1840) **1** : a picture or symbol used in a system of writing to represent a thing or an idea but not a particular word or phrase for it; *esp* : one that represents not the object pictured but some thing or idea that the object pictured is supposed to suggest **2** : LOGOGRAM — **ideo·gram·ic** *or* **ideo·gram·mic** \,ī-dē-ə-'gra-mik, ,ī-\ *adj* — **ideo·gram·mat·ic** \-dē-ō-grə-'ma-tik\ *adj*

ideo·graph \'ī-dē-ə-,graf, 'ī-\ *n* (1835) : IDEOGRAM — **ideo·graph·ic** \,ī-dē-ə-'gra-fik, ,ī-\ *adj* — **ideo·graph·i·cal·ly** \-fi-k(ə-)lē\ *adv*

ide·og·ra·phy \,ī-dē-'ä-grə-fē, ,ī-\ *n* (1836) **1** : the use of ideograms **2** : the representation of ideas by graphic symbols

ideo·log·i·cal \,ī-dē-ə-'lä-ji-kəl, ,i-\ *also* **ideo·log·ic** \-'lä-jik\ *adj* (1797) **1** : relating to or concerned with ideas **2** : of, relating to, or based on ideology — **ideo·log·i·cal·ly** \-'lä-ji-k(ə-)lē\ *adv*

ide·ol·o·gize \,ī-dē-'ä-lə-,jīz, ,i-\ *vt* **-gized; -giz·ing** (1860) : to give an ideological character or interpretation to; *esp* : to change or interpret in relation to a sociopolitical ideology often seen as biased or limited

ideo·logue *also* **idea·logue** \'ī-dē-ə-,lòg, -,läg\ *n* [F *idéologue*, backformation fr. *idéologie*] (1815) **1** : an impractical idealist : THEORIST **2** : an often blindly partisan advocate or adherent of a particular ideology

ide·ol·o·gy \,ī-dē-'ä-lə-jē, ,i-\ *also* **ide·al·o·gy** \-'ä-lə-jē, -'a-\ *n, pl* **-gies** [F *idéologie*, fr. *idéo-* + *-logie* -logy] (1813) **1** : visionary theorizing **2 a** : a systematic body of concepts esp. about human life or culture **b** : a manner or the content of thinking characteristic of an individual, group, or culture **c** : the integrated assertions, theories and aims that constitute a sociopolitical program — **ide·ol·o·gist** \-jist\ *n*

ideo·mo·tor \,ī-dē-ə-'mō-tər, ,i-\ *adj* [ISV] (1867) : not reflex but motivated by an idea ⟨~ muscular activity⟩

ides \'īdz\ *n pl but sing or pl in constr* [ME, fr. MF, fr. L *idus*] (14c) : the 15th day of March, May, July, or October or the 13th day of any other month in the ancient Roman calendar; *broadly* : this day and the seven days preceding it

-idin *or* **-idine** *n suffix* [ISV *-ide* + *-in, -ine*] : chemical compound related in origin or structure to another compound ⟨tolu*idine*⟩ ⟨guan*idine*⟩

idio- *comb form* [Gk, fr. *idios* — more at IDIOT] : one's own : personal : separate : distinct ⟨idioblast⟩

id·i·o·blast \'ī-dē-ə-,blast\ *n* [ISV] (1822) : a plant cell (as a sclereid) that differs markedly from neighboring cells — **id·io·blas·tic** \,ī-dē-ə-'blas-tik\ *adj*

id·i·o·cy \'ī-dē-ə-sē\ *n, pl* **-cies** (ca. 1529) **1** : extreme mental retardation commonly due to incomplete or abnormal development of the brain **2** : something notably stupid or foolish

id·i·o·graph·ic \,ī-dē-ə-'gra-fik\ *adj* [ISV] (ca. 1890) : relating to or dealing with something concrete, individual, or unique

id·i·o·lect \'ī-dē-ə-,lekt\ *n* [*idio-* + *-lect* (as in *dialect*)] (1948) : the language or speech pattern of one individual at a particular period of life — **id·io·lec·tal** \,ī-dē-ə-'lek-tᵊl\ *adj*

id·i·om \'ī-dē-əm\ *n* [MF & LL; MF *idiome*, fr. LL *idioma* individual peculiarity of language, fr. Gk *idiōmat-, idiōma*, fr. *idiousthai* to appropriate, fr. *idios*] (1588) **1 a** : the language peculiar to a people or to a district, community, or class : DIALECT **b** : the syntactical, grammatical, or structural form peculiar to a language **2** : an expression in the usage of a language that is peculiar to itself either grammatically (as *no, it wasn't me*) or in having a meaning that cannot be derived from the conjoined meanings of its elements (as *Monday week* for "the Monday a week after next Monday") **3** : a style or form of artistic expression that is characteristic of an individual, a period or movement, or a medium or instrument ⟨the modern jazz ~⟩; *broadly* : MANNER, STYLE ⟨a new culinary ~⟩

id·i·o·mat·ic \,ī-dē-ə-'ma-tik\ *adj* (1712) **1** : of, relating to, or conforming to idiom **2** : peculiar to a particular group, individual, or style — **id·i·o·mat·i·cal·ly** \-ti-k(ə-)lē\ *adv* — **id·i·o·mat·ic·ness** \-tik-nəs\ *n*

id·i·o·mor·phic \,ī-dē-ə-'mòr-fik\ *adj* [Gk *idiomorphos*, fr. *idio-* + *-morphos* -morphous] (1887) : having the proper form or shape — used of minerals whose crystalline growth has not been interfered with

---

\ə\ abut \ᵊ\ kitten, F table \ər\ further \a\ ash \ā\ ace \ä\ mop, mar \aù\ out \ch\ chin \e\ bet \ē\ easy \g\ go \i\ hit \ī\ ice \j\ job \ŋ\ sing \ō\ go \ò\ law \òi\ boy \th\ thin \t͟h\ the \ü\ loot \ù\ foot \y\ yet \zh\ vision \ä, k̲, ⁿ, œ, œ̄, ᵾ, ᵫ, ᵛ\ *see* Guide to Pronunciation

id·i·o·path·ic \ˌi-dē-ə-'pa-thik\ *adj* (1669) **1** : arising spontaneously or from an obscure or unknown cause : PRIMARY **2** : peculiar to the individual — **id·i·o·path·i·cal·ly** \-'pa-thi-k(ə-)lē\ *adv*

id·i·o·syn·cra·sy \ˌi-dē-ə-'siṇ-krə-sē\ *n, pl* **-sies** [Gk *idiosynkrasia*, fr. *idio-* + *synkerannynai* to blend, fr. *syn-* + *kerannynai* to mingle, mix — more at CRATER] (1604) **1 a** : a peculiarity of constitution or temperament : an individualizing characteristic or quality **b** : individual hypersensitiveness (as to a drug or food) **2** : characteristic peculiarity (as of temperament); *broadly* : ECCENTRICITY — **id·i·o·syn·crat·ic** \ˌi-dē-ō-(ˌ)sin-'kra-tik\ *adj* — **id·i·o·syn·crat·i·cal·ly** \-'kra-ti-k(ə-)lē\ *adv*

id·i·ot \'i-dē-ət\ *n* [ME, fr. L *idiota* ignorant person, fr. Gk *idiōtēs* one in a private station, layman, ignorant person, fr. *idios* one's own, private; akin to L *suus* one's own — more at SUICIDE] (14c) **1** : a person affected with idiocy; *esp* : a feebleminded person having a mental age not exceeding three years and requiring complete custodial care **2** : a foolish or stupid person — **idiot** *adj*

idiot box *n* (ca. 1955) : TELEVISION

id·i·ot·ic \ˌi-dē-'ä-tik\ *also* **id·i·ot·i·cal** \-'ä-ti-kəl\ *adj* (1713) **1** : characterized by idiocy **2** : showing complete lack of thought or common sense : FOOLISH — **id·i·ot·i·cal·ly** \-ti-k(ə-)lē\ *adv*

¹id·i·o·tism \'i-dē-ə-ˌti-zəm\ *n* [MF *idiotisme*, fr. L *idiotismus* common speech, fr. Gk *idiōtismos*, fr. *idiōtēs*] (1588) **1** *obs* : IDIOM 1 **2** : IDIOM 2

²id·i·ot·ism \'i-dē-ə-(ˌ)ti-zəm\ *n* [*idiot* + *-ism*] (ca. 1611) *archaic* : IDIOCY 2

idiot light *n* (1966) : a colored light on an instrument panel (as of an automobile) designed to give a warning (as of low oil pressure)

idiot sa·vant \'ē-ˌdyō-sä-'vän, *or same as* IDIOT *and* SAVANT *for respective sing and pl forms*\ *n, pl* **idiots savants** \-ˌdyō-sä-'vän(z)\ *or* **idiot savants** \-'vän(z)\ [F, lit., learned idiot] (1927) **1** : a mentally defective person who exhibits exceptional skill or brilliance in some limited field **2** : a person who is highly knowledgeable about one subject but knows little about anything else

-idium *n suffix, pl* **-idiums** *or* **-idia** [NL, fr. Gk *-idion*, dim. suffix] : small one (anther*idium*)

¹idle \'i-d³l\ *adj* **idler** \'id-lər, 'i-d³l-ər\; **idlest** \'id-ləst, 'i-d³l-əst\ [ME *idel*, fr. OE *idel*; akin to OHG *ital* worthless] (bef. 12c) **1** : lacking worth or basis : VAIN (~ chatter) (~ pleasure) **2** : not occupied or employed: as **a** : having no employment : INACTIVE (~ workers) **b** : not turned to normal or appropriate use (~ funds) (~ farmland) **c** : not scheduled to compete (the team will be ~ tomorrow) **3 a** : SHIFTLESS, LAZY **b** : having no evident lawful means of support *syn* see VAIN, INACTIVE — **idle·ness** \'i-d³l-nəs\ *n* — **idly** \'id-lē, 'i-d³l-ē\ *adv*

²idle *vb* **idled; idling** \'id-liṇ, 'i-d³l-iṇ\ *vi* (1592) **1 a** : to spend time in idleness **b** : to move idly **2** : to run at low power and often disconnected usu. so that power is not used for useful work (the engine is *idling*) ~ *vt* **1** : to pass in idleness **2** : to make idle (workers *idled* by a strike) **3** : to cause to idle — **idler** \'id-lər, 'i-d³l-ər\ *n*

idler pulley *n* (ca. 1890) : a guide or tightening pulley for a belt or chain

idler wheel *n* (1805) **1** : a wheel, gear, or roller used to transfer motion or to guide or support something **2** : IDLER PULLEY

idlesse \'id-ləs, id-'les\ *n* [ME, fr. *idle* + *-esse* (as in *richesse* wealth) — more at RICHES] (15c) : the quality or state of being idle : IDLENESS

ido·crase \'i-də-ˌkrās, 'i-, -ˌkrāz\ *n* [F, fr. Gk *eidos* form + *krasis* mixture, fr. *kerannynai* to mix — more at CRATER] (1804) : a mineral that is a complex silicate of calcium, magnesium, iron, and aluminum

idler wheel 1

idol \'i-d³l\ [ME, fr. OF *idole*, fr. LL *idolum*, fr. Gk *eidōlon* image, idol; akin to Gk *eidos* form — more at IDYLL] (13c) **1** : a representation or symbol of an object of worship; *broadly* : a false god **2 a** : a likeness of something **b** *obs* : PRETENDER, IMPOSTOR **3** : a form or appearance visible but without substance (an enchanted phantom, a lifeless ~ —P. B. Shelley) **4** : an object of extreme devotion (a movie ~); *also* : IDEAL 2 **5** : a false conception : FALLACY

idol·a·ter *or* **idol·a·tor** \ī-'dä-lə-tər\ *n* [ME *idolatrer*, fr. ME *idolatre*, fr. LL *idolatres*, fr. Gk *eidōlolatrēs*, fr. *eidōlon* + *-latrēs* -later] (14c) **1** : a worshiper of idols **2** : a person that admires intensely and often blindly one that is not usu. a subject of worship

idol·a·trous \ī-'dä-lə-trəs\ *adj* (1543) **1** : of or relating to idolatry **2** : having the character of idolatry (the religion of ~ nationalism — Aldous Huxley) **3** : given to idolatry — **idol·a·trous·ly** *adv* — **idol·a·trous·ness** *n*

idol·a·try \-trē\ *n, pl* **-tries** (13c) **1** : the worship of a physical object as a god **2** : immoderate attachment or devotion to something

idol·ize \'i-d³l-ˌīz\ *vb* **-ized; -iz·ing** *vt* (1598) : to worship as a god; *broadly* : to love or admire to excess (the common people whom he so *idolized* —*Times Lit. Supp.*) ~ *vi* : to practice idolatry — **idol·i·za·tion** \ˌi-d³l-ə-'zā-shən\ *n* — **idol·iz·er** \'i-d³l-ˌī-zər\ *n*

idyll *also* **idyl** \'i-d³l, chiefly Brit 'i-ˌdil\ *n* [L *idyllium*, fr. Gk *eidyllion*, fr. dim. of *eidos* form; akin to Gk *idein* to see — more at WIT] (1586) **1 a** : a simple descriptive work in poetry or prose that deals with rustic life or pastoral scenes or suggests a mood of peace and contentment **b** : a narrative poem (as Tennyson's *Idylls of the King*) treating an epic, romantic, or tragic theme **2 a** : a lighthearted carefree episode that is a fit subject for an idyll **b** : a romantic interlude

idyl·lic \ī-'dil-ik, chiefly Brit ˌ-\ *adj* (1856) **1** : of, relating to, or being an idyll **2** : pleasing or picturesque in natural simplicity — **idyl·li·cal·ly** \-'di-li-k(ə-)lē\ *adv*

-ie *also* **-y** *n suffix* [ME] **1** : little one : dear little one (bird*ie*) (sonn*y*) **2** : one belonging to : one having to do with (town*ie*) : one who is (preem*ie*) **3** : one of (such) a kind or quality (cut*ie*) (tough*ie*)

-ier — see -ER

¹if \'if, əf\ *conj* [ME, fr. OE *gif*; akin to OHG *ibu* if] (bef. 12c) **1** : in the event that **b** : allowing that **c** : on the assumption that **d** : on condition that **2** : WHETHER (asked ~ the mail had come) (I doubt ~ I'll pass the course) **3** — used as a function word to introduce an exclamation expressing a wish (~ it would only rain) **4** : even though

(an interesting ~ untenable argument) — **if anything** : on the contrary even : perhaps even (*if anything*, you ought to apologize)

²if \'if\ *n* (1513) **1** : CONDITION, STIPULATION (the question . . . depends on too many ~s to allow an answer —*Encounter*) **2** : SUPPOSITION

-iferous *adj comb form* [ME, fr. L *-ifer*, fr. *-i-* + *-fer* -ferous] : -FEROUS

iff \'if-³n(d)-'ön-lē-ˌif; 'if, *sometimes read with a prolonged* f\ *conj* [alter. of ¹*if*] (1955) : if and only if (two figures are congruent ~ one can be placed over the other so that they coincide)

if·fy \'i-fē\ *adj* [¹*if*] (1937) : abounding in contingencies or unknown qualities or conditions : UNCERTAIN (an ~ proposition) — **if·fi·ness** *n*

-ification *n suffix* [ME *-ificacioun*, fr. MF & L; MF *-ification*, fr. L *-ification-, -ificatio*, fr. *-i-* + *-ficatio* -fication] : -FICATION (desert*ification*)

-iform *adj comb form* [MF & L; MF *-iforme*, fr. L *-iformis*, fr. *-i-* + *-formis* -form] : -FORM (patell*iform*)

I formation *n* (1951) : an offensive football formation in which the running backs line up in a line directly behind the quarterback — compare T FORMATION

-ify *vb suffix* [ME *-ifien*, fr. OF *-ifier*, fr. L *-ificare*, fr. *-i-* + *-ficare* -fy] : -FY

IgA \ˌi-(ˌ)jē-'ā\ *n* [*immunoglobulin*] (1969) : a class of immunoglobulins found in external bodily secretions (as saliva, tears, and sweat)

Ig·bo \'ig-(ˌ)bō\ *var of* IBO

IgE \ˌi-(ˌ)jē-'ē\ *n* (1969) : a class of immunoglobulins that function esp. in allergic reactions

IgG \-'jē\ *n* (1969) : a class of immunoglobulins that includes the most common antibodies circulating in the blood

ig·loo \'i-(ˌ)glü\ *n, pl* **igloos** [Inuit *iglu* house] (1856) **1** : an Eskimo house usu. made of sod, wood, or stone when permanent or of blocks of snow or ice in the shape of a dome when built for temporary purposes **2** : a building or structure shaped like a dome

IgM \ˌi-(ˌ)jē-'em\ *n* (1969) : a class of immunoglobulins that includes antibodies that appear early in the immune response

ig·ne·ous \'ig-nē-əs\ *adj* [L *igneus*, fr. *ignis* fire; akin to Skt *agni* fire] (1664) **1** : of, relating to, or resembling fire : FIERY **2 a** : relating to, resulting from, or suggestive of the intrusion or extrusion of magma or volcanic activity **b** : formed by solidification of magma (~ rock)

ig·nes·cent \ig-'ne-s³nt\ *adj* [L *ignescent-, ignescens*, prp. of *ignescere* to catch fire, fr. *ignis*] (ca. 1828) : VOLATILE

ig·nim·brite \'ig-nəm-ˌbrīt\ *n* [G *Ignimbrit*, fr. L *ignis* + *imbr-* (fr. *imber* rain) + G *-it* ¹*-ite* — more at IMBRICATE] (1932) : a hard rock formed by solidification of chiefly fine deposits of volcanic ash

ig·nis fat·u·us \'ig-nəs-'fa-chə-wəs, -'fach-wəs\ *n, pl* **ig·nes fat·ui** \-ˌnēz-'fa-chə-ˌwī\ [ML, lit., foolish fire] (ca. 1563) **1** : a light that sometimes appears in the night over marshy ground and is often attributable to the combustion of gas from decomposed organic matter **2** : a deceptive goal or hope

ig·nite \ig-'nīt\ *vb* **ig·nit·ed; ig·nit·ing** [L *ignitus*, pp. of *ignire* to ignite, fr. *ignis*] *vt* (1666) **1** : to subject to fire or intense heat; *esp* : to render luminous by heat **2 a** : to set afire; *also* : KINDLE **b** : to cause (a fuel) to burn **3** : to heat up : EXCITE (oppression that *ignited* the hatred of the people) ~ *vi* **1** : to catch fire **2** : to begin to glow — **ig·nit·abil·i·ty** \ig-ˌni-tə-'bi-lə-tē\ *n* — **ig·nit·able** *also* **ig·nit·ible** \-'ni-tə-bəl\ *adj* — **ig·nit·er** *also* **ig·ni·tor** \-'ni-tər\ *n*

ig·ni·tion \ig-'ni-shən\ *n* (1612) **1** : the act or action of igniting: as **a** : the starting of a fire **b** : the heating of a plasma to a temperature high enough to sustain nuclear fusion **2** : the process or means (as an electric spark) of igniting a fuel mixture

ig·ni·tron \ig-'ni-ˌträn\ *n* [L *ignis* fire + E *-tron*] (1933) : a mercury-containing rectifier tube in which the arc is struck again at the beginning of each cycle by a special electrode separately energized by an auxiliary circuit

ig·no·ble \ig-'nō-bəl\ *adj* [ME, fr. MF, fr. L *ignobilis*, fr. *in-* + OL *gnobilis* noble] (15c) **1** : of low birth or common origin : PLEBEIAN **2** : characterized by baseness, lowness, or meanness *syn* see MEAN — **ig·no·bil·i·ty** \ˌig-nō-'bi-lə-tē\ *n* — **ig·no·ble·ness** \ig-'nō-bəl-nəs\ *n* — **ig·no·bly** \-blē *also* -bə-lē\ *adv*

ig·no·min·i·ous \ˌig-nə-'mi-nē-əs\ *adj* (15c) **1** : marked with or characterized by disgrace or shame : DISHONORABLE **2** : deserving of shame or infamy : DESPICABLE **3** : HUMILIATING, DEGRADING (suffered an ~ defeat) — **ig·no·min·i·ous·ly** *adv* — **ig·no·min·i·ous·ness** *n*

ig·no·mi·ny \'ig-nə-ˌmi-nē, -mə-nē *also* ig-'nä-mə-nē\ *n, pl* **-nies** [MF or L; MF *ignominie*, fr. L *ignominia*, fr. *ig-* (as in *ignorare* to be ignorant of, ignore) + *nomin-, nomen* name, repute — more at NAME] (1540) **1** : deep personal humiliation and disgrace **2** : disgraceful or dishonorable conduct, quality, or action *syn* see DISGRACE

ig·no·ra·mus \ˌig-nə-'rä-məs *also* -'ra-\ *n, pl* **-mus·es** *also* **-mi** \-mē\ [*Ignoramus*, ignorant lawyer in *Ignoramus* (1615), play by George Ruggle, fr. L, lit., we are ignorant of] (ca. 1616) : an utterly ignorant person : DUNCE

ig·no·rance \'ig-n(ə-)rən(t)s\ *n* (13c) : the state or fact of being ignorant

ig·no·rant \'ig-n(ə-)rənt\ *adj* (14c) **1 a** : destitute of knowledge or education (an ~ society); *also* : lacking knowledge or comprehension of the thing specified (parents ~ of modern mathematics) **b** : resulting from or showing lack of knowledge or intelligence (~ errors) **2** : UNAWARE, UNINFORMED — **ig·no·rant·ly** *adv* — **ig·no·rant·ness** *n*
syn IGNORANT, ILLITERATE, UNLETTERED, UNTUTORED, UNLEARNED mean not having knowledge. IGNORANT may imply a general condition or it may apply to lack of knowledge or awareness of a particular thing (an *ignorant* fool) (*ignorant* of nuclear physics). ILLITERATE applies to either an absolute or a relative inability to read and write (much of the population is still *illiterate*). UNLETTERED implies ignorance of the knowledge gained by reading (an allusion meaningless to the *unlettered*). UNTUTORED may imply lack of schooling in the arts and ways of civilization (strange monuments built by an *untutored* people). UNLEARNED suggests ignorance of advanced subjects (poetry not for academics but for the *unlearned* masses).

ig·no·ra·tio elen·chi \ˌig-nə-'rä-tē-ˌō-i-'leṇ-ˌkē\ *n* [L, lit., ignorance of proof] (1588) : a fallacy in logic of supposing a point proved or disproved by an argument proving or disproving something not at issue

ig·nore \ig-'nōr, -'nȯr\ *vt* **ig·nored; ig·nor·ing** [obs. *ignore* to be ignorant of, fr. F *ignorer*, fr. L *ignorare*, fr. *ignarus* ignorant, unknown, fr. *in-* + *gnoscere, noscere* to know — more at KNOW] (1801) **1** : to refuse to take notice of   **2** : to reject (a bill of indictment) as ungrounded *syn* see NEGLECT — **ig·nor·able** \-'nȯr-ə-bəl, -'nȯr-\ *adj* — **ig·nor·er** *n*

Igo·rot \ē-gə-'rōt\ *n, pl* **Igorot** *or* **Igorots** (1821)   **1** : a member of any of several related peoples of northwestern Luzon, Philippines   **2** : any of the Austronesian languages of the Igorot

Igraine \i-'grān\ *n* : the wife of Uther and mother of King Arthur

igua·na \i-'gwä-nə\ *n* [Sp, fr. Arawak & Carib *iwana*] (1555) : any of various large herbivorous typically dark-colored tropical American lizards (family Iguanidae) that have a serrated dorsal crest and are important as human food in their native habitat; *broadly* : any of various large lizards

iguan·odon \i-'gwä-nə-,dän\ *n* [NL *Iguanodont-, Iguanodon,* fr. Sp *iguana* + Gk *odṓn* tooth, fr. *odont-, odous* — more at TOOTH] (1830) : any of a genus (*Iguanodon*) of very large herbivorous dinosaurs of the early Cretaceous

IHS \,ī-,āch-'es\ [LL, part transliteration of Gk IHΣ, abbreviation for IHΣOYΣ *Iēsous* Jesus] — used as a Christian symbol and monogram for *Jesus*

ikat \'ē-,kät\ *n* [Malay, tying] (1927) : a fabric in which the yarns have been tie-dyed before weaving

ike·ba·na \,i-kä-'bä-nə, ,i-ki-, ,ē-\ *n* [Jp, fr. *ikeru* to keep alive, arrange + *hana* flower] (1901) : the Japanese art of flower arranging that emphasizes form and balance

ikon *var of* ICON

il- — see IN-

ilang–ilang *var of* YLANG-YLANG

¹-ile *adj suffix* [ME, fr. MF, fr. L *-ilis*] : tending to or capable of ⟨contractile⟩

²-ile *n suffix* [*-ile* (as in *quartile,* n.)] : segment of a (specified) size in a frequency distribution ⟨decile⟩

il·e·itis \,i-lē-'ī-təs\ *n* [NL] (ca. 1855) : inflammation of the ileum

il·e·um \'i-lē-əm\ *n, pl* **il·ea** \-lē-ə\ [NL, alter. of L *ilia,* pl., groin, viscera] (1682) : the last division of the small intestine extending between the jejunum and large intestine — **il·e·al** \-lē-əl\ *adj*

il·e·us \'i-lē-əs\ *n* [L, fr. Gk *eileos,* fr. *eilyein* to roll — more at VOLUBLE] (1693) : mechanical or functional obstruction of the bowel

ilex \'ī-,leks\ *n* [ME, fr. L] (14c)   **1** : HOLM OAK   **2** : HOLLY 1

il·i·ac \'i-lē-,ak\ *also* **il·i·al** \'i-lē-əl\ *adj* [LL *iliacus,* fr. L *ilium*] (1541) : of, relating to, or located near the ilium

Il·i·ad \'i-lē-əd, -,ad\ *n* [*Iliad,* ancient Greek epic poem attributed to Homer, fr. L *Iliad-, Ilias,* fr. Gk, fr. *Ilion* Troy] (1603)   **1 a** : a series of miseries or disastrous events   **b** : a series of exploits regarded as suitable for an epic   **2** : a long narrative; *esp* : an epic in the Homeric tradition — **Il·i·ad·ic** \,i-lē-'a-dik\ *adj*

il·i·um \'i-lē-əm\ *n, pl* **il·ia** \-lē-ə\ [NL, alter. of L *ilia*] (1706) : the dorsal, upper, and largest one of the three bones composing either lateral half of the pelvis

¹ilk \'ilk\ *pron* [ME, fr. OE *ilca,* fr. a prehistoric compound whose constituents are akin respectively to Goth *is* (akin to L *is* he, that) and OE *gelīc* like — more at ITERATE, LIKE] (bef. 12c) *chiefly Scot* : SAME — used with *that* esp. in the names of landed families

²ilk *n* (1790) : SORT, KIND ⟨the rejection of these books or others of like ~ —Kathleen Molz⟩

³ilk *pron* [ME, adj. & pron., fr. OE *ylc, ælc* — more at EACH] (bef. 12c) *chiefly Scot* : EACH

il·ka \'il-kə\ *adj* [ME, fr. *ilk* + *a* (indef. art.)] (13c) *chiefly Scot* : EACH, EVERY

¹ill \'il\ *adj* **worse** \'wərs\; **worst** \'wərst\ [ME, fr. ON *illr*] (12c)   **1 a** *chiefly Scot* : IMMORAL, VICIOUS   **b** : resulting from, accompanied by, or indicative of an evil or malevolent intention ⟨~ deeds⟩   **c** : attributing evil or an objectionable quality ⟨held an ~ opinion of his neighbors⟩   **2 a** : causing suffering or distress ⟨~ weather⟩   **b** *comparative also* **ill·er**   (1) : not normal or sound ⟨~ health⟩   (2) : not in good health; *also* : NAUSEATED   **3 a** : not suited to circumstances or not to one's advantage : UNLUCKY ⟨an ~ omen⟩   **b** : involving difficulty : HARD ⟨an ~ man to please⟩   **4 a** : not meeting an accepted standard ⟨~ manners⟩   **b** *archaic* : notably unskillful or inefficient   **5** : UNFRIENDLY, HOSTILE ⟨~ feeling⟩

²ill *adv* **worse; worst** (13c)   **1 a** : with displeasure or hostility   **b** : in a harsh manner   **c** : so as to reflect unfavorably ⟨spoke ~ of the neighbors⟩   **2** : in a reprehensible manner   **3** : HARDLY, SCARCELY ⟨can ~ afford such extravagances⟩   **4 a** : in an unfortunate manner : BADLY, UNLUCKILY ⟨~ fares the land . . . where wealth accumulates, and men decay —Oliver Goldsmith⟩   **b** : in a faulty, inefficient, insufficient, or unpleasant manner — often used in combination ⟨the methods used may be *ill*-adapted to the aims in view —R. M. Hutchins⟩

³ill *n* (13c)   **1** : the reverse of good : EVIL   **2 a** : MISFORTUNE, DISTRESS   **b**   (1) : AILMENT, SICKNESS   (2) : something that disturbs or afflicts : TROUBLE ⟨economic and social ~*s*⟩   **3** : something that reflects unfavorably ⟨spoke no ~ of him⟩

I'll \'i(ə)l\ (1567) : I will : I shall

ill–ad·vised \,i-ləd-'vīzd\ *adj* (ca. 1592) : resulting from or showing lack of wise and sufficient counsel or deliberation ⟨an ~ decision⟩ — **ill–ad·vis·ed·ly** \-'vī-zəd-lē\ *adv*

ill at ease *adj* (14c) : not feeling easy : UNCOMFORTABLE

il·la·tion \i-'lā-shən\ *n* [LL *illation-, illatio,* fr. L, action of bringing in, fr. *inferre* (pp. *illatus*) fr. bring in, fr. *in-* + *ferre* to carry — more at TOLERATE, BEAR] (1533)   **1** : the action of inferring : INFERENCE   **2** : a conclusion inferred

¹il·la·tive \'i-lə-tiv, i-'lā-\ *n* (1591)   **1** : a word (as *therefore*) or phrase (as *as a consequence*) introducing an inference   **2** : ILLATION 2

²illative *adj* (1611) : INFERENTIAL — **il·la·tive·ly** *adv*

il·laud·able \(,)i(l)-'lȯ-də-bəl\ *adj* [L *illaudabilis,* fr. *in-* + *laudabilis* laudable] (1589) : deserving no praise — **il·laud·ably** \-blē\ *adv*

ill–be·ing \'il-'bē-iŋ\ *n* (1840) : a condition of being deficient in health, happiness, or prosperity

ill–bod·ing \-'bō-diŋ\ *adj* (1591) : boding evil : INAUSPICIOUS

ill–bred \-'bred\ *adj* (1604) : badly brought up or showing bad upbringing : IMPOLITE

¹il·le·gal \(,)i(l)-'lē-gəl\ *adj* [MF or ML; MF *illegal,* fr. ML *illegalis,* fr. L *in-* + *legalis* legal] (1538) : not according to or authorized by law : UNLAWFUL, ILLICIT; *also* : not sanctioned by official rules (as of a game) — **il·le·gal·i·ty** \,i-li-'ga-lə-tē\ *n* — **il·le·gal·ly** \(,)i(l)-'lē-gə-lē\ *adv*

²illegal *n* (1939) : an illegal immigrant

il·le·gal·ize \(,)i(l)-'lē-gə-,līz\ *vt* (ca. 1818) : to make or declare illegal — **il·le·gal·i·za·tion** \-,lē-gə-lə-'zā-shən\ *n*

il·leg·i·ble \(,)i(l)-'le-jə-bəl\ *adj* (1640) : not legible : UNDECIPHERABLE ⟨~ writing⟩ — **il·leg·i·bil·i·ty** \-,le-jə-'bi-lə-tē\ *n* — **il·leg·i·bly** \-'le-jə-blē\ *adv*

il·le·git·i·ma·cy \,i-li-'ji-tə-mə-sē\ *n* (1680)   **1** : the quality or state of being illegitimate   **2** : BASTARDY 2

il·le·git·i·mate \-'ji-tə-mət\ *adj* (1536)   **1** : not recognized as lawful offspring; *specif* : born of parents not married to each other   **2** : not rightly deduced or inferred : ILLOGICAL   **3** : departing from the regular : ERRATIC   **4 a** : not sanctioned by law : ILLEGAL   **b** : not authorized by good usage   **c** *of a taxon* : published but not in accordance with the rules of the relevant international code — **il·le·git·i·mate·ly** *adv*

ill–fat·ed \'il-'fā-təd\ *adj* (1710)   **1** : having or destined to a hapless fate : UNFORTUNATE ⟨an ~ expedition⟩   **2** : that causes or marks the beginning of misfortune

ill–fa·vored \-'fā-vərd\ *adj* (ca. 1530)   **1** : unattractive in physical appearance; *esp* : having an ugly face   **2** : OFFENSIVE, OBJECTIONABLE

ill–got·ten \-'gä-t³n\ *adj* (1552) : acquired by illicit or improper means ⟨~ gains⟩

ill–hu·mored \'il-'hyü-mərd, -'yü-\ *adj* (1687) : SURLY, IRRITABLE — **ill–hu·mored·ly** *adv*

il·lib·er·al \(,)i(l)-'li-b(ə-)rəl\ *adj* [MF or L; MF, fr. L *illiberalis* ignoble, stingy, fr. L *in-* + *liberalis* liberal] (1535) : not liberal: as   **a** *archaic*   (1) : lacking a liberal education   (2) : lacking culture and refinement   **b** : not requiring the background of a liberal arts education ⟨~ occupations⟩   **c** *archaic* : not generous : STINGY   **d** : not broad-minded : BIGOTED   **e** : opposed to liberalism — **il·lib·er·al·i·ty** \-,li-bə-'ra-lə-tē\ *n* — **il·lib·er·al·ly** \-'li-b(ə-)rə-lē\ *adv* — **il·lib·er·al·ness** \-b(ə-)rəl-nəs\ *n*

il·lib·er·al·ism \-b(ə-)rə-,li-zəm\ *n* (1839) : opposition to or lack of liberalism

il·lic·it \(,)i(l)-'li-sət\ *adj* [L *illicitus,* fr. *in-* + *licitus* lawful — more at LICIT] (1506) : not permitted : UNLAWFUL — **il·lic·it·ly** *adv*

il·lim·it·able \(,)i(l)-'li-mə-tə-bəl\ *adj* (1596) : incapable of being limited or bounded : MEASURELESS ⟨the ~ reaches of space and time⟩ — **il·lim·it·abil·i·ty** \-,li-mə-tə-'bi-lə-tē\ *n* — **il·lim·it·able·ness** \-'li-mə-tə-bəl-nəs\ *n* — **il·lim·it·ably** \-blē\ *adv*

Il·li·nois \,i-lə-'nȯi *also* -'nȯiz\ *n, pl* **Illinois** [F, of Algonquian origin] (1703)   **1** *pl* : a confederacy of American Indian peoples of Illinois, Iowa, and Wisconsin   **2** : a member of any of the Illinois peoples

il·liq·uid \(,)i(l)-'lik-wəd\ *adj* (1913)   **1** : not being cash or readily convertible into cash ⟨~ holdings⟩   **2** : deficient in liquid assets ⟨an ~ bank⟩ — **il·li·quid·i·ty** \-,li-'kwi-də-tē\ *n*

il·lite \'i-,līt\ *n* [*Illinois,* state of U.S. + ¹-*ite*] (1937) : any of a group of clay minerals having essentially the crystal structure of muscovite — **il·lit·ic** \i-'li-tik\ *adj*

il·lit·er·a·cy \(,)i(l)-'li-t(ə-)rə-sē\ *n, pl* **-cies** (1660)   **1** : the quality or state of being illiterate; *esp* : inability to read or write   **2** : a mistake or crudity (as in speaking) typical of one who is illiterate

il·lit·er·ate \(,)i(l)-'li-t(ə-)rət\ *adj* [ME, fr. L *illiteratus,* fr. *in-* + *litteratus* literate] (15c)   **1** : having little or no education; *esp* : unable to read or write   **2 a** : showing or marked by a lack of familiarity with language and literature   **b** : violating approved patterns of speaking or writing   **3** : showing or marked by a lack of acquaintance with the fundamentals of a particular field of knowledge   *syn* see IGNORANT — **illiterate** *n* — **il·lit·er·ate·ly** *adv* — **il·lit·er·ate·ness** *n*

ill–man·nered \'il-'ma-nərd\ *adj* (15c) : having bad manners : RUDE

ill–na·tured \-'nā-chərd\ *adj* (1605)   **1** : MALEVOLENT, SPITEFUL   **2** : having a bad disposition : CROSS, SURLY — **ill–na·tured·ly** *adv*

ill·ness \'il-nəs\ *n* (ca. 1500)   **1** *obs*   **a** : WICKEDNESS   **b** : UNPLEASANTNESS   **2 a** : an unhealthy condition of body or mind   **b** : SICKNESS 2

il·lo·cu·tion·ary \,i-lə-'kyü-shə-,ner-ē, ,i(l)-lō-\ *adj* [²*in-* + *locution*] (1955) : relating to or being the communicative effect (as commanding or requesting) of an utterance ⟨"There's a snake under you" may have the ~ force of a warning⟩

il·log·ic \(,)i(l)-'lä-jik\ *n* [back-formation fr. *illogical*] (1856) : the quality or state of being illogical : ILLOGICALITY

il·log·i·cal \-ji-kəl\ *adj* (1588)   **1** : not observing the principles of logic   **2** : devoid of logic : SENSELESS — **il·log·i·cal·i·ty** \-,lä-ji-'ka-lə-tē\ *n* — **il·log·i·cal·ly** \-'lä-ji-k(ə-)lē\ *adv* — **il·log·i·cal·ness** \-kəl-nəs\ *n*

ill–sort·ed \'il-'sȯr-təd\ *adj* (1691)   **1** : not well matched ⟨he and his wife were an ~ pair —Lord Byron⟩   **2** *Scot* : much displeased

ill–starred \-'stärd\ *adj* (1604) : ILL-FATED, UNLUCKY ⟨an ~ venture⟩

ill–tem·pered \-'tem-pərd\ *adj* (1601) : ILL-NATURED, QUARRELSOME — **ill–tem·pered·ly** \-lē\ *adv*

ill–treat \-'trēt\ *vt* (1689) : to treat cruelly or improperly : MALTREAT — **ill–treat·ment** \-mənt\ *n*

il·lume \i-'lüm\ *vt* **il·lumed; il·lum·ing** (1602) : ILLUMINATE

il·lu·mi·nance \i-'lü-mə-nən(t)s\ *n* (ca. 1938) : ILLUMINATION 2

il·lu·mi·nant \-nənt\ *n* (1644) : an illuminating device or substance

¹il·lu·mi·nate \i-'lü-mə-nət\ *adj* (15c)   **1** *archaic* : brightened with light   **2** *archaic* : intellectually or spiritually enlightened

²il·lu·mi·nate \-,nāt\ *vt* **-nat·ed; -nat·ing** [ME, fr. L *illuminatus,* pp. of *illuminare,* fr. *in-* + *luminare* to light up, fr. *lumin-, lumen* light — more at LUMINARY] (15c)   **1 a** : to enlighten spiritually or intellectually   **b**   (1) : to supply or brighten with light   (2) : to make luminous or shining   **c** *archaic* : to set alight   **2** : to subject to radiation   **3** : to make clear : ELUCIDATE   **4** : to make illustrious or resplendent   **5** : to decorate (as a manuscript) with gold or silver or brilliant colors or with often elaborate designs or miniature pictures — **il·lu·mi·nat·ing·ly** \-,nā-tiŋ-lē\ *adv* — **il·lu·mi·na·tor** \-,nā-tər\ *n*

³il·lu·mi·nate \-nət\ *n* (1600) *archaic* : one having or claiming unusual enlightenment

il·lu·mi·na·ti \i-,lü-mə-'nä-tē\ *n pl* [It & NL; It, fr. NL, fr. L, pl. of *illuminatus*] (1599)   **1** *cap* : any of various groups claiming special

\ə\ abut \³\ kitten, F table \ər\ further \a\ ash \ā\ ace \ä\ mop, mar \aù\ out \ch\ chin \e\ bet \ē\ easy \g\ go \i\ hit \ī\ ice \j\ job \ŋ\ sing \ō\ go \ȯ\ law \ȯi\ boy \th\ thin \th\ the \ü\ loot \ù\ foot \y\ yet \zh\ vision \ä, k̲, ⁿ, œ, œ̄, œ, ūe, ūē, ᵞ\ *see* Guide to Pronunciation religious enlightenment **2 :** persons who are or who claim to be unusually enlightened

il·lu·mi·na·tion \i-,lü-mə-'nā-shən\ *n* (14c) **1 :** the action of illuminating or state of being illuminated: as **a :** spiritual or intellectual enlightenment **b** (1) **:** a lighting up (2) **:** decorative lighting or lighting effects **c :** decoration by the art of illuminating **2 :** the luminous flux per unit area on an intercepting surface at any given point **3 :** one of the decorative features used in the art of illuminating or in decorative lighting

il·lu·mi·na·tive \i-'lü-mə-,nā-tiv\ *adj* (1644) **:** of, relating to, or producing illumination : ILLUMINATING

il·lu·mine \i-'lü-mən\ *vt* **-mined; -min·ing** (14c) : ILLUMINATE — **il·lu·min·able** \-mə-nə-bəl\ *adj*

il·lu·mi·nism \-mə-,ni-zəm\ *n* (1798) **1 :** belief in or claim to a personal enlightenment not accessible to mankind in general **2** *cap* **:** beliefs or claims viewed as forming doctrine or principles of Illuminati — **il·lu·mi·nist** \-nist\ *n*

ill–us·age \'il-'yü-sij, -zij\ *n* (1593) : harsh, unkind, or abusive treatment

ill–use \-'yüz\ *vt* (1841) **:** to use badly : MALTREAT, ABUSE

il·lu·sion \i-'lü-zhən\ *n* [ME, fr. MF, fr. LL *illusion-, illusio*, fr. L, action of mocking, fr. *illudere* to mock at, fr. *in-* + *ludere* to play, mock — more at LUDICROUS] (14c) **1 a** *obs* **:** the action of deceiving **b** (1) **:** the state or fact of being intellectually deceived or misled : MISAPPREHENSION (2) **:** an instance of such deception **2 a** (1) **:** a misleading image presented to the vision (2) **:** something that deceives or misleads intellectually **b** (1) **:** perception of something objectively existing in such a way as to cause misinterpretation of its actual nature (2) **:** HALLUCINATION 1 (3) **:** a pattern capable of reversible perspective **3 :** a fine plain transparent bobbinet or tulle usu. made of silk and used for veils, trimmings, and dresses — **il·lu·sion·al** \-'lüzh-nəl, -'lü-zhə-nºl\ *adj*

il·lu·sion·ary \i-'lü-zhə-,ner-ē\ *adj* (1886) : ILLUSORY

il·lu·sion·ism \i-'lü-zhə-,ni-zəm\ *n* (1911) **:** the use of artistic techniques (as perspective or shading) to create the illusion of reality esp. in a work of art

il·lu·sion·ist \i-'lüzh-nist, -'lü-zhə-\ *n* (1850) **:** one who produces illusory effects: as **a :** one (as an artist) whose work is marked by illusionism **b :** a sleight-of-hand performer or a magician — **il·lu·sion·is·tic** \-,lü-zhə-'nis-tik\ *adj* — **il·lu·sion·is·ti·cal·ly** \-ti-k(ə-)lē\ *adv*

il·lu·sive \i-'lü-siv, -ziv\ *adj* (1606) : ILLUSORY — **il·lu·sive·ly** *adv* — **il·lu·sive·ness** *n*

il·lu·so·ry \i-'lüs-rē, -'lüz-; -'lü-sə-, -zə-\ *adj* (ca. 1631) **:** based on or producing illusion : DECEPTIVE ⟨~ hopes⟩ *syn* see APPARENT — **il·lu·so·ri·ly** \-rə-lē\ *adv* — **il·lu·so·ri·ness** \-rē-nəs\ *n*

il·lus·trate \'i-ləs-,trāt *also* i-'ləs-\ *vb* **-trat·ed; -trat·ing** [L *illustratus*, pp. of *illustrare*, fr. *in-* + *lustrare* to purify, make bright — more at LUSTER] *vt* (1526) **1** *obs* **a :** ENLIGHTEN **b :** to light up **2 a** *archaic* **:** to make illustrious **b** *obs* (1) **:** to make bright (2) **:** ADORN **3 a :** to make clear : CLARIFY **b :** to make clear by giving or by serving as an example or instance **c :** to provide with visual features intended to explain or decorate ⟨~ a book⟩ **4 :** to show clearly : DEMONSTRATE ~ *vi* **:** to give an example or instance — **il·lus·tra·tor** \'i-ləs-,trā-tər *also* i-'ləs-\ *n*

il·lus·tra·tion \,i-ləs-'trā-shən *also* i-,ləs-\ *n* (14c) **1 a :** the action of illustrating **:** the condition of being illustrated **b** *archaic* **:** the action of making illustrious or honored or distinguished **2 :** something that serves to illustrate: as **a :** an example or instance that helps make something clear **b :** a picture or diagram that helps make something clear or attractive *syn* see INSTANCE — **il·lus·tra·tion·al** \-shnəl, -shə-nºl\ *adj*

il·lus·tra·tive \i-'ləs-trə-tiv *also* 'i-lə-,strā-\ *adj* (1643) **:** serving, tending, or designed to illustrate ⟨~ examples⟩ — **il·lus·tra·tive·ly** *adv*

il·lus·tri·ous \i-'ləs-trē-əs\ *adj* [L *illustris*, prob. fr. *illustrare*] (1588) **1 :** notably or brilliantly outstanding because of dignity or achievements or actions : EMINENT **2** *archaic* **a :** shining brightly with light **b :** clearly evident *syn* see FAMOUS — **il·lus·tri·ous·ly** *adv* — **il·lus·tri·ous·ness** *n*

il·lu·vi·al \i-'lü-vē-əl\ *adj* (1924) **:** of, relating to, or marked by illuviation or illuviated materials or areas

il·lu·vi·a·tion \i-,lü-vē-'ā-shən\ *n* [²*in-* + *-luviation* (as in *eluviation*)] (1928) **:** accumulation of dissolved or suspended soil materials in one area or horizon as a result of eluviation from another — **il·lu·vi·at·ed** \i-'lü-vē-,ā-təd\ *adj*

ill will *n* (14c): unfriendly feeling *syn* see MALICE

ill–wish·er \'il-,wi-shər, -'wi-\ *n* (1607) **:** one that wishes ill to another

il·ly \i(l)-lē\ *adv* (15c) **:** not wisely or well : BADLY, ILL ⟨his ~ concealed pride⟩—Della Lutes⟩

Il·lyr·i·an \i-'lir-ē-ən\ *n* (1584) **1 :** a native or inhabitant of ancient Illyria **2 :** the poorly attested Indo-European languages of the Illyrians — see INDO-EUROPEAN LANGUAGES table — **Illyrian** *adj*

il·men·ite \'il-mə-,nīt\ *n* [G *Ilmenit*, fr. *Ilmen* range, Ural Mts., Russia] (ca. 1827) **:** a usu. massive iron-black mineral composed of iron, titanium, and oxygen that is a titanium ore

Ilo·ca·no *or* **Ilo·ka·no** \,ē-lə-'kä-(,)nō, ,i-\ *n, pl* **Ilocano** *or* **Ilocanos** *or* **Ilokano** *or* **Ilokanos** (1898) **1 :** a member of a major people of northern Luzon in the Philippines **2 :** the Austronesian language of the Ilocano people

im- — see IN-

I'm \'im\ (ca. 1594): I am

¹**im·age** \'i-mij\ *n* [ME, fr. OF, short for *imagene*, fr. L *imagin-, imago*; perh. akin to L *imitari* to imitate] (13c) **1 :** a reproduction or imitation of the form of a person or thing; *esp* **:** an imitation in solid form : STATUE **2 a :** the optical counterpart of an object produced by an optical device (as a lens or mirror) or an electronic device **b :** a likeness of an object produced on a photographic material **3 a :** exact likeness : SEMBLANCE ⟨God created man in his own ~ —Gen 1:27 (RSV)⟩ **b :** a person strikingly like another person ⟨she is the ~ of her mother⟩ **4 a :** a tangible or visible representation : INCARNATION ⟨the ~ of filial devotion⟩ **b** *archaic* **:** an illusory form : APPARITION **5 a** (1) **:** a mental picture of something not actually present : IMPRESSION (2) **:** a mental conception held in common by members of a group and symbolic of a basic attitude and orientation ⟨a disorderly courtroom can seriously tarnish a community's ~ of justice —Herbert Brownell⟩ **b :** IDEA, CONCEPT **6 :** a vivid or graphic representation or description **7 :** FIGURE OF SPEECH **8 :** a popular conception (as of a person, institution, or nation) projected esp. through the mass media ⟨promoting a corporate ~ of brotherly love and concern —R. C. Buck⟩ **9 :** a set of values given by a mathematical function (as a homomorphism) that corresponds to a particular subset of the domain

²**image** *vt* **im·aged; im·ag·ing** (14c) **1 :** to call up a mental picture of : IMAGINE **2 :** to describe or portray in language esp. in a vivid manner **3 a :** to create a representation of; *also* **:** to form an image of **b :** to represent symbolically **4 a :** REFLECT, MIRROR **b :** to make appear : PROJECT — **im·ag·er** \'i-mi-jər\ *n*

image orthicon *n* (1945): a highly sensitive television image tube

im·ag·ery \'i-mij-rē, -mi-jə-\ *n, pl* **-er·ies** (14c) **1 a :** the product of image makers : IMAGES; *also* **:** the art of making images **b :** pictures produced by an imaging system **2 :** figurative language **3 :** mental images; *esp* **:** the products of imagination

image tube *n* (1936) **:** an electron tube in which incident electromagnetic radiation (as light or infrared) produces a visible image on its fluorescent screen duplicating the original pattern of radiation — called also *image converter*

imag·in·able \i-'maj-nə-bəl, -'ma-jə-\ *adj* (14c) **:** capable of being imagined : CONCEIVABLE — **imag·in·able·ness** *n* — **imag·in·ably** \-blē\ *adv*

¹**imag·i·nal** \i-'ma-jə-nºl\ *adj* [*imagine* + ¹*-al*] (1647) **:** of or relating to imagination, images, or imagery

²**ima·gi·nal** \i-'ma-jə-nºl, -'mā-, -'mä-gə-\ *adj* [NL *imagin-, imago*] (1877) **:** of or relating to the insect imago

imag·i·nary \i-'ma-jə-,ner-ē\ *adj* (14c) **1 a :** existing only in imagination **:** lacking factual reality **b :** formed or characterized imaginatively or arbitrarily ⟨his canvases, chiefly ~, somber landscapes —Current Biog.⟩ **2 :** containing or relating to the imaginary unit ⟨~ roots⟩ — **imag·i·nari·ly** \i-,ma-jə-'ner-ə-lē\ *adv* — **imag·i·nari·ness** \-'ma-jə-,ner-ē-nəs\ *n*

syn IMAGINARY, FANCIFUL, VISIONARY, FANTASTIC, CHIMERICAL, QUIXOTIC mean unreal or unbelievable. IMAGINARY applies to something which is fictitious and purely the product of one's imagination ⟨an *imaginary* desert isle⟩. FANCIFUL suggests the free play of the imagination ⟨a teller of *fanciful* stories⟩. VISIONARY stresses impracticality or incapability of realization ⟨*visionary* schemes⟩. FANTASTIC implies incredibility or strangeness beyond belief ⟨a *fantastic* world inhabited by monsters⟩. CHIMERICAL combines the implication of VISIONARY and FANTASTIC ⟨*chimerical* dreams of future progress⟩. QUIXOTIC implies a devotion to romantic or chivalrous ideals unrestrained by ordinary prudence and common sense ⟨a *quixotic* crusade⟩.

imaginary number *n* (ca. 1911) **:** a complex number (as $2 + 3i$ in which the coefficient of the imaginary unit is not zero — called also *imaginary*; compare PURE IMAGINARY

imaginary part *n* (ca. 1929) **:** the part of a complex number (as $3i$ in $2 + 3i$) that has the imaginary unit as a factor

imaginary unit *n* (ca. 1911) **:** the positive square root of minus 1 denoted by i or $+\sqrt{i}$

imag·i·na·tion \i-,ma-jə-'nā-shən\ *n* [ME, fr. MF, fr. L *imagination-, imaginatio*, fr. *imaginari*] (14c) **1 :** the act or power of forming a mental image of something not present to the senses or never before wholly perceived in reality **2 a :** creative ability **b :** ability to confront and deal with a problem : RESOURCEFULNESS **c :** the thinking or active mind : INTEREST ⟨stories that fired the ~⟩ **3 a :** a creation of the mind; *esp* **:** an idealized or poetic creation **b :** fanciful or empty assumption

imag·i·na·tive \i-'maj-nə-tiv; -'ma-jə-,nā-, -nə-\ *adj* (14c) **1 a :** of, relating to, or characterized by imagination **b :** devoid of truth : FALSE **2 :** given to imagining **:** having a lively imagination **3 :** of or relating to images; *esp* **:** showing a command of imagery — **imag·i·na·tive·ly** *adv* — **imag·i·na·tive·ness** *n*

imag·ine \i-'ma-jən\ *vb* **imag·ined; imag·in·ing** \-'maj-niŋ, -'ma-jə-\ [ME, fr. MF *imaginer*, fr. L *imaginari*, fr. *imagin-, imago* image] *vt* (14c) **1 :** to form a mental image of (something not present) **2** *archaic* **:** PLAN, SCHEME **3 :** SUPPOSE, GUESS ⟨I ~ it will rain⟩ **4 :** to form a notion of without sufficient basis : FANCY ⟨~s himself to be a charming conversationalist⟩ ~ *vi* **1 :** to use the imagination **2 :** BELIEVE **3** *syn* see THINK

im·ag·ing \'i-mi-jiŋ\ *n* (1967) **:** the action or process of producing an image esp. by means other than visible light ⟨acoustic ~⟩ — compare MAGNETIC RESONANCE IMAGING

im·ag·ism \'i-mi-,ji-zəm\ *n, often cap* (1912) **:** a 20th century movement in poetry advocating free verse and the expression of ideas and emotions through clear precise images — **im·ag·ist** \-mi-jist\ *n or adj, often cap* — **im·ag·is·tic** \,i-mi-'jis-tik\ *adj* — **im·ag·is·ti·cal·ly** \-ti-k(ə-)lē\ *adv*

ima·go \i-'mā-(,)gō, -'mā-\ *n, pl* **imagoes** *or* **ima·gi·nes** \-'mā-gə-,nēz, -'mä-; -'mā-jə-, -'ma-\ [NL, fr. L, image] (ca. 1797) **1 :** an insect in its final, adult, sexually mature, and typically winged state **2 :** an idealized mental image of another person or the self

imam \i-'mäm, ē-', -'mam\ *n, often cap* [Ar *imām*] (1613) **1 :** the prayer leader of a mosque **2 :** a Muslim leader of the line of Ali held by Shiites to be the divinely appointed, sinless, infallible successors of Muhammad **3 :** any of various rulers that claim descent from Muhammad and exercise spiritual and temporal leadership over a Muslim region

imam·ate \-'mä-,māt, -'ma-\ *n, often cap* (ca. 1741) **1 :** the office of an imam **2 :** the region or country ruled over by an imam

ima·ret \i-'mär-ət\ *n* [Turk] (1613): an inn or hospice in Turkey

Ima·ri \i-'mär-ē\ *n* [*Imari*, Japan] (1875) **:** a multicolored Japanese porcelain usu. characterized by elaborate floral designs — **Imari** *adj*

im·bal·ance \(,)im-'ba-lən(t)s\ *n* (ca. 1890) **:** lack of balance **:** the state of being out of equilibrium or out of proportion ⟨a vitamin ~⟩ ⟨racial ~ in schools⟩ — **im·bal·anced** \-lən(t)st\ *adj*

im·be·cile \'im-bə-səl, -,sil\ *n* [F *imbécile*, n., fr. adj., weak, weak-minded, fr. L *imbecillus*] (1802) **1 :** a mentally deficient person; *esp* **:** a feebleminded person having a mental age of three to seven years and requiring supervision in the performance of routine daily tasks of self-care **2 :** FOOL, IDIOT — **imbecile** *or* **im·be·cil·ic** \,im-bə-'si-lik\ *adj*

im·be·cil·i·ty \ˌim-bə-'si-lə-tē\ *n, pl* **-ties** (1533) **1** : the quality or state of being imbecile or an imbecile **2 a** : utter foolishness; *also* : FUTILITY **b** : something that is foolish or nonsensical
im·bed *var of* EMBED
im·bibe \im-'bīb\ *vb* **im·bibed; im·bib·ing** [in sense 1, fr. ME *enbiben*, fr. MF *embiber*, fr. L *imbibere* to drink in, conceive, fr. *in-* + *bibere* to drink; in other senses, fr. L *imbibere* — more at POTABLE] *vt* (14c) **1** *archaic* : SOAK, STEEP **2 a** : to receive into the mind and retain ⟨~ moral principles⟩ **b** : to assimilate or take into solution **3 a** : DRINK **b** : to take in or up ⟨a sponge ~s moisture⟩ ~ *vi* **1** : DRINK **2 2 a** : to take in liquid **b** : to absorb or assimilate moisture, gas, light, or heat — **im·bib·er** *n*
im·bi·bi·tion \ˌim-bə-'bi-shən\ *n* (15c) : the act or action of imbibing; *esp* : the taking up of fluid by a colloidal system resulting in swelling — **im·bi·bi·tion·al** \-'bish-nəl, -'bi-shə-nᵊl\ *adj*
im·bit·ter *var of* EMBITTER
im·bo·som *var of* EMBOSOM
¹im·bri·cate \'im-bri-kət\ *adj* [LL *imbricatus*, pp. of *imbricare* to cover with pantiles, fr. L *imbric-, imbrex* pantile, fr. *imbr-, imber* rain; akin to Gk *ombros* rain] (ca. 1610) : lying lapped over each other in regular order ⟨~ scales⟩
²im·bri·cate \'im-brə-ˌkāt\ *vt* **-cat·ed; -cat·ing** (1784) : OVERLAP; *esp* : to overlap like roof tiles
im·bri·ca·tion \ˌim-brə-'kā-shən\ *n* (1713) **1** : an overlapping of edges (as of tiles or scales) **2** : a decoration or pattern showing imbrication

imbrication

im·bro·glio \im-'brōl-(ˌ)yō\ *n, pl* **-glios** [It, fr. *imbrogliare* to entangle, fr. MF *embrouiller* — more at EMBROIL] (1750) **1** : a confused mass **2 a** : an intricate or complicated situation (as in a drama or novel) **b** : an acutely painful or embarrassing misunderstanding **c** : a violently confused or bitterly complicated altercation : EMBROILMENT
im·brown *var of* EMBROWN
im·brue \im-'brü\ *vt* **im·brued; im·bru·ing** [ME *enbrewen*, prob. fr. MF *abrevrer, embevrer* to soak, drench, ultim. fr. L *bibere* to drink — more at POTABLE] (15c) : STAIN
im·brute \im-'brüt\ *vb* **im·brut·ed; im·brut·ing** *vi* (1634) : to sink to the level of a brute ~ *vt* : to degrade to the level of a brute
im·bue \-'byü\ *vt* **im·bued; im·bu·ing** [L *imbuere*] (1555) **1** : to permeate or influence as if by dyeing ⟨the spirit that ~s the new constitution⟩ **2** : to tinge or dye deeply **syn** see INFUSE
im·id·az·ole \ˌi-mə-'da-ˌzōl\ *n* [ISV] (1892) : a white crystalline heterocyclic base C₃H₄N₂ that is an antimetabolite related to histidine; *broadly* : any of various derivatives of this
im·ide \'i-ˌmīd\ *n* [ISV, alter. of *amide*] (1857) : a compound containing the NH group that is derived from ammonia by replacement of two hydrogen atoms by a metal or an equivalent of acid groups — compare AMIDE — **im·id·ic** \i-'mi-dik\ *adj*
im·i·do \'i-mə-ˌdō\ *adj* (1881) : relating to or containing the NH group or its substituted form NR united to one or two acid groups
im·ine \'i-ˌmēn\ *n* [ISV, alter. of *amine*] (1883) : a compound containing the NH group or its substituted form NR that is derived from ammonia by replacement of two hydrogen atoms by a hydrocarbon group or other nonacid organic group
im·i·no \'i-mə-ˌnō\ *adj* (1903) : relating to or containing the NH group or its substituted form NR united to a group other than an acid group
imip·ra·mine \i-'mi-prə-ˌmēn\ *n* [*imide* + *propyl* + *amine*] (1958) : a tricyclic antidepressant drug C₁₉H₂₄N₂
im·i·ta·ble \'i-mə-tə-bəl\ *adj* (1550) : capable or worthy of being imitated or copied
im·i·tate \'i-mə-ˌtāt\ *vt* **-tat·ed; -tat·ing** [L *imitatus*, pp. of *imitari* — more at IMAGE] (1534) **1** : to follow as a pattern, model, or example **2** : to be or appear like : RESEMBLE **3** : to produce a copy of : REPRODUCE **4** : MIMIC, COUNTERFEIT ⟨can ~ his father's booming voice⟩ **syn** see COPY — **im·i·ta·tor** \-ˌtā-tər\ *n*
¹im·i·ta·tion \ˌi-mə-'tā-shən\ *n* (14c) **1** : an act or instance of imitating **2** : something produced as a copy : COUNTERFEIT **3** : a literary work designed to reproduce the style of another author **4** : the repetition by one voice of a melody, phrase, or motive stated earlier in the composition by a different voice **5** : the quality of an object in possessing some of the nature or attributes of a transcendent idea **6** : the assumption of behavior observed in other individuals
²imitation *adj* (1840) : resembling something else that is usu. genuine and of better quality : not real ⟨~ leather⟩
im·i·ta·tive \'i-mə-ˌtā-tiv, *esp Brit* -tə-tiv\ *adj* (1584) **1 a** : marked by imitation ⟨acting is an ~ art⟩ **b** : reproducing or representing a natural sound : ONOMATOPOEIC ⟨"hiss" is an ~ word⟩ **c** : exhibiting mimicry **2** : inclined to imitate **3** : imitating something superior : COUNTERFEIT — **im·i·ta·tive·ly** *adv* — **im·i·ta·tive·ness** *n*
im·mac·u·la·cy \i-'ma-kyə-lə-sē\ *n* (1799) : the quality or state of being immaculate
im·mac·u·late \i-'ma-kyə-lət\ *adj* [ME *immaculat*, fr. L *immaculatus*, fr. *in-* + *maculatus* stained — more at MACULATE] (15c) **1** : having no stain or blemish : PURE **2** : containing no flaw or error **3 a** : spotlessly clean **b** : having no colored spots or marks ⟨petals ~⟩ — **im·mac·u·late·ly** *adv*
Immaculate Conception *n* (1687) **1** : the conception of the Virgin Mary in which as decreed in Roman Catholic dogma her soul was preserved free from original sin by divine grace **2** : December 8 observed as a Roman Catholic feast in commemoration of the Immaculate Conception
im·mane \i-'mān\ *adj* [L *immanis*, fr. *in-* + *manus* good — more at MATURE] (1602) *archaic* : HUGE; *also* : monstrous in character
im·ma·nence \'i-mə-nən(t)s\ *n* (1816) : the quality or state of being immanent : INHERENCE
im·ma·nen·cy \-nən(t)-sē\ *n* (1659) : IMMANENCE
im·ma·nent \-nənt\ *adj* [LL *immanent-, immanens*, prp. of *immanēre* to remain in place, fr. L *in-* + *manēre* to remain — more at MANSION] (1535) : remaining or operating within a domain of reality or realm of discourse : INHERENT; *specif* : having existence or effect only within the

mind or consciousness — compare TRANSCENDENT — **im·ma·nent·ly** *adv*
im·ma·nent·ism \-nən-ˌti-zəm\ *n* (1907) : any of several theories according to which God or an abstract mind or spirit pervades the world — **im·ma·nent·ist** \-nən-tist, -ˌnen-\ *n or adj* — **im·ma·nent·is·tic** \ˌi-mə-nən-'tis-tik\ *adj*
Im·man·u·el \i-'man-yə-wəl, -yəl\ *n* [ME *Emanuel*, fr. LL *Emmanuel*, fr. Gk *Emmanouēl*, fr. Heb *'immānū'ēl*, lit., with us is God] (15c) : MESSIAH 1
im·ma·te·ri·al \ˌi-mə-'tir-ē-əl\ *adj* [ME *immateriel*, fr. MF, fr. LL *immaterialis*, fr. L *in-* + LL *materialis* material] (14c) **1** : not consisting of matter : INCORPOREAL **2** : of no substantial consequence : UNIMPORTANT
im·ma·te·ri·al·ism \-ē-ə-ˌli-zəm\ *n* (1713) : a philosophical theory that material things have no reality except as mental perceptions — **im·ma·te·ri·al·ist** \-list\ *n*
im·ma·te·ri·al·i·ty \ˌi-mə-ˌtir-ē-'a-lə-tē\ *n, pl* **-ties** (1570) **1** : the quality or state of being immaterial **2** : something immaterial
im·ma·te·ri·al·ize \-'tir-ē-ə-ˌlīz\ *vt* (1661) : to make immaterial or incorporeal
im·ma·ture \ˌi-mə-'tur, -'tyur, -'chur\ *adj* [L *immaturus*, fr. *in-* + *maturus* mature] (1548) **1** *archaic* : PREMATURE **2 a** : lacking complete growth, differentiation, or development ⟨a thin ~ soil⟩ **b** : having the potential capacity to attain a definitive form or state : CRUDE, UNFINISHED ⟨a vigorous but ~ school of art⟩ **c** : exhibiting less than an expected degree of maturity ⟨emotionally ~ adults⟩ — **immature** *n* — **im·ma·ture·ly** *adv* — **im·ma·tu·ri·ty** \-'tur-ə-tē, -'tyur-, -'chur-\ *n*
im·mea·sur·able \(ˌ)i(m)-'mezh-rə-bəl, -'māzh-; -'me-zhə-rə-, -'mā-, -zhər-bəl\ *adj* (14c) : incapable of being measured; *broadly* : indefinitely extensive — **im·mea·sur·able·ness** *n* — **im·mea·sur·ably** \-blē\ *adv*
im·me·di·a·cy \i-'mē-dē-ə-sē, *Brit often* -'mē-jə-sē\ *n, pl* **-cies** (1605) **1** : the quality or state of being immediate **2** : something that is immediate — usu. used in pl.
im·me·di·ate \i-'mē-dē-ət, *Brit often* -'mē-jit\ *adj* [ME, fr. LL *immediatus*, fr. L *in-* + LL *mediatus* intermediate — more at MEDIATE] (15c) **1 a** : acting or being without the intervention of another object, cause, or agency : DIRECT ⟨the ~ cause of death⟩ **b** : present to the mind independently of other states or factors ⟨~ awareness⟩ **c** : involving or derived from a single premise ⟨an ~ inference⟩ **2** : being next in line or relation ⟨the ~ family⟩ **3 a** : existing without intervening space or substance ⟨brought into ~ contact⟩ **b** : being near at hand ⟨the ~ neighborhood⟩ **4 a** : occurring, acting, or accomplished without loss or interval of time : INSTANT ⟨an ~ need⟩ **b** (1) : near to or related to the present ⟨the ~ past⟩ (2) : of or relating to the here and now : CURRENT ⟨too busy with ~ concerns to worry about the future⟩ **5** : directly touching or concerning a person or thing ⟨the child's ~ world is the classroom⟩
immediate constituent *n* (1933) : any of the meaningful constituents directly forming a larger linguistic construction (as a phrase or sentence)
¹im·me·di·ate·ly \i-'mē-dē-ət-lē *also* -'mē-dit-, *Brit often* -'mē-jət-\ *adv* (15c) **1** : in direct connection or relation : DIRECTLY ⟨the parties ~ involved in the case⟩ ⟨the house ~ beyond this one⟩ **2** : without interval of time : STRAIGHTWAY
²immediately *conj* (1839) *chiefly Brit* : AS SOON AS
im·me·di·ate·ness *n* (1633) : IMMEDIACY 1
im·med·i·ca·ble \(ˌ)i(m)-'me-di-kə-bəl\ *adj* [L *immedicabilis*, fr. *in-* + *medicabilis* medicable] (1533) : INCURABLE ⟨wounds ~ —John Milton⟩ — **im·med·i·ca·bly** \-blē\ *adv*
Im·mel·mann \'i-məl-mən\ *n* [Max *Immelmann*] (1917) : a maneuver in which an airplane reverses direction by executing half of a loop upwards followed by half of a roll — called also *Immelmann turn*
im·me·mo·ri·al \ˌi-mə-'mōr-ē-əl, -'mȯr-\ *adj* [prob. fr. F *immémorial*, fr. MF, fr. ML *immemorialis* lacking memory, fr. L *in-* + *memorialis* memorial] (1602) : extending or existing since beyond the reach of memory, record, or tradition ⟨existing from time ~⟩ — **im·me·mo·ri·al·ly** \-ē-ə-lē\ *adv*
im·mense \i-'men(t)s\ *adj* [ME, fr. MF, fr. L *immensus* immeasurable, fr. *in-* + *mensus*, pp. of *metiri* to measure — more at MEASURE] (15c) **1** : marked by greatness esp. in size or degree; *esp* : transcending ordinary means of measurement ⟨the ~ and boundless universe⟩ **2** : supremely good : EXCELLENT **syn** see ENORMOUS — **im·mense·ly** *adv* — **im·mense·ness** *n*
im·men·si·ty \i-'men(t)-sə-tē\ *n, pl* **-ties** (15c) **1** : the quality or state of being immense **2** : something immense
im·men·su·ra·ble \(ˌ)i(m)-'men(t)s-rə-bəl, -'men(t)sh-; -'men(t)-sə-, -shə-\ *adj* [ME, fr. LL *immensurabilis*, fr. L *in-* + LL *mensurabilis* measurable — more at MENSURABLE] (15c) : IMMEASURABLE
im·merge \i-'mərj\ *vi* **im·merged; im·merg·ing** [L *immergere*] (1706) : to plunge into or immerse oneself in something
im·merse \i-'mərs\ *vt* **im·mersed; im·mers·ing** [ME, fr. L *immersus*, pp. of *immergere*, fr. *in-* + *mergere* to merge] (15c) **1** : to plunge into something that surrounds or covers; *esp* : to plunge or dip into a fluid **2** : ENGROSS, ABSORB ⟨completely *immersed* in his work⟩ **3** : to baptize by immersion
im·mers·ible \i-'mər-sə-bəl\ *adj* (ca. 1846) : capable of being totally submerged in water without damage to the heating element ⟨an ~ electric frying pan⟩
im·mer·sion \i-'mər-zhən, -shən\ *n* (15c) : an act of immersing : a state of being immersed; *specif* : baptism by complete submersion of the person in water
immersion heater *n* (1914) : a usu. electric unit that heats the liquid in which it is immersed
im·mesh \i-'mesh\ *var of* ENMESH
im·me·thod·i·cal \ˌi-mə-'thä-di-kəl\ *adj* (1605) : not methodical — **im·me·thod·i·cal·ly** \-k(ə-)lē\ *adv*

\ə\ abut \ᵊ\ kitten, F table \ər\ further \a\ ash \ā\ ace \ä\ mop, mar \aú\ out \ch\ chin \e\ bet \ē\ easy \g\ go \i\ hit \ī\ ice \j\ job \ŋ\ sing \ō\ go \ó\ law \ói\ boy \th\ thin \t̷h\ the \ü\ loot \ú\ foot \y\ yet \zh\ vision \ȧ, k̲, ⁿ, œ, œ̅, ue, ᵫ, ᵊ\ *see* Guide to Pronunciation

im·mi·grant \'i-mi-grǝnt\ *n* (1789) : one that immigrates: as **a** : a person who comes to a country to take up permanent residence **b** : a plant or animal that becomes established in an area where it was previously unknown — **immigrant** *adj*

im·mi·grate \'i-mǝ-,grāt\ *vb* **-grat·ed; -grat·ing** [L *immigratus*, pp. of *immigrare* to remove, go in, fr. *in-* + *migrare* to migrate] *vi* (ca. 1623) : to enter and usu. become established; *esp* : to come into a country of which one is not a native for permanent residence ~ *vt* : to bring in or send as immigrants — **im·mi·gra·tion** \,i-mǝ-'grā-shǝn\ *n* — **im·mi·gra·tion·al** \-shnǝl, -shǝ-nᵊl\ *adj*

im·mi·nence \'i-mǝ-nǝn(t)s\ *n* (1606) **1** : something imminent; *esp* : impending evil or danger **2** : the quality or state of being imminent

im·mi·nen·cy \-nǝn-sē\ *n* (1665) : IMMINENCE 2

im·mi·nent \'i-mǝ-nǝnt\ *adj* [L *imminent-, imminens*, prp. of *imminēre* to project, threaten, fr. *in-* + *-minēre* (akin to L *mont-, mons* mountain) — more at MOUNT] (1528) : ready to take place; *esp* : hanging threateningly over one's head ⟨was in ~ danger of being run over⟩ — **im·mi·nent·ly** *adv*

im·min·gle \i-'min-gǝl\ *vb* (1606) : BLEND, INTERMINGLE

im·mis·ci·ble \(,)i(m)-'mi-sǝ-bǝl\ *adj* (1671) : incapable of mixing or attaining homogeneity — **im·mis·ci·bil·i·ty** \-,mi-sǝ-'bi-lǝ-tē\ *n*

im·mit·i·ga·ble \(,)i(m)-'mi-ti-gǝ-bǝl\ *adj* [LL *immitigabilis*, fr. L *in-* + *mitigare* to mitigate] (1576) : not capable of being mitigated — **im·mit·i·ga·bly** \-blē\ *adv*

im·mit·tance \(,)i(m)-'mi-tᵊn(t)s\ *n* [*impedance* + ad*mittance*] (ca. 1948) : electrical admittance or impedance

im·mix \i-'miks\ *vt* [back-formation fr. *immixed* mixed in, fr. ME *immixte*, fr. L *immixtus*, pp. of *immiscēre*, fr. *in-* + *miscēre* to mix — more at MIX] (15c) : to mix intimately : COMMINGLE — **im·mix·ture** \-'miks-chǝr\ *n*

im·mo·bile \(,)i(m)-'mō-bǝl, -,bil *also* -,bēl\ *adj* [ME *in-mobill*, fr. L *immobilis*, fr. *in-* + *mobilis* mobile] (14c) **1** : incapable of being moved : FIXED **2** : not moving : MOTIONLESS ⟨keep the patient ~⟩ — **im·mo·bil·i·ty** \,i-(,)mō-'bi-lǝ-tē\ *n*

im·mo·bi·lism \i-'mō-bǝ-,li-zǝm\ *n* (1949) : a policy of extreme conservatism and opposition to change

im·mo·bi·lize \i-'mō-bǝ-,līz\ *vt* (1871) : to make immobile: as **a** : to prevent freedom of movement or effective use of ⟨the planes were immobilized by bad weather⟩ **b** : to reduce or eliminate motion of (the body or a part) by mechanical means or by strict bed rest **c** : to withhold (money or capital) from circulation — **im·mo·bi·li·za·tion** \-,mō-bǝ-lǝ-'zā-shǝn\ *n* — **im·mo·bi·liz·er** \'mō-bǝ-,lī-zǝr\ *n*

im·mod·er·a·cy \(,)i(m)-'mä-d(ǝ-)rǝ-sē\ *n* (1682) : lack of moderation

im·mod·er·ate \-d(ǝ-)rǝt\ *adj* [ME *immoderat*, fr. L *immoderatus*, fr. *in-* + *moderatus*, pp. of *moderare* to moderate] (14c) : exceeding just, usual, or suitable bounds ⟨~ pride⟩ ⟨an ~ appetite⟩ *syn* see EXCESSIVE — **im·mod·er·ate·ly** *adv* — **im·mod·er·ate·ness** *n* — **im·mod·er·a·tion** \(,)i(m)-,mä-dǝ-'rā-shǝn\ *n*

im·mod·est \(,)i(m)-'mä-dǝst\ *adj* [L *immodestus*, fr. *in-* + *modestus* modest] (ca. 1570) : not modest; *specif* : not conforming to the sexual mores of a particular time or place — **im·mod·est·ly** *adv* — **im·mod·es·ty** \-dǝ-stē\ *n*

im·mo·late \'i-mǝ-,lāt\ *vt* **-lat·ed; -lat·ing** [L *immolatus*, pp. of *immolare*, fr. *in-* + *mola* spelt grits; fr. the custom of sprinkling victims with sacrificial meal; akin to L *molere* to grind — more at MEAL] (1548) **1** : to offer in sacrifice; *esp* : to kill as a sacrificial victim **2** : to kill or destroy often by fire — **im·mo·la·tor** \-,lā-tǝr\ *n*

im·mo·la·tion \,i-mǝ-'lā-shǝn\ *n* (15c) **1** : the act of immolating : the state of being immolated **2** : something that is immolated

im·mor·al \(,)i(m)-'mȯr-ǝl, -'mär-\ *adj* (1660) : not moral; *broadly* : conflicting with generally or traditionally held moral principles — **im·mor·al·ly** \-ǝ-lē\ *adv*

im·mor·al·ist \-ǝ-list\ *n* (1697) : an advocate of immorality — **im·mor·al·ism** \-,li-zǝm\ *n*

im·mo·ral·i·ty \,i-(,)mȯ-'ra-lǝ-tē, ,i-mǝ-\ *n* (ca. 1566) **1** : the quality or state of being immoral; *esp* : UNCHASTITY **2** : an immoral act or practice

¹**im·mor·tal** \(,)i-'mȯr-tᵊl\ *adj* [ME, fr. L *immortalis*, fr. *in-* + *mortalis* mortal] (14c) **1** : exempt from death ⟨the ~ gods⟩ **2** : exempt from oblivion : IMPERISHABLE ⟨~ fame⟩ **3** : connected with or relating to immortality — **im·mor·tal·ly** \-tᵊl-ē\ *adv*

²**immortal** *n* (1684) **1 a** : one exempt from death **b** *pl, often cap* : the gods of the Greek and Roman pantheon **2 a** : a person whose fame is lasting **b** *cap* : any of the 40 members of the Académie Française

im·mor·tal·ise *Brit var of* IMMORTALIZE

im·mor·tal·i·ty \,i-,mȯr-'ta-lǝ-tē\ *n* (14c) : the quality or state of being immortal: **a** : unending existence **b** : lasting fame

im·mor·tal·ize \i-'mȯr-tᵊl-,īz\ *vt* **-ized; -iz·ing** (ca. 1566) : to make immortal — **im·mor·tal·i·za·tion** \-,mȯr-tᵊl-ǝ-'zā-shǝn\ *n* — **im·mor·tal·iz·er** \-'mȯr-tᵊl-,ī-zǝr\ *n*

im·mor·telle \,i-,mȯr-'tel\ *n* [F, fr. fem. of *immortel* immortal, fr. L *immortalis*] (1832) : EVERLASTING 3

im·mo·tile \(,)i(m)-'mō-tᵊl, -,tīl\ *adj* (1872) : lacking motility

¹**im·mov·able** \(,)i(m)-'mü-vǝ-bǝl\ *adj* (14c) **1** : incapable of being moved; *broadly* : not moving or not intended to be moved **2 a** : STEADFAST, UNYIELDING **b** : not capable of being moved emotionally — **im·mov·abil·i·ty** \,i-,mü-vǝ-'bi-lǝ-tē\ *n* — **im·mov·able·ness** \-'mü-vǝ-bǝl-nǝs\ *n* — **im·mov·ably** \-blē\ *adv*

²**immovable** *n* (1588) **1** : one that cannot be moved **2** *pl* : real property as opposed to movable property

im·mune \i-'myün\ *adj* [ME, fr. L *immunis*, fr. *in-* + *munia* services, obligations; akin to L *munus* service — more at MEAN] (15c) **1 a** : FREE, EXEMPT ⟨~ from further taxation⟩ **b** : marked by protection ⟨some criminal leaders are ~ from arrest⟩ **2** : not susceptible or responsive ⟨~ to all pleas⟩; *esp* : having a high degree of resistance to a disease ⟨~ to diphtheria⟩ **3 a** : having or producing antibodies or lymphocytes capable of reacting with a specific antigen ⟨an ~ serum⟩ **b** : produced by, involved in, or concerned with immunity or an immune response ⟨~ agglutinins⟩ ⟨~ globulins⟩ — **immune** *n*

immune response *n* (1953) : a bodily response to an antigen that occurs when lymphocytes identify the antigenic molecule as foreign and induce the formation of antibodies and lymphocytes capable of

reacting with it and rendering it harmless — called also *immune reaction*

immune system *n* (ca. 1919) : the bodily system that protects the body from foreign substances, cells, and tissues by producing the immune response and that includes esp. the thymus, spleen, lymph nodes, special deposits of lymphoid tissue (as in the gastrointestinal tract and bone marrow), lymphocytes including the B cells and T cells, and antibodies

im·mu·ni·ty \i-'myü-nǝ-tē\ *n, pl* **-ties** (14c) : the quality or state of being immune; *esp* : a condition of being able to resist a particular disease esp. through preventing development of a pathogenic microorganism or by counteracting the effects of its products

im·mu·nize \'i-myǝ-,nīz\ *vt* **-nized; -niz·ing** (1892) : to make immune — **im·mu·ni·za·tion** \,i-myǝ-nǝ-'zā-shǝn *also* ,i-,myü-nǝ-\ *n*

immuno- *comb form* [ISV, fr. *immune*] **1** : physiological immunity ⟨*immuno*logy⟩ **2** : immunologic ⟨*immuno*chemistry⟩ : immunologically ⟨*immuno*competent⟩ : immunology and ⟨*immuno*genetics⟩

im·mu·no·as·say \,i-myǝ-nō-'a-,sā, i-,myü-nō-, -a-'sā\ *n* (1959) : the identification of a substance (as a protein) based on its capacity to act as an antigen — **im·mu·no·as·say·able** \-a-'sā-ǝ-bǝl\ *adj*

im·mu·no·blot \'i-myǝ-nǝ-,blät, i-'myü-(,)nō-\ *n* (1982) : a blot in which a radioactively labeled antibody is used as the molecular probe — **im·mu·no·blot·ting** \-,blä-tiŋ\ *n*

im·mu·no·chem·is·try \,i-myǝ-nō-'ke-mǝ-strē, i-,myü-nō-\ *n* [ISV] (1907) : a branch of chemistry that deals with the chemical aspects of immunology — **im·mu·no·chem·i·cal** \-'ke-mi-kǝl\ *adj* — **im·mu·no·chem·i·cal·ly** \-k(ǝ-)lē\ *adv* — **im·mu·no·chem·ist** \-'ke-mist\ *n*

im·mu·no·com·pe·tence \-'käm-pǝ-tǝn(t)s\ *n* (1967) : the capacity for a normal immune response — **im·mu·no·com·pe·tent** \-tǝnt\ *adj*

im·mu·no·com·pro·mised \-'käm-prǝ-,mīzd\ *adj* (1979) : having the immune system impaired or weakened (as by drugs or illness) ⟨~ patients⟩

im·mu·no·cy·to·chem·is·try \-,sī-tō-'ke-mǝ-strē\ *n* (1960) : the application of biochemistry to cellular immunology — **im·mu·no·cy·to·chem·i·cal** \-'kǝ-mi-kǝl\ *adj* — **im·mu·no·cy·to·chem·i·cal·ly** \-'ke-mi-k(ǝ-)lē\ *adv*

im·mu·no·de·fi·cien·cy \-di-'fi-shǝn(t)-sē\ *n* (1969) : inability to produce a normal complement of antibodies or immunologically sensitized T cells esp. in response to specific antigens — **im·mu·no·de·fi·cient** \-shǝnt\ *adj*

im·mu·no·di·ag·no·sis \-,dī-ig-'nō-sǝs, -ǝg-\ *n* (1972) : diagnosis (as of cancer) by immunological methods — **im·mu·no·di·ag·nos·tic** \-'näs-tik\ *adj*

im·mu·no·dif·fu·sion \-di-'fyü-zhǝn\ *n* (1959) : any of several techniques for obtaining a precipitate between an antibody and its specific antigen by suspending one in a gel and letting the other migrate through it from a well or by letting both antibody and antigen migrate through the gel from separate wells to form an area of precipitation

im·mu·no·elec·tro·pho·re·sis \-ǝ-,lek-trǝ-fǝ-'rē-sǝs\ *n, pl* **-re·ses** \-,sēz\ (1958) : electrophoretic separation of proteins followed by identification by the formation of precipitates through specific immunologic reactions — **im·mu·no·elec·tro·pho·ret·ic** \-'re-tik\ *adj* — **im·mu·no·elec·tro·pho·ret·i·cal·ly** \-ti-k(ǝ-)lē\ *adv*

im·mu·no·flu·o·res·cence \-(,)flȯ-'re-sᵊn(t)s, -(,)flō-, -(,)flù(-ǝ)-\ *n* (1960) : the labeling of antibodies or antigens with fluorescent dyes esp. for the purpose of demonstrating the presence of a particular antigen or antibody in a tissue preparation or smear — **im·mu·no·flu·o·res·cent** \-sᵊnt\ *adj*

im·mu·no·gen \i-'myü-nǝ-jǝn, -,jen\ *n* [fr. *Immunogen*, a trademark] (1959) : an antigen that produces an immune response

im·mu·no·ge·net·ics \,i-myǝ-nō-jǝ-'ne-tiks, i-,myü-nō-\ *n pl but sing in constr* (1936) : a branch of immunology concerned with the interrelations of heredity, disease, and the immune system and its components (as antibodies) — **im·mu·no·ge·net·ic** \-tik\ *adj* — **im·mu·no·ge·net·i·cal·ly** \-ti-k(ǝ-)lē\ *adv* — **im·mu·no·ge·net·i·cist** \-jǝ-'ne-tǝ-sist\ *n*

im·mu·no·gen·ic \,i-myǝ-nō-'je-nik, i-,myü-nō-\ *adj* (ca. 1923) : relating to or producing an immune response ⟨~ substances⟩ — **im·mu·no·gen·e·sis** \-'je-nǝ-sǝs\ *n* — **im·mu·no·ge·nic·i·ty** \-jǝ-'ni-sǝ-tē\ *n*

im·mu·no·glob·u·lin \-'glä-byǝ-lǝn\ *n* (1953) : ANTIBODY

im·mu·no·he·ma·tol·o·gy \-,hē-mǝ-'tä-lǝ-jē\ *n* (1950) : a branch of immunology that deals with the immunologic properties of blood — **im·mu·no·he·ma·to·log·ic** \-,hē-mǝ-tᵊl-'ä-jik\ *or* **im·mu·no·he·ma·to·log·i·cal** \-'ä-ji-kǝl\ *adj* — **im·mu·no·he·ma·tol·o·gist** \-,hē-mǝ-'tä-lǝ-jist\ *n*

im·mu·no·his·to·chem·i·cal \-,his-tō-'ke-mi-kǝl\ *adj* (1960) : of or relating to the application of histochemical and immunologic methods to chemical analysis of living cells and tissues — **im·mu·no·his·to·chem·is·try** \-'ke-mǝ-strē\ *n*

im·mu·nol·o·gy \,i-myǝ-'nä-lǝ-jē\ *n* [ISV] (1910) : a science that deals with the immune system and the cell-mediated and humoral aspects of immunity and immune responses — **im·mu·no·log·ic** \-nǝ-'lä-jik\ *or* **im·mu·no·log·i·cal** \-'lä-ji-kǝl\ *adj* — **im·mu·no·log·i·cal·ly** \-ji-k(ǝ-)lē\ *adv* — **im·mu·nol·o·gist** \-myǝ-'nä-lǝ-jist\ *n*

im·mu·no·mod·u·la·tor \,i-myǝ-nō-'mä-jǝ-,lā-tǝr, i-,myü-nō-\ *n* (1977) : a substance that affects the functioning of the immune system — **im·mu·no·mod·u·la·to·ry** \-'mä-jǝ-lǝ-,tȯr-ē, -,tȯr-\ *adj*

im·mu·no·pa·thol·o·gy \-pǝ-'thä-lǝ-jē, -pa-\ *n* (1959) : a branch of medicine that deals with immune responses associated with disease — **im·mu·no·path·o·log·ic** \-,pa-thǝ-'lä-jik\ *or* **im·mu·no·path·o·log·i·cal** \-ji-kǝl\ *adj* — **im·mu·no·pa·thol·o·gist** \-pǝ-'thä-lǝ-jist, -pa-\ *n*

im·mu·no·pre·cip·i·ta·tion \-pri-,si-pǝ-'tä-shǝn\ *n* (1966) : precipitation of a complex of an antibody and its specific antigen — **im·mu·no·pre·cip·i·tate** \-'si-pǝ-tat, -pǝ-,tāt\ *n* — **im·mu·no·pre·cip·i·tate** \-pǝ-,tāt\ *vt*

im·mu·no·re·ac·tive \-rē-'ak-tiv\ *adj* (1966) : reacting to particular antigens or haptens ⟨~ lymphocytes⟩ — **im·mu·no·re·ac·tiv·i·ty** \-(,)rē-,ak-'ti-vǝ-tē\ *n*

im·mu·no·reg·u·la·to·ry \-'re-gyǝ-lǝ-,tȯr-ē, -,tȯr-\ *adj* (1971) : of or relating to the regulation of the immune system ⟨~ T cells⟩ — **im·mu·no·reg·u·la·tion** \-,re-gyǝ-'lā-shǝn, -gǝ-\ *n*

im·mu·no·sor·bent \-'sȯr-bǝnt\ *adj* (1966) : relating to or using a substrate consisting of a specific antibody or antigen chemically combined with an insoluble substance (as cellulose) to selectively remove the corresponding specific antigen or antibody from solution — **im-munosorbent** *n*

im·mu·no·sup·pres·sion \-sə-'pre-shən\ *n* (1963) : suppression (as by drugs) of natural immune responses — **im·mu·no·sup·press** \-sə-'pres\ *vt* — **im·mu·no·sup·pres·sant** \-'pre-sᵊnt\ *n or adj* — **im·mu·no·sup·pres·sive** \-'pre-siv\ *adj*

im·mu·no·ther·a·py \-'ther-ə-pē\ *n* [ISV] (ca. 1911) : treatment of or prophylaxis against disease by attempting to produce active or passive immunity — **im·mu·no·ther·a·peu·tic** \-,ther-ə-'pyü-tik\ *adj*

im·mure \i-'myùr\ *vt* **im·mured; im·mur·ing** [ML *immurare*, fr. L *in-* + *murus* wall — more at MUNITION] (1583) **1 a** : to enclose within or as if within walls **b** : IMPRISON **2** : to build into a wall; *esp* : to entomb in a wall — **im·mure·ment** \-'myùr-mənt\ *n*

im·mu·ta·ble \(ˌ)i(m)-'myü-tə-bəl\ *adj* [ME, fr. L *immutabilis*, fr. *in-* + *mutabilis* mutable] (15c) : not capable of or susceptible to change — **im·mu·ta·bil·i·ty** \-ˌmyü-tə-'bi-lə-tē\ *n* — **im·mu·ta·ble·ness** \'myü-tə-bəl-nəs\ *n* — **im·mu·ta·bly** \-blē\ *adv*

¹imp \'imp\ *n* [ME *impe*, fr. OE *impa*, fr. *impian* to imp] (bef. 12c) **1** *obs* : SHOOT, BUD; *also* : GRAFT **2 a** : a small demon : FIEND **b** : a mischievous child : URCHIN

²imp *vt* [ME, fr. OE *impian* to graft, fr. (assumed) VL *imputare*, fr. LL *impotus* grafted shoot, fr. Gk *emphytos* implanted, fr. *emphyein* to implant, fr. *em-* ²*en-* + *phyein* to bring forth — more at BE] (15c) **1** : to graft or repair (a wing, tail, or feather) with a feather to improve a falcon's flying capacity **2** : to equip with wings

¹im·pact \im-'pakt\ *vb* [L *impactus*, pp. of *impingere* to push against — more at IMPINGE] *vt* (1601) **1 a** : to fix firmly by or as if by packing or wedging **b** : to press together **2 a** : to have an impact on : impinge on **b** : to strike forcefully; *also* : to cause to strike forcefully ~ *vi* **1** : to have an impact **2** : to impinge or make contact esp. forcefully — **im·pac·tive** \im-'pak-tiv\ *adj* — **im·pac·tor** *also* **im·pact·er** \-tər\ *n*

²im·pact \'im-ˌpakt\ *n* (1781) **1 a** : an impinging or striking esp. of one body against another **b** : a forceful contact, collision, or onset; *also* : the impetus communicated in or as if in a collision **2** : the force of impression of one thing on another : a significant or major effect ⟨the ~ of science on our society⟩ ⟨an environmental ~ study⟩

impact crater *n* (1895) : CRATER 1b

im·pact·ed \im-'pak-təd\ *adj* (ca. 1616) **1 a** : packed or wedged in **b** : deeply entrenched : not easily changed or removed **2** *of a tooth* : wedged between the jawbone and another tooth **3** : of, relating to, or being an area (as a school district) providing tax-supported services to a population having a large proportion of federal employees and esp. those living or working on tax-exempt federal property ⟨aid to education in ~ areas⟩

im·pac·tion \im-'pak-shən\ *n* (1739) : the act of becoming or the state of being impacted; *esp* : lodgment of something (as feces) in a body passage or cavity

impact printer *n* (1968) : a printing device in which a printing element directly strikes a surface (as in a typewriter)

im·paint \im-'pānt\ *vt* (1596) *obs* : PAINT, DEPICT

im·pair \im-'par, -'per\ *vt* [ME *empeiren*, fr. MF *empeirer*, fr. (assumed) VL *impejorare*, fr. L *in-* + LL *pejorare* to make worse — more at PEJORATIVE] (14c) : to damage or make worse by or as if by diminishing in some material respect ⟨his health was ~ed by overwork⟩ ⟨the strike seriously ~ed community services⟩ *syn* see INJURE — **im·pair·er** *n* — **im·pair·ment** \-mənt\ *n*

im·paired \-'pard, -'perd\ *adj* (1605) : being in a less than perfect or whole condition: as **a** : handicapped or functionally defective — often used in combination ⟨hearing-*impaired*⟩ **b** *chiefly Canad* : DRUNK ⟨driving while ~⟩

im·pa·la \im-'pa-lə, -'pä-\ *n, pl* **impalas** *or* **impala** [Zulu] (1875) : a large brownish African antelope (*Aepyceros melampus*) that in the male has slender lyrate horns

im·pale \im-'pā(ə)l\ *vt* **im·paled; im·pal·ing** [MF & ML; MF *empaler*, fr. ML *impalare*, fr. L *in-* + *palus* stake — more at POLE] (1605) **1** : to join (coats of arms) on a heraldic shield divided vertically by a pale **2 a** : to pierce with or as if with something pointed; *esp* : to torture or kill by fixing on a sharp stake **b** : to fix in an inescapable or helpless position — **im·pale·ment** \-mənt\ *n* — **im·pal·er** \-'pā-lər\ *n*

im·pal·pa·ble \(ˌ)im-'pal-pə-bəl\ *adj* (1509) **1 a** : incapable of being felt by touch : INTANGIBLE ⟨the ~ aura of power that emanated from him —Osbert Sitwell⟩ **b** : so finely divided that no grains or grit can be felt ⟨rock worn to an ~ powder⟩ **2** : not readily discerned by the mind — **im·pal·pa·bil·i·ty** \-ˌpal-pə-'bi-lə-tē\ *n* — **im·pal·pa·bly** \-'pal-pə-blē\ *adv*

im·pan·el \im-'pa-nᵊl\ *vt* (15c) : to enroll in or on a panel ⟨~ a jury⟩

im·par·a·dise \im-'par-ə-ˌdīs, -ˌdīz\ *vt* **-dised; -dis·ing** (1592) : ENRAPTURE

im·par·i·ty \(ˌ)im-'par-ə-tē\ *n, pl* **-ties** [LL *imparitas*, fr. L *impar* unequal, fr. *in-* + *par* equal] (1563) : INEQUALITY, DISPARITY

im·part \im-'pärt\ *vt* [MF & L; MF *impartir*, fr. L *impartire*, fr. *in-* + *partire* to divide, part] (15c) **1** : to give, convey, or grant from or as if from a store ⟨her experience ~ed authority to her words⟩ ⟨the flavor ~ed by herbs⟩ **2** : to communicate the knowledge of : DISCLOSE ⟨~ed my scheme to no one⟩ — **im·par·ta·tion** \ˌim-ˌpär-'tā-shən\ *n* — **im·part·ment** \im-'pärt-mənt\ *n*

im·par·tial \(ˌ)im-'pär-shəl\ *adj* (1587) : not partial or biased : treating or affecting all equally *syn* see FAIR — **im·par·tial·i·ty** \-ˌpär-shē-'a-lə-tē, -ˌpär-'sha-\ *n* — **im·par·tial·ly** \-'pär-sh(ə-)lē\ *adv*

im·par·ti·ble \(ˌ)im-'pär-tə-bəl\ *adj* [LL *impartibilis*, fr. L *in-* + LL *partibilis* divisible, fr. L *partire*] (14c) : not partible : not subject to partition — **im·par·ti·bly** \-blē\ *adv*

im·pass·able \(ˌ)im-'pa-sə-bəl\ *adj* (1568) : incapable of being passed, traveled, crossed, or surmounted — **im·pass·abil·i·ty** \-ˌpa-sə-'bi-lə-tē\ *n* — **im·pass·able·ness** \-'pa-sə-bəl-nəs\ *n* — **im·pass·ably** \-blē\ *adv*

im·passe \'im-ˌpas, im-'\ *n* [F, fr. *in-* + *passer* to pass] (1851) **1 a** : a predicament affording no obvious escape **b** : DEADLOCK **2** : an impassable road or way : CUL-DE-SAC

im·pas·si·ble \(ˌ)im-'pa-sə-bəl\ *adj* [ME, fr. MF or LL; MF, fr. LL *impassibilis*, fr. L *in-* + LL *passibilis* passible] (14c) **1 a** : incapable of suffering or of experiencing pain : inaccessible to injury **2** : in-

capable of feeling : IMPASSIVE — **im·pas·si·bil·i·ty** \-ˌpa-sə-'bi-lə-tē\ *n* — **im·pas·si·bly** \-'pa-sə-blē\ *adv*

im·pas·sion \im-'pa-shən\ *vt* **im·pas·sioned; im·pas·sion·ing** \-sh(ə-)niŋ\ [prob. fr. It *impassionare*, fr. *in-* (fr. L) + *passione* passion, fr. LL *passion-, passio*] (1591) : to arouse the feelings or passions of

impassioned *adj* (1603) : filled with passion or zeal : showing great warmth or intensity of feeling

syn IMPASSIONED, PASSIONATE, ARDENT, FERVENT, FERVID, PERFERVID mean showing intense feeling. IMPASSIONED implies warmth and intensity without violence and suggests fluent verbal expression ⟨an *impassioned* plea for justice⟩. PASSIONATE implies great vehemence and often violence and wasteful diffusion of emotion ⟨a *passionate* denunciation⟩. ARDENT implies an intense degree of zeal, devotion, or enthusiasm ⟨an *ardent* supporter of human rights⟩. FERVENT stresses sincerity and steadiness of emotional warmth or zeal ⟨*fervent* good wishes⟩. FERVID suggests warmly and spontaneously and often feverishly expressed emotion ⟨*fervid* love letters⟩. PERFERVID implies the expression of exaggerated or overwrought feelings ⟨*perfervid* expressions of patriotism⟩.

im·pas·sive \(ˌ)im-'pa-siv\ *adj* (1605) **1 a** *archaic* : unsusceptible to pain **b** : unsusceptible to physical feeling : INSENSIBLE **c** : unsusceptible to or destitute of emotion : APATHETIC **2** : giving no sign of feeling or emotion : EXPRESSIONLESS — **im·pas·sive·ly** *adv* — **im·pas·sive·ness** *n* — **im·pas·siv·i·ty** \ˌim-ˌpa-'si-və-tē\ *n*

syn IMPASSIVE, STOIC, PHLEGMATIC, APATHETIC, STOLID mean unresponsive to something that might normally excite interest or emotion in action or facial expression ⟨met the news with an *impassive* look⟩. STOIC implies an apparent indifference to pleasure or esp. to pain often as a matter of principle or self-discipline ⟨was resolutely *stoic* even in adversity⟩. PHLEGMATIC implies a temperament or constitution hard to arouse ⟨a *phlegmatic* man unmoved by tears⟩. APATHETIC may imply a puzzling or deplorable indifference or inertness ⟨charitable appeals met an *apathetic* response⟩. STOLID implies an habitual absence of interest, responsiveness, or curiosity ⟨*stolid* workers wedded to routine⟩.

im·paste \im-'pāst\ *vt* [It *impastare*, fr. *in-* (fr. L) + *pasta* paste, fr. LL] (1576) *obs* : to make into a paste or crust

im·pas·to \im-'pas-(ˌ)tō, -'päs-\ *n, pl* **-tos** [It, fr. *impastare*] (1784) **1** : the thick application of a pigment to a canvas or panel in painting; *also* : the body of pigment so applied **2** : raised decoration on ceramic ware usu. of slip or enamel — **im·pas·toed** \-(ˌ)tōd\ *adj*

im·pa·tience \(ˌ)im-'pā-shən(t)s\ *n* (13c) : the quality or state of being impatient

im·pa·tiens \im-'pā-shənz, -shən(t)s\ *n* [NL, fr. L, impatient] (1885) : any of a widely distributed genus (*Impatiens*, family Balsaminaceae) of annual herbs with irregular spurred or saccate flowers and dehiscent capsules — compare TOUCH-ME-NOT

im·pa·tient \(ˌ)im-'pā-shənt\ *adj* [ME *impacient*, fr. MF, fr. L *impatient-, impatiens*, fr. *in-* + *patient-, patiens* patient] (14c) **1 a** : not patient : restless or short of temper esp. under irritation, delay, or opposition **b** : INTOLERANT ⟨~ of delay⟩ **2** : prompted or marked by impatience ⟨an ~ reply⟩ **3** : eagerly desirous : ANXIOUS ⟨~ to get home⟩ — **im·pa·tient·ly** *adv*

im·pawn \im-'pón, -'pän\ *vt* (1596) *archaic* : to put in pawn : PLEDGE

¹im·peach \im-'pēch\ *vt* [ME *empechen*, fr. MF *empeechier* to hinder, fr. LL *impedicare* to fetter, fr. L *in-* + *pedica* fetter, fr. *ped-, pes* foot — more at FOOT] (14c) **1 a** : to bring an accusation against **b** : to charge with a crime or misdemeanor; *specif* : to charge (a public official) before a competent tribunal with misconduct in office **2** : to cast doubt on; *esp* : to challenge the credibility or validity of ⟨~ the testimony of a witness⟩ **3** : to remove from office esp. for misconduct — **im·peach·able** \-'pē-chə-bəl\ *adj* — **im·peach·ment** \-'pēch-mənt\ *n*

²impeach *n* (1590) *obs* : CHARGE, IMPEACHMENT

im·pearl \im-'pər(-ə)l\ *vt* [prob. fr. MF *emperler*, fr. *en-* + *perle* pearl] (15c) : to form into pearls; *also* : to form of or adorn with pearls

im·pec·ca·ble \(ˌ)im-'pek-ə-bəl\ *adj* [L *impeccabilis*, fr. *in-* + *peccare* to sin] (1531) **1** : not capable of sinning or liable to sin **2** : free from fault or blame : FLAWLESS ⟨spoke ~ French⟩ — **im·pec·ca·bil·i·ty** \-ˌpe-kə-'bi-lə-tē\ *n* — **im·pec·ca·bly** \-'pe-kə-blē\ *adv*

im·pe·cu·nious \ˌim-pi-'kyü-nyəs, -nē-əs\ *adj* [¹*in-* + obs. E *pecunious* rich, fr. ME, fr. L *pecuniosus*, fr. *pecunia* money — more at FEE] (1596) : having very little or no money usu. habitually : PENNILESS — **im·pe·cu·ni·os·i·ty** \-ˌkyü-nē-'ä-sə-tē\ *n* — **im·pe·cu·nious·ly** *adv* — **im·pe·cu·nious·ness** *n*

im·ped·ance \im-'pē-dᵊn(t)s\ *n* (1886) : something that impedes : HINDRANCE: as **a** : the apparent opposition in an electrical circuit to the flow of an alternating current that is analogous to the actual electrical resistance to a direct current and that is the ratio of effective electromotive force to the effective current **b** : the ratio of the pressure to the volume displacement at a given surface in a sound-transmitting medium

im·pede \im-'pēd\ *vt* **im·ped·ed; im·ped·ing** [L *impedire*, fr. *in-* + *ped-, pes* foot — more at FOOT] (1605) : to interfere with or slow the progress of *syn* see HINDER — **im·ped·er** *n*

im·ped·i·ment \im-'pe-də-mənt\ *n* (14c) **1** : something that impedes; *esp* : an organic obstruction to speech **2** : a bar or hindrance (as lack of sufficient age) to a lawful marriage

im·ped·i·men·ta \(ˌ)im-ˌpe-də-'men-tə\ *n pl* [L, pl. of *impedimentum* impediment, fr. *impedire*] (1600) **1** : APPURTENANCES, EQUIPMENT **2** : things that impede

im·pel \im-'pel\ *vt* **im·pelled; im·pel·ling** [L *impellere*, fr. *in-* + *pellere* to drive — more at FELT] (15c) **1** : to urge or drive forward or on by or as if by the exertion of strong moral pressure : FORCE **2** : to impart motion to : PROPEL *syn* see MOVE

im·pel·ler *also* **im·pel·lor** \im-'pe-lər\ *n* (1685) **1** : one that impels **2** : ROTOR; *also* : a blade of a rotor

\ə\ abut \ᵊ\ kitten, F table \ər\ further \a\ ash \ā\ ace \ä\ mop, mar \aú\ out \ch\ chin \e\ bet \ē\ easy \g\ go \i\ hit \ī\ ice \j\ job \ŋ\ sing \ō\ go \ò\ law \òi\ boy \th\ thin \th̵\ the \ü\ loot \ú\ foot \y\ yet \zh\ vision \à, k̲, ⁿ, œ, œ̄, ᵫ, ūᵫ, ᵞ\ *see* Guide to Pronunciation

im·pend \im-'pend\ *vi* [L *impendēre*, fr. *in-* + *pendēre* to hang — more at PENDANT] (1599) **1 a** : to hover threateningly : MENACE **b** : to be about to occur **2** *archaic* : to hang suspended

im·pen·dent \im-'pen-dənt\ *adj* (1590) : being near at hand : APPROACHING

im·pen·e·tra·bil·i·ty \(,)im-,pe-nə-trə-'bi-lə-tē\ *n* (1665) **1** : the inability of two portions of matter to occupy the same space at the same time **2** : the quality or state of being impenetrable

im·pen·e·tra·ble \(,)im-'pe-nə-trə-bəl\ *adj* [ME *impenetrabel*, fr. MF *impenetrable*, fr. L *impenetrabilis*, fr. *in-* + *penetrabilis* penetrable] (15c) **1 a** : incapable of being penetrated or pierced **b** : inaccessible to knowledge, reason, or sympathy : IMPERVIOUS **2** : incapable of being comprehended : INSCRUTABLE — **im·pen·e·tra·bly** \-blē\ *adv*

im·pen·i·tence \(,)im-'pe-nə-tən(t)s\ *n* (1624) *archaic* : the quality or state of being impenitent

im·pen·i·tent \-tənt\ *adj* [ME, fr. LL *impaenitent-, impaenitens*, fr. L *in-* + *paenitent-, paenitens* penitent] (15c) : not penitent — **im·pen·i·tent·ly** *adv*

¹im·per·a·tive \im-'per-ə-tiv\ *adj* [ME *imperatyf*, fr. LL *imperativus*, fr. L *imperatus*, pp. of *imperare* to command — more at EMPEROR] (15c) **1 a** : of, relating to, or constituting the grammatical mood that expresses the will to influence the behavior of another **b** : expressive of a command, entreaty, or exhortation **c** : having power to restrain, control, and direct **2** : not to be avoided or evaded : NECESSARY ⟨an ∼ duty⟩ *syn* see MASTERFUL — **im·per·a·tive·ly** *adv* — **im·per·a·tive·ness** *n*

²imperative *n* (1530) **1** : the imperative mood or a verb form or verbal phrase expressing it **2** : something that is imperative: as **a** : COMMAND, ORDER **b** : RULE, GUIDE **c** : an obligatory act or duty **d** : an imperative judgment or proposition

im·pe·ra·tor \,im-pə-'rä-tər, -,tȯr\ *n* [L — more at EMPEROR] (ca. 1580) : a commander in chief or emperor of the ancient Romans — **im·per·a·to·ri·al** \(,)im-pə-ə-'tōr-ē-əl, -'tȯr-\ *adj*

im·per·ceiv·able \,im-pər-'sē-və-bəl\ *adj* (ca. 1617) *archaic* : IMPERCEPTIBLE

im·per·cep·ti·ble \,im-pər-'sep-tə-bəl\ *adj* [MF, fr. ML *imperceptibilis*, fr. L *in-* + LL *perceptibilis* perceptible] (15c) : not perceptible by a sense or by the mind : extremely slight, gradual, or subtle — **im·per·cep·ti·bly** \-'sep-tə-blē\ *adv*

im·per·cep·tive \,im-pər-'sep-tiv\ *adj* (1661) : not perceptive — **im·per·cep·tive·ness** *n*

im·per·cip·i·ence \-'si-pē-ən(t)s\ *n* (1891) : the quality or state of being imperceptive — **im·per·cip·i·ent** \-ənt\ *adj*

¹im·per·fect \(,)im-'pər-fikt\ *adj* [alter. of ME *imperfit*, fr. MF *imparfait*, fr. L *imperfectus*, fr. *in-* + *perfectus* perfect] (1570) **1** : not perfect: as **a** : DEFECTIVE **b** *of a flower* : having stamens or pistils but not both **c** : lacking or not involving sexual reproduction ⟨the ∼ stage of a fungus⟩ **2** : of, relating to, or constituting a verb tense used to designate a continuing state or an incomplete action in the past **3** : not enforceable at law — **im·per·fect·ly** \-fik(t)-lē\ *adv* — **im·per·fect·ness** \-fik(t)-nəs\ *n*

²imperfect *n* (1871) : an imperfect tense; *also* : the verb form expressing it

imperfect fungus *n* (ca. 1895) : any of various fungi (order Fungi Imperfecti syn. Deuteromycetes) of which only the conidial stage is known

im·per·fec·tion \,im-pər-'fek-shən\ *n* (14c) : the quality or state of being imperfect; *also* : FAULT, BLEMISH

im·per·fec·tive \,im-pər-'fek-tiv\ *adj* (1887) *of a verb form or aspect* : expressing action as incomplete or without reference to completion or as reiterated — compare PERFECTIVE — **imperfective** *n*

im·per·fo·rate \(,)im-'pər-f(ə-)rət, -fə-,rāt\ *adj* (1673) **1** : having no opening or aperture; *specif* : lacking the usual or normal opening **2** *of a stamp or a sheet of stamps* : lacking perforations or roulettes

¹im·pe·ri·al \im-'pir-ē-əl\ *adj* [ME, fr. MF, fr. LL *imperialis*, fr. L *imperium* command, empire] (14c) **1 a** : of, relating to, befitting, or suggestive of an empire or an emperor **b** (1) : of or relating to the United Kingdom as distinguished from the constituent parts (2) : of or relating to the Commonwealth and British Empire **2 a** : SOVEREIGN **b** : REGAL, IMPERIOUS **3** : of superior or unusual size or excellence **4** : belonging to the official British series of weights and measures — see WEIGHT table — **im·pe·ri·al·ly** \-ē-lē\ *adv*

²imperial *n* (ca. 1524) **1** *cap* : an adherent or soldier of the Holy Roman emperor **2** : EMPEROR **3** [F *impériale*; fr. the beard worn by Napoléon III] : a pointed beard growing below the lower lip **4** : something of unusual size or excellence

im·pe·ri·al·ism \im-'pir-ē-ə-,li-zəm\ *n* (1851) **1** : imperial government, authority, or system **2** : the policy, practice, or advocacy of extending the power and dominion of a nation esp. by direct territorial acquisitions or by gaining indirect control over the political or economic life of other areas; *broadly* : the extension or imposition of power, authority, or influence ⟨union ∼⟩ — **im·pe·ri·al·ist** \-list\ *n or adj* — **im·pe·ri·al·is·tic** \-,pir-ē-ə-'lis-tik\ *adj* — **im·pe·ri·al·is·ti·cal·ly** \-ti-k(ə-)lē\ *adv*

imperial moth *n* (ca. 1904) : a large American saturniid moth (*Eacles imperialis*) marked with yellow and lilac or purplish brown

im·per·il \im-'per-əl\ *vt* -**iled** *or* -**illed**; -**il·ing** *or* -**il·ling** (15c) : to bring into peril : ENDANGER — **im·per·il·ment** \-mənt\ *n*

im·pe·ri·ous \im-'pir-ē-əs\ *adj* [L *imperiosus*, fr. *imperium*] (1540) **1** : befitting or characteristic of one of eminent rank or attainments : COMMANDING, DOMINANT ⟨an ∼ manner⟩ **b** : marked by arrogant assurance : DOMINEERING **2** : intensely compelling : URGENT ⟨the ∼ problems of the new age —J. F. Kennedy⟩ *syn* see MASTERFUL — **im·pe·ri·ous·ly** *adv* — **im·pe·ri·ous·ness** *n*

im·per·ish·able \(,)im-'per-i-shə-bəl\ *adj* (1648) **1** : not perishable or subject to decay **2** : enduring or occurring forever ⟨∼ fame⟩ — **im·per·ish·abil·i·ty** \-,per-i-shə-'bi-lə-tē\ *n* — **imperishable** *n* — **im-**

imperial moth

per·ish·able·ness \-'per-i-shə-bəl-nəs\ *n* — **im·per·ish·ably** \-blē\ *adv*

im·pe·ri·um \im-'pir-ē-əm\ *n* [L — more at EMPIRE] (1651) **1 a** : supreme power or absolute dominion : CONTROL **b** : EMPIRE **2** : the right to command or to employ the force of the state : SOVEREIGNTY

im·per·ma·nence \(,)im-'pərm-nən(t)s, -'pər-mə-\ *n* (1796) : the quality or state of being impermanent

im·per·ma·nen·cy \-nən(t)-sē\ *n* (1648) : IMPERMANENCE

im·per·ma·nent \-nənt\ *adj* (1653) : not permanent : TRANSIENT — **im·per·ma·nent·ly** *adv*

im·per·me·able \(,)im-'pər-mē-ə-bəl\ *adj* [LL *impermeabilis*, fr. L *in-* + LL *permeabilis* permeable] (1697) : not permitting passage (as of a fluid) through its substance; *broadly* : IMPERVIOUS — **im·per·me·abil·i·ty** \-,pər-mē-ə-'bi-lə-tē\ *n*

im·per·mis·si·ble \,im-pər-'mi-sə-bəl\ *adj* (1858) : not permissible — **im·per·mis·si·bil·i·ty** \-,mi-sə-'bi-lə-tē\ *n* — **im·per·mis·si·bly** \-'mi-sə-blē\ *adv*

im·per·son·al \(,)im-'pərs-nəl, -'pər-s°n-əl\ *adj* [ME, fr. LL *impersonalis*, fr. L *in-* + *personalis* personal] (15c) **1 a** : denoting the verbal action of an unspecified agent and hence used with no expressed subject (as *methinks*) or with a merely formal subject (as *rained* in *it rained*) **b** *of a pronoun* : INDEFINITE **2 a** : having no personal reference or connection ⟨∼ criticism⟩ **b** : not engaging the human personality or emotions ⟨the machine as compared with the hand tool is an ∼ agency —John Dewey⟩ **c** : not existing as a person : not having human qualities or characteristics — **im·per·son·al·i·ty** \-,pər-s°n-'a-lə-tē\ *n* — **im·per·son·al·ly** \-'pərs-nə-lē, -'pər-s°n-ə-lē\ *adv*

im·per·son·al·ize \(,)im-'pərs-nə-,līz, -'pər-s°n-ə-\ *vt* (ca. 1899) : to make impersonal — **im·per·son·al·i·za·tion** \-,pərs-nə-lə-'zā-shən, -,pər-s°n-ə-\ *n*

im·per·son·ate \im-'pər-s°n-,āt\ *vt* -**at·ed**; -**at·ing** (1715) : to assume or act the character of : PERSONATE — **im·per·son·a·tion** \-,pər-s°n-'ā-shən\ *n* — **im·per·son·a·tor** \-'pər-s°n-,ā-tər\ *n*

im·per·ti·nence \(,)im-'pər-t°n-ən(t)s, -'pərt-nən(t)s\ *n* (1603) **1** : the quality or state of being impertinent: as **a** : IRRELEVANCE, INAPPROPRIATENESS **b** : INCIVILITY, INSOLENCE **2** : an instance of impertinence

im·per·ti·nen·cy \-ən(t)-sē, -nən(t)-\ *n, pl* -**cies** (1589) : IMPERTINENCE

im·per·ti·nent \(,)im-'pər-t°n-ənt, -'pərt-nənt\ *adj* [ME, fr. MF, fr. LL *impertinent-, impertinens*, fr. L *in-* + *pertinent-, pertinens*, prp. of *pertinēre* to pertain] (14c) **1** : not pertinent : IRRELEVANT **2 a** : not restrained within due or proper bounds esp. of propriety or good taste ⟨∼ curiosity⟩ **b** : given to or characterized by insolent rudeness ⟨an ∼ answer⟩ — **im·per·ti·nent·ly** *adv*

syn IMPERTINENT, OFFICIOUS, MEDDLESOME, INTRUSIVE, OBTRUSIVE mean given to thrusting oneself into the affairs of others. IMPERTINENT implies exceeding the bounds of propriety in showing interest or curiosity or in offering advice ⟨resented their *impertinent* interference⟩. OFFICIOUS implies the offering of services or attentions that are unwelcome or annoying ⟨*officious* friends made the job harder⟩. MEDDLESOME stresses an annoying and usu. prying interference in others' affairs ⟨a *meddlesome* landlord⟩. INTRUSIVE implies a tactless or otherwise objectionable thrusting into others' affairs ⟨tried to be helpful without being *intrusive*⟩. OBTRUSIVE stresses improper or offensive conspicuousness of interfering actions ⟨expressed an *obtrusive* concern for his safety⟩.

im·per·turb·able \,im-pər-'tər-bə-bəl\ *adj* [ME, fr. LL *imperturbabilis*, fr. L *in-* + *perturbare* to perturb] (15c) : marked by extreme calm, impassivity, and steadiness : SERENE *syn* see COOL — **im·per·turb·abil·i·ty** \-,tər-bə-'bi-lə-tē\ *n* — **im·per·turb·ably** \-'tər-bə-blē\ *adv*

im·per·vi·ous \(,)im-'pər-vē-əs\ *adj* [L *impervius*, fr. *in-* + *pervius* pervious] (1650) **1 a** : not allowing entrance or passage : IMPENETRABLE ⟨a coat ∼ to rain⟩ **b** : not capable of being damaged or harmed ⟨a carpet ∼ to rough treatment⟩ **2** : not capable of being affected or disturbed ⟨∼ to criticism⟩ — **im·per·vi·ous·ly** *adv* — **im·per·vi·ous·ness** *n*

im·pe·tig·i·nous \,im-pə-'ti-jə-nəs\ *adj* (1620) : of, relating to, or resembling impetigo ⟨∼ lesions⟩

im·pe·ti·go \,im-pə-'tē-(,)gō, -'tī-\ *n* [L, fr. *impetere* to attack — more at IMPETUS] (14c) : an acute contagious staphylococcal or streptococcal skin disease characterized by vesicles, pustules, and yellowish crusts

im·pe·trate \'im-pə-,trāt\ *vt* -**trat·ed**; -**trat·ing** [L *impetratus*, pp. of *impetrare*, fr. *in-* + *patrare* to accomplish — more at PERPETRATE] (ca. 1534) **1** : to obtain by request or entreaty **2** : to ask for : ENTREAT — **im·pe·tra·tion** \,im-pə-'trā-shən\ *n*

im·pet·u·os·i·ty \im-,pe-chə-'wä-sə-tē\ *n, pl* -**ties** (15c) **1** : the quality or state of being impetuous **2** : an impetuous action or impulse

im·pet·u·ous \im-'pech-wəs, -'pe-chə-\ *adj* [ME, fr. MF *impetueux*, fr. LL *impetuosus*, fr. L *impetus*] (14c) **1** : marked by impulsive vehemence or passion ⟨an ∼ temperament⟩ **2** : marked by force and violence of movement or action ⟨an ∼ wind⟩ *syn* see PRECIPITATE — **im·pet·u·ous·ly** *adv* — **im·pet·u·ous·ness** *n*

im·pe·tus \'im-pə-təs\ *n* [L, assault, impetus, fr. *impetere* to attack, fr. *in-* + *petere* to go to, seek — more at FEATHER] (1641) **1 a** (1) : a driving force : IMPULSE (2) : INCENTIVE, STIMULUS **b** : stimulation or encouragement resulting in increased activity **2** : the property possessed by a moving body in virtue of its mass and its motion — used of bodies moving suddenly or violently to indicate the origin and intensity of the motion

im·pi·e·ty \(,)im-'pī-ə-tē\ *n, pl* -**ties** (14c) **1** : the quality or state of being impious : IRREVERENCE **2** : an impious act

im·pinge \im-'pinj\ *vi* **im·pinged**; **im·ping·ing** [L *impingere*, fr. *in-* + *pangere* to fasten, drive in — more at PACT] (1605) **1** : to strike or dash esp. with a sharp collision ⟨I heard the rain ∼ upon the earth — James Joyce⟩ **2** : to have an effect : make an impression ⟨waiting for the germ of a new idea to ∼ upon my mind —Phyllis Bentley⟩ **3** : ENCROACH, INFRINGE ⟨∼ on other people's rights⟩ — **im·pinge·ment** \-'pinj-mənt\ *n*

im·pi·ous \'im-pē-əs, (,)im-'pī-\ *adj* [L *impius*, fr. *in-* + *pius* pious] (1542) : not pious : lacking in reverence or proper respect (as for God or one's parents) : IRREVERENT — **im·pi·ous·ly** *adv*

imp·ish \'im-pish\ *adj* (1652) : of, relating to, or befitting an imp; *esp* : MISCHIEVOUS — **imp·ish·ly** *adv* — **imp·ish·ness** *n*

im·pla·ca·ble \(,)im-'pla-kə-bəl, -'plā-\ *adj* [MF or L; MF, fr. L *implacabilis*, fr. *in-* + *placabilis* placable] (15c) : not placable : not capable of being appeased, significantly changed, or mitigated ⟨an ~ enemy⟩ — **im·pla·ca·bil·i·ty** \-ˌpla-kə-ˈbi-lə-tē, -ˌplä-\ *n* — **im·pla·ca·bly** \-ˈpla-kə-blē, -ˈplä-\ *adv*

¹im·plant \im-ˈplant\ *vt* (15c) **1 a** : to fix or set securely or deeply ⟨a ruby ~ed in the idol's forehead⟩ **b** : to set permanently in the consciousness or habit patterns : INCULCATE **2** : to insert in a living site (as for growth, slow release, or formation of an organic union) ⟨subcutaneously ~ed hormone pellets⟩ — **im·plant·able** \-ˈplan-tə-bəl\ *adj* — **im·plant·er** \im-ˈplan-tər\ *n*

syn IMPLANT, INCULCATE, INSTILL, INSEMINATE, INFIX mean to introduce into the mind. IMPLANT implies teaching that makes for permanence of what is taught ⟨*implanted* a love of reading in her students⟩. INCULCATE implies persistent or repeated efforts to impress on the mind ⟨tried to *inculcate* in him high moral standards⟩. INSTILL stresses gradual, gentle imparting of knowledge over a long period of time ⟨*instill* traditional values in your children⟩. INSEMINATE applies to a sowing of ideas in many minds so that they spread through a class or nation ⟨*inseminated* an unquestioning faith in technology⟩. INFIX stresses firmly inculcating a habit of thought ⟨*infixed* a chronic cynicism⟩.

²im·plant \ˈim-ˌplant\ *n* (1890) : something (as a graft or pellet) implanted in tissue

im·plan·ta·tion \ˌim-ˌplan-ˈtā-shən\ *n* (1578) **1 a** : the act or process of implanting something **b** : the state resulting from being implanted **2** *in placental mammals* : the process of attachment of the embryo to the maternal uterine wall

im·plau·si·ble \(ˌ)im-ˈplȯ-zə-bəl\ *adj* (ca. 1677) : not plausible : provoking disbelief — **im·plau·si·bil·i·ty** \-ˌplȯ-zə-ˈbi-lə-tē\ *n* — **im·plau·si·bly** \-ˈplȯ-zə-blē\ *adv*

im·plead \im-ˈplēd\ *vt* [ME *empleden*, fr. MF *emplaider*, fr. OF *emplaidier*, fr. *en-* + *plaidier* to plead] (14c) : to sue or prosecute at law

¹im·ple·ment \ˈim-plə-mənt\ *n* [ME, fr. LL *implementum* action of filling up, fr. L *implēre* to fill up, fr. *in-* + *plēre* to fill — more at FULL] (15c) **1** : an article serving to equip ⟨the ~s of religious worship⟩ **2** : a device used in the performance of a task **3** : one that serves as an instrument or tool ⟨the partnership agreement does not seem to be a very potent ~ —H. B. Hoffman⟩

syn IMPLEMENT, TOOL, INSTRUMENT, APPLIANCE, UTENSIL mean a relatively simple device for performing work. IMPLEMENT may apply to anything necessary to perform a task ⟨crude stone *implements*⟩ ⟨farm *implements*⟩. TOOL suggests an implement adapted to facilitate a definite kind or stage of work and suggests the need of skill more strongly than IMPLEMENT ⟨a carpenter's *tools*⟩. INSTRUMENT suggests a device capable of delicate or precise work ⟨the dentist's *instruments*⟩. APPLIANCE refers to a tool or instrument utilizing a power source and suggests portability or temporary attachment ⟨household *appliances*⟩. UTENSIL applies to a device used in domestic work or some routine unskilled activity ⟨kitchen *utensils*⟩.

²im·ple·ment \-ˌment\ *vt* (1806) **1** : CARRY OUT, ACCOMPLISH; *esp* : to give practical effect to and ensure of actual fulfillment by concrete measures **2** : to provide instruments or means of expression for — **im·ple·men·ta·tion** \ˌim-plə-mən-ˈtā-shən, -ˌmen-\ *n* — **im·ple·men·ter** *or* **im·ple·men·tor** \ˈim-plə-ˌmən-tər\ *n*

im·pli·cate \ˈim-plə-ˌkāt\ *vt* -**cat·ed**; -**cat·ing** [ME, to convey by implication, fr. ML *implicatus*, pp. of *implicare*, fr. L, to entwine, involve — more at EMPLOY] (15c) **1** : to involve as a consequence, corollary, or natural inference : IMPLY **2** *archaic* : to fold or twist together : ENTWINE **3 a** : to bring into intimate or incriminating connection **b** : to involve in the nature or operation of something

im·pli·ca·tion \ˌim-plə-ˈkā-shən\ *n* (15c) **1 a** : the act of implicating : the state of being implicated **b** : close connection; *esp* : an incriminating involvement **2 a** : the act of implying : the state of being implied **b** (1) : a logical relation between two propositions that fails to hold only if the first is true and the second is false (2) : a logical relationship between two propositions in which if the first is true the second is true (3) : a statement exhibiting a relation of implication **3** : something implied: as **a** : SUGGESTION **b** : a possible significance ⟨the book has political ~s⟩ — **im·pli·ca·tive** \ˈim-plə-ˌkā-tiv, im-ˈpli-kə-\ *adj* — **im·pli·ca·tive·ly** *adv* — **im·pli·ca·tive·ness** *n*

im·plic·it \im-ˈpli-sət\ *adj* [L *implicitus*, pp. of *implicare*] (1599) **1 a** : capable of being understood from something else though unexpressed : IMPLIED ⟨an ~ assumption⟩ **b** : involved in the nature or essence of something though not revealed, expressed, or developed : POTENTIAL ⟨a sculptor may see different figures ~ in a block of stone —John Dewey⟩ **c** *of a mathematical function* : defined by an expression in which the dependent variable and the one or more independent variables are not separated on opposite sides of an equation — compare EXPLICIT 4 **2** : being without doubt or reserve : UNQUESTIONING — **im·plic·it·ly** *adv* — **im·plic·it·ness** *n*

implicit differentiation *n* (ca. 1889) : the process of finding the derivative of a dependent variable in an implicit function by differentiating each term separately, by expressing the derivative of the dependent variable as a symbol, and by solving the resulting expression for the symbol

im·plode \im-ˈplōd\ *vb* **im·plod·ed**; **im·plod·ing** [²*in-* + *-plode* (as in *explode*)] *vi* (1881) **1 a** : to burst inward ⟨a blow causing a vacuum tube to ~⟩ **b** : to undergo violent compression ⟨massive stars which ~⟩ : to collapse inward as if from external pressure; *also* : to become greatly reduced as if from collapsing ~ *vt* : to cause to implode

im·plore \im-ˈplōr, -ˈplȯr\ *vt* **im·plored**; **im·plor·ing** [MF or L; MF *implorer*, fr. L *implorare*, fr. *in-* + *plorare* to cry out] (ca. 1540) **1** : to call upon in supplication : BESEECH **2** : to call or pray for earnestly : ENTREAT *syn* see BEG — **im·plor·ing·ly** *adv*

im·plo·sion \im-ˈplō-zhən\ *n* [²*in-* + *-plosion* (as in *explosion*)] (1877) **1** : the inrush of air in forming a suction stop **2** : the action of imploding **3** : the act or action of bringing to or as if to a center; *also* : INTEGRATION ⟨this ~ of cultures makes realistic for the first time the age-old vision of a world culture —Kenneth Keniston⟩ — **im·plo·sive** \-ˈplō-siv, -ziv\ *adj or n*

im·ply \im-ˈplī\ *vt* **im·plied**; **im·ply·ing** [ME *emplien*, fr. MF *emplier*, fr. L *implicare*] (14c) **1** *obs* : ENFOLD, ENTWINE **2** : to involve or indicate by inference, association, or necessary consequence rather than by direct statement ⟨rights ~ obligations⟩ **3** : to contain potentially **4** : to express indirectly ⟨his silence *implied* consent⟩ *syn* see SUGGEST *usage* see INFER

im·po·lite \ˌim-pə-ˈlīt\ *adj* [L *impolitus*, fr. *in-* + *politus* polite] (1739) : not polite : RUDE — **im·po·lite·ly** *adv* — **im·po·lite·ness** *n*

im·pol·i·tic \(ˌ)im-ˈpä-lə-ˌtik\ *adj* (ca. 1600) : not politic : RASH — **im·pol·i·tical** \-pə-ˈli-ti-kəl\ *adj* — **im·pol·it·i·cal·ly** \-ˈli-ti-k(ə-)lē\ *adv* — **im·pol·i·tic·ly** \-ˈpä-lə-ˌti-klē\ *adv*

im·pon·der·a·ble \(ˌ)im-ˈpän-d(ə-)rə-bəl\ *adj* [ML *imponderabilis*, fr. L *in-* + LL *ponderabilis* ponderable] (1794) : not ponderable : incapable of being weighed or evaluated with exactness — **im·pon·der·a·bil·i·ty** \-ˌpän-d(ə-)rə-ˈbi-lə-tē\ *n* — **imponderable** *n* — **im·pon·der·a·bly** \-ˈpän-d(ə-)rə-blē\ *adv*

im·pone \im-ˈpōn\ *vt* **im·poned**; **im·pon·ing** [L *imponere* to put upon, fr. *in-* + *ponere* to put — more at POSITION] (ca. 1623) *obs* : WAGER, BET

¹im·port \im-ˈpōrt, -ˈpȯrt, ˈim-ˌ\ *vb* [ME, fr. L *importare* to bring into, fr. *in-* + *portare* to carry — more at FARE] *vt* (15c) **1 a** : to bear or convey as meaning or portent : SIGNIFY **b** *archaic* : EXPRESS, STATE **c** : IMPLY **2** : to bring from a foreign or external source; *esp* : to bring (as merchandise) into a place or country from another country **3** *archaic* : to be of importance to ~ *vi* : to be of consequence : MATTER — **im·port·able** \im-ˈpōr-tə-bəl, -ˈpȯr-, ˈim-ˌ\ *adj* — **im·port·er** *n*

²im·port \ˈim-ˌpōrt, -ˌpȯrt\ *n* (ca. 1568) **1** : IMPORTANCE; *esp* : relative importance ⟨it is hard to determine the ~ of this decision⟩ **2** : PURPORT, SIGNIFICATION **3** : something that is imported **4** : IMPORTATION

im·por·tance \im-ˈpȯr-t²n(t)s, *esp Southern & NewEng* -tən(t)s, -dən(t)s\ *n* (1508) **1 a** : the quality or state of being important : CONSEQUENCE **b** : an important aspect or bearing : SIGNIFICANCE **2** *obs* : IMPORT, MEANING **3** *obs* : IMPORTUNITY **4** *obs* : a weighty matter *syn* IMPORTANCE, CONSEQUENCE, MOMENT, WEIGHT, SIGNIFICANCE mean a quality or aspect having great worth or significance. IMPORTANCE implies a value judgment of the superior worth or influence of something or someone ⟨a region with no cities of *importance*⟩. CONSEQUENCE generally implies importance because of probable or possible effects ⟨the style you choose is of little *consequence*⟩. MOMENT implies conspicuous or self-evident consequence ⟨a decision of great *moment*⟩. WEIGHT implies a judgment of the immediate relative importance of something ⟨the argument carried no *weight* with the judge⟩. SIGNIFICANCE implies a quality or character that should mark a thing as important but that is not self-evident and may or may not be recognized ⟨the treaty's *significance*⟩.

im·por·tan·cy \-t²n(t)-sē, -tən(t)-, -dən(t)-\ *n* (1540) *archaic* : IMPORTANCE

im·por·tant \im-ˈpȯr-t²nt, *esp Southern & NewEng* -tənt, -dənt\ *adj* [ME *importante*, fr. ML *important-, importans*, prp. of *importare* to signify, fr. L, to bring into] (15c) **1** : marked by or indicative of significant worth or consequence : valuable in content or relationship **2** *obs* : IMPORTUNATE, URGENT **3** : giving evidence of a feeling of self-importance *usage* see IMPORTANTLY

im·por·tant·ly \-lē\ *adv* (1647) **1** : in an important way ⟨contributed ~ to the language of the field —Ernst Mayr⟩ ⟨cleared his throat ~ and waited —E. K. Gann⟩ ⟨the real story is ~ different —Alexander Woollcott⟩ **2** : it is important that ⟨more ~ he stands a chance of having his publication barred —H. L. Mencken⟩

usage A number of commentators have objected to *importantly* as a sentence modifier (sense 2) and have recommended *important* instead. Actually both the adverb and the adjective are in reputable standard use in this function. *Important* is always used with *more* or *most* ⟨had bronze weapons and composite bows; more *important*, they utilized the horse and war chariot —Harry A. Gailey, Jr.⟩ ⟨second and most *important*, the book contains no important woman character —F. Scott Fitzgerald⟩. *Importantly* is somewhat more flexible in not requiring *more* or *most* ⟨sticks and, just as *importantly*, unsticks easily —Phoebe Hawkins⟩ ⟨*importantly*, the leaven in the mixture is quality —George O'Brien⟩.

im·por·ta·tion \ˌim-ˌpȯr-ˈtā-shən, -ˌpȯr-, -pər-\ *n* (1601) **1** : the act or practice of importing **2** : something imported

imported cabbageworm *n* (1892) : a small cosmopolitan white butterfly (*Pieris rapae*) or its larva which is a pest of cruciferous plants and esp. cabbage

imported fire ant *n* (ca. 1949) : either of two mound-building So. American fire ants (*Solenopsis richteri* and *S. invicta*) introduced into the southeastern U.S. that are agricultural pests and can produce stings requiring medical attention

im·por·tu·nate \im-ˈpȯr-chə-nət, -tyü-nət\ *adj* (1529) **1** : troublesomely urgent : overly persistent in request or demand **2** : TROUBLESOME — **im·por·tu·nate·ly** *adv* — **im·por·tu·nate·ness** *n*

¹im·por·tune \ˌim-pər-ˈtün, -ˈtyün; im-ˈpȯr-, -chən\ *adj* [ME, fr. MF & L; MF *importun*, fr. L *importunus*, fr. *in-* + *-portunus* (as in *opportunus* fit) — more at OPPORTUNE] (15c) **1** : IMPORTUNATE — **im·por·tune·ly** *adv*

²importune *vb* **-tuned**; **-tun·ing** *vt* (1530) **1 a** : to press or urge with troublesome persistence **b** *archaic* : to request or beg for urgently **2** : ANNOY, TROUBLE ~ *vi* : to beg, urge, or solicit persistently or troublesomely *syn* see BEG — **im·por·tun·er** *n*

im·por·tu·ni·ty \ˌim-pər-ˈtü-nə-tē, -ˈtyü-\ *n, pl* **-ties** (15c) **1** : the quality or state of being importunate **2** : an importunate request or demand

im·pose \im-ˈpōz\ *vb* **im·posed**; **im·pos·ing** [MF *imposer*, fr. L *imponere*, lit., to put upon (perf. indic. *imposui*), fr. *in-* + *ponere* to put — more at POSITION] *vt* (1581) **1 a** : to establish or apply by authority ⟨~ a tax⟩ ⟨~ new restrictions⟩ ⟨~ penalties⟩ **b** : to establish or bring about as if by force ⟨those limits *imposed* by our own inadequacies —C. H. Plimpton⟩ **2 a** : PLACE, SET **b** : to arrange (as pages) in the proper order for printing **3** : PASS OFF ⟨~ fake antiques on the public⟩ **4** : to force into the company or on the attention of another ⟨~ oneself on others⟩ ~ *vi* : to take unwarranted advantage of something ⟨*imposed* on his good nature⟩ — **im·pos·er** *n*

\ə\ abut \ᵊ\ kitten, F table \ər\ further \a\ ash \ā\ ace \ä\ mop, mar \au̇\ out \ch\ chin \e\ bet \ē\ easy \g\ go \i\ hit \ī\ ice \j\ job \ŋ\ sing \ō\ go \ȯ\ law \ȯi\ boy \th\ thin \t͟h\ the \ü\ loot \u̇\ foot \y\ yet \zh\ vision \à, k̲, ⁿ, œ, œ̄, ue, ᵫ, ᵞ\ *see* Guide to Pronunciation

im·pos·ing \im-ˈpō-ziŋ\ *adj* (1786) : impressive in size, bearing, dignity, or grandeur *syn* see GRAND — **im·pos·ing·ly** \-ziŋ-lē\ *adv*

im·po·si·tion \ˌim-pə-ˈzi-shən\ *n* (14c) **1** : something imposed: as **a** : LEVY, TAX **b** : an excessive or uncalled-for requirement or burden **2** : the act of imposing **3** : DECEPTION **4** : the order of arrangement of imposed pages

im·pos·si·bil·i·ty \(ˌ)im-ˌpä-sə-ˈbi-lə-tē\ *n* (14c) **1** : the quality or state of being impossible **2** : something impossible

im·pos·si·ble \(ˌ)im-ˈpä-sə-bəl\ *adj* [ME, fr. MF & L; MF, fr. L *impossibilis*, fr. *in-* + *possibilis* possible] (14c) **1 a** : incapable of being or of occurring **b** : felt to be incapable of being done, attained, or fulfilled : insuperably difficult **2 a** : extremely undesirable : UNACCEPTABLE **b** : extremely awkward or difficult to deal with — **im·pos·si·ble·ness** *n*

im·pos·si·bly \-blē\ *adv* (ca. 1580) **1** : not possibly **2** : to an improbable degree : UNBELIEVABLY ⟨an ~ green lawn⟩

¹im·post \ˈim-ˌpōst\ *n* [MF, fr. ML *impositum*, fr. L, neut. of *impositus*, pp. of *imponere*] (1568) : something imposed or levied : TAX

²impost *n* [F *imposte*, ultim. fr. L *impositus*] (1664) : a block, capital, or molding from which an arch springs — see ARCH illustration

im·pos·tor *or* **im·pos·ter** \im-ˈpäs-tər\ *n* [LL *impostor*, fr. L *imponere*] (1624) : one that assumes false identity or title for the purpose of deception

im·pos·tume \im-ˈpäs-ˌchüm\ *or* **im·pos·thume** \-ˌthüm, -ˌthyüm\ *n* [ME *emposteme*, ultim. fr. Gk *apostēma*, fr. *aphistanai* to remove, fr. *apo-* + *histanai* to cause to stand — more at STAND] (14c) *archaic* : ABSCESS

im·pos·ture \im-ˈpäs-chər\ *n* [LL *impostura*, fr. L *impositus, impostus*, pp. of *imponere*] (1537) **1** : the act or practice of deceiving by means of an assumed character or name **2** : an instance of imposture
  syn IMPOSTURE, FRAUD, SHAM, FAKE, HUMBUG, COUNTERFEIT mean a thing made to seem other than it is. IMPOSTURE applies to any situation in which a spurious object or performance is passed off as genuine ⟨their claim of environmental concern is an *imposture*⟩. FRAUD usu. implies a deliberate perversion of the truth ⟨the diary was exposed as a *fraud*⟩. SHAM applies to fraudulent imitation of a real thing or action ⟨condemned the election as a *sham*⟩. FAKE implies an imitation of or substitution for the genuine but does not necessarily imply dishonesty ⟨these jewels are *fakes*; the real ones are in the vault⟩. HUMBUG suggests elaborate pretense usu. so flagrant as to be transparent ⟨creating publicity by foisting *humbugs* on a gullible public⟩. COUNTERFEIT applies esp. to the close imitation of something valuable ⟨20-dollar bills that were *counterfeits*⟩.

im·po·tence \ˈim-pə-tən(t)s\ *n* (15c) : the quality or state of being impotent

im·po·ten·cy \-tən(t)-sē\ *n* (15c) : IMPOTENCE

im·po·tent \ˈim-pə-tənt\ *adj* [ME, fr. MF & L; MF, fr. L *impotent-, impotens*, fr. *in-* + *potent-, potens* potent] (14c) **1 a** : not potent : lacking in power, strength, or vigor : HELPLESS **b** : unable to copulate; *broadly* : STERILE — usu. used of males **2** *obs* : incapable of self-restraint : UNGOVERNABLE — **impotent** *n* — **im·po·tent·ly** *adv*

im·pound \im-ˈpaùnd\ *vt* (15c) **1 a** : to shut up in or as if in a pound : CONFINE **b** : to seize and hold in the custody of the law **c** : to take possession of ⟨she was dismissed and her manuscript ~ed —Jonathan Weiner⟩ **2** : to collect and confine (water) in or as if in a reservoir

im·pound·ment \-ˈpaùn(d)-mənt\ *n* (ca. 1665) **1** : the act of impounding : the state of being impounded **2** : a body of water formed by impounding

im·pov·er·ish \im-ˈpäv-rish, -ˈpä-və-\ *vt* [ME *enpoverisen*, fr. MF *empovriss-*, stem of *empovrir*, fr. *en-* + *povre* poor — more at POOR] (15c) **1** : to make poor **2** : to deprive of strength, richness, or fertility by depleting or draining of something essential *syn* see DEPLETE — **im·pov·er·ish·er** *n* — **im·pov·er·ish·ment** \-mənt\ *n*

impoverished *adj* (1950) *of a fauna or flora* : represented by few species or individuals

im·prac·ti·ca·ble \(ˌ)im-ˈprak-ti-kə-bəl\ *adj* (1653) **1** : IMPASSABLE ⟨an ~ road⟩ **2** : not practicable : incapable of being performed or accomplished by the means employed or at command — **im·prac·ti·ca·bil·i·ty** \-ˌprak-ti-kə-ˈbi-lə-tē\ *n* — **im·prac·ti·ca·bly** \-ˈprak-ti-kə-blē\ *adv*

im·prac·ti·cal \-ˈprak-ti-kəl\ *adj* (1865) : not practical: as **a** : not wise to put into or keep in practice or effect **b** : incapable of dealing sensibly or prudently with practical matters **c** : IMPRACTICABLE **d** : IDEALISTIC — **im·prac·ti·cal·i·ty** \-ˌprak-ti-ˈka-lə-tē\ *n* — **im·prac·ti·cal·ly** \-ˈprak-ti-k(ə-)lē\ *adv*

im·pre·cate \ˈim-pri-ˌkāt\ *vb* **-cat·ed; -cat·ing** [L *imprecatus*, pp. of *imprecari*, fr. *in-* + *precari* to pray — more at PRAY] *vt* (1613) : to invoke evil on : CURSE ~ *vi* : to utter curses

im·pre·ca·tion \ˌim-pri-ˈkā-shən\ *n* (15c) **1** : CURSE **2** : the act of imprecating — **im·pre·ca·to·ry** \ˈim-pri-kə-ˌtōr-ē, im-ˈpre-kə-, -ˌtȯr-\ *adj*

im·pre·cise \ˌim-pri-ˈsīs\ *adj* (1805) : not precise : INEXACT, VAGUE — **im·pre·cise·ly** *adv* — **im·pre·cise·ness** *n* — **im·pre·ci·sion** \-ˈsi-zhən\ *n*

im·preg·na·ble \im-ˈpreg-nə-bəl\ *adj* [ME *imprenable*, fr. MF, fr. *in-* + *prenable* vulnerable to capture, fr. *prendre* to take — more at PRIZE] (15c) **1** : incapable of being taken by assault : UNCONQUERABLE **2** : UNASSAILABLE; *also* : IMPENETRABLE — **im·preg·na·bil·i·ty** \(ˌ)im-ˌpreg-nə-ˈbi-lə-tē\ *n* — **im·preg·na·ble·ness** \im-ˈpreg-nə-bəl-nəs\ *n* — **im·preg·na·bly** \-blē\ *adv*

im·preg·nant \im-ˈpreg-nənt\ *n* (1926) : a substance used for impregnating another substance

¹im·preg·nate \im-ˈpreg-ˌnāt, ˈim-\ *vt* **-nat·ed; -nat·ing** [LL *impraegnatus*, pp. of *impraegnare*, fr. L *in-* + *praegnas* pregnant] (1605) **1 a** : to cause to be filled, imbued, permeated, or saturated **b** : to permeate thoroughly **2** : to make pregnant : FERTILIZE *syn* see SOAK — **im·preg·na·tion** \(ˌ)im-ˌpreg-ˈnā-shən\ *n* — **im·preg·na·tor** \im-ˈpreg-ˌnā-tər, ˈim-\ *n*

²im·preg·nate \im-ˈpreg-nət\ *adj* (1646) : being filled or saturated

im·pre·sa \im-ˈprā-zə, -sə\ *n* [It, lit., undertaking] (1588) : a device with a motto used in the 16th and 17th centuries; *broadly* : EMBLEM

im·pre·sa·rio \ˌim-prə-ˈsär-ē-ˌō, -ˈsar-, -ˈzär-\ *n*, *pl* **-ri·os** [It, fr. *impresa* undertaking, fr. *imprendere* to undertake, fr. (assumed) VL *imprehendere* — more at EMPRISE] (1746) **1** : the promoter, manager, or conductor of an opera or concert company **2** : a person who puts on or

sponsors an entertainment (as a television show or sports event) **3** : MANAGER, DIRECTOR

¹im·press \im-ˈpres\ *vb* [ME, fr. L *impressus*, pp. of *imprimere*, fr. *in-* + *premere* to press — more at PRESS] *vt* (14c) **1 a** : to apply with pressure so as to imprint **b** : to produce (as a mark) by pressure **c** : to mark by or as if by pressure or stamping **2 a** : to produce a vivid impression of **b** : to affect esp. forcibly or deeply : INFLUENCE **3** : TRANSFER, TRANSMIT ~ *vi* : to produce an impression *syn* see AFFECT — **im·press·ibil·i·ty** \-ˌpre-sə-ˈbi-lə-tē\ *n* — **im·press·ible** \-ˈpre-sə-bəl\ *adj*

²im·press \ˈim-ˌpres *also* im-ˈ\ *n* (1590) **1** : a characteristic or distinctive mark : STAMP ⟨the ~ of a fresh and vital intelligence is stamped ... in his work —Lytton Strachey⟩ **2** : IMPRESSION, EFFECT ⟨have an ~ on history⟩ **3** : the act of impressing **4 a** : a mark made by pressure : IMPRINT **b** : an image of something formed by or as if by pressure; *esp* : SEAL **c** : a product of pressure or influence

³im·press \im-ˈpres\ *vt* [²*in-* + ³*press*] (1596) **1** : to levy or take by force for public service; *esp* : to force into naval service **2 a** : to procure or enlist by forcible persuasion **b** : FORCE ⟨~ed him into a white coat for the Christmas festivities —Nancy Hale⟩

⁴im·press \ˈim-ˌpres *also* im-ˈ\ *n* (1602) : IMPRESSMENT

im·pres·sion \im-ˈpre-shən\ *n* (14c) **1 a** : a characteristic, trait, or feature resulting from some influence ⟨the ~ on behavior produced by the social milieu⟩ **b** : an effect of alteration or improvement ⟨the settlement left little ~ on the wilderness⟩ **c** : a telling image impressed on the senses or the mind **2** : the effect produced by impressing: as **a** : a stamp, form, or figure resulting from physical contact **b** : an imprint of the teeth and adjacent portions of the jaw for use in dentistry **c** : an esp. marked and often favorable influence or effect on feeling, sense, or mind **3** : the act of impressing: as **a** : affecting by stamping or pressing **b** : a communicating of a mold, trait, or character by an external force or influence **4 a** : the amount of pressure with which an inked printing surface deposits its ink on the paper **b** : one instance of the meeting of a printing surface and the material being printed; *also* : a single print or copy so made **c** : all the copies (as of a book) printed in one continuous operation from a single makeready **5** : an often indistinct or imprecise notion or remembrance **6 a** : the first coat of color in painting **b** : a coat of paint for ornament or preservation **7** : an imitation or representation of salient features in an artistic or theatrical medium; *esp* : an imitation in caricature of a noted personality as a form of theatrical entertainment *syn* see IDEA

im·pres·sion·able \im-ˈpre-sh(ə-)nə-bəl\ *adj* (1836) : capable of being easily impressed — **im·pres·sion·abil·i·ty** \-ˌpre-sh(ə-)nə-ˈbi-lə-tē\ *n*

im·pres·sion·ism \im-ˈpre-shə-ˌni-zəm\ *n* (1882) **1** *often cap* : a theory or practice in painting esp. among French painters of about 1870 of depicting the natural appearances of objects by means of dabs or strokes of primary unmixed colors in order to simulate actual reflected light **2 a** : the depiction (as in literature) of scene, emotion, or character by details intended to achieve a vividness or effectiveness more by evoking subjective and sensory impressions than by recreating an objective reality **b** : a style of musical composition designed to create subtle moods and impressions

im·pres·sion·ist \im-ˈpre-sh(ə-)nist\ *n* (1876) **1** *often cap* : one (as a painter) who practices or adheres to the theories of impressionism **2** : an entertainer who does impressions

im·pres·sion·is·tic \(ˌ)im-ˌpre-shə-ˈnis-tik\ *adj* (1886) **1** *or* **im·pres·sion·ist** \im-ˈpre-sh(ə-)nist\ *often cap* : of, relating to, or constituting impressionism **2** : based on or involving impression as distinct from expertise or fact ⟨intuitions and ~ anecdotal accounts —Sidney Hook⟩ — **im·pres·sion·is·ti·cal·ly** \(ˌ)im-ˌpre-shə-ˈnis-ti-k(ə-)lē\ *adv*

im·pres·sive \im-ˈpre-siv\ *adj* (1598) : making or tending to make a marked impression : having the power to excite attention, awe, or admiration *syn* see MOVING — **im·pres·sive·ly** *adv* — **im·pres·sive·ness** *n*

im·press·ment \im-ˈpres-mənt\ *n* (1787) : the act of seizing for public use or of impressing into public service

im·pres·sure \im-ˈpre-shər\ *n* (1600) *archaic* : a mark made by pressure : IMPRESSION

im·prest \ˈim-ˌprest\ *n* [obs. *imprest* to lend, prob. fr. It *imprestare*] (1568) : a loan or advance of money

im·pri·ma·tur \ˌim-prə-ˈmä-ˌtùr, im-ˈpri-mə-ˌtùr, -ˌtyùr\ *n* [NL, let it be printed, fr. *imprimere* to print, fr. L, to imprint, impress — more at IMPRESS] (1640) **1 a** : a license to print or publish esp. by Roman Catholic episcopal authority **b** : approval of a publication under circumstances of official censorship **2 a** : SANCTION, APPROVAL **b** : IMPRINT **c** : a mark of approval or distinction

im·pri·mis \im-ˈprī-məs, -ˈprē-\ *adv* [ME *imprimis*, fr. L *in primis* among the first (things)] (15c) : in the first place — used to introduce a list of items or considerations

¹im·print \im-ˈprint, ˈim-ˌ\ *vt* (14c) **1** : to mark by or as if by pressure : IMPRESS **2 a** : to fix indelibly or permanently (as on the memory) **b** : to subject to or induce by imprinting ⟨an ~ed preference⟩ ~ *vi* : to undergo imprinting — **im·print·er** \-ˈprin-tər, -ˌprin-\ *n*

²im·print \ˈim-ˌprint\ *n* [ME *enprent*, fr. MF *empreinte*, fr. fem. of *empreint*, pp. of *empreindre* to imprint, fr. L *imprimere*] (15c) : something imprinted or printed: as **a** : a mark or depression made by pressure ⟨the fossil ~ of a dinosaur's foot⟩ **b** : an identifying name (as of a publisher) placed conspicuously on a product; *also* : the name under which a publisher issues books **c** : an indelible distinguishing effect or influence

im·print·ing \ˈim-ˌprin-tiŋ, im-ˈ\ *n* (1937) : a rapid learning process that takes place early in the life of a social animal (as a greylag goose) and establishes a behavior pattern (as recognition of and attraction to its own kind or a substitute)

im·pris·on \im-ˈpri-zᵊn\ *vt* [ME, fr. OF *emprisoner*, fr. *en-* + *prison* prison] (14c) : to put in or as if in prison : CONFINE — **im·pris·on·ment** \-mənt\ *n*

im·prob·a·ble \(ˌ)im-ˈprä-bə-bəl, -ˈpräb-bəl\ *adj* [MF or L; MF, fr. L *improbabilis*, fr. *in-* + *probabilis* probable] (1598) : unlikely to be true or to occur; *also* : unlikely but real or true — **im·prob·a·bil·i·ty** \-ˌprä-bə-ˈbi-lə-tē\ *n* — **im·prob·a·bly** \-ˈprä-bə-blē, -ˈpräb-blē\ *adv*

¹im·promp·tu \im-ˈpräm(p)-(ˌ)tü, -(ˌ)tyü\ *n* [F, fr. *impromptu* extemporaneously, fr. L *in promptu* in readiness] (1683) **1** : something that is impromptu **2** : a musical composition suggesting improvisation

²im·promp·tu *adj* (1764) **1** : made, done, or formed on or as if on the spur of the moment : IMPROVISED **2** : composed or uttered without previous preparation : EXTEMPORANEOUS — **impromptu** *adv*

im·prop·er \(ˌ)im-ˈprä-pər\ *adj* [ME, fr. MF *impropre*, fr. L *improprius*, fr. *in-* + *proprius* proper] (15c) : not proper: as **a** : not in accord with fact, truth, or right procedure : INCORRECT ⟨∼ inference⟩ **b** : not regularly or normally formed or not properly so called **c** : not suited to the circumstances, design, or end ⟨∼ medicine⟩ **d** : not in accord with propriety, modesty, good manners, or good taste *syn* see INDECOROUS — **im·prop·er·ly** *adv* — **im·prop·er·ness** *n*

improper fraction *n* (1542) : a fraction whose numerator is equal to, larger than, or of equal or higher degree than the denominator

improper integral *n* (ca. 1942) : a definite integral whose region of integration is unbounded or includes a point at which the integrand is undefined or tends to infinity

im·pro·pri·e·ty \ˌim-p(r)ə-ˈprī-ə-tē\ *n, pl* **-ties** [F or LL; F *impropriété*, fr. LL *improprietat-*, *improprietas*, fr. L *improprius*] (1607) **1** : an improper or indecorous act or remark; *esp* : an unacceptable use of a word or of language **2** : the quality or state of being improper

im·prove \im-ˈprüv\ *vb* **im·proved; im·prov·ing** [AF *emprouer* to invest profitably, fr. OF *en-* + *prou* advantage, fr. LL *prode* — more at PROUD] *vt* (ca. 1529) **1** *archaic* : EMPLOY, USE **2 a** : to enhance in value or quality : make better **b** : to increase the value of (land or property) by making it more useful for humans (as by cultivation or the erection of buildings) **c** : to grade and drain (a road) and apply surfacing material other than pavement **3** : to use to good purpose ∼ *vi* **1** : to advance or make progress in what is desirable **2** : to make useful additions or amendments — **im·prov·abil·i·ty** \(ˌ)im-ˌprü-və-ˈbi-lə-tē\ *n* — **im·prov·able** \-ˈprü-və-bəl\ *adj* — **im·prov·er** *n*

syn IMPROVE, BETTER, HELP, AMELIORATE mean to make more acceptable or to bring nearer to a standard. IMPROVE and BETTER are general and interchangeable and apply to what can be made better whether it is good or bad ⟨measures to further *improve* the quality of medical care⟩ ⟨immigrants hoping to *better* their lot⟩. HELP implies a bettering that still leaves room for improvement ⟨a coat of paint would *help* that house⟩. AMELIORATE implies making more tolerable or acceptable conditions that are hard to endure ⟨tried to *ameliorate* the lives of people in the tenements⟩.

im·prove·ment \im-ˈprüv-mənt\ *n* (ca. 1550) **1** : the act or process of improving **2 a** : the state of being improved; *esp* : enhanced value or excellence **b** : an instance of such improvement : something that enhances value or excellence

im·prov·i·dence \(ˌ)im-ˈprä-və-dən(t)s, -ˌden(t)s\ *n* (15c) : the quality or state of being improvident

im·prov·i·dent \-dənt, -ˌdent\ *adj* [LL *improvident-*, *improvidens*, fr. L *in-* + *provident-*, *providens* provident] (1624) : not provident : not foreseeing and providing for the future — **im·prov·i·dent·ly** *adv*

im·pro·vi·sa·tion \(ˌ)im-ˌprä-və-ˈzā-shən, ˌim-prə-və- also ˌim-prə-(ˌ)vī-\ *n* (1786) **1** : the act or art of improvising **2** : something (as a musical or dramatic composition) improvised — **im·pro·vi·sa·tion·al** \-shnəl, -shə-nᵊl\ *adj* — **im·pro·vi·sa·tion·al·ly** *adv*

im·pro·vi·sa·tor \im-ˈprä-və-ˌzā-tər\ *n* (1795) : one that improvises — **im·prov·i·sa·to·ri·al** \(ˌ)im-ˌprä-və-zə-ˈtōr-ē-əl, -ˈtȯr-\ *adj* — **im·pro·vi·sa·to·ry** \im-ˈprä-və-zə-ˌtōr-ē, ˌim-prə-ˈvī-zə-, -ˌtȯr-\ *adj*

im·pro·vi·sa·to·re \(ˌ)im-ˌprä-və-zə-ˈtōr-ē, ˌim-prə-ˌvē-zə-, -ˈtȯr-\ *n, pl* **-to·ri** \-ˈtōr-ē, -ˈtȯr-\ *or* **-tores** [It *improvvisatore*, fr. *improvvisare*] (1765) : one that improvises (as verse) usu. extemporaneously

im·pro·vise \ˈim-prə-ˌvīz *also* ˌim-prə-ˈ\ *vb* **-vised; -vis·ing** [F *improviser*, It. *improvvisare*, fr. *improvviso* sudden, fr. L *improvisus*, lit., unforeseen, fr. *in-* + *provisus*, pp. of *providēre* to see ahead — more at PROVIDE] *vt* (1826) **1** : to compose, recite, play, or sing extemporaneously **2** : to make, invent, or arrange offhand **3** : to fabricate out of what is conveniently on hand ∼ *vi* : to improvise something — **im·pro·vis·er** *or* **im·pro·vi·sor** \-ˌvī-zər, -ˈvī-\ *n*

im·pru·dence \(ˌ)im-ˈprü-dᵊn(t)s\ *n* (15c) **1** : the quality or state of being imprudent **2** : an imprudent act

im·pru·dent \-dᵊnt\ *adj* [ME, fr. L *imprudent-*, *imprudens*, fr. *in-* + *prudent-*, *prudens* prudent] (14c) : not prudent : lacking discretion — **im·pru·dent·ly** *adv*

im·pu·dence \ˈim-pyə-dən(t)s\ *n* (14c) : the quality or state of being impudent

im·pu·dent \-dənt\ *adj* [ME, fr. L *impudent-*, *impudens*, fr. *in-* + *pudent-*, *pudens*, prp. of *pudēre* to feel shame] (14c) **1** *obs* : lacking modesty **2** : marked by contemptuous or cocky boldness or disregard of others : INSOLENT — **im·pu·dent·ly** *adv*

im·pu·dic·i·ty \ˌim-pyü-ˈdi-sə-tē\ *n* [MF *impudicité*, fr. L *impudicus* immodest, fr. *in-* + *pudicus* modest, fr. *pudēre*] (1528) : lack of modesty : SHAMELESSNESS

im·pugn \im-ˈpyün\ *vt* [ME, to assail, fr. MF *impugner*, fr. L *inpugnare*, fr. *in-* + *pugnare* to fight — more at PUNGENT] (14c) **1** : to assail by words or arguments : oppose or attack as false or lacking integrity **2** *obs* : ASSAIL **b** : RESIST — **im·pugn·able** \-ˈpyü-nə-bəl\ *adj* — **im·pugn·er** \-nər\ *n*

im·pu·is·sance \(ˌ)im-ˈpwi-sᵊn(t)s, (ˌ)im-ˈpyü-ə-sən(t)s; ˌim-pyü-ˈi-sᵊn(t)s\ *n* [ME, fr. MF, fr. *in-* + *puissance* puissance, power] (15c) : WEAKNESS, POWERLESSNESS

im·pu·is·sant \-sᵊnt, -sᵊnt\ *adj* [F] (1629) : WEAK, POWERLESS

¹im·pulse \ˈim-ˌpəls, im-ˈ\ *vt* **im·pulsed; im·puls·ing** (1611) : to give an impulse to

²im·pulse \ˈim-ˌpəls\ *n* [L *impulsus*, fr. *impellere* to impel] (1647) **1 a** : INSPIRATION, MOTIVATION **b** : a force so communicated as to produce motion suddenly ⟨∼ to⟩ : INCENTIVE **2 a** : the act of driving onward with sudden force : IMPULSION **b** : motion produced by such an impulse : IMPETUS **c** : a wave of excitation transmitted through tissues and esp. nerve fibers and muscles that results in physiological activity or inhibition **3 a** : a sudden spontaneous inclination or incitement to some usu. unpremeditated action **b** : a propensity or natural tendency usu. other than rational **4 a** : the product of the average value of a force and the time during which it acts : the change in momentum produced by the force **b** : PULSE 4a *syn* see MOTIVE

im·pul·sion \im-ˈpəl-shən\ *n* (15c) **1 a** : the act of impelling : the state of being impelled **b** : an impelling force **c** : an onward tendency derived from an impulsion **2** : IMPULSE 3a **3** : COMPULSION 2

im·pul·sive \im-ˈpəl-siv\ *adj* (15c) **1** : having the power of or actually driving or impelling **2** : actuated by or prone to act on impulse **3** : acting momentarily *syn* see SPONTANEOUS — **im·pul·sive·ly** *adv* — **im·pul·sive·ness** *n* — **im·pul·siv·i·ty** \-ˌpəl-ˈsi-və-tē\ *n*

im·pu·ni·ty \im-ˈpyü-nə-tē\ *n* [MF or L; MF *impunité*, fr. L *impunitat-*, *impunitas*, fr. *impune* without punishment, fr. *in-* + *poena* punishment — more at PAIN] (1532) : exemption or freedom from punishment, harm, or loss

im·pure \(ˌ)im-ˈpyu̇r\ *adj* [ME, fr. MF & L; MF, fr. L *impurus*, fr. *in-* + *purus* pure] (15c) : not pure: as **a** : LEWD, UNCHASTE **b** : containing something unclean : FOUL ⟨∼ water⟩ **c** : ritually unclean **d** : mixed or impregnated with an extraneous and usu. unwanted substance ⟨an ∼ chemical⟩ — **im·pure·ly** *adv* — **im·pure·ness** *n*

im·pu·ri·ty \(ˌ)im-ˈpyu̇r-ə-tē\ *n, pl* **-ties** (15c) **1** : something that is impure or makes something else impure **2** : the quality or state of being impure

im·pu·ta·tion \ˌim-pyə-ˈtā-shən\ *n* (1581) **1** : the act of imputing: as **a** : ATTRIBUTION, ASCRIPTION **b** : ACCUSATION **c** : INSINUATION **2** : something imputed — **im·pu·ta·tive** \im-ˈpyü-tə-tiv\ *adj* — **im·pu·ta·tive·ly** *adv*

im·pute \im-ˈpyüt\ *vt* **im·put·ed; im·put·ing** [ME *inputen*, fr. L *imputare*, fr. *in-* + *putare* to consider] (14c) **1** : to lay the responsibility or blame for often falsely or unjustly **2** : to credit to a person or a cause : ATTRIBUTE ⟨our vices as well as our virtues have been *imputed* to bodily derangement —B. N. Cardozo⟩ *syn* see ASCRIBE — **im·put·abil·i·ty** \-ˌpyü-tə-ˈbi-lə-tē\ *n* — **im·put·able** \-ˈpyü-tə-bəl\ *adj*

¹in \ˈin, ən, ᵊn\ *prep* [ME, fr. OE; akin to OHG *in* in, L *in*, Gk *en*] (bef. 12c) **1 a** — used as a function word to indicate inclusion, location, or position within limits ⟨∼ the lake⟩ ⟨wounded ∼ the leg⟩ ⟨∼ the summer⟩ **b** : INTO 1 ⟨went ∼ the house⟩ **2** — used as a function word to indicate means, medium, or instrumentality ⟨written ∼ pencil⟩ ⟨bound ∼ leather⟩ **3 a** — used as a function word to indicate limitation, qualification, or circumstance ⟨alike ∼ some respects⟩ ⟨left ∼ a hurry⟩ **b** : INTO 2a ⟨broke ∼ pieces⟩ **4** — used as a function word to indicate purpose ⟨said ∼ reply⟩ **5** — used as a function word to indicate the larger member of a ratio ⟨one ∼ six is eligible⟩

²in \ˈin\ *adv* (bef. 12c) **1 a** (1) : to or toward the inside esp. of a house or other building ⟨come ∼⟩ (2) : to or toward some destination or particular place ⟨flew ∼ on the first plane⟩ (3) : at close quarters : NEAR ⟨play close ∼⟩ **b** : so as to incorporate ⟨mix ∼ the flour⟩ — often used in combination ⟨built-*in* bookcases⟩ **c** : to or at an appropriate place ⟨fit a piece ∼⟩ **2 a** : within a particular place; *esp* : within the customary place of residence or business ⟨the doctor is ∼⟩ **b** : in the position of participant, insider, or officeholder — often used with *on* ⟨∼ on the joke⟩ **c** (1) : on good terms (2) : in a specified relation ⟨∼ bad with the boss⟩ (3) : in a position of assured or definitive success **d** : in vogue or season **e** *of an oil well* : in production **f** : in one's presence, possession, or control ⟨after the crops are ∼⟩ **g** : from a condition of indistinguishability to one of clarity ⟨fade ∼⟩ — **in for** : certain to experience ⟨*in for* a rude awakening⟩

³in \ˈin\ *adj* (1599) **1 a** : that is located inside or within ⟨the ∼ part⟩ **b** : that is in position, operation, or power ⟨the ∼ party⟩ **c** : INSIDE 2 **2** : that is directed or bound inward : INCOMING ⟨the ∼ train⟩ **3 a** : extremely fashionable ⟨the ∼ thing to do⟩ **b** : keenly aware of and responsive to what is new and smart ⟨the ∼ crowd⟩

⁴in \ˈin\ *n* (1764) **1** : one who is in office or power or on the inside ⟨a matter of ∼s versus outs⟩ **2** : INFLUENCE, PULL ⟨enjoyed some sort of ∼ with the commandant —Henriette Roosenburg⟩

¹in- *or* il- *or* im- *or* ir- *prefix* [ME, fr. MF, fr. L; akin to OE *un-*] : not : NON-, UN- — usu. il- before *l* ⟨*illogical*⟩, im- before *b, m,* or *p* ⟨*imbalance*⟩ ⟨*immoral*⟩ ⟨*impractical*⟩, ir- before *r* ⟨*irreducible*⟩, and in- before other sounds ⟨*inconclusive*⟩

²in- *or* il- *or* im- *or* ir- *prefix* [ME, fr. MF, fr. L, fr. *in* in, into] **1** : in : within : into : toward : on — usu. il- before *l* ⟨*illuviation*⟩, im- before *b, m,* or *p* ⟨*immingle*⟩, ir- before *r* ⟨*irradiance*⟩, and in- before other sounds ⟨*infiltrate*⟩ **2** : ¹EN- ⟨*imbrute*⟩ ⟨*imperil*⟩ ⟨*inspirit*⟩

¹-in *n suffix* [F *-ine*, fr. L *-ina*, fem. of *-īnus* of or belonging to — more at -EN] **1 a** : neutral chemical compound ⟨*piperine*⟩ **b** : enzyme ⟨*pancreatin*⟩ **c** : antibiotic ⟨*penicillin*⟩ **2** : ²INE 1a, b ⟨*epinephrin*⟩ **3** : pharmaceutical product ⟨*niacin*⟩

²-in *comb form* [*sit-in*] : organized public protest by means of or in favor of : demonstration ⟨*teach-in*⟩ ⟨*love-in*⟩

in·abil·i·ty \ˌi-nə-ˈbi-lə-tē\ *n* [ME *inabilite*, fr. MF *inhabilité*, fr. *in-* + *habilité* ability] (15c) : lack of sufficient power, resources, or capacity ⟨his ∼ to do math⟩

in ab·sen·tia \ˌin-ab-ˈsen(t)-sh(ē-)ə\ *adv* [L] (1886) : in absence ⟨gave him the award *in absentia*⟩

in·ac·ces·si·ble \ˌi-nik-ˈse-sə-bəl, ˌ(ˌ)i-ˌnak-\ *adj* [ME, fr. MF or LL; MF, fr. LL *inaccessibilis*, fr. L *in-* + LL *accessibilis* accessible] (15c) : not accessible — **in·ac·ces·si·bil·i·ty** \-ˌse-sə-ˈbi-lə-tē\ *n* — **in·ac·ces·si·bly** \-ˈse-sə-blē\ *adv*

in·ac·cu·ra·cy \(ˌ)i-ˈna-kyə-rə-sē, -k(ə-)rə-sē\ *n, pl* **-cies** (ca. 1755) **1** : the quality or state of being inaccurate **2** : MISTAKE, ERROR

in·ac·cu·rate \i-ˈna-kyə-rət, -k(ə-)rət\ *adj* (1738) : not accurate : FAULTY — **in·ac·cu·rate·ly** \-kyə-rət-lē, -k(ə-)rət-, -kyərt-\ *adv*

in·ac·tion \(ˌ)i-ˈnak-shən\ *n* (1707) : lack of action or activity : IDLENESS

in·ac·ti·vate \(ˌ)i-ˈnak-tə-ˌvāt\ *vt* (1906) : to make inactive — **in·ac·ti·va·tion** \-ˌnak-tə-ˈvā-shən\ *n*

in·ac·tive \(ˌ)i-ˈnak-tiv\ *adj* (1664) : not active: as **a** (1) : SEDENTARY (2) : INDOLENT, SLUGGISH **b** (1) : being out of use (2) : relating to or being members of the armed forces who are not performing or available for military duties ⟨*of a disease* : QUIESCENT **c** (1) : chemically inert (2) : optically neutral in polarized light **d** : biologically inert esp. because of the loss of some quality (as infectivity or antigenicity) — **in·ac·tive·ly** *adv* — **in·ac·tiv·i·ty** \-ˌnak-ˈti-və-tē\ *n*

syn INACTIVE, IDLE, INERT, PASSIVE, SUPINE mean not engaged in work or activity. INACTIVE applies to anyone or anything not in action or in

\ə\ abut \ᵊ\ kitten, F table \ər\ further \a\ ash \ā\ ace \ä\ mop, mar \au̇\ out \ch\ chin \e\ bet \ē\ easy \g\ go \i\ hit \ī\ ice \j\ job \ŋ\ sing \ō\ go \ȯ\ law \ȯi\ boy \th\ thin \th̲\ the \ü\ loot \u̇\ foot \y\ yet \zh\ vision \à, k̲, ⁿ, œ, œ̄, ue, ūe, ᵞ\ *see* Guide to Pronunciation operation or at work ⟨on *inactive* status as an astronaut⟩ ⟨*inactive* accounts⟩. IDLE applies to persons that are not busy or occupied or to their powers or their implements ⟨workers were *idle* in the fields⟩. INERT as applied to things implies powerlessness to move or to affect other things; as applied to persons it suggests an inherent or habitual indisposition to activity ⟨*inert* ingredients in drugs⟩ ⟨an *inert* citizenry⟩. PASSIVE implies immobility or lack of normally expected response to an external force or influence and often suggests deliberate submissiveness or self-control ⟨*passive* resistance⟩. SUPINE applies only to persons and commonly implies abjectness or indolence ⟨a *supine* willingness to play the fool⟩.

in·ad·e·qua·cy \(,)i-'na-di-kwə-sē\ *n, pl* **-cies** (1787) **1** : the quality or state of being inadequate **2** : INSUFFICIENCY, DEFICIENCY

in·ad·e·quate \-kwət\ *adj* (1671) : not adequate : INSUFFICIENT; *also* : not capable — **in·ad·e·quate·ly** *adv* — **in·ad·e·quate·ness** *n*

in·ad·mis·si·ble \,i-nəd-'mi-sə-bəl\ *adj* (1776) : not admissible — **in·ad·mis·si·bil·i·ty** \-,mi-sə-'bi-lə-tē\ *n* — **in·ad·mis·si·bly** \-'mi-sə-blē\ *adv*

in·ad·ver·tence \,i-nəd-'vər-t²n(t)s\ *n* [ME, fr. ML *inadvertentia*, fr. L *in-* + *advertent-*, *advertens*, prp. of *advertere* to advert] (15c) **1** : the fact or action of being inadvertent **2** : a result of inattention : OVERSIGHT

in·ad·ver·ten·cy \-t²n(t)-sē\ *n, pl* **-cies** (1592) : INADVERTENCE

in·ad·ver·tent \-t²nt\ *adj* [back-formation fr. *inadvertence*] (1653) **1** : not focusing the mind on a matter : INATTENTIVE **2** : UNINTENTIONAL — **in·ad·ver·tent·ly** *adv*

in·ad·vis·able \,i-nəd-'vī-zə-bəl\ *adj* (1870) : not advisable — **in·ad·vis·abil·i·ty** \-,vī-zə-'bi-lə-tē\ *n*

-inae *n pl suffix* [NL *-inae*, fr. L, fem. pl. of *-īnus*] : members of the subfamily of — in all names of zoological subfamilies in recent classifications ⟨*Felinae*⟩

in·alien·able \(,)i-'nāl-yə-nə-bəl, -'nā-lē-ə-nə-\ *adj* [prob. fr. F *inaliénable*, fr. *in-* + *aliénable* alienable] (ca. 1645) : incapable of being alienated, surrendered, or transferred ⟨~ rights⟩ — **in·alien·abil·i·ty** \-,nāl-yə-nə-'bi-lə-tē, -,nā-lē-ə-nə-\ *n* — **in·alien·ably** \-'nāl-yə-nə-blē, -'nā-lē-ə-nə-\ *adv*

in·al·ter·able \(,)i-'nȯl-t(ə-)rə-bəl\ *adj* (1541) : not alterable : UNALTERABLE — **in·al·ter·abil·i·ty** \-,nȯl-t(ə-)rə-'bi-lə-tē\ *n* — **in·al·ter·able·ness** \-'nȯl-t(ə-)rə-bəl-nəs\ *n* — **in·al·ter·ably** \-blē\ *adv*

in·amo·ra·ta \i-,na-mə-'rä-tə\ *n* [It *innamorata*, fr. fem. of *innamorato*, pp. of *innamorare* to inspire with love, fr. *in-* (fr. L) + *amore* love, fr. L *amor* — more at AMOROUS] (1651) : a woman with whom one is in love or has intimate relations

in–and–in \,in-ən(d)-'in\ *adv or adj* (1765) : in repeated generations of the same or closely related stock ⟨families . . . of one blood through mating or marrying ~ —F. H. Giddings⟩ ⟨~ breeding⟩

¹**inane** \i-'nān\ *adj* **inan·er; -est** [L *inanis*] (1662) **1** : EMPTY, INSUBSTANTIAL **2** : lacking significance, meaning, or point : SILLY *syn* see INSIPID — **inane·ly** *adv* — **inane·ness** \-'nān-nəs\ *n*

²**inane** *n* (1677) : void or empty space ⟨a voyage into the limitless ~ — V. G. Childe⟩

in·an·i·mate \(,)i-'na-nə-mət\ *adj* [ME, fr. LL *inanimatus*, fr. L *in-* + *animatus*, pp. of *animare* to animate] (15c) **1** : not animate : **a** : not endowed with life or spirit **b** : lacking consciousness or power of motion **2** : not animated or lively : DULL — **in·an·i·mate·ly** *adv* — **in·an·i·mate·ness** *n*

in·a·ni·tion \,i-nə-'ni-shən\ *n* (14c) : the quality or state of being empty: **a** : the loss of vitality that results from lack of food and water **b** : the absence or loss of social, moral, or intellectual vitality or vigor

inan·i·ty \i-'na-nə-tē\ *n, pl* **-ties** (1603) **1** : the quality or state of being inane: as **a** : lack of substance : EMPTINESS **b** : vapid, pointless, or fatuous character : SHALLOWNESS **2** : something that is inane

in·ap·par·ent \,i-nə-'par-ənt, -'per-\ *adj* (1626) : not apparent — **in·ap·par·ent·ly** *adv*

in·ap·peas·able \,i-nə-'pē-zə-bəl\ *adj* (1803) : UNAPPEASABLE

in·ap·pe·tence \(,)i-'na-pə-tən(t)s\ *n* (ca. 1691) : loss or lack of appetite

in·ap·pli·ca·ble \(,)i-'na-pli-kə-bəl *also* ,i-nə-'pli-kə-\ *adj* (1656) : not applicable : IRRELEVANT ⟨~ ,na-pli-kə-'bi-lə-tē *also* ,i-nə-,pli-kə-\ *n* — **in·ap·pli·ca·bly** \(,)i-'na-pli-kə-blē *also* ,i-nə-'pli-kə-\ *adv*

in·ap·po·site \(,)i-'na-pə-zət\ *adj* (1661) : not apposite — **in·ap·po·site·ly** *adv* — **in·ap·po·site·ness** *n*

in·ap·pre·cia·ble \,i-nə-'prē-shə-bəl, -'pri-sh(ē-)ə-bəl\ *adj* [prob. fr. F *inappréciable*, fr. MF *inappreciable*, fr. *in-* + *appreciable*] (1802) : too small to be perceived — **in·ap·pre·cia·bly** \-blē\ *adv*

in·ap·pre·cia·tive \,i-nə-'prē-shə-tiv, -'pri- *also* -'prē-shē-,ā-\ *adj* (1869) : not appreciative — **in·ap·pre·cia·tive·ly** *adv* — **in·ap·pre·cia·tive·ness** *n*

in·ap·proach·able \,i-nə-'prō-chə-bəl\ *adj* (ca. 1828) : not approachable : INACCESSIBLE

in·ap·pro·pri·ate \,i-nə-'prō-prē-ət\ *adj* (1804) : not appropriate : UNSUITABLE — **in·ap·pro·pri·ate·ly** *adv* — **in·ap·pro·pri·ate·ness** *n*

in·apt \(,)i-'napt\ *adj* (ca. 1670) : not apt: **a** : not suitable **b** : INEPT — **in·apt·ly** \-lē\ *adv* — **in·apt·ness** \-nəs\ *n*

in·ap·ti·tude \(,)i-'nap-tə-,tüd, -,tyüd\ *n* (1620) : lack of aptitude

in·ar·gu·able \,i-,när-gyə-wə-bəl\ *adj* (ca. 1875) : not arguable — **in·ar·gu·ably** \-blē\ *adv*

in·ar·tic·u·la·cy \,i-(,)när-'ti-kyə-lə-sē\ *n* (1921) : the quality or state of being inarticulate

¹**in·ar·tic·u·late** \-kyə-lət\ *adj* [LL *inarticulatus*, fr. L *in-* + *articulatus*, pp. of *articulare* to utter distinctly — more at ARTICULATE] (1603) **1 a** *of a sound* : uttered or formed without the definite articulations of intelligible speech **b** (1) : incapable of speech esp. under stress of emotion : MUTE (2) : incapable of being expressed by speech ⟨~ fear⟩ (3) : not voiced or expressed : UNSPOKEN ⟨society functions on many ~ premises⟩ **2** : incapable of giving coherent, clear, or effective expression to one's ideas or feelings **3** [NL *inarticulatus*, fr. L *in-* + NL *articulatus* articulate] : relating to, characteristic of, or being an inarticulate or its shell — **in·ar·tic·u·late·ly** *adv* — **in·ar·tic·u·late·ness** *n*

²**inarticulate** *n* (1952) : any of a class (Inarticulata) of brachiopods lacking a hinge connecting the two shell valves

in·ar·tis·tic \,i-när-'tis-tik\ *adj* (1859) **1** : not conforming to the principles of art **2** : not appreciative of art — **in·ar·tis·ti·cal·ly** \-ti-k(ə-)lē\ *adv*

in·as·much as \,i-nəz-'mə-chəz, -'mach-,az\ *conj* (14c) **1** : in the degree that : INSOFAR AS **2** : in view of the fact that : SINCE

in·at·ten·tion \,i-nə-'ten(t)-shən\ *n* (ca. 1670) : failure to pay attention

in·at·ten·tive \-'ten-tiv\ *adj* (1692) : not attentive — **in·at·ten·tive·ly** *adv* — **in·at·ten·tive·ness** *n*

in·au·di·ble \(,)i-'nȯ-də-bəl\ *adj* [LL *inaudibilis*, fr. L *in-* + LL *audibilis* audible] (1601) : not audible — **in·au·di·bil·i·ty** \(,)i-,nȯ-də-'bi-lə-tē\ *n* — **in·au·di·bly** \(,)i-'nȯ-də-blē\ *adv*

¹**in·au·gu·ral** \i-'nȯ-gyə-rəl, -g(ə-)rəl\ *adj* (1689) **1** : of or relating to an inauguration **2** : marking a beginning : first in a projected series

²**inaugural** *n* (1832) **1** : an inaugural address **2** : INAUGURATION

in·au·gu·rate \i-'nȯ-gyə-,rāt, -gə-,rāt\ *vt* **-rat·ed; -rat·ing** [L *inauguratus*, pp. of *inaugurare* to practice augury, fr. *in-* + *augurare* to augur; fr. the rites connected with augury] (1606) **1** : to induct into an office with suitable ceremonies **2 a** : to dedicate ceremoniously : observe formally the beginning of **b** : to bring about the beginning of *syn* see BEGIN — **in·au·gu·ra·tor** \-,rā-tər\ *n*

in·au·gu·ra·tion \-,nȯ-gyə-'rā-shən, -gə-\ *n* (1569) : an act of inaugurating; *esp* : a ceremonial induction into office

Inauguration Day *n* (1829) : January 20 following a presidential election on which the president of the U.S. is inaugurated

in·aus·pi·cious \,i-,nȯ-'spi-shəs\ *adj* (1592) : not auspicious — **in·aus·pi·cious·ly** *adv* — **in·aus·pi·cious·ness** *n*

in·au·then·tic \,i-,nȯ-'then-tik\ *adj* (1860) : not authentic — **in·au·then·tic·i·ty** \,i-,nȯ-,then-'ti-sə-tē, -thən-\ *n*

in–be·tween \,i-bi-'twēn\ *adj or n* (1815) : INTERMEDIATE

in between *adv or prep* (1892) : BETWEEN

¹**in·board** \'in-,bȯrd, -,bȯrd\ *adv* (1830) **1** : inside the line of a ship's bulwarks or hull **2** : toward the center line of a vehicle or craft (as a ship or aircraft)

²**inboard** *adj* (1847) **1** : located inboard ⟨an ~ engine⟩ ⟨an ~ spoiler⟩ **2** *of a boat* : having an inboard engine

³**inboard** *n* (1950) : a boat with an inboard motor

in·born \'in-'bȯrn\ *adj* (1513) **1** : present from or as if from birth **2** : HEREDITARY, INHERITED *syn* see INNATE

in·bound \'in-,baȯnd\ *adj* (1894) : inward bound

in·bounds \'in-'baȯn(d)z\ *adj* (1968) : involving putting a basketball in play by passing it onto the court from out of bounds

inbounds line *n* (ca. 1961) : either of two broken lines running the length of a football field at right angles to the yard lines

in·breathe \'in-,brēth\ *vt* (14c) : to breathe (something) in : INHALE

in·bred \'in-'bred\ *adj* (ca. 1592) **1** : rooted and ingrained in one's nature as deeply as if implanted by heredity ⟨an ~ love of freedom⟩ **2** [fr. pp. of *inbreed*] : subjected to or produced by inbreeding *syn* see INNATE — **in·bred** \'in-,bred\ *n*

in·breed \'in-'brēd\ *vb* **-bred** \-'bred\; **-breed·ing** *vt* (1599) : to subject to inbreeding ~ *vi* : to engage in inbreeding

in·breed·ing \'in-,brē-diŋ\ *n* (ca. 1842) **1** : the interbreeding of closely related individuals esp. to preserve and fix desirable characters of and to eliminate unfavorable characters from a stock **2** : confinement to a narrow range or a local or limited field of choice

in·built \'in-'bilt\ *adj* (1923) *chiefly Brit* : BUILT-IN

In·ca \'iŋ-kə\ *n* [Sp, fr. Quechua *inka* ruler of the Inca empire] (1594) **1 a** : a member of the Quechuan peoples of Peru maintaining an empire until the Spanish conquest **b** : a king or noble of the Inca empire **2** : a member of any people under Inca influence — **In·ca·ic** \in-'kā-ik\ *adj* — **In·can** \'iŋ-kən\ *adj*

in·cal·cu·la·ble \(,)in-'kal-kyə-lə-bəl\ *adj* (1795) : not capable of being calculated: as **a** : very great **b** : not predictable : UNCERTAIN — **in·cal·cu·la·bil·i·ty** \-,kal-kyə-lə-'bi-lə-tē\ *n* — **in·cal·cu·la·bly** \-'kal-kyə-lə-blē\ *adv*

in·ca·les·cence \,in-kə-'le-s²n(t)s, ,iŋ-\ *n* [L *incalescere* to become warm, fr. *in-* + *calescere* to become warm, incho. of *calēre* to be warm — more at LEE] (1646) : a growing warm or ardent — **in·ca·les·cent** \-s²nt\ *adj*

in camera *adv* [NL, lit., in a chamber] (1882) : in private : SECRETLY

in·can·desce \,in-kən-'des *also* -(,)kan-\ *vi* **-desced; -desc·ing** [L *candescere*] (1874) : to be or become incandescent

in·can·des·cence \,in-kən-'de-s²n(t)s *also* -(,)kan-\ *n* (1656) : the quality or state of being incandescent; *esp* : emission by a hot body of radiation that makes it visible

in·can·des·cent \-s²nt\ *adj* [prob. fr. F, fr. L *incandescent-, incandescens*, prp. of *incandescere* to become hot, fr. *in-* + *candescere* to become hot, fr. *candēre* to glow — more at CANDID] (1794) **1 a** : white, glowing, or luminous with intense heat **b** : strikingly bright, radiant, or clear **c** : marked by brilliance esp. of expression ⟨~ wit⟩ **d** : characterized by glowing zeal : ARDENT ⟨~ affection⟩ **2 a** : of, relating to, or being light produced by incandescence **b** : producing light by incandescence — **in·can·des·cent·ly** *adv*

incandescent lamp *n* (1881) : an electric lamp in which a filament gives off light when heated to incandescence by an electric current — called also *incandescent, incandescent bulb, incandescent lightbulb, lightbulb*

in·cant \in-'kant\ *vi* [L *incantāre*] (1945) : RECITE, UTTER

in·can·ta·tion \,in-,kan-'tā-shən\ *n* [ME *incantacioun*, fr. MF *incantation*, fr. LL *incantation-, incantatio*, fr. L *incantare* to enchant — more at ENCHANT] (14c) : a use of spells or verbal charms spoken or sung as a part of a ritual of magic; *also* : a written or recited formula of words designed to produce a particular effect — **in·can·ta·tion·al** \-shnəl, -shə-n²l\ *adj* — **in·can·ta·to·ry** \in-'kan-tə-,tȯr-ē, -,tȯr-\ *adj*

in·ca·pa·ble \(,)in-'kā-pə-bəl\ *adj* [MF, fr. *in-* + *capable* capable] (1594) **1** : lacking capacity, ability, or qualification for the purpose or

incandescent lamp: *1* bulb containing gas, *2* filament, *3* connecting and supporting wires, *4* exhaust tube, *5* screw base, *6* base contact end in view: as **a** *archaic* : not able to take in, hold, or keep **b** *archaic* : not receptive **c** : not being in a state or of a kind to admit : INSUSCEPTIBLE **d** : not able or fit for the doing or performance : INCOMPETENT **2** : lacking legal qualification or power (as by reason of mental incompetence) : DISQUALIFIED — **in·ca·pa·bil·i·ty** \-₁kā-pə-'bi-lə-tē\ n — **in·ca·pa·ble·ness** \-'kā-pə-bəl-nəs\ n — **in·ca·pa·bly** \-blē\ adv

in·ca·pac·i·tate \₁in-kə-'pa-sə-₁tāt\ vt **-tat·ed; -tat·ing** (1657) **1** : to make legally incapable or ineligible **2** : to deprive of capacity or natural power : DISABLE — **in·ca·pac·i·ta·tion** \-₁pa-sə-'tā-shən\ n

in·ca·pac·i·ty \₁in-kə-'pa-sə-tē, -'pas-tē\ n, pl **-ties** [F incapacité, fr. MF, fr. in- + capacité capacity] (1611) : the quality or state of being incapable; esp : lack of physical or intellectual power or of natural or legal qualifications

in·car·cer·ate \in-'kär-sə-₁rāt\ vt **-at·ed; -at·ing** [L incarceratus, pp. of incarcerare, fr. in- + carcer prison] (1560) **1** : to put in prison **2** : to subject to confinement — **in·car·cer·a·tion** \(₁)in-₁kär-sə-'rā-shən\ n

in·car·di·na·tion \(₁)in-₁kär-dᵊn-'ā-shən\ n [LL incardination-, incardinatio, fr. incardinare to ordain as chief priest, fr. L in- ²in- + LL cardinalis principal — more at CARDINAL] (1897) : the formal acceptance by a diocese of a clergyman from another diocese

¹in·car·na·dine \in-'kär-nə-₁dīn, -₁dēn, -dən\ adj [MF incarnadin, fr. OIt incarnadino, fr. incarnato flesh-colored, fr. LL incarnatus] (1591) **1** : having the pinkish color of flesh **2** : RED; esp : BLOODRED

²incarnadine vt **-dined; -din·ing** (1605) : to make incarnadine : REDDEN

¹in·car·nate \in-'kär-nət, -₁nāt\ adj [ME incarnat, fr. LL incarnatus, pp. of incarnare to incarnate, fr. L in- + carn-, caro flesh — more at CARNAL] (14c) **1 a** : invested with bodily and esp. human nature and form **b** : made manifest or comprehensible : EMBODIED (a fiend ∼) **2** : INCARNADINE (∼ clover)

²in·car·nate \in-'kär-₁nāt, 'in-₁\ vt **-nat·ed; -nat·ing** (1533) **1** : to make incarnate: as **a** : to give bodily form and substance to **b** (1) : to give a concrete or actual form to : ACTUALIZE (2) : to constitute an embodiment or type of (no one culture ∼s every important human value — Denis Goulet)

in·car·na·tion \₁in-(₁)kär-'nā-shən\ n (14c) **1 a** (1) : the embodiment of a deity or spirit in some earthly form (2) cap : the union of divinity with humanity in Jesus Christ **b** : a concrete or actual form of a quality or concept; esp : a person showing a trait or typical character to a marked degree (she is the ∼ of goodness) **2** : the act of incarnating : the state of being incarnate **3** : a particular physical form or state : VERSION (in another ∼ he might be a first vice-president — Walter Teller) (TV and movie ∼s of the story)

in·case var of ENCASE

in case conj (14c) **1** : IF (in case we are surprised, keep by me — Washington Irving) **2** : as a precaution against the event that (carries a gun in case he is attacked)

in·cau·tion \(₁)in-'kȯ-shən\ n (ca. 1720) : lack of caution : HEEDLESSNESS

in·cau·tious \-shəs\ adj (ca. 1703) : lacking in caution : CARELESS — **in·cau·tious·ly** adv — **in·cau·tious·ness** n

in·cen·di·a·rism \in-'sen-dē-ə-₁ri-zəm\ n (ca. 1710) : incendiary action or behavior

¹in·cen·di·ary \in-'sen-dē-₁er-ē, -'sen-də-rē, -dyə-\ n, pl **-ar·ies** [ME, fr. L incendiarius, fr. incendium conflagration, fr. incendere] (15c) **1 a** : a person who deliberately sets fire to a building or other property **b** : an incendiary agent (as a bomb) **2** : a person who excites factions, quarrels, or sedition : AGITATOR

²incendiary adj (15c) **1** : of, relating to, or involving a deliberate burning of property **2** : tending to excite or inflame : INFLAMMATORY (∼ speeches) **3 a** : igniting combustible materials spontaneously **b** : of, relating to, or being a weapon (as a bomb) designed to start fires

¹in·cense \'in-₁sen(t)s\ n [ME encens, fr. OF, fr. LL incensum, fr. L, neut. of incensus, pp. of incendere to set on fire, fr. in- + -cendere to burn; akin to L candēre to glow — more at CANDID] (13c) **1** : material used to produce a fragrant odor when burned **2** : the perfume exhaled from some spices and gums when burned; broadly : a pleasing scent **3** : pleasing attention : FLATTERY

²incense vt **in·censed; in·cens·ing** (13c) **1** : to apply or offer incense to **2** : to perfume with incense

³in·cense \in-'sen(t)s\ vt **in·censed; in·cens·ing** [ME encensen, fr. MF incenser, fr. L incensus] (15c) **1** archaic : to cause (a passion or emotion) to become aroused **2** : to arouse the extreme anger or indignation of

in·cen·ter \'in-₁sen-tər\ n [inscribe + ¹center] (ca. 1890) : the single point in which the three bisectors of the interior angles of a triangle intersect and which is the center of the inscribed circle

in·cen·tive \in-'sen-tiv\ n [ME, fr. LL incentivum, fr. neut. of incentivus stimulating, fr. L, setting the tune, fr. incentus, pp. of incinere to set the tune, fr. in- + canere to sing — more at CHANT] (15c) : something that incites or has a tendency to incite to determination or action syn see MOTIVE — **incentive** adj

in·cep·tion \in-'sep-shən\ n [ME incepcion, fr. L inception-, inceptio, fr. incipere to begin, fr. in- + capere to take] (15c) : an act, process, or instance of beginning : COMMENCEMENT syn see ORIGIN

¹in·cep·tive \in-'sep-tiv\ n (1612) : an inchoative verb

²inceptive adj (1656) **1** : INCHOATIVE **2** : of or relating to a beginning — **in·cep·tive·ly** adv

in·cer·ti·tude \(₁)in-'sər-tə-₁tüd, -₁tyüd\ n [ME, fr. MF, fr. LL incertitudo, fr. L in- + LL certitudo certitude] (15c) : UNCERTAINTY: **a** : absence of assurance or confidence : DOUBT **b** : the quality or state of being unstable or insecure

in·ces·san·cy \(₁)in-'se-sᵊn(t)-sē\ n (1615) : the quality or state of being incessant

in·ces·sant \(₁)in-'se-sᵊnt\ adj [ME incessaunt, fr. LL incessant-, incessans, fr. L in- + cessant-, cessans, prp. of cessare to delay — more at CEASE] (15c) : continuing or following without interruption : UNCEASING syn see CONTINUAL — **in·ces·sant·ly** adv

in·cest \'in-₁sest\ n [ME, fr. L incestus sexual impurity, fr. incestus impure, fr. in- + castus pure — more at CASTE] (13c) : sexual intercourse between persons so closely related that they are forbidden by law to marry; also : the statutory crime of such a relationship

in·ces·tu·ous \in-'ses-chə-wəs, -'sesh-\ adj (1532) **1** : constituting or involving incest **2** : guilty of incest — **in·ces·tu·ous·ly** adv — **in·ces·tu·ous·ness** n

¹inch \'inch\ n [ME, fr. OE ynce, fr. L uncia — more at OUNCE] (bef. 12c) **1** : a unit of length equal to ¹/₃₆ yard — see WEIGHT table **2 a** : a small amount, distance, or degree (is like cutting a dog's tail off by ∼es —Milton Friedman) **3** pl : STATURE, HEIGHT **4 a** : a fall (as of rain or snow) sufficient to cover a surface or to fill a gauge to the depth of one inch **b** : a degree of atmospheric or other pressure sufficient to balance the weight of a column of liquid (as mercury) one inch high in a barometer or manometer — **every inch** : to the utmost degree (looks every inch a winner) — **within an inch of** : almost to the point of

²inch vi (1599) : to move by small degrees : progress slowly (the long line of people ∼ing up the stairs) ∼ vt : to cause to move slowly (sooner or later they begin ∼ing prices back up —Forbes)

³inch n [ME (Sc dial.), fr. ScGael innis] (15c) chiefly Scot : ISLAND

inched \'incht\ adj (1605) : measuring a specified number of inches

-inch·er \'in-chər\ n comb form : one that has a dimension of a specified number of inches (a four-incher)

inch-meal \'inch-₁mēl, -'mē(ə)l\ adv [¹inch + -meal (as in piecemeal)] (1530) : LITTLE BY LITTLE, GRADUALLY

in·cho·ate \in-'kō-ət, 'in-kə-₁wāt\ adj [L inchoatus, pp. of inchoare to start work on, perh. fr. in- + cohum part of a yoke to which the beam of a plow is fitted] (1534) : being only partly in existence or operation; esp : imperfectly formed or formulated : FORMLESS (misty, ∼ suspicions that all is not well with the nation —J. M. Perry) — **in·cho·ate·ly** adv — **in·cho·ate·ness** n

in·cho·a·tive \in-'kō-ə-tiv\ adj (ca. 1631) **1** : INITIAL, FORMATIVE (the ∼ stages) **2** : denoting the beginning of an action, state, or occurrence — used of verbs — **inchoative** n — **in·cho·a·tive·ly** adv

inch·worm \'inch-₁wərm\ n (ca. 1861) : LOOPER 1

in·ci·dence \'in(t)-sə-dən(t)s, -₁den(t)s\ n (1626) **1 a** : ANGLE OF INCIDENCE **b** : the arrival of something (as a projectile or a ray of light) at a surface **2 a** : an act or the fact or manner of falling upon or affecting : OCCURRENCE **b** : rate of occurrence or influence (a high ∼ of crime)

¹in·ci·dent \'in(t)-sə-dənt, -₁dent\ n [ME, fr. MF, fr. ML incident-, incidens, fr. L, prp. of incidere to fall into, fr. in- + cadere to fall — more at CHANCE] (15c) **1** : something dependent on or subordinate to something else of greater or principal importance **2 a** : an occurrence of an action or situation that is a separate unit of experience : HAPPENING **b** : an accompanying minor occurrence or condition : CONCOMITANT **3** : an action likely to lead to grave consequences esp. in diplomatic matters (a serious border ∼) syn see OCCURRENCE

²incident adj (15c) **1** : occurring or likely to occur esp. as a minor consequence or accompaniment (the confusion ∼ to moving day) **2** : dependent on or relating to another thing in law **3** : falling or striking on something (∼ light rays)

¹in·ci·den·tal \₁in(t)-sə-'den-tᵊl\ adj (1616) **1** : being likely to ensue as a chance or minor consequence (social obligations ∼ to the job) **2** : occurring merely by chance or without intention or calculation

²incidental n (1707) **1** pl : minor items (as of expense) that are not particularized **2** : something that is incidental

in·ci·den·tal·ly \-'den-tᵊl-ē, esp for 2 -'dent-lē\ adv (1665) **1** : in an incidental manner : not intentionally (the arrant nonsense of some of his statements is ∼ hilarious —John Lahr) **2** : by way of interjection or digression : by the way (fortunate in having a good teacher . . . — still living, ∼ —John Fischer)

incidental music n (1864) : descriptive music played during a play to project a mood or to accompany stage action

in·cin·er·ate \in-'si-nə-₁rāt\ vt **-at·ed; -at·ing** [ML incineratus, pp. of incinerare, fr. L in- + ciner-, cinis ashes; akin to Gk konis dust, ashes] (1555) : to cause to burn to ashes — **in·cin·er·a·tion** \-₁si-nə-'rā-shən\ n

in·cin·er·a·tor \in-'si-nə-₁rā-tər\ n (1883) : one that incinerates; esp : a furnace or a container for incinerating waste materials

in·cip·i·ence \in-'si-pē-ən(t)s\ n (ca. 1864) : INCIPIENCY

in·cip·i·en·cy \-ən(t)-sē\ n (1817) : the state or fact of being incipient : BEGINNING

in·cip·i·ent \-ənt\ adj [L incipient-, incipiens, prp. of incipere to begin — more at INCEPTION] (1669) : beginning to come into being or to become apparent (an ∼ solar system) (evidence of ∼ racial tension) — **in·cip·i·ent·ly** adv

in·ci·pit \'in(t)-sə-pət, 'iŋ-kə-₁pit; in-'si-pət, -'ki-\ n [L, it begins, fr. incipere] (1897) : the first part : BEGINNING; specif : the opening words of a text of a medieval manuscript or early printed book

in·ci·sal \in-'sī-zəl, -səl\ adj (1903) : of, relating to, involving, or being the cutting edge or surface of a tooth (as an incisor)

in·cise \in-'sīz, -'sīs\ vt **in·cised; in·cis·ing** [MF or L; MF inciser, fr. L incisus, pp. of incidere, fr. in- + caedere to cut] (1567) **1** : to cut into **2 a** : to carve figures, letters, or devices into : ENGRAVE **b** : to carve (as an inscription) into a surface

incised adj (15c) **1** : cut in : ENGRAVED; esp : decorated with incised figures **2** : having a margin that is deeply and sharply notched (an ∼ leaf)

in·ci·sion \in-'si-zhən\ n (14c) **1 a** : CUT, GASH; specif : a wound made esp. in surgery by incising the body **b** : a marginal notch (as in a leaf) **2** : an act of incising something **3** : the quality or state of being incisive

in·ci·sive \in-'sī-siv\ adj (ca. 1850) : impressively direct and decisive (as in manner or presentation) — **in·ci·sive·ly** adv — **in·ci·sive·ness** n

in·ci·sor \in-'sī-zər\ n (1666) : a front tooth typically adapted for cutting; esp : one of the cutting teeth in mammals located between the canines when canines are present — see TOOTH illustration

in·ci·ta·tion \₁in-₁sī-'tā-shən, ₁in(t)-sə-\ n (15c) **1** : an act of inciting : STIMULATION **2** : something that incites to action : INCENTIVE

\ə\ abut \ᵊ\ kitten, F table \ər\ further \a\ ash \ā\ ace \ä\ mop, mar \au̇\ out \ch\ chin \e\ bet \ē\ easy \g\ go \i\ hit \ī\ ice \j\ job \ŋ\ sing \ō\ go \ȯ\ law \ȯi\ boy \th\ thin \t͟h\ the \ü\ loot \u̇\ foot \y\ yet \zh\ vision \à, k̲, ⁿ, œ, œ̄, ᵫ, ᵫ̄, ʸ\ see Guide to Pronunciation

in·cite \in-'sīt\ *vt* **in·cit·ed; in·cit·ing** [MF *inciter,* fr. L *incitare,* fr. *in-* + *citare* to put in motion — more at CITE] (15c) : to move to action : stir up : spur on : urge on — **in·cit·ant** \-'sī-tⁿnt\ *n* — **in·cite·ment** \-'sīt-mənt\ *n* — **in·cit·er** *n*
syn INCITE, INSTIGATE, ABET, FOMENT mean to spur to action. INCITE stresses a stirring up and urging on, and may or may not imply initiating ⟨*inciting* a riot⟩. INSTIGATE definitely implies responsibility for initiating another's action and often connotes underhandedness or evil intention ⟨*instigated* a conspiracy⟩. ABET implies both assisting and encouraging ⟨*aiding* and *abetting* the enemy⟩. FOMENT implies persistence in goading ⟨*fomenting* rebellion⟩.
in·ci·vil·i·ty \in(t)-sə-'vi-lə-tē\ *n* [MF *incivilité,* fr. LL *incivilitat-, incivilitas,* fr. *incivilis,* fr. L *in-* + *civilis* civil] (1584) **1** : the quality or state of being uncivil **2** : a rude or discourteous act
in·clem·en·cy \(,)in-'kle-mən(t)-sē\ *n* (1559) : the quality or state of being inclement
in·clem·ent \(,)in-'kle-mənt, 'in-klə-\ *adj* [L *inclement-, inclemens,* fr. *in-* + *clement-, clemens* clement] (1621) : lacking mildness: as   **a** *archaic* : severe in temper or action : UNMERCIFUL   **b** : physically severe : STORMY ⟨~ weather⟩ — **in·clem·ent·ly** *adv*
in·clin·able \in-'klī-nə-bəl\ *adj* (15c) : having a tendency or inclination; *also* : disposed to favor or think well of
in·cli·na·tion \,in-klə-'nā-shən, ,iŋ-\ *n* (14c)   **1 a** *obs* : natural disposition : CHARACTER   **b** : a particular disposition of mind or character : PROPENSITY; *esp* : LIKING ⟨had little ~ for housekeeping⟩   **2** : an act or the action of bending or inclining: as   **a** : BOW, NOD   **b** : a tilting of something   **3 a** : a deviation from the true vertical or horizontal : SLANT; *also* : the degree of such deviation   **b** : an inclined surface : SLOPE   **c** (1) : the angle determined by two lines or planes   (2) : the angle made by a line with the x-axis measured counterclockwise from the positive direction of that axis ⟨the clutch has an ~ to slip⟩ — **in·cli·na·tion·al** \-shnəl, -shə-nⁿl\ *adj*
¹in·cline \in-'klīn\ *vb* **in·clined; in·clin·ing** [ME, fr. MF *incliner,* fr. L *inclinare,* fr. *in-* + *clinare* to lean — more at LEAN] *vi* (14c)   **1** : to bend the head or body forward : BOW   **2** : to lean, tend, or become drawn toward an opinion or course of conduct   **3** : to deviate from a line, direction, or course; *specif* : to deviate from the vertical or horizontal ~ *vt*   **1** : to cause to stoop or bow : BEND   **2** : to have influence on : PERSUADE ⟨his love of books *inclined* him toward a literary career⟩   **3** : to give a bend or slant to — **in·clin·er** *n*
syn INCLINE, BIAS, DISPOSE, PREDISPOSE mean to influence one to have or take an attitude toward something. INCLINE implies a tendency to favor one of two or more actions or conclusions ⟨I *incline* to agree⟩. BIAS suggests a settled and predictable leaning in one direction and connotes unfair prejudice ⟨the experience *biased* him against foreigners⟩. DISPOSE suggests an affecting of one's mood or temper so as to incline one toward something ⟨her nature *disposes* to trust others⟩. PREDISPOSE implies the operation of a disposing influence well in advance of the opportunity to manifest itself ⟨does fictional violence *predispose* them to accept real violence?⟩.
²in·cline \in-'klīn\ *n* (1846) : an inclined plane : GRADE, SLOPE
in·clined \in-'klīnd, 2 *also* 'in-\ *adj* (14c)   **1** : having inclination, disposition, or tendency   **2 a** : having a leaning or slope   **b** : making an angle with a line or plane
inclined plane *n* (1710) : a plane surface that makes an oblique angle with the plane of the horizon
in·clin·ing \in-'klī-niŋ\ *n* (14c)   **1** : INCLINATION   **2** *archaic* : PARTY, FOLLOWING
in·cli·nom·e·ter \,in-klə-'nä-mə-tər, ,iŋ-; ,in-,klī-\ *n* (1852) : an instrument for indicating the inclination to the horizontal of an axis (as of an airplane)
in·clip \in-'klip\ *vt* (1608) *archaic* : CLASP, ENCLOSE
inclose, inclosure *var of* ENCLOSE, ENCLOSURE
in·clude \in-'klüd\ *vt* **in·clud·ed; in·clud·ing** [ME, fr. L *includere,* fr. *in-* + *claudere* to close — more at CLOSE] (15c)   **1** : to shut up : EN-CLOSE   **2** : to take in or comprise as a part of a whole   **3** : to contain between or within ⟨two sides and the *included* angle⟩ — **in·clud·able** *or* **in·clud·ible** \-'klü-də-bəl\ *adj*
syn INCLUDE, COMPREHEND, EMBRACE, INVOLVE mean to contain within as part of the whole. INCLUDE suggests the containment of something as a constituent, component, or subordinate part of a larger whole ⟨the price of dinner *includes* dessert⟩. COMPREHEND implies that something comes within the scope of a statement or definition ⟨his system *comprehends* all history⟩. EMBRACE implies a gathering of separate items within a whole ⟨her faith *embraces* both Christian and non= Christian beliefs⟩. INVOLVE suggests inclusion by virtue of the nature of the whole, whether by being its natural or inevitable consequence ⟨the new job *involves* a lot of detail⟩.
in·clu·sion \in-'klü-zhən\ *n* [L *inclusion-, inclusio,* fr. *includere*] (1600)   **1** : the act of including : the state of being included   **2** : something that is included: as   **a** : a gaseous, liquid, or solid foreign body enclosed in a mass (as of a mineral)   **b** : a passive usu. temporary product of cell activity (as a starch grain) within the cytoplasm or nucleus   **3** : a relation between two classes that exists when all members of the first are also members of the second — compare MEMBERSHIP 3
inclusion body *n* (ca. 1919) : an inclusion, abnormal structure, or foreign cell within a cell; *specif* : an intracellular body that is characteristic of some virus diseases and that is the site of virus multiplication
in·clu·sive \in-'klü-siv, -ziv\ *adj* (15c)   **1** : comprehending stated limits or extremes ⟨from Monday to Friday ~⟩   **2 a** : broad in orientation or scope   **b** : covering or intended to cover all items, costs, or services — **in·clu·sive·ly** *adv* — **in·clu·sive·ness** *n*
inclusive disjunction *n* (1942) : a complex sentence in logic that is true when either or both of its constituent propositions are true — see TRUTH TABLE table
inclusive of *prep* (1709) : including or taking into account ⟨the cost of building *inclusive of* materials⟩
in·co·erc·ible \,in-kō-'ər-sə-bəl\ *adj* (1710) : incapable of being controlled, checked, or confined
in·cog·i·tant \in-'kä-jə-tənt\ *adj* [L *incogitant-, incogitans,* fr. *in-* + *cogitant-, cogitans,* prp. of *cogitare* to cogitate] (1628) : THOUGHTLESS, INCONSIDERATE

in·cog·ni·ta \,in-,käg-'nē-tə *also* in-'käg-nə-tə\ *adv or adj* [It, fem. of *incognito*] (1638) : INCOGNITO — used only of a woman — **incognita** *n*
¹in·cog·ni·to \,in-,käg-'nē-(,)tō *also* in-'käg-nə-,tō\ *adv or adj* [It, fr. L *incognitus* unknown, fr. *in-* + *cognitus,* pp. of *cognoscere* to know — more at COGNITION] (1635) : with one's identity concealed
²incognito *n, pl* **-tos** (1638)   **1** : one appearing or living incognito   **2** : the state or assumed identity of one living or traveling incognito or incognita
in·cog·ni·zant \(,)in-'käg-nə-zənt\ *adj* (1837) : lacking awareness or consciousness — **in·cog·ni·zance** \-zən(t)s\ *n*
in·co·her·ence \,in-kō-'hir-ən(t)s, -'her-\ *n* (1611)   **1** : the quality or state of being incoherent   **2** : something that is incoherent
in·co·her·ent \-ənt\ *adj* (1626)   **1** : lacking coherence: as   **a** : lacking cohesion : LOOSE   **b** : lacking orderly continuity, arrangement, or relevance : INCONSISTENT   **2** : lacking clarity or intelligibility : INCOMPRE-HENSIBLE — **in·co·her·ent·ly** *adv*
in·com·bus·ti·ble \,in-kəm-'bəs-tə-bəl\ *adj* [ME, prob. fr. MF, fr. *in-* + *combustible* combustible] (15c) : not combustible : incapable of being burned — **in·com·bus·ti·bil·i·ty** \-,bəs-tə-'bi-lə-tē\ *n* — **incombustible** *n*
in·come \'in-,kəm *also* 'in-kəm *or* 'iŋ-kəm\ *n* (14c)   **1** : a coming in : ENTRANCE, INFLUX ⟨fluctuations in the nutrient ~ of a body of water⟩   **2** : a gain or recurrent benefit usu. measured in money that derives from capital or labor; *also* : the amount of such gain received in a period of time ⟨has an ~ of $20,000 a year⟩
income account *n* (1869) : a financial statement of a business showing the details of revenues, costs, expenses, losses, and profits for a given period — called also *income statement*
income bond *n* (ca. 1864) : a bond that pays interest at a rate based on the issuer's earnings
income tax *n* (1799) : a tax on the net income of an individual or a business
¹in·com·ing \'in-,kə-miŋ\ *n* (14c)   **1** : the act of coming in : ARRIVAL   **2** : INCOME — usu. used in pl.
²incoming *adj* (1753)   **1** : coming in : ARRIVING ⟨an ~ ship⟩ ⟨~ mail⟩   **2** : taking a new place or position esp. as part of a succession ⟨the ~ president⟩   **3** : just starting or beginning ⟨the ~ year⟩
in·com·men·su·ra·ble \,in-kə-'men(t)s-rə-bəl, -'men(t)sh-; -'men(t)-sə-, -shə-\ *adj* (1570) : not commensurable; *broadly* : lacking a basis of comparison in respect to a quality normally subject to comparison — **in·com·men·su·ra·bil·i·ty** \-,men(t)s-rə-'bi-lə-tē, -,men(t)sh-; -,men(t)-sə-, -shə-\ *n* — **incommensurable** *n* — **in·com·men·su·ra·bly** \-'men(t)s-rə-blē, -'men(t)sh-; -'men(t)-sə-, -shə-\ *adv*
in·com·men·su·rate \-'men(t)s-rət, -'men(t)sh-; -'men(t)-sə-, -shə-\ *adj* (1650) : not commensurate: as   **a** : INCOMMENSURABLE   **b** : INADE-QUATE   **c** : DISPROPORTIONATE
in·com·mode \,in-kə-'mōd\ *vt* **-mod·ed; -mod·ing** [MF *incommoder,* fr. L *incommodare,* fr. *incommodus* inconvenient, fr. *in-* + *commodus* convenient — more at COMMODE] (1598) : to give inconvenience or distress to : DISTURB
in·com·mo·di·ous \,in-kə-'mō-dē-əs\ *adj* (1551) : not commodious : INCONVENIENT — **in·com·mo·di·ous·ly** *adv* — **in·com·mo·di·ous·ness** *n*
in·com·mod·i·ty \-'mä-də-tē\ *n* (15c) : a source of inconvenience : DISADVANTAGE
in·com·mu·ni·ca·ble \,in-kə-'myü-ni-kə-bəl\ *adj* [MF or LL; MF, fr. LL *incommunicabilis,* fr. L *in-* + LL *communicabilis* communicable] (1568) : not communicable: as   **a** : incapable of being communicated or imparted   **b** : UNCOMMUNICATIVE — **in·com·mu·ni·ca·bil·i·ty** \-,myü-ni-kə-'bi-lə-tē\ *n* — **in·com·mu·ni·ca·bly** \-'myü-ni-kə-blē\ *adv*
in·com·mu·ni·ca·do \-,myü-nə-'kä-(,)dō\ *adv or adj* [Sp *incomunicado,* fr. pp. of *incomunicar* to deprive of communication, fr. *in-* (fr. L) + *comunicar* to communicate, fr. L *communicare*] (1844) : without means of communication; *also* : in solitary confinement
in·com·mu·ni·ca·tive \-'myü-nə-,kā-tiv, -ni-kə-tiv\ *adj* (1670) : UN-COMMUNICATIVE
in·com·mut·able \,in-kə-'myü-tə-bəl\ *adj* [ME, fr. L *incommutabilis,* fr. *in-* + *commutabilis* commutable] (15c) : not commutable: as   **a** : not interchangeable   **b** : UNCHANGEABLE — **in·com·mut·ably** \-blē\ *adv*
in·com·pa·ra·ble \(,)in-'käm-p(ə-)rə-bəl, ÷,in-kəm-'par-ə-\ *adj* [ME, fr. MF, fr. L *incomparabilis,* fr. *in-* + *comparabilis* comparable] (15c)   **1** : eminent beyond comparison : MATCHLESS   **2** : not suitable for comparison — **in·com·pa·ra·bil·i·ty** \(,)in-,käm-p(ə-)rə-'bi-lə-tē, ÷,in-kəm-,par-ə-\ *n* — **in·com·pa·ra·bly** \(,)in-'käm-p(ə-)rə-blē, ÷,in-kəm-'par-ə-\ *adv*
in·com·pat·i·bil·i·ty \,in-kəm-,pa-tə-'bi-lə-tē\ *n, pl* **-ties** (1611)   **1 a** : the quality or state of being incompatible   **b** : lack of interfertility between two plants   **2** *pl* : mutually antagonistic things or qualities
in·com·pat·i·ble \,in-kəm-'pa-tə-bəl\ *adj* [ME, fr. MF & ML; MF, fr. ML *incompatibilis,* fr. L *in-* + ML *compatibilis* compatible] (15c)   **1** : incapable of being held by one person at one time — used of offices that make conflicting demands on the holder   **2** : not compatible: as   **a** : incapable of association or harmonious coexistence ⟨~ colors⟩   **b** : unsuitable for use together because of undesirable chemical or physiological effects ⟨~ drugs⟩   **c** : not both true ⟨~ propositions⟩   **d** : incapable of blending into a stable homogeneous mixture — **incompatible** *n* — **in·com·pat·i·bly** \-blē\ *adv*
in·com·pe·tence \(,)in-'käm-pə-tən(t)s\ *n* (1663) : the state or fact of being incompetent
in·com·pe·ten·cy \-tən-sē\ *n* (1611) : INCOMPETENCE
in·com·pe·tent \(,)in-'käm-pə-tənt\ *adj* [MF *incompétent,* fr. *in-* + *compétent* competent] (1597)   **1** : not legally qualified   **2** : inadequate to or unsuitable for a particular purpose   **3 a** : lacking the qualities needed for effective action   **b** : unable to function properly ⟨~ heart valves⟩ — **incompetent** *n* — **in·com·pe·tent·ly** *adv*
in·com·plete \,in-kəm-'plēt\ *adj* [ME *incompleet,* fr. LL *incompletus,* fr. L *in-* + *completus* complete] (14c)   **1** : not complete : UNFINISHED: as   **a** : lacking a part; *esp* : lacking one or more sets of floral organs   **b** *of insect metamorphosis* : characterized by the absence of a pupal stage between the immature stages and the adult of an insect in which the young usu. resemble the adult — compare COMPLETE 5   **2** *of a football*

pass : not legally caught — **in·com·plete·ly** *adv* — **in·com·plete·ness** *n*

in·com·pli·ant \ˌin-kəm-'plī-ənt\ *adj* (1647) : not compliant or pliable

in·com·pre·hen·si·ble \(ˌ)in-ˌkäm-pri-'hen(t)-sə-bəl\ *adj* [ME, fr. L *incomprehensibilis*, fr. *in-* + *comprehensibilis* comprehensible] (14c) **1** *archaic* : having or subject to no limits **2** : impossible to comprehend : UNINTELLIGIBLE — **in·com·pre·hen·si·bil·i·ty** \-ˌhen(t)-sə-'bi-lə-tē\ *n* — **in·com·pre·hen·si·ble·ness** *n* — **in·com·pre·hen·si·bly** \-'hen(t)-sə-blē\ *adv*

in·com·pre·hen·sion \-'hen(t)-shən\ *n* (1605) : lack of comprehension or understanding

in·com·press·ible \ˌin-kəm-'pre-sə-bəl\ *adj* (ca. 1736) : incapable of or resistant to compression

in·com·put·able \ˌin-kəm-'pyü-tə-bəl\ *adj* (1606) : not computable : very great — **in·com·put·ably** \-blē\ *adv*

in·con·ceiv·able \ˌin-kən-'sē-və-bəl\ *adj* (ca. 1631) : not conceivable: as **a** : impossible to comprehend **b** : UNBELIEVABLE — **in·con·ceiv·abil·i·ty** \-ˌsē-və-'bi-lə-tē\ *n* — **in·con·ceiv·able·ness** \-'sē-və-bəl-nəs\ *n* — **in·con·ceiv·ably** \-blē\ *adv*

in·con·cin·ni·ty \ˌin-kən-'si-nə-tē\ *n* [L *inconcinnitas*, fr. *in-* + *concinnitas* concinnity] (ca. 1616) : lack of suitability or congruity : INELEGANCE

in·con·clu·sive \ˌin-kən-'klü-siv, -ziv\ *adj* (1707) : leading to no conclusion or definite result — **in·con·clu·sive·ly** *adv* — **in·con·clu·sive·ness** *n*

in·con·dite \in-'kän-dət, -ˌdīt\ *adj* [L *inconditus*, fr. *in-* + *conditus*, pp. of *condere* to put together, fr. *com-* + *-dere* to put — more at DO] (1539) : badly put together : CRUDE

in·con·for·mi·ty \ˌin-kən-'fȯr-mə-tē\ *n* (1594) : NONCONFORMITY

in·con·gru·ence \ˌin-kən-'grü-ən(t)s, (ˌ)in-'käŋ-grə-wən(t)s\ *n* (1610) : INCONGRUITY

in·con·gru·ent \-ənt, -wənt\ *adj* [ME, fr. L *incongruent-, incongruens*, fr. *in-* + *congruent-, congruens* congruent] (15c) : not congruent ⟨~ triangles⟩ — **in·con·gru·ent·ly** *adv*

in·con·gru·i·ty \ˌin-kən-'grü-ə-tē, -ˌkän-\ *n, pl* **-ties** (ca. 1532) **1** : the quality or state of being incongruous **2** : something that is incongruous

in·con·gru·ous \(ˌ)in-'käŋ-grə-wəs\ *adj* [LL *incongruus*, fr. L *in-* + *congruus* congruous] (1611) : lacking congruity: as **a** : not harmonious : INCOMPATIBLE ⟨~ colors⟩ **b** : not conforming : DISAGREEING ⟨conduct ~ with principle⟩ **c** : inconsistent within itself ⟨an ~ story⟩ **d** : lacking propriety : UNSUITABLE ⟨~ manners⟩ — **in·con·gru·ous·ly** *adv* — **in·con·gru·ous·ness** *n*

in·con·scient \(ˌ)in-'kän(t)-shənt\ *adj* [prob. fr. F, fr. *in-* + *conscient* mindful, fr. L *conscient-, consciens*, prp. of *conscire* to be conscious — more at CONSCIENCE] (1885) : UNCONSCIOUS, MINDLESS

in·con·sec·u·tive \ˌin-kən-'se-kyə-tiv, -kə-tiv\ *adj* (1831) : not consecutive : the quality or state of being inconsequent

in·con·se·quence \(ˌ)in-'kän(t)-sə-ˌkwen(t)s, -si-kwən(t)s\ *n* (1588) : the quality or state of being inconsequent

in·con·se·quent \-ˌkwent, -kwənt\ *adj* [LL *inconsequent-, inconsequens*, fr. L *in-* + *consequent-, consequens* consequent] (1579) **1 a** : lacking reasonable sequence : ILLOGICAL **b** : INCONSECUTIVE **2** : INCONSEQUENTIAL **3** : IRRELEVANT — **in·con·se·quent·ly** *adv*

in·con·se·quen·tial \(ˌ)in-ˌkän(t)-sə-'kwen(t)-shəl\ *adj* (1621) **1 a** : ILLOGICAL **b** : IRRELEVANT **2** : of no significance : UNIMPORTANT — **in·con·se·quen·ti·al·i·ty** \-ˌkwen(t)-shē-'a-lə-tē\ *n* — **in·con·se·quen·tial·ly** \-'kwen(t)-shlē, -'kwen(t)-shə-\ *adv*

in·con·sid·er·able \ˌin-kən-'si-d(ə-)rə-bəl, -'si-drə-bəl\ *adj* [F, fr. *in-* + *considerable* considerable, fr. ML *considerabilis*] (1637) : not considerable : TRIVIAL — **in·con·sid·er·able·ness** *n* — **in·con·sid·er·ably** \-blē\ *adv*

in·con·sid·er·ate \ˌin-kən-'si-d(ə-)rət\ *adj* [ME *inconsyderatt*, fr. L *inconsideratus*, fr. *in-* + *consideratus* considerate] (15c) **1 a** : HEEDLESS, THOUGHTLESS **b** : careless of the rights or feelings of others **2** : not adequately considered : ILL-ADVISED — **in·con·sid·er·ate·ly** *adv* — **in·con·sid·er·ate·ness** *n* — **in·con·sid·er·ation** \-ˌsi-də-'rā-shən\ *n*

in·con·sis·tence \ˌin-kən-'sis-tən(t)s\ *n* (1643) : INCONSISTENCY

in·con·sis·ten·cy \ˌin-kən-'sis-tən(t)-sē\ *n* (1647) **1** : an instance of being inconsistent **2** : the quality or state of being inconsistent

in·con·sis·tent \-tənt\ *adj* (1646) : lacking consistency: as **a** : not compatible with another fact or claim ⟨~ statements⟩ **b** : containing incompatible elements ⟨an ~ argument⟩ **c** : incoherent or illogical in thought or actions : CHANGEABLE **d** : not satisfiable by the same set of values for the unknowns ⟨~ equations⟩ ⟨~ inequalities⟩ — **in·con·sis·tent·ly** *adv*

in·con·sol·able \ˌin-kən-'sō-lə-bəl\ *adj* [L *inconsolabilis*, fr. *in-* + *consolabilis* consolable] (1596) : incapable of being consoled : DISCONSOLATE — **in·con·sol·able·ness** *n* — **in·con·sol·ably** \-blē\ *adv*

in·con·so·nance \(ˌ)in-'kän(t)-s(ə-)nən(t)s\ *n* (ca. 1811) : lack of consonance or harmony : DISAGREEMENT

in·con·so·nant \-s(ə-)nənt\ *adj* (1658) : not consonant : DISCORDANT

in·con·spic·u·ous \ˌin-kən-'spi-kyə-wəs\ *adj* [L *inconspicuus*, fr. *in-* + *conspicuus* conspicuous] (1648) : not readily noticeable — **in·con·spic·u·ous·ly** *adv* — **in·con·spic·u·ous·ness** *n*

in·con·stan·cy \(ˌ)in-'kän(t)-stən(t)-sē\ *n* (1526) : the quality or state of being inconstant

in·con·stant \-stənt\ *adj* [ME, fr. MF, fr. L *inconstant-, inconstans*, fr. *in-* + *constant-, constans* constant] (15c) : likely to change frequently without apparent or cogent reason — **in·con·stant·ly** *adv*
  syn INCONSTANT, FICKLE, CAPRICIOUS, MERCURIAL, UNSTABLE mean lacking firmness or steadiness (as in purpose or devotion). INCONSTANT implies an incapacity for steadiness and an inherent tendency to change ⟨an *inconstant* friend⟩. FICKLE suggests unreliability because of perverse changeability and incapacity for steadfastness ⟨performers discover how *fickle* fans can be⟩. CAPRICIOUS suggests motivation by sudden whim or fancy and stresses unpredictability ⟨an utterly *capricious* critic⟩. MERCURIAL implies a rapid changeability in mood ⟨made anxious by her boss's *mercurial* temperament⟩. UNSTABLE implies an incapacity for remaining in a fixed position or steady course and applies esp. to a lack of emotional balance ⟨too *unstable* to hold a job⟩.

in·con·sum·able \ˌin-kən-'sü-mə-bəl\ *adj* (1646) : not capable of being consumed — **in·con·sum·ably** \-blē\ *adv*

in·con·test·able \ˌin-kən-'tes-tə-bəl\ *adj* [F, fr. *in-* + *contestable*, fr. *contester* to contest] (1673) : not contestable : INDISPUTABLE — **in·con·test·abil·i·ty** \-ˌtes-tə-'bi-lə-tē\ *n* — **in·con·test·ably** \-'tes-tə-blē\ *adv*

in·con·ti·nence \(ˌ)in-'kän-t²n-ən(t)s\ *n* (14c) : the quality or state of being incontinent: as **a** : failure to restrain sexual appetite : UNCHASTITY **b** : inability of the body to control the evacuative functions

in·con·ti·nen·cy \-ən(t)-sē\ *n* (15c) : INCONTINENCE

¹**in·con·ti·nent** \(ˌ)in-'kän-t²n-ənt\ *adj* [ME, fr. MF or L; MF, fr. L *incontinent-, incontinens*, fr. *in-* + *continent-, continens* continent] (14c) : not continent: as **a** (1) : lacking self-restraint (2) : not being under control **b** : unable to retain a bodily discharge (as urine) voluntarily

²**incontinent** *adv* [ME, fr. MF, fr. LL *in continenti*] (15c) : ¹INCONTINENTLY

¹**in·con·ti·nent·ly** *adv* (15c) : without delay : IMMEDIATELY

²**incontinently** *adv* (ca. 1552) : in an incontinent or unrestrained manner: as **a** : without moral restraint : LEWDLY **b** : without due or reasonable consideration

in·con·trol·la·ble \ˌin-kən-'trō-lə-bəl\ *adj* (1599) : UNCONTROLLABLE

in·con·tro·vert·ible \(ˌ)in-ˌkän-trə-'vər-tə-bəl\ *adj* (1646) : not open to question : INDISPUTABLE ⟨~ evidence⟩ — **in·con·tro·vert·ibly** \-blē\ *adv*

¹**in·con·ve·nience** \ˌin-kən-'vē-nyən(t)s\ *n* [ME, harm, damage, fr. LL *inconvenientia*, fr. L *inconvenient-, inconveniens*] (1547) **1** : something that is inconvenient **2** : the quality or state of being inconvenient

²**inconvenience** *vt* **-nienced; -nienc·ing** (ca. 1656) : to subject to inconvenience : put to trouble

in·con·ve·nien·cy \ˌin-kən-'vē-nyən(t)-sē\ *n, pl* **-cies** (ca. 1552) : INCONVENIENCE

in·con·ve·nient \ˌin-kən-'vē-nyənt\ *adj* [ME, fr. MF, fr. L *inconvenient-, inconveniens*, fr. *in-* + *convenient-, conveniens* convenient] (1651) : not convenient esp. in giving trouble or annoyance : INOPPORTUNE — **in·con·ve·nient·ly** *adv*

in·con·vert·ible \-'vər-tə-bəl\ *adj* [prob. fr. LL *inconvertibilis*, fr. L *in-* + *convertibilis* convertible] (1646) : not convertible: as **a** *of paper money* : not exchangeable for coin **b** *of a currency* : not exchangeable for a foreign currency — **in·con·vert·ibil·i·ty** \-ˌvər-tə-'bi-lə-tē\ *n* — **in·con·vert·ibly** \-'vər-tə-blē\ *adv*

in·con·vinc·ible \ˌin-kən-'vin(t)-sə-bəl\ *adj* (1674) : incapable of being convinced

in·co·or·di·na·tion \-(ˌ)kō-ˌȯr-d²n-'ā-shən\ *n* (1876) : lack of coordination esp. of muscular movements resulting from loss of voluntary control

¹**in·cor·po·rate** \in-'kȯr-pə-ˌrāt\ *vb* **-rat·ed; -rat·ing** [ME, fr. LL *incorporatus*, pp. of *incorporare*, fr. L *in-* + *corpor-, corpus* body — more at MIDRIFF] *vt* (14c) **1 a** : to unite or work into something already existent so as to form an indistinguishable whole **b** : to blend or combine thoroughly **2 a** : to form into a legal corporation **b** : to admit to membership in a corporate body **3** : to give material form to : EMBODY ~ *vi* **1** : to unite in or as one body **2** : to form or become a corporation — **in·cor·po·ra·ble** \-p(ə-)rə-bəl\ *adj* — **in·cor·po·ra·tion** \-ˌkȯr-pə-'rā-shən\ *n* — **in·cor·po·ra·tive** \-'kȯr-pə-ˌrā-tiv, -p(ə-)rə-tiv\ *adj* — **in·cor·po·ra·tor** \-pə-ˌrā-tər\ *n*

²**in·cor·po·rate** \in-'kȯr-p(ə-)rət\ *adj* (14c) : INCORPORATED

in·cor·po·rat·ed \-pə-ˌrā-təd\ *adj* (1599) **1** : united in one body **2** : formed into a legal corporation

in·cor·po·re·al \ˌin-(ˌ)kȯr-'pȯr-ē-əl, -'pȯr-\ *adj* [ME *incorporealle*, fr. L *incorporeus*, fr. *in-* + *corporeus* corporeal] (15c) **1** : not corporeal : having no material body or form **2** : of, relating to, or constituting a right that is based on property (as bonds or patents) which has no intrinsic value — **in·cor·po·re·al·ly** \-ə-lē\ *adv*

in·cor·po·re·ity \(ˌ)in-ˌkȯr-pə-'rē-ə-tē\ *n* (1601) : the quality or state of being incorporeal : IMMATERIALITY

in·cor·rect \ˌin-kə-'rekt\ *adj* [ME, fr. MF or L; MF, fr. L *incorrectus*, fr. *in-* + *correctus* correct] (15c) **1** *obs* : not corrected or chastened **2 a** : INACCURATE, FAULTY **b** : not true : WRONG **3** : UNBECOMING, IMPROPER — **in·cor·rect·ly** \-'rekt-lē\ *adv* — **in·cor·rect·ness** \-nəs\ *n*

in·cor·ri·gi·ble \in-'kȯr-ə-jə-bəl, -'kär-\ *adj* [ME, fr. L *incorrigibilis*, fr. L *in-* + *corrigere* to correct — more at CORRECT] (14c) : incapable of being corrected or amended: as **a** (1) : not reformable : DEPRAVED (2) : DELINQUENT **b** : not manageable : UNRULY **c** : UNALTERABLE, INVETERATE — **in·cor·ri·gi·bil·i·ty** \-ˌkȯr-ə-jə-'bi-lə-tē, -ˌkär-\ *n* — **incorrigible** *n* — **in·cor·ri·gi·ble·ness** \-'kȯr-ə-jə-bəl-nəs, -'kär-\ *n* — **in·cor·ri·gi·bly** \-blē\ *adv*

in·cor·rupt \ˌin-kə-'rəpt\ *also* **in·cor·rupt·ed** \-'rəp-təd\ *adj* [ME, fr. L *incorruptus*, fr. *in-* + *corruptus* corrupt] (14c) : free from corruption: as **a** *obs* : not affected with decay **b** : not defiled or depraved : UPRIGHT **c** : free from error — **in·cor·rupt·ly** \-'rəp(t)-lē\ *adv* — **in·cor·rupt·ness** \-nəs\ *n*

in·cor·rupt·ible \ˌin-kə-'rəp-tə-bəl\ *adj* (14c) : incapable of corruption: as **a** : not subject to decay or dissolution **b** : incapable of being bribed or morally corrupted — **in·cor·rupt·ibil·i·ty** \-ˌrəp-tə-'bi-lə-tē\ *n* — **incorruptible** *n* — **in·cor·rupt·ibly** \-'rəp-tə-blē\ *adv*

in·cor·rup·tion \ˌin-kə-'rəp-shən\ *n* (14c) *archaic* : the quality or state of being free from physical decay

¹**in·crease** \in-'krēs, 'in-ˌ\ *vb* **in·creased; in·creas·ing** [ME *encresen*, fr. MF *encreistre*, fr. L *increscere*, fr. *in-* + *crescere* to grow — more at CRESCENT] *vi* (14c) **1** : to become progressively greater (as in size, amount, number, or intensity) **2** : to multiply by the production of young ~ *vt* **1** : to make greater : AUGMENT **2** *obs* : ENRICH — **in·creas·able** \-'krē-sə-bəl, -zə-bəl\ *adj* — **in·creas·er** *n*
  syn INCREASE, ENLARGE, AUGMENT, MULTIPLY mean to make or become greater. INCREASE used intransitively implies progressive growth in size, amount, or intensity ⟨his waistline *increased* with age⟩ used transitively it may imply simple not necessarily progressive addition ⟨*increased* her landholdings⟩. ENLARGE implies expansion or extension that makes greater in size or capacity ⟨*enlarged* the kitchen⟩. AUGMENT

\ə\ abut \ᵊ\ kitten, F table \ər\ further \a\ ash \ā\ ace \ä\ mop, mar
\aù\ out \ch\ chin \e\ bet \ē\ easy \g\ go \i\ hit \ī\ ice \j\ job
\ŋ\ sing \ō\ go \ȯ\ law \ȯi\ boy \th\ thin \th\ the \ü\ loot \ù\ foot
\y\ yet \zh\ vision \à, k̲, ⁿ, œ, œ̄, ue, ūe, ᵞ\ *see* Guide to Pronunciation

implies addition to what is already well grown or well developed ⟨the inheritance *augmented* his fortune⟩. MULTIPLY implies increase in number by natural generation or by indefinite repetition of a process ⟨with each attempt the problems *multiplied*⟩.

²in·crease \'in-ˌkrēs, in-'\ *n* (14c) **1** : the act or process of increasing: as **a** : addition or enlargement in size, extent, or quantity **b** *obs* : PROPAGATION **2** : something that is added to an original stock or amount by augmentation or growth (as offspring, produce, profit)

in·creas·ing·ly \in-'krē-siŋ-lē, 'in-ˌkrē-\ *adv* (14c) : to an increasing degree

in·cre·ate \ˌin-krē-'āt, in-'krē-ət\ *adj* [ME *increat*, fr. LL *increatus*, fr. L *in-* + *creatus*, pp. of *creare* to create] (15c) : UNCREATED

in·cred·i·ble \(ˌ)in-'kre-də-bəl\ *adj* [ME, fr. L *incredibilis*, fr. *in-* + *credibilis* credible] (15c) : too extraordinary and improbable to be believed; *also* : hard to believe — **in·cred·i·bil·i·ty** \-ˌkre-də-'bi-lə-tē\ *n* — **in·cred·i·ble·ness** \-'kre-də-bəl-nəs\ *n*

in·cred·i·bly \-blē\ *adv* (ca. 1500) **1** : in an incredible manner **2** : EXTREMELY ⟨~ difficult⟩

in·cre·du·li·ty \ˌin-kri-'dü-lə-tē, -'dyü-\ *n* (15c) : the quality or state of being incredulous : DISBELIEF

in·cred·u·lous \(ˌ)in-'kre-jə-ləs, -dyə-ləs\ *adj* [L *incredulus*, fr. *in-* + *credulus* credulous] (1579) **1** : unwilling to admit or accept what is offered as true : not credulous : SKEPTICAL **2** : INCREDIBLE **3** : expressing incredulity — **in·cred·u·lous·ly** *adv*
usage Sense 2 has been revived in this century after a couple of centuries of disuse. Although it is a sense with good literary precedent—among others Shakespeare used it—many people think it is a result of confusion with *incredible*, which is still the usual word in this sense.

in·cre·ment \'iŋ-krə-mənt, 'in-\ *n* [ME, fr. L *incrementum*, fr. *increscere* to increase] (15c) **1** : the action or process of increasing esp. in quantity or value : ENLARGEMENT **2 a** : something gained or added **b** : one of a series of regular consecutive additions **c** : a minute increase in quantity **3** : the amount or degree by which something changes; *esp* : the amount of positive or negative change in the value of one or more of a set of variables — **in·cre·men·tal** \ˌiŋ-krə-'men-tᵊl, ˌin-\ *adj* — **in·cre·men·tal·ly** \-tᵊl-ē\ *adv*

in·cre·men·tal·ism \ˌiŋ-krə-'men-tᵊl-ˌi-zəm\ *n* (1966) : a policy or advocacy of a policy of political or social change by degrees : GRADUALISM — **in·cre·men·tal·ist** \-tᵊl-ist\ *n*

incremental repetition *n* (1918) : repetition in each stanza (as of a ballad) of part of the preceding stanza usu. with a slight change in wording for dramatic effect

in·cres·cent \in-'kre-sᵊnt\ *adj* [L *increscent-, increscens*, prp. of *increscere*] (ca. 1658) : becoming gradually greater : WAXING ⟨the ~ moon⟩

in·crim·i·nate \in-'kri-mə-ˌnāt\ *vt* **-nat·ed; -nat·ing** [LL *incriminatus*, pp. of *incriminare*, fr. L *in-* + *crimin-, crimen* crime] (ca. 1736) : to charge with or show evidence or proof of involvement in a crime or fault — **in·crim·i·na·tion** \-ˌkri-mə-'nā-shən\ *n* — **in·crim·i·na·to·ry** \-'krim-nə-ˌtōr-ē, -'kri-mə-, -ˌtôr-\ *adj*

incrust *var of* ENCRUST

in·crus·ta·tion \ˌin-ˌkrəs-'tā-shən\ *n* [L *incrustation-, incrustatio*, fr. *incrustare* to encrust] (1644) **1 a** : a crust or hard coating **b** : a growth or accumulation (as of habits, opinions, or customs) resembling a crust **2** : the act of encrusting : the state of being encrusted **3 a** : OVERLAY **b** : INLAY

in·cu·bate \'iŋ-kyə-ˌbāt, 'in-\ *vb* **-bat·ed; -bat·ing** [L *incubatus*, pp. of *incubare*, fr. *in-* + *cubare* to lie] *vt* (ca. 1721) **1** : to sit on (eggs) so as to hatch by the warmth of the body; *also* : to maintain (as an embryo or a chemically active system) under conditions favorable for hatching, development, or reaction **2** : to cause (as an idea) to develop ~ *vi* **1** : to sit on eggs **2** : to undergo incubation — **in·cu·ba·tive** \-ˌbā-tiv\ *adj* — **in·cu·ba·to·ry** \-kyə-bə-ˌtōr-ē, -ˌtôr-; -ˌbā-tə-rē\ *adj*

in·cu·ba·tion \ˌiŋ-kyə-'bā-shən, ˌin-\ *n* (1646) **1** : the act or process of incubating **2** : INCUBATION PERIOD

incubation period *n* (1879) : the period between the infection of an individual by a pathogen and the manifestation of the disease it causes

in·cu·ba·tor \'iŋ-kyə-ˌbā-tər, 'in-\ *n* (1857) : one that incubates: as **a** : an apparatus by which eggs are hatched artificially **b** : an apparatus with a chamber used to provide controlled environmental conditions esp. for the cultivation of microorganisms or the care and protection of premature or sick babies

in·cu·bus \'iŋ-kyə-bəs, 'in-\ *n, pl* **-bi** \-ˌbī, -ˌbē\ *also* **-bus·es** [ME, fr. LL, fr. L *incubare*] (13c) **1** : an evil spirit that lies on persons in their sleep; *esp* : one that has sexual intercourse with women while they are sleeping — compare SUCCUBUS **2** : NIGHTMARE **3** : one that oppresses or burdens like a nightmare

in·cul·cate \in-'kəl-ˌkāt, 'in-(ˌ)\ *vt* **-cat·ed; -cat·ing** [L *inculcatus*, pp. of *inculcare*, lit., to tread on, fr. *in-* + *calcare* to trample, fr. *calc-, calx* heel] (1550) : to teach and impress by frequent repetitions or admonitions **syn** see IMPLANT — **in·cul·ca·tion** \ˌin-(ˌ)kəl-'kā-shən\ *n* — **in·cul·ca·tor** \in-'kəl-ˌkā-tər, 'in-(ˌ)\ *n*

in·cul·pa·ble \(ˌ)in-'kəl-pə-bəl\ *adj* (15c) : free from guilt : BLAMELESS

in·cul·pate \in-'kəl-ˌpāt, 'in-(ˌ)\ *vt* **-pat·ed; -pat·ing** [LL *inculpatus*, fr. L *in-* + *culpatus*, pp. of *culpare* to blame, fr. *culpa* guilt] (1799) : INCRIMINATE — **in·cul·pa·tion** \ˌin-(ˌ)kəl-'pā-shən\ *n* — **in·cul·pa·to·ry** \in-'kəl-pə-ˌtōr-ē, -ˌtôr-\ *adj*

in·cult \in-'kəlt\ *adj* [L *incultus*, fr. *in-* + *cultus*, pp. of *colere* to cultivate — more at WHEEL] (1599) : COARSE, UNCULTURED

in·cum·ben·cy \in-'kəm-bən(t)-sē\ *n, pl* **-cies** (ca. 1608) **1** : something that is incumbent : DUTY **2** : the quality or state of being incumbent **3** : the sphere of action or period of office of an incumbent

¹in·cum·bent \in-'kəm-bənt\ *n* [ME, fr. L *incumbent-, incumbens*, prp. of *incumbere* to lie down on, fr. *in-* + *-cumbere* to lie down; akin to *cubare* to lie] (15c) **1** : the holder of an office or ecclesiastical benefice **2** : OCCUPANT

²incumbent *adj* (1567) **1** : imposed as a duty : OBLIGATORY **2** : having the status of an incumbent; *esp* : occupying a specified office **3** : lying or resting on something else **4** : bent over so as to rest on or touch an underlying surface

incumber *var of* ENCUMBER

in·cu·na·ble \in-'kyü-nə-bəl\ *n* [F, fr. NL *incunabulum*] (1886) : INCUNABULUM

in·cu·nab·u·lum \ˌin-kyə-'na-byə-ləm, ˌiŋ-\ *n, pl* **-la** \-lə\ [NL, fr. L *incunabula*, pl., bands holding the baby in a cradle, fr. *in-* + *cunae*

cradle] (ca. 1859) **1** : a book printed before 1501 **2** : a work of art or of industry of an early period

in·cur \in-'kər\ *vt* **in·curred; in·cur·ring** [ME *incurren*, fr. L *incurrere*, lit., to run into, fr. *in-* + *currere* to run — more at CAR] (15c) : to become liable or subject to : bring down upon oneself ⟨~ expenses⟩

in·cur·able \(ˌ)in-'kyûr-ə-bəl\ *adj* [ME, fr. MF or LL; MF, fr. LL *incurabilis*, fr. L *in-* + *curabilis* curable] (14c) : not curable ⟨an ~ disease⟩; *broadly* : not likely to be changed or corrected ⟨~ optimism⟩ — **incurable** *n* — **in·cur·ably** \-blē\ *adv*

in·cu·ri·ous \(ˌ)in-'kyûr-ē-əs\ *adj* [L *incuriosus*, fr. *in-* + *curiosus* curious] (ca. 1618) : lacking a normal or usual curiosity : UNINTERESTED ⟨a blank ~ stare⟩ **syn** see INDIFFERENT — **in·cu·ri·os·i·ty** \-ˌkyûr-ē-'ä-sə-tē\ *n* — **in·cu·ri·ous·ly** \-'kyûr-ē-əs-lē\ *adv* — **in·cu·ri·ous·ness** *n*

in·cur·rence \in-'kər-ən(t)s, -'kə-rən(t)s\ *n* (ca. 1656) : the act or process of incurring

in·cur·rent \-ənt, -rənt\ *adj* [L *incurrent-, incurrens*, prp. of *incurrere*] (ca. 1856) : giving passage to a current that flows inward

in·cur·sion \in-'kər-zhən\ *n* [ME, fr. MF or L; MF, fr. L *incursion-, incursio*, fr. *incurrere*] (15c) **1** : a hostile entrance into a territory : RAID **2** : an entering in or into (as an activity or undertaking) ⟨his only ~ into the arts⟩

in·cur·vate \'in-ˌkər-ˌvāt, (ˌ)in-'kər-\ *vt* **-vat·ed; -vat·ing** (1578) : to cause to curve inward : BEND — **in·cur·vate** \'in-ˌkər-ˌvāt, (ˌ)in-'kər-vət\ *adj* — **in·cur·va·tion** \ˌin-ˌkər-'vā-shən\ *n* — **in·cur·va·ture** \(ˌ)in-'kər-və-ˌchûr, -chər, -ˌtyûr, -ˌtûr\ *n*

in·curve \(ˌ)in-'kərv, 'in-ˌ\ *vt* [L *incurvare*, fr. *in-* + *curvare* to curve, fr. *curvus* curved — more at CURVE] (1610) : to bend so as to curve inward

in·cus \'iŋ-kəs\ *n, pl* **in·cu·des** \iŋ-'kyü-(ˌ)dēz, 'iŋ-kyə-ˌdēz\ [NL, fr. L, anvil, fr. *incudere*] (1669) : the middle bone of a chain of three small bones in the ear of a mammal — called also *anvil;* see EAR illustration

in·cuse \in-'kyüz, -'kyüs\ *adj* [L *incusus*, pp. of *incudere* to stamp, strike, fr. *in-* + *cudere* to beat — more at HEW] (1818) : formed by stamping or punching in — used chiefly of old coins or features of their design

Ind \'ind, 'īnd\ *n* (13c) **1** *archaic* : India **2** *obs* : Indies

ind- *or* **indo-** *comb form* [ISV, fr. L *indicum* — more at INDIGO] **1** : indigo ⟨*indoxyl*⟩ **2** : resembling indigo (as in color) ⟨*indophenol*⟩

in·da·ba \in-'dä-bə\ *n* [Zulu *indaba* affair] (1827) *chiefly SoAfr* : CONFERENCE, PARLEY

in·da·gate \'in-də-ˌgāt\ *vt* **-gat·ed; -gat·ing** [L *indagatus*, pp. of *indagare*, fr. *indago* ring of hunters encircling game, act of searching, fr. OL *indu* in + L *agere* to drive — more at END, AGENT] (ca. 1623) : to search into : INVESTIGATE — **in·da·ga·tion** \ˌin-də-'gā-shən\ *n* — **in·da·ga·tor** \'in-də-ˌgā-tər\ *n*

in·debt·ed \in-'de-təd\ *adj* [ME *indetted*, fr. OF *endeté*, pp. of *endeter* to involve in debt, fr. *en-* + *dete* debt] (13c) **1** : owing gratitude or recognition to another : BEHOLDEN **2** : owing money

in·debt·ed·ness *n* (1647) **1** : the condition of being indebted **2** : something (as an amount of money) that is owed

in·de·cen·cy \(ˌ)in-'dē-sᵊn(t)-sē\ *n* (1589) **1** : the quality or state of being indecent **2** : something (as a word or action) that is indecent

in·de·cent \-sᵊnt\ *adj* [MF or L; MF *indécent*, fr. L *indecent-, indecens*, fr. *in-* + *decent-, decens* decent] (ca. 1587) : not decent; *esp* : grossly unseemly or offensive to manners or morals — **in·de·cent·ly** *adv*

indecent assault *n* (1861) : an immoral act or series of acts exclusive of rape committed against another person without consent

indecent exposure *n* (1851) : intentional exposure of part of one's body (as the genitals) in a place where such exposure is likely to be an offense against the generally accepted standards of decency

in·de·ci·pher·able \ˌin-di-'sī-f(ə-)rə-bəl\ *adj* (1802) : incapable of being deciphered

in·de·ci·sion \ˌin-di-'si-zhən\ *n* [F *indécision*, fr. *indécis* undecided, fr. LL *indecisus*, fr. L *in-* + *decisus*, pp. of *decidere* to decide] (ca. 1763) : a wavering between two or more possible courses of action : IRRESOLUTION

in·de·ci·sive \ˌin-di-'sī-siv\ *adj* (1726) **1** : not decisive : INCONCLUSIVE **2** : marked by or prone to indecision : IRRESOLUTE **3** : not clearly marked out : INDEFINITE — **in·de·ci·sive·ly** *adv* — **in·de·ci·sive·ness** *n*

in·de·clin·able \ˌin-di-'klī-nə-bəl\ *adj* [ME, fr. MF, fr. LL *indeclinabilis*, fr. L *in-* + LL *declinabilis* capable of being inflected, fr. L *declinare* to inflect — more at DECLINE] (14c) : having no grammatical inflections

in·de·com·pos·able \ˌin-ˌdē-kəm-'pō-zə-bəl\ *adj* (1807) : not capable of being separated into component parts or elements

in·de·co·rous \(ˌ)in-'de-k(ə-)rəs; ˌin-di-'kōr-əs, -'kôr-\ *adj* [L *indecorus*, fr. *in-* + *decorus* decorous] (1682) : not decorous : conflicting with accepted standards of good conduct or good taste — **in·de·co·rous·ly** *adv* — **in·de·co·rous·ness** *n*
syn INDECOROUS, IMPROPER, UNSEEMLY, UNBECOMING, INDELICATE mean not conforming to what is accepted as right, fitting, or in good taste. INDECOROUS suggests a violation of accepted standards of good manners ⟨*indecorous* behavior⟩. IMPROPER applies to a broader range of transgressions of rules not only of social behavior but of ethical practice or logical procedure or prescribed method ⟨*improper* use of campaign contributions⟩. UNSEEMLY adds a suggestion of special inappropriateness to a situation or an offensiveness to good taste ⟨remarried with *unseemly* haste⟩. UNBECOMING suggests behavior or language that does not suit one's character or status ⟨conduct *unbecoming* to an officer⟩. INDELICATE implies a lack of modesty or of tact or of refined perception of feeling ⟨*indelicate* expressions for bodily functions⟩.

in·de·co·rum \ˌin-di-'kōr-əm, -'kôr-\ *n* [L, neut. of *indecorus*] (1575) **1** : something that is indecorous **2** : lack of decorum : IMPROPRIETY

in·deed \in-'dēd\ *adv* (14c) **1** : without any question : TRULY, UNDENIABLY — often used interjectionally to express irony or disbelief or surprise **2** : in reality **3** : all things considered : as a matter of fact

in·de·fat·i·ga·ble \ˌin-di-'fa-ti-gə-bəl\ *adj* [MF, fr. L *indefatigabilis*, fr. *in-* + *defatigare* to fatigue, fr. *de-* + *fatigare* to fatigue] (1611) : incapable of being fatigued : UNTIRING — **in·de·fat·i·ga·bil·i·ty** \-ˌfa-ti-gə-'bi-lə-tē\ *n* — **in·de·fat·i·ga·ble·ness** \-'fa-ti-gə-bəl-nəs\ *n* — **in·de·fat·i·ga·bly** \-blē\ *adv*

in·de·fea·si·ble \ˌin-di-'fē-zə-bəl\ *adj* (1548) : not capable of being annulled or voided or undone ⟨an ~ right⟩ — **in·de·fea·si·bil·i·ty** \-ˌfē-zə-'bi-lə-tē\ *n* — **in·de·fea·si·bly** \-'fē-zə-blē\ *adv*

in·de·fec·ti·ble \-'fek-tə-bəl\ *adj* (1659) **1** : not subject to failure or decay : LASTING **2** : free of faults : FLAWLESS — **in·de·fec·ti·bil·i·ty** \-,fek-tə-'bi-lə-tē\ *n* — **in·de·fec·ti·bly** \-'fek-tə-blē\ *adv*

in·de·fen·si·ble \-'fen(t)-sə-bəl\ *adj* (1529) **1 a** : incapable of being maintained as right or valid : UNTENABLE **b** : incapable of being justified or excused : INEXCUSABLE **2** : incapable of being protected against physical attack — **in·de·fen·si·bil·i·ty** \-,fen(t)-sə-'bi-lə-tē\ *n* — **in·de·fen·si·ble** \-'fen(t)-sə-blē\ *adv*

in·de·fin·able \-'fī-nə-bəl\ *adj* (1810) : incapable of being precisely described or analyzed — **indefinable** *n* — **in·de·fin·able·ness** \-'fī-nə-bəl-nəs\ *n* — **in·de·fin·ably** \-blē\ *adv*

in·def·i·nite \(,)in-'def-nət, -'de-fə-\ *adj* [L *indefinitus,* fr. *in-* + *definitus* definite] (1530) : not definite: as **a** : typically designating an unidentified, generic, or unfamiliar person or thing ⟨the ~ articles *a* and *an*⟩ ⟨~ pronouns⟩ **b** : not precise : VAGUE **c** : having no exact limits **d** *of floral organs* : numerous and difficult to ascertain in number — **indefinite** *n* — **in·def·i·nite·ly** *adv* — **in·def·i·nite·ness** *n*

indefinite integral *n* (ca. 1877) : any function whose derivative is a given function

in·de·his·cent \,in-di-'his-ᵊnt\ *adj* (1832) : remaining closed at maturity ⟨~ fruits⟩ — **in·de·his·cence** \-s²n(t)s\ *n*

in·del·i·ble \in-'de-lə-bəl\ *adj* [ME *indelyble,* fr. ML *indelibilis,* alter. of L *indelebilis,* fr. *in-* + *delēre* to delete] (15c) **1 a** : that cannot be removed, washed away, or erased **b** : making marks that cannot easily be removed ⟨an ~ pencil⟩ **2 a** : LASTING ⟨~ memories⟩ **b** : UNFORGETTABLE, MEMORABLE ⟨an ~ performance⟩ — **in·del·i·bil·i·ty** \(,)in-,de-lə-'bi-lə-tē\ *n* — **in·del·i·bly** \in-'de-lə-blē\ *adv*

in·del·i·ca·cy \(,)in-'de-li-kə-sē\ *n* (1712) **1** : the quality or state of being indelicate **2** : something that is indelicate

in·del·i·cate \-li-kət\ *adj* (1742) : not delicate: **a** (1) : lacking in or offending against propriety : IMPROPER (2) : verging on the indecent : COARSE **b** : marked by a lack of feeling for the sensibilities of others : TACTLESS *syn* see INDECOROUS — **in·del·i·cate·ly** *adv* — **in·del·i·cate·ness** *n*

in·dem·ni·fi·ca·tion \in-,dem-nə-fə-'kā-shən\ *n* (1732) **1 a** : the action of indemnifying **b** : the condition of being indemnified **2** : INDEMNITY 2b

in·dem·ni·fy \in-'dem-nə-,fī\ *vt* **-fied; -fy·ing** [L *indemnis* unharmed, fr. *in-* + *damnum* damage] (ca. 1611) **1** : to secure against hurt, loss, or damage **2** : to make compensation to for incurred hurt, loss, or damage *syn* see PAY — **in·dem·ni·fi·er** \-,fī(-ə)r\ *n*

in·dem·ni·ty \in-'dem-nə-tē\ *n, pl* **-ties** (15c) **1 a** : security against hurt, loss, or damage **b** : exemption from incurred penalties or liabilities **2 a** : INDEMNIFICATION 1 **b** : something that indemnifies

in·de·mon·stra·ble \,in-di-'män(t)-strə-bəl, (,)in-'dem-ən-strə-\ *adj* (1570) : incapable of being demonstrated : not subject to proof — **in·de·mon·stra·bly** \-blē\ *adv*

¹in·dent \in-'dent\ *vb* [ME, fr. MF *endenter,* fr. OF, fr. *en-* + *dent* tooth, fr. L *dent-, dens* — more at TOOTH] *vt* (14c) **1 a** : to divide (a document) so as to produce sections with irregular edges that can be matched for authentication **b** : to draw up (as a deed) in two or more exactly corresponding copies **2** : to notch the edge of : make jagged **3** : INDENTURE **4** : to set (as a line of a paragraph) in from the margin **5** *chiefly Brit* : to order by an indent ~ *vi* **1** *obs* : to make a formal or express agreement **2** : to form an indentation **3** *chiefly Brit* : to make out an indent for something — **in·dent·er** — **indent on** **1** *chiefly Brit* : to make a requisition on **2** *chiefly Brit* : to draw on

²in·dent \in-'dent, 'in-,\ *n* (15c) **1** : INDENTURE 1 **b** : a certificate issued by the U.S. at the close of the American Revolution for the principal or interest on the public debt **2** *chiefly Brit* : an official requisition **b** : a purchase order for goods esp. when sent from a foreign country **3** : INDENTION

³in·dent \in-'dent\ *vt* [ME *endenten,* fr. *en-* + *denten* to dent] (15c) **1** : to force inward so as to form a depression **2** : to form a dent in — **in·dent·er** *n*

⁴in·dent \in-'dent, 'in-,\ *n* (1596) : INDENTATION

in·den·ta·tion \,in-,den-'tā-shən\ *n* (ca. 1728) **1 a** : an angular cut in an edge : NOTCH **b** : a recess in a surface **2** : the action of indenting : the condition of being indented **3** : DENT **4** : INDENTION 2b

in·den·tion \in-'den(t)-shən\ *n* (1763) **1** *archaic* : INDENTATION 1 **2 a** : the action of indenting : the condition of being indented **b** : the blank space produced by indenting

¹in·den·ture \in-'den(t)-shər\ *n* [ME *endenture,* fr. MF, fr. *endenter*] (14c) **1 a** (1) : a document or a section of a document that is indented (2) : a formal or official document usu. executed in two or more copies (3) : a contract binding one person to work for another for a given period of time — usu. used in pl. **b** : a formal certificate (as an inventory or voucher) prepared for purposes of control **c** : a document stating the terms under which a security (as a bond) is issued **2** : INDENTATION 1 **3** [³*indent*] : DENT

²indenture *vt* **in·den·tured; in·den·tur·ing** \-'den(t)-shriŋ, -'den(t)-shə-riŋ\ (1676) : to bind (as an apprentice) by or as if by indentures

indentured servant *n* (1723) : a person who signs and is bound by indentures to work for another for a specified time esp. in return for payment of travel expenses and maintenance

in·de·pen·dence \,in-də-'pen-dən(t)s\ *n* (1640) **1** : the quality or state of being independent **2** *archaic* : COMPETENCE 1

Independence Day *n* (1791) : a civil holiday for the celebration of the anniversary of the beginnings of national independence; *specif* : July 4 observed as a legal holiday in the U.S. in commemoration of the adoption of the Declaration of Independence in 1776

in·de·pen·den·cy \,in-də-'pen-dən(t)-sē\ *n* (ca. 1611) **1** : INDEPENDENCE 1 **2** *cap* : the Independent polity or movement **3** : an independent political unit

¹in·de·pen·dent \,in-də-'pen-dənt\ *adj* (1611) **1** : not dependent: as **a** (1) : not subject to control by others : SELF-GOVERNING (2) : not affiliated with a larger controlling unit **b** (1) : not requiring or relying on something else : not contingent ⟨an ~ conclusion⟩ (2) : not looking to others for one's opinions or for guidance in conduct (3) : not bound by or committed to a political party **c** (1) : not requiring or relying on others (as for care or livelihood) ⟨~ of her parents⟩ (2) : being enough to free one from the necessity of working for a living ⟨a man of ~ means⟩ **d** : showing a desire for freedom ⟨an ~ manner⟩

e (1) : not determined by or capable of being deduced or derived from or expressed in terms of members (as axioms or equations) of the set under consideration; *esp* : having linear independence ⟨an ~ set of vectors⟩ (2) : having the property that the joint probability (as of events or samples) or the joint probability density function (as of random variables) equals the product of the probabilities or probability density functions of separate occurrence **2** *cap* : of or relating to the Independents **3 a** : MAIN 5 ⟨an ~ clause⟩ **b** : neither deducible from nor incompatible with another statement ⟨~ postulates⟩ *syn* see FREE — **in·de·pen·dent·ly** *adv*

²independent *n* (1644) **1** *cap* : a sectarian of an English religious movement for congregational autonomy originating in the late 16th century, giving rise to Congregationalists, Baptists, and Friends, and forming one of the major political groupings of the period of Cromwell **2** : one that is independent; *esp, often cap* : one that is not bound by or definitively committed to a political party

independent assortment *n* (ca. 1948) : formation of random combinations of chromosomes in meiosis and of genes on different pairs of homologous chromosomes by the passage according to the laws of probability of one of each diploid pair of homologous chromosomes into each gamete independently of each other pair

independent variable *n* (1852) : a mathematical variable whose value is specified first and determines the value of one or more other values in an expression or function

in—depth \('(,)in-'depth\ *adj* (1965) : COMPREHENSIVE, THOROUGH ⟨an ~ study⟩

in·de·scrib·able \,in-di-'skrī-bə-bəl\ *adj* (1794) **1** : that cannot be described ⟨an ~ sensation⟩ **2** : surpassing description ⟨~ joy⟩ — **in·de·scrib·able·ness** — **in·de·scrib·ably** \-blē\ *adv*

in·de·struc·ti·ble \-'strək-tə-bəl\ *adj* [prob. fr. LL *indestructibilis,* fr. L *in-* + *destructus,* pp. of *destruere* to tear down — more at DESTROY] (1667) : incapable of being destroyed, ruined, or rendered ineffective — **in·de·struc·ti·bil·i·ty** \-,strək-tə-'bi-lə-tē\ *n* — **in·de·struc·ti·ble·ness** \-'strək-tə-bəl-nəs\ *n* — **in·de·struc·ti·bly** \-blē\ *adv*

in·de·ter·min·able \,in-di-'tərm-nə-bəl, -'tər-mə-\ *adj* (15c) **1** : incapable of being definitely decided or settled **2** : incapable of being definitely fixed or ascertained — **in·de·ter·min·ably** \-blē\ *adv*

in·de·ter·mi·na·cy \-nə-sē\ *n* (1649) : the quality or state of being indeterminate

indeterminacy principle *n* (ca. 1928) : UNCERTAINTY PRINCIPLE

in·de·ter·mi·nate \,in-di-'tərm-nət, -'tər-mə-\ *adj* [ME *indeterminat,* fr. LL *indeterminatus,* fr. L *in-* + *determinatus,* pp. of *determinare* to determine] (14c) **1 a** : not definitely or precisely determined or fixed : VAGUE **b** : not known in advance **c** : not leading to a definite end or result **2** : having an infinite number of solutions ⟨a system of ~ equations⟩ **3** : being one of the seven undefined mathematical expressions

$$\frac{0}{0}, \frac{\infty}{\infty}, \infty \cdot 0, 1^\infty, 0^0, \infty^0, \infty - \infty$$

4 : characterized by sequential flowering from the lateral or basal buds to the central or uppermost buds; *also* : characterized by growth in which the main stem continues to elongate indefinitely without being limited by a terminal inflorescence — compare DETERMINATE 4 — **in·de·ter·mi·nate·ly** *adv* — **in·de·ter·mi·nate·ness** *n* — **in·de·ter·mi·na·tion** \-,tər-mə-'nā-shən\ *n*

in·de·ter·min·ism \-'tər-mə-,ni-zəm\ *n* (1874) **1 a** : a theory that the will is free and that deliberate choice and actions are not determined by or predictable from antecedent causes **b** : a theory that holds that not every event has a cause **2** : the quality or state of being indeterminate; *esp* : UNPREDICTABILITY — **in·de·ter·min·ist** \-'tərm-nist, -'tər-mə-\ *n* — **in·de·ter·min·is·tic** \-,tər-mə-'nis-tik\ *adj*

¹in·dex \'in-,deks\ *n, pl* **in·dex·es** or **in·di·ces** \-də-,sēz\ [L *indic-, index,* fr. *indicare* to indicate] (1571) **1 a** : a device (as the pointer on a scale or the gnomon of a sundial) that serves to indicate a value or quantity **b** : something (as a physical feature or a mode of expression) that leads one to a particular fact or conclusion : INDICATION **2** : a list (as of bibliographical information or citations to a body of literature) arranged usu. in alphabetical order of some specified datum (as author, subject, or keyword): as **a** : a list of items (as topics or names) treated in a printed work that gives for each item the page number where it may be found **b** : THUMB INDEX **c** : a bibliographical analysis of groups of publications that is usu. published periodically **3** : a list of restricted or prohibited material; *specif, cap* : a list of books the reading of which is prohibited or restricted for Roman Catholics by the church authorities **4** *pl usu* **indices** : a number or symbol or expression (as an exponent) associated with another to indicate a mathematical operation to be performed or to indicate use or position in an arrangement **5** : a character ☞ used to direct attention to a note or paragraph — called also *fist* **6 a** : a number (as a ratio) derived from a series of observations and used as an indicator or measure; *specif* : INDEX NUMBER **b** : the ratio of one dimension of a thing (as an anatomical structure) to another dimension

²index *vt* (1720) **1 a** : to provide with an index **b** : to list in an index ⟨all persons and places mentioned are carefully ~ed⟩ **2** : to serve as an index of **3** : to regulate (as wages, prices, or interest rates) by indexation ~ *vi* : to index something — **in·dex·er** *n*

in·dex·ation \,in-dek-'sā-shən\ *n* (1960) : a system of economic control in which certain variables (as wages and interest) are tied to a cost-of-living index so that both rise or fall at the same rate and the detrimental effect of inflation is theoretically eliminated

index finger *n* (1849) : FOREFINGER

index fossil *n* (1900) : a fossil usu. with a narrow time range and wide spatial distribution that is used in the identification of related geologic formations

³in·dex·i·cal \(,)in-'dek-si-kəl\ *adj* (ca. 1828) **1** : of or relating to an index **2 a** : varying in reference with the individual speaker ⟨the ~

\ə\ abut \ᵊ\ kitten, F table \ər\ further \a\ ash \ā\ ace \ä\ mop, mar \au̇\ out \ch\ chin \e\ bet \ē\ easy \g\ go \i\ hit \ī\ ice \j\ job \ŋ\ sing \ō\ go \ȯ\ law \ȯi\ boy \th\ thin \t͟h\ the \ü\ loot \u̇\ foot \y\ yet \zh\ vision \ä, k̲, ⁿ, œ, œ̄, ᵫ, ᵫ̄, ᵊ\ see Guide to Pronunciation

words *I, here, now*⟩   **b** : associated with or identifying an individual speaker ⟨∼ features of speech⟩
²indexical *n* (1971) : an indexical word, sign, or feature
indexing *n* (1957) : INDEXATION
index number *n* (ca. 1896) : a number used to indicate change in magnitude (as of cost or price) as compared with the magnitude at some specified time usu. taken as 100
index of refraction (1829) : the ratio of the speed of radiation (as light) in one medium (as a vacuum) to that in another medium
indi- — see IND-
In·dia \'in-dē-ə\ (ca. 1952) — a communications code word for the letter *i*
india ink *n, often cap 1st I* (1665) **1** : a solid black pigment (as specially prepared lampblack) used in drawing and lettering **2** : a fluid ink consisting usu. of a fine suspension of india ink in a liquid
In·dia·man \'in-dē-ə-mən\ *n* (1709) : a merchant ship formerly used in trade with India; *esp* : a large sailing ship used in this trade
In·di·an \'in-dē-ən, *dial* -jən *or* -din\ *n* (14c) **1 a** : a native or inhabitant of India or of the East Indies **b** : a person of Indian descent **2 a** [fr. the belief held by Columbus that the lands he discovered were part of Asia] : AMERICAN INDIAN **b** : one of the native languages of American Indians — **Indian** *adj* — **In·di·an·ness** *n*
Indian agent *n* (1807) : an official representative of the U.S. federal government to American Indian tribes esp. on reservations
Indian club *n* (1857) : a usu. wooden club shaped like a large bottle or tenpin that is swung for gymnastic exercise
Indian corn *n* (1617) **1** : a tall widely cultivated American cereal grass (*Zea mays*) bearing seeds on elongated ears **2** : the ears of Indian corn; *also* : its edible seeds
Indian elephant *n* (1607) : ELEPHANT 1b
Indian file *n* (1758) : SINGLE FILE
Indian giver *n* (ca. 1848) : a person who gives something to another and then takes it back or expects an equivalent in return — **Indian giving** *n*
Indian hemp *n* (1619) **1** : an American dogbane (*Apocynum cannabinum*) with milky juice, tough fibrous bark, and an emetic and cathartic root **2** : HEMP 1
In·di·an·ism \'in-dē-ə-ni-zəm\ *n* (1651) **1** : the qualities or culture distinctive of American Indians **2** : policy designed to further the interests or culture of American Indians — **In·di·an·ist** \-nist\ *adj or n*
In·di·an·ize \'in-dē-ə-nīz\ *vt* **-ized; -izing** (1702) **1** : to cause to acquire or conform to the characteristics, culture, or usage of American Indians or of India **2** : to bring (as a region) under the cultural or political influence or control of India — **In·di·an·i·za·tion** \,in-dē-ə-(,)nī-'zā-shən\ *n*
Indian licorice *n* (ca. 1890) : ROSARY PEA 1
Indian meal *n* (1609) : CORNMEAL
Indian paintbrush *n* (ca. 1892) **1** : any of a genus (*Castilleja*) of herbaceous plants of the snapdragon family that have brightly colored bracts — called also *painted cup* **2** : ORANGE HAWKWEED
Indian pipe *n* (ca. 1818) : a waxy white saprophytic herb (*Monotropa uniflora*) of the family Monotropaceae, the Indian-pipe family) of Asia and No. America having leaves reduced to scales
Indian pudding *n* (1722) : a baked pudding made chiefly of cornmeal, milk, and molasses
Indian red *n* (ca. 1753) **1** : any of various usu. dark red pigments consisting chiefly of iron oxide **2** : a strong or moderate reddish brown
Indian sign *n* (1910) : HEX, SPELL
Indian summer *n* (1778) **1** : a period of warm or mild weather in late autumn or early winter **2** : a happy or flourishing period occurring toward the end of something ⟨life in the *Indian summer* of Czarist Russia —John Davenport⟩

Indian paintbrush

Indian tobacco *n* (ca. 1618) **1** : an American wild lobelia (*Lobelia inflata*) with small blue or white flowers **2** : a wild tobacco (*Nicotiana bigelovii*) found in dry valleys from southern California to southern Oregon
In·di·an–wres·tle \'in-dē-ən-,re-səl, -,ra-\ *vi* [back-formation fr. *Indian wrestling*] (1938) : to engage in Indian wrestling
Indian wrestling *n* (1913) **1** : wrestling in which two people lie side by side on their backs in reversed position locking their near arms and raising and locking the corresponding legs and attempt to force each other's leg down and turn the other wrestler facedown **2** : wrestling in which two people stand face to face gripping usu. their right hands and setting the outsides of the corresponding feet together and attempt to force each other off balance **3** : ARM WRESTLING
India paper *n* (1768) **1** : a thin absorbent paper used esp. for proving inked intaglio surfaces (as steel engravings) **2** : a thin tough opaque printing paper
india rubber *n, often cap I* (1790) : ¹RUBBER 2a
In·dic \'in-dik\ *adj* (1877) **1** : of or relating to the subcontinent of India : INDIAN **2** : of, relating to, or constituting the Indo-Aryan branch of the Indo-European languages — **Indic** *n*
in·di·can \'in-di-,kan\ *n* [*L indicum* indigo — more at INDIGO] (1859) **1** : an indigo-forming substance $C_8H_7NO_4S$ found as a salt in urine and other animal fluids; *also* : its potassium salt $C_8H_6KNO_4S$ **2** : a glucoside $C_{14}H_{17}NO_6$ occurring esp. in the indigo plant and being a source of natural indigo
in·di·cant \'in-di-kənt\ *n* (1623) : something that serves to indicate
in·di·cate \'in-də-,kāt\ *vt* **-cat·ed; -cat·ing** [L *indicatus*, pp. of *indicare*, fr. *in-* + *dicare* to proclaim, dedicate — more at DICTION] (ca. 1609) **1 a** : to point out or point to **b** : to be a sign, symptom, or index of ⟨the high fever ∼*s* a serious condition⟩ **c** : to demonstrate or suggest the necessity or advisability of ⟨*indicated* the need for a new school⟩ **2** : to state or express briefly ⟨*indicated* a desire to cooperate⟩
in·di·ca·tion \,in-də-'kā-shən\ *n* (15c) **1 a** : something that serves to indicate **b** : something that is indicated as advisable or necessary **2** : the action of indicating — **in·di·ca·tion·al** \-shnəl, -shə-nᵊl\ *adj*
¹in·dic·a·tive \in-'di-kə-tiv\ *adj* (15c) **1** : of, relating to, or constituting a verb form or set of verb forms that represents the denoted act or state as an objective fact ⟨the ∼ mood⟩ **2** : serving to indicate ⟨actions ∼ of fear⟩ — **in·dic·a·tive·ly** *adv*
²indicative *n* (1530) **1** : the indicative mood of a language **2** : a form in the indicative mood
in·di·ca·tor \'in-də-,kā-tər\ *n* (1666) **1** : one that indicates: as **a** : an index hand (as on a dial) : POINTER **b** (1) : GAUGE 2b, DIAL 4a (2) : an instrument for automatically making a diagram that indicates the pressure in and volume of the working fluid of an engine throughout the cycle **2 a** : a substance (as litmus) used to show visually (as by change of color) the condition of a solution with respect to the presence of a particular material (as a free acid or alkali) **b** : TRACER 4b **3** : an organism or ecological community so strictly associated with particular environmental conditions that its presence is indicative of the existence of these conditions **4** : any of a group of statistical values (as level of employment) that taken together give an indication of the health of the economy — **in·dic·a·to·ry** \in-'di-kə-,tōr-ē, -,tōr-\ *adj*
indices *pl of* INDEX
in·di·cia \in-'di-sh(ē-)ə\ *n pl* [L, pl. of *indicium* sign, fr. *indicare*] (ca. 1626) **1** : distinctive marks : INDICATIONS **2** : postal markings often imprinted on mail or on labels to be affixed to mail
in·dict \in-'dīt\ *vt* [alter. of earlier *indite*, fr. ME *inditen*, fr. AF *enditer*, fr. OF, to write down — more at INDITE] (ca. 1626) **1** : to charge with a fault or offense : CRITICIZE, ACCUSE **2** : to charge with a crime by the finding or presentment of a jury (as a grand jury) in due form of law — **in·dict·er** *or* **in·dict·or** \-'dī-tər\ *n*
in·dict·able \-'dī-tə-bəl\ *adj* (ca. 1706) **1** : subject to being indicted : liable to indictment **2** : making one liable to indictment ⟨an ∼ offense⟩
in·dic·tion \in-'dik-shən\ *n* [ME *indiccioun*, fr. LL *indiction-, indictio*, fr. L, proclamation, fr. *indicere* to proclaim, fr. *in-* + *dicere* to say — more at DICTION] (14c) : a 15-year cycle used as a chronological unit in several ancient and medieval systems
in·dict·ment \in-'dīt-mənt\ *n* (14c) **1 a** : the action or the legal process of indicting **b** : the state of being indicted **2** : a formal written statement framed by a prosecuting authority and found by a jury (as a grand jury) charging a person with an offense **3** : an expression of strong disapproval ⟨an ∼ of contemporary morality⟩
in·die \'in-dē\ *n* [by shortening & alter. fr. *independent*] (1928) : something (as an unaffiliated record or motion-picture production company) independent — **indie** *adj*
in·dif·fer·ence \in-'di-fərn(t)s, -,f(ə-)rən(t)s\ *n* (15c) **1** : the quality, state, or fact of being indifferent **2** *archaic* : lack of difference or distinction between two or more things **3** : absence of compulsion to or toward one thing or another
in·dif·fer·en·cy \-'fərn(t)-sē, -,f(ə-)rən(t)-sē\ *n* (15c) *archaic* : INDIFFERENCE
in·dif·fer·ent \in-'di-fərnt, -,f(ə-)rənt\ *adj* [ME, fr. MF or L; MF, regarded as neither good nor bad, fr. L *indifferent-, indifferens*, fr. *in-* + *different-, differens*, prp. of *differre* to be different — more at DIFFER] (14c) **1** : marked by impartiality : UNBIASED **2 a** : that does not matter one way or the other **b** : of no importance or value one way or the other **3 a** : marked by no special liking for or dislike of something ⟨∼ about which task he was given⟩ **b** : marked by a lack of interest, enthusiasm, or concern for something : APATHETIC ⟨∼ to suffering and poverty⟩ **4** : being neither excessive nor inadequate : MODERATE ⟨hills of ∼ size⟩ **5 a** : being neither good nor bad : MEDIOCRE ⟨does ∼ work⟩ **b** : being neither right nor wrong **6** : characterized by lack of active quality : NEUTRAL **7 a** : not differentiated **b** : capable of development in more than one direction; *esp* : not yet embryologically determined — **in·dif·fer·ent·ly** *adv*
    syn INDIFFERENT, UNCONCERNED, INCURIOUS, ALOOF, DETACHED, DISINTERESTED mean not showing or feeling interest. INDIFFERENT implies neutrality of attitude from lack of inclination, preference, or prejudice ⟨*indifferent* to the dictates of fashion⟩. UNCONCERNED suggests a lack of sensitivity or regard for others' needs or troubles ⟨*unconcerned* about the homeless⟩. INCURIOUS implies an inability to take a normal interest due to dullness of mind or to self-centeredness ⟨*incurious* about the world⟩. ALOOF suggests a cool reserve arising from a sense of superiority or disdain for inferiors or from shyness ⟨*aloof* from his coworkers⟩. DETACHED implies an objective attitude achieved through absence of prejudice or selfishness ⟨observed family gatherings with *detached* amusement⟩. DISINTERESTED implies a circumstantial freedom from concern for personal or esp. financial advantage that enables one to judge or advise without bias ⟨judged by a panel of *disinterested* observers⟩.
in·dif·fer·ent·ism \-'fərn-,ti-zəm, -,f(ə-)rən-\ *n* (1827) : INDIFFERENCE; *specif* : belief that all religions are equally valid — **in·dif·fer·ent·ist** \-'fərn-tist, -,f(ə-)rən-\ *n*
in·di·gence \'in-di-jən(t)s\ *n* (14c) : a level of poverty in which real hardship and deprivation are suffered and comforts of life are wholly lacking **syn** see POVERTY
in·di·gene \'in-də-,jēn\ *also* **in·di·gen** \-di-jən, -də-,jen\ *n* [L *indigena*] (1598) : NATIVE
in·di·ge·nize \in-'di-jə-,nīz\ *vt* **-nized; -niz·ing** (1951) : to cause to have indigenous characteristics — **in·dig·e·ni·za·tion** \-,di-jə-nə-'zā-shən, -,nī-\ *n*
in·dig·e·nous \in-'di-jə-nəs\ *adj* [LL *indigenus*, fr. L *indigena*, n., native, fr. OL *indu, endo* in, within + L *gignere* to beget — more at END-, KIN] (1646) **1** : having originated in and being produced, growing, living, or occurring naturally in a particular region or environment **2** : INNATE, INBORN **syn** see NATIVE — **in·dig·e·nous·ly** *adv* — **in·dig·e·nous·ness** *n*
in·di·gent \'in-di-jənt\ *adj* [ME, fr. MF, fr. L *indigent-, indigens*, prp. of *indigēre* to need, fr. OL *indu* + L *egēre* to need; perh. akin to OHG *ekrōdi* thin] (15c) **1** : suffering from indigence : IMPOVERISHED **2 a** *archaic* : DEFICIENT **b** *archaic* : totally lacking in something specified — **indigent** *n*
in·di·gest·ed \,in-(,)dī-'jes-təd, -də-\ *adj* (1587) : not carefully thought out or arranged : FORMLESS
in·di·gest·ible \-'jes-tə-bəl\ *adj* [ME, fr. LL *indigestibilis*, fr. L *in-* + LL *digestibilis* digestible] (15c) : not digestible : not easily digested — **in·di·gest·ibil·i·ty** \-,jes-tə-'bi-lə-tē\ *n* — **indigestible** *n*
in·di·ges·tion \-'jes-chən, -'jesh-\ *n* (14c) **1** : inability to digest or difficulty in digesting something **2** : a case or attack of indigestion

in·dign \in-'dīn\ *adj* [ME *indigne*, fr. MF, fr. L *indignus*] (14c) **1** *archaic* : UNWORTHY, UNDESERVING **2** *obs* : UNBECOMING, DISGRACEFUL

in·dig·nant \in-'dig-nənt\ *adj* [L *indignant-*, *indignans*, prp. of *indignari* to be indignant, fr. *indignus* unworthy, fr. *in-* + *dignus* worthy — more at DECENT] (1590) : filled with or marked by indignation ⟨became ~ at the accusation⟩ — **in·dig·nant·ly** *adv*

in·dig·na·tion \ˌin-dig-'nā-shən\ *n* (14c) : anger aroused by something unjust, unworthy, or mean *syn* see ANGER

in·dig·ni·ty \in-'dig-nə-tē\ *n, pl* **-ties** [L *indignitat-*, *indignitas*, fr. *indignus*] (1584) **1 a** : an act that offends against a person's dignity or self-respect : INSULT **b** : humiliating treatment **2** *obs* : lack or loss of dignity or honor

in·di·go \'in-di-ˌgō\ *n, pl* **-gos** *or* **-goes** [It dial., fr. L *indicum*, fr. Gk *indikon*, fr. neut. of *indikos* Indic, fr. *Indos* India] (1555) **1 a** : a blue vat dye obtained from plants (as indigo plants) **b** : the principal coloring matter $C_{16}H_{10}N_2O_2$ of natural indigo usu. synthesized as a blue powder with a coppery luster **2** : INDIGO PLANT **3** : a deep reddish blue

indigo bunting *n* (1783) : a common small American finch (*Passerina cyanea*) of which the male is largely indigo-blue in spring and summer

indigo plant *n* (1757) : a plant that yields indigo; *esp* : any of a genus (*Indigofera*) of leguminous herbs

indigo snake *n* (ca. 1885) : a large blue-black or brownish colubrid snake (*Drymarchon corais*) of the southeastern U.S. and Texas to Argentina — called also *gopher snake*

in·di·go·tin \in-'di-gə-tən, ˌin-di-'gō-tᵊn\ *n* [F *indigotine*, irreg. fr. *indigo* indigo] (1838) : INDIGO 1b

in·di·rect \ˌin-də-'rekt, -(ˌ)dī-\ *adj* [ME, fr. ML *indirectus*, fr. L *in-* + *directus* direct — more at DRESS] (14c) : not direct: as **a** (1) : deviating from a direct line or course : ROUNDABOUT (2) : not going straight to the point ⟨an ~ accusation⟩ (3) : being or involving proof of a proposition or theorem by demonstration that its negation leads to an absurdity or contradiction **b** : not straightforward and open : DECEITFUL **c** : not directly aimed at or achieved ⟨~ consequences⟩ **d** : stating what a real or supposed original speaker said with changes in wording that conform the statement grammatically to the sentence in which it is included ⟨~ discourse⟩ ⟨an ~ question⟩ **e** : not effected by the action of the people or the electorate ⟨~ government representation⟩ — **in·di·rect·ly** \-'rek(t)-lē\ *adv* — **in·di·rect·ness** \-nəs\ *n*

indirect cost *n* (ca. 1909) : a cost that is not identifiable with a specific product, function, or activity

indirect evidence *n* (1824) : evidence that establishes immediately collateral facts from which the main fact may be inferred : CIRCUMSTANTIAL EVIDENCE

in·di·rec·tion \ˌin-də-'rek-shən, -(ˌ)dī-\ *n* (1590) **1 a** : indirect action or procedure **b** : lack of direction : AIMLESSNESS **2 a** : lack of straightforwardness and openness : DECEITFULNESS **b** : something (as an act or statement) marked by lack of straightforwardness ⟨hated diplomatic ~s —*Rev. of Reviews*⟩

indirect lighting *n* (1922) : lighting in which the light emitted by a source is diffusely reflected (as by the ceiling)

indirect object *n* (1879) : a grammatical object representing the secondary goal of the action of its verb (as *her* in "I gave her the book")

in·di·scern·ible \in-di-'sər-nə-bəl, -'zər-\ *adj* (1635) : incapable of being discerned : not recognizable as distinct

in·dis·ci·plin·able \(ˌ)in-ˌdi-sə-'pli-nə-bəl, -'di-sə-plə-\ *adj* (1600) : not subject to or capable of being disciplined

in·dis·ci·pline \(ˌ)in-'di-sə-plən\ *n* (1783) : lack of discipline — **in·dis·ci·plined** \-plənd, -(ˌ)plind\ *adj*

in·dis·cov·er·able \in-dis-'kəv-rə-bəl, -'kə-və-\ *adj* (1640) : not discoverable

in·dis·creet \ˌin-di-'skrēt\ *adj* [ME *indiscrete*, fr. MF & LL; MF *indiscret*, fr. LL *indiscretus*, fr. L, indistinguishable, fr. *in-* + *discretus*, pp. of *discernere* to separate — more at DISCERN] (15c) : not discreet : IMPRUDENT — **in·dis·creet·ly** *adv* — **in·dis·creet·ness** *n*

in·dis·cre·tion \ˌin-di-'skre-shən\ *n* (14c) **1** : lack of discretion : IMPRUDENCE ⟨dietary ~⟩ **2 a** : something (as an act or remark) marked by lack of discretion **b** : an act at variance with the accepted morality of a society ⟨resigned because of financial ~s⟩

in·dis·crim·i·nate \ˌin-dis-'krim-nət, -'kri-mə-\ *adj* (ca. 1598) **1 a** : not marked by careful distinction : deficient in discrimination and discernment ⟨~ reading habits⟩ ⟨~ mass destruction⟩ **b** : HAPHAZARD, RANDOM ⟨~ application of a law⟩ **2 a** : PROMISCUOUS, UNRESTRAINED ⟨~ sexual behavior⟩ **b** : HETEROGENEOUS, MOTLEY ⟨an ~ collection⟩ — **in·dis·crim·i·nate·ly** *adv* — **in·dis·crim·i·nate·ness** *n*

in·dis·crim·i·nat·ing \-'kri-mə-ˌnā-tiŋ\ *adj* (ca. 1767) : not discriminating — **in·dis·crim·i·nat·ing·ly** \-tiŋ-lē\ *adv*

in·dis·crim·i·na·tion \-ˌkri-mə-'nā-shən\ *n* (1649) : lack of discrimination

in·dis·pens·able \ˌin-di-'spen(t)-sə-bəl\ *adj* (1653) **1** : not subject to being set aside or neglected ⟨an ~ obligation⟩ **2** : absolutely necessary : ESSENTIAL ⟨an ~ member of the staff⟩ — **in·dis·pens·abil·i·ty** \-ˌspen(t)-sə-'bi-lə-tē\ *n* — **indispensable** *n* — **in·dis·pens·able·ness** \-'spen(t)-sə-bəl-nəs\ *n* — **in·dis·pens·ably** \-blē\ *adv*

in·dis·pose \ˌin-di-'spōz\ *vt* **-posed; -pos·ing** [prob. back-formation fr. *indisposed*] (1657) **1 a** : to make unfit : DISQUALIFY **b** : to make averse : DISINCLINE **2** *archaic* : to cause to be in poor physical health

in·dis·posed \-'spōzd\ *adj* (15c) **1** : slightly ill **2** : AVERSE

in·dis·po·si·tion \ˌin-ˌdis-pə-'zi-shən\ *n* (15c) : the condition of being indisposed: **a** : DISINCLINATION **b** : a usu. slight illness

in·dis·put·able \ˌin-di-'spyü-tə-bəl, (ˌ)in-'dis-pyə-\ *adj* [LL *indisputabilis*, fr. L *in-* + *disputabilis* disputable] (1551) : not disputable : UNQUESTIONABLE ⟨~ proof⟩ — **in·dis·put·able·ness** *n* — **in·dis·put·ably** \-blē\ *adv*

in·dis·so·cia·ble \ˌin-di-'sō-sh(ē-)ə-bəl, -sē-ə-\ *adj* (1855) : not dissociated : INSEPARABLE — **in·dis·so·cia·bly** \-blē\ *adv*

in·dis·sol·u·ble \ˌin-di-'säl-yə-bəl\ *adj* (1542) : not dissoluble; *esp* : incapable of being annulled, undone, or broken : PERMANENT ⟨an ~ contract⟩ — **in·dis·sol·u·bil·i·ty** \-ˌsäl-yə-'bi-lə-tē\ *n* — **in·dis·sol·u·ble·ness** \-'säl-yə-bəl-nəs\ *n* — **in·dis·sol·u·bly** \-blē\ *adv*

in·dis·tinct \ˌin-di-'stiŋ(k)t\ *adj* [L *indistinctus*, fr. *in-* + *distinctus* distinct] (1526) : not distinct: as **a** : not sharply outlined or separable : BLURRED ⟨~ figures in the fog⟩ **b** : FAINT, DIM ⟨an ~ light in the distance⟩ **c** : not clearly recognizable or understandable : UNCERTAIN

— **in·dis·tinct·ly** \-'stiŋ(k)t-lē, -'stiŋ-klē\ *adv* — **in·dis·tinct·ness** \-'stiŋ(k)t-nəs, -'stiŋk-nəs\ *n*

in·dis·tinc·tive \-'stiŋ(k)-tiv\ *adj* (1846) : lacking distinctive qualities

in·dis·tin·guish·able \ˌin-di-'stiŋ-gwi-shə-bəl, -'stiŋ-wi-\ *adj* (1606) : not distinguishable: as **a** : indeterminate in shape or structure **b** : not clearly recognizable or understandable **c** : lacking identifying or individualizing qualities — **in·dis·tin·guish·abil·i·ty** \-ˌstiŋ-gwi-shə-'bi-lə-tē, -ˌstiŋ-wi-\ *n* — **in·dis·tin·guish·ably** \-blē\ *adv*

in·dite \in-'dīt\ *vt* **in·dit·ed; in·dit·ing** [ME *enditen*, fr. OF *enditer* to write down, proclaim, fr. (assumed) VL *indictare* to proclaim, freq. of L *indicere* to proclaim, fr. *in-* + *dicere* to say — more at DICTION] (14c) **1 a** : MAKE UP, COMPOSE ⟨~ a poem⟩ **b** : to give literary or formal expression to **c** : to put down in writing ⟨~ a message⟩ **2** *obs* : DICTATE — **in·dit·er** *n*

in·di·um \'in-dē-əm\ *n* [ISV *ind-* + NL *-ium*] (1864) : a malleable fusible silvery metallic element that is chiefly trivalent, occurs esp. in sphalerite ores, and is used as a plating for bearings, in alloys having a low melting point, and in the making of transistors — see ELEMENT table

indium antimonide *n* (1957) : a synthetic compound InSb of indium and antimony that is a semiconducting and photosensitive material and is used esp. in infrared photodetectors

¹in·di·vid·u·al \ˌin-də-'vij-wəl, -'vi-jə-wəl, -'vi-jəl\ *adj* [ML *individualis*, fr. L *individuus* indivisible, fr. *in-* + *dividuus* divided, fr. *dividere* to divide] (15c) **1** *obs* : INSEPARABLE **2 a** : of, relating to, or distinctively associated with an individual ⟨an ~ effort⟩ **b** : being an individual or existing as an indivisible whole **c** : intended for one person ⟨an ~ serving⟩ **3** : existing as a distinct entity : SEPARATE **4** : having marked individuality ⟨an ~ style⟩ *syn* see SPECIAL, CHARACTERISTIC — **in·di·vid·u·al·ly** *adv*

²individual *n* (1605) **1 a** : a particular being or thing as distinguished from a class, species, or collection: as (1) : a single human being as contrasted with a social group or institution ⟨a teacher who works with ~s⟩ (2) : a single organism as distinguished from a group **b** : a particular person ⟨are you the ~ I spoke with on the telephone?⟩ **2** : an indivisible entity **3** : the reference of a name or variable of the lowest logical type in a calculus

in·di·vid·u·al·ise *Brit var of* INDIVIDUALIZE

in·di·vid·u·al·ism \ˌin-də-'vij-wə-ˌli-zəm, -'vi-jə-wə-, -'vi-jə-ˌli-\ *n* (1827) **1 a** (1) : a doctrine that the interests of the individual are or ought to be ethically paramount; *also* : conduct guided by such a doctrine (2) : the conception that all values, rights, and duties originate in individuals **b** : a theory maintaining the political and economic independence of the individual and stressing individual initiative, action, and interests; *also* : conduct or practice guided by such a theory **2 a** : INDIVIDUALITY **b** : an individual peculiarity : IDIOSYNCRASY

in·di·vid·u·al·ist \-list\ *n* (1840) **1** : one that pursues a markedly independent course in thought or action **2** : one that advocates or practices individualism — **individualist** *or* **in·di·vid·u·al·is·tic** \-ˌvi-jə-wə-'lis-tik, -ˌvi-jə-wə-, -ˌvi-jə-'lis-\ *adj* — **in·di·vid·u·al·is·ti·cal·ly** \-'lis-ti-k(ə-)lē\ *adv*

in·di·vid·u·al·i·ty \-ˌvi-jə-'wa-lə-tē\ *n, pl* **-ties** (1614) **1 a** : total character peculiar to and distinguishing an individual from others **b** : PERSONALITY **2** *archaic* : the quality or state of being indivisible **3** : separate or distinct existence **4** : INDIVIDUAL, PERSON

in·di·vid·u·al·ize \-'vij-wə-ˌlīz, -'vi-jə-wə-, -'vi-jə-ˌliz\ *vt* **-ized; -iz·ing** (1637) **1** : to make individual in character **2** : to treat or notice individually : PARTICULARIZE **3** : to adapt to the needs or special circumstances of an individual ⟨~ teaching according to student ability⟩ — **in·di·vid·u·al·i·za·tion** \-ˌvij-wə-lə-'zā-shən, -ˌvi-jə-wə-, -ˌvi-jə-lə-\ *n*

individual medley *n* (ca. 1949) : a swimming race in which each contestant swims each part of the course with a different stroke

individual retirement account *n* (1974) : IRA

in·di·vid·u·ate \ˌin-də-'vi-jə-ˌwāt\ *vt* **-at·ed; -at·ing** (1614) **1** : to give individuality to **2** : to form into a distinct entity

in·di·vid·u·a·tion \-ˌvi-jə-'wā-shən\ *n* (1628) **1** : the act or process of individuating: as **a** (1) : the development of the individual from the universal (2) : the determination of the individual in the general **b** : the process by which individuals in society become differentiated from one another **c** : regional differentiation along a primary embryonic axis **2** : the state of being individuated; *specif* : INDIVIDUALITY

in·di·vis·i·ble \ˌin-də-'vi-zə-bəl\ *adj* [ME, fr. LL *indivisibilis*, fr. L *in-* + LL *divisibilis* divisible] (14c) : not divisible — **in·di·vis·i·bil·i·ty** \-ˌvi-zə-'bi-lə-tē\ *n* — **indivisible** *n* — **in·di·vis·i·bly** \-'vi-zə-blē\ *adv*

indo- *see* IND.

Indo- *comb form* [Gk, fr. *Indos* India] **1** : India or the East Indies ⟨*Indo*-Pakistani⟩ **2** : Indo-European ⟨*Indo*-Hittite⟩

In·do–Ar·y·an \ˌin-dō-'ar-ē-ən, -'er-; -'är-yən\ *n* (1881) **1** : a member of one of the peoples of the Indian subcontinent speaking an Indo-European language **2** : one of the early Indo-European invaders of southern Asia **3** : a branch of the Indo-European language family that includes Hindi, Bengali, Punjabi, and other languages spoken primarily in India, Pakistan, Bangladesh, and Sri Lanka — see INDO-EUROPEAN LANGUAGES table — **Indo–Aryan** *adj*

In·do–Chi·nese \-ˌchī-'nēz, -'nēs\ *n* (ca. 1934) **1** : a native or inhabitant of Indochina **2** : SINO-TIBETAN — **Indo–Chinese** *adj*

in·doc·ile \(ˌ)in-'dä-səl *also* -ˌsīl, esp Brit -'dō-ˌsīl\ *adj* [MF, fr. L *indocilis*, fr. *in-* + *docilis* docile] (1603) : unwilling or indisposed to be taught or disciplined : INTRACTABLE — **in·do·cil·i·ty** \ˌin-dä-'si-lə-tē, -dō-\ *n*

in·doc·tri·nate \in-'däk-trə-ˌnāt\ *vt* **-nat·ed; -nat·ing** [prob. fr. ME *endoctrinen*, fr. MF *endoctriner*, fr. OF, fr. *en-* + *doctrine* doctrine] (1626) **1** : to instruct esp. in fundamentals or rudiments : TEACH **2** : to imbue with a usu. partisan or sectarian opinion, point of view, or principle — **in·doc·tri·na·tion** \ˌin-ˌdäk-trə-'nā-shən\ *n* — **in·doc·tri·na·tor** \in-'däk-trə-ˌnā-tər\ *n*

\ə\ abut \ᵊ\ kitten, F table \ər\ further \a\ ash \ā\ ace \ä\ mop, mar \aů\ out \ch\ chin \e\ bet \ē\ easy \g\ go \i\ hit \ī\ ice \j\ job \ŋ\ sing \ō\ go \ȯ\ law \ȯi\ boy \th\ thin \t͟h\ the \ü\ loot \ů\ foot \y\ yet \zh\ vision \à, k̲, ⁿ, œ, œ̄, ս, ս̄, ᵜ\ *see* Guide to Pronunciation

¹**In·do-Eu·ro·pe·an** \,in-dō-,yur̄-ə-'pē-ən\ *adj* (1814) : of, relating to, or constituting the Indo-European languages

²**Indo-European** *n* (1864) **1 :** INDO-EUROPEAN LANGUAGES **2 a :** an unrecorded prehistoric language from which the Indo-European languages are descended **b :** a member of the people speaking this language

In·do-Eu·ro·pe·an·ist \-,yur̄-ə-'pē-ə-nist\ *n* (1926) : a specialist in Indo-European linguistics

Indo-European languages *n pl* (1864) : a family of languages comprising those spoken in most of Europe and in the parts of the world colonized by Europeans since 1500 and also in Persia, the subcontinent of India, and some other parts of Asia

In·do-Ger·man·ic \,in-dō-jər-'ma-nik\ *adj* (1835) : INDO-EUROPEAN — **Indo-Germanic** *n*

In·do-Hit·tite \-'hi-,tīt\ *n* (1930) **1 :** a hypothetical parent language of Indo-European and Anatolian **2 :** a language family including Indo-European and Anatolian — **Indo-Hittite** *adj*

In·do-Ira·ni·an \-ir-'ä-nē-ən\ *adj* (1876) : of, relating to, or constituting a subfamily of the Indo-European languages that consists of the Indo-Aryan and the Iranian branches — see INDO-EUROPEAN LANGUAGES table — **Indo-Iranian** *n*

in·dole \'in-,dōl\ *n* [ISV *ind-* + *-ole*] (1869) : a crystalline compound C₈H₇N that is a decomposition product of proteins containing tryptophan, that can be made synthetically, and that is used in perfumes; *also* : a derivative of indole

in·dole·ace·tic acid \,in-(,)dō-lə-'sē-tik-\ *n* (1937) : a crystalline plant hormone C₁₀H₉NO₂ that is a naturally occurring auxin promoting growth and rooting of plants — called *also heteroauxin*

in·dole·bu·tyr·ic acid \,in-(,)dōl-byü-'tir-ik-\ *n* (1936) : a crystalline acid C₁₂H₁₃NO₂ similar to indoleacetic acid in its effects on plants

in·do·lence \'in-də-lən(t)s\ *n* (1710) : inclination to laziness : SLOTH

in·do·lent \-lənt\ *adj* [LL *indolent-, indolens* insensitive to pain, fr. L *in-* + *dolent-, dolens,* prp. of *dolēre* to feel pain] (1663) **1 a :** causing little or no pain **b :** slow to develop or heal **2 a :** averse to activity, effort, or movement : habitually lazy **b :** conducing to or encouraging laziness ⟨~ heat⟩ **c :** exhibiting indolence ⟨an ~ sigh⟩ *syn* see LAZY — **in·do·lent·ly** *adv*

In·dol·o·gy \(,)in-'dä-lə-jē\ *n* (1888) : the study of India and its people — **In·dol·o·gist** \-jist\ *n*

in·do·meth·a·cin \,in-dō-'me-thə-sən\ *n* [*indole* + *meth-* + *ac*etic acid + ¹-*in*] (1963) : a nonsteroidal drug C₁₉H₁₆ClNO₄ with anti-inflammatory, analgesic, and antipyretic properties used esp. in treating arthritis

in·dom·i·ta·ble \in-'dä-mə-tə-bəl\ *adj* [LL *indomitabilis,* fr. L *in-* + *domitare* to tame — more at DAUNT] (1830) : incapable of being subdued : UNCONQUERABLE ⟨~ courage⟩ — **in·dom·i·ta·bil·i·ty** \(,)in-,dä-mə-tə-'bi-lə-tē\ *n* — **in·dom·i·ta·ble·ness** \in-'dä-mə-tə-bəl-nəs\ *n* — **in·dom·i·ta·bly** \-blē\ *adv*

In·do·ne·sian \,in-də-'nē-zhən, -shən\ *n* (1850) **1 :** a native or inhabitant of the Malay Archipelago **2 a :** a native or inhabitant of the Republic of Indonesia **b :** the language based on Malay that is the national language of the Republic of Indonesia — **Indonesian** *adj*

in·door \'in-,dōr, -,dȯr\ *adj* (1711) **1 :** of or relating to the interior of a building **2 :** living, located, or carried on within a building ⟨an ~ sport⟩

in·doors \'in-,dōrz, (,)in-, -,dȯrz\ *adv* (1832) : in or into a building

in·do·phe·nol \,in-dō-'fē-,nȯl, -,nōl, ,in-(,)dō-fi-'\ *n* [ISV] (ca. 1881) : any of various blue or green dyes

in·dorse, in·dorse·ment *var of* ENDORSE, ENDORSEMENT

in·dox·yl \in-'däk-səl\ *n* [ISV *ind-* + *hydroxyl*] (ca. 1886) : a crystalline compound C₈H₇NO found in plants and animals or synthesized as a step in indigo manufacture

in·draft \'in-,draft, -,dräft\ *n* (1594) **1 :** an inward flow or current (as of air or water) **2 :** a drawing or pulling in

in·drawn \'in-,drȯn\ *adj* (1751) **1 :** ALOOF, RESERVED **2 :** drawn in

in·dri \'in-drē\ *n, pl* **indris** [F, fr. Malagasy *indry* look!] (1839) : a large black-and-white Madagascan lemur (*Indri indri*) that is about two feet long with a rudimentary tail

in·du·bi·ta·ble \(,)in-'dü-bə-tə-bəl, -'dyü-\ *adj* [ME *indubitabyll,* fr. L *indubitabilis,* fr. *in-* + *dubitabilis* dubitable] (15c) : too evident to be doubted : UNQUESTIONABLE — **in·du·bi·ta·bil·i·ty** \-,dü-bə-tə-'bi-lə-tē, -,dyü-\ *n* — **in·du·bi·ta·ble·ness** \-'dü-bə-tə-bəl-nəs, -'dyü-\ *n* — **in·du·bi·ta·bly** \-blē\ *adv*

in·duce \in-'düs, -'dyüs\ *vt* **in·duced; in·duc·ing** [ME, fr. L *inducere,* fr. *in-* + *ducere* to lead — more at TOW] (14c) **1 a :** to move by persuasion or influence **b :** to call forth or bring about by influence or stimulation **2 a :** EFFECT, CAUSE **b :** to cause the formation of **c :** to produce (as an electric current) by induction **3 :** to determine by induction; *specif :* to infer from particulars

in·duce·ment \in-'düs-mənt, -'dyüs-\ *n* (1594) **1 :** a motive or consideration that leads one to action or to additional or more effective actions **2 :** the act or process of inducing **3 :** matter presented by way of introduction or background to explain the principal allegations of a legal cause, plea, or defense *syn* see MOTIVE

in·duc·er \-'dü-sər, -'dyü-\ *n* (1554) : one that induces; *esp* : a substance that is capable of activating a structural gene by combining with and inactivating a genetic repressor

in·duc·ible \in-'dü-sə-bəl, -'dyü-\ *adj* (ca. 1677) : capable of being induced; *esp* : formed by a cell in response to the presence of its substrate ⟨~ enzymes⟩ — compare CONSTITUTIVE — **in·duc·ibil·i·ty** \-,dü-sə-'bi-lə-tē, -,dyü-\ *n*

in·duct \in-'dəkt\ *vt* [ME, fr. ML *inductus,* pp. of *inducere,* fr. L] (14c) **1 :** to put in formal possession (as of a benefice or office) : INSTALL ⟨was ~*ed* as president of the college⟩ **2 a :** to admit as a member ⟨~*ed* into a scholastic society⟩ **b :** INTRODUCE, INITIATE **c :** to enroll for military training or service (as under a selective service act) **3 :** LEAD, CONDUCT

in·duc·tance \in-'dək-tən(t)s\ *n* (1886) **1 a :** a property of an electric circuit by which an electromotive force is induced in it by a variation of current either in the circuit itself or in a neighboring circuit **b :** the measure of this property that is equal to the ratio of the induced electromotive force to the rate of change of the inducing current **2 :** a circuit or a device possessing inductance

in·duct·ee \(,)in-,dək-'tē, in-'dək-,\ *n* (1940) : one who is inducted

in·duc·tion \in-'dək-shən\ *n* (14c) **1 a :** the act or process of inducting (as into office) **b :** an initial experience : INITIATION **c :** the formality by which a civilian is inducted into military service **2 a** (1) : inference of a generalized conclusion from particular instances — compare DEDUCTION 2a (2) : a conclusion arrived at by induction **b** : mathematical demonstration of the validity of a law concerning all the positive integers by proving that it holds for the integer 1 and that if it holds for all the integers preceding a given integer it must hold for the next following integer **3 :** a preface, prologue, or introductory scene esp. of an early English play **4 a :** the act of bringing forward or adducing (as facts or particulars) **b :** the act of causing or bringing on or about **c :** the process by which an electrical conductor becomes electrified when near a charged body, by which a magnetizable body becomes magnetized when in a magnetic field or in the magnetic flux set up by a magnetomotive force, or by which an electromotive force is produced in a circuit by varying the magnetic field linked with the circuit **d :** the inspiration of the fuel-air charge from the carburetor into the combustion chamber of an internal-combustion engine **e** : the sum of the processes by which the fate of embryonic cells is determined and morphogenetic differentiation brought about

induction coil *n* (1837) : an apparatus for obtaining intermittent high voltage consisting of a primary coil through which the direct current flows, an interrupter, and a secondary coil of a larger number of turns in which the high voltage is induced

induction heating *n* (1919) : heating of material by means of an electric current that is caused to flow through the material or its container by electromagnetic induction

induction motor *n* (1897) : an alternating-current motor in which torque is produced by the reaction between a varying magnetic field generated in the stator and the current induced in the coils of the rotor

in·duc·tive \in-'dək-tiv\ *adj* (15c) **1 :** leading on : INDUCING **2 :** of, relating to, or employing mathematical or logical induction ⟨~ reasoning⟩ **3 :** of or relating to inductance or electrical induction **4 :** INTRODUCTORY **5 :** involving the action of an embryological inductor : tending to produce induction — **in·duc·tive·ly** *adv*

in·duc·tor \in-'dək-tər\ *n* (1652) **1 :** one that inducts **2 a :** a part of an electrical apparatus that acts upon another or is itself acted upon by induction **b :** REACTOR 2 **3 :** ORGANIZER 2

in·due *var of* ENDUE

in·dulge \in-'dəlj\ *vb* **in·dulged; in·dulg·ing** [L *indulgēre* to be complaisant] *vt* (ca. 1623) **1 a :** to give free rein to **b :** to take unrestrained pleasure in : GRATIFY **2 a :** to yield to the desire of : HUMOR **b :** to treat with excessive leniency, generosity, or consideration ~ *vi* : to indulge oneself — **in·dulg·er** *n*

syn INDULGE, PAMPER, HUMOR, SPOIL, BABY, MOLLYCODDLE mean to show undue favor to a person's desires and feelings. INDULGE implies excessive compliance and weakness in gratifying another's or one's own desires ⟨indulged myself with food at the slightest excuse⟩. PAMPER implies inordinate gratification of desire for luxury and comfort with consequent enervating effect ⟨pampered by the amenities of modern living⟩. HUMOR stresses a yielding to a person's moods or whims ⟨humored him by letting him tell the story⟩. SPOIL stresses the injurious effects on character by indulging or pampering ⟨foolish parents spoil their children⟩. BABY suggests excessive care, attention, or solicitude ⟨babying students by grading too easily⟩. MOLLYCODDLE suggests an excessive degree of care and attention to another's health or welfare ⟨refused to mollycoddle her malingering son⟩.

in·dul·gence \in-'dəl-jən(t)s\ *n* (14c) **1 :** remission of part or all of the temporal and esp. purgatorial punishment that according to Roman Catholicism is due for sins whose eternal punishment has been remitted and whose guilt has been pardoned (as through the sacrament of reconciliation) **2 :** the act of indulging : the state of being indulgent **3 a** : an indulgent act **b :** an extension of time for payment or performance granted as a favor **4 a :** the act of indulging in something; *esp* : SELF-INDULGENCE **b :** something indulged in ⟨walk off gastronomic ~s —Barbara L. Michaels⟩

in·dul·gent \in-'dəl-jənt\ *adj* [L *indulgent-, indulgens,* prp. of *indulgēre*] (1509) : indulging or characterized by indulgence; *esp* : LENIENT — **in·dul·gent·ly** *adv*

in·dult \'in-,dəlt, in-'\ *n* [ME (Sc), fr. ML *indultum,* fr. LL, grant, fr. L, neut. of *indultus,* pp. of *indulgēre*] (15c) : a special often temporary dispensation granted in the Roman Catholic Church

¹**in·du·rate** \'in-də-rət, -dyə-; in-'dur̄-ət, -'dyur̄-\ *adj* (14c) : physically or morally hardened

²**in·du·rate** \'in-də-,rāt, -dyə-\ *vb* **-rat·ed; -rat·ing** [L *induratus,* pp. of *indurare,* fr. *in-* + *durare* to harden, fr. *durus* hard — more at DURING] *vt* (1538) **1 :** to make unfeeling, stubborn, or obdurate **2 :** to make hardy : INURE **3 :** to make hard ⟨great heat ~s clay⟩ **4 :** to establish firmly : CONFIRM ~ *vi* **1 :** to grow hard : HARDEN **2 :** to become established

in·du·rat·ed \-,rä-təd\ *adj* (1604) : having become firm or hard esp. by increase of fibrous elements ⟨~ tissue⟩

in·du·ra·tion \,in-də-'rä-shən, -dyə-\ *n* (14c) : the process of or condition produced by growing hard; *specif :* sclerosis esp. when associated with inflammation — **in·du·ra·tive** \'in-də-,rä-tiv, -dyə-; in-'dur̄-ə-, -'dyur̄-\ *adj*

in·du·si·um \in-'dü-zē-əm, -'dyü-; -zhē-\ *n, pl* **-sia** \-zē-ə, -zhē-\ [NL, fr. L, tunic] (1807) : an investing outgrowth or membrane: as **a :** an outgrowth of a fern frond that invests the sori **b :** the annulus of a fungus esp. when large and full

¹**in·dus·tri·al** \in-'dəs-trē-əl\ *adj* (15c) **1 :** of or relating to industry **2** : derived from human industry ⟨~ wealth⟩ **3 :** engaged in industry ⟨the ~ classes⟩ **4 :** used in or developed for use in industry ⟨~ diamonds⟩; *also* : HEAVY-DUTY ⟨an ~ zipper⟩ **5 :** characterized by highly developed industries ⟨an ~ nation⟩ — **in·dus·tri·al·ly** \-trē-ə-lē\ *adv*

²**industrial** *n* (1865) **1 a :** one that is employed in industry **b :** a company engaged in industrial production or service **2 :** a stock or bond issued by an industrial corporation or enterprise

industrial action *n* (ca. 1931) *Brit :* JOB ACTION

industrial archaeology *n* (1951) : the study of the buildings, machinery, and equipment of the industrial revolution — **industrial archaeologist** *n*

INDO-EUROPEAN LANGUAGES

BRANCH	GROUP	LANGUAGES AND MAJOR DIALECTS[1]			PROVENIENCE
		ANCIENT	MEDIEVAL	MODERN	
	Anatolian	*Hittite, Lydian, Lycian Luwian, Palaic Hieroglyphic Luwian*			ancient Asia Minor
INDO-IRANIAN	Kafiri (Nuristani)			languages of eastern Afghanistan	Afghanistan
INDO-IRANIAN — Indo-Aryan	Sanskritic	*Sanskrit, Pali* *Prakrits*	*Prakrits*		India
				Shina, Khowar	Upper Indus valley
				Kashmiri	Kashmir
				Lahnda	western Punjab
				Sindhi	Sind
				Panjabi	Punjab
				Rajasthani	Rajasthan
				Gujarati	Gujarat
				Marathi	western India
				Konkani	western India
				Oriya	Orissa
				Bengali	Bangladesh, West Bengal
				Assamese	Assam
				Bhojpuri	Bihar, Uttar Pradesh
				Hindi	northern India
				Urdu	Pakistan, India
				Nepali	Nepal
				Sinhalese	Sri Lanka
				Romany	uncertain
INDO-IRANIAN — Iranian	West	*Old Persian*	*Pahlavi* Persian		Persia Iran
				Persian	Iran
				Kurdish	Iran, Iraq, Turkey
				Baluchi	Pakistan
				Tajiki	Tajikistan
	East	*Avestan*			ancient Persia
			Sogdian, Khotanese		central Asia
				Pashto	Afghanistan, Pakistan
				Ossetic	Caucasus
	Armenian		Armenian	Armenian	Asia Minor, Caucasus
Greek or Hellenic		*Greek*	*Greek*	Greek	Greece, the eastern Mediterranean
BALTO-SLAVIC — Baltic			*Old Prussian*		East Prussia
				Lithuanian	Lithuania
				Latvian	Latvia
BALTO-SLAVIC — Slavic	South		*Old Church Slavonic*		
				Slovene	Slovenia
				Serbo-Croatian	Croatia, Bosnia and Herzegovina, Serbia, Montenegro
				Macedonian	Macedonia
				Bulgarian	Bulgaria
	West			Czech, Slovak	Czechoslovakia
				Polish, Kashubian	Poland
				Wendish, *Polabian*	Germany
	East		*Old Russian*	Russian	Russia
				Ukrainian	Ukraine
				Belorussian	Belarus
	Albanian			Albanian	Albania, Serbia, Macedonia
Scantily recorded and of uncertain affinities within Indo-European		*Ligurian, Messapian, Illyrian, Thracian, Phrygian*			ancient Italy Balkans Asia Minor
	Tocharian		*Tocharian A* *Tocharian B*		central Asia
GERMANIC	East		*Gothic*		eastern Europe
	North		*Old Norse*	Icelandic	Iceland
				Faeroese	Faeroe Islands
				Norwegian	Norway
				Swedish	Sweden
				Danish	Denmark
	West		*Old High German* *Middle High German*	German	Germany, Switzerland, Austria
				Yiddish	Germany, eastern Europe
			Old Saxon *Middle Low German*	Low German	northern Germany
			Middle Dutch	Dutch	Netherlands
				Afrikaans	South Africa
				Flemish	Belgium
			Old Frisian	Frisian	Netherlands, Germany
			Old English *Middle English*	English	England
ITALIC		*Venetic, Oscan, Umbrian, Faliscan* Latin			ancient Italy
				Portuguese	Portugal
				Spanish	Spain
				Judeo-Spanish	Mediterranean lands
				Catalan	Spain (Catalonia)
			Old Provençal	Provençal	southern France
			Old French *Middle French*	French	France, Belgium, Switzerland
				Italian	Italy, Switzerland
				Rhaeto-Romance	Switzerland, Italy
				Sardinian	Sardinia
				Dalmatian	Adriatic coast
				Romanian	Romania, Balkans
CELTIC	Continental	*Gaulish*			Gaul
	Goidelic		*Old Irish* *Middle Irish*	Irish	Ireland
				Scottish Gaelic	Scotland
				Manx	Isle of Man
	Brythonic		*Old Welsh* *Middle Welsh*	Welsh	Wales
			Old Cornish	Cornish	Cornwall
			Old Breton	Breton	Brittany

[1] Italics denote dead languages. Languages listed in roman type in the ancient or medieval column survive only in some special use, as in literary composition or liturgy.

industrial arts *n pl but sing in constr* (ca. 1925) : a subject taught in elementary and secondary schools that aims at developing manual skill and familiarity with tools and machines

industrial engineering *n* (ca. 1924) : engineering that deals with the design, improvement, and installation of integrated systems (as of people, materials, and energy) in industry — **industrial engineer** *n*

in·dus·tri·al·ise *Brit var of* INDUSTRIALIZE

in·dus·tri·al·ism \in-'dəs-trē-ə-ˌli-zəm\ *n* (1831) : social organization in which industries and esp. large-scale industries are dominant

in·dus·tri·al·ist \-list\ *n* (1864) : one owning or engaged in the management of an industry : MANUFACTURER

in·dus·tri·al·ize \in-'dəs-trē-ə-ˌlīz\ *vb* **-ized; -iz·ing** *vt* (1882) : to make industrial ⟨~ an agricultural region⟩ ~ *vi* : to become industrial — **in·dus·tri·al·i·za·tion** \-ˌdəs-trē-ə-lə-'zā-shən\ *n*

industrial melanism *n* (1943) : genetically determined melanism as a population phenomenon esp. in moths in which the proportion of dark individuals tends to increase due to differential predation esp. by birds which more easily find and eat lighter-colored individuals in habitats darkened by industrial pollution

industrial psychology *n* (1917) : the application of the findings and methods of experimental, clinical, and social psychology to industrial concerns — **industrial psychologist** *n*

industrial relations *n pl* (1904) : the dealings or relationships of a usu. large business or industrial enterprise with its own workers, with labor in general, with governmental agencies, or with the public

industrial revolution *n* (1848) : a rapid major change in an economy (as in England in the late 18th century) marked by the general introduction of power-driven machinery or by an important change in the prevailing types and methods of use of such machines

industrial school *n* (1853) : a school specializing in the teaching of industrial arts; *specif* : one for juvenile delinquents

industrial sociology *n* (1948) : sociological analysis directed at institutions and social relationships within and largely controlled or affected by industry

in·dus·tri·al–strength \in-'dəs-trē-əl-'stren(k)th, -'stren(t)th\ *adj* (1976) : of industrial quality; *also* : marked by more than usual power or durability ⟨~ boots⟩ ⟨an ~ voice⟩

industrial union *n* (1902) : a labor union open to workers in an industry irrespective of their occupation or craft — compare CRAFT UNION

in·dus·tri·ous \in-'dəs-trē-əs\ *adj* (15c) **1** *obs* : SKILLFUL, INGENIOUS **2** : persistently active : ZEALOUS **3** : constantly, regularly, or habitually occupied : DILIGENT *syn* see BUSY — **in·dus·tri·ous·ly** *adv* — **in·dus·tri·ous·ness** *n*

in·dus·try \'in-(ˌ)dəs-trē\ *n, pl* **-tries** [ME *industrie* skill, employment involving skill, fr. MF, fr. L *industria* diligence, fr. *industrius* diligent, fr. OL *indostruus*, perh. fr. *indu* in + *-struus* (akin to L *struere* to build) — more at END, STREW] (15c) **1** : diligence in an employment or pursuit; *esp* : steady or habitual effort **2 a** : systematic labor esp. for some useful purpose or the creation of something of value **b** : a department or branch of a craft, art, business, or manufacture; *esp* : one that employs a large personnel and capital esp. in manufacturing **c** : a distinct group of productive or profit-making enterprises ⟨the banking ~⟩ **d** : manufacturing activity as a whole ⟨the nation's ~⟩ **3** : work devoted to the study of a particular subject or author ⟨the Shakespeare ~⟩ *syn* see BUSINESS

in·dwell \in-'dwel, 'in-ˌ\ *vi* (14c) : to exist as an inner activating spirit, force, or principle ~ *vt* : to exist within as an activating spirit, force, or principle — **in·dwell·er** *n*

in·dwell·ing \'in-ˌdwe-liŋ\ *adj* (1646) **1** : being an inner activating or guiding force **2** : left within a bodily organ or passage esp. to promote drainage — used of an implanted tube (as a catheter)

¹-ine *adj suffix* **1** [ME *-in, -ine*, fr. MF & L; MF *-in*, fr. L *-inus* — more at -EN] : of or relating to ⟨estuar*ine*⟩ **2** [ME *-in, -ine*, fr. MF & L; MF *-in*, fr. L *-inus*, fr. Gk *-inos* — more at -EN] : made of : like ⟨opal*ine*⟩

²-ine *n suffix* [ME *-in, -ine*, fr. MF & L; MF *-ine*, fr. L *-ina*, fr. fem. of *-inus*, adj. suffix] **1** : chemical substance: as **a** : halogen element ⟨chlor*ine*⟩ **b** : basic or base-containing carbon compound that contains nitrogen ⟨quin*ine*⟩ ⟨cyst*ine*⟩ **c** : mixture of compounds (as of hydrocarbons) ⟨gasol*ine*⟩ **d** : hydride ⟨ars*ine*⟩ **2** : -IN 1a **3** : commercial product or material ⟨glass*ine*⟩

in·ebri·ant \i-'nē-brē-ənt\ *n* (1819) : INTOXICANT

¹in·ebri·ate \i-'nē-brē-ˌāt\ *vt* **-at·ed; -at·ing** [L *inebriatus*, pp. of *inebriare*, fr. *in-* + *ebriare* to intoxicate, fr. *ebrius* drunk] (15c) **1** : to exhilarate or stupefy as if by liquor **2** : to make drunk : INTOXICATE — **in·ebri·a·tion** \-ˌnē-brē-'ā-shən\ *n*

²in·ebri·ate \i-'nē-brē-ət, -ˌāt\ *adj* (15c) **1** : affected by alcohol : DRUNK **2** : addicted to excessive drinking

³in·ebri·ate \-ət\ *n* (ca. 1796) : one who is drunk; *esp* : DRUNKARD

in·ebri·at·ed \-brē-ˌā-təd\ *adj* (1609) : exhilarated or confused by or as if by alcohol : INTOXICATED

in·ebri·ety \ˌi-ni-'brī-ə-tē\ *n* [prob. blend of *inebriation* and *ebriety* drunkenness] (1801) : the state of being inebriated : DRUNKENNESS

in·ed·i·ble \(ˌ)i-'ne-də-bəl\ *adj* (1822) : not fit to be eaten

in·ed·u·ca·ble \(ˌ)i-'ne-jə-kə-bəl\ *adj* (1884) : incapable of being educated — **in·ed·u·ca·bil·i·ty** \-ˌne-jə-kə-'bi-lə-tē\ *n*

in·ef·fa·ble \(ˌ)i-'ne-fə-bəl\ *adj* [ME, fr. MF, fr. L *ineffabilis*, fr. *in-* + *effabilis* capable of being expressed, fr. *effari* to speak out, fr. *ex-* + *fari* to speak — more at BAN] (14c) **1 a** : incapable of being expressed in words : INDESCRIBABLE ⟨~ joy⟩ **b** : UNSPEAKABLE ⟨~ disgust⟩ **2** : not to be uttered : TABOO ⟨the ~ name of Jehovah⟩ — **in·ef·fa·bil·i·ty** \-ˌne-fə-'bi-lə-tē\ *n* — **in·ef·fa·ble·ness** \-'ne-fə-bəl-nəs\ *n* — **in·ef·fa·bly** \-blē\ *adv*

in·ef·face·able \ˌi-nə-'fā-sə-bəl\ *adj* [prob. fr. F *ineffaçable*, fr. MF, fr. *in-* + *effaçable* effaceable] (1804) : not effaceable : INERADICABLE — **in·ef·face·abil·i·ty** \-ˌfā-sə-'bi-lə-tē\ *n* — **in·ef·face·ably** \-'fā-sə-blē\ *adv*

in·ef·fec·tive \ˌi-nə-'fek-tiv\ *adj* (1649) **1** : not producing an intended effect : INEFFECTUAL ⟨~ lighting⟩ **2** : not capable of performing efficiently or as expected : INCAPABLE ⟨an ~ executive⟩ — **in·ef·fec·tive·ly** *adv* — **in·ef·fec·tive·ness** *n*

in·ef·fec·tu·al \ˌi-nə-'fek-chə(-wə)l, -'feksh-wəl\ *adj* (15c) **1** : not producing the proper or intended effect : FUTILE **2** : INEFFECTIVE 2 — **in·ef·fec·tu·al·i·ty** \-ˌfek-chə-'wa-lə-tē\ *n* — **in·ef·fec·tu·al·ly** \-'fek-chə(-wə)-lē, -'feksh-wə-lē\ *adv* — **in·ef·fec·tu·al·ness** *n*

in·ef·fi·ca·cious \(ˌ)i-ˌne-fə-'kā-shəs\ *adj* (1658) : lacking the power to produce a desired effect : INEFFECTIVE — **in·ef·fi·ca·cious·ly** *adv* — **in·ef·fi·ca·cious·ness** *n*

in·ef·fi·ca·cy \(ˌ)i-'ne-fi-kə-sē\ *n* [LL *inefficacia*, fr. L *inefficac-, inefficax* inefficacious, fr. *in-* + *efficac-, efficax* efficacious] (ca. 1615) : lack of power to produce a desired effect

in·ef·fi·cien·cy \ˌi-nə-'fi-shən(t)-sē\ *n, pl* **-cies** (1749) **1** : the quality or state of being inefficient **2** : something that is inefficient

in·ef·fi·cient \-'fi-shənt\ *adj* (1750) : not efficient: as **a** : not producing the effect intended or desired **b** : wasteful of time or energy ⟨~ operating procedures⟩ **c** : INCAPABLE, INCOMPETENT ⟨an ~ worker⟩ — **inefficient** *n* — **in·ef·fi·cient·ly** *adv*

in·e·gal·i·tar·i·an \ˌi-ni-ˌga-lə-'ter-ē-ən\ *adj* (1940) : marked by disparity in social and economic standing

in·elas·tic \ˌi-nə-'las-tik\ *adj* (1748) : not elastic: as **a** : slow to react or respond to changing conditions **b** : INFLEXIBLE, UNYIELDING — **in·elas·tic·i·ty** \ˌi-ni-ˌlas-'ti-s(ə-)tē, (ˌ)i-ˌnē-ˌlas-\ *n*

inelastic collision *n* (1937) : a collision in which part of the kinetic energy of the colliding particles changes into another form of energy (as radiation)

inelastic scattering *n* (1938) : a scattering of particles as the result of inelastic collision in which the total kinetic energy of the colliding particles changes

in·el·e·gance \(ˌ)i-'ne-li-gən(t)s\ *n* (1726) : lack of elegance

in·el·e·gant \-gənt\ *adj* [MF, fr. L *inelegant-, inelegans* elegant, fr. *in-* + *elegant-, elegans* elegant] (ca. 1570) : lacking in refinement, grace, or good taste — **in·el·e·gant·ly** *adv*

in·el·i·gi·ble \(ˌ)i-'ne-lə-jə-bəl\ *adj* [F *inéligible*, fr. *in-* + *éligible* eligible] (1770) : not eligible: as **a** : not qualified for an office or position **b** : not permitted under football rules to catch a forward pass — **in·el·i·gi·bil·i·ty** \-ˌne-lə-jə-'bi-lə-tē\ *n* — **ineligible** *n*

in·el·o·quent \(ˌ)i-'ne-lə-kwənt\ *adj* (ca. 1530) : not eloquent — **in·el·o·quent·ly** *adv*

in·eluc·ta·ble \ˌi-ni-'lək-tə-bəl\ *adj* [L *ineluctabilis*, fr. *in-* + *eluctari* to struggle clear of, fr. *ex-* + *luctari* to struggle, wrestle; akin to L *luxus* dislocated — more at LOCK] (ca. 1623) : not to be avoided, changed, or resisted : INEVITABLE — **in·eluc·ta·bil·i·ty** \-ˌlək-tə-'bi-lə-tē\ *n* — **in·eluc·ta·bly** \-'lək-tə-blē\ *adv*

in·elud·ible \ˌi-ni-'lü-də-bəl\ *adj* (1662) : INESCAPABLE

in·enar·ra·ble \ˌi-ni-'nar-ə-bəl\ *adj* [ME, fr. MF, fr. L *inenarrabilis*, fr. *in-* + *enarrare* to explain in detail, fr. *e-* + *narrare* to narrate] (15c) : incapable of being narrated : INDESCRIBABLE

in·ept \i-'nept\ *adj* [MF *inepte*, fr. L *ineptus*, fr. *in-* + *aptus* apt] (1542) **1** : lacking in fitness or aptitude : UNFIT **2** : lacking sense or reason : FOOLISH **3** : not suitable to the time, place, or occasion : inappropriate often to an absurd degree **4** : generally incompetent : BUNGLING *syn* see AWKWARD — **in·ept·ly** \-'nep(t)-lē\ *adv* — **in·ept·ness** \-nəs\ *n*

in·ep·ti·tude \(ˌ)i-'nep-tə-ˌtüd, -ˌtyüd\ *n* [L *ineptitudo*, fr. *ineptus*] (1615) : the quality or state of being inept; *esp* : INCOMPETENCE

in·equal·i·ty \ˌi-ni-'kwä-lə-tē\ *n* [ME *inequalite*, fr. MF *inequalité*, fr. L *inaequalitat-, inaequalitas*, fr. *inaequalis* unequal, fr. *in-* + *aequalis* equal] (15c) **1** : the quality of being unequal or uneven: as **a** : lack of evenness **b** : social disparity **c** : disparity of distribution or opportunity **d** : the condition of being variable : CHANGEABLENESS **2** : an instance of being unequal **3** : a formal statement of inequality between two quantities usu. separated by a sign of inequality (as <, >, or ≠ signifying respectively *is less than, is greater than,* or *is not equal to*)

in·eq·ui·ta·ble \(ˌ)i-'ne-kwə-tə-bəl\ *adj* (1667) : not equitable : UNFAIR — **in·eq·ui·ta·bly** \-blē\ *adv*

in·eq·ui·ty \(ˌ)i-'ne-kwə-tē\ *n* (1556) **1** : INJUSTICE, UNFAIRNESS **2** : an instance of injustice or unfairness

in·equi·valve \(ˌ)i-'nē-kwə-ˌvalv\ *also* **in·equi·valved** \-ˌvalvd\ *adj* (1776) : having the valves unequal in size and form — used of a bivalve mollusk or shell

in·erad·i·ca·ble \ˌi-ni-'ra-di-kə-bəl\ *adj* (1818) : incapable of being eradicated — **in·erad·i·ca·bil·i·ty** \-ˌra-di-kə-'bi-lə-tē\ *n* — **in·erad·i·ca·bly** \-'ra-di-kə-blē\ *adv*

in·er·ran·cy \i-'ner-ən(t)-sē\ *n* (ca. 1834) : exemption from error : INFALLIBILITY ⟨the question of biblical ~⟩

in·er·rant \-ənt\ *adj* [L *inerrant-, inerrans*, fr. *in-* + *errant-, errans*, prp. of *errare* to err] (1837) : free from error

in·ert \i-'nərt\ *adj* [L *inert-, iners* unskilled, idle, fr. *in-* + *art-, ars* skill — more at ARM] (1647) **1** : lacking the power to move **2** : very slow to move or act : SLUGGISH **3** : deficient in active properties; *esp* : lacking a usual or anticipated chemical or biological action *syn* see INACTIVE — **inert** *n* — **in·ert·ly** *adv* — **in·ert·ness** *n*

inert gas *n* (1898) : NOBLE GAS

in·er·tia \i-'nər-shə, -shē-ə\ *n* [NL, fr. L, lack of skill, fr. *inert-, iners*] (1713) **1 a** : a property of matter by which it remains at rest or in uniform motion in the same straight line unless acted upon by some external force **b** : an analogous property of other physical quantities (as electricity) **2** : indisposition to motion, exertion, or change : INERTNESS — **in·er·tial** \-shəl\ *adj* — **in·er·tial·ly** \-'nər-shə-lē\ *adv*

inertial guidance *n* (ca. 1948) : guidance (as of an aircraft or spacecraft) by means of self-contained automatically controlling devices that respond to inertial forces — called also *inertial navigation*

in·es·cap·able \ˌi-nə-'skā-pə-bəl\ *adj* (1792) : incapable of being avoided, ignored, or denied : INEVITABLE — **in·es·cap·ably** \-blē\ *adv*

in·es·sen·tial \ˌi-nə-'sen(t)-shəl\ *adj* (1677) **1** : having no essence **2** : not essential : UNESSENTIAL — **inessential** *n*

in·es·ti·ma·ble \(ˌ)i-'nes-tə-mə-bəl\ *adj* [ME, fr. MF, fr. L *inaestimabilis*, fr. *in-* + *aestimabilis* estimable] (14c) **1** : incapable of being estimated or computed ⟨storms caused ~ damage⟩ **2** : too valuable or excellent to be measured or appreciated ⟨has performed an ~ service for his country⟩ — **in·es·ti·ma·bly** \-blē\ *adv*

in·ev·i·ta·ble \i-'ne-və-tə-bəl\ *adj* [ME, fr. L *inevitabilis*, fr. *in-* + *evitabilis* evitable] (14c) : incapable of being avoided or evaded — **in·ev·i·ta·bil·i·ty** \-ˌne-və-tə-'bi-lə-tē\ *n* — **in·ev·i·ta·ble·ness** \-'ne-və-tə-bəl-nəs\ *n*

in·ev·i·ta·bly \-blē\ *adv* (15c) **1** : in an inevitable way **2** : as is to be expected ⟨~, it rained⟩

in·ex·act \ˌi-nig-'zakt\ *adj* [F, fr. *in-* + *exact* exact] (ca. 1828) **1** : not precisely correct or true : INACCURATE ⟨an ~ translation⟩ **2** : not rigorous and careful ⟨an ~ thinker⟩ — **in·ex·act·ly** \-'zak(t)-lē\ *adv* — **in·ex·act·ness** \-nəs\ *n*

in·ex·ac·ti·tude \(,)i-,nig-'zak-tə-,tüd, -,tyüd\ *n* [F, fr. *inexact*] (1782) **1** : lack of exactitude or precision **2** : an instance of inexactness

in ex·cel·sis \in-ik-'sel-səs *also* -'chel-\ *adv* [LL, on high] (1602) : in the highest degree

in·ex·cus·able \,in-ik-'skyü-zə-bəl\ *adj* [ME, fr. L *inexcusabilis*, fr. *in-* + *excusabilis* excusable] (15c) : being without excuse or justification — **in·ex·cus·able·ness** *n* — **in·ex·cus·ably** \-blē\ *adv*

in·ex·haust·ible \,i-nig-'zȯ-stə-bəl\ *adj* (1601) : not exhaustible: as **a** : incapable of being used up ⟨~ riches⟩ **b** : incapable of being wearied or worn out ⟨an ~ hiker⟩ — **in·ex·haust·ibil·i·ty** \-,zȯ-stə-'bi-lə-tē\ *n* — **in·ex·haust·ible·ness** \-'zȯ-stə-bəl-nəs\ *n* — **in·ex·haust·ibly** \-blē\ *adv*

in·ex·is·tence \,i-nig-'zis-tən(t)s\ *n* (ca. 1623) : absence of existence : NONEXISTENCE

in·ex·is·tent \-tənt\ *adj* [LL *inexsistent-, inexsistens*, fr. L *in-* + *exsistent-, exsistens*, prp. of *exsistere* to exist] (1646) : not having existence : NONEXISTENCE

in·ex·o·ra·ble \(,)i-'neks-rə-bəl, -'nek-sə-, -'neg-zə-rə-\ *adj* [L *inexorabilis*, fr. *in-* + *exorabilis* pliant, fr. *exorare* to prevail upon, fr. *ex-* + *orare* to speak — more at ORATION] (1553) : not to be persuaded or moved by entreaty : RELENTLESS — **in·ex·o·ra·bil·i·ty** \(,)i-,neks-rə-'bi-lə-tē, -,nek-sə-, -,neg-zə-\ *n* — **in·ex·o·ra·ble·ness** \-'neks-rə-bəl-nəs, -'nek-sə-, -'neg-zə-\ *n* — **in·ex·o·ra·bly** \-blē\ *adv*

in·ex·pe·di·ence \,i-nik-'spē-dē-ən(t)s\ *n* (1608) : INEXPEDIENCY

in·ex·pe·di·en·cy \-ən(t)-sē\ *n* (1641) : the quality or fact of being inexpedient

in·ex·pe·di·ent \-ənt\ *adj* (1608) : not expedient : INADVISABLE — **in·ex·pe·di·ent·ly** *adv*

in·ex·pen·sive \,i-nik-'spen(t)-siv\ *adj* (ca. 1846) : reasonable in price : CHEAP — **in·ex·pen·sive·ly** *adv* — **in·ex·pen·sive·ness** *n*

in·ex·pe·ri·ence \,i-nik-'spir-ē-ən(t)s\ *n* [MF, fr. LL *inexperientia*, fr. L *in-* + *experientia* experience] (1598) **1** : lack of practical experience **2** : lack of knowledge of the ways of the world — **in·ex·pe·ri·enced** \-ən(t)st\ *adj*

in·ex·pert \(,)i-'nek-,spərt, ,i-nik-'\ *adj* [ME, fr. MF, fr. L *inexpertus*, fr. *in-* + *expertus* expert] (15c) : not expert : UNSKILLED — **in·ex·pert** \-'nek-,spərt\ *n* — **in·ex·pert·ly** \-'nek-,spərt-lē, ,i-nik-'\ *adv* — **in·ex·pert·ness** *n*

in·ex·pi·a·ble \(,)i-'nek-spē-ə-bəl\ *adj* [ME *inexpyable*, fr. L *inexpiabilis*, fr. *in-* + *expiare* to expiate] (15c) **1** : not capable of being atoned for **2** *obs* : IMPLACABLE, UNAPPEASABLE — **in·ex·pi·a·bly** \-blē\ *adv*

in·ex·plain·able \,i-nik-'splā-nə-bəl\ *adj* (ca. 1923) : INEXPLICABLE

in·ex·pli·ca·ble \,i-nik-'spli-kə-bəl, (,)i-'nek-(,)spli-\ *adj* [ME, fr. MF, fr. L *inexplicabilis*, fr. *in-* + *explicabilis* explicable] (15c) : incapable of being explained, interpreted, or accounted for — **in·ex·pli·ca·bil·i·ty** \,i-nik-,spli-kə-'bi-lə-tē, (,)i-,nek-(,)spli-\ *n* — **in·ex·pli·ca·ble·ness** \,i-nik-'spli-kə-bəl-nəs, (,)i-'nek-(,)spli-\ *n* — **in·ex·pli·ca·bly** \-blē\ *adv*

in·ex·plic·it \,i-nik-'splis-ət\ *adj* (ca. 1812) : not explicit

in·ex·press·ible \-'spre-sə-bəl\ *adj* (1625) : not capable of being expressed : INDESCRIBABLE — **in·ex·press·ibil·i·ty** \-,spre-sə-'bi-lə-tē\ *n* — **in·ex·press·ible·ness** \-'spre-sə-bəl-nəs\ *n* — **in·ex·press·ibly** \-blē\ *adv*

in·ex·pres·sive \-'spre-siv\ *adj* (1652) **1** *archaic* : INEXPRESSIBLE **2** : lacking expression or meaning ⟨an ~ face⟩ — **in·ex·pres·sive·ly** *adv* — **in·ex·pres·sive·ness** *n*

in·ex·pug·na·ble \,i-nik-'spəg-nə-bəl, -'spyü-nə-\ *adj* [ME *inexpungnabull*, fr. MF, fr. L *inexpugnabilis*, fr. *in-* + *expugnare* to take by storm, fr. *ex-* + *pugnare* to fight — more at PUNGENT] (15c) **1** : incapable of being subdued or overthrown : IMPREGNABLE ⟨an ~ position⟩ **2** : STABLE, FIXED ⟨~ hatred⟩ — **in·ex·pug·na·ble·ness** *n* — **in·ex·pug·na·bly** \-blē\ *adv*

in·ex·pung·ible \,i-nik-'spən-jə-bəl\ *adj* [*in-* + *expunge*] (1888) : incapable of being obliterated

in ex·ten·so \,in-ik-'sten(t)-(,)sō\ *adv* [ML] (1826) : at full length ⟨the passage was quoted *in extenso*⟩

in·ex·tin·guish·able \,i-nik-'stiŋ-gwi-shə-bəl, -'stiŋ-wi-\ *adj* (15c) : not extinguishable : UNQUENCHABLE ⟨an ~ flame⟩ ⟨an ~ longing⟩ — **in·ex·tin·guish·ably** \-blē\ *adv*

in ex·tre·mis \,in-ik-'strē-məs, -ik-'strä-\ *adv* [L] (ca. 1530) : in extreme circumstances; *esp* : at the point of death

in·ex·tri·ca·ble \,i-nik-'stri-kə-bəl, (,)i-'nek-(,)stri-\ *adj* [ME, fr. MF or L; MF, fr. L *inextricabilis*, fr. *in-* + *extricabilis* extricable] (15c) **1** : forming a maze or tangle from which it is impossible to get free **2** a : incapable of being disentangled or untied ⟨a ~ knot⟩ **b** : not capable of being solved — **in·ex·tri·ca·bil·i·ty** \,i-nik-,stri-kə-'bi-lə-tē, (,)i-,nek-(,)stri-\ *n* — **in·ex·tri·ca·bly** \,i-nik-'stri-kə-blē, (,)i-'nek-(,)stri-\ *adv*

in·fal·li·ble \(,)in-'fa-lə-bəl\ *adj* [ME, fr. ML *infallibilis*, fr. L *in-* + LL *fallibilis* fallible] (15c) **1** : incapable of error : UNERRING ⟨an ~ memory⟩ **2** : not liable to mislead, deceive, or disappoint : CERTAIN ⟨an ~ remedy⟩ **3** : incapable of error in defining doctrines touching faith or morals — **in·fal·li·bil·i·ty** \-,fa-lə-'bi-lə-tē\ *n* — **in·fal·li·bly** \-'fa-lə-blē\ *adv*

in·fall·ing \'in-,fȯ-liŋ\ *adj* (1964) : moving under the influence of gravity toward a celestial object (as a black hole) — **in·fall** \-,fȯl\ *n*

in·fa·mous \'in-fə-məs\ *adj* [ME, fr. L *infamis*, fr. *in-* + *fama* fame] (14c) **1** : having a reputation of the worst kind **2** : causing or bringing infamy : DISGRACEFUL **3** : convicted of an offense bringing infamy — **in·fa·mous·ly** *adv*

in·fa·my \-mē\ *n, pl* **-mies** (15c) **1** : evil reputation brought about by something grossly infamous, shocking, or brutal **2** a : an extreme and publicly known criminal or evil act **b** : the state of being infamous **syn** see DISGRACE

in·fan·cy \'in-fən(t)-sē\ *n, pl* **-cies** (14c) **1** : early childhood **2** : a beginning or early period of existence **3** : the legal status of an infant

¹in·fant \'in-fənt\ *n* [ME *enfaunt*, fr. MF *enfant*, fr. L *infant-, infans*, fr. *infant-, infans*, adj., incapable of speech, young, fr. *in-* + *fant-, fans*, prp. of *fari* to speak — more at BAN] (14c) **1** : a child in the first period of life **2** : a person who is not of full age : MINOR

²infant *adj* (ca. 1586) **1** : intended for young children **2** : being in an early stage of development **3** : of, relating to, or being in infancy

in·fan·ta \in-'fan-tə, -'fän-\ *n* [Sp & Pg, fem. of *infante*] (1593) : a daughter of a Spanish or Portuguese monarch

in·fan·te \in-'fan-tē, -'fän-(,)tā\ *n* [Sp & Pg, lit., infant, fr. L *infant-, infans*] (1555) : a younger son of a Spanish or Portuguese monarch

in·fan·ti·cide \in-'fan-tə-,sīd\ *n* [LL *infanticidium*, fr. L *infant-, infans* + *-i-* + *-cidium* -cide] (ca. 1656) **1** : the killing of an infant **2** [LL *infanticida*, fr. L *infant-, infans* + *-i-* + *-cida* -cide] : one who kills an infant — **in·fan·ti·ci·dal** \-,fan-tə-'si-d⁸l\ *adj*

in·fan·tile \'in-fən-,tīl, -t⁸l, -,tēl, -(,)til\ *adj* (1696) **1** : of or relating to infants or infancy **2** : suitable to or characteristic of an infant; *esp* : very immature — **in·fan·til·i·ty** \,in-fən-'ti-lə-tē\ *n*

infantile paralysis *n* (1843) : POLIOMYELITIS

in·fan·til·ism \'in-fən-,tī-,li-zəm, -tə-,li-; in-'fan-t⁸l-,i-\ *n* (1895) **1** : retention of childish physical, mental, or emotional qualities in adult life; *esp* : failure to attain sexual maturity **2** : an act or expression that indicates lack of maturity

in·fan·til·ize \'in-fən-,tī-,līz, -fən-t⁸l-,īz; in-'fan-t⁸l-,īz\ *vt* **-ized; -iz·ing** (1943) **1** : to make or keep infantile **2** : to treat as if infantile — **in·fan·til·i·za·tion** \,in-fən-,tī-lə-'zā-shən, -fən-t⁸l-ə-; in-,fan-t⁸l-ə-\ *n*

in·fan·tine \'in-fən-,tīn, -,tēn\ *adj* (1603) : INFANTILE, CHILDISH

in·fan·try \'in-fən-trē\ *n, pl* **-tries** [MF & OIt; MF *infanterie*, fr. OIt *infanteria*, fr. *infante* boy, foot soldier, fr. L *infant-, infans*] (1579) **1** a : soldiers trained, armed, and equipped to fight on foot **b** : a branch of an army composed of these soldiers **2** : an infantry regiment or division

in·fan·try·man \-trē-mən\ *n* (1883) : an infantry soldier

infant school *n* (1824) *Brit* : a school for children aged five to seven or eight

in·farct \'in-,färkt, in-'\ *n* [L *infarctus*, pp. of *infarcire* to stuff, fr. *in-* + *farcire* to stuff] (1873) : an area of necrosis in a tissue or organ resulting from obstruction of the local circulation by a thrombus or embolus — **in·farct·ed** \in-'färk-təd\ *adj* — **in·farc·tion** \in-'färk-shən\ *n*

in·fare \'in-,far, -,fer\ *n* [ME, entrance, fr. OE *infær*, fr. *in* + *fær* way, fr. *faran* to go — more at FARE] (1595) *chiefly dial* : a reception for a newly married couple

¹in·fat·u·ate \in-'fa-chə-wət\ *adj* (15c) : being in an infatuated state or condition

²in·fat·u·ate \-,wāt\ *vt* **-at·ed; -at·ing** [L *infatuatus*, pp. of *infatuare*, fr. *in-* + *fatuus* fatuous] (1533) **1** : to cause to be foolish : deprive of sound judgment **2** : to inspire with a foolish or extravagant love or admiration — **in·fat·u·a·tion** \-,fa-chə-'wā-shən\ *n*

in·fau·na \'in-,fȯ-nə, -,fä-\ *n* [NL, fr. ²*in-* + *fauna*] (1914) : benthic fauna living in the substrate and esp. in a soft sea bottom — compare EPIFAUNA — **in·fau·nal** \-,fȯ-n⁸l, -,fä-\ *adj*

in·fea·si·ble \(,)in-'fē-zə-bəl\ *adj* (1533) : not feasible : IMPRACTICABLE — **in·fea·si·bil·i·ty** \-,fē-zə-'bi-lə-tē\ *n*

in·fect \in-'fekt\ *vt* [ME, fr. L *infectus*, pp. of *inficere*, fr. *in-* + *facere* to make, do — more at DO] (14c) **1** : to contaminate with a disease-producing substance or agent (as bacteria) **2** a : to communicate a pathogen or a disease to **b** *of a pathogenic organism* : to invade (an individual or organ) usu. by penetration **c** *of a computer virus* : to become transmitted and copied to (as a computer) **3** a : CONTAMINATE, CORRUPT ⟨the inflated writing that ~s such stories⟩ **b** : to work upon or seize upon so as to induce sympathy, belief, or support ⟨trying to ~ their salespeople with their enthusiasm⟩ — **in·fec·tor** \-'fek-tər\ *n*

in·fec·tion \in-'fek-shən\ *n* (14c) **1** : the act or result of affecting injuriously **2** : an infective agent or material contaminated with an infective agent **3** a : the state produced by the establishment of an infective agent in or on a suitable host **b** : a disease resulting from infection **4** : an act or process of infecting; *also* : the establishment of a pathogen in its host after invasion **5** : the communication of emotions or qualities through example or contact

in·fec·tious \-shəs\ *adj* (1542) **1** a : capable of causing infection **b** : communicable by infection — compare CONTAGIOUS **2** : that corrupts or contaminates **3** : spreading or capable of spreading rapidly to others ⟨their enthusiasm was ~⟩ ⟨an ~ grin⟩ — **in·fec·tious·ly** *adv* — **in·fec·tious·ness** *n*

infectious hepatitis *n* (ca. 1941) : HEPATITIS A

infectious mononucleosis *n* (1920) : an acute infectious disease associated with Epstein-Barr virus and characterized by fever, swelling of lymph nodes, and lymphocytosis

in·fec·tive \in-'fek-tiv\ *adj* (14c) **1** : producing or capable of producing infection **2** : affecting others : INFECTIOUS — **in·fec·tiv·i·ty** \(,)in-,fek-'ti-və-tē\ *n*

in·fe·lic·i·tous \,in-fi-'li-sə-təs\ *adj* (1835) : not appropriate in application or expression — **in·fe·lic·i·tous·ly** *adv*

in·fe·lic·i·ty \-sə-tē\ *n, pl* **-ties** [ME *infelicite* unhappiness, fr. L *infelicitas*, fr. *infelic-, infelix* unhappy, fr. *in-* + *felic-, felix* fruitful — more at FEMININE] (1617) **1** : the quality or state of being infelicitous **2** : something that is infelicitous

in·fer \in-'fər\ *vb* **in·ferred; in·fer·ring** [MF or L; MF *inferer*, fr. L *inferre*, lit., to carry or bring into, fr. *in-* + *ferre* to carry — more at BEAR] *vt* (1528) **1** : to derive as a conclusion from facts or premises ⟨we see smoke and ~ fire —L. A. White⟩ — compare IMPLY **2** : GUESS, SURMISE ⟨your letter . . . allows me to ~ that you are as well as ever — O. W. Holmes †1935⟩ **3** a : to involve as a normal outcome of thought **b** : to point out : INDICATE ⟨this doth ~ the zeal I had to see him —Shak.⟩ **4** : SUGGEST, HINT ⟨another survey . . . ~s that two-thirds of all present computer installations are not paying for themselves —H. R. Chellman⟩ ~ *vi* : to draw inferences ⟨men . . . have observed, inferred, and reasoned . . . to all kinds of results —John Dewey⟩ — **in·fer·able** *also* **in·fer·ri·ble** \in-'fər-ə-bəl\ *adj* — **in·fer·rer** \-'fər-ər\ *n*

syn INFER, DEDUCE, CONCLUDE, JUDGE, GATHER mean to arrive at a mental conclusion. INFER implies arriving at a conclusion by reasoning from evidence; if the evidence is slight, the term comes close to *surmise* ⟨from that remark, I *inferred* that they knew each other⟩. DEDUCE often adds to INFER the special implication of drawing a particular inference from a generalization ⟨denied we could *deduce* anything important from human mortality⟩. CONCLUDE implies arriving at a necessary inference at the end of a chain of reasoning ⟨*concluded* that only the accused could be guilty⟩. JUDGE stresses a weighing of the evidence on which a conclusion is based ⟨*judge* people by their actions⟩. GATHER suggests an intuitive forming of a conclusion from implications ⟨*gathered* their desire to be alone without a word⟩.

usage Sir Thomas More is the first writer known to have used both *infer* and *imply* in their approved senses (1528). He is also the first to have used *infer* in a sense close in meaning to *imply* (1533). Both of these uses of *infer* coexisted without comment until some time around the end of World War I. Since then, senses 3 and 4 of *infer* have been frequently condemned as an undesirable blurring of a useful distinction. The actual blurring has been done by the commentators. Sense 3, descended from More's use of 1533, does not occur with a personal subject. When objections arose, they were to a use with a personal subject (now sense 4). Since dictionaries did not recognize this use specifically, the objectors assumed that sense 3 was the one they found illogical, even though it had been in respectable use for four centuries. The actual usage condemned was a spoken one never used in logical discourse. At present sense 4 is found in print chiefly in letters to the editor and other informal prose, not in serious intellectual writing. The controversy over sense 4 has apparently reduced the frequency of use of sense 3.

in-fer-ence \'in-f(ə-)rən(t)s, -fərn)t)s\ *n* (1594)   **1** : the act or process of inferring: as   **a** : the act of passing from one proposition, statement, or judgment considered as true to another whose truth is believed to follow from that of the former   **b** : the act of passing from statistical sample data to generalizations (as of the value of population parameters) usu. with calculated degrees of certainty   **2** : something that is inferred; *esp* : a proposition arrived at by inference   **3** : the premises and conclusion of a process of inferring

in-fer-en-tial \ˌin-fə-'ren(t)-shəl\ *adj* [ML *inferentia*, fr. L *inferent-, inferens*, prp. of *inferre*] (1657)   **1** : relating to, involving, or resembling inference   **2** : deduced or deducible by inference — **in-fer-en-tial-ly** \-'ren(t)-sh(ə-)lē\ *adv* (1691)   : by way of inference : through inference

in-fe-ri-or \in-'fir-ē-ər\ *adj* [ME, fr. L, compar. of *inferus* lower — more at UNDER] (15c)   **1** : situated lower down : LOWER   **2 a** : of low or lower degree or rank   **b** : of poor quality : MEDIOCRE   **3** : of little or less importance, value, or merit ⟨always felt ∼ to his older brother⟩   **4 a** : situated below another and esp. another similar superior part of an upright body   **b** : situated in a relatively low posterior or ventral position in a quadrupedal body   **c** (1) : situated below another plant part or organ   (2) : ABAXIAL   **5** : relating to or being a subscript — **infe-rior** *n* — **in-fe-ri-or-i-ty** \(ˌ)in-ˌfir-ē-'ȯr-ə-tē, -'är-\ *n* — **in-fe-ri-or-ly** \in-'fir-ē-ər-lē\ *adv*

inferior conjunction *n* (1833) : a conjunction of an inferior planet with the sun in which the planet is aligned between the earth and the sun

inferiority complex *n* (1922)   **1** : an acute sense of personal inferiority often resulting either in timidity or through overcompensation in exaggerated aggressiveness   **2** : a collective sense of cultural, regional, or national inferiority

inferior planet *n* (1658) : either of the planets Mercury and Venus whose orbits lie within that of the earth

in-fer-nal \in-'fər-nᵊl\ *adj* [ME, fr. MF, fr. LL *infernalis*, fr. *infernus* hell, fr. L, lower, fr. *inferus*] (14c)   **1** : of or relating to a nether world of the dead   **2 a** : of or relating to hell   **b** : HELLISH, DIABOLICAL   **3** : DAMNABLE ⟨an ∼ nuisance⟩ — **in-fer-nal-ly** \-nᵊl-ē\ *adv*

infernal machine *n* (1810) : a machine or apparatus maliciously designed to explode and destroy life or property; *esp* : a concealed or disguised bomb

in-fer-no \in-'fər-(ˌ)nō\ *n, pl* **-nos** [It, hell, fr. LL *infernus*] (1834) : a place or a state that resembles or suggests hell ⟨the ∼ of war⟩; *also* : intense heat ⟨the roaring ∼ of the blast furnace⟩

in-fer-tile \(')in-'fər-tᵊl\ *adj* [MF, fr. LL *infertilis*, fr. L *in-* + *fertilis* fertile] (1597): not fertile or productive ⟨∼ eggs⟩ ⟨∼ fields⟩ — **in-fer-til-i-ty** \ˌin-(ˌ)fər-'ti-lə-tē\ *n*

in-fest \in-'fest\ *vt* [F *infester*, fr. L *infestare*, fr. *infestus* hostile] (1602)   **1** : to spread or swarm in or over in a troublesome manner ⟨a slum ∼ed with crime⟩ ⟨shark-*infested* waters⟩   **2** : to live in or on as a parasite — **in-fes-tant** \-'fes-tənt\ *n* — **in-fes-ta-tion** \ˌin-ˌfes-'tā-shən\ *n* — **in-fest-er** \in-'fes-tər\ *n*

in-fi-del \'in-fə-dᵊl, -fə-ˌdel\ *n* [ME *infidele*, fr. MF, fr. LL *infidelis* unbelieving, fr. L, unfaithful, fr. *in-* + *fidelis* faithful — more at FIDELITY] (15c)   **1** : one who is not a Christian or who opposes Christianity   **2 a** : an unbeliever with respect to a particular religion   **b** : one who acknowledges no religious belief   **3** : a disbeliever in something specified or understood — **infidel** *adj*

in-fi-del-i-ty \ˌin-fə-'de-lə-tē, -(ˌ)fī-\ *n, pl* **-ties** (15c)   **1** : lack of belief in a religion   **2 a** : unfaithfulness to a moral obligation : DISLOYALTY   **b** : marital unfaithfulness or an instance of it

in-field \'in-ˌfēld\ *n* (1606)   **1** : a field near a farmhouse   **2 a** : the area of a baseball field enclosed by the three bases and home plate   **b** : the defensive positions comprising first base, second base, shortstop, and third base; *also* : the players who play these positions   **3** : the area enclosed by a racetrack or running track

in-field-er \-ˌfēl-dər\ *n* (1867) : a baseball player who plays in the infield

infield hit *n* (1912) : a base hit on a ball that does not leave the infield

infield out *n* (1926) : a ground ball on which the batter is put out by an infielder

in-fight-ing \'in-ˌfī-tiŋ\ *n* (1816)   **1** : fighting or boxing at close quarters   **2** : rough-and-tumble fighting   **3** : prolonged and often bitter dissension or rivalry among members of a group or organization ⟨bureaucratic ∼⟩ — **in-fight** \'in-ˌfīt\ *vi* — **in-fight-er** \-ˌfī-tər\ *n*

in-fil-trate \in-'fil-ˌtrāt, 'in-(ˌ)\ *vb* **-trat-ed; -trat-ing** *vt* (1758)   **1** : to cause (as a liquid) to permeate something by penetrating its pores or interstices   **2** : to pass into or through (a substance) by filtering or

permeating   **3** : to pass (troops) singly or in small groups through gaps in the enemy line   **4** : to enter or become established in gradually or unobtrusively usu. for subversive purposes ⟨the intelligence staff had been *infiltrated* by spies⟩   ∼ *vi* : to enter, permeate, or pass through a substance or area by filtering or by insinuating gradually — **infiltrate** *n* — **in-fil-tra-tion** \ˌin-(ˌ)fil-'trā-shən\ *n* — **in-fil-tra-tive** \'in-(ˌ)fil-ˌtrā-tiv, in-'fil-trə-\ *adj* — **in-fil-tra-tor** \in-'fil-ˌtrā-tər, 'in-(ˌ)\ *n*

¹in-fi-nite \'in-fə-nət\ *adj* [ME *infinit*, fr. MF or L; MF, fr. L *infinitus*, fr. *in-* + *finitus* finite] (14c)   **1** : extending indefinitely : ENDLESS ⟨∼ space⟩   **2** : immeasurably or inconceivably great or extensive : INEXHAUSTIBLE ⟨∼ patience⟩   **3** : subject to no limitation or external determination   **4 a** : extending beyond, lying beyond, or being greater than any preassigned finite value however large ⟨∼ number of positive numbers⟩   **b** : extending to infinity ⟨∼ plane surface⟩   **c** : characterized by an infinite number of elements or terms ⟨an ∼ set⟩ ⟨an ∼ series⟩ — **in-fi-nite-ly** *adv* — **in-fi-nite-ness** *n*

²infinite *n* (1535) : something that is infinite (as in extent, duration, or number)

¹in-fin-i-tes-i-mal \(ˌ)in-ˌfi-nə-'te-sə-məl, -zə-məl\ *n* [NL *infinitesimus* infinite in rank, fr. L *infinitus*] (1706) : an infinitesimal quantity or variable

²infinitesimal *adj* (1710)   **1** : taking on values arbitrarily close to but greater than zero   **2** : immeasurably or incalculably small — **in-fin-i-tes-i-mal-ly** \-mə-lē\ *adv*

infinitesimal calculus *n* (1801) : CALCULUS 1b

¹in-fin-i-tiv-al \(ˌ)in-ˌfi-nə-'tī-vəl\ *adj* (1869) : relating to the infinitive

¹in-fin-i-tive \in-'fi-nə-tiv\ *adj* [ME *infinityf*, fr. LL *infinitivus*, fr. L *infinitus*] (15c) : formed with the infinitive — **in-fin-i-tive-ly** *adv*

²infinitive *n* (1530) : a verb form normally identical in English with the first person singular that performs some functions of a noun and at the same time displays some characteristics of a verb and that is used with *to* (as in "I asked him *to go*") except with auxiliary and various other verbs (as in "no one saw him *leave*")

in-fin-i-tude \in-'fi-nə-ˌtüd, -ˌtyüd\ *n* (1641)   **1** : the quality or state of being infinite : INFINITENESS   **2** : something that is infinite esp. in extent   **3** : an infinite number or quantity

in-fin-i-ty \in-'fi-nə-tē\ *n, pl* **-ties** (14c)   **1 a** : the quality of being infinite   **b** : unlimited extent of time, space, or quantity : BOUNDLESSNESS   **2** : an indefinitely great number or amount ⟨an ∼ of stars⟩   **3 a** : the limit of the value of a function or variable when it tends to become numerically larger than any preassigned finite number   **b** : a part of a geometric magnitude that lies beyond any part whose distance from a given reference position is finite ⟨do parallel lines ever meet if they extend to ∼⟩   **c** : a transfinite number (as aleph-null)   **4** : a distance so great that the rays of light from a point source at that distance may be regarded as parallel

in-firm \in-'fərm\ *adj* [ME, fr. L *infirmus*, fr. *in-* + *firmus* firm] (14c)   **1** : of poor or deteriorated vitality; *esp* : feeble from age   **2** : weak of mind, will, or character : IRRESOLUTE, VACILLATING   **3** : not solid or stable : INSECURE   *syn* see WEAK — **in-firm-ly** *adv*

in-fir-ma-ry \in-'fərm-rē, -'fər-mə-\ *n, pl* **-ries** (15c) : a place where the infirm or sick are lodged for care and treatment

in-fir-mi-ty \in-'fər-mə-tē\ *n, pl* **-ties** (14c)   **1 a** : the quality or state of being infirm   **b** : the condition of being feeble : FRAILTY   **2** : DISEASE, MALADY   **3** : a personal failing : FOIBLE ⟨one of the besetting *infirmities* of living creatures is egotism —A. J. Toynbee⟩

¹in-fix \'in-ˌfiks, in-'\ *vt* [L *infixus*, pp. of *infigere*, fr. *in-* + *figere* to fasten — more at FIX] (1502)   **1** : to fasten or fix by piercing or thrusting in   **2** : to impress firmly in the consciousness or disposition   **3** : to insert (as a sound or letter) as an infix   *syn* see IMPLANT — **in-fix-ation** \ˌin-(ˌ)fik-'sā-shən\ *n*

²in-fix \'in-ˌfiks\ *n* (1881) : a derivational or inflectional affix appearing in the body of a word (as Sanskrit *-n-* in *vindami* "I know") as contrasted with *vid* "to know")

³in-fix *same as* ²\ *adj* (1971) : characterized by placement of a binary operator between the operands ⟨*a* + *b* is expressed in ∼ notation⟩ — compare POSTFIX, PREFIX

in fla-gran-te de-lic-to \ˌin-flə-ˌgrän-tē-di-'lik-(ˌ)tō, -ˌgran-\ *adv* (1772) : FLAGRANTE DELICTO

in-flame \in-'flām\ *vb* **in-flamed; in-flam-ing** [ME *enflamen*, fr. MF *enflamer*, fr. L *inflammare*, fr. *in-* + *flamma* flame] *vt* (14c)   **1 a** : to excite to excessive or uncontrollable action or feeling   **b** : to make more heated or violent : INTENSIFY ⟨insults served only to ∼ the feud⟩   **2** : to set on fire : KINDLE   **3** : to cause to redden or grow hot from anger or excitement   **4** : to cause inflammation in (bodily tissue)   ∼ *vi*   **1** : to burst into flame   **2** : to become excited or angered   **3** : to become affected with inflammation — **in-flam-er** *n*

in-flam-ma-ble \in-'fla-mə-bəl\ *adj* [F, fr. ML *inflammabilis*, fr. L *inflammare*] (1605)   **1** : FLAMMABLE   **2** : easily inflamed, excited, or angered : IRASCIBLE — **in-flam-ma-bil-i-ty** \-ˌfla-mə-'bi-lə-tē\ *n* — **inflammable** *n* — **in-flam-ma-ble-ness** \-'fla-mə-bəl-nəs\ *n* — **in-flam-ma-bly** \-blē\ *adv*

in-flam-ma-tion \ˌin-flə-'mā-shən\ *n* (15c)   **1** : a local response to cellular injury that is marked by capillary dilatation, leukocytic infiltration, redness, heat, and pain and that serves as a mechanism initiating the elimination of noxious agents and of damaged tissue   **2** : the act of inflaming : the state of being inflamed

in-flam-ma-to-ry \in-'fla-mə-ˌtōr-ē, -ˌtȯr-\ *adj* (ca. 1711)   **1** : tending to excite anger, disorder, or tumult : SEDITIOUS   **2** : tending to inflame or excite the senses   **3** : accompanied by or tending to cause inflammation — **in-flam-ma-to-ri-ly** \-ˌfla-mə-ˌtōr-ə-lē, -ˌtȯr-\ *adv*

in-flat-able \in-'flā-tə-bəl\ *adj* (1878) : capable of being inflated ⟨an ∼ boat⟩ — **inflatable** *n*

in-flate \in-'flāt\ *vb* **in-flat-ed; in-flat-ing** [ME, fr. L *inflatus*, pp. of *inflare*, fr. *in-* + *flare* to blow — more at BLOW] *vt* (15c)   **1** : to swell or distend with air or gas   **2** : to puff up : ELATE   **3** : to expand or increase abnormally or imprudently   ∼ *vi* : to become inflated   *syn* see EXPAND — **in-fla-tor** or **in-flat-er** \-'flā-tər\ *n*

inflated *adj* (1652)   **1** : elaborated or heightened by artificial or empty means ⟨an ∼ style of writing⟩   **2** : distended with air or gas   **3** : expanded to an abnormal or unjustifiable volume or level ⟨∼ prices⟩   **4** : being hollow and enlarged or distended

in-fla-tion \in-'flā-shən\ *n* (14c)   **1** : an act of inflating : a state of being inflated: as   **a** : DISTENSION   **b** : a hypothetical extremely brief period of very rapid expansion of the universe immediately following the big bang   c : empty pretentiousness : POMPOSITY 2 : an increase in the volume of money and credit relative to available goods and services resulting in a continuing rise in the general price level

in·fla·tion·ary \-shə-ˌner-ē\ adj (1920) : of, characterized by, or productive of inflation

inflationary spiral n (1931) : a continuous rise in prices that is sustained by the tendency of wage increases and cost increases to react on each other

in·fla·tion·ism \in-'flā-shə-ˌni-zəm\ n (1919) : the policy of economic inflation — **in·fla·tion·ist** \-sh(ə-)nist\ n or adj

in·flect \in-'flekt\ vb [ME, fr. L inflectere, fr. in- + flectere to bend] vt (15c) 1 : to turn from a direct line or course : CURVE 2 : to vary (a word) by inflection : DECLINE, CONJUGATE 3 : to change or vary the pitch of (as the voice) ~ vi : to become modified by inflection — **in·flect·able** \-'flek-tə-bəl\ adj — **in·flec·tive** \-'flek-tiv\ adj

in·flec·tion \in-'flek-shən\ n (1531) 1 : the act or result of curving or bending : BEND 2 : change in pitch or loudness of the voice 3 a : the change of form that words undergo to mark such distinctions as those of case, gender, number, tense, person, mood, or voice b : a form, suffix, or element involved in such variation c : ACCIDENCE 4 a : change in curvature of an arc or curve from concave to convex or conversely b : INFLECTION POINT

in·flec·tion·al \-shnəl, -shə-nᵊl\ adj (1832) : of, relating to, or characterized by inflection ⟨an ~ suffix⟩ — **in·flec·tion·al·ly** adv

inflection point n (ca. 1721) : a point on a curve that separates an arc concave upward from one concave downward and vice versa

in·flexed \in-'flekst\ adj [L inflexus, pp. of inflectere] (1661) : bent or turned abruptly inward or downward or toward the axis ⟨~ petals⟩

in·flex·i·ble \(ˌ)in-'flek-sə-bəl\ adj [ME, fr. L inflexibilis, fr. in- + flexibilis flexible] (14c) 1 : rigidly firm in will or purpose : UNYIELDING 2 : not readily bent : lacking or deficient in suppleness 3 : incapable of change : UNALTERABLE — **in·flex·i·bil·i·ty** \-ˌflek-sə-'bi-lə-tē\ n — **in·flex·i·ble·ness** \-'flek-sə-bəl-nəs\ n — **in·flex·i·bly** \-blē\ adv
syn INFLEXIBLE, OBDURATE, ADAMANT mean unwilling to alter a predetermined course or purpose. INFLEXIBLE implies rigid adherence or even slavish conformity to principle ⟨inflexible in their demands⟩. OBDURATE stresses hardness of heart and insensitivity to appeals for mercy or the influence of divine grace ⟨obdurate in his refusal to grant clemency⟩. ADAMANT implies utter immovability in the face of all temptation or entreaty ⟨adamant that the work should continue⟩.
syn see in addition STIFF

in·flex·ion chiefly Brit var of INFLECTION

in·flict \in-'flikt\ vt [L inflictus, pp. of infligere, fr. in- + fligere to strike — more at PROFLIGATE] (1566) 1 : AFFLICT 2 a : to give by or as if by striking ⟨~ pain⟩ b : to cause (something unpleasant) to be endured ⟨~ my annual message upon the church —Mark Twain⟩ — **in·flict·er** or **in·flic·tor** \-'flik-tər\ n — **in·flic·tive** \-tiv\ adj

in·flic·tion \in-'flik-shən\ n (1534) 1 : the act of inflicting 2 : something (as punishment or suffering) that is inflicted

in–flight \'in-'flīt, ˌ)in-\ adj (1944) : made, carried out, or provided for use or enjoyment while in flight ⟨~ movies⟩

in·flo·res·cence \ˌin-flə-'re-sᵊn(t)s\ n [NL inflorescentia, fr. LL inflorescent-, inflorescens, prp. of inflorescere to begin to bloom, fr. L in- + florescere to begin to bloom — more at FLORESCENCE] (1760) 1 a (1) : the mode of development and arrangement of flowers on an axis (2) : a floral axis with its appendages; also : a flower cluster b : a cluster of reproductive organs on a moss usu. subtended by a bract 2 : the budding and unfolding of blossoms : FLOWERING

inflorescence 1a(1): *1* raceme, *2* corymb, *3* umbel, *4* compound umbel, *5* capitulum, *6* spike, *7* compound spike, *8* panicle, *9* cyme

in·flow \'in-ˌflō\ n (1839) : a flowing in ⟨the ~ of air⟩ ⟨an ~ of funds⟩

¹in·flu·ence \'in-ˌflü-ən(t)s, esp Southern in-'\ n [ME, fr. MF, fr. ML influentia, fr. L influent-, influens, prp. of influere to flow in, fr. in- + fluere to flow — more at FLUID] (14c) 1 a : an ethereal fluid held to flow from the stars and to affect the actions of humans b : an emanation of occult power held to derive from stars 2 : an emanation of spiritual or moral force 3 a : the act or power of producing an effect without apparent exertion of force or direct exercise of command b : corrupt interference with authority for personal gain 4 : the power or capacity of causing an effect in indirect or intangible ways : SWAY 5 : one that exerts influence — **under the influence** : affected by alcohol : DRUNK ⟨was arrested for driving under the influence⟩
syn INFLUENCE, AUTHORITY, PRESTIGE, WEIGHT, CREDIT mean power exerted over the minds or behavior of others. INFLUENCE may apply to a force exercised and received consciously or unconsciously ⟨used her influence to get the bill passed⟩. AUTHORITY implies the power of winning devotion or allegiance or of compelling acceptance and belief ⟨his opinions lacked authority⟩. PRESTIGE implies the ascendancy given by conspicuous excellence or reputation for superiority ⟨the prestige of the newspaper⟩. WEIGHT implies measurable or decisive influence in determining acts or choices ⟨their wishes obviously carried much weight⟩. CREDIT suggests influence that arises from the confidence of others ⟨his credit with the press⟩.

²influence vt **-enced; -enc·ing** (1658) 1 : to affect or alter by indirect or intangible means : SWAY 2 : to have an effect on the condition or development of : MODIFY   syn see AFFECT — **in·flu·ence·able** \-ən(t)-sə-bəl\ adj

¹in·flu·ent \'in-ˌflü-ənt, in-'\ adj (15c) : flowing in

²influent n (1859) 1 : something that flows in: as a : a tributary stream b : fluid input into a reservoir or process 2 : a factor (as a particular animal) modifying the balance and stability of an ecological community

in·flu·en·tial \ˌin-(ˌ)flü-'en(t)-shəl\ adj (1570) : exerting or possessing influence — **in·flu·en·tial·ly** \-'en(t)-sh(ə-)lē\ adv

²influential n (1831) : one who has great influence

in·flu·en·za \ˌin-(ˌ)flü-'en-zə\ n [It, lit., influence, fr. ML influentia; fr. the belief that epidemics were due to the influence of the stars] (1743) 1 : an acute highly contagious virus disease caused by various strains of a myxovirus (family Orthomyxoviridae) and characterized by sudden onset, fever, prostration, severe aches and pains, and progressive inflammation of the respiratory mucous membrane; broadly : a human respiratory infection of undetermined cause 2 : any of numerous febrile usu. virus diseases of domestic animals marked by respiratory symptoms, inflammation of mucous membranes, and often systemic involvement — **in·flu·en·zal** \-zəl\ adj

in·flux \'in-ˌfləks\ n [ML influxus, fr. L influere] (1626) : a coming in ⟨an ~ of tourists⟩

in·fo \'in-(ˌ)fō\ n (1913) : INFORMATION

in·fold \in-'fōld\ vt (15c) : ENFOLD, ENVELOP ~ vi : to fold inward or toward one another

in·fo·mer·cial \'in-(ˌ)fō-ˌmər-shəl, -fə-\ n [information + ²commercial] (1981) : a television program that is an extended advertisement often including a discussion or demonstration

in·form \in-'fórm\ vb [ME, fr. MF enformer, fr. L informare, fr. in- + forma form] vt (14c) 1 obs : to give material form to 2 a : to give character or essence to ⟨the principles which ~ modern teaching⟩ b : to be the characteristic quality of : ANIMATE ⟨the compassion that ~s her work⟩ 3 obs : GUIDE, DIRECT 4 obs : to make known 5 : to communicate knowledge to ⟨~ a prisoner of his rights⟩ ~ vi 1 : to impart information or knowledge 2 : to give information (as of another's wrongdoing) to an authority
syn INFORM, ACQUAINT, APPRISE, NOTIFY mean to make one aware of something. INFORM implies the imparting of knowledge esp. of facts or occurrences ⟨informed us of the crisis⟩. ACQUAINT lays stress on introducing to or familiarizing with ⟨acquaint yourself with the keyboard⟩. APPRISE implies communicating something of special interest or importance ⟨keep us apprised of the situation⟩. NOTIFY implies sending notice of something requiring attention or demanding action ⟨notified the witness when to appear⟩.

in·for·mal \(ˌ)in-'fór-məl\ adj (1585) 1 : marked by the absence of formality or ceremony ⟨an ~ meeting⟩ ⟨an ~ group⟩ 2 : characteristic of or appropriate to ordinary, casual, or familiar use ⟨~ English⟩ ⟨~ clothes⟩ — **in·for·mal·i·ty** \-(ˌ)fór-'ma-lə-tē, -fər-\ n — **in·for·mal·ly** \-'fór-mə-lē\ adv

in·for·mant \in-'fór-mənt\ n (1693) : a person who gives information: as a : INFORMER b : one who supplies cultural or linguistic data in response to interrogation by an investigator

in for·ma pau·pe·ris \ˌin-'fór-mə-'pó-pə-rəs, -'pau̇-\ adj or adv [L, in the form of a pauper] (1592) : as a poor person

in·for·mat·ics \ˌin-fər-'ma-tiks\ n pl but sing in constr [ISV information + -ics] (ca. 1967) chiefly Brit : INFORMATION SCIENCE

in·for·ma·tion \ˌin-fər-'mā-shən\ n (14c) 1 : the communication or reception of knowledge or intelligence 2 a (1) : knowledge obtained from investigation, study, or instruction (2) : INTELLIGENCE, NEWS (3) : FACTS, DATA b : the attribute inherent in and communicated by one of two or more alternative sequences or arrangements of something (as nucleotides in DNA or binary digits in a computer program) that produce specific effects c (1) : a signal or character (as in a communication system or computer) representing data (2) : something (as a message, experimental data, or a picture) which justifies change in a construct (as a plan or theory) that represents physical or mental experience or another construct d : a quantitative measure of the content of information; specif : a numerical quantity that measures the uncertainty in the outcome of an experiment to be performed 3 : the act of informing against a person 4 : a formal accusation of a crime made by a prosecuting officer as distinguished from an indictment presented by a grand jury — **in·for·ma·tion·al** \-shnəl, -shə-nᵊl\ adj — **in·for·ma·tion·al·ly** adv

information retrieval n (1950) : the techniques of storing and recovering and often disseminating recorded data esp. through the use of a computerized system

information science n (1960) : the collection, classification, storage, retrieval, and dissemination of recorded knowledge treated both as a pure and as an applied science

information theory n (1950) : a theory that deals statistically with information, with the measurement of its content in terms of its distinguishing essential characteristics or by the number of alternatives from which it makes a choice possible, and with the efficiency of processes of communication between humans and machines

in·for·ma·tive \in-'fór-mə-tiv\ adj (1655) : imparting knowledge : INSTRUCTIVE — **in·for·ma·tive·ly** adv — **in·for·ma·tive·ness** n

in·for·ma·to·ry \-mə-ˌtór-ē, -ˌtór-\ adj (ca. 1879) : conveying information — **in·for·ma·to·ri·ly** \in-ˌfór-mə-'tór-ə-lē, -'tór-\ adv

in·formed \in-'fórmd\ adj (15c) 1 a : having information ⟨~ sources⟩ ⟨~ observers⟩ b : based on possession of information ⟨an ~ opinion⟩ 2 : EDUCATED, KNOWLEDGEABLE ⟨what the ~ person should know⟩ — **in·formed·ly** \-'fór-məd-lē, -'fór-məd-lē\ adv

informed consent n (ca. 1967) : consent to surgery by a patient or to participation in a medical experiment by a subject after achieving an understanding of what is involved

\a\ abut \ᵊ\ kitten, F table \ər\ further \a\ ash \ā\ ace \ä\ mop, mar \au̇\ out \ch\ chin \e\ bet \ē\ easy \g\ go \i\ hit \ī\ ice \j\ job \ŋ\ sing \ō\ go \ȯ\ law \ȯi\ boy \th\ thin \th\ the \ü\ loot \u̇\ foot \y\ yet \zh\ vision \à, ḵ, ⁿ, œ, œ̄, ᵫ, ᵫ̄, ᵊ\ see Guide to Pronunciation

in·form·er \in-'fȯr-mər\ n (14c) **1** : one that imparts knowledge or news **2** : one that informs against another; *specif* : one who makes a practice esp. for a financial reward of informing against others for violations of penal laws

in·fo·tain·ment \in-(,)fō-'tān-mənt\ n [*information* + enter*tainment*] (1982) : a television program that presents information (as news) in a manner intended to be entertaining

in·fra \'in-frə also -,frä\ adv [L] (ca. 1740) : later in this writing : BELOW ⟨for additional examples see ∼⟩

infra· prefix [L *infra* — more at UNDER] **1** : below ⟨*infra*human⟩ ⟨*infra*sonic⟩ **2** : within ⟨*infra*specific⟩ **3** : below in a scale or series ⟨*infra*red⟩

in·frac·tion \in-'frak-shən\ n [ME, fr. ML *infraction-, infractio,* fr. L, subduing, fr. *infringere* to break — more at INFRINGE] (15c) : the act of infringing : VIOLATION — **in·fract** \in-'frakt\ vt

in·fra dig \'in-frə-'dig, -,(,)frä\ adj [short for L *infra dignitatem*] (1824) : being beneath one's dignity : UNDIGNIFIED ⟨while his work . . . was financially profitable, it was just a bit *infra dig*—John McCarten⟩

in·fra·hu·man \,in-frə-'hyü-mən, -,(,)frä-, -'yü-\ adj (1847) : less or lower than human ⟨∼ primates⟩ — **infrahuman** n

in·fran·gi·ble \(,)in-'fran-jə-bəl\ adj [MF, fr. LL *infrangibilis,* fr. L *in-* + *frangere* to break — more at BREAK] (1597) **1** : not capable of being broken or separated into parts **2** : not to be infringed or violated — **in·fran·gi·bil·i·ty** \-,fran-jə-'bi-lə-tē\ n — **in·fran·gi·bly** \-'fran-jə-blē\ adv

in·fra·red \,in-frə-'red, -,(,)frä-, -fə-\ adj (1881) **1** : situated outside the visible spectrum at its red end — used of radiation having a wavelength between about 700 nanometers and 1 millimeter **2** : relating to, producing, or employing infrared radiation ⟨∼ therapy⟩ **3** : sensitive to infrared radiation ⟨∼ photographic film⟩ — **infrared** n

in·fra·son·ic \,in-frə-'sä-nik, -,(,)frä-\ adj (1927) **1** : having or relating to a frequency below the audibility range of the human ear **2** : utilizing or produced by infrasonic waves or vibrations

in·fra·spe·cif·ic \-spi-'si-fik\ adj (1939) : included within a species ⟨∼ variability⟩

in·fra·struc·ture \'in-frə-,strək-chər, -,(,)frä-\ n (1927) **1** : the underlying foundation or basic framework (as of a system or organization) **2** : the permanent installations required for military purposes **3** : the system of public works of a country, state, or region; *also* : the resources (as personnel, buildings, or equipment) required for an activity

in·fre·quence \(,)in-'frē-kwən(t)s\ n (1644) : INFREQUENCY

in·fre·quen·cy \-kwən(t)-sē\ n (1677) : rarity of occurrence

in·fre·quent \(,)in-'frē-kwənt\ adj [L *infrequent-, infrequens,* fr. *in-* + *frequent-, frequens* frequent] (1531) **1** : seldom happening or occurring : RARE **2** : placed or occurring at wide intervals in space or time ⟨a slope scattered with ∼ pines⟩ ⟨∼ visits⟩ — **in·fre·quent·ly** adv
  syn INFREQUENT, UNCOMMON, SCARCE, RARE, SPORADIC mean not common or abundant. INFREQUENT implies occurrence at wide intervals in space or time ⟨*infrequent* family visits⟩. UNCOMMON suggests a frequency below normal expectation ⟨smallpox is now *uncommon* in many countries⟩. SCARCE implies falling short of a standard or required abundance ⟨jobs were *scarce* during the Depression⟩. RARE suggests extreme scarcity or infrequency and often implies consequent high value ⟨*rare* first editions⟩. SPORADIC implies occurrence in scattered instances or isolated outbursts ⟨*sporadic* cases of influenza⟩.

in·fringe \in-'frinj\ vb *in·fringed; in·fring·ing* [ML *infringere,* fr. L, to break, crush, fr. *in-* + *frangere* to break — more at BREAK] vt (1533) **1** : to encroach upon in a way that violates law or the rights of another ⟨∼ a patent⟩ **2** *obs* : DEFEAT, FRUSTRATE ∼ vi : ENCROACH — used with *on* or *upon* ⟨∼ on our rights⟩ *syn* see TRESPASS — **in·fring·er** n

in·fringe·ment \in-'frinj-mənt\ n (1628) **1** : the act of infringing : VIOLATION **2** : an encroachment or trespass on a right or privilege

in·fun·dib·u·lar \,in-(,)fən-'di-byə-lər\ adj (1795) **1** : INFUNDIBULIFORM

in·fun·dib·u·li·form \-lə-,fȯrm\ adj [NL *infundibulum* + E *-iform*] (1752) : having the form of a funnel or cone

in·fun·dib·u·lum \-ləm\ n, pl **-la** \-lə\ [NL, fr. L, funnel — more at FUNNEL] (1543) : any of various funnel-shaped organs or parts: as **a** : the hollow conical process of gray matter by which the pituitary gland is continuous with the brain **b** : the calyx of a kidney **c** : the abdominal opening of a fallopian tube

¹in·fu·ri·ate \in-'fyu̇r-ē-,āt\ vt **-at·ed; -at·ing** [ML *infuriatus,* pp. of *infuriare,* fr. L *in-* + *furia* fury] (1667) : to make furious — **in·fu·ri·at·ing·ly** \-,ā-tiŋ-lē\ adv — **in·fu·ri·a·tion** \-,fyu̇r-ē-'ā-shən\ n

²in·fu·ri·ate \in-'fyu̇r-ē-ət\ adj (1667) : furiously angry

in·fuse \in-'fyüz\ vt *in·fused; in·fus·ing* [ME, to pour in, fr. MF & L; MF *infuser,* fr. L *infusus,* pp. of *infundere* to pour in, fr. *in-* + *fundere* to pour — more at FOUND] (1526) **1 a** : to cause to be permeated with something (as a principle or quality) that alters usu. for the better ⟨∼ the team with confidence⟩ **b** : INTRODUCE, INSINUATE ⟨a new spirit was *infused* into American art —*Amer. Guide Series: N.Y.*⟩ **2** : INSPIRE, ANIMATE ⟨the sense of purpose that *infuses* scientific research⟩ **3** : to steep in liquid (as water) without boiling so as to extract the soluble constituents or principles — **in·fus·er** n
  syn INFUSE, SUFFUSE, IMBUE, INGRAIN, INOCULATE, LEAVEN mean to introduce one thing into another so as to affect it throughout. INFUSE implies a pouring in of something that gives new life or significance ⟨new members *infused* enthusiasm into the club⟩. SUFFUSE implies a spreading through of something that gives an unusual color or quality ⟨a room *suffused* with light⟩. IMBUE implies the introduction of a quality that fills and permeates the whole being ⟨*imbue* students with intellectual curiosity⟩. INGRAIN, used only in the passive or past participle, suggests the deep implanting of a quality or trait ⟨clung to *ingrained* habits⟩. INOCULATE implies an imbuing or implanting with a germinal idea and often suggests surreptitiousness or subtlety ⟨an electorate *inoculated* with dangerous ideas⟩. LEAVEN implies introducing something that enlivens, tempers, or markedly alters the total quality ⟨a serious play *leavened* with comic moments⟩.

in·fus·ible \(,)in-'fyü-zə-bəl\ adj (1555) : incapable of being fused : very difficult to fuse — **in·fus·ibil·i·ty** \-,fyü-zə-'bi-lə-tē\ n — **in·fus·ible·ness** \-'fyü-zə-bəl-nəs\ n

in·fu·sion \in-'fyü-zhən\ n (15c) **1** : the act or process of infusing **2** : a product obtained by infusing **3** : the continuous slow introduction of a solution esp. into a vein

in·fu·so·ri·al earth \,in-fyü-'zȯr-ē-əl-, -'sȯr-, -'zȯr-, -'sȯr-\ n (1882) : KIESELGUHR

in·fu·so·ri·an \-ē-ən\ n [ultim. fr. L *infusus*] (1859) : any of a heterogeneous group of minute organisms found esp. in decomposing infusions of organic matter; *esp* : a ciliated protozoan — **infusorian** adj

¹-ing \iŋ *also* ēŋ; *in some dialects & in other dialects informally* in, ən *also* ēn; *after certain consonants* ⁿn, ⁿm, ⁿŋ\ n *suffix* [ME, fr. OE *-ung, -ing,* suffix forming nouns from verbs; akin to OHG *-ung,* suffix forming nouns from verbs] **1** : action or process ⟨*running*⟩ ⟨*sleeping*⟩ : instance of an action or process ⟨a *meeting*⟩ **2 a** : product or result of an action or process ⟨an *engraving*⟩ — often in pl. ⟨*earnings*⟩ **b** : something used in an action or process ⟨a bed *covering*⟩ ⟨the *lining* of a coat⟩ **3** : action or process connected with (a specified thing) ⟨*boating*⟩ **4** : something connected with, consisting of, or used in making (a specified thing) ⟨*scaffolding*⟩ ⟨*shirting*⟩ **5** : something related to (a specified concept) ⟨*offing*⟩

²-ing n *suffix* [ME, fr. OE *-ing, -ung;* akin to OHG *-ing* one of a (specified) kind] : one of a (specified) kind ⟨*sweeting*⟩

³-ing *vb suffix or adj suffix* [ME, prob. fr. ¹*-ing*] — used to form the present participle ⟨*sailing*⟩ and sometimes to form an adjective resembling a present participle but not derived from a verb ⟨*swashbuckling*⟩
  usage Though the pronunciation of *-ing* with the consonant \n\, misleadingly referred to as "dropping the *g,*" is often deprecated, this pronunciation is frequently heard. It is not known for certain why the Middle English present participle ending *-ende* was replaced by *-ing.* Analogy with the earlier noun suffix *-ing* prob. had something to do with it. In early Modern English, present participles were regularly formed with *-ing* pronounced \iŋ\ (as can still be heard in a few dialects) and later \iŋ\. Evidence also shows that some speakers used \in\ and by the 18th century this pronunciation became widespread. Though teachers (with some success) campaigned against it, \in\ remained a feature of the speech of many of the best speakers in Britain and the U.S. well into this century. It has by now lost its respectability, at least when attention is drawn to it, but throughout the U.S. it persists largely unnoticed and in some dialects it predominates over \iŋ\.

in·gath·er \in-'ga-thər, 'in-,\ vt (1557) : to gather in ∼ vi : ASSEMBLE — **in·gath·er·ing** \-,gath-riŋ, -,geth-; -,ga-thə-, -,ge-\ n

in·ge·nious \in-'jēn-yəs\ adj [ME *ingenyous,* fr. MF *ingenieux,* fr. L *ingeniosus,* fr. *ingenium* natural capacity — more at ENGINE] (15c) **1** *obs* : showing or calling for intelligence, aptitude, or discernment **2** : marked by especial aptitude at discovering, inventing, or contriving **3** : marked by originality, resourcefulness, and cleverness in conception or execution ⟨an ∼ contraption⟩ *syn* see CLEVER — **in·ge·nious·ly** adv — **in·ge·nious·ness** n

in·ge·nue *or* **in·gé·nue** \'an-jə-,nü, 'än-; 'aⁿ-zhə-, 'äⁿ-\ n [F *ingénue,* fem. of *ingénu* ingenuous, fr. L *ingenuus*] (1848) **1** : a naive girl or young woman **2** : the stage role of an ingenue; *also* : an actress playing such a role

in·ge·nu·i·ty \,in-jə-'nü-ə-tē, -'nyü-\ n, pl **-ties** (ca. 1592) **1** *obs* : CANDOR, INGENUOUSNESS **2 a** : skill or cleverness in devising or combining : INVENTIVENESS **b** : cleverness or aptness of design or contrivance **3** : an ingenious device or contrivance

¹in·gen·u·ous \in-'jen-yə-wəs\ adj [by alter.] (1588) *obs* : INGENIOUS

²ingenuous adj [L *ingenuus* native, free born, fr. *in-* + *gignere* to beget — more at KIN] (1588) **1** *obs* : NOBLE, HONORABLE **2 a** : showing innocent or childlike simplicity and candidness **b** : lacking craft or subtlety *syn* see NATURAL — **in·gen·u·ous·ly** adv — **in·gen·u·ous·ness** n

in·gest \in-'jest\ vt [L *ingestus,* pp. of *ingerere* to carry in, fr. *in-* + *gerere* to bear] (1620) : to take in for or as if for digestion — **in·gest·ible** \-'jes-tə-bəl\ adj — **in·ges·tion** \-'jes-chən, -'jesh-\ n — **in·ges·tive** \-'jes-tiv\ adj

in·ges·ta \in-'jes-tə\ n pl [NL, fr. L, neut. pl. of *ingestus*] (1727) : material taken into the body by way of the digestive tract

in·gle \'iŋ-gəl, 'iŋ-əl\ n [ScGael *aingeal*] (1508) **1** : a fire in a fireplace **2** : FIREPLACE **3** : CORNER, ANGLE

in·gle·nook \-,nu̇k\ n (1772) : a nook by a large open fireplace; *also* : a bench or settle occupying this nook

in·glo·ri·ous \(,)in-'glōr-ē-əs, -'glȯr-\ adj [L *inglorius,* fr. *in-* + *gloria* glory] (1573) **1** : SHAMEFUL, IGNOMINIOUS **2** : not glorious : lacking fame or honor — **in·glo·ri·ous·ly** adv — **in·glo·ri·ous·ness** n

in·got \'iŋ-gət\ n [ME, perh. modif. of MF *lingot* ingot of metal, incorrectly divided as *l'ingot,* as if fr. *le* the, fr. L *ille* that] (14c) **1** : a mold in which metal is cast **2** : a mass of metal cast into a convenient shape for storage or transportation to be later processed

ingot iron n (1877) : iron containing only small proportions of impurities (as less than 0.05 percent carbon)

¹in·grain \(,)in-'grān\ vt (ca. 1641) : to work indelibly into the natural texture or mental or moral constitution *syn* see INFUSE

²in·grain \'in-,grān\ adj (1766) **1 a** : made of fiber that is dyed before being spun into yarn **b** : made of yarn that is dyed before being woven or knitted **2** : thoroughly worked in : INNATE

³in·grain \'in-,grān\ n (ca. 1890) : innate quality or character

in·grained \'in-,grānd, (,)in-'\ adj (1599) **1** : worked into the grain or fiber **2** : forming a part of the essence or inmost being : DEEP-SEATED ⟨∼ prejudice⟩ — **in·grained·ly** \'in-,grā-nəd-lē, 'in-,gränd-lē, (,)in-'\ adv

in·grate \'in-,grāt\ n [L *ingratus* ungrateful, fr. *in-* + *gratus* grateful — more at GRACE] (1622) : an ungrateful person

in·gra·ti·ate \in-'grā-shē-,āt\ vt **-at·ed; -at·ing** [²*in-* + L *gratia* grace] (1622) : to gain favor or favorable acceptance for by deliberate effort — usu. used with *with* ⟨∼ themselves with the community leaders — William Attwood⟩ — **in·gra·ti·a·tion** \-,grā-shē-'ā-shən\ n — **in·gra·tia·to·ry** \-'grā-sh(ē-)ə-,tōr-ē, -,tȯr-\ adj

ingratiating adj (1655) **1** : capable of winning favor : PLEASING ⟨∼ smile⟩ **2** : intended or adopted in order to gain favor : FLATTERING — **in·gra·ti·at·ing·ly** \-'grā-shē-,ā-tiŋ-lē\ adv

in·grat·i·tude \(,)in-'gra-tə-,tüd, -,tyüd\ n [ME, fr. MF, fr. ML *ingratitudo,* fr. L *in-* + LL *gratitudo* gratitude] (14c) : forgetfulness of or poor return for kindness received : UNGRATEFULNESS

in·gre·di·ent \in-'grē-dē-ənt\ n [ME, fr. L *ingredient-, ingrediens,* prp. of *ingredi* to go into, fr. *in-* + *gradi* to go — more at GRADE] (15c) : something that enters into a compound or is a component part of any combination or mixture : CONSTITUENT *syn* see ELEMENT — **ingredi-ent** *adj*

in·gress \'in-ˌgres\ *n* [ME, fr. L *ingressus*, fr. *ingredī*] (15c) **1** : the act of entering : ENTRANCE **2** : the power or liberty of entrance or access — **in·gres·sion** \in-'gre-shən\ *n*

in·gres·sive \in-'gre-siv\ *adj* (1649) **1** : of, relating to, or involving ingress; *esp* : produced by ingress of air into the vocal tract ⟨∼ sounds⟩ **2** : INCHOATIVE **2** — **ingressive** *n* — **in·gres·sive·ness** *n*

in-group \'in-ˌgrüp\ *n* (1907) **1** : a group with which one feels a sense of solidarity or community of interests — compare OUT-GROUP **2** : CLIQUE

in·grow·ing \'in-ˌgrō-iŋ\ *adj* (1869) : growing or tending inward

in·grown \-ˌgrōn\ *adj* (1670) **1** : grown in; *specif* : having the free tip or edge embedded in the flesh ⟨an ∼ toenail⟩ **2** : having the direction of growth or activity or interest inward rather than outward : WITH-DRAWN — **in·grown·ness** \(ˌ)in-'grōn-nəs\ *n*

in·growth \'in-ˌgrōth\ *n* (1870) **1** : a growing inward (as to fill a void) **2** : something that grows in or into a space

in·gui·nal \'iŋ-gwə-nᵊl\ *adj* [ME *inguynale*, fr. L *inguinalis*, fr. *inguin-, inguen* groin — more at ADEN-] (15c) : of, relating to, or situated in the region of the groin or in either of the lowest lateral regions of the abdomen ⟨∼ hernia⟩

in·gur·gi·tate \in-'gər-jə-ˌtāt\ *vt* **-tat·ed; -tat·ing** [L *ingurgitatus*, pp. of *ingurgitare*, fr. *in-* + *gurgit-, gurges* whirlpool — more at VORACIOUS] (ca. 1570) : to swallow greedily or in large quantities : GUZZLE — **in·gur·gi·ta·tion** \(ˌ)in-ˌgər-jə-'tā-shən\ *n*

in·hab·it \in-'ha-bət\ *vb* [ME *enhabiten*, fr. MF & L; MF *enhabiter*, fr. L *inhabitare*, fr. *in-* + *habitare* to dwell, freq. of *habēre* to have — more at GIVE] *vt* (14c) **1** : to occupy as a place of settled residence or habitat : live in ⟨∼ a small house⟩ **2** : to be present in or occupy in any manner or form ⟨the human beings who ∼ this tale —Al Newman⟩ ∼ *vi, archaic* : to have residence in a place : DWELL — **in·hab·it·able** \-bə-tə-bəl\ *adj* — **in·hab·it·er** *n*

in·hab·it·an·cy \in-'ha-bə-tən(t)-sē\ *n* (1681) : INHABITATION

in·hab·i·tant \in-'ha-bə-tənt\ *n* (15c) : one that occupies a particular place regularly, routinely, or for a period of time ⟨∼s of large cities⟩ ⟨the tapeworm is an ∼ of the intestine⟩

in·hab·i·ta·tion \in-ˌha-bə-'tā-shən\ *n* (15c) : the act of inhabiting : the state of being inhabited

inhabited *adj* (15c) : having inhabitants

in·hal·ant \in-'hā-lənt\ *n* (ca. 1834) : something (as an allergen or medication) that is inhaled — **inhalant** *adj*

in·ha·la·tion \ˌin-hə-'lā-shən, ˌi-nᵊl-'ā-\ *n* (ca. 1623) **1** : the act or an instance of inhaling **2** : material (as medication) to be taken in by inhaling — **in·ha·la·tion·al** \-shnəl, -shə-nᵊl\ *adj*

in·ha·la·tor \'in-hə-ˌlā-tər, 'i-nᵊl-ˌā-\ *n* (1925) : a device providing a mixture of oxygen and carbon dioxide for breathing that is used esp. in conjunction with artificial respiration

in·hale \in-'hā(ə)l\ *vb* **in·haled; in·hal·ing** [*in-* + *exhale*] *vt* (1725) **1** : to draw in by breathing **2** : to take in eagerly or greedily ⟨inhaled about four meals at once —Ring Lardner⟩ ∼ *vi* : to breathe in — **in·hale** \in-', -in-ˌ\ *n*

in·hal·er \in-'hā-lər\ *n* (1778) **1** : a device by means of which medicinal material is inhaled **2** : one that inhales

in·har·mon·ic \ˌin-(ˌ)här-'mä-nik\ *adj* (ca. 1828) : not harmonic

in·har·mo·ni·ous \-'mō-nē-əs\ *adj* (1711) **1** : not harmonious : DIS-CORDANT **2** : not fitting or congenial : CONFLICTING — **in·har·mo·ni·ous·ly** *adv* — **in·har·mo·ni·ous·ness** *n*

in·har·mo·ny \(ˌ)in-'här-mə-nē\ *n* (1799) : DISCORD

in·here \in-'hir\ *vi* or **in·hered; in·her·ing** [L *inhaerēre*, fr. *in-* + *haerēre* to adhere] (15c) : to be inherent

in·her·ence \in-'hir-ən(t)s, -'her-\ *n* (1577) : the quality, state, or fact of inhering

in·her·ent \-ənt\ *adj* [L *inhaerent-, inhaerens*, prp. of *inhaerēre*] (1581) : involved in the constitution or essential character of something : belonging by nature or habit : INTRINSIC — **in·her·ent·ly** *adv*

in·her·it \in-'her-ət\ *vb* [ME *enheriten* to make one an heir, inherit, fr. MF *enheriter* to make one an heir, fr. LL *inhereditare*, fr. L *in-* + *hereditas* inheritance — more at HEREDITY] *vt* (14c) **1** : to come into possession of or receive esp. as a right or divine portion ⟨and every one who has left houses or brothers or sisters . . . for my name's sake, will receive a hundredfold, and ∼ eternal life —Mt 19:29 (RSV)⟩ **2 a** : to receive from an ancestor as a right or title descendible by law at the ancestor's death **b** : to receive as a devise or legacy **3** : to receive from ancestors by genetic transmission ⟨∼ a strong constitution⟩ **4** : to have in turn or receive as if from an ancestor ⟨∼ed the problem from his predecessor⟩ ∼ *vi* : to take or hold a possession or rights by inheritance — **in·her·i·tor** \-ə-tər\ *n* — **in·her·i·tress** \-ə-trəs\ *or* **in·her·i·trix** \-ə-(ˌ)triks\ *n*

in·her·it·able \in-'her-ə-tə-bəl\ *adj* (15c) **1** : capable of being inherited : TRANSMISSIBLE **2** : capable of taking by inheritance — **in·her·it·abil·i·ty** \-ˌher-ə-tə-'bi-lə-tē\ *n* — **in·her·it·able·ness** \-'her-ə-tə-bəl-nəs\ *n*

in·her·i·tance \in-'her-ə-tən(t)s\ *n* (14c) **1 a** : the act of inheriting property **b** : the reception of genetic qualities by transmission from parent to offspring **c** : the acquisition of a possession, condition, or trait from past generations **2** : something that is or may be inherited **3 a** : TRADITION **b** : a valuable possession that is a common heritage from nature **4** *obs* : POSSESSION

inheritance tax *n* (1841) **1** : an excise in the form of a percentage of the value of the property received that is levied on the privilege of an heir to inherit property **2** : DEATH TAX; *esp* : ESTATE TAX

in·hib·in \in-'hi-bən\ *n* [L *inhibēre* to inhibit + E *-in*] (1932) : a human hormone that is secreted by Sertoli cells in the male and granulosa cells in the female and that inhibits the secretion of follicle-stimulating hormone

in·hib·it \in-'hi-bət\ *vb* [ME, fr. L *inhibitus*, pp. of *inhibēre*, fr. *in-* + *habēre* to have — more at HABIT] *vt* (15c) **1** : to prohibit from doing something **2 a** : to hold in check : RESTRAIN **b** : to discourage from free or spontaneous activity esp. through the operation of inner psychological impediments or of social controls ∼ *vi* : to cause inhibition *syn* see FORBID — **in·hib·i·tive** \-bə-tiv\ *adj* — **in·hib·i·to·ry** \-bə-ˌtōr-ē, -ˌtor-\ *adj*

in·hi·bi·tion \ˌin-hə-'bi-shən, ˌi-nə-\ *n* (14c) **1 a** : the act of inhibiting

: the state of being inhibited **b** : something that forbids, debars, or restricts **2** : an inner impediment to free activity, expression, or functioning: as **a** : a psychic activity imposing restraint upon another activity **b** : a restraining of the function of a bodily organ or an agent (as an enzyme)

in·hib·i·tor \in-'hi-bə-tər\ *n* (ca. 1611) : one that inhibits; *esp* : an agent that slows or interferes with a chemical action

in·hold·ing \'in-ˌhōl-diŋ\ *n* (1947) : privately owned land inside the boundary of a national park

in·ho·mo·ge·ne·i·ty \(ˌ)in-ˌhō-mə-jə-'nē-ə-tē, -'nā- also ÷-'nī-; *esp Brit* -ˌhä-mə-\ *n, pl* **-ties** (1899) **1** : the condition of not being homogeneous **2** : a part that is not homogeneous with the larger uniform mass in which it occurs; *esp* : a localized collection of matter in the universe — **in·ho·mo·ge·neous** \-'jē-nē-əs, -nyəs\ *adj*

in·hos·pi·ta·ble \ˌin-(ˌ)hä-'spi-tə-bəl, (ˌ)in-'häs-(ˌ)pi-\ *adj* (ca. 1570) **1** : not showing hospitality : not friendly or receptive **2** : providing no shelter or sustenance — **in·hos·pi·ta·ble·ness** *n* — **in·hos·pi·ta·bly** \-blē\ *adv*

in·hos·pi·tal·i·ty \(ˌ)in-ˌhäs-pə-'ta-lə-tē\ *n* (ca. 1576) : the quality or state of being inhospitable

in–house \'in-ˌhaus, -'haus\ *adj* (ca. 1956) : existing, originating, or carried on within a group or organization or its facilities : not outside ⟨an ∼ publication⟩ ⟨a company's ∼ staff⟩ — **in–house** *adv*

in·hu·man \(ˌ)in-'hyü-mən, -'yü-\ *adj* [ME *inhumayne*, fr. MF & L; MF *inhumain*, fr. L *inhumanus*, fr. *in-* + *humanus* human] (15c) **1 a** : lacking pity, kindness, or mercy : SAVAGE ⟨an ∼ tyrant⟩ **b** : COLD, IMPERSONAL ⟨his usual quiet, almost ∼ courtesy —F. Tennyson Jesse⟩ **c** : not worthy of or conforming to the needs of human beings ⟨∼ living conditions⟩ **2** : of or suggesting a nonhuman class of beings — **in·hu·man·ly** *adv* — **in·hu·man·ness** \-mən-nəs\ *n*

in·hu·mane \ˌin-(ˌ)hyü-'mān, -(ˌ)yü-\ *adj* [MF *inhumain* & L *inhumanus*] (1599) : not humane : INHUMAN **1** — **in·hu·mane·ly** *adv*

in·hu·man·i·ty \-'ma-nə-tē\ *n, pl* **-ties** (15c) **1 a** : the quality or state of being cruel or barbarous **b** : a cruel or barbarous act **2** : absence of warmth or geniality : IMPERSONALITY

in·hume \in-'hyüm\ *vt* **in·humed; in·hum·ing** [prob. fr. F *inhumer*, fr. ML *inhumare*, fr. L *in-* + *humus* earth — more at HUMBLE] (1604) : BURY, INTER — **in·hu·ma·tion** \ˌin-hyü-'mā-shən\ *n*

in·im·i·cal \i-'ni-mi-kəl\ *adj* [LL *inimicalis*, fr. L *inimicus* enemy — more at ENEMY] (1573) **1** : being adverse often by reason of hostility or malevolence **2 a** : having the disposition of an enemy : HOSTILE **b** : reflecting or indicating hostility : UNFRIENDLY — **in·im·i·cal·ly** \-mi-k(ə-)lē\ *adv*

in·im·i·ta·ble \(ˌ)i-'ni-mə-tə-bəl\ *adj* [ME, fr. MF or L; MF, fr. L *inimitabilis*, fr. *in-* + *imitabilis* imitable] (15c) : not capable of being imitated : MATCHLESS — **in·im·i·ta·ble·ness** *n* — **in·im·i·ta·bly** \-blē\ *adv*

in·i·on \'i-nē-ˌän, -ən\ *n* [NL, fr. Gk, back of the head, dim. of *in-, is* sinew, tendon] (ca. 1811) : the external occipital protuberance of the skull

in·iq·ui·tous \i-'ni-kwə-təs\ *adj* (1726) : characterized by iniquity *syn* see VICIOUS — **in·iq·ui·tous·ly** *adv* — **in·iq·ui·tous·ness** *n*

in·iq·ui·ty \-kwə-tē\ *n, pl* **-ties** [ME *iniquite*, fr. MF *iniquité*, fr. L *iniquitat-, iniquitas*, fr. *iniquus* uneven, fr. *in-* + *aequus* equal] (14c) **1** : gross injustice : WICKEDNESS **2** : a wicked act or thing : SIN

¹ini·tial \i-'ni-shəl\ *adj* [MF & L; MF, fr. L *initialis*, fr. *initium* beginning, fr. *inire* to go into, fr. *in-* + *ire* to go — more at ISSUE] (1526) **1** : of or relating to the beginning : INCIPIENT **2** : placed at the beginning : FIRST — **ini·tial·ly** \i-'ni-sh(ə-)lē\ *adv* — **ini·tial·ness** \i-'ni-shəl-nəs\ *n*

²initial *n* (1627) **1 a** : the first letter of a name **b** *pl* : the first letter of each word in a full name ⟨found that their ∼s were identical⟩ **2** : a large letter beginning a text or a division or paragraph **3** : ANLAGE, PRECURSOR; *specif* : a meristematic cell

³initial *vt* **ini·tialed** *or* **ini·tialled; ini·tial·ing** *or* **ini·tial·ling** \i-'ni-sh(ə-)liŋ\ (ca. 1864) **1** : to affix an initial to **2** : to authenticate or give preliminary approval to by affixing the initials of an authorizing representative

ini·tial·ism \i-'ni-shə-ˌli-zəm\ *n* (1899) : an acronym formed from initial letters

ini·tial·ize \-ˌlīz\ *vt* **-ized; -iz·ing** (1957) : to set (as a computer program counter) to a starting position, value, or configuration — **ini·tial·i·za·tion** \i-ˌni-sh(ə-)lə-'zā-shən\ *n*

initial rhyme *n* (1838) : ALLITERATION

initial side *n* (1957) : a stationary straight line that contains a point about which another straight line is rotated to form an angle — compare TERMINAL SIDE

¹ini·ti·ate \i-'ni-shē-ˌāt\ *vt* **-at·ed; -at·ing** [LL *initiatus*, pp. of *initiare*, fr. L, to induct, fr. *initium*] (ca. 1573) **1** : to cause or facilitate the beginning of : set going ⟨∼ a program of reform⟩ ⟨enzymes that ∼ fermentation⟩ **2** : to induct into membership by or as if by special rites **3** : to instruct in the rudiments or principles of something : IN-TRODUCE *syn* see BEGIN — **ini·ti·a·tor** \-ˌā-tər\ *n*

²ini·ti·ate \i-'ni-sh(ē-)ət\ *adj* (1605) **1** *obs* : relating to an initiate **2 a** : initiated or properly admitted (as to membership or an office) **b** : instructed in some secret knowledge

³ini·ti·ate \i-'ni-sh(ē-)ət\ *n* (1811) **1** : a person who is undergoing or has undergone an initiation **2** : a person who is instructed or adept in some special field

ini·ti·a·tion \i-ˌni-shē-'ā-shən\ *n* (1583) **1 a** : the act or an instance of initiating **b** : the process of being initiated **c** : the rites, ceremonies, ordeals, or instructions with which one is made a member of a sect or society or is invested with a particular function or status **2** : the condition of being initiated into some experience or sphere of activity : KNOWLEDGEABLENESS

¹ini·tia·tive \i-'ni-shə-tiv *also* -shē-ə-tiv\ *adj* (1795) : of or relating to initiation : INTRODUCTORY, PRELIMINARY

\ə\ abut \ᵊ\ kitten, F table \ər\ further \a\ ash \ā\ ace \ä\ mop, mar \aú\ out \ch\ chin \e\ bet \ē\ easy \g\ go \i\ hit \ī\ ice \j\ job \ŋ\ sing \ō\ go \o\ law \oi\ boy \th\ thin \th\ the \ü\ loot \ú\ foot \y\ yet \zh\ vision \à, ḵ, ⁿ, œ, œ̄, ue, ūe, ʸ\ *see* Guide to Pronunciation

²**initiative** n (1793) **1 :** an introductory step ⟨took the ~ in attempting to settle the issue⟩ **2 :** energy or aptitude displayed in initiation of action : ENTERPRISE ⟨showed great ~⟩ **3 a :** the right to initiate legislative action **b :** a procedure enabling a specified number of voters by petition to propose a law and secure its submission to the electorate or to the legislature for approval — compare REFERENDUM 1 — **on one's own initiative :** at one's own discretion : independently of outside influence or control

ini·tia·to·ry \i-'ni-sh(ē-)ə-,tōr-ē, -,tȯr-\ adj (ca. 1615) **1 :** constituting a beginning **2 :** tending or serving to initiate

in·ject \in-'jekt\ vt [L injectus, pp. of inicere, fr. in- + jacere to throw — more at JET] (1601) **1 a :** to introduce into something forcefully ⟨~ fuel into an engine⟩ **b :** to force a fluid into (as for medical purposes) **2 :** to introduce as an element or factor in or into some situation or subject ⟨condemning any attempt to ~ religious bigotry into the campaign —Current Biog.⟩ — **in·ject·able** \-'jek-tə-bəl\ adj or n — **in·jec·tor** \-'jek-tər\ n

in·jec·tant \-'jek-tənt\ n (1950) **:** a substance that is injected into something

in·jec·tion \in-'jek-shən\ n (15c) **1 a :** an act or instance of injecting **b :** the placing of an artificial satellite or a spacecraft into an orbit or on a trajectory; also : the time or place at which injection occurs **2 :** something (as a medication) that is injected **3 :** a mathematical function that is a one-to-one mapping — compare BIJECTION, SURJECTION

injection molding n (1932) **:** a method of forming articles (as of plastic) by heating the molding material until it can flow and injecting it into a mold — **injection–molded** adj

in·jec·tive \in-'jek-tiv\ adj (1952) **:** being a one-to-one mathematical function

in–joke \'in-,jōk, -'jōk\ n (1964) **:** a joke for or about a select group of people

in·ju·di·cious \,in-jù-'di-shəs\ adj (1649) **:** not judicious : INDISCREET, UNWISE — **in·ju·di·cious·ly** adv — **in·ju·di·cious·ness** n

in·junc·tion \in-'jəŋ(k)-shən\ n [ME injunccion, fr. MF & LL; MF injonction, fr. LL injunction-, injunctio, fr. L injungere to enjoin — more at ENJOIN] (15c) **1 :** the act or an instance of enjoining : ORDER, ADMONITION **2 :** a writ granted by a court of equity whereby one is required to do or to refrain from doing a specified act — **in·junc·tive** \-'jəŋ(k)-tiv\ adj

in·jure \'in-jər\ vt **in·jured; in·jur·ing** \'inj-riŋ, 'in-jə-\ [ME enjuren, fr. MF enjurier, fr. L injuriare, fr. L injuria injury] (15c) **1 a :** to do an injustice to : WRONG **b :** to harm, impair, or tarnish the standing of **c :** to give pain to ⟨~ a person's pride⟩ **2 a :** to inflict bodily hurt on **b :** to impair the soundness of **c :** to inflict material damage or loss on — **in·jur·er** \'in-jər-ər\ n

syn INJURE, HARM, HURT, DAMAGE, IMPAIR, MAR mean to affect injuriously. INJURE implies the inflicting of anything detrimental to one's looks, comfort, health, or success ⟨badly injured in an accident⟩. HARM often stresses the inflicting of pain, suffering, or loss ⟨careful not to harm the animals⟩. HURT implies inflicting a wound to the body or to the feelings ⟨hurt by their callous remarks⟩. DAMAGE suggests injury that lowers value or impairs usefulness ⟨a table damaged in shipping⟩. IMPAIR suggests a making less complete or efficient by deterioration or diminution ⟨years of smoking had impaired his health⟩. MAR applies to injury that spoils perfection (as of a surface) or causes disfigurement ⟨the text is marred by many typos⟩.

in·ju·ri·ous \in-'jùr-ē-əs\ adj (15c) **1 :** inflicting or tending to inflict injury : DETRIMENTAL ⟨~ to health⟩ **2 :** ABUSIVE, DEFAMATORY ⟨speak not ~ words —George Washington⟩ — **in·ju·ri·ous·ly** adv — **in·ju·ri·ous·ness** n

in·ju·ry \'inj-rē, 'in-jə-\ n, pl **-ries** [ME injurie, fr. L injuria, fr. injurus injurious, fr. in- + jur-, jus right — more at JUST] (14c) **1 a :** an act that damages or hurts : WRONG **b :** violation of another's rights for which the law allows an action to recover damages **2 :** hurt, damage, or loss sustained syn see INJUSTICE

in·jus·tice \(,)in-'jəs-təs\ n [ME, fr. MF, fr. L injustitia, fr. injustus unjust, fr. in- + justus just] (14c) **1 :** absence of justice : violation of right or of the rights of another : UNFAIRNESS **2 :** an unjust act : WRONG

syn INJUSTICE, INJURY, WRONG, GRIEVANCE mean an act that inflicts undeserved hurt. INJUSTICE applies to any act that involves unfairness to another or violation of his rights ⟨the injustices suffered by the lower classes⟩. INJURY applies in law specif. to an injustice for which one may sue to recover compensation ⟨libel constitutes a legal injury⟩. WRONG applies also in law to any act punishable according to the criminal code; it may apply more generally to any flagrant injustice ⟨determined to right society's wrongs⟩. GRIEVANCE applies to any circumstance or condition that constitutes an injustice to the sufferer and gives just ground for complaint ⟨investigating employee grievances⟩.

¹**ink** \'iŋk\ n, often attrib [ME enke, fr. OF, fr. LL encaustum, fr. neut. of L encaustum burned in, fr. Gk enkauston, verbal of enkaiein to burn in — more at ENCAUSTIC] (13c) **1 :** a colored usu. liquid material for writing and printing **2 :** the black protective secretion of a cephalopod **3** slang : PUBLICITY 2d — **ink·i·ness** \'iŋ-kē-nəs\ n — **inky** \'iŋ-kē\ adj

²**ink** vt (1562) **1 :** to put ink on ⟨~ a pen⟩; also : to draw or write on in ink **2 :** SIGN 2a ⟨~ed a new contract⟩ **b :** SIGN 4

ink·ber·ry \'iŋk-,ber-ē\ n [fr. the use of the berries for making ink] (1765) **1 a :** a holly (Ilex glabra) of eastern No. America with evergreen oblong leathery leaves and small usu. black berries **b :** POKEWEED **2 :** the fruit of an inkberry

ink·blot test \'iŋk-,blät-\ n (1928) **:** any of several psychological tests (as a Rorschach test) based on the interpretation of irregular figures (as blots of ink)

¹**ink·horn** \'iŋk-,hȯrn\ n (14c) **:** a small portable bottle (as of horn) for holding ink

²**inkhorn** adj (1543) **:** ostentatiously learned : PEDANTIC ⟨~ terms⟩

in–kind \'in-'kīnd\ adj (1973) **:** consisting of something (as goods or commodities) other than money ⟨in-kind relief for the poor⟩

ink–jet \'iŋk-'jet\ adj (1976) **:** of, relating to, or being a dot matrix printer in which electrically charged droplets of ink are projected onto the paper

in·kle \'iŋ-kəl\ n [origin unknown] (1541) **:** a colored linen tape or braid woven on a very narrow loom and used for trimming; also : the thread used

in·kling \'iŋ-kliŋ\ n [ME yngkiling whisper, mention, prob. fr. inclen to hint at; akin to OE inca suspicion] (1513) **1 :** a slight indication or suggestion : HINT, CLUE ⟨there was no path—no ~ even of a track —New Yorker⟩ **2 :** a slight knowledge or vague notion ⟨had not the faintest ~ of what it was all about —H. W. Carter⟩

ink·stand \'iŋk-,stand\ n (1773) **:** INKWELL; also : a stand with fittings for holding ink and pens

ink·stone \'iŋk-,stōn\ n (ca. 1889) **:** a stone used in Chinese art and calligraphy on which dry ink and water are mixed

ink·well \'iŋk-,wel\ n (ca. 1875) **:** a container (as in a desk) for ink

inky cap n (1923) **:** a mushroom (genus Coprinus, esp. C. atramentarius) whose pileus deliquesces into an inky fluid after the spores have matured — called also ink cap

inky cap

in·laid \'in-'lād\ adj (1598) **1 a :** set into a surface in a decorative design ⟨tables with ~ marble⟩ **b :** decorated with a design or material set into a surface ⟨a table with an ~ top⟩ **2** of linoleum : having a design that goes all the way through to the backing

¹**in·land** \'in-,land, -lənd\ adj (1546) **1** chiefly Brit : not foreign : DOMESTIC **2 :** of or relating to the interior of a country

²**inland** n (1573) **:** the interior part of a country

³**inland** adv (1600) **:** into or toward the interior

in·land·er \'in-,lan-dər, -lən-\ n (1610) **:** one who lives inland

in–law \'in-,lȯ\ n [mother-in-law, etc.] (1894) **:** a relative by marriage

¹**in·lay** \(,)in-'lā, 'in-,\ vt **in·laid** \-'lād, -,lād\; **in·lay·ing** (1596) **1 a :** to set into a surface or ground material **b :** to adorn with insertions **c :** to insert (as a color plate) into a mat or other reinforcement **2 :** to rub, beat, or fuse (as wire) into an incision in metal, wood, or stone — **in·lay·er** n

²**in·lay** \'in-,lā\ n (1667) **1 :** inlaid work or a decorative inlaid pattern **2 :** a tooth filling shaped to fit a cavity and then cemented into place

in·let \'in-,let, -lət\ n [fr. its letting water in] (ca. 1576) **1 a :** a bay or recess in the shore of a sea, lake, or river; also : CREEK **b :** a narrow water passage between peninsulas or through a barrier island leading to a bay or lagoon **2 :** a way of entering; esp : an opening for intake

in·li·er \'in-,lī(-ə)r\ n [²in + outlier] (ca. 1859) **1 :** a mass of rock whose outcrop is surrounded by rock of younger age **2 :** a distinct area or formation completely surrounded by another; also : ENCLAVE

in–line \'in-'līn, ,in-\ adj or adv (1929) **:** having the parts or units arranged in a straight line; also : being so arranged

in–line engine \(,)in-'līn-, ,in-\ n (1929) **:** an internal combustion engine in which the cylinders are arranged in one or more straight lines

in–line skate n (1989) **:** a roller skate whose four wheels are set in-line for greater speed and maneuverability — **in–line skating** n

¹**in lo·co pa·ren·tis** \in-'lō-kō-pə-'ren-təs\ adv [L] (1828) **:** in the place of a parent

²**in loco parentis** n (1968) **:** regulation or supervision by an administrative body (as at a university) acting in loco parentis

in·ly \'in-lē\ adv (bef. 12c) **1 :** INWARDLY **2 :** in a manner suggesting great depth of knowledge or understanding : THOROUGHLY

in·mate \'in-,māt\ n (1589) **:** any of a group occupying a single place of residence; esp : a person confined (as in a prison or hospital)

in me·di·as res \,in-'me-dē-əs-'räs, -'mē-dē-əs-'rēz\ adv [L, lit., into the midst of things] (1786) **:** in or into the middle of a narrative or plot

in me·mo·ri·am \,in-mə-'mōr-ē-əm, -'mȯr-\ prep [L] (1850) **:** in memory of — used esp. in epitaphs

in–mi·grant \'in-,mī-grənt\ n (1942) **:** one that in-migrates

in–mi·grate \'in-,mī-,grāt\ vi (1942) **:** to move into or come to live in a region or community esp. as part of a large-scale and continuing movement of population — compare OUT-MIGRATE — **in–mi·gra·tion** \,in-mī-'grā-shən\ n

in·most \'in-,mōst\ adj [ME, fr. OE innemest, superl. of inne, adv., in, within, fr. in, adv.] (bef. 12c) **:** deepest within : farthest from the outside

¹**inn** \'in\ n [ME, fr. OE; akin to ON inni dwelling, inn, OE in, adv.] (bef. 12c) **1 a :** an establishment for the lodging and entertaining of travelers **b :** TAVERN **2 :** a residence formerly provided for British students in London and esp. for students of law

²**inn** vi (14c) **:** to put up at an inn

in·nards \'i-nərdz\ n pl [alter. of inwards] (ca. 1825) **1 :** the internal organs of a human being or animal; esp : VISCERA **2 :** the internal parts esp. of a structure or mechanism

in·nate \i-'nāt, 'i-,\ adj [ME innat, fr. L innatus, pp. of innasci to be born in, fr. in- + nasci to be born — more at NATION] (15c) **1 :** existing in, belonging to, or determined by factors present in an individual from birth : NATIVE, INBORN ⟨~ behavior⟩ **2 :** belonging to the essential nature of something : INHERENT **3 :** originating in or derived from the mind or the constitution of the intellect rather than from experience — **in·nate·ly** adv — **in·nate·ness** n

syn INNATE, INBORN, INBRED, CONGENITAL, HEREDITARY mean not acquired after birth. INNATE applies to qualities or characteristics that are part of one's inner essential nature ⟨an innate sense of fair play⟩. INBORN suggests a quality or tendency either actually present at birth or so marked and deep-seated as to seem so ⟨her inborn love of nature⟩. INBRED suggests something either acquired from parents by heredity or so deeply rooted and ingrained as to seem acquired in that way ⟨inbred political loyalties⟩. CONGENITAL and HEREDITARY refer to what is acquired before or at birth, the former to things acquired during fetal development and the latter to things transmitted from one's ancestors ⟨a congenital heart murmur⟩ ⟨eye color is hereditary⟩.

in·ner \'i-nər\ adj [ME, fr. OE innera, compar. of inne within] (bef. 12c) **1 a :** situated farther in ⟨the ~ bark⟩ **b :** being near a center esp. of influence ⟨the ~ circles of political power⟩ **2 :** of or relating to the mind or spirit ⟨the ~ life⟩ — **inner** n — **in·ner·ly** adv

inner city *n* (1961) : the usu. older, poorer, and more densely populated central section of a city — **inner–city** *adj*

in·ner–di·rect·ed \'i-nər-də-'rek-təd, -(,)di-\ *adj* (1950) : directed in thought and action by one's own scale of values as opposed to external norms

inner ear *n* (ca. 1923) : the essential organ of hearing and equilibrium that is located in the temporal bone, is innervated by the auditory nerve, and includes the vestibule, the semicircular canals, and the cochlea

inner light *n, often cap I&L* (1856) : a divine presence held (as in Quaker doctrine) to enlighten and guide the soul

¹**in·ner·most** \'i-nər-,mōst\ *adj* (14c) : farthest inward : INMOST

²**innermost** *n* (14c) : the inmost part

inner planet *n* (1951) : any of the planets Mercury, Venus, Earth, and Mars whose orbits are within the asteroid belt

inner product *n* (ca. 1911) : SCALAR PRODUCT

in·ner·sole \'i-nər-'sōl\ *n* (ca. 1892) : INSOLE

inner space *n* (1958) **1** : space at or near the earth's surface and esp. under the sea **2** : one's inner self

in·ner·spring \'i-nər-'spriŋ\ *adj* (1928) : having coil springs inside a padded casing ⟨~ mattress⟩

inner tube *n* (1895) : an airtight rubber tube inside a pneumatic tire to hold air under pressure

in·ner·vate \i-'nər-,vāt, 'i-(,)nər-\ *vt* **-vat·ed; -vat·ing** (1870) : to supply with nerves — **in·ner·va·tion** \,i-(,)nər-'vā-shən, i-,nər-\ *n*

in·ning \'i-niŋ\ *n* [²*in* + ¹-*ing*] (1735) **1 a** *pl but sing or pl in constr* : a division of a cricket match **b** : a division of a baseball game consisting of a turn at bat for each team; *also* : a baseball team's turn at bat ending with the third out **c** : a player's turn (as in horseshoes, pool, or croquet) **2** : a chance or opportunity for action or accomplishment — usu. used in pl. but sing. or pl. in constr. ⟨that momentous ~s which was to project him into world politics —*Times Lit. Supp.*⟩

inn·keep·er \'in-,kē-pər\ *n* (15c) **1** : a proprietor of an inn **2** : HOTELMAN

in·no·cence \'i-nə-sən(t)s\ *n* (14c) **1 a** : freedom from guilt or sin through being unacquainted with evil : BLAMELESSNESS **b** : CHASTITY **c** : freedom from legal guilt of a particular crime or offense **d** (1) : freedom from guile or cunning : SIMPLICITY (2) : lack of worldly experience or sophistication **e** : lack of knowledge : IGNORANCE ⟨written in entire ~ of the Italian language —E. R. Bentley⟩ **2** : one that is innocent **3** : BLUET

in·no·cen·cy \-sən(t)-sē\ *n, pl* **-cies** (14c) : INNOCENCE; *also* : an innocent action or quality

in·no·cent \'i-nə-sənt\ *adj* [ME, fr. MF, fr. L *innocent-, innocens*, fr. *in-* + *nocent-, nocens* wicked, fr. prp. of *nocēre* to harm — more at NOXIOUS] (14c) **1 a** : free from guilt or sin esp. through lack of knowledge : BLAMELESS ⟨an ~ child⟩ **b** : harmless in effect or intention ⟨searching for a hidden motive in even the most ~ conversation —Leonard Wibberley⟩; *also* : CANDID ⟨gave me an ~ gaze⟩ **c** : free from legal guilt or fault; *also* : LAWFUL ⟨a wholly ~ transaction⟩ **2 a** : lacking or reflecting a lack of sophistication, guile, or self-consciousness : ARTLESS, INGENUOUS **b** : IGNORANT ⟨almost entirely ~ of Latin —C. L. Wrenn⟩; *also* : UNAWARE ⟨perfectly ~ of the confusion he had created —B. R. Haydon⟩ **3** : lacking or deprived of something ⟨her face ~ of cosmetics —Marcia Davenport⟩ — **innocent** *n* — **in·no·cent·ly** *adv*

in·noc·u·ous \i-'nä-kyə-wəs\ *adj* [L *innocuus*, fr. *in-* + *nocēre*] (1598) **1** : producing no injury : HARMLESS **2** : not likely to give offense or to arouse strong feelings or hostility : INOFFENSIVE, INSIPID — **in·noc·u·ous·ly** *adv* — **in·noc·u·ous·ness** *n*

in·nom·i·nate \i-'nä-mə-nət\ *adj* [LL *innominatus*, fr. L *in-* + *nominatus*, pp. of *nominare* to nominate] (1638) : having no name : UNNAMED; *also* : ANONYMOUS

innominate artery *n* (1870) : BRACHIOCEPHALIC ARTERY

innominate bone *n* (1866) : the large flaring bone that constitutes a lateral half of the pelvis in mammals and is composed of the ilium, ischium, and pubis which are fused into one bone in the adult

innominate vein *n* (1876) : BRACHIOCEPHALIC VEIN

in·no·vate \'i-nə-,vāt\ *vb* **-vat·ed; -vat·ing** [L *innovatus*, pp. of *innovare*, fr. *in-* + *novus* new — more at NEW] *vt* (1548) **1** : to introduce as or as if new **2** *archaic* : to effect a change in ⟨the dictates of my father were . . . not to be altered, innovated, or even discussed —Sir Walter Scott⟩ ~ *vi* : to make changes : do something in a new way — **in·no·va·tor** \-,vā-tər\ *n* — **in·no·va·to·ry** \'i-nə-və-,tōr-ē, -,tōr-; 'i-nə-,vā-tə-rē\ *adj*

in·no·va·tion \,i-nə-'vā-shən\ *n* (15c) **1** : the introduction of something new **2** : a new idea, method, or device : NOVELTY — **in·no·va·tion·al** \-shnəl, -shə-n³l\ *adj*

in·no·va·tive \'i-nə-,vā-tiv\ *adj* (1608) : characterized by, tending to, or introducing innovations — **in·no·va·tive·ly** *adv* — **in·no·va·tive·ness** *n*

Inns of Court (15c) **1** : the four sets of buildings in London belonging to four societies of students and practitioners of the law **2** : the four societies that alone admit to practice at the English bar

in·nu·en·do \,in-yə-'wen-(,)dō\ *n, pl* **-dos** or **-does** [L, by hinting, fr. *innuere* to hint, fr. *in-* + *nuere* to nod — more at NUMEN] (1678) **1 a** : an oblique allusion : HINT, INSINUATION; *esp* : a veiled or equivocal reflection on character or reputation **b** : the use of such allusions ⟨resorting to ~⟩ **2** : a parenthetical explanation introduced into the text of a legal document

In·nu·it *var of* INUIT

in·nu·mer·a·ble \i-'nüm-rə-bəl, -'nyüm-; -'n(y)ü-mə-\ *adj* [ME, fr. L *innumerabilis*, fr. *in-* + *numerabilis* numerable] (14c) : too many to be numbered : COUNTLESS; *also* : very many — **in·nu·mer·a·bly** \-blē\ *adv*

in·nu·mer·ate \-rət\ *adj* (1959) : marked by an ignorance of mathematics and the scientific approach — **in·nu·mer·a·cy** \-rə-sē\ *n* — **innumerate** *n*

in·nu·mer·ous \-rəs\ *adj* [L *innumerus*, fr. *in-* + *numerus* number] (1531) : INNUMERABLE

in·ob·ser·vance \,i-nəb-'zər-vən(t)s\ *n* [F & L; F, fr. L *inobservantia*, fr. *in-* + *observantia* observance] (1611) **1** : lack of attention : HEEDLESSNESS **2** : failure to fulfill : NONOBSERVANCE — **in·ob·ser·vant** \-vənt\ *adj*

in·oc·u·lant \i-'nä-kyə-lənt\ *n* (1898) : INOCULUM

in·oc·u·late \i-'nä-kyə-,lāt\ *vt* **-lat·ed; -lat·ing** [ME, to insert a bud in a plant, fr. L *inoculatus*, pp. of *inoculare*, fr. *in-* + *oculus* eye, bud — more at EYE] (1721) **1 a** : to introduce a microorganism into ⟨~ mice with anthrax⟩ ⟨beans *inoculated* with nitrogen-fixing bacteria⟩ **b** : to introduce (as a microorganism) into a suitable situation for growth **c** : to introduce immunologically active material (as an antibody or antigen) into esp. in order to treat or prevent a disease ⟨~ children against diphtheria⟩ **2** : to introduce something into the mind of **3** : to protect as if by inoculation *syn* see INFUSE — **in·oc·u·la·tive** \-,lā-tiv\ *adj* — **in·oc·u·la·tor** \-,lā-tər\ *n*

in·oc·u·la·tion \i-,nä-kyə-'lā-shən\ *n* (1714) **1** : the act or process of or an instance of inoculating; *esp* : the introduction of a pathogen or antigen into a living organism to stimulate the production of antibodies **2** : INOCULUM

in·oc·u·lum \i-'nä-kyə-ləm\ *n, pl* **-la** \-lə\ [NL, fr. L *inoculare*] (1902) : material used for inoculation

in·of·fen·sive \,i-nə-'fen(t)-siv\ *adj* (1646) **1** : causing no harm or injury **2 a** : giving no provocation : PEACEABLE **b** : not objectionable to the senses — **in·of·fen·sive·ly** *adv* — **in·of·fen·sive·ness** *n*

in·op·er·a·ble \(,)i-'nä-p(ə-)rə-bəl\ *adj* [prob. fr. F *inopérable*] (1886) **1** : not treatable or remediable by surgery ⟨~ cancer⟩ **2** : INOPERATIVE

in·op·er·a·tive \-'nä-p(ə-)rə-tiv, -'nä-pə-,rā-\ *adj* (ca. 1631) : not operative: as **a** : not functioning ⟨an ~ clock⟩ **b** : having no effect or force ⟨an ~ law⟩ — **in·op·er·a·tive·ness** *n*

in·oper·cu·late \,i-nō-'pər-kyə-lət\ *adj* (ca. 1836) : having no operculum — **inoperculate** *n*

in·op·por·tune \(,)i-,nä-pər-'tün, -'tyün\ *adj* [L *inopportunus*, fr. *in-* + *opportunus* opportune] (ca. 1507) : INCONVENIENT, UNSEASONABLE — **in·op·por·tune·ly** *adv* — **in·op·por·tune·ness** \-'t(y)ün-nəs\ *n*

in order that *conj* (1711) : THAT 2a(1)

in·or·di·nate \i-'nòrd-³n-ət, -'nòrd-nət\ *adj* [ME *inordinat*, fr. L *inordinatus*, fr. *in-* + *ordinatus*, pp. of *ordinare* to arrange — more at ORDAIN] (14c) **1** *archaic* : DISORDERLY, UNREGULATED **2** : exceeding reasonable limits : IMMODERATE *syn* see EXCESSIVE — **in·or·di·nate·ly** *adv* — **in·or·di·nate·ness** *n*

in·or·gan·ic \,i-(,)nòr-'ga-nik\ *adj* (1794) **1 a** (1) : being or composed of matter other than plant or animal : MINERAL (2) : forming or belonging to the inanimate world **b** : of, relating to, or dealt with by a branch of chemistry concerned with substances not usu. classed as organic **2** : not arising from natural growth : ARTIFICIAL; *also* : lacking structure, character, or vitality ⟨dull ~ things, without individuality or prestige —John Buchan⟩ — **in·or·gan·i·cal·ly** \-ni-k(ə-)lē\ *adv*

in·os·cu·late \i-'näs-kyə-,lāt\ *vb* **-lat·ed; -lat·ing** [²*in-* + *osculate*] (1671) : JOIN, UNITE — **in·os·cu·la·tion** \(,)i-,näs-kyə-'lā-shən\ *n*

ino·si·tol \i-'nō-sə-,tòl, ī-'nō-, -,tōl\ *n* [ISV, fr. *inosite* inositol, fr. Gk *in-*, *is* sinew + ISV ²-*ose* + ¹-*ite*] (1891) : any of several crystalline stereoisomeric cyclic alcohols $C_6H_{12}O_6$; *esp* : MYOINOSITOL

ino·tro·pic \,ē-nə-'trō-pik, ,i-nə-, -'trä-\ *adj* [ISV *ino-* (fr. Gk *in-*, *is* sinew) + -*tropic*] (1903) : relating to or influencing the force of muscular contractions

in·pa·tient \'in-,pā-shənt\ *n* (1760) : a hospital patient who receives lodging and food as well as treatment — compare OUTPATIENT

in per·so·nam \,in-pər-'sō-,nam, -,näm\ *adv or adj* [LL, against a person] (ca. 1860) : against a person for the purpose of imposing a liability or obligation — used esp. of legal actions, judgments, or jurisdiction; compare IN REM

in pet·to \in-'pe-(,)tō\ *adv or adj* [It, lit., in the breast] (ca. 1674) **1** : in private : SECRETLY **2** : in miniature

in·pour·ing \'in-,pōr-iŋ, -,pòr-\ *n* (1721) : INRUSH

in–print \'in-'print\ *adj* (1950) : being in print

in–pro·cess \(,)in-'prä-,ses, -'prō-, -səs\ *adj* (1925) : of, relating to, or being goods in manufacture as distinguished from raw materials or from finished products

in pro·pria per·so·na \in-'prō-prē-ə-pər-'sō-nə\ *adv* [ML] (1654) : in one's own person or character : PERSONALLY; *esp* : without the assistance of an attorney

¹**in·put** \'in-,pùt\ *n* (1753) **1** : something that is put in: as **a** : an amount put in ⟨increased ~ of fertilizer increases crop yield⟩ **b** : power or energy put into a machine or system for storage, conversion in kind, or conversion of characteristics usu. with the intent of sizable recovery in the form of output **c** : a component of production (as land, labor, or raw materials) **d** : information fed into a data processing system or computer **e** : ADVICE, OPINION, COMMENT **2** : the means by which or the point at which an input (as of energy, material, or data) is made **3** : the act or process of putting in

²**input** *vt* **in·put·ted** or **input; in·put·ting** (1946) : to enter (as data) into a computer or data processing system

in·quest \'in-,kwest\ *n* [ME, fr. OF *enqueste*, fr. (assumed) VL *in-quaesta*, fem. of *inquaestus*, pp. of *inquaerere* to inquire] (13c) **1 a** : a judicial or official inquiry or examination esp. before a jury ⟨a coroner's ~⟩ **b** : a body of people (as a jury) assembled to hold such an inquiry **c** : the finding of the jury upon such inquiry or the document recording it **2** : INQUIRY, INVESTIGATION

in·qui·etude \(,)in-'kwī-ə-,tüd, -,tyüd\ *n* [ME, fr. MF or LL; MF, fr. LL *inquietudo*, fr. L *inquietus* disturbed, fr. *in-* + *quietus* quiet] (15c) : disturbed state : DISQUIETUDE

in·qui·line \'in-kwə-,līn, 'iŋ-, -lən\ *n* [L *inquilinus* tenant, lodger, fr. *in-* + *colere* to cultivate, dwell — more at WHEEL] (1879) : an animal that lives habitually in the nest or abode of some other species

in·quire \in-'kwīr\ *vb* **in·quired; in·quir·ing** [ME *enquiren*, fr. OF *enquerre*, fr. (assumed) VL *inquaerere*, alter. of L *inquirere*, fr. *in-* + *quaerere* to seek] *vt* (13c) **1** : to ask about ⟨some kindred spirit shall ~ thy fate —Thomas Gray⟩ **2** : to search into : INVESTIGATE ~ *vi* **1** : to put a question : seek for information by questioning ⟨*inquired* about the horses⟩ **2** : to make investigation or inquiry — often used

---

\ə\ abut \ᵊ\ kitten, F table \ər\ further \a\ ash \ā\ ace \ä\ mop, mar
\aù\ out \ch\ chin \e\ bet \ē\ easy \g\ go \i\ hit \ī\ ice \j\ job
\ŋ\ sing \ō\ go \ò\ law \òi\ boy \th\ thin \t̲h̲\ the \ü\ loot \ù\ foot
\y\ yet \zh\ vision \ä, k̲, ⁿ, œ, œ̄, ᵾ, ᵿ, ᵊ\ *see* Guide to Pronunciation

with *into* *syn* see ASK — **in·quir·er** *n* — **in·quir·ing·ly** \-'kwī-riŋ-lē\ *adv* — **inquire after** : to ask about the health of
in·qui·ry \in-'kwir-ē, 'in-.; 'in-kwə-rē, 'in-; 'in-.kwir-ē\ *n, pl* **-ries** (15c) **1** : examination into facts or principles : RESEARCH **2** : a request for information **3** : a systematic investigation often of a matter of public interest
in·qui·si·tion \.in-kwə-'zi-shən, .iŋ-\ *n* [ME *inquisicioun*, fr. MF *inquisition*, fr. L *inquisition-, inquisitio*, fr. *inquirere*] (14c) **1** : the act of inquiring : EXAMINATION **2** : a judicial or official inquiry or examination usu. before a jury; *also* : the finding of the jury **3 a** *cap* : a former Roman Catholic tribunal for the discovery and punishment of heresy **b** : an investigation conducted with little regard for individual rights **c** : a severe questioning — **in·qui·si·tion·al** \-'zi-sh(ə-)nᵊl\ *adj*
in·quis·i·tive \in-'kwi-zə-tiv\ *adj* (14c) **1** : given to examination or investigation **2** : inclined to ask questions; *esp* : inordinately or improperly curious about the affairs of others *syn* see CURIOUS — **in·quis·i·tive·ly** *adv* — **in·quis·i·tive·ness** *n*
in·quis·i·tor \in-'kwi-zə-tər\ *n* (1504) : one who inquires or makes inquisition; *esp* : one who is unduly harsh, severe, or hostile in making an inquiry — **in·quis·i·to·ri·al** \-.kwi-zə-'tōr-ē-əl, -'tȯr-\ *adj* — **in·quis·i·to·ri·al·ly** \-ē-ə-lē\ *adv*
in re \in-'rā, -'rē\ *prep* [L] (1877) : in the matter of : CONCERNING, RE — often used in the title or name of a law case
in rem \in-'rem\ *adv or adj* [LL] (ca. 1860) : against a thing (as a right, status, or property) — used esp. of legal actions, judgments, or jurisdiction; compare IN PERSONAM
in–residence *adj* (1845) : being officially associated with an organization in a specified capacity — usu. used in combination ⟨writer-*in-residence* at the university⟩
in·ro \'in-.rō\ *n, pl* **inro** [Jp *inrō*] (1617) : a small compartmented and usu. ornamented container hung from an obi to hold small objects (as medicines and perfumes)
in·road \'in-.rōd\ *n* (1548) **1** : a sudden hostile incursion : RAID **2** : an advance or penetration often at the expense of someone or something — usu. used in pl.
in·rush \'in-.rəsh\ *n* (1817) : a crowding or flooding in
in·sa·lu·bri·ous \.in-sə-'lü-brē-əs\ *adj* [L *insalubris*, fr. *in-* + *salubris* healthful — more at SAFE] (1615) : not conducive to health : UNWHOLESOME ⟨an ~ climate⟩ — **in·sa·lu·bri·ty** \-brə-tē\ *n*
ins and outs \.in-zən(d)-'aůts\ *n pl* (ca. 1670) **1** : characteristic peculiarities or technicalities **2** : RAMIFICATIONS
in·sane \(.)in-'sān\ *adj* [L *insanus*, fr. *in-* + *sanus* sane] (ca. 1550) **1** : mentally disordered : exhibiting insanity **2** : used by, typical of, or intended for insane persons ⟨an ~ asylum⟩ **3** : ABSURD ⟨an ~ scheme for making money⟩ — **in·sane·ly** *adv* — **in·sane·ness** \-'sān-nəs\ *n*
in·san·i·tary \(.)in-'sa-nə-.ter-ē\ *adj* (1874) : unclean enough to endanger health : CONTAMINATED — **in·san·i·ta·tion** \.in-.sa-nə-'tā-shən\ *n*
in·san·i·ty \in-'sa-nə-tē\ *n, pl* **-ties** (1590) **1 a** : a deranged state of the mind usu. occurring as a specific disorder (as schizophrenia) and usu. excluding such states as mental retardation, psychoneurosis, and various character disorders **b** : a mental disorder **2** : such unsoundness of mind or lack of understanding as prevents one from having the mental capacity required by law to enter into a particular relationship, status, or transaction or as removes one from criminal or civil responsibility **3 a** : extreme folly or unreasonableness **b** : something utterly foolish or unreasonable
in·sa·tia·ble \(.)in-'sā-shə-bəl\ *adj* [ME *insaciable*, fr. MF, fr. L *insatiabilis*, fr. *in-* + *satiare* to satisfy — more at SATIATE] (15c) : incapable of being satisfied : QUENCHLESS ⟨had an ~ desire for wealth⟩ — **in·sa·tia·bil·i·ty** \(.)in-.sā-shə-'bi-lə-tē\ *n* — **in·sa·tia·ble·ness** \(.)in-'sā-shə-bəl-nəs\ *n* — **in·sa·tia·bly** \-blē\ *adv*
in·sa·tiate \(.)in-'sā-sh(ē-)ət\ *adj* (15c) : INSATIABLE — **in·sa·tiate·ly** *adv* — **in·sa·tiate·ness** *n*
in·scribe \in-'skrīb\ *vt* [ME, fr. L *inscribere*, fr. *in-* + *scribere* to write — more at SCRIBE] (15c) **1 a** : to write, engrave, or print as a lasting record **b** : to enter on a list : ENROLL **2 a** : to write, engrave, or print characters upon **b** : to autograph or address (a book) as a gift **3** : to dedicate to someone **4** : to draw within a figure so as to touch in as many places as possible ⟨a regular polygon *inscribed* in a circle⟩ **5** *Brit* : to register the name of the holder of (a security) — **in·scrib·er** *n*
in·scrip·tion \in-'skrip-shən\ *n* [ME *inscripcioun*, fr. L *inscription-, inscriptio*, fr. *inscribere*] (14c) **1 a** : something that is inscribed; *also* : SUPERSCRIPTION **b** : EPIGRAPH **2 c** : the wording on a coin, medal, seal, or currency note **2** : the dedication of a book or work of art **3 a** : the act of inscribing **b** : the entering of a name on or as if on a list : ENROLLMENT **4** *Brit* **a** : the act of inscribing securities **b** *pl* : inscribed securities — **in·scrip·tion·al** \-shnəl, -shə-nᵊl\ *adj*
in·scrip·tive \in-'skrip-tiv\ *adj* (1740) : relating to or constituting an inscription — **in·scrip·tive·ly** *adv*
in·scroll \in-'skrōl\ *vt* (1596) *archaic* : to write on a scroll : RECORD
in·scru·ta·ble \in-'skrü-tə-bəl\ *adj* [ME, fr. LL *inscrutabilis*, fr. L *in-* + *scrutari* to search — more at SCRUTINY] (15c) : not readily investigated, interpreted, or understood : MYSTERIOUS — **in·scru·ta·bil·i·ty** \-.skrü-tə-'bi-lə-tē\ *n* — **in·scru·ta·ble·ness** \-'skrü-tə-bəl-nəs\ *n* — **in·scru·ta·bly** \-blē\ *adv*
in·sculp \in-'skəlp\ *vt* [ME, fr. L *insculpere*, fr. *in-* + *scalpere* to scratch, carve — more at SHELF] (15c) *archaic* : ENGRAVE, SCULPTURE
in·seam \'in-.sēm\ *n* (1886) : the seam on the inside of the leg of a pair of pants; *also* : the length of this seam
in·sect \'in-.sekt\ *n* [L *insectum*, fr. neut. of *insectus*, pp. of *insecare* to cut into, fr. *in-* + *secare* to cut — more at SAW] (1601) **1 a** : any of numerous small invertebrate animals (as spiders or centipedes) that are more or less obviously segmented **b** : any of a class (Insecta) of arthropods (as bugs or bees) with well-defined head, thorax, and abdomen, only three pairs of legs, and typically one or two pairs of wings **2** : a trivial or contemptible person — **insect** *adj*
in·sec·ta·ry \'in-.sek-tə-rē, in-'\ *n, pl* **-ries** (1888) : a place for the keeping or rearing of living insects
in·sec·ti·cid·al \(.)in-.sek-tə-'sī-dᵊl\ *adj* (1857) **1** : destroying or controlling insects **2** : of or relating to an insecticide — **in·sec·ti·cid·al·ly** \-dᵊl-ē\ *adv*
in·sec·ti·cide \in-'sek-tə-.sīd\ *n* [ISV] (1865) : an agent that destroys insects

insect 1b: *1* labial palpus, *2* maxillary palpus, *3* simple eye, *4* antenna, *5* compound eye, *6* prothorax, *7* tympanum, *8* wing, *9* ovipositor, *10* spiracles, *11* abdomen, *12* metathorax, *13* mesothorax

in·sec·tile \(.)in-'sek-tᵊl, -.tīl, -(.)tīl\ *adj* (ca. 1626) : being or suggestive of an insect
in·sec·ti·vore \in-'sek-tə-.vōr, -.vȯr\ *n* [NL *Insectivora*, fr. L *insectum* + *-vorus* -vorous] (1840) **1** : any of an order (Insectivora) of mammals comprising forms (as moles, shrews, and hedgehogs) that are mostly small, insectivorous, and nocturnal **2** : an insectivorous plant or animal
in·sec·tiv·o·rous \.in-.sek-'tiv-rəs, -'ti-və-\ *adj* (1661) : depending on insects as food
in·se·cure \.in-si-'kyůr\ *adj* [ML *insecurus*, fr. L *in-* + *securus* secure] (1649) **1** : not confident or sure : UNCERTAIN ⟨feeling somewhat ~ of his reception⟩ **2** : not adequately guarded or sustained : UNSAFE ⟨an ~ investment⟩ **3** : not firmly fastened or fixed : SHAKY ⟨the hinge is loose and ~⟩ **4 a** : not highly stable or well-adjusted ⟨an ~ marriage⟩ **b** : deficient in assurance : beset by fear and anxiety ⟨always felt ~ in a group of strangers⟩ — **in·se·cure·ly** *adv* — **in·se·cure·ness** *n* — **in·se·cu·ri·ty** \-'kyůr-ə-tē\ *n*
in·sel·berg \'in(t)-səl-.bərg, 'in-zəl-, -.berg\ *n, pl* **-bergs** *also* **-ber·ge** \-.bər-gə, -.ber-\ [G, fr. *Insel* island + *Berg* mountain] (1913) : an isolated mountain
in·sem·i·nate \in-'se-mə-.nāt\ *vt* **-nat·ed; -nat·ing** [L *inseminatus*, pp. of *inseminare*, fr. *in-* + *semin-, semen* seed — more at SEMEN] (ca. 1623) **1** : SOW **2** : to introduce semen into the genital tract of (a female) *syn* see IMPLANT — **in·sem·i·na·tion** \-.se-mə-'nā-shən\ *n*
in·sem·i·na·tor \-'se-mə-.nā-tər\ *n* (1944) : one that inseminates cattle artificially
in·sen·sate \(.)in-'sen-.sāt, -sət\ *adj* [LL *insensatus*, fr. L *in-* + LL *sensatus* having sense, fr. L *sensus* sense] (15c) **1** : lacking sense or understanding; *also* : FOOLISH **2** : lacking animate awareness or sensation **3** : lacking humane feeling : BRUTAL — **in·sen·sate·ly** *adv*
in·sen·si·ble \(.)in-'sen(t)-sə-bəl\ *adj* [ME, fr. MF & L; MF, fr. L *insensibilis*, fr. *in-* + *sensibilis* sensible] (14c) **1** : IMPERCEPTIBLE ⟨dampened by an ~ dew⟩; *broadly* : SLIGHT, GRADUAL ⟨~ motion⟩ **2** : incapable or bereft of feeling or sensation: as **a** : not endowed with life or spirit : INSENTIENT ⟨~ earth⟩ **b** : UNCONSCIOUS ⟨knocked ~ by a sudden blow⟩ **c** : lacking sensory perception or ability to react ⟨~ to pain⟩ **3 a** : lacking emotional response : APATHETIC, INDIFFERENT ⟨~ to fear⟩ **b** : UNAWARE ⟨~ of their danger⟩ **4** *archaic* : STUPID, SENSELESS **5** : not intelligible : MEANINGLESS **6** : lacking delicacy or refinement — **in·sen·si·bil·i·ty** \(.)in-.sen(t)-sə-'bi-lə-tē\ *n* — **in·sen·si·ble·ness** \(.)in-'sen(t)-sə-bəl-nəs\ *n* — **in·sen·si·bly** \(.)in-'sen(t)-sə-blē\ *adv*
in·sen·si·tive \(.)in-'sen(t)-s(ə-)tiv\ *adj* (1834) **1 a** : not responsive or susceptible ⟨~ to the demands of the public⟩ **b** : lacking feeling or tact ⟨so ~ as to laugh at someone in pain⟩ **2** : not physically or chemically sensitive — **in·sen·si·tive·ly** *adv* — **in·sen·si·tive·ness** *n* — **in·sen·si·tiv·i·ty** \(.)in-.sen(t)-sə-'ti-və-tē\ *n*
in·sen·tient \(.)in-'sen(t)-sh(ē-)ənt\ *adj* (1764) : lacking perception, consciousness, or animation — **in·sen·tience** \-sh(ē-)ən(t)s\ *n*
in·sep·a·ra·ble \(.)in-'se-p(ə-)rə-bəl\ *adj* [ME, fr. L *inseparabilis*, fr. *in-* + *separabilis* separable] (14c) : incapable of being separated or disjoined — **in·sep·a·ra·bil·i·ty** \(.)in-.se-p(ə-)rə-'bi-lə-tē\ *n* — **insepa·rable** *n* — **in·sep·a·ra·ble·ness** \(.)in-'se-p(ə-)rə-bəl-nəs\ *n* — **in·sep·a·ra·bly** \-blē\ *adv*
¹in·sert \in-'sərt\ *vb* [L *insertus*, pp. of *inserere*, fr. *in-* + *serere* to join — more at SERIES] *vt* (1529) **1** : to put or thrust in ⟨~ the key in the lock⟩ ⟨~ a spacecraft into orbit⟩ **2** : to put or introduce into the body of something : INTERPOLATE ⟨~ a change in a manuscript⟩ **3** : to set in and make fast; *esp* : to insert by sewing between two cut edges **4** : to place into action (as in a game) ⟨~ a new pitcher⟩ ~ *vi, of a muscle* : to be in attachment to the part to be moved *syn* see INTRODUCE — **in·sert·er** *n*
²in·sert \'in-.sərt\ *n* (ca. 1889) : something that is inserted or is for insertion; *esp* : written or printed material inserted (as between the leaves of a book)
in·ser·tion \in-'sər-shən\ *n* (1539) **1** : something that is inserted: as **a** : the part of a muscle that inserts **b** : the mode or place of attachment of an organ or part **c** : embroidery or needlework inserted as ornament between two pieces of fabric **d** : a section of genetic material that is inserted into an existing gene sequence **2 a** : the act or process of inserting **b** : the mutational process producing a genetic insertion — **in·ser·tion·al** \-shnəl, -shə-nᵊl\ *adj*
in–ser·vice \'in-'sər-vəs\ *adj* (1928) **1** : going on or continuing while one is fully employed ⟨~ teacher education workshops⟩ **2** : of, relating to, or being one that is fully employed ⟨~ police officers⟩
¹in·set \'in-.set\ *n* (1559) **1 a** : a place where something flows in : CHANNEL **b** : a setting or flowing in **2** : something that is inset: as **a** : a small graphic representation (as a map or picture) set within a larger one **b** : a piece of cloth set into a garment (as for decoration) **c** : a part or section of a utensil that fits into an outer part
²in·set \'in-.set, in-'\ *vt* **inset** *or* **in·set·ted; in·set·ting** (1658) **1** : SET IN; *esp* : to insert within something else in such a way as to be visible **2** : to provide with an inset
¹in·shore \'in-.shōr, -'shȯr\ *adj* (1701) **1** : situated, living, or carried on near shore **2** : moving toward shore ⟨an ~ current⟩

²**in·shore** *adv* (1748) : to or toward shore ⟨boats driven ~ by the storm⟩

¹**in·side** \(ˌ)in-ˈsīd, ˈin-ˌ\ *n* (14c)   **1 a** : an interior or internal part or place : the part within   **b** : inward nature, thoughts, or feeling ⟨ : VISCERA, ENTRAILS — usu. used in pl.   **2** : an inner side or surface   **3 a** : a position of power, trust, or familiarity ⟨only someone on the ~ could have told⟩   **b** : confidential information ⟨has the ~ on what happened at the convention⟩   **4** : the area nearest a specified or implied point of reference: as   **a** : the side of home plate nearest the batter   **b** : the middle portion of a playing area   **c** : the area near or underneath the basket in basketball

²**inside** *adv* (15c)   **1** : on the inner side   **2** : in or into the interior   **3** : to or on the inside   **4** : in prison

³**inside** *adj* (1611)   **1** : of, relating to, or being on or near the inside ⟨an ~ pitch⟩   **2 a** : relating or known to a select group ⟨~ information⟩   **b** : BEHIND-THE-SCENES

⁴**inside** *prep* (1791)   **1 a** : in or into or as if in or into the interior of   **b** : on the inner side of   **2** : WITHIN ⟨~ an hour⟩

inside address *n* (ca. 1941) : ADDRESS 5c

inside of *prep* (1839) : INSIDE

inside out *adv* (ca. 1600)   **1** : in such a manner that the inner surface becomes the outer ⟨turned the shirt *inside out*⟩   **2** : to a thorough degree ⟨knows the subject *inside out*⟩   **3** : in or into a state of disarray often involving drastic reorganization ⟨turned the business *inside out*⟩

in·sid·er \(ˌ)in-ˈsī-dər, ˈin-ˌ\ *n* (1848) : a person recognized or accepted as a member of a group, category, or organization: as   **a** : a person who is in a position of power or has access to confidential information   **b** : one (as an officer or director) who is in a position to have special knowledge of the affairs of or to influence the decisions of a company

insider trading *n* (1966) : the illegal use of insider information for profit in financial trading

inside track *n* (1857) : an advantageous competitive position ⟨the owner's son has the *inside track* for the job⟩

in·sid·i·ous \in-ˈsi-dē-əs\ *adj* [L *insidiosus*, fr. *insidiae* ambush, fr. *insidēre* to sit in, sit on, fr. *in-* + *sedēre* to sit — more at SIT] (1545)   **1 a** : awaiting a chance to entrap : TREACHEROUS   **b** : harmful but enticing : SEDUCTIVE ⟨~ drugs⟩   **2 a** : having a gradual and cumulative effect : SUBTLE ⟨the ~ pressures of modern life⟩   **b** *of a disease* : developing so gradually as to be well established before becoming apparent — **in·sid·i·ous·ly** *adv* — **in·sid·i·ous·ness** *n*

in·sight \ˈin-ˌsīt\ *n* (13c)   **1** : the power or act of seeing into a situation : PENETRATION   **2** : the act or result of apprehending the inner nature of things or of seeing intuitively   *syn* see DISCERNMENT

in·sight·ful \ˈin-ˌsīt-fəl, in-ˈ\ *adj* (1907) : exhibiting or characterized by insight — **in·sight·ful·ly** *adv*

in·sig·nia \in-ˈsig-nē-ə\ *or* **in·sig·ne** \-(ˌ)nē\ *n, pl* **-nia** *or* **-ni·as** [L *insignia*, pl. of *insigne* mark, badge, fr. neut. of *insignis* marked, distinguished, fr. *in-* + *signum* mark — more at SIGN] (1648)   **1 a** : a badge of authority or honor   **2** : a distinguishing mark or sign

in·sig·nif·i·cance \ˌin(t)-sig-ˈni-fi-kən(t)s\ *n* (1699) : the quality or state of being insignificant

in·sig·nif·i·can·cy \-kən(t)-sē\ *n, pl* **-cies** (1651)   **1** : INSIGNIFICANCE   **2** : an insignificant thing or person

in·sig·nif·i·cant \-kənt\ *adj* (1651) : not significant: as   **a** : lacking meaning or import : INCONSEQUENTIAL   **b** : not worth considering : UNIMPORTANT   **c** : lacking weight, position, or influence : CONTEMPTIBLE   **d** : small in size, quantity, or number — **in·sig·nif·i·cant·ly** *adv*

in·sin·cere \ˌin-sin-ˈsir, -sən-\ *adj* [L *insincerus*, fr. *in-* + *sincerus* sincere] (1634) : not sincere : HYPOCRITICAL — **in·sin·cere·ly** *adv* — **in·sin·cer·i·ty** \-ˈser-ə-tē *also* -ˈsir-\ *n*

in·sin·u·ate \in-ˈsin-yə-ˌwāt\ *vb* **-at·ed; -at·ing** [L *insinuatus*, pp. of *insinuare*, fr. *in-* + *sinuare* to bend, curve, fr. *sinus* curve] *vt* (1529)   **1 a** : to introduce (as an idea) gradually or in a subtle, indirect, or covert way ⟨~ doubts into a trusting mind⟩   **b** : to impart or communicate with artful or oblique reference   **2** : to introduce (as oneself) by stealthy, smooth, or artful means   ~ *vi*   **1** *archaic* : to enter gently, slowly, or imperceptibly : CREEP   **2** *archaic* : to ingratiate oneself   *syn* see INTRODUCE, SUGGEST — **in·sin·u·a·tive** \-ˌwā-tiv\ *adj* — **in·sin·u·a·tor** \-ˌwā-tər\ *n*

insinuating *adj* (1591)   **1** : winning favor and confidence by imperceptible degrees : INGRATIATING   **2** : tending gradually to cause doubt, distrust, or change of outlook often in a slyly subtle manner ⟨~ remarks⟩ — **in·sin·u·at·ing·ly** *adv*

in·sin·u·a·tion \(ˌ)in-ˌsin-yə-ˈwā-shən\ *n* (1526)   **1** : the act or process of insinuating   **2** : something that is insinuated; *esp* : a sly, subtle, and usu. derogatory utterance

in·sip·id \in-ˈsi-pəd\ *adj* [F & LL; F *insipide*, fr. LL *insipidus*, fr. L *in-* + *sapidus* savory, fr. *sapere* to taste — more at SAGE] (1609)   **1** : lacking taste or savor : TASTELESS   **2** : lacking in qualities that interest, stimulate, or challenge : DULL, FLAT — **in·si·pid·i·ty** \ˌin-sə-ˈpi-də-tē\ *n* — **in·sip·id·ly** \in-ˈsi-pəd-lē\ *adv*
   syn INSIPID, VAPID, FLAT, JEJUNE, BANAL, INANE mean devoid of qualities that make for spirit and character. INSIPID implies a lack of sufficient taste or savor to please or interest ⟨an *insipid* romance with platitudes on every page⟩. VAPID suggests a lack of liveliness, force, or spirit ⟨an exciting story given a *vapid* treatment⟩. FLAT applies to things that have lost their sparkle or zest ⟨although well-regarded in its day, the novel now seems *flat*⟩. JEJUNE suggests a lack of rewarding or satisfying substance ⟨a *jejune* and gassy speech⟩. BANAL stresses the complete absence of freshness, novelty, or immediacy ⟨a *banal* tale of unrequited love⟩. INANE implies a lack of any significant or convincing quality ⟨an *inane* interpretation of the play⟩.

in·sist \in-ˈsist\ *vb* [MF or L; MF *insister*, fr. L *insistere* to stand upon, persist, fr. *in-* + *sistere* to take a stand; akin to L *stare* to stand — more at STAND] *vi* (1586)   **1** : to be emphatic, firm, or resolute about something intended, demanded, or required ⟨they ~ on going⟩   **2** *archaic* : PERSIST   ~ *vt* : to maintain in a persistent or positive manner ⟨~ed that the story was true⟩

in·sis·tence \in-ˈsis-tən(t)s\ *n* (15c)   **1** : the act or an instance of insisting   **2** : the quality or state of being insistent : URGENCY

in·sis·ten·cy \-tən(t)-sē\ *n, pl* **-cies** (1859) : INSISTENCE

in·sis·tent \in-ˈsis-tənt\ *adj* [L *insistent-, insistens*, prp. of *insistere*] (1868)   **1** : disposed to insist : PERSISTENT   **2** : compelling attention ⟨the ~ pounding of the waves⟩ — **in·sis·tent·ly** *adv*

in si·tu \(ˌ)in-ˈsī-(ˌ)tü, -ˈsi-, -(ˌ)tyü *also* -ˈsē-, -(ˌ)chü\ *adv or adj* [L, in position] (1740) : in the natural or original position or place

in·so·bri·e·ty \ˌin-sə-ˈbrī-ə-tē, -sō-\ *n* (ca. 1611) : lack of sobriety or moderation; *esp* : intemperance in drinking

in·so·cia·ble \(ˌ)in-ˈsō-shə-bəl\ *adj* [L *insociabilis*, fr. *in-* + *sociabilis* sociable] (1588) : not sociable — **in·so·cia·bil·i·ty** \-(ˌ)sō-shə-ˈbi-lə-tē\ *n* — **in·so·cia·bly** \-ˈsō-shə-blē\ *adv*

in·so·far \ˌin-sə-ˈfär\ *adv* (1596) : to such extent or degree

insofar as *conj* (15c) : to the extent or degree that

in·so·la·tion \ˌin-(ˌ)sō-ˈlā-shən\ *n* [F or L; F, fr. L *insolation-, insolatio*, fr. *insolare* to expose to the sun, fr. *in-* + *sol* sun — more at SOLAR] (1617)   **1** : exposure to the sun's rays : SUNSTROKE   **3 a** : solar radiation that has been received   **b** : the rate of delivery of direct solar radiation per unit of horizontal surface; *broadly* : that relating to total solar radiation

in·sole \ˈin-ˌsōl\ *n* (ca. 1861)   **1** : an inside sole of a shoe   **2** : a loose thin strip placed inside a shoe for warmth or comfort

in·so·lence \ˈin(t)-s(ə-)lən(t)s\ *n* (14c)   **1** : the quality or state of being insolent   **2** : an instance of insolent conduct or treatment

in·so·lent \-s(ə-)lənt\ *adj* [ME, fr. L *insolent-, insolens* unaccustomed, overbearing, fr. *in-* + *solens*, prp. of *solēre* to be accustomed; perh. akin to L *sodalis* comrade — more at SIB] (14c)   **1** : insultingly contemptuous in speech or conduct : OVERBEARING   **2** : exhibiting boldness or effrontery : IMPUDENT   *syn* see PROUD — **insolent** *n* — **in·so·lent·ly** *adv*

in·sol·u·bi·lize \(ˌ)in-ˈsäl-yə-bə-ˌlīz\ *vt* (1897) : to make insoluble — **in·sol·u·bi·li·za·tion** \-ˌsäl-yə-bə-lə-ˈzā-shən\ *n*

in·sol·u·ble \(ˌ)in-ˈsäl-yə-bəl\ *adj* [ME *insolible*, fr. L *insolubilis*, fr. *in-* + *solvere* to free, dissolve — more at SOLVE] (14c) : not soluble: as   **a** *archaic* : INDISSOLUBLE   **b** : having or admitting of no solution or explanation   **c** : incapable of being dissolved in a liquid; *also* : soluble only with difficulty or to a slight degree — **in·sol·u·bil·i·ty** \-ˌsäl-yə-ˈbi-lə-tē\ *n* — **insoluble** *n* — **in·sol·u·ble·ness** \-ˈsäl-yə-bəl-nəs\ *n* — **in·sol·u·bly** \-blē\ *adv*

in·solv·able \(ˌ)in-ˈsäl-və-bəl, -ˈsòl-\ *adj* (1693) : admitting no solution ⟨an apparently ~ problem⟩ — **in·solv·ably** \-blē\ *adv*

in·sol·vent \(ˌ)in-ˈsäl-vənt, -ˈsòl-\ *adj* (1591)   **1 a** (1) : unable to pay debts as they fall due in the usual course of business   (2) : having liabilities in excess of a reasonable market value of assets held   **b** : insufficient to pay all debts ⟨an ~ estate⟩   **c** : not up to a normal standard or complement : IMPOVERISHED   **2** : relating to or for the relief of insolvents — **in·sol·ven·cy** \-vən(t)-sē\ *n* — **insolvent** *n*

in·som·nia \in-ˈsäm-nē-ə\ *n* [L, fr. *insomnis* sleepless, fr. *in-* + *somnus* sleep — more at SOMNOLENT] (ca. 1623) : prolonged and usu. abnormal inability to obtain adequate sleep — **in·som·ni·ac** \-nē-ˌak\ *adj or n*

in·so·much as \ˌin(t)-sō-ˈməch-\ *conj* (14c) : INASMUCH AS

insomuch that *conj* (14c) : SO 1

in·sou·ci·ance \in-ˈsü-sē-ən(t)s, aⁿ-süs-yäⁿs\ *n* [F, fr. *in-* + *soucier* to trouble, disturb, fr. L *sollicitare* — more at SOLICIT] (1799) : light-hearted unconcern : NONCHALANCE — **in·sou·ci·ant** \in-ˈsü-sē-ənt, aⁿ-süs-yäⁿ\ *adj* — **in·sou·ci·ant·ly** \in-ˈsü-sē-ənt-lē\ *adv*

in·soul *var of* ENSOUL

in·span \in-ˈspan, ˈin-ˌ\ *vb* [Afrik, fr. D *inspannen*] (ca. 1827) *chiefly SoAfr* : YOKE, HARNESS

in·spect \in-ˈspekt\ *vb* [L *inspectus*, pp. of *inspicere*, fr. *in-* + *specere* to look — more at SPY] *vt* (ca. 1623)   **1** : to view closely in critical appraisal : look over   **2** : to examine officially ⟨~s the barracks every Friday⟩   ~ *vi* : to make an inspection   *syn* see SCRUTINIZE — **in·spec·tive** \-ˈspek-tiv\ *adj*

in·spec·tion \in-ˈspek-shən\ *n* (14c)   **1 a** : the act of inspecting   **b** : recognition of a familiar pattern leading to immediate solution of a mathematical problem ⟨solve an equation by ~⟩   **2** : a checking or testing of an individual against established standards

inspection arms *n* [fr. the command *inspection arms!*] (ca. 1884) : a position in the manual of arms in which the rifle is held at port arms with the chamber open for inspection; *also* : a command to assume this position

in·spec·tor \in-ˈspek-tər\ *n* (1602)   **1** : a person employed to inspect something   **2 a** : a police officer who is in charge of usu. several precincts and ranks below a superintendent or deputy superintendent   **b** : a person appointed to oversee a polling place — **in·spec·tor·ship** \-ˌship\ *n*

in·spec·tor·ate \in-ˈspek-t(ə-)rət\ *n* (1762)   **1** : the office, position, work, or district of an inspector   **2** : a body of inspectors

inspector general *n* (1702) : a person who heads an inspectorate or a system of inspection (as of an army)

in·sphere *var of* ENSPHERE

in·spi·ra·tion \ˌin(t)-spə-ˈrā-shən, -(ˌ)spi-\ *n* (14c)   **1 a** : a divine influence or action on a person believed to qualify him or her to receive and communicate sacred revelation   **b** : the action or power of moving the intellect or emotions   **c** : the act of influencing or suggesting opinions   **2** : the act of drawing in; *specif* : the drawing of air into the lungs   **3 a** : the quality or state of being inspired   **b** : something that is inspired ⟨a scheme that was pure ~⟩   **4** : an inspiring agent or influence — **in·spi·ra·tion·al** \-shnəl, -shə-nᵊl\ *adj* — **in·spi·ra·tion·al·ly** *adv*

in·spi·ra·tor \ˈin(t)-spə-ˌrā-tər, -(ˌ)spi-\ *n* (1624) : one that inspires ⟨teachers who are ~s of the young⟩

in·spi·ra·to·ry \in-ˈspī-rə-ˌtōr-ē, ˈin(t)-sp(ə-)rə-, -ˌtòr-\ *adj* (1773) : of, relating to, used for, or associated with inspiration

in·spire \in-ˈspīr\ *vb* **in·spired; in·spir·ing** [ME, fr. MF & L; MF *inspirer*, fr. L *inspirare*, fr. *in-* + *spirare* to breathe] *vt* (14c)   **1 a** : to influence, move, or guide by divine or supernatural inspiration   **b** : to exert an animating, enlivening, or exalting influence on ⟨was particularly *inspired* by the Romanticists⟩   **c** : to spur on : IMPEL, MOTIVATE ⟨threats don't necessarily ~ people to work⟩   **d** : AFFECT ⟨seeing the old room again *inspired* him with nostalgia⟩   **2 a** *archaic* : to breathe

\ə\ abut \ᵊ\ kitten, F table \ər\ further \a\ ash \ā\ ace \ä\ mop, mar \aù\ out \ch\ chin \e\ bet \ē\ easy \g\ go \i\ hit \ī\ ice \j\ job \ŋ\ sing \ō\ go \ò\ law \òi\ boy \th\ thin \t̷h\ the \ü\ loot \ù\ foot \y\ yet \zh\ vision \à, ḵ, ⁿ, œ, œ̄, ᵫ, ᵾ̄, ᶦ\ *see* Guide to Pronunciation or blow into or upon **b** *archaic* : to infuse (as life) by breathing **3 a** : to communicate to an agent supernaturally **b** : to draw forth or bring out ⟨thoughts *inspired* by a visit to the cathedral⟩ **4** : INHALE 1 **5 a** : BRING ABOUT, OCCASION ⟨the book was *inspired* by his travels in the Far East⟩ **b** : INCITE **6** : to spread (rumor) by indirect means or through the agency of another ∼ *vi* : INHALE — **in·spir·er** *n*

inspired *adj* (15c) : outstanding or brilliant in a way or to a degree suggestive of divine inspiration ⟨gave an ∼ performance⟩

inspiring *adj* (1717) : having an animating or exalting effect

in·spir·it \in-'spir-ət\ *vt* (15c) : to fill with spirit **syn** see ENCOURAGE — **in·spir·it·ing·ly** \-ə-tiŋ-lē\ *adv*

in·spis·sate \in-'spi-ˌsāt, 'in(t)-spə-ˌsāt\ *vt* **-sat·ed; -sat·ing** [LL *inspissatus*, pp. of *inspissare*, fr. L *in-* + *spissus* slow, dense; akin to Gk *spidnos* compact, Lith *spisti* to form a swarm] (1626) : to make thick or thicker — **in·spis·sa·tion** \ˌin(t)-spə-'sā-shən, (ˌ)in-ˌspi-'sā-\ *n* — **in·spis·sa·tor** \in-'spi-ˌsā-tər, 'in(t)-spə-ˌsā-\ *n*

in·spis·sat·ed \in-'spi-ˌsā-təd, 'in(t)-spə-ˌsā-\ *adj* (1603) : thickened in consistency; *broadly* : made or having become thick, heavy, or intense

in·sta·bil·i·ty \ˌin(t)-stə-'bi-lə-tē\ *n* (15c) : the quality or state of being unstable; *esp* : lack of emotional or mental stability

in·sta·ble \(ˌ)in-'stā-bəl\ *adj* [MF or L; MF, fr. L *instabilis*, fr. *in-* + *stabilis* stable] (15c) : UNSTABLE

in·stall *also* **in·stal** \in-'stól\ *vt* **in·stalled; in·stall·ing** [ME, fr. MF *installer*, fr. ML *installare*, fr. L *in-* + ML *stallum* stall, fr. OHG *stal*] (15c) **1 a** : to place in an office or dignity by seating in a stall or official seat **b** : to induct into an office, rank, or order ⟨∼ed the new president⟩ **2** : to establish in an indicated place, condition, or status ⟨∼ing herself in front of the fireplace⟩ **3** : to set up for use or service ⟨had an exhaust fan ∼ed in the kitchen⟩ — **in·stall·er** *n*

in·stal·la·tion \ˌin(t)-stə-'lā-shən\ *n* (15c) **1** : the act of installing : the state of being installed **2** : something that is installed for use **3** : a military camp, fort, or base

¹in·stall·ment *also* **in·stal·ment** \in-'stól-mənt\ *n* (1589) : INSTALLATION 1

²installment *also* **instalment** *n* [alter. of earlier *estallment* payment by installment, deriv. of OF *estaler* to place, fix, fr. *estal* place, of Gmc origin; akin to OHG *stal* place, stall] (1776) **1** : one of the parts into which a debt is divided when payment is made at intervals **2 a** : one of several parts (as of a publication) presented at intervals **b** : one part of a serial story — **installment** *adj*

installment plan *n* (1876) : a system of paying for goods by installments

¹in·stance \'in(t)-stən(t)s\ *n* (14c) **1 a** *archaic* : urgent or earnest solicitation **b** : INSTIGATION, REQUEST ⟨am writing to you at the ∼ of my client⟩ **c** *obs* : an impelling cause or motive **2 a** *archaic* : EXCEPTION **b** : an individual illustrative of a category or brought forward in support or disproof of a generalization **c** *obs* : TOKEN, SIGN **3** : the institution and prosecution of a lawsuit : SUIT **4** : a step, stage, or situation viewed as part of a process or series of events ⟨prefers, in this ∼, to remain anonymous —*Times Lit. Supp.*⟩ — **for in·stance** \fə-'rin(t)-stən(t)s, 'frin(t)-\ : as an instance or example ⟨older people like my grandmother, *for instance*⟩

syn INSTANCE, CASE, ILLUSTRATION, EXAMPLE, SAMPLE, SPECIMEN mean something that exhibits distinguishing characteristics in its category. INSTANCE applies to any individual person, act, or thing that may be offered to illustrate or explain ⟨an *instance* of history repeating itself⟩. CASE is used to direct attention to a real or assumed occurrence or situation that is to be considered, studied, or dealt with ⟨a *case* of mistaken identity⟩. ILLUSTRATION applies to an instance offered as a means of clarifying or illuminating a general statement ⟨a telling *illustration* of Murphy's Law⟩. EXAMPLE applies to a typical, representative, or illustrative instance or case ⟨a typical *example* of bureaucratic waste⟩. SAMPLE implies a part or unit taken at random from a larger whole and so presumed to be typical of its qualities ⟨show us a *sample* of your work⟩. SPECIMEN applies to any example or sample whether representative or merely existent and available ⟨one of the finest *specimens* of the jeweler's art⟩.

²instance *vt* **in·stanced; in·stanc·ing** (1601) **1** : to illustrate or demonstrate by an instance **2** : to mention as a case or example : CITE

in·stan·cy \'in(t)-stən(t)-sē\ *n, pl* **-cies** (1515) **1** : URGENCY, INSISTENCE **2** : nearness of approach : IMMINENCE **3** : immediacy of occurrence or action : INSTANTANEOUSNESS

¹in·stant \'in(t)-stənt\ *n* [ME, fr. ML *instant-, instans*, fr. *instant-, instans*, adj., instant, fr. L] (14c) **1** : an infinitesimal space of time; *esp* : a point in time separating two states ⟨at the ∼ of death⟩ **2** : the present or current month

²instant *adj* [ME, fr. MF or L; MF, fr. L *instant-, instans*, fr. prp. of *instare* to stand upon, urge, fr. *in-* + *stare* to stand — more at STAND] (15c) **1** : IMPORTUNATE, URGENT **2 a** : PRESENT, CURRENT ⟨previous felonies not related to the ∼ crime⟩ **b** : of or occurring in the present month **3** : IMMEDIATE, DIRECT ⟨the play was an ∼ success⟩ **4 a** (1) : premixed or precooked for easy final preparation ⟨∼ pudding⟩ (2) : appearing in or as if in ready-to-use form ⟨∼ culture⟩ **b** : immediately soluble in water ⟨∼ coffee⟩ **5** : produced or occurring with or as if with extreme rapidity and ease — **in·stant·ness** *n*

in·stan·ta·neous \ˌin(t)-stən-'tā-nē-əs, -nyəs\ *adj* [ML *instantaneus*, fr. *instant-, instans*, n.] (1651) **1** : done, occurring, or acting without any perceptible duration of time ⟨death was ∼⟩ **2** : done without any delay being purposely introduced ⟨took ∼ action to correct the abuse⟩ **3** : occurring or present at a particular instant ⟨∼ velocity⟩ — **in·stan·ta·ne·ity** \ˌin-ˌstan-tⁿ-'ē-ə-tē, ˌin(t)-stən-tə-'nē-\ *n* — **in·stan·ta·neous·ly** \ˌin(t)-stən-'tā-nē-əs-lē, -nyəs-lē\ *adv* — **in·stan·ta·neous·ness** *n*

in·stan·ter \in-'stan-tər\ *adv* [ML, fr. *instant-, instans*] (1688) : at once

in·stan·ti·ate \in-'stan(t)-shē-ˌāt\ *vt* **-at·ed; -at·ing** (1949) : to represent (an abstraction) by a concrete instance ⟨heroes ∼ ideals —W. J. Bennett⟩ — **in·stan·ti·a·tion** \-ˌstan(t)-shē-'ā-shən\ *n*

¹in·stant·ly \'in(t)-stənt-lē\ *adv* (15c) **1** : with importunity : URGENTLY **2** : without the least delay : IMMEDIATELY

²instantly *conj* (1793) : as soon as ⟨he ran across the grass ∼ he perceived his mother —W. M. Thackeray⟩

instant replay *n* (1966) : a videotape recording of an action (as a play in football) that can be played back (as in slow motion) immediately

after the action has been completed; *also* : the playing of such a recording

in·star \'in-ˌstär\ *n* [NL, fr. L, equivalent] (1895) : a stage in the life of an arthropod (as an insect) between two successive molts; *also* : an individual in a specified instar

in·state \in-'stāt\ *vt* (1603) **1** *obs* **a** : INVEST, ENDOW **b** : BESTOW, CONFER **2** : to set or establish in a rank or office : INSTALL

in sta·tu quo \in-ˌstā-(ˌ)tü-'kwō, -ˌsta-; -ˌsta-(ˌ)chü-\ *adv* [NL, lit., in the state in which] (1602) : in the former or same state

in·stau·ra·tion \ˌin-ˌstó-'rā-shən, ˌin(t)-stə-\ *n* [L *instauration-, instauratio*, fr. *instaurare* to renew, restore — more at STORE] (ca. 1603) **1** : restoration after decay, lapse, or dilapidation **2** : an act of instituting or establishing something

in·stead \in-'sted\ *adv* (1667) **1** : as a substitute or equivalent ⟨was going to write but called ∼⟩ **2** : as an alternative to something expressed or implied : RATHER ⟨longed ∼ for a quiet country life⟩

instead of \in-'ste-də(v), -'sti-\ *prep* [ME *in sted of*] (13c) : in place of : as a substitute for or alternative to

in·step \'in-ˌstep\ *n* (15c) **1** : the arched middle portion of the human foot in front of the ankle joint; *esp* : its upper surface **2** : the part of a shoe or stocking that fits over the instep

in·sti·gate \'in(t)-stə-ˌgāt\ *vt* **-gat·ed; -gat·ing** [L *instigatus*, pp. of *instigare* — more at STICK] (1542) : to goad or urge forward : PROVOKE **syn** see INCITE — **in·sti·ga·tion** \ˌin(t)-stə-'gā-shən\ *n* — **in·sti·ga·tive** \'in(t)-stə-ˌgā-tiv\ *adj* — **in·sti·ga·tor** \-ˌgā-tər\ *n*

in·still *also* **in·stil** \in-'stil\ *vt* **in·stilled; in·still·ing** [ME, fr. MF & L; MF *instiller*, fr. L *instillare*, fr. *in-* + *stillare* to drip, fr. *stilla* drop] (15c) **1** : to cause to enter drop by drop ⟨∼ medication into the infected eye⟩ **2** : to impart gradually ⟨∼ing a love of learning in children⟩ **syn** see IMPLANT — **in·stil·la·tion** \ˌin(t)-stə-'lā-shən, -ˌ(ˌ)sti-\ *n* — **in·still·er** \in-'sti-lər\ *n* — **in·still·ment** \-mənt\ *n*

¹in·stinct \'in-ˌstiŋ(k)t\ *n* [ME, fr. L *instinctus* impulse, fr. *instinguere* to incite; akin to L *instigare* to instigate] (15c) **1** : a natural or inherent aptitude, impulse, or capacity ⟨had an ∼ for the right word⟩ **2 a** : a largely inheritable and unalterable tendency of an organism to make a complex and specific response to environmental stimuli without involving reason **b** : behavior that is mediated by reactions below the conscious level — **in·stinc·tu·al** \in-'stiŋ(k)-chə-wəl, -chəl, -shwəl\ *adj* — **in·stinc·tu·al·ly** *adv*

²in·stinct \in-'stiŋ(k)t, 'in-ˌ\ *adj* (1667) **1** *obs* : impelled by an inner or animating or exciting agency **2** : profoundly imbued : INFUSED ⟨my mood, ∼ with romance —S. J. Perelman⟩

in·stinc·tive \in-'stiŋ(k)-tiv\ *adj* (15c) **1** : of, relating to, or being instinct **2** : prompted by natural instinct or propensity : arising spontaneously ⟨an ∼ fear of innovation —V. L. Parrington⟩ **syn** see SPONTANEOUS — **in·stinc·tive·ly** *adv*

¹in·sti·tute \'in(t)-stə-ˌtüt, -ˌtyüt\ *vt* **-tut·ed; -tut·ing** [ME, fr. L *institutus*, pp. of *instituere*, fr. *in-* + *statuere* to set up — more at STATUTE] (14c) **1** : to establish in a position or office **2 a** : to originate and get established : ORGANIZE ⟨instituted reading clinics⟩ **b** : to set going : INAUGURATE ⟨instituting an investigation of the charges⟩ — **in·sti·tut·er** *or* **in·sti·tu·tor** \-ˌtü-tər, -ˌtyü-\ *n*

²institute *n* (1546) : something that is instituted: as **a** (1) : an elementary principle recognized as authoritative (2) *pl* : a collection of such principles and precepts; *esp* : a legal compendium **b** : an organization for the promotion of a cause : ASSOCIATION ⟨a research ∼⟩ ⟨an ∼ for the blind⟩ **c** : an educational institution and esp. one devoted to technical fields **d** : a usu. brief intensive course of instruction on selected topics relating to a particular field ⟨an urban studies ∼⟩

in·sti·tu·tion \ˌin(t)-stə-'tü-shən, -'tyü-\ *n* (14c) **1** : an act of instituting : ESTABLISHMENT **2 a** : a significant practice, relationship, or organization in a society or culture ⟨the ∼ of marriage⟩; *also* : something or someone firmly associated with a place or thing ⟨she has become an ∼ in the theater⟩ **b** : an established organization or corporation (as a college or university) esp. of a public character; *also* : ASYLUM 4 — **in·sti·tu·tion·al** \-shnəl, -shə-nⁿl\ *adj* — **in·sti·tu·tion·al·ly** *adv*

in·sti·tu·tion·al·ise *Brit var of* INSTITUTIONALIZE

in·sti·tu·tion·al·ism \-shnə-ˌli-zəm, -shə-nⁿl-ˌi-zəm\ *n* (1862) **1** : emphasis on organization (as in religion) at the expense of other factors **2** : public institutional care of handicapped, delinquent, or dependent persons **3** : an economic school of thought that emphasizes the role of social institutions in influencing economic behavior — **in·sti·tu·tion·al·ist** \-shnə-list, -shə-nⁿl-ist\ *n*

in·sti·tu·tion·al·ize \-shnə-ˌliz, -shə-nⁿl-ˌiz\ *vt* **-ized; -iz·ing** (1865) **1** : to make into an institution : give character of an institution to ⟨institutionalized housing⟩; *esp* : to incorporate into a structured and often highly formalized system ⟨institutionalized values⟩ **2** : to put in the care of an institution ⟨∼ alcoholics⟩ — **in·sti·tu·tion·al·i·za·tion** \-ˌtü-shnə-lə-'zā-shən, -shə-nⁿl-ə-'zā-\ *n*

in-store \'in-ˌstór, -ˌstòr\ *adj* (1961) : relating to or being an operation or activity located or taking place inside a store ⟨∼ consumer survey⟩

in·struct \in-'strəkt\ *vt* [ME, fr. L *instructus*, pp. of *instruere*, fr. *in-* + *struere* to build — more at STRUCTURE] (15c) **1** : to give knowledge to : TEACH, TRAIN **2** : to provide with authoritative information or advice ⟨the judge ∼ed the jury⟩ **3** : to give an order or command to : DIRECT **syn** see TEACH, COMMAND

in·struc·tion \in-'strək-shən\ *n* (15c) **1 a** : PRECEPT ⟨prevailing cultural ∼s⟩ **b** : a direction calling for compliance : ORDER — usu. used in pl. ⟨had ∼s not to admit strangers⟩ **c** *pl* : an outline or manual of technical procedure : DIRECTIONS **d** : a code that tells a computer to perform a particular operation **2** : the action, practice, or profession of teaching — **in·struc·tion·al** \-shnəl, -shə-nⁿl\ *adj*

in·struc·tive \in-'strək-tiv\ *adj* (1611) : carrying a lesson : ENLIGHTENING — **in·struc·tive·ly** *adv* — **in·struc·tive·ness** *n*

in·struc·tor \in-'strək-tər\ *n* (15c) : one that instructs : TEACHER; *esp* : a college teacher below professorial rank — **in·struc·tor·ship** \-ˌship\ *n*

in·struc·tress \-'strək-trəs\ *n* (1630) : a woman who is an instructor

¹in·stru·ment \'in(t)-strə-mənt\ *n* [ME, fr. L *instrumentum*, fr. *instruere* to arrange, instruct] (14c) **1** : a device used to produce music **2 a** : a means whereby something is achieved, performed, or furthered **b** : one used by another as a means or aid : DUPE, TOOL **3** : IMPLEMENT; *esp* : one designed for precision work **4** : a formal legal document (as a deed, bond, or agreement) **5 a** : a measuring device for determining the present value of a quantity under observation **b** : an electrical or mechanical device used in navigating an airplane; *esp* : such a device used as the sole means of navigating *syn* see IMPLEMENT

²**in·stru·ment** \-,ment\ *vt* (1752) **1** : to address a legal instrument to **2** : to score for musical performance : ORCHESTRATE **3** : to equip with instruments esp. for measuring and recording data ⟨an *instrumented* spacecraft⟩

in·stru·men·tal \,in(t)-strə-'men-t³l\ *adj* (14c) **1 a** : serving as a means, agent, or tool ⟨was ~ in organizing the strike⟩ **b** : of, relating to, or done with an instrument or tool **2** : relating to, composed for, or performed on a musical instrument **3** : of, relating to, or being a grammatical case or form expressing means or agency **4** : of or relating to instrumentalism **5** : OPERANT 3 ⟨~ learning⟩ ⟨~ conditioning⟩ — **instrumental** *n* — **in·stru·men·tal·ly** \-t³l-ē\ *adv*

in·stru·men·tal·ism \-,i-zəm\ *n* (1909) : a doctrine that ideas are instruments of action and that their usefulness determines their truth

in·stru·men·tal·ist \-ist\ *n* (1823) **1** : a player on a musical instrument **2** : an exponent of instrumentalism — **instrumentalist** *adj*

in·stru·men·tal·i·ty \,in(t)-strə-mən-'ta-lə-tē, -,men-\ *n, pl* **-ties** (1651) **1** : the quality or state of being instrumental **2** : MEANS, AGENCY

in·stru·men·ta·tion \,in(t)-strə-mən-'tā-shən, -,men-\ *n* (1845) **1** : the arrangement or composition of music for instruments esp. for a band or orchestra **2** : the use or application of instruments (as for observation, measurement, or control) **3** : instruments for a particular purpose; *also* : a selection or arrangement of instruments

instrument flying *n* (1928) : navigation of an airplane by instruments only

instrument landing *n* (1938) : a landing made with limited visibility by means of instruments and by ground radio direction

instrument panel *n* (1922) : a panel on which instruments are mounted; *esp* : DASHBOARD 2

in·sub·or·di·nate \,in(t)-sə-'bȯr-d³n-ət, -'bȯrd-nət\ *adj* (ca. 1828) : disobedient to authority — **insubordinate** *n* — **in·sub·or·di·nate·ly** *adv* — **in·sub·or·di·na·tion** \-,bȯr-d³n-'ā-shən\ *n*

in·sub·stan·tial \,in(t)-səb-'stan(t)-shəl\ *adj* [prob. fr. F *insubstantiel*, fr. LL *insubstantialis*, fr. L *in-* + LL *substantialis* substantial] (1607) : not substantial: as **a** : lacking substance or material nature **b** : lacking firmness or solidity : FLIMSY — **in·sub·stan·ti·al·i·ty** \-,stan(t)-shē-'a-lə-tē\ *n*

in·suf·fer·able \(,)in-'sə-f(ə-)rə-bəl\ *adj* (15c) : not to be endured : IN-TOLERABLE ⟨an ~ bore⟩ — **in·suf·fer·able·ness** *n* — **in·suf·fer·ably** \-blē\ *adv*

in·suf·fi·cien·cy \,in(t)-sə-'fi-shən(t)-sē\ *n, pl* **-cies** (1526) **1** : the quality or state of being insufficient: as **a** : lack of mental or moral fitness : INCOMPETENCE ⟨the ~ of this person for public office⟩ **b** : lack of adequate supply ⟨~ of provisions⟩ **c** : lack of physical power or capacity; *specif* : inability of an organ or body part to function normally **2** : something that is insufficient or falls short of expectations

in·suf·fi·cient \,in(t)-sə-'fi-shənt\ *adj* [ME, fr. MF, fr. LL *insufficient-*, *insufficiens*, fr. L *in-* + *sufficient-*, *sufficiens* sufficient] (14c) : not sufficient : INADEQUATE; *esp* : lacking adequate power, capacity, or competence — **in·suf·fi·cient·ly** *adv*

in·suf·fla·tion \,in(t)-sə-'flā-shən, in,sə-'flā-\ *n* [ME *insufflacion*, fr. MF *insufflation*, fr. LL *insufflation-*, *insufflatio*, fr. *insufflare* to blow upon, fr. L *in-* + *sufflare* to inflate, fr. *sub-* + *flare* to blow — more at BLOW] (15c) : an act or the action of blowing on, into, or in: as **a** : a Christian ceremonial rite of exorcism performed by breathing on a person **b** : the act of blowing something (as a gas, powder, or vapor) into a body cavity — **in·suf·flate** \'in(t)-sə-,flāt, in-'sə-,flāt\ *vt* — **in·suf·fla·tor** \-,flā-tər\ *n*

in·su·lant \'in(t)-sə-lənt\ *n* (ca. 1929) *chiefly Brit* : INSULATION 2

in·su·lar \'in(t)-sə-lər, -syù-, 'in-shə-lər\ *adj* [LL *insularis*, fr. L *insula* island] (1611) **1 a** : of, relating to, or constituting an island **b** : dwelling or situated on an island ⟨~ residents⟩ **2** : characteristic of an isolated people; *esp* : being, having, or reflecting a narrow provincial viewpoint **3** : of or relating to an island of cells or tissue — **in·su·lar·ism** \-lə,ri-zəm\ *n* — **in·su·lar·i·ty** \,in(t)-sù-'lar-ə-tē, -syù-, ,in-shə-'lar-\ *n* — **in·su·lar·ly** \'in(t)-sù-lər-lē, -syù-, 'in-shə-\ *adv*

in·su·late \'in(t)-sə-,lāt\ *vt* **-lat·ed; -lat·ing** [L *insula*] (ca. 1741) : to place in a detached situation : ISOLATE; *esp* : to separate from conducting bodies by means of nonconductors so as to prevent transfer of electricity, heat, or sound

in·su·la·tion \,in(t)-sə-'lā-shən\ *n* (1798) **1 a** : the action of insulating **b** : the state of being insulated **2** : material used in insulating

in·su·la·tor \'in(t)-sə-,lā-tər\ *n* (1801) : one that insulates: as **a** : a material that is a poor conductor (as of electricity or heat) — compare SEMICONDUCTOR **b** : a device made of an electrical insulating material and used for separating or supporting conductors

in·su·lin \'in(t)-s(ə-)lən\ *n* [NL *insula* islet (of Langerhans), fr. L, island] (1914) : a protein pancreatic hormone secreted by the islets of Langerhans that is essential esp. for the metabolism of carbohydrates and is used in the treatment and control of diabetes mellitus

insulin shock *n* (1925) : hypoglycemia associated with the presence of excessive insulin in the system and characterized by progressive development of coma

¹**in·sult** \in-'səlt\ *vb* [MF or L; MF *insulter*, fr. L *insultare*, lit., to spring upon, fr. *in-* + *saltare* to leap — more at SALTATION] *vi* (1540) *archaic* : to behave with pride or arrogance : VAUNT ~ *vt* : to treat with insolence, indignity, or contempt : AFFRONT; *also* : to affect offensively or damagingly ⟨doggerel that ~s the reader's intelligence⟩ *syn* see OF-FEND — **in·sult·er** *n* — **in·sult·ing·ly** \in-'səl-tiŋ-lē\ *adv*

²**in·sult** \'in-,səlt\ *n* (1671) **1** : a gross indignity **2** : injury to the body or one of its parts; *also* : something that causes or has a potential for causing such insult ⟨pollution and other environmental ~s⟩

in·su·per·a·ble \(,)in-'sü-p(ə-)rə-bəl\ *adj* [ME, fr. MF & L; MF, fr. L *insuperabilis*, fr. *in-* + *superare* to surmount, fr. *super* over — more at OVER] (14c) : incapable of being surmounted, overcome, passed over, or solved ⟨~ difficulties⟩ — **in·su·per·a·bly** \-blē\ *adv*

in·sup·port·a·ble \,in(t)-sə-'pōr-tə-bəl, -'pȯr-\ *adj* [MF or LL; MF, fr. LL *insupportabilis*, fr. L *in-* + *supportare* to support] (ca. 1530) : not supportable: as **a** : more than can be endured ⟨~ pain⟩ **b** : impossible to justify ⟨~ charges⟩ — **in·sup·port·a·bly** \-blē\ *adv*

in·sup·press·ible \,in(t)-sə-'pre-sə-bəl\ *adj* (1610) : IRREPRESSIBLE

in·sur·able \in-'shùr-ə-bəl\ *adj* (1810) : that may be insured — **in·sur·abil·i·ty** \-,shùr-ə-'bi-lə-tē\ *n*

¹**in·sur·ance** \in-'shùr-ən(t)s *also* 'in-,\ *n* (1651) **1 a** : the business of insuring persons or property **b** : coverage by contract whereby one party undertakes to indemnify or guarantee another against loss by a specified contingency or peril **c** : the sum for which something is insured **2** : a means of guaranteeing protection or safety ⟨the contract is your ~ against price changes⟩

²**insurance** *adj* (1954) : being a score that adds to a team's lead and makes it impossible for the opposing team to tie the game with its next score ⟨~ run⟩

in·sure \in-'shùr\ *vb* **in·sured; in·sur·ing** [ME, to assure, prob. alter. of *assuren*] *vt* (1635) **1** : to provide or obtain insurance on or for **2** : to make certain esp. by taking necessary measures and precautions ~ *vi* : to contract to give or take insurance *syn* see ENSURE

insured *n* (1681) : a person whose life or property is insured

in·sur·er \in-'shùr-ər\ *n* (1654) : one that insures; *specif* : an insurance underwriter

in·sur·gence \in-'sər-jən(t)s\ *n* (1847) : an act or the action of being insurgent : INSURRECTION

in·sur·gen·cy \-jən(t)-sē\ *n, pl* **-cies** (1803) **1** : the quality or state of being insurgent; *specif* : a condition of revolt against a government that is less than an organized revolution and that is not recognized as belligerency **2** : INSURGENCE

¹**in·sur·gent** \-jənt\ *n* [L *insurgent-*, *insurgens*, prp. of *insurgere* to rise up, fr. *in-* + *surgere* to rise — more at SURGE] (1765) **1** : a person who revolts against civil authority or an established government; *esp* : a rebel not recognized as a belligerent **2** : one who acts contrary to the policies and decisions of one's own political party

²**insurgent** *adj* (1814) : rising in opposition to civil authority or established leadership : REBELLIOUS — **in·sur·gent·ly** *adv*

in·sur·mount·able \,in(t)-sər-'maùn-tə-bəl\ *adj* (1690) : incapable of being surmounted : INSUPERABLE ⟨~ problems⟩ — **in·sur·mount·ably** \-blē\ *adv*

in·sur·rec·tion \,in(t)-sə-'rek-shən\ *n* [ME, fr. MF, fr. LL *insurrection-*, *insurrectio*, fr. *insurgere* to rise up] (15c) : an act or instance of revolting against civil authority or an established government *syn* see REBELLION — **in·sur·rec·tion·al** \-shnəl, -shə-n³l\ *adj* — **in·sur·rec·tion·ary** \-shə-,ner-ē\ *adj or n* — **in·sur·rec·tion·ist** \-sh(ə-)nist\ *n*

in·sus·cep·ti·ble \,in(t)-sə-'sep-tə-bəl\ *adj* (1603) : not susceptible ⟨~ to flattery⟩ — **in·sus·cep·ti·bil·i·ty** \-,sep-tə-'bi-lə-tē\ *n* — **in·sus·cep·ti·bly** \,in(t)-'sep-tə-blē\ *adv*

in·tact \in-'takt\ *adj* [ME *intacte*, fr. L *intactus*, fr. *in-* + *tactus*, pp. of *tangere* to touch — more at TANGENT] (15c) **1** : untouched esp. by anything that harms or diminishes : ENTIRE, UNINJURED **2** *of a living body or its parts* : having no relevant component removed or destroyed: **a** : physically virginal **b** : not castrated *syn* see PERFECT — **in·tact·ness** \-'tak(t)-nəs\ *n*

in·ta·glio \in-'tal-(,)yō, -'täl-; -'ta-glē-,ō, -'tä-\ *n, pl* **-glios** [It, fr. *intagliare* to engrave, cut, fr. ML *intaliare*, fr. L *in-* + LL *taliare* to cut — more at TAILOR] (1644) **1 a** : an engraving or incised figure in stone or other hard material depressed below the surface so that an impression from the design yields an image in relief **b** : the art or process of executing intaglios **c** : printing (as in die stamping and gravure) done from a plate in which the image is sunk below the surface **2** : something (as a gem) carved in intaglio

intaglio 1a

in·take \'in-,tāk\ *n* (15c) **1** : an opening through which fluid enters an enclosure **2 a** : a taking in **b** (1) : the amount taken in (2) : something (as energy) taken in : INPUT

¹**in·tan·gi·ble** \(,)in-'tan-jə-bəl\ *adj* [F or ML; F, fr. ML *intangibilis*, fr. L *in-* + LL *tangibilis* tangible] (1640) : not tangible : IMPALPABLE — **in·tan·gi·bil·i·ty** \-,tan-jə-'bi-lə-tē\ *n* — **in·tan·gi·ble·ness** \-'tan-jə-bəl-nəs\ *n* — **in·tan·gi·bly** \-blē\ *adv*

²**intangible** *n* (1914) : something intangible; *specif* : an asset (as goodwill) that is not corporeal

in·tar·sia \in-'tär-sē-ə\ *n* [G, modif. of It *intarsio*] (1867) **1** : a mosaic usu. of wood fitted into a support; *also* : the art or process of making such a mosaic **2** : a colored design knitted on both sides of a fabric (as in a sweater)

in·te·ger \'in-ti-jər\ *n* [L, adj., whole, entire — more at ENTIRE] (1571) **1** : any of the natural numbers, the negatives of these numbers, or zero **2** : a complete entity

in·te·gra·ble \'in-ti-grə-bəl\ *adj* (ca. 1741) : capable of being integrated ⟨~ functions⟩ — **in·te·gra·bil·i·ty** \,in-ti-grə-'bi-lə-tē\ *n*

¹**in·te·gral** \'in-ti-grəl *(usu so in mathematics)*; in-'te-grəl *also* -'tē- *also* ÷'in-trə-gəl\ *adj* (1551) **1** : essential to completeness : CONSTITU-ENT ⟨an ~ part of the curriculum⟩ **b** (1) : being, containing, or relating to one or more mathematical integers (2) : relating to or concerned with mathematical integrals or integration **c** : formed as a unit with another part ⟨a seat with ~ headrest⟩ **2** : composed of integral parts **3** : lacking nothing essential : ENTIRE — **in·te·gral·i·ty** \,in-tə-'gra-lə-tē\ *n* — **in·te·gral·ly** \'in-ti-grə-lē; in-'te-grə- *also* -'tē-\ *adv*

²**integral** *n* (ca. 1741) : the result of a mathematical integration — compare DEFINITE INTEGRAL, INDEFINITE INTEGRAL

integral calculus *n* (ca. 1741) : a branch of mathematics concerned with the theory and applications (as in the determination of lengths, areas, and volumes and in the solution of differential equations) of integrals and integration

integral domain *n* (1937) : a mathematical ring in which multiplication is commutative, which has a multiplicative identity element, and which contains no pair of nonzero elements whose product is zero ⟨the

\ə\ abut \³\ kitten, F table \ər\ further \a\ ash \ā\ ace \ä\ mop, mar \aù\ out \ch\ chin \e\ bet \ē\ easy \g\ go \i\ hit \ī\ ice \j\ job \ŋ\ sing \ō\ go \ò\ law \òi\ boy \th\ thin \th\ the \ü\ loot \ù\ foot \y\ yet \zh\ vision \ä, k̲, ⁿ, œ, œ̄, ue, ūe, ᵞ\ see Guide to Pronunciation integers under the operations of addition and multiplication form an *integral domain*⟩

in·te·grand \'in-tə-ˌgrand\ n [L *integrandus*, gerundive of *integrare*] (1897) : a mathematical expression to be integrated

in·te·grate \'in-tə-ˌgrāt\ vb **-grat·ed; -grat·ing** [L *integratus*, pp. of *integrare*, fr. *integr-*, *integer*] vt (1638) **1** : to form, coordinate, or blend into a functioning or unified whole : UNITE **2** : to find the integral of (as a function or equation) **3 a** : to unite with something else **b** : to incorporate into a larger unit **4 a** : to end the segregation of and bring into equal membership in society or an organization **b** : DESEGREGATE ⟨∼ school districts⟩ ∼ vi : to become integrated

integrated adj (1922) **1** : marked by the unified control of all aspects of industrial production from raw materials through distribution of finished products ⟨∼ companies⟩ ⟨∼ production⟩ **2** : characterized by integration and esp. racial integration ⟨an ∼ society⟩ ⟨∼ schools⟩

integrated circuit n (1962) : a tiny complex of electronic components and their connections that is produced in or on a small slice of material (as silicon) — **integrated circuitry** n

in·te·gra·tion \ˌin-tə-'grā-shən\ n (1620) **1** : the act or process or an instance of integrating: as **a** : incorporation as equals into society or an organization of individuals of different groups (as races) **b** : coordination of mental processes into a normal effective personality or with the individual's environment **2 a** : the operation of finding a function whose differential is known. **b** : the operation of solving a differential equation

in·te·gra·tion·ist \-sh(ə-)nist\ n (1951) : a person who believes in, advocates, or practices social integration — **integrationist** adj

in·te·gra·tive \'in-tə-ˌgrā-tiv\ adj (1862) : serving to integrate or favoring integration : directed toward integration

in·te·gra·tor \-ˌgrā-tər\ n (1876) : one that integrates; esp : a device or computer unit that totalizes variable quantities in a manner comparable to mathematical integration

in·teg·ri·ty \in-'te-grə-tē\ n [ME *integrite*, fr. MF & L; MF *integrité*, fr. L *integritat-*, *integritas*, fr. *integr-*, *integer* entire] (14c) **1** : firm adherence to a code of esp. moral or artistic values : INCORRUPTIBILITY **2** : an unimpaired condition : SOUNDNESS **3** : the quality or state of being complete or undivided : COMPLETENESS *syn* see HONESTY

in·teg·u·ment \in-'te-gyə-mənt\ n [L *integumentum*, fr. *integere* to cover, fr. *in-* + *tegere* to cover — more at THATCH] (ca. 1611) : something that covers or encloses; esp : an enveloping layer (as a skin, membrane, or husk) of an organism or one of its parts — **in·teg·u·men·ta·ry** \-ˌment-(ə-)rē\ adj

in·tel·lect \'in-tᵊl-ˌekt\ n [ME, fr. MF or L; MF, fr. L *intellectus*, fr. *intellegere* to understand — more at INTELLIGENT] (14c) **1 a** : the power of knowing as distinguished from the power to feel and to will : the capacity for knowledge **b** : the capacity for rational or intelligent thought esp. when highly developed **2** : a person with great intellectual powers

in·tel·lec·tion \ˌin-tᵊl-'ek-shən\ n (1579) **1** : an act of the intellect : THOUGHT **2** : exercise of the intellect : REASONING

in·tel·lec·tive \-'ek-tiv\ adj (15c) : having, relating to, or belonging to the intellect : RATIONAL — **in·tel·lec·tive·ly** adv

¹in·tel·lec·tu·al \ˌin-tᵊl-'ek-chə-wəl, -chəl, -shwəl\ adj (14c) **1 a** : of or relating to the intellect or its use **b** : developed or chiefly guided by the intellect rather than by emotion or experience : RATIONAL **c** : requiring use of the intellect **2 a** : given to study, reflection, and speculation **b** : engaged in activity requiring the creative use of the intellect — **in·tel·lec·tu·al·i·ty** \-ˌek-chə-wə-'la-lə-tē\ n — **in·tel·lec·tu·al·ly** \-'ek-chə-wə-lē, -chə-lē, -shwə-lē\ adv — **in·tel·lec·tu·al·ness** \-'ek-chə-wəl-nəs, -chəl-, -shwəl-\ n

²intellectual n (1615) **1** pl, archaic : intellectual powers **2** : an intellectual person

in·tel·lec·tu·al·ism \ˌin-tᵊl-'ek-chə-wə-ˌli-zəm, -chə-ˌli-, -shwə-ˌli-\ n (1838) : devotion to the exercise of intellect or to intellectual pursuits — **in·tel·lec·tu·al·ist** \-list\ n or adj — **in·tel·lec·tu·al·is·tic** \-ˌek-chə-wə-'lis-tik, -chə-'lis-, -shwə-'lis-\ adj

in·tel·lec·tu·al·ize \ˌin-tᵊl-'ek-chə-wə-ˌlīz, -chə-ˌlīz, -shwə-ˌlīz\ vt *-ized; -iz·ing* (ca. 1819) : to give rational form or content to — **in·tel·lec·tu·al·i·za·tion** \-ˌek-chə-wə-lə-'zā-shən, -chə-lə-, -shwə-lə-\ n — **in·tel·lec·tu·al·iz·er** \-'ek-chə-wə-ˌlī-zər, -chə-ˌlī-, -shwə-ˌlī-\ n

in·tel·li·gence \in-'te-lə-jən(t)s\ n [ME, fr. MF, fr. L *intelligentia*, fr. *intelligent-*, *intelligens* intelligent] (14c) **1 a** (1) : the ability to learn or understand or to deal with new or trying situations : REASON; *also* : the skilled use of reason (2) : the ability to apply knowledge to manipulate one's environment or to think abstractly as measured by objective criteria (as tests) **b** *Christian Science* : the basic eternal quality of divine Mind **c** : mental acuteness : SHREWDNESS **2 a** : an intelligent entity; *esp* : ANGEL **b** : intelligent minds or mind ⟨cosmic ∼⟩ **3** : the act of understanding : COMPREHENSION **4 a** : INFORMATION, NEWS **b** : information concerning an enemy or possible enemy or an area; *also* : an agency engaged in obtaining such information **5** : the ability to perform computer functions

intelligence quotient n (1916) : a number used to express the apparent relative intelligence of a person that is the ratio multiplied by 100 of the mental age as reported on a standardized test to the chronological age

in·tel·li·genc·er \in-'te-lə-jən(t)-sər; -'te-lə-ˌjen(t)-, -ˌte-lə-'\ n (1581) **1** : a secret agent : SPY **2** : a bringer of news : REPORTER

intelligence test n (1914) : a test designed to determine the relative mental capacity of a person

in·tel·li·gent \in-'te-lə-jənt\ adj [L *intelligent-*, *intelligens*, prp. of *intelligere*, *intellegere* to understand, fr. *inter-* + *legere* to gather, select — more at LEGEND] (1509) **1 a** : having or indicating a high or satisfactory degree of intelligence and mental capacity **b** : revealing or reflecting good judgment or sound thought : SKILLFUL **2 a** : possessing intelligence **b** : guided or directed by intellect : RATIONAL **3 a** : guided or controlled by a computer; *esp* : using a built-in microprocessor for automatic operation, for processing of data, or for achieving greater versatility — compare DUMB 7 **b** : able to produce printed material from digital signals ⟨an ∼ copier⟩ — **in·tel·li·gen·tial** \-ˌte-lə-'jen(t)-shəl\ adj — **in·tel·li·gent·ly** \-'te-lə-jənt-lē\ adv

syn INTELLIGENT, CLEVER, ALERT, QUICK-WITTED mean mentally keen or quick. INTELLIGENT stresses success in coping with new situations and solving problems ⟨an *intelligent* person could assemble it fast⟩. CLEVER

implies native ability or aptness and sometimes suggests a lack of more substantial qualities ⟨*clever* with words⟩. ALERT stresses quickness in perceiving and understanding ⟨*alert* to new technology⟩. QUICK-WITTED implies promptness in finding answers in debate or in devising expedients in moments of danger or challenge ⟨no match for his *quick-witted* opponent⟩.

in·tel·li·gent·sia \in-ˌte-lə-'jen(t)-sē-ə, -'gen(t)-\ n [Russ *intelligentsiya*, fr. L *intelligentia* intelligence] (1907) : intellectuals who form an artistic, social, or political vanguard or elite

in·tel·li·gi·ble \in-'te-lə-jə-bəl\ adj [ME, fr. L *intelligibilis*, fr. *intelligere*] (14c) **1** : apprehensible by the intellect only **2** : capable of being understood or comprehended — **in·tel·li·gi·bil·i·ty** \-ˌte-lə-jə-'bi-lə-tē\ n — **in·tel·li·gi·ble·ness** \-'te-lə-jə-bəl-nəs\ n — **in·tel·li·gi·bly** \-blē\ adv

in·tem·per·ance \(ˌ)in-'tem-p(ə-)rən(t)s\ n (15c) : lack of moderation; *esp* : habitual or excessive drinking of intoxicants

in·tem·per·ate \-p(ə-)rət\ adj [ME *intemperat*, fr. L *intemperatus*, fr. *in-* + *temperatus*, pp. of *temperare* to temper] (14c) : not temperate ⟨∼ criticism⟩; *esp* : given to excessive use of intoxicating liquors — **in·tem·per·ate·ly** adv — **in·tem·per·ate·ness** n

in·tend \in-'tend\ vb [ME *entenden*, *intenden*, fr. MF *entendre* to purpose, fr. L *intendere* to stretch out, direct, aim at, fr. *in-* + *tendere* to stretch — more at THIN] vt (14c) **1** : to direct the mind on **2** archaic : to proceed on (a course) **3 a** : SIGNIFY, MEAN **b** : to refer to **4 a** : to have in mind as a purpose or goal : PLAN **b** : to design for a specified use or future ∼ vi, archaic : SET OUT, START — **in·tend·er** n

¹intended adj (15c) **1** : expected to be such in the future ⟨an ∼ career⟩ ⟨his ∼ bride⟩ **2** : INTENTIONAL — **in·tend·ed·ly** adv

²intended n (1767) : the person to whom another is engaged

intending adj (1788) : PROSPECTIVE, ASPIRING ⟨an ∼ teacher⟩

in·tend·ment \in-'ten(d)-mənt\ n (14c) : the true meaning or intention esp. of a law

in·ten·er·ate \in-'te-nə-ˌrāt\ vt *-at·ed; -at·ing* [²*in-* + L *tener* soft, tender — more at TENDER] (1595) : to make tender : SOFTEN — **in·ten·er·a·tion** \-ˌte-nə-'rā-shən\ n

in·tense \in-'ten(t)s\ adj [ME, fr. MF, fr. L *intensus*, fr. pp. of *intendere* to stretch out] (15c) **1 a** : existing in an extreme degree ⟨the excitement was ∼⟩ ⟨∼ pain⟩ **b** : having or showing a characteristic in extreme degree ⟨∼ colors⟩ **2** : marked by or expressive of great zeal, energy, determination, or concentration ⟨∼ effort⟩ **3 a** : exhibiting strong feeling or earnestness of purpose ⟨an ∼ student⟩ **b** : deeply felt — **in·tense·ly** adv — **in·tense·ness** n

in·ten·si·fi·er \in-'ten(t)-sə-ˌfi(-ə)r\ n (1835) : one that intensifies; *esp* : INTENSIVE

in·ten·si·fy \in-'ten(t)-sə-ˌfī\ vb *-fied; -fy·ing* vt (1817) **1** : to make intense or more intensive : STRENGTHEN **2 a** : to increase the density and contrast of (a photographic image) by chemical treatment **b** : to make more acute : SHARPEN ∼ vi : to become intense or more intensive : grow stronger or more acute — **in·ten·si·fi·ca·tion** \-ˌten(t)s-fə-'kā-shən, -ˌten(t)-sə-\ n

in·ten·sion \in-'ten(t)-shən\ n (1604) **1** : INTENSITY **2** : CONNOTATION **3** — **in·ten·sion·al** \-'tench-nəl, -'ten(t)-shə-nᵊl\ adj — **in·ten·sion·al·i·ty** \-ˌten(t)-shə-'na-lə-tē\ n — **in·ten·sion·al·ly** \-'tench-nə-lē, -'ten(t)-shə-nᵊl-ē\ adv

in·ten·si·ty \in-'ten(t)-sə-tē\ n, pl *-ties* (1665) **1** : the quality or state of being intense; *esp* : extreme degree of strength, force, energy, or feeling **2** : the magnitude of a quantity (as force or energy) per unit (as of area, charge, mass, or time) **3** : SATURATION 4a

¹in·ten·sive \in-'ten(t)-siv\ adj (15c) **1** : of, relating to, or marked by intensity or intensification: as **a** : highly concentrated ⟨∼ study⟩ **b** : tending to strengthen or increase; *esp* : tending to give force or emphasis ⟨∼ adverb⟩ **c** : constituting or relating to a method designed to increase productivity by the expenditure of more capital and labor rather than by increase in scope ⟨∼ farming⟩ — **in·ten·sive·ly** adv — **in·ten·sive·ness** n

²intensive n (1813) : an intensive linguistic element

intensive care n (1963) : special medical equipment and services for taking care of seriously ill patients ⟨heart patients in *intensive care*⟩ ⟨an *intensive care* unit⟩

¹in·tent \in-'tent\ n [ME *entent*, fr. OF, fr. LL *intentus*, fr. L, act of stretching out, fr. *intendere*] (13c) **1 a** : the act or fact of intending : PURPOSE; *esp* : the design or purpose to commit a wrongful or criminal act ⟨admitted wounding him with ∼⟩ **b** : the state of mind with which an act is done : VOLITION **2** : a usu. clearly formulated or planned intention : AIM **3 a** : MEANING, SIGNIFICANCE **b** : CONNOTATION 3 *syn* see INTENTION

²intent adj [L *intentus*, fr. pp. of *intendere*] (14c) **1** : directed with strained or eager attention : CONCENTRATED **2** : having the mind, attention, or will concentrated on something or some end or purpose ⟨∼ on their work⟩ — **in·tent·ly** adv — **in·tent·ness** n

in·ten·tion \in-'ten(t)-shən\ n (14c) **1** : a determination to act in a certain way : RESOLVE **2** : IMPORT, SIGNIFICANCE **3 a** : what one intends to do or bring about **b** : the object for which a prayer, mass, or pious act is offered **4** : a process or manner of healing of incised wounds **5** : CONCEPT; *esp* : a concept considered as the product of attention directed to an object of knowledge **6** pl : purpose with respect to marriage

syn INTENTION, INTENT, PURPOSE, DESIGN, AIM, END, OBJECT, OBJECTIVE, GOAL mean what one intends to accomplish or attain. INTENTION implies little more than what one has in mind to do or bring about ⟨announced his *intention* to marry⟩. INTENT suggests clearer formulation or greater deliberateness ⟨the clear *intent* of the statute⟩. PURPOSE suggests a more settled determination ⟨being successful was her *purpose* in life⟩. DESIGN implies a more carefully calculated plan ⟨the order of events came by accident, not *design*⟩. AIM adds to these implications of effort directed toward attaining or accomplishing ⟨her *aim* was to raise film to an art form⟩. END stresses the intended effect of action often in distinction or contrast to the action or means as such ⟨willing to use any means to achieve his *end*⟩. OBJECT may equal END but more often applies to a more individually determined wish or need ⟨his constant *object* was the achievement of pleasure⟩. OBJECTIVE implies something tangible and immediately attainable ⟨their *objective* is to seize the oil fields⟩. GOAL suggests something attained only by prolonged effort and hardship ⟨worked years to reach her *goals*⟩.

in·ten·tion·al \in-'tench-nəl, -'ten(t)-shə-n°l\ *adj* (ca. 1727) **1** : done by intention or design : INTENDED ⟨~ damage⟩ **2 a** : of or relating to epistemological intention **b** : having external reference *syn* see VOLUNTARY — **in·ten·tion·al·i·ty** \-,ten(t)-shə-'na-lə-tē\ *n* — **in·ten·tion·al·ly** \in-'tench-nə-lē, -'ten(t)-shə-n°l-ē\ *adv*

in·ter \in-'tər\ *vt* **in·terred; in·ter·ring** [ME *enteren*, fr. MF *enterrer*, fr. (assumed) VL *interrare*, fr. *in-* + L *terra* earth — more at TERRACE] (14c) : to deposit (a dead body) in the earth or in a tomb

inter- *prefix* [ME *inter-, enter-*, fr. MF & L; MF *inter-, entre-*, fr. L *inter-*, fr. *inter*; akin to OHG *untar* among, Gk *enteron* intestine, OE *in* in] **1** : between : among : in the midst ⟨*inter*crop⟩ ⟨*inter*penetrate⟩ ⟨*inter*stellar⟩ **2** : reciprocal ⟨*inter*relation⟩ : reciprocally ⟨*inter*marry⟩ **3** : located between ⟨*inter*face⟩ **4** : carried on between ⟨*inter*national⟩ **5** : occurring between ⟨*inter*borough⟩ : intervening ⟨*inter*glacial⟩ **6** : shared by, involving, or derived from two or more ⟨*inter*faith⟩ **7** : between the limits of : within ⟨*inter*tropical⟩ **8** : existing between ⟨*inter*communal⟩ ⟨*inter*company⟩

in·ter·Af·ri·can	in·ter·do·min·ion	in·ter·par·ish
in·ter·agen·cy	in·ter·elec·trode	in·ter·pa·ro·chi·al
in·ter·al·le·lic	in·ter·elec·tron	in·ter·par·ox·ys·mal
in·ter·Amer·i·can	in·ter·elec·tron·ic	in·ter·par·ti·cle
in·ter·an·i·ma·tion	in·ter·ep·i·dem·ic	in·ter·par·ty
in·ter·an·nu·al	in·ter·eth·nic	in·ter·per·cep·tu·al
in·ter·as·so·ci·a·tion	in·ter·fac·ul·ty	in·ter·per·me·ate
in·ter·atom·ic	in·ter·fa·mil·ial	in·ter·pha·lan·ge·al
in·ter·avail·abil·i·ty	in·ter·fam·i·ly	in·ter·plan·e·tary
in·ter·bank	in·ter·fi·ber	in·ter·plu·vi·al
in·ter·ba·sin	in·ter·firm	in·ter·point
in·ter·bed	in·ter·flow	in·ter·pop·u·la·tion
in·ter·be·hav·ior	in·ter·flu·vi·al	in·ter·pop·u·la·tion·al
in·ter·be·hav·ior·al	in·ter·fold	in·ter·pro·fes·sion·al
in·ter·bor·ough	in·ter·fra·ter·ni·ty	in·ter·pro·vin·cial
in·ter·branch	in·ter·gang	in·ter·psy·chic
in·ter·cal·i·bra·tion	in·ter·gen·er·a·tion	in·ter·re·gion·al
in·ter·cam·pus	in·ter·gen·er·a·tion·al	in·ter·re·li·gious
in·ter·caste	in·ter·gen·er·ic	in·ter·re·nal
in·ter·cell	in·ter·graft	in·ter·row
in·ter·cel·lu·lar	in·ter·gran·u·lar	in·ter·school
in·ter·chain	in·ter·group	in·ter·sec·tion·al
in·ter·chan·nel	in·ter·hemi·spher·ic	in·ter·seg·ment
in·ter·chro·mo·som·al	in·ter·in·di·vid·u·al	in·ter·seg·men·tal
in·ter·church	in·ter·in·dus·try	in·ter·sen·so·ry
in·ter·city	in·ter·in·flu·ence	in·ter·so·ci·etal
in·ter·clan	in·ter·in·sti·tu·tion·al	in·ter·so·ci·ety
in·ter·class	in·ter·in·volve	in·ter·stage
in·ter·club	in·ter·ion·ic	in·ter·sta·tion
in·ter·clus·ter	in·ter·is·land	in·ter·stim·u·la·tion
in·ter·coast·al	in·ter·ju·ris·dic·tion·al	in·ter·stim·u·lus
in·ter·co·lo·nial	in·ter·la·cus·trine	in·ter·strain
in·ter·com·mu·nal	in·ter·lam·i·nar	in·ter·strand
in·ter·com·mu·ni·ty	in·ter·lay	in·ter·strat·i·fi·ca·tion
in·ter·com·pa·ny	in·ter·lay·er	in·ter·strat·i·fy
in·ter·com·pare	in·ter·lend	in·ter·sub·sti·tut·abil·i·ty
in·ter·com·pre·hen·si·bil·i·ty	in·ter·li·brary	in·ter·sub·sti·tut·able
in·ter·cor·po·rate	in·ter·lin·er	in·ter·sys·tem
in·ter·cor·re·late	in·ter·lob·u·lar	in·ter·term
in·ter·cor·re·la·tion	in·ter·lo·cal	in·ter·ter·mi·nal
in·ter·cor·ti·cal	in·ter·male	in·ter·ter·ri·to·ri·al
in·ter·coun·try	in·ter·mar·gin·al	in·ter·trans·lat·able
in·ter·coun·ty	in·ter·mem·brane	in·ter·tri·al
in·ter·cou·ple	in·ter·min·is·te·ri·al	in·ter·trib·al
in·ter·cra·ter	in·ter·mi·tot·ic	in·ter·troop
in·ter·crys·tal·line	in·ter·mo·lec·u·lar	in·ter·union
in·ter·cul·tur·al	in·ter·mo·lec·u·lar·ly	in·ter·unit
in·ter·cul·tur·al·ly	in·ter·moun·tain	in·ter·uni·ver·si·ty
in·ter·cul·ture	in·ter·nu·cle·ar	in·ter·ur·ban
in·ter·deal·er	in·ter·nu·cle·on	in·ter·val·ley
in·ter·de·nom·i·na·tion·al	in·ter·nu·cle·on·ic	in·ter·ven·tric·u·lar
in·ter·de·part·men·tal	in·ter·nu·cle·o·tide	in·ter·ver·te·bral
in·ter·de·part·men·tal·ly	in·ter·ob·serv·er	in·ter·vil·lage
in·ter·de·pend	in·ter·ocean	in·ter·vis·i·bil·i·ty
in·ter·de·pen·dence	in·ter·oce·an·ic	in·ter·vis·i·ble
in·ter·de·pen·den·cy	in·ter·of·fice	in·ter·vis·i·ta·tion
in·ter·de·pen·dent	in·ter·op·er·a·tive	in·ter·war
in·ter·de·pen·dent·ly	in·ter·or·bit·al	in·ter·work
in·ter·di·a·lec·tal	in·ter·or·gan	in·ter·work·ing
in·ter·dis·trict	in·ter·or·ga·ni·za·tion·al	in·ter·zon·al
in·ter·di·vi·sion·al	in·ter·pan·dem·ic	in·ter·zone

in·ter·a·bang *var of* INTERROBANG

in·ter·act \,in-tə-'rakt\ *vi* (1839) : to act upon one another

in·ter·ac·tant \-'rak-tənt\ *n* (1949) : one that interacts

in·ter·ac·tion \,in-tə-'rak-shən\ *n* (1832) : mutual or reciprocal action or influence — **in·ter·ac·tion·al** \-shnəl, -shə-n°l\ *adj*

in·ter·ac·tive \-'rak-tiv\ *adj* (1832) **1** : mutually or reciprocally active **2** : of, relating to, or being a two-way electronic communication system (as a telephone, cable television, or a computer) that involves a user's orders (as for information or merchandise) or responses (as to a poll) — **in·ter·ac·tive·ly** *adv*

in·ter alia \,in-tər-'ā-lē-ə, -'ä-\ *adv* [L] (1665) : among other things

in·ter ali·os \-lē-,ōs\ *adv* [L] (ca. 1670) : among other persons

in·ter·al·lied \,in-tər-'a-,līd, -ə-'līd\ *adj* (1917) : relating to, composed of, or involving allies

in·ter·breed \,in-tər-'brēd\ *vb* **-bred** \-'bred\; **-breed·ing** *vi* (1859) : to breed together: as **a** : CROSSBREED **b** : to breed within a closed population ~ *vt* : to cause to breed together

in·ter·ca·la·ry \in-'tər-kə-,ler-ē, ,in-tər-'ka-lə-rē\ *adj* [L *intercalarius*, fr.

intercalare] (1614) **1 a** : inserted in a calendar ⟨an ~ day⟩ **b** *of a year* : containing an intercalary period (as a day or month) **2** : inserted between other things or parts : INTERPOLATED

in·ter·ca·late \in-'tər-kə-,lāt\ *vt* **-lat·ed; -lat·ing** [L *intercalatus*, pp. of *intercalare*, fr. *inter-* + *calare* to proclaim, call — more at LOW] (1603) **1** : to insert (as a day) in a calendar **2** : to insert between or among existing elements or layers *syn* see INTRODUCE — **in·ter·ca·la·tion** \-,tər-kə-'lā-shən\ *n*

in·ter·cede \,in-tər-'sēd\ *vi* **-ced·ed; -ced·ing** [L *intercedere*, fr. *inter-* + *cedere* to go] (1597) : to intervene between parties with a view to reconciling differences : MEDIATE *syn* see INTERPOSE — **in·ter·ced·er** *n*

in·ter·cen·sal \,in-tər-'sen(t)-səl\ *adj* (1887) : occurring between censuses ⟨~ estimates⟩ ⟨~ period⟩

[1]in·ter·cept \,in-tər-'sept\ *vt* [ME, fr. L *interceptus*, pp. of *intercipere*, fr. *inter-* + *capere* to take, seize — more at HEAVE] (15c) **1** *obs* : PREVENT, HINDER **2 a** : to stop, seize, or interrupt in progress or course or before arrival **b** : to receive (a communication or signal directed elsewhere) usu. secretly **3** *obs* : to interrupt communication or connection with **4** : to include (part of a curve, surface, or solid) between two points, curves, or surfaces ⟨the part of a circumference ~ed between two radii⟩ **5 a** : to gain possession of (an opponent's pass) **b** : to intercept a pass thrown by (an opponent)

[2]in·ter·cept \'in-tər-,sept\ *n* (1821) **1** : the distance from the origin to a point where a graph crosses a coordinate axis **2** : INTERCEPTION; *esp* : the interception of a missile by an interceptor or of a target by a missile **3** : a message, code, or signal that is intercepted (as by monitoring radio communications)

in·ter·cep·tion \,in-tər-'sep-shən\ *n* (15c) **1 a** : the action of intercepting **b** : the state of being intercepted **2** : something that is intercepted; *esp* : an intercepted forward pass

in·ter·cep·tor *also* **in·ter·cept·er** \,in-tər-'sep-tər\ *n* (1598) : one that intercepts; *specif* : a light high-speed fast-climbing fighter plane or missile designed for defense against raiding bombers or missiles

in·ter·ces·sion \,in-tər-'se-shən\ *n* [ME, fr. MF or L; MF, fr. L *intercession-, intercessio*, fr. *intercedere*] (15c) **1** : the act of interceding **2** : prayer, petition, or entreaty in favor of another — **in·ter·ces·sion·al** \-'sesh-nəl, -'se-shə-n°l\ *adj* — **in·ter·ces·sor** \'se-sər\ *n* — **in·ter·ces·so·ry** \-'ses-rē, -'se-sə-rē\ *adj*

[1]in·ter·change \,in-tər-'chānj\ *vb* [ME *entrechaungen*, fr. MF *entrechangier*, fr. OF, fr. *entre- inter-* + *changier* to change] *vt* (14c) **1** : to put each of (two things) in the place of the other **2** : EXCHANGE ~ *vi* : to change places mutually — **in·ter·chang·er** *n*

[2]in·ter·change \'in-tər-,chānj\ *n* (15c) **1** : the act, process, or an instance of interchanging : EXCHANGE **2** : a junction of two or more highways by a system of separate levels that permit traffic to pass from one to another without the crossing of traffic streams

in·ter·change·able \,in-tər-'chān-jə-bəl\ *adj* (14c) : capable of being interchanged; *esp* : permitting mutual substitution ⟨~ parts⟩ — **in·ter·change·abil·i·ty** \-,chān-jə-'bi-lə-tē\ *n* — **in·ter·change·able·ness** \-'chān-jə-bəl-nəs\ *n* — **in·ter·change·ably** \-blē\ *adv*

in·ter·col·le·giate \,in-tər-kə-'lē-jət, -jē-ət\ *adj* (ca. 1874) : existing, carried on, or participating in activities between colleges ⟨~ athletics⟩

in·ter·co·lum·ni·a·tion \,in-tər-kə-,ləm-nē-'ā-shən\ *n* [L *intercolumnium* space between two columns, fr. *inter-* + *columna* column] (1624) **1** : the clear space between the columns of a series **2** : the system of spacing of the columns of a colonnade

in·ter·com \'in-tər-,käm\ *n* [short for *intercommunication system*] (1940) : a two-way communication system with a microphone and loudspeaker at each station for localized use

in·ter·com·mu·ni·cate \,in-tər-kə-'myü-nə-,kāt\ *vi* (1586) **1** : to exchange communication with one another **2** : to afford passage from one to another — **in·ter·com·mu·ni·ca·tion** \-,myü-nə-'kā-shən\ *n*

intercommunication system *n* (1911) : INTERCOM

in·ter·com·mu·nion \,in-tər-kə-'myü-nyən\ *n* (1921) : interdenominational participation in communion

in·ter·con·nect \,in-tər-kə-'nekt\ *vt* (1865) : to connect with one another ~ *vi* : to be or become mutually connected — **in·ter·con·nec·tion** \-'nek-shən\ *n*

interconnected *adj* (1865) **1** : mutually joined or related ⟨~ highways⟩ ⟨~ political issues⟩ **2** : having internal connections between the parts or elements — **in·ter·con·nec·ted·ness** *n*

in·ter·con·ti·nen·tal \,in-tər-,kän-t°n-'en-t°l\ *adj* (ca. 1855) **1** : extending among continents or carried on between continents **2** : capable of traveling between continents ⟨~ ballistic missile⟩

in·ter·con·ver·sion \,in-tər-kən-'vər-zhən, -shən\ *n* (1865) : mutual conversion ⟨~ of chemical compounds⟩ — **in·ter·con·vert** \-'vərt\ *vt* — **in·ter·con·vert·ibil·i·ty** \-,vər-tə-'bi-lə-tē\ *n* — **in·ter·con·vert·ible** \-'vər-tə-bəl\ *adj*

in·ter·cool·er \,in-tər-'kü-lər\ *n* (1899) : a device for cooling a fluid (as air) between successive heat-generating processes

in·ter·cos·tal \,in-tər-'käs-t°l\ *adj* [NL *intercostalis*, fr. L *inter-* + *costa* rib — more at COAST] (1597) : situated or extending between the ribs ⟨~ spaces⟩ ⟨~ muscles⟩ — **intercostal** *n*

in·ter·course \'in-tər-,kōrs, -,kȯrs\ *n* [ME *intercurse*, prob. fr. MF *entrecours*, fr. ML *intercursus*, fr. L, act of running between, fr. *intercurrere* to run between, fr. *inter-* + *currere* to run — more at CAR] (15c) **1** : connection or dealings between persons or groups **2** : exchange esp. of thoughts or feelings : COMMUNION **3** : physical sexual contact between individuals that involves the genitalia of at least one person ⟨heterosexual ~⟩ ⟨anal ~⟩ ⟨oral ~⟩; *esp* : SEXUAL INTERCOURSE 1

in·ter·crop \,in-tər-'kräp, 'in-tər-,\ *vt* (1898) : to grow a crop in between (another) ~ *vi* : to grow two or more crops simultaneously (as in alternate rows) on the same plot — **in·ter·crop** \'in-tər-,kräp\ *n*

[1]in·ter·cross \,in-tər-'krȯs\ *vb* (1711) : CROSS

[2]in·ter·cross \'in-tər-,krȯs\ *n* (1859) : an instance or a product of crossbreeding

---

\ə\ abut \°\ kitten, F table \ər\ further \a\ ash \ā\ ace \ä\ mop, mar \aȯ\ out \ch\ chin \e\ bet \ē\ easy \g\ go \i\ hit \ī\ ice \j\ job \ŋ\ sing \ō\ go \ȯ\ law \ȯi\ boy \th\ thin \th̲\ the \ü\ loot \u̇\ foot \y\ yet \zh\ vision \à, k̲, ⁿ, œ, œ̄, ᴜ, ᴜ̄, ᵞ\ *see* Guide to Pronunciation

in·ter·cur·rent \,in-tər-'kər-ənt, -'kə-rənt\ *adj* [L *intercurrent-, intercurrens*, prp. of *intercurrere*] (1611) : occurring during and modifying the course of another disease ⟨an ∼ infection⟩

in·ter·cut \,in-tər-'kət\ *vt* (1938) **1** : to insert (a contrasting camera shot) into a take by cutting **2** : to insert a contrasting camera shot into (a take) by cutting ∼ *vi* : to alternate contrasting camera shots by cutting

in·ter·den·tal \,in-tər-'den-t³l\ *adj* (ca. 1874) **1** : situated or intended for use between the teeth **2** : formed with the tip of the tongue between the upper and lower front teeth — **in·ter·den·tal·ly** \-t³l-ē\ *adv*

¹**in·ter·dict** \'in-tər-,dikt\ *n* [ME, alter. of *entredit*, fr. OF, fr. L *interdictum* prohibition, fr. neut. of *interdictus*, pp. of *interdicere* to interpose, forbid, fr. *inter-* + *dicere* to say — more at DICTION] (15c) **1** : a Roman Catholic ecclesiastical censure withdrawing most sacraments and Christian burial from a person or district **2** : a prohibitory decree : PROHIBITION

²**in·ter·dict** \,in-tər-'dikt\ *vt* (15c) **1** : to lay under or prohibit by an interdict **2** : to forbid in a usu. formal or authoritative manner **3** : to destroy, damage, or cut off (as an enemy line of supply) by firepower to stop or hamper an enemy *syn* see FORBID — **in·ter·dic·tion** \-'dik-shən\ *n* — **in·ter·dic·tive** \-'dik-tiv\ *adj* — **in·ter·dic·tor** \-tər\ *n* — **in·ter·dic·to·ry** \-t(ə-)rē\ *adj*

in·ter·dif·fu·sion \-di-'fyü-zhən\ *n* (ca. 1872) : the process of diffusing and mixing freely so as to approach a homogeneous mixture — **in·ter·dif·fuse** \-'fyüz\ *vi*

in·ter·dig·i·tate \-'di-jə-,tāt\ *vi* **-tat·ed; -tat·ing** [*inter-* + L *digitus* finger — more at TOE] (ca. 1849) : to become interlocked like the fingers of folded hands — **in·ter·dig·i·ta·tion** \-,di-jə-'tā-shən\ *n*

in·ter·dis·ci·plin·ary \-'di-sə-plə-,ner-ē\ *adj* (1926) : involving two or more academic, scientific, or artistic disciplines

¹**in·ter·est** \'in-t(ə-)rəst; 'in-tə-,rest, -,trest; 'in-tərst\ *n* [ME, prob. alter. of earlier *interesse*, fr. AF & ML; AF, fr. ML, fr. L, to be between, make a difference, concern, fr. *inter-* + *esse* to be — more at IS] (15c) **1 a** (1) : right, title, or legal share in something (2) : participation in advantage and responsibility **b** : BUSINESS, COMPANY **2 a** : a charge for borrowed money generally a percentage of the amount borrowed **b** : an excess above what is due or expected ⟨returned the insults with ∼⟩ **3** : ADVANTAGE, BENEFIT; *also* : SELF-INTEREST **4** : SPECIAL INTEREST **5 a** : a feeling that accompanies or causes special attention to an object or class of objects : CONCERN **b** : something that arouses such attention **c** : a quality in a thing arousing interest

²**interest** *vt* (1608) **1** : to induce or persuade to participate or engage **2** : to engage the attention or arouse the interest of

in·ter·est·ed *adj* (1602) **1** : having the attention engaged ⟨∼ listeners⟩ **2** : being affected or involved ⟨∼ parties⟩ — **in·ter·est·ed·ly** *adv*

interest group *n* (1908) : a group of persons having a common identifying interest that often provides a basis for action

in·ter·est·ing \'in-t(ə-)rəs-tiŋ; 'in-tə-,res-, 'in-,tres-; 'in-tərs-\ *adj* (1768) : holding the attention : arousing interest — **in·ter·est·ing·ness** *n*

in·ter·est·ing·ly \-lē\ *adv* (1811) **1** : in an interesting manner **2** : as a matter of interest

¹**in·ter·face** \'in-tər-,fās\ *n* (1882) **1** : a surface forming a common boundary of two bodies, spaces, or phases ⟨an oil-water ∼⟩ **2 a** : the place at which independent and often unrelated systems meet and act on or communicate with each other ⟨the man-machine ∼⟩ **b** : the means by which interaction or communication is achieved at an interface — **in·ter·fa·cial** \,in-tər-'fā-shəl\ *adj*

²**interface** *vt* (1962) **1** : to connect by means of an interface ⟨∼ a machine with a computer⟩ **2** : to serve as an interface for ∼ *vi* **1** : to become interfaced **2** : to interact or coordinate harmoniously

in·ter·fac·ing \-,fā-siŋ\ *n* (1942) : fabric sewn between the facing and the outside of a garment (as in a collar or cuff) for stiffening and shape retention

in·ter·faith \,in-tər-'fāth\ *adj* (1932) : involving persons of different religious faiths

in·ter·fere \,in-tə(r)-'fir\ *vi* **-fered; -fer·ing** [ME *enterferen*, fr. MF (s')*entreferir* to strike one another, fr. OF, fr. *entre-* inter- + *ferir* to strike, fr. L *ferire* — more at BORE] (15c) **1** : to interpose in a way that hinders or impedes : come into collision or be in opposition **2** : to strike one foot against the opposite foot or ankle in walking or running — used esp. of horses **3** : to enter into or take a part in the concerns of others **4** : to act reciprocally so as to augment, diminish, or otherwise affect one another — used of waves *syn* see INTERPOSE — **in·ter·fer·er** *n*

in·ter·fer·ence \-'fir-ən(t)s\ *n* (1783) **1 a** : the act or process of interfering **b** : something that interferes : OBSTRUCTION **2** : the mutual effect on meeting of two wave trains (as of light or sound) that constitutes alternating areas of increased and decreased amplitude (as light and dark lines or louder and softer sound) **3 a** : the legal blocking of an opponent in football to make way for the ballcarrier **b** : the illegal hindering of an opponent in sports **4** : partial or complete inhibition or sometimes facilitation of other genetic crossovers in the vicinity of a chromosomal locus where a preceding crossover has occurred **5 a** : confusion of a received radio signal due to the presence of noise (as atmospherics) or signals from two or more transmitters on a single frequency **b** : something that produces such confusion **6** : the disturbing effect of new learning on the performance of previously learned behavior with which it is inconsistent — **in·ter·fer·en·tial** \-fə-'ren(t)-shəl, -,fer-'en(t)-\ *adj*

in·ter·fer·o·gram \,in-tə(r)-'fir-ə-,gram\ *n* (1921) : a photographic record made by an apparatus for recording optical interference phenomena

in·ter·fer·om·e·ter \,in-tə(r)-fə-'rä-mə-tər, -,fi-'rä-\ *n* [ISV] (1897) : an instrument that utilizes the interference of waves (as of light) for precise determinations (as of distance or wavelength) — **in·ter·fer·o·met·ric** \-,fir-ə-'me-trik\ *adj* — **in·ter·fer·o·met·ri·cal·ly** \-tri-k(ə-)lē\ *adv* — **in·ter·fer·om·e·try** \-fə-'rä-mə-trē, -,fi-'rä-\ *n*

in·ter·fer·on \,in-tə(r)-'fir-,än\ *n* [*interfere* + ²-*on*] (1957) : any of a group of heat-stable soluble basic antiviral glycoproteins of low molecular weight that are produced usu. by cells exposed to the action of a virus, sometimes to the action of another intracellular parasite (as a bacterium), or experimentally to the action of some chemicals

in·ter·fer·tile \,in-tər-'fər-t³l\ *adj* (1899) : capable of interbreeding — **in·ter·fer·til·i·ty** \-(,)fər-'ti-lə-tē\ *n*

---

in·ter·file \,in-tər-'fi(ə)l\ *vt* (1950) : to arrange in or add to a file : FILE

in·ter·fluve \'in-tər-,flüv\ *n* [*inter-* + L *fluvius* river — more at FLUVIAL] (1895) : the area between adjacent streams flowing in the same direction

in·ter·fuse \,in-tər-'fyüz\ *vb* [L *interfusus*, pp. of *interfundere* to pour between, fr. *inter-* + *fundere* to pour — more at FOUND] *vt* (1593) **1** : to combine by fusing : BLEND **2** : to add as if by fusing : INFUSE ∼ *vi* : BLEND, FUSE — **in·ter·fu·sion** \-'fyü-zhən\ *n*

in·ter·ga·lac·tic \,in-tər-gə-'lak-tik\ *adj* (1928) **1** : situated in or relating to the spaces between galaxies **2** : of, relating to, or occurring in outer space ⟨∼ battles⟩

in·ter·gla·cial \-'glā-shəl\ *n* (1867) : a warm period between glacial epochs — **interglacial** *adj*

in·ter·gov·ern·men·tal \-'gə-vər(n)-'men-t³l\ *adj* (1927) : existing or occurring between two or more governments or levels of government

in·ter·gra·da·tion \-grā-'dā-shən, -grə-\ *n* (1874) : the condition of an individual or population that intergrades — **in·ter·gra·da·tion·al** \-shnəl, -shə-n³l\ *adj*

¹**in·ter·grade** \,in-tər-'grād\ *vi* (1874) : to merge gradually one with another through a continuous series of intermediate forms

²**in·ter·grade** \'in-tər-,grād\ *n* (1888) : an intermediate form

in·ter·growth \'in-tər-,grōth\ *n* (1844) : a growing between or together; *also* : the product of such growth

¹**in·ter·im** \'in-tə-rəm\ *n* [L, adv., meanwhile, fr. *inter* between — more at INTER-] (ca. 1580) : an intervening time : INTERVAL

²**interim** *adj* (1604) : done, made, appointed, or occurring for an interim

¹**in·te·ri·or** \in-'tir-ē-ər\ *adj* [MF & L; MF, fr. L, compar. of (assumed) OL *interus* inward, on the inside; akin to L *inter*] (15c) **1** : lying, occurring, or functioning within the limiting boundaries : INNER ⟨an ∼ point of a triangle⟩ **2** : belonging to mental or spiritual life ⟨a simple ∼ piety⟩ **3** : belonging to the inner constitution or concealed nature of something ⟨∼ meaning of a poem⟩ **4** : lying away or remote from the border or shore — **in·te·ri·or·ly** \in-'tir-ē-ər-lē\ *adv*

²**interior** *n* (1596) **1** : the inner or spiritual nature : CHARACTER **2** : the interior part (as of a country or island) **3** : the internal or inner part of a thing : INSIDE **4** : the internal affairs of a state or nation **5** : a representation (as in a play or movie) of the interior of a building

interior angle *n* (1756) **1** : the inner of the two angles formed where two sides of a polygon come together **2** : any of the four angles formed in the area between a pair of parallel lines when a third line cuts them

interior decoration *n* (1807) : INTERIOR DESIGN

interior decorator *n* (1867) : INTERIOR DESIGNER, DECORATOR

interior design *n* (1927) : the art or practice of planning and supervising the design and execution of architectural interiors and their furnishings

agh, bgh, ghd, ghc
interior angle 2

interior designer *n* (1938) : one who specializes in interior design

in·te·ri·or·ise *Brit var of* INTERIORIZE

in·te·ri·or·i·ty \(,)in-,tir-ē-'ór-ə-tē, -'är-\ *n* (1701) : interior quality or character; *also* : inner life or substance ⟨characters that lack ∼⟩

in·te·ri·or·ize \in-'tir-ē-ə-,riz\ *vt* **-ized; -iz·ing** (1906) : to make interior; *esp* : to make a part of one's own inner being or mental structure — **in·te·ri·or·iza·tion** \-,tir-ē-ə-rə-'zā-shən\ *n*

interior monologue *n* (1922) : a usu. extended representation in monologue of a fictional character's thought and feeling

in·ter·ject \,in-tər-'jekt\ *vt* [L *interjectus*, pp. of *intericere*, fr. *inter-* + *jacere* to throw — more at JET] (1588) : to throw in between or among other things : INTERPOLATE ⟨∼ a remark⟩ *syn* see INTRODUCE — **in·ter·jec·tor** \-'jek-tər\ *n* — **in·ter·jec·to·ry** \-t(ə-)rē\ *adj*

in·ter·jec·tion \,in-tər-'jek-shən\ *n* (15c) **1 a** : the act of uttering exclamations : EJACULATION **b** : the act of putting in between : INTERPOSITION **2** : an ejaculatory utterance usu. lacking grammatical connection: **a** : a word or phrase used in exclamation (as *Heavens! Dear me!*) **b** : a cry or inarticulate utterance (as *Alas! ouch! phooey! ugh!*) expressing an emotion **3** : something that is interjected or that interrupts

in·ter·jec·tion·al \-shnəl, -shə-n³l\ *adj* (1761) **1** : of, relating to, or constituting an interjection : EJACULATORY **2** : thrown in between other words : PARENTHETICAL — **in·ter·jec·tion·al·ly** *adv*

in·ter·lace \,in-tər-'lās\ *vb* [ME *entrelacen*, fr. MF *entrelacer*, fr. OF *entrelacier*, fr. *entre-* inter- + *lacier* to lace] *vt* (14c) **1** : to unite by or as if by lacing together : INTERWEAVE **2** : to vary by alternation or intermixture : INTERSPERSE ⟨narrative *interlaced* with anecdotes⟩ ∼ *vi* : to cross one another as if woven together : INTERTWINE — **in·ter·lace·ment** \-mənt\ *n*

in·ter·lard \,in-tər-'lärd\ *vt* [MF *entrelarder*, fr. OF, fr. *entre* inter- + *larder* to lard, fr. *lard*, fr. L *lardum*] (ca. 1587) : to vary by intermixture : INTERSPERSE, INTERLACE

in·ter·leave \,in-tər-'lēv\ *vt* **-leaved; -leav·ing** (1668) : to arrange in or as if in alternate layers

in·ter·leu·kin \,in-tər-'lü-kən\ *n* [*inter-* + *leuk-* + ¹-*in*] (1979) : any of several compounds of low molecular weight that are produced by lymphocytes, macrophages, and monocytes and that function esp. in regulation of the immune system and esp. cell-mediated immunity

in·ter·leu·kin-1 \-'wən\ *n* (1979) : an interleukin produced esp. by monocytes and macrophages that regulates immune responses by activating lymphocytes and mediates other biological processes (as the onset of fever) usu. associated with infection and inflammation

in·ter·leu·kin-2 \-'tü\ *n* (1979) : an interleukin produced by antigen-stimulated helper T cells in the presence of interleukin-1 that induces proliferation of immune cells (as T cells and B cells) and is used experimentally esp. in treating certain cancers

¹**in·ter·line** \,in-tər-'līn\ *vt* [ME *enterlinen*, fr. ML *interlineare*, fr. L *inter-* + *linea* line] (15c) : to insert between lines already written or printed — **in·ter·lin·e·a·tion** \-,li-nē-'ā-shən\ *n*

²**interline** *vt* [ME, fr. *inter-* + *linen* to line] (15c) : to provide (a garment) with an interlining

³**interline** *adj* (1897) : relating to, involving, or carried by two or more transportation lines

¹in·ter·lin·ear \,in-tər-'li-nē-ər\ adj [ME interliniare, fr. ML interlinearis, fr. L inter- + linea line] (15c) 1 : inserted between lines already written or printed 2 : written or printed in different languages or texts in alternate lines — in·ter·lin·ear·ly adv

²interlinear n (1850) : a book having interlinear matter; esp : a book in a foreign language with interlinear translation

in·ter·lin·ing \'in-tər-,lī-niŋ\ n (1881) : a lining (as of a coat) sewn between the ordinary lining and the outside fabric

in·ter·link \,in-tər-'liŋk\ vt (1587) : to link together — in·ter·link \'in-tər-,liŋk\ n

¹in·ter·lock \,in-tər-'läk\ vi (1632) : to become locked together or interconnected ~ vt 1 : to lock together : UNITE 2 : to connect so that the motion or operation of any part is constrained by another

²in·ter·lock \'in-tər-,läk\ n (1874) 1 : the quality, state, sense, or an instance of being interlocked 2 : an arrangement in which the operation of one part or mechanism automatically brings about or prevents the operation of another ⟨a safety ~⟩ 3 a : a stretchable fabric made on a circular knitting machine and consisting of two ribbed fabrics joined by interlocking b : a garment made of interlock

in·ter·loc·u·tor \,in-tər-'lä-kyə-tər\ n [L interloqui to speak between, issue an interlocutory decree, fr. inter- + loqui to speak] (1514) 1 : one who takes part in dialogue or conversation 2 : a man in the middle of the line in a minstrel show who questions the end men and acts as leader

in·ter·loc·u·to·ry \-kyə-,tōr-ē, -,tȯr-\ adj (15c) : pronounced during the progress of a legal action and having only provisional force ⟨~ decree⟩

in·ter·lope \,in-tər-'lōp, 'in-tər-,\ vi -loped; -lop·ing [prob. back-formation fr. interloper, fr. inter- + -loper (akin to MD lopen to run, OE hlēapan to leap) — more at LEAP] (1615) 1 : to encroach on the rights (as in trade) of others 2 : INTRUDE, INTERFERE

in·ter·lop·er \'in-tər-,lō-pər, ,in-tər-'\ n (ca. 1590) : one that interlopes: as a : an illegal or unlicensed trader b : one that intrudes in a place or sphere of activity

in·ter·lude \'in-tər-,lüd\ n [ME enterlude, fr. ML interludium, fr. L inter- + ludus play — more at LUDICROUS] (14c) 1 : a usu. short simple play or dramatic entertainment 2 : an intervening or interruptive period, space, or event : INTERVAL 3 : a musical composition inserted between the parts of a longer composition, a drama, or a religious service

in·ter·lu·nar \,in-tər-'lü-nər\ also in·ter·lu·na·ry \-nə-rē\ adj [prob. fr. MF interlunaire, fr. L interlunium interlunar period, fr. inter- + luna moon — more at LUNAR] (1598) : relating to the interval between old and new moon when the moon is invisible

in·ter·mar·riage \,in-tər-'mar-ij\ n (1579) 1 : ENDOGAMY 2 : marriage between members of different groups

in·ter·mar·ry \-'mar-ē\ vi (1574) 1 a : to marry each other b : to marry within a group 2 : to become connected by intermarriage

in·ter·med·dle \,in-tər-'me-dᵊl\ vi [ME entermedlen, fr. MF entremedler, fr. OF, fr. entre- inter- + medler to mix — more at MEDDLE] (15c) : to meddle impertinently and officiously and usu. so as to interfere — in·ter·med·dler \-'med-lər, -'me-dᵊl-ər\ n

in·ter·me·di·a·cy \,in-tər-'mē-dē-ə-sē\ n (1713) 1 : the act or action of intermediating 2 : the quality or state of being intermediate

¹in·ter·me·di·ary \,in-tər-'mē-dē-,er-ē\ adj (1788) 1 : INTERMEDIATE 2 : acting as a mediator ⟨an ~ agent⟩ ⟨an ~ particle⟩

²intermediary n, pl -ar·ies (1791) 1 a : MEDIATOR, GO-BETWEEN b : MEDIUM, MEANS 2 : an intermediate form, product, or stage

¹in·ter·me·di·ate \,in-tər-'mē-dē-ət\ adj [ML intermediatus, fr. L intermedius, fr. inter- + medius mid, middle — more at MID] (15c) 1 : being or occurring at the middle place, stage, or degree or between extremes 2 : of or relating to an intermediate school ⟨an ~ curriculum⟩ — in·ter·me·di·ate·ly adv — in·ter·me·di·ate·ness n

²intermediate n (1650) 1 : one that is intermediate 2 : MEDIATOR, GO-BETWEEN 3 a : a chemical compound synthesized from simpler compounds and usu. intended to be used in later syntheses of more complex products b : a usu. short-lived chemical species formed in a reaction as an intermediate step between the starting material and the final product 4 : an automobile larger than a compact but smaller than a full-sized automobile

³in·ter·me·di·ate \-dē-,āt\ vi [ML intermediatus, pp. of intermediare, fr. L inter- + LL mediare to mediate] (1610) 1 : INTERVENE, INTERPOSE 2 : to act as an intermediate

intermediate host n (1878) 1 : a host which is normally used by a parasite in the course of its life cycle and in which it may multiply asexually but not sexually — compare DEFINITIVE HOST 2 a : RESERVOIR 3 b : VECTOR

intermediate school n (1842) 1 : JUNIOR HIGH SCHOOL 2 : a school usu. comprising grades 4 to 6

intermediate vector boson n (1968) : any of three particles that mediate the weak force — called also intermediate boson; compare w PARTICLE, Z PARTICLE

in·ter·me·di·a·tion \,in-tər-,mē-dē-'ā-shən\ n (1602) : the act of coming between : INTERVENTION, MEDIATION

in·ter·me·din \,in-tər-'mē-dᵊn\ n (1932) : MELANOCYTE-STIMULATING HORMONE

in·ter·ment \in-'tər-mənt\ n (14c) : the act or ceremony of interring

in·ter·mesh \,in-tər-'mesh\ vi (ca. 1903) : INTERLOCK ~ vt : to mesh together : INTERLOCK

in·ter·me·tal·lic \,in-tər-mə-'ta-lik\ adj (1900) : composed of two or more metals or of a metal and a nonmetal; esp : being an alloy having a characteristic crystal structure and usu. a definite composition ⟨~ compound⟩ — intermetallic n

in·ter·mez·zo \,in-tər-'met-(,)sō, -'med-(,)zō\ n, pl -zi \-(,)sē, -(,)zē\ or -zos [It, ultim. fr. L intermedius intermediate] (1771) 1 : a short light entr'acte 2 a : a movement coming between the major sections of an extended musical work (as an opera) b : a short independent instrumental composition 3 : a usu. brief interlude or diversion

in·ter·mi·na·ble \(,)in-'tər-mə-nə-bəl, -'tər-mə-\ adj [ME, fr. LL interminabilis, fr. L in- + terminare to terminate] (15c) : having or seeming to have no end; esp : wearisomely protracted ⟨a ~ sermon⟩ — in·ter·mi·na·ble·ness n — in·ter·mi·na·bly \-blē\ adv

in·ter·min·gle \,in-tər-'miŋ-gəl\ vb (15c) : INTERMIX

in·ter·mis·sion \,in-tər-'mi-shən\ n [ME intermyssyown, fr. L intermis-

sion-, intermissio, fr. intermittere] (15c) 1 : the act of intermitting : the state of being intermitted 2 : an interval between the parts of an entertainment (as the acts of a play) — in·ter·mis·sion·less adj

in·ter·mit \'in-'mit\ vb -mit·ted; -mit·ting [L intermittere, fr. inter- + mittere to send] vt (ca. 1542) : to cause to cease for a time or at intervals : DISCONTINUE ~ vi : to be intermittent — in·ter·mit·ter n

in·ter·mit·tence \-'mi-tən(t)s\ n (1796) : the quality or state of being intermittent

in·ter·mit·ten·cy \-'mi-tən(t)-sē\ n (1662) : INTERMITTENCE

in·ter·mit·tent \-'mi-tᵊnt\ adj [L intermittent-, intermittens, prp. of intermittere] (1601) : coming and going at intervals : not continuous ⟨~ rain⟩; also : OCCASIONAL ⟨~ trips abroad⟩ — in·ter·mit·tent·ly adv

in·ter·mix \,in-tər-'miks\ vb [back-formation fr. obs. intermixt intermingled, fr. L intermixtus, pp. of intermiscēre to intermix, fr. inter- + miscēre to mix — more at MIX] vt (1542) : to mix together ~ vi : to become mixed together — in·ter·mix·ture \-'miks-chər\ n

in·ter·mod·al \'in-'mō-dəl\ adj (1963) 1 : being or involving transportation by more than one form of carrier during a single journey 2 : used for intermodal transport

in·ter·mod·u·la·tion \-,mä-jə-'lā-shən\ n [ISV] (1931) : the production in an electrical device of currents having frequencies equal to the sums and differences of frequencies supplied to the device or of their harmonics

in·ter·mon·tane \,in-tər-'män-,tān\ or in·ter·mont \'in-tər-,mänt\ adj [L mont-, mons mount] (1807) : situated between mountains ⟨an ~ basin⟩

¹in·tern or in·terne \in-'tərn, 'in-,\ adj [MF interne, fr. L internus] (ca. 1500) archaic : INTERNAL

²in·tern \'in-,tərn, in-'\ vt (1866) : to confine or impound esp. during a war ⟨~ enemy aliens⟩ — in·tern·ee \,(,)in-,tər-'nē\ n — in·tern·ment \in-'tərn-mənt, 'in-,\ n

³in·tern also in·terne \'in-,tərn\ n [F interne, fr. interne, adj.] (ca. 1879) : an advanced student or graduate usu. in a professional field (as medicine or teaching) gaining supervised practical experience (as in a hospital or classroom) — in·tern·ship \-,ship\ n

⁴in·tern \-,tərn\ vi (ca. 1928) : to act as an intern

in·ter·nal \in-'tər-nᵊl, 'in-,\ adj [ME internalle, fr. L internus; akin to L inter between] (15c) 1 a (1) : situated or situated within the limits or surface of something: as a (1) : situated near the inside of the body (2) : situated on the side toward the median plane of the body b : of, relating to, or occurring within the confines of an organized structure (as a club, company, or state) ⟨~ affairs⟩ 2 : relating or belonging to or existing within the mind 3 : INTRINSIC, INHERENT ⟨~ evidence of forgery in a document⟩ 4 : present or arising within an organism or one of its parts ⟨~ stimulus⟩ 5 : applied or intended for application through the stomach by being swallowed ⟨an ~ remedy⟩ — in·ter·nal·i·ty \,in-,tər-'na-lə-tē\ n — in·ter·nal·ly \in-'tər-nᵊl-ē\ adv

internal combustion engine n (1884) : a heat engine in which the combustion that generates the heat takes place inside the engine proper instead of in a furnace

in·ter·nal·ise Brit var of INTERNALIZE

in·ter·nal·ize \in-'tər-nᵊl-,īz\ vt -ized; -iz·ing (1884) : to give a subjective character to; specif : to incorporate (as values or patterns of culture) within the self as conscious or subconscious guiding principles through learning or socialization — in·ter·nal·i·za·tion \-,tər-nᵊl-ə-'zā-shən\ n

internal medicine n (ca. 1904) : a branch of medicine that deals with the diagnosis and treatment of diseases not requiring surgery

internal respiration n (ca. 1890) : an exchange of gases between the cells of the body and the blood by way of the fluid bathing the cells — compare EXTERNAL RESPIRATION

internal rhyme n (1903) : rhyme between a word within a line and another either at the end of the same line or within another line

internal secretion n (1895) : HORMONE

¹in·ter·na·tion·al \,in-tər-'nash-nəl, -'na-shə-nᵊl\ adj (1780) 1 : of, relating to, or affecting two or more nations ⟨~ trade⟩ 2 : of, relating to, or constituting a group or association having members in two or more nations ⟨~ movement⟩ 3 : active, known, or reaching beyond national boundaries ⟨an ~ reputation⟩ — in·ter·na·tion·al·i·ty \-,na-shə-'na-lə-tē\ n — in·ter·na·tion·al·ly \-'nash-nə-lē, -'na-shə-nᵊl-ē\ adv

²international n (1870) : one that is international; esp : an organization of international scope

international date line n (ca. 1909) : an arbitrary line approximately along the 180th meridian designated as the place where each calendar day begins

in·ter·na·tion·al·ise Brit var of INTERNATIONALIZE

in·ter·na·tion·al·ism \-'nash-nə-,li-zəm, -'na-shə-nᵊl-,i-zəm\ n (1851) 1 : international character, principles, interests, or outlook 2 a : a policy of cooperation among nations b : an attitude or belief favoring such a policy — in·ter·na·tion·al·ist \-list, -ist\ n or adj

in·ter·na·tion·al·ize \,in-tər-'nash-nə-,līz, -'na-shə-nᵊl-,īz\ vt (ca. 1864) : to make international; also : to place under international control ⟨a proposal to ~ the city⟩ — in·ter·na·tion·al·i·za·tion \-,nash-nə-lə-'zā-shən, -,na-shə-nᵊl-ə-\ n

international law n (ca. 1828) : a body of rules that control or affect the rights of nations in their relations with each other

International Phonetic Alphabet n (1898) : IPA

international pitch n (1904) : a tuning standard of 440 vibrations per second for A above middle C

international relations n pl but sing in constr (1951) : a branch of political science concerned with relations between nations and primarily with foreign policies

International Scientific Vocabulary n (ca. 1959) : a part of the vocabulary of the sciences and other specialized studies that consists of words or other linguistic forms current in two or more languages and

\ə\ abut \ᵊ\ kitten, F table \ər\ further \a\ ash \ā\ ace \ä\ mop, mar \au̇\ out \ch\ chin \e\ bet \ē\ easy \g\ go \i\ hit \ī\ ice \j\ job \ŋ\ sing \ō\ go \ȯ\ law \ȯi\ boy \th\ thin \t̲h̲\ the \ü\ loot \u̇\ foot \y\ yet \zh\ vision \á, k̲, ⁿ, œ, œ̄, ue, ūe, ʸ\ see Guide to Pronunciation differing from New Latin in being adapted to the structure of the individual languages in which they appear

International Style *n* (1932)   **1** : a style in European art of the 14th and early 15th centuries marked by sinuous line, rich color, and decorative surface detail   **2** : a style in architecture developed in the 1920s that uses modern materials (as steel, glass, and reinforced concrete), expresses structure directly, and eliminates nonstructural ornament

International System of Units *n* (1961) : a system of units based on the metric system and developed and refined by international convention esp. for scientific work

international unit *n* (1922) : a quantity of a biologic (as a vitamin) that produces a particular biological effect agreed upon as an international standard

in·ter·ne·cine \,in-tər-'ne-,sēn, -'nē-s*ə*n, -'nē-,sīn, -nə-'sēn; in-'tər-nə-,sēn\ *adj* [L *internecinus*, fr. *internecare* to destroy, kill, fr. *inter-* + *necare* to kill, fr. *nec-, nex* violent death — more at NOXIOUS] (1663)   **1** : marked by slaughter : DEADLY; *esp* : mutually destructive   **2** : of, relating to, or involving conflict within a group ⟨bitter ∼ feuds⟩

in·ter·neu·ron \,in-tər-'nur-,än, -'nyur-\ *n* (1939) : an internuncial neuron — **in·ter·neu·ro·nal** \-'nur-ə-n*ə*l, -'nyur-; -,nu-'rō-, -nyu-'\ *adj*

in·ter·nist \'in-,tər-nist\ *n* (1904) : a specialist in internal medicine

in·ter·node \'in-tər-,nōd\ *n* [L *internodium*, fr. *inter-* + *nodus* knot] (1667) : an interval or part between two nodes (as of a stem) — **in·ter·nod·al** \,in-tər-'nō-d*ə*l\ *adj*

in·ter·nun·ci·al \,in-tər-'nən(t)-sē-əl, -'nun(t)-\ *adj* (1845)   **1** : of or relating to an internuncio   **2** : serving to link sensory and motor neurons

in·ter·nun·cio \,in-tər-'nən(t)-sē-,ō, -'nun(t)-\ *n* [It *internunzio,* fr. L *internuntius, internuncius,* fr. *inter-* + *nuntius, nuncius* messenger] (1641)   **1** : a messenger between two parties : GO-BETWEEN   **2** : a papal legate of lower rank than a nuncio

in·ter·o·cep·tive \,in-tə-rō-'sep-tiv\ *adj* [*interior* + *-o-* + *-ceptive* (as in *receptive*)] (ca. 1921) : of, relating to, or being stimuli arising within the body and esp. in the viscera

in·ter·o·cep·tor \-'tər\ *n* (1906) : a sensory receptor excited by interoceptive stimuli

in·ter·op·er·a·bil·i·ty \,in-tə-,rä-p(ə-)rə-'bi-lə-tē\ *n* (1977) : ability of a system (as a weapons system) to use the parts or equipment of another system — **in·ter·op·er·a·ble** \-'rä-p(ə-)rə-bəl\ *adj*

in·ter·pel·late \in-tər-'pe-,lāt, -pə-'lāt\ *vt* **-lat·ed; -lat·ing** [L *interpellatus,* pp. of *interpellare* to interrupt, fr. *inter-* + *-pellare* (fr. *pellere* to drive) — more at FELT] (1874) : to question (as a foreign minister) formally concerning an official action or policy or personal conduct — **in·ter·pel·la·tion** \-pə-'lā-shən\ *n* — **in·ter·pel·la·tor** \-'pe-,lā-tər, -pə-'lā-\ *n*

in·ter·pen·e·trate \,in-tər-'pe-nə-,trāt\ *vi* (ca. 1810) : to penetrate mutually ∼ *vt* : to penetrate between, within, or throughout : PERMEATE — **in·ter·pen·e·tra·tion** \-,pe-nə-'trā-shən\ *n*

in·ter·per·son·al \-'pərs-nəl, -'pər-s*ə*n-əl\ *adj* (1842) : being, relating to, or involving relations between persons — **in·ter·per·son·al·ly** *adv*

in·ter·phase \'in-tər-,fāz\ *n* (1913) : the interval between the end of one mitotic or meiotic division and the beginning of another

in·ter·plant \,in-tər-'plant\ *vt* (1911) : to plant a crop between (plants of another kind); *also* : to set out young trees among (existing growth)

in·ter·play \'in-tər-,plā\ *n* (1862) : INTERACTION ⟨the ∼ of opposing forces⟩ — **in·ter·play** \,in-tər-', in-tər-,\ *vi*

in·ter·plead \,in-tər-'plēd\ *vi* [AF *enterpleder,* fr. *enter-* inter- + *pleder* to plead, fr. OF *plaidier* — more at PLEAD] (1567) : to go to trial with each other in order to determine a right on which the action of a third party depends

¹in·ter·plead·er \-'plē-dər\ *n* [AF *enterpleder,* fr. *enterpleder,* v.] (1567) : a proceeding to enable a person to compel parties making the same claim against him to litigate the matter between themselves

²interpleader *n* (ca. 1846) : one that interpleads

in·ter·po·late \in-'tər-pə-,lāt\ *vb* **-lat·ed; -lat·ing** [L *interpolatus,* pp. of *interpolare* to refurbish, alter, interpolate, fr. *inter-* + *-polare* (fr. *polire* to polish)] *vt* (1612)   **1 a** : to alter or corrupt (as a text) by inserting new or foreign matter   **b** : to insert (words) into a text or into a conversation   **2** : to insert between other things or parts : INTERCALATE   **3** : to estimate values of (a function) between two known values ∼ *vi* : to make insertions (as of estimated values) — **in·ter·po·la·tion** \-,tər-pə-'lā-shən\ *n* — **in·ter·po·la·tive** \-'tər-pə-,lā-tiv\ *adj* — **in·ter·po·la·tor** \-,lā-tər\ *n*

in·ter·pose \,in-tər-'pōz\ *vb* **-posed; -pos·ing** [MF *interposer,* fr. L *interponere* (perf. indic. *interposui*), fr. *inter-* + *ponere* to put — more at POSITION] *vt* (1582)   **1 a** : to place in an intervening position   **b** : to put (oneself) between : INTRUDE   **2** : to put forth by way of interference or intervention   **3** : to introduce or throw in between the parts of a conversation or argument ∼ *vi*   **1** : to be or come between   **2** : to step in between parties at variance : INTERVENE   **3** : INTERRUPT — **in·ter·pos·er** *n*

syn INTERPOSE, INTERFERE, INTERVENE, MEDIATE, INTERCEDE mean to come or go between. INTERPOSE often implies no more than this ⟨*interposed* herself between him and the door⟩. INTERFERE implies hindering ⟨noise *interfered* with my concentration⟩. INTERVENE may imply an occurring in space or time between two things or a stepping in to stop a conflict ⟨quarreled until the manager *intervened*⟩. MEDIATE implies intervening between hostile factions ⟨*mediated* between the parties⟩. INTERCEDE implies acting in behalf of an offender in begging mercy or forgiveness ⟨*interceded* on our behalf⟩. *syn* see in addition INTRODUCE

in·ter·po·si·tion \-pə-'zi-shən\ *n* (14c)   **1 a** : the act of interposing   **b** : the action of a state whereby its sovereignty is placed between its citizens and the federal government   **2** : something interposed

in·ter·pret \in-'tər-prət, -pət\ *vb* [ME, fr. MF & L; MF *interpreter,* fr. L *interpretari,* fr. *interpret-, interpres* agent, negotiator, interpreter] *vt* (14c)   **1** : to explain or tell the meaning of : present in understandable terms   **2** : to conceive in the light of individual belief, judgment, or circumstance : CONSTRUE   **3** : to represent by means of art : bring to realization by performance or direction ⟨∼s a role⟩ ∼ *vi* : to act as an interpreter between speakers of different languages *syn* see EXPLAIN — **in·ter·pret·abil·i·ty** \-,tər-prə-tə-'bi-lə-tē, -pə-tə-\ *n* — **in·ter·pret·able** \-'tər-prə-tə-bəl, -pə-tə-\ *adj*

in·ter·pre·ta·tion \in-,tər-prə-'tā-shən, -pə-\ *n* (14c)   **1** : the act or the result of interpreting : EXPLANATION   **2** : a particular adaptation or version of a work, method, or style   **3** : a teaching technique that combines factual with stimulating explanatory information ⟨natural history ∼ program⟩ — **in·ter·pre·ta·tion·al** \-shnəl, -shə-n*ə*l\ *adj* — **in·ter·pre·ta·tive** \in-'tər-prə-,tā-tiv *also* -prə-tə-tiv\ *adj* — **in·ter·pre·ta·tive·ly** *adv* — **in·ter·pre·tive** \-'tər-prə-tiv, -pə-\ *adj* — **in·ter·pre·tive·ly** *adv*

in·ter·pret·er \in-'tər-prə-tər, -pə-\ *n* (14c)   **1** : one that interprets: as **a** : one who translates orally for parties conversing in different languages   **b** : one who explains or expounds   **2 a** : a machine that prints on punched cards the symbols recorded in them by perforations   **b** : a computer program that translates an instruction into machine language and executes it before going to the next instruction

in·ter·prox·i·mal \,in-tər-'präk-sə-məl\ *adj* (1897) : situated or used in the areas between adjoining teeth ⟨∼ space⟩

in·ter·pu·pil·lary \,in-tər-'pyü-pə-,ler-ē\ *adj* (ca. 1904) : extending between the pupils of the eyes; *also* : extending between the centers of a pair of spectacle lenses ⟨∼ distance⟩

in·ter·ra·cial \-'rā-shəl\ *adj* (1888) : of, involving, or designed for members of different races — **in·ter·ra·cial·ly** \-shə-lē\ *adv*

interred *past and past part of* INTER

in·ter·reg·num \,in-tə-'reg-nəm\ *n, pl* **-nums** *or* **-na** \-nə\ [L, fr. *inter-* + *regnum* reign — more at REIGN] (1590)   **1** : the time during which a throne is vacant between two successive reigns or regimes   **2** : a period during which the normal functions of government or control are suspended   **3** : a lapse or pause in a continuous series

in·ter·re·late \,in-tə(r)-ri-'lāt\ *vt* (1888) : to bring into mutual relation ∼ *vi* : to have mutual relationship — **in·ter·re·la·tion** \-'lā-shən\ *n* — **in·ter·re·la·tion·ship** \-,ship\ *n*

in·ter·re·lat·ed \-'lā-təd\ *adj* (1827) : having a mutual or reciprocal relation — **in·ter·re·lat·ed·ly** *adv* — **in·ter·re·lat·ed·ness** *n*

interring *pres part of* INTER

in·ter·ro·bang \in-'ter-ə-,baŋ\ *n* [*interrogation* (point) + *bang* (printers' slang for *exclamation point*)] (1967) : a punctuation mark ? designed for use esp. at the end of an exclamatory rhetorical question

in·ter·ro·gate \in-'ter-ə-,gāt\ *vt* **-gat·ed; -gat·ing** [L *interrogatus,* pp. of *interrogare,* fr. *inter-* + *rogare* to ask — more at RIGHT] (15c)   **1** : to question formally and systematically   **2** : to give or send out a signal to (as a transponder or computer) for triggering an appropriate response   *syn* see ASK — **in·ter·ro·ga·tee** \-,ter-ə-(,)gä-'tē\ *n* — **in·ter·ro·ga·tion** \-,ter-ə-'gä-shən\ *n* — **in·ter·ro·ga·tion·al** \-shnəl, -shə-n*ə*l\ *adj*

interrogation point *n* (ca. 1864) : QUESTION MARK

¹in·ter·rog·a·tive \,in-tə-'rä-gə-tiv\ *adj* (15c)   **1 a** : used in a question   **b** : having the form or force of a question   **2** : INQUISITIVE, QUESTIONING — **in·ter·rog·a·tive·ly** *adv*

²interrogative *n* (1522)   **1** : a word (as *who, what, which*) or a particle (as Latin *-ne*) used in asking questions   **2** : QUESTION 1a

in·ter·ro·ga·tor \in-'ter-ə-,gā-tər\ *n* (1751)   **1** : one that interrogates   **2** : a radio transmitter and receiver for sending out a signal that triggers a transponder and for receiving and displaying the reply

¹in·ter·rog·a·to·ry \,in-tə-'rä-gə-,tōr-ē, -,tȯr-\ *n, pl* **-ries** (1533) : a formal question or inquiry; *esp* : a written question required to be answered under direction of a court

²interrogatory *adj* (1576) : INTERROGATIVE

in·ter·ro·gee \in-,ter-ə-'gē\ *n* (1919) : one who is interrogated

¹in·ter·rupt \,in-tə-'rəpt\ *vb* [ME, fr. L *interruptus,* pp. of *interrumpere,* fr. *inter-* + *rumpere* to break — more at REAVE] *vt* (15c)   **1** : to stop or hinder by breaking in   **2** : to break the uniformity or continuity of ∼ *vi* : to break in upon an action; *esp* : to break in with questions or remarks while another is speaking — **in·ter·rupt·ible** \-'rəp-tə-bəl\ *adj* — **in·ter·rup·tion** \-'rəp-shən\ *n* — **in·ter·rup·tive** \-'rəp-tiv\ *adv*

²interrupt \,in-tə-'rəpt, 'in-tə-,\ *n* (1957) : a feature of a computer that permits the execution of a program to be interrupted in order to perform a special set of operations; *also* : the interruption itself

in·ter·rupt·er *also* **in·ter·rup·tor** \,in-tə-'rəp-tər\ *n* (ca. 1512) : one that interrupts; *esp* : a device for interrupting an electric current usu. automatically

in·ter·scho·las·tic \,in-tər-skə-'las-tik\ *adj* (1879) : existing or carried on between schools ⟨∼ athletics⟩

in·ter se \,in-tər-'sā, -'sē\ *adv or adj* [L] (1845) : among or between themselves

in·ter·sect \,in-tər-'sekt\ *vb* [L *intersectus,* pp. of *intersecare,* fr. *inter-* + *secare* to cut — more at SAW] *vt* (1615) : to pierce or divide by passing through or across : CROSS ∼ *vi*   **1** : to meet and cross at a point   **2** : to share a common area : OVERLAP

in·ter·sec·tion \,in-tər-'sek-shən, *esp in sense* 2 'in-tər-,\ *n* (1559)   **1** : the act or process of intersecting   **2** : a place or area where two or more things (as streets) intersect   **3 a** : the set of elements common to two or more sets; *esp* : the set of points common to two geometric configurations   **b** : the operation of finding the intersection of two or more sets

a intersection 3a

in·ter·ser·vice \,in-tər-'sər-vəs\ *adj* (1946) : existing between or relating to two or more of the armed services ⟨∼ rivalry⟩

in·ter·ses·sion \'in-tər-,se-shən\ *n* (1932) : a period between two academic sessions or terms sometimes utilized for brief concentrated courses

in·ter·sex \'in-tər-,seks\ *n* [ISV] (1910) : an intersexual individual

in·ter·sex·u·al \,in-tər-'sek-shə-wəl, -shwəl, -shəl\ *adj* [ISV] (ca. 1866)   **1** : existing between sexes ⟨∼ hostility⟩   **2** : intermediate in sexual characters between a typical male and a typical female — **in·ter·sex·u·al·i·ty** \-,sek-shə-'wa-lə-tē\ *n* — **in·ter·sex·u·al·ly** \-'sek-shə-wə-lē, -shwə-lē, -shə-lē\ *adv*

¹in·ter·space \'in-tər-,spās\ *n* (15c) : an intervening space : INTERVAL

²in·ter·space \,in-tər-'spās\ *vt* (1685) : to occupy or fill the space between

in·ter·spe·cif·ic \,in-tər-spi-'si-fik\ *also* **in·ter·spe·cies** \-'spē-(,)shēz, -,(,)sēz\ *adj* (1889) : existing, occurring, or arising between species ⟨∼ hybrid⟩

in·ter·sperse \,in-tər-'spərs\ *vt* **-spersed; -spers·ing** [L *interspersus* interspersed, fr. *inter-* + *sparsus*, pp. of *spargere* to scatter — more at SPARK] (1566) **1** : to place something at intervals in or among **2** : to insert at intervals among other things ⟨*interspersing* drawings throughout the text⟩ — **in·ter·sper·sion** \-'spər-zhən, -shən\ *n*

in·ter·sta·di·al \,in-tər-'stā-dē-əl\ *n* [ISV *inter-* + NL *stadium* stage, phase, fr. L — more at STADIUM] (1914) : a subdivision within a glacial stage marking a temporary retreat of the ice

¹in·ter·state \,in-tər-'stāt\ *adj* (1844) : of, connecting, or existing between two or more states esp. of the U.S. ⟨~ commerce⟩

²in·ter·state \'in-tər-,stāt\ *n* (1968) : any of a system of expressways connecting most major U.S. cities — called also *interstate highway*

in·ter·stel·lar \-'ste-lər\ *adj* (1626) : located, taking place, or traveling among the stars esp. of the Milky Way galaxy

in·ter·ster·ile \-'ster-əl, *chiefly Brit* -,il\ *adj* (1916) : incapable of producing offspring by interbreeding — **in·ter·ste·ril·i·ty** \-stə-'ri-lə-tē\ *n*

in·ter·stice \in-'tər-stəs\ *n, pl* **-stic·es** \-stə-,sēz, -stə-səz\ [ME, fr. L *interstitium*, fr. *inter-* + *-stit-, -stes* standing (as in *superstes* standing over) — more at SUPERSTITION] (15c) **1 a** : a space that intervenes between things; *esp* : one between closely spaced things **b** : a gap or break in something generally continuous ⟨the ~s of society⟩ ⟨passages of genuine literary merit in the ~s of the ludicrous . . . plots —Joyce Carol Oates⟩ **2** : a short space of time between events

in·ter·sti·tial \,in-tər-'sti-shəl\ *adj* (1646) **1** : relating to or situated in the interstices **2 a** : situated within but not restricted to or characteristic of a particular organ or tissue — used esp. of fibrous tissue **b** : affecting the interstitial tissues of an organ or part **3** : being or relating to a crystalline compound in which usu. small atoms or ions of a nonmetal occupy holes between the larger metal atoms or ions in the crystal lattice — **in·ter·sti·tial·ly** \-shə-lē\ *adv*

in·ter·sub·jec·tive \,in-tər-səb-'jek-tiv\ *adj* (1899) **1** : involving or occurring between separate conscious minds ⟨~ communication⟩ **2** : accessible to or capable of being established for two or more subjects : OBJECTIVE — **in·ter·sub·jec·tive·ly** *adv* — **in·ter·sub·jec·tiv·i·ty** \-(,)səb-,jek-'ti-və-tē\ *n*

in·ter·tes·ta·men·tal \-,tes-tə-'men-t⁹l\ *adj* (1929) : of, relating to, or forming the period of two centuries between the composition of the last book of the Old Testament and the first book of the New Testament

in·ter·tid·al \-'tī-d⁹l\ *adj* (1883) : of, relating to, or being the part of the littoral zone above low-tide mark — **in·ter·tid·al·ly** \-d⁹l-ē\ *adv*

in·ter·tie \'in-tər-,tī\ *n* (1951) : an interconnection permitting passage of current between two or more electric utility systems

in·ter·till \,in-tər-'til\ *vt* (1912) : to cultivate between the rows of (a crop) — **in·ter·till·age** \-'ti-lij\ *n*

in·ter·trop·i·cal \-'trä-pi-kəl\ *adj* (1794) **1** : situated between or within the tropics **2** : relating to regions within the tropics : TROPICAL

in·ter·twine \-'twīn\ *vt* (1641) : to unite by twining one with another ~ *vi* : to twine about one another; *also* : to become mutually involved — **in·ter·twine·ment** \-mənt\ *n*

in·ter·twist \-'twist\ *vb* (ca. 1659) : INTERTWINE — **in·ter·twist** \'in-tər-,twist\ *n*

in·ter·val \'in-tər-vəl\ *n* [ME *intervalle*, fr. MF, fr. L *intervallum* space between ramparts, interval, fr. *inter-* + *vallum* rampart — more at WALL] (14c) **1 a** : a space of time between events or states **b** *Brit* : INTERMISSION **2 a** : a space between objects, units, points, or states **b** : difference in pitch between tones **3** : a set of real numbers between two numbers either including or excluding one or both of them **4** : one of a series of fast-paced runs interspersed with jogging for training (as of a runner) — **in·ter·val·lic** \,in-tər-'va-lik\ *adj*

in·ter·vale \'in-tər-vəl, -,vāl\ *n* [obs. *intervale* interval] (1647) *chiefly NewEng* : BOTTOMLAND

in·ter·val·om·e·ter \,in-tər-və-'lä-mə-tər\ *n* (1933) : a device that operates a control (as for a camera shutter) at regular intervals

in·ter·vene \,in-tər-'vēn\ *vi* **-vened; -ven·ing** [L *intervenire* to come between, fr. *inter-* + *venire* to come — more at COME] (1587) **1** : to occur, fall, or come between points of time or events **2** : to enter or appear as an irrelevant or extraneous feature or circumstance **3** : to come in or between by way of hindrance or modification ⟨~ to stop a fight⟩ **4** : to occur or lie between two things **5 a** : to become a third party to a legal proceeding begun by others for the protection of an alleged interest **b** : to interfere usu. by force or threat of force in another nation's internal affairs esp. to compel or prevent an action or to maintain or alter a condition *syn* see INTERPOSE — **in·ter·ven·tion** \-'ven(t)-shən\ *n*

in·ter·ve·nor \-'vē-nər, -,nòr\ *or* **in·ter·ven·er** \-'vē-nər\ *n* (1621) : one who intervenes; *esp* : one who intervenes as a third party in a legal proceeding

in·ter·ven·tion·ism \-'ven(t)-shə-,ni-zəm\ *n* (1923) : the theory or practice of intervening; *specif* : governmental interference in economic affairs at home or in political affairs of another country — **in·ter·ven·tion·ist** \-'vench-nist, -'ven(t)-shə-nist\ *n or adj*

in·ter·ver·te·bral disk \,in-tər-'vər-tə-brəl-, -,(,)vər-tē-\ *n* (ca. 1860) : any of the tough elastic disks that are interposed between the centra of adjoining vertebrae and that consist of an outer fibrous ring enclosing an inner pulpy nucleus

in·ter·view \'in-tər-,vyü\ *n* [MF *entrevue*, fr. (s')*entrevoir* to see one another, meet, fr. *entre-* inter- + *voir* to see — more at VIEW] (1514) **1** : a formal consultation usu. to evaluate qualifications (as of a prospective student or employee) **2 a** : a meeting at which information is obtained (as by a reporter, television commentator, or pollster) from a person **b** : a report or reproduction of information so obtained **3** : INTERVIEWEE — **interview** *vb* — **in·ter·view·er** *n*

in·ter·view·ee \,in-tər-(,)vyü-'ē\ *n* (1884) : one who is interviewed

in·ter vi·vos \'in-tər-'vē-,vōs, -'vī-\ *adv or adj* [LL] (1837) : between living persons ⟨transaction *inter vivos*⟩; *esp* : from one living person to another ⟨*inter vivos* gifts⟩ ⟨property transferred *inter vivos*⟩

in·ter·vo·cal·ic \,in-tər-vō-'ka-lik\ *adj* (1887) : immediately preceded and immediately followed by a vowel — **in·ter·vo·cal·i·cal·ly** \-li-k(ə-)lē\ *adv*

in·ter·weave \,in-tər-'wēv\ *vb* **-wove** \-'wōv\ *also* **-weaved; -wo·ven** \-'wō-vən\ *also* **-weaved; -weav·ing** *vt* (1598) **1** : to weave together **2** : to mix or blend together ⟨*interweaving* his own insights . . . with letters and memoirs —Phoebe Adams⟩ ~ *vi* : INTERTWINE, INTERMIN-

GLE — **in·ter·weave** \'in-tər-,wēv\ *n* — **in·ter·wo·ven** \,in-tər-'wō-vən\ *adj*

in·tes·ta·cy \in-'tes-tə-sē\ *n* (1767) : the quality or state of being or dying intestate

¹in·tes·tate \in-'tes-,tāt, -tət\ *adj* [ME, fr. L *intestatus*, fr. *in-* + *testatus* testate] (14c) **1** : having made no valid will ⟨died ~⟩ **2** : not disposed of by will ⟨an ~ estate⟩

²intestate *n* (1658) : one who dies intestate

in·tes·ti·nal \in-'tes-tə-n⁹l, -'tes(t)-nəl, -'te-s⁹n-əl, *Brit often* ,in-(,)tes-'tī-n⁹l\ *adj* (15c) **1** : affecting or occurring in the intestine; *also* : living in the intestine **2** : of, relating to, or being the intestine — **in·tes·ti·nal·ly** *adv*

intestinal fortitude *n* [euphemism for *guts*] (ca. 1937) : COURAGE, STAMINA

¹in·tes·tine \in-'tes-tən\ *adj* [ME, fr. MF or L; MF *intestin*, fr. L *intestinus*, fr. *intus* within — more at ENT.] (15c) : INTERNAL; *specif* : of or relating to the internal affairs of a state or country ⟨~ war⟩

²intestine *n* [ME, fr. MF *intestin*, fr. L *intestinum*, fr. neut. of *intestinus*] (15c) : the tubular part of the alimentary canal that extends from the stomach to the anus

in·ti \'in-tē\ *n* [Quechua, sun] (1985) : the basic monetary unit of Peru from 1985 to 1990

in·ti·ma \'in-tə-mə\ *n, pl* **-mae** \-,mē, -,mī\ *or* **-mas** [NL, fr. L, fem. of *intimus*] (1873) : the innermost coat of an organ (as a blood vessel) consisting usu. of an endothelial layer backed by connective tissue and elastic tissue — **in·ti·mal** \-məl\ *adj*

in·ti·ma·cy \'in-tə-mə-sē\ *n, pl* **-cies** (1641) **1** : the state of being intimate : FAMILIARITY **2** : something of a personal or private nature

¹in·ti·mate \'in-tə-,māt\ *vt* **-mat·ed; -mat·ing** [LL *intimatus*, pp. of *intimare* to put in, announce, fr. L *intimus* innermost, superl. of (assumed) OL *interus* inward — more at INTERIOR] (1522) **1** : to make known esp. publicly or formally : ANNOUNCE **2** : to communicate delicately and indirectly : HINT *syn* see SUGGEST — **in·ti·mat·er** *n* — **in·ti·ma·tion** \,in-tə-'mā-shən\ *n*

²in·ti·mate \'in-tə-mət\ *adj* [alter. of obs. *intime*, fr. L *intimus*] (1632) **1 a** : INTRINSIC, ESSENTIAL **b** : belonging to or characterizing one's deepest nature **2** : marked by very close association, contact, or familiarity ⟨~ knowledge of the law⟩ **3 a** : marked by a warm friendship developing through long association **b** : suggesting informal warmth or privacy ⟨~ clubs⟩ **4** : of a very personal or private nature — **in·ti·mate·ly** *adv* — **in·ti·mate·ness** *n*

³in·ti·mate \'in-tə-mət\ *n* (1659) : an intimate friend or confidant

in·tim·i·date \in-'ti-mə-,dāt\ *vt* **-dat·ed; -dat·ing** [ML *intimidatus*, pp. of *intimidare*, fr. L *in-* + *timidus* timid] (1646) **1** : to make timid or fearful : FRIGHTEN; *esp* : to compel or deter by or as if by threats — **in·tim·i·dat·ing·ly** \-,dā-tiŋ-lē\ *adv* — **in·tim·i·da·tion** \,ti-mə-'dā-shən\ *n* — **in·tim·i·da·tor** \-'ti-mə-,dā-tər\ *n*

syn INTIMIDATE, COW, BULLDOZE, BULLY, BROWBEAT mean to frighten into submission. INTIMIDATE implies inducing fear or a sense of inferiority into another ⟨*intimidated* by so many other bright freshmen⟩. COW implies reduction to a state where the spirit is broken or all courage is lost ⟨not at all *cowed* by the odds against making it in show business⟩. BULLDOZE implies an intimidating or an overcoming of resistance usu. by urgings, demands, or threats ⟨*bulldozed* the city council into approving the plan⟩. BULLY implies intimidation through threats, insults, or aggressive behavior ⟨*bullied* into giving up their lunch money⟩. BROWBEAT implies a cowing through arrogant, scornful, contemptuous, or insolent treatment ⟨*browbeat* the witness into a contradiction⟩.

in·tim·i·da·to·ry \-'ti-mə-də-,tōr-ē, -,tòr-\ *adj* (ca. 1846) : tending to intimidate

in·tinc·tion \in-'tiŋ(k)-shən\ *n* [LL *intinction-, intinctio* baptism, fr. L *intingere* to dip in, fr. *in-* + *tingere* to dip, moisten — more at TINGE] (1872) : the administration of the sacrament of Communion by dipping the bread in the wine and giving both together to the communicant

in·tine \'in-,tēn\ *n* [prob. fr. G, fr. L *intus* within + NL *in-* fibrous tissue, fr. Gk *in-, is* tendon] (1835) : the inner mostly cellulose wall of a spore (as a pollen grain)

in·tit·ule \in-'ti-(,)chü(ə)l\ *vt* **-uled; -ul·ing** [MF *intituler*, fr. LL *intitulare*, fr. L *in-* + *titulus* title] (15c) *Brit* : to furnish (as a legislative act) with a title or designation

in·to \in-(,)tü, -tə\ *prep* [ME, fr. OE *intō*, fr. *in-* ²*in* + *tō* to] (bef. 12c) **1** — used as a function word to indicate entry, introduction, insertion, superposition, or inclusion ⟨came ~ the house⟩ ⟨enter ~ an alliance⟩ **2 a** : to the state, condition, or form of ⟨got ~ trouble⟩ **b** : to the occupation, action, or possession of ⟨go ~ farming⟩ **c** : involved with or interested in ⟨~ hard drugs⟩ ⟨~ Latin epigrammatists⟩ **3** — used as a function word to indicate a period of time or an extent of space part of which is passed or occupied ⟨far ~ the night⟩ **4** : in the direction of ⟨looking ~ the sun⟩ **5** : to a position of contact with : AGAINST ⟨ran ~ a wall⟩ **6** — used as a function word to indicate the dividend in division ⟨dividing 3 ~ 6 gives 2⟩

in·tol·er·a·ble \(,)in-'täl-rə-bəl, -'tä-lə-rə-, -'tä-lər-bəl\ *adj* [ME, fr. L *intolerabilis*, fr. *in-* + *tolerabilis* tolerable] (15c) **1** : not tolerable : UNBEARABLE ⟨~ pain⟩ **2** : EXCESSIVE — **in·tol·er·a·bil·i·ty** \-,täl-rə-'bi-lə-tē, -,tä-lə-rə-, -,tä-lər-'\ *n* — **in·tol·er·a·ble·ness** \-'täl-rə-bəl-nəs, -'tä-lə-rə-, -'tä-lər-bəl-\ *n* — **in·tol·er·a·bly** \-blē\ *adv*

in·tol·er·ance \(,)in-'täl-rən(t)s, -'tä-lə-\ *n* (1765) : the quality or state of being intolerant; *esp* : exceptional sensitivity (as to a drug)

in·tol·er·ant \-rənt\ *adj* (ca. 1735) **1** : unable or unwilling to endure ⟨a plant ~ of direct sunlight⟩ ⟨~ of criticism⟩ **2 a** : unwilling to grant equal freedom of expression esp. in religious matters : BIGOTED **b** : unwilling to grant or share social, political, or professional rights — **in·tol·er·ant·ly** *adv* — **in·tol·er·ant·ness** *n*

in·to·nate \'in-tə-,nāt, -(,)tō-\ *vt* **-nat·ed; -nat·ing** (1795) : INTONE, UTTER

\ə\ abut \ᵊ\ kitten, F table \ər\ further \a\ ash \ā\ ace \ä\ mop, mar \au̇\ out \ch\ chin \e\ bet \ē\ easy \g\ go \i\ hit \ī\ ice \j\ job \ŋ\ sing \ō\ go \ȯ\ law \ȯi\ boy \th\ thin \t͟h\ the \ü\ loot \u̇\ foot \y\ yet \zh\ vision \ä, ḵ, ⁿ, œ, œ̄, ᵫ, ᵫ̄, ᵞ\ *see* Guide to Pronunciation

in·to·na·tion \ˌin-tə-ˈnā-shən, -ˌtō-\ *n* (1620) **1** : the act of intoning and esp. of chanting **2** : something that is intoned; *specif* : the opening tones of a Gregorian chant **3** : the ability to play or sing notes in tune **4** : manner of utterance; *specif* : the rise and fall in pitch of the voice in speech — **in·to·na·tion·al** \-shnəl, -shə-nᵊl\ *adj*

in·tone \in-ˈtōn\ *vb* **in·toned; in·ton·ing** [ME *entonen*, fr. MF *entoner*, fr. ML *intonare*, fr. L *in-* + *tonus* tone] *vt* (15c) : to utter in musical or prolonged tones : recite in singing tones or in a monotone ~ *vi* : to utter something in singing tones or in monotone — **in·ton·er** *n*

in to·to \in-ˈtō-(ˌ)tō\ *adv* [L, on the whole] (1796) : TOTALLY, ENTIRELY

in·tox·i·cant \in-ˈtäk-si-kənt\ *n* (1863) : something that intoxicates; *esp* : an alcoholic drink — **intoxicant** *adj*

¹**in·tox·i·cate** \-si-kət\ *adj* (15c) *archaic* : INTOXICATED

²**in·tox·i·cate** \-sə-ˌkāt\ *vt* **-cat·ed; -cat·ing** [ME, fr. ML *intoxicatus*, pp. of *intoxicare*, fr. L *in-* + *toxicum* poison — more at TOXIC] (15c) **1** : POISON **2 a** : to excite or stupefy by alcohol or a drug esp. to the point where physical and mental control is markedly diminished **b** : to excite or elate to the point of enthusiasm or frenzy

in·tox·i·cat·ed \-sə-ˌkā-təd\ *adj* (1576) : affected by or as if by alcohol : DRUNK — **in·tox·i·cat·ed·ly** \-ˌkā-təd-lē\ *adv*

in·tox·i·ca·tion \in-ˌtäk-sə-ˈkā-shən\ *n* (15c) **1** : an abnormal state that is essentially a poisoning ⟨intestinal ~⟩ **2 a** : the condition of being drunk : INEBRIATION **b** : a strong excitement or elation

in·tra- \ˈin-trə, -(ˌ)trä\ *prefix* [LL, fr. L *intra*, fr. (assumed) OL *interus*, adj., inward — more at INTERIOR] **1 a** : within ⟨intragalactic⟩ **b** : during ⟨intraday⟩ **c** : between layers of ⟨intradermal⟩ **2** : INTRO- ⟨an *intra*muscular injection⟩

in·tra·ar·te·ri·al \-är-ˈtir-ē-əl\ *adj* (1897) : situated or occurring within, administered into, or involving entry by way of an artery — **in·tra·ar·te·ri·al·ly** \-ē-ə-lē\ *adv*

in·tra·ar·tic·u·lar \-är-ˈti-kyə-lər\ *adj* (ca. 1888) : situated within, occurring within, or administered by entry into a joint

in·tra·car·di·ac \-ˈkär-dē-ˌak\ *also* **in·tra·car·di·al** \-dē-əl\ *adj* (1876) : situated or occurring within or introduced or involving entry into the heart ⟨~ surgery⟩ ⟨an ~ catheter⟩ — **in·tra·car·di·al·ly** \-dē-ə-lē\ *adv*

in·tra·cel·lu·lar \ˈsel-yə-lər\ *adj* (1876) : existing, occurring, or functioning within a cell ⟨~ parasites⟩ — **in·tra·cel·lu·lar·ly** *adv*

in·tra·ce·re·bral \-sə-ˈrē-brəl, -ˈser-ə-\ *adj* (1881) : situated in, introduced into, or made into the cerebrum ⟨~ injections⟩ ⟨~ bleeding⟩ — **in·tra·ce·re·bral·ly** \-brə-lē\ *adv*

in·tra·com·pa·ny \-ˈkəmp-nē, -ˈkəm-pə-\ *adj* (1926) : occurring within or taking place between branches or employees of a company ⟨~ income⟩

in·tra·cra·ni·al \-ˈkrā-nē-əl\ *adj* (ca. 1849) : existing or occurring within the cranium; *also* : affecting or involving intracranial structures — **in·tra·cra·ni·al·ly** \-nē-ə-lē\ *adv*

in·trac·ta·ble \(ˌ)in-ˈtrak-tə-bəl\ *adj* [L *intractabilis*, fr. *in-* + *tractabilis* tractable] (1531) **1** : not easily governed, managed, or directed : OBSTINATE **2** : not easily manipulated or wrought ⟨~ metal⟩ **3** : not easily relieved or cured ⟨~ pain⟩ *syn* see UNRULY — **in·trac·ta·bil·i·ty** \(ˌ)in-ˌtrak-tə-ˈbi-lə-tē\ *n* — **in·trac·ta·bly** \-blē\ *adv*

in·tra·cu·ta·ne·ous \ˌin-trə-kyù-ˈtā-nē-əs, -(ˌ)trä-\ *adj* (1885) : INTRADERMAL — **in·tra·cu·ta·ne·ous·ly** *adv*

in·tra·day \ˈin-trə-ˌdā, -(ˌ)trä-\ *adj* (1950) : occurring in the course of a single day ⟨the market showed wide ~ fluctuations⟩

in·tra·der·mal \in-trə-ˈdər-məl, -(ˌ)trä-\ *adj* (ca. 1900) : situated, occurring, or done within or between the layers of the skin; *also* : administered by entering the skin ⟨~ injections⟩ — **in·tra·der·mal·ly** \-mə-lē\ *adv*

intradermal test *n* (1916) : a test for immunity or hypersensitivity made by injecting a minute amount of diluted antigen into the skin

in·tra·dos \ˈin-trə-ˌdäs, -ˌdō; in-ˈträ-ˌdäs\ *n, pl* **-dos** \-ˌdōz, -ˌdäs\ *or* **-dos·es** \-ˌdä-səz\ [F, fr. L *intra* within + F *dos* back — more at DOSSIER] (1772) : the interior curve of an arch — see ARCH illustration

in·tra·ga·lac·tic \ˌin-trə-gə-ˈlak-tik, -(ˌ)trä-\ *adj* (1964) : situated or occurring within the confines of a single galaxy

in·tra·gen·ic \-ˈje-nik\ *adj* (1937) : being or occurring within a gene ⟨~ recombination⟩ ⟨~ mutation⟩

in·tra·mo·lec·u·lar \-mə-ˈle-kyə-lər\ *adj* [ISV] (1884) : existing or acting within the molecule; *also* : formed by reaction between different parts of the same molecule — **in·tra·mo·lec·u·lar·ly** *adv*

in·tra·mu·ral \-ˈmyùr-əl\ *adj* (1846) **1 a** : being or occurring within the limits usu. of a community, organization, or institution **b** : competed only within the student body ⟨~ sports⟩ **2** : situated or occurring within the substance of the walls of an organ — **in·tra·mu·ral·ly** \-ə-lē\ *adv*

in·tra·mus·cu·lar \-ˈməs-kyə-lər\ *adj* [ISV] (1874) : situated in, occurring in, or administered by entering a muscle — **in·tra·mus·cu·lar·ly** *adv*

in·tra·na·sal \-ˈnā-zəl\ *adj* (1886) : lying within or administered by way of the nasal structures — **in·tra·na·sal·ly** \-ˈnāz-lē, -ˈnā-zə-\ *adv*

in·tran·si·geance \in-ˈtran(t)-sə-jən(t)s, -ˈtran-zə-\ *n* [F] (1899) : INTRANSIGENCE — **in·tran·si·geant** \-jənt\ *adj or n* — **in·tran·si·geant·ly** *adv*

in·tran·si·gence \-jən(t)s\ *n* (1882) : the quality or state of being intransigent

in·tran·si·gent \-jənt\ *adj* [Sp *intransigente*, fr. *in-* + *transigente*, prp. of *transigir* to compromise, fr. L *transigere* to come to an agreement — more at TRANSACT] (ca. 1879) **1 a** : refusing to compromise or to abandon an extreme position or attitude : UNCOMPROMISING **b** : IRRECONCILABLE **2** : characteristic of an intransigent person — **intransigent** *n* — **in·tran·si·gent·ly** *adv*

in·tran·si·tive \(ˌ)in-ˈtran(t)-sə-tiv, -ˈtran-zə-; -ˈtran(t)s-tiv\ *adj* [LL *intransitivus*, fr. L *in-* + LL *transitivus* transitive] (1612) : not transitive; *esp* : characterized by not having or containing a direct object ⟨an ~ verb⟩ — **in·tran·si·tive·ly** *adv* — **in·tran·si·tive·ness** *n* — **in·tran·si·tiv·i·ty** \(ˌ)in-ˌtran(t)-sə-ˈti-və-tē, -ˌtran-zə-\ *n*

in·tra·oc·u·lar \ˌin-trə-ˈä-kyə-lər, -(ˌ)trä-\ *adj* [ISV] (1826) : implanted in, occurring in, or administered by entering the eyeball — **in·tra·oc·u·lar·ly** *adv*

in·tra·per·i·to·ne·al \ˌin-trə-ˌper-ə-tᵊn-ˈē-əl\ *adj* (ca. 1836) : existing within or administered by entering the peritoneum — **in·tra·per·i·to·ne·al·ly** \-ˈē-ə-lē\ *adv*

in·tra·per·son·al \-ˈpərs-nəl, -ˈpər-sᵊn-əl\ *adj* (1909) : occurring within the individual mind or self ⟨~ concerns of the aged⟩

in·tra·plate \ˈin-trə-ˌplāt, -(ˌ)trä-\ *adj* (1973) : relating to or occurring within the interior of a tectonic plate ⟨an ~ earthquake⟩

in·tra·pop·u·la·tion \ˈin-trə-ˌpä-pyə-ˈlā-shən, -(ˌ)trä-\ *adj* (1959) : occurring within or taking place between members of a population

in·tra·pre·neur \ˌin-trə-prə-ˈnər, -ˈnùr, -ˈnyùr\ *n* [*intra-* + *entrepreneur*] (1982) : a corporate executive who develops new enterprises within the corporation — **in·tra·pre·neur·ial** \-ˈnər-ē-əl, -ˈn(y)ùr-\ *adj*

in·tra·psy·chic \in-trə-ˈsī-kik, -(ˌ)trä-\ *adj* (1917) : being or occurring within the psyche, mind, or personality — **in·tra·psy·chi·cal·ly** \-ki-k(ə-)lē\ *adv*

in·tra·spe·cies \-ˈspē-(ˌ)shēz, -(ˌ)sēz\ *adj* (1927) : INTRASPECIFIC

in·tra·spe·cif·ic \-spi-ˈsi-fik\ *adj* (1919) : occurring within a species or involving members of one species

in·tra·state \-ˈstāt\ *adj* (1903) : existing or occurring within a state

in·tra·the·cal \-ˈthē-kəl\ *adj* (1887) : introduced into or occurring in the space under the arachnoid membrane of the brain or spinal cord — **in·tra·the·cal·ly** \-k(ə-)lē\ *adv*

in·tra·tho·rac·ic \-thə-ˈra-sik\ *adj* [ISV] (1862) : situated or occurring within the thorax ⟨~ pressure⟩ — **in·tra·tho·rac·i·cal·ly** *adv*

in·tra·uter·ine \-ˈyü-tə-rən, -ˌrīn\ *adj* [ISV] (ca. 1836) : situated, used, or occurring within the uterus; *also* : involving the part of development that takes place in the uterus

intrauterine device *n* (1964) : a device inserted and left in the uterus to prevent effective conception — called also *intrauterine contraceptive device*, IUD

in·tra·vas·cu·lar \ˌin-trə-ˈvas-kyə-lər, -(ˌ)trä-\ *adj* (1876) : situated in, occurring in, or administered by entry into a blood vessel ⟨~ thrombosis⟩ ⟨an ~ injection⟩ — **in·tra·vas·cu·lar·ly** *adv*

in·tra·ve·nous \ˌin-trə-ˈvē-nəs\ *adj* [ISV] (ca. 1849) : situated, performed, or occurring within or entering by way of a vein; *also* : used in intravenous procedures — **in·tra·ve·nous·ly** *adv*

in·tra·ven·tric·u·lar \ˌin-trə-ven-ˈtri-kyə-lər, -(ˌ)trä-\ *adj* (1882) : situated within, occurring within, or administered into a ventricle — **in·tra·ven·tric·u·lar·ly** *adv*

in·tra·vi·tal \-ˈvī-tᵊl\ *adj* [ISV] (ca. 1890) **1** : performed upon or found in a living subject **2** : having or utilizing the property of staining cells without killing them — compare SUPRAVITAL — **in·tra·vi·tal·ly** \-tᵊl-ē\ *adv*

in·tra·vi·tam \-ˈvī-ˌtam, -ˈwē-ˌtäm\ *adj* [NL *intra vitam* during life] (1881) : INTRAVITAL

in·tra·zon·al \-ˈzō-nᵊl, -(ˌ)trä-\ *adj* (1927) : of, relating to, or being a soil or a major soil group marked by relatively well-developed characteristics that are determined primarily by essentially local factors (as the parent material) rather than climate and vegetation — compare AZONAL, ZONAL

intreat *archaic var of* ENTREAT

intrench *var of* ENTRENCH

in·trep·id \in-ˈtre-pəd\ *adj* [L *intrepidus*, fr. *in-* + *trepidus* alarmed — more at TREPIDATION] (1697) : characterized by resolute fearlessness, fortitude, and endurance — **in·tre·pid·i·ty** \ˌin-trə-ˈpi-də-tē\ *n* — **in·trep·id·ly** \in-ˈtre-pəd-lē\ *adv* — **in·trep·id·ness** *n*

in·tri·ca·cy \ˈin-tri-kə-sē\ *n, pl* **-cies** (1602) **1** : the quality or state of being intricate **2** : something intricate ⟨the *intricacies* of a plot⟩

in·tri·cate \ˈin-tri-kət\ *adj* [ME, fr. L *intricatus*, pp. of *intricare* to entangle, fr. *in-* + *tricae* trifles, complications] (15c) **1** : having many parts complexly interrelating parts or elements : COMPLICATED **2** : difficult to resolve or analyze *syn* see COMPLEX — **in·tri·cate·ly** *adv* — **in·tri·cate·ness** *n*

in·tri·gant *or* **in·tri·guant** \ˌin-trē-ˈgänt, ˌan-, -ˈgänⁿ\ *n* [F *intrigant*, fr. It *intrigante*, prp. of *intrigare*] (1781) : one that intrigues

¹**in·trigue** \in-ˈtrēg\ *vb* **in·trigued; in·tri·gu·ing** [F *intriguer*, fr. It *intrigare*, fr. L *intricare*] *vt* (1612) **1** : CHEAT, TRICK **2** : to accomplish by intrigue ⟨*intrigued* myself into the club⟩ **3** *obs* : ENTANGLE **4** : to arouse the interest, desire, or curiosity of ⟨*intrigued* by the tale⟩ ~ *vi* : to carry on an intrigue; *esp* : PLOT, SCHEME — **in·trigu·er** *n*

²**in·trigue** \ˈin-ˌtrēg, in-ˈ\ *n* (1647) **1 a** : a secret scheme : MACHINATION **b** : the practice of engaging in intrigues **2** : a clandestine love affair *syn* see PLOT

in·tri·gu·ing \in-ˈtrē-giŋ\ *adj* (1909) : engaging the interest to a marked degree : FASCINATING — **in·tri·gu·ing·ly** \-giŋ-lē\ *adv*

in·trin·sic \in-ˈtrin-zik, -ˈtrin(t)-sik\ *adj* [MF *intrinsèque* internal, fr. LL *intrinsecus*, fr. L, adv., inwardly; akin to L *intra* within — more at INTRA-] (1642) **1 a** : belonging to the essential nature or constitution of a thing ⟨the ~ worth of a gem⟩ ⟨the ~ brightness of a star⟩ **b** : being or relating to a semiconductor in which the concentration of charge carriers is characteristic of the material itself instead of the content of any impurities it contains **2 a** : originating or due to causes within a body, organ, or part ⟨an ~ metabolic disease⟩ **b** : originating and included wholly within an organ or part ⟨~ muscles⟩ — compare EXTRINSIC 1b — **in·trin·si·cal·ly** \-zi-k(ə-)lē, -si-\ *adv*

in·trin·si·cal \-zi-kəl, -si-\ *adj* (ca. 1548) *archaic* : INTRINSIC

intrinsic factor *n* (1930) : a substance produced by normal gastrointestinal mucosa that facilitates absorption of vitamin B_{12}

in·tro \ˈin-(ˌ)trō\ *n, pl* **intros** (ca. 1899) : INTRODUCTION

intro- *prefix* [ME, fr. MF, fr. L, fr. *intro* inside, to the inside, fr. (assumed) OL *interus*, adj., inward] **1** : in : into ⟨introjection⟩ **2** : inward : within ⟨introvert⟩ — compare EXTRO-

in·tro·duce \ˌin-trə-ˈdüs, -ˈdyüs\ *vt* **-duced; -duc·ing** [ME, fr. L *introducere*, fr. *intro-* + *ducere* to lead — more at TOW] (15c) **1** : to lead or bring in esp. for the first time **2 a** : to bring into play **b** : to bring into practice or use : INSTITUTE **3** : to lead to or make known by a formal act, announcement, or recommendation: as **a** : to cause to be acquainted **b** : to present formally at court or into society **c** : to present or announce formally or officially or by an official reading **d** : to make preliminary explanatory or laudatory remarks about ⟨~ to bring (as an actor or singer) before the public for the first time **4** : PLACE, INSERT **5** : to bring to a knowledge of something — **in·tro·duc·er** *n*

syn INTRODUCE, INSERT, INSINUATE, INTERPOLATE, INTERCALATE, INTERPOSE, INTERJECT mean to put between or among others. INTRODUCE is a general term for bringing or placing a thing or person into a group or body already in existence ⟨*introduced* a new topic into the conversation⟩. INSERT implies putting into a fixed or open space between or among ⟨*inserted* a clause in the contract⟩. INSINUATE implies introducing gradually or by gentle pressure ⟨*insinuated* himself into the group⟩. INTERPOLATE applies to the inserting of something extraneous or spurious ⟨*interpolated* her own comments into the report⟩. INTERCALATE suggests an intrusive inserting of something in an existing series or sequence ⟨new chapters *intercalated* with the old⟩. INTERPOSE suggests inserting an obstruction or cause of delay ⟨*interpose* barriers to communication⟩. INTERJECT implies an abrupt or forced introduction ⟨*interjected* a question⟩.

in·tro·duc·tion \,in-trə-'dək-shən\ *n* [ME *introduccioun* act of introducing, fr. MF *introduction*, fr. L *introduction-*, *introductio*, fr. *introducere*] (14c) **1** : something that introduces: as **a** (1) : a part of a book or treatise preliminary to the main portion (2) : a preliminary treatise or course of study **b** : a short introductory musical passage **2** : the act or process of introducing : the state of being introduced **3** : a putting in : INSERTION **4** : something introduced; *specif* : a new or exotic plant or animal

in·tro·duc·to·ry \,in-trə-'dək-t(ə-)rē\ *adj* (1605) : of, relating to, or being a first step that sets something going or in proper perspective ⟨an ∼ course in calculus⟩ — **in·tro·duc·to·ri·ly** \-t(ə-)rə-lē\ *adv*

in·tro·gres·sion \,in-trə-'gre-shən\ *n* [*intro-* + *-gression* (as in *regression*)] (1938) : the entry or introduction of a gene from one gene complex into another — **in·tro·gres·sant** \-'gre-s³nt\ *adj or n* — **in·tro·gres·sive** \-'gre-siv\ *adj*

in·troit \'in-,tròit, -,trō-ət, in-'\ *n* [ME, fr. MF *introite*, fr. ML *introitus*, fr. L, entrance, fr. *introire* to go in, fr. *intro-* + *ire* to go — more at ISSUE] (15c) **1** *often cap* : the first part of the traditional proper of the Mass consisting of an antiphon, verse from a psalm, and the Gloria Patri **2** : a piece of music sung or played at the beginning of a worship service

in·tro·ject \,in-trə-'jekt\ *vt* [back-formation fr. *introjection*, fr. ISV *intro-* + *projection*] (1925) : to incorporate (attitudes or ideas) into one's personality unconsciously — **in·tro·jec·tion** \-'jek-shən\ *n*

in·tro·mis·sion \,in-trə-'mi-shən\ *n* [F, fr. MF, fr. ML *intromission-*, *intromissio*, fr. L *intromittere*] (1601) : the act or process of intromitting; *esp* : the insertion or period of insertion of the penis in the vagina in copulation

in·tro·mit \-'mit\ *vt* **-mit·ted; -mit·ting** [L *intromittere*, fr. *intro-* + *mittere* to send] (ca. 1588) : to send or put in : INSERT — **in·tro·mit·tent** \-'mi-t³nt\ *adj* — **in·tro·mit·ter** \-tər\ *n*

in·tron \'in-,trän\ *n* [*intervening* sequence + *²-on*] (1978) : a polynucleotide sequence in a nucleic acid that does not code information for protein synthesis and is removed before translation of messenger RNA — compare EXON

in·trorse \'in-,tròrs\ *adj* [L *introrsus*, adv., inward, fr. *intro-* + *versus* toward, fr. pp. of *vertere* to turn — more at WORTH] (1842) : facing inward or toward the axis of growth ⟨an ∼ anther⟩

in·tro·spec·tion \,in-trə-'spek-shən\ *n* [L *introspectus*, pp. of *introspicere* to look inside, fr. *intro-* + *specere* to look — more at SPY] (ca. 1677) : a reflective looking inward : an examination of one's own thoughts and feelings — **in·tro·spect** \-'spekt\ *vb* — **in·tro·spec·tion·al** \-'spek-shnəl, -shə-n³l\ *adj* — **in·tro·spec·tive** \-'spek-tiv\ *adj* — **in·tro·spec·tive·ly** *adv* — **in·tro·spec·tive·ness** *n*

in·tro·spec·tion·ism \-shə-,ni-zəm\ *n* (1922) : a doctrine that psychology must be based essentially on data derived from introspection — compare BEHAVIORISM — **in·tro·spec·tion·ist** \-sh(ə-)nist\ *n or adj* — **in·tro·spec·tion·is·tic** \-,spek-shə-'nis-tik\ *adj* — **introspectionist** *n*

in·tro·ver·sion \,in-trə-'vər-zhən, -shən\ *n* [*intro-* + *-version* (as in *diversion*)] (1654) **1** : the act of introverting : the state of being introverted **2** : the state or tendency toward being wholly or predominantly concerned with and interested in one's own mental life — **in·tro·ver·sive** \-'vər-siv, -ziv\ *adj* — **in·tro·ver·sive·ly** *adv*

¹in·tro·vert \'in-trə-,vərt\ *vt* [*intro-* + *-vert* (as in *divert*)] (1669) : to turn inward or in upon itself: as **a** : to concentrate or direct upon oneself **b** : to produce psychological introversion in

²introvert *n* (1883) **1** : something (as the retractile proboscis of some worms) that is or can be drawn in esp. by invagination **2** : one whose personality is characterized by introversion; *broadly* : a reserved or shy person

in·trude \in-'trüd\ *vb* **in·trud·ed; in·trud·ing** [ME, fr. L *intrudere* to thrust in, fr. *in-* + *trudere* to thrust — more at THREAT] *vi* (15c) **1** : to thrust oneself in without invitation, permission, or welcome **2** : to enter as a geological intrusion ∼ *vt* **1** : to thrust or force in or upon someone or something esp. without permission, welcome, or fitness **2** : to cause to enter as if by force — **in·trud·er** *n*

in·tru·sion \in-'trü-zhən\ *n* [ME, fr. MF, fr. ML *intrusion-*, *intrusio*, fr. L *intrudere*] (15c) **1** : the act of intruding or the state of being intruded; *esp* : the act of wrongfully entering upon, seizing, or taking possession of the property of another **2** : the forcible entry of molten rock or magma into or between other rock formations; *also* : the intruded magma

in·tru·sive \in-'trü-siv, -ziv\ *adj* (15c) **1 a** : characterized by intrusion **b** : intruding where one is not welcome or invited **2 a** : projecting inward ⟨an ∼ arm of the sea⟩ **b** (1) *of a rock* : having been forced while in a plastic state into cavities or between layers (2) : PLUTONIC **3** : having nothing that corresponds to a sound or letter in orthography or etymon ⟨∼ \t\ in \'mints\ for *mince*⟩ **syn** see IMPERTINENT — **intrusive** *n* — **in·tru·sive·ly** *adv* — **in·tru·sive·ness** *n*

intrust *var of* ENTRUST

in·tu·ba·tion \,in-(,)tü-'bā-shən, -(,)tyü-, -tə-\ *n* (1887) : the introduction of a tube into a hollow organ (as the trachea) — **in·tu·bate** \'in-(,)tü-,bāt, -(,) tyü-, -tə-\ *vt*

in·tu·it \in-'tü-ət, -'tyü-\ *vt* (1855) : to apprehend by intuition — **in·tu·it·able** \-ə-tə-bəl\ *adj*

in·tu·ition \,in-tù-'wi-shən, -tyù-\ *n* [ME *intuycyon*, fr. LL *intuition-*, *intuitio* act of contemplating, fr. L *intuēri* to look at, contemplate, fr. *in-* + *tuēri* to look at] (15c) **1** : quick and ready insight **2 a** : immediate apprehension or cognition **b** : knowledge or conviction gained by intuition **c** : the power or faculty of attaining to direct knowledge or cognition without evident rational thought and inference — **in·tu·i·tion·al** \-'wish-nəl, -'wi-shə-n³l\ *adj*

in·tu·i·tion·ism \,in-tù-'wi-shə-,ni-zəm\ *n* (1847) **1 a** : a doctrine that objects of perception are intuitively known to be real **b** : a doctrine that there are basic truths intuitively known **2** : a doctrine that right or wrong or fundamental principles about what is right and wrong can be intuited **3** : a philosophical thesis that human beings have a direct intuitive understanding of mathematics and that rejects the principle that every mathematical statement must be true or false — **in·tu·i·tion·ist** \-sh(ə-)nist\ *adj or n*

in·tu·i·tive \in-'tü-ə-tiv, -'tyü-\ *adj* (1621) **1 a** : known or perceived by intuition : directly apprehended ⟨had an ∼ awareness of his sister's feelings⟩ **b** : knowable by intuition **2** : knowing or perceiving by intuition **3** : possessing or given to intuition or insight ⟨an ∼ mind⟩ — **in·tu·i·tive·ly** *adv* — **in·tu·i·tive·ness** *n*

in·tu·mes·cence \,in-tü-'me-s³n(t)s, -tyü-\ *n* [F, fr. L *intumescere* to swell up, fr. *in-* + *tumescere* to swell — more at TUMESCENCE] (ca. 1656) : a swollen or enlarged part of a plant or animal; *also* : the process of swelling up or enlarging

in·tu·mes·cent \-s³nt\ *adj* (1953) *of paint* : swelling and charring when exposed to flame

in·tus·sus·cept \,in-tə-sə-'sept\ *vb* [back-formation fr. *intussusception*] *vt* (1802) : to take in by or cause to undergo intussusception; *esp* : INVAGINATE ∼ *vi* : to undergo intussusception

in·tus·sus·cep·tion \-'sep-shən\ *n* [L *intus* within + *susception-*, *susceptio* action of undertaking, fr. *suscipere* to take up — more at SUSCEPTIBLE] (1707) **1** : a drawing in of something from without: as **a** : INVAGINATION; *esp* : the slipping of a length of intestine into an adjacent portion usu. producing obstruction **b** : the assimilation of new material and its dispersal among preexistent matter — **in·tus·sus·cep·tive** \-'sep-tiv\ *adj*

In·u·it \'i-nü-wət, -nyü-\ *n* [Inuit *inuit*, pl. of *inuk* person] (1765) **1** *pl* **Inuit** *or* **Inuits** **a** (1) : the Eskimo people of No. America and Greenland (2) : the Eskimo people of Canada **b** : a member of such people **2** : ESKIMO 2 **b** : the group of Eskimo dialects spoken from northwestern Canada to Greenland

Inuk·ti·tut \i-'nük-tə-,tüt\ *n* (1974) : the group of Eskimo dialects spoken by the Inuit of central and eastern arctic Canada

in·u·lin \'in-yə-lən\ *n* [prob. fr. G *Inulin*, fr. L *inula* elecampane] (1813) : a tasteless white polysaccharide found esp. dissolved in the sap of the roots and rhizomes of composite plants

in·unc·tion \i-'nən(k)-shən\ *n* [ME, fr. L *inunction-*, *inunctio*, fr. *inunguere* to anoint — more at ANOINT] (15c) : an act of applying oil or ointment : ANOINTING

in·un·date \'i-(,)nən-,dāt\ *vt* **-dat·ed; -dat·ing** [L *inundatus*, pp. of *inundare*, fr. *in-* + *unda* wave — more at WATER] (1590) **1** : to cover with a flood : OVERFLOW **2** : OVERWHELM — **in·un·da·tion** \,i-(,)nən-'dā-shən\ *n* — **in·un·da·tor** \'i-(,)nən-,dā-tər\ *n* — **in·un·da·to·ry** \i-'nən-də-,tòr-ē, -,tòr-\ *adj*

Inu·pi·at \i-'nü-pē-,ät, -'nyü-\ *also* **Inu·pi·aq** \-,äk\ *n* [Inupiat *in³upiaq*, pl. *in³upiat*, lit., real person] (1967) **1** *pl* **Inupiat** *or* **Inupiats** *also* **Inupiaq** *or* **Inupiaqs** : a member of the Eskimo people of northern Alaska **2** : the language of the Inupiat people

in·ure \i-'nùr, -'nyùr\ *vb* **in·ured; in·ur·ing** [ME *enuren*, fr. *en-* + *ure*, n., use, custom, fr. MF *uevre* work, practice, fr. L *opera* work — more at OPERA] *vt* (15c) : to accustom to accept something undesirable ∼ *vi* : to become of advantage — **in·ure·ment** \-mənt\ *n*

in·urn \i-'nərn\ *vt* (1602) **1** : ENTOMB **2** : to place (as cremated remains) in an urn

in utero \in-'yü-tə-,rō\ *adv or adj* [L] (1713) : in the uterus : before birth ⟨a disease acquired *in utero*⟩ ⟨an *in utero* diagnosis⟩

in·utile \(,)in-'yü-t³l, -,til\ *adj* [ME, fr. MF, fr. L *inutilis*, fr. *in-* + *utilis* useful — more at UTILITY] (15c) : USELESS, UNUSABLE — **in·util·i·ty** \,in-yü-'ti-lə-tē\ *n*

in vac·uo \in-'va-kyə-,wō\ *adv* [NL] (1660) : in a vacuum

in·vade \in-'vād\ *vt* **in·vad·ed; in·vad·ing** [ME, fr. L *invadere*, fr. *in-* + *vadere* to go — more at WADE] (15c) **1** : to enter for conquest or plunder **2** : to encroach upon : INFRINGE **3 a** : to spread over or into as if invading : PERMEATE ⟨doubts ∼ his mind⟩ **b** : to affect injuriously and progressively ⟨gangrene ∼s healthy tissue⟩ **syn** see TRESPASS — **in·vad·er** *n*

in·vag·i·nate \in-'va-jə-,nāt\ *vb* **-nat·ed; -nat·ing** [ML *invaginatus*, pp. of *invaginare*, fr. L *in-* + *vagina* sheath] *vt* (ca. 1656) **1** : ENCLOSE, SHEATHE **2** : to fold in so that an outer becomes an inner surface ∼ *vi* : to undergo invagination

in·vag·i·na·tion \-,va-jə-'nā-shən\ *n* (ca. 1658) **1** : an act or process of invaginating; *esp* : the formation of a gastrula by an infolding of part of the wall of the blastula **2** : an invaginated part

¹in·val·id \(,)in-'va-ləd\ *adj* [L *invalidus* weak, fr. *in-* + *validus* strong — more at VALID] (1542) : not valid: **a** : being without foundation or force in fact, truth, or law **b** : logically inconsequent — **in·val·id·ly** \-lē\ *adv*

²in·va·lid \'in-və-ləd, *Brit usu* -,lēd\ *adj* [L & F; F *invalide*, fr. L *invalidus*] (1642) **1** : suffering from disease or disability : SICKLY **2** : of, relating to, or suited to one that is sick

³invalid *same as ²*\ *n* (1709) : one that is sickly or disabled

⁴in·va·lid \'in-və-ləd, -,lid, *Brit usu* -,lēd *or* ,in-və-'lēd\ *vt* (1787) **1** : to remove from active duty by reason of sickness or disability **2** : to make sickly or disabled

in·val·i·date \(,)in-'va-lə-,dāt\ *vt* (1649) : to make invalid; *esp* : to weaken or destroy the cogency of **syn** see NULLIFY — **in·val·i·da·tion** \-,va-lə-'dā-shən\ *n* — **in·val·i·da·tor** \(,)in-'va-lə-,dā-tər\ *n*

in·va·lid·ism \'in-və-lə-,di-zəm\ *n* (1794) : a chronic condition of being an invalid

in·va·lid·i·ty \,in-və-'li-də-tē, -va-\ *n, pl* **-ties** (ca. 1550) **1** : lack of validity or cogency **2** : incapacitating bodily disability; *also* : INVALIDISM

in·valu·able \(,)in-'val-yə-bəl, -yə-wə-bəl\ *adj* [¹*in-* + *value*, v. + *-able*] (1576) : valuable beyond estimation : PRICELESS — **in·valu·able·ness** *n* — **in·valu·ably** \-blē\ *adv*

\ə\ abut \³\ kitten, F table \ər\ further \a\ ash \ā\ ace \ä\ mop, mar \aù\ out \ch\ chin \e\ bet \ē\ easy \g\ go \i\ hit \ī\ ice \j\ job \ŋ\ sing \ō\ go \ò\ law \òi\ boy \th\ thin \tẖ\ the \ü\ loot \ù\ foot \y\ yet \zh\ vision \á, k̲, ⁿ, œ, œ̄, ᵫ, ᵲᴇ, �\ see Guide to Pronunciation

in·var \'in-,vär\ *n, often cap* [fr. *Invar*, a trademark] (1902) : an iron‑nickel alloy that expands little on heating

in·vari·able \(,)in-'ver-ē-ə-bəl, -'var-\ *adj* (15c) : not changing or capable of change : CONSTANT — **in·vari·abil·i·ty** \-,ver-ē-ə-'bi-lə-tē, -,var-\ *n* — **invariable** *n* — **in·vari·ably** \-blē\ *adv*

in·vari·ance \(,)in-'ver-ē-ən(t)s, -'var-\ *n* (1878) : the quality or state of being invariant

in·vari·ant \-ənt\ *adj* (1874) : CONSTANT, UNCHANGING; *specif* : unchanged by specified mathematical or physical operations or transformations 〈~ factor〉 — **invariant** *n*

in·va·sion \in-'vā-zhən\ *n* [ME *invasioune*, fr. MF *invasion*, fr. LL *invasion-, invasio*, fr. L *invadere* to invade] (15c) 1 : an act of invading; *esp* : incursion of an army for conquest or plunder 2 : the incoming or spread of something usu. hurtful

in·va·sive \-siv, -ziv\ *adj* (1598) 1 : of, relating to, or characterized by military aggression 2 : tending to spread; *esp* : tending to invade healthy tissue 〈~ cancer cells〉 3 : tending to infringe 4 : involving entry into the living body (as by incision or by insertion of an instrument) 〈~ diagnostic techniques〉 — **in·va·sive·ness** *n*

¹in·vec·tive \in-'vek-tiv\ *adj* [ME *invectif*, fr. MF, fr. L *invectivus*, fr. *invectus*, pp. of *invehere*] (15c) : of, relating to, or characterized by insult or abuse — **in·vec·tive·ly** *adv* — **in·vec·tive·ness** *n*

²invective *n* (1523) 1 : an abusive expression or speech 2 : insulting or abusive language : VITUPERATION *syn* see ABUSE

in·veigh \in-'vā\ *vi* [L *invehi* to attack, inveigh, pass. of *invehere* to carry in, fr. *in-* + *vehere* to carry — more at WAY] (1529) : to protest or complain bitterly or vehemently : RAIL — **in·veigh·er** *n*

in·vei·gle \in-'vā-gəl *sometimes* -'vē-\ *vt* **in·vei·gled**; **in·vei·gling** \-g(ə-)liŋ\ [modif. of MF *aveugler* to blind, hoodwink, fr. OF *avogler*, fr. *avogle* blind, fr. ML *ab oculis*, lit., lacking eyes] (1539) 1 : to win over by wiles : ENTICE 2 : to acquire by ingenuity or flattery *syn* see LURE — **in·vei·gle·ment** \-gəl-mənt\ *n* — **in·vei·gler** \-g(ə-)lər\ *n*

in·vent \in-'vent\ *vt* [ME, fr. L *inventus*, pp. of *invenire* to come upon, find, fr. *in-* + *venire* to come — more at COME] (15c) 1 *archaic* : FIND, DISCOVER 2 : to devise by thinking : FABRICATE 3 : to produce (as something useful) for the first time through the use of the imagination or of ingenious thinking and experiment — **in·ven·tor** \-'ven-tər\ *n* — **in·ven·tress** \-'ven-trəs\ *n*

in·ven·tion \in-'ven(t)-shən\ *n* (14c) 1 : DISCOVERY, FINDING 2 : productive imagination : INVENTIVENESS 3 **a** : something invented: as (1) : a product of the imagination; *esp* : a false conception (2) : a device, contrivance, or process originated after study and experiment **b** : a short keyboard composition featuring two or three part counterpoint 4 : the act or process of inventing

in·ven·tive \in-'ven-tiv\ *adj* (15c) 1 : adept or prolific at producing inventions : CREATIVE 2 : characterized by invention — **in·ven·tive·ly** *adv* — **in·ven·tive·ness** *n*

¹in·ven·to·ry \'in-vən-,tōr-ē, -,tor-\ *n, pl* **-ries** (1523) 1 **a** : an itemized list of current assets: as (1) : a catalog of the property of an individual or estate (2) : a list of goods on hand **b** : a survey of natural resources **c** : a list of traits, preferences, attitudes, interests, or abilities used to evaluate personal characteristics or skills 2 : the quantity of goods or materials on hand : STOCK 3 : the act or process of taking an inventory — **in·ven·to·ri·al** \,in-vən-'tōr-ē-əl\ *adj* — **in·ven·to·ri·al·ly** \-ē-ə-lē\ *adv*

²inventory *vt* **-ried**; **-ry·ing** (1602) : to make an inventory of : CATALOG

in·ver·ness \,in-vər-'nes\ *n* [*Inverness, Scotland*] (1863) : a loose belted coat having a cape with a close-fitting round collar

¹in·verse \(,)in-'vərs, 'in-,\ *adj* [L *inversus*, fr. pp. of *invertere*] (15c) 1 : opposite in order, nature, or effect 2 : being an inverse function 〈~ sine〉

²inverse *n* (ca. 1681) 1 : something of a contrary nature or quality : OPPOSITE, REVERSE 2 : a proposition or theorem formed by contradicting both the subject and predicate or both the hypothesis and conclusion of a given proposition or theorem 〈the ~ of "if A then B" is "if not-A then not-B"〉 — compare CONTRAPOSITIVE 3 **a** : INVERSE FUNCTION; *also* : an operation (as subtraction) that undoes the effect of another operation **b** : a set element that is related to another element in such a way that the result of applying a given binary operation to them is an identity element of the set

inverse function *n* (1816) : a function that is derived from a given function by interchanging the two variables — compare LOGARITHMIC FUNCTION

in·verse·ly \'in-,vərs-lē, (,)in-'\ *adv* (1660) 1 : in an inverse order or manner 2 : in the manner of inverse variation 〈varies ~〉

inversely proportional *adj* (ca. 1890) : related by inverse variation — compare DIRECTLY PROPORTIONAL

inverse square law *n* (1921) : a statement in physics: a given physical quantity (as illumination) varies with the distance from the source inversely as the square of the distance

inverse variation *n* (1936) 1 : mathematical relationship between two variables which can be expressed by an equation in which the product of two variables is equal to a constant 2 : an equation or function expressing inverse variation — compare DIRECT VARIATION

in·ver·sion \in-'vər-zhən, -shən\ *n* (1586) 1 : a reversal of position, order, form, or relationship: as **a** (1) : a change in normal word order; *esp* : the placement of a verb before its subject (2) : the process or result of changing or reversing the relative positions of the notes of a musical interval, chord, or phrase **b** : the condition of being turned inward or inside out **c** : a breaking off of a chromosome section and its subsequent reattachment in inverted position; *also* : a chromosomal section that has undergone this process 2 : the act or process of inverting 3 **a** : a change in the order of the terms of a mathematical proportion effected by inverting each ratio **b** : the operation of forming the inverse of a magnitude, a function, an operation, or an element 4 **a** : the conversion of dextrorotatory sucrose into a levorotatory mixture of glucose and fructose **b** : a change from one stereochemical figuration at a chiral center in a usu. organic molecule to the opposite configuration that is brought about by a reaction in which a substitution of one group is made for a different group 5 : HOMOSEXUALITY 6 : an increase of temperature with height through a layer of air

in·ver·sive \-'vər-siv, -ziv\ *adj* (1875) : marked by inversion

¹in·vert \in-'vərt\ *vt* [L *invertere*, fr. *in-* + *vertere* to turn — more at WORTH] (1533) 1 **a** : to reverse in position, order, or relationship **b** : to subject to inversion 2 **a** : to turn inside out or upside down **b** : to turn inward 3 : to find the mathematical reciprocal of 〈to divide using fractions, ~ the divisor and multiply〉 *syn* see REVERSE

²in·vert \'in-,vərt\ *n* (1838) : one characterized by inversion; *esp* : HOMOSEXUAL

in·ver·tase \in-'vər-,tās, -,tāz; 'in-vər-,\ *n* [ISV] (1887) : an enzyme that catalyzes the hydrolysis of sucrose

in·ver·te·brate \(,)in-'vər-tə-brət, -,brāt\ *adj* [NL *invertebratus*, fr. L *in-* + NL *vertebratus* vertebrate] (1838) 1 : lacking a spinal column; *also* : of or relating to invertebrate animals 2 : lacking in strength or vitality : WEAK — **invertebrate** *n*

inverted comma *n* (1789) *chiefly Brit* : QUOTATION MARK

in·vert·er \in-'vər-tər\ *n* (1611) 1 : one that inverts 2 : a device for converting direct current into alternating current

in·vert·ible \in-'vər-tə-bəl\ *adj* (1881) : capable of being inverted or subjected to inversion 〈an ~ matrix〉

invert sugar *n* (1880) : a mixture of dextrose and levulose found in fruits or produced artificially by the inversion of sucrose

¹in·vest \in-'vest\ *vt* [L *investire* to clothe, surround, fr. *in-* + *vestis* garment — more at WEAR] (ca. 1534) 1 [ML *investire*, fr. L, to clothe] **a** : to array in the symbols of office or honor **b** : to furnish with power or authority **c** : to grant someone control or authority over : VEST 2 : to cover completely : ENVELOP 3 : CLOTHE, ADORN 4 [MF *investir*, fr. OIt *investire*, fr. L, to surround] : to surround with troops or ships so as to prevent escape or entry 5 : to endow with a quality : INFUSE

²invest *vb* [It *investire* to clothe, invest money, fr. L, to clothe] *vt* (1613) 1 : to commit (money) in order to earn a financial return 2 : to make use of for future benefits or advantages ~ *vi* : to make an investment — **in·vest·able** \-'ves-tə-bəl\ *adj* — **in·ves·tor** \-'ves-tər\ *n*

in·ves·ti·gate \in-'ves-tə-,gāt\ *vb* **-gat·ed**; **-gat·ing** [L *investigatus*, pp. of *investigare* to track, investigate, fr. *in-* + *vestigium* footprint, track] *vt* (ca. 1510) : to observe or study by close examination and systematic inquiry ~ *vi* : to make a systematic examination; *esp* : to conduct an official inquiry — **in·ves·ti·ga·tion** \-,ves-tə-'gā-shən\ *n* — **in·ves·ti·ga·tion·al** \-shnəl, -shə-n⁷l\ *adj* — **in·ves·ti·ga·tive** \'ves-tə-,gā-tiv\ *adj* — **in·ves·ti·ga·tor** \-,gā-tər\ *n* — **in·ves·ti·ga·to·ry** \'ves-ti-gə-,tōr-ē, -,tor-\ *adj*

in·ves·ti·ture \in-'ves-tə-,chúr, -chər, -,tyùr, -,tùr\ *n* [ME, fr. ML *investitura*, fr. *investitus*, pp. of *investire*] (14c) 1 : the act of establishing in office or ratifying 2 : something that covers or adorns

¹in·vest·ment \in-'ves(t)-mənt\ *n* [*¹invest*] (1597) 1 *archaic* : VESTMENT **b** : an outer layer : ENVELOPE 2 : INVESTITURE 1 3 : BLOCKADE, SIEGE

²investment *n* [*²invest*] (1615) : the outlay of money usu. for income or profit : capital outlay; *also* : the sum invested or the property purchased

investment company *n* (ca. 1917) : a company whose primary business is holding securities of other companies purely for investment purposes — compare HOLDING COMPANY

in·vet·er·a·cy \in-'ve-t(ə-)rə-sē\ *n* [*inveterate* + *-cy*] (ca. 1719) : the quality or state of being obstinate or persistent : TENACITY

in·vet·er·ate \in-'ve-t(ə-)rət\ *adj* [ME, fr. L *inveteratus*, fr. pp. of *inveterare* to age (v.t.), fr. *in-* + *veter-, vetus* old — more at WETHER] (14c) 1 : firmly established by long persistence 〈the ~ tendency to overlook the obvious〉 2 : confirmed in a habit : HABITUAL 〈an ~ liar〉 — **in·vet·er·ate·ly** *adv*

syn INVETERATE, CONFIRMED, CHRONIC mean firmly established. INVETERATE applies to a habit, attitude or feeling of such long existence as to be practically ineradicable or unalterable 〈an *inveterate* smoker〉. CONFIRMED implies a growing stronger and firmer with time so as to resist change or reform 〈a *confirmed* bachelor〉. CHRONIC suggests something that is persistent or endlessly recurrent and troublesome 〈a *chronic* complainer〉.

in·vi·a·ble \(,)in-'vī-ə-bəl\ *adj* [ISV] (1918) : incapable of surviving esp. because of a deleterious genetic constitution — **in·vi·a·bil·i·ty** \-,vī-ə-'bi-lə-tē\ *n*

in·vid·i·ous \in-'vi-dē-əs\ *adj* [L *invidiosus* envious, invidious, fr. *invidia* envy — more at ENVY] (1606) 1 : tending to cause discontent, animosity, or envy 〈the ~ task of arbitration〉 2 : ENVIOUS 3 **a** : of an unpleasant or objectionable nature : OBNOXIOUS 〈~ remarks〉 **b** : of a kind to cause harm or resentment 〈an ~ comparison〉 *syn* see REPUGNANT — **in·vid·i·ous·ly** *adv* — **in·vid·i·ous·ness** *n*

in·vig·i·late \in-'vi-jə-,lāt\ *vb* **-lat·ed**; **-lat·ing** [L *invigilatus*, pp. of *invigilare* to stay awake, be watchful, fr. *in-* + *vigilare* to stay awake — more at VIGILANT] *vi* (1553) : to keep watch; *esp, Brit* : to supervise students at an examination ~ *vt* : SUPERVISE, MONITOR — **in·vig·i·la·tion** \-,vi-jə-'lā-shən\ *n* — **in·vig·i·la·tor** \-'vi-jə-,lā-tər\ *n*

in·vig·o·rate \in-'vi-gə-,rāt\ *vt* **-rat·ed**; **-rat·ing** [prob. fr. *in-* + *vigor*] (1646) : to give life and energy to : ANIMATE; *also* : STIMULATE 1 — **in·vig·o·rat·ing·ly** \-,rā-tiŋ-lē\ *adv* — **in·vig·o·ra·tion** \-,vi-gə-'rā-shən\ *n* — **in·vig·o·ra·tor** \-'vi-gə-,rā-tər\ *n*

in·vin·ci·ble \(,)in-'vin(t)-sə-bəl\ *adj* [ME, fr. MF, fr. LL *invincibilis*, fr. L *in-* + *vincere* to conquer — more at VICTOR] (15c) : incapable of being conquered, overcome, or subdued — **in·vin·ci·bil·i·ty** \-,vin(t)-sə-'bi-lə-tē\ *n* — **in·vin·ci·ble·ness** \-'vin(t)-sə-bəl-nəs\ *n* — **in·vin·ci·bly** \-blē\ *adv*

in·vi·o·la·ble \(,)in-'vī-ə-lə-bəl\ *adj* [ME, fr. MF or L; MF, fr. L *inviolabilis*, fr. *in-* + *violare* to violate] (15c) 1 : secure from violation or profanation 2 : secure from assault or trespass : UNASSAILABLE — **in·vi·o·la·bil·i·ty** \-,vī-ə-lə-'bi-lə-tē\ *n* — **in·vi·o·la·ble·ness** \-'vī-ə-lə-bəl-nəs\ *n* — **in·vi·o·la·bly** \-blē\ *adv*

in·vi·o·la·cy \(,)in-'vī-ə-lə-sē\ *n* (ca. 1846) : the quality or state of being inviolate

in·vi·o·late \-'vī-ə-lət\ *adj* (15c) : not violated or profaned; *esp* : PURE — **in·vi·o·late·ly** *adv* — **in·vi·o·late·ness** *n*

in·vis·cid \(,)in-'vi-səd\ *adj* (ca. 1889) 1 : having zero viscosity 2 : of or relating to an inviscid fluid 〈~ flow〉

in·vis·i·ble \(,)in-'vi-zə-bəl\ *adj* [ME, fr. MF, fr. L *invisibilis*, fr. *in-* + *visibilis* visible] (14c) 1 **a** : incapable by nature of being seen **b** : inaccessible to view : HIDDEN 2 : IMPERCEPTIBLE, INCONSPICUOUS 3 **a** : not appearing in published financial statements **b** : not reflected in statistics — **in·vis·i·bil·i·ty** \-,vi-zə-'bi-lə-tē\ *n* — **invisible** *n* — **in·vis·i·ble·ness** \-'vi-zə-bəl-nəs\ *n* — **in·vis·i·bly** \-blē\ *adv*

in·vi·ta·tion \,in-və-'tā-shən\ *n* (15c)   **1 a :** the act of inviting   **b :** an often formal request to be present or participate   **2 :** INCENTIVE, INDUCEMENT

in·vi·ta·tion·al \-shnəl, -shə-nᵊl\ *adj* (1922)   **1 :** prepared or entered in response to a request ⟨an ~ article⟩   **2 :** limited to invited participants ⟨an ~ tournament⟩ — **invitational** *n*

¹in·vi·ta·to·ry \in-'vī-tə-,tōr-ē, -,tȯr-\ *adj* (14c) : containing an invitation

²invitatory *n, pl* **-ries** (14c) : an invitatory psalm or antiphon

¹in·vite \in-'vīt\ *vt* **in·vit·ed; in·vit·ing** [MF or L; MF *inviter,* fr. L *invitare*] (1533)   **1 a :** to offer an incentive or inducement to : ENTICE   **b :** to increase the likelihood of   **2 a :** to request the presence or participation of   **b :** to request formally   **c :** to urge politely : WELCOME — **in·vit·er** *n*

²in·vite \'in-,vīt\ *n* (1659) : INVITATION 1

in·vit·ee \,in-və-'tē, -,vī-\ *n* (1803) : an invited person

inviting \in-'vī-tiŋ\ *adj* (1604) : ATTRACTIVE, TEMPTING — **in·vit·ing·ly** \-tiŋ-lē\ *adv*

in vi·tro \in-'vē-(,)trō, -'vi-\ *adv or adj* [NL, lit., in glass] (ca. 1894) : outside the living body and in an artificial environment

in vi·vo \in-'vē-(,)vō\ *adv or adj* [NL, lit., in the living] (1901) : in the living body of a plant or animal

in·vo·cate \'in-və-,kāt\ *vt* (1526) *archaic* : INVOKE

in·vo·ca·tion \,in-və-'kā-shən\ *n* [ME *invocacioun,* fr. MF *invocation,* fr. L *invocation-, invocatio,* fr. *invocare*] (14c)   **1 a :** the act or process of petitioning for help or support; *specif, often cap* **:** a prayer of entreaty (as at the beginning of a service of worship)   **b :** a calling upon for authority or justification   **2 :** a formula for conjuring : INCANTATION   **3 :** an act of legal or moral implementation : ENFORCEMENT — **in·vo·ca·tion·al** \-shnəl, -shə-nᵊl\ *adj* — **in·voc·a·to·ry** \in-'vä-kə-,tōr-ē, -,tȯr-\ *adj*

¹in·voice \'in-,vȯis\ *n* [modif. of MF *envois,* pl. of *envoi* message — more at ENVOI] (1560)   **1 :** an itemized list of goods shipped usu. specifying the price and the terms of sale : BILL   **2 :** a consignment of merchandise

²invoice *vt* **in·voiced; in·voic·ing** (1698) : to send an invoice for or to

in·voke \in-'vōk\ *vt* **in·voked; in·vok·ing** [ME, fr. MF *invoquer,* fr. L *invocare,* fr. *in-* + *vocare* to call, fr. *voc-, vox* voice — more at VOICE] (15c)   **1 a :** to petition for help or support   **b :** to appeal to or cite as authority   **2 :** to call forth by incantation : CONJURE   **3 :** to make an earnest request for : SOLICIT   **4 :** to put into effect or operation : IMPLEMENT   **5 :** BRING ABOUT, CAUSE — **in·vok·er** *n*

in·vo·lu·cre \'in-və-,lü-kər\ *n* [F, fr. NL *involucrum*] (1794) : one or more whorls of bracts situated below and close to a flower, flower cluster, or fruit — **in·vo·lu·cral** \,in-və-'lü-krəl\ *adj* — **in·vo·lu·crate** \-krət, -,krāt\ *adj*

in·vo·lu·crum \,in-və-'lü-krəm\ *n, pl* **-cra** \-krə\ [NL, sheath, involucre, fr. L, wrapper, fr. *involvere* to wrap] (ca. 1677) : a surrounding envelope or sheath

in·vol·un·tary \(,)in-'vä-lən-,ter-ē\ *adj* [ME *involuntari,* fr. LL *involuntarius,* fr. L *in-* + *voluntarius* voluntary] (15c)   **1 :** done contrary to or without choice   **2 :** COMPULSORY   **3 :** not subject to control of the will : REFLEX — **in·vol·un·tari·ly** \,vä-lən-'ter-ə-lē\ *adv* — **in·vol·un·tari·ness** \-'vä-lən-,ter-ē-nəs\ *n*

involuntary manslaughter *n* (ca. 1879) : manslaughter resulting from the failure to perform a legal duty expressly required to safeguard human life, from the commission of an unlawful act not constituting a felony, or from the commission of a lawful act in a negligent or improper manner

involuntary muscle *n* (1840) : muscle governing reflex functions and not under direct voluntary control; *esp* **:** SMOOTH MUSCLE

¹in·vo·lute \'in-və-,lüt\ *adj* [L *involutus* concealed, fr. pp. of *involvere*] (1661)   **1 a :** curled spirally   **b** (1) **:** curled or curved inward   (2) **:** having the edges rolled over the upper surface toward the midrib ⟨an ~ leaf⟩   **c :** having the form of an involute ⟨a gear with ~ teeth⟩   **2 :** INVOLVED, INTRICATE

²involute *n* (ca. 1796) : a curve traced by a point on a thread kept taut as it is unwound from another curve ⟨~ of a circle⟩

³in·vo·lute \,in-və-'lüt\ *vi* **-lut·ed; -lut·ing** (1816)   **1 :** to become involute   **2 a :** to return to a former condition   **b :** to become cleared up : DISAPPEAR

in·vo·lu·tion \,in-və-'lü-shən\ *n* [L *involution-, involutio,* fr. *involvere*] (ca. 1611)   **1 a** (1) **:** the act or an instance of enfolding or entangling : INVOLVEMENT   (2) **:** an involved grammatical construction usu. characterized by the insertion of clauses between the subject and predicate   **b :** COMPLEXITY, INTRICACY   **2 :** EXPONENTIATION   **3 a :** an inward curvature or penetration   **b :** the formation of a gastrula by ingrowth of cells formed at the dorsal lip   **4 :** a shrinking or return to a former size   **5 :** the regressive alterations of a body or its parts characteristic of the aging process; *specif* **:** decline marked by a decrease of bodily vigor and in women by menopause — **in·vo·lu·tion·al** \-shnəl, -shə-nᵊl\ *adj*

in·volve \in-'välv, -'vȯlv *also* -'väv *or* -'vȯv\ *vt* **in·volved; in·volv·ing** [ME, to roll up, wrap, fr. L *involvere,* fr. *in-* + *volvere* to roll — more at VOLUBLE] (14c)   **1** *archaic* **:** to enfold or envelop so as to encumber   **2 a :** to engage as a participant ⟨workers *involved* in building a house⟩   **b :** to oblige to take part ⟨right of Congress to ~ the nation in war⟩   **c :** to occupy (as oneself) absorbingly; *esp* **:** to commit (as oneself) emotionally ⟨was *involved* with a married man⟩   **3 :** to surround as if with a wrapping : ENVELOP   **4** *archaic* **:** to wind, coil, or wreathe about   **b :** to relate closely : CONNECT   **5 a :** to have within or as part of itself : INCLUDE   **b :** to require as a necessary accompaniment : ENTAIL   **c :** to have an effect on   *syn* see INCLUDE — **in·volve·ment** \-'välv-mənt, -'vȯlv-\ *n* — **in·volv·er** *n*

in·volved \-'välvd, -'vȯlvd *also* -'vävd *or* -'vȯvd\ *adj* (15c)   **1 :** INVO-

involute *a, p, p, p, p* traced by any point *p* of the thread *t* unwinding from curve *c*

LUTE, TWISTED   **2 a :** marked by extreme and often needless or excessive complexity   **b :** difficult to deal with because of complexity or disorder   **3 :** being affected or implicated   *syn* see COMPLEX — **in·volv·ed·ly** \-'väl-vəd-lē, -'vȯl- *also* -'vä-vəd- *or* -'vȯ-\ *adv*

in·vul·ner·a·ble \(,)in-'vəl-n(ə-)rə-bəl, -nər-bəl\ *adj* [L *invulnerabilis,* fr. *in-* + *vulnerare* to wound — more at VULNERABLE] (1595)   **1 :** incapable of being wounded, injured, or harmed   **2 :** immune to or proof against attack : IMPREGNABLE — **in·vul·ner·a·bil·i·ty** \-,vəl-n(ə-)rə-'bi-lə-tē\ *n* — **in·vul·ner·a·ble·ness** \-'vəl-n(ə-)rə-bəl-nəs, -nər-bəl-\ *n* — **in·vul·ner·a·bly** \-blē\ *adv*

¹in·ward \'in-wərd\ *adj* [ME, fr. OE *inweard* (akin to OHG *inwert*), fr. *in* + *-weard* ward] (bef. 12c)   **1 :** situated on the inside : INNER   **2 a :** of or relating to the mind or spirit ⟨~ peace⟩   **b :** absorbed in one's own mental or spiritual life : INTROSPECTIVE   **3 :** marked by close acquaintance : FAMILIAR   **4 :** directed toward the interior

²inward *or* **in·wards** \-wərdz\ *adv* (bef. 12c)   **1 :** toward the inside, center, or interior   **2 :** toward the inner being

³inward *n* (bef. 12c)   **1 :** something that is inward   **2 in·wards** \'in-ərdz, -wərdz\ *pl* **:** INNARDS

Inward Light *n* (1706) : INNER LIGHT

in·ward·ly \'in-wərd-lē\ *adv* (bef. 12c)   **1 :** in the innermost being : MENTALLY, SPIRITUALLY   **2 a :** beneath the surface : INTERNALLY ⟨bled ~⟩   **b :** to oneself : PRIVATELY ⟨cursed ~⟩

in·ward·ness *n* (14c)   **1 :** internal quality or substance   **2 :** close acquaintance : FAMILIARITY   **3 :** fundamental nature : ESSENCE   **4 :** absorption in one's own mental or spiritual life

in·weave \(,)in-'wēv\ *vt* **-wove** \-'wōv\ *also* **-weaved; -wo·ven** \-'wō-vən\ *also* **-weaved; -weav·ing** (15c) : INTERWEAVE, INTERLACE

in·wrought \(,)in-'rȯt, 'in-,\ *adj* (1637)   **1 :** having decoration worked in : ORNAMENTED; *esp* **:** decorated with embroidery   **2 :** worked in esp. as decoration

in–your–face *adj* (1982) : characterized by or being bold and often arrogant aggressiveness ⟨~ basketball⟩

Io \'ī-(,)ō\ *n* [L, fr. Gk *Iō*] : a maiden loved by Zeus and changed by him into a heifer so that she might escape the jealous rage of Hera

iod- *or* **iodo-** *comb form* [F *iode*] : iodine ⟨*iodize*⟩ ⟨*iodoform*⟩

io·date \'ī-ə-,dāt, -dət\ *n* [F, fr. *iode*] (1826) : a salt of iodic acid

iod·ic acid \ī-'ä-dik-\ *n* [F *iodique,* fr. *iode*] (1826) : a crystalline oxidizing solid HIO₃ formed by oxidation of iodine

io·dide \'ī-ə-,dīd\ *n* [ISV] (1822) : a salt of hydriodic acid; *also* **:** the univalent anion I− of such a salt

io·din·ate \'ī-ə-də-,nāt\ *vt* **-at·ed; -at·ing** (1908) : to treat or cause to combine with iodine or a compound of iodine — **io·din·a·tion** \,ī-ə-də-'nā-shən\ *n*

io·dine \'ī-ə-,dīn, -dᵊn, -,dēn\ *n, often attrib* [F *iode,* fr. Gk *ioeidēs* violet colored, fr. *ion* violet] (1814)   **1 :** a nonmetallic halogen element obtained usu. as heavy shining blackish gray crystals and used esp. in medicine, photography, and analysis — see ELEMENT table   **2 :** a tincture of iodine used esp. as a topical antiseptic

io·dise *Brit var of* IODIZE

io·dize \'ī-ə-,dīz\ *vt* **io·dized; io·diz·ing** (1841) : to treat with iodine or an iodide ⟨*iodized* salt⟩

io·do·form \ī-'ō-də-,fȯrm, -'ä-\ *n* [ISV *iod-* + *-form* (as in *chloroform*)] (1838) : a yellow crystalline volatile compound CHI₃ with a penetrating persistent odor that is used as an antiseptic dressing

io·do·phor \-,fȯr\ *n* [*iod-* + Gk *-phoros* carrier — more at -PHORE] (1952) : a complex of iodine and a surface-active agent that releases iodine gradually and serves as a disinfectant

io·dop·sin \,ī-ə-'däp-sən\ *n* [*iod-* (fr. Gk *ioeidēs* violet colored) + Gk *opsis* sight, vision + E *-in* — more at OPTIC] (1938) : a photosensitive violet pigment in the retinal cones that is similar to rhodopsin but more labile, is formed from vitamin A, and is important in daylight vision

io moth \'ī-,ō-\ *n* [L *Io*] (1870) : a chiefly No. American saturniid moth (*Automeris io*) having a large circular eyelike spot on the upper surface of each hind wing and a larva with stinging spines

ion \'ī-ən, 'ī-,än\ *n* [Gk, neut. of *ion,* prp. of *ienai* to go — more at ISSUE] (ca. 1834)   **1 :** an atom or group of atoms that carries a positive or negative electric charge as a result of having lost or gained one or more electrons   **2 :** a charged subatomic particle (as a free electron)

-ion *n suffix* [ME *-ioun, -ion,* fr. OF *-ion,* fr. L *-ion-, -io*]   **1 a :** act or process ⟨*validation*⟩   **b :** result of an act or process ⟨*regulation*⟩   **2 :** state or condition ⟨*hydration*⟩

ion engine *n* (1958) : a reaction engine deriving thrust from the ejection of a stream of ionized particles

ion exchange *n* (1923) : a reversible interchange of one kind of ion present on an insoluble solid with another of like charge present in a solution surrounding the solid with the reaction being used esp. for softening or demineralizing water, the purification of chemicals, or the separation of substances — **ion exchanger** *n*

ion exchange resin *n* (1943) : an insoluble material of high molecular weight that contains groups which can be exchanged with ions in a solution with which it is in contact

Io·ni·an \ī-'ō-nē-ən\ *n* [*Ionia,* Asia Minor] (1550)   **1 :** a member of any of the Greek peoples who settled on the islands of the Aegean Sea and the western shore of Asia Minor toward the end of the second millennium B.C.   **2 :** a native or inhabitant of Ionia — **Ionian** *adj*

ion·ic \ī-'ä-nik\ *adj* [ISV] (1890)   **1 :** of, relating to, existing as, or characterized by ions ⟨~ gases⟩ ⟨the ~ charge⟩   **2 :** based on or functioning by means of ions ⟨~ conduction⟩ ⟨an ~ lattice⟩ — **ion·ic·i·ty** \,ī-ə-'ni-sə-tē\ *n*

¹Ion·ic \ī-'ä-nik\ *adj* [L & MF; MF *ionique,* fr. L *ionicus,* fr. Gk *iōnikos,* fr. *Iōnia* Ionia] (1585)   **1 :** of or relating to the ancient Greek architectural order distinguished esp. by fluted columns on bases and scroll volutes in its capitals — see ORDER illustration   **2 :** of or relating to Ionia or the Ionians

²Ionic *n* (1668) : a dialect of ancient Greek spoken esp. in Ionia and the Cyclades

---

\ə\ abut \ᵊ\ kitten, F table \ər\ further \a\ ash \ā\ ace \ä\ mop, mar \aú\ out \ch\ chin \e\ bet \ē\ easy \g\ go \i\ hit \ī\ ice \j\ job \ŋ\ sing \ō\ go \ȯ\ law \ȯi\ boy \th\ thin \t͟h\ the \ü\ loot \ú\ foot \y\ yet \zh\ vision \à, k͓, ⁿ, œ, œ̄, ɶ, ᵫ, �465\ *see* Guide to Pronunciation

ionic bond *n* (1939) : a chemical bond formed between oppositely charged species because of their mutual electrostatic attraction

ion·ise *Brit var of* IONIZE

io·ni·um \ī-'ō-nē-əm\ *n* [*ion*; fr. its ionizing action] (1907) : a natural radioactive isotope of thorium having a mass number of 230

ionization chamber *n* (1904) : a partially evacuated tube provided with electrodes so that its conductivity due to the ionization of the residual gas reveals the presence of ionizing radiation

ion·ize \'ī-ə-₁nīz\ *vb* **ion·ized; ion·iz·ing** [ISV] *vt* (1898) : to convert wholly or partly into ions ~ *vi* : to become ionized — **ion·iz·able** \-₁nī-zə-bəl\ *adj* — **ion·i·za·tion** \₁ī-ə-nə-'zā-shən\ *n* — **ion·iz·er** \'ī-ə-₁nī-zər\ *n*

ion·o·phore \ī-'ä-nə-₁fōr, -₁fȯr\ *n* (ca. 1955) : a compound that facilitates transmission of an ion (as of calcium) across a lipid barrier (as in a cell membrane) by combining with the ion or by increasing the permeability of the barrier to it

ion·o·sphere \ī-'ä-nə-₁sfir\ *n* (1926) : the part of the earth's atmosphere in which ionization of atmospheric gases affects the propagation of radio waves, which extends from about 30 miles (50 kilometers) to the exosphere, which is divided into regions of one or more layers whose altitudes and degrees of ionization vary with time of day, season, and solar cycle, and which is contiguous with the upper portion of the mesosphere and the thermosphere; *also* : a comparable region of charged particles surrounding another celestial body (as Venus) — **ion·o·spher·ic** \₁ī-₁ä-nə-'sfir-ik, -'sfer-\ *adj* — **ion·o·spher·i·cal·ly** \-i-k(ə-)lē\ *adv*

ion·to·pho·re·sis \(₁)ī-₁än-tə-fə-'rē-səs\ *n*, *pl* **-re·ses** \-₁sēz\ [NL, fr. *ionto-* ion (fr. Gk *iont-, ion,* prp. of *ienai*) + *-phoresis*] (1909) : the introduction of an ionized substance (as a drug) through intact skin by the application of a direct electric current — **ion·to·pho·ret·ic** \-'re-tik\ *adj* — **ion·to·pho·ret·i·cal·ly** \-ti-k(ə-)lē\ *adv*

io·ta \ī-'ō-tə\ *n* [L, fr. Gk *iōta,* of Sem origin; akin to Heb *yōdh* yod] (1607) **1** : the 9th letter of the Greek alphabet — see ALPHABET table **2** : an infinitesimal amount — JOT

IOU \₁ī-(₁)ō-'yü\ *n* [fr. the pronunciation of *I owe you*] (1795) **1** : a paper that has on it the letters IOU, a stated sum, and a signature and that is given as an acknowledgment of debt **2** : DEBT, OBLIGATION

-ious *adj suffix* [ME, partly fr. OF *-ious, -ieux,* fr. L *-iosus,* fr. *-i-,* penultimate vowel of some noun stems + *-osus* -ous; partly fr. L *-ius,* adj. suffix] : -OUS

IPA \₁ī-(₁)pē-'ā\ *n* [*International Phonetic Alphabet*] (1933) : an alphabet designed to represent each human speech sound with a unique symbol

ip·e·cac \'i-pi-₁kak\ *or* **ipe·ca·cu·an·ha** \₁i-pi-₁ka-kyə-'wä-nə, -nyə\ *n* [Pg *ipecacuanha,* fr. Tupi *ipekaaguéne*] (1682) **1** : the dried rhizome and roots of either of two tropical American plants (*Cephaelis acuminata* and *C. ipecacuanha*) of the madder family used esp. as a source of emetine; *also* : either of these plants **2** : an emetic and expectorant drug that contains emetine and is prepared from ipecac esp. as a syrup for use in treating accidental poisoning

Iph·i·ge·nia \₁i-fə-jə-'nī-ə\ *n* [L, fr. Gk *Iphigeneia*] : a daughter of Agamemnon nearly sacrificed by him to Artemis but saved by her and made a priestess

ipro·ni·a·zid \₁ī-prə-'nī-ə-zəd\ *n* [blend of *isoniazid* and *propyl*] (1952) : a derivative $C_9H_{13}N_3O$ of isoniazid that is used as a monoamine oxidase inhibitor and was formerly used in treating tuberculosis

ip·se dix·it \₁ip-sē-'dik-sət\ *n* [L, he himself said it] (15c) : an assertion made but not proved : DICTUM

ip·si·lat·er·al \₁ip-si-'la-t(ə-)rəl\ *adj* [ISV, fr. L *ipse* self, himself + *later-, latus* side] (1907) : situated or appearing on or affecting the same side of the body — **ip·si·lat·er·al·ly** \-t(ə-)rə-lē\ *adv*

ip·so·si·ma ver·ba \ip-'si-sə-mə-'vər-bə\ *n pl* [NL, lit., the selfsame words] (1807) : the exact language used by someone quoted

ip·so fac·to \'ip-(₁)sō-'fak-(₁)tō\ *adv* [NL, lit., by the fact itself] (1548) : by that very fact or act : as an inevitable result

IQ \₁ī-'kyü\ *n* (1920) : INTELLIGENCE QUOTIENT

ir- — see IN-

IRA \₁ī-(₁)är-'ā; 'ī-rə\ *n, pl* **IRAs** [*individual retirement account*] (1974) : a savings account in which a person may deposit up to a stipulated amount each year with the deposits deductible from taxable income and both deposits and interest taxable after the person's retirement

Ira·ni·an \i-'rä-nē-ən, -'ra-, -'rä-; ī-\ *n* (1789) **1** : a native or inhabitant of Iran **2** : a branch of the Indo-European family of languages that includes Persian — see INDO-EUROPEAN LANGUAGES table — **Iranian** *adj*

iras·ci·ble \i-'ra-sə-bəl\ *adj* [MF, fr. LL *irascibilis,* fr. L *irasci* to become angry, be angry, fr. *ira*] (ca. 1530) : marked by hot temper and easily provoked anger — **iras·ci·bil·i·ty** \-₁ra-sə-'bi-lə-tē\ *n* — **iras·ci·ble·ness** \i-'ra-sə-bəl-nəs\ *n* — **iras·ci·bly** \-blē\ *adv*

irate \ī-'rāt, 'ī-,, i-'rāt\ *adj* (1838) **1** : roused to ire ⟨an ~ taxpayer⟩ **2** : arising from anger ⟨~ words⟩ — **irate·ly** *adv* — **irate·ness** *n*

ire \'ī(ə)r\ *n* [ME, fr. MF, fr. L *ira;* perh. akin to Gk *oistros* gadfly, frenzy] (14c) : intense and usu. openly displayed anger **syn** see ANGER — **ire** *vt* — **ire·ful** \-fəl\ *adj*

iren·ic \ī-'re-nik, -'rē-\ *adj* [Gk *eirēnikos,* fr. *eirēnē* peace] (ca. 1864) : favoring, conducive to, or operating toward peace, moderation, or conciliation — **iren·i·cal·ly** \'re-ni-k(ə-)lē, -'rē-\ *adv*

irid- *or* **irido-** *comb form* **1** [L *irid-, iris*] : rainbow ⟨*irid*escent⟩ **2** [NL *irid-, iris*] : iris of the eye ⟨*irid*ology⟩

ir·i·des·cence \₁ir-ə-'de-sᵊn(t)s\ *n* (1804) **1** : a lustrous rainbowlike play of color caused by differential refraction of light waves (as from an oil slick, soap bubble, or fish scales) that tends to change as the angle of view changes **2** : a lustrous or attractive quality or effect ⟨the agglomeration of power which . . . gives them a certain ~ of glamor and superiority —Margaret Landon⟩

ir·i·des·cent \-sᵊnt\ *adj* (1791) : having or exhibiting iridescence — **ir·i·des·cent·ly** *adv*

irid·ic \i-'ri-dik, ī-'ri-dik\ *adj* (ca. 1890) : of or relating to the iris of the eye

irid·i·um \i-'ri-dē-əm\ *n* [NL, fr. L *irid-, iris;* fr. the colors produced by its dissolving in hydrochloric acid] (1804) : a silver-white hard brittle very heavy metallic element — see ELEMENT table

ir·i·dol·o·gy \₁ī-rə-'dä-lə-jē\ *n, pl* **-gies** (ca. 1923) : the study of the iris of the eye for indications of bodily health and disease — **ir·i·dol·o·gist** \-jist\ *n*

ir·id·os·mine \₁ir-ə-'däz-₁mēn\ *n* [G, fr. NL *iridium + osmium*] (1827) : a mineral that is a native iridium osmium alloy usu. containing some rhodium and platinum

¹iris \'ī-rəs\ *n, pl* **iris·es** *or* **iri·des** \'ī-rə-₁dēz, 'ir-ə-\ [ME, fr. L *irid-, iris* rainbow, iris plant, fr. Gk, rainbow, iris plant, iris of the eye — more at WIRE] (15c) **1** : RAINBOW **2** [NL *irid-, iris,* fr. Gk] **a** : the opaque contractile diaphragm perforated by the pupil and forming the colored portion of the eye — see EYE illustration **b** : IRIS DIAPHRAGM; *also* : a similar device with a circular opening that can be varied in size **3** *or pl* **iris** [NL *Irid-, Iris,* genus name, fr. L] : any of a large genus (*Iris* of the family Iridaceae, the iris family) of perennial herbaceous plants with linear usu. basal leaves and large showy flowers

²iris *vt* (1816) : to make iridescent

Iris \'ī-rəs\ *n* [L, fr. Gk] : the Greek goddess of the rainbow and a messenger of the gods

iris diaphragm *n* (1867) : an adjustable diaphragm of thin opaque plates that can be turned by a ring so as to change the diameter of a central opening usu. to regulate the aperture of a lens

Irish \'ī-rish\ *n* [ME, fr. (assumed) OE *Īrisc,* fr. *Īras* Irishmen, of Celt origin; akin to OIr *Ériu* Ireland] (13c) **1** *pl in constr* : natives or inhabitants of Ireland or their descendants esp. when of Celtic speech or culture **2 a** : the Celtic language of Ireland esp. as used since the later medieval period **b** : English spoken by the Irish **3** : IRISH WHISKEY — **Irish** *adj*

iris diaphragm

Irish bull *n* (1802) : an incongruous statement (as "it was hereditary in his family to have no children")

Irish coffee *n* (1950) : hot sugared coffee and Irish whiskey topped with whipped cream

Irish confetti *n* (1922) : a rock or brick used as a missile

Irish Gaelic *n* (1891) : IRISH 2a

Irish·ism \'ī-ri-₁shi-zəm\ *n* (1734) **1** : a word, phrase, or expression characteristic of the Irish **2** : IRISH BULL

Irish·ly \'ī-rish-lē\ *adv* (1571) : in a manner characteristic of the Irish

Irish mail *n* (1908) : a 3- or 4-wheeled toy vehicle activated by a hand lever

Irish·man \'ī-rish-mən\ *n* (13c) **1** : a native or inhabitant of Ireland **2** : one that is of Irish descent

Irish moss *n* (1845) **1** : the dried and bleached plants of a red alga (esp. *Chondrus crispus*) used as an agent for thickening or emulsifying or as a demulcent **2** : a red alga that is a source of Irish moss — called also *carrageen*

Irish·ness \'ī-rish-nəs\ *n* (1804) : the fact or quality of being Irish

Irish potato *n* (1664) : POTATO 2b

Irish·ry \'ī-rish-rē\ *n, pl* **-ries** (14c) **1** : IRISH 1 **2 a** : Irish quality or character **b** : an Irish peculiarity or trait

Irish setter *n* (1866) : any of a breed of bird dogs generally comparable to English setters but with a mahogany-red coat

Irish stew *n* (1814) : a stew having as its principal ingredients meat (as lamb), potatoes, and onions in a thick gravy

Irish terrier *n* (1857) : any of a breed of active medium-sized terriers developed in Ireland and characterized by a dense close usu. reddish wiry coat

Irish water spaniel *n* (1885) : any of a breed of large retrievers characterized by a topknot, a heavy curly coat which is dark liver in color, and a short-haired tail

Irish whiskey *n* (1798) : whiskey made in Ireland chiefly of barley

Irish wolfhound *n* (1880) : any of a breed of very tall heavily built hounds having a rough wiry coat

Irish·wom·an \'ī-rish-₁wu̇-mən\ *n* (15c) : a woman born in Ireland or of Irish descent

iri·tis \ī-'rī-təs\ *n* [NL, irreg. fr. *iris*] (1818) : inflammation of the iris of the eye

¹irk \'ərk\ *vt* [ME] (15c) : to make weary, irritated, or bored **syn** see ANNOY

²irk *n* (ca. 1570) **1** : the fact of being annoying **2** : a source of annoyance

irk·some \'ərk-səm\ *adj* (15c) : tending to irk : TEDIOUS ⟨an ~ task⟩ — **irk·some·ly** *adv* — **irk·some·ness** *n*

Irish wolfhound

iro·ko \ə-'rō-(₁)kō\ *n* [Yoruba *irókò*] (1890) : a large tropical western African tree (*Chlorophora excelsa*) of the mulberry family having strong streaky insect-resistant wood which is often used as a teak substitute; *also* : this wood

¹iron \'ī(-ə)rn\ *n* [ME, fr. OE *īsern, īren;* akin to OHG *īsarn* iron] (bef. 12c) **1** : a heavy malleable ductile magnetic silver-white metallic element that readily rusts in moist air, occurs native in meteorites and combined in most igneous rocks, is the most used of metals, and is vital to biological processes — see ELEMENT table **2** : something made of iron: as **a** *pl* : shackles for the hands or legs **b** : a heated metal implement used for branding or cauterizing **c** : a household device usu. with a flat metal base that is heated to smooth, finish, or press (as cloth) **d** : STIRRUP — usu. used in pl. **e** : any of a series of numbered golf clubs having relatively thin metal heads — compare WOOD 3 **3** : great strength, hardness, or determination — **iron in the fire 1** : a matter requiring close attention **2** : a prospective course of action

²iron *adj* (bef. 12c) **1** : of, relating to, or made of iron **2** : resembling iron **3 a** : strong and healthy : ROBUST **b** : INFLEXIBLE, UNRELENTING ⟨~ determination⟩ **c** : holding or binding fast ⟨an ~ grip⟩ — **iron·ness** \'ī(-ə)rn-nəs\ *n*

³iron *vt* (15c) **1** : to furnish or cover with iron **2** : to shackle with irons **3 a** : to smooth with or as if with a heated iron ⟨~ a shirt⟩ **b** : to remove (as wrinkles) by ironing ~ *vi* : to smooth or press cloth or clothing with a heated iron

Iron Age n (1879) : the period of human culture characterized by the smelting of iron and its use in industry beginning somewhat before 1000 B.C. in western Asia and Egypt

iron·bark \ˈī(-ə)rn-ˌbärk\ n (1799) : any of several Australian eucalypti having hard gray bark and heavy hard durable wood used esp. in heavy construction; *also* : this wood

iron·bound \-ˈbaund\ adj (14c) : bound with or as if with iron: as **a** : HARSH, RUGGED ⟨~ coast⟩ **b** : STERN, RIGOROUS ⟨~ traditions⟩

¹**iron·clad** \-ˈklad\ adj (ca. 1847) **1** : sheathed in iron armor — used esp. of naval vessels **2** : so firm or secure as to be unbreakable: as **a** : BINDING ⟨an ~ oath⟩ **b** : having no obvious weakness ⟨an ~ case against the defendant⟩

²**iron·clad** \-ˌklad\ n (1862) : an armored naval vessel esp. of the mid to late nineteenth century

iron curtain n (1819) **1** : an impenetrable barrier ⟨the *iron curtain* between the ego and the unconscious —C. J. Rolo⟩ **2** : a political, military, and ideological barrier that cuts off and isolates an area; *specif, often cap* : one isolating an area under Soviet control

iron·er \ˈī(-ə)rn-ər\ n (1773) : one that irons; *specif* : MANGLE

iron·fisted \ˈī(-ə)rn-ˈfis-təd\ adj (1599) **1** : STINGY, MISERLY **2** : being both harsh and ruthless ⟨~ methods⟩

iron gray n (bef. 12c) : a slightly greenish dark gray

iron hand n (1703) : stern or rigorous control ⟨ruled with an *iron hand*⟩ — **iron-hand·ed** \ˈī(-ə)rn-ˈhan-dəd\ adj

iron·heart·ed \ˈī(-ə)rn-ˈhär-təd\ adj (1600) : CRUEL, HARD-HEARTED

iron horse n (1840) : LOCOMOTIVE 1; esp : a steam locomotive

iron·ic \ī-ˈrä-nik also i-ˈrä-\ or **iron·i·cal** \-ni-kəl\ adj (1576) **1** : relating to, containing, or constituting irony **2** : given to irony *syn* see SARCASTIC — **iron·i·cal·ness** \-ni-kəl-nəs\ n

iron·i·cal·ly \-ni-k(ə-)lē\ adv (1576) **1** : in an ironic manner **2** : it is ironic, curious, or surprising

iron·ing \ˈī(-ə)r-niŋ\ n (ca. 1710) **1** : the action or process of smoothing or pressing with or as if with a heated iron **2** : clothes ironed or to be ironed

ironing board n (1843) : a flat padded cloth-covered surface on which clothes are ironed

iro·nist \ˈī-rə-nist\ n (1727) : one who uses irony esp. in the development of a literary work or theme

iro·nize \-ˌnīz\ vb **-nized; -niz·ing** vt (1602) : to make ironic in appearance or effect ~ vi : to use irony: speak or behave ironically

iron lung n (1932) : a device for artificial respiration in which rhythmic alternations in the air pressure in a chamber surrounding a patient's chest force air into and out of the lungs

iron maiden n (ca. 1895) : a supposed medieval torture device consisting of a hollow iron statue or coffin in the shape of a woman that is lined with spikes which impale the enclosed victim

iron man n (1914) : a man of unusual physical endurance

iron·mas·ter \ˈī(-ə)rn-ˌmas-tər\ n (1674) : a manufacturer of iron

iron·mon·ger \-ˌməŋ-gər, -ˌmäŋ-\ n (14c) Brit : a dealer in iron and hardware

iron·mon·gery \-g(ə-)rē\ n (1711) : something made of metal; esp, Brit : HARDWARE 1

iron out vt (1870) **1** : to make smooth or flat by or as if by pressing **2** : to resolve or work out a solution to ⟨*ironed out* their differences⟩

iron oxide n (1885) : any of several oxides of iron: as **a** : FERRIC OXIDE **b** : FERROUS OXIDE

iron pyrites n (ca. 1817) : PYRITE — called also *iron pyrite*

iron ration n (1870) : an emergency ration

iron·side \-ˌsīd\ n (13c) : a man of great strength or bravery

iron·stone \ˈī(-ə)rn-ˌstōn\ n (1522) **1** : a hard sedimentary rock rich in iron; esp : a siderite in a coal region **2** : IRONSTONE CHINA

ironstone china n (1825) : a hard heavy durable white pottery developed in England early in the 19th century

iron sulfide n (1885) : any of several sulfides of iron

iron·ware \ˈī(-ə)rn-ˌwar, -ˌwer\ n (15c) : articles made of iron

iron·weed \-ˌwēd\ n (1819) : any of several mostly weedy American composite plants (genus *Vernonia*) usu. having alternate leaves and perfect red, purple, or white tubular flowers in terminal cymose heads

iron·wood \-ˌwud\ n (1657) **1** : any of numerous trees and shrubs (as a hornbeam or hop hornbeam) with exceptionally tough or hard wood **2** : the wood of an ironwood

iron·work \-ˌwərk\ n (15c) **1** : work in iron; *also* : something made of iron **2** pl but sing or pl in constr : a mill or building where iron or steel is smelted or heavy iron or steel products are made — **iron·work·er** \-ˌwər-kər\ n

iro·ny \ˈī-rə-nē also ˈī(-ə)r-nē\ n, pl **-nies** [L *ironia*, fr. Gk *eirōnia*, fr. *eirōn* dissembler] (1502) **1** : a pretense of ignorance and of willingness to learn from another assumed in order to make the other's false conceptions conspicuous by adroit questioning — called also *Socratic irony* **2 a** : the use of words to express something other than and esp. the opposite of the literal meaning **b** : a usu. humorous or sardonic literary style or form characterized by irony **c** : an ironic expression or utterance **3 a** (1) : incongruity between the actual result of a sequence of events and the normal or expected result (2) : an event or result marked by such incongruity **b** : incongruity between a situation developed in a drama and the accompanying words or actions that is understood by the audience but not by the characters in the play — called also *dramatic irony, tragic irony* *syn* see WIT

Ir·o·quoi·an \ˌir-ə-ˈkwöi-ən\ n (1697) **1** : a member of any of the peoples constituting the Iroquois **2** : an American Indian language family of eastern No. America including Cayuga, Cherokee, Mohawk, Onondaga, Oneida, Seneca, and Tuscarora — **Iroquoian** adj

Ir·o·quois \ˈir-ə-ˌkwöi also -ˌkwä\ n, pl **Iroquois** \-ˌkwöi(z), -ˌkwä(z)\ [F, prob. of Algonquian origin] (1666) **1** pl : an American Indian confederacy orig. of New York consisting of the Cayuga, Mohawk, Oneida, Onondaga, and Seneca and later including the Tuscarora **2** : a member of any of the Iroquois peoples

ir·ra·di·ance \ir-ˈrā-dē-ən(t)s\ n (1667) **1** : RADIANCE 1 **2** : the density of radiation incident on a given surface usu. expressed in watts per square centimeter or square meter

ir·ra·di·ate \ir-ˈrā-dē-ˌāt\ vb **-at·ed; -at·ing** [L *irradiatus*, pp. of *irradiare*, fr. *in-* + *radius* ray] vt (1603) **1 a** : to cast rays of light upon : ILLUMINATE **b** : to enlighten intellectually or spiritually **c** : to affect or treat by radiant energy (as heat); *specif* : to treat by exposure to radiation **2** : to emit like rays of light : RADIATE ⟨*irradiating* strength and comfort⟩ ~ vi, *archaic* : to emit rays : SHINE — **ir·ra·di·a·tive** \-ˌā-tiv\ adj — **ir·ra·di·a·tor** \-ˌā-tər\ n

ir·ra·di·a·tion \i-ˌrā-dē-ˈā-shən\ n (1901) **1** : exposure to radiation (as X rays or alpha particles) **2** : application of radiation (as X rays or ultraviolet light) esp. for therapeutic purposes

ir·rad·i·ca·ble \i-ˈrad-i-kə-bəl\ adj [ML *irradicabilis*, fr. L *in-* + *radic-, radix* root — more at ROOT] (1728) : impossible to eradicate : DEEP-ROOTED — **ir·rad·i·ca·bly** \-blē\ adv

ir·ra·tio·nal \i-ˈra-sh(ə-)nəl, (ˌ)i(r)-\ adj [ME, fr. L *irrationalis*, fr. *in-* + *rationalis* rational] (14c) : not rational: as **a** (1) : not endowed with reason or understanding (2) : lacking usual or normal mental clarity or coherence **b** : not governed by or according to reason ⟨~ fears⟩ **c** *Greek & Latin prosody* (1) *of a syllable* : having a quantity other than that required by the meter (2) *of a foot* : containing such a syllable **d** (1) : being an irrational number ⟨an ~ root of an equation⟩ (2) : having a numerical value that is an irrational number ⟨a length that is ~⟩ — **ir·ra·tio·nal·i·ty** \-ˌra-shə-ˈna-lə-tē\ n — **ir·ra·tio·nal·ly** \-ˈra-sh(ə-)nə-lē\ adv

²**irrational** n (1646) **1** : an irrational being **2** : IRRATIONAL NUMBER

ir·ra·tio·nal·ism \i-ˈra-sh(ə-)nə-ˌli-zəm\ n (1811) : a system emphasizing intuition, instinct, feeling, or faith rather than reason or holding that the universe is governed by irrational forces **2** : the quality or state of being irrational — **ir·ra·tio·nal·ist** \-list\ n or adj — **ir·ra·tio·nal·is·tic** \-ˌra-sh(ə-)nə-ˈlis-tik\ adj

irrational number n (1551) : a number that can be expressed as an infinite decimal with no set of consecutive digits repeating itself indefinitely and that cannot be expressed as the quotient of two integers

ir·re·al \i-ˈrē(-ə)l, (ˌ)i(r)-, -ˈri(-ə)l\ adj (1944) : not real

ir·re·al·i·ty \ˌir-ē-ˈa-lə-tē\ n (1803) : UNREALITY

ir·re·claim·able \ˌir-i-ˈklā-mə-bəl\ adj (1662) : incapable of being reclaimed — **ir·re·claim·ably** \-blē\ adv

¹**ir·rec·on·cil·able** \i-ˌre-kən-ˈsī-lə-bəl, i-ˈre-kən-ˌ, ˌi(r)-\ adj (1599) : impossible to reconcile — **ir·rec·on·cil·abil·i·ty** \-ˌre-kən-ˌsī-lə-ˈbi-lə-tē\ n — **ir·rec·on·cil·able·ness** \-ˌre-kən-ˈsī-lə-bəl-nəs, -ˈre-kən-ˌ\ n — **ir·rec·on·cil·ably** \-blē\ adv

²**irreconcilable** n (1748) : one that is irreconcilable; esp : a member of a group (as a political party) opposing compromise or collaboration

ir·re·cov·er·able \ˌir-i-ˈkəv-rə-bəl, -ˈkə-və-\ adj (15c) : not capable of being recovered or rectified : IRREPARABLE — **ir·re·cov·er·able·ness** n — **ir·re·cov·er·ably** \-blē\ adv

ir·re·cu·sa·ble \ˌir-i-ˈkyü-zə-bəl\ adj [LL *irrecusabilis*, fr. L *in-* + *recusare* to reject, refuse — more at RECUSANT] (1776) : not subject to exception or rejection — **ir·re·cu·sa·bly** \-blē\ adv

ir·re·deem·able \ˌir-i-ˈdē-mə-bəl\ adj (1698) **1** : not redeemable: as **a** : not terminable by payment of the principal ⟨~ bond⟩ **b** : INCONVERTIBLE **2** : being beyond remedy : HOPELESS ⟨~ mistakes⟩ — **ir·re·deem·ably** \-blē\ adv

ir·re·den·ta \ˌir-i-ˈden-tə\ n [It *Italia irredenta*, lit., unredeemed Italy, Italian-speaking territory not incorporated in Italy] (1914) : a territory historically or ethnically related to one political unit but under the political control of another

ir·re·den·tism \-ˈden-ˌti-zəm\ n (1883) : a political principle or policy directed toward the incorporation of irredentas within the boundaries of their historically or ethnically related political unit — **ir·re·den·tist** \-ˈden-tist\ n or adj

ir·re·duc·ible \ˌir-i-ˈdü-sə-bəl, -ˈdyü-\ adj (1633) : impossible to transform into or restore to a desired or simpler condition ⟨an ~ matrix⟩; *specif* : incapable of being factored into polynomials of lower degree with coefficients in some given field (as the rational numbers) or integral domain (as the integers) ⟨an ~ equation⟩ — **ir·re·duc·ibil·i·ty** \-ˌdü-sə-ˈbi-lə-tē, -ˌdyü-\ n — **ir·re·duc·ibly** \-ˈdü-sə-blē, -ˈdyü-\ adv

ir·re·flex·ive \ˌir-i-ˈflek-siv\ adj (ca. 1890) : being a relation for which the reflexive property does not hold for any element of a given set

ir·re·form·able \ˌir-i-ˈför-mə-bəl\ adj (1609) **1** : incapable of being reformed : INCORRIGIBLE **2** : not subject to revision or alteration ⟨~ dogma⟩ — **ir·re·form·abil·i·ty** \-ˌför-mə-ˈbi-lə-tē\ n

ir·re·fra·ga·ble \i-ˈre-frə-gə-bəl, (ˌ)i(r)-; ˌir-i-ˈfra-gə-\ adj [LL *irrefragabilis*, fr. L *in-* + *refragari* to oppose, fr. *re-* + *-fragari* (as in *suffragari* to vote for); akin to L *suffragium* suffrage] (1533) **1** : impossible to refute ⟨~ arguments⟩ **2** : impossible to break or alter ⟨~ rules⟩ — **ir·re·fra·ga·bil·i·ty** \i-ˌre-frə-gə-ˈbi-lə-tē, (ˌ)i(r)-; ˌir-i-ˌfra-gə-\ n — **ir·re·fra·ga·bly** \i-ˈre-frə-gə-blē, (ˌ)i(r)-; ˌir-i-ˈfra-gə-\ adv

ir·re·fut·able \ˌir-i-ˈfyü-tə-bəl; i-ˈre-fyə-tə-, (ˌ)i(r)-\ adj [LL *irrefutabilis*, fr. L *in-* + *refutare* to refute] (1620) : impossible to refute : INCONTROVERTIBLE ⟨~ proof⟩ — **ir·re·fut·abil·i·ty** \ˌir-i-ˌfyü-tə-ˈbi-lə-tē; i-ˌre-fyə-tə-, (ˌ)i(r)-\ n — **ir·re·fut·ably** \ˌir-i-ˈfyü-tə-blē; i-ˈre-fyə-tə-, (ˌ)i(r)-\ adv

ir·re·gard·less \ˌir-i-ˈgärd-ləs\ adv [prob. blend of *irrespective* and *regardless*] (ca. 1912) *nonstand* : REGARDLESS

usage Irregardless originated in dialectal American speech in the early 20th century. Its fairly widespread use in speech called it to the attention of usage commentators as early as 1927. The most frequently repeated remark about it is that "there is no such word." There is such a word, however. It is still used primarily in speech, although it can be found from time to time in edited prose. Its reputation has not risen over the years, and it is still a long way from general acceptance. Use *regardless* instead.

¹**ir·reg·u·lar** \i-ˈre-gyə-lər, (ˌ)i(r)-\ adj [ME *irreguler*, fr. MF, fr. LL *irregularis* not in accordance with rule, fr. L *in-* + *regularis* regular] (14c) **1 a** : not being or acting in accord with laws, rules, or established custom ⟨~ conduct⟩ **b** : not conforming to the usual pattern of inflection ⟨~ verbs⟩; *specif* : STRONG 16 **c** : not following a usual or prescribed procedure; *esp, Brit* : celebrated without either proclamation or publication of intention to marry ⟨~ marriage⟩ **2** : not belonging to or a part of a regular organized group; *specif* : not belonging to a regular army but raised for a special purpose ⟨~ troops⟩

\ə\ abut \ᵊ\ kitten, F table \ər\ further \a\ ash \ā\ ace \ä\ mop, mar
\au̇\ out \ch\ chin \e\ bet \ē\ easy \g\ go \i\ hit \ī\ ice \j\ job
\ŋ\ sing \ō\ go \ȯ\ law \ȯi\ boy \th\ thin \t͟h\ the \ü\ loot \u̇\ foot
\y\ yet \zh\ vision \à, k̲, ⁿ, œ, œ̄, ᴜᴇ, ᵫ, ᵞ\ see Guide to Pronunciation

3 a : lacking perfect symmetry or evenness ⟨an ~ coastline⟩ **b :** ZY-GOMORPHIC ⟨~ flowers⟩ **4 :** lacking continuity or regularity esp. of occurrence or activity ⟨~ employment⟩ — **ir·reg·u·lar·ly** *adv*
syn IRREGULAR, ANOMALOUS, UNNATURAL mean not conforming to rule, law, or custom. IRREGULAR implies not conforming to a law or regulation imposed for the sake of uniformity in method, practice, or conduct ⟨concerned about his *irregular* behavior⟩. ANOMALOUS implies not conforming to what might be expected because of the class or type to which it belongs or the laws that govern its existence ⟨her drive made her an *anomalous* figure in a sleepy organization⟩. UNNATURAL suggests what is contrary to nature or to principles or standards felt to be essential to the well-being of civilized society ⟨prisoners treated with *unnatural* cruelty⟩.
²**irregular** *n* (15c) : one that is irregular: as **a :** a soldier who is not a member of a regular military force **b :** merchandise that has minor defects or that falls next below the manufacturer's standard for firsts
ir·reg·u·lar·i·ty \i-ˌre-gyə-ˈla-rə-tē, ˌi(r)-\ *n, pl* **-ties** [ME *irregularite,* fr. MF *irregularité,* fr. ML *irregularitat-, irregularitas,* fr. LL *irregularis*] (14c) **1 :** something that is irregular (as improper or dishonest conduct) ⟨alleged *irregularities* in the city government⟩ **2 :** the quality or state of being irregular **3 :** CONSTIPATION
ir·rel·a·tive \-ˈre-lə-tiv\ *adj* (1640) : not relative: **a :** not related **b :** IRRELEVANT — **ir·rel·a·tive·ly** *adv*
ir·rel·e·vance \-ˈre-lə-vən(t)s\ *n* (1847) **1 :** the quality or state of being irrelevant **2 :** something irrelevant
ir·rel·e·van·cy \-vən(t)-sē\ *n, pl* **-cies** (1592) : IRRELEVANCE
ir·rel·e·vant \-vənt\ *adj* (1786) : not relevant : INAPPLICABLE ⟨that statement is ~ to your argument⟩ — **ir·rel·e·vant·ly** *adv*
ir·re·li·gion \ˌir-i-ˈli-jən\ *n* [MF or LL; MF, fr. LL *irreligion-, irreligio,* fr. L *in-* + *religion-, religio* religion] (1598) : the quality or state of being irreligious — **ir·re·li·gion·ist** \-ˈlij-nist, -ˈli-jə-\ *n*
ir·re·li·gious \-ˈli-jəs\ *adj* (15c) **1 :** neglectful of religion : lacking religious emotions, doctrines, or practices ⟨so ~ that they exploit popular religion for professional purposes —G. B. Shaw⟩ **2 :** indicating lack of religion — **ir·re·li·gious·ly** *adv*
ir·re·me·able \i-ˈrē-mē-ə-bəl, ˌi(r)-\ *adj* [L *irremeabilis,* fr. *in-* + *remeare* to go back, fr. *re-* + *meare* to go — more at PERMEATE] (1569) : offering no possibility of return
ir·re·me·di·a·ble \ˌir-i-ˈmē-dē-ə-bəl\ *adj* [ME, fr. L *irremediabilis,* fr. *in-* + *remediabilis* remediable] (15c) : not remediable; *specif* : INCURABLE — **ir·re·me·di·a·ble·ness** *n* — **ir·re·me·di·a·bly** \-blē\ *adv*
ir·re·mov·able \-ˈmü-və-bəl\ *adj* (1598) : not removable — **ir·re·mov·abil·i·ty** \-ˌmü-və-ˈbi-lə-tē\ *n* — **ir·re·mov·ably** \-ˈmü-və-blē\ *adv*
ir·rep·a·ra·ble \i-ˈre-p(ə-)rə-bəl, ˌi(r)- *also* ÷ˌir-(r)ə-ˈpar-ə-bəl\ *adj* [ME, fr. MF, fr. L *irreparabilis,* fr. *in-* + *reparabilis* reparable] (15c) : not reparable : IRREMEDIABLE ⟨~ damage⟩ — **ir·rep·a·ra·ble·ness** *n* — **ir·rep·a·ra·bly** \-blē\ *adv*
ir·re·peal·able \ˌir-i-ˈpē-lə-bəl\ *adj* (1633) : not repealable — **ir·re·peal·abil·i·ty** \-ˌpē-lə-ˈbi-lə-tē\ *n*
ir·re·place·able \-ˈplā-sə-bəl\ *adj* (1807) : not replaceable — **ir·re·place·abil·i·ty** \-ˌplā-sə-ˈbi-lə-tē\ *n* — **ir·re·place·able·ness** \-ˈplā-sə-bəl-nəs\ *n* — **ir·re·place·ably** \-blē\ *adv*
ir·re·press·ible \-ˈpre-sə-bəl\ *adj* (1811) : impossible to repress, restrain, or control ⟨~ curiosity⟩ — **ir·re·press·ibil·i·ty** \-ˌpre-sə-ˈbi-lə-tē\ *n* — **ir·re·press·ibly** \-ˈpre-sə-blē\ *adv*
ir·re·proach·able \-ˈprō-chə-bəl\ *adj* (1634) : not reproachable : BLAMELESS, IMPECCABLE ⟨~ conduct⟩ — **ir·re·proach·abil·i·ty** \-ˌprō-chə-ˈbi-lə-tē\ *n* — **ir·re·proach·able·ness** \-ˈprō-chə-bəl-nəs\ *n* — **ir·re·proach·ably** \-blē\ *adv*
ir·re·pro·duc·ible \i-ˌrē-prə-ˈdü-sə-bəl, ˌi(r)-, -ˈdyü-\ *adj* (1868) : not reproducible — **ir·re·pro·duc·ibil·i·ty** \-ˌdü-sə-ˈbi-lə-tē, -ˌdyü-\ *n*
ir·re·sist·ible \ˌir-i-ˈzis-tə-bəl\ *adj* (1597) : impossible to resist ⟨an ~ attraction⟩ — **ir·re·sist·ibil·i·ty** \-ˌzis-tə-ˈbi-lə-tē\ *n* — **ir·re·sist·ible·ness** \-ˈzis-tə-bəl-nəs\ *n* — **ir·re·sist·ibly** \-blē\ *adv*
ir·re·sol·u·ble \-ˈzäl-yə-bəl\ *adj* [L *irresolubilis,* fr. *in-* + *resolvere* to resolve] (1666) **1** *archaic* : INDISSOLUBLE **2 :** having or admitting of no solution or explanation
ir·res·o·lute \i-ˈre-zə-ˌlüt, ˌi(r)-, -lət\ *adj* (1579) : uncertain how to act or proceed : VACILLATING — **ir·res·o·lute·ly** \-ˌlüt-lē, -lət-; -ˌre-zə-ˈlüt-\ *adv* — **ir·res·o·lute·ness** \-ˌlüt-nəs, -lət-, -ˈlüt-\ *n* — **ir·res·o·lu·tion** \-ˌre-zə-ˈlü-shən\ *n*
ir·re·solv·able \ˌir-i-ˈzäl-və-bəl, -ˈzȯl-\ *adj* (1660) : incapable of being resolved; *also* : not analyzable
ir·re·spec·tive of \ˌir-i-ˈspek-tiv-\ *prep* (1839) : REGARDLESS OF ⟨free public schools open to all *irrespective* of race, color, or creed —J. B. Conant⟩
¹**ir·re·spon·si·ble** \ˌir-i-ˈspän(t)-sə-bəl\ *adj* (1648) : not responsible: as **a :** not answerable to higher authority ⟨an ~ dictatorship⟩ **b :** said or done with no sense of responsibility ⟨~ accusations⟩ **c :** lacking a sense of responsibility **d :** unable esp. mentally or financially to bear responsibility — **ir·re·spon·si·bil·i·ty** \ˌir-i-ˌspän(t)-sə-ˈbi-lə-tē\ *n* — **ir·re·spon·si·ble·ness** \ir-i-ˈspän(t)-sə-bəl-nəs\ *n* — **ir·re·spon·si·bly** \-blē\ *adv*
²**irresponsible** *n* (1894) : one that is irresponsible
ir·re·spon·sive \ˌir-i-ˈspän(t)-siv\ *adj* (ca. 1846) : not responsive; *esp* : not able, ready, or inclined to respond — **ir·re·spon·sive·ness** *n*
ir·re·triev·able \ˌir-i-ˈtrē-və-bəl\ *adj* (1702) : not retrievable : impossible to regain or recover — **ir·re·triev·abil·i·ty** \-ˌtrē-və-ˈbi-lə-tē\ *n* — **ir·re·triev·ably** \-i-ˈtrē-və-blē\ *adv*
ir·rev·er·ence \i-ˈrev-rəns, ˌi(r)-, -ˈre-və-; -ˈre-vərn(t)s\ *n* (14c) **1** : lack of reverence **2 :** an irreverent act or utterance
ir·rev·er·ent \-rənt; -vərnt\ *adj* [ME, fr. L *irreverent-, irreverens,* fr. *in-* + *reverent-, reverens* reverent] (15c) : lacking proper respect or seriousness; *also* : SATIRIC — **ir·rev·er·ent·ly** *adv*
ir·re·vers·ible \ˌir-i-ˈvər-sə-bəl\ *adj* (1630) : not reversible — **ir·re·vers·ibil·i·ty** \-ˌvər-sə-ˈbi-lə-tē\ *n* — **ir·re·vers·ibly** \-ˈvər-sə-blē\ *adv*
ir·rev·o·ca·ble \i-ˈre-və-kə-bəl, ˌi(r)- *sometimes* ˌir-(r)ə-ˈvō-kə-\ *adj* [ME, fr. L *irrevocabilis,* fr. *in-* + *revocabilis* revocable] (14c) : not possible to revoke : UNALTERABLE ⟨an ~ decision⟩ — **ir·rev·o·ca·bil·i·ty** \-ˌre-və-kə-ˈbi-lə-tē, -ˌre-və-; ˌir-(r)ə-ˌvō-kə-\ *n* — **ir·rev·o·ca·ble·ness** \-ˈre-və-kə-bəl-nəs, ˌir-(r)ə-ˈvō-kə-\ *n* — **ir·rev·o·ca·bly** \-blē\ *adv*
ir·ri·den·ta *var of* IRREDENTA
ir·ri·gate \ˈir-ə-ˌgāt\ *vb* **-gat·ed; -gat·ing** [L *irrigatus,* pp. of *irrigare,* fr. *in-* + *rigare* to water; perh. akin to OHG *regan* rain — more at

RAIN] *vt* (1615) **1 :** WET, MOISTEN: as **a :** to supply (as land) with water by artificial means **b :** to flush (a body part) with a stream of liquid (as in removing a foreign body or medicating) **2 :** to refresh as if by watering ~ *vi* : to practice irrigation — **ir·ri·ga·tion** \ˌir-ə-ˈgā-shən\ *n* — **ir·ri·ga·tor** \ˈir-ə-ˌgā-tər\ *n*
ir·ri·ta·bil·i·ty \ˌir-ə-tə-ˈbi-lə-tē\ *n, pl* **-ties** (1755) **1 :** the property of protoplasm and living organisms that permits them to react to stimuli **2 :** the quality or state of being irritable: as **a :** quick excitability to annoyance, impatience, or anger : PETULANCE **b :** abnormal or excessive excitability of an organ or part of the body
ir·ri·ta·ble \ˈir-ə-tə-bəl\ *adj* (1662) : capable of being irritated: as **a :** easily exasperated or excited **b :** responsive to stimuli — **ir·ri·ta·ble·ness** *n* — **ir·ri·ta·bly** \-blē\ *adv*
¹**ir·ri·tant** \ˈir-ə-tənt\ *adj* (1636) : causing irritation; *specif* : tending to produce physical irritation
²**irritant** *n* (1802) : something that irritates or excites
ir·ri·tate \ˈir-ə-ˌtāt\ *vb* **-tat·ed; -tat·ing** [L *irritatus,* pp. of *irritare*] *vt* (1598) **1 :** to provoke impatience, anger, or displeasure in : ANNOY **2** : to induce irritability in or of ~ *vi* : to cause or induce displeasure or irritation — **ir·ri·tat·ing·ly** \-ˌtā-tiŋ-lē\ *adv*
syn IRRITATE, EXASPERATE, NETTLE, PROVOKE, RILE, PEEVE mean to excite a feeling of anger or annoyance. IRRITATE implies an often gradual arousing of angry feelings that may range from mere impatience to rage ⟨constant nagging that *irritated* me greatly⟩. EXASPERATE suggests galling annoyance and the arousing of extreme impatience ⟨his *exasperating* habit of putting off needed decisions⟩. NETTLE suggests a sharp but passing annoyance or stinging ⟨your pompous attitude *nettled* several people⟩. PROVOKE implies an arousing of strong annoyance that may excite to action ⟨remarks made solely to *provoke* her⟩. RILE implies inducing an angry or resentful agitation ⟨the new work schedules *riled* the employees⟩. PEEVE suggests arousing fretful often petty or querulous irritation ⟨a toddler *peeved* at being refused a cookie⟩.
irritated *adj* (1595) : subjected to irritation; *esp* : roughened, reddened, or inflamed by an irritant ⟨~ eyes⟩
ir·ri·ta·tion \ˌir-ə-ˈtā-shən\ *n* (15c) **1 a :** the act of irritating **b** : something that irritates **c :** the state of being irritated **2 :** a condition of irritability, soreness, roughness, or inflammation of a bodily part
ir·ri·ta·tive \ˈir-ə-ˌtā-tiv\ *adj* (1644) **1 :** serving to excite : IRRITATING **2** : accompanied with or produced by irritation ⟨~ coughing⟩
ir·ro·ta·tion·al \ˌir-(r)ō-ˈtā-shnəl, -shə-nᵊl\ *adj* (1875) **1 :** not rotating or involving rotation ⟨an ~ electric field⟩ **2 :** free of vortices ⟨~ flow⟩
ir·rupt \i-ˈrəpt\ *vi* [L *irruptus,* pp. of *irrumpere,* fr. *in-* + *rumpere* to break — more at REAVE] (1886) **1 :** to rush in forcibly or violently **2** *of a natural population* : to undergo a sudden upsurge in numbers esp. when natural ecological balances and checks are disturbed **3 :** ERUPT 1c ⟨the crowd ~*ed* in a fervor of patriotism —*Time*⟩ — **ir·rup·tion** \-ˈrəp-shən\ *n*
ir·rup·tive \-ˈrəp-tiv\ *adj* (1593) : irrupting or tending to irrupt — **ir·rup·tive·ly** *adv*
is [ME, fr. OE; akin to OHG *ist* is (fr. *sīn* to be), L *est* (fr. *esse* to be), Gk *esti* (fr. *einai* to be)] *pres 3d sing* of BE, *dial pres 1st & 2d sing* of BE, *substand pres pl* of BE
is- or **iso-** *comb form* [LL, fr. Gk, fr. *isos* equal] **1 :** equal : homogeneous : uniform ⟨*isentropic*⟩ **2 :** isomeric ⟨*isocyanate*⟩ **3 :** for or from different individuals of the same species ⟨*iso*agglutinin⟩
Isaac \ˈī-zik, -zək\ *n* [LL, fr. Heb *Yishāq*] : the son of Abraham and father of Jacob according to the account in Genesis
Isa·iah \ī-ˈzā-ə, *chiefly Brit* -ˈzī-\ *n* [Heb *Yĕshaʿăyāhū*] **1 :** a major Hebrew prophet in Judah about 740 to 701 B.C. **2 :** a prophetic book of canonical Jewish and Christian Scripture — see BIBLE table
Isa·ias \-əs\ *n* [LL, fr. Gk *Ēsaias,* fr. Heb *Yĕshaʿăyāhū*] : ISAIAH
is·al·lo·bar \(ˌ)ī-ˈsa-lə-ˌbär\ *n* [ISV *is-* + *all-* + *-bar* (as in *isobar*)] (1909) : an imaginary line or a line on a chart connecting the places of equal change of atmospheric pressure within a specified time — **is·al·lo·bar·ic** \ī-ˌsa-lə-ˈbar-ik, -ˈber-\ *adj*
is·chae·mia *chiefly Brit var of* ISCHEMIA
is·che·mia \is-ˈkē-mē-ə\ *n* [NL *ischaemia,* fr. *ischaemus* styptic, fr. Gk *ischaimos,* fr. *ischein* to restrain (akin to Gk *echein* to hold) + *haima* blood — more at SCHEME] (ca. 1860) : localized tissue anemia due to obstruction of the inflow of arterial blood — **is·che·mic** \-mik\ *adj*
is·chi·um \ˈis-kē-əm\ *n, pl* **is·chia** \-ə\ [L, hip joint, fr. Gk *ischion*] (1646) : the dorsal and posterior of the three principal bones composing either half of the pelvis — **is·chi·al** \-əl\ *adj*
-ise *vb suffix, chiefly Brit* : -IZE
is·en·tro·pic \ˌī-sᵊn-ˈtrō-pik, -ˈträ-\ *adj* (1873) : of or relating to equal or constant entropy; *esp* : taking place without change of entropy — **is·en·tro·pi·cal·ly** \-ˈtrō-pi-k(ə-)lē, -ˈträ-\ *adv*
Iseult \is-ˈült, iz-\ *n* [OF *Isolt, Iseut*] : ISOLDE
-ish *adj suffix* [ME, fr. OE *-isc;* akin to OHG *-isc,* -ish, Gk *-iskos,* dim. suffix] **1 :** of, relating to, or being — chiefly in adjectives indicating nationality or ethnic group ⟨Finn*ish*⟩ **2 a :** characteristic of ⟨boy*ish*⟩ ⟨Pollyanna*ish*⟩ **b :** inclined or liable to ⟨book*ish*⟩ ⟨qualm*ish*⟩ **3 a** : having a touch or trace of ⟨purpl*ish*⟩: somewhat ⟨dark*ish*⟩ **b :** having the approximate age of ⟨forty*ish*⟩
Ish·ma·el \ˈish-(ˌ)mā-əl, -mē-\ *n* [Heb *Yishmāʿēl*] **1 :** the outcast son of Abraham and Hagar according to the account in Genesis **2 :** a social outcast
Ish·ma·el·ite \-ə-ˌlīt\ *n* (14c) **1 :** a descendant of Ishmael **2 :** ISHMAEL 2 — **Ish·ma·el·it·ish** \-ˌlī-tish\ *adj* — **Ish·ma·el·it·ism** \-ˌlī-ˌti-zəm\ *n*
isin·glass \ˈī-zᵊn-ˌglas, ˈī-ziŋ-\ *n* [prob. by folk etymology fr. obs. D *huizenblas,* fr. MD *huusblase,* fr. *huus* sturgeon + *blase* bladder] (1545) **1 :** a semitransparent whitish very pure gelatin prepared from the air bladders of fishes (as sturgeons) and used esp. as a clarifying agent in jellies and glue **2 :** MICA
Isis \ˈī-səs\ *n* [L *Isid-, Isis,* fr. Gk, fr. Egypt *ʾst*] : an Egyptian nature goddess and wife and sister of Osiris
Is·lam \is-ˈläm, iz-, -ˈlam, ˈis-ˌ, ˈiz-ˌ\ *n* [Ar *islām* submission (to the will of God)] (1817) **1 :** the religious faith of Muslims including belief in Allah as the sole deity and in Muhammad as his prophet **2 a :** the civilization erected upon Islamic faith **b :** the group of modern na-

tions in which Islam is the dominant religion — **Is·lam·ic** \is-'lä-mik, iz-, -'la-\ *adj* — **Is·lam·ics** \-miks\ *n pl but sing or pl in constr*
Islamic calendar *n* (1974) : a lunar calendar reckoned from the Hegira in A.D. 622 and organized in cycles of 30 years — see MONTH table
Islamic era *n* (1975) : the era used in Muslim countries for numbering Islamic calendar years since the Hegira
Is·lam·ism \is-'lä-,mi-zəm, iz-, -'la-; 'iz-lə-\ *n* (1747) : the faith, doctrine, or cause of Islam — **Is·lam·ist** \-mist\ *n*
Is·lam·ize \'iz-lə-,mīz; is-'lä-,mīz, iz-, -'la-\ *vt* **-ized; -iz·ing** (ca. 1846) : to make Islamic; *esp* : to convert to Islam — **Is·lam·i·za·tion** \,iz-lə-mə-'zā-shən; is-,lä-mə-, iz-, -,la-\ *n*
¹is·land \'ī-lənd\ *n* [alter. (influenced by OF *isle*) of earlier *iland*, fr. ME, fr. OE *igland* (akin to ON *eyland*), fr. *ig* island (akin to OE *ēa* river, L *aqua* water) + *land* land] (bef. 12c) **1 a** : a tract of land surrounded by water and smaller than a continent **2** : something resembling an island esp. in its isolated or surrounded position: as **a** : a usu. raised area within a thoroughfare, parking lot, or driveway used esp. to separate or direct traffic **b** : a superstructure on the deck of a ship (as an aircraft carrier) **c** : a kitchen counter that is approachable from all sides **3** : an isolated group or area; *esp* : an isolated ethnological group
²island *vt* (1661) **1 a** : to make into or as if into an island **b** : to dot with or as if with islands **2** : ISOLATE
is·land·er \'ī-lən-dər\ *n* (ca. 1550) : a native or inhabitant of an island
is·land–hop \'ī-lənd-,häp\ *vi* (1944) : to travel from island to island in a chain
island universe *n* (1867) : a galaxy other than the Milky Way
¹isle \'ī(ə)l\ *n* [ME, fr. OF, fr. L *insula*] (13c) : ISLAND; *esp* : ISLET
²isle *vt* **isled; isl·ing** (ca. 1576) **1** : to make an isle of **2** : to place on or as if on an isle
is·let \'ī-lət\ *n* (1538) : a little island
islet of Lang·er·hans \-'läŋ-ər-,hänz, -,hän(t)s\ [Paul *Langerhans* †1888 Ger. physician] (1896) : any of the groups of small slightly granular endocrine cells that form anastomosing trabeculae among the tubules and alveoli of the pancreas and secrete insulin and glucagon — called also *islet*
ism \'i-zəm\ *n* [-ism] (1680) : a distinctive doctrine, cause, or theory
-ism *n suffix* [ME -*isme*, fr. MF & L; MF, partly fr. L -*isma* (fr. Gk) & partly fr. L -*ismus*, fr. Gk -*ismos*; Gk -*isma* & -*ismos*, fr. verbs in -*izein* -ize] **1 a** : act : practice : process ⟨critic*ism*⟩ ⟨plagiar*ism*⟩ **b** : manner of action or behavior characteristic of a (specified) person or thing ⟨animal*ism*⟩ **c** : prejudice or discrimination on the basis of a (specified) attribute ⟨rac*ism*⟩ ⟨sex*ism*⟩ **2 a** : state : condition : property ⟨barbarian*ism*⟩ **b** : abnormal state or condition resulting from excess of a (specified) thing ⟨alcohol*ism*⟩ or marked by resemblance to (such) a person or thing ⟨mongol*ism*⟩ **3 a** : doctrine : theory : cult ⟨Buddh*ism*⟩ **b** : adherence to a system or a class of principles ⟨stoic*ism*⟩ **4** : characteristic or peculiar feature or trait ⟨colloquial*ism*⟩
isn't \'i-z²nt, -²n, *dial also* 'i-d²n(t) *or* 'in(t)\ (1710) : is not
iso- — see IS-
iso·ag·glu·ti·nin \,ī-(,)sō-ə-'glü-t²n-ən\ *n* (ca. 1903) : an agglutinin from one individual that is specific for a cell type (as of red blood cells) possessed by some individuals of the same species
iso·al·lox·a·zine \-ə-'läk-sə-,zēn\ *n* [*is-* + *all*antoic + *ox*alic + *az*ine] (1936) : a yellow solid $C_{10}H_6N_4O_2$ that is the precursor of various flavins (as riboflavin)
iso·an·ti·body \-an-ti-,bä-dē\ *n* (1919) : ALLOANTIBODY
iso·an·ti·gen \-'an-ti-jən\ *n* [ISV] (1936) : ALLOANTIGEN — **iso·an·ti·gen·ic** \-,an-ti-'je-nik\ *adj*
iso·bar \'ī-sə-,bär\ *n* [ISV *is-* + *-bar* (fr. Gk *baros* weight); akin to Gk *barys* heavy — more at GRIEVE] (ca. 1864) **1** : an imaginary line or a line on a map or chart connecting or marking places on the surface of the earth where the height of the barometer reduced to sea level is the same either at a given time or for a certain period **2** : one of two or more atoms or elements having the same atomic weights or mass numbers but different atomic numbers
iso·bar·ic \,ī-sə-'bär-ik, -'bar-\ *adj* [ISV] (1878) **1** : of or relating to an isobar **2** : characterized by constant or equal pressure ⟨an ~ process⟩
iso·bu·tane \,ī-sō-'byü-,tān\ *n* [ISV] (1876) : a gaseous branched-chain hydrocarbon $(CH_3)_3CH$ isomeric with normal butane that is used esp. as a fuel
iso·bu·tyl·ene \-'byü-t²l-,ēn\ *n* [ISV] (1872) : a gaseous butylene C_4H_8 used esp. in making butyl rubber and gasoline components
iso·ca·lor·ic \-kə-'lȯr-ik, -'lȯr-, -'lär-; -'ka-lə-rik\ *adj* (1922) : having similar caloric values ⟨~ diets⟩
iso·car·box·az·id \-,kär-'bäk-sə-zəd\ *n* [*is-* + *carb-* + *ox-* + *hydra*zide] (1959) : an antidepressant drug $C_{12}H_{13}N_3O_2$
iso·chro·mo·some \,ī-sə-'krō-mə-,sōm, -,zōm\ *n* (1939) : a chromosome produced by transverse splitting of the centromere so that both arms are derived from the dyad on one side of the centromere of the parental chromosome and each arm has identical genes arranged in the same order counting away from the centromere
iso·chron \'ī-sə-,krän\ *or* **iso·chrone** \-,krōn\ *n* [ISV *is-* + -*chron* (fr. Gk *chronos* time)] (1881) : an imaginary line or a line on a chart connecting points at which an event occurs simultaneously or which represents the same time or time difference
iso·chro·nal \ī-'sä-krə-n²l, ,ī-sə-'krō-\ *adj* [Gk *isochronos*, fr. *is-* + *chronos* time] (1680) : uniform in time : having equal duration : recurring at regular intervals — **iso·chro·nal·ly** \-n²l-ē\ *adv* — **iso·chro·nism** \ī-'sä-krə-,ni-zəm, ,ī-sə-'krō-\ *n*
iso·chro·nous \ī-'sä-krə-nəs, ,ī-sə-'krō-\ *adj* [Gk *isochronos*] (1706) : ISOCHRONAL — **iso·chro·nous·ly** *adv*
iso·cit·ric acid \,ī-sə-'si-trik-\ *n* (1869) : a crystalline isomer of citric acid that occurs esp. as an intermediate stage in the Krebs cycle
iso·cy·a·nate \,ī-sō-'sī-ə-,nāt, -nət\ *n* [ISV] (1872) : an ester of isomeric cyanic acid used esp. in plastics and adhesives
iso·cy·clic \'si-klik, -'sī-\ *adj* [ISV] (1900) : having or being a ring composed of atoms of only one element; *esp* : CARBOCYCLIC
iso·di·a·met·ric \-,dī-ə-'me-trik\ *adj* [ISV] (ca. 1879) : having equal diameters
iso·dose \'ī-sə-,dōs\ *adj* [ISV] (1922) : of or relating to points or zones in a medium that receive equal doses of radiation
iso·elec·tric \,ī-sō-i-'lek-trik\ *adj* [ISV] (1877) **1** : having or representing zero difference of electric potential **2** : being the pH at which the electrolyte will not migrate in an electrical field ⟨the ~ point of a protein⟩
isoelectric focusing *n* (1971) : an electrophoretic technique for separating proteins by causing them to migrate under the influence of an electric field through a medium (as a gel) having a pH gradient to locations with pH values corresponding to their isoelectric points
iso·elec·tron·ic \-i-,lek-'trä-nik\ *adj* [ISV] (1926) : having the same number of electrons or valence electrons — **iso·elec·tron·i·cal·ly** \-ni-k(ə-)lē\ *adv*
iso·en·zyme \-'en-,zīm\ *n* (1960) : any of two or more chemically distinct but functionally similar enzymes — **iso·en·zy·mat·ic** \-,en-zə-'ma-tik, -,zī-\ *adj* — **iso·en·zy·mic** \-en-'zī-mik\ *adj*
iso·ga·mete \-'ga-,mēt *also* -gə-'mēt\ *n* [ISV] (1891) : a gamete indistinguishable in form or size or behavior from another gamete with which it can unite to form a zygote — **iso·ga·met·ic** \-gə-'me-tik\ *adj*
isog·a·mous \ī-'sä-gə-məs\ *adj* [prob. fr. (assumed) NL *isogamus*, fr. *is-* + -*gamous* -gamous] (1887) : having or involving isogametes — compare HETEROGAMOUS — **isog·a·my** \-mē\ *n*
iso·ge·ne·ic \,ī-sō-jə-'nē-ik, -'nā-\ *adj* [alter. of *isogenic*] (1963) : SYNGENEIC ⟨an ~ graft⟩
iso·gen·ic \-'je-nik\ *adj* [*is-* + *gene* + ¹-*ic*] (ca. 1931) : characterized by essentially identical genes ⟨identical twins are ~⟩
iso·gloss \'ī-sə-,gläs, -,glȯs\ *n* [ISV *is-* + Gk *glōssa* language — more at GLOSS] (1925) **1** : a boundary line between places or regions that differ in a particular linguistic feature **2** : a line on a map representing an isogloss — **iso·gloss·al** \,ī-sə-'glä-səl, -'glȯ-\ *adj* — **iso·gloss·ic** \-'glä-sik, -'glȯ-\ *adj*
iso·gon·ic \,ī-sə-'gä-nik\ *adj* [*isogony*, fr. *is-* + -*gony*] (1924) : exhibiting equivalent relative growth of parts such that size relations remain constant — **isog·o·ny** \ī-'sä-gə-nē\ *n*
isogonic line *n* (ca. 1859) : an imaginary line or a line on a map joining points on the earth's surface at which the magnetic declination is the same — called also *isogonal*
iso·graft \'ī-sə-,graft\ *n* (1958) : a homograft between genetically identical or nearly identical individuals — **isograft** *vt*
iso·gram \'ī-sə-,gram\ *n* (1889) : ISOLINE
iso·hy·et \,ī-sō-'hī-ət\ *n* [ISV *is-* + Gk *hyetos* rain, fr. *hyein* to rain; prob. akin to Toch B *swese* rain] (1899) : a line on a map or chart connecting areas of equal rainfall — **iso·hy·et·al** \-ə-t²l\ *adj*
iso·la·ble \'ī-sə-lə-bəl *also* 'i-\ *also* **iso·lat·able** \,ī-sə-'lā-tə-bəl *also* ,i-\ *adj* (ca. 1885) : capable of being isolated
¹iso·late \'ī-sə-,lāt *also* 'i-\ *vt* **-lat·ed; -lat·ing** [back-formation fr. *isolated* set apart, fr. F *isolé*, fr. It *isolato*, fr. *isola* island, fr. L *insula*] (1807) **1** : to set apart from others; *also* : QUARANTINE **2** : to select from among others; *esp* : to separate from another substance so as to obtain pure or in a free state **3** : INSULATE — **iso·la·tor** \-,lā-tər\ *n*
²iso·late \-lət, -,lāt\ *adj* (1819) : being alone : SOLITARY, ISOLATED
³iso·late \-lət, -,lāt\ *n* (1890) **1** : a product of isolating : an individual, population, or kind obtained by or resulting from selection or separation **2** : an individual socially withdrawn or removed from society
isolated *adj* (1763) **1** : occurring alone or once : UNIQUE **2** : SPORADIC
iso·la·tion \,ī-sə-'lā-shən *also* ,i-\ *n* (1833) : the action of isolating : the condition of being isolated *syn* see SOLITUDE
iso·la·tion·ism \-shə-,ni-zəm\ *n* (1922) : a policy of national isolation by abstention from alliances and other international political and economic relations — **iso·la·tion·ist** \-sh(ə-)nist\ *n or adj*
Isol·de \i-'zȯl-də, -'sȯl-\ *n* [G, fr. OF *Isolt, Iseut*] **1** : an Irish princess married to King Mark of Cornwall and loved by Tristram **2** : the daughter of the King of Brittany and wife of Tristram
iso·leu·cine \,ī-sō-'lü-,sēn\ *n* [ISV] (1903) : a crystalline essential amino acid $C_6H_{13}NO_2$ isomeric with leucine
iso·line \'ī-(,)sō-,līn\ *n* (1944) : a line on a map or chart along which there is a constant value (as of temperature or rainfall)
iso·mer \'ī-sə-mər\ *n* [ISV, back-formation fr. *isomeric*] (1866) **1** : one of two or more compounds, radicals, or ions that contain the same number of atoms of the same elements but differ in structural arrangement and properties **2** : a nuclide isomeric with one or more others
isom·er·ase \ī-'sä-mə-,rās, -,rāz\ *n* (1927) : an enzyme that catalyzes the conversion of its substrate to an isomeric form
iso·mer·ic \,ī-sə-'mer-ik\ *adj* [G *isomerisch*, fr. Gk *isomerēs* equally divided, fr. *is-* + *meros* part — more at MERIT] (1838) : of, relating to, or exhibiting isomerism
isom·er·ism \ī-'sä-mə-,ri-zəm\ *n* (1839) **1** : the relationship of two or more chemical species that are isomers **2** : the relation of two or more nuclides with the same mass numbers and atomic numbers but different energy states and rates of radioactive decay
isom·er·ize \ī-'sä-mə-,rīz\ *vb* **-ized; -iz·ing** *vi* (1891) : to become changed into an isomeric form ~ *vt* : to cause to isomerize — **isom·er·i·za·tion** \-,sä-mə-rə-'zā-shən\ *n*
iso·met·ric \,ī-sə-'me-trik\ *adj* (ca. 1855) **1** : of, relating to, or characterized by equality of measure; *esp* : relating to or being a crystallographic system characterized by three equal axes at right angles **2** : of, relating to, involving, or being muscular contraction (as in isometrics) against resistance, without significant shortening of muscle fibers, and with marked increase in muscle tone — compare ISOTONIC — **iso·met·ri·cal·ly** \-tri-k(ə-)lē\ *adv*
isometric line *n* (ca. 1911) **1** : a line representing changes of pressure or temperature under conditions of constant volume **2** : a line (as a contour line) drawn on a map and indicating a true constant value throughout its extent
iso·met·rics \,ī-sə-'me-triks\ *n pl but sing or pl in constr* (1962) : exercise or a system of exercises in which opposing muscles are so contracted that there is little shortening but great increase in tone of muscle fibers involved
isom·e·try \ī-'sä-mə-trē\ *n, pl* **-tries** (1941) : a mapping of a metric space onto another or onto itself so that the distance between any two

\ə\ abut \²\ kitten, F table \ər\ further \a\ ash \ā\ ace \ä\ mop, mar
\au̇\ out \ch\ chin \e\ bet \ē\ easy \g\ go \i\ hit \ī\ ice \j\ job
\ŋ\ sing \ō\ go \ȯ\ law \ȯi\ boy \th\ thin \t̲h̲\ the \ü\ loot \u̇\ foot
\y\ yet \zh\ vision \à, k̲, ⁿ, œ, œ̄, ᴜᴇ, ᵫ, ¹\ *see* Guide to Pronunciation

points in the original space is the same as the distance between their images in the second space ⟨rotation and translation are *isometries* of the plane⟩

iso·mor·phic \ˌī-sə-'mȯr-fik\ *adj* (1862) **1 a :** being of identical or similar form, shape, or structure ⟨~ crystals⟩ **b :** having sporophytic and gametophytic generations alike in size and shape **2 :** related by an isomorphism ⟨~ mathematical rings⟩ — **iso·mor·phi·cal·ly** \-fi-k(ə-)lē\ *adv*

iso·mor·phism \ˌī-sə-'mȯr-ˌfi-zəm\ *n* [ISV] (ca. 1828) **1 :** the quality or state of being isomorphic: as **a :** similarity in organisms of different ancestry resulting from convergence **b :** similarity of crystalline form between chemical compounds **2 :** a one-to-one correspondence between two mathematical sets; *esp* : a homomorphism that is one-to-one — compare ENDOMORPHISM

iso·mor·phous \ˌī-sə-'mȯr-fəs\ *adj* (ca. 1828) : ISOMORPHIC 1a — **iso·morph** \'ī-sə-ˌmȯrf\ *n*

iso·ni·a·zid \ˌī-sə-'nī-ə-zəd\ *n* [*is*- + *nicotinic* acid + hydr*azide*] (1952) : a crystalline compound $C_6H_7N_3O$ used in treating tuberculosis

iso·oc·tane \ˌī-sō-'äk-ˌtān\ *n* [ISV] (1909) : an octane of branched= chain structure or a mixture of such octanes; *esp* : a flammable liquid octane used in determining the octane number of fuels

iso·pach \'ī-sə-ˌpak\ *n* [*is*- + -*pach* (fr. Gk *pachys* thick) — more at PACHYDERM] (ca. 1918) : an isoline that connects points of equal thickness of a geological stratum formation or group of formations

iso·phote \'ī-sə-ˌfōt\ *n* [ISV *is*- + -*phote* (fr. Gk *phōt-, phōs* light) — more at FANCY] (ca. 1909) : a curve on a chart joining points of equal light intensity from a given source — **iso·phot·al** \ˌī-sə-'fō-təl\ *adj*

iso·pi·es·tic \ˌī-sō-pē-'es-tik, -ˌpī-\ *adj* [*is*- + Gk *piestos*, verbal of *piezein* to press — more at PIEZO-] (1873) : of, relating to, or marked by equal pressure

iso·pleth \'ī-sə-ˌpleth\ *n* [ISV *is*- + Gk *plēthos* quantity; akin to Gk *plēthein* to be full — more at FULL] (1908) **1 :** an isoline on a graph showing the occurrence or frequency of a phenomenon as a function of two variables **2 :** a line on a map connecting points at which a given variable has a specified constant value — **iso·pleth·ic** \ˌī-sə-'ple-thik\ *adj*

iso·pod \'ī-sə-ˌpäd\ *n* [ultim. fr. Gk *is*- + *pod-, pous* foot — more at FOOT] (ca. 1835) : any of a large order (Isopoda) of small sessile-eyed crustaceans with the body composed of seven free thoracic segments each bearing a pair of similar legs — **isopod** *adj*

iso·pren·a·line \ˌī-sə-'pren-ᵊl-ən\ *n* [prob. fr. *isopropyl* + *adrenaline*] (1951) : ISOPROTERENOL

iso·prene \'ī-sə-ˌprēn\ *n* [prob. fr. *is*- + *propyl* + -*ene*] (1860) : a flammable liquid unsaturated hydrocarbon C_5H_8 used esp. in synthetic rubber

iso·pren·oid \ˌī-sə-'prē-ˌnȯid\ *adj* (1940) : relating to, containing, or being a branched-chain grouping characteristic of isoprene

iso·pro·pyl \ˌī-sə-'prō-pəl\ *n, often attrib* [ISV] (1866) : the alkyl radical isomeric with normal propyl — often used in combination

isopropyl alcohol *n* (1872) : a volatile flammable alcohol C_3H_8O used esp. as a solvent and rubbing alcohol

iso·pro·ter·e·nol \ˌī-sə-prō-'ter-ə-ˌnȯl, -ˌnōl, -ˌnȯl\ *n* [*isopropyl* + *arterenol* norepinephrine, fr. *Arterenol*, a trademark] (1957) : a drug $C_{11}H_{17}NO_3$ used in the treatment of asthma

iso·pyc·nic \ˌī-sō-'pik-nik\ *adj* [*is*- + Gk *pyknos* dense] (ca. 1890) **1 :** of, relating to, or marked by equal or constant density **2 :** being or produced by a technique (as centrifugation) in which the components of a mixture are separated on the basis of differences in density

isos·ce·les \ī-'säs-ˌlēz, -ˌsä-sə-\ *adj* [LL *isosceles* having two equal sides, fr. Gk *isoskelēs*, fr. *is*- + *skelos* leg; perh. akin to OE *sceol* wry] (1551) **1** *of a triangle* : having two equal sides — see TRIANGLE illustration **2** *of a trapezoid* : having the two nonparallel sides equal

is·os·mot·ic \ˌī-ˌsäz-'mä-tik, -ˌsäs-\ *adj* [ISV] (1895) : of, relating to, or exhibiting equal osmotic pressure ⟨~ solutions⟩ — **is·os·mot·i·cal·ly** \-'mä-ti-k(ə-)lē\ *adv*

iso·spin \'ī-sə-ˌspin\ *n* (1961) : a quantum characteristic of a group of closely related subatomic particles (as a proton and a neutron) handled mathematically like ordinary spin with the possible orientations in a hypothetical space specifying the number of particles of differing electric charge comprising the group — called also *isotopic spin*

isos·ta·sy \ī-'säs-tə-sē\ *n* [ISV *is*- + Gk -*stasia* condition of standing, fr. *histanai* to cause to stand — more at STAND] (1889) **1 :** general equilibrium in the earth's crust maintained by a yielding flow of rock material beneath the surface under gravitative stress **2 :** the quality or state of being subjected to equal pressure from every side — **iso·stat·ic** \ˌī-sə-'sta-tik\ *adj* — **iso·stat·i·cal·ly** \-'sta-ti-k(ə-)lē\ *adv*

iso·tach \ˌī-sə-ˌtak\ *n* [ISV *is*- + -*tach* (fr. Gk *tachys* quick)] (1947) : a line on a map or chart connecting points of equal wind speed

iso·tac·tic \ˌī-sə-'tak-tik\ *adj* (1955) : having or relating to a stereochemical regularity of structure in the repeating units of a polymer — compare ATACTIC

iso·therm \'ī-sə-ˌthərm\ *n* [F *isotherme*, adj.] (1859) **1 :** a line on a map or chart of the earth's surface connecting points having the same temperature at a given time or the same mean temperature for a given period **2 :** a line on a chart representing changes of volume or pressure under conditions of constant temperature

iso·ther·mal \ˌī-sə-'thər-məl\ *adj* [F *isotherme*, fr. *is*- + -*therme* (fr. Gk *thermos* hot) — more at THERM] (1826) **1 :** of, relating to, or marked by equality of temperature **2 :** of, relating to, or marked by changes of volume or pressure under conditions of constant temperature — **iso·ther·mal·ly** \-mə-lē\ *adv*

iso·ton·ic \ˌī-sə-'tä-nik\ *adj* [ISV] (1891) **1 :** of, relating to, or being muscular contraction in the absence of significant resistance, with marked shortening of muscle fibers, and great increase in muscle tone — compare ISOMETRIC **2 :** ISOSMOTIC — used of solutions — **iso·ton·i·cal·ly** \-ni-k(ə-)lē\ *adv* — **iso·to·nic·i·ty** \-tō-'ni-sə-tē\ *n*

iso·tope \'ī-sə-ˌtōp\ *n* [*is*- + Gk *topos* place] (1913) **1 :** any of two or more species of atoms of a chemical element with the same atomic number and nearly identical chemical behavior but with differing atomic mass or mass number and different physical properties **2 :** NUCLIDE — **iso·top·ic** \ˌī-sə-'tä-pik, -'tō-\ *adj* — **iso·top·i·cal·ly** \-'tä-pi-k(ə-)lē, -'tō-\ *adv*

isotopic spin *n* (1937) : ISOSPIN

iso·tro·pic \ˌī-sə-'trō-pik, -'trä-\ *adj* [ISV] (ca. 1860) : exhibiting properties (as velocity of light transmission) with the same values when measured along axes in all directions ⟨an ~ crystal⟩ — **isot·ro·py** \ī-'sä-trə-pē\ *n*

iso·zyme \'ī-sə-ˌzīm\ *n* (1959) : ISOENZYME — **iso·zy·mic** \ˌī-sə-'zī-mik\ *adj*

Is·ra·el \'iz-rē-əl, -(ˌ)rā- *also* 'is- *or* 'iz-rəl\ *n* [ME, fr. OE, fr. LL, fr. Gk *Israēl*, fr. Heb *Yiśrā'ēl*] **1 :** JACOB 2 **2 :** the Jewish people **3 :** a people chosen by God — **Israel** *adj*

¹Is·rae·li \iz-'rā-lē *also* ˌiz-rə-'ā-lē\ *adj* [NHeb *yiśrē'ēlī*, fr. Heb, Israelite, n. & adj., fr. *Yiśrā'ēl*] (1948) : of or relating to the people or the republic of Israel

²Israeli *n, pl* **Israelis** *also* **Israeli** (1948) : a native or inhabitant of the republic of Israel

¹Is·ra·el·ite \'iz-r(ē-)ə-ˌlīt\ *n* [ME, fr. LL *Israelita*, fr. Gk *Israēlitēs*, fr. *Israēl*] (14c) : a descendant of the Hebrew patriarch Jacob; *specif* : a native or inhabitant of the ancient northern kingdom of Israel

²Israelite *adj* (1851) : of or relating to Israel or to the Israelites

Is·sa·char \'i-sə-ˌkär\ *n* [LL, fr. Gk, fr. Heb *Yiśśākhār*] : a son of Jacob and the traditional eponymous ancestor of one of the tribes of Israel

is·sei \(ˌ)ē-'sā, 'ē-ˌsā\ *n, pl* **issei** *often cap* [Jp, lit., first generation] (1937) : a Japanese immigrant esp. to the U.S.

is·su·able \'i-shü-ə-bəl\ *adj* (ca. 1570) **1 :** open to contest, debate, or litigation **2 :** authorized for issue ⟨bonds ~ under the merger terms⟩ **3 :** possible as a result or consequence — **is·su·ably** \-blē\ *adv*

is·su·ance \'i-shə-wən(t)s\ *n* (1863) : ISSUE 2, 9a

is·su·ant \-wənt\ *adj* (1610) **1** *of a heraldic animal* : rising with only the upper part visible **2** *archaic* : coming forth : EMERGING

¹is·sue \'i-(ˌ)shü, *chiefly Southern* 'i-shə, *chiefly Brit* 'is-(ˌ)yü\ *n* [ME, exit, proceeds, fr. MF, fr. OF, fr. *issir* to come out, go out, fr. L *exire* to go out, fr. *ex*- + *ire* to go; akin to Goth *iddja* he went, Gk *ienai* to go, Skt *eti* he goes] (14c) **1** *pl* : proceeds from a source of revenue (as an estate) **2 :** the action of going, coming, or flowing out : EGRESS, EMERGENCE **3 :** a means or place of going out : EXIT, OUTLET **4 :** OFFSPRING, PROGENY ⟨died without ~⟩ **5 a :** a final outcome that usu. constitutes a solution (as of a problem) or resolution (as of a difficulty) **b** *obs* : a final conclusion or decision about something arrived at after consideration **c** *archaic* : TERMINATION, END ⟨hope that his enterprise would have a prosperous ~ —T. B. Macaulay⟩ **6 a :** a matter that is in dispute between two or more parties **b :** the point at which an unsettled matter is ready for a decision ⟨brought the matter to an ~⟩ **7 :** a discharge (as of blood) from the body **8 a :** something coming forth from a specified source ⟨~s of a disordered imagination⟩ **b :** DEED **9 a :** the act of publishing or officially giving out or making available ⟨the next ~ of commemorative stamps⟩ ⟨~ of supplies by the quartermaster⟩ **b :** the thing or the whole quantity of things given out at one time ⟨read the latest ~⟩ — **is·sue·less** \'i-shü-ləs\ *adj* — **at issue 1 :** in a state of controversy : in disagreement **2** *also* **in issue** : under discussion or in dispute

²issue *vb* **is·sued; is·su·ing** *vi* (14c) **1 a :** to go, come, or flow out **b :** to come forth : EMERGE **c :** to come to an issue of law or fact in pleading **2 :** ACCRUE ⟨profits *issuing* from the sale of the stock⟩ **3 :** to descend from a specified parent or ancestor **4 :** to be a consequence or final outcome : EMANATE, RESULT **5 :** to appear or become available through being officially put forth or distributed **6 :** EVENTUATE, TERMINATE ~ *vt* **1 :** to cause to come forth : DISCHARGE, EMIT **2 a :** to put forth or distribute usu. officially ⟨government *issued* a new airmail stamp⟩ ⟨~ orders⟩ **b :** to send out for sale or circulation : PUBLISH ⟨*Brit* : PROVIDE 2b, SUPPLY *syn* see SPRING — **is·su·er** *n*

¹-ist *n suffix* [ME -*iste*, fr. OF & L; OF -*iste*, fr. L -*ista*, -*istes*, fr. Gk -*istēs*, fr. verbs in -*izein* -ize] **1 a :** one that performs a (specified) action ⟨cyclist⟩ : one that makes or produces a (specified) thing ⟨novelist⟩ **b :** one that plays a (specified) musical instrument ⟨harpist⟩ **c :** one that operates a (specified) mechanical instrument or contrivance ⟨automobilist⟩ **2 :** one that specializes in a (specified) art or science or skill ⟨geologist⟩ ⟨ventriloquist⟩ **3 :** one that adheres to or advocates a (specified) doctrine or system or code of behavior ⟨socialist⟩ ⟨royalist⟩ ⟨hedonist⟩ or that of a (specified) individual ⟨Calvinist⟩ ⟨Darwinist⟩

²-ist *adj suffix* : of, relating to, or characteristic of ⟨elitist⟩

¹isth·mi·an \'is-mē-ən\ *n* (1601) **1 :** a native or inhabitant of an isthmus **2** *cap* : a native or inhabitant of the Isthmus of Panama

²isthmian *adj* (1603) : of, relating to, or situated in or near an isthmus: as **a** *often cap* : of or relating to the Isthmus of Corinth in Greece or the games held there in ancient times **b** *often cap* : of or relating to the Isthmus of Panama connecting the No. American and So. American continents

isth·mic \'is-mik\ *adj* (1585) : of or relating to an anatomical isthmus

isth·mus \'is-məs\ *n* [L, fr. Gk *isthmos*] (1555) **1 :** a narrow strip of land connecting two larger land areas **2 :** a narrow anatomical part or passage connecting two larger structures or cavities

is·tle \'ist-lē\ *n* [AmerSp *ixtle*, fr. Nahuatl *ichtli*] (1883) : a strong fiber (as for cordage or basketwork) from various tropical American plants (as of the genus *Agave*)

¹it \'it, ət\ *pron* [ME, fr. OE *hit* — more at HE] (bef. 12c) **1 :** that one — used as subject or direct object or indirect object of a verb or object of a preposition usu. in reference to a lifeless thing ⟨took a quick look at the house and noticed ~ was very old⟩, a plant ⟨there is a rosebush near the fence and ~ is now blooming⟩, a person or animal whose sex is unknown or disregarded ⟨don't know who ~ is⟩, a group of individuals or things, or an abstract entity ⟨beauty is everywhere and ~ is a source of joy⟩; compare HE, ITS, SHE, THEY **2** — used as subject of an impersonal verb that expresses a condition or action without reference to an agent ⟨~ is raining⟩ **3 a** — used as anticipatory subject or object of a verb ⟨~ is necessary to repeat the whole thing⟩; often used to shift emphasis to a part of a statement other than the subject ⟨~ was in this city that the treaty was signed⟩ **b** — used with many verbs as a direct object with little or no meaning ⟨footed ~ back to camp⟩ **4** — used to refer to an explicit or implicit state of affairs or circumstances ⟨how is ~ going⟩ **5 :** a crucial or climactic point ⟨this is ~⟩

²it \'it\ *n* (1842) : the player in a game who performs the principal action of the game (as trying to find others in hide-and-seek)

it·a·con·ic acid \ˌit-ə-'kä-nik-\ *n* [ISV, anagram of *aconitic* acid, $C_3H_3(COOH)_3$, fr. *aconite*] (ca. 1872) : a crystalline dicarboxylic acid $C_5H_6O_4$ obtained usu. by fermentation of sugars with molds (genus *Aspergillus*) and used as a monomer for polymers and polyesters

¹**Ital·ian** \ə-'tal-yən, i- *also* ͵ī-\ *n* (14c) **1 a :** a native or inhabitant of Italy **b :** a person of Italian descent **2 :** the Romance language of the Italians
²**Italian** *adj* (15c) **:** of, relating to, or characteristic of Italy, the Italians, or Italian
ital·ian·ate \-yə-͵nāt\ *vt* **-at·ed; -at·ing** *often cap* (1553) **:** ITALIANIZE
Ital·ian·ate \-nət, -͵nāt\ *adj* (1572) **:** Italian in quality or characteristics
Italian dressing *n* (ca. 1902) **:** a salad dressing flavored esp. with garlic and oregano
Italian greyhound *n* (1743) **:** any of a breed of toy dogs resembling the standard greyhound in miniature

Italian greyhound

ital·ian·ise *often cap, Brit var of* ITALIANIZE
Ital·ian·ism \ə-'tal-yə-͵ni-zəm, i- *also* ī-\ *n* (1594) **1 a :** a quality characteristic of Italy or the Italian people **b :** a characteristic feature of Italian occurring in another language **2 a :** specialized interest in or emulation of Italian qualities or achievements **b :** promotion or love of Italian policies or ideals
ital·ian·ize \ə-'tal-yə-͵nīz, i- *also* ī-\ *vb* **-ized; -iz·ing** *often cap, vi* (ca. 1611) **:** to act Italian; *specif* **:** to follow the style or technique of recognized Italian painters ~ *vt* **:** to make Italian (as in appearance or behavior) — **Ital·ian·i·za·tion** \-͵tal-yə-nə-'zā-shən\ *n*
Italian sandwich *n* (ca. 1953) **:** SUBMARINE 2
Italian sonnet *n* (1879) **:** a sonnet consisting of an octave rhyming *abba abba* and a sestet rhyming in any of various patterns (as *cde cde* or *cdc dcd*) — called also *Petrarchan sonnet*
¹**ital·ic** \ə-'ta-lik, i-, ī-\ *adj* (1612) **1 a :** of or relating to a type style with characters that slant upward to the right (as in *"these words are italic"*) — compare ROMAN **b :** of or relating to a style of slanted cursive handwriting developed in the 15th and 16th centuries **2** *cap* **:** of or relating to ancient Italy, its peoples, or their Indo-European languages
²**italic** *n* (1676) **1 :** an italic character or type **2** *cap* **:** a branch of the Indo-European language family that includes Latin, Oscan, and Umbrian — see INDO-EUROPEAN LANGUAGES table
ital·i·cise *Brit var of* ITALICIZE
ital·i·cize \ə-'ta-lə-͵sīz, i-, ī-\ *vt* **-cized; -ciz·ing** (1795) **1 :** to print in italics or underscore with a single line **2 :** EMPHASIZE (the microphone ~s every curdled top note —P. G. Davis) — **ital·i·ci·za·tion** \-͵ta-lə-sə-'zā-shən\ *n*
Ita·lo- \i-'ta-lō *also* 'i-t⁽ᵊ⁾l-ō\ *comb form* **1 :** Italian (*Italo*phile) **2 :** Italian and (*Italo*-Austrian)
Ita·lo·phile \i-'ta-lə-͵fīl\ *adj* (ca. 1902) **:** friendly to or favoring what is Italian — **Italophile** *n*
¹**itch** \'ich\ *vb* [ME *icchen*, fr. OE *giccan;* akin to OHG *jucchen* to itch] *vi* (bef. 12c) **1 a :** to have an itch (her arm ~*ed*) **b :** to produce an itchy sensation (long underwear that ~*es*) **2 :** to have a restless desire or hankering for something (were ~*ing* to go outside) ~ *vt* **1 :** to cause to itch **2 :** VEX, IRRITATE
²**itch** *n* (bef. 12c) **1 a :** an uneasy irritating sensation in the upper surface of the skin usu. held to result from mild stimulation of pain receptors **b :** a skin disorder accompanied by such a sensation; *esp* **:** a contagious eruption caused by a mite (*Sarcoptes scabiei*) that burrows in the skin and causes intense itching **2 a :** a restless usu. constant often compulsive desire (an ~ to travel) **b :** LUST, PRURIENCE — **itch·i·ness** \'i-chē-nəs\ *n* — **itchy** \'i-chē\ *adj*
it'd \'i-təd, ͵id\ (1859) **:** it had **:** it would
¹**-ite** *n suffix* [ME, fr. OF & L; OF, fr. L *-ita, -ites,* fr. Gk *-itēs*] **1 a :** native **:** resident (Brooklyn*ite*) **b :** descendant (Ephraim*ite*) **c :** adherent **:** follower (Jacob*ite*) (Puscy*ite*) **2 a** (1) **:** product (metabol*ite*) (2) **:** commercially manufactured product (ebon*ite*) **b** : -ITOL (mann*ite*) **3** [NL *-ites,* fr. L] **:** fossil (ammon*ite*) **4 :** mineral (erythr*ite*) **:** rock (anorthos*ite*) **5** [F, fr. L, *-ita, -ites*] **:** segment or constituent part of a body or of a bodily part (som*ite*) (dendr*ite*)
²**-ite** *n suffix* [F, alter. of *-ate* -ate, fr. NL *-atum*] **:** salt or ester of an acid with a name ending in *-ous* (nitr*ite*)
¹**item** \'ī-,tem, 'ī-təm\ *adv* [ME, fr. L, fr. *ita* thus] (14c) **:** and in addition **:** ALSO — used to introduce each article in a list or enumeration
²**item** \'ī-təm\ *n* (1571) **1** *obs* **:** WARNING, HINT **2 :** a distinct part in an enumeration, account, or series **:** ARTICLE **3 :** an object of attention, concern, or interest **4 :** a separate piece of news or information **5 :** a couple in a romantic or sexual relationship
syn ITEM, DETAIL, PARTICULAR mean one of the distinct parts of a whole. ITEM applies to each thing specified separately in a list or in a group of things that might be listed or enumerated (every *item* on the list). DETAIL applies to one of the small component parts of a larger whole such as a task, building, painting, narration, or process (leave the *details* to others). PARTICULAR stresses the smallness, singleness, and esp. the concreteness of a detail or item (a description that included few *particulars*).
³**item** \'ī-təm\ *vt* (1601) **1** *archaic* **:** COMPUTE, RECKON **2** *archaic* **:** to set down the particular details of
item·ise *Brit var of* ITEMIZE
item·i·za·tion \͵ī-tə-mə-'zā-shən\ *n* (1894) **:** the act of itemizing; *also* **:** an itemized list
item·ize \'ī-tə-͵mīz\ *vt* **-ized; -iz·ing** (1857) **:** to set down in detail or by particulars **:** LIST (*itemized* all expenses)
it·er·ance \'i-tə-rən(t)s\ *n* (1604) **:** REPETITION
it·er·ant \-rənt\ *adj* (1626) **:** marked by repetition, reiteration, or recurrence (~ echoes)
it·er·ate \'i-tə-͵rāt\ *vt* **-at·ed; -at·ing** [L *iteratus,* pp. of *iterare,* fr. *iterum* again; akin to L *is* he, that, *ita* thus, Skt *itara* the other, *iti* thus] (1533) **:** to say or do again or again and again **:** REITERATE
it·er·a·tion \͵i-tə-'rā-shən\ *n* (15c) **1 :** the action or a process of iterat-

ing or repeating: as **a :** a procedure in which repetition of a sequence of operations yields results successively closer to a desired result **b :** the repetition of a sequence of computer instructions a specified number of times or until a condition is met — compare RECURSION **2 :** one execution of a sequence of operations or instructions in an iteration
it·er·a·tive \'i-tə-͵rā-tiv, -rə-\ *adj* (15c) **:** involving repetition: as **a :** expressing repetition of a verbal action **b :** relating to or being iteration of an operation or procedure — **it·er·a·tive·ly** *adv*
ithy·phal·lic \͵i-thi-'fa-lik\ *adj* [LL *ithyphallicus,* fr. Gk *ithyphallikos,* fr. *ithyphallos* erect phallus, fr. *ithys* straight + *phallos* phallus] (1795) **1 :** of or relating to the phallus carried in procession in ancient festivals of Bacchus **2 a :** having an erect penis — usu. used of figures in an art representation **b :** OBSCENE, LEWD
itin·er·an·cy \i-'ti-nə-rən(t)-sē\ *n* (1789) **1 :** a system (as in the Methodist Church) of rotating ministers who itinerate **2 a :** the act of itinerating **b :** the state of being itinerant
itin·er·ant \-rənt\ *adj* [LL *itinerant-, itinerans,* prp. of *itinerari* to journey, fr. L *itiner-, iter* journey, way; akin to Hitt *itar* way, L *ire* to go — more at ISSUE] (ca. 1576) **:** traveling from place to place; *esp* **:** covering a circuit (~ preacher) — **itinerant** *n* — **itin·er·ant·ly** *adv*
itin·er·ary \i-'ti-nə-͵rer-ē, ə-, *chiefly Brit* ÷-'ti-nə-rē\ *n,* **pl -ar·ies** (15c) **1 :** the route of a journey or tour or the proposed outline of one **2 :** a travel diary **3 :** a traveler's guidebook — **itinerary** *adj*
itin·er·ate \i-'ti-nə-͵rāt, ə-\ *vi* **-at·ed; -at·ing** (1775) **:** to travel a preaching or judicial circuit — **itin·er·a·tion** \-͵ti-nə-'rā-shən\ *n*
-itious *adj suffix* [L *-icius, -itius*] **:** of, relating to, or having the characteristics of (excrement*itious*)
-itis *n suffix, pl* **-itises** *also* **-itides** *or* **-ites** [NL, fr. L & Gk; L, fr. Gk, fr. fem. of *-itēs -ite*] **1 :** disease or inflammation (bronch*itis*) **2** *pl usu* **-itises :** condition likened to a disease — chiefly in nonce formations (television*itis*)
it'll \'i-t⁽ᵊ⁾l\ (1824) **:** it will **:** it shall
-itol *n suffix* [ISV ¹*-ite* + ¹*-ol*] **:** polyhydroxy alcohol usu. related to a sugar (mann*itol*)
its \'its, əts\ *adj* (1598) **:** of or relating to it or itself esp. as possessor, agent, or object of an action (going to ~ kennel) (a child proud of ~ first drawings) (~ final enactment into law)
it's \'its, əts\ (ca. 1555) **:** it is **:** it has
it·self \it-'self, ət-, *Southern also* -'sef\ *pron* (bef. 12c) **1 :** that identical one — compare IT 1; used reflexively (watched the cat giving ~ a bath), for emphasis (the letter ~ was missing), or in absolute constructions (~ a splendid specimen of classic art, it has been exhibited throughout the world) **2 :** its normal, healthy, or sane condition — **in itself :** in its own nature **:** INTRINSICALLY (was not *in itself* bad)
it·ty–bit·ty \'i-tē-'bi-tē\ *or* **it·sy–bit·sy** \'it-sē-'bit-sē\ *adj* [prob. fr. baby talk for *little bit*] (1938) **:** extremely small **:** TINY
-ity *n suffix, pl* **-ities** [ME *-ite,* fr. OF or L; OF *-ité,* fr. L *-itat-, -itas,* fr. *-i-* (stem vowel of adjs.) + *-tat-, -tas* -ity; akin to Gk *-tēt-, -tēs* -ity] **:** quality **:** state **:** degree (alkalin*ity*) (theatrical*ity*)
IUD \͵i-(͵)yü-'dē\ *n* (1965) **:** INTRAUTERINE DEVICE
-ium *n suffix* [NL, fr. L, ending of some neut. nouns] **a :** a chemical element (sod*ium*) **b :** cation (tetrazol*ium*) **2** *pl* **-iums** *or* **-ia** [NL, fr. L, fr. Gk *-ion*]**:** small one **:** mass — esp. in botanical terms (pol·lin*ium*)
IV \͵i-'vē\ *n, pl* **IVs** [*intravenous*] (ca. 1955) **:** an apparatus used to administer an intravenous injection or feeding; *also* **:** such an injection or feeding
-ive *adj suffix* [ME *-if, -ive,* fr. MF & L; MF *-if,* fr. L *-ivus*] **:** that performs or tends toward an (indicated) action (amus*ive*)
I've \'īv\ (1586) **:** I have
iver·mec·tin \͵i-vər-'mek-tən\ *n* [perh. fr. d*i*- + NL a*vermitilis* (specific epithet of *Streptomyces avermitilis,* bacterium from which it is derived) + E *-ect-* (of unknown origin) + ¹*-in*] (1981) **:** a drug mixture of two structurally similar semisynthetic lactones that is used in veterinary medicine as an anthelmintic, acaricide, and insecticide and in human medicine to treat onchocerciasis
ivied \'i-vēd\ *adj* (ca. 1771) **1 :** overgrown with ivy **2 :** ACADEMIC
ivo·ry \'īv-rē, 'ī-və-rē\ *n, pl* **-ries** [ME *ivorie,* fr. OF *ivoire,* fr. L *eboreus* of ivory, fr. *ebor-, ebur* ivory, fr. Egypt *'b, 'bw* elephant, ivory] (13c) **1 a :** the hard creamy-white modified dentine that composes the tusks of a tusked mammal (as an elephant, walrus, or narwhal) **b :** a tusk that yields ivory **2 :** a variable color averaging a pale yellow **3** *slang* **:** TOOTH **4 :** something (as a piano key) made of ivory or of a similar substance — **ivory** *adj*
ivo·ry·bill \-͵bil\ *n* (1787) **:** IVORY-BILLED WOODPECKER
ivo·ry–billed woodpecker \-'bild-\ *n* (1811) **:** a very large black-and≠ white woodpecker (*Campephilus principalis*) of the southeastern U.S. and Cuba that has a showy red crest in the male and is presumed extinct in the U.S.
ivory black *n* (1634) **:** a fine black pigment made by calcining ivory
ivory nut *n* (ca. 1847) **:** the nutlike seed of a So. American palm (*Phytelephas macrocarpa*) containing a very hard endosperm used for carving and turning — compare VEGETABLE IVORY
ivory tower *n* [trans. of F *tour d'ivoire*] (1911) **1 :** an impractical often escapist attitude marked by aloof lack of concern with or interest in practical matters or urgent problems **2 :** a secluded place that affords the means of treating practical issues with an impractical often escapist attitude; *esp* **:** a place of learning — **ivory–tower** *adj* — **ivo·ry–tow·er·ish** \-'taü-(ə-)rish\ *adj*
ivo·ry–tow·ered \-'taü-(ə-)rd\ *adj* (1937) **:** divorced from reality and practical matters (an ~ recluse)
¹**ivy** \'i-vē\ *n, pl* **ivies** [ME, fr. OE *ifig;* akin to OHG *ebah* ivy] (bef. 12c) **1 :** a widely cultivated ornamental climbing or prostrate or sometimes shrubby chiefly Eurasian vine (*Hedera helix*) of the ginseng family with evergreen leaves, small yellowish flowers, and black berries **2 :** POISON IVY **3** *often cap* **:** an Ivy League college

\ə\ abut \ᵊ\ kitten, F table \ər\ further \a\ ash \ā\ ace \ä\ mop, mar \aủ\ out \ch\ chin \e\ bet \ē\ easy \g\ go \i\ hit \ī\ ice \j\ job \ŋ\ sing \ō\ go \ò\ law \òi\ boy \th\ thin \t͟h\ the \ü\ loot \ủ\ foot \y\ yet \zh\ vision \à, k̲, ⁿ, œ, œ̄, ue, ue̅, ᵇ\ *see* Guide to Pronunciation

²**ivy** *adj* [fr. the prevalence of ivy-covered buildings on the campuses of older U.S. colleges] (1933) **1** : ACADEMIC **2** : IVY LEAGUE

Ivy League *adj* (1939) **1** : of, relating to, or characteristic of a group of long-established eastern U.S. colleges widely regarded as high in scholastic and social prestige **2** : of, relating to, or characteristic of the students of Ivy League colleges

Ivy Leaguer *n* (1943) : a student at or a graduate of an Ivy League college

iwis \ē-'wis, ī-\ *adv* [ME, fr. OE *gewis* certain; akin to OHG *giwisso* certainly, OE *witan* to know — more at WIT] (12c) *archaic* : SURELY

Ix·i·on \ik-'sī-ən\ *n* [L, fr. Gk *Ixīōn*] : a Thessalian king bound by Zeus to a burning wheel in Tartarus for attempting to seduce Hera

ix·o·did \'ik-sə-,did, ik-'sō-dəd\ *adj* [ultim. fr. Gk *ixōdēs* sticky, fr. *ixos* birdlime] (ca. 1909) : of, relating to, or being a typical tick (family Ixodidae) — **ixodid** *n*

Iyar \'ē-,yär\ *n* [Heb *Iyyār*] (1737) : the 8th month of the civil year or the 2d month of the ecclesiastical year in the Jewish calendar — see MONTH table

-i·za·tion \ə-'zā-shən *also* (,)ī-'zā-\ *n suffix* : action, process, or result of making ⟨socialization⟩

-ize *vb suffix* [ME *-isen*, fr. OF *-iser*, fr. LL *-izare*, fr. Gk *-izein*] **1 a** (1) : cause to be or conform to or resemble ⟨systemize⟩ ⟨Americanize⟩ : cause to be formed into ⟨unionize⟩ (2) : subject to a (specified) action ⟨plagiarize⟩ (3) : impregnate or treat or combine with ⟨aluminize⟩ **b** : treat like ⟨idolize⟩ **c** : treat according to the method of ⟨bowdlerize⟩ **2 a** : become : become like ⟨crystallize⟩ **b** : be productive in or of ⟨hypothesize⟩ : engage in a (specified) activity ⟨philosophize⟩ **c** : adopt or spread the manner of activity or the teaching of ⟨Platonize⟩
usage The suffix *-ize* has been productive in English since the time of Thomas Nashe (1567–1601), who claimed credit for introducing it into English to remedy the surplus of monosyllabic words. Almost any noun or adjective can be made into a verb by adding *-ize* ⟨hospitalize⟩ ⟨familiarize⟩; many technical terms are coined this way ⟨oxidize⟩ as well as verbs of ethnic derivation ⟨Americanize⟩ and verbs derived from proper names ⟨bowdlerize⟩ ⟨mesmerize⟩. Nashe noted in 1591 that his coinages in *-ize* were being complained about, and to this day new words in *-ize* ⟨finalize⟩ ⟨prioritize⟩ are sure to draw critical fire.

iz·zard \'i-zərd\ *n* [alter. of earlier *ezod, ezed*, prob. fr. MF *et zede* and Z] (ca. 1726) *chiefly dial* : the letter z

---

J

j \'jā\ *n, pl* **j's** *or* **js** \'jāz\ *often cap, often attrib* (15c) **1 a** : the 10th letter of the English alphabet **b** : a speech counterpart of orthographic *j* **2 a** : a graphic device for reproducing the letter *j* **b** : a unit vector parallel to the y-axis **3** : one designated *j* esp. as the 10th in order or class **4** : something shaped like the letter J

¹**jab** \'jab\ *vb* **jabbed; jab·bing** [alter. of *job* to strike] *vt* (1827) **1 a** : to pierce with or as if with a sharp object : STAB **b** : to poke quickly or abruptly : THRUST **2** : to strike with a short straight blow ~ *vi* **1** : to make quick or abrupt thrusts with a sharp object **2** : to strike a person with a short straight blow

²**jab** *n* (1872) : an act of jabbing; *esp* : a short straight boxing punch delivered with the leading hand

¹**jab·ber** \'ja-bər\ *vb* **jab·bered; jab·ber·ing** \'ja-b(ə-)riŋ\ [ME *jaberen*, of imit. origin] *vi* (15c) : to talk rapidly, indistinctly, or unintelligibly ~ *vt* : to speak rapidly or indistinctly — **jab·ber·er** \'ja-bər-ər\ *n*

²**jabber** *n* (1727) : GIBBERISH, CHATTER

jab·ber·wocky \'ja-bər-,wä-kē\ *n* [*Jabberwocky*, nonsense poem by Lewis Carroll] (1908) : meaningless speech or writing

jab·i·ru \,zha-bə-'rü\ *n* [Pg, fr. Tupi *jabirú*] (1774) : any of several large tropical storks

jab·o·ran·di \,zha-bə-,ran-'dē, -'ran-dē\ *n* [Pg, fr. Tupi *yaborandí*] (ca. 1875) : the dried leaves of two So. American shrubs (*Pilocarpus jaborandi* and *P. microphyllus*) of the rue family that are a source of pilocarpine

ja·bot \zha-'bō, 'ja-,bō\ *n* [F] (1823) **1** : a fall of lace or cloth attached to the front of a neckband and worn esp. by men in the 18th century **2** : a pleated frill of cloth or lace attached down the center front of a woman's blouse or dress

ja·bo·ti·ca·ba \zhə-,bü-ti-'kä-bə\ *n* [Pg, fr. Tupi] (1824) : a Brazilian tree (*Myrciaria cauliflora*) of the myrtle family cultivated in warm regions for its edible usu. purplish fruit

ja·cal \hə-'käl\ *n, pl* **ja·ca·les** \-'kä-(,)läs\ *also* **ja·cals** [MexSp, fr. Nahuatl *xahcalli*] (1838) : a hut in Mexico and southwestern U.S. with a thatched roof and walls made of upright poles or sticks covered and chinked with mud or clay

jac·a·mar \'zha-kə-,mär\ *n* [F, fr. Tupi *jacamáciri*] (1825) : any of a family (Galbulidae) of usu. iridescent green or bronze insectivorous birds of Central and So. American tropical forests

ja·ca·na \jə-'kä-nə, zha-sᵊn-'aⁿ\ *n* [Pg *jaçanã*, fr. Tupi & Guarani] (ca. 1753) : any of a family (Jacanidae) of long-legged and long-toed tropical wading birds that frequent coastal freshwater marshes and ponds

jac·a·ran·da \,ja-kə-'ran-də\ *n* [NL, fr. Pg *jacarandá*] (ca. 1753) : any of a genus (*Jacaranda*) of pinnate-leaved tropical American trees of the trumpet-creeper family with showy usu. blue flowers in panicles

ja·cinth \'jā-sᵊn(t)th, 'ja-\ *n* [ME *iacinct*, fr. OF *jacinthe*, fr. L *hyacinthus*, a flowering plant, a gem] (13c) **1** : HYACINTH **2** : a gem more nearly orange in color than a hyacinth

¹**jack** \'jak\ *n* [ME *Jacke*, familiar term of address to a social inferior, nickname for *Johan* John] (1548) **1 a** : MAN — usu. used as an intensive in such phrases as *every man jack* **b** *often cap* : SAILOR **c** (1) : SERVANT, LABORER (2) : LUMBERJACK **2** : any of various usu. mechanical devices: as **a** : a device for turning a spit **b** : a usu. portable mechanism or device for exerting pressure or lifting a heavy body a short distance **3** : something that supports or holds in position: as **a** : an iron bar at a topgallant masthead to support a royal mast and spread the royal shrouds **b** : a wooden brace fastened behind a scenic unit in a stage set to prop it up **4 a** : any of several fishes; *esp* : any

jabot 1

of various carangids **b** : a male donkey **c** : JACKRABBIT **d** : any of several birds (as a jackdaw) **5 a** : a small white target ball in lawn bowling **b** : a small national flag flown by a ship **c** (1) *pl but sing in constr* : a game played with a set of small objects that are tossed, caught, and moved in various figures (2) : a small 6-pointed metal object used in the game of jacks **6 a** : a playing card carrying the figure of a soldier or servant and ranking usu. below the queen **b** : JACKPOT 1a(2) **7** *slang* : MONEY **8** : a female fitting in an electric circuit used with a plug to make a connection with another circuit **9 a** : APPLEJACK **b** : BRANDY **10** : JACKKNIFE 2 **11** : MONTEREY JACK

²**jack** *vi* (ca. 1841) : to hunt or fish at night with a jacklight ~ *vt* **1** : to hunt for at night with a jacklight **2 a** : to move or lift by or as if by a jack **b** : to raise the level of — usu. used with *up* ⟨~ up the price⟩ **c** : to take to task — **jack·er** *n*

jack·al \'ja-kəl *also* -,kȯl\ *n* [Turk *çakal*, fr. Per *shagāl*, of Indo-Aryan origin; akin to Skt *sṛgāla* jackal] (1603) **1** : any of several small omnivorous canids (as *Canis aureus*) of Africa and Asia having large ears, long legs, and bushy tails **2 a** : a person who performs routine or menial tasks for another **b** : a person who serves or collaborates with another esp. in the commission of base acts

Jack-a-Lent \'ja-kə-,lent\ *n* [¹*jack* + *a* (of) + *Lent*] (1598) **1** : a small stuffed puppet set up to be pelted for fun in Lent **2** : a simple or insignificant person

jack·a·napes \'ja-kə-,nāps\ *n* [ME *Jack Napis*, nickname for William de la Pole †1450 duke of Suffolk] (1526) **1** : MONKEY, APE **2 a** : an impudent or conceited fellow **b** : a saucy or mischievous child

jack·ass \'jak-,as\ *n* (1727) **1** : DONKEY; *esp* : a male donkey **2 a** : stupid person : FOOL

jack·ass·ery \jak-,a-sə-rē, -,as-rē\ *n, pl* **-er·ies** (1833) : foolish action or behavior

jack bean *n* (1885) : a bushy annual tropical American legume (genus *Canavalia*); *esp* : a plant (*C. ensiformis*) grown esp. for forage

jack·boot \'jak-,büt\ *n* (1686) **1** : a heavy military boot made of glossy black leather extending above the knee and worn esp. during the 17th and 18th centuries **2** : the spirit or policy of militarism or totalitarianism **3** : a laceless military boot reaching to the calf

jack·boot·ed \-,bü-təd\ *adj* (1846) **1** : wearing jackboots **2** : ruthlessly and violently oppressive ⟨~ force⟩

jack cheese *n, often cap J* [alter. of David *Jacks*, 19th cent. California landowner] (1912) : MONTEREY JACK

jack crevalle *n* (1948) : a carangid fish (*Caranx hippos*) that is an important food fish along the west coast of Florida

jack·daw \'jak-,dȯ\ *n* (1543) **1** : a common black and gray bird (*Corvus monedula*) of Eurasia and northern Africa that is related to but smaller than the common crow **2** : GRACKLE 1

¹**jack·et** \'ja-kət\ *n* [ME *jaket*, fr. MF *jaquet*, dim. of *jaque* short jacket, fr. *jacque* peasant, fr. the name *Jacques* James] (15c) **1 a** : a garment for the upper body usu. having a front opening, collar, lapels, sleeves, and pockets **b** : something worn or fastened around the body but not for use as clothing **2 a** (1) : the natural covering of an animal (2) : the fur or wool of a mammal **b** : the skin of a potato **3** : an outer covering or casing: as **a** (1) : a thermally nonconducting cover (2) : a covering that encloses an intermediate space through which a temperature-controlling fluid circulates (3) : a tough cold-worked metal casing that forms the outer shell of a built-up bullet **b** (1) : a wrapper or open envelope for a document (2) : an envelope for enclosing registered mail during delivery from one post office to another **c** (1) : a detachable protective cover for a book (2) : a paper or paperboard envelope for a phonograph record — **jack·et·less** \-ləs\ *adj*

²**jacket** *vt* (1856) : to put a jacket on : enclose in or with a jacket

Jack Frost *n* (1826) : frost or frosty weather personified

jack·fruit \'jak-,früt\ *n* [Pg *jaca* jackfruit, fr. Malayalam *cakka*] (1830) : a large tropical Asian tree (*Artocarpus heterophyllus*) related to the breadfruit that yields a fine-grained yellow wood and immense fruits which contain an edible pulp and nutritious seeds; *also* : its fruit

jack·ham·mer \'jak-,ha-mər\ *n* (1916) **1** : a pneumatically operated percussive rock-drilling tool usu. held in the hands **2** : a device in which a tool (as a chisel for breaking up pavements) is driven percussively by compressed air — **jackhammer** *vb*

jack-in-the-box \'ja-kən-ˌthə-ˌbäks\ *n, pl* **jack-in-the-box-es** *or* **jacks-in-the-box** (1702) : a toy consisting of a small box out of which a figure (as of a clown's head) springs when the lid is raised

jack-in-the-pul-pit \ˌja-kən-thə-'pùl-ˌpit, -pət *also* -'pəl-\ *n, pl* **jack-in-the-pulpits** *or* **jacks-in-the-pulpit** (1837) : an American spring-flowering woodland herb (*Arisaema triphyllum* syn. *A. atrorubens*) of the arum family having an upright club-shaped spadix arched over by a green and purple spathe

¹jack-knife \'jak-ˌnīf\ *n* (1711) **1** : a large strong pocketknife **2** : a dive executed headfirst in which the diver bends from the waist and touches the ankles while holding the knees unbent and then straightens out

²jackknife *vt* (1806) **1** : to cut with a jackknife **2** : to cause to double up like a jackknife ~ *vi* **1** : to double up like a jackknife **2** : to turn and form an angle of 90 degrees or less with each other — used esp. of a tractor-trailer combination

jack-leg \'jak-ˌleg, -ˌläg\ *adj* [*jack* + *-leg* (as in *blackleg*)] (1850) **1 a** : lacking skill or training : AMATEUR ⟨a ~ carpenter⟩ **b** : characterized by unscrupulousness, dishonesty, or lack of professional standards ⟨a ~ lawyer⟩ **2** : designed as a temporary expedient : MAKESHIFT — **jackleg** *n*

jack-light \-ˌlīt\ *n* (ca. 1841) : a light used esp. in hunting or fishing at night

jack mackerel *n* (1882) : a California carangid food fish (*Trachurus symmetricus*) that is iridescent green or bluish above and silvery below

jack-of-all-trades \ˌja-kə-ˌvòl-'trädz\ *n, pl* **jacks-of-all-trades** (1618) : a person who can do passable work at various tasks : a handy versatile person

jack off *vb* [prob. alter. of *jerk off*] (1959) : MASTURBATE — usu. considered vulgar

jack-o'-lan-tern \'ja-kə-ˌlan-tərn\ *n* (1750) **1** : IGNIS FATUUS **2** : a lantern made of a pumpkin cut to look like a human face **3** : a large orangish gill fungus (*Omphalotus olearius* syn. *Clitocybe illudens*) that is poisonous and luminescent

jack pine *n* (1883) : a slender pine (*Pinus banksiana*) of northern No. America that has two stout needles in each fascicle and wood used esp. for pulpwood

jack plane *n* (ca. 1816) : a medium-sized general-purpose plane used in carpentry and joinery

jack-pot \'jak-ˌpät\ *n* (1881) **1 a** (1) : a hand or game of draw poker in which a pair of jacks or better is required to open (2) : a large pot (as in poker) formed by the accumulation of stakes from previous play **b** (1) : a combination on a slot machine that wins a top prize or all the coins available for paying out (2) : the sum so won **c** : a large fund of money or other reward formed by the accumulation of unwon prizes **2** : an impressive often unexpected success or reward **3** *chiefly West* : a tight spot : JAM

jack-rab-bit \-ˌra-bət\ *n* [*jack* (jackass) + *rabbit*; fr. its long ears] (1863) : any of several large hares (genus *Lepus*) of western No. America having very long ears and long hind legs

Jack Russell terrier \'jak-'rə-səl-\ *n* [*Jack* (John) *Russell* †1883 Eng. clergyman & dog breeder] (1961) : any of a breed of small terriers having a usu. white coat with brown, black, or tricolor markings — called also *Jack Russell*

jack salmon *n* (1871) **1** : WALLEYE 3 **2** : GRILSE

jack-screw \'jak-ˌskrü\ *n* (1769) : SCREW JACK

jack-smelt \-ˌsmelt\ *n* (1949) : a large silversides (*Atherinopsis californiensis*) of the Pacific coast of No. America that is the chief commercial smelt of the California markets

Jack-son Day \'jak-sən-\ *n* [Andrew *Jackson*; fr. his defense of New Orleans] (1885) : January 8 celebrated as a legal holiday in Louisiana to commemorate the successful defense of New Orleans in 1815

jack stand *n* (1968) : a stand whose height may be adjusted and fixed by a pin and which is used to support an automobile that is then raised by a jack

jack-stay \-ˌstā\ *n* (ca. 1840) **1** : an iron rod, wooden bar, or wire rope along a yard of a ship to which the sails are fastened **2** : a support of wood, iron, or rope running up a mast on which the parrel of a yard travels

jack-straw \'jak-ˌstrò\ *n* (1801) **1** *pl but sing in constr* : a game in which a set of straws or thin strips is let fall in a heap with each player in turn trying to remove one at a time without disturbing the rest **2** : one of the pieces used in the game jackstraws

jack-tar \-'tär\ *n, often cap* (1781) : SAILOR

jack-up \'jak-ˌəp\ *n* (1965) : a drilling rig used in offshore drilling whose drilling platform is a barge from which legs are lowered to the bottom when over the drill site and which is raised above the water and supported on the legs to conduct drilling operations

Ja-cob \'jā-kəb\ *n* [LL, fr. Gk *Iacōb*, fr. Heb *Ya'ăqōbh*] **1** : a son of Isaac and Rebekah, the twin brother of Esau, and heir of God's promise of blessing to Abraham **2** : the ancient Hebrew nation

Jac-o-be-an \ˌja-kə-'bē-ən\ *adj* [NL *Jacobaeus*, fr. *Jacobus* James] (1844) : of, relating to, or characteristic of James I of England or his age — **Jacobean** *n*

jacobean lily *n, often cap J* [LL *Jacobus* (St. James)] (ca. 1774) : a Mexican bulbous herb (*Sprekelia formosissima*) of the amaryllis family cultivated for its bright red solitary flower

Ja-co-bi-an \jə-'kō-bē-ən, yä-\ *n* [K. G. J. *Jacobi* †1851 Ger. mathematician] (1881) : a determinant defined for a finite number of functions of the same number of variables in which each row consists of the first partial derivatives of the same function with respect to each of the variables

Jac-o-bin \'ja-kə-bən\ *n* [ME, fr. MF, fr. ML *Jacobinus*, fr. LL *Jacobus* (St. James); fr. the location of the first Dominican convent in the street of St. James, Paris] (14c) **1** : DOMINICAN **2** [F, fr. *Jacobin* Dominican; fr. the group's founding in the Dominican convent in Paris]**:** a member of an extremist or radical political group; *esp* : a member of such a group advocating egalitarian democracy and engaging in terrorist activities during the French Revolution of 1789 — **Jac-o-bin-ic** \ˌja-kə-'bi-nik\ *or* **Jac-o-bin-i-cal** \-ni-kəl\ *adj* — **Jac-o-bin-ism** \'ja-kə-bə-ˌni-zəm\ *n*

¹Jac-o-bite \'ja-kə-ˌbīt\ *n* [ME, fr. ML *Jacobita*, fr. *Jacobus* Baradaeus

---

(Jacob Baradai) †578 Syrian monk] (15c) : a member of any of various Monophysite Eastern churches; *esp* : a member of the Monophysite Syrian church

²Jacobite *n* [*Jacobus* (James II)] (1689) : a partisan of James II of England or of the Stuarts after the revolution of 1688 — **Jac-o-bit-i-cal** \ˌja-kə-'bi-ti-kəl\ *or* **Jac-o-bit-ism** \'ja-kə-ˌbī-ˌti-zəm\ *n*

Ja-cob's ladder \'jā-kəbz-\ *n* [fr. the ladder seen in a dream by Jacob in Gen 28:12] (1733) **1** : any of a genus (*Polemonium*) of herbs of the phlox family that have pinnate leaves, an herbaceous calyx, a bell-shaped corolla with stamens with their filaments bent downward, and a several-seeded capsule; *esp* : a perennial (*P. caeruleum*) of European origin with bright blue or occas. white flowers **2** : a marine ladder of rope or chain with wooden or iron rungs

Ja-cob-son's organ \'jā-kəb-sənz-\ *n* [Ludvig L. *Jacobson* †1843 Dan. anatomist] (1885) : either of a pair of small pits that are situated one on either side of the nasal septum (as in higher vertebrates) or in the buccal cavity and that are rudimentary in humans but developed in reptiles, amphibians, and some mammals as chemoreceptors

Ja-co-bus \jə-'kō-bəs\ *n* [*Jacobus* (James I), during whose reign unites were coined] (1612) : UNITE

jac-o-net \'ja-kə-ˌnet\ *n* [modif. of Urdu *jagannāthī*] (1769) : a lightweight cotton cloth used for clothing and bandages

jac-quard \'ja-ˌkärd\ *n, often cap, often attrib* [Joseph *Jacquard*] (1841) **1 a** : the control mechanism of a Jacquard loom **b** : JACQUARD LOOM **2** : a fabric of intricate variegated weave or pattern

Jacquard loom *n* (1851) : a loom designed to weave fabrics of intricate design whose control mechanism makes use of cards with holes punched in them

jac-que-rie \ˌzhä-kə-'rē, ˌzha-\ *n, often cap* [MF, fr. the French peasant revolt in 1358, fr. *jacque* peasant — more at JACKET] (1523) : a peasants' revolt

jac-ti-ta-tion \ˌjak-tə-'tā-shən\ *n* [LL *jactitation-, jactitatio*, fr. *jactitare*, freq. of L *jactare* to throw — more at JET] (1665) : a tossing to and fro or jerking and twitching of the body

Ja-cuz-zi \jə-'kü-zē\ *trademark* — used for a whirlpool bath and a recreational bathing tub or pool

¹jade \'jād\ *n* [ME] (14c) **1** : a broken-down, vicious, or worthless horse **2 a** : a disreputable woman **b** : a flirtatious girl

²jade *vb* **jad-ed; jad-ing** *vt* (1598) **1 a** : to wear out by overwork or abuse **b** : to tire or dull through repetition or excess **2** *obs* : to make ridiculous ~ *vi* : to become weary or dulled *syn* see TIRE

³jade *n* [F, fr. obs. Sp (*piedra de la*) *ijada*, lit., loin stone, ultim. fr. L *ilia*, pl., flanks; fr. the belief that jade cures renal colic] (1657) **1** : either of two tough compact typically green gemstones that take a high polish: **a** : JADEITE **b** : NEPHRITE **2** : a sculpture or artifact of jade **3** : JADE GREEN

jaded *adj* (1600) **1** : fatigued by overwork : EXHAUSTED **2** : dulled by experience or by surfeit — **jad-ed-ly** *adv* — **jad-ed-ness** *n*

jade green *n* (1892) : a light bluish green

jade-ite \'jā-ˌdīt\ *n* [F] (1865) : a monoclinic mineral that is a silicate of sodium and aluminum and is a jade — **ja-dit-ic** \jā-'di-tik\ *adj*

jade plant *n* (1944) : any of several succulent plants (genus *Crassula*) of the orpine family cultivated as foliage plants

jae-ger \'yā-gər\ *n* [G *Jäger*] (1809) **1 a** : HUNTER, HUNTSMAN **b** : one attending a person of rank or wealth and wearing hunter's costume **2** : any of several large dark-colored birds (genus *Stercorarius* of the family Stercorariidae) of northern seas that are strong fliers and that tend to harass weaker birds until they drop or disgorge their prey

¹jag \'jag\ *vb* **jagged; jag-ging** [ME *jaggen*] *vt* (15c) **1** *chiefly dial* : PRICK, STAB **2** : to cut indentations into; *also* : to form teeth on (a saw) by cutting indentations ~ *vi* **1** : PRICK, THRUST **2** : to move in jerks — **jag-ger** *n*

²jag *n* (1578) : a sharp projecting part : BARB

³jag *n* [origin unknown] (1597) **1** : a small load **2 a** : a state or feeling of exhilaration or intoxication usu. induced by liquor **b** : SPREE ⟨a crying ~⟩

jag-ged \'ja-gəd\ *adj* (1577) **1** : having a sharply uneven edge or surface **2** : having a harsh, rough, or irregular quality — **jag-ged-ly** *adv* — **jag-ged-ness** *n*

jag-gery \'ja-gə-rē\ *n* [Pg *jágara*, prob. fr. Malayalam *chakkara* sugar] (1598) : an unrefined brown sugar made from palm sap

jag-gy \'ja-gē\ *adj* (1717) : JAGGED, NOTCHED

jag-uar \'ja-ˌgwär, -gyə-ˌwär, -gwər, *esp Brit* 'ja-gyə-wər\ *n* [Sp *yaguar* & Pg *jaguar*, fr. Guarani *yaguara* & Tupi *jaguara*] (1604) : a large cat (*Panthera onca* syn. *Felis onca*) chiefly of Central and So. America that is larger and stockier than the leopard and is brownish yellow or buff with black spots

jag-ua-run-di \ˌzha-gwə-'rən-dē\ *also* **jag-ua-ron-di** \-rän-\ *n* [AmerSp, fr. Guarani *yaguaruindí*] (ca. 1885) : a slender long-tailed short-legged black, gray, or reddish wildcat (*Felis yagouaroundi*) chiefly of Central and So. America

Jah \'jä\ *n* [Heb *Yāh*] (1975) : the Supreme Being of Rastafarianism

Jah-veh \'yä-(ˌ)vä\ *var of* YAHWEH

jai alai \'hī-ˌlī, ˌhī-ə-'lī\ *n* [Sp, fr. Basque, fr. *jai* festival + *alai* merry] (1903) : a court game somewhat like handball played usu. by two or four players with a ball and a long curved wicker basket strapped to the wrist

¹jail \'jā(ə)l\ *n* [ME *jaiole*, fr. OF, fr. LL *caveola*, dim. of L *cavea* cage — more at CAGE] (13c) **1** : a place of confinement for persons held in lawful custody; *specif* : such a place under the jurisdiction of a local government (as a county) for the confinement of persons awaiting trial or those convicted of minor crimes — compare PRISON **2** : confinement in a jail

²jail *vt* (1604) : to confine in or as if in a jail

jail-bait \'jā(ə)l-ˌbāt\ *n* (1930) : a girl under the age of consent with whom sexual intercourse is unlawful and constitutes statutory rape

---

\ə\ abut \ᵊ\ kitten, F table \ər\ further \a\ ash \ā\ ace \ä\ mop, mar \au̇\ out \ch\ chin \e\ bet \ē\ easy \g\ go \i\ hit \ī\ ice \j\ job \ŋ\ sing \ō\ go \ȯ\ law \ȯi\ boy \th\ thin \t͟h\ the \ü\ loot \u̇\ foot \y\ yet \zh\ vision \ä, ḵ, ⁿ, œ, œ̄, ᵫ, ᵾ, ᵫ̄, ᴼ\ *see* Guide to Pronunciation

jail·bird \-ˌbərd\ n (1603) : a person confined in jail; specif : an habitual criminal

jail·break \-ˌbrāk\ n (1910) : a forcible escape from jail

jail·er or **jail·or** \'jā-lər\ n (13c) **1 :** a keeper of a jail **2 :** one that restricts another's liberty as if by imprisonment

jail·house \'jā(ə)l-ˌhaús\ n (1812) : JAIL 1

jailhouse lawyer n (1969) : a prison inmate self-taught in the law who tries to gain release through legal maneuvers or who advises fellow inmates in their legal problems

Jain \'jīn\ or **Jai·na** \'jī-nə\ n [Hindi Jain, fr. Skt Jaina] (1805) : an adherent of Jainism

Jain·ism \'jī-ˌni-zəm\ n (1858) : a religion of India originating in the 6th century B.C. and teaching liberation of the soul by right knowledge, right faith, and right conduct

jake \'jāk\ adj [origin unknown] (1914) slang : ALL RIGHT, FINE

jake leg \'jāk-ˌleg, -ˌlāg\ n [jake grain alcohol flavored with an alcoholic extract of ginger] (1932) : a paralysis caused by drinking improperly distilled or contaminated liquor

jakes \'jāks\ n pl but sing or pl in constr [perh. fr. F Jacques James] (1538) : PRIVY 1

jal·ap \'ja-ləp, 'jä-\ n [F & Sp; F jalap, fr. Sp jalapa, fr. Jalapa, Mexico] (1644) **1 a :** the dried tuberous root of a Mexican plant (Ipomoea purga syn. Exogonium purga) of the morning-glory family; also : a powdered purgative drug prepared from it that contains resinous glycosides **b :** the root or derived drug of plants related to the one supplying jalap **2 :** a plant yielding jalap

ja·la·pe·ño also **ja·la·pe·no** \ˌhä-lə-'pā-(ˌ)nyō, ˌha-, -'pā-(ˌ)nō, -'pē-(ˌ)nō\ n, pl **-ños** also **-nos** [MexSp, fr. jalapeño, adj., of Jalapa] (1939) : a small plump dark green Mexican hot pepper — called also jalapeño pepper

ja·lopy \jə-'lä-pē\ n, pl **ja·lop·ies** [origin unknown] (1928) : a dilapidated old vehicle (as an automobile)

jal·ou·sie \'ja-lə-sē\ n [F, lit., jealousy, fr. OF jelous jealous] (1766) **1** : a blind with adjustable horizontal slats for admitting light and air while excluding direct sun and rain **2 :** a window made of adjustable glass louvers that control ventilation

¹jam \'jam\ vb **jammed; jam·ming** [origin unknown] vi (1706) **1 a** : to become blocked or wedged **b :** to become unworkable through the jamming of a movable part **c :** to force one's way into a restricted space **3 :** to take part in a jam session ~ vt **1 a :** to press into a close or tight position ⟨~ his hat on⟩ **b** (1) **:** to cause to become wedged so as to be unworkable ⟨~ the typewriter keys⟩ (2) **:** to make unworkable by jamming **c :** to block passage of : OBSTRUCT **d :** to fill often to excess : PACK ⟨the crowd jammed the theater⟩ **2 :** to push forcibly; esp : to apply (brakes) suddenly and forcibly — used with on **3 :** CRUSH, BRUISE **4 a :** to make unintelligible by sending out interfering signals or messages **b :** to make (as a radar apparatus) ineffective by jamming signals or by causing reflection of radar waves **5 :** to pitch inside to (a batter) — **jam·mer** \'ja-mər\ n

²jam n (1805) **1 a :** an act or instance of jamming **b :** a crowded mass that impedes or blocks ⟨a traffic ~⟩ **2 a :** the quality or state of being jammed **b :** the pressure or congestion of a crowd : CRUSH **3** : a difficult state of affairs : FIX ⟨got into a ~⟩ **4 :** JAM SESSION **5** : DUNK SHOT

³jam n [prob. fr. ¹jam] (ca. 1736) **:** a food made by boiling fruit and sugar to a thick consistency — **jam·my** \'ja-mē\ adj

Jamaica rum n (ca. 1900) **:** a heavy-bodied rum made by slow fermentation and marked by a pungent bouquet

jamb \'jam\ n [ME jambe, fr. MF, lit., leg, fr. LL gamba — more at GAMBIT] (14c) **1 :** an upright piece or surface forming the side of an opening (as for a door, window, or fireplace) **2 :** a projecting columnar part or mass

jam·ba·laya \ˌjəm-bə-'lī-ə\ n [LaF, fr. Prov jambalaia] (1872) **1 :** rice cooked usu. with ham, sausage, chicken, shrimp, or oysters and seasoned with herbs **2 :** a mixture of diverse elements ⟨curious ~s of competing elements —Neil Hickey⟩

jam·beau \'jam-(ˌ)bō\ n, pl **jam·beaux** \-(ˌ)bōz\ [ME, fr. (assumed) AF, fr. MF jambe] (14c) **:** a piece of medieval armor for the leg below the knee — see ARMOR illustration

jam·bo·ree \ˌjam-bə-'rē\ n [origin unknown] (1864) **1 :** a noisy or unrestrained carouse **2 a :** a large festive gathering **b :** a national or international camping assembly of Boy Scouts **3 :** a long mixed program of entertainment

James \'jāmz\ n [ME, fr. MF, fr. (assumed) VL Jacomus, alter. of LL Jacobus, Jacob Jacob] **1 :** an apostle, son of Zebedee, and brother of the apostle John according to the Gospel accounts **2 :** an apostle and son of Alphaeus according to the Gospel accounts — called also James the Less **3 :** a brother of Jesus traditionally held to be the author of the New Testament Epistle of James **4 :** a moral lecture addressed to early Christians and included as a book in the New Testament — see BIBLE table

jam·mies \'ja-mēz\ n pl [by shortening & alter.] (1973) : PAJAMAS 2

jam-pack \'jam-ˈpak\ vt (1924) : to pack tightly or to excess

Jams \'jamz\ trademark — used for knee-length loose-fitting swim trunks

jam session n [²jam] (1933) : an often impromptu performance by a group esp. of jazz musicians that is characterized by improvisation

Jam·shid or **Jam·shyd** \jam-'shēd\ n [Per Jamshīd] : an early legendary king of Persia who reigned for 700 years

jam—up \'jam-ˌəp\ n (1941) : JAM 1

Jane Doe \'jän-'dō\ n (1936) : a female party to legal proceedings whose true name is unknown

Jane·ite \'jā-ˌnīt\ n (1896) : an enthusiastic admirer of Jane Austen's writings

¹jan·gle \'jaŋ-gəl\ vb **jan·gled; jan·gling** \-g(ə-)liŋ\ [ME, fr. MF jangler, of Gmc origin; akin to MD jangelen to grumble] vi (14c) **1 :** to talk idly **2 :** to quarrel verbally **3 :** to make a harsh or discordant often ringing sound ⟨keys jangling in my pocket⟩ ~ vt **1 :** to utter or sound in a discordant, babbling, or chattering way **2 a :** to cause to sound harshly or inharmoniously **b :** to excite to tense irritation ⟨jangled nerves⟩ — **jan·gler** \-g(ə-)lər\ n

²jangle n (14c) **1 :** idle talk **2 :** noisy quarreling **3 :** a discordant often ringing sound : DISCORD

jan·gly \'jaŋ-g(ə-)lē\ adj (1892) : marked by jangling : having a jangling quality ⟨~ earrings⟩ ⟨~ guitar music⟩

jan·is·sary or **jan·i·zary** \'ja-nə-ˌser-ē, -ˌzer-\ n, pl **-sar·ies** or **-zar·ies** [It gianizzero, fr. Turk yeniçeri, fr. yeni new + çeri soldier] (1529) **1** often cap **:** a soldier of an elite corps of Turkish troops organized in the 14th century and abolished in 1826 **2 :** a member of a group of loyal or subservient troops, officials, or supporters

jan·i·tor \'ja-nə-tər\ n [L, fr. janus arch, gate] (1629) **1 :** DOORKEEPER **2 :** one who keeps the premises of a building (as an apartment or office) clean, tends the heating system, and makes minor repairs — **jan·i·to·ri·al** \ˌja-nə-'tōr-ē-əl, -'tor-\ adj

Jan·sen·ism \'jan(t)-sə-ˌni-zəm\ n [F jansénisme, fr. Cornelis Jansen] (ca. 1656) **1 :** a system of doctrine based on moral determinism, defended by various reformist factions among 17th. and 18th century western European Roman Catholic clergy, religious, and scholars, and condemned as heretical by papal authority **2 :** a puritanical attitude (as toward sex) — **Jan·sen·ist** \-nist\ n — **Jan·sen·is·tic** \ˌjan(t)-sə-'nis-tik\ adj

Jan·u·ary \'jan-yə-ˌwer-ē\ n, pl **-ar·ies** or **-ar·ys** [ME Januarie, fr. L Januarius, 1st month of the ancient Roman year, fr. Janus] (14c) **:** the 1st month of the Gregorian calendar

Ja·nus \'jā-nəs\ n [L] **:** a Roman god that is identified with doors, gates, and all beginnings and that is represented artistically with two opposite faces

Janus—faced \-ˌfāst\ adj (1682) **:** having two contrasting aspects; esp : DUPLICITOUS, TWO-FACED

Janus green n [prob. fr. Janus, a trademark] (1898) **:** a basic azine dye used esp. as a biological stain (as for mitochondria)

Jap \'jap\ n or adj (1860) : JAPANESE — usu. used disparagingly

JAP \'jap\ n (ca. 1973) : JEWISH AMERICAN PRINCESS — usu. used disparagingly

ja·pan \jə-'pan\ adj (1673) **:** of, relating to, or originating in Japan **:** of a kind or style characteristic of Japanese workmanship

²japan n (1688) **1 a :** any of several varnishes yielding a hard brilliant finish **b :** a hard dark coating containing asphalt and a drier that is used esp. on metal and fixed by heating — called also japan black **2** : work (as lacquer ware) finished and decorated in the Japanese manner

³japan vt **ja·panned; ja·pan·ning** (1688) **1 :** to cover with or as if with a coat of japan **2 :** to give a high gloss to — **ja·pan·ner** n

Jap·a·nese \ˌja-pə-'nēz, -'nēs\ n, pl **Japanese** (1604) **1 a :** a native or inhabitant of Japan **b :** a person of Japanese descent **2 :** the language of the Japanese — **Japanese** adj

Japanese an·drom·e·da \-ˌan-'drä-mə-də\ n [NL Andromeda, genus of plants, fr. L Andromeda, Ethiopian princess, fr. Gk Andromedē] (1948) **:** a shrubby evergreen Asian heath (Pieris japonica) with glossy leaves and drooping clusters of usu. whitish flowers

Japanese beetle n (1900) **:** a small metallic green and brown scarab beetle (Popillia japonica) that has been introduced into America from Japan and as a grub feeds on the roots of grasses and decaying vegetation and as an adult eats foliage and fruits

Japanese cedar n (ca. 1880) **:** a large evergreen tree (Cryptomeria japonica) grown esp. in China and Japan for its valuable soft wood

Japanese iris n (1883) **:** any of various beardless garden irises (esp. Iris kaempferi) with very large showy flowers

Japanese lacquer n (1876) : LACQUER 1b

Japanese maple n (1898) **:** a maple (Acer palmatum) of Japan, China, and Korea with purple flowers and usu. deeply parted leaves that is widely cultivated as a shrub or small tree

Japanese millet n (1900) **:** a coarse annual grass (Echinochloa frumentacea) cultivated esp. in Asia for its edible seeds

Japanese plum n (1893) **:** a tree (Prunus salicina) native to China and cultivated in Japan that bears Japanese plums; also : the large usu. yellow to light red fruit of a Japanese plum

Japanese quail n (1963) **:** a quail (Coturnix japonica syn. C. coturnix japonica) from China and Japan that is often used in laboratory research

Japanese quince n (1900) **:** a hardy Chinese ornamental shrub (Chaenomeles speciosa syn. C. lagenaria) of the rose family with scarlet, pink, or white flowers

Japanese spurge n (1924) **:** a low Japanese herb or subshrub (Pachysandra terminalis) of the box family often used as a ground cover

Jap·a·nize \'ja-pə-ˌnīz\ vt **-nized; -niz·ing** (1890) **1 :** to make Japanese **2 :** to bring (as an area or industry) under the influence of Japan — **Jap·a·ni·za·tion** \ˌja-pə-nə-'zā-shən\ n

Japan wax n (1859) **:** a yellowish fat obtained from the berries of several sumacs (as Rhus verniciflua and R. succedanea) and used chiefly in polishes

¹jape \'jāp\ vb **japed; jap·ing** [ME] vi (14c) **:** to say or do something jokingly or mockingly ~ vt **:** to make mocking fun of — **jap·er** \'jā-pər\ n — **jap·ery** \'jā-p(ə-)rē\ n

²jape n (14c) **:** something designed to arouse amusement or laughter: as **a :** an amusing literary or dramatic production **b :** GIBE

Ja·pheth \'jā-fəth\ n [L Japheth or Gk Iapheth, fr. Heb Yepheth] : a son of Noah held to be the progenitor of the Medes and Greeks

ja·po·nais·e·rie \ˌzhä-pō-ne-zə-'rē, -nez-'rē\ n, often cap [F, fr. japonais Japanese] (1896) **:** a style in art reflecting Japanese qualities or motifs; also : an object or decoration in this style

ja·pon·i·ca \jə-'pä-ni-kə\ n [NL, fr. fem. of Japonicus Japanese, fr. Japonia Japan] (1819) : JAPANESE QUINCE

¹jar \'jär\ vb **jarred; jar·ring** [prob. fr. imit. origin] vi (1526) **1 a** : to make a harsh or discordant sound **b :** to have a harshly disagreeable or disconcerting effect **c :** to be out of harmony; specif : BICKER **2 :** to undergo severe vibration ~ vt **:** to cause to jar: as **a :** to affect disagreeably : UNSETTLE **b :** to make unstable : SHAKE — **jar·ring·ly** \'jär-iŋ-lē\ adv

²jar n (1537) **1 a :** a state or manifestation of discord or conflict **b** : a harsh grating sound **2 a :** a sudden or unexpected shake **b :** an unsettling shock **c :** an unpleasant break or conflict in rhythm, flow, or transition

³jar n [MF jarre, fr. OProv jarra, fr. Ar jarrah earthen water vessel] (1592) **1 :** a widemouthed container made typically of earthenware or glass **2 :** as much as a jar will hold — **jar·ful** \-ˌful\ n

⁴jar *n* [alter. of earlier *char* turn, fr. ME — more at CHARE] (1674) *archaic* : the position of being ajar — usu. used in the phrase *on the jar*
jar·di·niere *or* **jar·di·nière** \,jär-d°n-'ir, ,zhär-d°n-'yer, -'er\ *n* [F *jardinière*, lit., female gardener] (1841) **1 a** : an ornamental stand for plants or flowers **b** : a large usu. ceramic flowerpot holder **2** : a garnish for meat consisting of several cooked vegetables cut into pieces
¹jar·gon \'jär-gən, -,gän\ *n* [ME, fr. MF] (14c) **1 a** : confused unintelligible language **b** : a strange, outlandish, or barbarous language or dialect **c** : a hybrid language or dialect simplified in vocabulary and grammar and used for communication between peoples of different speech **2** : the technical terminology or characteristic idiom of a special activity or group **3** : obscure and often pretentious language marked by circumlocutions and long words — **jar·gon·ish** \-gə-nish\ *adj* — **jar·gon·is·tic** \,jär-gə-'nis-tik\ *adj*
²jargon *vi* (14c) **1** : TWITTER, WARBLE **2** : JARGONIZE
jar·gon·ize \'jär-gə-,nīz\ *vb* **-ized; -iz·ing** *vi* (1803) : to speak or write jargon ~ *vt* **1** : to express in jargon **2** : to make into jargon
jar·goon \jär-'gün\ *or* **jar·gon** \-'gän\ *n* [F *jargon* — more at ZIRCON] (1769) : a colorless, pale yellow, or smoky zircon
jar·head \'jär-,hed\ *n* (ca. 1960) *slang* : MARINE 2
jarl \'yär(-ə)l\ *n* [ON — more at EARL] (1820) : a Scandinavian noble ranking immediately below the king
jar·rah \'jar-ə\ *n* [Nyungar (Australian aboriginal language of southwest Western Australia) *jarily*] (ca. 1866) : a eucalyptus (*Eucalyptus marginata*) of western Australia with rough bark and alternate leaves; *also* : its wood
jas·mine \'jaz-mən\ *n* [F *jasmin*, fr. Ar *yāsamīn*, fr. Per] (1562) **1 a** : any of numerous often climbing shrubs (genus *Jasminum*) of the olive family that usu. have extremely fragrant flowers; *esp* : a tall-climbing semievergreen Asian shrub (*J. officinale*) with fragrant white flowers from which oil is extracted for use in perfumes **b** : any of numerous plants having sweet-scented flowers; *esp* : YELLOW JESSAMINE **2** : a light yellow
Ja·son \'jā-s°n\ *n* [L *Iason*, fr. Gk *Iasōn*] : a legendary Greek hero distinguished for his successful quest of the Golden Fleece
jas·per \'jas-pər\ *n* [ME *jaspre*, fr. MF, fr. L *jaspis*, fr. Gk *iaspis*, of Sem origin; akin to Heb *yāshĕpheh* jasper] (14c) **1** : an opaque cryptocrystalline quartz of any of several colors; *esp* : green chalcedony **2** : colored stoneware with raised white decoration **3** : a blackish green — **jas·pery** \-pə-rē\ *adj*
jas·per·ware \'jas-pər-,war, -wer\ *n* (1863) : JASPER 2
jas·sid \'ja-səd\ *n* [ultim. fr. Gk *Iasos*, town in Asia Minor] (1892) : any of numerous small leafhoppers that include many economically significant pests of cultivated plants; *broadly* : LEAFHOPPER
Jat \'jät\ *n* [Hindi *Jāṭ*] (1622) : a member of an Indo-Aryan people of the Punjab and Uttar Pradesh
jaunce \'jȯn(t)s, 'jän(t)s\ *vi* [origin unknown] (1593) *archaic* : PRANCE
jaun·dice \'jȯn-dəs, 'jän-\ *n* [ME *jaundis*, fr. MF *jaunisse*, fr. *jaune* yellow, fr. L *galbinus* greenish yellow] (14c) **1** : yellowish pigmentation of the skin, tissues, and body fluids caused by the deposition of bile pigments **2** : a disease or abnormal condition characterized by jaundice **3** : a state or attitude characterized by satiety, distaste, or hostility
jaun·diced \-dəst\ *adj* (1640) **1** : affected with or as if with jaundice **2** : exhibiting or influenced by envy, distaste, or hostility ⟨a ~ eye⟩
¹jaunt \'jȯnt, 'jänt\ *vi* [origin unknown] (1575) **1** *archaic* : to trudge about **2** : to make a usu. short journey for pleasure
²jaunt *n* (1592) **1** *archaic* : a tiring trip **2** : an excursion undertaken esp. for pleasure
jaunting car *n* (1801) : a light 2-wheeled open horse-drawn vehicle used esp. in Ireland with lengthwise seats placed face-to-face or back to back
jaun·ty \'jȯn-tē, 'jän-\ *adj* **jaun·ti·er; -est** [modif. of F *gentil*] (1662) **1** *archaic* **a** : GENTEEL **b** : STYLISH **2** : sprightly in manner or appearance : LIVELY — **jaun·ti·ly** \'jȯn-t°l-ē, 'jän-\ *adv* — **jaun·ti·ness** \'jȯn-tē-nəs, 'jän-\ *n*
ja·va \'jä-və, 'jä-, -vē\ *n, often cap* [*Java*, island of Indonesia] (1850) : COFFEE
Ja·va man \'jä-və-, 'ja-\ *n* (1911) : a Pleistocene hominid known from fragmentary skeletons found in Trinil and Djetis, Java and now classified with the pithecanthropines
Ja·va·nese \,ja-və-'nēz, ,jä-, -'nēs\ *n, pl* **Javanese** [*Java* + *-nese* (as in *Japanese*)] (1704) **1** : a member of an Indonesian people inhabiting the island of Java **2** : an Austronesian language of the Javanese people — **Javanese** *adj*
jav·e·lin \'jav-lən, 'ja-və-\ *n* [ME *chafeveleyn*, fr. MF *javeline*, alter. of *javelot*, of Celt origin; akin to OIr *gabul* forked stick] (15c) **1** : a light spear thrown as a weapon of war or in hunting **2** : a slender usu. metal shaft at least 260 centimeters long that is thrown for distance in a field event
ja·ve·li·na \,hä-və-'lē-nə\ *n* [AmerSp *jabalina*, fr. Sp, fem. of *jabalí* wild boar, fr. Ar *jabalī*] (1822) : PECCARY
Ja·velle water \zha-'vel, zhə-\ *n* [*Javel*, former village in France] (1890) : an aqueous solution of sodium hypochlorite used as a disinfectant or a bleaching agent
¹jaw \'jȯ\ *n* [ME] (14c) **1 a** : either of two complex cartilaginous or bony structures in most vertebrates that border the mouth, support the soft parts enclosing it, usu. bear teeth on their oral margin, and are an upper that is more or less firmly fused with the skull and a lower that is hinged, movable, and articulated with the temporal bone of either side **b** : the parts constituting the walls of the mouth and serving to open and close it — usu. used in pl. **c** : any of various organs of invertebrates that perform the function of the vertebrate jaws **2** : something resembling the jaw of an animal: as **a** : one of the sides of a narrow pass or channel **b** : either of two or more opposable parts that open and close for holding or crushing something between them **3 a** : a space lying between or as if between open jaws ⟨escaped out of the ~s of the whale⟩ **b** : a position or situation in which one is threatened ⟨rode into the ~s of danger⟩ **4** : a friendly chat

²jaw *vi* (1748) : to talk esp. abusively, indignantly, or long-windedly ~ *vt* : to talk to in a scolding or boring manner
jaw·bone \'jȯ-,bōn\ *n* (15c) : JAW 1a; *esp* : MANDIBLE
jaw·bon·ing \-,bō-niŋ\ *n* (1969) : the use of public appeals (as by a president) to influence the actions esp. of business and labor leaders; *broadly* : the use of spoken persuasion — **jaw·bone** \-,bōn\ *vt*
jaw·break·er \-,brā-kər\ *n* (1839) **1** : a word difficult to pronounce **2** : a round hard candy
jawed \'jȯd\ *adj* (ca. 1529) : having jaws ⟨~ fishes⟩ — usu. used in combination ⟨square-*jawed*⟩ ⟨a 3-*jawed* chuck⟩
jaw·less fish \'jȯ-ləs-\ *n* (ca. 1941) : any of the taxonomic group (Agnatha) of primitive vertebrates without jaws including cyclostomes and extinct related forms — compare BONY FISH, CARTILAGINOUS FISH
jaw·line \'jȯ-,līn\ *n* (1924) : the outline of the lower jaw
¹jay \'jā\ *n* [ME, fr. MF *jai*, fr. LL *gaius*] (14c) **1 a** : a predominantly fawn-colored Old World bird (*Garrulus glandarius*) of the crow family with a black-and-white crest and wings marked with black, white, and blue **b** : any of various usu. crested and largely blue chiefly New World birds that are related to the common Old World jay and have roving habits and harsh voices **2 a** : an impertinent chatterer **b** : DANDY 1 **c** : GREENHORN **3** : a moderate blue
²jay *n* (ca. 1889) **1** : the letter *j* **2** : JOINT 4
jay·bird \'jā-,bərd\ *n* (1661) : ¹JAY 1, 2
Jay·cee \jā-'sē\ *n* [fr. the initials of Junior Citizens, former name of the organization] (1938) : a member of a major national and international civic organization
jay·gee \jā-'jē\ *n* [junior grade] (1943) : LIEUTENANT JUNIOR GRADE
jay·hawk·er \'jā-,hȯ-kər\ *n* (1858) **1 a** *often cap* : a member of a band of antislavery guerrillas in Kansas and Missouri before and during the Civil War **b** : BANDIT **2** *cap* : a native or resident of Kansas — used as a nickname
jay·vee \jā-'vē\ *n* [junior varsity] (1937) **1** : JUNIOR VARSITY **2** : a member of a junior varsity team
jay·walk \'jā-,wȯk\ *vi* (1919) : to cross a street carelessly or in an illegal manner so as to be endangered by traffic — **jay·walk·er** *n*
¹jazz \'jaz\ *n, often attrib* [origin unknown] (1913) **1 a** : American music developed esp. from ragtime and blues and characterized by propulsive syncopated rhythms, polyphonic ensemble playing, varying degrees of improvisation, and often deliberate distortions of pitch and timbre **b** : popular dance music influenced by jazz and played in a loud rhythmic manner **2** : empty talk : HUMBUG ⟨spouted all the scientific ~ —Pete Martin⟩ **3** : similar but unspecified things : STUFF ⟨that wind, and the waves, and all that ~ —John Updike⟩ — **jazz·like** \-,līk\ *adj*
²jazz *vt* (1917) **1 a** : ENLIVEN — usu. used with *up* **b** : ACCELERATE **2** : to play in the manner of jazz ~ *vi* **1** : to go here and there : GAD **2** : to dance to or play jazz
jazz·man \'jaz-,man, -mən\ *n* (1926) : a jazz musician
jazz-rock \-'räk\ *n* (1968) : a blend of jazz and rock music
jazzy \'ja-zē\ *adj* **jazz·i·er; -est** (1919) **1** : having the characteristics of jazz **2** : marked by unrestraint, animation, or flashiness — **jazz·i·ly** \'ja-zə-lē\ *adv* — **jazz·i·ness** \'ja-zē-nəs\ *n*
J-bar lift \'jā-,bär-\ *n* (1954) : a ski lift having a series of J-shaped bars each of which pulls one skier
jeal·ous \'je-ləs\ *adj* [ME *jelous*, fr. OF, fr. (assumed) VL *zelosus*, fr. LL *zelus* zeal — more at ZEAL] (13c) **1 a** : intolerant of rivalry or unfaithfulness **b** : disposed to suspect rivalry or unfaithfulness **2** : hostile toward a rival or one believed to enjoy an advantage **3** : vigilant in guarding a possession ⟨new colonies were ~ of their new independence —Scott Buchanan⟩ — **jeal·ous·ly** *adv* — **jeal·ous·ness** *n*
jeal·ou·sy \'je-lə-sē\ *n, pl* **-sies** (13c) **1** : a jealous disposition, attitude, or feeling **2** : zealous vigilance
jean \'jēn\ *n* [short for *jean fustian*, fr. ME *Gene* Genoa, Italy + *fustian*] (1577) **1** : a durable twilled cotton cloth used esp. for sportswear and work clothes **2** : pants that are usu. close-fitting and made esp. of jean or denim — usu. used in pl.
¹jeep \'jēp\ *n* [prob. fr. *g. p.* (abbr. of *general purpose*)] (1940) : a small general-purpose motor vehicle with 80-inch wheelbase, ¼-ton capacity, and four-wheel drive used by the U.S. army in World War II; *also* : a similar but larger and more powerful U.S. army vehicle
²jeep *vi* (1942) : to travel by jeep
Jeep *trademark* — used for a civilian automotive vehicle
jee·pers \'jē-pərz\ *also* **jee·pers cree·pers** \-'krē-pərz\ *interj* [jeepers, euphemism for *Jesus*; jeepers creepers, euphemism for *Jesus Christ*] (1927) — used as a mild oath
jeep·ney \'jēp-nē\ *n* [*jeep* + *jitney*] (ca. 1949) : a Philippine jitney bus converted from a jeep
¹jeer \'jir\ *vb* [origin unknown] *vi* (1561) : to speak or cry out with derision or mockery ~ *vt* : to deride with jeers : TAUNT **syn** see SCOFF — **jeer·er** *n* — **jeer·ing·ly** \-iŋ-lē\ *adv*
²jeer *n* (1625) : a jeering remark or sound : TAUNT
jeez \'jēz\ *interj* [euphemism for *Jesus*] (1923) — used as a mild oath or introductory expletive (as to express surprise)
je·fe \'hā-(,)fā, 'he-; 'he-fē\ *n* [Sp, fr. F *chef*, fr. MF *chief* — more at CHIEF] (1903) : CHIEF, LEADER
Jef·fer·son Da·vis's Birthday \'je-fər-sən-'dā-və-səz-\ *n* (1929) : the first Monday in June observed as a legal holiday in many Southern states
Jef·fer·son Day \'je-fər-sən-\ *n* (1936) : April 13 observed as a holiday in Alabama in commemoration of Thomas Jefferson's birthday
Jef·frey pine \'je-frē-\ *n* [John *Jeffrey* †1854 Scot. botanical explorer] (1858) : a pine (*Pinus jeffreyi*) of the western U.S. having long needles in groups of three
je·had *var of* JIHAD
Je·hosh·a·phat \ji-'hä-sə-,fat, -shə-\ *n* [Heb *Yĕhōshāphāth*] : a king of Judah who brought Judah into an alliance with the northern kingdom of Israel in the 9th century B.C.

jasmine 1a

\ə\ abut \ə\ kitten, F table \ər\ further \a\ ash \ā\ ace \ä\ mop, mar \aú\ out \ch\ chin \e\ bet \ē\ easy \g\ go \i\ hit \ī\ ice \j\ job \ŋ\ sing \ō\ go \ȯ\ law \ȯi\ boy \th\ thin \th\ the \ü\ loot \ú\ foot \y\ yet \zh\ vision \à, ḵ, ⁿ, œ, œ̄, ᵫ, ū̄, ᵫ̄\ *see* Guide to Pronunciation

Je·ho·vah \ji-'hō-və\ *n* [NL, reading (as *Yĕhōwāh*) of Heb *yhwh* Yahweh with the vowel points of '*adhōnāy* my lord] (1530) : GOD 1

Jehovah's Witness *n* (1932) : a member of a group that witness by distributing literature and by personal evangelism to beliefs in the theocratic rule of God, the sinfulness of organized religions and governments, and an imminent millennium

je·hu \'jē-(ˌ)hyü, -(ˌ)hü\ *n* [Heb *Yēhū*] **1** *cap* : a king of Israel in the 9th century B.C. who according to the account in II Kings had Jezebel killed in accordance with Elijah's prophecy **2** : a driver of a coach or cab

je·ju·nal \ji-'jü-n²l\ *adj* (ca. 1887) : of or relating to the jejunum

je·june \ji-'jün\ *adj* [L *jejunus* empty of food, hungry, meager] (1646) **1** : lacking nutritive value 〈~ diets〉 **2** : devoid of significance or interest : DULL 〈~ lectures〉 **3** : JUVENILE, PUERILE 〈~ reflections on life and art〉 *syn* see INSIPID — **je·june·ly** *adv* — **je·june·ness** \-'jün-nəs\ *n*

je·ju·num \ji-'jü-nəm\ *n* [ME, fr. ML, fr. neut. of L *jejunus*] (14c) : the section of the small intestine that comprises the first two fifths beyond the duodenum and that is larger, thicker-walled, and more vascular and has more circular folds than the ileum

Je·kyll and Hyde \'je-kə-lən-'hīd *also* 'jē- *or* 'jā-\ [Dr. Jekyll & Mr. Hyde, representing the two-sided personality of the protagonist in *The Strange Case of Dr. Jekyll and Mr. Hyde* (1886) by R. L. Stevenson] (ca. 1922) : one having a two-sided personality one side of which is good and the other evil

jell \'jel\ *vb* [back-formation fr. *jelly*] *vi* (1869) **1** : to come to the consistency of jelly : CONGEAL, SET **2** : to take shape and achieve distinctness : become cohesive 〈~ *vt* : to cause to jell

jellied gasoline *n* (1944) : NAPALM

Jell-O \'je-(ˌ)lō\ *trademark* — used for a gelatin dessert usu. with the flavor and color of fruit

¹jel·ly \'je-lē\ *n, pl* **jellies** [ME *gelly*, fr. MF *gelee*, fr. fem. of *gelé*, pp. of *geler* to freeze, congeal, fr. L *gelare* — more at COLD] (14c) **1** : a soft somewhat elastic food product made usu. with gelatin or pectin; *esp* : a fruit product made by boiling sugar and the juice of fruit **2** : a substance resembling jelly in consistency **3** : a state of fear or irresolution **4** : a shapeless structureless mass : PULP — **jel·ly·like** \-ˌlīk\ *adj*

²jelly *vb* **jel·lied; jel·ly·ing** *vi* (1590) **1** : JELL **2** : to make jelly 〈~ *vt* : to bring to the consistency of jelly

jelly bean *n* (1905) : a sugar-glazed bean-shaped candy

jel·ly·fish \'je-lē-ˌfish\ *n* (1841) **1 a** : a free-swimming marine coelenterate that is the sexually reproducing form of a hydrozoan or scyphozoan and has a nearly transparent saucer-shaped body and extensile marginal tentacles studded with stinging cells **b** : SIPHONOPHORE **c** : CTENOPHORE **2** : a person lacking backbone or firmness

jelly roll *n* (1895) : a thin sheet of sponge cake spread with jelly and rolled up

jel·u·tong \'je-lə-ˌtȯŋ\ *n* [Malay *jĕlutong*] (ca. 1836) **1** : any of several trees (genus *Dyera*) of the dogbane family **2** : the resinous rubbery latex of a jelutong (esp. *Dyera costulata*) used esp. as a chicle substitute

jem·my \'je-mē\ *n, pl* **jemmies** [fr. the name *Jemmy*] (ca. 1811) *Brit* : JIMMY

je ne sais quoi \zhə-nə-ˌsā-'kwä\ *n* [F, lit., I know not what] (ca. 1656) : something that cannot be adequately described or expressed

jen·net \'he-nə, 'je-nət\ *n* [ME *genett*, fr. MF *genet*, fr. Catal, Zenete (member of a Berber people), horse] (15c) **1** : a small Spanish horse **2 a** : a female donkey **b** : HINNY

jen·ny \'je-nē\ *n, pl* **jennies** [fr. the name *Jenny*] (1600) **1 a** : a female donkey 〈~ wren〉 **b** : a female donkey **2** : SPINNING JENNY

je·on \(ˌ)jä-'ȯn\ *n, pl* **jeon** [Korean *chŏn*] (ca. 1969) : the chon of South Korea

jeop·ard \'je-pərd\ *vt* [ME, back-formation fr. *jeopardie*] (14c) : JEOPARDIZE

jeop·ar·dise *Brit var of* JEOPARDIZE

jeop·ar·dize \'je-pər-ˌdīz\ *vt* **-dized; -diz·ing** (1582) : to expose to danger or risk : IMPERIL

jeop·ar·dy \'je-pər-dē\ *n* [ME *jeopardie*, fr. AF *juparti*, fr. OF *jeu parti* alternative, lit., divided game] (14c) **1** : exposure to or imminence of death, loss, or injury : DANGER **2** : the danger that an accused person is subjected to when on trial for a criminal offense

je·quir·i·ty bean \jə-'kwir-ə-tē-\ *n* [F *jékwirity*] (ca. 1889) **1** : the poisonous scarlet and black seed of the rosary pea often used for beads **2** : ROSARY PEA 1

jer·boa \jər-'bō-ə, jer-\ *n* [NL, fr. Ar *yarbū*'] (1662) : any of several social nocturnal Old World jumping rodents (family Dipodidae) with long hind legs and long tail

jer·e·mi·ad \ˌjer-ə-'mī-əd, -ˌad\ *n* [F *jérémiade*, fr. *Jérémie* Jeremiah, fr. LL *Jeremias*] (1780) : a prolonged lamentation or complaint; *also* : a cautionary or angry harangue

Jer·e·mi·ah \-'mī-ə\ *n* [LL *Jeremias*, fr. Gk *Hieremias*, fr. Heb *Yirmĕyāh*] **1** : a major Hebrew prophet of the 6th and 7th centuries B.C. **2** : one who is pessimistic about the present and foresees a calamitous future **3** : a prophetic book of canonical Jewish and Christian Scripture — see BIBLE table

Jer·e·mi·as \-'mī-əs\ *n* [LL] : JEREMIAH

¹jerk \'jərk\ *n* [prob. alter. of *yerk*] (1575) **1** : a single quick motion of short duration **2 a** : jolting, bouncing, or thrusting motions **b** : a tendency to produce spasmodic motions **3 a** : an involuntary spasmodic muscular movement due to reflex action **b** *pl* : involuntary twitchings due to nervous excitement **4** : an annoyingly stupid or foolish person **5** : the pushing of a weight from shoulder height to a position overhead in weight lifting

²jerk *vt* (1589) **1** : to give a quick suddenly arrested push, pull, or twist to **2** : to propel or move with or as if with a quick suddenly arrested motion **3** : to mix and serve (as sodas) behind a soda fountain 〈~ *vi* **1** : to make a sudden spasmodic motion **2** : to move in short abrupt motions or with frequent jolts — **jerk·er** *n*

³jerk *vt* [back-formation fr. ¹*jerky*] (1707) : to preserve (meat) in long sun-dried slices

jerk around *vt* (1941) : to treat badly esp. by being underhanded or inconsistent

jer·kin \'jər-kən\ *n* [origin unknown] (1519) : a close-fitting hip-length usu. sleeveless jacket

jerk off *vb* (ca. 1904) : MASTURBATE — usu. considered vulgar

jerk·wa·ter \'jərk-ˌwȯ-tər, -ˌwä-\ *adj* [fr. *jerkwater* rural train] (1888) **1** : remote and unimportant 〈~ towns〉 **2** : TRIVIAL

¹jer·ky \'jər-kē\ *n* [Sp *charqui*, fr. Quechua *ch'arki*] (1850) : jerked meat

²jerky \'jər-kē\ *adj* **jerk·i·er; -est** (1858) **1 a** : moving along with or marked by fits and starts **b** : characterized by abrupt transitions **2** : INANE, FOOLISH — **jerk·i·ly** \-kə-lē\ *adv* — **jerk·i·ness** \-kē-nəs\ *n*

jer·o·bo·am \ˌjer-ə-'bō-əm\ *n* [*Jeroboam* I †*ab* 912 B.C. king of the northern kingdom of Israel] (1816) : an oversize wine bottle holding about three liters

jer·ri·can *or* **jerry can** \'jer-ē-ˌkan\ *n* [*Jerry* + *can*; fr. its German design] (1943) : a narrow flat-sided liquid container holding five gallons (about 19 liters)

Jer·ry \'jer-ē\ *n, pl* **Jerries** [by shortening & alter.] (1898) *chiefly Brit* : GERMAN

jer·ry–build \'jer-ē-ˌbild\ *vt* **-built** \-ˌbilt\; **-build·ing** [back-formation fr. *jerry-built*] (1885) : to build cheaply and flimsily — **jer·ry–build·er** *n*

jer·ry–built *adj* [origin unknown] (1869) **1** : built cheaply and unsubstantially **2** : carelessly or hastily put together

jer·sey \'jər-zē\ *n, pl* **jerseys** [*Jersey*, one of the Channel Islands] (1587) **1** : a plain weft-knitted fabric made of wool, cotton, nylon, rayon, or silk and used esp. for clothing **2** : any of various close-fitting usu. circular-knitted garments esp. for the upper body **3** *often cap* : any of a breed of small short-horned predominantly yellowish brown or fawn dairy cattle noted for their rich milk

Jersey pine *n* (1743) : VIRGINIA PINE

Je·ru·sa·lem artichoke \jə-ˌrü-s(ə-)ləm-, -ˌrüz-ləm-, -'rü-zə-\ *n* [*Jerusalem* by folk etymology fr. It *girasole* girasole] (1641) : a perennial American sunflower (*Helianthus tuberosus*) widely cultivated for its tubers that are used as a vegetable and as a livestock feed

Jerusalem cherry *n* [*Jerusalem*, Palestine] (1580) : either of two plants (*Solanum pseudocapsicum* and *S. capsicastrum*) of the nightshade family cultivated as ornamental houseplants for their orange to red berries

Jerusalem cricket *n* (1947) : a large-headed burrowing nocturnal orthopteran insect (*Stenopelmatus fuscus*) of the southwestern U.S.

Jerusalem thorn *n* (1866) : a tropical American leguminous spiny shrub or shrubby tree (*Parkinsonia aculeata*) with pinnate leaves and showy racemose yellow flowers that is widely cultivated

Jerusalem cricket

jess \'jes\ *n* [ME *ges*, fr. MF *gies*, fr. pl. of *jet* throw, fr. *jeter* to throw — more at JET] (14c) : a short strap secured on the leg of a hawk and usu. provided with a ring for attaching a leash — **jessed** \'jest\ *adj*

jes·sa·mine \'jes-mən, 'jes-ə-\ *var of* JASMINE

Jes·se \'je-sē\ *n* [Heb *Yishay*] : the father of David, king of Israel, according to the account in I Samuel

jest \'jest\ *n* [ME *geste* idle tale, story in verse, fr. OF, fr. L *gesta* deeds, fr. neut. pl. of *gestus*, pp. of *gerere* to bear, wage] (ca. 1548) **1** : an utterance (as a jeer or quip) intended to be taken as mockery or humor **2 a** : PRANK **b** : a ludicrous circumstance or incident **3 a** : a frivolous mood or manner (spoken in ~) **b** : gaiety and merriment **4** : LAUGHINGSTOCK *syn* see FUN — **jest** *vb*

jest·er \'jes-tər\ *n* (14c) **1** : FOOL 2a **2** : one given to jests

Je·su·it \'je-zü-ət, -zhü- *also* -zyü-\ *n* [NL *Jesuita*, fr. LL *Jesus*] (1559) **1** : a member of the Roman Catholic Society of Jesus founded by St. Ignatius Loyola in 1534 and devoted to missionary and educational work **2** : one given to intrigue or equivocation — **je·su·it·ic** \ˌje-zü-'(w)i-tik, -zhü-, -zyü-\ *or* **je·su·it·i·cal** \-ti-kəl\ *adj, often cap* — **je·su·it·i·cal·ly** \-ti-k(ə-)lē\ *adv, often cap* — **je·su·it·ism** \'je-zü-ə-ˌti-zəm, -zhü-, -zyü-\ *or* **je·su·it·ry** \-ə-trē\ *n, often cap*

Je·sus \'jē-zəs, -zəz *also* -ˌzəs and -ˌzəz\ *n* [LL, fr. Gk *Iēsous*, fr. Heb *Yēshūa*'] **1** : the Jewish religious teacher whose life, death, and resurrection as reported by the Evangelists are the basis of the Christian message of salvation — called also *Jesus Christ* **2** *Christian Science* : the highest human corporeal concept of the divine idea rebuking and destroying error and bringing to light man's immortality

¹jet \'jet\ *n* [ME, fr. MF *jaiet*, fr. L *gagates*, fr. Gk *Gagas*, *Gagas*, town and river in Asia Minor] (14c) **1** : a compact velvet-black coal that takes a good polish and is often used for jewelry **2** : an intense black

²jet *adj* (1716) : of the color jet

³jet *vb* **jet·ted; jet·ting** [F *jeter*, lit., to throw, fr. MF, fr. L *jactare* to throw, freq. of *jacere* to throw; akin to Gk *hienai* to send] *vi* (1692) : to spout forth : GUSH 〈~ *vt* : to emit in a stream : SPOUT

⁴jet *n* (ca. 1696) **1 a** (1) : a usu. forceful stream of fluid (as water or gas) discharged from a narrow opening or a nozzle (2) : a narrow stream of material (as plasma) emanating or appearing to emanate from a celestial object (as a radio galaxy) **b** : a nozzle for a jet of fluid **2** : something issuing as if in a jet 〈talk poured from her in a brilliant ~ —*Time*〉 **3 a** : JET ENGINE **b** : an airplane powered by one or more jet engines **4** : a long narrow current of high-speed winds (as a jet stream) — **jet·like** \-ˌlīk\ *adj*

⁵jet *vi* **jet·ted; jet·ting** (1949) **1** : to travel by jet airplane **2** : to move or progress by or as if by jet propulsion

jet–bead \'jet-ˌbēd\ *n* (ca. 1930) : a shrub (*Rhodotypos scandens*) that has black shining fruit and is used as an ornamental

jet–black \-'blak\ *adj* (15c) : black as jet

je·té \zhə-'tā\ *n* [F, fr. pp. of *jeter*] (1830) : a springing jump in ballet made from one foot to the other in any direction

jet engine *n* (1943) : an engine that produces motion as a result of the rearward discharge of a jet of fluid; *specif* : an airplane engine that uses atmospheric oxygen to burn fuel and produces a rearward discharge of heated air and exhaust gases — see AIRPLANE illustration

jet lag *n* (1969) : a condition that is characterized by various psychological and physiological effects (as fatigue and irritability), occurs following long flight through several time zones, and prob. results from disruption of circadian rhythms in the human body — **jet–lagged** \'jet-ˌlagd\ *adj*

jet·lin·er \'jet-ˌlī-nər\ *n* (1949) : a jet-propelled airliner

jet·port \'jet-ˌpȯrt, -ˌpȯrt\ *n* (1961) : an airport designed to handle jet airplanes

jet–pro·pelled \'jet-prə-'peld\ *adj* (1877) **1** : moving by jet propulsion **2** : suggestive of the speed and force of a jet airplane

jet propulsion *n* (1867) : propulsion of a body produced by the forwardly directed forces of the reaction resulting from the rearward discharge of a jet of fluid; *esp* : propulsion of an airplane by jet engines

jet·sam \'jet-səm\ *n* [alter. of *jettison*] (1570) **1** : the part of a ship, its equipment, or its cargo that is cast overboard to lighten the load in time of distress and that sinks or is washed ashore **2** : FLOTSAM 2

jet set *n* (1951) : an international social group of wealthy individuals who frequent fashionable resorts — **jet–set·ter** \-ˌse-tər\ *n* — **jet–set·ting** \-ˌse-tiŋ\ *adj*

jet stream *n* (1947) : a long narrow meandering current of high-speed winds near the tropopause blowing from a generally westerly direction and often exceeding a speed of 250 miles (402 kilometers) per hour

¹**jet·ti·son** \'je-tə-sən, -zən\ *n* [ME *jetteson*, fr. AF *getteson*, fr. OF *getaison* action of throwing, fr. L *jactation-, jactatio*, fr. *jactare* — more at JET] (15c) : a voluntary sacrifice of cargo to lighten a ship's load in time of distress

²**jettison** *vt* (1848) **1** : to make jettison of **2** : to get rid of as superfluous or encumbering : DISCARD **3** : to drop from an airplane or spacecraft in flight — **jet·ti·son·able** \-sə-nə-bəl, -zə-\ *adj*

¹**jet·ty** \'je-tē\ *n, pl* **jetties** [ME *jette*, fr. MF *jetee*, fr. fem. of *jeté*, pp. of *jeter* to throw — more at JET] (15c) **1 a** : a structure extended into a sea, lake, or river to influence the current or tide or to protect a harbor **b** : a protecting frame of a pier **2** : a landing wharf

²**jetty** *vi* **jet·tied; jet·ty·ing** (1598) : PROJECT, JUT

³**jetty** *adj* (1586) : black as jet

jeu d'es·prit \zhœ-des-prē\ *n, pl* **jeux d'esprit** \same\ [F, lit., play of the mind] (1712) : a witty comment or composition

jeu·nesse do·rée \zhœ-nes-dȯ-rā\ *n* [F, gilded youth] (1836) : young people of wealth and fashion

Jew \'jü\ *n* [ME, fr. OF *gyu*, fr. L *Judaeus*, fr. Gk *Ioudaios*, fr. Heb *Yĕhūdhī*, fr. *Yĕhūdhāh* Judah, Jewish kingdom] (13c) **1 a** : a member of the tribe of Judah **b** : ISRAELITE **2** : a member of a nation existing in Palestine from the 6th century B.C. to the 1st century A.D. **3** : a person belonging to a continuation through descent or conversion of the ancient Jewish people **4** : one whose religion is Judaism

¹**jew·el** \'jü-əl, 'jül *also* 'jü(ə)l\ *n, often attrib* [ME *juel*, fr. OF, prob. dim. of *jeu* game, play, fr. L *jocus* game, joke — more at JOKE] (13c) **1** : an ornament of precious metal often set with stones or decorated with enamel and worn as an accessory of dress **2** : one that is highly esteemed **3** : a precious stone : GEM **4** : a bearing for a pivot (as in a watch) made of crystal, glass, or a gem — **jew·el·like** \-ˌlīk\ *adj*

²**jewel** *vt* **-eled** *or* **-elled; -el·ing** *or* **-el·ling** (1601) **1** : to adorn or equip with jewels **2** : to give beauty to as if with jewels : EMBELLISH

jewel box *n* (1831) **1** : a small box or case designed to hold jewelry **2** : something small and exquisite **3** : a clear plastic case for a compact disc

jew·el·er *or* **jew·el·ler** \'jü-ə-lər, 'jü-lər *also* 'jü(-ə)-lər\ *n* (14c) **1** : one who makes or repairs jewelry **2** : one who deals in jewelry, precious stones, watches, and usu. silverware and china

jew·el·lery *chiefly Brit var of* JEWELRY

jew·el·ry \'jü-əl-rē, 'jül-rē, 'jü(-ə)l-\ *n* (14c) : JEWELS; *esp* : objects of precious metal often set with gems and worn for personal adornment

jew·el·weed \-ˌwēd\ *n* (1818) : TOUCH-ME-NOT

Jew·ess \'jü-əs\ *n* (14c) : a Jewish girl or woman — sometimes taken to be offensive

jew·fish \'jü-ˌfish\ *n* (1679) : any of various large groupers (esp. *Epinephelus itajara*) that are usu. dusky green, brown, or blackish, thickheaded, and rough-scaled

Jew·ish \'jü-ish\ *adj* (ca. 1546) : of, relating to, or characteristic of the Jews; *also* : being a Jew — **Jew·ish·ly** *adv* — **Jew·ish·ness** *n*

Jewish American Princess *n* (1979) : a stereotypical well-to-do or spoiled American Jewish girl or woman — called also *Jewish Princess*; often used disparagingly

Jewish calendar *n* (ca. 1888) : a calendar in use among Jewish peoples that is reckoned from the year 3761 B.C. and dates in its present form from about A.D. 360 — see MONTH table

JEWISH YEARS 5754–5773

JEWISH YEAR		A.D.	JEWISH YEAR		A.D.
5754	begins	Sept. 16, 1993	5764	begins	Sept. 27, 2003
5755	begins	Sept. 6, 1994	5765	begins	Sept. 16, 2004
5756	begins	Sept. 25, 1995	5766	begins	Oct. 4, 2005
5757	begins	Sept. 14, 1996	5767	begins	Sept. 23, 2006
5758	begins	Oct. 2, 1997	5768	begins	Sept. 13, 2007
5759	begins	Sept. 21, 1998	5769	begins	Sept. 30, 2008
5760	begins	Sept. 11, 1999	5770	begins	Sept. 19, 2009
5761	begins	Sept. 30, 2000	5771	begins	Sept. 9, 2010
5762	begins	Sept. 18, 2001	5772	begins	Sept. 29, 2011
5763	begins	Sept. 7, 2002	5773	begins	Sept. 17, 2012

Jew·ry \'jü(-ə)r-ē, 'jü-rē\ *n* (14c) **1** *pl* **Jewries** : a community of Jews **2** : the Jewish people

Jew's harp *or* **Jews' harp** \'jüz-ˌhärp, 'jüs-\ *n* (1595) : a small lyre-shaped instrument that when held between the teeth gives tones from a metal tongue struck by the finger

Jez·e·bel \'je-zə-ˌbel\ *n* [Heb *Izebhel*] **1** : the Phoenician wife of Ahab who according to the account in I and II Kings pressed the cult of Baal on the Israelite kingdom but was finally killed in accordance with Elijah's prophecy **2** *often not cap* : an impudent, shameless, or morally unrestrained woman

JHVH *var of* YHWH

jiao \jē-'au̇\ *n* [Chin (Beijing) *jiǎo*] (1949) : a monetary unit of the People's Republic of China equal to ¹/₁₀ yuan

¹**jib** \'jib\ *n* [origin unknown] (1661) : a triangular sail set on a stay extending usu. from the head of the foremast to the bowsprit or the jibboom; *also* : the small triangular headsail on a sloop — see SAIL illustration

Jew's harp

²**jib** *n* [prob. by shortening & alter. fr. *gibbet*] (1764) **1** : the projecting arm of a crane **2** : a derrick boom

³**jib** *vi* **jibbed; jib·bing** [prob. fr. *jib* to shift from one side of a ship to the other, perh. fr. ¹*jib*] (1811) : to refuse to proceed further : BALK — **jib·ber** *n*

jib–boom \'ji(b)-'büm\ *n* [¹*jib* + *boom*] (1748) : a spar that forms an extension of the bowsprit

¹**jibe** \'jīb\ *var of* GIBE

²**jibe** *vb* **jibed; jib·ing** [perh. modif. of D *gijben*] *vi* (1693) **1** : to shift suddenly and forcibly from one side to the other — used of a fore-and-aft sail **2** : to change a vessel's course when sailing with the wind so that as the stern passes through the eye of the wind the boom swings to the opposite side ~ *vt* : to cause to jibe

³**jibe** *vi* **jibed; jib·ing** [origin unknown] (1813) : to be in accord : AGREE

ji·ca·ma \'hē-kə-mə\ *n* [MexSp *jícama*, fr. Nahuatl *xīcamatl*] (ca. 1909) : an edible starchy tuberous root of a leguminous tropical American vine (*Pachyrhizus erosus*)

Ji·ca·ri·lla \ˌhē-kə-'rē-yə\ *n, pl* **Jicarilla** *or* **Jicarillas** [AmerSp *apaches de la xicarilla*, lit., gourd-cup Apaches, fr. *Cerro de la Xicarilla*, lit., gourd-cup peak, unidentified mountain in Jicarilla territory] (1850) **1** : a member of an Apache people orig. of southeastern Colorado, northern New Mexico, and adjacent areas and now living chiefly in northern New Mexico **2** : the language of the Jicarilla people

jiff \'jif\ *n* (1797) : JIFFY

jif·fy \'ji-fē\ *n, pl* **jiffies** [origin unknown] (1779) : MOMENT, INSTANT ⟨ready in a ~⟩

¹**jig** \'jig\ *n* [perh. fr. MF *giguer* to frolic, fr. *gigue* fiddle, of Gmc origin; akin to OHG *giga* fiddle; akin to ON *geiga* to turn aside] (ca. 1560) **1 a** : any of several lively springy dances in triple rhythm **b** : music to which a jig may be danced **2** : TRICK, GAME — used chiefly in the phrase *the jig is up* **3 a** : any of several fishing devices that are jerked up and down or drawn through the water **b** : a device used to maintain mechanically the correct positional relationship between a piece of work and the tool or between parts of work during assembly **c** : a device in which crushed ore is concentrated or coal is cleaned by agitating in water — **in jig time** : in a short time : QUICKLY

²**jig** *vb* **jigged; jig·ging** *vi* (1604) **1 a** : to move with rapid jerky motions **b** : to dance a jig **2** : to fish with a jig ~ *vt* **1** : to dance in the rapid lively manner of a jig **2 a** : to give a rapid jerky motion to **b** : to separate (a mineral or ore from waste) with a jig **3** : to catch (a fish) with a jig **4** : to machine by means of a jig-controlled tool operation

³**jig** *n* [short for *jigaboo* black person] (1927) : BLACK 4 — usu. taken to be offensive

¹**jig·ger** \'ji-gər\ *n* (1675) **1** : one that jigs or operates a jig **2** : any of several sails **3** : JIG 3a **4 a** (1) : a mechanical device usu. with a jerky reciprocating motion (2) : a mold or a machine incorporating a revolving mold on which ceramic items (as plates) are formed **b** : GADGET, DOODAD **5** : a measure used in mixing drinks that usu. holds 1 to 2 ounces (30 to 60 milliliters)

²**jigger** *n* [perh. fr. Wolof *jiga* insect] (1781) : CHIGGER

³**jigger** *vb* [freq. of ²*jig*] *vi* (1867) : to jerk up and down ~ *vt* : to alter or rearrange esp. by manipulating ⟨~ an election district⟩

jig·gery–pok·ery \ˌji-gər-ē-'pō-kər-ē\ *n* [prob. alter. of Sc *joukery-pawkery*, fr. *jouk* to dodge, cheat + *pawk* trick, wile] (ca. 1892) : underhanded manipulation or dealings : TRICKERY

jig·gle \'ji-gəl\ *vb* **jig·gled; jig·gling** \-g(ə-)liŋ\ [freq. of ²*jig*] *vt* (1836) : to cause to move with quick little jerks or oscillating motions ~ *vi* : to move from or as if from being jiggled — **jiggle** *n* — **jig·gly** \-g(ə-)lē\ *adj*

¹**jig·saw** \'jig-ˌsȯ\ *n* (1873) **1** : a machine saw with a narrow vertically reciprocating blade for cutting curved and irregular lines or ornamental patterns in openwork **2** : SCROLL SAW 1 **3** : JIGSAW PUZZLE

²**jigsaw** *vt* (1873) **1** : to cut or form by or as if by a jigsaw **2** : to arrange or place in an intricate or interlocking way

³**jigsaw** *adj* (1884) : suggesting a jigsaw puzzle or its separate pieces

jigsaw puzzle *n* (1919) : a puzzle consisting of small irregularly cut pieces that are to be fitted together to form a picture; *also* : something suggesting a jigsaw puzzle

ji·had \ji-'häd, *chiefly Brit* -'had\ *n* [Ar *jihād*] (1869) **1** : a holy war waged on behalf of Islam as a religious duty **2** : a crusade for a principle or belief

jil·lion \'jil-yən\ *n* [*j* + *-illion* (as in *million*)] (ca. 1942) : an indeterminately large number — **jillion** *adj*

¹**jilt** \'jilt\ *vt* (1673) : to drop (a lover) capriciously or unfeelingly — **jilt·er** *n*

²**jilt** *n* [alter. of *jillet* flirtatious girl] (ca. 1674) : one who jilts a lover

jim crow \'jim-'krō\ *n, often cap J&C* [*Jim Crow*, stereotype black man in a 19th cent. song-and-dance act] (1838) **1** : BLACK 4 — usu. taken to be offensive **2** : ethnic discrimination esp. against blacks by legal enforcement or traditional sanctions — **jim crow** *adj, often cap J&C* — **jim crow·ism** \-ˌji-zəm\ *n, often cap J&C*

jim–dan·dy \'jim-'dan-dē\ *n* [fr. the name *Jim*] (1887) : something excellent of its kind

jim-jams \'jim-ˌjamz\ *n pl* [perh. alter. of *delirium tremens*] (1852) : JITTERS

jim·mies \'ji-mēz\ *n pl* [origin unknown] (ca. 1947) : tiny rod-shaped bits of usu. chocolate-flavored candy often sprinkled on ice cream

\ə\ abut \ᵊ\ kitten, F table \ər\ further \a\ ash \ā\ ace \ä\ mop, mar
\au̇\ out \ch\ chin \e\ bet \ē\ easy \g\ go \i\ hit \ī\ ice \j\ job
\ŋ\ sing \ō\ go \ȯ\ law \ȯi\ boy \th\ thin \t̷h\ the \ü\ loot \u̇\ foot
\y\ yet \zh\ vision \ä, k̲, ⁿ, œ, œ̄, ᵫ, ᵫ̄, ᵧ\ *see* Guide to Pronunciation

¹**jim·my** \'ji-mē\ *n, pl* **jimmies** [fr. the name *Jimmy*] (1848) : a short crowbar

²**jimmy** *vt* **jim·mied; jim·my·ing** (1893) : to force open with or as if with a jimmy ⟨the burglar *jimmied* a window⟩

jim·son·weed \'jim(p)-sən-ˌwēd\ *n, often cap* [*Jamestown*, Va.] (1832) : a poisonous tall coarse annual weed (*Datura stramonium*) of the nightshade family with rank-smelling foliage and large white or violet trumpet-shaped flowers succeeded by globose prickly fruits

¹**jin·gle** \'jiŋ-gəl\ *vb* **jin·gled; jin·gling** \-g(ə-)liŋ\ [ME *ginglen*, of imit. origin] *vi* (14c) **1** : to make a light clinking or tinkling sound **2** : to rhyme or sound in a catchy repetitious manner ~ *vt* : to cause to jingle — **jin·gler** \-g(ə-)lər\ *n*

²**jingle** *n* (1599) **1 a** : a light clinking or tinkling sound **b** : a catchy repetition of sounds in a poem **2** : something that jingles **b** : a short verse or song marked by catchy repetition — **jin·gly** \-g(ə-)lē\ *adj*

¹**jin·go** \'jiŋ-(ˌ)gō\ *interj* [prob. euphemism for *Jesus*] (1694) — used as a mild oath usu. in the phrase *by jingo*

²**jingo** *n, pl* **jingoes** [fr. the fact that the phrase *by jingo* appeared in the refrain of a chauvinistic song] (1878) : one characterized by jingoism — **jin·go·ish** \-ish\ *adj*

jin·go·ism \'jiŋ-(ˌ)gō-ˌi-zəm\ *n* (1878) : extreme chauvinism or nationalism marked esp. by a belligerent foreign policy — **jin·go·ist** \-ist\ *n or adj* — **jin·go·is·tic** \ˌjiŋ-gō-'is-tik\ *adj* — **jin·go·is·ti·cal·ly** \-ti-k(ə-)lē\ *adv*

¹**jink** \'jiŋk\ *vi* [origin unknown] (1785) : to move quickly or unexpectedly with sudden turns and shifts (as in dodging)

²**jink** *n* (1786) **1** : a quick evasive turn : SLIP **2** *pl* : PRANKS, FROLICS; *esp* : HIGH JINKS

jin·ni \'jē-nē, 'ji-, jə-'nē\ *or* \'jin\ *n, pl* **jinn** *or* **jinns** [Ar *jinnīy* demon] (1684) **1** : one of a class of spirits that according to Muslim demonology inhabit the earth, assume various forms, and exercise supernatural power **2** : GENIE 2

jin·rick·sha *or* **jin·rik·i·sha** \jin-'rik-ˌshò\ *n* [Jp] (1874) : RICKSHA

¹**jinx** \'jiŋ(k)s\ *n* [perh. alter. of *jynx* wryneck; fr. the use of wrynecks in witchcraft] (1911) : one that brings bad luck; *also* : the state or spell of bad luck brought on by a jinx

²**jinx** *vt* (1917) : to foredoom to failure or misfortune : bring bad luck to

ji·pi·ja·pa \ˌhē-pē-'hä-pə\ *n* [Sp, fr. *Jipijapa*, Ecuador] (1858) **1** : a Central and So. American plant (*Carludovica palmata* of the family Cyclanthaceae) resembling a palm **2** : PANAMA

jit·ney \'jit-nē\ *n, pl* **jitneys** [origin unknown] (1903) **1** *slang* : NICKEL 2a(1) **2** [fr. the original 5 cent fare]: BUS 1a; *esp* : a small bus that carries passengers over a regular route on a flexible schedule

¹**jit·ter** \'ji-tər\ *n* [origin unknown] (1929) **1** *pl* : a sense of panic or extreme nervousness ⟨had a bad case of the ~s before his performance⟩ **2** : the state of mind or the movement of one that jitters **3** : irregular random movement (as of a pointer or an image on a television screen); *also* : vibratory motion

²**jitter** *vi* (1931) **1** : to be nervous or act in a nervous way **2** : to make continuous fast repetitive movements

¹**jit·ter·bug** \'ji-tər-ˌbəg\ *n* (1938) **1** : a jazz variation of the two-step in which couples swing, balance, and twirl in standardized patterns and often with vigorous acrobatics **2** : one who dances the jitterbug

²**jitterbug** *vi* (1939) **1** : to dance the jitterbug **2** : to move around or back and forth with quick often jerky movements esp. to confuse or disconcert an opponent in sports

jit·tery \'ji-tə-rē\ *adj* (1931) **1** : suffering from the jitters **2** : marked by jittering movements — **jit·ter·i·ness** \-nəs\ *n*

jiu·jit·su, jiu·jut·su *var of* JUJITSU

¹**jive** \'jīv\ *n* [origin unknown] (1928) **1** : swing music or the dancing performed to it **2 a** : glib, deceptive, or foolish talk **b** : the jargon of hipsters **c** : a special jargon of difficult or slang terms — **jivey** \'jī-vē\ *adj*

²**jive** *vb* **jived; jiv·ing** *vt* (1928) **1** : TEASE 3, CAJOLE **2** : SWING 5 ~ *vi* **1** : KID 2 : to dance to or play jive

³**jive** *adj* (1953) *slang* : PHONY

jo \'jō\ *n, pl* **joes** [alter. of *joy*] (ca. 1529) *chiefly Scot* : SWEETHEART, DEAR

¹**job** \'jäb\ *n* [perh. fr. obs. E *job* lump] (ca. 1627) **1 a** : a piece of work; *esp* : a small miscellaneous piece of work undertaken on order at a stated rate **b** : the object or material on which work is being done **c** : something produced by or as if by work ⟨do a better ~ next time⟩ **d** : an example of a usu. specified type : ITEM ⟨this ~ is round-necked and sleeveless —Lois Long⟩ **2 a** : something done for private advantage ⟨suspected the whole incident was a put-up ~⟩ **b** : a criminal enterprise; *specif* : ROBBERY **c** : a damaging or destructive bit of work ⟨did a ~ on him⟩ **3 a** (1) : something that has to be done : TASK (2) : an undertaking requiring unusual exertion ⟨it was a real ~ to talk over that noise⟩ **b** : a specific duty, role, or function **c** : a regular remunerative position **d** *chiefly Brit* : state of affairs — used with *bad* or *good* ⟨it was a good ~ you didn't hit the old man —E. L. Thomas⟩ *syn* see TASK — **on the job** : at work

²**job** *vb* **jobbed; job·bing** *vi* (1694) **1** : to do odd or occasional pieces of work for hire **2** : to carry on public business for private gain **3** : to carry on the business of a middleman or wholesaler ~ *vt* **1** : to buy and sell (as stock) for profit : SPECULATE **2** : to hire or let by the job or for a period of service **3** : to get, deal with, or effect by jobbery **4** : to do or cause to be done by separate portions or lots : SUBCONTRACT **5** : to penalize or deprive unfairly

³**job** *adj* (1710) **1** *Brit* : that is for hire for a given service or period **2** : used in, engaged in, or done as job work ⟨a ~ shop⟩ **3** : of or relating to a job or to employment ⟨a guarantee of ~ security⟩

Job \'jōb\ *n* [L, fr. Gk *Iōb*, fr. Heb *Iyyōbh*] **1** : the hero of the book of Job who endures afflictions with fortitude and faith **2** : a narrative and poetic book of canonical Jewish and Christian Scripture — see BIBLE table

job action *n* (ca. 1968) : a temporary action (as a slowdown) by workers as a protest and means of forcing compliance with demands

job·ber \'jä-bər\ *n* (1670) : one that jobs: as **a** (1) : WHOLESALER; *specif* : a wholesaler who operates on a small scale or who sells only to retailers and institutions (2) : STOCKJOBBER **b** : a person who works by the job

job·bery \'jä-b(ə-)rē\ *n* (1832) : the act or practice of jobbing; *esp* : corruption in public office

job·hold·er \'jäb-ˌhōl-dər\ *n* (1904) : a person having a regular job

job–hop·ping \-ˌhä-piŋ\ *n* (ca. 1952) : the practice of moving from job to job — **job–hop·per** \-ˌhä-pər\ *n*

job·less \'jäb-ləs\ *adj* (1919) **1** : having no job **2** : of or relating to those having no job — **job·less·ness** *n*

job lot *n* (1851) **1** : a miscellaneous collection of goods for sale as a lot usu. to a retailer **2** : a miscellaneous and usu. inferior collection or group

Job's comforter \'jōbz-\ *n* [fr. the tone of the speeches made to Job by his friends] (1738) : a person who discourages or depresses while seemingly giving comfort and consolation

Job's tears *n pl* (1597) **1** : hard pearly white seeds often used as beads **2** *sing in constr* : an Asian grass (*Coix lacryma-jobi*) whose seeds are Job's tears

Jo·cas·ta \jō-'kas-tə\ *n* [L, fr. Gk *Iokastē*] : a queen of Thebes who marries Oedipus not knowing that he is her son

Job's tears 2

¹**jock** \'jäk\ *n* (1826) **1** : JOCKEY **2** : DISC JOCKEY

²**jock** *n* [*jockstrap*] (1922) **1** : ATHLETIC SUPPORTER **2** : ATHLETE; *esp* : a college athlete

¹**jock·ey** \'jä-kē\ *n, pl* **jockeys** [*Jockey*, Sc nickname for *John*] (1670) **1** : a person who rides or drives a horse esp. as a professional in a race **2** : a person who operates or works with a specified vehicle, device, or object : OPERATOR ⟨an accountant, a pencil ~ — with almost no association with the out-of-doors —James Selder⟩

²**jockey** *vb* **jock·eyed; jock·ey·ing** *vt* (1708) **1** : to deal shrewdly or fraudulently with **2 a** : to ride or drive (a horse) as a jockey **b** : DRIVE, OPERATE **3 a** : to maneuver or manipulate by adroit or devious means ⟨was ~ed out of the job⟩ **b** : to change the position of by a series of movements ⟨~ a truck into position⟩ ~ *vi* **1** : to act as a jockey **2** : to maneuver for advantage — often used in the phrase *jockey for position*

jockey club *n* (1775) : an association for the promotion and regulation of horse racing

jock itch *n* [²*jock*] (1950) : ringworm of the crotch : TINEA CRURIS

jock·strap \'jäk-ˌstrap\ *n* [E slang *jock* penis + E *strap*] (1886) : ATHLETIC SUPPORTER

jo·cose \jō-'kōs, jə-\ *adj* [L *jocosus*, fr. *jocus* joke] (1673) **1** : given to joking : MERRY **2** : characterized by joking : HUMOROUS *syn* see WITTY — **jo·cose·ly** *adv* — **jo·cose·ness** *n* — **jo·cos·i·ty** \jō-'kä-sə-tē, jə-\ *n*

joc·u·lar \'jä-kyə-lər\ *adj* [L *jocularis*, fr. *joculus*, dim. of *jocus*] (1626) **1** : given to jesting : habitually jolly or jocund **2** : characterized by jesting : PLAYFUL — **joc·u·lar·i·ty** \ˌjä-kyə-'lar-ə-tē\ *n* — **joc·u·lar·ly** \'jä-kyə-lər-lē\ *adv*

jo·cund \'jä-kənd *also* 'jō-(ˌ)kənd\ *adj* [ME, fr. LL *jocundus*, alter. of L *jucundus*, fr. *juvare* to help] (14c) : marked by or suggestive of high spirits and lively mirthfulness ⟨a poet could not but be gay, in such a ~ company —William Wordsworth⟩ *syn* see MERRY — **jo·cun·di·ty** \jō-'kən-də-tē, jä-\ *n* — **jo·cund·ly** \'jä-kənd-lē, 'jō-(ˌ)\ *adv*

jodh·pur \'jäd-(ˌ)pər\ *n* [*Jodhpur*, India] (1899) **1** *pl* : riding breeches cut full through the hips and close-fitting from knee to ankle **2** : an ankle-high boot fastened with a strap that is buckled at the side — called also *jodhpur boot*

joe \'jō\ *n, often cap* [fr. *Joe*, nickname for *Joseph*] (1846) : FELLOW, GUY ⟨an average ~⟩

Jo·el \'jō(-ə)l\ *n* [L, fr. Gk *Iōēl*, fr. Heb *Yō'ēl*] **1** : the traditionally assumed author of the book of Joel **2** : a narrative and apocalyptic book of canonical Jewish and Christian Scripture — see BIBLE table

joe–pye weed \'jō-ˌpī-\ *n* [origin unknown] (ca. 1818) : any of several tall American perennial composite herbs (esp. *Eupatorium maculatum* and *E. purpureum*) with whorled leaves and corymbose heads of typically purple tubular flowers

jo·ey \'jō-ē\ *n* [origin unknown] (1839) *Austral* : a baby animal; *esp* : a baby kangaroo

¹**jog** \'jäg, 'jȯg\ *vb* **jogged; jog·ging** [prob. alter. of *shog*] *vt* (1548) **1** : to give a slight shake or push to : NUDGE **2** : to rouse to alertness ⟨*jogged* his memory⟩ **3** : to cause (as a horse) to go at a jog **4** : to align the edges of (piled sheets of paper) by hitting or shaking against a flat surface ~ *vi* **1** : to move up and down or about with a short heavy motion ⟨his . . . holster *jogging* against his hip —Thomas Williams⟩ **2** : to run or ride at a slow trot **b** : to go at a slow, leisurely, or monotonous pace : TRUDGE

²**jog** *n* (1635) **1** : a slight shake : PUSH **2** : a movement, pace, or instance of jogging (as for exercise) : a horse's slow measured trot

³**jog** *n* [prob. alter. of ²*jag*] (1715) **1 a** : a projecting or retreating part (as of a line or surface) **b** : the space in the angle of a jog **2** : a brief abrupt change in direction

⁴**jog** *vi* **jogged; jog·ging** (1953) : to make a jog ⟨the road ~s to the right⟩

jog·ger \'jä-gər, 'jȯ-\ *n* (ca. 1700) **1** : one that jogs **2** : a device for jogging piled sheets of paper

¹**jog·gle** \'jä-gəl\ *vb* **jog·gled; jog·gling** \-g(ə-)liŋ\ [freq. of ¹*jog*] (1513) : to shake slightly ~ *vi* : to move shakily or jerkily — **jog·gler** \-g(ə-)lər\ *n*

²**joggle** *n* (ca. 1727) : ²JOG 2a

³**joggle** *n* [dim. of ³*jog*] (1793) **1** : a notch or tooth in a joining surface (as of a piece of building material) to prevent slipping **2** : a dowel for joining two adjacent blocks of masonry

⁴**joggle** *vt* **jog·gled; jog·gling** \'jä-g(ə-)liŋ\ (1820) : to join by means of a joggle so as to prevent sliding apart

jog trot *n* (1796) **1** : ²JOG 2b **2** : a routine habit or course of action

Jo·han·nine \jō-'ha-ˌnīn, -nən\ *adj* [LL *Johannes* John] (1861) : of, relating to, or characteristic of the apostle John or the New Testament books ascribed to him

Jo·han·nis·berg Riesling \yō-'hä-nəs-ˌberg-\ *n* [*Johannisberg*, village in Germany] (1976) : a Riesling produced in the U.S. (as in California)

john \'jän\ *n* [fr. the name *John*] (1856)   **1** : TOILET   **2** : a prostitute's client

John \'jän\ *n* [LL *Johannes*, fr. Gk *Iōannēs*, fr. Heb *Yōhānān*]   **1** : a Jewish prophet who according to Gospel accounts foretold Jesus's messianic ministry and baptized him — called also *John the Baptist*   **2** : an apostle who according to various Christian traditions wrote the fourth Gospel, the three Johannine Epistles, and the Book of Revelation   **3** : the fourth Gospel in the New Testament — see BIBLE table   **4** : any of three short didactic letters addressed to early Christians and included in the New Testament — see BIBLE table

John Barleycorn *n* (ca. 1620) : alcoholic liquor personified

john·boat \'jän-ˌbōt\ *n* [fr. the name *John*] (1905) : a narrow flat-bottomed square-ended boat usu. propelled by a pole or paddle and used on inland waterways

John Bull \-'bu̇l\ *n* [*John Bull*, character typifying the English nation in *The History of John Bull* (1712) by John Arbuthnot] (1778)   **1** : the English nation personified : the English people   **2** : a typical Englishman — **John Bull·ish** \-'bu̇-lish\ *adj* — **John Bull·ish·ness** *n* — **John Bull·ism** \-ˌli-zəm\ *n*

John Doe \-'dō\ *n* (1768)   **1** : a party to legal proceedings whose true name is unknown   **2** : an average man

John Do·ry \-'dōr-ē, -'dȯr-\ *n, pl* **John Dories** [earlier *dory*, fr. ME *dorre*, fr. MF *doree*, lit., gilded one] (1754) : a common yellow to olive food fish (*Zeus faber*) of Europe and Africa with an oval compressed body, long dorsal spines, and a dark spot on each side; *also* : a closely related and possibly identical fish (*Z. capensis*) widely distributed in southern seas

Joh·ne's disease \'yō-nəz-\ *n* [Heinrich A. *Johne* †1910 Ger. bacteriologist] (1907) : a chronic often fatal contagious enteritis of ruminants and esp. of cattle that is caused by a bacterium (*Mycobacterium paratuberculosis*) and is characterized by persistent diarrhea and gradual emaciation

John Han·cock \'jän-'han-ˌkäk\ *n* [*John Hancock*; fr. the prominence of his signature on the Declaration of Independence] (1903) : an autograph signature

John Hen·ry \-'hen-rē\ *n* [fr. the name *John Henry*, fr. confusion with *John Hancock*] (1914) : an autograph signature

John Mark *n* : MARK 1a

john·ny \'jä-nē\ *n, pl* **johnnies** [fr. the name *Johnny*] (1673)   **1** *often cap* : FELLOW, GUY   **2** : a short-sleeved collarless gown that is open in the back and is worn by persons (as hospital patients) undergoing medical examination or treatment

john·ny·cake \'jä-nē-ˌkāk\ *n* [prob. fr. the name *Johnny*] (1739) : a bread made with cornmeal

John·ny–come–late·ly \'jä-nē-(ˌ)kəm-'lāt-lē\ *n, pl* **Johnny–come–latelies** *or* **Johnnies–come–lately** (1839)   **1** : a late or recent arrival : NEWCOMER   **2** : UPSTART ⟨established families tend to hold themselves above the *Johnny-come-latelies* —William Zeckendorf †1976⟩

John·ny–jump–up \'jä-nē-ˌjəmp-ˌəp\ *n* (1842)   **1** : a common and long-cultivated European viola (*Viola tricolor*) which has short-spurred flowers usu. blue or purple mixed with white and yellow and from which most of the garden pansies are derived; *broadly* : any of various small-flowered cultivated pansies   **2** : any of various American violets

John·ny–on–the–spot \'jä-nē-ˌȯn-thə-'spät, -ˌän-\ *n* (1896) : a person who is on hand and ready to perform a service or respond to an emergency

Johnny Reb \-'reb\ *n* [fr. the name *Johnny* + *reb* rebel] (1865) : a Confederate soldier

John·son·ese \ˌjän(t)-sə-'nēz, -'nēs\ *n* [Samuel *Johnson*] (1843) : a literary style characterized by balanced phraseology and Latinate diction

john·son·grass \'jän(t)-sən-ˌgras\ *n, often cap* [William *Johnston* †1859 Am. agriculturist] (1884) : a tall perennial sorghum (*Sorghum halepense*) orig. of the Mediterranean region that is widely used for forage in warm areas and often becomes naturalized

joie de vi·vre \ˌzhwä-də-'vēvrᵊ\ *n* [F, lit., joy of living] (1889) : keen or buoyant enjoyment of life

¹join \'join\ *vb* [ME, fr. OF *joindre*, fr. L *jungere* — more at YOKE] *vt* (13c)   **1 a** : to put or bring together so as to form a unit ⟨~ two blocks of wood with glue⟩   **b** : to connect (as points) by a line   **c** : ADJOIN   **2** : to put or bring into close association or relationship ⟨~ed in marriage⟩   **3** : to engage in (battle)   **4 a** : to come into the company of ⟨~ed us for lunch⟩   **b** : to associate oneself with ⟨~ed the church⟩ ~ *vi*   **1 a** : to come together so as to be connected ⟨nouns ~ to form compounds⟩   **b** : ADJOIN ⟨the two estates ~⟩   **2** : to come into close association or relationship: as   **a** : to form an alliance   **b** : to become a member of a group   **c** : to take part in a collective activity ⟨~ in singing⟩ — **join·able** \'joi-nə-bəl\ *adj*

syn JOIN, COMBINE, UNITE, CONNECT, LINK, ASSOCIATE, RELATE mean to bring or come together into some manner of union. JOIN implies a bringing into contact or conjunction of any degree of closeness ⟨*joined* forces in an effort to win⟩. COMBINE implies some merging or mingling with corresponding loss of identity of each unit ⟨*combined* jazz and rock to create a new music⟩. UNITE implies somewhat greater loss of separate identity ⟨the colonies *united* to form a republic⟩. CONNECT suggests a loose or external attachment with little or no loss of identity ⟨a mutual defense treaty *connected* the two nations⟩. LINK may imply strong connection or inseparability of elements still retaining identity ⟨a name forever *linked* with liberty⟩. ASSOCIATE stresses the mere fact of frequent occurrence or existence together in space or in logical relation ⟨opera is popularly *associated* with high society⟩. RELATE suggests the existence of a real or presumed logical connection ⟨*related* what he observed to what he already knew⟩.

²join *n* (1825)   **1** : JOINT   **2** : UNION 2d

join·der \'join-dər\ *n* [F *joindre* to join, fr. OF] (1601)   **1** : CONJUNCTION 1   **2 a** (1) : a joining of parties as plaintiffs or defendants in a suit   (2) : a joining of causes of action or defense   **b** : acceptance of an issue tendered

join·er \'joi-nər\ *n* (14c) : one that joins: as   **a** : a person whose occupation is to construct articles by joining pieces of wood   **b** : a gregarious or civic-minded person who joins many organizations

join·ery \'joi-nə-rē, 'join-rē\ *n* (1678)   **1** : the art or trade of a joiner   **2** : work done by a joiner

join·ing \'joi-niŋ\ *n* (14c)   **1** : the act or an instance of joining one thing to another : JUNCTURE   **2 a** : the place or manner of being joined together   **b** : something that joins two things together

¹joint \'joint\ *n* [ME *jointe*, fr. OF, fr. *joindre*] (13c)   **1 a** (1) : the point of contact between elements of an animal skeleton with the parts that surround and support it   (2) : NODE 5b   **b** : a part or space included between two articulations, knots, or nodes   **c** : a large piece of meat for roasting   **2 a** : a place where two things or parts are joined   **b** : a space between the adjacent surfaces of two bodies joined and held together (as by cement or mortar)   **c** : a fracture or crack in rock not accompanied by dislocation   **d** : the flexing part of a cover along either backbone edge of a book   **e** : the junction of two or more members of a framed structure   **f** : a union formed by two abutting rails in a track including the elements (as bars and bolts) necessary to hold the abutting rails together   **g** : an area at which two ends, surfaces, or edges are attached   **3 a** : a shabby or disreputable place of entertainment   **b** : PLACE, ESTABLISHMENT ⟨a ~ slang⟩ : PRISON 2   **4** : a marijuana cigarette — **joint·ed** \'join-təd\ *adj* — **joint·ed·ly** *adv* — **joint·ed·ness** *n* — **out of joint**   **1 a** *of a bone* : having the head slipped from its socket   **b** : at variance   **2 a** : DISORDERED 2a   **b** : being out of humor : DISSATISFIED

²joint *adj* [ME, fr. MF, fr. pp. of *joindre*, fr. OF] (14c)   **1** : UNITED, COMBINED ⟨the ~ influences of culture and climate⟩   **2** : common to two or more: as   **a** (1) : involving the united activity of two or more ⟨a ~ effort⟩   (2) : constituting an activity, operation, or organization in which elements of more than one armed service participate ⟨~ maneuvers⟩   (3) : constituting an action or expression of two or more governments ⟨~ peace talks⟩   **b** : shared by or affecting two or more ⟨a ~ fine⟩   **3** : united, joined, or sharing with another (as in a right or status) ⟨~ heirs⟩   **4** : being a function of or involving two or more variables and esp. random variables — **joint·ly** *adv*

³joint *vb* [¹*joint*] *vt* (1530)   **1** : to separate the joints of (as meat)   **2 a** : to unite by a joint : fit together   **b** : to provide with a joint : ARTICULATE   **c** : to prepare (as a board) for joining by planing the edge ~ *vi*   **1** : to fit as if by joints ⟨the stones ~ neatly⟩   **2** : to form joints as a stage in growth — used esp. of small grains

Joint Chiefs of Staff (1946) : a military advisory group composed of the chiefs of staff of the army and air force, the chief of naval operations, and sometimes the commandant of the marine corps

joint·er \'join-tər\ *n* (1678) : one that joints; *esp* : any of various tools used in making joints

joint grass *n* (1835) : a coarse creeping grass (*Paspalum distichum*) with jointed stems that is used for fodder and for erosion control

joint resolution *n* (1838) : a resolution passed by both houses of a legislative body that has the force of law when signed by or passed over the veto of the executive

join·tress \'join-trəs\ *n* (1602) : a woman having a legal jointure

joint–stock company *n* (1776) : a company or association consisting of individuals organized to conduct a business for gain and having a joint stock of capital represented by shares owned without the consent of the members and transferable without the consent of the group

join·ture \'join-chər\ *n* (14c)   **1 a** : an act of joining : the state of being joined   **b** : JOINT   **2 a** : an estate settled on a wife to be taken by her in lieu of dower   **b** : a settlement on the wife of a freehold estate for her lifetime

joint·worm \'join-ˌwərm\ *n* (1851) : the larva of any of several small chalcid wasps (genus *Harmolita*) that attacks the stems of grain and causes swellings like galls at or just above the first joint

joist \'joist\ *n* [ME *joiste*, fr. MF *giste*, fr. (assumed) VL *jacitum*, fr. L *jacēre* to lie — more at ADJACENT] (15c) : any of the small timbers or metal beams ranged parallel from wall to wall in a structure to support a floor or ceiling

jo·jo·ba \hə-'hō-bə\ *n* [MexSp] (1923) : a shrub or small tree (*Simmondsia chinensis* syn. *S. californica*) of the box family of southwestern No. America with edible seeds that yield a valuable liquid wax

¹joke \'jōk\ *n* [L *jocus*; perh. akin to OHG *gehan* to say, Skt *yācati* he asks] (1670)   **1 a** : something said or done to provoke laughter; *esp* : a brief oral narrative with a climactic humorous twist   **b** (1) : the humorous or ridiculous element in something   (2) : an instance of jesting : KIDDING ⟨can't take a ~⟩   **c** : PRACTICAL JOKE   **d** : LAUGHINGSTOCK   **2** : something not to be taken seriously : a trifling matter ⟨consider his skiing a ~ —Harold Callender⟩ — often used in negative construction ⟨it is no ~ to be lost in the desert⟩

²joke *vb* **joked; jok·ing** *vi* (1670) : to make jokes : JEST ~ *vt* : to make the object of a joke : KID — **jok·ing·ly** \'jō-kiŋ-lē\ *adv*

jok·er \'jō-kər\ *n* (1729)   **1 a** : a person given to joking : WAG   **b** : FELLOW, GUY; *esp* : an insignificant, obnoxious, or incompetent person ⟨a shame to let a ~ like this win —Harold Robbins⟩   **2** : a playing card added to a pack as a wild card or as the highest-ranking card   **3 a** (1) : an ambiguous or apparently immaterial clause inserted in a legislative bill to make it inoperative or uncertain in some respect   (2) : an unsuspected, misleading, or misunderstood clause, phrase, or word in a document that nullifies or greatly alters it   **b** : something (as an expedient or stratagem) held in reserve to gain an end or escape from a predicament   **c** : an unsuspected or not readily apparent fact, factor, or condition that thwarts or nullifies a seeming advantage

jok·ey *also* **joky** \'jō-kē\ *adj* **jok·i·er; -est** (ca. 1825)   **1** : given to joking   **2** : HUMOROUS, COMICAL   **3** : amusingly ridiculous : LAUGHABLE — **jok·i·ly** \-kə-lē\ *adv* — **jok·i·ness** \-kē-nəs\ *n*

jol·li·fi·ca·tion \ˌjä-li-fə-'kā-shən\ *n* (1809) : FESTIVITY, MERRYMAKING

jol·li·ty \'jä-lə-tē\ *n, pl* **-ties** (14c)   **1** : the quality or state of being jolly : MERRIMENT   **2** *Brit* : a festive gathering

¹jol·ly \'jä-lē\ *adj* **jol·li·er; -est** [ME *joli*, fr. OF] (14c)   **1 a** (1) : full of high spirits : JOYOUS   (2) : given to conviviality : JOVIAL   **b** : expressing, suggesting, or inspiring gaiety : CHEERFUL   **2** : extremely pleasant or agreeable : SPLENDID   **syn** see MERRY

\ə\ abut \ᵊ\ kitten, F table \ər\ further \a\ ash \ā\ ace \ä\ mop, mar \au̇\ out \ch\ chin \e\ bet \ē\ easy \g\ go \i\ hit \ī\ ice \j\ job \ŋ\ sing \ō\ go \ȯ\ law \ȯi\ boy \th\ thin \th̲\ the \ü\ loot \u̇\ foot \y\ yet \zh\ vision \à, k̲, ⁿ, œ, œ̄, ɯ, ᵮ, ᵊ\ see Guide to Pronunciation

²**jolly** *adv* (1549) : VERY ⟨would . . . do as they were ~ well told —John Stockbridge⟩

³**jolly** *vb* **jol·lied; jol·ly·ing** *vi* (1610) : to engage in good-natured banter ~ *vt* : to put or try to put in good humor esp. to gain an end

⁴**jolly** *n, pl* **jollies** (1905) **1** *chiefly Brit* : a good time : JOLLIFICATION **2** *pl* : KICKS ⟨get their *jollies* by reenacting famous murders —H. F. Waters⟩

jol·ly boat \'jä-lē-\ *n* [origin unknown] (ca. 1741) : a ship's boat of medium size used for general-purpose work

Jol·ly Rog·er \'jä-lē-'rä-jər\ *n* [prob. fr. ¹*jolly* + the name *Roger*] (ca. 1785) : a black flag with a white skull and crossbones formerly used by pirates as their ensign

¹**jolt** \'jōlt\ *vb* [prob. blend of obs. *joll* to strike and *jot* to bump] *vt* (1596) **1** : to cause to move with a sudden jerky motion **2** : to give a knock or blow to; *specif* : to jar with a quick or hard blow **3 a** : to disturb the composure of ⟨crudely ~*ed* out of that mood —Virginia Woolf⟩ **b** : to interfere with roughly, abruptly, and disconcertingly ⟨determination to pursue his own course was ~*ed* badly —F. L. Paxson⟩ ~ *vi* : to move with a sudden jerky motion — **jolt·er** *n*

²**jolt** *n* (1599) **1** : an abrupt sharp jerky blow or movement **2 a** (1) : a sudden feeling of shock, surprise, or disappointment (2) : an event or development causing such a feeling ⟨the defeat was quite a ~⟩ **b** : a serious check or reverse ⟨a severe financial ~⟩ **3** : a small potent or bracing portion ⟨a ~ of horseradish⟩ — **jolty** \'jōl-tē\ *adj*

jolt-wag·on \'jōlt-,wa-gən\ *n* (1886) *Midland* : a farm wagon

Jo·nah \'jō-nə, *3 is also* -nər\ *n* [Heb *Yōnāh*] **1** : an Israelite prophet who according to the account in the book of Johah resisted a divine call to repentance to the people of Nineveh, was swallowed and vomited by a great fish, and eventually carried out his mission **2** : a narrative book of canonical Jewish and Christian Scripture — see BIBLE table **3** : one believed to bring bad luck

Jo·nas \'jō-nəs\ *n* [LL, fr. Heb *Yōnāh*] : JONAH

Jon·a·than \'jä-nə-thən\ *n* [Heb *Yōnāthān*] **1** : a son of Saul and friend of David according to the account in I Samuel **2** : AMERICAN; *esp* : a New Englander **3** : any of a variety of red-skinned apple

jon·gleur \zhōⁿ-'glər\ *n* [F, fr. OF *jogleour* — more at JUGGLER] (1779) : an itinerant medieval entertainer proficient in juggling, acrobatics, music, and recitation

jon·quil \'jän-kwəl, 'jäŋ-\ *n* [F *jonquille*, fr. Sp *junquillo*, dim. of *junco* reed, fr. L *juncus*] (1629) : a Mediterranean perennial bulbous herb (*Narcissus jonquilla*) of the amaryllis family with long linear leaves that is widely cultivated for its yellow or white fragrant short-tubed clustered flowers — compare DAFFODIL

Jor·dan almond \'jòr-dⁿn-\ *n* [ME *jardin almande*, fr. MF *jardin* garden + ME *almande* almond] (1615) : a large Spanish almond esp. when salted or coated with sugar of various colors

Jor·dan curve \zhòr-'dä²-, 'jòr-dⁿn-\ *n* [Camille *Jordan* †1922 Fr. mathematician] (1900) : SIMPLE CLOSED CURVE

Jordan curve theorem *n* (1947) : a fundamental theorem of topology: every simple closed curve divides the plane into two regions for which it is the common boundary

jo·rum \'jòr-əm, 'jòr-\ *n* [perh. fr. *Joram* in the Bible who "brought with him vessels of silver" (2 Sam 8:10—AV)] (1730) : a large drinking vessel or its contents

jo·seph \'jō-zəf *also* -səf\ *n* [L, fr. Gk *Iōsēph*, fr. Heb *Yōsēph*] **1** *cap* **a** : a son of Jacob who according to the account in Genesis rose to high political office in Egypt after being sold into slavery by his brothers **b** : the husband of Mary the mother of Jesus according to the Gospel accounts **2** : a long cloak worn esp. by women in the 18th century

Jo·seph·ite \-zə-,fīt, -sə-\ *n* (1890) : a member of St. Joseph's Society of the Sacred Heart founded in 1871 in Baltimore, Md. and devoted to missionary work among black Americans

Joseph of Ar·i·ma·thea \-,ar-ə-mə-'thē-ə\ *n* : a rich councillor of the Sanhedrin who according to the Gospel accounts placed the body of Jesus in his own tomb and according to medieval legend took the Holy Grail to England

Jo·seph·son junction \'jō-zəf-sən- *also* -səf-sən-\ *n* [Brian D. *Josephson*] (1965) : an electronic fast-switching device that consists of two layers of superconducting metal separated by a thin layer of insulator through which low current flows but increased current causes the insulator to block the flow

¹**josh** \'jäsh\ *vb* [origin unknown] *vt* (1852) : to tease good-naturedly : KID ~ *vi* : to engage in banter : JOKE — **josh·er** *n*

²**josh** *n* (1878) : a good-humored joke : JEST

Josh·ua \'jä-sh(ə-)wə\ *n* [Heb *Yĕhōshūaʿ*] **1** : the divinely commissioned successor of Moses and military leader of the Israelites during the conquest of Canaan according to the account in the book of Joshua **2** : a mainly narrative book of canonical Jewish and Christian Scripture — see BIBLE table

Joshua tree *n* (1884) : a tall branched arborescent yucca (*Yucca brevifolia*) of the southwestern U.S. that has clustered greenish white flowers

Joshua tree

¹**jos·tle** \'jä-səl\ *vb* **jos·tled; jos·tling** \-s(ə-)liŋ\ [alter. of *justle*, freq. of ¹*joust*] *vi* (1546) **1 a** : to come in contact or into collision **b** : to make one's way by pushing and shoving **c** : to exist in close proximity **2** : to vie in gaining an objective : CONTEND ~ *vt* **1 a** : to come in contact or into collision with **b** : to force by pushing : ELBOW **c** : to stir up : AGITATE **d** : to exist in close proximity with **2** : to vie with in attaining an objective

²**jostle** *n* (1611) **1** : a jostling encounter or experience **2** : the state of being crowded or jostled together

Jos·ue \'jä-shü-(,)ē\ *n* [LL, fr. Heb *Yĕhōshūaʿ*] : JOSHUA

¹**jot** \'jät\ *n* [L *iota, jota* iota] (1500) : the least bit : IOTA

²**jot** *vt* **jot·ted; jot·ting** (1721) : to write briefly or hurriedly : set down in the form of a note ⟨~ this down⟩

jotting *n* (1814) : a brief note : MEMORANDUM

Jo·tun *also* **Jo·tunn** \'yōt-ⁿn, -,tún\ *n* [ON *jotunn*] : a member of a race of giants in Norse mythology

Jo·tun·heim *also* **Jo·tunn·heim** \-,hīm, -,häm\ *n* [ON *Jotunheimar*] : the home of the Jotuns in Norse mythology

jou·al \zhü-'al, -'äl, -'ál\ *n* [CanF, rendering of a nonstandard pron. of F *cheval* horse] (1962) : spoken Canadian French; *esp* : the local forms of the spoken French of Quebec that differ the most from prescribed forms

joule \'jü(ə)l *also* ÷'jaú(ə)l\ *n* [James P. *Joule*] (1882) : a unit of work or energy equal to the work done by a force of one newton acting through a distance of one meter

¹**jounce** \'jaún(t)s\ *vb* **jounced; jounc·ing** [ME] *vi* (15c) : to move in an up-and-down manner : BOUNCE ~ *vt* : to cause to jounce

²**jounce** *n* (ca. 1787) : JOLT

jouncy \'jaún(t)-sē\ *adj* **jounc·i·er; -est** (1943) : marked by a jouncing motion or effect

jour·nal \'jər-nⁿl\ *n* [ME, service book containing the day hours, fr. MF *journal*, adj., daily, fr. L *diurnalis*, fr. *diurnus* of the day, fr. *dies* day — more at DEITY] (15c) **1 a** : a record of current transactions; *esp* : a book of original entry in double-entry bookkeeping **b** : an account of day-to-day events **c** : a record of experiences, ideas, or reflections kept regularly for private use **d** : a record of transactions kept by a deliberative or legislative body **e** : LOG 3, 4 **2 a** : a daily newspaper **b** : a periodical dealing esp. with matters of current interest **3** : the part of a rotating shaft, axle, roll, or spindle that turns in a bearing

journal box *n* (ca. 1859) : a metal housing to support and protect a journal bearing

jour·nal·ese \,jər-nⁿl-'ēz, -'ēs\ *n* (1882) : a style of writing held to be characteristic of newspapers

jour·nal·ism \'jər-nⁿl-,i-zəm\ *n* (1833) **1 a** : the collection and editing of news for presentation through the media **b** : the public press **c** : an academic study concerned with the collection and editing of news or the management of a news medium **2 a** : writing designed for publication in a newspaper or magazine **b** : writing characterized by a direct presentation of facts or description of events without an attempt at interpretation **c** : writing designed to appeal to current popular taste or public interest

jour·nal·ist \-nⁿl-ist\ *n* (1693) **1 a** : a person engaged in journalism; *esp* : a writer or editor for a news medium **b** : a writer who aims at a mass audience **2** : a person who keeps a journal

jour·nal·is·tic \,jər-nⁿl-'is-tik\ *adj* (1829) : of, relating to, or characteristic of journalism or journalists — **jour·nal·is·ti·cal·ly** \-ti-k(ə-)lē\ *adv*

jour·nal·ize \'jər-nⁿl-,īz\ *vb* **-ized; -iz·ing** *vt* (1766) : to record in a journal ~ *vi* **1** : to keep a journal in accounting **2** : to keep a personal journal — **jour·nal·iz·er** *n*

¹**jour·ney** \'jər-nē\ *n, pl* **journeys** [ME, fr. OF *journee* day's journey, fr. *jour* day, fr. LL *diurnum*, fr. L, neut. of *diurnus*] (13c) **1** : travel or passage from one place to another : TRIP **2** *chiefly dial* : a day's travel **3** : something suggesting travel or passage from one place to another ⟨the ~ from youth to maturity⟩ ⟨a ~ through time⟩

²**journey** *vb* **jour·neyed; jour·ney·ing** *vi* (14c) : to go on a journey : TRAVEL ~ *vt* : to travel over or through — **jour·ney·er** *n*

jour·ney·man \-mən\ *n* [ME, fr. *journey* journey, a day's labor + *man*] (15c) **1** : a worker who has learned a trade and works for another person usu. by the day **2** : an experienced reliable worker or performer esp. as distinguished from one who is brilliant or colorful ⟨a good ~ trumpeter —*New Yorker*⟩ ⟨a ~ outfielder⟩

jour·ney·work \-,wərk\ *n* (1601) **1** : work done by a journeyman **2** : HACKWORK

¹**joust** \'jaúst *sometimes* 'jäst *or* 'jüst\ *vi* [ME, fr. MF *juster* to unite, joust, fr. (assumed) VL *juxtare*, fr. L *juxta* near; akin to L *jungere* to join — more at YOKE] (14c) **1 a** : to fight on horseback as a knight or man-at-arms **b** : to engage in combat with lances on horseback **2** : to engage in personal combat or competition — **joust·er** *n*

²**joust** *n* (14c) **1 a** : a combat on horseback between two knights with lances esp. as part of a tournament **b** *pl* : TOURNAMENT **2** : a personal combat or competition : STRUGGLE

Jove \'jōv\ *n* [L *Jov-, Juppiter*] : JUPITER — often used interjectionally to express surprise or agreement esp. in the phrase *by Jove*

jo·vial \'jō-vē-əl, -vyəl\ *adj* (1592) **1** *cap* : of or relating to Jove **2** : markedly good-humored esp. as evidenced by jollity and conviviality *syn* see MERRY — **jo·vi·al·i·ty** \,jō-vē-'a-lə-tē\ *n* — **jo·vial·ly** \'jō-vē-ə-lē, -vyə-\ *adv*

Jo·vi·an \'jō-vē-ən\ *adj* (1530) : of, relating to, or characteristic of the god or planet Jupiter

jow \'jaú\ *n* [ME *jollen* to knock] (1515) *chiefly Scot* : STROKE, TOLL

jo·war \jə-'wär\ *n* [Hindi *joār, juwār*, fr. Skt *yavākāra* barley-shaped, fr. *yava* barley + *karoti* he makes] (1800) : DURRA

¹**jowl** \'jaú(ə)l *sometimes* 'jōl\ *n* [alter. of ME *choll*] (15c) : a cut of fish consisting of the head and usu. adjacent parts

²**jowl** *n* [alter. of ME *cholle*, prob. fr. OE *ceole* throat — more at GLUTTON] (1591) : usu. slack flesh (as a dewlap, wattle, or the pendulous part of a double chin) associated with the cheeks, lower jaw, or throat

³**jowl** *n* [alter. of ME *chavel*, fr. OE *ceafl*; akin to MHG *kivel* jaw, Av *zafar-* mouth] (1598) **1 a** : JAW; *esp* : MANDIBLE **b** : one of the lateral halves of the mandible **2 a** : CHEEK 1 **b** : the cheek meat of a hog ⟨a dinner of boiled ~s⟩

jowly \'jaú-lē *sometimes* 'jō-\ *adj* **jowl·i·er; -est** (ca. 1873) : having marked jowls : having full or saggy flesh about the lower cheeks and jaw area ⟨elderly man with a disillusioned ~ face —John Dos Passos⟩

¹**joy** \'jòi\ *n* [ME, fr. OF *joie*, fr. L *gaudia*, pl. of *gaudium*, fr. *gaudēre* to rejoice; prob. akin to Gk *gēthein* to rejoice] (13c) **1 a** : the emotion evoked by well-being, success, or good fortune or by the prospect of possessing what one desires : DELIGHT **b** : the expression or exhibition of such emotion : GAIETY **2** : a state of happiness or felicity : BLISS **3** : a source or cause of delight — **joy·less** \-ləs\ *adj* — **joy·less·ly** *adv* — **joy·less·ness** *n*

²**joy** *vi* (14c) : to experience great pleasure or delight : REJOICE ~ *vt* **1** *archaic* : GLADDEN **2** *archaic* : ENJOY

joy·ance \'jòi-ən(t)s\ n (ca. 1586) archaic : DELIGHT, ENJOYMENT
joy·ful \'jòi-fəl\ adj (13c) : experiencing, causing, or showing joy : HAPPY — **joy·ful·ly** \-fə-lē\ adv — **joy·ful·ness** n
joy·ous \'jòi-əs\ adj (14c) : JOYFUL — **joy·ous·ly** adv — **joy·ous·ness** n
joy·pop \'jòi-,päp\ vi (1953) : to use habit-forming drugs occasionally or irregularly without becoming addicted — **joy·pop·per** n
joy·ride \'jòi-,rīd\ n (1909) **1** : a ride taken for pleasure (as in a car or aircraft); esp : an automobile ride marked by reckless driving (as in a stolen car) **2** : conduct or action resembling a joyride esp. in disregard of cost or consequences — **joyride** vi — **joy·rid·er** \-,rī-dər\ n — **joy·rid·ing** n
joy·stick \-,stik\ n [perh. fr. E slang joystick penis] (1910) **1** : a lever in an airplane that operates the elevators by a fore-and-aft motion and the ailerons by a side-to-side motion **2** : a control for any of various devices (as a computer display) that resembles an airplane's joystick esp. in being capable of motion in two or more directions
J/psi particle \,jā-'sī-, -'psi-\ n (1977) : an unstable neutral fundamental particle of the meson group that has about 6000 times the mass of an electron — called also J particle, psi particle
ju·ba \'jü-bə\ n [origin unknown] (1834) : a dance of Southern plantation blacks accompanied by complexly rhythmic hand clapping and slapping of the knees and thighs
Ju·bal \'jü-bəl\ n [Heb Yūbhāl] : a descendant of Cain who according to the account in Genesis is the father of those who play the harp and organ
ju·bi·lance \'jü-bə-lən(t)s\ n (1864) : JUBILATION 1
ju·bi·lant \'jü-bə-lənt\ adj (1667) : EXULTANT — **ju·bi·lant·ly** adv
ju·bi·lar·i·an \,jü-bə-'ler-ē-ən, -'lar-\ n (1782) : one celebrating a jubilee
ju·bi·late \'jü-bə-,lāt\ vi -lat·ed; -lat·ing [L jubilatus, pp. of jubilare; akin to MHG jū (exclamation of joy), Gk iygē shout] (ca. 1641) : REJOICE
Ju·bi·la·te \,yü-bə-'lä-,tā, ,jü-\ n [L, 2d pers. pl. imper. of jubilare] (1549) **1 a** : the 100th Psalm in the Authorized Version **b** not cap : a joyous song or outburst **2** : the third Sunday after Easter
ju·bi·la·tion \,jü-bə-'lā-shən\ n (14c) : an act of rejoicing : the state of being jubilant **2** : an expression of great joy
¹ju·bi·lee \'jü-bə-(,)lē, ,jü-bə-'lē\ n [ME, fr. MF & LL; MF jubilé, fr. LL jubilaeus, modif. of LGk iōbēlaios, fr. Heb yōbhēl ram's horn, jubilee] (14c) **1** often cap : a year of emancipation and restoration provided by ancient Hebrew law to be kept every 50 years by the emancipation of Hebrew slaves, restoration of alienated lands to their former owners, and omission of all cultivation of the land **2 a** : a special anniversary; esp : a 50th anniversary **b** : a celebration of such an anniversary **3 a** : a period of time proclaimed by the Roman Catholic pope ordinarily every 25 years as a time of special solemnity **b** : a special plenary indulgence granted during a year of jubilee to Roman Catholics who perform certain specified works of repentance and piety **4 a** : JUBILATION **b** : a season of celebration **5** : an Afro-American religious song usu. referring to a time of future happiness
²jubilee adj, often cap (1951) : FLAMBÉ ⟨cherries ∼⟩
Ju·dah \'jü-də\ n [Heb Yěhūdhāh] : a son of Jacob and the traditional eponymous ancestor of one of the tribes of Israel
Ju·da·ic \jü-'dā-ik\ also **Ju·da·ical** \-'dā-ə-kəl\ adj [ME Judeical, fr. L judaicus, fr. Gk ioudaikos, fr. Ioudaios Jew — more at JEW] (15c) : of, relating to, or characteristic of Jews or Judaism
Ju·da·ica \-'dā-ə-kə\ n pl [L, neut. pl. of Judaicus] (1923) : literary or historical materials relating to Jews or Judaism
Ju·da·ism \'jü-də-,i-zəm, 'jü-dē-, 'jü-(,)dā-, Brit also 'jü-,dī-zəm\ n (14c) **1** : a religion developed among the ancient Hebrews and characterized by belief in one transcendent God who has revealed himself to Abraham, Moses, and the Hebrew prophets and by a religious life in accordance with Scriptures and rabbinic traditions **2** : conformity to Jewish rites, ceremonies, and practices **3** : the cultural, social, and religious beliefs and practices of the Jews **4** : the whole body of Jews : the Jewish people
Ju·da·ist \'jü-də-ist, 'jü-dē-, jü-'dā-\ n (ca. 1846) : one that believes in or practices Judaism — **Ju·da·is·tic** \,jü-də-'is-tik, jü-dē-, jü-(,)dā-\ adj
Ju·da·ize \'jü-də-,īz, 'jü-dē-, 'jü-(,)dā-\ vb -ized; -iz·ing vi (1582) : to adopt the customs, beliefs, or character of a Jew ∼ vt : to make Jewish — **Ju·da·i·za·tion** \,jü-də-ə-'zā-shən, ,jü-dē-ə-, jü-(,)dā-ə-\ n — **Ju·da·iz·er** \'jü-də-,ī-zər, 'jü-dē-, 'jü-(,)dā-\ n
Ju·das \'jü-dəs\ n [LL, fr. Gk Ioudas, fr. Heb Yěhūdhāh] **1 a** : the apostle who in the Gospel accounts betrayed Jesus : a son of James and one of the twelve apostles **2** : TRAITOR; esp : one who betrays under the guise of friendship **3** not cap : PEEPHOLE — called also judas hole, judas window
Judas Is·car·i·ot \-is-'kar-ē-ət\ n [LL Judas Iscariotes, fr. Gk Ioudas Iskariōtēs] : JUDAS 1a
Judas tree n [fr. the belief that Judas Iscariot hanged himself from a tree of this kind] (1668) : any of a genus (Cercis) of leguminous trees and shrubs (as a redbud) often cultivated for their showy flowers; esp : a Eurasian tree (C. siliquastrum) with purplish rosy flowers
¹jud·der \'jə-dər\ vi [prob. alter. of shudder] (1931) chiefly Brit : to vibrate with intensity ⟨the engine stalled and kept ∼ing —Roy Spicer⟩
²judder n (1935) chiefly Brit : the action or sound of juddering
Jude \'jüd\ n [LL Judas] **1** : the author of the New Testament Epistle of Jude **2** : a short hortatory epistle addressed to early Christians and included as a book in the New Testament — see BIBLE table
Ju·deo-Chris·tian \jü-,dā-ō-'kris-chən, -'krish- also ,jü-dē-ō- or jü-,dē-ō-\ adj [L Judaeus Jew — more at JEW] (1899) : having historical roots in both Judaism and Christianity
Ju·deo-Span·ish \-'spa-nish\ n (1851) : the Romance language of Sephardic Jews esp. in the Balkans and Asia Minor
¹judge \'jəj\ vb **judged; judg·ing** [ME juggen, fr. OF jugier, fr. L judicare, fr. judic-, judex judge, fr. jus right, law + dicere to decide, say — more at JUST, DICTION] vt (13c) **1** : to form an opinion about through careful weighing of evidence and testing of premises **2** : to sit in judgment on : TRY **3** : to determine or pronounce after inquiry and deliberation **4** : GOVERN, RULE — used of a Hebrew tribal leader **5** : to form an estimate or evaluation of; esp : to form a negative opinion about ⟨shouldn't ∼ him because of his accent⟩ **6** : to hold as an opin-

ion : GUESS, THINK ⟨I ∼ she knew what she was doing⟩ ∼ vi **1** : to form an opinion **2** : to decide as a judge syn see INFER — **judg·er** n
²judge n [ME juge, fr. MF, fr. L judex] (14c) : one who judges: as **a** : a public official authorized to decide questions brought before a court **b** often cap : a tribal hero exercising leadership among the Hebrews after the death of Joshua **c** : one appointed to decide in a contest or competition : UMPIRE **d** : one who gives an authoritative opinion **e** : CRITIC — **judge·ship** \-,ship\ n
judge advocate n (1748) **1** : an officer assigned to the judge advocate general's corps or department **2** : a staff officer serving as legal adviser to a military commander
judge advocate general n (1862) : the senior legal officer and chief legal adviser in the army, air force, or navy
Judg·es \'jə-jəz\ n : a narrative and historical book of Jewish and Christian Scripture — see BIBLE table
judg·mat·ic \,jəj-'ma-tik\ or **judg·mat·i·cal** \-ti-kəl\ adj [prob. irreg. fr. judgment] (1826) : JUDICIOUS — **judg·mat·i·cal·ly** \-ti-k(ə-)lē\ adv
judg·ment or **judge·ment** \'jəj-mənt\ n (13c) **1 a** : a formal utterance of an authoritative opinion **b** : an opinion so pronounced **2 a** : a formal decision given by a court **b** (1) : an obligation (as a debt) created by the decree of a court (2) : a certificate evidencing such a decree **3 a** cap : the final judging of mankind by God **b** : a divine sentence or decision; specif : a calamity held to be sent by God **4 a** : the process of forming an opinion or evaluation by discerning and comparing **b** : an opinion or estimate so formed **5 a** : the capacity for judging : DISCERNMENT **b** : the exercise of this capacity **6** : a proposition stating something believed or asserted syn see SENSE
judg·men·tal \,jəj-'men-t³l\ adj (1909) **1** : of, relating to, or involving judgment **2** : characterized by a tendency to judge harshly — **judg·men·tal·ly** \-ē\ adv
judgment day n (1591) **1** cap J&D : the day of God's judgment of mankind at the end of the world according to various theologies **2** : a day of final judgment
ju·di·ca·to·ry \'jü-di-kə-,tōr-ē, -,tòr-\ n, pl -ries (ca. 1575) **1** : JUDICIARY 1a **2** : JUDICATURE 2
ju·di·ca·ture \'jü-di-kə-,chùr, -chər, -,tyùr, -,tùr\ n [MF, fr. ML judicatura, fr. L judicatus, pp. of judicare] (ca. 1530) **1** : the action of judging : the administration of justice **2** : a court of justice **3** : JUDICIARY 1
ju·di·cial \jü-'di-shəl\ adj [ME, fr. L judicialis, fr. judicium judgment, fr. judex] (14c) **1 a** : of or relating to a judgment, the function of judging, the administration of justice, or the judiciary ⟨∼ processes⟩ **b** : belonging to the branch of government that is charged with trying all cases that involve the government and with the administration of justice within its jurisdiction — compare EXECUTIVE, LEGISLATIVE **2** : ordered or enforced by a court ⟨∼ decisions⟩ **3** : of, characterized by, or expressing judgment : CRITICAL 1b **4** : arising from a judgment of God **5** : belonging or appropriate to a judge or the judiciary — **ju·di·cial·ly** \-'di-sh(ə-)lē\ adv
judicial review n (ca. 1924) **1** : REVIEW 5 **2** : a constitutional doctrine that gives to a court system the power to annul legislative or executive acts which the judges declare to be unconstitutional
ju·di·cia·ry \jü-'di-shē-,er-ē, -'di-shə-rē\ n [judiciary, adj., fr. L judiciarius judicial, fr. judicium] (1787) **1 a** : a system of courts of law **b** : the judges of these courts **2 a** : a branch of government in which judicial power is vested — **judiciary** adj
ju·di·cious \jü-'di-shəs\ adj (1598) : having, exercising, or characterized by sound judgment : DISCREET syn see WISE — **ju·di·cious·ly** adv — **ju·di·cious·ness** n
Ju·dith \'jü-dəth\ n [LL, fr. Gk Ioudith, fr. Heb Yěhūdhīth] **1** : the Jewish heroine who saves the city of Bethulia in the book of Judith **2** : a book of Scripture included in the Roman Catholic canon of the Old Testament and in the Protestant Apocrypha — see BIBLE table
ju·do \'jü-(,)dō\ n [Jp jūdō, fr. jū weakness, gentleness + dō art] (1889) : a sport developed from jujitsu that emphasizes the use of quick movement and leverage to throw an opponent — **judo·ist** \-,ō-ist\ n
¹jug \'jəg\ n [perh. fr. Jug, nickname for Joan] (1538) **1 a** chiefly Brit : a small pitcher **b** (1) : a large deep usu. earthenware or glass container with a narrow mouth and a handle **c** : the contents of such a container : JUGFUL **2** : JAIL, PRISON
²jug vt **jugged; jug·ging** (1747) **1** : to stew (as a hare) in an earthenware vessel **2** : JAIL, IMPRISON
ju·gate \'jü-,gāt, -gət\ adj [NL jugum yoke] (ca. 1887) **1** : having parts arranged in pairs : PAIRED **2** : having a jugum
jug band n (ca. 1933) : a band that uses primitive or improvised instruments (as jugs, washboards, and kazoos) to play blues, jazz, and folk music
jug·ful \'jəg-,fùl\ n (1831) **1** : as much as a jug will hold **2** : a great deal — used in the phrase not by a jugful
jug·ger·naut \'jə-gər-,nòt, -,nät\ n [Hindi Jagannāth, lit., lord of the world, title of Vishnu] (1841) **1** chiefly Brit : a large heavy truck **2** : a massive inexorable force, campaign, movement, or object that crushes whatever is in its path ⟨an advertising ∼⟩ ⟨a political ∼⟩
¹jug·gle \'jə-gəl\ vb **jug·gled; jug·gling** \-g(ə-)liŋ\ [ME jogelen, fr. MF jogler to joke, fr. L joculari, fr. joculus, dim. of jocus joke] vi (15c) **1** : to perform the tricks of a juggler **2** : to engage in manipulation esp. in order to achieve a desired end ∼ vt **1 a** : to practice deceit or trickery on : BEGUILE **b** : to manipulate or rearrange esp. in order to achieve a desired end ⟨∼ an account to hide a loss⟩ **2 a** : to toss in the manner of a juggler **b** : to hold or balance precariously **3** : to handle or deal with usu. several things (as obligations) at one time so as to satisfy often competing requirements ⟨∼ the responsibilities of family life and full-time job —Jane S. Gould⟩
²juggle n (1664) : an act or instance of juggling: **a** : a trick of magic **b** : a show of manual dexterity **c** : an act of manipulation esp. to achieve a desired end
jug·gler \'jə-g(ə-)lər\ n [ME jogelour, fr. OE geogelere jester, fr. OF

\ə\ abut \ʰ\ kitten, F table \ər\ further \a\ ash \ā\ ace \ä\ mop, mar
\aù\ out \ch\ chin \e\ bet \ē\ easy \g\ go \i\ hit \ī\ ice \j\ job
\ŋ\ sing \ō\ go \ò\ law \òi\ boy \th\ thin \t̲h̲\ the \ü\ loot \ù\ foot
\y\ yet \zh\ vision \á, k̲, ⁿ, œ, œ̄, ue, ūe, ᵁ\ see Guide to Pronunciation

jogleour, fr. L *joculator*, fr. *joculari*] (14c) **1 a** : one who performs tricks or acts of magic or deftness **b** : one skilled in keeping several objects in motion in the air at the same time by alternately tossing and catching them **2** : one who manipulates esp. in order to achieve a desired end

jug·glery \'jə-glə-rē\ *n* (14c) **1** : the art or practice of a juggler **2** : manipulation or trickery esp. to achieve a desired end

¹jug·u·lar \'jə-gyə-lər *also* 'jü- *also* -g(ə-)lər\ *adj* [LL *jugularis*, fr. L *jugulum* collarbone, throat, fr. *jugum* yoke] (1597) **1** : of or relating to the throat or neck **2** : of or relating to the jugular vein

²jugular *n* (1615) **1** : JUGULAR VEIN **2** : the most vital or vulnerable part of something ⟨showed an instinct for the ~ in competition⟩

jugular vein *n* (1597) : any of several veins of each side of the neck that return blood from the head

ju·gum \'jü-gəm\ *n, pl* **ju·ga** \-gə\ *or* **jugums** [NL, fr. L, yoke — more at YOKE] (1893) : the most posterior and basal portion of an insect's wing modified in some lepidopterans into a lobe that couples the fore and hind wings during flight

jug wine *n* (1972) : table wine sold in large bottles

¹juice \'jüs\ *n* [ME *jus*, fr. OF, broth, juice, fr. L; akin to ON *ostr* cheese, Gk *zymē* leaven, Skt *yūṣa* broth] (14c) **1** : the extractable fluid contents of cells or tissues **2 a** *pl* : the natural fluids of an animal body **b** : the liquid or moisture contained in something **3 a** : the inherent quality of a thing : ESSENCE **b** : STRENGTH, VIGOR, VITALITY **4** : a medium (as electricity or gasoline) that supplies power **5** *slang* : LIQUOR **6** *slang* : exorbitant interest exacted of a borrower under the threat of violence **7** *slang* : INFLUENCE, CLOUT **8** : a motivating, inspiring, or enabling force or factor ⟨creative ~s⟩ — **juice·less** \'jüs-ləs\ *adj*

²juice *vt* **juiced; juic·ing** (1603) **1** : to add juice to **2** : to extract the juice of

juiced \'jüst\ *adj* (1592) **1** : containing juice — usu. used in combination ⟨precious-*juiced* flowers —Shak.⟩ **2** *slang* : DRUNK 1a

juice·head \'jüs-,hed\ *n* (1955) *slang* : ALCOHOLIC

juic·er \'jü-sər\ *n* (1938) **1** : an appliance for extracting juice from fruit or vegetables **2** *slang* : a heavy or habitual drinker

juice up *vt* (1955) : to give life, energy, or spirit to

juicy \'jü-sē\ *adj* **juic·i·er; -est** (15c) **1** : having much juice : SUCCULENT **2** : rewarding or profitable esp. financially : FAT ⟨~ contract⟩ ⟨a ~ dramatic role⟩ **3 a** : rich in interest : COLORFUL ⟨~ details⟩ **b** : SENSATIONAL, RACY ⟨a ~ scandal⟩ **c** : full of vitality : LUSTY — **juic·i·ly** \-sə-lē\ *adv* — **juic·i·ness** \-sē-nəs\ *n*

ju·jit·su *or* **ju·jut·su** \jü-'jit-(,)sü\ *n* [Jp *jūjutsu*, fr. *jū* weakness, gentleness + *jutsu* art, skill] (1875) : an art of weaponless fighting employing holds, throws, and paralyzing blows to subdue or disable an opponent

ju·ju \'jü-(,)jü\ *n* [of W. African origin; akin to Hausa *jùju* fetish] (1894) **1** : a fetish, charm, or amulet of West African peoples **2** : the magic attributed to or associated with jujus

ju·jube \'jü-jüb, *esp for 2* 'jü-jü-,bē\ *n* [ME, fr. ML *jujuba*, alter. of L *zizyphum*, fr. Gk *zizyphon*] (14c) **1 a** : an edible drupaceous fruit of any of several trees (genus *Ziziphus*) of the buckthorn family; *esp* : one of an Asian tree (Z. *jujuba*) **b** : a tree producing this fruit **2** : a fruit-flavored gumdrop or lozenge

juke \'jük\ *vb* **juked; juk·ing** [prob. alter. of E dial. *jouk* to cheat, deceive] *vt* (1967) : to fake out of position (as in football) ~ *vi* : to juke someone

juke·box \'jük-,bäks\ *n* [*juke* brothel, akin to Gullah *juke* disorderly, of W. African origin; akin to Bambara *dzugu* wicked] (1939) : a coin-operated phonograph or compact-disc player that automatically plays recordings selected from its list

juke joint *n* (1937) : a small inexpensive establishment for eating, drinking, or dancing to the music of a jukebox

ju·lep \'jü-ləp\ *n* [ME, fr. MF, fr. Ar *julāb*, fr. Per *gulāb*, fr. *gul* rose + *āb* water] (14c) **1** : a drink consisting of sweet syrup, flavoring, and water **2** : a drink consisting of a liquor (as bourbon or brandy) and sugar poured over crushed ice and garnished with mint

Ju·lian calendar \'jül-yən-\ *n* [L *Julianus*, fr. Gaius *Julius* Caesar] (ca. 1771) : a calendar introduced in Rome in 46 B.C. establishing the 12-month year of 365 days with each fourth year having 366 days and the months each having 31 or 30 days except for February which has 28 or in leap years 29 days — compare GREGORIAN CALENDAR

¹ju·li·enne \,jü-lē-'en, zhü-\ *n* [F, short for *potage à la julienne*, prob. fr. *Julienne* woman's name] (1841) **1** : a consommé containing julienned vegetables **2 a** : food (as meat or vegetables) that has been julienned **b** : a preparation or garnish of julienned food ⟨a ~ of leeks⟩ — **julienne** *adj*

²julienne *vt* **-enned; -en·ning** (ca. 1930) : to slice into thin strips the size of matchsticks ⟨wash and ~ the carrots⟩

Ju·liet \'jül-yət; ,jü-lē-'et, 'jü-lē-,\ *n* : the heroine of Shakespeare's tragedy *Romeo and Juliet* who dies for love of Romeo

Ju·li·ett \,jü-lē-'et\ [prob. irreg. fr. *Juliet*] (1952) — a communications code word for the letter *j*

Ju·ly \ju-'lī\ *n* [ME *Julie*, fr. OE *Julius*, fr. L, fr. Gaius *Julius* Caesar] (13c) : the 7th month of the Gregorian calendar

Ju·ma·da \ü-'ma-də\ *n* [Ar *Jumādá*] (1771) : either of two months of the Islamic year: **a** : the 5th month **b** : the 6th month — see MONTH table

¹jum·ble \'jəm-bəl\ *vb* **jum·bled; jum·bling** \-b(ə-)liŋ\ [perh. imit.] *vi* (ca. 1529) : to move in a confused or disordered manner ~ *vt* : to mix into a confused or disordered mass — often used with *up*

²jumble *n* (1661) **1 a** : a mass of things mingled together without order or plan : HODGEPODGE **b** : a state of confusion **2** *Brit* : articles for a rummage sale

³jumble *n* [origin unknown] (1615) : a small thin usu. ring-shaped sugared cookie or cake

jumble sale *n* (1898) *Brit* : RUMMAGE SALE

jum·bo \'jəm-(,)bō\ *n, pl* **jumbos** [*Jumbo*, a huge elephant exhibited by P. T. Barnum] (1883) : a very large specimen of its kind — **jumbo** *adj*

¹jump \'jəmp\ *vb* [prob. akin to LG *gumpen* to jump] (1530) **1 a** : to spring into the air : LEAP; *esp* : to spring free from the ground or other base by the muscular action of feet and legs **b** : to move suddenly or involuntarily : START **c** : to move over a position occupied by an opponent's piece in a board game often thereby capturing the piece

d : to undergo a vertical or lateral displacement owing to improper alignment of the film on a projector mechanism **e** : to start out or forward : BEGIN — usu. used with *off* ⟨~ off to a big lead⟩ **f** : to move energetically : HUSTLE **g** : to go from one sequence of instructions in a computer program to another ⟨~ to a subroutine⟩ **2** : COINCIDE, AGREE **3 a** : to move haphazardly or irregularly : shift abruptly ⟨~ed from job to job⟩ **b** : to change or abandon employment esp. in violation of contract **c** : to rise suddenly in rank or status **d** : to undergo a sudden sharp change in value ⟨prices ~ed⟩ **e** : to make a jump in bridge **f** : to make a hurried judgment ⟨~ to conclusions⟩ **g** : to show eagerness ⟨~ed at the chance⟩ **h** : to enter eagerly ⟨~ on the bandwagon⟩ **4** : to make a sudden physical or verbal attack ⟨~ed on him for his criticism⟩ **5** : to bustle with activity ⟨the bar was ~ing with young people⟩ ~ *vt* **1 a** : to leap over ⟨~ a hurdle⟩ **b** : to move over (a piece) in a board game **c** : to act, move, or begin before (as a signal) ⟨~ the green light⟩ **d** : to leap aboard ⟨~ a freight⟩ **2** *obs* : RISK, HAZARD **3 a** : to escape from : AVOID ⟨~ town without paying their bills —Hamilton Basso⟩ **c** : to depart from (a normal course) ⟨~ the track⟩ **4 a** : to make a sudden physical or verbal attack on **b** : to occupy illegally ⟨~ a mining claim⟩ **5 a** (1) : to cause to leap (2) : to cause (game) to break cover : START, FLUSH **b** : to elevate in rank or status **c** : to raise (a bridge partner's bid) by more than one rank **d** : to increase suddenly and sharply — **jump bail** : to abscond after being released from prison on bail — **jump ship** **1** : to leave the company of a ship without authority **2** : to desert a cause or party esp. abruptly : DEFECT — **jump the gun** **1** : to start in a race before the starting signal **2** : to act, move, or begin something before the proper time — **jump the queue** *Brit* : to advance directly to or as if to the head of a line

²jump *adv* (1539) *obs* : EXACTLY, PAT

³jump *n* (ca. 1552) **1 a** (1) : an act of jumping : LEAP (2) : any of several sports competitions featuring a leap, spring, or bound (3) : a space cleared or covered by a leap (4) : an obstacle to be jumped over or from **b** : a sudden involuntary movement : START **c** : a move made in a board game by jumping **d** : a transfer from one sequence of instructions in a computer program to a different sequence ⟨conditional ~⟩ **2** *obs* : VENTURE **3 a** (1) : a sharp sudden increase (2) : a bid in bridge of more tricks than are necessary to overcall the preceding bid — compare SHIFT **b** : an abrupt change or transition **c** (1) : a quick short journey (2) : one in a series of moves from one place to another **4** : an advantage at the start ⟨desirous of getting the ~ on the competition —Elmer Davis⟩

jump ball *n* (1924) : a method of putting a basketball into play by tossing it into the air between two opponents who jump up and attempt to tap the ball to a teammate

jump boot *n* (1942) : a boot worn esp. by paratroopers

jump cut *n* (1948) : a sudden often jarring cut from one shot or scene to another without intervening devices (as fade-outs or dissolves); *broadly* : an abrupt transition (as in a narrative) — **jump-cut** \'jəmp-,kət\ *vb*

¹jump·er \'jəm-pər\ *n* (1611) **1** : a person who jumps **2 a** : any of various devices operating with a jumping motion **b** : any of several sleds **c** : a short wire used to close a break or cut out part of a circuit **3** : any of several jumping animals; *esp* : a saddle horse trained to jump obstacles **4** : JUMP SHOT

²jump·er \'jəm-pər\ *n* [prob. fr. E dial. *jump* jumper] (1853) **1** : a loose blouse or jacket worn by workmen **2** : a sleeveless one-piece dress worn usu. with a blouse **3** : a child's coverall — usu. used in pl. **4** *chiefly Brit* : SWEATER 2

jumper cables *n pl* (ca. 1926) : a pair of heavy-duty electrical cables with alligator clamps used to make a connection for jump-starting a vehicle

jump hook *n* (1982) : a hook shot in which the player jumps before releasing the ball

jumping bean *n* (ca. 1889) : a seed of any of several Mexican shrubs (genera *Sebastiania* and *Sapium*) of the spurge family that tumbles about because of the movements of the larva of a small moth (*Carpocapsa saltitans*) inside it

jumping jack *n* (1883) **1** : a toy figure of a man jointed and made to jump or dance by means of strings or a sliding stick **2** : a conditioning exercise performed from a standing position by jumping to a position with legs spread and hands touching overhead and then to the original position — called also *side-straddle hop*

jumping mouse *n* (1826) : any of several small hibernating No. American rodents (family Zapodidae) with long hind legs and tail and no cheek pouches

jumping-off place \,jəm-piŋ-'of-\ *n* (1826) **1** : a remote or isolated place **2** : a place or point from which an enterprise, investigation, or discussion is launched — called also *jumping-off point*

jumping plant louse *n* (ca. 1901) : any of numerous plant lice (family Psyllidae) with the femurs thickened and adapted for leaping

jumping spider *n* (1813) : any of a family (Salticidae) of small spiders that stalk and leap upon their prey

jump jet *n* (1964) : a military jet aircraft with vertical takeoff and landing capability

jump-off \'jəm-,of\ *n* (1917) **1** : the start of a race or an attack **2** : a jumping competition to break a tie at the end of regular competition (as in a horse show)

jump pass *n* (ca. 1948) : a pass made by a player (as in football or basketball) while jumping

jump rope *n* (1834) : a rope used for exercises and children's games that involve jumping over the usu. twirling rope each time it reaches its lowest point; *also* : a game played with a jump rope

jump seat *n* (ca. 1864) **1** : a movable carriage seat **2** : a folding seat between the front and rear seats of a passenger automobile

jump shot *n* (1948) : a shot in basketball made by jumping into the air and releasing the ball with one or both hands at the peak of the jump

jump-start \'jəmp-'stärt\ *vt* (1973) **1** : to start (an engine or vehicle) by temporary connection to an external power source (as another vehicle's battery) **2 a** : to get off to a speedy start ⟨advertising can ~ a political campaign⟩ **b** : to impart fresh or renewed energy to : ENERGIZE ⟨a plan to ~ the stagnant economy⟩ — **jump start** *n*

jump·suit \'jəmp-ˌsüt\ n (1944) **1 :** a coverall worn by parachutists for jumping **2 :** a one-piece garment consisting of a blouse or shirt with attached trousers or shorts
jumpy \'jəm-pē\ adj **jump·i·er; -est** (1869) **1 :** characterized by jumps or sudden variations **2 :** NERVOUS, JITTERY — **jump·i·ness** n
jun \'jən\ n, pl **jun** [Korean chŏn] (1966) **:** the chon of North Korea
jun·co \'jəŋ-(ˌ)kō\ n, pl **juncos** or **juncoes** [NL, fr. Sp, reed — more at JONQUIL] (1887) **:** any of a genus (Junco) of small widely distributed American finches usu. having a pink bill, ashy gray head and back, and conspicuous white lateral tail feathers
junc·tion \'jəŋ(k)-shən\ n [L junction-, junctio, fr. jungere to join — more at YOKE] (1711) **1 :** an act of joining **:** the state of being joined **2 a :** place or point of meeting **b :** an intersection of roads esp. where one terminates **c :** a point (as in a thermocouple) at which dissimilar metals make contact **d :** an interface in a semiconductor device between regions with different electrical characteristics **3 :** something that joins — **junc·tion·al** \-shnəl, -shə-nᵊl\ adj
junc·tur·al \'jəŋ(k)-chə-rəl, 'jəŋ(k)-shrəl\ adj (1942) **:** of or relating to phonetic juncture
junc·ture \'jəŋ(k)-chər\ n (14c) **1 a :** JOINT, CONNECTION **b :** the manner of transition or mode of relationship between two consecutive sounds in speech **2 :** an instance of joining **:** UNION, JUNCTION **3 :** a point of time; esp **:** one made critical by a concurrence of circumstances **syn** JUNCTURE, EXIGENCY, EMERGENCY, CONTINGENCY, PINCH, STRAITS, CRISIS mean a critical or crucial time or state of affairs. JUNCTURE stresses the significant concurrence or convergence of events ⟨an important juncture in our country's history⟩. EXIGENCY stresses the pressure of restrictions or urgency of demands created by a special situation ⟨provide for exigencies⟩. EMERGENCY applies to a sudden unforeseen situation requiring prompt action to avoid disaster ⟨the presence of mind needed to deal with emergencies⟩. CONTINGENCY implies an emergency or exigency that is regarded as possible but uncertain of occurrence ⟨contingency plans⟩. PINCH implies urgency or pressure for action to a less intense degree than EXIGENCY or EMERGENCY ⟨come through in a pinch⟩. STRAITS applies to a troublesome situation from which escape is extremely difficult ⟨in dire straits⟩. CRISIS applies to a juncture whose outcome will make a decisive difference ⟨a crisis of confidence⟩.
June \'jün\ n [ME, fr. MF & L; MF Juin, fr. L Junius] (14c) **:** the 6th month of the Gregorian calendar
June·ber·ry \'jün-ˌber-ē\ n (ca. 1810) **:** SERVICEBERRY
june bug n, often cap J (1829) **:** any of numerous rather large leaf-eating scarab beetles (subfamily Melolonthinae) that fly chiefly in late spring and have larvae that are white grubs which live in soil and feed chiefly on the roots of grasses and other plants — called also june beetle
Jung·ian \'yuŋ-ē-ən\ adj (ca. 1930) **:** of, relating to, or characteristic of C. G. Jung or his psychological doctrines — **Jungian** n
jun·gle \'jəŋ-gəl\ n, often attrib [Hindi jaṅgal forest, fr. Skt jaṅgala desert region] (1776) **1 a :** an impenetrable thicket or tangled mass of tropical vegetation **b :** a tract overgrown with thickets or masses of vegetation **2 :** a hobo camp **3 a** (1) **:** a confused or disordered mass of objects **:** JUMBLE (2) **:** something that baffles or frustrates by its tangled or complex character **:** MAZE ⟨the ~ of housing laws — Bernard Taper⟩ **b :** a place of ruthless struggle for survival ⟨the city is a ~ where no one is safe after dark —Stuart Chase⟩ — **jun·gle·like** \-gə(l)-ˌlīk\ adj — **jun·gly** \-g(ə-)lē\ adj
jun·gled \-gəld\ adj (1842) **:** abounding in jungle ⟨a ~ island⟩
jungle fowl n (ca. 1825) **:** any of several Asian wild birds (genus Gallus) related to the pheasants; esp **:** a bird (G. gallus) of southeastern Asia from which domestic fowls have prob. descended
jungle gym n [fr. Junglegym, a trademark] (1923) **:** a structure of vertical and horizontal bars for use by children at play
¹ju·nior \'jün-yər\ adj [L, compar. of juvenis young — more at YOUNG] (13c) **1 a :** less advanced in age **:** YOUNGER — used chiefly to distinguish a son with the same given name as his father **b** (1) **:** YOUTHFUL (2) **:** designed for young people and esp. adolescents **c :** of more recent date and therefore inferior or subordinate ⟨a ~ lien⟩ **2 a :** lower in standing or rank ⟨~ partners⟩ **b :** duplicating or suggesting one a smaller scale something typically large or powerful ⟨a ~ gale⟩ **3 :** of or relating to juniors or the class of juniors at an educational institution ⟨the ~ prom⟩
²junior n [L, n. & adj.] (1526) **1 a** (1) **:** a person who is younger than another ⟨a man six years my ~⟩ (2) **:** a male child **:** SON (3) **:** a young person **b :** a clothing size for women and girls with slight figures **2 a :** a person holding a lower position in a hierarchy of ranks **b :** a student in the next-to-the-last year before graduating from an educational institution **3** cap **:** a member of a program of the Girl Scouts for girls in the third through sixth grades in school
ju·nior·ate \'jün-yə-ˌrāt, -rət\ n (1845) **1 :** a course of high school or college study for candidates for the priesthood, brotherhood, or sisterhood; specif **:** one preparatory to the course in philosophy **2 :** a seminary for juniorate training
junior college n (1899) **:** an educational institution that offers two years of studies corresponding to those in the first two years of a four-year college and that often offers technical, vocational, and liberal studies to the adults of a community
junior high school n (1909) **:** a school usu. including grades 7 to 9 — called also junior high
Junior Leaguer n (1938) **:** a member of a league of young women organized for volunteer service to civic and social organizations
junior miss n (1927) **1 :** an adolescent girl **2 :** JUNIOR 1b
junior varsity n (1949) **:** a team composed of members lacking the experience or qualification required for the varsity
ju·ni·per \'jü-nə-pər\ n [ME junipere, fr. L juniperus] (14c) **1 :** any of numerous evergreen shrubs or trees (genus Juniperus) of the cypress family with leaves resembling needles or scales and female cones usu. resembling berries **2 :** any of several coniferous trees resembling true junipers
juniper oil n (ca. 1889) **:** an acrid essential oil obtained from the fruit of a common juniper (Juniperus communis) and used esp. in gin and liqueurs
juniper tar n (ca. 1930) **:** a tarry liquid used locally in treating skin diseases and obtained by distillation from the wood of a Eurasian juniper (Juniperus oxycedrus) — called also cade oil, juniper tar oil

¹junk \'jəŋk\ n [ME jonke] (14c) **1 :** pieces of old cable or cordage used esp. to make gaskets, mats, swabs, or oakum **2 a** (1) **:** old iron, glass, paper, or other waste that may be used again in some form (2) **:** secondhand, worn, or discarded articles (3) **:** CLUTTER 1b **b :** something of poor quality **:** TRASH **c :** something of little meaning, worth, or significance **3** slang **:** NARCOTICS; esp **:** HEROIN **4 :** JUNK BOND **5 :** baseball pitches other than fastballs (as curveballs or change-ups) — **junky** \'jəŋ-kē\ adj
²junk vt (1916) **:** to get rid of as worthless **:** SCRAP **syn** see DISCARD
³junk n [Pg junco, fr. Jav joṅ] (1613) **:** any of various ships of Chinese waters with bluff lines, a high poop and overhanging stem, little or no keel, high pole masts, and a deep rudder

junk

junk art n (1962) **:** three-dimensional art made from discarded material (as metal, mortar, glass, or wood) — **junk artist** n
junk bond n (1976) **:** a high-risk bond that offers a high yield and is often issued to finance a takeover of a company
junk·er \'jəŋ-kər\ n [¹junk + ²-er] (1944) **:** something (as an automobile) of such age and condition as to be ready for scrapping
Jun·ker \'yuȯŋ-kər\ n [G, fr. OHG juncherro, lit., young lord] (1554) **:** a member of the Prussian landed aristocracy — **Jun·ker·dom** \-kər-dəm\ n — **Jun·ker·ism** \-kə-ˌri-zəm\ n
¹jun·ket \'jəŋ-kət\ n [ME ioncate, ultim. fr. (assumed) VL juncata, fr. L juncus rush] (15c) **1 :** a dessert of sweetened flavored milk set with rennet **2 a :** a festive social affair **b :** TRIP, JOURNEY; esp **:** a trip made by an official at public expense
²junket vi (1555) **1 :** FEAST, BANQUET **2 :** to go on a junket — **jun·ke·teer** \ˌjəŋ-kə-'tir\ or **jun·ket·er** \'jəŋ-kə-tər\ n
junk food n (1971) **1 :** food that is high in calories but low in nutritional content **2 :** something that is appealing or enjoyable but of little or no real value ⟨the ultimate in junk food for young minds — Cleveland Amory⟩
junk·ie also **junky** \'jəŋ-kē\ n, pl **junk·ies** (1923) **1** slang **a :** a narcotics peddler or addict **b :** a person who derives inordinate pleasure from or who is dependent on something ⟨sugar ~⟩ ⟨television news ~⟩ **2 :** a junk dealer
junk mail n (1954) **:** third-class mail (as advertising circulars) that is often addressed to "occupant" or "resident"
junk sculpture n (1965) **:** JUNK ART
junk·yard \'jəŋk-ˌyärd\ n (1880) **:** a yard used to store sometimes resalable junk
Ju·no \'jü-(ˌ)nō\ n **:** the wife of Jupiter, queen of heaven, and goddess of light, birth, women, and marriage — compare HERA
Ju·no·esque \ˌjü-(ˌ)nō-'esk\ adj (1888) **:** marked by stately beauty
jun·ta \'huṅ-tə, 'jən-, 'hən-\ n [Sp, fr. fem. of junto joined, fr. L junctus, pp. of jungere to join — more at YOKE] (1622) **1 :** a council or committee for political or governmental purposes; esp **:** a group of persons controlling a government esp. after a revolutionary seizure of power **2 :** JUNTO
jun·to \'jən-(ˌ)tō\ n, pl **juntos** [prob. alter. of junta] (1623) **:** a group of persons joined for a common purpose
Ju·pi·ter \'jü-pə-tər\ n [L] **1 :** the chief Roman god, husband of Juno, and god of light, of the sky and weather, and of the state and its welfare and its laws — compare ZEUS **2 :** the largest of the planets and fifth in order from the sun — see PLANET table
ju·ral \'jur-əl\ adj [L jur-, jus law] (1635) **1 :** of or relating to law **2 :** of or relating to rights or obligations — **ju·ral·ly** \-ə-lē\ adv
Ju·ras·sic \ju̇-'ra-sik\ adj [F jurassique, fr. Jura mountain range] (1831) **:** of, relating to, or being the period of the Mesozoic era between the Triassic and the Cretaceous or the corresponding system of rocks marked by the presence of dinosaurs and the first appearance of birds — see GEOLOGIC TIME table — **Jurassic** n
ju·rat \'ju̇r-ˌat\ n [short for L juratum (est) it has been sworn, 3d sing. perf. pass. of jurare to swear — more at JURY] (1796) **:** a certificate added to an affidavit stating when, before whom, and where it was made
ju·rel \hü-'rel\ n [Sp] (1772) **:** any of several food fishes (family Carangidae) of warm seas
ju·rid·i·cal \ju̇-'ri-di-kəl\ also **ju·rid·ic** \-dik\ adj [L juridicus, fr. jur-, jus + dicere to say — more at DICTION] (1502) **1 :** of or relating to the administration of justice or the office of a judge **2 :** of or relating to law or jurisprudence **:** LEGAL — **ju·rid·i·cal·ly** \-di-k(ə-)lē\ adv
ju·ris·con·sult \ˌju̇r-əs-'kän-ˌsəlt, -kən-ˌ\ n [L jurisconsultus, fr. juris (gen. of jus) + consultus, pp. of consulere to consult] (1605) **:** JURIST; esp **:** one learned in international and public law
ju·ris·dic·tion \ˌju̇r-əs-'dik-shən\ n [ME jurisdiccioun, fr. MF & L; MF juridiction, fr. L jurisdiction-, jurisdictio, fr. juris + diction-, dictio act of saying — more at DICTION] (14c) **1 :** the power, right, or authority to interpret and apply the law **2 a :** the authority of a sovereign power to govern or legislate **b :** the power or right to exercise authority **:** CONTROL **3 :** the limits or territory within which authority may be exercised **syn** see POWER — **ju·ris·dic·tion·al** \-shnəl, -shə-nᵊl\ adj — **ju·ris·dic·tion·al·ly** adv
Ju·ris Doctor \'ju̇r-əs-\ n [L, doctor of law] (1969) **:** a degree equivalent to bachelor of laws
ju·ris·pru·dence \ˌju̇r-əs-'prü-dᵊn(t)s\ n (ca. 1656) **1 a :** a system or body of law **b :** the course of court decisions **2 :** the science or philosophy of law **3 :** a department of law ⟨medical ~⟩ — **ju·ris·pru-**

\ə\ abut \ᵊ\ kitten, F table \ər\ further \a\ ash \ā\ ace \ä\ mop, mar \au̇\ out \ch\ chin \e\ bet \ē\ easy \g\ go \i\ hit \ī\ ice \j\ job \ŋ\ sing \ō\ go \ȯ\ law \ȯi\ boy \th\ thin \t͟h\ the \ü\ loot \u̇\ foot \y\ yet \zh\ vision \ȧ, ḵ, ⁿ, œ, œ̄, ᴜᴇ, ᵫ̄, ʸ\ see Guide to Pronunciation

den·tial \-prü-'den(t)-shəl\ *adj* — **ju·ris·pru·den·tial·ly** \-'den(t)-sh(ə-)lē\ *adv*

ju·ris·pru·dent \-'prü-d°nt\ *n* [LL *jurisprudent-, jurisprudens,* fr. L *juris* + *prudent-, prudens* skilled, prudent] (1628) : JURIST

ju·rist \'jùr-ist\ *n* [MF *juriste,* fr. ML *jurista,* fr. L *jur-, jus*] (15c) : one having a thorough knowledge of law; *esp* : JUDGE

ju·ris·tic \jù-'ris-tik\ *adj* (1831) **1** : of or relating to a jurist or jurisprudence **2** : of, relating to, or recognized in law — **ju·ris·ti·cal·ly** \-ti-k(ə-)lē\ *adv*

ju·ror \'jùr-ər, 'jùr-,òr\ *n* (14c) **1 a** : a member of a jury **b** : a person summoned to serve on a jury **2** : a person who takes an oath (as of allegiance)

¹ju·ry \'jùr-ē\ *n, pl* **juries** [ME *jure,* fr. AF *juree,* fr. OF *jurer* to swear, fr. L *jurare,* fr. *jur-, jus*] (15c) **1** : a body of persons sworn to give a verdict on some matter submitted to them; *esp* : a body of persons legally selected and sworn to inquire into any matter of fact and to give their verdict according to the evidence **2** : a committee for judging and awarding prizes at a contest or exhibition **3** : one (as the public or test results) that will decide — used esp. in the phrase *the jury is still out*

²jury *adj* [origin unknown] (1616) : improvised for temporary use esp. in an emergency : MAKESHIFT ⟨a ~ mast⟩ ⟨a ~ rig⟩

³jury *vt* **jur·ied; jury·ing** (1947) : to select material as appropriate for exhibition in (as an art show) — used chiefly as a participle ⟨a *juried* show⟩

ju·ry-rig \'jùr-ē-,rig, -'rig\ *vt* [²*jury*] (1788) : to erect, construct, or arrange in a makeshift fashion

jus gen·ti·um \'yüs-'gen-tē-əm\ *n* [L, law of nations] (1548) : INTERNATIONAL LAW

jus san·gui·nis \-'säŋ-gwə-nəs\ *n* [L, right of blood] (1902) : a rule that a child's citizenship is determined by its parents' citizenship

jus·sive \'jə-siv\ *n* [L *jussus,* pp. of *jubēre* to order; akin to Gk *hysminē* battle] (1846) : a word, form, case, or mood expressing command — **jussive** *adj*

jus so·li \'yüs-'sō-,lē\ *n* [L, right of the soil] (1902) : a rule that the citizenship of a child is determined by the place of its birth

¹just \'jəst, 'jüst\ *var of* JOUST

²just \'jəst\ *adj* [ME, fr. MF & L; MF *juste,* fr. L *justus,* fr. *jus* right, law; akin to Skt *yos* welfare] (14c) **1 a** : having a basis in or conforming to fact or reason : REASONABLE ⟨a ~ but not a generous decision⟩ **b** *archaic* : faithful to an original **c** : conforming to a standard of correctness : PROPER ⟨~ proportions⟩ **2 a** (1) : acting or being in conformity with what is morally upright or good : RIGHTEOUS ⟨a ~ war⟩ (2) : being what is merited : DESERVED ⟨a ~ punishment⟩ **b** : legally correct : LAWFUL ⟨~ title to an estate⟩ *syn* see FAIR, UPRIGHT — **just·ly** *adv* — **just·ness** \'jəs(t)-nəs\ *n*

³just \'jəst, 'jist, 'jest *also without* t\ *adv* (15c) **1 a** : EXACTLY, PRECISELY ⟨~ right⟩ **b** : very recently ⟨the bell ~ rang⟩ **2 a** : by a very small margin : BARELY ⟨~ too late⟩ **b** : IMMEDIATELY, DIRECTLY ⟨~ west of here⟩ **3 a** : ONLY, SIMPLY ⟨~ last year⟩ ⟨~ be yourself⟩ **b** : QUITE, VERY ⟨~ wonderful⟩ **4** : PERHAPS, POSSIBLY ⟨it ~ might work⟩ — **just about** : ALMOST ⟨the work is *just about* done⟩

just-folks \'jəs(t)-'fōks\ *adj* (1952) : marked by the absence of formality or sophistication : UNPRETENTIOUS ⟨her ~ manner⟩

jus·tice \'jəs-təs\ *n* [ME, fr. OE & OF; OE *justice,* fr. OF *justice,* fr. L *justitia,* fr. *justus*] (12c) **1 a** : the maintenance or administration of what is just esp. by the impartial adjustment of conflicting claims or the assignment of merited rewards or punishments **b** : JUDGE **c** : the administration of law; *esp* : the establishment or determination of rights according to the rules of law or equity **2 a** : the quality of being just, impartial, or fair **b** (1) : the principle or ideal of just dealing or right action (2) : conformity to this principle or ideal : RIGHTEOUSNESS **c** : the quality of conforming to law **3** : conformity to truth, fact, or reason : CORRECTNESS

justice of the peace (15c) : a local magistrate empowered chiefly to administer summary justice in minor cases, to commit for trial, and to administer oaths and perform marriages

jus·ti·cia·ble \,jə-'sti-sh(ē-)ə-bəl\ *adj* (15c) **1** : liable to trial in a court of justice ⟨a ~ offense⟩ **2** : capable of being decided by legal principles or by a court of justice — **jus·ti·cia·bil·i·ty** \,jə-,sti-sh(ē-)ə-'bi-lə-tē\ *n*

jus·ti·ci·ar \jə-'sti-shē-ər, -,är\ *n* [ME, fr. ML *justitiarius,* fr. L *justitia*] (ca. 1580) : the chief political and judicial officer of the Norman and later kings of England until the 13th century

jus·ti·fi·a·ble \'jəs-tə-,fī-ə-bəl\ *adj* (1561) : capable of being justified : EXCUSABLE ⟨~ family pride —*Current Biog.*⟩ — **jus·ti·fi·abil·i·ty** \,jəs-tə-,fī-ə-'bi-lə-tē\ *n* — **jus·ti·fi·ably** \'jəs-tə-,fī-ə-blē\ *adv*

jus·ti·fi·ca·tion \,jəs-tə-fə-'kā-shən\ *n* (14c) **1** : the act, process, or state of being justified by God **2 a** : the act or an instance of justifying : VINDICATION **b** : something that justifies **3** : the process or result of justifying lines of text

jus·ti·fi·ca·tive \'jəs-tə-fə-,kā-tiv\ *adj* (1611) : JUSTIFICATORY

jus·ti·fi·ca·to·ry \,jəs-'ti-fi-kə-,tōr-ē, -,tòr-; 'jəs-tə-fə-,kā-tə-rē\ *adj* (1579) : tending or serving to justify : VINDICATORY

jus·ti·fy \'jəs-tə-,fī\ *vb* **-fied; -fy·ing** [ME *justifien,* fr. MF or LL; MF *justifier,* fr. LL *justificare,* fr. L *justus*] *vt* (14c) **1 a** : to prove or show to be just, right, or reasonable **b** (1) : to show to have had a sufficient legal reason (2) : to qualify (oneself) as a surety by taking oath to the ownership of sufficient property **2 a** *archaic* : to administer justice to **b** *archaic* : ABSOLVE **c** : to judge, regard, or treat as righteous and worthy of salvation **3 a** : to space (as lines of text) so that the lines come out even at the margin **b** : to make even by justifying ⟨*justified* margins⟩ ~ *vi* **1 a** : to show a sufficient lawful reason for an act done **b** : to qualify as bail or surety **2** : to justify lines of text *syn* see MAINTAIN — **jus·ti·fi·er** \-,fī(-ə)r\ *n*

just–in–time *n, often attrib* (1981) : a manufacturing strategy wherein parts are produced or delivered only as needed

¹jut \'jət\ *vb* **jut·ted; jut·ting** [perh. short for ²*jutty*] *vi* (ca. 1573) : to extend out, up, or forward : PROJECT ⟨mountains *jutting* into the sky⟩ ⟨a *jutting* jaw⟩ ~ *vt* : to cause to project

²jut *n* (1786) : something that juts : PROJECTION

jute \'jüt\ *n* [Bengali *jhuto*] (1746) : the glossy fiber of either of two East Indian plants (*Corchorus olitorius* and *C. capsularis*) of the linden family used chiefly for sacking, burlap, and twine; *also* : a plant producing jute

Jute \'jüt\ *n* [ME, fr. ML *Jutae* Jutes, of Gmc origin; akin to OE *Eotenas* Jutes] (14c) : a member of a Germanic people invading England from the Continent and settling in Kent in the 5th century — **Jut·ish** \'jü-tish\ *adj*

¹jut·ty \'jə-tē\ *n, pl* **jutties** [ME] (15c) **1** *archaic* : JETTY **2** : a projecting part of a building

²jutty *vt* **jut·tied; jut·ty·ing** (1599) *obs* : to project beyond

ju·ve·nes·cence \,jü-və-'ne-s°n(t)s\ *n* (1800) : the state of being youthful or of growing young — **ju·ve·nes·cent** \-s°nt\ *adj*

¹ju·ve·nile \'jü-və-,nīl, -n°l\ *adj* [F or L; F *juvénile,* fr. L *juvenilis,* fr. *juvenis* young person — more at YOUNG] (1625) **1 a** : physiologically immature or undeveloped : YOUNG **b** : derived from sources within the earth and coming to the surface for the first time — used esp. of water and gas **2** : of, relating to, characteristic of, or suitable for children or young people ⟨~ books⟩ **3** : reflecting psychological or intellectual immaturity : CHILDISH

²juvenile *n* (1733) **1 a** : a young person : YOUTH **b** : a book for children or young people **2 a** : a young individual resembling an adult of its kind except in size and reproductive activity: as **a** : a fledged bird not yet in adult plumage **b** : a 2-year-old racehorse **3** : an actor or actress who plays youthful parts

juvenile court *n* (1899) : a court that has special jurisdiction over delinquent and dependent children usu. up to the age of 18

juvenile delinquency *n* (1816) **1** : conduct by a juvenile characterized by antisocial behavior that is beyond parental control and therefore subject to legal action **2** : a violation of the law committed by a juvenile and not punishable by death or life imprisonment — **juvenile delinquent** *n*

juvenile hormone *n* (1940) : an insect hormone that is secreted by the corpora allata, inhibits maturation to the imago, and plays a role in reproduction

juvenile officer *n* (1954) : a police officer charged with the detection, prosecution, and care of juvenile delinquents

ju·ve·nil·ia \,jü-və-'ni-lē-ə\ *n pl* [L, neut. pl. of *juvenilis*] (1622) **1** : compositions produced in the artist's or author's youth **2** : artistic or literary compositions suited to or designed for the young

ju·ve·nil·i·ty \,jü-və-'ni-lə-tē\ *n, pl* **-ties** (ca. 1623) **1** : the quality or state of being juvenile : YOUTHFULNESS **2 a** : immaturity of thought or conduct **b** : an instance of being juvenile

jux·ta·pose \'jək-stə-,pōz\ *vt* **-posed; -pos·ing** [prob. back-formation fr. *juxtaposition*] (1851) : to place side by side ⟨~ unexpected combinations of colors, shapes and ideas —J. F. T. Bugental⟩

juxtaposed *adj* (1855) : placed side by side : being in juxtaposition *syn* see ADJACENT

jux·ta·po·si·tion \,jək-stə-pə-'zi-shən\ *n* [L *juxta* near + E *position* — more at JOUST] (1654) : the act or an instance of placing two or more things side by side; *also* : the state of being so placed — **jux·ta·po·si·tion·al** \-'zish-nəl, -'zi-shə-n°l\ *adj*

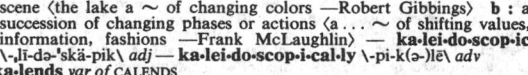

k \'kā\ *n, pl* **k's** *or* **ks** \'kāz\ *often cap, often attrib* (bef. 12c) **1 a :** the 11th letter of the English alphabet **b :** a graphic representation of this letter **c :** a speech counterpart of orthographic *k* **2 :** a graphic device for reproducing the letter *k* **3 :** one designated *k* esp. as the 11th in order or class **4 :** something shaped like the letter K **5 :** a unit vector parallel to the z-axis **6** [*kilo-*] **:** THOUSAND ⟨a salary of $24K⟩ **7** [*kilo-*]**:** a unit of computer storage capacity equal to 1024 bytes ⟨a computer memory of 64K⟩ **8** *cap* **:** STRIKEOUT

Kaa·ba \'kä-bə\ *n* [Ar *ka'bah,* lit., cubic building] (1734) **:** a small stone building in the court of the Great Mosque at Mecca that contains a sacred black stone and is the goal of Islamic pilgrimage and the point toward which Muslims turn in praying

ka·ba·la *or* **kab·ba·la** *or* **kab·ba·lah** *var of* CABALA

ka·bob \kə-'bäb *also* 'kä-,\ *n* [Per, Hindi, Ar & Turk; Per & Hindi *kabāb,* fr. Ar, fr. Turk *kebap*] (1673) **:** cubes of meat (as lamb or beef) marinated and cooked with vegetables (as onions, tomatoes, and green peppers) usu. on a skewer

Ka·bu·ki \kə-'bü-kē, 'kä-bù-(,)kē\ *n* [Jp] (1899) **:** traditional Japanese popular drama with singing and dancing performed in a highly stylized manner

Ka·byle \kə-'bī(ə)l\ *n* [Ar *qabā'il,* pl. of *qabīlah* tribe] (1738) **1 :** a member of a Berber people living in the mountainous coastal area east of Algiers **2 :** the Berber language of the Kabyles

ka·chi·na \kə-'chē-nə\ *n* [Hopi *qacína*] (1888) **1 :** one of the deified ancestral spirits believed among the Hopi and other Pueblo Indians to visit the pueblos at intervals **2 :** one of the elaborately masked kachina impersonators that dance at agricultural ceremonies **3 :** a doll representing a kachina

kad·dish \'kä-dish\ *n, often cap* [Aram *qaddīsh* holy] (1613) **:** a Jewish prayer recited in the daily ritual of the synagogue and by mourners at public services after the death of a close relative

kaf·fee·klatsch \'kò-fē-,klach, 'kä-fē-, -,kläch, -,klòch\ *n, often cap* [G, fr. *Kaffee* coffee + *Klatsch* gossip] (1888) **:** an informal social gathering for coffee and conversation

Kaf·fir *or* **Kaf·ir** \'ka-fər\ *n* [Ar *kāfir* infidel] (1778) **1** *archaic* **:** a member of a group of southern African Bantu-speaking peoples **2** *often not cap, chiefly SoAfr* **:** a black African — usu. used disparagingly

kaf·fi·yeh \kə-'fē-ə\ *n* [Ar *kūfiyah, kaffiyah,* fr. al-*Kufah* Al Kufa, town in Iraq] (ca. 1817) **:** an Arab headdress consisting of a square of cloth folded to form a triangle and held on by a cord

kaf·ir \'ka-fər\ *n* (ca. 1785) **:** a grain sorghum (*Sorghum caffrorum*) with stout short-jointed somewhat juicy stalks and erect heads

Kaf·ir \'ka-fər\ *n* [Ar *kāfir*] (1759) **:** a member of a group of peoples of the Hindu Kush in northeastern Afghanistan

Kaf·iri \'ka-fə-rē\ *n* (1901) **:** the group of languages spoken by the Kafirs that constitutes a distinct branch of Indo-Iranian — see INDO-EUROPEAN LANGUAGES table

Kaf·ka·esque \,käf-kə-'esk, ,kaf-\ *adj* (1946) **:** of, relating to, or suggestive of Franz Kafka or his writings; *esp* **:** having a nightmarishly complex, bizarre, or illogical quality ⟨~ bureaucratic delays⟩

kaf·tan *var of* CAFTAN

ka·hu·na \kə-'hü-nə\ *n* [Hawaiian] (1886) **:** a Hawaiian witch doctor

kai·nite \'kī-,nīt, 'kä-\ *also* **kai·nit** \ki-'nēt\ *n* [G *Kainit,* fr. Gk *kainos* new — more at RECENT] (1868) **:** a natural salt KMg(SO₄)Cl·3H₂O consisting of a hydrous sulfate and chloride of magnesium and potassium that is used as a fertilizer and as a source of potassium and magnesium compounds

kai·ser \'kī-zər\ *n* [ME, fr. ON *keisari;* akin to OHG *keisur* emperor; both fr. a prehistoric Gmc word borrowed fr. L *Caesar,* cognomen of the Emperor Augustus] (13c) **:** EMPEROR; *esp* **:** the ruler of Germany from 1871 to 1918 — **kai·ser·dom** \-zər-dəm\ *n* — **kai·ser·ism** \-zə-,ri-zəm\ *n*

kai·se·rin \'kī-zə-rən\ *n* [G, fem. of *Kaiser*] (ca. 1888) **:** the wife of a kaiser

kaiser roll *n* (ca. 1898) **:** a crusty roll often used for sandwiches

ka·ka \'kä-kə\ *n* [Maori] (ca. 1774) **:** an olive brown New Zealand parrot (*Nestor meridionalis*) with gray and red markings

ka·ka·po \,kä-kə-'pō\ *n, pl* **-pos** [Maori] (1843) **:** a large chiefly nocturnal burrowing New Zealand parrot (*Strigops habroptilus*) that has green and brown barred plumage and well-developed wings with little power of flight

ka·ke·mo·no \,kä-ki-'mō-(,)nō\ *n, pl* **-nos** [Jp] (1890) **:** a vertical Japanese ornamental pictorial or calligraphic scroll

ka·ki·e·mon \,kä-kē-'ā-,män\ *n, often cap* [Sakaida *Kakiemon fl* 1650 Japanese potter] (1890) **:** a Japanese porcelain decorated with enamel

ka·la–azar \,kä-lə-ə-'zär, ,kä-\ *n* [Hindi *kālā-āzār* black disease, fr. Hindi *kālā* black + Per *āzār* disease] (1882) **:** a severe infectious disease chiefly of tropical areas that is marked by fever, progressive anemia, leukopenia, and enlargement of the spleen and liver and caused by a flagellate (*Leishmania donovani*) transmitted by the bite of sand flies

ka·lan·choe \,ka-lən-'kō-ē *also* kə-'laŋ-kə-(,)wē *or* 'ka-lən-,chō\ *n* [NL] (1830) **:** any of a genus (*Kalanchoe*) of chiefly African tropical succulent herbs or shrubs of the orpine family often cultivated as ornamentals — compare BRYOPHYLLUM

kale \'kā(ə)l\ *n* [Sc, fr. ME (northern) *cal,* fr. OE *cāl* — more at COLE] (14c) **1 a :** COLE **b :** a hardy cabbage (*Brassica oleracea acephala*) with curled often finely incised leaves that do not form a dense head **2** *slang* **:** MONEY

ka·lei·do·scope \kə-'lī-də-,skōp\ *n* [Gk *kalos* beautiful + *eidos* form + E *-scope* — more at IDYLL] (1817) **1 :** an instrument containing loose bits of colored material (as glass or plastic) between two flat plates and two plane mirrors so placed that changes of position of the bits of material are reflected in an endless variety of patterns **2 :** something resembling a kaleidoscope: as **a :** a variegated changing pattern or

kachina 3

---

scene ⟨the lake a ~ of changing colors —Robert Gibbings⟩ **b :** a succession of changing phases or actions ⟨a . . . ~ of shifting values, information, fashions —Frank McLaughlin⟩ — **ka·lei·do·scop·ic** \-,lī-də-'skä-pik\ *adj* — **ka·lei·do·scop·i·cal·ly** \-pi-k(ə-)lē\ *adv*

ka·lends *var of* CALENDS

kal·li·din \'ka-lə-dən\ *n* [G, fr. *Kallīkrein* + Pept*id* peptide + *-in*] (1950) **:** either of two vasodilator kinins formed from blood plasma globulin by the action of kallikrein: **a :** BRADYKININ **b :** one with a terminal lysine amino-acid residue added to bradykinin

kal·li·krein \,ka-lə-'krē-ən, kə-'li-krē-ən\ *n* [G, fr. Gk *kallikreas* sweetbread, pancreas, fr. *kalli-* beautiful (fr. *kallos* beauty) + *kreas* flesh — more at RAW] (1930) **:** a hypotensive protease that liberates kinins from blood plasma proteins and is used therapeutically for vasodilation

Kal·muck *or* **Kal·muk** \'kal-,mək, kal-\ *or* **Kal·myk** \kal-'mik\ *n* [Russ *kalmyk,* fr. Volga Tatar *kalmȳk*] (1613) **1 :** a member of a Buddhist Mongol people orig. of Dzungaria living mainly northwest of the Caspian Sea in Russia **2 :** the Mongolian language of the Kalmucks

Ka·ma \'kä-mə\ *n* [Skt *Kāma,* fr. *kāma* love] **:** the Hindu god of love

ka·ma·ai·na \,kä-mə-ə-'ī-nə\ *n* [Hawaiian *kama'āina,* fr. *kama* child + *'āina* land] (1903) **:** one who has lived in Hawaii for a long time

kame \'kām\ *n* [Sc, kame, comb, fr. ME (northern) *camb* comb, fr. OE] (1795) **:** a short ridge, hill, or mound of stratified drift deposited by glacial meltwater

Ka·me·ha·me·ha Day \kə-,mā-ə-'mā-(,)hä-\ *n* (1925) **:** June 11 observed as a holiday in Hawaii in commemoration of the birthday of Kamehameha I

¹ka·mi·ka·ze \,kä-mi-'kä-zē\ *n* [Jp, lit., divine wind] (1945) **1 a :** a member of a Japanese air attack corps in World War II assigned to make a suicidal crash on a target (as a ship) **2 :** an airplane containing explosives to be flown in a suicide crash on a target

²kamikaze *adj* (1945) **1 :** of, relating to, being, or resembling a kamikaze **2 :** having or showing reckless disregard for safety or personal welfare

kam·pong \'käm-,pòŋ, 'kam-\ *n* [Malay] (1844) **:** a hamlet or village in a Malay-speaking country

ka·na \'kä-nə\ *n, pl* **kana** *often attrib* [Jp] (1727) **:** a Japanese system of syllabic writing having characters that can be used exclusively for writing foreign words or in combination with kanji (as for indicating pronunciations or grammatical inflections); *also* **:** a single character belonging to the kana system — compare HIRAGANA, KATAKANA

Ka·nak \kə-'näk, -'nak\ *n* [F *canaque,* prob. fr. E *Kanaka* South Sea islander, fr. Hawaiian, person] (1910) **:** a native Melanesian inhabitant of New Caledonia

kana·my·cin \,ka-nə-'mī-s²n\ *n* [NL *kanamyceticus,* specific epithet of *Streptomyces kanamyceticus*] (1957) **:** a broad-spectrum antibiotic from a Japanese soil streptomyces (*Streptomyces kanamyceticus*)

Kan·a·rese \,ka-nə-'rēz, -'rēs\ *n, pl* **Kanarese** [*Kanara,* India] (1847) **1 :** KANNADA **2 :** a member of a Kannada-speaking people of Karnataka, southern India

kan·ban \'kän-,bän\ *n, often attrib* [Jp, sign, placard; fr. the cards used on assembly lines to signal that parts are needed] (1982) **:** JUST-IN-TIME

kan·ga·roo \,kaŋ-gə-'rü\ *n, pl* **-roos** [Guugu Yimidhirr (Australian aboriginal language of northern Queensland) *gaŋurru*] (1770) **:** any of various herbivorous leaping marsupial mammals (family Macropodidae) of Australia, New Guinea, and adjacent islands with a small head, large ears, long powerful hind legs, a long thick tail used as a support and in balancing, and rather small forelegs not used in progression

kangaroo court *n* (1853) **1 :** a mock court in which the principles of law and justice are disregarded or perverted **2 :** a court characterized by irresponsible, unauthorized, or irregular status or procedures **3 :** judgment or punishment given outside of legal procedure

kangaroo rat *n* (1867) **:** any of a genus (*Dipodomys*) of pouched nocturnal burrowing rodents of arid parts of the western U.S. and Mexico

kan·ji \'kän-(,)jē\ *n, pl* **kanji** *often attrib* [Jp] (1920) **:** a Japanese system of writing that utilizes characters borrowed or adapted from Chinese writing; *also* **:** a single character belonging to the kanji system — compare KANA

Kan·na·da \'kä-nə-də *also* 'ka-\ *n* [Kannada *kannada*] (1856) **:** the major Dravidian language of Karnataka, southern India

kangaroo rat

kan·te·le \'kän-tə-lə\ *n* [Finn] (ca. 1903) **:** a traditional Finnish zither orig. having five strings but now having as many as thirty

ka·o·lin \'kā-ə-lən\ *n* [F *kaolin,* fr. *Gaoling* hill in China] (ca. 1741) **:** a fine usu. white clay that is used in ceramics and refractories, as a filler or extender, and in medicine esp. as an adsorbent in the treatment of diarrhea

ka·o·lin·ite \-lə-,nīt\ *n* (1867) **:** a mineral consisting of a hydrous silicate of aluminum that constitutes the principal mineral in kaolin — **ka·o·lin·it·ic** \,kā-ə-lə-'ni-tik\ *adj*

ka·on \'kā-,än\ *n* [ISV *ka* kay (fr. *K-meson,* its earlier name) + ²-*on*] (1958) **:** an unstable meson that occurs in both charged and neutral forms and is about 970 times more massive than an electron

ka·pell·mei·ster \kə-'pel-,mī-stər, kä-\ *n, often cap* [G, fr. *Kapelle* choir + *Meister* master] (1838) **:** the director of a choir or orchestra

kaph \'käf, 'kóf\ *n* [Heb, lit., palm of the hand] (ca. 1823) **:** the 11th letter of the Hebrew alphabet — see ALPHABET table

ka·pok \'kā-,päk\ *n* [Malay] (ca. 1750) **:** a mass of silky fibers that clothe the seeds of the ceiba tree and are used esp. as a filling for mattresses, life preservers, and sleeping bags and as insulation

Ka·po·si's sarcoma \'ka-pə-sēz- *also* -shēz-, kə-'pō-sēz-\ *n* [Moritz *Kaposi* †1902 Hung. dermatologist] (1916) **:** a neoplastic disease asso-

---

\a\ abut \²\ kitten, F table \ər\ further \a\ ash \ā\ ace \ä\ mop, mar \aú\ out \ch\ chin \e\ bet \ē\ easy \g\ go \i\ hit \ī\ ice \j\ job \ŋ\ sing \ō\ go \ò\ law \òi\ boy \th\ thin \t͟h\ the \ü\ loot \ù\ foot \y\ yet \zh\ vision \ä, k̲, ⁿ, œ, œ̄, ᵫ, ᵫ̄, �究\ *see* Guide to Pronunciation ciated esp. with AIDS, affecting esp. the skin and mucous membranes, and characterized usu. by the formation of pink to reddish-brown or bluish plaques, macules, papules, or nodules

kap·pa \'ka-pə\ n [ME, fr. Gk, of Sem origin; akin to Heb *kaph*] (15c) : the 10th letter of the Greek alphabet — see ALPHABET table

ka·put also **ka·putt** \kə-'put, kä-, -'püt\ adj [G *kaputt*, fr. F *capot* not having made a trick at piquet] (1895) **1** : utterly finished, defeated, or destroyed **2** : unable to function : USELESS ⟨my battery went ∼ — Henry James Jr.⟩ **3** : hopelessly outmoded

kar·a·bi·ner var of CARABINER

Kara·ism \'kar-ə-‚i-zəm\ n [LHeb *qĕrāïm* Karaites, fr. Heb *qārā* to read] (ca. 1883) : a Jewish doctrine originating in Baghdad in the 8th century that rejects rabbinism and talmudism and bases its tenets on Scripture alone — **Kara·ite** \-‚īt\ n

kar·a·kul \'kar-ə-kəl\ n [*Karakul*, village in Uzbekistan] (1853) **1** often cap : any of a breed of hardy fat-tailed sheep from Uzbekistan with a narrow body and coarse wiry fur **2** : the tightly curled glossy coat of the newborn lamb of a karakul valued as fur

kar·a·o·ke \‚kar-ē-'ō-kē, kə-'rō-kē, ‚kä-rä-'ō-(‚)kā\ n [Jp, fr. *kara* empty + *ōke*, short for *ōkesutora* orchestra] (1982) : a device that plays instrumental accompaniments for a selection of songs to which the user sings along and that records the user's singing with the music

kar·at \'kar-ət\ n [ME, prob. fr. MF *carat*, fr. ML *carratus* unit of weight for precious stones — more at CARAT] (15c) : a unit of fineness for gold equal to ¹/₂₄ part of pure gold in an alloy

ka·ra·te \kə-'rä-tē\ n [Jp, fr. *kara* empty + *te* hand] (1955) : an Oriental art of self-defense in which an attacker is disabled by crippling kicks and punches — **ka·ra·te·ist** \-ist\ n

ka·ra·ya gum \kə-'rī-ə-\ n [Hindi *karāyal* resin] (1916) : any of several vegetable gums similar to tragacanth and often used as substitutes for it that are obtained from tropical Asian trees (genera *Sterculia* of the family Sterculiaceae and *Cochlospermum* of the family Bixaceae); esp : one derived from an Indian tree (*S. urens*)

Ka·re·lian \kə-'rē-lē-ən, -'rēl-yən\ n (1855) **1** : a native or inhabitant of Karelia **2** : the Finno-Ugric language of the Karelians — **Karelian** adj

Ka·ren \kə-'ren\ n, pl **Karen** or **Karens** (1833) **1** : a member of a group of peoples of eastern and southern Myanmar **2 a** : a group of languages spoken by the Karen peoples **b** : a language of this group

kar·ma \'kär-mə also 'kər-\ n [Skt *karma* fate, work] (1827) **1** often cap : the force generated by a person's actions held in Hinduism and Buddhism to perpetuate transmigration and in its ethical consequences to determine the nature of the person's next existence **2** : VIBRATION 4 — **kar·mic** \-mik\ adj

ka·roo or **kar·roo** \kə-'rü\ n, pl **karoos** or **karroos** [Afrik *karo*] (1789) : a dry tableland of southern Africa

ka·ross \kə-'räs\ n [Afrik *karos*] (1785) : a simple garment or rug of skins used esp. by native tribesmen of southern Africa

karst \'kärst\ n [G] (1902) : an irregular limestone region with sinks, underground streams, and caverns — **karst·ic** \'kär-stik\ adj

kart \'kärt\ n [prob. fr. *GoKart*, a trademark] (1959) : a miniature motorcar used esp. in racing — **kart·ing** n

kary- or **karyo-** also **cary-** or **caryo-** comb form [NL, fr. Gk *karyon* nut — more at CAREEN] **1** : nucleus of a cell ⟨*karyo*kinesis⟩ **2** : nut : kernel ⟨*caryo*psis⟩

kar·y·og·a·my \‚kar-ē-'ä-gə-mē\ n, pl **-mies** (1891) : the fusion of cell nuclei (as in fertilization)

kar·y·o·ki·ne·sis \‚kar-ē-ō-kə-'nē-səs, -kī-\ n [NL] (1882) **1** : the nuclear phenomena characteristic of mitosis **2** : the whole process of mitosis — **kar·y·o·ki·net·ic** \-'ne-tik\ adj

kar·y·ol·o·gy \‚kar-ē-'ä-lə-jē\ n [ISV] (1895) **1** : the minute cytological characteristics of the cell nucleus esp. with regard to the chromosomes **2** : a branch of cytology concerned with the karyology of cell nuclei — **kar·y·o·log·i·cal** \-ē-ə-'lä-ji-kəl\ also **kar·y·o·log·ic** \-jik\ adj

kar·y·o·lymph \'kar-ē-ō-‚lim(p)f\ n [ISV] (1899) : NUCLEAR SAP

kar·y·o·some \'kar-ē-ə-‚sōm\ n [ISV] (1889) : a mass of chromatin in a cell nucleus that resembles a nucleolus

¹kar·y·o·type \'kar-ē-ə-‚tīp\ n [ISV] (1929) : the chromosomal characteristics of a cell; also : the chromosomes themselves or a representation of them — **kar·y·o·typ·ic** \‚kar-ē-ə-'ti-pik\ adj — **kar·y·o·typ·i·cal·ly** \-pi-k(ə-)lē\ adv

²karyotype vt : to determine the karyotype of

Kas·bah var of CASBAH

ka·sha \'kä-shə, 'ka-\ n [Russ] (1808) **1** : a porridge made usu. from buckwheat groats **2** : kasha grain before cooking

Ka·shan \kə-'shän\ n [*Kashan*, Iran] (1920) : an Oriental rug with floral motifs in soft colors

Kash·mir var of CASHMERE

Kash·miri \kash-'mir-ē, kazh-\ n, pl **Kashmiris** or **Kashmiri** (1880) **1** : an Indo-Aryan language spoken in Kashmir **2** : a native or inhabitant of Kashmir

kash·ruth or **kash·rut** \kä-'shrüt, -'shrüth\ n [Heb *kashrūth*, lit., fitness] (1907) **1** : the Jewish dietary laws **2** : the state of being kosher

Ka·shu·bi·an \kə-'shü-bē-ən\ n [*Kashube* a member of a Slavic people] (1919) : a Slavic language spoken in the vicinity of Gdansk

kat var of KHAT

ka·ta \'kä-(‚)tä\ n, pl **kata** or **katas** [Jp, lit., model, pattern] (1945) : a set combination of positions and movements (as in karate) performed as an exercise

kat·a·bat·ic \‚ka-tə-'ba-tik\ adj [Gk *katabatos* descending, verbal of *katabainein* to go down, fr. *kata-* cata- + *bainein* to go — more at COME] (1918) : relating to or being a wind produced by the flow of cold dense air down a slope (as of a mountain or glacier) in an area subject to radiational cooling

ka·ta·ka·na \‚kä-tə-'kä-nə\ n [Jp, fr. *kata* part + *kana* kana] (1727) : the form of Japanese syllabic writing used esp. for scientific terms, official documents, and words adopted from other languages — compare HIRAGANA

ka·tchi·na or **ka·tci·na** var of KACHINA

Ka·tha·re·vu·sa \‚kä-thə-'re-vu-‚sä\ n [NGk *kathareuousa*, fr. Gk, fem. of *kathareuōn*, prp. of *kathareuein* to be pure, fr. *katharos* pure] (1936) : modern Greek conforming to classic Greek usage

ka·thar·sis var of CATHARSIS

ka·ty·did \'kä-tē-‚did\ n [imit.] (1784) : any of several large green American long-horned grasshoppers usu. having stridulating organs on the forewings of the males that produce a loud shrill sound

kat·zen·jam·mer \'kat-sən-‚ja-mər\ n [G, fr. *Katze* cat + *Jammer* distress] (1849) **1** : HANGOVER **2** : DISTRESS 2 **3** : a discordant clamor

kau·ri \'kau̇(-ə)r-ē\ n [Maori *kawri*] (1823) **1** : any of various trees (genus *Agathis*) of the araucaria family; esp : a tall timber tree (*A. australis*) of New Zealand having fine white straight-grained wood **2** : a light-colored to brown resin from the kauri tree found as a fossil in the ground or collected from living trees and used esp. in varnishes and linoleum — called also *kauri gum, kauri resin*

ka·va \'kä-və\ n [Tongan & Marquesan, lit., bitter] (1810) **1** : an Australasian shrubby pepper (*Piper methysticum*) from whose crushed root an intoxicating beverage is made **2** : the beverage made from kava

kay \'kā\ n (14c) : the letter *k*

Kay \'kā\ n : a boastful overbearing knight of the Round Table who is foster brother and seneschal of King Arthur

kay·ak \'kī-‚ak\ n [Inuit *qayaq*] (1757) **1** : an Eskimo canoe made of a frame covered with skins except for a small opening in the center and propelled by a double-bladed paddle **2** : a portable boat styled like an Eskimo kayak — **kay·ak·er** \-‚a-kər\ n — **kay·ak·ing** \-kiŋ\ n

¹kayo \(‚)kā-'ō, 'kā-(‚)ō\ n [pronunciation of KO, abbr.] (1920) : KNOCKOUT

²kayo vt **kay·oed; kayo·ing** (1923) : KNOCK OUT

Ka·zak \kə-'zak, -'zäk\ n [*Kazak* (Kazakh), town in Azerbaijan] (1900) : an Oriental rug in bold colors with geometric designs or stylized plant and animal forms

Ka·zakh \kə-'zak, -'zäk\ n [Russ *kazakh*, fr. Kazakh *kazak*] (1832) **1** : a member of a Turkic people of Kazakhstan and other countries of central Asia **2** : the language of the Kazakhs

ka·zoo \kə-'zü\ n, pl **kazoos** [imit.] (1884) : an instrument that imparts a buzzing quality to the human voice and that usu. consists of a small metal or plastic tube with a side hole covered by a thin membrane

K-band \'kā-\ n (ca. 1948) : a segment of the radio spectrum that lies between 10.9 GHz and 36.0 GHz and spans the upper superhigh-frequency and lower extremely-high-frequency bands and that is used esp. for police radars, satellite communication, and astronomical observation

kea \'kē-ə\ n [Maori] (1862) : a large mostly dull green New Zealand parrot (*Nestor notabilis*) that is normally insectivorous but sometimes destroys sheep by slashing the back to feed on the kidney fat

ke·bab or **ke·bob** var of KABOB

keb·buck or **keb·bock** \'ke-bək\ n [ME (Sc dial.) *cabok*, fr. ScGael *ceapag*] (15c) dial Brit : a whole wheel or ball of cheese

¹kedge \'kej\ vt **kedged; kedg·ing** [ME *caggen*] (1627) : to move (a ship) by means of a line attached to a kedge dropped at the distance and in the direction desired

²kedge n (ca. 1769) : a small anchor used esp. in kedging

ked·ge·ree \'ke-jə-rē\ n [Hindi *khicarī*, fr. Skt *khiccā*] (1662) **1** : an Indian dish of seasoned rice, beans, lentils, and sometimes smoked fish **2** : cooked or smoked fish, rice, hard-boiled eggs, and seasoning heated in cream

¹keek \'kēk\ vi [ME *kiken*] (14c) chiefly Scot : PEEP, LOOK

²keek n (1721) chiefly Scot : PEEP, LOOK

¹keel \'kē(ə)l\ vb [ME *kelen*, fr. OE *cēlan*, fr. *cōl* cool] (bef. 12c) chiefly dial : COOL

²keel n [ME *kele*, fr. MD *kiel*; akin to OE *cēol* ship] (14c) : a flat-bottomed barge used esp. on the Tyne to carry coal

³keel n [ME *kele*, fr. ON *kjǫlr*; akin to OE *ceole* throat, beak of a ship — more at GLUTTON] (14c) **1 a** : the chief structural member of a boat or ship that extends longitudinally along the center of its bottom and that often projects from the bottom; also : this projection **b** : SHIP **2** : a projection suggesting a keel; esp : CARINA — **keeled** \'kē(ə)ld\ adj — **keel·less** \'kē(ə)l-ləs\ adj

⁴keel vi (1832) **1** : to fall in or as if in a faint — usu. used with over **2** : to heel or lean precariously

⁵keel n [ME (Sc dial.) *keyle*] (15c) chiefly dial : RED OCHER

keel·boat \'kē(ə)l-‚bōt\ n (1695) : a shallow covered keeled riverboat that is usu. rowed, poled, or towed and that is used for freight

keel·haul \-‚hȯl\ vt [D *kielhalen*, fr. *kiel* keel + *halen* to haul] (1666) **1** : to haul under the keel of a ship as punishment or torture **2** : to rebuke severely

keel·son \'kel-sən, 'kē(ə)l-\ n [ME *kelswayn*, prob. of Scand origin; akin to Sw *kölsvin* keelson] (1598) : a longitudinal structure running above and fastened to the keel of a ship in order to stiffen and strengthen its framework

¹keen \'kēn\ adj [ME *kene* brave, sharp, fr. OE *cēne* brave; akin to OHG *kuoni* brave] (13c) **1 a** : having a fine edge or point : SHARP ⟨a ∼ sword⟩ **b** : affecting one as if by cutting ⟨∼ sarcasm⟩ **c** : pungent to the sense ⟨a ∼ scent⟩ **2 a** (1) : showing a quick and ardent responsiveness : ENTHUSIASTIC ⟨a ∼ swimmer⟩ (2) : EAGER ⟨was ∼ to begin⟩ **b** of emotion or feeling : INTENSE ⟨the ∼ delight in the chase — F. W. Maitland⟩ **3 a** : intellectually alert : having or characteristic of a quick penetrating mind ⟨a ∼ student⟩ ⟨a ∼ awareness of the problem⟩; also : shrewdly astute ⟨∼ bargainers⟩ **b** : sharply contested ⟨∼ debate⟩ **c** : extremely sensitive in perception ⟨∼ eyes⟩ **4** : WONDERFUL, EXCELLENT *syn* see SHARP, EAGER — **keen·ly** adv — **keen·ness** \-nəs\ n

²keen n (1830) : a lamentation for the dead uttered in a loud wailing voice or sometimes in a wordless cry

³keen vb [Ir *caoinim* I lament] vi (1845) **1 a** : to lament with a keen **b** : to make a sound suggestive of a keen **2** : to lament, mourn, or complain loudly ∼ vt : to utter by keening — **keen·er** n

¹keep \'kēp\ vb **kept** \'kept\; **keep·ing** [ME *kepen*, fr. OE *cēpan*; perh. akin to OHG *chapfēn* to look] vt (bef. 12c) **1** : to take notice of by appropriate conduct : FULFILL: as **a** : to be faithful to ⟨∼ a promise⟩ **b** : to act fittingly in relation to ⟨∼ the Sabbath⟩ **c** : to conform to in habits or conduct ⟨∼ late hours⟩ **d** : to stay in accord with (a beat) ⟨∼ time⟩ **2** : PRESERVE, MAINTAIN: as **a** : to watch over and defend ⟨∼ us from harm⟩ **b** (1) : to take care of : TEND ⟨∼ a garden⟩ (2) : SUPPORT (3) : to maintain in a good, fitting, or orderly condition —

usu. used with *up* **c** : to continue to maintain ⟨~ watch⟩ **d** (1) : to cause to remain in a given place, situation, or condition ⟨~ him waiting⟩ (2) : to preserve (food) in an unspoiled condition **e** : to have or maintain in one's service or at one's disposal ⟨~ a mistress⟩ — often used with *on* ⟨kept the cook on⟩; *also* : to lodge or feed for pay ⟨~ boarders⟩ **f** (1) : to maintain a record in ⟨~ a diary⟩ (2) : to enter in a book ⟨~ records⟩ **g** : to have customarily in stock for sale **3 a** : to restrain from departure or removal : DETAIN ⟨~ children in after school⟩ **b** : HOLD BACK, RESTRAIN ⟨~ them from going⟩ ⟨kept him back with difficulty⟩ **c** : SAVE, RESERVE ⟨~ some for later⟩ ⟨kept some out for a friend⟩ **d** : to refrain from revealing ⟨~ a secret⟩ **4 a** : to retain in one's possession or power ⟨kept the money we found⟩ **b** : to refrain from granting, giving, or allowing ⟨kept the news back⟩ **c** : to have in control ⟨~ your temper⟩ **5** : to confine oneself to ⟨~ my room⟩ **6 a** : to stay or continue in ⟨~ the path⟩ ⟨~ your seat⟩ **b** : to stay or remain on or in usu. against opposition : HOLD ⟨kept her ground⟩ **7** : CONDUCT, MANAGE ⟨~ a tearoom⟩ ~ *vi* **1** *chiefly Brit* : LIVE, LODGE **2 a** : to maintain a course, direction, or progress ⟨~ to the right⟩ **b** : to continue usu. without interruption ⟨~ talking⟩ ⟨~ quiet⟩ **c** : to persist in a practice ⟨kept smiling⟩ ⟨kept bothering them⟩ ⟨kept on smoking in spite of warnings⟩ **3** : STAY, REMAIN ⟨~ out of the way⟩ ⟨~ off the grass⟩: as **a** : to stay even — usu. used with *up* ⟨~ up with the Joneses⟩ **b** : to remain in good condition ⟨meat will ~ in the freezer⟩ **c** : to remain secret ⟨the secret would ~⟩ **d** : to call for no immediate action ⟨the matter will ~ until morning⟩ **4** : AB-STAIN, REFRAIN ⟨can't ~ from talking⟩ **5** : to be in session ⟨school will ~ through the winter —W. M. Thayer⟩ **6** *of a quarterback* : to retain possession of a football esp. after faking a handoff — **keep an eye on** : WATCH — **keep at** : to persist in doing or concerning oneself with — **keep company** : to go together as frequent companions or in courtship — **keep house** : to manage a household — **keep one's distance** *or* **keep at a distance** : to stay aloof : maintain a reserved attitude — **keep one's eyes open** *or* **keep one's eyes peeled** : to be on the alert : be watchful — **keep one's hand in** : to keep in practice — **keep pace** : to stay even; *also* : KEEP UP — **keep step** : to keep in step — **keep to** **1 a** : to stay in **b** : to limit oneself to **2** : to abide by — **keep to oneself** **1** : to keep secret ⟨kept the facts *to myself*⟩ **2** : to remain solitary or apart from other people

syn KEEP, OBSERVE, CELEBRATE, COMMEMORATE mean to notice or honor a day, occasion, or deed. KEEP stresses the idea of not neglecting or violating ⟨kept the Sabbath by refraining from work⟩. OBSERVE suggests marking the occasion by ceremonious performance ⟨not all holidays are *observed* nationally⟩. CELEBRATE suggests acknowledging an occasion by festivity ⟨traditionally *celebrates* Thanksgiving with a huge dinner⟩. COMMEMORATE suggests that an occasion is marked by observances that remind one of the origin and significance of the day ⟨commemorate Memorial Day with the laying of wreaths⟩.

syn KEEP, RETAIN, DETAIN, WITHHOLD, RESERVE mean to hold in one's possession or under one's control. KEEP may suggest a holding securely in one's possession, custody, or control ⟨keep this while I'm gone⟩. RETAIN implies continued keeping, esp. against threatened seizure or forced loss ⟨managed to *retain* their dignity even in poverty⟩. DETAIN suggests a delay in letting go ⟨detained them for questioning⟩. WITHHOLD implies restraint in letting go or a refusal to let go ⟨withheld information from the authorities⟩. RESERVE suggests a keeping in store for future use ⟨reserve some of your energy for the last mile⟩.

²**keep** *n* (1579) **1 a** *archaic* : CUSTODY, CHARGE **b** : MAINTENANCE **2** : one that keeps or protects: as **a** : FORTRESS, CASTLE; *specif* : the strongest and securest part of a medieval castle **b** : one whose job is to keep or tend **c** : PRISON, JAIL **3** : the means or provisions by which one is kept ⟨earned his ~⟩ **4** : KEEPER 4 — **for keeps** **1 a** : with the provision that one keep what one has won ⟨played marbles *for keeps*⟩ **b** : with deadly seriousness **2** : for an indefinitely long time : PERMA-NENTLY ⟨with the result of ending the matter

keep back *vi* (1837) : to refrain from approaching or advancing near something ⟨police asked the spectators to *keep back*⟩

keep down *vt* (1581) **1** : to keep in control ⟨keep expenses *down*⟩ **2** : to prevent from growing, advancing, or succeeding

keep·er \'kē-pər\ *n* (14c) **1** : one that keeps: as **a** : PROTECTOR **b** : GAMEKEEPER **c** : WARDEN **d** : CUSTODIAN **e** *chiefly Brit* : CURATOR **2** : any of various devices for keeping something in position **3 a** : one fit or suitable for keeping; *esp* : a fish large enough to be legally caught and kept **b** : a domestic animal considered with respect to how easy it is to care for ⟨an easy ~⟩ **4** : an offensive football play in which the quarterback runs with the ball

keep·ing \'kē-piŋ\ *n* (14c) **1** : the act of one that keeps: as **a** : CUS-TODY, MAINTENANCE **b** : OBSERVANCE **c** : a reserving or preserving for future use **2 a** : the means by which something is kept : SUPPORT, PROVISION **b** : the state of being kept or the condition in which something is kept ⟨the house is in good ~⟩ **3** : CONFORMITY ⟨in ~ with good taste⟩ ⟨out of ~ with the decor⟩

keep·sake \'kēp-ˌsāk\ *n* [¹keep + -sake (as in *namesake*)] (1790) : something kept or given to be kept as a memento

keep up *vt* (15c) **1** : to persist or persevere in ⟨kept *up* the good work⟩; *also* : MAINTAIN, SUSTAIN ⟨keep standards *up*⟩ ~ *vi* **1** : to keep adequately informed or up-to-date ⟨keep *up* on international affairs⟩ **2** : to continue without interruption ⟨rain kept *up* all night⟩ **3** : to maintain contact or relations with ⟨keep *up* with old friends⟩

kees·hond \'kās-ˌhȯnt\ *n, pl* **kees·hon·den** \-ˌhȯn-dən\ [D, prob. fr. *Kees*, nickname for *Cornelis* Cornelius + *hond* dog, fr. MD; akin to OE *hund* hound] (1926) : any of a Dutch breed of compact medium-sized dogs that have a dense heavy grayish coat and a foxy head

kef \'kef, 'kef, 'kāf\ *n* [Ar *kayf* pleasure] (1808) **1** : a state of dreamy tranquillity **2** : smoking material (as marijuana) that produces kef

kef·fi·yeh *var of* KAFFIYEH

ke·fir \ke-'fir, 'kē-fər, 'ke-\ *n* [Russ] (1884) : a beverage of fermented cow's milk

keg \'keg, *dial* 'kag, 'kāg\ *n* [ME *kag*, of Scand origin; akin to ON *kaggi* keg] (ca. 1632) **1** : a small cask or barrel having a capacity of 30 gallons (136.4 liters) or less **2** : the contents of a keg

keg·ler \'ke-glər, 'kā-\ *n* [G, fr. *kegeln* to bowl, fr. *Kegel* bowling pin, fr. OHG *kegil* stake, peg] (1932) : ¹BOWLER

keg·ling \'ke-gliŋ, 'kā-\ *n* (1938) : BOWLING

keis·ter \'kēs-tər, 'kīs-\ *or* **kees·ter** \'kēs-\ *n* [E slang *keister* satchel] (1931) *slang* : BUTTOCKS

ke·lim *var of* KILIM

kel·ly green \'ke-lē-\ *n, often cap K* [fr. the common Irish name *Kelly*; fr. the association of Ireland with the color green] (ca. 1935) : a strong yellowish green

ke·loid \'kē-ˌlȯid\ *n* [F *kéloïde*, fr. Gk *chēlē* claw] (1854) : a thick scar resulting from excessive growth of fibrous tissue — **keloid** *adj* — **ke·loi·dal** \kē-'lȯi-d²l\ *adj*

kelp \'kelp\ *n* [ME *culp*] (14c) **1 a** : any of various large brown seaweeds (order Laminariales) **b** : a mass of large seaweeds **2** : the ashes of seaweed used esp. as a source of iodine

kelp bass *n* (ca. 1936) : a mottled sea bass (*Paralabrax clathratus*) that occurs along the Pacific coast of the U.S. and is an important sport fish

¹**kel·pie** \'kel-pē\ *n* [perh. fr. ScGael *cailpeach*, *colpach* heifer, colt] (1747) : a water sprite of Scottish folklore that delights in or brings about the drowning of wayfarers

²**kelpie** *n* [*Kelpie*, name of a dog of this breed] (1903) : any of a breed of energetic working dogs developed in Australia from British sheepdogs

Kelt \'kelt\, **Kelt·ic** \'kel-tik\ *var of* CELT, CELTIC

kel·vin \'kel-vən\ *n* (1968) : the base unit of temperature in the International System of Units that is equal to 1/273.16 of the Kelvin scale temperature of the triple point of water

Kelvin *adj* [William Thomson, Lord *Kelvin*] (1908) : relating to, conforming to, or having a thermometric scale on which the unit of measurement equals the Celsius degree and according to which absolute zero is 0 K, the equivalent of −273.15°C

kemp \'kemp\ *n* [ME *kempe* coarse hair, prob. of Scand origin; akin to ON *kampr* mustache; akin to OE *cenep* mustache] (1641) : a coarse fiber esp. of wool that is usu. short, wavy, and white, has little affinity for dye, and is used in mixed wools

Kemp's ridley \'kemps-\ *n* [Richard M. *Kemp* *fl* 1873 Am. amateur naturalist] (1979) : RIDLEY a

kempt \'kem(p)t\ *adj* [back-formation fr. *unkempt*] (1929) : neatly kept : TRIM

¹**ken** \'ken\ *vb* **kenned; ken·ning** [ME *kennen*, fr. OE *cennan* to make known & ON *kenna* to perceive; both akin to OE *can* know — more at CAN] *vt* (13c) **1** *archaic* : SEE **2** *chiefly dial* : RECOGNIZE **3** *chiefly Scot* : KNOW ~ *vi, chiefly Scot* : KNOW

²**ken** *n* (1590) **1 a** : the range of vision : SIGHT, VIEW ⟨'tis double death to drown in ~ of shore —Shak.⟩ **2** : the range of perception, understanding, or knowledge ⟨abstract words that are beyond the ~ of young children —Lois M. Rettie⟩

ke·naf \kə-'naf\ *n* [Per] (1891) : an African hibiscus (*Hibiscus cannabinus*) widely cultivated for its fiber; *also* : the fiber used esp. for cordage

Ken·dal green \'ken-d²l-\ *n* [*Kendal*, England] (1514) : a green woolen cloth resembling homespun or tweed

ken·do \'ken-(ˌ)dō\ *n* [Jp *kendō*, fr. *ken* sword + *dō* art] (1921) : a Japanese sport of fencing with bamboo swords

¹**ken·nel** \'ke-n²l\ *n* [ME *kenel*, ultim. fr. (assumed) VL *canile*, fr. L *canis* dog — more at HOUND] (14c) **1 a** : a shelter for a dog or cat **b** : an establishment for the breeding or boarding of dogs or cats **2** : a pack of dogs

²**kennel** *vb* **-neled** *or* **-nelled; -nel·ing** *or* **-nel·ling** *vi* (1552) : to take shelter in or as if in a kennel ~ *vt* : to put or keep in or as if in a kennel

³**kennel** *n* [alter. of *cannel* gutter] (15c) : a gutter in a street

¹**ken·ning** \'ke-niŋ\ *n* [ME, sight, view, fr. gerund of *kennen*] (1786) *chiefly Scot* : a perceptible but small amount

²**kenning** *n* [ON, fr. *kenna*] (1883) : a metaphorical compound word or phrase (as *swan-road* for *ocean*) used esp. in Old English and Old Norse poetry

ke·no \'kē-(ˌ)nō\ *n* [F *quine*, set of five winning numbers in a lottery + E -*o* (as in *lotto*)] (1814) : a game resembling bingo

ken·speck·le \'ken-ˌspe-kəl\ *adj* [prob. of Scand origin; akin to Norw *kjennspak* quick to recognize] (1616) *chiefly Scot* : CONSPICUOUS

kent·ledge \'kent-lij\ *n* [origin unknown] (1607) : pig iron or scrap metal used as ballast

Ken·tucky bluegrass \kən-'tə-kē-\ *n* [*Kentucky*, state of U.S.] (1849) : a valuable Old World pasture and meadow grass (*Poa pratensis*) naturalized in America — called also *bluegrass*

Kentucky coffee tree *n* (1875) : a tall No. American leguminous tree (*Gymnocladus dioica*) with bipinnate leaves and large woody brown pods whose seeds have been used as a substitute for coffee

Kentucky rifle *n* (1832) : a muzzle-loading long-barreled flintlock rifle developed in the 18th century in Pennsylvania and used extensively on the American frontier

Ke·ogh plan \'kē-(ˌ)ō-\ *n* [Eugene James *Keogh* †1989 Am. politician] (1974) : an individual retirement account for the self-employed

ke·pi \'kā-pē, 'ke-\ *also* **ké·pi** \'kā-\ *n* [F *képi*, fr. G dial. (Switzerland) *käppi* cap] (1861) : a military cap with a round flat top sloping toward the front and a visor

kept *past and past part of* KEEP

kerat- *or* **kerato-** *comb form* [ISV, fr. Gk *kerato-*, *keras* horn — more at HORN] : cornea ⟨keratitis⟩

ker·a·tin \'ker-ə-t²n\ *n* [ISV] (ca. 1849) : any of various sulfur-containing fibrous proteins that form the chemical basis of horny epidermal tissues (as hair and nails) — **ke·ra·ti·nous** \kə-'ra-t²n-əs\ *adj*

ke·ra·ti·ni·za·tion \ˌker-ə-tə-nə-'zā-shən, kə-ˌra-t²n-ə-\ *n* (ca. 1887) : conversion into keratin or keratinous tissue — **ke·ra·ti·nize** \'ker-ə-tə-ˌnīz, kə-'ra-t²n-ˌīz\ *vb*

ke·ra·ti·no·phil·ic \ˌker-ə-tə-nə-'fi-lik, kə-ˌra-t²n-ə-\ *adj* (1946) : exhibiting affinity for keratin (as in hair, skin, feathers, or horns) — used chiefly of fungi capable of growing on such materials

ker·a·ti·tis \ˌker-ə-'tī-təs\ *n, pl* **-tit·i·des** \-'ti-tə-ˌdēz\ [NL] (1858) : inflammation of the cornea of the eye

---

\ə\ abut \ᵊ\ kitten, F table \ər\ further \a\ ash \ā\ ace \ä\ mop, mar \aủ\ out \ch\ chin \e\ bet \ē\ easy \g\ go \i\ hit \ī\ ice \j\ job \ŋ\ sing \ō\ go \ȯ\ law \ȯi\ boy \th\ thin \t̲h̲\ the \ü\ loot \ủ\ foot \y\ yet \zh\ vision \à, k̲, ⁿ, œ, œ̄, ue, u̇e, ᵊ\ *see* Guide to Pronunciation

ker·a·to·con·junc·ti·vi·tis \'ker-ə-(,)tō-kən-jəŋ(k)-tə-'vī-təs\ *n* [NL] (1887) : combined inflammation of the cornea and conjunctiva

ker·a·to·plas·ty \'ker-ə-tō-,plas-tē\ *n, pl* **-ties** (ca. 1857) : plastic surgery on the cornea; *esp* : corneal grafting

ker·a·to·sis \,ker-ə-'tō-səs\ *n, pl* **-to·ses** \-,sēz\ [NL] (1885) : an area of skin marked by overgrowth of horny tissue — **ker·a·tot·ic** \-'tä-tik\ *adj*

kerb \'kərb\ *n* (1805) *Brit* : CURB 5

ker·chief \'kər-chəf, -,chēf\ *n, pl* **kerchiefs** \-chəfs, -,chēfs\ *also* **kerchieves** \-,chēvz\ [ME *courchef*, fr. OF *cuevrechief*, fr. *covrir* to cover + *chief* head — more at CHIEF] (13c) 1 : a square of cloth used as a head covering or worn as a scarf around the neck 2 : HANDKERCHIEF 1 — **ker·chiefed** \-chəft, -,chēft\ *adj*

kerf \'kərf\ *n* [ME, action of cutting, fr. OE *cyrf*; akin to OE *ceorfan* to carve — more at CARVE] (1523) 1 : a slit or notch made by a saw or cutting torch 2 : the width of cut made by a saw or cutting torch

ker·fuf·fle \kər-'fə-fəl\ *n* [alter. of *carfuffle*, fr. Sc *car*- (prob. fr. ScGael *cearr* wrong, awkward) + *fuffle* to become disheveled] (1946) *chiefly Brit* : DISTURBANCE, FUSS

Ker·man \kər-'män, ker-\ *var of* KIRMAN

ker·mes \'kər-(,)mēz\ *n* [F *kermès*, fr. Ar *qirmiz*] (1603) : the dried bodies of the females of various scale insects (genus *Kermes*) that are found on a Mediterranean oak (*Quercus coccifera*) and constitute a red dyestuff; *also* : the dye

ker·mis \'kər-məs\ *or* **ker·mess** \-məs, -,mes\ *or* **ker·messe** \-məs, -,mes\ *n* [D *kermis*, fr. MD *kercmisse*, fr. *kerc, kerke* church + *misse* mass, church festival] (1577) 1 : an outdoor festival of the Low Countries 2 : a fair held usu. for charitable purposes

¹kern *or* **kerne** \'kərn, 'kern\ *n* [ME *kerne*, fr. MIr *cethern* band of soldiers] (15c) 1 : a light-armed foot soldier of medieval Ireland or Scotland 2 : YOKEL

²kern \'kərn\ *n* [F *carne* corner, fr. F dial., fr. L *cardin-, cardo* hinge] (1683) : a part of a typeset letter that projects beyond its side bearings

ker·nel \'kər-nᵊl\ *n* [ME, fr. OE *cyrnel*, dim. of *corn*] (bef. 12c) 1 *chiefly dial* : a fruit seed 2 : the inner softer part of a seed, fruit stone, or nut 3 : a whole seed of a cereal ⟨a ~ of corn⟩ 4 : a central or essential part : GERM ⟨like many stereotypes . . . this one too contains some ~s of truth —S. M. Lyman⟩ 5 : a subset of the elements of one set (as a group) that a function (as a homomorphism) maps onto an identity element of another set

kern·ite \'kər-,nīt\ *n* [Kern Co., Calif.] (1927) : a mineral that consists of a hydrous borate of sodium and is an important source of borax

ker·o·gen \'ker-ə-jən\ *n* [Gk *kēros* wax + E *-gen* — more at CERUMEN] (1906) : bituminous material occurring in shale and yielding oil when heated

ker·o·sene *or* **ker·o·sine** \'ker-ə-,sēn, ,ker-ə-', 'kar-, ,kar-\ *n* [Gk *kēros* + E *-ene* (as in *camphene*)] (1854) : a flammable hydrocarbon oil usu. obtained by distillation of petroleum and used for a fuel and as a solvent and thinner

ker·ria \'ker-ē-ə\ *n* [NL, fr. William Kerr †1814 Eng. gardener] (1823) : a shrub (*Kerria japonica*) of the rose family that is native to China and Japan and has solitary yellow and often double flowers

ker·ry \'ker-ē\ *n, pl* **kerries** *often cap* [County *Kerry*, Ireland] (1829) : any of an Irish breed of small hardy black dairy cattle

Kerry blue terrier *n* (1922) : any of an Irish breed of medium-sized terriers with a long squarish head, deep chest, and silky bluish coat

ker·sey \'kər-zē\ *n, pl* **kerseys** [ME, fr. *Kersey*, England] (14c) 1 a : a coarse ribbed woolen cloth for hose and work clothes b : a heavy wool or wool and cotton fabric used esp. for uniforms and coats 2 : a garment of kersey

ker·sey·mere \'kər-zē-,mir\ *n* [alter. of *cassimere*] (1798) : a fine woolen fabric with a close nap made in fancy twill weaves

ke·ryg·ma \kə-'rig-mə\ *n* [Gk *kērygma*, fr. *kēryssein* to proclaim, fr. *kēryx* herald — more at CADUCEUS] (1889) : the apostolic proclamation of salvation through Jesus Christ — **ker·yg·mat·ic** \,ker-ig-'ma-tik\ *adj*

kes·trel \'kes-trəl\ *n* [ME *castrel*, fr. MF *crecerelle*, fr. *crecelle* rattle; fr. its cry] (15c) : any of various small chiefly Old World falcons (genus *Falco*) that usu. hover in the air while searching for prey: as a : a common Eurasian falcon (*F. tinnunculus*) b : an American falcon (*F. sparverius*) having a reddish brown back and tail and bluish gray wings

ket- *or* **keto-** *comb form* [ISV] : ketone ⟨*ketosis*⟩

ketch \'kech\ *n* [alter. of *catch*, fr. ME *cache*] (ca. 1649) : a fore-and-aft rigged vessel similar to a yawl but with a larger mizzen and with the mizzenmast stepped farther forward

ketch·up \'ke-chəp, 'ka-\ *n* [Malay *kēchap* fish sauce] (ca. 1690) : a seasoned pureed condiment usu. made from tomatoes

ke·tene \'kē-,tēn\ *n* [ISV] (1907) : a colorless poisonous gas C_2H_2O of penetrating odor used esp. as an acetylating agent; *also* : any of various derivatives of this compound

ke·to \'kē-(,)tō\ *adj* [*ket-*] (1891) : of or relating to a ketone; *also* : containing a ketone group

ke·to·gen·e·sis \,kē-tō-'je-nə-səs\ *n* [NL] (1915) : the production of ketone bodies (as in diabetes) — **ke·to·gen·ic** \-'je-nik\ *adj*

ketch

ke·to·glu·tar·ic acid \-glü-'tar-ik-\ *n* (1908) : either of two crystalline keto derivatives $C_5H_6O_5$ of glutaric acid; *esp* : the alpha keto isomer formed in various metabolic processes (as the Krebs cycle)

ke·tone \'kē-,tōn\ *n* [G *Keton*, alter. of *Aceton* acetone] (1851) : an organic compound (as acetone) with a carbonyl group attached to two carbon atoms — **ke·ton·ic** \kē-'tä-nik\ *adj*

ketone body *n* (1915) : any of the three compounds acetoacetic acid, acetone, and beta-hydroxybutyric acid which are normal intermediates in lipid metabolism and accumulate in the blood and urine in abnormal amounts in conditions of impaired metabolism (as diabetes mellitus)

ke·tose \'kē-,tōs, -,tōz\ *n* [ISV] (1902) : a sugar (as fructose) containing one ketone group per molecule

ke·to·sis \kē-'tō-səs\ *n* [NL] (1917) : an abnormal increase of ketone bodies in the body — **ke·tot·ic** \-'tä-tik\ *adj*

ke·to·ste·roid \,kē-tō-'stir-,óid *also* -'ster-\ *n* [ISV] (1939) : a steroid (as cortisone or estrone) containing a ketone group

ket·tle \'ke-tᵊl\ *n* [ME *ketel*, fr. ON *ketill* (akin to OE *cietel* kettle), both fr. a prehistoric Gmc word borrowed fr. L *catillus*, dim. of *catinus* bowl] (13c) 1 : a metallic vessel usu. used for boiling liquids; *esp* : TEAKETTLE 2 : KETTLEDRUM 3 a : POTHOLE 1b b : a steep-sided hollow without surface drainage esp. in a deposit of glacial drift

ket·tle·drum \-,drəm\ *n* (1602) : a percussion instrument that consists of a hollow brass, copper, or fiberglass hemisphere with a calfskin or plastic head whose tension can be changed to vary the pitch

kettle of fish (1742) 1 : a bad state of affairs : MESS 2 : something to be considered or reckoned with : MATTER ⟨books and discs . . . were two very different *kettles of fish* —Roland Gelatt⟩

Kew·pie \'kyü-pē\ *trademark* — used for a small chubby doll with a topknot of hair

¹key \'kē\ *n* [ME, fr. OE *cǣg*; akin to OFris *kēi* key] (bef. 12c) 1 a : a usu. metal instrument by which the bolt of a lock is turned b : any of various devices having the form or function of such a key 2 a : a means of gaining or preventing entrance, possession, or control b : an instrumental or deciding factor 3 a : something that gives an explanation or identification or provides a solution ⟨the ~ to a riddle⟩ b : a list of words or phrases giving an explanation of symbols or abbreviations c : an aid to interpretation or identification : CLUE d : an arrangement of the salient characters of a group of plants or animals or of taxa designed to facilitate identification e : a map legend 4 a (1) : COTTER PIN (2) : COTTER b : a keystone in an arch c : a small piece of wood or metal used as a wedge or for preventing motion between parts 5 a : one of the levers of a keyboard musical instrument that actuates the mechanism and produces the tones b : a lever that controls a vent in the side of a woodwind instrument or a valve in a brass instrument c : a part to be depressed by a finger that serves as one unit of a keyboard 6 : SAMARA 7 : a system of tones and harmonies generated from a hierarchical scale of seven tones based on a tonic ⟨the ~ of G major⟩ 8 a : characteristic style or tone b : the tone or pitch of a voice c : the predominant tone of a photograph with respect to its lightness or darkness 9 : a decoration or charm resembling a key 10 : a small switch for opening or closing an electric circuit ⟨a telegraph ~⟩ 11 : the set of instructions governing the encipherment and decipherment of messages 12 : a free-throw area in basketball — **keyed** \'kēd\ *adj* — **key·less** \'kē-ləs\ *adj*

²key *vt* (14c) 1 : to lock with or as if with a key : FASTEN: as a : to secure (as a pulley on a shaft) by a key b : to finish off (an arch) by inserting a keystone 2 : to regulate the musical pitch of 3 : to bring into harmony or conformity : make appropriate : ATTUNE ⟨remarks ~ed to a situation⟩ 4 : to identify (a biological specimen) by a key 5 : to provide with identifying or explanatory cross-references ⟨instructions ~ed to accompanying drawings —John Gartner⟩ 6 : to make nervous, tense, or excited — usu. used with *up* ⟨was ~ed up over her impending operation⟩ 7 : KEYBOARD — often used with *in* ~ *vi* 1 : to use a key 2 : to observe the position or movement of an opposing player in football in order to anticipate the play — usu. used with *on* 3 : KEYBOARD

³key *adj* (1913) : IMPORTANT, FUNDAMENTAL ⟨~ issues⟩

⁴key *n* [Sp *cayo*, fr. Taino] (1697) : a low island or reef; *specif* : any of the coral islets off the southern coast of Florida

⁵key *n* [by shortening & alter. fr. *kilo*] (1968) *slang* : a kilogram esp. of marijuana or heroin

¹key·board \'kē-,bórd, -,bórd\ *n* (1819) 1 : a bank of keys on a musical instrument (as a piano) that usu. consists of seven white and five raised black keys to the octave 2 : an assemblage of systematically arranged keys by which a machine or device is operated 3 : a board on which keys for locks are hung

²keyboard *vt* (1961) : to capture or set (as data or text) by means of a keyboard ~ *vi* : to operate a machine (as for typesetting) by means of a keyboard — **key·board·er** *n*

key·board·ist \'kē-,bór-dist, -,bór-\ *n* (1973) : a person who plays a keyboard musical instrument

key·but·ton \'kē-,bə-tᵊn\ *n* (ca. 1920) : KEY 5c

key club *n* [fr. the key to the premises provided to each member] (1962) : an informal private club serving liquor and providing entertainment

key deer *n, often cap* K (1950) : a very small rare white-tailed deer (*Odocoileus virginianus clavium*) native to the Florida Keys

key grip \,kē-\ *n* (1979) : the technician in charge of moving and setting up camera tracks and scenery in a motion-picture or television production

¹key·hole \'kē-,hōl\ *n* (ca. 1592) 1 : a hole for receiving a key 2 : KEY 12

²keyhole *adj* (1937) 1 : revealingly intimate ⟨a ~ report⟩ 2 : intent on revealing intimate details ⟨~ columnists⟩

keyhole saw *n* (1777) : a narrow pointed fine-toothed handsaw used for cutting curves of short radius

key light *n* (ca. 1937) : the main light illuminating a photographic subject

key lime *n, often cap* K (1929) : a lime grown esp. in the Florida Keys and adjacent areas

key lime pie *n, often cap* K (1954) : a usu. meringue-topped lime custard pie traditionally made with key limes

Keynes·ian·ism \'kān-zē-ə-,ni-zəm\ *n* (1946) : the economic theories and programs ascribed to John M. Keynes and his followers; *specif* : the advocacy of monetary and fiscal programs by government to increase employment and spending — **Keynes·ian** \'kān-zē-ən\ *n or adj*

¹key·note \'kē-,nōt\ *n* (1776) 1 : the first and harmonically fundamental tone of a scale 2 : the fundamental or central fact, idea, or mood ⟨sadness is the ~ of this little collection —*Books Abroad*⟩

²keynote *vt* (1914) 1 : to set the keynote of 2 : to deliver the keynote address at — **key·not·er** *n*

keynote address *n* (ca. 1908) : an address designed to present the issues of primary interest to an assembly (as a political convention) and often to arouse unity and enthusiasm — called also *keynote speech*

keynote speaker *n* (1950) : one who delivers a keynote address

key·pad \'kē-,pad\ *n* (1975) : a small often handheld keyboard

¹key·punch \'kē-,pənch\ *n* (1918) : a machine with a keyboard used to cut holes or notches in punched cards

²keypunch *vt* (1959) : to enter (data) on punched cards with a key-punch — **key·punch·er** *n*

key signature *n* (1875) : the sharps or flats placed after a clef in music to indicate the key

key·stone \'kē-,stōn\ *n* (ca. 1637) **1** : the wedge-shaped piece at the crown of an arch that locks the other pieces in place — see ARCH illustration **2** : something on which associated things depend for support ⟨determination, a ∼ of the puritan ethic —L. S. Lewis⟩

¹key·stroke \-,strōk\ *n* (ca. 1910) : the act or an instance of depressing a key on a keyboard

²keystroke *vt* (1966) : KEYBOARD

key·way \-,wā\ *n* (ca. 1864) **1** : a groove or channel for a key **2** : the aperture for the key in a lock having a flat metal key

key word *n* (1859) : a word that is a key: as **a** : a word exemplifying the meaning or value of a letter or symbol **b** *usu* **key·word** \-,wərd\ : a significant word from a title or document used as an index to content

khad·dar \'kä-dər\ *or* **kha·di** \'kä-dē\ *n* [Hindi *khādar, khādī*] (ca. 1885) : homespun cotton cloth of India

kha·ki \'ka-kē, 'kä-kē, *Canad often* 'kär-\ *n* [Hindi *khākī* dust-colored, fr. *khāk* dust, fr. Per] (1857) **1** : a light yellowish brown **2 a** : a khaki‐colored cloth made usu. of cotton or wool and used esp. for military uniforms **b** : a garment of this cloth; *esp* : a military uniform — usu. used in pl. — **khaki** *adj*

Khal·kha \'kal-kə, 'kal-kə\ *n* (1873) **1** : a member of a Mongol people of Outer Mongolia **2** : the language of the Khalkha people used as the official language of the Mongolian People's Republic

kham·sin \kam-'sēn\ *n* [Ar *rīḥ al-khamsīn* the wind of the fifty (days between Easter and Pentecost)] (1685) : a hot southerly Egyptian wind

¹khan \'kän *also* 'kan\ *n* [ME *caan*, fr. MF, of Turkic origin; akin to Turk *han* prince] (15c) **1** : a medieval sovereign of China and ruler over the Turkish, Tatar, and Mongol tribes **2** : a local chieftain or man of rank in some countries of central Asia

²khan *n* [Ar *khān*] (1614) : a caravansary or rest house in some Asian countries

khan·ate \'kä-,nāt *also* 'ka-\ *n* (1799) : the state or jurisdiction of a khan

khap·ra beetle \'ka-prə-, 'kä-\ *n* [Hindi *khaprā*, lit., destroyer] (1928) : a dermestid beetle (*Trogoderma granarium*) that is native to the Indian subcontinent and is now a serious pest of stored grain in most parts of the world

khat \'kät\ *n* [Ar *qāt*] (1858) : a shrub (*Catha edulis*) cultivated in the Middle East and Africa for its leaves and buds that are the source of an habituating stimulant when chewed or used as a tea

khe·dive \kə-'dēv\ *n* [F *khédive*, fr. Turk *hidiv*] (1867) : a ruler of Egypt from 1867 to 1914 governing as a viceroy of the sultan of Turkey — **khe·div·ial** \-'dē-vē-əl\ *or* **khe·div·al** \-'dē-vəl\ *adj*

Khmer \kə-'mer\ *n, pl* **Khmer** *or* **Khmers** (1876) **1** : a member of an aboriginal people of Cambodia **2** : the Mon-Khmer language of the Khmer people that is the official language of Cambodia — **Khmer** *adj*

Khoi·khoi \'kȯi-,kȯi\ *n, pl* **Khoikhoi** (1791) : HOTTENTOT

Khoi·san \'kȯi-,sän, -'sän\ *n* [*Khoikhoi* + *San*] (1930) **1** : a group of African peoples speaking Khoisan languages **2** : a family of African languages comprising principally Hottentot and the Bushman languages

khoum \'küm, 'kúm\ *n* [modif. of Ar *khums*, lit., one fifth] (1973) — see *ouguiya* at MONEY table

Kho·war \'kō-,wär\ *n* (1882) : an Indo-Aryan language of northwest Pakistan

ki·ang \kē-'äŋ\ *n* [Tibetan *rkyaṅ*] (1869) : an Asian wild ass (*Equus hemionus kiang* syn. *E. kiang*) usu. with reddish back and sides and white underparts, muzzle, and belly

kiaugh \'kyäk\ *n* [origin unknown] (1786) *Scot* : TROUBLE, ANXIETY

kib·be *or* **kib·beh** *or* **kib·bi** \'ki-bē\ *n* [Ar *kubbah*] (1937) : a Near Eastern dish of ground lamb and bulgur that is eaten cooked or raw

¹kib·ble \'ki-bəl\ *vt* **kib·bled**; **kib·bling** \-b(ə-)liŋ\ [origin unknown] (ca. 1790) : to grind coarsely ⟨*kibbled* dog biscuit⟩ ⟨*kibbled* grain⟩

²kibble *n* (1942) : coarsely ground meal or grain (as for animal feed)

kib·butz \ki-'búts, -'büts\ *n, pl* **kib·but·zim** \-,bùt-'sēm, -,büt-\ [NHeb *qibbūṣ*] (1944) : a communal farm or settlement in Israel

kib·butz·nik \-'bùt-snik, -'büt-\ *n* [Yiddish *kibutsnik*, fr. *kibuts* kibbutz (fr. NHeb *qibbūṣ*) + -*nik*, agent suffix] (1947) : a member of a kibbutz

kibe \'kīb\ *n* [ME] (14c) : an ulcerated chilblain esp. on the heel

ki·bitz *also* **kib·bitz** \'ki-bəts, kə-'bits\ *vb* [Yiddish *kibetsn*] *vi* (1927) : to act as a kibitzer ∼ *vt* : to observe as a kibitzer; *esp* : to be a kibitzer at ⟨∼ a card game⟩

ki·bitz·er *also* **kib·bitz·er** \'ki-bət-sər, kə-'bit-\ *n* (1922) : one who looks on and often offers unwanted advice or comment esp. at a card game; *broadly* : one who offers opinions

ki·bosh \'kī-,bäsh, kī-'\ *n* [origin unknown] (1836) : something that serves as a check or stop ⟨put the ∼ on that⟩ — **kibosh** *vt*

¹kick \'kik\ *vb* [ME *kiken*] *vi* (14c) **1 a** : to strike out with the foot or feet **b** : to make a kick in football **2 a** : to show opposition : RESIST, REBEL **b** : to protest strenuously or urgently : express grave discontent; *broadly* : COMPLAIN **3** : to function with vitality and energy ⟨alive and ∼ing⟩ **4** *of a firearm* : to recoil when fired **5** : to go from one place to another as circumstance or whim dictates ∼ *vt* **1 a** : to strike, thrust, or hit with the foot **b** : to strike suddenly and forcefully as if with the foot **c** : to remove from a position or status ⟨∼ed him off the team⟩ **2** : to score by kicking a ball **3** : to heap reproaches upon (oneself) ⟨∼ed themselves for not going⟩ **4** : to free oneself of (as a drug habit) — **kick·able** \'ki-kə-bəl\ *adj* — **kick ass** : to kick butt — often considered vulgar — **kick butt** : to use forceful or coercive measures in order to achieve a purpose; *also* : to succeed or win overwhelmingly — **kick over the traces** : to cast off restraint, authority, or control — **kick the bucket** : DIE — **kick up one's heels 1** : to

show sudden delight **2** : to have a lively time — **kick upstairs** : to promote to a higher but less desirable position

²kick *n* (1530) **1 a** : a blow or sudden forceful thrust with the foot; *specif* : a sudden propelling of a ball with the foot **b** : the power to kick **c** : a rhythmic motion of the legs used in swimming **d** : a burst of speed in racing **2 a** : a sudden forceful jolt or thrust suggesting a kick; *esp* : the recoil of a gun **3** : POCKET, WALLET **4 a** : a feeling or expression of opposition or objection ⟨a ∼ against the administration⟩ **b** : the grounds for objection **5 a** : an effect suggestive of a kick ⟨chili with a ∼⟩ **b** : a stimulating or pleasurable effect or experience **c** : pursuit of an absorbing or obsessive new interest ⟨a skiing ∼⟩ **6** : a sudden and striking surprise, revelation, or turn of events

kick around *vi* (1839) **1** : to wander or pass time aimlessly **2** : to lie about mostly unnoticed or forgotten ∼ *vt* **1** : to treat in an inconsiderate or high-handed fashion **2** : to consider, examine, or discuss from various angles

kick–ass \'kik-,as\ *adj* (1970) : strikingly tough, aggressive, or uncompromising — often considered vulgar

kick·back \'kik-,bak\ *n* (1920) **1** : a sharp violent reaction **2** : a return of a part of a sum received often because of confidential agreement or coercion ⟨every city contract had been let with a ten percent ∼ to city officials —D. K. Shipler⟩

kick·board \-,bōrd, -,bȯrd\ *n* (1949) : a buoyant rectangular board held by a swimmer while developing kicking techniques

kick·box·ing \-,bäk-siŋ\ *n* (1971) : boxing in which boxers are permitted to kick with bare feet as in karate — **kick·box·er** \-sər\ *n*

kick·er *n* (ca. 1580) **1** : one that kicks or kicks something **2** : KICK 6

kick in *vt* (1908) : CONTRIBUTE ∼ *vi* **1** *slang* : DIE **2** : to make a contribution

kick·off \'kik-,ȯf\ *n* (1857) **1** : a kick that puts the ball into play in a football or soccer game **2** : COMMENCEMENT 1 ⟨the campaign ∼⟩

kick off *vi* (1857) **1** : to start or resume play in football by a placekick **2** : to begin proceedings **3** *slang* : DIE ∼ *vt* : to mark the beginning of

kick out *vt* (1697) : to dismiss or eject forcefully or summarily

kick over *vi* (1951) : to begin to fire — used of an internal combustion engine ∼ *vt* : TURN OVER 1b

kick pleat *n* (1926) : a short inverted pleat (as at the bottom of a skirt) used to give breadth

kick·shaw \'kik-,shȯ\ *n* [by folk etymology fr. F *quelque chose* something] (1597) **1** : a fancy dish : DELICACY **2** : TRINKET, GEWGAW

kick·stand \'kik-,stand\ *n* [fr. its being put in position by a kick] (1947) : a swiveling metal bar or rod for holding up a 2-wheeled vehicle (as a bicycle) when not in use

kick turn *n* (1910) : a standing half turn in skiing made by swinging one ski high with a jerk and planting it in the desired direction and then lifting the other ski into a parallel position

kick·up \'kik-,əp\ *n* (ca. 1793) : a noisy quarrel : ROW

kick up *vt* (1756) **1** : to stir up : PROVOKE ⟨*kick up* a fuss⟩ **2** : to cause to rise upward ⟨clouds of dust *kicked up* by passing cars⟩ ∼ *vi* : to give evidence of disorder

kicky \'ki-kē\ *adj* (1966) : providing a kick or thrill : EXCITING; *also* : excitingly fashionable

¹kid \'kid\ *n* [ME *kide*, of Scand origin; akin to ON *kith* kid] (13c) **1 a** : a young goat **b** : a young individual of various animals related to the goat **2 a** : the flesh, fur, or skin of a kid **b** : something made of kid **3** : a young person; *esp* : CHILD — often used as a generalized reference to one esp. younger or less experienced ⟨the ∼ on the pro golf tour⟩ ⟨poor ∼⟩ — **kid·dish** \'ki-dish\ *adj*

²kid *vi* **kid·ded**; **kid·ding** (15c) : to bring forth young — used of a goat or an antelope

³kid *vb* **kid·ded**; **kid·ding** [prob. fr. ¹*kid*] *vt* (1902) **1** : to deceive as a joke ⟨it's the truth; I wouldn't ∼ you⟩ **2** : to make fun of ∼ *vi* : to engage in good-humored fooling or horseplay — often used with *around* — **kid·der** *n* — **kid·ding·ly** \'ki-diŋ-lē\ *adv*

Kid·der·min·ster \'ki-dər-,min(t)-stər\ *n* [*Kidderminster*, England] (1836) : an ingrain carpet — called also *Kidderminster carpet*

kid·die *or* **kid·dy** \'ki-dē\ *n, pl* **kiddies** *often attrib* [¹*kid*] (1889) : a small child

kid·dush \'ki-dəsh, -dish; ki-'düsh\ *n* [LHeb *qiddūsh* sanctification] (1753) : a ceremonial blessing pronounced over wine or bread in a Jewish home or synagogue on a holy day (as the Sabbath)

kid–glove \'kid-'gləv\ *adj* (1888) : marked by extreme care or deference ⟨∼ treatment⟩

kid glove *n* (1832) : a dress glove made of kid leather — **kid–gloved** \'kid-'gləvd\ *adj* — **with kid gloves** : with special consideration

kid leather *n* (1687) **1** : a soft pliable leather made from kidskin **2** : a glove leather made from lambskin or goatskin

kid·nap \'kid-,nap\ *vt* **-napped** *or* **-naped** \-,napt\; **-nap·ping** *or* **-nap·ing** [prob. back-formation fr. *kidnapper*, fr. *kid* + obs. *napper* thief] (1682) : to seize and detain or carry away by unlawful force or fraud and often with a demand for ransom — **kid·nap·pee** *or* **kid·nap·ee** \,kid-,na-'pē\ *n* — **kid·nap·per** *or* **kid·nap·er** *n*

kid·ney \'kid-nē\ *n, pl* **kidneys** [ME] (14c) **1 a** : one of a pair of vertebrate organs situated in the body cavity near the spinal column that excrete waste products of metabolism, in humans are bean-shaped organs about 4½ inches (11½ centimeters) long lying behind the peritoneum in a mass of fatty tissue, and consist chiefly of nephrons by which urine is secreted, collected, and discharged into a main cavity whence it is conveyed by the ureter to the bladder **b** : any of various excretory organs of invertebrate animals **2** : the kidney of an animal eaten as food **3** : sort or kind esp. with regard to temperament ⟨a nice helpful guy, of a different ∼ entirely from the . . . Secret Police —Paula Lecler⟩

kidney bean *n* (1548) **1** : an edible and nutritious seed of any cultivated bean of the common species (*Phaseolus vulgaris*); *esp* : a large dark red bean seed **2** : a plant bearing kidney beans

kidney stone *n* (1946) : a calculus in the kidney

\ə\ abut \ᵊ\ kitten, F table \ər\ further \a\ ash \ā\ ace \ä\ mop, mar
\au̇\ out \ch\ chin \e\ bet \ē\ easy \g\ go \i\ hit \ī\ ice \j\ job
\ŋ\ sing \ō\ go \ȯ\ law \ȯi\ boy \th\ thin \t͟h\ the \ü\ loot \ú\ foot
\y\ yet \zh\ vision \à, k̲, ⁿ, œ, œ̄, ᵫ, ᵫ̄, ᵊ\ *see* Guide to Pronunciation

kid·skin \'kid-ˌskin\ *n* (14c) : the skin of a young or sometimes a mature goat; *also* : KID LEATHER

kid stuff *n* (1929) **1** : something befitting or appropriate only to children   **2** : something extremely simple or easy

kiel·ba·sa \kēl-'bä-sə, kil- *also* ki-'bä-sə\ *n, pl* **-basas** *also* **-ba·sy** \-'bä-sē\ [Pol *kiełbasa*] (ca. 1939) : a smoked sausage of Polish origin

kie·sel·guhr \'kē-zəl-ˌgur\ *n* [G *Kieselgur*] (1875) : loose or porous diatomite

kie·ser·ite \'kē-zə-ˌrīt\ *n* [G *Kieserit*, fr. Dietrich *Kieser* †1862 Ger. physician] (1862) : a mineral that is a white hydrous magnesium sulfate

kif \'kif, 'kēf\ *var of* KEF

kike \'kīk\ *n* [origin unknown] (1904) : JEW — usu. taken to be offensive

Ki·ku·yu \kē-'kü-(ˌ)yü\ *n, pl* **Kikuyu** *or* **Kikuyus** (1894) **1** : a member of a Bantu-speaking people of Kenya   **2** : the Bantu language of the Kikuyu people

kil·der·kin \'kil-dər-kən\ *n* [ME, fr. MD *kindekijn*, fr. ML *quintale* quintal] (14c) **1** : an English unit of capacity equal to ½ barrel   **2** : CASK

ki·lim \kē-'lēm\ *n* [Turk, fr. Pers *kilīm*] (1881) : a pileless handwoven reversible rug or covering made in Turkey, Kurdistan, the Caucasus, Iran, and western Turkestan

¹kill \'kil\ *vb* [ME, perh. fr. (assumed) OE *cyllan*; akin to OE *cwellan* to kill — more at QUELL] *vt* (14c) **1 a** : to deprive of life   **b** (1) : to slaughter (as a hog) for food   (2) : to convert a food animal into (a kind of meat) by slaughtering   **2 a** : to put an end to ⟨~ competition⟩   **b** : DEFEAT, VETO ⟨~ed the amendment⟩   **c** : to mark for omission; *also* : DELETE   **3 a** : to destroy the vital or essential quality of ⟨~ed the pain with drugs⟩   **b** : to cause to stop ⟨~ the motor⟩   **c** : to check the flow of current through   **4** : to make a markedly favorable impression on ⟨she ~ed the audience⟩   **5** : to get through uneventfully ⟨~ time⟩; *also* : to get through (the time of a penalty) without being scored on ⟨~ a penalty⟩   **6 a** : to cause extreme pain to   **b** : to tire almost to the point of collapse   **7** : to hit (a shot) so hard in various games that a return is impossible   **8** : to consume (as a drink) totally ~ *vi* **1** : to deprive one of life   **2** : to make a markedly favorable impression ⟨was dressed to ~⟩

syn KILL, SLAY, MURDER, ASSASSINATE, DISPATCH, EXECUTE mean to deprive of life. KILL merely states the fact of death caused by an agency in any manner ⟨*killed* in an accident⟩ ⟨frost *killed* the plants⟩. SLAY is a chiefly literary term implying deliberateness and violence but not necessarily motive ⟨*slew* thousands of the Philistines⟩. MURDER specif. implies stealth and motive and premeditation and therefore full moral responsibility ⟨convicted of *murdering* a rival⟩. ASSASSINATE applies to deliberate killing openly or secretly often for political motives ⟨terrorists *assassinated* the Senator⟩. DISPATCH stresses quickness and directness in putting to death ⟨*dispatched* the sentry with one bullet⟩. EXECUTE stresses putting to death as a legal penalty ⟨*executed* by lethal gas⟩.

²kill *n* (1814) **1** : an act or instance of killing   **2** : something killed: as   **a** (1) : an animal shot in a hunt   (2) : animals killed in a hunt, season, or particular period of time   **b** : an enemy unit (as an airplane or ship) destroyed by military action   **c** : a return shot in any of various games (as badminton, handball, or table tennis) that is too hard for an opponent to handle

³kill *n, often cap* [D *kil*] (1669) : CHANNEL, CREEK — used chiefly in place names in Delaware, Pennsylvania, and New York

kill·deer \'kil-ˌdir\ *n, pl* **killdeers** *or* **killdeer** [imit.] (1731) : an American plover (*Charadrius vociferus*) characterized by two black breast bands and a plaintive penetrating cry

¹kill·er \'ki-lər\ *n* (15c) **1** : one that kills   **2** : KILLER WHALE   **3 a** : one that has a forceful, violent, or striking impact   **b** : one that is extremely difficult to deal with

²killer *adj* (1951) **1** : strikingly impressive or effective ⟨a ~ smile⟩ ⟨a ~ résumé⟩   **2** : extremely difficult to deal with ⟨a ~ fastball⟩; *also* : causing death or devastation ⟨a ~ tornado⟩

killdeer

killer bee *n* (1976) : AFRICANIZED BEE

killer cell *n* (1972) : a T cell that functions in cell-mediated immunity by destroying a cell (as a tumor cell) having a specific antigenic molecule on its surface — called also *killer T cell*

killer instinct *n* (1931) : an aggressive tenacious urge for domination in a struggle to attain a set goal

killer whale *n* (1884) : a small gregarious whale (*Orcinus orca*) that is black with a white ventral side and white oval-shaped patches behind the eyes and attains a length of 20 to 30 feet (6.1 to 9.1 meters) — called also *orca*

kil·li·fish \'ki-li-ˌfish\ *n* [*killie* killifish (perh. fr. ³*kill*) + *fish*] (1836) **1** : any of a family (Cyprinodontidae) of numerous small oviparous fishes much used as bait and in mosquito control   **2** : any of a family (Poeciliidae) of live-bearers

¹kill·ing \'ki-liŋ\ *n* (15c) **1** : the act of one that kills   **2** : KILL 2a   **3** : a sudden notable gain or profit

²killing *adj* (15c) **1** : that kills or relates to killing   **2** : highly amusing   **3** : extremely difficult to deal with ⟨the suspense is ~⟩; *also* : calling for great strength, stamina, or endurance ⟨a ~ schedule⟩ — **kill·ing·ly** \-lē\ *adv*

kill·joy \'kil-ˌjoi\ *n* (1776) : one who spoils the pleasure of others

kill off *vt* (1607) : to destroy in large numbers or totally

kiln \'kiln, 'kil\ *n* [ME *kilne*, fr. OE *cyln*, fr. L *culina* kitchen, fr. *coquere* to cook — more at COOK] (bef. 12c) : an oven, furnace, or heated enclosure used for processing a substance by burning, firing, or drying — **kiln** *vt*

ki·lo \'kē-(ˌ)lō *also* 'ki-\ *n, pl* **kilos** (1870) : KILOGRAM

Kilo (1952) — a communications code word for the letter *k*

kilo- *comb form* [F, modif. of Gk *chilioi*] : thousand ⟨*kilo*ton⟩

ki·lo·bar \'kē-lə-ˌbär, 'ki-lə-\ *n* [ISV] (1926) : a unit of pressure equal to 1000 bars

ki·lo·base \-ˌbās\ *n* (1975) : a unit of measure of the length of a nucleic-acid chain that equals one thousand base pairs

ki·lo·bit \-ˌbit\ *n* [ISV] (1961) **1** : 1000 bits   **2** : 1024 bits

ki·lo·byte \-ˌbīt\ *n* [fr. the fact that 1024 (2¹⁰) is the power of 2 closest to 1000] (1970) : 1024 bytes

ki·lo·cal·o·rie \-ˌka-lə-rē, -ˌkal-rē\ *n* [ISV] (1894) : CALORIE 1b

ki·lo·cy·cle \'ki-lə-ˌsī-kəl\ *n* [ISV] (1921) : 1000 cycles; *esp* : KILOHERTZ

ki·lo·gauss \'kē-lə-ˌgaus, 'ki-lə-\ *n* [ISV] (1895) : 1000 gauss

ki·lo·gram \-ˌgram\ *n* [F *kilogramme*, fr. *kilo-* + *gramme* gram] (1797) **1** : the base unit of mass in the International System of Units that is equal to the mass of a prototype agreed upon by international convention and that is nearly equal to the mass of 1000 cubic centimeters of water at the temperature of its maximum density — see METRIC SYSTEM table   **2** : a unit of force equal to the weight of a kilogram mass under a gravitational attraction equal to that of the earth

kilogram-meter *n* (1886) : the meter-kilogram-second gravitational unit of work and energy equal to the work done by a kilogram force acting through a distance of one meter in the direction of the force : about 7.235 foot-pounds

ki·lo·hertz \'ki-lə-ˌhərts, 'kē-lə-, -ˌherts\ *n* [ISV] (1929) : 1000 hertz

ki·lo·joule \-ˌjü(ə)l\ *n* [ISV] (ca. 1889) : 1000 joules

kilo·li·ter \'ki-lə-ˌlē-tər\ *n* [F *kilolitre*, fr. *kilo-* + *litre* liter] (1810) — see METRIC SYSTEM table

ki·lo·me·ter \÷-kə-'lä-mə-tər, ÷-ki-; 'ki-lə-ˌmē-tər\ *n* [F *kilomètre*, fr. *kilo-* + *mètre* meter] (1810) — see METRIC SYSTEM table
   usage In No. American speech *kilometer* is most often pronounced with primary stress on the second syllable. This pronunciation is also heard frequently in British speech. Those who object to second syllable stress say that the first syllable should be stressed in accord with the stress patterns of *centimeter*, *millimeter*, etc. However, the pronunciation of *kilometer* does not parallel that of other metric compounds. From 1828 to 1841 Noah Webster indicated only second syllable stress, and his successor added a first syllable stress variant in the first Merriam-Webster dictionary of 1847. Thus, both pronunciations are venerable. Most scientists use second syllable stress, although first syllable stress seems to occur with a higher rate of frequency among scientists than among nonscientists.

ki·lo·par·sec \'ki-lə-ˌpär-ˌsek, 'kē-lə-\ *n* (1922) : 1000 parsecs

ki·lo·pas·cal \'ki-lə-ˌpas-'kal\ *n* (1978) : 1000 pascals

ki·lo·rad \'ki-lə-ˌrad\ *n* [ISV] (1965) : 1000 rads

ki·lo·ton \-ˌtən *also* -ˌtän\ *n* (1950) **1** : 1000 tons   **2** : an explosive force equivalent to that of 1000 tons of TNT

ki·lo·volt \-ˌvōlt\ *n* [ISV] (ca. 1898) : a unit of potential difference equal to 1000 volts

kilo·watt \'ki-lə-ˌwät\ *n* [ISV] (1884) : 1000 watts

kilowatt-hour *n* (1892) : a unit of work or energy equal to that expended by one kilowatt in one hour or to 3.6 million joules

¹kilt \'kilt\ *vb* [ME, of Scand origin; akin to ON *kjalta* lap, fold of a gathered skirt] *vt* (14c) **1** *chiefly dial* : to tuck up (as a skirt)   **2** : to equip with a kilt ~ *vi* : to move nimbly

²kilt *n* (ca. 1730) **1** : a knee-length pleated skirt usu. of tartan worn by men in Scotland and by Scottish regiments in the British armies   **2** : a garment that resembles a Scottish kilt

kil·ter \'kil-tər\ *n* [origin unknown] (1628) : proper or usual state or condition ⟨out of ~⟩

kilt·ie \'kil-tē\ *n* (1842) **1** *or* **kilty** : one who wears a kilt   **2** : a shoe with a long slashed tongue that folds over the instep; *also* : such a tongue

kim·ber·lite \'kim-bər-ˌlīt\ *n* [*Kimberley*, So. Africa + ¹-*ite*] (1887) : an agglomerate biotite-peridotite that occurs in pipes esp. in southern Africa and that often contains diamonds

Kim·bun·du \kim-'bun-(ˌ)dü\ *n* (ca. 1895) : a Bantu language of northern Angola

kim·chi *also* **kim·chee** \'kim-chē\ *n* [Korean *kimch'i*] (1898) : a vegetable pickle seasoned with garlic, red pepper, and ginger that is the national dish of Korea

ki·mo·no \kə-'mō-(ˌ)nō, -nə\ *n, pl* **-nos** [Jp, clothes, fr. *ki* wearing + *mono* thing] (1886) **1** : a long robe with wide sleeves traditionally worn with a broad sash as an outer garment by the Japanese   **2** : a loose dressing gown or jacket — **ki·mo·noed** \-(ˌ)nōd, -nəd\ *adj*

¹kin \'kin\ *n* [ME, fr. OE *cynn*; akin to OHG *chunni* race, L *genus* birth, race, kind, Gk *genos*, L *gignere* to beget, Gk *gignesthai* to be born] (bef. 12c) **1** : a group of persons of common ancestry : CLAN   **2 a** : one's relatives : KINDRED   **b** : KINSMAN ⟨he wasn't any ~ to you — Jean Stafford⟩   **3** *archaic* : KINSHIP

²kin *adj* (1597) : KINDRED, RELATED

-kin \kən\ *also* **-kins** \kənz\ *n suffix* [ME, fr. MD -*kin*; akin to OHG -*chīn*, dim. suffix] : little ⟨cat*kin*⟩ ⟨baby*kins*⟩

ki·na \'kē-nə\ *n* [New Guinea Pidgin, lit., a kind of shell] (1975) — see MONEY table

ki·nase \'kī-ˌnās, -ˌnāz\ *n* [ISV, fr. *kinetic*] (1947) : an enzyme that catalyzes the transfer of phosphate groups from a high-energy phosphate-containing molecule (as ATP) to a substrate

¹kind \'kīnd\ *n* [ME *kinde*, fr. OE *cynd*; akin to OE *cynn* kin] (bef. 12c) **1 a** *archaic* : NATURE   **b** *archaic* : FAMILY, LINEAGE   **2** *archaic* : MANNER   **3** : fundamental nature or quality : ESSENCE   **4 a** : a group united by common traits or interests : CATEGORY   **b** : a specific or recognized variety ⟨what ~ of car do you drive⟩   **c** : a doubtful or barely admissible member of a category ⟨a ~ of gray⟩   **5 a** : goods or commodities as distinguished from money ⟨payment in ~⟩   **b** : the equivalent of what has been offered or received   *syn* see TYPE — **all kinds of** **1** : MANY ⟨likes *all kinds of* sports⟩   **2** : plenty of ⟨has *all kinds of* time⟩

²kind *adj* (14c) **1** *chiefly dial* : AFFECTIONATE, LOVING   **2 a** : of a sympathetic or helpful nature   **b** : of a forbearing nature : GENTLE   **c** : arising from or characterized by sympathy or forbearance ⟨a ~ act⟩   **3** : of a kind to give pleasure or relief

kin·der·gar·ten \'kin-də(r)-ˌgär-tᵊn, -dᵊn\ *n* [G, fr. *Kinder* children + *Garten* garden] (1852) : a school or class for children usu. from four to six years old

kin·der·gart·ner \-ˌgärt-nər, -ˌgärd-\ *also* **kin·der·gar·ten·er** \-ˌgärt-ᵊn-ər, -dᵊn-\ *n* (1889) **1** : a teacher at a kindergarten   **2** : a child attending or of an age to attend kindergarten

kind·heart·ed \ˌkīnd-'här-təd\ *adj* (1535) : marked by a sympathetic nature — **kind·heart·ed·ly** *adv* — **kind·heart·ed·ness** *n*

¹**kin·dle** \'kin-d⁹l\ *vb* **kin·dled; kin·dling** \'kin(d)-liŋ, 'kin-d⁹l-iŋ\ [ME, prob. modif. of ON *kynda;* akin to OHG *cuntes*al fire] *vt* (13c) **1** : to start (a fire) burning : LIGHT **2 a** : to stir up : AROUSE ⟨~ interest⟩ **b** : to bring into being : START **3** : to cause to glow : ILLUMINATE ~ *vi* **1** : to catch fire **2 a** : to flare up **b** : to become animated **3** : to become illuminated — **kin·dler** \'kin(d)-lər, 'kin-d⁹l-ər\ *n*

²**kindle** *vb* **kin·dled; kin·dling** [ME, fr. *kindle* young animal, prob. fr. *kinde,* n., kind] *vt* (13c) : BEAR — used esp. of a rabbit ~ *vi* : to bring forth young — used esp. of a rabbit

kind·less \'kin(d)-ləs\ *adj* (13c) **1** *obs* : INHUMAN **2** : DISAGREEABLE, UNCONGENIAL — **kind·less·ly** *adv*

kind·li·ness \'kin(d)-lē-nəs\ *n* (15c) **1** : the quality or state of being kindly **2** : a kindly deed

kin·dling \'kin(d)-liŋ, 'kin-lən\ *n* (1513) : easily combustible material for starting a fire

¹**kind·ly** \'kin(d)-lē\ *adj* **kind·li·er; -est** [ME, fr. OE *cyndelīc,* fr. *cynd*] (bef. 12c) **1 a** *obs* : NATURAL **b** *archaic* : LAWFUL **2** : of an agreeable or beneficial nature : PLEASANT ⟨~ climate⟩ **3** : of a sympathetic or generous nature

²**kindly** *adv* (bef. 12c) **1 a** : in the normal way : NATURALLY ⟨old wounds which had healed ~ *—Amer. Mercury*⟩ **b** : READILY ⟨did not take ~ to suggestions⟩ **2 a** : in a kind manner : SYMPATHETICALLY **b** : as a gesture of goodwill ⟨would take it ~ if you would put in a good word⟩ **c** : in a gracious manner : COURTEOUSLY ⟨they ~ invited us along⟩ **d** : as a matter of courtesy : PLEASE ⟨would you ~ order me a cab⟩ **3** *chiefly Southern* : SOMEWHAT, KIND OF ⟨it's ~ embarrassing —Walter Davis⟩

kind·ness \'kin(d)-nəs\ *n* (13c) **1 a** : a kind deed : FAVOR **2 a** : the quality or state of being kind **b** *archaic* : AFFECTION

kind of *adv* (1775) **1** : to a moderate degree : SOMEWHAT ⟨it's *kind of* late to begin⟩ **2** : in a way that approximates : MORE OR LESS ⟨*kind of* sneaked up on us⟩

¹**kin·dred** \'kin-drəd\ *n* [ME, fr. *kin* + OE *ræden* condition, fr. *rǣdan* to advise, read] (12c) **1 a** : a group of related individuals **b** : one's relatives **2** : family relationship : KINSHIP

²**kindred** *adj* (14c) **1** : of a similar nature or character : LIKE **2** : of the same ancestry

kine \'kīn\ *archaic pl of* COW

kin·e·ma \'ki-nə-mə\ *Brit var of* CINEMA

ki·ne·mat·ics \ˌki-nə-'ma-tiks *also* ˌkī-\ *n pl but sing in constr* [F *cinématique,* fr. Gk *kinēmat-, kinēma* motion, fr. *kinein* to move] (1840) : a branch of dynamics that deals with aspects of motion apart from considerations of mass and force — **ki·ne·mat·ic** \-tik\ *or* **ki·ne·mat·i·cal** \-ti-kəl\ *adj* — **ki·ne·mat·i·cal·ly** \-ti-k(ə-)lē\ *adv*

¹**ki·ne·scope** \'ki-nə-ˌskōp *also* 'kī-\ *n* [fr. *Kinescope,* a trademark] (1930) **1** : PICTURE TUBE **2** : a motion picture made from an image on a picture tube

²**kinescope** *vt* **-scoped; -scop·ing** (1949) : to make a kinescope of

ki·ne·sics \kə-'nē-siks, ki-, -ziks\ *n pl but sing in constr* [Gk *kinēsis* motion + E *-ics*] (1952) : a systematic study of the relationship between nonlinguistic body motions (as blushes, shrugs, or eye movement) and communication

ki·ne·si·ol·o·gy \kə-ˌnē-sē-'ä-lə-jē, kī-, -zē-\ *n* [Gk *kinēsis*] (1894) : the study of the principles of mechanics and anatomy in relation to human movement

ki·ne·sis \kə-'nē-səs, kī-\ *n, pl* **ki·ne·ses** \-ˌsēz\ [NL, fr. Gk *kinēsis*] (1905) : a movement that lacks directional orientation and depends upon the intensity of stimulation

-kinesis *n comb form, pl* **-kineses** [NL, fr. Gk *kinēsis,* fr. *kinein* to move; akin to L *ciēre* to move] **1** : division ⟨karyo*kinesis*⟩ **2** : production of motion ⟨tele*kinesis*⟩

kin·es·the·sia \ˌki-nəs-'thē-zh(ē-)ə, ˌkī-\ *or* **kin·es·the·sis** \-'thē-səs\ *n, pl* **-the·sias** *or* **-the·ses** \-ˌsēz\ [NL, fr. Gk *kinein* + *aisthēsis* perception — more at ANESTHESIA] (1880) : a sense mediated by end organs located in muscles, tendons, and joints and stimulated by bodily movements and tensions; *also* : sensory experience derived from this sense — **kin·es·thet·ic** \-'the-tik\ *adj* — **kin·es·thet·i·cal·ly** \-ti-k(ə-)lē\ *adv*

kinet- *or* **kineto-** *comb form* [Gk *kinētos* moving] : movement : motion ⟨*kineto*some⟩

ki·net·ic \kə-'ne-tik *also* kī-\ *adj* [Gk *kinētikos,* fr. *kinētos,* fr. *kinein*] (1864) **1** : of or relating to the motion of material bodies and the forces and energy associated therewith **2 a** : ACTIVE, LIVELY **b** : DYNAMIC, ENERGIZING **3** : of or relating to kinetic art — **ki·net·i·cal·ly** \-ti-k(ə-)lē\ *adv*

kinetic art *n* (1961) : art (as sculpture or assemblage) having mechanical parts which can be set in motion — **kinetic artist** *n*

kinetic energy *n* (1870) : energy associated with motion

ki·net·i·cist \kə-'ne-tə-sist *also* kī-\ *n* (1960) **1** : a specialist in kinetics **2** : a person who works in kinetic art : KINETIC ARTIST

ki·net·ics \kə-'ne-tiks *also* kī-\ *n pl but sing or pl in constr* (ca. 1859) **1 a** : a branch of science that deals with the effects of forces upon the motions of material bodies or with changes in a physical or chemical system **b** : the rate of change in such a system **2** : the mechanism by which a physical or chemical change is effected

kinetic theory *n* (1864) : either of two theories in physics based on the fact that the minute particles of a substance are in vigorous motion: **a** : a theory that the particles of a gas move in straight lines with high average velocity, continually encounter one another and thus change their individual velocities and directions, and cause pressure by their impact against the walls of a container — called also *kinetic theory of gases* **b** : a theory that the temperature of a substance increases with an increase in either the average kinetic energy of the particles or the average potential energy of separation (as in fusion) of the particles or in both when heat is added — called also *kinetic theory of heat*

ki·ne·tin \'kī-nə-tin\ *n* (1955) : a cytokinin $C_{10}H_9N_5O$ that increases mitosis and callus formation

ki·net·o·chore \kə-'nē-tə-ˌkōr, kī-, -ˌkȯr\ *n* [*kinet-* + Gk *chōros* place] (1934) : CENTROMERE

ki·net·o·plast \kə-'nē-tə-ˌplast, kī-\ *n* [ISV] (1925) : an extranuclear cell organelle within a mitochondrion esp. of trypanosomes that contains DNA

ki·net·o·scope \kə-'ne-tə-ˌskōp, kī-\ *n* [fr. *Kinetoscope,* a trademark] (1894) : a device for viewing through a magnifying lens a sequence of pictures on an endless band of film moved continuously over a light source and a rapidly rotating shutter that creates an illusion of motion

ki·net·o·some \-ˌsōm\ *n* (1912) : BASAL BODY

kin·folk \'kin-ˌfōk\ *or* **kinfolks** *n pl* (1873) : RELATIVES

king \'kiŋ\ *n* [ME, fr. OE *cyning;* akin to OHG *kuning* king, OE *cynn* kin] (bef. 12c) **1 a** : a male monarch of a major territorial unit; *esp* : one whose position is hereditary and who rules for life **b** : a paramount chief **2** *cap* : GOD, CHRIST **3** : one that holds a preeminent position; *esp* : a chief among competitors **4** : the principal piece of each color in chess having the power to move ordinarily one square in any direction and to capture opposing pieces but being obliged never to enter or remain in check **5** : a playing card marked with a stylized figure of a king **6** : a checker that has been crowned

king·bird \-ˌbərd\ *n* (1778) : any of various American tyrant flycatchers (genus *Tyrannus*)

king·bolt \-ˌbōlt\ *n* (1825) : a vertical bolt by which the forward axle and wheels of a vehicle or the trucks of a railroad car are connected with the other parts

King Charles spaniel \-'chär(-ə)lz-\ *n* [*Charles* II of England] (1833) : an English toy spaniel having a black and tan coat

king cobra *n* (1894) : a large cobra (*Ophiophagus hannah* syn. *Naja hannah*) of southeastern Asia and the Philippines that may attain a length of 18 feet (5.5 meters)

king crab *n* (1698) **1** : HORSESHOE CRAB **2** : any of several very large crabs; *esp* : one (*Paralithoides camtschaticus*) of the No. Pacific caught commercially for food

king·craft \'kiŋ-ˌkraft\ *n* (1643) : the art of governing as a king

king·cup \-ˌkəp\ *n* (1538) : any of several plants of the buttercup family; *esp* : MARSH MARIGOLD

king·dom \'kiŋ-dəm\ *n* (bef. 12c) **1** *archaic* : KINGSHIP **2** : a politically organized community or major territorial unit having a monarchical form of government headed by a king or queen **3** *often cap* **a** : the eternal kingship of God **b** : the realm in which God's will is fulfilled **4 a** : a realm or region in which something is dominant **b** : an area or sphere in which one holds a preeminent position **5 a** : one of the three primary divisions into which natural objects are commonly classified — compare ANIMAL KINGDOM, MINERAL KINGDOM, PLANT KINGDOM **b** : a major category (as Plantae or Protista) in biological taxonomy that ranks above the phylum and is the highest and most encompassing group

king cobra

kingdom come *n* [fr. the phrase "Thy *kingdom come*" (Mt 6:10)] (1785) : the next world : HEAVEN

king·fish \'kiŋ-ˌfish\ *n* (1750) **1** : any of several marine croakers (family Sciaenidae) **a** : any of three fishes (*Menticirrhus americanus, M. littoralis,* and *M. saxatilis*) of shallow coastal waters of the Atlantic Ocean **b** : a small silvery food and sport fish (*Genyonemus lineatus*) of inshore waters esp. of California — called also *white croaker* **2** : KING MACKEREL **3** : an undisputed master in an area or group

king·fish·er \-ˌfi-shər\ *n* (15c) : any of numerous nonpasserine birds (family Alcedinidae) that are usu. crested and bright-colored with a short tail and a long stout sharp bill

King James Version \-'jämz-\ *n* [*James* I of England] (ca. 1889) : AUTHORIZED VERSION

king·let \'kiŋ-lət\ *n* (1603) **1** : a weak or petty king **2** : any of several small birds (genus *Regulus*) that are related to the gnatcatchers

king·ly \'kiŋ-lē\ *adj* **king·li·er; -est** (14c) **1** : having royal rank **2** : of, relating to, or befitting a king **3** : MONARCHICAL — **king·li·ness** *n* — **kingly** *adv*

king mackerel *n* (ca. 1930) : a mackerel (*Scomberomorus cavalla*) that is noted esp. as a fighting sport fish

king·mak·er \'kiŋ-ˌmā-kər\ *n* (1599) : one having great influence over the choice of candidates for political office

king of arms (15c) : an officer of arms of the highest rank

king penguin *n* (1885) : a large penguin (*Aptenodytes patagonica*) chiefly of subantarctic regions

king·pin \'kiŋ-ˌpin\ *n* (1801) **1** : any of several bowling pins: as **a** : HEADPIN **b** : the pin that stands in the middle of a triangular arrangement of bowling pins **2** : the chief person in a group or undertaking **3 a** : KINGBOLT **b** : a pin connecting the two parts of a knuckle joint (as in an automobile steering linkage)

king post *n* (1776) : a vertical member connecting the apex of a triangular truss (as of a roof) with the base

Kings \'kiŋz\ *n pl but sing in constr* **1** : either of two narrative and historical books of canonical Jewish and Christian Scripture — see BIBLE table **2** : any of four narrative and historical books in the former Roman Catholic canon of the Old Testament

king salmon *n* (1881) : CHINOOK SALMON

King's Bench *n* (14c) : a division in the English superior courts system that hears civil and criminal cases

King's Counsel *n* (1689) : a barrister selected to serve as counsel to the British crown

King's English *n* (1553) : standard, pure, or correct English speech or usage

king's evil *n, often cap K&E* [fr. the former belief that it could be healed by a king's touch] (14c) : SCROFULA

king·ship \'kiŋ-ˌship\ *n* (14c) **1** : the position, office, or dignity of a king **2** : the personality of a king **3** : government by a king

---

\ə\ abut \ᵊ\ kitten, F table \ər\ further \a\ ash \ā\ ace \ä\ mop, mar \au̇\ out \ch\ chin \e\ bet \ē\ easy \g\ go \i\ hit \ī\ ice \j\ job \ŋ\ sing \ō\ go \ȯ\ law \ȯi\ boy \th\ thin \th̲\ the \ü\ loot \u̇\ foot \y\ yet \zh\ vision \à, k̲, ⁿ, œ, œ̄, ɶ, ūē, ᵞ\ *see* Guide to Pronunciation

king·side \-ˌsīd\ n (1941) : the side of a chessboard containing the file on which the king sits at the beginning of the game

king–size \-ˌsīz\ or **king–sized** \-ˌsīzd\ adj (1942) **1** : longer than the regular or standard size ⟨a ~ cigarette⟩ **2** : unusually large **3** a : having dimensions of approximately 76 inches by 80 inches (about 1.9 by 2.0 meters) — used of a bed; compare FULL-SIZE, QUEEN-SIZE, TWIN-SIZE **b** : of a size that fits a king-size bed ⟨~ sheets⟩

king snake n (1709) : any of numerous brightly marked colubrid snakes (genus Lampropeltis) chiefly of No. and Central America

king's ransom n (ca. 1590) : a very large sum

king·wood \-ˌwu̇d\ n (ca. 1851) : the wood of any of several tropical American leguminous trees (esp. genus Dalbergia); esp : the wood of a Brazilian tree (D. cearensis) used esp. for furniture

ki·nin \ˈkī-nən\ n [Gk kinein to move, stimulate + E ¹-in — more at -KINESIS] (1954) **1** : any of various polypeptide hormones that are formed locally in the tissues and cause dilation of blood vessels and contraction of smooth muscle **2** : CYTOKININ

¹kink \ˈkiŋk\ n [D; akin to MLG kinke kink] (1678) **1** : a short tight twist or curl caused by a doubling or winding of something upon itself **2** a : a mental or physical peculiarity : ECCENTRICITY, QUIRK **b** : WHIM **3** : a clever unusual way of doing something **4** : a cramp in some part of the body **5** : an imperfection likely to cause difficulties in the operation of something

²kink vi (1697) : to form a kink ~ vt : to make a kink in

kin·ka·jou \ˈkiŋ-kə-ˌjü\ n [F, alter. of quincajou wolverine, of Algonquian origin; akin to Ojibwa kwi·nkwaʔake· wolverine] (1796) : a nocturnal arboreal omnivorous mammal (Potos flavus) found from Mexico to So. America that is related to the raccoon and has a long prehensile tail, large eyes, and yellowish brown fur

kinky \ˈkiŋ-kē\ adj **kink·i·er**; **-est** (1844) **1** : closely twisted or curled **2** : relating to, having, or appealing to unconventional tastes esp. in sex; also : sexually deviant **3** : OUTLANDISH, FAR-OUT — **kink·i·ly** \ˈkiŋ-kə-lē\ adv — **kink·i·ness** \ˈkiŋ-kē-nəs\ n

kin·ni·kin·nick \ˌki-ni-kə-ˈnik, ˈki-ni-kə-ˌ\ n [of Algonquian origin; akin to Massachuset kinukkinuk mixture] (1799) : a mixture of dried leaves and bark and sometimes tobacco smoked by the Indians and pioneers esp. in the Ohio valley; also : a plant (as a sumac or dogwood) used in it

-kins — see -KIN

kins·folk \ˈkinz-ˌfōk\ n pl (15c) : RELATIVES

kin·ship \ˈkin-ˌship\ n (1833) : the quality or state of being kin : RELATIONSHIP

kins·man \ˈkinz-mən\ n (12c) : RELATIVE; specif : a male relative

kins·wom·an \-ˌwu̇-mən\ n (14c) : a female relative

ki·osk \ˈkē-ˌäsk\ n [Turk köşk, fr. Per kūshk portico] (1625) **1** : an open summerhouse or pavilion **2** : a small structure with one or more open sides that is used to vend merchandise (as newspapers) or services (as film developing)

Ki·o·wa \ˈkī-ə-ˌwȯ, -ˌwä, -ˌwä\ n, pl **Kiowa** or **Kiowas** (1808) **1** : a member of an American Indian people of what are now Colorado, Kansas, New Mexico, Oklahoma, and Texas **2** : the language of the Kiowa people

¹kip \ˈkip\ n [obs. D; akin to MLG kip bundle of hides] (ca. 1525) : a bundle of undressed hides of young or small animals; also : one of the hides

²kip n [perh. fr. Dan kippe cheap tavern] (1879) **1** : BED ⟨ready for the ~ after this screwball day —K. M. Dodson⟩ **2** chiefly Brit : SLEEP, NAP ⟨roused the . . . family from their ~ —Sylvia Margolis⟩

³kip vi **kipped; kip·ping** (ca. 1889) Brit : SLEEP — sometimes used with down ⟨~ down on a spare bed —Alice Glenday⟩

⁴kip n [kilo- + pound] (1914) : a unit of weight equal to 1000 pounds (4448 newtons) used to express deadweight load

⁵kip \ˈkip, ˈgip\ n, pl **kip** or **kips** [Lao ki:p, lit., ingot] (1955) — see MONEY table

¹kip·per \ˈki-pər\ n [ME kypre, fr. OE cypera; akin to OE coper copper] (bef. 12c) **1** : a male salmon or sea trout during or after the spawning season **2** : a kippered herring or salmon

²kipper vt **kip·pered; kip·per·ing** \-p(ə-)riŋ\ (1773) : to cure (split dressed fish) by salting and smoking — **kip·per·er** \-pər-ər\ n

Kir·ghiz \kir-ˈgēz\ n, pl **Kirghiz** or **Kir·ghiz·es** [Kirghiz kïrğïz] (1600) **1** : a member of a Turkic people of Kyrgyzstan and adjacent areas of central Asia **2** : the language of the Kirghiz

kirk \ˈkirk, ˈkərk\ n [ME (northern dial.), fr. ON kirkja, fr. OE cirice — more at CHURCH] (12c) **1** chiefly Scot : CHURCH **2** cap : the national church of Scotland as distinguished from the Church of England or the Episcopal Church in Scotland

Kir·li·an photography \ˈkir-lē-ən-\ n [Semyon D. & Valentina K. Kirlian fl1939 Soviet inventors] (1972) : a process in which an image is obtained by application of a high-frequency electric field to an object so that it radiates a characteristic pattern of luminescence that is recorded on photographic film — **Kirlian photograph** n

Kir·man \kər-ˈmän, kir-\ n [Kirman, province in Iran] (1876) : a Persian carpet or rug characterized by elaborate fluid designs and soft colors

kir·mess \ˈkər-məs\ var of KERMIS

kirsch \ˈkirsh\ n [G, short for Kirschwasser, fr. Kirsche cherry + Wasser water] (1869) : a dry colorless brandy distilled from the fermented juice of the black morello cherry

Kirt·land's warbler \ˈkərt-lən(d)z-\ n [Jared P. Kirtland †1877 Am. naturalist] (1858) : a rare warbler (Dendroica kirtlandii) of northeastern No. America that breeds in Michigan and winters in the Bahamas

kir·tle \ˈkər-tʔl\ n [ME kirtel, fr. OE cyrtel, fr. (assumed) OE curt short, fr. L curtus shortened — more at SHEAR] (bef. 12c) **1** : a tunic or coat worn by men esp. in the Middle Ages **2** : a long gown or dress worn by women

kish·ke also **kish·ka** \ˈkish-kə\ n [Yiddish kishke gut, sausage, of Slavic origin; akin to Pol kiszka gut, sausage] (ca. 1936) : beef or fowl casing stuffed (as with meat, flour, and spices) and cooked

Kis·lev \ˈkis-lēv\ n [Heb Kislēw] (14c) : the 3d month of the civil year or the 9th month of the ecclesiastical year in the Jewish calendar — see MONTH table

kis·met \ˈkiz-ˌmet, -mət\ n, often cap [Turk, fr. Ar qismah portion, lot] (1834) : FATE 1, 2a

¹kiss \ˈkis\ vb [ME, fr. OE cyssan; akin to OHG kussen to kiss] vt (bef.

12c) 1 : to touch with the lips esp. as a mark of affection or greeting **2** : to touch gently or lightly ⟨wind gently ~ing the trees⟩ ~ vi **1** : to salute or caress one another with the lips **2** : to come in gentle contact — **kiss·able** \ˈki-sə-bəl\ adj — **kiss ass** : to act obsequiously esp. to gain favor — usu. considered vulgar — **kiss good–bye 1** : LEAVE **2** : to resign oneself to the loss of

²kiss n (bef. 12c) **1** : a caress with the lips **2** : a gentle touch or contact **3** a : a small drop cookie made of meringue **b** : a bite-size piece of candy often wrapped in paper or foil **4** : an expression of affection (sent him ~es in her letter)

kiss–and–tell \ˈkis-ʔn(d)-ˈtel\ adj (1949) : telling details of private matters ⟨kiss-and-tell autobiographies⟩

kiss·er \ˈki-sər\ n (1537) **1** : one that kisses **2** slang **a** : MOUTH **b** : FACE

kissing bug n (1899) : CONENOSE

kissing cousin n (1941) **1** : a person and esp. a relative whom one knows well enough to kiss more or less formally upon meeting **2** : one that is closely related in kind to something else

kissing disease n [fr. the belief that it is frequently transmitted by kissing] (1962) : INFECTIOUS MONONUCLEOSIS

kiss of death [fr. the kiss with which Judas betrayed Jesus (Mk 14:44–46)] (1943) : something (as an act or association) ultimately causing ruin

kiss off vt (ca. 1935) : to dismiss lightly ⟨kisses the other performers off as mere amateurs⟩ — **kiss–off** \ˈki-ˌsȯf\ n

kiss of life (1961) chiefly Brit : artificial respiration by the mouth-to-mouth method

kiss of peace n (ca. 1898) : a ceremonial kiss, embrace, or handclasp used in Christian liturgies and esp. the Eucharist as a sign of fraternal unity

kist \ˈkist\ n [ME kiste, fr. ON kista, ultim. fr. L cista — more at CHEST] (14c) chiefly Scot & SoAfr : CHEST 1b

¹kit \ˈkit\ n [ME] (14c) **1** dial Brit : a wooden tub **2** a (1) : a collection of articles usu. for personal use ⟨a travel ~⟩ (2) : a set of tools or implements ⟨a carpenter's ~⟩ (3) : a set of parts to be assembled or worked up ⟨model-airplane ~⟩ (4) : a packaged collection of related material ⟨convention ~⟩ (5) chiefly Brit : GEAR ⟨run over to my billet and get some overnight ~ —Lionel Shapiro⟩ **b** : a container for any of such sets or collections **3** : a group of persons or things — usu. used in the phrase the whole kit and caboodle

²kit vt **kit·ted; kit·ting** (1919) chiefly Brit : EQUIP, OUTFIT — often used with up or out

³kit n [origin unknown] (1519) : a small narrow violin

⁴kit n (1562) **1** : KITTEN **2** : a young or undersized fur-bearing animal; also : its pelt

kit bag n [¹kit] (1893) **1** : KNAPSACK **2** : a suitcase usu. with sides that fasten at the top or open to the full width of the bag

kitch·en \ˈki-chən\ n [ME kichene, fr. OE cycene, fr. LL coquina, fr. L coquere to cook — more at COOK] (bef. 12c) **1** : a place (as a room) with cooking facilities **2** : the personnel that prepares, cooks, and serves food **3** : CUISINE

kitchen cabinet n (1832) **1** : an informal group of advisers to one in a position of power (as the head of a government) **2** : a cupboard with drawers and shelves for use in a kitchen

kitch·en·ette \ˌki-chə-ˈnet\ n (1903) : a small kitchen or an alcove containing cooking facilities

kitchen garden n (1580) : a garden in which plants (as vegetables or herbs) for use in the kitchen are cultivated

kitchen midden n (1863) : a refuse heap; specif : a mound marking the site of a primitive human habitation

kitchen police n (ca. 1917) **1** : KP **2** : the work of KPs

kitch·en–sink \-ˈsiŋk\ adj (1941) **1** chiefly Brit : portraying or emphasizing the squalid aspects of modern life ⟨the ~ realism of contemporary British drama —Current Biog.⟩ **2** : being or made up of a hodgepodge of disparate elements or ingredients

kitch·en·ware \-ˌwar, -ˌwer\ n (1722) : utensils and appliances for use in a kitchen

¹kite \ˈkīt\ n [ME, fr. OE cȳta; akin to MHG kūze owl] (bef. 12c) **1** : any of various usu. small hawks (family Accipitridae) with long narrow wings and often a notched or forked tail **2** : a person who preys on others **3** : a light frame covered usu. with paper or cloth, often provided with a balancing tail, and designed to be flown in the air at the end of a long string **4** : a check drawn against uncollected funds in a bank account or fraudulently raised before cashing **5** : a light sail used in a light breeze usu. in addition to the regular working sails; esp : SPINNAKER — **kite–like** adj

²kite vb **kit·ed; kit·ing** vt (1839) **1** : to use (a bad check) to get credit or money **2** : to cause to soar ⟨kited the prices they charged wealthy clients⟩ ~ vi **1** a : to go in a rapid, carefree, or flighty manner **b** : to rise rapidly : SOAR ⟨the prices of necessities continue to ~⟩ **2** : to get money or credit by a kite

kit fox n [⁴kit] (1805) **1** a : SWIFT FOX **b** : a fox (Vulpes macrotis) of the southwestern U.S. and Mexico with exceptionally large ears and a black tip on the tail **2** : the fur or pelt of a kit fox

kith \ˈkith\ n [ME, fr. OE cȳthth; akin to cūth known — more at UNCOUTH] (bef. 12c) : familiar friends, neighbors, or relatives ⟨~ and kin⟩

kith·a·ra \ˈki-thə-rə\ n [ME cithara, fr. L, fr. Gk kithara] (14c) : an ancient Greek stringed instrument similar to but larger than the lyre and having a box-shaped resonator

kithe \ˈkīth\ vb **kithed; kith·ing** [ME, fr. OE cȳthan, fr. cūth] vt (bef. 12c) chiefly Scot : to make known ~ vi, chiefly Scot : to become known

kitsch \ˈkich\ n [G, kitsch, trash] (1925) : something that appeals to popular or lowbrow taste and is often of poor quality — **kitsch** adj — **kitschy** \ˈki-chē\ adj

¹kit·ten \ˈki-tʔn\ n [ME kitoun, fr. (assumed) ONF caton, dim. of cat, fr. LL cattus] (14c) : a young cat; also : an immature individual of various other small mammals

²kitten vi **kit·tened; kit·ten·ing** \ˈkit-niŋ, ˈki-tʔn-iŋ\ (15c) : to give birth to kittens

kit·ten·ish \ˈkit-nish, ˈki-tʔn-ish\ adj (1754) : resembling a kitten; esp : coyly playful — **kit·ten·ish·ly** adv — **kit·ten·ish·ness** n

kit·ti·wake \ˈki-tē-ˌwāk\ n [imit.] (1661) : either of two cliff-nesting gulls (Rissa tridactyla and R. brevirostris) that winter on the open ocean

¹kit·tle \'kit-ᵊl\ *vt* **kit·tled; kit·tling** \'kit-liŋ, 'ki-tᵊl-iŋ\ [ME (northern dial.) *kytyllen*] (bef. 12c) **1** *chiefly Scot* : TICKLE **2** *chiefly Scot* : PERPLEX

²kittle *adj* (1568) *chiefly Scot* : TICKLISH 2, TOUCHY

¹kit·ty \'ki-tē\ *n, pl* **kitties** (1719) : CAT 1a; *esp* : KITTEN

²kitty *n, pl* **kitties** [¹*kit*] (ca. 1887) **1** : a fund in a poker game made up of contributions from each pot **2** : a sum of money or collection of goods often made up of small contributions : POOL

kit·ty–cor·ner *or* **kit·ty–cor·nered** *var of* CATERCORNER

ki·va \'kē-və\ *n* [Hopi *kíva*] (1871) : a Pueblo Indian ceremonial structure that is usu. round and partly underground

Ki·wa·ni·an \kə-'wä-nē-ən\ *n* [*Kiwanis* (*Club*)] (1921) : a member of a major national and international service club

ki·wi \'kē-(ˌ)wē\ *n* [Maori] (1835) **1** : any of a small genus (*Apteryx*) of flightless New Zealand birds with rudimentary wings, stout legs, a long bill, and grayish brown hairlike plumage **2** *cap* : a native or resident of New Zealand — used as a nickname **3** : KIWIFRUIT

ki·wi·fruit \-ˌfrüt\ *n* (1966) : the fruit of a Chinese gooseberry

Klam·ath weed \'kla-məth-\ *n* [*Klamath* (*River*)] (1922) : a European yellow-flowered perennial Saint John's-wort (*Hypericum perforatum*) that is naturalized in No. America esp. in rangelands

kiwi 1

Klan \'klan\ *n* [(*Ku Klux*) *Klan*] (1867) : an organization of Ku Kluxers; *also* : a subordinate unit of such an organization — **Klan·ism** \-ˌi-zəm\ *n* — **Klans·man** \'klanz-mən\ *n*

klatch *or* **klatsch** \'klach, 'kläch\ *n* [G *Klatsch* gossip] (1941) : a gathering characterized usu. by informal conversation

klav·ern \'kla-vərn\ *n, often cap* [blend of *Klan* and *cavern*] (ca. 1924) : a local unit of the Klan

Klax·on \'klak-sən\ *trademark* — used for an electrically operated horn or warning signal

kleb·si·el·la \ˌkleb-zē-'e-lə\ *n* [NL, fr. Edwin *Klebs* †1913 Ger. pathologist] (1928) : any of a genus (*Klebsiella*) of nonmotile gram-negative frequently encapsulated bacterial rods

Klee·nex \'klē-ˌneks\ *trademark* — used for a cleansing tissue

Klein bottle \'klīn-\ *n* [Felix *Klein* †1925 Ger. mathematician] (1941) : a one-sided surface that is formed by passing the narrow end of a tapered tube through the side of the tube and flaring this end out to join the other end

klepht \'kleft\ *n, often cap* [NGk *klephtēs*, lit., robber, fr. Gk *kleptēs*, *kleptein*] (1820) : a Greek belonging to any of several independent guerrilla communities formed after the Turkish conquest of Greece — **kleph·tic** \'klef-tik\ *adj, often cap*

klepto– *comb form* [Gk, fr. *kleptein* to steal; akin to Goth *hlifan* to steal, L *clepere*] : stealing : theft ⟨*kleptomania*⟩

klep·to·ma·nia \ˌklep-tə-'mā-nē-ə, -nyə\ *n* [NL] (1830) : a persistent neurotic impulse to steal esp. without economic motive

klep·to·ma·ni·ac \-nē-ˌak\ *n* (1861) : a person evidencing kleptomania

klez·mer \'klez-mər\ *n, pl* **klez·mo·rim** \(ˌ)klez-'mòr-əm\ [Yiddish, fr. Heb *kēlēy zemer* musical instruments] (1949) **1** : a Jewish instrumentalist esp. of traditional eastern European music **2** : the music played by klezmorim

klieg light *or* **kleig light** \'klēg-\ *n* [John H. *Kliegl* †1959 & Anton T. *Kliegl* †1927 German-born Am. lighting experts] (1919) : a carbon arc lamp used esp. in making motion pictures

Kline·fel·ter's syndrome \'klīn-ˌfel-tərz-\ *n* [Harry F. *Klinefelter* b1912 Am. physician] (1950) : an abnormal condition in a male characterized by usu. two X and one Y chromosomes, infertility, and smallness of the testicles

klis·ter \'klis-tər\ *n* [Norw., lit., paste, fr. MLG *klíster*] (1936) : a soft wax used on skis

kloof \'klüf\ *n* [Afrik] (1731) *SoAfr* : a deep glen : RAVINE

kludge \'klüj\ *or* **kluge** \'klüj, 'klü-jē\ *n* [origin unknown] (1962) : a system and esp. a computer system made up of poorly matched components

klutz \'kləts\ *n* [Yiddish *klots*, lit., wooden beam, fr. MHG *kloz* lumpy mass — more at CLOUT] (1960) : a clumsy person — **klutz·i·ness** \'klət-sē-nəs\ *n* — **klutzy** \'klət-sē\ *adj*

kly·stron \'klī-ˌsträn\ *n* [fr. *Klystron*, a trademark] (1939) : an electron tube in which bunching of electrons is produced by electric fields and which is used for the generation and amplification of ultrahigh-frequency current

K–me·son \'kā-\ *n* (1951) : KAON

knack \'nak\ *n* [ME *knak*] (14c) **1 a** : a clever trick or stratagem **b** : a clever way of doing something **2** : a special ready capacity that is hard to analyze or teach **3** *archaic* : an ingenious device; *broadly* : TOY, KNICKKNACK **syn** see GIFT

knack·er \'na-kər\ *n* [prob. fr. E dial., saddlemaker] (1812) **1** *Brit* : a buyer of worn-out domestic animals or their carcasses for use esp. as animal food or fertilizer **2** *Brit* : a buyer of old structures for their constituent materials

knack·ered \'na-kərd\ *adj* [E slang *knacker* to kill, tire, perh. fr. *knacker*, n.] (1886) *Brit* : TIRED, EXHAUSTED

knack·wurst *var of* KNOCKWURST

¹knap \'nap\ *n* [ME, fr. OE *cnæp*; akin to OE *cnotta* knot] (bef. 12c) **1** *chiefly dial* : a crest of a hill : SUMMIT **2** *chiefly dial* : a small hill

²knap *vt* **knapped; knap·ping** [ME *knappen*, of imit. origin] (15c) **1** *dial Brit* : ²RAP **1 2** : to break with a quick blow; *esp* : to shape (as flints) by breaking off pieces **3** *dial Brit* : SNAP, CROP **4** *dial Brit* : CHATTER — **knap·per** *n*

knap·sack \'nap-ˌsak\ *n* [LG *knappsack* or D *knapzak*, fr. LG & D *knappen* to make a snapping noise, eat + LG *sack* or D *zak* sack] (1603) : a bag (as of canvas or nylon) strapped on the back and used for carrying supplies or personal belongings — **knap·sacked** \-ˌsakt\ *adj*

knap·weed \-ˌwēd\ *n* [ME *knopwed*, fr. *knop* knop + *wed* weed] (15c) : any of various weedy centaureas; *esp* : a widely naturalized European

perennial (*Centaurea nigra*) with tough wiry stems and knobby heads of purple flowers

knave \'nāv\ *n* [ME, fr. OE *cnafa*; akin to OHG *knabo* boy] (bef. 12c) **1** *archaic* **a** : a boy servant **b** : a male servant **c** : a man of humble birth or position **2** : a tricky deceitful fellow **3** : JACK 6a

knav·ery \'nā-və-rē, 'nāv-rē\ *n, pl* **-er·ies** (1528) **1 a** : RASCALITY **b** : a roguish or mischievous act **2** *obs* : roguish mischief

knav·ish \'nā-vish\ *adj* (14c) : of, relating to, or characteristic of a knave; *esp* : DISHONEST — **knav·ish·ly** *adv*

knead \'nēd\ *vt* [ME *kneden*, fr. OE *cnedan*; akin to OHG *knetan* to knead] (bef. 12c) **1 a** : to work and press into a mass with or as if with the hands ⟨~*ing* dough⟩ **b** : to manipulate or massage with a kneading motion ⟨~*ed* sore neck muscles⟩ **2** : to form or shape by or as if by kneading — **knead·able** \'nē-də-bəl\ *adj* — **knead·er** *n*

¹knee \'nē\ *n, often attrib* [ME, fr. OE *cnēow*; akin to OHG *kneo* knee, L *genu*, Gk *gony*] (bef. 12c) **1 a** : a joint in the middle part of the human leg that is the articulation between the femur, tibia, and patella; *also* : the part of the leg that includes this joint **b** (1) : the joint in the hind leg of a four-footed vertebrate that corresponds to the human knee (2) : the carpal joint of the foreleg of a four-footed vertebrate **c** : the tarsal joint of a bird **d** : the joint between the femur and tibia of an insect **2** : something resembling the human knee: as **a** : a piece of timber naturally or artificially bent for use in supporting structures coming together at an angle (as the deck beams of a ship) **b** : a rounded or conical process rising from the roots of various swamp-growing trees ⟨cypress ~⟩ **3** : the part of a garment covering the knee **4** : a blow with the bent knee — **kneed** \'nēd\ *adj* — **to one's knees** : into a state of submission or defeat

²knee *vt* **kneed; knee·ing** (bef. 12c) **1** *archaic* : to bend the knee to **2** : to strike with the knee

knee breeches *n pl* (1833) : BREECH 1a

knee·cap \'nē-ˌkap\ *n* (1869) : PATELLA

knee·cap·ping \'nē-ˌka-piŋ\ *n* (1974) : the terroristic act or practice of maiming a person's knees (as by gunshot) — **kneecap** *vt*

knee–deep \-'dēp\ *adj* (15c) **1 a** : sunk to the knees ⟨~ in mud⟩ **b** : deeply engaged or occupied ⟨~ in work⟩ **2** : KNEE-HIGH

knee–high \-'hī\ *adj* (1743) **1** : rising or reaching upward to the knees ⟨~ stockings⟩ — **knee–high** \-ˌhī\ *n*

knee·hole \-ˌhōl\ *n* (1893) : an open space (as under a desk) for the knees

knee–jerk \'nē-ˌjərk, -'jərk\ *adj* (1951) : readily predictable : AUTOMATIC ⟨~ reactions⟩; *also* : reacting in a readily predictable way ⟨~ liberals⟩

knee jerk *n* (1876) : an involuntary forward kick produced by a light blow on the tendon below the patella

kneel \'nē(ə)l\ *vi* **knelt** \'nelt\ *or* **kneeled; kneel·ing** [ME *knelen*, fr. OE *cnēowlian*; akin to OE *cnēow* knee] (bef. 12c) : to bend the knee : fall or rest on the knees

kneel·er \'nē-lər\ *n* (14c) **1** : one that kneels **2** : something (as a cushion or board) to kneel on

knee·pan \'nē-ˌpan\ *n* (15c) : PATELLA

knee–slap·per \-ˌsla-pər\ *n* (1966) : an extremely funny joke, line, or story

knee·sock \-ˌsäk\ *n* (1964) : a knee-high sock

¹knell \'nel\ *vb* [ME, fr. OE *cnyllan*; akin to MHG *erknellen* to toll] *vt* (bef. 12c) : to summon or announce by or as if by a knell ~ *vi* **1** : to ring esp. for a death, funeral, or disaster : TOLL **2** : to sound in an ominous manner or with an ominous effect

²knell *n* (bef. 12c) **1** : a stroke or sound of a bell esp. when rung slowly (as for a death, funeral, or disaster) **2** : an indication of the end or the failure of something ⟨sounded the death ~ for our hopes⟩

knew *past of* KNOW

knick·er·bock·er \'ni-kə(r)-ˌbä-kər\ *n* [Diedrich *Knickerbocker*, fictitious author of *History of New York* (1809) by Washington Irving] (1848) **1** *cap* : a descendant of the early Dutch settlers of New York; *broadly* : a native or resident of the city or state of New York — used as a nickname **2** *pl* : KNICKERS

knick·ers \'ni-kərz\ *n pl* [short for *knickerbockers*] (1881) **1** : loose-fitting short pants gathered at the knee **2** *chiefly Brit* : UNDERPANTS

knick·knack \'nik-ˌnak\ *n* [redupl. of *knack*] (1682) : a small trivial article usu. intended for ornament

¹knife \'nīf\ *n, pl* **knives** \'nīvz\ *often attrib* [ME *knif*, fr. OE *cnif*, perh. fr. ON *knifr*; akin to MLG *knif* knife] (bef. 12c) **1 a** : a cutting instrument consisting of a sharp blade fastened to a handle **b** : a weapon resembling a knife **2** : a sharp cutting blade or tool in a machine **3** : SURGERY **4** — usu. used in the phrase *under the knife* — **knife·like** \'nīf-ˌlīk\ *adj*

²knife *vb* **knifed; knif·ing** *vt* (1865) **1** : to use a knife on; *specif* : to stab, slash, or wound with a knife **2** : to cut, mark, or spread with a knife **3** : to try to defeat by underhanded means **4** : to move like a knife in ⟨birds *knifing* the autumn sky⟩ ~ *vi* : to cut a way with or as if with a knife blade ⟨the cruiser *knifed* through the heavy seas⟩

knife–edge \'nīf-ˌej\ *n* (1818) **1** : a sharp wedge of steel or other hard material used as a fulcrum for a lever beam in a precision instrument **2** : a sharp narrow knifelike edge

knife–point \-ˌpòint\ *n* (ca. 1911) : the point of a knife — **at knife-point** : under a threat of being knifed

knight \'nīt\ *n* [ME, fr. OE *cniht* man-at-arms, boy, servant; akin to OHG *kneht* youth, military follower] (bef. 12c) **1 a** (1) : a mounted man-at-arms serving a feudal superior; *esp* : a man ceremonially inducted into special military rank usu. after completing service as page and squire (2) : a man honored by a sovereign for merit and in Great Britain ranking below a baronet (3) : a person of antiquity equal to a knight in rank **b** : a man devoted to the service of a lady as her attendant or champion **c** : a member of an order or society **2** : either of two pieces of the same color in a set of chessmen having the power to

---

\ə\ abut \ᵊ\ kitten, F table \ər\ further \a\ ash \ā\ ace \ä\ mop, mar \aù\ out \ch\ chin \e\ bet \ē\ easy \g\ go \i\ hit \ī\ ice \j\ job \ŋ\ sing \ō\ go \ò\ law \òi\ boy \th\ thin \t͟h\ the \ü\ loot \ù\ foot \y\ yet \zh\ vision \à, k̟, ⁿ, œ, œ̄, ᴜᴇ, ᴜ̄ᴇ, ᵜ\ see Guide to Pronunciation make an L-shaped move of two squares in one row and one square in a perpendicular row over squares that may be occupied

²**knight** vt (13c) : to make a knight of

knight–er·rant \'nīt-'er-ənt\ n, pl **knights–errant** (14c) : a knight traveling in search of adventures in which to exhibit military skill, prowess, and generosity

knight–er·rant·ry \-'er-ən-trē\ n, pl **knight–errantries** (1654) 1 : the practice or actions of a knight-errant 2 : quixotic conduct

knight·hood \'nīt-,hůd\ n (13c) 1 : the rank, dignity, or profession of a knight 2 : the qualities befitting a knight : CHIVALRY 3 : knights as a class or body

knight·ly \'nīt-lē\ adj (14c) 1 : of, relating to, or characteristic of a knight 2 : made up of knights — **knight·li·ness** n — **knightly** adv

Knight of Co·lum·bus \-kə-'ləm-bəs\ n, pl **Knights of Columbus** [Christopher *Columbus*] (1882) : a member of a benevolent and fraternal society of Roman Catholic men

Knight of Pyth·i·as \-'pi-thē-əs\ n, pl **Knights of Pythias** (1869) : a member of a secret benevolent and fraternal order

Knight of the Mac·ca·bees \-'ma-kə-,bēz\ n, pl **Knights of the Maccabees** (1922) : a member of a secret benevolent society

Knight Templar n, pl **Knights Templars** or **Knights Templar** (1610) 1 : TEMPLAR 1 2 : a member of an order of Freemasonry conferring three orders in the York rite

knish \kə-'nish\ n [Yiddish, fr. Pol knysz] (1916) : a small round or square of dough stuffed with a filling (as potato) and baked or fried

¹**knit** \'nit\ vb **knit** or **knit·ted; knit·ting** [ME knitten, fr. OE cnyttan; akin to OE cnotta knot] vt (bef. 12c) 1 chiefly dial : to tie together 2 a : to link firmly or closely ⟨knitted my hands⟩ b : to cause to grow together ⟨time and rest will ~ a fractured bone⟩ c : to contract into wrinkles ⟨knitted her brow⟩ 3 : to form by interlacing yarn or thread in a series of connected loops with needles ~ vi 1 : to make knitted fabrics or objects 2 a : to become compact b : to grow together c : to become drawn together — **knit·ter** n

²**knit** n (1596) : KNIT STITCH; also : a knit fabric

knit stitch n (ca. 1885) : a basic knitting stitch usu. made with the yarn at the back of the work by inserting the right needle into the front part of a loop on the left needle from the left side, catching the yarn with the point of the right needle, and bringing it through the first loop to form a new loop — compare PURL STITCH

knit·ting n (15c) 1 : the action or method of one that knits 2 : work done or being done by one that knits

knit·wear \'nit-,war, -,wer\ n (1926) : knitted clothing

knob \'näb\ n [ME knobbe; akin to MLG knubbe knob] (bef. 12c) 1 a : a rounded protuberance : LUMP b : a small rounded ornament or handle 2 : a rounded usu. isolated hill or mountain — **knobbed** \'näbd\ adj — **knob·by** \'nä-bē\ adj

knob·bly \'nä-b(ə-)lē\ adj (1859) : having very small knobs ⟨a ~ mattress⟩

knob·ker·rie \'näb-,ker-ē\ n [Afrik knopkierie, fr. knop knob + kierie club] (1844) : a short wooden club with a knob at one end used as a missile or in close attack esp. by Zulus of southern Africa

¹**knock** \'näk\ vb [ME knoken, fr. OE cnocian; akin to MHG knochen to press] vi (bef. 12c) 1 : to strike something with a sharp blow 2 : to collide with something 3 a : BUSTLE ⟨heard them ~ing around in the kitchen⟩ b : WANDER ⟨~ed about Europe all summer⟩ 4 a : to make a pounding noise b : to have engine knock 5 : to find fault ~ vt 1 a (1) : to strike sharply (2) : to drive, force, or make by or as if by so striking b : to set forcibly in motion with a blow 2 : to cause to collide 3 : to find fault with ⟨always ~ing those in authority⟩ — **knock cold** : KNOCK OUT 2a(1) — **knock dead** : to move strongly esp. to admiration or applause ⟨a comedian who really knocks them dead⟩ — **knock for a loop** 1 a : OVERCOME ⟨knocked my opponent for a loop⟩ b : DEMOLISH ⟨knocked our idea for a loop⟩ 2 : DUMBFOUND, AMAZE ⟨the news knocked them for a loop⟩ — **knock one's socks off** : to overwhelm or amaze one ⟨a performance that will knock your socks off⟩ — **knock together** : to make or assemble esp. hurriedly or in a makeshift way ⟨knocked together my own bookcase⟩

²**knock** n (14c) 1 a : a sharp blow : RAP, HIT ⟨a loud ~ on the door⟩ b (1) : a severe misfortune or hardship (2) : SETBACK, REVERSAL 2 a : a pounding noise b : a sharp repetitive metallic noise caused by abnormal ignition in an automobile engine 3 : a harsh and often petty criticism ⟨likes praise but can't stand the ~s⟩

knock·about \'nä-kə-,baůt\ adj (1880) 1 : suitable for rough use ⟨~ clothing⟩ 2 a : being noisy and rough : BOISTEROUS ⟨~ games⟩ b : characterized by boisterous antics and often extravagant burlesque ⟨~ comedy⟩ 3 of a sailing vessel : having a simplified rig marked by absence of bowsprit and topmast ⟨a ~ sloop⟩ — **knockabout** n

knock back vt (ca. 1931) : DRINK, SWALLOW; specif : to toss down (an alcoholic beverage)

¹**knock–down** \'näk-,daůn\ adj (1690) 1 : having such force as to strike down or overwhelm ⟨a bewildering assortment of ~ arguments —J. W. Krutch⟩ 2 : that can easily be assembled or disassembled ⟨a ~ table⟩ 3 chiefly Brit : extremely low : REDUCED ⟨~ prices⟩

²**knockdown** n (1809) 1 : the action of knocking down 2 : something (as a blow) that strikes down or overwhelms 3 : something (as a piece of furniture) that can be readily assembled or disassembled

knock down \-'daůn\ vt (15c) 1 : to strike to the ground with or as if with a sharp blow : FELL 2 : to dispose of (an item) to a bidder at an auction sale 3 : to take apart : DISASSEMBLE 4 : to receive as income or salary ⟨positions where they were able to knock down good money —Infantry Jour.⟩ 5 : REDUCE

knock–down–drag–out or **knock–down–and–drag–out** adj (1834) : marked by extreme violence or bitterness and by the showing of no mercy ⟨~ political debates⟩ — **knock–down–drag–out** n

knock·er \'nä-kər\ n (14c) 1 : one that knocks: as a : a metal ring, bar, or hammer hinged to a door for use in knocking b : a persistently pessimistic critic 2 : BREAST — usu. used in pl.; often considered vulgar

knock–knee \'näk-'nē, -,nē\ n (1879) : a condition in which the legs curve inward at the knees — **knock–kneed** \-'nēd\ adj

knock–off \'näk-,ȯf\ n (1966) : a copy that sells for less than the original; broadly : a copy or imitation of someone or something popular

knock off vi (1649) : to stop doing something ~ vt 1 : to do hurriedly or routinely ⟨knocked off one painting after another⟩ 2 : DIS-

CONTINUE, STOP ⟨knocked off work at five⟩ 3 : DEDUCT ⟨knocked off a little to make the price more attractive⟩ 4 a : KILL ⟨knocked off two men . . . on mercenary grounds —Lewis Baker⟩ b : OVERCOME, DEFEAT ⟨knocked off each center of rebellion⟩ 5 : ROB ⟨knocked off a couple of banks⟩ 6 : to make a knockoff of : COPY, IMITATE ⟨knocks off popular dress designs⟩

knock·out \'näk-,aůt\ n (1887) 1 a : the act of knocking out : the condition of being knocked out b (1) : the termination of a boxing match when one boxer has been knocked down and is unable to rise and resume boxing within a specified time (2) : TECHNICAL KNOCKOUT c : a blow that knocks out an opponent 2 : something sensationally striking, appealing, or attractive — **knockout** adj

knock out vt (1856) 1 : to produce roughly or hastily 2 a (1) : to defeat (a boxing opponent) by a knockout (2) : to make unconscious ⟨the drug knocked him out⟩ b : to make inoperative or useless ⟨electricity was knocked out by the storm⟩ c : to get rid of : ELIMINATE ⟨knocked out illegal gambling⟩ 3 : to tire out : EXHAUST ⟨knocked themselves out with work⟩ 4 : to cause (an opposing pitcher) to be removed from a baseball game by a batting rally

knockout drops n pl (1895) : drops of a solution of a drug (as chloral hydrate) put into a drink to produce unconsciousness or stupefaction

knock over vt (ca. 1814) 1 a (1) : to strike to the ground : FELL (2) : OVERWHELM ⟨was knocked over by the news⟩ b : ELIMINATE ⟨knocked over every difficulty⟩ 2 a : STEAL; esp : HIJACK ⟨knocks over a truckload of merchandise —J. B. Martin⟩ b : ROB ⟨knocking over a bank⟩

knock up vt (1663) 1 Brit : ROUSE, SUMMON 2 : to make pregnant — sometimes considered vulgar

knock·wurst \'näk-(,)wərst also -,vů(r)st, sometimes -,vùsht\ n [G Knackwurst, fr. knacken to crackle (of imit. origin) + Wurst wurst] (ca. 1929) : a short thick heavily seasoned sausage

¹**knoll** \'nōl\ n [ME knol, fr. OE cnoll; akin to ON knollr mountaintop] (bef. 12c) : a small round hill : MOUND

²**knoll** vb [ME, prob. alter. of knellen to knell] (15c) archaic : KNELL

knop \'näp\ n [ME, fr. OE -cnoppa knob] (bef. 12c) : a usu. ornamental knob — **knopped** \'näpt\ adj

¹**knot** \'nät\ n [ME, fr. OE cnotta; akin to OHG knoto knot] (bef. 12c) 1 a : an interlacement of the parts of one or more flexible bodies forming a lump or knob b : the lump or knob so formed c : a tight constriction or the sense of constriction ⟨my stomach was all in ~s⟩ 2 : something hard to solve : PROBLEM ⟨a matter full of legal ~s⟩ 3 : a bond of union; esp : the marriage bond 4 a : a protuberant lump or swelling in tissue ⟨a ~ in a gland⟩ b : the base of a woody branch enclosed in the stem from which it arises; also : its section in lumber 5 : a cluster of persons or things : GROUP 6 : an ornamental bow of ribbon : COCKADE 7 a : a division of the log's line serving to measure a ship's speed b (1) : one nautical mile per hour (2) : one nautical mile — not used technically

²**knot** vb **knot·ted; knot·ting** vt (1547) 1 : to tie in or with a knot : form knots in 2 : to unite closely or intricately : ENTANGLE 3 : TIE 4b ⟨knotted the score⟩ ~ vi : to form knots — **knot·ter** n

³**knot** n, pl **knots** or **knot** [ME knott] (15c) : either of two sandpipers (Calidris canutus and C. tenuirostris) that breed in the Arctic and winter in temperate or warm parts of the New and Old World

knot garden n (1519) : an elaborately designed garden esp. of flowers or herbs

knot·grass \'nät-,gras\ n (1538) 1 : a cosmopolitan weed (Polygonum aviculare) of the buckwheat family with jointed stems, prominent sheathing stipules, and minute flowers; broadly : any of several congeneric plants 2 : any of several grasses with markedly jointed stems; esp : JOINT GRASS

knot 1b: 1 Blackwall hitch, 2 carrick bend, 3 clove hitch, 4 cat's-paw, 5 figure eight, 6 granny knot, 7 bowline, 8 overhand knot, 9 fisherman's bend, 10 half hitch, 11 square knot, 12 slip knot, 13 stevedore knot, 14 true lover's knot, 15 surgeon's knot, 16 Turk's head, 17 sheet bend, 18 timber hitch, 19 seizing, 20 rolling hitch, 21 sheepshank

knot·hole \-,hōl\ n (1726) : a hole in a board or tree trunk where a knot or branch has come out

knot·ted \'nä-təd\ adj (12c) 1 : tied in or with a knot 2 : full of knots : GNARLED 3 : KNOTTY 4 : ornamented with knots or knobs

knot·ty \'nä-tē\ adj **knot·ti·er; -est** (13c) : marked by or full of knots; esp : so full of difficulties and complications as to be likely to defy solution ⟨a ~ problem⟩ syn see COMPLEX — **knot·ti·ness** n

knotty pine n (ca. 1898) : pine wood that has a decorative distribution of knots and is used esp. for interior finish

knot·weed \'nät-,wēd\ n (1884) : any of several herbs (genus Polygonum) of the buckwheat family with leaves and bracts jointed and having a very short petiole; broadly : POLYGONUM

knout \'naůt, sometimes 'nůt\ n [Russ knut, of Scand origin; akin to ON knútr knot; akin to OE cnotta] (1716) : a whip used for flogging — **knout** vt

¹**know** \'nō\ vb **knew** \'nü also 'nyü\; **known** \'nōn\; **know·ing** [ME, fr. OE cnāwan; akin to OHG bichnāan to recognize, L gnoscere, noscere

to come to know, Gk *gignōskein*] *vt* (bef. 12c) **1 a** (1) : to perceive directly : have direct cognition of (2) : to have understanding of ⟨importance of ∼*ing* oneself⟩ (3) : to recognize the nature of : DISCERN **b** (1) : to recognize as being the same as something previously known (2) : to be acquainted or familiar with (3) : to have experience of **2 a** : to be aware of the truth or factuality of : be convinced or certain of **b** : to have a practical understanding of ⟨∼*s* how to write⟩ **3** *archaic* : to have sexual intercourse with ∼ *vi* **1** : to have knowledge : to be or become cognizant — sometimes used interjectionally with *you* esp. as a filler in informal speech — **know·able** \'nō-ə-bəl\ *adj* — **know·er** \'nō(-ə)r\ *n* — **know from** : to have knowledge of ⟨didn't *know from* sibling rivalry —Penny Marshall⟩
²know *n* (1592) : KNOWLEDGE — **in the know** : in possession of exclusive knowledge or information; *broadly* : WELL-INFORMED
know–all \'nō-,ól\ *n* (ca. 1864) *chiefly Brit* : KNOW-IT-ALL
know–how \'nō-,haù\ *n* (1838) : knowledge of how to do something smoothly and efficiently : EXPERTISE
¹know·ing \'nō-iŋ\ *n* (14c) : ACQUAINTANCE, COGNIZANCE
²knowing *adj* **1** : having or reflecting knowledge, information, or intelligence **2 a** : shrewdly and keenly alert : ASTUTE **b** : indicating possession of exclusive inside knowledge or information ⟨a ∼ smile⟩ **3** : COGNITIVE **4** : DELIBERATE ⟨∼ interference in the affairs of another⟩ — **know·ing·ly** *adv* — **know·ing·ness** *n*
know–it–all \'nō-ət-,ól\ *n* (1895) : one who claims to know everything; *also* : one who disdains advice — **know–it–all** *adj*
knowl·edge \'nä-lij\ *n* [ME *knowlege*, fr. *knowlechen* to acknowledge, irreg. fr. *knowen*] (14c) **1** *obs* : COGNIZANCE **2 a** (1) : the fact or condition of knowing something with familiarity gained through experience or association (2) : acquaintance with or understanding of a science, art, or technique **b** (1) : the fact or condition of being aware of something (2) : the range of one's information or understanding ⟨answered to the best of my ∼⟩ **c** : the circumstance or condition of apprehending truth or fact through reasoning : COGNITION **d** : the fact or condition of having information or of being learned ⟨a man of unusual ∼⟩ **3** *archaic* : SEXUAL INTERCOURSE **4 a** : the sum of what is known : the body of truth, information, and principles acquired by mankind **b** *archaic* : a branch of learning
syn KNOWLEDGE, LEARNING, ERUDITION, SCHOLARSHIP mean what is or can be known by an individual or by mankind. KNOWLEDGE applies to facts or ideas acquired by study, investigation, observation, or experience ⟨rich in the *knowledge* of human nature⟩. LEARNING applies to knowledge acquired esp. through formal, often advanced, schooling ⟨a book that demonstrates vast *learning*⟩. ERUDITION strongly implies the acquiring of profound, recondite, or bookish learning ⟨an *erudition* unusual even in a scholar⟩. SCHOLARSHIP implies the possession of learning characteristic of the advanced scholar in a specialized field of study or investigation ⟨a work of first-rate literary *scholarship*⟩.
knowl·edge·able \'nä-lij-ə-bəl\ *adj* (1829) : having or exhibiting knowledge or intelligence — **knowl·edge·abil·i·ty** \,nä-li-jə-'bi-lə-tē\ *n* — **knowl·edge·able·ness** *n* — **knowl·edge·ably** \-blē\ *adv*
knowledge engineering *n* (1980) : a branch of artificial intelligence that emphasizes the development and use of expert systems — **knowledge engineer** *n*
known \'nōn\ *adj* (13c) : familiar : generally recognized ⟨a ∼ authority on art⟩
know–noth·ing \'nō-,nə-thiŋ\ *n* (1827) **1 a** : IGNORAMUS **b** : AGNOSTIC **2** *cap K&N* : a member of a 19th century secret American political organization hostile to the political influence of recent immigrants and Roman Catholics
know–noth·ing·ism \-thiŋ-,i-zəm\ *n* (1854) **1** *cap K&N* : the principles and policies of the Know-Nothings **2** : the condition of knowing nothing or desiring to know nothing or the conviction that nothing can be known with certainty esp. in religion or morality **3** *often cap K&N* : a mid-twentieth century political attitude characterized by anti=intellectualism, exaggerated patriotism, and fear of foreign subversive influences
knub·by *var of* NUBBY
¹knuck·le \'nə-kəl\ *n* [ME *knokel*; akin to MHG *knöchel* knuckle] (14c) **1 a** : the rounded prominence formed by the ends of the two adjacent bones at a joint — used esp. of those at the joints of the fingers **b** : the joint of a knuckle **2** : a cut of meat consisting of the tarsal or carpal joint with the adjoining flesh **3** : something resembling a knuckle: as **a** (1) : one of the joining parts of a hinge through which a pin or rivet passes (2) : KNUCKLE JOINT **b** : the meeting of two surfaces at a sharp angle (as in a roof) **c** : a pivotal point **4** *pl* : a set of metal finger rings or guards attached to a transverse piece and worn over the front of the doubled fist for use as a weapon — called also **brass knuckles** — **knuck·led** *adj*
²knuckle *vb* **knuck·led; knuck·ling** \'nə-k(ə-)liŋ\ *vi* (1740) : to place the knuckles on the ground in shooting a marble ∼ *vt* : to press or rub with the knuckles
knuck·le·ball \'nə-kəl-,ból\ *n* (1910) : a baseball pitch in which the ball is gripped with the knuckles or the tips of the fingers pressed against the top and thrown with little speed or spin — **knuck·le·ball·er** \-,bó-lər\ *n*
knuck·le·bone \'nək-əl-,bōn\ *n* (1577) **1** : a bone (as a metatarsus or metacarpus of a sheep) used in games and formerly in divination **2** *pl but sing in constr* : a game played with knucklebones or jacks
knuckle down *vi* (ca. 1864) : to apply oneself earnestly
knuck·le·dust·er \'nə-kəl-,dəs-tər\ *n* (1858) : KNUCKLE 4
knuck·le·head \-,hed\ *n* (1942) : DUMBBELL 2 — **knuck·le·head·ed** \-,hed-əd\ *adj*
knuckle joint *n* (ca. 1864) : a hinge joint in which a projection with an eye on one piece enters a jaw between two corresponding projections with eyes on another piece and is retained by a pin or rivet
knuck·ler \'nə-k(ə-)lər\ *n* (1928) : KNUCKLEBALL
knuckle under *vi* (1869) : GIVE IN, SUBMIT
knur \'nər\ *n* [ME *knorre*; akin to MHG *knorre* burl] (14c) : a hard excrescence (as on a tree trunk) : GNARL
knurl \'nərl\ *n* [prob. blend of *knur* and *gnarl*] (1608) **1** : a small protuberance, excrescence, or knob **2** : one of a series of small ridges

knuckle joint

or beads on a metal surface to aid in gripping — **knurled** \'nər(-ə)ld\ *adj* — **knurly** \'nər-lē\ *adj*
¹KO \(,)kā-'ō, 'kā-(,)ō\ *n* [*knock out*] (1911) : KNOCKOUT
²KO *vt* **KO'd** \kā-'ōd, 'kā-(,)ōd\; **KO'·ing** \-'ō-iŋ, -(,)ō-\ (1926) : to knock out (as in boxing)
koa \'kō-ə\ *n* [Hawaiian] (1850) **1** : a Hawaiian timber tree (*Acacia koa*) with crescent-shaped leaves and white flowers borne in small round heads **2** : the fine-grained red wood of the koa used esp. for furniture
ko·ala \kō-'wä-lə, kō-'ä-\ *n* [Dharuk (Australian aboriginal language of the Port Jackson area) *gulawan*] (1803) : an Australian arboreal marsupial (*Phascolarctos cinereus*) that has a broad head, large hairy ears, dense gray fur, and sharp claws and feeds on eucalyptus leaves — called also **koala bear**
ko·an \'kō-,än\ *n* [Jp *kōan*, fr. *kō* public + *an* proposition] (1945) : a paradox to be meditated upon that is used to train Zen Buddhist monks to abandon ultimate dependence on reason and to force them into gaining sudden intuitive enlightenment
ko·bo \'kō-(,)bō\ *n*, *pl* **kobo** [alter. of ¹*copper*] (1972) — see *naira* at MONEY table
ko·bold \'kō-,bóld\ *n* [G — more as COBALT] (1830) **1** : a gnome that in German folklore inhabits underground places **2** : an often mischievous domestic spirit of German folklore
Ko·di·ak bear \'kō-dē-,ak-\ *n* [*Kodiak* Island, Alaska] (1899) : a large brown bear of the southern coast of Alaska and adjacent islands
kohl \'kōl\ *n* [Ar *kuḥl*] (1799) : a preparation used esp. in Arabia and Egypt to darken the edges of the eyelids
kohl·ra·bi \kōl-'rä-bē *also* -'ra-\ *n*, *pl* **-bies** [G, fr. It *cavolo rapa*, fr. *cavolo* cabbage + *rapa* turnip] (1807) : any of a race of cabbages (*Brassica oleracea gongylodes*) having a greatly enlarged, fleshy, turnip=shaped edible stem
koi \'kói\ *n*, *pl* **koi** [Jp] (1727) : a carp (*Cyprinus carpio*) bred esp. in Japan for large size and a variety of colors and often stocked in ornamental ponds
koi·ne *also* **koi·né** \kói-'nā, 'kói-; kē-'nē\ *n* [Gk *koinē*, fr. fem. of *koinos* common] (1909) **1** *cap* : the Greek language commonly spoken and written in eastern Mediterranean countries in the Hellenistic and Roman periods **2** : a dialect or language of a region that has become the common or standard language of a larger area
ko·kan·ee \kō-'ka-nē\ *n* [perh. fr. Shuswap (Salishan language of British Columbia) *kəknǽw*] (1875) : a small landlocked sockeye salmon — called also **kokanee salmon**
kok–sa·ghyz *or* **kok–sa·gyz** \,kōk-sə-'gēz, ,käk-, -'giz\ *n* [Russ *kok=sagyz*] (1932) : a perennial Asian dandelion (*Taraxacum kok-saghyz*) cultivated for its fleshy roots that have a high rubber content
ko·la *var of* COLA
kola nut \'kō-lə-\ *n* [*kola*, perh. modif. of Malinke *kolo* kola nut] (1868) : the bitter caffeine-containing chestnut-sized seed of a kola tree used esp. as a masticatory and in beverages
kola tree *n* (1937) : an African tree (genus *Cola*, esp. *C. nitida* and *C. acuminata* of the family Sterculiaceae) cultivated in various tropical areas for its kola nuts
ko·lin·sky \kə-'lin(t)-skē\ *n*, *pl* **-skies** [origin unknown] (1851) **1** : any of several Asian minks (esp. *Mustela siberica*) **2** : the fur or pelt of a kolinsky
kol·khoz \käl-'kóz, -'kòs\ *n*, *pl* **kol·kho·zy** \-'kò-zē\ *or* **kol·khoz·es** \-'kò-zəz\ [Russ, fr. *kollektivnoe khozyaistvo* collective farm] (1921) : a collective farm of the U.S.S.R.
kol·khoz·nik \käl-'kóz-nik\ *n*, *pl* **-ni·ki** \-ni-kē\ *or* **-niks** [Russ, fr. *kolkhoz* + -*nik*, agent suffix] (1944) : a member of a kolkhoz
Kol Ni·dre \kōl-'ni-(,)drā, kól-, -drə; -ni-'drā\ *n* [Aram *kol nidhrē* all the vows; fr. the opening phrase of the prayer] (1881) : a formula for the annulment of private vows chanted in the synagogue on the eve of Yom Kippur
ko·lo \'kō-(,)lō\ *n*, *pl* **kolos** [Serbo-Croatian, lit., circle, wheel; akin to Gk *kyklos* circle — more at WHEEL] (1910) : a central European folk dance in which dancers form a circle and progress slowly to right or left while one or more dancers perform elaborate steps in the center
ko·mat·ik \kō-'ma-tik\ *n* [Inuit *qamutik*] (ca. 1824) : an Eskimo sledge with wooden runners and crossbars lashed with rawhide
Ko·mo·do dragon \kə-'mō-dō-\ *n* [*Komodo* Island, Indonesia] (1927) : an Indonesian monitor lizard (*Varanus komodoensis*) that is the largest of all known lizards and may attain a length of 10 feet (3 meters)
ko·mon·dor \'kä-mən-,dòr, 'kō-\ *n*, *pl* **-dors** *or* **-dor·ok** \-,dòr-ək\ [Hung] (1931) : any of a breed of large powerful shaggy-coated white dogs of Hungarian origin that are used to guard sheep
Kom·so·mol \'käm-sə-,mòl, -,mól\ *n* [Russ, fr. *Kommunisticheskii Soyuz Molodezhi* Communist Union of Youth] (1925) : a Russian Communist youth organization
Kon·go \'käŋ-(,)gō\ *n*, *pl* **Kongo** *or* **Kongos** (ca. 1902) **1** : a member of a Bantu people of the lower Congo river **2** : the Bantu language of the Kongo people
Kon·ka·ni \'käŋ-kə-(,)nē\ *n* [Marathi *Koṅkaṇī*] (1873) : an Indo-Aryan language of the west coast of India
koo·doo *var of* KUDU
kook \'kük\ *n* [by shortening & alter. fr. *cuckoo*] (1960) : one whose ideas or actions are eccentric, fantastic, or crazy : SCREWBALL
kook·a·bur·ra \'kú-kə-,bər-ə, -,bə-rə\ *n* [Wiradhuri (Australian aboriginal language of central New South Wales) *gugubarra*] (1834) : a brownish kingfisher (*Dacelo novaeguineae* syn. *D. gigas*) of Australia that is about the size of a crow and has a call resembling loud laughter — called also **laughing jackass**
kooky *also* **kook·ie** \'kü-kē\ *adj* **kook·i·er; -est** (1959) : having the characteristics of a kook : CRAZY, OFFBEAT — **kook·i·ness** *n*
ko·peck *or* **ko·pek** \'kō-,pek\ *n* [Russ *kopeǐka*] (1698) — see *ruble* at MONEY table
koph *var of* QOPH

\ə\ abut \'\ kitten, F table \ər\ further \a\ ash \ā\ ace \ä\ mop, mar \aù\ out \ch\ chin \e\ bet \ē\ easy \g\ go \i\ hit \ī\ ice \j\ job \ŋ\ sing \ō\ go \ò\ law \òi\ boy \th\ thin \t̲h̲\ the \ü\ loot \ù\ foot \y\ yet \zh\ vision \á, k̲, ⁿ, œ, œ̄, ᵫ, ᵫ̄, ᵊ\ *see* Guide to Pronunciation

kop·je or **kop·pie** \'kä-pē\ n [Afrik koppie] (1848) : a small hill esp. on the African veld

kor var of COR

Ko·ran \kə-'ran, -'rän; 'kȯr-,an, 'kȯr-\ n [Ar qur'ān] (ca. 1615) : the book composed of sacred writings accepted by Muslims as revelations made to Muhammad by Allah through the angel Gabriel — **Ko·ran·ic** \kə-'ra-nik\ adj

Ko·rat \kō-'rät, kō-\ n [Korat province, Thailand] (1967) : any of a breed of shorthaired domestic cats originating in Thailand and having a heart-shaped face, a silver-blue coat, and green eyes

ko·re \'kȯ-(,)rä, 'kō-\ n, pl **ko·rai** \-,ri, -(,)rä\ [Gk korē girl; akin to Gk koros boy — more at CRESCENT] (1920) : an ancient Greek statue of a clothed young woman standing with feet together

Ko·re·an \kə-'rē-ən, esp Southern (,)kō-\ n (1600) **1** : a native or inhabitant of Korea **2** : the language of the Korean people — **Korean** adj

ko·ru·na \'kȯr-ə-,nä, 'kär-\ n, pl **ko·ru·ny** \-ə-nē\ or **korunas** or **ko·run** \'kȯr-ən, 'kär-\ [Czech, lit., crown, fr. L corona — more at CROWN] (1930) — see MONEY table

¹ko·sher \'kō-shər\ adj [Yiddish, fr. Heb kāshēr fit, proper] (1851) **1 a** : sanctioned by Jewish law; esp : ritually fit for use ⟨~ meat⟩ **b** : selling or serving food ritually fit according to Jewish law ⟨a ~ restaurant⟩ **2** : being proper, acceptable, or satisfactory ⟨found things going on that were not ~ —Homer Bigart⟩

²kosher vt **ko·shered; ko·sher·ing** \-sh(ə-)riŋ\ (1871) : to make kosher

³kosher n (1886) : the observance of kosher practices — used in the phrase keep kosher

ko·to \'kō-(,)tō\ n [Jp] (1795) : a long Japanese zither having 13 silk strings

kou·miss \kü-'mis, 'kü-məs\ n [Russ kumys, of Turkic origin; akin to Turk kımız koumiss] (1598) : a beverage of fermented mare's milk made orig. by the nomadic peoples of central Asia

kou·prey \'kü-,prā\ n [Khmer ko:prey] (1940) : a short-haired ox (Bos sauveli) of forests of Cambodia, Thailand, and Vietnam having a large dewlap

kou·ros \'kü-,rōs\ n, pl **kou·roi** \-(,)rȯi\ [Gk kouros, koros boy — more at CRESCENT] (1920) : an ancient Greek statue of a nude male youth standing with the left leg forward and arms at the sides

¹kow·tow \(,)kaù-'taù, 'kaù-,\ n [Chin (Beijing) kòutóu, fr. kòu to knock + tóu head] (1804) : an act of kowtowing

²kowtow vi (1826) **1** : to show obsequious deference : FAWN **2** : to kneel and touch the forehead to the ground in token of homage, worship, or deep respect

KP \,kä-'pē\ n [kitchen police] (1918) **1** : an enlisted man detailed to assist the cooks in a military mess **2** : the work of KPs

¹kraal \'krȯl, 'kräl\ n [Afrik, fr. Pg curral pen for cattle, enclosure, fr. (assumed) VL currale enclosure for vehicles — more at CORRAL] (1731) **1 a** : a village of southern African natives **b** : the native village community **2** : an enclosure for animals esp. in southern Africa

²kraal vt (1827) : to pen in a kraal

kraft \'kräft, 'kraft\ n, often attrib [G, lit., strength, fr. OHG — more at CRAFT] (1906) : a strong paper or paperboard made from wood pulp produced from wood chips boiled in an alkaline solution containing sodium sulfate

krait \'krīt\ n [Hindi karait] (1874) : any of a genus (Bungarus) of brightly banded extremely venomous nocturnal elapid snakes of Pakistan, India, southeastern Asia, and adjacent islands

kra·ken \'krä-kən\ n [Norw dial.] (1755) : a fabulous Scandinavian sea monster

kra·ter \'krā-tər, krä-'ter\ n [Gk kratēr — more at CRATER] (ca. 1736) : a jar or vase of classical antiquity having a large round body and a wide mouth and used for mixing wine and water

K ration \'kā-\ n [A. B. Keys b1904 Am. physiologist] (ca. 1940) : a lightweight packaged ration of emergency foods developed for the U.S. armed forces in World War II

kraut \'kraùt\ n [G, cabbage, fr. OHG krūt] (1855) **1** : SAUERKRAUT **2** often cap : GERMAN — usu. used disparagingly

Krebs cycle \'krebz-\ n [H. A. Krebs] (1941) : a sequence of reactions in the living organism in which oxidation of acetic acid or acetyl equivalent provides energy for storage in phosphate bonds (as in ATP) — called also citric acid cycle, tricarboxylic acid cycle

krem·lin \'krem-lən\ n [obs. G Kremelien the citadel of Moscow, ultim. fr. ORuss kremlǐ] (1662) **1** : the citadel of a Russian city **2** cap [the Kremlin, citadel of Moscow and seat of government of Russia and formerly of the U.S.S.R.] : the Russian government

krem·lin·ol·o·gy \,krem-lə-'nä-lə-jē\ n, often cap (1958) : the study of the policies and practices of the Soviet government — **krem·lin·ol·o·gist** \-jist\ n, often cap

krep·lach \'krep-lәk, -,läk\ n [Yiddish kreplekh, pl. of krepl filled dumpling] (ca. 1892) : square or triangular dumplings filled with ground meat or cheese, boiled or fried, and usu. served in soup

kreu·zer \'krȯit-sər\ n [G, fr. Kreuz cross; fr. its markings] (1547) : a small coin formerly used in Austria and Germany

krill \'kril\ n [Norw kril fry of fish] (1907) : planktonic crustaceans and larvae (order Euphausiacea) that constitute the principal food of baleen whales

krim·mer \'kri-mər\ n [G, fr. Krim Crimea] (1834) : a gray fur made from the pelts of young lambs of the Crimean Peninsula region

Krio \'krē-ō\ n [Krio, speaker of Krio, Krio language, perh. fr. Yoruba Kiriyó Christian, ultim. fr. Pg crioulo Creole] (1955) : an English-based creole spoken in Sierra Leone

kris \'krēs\ n [Malay kĕris] (ca. 1580) : a Malay or Indonesian dagger with a ridged serpentine blade

Krish·na \'krish-nə, 'krēsh-\ n [Skt Kṛṣṇa] (1864) : a deity or deified hero of later Hinduism worshiped as an incarnation of Vishnu

Krish·na·ism \-,i-zəm\ n (1885) : a widespread form of Hindu religion characterized by the worship of Krishna

Kriss Krin·gle \'kris-'kriŋ-gəl\ n [modif. of G Christkindl Christ child, Christmas gift, dim. of Christkind Christ child] (1830) : SANTA CLAUS

¹kro·na \'krō-nə\ n, pl **kro·nor** \-,nȯr, -nər\ [Sw, lit., crown] (1875) — see MONEY table

²kro·na \'krō-nə\ n, pl **kro·nur** \-nər\ [Icel krōna, lit., crown] (1886) — see MONEY table

¹kro·ne \'krō-nə\ n, pl **kro·ner** \-nər\ [Dan, lit., crown] (1885) — see MONEY table

²kro·ne \'krō-nə\ n, pl **kro·nen** \-nən\ [G, lit., crown] (1895) **1** : the basic monetary unit of Austria from 1892 to 1925 **2** : a coin representing one krone

Kro·neck·er delta \'krō-,ne-kər-\ n [Leopold Kronecker †1891 Ger. mathematician] (1926) : a function of two variables that is 1 when the variables have the same value and is 0 when they have different values

Kru·ger·rand \'krü-gə(r)-,rand, -,ränd, -,ränt\ n [S.J.P. Kruger + rand] (1967) : a one-ounce gold coin of the Republic of So. Africa

krumm·holz \'krùm-,hōlts\ n, pl **krummholz** [G, fr. krumm crooked + Holz wood] (1903) : stunted forest characteristic of timberline

krumm·horn also **krum·horn** \'krȯm-,hȯrn\ n [G Krummhorn, fr. krumm curved + Horn horn] (ca. 1696) : a Renaissance double-reed woodwind instrument consisting of a curved boxwood tube and having a pierced cap covering the reed

kryp·ton \'krip-,tän\ n [Gk, neut. of kryptos hidden — more at CRYPT] (1898) : a colorless relatively inert gaseous element found in air at about one part per million and used esp. in electric lamps — see ELEMENT table

Ksha·tri·ya \'ksha-trē-ə, 'cha-\ n [Skt kṣatriya, fr. kṣatra dominion — more at CHECK] (1794) : a Hindu of an upper caste traditionally assigned to governing and military occupations

Ku·che·an \'kü-chē-ən, 'kü-\ n [Kuche, Kucha, Sinkiang, China] (ca. 1934) : TOCHARIAN B

ku·chen \'kü-kən, -kən\ n, pl **kuchen** [G, cake, fr. OHG kuocho — more at CAKE] (1854) : any of various coffee cakes made from sweet yeast dough

ku·do \'kü-(,)dō, 'kyü-\ n, pl **kudos** [back-formation fr. kudos (taken as a pl.)] (1926) **1** : AWARD, HONOR ⟨a score of honorary degrees and . . . other ~s —Time⟩ **2** : COMPLIMENT, PRAISE ⟨to all three should go some kind of special ~ for refusing to succumb —Al Hine⟩

usage Some commentators hold that since kudos is a singular word it cannot be used as a plural and that the word kudo is impossible. But kudo does exist; it is simply one of the most recent words created by back-formation from another word misunderstood as a plural. Kudos was introduced into English in the 19th century; it was used in contexts where a reader unfamiliar with Greek could not be sure whether it was singular or plural. By the 1920s it began to appear as a plural, and about 25 years later kudo began to appear. It may have begun as a misunderstanding, but then so did cherry and pea.

ku·dos \'kü-,däs, 'kyü-, -,dōs\ n [Gk kydos] (1831) **1** : fame and renown resulting from an act or achievement : PRESTIGE **2** : praise given for achievement

ku·du \'kü-(,)dü\ n, pl **kudu** or **kudus** [Afrik koedoe] (1777) : a large grayish brown African antelope (Tragelaphus strepsiceros) with large annulated spirally twisted horns; also : a related antelope (T. imberbis)

kud·zu \'kùd-(,)zü, 'kəd-\ n [Jp kuzu] (1876) : an Asian leguminous vine (Pueraria lobata syn. P. thunbergiana) that is used for forage and erosion control and that is often a serious weed in the southeastern U.S.

ku·gel \'kü-gəl\ n [Yiddish kugl, fr. MHG kugel ball — more at CUDGEL] (1846) : a baked pudding (as of potatoes or noodles) usu. served as a side dish

Ku Klux·er \'kü-'klək-sər also 'kyü- or 'klü-\ n (1880) : a member of the Ku Klux Klan — **Ku Klux·ism** \-'klək-,si-zəm\ n

Ku Klux Klan \'kü-'kləks-'klan also 'kyü- or 'klü-\ n (1867) **1** : a post-Civil War secret society advocating white supremacy **2** : a 20th century secret fraternal group held to confine its membership to American-born white Christians

ku·lak \'kü-,lak, -,läk, kü-'\ n [Russ, lit., fist] (1877) **1** : a prosperous or wealthy peasant farmer in 19th century Russia **2** : a farmer characterized by Communists as having excessive wealth

kul·tur \kül-'tür\ n, often cap [G, fr. L cultura culture] (1914) **1** : CULTURE 5 **2** : culture emphasizing practical efficiency and individual subordination to the state **3** : German culture held to be superior esp. by militant Nazi and Hohenzollern expansionists

Kul·tur·kampf \-,käm(p)f\ n [G, fr. Kultur + Kampf conflict] (1879) : conflict between civil government and religious authorities esp. over control of education and church appointments

ku·miss var of KOUMISS

küm·mel \'ki-məl\ n [G, lit., caraway seed, fr. OHG kumin cumin] (1864) : a colorless liqueur flavored principally with caraway seeds

kum·quat \'kəm-,kwät\ n [Chin (Guangdong) gām-gwāt, fr. gām gold + gwāt citrus fruit] (1699) : any of several small yellow to orange citrus fruits with sweet spongy rind and somewhat acid pulp that are used chiefly for preserves; also : a tree or shrub (genus Fortunella) of the rue family that bears kumquats

kun·da·li·ni \,kùn-də-'lē-nē, ,kən-\ n, often cap [Skt kundalinī, fr. fem. of kundalin circular, coiled, fr. kundala ring] (1905) : the yogic life force that is held to lie coiled at the base of the spine until it is aroused and sent to the head to trigger enlightenment

Kung \'kùŋ, 'küŋ; in !Kung the initial sound is a type of click\ n, pl **Kung** (1926) **1** : a member of a people of southern Africa — usu. preceded in writing by ! **2** : the Khoisan language of the !Kung people — usu. preceded in writing by !

kung fu \,kəŋ-'fü, ,kùŋ-, ,küŋ-\ n [Chin (Beijing) gōngfu skill, art] (1966) : any of various Chinese arts of self-defense like karate

kunz·ite \'kùn(t)-,sīt\ n [G. F. Kunz †1932 Am. gem expert] (1903) : a spodumene that occurs in pinkish lilac crystals and is used as a gem

Kurd \'kùrd, 'kərd\ n (1595) : a member of a pastoral and agricultural people who inhabit a plateau region in adjoining parts of Turkey, Iran, Iraq, Syria, Armenia, and Azerbaijan — **Kurd·ish** \'kùr-dish, 'kər-\ adj

Kurdish n (1813) : the Iranian language of the Kurds

Kur·di·stan \,kùr-də-'stan, ,kər-\ n [Kurdistan, Asia] (1904) : an Oriental rug woven by the Kurds and noted for fine colors

kur·gan \kùr-'gän, -'gan\ n [Russ, of Turkic origin; akin to Turk kurgan fortress, castle] (1889) : a burial mound of eastern Europe or Siberia

kur·ra·jong \'kər-ə-,jȯŋ, 'kə-rə-, -,jäŋ\ n [Dharuk (Australian aboriginal language of the Port Jackson area) garajuŋ] (1823) : any of several Australian trees or shrubs (family Sterculiaceae) having strong bast fiber used by Australian aborigines; *esp* : a widely planted shelter and forage tree (*Brachychiton populneum*)

kur·to·sis \(,)kər-'tō-səs\ *n* [Gk *kyrtōsis* convexity, fr. *kyrtos* convex — more at CURVE] (1905) : the peakedness or flatness of the graph of a frequency distribution esp. with respect to the concentration of values near the mean as compared with the normal distribution

ku·ru \'kür-(,)ü\ *n* [Fore (language of eastern highland Papua New Guinea)] (1957) : a rare progressive fatal encephalopathy that is caused by a slow virus, resembles Creutzfeldt-Jakob disease, and occurs among tribesmen in eastern New Guinea

ku·rus \kə-'rüsh\ *n, pl* **kurus** [Turk *kuruş*] (1882) — see lira at MONEY table

Ku·te·nai \'kü-t²n-,ā, -,ē\ *n, pl* **Kutenai** *or* **Kutenais** (1801) **1** : a member of an American Indian people of the Rocky Mountains in both the U.S. and Canada **2** : the language of the Kutenai people

kvass \'kväs, 'kfäs\ *n* [Russ *kvas*] (ca. 1553) : a slightly alcoholic beverage of eastern Europe made from fermented mixed cereals and often flavored

¹kvetch \'kvech, 'kfech\ *vi* [Yiddish *kvetshn*, lit., to squeeze, pinch, fr. MHG *quetschen*] (ca. 1952) : to complain habitually : GRIPE

²kvetch *n* (1964) **1** : an habitual complainer **2** : COMPLAINT 1 — **kvetchy** \'kve-chē, 'kfe-\ *adj*

Kwa \'kwä\ *n* (1857) : a branch of the Niger-Congo language family that is spoken along the African coast and its hinterland from the Ivory Coast to southwestern Nigeria

kwa·cha \'kwä-chə\ *n, pl* **kwacha** [Bemba or Chichewa (Bantu language of Malawi), lit., it dawns] (1966) — see MONEY table

Kwa·ki·utl \,kwä-kē-'yü-t²l, ,kwä-'kyü-\ *n, pl* **Kwakiutl** (1848) **1** : a member of an American Indian people of the Canadian Pacific coast **2** : the language of the Kwakiutl people

kwan·za \'kwän-zə\ *n, pl* **kwanzas** *or* **kwanza** [*Kwanza* (Cuanza), river in Angola] (1978) — see MONEY table

Kwan·za *or* **Kwan·zaa** \'kwän-zə\ *n* [Swahili *kwanza* first] (1972) : an African-American festival held in late December

kwash·i·or·kor \,kwä-shē-'òr-kər, -òr-'kòr\ *n* [Ga (Kwa language of coastal Ghana) *kwàsɔ̀kɔ́* influence a child is said to be under when a second child comes] (1935) : severe malnutrition in infants and children that is caused by a diet high in carbohydrate and low in protein

KWIC \'kwik\ *n* [keyword in context] (1959) : a computer-generated index alphabetized on a keyword that appears within a brief context

ky·ack \'kī-,ak\ *n* [origin unknown] (1901) : a packsack to be swung on either side of a packsaddle

ky·a·nite \'kī-ə-,nīt\ *n* [G *Zyanit*, fr. Gk *kyanos* dark blue enamel, lapis lazuli] (1794) : an aluminum silicate Al₂SiO₅ that occurs usu. in blue thin-bladed triclinic crystals and crystalline aggregates and is sometimes used as a gemstone

kyat \'chät\ *n* [Burmese *cᵛat*] (1952) — see MONEY table

ky·bosh *chiefly Brit var of* KIBOSH

ky·mo·gram \'kī-mə-,gram\ *n* [ISV] (1923) : a record made by a kymograph

ky·mo·graph \-,graf\ *n* [Gk *kyma* wave + ISV *-graph* — more at CYME] (1872) : a device which graphically records motion or pressure (as of blood) — **ky·mo·graph·ic** \,kī-mə-'gra-fik\ *adj* — **ky·mog·ra·phy** \kī-'mä-grə-fē\ *n*

Kym·ric *var of* CYMRIC

ky·pho·sis \kī-'fō-səs\ *n* [NL, fr. Gk *kyphōsis*, fr. *kyphos* humpbacked] (1847) : abnormal backward curvature of the spine — **ky·phot·ic** \-'fä-tik\ *adj*

ky·rie \'kir-ē-,ā\ *n, often cap* [ME, fr. ML, fr. LL *kyrie eleison*, transliteration of Gk *kyrie eleēson* Lord, have mercy] (14c) : a short liturgical prayer that begins with or consists of the words "Lord, have mercy"

ky·rie elei·son \'kir-ē-,ā-ə-'lā-(ə-),sän, -(ə-)sən *also* 'kir-ē-ə-'lā-\ *n, often cap K&E* (13c) : KYRIE

kyte \'kīt\ *n* [prob. fr. LG *küt* bowel] (ca. 1540) *chiefly Scot* : BELLY 1, 2

kythe *var of* KITHE

---

l \'el\ *n, pl* **l's** *or* **ls** \'elz\ *often cap, often attrib* (bef. 12c) **1 a** : the 12th letter of the English alphabet **b** : a graphic representation of this letter **c** : a speech counterpart of orthographic *l* **2** : fifty — see NUMBER table **3** : a graphic device for reproducing the letter *l* **4** : one designated *l* esp. as the 12th in order or class **5** : something shaped like the letter L; *specif* : ²ELL 1 **6** : ²EL

l- *prefix* [ISV, fr. *lev-*] **1** \,lē-(,)vō, ,el, 'el\ : levorotatory ⟨*l*-tartaric acid⟩ **2** \,el, 'el\ : having a similar configuration at a selected carbon atom to the configuration of levorotatory glyceraldehyde — usu. printed as a small capital ⟨L-fructose⟩

¹la \'lò, 'lä\ *interj* [ME (northern dial.), fr. OE *lā*] (bef. 12c) *chiefly dial* — used for emphasis or expressing surprise

²la \'lä\ *n* [ME, fr. ML, fr. the syllable sung to this note in a medieval hymn to St. John the Baptist] (14c) : the 6th tone of the diatonic scale in solmization

laa·ger \'lä-gər\ *n* [obs. Afrik *lager* (now *laer*), fr. G *Lager*, fr. OHG *legar* couch — more at LAIR] (1850) **1** *SoAfr* : CAMP; *esp* : an encampment protected by a circle of wagons or armored vehicles **2** : a defensive position, policy, or attitude — **laager** *vi*

laa·ri \'lä-(,)rē\ *n, pl* **laari** [prob. fr. Divehi (Indo-Aryan language of the Maldive Islands), fr. Pers *lārī* piece of silver wire used as currency] (1983) — see rufiyaa at MONEY table

lab \'lab\ *n* (ca. 1895) : LABORATORY

Lab \'lab\ *n* (1957) : LABRADOR RETRIEVER

la·ba·no·ta·tion \,la-bə-nō-'tā-shən, ,la-; lə-,bä-(,)nō-\ *n* [Rudolf Laban †1958 Hung. dance theorist + E *notation*] (1952) : a method of recording bodily movement (as in dance) on a staff by means of symbols (as of direction) that can be aligned with musical accompaniment

lab·a·rum \'la-bə-rəm\ *n* [LL] (1606) : an imperial standard of the later Roman emperors resembling the vexillum; *esp* : the standard bearing the Chi-Rho adopted by Constantine after his conversion to Christianity

lab·da·num \'lab-də-nəm\ *n* [ML *lapdanum*] (14c) : a soft dark fragrant bitter oleoresin derived from various rockroses (genus *Cistus*) and used in making perfumes

¹la·bel \'lā-bəl\ *n* [ME, fr. MF] (14c) **1** *archaic* : BAND, FILLET; *specif* : one attached to a document to hold an appended seal **2** : a heraldic charge that consists of a narrow horizontal band with usu. three pendants **3 a** : a slip (as of paper or cloth) inscribed and affixed to something for identification or description **b** : written or printed matter accompanying an article to furnish identification or other information **c** : a descriptive or identifying word or phrase: as **(1)** : EPITHET **(2)** : a word or phrase used with a dictionary definition to provide additional information **d** : a usu. radioactive isotope used in labeling **4** : an adhesive stamp (as for postage or revenue) **5 a (1)** : a brand of commercial recordings issued under a usu. trademarked name **(2)** : a recording so issued **(3)** : a company issuing such recordings **b** : the brand name of a retail store selling clothing, a clothing manufacturer, or a fashion designer

²label *vt* **la·beled** *or* **la·belled; la·bel·ing** *or* **la·bel·ling** \'lā-b(ə-)liŋ\

(1601) **1 a** : to affix a label to **b** : to describe or designate with or as if with a label **2 a** : to distinguish (an element or atom) by using an isotope distinctive in some manner (as in mass or radioactivity) **b** : to distinguish (as a compound or cell) by introducing a traceable constituent (as a dye or labeled atom) — **la·bel·able** \'lā-bə-lə-bəl\ *adj* — **la·bel·er** \'lā-b(ə-)lər\ *n*

la·bel·lum \lə-'be-ləm\ *n, pl* **la·bel·la** \-lə\ [NL, fr. L, dim. of *labrum* lip — more at LIP] (1830) **1** : the median and usu. most morphologically distinct member of the corolla of an orchid **2** : a terminal part of the labium or labrum of various insects

labia *pl of* LABIUM

¹la·bi·al \'lā-bē-əl\ *adj* [ML *labialis*, fr. L *labium* lip] (1594) **1** : uttered with the participation of one or both lips ⟨the ~ sounds \f\, \p\, and \ü\⟩ **2** : of, relating to, or situated near the lips or labia — **la·bi·al·ly** \-ə-lē\ *adv*

²labial *n* (1668) : a labial consonant

la·bi·al·ize \'lā-bē-ə-,līz\ *vt* **-ized; -iz·ing** (1867) : to make labial : ROUND 1b(2) — **la·bi·al·i·za·tion** \,lā-bē-ə-lə-'zā-shən, -byə-lə-\ *n*

la·bia ma·jo·ra \'lā-bē-ə-mə-'jòr-ə, -'jòr-\ *n pl* [NL, lit., larger lips] (1838) : the outer fatty folds of the vulva bounding the vestibule

labia mi·no·ra \-mə-'nòr-ə, -'nòr-\ *n pl* [NL, lit., smaller lips] (1838) : the inner highly vascular largely connective-tissue folds of the vulva bounding the vestibule

¹la·bi·ate \'lā-bē-ət, -bē-,āt\ *adj* [NL *labiatus*, fr. L *labium*] (1706) **1** : having the limb of a tubular corolla or calyx divided into two unequal parts projecting one over the other like lips ⟨mints and the snapdragon are ~⟩ **2** : of or relating to the mint family

²labiate *n* (1845) : a plant of the mint family

la·bile \'lā-,bīl, -bəl\ *adj* [F, fr. MF, prone to err, fr. LL *labilis*, fr. L *labi* to slip — more at SLEEP] (1603) **1** : readily or continually undergoing chemical, physical, or biological change or breakdown : UNSTABLE ⟨a ~ mineral⟩ **2** : readily open to change — **la·bil·i·ty** \lā-'bi-lə-tē\ *n*

labio- *comb form* [L *labium*] : labial and ⟨*labiodental*⟩

la·bio·den·tal \,lā-bē-ō-'den-t²l\ *adj* (1669) : uttered with the participation of the lip and teeth ⟨the ~ sounds \f\ and \v\⟩ — **labiodental** *n*

la·bio·ve·lar \-'vē-lər\ *adj* [ISV] (1894) : both labial and velar ⟨the ~ sound \w\⟩ — **labiovelar** *n*

la·bi·um \'lā-bē-əm\ *n, pl* **la·bia** \-ə\ [NL, fr. L, lip — more at LIP] (1634) **1** : any of the folds at the margin of the vulva — compare LABIA MAJORA, LABIA MINORA **2** : the lower lip of a labiate corolla **3 a** : a lower mouthpart of an insect that is formed by the second pair of maxillae united in the middle line **b** : a liplike part of various invertebrates

¹la·bor \'lā-bər\ *n* [ME, fr. MF, fr. L *labor*; perh. akin to L *labare* to totter, *labi* to slip — more at SLEEP] (14c) **1 a** : expenditure of physical or mental effort esp. when difficult or compulsory **b (1)** : human activity that provides the goods or services in an economy **(2)** : the

---

\ə\ abut \²\ kitten, F table \ər\ further \a\ ash \ā\ ace \ä\ mop, mar
\aú\ out \ch\ chin \e\ bet \ē\ easy \g\ go \i\ hit \ī\ ice \j\ job
\ŋ\ sing \ō\ go \ò\ law \òi\ boy \th\ thin \t̲h̲\ the \ü\ loot \ú\ foot
\y\ yet \zh\ vision \à, k̲, ⁿ, œ, œ̄, ue, ūe, ᵛ\ see Guide to Pronunciation

services performed by workers for wages as distinguished from those rendered by entrepreneurs for profits **c** : the physical activities involved in giving birth; *also* : the period of such labor **2** : an act or process requiring labor : TASK **3** : a product of labor **4 a** : an economic group comprising those who do manual labor or work for wages **b** (1) : workers employed in an establishment (2) : workers available for employment **c** : the organizations or officials representing groups of workers **5** *usu* **Labour** : the Labour party of the United Kingdom or of another nation of the Commonwealth *syn* see WORK

²**labor** *vb* **la·bored; la·bor·ing** \-b(ə-)riŋ\ *vi* (14c) **1** : to exert one's powers of body or mind esp. with painful or strenuous effort : WORK **2** : to move with great effort ⟨the truck ~ed up the hill⟩ **3** : to be in the labor of giving birth **4** : to suffer from some disadvantage or distress ⟨~ under a delusion⟩ **5** *of a ship* : to pitch or roll heavily ~ *vt* **1** *archaic* **a** : to spend labor on or produce by labor **b** : to strive to effect or achieve **2** : to treat or work out in often laborious detail ⟨~ the obvious⟩ **3** : DISTRESS, BURDEN **4** : to cause to labor

³**labor** *adj* (1640) **1** : of or relating to labor **2** *cap* : of, relating to, or constituting a political party held to represent the interests of workers or made up largely of organized labor groups

lab·o·ra·to·ry \'la-b(ə-)rə-,tōr-ē, -,tór- *sometimes* 'la-bə(r)-, or lə-'bór-ə-,, *Brit usu* lə-'bär-ə-t(ə-)rē\ *n, pl* **-ries** *often attrib* [ML *laboratorium,* fr. L *laborare* to labor, fr. *labor*] (1605) **1 a** : a place equipped for experimental study in a science or for testing and analysis; *broadly* : a place providing opportunity for experimentation, observation, or practice in a field of study **b** : a place like a laboratory for testing, experimentation, or practice ⟨the ~ of the mind⟩ **2** : an academic period set aside for laboratory work

labor camp *n* (1900) **1** : a penal colony where forced labor is performed **2** : a camp for migratory laborers

Labor Day *n* (1886) : a day set aside for special recognition of working people: as **a** : the first Monday in September observed in the U.S. and Canada as a legal holiday **b** : May 1 in many countries

la·bored \'lā-bərd\ *adj* (1608) **1** : produced or performed with labor ⟨~ breathing⟩; *also* : lacking ease of expression ⟨a ~ speech⟩

la·bor·er \-bər-ər\ *n* (14c) : one that labors; *specif* : a person who does unskilled physical work for wages

labor force *n* (1911) : WORK FORCE

la·bor–in·ten·sive \'lā-bər-in-,ten(t)-siv\ *adj* (1953) : having high labor costs per unit of output; *esp* : requiring greater expenditure on labor than on capital

la·bo·ri·ous \lə-'bór-ē-əs, -'bor-\ *adj* (14c) **1** : devoted to labor : INDUSTRIOUS **2** : involving or characterized by hard or toilsome effort : LABORED — **la·bo·ri·ous·ly** *adv* — **la·bo·ri·ous·ness** *n*

la·bor·ite \'lā-bə-,rīt\ *n* (1889) **1** : a member of a group favoring the interests of labor **2** *cap* **a** : a member of a political party devoted chiefly to the interests of labor **b** *usu* **La·bour·ite** : a member of the British Labour party

la·bor·sav·ing \'lā-bər-,sā-viŋ\ *adj* (ca. 1779) : adapted to replace or decrease human and esp. manual labor

labor union *n* (1866) : an organization of workers formed for the purpose of advancing its members' interests in respect to wages, benefits, and working conditions

la·bour *chiefly Brit var of* LABOR

lab·ra·dor·ite \'la-brə-,dòr-,īt\ *n* [*Labrador* Peninsula, Canada] (1814) : a triclinic feldspar showing a play of several colors

Lab·ra·dor retriever \'la-brə-,dòr-\ *n* [*Labrador,* Newfoundland] (1910) : any of a breed of compact, strongly built retrievers largely developed in England from stock originating in Newfoundland and having a short dense black, yellow, or chocolate coat — called also *Lab, Labrador*

Labrador tea *n* (1767) : a low-growing ericaceous evergreen shrub (*Ledum groenlandicum*) chiefly of northern No. America with white or creamy bell-shaped flowers and leaves sometimes used in making tea; *also* : a related Rocky Mountain shrub (*L. glandulosum*)

la·bret \'lā-brət\ *n* [L *labrum*] (1857) : an ornament worn in a perforation of the lip

la·brum \'lā-brəm\ *n* [NL, fr. L, lip, edge — more at LIP] (1826) : an upper or anterior mouthpart of an arthropod consisting of a single median piece in front of or above the mandibles

la·bur·num \lə-'bər-nəm\ *n* [NL, fr. L] (1567) : any of a small genus (*Laburnum* and esp. *L. anagyroides*) of poisonous leguminous shrubs and trees of Eurasia with pendulous racemes of bright yellow flowers

lab·y·rinth \'la-bə-,rin(t)th, -rən(t)th\ *n* [ME *laborintus,* fr. L *labyrinthus,* fr. Gk *labyrinthos*] (14c) **1 a** : a place constructed of or full of intricate passageways and blind alleys **b** : a maze (as in a garden) formed by paths separated by high hedges **2** : something extremely complex or tortuous in structure, arrangement, or character : INTRICACY, PERPLEXITY ⟨a ~ of swamps and channels⟩ ⟨guided them through the ~s of city life —Paul Blanshard⟩ **3** : a tortuous anatomical structure; *esp* : the internal ear or its bony or membranous part

lab·y·rin·thi·an \,la-bə-'rin(t)-thē-ən\ *adj* (1588) : LABYRINTHINE

lab·y·rin·thine \-'rin(t)-thən; -'rin-,thīn, -,thēn\ *adj* (1632) **1** : of, relating to, or resembling a labyrinth : INTRICATE, INVOLVED **2** : of, relating to, affecting, or originating in the internal ear ⟨~ lesions⟩

lab·y·rin·tho·dont \-'rin(t)-thə-,dänt\ *n* [NL *Labyrinthodontia,* fr. Gk *labyrinthos* + *odont-, odous* tooth — more at TOOTH] (ca. 1852) : any of a superorder (Labyrinthodontia) of extinct amphibians of the Late Paleozoic and Early Mesozoic typically having bodies resembling salamanders or crocodiles and considered to be the earliest tetrapod vertebrates — **labyrinthodont** *adj*

lac \'lak\ *n* [Per *lak* & Hindi *lākh,* fr. Skt *lākṣā*] (1598) : a resinous substance secreted by a scale insect (*Laccifer lacca*) and used chiefly in the form of shellac

lac·co·lith \'la-kə-,lith\ *n* [Gk *lakkos* pond, reservoir + E *-lith* — more at LAKE] (1879) : a mass of igneous rock that is intruded between sedimentary beds and typically causes a domical bulging of the overlying strata — **lac·co·lith·ic** \,la-kə-'li-thik\ *adj*

¹**lace** \'lās\ *vb* **laced; lac·ing** [ME, fr. OF *lacier,* fr. L *laqueare* to ensnare, fr. *laqueus*] *vt* (13c) **1** : to draw together the edges of by or as if by a lace passed through eyelets **2** : to draw or pass (as a lace) through something (as eyelets) **3** : to confine or compress by tightening laces of a garment **4 a** : to adorn with or as if with lace **b** : to mark with streaks of color **5** : BEAT, LASH **6 a** : to add a dash of

liquor to **b** : to add to something to impart pungency, savor, or zest ⟨a sauce *laced* with garlic⟩ ⟨conversation *laced* with sarcasm⟩ **c** : to adulterate with a substance ⟨*laced* a guard's coffee with a sedative⟩ ~ *vi* : to admit of being tied or fastened with a lace — **lac·er** *n*

²**lace** *n* [ME, fr. MF *laz,* fr. L *laqueus* snare] (14c) **1** : a cord or string used for drawing together two edges (as of a garment or a shoe) **2** : an ornamental braid for trimming coats or uniforms **3** : an openwork usu. figured fabric made of thread or yarn and used for trimmings, household coverings, and entire garments — **laced** \'lāst\ *adj* — **lace·less** \'lās-ləs\ *adj* — **lace·like** \'lās-,līk\ *adj*

lace–curtain *adj* (1934) : copying middle-class attributes : aspiring to middle-class standing

¹**lac·er·ate** \'la-sə-,rāt\ *vt* **-at·ed; -at·ing** [ME, fr. L *laceratus,* pp. of *lacerare* to tear; akin to Gk *lakis* tear] (15c) **1** : to tear or rend roughly **2** : to cause sharp mental or emotional pain to : DISTRESS — **lac·er·a·tive** \-,rā-tiv\ *adj*

²**lac·er·ate** \-rət, -,lōs·rət *or* **lac·er·at·ed** \-,rā-təd\ *adj* (1542) **1 a** : torn jaggedly : MANGLED **b** : extremely harrowed or distracted **2** : having the edges deeply and irregularly cut ⟨a ~ petal⟩

lac·er·a·tion \,la-sə-'rā-shən\ *n* (1597) **1** : the act of lacerating **2** : a torn and ragged wound

lace·wing \'lās-,wiŋ\ *n* (1854) : any of various neuropterous insects (as genera *Chrysopa* and *Hemerobius*) having delicate lace-like wing venation, usu. long antennae, and often brilliant eyes — called also *lacewing fly*

lacewing

lace·work \'lās-,wərk\ *n* (1849) : objects or patterns consisting of or resembling lace

lac·ey *var of* LACY

la·ches \'la-chəz, 'lā-\ *n, pl* **laches** [ME *lachesse,* fr. MF *laschesse,* fr. OF *lasche* lax, ultim. fr. L *laxare* to loosen — more at LEASE] (14c) : negligence in the observance of duty or opportunity; *specif* : undue delay in asserting a legal right or privilege

lach·ry·mal *or* **lac·ri·mal** \'la-krə-məl\ *adj* [MF or ML; MF *lacrymal,* fr. ML *lacrimalis,* fr. L *lacrima* tear, fr. OL *dacrima,* prob. fr. Gk *dakry* — more at TEAR] (15c) **1** *usu* **lacrimal** : of, relating to, or being glands that produce tears **2** : of, relating to, or marked by tears

lach·ry·mose \-,mōs\ *adj* [L *lacrimosus,* fr. *lacrima*] (ca. 1727) **1** : given to tears or weeping : TEARFUL **2** : tending to cause tears : MOURNFUL — **lach·ry·mose·ly** *adv* — **lach·ry·mos·i·ty** \,la-krə-'mä-sə-tē\ *n*

lac·ing \'lā-siŋ\ *n* (14c) **1** : the action of one that laces **2** : something that laces : LACE **3** : a contrasting marginal band of color (as on a feather) **4 a** : a dash of liquor in a food or beverage **b** : a trace or sprinkling that adds spice or flavor **5** : a decisive defeat

la·cin·i·ate \lə-'si-nē-ət, -,āt\ *adj* [L *lacinia* flap; akin to L *lacerare*] (ca. 1760) : bordered with a fringe; *esp* : cut into deep irregular usu. pointed lobes ⟨~ petals⟩ — **la·cin·i·a·tion** \-,si-nē-'ā-shən\ *n*

¹**lack** \'lak\ *vi* (13c) **1** : to be deficient or missing ⟨time is ~*ing* for a full explanation⟩ **2** : to be short or have need of something ⟨he will not ~ for advisers⟩ ~ *vt* : to stand in need of : suffer from the absence or deficiency of ⟨~ the necessities of life⟩

²**lack** *n* [ME *lak;* akin to MD *lak* lack, ON *lakr* defective] (14c) **1** : the fact or state of being wanting or deficient **2** : something that is lacking or is needed

lack·a·dai·si·cal \,la-kə-'dā-zi-kəl\ *adj* [irreg. fr. *lackaday* + *-ical*] (1768) : lacking life, spirit, or zest : LANGUID — **lack·a·dai·si·cal·ly** \-k(ə-)lē\ *adv*

lack·a·day \'la-kə-,dā\ *interj* [by alter. & shortening fr. *alack the day*] (1695) *archaic* — used to express regret or deprecation

¹**lack·ey** \'la-kē\ *n, pl* **lackeys** [MF *laquais*] (1523) **1 a** : FOOTMAN 2, SERVANT **b** : someone who does menial tasks or runs errands for another **2** : a servile follower : TOADY

²**lackey** *vb* **lack·eyed; lack·ey·ing** *vi* (1568) *obs* : to act as a lackey : TOADY ~ *vt* : to wait upon or serve obsequiously

lack·lus·ter \'lak-,ləs-tər\ *adj* (1600) : lacking in sheen, brilliance, or vitality : DULL, MEDIOCRE — **lackluster** *n*

la·con·ic \lə-'kä-nik\ *adj* [L *laconicus* Spartan, fr. Gk *lakōnikos;* fr. the Spartan reputation for terseness of speech] (1589) : using or involving the use of a minimum of words : concise to the point of seeming rude or mysterious *syn* see CONCISE — **la·con·i·cal·ly** \-ni-k(ə-)lē\ *adv*

lac·o·nism \'la-kə-,ni-zəm\ *n* (1570) **1** : brevity or terseness of expression or style **2** : a laconic expression

¹**lac·quer** \'la-kər\ *n* [Pg *lacré* sealing wax, fr. *laca* lac, fr. Ar *lakk,* fr. Per *lak* — more at LAC] (1592) **1 a** : a spirit varnish (as shellac) **b** : any of various durable natural varnishes; *esp* : a varnish obtained from an Asian sumac (*Rhus verniciflua*) — called also *Japanese lacquer* **2** : any of various clear or colored synthetic organic coatings that typically dry to form a film by evaporation of the solvent; *esp* : a solution of a cellulose derivative (as nitrocellulose)

²**lacquer** *vt* **lac·quered; lac·quer·ing** \-k(ə-)riŋ\ (1688) **1** : to coat with or as if with lacquer **2** : to give a smooth finish or appearance to : make glossy — **lac·quer·er** \-kər-ər\ *n*

lac·quer·ware \-,war, -,wer\ *n* (1697) : a decorative article usu. made of wood and coated with lacquer; *also* : such articles or ware collectively

lac·quer·work \-,wərk\ *n* (ca. 1901) : LACQUERWARE

lac·ri·ma·tion \,la-krə-'mā-shən\ *n* (1572) : the secretion of tears esp. when abnormal or excessive

lac·ri·ma·tor *or* **lach·ry·ma·tor** \'la-krə-,mā-tər\ *n* [L *lacrimare* to weep, fr. *lacrima* tear — more at LACHRYMAL] (1918) : a tear-producing substance (as tear gas)

la·crosse \lə-'krós\ *n* [CanF *la crosse,* lit., the crosier] (1718) : a goal game in which players use a long-handled stick that has a triangular head with a mesh pouch for catching, carrying, and throwing the ball

lact- *or* **lacti-** *or* **lacto-** *comb form* [F & L; F, fr. L, fr. *lact-, lac* — more at GALAXY] **1** : milk ⟨*lacto*globulin⟩ **2 a** : lactic acid ⟨*lactate*⟩ **b** : lactose ⟨*lactase*⟩

lact·al·bu·min \‚lak-‚tal-'byü-mən\ n [ISV] (ca. 1857) : an albumin that is obtained from whey and is similar to serum albumin

lac·tase \'lak-‚tās, -‚tāz\ n [ISV] (1891) : an enzyme that hydrolyzes beta-galactosides (as lactose) and occurs esp. in the intestines of young mammals and in yeasts

¹lac·tate \'lak-‚tāt\ n (ca. 1794) : a salt or ester of lactic acid

²lactate vi **lac·tat·ed; lac·tat·ing** [L lactatus, pp. of lactare, fr. lact-, lac] (ca. 1889) : to secrete milk — **lac·ta·tion** \lak-'tā-shən\ n — **lac·ta·tion·al** \-shnəl, -shə-n³l\ adj

¹lac·te·al \'lak-tē-əl\ adj [L lacteus of milk, fr. lact-, lac] (ca. 1658) 1 : relating to, consisting of, producing, or resembling milk 2 a : conveying or containing a milky fluid b : of or relating to the lacteals

²lacteal n (1680) : any of the lymphatic vessels arising from the villi of the small intestine and conveying chyle to the thoracic duct

lac·tic \'lak-tik\ adj (1790) 1 a : of or relating to milk b : obtained from sour milk or whey 2 : involving the production of lactic acid

lactic acid (1790) : a hygroscopic organic acid $C_3H_6O_3$ present normally in tissue, produced in carbohydrate matter usu. by bacterial fermentation, and used esp. in food and medicine and in industry

lac·tif·er·ous \lak-'ti-f(ə-)rəs\ adj [F or LL; F lactifère, fr. LL lactifer, fr. L lact-, lac + -fer] (ca. 1674) 1 : yielding a milky juice 〈∼ plants〉 2 : secreting or conveying milk

lac·to·ba·cil·lus \‚lak-tō-bə-'si-ləs\ n [NL] (1924) : any of a genus (Lactobacillus) of lactic-acid-forming bacteria

lac·to·gen·ic \‚lak-tə-'je-nik\ adj (1933) : inducing lactation 〈∼ hormones〉

lac·to·glob·u·lin \-'glä-byə-lən\ n (1885) : a crystalline protein fraction that is obtained from the whey of milk

lac·tone \'lak-‚tōn\ n [ISV] (1880) : any of various cyclic esters formed from hydroxy acids — **lac·ton·ic** \lak-'tä-nik\ adj

lac·tose \'lak-‚tōs, -‚tōz\ n [ISV] (1858) : a disaccharide sugar $C_{12}H_{22}O_{11}$ that is present in milk and yields glucose and galactose upon hydrolysis and yields esp. lactic acid upon fermentation

la·cu·na \lə-'kü-nə, -'kyü-\ n, pl **la·cu·nae** \-'kyü-(‚)nē, -'kü-‚nī\ or **la·cu·nas** \-'kü-nəz, -'kyü-\ [L, pool, pit, gap — more at LAGOON] (1652) 1 : a blank space or a missing part : GAP 2 : a small cavity, pit, or discontinuity in an anatomical structure — **la·cu·nar** \-'kü-nər, -'kyü-\ also **la·cu·nate** \lə-'kü-nət, -'kyü-, -‚nāt; 'la-kyə-‚nāt\ adj

la·cus·trine \lə-'kəs-trən\ adj [F or It lacustre, fr. L lacus lake] (1830) : of, relating to, formed in, living in, or growing in lakes 〈∼ deposits〉 〈∼ faunas〉

lacy \'lā-sē\ adj **lac·i·er; -est** (1804) : resembling or consisting of lace

lad \'lad\ n [ME ladde] (14c) 1 : a male person of any age between early boyhood and maturity : BOY, YOUTH 2 : FELLOW, CHAP

lad·a·num \'la-d³n-əm, 'lad-nəm\ var of LABDANUM

lad·der \'la-dər\ n, often attrib [ME, fr. OE hlæder; akin to OHG leitara ladder, OE hlinian to lean — more at LEAN] (bef. 12c) 1 : a structure for climbing up or down that consists essentially of two long sidepieces joined at intervals by crosspieces on which one may step 2 : something that resembles a ladder in form or use; esp : RUN 11a 3 : a series of usu. ascending steps or stages : SCALE 〈climbing up the corporate ∼〉 — **lad·der·like** \-‚līk\ adj

lad·der–back \-‚bak\ adj (1908) of furniture : having a back consisting of two upright posts connected by horizontal slats

ladder truck (1889) : HOOK AND LADDER TRUCK

lad·die \'la-dē\ n (1546) : a young lad

lade \'lād\ vb **lad·ed; lad·ed** or **lad·en** \'lā-d³n\; **lad·ing** [ME, fr. OE hladan; akin to OHG hladan to load, OCS klasti to place] vt (bef. 12c) 1 a : to put a load or burden on or in : LOAD b : to put or place as a load esp. for shipment : SHIP c : to load heavily or oppressively 2 : DIP, LADLE ∼ vi 1 : to take on cargo : LOAD 2 : to take up or convey a liquid by dipping

¹lad·en \'lā-d³n\ vt **lad·ened; lad·en·ing** \'lād-niŋ, 'lā-d³n-iŋ\ (1514) : LADE

²laden adj (bef. 12c) : carrying a load or burden

la–di–da \‚lä-dē-'dä\ also **la–de–da** adj [perh. alter. of lardy-dardy foppish] (1895) : affectedly refined in manners or tastes : PRETENTIOUS, ELEGANT

la·dies \'lā-dēz\ n pl but sing or pl in constr (1918) chiefly Brit : LADIES' ROOM

ladies' man also **lady's man** n (1784) : a man who shows a marked fondness for the company of women or is esp. attentive to women

ladies' room n (1870) : a room equipped with lavatories and toilets for the use of women

ladies' tresses n pl but sing or pl in constr (1548) : any of a widely distributed genus (Spiranthes) of terrestrial orchids with slender often twisted spikes of white irregular flowers

La·din \lə-'dēn\ n [Rhaeto-Romance, fr. L Latinum Latin] (1877) 1 a : a Rhaeto-Romance dialect of Alto Adige in northern Italy b : the Rhaeto-Romance dialects of the Engadine Valley in Switzerland 2 : one speaking Ladin as a mother tongue

lad·ing \'lā-diŋ\ n (1500) 1 a : LOADING 1 b : an act of bailing, dipping, or ladling 2 : CARGO, FREIGHT

la·di·no \lə-'dē-nō, -'nos [Sp, lit., Latin, fr. L latinus] (1877) 1 often cap [AmerSp] : a westernized Spanish-speaking Latin American; esp : MESTIZO 2 cap [Judeo-Spanish, fr. OSp] : JUDEO-SPANISH

la·di·no clover \lə-'dī-(‚)nō-, -nə-\ n [perh. irreg. fr. Lodi, Italy + It -ino, adj. suffix] (1924) : a large nutritious rapidly growing clover that is a variety of white clover and is widely planted esp. for forage — called also ladino

¹la·dle \'lā-d³l\ n [ME ladel, fr. OE hlædel, fr. hladan] (bef. 12c) 1 : a deep-bowled long-handled spoon used esp. for dipping up and conveying liquids 2 : something resembling a ladle in form or function

²ladle vt **la·dled; la·dling** \'lād-liŋ, 'lā-d³l-iŋ\ (1525) : to take up and convey in or as if in a ladle

la dol·ce vi·ta \(‚)lä-‚dōl-(‚)chā-'vē-(‚)tä\ var of DOLCE VITA

la·dy \'lā-dē\ n, pl **ladies** often attrib [ME, fr. OE hlæfdige, fr. hlāf bread + -dige (akin to dæge kneader of bread) — more at LOAF, DAIRY] (bef. 12c) 1 : a woman having proprietary rights or authority esp. as a feudal superior b : a woman receiving the homage or devotion of a knight or lover 2 cap : VIRGIN MARY — usu. used with Our 3 a : a woman of superior social position b : a woman of refinement and gentle manners c : WOMAN, FEMALE — often used in a courteous reference 〈show the ∼ to a seat〉 or usu. in the pl. in address 〈ladies and

gentlemen〉 4 a : WIFE b : GIRLFRIEND, MISTRESS 5 a : any of various titled women in Great Britain — used as the customary title of (1) a marchioness, countess, viscountess, or baroness or (2) the wife of a knight, baronet, member of the peerage, or one having the courtesy title of lord and used as a courtesy title for the daughter of a duke, marquess, or earl b : a female member of an order of knighthood — compare DAME

la·dy·bug \'lā-dē-‚bəg\ n [Our Lady, the Virgin Mary] (1699) : any of numerous small nearly hemispherical often brightly colored beetles (family Coccinellidae) of temperate and tropical regions that usu. feed both as larvae and adults on other insects — called also lady beetle, ladybird, ladybird beetle

lady chapel n, often cap L&C (15c) : a chapel dedicated to the Virgin Mary

Lady Day n (13c) : ANNUNCIATION 1

la·dy·fin·ger \'lā-dē-‚fiŋ-gər\ n (1820) : a small finger-shaped sponge cake

la·dy·fish \-‚fish\ n (1712) 1 : BONEFISH 1 2 : a large silvery food and sport fish (Elops saurus) that resembles a herring but is related to the tarpon

la·dy–in–wait·ing \'lā-dē-in-'wā-tiŋ\ n, pl **ladies–in–waiting** (1862) : a lady of a queen's or a princess's household appointed to wait on her

la·dy–kill·er \'lā-dē-‚ki-lər\ n (ca. 1810) : a man who is extremely attractive to women

la·dy·kin \'lā-dē-kən\ n (1853) : a little lady

la·dy·like \-‚līk\ adj (1586) 1 : becoming or suitable to a lady 2 : resembling a lady in appearance or manners : WELL-BRED 3 a : feeling or showing too much concern about elegance or propriety 〈∼ embarrassment at not being the wife of a real doctor —Lewis Vogler〉 b : lacking in strength, force, or virility

la·dy–love \'lā-dē-‚ləv, ‚lä-dē-'\ n (1733) : SWEETHEART, MISTRESS

lady of the house (1816) : the chief female in a household

Lady of the Lake (15c) : VIVIAN

la·dy·ship \'lā-dē-‚ship\ n (13c) : the condition of being a lady : rank of lady — used as a title for a woman having the rank of lady 〈her Ladyship is not at home〉 〈if your Ladyship please〉

lady's slipper n (1597) : any of several No. American temperate-zone orchids (as of the genus Cypripedium) having flowers whose shape suggests a slipper — called also lady slipper

la·dy's–smock \-‚smäk\ n (1588) : CUCKOOFLOWER 1

lady's thumb n (1837) : a widely distributed weedy annual herb (Polygonum persicaria) that has large lanceolate leaves often with a blackish blotch suggesting a thumbprint

La·er·tes \lā-'ər-tēz\ n [L, fr. Gk Laertēs] 1 : the father of Odysseus in Greek mythology 2 : the son of Polonius and brother of Ophelia in Shakespeare's Hamlet

Lae·ta·re Sunday \lā-'tär-ē-, -'tar-\ n [L laetare, sing. imper. of laetari to rejoice] (ca. 1870) : the fourth Sunday in Lent

la·e·trile \'lā-ə-(‚)tril, -trəl\ n, often cap [laevorotary (levorotatory) + nitrile] (1953) : a drug derived esp. from apricot pits that contains amygdalin and has been used in the treatment of cancer although of unproved effectiveness

¹lag \'lag\ n [prob. of Scand origin; akin to Norw dial. lagga to go slowly] (1514) 1 : one that lags or is last 2 a : the act or the condition of lagging b : comparative slowness or retardation c (1) : an amount of lagging or the time during which lagging continues (2) : a space of time esp. between related events or phenomena : INTERVAL 3 : the action of lagging for opening shot (as in marbles or billiards)

²lag vi **lagged; lag·ging** (1530) 1 a : to stay or fall behind : LINGER, LOITER b : to move, function, or develop with comparative slowness c : to become retarded in attaining maximum value 2 : to slacken or weaken gradually : FLAG 3 : to toss or roll a marble toward a line or a cue ball toward the head cushion to determine order of play ∼ vt 1 : to lag behind 〈current that ∼s the voltage〉 2 : to pitch or shoot (as a coin or marble) at a mark syn see DELAY — **lag·ger** n

³lag adj (1552) : LAST, HINDMOST

⁴lag n [prob. of Scand origin; akin to ON logg rim of a barrel] (1672) 1 : a barrel stave 2 : a stave, slat, or strip (as of wood or asbestos) forming part of a covering for a cylindrical object

⁵lag vt **lagged; lag·ging** (1870) : to cover or provide with lags

⁶lag vt **lagged; lag·ging** [origin unknown] (ca. 1812) 1 slang chiefly Brit : to transport or jail for crime 2 slang chiefly Brit : ARREST

⁷lag n (ca. 1812) 1 slang chiefly Brit a : a person transported for crime b : CONVICT c : an ex-convict 2 slang chiefly Brit : a jail sentence : STRETCH

lag·an \'la-gən\ also **lag·end** \-gənd\ n [MF lagan or ML laganum debris washed up from the sea] (1641) : goods thrown into the sea with a buoy attached so that they may be found again

Lag b'Omer \'läg-'bō-mər, ‚läg-bə-'ō-\ n [Heb, 33d in Omer] (ca. 1904) : a Jewish holiday falling on the 33d day of the Omer and commemorating the heroism of Bar Kokhba and Akiba ben Joseph

la·ger \'lä-gər\ n [G Lagerbier beer made for storage, fr. Lager storehouse + Bier beer] (ca. 1853) : a light beer brewed by slow fermentation and matured under refrigeration

¹lag·gard \'la-gərd\ adj (1702) : lagging or tending to lag : DILATORY — **lag·gard·ly** adv or adj — **lag·gard·ness** n

²laggard n (1808) : one that lags or lingers

lag·ging \'la-giŋ\ n (1794) : a lag or material used for making lags: as a : material for thermal insulation esp. around a cylindrical object b : planking used esp. for preventing cave-ins in earthwork or for supporting an arch during construction

la·gniappe \'lan-‚yap, lan-'\ n [AmerF, fr. AmerSp la ñapa the lagniappe] (1849) : a small gift given a customer by a merchant at the time of a purchase; broadly : something given or obtained gratuitously or by way of good measure

lago·morph \'la-gə-‚mȯrf\ n [ultim. fr. Gk lagōs hare + morphē form] (1882) : any of an order (Lagomorpha) of gnawing herbivorous mam-

\ə\ abut \³\ kitten, F table \ər\ further \a\ ash \ā\ ace \ä\ mop, mar \aú\ out \ch\ chin \e\ bet \ē\ easy \g\ go \i\ hit \ī\ ice \j\ job \ŋ\ sing \ō\ go \ȯ\ law \ȯi\ boy \th\ thin \th\ the \ü\ loot \ú\ foot \y\ yet \zh\ vision \ä, k̲, ⁿ, œ, œ̄, ue, ūe, ᵞ\ see Guide to Pronunciation mals having two pairs of incisors in the upper jaw one behind the other and comprising the rabbits, hares, and pikas

la·goon \lə-'gün\ *n* [F & It; F *lagune*, fr. It *laguna*, fr. L *lacuna* pit, pool, fr. *lacus* lake] (1673) **1 :** a shallow sound, channel, or pond near or communicating with a larger body of water **2 :** a shallow artificial pool or pond (as for the processing of sewage or storage of a liquid) — **la·goon·al** \-'gü-nᵊl\ *adj*

La·grang·ian \lə-'grän-jē-ən, -'grän-zhē-\ *n* [Joseph-Louis *Lagrange*] (1938) **:** a function that describes the state of a dynamic system in terms of position coordinates and their time derivatives and that is equal to the difference between the potential energy and kinetic energy — compare HAMILTONIAN

la·har \'lä-,här\ *n* [Jav] (1929) **:** a mudflow composed of volcanic debris and water

lah–de–dah, lah–dee–dah, lah–di–dah *var of* LA-DI-DA

Lahn·da \'län-də\ *n* (1901) **:** an Indo-Aryan language of eastern Pakistan

la·ical \'lā-ə-kəl\ *or* **la·ic** \'lā-ik\ *adj* [LL *laicus*, fr. LGk *laïkos*, fr. Gk, of the people, fr. *laos* people] (ca. 1587) **:** of or relating to the laity **:** SECULAR — **laic** *n* — **la·ical·ly** \'lā-ə-k(ə-)lē\ *adv*

la·i·cism \'lā-ə-,si-zəm\ *n* (ca. 1909) **:** a political system characterized by the exclusion of ecclesiastical control and influence

la·i·cize \'lā-ə-,sīz\ *vt* **la·i·cized; la·i·ciz·ing** (1870) **1 :** to reduce to lay status **2 :** to put under the direction of or open to the laity — **la·i·ci·za·tion** \,lā-ə-sə-'zā-shən\ *n*

laid *past and past part of* LAY

laid–back \'lād-'bak, ,lād-\ *adj* (1969) **:** having a relaxed style or character (~ music) — **laid–back·ness** \-nəs\ *n*

laid paper \'lād-\ *n* (1839) **:** paper watermarked with fine lines running across the grain — compare WOVE PAPER

laigh \'läk\ *Scot var of* LOW

lain *past part of* LIE

¹lair \'lar, 'ler\ *n* [ME, fr. OE *leger*; akin to OHG *legar* bed, OE *licgan* to lie — more at LIE] (bef. 12c) **1** *dial Brit* **:** a resting or sleeping place **:** BED **2 a :** the resting or living place of a wild animal **:** DEN **b :** a refuge or place for hiding

²lair *vb* [Sc *lair* mire] *vt* (ca. 1560) *chiefly Scot* **:** to cause to sink in mire ~ *vi, chiefly Scot* **:** WALLOW

laird \'lard, 'lerd\ *n* [ME (northern dial.) *lord, lard* lord] (14c) *chiefly Scot* **:** a landed proprietor — **laird·ly** \-lē\ *adj*

lais·ser–faire *chiefly Brit var of* LAISSEZ-FAIRE

lais·ser–pas·ser *chiefly Brit var of* LAISSEZ-PASSER

lais·sez–faire \,le-sā-'far, ,lā-, -,zā-, -'fer\ *n* [F *laissez faire*, imper. of *laisser faire* to let (people) do (as they choose)] (1825) **1 :** a doctrine opposing governmental interference in economic affairs beyond the minimum necessary for the maintenance of peace and property rights **2 :** a philosophy or practice characterized by a usu. deliberate abstention from direction or interference esp. with individual freedom of choice and action — **laissez–faire** *adj*

lais·sez–pas·ser \-,pa-'sā\ *n* [F, fr. *laissez passer* let (someone) pass] (1914) **:** PERMIT, PASS

lai·tance \'lā-tᵊn(t)s\ *n* [F, fr. *lait* milk, fr. L *lact-, lac* — more at GALAXY] (ca. 1902) **:** an accumulation of fine particles on the surface of fresh concrete due to an upward movement of water (as when excessive mixing water is used)

la·ity \'lā-ə-tē\ *n* [⁵*lay*] (15c) **1 :** the people of a religious faith as distinguished from its clergy **2 :** the mass of the people as distinguished from those of a particular profession or those specially skilled

La·ius \'lā-əs, 'lī-əs\ *n* [L, fr. Gk *Laïos*] **:** a king of Thebes slain by his son Oedipus in fulfillment of an oracle

¹lake \'lāk\ *n, often attrib* [ME, fr. OF *lac* lake, fr. L *lacus*; akin to OE *lagu* sea, Gk *lakkos* pond] (12c) **:** a considerable inland body of standing water; *also* **:** a pool of other liquid (as lava, oil, or pitch) — **lake·like** \-,līk\ *adj*

²lake *n* [F *laque* lac, fr. OProv *laca*, fr. Ar *lakk* — more at LACQUER] (1598) **1 a :** a purplish red pigment prepared from lac or cochineal **b :** any of numerous usu. bright translucent organic pigments composed essentially of a soluble dye absorbed on or combined with an inorganic carrier **2 :** CARMINE 2 — **laky** \'lā-kē\ *adj*

³lake *vb* **laked; lak·ing** *vt* (1903) **:** to cause (blood) to undergo a physiological change in which the hemoglobin becomes dissolved in the plasma ~ *vi, of blood* **:** to undergo the process by which hemoglobin becomes dissolved in the plasma

lake dwelling *n* (1863) **:** a dwelling built on piles in a lake; *specif* **:** one built in prehistoric times — **lake dweller** *n*

lake·front \'lāk-,frᵊnt\ *n* (1880) **:** an area fronting on a lake

lake herring *n* (1842) **:** a cisco (*Coregonus artedii*) found from Lake Memphremagog to Lake Superior and northward and important as a commercial food fish

Lake·land terrier \'lāk-lənd-, -,land-\ *n* [*Lakeland*, England] (1928) **:** any of an English breed of rather small harsh-coated terriers

lak·er \'lā-kər\ *n* (1823) **:** one associated with a lake; *esp* **:** a fish living in or taken from a lake

lake·shore \'lāk-,shōr, -,shȯr\ *n* (1798) **:** the shore of a lake; *also* **:** LAKEFRONT

lake·side \-,sīd\ *n* (1560) **:** LAKEFRONT

lake trout *n* (1668) **:** any of various trout and salmon found in lakes; *esp* **:** MACKINAW TROUT

lakh \'läk, 'lak\ *n* [Hindi *lākh*] (1599) **1 :** one hundred thousand ⟨50 ~s of rupees⟩ **2 :** a great number — **lakh** *adj*

La·ko·ta \lə-'kō-tə\ *n, pl* **Lakota** *also* **Lakotas** (1927) **1 :** a member of a western division of the Dakota peoples **2 :** a dialect of Dakota

-lalia *n comb form* [NL, fr. Gk *lalia* chatter, fr. *lalein* to chat] **:** speech disorder (of a specified type) ⟨echo*lalia*⟩

lal·lan \'la-lən\ *or* **lal·land** \-lən(d)\ *Scot var of* LOWLAND

Lal·lans \'la-lənz\ *n* (1785) **:** Scots as spoken and written in the lowlands of Scotland

Lal·ly \'la-lē\ *trademark* — used for a concrete-filled cylindrical steel structural column

lal·ly-gag *var of* LOLLYGAG

¹lam \'lam\ *vb* **lammed; lam·ming** [of Scand origin; akin to ON *lemja* to thrash; akin to OE *lama* lame] (1595) *vt* **:** to beat soundly **:** THRASH ~ *vi* **1 :** STRIKE, THRASH **2 :** to flee hastily **:** SCRAM

²lam *n* (1897) **:** sudden or hurried flight esp. from the law ⟨on the ~⟩

la·ma \'lä-mə\ *n* [Tibetan *blama*] (1654) **:** a Lamaist monk

La·ma·ism \'lä-mə-,i-zəm\ *n* (1817) **:** the Mahayana Buddhism of Tibet and Mongolia marked by tantric and shamanistic ritual and a dominant monastic hierarchy headed by the Dalai Lama — **La·ma·ist** \-mə-ist\ *n or adj* — **La·ma·is·tic** \,lä-mə-'is-tik\ *adj*

La·marck·ism \lə-'mär-,ki-zəm\ *n* [J.-B. de Monet de *Lamarck*] (1884) **:** a theory of organic evolution asserting that environmental changes cause structural changes in animals and plants that are transmitted to offspring — **La·marck·ian** \-kē-ən\ *adj*

la·ma·sery \'lä-mə-,ser-ē\ *n, pl* **-ser·ies** [F *lamaserie*, fr. *lama* + Per *sarāi* palace] (1849) **:** a monastery of lamas

La·maze \lə-'mäz\ *adj* [Fernand *Lamaze* †1957 Fr. obstetrician] (1965) **:** relating to or being a method of childbirth that involves psychological and physical preparation by the mother in order to suppress pain and facilitate delivery without drugs

¹lamb \'lam\ *n* [ME, fr. OE; akin to OHG *lamb* lamb] (bef. 12c) **1 a :** a young sheep; *esp* **:** one that is less than one year old or without permanent teeth **b :** the young of various animals (as the smaller antelopes) other than sheep **2 a :** a gentle or weak person **b :** DEAR, PET **c :** a person easily cheated or deceived esp. in trading securities **3 a :** the flesh of a lamb used as food **b :** LAMBSKIN — **lamb·like** \-,līk\ *adj* — **lamby** \'la-mē\ *adj*

²lamb *vi* (1611) **:** to bring forth a lamb ~ *vt* **1 :** to bring forth (a lamb) **2 :** to tend (ewes) at lambing time — **lamb·er** \'la-mər\ *n*

lam·baste *or* **lam·bast** \(,)lam-'bāst, -'bast; 'lam-,\ *vt* [prob. fr. ¹*lam* + *baste*] (1637) **1 :** to assault violently **:** BEAT, WHIP **2 :** to attack verbally **:** CENSURE

lamb·da \'lam-də\ *n* [ME, fr. Gk, of Sem origin; akin to Heb *lāmedh* lamed] (15c) **1 :** the 11th letter of the Greek alphabet — see ALPHABET table **2 :** an uncharged unstable elementary particle that has a mass 2183 times that of an electron and that decays typically into a nucleon and a pion

lam·ben·cy \'lam-bən(t)-sē\ *n, pl* **-cies** (1817) **:** the quality, state, or an instance of being lambent

lam·bent \'lam-bənt\ *adj* [L *lambent-, lambens*, prp. of *lambere* to lick — more at LAP] (1647) **1 :** playing lightly on or over a surface **2 :** softly bright or radiant **3 :** marked by lightness or brilliance esp. of expression — **lam·bent·ly** *adv*

lam·bert \'lam-bərt\ *n* [Johann H. *Lambert* †1777 Ger. physicist & philosopher] (1915) **:** the centimeter-gram-second unit of brightness equal to the brightness of a perfectly diffusing surface that radiates or reflects one lumen per square centimeter

lamb·kill \'lam-,kil\ *n* (1790) **:** SHEEP LAUREL

lam·bre·quin \'lam-bər-kən, -bri-kən\ *n* [F] (ca. 1725) **1 :** a scarf used to cover a knight's helmet **2 :** a short decorative drapery for a shelf edge or for the top of a window casing **:** VALANCE

Lam·brus·co \lam-'brü-(,)skō, -'brü-\ *n* [It, fr. L *labruscum* fruit of the wild grape *Vitis labrusca*] (1943) **:** a fruity and fizzy red Italian table wine

lamb's ears *n pl but usu sing in constr* (1930) **:** a widely cultivated perennial herb (*Stachys byzantina* syn. *S. olympica*) of the mint family that occurs in southwestern Asia and has leaves covered with densely matted hairs

lamb·skin \'lam-,skin\ *n* (14c) **:** a lamb's skin or a small fine-grade sheepskin or the leather made from either; *specif* **:** such a skin dressed with the wool on and used esp. for winter clothing

lamb's lettuce *n* (1597) **:** CORN SALAD

lamb's–quar·ter \'lamz-,kwȯ(r)-tər, -,kȯ(r)-\ *n* (1773) **1 :** a goosefoot (*Chenopodium album*) having glaucous foliage that is sometimes used as greens — usu. used in pl. but sing. or pl. in constr. **2 :** any of several oraches — usu. used in pl. but sing. or pl. in constr.

¹lame \'lām\ *adj* **lam·er; lam·est** [ME, fr. OE *lama*; akin to OHG *lam* lame, Lith *limti* to break down] (bef. 12c) **1 a :** having a body part and esp. a limb so disabled as to impair freedom of movement **b :** marked by stiffness and soreness ⟨a ~ shoulder⟩ **2 :** lacking needful or desirable substance **:** WEAK, INEFFECTUAL ⟨a ~ excuse⟩ **3** *slang* **:** not being in the know **:** SQUARE — **lame·ly** *adv* — **lame·ness** *n*

²lame *vt* **lamed; lam·ing** (14c) **1 :** to make lame **:** CRIPPLE **2 :** to make weak or ineffective **:** DISABLE

³lame *n* (1959) *slang* **:** a person who is not in the know **:** SQUARE

⁴lame \'läm, 'lam\ *n* [MF, fr. L *lamina*] (1586) **1 :** a thin plate esp. of metal **:** LAMINA **2 :** small overlapping steel plates joined to slide on one another (as in medieval armor)

la·mé \lä-'mā, la-\ *n* [F] (1922) **:** a brocaded clothing fabric made from any of various fibers combined with tinsel filling threads

lame·brain \'lām-,brān\ *n* (1944) **:** a dull-witted person **:** DOLT — **lamebrain** *or* **lame·brained** \-'brānd\ *adj*

la·med \'lä-,med\ *n* [Heb *lāmedh*, lit., ox goad] (1665) **:** the 12th letter of the Hebrew alphabet — see ALPHABET table

lame duck *n* (1761) **1 :** one that is weak or that falls behind in ability or achievement; *esp, chiefly Brit* **:** an ailing company **2 :** an elected official or group continuing to hold political office during the period between the election and the inauguration of a successor **3 :** one whose position or term of office will soon end — **lame–duck** \'lām-'dək\ *adj*

lamell- *or* **lamelli-** *comb form* [NL, fr. *lamella*] **:** lamella ⟨*lamelli*form⟩

la·mel·la \lə-'me-lə\ *n, pl* **la·mel·lae** \-'me-(,)lē, -,lī\ *also* **lamellas** [NL, fr. L, dim. of *lamina* thin plate] (1678) **:** a thin flat scale, membrane, or layer: as **1 :** one of the thin plates composing the gills of a bivalve mollusk **b :** a gill of a mushroom

lamb 3a: *A* wholesale cuts: *1* leg, *2* loin, *3* rack, *4* breast, *5* shank, *6* shoulder; *B* retail cuts: *a* leg, *b* sirloin chops and roast, *c* loin chops, rolled loin roast, *d* patties and chopped roast, *e* rib chops, crown roast, *f* riblets, stew, and stuffed or rolled breast, *g* shoulder roast, shoulder chops, *h* neck slices, *i* shanks, *j* blade chops, *k* arm chops

la·mel·lar \lə-'me-lər\ *adj* (1794) **1** : composed of or arranged in lamellae **2** : LAMELLIFORM

la·mel·late \lə-'me-lət, 'la-mə-ˌlāt\ *adj* (1826) **1** : composed of or furnished with lamellae **2** : LAMELLIFORM — **la·mel·late·ly** *adv*

la·mel·li·branch \lə-'me-lə-ˌbraŋk\ *n, pl* **-branchs** [NL *Lamellibranchia*, fr. *lamell-* + L *branchia* gill] (1855) : any of a class (Lamellibranchia) of bivalve mollusks (as clams, oysters, and mussels) that have the body bilaterally symmetrical, compressed, and enclosed within the mantle and that build up a shell whose right and left parts are connected by a hinge over the animal's back — **lamellibranch** *adj*

la·mel·li·corn \lə-'me-lə-ˌkȯrn\ *adj* [ultim. fr. NL *lamella* + L *cornu* horn — more at HORN] (ca. 1842) : of, relating to, or belonging to a superfamily (Scarabaeoidea syn. Lamellicornia) of beetles (as a scarab or stag beetle) characterized by 5-jointed tarsi and club-tipped antennae often angled like an elbow — **lamellicorn** *n*

la·mel·li·form \-ˌfȯrm\ *adj* (1819) : having the form of a thin plate

¹la·ment \lə-'ment\ *vb* [ME *lementen*, fr. MF & L; MF *lamenter*, fr. L *lamentari*, fr. *lamentum*, n., lament] *vi* (15c) **1** : to mourn aloud : WAIL ~ *vt* **1** : to express sorrow, mourning, or regret for often demonstratively : MOURN **2** : to regret strongly *syn* see DEPLORE

²lament *n* (1591) **1** : a crying out in grief : WAILING **2** : DIRGE, ELEGY **3** : COMPLAINT

la·men·ta·ble \'la-mən-tə-bəl, ÷lə-'men-\ *adj* (15c) **1** : that is to be regretted or lamented : DEPLORABLE **2** : expressing grief : MOURNFUL — **la·men·ta·ble·ness** *n* — **la·men·ta·bly** \-blē\ *adv*

lam·en·ta·tion \ˌla-mən-'tā-shən\ *n* (14c) : an act or instance of lamenting

Lam·en·ta·tions \-shənz\ *n pl but sing in constr* : a poetic book on the fall of Jerusalem in canonical Jewish and Christian Scripture — see BIBLE table

la·ment·ed \lə-'men-təd\ *adj* (1611) : mourned for — **la·ment·ed·ly** *adv*

la·mia \'lā-mē-ə\ *n* [ME, fr. L, fr. Gk, devouring monster; akin to Gk *lamyros* gluttonous] (14c) : a female demon : VAMPIRE

lamin- *comb form* : lamina ⟨*laminar*⟩

lam·i·na \'la-mə-nə\ *n, pl* **-nae** \-ˌnē, -ˌnī\ *or* **-nas** [L] (ca. 1656) **1** : a thin plate or scale : LAYER **2** : the expanded part of a foliage leaf **3** : one of the narrow thin parallel plates of soft vascular sensitive tissue that cover the flesh within the wall of a hoof

lam·i·nal \'la-mə-n²l\ *adj* (1825) **1** : LAMINAR **2** : produced with the blade of the tongue (as \sh\, \zh\, \ch\, \j\, or \y\) — compare APICAL

lamina pro·pria \-'prō-prē-ə\ *n, pl* **laminae pro·pri·ae** \-prē-ˌē, -ˌī\ [NL, lit., proper lamina] (1937) : a highly vascular layer of connective tissue under the basement membrane lining a layer of epithelium

lam·i·nar \'la-mə-nər\ *adj* (1811) : arranged in, consisting of, or resembling laminae

laminar flow *n* (1935) : streamline flow in a fluid near a solid boundary — compare TURBULENT FLOW

lam·i·nar·ia \ˌla-mə-'ner-ē-ə, -'nar-\ *n* [NL, fr. L *lamina*] (1848) : any of a genus (*Laminaria*) of large chiefly perennial kelps with an unbranched cylindrical or flattened stipe and a smooth or convoluted blade; *broadly* : any of various related kelps (order Laminariales) — **lam·i·nar·i·an** \-ē-ən\ *adj or n*

lam·i·nar·in \ˌla-mə-'ner-ən, -'nar-\ *n* [ISV *laminar-* (fr. NL *Laminaria*) + ¹*-in*] (ca. 1931) : a polysaccharide that is found in various brown algae and yields only glucose on hydrolysis

¹lam·i·nate \'la-mə-ˌnāt\ *vb* **-nat·ed; -nat·ing** *vt* (1665) **1** : to roll or compress into a thin plate **2** : to separate into laminae **3 a** : to make (as a windshield) by uniting superposed layers of one or more materials **b** : to unite (layers of material) by an adhesive or other means ~ *vi* : to divide into laminae — **lam·i·na·tor** \-ˌnā-tər\ *n*

²lam·i·nate \-nət, -ˌnāt\ *adj* (1668) **1** : consisting of laminae **2** : bearing or covered with laminae

³lam·i·nate \-nət, -ˌnāt\ *n* (1939) : a product made by laminating

lam·i·nat·ed \-ˌnā-təd\ *adj* (1665) **1** : LAMINATE 1 **2 a** : composed of layers of firmly united material **b** : made by bonding or impregnating superposed layers (as of paper, wood, or fabric) with resin and compressing under heat

lam·i·na·tion \ˌla-mə-'nā-shən\ *n* (ca. 1676) **1** : the process of laminating **2** : the state of being laminated **3** : a laminated structure **4** : LAMINA

lam·i·ni·tis \ˌla-mə-'nī-təs\ *n* [NL] (1843) : inflammation of the laminae esp. in the hoof of a horse — called also *founder*

Lam·mas \'la-məs\ *n* [ME *Lammasse*, fr. OE *hlāfmæsse*, fr. *hlāf* loaf, bread + *mæsse* mass; fr. the fact that formerly loaves from the first ripe grain were consecrated on this day] (bef. 12c) **1** : August 1 orig. celebrated in England as a harvest festival — called also *Lammas Day* **2** : the time of the year around Lammas Day

Lam·mas·tide \-ˌtīd\ *n* (14c) : LAMMAS 2

lam·mer·gei·er *or* **lam·mer·gey·er** \'la-mər-ˌgī(-ə)r\ *n* [G *Lämmergeier*, fr. *Lämmer* lambs + *Geier* vulture] (1817) : a large Old World vulture (*Gypaetus barbatus*) that occurs in mountain regions and in flight resembles a huge falcon

lamp \'lamp\ *n* [ME, fr. OF *lampe*, fr. L *lampas*, fr. Gk, fr. *lampein* to shine; akin to Hitt *lap-* to burn] (13c) **1 a** : any of various devices for producing light or sometimes heat: as **(1)** : a vessel with a wick for burning an inflammable liquid (as oil) to produce light **(2)** : a glass bulb or tube that emits light produced by electricity (as an incandescent lamp or fluorescent lamp) **b** : a decorative appliance housing a lamp that is usu. covered by a shade **2** : a celestial body **3** : a source of intellectual or spiritual illumination **4** : EYE 1a — usu. used in pl.

lamp·black \-ˌblak\ *n* (1598) : a finely powdered black soot deposited in incomplete combustion of carbonaceous materials and used chiefly as a pigment (as in paints, enamels, and printing inks)

lamp·brush chromosome \'lamp-ˌbrəsh-\ *n* (1911) : a greatly enlarged diplotene chromosome that has apparently filamentous granular loops extending from the chromomeres and is characteristic of some animal oocytes

lamp·light \'lamp-ˌlīt\ *n* (14c) : the light of a lamp

lamp·light·er \-ˌlī-tər\ *n* (1750) : one that lights a lamp

¹lam·poon \lam-'pün\ *n* [F *lampon*] (1645) : SATIRE 1; *specif* : a harsh satire usu. directed against an individual

²lampoon *vt* (ca. 1657) : to make the subject of a lampoon : RIDICULE — **lam·poon·er** *n* — **lam·poon·ery** \-'pü-nə-rē, -'pün-rē\ *n*

lamp·post \'lam(p)-ˌpōst\ *n* (1790) : a post supporting a usu. outdoor lamp or lantern

lam·prey \'lam-prē, -ˌprā\ *n, pl* **lampreys** [ME, fr. OF *lampreie*, fr. ML *lampreda*] (14c) : any of a family (Petromyzontidae) of eel-shaped freshwater or anadromous jawless fishes that include those cyclostomes having well-developed eyes and a large disk-shaped suctorial mouth armed with horny teeth — called also *lamprey eel*

lamp·shell \'lamp-ˌshel\ *n* [fr. the resemblance of the shell and its protruding peduncle to an ancient oil lamp with the wick protruding] (1854) : BRACHIOPOD

lam·ster \'lam(p)-stər\ *also* **lam·is·ter** \'la-mə-stər\ *n* [²*lam* + *-ster*] (1904) : a fugitive esp. from the law

LAN \'lan, ˌel-(ˌ)ā-'en\ *n* (1982) : LOCAL AREA NETWORK

la·nai \lə-'nī, lä-\ *n* [Hawaiian *lānai*] (1823) : PORCH, VERANDA

Lan·ca·shire \'laŋ-kə-ˌshir, -shər\ *n* [*Lancashire*, England] (1896) : a moist crumbly white English cheese that is used esp. in cooking

Lan·cas·tri·an \laŋ-'kas-trē-ən, lan-\ *adj* [John of Gaunt, duke of Lancaster] (1612) : of or relating to the English royal house that ruled from 1399 to 1461

¹lance \'lan(t)s\ *n* [ME, fr. OF, fr. L *lancea*] (14c) **1** : a steel-tipped spear carried by mounted knights or light cavalry **2** : any of various sharp objects suggestive of a lance: as **a** : LANCET **b** : a spear used for killing whales or fish **3** : LANCER 1b

²lance *vb* **lanced; lanc·ing** [ME, fr. MF *lancer*, fr. LL *lanceare*, fr. L *lancea*] *vt* (14c) **1 a** : to pierce with or as if with a lance **b** : to open with or as if with a lancet ⟨~ a boil⟩ **2** : to throw forward : HURL ~ *vi* : to move forward quickly

lance corporal *n* [*lance* (as in obs. *lancepesade* lance corporal, fr. MF *lancepessade*)] (1786) : an enlisted man in the marine corps ranking above a private first class and below a corporal

lance·let \'lan(t)-slət\ *n* (ca. 1836) : any of a subphylum (Cephalochordata) of small translucent marine primitive chordate animals that are fishlike in appearance and usu. live partially buried on the ocean floor — called also *amphioxus*

Lan·ce·lot \'lan(t)-sə-ˌlät, 'län(t)-, -s(ə-)lət\ *n* : a knight of the Round Table and lover of Queen Guinevere

lan·ce·o·late \'lan(t)-sē-ə-ˌlāt\ *adj* [LL *lanceolatus*, fr. L *lanceola*, dim. of *lancea*] (ca. 1760) : shaped like a lance head; *specif* : tapering to a point at the apex and sometimes at the base ⟨~ leaves⟩ ⟨~ prisms⟩ — see LEAF illustration

lanc·er \'lan(t)-sər\ *n* (1590) **1 a** : one who carries a lance **b** : a member of a military unit formerly composed of light cavalry armed with lances **2** *pl but sing in constr* : a set of five quadrilles each in a different meter **b** : the music for such dances

lan·cet \'lan(t)-sət\ *n* (15c) **1** : a sharp-pointed and commonly 2-edged surgical instrument used to make small incisions **2 a** : LANCET WINDOW **b** : LANCET ARCH

lancet arch *n* (ca. 1823) : an acutely pointed arch — see ARCH illustration

lan·cet·ed \'lan(t)-sə-təd\ *adj* (1855) : having a lancet arch or lancet windows

lancet window *n* (1781) : a high narrow window with an acutely pointed head and without tracery

lance·wood \'lan(t)s-ˌwúd\ *n* (1697) : a tough elastic wood used esp. for shafts, fishing rods, and bows; *also* : a tree (esp. *Oxandra lanceolata*) yielding this wood

lan·ci·nat·ing \'lan(t)-sə-ˌnā-tiŋ\ *adj* [*lancinate* to pierce, fr. L *lancinatus*, pp. of *lancinare*; akin to L *lacerare* to rend — more at LACERATE] (1762) : characterized by piercing or stabbing sensations ⟨~ pain⟩

¹land \'land\ *n, often attrib* [ME, fr. OE; akin to OHG *lant* land, MIr *lann*] (bef. 12c) **1 a** : the solid part of the surface of the earth; *also* : a corresponding part of a celestial body (as the moon) **b** : ground or soil of a specified situation, nature, or quality ⟨dry ~⟩ **c** : the surface of the earth and all its natural resources **2 a** : a portion of the earth's solid surface distinguishable by boundaries or ownership ⟨bought ~ in the country⟩: as **a** : COUNTRY ⟨campaigned across the ~⟩ **b** : a rural area characterized by farming or ranching; *also* : farming or ranching as a way of life ⟨wanted to move back to the ~⟩ **3** : REALM, DOMAIN ⟨in the ~ of dreams⟩ — sometimes used in combination ⟨television*land*⟩ **4** : the people of a country ⟨the ~ rose in rebellion⟩ **5** : an area of a partly machined surface that is left without machining — **land·less** \'land-ləs\ *adj* — **land·less·ness** \-nəs\ *n*

²land *vt* (13c) **1** : to set or put on shore from a ship : DISEMBARK **2 a** : to set down after conveying **b** : to cause to reach or come to rest in a particular place ⟨never ~*ed* a punch⟩ **c** : to bring to a specified condition ⟨his carelessness ~*ed* him in trouble⟩ **d** : to bring (as an airplane) to a landing **3 a** : to catch and bring in (as a fish) **b** : GAIN, SECURE ⟨~ a job⟩ ~ *vi* **1 a** : to go ashore from a ship : DISEMBARK **b** *of a ship or boat* : to touch at a place on shore **2 a** : to come to the end of a course or to a stage in a journey : ARRIVE ⟨took the wrong subway and ~*ed* on the other side of town⟩ **b** : to come to be in a condition or situation ⟨~*ed* in jail⟩ **c** : to strike or meet a surface (as after a fall) ⟨~*ed* on my head⟩ **d** : to alight on a surface

lan·dau \'lan-ˌdau, -ˌdȯ\ *n* [*Landau*, Bavaria, Germany] (1743) : a four-wheel carriage with a top divided into two sections that can be let down, thrown back, or removed and with a raised seat outside for the driver

lan·dau·let \ˌlan-dᵊl-'et\ *n* (1794) : a small landau

land bank *n* (1696) : a bank that provides financing for land development and for farm mortgages

landau

land·ed \'lan-dəd\ *adj* (15c) **1** : having an estate in land ⟨~ proprietors⟩ **2** : consisting in or derived from land or real estate ⟨~ wealth⟩

\ə\ abut \²\ kitten, F table \ər\ further \a\ ash \ā\ ace \ä\ mop, mar \aú\ out \ch\ chin \e\ bet \ē\ easy \g\ go \i\ hit \ī\ ice \j\ job \ŋ\ sing \ō\ go \ȯ\ law \ȯi\ boy \th\ thin \th\ the \ü\ loot \ú\ foot \y\ yet \zh\ vision \á, k̲, ⁿ, œ, œ̄, ᵫ, ūͤ, ᵉ\ see Guide to Pronunciation

land·er \'lan-dər\ n (1859) : one that lands; esp : a space vehicle that is designed to land on a celestial body (as the moon or a planet)
land·fall \'lan(d)-ˌfȯl\ n (1627) **1** : a sighting or making of land after a voyage or flight **2** : the land first sighted on a voyage or flight
land·fill \-ˌfil\ n (1942) **1** : a system of trash and garbage disposal in which the waste is buried between layers of earth to build up low-lying land — called also *sanitary landfill* **2** : an area built up by landfill
land·form \-ˌfȯrm\ n (1893) : a natural feature of a land surface
land·grab \-ˌgrab\ n (1860) : a usu. swift acquisition of land often by fraud or force — **land—grab·ber** \-ˌgra-bər\ n
land grant n (1862) : a grant of land made by the government esp. for roads, railroads, or agricultural colleges
land·hold·er \'land-ˌhōl-dər\ n (15c) : a holder or owner of land
land·hold·ing \-ˌhōl-diŋ\ n (ca. 1890) **1** : the state or fact of holding or owning land **2** : property in land — **landholding** adj
land·ing n (15c) **1** : an act or process of one that lands; esp : a going or bringing to a surface (as land or shore) after a voyage or flight **2** : a place for discharging and taking on passengers and cargo **3** : a level part of a staircase (as at the end of a flight of stairs)
landing craft n (1940) : any of numerous naval craft designed for conveying troops and equipment from a transport to a beach in an amphibious assault
landing field n (ca. 1920) : a field where aircraft may land and take off
landing gear n (1911) : the part that supports the weight of an airplane or spacecraft when in contact with the land or water
landing strip n (1930) : AIRSTRIP
land·la·dy \'land-ˌlā-dē\ n (ca. 1536) : a woman who is a landlord
land·line \-ˌlīn\ n (1865) : a line of communication (as by telephone cable) on land
land·locked \-ˌläkt\ adj (1622) **1** : enclosed or nearly enclosed by land ⟨a ~ country⟩ **2** : confined to fresh water by some barrier ⟨~ salmon⟩
land·lord \-ˌlȯrd\ n (bef. 12c) **1** : the owner of property (as land, houses, or apartments) that is leased or rented to another **2** : the master of an inn or lodging house : INNKEEPER
land·lord·ism \-ˌlȯr-ˌdi-zəm\ n (1844) : an economic system or practice by which ownership of land is vested in one who leases it to cultivators
land·lub·ber \-ˌlə-bər\ n (ca. 1700) : LANDSMAN 2 ⟨clumsy ~s learning to sail⟩ — **land·lub·ber·li·ness** \-bər-lē-nəs\ n — **land·lub·ber·ly** \-bər-lē\ adj — **land·lub·bing** \-biŋ\ adj
land·mark \-ˌmärk\ n (bef. 12c) **1** : an object (as a stone or tree) that marks the boundary of land **2 a** : a conspicuous object on land that marks a locality **b** : an anatomical structure used as a point of orientation in locating other structures **3** : an event or development that marks a turning point or a stage **4** : a structure (as a building) of unusual historical and usu. aesthetic interest; esp : one that is officially designated and set aside for preservation
land·mass \-ˌmas\ n (1856) : a large area of land ⟨continental ~es⟩
land mine n (1890) **1** : a mine placed on or just below the surface of the ground and designed to be exploded by the weight of vehicles or troops passing over it **2** : BOOBY TRAP 1
land office n (1681) : a government office in which entries upon and sales of public land are registered
land—office business n (1839) : extensive and rapid business ⟨money changers . . . did a *land-office business* on payday —F. J. Haskin⟩
land·own·er \'land-ˌō-nər\ n (ca. 1733) : an owner of land — **land·own·er·ship** \-ˌship\ n — **land·own·ing** \-ˌō-niŋ\ adj or n
land—poor \'lan(d)-ˌpu̇r\ adj (1873) : owning so much unprofitable or encumbered land as to lack funds to develop the land or pay the charges due on it
Land·ra·ce \'län-ˌrä-sə\ n [Dan. fr. *land* + *race*] (1935) : a swine of any of several breeds locally developed in northern Europe
land reform n (1846) : measures designed to effect a more equitable distribution of agricultural land esp. by governmental action; also : the resulting redistribution
¹**land·scape** \'lan(d)-ˌskāp\ n, often attrib [D *landschap*, fr. *land* + *-schap* -ship] (1598) **1 a** : a picture representing a view of natural inland scenery **b** : the art of depicting such scenery **2 a** : the landforms of a region in the aggregate **b** : a portion of territory that can be viewed at one time from one place **c** : a particular area of activity : SCENE ⟨political ~⟩ **3** obs : VISTA, PROSPECT
²**landscape** vb **land·scaped; land·scap·ing** vt (1914) : to modify or ornament (a natural landscape) by altering the plant cover ~ vi : to engage in landscape gardening — **land·scap·er** n
landscape architect n (1863) : one who develops land for human use and enjoyment through effective placement of structures, vehicular and pedestrian ways, and plantings — **landscape architecture** n
landscape gardener n (ca. 1763) : one who is engaged in the development and decorative planting of gardens and grounds — **landscape gardening** n
land·scap·ist \'lan(d)-ˌskā-pist\ n (1843) : a painter of landscapes
¹**land·slide** \'lan(d)-ˌslīd\ n (1838) **1** : the usu. rapid downward movement of a mass of rock, earth, or artificial fill on a slope; also : the mass that moves down **2 a** : a great majority of votes for one side **b** : an overwhelming victory
²**landslide** vi **-slid** \-ˌslid\; **-slid·ing** \-ˌslī-diŋ\ (1926) **1** : to produce a landslide **2** : to win an election by a heavy majority
land·slip \-ˌslip\ n (1679) : LANDSLIDE 1
Lands·mål or **Lands·maal** \'län(t)s-ˌmȯl\ n [Norw. fr. *land* country + *mål* speech] (1886) : NYNORSK
lands·man \'lan(d)z-mən\ n (1598) **1** : a fellow countryman **2** : one who lives on the land; esp : one who knows little or nothing of the sea or seamanship
land·ward \'land-wərd\ adv or adj (15c) : to or toward the land
land yacht n (1928) : a 3-wheel wind-driven recreation vehicle consisting usu. of a bare-frame structure and a single sail and used esp. on areas of firmly packed sand
¹**lane** \'lān\ n [ME, fr. OE *lanu*; akin to MD *lane* lane] (bef. 12c) **1 a** : a narrow passageway between fences or hedges **2** : a relatively narrow way or track: as **a** : an ocean route used by or prescribed for ships **b** : a strip of roadway for a single line of vehicles ⟨ : AIR LANE⟩ **d** : any of several parallel courses on a track or swimming pool in which a competitor must stay during a race **e** : an unmarked lengthwise divi-

sion of a playing area which defines the playing zone of a particular player **f** : a narrow hardwood surface having pins at one end and a shallow channel along each side that is used in bowling **g** : FREE THROW LANE
²**lane** Scot var of LONE
lane·way \'lān-ˌwā\ n (1882) Brit : LANE
lang·bein·ite \'laŋ-ˌbī-ˌnīt\ n [G *Langbeinit*, fr. A. *Langbein*, 19th cent. Ger. chemist] (ca. 1897) : a mineral that is a double sulfate of potassium and magnesium used in the fertilizer industry
lang·lauf \'läŋ-ˌlau̇f\ n [G, fr. *lang* + *Lauf* race] (1927) : cross=country running or racing on skis — **lang·lauf·er** \-ˌlau̇-fər\ n
lang·ley \'laŋ-lē\ n, pl **langleys** [Samuel P. *Langley*] (1947) : a unit of solar radiation equivalent to one gram calorie per square centimeter of irradiated surface
Lan·go·bard \'laŋ-gə-ˌbärd\ n [L *Langobardus*] (1788) : LOMBARD 1a — **Lan·go·bar·dic** \ˌlaŋ-gə-'bär-dik\ adj
lan·gouste \län-'güst\ n [F, grasshopper, lobster, fr. OF *languste*, fr. OProv *langosta*, fr. (assumed) VL *lacusta*, alter. of L *locusta*] (1832) : SPINY LOBSTER
lan·gous·tine \ˌlaŋ-gə-'stēn\ also **lan·gos·ti·no** \ˌlaŋ-gə-'stē-(ˌ)nō\ n, pl **-tines** also **-ti·nos** [*langoustine*, fr. F, dim. of *langouste*; *langostino*, fr. Sp, dim. of *langosta* spiny lobster, locust, fr. (assumed) VL *lacusta*] (1915) : any of several small lobsters (genera *Nephropsis* and *Metanephrops* of the family Nephropidae) widely used for food
¹**lang syne** \(ˌ)laŋ-'zīn, -'sīn\ adv [ME (Sc), fr. *lang* long + *syne* since] (15c) chiefly Scot : at a distant time in the past
²**lang syne** n (1694) chiefly Scot : times past ⟨should auld acquaintance be forgot, and days o' auld *lang syne* —Robert Burns⟩
lan·guage \'laŋ-gwij, -wij\ n [ME, fr. OF, fr. *langue* tongue, language, fr. L *lingua* — more at TONGUE] (14c) **1 a** : the words, their pronunciation, and the methods of combining them used and understood by a community **b** (1) : audible, articulate, meaningful sound as produced by the action of the vocal organs (2) : a systematic means of communicating ideas or feelings by the use of conventionalized signs, sounds, gestures, or marks having understood meanings (3) : the suggestion by objects, actions, or conditions of associated ideas or feelings ⟨~ in their very gesture —Shak.⟩ (4) : the means by which animals communicate (5) : a formal system of signs and symbols (as FORTRAN or a calculus in logic) including rules for the formation and transformation of admissible expressions (6) : MACHINE LANGUAGE 1 **2 a** : form or manner of verbal expression; specif : STYLE **b** : the vocabulary and phraseology belonging to an art or a department of knowledge **c** : PROFANITY **3** : the study of language esp. as a school subject

HOME LANGUAGES WITH OVER FORTY MILLION SPEAKERS[1]

LANGUAGE	MILLIONS	LANGUAGE	MILLIONS
Mandarin Chinese	865	Korean	70
English	334	Marathi	68
Spanish	283	Italian	68
Arabic	197	Tamil	65
Bengali	181	French	65
Hindi and Urdu	172	Vietnamese	61
Portuguese	161	Awadhi[2]	61
Russian	156	Bhojpuri	58
Japanese	125	Southern Min Chinese[3]	55
German	104	Turkish	52
Wu Chinese	94	Ukrainian	50
Panjabi	76	Thai and Lao	47
Javanese	76	Polish	42
Telugu	72	Gujarati	41
Cantonese	70	Persian	40

[1] Compiled by William W. Gage, using information supplied in *Ethnologue: Languages of the World*, 11th ed. (Dallas: Summer Institute of Linguistics, 1988). Home language used here means the language usually spoken at home.
[2] Indo-Aryan language of eastern and central Uttar Pradesh.
[3] Group of Chinese dialects esp. of Xiamen, Shantou, and Taiwan.

language arts n pl (1948) : the subjects (as reading, spelling, literature, and composition) that aim at developing the student's comprehension and capacity for use of written and oral language
langue \läⁿg\ n [F, lit., language] (1924) : language viewed abstractly as a system of forms and conventions used for communication in a community; also : COMPETENCE 3 — compare PAROLE
langue d'oc \läŋ-'dȯk, läŋg-'dȯk\ n [F, fr. OF, lit., language of *oc*; fr. the Provençal use of the word *oc* for "yes"] (1703) : PROVENÇAL 2
langue d'oïl \läŋ-'dȯi(ə)l, -'dȯi; läŋ-dȯ-ēl, -dȯil\ n [F, fr. OF, lit., language of *oïl*; fr. the French use of the word *oil* for "yes"] (1703) : FRENCH 1
lan·guet \'laŋ-gwət, laŋ-'gwet\ n [ME, fr. MF *languete*, dim. of *langue*] (15c) : something resembling the tongue in form or function
lan·guid \'laŋ-gwəd\ adj [MF *languide*, fr. L *languidus*, fr. *languēre* to languish — more at SLACK] (1597) **1** : drooping or flagging from or as if from exhaustion : WEAK **2** : sluggish in character or disposition : LISTLESS **3** : lacking force or quickness of movement : SLOW — **lan·guid·ly** adv — **lan·guid·ness** n
lan·guish \'laŋ-gwish\ vi [ME, fr. MF *languiss-*, stem of *languir*, fr. (assumed) VL *languire*, fr. L *languēre*] (14c) **1 a** : to be or become feeble, weak, or enervated **b** : to be or live in a state of depression or decreasing vitality **2 a** : to become dispirited : PINE ⟨~ing in prison⟩ **b** : to suffer neglect ⟨the bill ~ed in the Senate for eight months⟩ **3** : to assume an expression of grief or emotion appealing for sympathy — **lan·guish·er** n — **lan·guish·ing·ly** \-gwi-shiŋ-lē\ adv — **lan·guish·ment** \-gwish-mənt\ n
lan·guor \'laŋ-gər also -ər\ n [ME, fr. MF, fr. L, fr. *languēre*] (14c) **1** : weakness or weariness of body or mind **2** : listless indolence or inertia *syn* see LETHARGY
lan·guor·ous \'laŋ-gə-rəs, -grəs also -ə-rəs\ adj (15c) **1** : producing or tending to produce languor ⟨a ~ climate⟩ **2** : full of or characterized by languor — **lan·guor·ous·ly** adv

lan·gur \läṅ-'gu̇r\ *n* [Hindi *lāgūr*] (1825) : any of several slender long-tailed Asian monkeys (subfamily Colobinae)

lank \'laṅk\ *adj* [ME, fr. OE *hlanc*; akin to OHG *hlanca* loin] (bef. 12c) **1** : not well filled out — SLENDER, THIN ⟨~ cattle⟩ **2** : insufficient in quantity, degree, or extent ⟨~ grass⟩ **3** : hanging straight and limp without spring or curl ⟨~ hair⟩ *syn* see LEAN — **lank·ly** *adv* — **lank·ness** *n*

lanky \'laṅ-kē\ *adj* **lank·i·er; -est** (1818) : ungracefully tall and thin *syn* see LEAN — **lank·i·ly** \-kə-lē\ *adv* — **lank·i·ness** \-kē-nəs\ *n*

lan·ner \'la-nər\ *n* [ME *laner*, fr. MF *lanier*] (14c) : a falcon (*Falco biarmicus*) of southern Europe, southwestern Asia, and Africa; *specif* : a female lanner

lan·ner·et \₁la-nə-'ret\ *n* (15c) : a male lanner

lan·o·lin \'la-nᵊl-ən\ *n* [L *lana* wool + ISV ³*-ol* + ¹*-in*] (1885) : wool grease esp. when refined for use in ointments and cosmetics

lan·ta·na \lan-'tä-nə\ *n* [NL, fr. It dial., viburnum] (1791) : any of a genus (*Lantana*) of tropical shrubs of the vervain family with showy heads of small bright flowers

lan·tern \'lan-tərn\ *n, often attrib* [ME *lanterne*, fr. OF, fr. L *lanterna*, fr. Gk *lamptēr*, fr. *lampein* to shine — more at LAMP] (13c) **1** : a usu. portable protective case for a light with transparent openings — compare CHINESE LANTERN **2 a** *obs* : LIGHTHOUSE **b** : the chamber in a lighthouse containing the light **c** : a structure with glazed or open sides above an opening in a roof for light or ventilation **d** : a small tower or cupola or one stage of a cupola **3** : PROJECTOR 2b

lantern fish *n* (ca. 1753) : any of a family (Myctophidae) of small deep-sea bony fishes that have a large mouth, large eyes, and usu. numerous photophores

lantern fly *n* (ca. 1753) : any of several large brightly marked homopterous insects (family Fulgoridae) having the front of the head prolonged into a hollow structure

lantern jaw *n* (1711) : an undershot jaw — **lan·tern–jawed** \'lan-tərn-₁jȯd\ *adj*

lantern pinion *n* (ca. 1859) : a gear pinion having cylindrical bars instead of teeth

lan·tha·nide \'lan(t)-thə-₁nīd\ *n* [ISV] (1926) : any in a series of elements of increasing atomic numbers beginning with lanthanum (57) or cerium (58) and ending with lutetium (71) — see PERIODIC TABLE table

lan·tha·num \-nəm\ *n* [NL, fr. Gk *lanthanein* to escape notice — more at LATENT] (1841) : a white soft malleable metallic element that occurs in rare-earth minerals — see ELEMENT table

lant·horn \'lan-tərn\ *n* (1587) *chiefly Brit* : LANTERN

la·nu·gi·nous \lə-'nü-jə-nəs, -'nyü-\ *adj* [L *lanuginosus*, fr. *lanugin-, lanugo*] (1575) : covered with down or fine soft hair : DOWNY

la·nu·go \lə-'nü-(₁)gō, -'nyü-\ *n* [L, down, fr. *lana* wool — more at WOOL] (15c) : a dense cottony or downy growth; *specif* : the soft woolly hair that covers the fetus of some mammals

lan·yard \'lan-yərd\ *n* [ME *lanyer* thong, strap, fr. MF *laniere*] (1626) **1** : a piece of rope or line for fastening something in a ship; *esp* : one of the pieces passing through deadeyes to extend shrouds or stays **2 a** : a cord or strap to hold something (as a knife or a whistle) and usu. worn around the neck **b** : a cord worn as a symbol of a military citation **3** : a strong line used to activate a system (as in firing a cannon or sounding a whistle)

Lao \'lau̇\ *n, pl* **Lao** *or* **Laos** \'lau̇z\ (1808) **1** : a member of a Buddhist people living in Laos and adjacent parts of northeastern Thailand **2** : the Thai language of the Lao people — **Lao** *adj*

La·oc·o·ön \lā-'ä-kə-₁wän\ *n* [L, fr. Gk *Laokoōn*] : a Trojan priest killed with his sons by two sea serpents after warning the Trojans against the wooden horse

La·od·i·ce·an \lā-₁ä-də-'sē-ən, ₁lā-ō-də-\ *adj* [fr. the reproach to the church of the Laodiceans in Rev 3:15–16] (1633) : lukewarm or indifferent in religion or politics — **Laodicean** *n*

Lao·tian \lā-'ō-shən, 'lau̇-shən\ *n* [prob. fr. F *laotien*, adj. & n., fr. *Lao*] (1847) : LAO — **Laotian** *adj*

¹lap \'lap\ *n* [ME *lappe*, fr. OE *læppa* flap] (bef. 12c) **1 a** : a loose overlapping or hanging panel or flap esp. of a garment **b** *archaic* : the skirt of a coat or dress **2 a** : the clothing that lies on the knees, thighs, and lower part of the trunk when one sits **b** : the front part of the lower trunk and thighs of a seated person **3** : responsible custody : CONTROL ⟨going to drop the whole thing in your ~ —Hamilton Basso⟩ — **lap·ful** \'lap-₁fu̇l\ *n* — **the lap of luxury** : an environment of great ease, comfort, and wealth ⟨was reared in *the lap of luxury*⟩

²lap *vb* **lapped; lap·ping** *vt* (14c) **1 a** : to fold over or around something : WIND **b** : to envelop entirely : SWATHE **2** : to fold over esp. into layers **3** : to hold protectively in or as if in the lap : CUDDLE **4 a** : to place over and cover a part of : OVERLAP ⟨~ shingles on a roof⟩ **b** : to join (as two boards) by a lap joint **5 a** : to dress, smooth, or polish (as a metal surface) to a high degree of refinement or accuracy **b** : to shape or fit by working two surfaces together with or without abrasives until a very close fit is produced **6 a** : to overtake and thereby lead or increase the lead over (another contestant) by a full circuit of a racecourse **b** : to complete the circuit of (a racecourse) ~ *vi* **1** : FOLD, WIND **2 a** : to project beyond or spread over something **b** : to lie partly over or alongside of something or of one another : OVERLAP **3** : to traverse a course — **lap·per** *n*

³lap *n* (1800) **1 a** : the amount by which one object overlaps or projects beyond another **b** : the part of an object that overlaps another **2** : a smoothing and polishing tool usu. consisting of a piece of wood, leather, felt, or soft metal in a special shape used with or without an embedded abrasive **3** : a doubling or layering of a flexible substance (as fibers or paper) **4 a** : the act or an instance of traversing a course (as a racing track or swimming pool); *also* : the distance covered **b** : one segment of a larger unit (as a journey) **c** : one complete turn (as of a rope around a drum)

⁴lap *vb* **lapped; lap·ping** [ME, fr. OE *lapian*; akin to OHG *laffan* to lick, L *lambere*, Gk *laphyssein* to devour] *vi* (bef. 12c) **1** : to take in food or drink with the tongue **2 a** : to make a gentle intermittent splashing sound **b** : to move in little waves : WASH ~ *vt* **1 a** : to take in (food or drink) with the tongue **b** : to take in or absorb eagerly or quickly — used with *up* ⟨the crowd *lapped* up every word he said⟩ **2** : to flow or splash against in little waves — **lap·per** *n*

⁵lap *n* (14c) **1 a** : an act or instance of lapping **b** : the amount that can be carried to the mouth by one lick or scoop of the tongue **2** : a thin or weak beverage or food **3** : a gentle splashing sound

laparo- *comb form* [Gk *lapara* flank, fr. *laparos* slack] : abdominal wall ⟨*laparotomy*⟩

lap·a·ro·scope \'la-p(ə-)rə-₁skōp\ *n* [ISV] (ca. 1923) : a fiberoptic instrument inserted through an incision in the abdominal wall and used to examine visually the interior of the peritoneal cavity

lap·a·ros·co·py \₁la-pə-'räs-kə-pē\ *n, pl* **-pies** (1916) **1** : visual examination of the abdomen by means of a laparoscope **2** : an operation involving laparoscopy; *esp* : one for sterilization of the female or for removal of ova that involves use of a laparoscope to guide surgical procedures within the abdomen — **lap·a·ro·scop·ic** \-rə-'skä-pik\ *adj* — **lap·a·ros·co·pist** \₁la-pə-'räs-kə-pist\ *n*

lap·a·rot·o·my \₁la-pə-'rä-tə-mē\ *n, pl* **-mies** (1878) : surgical section of the abdominal wall

lap belt *n* (1952) : a seat belt that fastens across the lap

lap·board \'lap-₁bȯrd, -₁bȯrd\ *n* (1804) : a board used on the lap as a table or desk

lap·dog \-₁dȯg\ *n* (1645) **1** : a small dog that may be held in the lap **2** : a servile dependent or follower

la·pel \lə-'pel\ *n* [dim. of ¹*lap*] (1789) : the part of a garment that is turned back; *specif* : the fold of the front of a coat that is usu. a continuation of the collar — **la·pelled** *or* **la·peled** *adj*

lap·i·dar·i·an \₁la-pə-'der-ē-ən\ *adj* (1683) : LAPIDARY 1

¹lap·i·dary \'la-pə-₁der-ē\ *n, pl* **-dar·ies** (14c) **1** : a cutter, polisher, or engraver of precious stones usu. other than diamonds **2** : the art of cutting gems

²lapidary *adj* [L *lapidarius* of stone, fr. *lapid-, lapis* stone] (1724) **1** : having the elegance and precision associated with inscriptions on monumental stone ⟨the ~ phrasing... and subtle condensations of emotions... reward attentive reading —G. A. Cardwell⟩ **2 a** : sculptured in or engraved on stone **b** : of or relating to precious stones or the art of cutting them

la·pil·lus \lə-'pi-ləs\ *n, pl* **-li** \-₁lī, -(₁)lē\ [L, dim. of *lapis*] (1747) : a small stony or glassy fragment of lava ejected in a volcanic eruption

lap·in \'la-pən\ *n* [F] (1905) **1** : RABBIT; *specif* : a castrated male rabbit **2** : rabbit fur usu. sheared and dyed

la·pis la·zu·li \₁lap-əs-'la-zə-lē, -'la-zhə-\ *n* [ME, fr. ML, fr. L *lapis* + ML *lazuli*, gen. of *lazulum* lapis lazuli, fr. Ar *lāzaward* — more at AZURE] (15c) : a semiprecious stone that is usu. rich azure blue and is essentially a complex silicate often with spangles of iron pyrites — called also *lapis*

lap joint *n* (1823) : a joint made by overlapping two ends or edges and fastening them together — **lap–joint·ed** \'lap-₁jȯin-təd\ *adj*

La·place transform \lə-'pläs-, -'plas-\ [Pierre Simon, Marquis de *Laplace*] (1942) : a transformation of a function *f(x)* into the function

$$g(t) = \int_0^\infty e^{-xt} f(x) dx$$

that is useful esp. in reducing the solution of an ordinary linear differential equation with constant coefficients to the solution of a polynomial equation

Lapp \'lap\ *n* [Sw] (1859) **1** : a member of a people of northern Scandinavia, Finland, and the Kola Peninsula of northern Russia who are traditionally fishermen, nomadic herders of caribou, and hunters of sea mammals **2** : any or all of the closely related Finno-Ugric languages of the Lapps — **Lapp·ish** *adj or n*

lap·pet \'la-pət\ *n* (1573) **1** : a fold or flap on a garment or headdress **2** : a flat overlapping or hanging piece

lap robe *n* (ca. 1866) : a covering (as a blanket) for the legs, lap, and feet esp. of a passenger in a car or carriage

Lap·sang souchong \'läp-₁säṅ-, 'lap-₁saṅ-\ *n* [origin unknown] (ca. 1878) : a souchong tea having a pronounced smoky flavor and aroma

¹lapse \'laps\ *n* [L *lapsus*, fr. *labi* to slip — more at SLEEP] (1526) **1 a** : a slight error typically due to forgetfulness or inattention ⟨a ~ in table manners⟩ **b** : a temporary deviation or fall esp. from a higher to a lower state ⟨a ~ from grace⟩ **2** : a becoming less : DECLINE **3 a** (1) : the termination of a right or privilege through neglect to exercise it within some limit of time (2) : termination of coverage for nonpayment of premiums **b** : INTERRUPTION, DISCONTINUANCE ⟨returned to college after a ~ of several years⟩ **4** : an abandonment of religious faith : APOSTASY **5** : a passage of time; *also* : INTERVAL *syn* see ERROR

²lapse *vb* **lapsed; laps·ing** *vi* (1611) **1 a** : to fall from an attained and usu. high level (as of morals or manners) to one much lower; *also* : to depart from an accepted pattern or standard **b** : to sink or slip gradually : SUBSIDE ⟨*lapsed* into unconsciousness⟩ **2** : to go out of existence : CEASE ⟨after a few polite exchanges, the conversation *lapsed*⟩ **3** : to pass from one proprietor to another or from an original owner by omission or negligence ⟨allowed the insurance policy to ~⟩ **4 a** : to glide along : PASS ⟨time ~s⟩ ~ *vt* : to let slip : FORFEIT ⟨all of those who have *lapsed* their membership —*AAUP Bull.*⟩ — **laps·er** *n*

lapsed *adj* (1638) *of a person* : having given up or allowed the lapse of a former position, relationship, or commitment ⟨a ~ Catholic⟩

lapse rate *n* (1918) : the adiabatic rate of decrease of atmospheric temperature with increasing altitude

lap·strake \'lap-₁strāk\ *adj* (1771) : CLINKER-BUILT

lap·top \'lap-₁täp\ *adj* (1984) : of a size and design that makes operation and use on one's lap convenient ⟨a ~ personal computer⟩ — compare DESKTOP — **laptop** *n*

La·pu·tan \lə-'pyü-tᵊn\ *n* : an inhabitant of a flying island in Swift's *Gulliver's Travels* characterized by a neglect of useful occupations and a devotion to visionary projects — **Laputan** *adj*

lap·wing \'lap-₁wiṅ\ *n* [ME, by folk etymology fr. OE *hlēapewince*; akin to OE *hlēapan* to leap and to OE *wincian* to wink] (14c) : a crested Old World plover (*Vanellus vanellus*) noted for its slow irregular flapping flight and shrill wailing cry; *also* : any of several related plovers

\ə\ abut \ᵊ\ kitten, F table \ər\ further \a\ ash \ā\ ace \ä\ mop, mar \au̇\ out \ch\ chin \e\ bet \ē\ easy \g\ go \i\ hit \ī\ ice \j\ job \ṅ\ sing \ō\ go \ȯ\ law \ȯi\ boy \th\ thin \th̲\ the \ü\ loot \u̇\ foot \y\ yet \zh\ vision \a̲, k̲, ⁿ, œ, œ̄, ᴜᴇ, ᵾ, ʸ\ *see* Guide to Pronunciation

Lar \'lär\ *n, pl* **Lar·es** \'lar-(,)ēz, 'ler-\ [L — more at LARVA] : a tutelary god or spirit associated with Vesta and the Penates as a guardian of the household by the ancient Romans

lar·board \'lär-bərd\ *n* [ME *ladeborde*] (14c) : ⁵PORT — **larboard** *adj*

lar·ce·ner \'lärs-nər, 'lär-s³n-ər\ *n* (ca. 1635) : LARCENIST

lar·ce·nist \-nist, -s³n-ist\ *n* (1803) : a person who commits larceny

lar·ce·nous \-nəs, -s³n-əs\ *adj* (1742) **1** : having the character of or constituting larceny **2** : committing larceny — **lar·ce·nous·ly** *adv*

lar·ce·ny \-nē, -s³n-ē\ *n, pl* **-nies** [ME, fr. MF *larcin* theft, fr. L *latrocinium* robbery, fr. *latron-, latro* mercenary soldier, prob. fr. (assumed) Gk *latrōn*, fr. Gk *latron* pay] (15c) : the unlawful taking of personal property with intent to deprive the rightful owner of it permanently

larch \'lärch\ *n* [prob. fr. G *Lärche*, fr. MHG *lerche*, fr. L *laric-, larix*] (1548) : any of a genus (*Larix*) of trees of the pine family with short fascicled deciduous leaves; *also* : the wood of a larch

¹**lard** \'lärd\ *vt* (14c) **1 a** : to dress (meat) for cooking by inserting or covering with something (as strips of fat) **b** : to cover or soil with grease **2** : to decorate or intersperse with something (the book is ~ed with anecdotes) **3** *obs* : to make rich with or as if with fat

²**lard** *n* [ME, fr. MF, fr. L *lardum, laridum*; perh. akin to Gk *larinos* fat] (14c) : a soft white solid or semisolid fat obtained by rendering fatty tissue of the hog — **lardy** \'lär-dē\ *adj*

lar·der \'lär-dər\ *n* [ME, fr. MF *lardier*, fr. *lard*] (14c) **1** : a place where food is stored : PANTRY **2** : a supply of food

lar·doon \lär-'dün\ *or* **lar·don** \'lär-,dän\ *n* [ME, fr. MF *lardon* piece of fat pork, fr. *lard*] (14c) : a strip (as of salt pork) with which meat is larded

lares and penates *see* LAR, PENATES\ *n pl* (1775) **1** : household gods **2** : personal or household effects

¹**large** \'lärj\ *adj* **larg·er; larg·est** [ME, fr. OF, fr. L *largus*] (12c) **1** *obs* : LAVISH **2** *obs* **a** : AMPLE, ABUNDANT **b** : EXTENSIVE, BROAD **3** : having more than usual power, capacity, or scope : COMPREHENSIVE (take the ~ view) (will take a *larger* role in the negotiations) **4 a** : exceeding most other things of like kind esp. in quantity or size : BIG **b** : dealing in great numbers or quantities (a ~ and highly profitable business) **5** *obs* **a** *of language or expression* : COARSE, VULGAR **b** : lax in conduct : LOOSE **6** *of a wind* : FAVORABLE **7** : EXTRAVAGANT, BOASTFUL (~ talk) — **large·ness** *n* — **larg·ish** \'lär-jish\ *adj*

²**large** *adv* (14c) **1** *obs* : in abundance : AMPLY, LIBERALLY **2** : with the wind abaft the beam

³**large** *n* (14c) *obs* : LIBERALITY, GENEROSITY — **at large 1 a** : free of restraint or confinement (the escaped prisoner is still *at large*) **b** : without a specific subject or assignment (critic *at large*) **2** : at length **3** : in a general way **4** : as a whole (society *at large*) **5** : as the political representative of or to a whole area rather than of one of its subdivisions — used in combination with a preceding noun (a congressman-*at-large*) — **in the large** : on a large scale : in general

large calorie *n* (ca. 1909) : CALORIE 1b

large·heart·ed \,lärj-'här-təd\ *adj* (1645) : having a generous disposition : SYMPATHETIC — **large·heart·ed·ness** *n*

large intestine *n* (1823) : the more terminal division of the vertebrate intestine that is wider and shorter than the small intestine, typically divided into cecum, colon, and rectum, and concerned esp. with the resorption of water and the formation of feces

large·ly \'lärj-lē\ *adv* (13c) : in a large manner; *esp* : to a large extent : MOSTLY, PRIMARILY

large–mind·ed \,lärj-'mīn-dəd\ *adj* (1725) : generous or comprehensive in outlook, range, or capacity — **large–mind·ed·ly** *adv* — **large–mind·ed·ness** *n*

large–mouth bass \'lärj-,mauth-\ *n* (1941) : a large black bass (*Micropterus salmoides*) that is blackish green above and lighter below and has the maxillary bones of the upper jaw extending behind the eyes — called also **largemouth, largemouth black bass**

large–print \-'print\ *adj* (1968) : being set in a large size of type (as 14 point or larger) esp. for use by the partially sighted (~ books)

larger–than–life *adj* (1950) : of the sort legends are made of (~ heroes)

large–scale integration *n* (1966) : the process of placing a large number of circuits on a small chip

lar·gesse *or* **lar·gess** \lär-'zhes, lär-'jes *also* 'lär-,jes\ *n* [ME *largesse*, fr. OF, fr. *large*] (13c) **1** : liberal giving (as of money) to or as if to an inferior; *also* : something so given **2** : GENEROSITY

¹**lar·ghet·to** \lär-'ge-(,)tō\ *n, pl* **-tos** (ca. 1724) : a movement played larghetto

²**larghetto** *adv or adj* [It, somewhat slow, fr. *largo*] (ca. 1801) : slower than andante but not so slow as largo — used as a direction in music

¹**lar·go** \'lär-(,)gō\ *adv or adj* [It, slow, broad, fr. L *largus* abundant] (1683) : at a very slow tempo — used as a direction in music

²**largo** *n, pl* **largos** (ca. 1724) : a largo movement

lar·i·at \'lar-ē-ət, 'ler-\ *n* [AmerSp *la reata* the lasso, fr. Sp *la* (the (fem. of *el,* fr. L *ille* that) + AmerSp *reata* lasso, fr. Sp *reatar* to tie again, fr. *re-* + *atar* to tie, fr. L *aptare* to fit — more at ADAPT] (1832) : a long light rope (as of hemp or leather) used with a running noose to catch livestock or with or without the noose to tether grazing animals : LASSO

¹**lark** \'lärk\ *n* [ME *laveroc, laverke*, fr. OE *lāwerce*; akin to OHG *lērihha* lark] (bef. 12c) : any of a family (Alaudidae) of chiefly Old World songbirds that are usu. brownish in color; *esp* : SKYLARK — compare MEADOWLARK

²**lark** *n* [³*lark*] (ca. 1811) : something done solely for fun or adventure (ran for office on a ~)

³**lark** *vi* [prob. alter. of *lake* to frolic] (1813) : to engage in harmless fun or mischief — often used with *about* — **lark·er** *n*

lark·spur \'lärk-,spər\ *n* (1578) **1** : DELPHINIUM **2** : any of the delphiniums that are annuals, have the upper two petals of the corolla united and the bottom two missing, are now often placed in a separate genus (*Consolida*), and include several widely cultivated forms

larky \'lär-kē\ *adj* **lark·i·er; -est** (1841) **1** : given to or ready for larking : SPORTIVE **2** : resulting from a lark — **lark·i·ness** \-nəs\ *n*

lar·ri·gan \'lar-i-gən\ *n* [origin unknown] (1886) : an oil-tanned moccasin with a leg often reaching the knee

lar·ri·kin \'lar-i-kən\ *n* [origin unknown] (1868) *chiefly Austral* : HOODLUM, ROWDY — **larrikin** *adj*

¹**lar·rup** \'lar-əp\ *n* [origin unknown] (ca. 1820) *dial* : ⁵BLOW

²**larrup** *vt* (ca. 1823) **1** *dial* : to flog soundly : WHIP **2** *dial* : to defeat decisively : TROUNCE ~ *vi, dial* : to move indolently or clumsily

la·rum \'lär-əm, 'lar-\ *n* [short for *alarum*] (15c) *archaic* : ALARM

lar·va \'lär-və\ *n, pl* **lar·vae** \-(,)vē, -,vī\ *also* **larvas** [NL, fr. L, specter, mask; akin to L *lar* Lar] (1768) **1** : the immature, wingless, and often wormlike feeding form that hatches from the egg of many insects, alters chiefly in size while passing through several molts, and is finally transformed into a pupa or chrysalis from which the adult emerges **2** : the early form of an animal (as a frog or sea urchin) that at birth or hatching is fundamentally unlike its parent and must metamorphose before assuming the adult characters — **lar·val** \-vəl\ *adj*

lar·vi·cide \'lär-və-,sīd\ *n* (ca. 1888) : an agent for killing larval pests — **lar·vi·cid·al** \,lär-və-'sī-d³l\ *adj*

laryng- *or* laryngo- *comb form* [NL, fr. Gk, fr. *laryng-, larynx*] : larynx (*laryngitis*)

¹**la·ryn·geal** \lə-'rin-jəl *also* -jē-əl; ,lar-ən-'jē-əl\ *adj* (1795) **1** : of, relating to, or used on the larynx **2** : produced by or with constriction of the larynx (~ articulation of sounds)

²**laryngeal** *n* (ca. 1902) **1** : an anatomical part (as a nerve or artery) that supplies or is associated with the larynx **2 a** : a laryngeal sound **b** : any of a set of several conjectured phonemes reconstructed for Proto-Indo-European chiefly on indirect evidence

lar·yn·gec·to·mee \,lar-ən-,jek-tə-'mē\ *n* (1956) : a person who has undergone laryngectomy

lar·yn·gec·to·my \-'jek-tə-mē\ *n, pl* **-mies** (ca. 1888) : surgical removal of all or part of the larynx — **lar·yn·gec·to·mized** \-tə-,mīzd\ *adj*

lar·yn·gi·tis \,lar-ən-'jī-təs\ *n* [NL] (ca. 1834) : inflammation of the larynx — **lar·yn·git·ic** \-'ji-tik\ *adj*

lar·yn·gol·o·gy \,lar-ən-'gä-lə-jē\ *n* [ISV] (ca. 1842) : a branch of medicine dealing with diseases of the larynx and nasopharynx

la·ryn·go·scope \lə-'rin-gə-,skōp, -'rin-jə-\ *n* [ISV] (1860) : an instrument for examining the interior of the larynx — **lar·yn·gos·co·py** \,lar-ən-'gäs-kə-pē\ *n*

lar·ynx \'lar-iŋ(k)s\ *n, pl* **la·ryn·ges** \lə-'rin-(,)jēz\ *or* **lar·ynx·es** [NL *laryng-, larynx*, fr. Gk] (1578) : the modified upper part of the trachea of air-breathing vertebrates that in humans, most other mammals, and a few lower forms contains the vocal cords

la·sa·gna \lə-'zän-yə\ *n* [It *lasagna*, fr. (assumed) VL *lasania* cooking pot, its contents, fr. L *lasanum* chamber pot, fr. Gk *lasanon*] (1846) **1** *also* **la·sa·gne** \-yə\ : pasta in the form of broad often ruffled ribbons **2** : a baked dish consisting chiefly of layers of boiled lasagna, cheese, and a seasoned sauce of tomatoes and usu. meat

las·car \'las-kər\ *n* [Hindi *lashkar* army] (1615) : an Indian sailor, army servant, or artilleryman

las·civ·i·ous \lə-'si-vē-əs\ *adj* [LL *lasciviosus*, fr. L *lascivia* wantonness, fr. *lascivus* wanton — more at LUST] (15c) : LEWD, LUSTFUL — **las·civ·i·ous·ly** *adv* — **las·civ·i·ous·ness** *n*

lase \'lāz\ *vi* **lased; las·ing** [back-formation fr. *laser*] (1962) : to emit coherent light

la·ser \'lā-zər\ *n, often attrib* [*l*ight *a*mplification by *s*timulated *e*mission of *r*adiation] (1960) : a device that utilizes the natural oscillations of atoms or molecules between energy levels for generating coherent electromagnetic radiation usu. in the ultraviolet, visible, or infrared regions of the spectrum

laser disc *n* (1980) : OPTICAL DISK; *esp* : one on which programs are recorded for playback on a television set

laser printer *n* (1979) : a high-resolution printer for computer output that xerographically prints an image formed by a laser

¹**lash** \'lash\ *vb* [ME] (14c) **1** : to move violently or suddenly : DASH **2** : to thrash or beat violently (rain ~ed at the windowpanes) **3** : to make a verbal attack or retort — usu. used with *out* ~ *vt* **1 a** : to whip or fling about violently (the big cat ~ed its tail about threateningly) **b** : to strike or beat with or as if with a whip (waves ~ed the shore) **2 a** : to assail with stinging words **b** : DRIVE, WHIP (~ed them into a fury with his fiery speech) — **lash·er** *n*

²**lash** *n* (14c) **1 a** (1) : a stroke with or as if with a whip (2) : the flexible part of a whip; *also* : WHIP **b** : punishment by whipping **2 a** : a beating, whipping, or driving force **3** : a stinging rebuke **4** : EYELASH **5** : the clearance or play between adjacent movable mechanical parts

³**lash** *vt* [ME *lasschyn* to lace, fr. MF *lacier* — more at LACE] (1624) : to bind with or as if with a line — **lash·er** *n*

lash·ing *n* (1669) : something used for binding, wrapping, or fastening

lash·ings \'la-shiŋz, -shǝnz\ *also* **lash·ins** \-shǝnz\ *n pl* [fr. gerund of ¹*lash*] (1829) *chiefly Brit* : a great plenty ? ABUNDANCE (piles of bread and butter and ~ of tea —Molly Weir)

lash–up \'lash-,əp\ *n* [³*lash*] (1898) **1** : something hastily put together or improvised **2** : OUTFIT 3

L–as·par·a·gi·nase \'el-as-'par-ə-jə-,nās, -,nāz\ *n* (1962) : an enzyme that breaks down the physiologically commoner form of asparagine, is obtained esp. from bacteria, and is used esp. to treat leukemia

lass \'las\ *n* [ME *las*] (14c) **1** : a young woman : GIRL **2** : SWEETHEART

Las·sa fever \'la-sǝ-\ *n* [*Lassa*, village in Nigeria] (1970) : a virus disease esp. of Africa that is characterized by a high fever, headaches, mouth ulcers, muscle aches, small hemorrhages under the skin, heart and kidney failure, and a high mortality rate

lass·ie \'la-sē\ *n* (1725) : LASS 1

las·si·tude \'la-sə-,tüd, -,tyüd\ *n* [MF, fr. L *lassitudo*, fr. *lassus* weary; prob. akin to OE *lǣt* late — more at LATE] (15c) **1** : a condition of weariness or debility : FATIGUE **2** : a condition of listlessness : LANGUOR *syn* see LETHARGY

¹**las·so** \'la-(,)sō, la-'sü\ *vt* (1807) : to capture with or as if with a lasso : ROPE — **las·so·er** *n*

²**lasso** *n, pl* **lassos** *or* **lassoes** [Sp *lazo*, fr. L *laqueus* snare] (1808) : a rope or long thong of leather with a noose used esp. for catching horses and cattle : LARIAT

¹**last** \'last\ *vb* [ME, fr. OE *lǣstan* to last, follow; akin to OE *lāst* footprint] *vi* (bef. 12c) **1** : to continue in time **2 a** : to remain fresh or unimpaired : ENDURE **b** : to manage to continue (as in a course of action) **c** : to continue to live ~ *vt* **1** : to continue in existence or action as long as or longer than — often used with *out* ⟨couldn't ~ out the training program⟩ **2** : to be enough for the needs of ⟨the supplies will ~ them a week⟩ *syn* see CONTINUE — **last·er** *n*

²**last** *n* [ME, fr. OE *lǣste*, fr. *lāst* footprint; akin to OHG *leist* shoemaker's last, L *lira* furrow — more at LEARN] (bef. 12c) : a form (as of metal or plastic) which is shaped like the human foot and over which a shoe is shaped or repaired

³**last** *vt* (ca. 1859) : to shape with a last — **last·er** *n*

⁴**last** *adv* [ME, fr. OE *latost*, superl. of *lǣt* late] (bef. 12c) **1** : after all others : at the end ⟨came ~ and left first⟩ **2** : most lately ⟨saw him ~ in Rome⟩ **3** : in conclusion ⟨~, let's consider the social aspect⟩

⁵**last** *adj* (13c) **1 a** : following all the rest ⟨he was the ~ one out⟩ **b** : being the only remaining ⟨our ~ dollar⟩ **2 a** : belonging to the final stage (as of life) ⟨his ~ hours on earth⟩ **b** : administered to the seriously sick or dying ⟨the ~ rites of the church⟩ **3 a** : next before the present : most recent ⟨~ week⟩ ⟨his ~ book was a failure⟩ **b** : most up-to-date : LATEST ⟨it's the ~ thing in fashion⟩ **4 a** : lowest in rank or standing; *also* : WORST **b** : farthest from a specified quality, attitude, or likelihood ⟨would be the ~ person to fall for flattery⟩ **5 a** : CONCLUSIVE ⟨there is no ~ answer to the problem⟩ **b** : highest in degree : SUPREME, ULTIMATE **c** : DISTINCT, SEPARATE — used as an intensive ⟨ate every ~ piece of food⟩ — **last·ly** *adv*

syn LAST, FINAL, TERMINAL, EVENTUAL, ULTIMATE mean following all others (as in time, order, or importance). LAST applies to something that comes at the end of a series but does not always imply that the series is completed or stopped ⟨*last* page of a book⟩ ⟨*last* news we had of him⟩. FINAL applies to that which definitely closes a series, process, or progress ⟨*final* day of school⟩. TERMINAL may indicate a limit of extension, growth, or development ⟨*terminal* phase of a disease⟩. EVENTUAL applies to something that is bound to follow sooner or later as the final effect of causes already operating ⟨*eventual* defeat of the enemy⟩. ULTIMATE implies the last degree or stage of a long process beyond which further progress or change is impossible ⟨the *ultimate* collapse of the system⟩.

⁶**last** *n* (13c) : something that is last — **at last** *or* **at long last** : at the end of a period of time : FINALLY ⟨*at last* you've come home⟩

last–ditch \'last(t)-,dich, -'dich\ *adj* (1937) **1** : fought or conducted from the last ditch : waged with desperation or unyielding defiance ⟨~ resistance⟩ **2** : made as a final effort esp. to avert disaster ⟨a ~ attempt to raise the money⟩

last ditch *n* (ca. 1715) : a place of final defense or resort

last–gasp \'last(t)-'gasp\ *adj* (1921) : done or coming at the very end — **last gasp** *n*

last hurrah *n* [fr. *The Last Hurrah* (1956) by Edwin O'Connor †1968 Am. novelist] (1966) : a final often valedictory effort, production, or appearance ⟨his unsuccessful Senate run was his *last hurrah* —R. W. Daly⟩

last–in first–out *adj* (1940) : of, relating to, or being a method of inventory accounting that values stock on hand according to costs at the time of acquisition and not according to the cost of replacement

¹**last·ing** *adj* (12c) : existing or continuing a long while : ENDURING — **last·ing·ly** \'las-tiŋ-lē\ *adv* — **last·ing·ness** *n*

syn LASTING, PERMANENT, DURABLE, STABLE mean enduring for so long as to seem fixed or established. LASTING implies a capacity to continue indefinitely ⟨a book that left a *lasting* impression on me⟩. PERMANENT adds usu. the implication of being designed or planned to stand or continue indefinitely ⟨*permanent* living arrangements⟩. DURABLE implies power to resist destructive agencies ⟨*durable* fabrics⟩. STABLE implies lastingness because of resistance to being overturned or displaced ⟨a *stable* government⟩.

²**lasting** *n* (15c) **1** *archaic* : long life **2** : a sturdy cotton or worsted cloth used esp. in shoes and luggage

Last Judgment *n* (14c) : the judgment of mankind before God at the end of the world

last minute *n* (1920) : the moment just before some climactic, decisive, or disastrous event

last name *n* (1897) : SURNAME 2

last rites *n* (1922) : EXTREME UNCTION

last straw *n* [fr. the fable of the last straw that broke the camel's back when added to its burden] (1848) : the last of a series (as of events or indignities) that brings one beyond the point of endurance

Last Supper *n* (14c) : the supper eaten by Jesus and his disciples on the night of his betrayal

Last Things *n pl* [trans. of ML *Novissima*] (1522) : events (as the resurrection and divine judgment of all humankind) marking the end of the world : eschatological happenings

last word *n* (1563) **1** : the final remark in a verbal exchange **2 a** : the power of final decision **b** : a definitive statement or treatment ⟨this study will surely be the *last word* on the subject for many years⟩ **3** : the most advanced, up-to-date, or fashionable exemplar of its kind ⟨the *last word* in sports cars⟩

lat \'lat\ *n* [Latvian *lats*, fr. *Latvija* Latvia] (1923) — see MONEY table

lat·a·kia \,la-tə-'kē-ə\ *n* [*Latakia*, seaport in Syria] (1833) : a highly aromatic Turkish smoking tobacco

¹**latch** \'lach\ *vi* [ME *lachen*, fr. OE *lǣccan*; perh. akin to Gk *lambanein* to take, seize] (13c) **1** : to lay hold with or as if with the hands or arms — used with *on* or *onto* **2** : to associate oneself intimately and often artfully — used with *on* or *onto* ⟨~ed onto a rich widow⟩

²**latch** *n* (13c) : any of various devices in which mating mechanical parts engage to fasten but usu. not to lock something: **a** : a fastener (as for a door) consisting essentially of a pivoted bar that falls into a notch **b** : a fastener (as for a door) in which a spring slides a bolt into a hole; *also* : NIGHT LATCH

³**latch** *vt* (15c) : to make fast with or as if with a latch

latch·et \'la-chət\ *n* [ME *lachet*, fr. MF, shoestring, fr. *laz* snare, fr. L *laqueus*] (15c) : a narrow leather strap, thong, or lace that fastens a shoe or sandal on the foot

latch·key \'lach-,kē\ *n* (1825) : a key to an outside and esp. a front door

latchkey child *n* (1944) : a young child of working parents who must spend part of the day unsupervised (as at home) — called also *latchkey kid*

latch·string \-,striŋ\ *n* (1791) : a string on a latch that may be left hanging outside the door to permit the raising of the latch from the outside or drawn inside to prevent intrusion

¹**late** \'lāt\ *adj* **lat·er**; **lat·est** [ME, late, slow, fr. OE *lǣt*; akin to OHG *laz* slow, OE *lǣtan* to let] (bef. 12c) **1 a** : coming or remaining after the due, usual, or proper time ⟨a ~ spring⟩ (2) : of, relating to, or imposed because of tardiness **b** : of or relating to an advanced stage in point of time or development ⟨the ~ Middle Ages⟩; *esp* : far advanced toward the close of the day or night ⟨~ hours⟩ **2 a** : living comparatively recently — used of persons ⟨the ~ John Doe⟩ and often with reference to a specific relationship or status ⟨his ~ wife⟩ **b** : being something or holding some position or relationship recently but not now ⟨the ~ belligerents⟩ **c** : made, appearing, or happening just previous to the present time esp. as the most recent of a succession ⟨our ~ quarrel⟩ *syn* see DEAD — **late·ness** *n*

²**late** *adv* **lat·er**; **lat·est** (bef. 12c) **1 a** : after the usual or proper time ⟨got to work ~⟩ **b** : at or to an advanced point of time **2** : not long ago : RECENTLY ⟨a man ~ of Chicago⟩ — **of late** : in the period shortly or immediately preceding : RECENTLY ⟨has been sick *of late*⟩

late blight *n* (1900) : a disease of solanaceous plants (as the potato and tomato) that is caused by a fungus (*Phytophthora infestans*) and is characterized by decay of stems, leaves, and in the potato also of tubers

late·com·er \'lāt-,kə-mər\ *n* (1892) : one that arrives late; *also* : a recent arrival

lat·ed \'lā-təd\ *adj* (ca. 1592) : BELATED

¹**la·teen** \la-'tēn\ *adj* [F (*voile*) *latine*, lit., Latin (Mediterranean) sail] (ca. 1741) : being or relating to a rig used esp. on the north coast of Africa and characterized by a triangular sail extended by a long spar slung to a low mast

²**lateen** *n* (ca. 1775) **1** *also* **la·teen·er** \-'tē-nər\ : a lateen-rigged ship **2** : a lateen sail

Late Greek *n* (ca. 1889) : the Greek language as used in the 3d to 6th centuries

Late Hebrew *n* (1951) : the Hebrew language used by writers from about the 2d century B.C. to the early Middle Ages

Late Latin *n* (1888) : the Latin language used by writers in the 3d to 6th centuries

late·ly \'lāt-lē\ *adv* (15c) : of late : RECENTLY ⟨has been friendlier ~⟩

lat·en \'lāt-ᵊn\ *vb* **lat·ened**; **lat·en·ing** \'lāt-niŋ, 'lā-tᵊn-iŋ\ *vi* (1880) : to grow late ~ *vt* : to cause to grow late

la·ten·cy \'lā-tᵊn(t)-sē\ *n, pl* **-cies** (ca. 1638) **1** : the quality or state of being latent : DORMANCY **2** : something latent **3** : a stage of personality development that extends from about the age of five to the beginning of puberty and during which sexual urges often appear to lie dormant **4** : LATENT PERIOD 2

latency period *n* (1910) **1** : LATENCY 3 **2** : LATENT PERIOD

La Tène \lä-'ten, -'tän\ *adj* [*La Tène*, shallows of the Lake of Neuchâtel, Switzerland] (1901) : of or relating to the later period of the Iron Age in Europe assumed to date from 500 B.C. to A.D. 1

la·ten·si·fi·ca·tion \lā-,ten(t)-sə-fə-'kā-shən, lə-\ *n* [blend of ¹*latent* and *intensification*] (1940) : intensification of a latent photographic image by chemical treatment or exposure to light of low intensity

¹**la·tent** \'lā-tᵊnt\ *adj* [ME, fr. L *latent-, latens*, fr. prp. of *latēre* to lie hidden; akin to Gk *lanthanein* to escape notice] (15c) : present and capable of becoming though not now visible, obvious, or active ⟨a ~ infection⟩ — **la·tent·ly** *adv*

syn LATENT, DORMANT, QUIESCENT, POTENTIAL mean not now showing signs of activity or existence. LATENT applies to a power or quality that has not yet come forth but may emerge and develop ⟨a *latent* desire for success⟩. DORMANT suggests the inactivity of something (as a feeling or power) as though sleeping ⟨their passion had lain *dormant*⟩. QUIESCENT suggests a usu. temporary cessation of activity ⟨the disease was *quiescent*⟩. POTENTIAL applies to what does not yet have existence or effect but is likely soon to have ⟨a *potential* disaster⟩.

²**latent** *n* (1923) : a fingerprint (as at the scene of a crime) that is scarcely visible but can be developed for study

latent heat *n* (ca. 1757) : heat given off or absorbed in a process (as fusion or vaporization) other than a change of temperature

latent period *n* (1837) **1** : the incubation period of a disease **2** : the interval between stimulation and response

latent root *n* (1883) : an eigenvalue of a matrix

lat·er \'lā-tər\ *adv* (13c) : at some time subsequent to a given time : SUBSEQUENTLY, AFTERWARD ⟨four months ~⟩ ⟨they ~ regretted their decision⟩ — often used with *on* ⟨experience that will be useful ~ *on*⟩

-later *n comb form* [ME *-later*, fr. MF *-latre*, fr. LL *-latres*, fr. Gk *-latrēs*; akin to Gk *latron* pay] : worshiper ⟨biblio*later*⟩

lat·er·ad \'la-tə-,rad\ *adv* [L *later-, latus*] (1814) : toward the side

¹**lat·er·al** \'la-tə-rəl *also* 'la-trəl\ *adj* [ME *laterale*, fr. L *lateralis*, fr. *later-, latus* side] (15c) **1** : of or relating to the side **2** : situated on, directed toward, or coming from the side **3** : extending from side to side ⟨~ axis of an airplane⟩ **4** : produced with passage of breath around the side of a constriction formed with the tongue ⟨\l\ is ~⟩ — **lat·er·al·ly** *adv*

²**lateral** *n* (1851) **1** : a branch from the main part (as in an irrigation or electrical system) **2** : a pass in football thrown parallel to the line of scrimmage or in a direction away from the opponent's goal **3** : a lateral speech sound

³**lateral** *vi* (1944) : to throw a lateral

lateral bud *n* (ca. 1892) : a bud that develops in the axil between a petiole and a stem

---

\ə\ abut \ᵊ\ kitten, F table \ər\ further \a\ ash \ā\ ace \ä\ mop, mar \aú\ out \ch\ chin \e\ bet \ē\ easy \g\ go \i\ hit \ī\ ice \j\ job \ŋ\ sing \ō\ go \ò\ law \òi\ boy \th\ thin \t̲h̲\ the \ü\ loot \ú\ foot \y\ yet \zh\ vision \à, k̲, ⁿ, œ, œ̄, ᵫ, ᵫ̄, ᵊ\ *see* Guide to Pronunciation

lat·er·al·i·za·tion \,la-tə-rə-lə-'zā-shən, ,la-trə-\ *n* (ca. 1899) : localization of function or activity (as of verbal processes in the brain) on one side of the body in preference to the other — **lat·er·al·ize** \'la-tə-rə-,līz, 'la-trə-\ *vt*

lateral line *n* (1870) : a canal along the side of a fish containing pores that open into tubes supplied with sense organs sensitive to low vibrations; *also* : one of these tubes or sense organs

lat·er·ite \'la-tə-,rīt\ *n* [L *later* brick] (1807) : a residual product of rock decay that is red in color and has a high content in the oxides of iron and hydroxide of aluminum — **lat·er·it·ic** \,la-tə-'ri-tik\ *adj*

lat·er·i·za·tion \,la-tə-rə-'zā-shən\ *n* (ca. 1882) : the process of conversion of rock to laterite

¹**lat·est** \'lā-təst\ *adj* (1588) **1** *archaic* : LAST **2** : most recent ⟨the ~ news⟩ ⟨the ~ style⟩

²**latest** *n* (1884) **1** : the latest acceptable time — usu. used in the phrase *at the latest* **2** : something that is the most recent or currently fashionable ⟨the ~ in diving techniques⟩

late·wood \'lāt-,wùd\ *n* (ca. 1933) : SUMMERWOOD

la·tex \'lā-,teks\ *n, pl* **la·ti·ces** \'lā-tə-,sēz, 'la-\ *or* **la·tex·es** [NL *latic-, latex,* fr. L, fluid] (1835) **1** : a milky usu. white fluid that is produced by cells of various seed plants (as of the milkweed, spurge, and poppy families) and is the source of rubber, gutta-percha, chicle, and balata **2** : a water emulsion of a synthetic rubber or plastic obtained by polymerization and used esp. in coatings (as paint) and adhesives

lath \'lath *also* 'lath\ *n, pl* **laths** *or* **lath** [ME, fr. (assumed) OE *læthth-;* akin to OHG *latta* lath, W *llath* lath] (13c) **1** : a thin narrow strip of wood nailed to rafters, joists, or studding as a groundwork for slates, tiles, or plaster **2** : a building material in sheets used as a base for plaster **3** : a quantity of laths — **lath** *vt*

¹**lathe** \'lāth\ *n* [prob. fr. ME *lath* supporting stand] (ca. 1611) : a machine in which work is rotated about a horizontal axis and shaped by a fixed tool

²**lathe** *vt* **lathed; lath·ing** (ca. 1903) : to cut or shape with a lathe

¹**lath·er** \'la-thər\ *n* [(assumed) ME, fr. OE *lēathor;* akin to L *lavere* to wash — more at LYE] (bef. 12c) **1 a** : a foam or froth formed when a detergent (as soap) is agitated in water **b** : foam or froth from profuse sweating (as on a horse) **2** : an agitated or overwrought state : DITHER — **lath·ery** \-th(ə-)rē\ *adj*

²**lather** *vb* **lath·ered; lath·er·ing** \-th(ə-)riŋ\ *vt* (bef. 12c) **1** : to spread lather over **2** : to beat severely : FLOG ~ *vi* : to form a lather or a froth like lather — **lath·er·er** \-thər-ər\ *n*

lath·y·rism \'la-thə-,ri-zəm\ *n* [NL *Lathyros,* fr. Gk *lathyros,* a type of pea] (ca. 1888) : a diseased condition of humans, domestic animals, and esp. horses that results from poisoning by a substance found in some legumes (genus *Lathyrus* and esp. *L. sativus*) and is characterized esp. by spastic paralysis of the hind or lower limbs

lath·y·rit·ic \,la-thə-'ri-tik\ *adj* (1960) : of, relating to, affected with, or characteristic of lathyrism ⟨~ rats⟩ ⟨~ cartilage⟩

latices *pl of* LATEX

la·tic·i·fer \lā-'ti-sə-fər\ *n* [ISV *latici-* (fr. NL *latic-, latex*) + *-fer*] (ca. 1928) : a plant cell or vessel that contains latex

la·ti·fun·dio \,lä-tə-'fün-dē-,ō\ *n, pl* **-di·os** [Sp, fr. L *latifundium*] (ca. 1902) : a latifundium in Spain or Latin America

lat·i·fun·di·um \,la-tə-'fən-dē-əm\ *n, pl* **-dia** \-dē-ə\ [L, fr. *latus* wide + *fundus* piece of landed property, foundation, bottom — more at BOTTOM] (1630) : a great landed estate with primitive agriculture and labor often in a state of partial servitude

lat·i·go \'la-ti-,gō\ *n, pl* **-gos** *also* **-goes** [Sp *látigo*] (1873) *chiefly West* : a long strap on a saddletree of a western saddle to adjust the cinch

¹**Lat·in** \'la-t°n\ *adj* [ME, fr. OE, fr. L *Latinus,* fr. *Latium,* ancient country of Italy] (bef. 12c) **1 a** : of, relating to, or composed in Latin **b** : ROMANCE **2** : of or relating to Latium or the Latins **3** : of or relating to the part of the Catholic Church that until recently used a Latin rite and forms the patriarchate of the pope **4** : of or relating to the peoples or countries using Romance languages; *specif* : of or relating to the peoples or countries of Latin America

²**Latin** *n* (bef. 12c) **1** : the Italic language of ancient Latium and of Rome and until modern times the dominant language of school, church, and state in western Europe — see INDO-EUROPEAN LANGUAGES table **2** : a member of the people of ancient Latium **3** : a Catholic of the Latin rite **4** : a member of one of the Latin peoples; *specif* : a native or inhabitant of Latin America **5** : LATIN ALPHABET

Latin alphabet *n* (1823) : an alphabet that was used for writing Latin and that has been modified for writing many modern languages

Latin Americanist *n* (1972) : a specialist in Latin American civilization

Lat·in·ate \'la-t°n-,āt\ *adj* (1904) : of, relating to, resembling, or derived from Latin

Latin cross *n* (1797) : a figure of a cross having a long upright shaft and a shorter crossbar traversing it above the middle — see CROSS illustration

Lat·in·ism \'la-t°n-,i-zəm\ *n* (ca. 1570) **1** : a characteristic feature of Latin occurring in another language **2** : Latin quality or character

Lat·in·ist \'la-t°n-ist, 'lat-nist\ *n* (15c) : a specialist in the Latin language or Roman culture

la·tin·i·ty \la-'ti-nə-tē, lə-\ *n, often cap* (1619) **1** : a manner of speaking or writing Latin **2** : LATINISM 2

lat·in·ize \'la-t°n-,īz\ *vb* **-ized; -iz·ing** *often cap, vt* (1589) **1 a** *obs* : to translate into Latin **b** : to give a Latin form to **c** : to introduce Latinisms into **d** : ROMANIZE 2 **2** : to make Latin or Italian in doctrine, ideas, or traits; *specif* : to cause to resemble the Roman Catholic Church ~ *vi* **1** : to use Latinisms **2** : to exhibit the influence of the Romans or of the Roman Catholic Church — **lat·in·i·za·tion** \,la-t°n-ə-'zā-shən, ,lat-nə-\ *n*

La·ti·no \lə-'tē-(,)nō\ *n, pl* **-nos** [AmerSp, prob. short for *latinoamericano* Latin American] (1946) **1** : a native or inhabitant of Latin America **2** : a person of Latin-American origin living in the U.S. — **Latino** *adj*

Latin square *n* (1890) : a square array which contains *n* different elements with each element occurring *n* times but with no element occurring twice in the same column or row and which is used esp. in the statistical design of experiments (as in agriculture)

lat·ish \'lā-tish\ *adj* (1611) : somewhat late

lat·i·tude \'la-tə-,tüd, -,tyüd\ *n* [ME, fr. L *latitudin-, latitudo,* fr. *latus*

wide; akin to OCS *postilati* to spread] (14c) **1** *archaic* : extent or distance from side to side : WIDTH **2** : angular distance from some specified circle or plane of reference: as **a** : angular distance north or south from the earth's equator measured through 90 degrees **b** : angular distance of a celestial body from the ecliptic **c** : a region or locality as marked by its latitude **3 a** *archaic* : SCOPE, RANGE **b** : the range of exposures within which a film or plate will produce a negative or positive of satisfactory quality **4** : freedom of action or choice — **lat·i·tu·di·nal** \,la-tə-'tüd-nəl, -'tyüd-; -'tü-d°n-əl, -'tyü-\ *adj* — **lat·i·tu·di·nal·ly** *adv*

latitude 2a: hemisphere marked with parallels of latitude

lat·i·tu·di·nar·i·an \,la-tə-,tü-d°n-'er-ē-ən, -,tyü-\ *n* (1662) : a person who is broad and liberal in standards of religious belief and conduct — **latitudinarian** *adj* — **lat·i·tu·di·nar·i·an·ism** \-ē-ə-,ni-zəm\ *n*

lat·ke \'lät-kə\ *n* [Yiddish, pancake, fr. Ukrainian *oladka*] (1927) : POTATO PANCAKE

lat·o·sol \'la-tə-,sòl\ *n* [irreg. fr. L *later* brick + E *-sol* (as in *podsol,* var. of *podzol*)] (1949) : a leached red and yellow tropical soil — **lat·o·sol·ic** \,la-tə-'sò-lik\ *adj*

la·trine \lə-'trēn\ *n* [F, fr. L *latrina,* contr. of *lavatrina,* fr. *lavare* to wash — more at LYE] (1642) **1** : a receptacle (as a pit in the earth) for use as a toilet **2** : TOILET

-latry *n comb form* [ME *-latrie,* fr. OF, fr. LL *-latria,* fr. Gk, fr. *latreia;* akin to Gk *latron* pay] : worship ⟨heliolatry⟩

lat·te \'lä-(,)tā\ *n* (1991) : CAFFE LATTE

lat·ten \'la-t°n\ *n* [ME *laton,* fr. MF] (14c) : a yellow alloy identical to or resembling brass typically hammered into thin sheets and formerly much used for church utensils

lat·ter \'la-tər\ *adj* [ME, fr. OE *lætra,* compar. of *læt* late] (bef. 12c) **1 a** : belonging to a subsequent time or period : more recent ⟨the ~ stages of growth⟩ **b** : of or relating to the end ⟨in their ~ days⟩ **c** : RECENT, PRESENT ⟨affected by ~ calamities⟩ **2** : of, relating to, or being the second of two groups or things or the last of several groups or things referred to ⟨of ham and beef the ~ meat is cheaper today⟩ ⟨of ham and beef the ~ is cheaper today⟩

lat·ter–day \'la-tər-,dā\ *adj* (1850) **1** : of present or recent times ⟨~ prophets⟩ **2** : of a later or subsequent time

Latter–day Saint *n, often cap D* (1834) : a member of any of several religious bodies tracing their origin to Joseph Smith in 1830 and accepting the Book of Mormon as divine revelation : MORMON

lat·ter·ly *adv* (1734) **1** : LATER **2** : of late : RECENTLY

lat·tice \'la-təs\ *n* [ME *latis,* fr. MF *lattis*] (14c) **1 a** : a framework or structure of crossed wood or metal strips **b** : a window, door, or gate having a lattice **c** : a network or design resembling a lattice **2** : a regular geometrical arrangement of points or objects over an area or in space; *specif* : the arrangement of atoms in a crystal **3** : a mathematical set that has some elements ordered and that is such that for any two elements there exists a greatest element in the subset of all elements less than or equal to both and a least element in the subset of all elements greater than or equal to both — **lattice** *vt* — **lat·ticed** \-tist\ *adj*

lattice girder *n* (1852) : a girder with top and bottom flanges connected by a latticework web

lat·tice·work \'la-təs-,wərk\ *n* (15c) : a lattice or work made of lattices

la·tus rec·tum \'la-təs-'rek-təm\ *n* [NL, lit., straight side] (1702) : a chord of a conic section (as an ellipse) that passes through a focus and is parallel to the directrix

Lat·vi·an \'lat-vē-ən\ *n* (1924) **1** : the Baltic language of the Latvian people **2** : a native or inhabitant of Latvia — **Latvian** *adj*

lau·an \'lü-,än, lü-'; laü-'än\ *n* [Tag *lawaan*] (1894) : any of various Philippine timbers (as of the genera *Shorea* and *Parashorea*) that are light yellow to reddish brown or brown and include some which enter commerce as Philippine mahogany

¹**laud** \'lòd\ *n* [ME *laudes* (pl.), fr. ML, fr. L, pl. of *laud-, laus* praise] (14c) **1** *pl but sing or pl in constr, often cap* : an office of solemn praise to God forming with matins the first of the canonical hours **2** : PRAISE, ACCLAIM

²**laud** *vt* [L *laudare,* fr. *laud-, laus*] (14c) : PRAISE, EXTOL

laud·able \'lò-də-bəl\ *adj* (15c) : worthy of praise : COMMENDABLE — **laud·able·ness** \'lò-də-bəl-nəs\ *n* — **laud·ably** \-blē\ *adv*

lau·da·num \'lòd-nəm, 'lò-d°n-əm\ *n* [NL] (ca. 1603) **1** : any of various formerly used preparations of opium **2** : a tincture of opium

lau·da·tion \lò-'dā-shən\ *n* (15c) : the act of praising : EULOGY

lau·da·tive \'lò-də-tiv\ *adj* (15c) : LAUDATORY

lau·da·to·ry \'lò-də-,tòr-ē, -,tór-\ *adj* (1555) : of, relating to, or expressing praise

¹**laugh** \'laf, 'laf\ *vb* [ME, fr. OE *hliehhan;* akin to OHG *lachēn* to laugh] *vi* (bef. 12c) **1 a** : to show mirth, joy, or scorn with a smile and chuckle or explosive sound **b** : to find amusement or pleasure in something ⟨~ed at his own clumsiness⟩ **c** : to become amused or derisive ⟨a very skeptical public ~ed at our early efforts — Graenum Berger⟩ **2 a** : to produce the sound or appearance of laughter ⟨a ~ing brook⟩ **b** : to be of a kind that inspires joy ~ *vt* **1** : to influence or move by laughter ⟨~ed the bad singer off the stage⟩ **2** : to utter with a laugh — **laugh·ing·ly** \'la-fiŋ-lē, 'là-\ *adv*

²**laugh** *n* (1690) **1** : the act of laughing **2 a** : a cause for derision or merriment : JOKE **b** : an expression of scorn or mockery : JEER **3** *pl* : DIVERSION, SPORT ⟨play baseball just for ~s⟩

laugh·able \'la-fə-bəl, 'là-\ *adj* (1596) : of a kind to provoke laughter or sometimes derision : amusingly ridiculous — **laugh·able·ness** *n* — **laugh·ably** \-blē\ *adv*

syn LAUGHABLE, LUDICROUS, RIDICULOUS, COMIC, COMICAL mean provoking laughter or mirth. LAUGHABLE applies to anything occasioning laughter ⟨*laughable* attempts at waterskiing⟩. LUDICROUS suggests absurdity or preposterousness that excites both laughter and scorn ⟨a spy thriller with a *ludicrous* plot⟩. RIDICULOUS suggests extreme absurdity, foolishness, or contemptibility ⟨a *ridiculous* portrayal of wartime combat⟩. COMIC applies esp. to that which arouses thoughtful amusement ⟨a *comic* character⟩. COMICAL applies to that which arouses spontaneous hilarity ⟨you looked *comical*⟩.

laugh·er \'la-fər, 'lȧ-\ *n* (15c) **1 :** one that laughs **2 :** something (as a game) that is easily won or handled

laughing gas *n* (ca. 1842) : NITROUS OXIDE

laughing gull *n* (1789) : an American gull (*Larus atricilla*) having a black head in breeding plumage and black wing tips blending into the gray upper side of the wings

laughing jackass *n* (1798) : KOOKABURRA

laughing matter *n* (ca. 1583) : something not to be taken seriously — usu. used in the phrase *no laughing matter*

laugh·ing·stock \'la-fiŋ-,stäk, 'lȧ-\ *n* (1533) : an object of ridicule

laugh off *vt* (1715) : to minimize by treating as amusingly or absurdly trivial

laugh·ter \'laf-tər, 'lȧf-\ *n* [ME, fr. OE *hleahtor;* akin to OE *hliehhan*] (bef. 12c) **1 :** a sound of or as if of laughing **2** *archaic* : a cause of merriment

laugh track *n* (1962) : laughter to accompany dialogue or action (as of a television program)

launce \'lȯn(t)s, 'län(t)s\ *n* [prob. fr. ¹*lance*] (1623) : SAND LANCE

¹launch \'lȯnch, 'länch\ *vb* [ME, fr. ONF *lancher,* fr. LL *lanceare* to wield a lance — more at LANCE] *vt* (14c) **1 a :** to throw forward : HURL **b :** to release, catapult, or send off (a self-propelled object) ⟨~ a rocket⟩ **2 a :** to set (a boat or ship) afloat **b :** to give (a person) a start ⟨~ed in a new career⟩ **c** (1) : to originate or set in motion : INITIATE, INTRODUCE (2) : to get off to a good start ~ *vi* **1 a :** to spring forward : TAKE OFF **b :** to throw oneself energetically : PLUNGE **2 a** *archaic* : to slide down the ways **b :** to make a start

²launch *n* (1749) : an act or instance of launching

³launch *n* [Sp or Pg; Sp *lancha,* fr. Pg] (1697) **1 :** a large boat that operates from a ship **2 :** a small motorboat that is open or that has the forepart of the hull covered

launch·er \'lȯn-chər, 'län-\ *n* (1911) : one that launches: as **a :** a device for firing grenades **b :** a device for launching a missile **c** : LAUNCH VEHICLE

launching pad *n* (1951) **1 :** LAUNCHPAD **2 :** SPRINGBOARD 2

launch·pad \'lȯnch-,pad, 'länch-\ *n* (1958) : a nonflammable platform from which a rocket, launch vehicle, or guided missile can be launched

launch vehicle *n* (ca. 1960) : a rocket used to launch a satellite or spacecraft

launch window *n* (1962) : WINDOW 8

¹laun·der \'lȯn-dər, 'län-\ *vb* **laun·dered; laun·der·ing** \-d(ə-)riŋ\ [ME *launder,* n.] *vt* (1664) **1 :** to wash (as clothes) in water **2 :** to make ready for use by washing and ironing ⟨a freshly ~ed shirt⟩ **3** : to transfer (as illegally obtained money or investments) through an outside party to conceal the true source ~ *vi* : to wash or wash and iron clothing or household linens — **laun·der·er** \-dər-ər\ *n*

²launder *n* [ME, launderer, fr. MF *lavandier,* fr. ML *lavandarius,* fr. L *lavandus,* gerundive of *lavare* to wash — more at LYE] (1667) : TROUGH; *esp* : a box conduit conveying particulate material suspended in water in ore dressing

laun·der·ette \,lȯn-də-'ret, ,län-\ *also* **laun·drette** \-'dret\ *n* [fr. *Launderette,* a service mark] (ca. 1948) : a self-service laundry

laun·dress \'lȯn-drəs, 'län-\ *n* (1550) : a woman who is a laundry worker

Laun·dro·mat \'lȯn-drə-,mat, 'län-\ *service mark* — used for a self-service laundry

laun·dry \'lȯn-drē, 'län-\ *n, pl* **laundries** (14c) **1 a :** a room for doing the family wash **b :** a commercial laundering establishment **2** : clothes or linens that have been or are to be laundered

laundry list *n* (1958) : a usu. long list of items ⟨the *laundry list* of new consumer-protection bills — N. C. Miller⟩

laun·dry·man \-mən\ *n* (1708) : a man who is a laundry worker

Laun·fal \'lȯn-fəl, 'län-\ *n* : a knight of the Round Table in late Arthurian legend

lau·ra \'läv-rə\ *n* [LGk, fr. Gk, lane] (ca. 1752) : a monastery of an Eastern church

¹lau·re·ate \'lȯr-ē-ət, 'lär-\ *n* [ME, crowned with laurel as a distinction, fr. L *laureatus,* fr. *laurea* laurel wreath, fr. fem. of *laureus* of laurel, fr. *laurus*] (ca. 1529) : the recipient of honor or recognition for achievement in an art or science; *specif* : POET LAUREATE — **laureate** *adj* — **lau·re·ate·ship** \-,ship\ *n*

²lau·re·ate \'lȯr-ē-,āt, 'lär-\ *vt* **-at·ed; -at·ing** (ca. 1610) **1 :** to crown with or as if with a laurel wreath for excellence or achievement **2 :** to appoint to the office of poet laureate — **lau·re·ation** \,lȯr-ē-'ā-shən, ,lär-\ *n*

¹lau·rel \'lȯr-əl, 'lär-\ *n* [ME *lorel,* fr. OF *lorier,* fr. *lor* laurel, fr. L *laurus*] (14c) **1 :** any of a genus (*Laurus* of the family Lauraceae, the laurel family) of evergreen trees that have alternate entire leaves, small tetramerous flowers surrounded by bracts, and fruits that are ovoid berries; *specif* : a tree (*L. nobilis*) of southern Europe with foliage used by the ancient Greeks to crown victors in the Pythian games **2 :** a tree or shrub that resembles the true laurel; *esp* : MOUNTAIN LAUREL **3 :** a crown of laurel : HONOR — usu. used in pl.

²laurel *vt* **-reled** *or* **-relled; -rel·ing** *or* **-rel·ling** (1631) : to deck or crown with laurel

lau·ric acid \'lȯr-ik-, 'lär-\ *n* [ISV, fr. L *laurus*] (1873) : a crystalline fatty acid $C_{12}H_{24}O_2$ found esp. in coconut oil and used in making soaps, esters, and lauryl alcohol

lau·ryl alcohol \'lȯr-əl-, 'lär-\ *n* (1922) : a compound $C_{12}H_{26}O$; *also* : a liquid mixture of this and other alcohols used esp. in making detergents

la·va \'lä-və, 'la-\ *n* [It, ultim. fr. L *labes* fall; akin to L *labi* to slide — more at SLEEP] (1759) : molten rock that issues from a volcano or from a fissure in the earth's surface; *also* : such rock that has cooled and hardened — **la·va·like** \-,līk\ *adj*

la·va·bo \lə-'vä-(,)bō\ *n, pl* **-bos** [L, I shall wash, fr. *lavare*] (ca. 1858) **1** *often cap* : a ceremony at Mass in which the celebrant washes his hands after offering the oblations and says Psalm 25:6–12 (DV) **2 a** : a washbasin and a tank with a spigot that are fastened to a wall **b** : this combination used as a planter

la·vage \lə-'väzh, *Brit usu* 'la-vij\ *n* [F, fr. MF, fr. *laver* to wash, fr. L *lavare*] (ca. 1895) : WASHING; *esp* : the therapeutic washing out of an organ

la·va·la·va \,lä-və-'lä-və\ *n* [Samoan, clothing] (ca. 1891) : a rectangular cloth of cotton print worn like a kilt or skirt in Polynesia and esp. in Samoa

la·va·liere *or* **la·val·liere** \,lä-və-'lir, ,la-\ *n* [F *lavallière* necktie with a large knot] (1906) : a pendant on a fine chain that is worn as a necklace

la·va·lier microphone \,lä-və-'lir-, ,la-\ *or* **lavaliere microphone** *same*\ *n* (ca. 1962) : a small microphone hung around the neck of the user

la·va·tion \lā-'vā-shən\ *n* [L *lavation-, lavatio,* fr. *lavare*] (15c) : the act or an instance of washing or cleansing

lav·a·to·ry \'la-və-,tōr-ē, -,tȯr-, *Brit* -və-t(ə-)rē\ *n, pl* **-ries** [ME *lavatorie,* fr. ML *lavatorium,* fr. L *lavare* to wash — more at LYE] (14c) **1 :** a vessel (as a basin) for washing; *esp* : a fixed bowl or basin with running water and drainpipe for washing **2 :** a room with conveniences for washing and usu. with one or more toilets **3 :** TOILET 3b — **lavatory** *adj*

¹lave \'lāv\ *n* [ME (northern dial.), fr. OE *lāf;* akin to OE be*lifan* to remain — more at LEAVE] (bef. 12c) *chiefly dial* : something that is left : RESIDUE

²lave *vb* **laved; lav·ing** [ME, fr. OE *lafian,* fr. L *lavare*] *vt* (bef. 12c) **1 a :** WASH, BATHE **b :** to flow along or against **2 :** POUR ~ *vi, archaic* : to wash oneself : BATHE

lav·en·der \'la-vən-dər\ *n* [ME *lavendre,* fr. AF, fr. ML *lavandula*] (13c) **1 a :** a Mediterranean mint (*Lavandula angustifolia* syn. *L. officinalis*) widely cultivated for its narrow aromatic leaves and spikes of lilac-purple flowers which are dried and used in sachets **b :** any of several plants congeneric with true lavender and used similarly but often considered inferior **2 :** a pale purple

²lavender *vt* **lav·en·dered; lav·en·der·ing** \-d(ə-)riŋ\ (1820) : to sprinkle or perfume with lavender

¹la·ver \'lā-vər\ *n* [ME *lavour,* fr. MF *lavoir,* fr. ML *lavatorium*] (1535) : a large basin used for ceremonial ablutions in the ancient Jewish Tabernacle and Temple worship

²la·ver \'lā-vər, 'lä-\ *n* [NL, fr. L, a water plant] (1611) : any of several common red algae (genus *Porphyra*) with fronds used for stewing or pickling

La·vin·ia \lə-'vi-nē-ə\ *n* [L] : a daughter of King Latinus in Virgil's *Aeneid* who is betrothed to Turnus but marries Aeneas

¹lav·ish \'la-vish\ *adj* [ME *lavas* abundance, fr. MF *lavasse* downpour of rain, fr. *laver* to wash — more at LAVAGE] (15c) **1 :** expending or bestowing profusely : PRODIGAL **2 a :** expended or produced in abundance **b :** marked by profusion or excess *syn* see PROFUSE — **lav·ish·ly** *adv* — **lav·ish·ness** *n*

²lavish *vt* (1542) : to expend or bestow with profusion : SQUANDER

lav·rock \'lä-rək, 'lav-\ *or* **la·ver·ock** \'la-və-\ *n* [ME *laverok,* fr. OE *lāwerce*] (14c) *chiefly Scot* : LARK

law \'lȯ\ *n* [ME, fr. OE *lagu,* of Scand origin; akin to ON *lǫg* law; akin to OE *licgan* to lie — more at LIE] (bef. 12c) **1 a** (1) : a binding custom or practice of a community : a rule of conduct or action prescribed or formally recognized as binding or enforced by a controlling authority (2) : the whole body of such customs, practices, or rules (3) : COMMON LAW **b** (1) : the control brought about by the existence or enforcement of such law (2) : the action of laws considered as a means of redressing wrongs; *also* : LITIGATION (3) : the agency of or an agent of established law **c** : a rule or order that it is advisable or obligatory to observe **d** : something compatible with or enforceable by established law **e** : CONTROL, AUTHORITY **2 a** *often cap* : the revelation of the will of God set forth in the Old Testament **b** *cap* : the first part of the Jewish scriptures : PENTATEUCH, TORAH — see BIBLE table **3 :** a rule of construction or procedure ⟨the ~s of poetry⟩ **4** : the whole body of laws relating to one subject **5 a :** the legal profession **b :** law as a department of knowledge : JURISPRUDENCE **c** : legal knowledge **6 a :** a statement of an order or relation of phenomena that so far as is known is invariable under the given conditions **b :** a general relation proved or assumed to hold between mathematical or logical expressions — **at law :** under or within the provisions of the law ⟨enforceable *at law*⟩

syn LAW, RULE, REGULATION, PRECEPT, STATUTE, ORDINANCE, CANON mean a principle governing action or procedure. LAW implies imposition by a sovereign authority and the obligation of obedience on the part of all subject to that authority ⟨obey the *law*⟩. RULE applies to more restricted or specific situations ⟨the *rules* of the game⟩. REGULATION implies prescription by authority in order to control an organization or system ⟨*regulations* affecting nuclear power plants⟩. PRECEPT commonly suggests something advisory and not obligatory communicated typically through teaching ⟨the *precepts* of effective writing⟩. STATUTE implies a law enacted by a legislative body ⟨a *statute* requiring the use of seat belts⟩. ORDINANCE applies to an order governing some detail of procedure or conduct enforced by a limited authority such as a municipality ⟨a city *ordinance*⟩. CANON suggests in nonreligious use a principle or rule of behavior or procedure commonly accepted as a valid guide ⟨the *canons* of good taste⟩. *syn* see in addition HYPOTHESIS

²law *vi* (ca. 1550) : LITIGATE ~ *vt, chiefly dial* : to sue or prosecute at law

law–abid·ing \'lȯ-ə-,bī-diŋ\ *adj* (1834) : abiding by or obedient to the law — **law–abid·ing·ness** *n*

law·break·er \'lȯ-,brā-kər\ *n* (15c) : one who violates the law — **law·break·ing** \-kiŋ\ *adj or n*

law·ful \'lȯ-fəl\ *adj* (14c) **1 :** being in harmony with the law ⟨a ~ judgment⟩ **b :** constituted, authorized, or established by law : RIGHTFUL ⟨~ institutions⟩ **2 :** LAW-ABIDING ⟨~ citizens⟩ — **law·ful·ly** \-f(ə-)lē\ *adv* — **law·ful·ness** \-fəl-nəs\ *n*

syn LAWFUL, LEGAL, LEGITIMATE, LICIT mean being in accordance with law. LAWFUL may apply to conformity with law of any sort (as natural, divine, common, or canon) ⟨the *lawful* sovereign⟩. LEGAL applies to

\ə\ abut \ᵊ\ kitten, F table \ər\ further \a\ ash \ā\ ace \ä\ mop, mar
\aú\ out \ch\ chin \e\ bet \ē\ easy \g\ go \i\ hit \ī\ ice \j\ job
\ŋ\ sing \ō\ go \ȯ\ law \ȯi\ boy \th\ thin \t͟h\ the \ü\ loot \ù\ foot
\y\ yet \zh\ vision \ȧ, k̲, ⁿ, œ, œ̄, ᴜe, ūe, ᶤ\ *see* Guide to Pronunciation

what is sanctioned by law or in conformity with the law, esp. as it is written or administered by the courts ⟨*legal* residents of the state⟩. LEGITIMATE may apply to a legal right or status but also, in extended use, to a right or status supported by tradition, custom, or accepted standards ⟨a perfectly *legitimate* question about finances⟩. LICIT applies to a strict conformity to the provisions of the law and applies esp. to what is regulated by law ⟨the *licit* use of the drug by hospitals⟩.

law·giv·er \ˈlȯ-ˌgi-vər\ *n* (14c) **1 :** one who gives a code of laws to a people **2 :** LEGISLATOR

law·less \ˈlȯ-ləs\ *adj* (12c) **1 :** not regulated by or based on law **2 a :** not restrained or controlled by law **:** UNRULY **b :** ILLEGAL — **law·less·ly** *adv* — **law·less·ness** *n*

law·mak·er \ˈlȯ-ˌmā-kər\ *n* (14c) **:** one that makes laws **:** LEGISLATOR — **law·mak·ing** \-ˌkiŋ\ *n*

law·man \ˈlȯ-mən\ *n* (1944) **:** a law-enforcement officer (as a sheriff or marshal)

law merchant *n, pl* **laws merchant** (15c) **:** the legal rules formerly applied to cases arising in commercial transactions

¹lawn \ˈlȯn, ˈlän\ *n* [ME *launde*, fr. MF *lande* heath, of Celt origin; akin to MIr *lann* land — more at LAND] (14c) **1** *archaic* **:** an open space between woods **:** GLADE **2 :** ground (as around a house or in a garden or park) that is covered with grass and is kept mowed **3 :** a relatively even layer of bacteria covering the surface of a culture medium — **lawn** *or* **lawny** \ˈlȯ-nē, ˈlä-\ *adj*

²lawn *n* [ME, fr. *Laon*, France] (15c) **:** a fine sheer linen or cotton fabric of plain weave that is thinner than cambric — **lawny** *adj*

lawn bowling *n* (ca. 1929) **:** a bowling game played on a green with wooden balls which are rolled at a jack

lawn mower (1869) **:** a machine for cutting grass on lawns

lawn tennis *n* (1874) **:** TENNIS 2

law of averages (ca. 1929) **:** the commonsense observation that probability influences everyday life so that over the long term the possible outcomes of a repeated event occur with specific frequencies

law of definite proportions (ca. 1909) **:** a statement in chemistry: every definite compound always contains the same elements in the same proportions by weight

law of dominance (1942) **:** MENDEL'S LAW 3

law of independent assortment (1943) **:** MENDEL'S LAW 2

law of large numbers (1911) **:** a theorem in mathematical statistics: the probability that the absolute value of the difference between the mean of a population sample and the mean of the population from which it is drawn is greater than an arbitrarily small amount approaches zero as the size of the sample approaches infinity

Law of Moses (14c) **:** PENTATEUCH, TORAH

law of nations (ca. 1548) **:** INTERNATIONAL LAW

law of parsimony (1837) **:** OCCAM'S RAZOR

law of segregation (ca. 1909) **:** MENDEL'S LAW 1

law of war (1947) **:** the code that governs or one of the rules that govern the rights and duties of belligerents in international war

law·ren·ci·um \lȯ-ˈren(t)-sē-əm\ *n* [NL, fr. Ernest O. *Lawrence*] (1961) **:** a short-lived radioactive element that is produced artificially from californium — see ELEMENT table

law·suit \ˈlȯ-ˌsüt\ *n* (1624) **:** a suit in law **:** a case before a court

law·yer \ˈlȯ-yər, ˈlȯi-ər\ *n* (14c) **:** one whose profession is to conduct lawsuits for clients or to advise as to legal rights and obligations in other matters — **law·yer·like** \-ˌlīk\ *adj* — **law·yer·ly** \-lē\ *adj*

law·yer·ing \ˈlȯ-yə-riŋ, ˈlȯi-ə-\ *n* (1676) **:** the profession or work of a lawyer

lax \ˈlaks\ *adj* [ME, fr. L *laxus* loose — more at SLACK] (14c) **1** *a of the bowels* **:** LOOSE, OPEN **b :** having loose bowels **2 :** deficient in firmness **:** not stringent ⟨~ control⟩ ⟨a ~ foreman⟩ **3 a :** not tense, firm, or rigid **:** SLACK ⟨a ~ rope⟩ **b :** having an open or loose texture **c :** having the constituents spread apart ⟨a ~ flower cluster⟩ **4 :** articulated with the muscles involved in a relatively relaxed state (as the vowel \i\ in contrast with the vowel \ē\) *syn* see NEGLIGENT — **lax·a·tion** \lak-ˈsā-shən\ *n* — **lax·ly** \ˈlaks-lē\ *adv* — **lax·ness** *n*

¹lax·a·tive \ˈlak-sə-tiv\ *adj* [ME *laxatif*, fr. ML *laxativus*, fr. L *laxatus*, pp. of *laxare* to loosen, fr. *laxus*] (14c) **:** having a tendency to loosen or relax; *specif* **:** relieving constipation

²laxative *n* (14c) **:** a usu. mild laxative drug

lax·i·ty \ˈlak-sə-tē\ *n* (1528) **:** the quality or state of being lax

¹lay \ˈlā\ *vb* **laid** \ˈlād\; **lay·ing** [ME *leyen*, fr. OE *lecgan*; akin to OE *licgan* to lie — more at LIE] *vt* (bef. 12c) **1 :** to beat or strike down with force **2 a :** to put or set down **b :** to place for rest or sleep; *esp* **:** BURY **3 :** to bring forth and deposit (an egg) **4 :** CALM, ALLAY ⟨~ the dust⟩ **5 :** BET, WAGER **6 :** to press down giving a smooth and even surface **7 a :** to dispose or spread over or on a surface ⟨~ track⟩ ⟨~ plaster⟩ **b :** to set in order or position ⟨~ a table for dinner⟩ ⟨~ brick⟩ **c :** to put (strands) in place and twist to form a rope, hawser, or cable; *also* **:** to make by so doing ⟨~ up rope⟩ **8 a :** to impose as a duty, burden, or punishment ⟨~ a tax⟩ **b :** to put as a burden of reproach ⟨*laid* the blame on her⟩ **c :** to advance as an accusation **:** IMPUTE ⟨the disaster was *laid* to faulty inspection⟩ **9 :** to place (something immaterial) on something ⟨~ stress on grammar⟩ **10 :** PREPARE, CONTRIVE ⟨a well-*laid* plan⟩ **11 a :** to bring against or into contact with something **:** APPLY ⟨*laid* the watch to his ear⟩ **b :** to prepare or position for action or operation ⟨~ a fire in the fireplace⟩; *also* **:** to adjust (a gun) to the proper direction and elevation **12 :** to bring to a specified condition ⟨~ waste the land⟩ **13 a :** ASSERT, ALLEGE ⟨~ claim to an estate⟩ **b :** to submit for examination and judgment ⟨*laid* her case before the commission⟩ **14 :** to copulate with — sometimes considered vulgar ~ *vi* **1 :** to produce and deposit eggs **2** *nonstand* **:** ¹LIE **3 :** WAGER, BET **4** *dial* **:** PLAN, PREPARE **5 a :** to apply oneself vigorously ⟨*laid* to his oars⟩ **b :** to proceed to a specified place or position on a ship ⟨~ aloft⟩ — **lay on the table 1 :** to remove (a parliamentary motion) from consideration indefinitely **2** *Brit* **:** to put (as legislation) on the agenda

usage LAY has been used intransitively in the sense of "lie" since the 14th century. The practice was unremarked until around 1770; attempts to correct it have been a fixture of schoolbooks ever since. Generations of teachers and critics have succeeded in taming most literary and learned writing, but intransitive *lay* persists in familiar speech and is a bit more common in general prose than one might suspect. Much of the problem lies in the confusing similarity of the principal parts of the two words. Another influence may be a folk belief that *lie* is for people and *lay* is for things. Some commentators are ready to abandon the distinction, suggesting that *lay* is on the rise socially. But if it does rise to respectability, it is sure to do so slowly: many people have invested effort in learning to keep *lie* and *lay* distinct. Remember that even though many people do use *lay* for *lie*, others will judge you unfavorably if you do.

²lay *n* (1590) **1 :** COVERT, LAIR **2 :** something (as a layer) that lies or is laid **3 a :** line of action **:** PLAN **b :** line of work **:** OCCUPATION **4 a :** terms of sale or employment **:** PRICE **b :** share of profit (as on a whaling voyage) paid in lieu of wages **5 a :** the amount of advance of any point in a rope strand for one turn **b :** the nature of a fiber rope as determined by the amount of twist, the angle of the strands, and the angle of the threads in the strands **6 :** the way in which a thing lies or is laid in relation to something else ⟨the ~ of the land⟩ **7 :** the state of one that lays eggs ⟨hens coming into ~⟩ **8 a :** a partner in sexual intercourse — usu. considered vulgar **b :** SEXUAL INTERCOURSE — usu. considered vulgar

³lay *past of* LIE

⁴lay *n* [ME, fr. OF *lai*] (13c) **1 :** a simple narrative poem **:** BALLAD **2 :** MELODY, SONG

⁵lay *adj* [ME, fr. MF *lai*, fr. LL *laicus*, fr. Gk *laikos* of the people, fr. *laos* people] (15c) **1 :** of or relating to the laity **:** not ecclesiastical **2 :** of or relating to members of a religious house occupied with domestic or manual work ⟨a ~ brother⟩ **3 :** not of a particular profession ⟨the ~ public⟩; *also* **:** lacking extensive knowledge of a particular subject

lay·about \ˈlā-ə-ˌbaut\ *n* (1932) **:** a lazy shiftless person **:** IDLER

lay·away \ˈlā-ə-ˌwā\ *n* (1944) **:** a purchasing agreement by which a retailer agrees to hold merchandise secured by a deposit until the price is paid in full by the customer

lay away *vt* (ca. 1928) **:** to put aside for future use or delivery

lay-by \ˈlā-ˌbī\ *n* (1939) **1** *Brit* **:** TURNOUT 4b **2 :** the final operation (as a last cultivating) in the growing of a field crop

lay by *vt* (15c) **1 :** to lay aside **:** DISCARD **2 :** to store for future use **:** SAVE **3 :** to cultivate (as corn) for the last time

lay day *n* (1845) **1 :** one of the days allowed by the charter for loading or unloading a vessel **2 :** a day of delay in port

lay down *vt* (13c) **1 :** to give up **:** SURRENDER ⟨*lay down* your arms⟩ **2 a :** ESTABLISH, PRESCRIBE ⟨*lay down* a scale for a meal⟩ **b :** to assert or command dogmatically ⟨*lay down* the law⟩ **3 :** STORE, PRESERVE **4 a :** to direct toward a target ⟨*lay down* a barrage⟩ **b :** to hit along the ground ⟨*laid down* a sacrifice bunt⟩ ~ *vi, nonstand* **:** to lie down

¹lay·er \ˈlā-ər, ˈle(-ə)r\ *n* (13c) **1 :** one that lays (as a worker who lays brick or a hen that lays eggs) **2 a :** one thickness, course, or fold laid or lying over or under another **b :** STRATUM **c :** HORIZON 2 **3 a :** a branch or shoot of a plant that roots while still attached to the parent plant **b :** a plant developed by layering — **lay·ered** \ˈlā-ərd, ˈle(-ə)rd\ *adj*

²layer *vt* (1832) **1 :** to propagate (a plant) by means of layers **2 a :** to place as a layer **b :** to place a layer on top of **c :** to form or arrange in layers ~ *vi* **1 a :** to separate into layers **b :** to form out of superimposed layers **2** *of a plant* **:** to form roots where a stem comes in contact with the ground

lay·er·age \ˈlā-ə-rij, ˈle-ə-\ *n* (1902) **:** the practice, art, or process of rooting plants by layering

lay·ette \lā-ˈet\ *n* [F, fr. MF, dim. of *laye* box, fr. MD *lade*; akin to OE *hladan* to load — more at LADE] (1839) **:** a complete outfit of clothing and equipment for a newborn infant

lay figure *n* [obs. E *layman* lay figure, fr. D *leeman*] (1795) **1 :** a jointed model of the human body used by artists to show the disposition of drapery **2 :** a person likened to a dummy or puppet

lay in *vt* (1579) **:** LAY BY, SAVE

laying on of hands (15c) **:** the act of laying hands on a person's head to confer a spiritual blessing (as in Christian ordination, confirmation, or faith healing)

lay·man \ˈlā-mən\ *n* (15c) **1 :** a person who is not a member of the clergy **2 :** a person who does not belong to a particular profession or who is not expert in some field

lay·off \ˈlā-ˌȯf\ *n* (1889) **1 :** a period of inactivity or idleness **2 :** the act of laying off an employee or a workforce; *also* **:** SHUTDOWN

lay off *vt* (1748) **1 :** to mark or measure off **2 :** to cease to employ (a worker) often temporarily **3** *of a bookie* **:** to place all or part of (an accepted bet) with another bookie to reduce the risk **4 a :** to leave undisturbed **b :** AVOID, QUIT ~ *vi* **1 :** to stop doing or taking something **2 :** to leave one alone ⟨wish you'd just *lay off*⟩

lay on *vt* (1600) **1 :** to apply by or as if by spreading on a surface ⟨*laying* it on thick⟩ **b :** PROVIDE, ARRANGE ⟨food *laid on* in abundance⟩ **c :** HAND OUT ⟨*laid on* awards⟩ **2** *chiefly Brit* **:** HIRE ~ *vi* **:** ATTACK, BEAT

lay·out \ˈlā-ˌaut\ *n* (1852) **1 :** the plan or design or arrangement of something that is laid out: as **a :** DUMMY 5b **b :** final arrangement of matter to be reproduced esp. by printing **2 :** the act or process of planning or laying out in detail **3 a :** something that is laid out ⟨a model train ~⟩ **b :** land or structures or rooms used for a particular purpose ⟨a cattle-ranching ~⟩; *also* **:** PLACE **c :** a set or outfit esp. of tools

lay out *vt* (15c) **1 :** DISPLAY, EXHIBIT **2 :** SPEND **3 a :** to prepare (a corpse) for viewing **b :** to knock flat or unconscious **4 :** to plan in detail ⟨*lay out* a campaign⟩ **5 :** ARRANGE, DESIGN **6 :** to mark (work) for drilling, machining, or filing

lay·over \ˈlā-ˌō-vər\ *n* (1873) **:** STOPOVER

lay over *vt* (1838) **:** POSTPONE ~ *vi* **:** to make a stopover

lay·peo·ple \ˈlā-ˌpē-pəl\ *n pl* (15c) **:** LAYPERSONS

lay·per·son \-ˌpər-s⁰n\ *n* (1972) **:** a member of the laity

lay reader *n* (1751) **:** an Anglican or Roman Catholic layman authorized to conduct parts of the church services not requiring a clergyman

lay to *vi* (1796) **:** LIE TO ~ *vt* **:** to bring (a ship) into the wind and hold stationary

lay-up \ˈlā-ˌəp\ *n* (1925) **1 :** the action of laying up or the condition of being laid up **2 :** a shot in basketball made from near the basket usu. by playing the ball off the backboard

lay up *vt* (14c) **1 :** to store up **:** LAY BY **2 :** to disable or confine with illness or injury **3 :** to take out of active service

lay·wom·an \'lā-,wu̇-mən\ n (1529) : a woman who is a member of the laity

la·zar \'la-zər, 'lā-\ n [ME, fr. ML *lazarus*, fr. LL *Lazarus*] (14c) : a person afflicted with a repulsive disease; *specif* : LEPER

laz·a·ret·to \,la-zə-'re-(,)tō\ *or* **laz·a·ret** \-'ret\ *also* **laz·a·rette** \-'ret\ *n, pl* **-rettos** *or* **-rets** *also* **-rettes** [It *lazzaretto*, alter. of *Nazaretto*, quarantine station in Venice, fr. *Santa Maria di Nazareth*, church on the island where it was located] (1549) **1** *usu* **lazaretto** : an institution (as a hospital) for those with contagious diseases **2** : a building or a ship used for detention in quarantine **3** *usu* **lazaret** : a space in a ship between decks used as a storeroom

La·za·rist \'la-zə-rist, lə-'zär-ist\ n [College of St. *Lazare*, Paris, former home of the congregation] (1747) : VINCENTIAN

Laz·a·rus \'laz-rəs, 'la-zə-\ n [LL, fr. Gk *Lazaros*, fr. Heb *El'āzār*] **1** : a brother of Mary and Martha raised by Jesus from the dead according to the account in John 11 **2** : the diseased beggar in the parable of the rich man and the beggar found in Luke 16

laze \'lāz\ vb **lazed; laz·ing** [back-formation fr. *lazy*] vi (ca. 1592) : to act or lie lazily : IDLE ∼ vt : to pass (time) in idleness or relaxation — **laze** n

la·zu·lite \'la-zyü-,līt, -zhə-\ n [G *Lazulith*, fr. ML *lazulum* lapis lazuli] (1807) : an often crystalline azure-blue mineral that is a hydrous phosphate of aluminum, iron, and magnesium

1la·zy \'lā-zē\ *adj* **la·zi·er; -est** [perh. fr. MLG *lasich* feeble; akin to MHG er*leswen* to become weak] (1549) **1 a** : disinclined to activity or exertion : not energetic or vigorous **b** : encouraging inactivity or indolence ⟨a ∼ summer day⟩ **2** : moving slowly : SLUGGISH **3** : DROOPY, LAX ⟨a rabbit with ∼ ears⟩ **4** : placed on its side ⟨∼ E livestock brand⟩ **5** : not rigorous or strict ⟨∼ scholarship⟩ — **la·zi·ly** \-zə-lē\ *adv* — **la·zi·ness** \-zē-nəs\ n — **la·zy·ish** \-zē-ish\ *adj*

syn LAZY, INDOLENT, SLOTHFUL mean not easily aroused to activity. LAZY suggests a disinclination to work or to take trouble ⟨convenience foods for *lazy* cooks⟩. INDOLENT suggests a love of ease and a settled dislike of movement or activity ⟨the heat made us all *indolent*⟩. SLOTHFUL implies a temperamental inability to act promptly or speedily when action or speed is called for ⟨fired for being *slothful* about filling orders⟩.

2lazy vi **la·zied; la·zy·ing** (1612) : to move or lie lazily : LAZE

la·zy·bones \'lā-zē-,bōnz\ n pl but sing or pl in constr (1592) : a lazy person

lazy eye n (1939) : AMBLYOPIA; *also* : an eye affected with amblyopia

lazy Su·san \-'sü-z³n\ n (1917) : a revolving tray used for serving food, condiments, or relishes

lazy tongs n pl (1836) : a series of jointed and pivoted bars capable of great extension used to pick up or handle something at a distance

lazy tongs

LCD \,el-(,)sē-'dē\ n [*liquid crystal display*] (1973) : a constantly operating display (as of the time in a digital watch) that consists of segments of a liquid crystal whose reflectivity varies according to the voltage applied to them

LD₅₀ \,el-,dē-'fif-tē\ n [*lethal dose*] (1942) : the amount of a toxic agent (as a poison, virus, or radiation) that is sufficient to kill 50% of a population of animals usu. within a certain time

LDL \,el-(,)dē-'el\ n [*low-density lipoprotein*] (1976) : a cholesterol-rich protein-poor lipoprotein of blood plasma correlated with increased risk of atherosclerosis — compare HDL

L–do·pa \'el-'dō-pə\ n (1939) : the levorotatory form of dopa that is obtained esp. from broad beans or prepared synthetically, stimulates the production of dopamine in the brain, and is used in treating Parkinson's disease

lea *or* **ley** \'lē, 'lā\ n [ME *leye*, fr. OE *lēah*; akin to OHG *lōh* thicket, L *lucus* grove, *lux* light — more at LIGHT] (bef. 12c) **1** : GRASSLAND, PASTURE **2** *usu* **ley** : arable land used temporarily for hay or grazing

1leach \'lēch\ *var of* LEECH

2leach vb [*leach* vessel through which water is passed to extract lye] vt (1796) **1** : to dissolve out by the action of a percolating liquid ⟨∼ out alkali from ashes⟩ **2** : to subject to the action of percolating liquid (as water) in order to separate the soluble components **3 a** : to remove (nutritive or harmful elements) from soil by percolation **b** : to draw out or remove as if by percolation ⟨all meaning has been ∼ed from my life⟩ ∼ vi : to pass out or through by percolation — **leach·abil·i·ty** \,lē-chə-'bi-lə-tē\ n — **leach·able** \'lē-chə-bəl\ *adj* — **leach·er** n

leach·ate \'lēch-,āt\ n (1934) : a solution or product obtained by leaching

1lead \'lēd\ vb **led** \'led\; **lead·ing** [ME *leden*, fr. OE *lǣdan*; akin to OHG *leiten* to lead, OE *līthan* to go] vt (bef. 12c) **1 a** : to guide on a way esp. by going in advance **b** : to direct on a course or in a direction **c** : to serve as a channel for ⟨a pipe ∼s water to the house⟩ **2** : to go through : LIVE ⟨∼ a quiet life⟩ **3 a** (1) : to direct the operations, activity, or performance of ⟨∼ an orchestra⟩ (2) : to have charge of ⟨∼ a campaign⟩ (3) : to suggest to (a witness) the answer desired by asking leading questions **b** (1) : to go at the head of ⟨∼ a parade⟩ (2) : to be first in or among ⟨∼ the league⟩ (3) : to have a margin over ⟨*led* his opponent⟩ **4** : to bring to some conclusion or condition ⟨*led* to believe otherwise⟩ **5** : to begin play with ⟨∼ trumps⟩ **6 a** : to aim in front of (a moving object) ⟨∼ a duck⟩ **b** : to pass a ball or puck just in front of (a moving teammate) ∼ vi **1 a** : to guide someone or something along a way **b** : to lie, run, or open in a specified place or direction ⟨path ∼s uphill⟩ **c** : to guide a dance partner through the steps of a dance **2 a** : to be first **b** (1) : BEGIN, OPEN (2) : to play the first card of a trick, round, or game **3** : to tend toward or have a result ⟨study ∼*ing* to a degree⟩ **4** : to direct the first of a series of blows at an opponent in boxing *syn* see GUIDE — **lead one down the garden path** *also* **lead one up the garden path** : HOODWINK, DECEIVE

2lead n (15c) **1 a** (1) : LEADERSHIP (2) : EXAMPLE, PRECEDENT **b** (1) : position at the front : VANGUARD (2) : INITIATIVE **2 a** : the act or privilege of leading in cards; *also* : the card or suit led **c** : a margin or measure of advantage or superiority or position in advance **2** : one that leads: as **a** : LODE 1 **b** : a channel of water esp. through a field of ice **c** : INDICATION, CLUE **d** : a principal role in a dramatic production; *also* : one who plays such a role **e** : LEASH 1 **f** (1) : an introductory

section of a news story (2) : a news story of chief importance **3** : an insulated electrical conductor connected to an electrical device **4** : the course of a rope from end to end **5** : the amount of axial advance of a point accompanying a complete turn of a thread (as of a screw or worm) **6** : a position taken by a base runner off a base toward the next **7** : the first punch of a series or an exchange of punches in boxing — **lead·less** \-ləs\ *adj*

3lead *adj* (1828) : acting or serving as a lead or leader ⟨a ∼ article⟩

4lead \'led\ n, *often attrib* [ME *leed*, fr. OE *lēad*; akin to MHG *lōt* lead] (bef. 12c) **1** : a heavy soft malleable ductile plastic but inelastic bluish white metallic element found mostly in combination and used esp. in pipes, cable sheaths, batteries, solder, and shields against radioactivity — see ELEMENT table **2 a** : a plummet for sounding at sea **b** *pl, Brit* : a usu. flat lead roof **c** *pl* : lead framing for panes in windows **d** : a thin strip of metal used to separate lines of type in printing **3 a** : a thin stick of marking substance in or for a pencil **b** : WHITE LEAD **4** : BULLETS, PROJECTILES **5** : TETRAETHYL LEAD — **lead·less** \-ləs\ *adj*

5lead \'led\ vt (14c) **1** : to cover, line, or weight with lead **2** : to fix (window glass) in position with leads **3** : to put space between the lines of (typeset matter) **4** : to treat or mix with lead or a lead compound ⟨∼ed gasoline⟩

lead acetate n (1885) : an acetate of lead; *esp* : a poisonous soluble salt $PbC_4H_6O_4{\cdot}3H_2O$

lead arsenate n (ca. 1903) : an arsenate of lead: as **a** : an acid salt $PbHAsO_4$ used esp. as an insecticide **b** : a neutral salt $Pb_3(AsO_4)_2$ used esp. as an insecticide

lead azide n (1918) : a crystalline explosive compound $Pb(N_3)_2$ used as a detonating agent

lead carbonate n (1873) : a carbonate of lead; *esp* : a poisonous basic salt $Pb_3(OH)_2(CO_3)_2$ used esp. as a white pigment

lead chromate n (ca. 1885) : a chromate of lead; *esp* : CHROME YELLOW

lead dioxide n (1885) : a poisonous compound PbO_2 used esp. as an oxidizing agent and as an electrode in batteries

lead·en \'le-d³n\ *adj* (bef. 12c) **1 a** : made of lead **b** : of the color of lead : dull gray **2 a** : oppressively heavy **b** : SLUGGISH **c** : lacking spirit or animation — **lead·en·ly** *adv* — **lead·en·ness** \-d³n-(n)əs\ n

lead·er \'lē-dər\ n (14c) **1** : something that leads: as **a** : a primary or terminal shoot of a plant **b** : TENDON, SINEW **c** *pl* : dots or hyphens (as in an index) used to lead the eye horizontally : ELLIPSIS 2 **d** *chiefly Brit* : a newspaper editorial **e** (1) : something for guiding fish into a trap (2) : a short length of material for attaching the end of a fishing line to a lure or hook **f** : LOSS LEADER **g** : something that ranks first **h** : a blank section at the beginning or end of a reel of film or recorded tape **2** : a person who leads: as **a** : GUIDE, CONDUCTOR **b** (1) : a person who directs a military force or unit (2) : a person who has commanding authority or influence **c** (1) : the principal officer of a British political party (2) : a party member chosen to manage party activities in a legislative body (3) : such a party member presiding over the whole legislative body when the party constitutes a majority **d** (1) : CONDUCTOR c (2) : a first or principal performer of a group **3** : a horse placed in advance of the other horses of a team — **lead·er·less** \-ləs\ *adj*

leader of the opposition (1771) : the principal member of the opposition party in a British legislative body who is given the status of a salaried government official and an important role in organizing the business of the house

lead·er·ship \'lē-dər-,ship\ n (1821) **1** : the office or position of a leader **2** : capacity to lead **3** : the act or an instance of leading **4** : LEADERS

lead glass n (1856) : glass containing a high proportion of lead oxide and having extraordinary clarity and brilliance

lead–in \'lēd-,in\ n (1913) : something that leads into something else ⟨a ∼ to the commercial⟩ — **lead–in** *adj*

lead·ing \'lē-diŋ\ *adj* (1597) **1** : coming or ranking first : FOREMOST **2** : exercising leadership **3** : providing direction or guidance ⟨a ∼ question⟩ **4** : given most prominent display ⟨the ∼ story⟩

leading edge n (1877) **1** : the foremost edge of an airfoil **2** : the forward part of something that moves or seems to move

leading lady n (1874) : an actress who plays the leading female role (as in a play or movie)

leading man n (1827) : an actor who plays the leading male role (as in a play or movie)

leading tone n (ca. 1889) : the seventh tone of a diatonic scale — called also *leading note*

lead line \'led-\ n (15c) : SOUNDING LINE

lead·man \'lēd-,man, -mən\ n (1939) : a worker in charge of other workers

lead monoxide n (ca. 1909) : a yellow to brownish red poisonous compound PbO used in rubber manufacture and glassmaking

lead-off \'lēd-,ȯf\ n (ca. 1886) **1** : a beginning or leading action **2** : one that leads off — **leadoff** *adj*

lead off \'lēd-\ vt (1817) **1** : to make a start on : OPEN **2** : to bat first for a baseball team in (an inning) ∼ vi : BEGIN; *also* : to come on or perform first

lead on vt (1598) : to entice or induce to proceed in a course esp. when unwise or mistaken

lead oxide n (ca. 1926) : any of several oxides of lead; *esp* : LEAD MONOXIDE

lead pencil \'led-\ n (1688) : a pencil using graphite as the marking material

lead-pipe \'led-'pīp\ *adj* (1898) : CERTAIN, GUARANTEED ⟨a ∼ cinch⟩

lead-plant \'led-,plant\ n (ca. 1833) : a leguminous shrub (*Amorpha canescens*) of the western U.S. that has hoary pinnate leaves and bears dull-colored racemose flowers

lead poisoning n (ca. 1842) : chronic intoxication that is produced by the absorption of lead into the system and is characterized by severe colicky pains, a dark line along the gums, and local muscular paralysis

---

\ə\ abut \ᵊ\ kitten, F table \ər\ further \a\ ash \ā\ ace \ä\ mop, mar \au̇\ out \ch\ chin \e\ bet \ē\ easy \g\ go \i\ hit \ī\ ice \j\ job \ŋ\ sing \ō\ go \ȯ\ law \ȯi\ boy \th\ thin \t̲h̲\ the \ü\ loot \u̇\ foot \y\ yet \zh\ vision \à, k̲, ⁿ, œ, œ̄, ʉ, ᵁ, ᵞ\ see Guide to Pronunciation

lead·screw \ˈlēd-ˌskrü\ n (ca. 1889) : a threaded rod on which a mechanism travels and can be positioned precisely

leads·man \ˈledz-mən\ n (1857) : a man who uses a sounding lead to determine depth of water

lead sulfide n (ca. 1898) : an insoluble black compound PbS that occurs naturally as galena and is used in photoconductive cells

lead time \ˈlēd-\ n (1944) : the time between the beginning of a process or project and the appearance of its results

lead–up \ˈlēd-ˌəp\ n (1942) : something that leads up to or prepares the way for something else

lead up \ˈlēd-\ vi (1861) **1** : to prepare the way **2** : to make a gradual or indirect approach to a topic

lead·work \ˈled-ˌwərk\ n (1641) : articles made of or work done in lead

leady \ˈle-dē\ adj lead·i·er; -est (14c) : containing or resembling lead

¹**leaf** \ˈlēf\ n, pl **leaves** \ˈlēvz\ also **leafs** \ˈlēfs\ often attrib [ME leef, fr. OE lēaf; akin to OHG loub leaf] (bef. 12c) **1 a** (1) : a lateral outgrowth from a plant stem that is typically a flattened expanded variably shaped greenish organ, constitutes a unit of the foliage, and functions primarily in food manufacture by photosynthesis **b** : a modified leaf primarily engaged in functions other than food manufacture **b** (1) : FOLIAGE ⟨trees in full ~⟩ (2) : the leaves of a plant as an article of commerce **2** : something suggestive of a leaf: as **a** : a part of a book or folded sheet containing a page on each side **b** (1) : a part (as of window shutters, folding doors, or gates) that slides or is hinged (2) : the movable parts of a table top **c** (1) : a thin sheet or plate of any substance : LAMINA (2) : metal (as gold or silver) in sheets usu. thinner than foil (3) : one of the plates of a leaf spring — **leaf·less** \ˈlēf-ləs\ adj — **leaf·like** \ˈlēf-ˌlīk\ adj

²**leaf** vi (1611) **1** : to shoot out or produce leaves **2** : to turn over pages ⟨~ through a book⟩ ~ vt : to turn over the pages of

leaf·age \ˈlē-fij\ n (1599) **1** : FOLIAGE **2** : the representation of leafage (as in architecture)

leaf bud n (1664) : a bud that develops into a leafy shoot and does not produce flowers

leaf butterfly n (1882) : any of a genus (Kallima) of nymphalid butterflies of southern Asia and the East Indies that mimic leaves

forms of leaf 1a(1): 1 needle-shaped, 2 linear, 3 lanceolate, 4 elliptical, 5 ensiform, 6 oblong, 7 oblanceolate with acuminate tip, 8 ovate with acute tip, 9 obovate, 10 spatulate, 11 fiddle-shaped, 12 cuneate, 13 deltoid, 14 cordate, 15 reniform, 16 orbiculate, 17 runcinate, 18 lyrate, 19 peltate, 20 hastate, 21 sagittate, 22 odd-pinnate, 23 abruptly pinnate, 24 trifoliolate, 25, 26 palmate

leaf curl n (1899) : a plant disease caused by a fungus (genus Taphrina) or virus and characterized by curling of leaves; esp : PEACH LEAF CURL

leafed \ˈlēft\ adj (1552) : LEAVED

leaf fat n (ca. 1725) : the fat that lines the abdominal cavity and encloses the kidneys; esp : that of a hog used in the manufacture of lard

leaf·hop·per \ˈlēf-ˌhä-pər\ n (1852) : any of a family (Cicadellidae) of small leaping homopterous insects that suck the juices of plants

leaf lard n (ca. 1847) : high-quality lard made from leaf fat

¹**leaf·let** \ˈlēf-lət\ n (1787) **1 a** : one of the divisions of a compound leaf **b** : a small or young foliage leaf **2** : a leaflike organ or part **3** : a usu. folded printed sheet intended for free distribution

²**leaflet** vb -let·ed or -let·ted; -let·ing or -let·ting vi (1962) : to hand out leaflets ~ vt : to hand out leaflets to — **leaf·le·teer** \ˌlēf-lə-ˈtir\ n

leaf miner n (1830) : any of various small insects (as moths or dipteran flies) that in the larval stages burrow and eat the parenchyma of leaves

leaf mold n (1845) **1** : a compost or layer composed chiefly of decayed vegetable matter **2** : a mold or mildew that affects foliage

leaf roll n (1916) : a virus disease of the potato that is transmitted by aphids and is characterized by an upward rolling of the leaf margins, smaller tubers, and netlike necrotic areas in the phloem

leaf roller n (1830) : any of various lepidopterans whose larvae make a nest by rolling up plant leaves

leaf rust n (1865) : a rust disease of plants and esp. of wheat that affects primarily the leaves

leaf scar n (1835) : the mark left on a stem after a leaf falls

leaf scorch n (ca. 1909) : any of various plant diseases characterized by a burned or scorched appearance of the foliage

leaf spot n (ca. 1895) : any of various plant diseases characterized by discolored often circular spots on the leaves

leaf spring n (ca. 1893) : a spring made of superposed strips or leaves

leaf·stalk \ˈlēf-ˌstȯk\ n (ca. 1776) : PETIOLE

leaf trace n [³trace] (1875) : a trace associated with a leaf

leafy \ˈlē-fē\ adj leaf·i·er; -est (15c) **1 a** : furnished with or abounding in leaves ⟨~ woodlands⟩ **b** : having broad-bladed leaves ⟨mosses, grasses, and ~ plants⟩ **c** : consisting chiefly of leaves ⟨~ vegetables⟩ **2** : resembling a leaf; specif : LAMINATE

leafy liverwort n (1922) : any of an order (Jungermanniales) of usu. epiphytic liverworts with a leafy gametophyte that has one ventral and two dorsal rows of leaves on the stem

leafy spurge n (ca. 1889) : a tall perennial European herb (Euphorbia esula) that is naturalized in the northern U.S. and Canada

¹**league** \ˈlēg\ n [ME leuge, lege, fr. LL leuga] (14c) **1** : any of various units of distance from about 2.4 to 4.6 statute miles (3.9 to 7.4 kilometers) **2** : a square league

²**league** n [ME (Sc) ligg, fr. MF ligue, fr. OIt liga, fr. ligare to bind, fr. L — more at LIGATURE] (15c) **1 a** : an association of nations or other political entities for a common purpose **b** (1) : an association of

persons or groups united by common interests or goals (2) : a group of sports teams that regularly play one another **c** : an informal alliance **2** : CLASS, CATEGORY

³**league** vb leagued; leagu·ing vt (1604) : to unite in a league ~ vi : to form a league

lea·guer \ˈlē-gər\ n [D leger; akin to OHG legar bed — more at LAIR] (1577) **1** : a military camp **2** : SIEGE

²**leaguer** vt (ca. 1720) archaic : BESIEGE, BELEAGUER

³**leagu·er** \ˈlē-gər\ n [²league] (1591) : a member of a league

¹**leak** \ˈlēk\ vb [ME leken, fr. ON leka; akin to OE leccan to moisten, MIr legaid it melts] vi (14c) **1 a** : to enter or escape through an opening usu. by a fault or mistake ⟨fumes ~ in⟩ **b** : to let a substance or light in or out through an opening **2 a** : to become known despite efforts at concealment **b** : to be the source of an information leak ~ vt **1** : to permit to enter or escape through or as if through a leak **2** : to give out (information) surreptitiously ⟨~ed the story to the press⟩ — **leak·er** \ˈlē-kər\ n

²**leak** n (15c) **1 a** : a crack or hole that usu. by mistake admits or lets escape **b** : something that permits the admission or escape of something else usu. with prejudicial effect **2** : the act, process, or an instance of leaking **3** : an act of urinating — used esp. in the phrase take a leak; sometimes considered vulgar — **leak·proof** \ˈlēk-ˌprüf\ adj

leak·age \ˈlē-kij\ n (15c) **1 a** : the act or process or an instance of leaking **b** : loss of electricity esp. due to faulty insulation **2** : something or the amount that leaks

leaky \ˈlē-kē\ adj leak·i·er; -est (15c) : permitting fluid to leak in or out — **leak·i·ly** \-kə-lē\ adv — **leak·i·ness** \-kē-nəs\ n

leal \ˈlē(ə)l\ adj [ME leel, fr. MF leial, leel — more at LOYAL] (14c) chiefly Scot : LOYAL, TRUE — **leal·ly** \ˈlē-ə(l)-lē, ˈlēl-lē\ adv

¹**lean** \ˈlēn\ vb leaned \ˈlēnd, chiefly Brit ˈlent\; lean·ing \ˈlē-niŋ\ [ME lenen, fr. OE hleonian; akin to OHG hlinēn to lean, Gk klinein, L clinare] vi (12c) **1 a** : to incline, deviate, or bend from a vertical position **b** : to cast one's weight to one side for support **2** : to rely for support or inspiration **3** : to incline in opinion, taste, or desire ~ vt : to cause to lean : INCLINE — **lean on** : to apply pressure to

²**lean** n (1776) : the act or an instance of leaning : INCLINATION

³**lean** adj [ME lene, fr. OE hlæne] (bef. 12c) **1 a** : lacking or deficient in flesh **b** : containing little or no fat **2** : lacking richness, sufficiency, or productiveness **3** : deficient in an essential or important quality or ingredient: as **a** of ore : containing little valuable mineral **b** : low in combustible component — used esp. of fuel mixtures **4** : characterized by economy (as of style, expression, or operation) — **lean·ly** adv — **lean·ness** \ˈlēn-nəs\ n

syn LEAN, SPARE, LANK, LANKY, GAUNT, RAWBONED, SCRAWNY, SKINNY mean thin because of an absence of excess flesh. LEAN stresses lack of fat and of curving contours ⟨a lean racehorse⟩. SPARE suggests leanness from abstemious living or constant exercise ⟨the gymnast's spare figure⟩. LANK implies tallness as well as leanness ⟨the lank legs of the heron⟩. LANKY suggests awkwardness and loose-jointedness as well as thinness ⟨a lanky youth, all arms and legs⟩. GAUNT implies marked thinness or emaciation as from overwork or suffering ⟨a prisoner's gaunt face⟩. RAWBONED suggests a large ungainly build without implying undernourishment ⟨a rawboned farmer⟩. SCRAWNY and SKINNY imply an extreme leanness that suggests deficient strength and vitality ⟨a scrawny chicken⟩ ⟨skinny street urchins⟩.

⁴**lean** vt (bef. 12c) : to make lean

⁵**lean** n (15c) : the part of meat that consists principally of lean muscle

Le·an·der \lē-ˈan-dər\ n [L, fr. Gk Leandros] : a youth in Greek mythology who swims the Hellespont nightly to visit Hero and who ultimately drowns in one of the crossings

lean·ing \ˈlē-niŋ\ n (15c) : a definite but not decisive attraction or tendency — often used in pl.

syn LEANING, PROPENSITY, PROCLIVITY, PENCHANT mean a strong instinct or liking for something. LEANING suggests a liking or attraction not strong enough to be decisive or uncontrollable ⟨a student with artistic leanings⟩. PROPENSITY implies a deeply ingrained and usu. irresistible inclination ⟨a propensity to offer advice⟩. PROCLIVITY suggests a strong natural proneness usu. to something objectionable or evil ⟨a proclivity for violence⟩. PENCHANT implies a strongly marked taste in the person or an irresistible attraction in the object ⟨a penchant for taking risks⟩.

leant \ˈlent\ chiefly Brit past of LEAN

¹**lean–to** \ˈlēn-ˌtü\ n, pl **lean-tos** \-ˌtüz\ (15c) **1** : a wing or extension of a building having a lean-to roof **2** : a rough shed or shelter with a lean-to roof

²**lean–to** adj (1649) : having only one slope or pitch ⟨~ roof⟩ — see ROOF illustration

¹**leap** \ˈlēp\ vb leaped or leapt \ˈlēpt also ˈlept\; leap·ing \ˈlē-piŋ\ [ME lepen, fr. OE hlēapan; akin to OHG hlouffan to run] vi (bef. 12c) **1** : to spring free from or as if from the ground : JUMP ⟨~ over a fence⟩ ⟨a fish ~s out of the water⟩ **2 a** : to pass abruptly from one state or topic to another **b** : to act precipitately ⟨~ed at the chance⟩ ~ vt : to pass over by leaping — **leap·er** \ˈlē-pər\ n

²**leap** n (bef. 12c) **1 a** : an act of leaping : SPRING, BOUND **b** (1) : a place leaped over or from (2) : the distance covered by a leap **2 a** : a sudden passage or transition ⟨a great ~ forward⟩ **b** : a chance made in an area of ultimate concern ⟨a ~ of faith⟩ — **by leaps and bounds** : with extraordinary rapidity

¹**leap·frog** \ˈlēp-ˌfrȯg, -ˌfräg\ n (1599) : a game in which one player bends down and is vaulted over by another player

²**leapfrog** vb leap·frogged; leap·frog·ging vi (1872) : to leap or progress in or as if in leapfrog ~ vt **1** : to go ahead of (each other) in turn; specif : to advance (two military units) by keeping one unit in action while moving the other unit past it to a position farther in front **2** : to evade by or as if by a bypass

leap second n (1971) : an intercalary second added to Coordinated Universal Time to compensate for the slowing of the earth's rotation and keep Coordinated Universal Time in synchrony with solar time

leap year n (14c) **1** : a year in the Gregorian calendar containing 366 days with February 29 as the extra day **2** : an intercalary year in any calendar

Lear \ˈlir\ n : a legendary king of Britain and hero of Shakespeare's tragedy King Lear

learn \'lərn\ *vb* **learned** \'lərnd, 'lərnt\; **learn·ing** [ME *lernen,* fr. OE *leornian;* akin to OHG *lernēn* to learn, OE *last* footprint, L *lira* furrow, track] *vt* (bef. 12c) **1 a** (1) : to gain knowledge or understanding of or skill in by study, instruction, or experience ⟨~ a trade⟩ (2) : MEMORIZE ⟨~ the lines of a play⟩ **b** : to come to be able ⟨~ to dance⟩ **c** : to come to realize ⟨~*ed* that honesty paid⟩ **2 a** *nonstand* : TEACH **b** *obs* : to inform of something **3** : to come to know : HEAR ⟨we just ~*ed* that he was ill⟩ ~ *vi* : to acquire knowledge or skill or a behavioral tendency   *syn* see DISCOVER — **learn·able** \'lər-nə-bəl\ *adj* — **learn·er** *n*
   usage Learn in the sense of "teach" dates from the 13th century and was standard until at least the early 19th ⟨made them drunk with true Hollands—and then *learned* them the art of making bargains — Washington Irving⟩. But by Mark Twain's time it was receding to a speech form associated chiefly with the less educated ⟨never done nothing for three months but set in his back yard and *learn* that frog to jump —Mark Twain⟩. The present-day status of *learn* has not risen. This use persists in speech, but in writing it appears mainly in the representation of such speech or its deliberate imitation for effect.
learned *adj* (14c) **1** \'lər-nəd\ : characterized by or associated with learning : ERUDITE **2** \'lərnd, 'lərnt\ : acquired by learning ⟨~ behavior⟩ — **learn·ed·ly** \'lər-nəd-lē\ *adv* — **learn·ed·ness** \'lər-nəd-nəs\ *n*
learn·ing *n* (bef. 12c) **1** : the act or experience of one that learns **2** : knowledge or skill acquired by instruction or study **3** : modification of a behavioral tendency by experience (as exposure to conditioning)   *syn* see KNOWLEDGE
learning curve *n* (1922) : a curve plotting performance against practice; *esp* : one graphing decline in unit costs with cumulative output
learning disabled *adj* (1973) : having difficulty in learning a basic scholastic skill because of a disorder (as dyslexia or attention deficit disorder) that interferes with the learning process — **learning disability** *n*
learnt \'lərnt\ *chiefly Brit past and past part of* LEARN
leary *var of* LEERY
¹lease \'lēs\ *n* [ME *les,* fr. AF, fr. *lesser*] (14c) **1** : a contract by which one conveys real estate, equipment, or facilities for a specified term and for a specified rent; *also* : the act of such conveyance or the term for which it is made **2** : a piece of land or property that is leased **3** : a continuance or opportunity for continuance ⟨a new ~ on life⟩
²lease *vt* **leased; leas·ing** [AF *lesser,* fr. OF *laissier* to let go, fr. L *laxare* to loosen, fr. *laxus* slack — more at SLACK] (ca. 1570) **1** : to grant by lease **2** : to hold under a lease   *syn* see HIRE — **leas·able** \'lē-sə-bəl\ *adj*
lease·back \'lēs-,bak\ *n* (1947) : the sale of property with the understanding that the seller can lease it from the new owner
lease·hold \'lēs-,hōld\ *n* (1720) **1** : a tenure by lease **2** : property held by lease — **lease·hold·er** *n*
leash \'lēsh\ *n* [ME *lees, leshe,* fr. MF *laisse,* fr. OF *laissier*] (14c) **1 a** : a line for leading or restraining an animal **b** : something that restrains **2 a** : a set of three animals (as greyhounds, foxes, bucks, or hares) **b** : a set of three — **leash** *vt*
leash law *n* (1966) : an ordinance requiring dogs to be restrained when not confined to their owner's property
leas·ing \'lē-sin, -zin\ *n* [ME *lesing,* fr. OE *lēasung,* fr. *lēasian* to lie, fr. *lēas* false] (bef. 12c) *archaic* : the act of lying; *also* : LIE, FALSEHOOD
¹least \'lēst\ *adj, superlative of* ¹LITTLE [ME *leest,* fr. OE *lǣst,* superl. of *lǣssa* less] (bef. 12c) **1** : lowest in importance or position **2 a** : smallest in size or degree **b** : being a member of a kind distinguished by diminutive size ⟨~ bittern⟩ **c** : smallest possible : SLIGHTEST
²least *n* (12c) : one that is least — **at least 1** : at the minimum **2** : in any case
³least *adv, superlative of* ²LITTLE (13c) : in the smallest or lowest degree — **least of all** : especially not ⟨no one, *least of all* the children, paid attention⟩
least common denominator *n* (1875) : the least common multiple of two or more denominators
least common multiple *n* (1823) **1** : the smallest common multiple of two or more numbers **2** : the common multiple of lowest degree of two or more polynomials
least squares *n pl* (1825) : a method of fitting a curve to a set of points representing statistical data in such a way that the sum of the squares of the distances of the points from the curve is a minimum
least·ways \'lēst-,wāz\ *adv* (14c) *dial* : at least
least·wise \-,wīz\ *adv* (15c) : at least
¹leath·er \'le-thər\ *n* [ME *lether,* fr. OE *lether-;* akin to OHG *leder* leather, OIr *lethar*] (13c) **1** : animal skin dressed for use **2** : the flap of the ear of a dog — see DOG illustration **3** : something wholly or partly made of leather — **leather** *adj* — **leath·er·like** \-,līk\ *adj*
²leather *vt* **leath·ered; leath·er·ing** \'le-thə-rin, 'leth-rin\ (13c) **1** : to cover with leather **2** : to beat with a strap : THRASH
leath·er·back \'le-thər-,bak\ *n* (ca. 1855) : the largest existing sea turtle (*Dermochelys coriacea*) distinguished by its flexible carapace composed of a mosaic of small bones embedded in a thick leathery skin

leath·er·ette \,le-thə-'ret\ *n, often attrib* [fr. *Leatherette,* a trademark] (ca. 1879) : simulated leather
leath·er·leaf \'le-thər-,lēf\ *n* (ca. 1818) : a north temperate ericaceous bog shrub (*Chamaedaphne calyculata*) with evergreen coriaceous leaves and small white cylindrical flowers

leatherback

leath·ern \'le-thərn\ *adj* (bef. 12c) : made of, consisting of, or resembling leather
leath·er·neck \-thər-,nek\ *n* [fr. the leather collar formerly part of the uniform] (ca. 1914) : a member of the U.S. Marine Corps
leath·er·wood \'le-thər-,wùd\ *n* (1743) **1** : a small tree (*Dirca palustris*) of the mezereon family with pliant stems and yellow flowers **2** : a small tree (*Cyrilla racemiflora*) of the southeastern U.S. related to the titi
leath·ery \'le-thə-rē, 'leth-rē\ *adj* (ca. 1552) : resembling leather in appearance or consistency

¹leave \'lēv\ *vb* **left** \'left\; **leav·ing** [ME *leven,* fr. OE *lǣfan;* akin to OHG *verleiben* to leave, OE *belīfan* to be left over, and perh. to Lith *lipti* to adhere, Gk *lipos* grease, fat] *vt* (bef. 12c) **1 a** (1) : BEQUEATH, DEVISE ⟨*left* a fortune to his son⟩ (2) : to have remaining after one's death ⟨~*s* a widow and two children⟩ **b** : to cause to remain as a trace or aftereffect ⟨oil ~*s* a stain⟩ ⟨the wound *left* an ugly scar⟩ **2 a** : to cause or allow to be or remain in a specified condition ⟨~ the door open⟩ ⟨his manner *left* me cold⟩ **b** : to fail to include or take along ⟨*left* the notes at home⟩ ⟨the movie ~*s* a lot out⟩ **c** : to have as a remainder ⟨4 from 7 ~*s* 3⟩ **d** : to permit to be or remain subject to another's action or control ⟨just ~ everything to me⟩ **e** : LET **f** : to cause or allow to be or remain available ⟨~ room for expansion⟩ ⟨wanted to ~ himself an out⟩ **3 a** : to go away from : DEPART ⟨~ the room⟩ **b** : DESERT, ABANDON ⟨*left* his wife⟩ **c** : to terminate association with : withdraw from ⟨*left* school before graduation⟩ **4** : to put, deposit, or deliver before or in the process of departing ⟨someone *left* a package for you⟩ ~ *vi* : SET OUT, DEPART — **leav·er** *n* — **leave alone** : to refrain from bothering or using
   usage Leave (sense 2e) with the infinitive but without *to* ⟨*leave* it be⟩ is a mostly spoken idiom used in writing esp. for humorous effect. It is not often criticized in British English, but American commentators, adhering to an opinion first expressed in 1881, still dislike it.
²leave *n* [ME *leve,* fr. OE *lēaf;* akin to MHG *loube* permission, OE *alȳfan* to allow — more at BELIEVE] (bef. 12c) **1 a** : permission to do something **b** : authorized esp. extended absence from duty or employment **2** : an act of leaving : DEPARTURE
³leave *vi* **leaved; leav·ing** [ME *leven,* fr. *leef* leaf] (14c) : LEAF
leaved *adj* (13c) : having leaves — usu. used in combination ⟨palmate-*leaved*⟩ ⟨a four-*leaved* clover⟩
¹leav·en \'le-vən\ *n* [ME *levain,* fr. MF, fr. (assumed) VL *levamen,* fr. L *levare* to raise — more at LEVER] (14c) **1 a** : a substance (as yeast) used to produce fermentation in dough or a liquid; *esp* : SOURDOUGH **b** : a material (as baking powder) used to produce a gas that lightens dough or batter **2** : something that modifies or lightens
²leaven *vt* **leav·ened; leav·en·ing** \'lev-nin, 'le-və-\ (15c) **1** : to raise (as bread) with a leaven **2** : to mingle or permeate with some modifying, alleviating, or vivifying element   *syn* see INFUSE
leavening *n* (ca. 1626) : a leavening agent : LEAVEN
leave of absence (1771) **1** : permission to be absent from duty or employment **2** : LEAVE 1b
leave off *vb* (14c) : STOP, CEASE
leaves *pl of* LEAF
leave–tak·ing \'lēv-,tā-kin\ *n* (14c) : DEPARTURE, FAREWELL
leav·ings \'lē-vinz\ *n pl* (14c) : REMNANTS, RESIDUE
le·bens·raum \'lā-bənz-,raúm, -bən(t)s-\ *n, often cap* [G, fr. *Leben* living, life + *Raum* space] (1905) **1** : territory believed esp. by Nazis to be necessary for national existence or economic self-sufficiency **2** : space required for life, growth, or activity
¹lech \'lech\ *n* (ca. 1830) **1** : LETCH, LUST **2** : LECHER
²lech *vi* (1911) : LUST
lech·er \'le-chər\ *n* [ME *lechour,* fr. OF *lecheor,* fr. *lechier* to lick, live in debauchery, of Gmc origin; akin to OHG *leckōn* to lick — more at LICK] (13c) : a man who engages in lechery
lech·er·ous \'le-chə-rəs, 'lech-rəs\ *adj* (14c) : given to or suggestive of lechery — **lech·er·ous·ly** *adv* — **lech·er·ous·ness** *n*
lech·ery \-rē\ *n* (13c) : inordinate indulgence in sexual activity : LASCIVIOUSNESS
le·chwe \'lēch-wē\ *n, pl* **lechwe** *or* **lechwes** [prob. fr. Sesotho *lets'a*] (1857) : an antelope (*Kobus leche*) that inhabits wetlands of southern Africa; *also* : a related antelope (*K. megaceros*) of the Nile Valley in Sudan and Ethiopia
lec·i·thin \'le-sə-thən\ *n* [ISV, fr. Gk *lekithos* yolk of an egg] (1861) : any of several waxy hygroscopic phospholipids that are widely distributed in animals and plants, form colloidal solutions in water, and have emulsifying, wetting, and antioxidant properties; *also* : a mixture of or substance rich in lecithins
lec·i·thin·ase \-thə-,nās, -,nāz\ *n* (1910) : PHOSPHOLIPASE
lec·tern \'lek-tərn\ *n* [ME *lettorne,* fr. MF *letrun,* fr. ML *lectorinum,* fr. L *lector* reader, fr. *legere* to read — more at LEGEND] (14c) : a stand used to support a book in a convenient position for a standing reader; *esp* : one from which scripture lessons are read in a church service
lec·tion \'lek-shən\ *n* [LL *lection-, lectio,* fr. L, act of reading — more at LESSON] (1608) **1** : a liturgical lesson for a particular day **2** [NL *lection-, lectio,* fr. L] : a variant reading of a text
lec·tion·ary \'lek-shə-,ner-ē\ *n, pl* **-ar·ies** (1780) : a book or list of lections for the church year
lec·tor \'lek-tər, -,tòr\ *n* [ME, fr. LL, reader of the lessons in a church service, fr. L, reader, fr. *legere*] (14c) : one who assists at a worship service chiefly by reading a lesson
lec·to·type \'lek-tə-,tīp\ *n* [Gk *lektos* chosen (fr. *legein* to gather, choose) + E *type* — more at LEGEND] (ca. 1905) : a specimen chosen as the type of a species or subspecies if the author of the name fails to designate a type
¹lec·ture \'lek-chər, -shər\ *n* [ME, act of reading, fr. LL *lectura,* fr. L *lectus,* pp. of *legere*] (15c) **1** : a discourse given before an audience or class esp. for instruction **2** : a formal reproof — **lec·ture·ship** \-,ship\ *n*
²lecture *vb* **lec·tured; lec·tur·ing** \'lek-chə-rin, 'lek-shrin\ *vi* (ca. 1590) : to deliver a lecture or a course of lectures ~ *vt* **1** : to deliver a lecture to **2** : to reprove formally — **lec·tur·er** \-chər-ər, -shrər\ *n*
led *past and past part of* LEAD
LED \,el-(,)ē-'dē\ *n* [light-emitting diode] (1968) : a semiconductor diode that emits light when a voltage is applied to it and that is used in an electronic display (as for a digital watch)
Le·da \'lē-də\ *n* [L, fr. Gk *Lēda*] : the mother of Clytemnestra and Castor by her husband Tyndareus and of Helen and Pollux by Zeus who comes to her in the form of a swan

---

\ə\ abut \ᵊ\ kitten, F table \ər\ further \a\ ash \ā\ ace \ä\ mop, mar \aú\ out \ch\ chin \e\ bet \ē\ easy \g\ go \i\ hit \ī\ ice \j\ job \ŋ\ sing \ō\ go \ò\ law \òi\ boy \th\ thin \th\ the \ü\ loot \ù\ foot \y\ yet \zh\ vision \à, k̲, ⁿ, œ, œ̄, ᵫ, ᵿ, ʸ\ *see* Guide to Pronunciation

le·der·ho·sen \'lā-dər-ˌhō-z°n\ *n pl* [G, fr. MHG *lederhose*, fr. *leder* leather + *hose* trousers] (1936) : leather shorts often with suspenders worn esp. in Bavaria

ledge \'lej\ *n* [ME *legge* bar of a gate] (1535) **1** : a raised or projecting edge or molding intended to protect or check ⟨a window ∼⟩ **2** : an underwater ridge or reef esp. near the shore **3 a** : a narrow flat surface or shelf; *esp* : one that projects from a wall of rock **b** : rock that is solid or continuous enough to form ledges : BEDROCK ⟨the field was full of ∼⟩ **4** : LODE, VEIN — **ledgy** \'le-jē\ *adj*

led·ger \'le-jər\ *n* [ME *legger*, prob. fr. *leyen*, *leggen* to lay] (1588) **1** : a book containing accounts to which debits and credits are posted from books of original entry **2** : a horizontal timber secured to the uprights of scaffolding to support the putlog

ledger line (1700) : a short line added above or below a musical staff to extend its range

¹lee \'lē\ *n* [ME, fr. OE *hlēo*; perh. akin to OHG *lāo* lukewarm, L *calēre* to be warm] (bef. 12c) **1** : protecting shelter **2** : the side (as of a ship) that is sheltered from the wind

²lee *adj* (15c) **1** : of or relating to the side sheltered from the wind — compare WEATHER **2** : facing in the direction of motion of an overriding glacier — used esp. of a hillside

lee·board \'lē-ˌbōrd, -ˌbȯrd\ *n* (1691) : either of the wood or metal planes attached outside the hull of a sailboat to prevent leeway

¹leech \'lēch\ *n* [ME *leche*, fr. OE *lǣce*; akin to OHG *lāhhi* physician] (bef. 12c) **1** *archaic* : PHYSICIAN, SURGEON **2** [fr. its former use by physicians for bleeding patients] **a** : any of numerous carnivorous or bloodsucking usu. freshwater annelid worms (class Hirudinea) that have typically a flattened lanceolate segmented body with a sucker at each end **3** : a hanger-on who seeks advantage or gain *syn* see PARASITE — **leech·like** \-ˌlīk\ *adj*

²leech *vt* (1828) **1** : to bleed by the use of leeches **2** : to drain the substance of : EXHAUST ∼ *vi* : to attach oneself to a person as a leech

³leech *n* [ME *leche*, fr. MLG *lik* boltrope — more at LIGATURE] (15c) **1** : either vertical edge of a square sail **2** : the after edge of a fore-and-aft sail

leek \'lēk\ *n* [ME, fr. OE *lēac*; akin to OHG *louh* leek] (bef. 12c) : a biennial garden herb (*Allium ampeloprasum porrum*) of the lily family grown for its mildly pungent succulent linear leaves and esp. for its thick cylindrical stalk

¹leer \'lir\ *vi* [prob. fr. obs. *leer* cheek] (1530) : to cast a sidelong glance; *esp* : to give a leer — **leer·ing·ly** \-iŋ-lē\ *adv*

²leer *n* (1598) : a lascivious, knowing, or wanton look

leery \'lir-ē\ *adj* (1718) : SUSPICIOUS, WARY — often used with *of*

lees \'lēz\ *n pl* [ME *lie*, fr. MF, fr. ML *lia*] (14c) : the sediment of a liquor (as wine) during fermentation and aging : DREGS

Lee's Birthday \'lēz-\ *n* [Robert E. *Lee*] (1910) : January 19 or the third Monday in January observed as a legal holiday in many southern states

lee shore *n* (ca. 1580) : a shore lying off a ship's leeward side and constituting a severe danger in storm

¹lee·ward \'lē-wərd, *esp naut* 'lü-ərd\ *n* (1549) : the lee side

²leeward *adj* (1666) : being in or facing the direction toward which the wind is blowing; *also* : being the side opposite the windward

lee·way \'lē-ˌwā\ *n* (1669) **1 a** : off-course lateral movement of a ship when under way **b** : the angle between the heading and the track of an airplane **2** : an allowable margin of freedom or variation : TOLERANCE

¹left \'left\ *adj* [ME, fr. OE, weak; akin to MLG *lucht* left; fr. the left hand's being the weaker in most individuals] (13c) **1 a** : of, relating to, situated on, or being the side of the body in which the heart is mostly located **b** : located nearer to the left hand than to the right **c** (1) : located on the left of an observer facing in the same direction as the object specified ⟨stage ∼⟩ (2) : located on the left when facing downstream ⟨the ∼ bank of a river⟩ **2** *often cap* : of, adhering to, or constituted by the left esp. in politics — **left** *adv*

²left *n* (13c) **1 a** : the left hand **b** : the location or direction of the left side **c** : the part on the left side **2 a** : LEFT FIELD **b** : a blow struck with the left fist **3** *often cap* **a** : the part of a legislative chamber located to the left of the presiding officer **b** : the members of a continental European legislative body occupying the left as a result of holding more radical political views than other members **4** *cap* **a** : those professing views usu. characterized by desire to reform or overthrow the established order esp. in politics and usu. advocating change in the name of the greater freedom or well-being of the common man **b** : a radical as distinguished from a conservative position

³left *past and past part of* LEAVE

left–bank *adj*, *often cap L&B* (1929) : of, relating to, situated in, or characteristic of the bohemian district of Paris on the left bank of the Seine River

left field *n* (1857) **1** : the position of the player defending left field **2** : the part of the baseball outfield to the left looking out from the plate **3** : a state or position far from the mainstream (as of prevailing opinion) ⟨they were really out in *left field* with that idea⟩ : a source of the unexpected or illogical ⟨that question came out of *left field*⟩ — **left fielder** *n*

left–hand \'left-ˌhand, 'lef-ˌtand\ *adj* (1598) **1** : situated on the left **2** : LEFT-HANDED

left–hand·ed \-ˈhan-dəd, -ˈtan-\ *adj* (14c) **1** : using the left hand habitually or more easily than the right; *also* : swinging from left to right ⟨a ∼ batter⟩ **2** : relating to, designed for, or done with the left hand **3** : MORGANATIC **4 a** : CLUMSY, AWKWARD **b** : INSINCERE, BACKHANDED, DUBIOUS ⟨a ∼ compliment⟩ **5 a** : having a direction contrary to that of the hands of a watch viewed from in front : COUNTERCLOCKWISE **b** : having a spiral structure or form that ascends or advances to the left ⟨a ∼ rope⟩ — **left–handed** *adv* — **left–hand·ed·ly** *adv* — **left–hand·ed·ness** *n*

left–hand·er \-ˈhan-dər, -ˈtan-\ *n* (1881) : a left-handed person

left·ish \'lef-tish\ *adj* (1934) : showing leftist tendencies

left·ism \'lef-ˌti-zəm\ *n* (1920) **1** : the principles and views of the Left; *also* : the movement embodying these principles **2** : advocacy of or adherence to the doctrines of the Left — **left·ist** \-tist\ *n or adj*

¹left·over \'left-ˌō-vər\ *n* (1891) **1** : something that remains unused or unconsumed; *esp* : leftover food served at a later meal — usu. used in pl. **2** : an anachronistic survival : VESTIGE

²left·over *adj* (1897) : not consumed or used ⟨∼ food⟩ ⟨∼ space⟩

left shoulder arms *n* [fr. the command *left shoulder arms!*] (ca. 1918) : a position in the manual of arms in which the butt of the rifle is held in the left hand with the barrel resting on the left shoulder; *also* : a command to assume this position

left·ward \'left-wərd\ *adj or adv* (15c) : being toward or on the left

left wing *n* (1884) **1** : the leftist division of a group (as a political party) **2** : LEFT 4a — **left–wing** *adj* — **left–wing·er** \'left-'wiŋ-ər\ *n*

lefty \'lef-tē\ *n, pl* **left·ies** (1886) **1** : LEFT-HANDER **2** : an advocate of leftism — **lefty** *adj*

¹leg \'leg *also* 'lāg\ *n* [ME, fr. ON *leggr*] (14c) **1** : a limb of an animal used esp. for supporting the body and for walking: as **a** (1) : one of the paired vertebrate limbs that in bipeds extend from the top of the thigh to the foot (2) : the part of such a limb between the knee and foot **b** : the back half of a hindquarter of a meat animal **c** : one of the rather generalized segmental appendages of an arthropod used in walking and crawling **2 a** : a pole or bar serving as a support or prop ⟨the ∼s of a tripod⟩ **b** : a branch of a forked or jointed object ⟨the ∼s of a compass⟩ **3 a** : the part of an article of clothing that covers the leg **b** : the part of the upper (as of a boot) that extends above the ankle **4** : OBEISANCE, BOW — used chiefly in the phrase *to make a leg* **5** : a side of a right triangle that is not the hypotenuse; *also* : a side of an isosceles triangle that is not the base **6 a** : the course and distance sailed by a boat on a single tack **b** : a portion of a trip : STAGE **c** : one section of a relay race **d** : one of several events or games necessary to be won to decide a competition ⟨won the first two ∼s of horse racing's Triple Crown⟩ **7** : a branch or part of an object or system — **leg·less** \-ləs\ *adj* — **a leg to stand on** : SUPPORT; *esp* : a basis for one's position in a controversy — **on one's last legs** : at or near the end of one's resources : on the verge of failure, exhaustion, or ruin

²leg *vi* **legged**; **leg·ging** (1601) : to use the legs in walking; *esp* : RUN

leg·a·cy \'le-gə-sē\ *n, pl* **-cies** [ME *legacie* office of a legate, bequest, fr. MF or ML; MF, office of a legate, fr. ML *legatia*, fr. L *legatus*] (15c) **1** : a gift by will esp. of money or other personal property : BEQUEST **2** : something transmitted by or received from an ancestor or predecessor or from the past ⟨the ∼ of the ancient philosophers⟩

¹le·gal \'lē-gəl\ *adj* [MF, fr. L *legalis*, fr. *leg-, lex* law] (ca. 1500) **1** : of or relating to law **2 a** : deriving authority from or founded on law : DE JURE **b** : having a formal status derived from law often without a basis in actual fact : TITULAR ⟨a corporation is a ∼ but not a real person⟩ **c** : established by law; *esp* : STATUTORY **3** : conforming to or permitted by law or established rules **4** : recognized or made effective by a court of law as distinguished from a court of equity **5** : of, relating to, or having the characteristics of the profession of law or of one of its members **6** : created by the constructions of the law ⟨a ∼ fiction⟩ *syn* see LAWFUL — **le·gal·ly** \-gə-lē\ *adv*

²legal *n* (1526) : one that conforms to rules or the law

legal age *n* (ca. 1904) : the age at which a person enters into full adult legal rights and responsibilities (as of making contracts or wills)

legal aid *n* (1890) : aid provided by an organization established esp. to serve the legal needs of the poor

legal eagle *n* (1942) : LAWYER

le·gal·ese \ˌlē-gə-'lēz, -'lēs\ *n* (1914) : the specialized language of the legal profession ⟨replaced ∼ with plain talk —Steve Weinberg⟩

legal holiday *n* (1867) : a holiday established by legal authority and marked by restrictions on work and transaction of official business

le·gal·ise *Brit var of* LEGALIZE

le·gal·ism \'lē-gə-ˌli-zəm\ *n* (1838) **1** : strict, literal, or excessive conformity to the law or to a religious or moral code ⟨the institutionalized ∼ that restricts free choice⟩ **2** : a legal term or rule

le·gal·ist \-list\ *n* (1646) **1** : an advocate or adherent of moral legalism **2** : one that views things from a legal standpoint; *esp* : one that places primary emphasis on legal principles or on the formal structure of governmental institutions — **le·gal·is·tic** \ˌlē-gə-'lis-tik\ *adj* — **le·gal·is·ti·cal·ly** \-ti-k(ə-)lē\ *adv*

le·gal·i·ty \li-'ga-lə-tē\ *n, pl* **-ties** (15c) **1** : attachment to or observance of law **2** : the quality or state of being legal : LAWFULNESS **3** *pl* : obligations imposed by law

le·gal·ize \'lē-gə-ˌlīz\ *vt* **-ized**; **-iz·ing** (ca. 1716) : to make legal; *esp* : to give legal validity or sanction to — **le·gal·i·za·tion** \ˌlē-gə-lə-'zā-shən\ *n* — **le·gal·iz·er** \'lē-gə-ˌlī-zər\ *n*

legal pad *n* (1967) : a writing tablet of ruled yellow paper that is usu. 8.5 by 14 inches (22 by 36 centimeters)

legal reserve *n* (ca. 1902) : the minimum amount of bank deposits or life insurance company assets required by law to be kept as reserves

legal tender *n* (1739) : money that is legally valid for the payment of debts and that must be accepted for that purpose when offered

¹leg·ate \'le-gət\ *n* [ME, fr. MF & L; MF *legat*, fr. L *legatus* deputy, emissary, fr. pp. of *legare* to depute, send as emissary, bequeath, fr. *leg-, lex*] (12c) : a usu. official emissary — **leg·ate·ship** \-ˌship\ *n*

²le·gate \li-'gāt\ *vt* **le·gat·ed**; **le·gat·ing** [*legatus*, pp. of *legare* to bequeath] (15c) : BEQUEATH 1 — **le·ga·tor** \-'gā-tər\ *n*

leg·a·tee \ˌle-gə-'tē\ *n* (ca. 1688) : one to whom a legacy is bequeathed or a devise is given

leg·a·tine \'le-gə-ˌtēn, -ˌtīn\ *adj* (1611) : of, headed by, or enacted under the authority of a legate

le·ga·tion \li-'gā-shən\ *n* (14c) **1** : the sending forth of a legate **2** : a body of deputies sent on a mission; *specif* : a diplomatic mission in a foreign country headed by a minister **3** : the official residence and office of a diplomatic minister in a foreign country

¹le·ga·to \li-'gä-(ˌ)tō\ *adv or adj* [It, lit., tied] (ca. 1811) : in a manner that is smooth and connected (as between successive tones) — used esp. as a direction in music

²legato *n* (1885) : a smooth and connected manner of performance (as of music); *also* : a passage of music so performed

leg·end \'le-jənd\ *n* [ME *legende*, fr. MF & ML; MF *legende*, fr. ML *legenda*, fr. L, fem. of *legendus*, gerundive of *legere* to gather, select, read; akin to Gk *legein* to gather, say, *logos* speech, word, reason] (14c) **1 a** : a story coming down from the past; *esp* : one popularly regarded as historical although not verifiable **b** : a body of such stories ⟨a place in the ∼ of the frontier⟩ **c** : a popular myth of recent origin **d** : a person or thing that inspires legends **e** : the subject of a legend ⟨its violence was ∼ even in its own time —William Broyles Jr.⟩ **2 a**

: an inscription or title on an object (as a coin)   **b :** CAPTION 2b   **c :** an explanatory list of the symbols on a map or chart

leg·end·ary \'le-jən-ˌder-ē\ *adj* (1587) **1 :** of, relating to, or characteristic of legend or a legend   **2 :** WELL-KNOWN, FAMOUS *syn* see FICTITIOUS — **leg·en·dari·ly** \ˌle-jən-'der-ə-lē\ *adv*

leg·end·ry \'le-jən-drē\ *n* (1849) **:** a body of legends

leg·er \'le-jər\ *var of* LEDGER

leg·er-de·main \ˌle-jər-də-'mān\ *n* [ME, fr. MF *leger de main* light of hand] (15c) **1 :** SLEIGHT OF HAND   **2 :** a display of skill or adroitness

le·ger·i·ty \lə-'jer-ə-tē, le-\ *n* [MF *legereté*, fr. OF, lightness, fr. *leger* light, fr. (assumed) VL *leviarius*, fr. L *levis* — more at LIGHT] (1561) **:** alert facile quickness of mind or body

leger line *n* (ca. 1775) **:** LEDGER LINE

leges *pl of* LEX

leg·ged \'le-gəd *also* 'lā-, Brit *usu* 'legd\ *adj* (15c) **:** having a leg or legs esp. of a specified kind or number — often used in combination ⟨a four-*legged* animal⟩

leg·ging *or* **leg·gin** \'le-gən *also* 'lā-, -gin\ *n* (1751) **:** a covering (as of leather or cloth) for the leg — usu. used in pl.; *also* **:** TIGHTS

leg·gy \'le-gē *also* 'lā-\ *adj* **leg·gi·er; -est** (1787) **1 :** having disproportionately long legs   **2 :** having long and attractive legs   **3 :** SPINDLY — used of a plant — **leg·gi·ness** \-nəs\ *n*

leg·hold trap \'leg-ˌhōld-\ *n* (1973) **:** a jawed usu. steel trap that is used to hold a wild mammal and operates by springing closed and clamping onto the leg of the animal that steps on it

leg·horn \'leg-ˌhȯrn; 'le-ˌgȯrn, -gərn\ *n* [*Leghorn*, Italy] (1740) **1   a :** a fine plaited straw made from an Italian wheat   **b :** a hat of this straw   **2 :** any of a Mediterranean breed of small hardy fowls noted for their large production of white eggs

leg·i·ble \'le-jə-bəl\ *adj* [ME, fr. LL *legibilis*, fr. L *legere* to read] (14c) **1 :** capable of being read or deciphered   **2 :** capable of being discovered or understood — **leg·i·bil·i·ty** \ˌle-jə-'bi-lə-tē\ *n* — **leg·i·bly** \'le-jə-blē\ *adv*

¹**le·gion** \'lē-jən\ *n* [ME, fr. OF, fr. L *legion-, legio*, fr. *legere* to gather — more at LEGEND] (13c) **1 :** the principal unit of the Roman army comprising 3000 to 6000 foot soldiers with cavalry   **2 :** a large military force; *esp* **:** ARMY 1a   **3 :** a very large number **:** MULTITUDE   **4 :** a national association of ex-servicemen

²**legion** *adj* (1678) **:** MANY, NUMEROUS ⟨the problems are ~⟩

¹**le·gion·ary** \'lē-jə-ˌner-ē\ *adj* [L *legionarius*, fr. *legion-, legio*] (15c) **:** of, relating to, or constituting a legion

²**legionary** *n*, *pl* **-ar·ies** (1598) **:** LEGIONNAIRE

le·gion·naire \ˌlē-jə-'nar, -'ner\ *n* [F *légionnaire*, fr. L *legionarius*] (1818) **:** a member of a legion

Legionnaires' disease \-'narz-, -'nerz-\ *also* **Legionnaire's disease** *n* [fr. its first recognized occurrence at an American Legion convention in 1976] (1976) **:** a lobar pneumonia caused by a bacterium (*Legionella pneumophila*)

Legion of Honor (1827) **:** a French order conferred as a reward for civil or military merit

Legion of Merit (1943) **:** a U.S. military decoration awarded for exceptionally meritorious conduct in the performance of outstanding services

leg·is·late \'le-jəs-ˌlāt\ *vb* **-lat·ed; -lat·ing** [back-formation fr. *legislator*] *vi* (1805) **:** to perform the function of legislation; *specif* **:** to make or enact laws ~ *vt* **:** to cause, create, provide, or bring about by or as if by legislation

leg·is·la·tion \ˌle-jəs-'lā-shən\ *n* (ca. 1655) **1 :** the action of legislating; *specif* **:** the exercise of the power and function of making rules (as laws) that have the force of authority by virtue of their promulgation by an official organ of a state or other organization   **2 :** the enactments of a legislator or a legislative body   **3 :** a matter of business for or under consideration by a legislative body

¹**leg·is·la·tive** \'le-jəs-ˌlā-tiv, -lə-\ *adj* (ca. 1641) **1   a :** having the power or performing the function of legislating   **b :** belonging to the branch of government that is charged with such powers as making laws, levying and collecting taxes, and making financial appropriations — compare EXECUTIVE, JUDICIAL   **2   a :** of or relating to a legislature ⟨~ committees⟩   **b :** composed of members of a legislature ⟨~ caucus⟩   **c :** created by a legislature esp. as distinguished from an executive or judicial body   **d :** designed to assist a legislature or its members ⟨a ~ research agency⟩   **3 :** of, concerned with, or created by legislation — **leg·is·la·tive·ly** *adv*

²**legislative** *n* (1642) **:** the body or department exercising the power and function of legislating **:** LEGISLATURE

legislative assembly *n*, *often cap L&A* (1836) **1 :** a bicameral legislature (as in an American state)   **2 :** the lower house of a bicameral legislature   **3 :** a unicameral legislature; *esp* **:** one in a Canadian province

legislative council *n*, *often cap L&C* (1787) **1 :** a permanent committee chosen from both houses that meets between sessions of a state legislature to study state problems and plan a legislative program   **2 :** a unicameral legislature (as in a British colony)   **3 :** the upper house of a British bicameral legislature

leg·is·la·tor \'le-jəs-ˌlā-ˌtȯr, -ˌlā-tər *also* ˌle-jəs-'lā-ˌtȯr\ *n* [L *legis lator*, lit., proposer of a law, fr. *legis* (gen. of *lex* law) + *lator* proposer, fr. *ferre* (pp. *latus*) to carry, propose — more at TOLERATE, BEAR] (1603) **:** one that makes laws esp. for a political unit; *esp* **:** a member of a legislative body — **leg·is·la·to·ri·al** \ˌle-jəs-lə-'tȯr-ē-əl, -'tȯr-\ *adj* — **leg·is·la·tor·ship** \'le-jəs-ˌlā-tər-ˌship\ *n*

leg·is·la·ture \'le-jəs-ˌlā-chər *also* ˌle-jəs-', Brit *often* 'le-jəs-lə-\ *n* (ca. 1676) **:** a body of persons having the power to legislate; *specif* **:** an organized body having the authority to make laws for a political unit

le·gist \'lē-jist\ *n* [ME, fr. MF *legiste*, fr. ML *legista*, fr. L *leg-, lex*] (15c) **:** a specialist in law; *esp* **:** one learned in Roman or civil law

le·git \li-'jit\ *adj* (1908) *slang* **:** LEGITIMATE

le·git·i·ma·cy \li-'ji-tə-mə-sē\ *n* (1691) **:** the quality or state of being legitimate

¹**le·git·i·mate** \li-'ji-tə-mət\ *adj* [ME *legitimat*, fr. ML *legitimatus*, pp. of *legitimare* to legitimate, fr. L *legitimus* legitimate, fr. *leg-, lex* law] (15c) **1   a :** lawfully begotten; *specif* **:** born in wedlock   **b :** having full filial rights and obligations by birth ⟨a ~ child⟩   **2 :** being exactly as purposed **:** neither spurious nor false ⟨a ~ grievance⟩ ⟨a ~ practitioner⟩   **3   a :** accordant with law or with established legal forms and requirements ⟨a ~ government⟩   **b :** ruling by or based on the strict

principle of hereditary right ⟨a ~ king⟩   **4 :** conforming to recognized principles or accepted rules and standards ⟨~ advertising expenditure⟩ ⟨~ inference⟩   **5 :** relating to plays acted by professional actors but not including revues, burlesque, or some forms of musical comedy ⟨the ~ theater⟩ *syn* see LAWFUL — **le·git·i·mate·ly** *adv*

²**le·git·i·mate** \-ˌmāt\ *vt* **-mat·ed; -mat·ing** (1531) **:** to make legitimate: **a** (1) **:** to give legal status or authorization to (2) **:** to show or affirm to be justified   **b :** to put (a bastard) in the state of a legitimate child before the law by legal means — **le·git·i·ma·tion** \-ˌji-tə-'mā-shən\ *n* — **le·git·i·mat·or** \-'ji-tə-ˌmā-tər\ *n*

le·git·i·ma·tize \li-'ji-tə-mə-ˌtīz\ *vt* **-tized; -tiz·ing** (1791) **:** LEGITIMATE

le·git·i·mise *Brit var of* LEGITIMIZE

le·git·i·mism \li-'ji-tə-ˌmi-zəm\ *n*, *often cap* (1877) **:** adherence to the principles of political legitimacy or to a person claiming legitimacy — **le·git·i·mist** \-mist\ *n*, *often cap* — **legitimist** *adj*

le·git·i·mize \-ˌmīz\ *vt* **-mized; -miz·ing** (1848) **:** LEGITIMATE — **le·git·i·mi·za·tion** \-ˌji-tə-mə-'zā-shən\ *n* — **le·git·i·miz·er** \-'ji-tə-ˌmī-zər\ *n*

leg·man \'leg-ˌman *also* 'lāg-\ *n* (1923) **1 :** a reporter assigned usu. to gather information   **2 :** an assistant who performs various subordinate tasks (as gathering information or running errands)

leg-of-mut·ton *or* **leg-o'-mut·ton** \ˌle-gə(v)-'mə-t³n *also* ˌlāg-\ *adj* (1840) **:** having the approximately triangular shape or outline of a leg of mutton ⟨~ sleeve⟩ ⟨~ sail⟩

leg out *vt* (1965) **:** to make (as a base hit) by fast running

leg-pull \'leg-ˌpul *also* 'lāg-\ *n* [fr. the phrase *to pull one's leg*] (1915) **:** a humorous deception or hoax

leg·room \-ˌrüm, -ˌrum\ *n* (1926) **:** space in which to extend the legs while seated

le·gume \'le-ˌgyüm, li-'gyüm\ *n* [F *légume*, fr. L *legumin-, legumen* leguminous plant, fr. *legere* to gather — more at LEGEND] (1676) **1   a :** the fruit or seed of leguminous plants (as peas or beans) used for food   **b :** a vegetable used for food   **2 :** any of a large family (Leguminosae syn. Fabaceae) of dicotyledonous herbs, shrubs, and trees having fruits that are legumes (sense 3) or loments, bearing nodules on the roots that contain nitrogen-fixing bacteria, and including important food and forage plants (as peas, beans, or clovers)   **3 :** a dry dehiscent one-celled fruit developed from a simple superior ovary and usu. dehiscing into two valves with the seeds attached to the ventral suture **:** POD

le·gu·mi·nous \li-'gyü-mə-nəs, le-\ *adj* (15c) **1 :** of, relating to, or consisting of plants that are legumes   **2 :** resembling a legume

leg up *n* (1837) **1 :** a helping hand **:** BOOST   **2 :** HEAD START

leg warmer *n* (1974) **:** a usu. knitted covering for the leg

leg·work \'leg-ˌwȯrk *also* 'lāg-\ *n* (1891) **:** active physical work (as in gathering information) that forms the basis of more creative or mentally exacting work (as writing a book)

le·hua \lā-'hü-ə\ *n* [Hawaiian] (1888) **:** a common very showy chiefly Polynesian tree (*Metrosideros collinus*) of the myrtle family having bright red flowers and a hard wood; *also* **:** its flower

¹**lei** \'lā, 'lā-ˌē\ *n* [Hawaiian] (1843) **:** a wreath or necklace usu. of flowers or leaves

²**lei** \'lā\ *pl of* LEU

Leices·ter \'les-tər\ *n* [*Leicester*, county in England] (1798) **1 :** an individual of either of two English breeds of white-faced long-wool sheep raised esp. for mutton   **2 :** a hard usu. orange-colored cheese similar to cheddar

leish·man·ia \lēsh-'ma-nē-ə\ *n* [NL, fr. Sir W. B. *Leishman* †1926 Brit. medical officer] (1914) **:** any of a genus (*Leishmania*) of flagellate protozoans that are parasitic in the tissues of vertebrates; *broadly* **:** an organism resembling the leishmanias that is included in the family (Trypanosomatidae) to which they belong — **leish·man·i·al** \-nē-əl\ *adj*

leish·man·i·a·sis \ˌlēsh-mə-'nī-ə-səs\ *n* [NL] (1912) **:** infection with or disease caused by leishmanias

leis·ter \'lēs-tər\ *n* [of Scand origin; akin to ON *ljōstr* leister] (ca. 1534) **:** a spear armed with three or more barbed prongs for catching fish

lei·sure \'lē-zhər, 'le-, 'lā-\ *n* [ME *leisure*, fr. MF *leisir*, fr. *leisir* to be permitted, fr. L *licēre*] (14c) **1 :** freedom provided by the cessation of activities; *esp* **:** time free from work or duties   **2 :** EASE, LEISURELINESS — **leisure** *adj* **:** at leisure *or* at one's leisure **:** in one's leisure time **:** at one's convenience ⟨read the book *at her leisure*⟩

lei·sured \-zhərd\ *adj* (1631) **:** having leisure **:** LEISURELY

¹**lei·sure·ly** \-zhər-lē\ *adv* (15c) **:** without haste **:** DELIBERATELY

²**leisurely** *adj* (1604) **:** characterized by leisure **:** UNHURRIED — **lei·sure·li·ness** *n*

leisure suit *n* (1975) **:** a suit consisting of a shirt jacket and matching trousers for informal wear

leit·mo·tiv *or* **leit·mo·tif** \'līt-mō-ˌtēf\ *n* [G *Leitmotiv*, fr. *leiten* to lead + *Motiv* motive] (ca. 1876) **1 :** an associated melodic phrase or figure that accompanies the reappearance of an idea, person, or situation esp. in a Wagnerian music drama   **2 :** a dominant recurring theme

¹**lek** \'lek\ *n* [Sw, short for *lekställe* mating ground, fr. *lek* mating, sport + *ställe* place] (1871) **:** an assembly area where animals (as the prairie chicken) carry on display and courtship behavior

²**lek** *n*, *pl* **leks** *or* **le·ke** \'le-kə\ *also* **lek** *or* **le·ku** \'le-(ˌ)kü\ [Alb] (1927) — see MONEY table

lek·var \'lek-ˌvär\ *n* [Hung *lekvár* jam] (ca. 1958) **:** a prune butter used as a pastry filling

le·man \'le-mən, 'lē-\ *n* [ME *lefman, leman*, fr. *lef* lief] (13c) *archaic* **:** SWEETHEART, LOVER; *esp* **:** MISTRESS

¹**lem·ma** \'le-mə\ *n*, *pl* **lemmas** *or* **lem·ma·ta** \-mə-tə\ [L, fr. Gk *lēmma* thing taken, assumption, fr. *lambanein* to take — more at LATCH] (1570) **1 :** an auxiliary proposition used in the demonstration of another proposition   **2 :** the argument or theme of a composition prefixed as a title or introduction; *also* **:** the heading or theme of a comment or note on a text   **3 :** a glossed word or phrase

---

\ə\ abut \'ə\ kitten, F table \ər\ further \a\ ash \ā\ ace \ä\ mop, mar \au̇\ out \ch\ chin \e\ bet \ē\ easy \g\ go \i\ hit \ī\ ice \j\ job \ŋ\ sing \ō\ go \ȯ\ law \ȯi\ boy \th\ thin \th̲\ the \ü\ loot \u̇\ foot \y\ yet \zh\ vision \à, k̲, ⁿ, œ, œ̄, ue, ūe, ᵜ\ see Guide to Pronunciation

²**lem·ma** *n* [Gk, husk, fr. *lepein* to peel — more at LEPER] (1906) : the lower of the two bracts enclosing the flower in the spikelet of grasses

lem·ming \'le-miŋ\ *n* [Norw] (1713) : any of various small short-tailed furry-footed rodents (as genera *Lemmus* and *Dicrostonyx*) of circumpolar distribution that are notable for the recurrent mass migrations of a European form (*L. lemmus*) which often continue into the sea where vast numbers are drowned — **lem·ming-like** \-,lik\ *adj*

lem·nis·cate \lem-'nis-kət\ *n* [NL lemniscata, fr. fem. of L *lemniscatus* with hanging ribbons, fr. *lemniscus*] (ca. 1781) : a figure-eight shaped curve whose equation in polar coordinates is ρ² = a² cos 2θ or ρ² = a² sin 2θ

lem·nis·cus \lem-'nis-kəs\ *n, pl* **-nis·ci** \-'nis-,kī, -,kē; -'ni-,sī\ [NL, fr. L, ribbon, fr. Gk *lēmniskos*] (ca. 1905) : a band of fibers and esp. nerve fibers — **lem·nis·cal** \-kəl\ *adj*

¹**lem·on** \'le-mən\ *n* [ME *lymon*, fr. MF *limon*, fr. ML *limon-, limo*, fr. Ar *laymūn*] (15c) **1 a** : an acid fruit that is botanically a many-seeded pale yellow oblong berry and is produced by a small thorny tree (*Citrus limon*) **b** : a tree that bears lemons **2** : one (as an automobile) that is unsatisfactory or defective — **lem·ony** \'le-mə-nē\ *adj*

²**lemon** *adj* (1598) **1** : of the color lemon yellow **2 a** : containing lemon **b** : having the flavor or scent of lemon

lem·on·ade \,le-mə-'nād\ *n* (1604) : a beverage of sweetened lemon juice mixed with water

lemon balm *n* (ca. 1888) : a bushy perennial Old World mint (*Melissa officinalis*) often cultivated for its fragrant lemon-flavored leaves

lemon 1: branch with fruit and flowers

lem·on·grass \'le-mən-,gras\ *n* (1801) : a grass (*Cymbopogon citratus*) of robust habit that grows in tropical regions, is used as an herb, and is the source of an essential oil with an odor of lemon or verbena

lemon law *n* (1982) : a law offering car buyers relief (as by repair, replacement, or refund) for defects detected during a specified period after purchase

lemon shark *n* (1942) : a medium-sized requiem shark (*Negaprion brevirostris*) of the warm Atlantic that is yellowish brown to gray above with yellow or greenish sides

lemon sole *n* (1876) : any of several flatfishes and esp. flounders: as **a** : a bottom-dwelling flounder (*Microstomus kitt*) of the northeastern Atlantic that is an important food fish **b** : WINTER FLOUNDER

lemon yellow *n* (1807) : a brilliant greenish yellow color

lem·pi·ra \lem-'pir-ə\ *n* [AmerSp, fr. *Lempira*, 16th cent. Indian chief] (ca. 1934) — see MONEY table

le·mur \'lē-mər\ *n* [NL, fr. L *lemures*, pl., ghosts] (1795) : any of various arboreal chiefly nocturnal mammals that were formerly widespread but are now largely confined to Madagascar, are related to the monkeys but are usu. regarded as constituting a distinct superfamily (Lemuroidea), and usu. have a muzzle like a fox, large eyes, very soft woolly fur, and a long furry tail

le·mu·res \'le-mə-,rās, 'lem-yə-,rēz\ *n pl* [L] (1555) : spirits of the unburied dead exorcised from homes in early Roman religious rites

lend \'lend\ *vb* **lent** \'lent\; **lend·ing** [ME *lenen, lenden*, fr. OE *lǣnan*, fr. *lǣn* loan — more at LOAN] *vt* (bef. 12c) **1 a** : to give for temporary use on condition that the same or its equivalent be returned **b** : to let out (money) for temporary use on condition of repayment with interest **2 a** : to give the assistance or support of : AFFORD, FURNISH ⟨a dispassionate and scholarly manner which ∼s great force to his criticisms —*Times Lit. Supp.*⟩ **b** : to adapt or apply (oneself) readily : ACCOMMODATE ⟨a topic that ∼s itself admirably to class discussion⟩ ∼ *vi* : to make a loan **usage** see LOAN — **lend·able** \'len-də-bəl\ *adj* — **lend·er** *n*

lemur

lending library *n* (1708) : a library from which materials are lent; *esp* : RENTAL LIBRARY

lend–lease \'lend-'lēs\ *n* [U.S. *Lend-Lease* Act (1941)] (1941) : the transfer of goods and services to an ally to aid in a common cause with payment made by a return of the original items or their use in the cause or by a similar transfer of other goods and services — **lend–lease** *vt*

length \'leŋ(k)th, 'len(t)th\ *n, pl* **lengths** \'leŋ(k)ths, 'len(t)ths, 'leŋ(k)s\ [ME *lengthe*, fr. OE *lengthu*, fr. *lang* long] (bef. 12c) **1 a** : the longer or longest dimension of an object **b** : a measured distance or dimension ⟨10 feet in ∼⟩ — see METRIC SYSTEM table, WEIGHT table **c** : the quality or state of being long **2 a** : duration or extent in time **b** : relative duration or stress of a sound **3 a** : distance or extent in space **b** : the length of something taken as a unit of measure ⟨his horse led by a ∼⟩ **4** : the degree to which something (as a course of action or a line of thought) is carried — often used in pl. ⟨went to great ∼s to learn the truth⟩ **5 a** : a long expanse or stretch **b** : a piece constituting or usable as part of a whole or of a connected series : SECTION ⟨a ∼ of pipe⟩ **6** : a vertical dimension of an article of clothing — **at length 1** : FULLY, COMPREHENSIVELY **2** : at last : FINALLY

length·en \'leŋ(k)-thən, 'len(t)-\ *vb* **length·ened**; **length·en·ing** \'leŋ(k)th-niŋ, 'len(t)th-; 'leŋ(k)-thə-, 'len(t)-\ *vt* (14c) : to make longer ∼ *vi* : to grow longer **syn** see EXTEND — **length·en·er** \'leŋ(k)th-nər, 'len(t)th-; 'leŋ(k)-thə-, 'len(t)-\ *n*

length·ways \'leŋ(k)th-,wāz, 'len(t)th-\ *adv* (1599) : LENGTHWISE

length·wise \-,wīz\ *adv* (ca. 1580) : in the direction of the length : LONGITUDINALLY — **lengthwise** *adj*

lengthy \'leŋ(k)-thē, 'len(t)-\ *adj* **length·i·er**; **-est** (1689) **1** : protracted excessively : OVERLONG **2** : EXTENDED, LONG — **length·i·ly** \-thə-lē\ *adv* — **length·i·ness** \-thē-nəs\ *n*

le·nience \'lē-nyən(t)s, -nē-ən(t)s\ *n* (1796) : LENIENCY

le·nien·cy \'lē-nē-ən(t)-sē, -nyən(t)-sē\ *n, pl* **-cies** (1780) **1** : the quality or state of being lenient **2** : a lenient disposition or practice **syn** see MERCY

le·nient \'lē-nē-ənt, -nyənt\ *adj* [L *lenient-, leniens*, prp. of *lenire* to soften, soothe, fr. *lenis* soft, mild; prob. akin to Lith *lénas* tranquil — more at LET] (1652) **1** : exerting a soothing or easing influence : relieving pain or stress **2** : of mild and tolerant disposition; *esp* : INDULGENT — **le·nient·ly** *adv*

Leni–Len·a·pe *or* **Len·ni–Len·a·pe** \,le-nē-'le-nə-pē, -lə-'nä-pē\ *n* [Delaware (Unami dialects) *lǎni-lǒnáp'e*] (ca. 1782) : DELAWARE 1

Le·nin·ism \'le-nə-,ni-zəm\ *n* (1918) : the political, economic, and social principles and policies advocated by Lenin; *esp* : the theory and practice of communism developed by or associated with Lenin — **Le·nin·ist** \-nist\ *n or adj* — **Le·nin·ite** \-,nīt\ *n or adj*

le·nis \'lē-nəs, 'lā-\ *adj* [NL, fr. L, mild, smooth] (ca. 1897) : produced with an articulation that is lax in relation to another speech sound ⟨\t\ in *gutter* is ∼, \t\ in *toe* is fortis⟩

len·i·tion \lə-'ni-shən\ *n* [L *lenire*] (1912) : the change from fortis to lenis articulation

len·i·tive \'le-nə-tiv\ *adj* [ME *lenitif*, fr. MF, fr. ML *lenitivus*, fr. L *lenitus*, pp. of *lenire*] (15c) : alleviating pain or harshness : SOOTHING — **lenitive** *n* — **len·i·tive·ly** *adv*

len·i·ty \'le-nə-tē\ *n* (1548) : the quality or state of being lenient : CLEMENCY

le·no \'lē-(,)nō\ *n* [perh. fr. F *linon* linen fabric, lawn, fr. MF *lin* flax, linen, fr. L *linum* flax] (1821) **1** : an open weave in which pairs of warp yarns cross one another and thereby lock the filling yarn in position **2** : a fabric made with a leno weave

¹**lens** *also* **lense** \'lenz\ *n* [NL *lent-, lens*, fr. L, lentil; fr. its shape] (1693) **1 a** : a piece of transparent material (as glass) that has two opposite regular surfaces either both curved or one curved and the other plane and that is used either singly or combined in an optical instrument for forming an image by focusing rays of light **b** : a combination of two or more simple lenses **c** : a piece of glass or plastic used (as in safety goggles or sunglasses) to protect the eye **2** : a device for directing or focusing radiation other than light (as sound waves, radio microwaves, or electrons) **3** : something shaped like a double-convex optical lens ⟨∼ of sandstone⟩ **4** : a highly transparent biconvex lens-shaped or nearly spherical body in the eye that focuses light rays (as upon the retina) — see EYE illustration **5** : something that facilitates and influences perception, comprehension, or evaluation ⟨the author's own ∼ seems blurred by bias —Seymour Topping⟩ — **lensed** \'lenzd\ *adj* — **lens·less** \'lenz-ləs\ *adj*

²**lens** *vt* (1942) : to make a motion picture of : FILM

lens·man \-mən, -,man\ *n* (1938) : PHOTOGRAPHER

Lent \'lent\ *n* [ME *lente* springtime, Lent, fr. OE *lencten*; akin to OHG *lenzin* spring] (13c) : the 40 weekdays from Ash Wednesday to Easter observed by the Roman Catholic, Eastern, and some Protestant churches as a period of penitence and fasting

len·ta·men·te \,len-tə-'men-(,)tā\ *adv or adj* [It, fr. *lento* slow] (1724) : LENTO

len·tan·do \len-'tän-(,)dō\ *adv or adj* [It] (ca. 1847) : becoming slower — used as a direction in music

Lent·en \'len-t⁺n\ *adj* (bef. 12c) : of, relating to, or suitable for Lent; *esp* : MEAGER ⟨∼ fare⟩

len·tic \'len-tik\ *adj* [L *lentus* sluggish] (ca. 1938) : of, relating to, or living in still waters (as lakes, ponds, or swamps) — compare LOTIC

len·ti·cel \'len-tə-,sel\ *n* [NL *lenticella*, dim. of L *lent-, lens* lentil] (ca. 1864) : a loose aggregation of cells which penetrates the surface (as of a stem) of a woody plant and through which gases are exchanged between the atmosphere and the underlying tissues

len·tic·u·lar \len-'ti-kyə-lər\ *adj* [ME, fr. L *lenticularis* lentil-shaped, fr. *lenticula* lentil] (15c) **1** : having the shape of a double-convex lens **2** : of or relating to a lens **3** : provided with or utilizing lenticules ⟨a ∼ screen⟩

len·ti·cule \'len-tə-,kyü(ə)l\ *n* [L *lenticula*] (1942) **1** : any of the minute lenses on the base side of a film used in stereoscopic or color photography **2** : any of the tiny corrugations or grooves molded or embossed into the surface of a projection screen

len·til \'len-t⁺l\ *n* [ME, fr. OF *lentille*, fr. L *lenticula*, dim. of *lent-, lens*] (13c) **1** : a widely cultivated Eurasian annual leguminous plant (*Lens culinaris*) with flattened edible seeds and leafy stalks used as fodder **2** : the seed of the lentil

len·tis·si·mo \len-'ti-sə-,mō\ *adv or adj* [It, superl. of *lento*] (ca. 1903) : at a very slow tempo — used as a direction in music

len·ti·vi·rus \,len-tə-'vī-rəs\ *n* [NL, fr. L *lentus* slow + NL *virus*] (1982) : any of a group of retroviruses that cause slowly progressive often fatal animal diseases

len·to \'len-(,)tō\ *adv or adj* [It, fr. *lento*, adj., slow, fr. L *lentus* pliant, sluggish, slow — more at LITHE] (ca. 1724) : at a slow tempo — used esp. as a direction in music

Leo \'lē-(,)ō\ *n* [L (gen. *Leonis*), lit., lion — more at LION] **1** : a northern constellation east of Cancer **2 a** : the 5th sign of the zodiac in astrology — see ZODIAC table **b** : one born under this sign — **Le·o·nine** \'lē-ə-,nīn\ *adj*

le·one \lē-'ōn\ *n, pl* **leones** *or* **leone** [Sierra Leone] (1964) — see MONEY table

Le·o·nid \'lē-ə-nid\ *n, pl* **Leonids** *or* **Le·on·i·des** \lē-'ä-nə-,dēz\ [Leon-, Leo; fr. their appearing to radiate from a point in Leo] (1876) : any of the meteors in a meteor shower occurring every year about November 14

le·o·nine \'lē-ə-,nīn\ *adj* [ME, fr. L *leoninus*, fr. *leon-, leo*] (14c) : of, relating to, or suggestive of, or resembling a lion

leop·ard \'le-pərd\ *n* [ME, fr. OF *leupart*, fr. LL *leopardus*, fr. Gk *leopardos*, fr. *leōn* lion + *pardos* leopard] (13c) **1** : a large strong cat (*Panthera pardus*) of southern Asia and Africa that is adept at climbing and is usu. tawny or buff with black spots arranged in rosettes — called also *panther* **2** : a heraldic representation of a lion passant guardant — **leop·ard·ess** \-pər-dəs\ *n*

leopard frog *n* (1839) : a common No. American frog (*Rana pipiens*) that is bright green or brown with large black white-margined blotches on the back; *also* : a similar frog (*R. sphenocephala*) of the southeastern U.S.

leopard seal n (1893) : a spotted slate gray seal (*Hydrurga leptonyx*) of the southern Atlantic to the southern Pacific that often feeds on other seals

le·o·tard \'lē-ə-ˌtärd\ n [Jules Léotard, †1870 Fr. aerial gymnast] (1886) : a close-fitting one-piece garment worn esp. by dancers, acrobats, and aerialists; *also* : TIGHTS — often used in pl. — **le·o·tard·ed** \-ˌtär-dəd\ *adj*

Lep·cha \'lep-chə\ n, pl **Lepcha** or **Lepchas** (1819) **1** : a member of a people of Sikkim, India **2** : the Tibeto-Burman language of the Lepcha people

lep·er \'le-pər\ n [ME, fr. *lepre* leprosy, fr. MF, fr. LL *lepra*, fr. Gk, fr. *lepein* to peel; perh. akin to Lith *lopas* piece, scrap] (14c) **1** : a person affected with leprosy **2** : a person shunned for moral or social reasons

lepid- or **lepido-** *comb form* [NL, fr. Gk, fr. *lepid-*, *lepis* scale, fr. *lepein*] : flake : scale ⟨*Lepidoptera*⟩

le·pid·o·lite \li-'pi-d°l-ˌīt\ n [G *Lepidolith*, fr. *lepid-* + *-lith*] (ca. 1796) : a variable mineral that consists of a mica containing lithium and is used esp. in glazes and enamels

lep·i·dop·tera \ˌle-pə-'däp-tə-rə\ n pl (ca. 1773) : insects that are lepidopterans

lep·i·dop·ter·an \-rən\ n [NL *Lepidoptera*, fr. *lepid-* + Gk *pteron* wing — more at FEATHER] (ca. 1901) : any of a large order (Lepidoptera) of insects comprising the butterflies, moths, and skippers that as adults have four broad or lanceolate wings usu. covered with minute overlapping and often brightly colored scales and that as larvae are caterpillars — **lepidopteran** *adj* — **lep·i·dop·ter·ous** \-tə-rəs\ *adj*

lep·i·dop·ter·ist \-tə-rist\ n (1826) : a specialist in lepidopterology

lep·i·dop·ter·ol·o·gy \-ˌdäp-tə-'rä-lə-jē\ n (1898) : a branch of entomology concerned with lepidopterans — **lep·i·dop·ter·o·log·i·cal** \-tə-rə-'lä-ji-kəl\ *adj* — **lep·i·dop·ter·ol·o·gist** \-tə-'rä-lə-jist\ n

lep·i·dote \'le-pə-ˌdōt\ n [Gk *lepidōtos* scaly, fr. *lepid-*, *lepis*] (ca. 1836) : a rhododendron covered with scurf or scurfy scales

lep·re·chaun \'lep-rə-ˌkän, -ˌkòn\ n [Ir *leipreachán*] (1604) : a mischievous elf of Irish folklore usu. believed to reveal the hiding place of treasure if caught — **lep·re·chaun·ish** \-ˌkä-nish, -ˌkò-\ *adj*

le·pro·ma·tous \le-'prä-mə-təs, -'prō-\ *adj* [NL *lepromat-*, *leproma* leprous lesion, fr. LL *lepra*] (1898) : characterized by, exhibiting, or being leprosy with infective superficial granulomatous nodules

lep·ro·sar·i·um \ˌle-prə-'ser-ē-əm\ n, pl **-i·ums** or **-ia** \-ē-ə\ [ML, fr. LL *leprosus*] (ca. 1846) : a hospital for leprosy patients

lep·ro·sy \'le-prə-sē\ n [ME *lepruse*, fr. *leprous*] (15c) **1** : a chronic disease caused by a bacillus (*Mycobacterium leprae*) and characterized by the formation of nodules or of macules that enlarge and spread accompanied by loss of sensation with eventual paralysis, wasting of muscle, and production of deformities and mutilations **2** : a morally or spiritually harmful influence — **lep·rot·ic** \le-'prä-tik\ *adj*

lep·rous \'le-prəs\ *adj* [ME, fr. LL *leprosus* leprous, fr. *lepra* leprosy — more at LEPER] (13c) **1** a : infected with leprosy **b** : of, relating to, or resembling leprosy or a leper **2** : SCALY, SCURFY — **lep·rous·ly** *adv*

-lepsy *n comb form* [MF *-lepsie*, fr. LL *-lepsia*, fr. Gk *-lēpsia*, fr. *lēpsis*, fr. *lambanein* to take, seize — more at LATCH] : taking : seizure ⟨narcolepsy⟩

lep·to·ceph·a·lus \ˌlep-tə-'se-fə-ləs\ n, pl **-li** \-ˌlī, -ˌlē\ [NL, fr. Gk *leptos* + *kephalē* head — more at CEPHALIC] (1769) : a long thin small-headed transparent pelagic first larva of various eels

¹lep·ton \lep-'tän\ n, pl **lep·ta** \-'tä\ [NGk, fr. Gk, a small coin, fr. neut. of *leptos* peeled, slender, small, fr. *lepein* to peel — more at LEPER] (ca. 1741) — see *drachma* at MONEY table

²lep·ton \'lep-ˌtän\ n [Gk *leptos* + E *²-on*] (ca. 1929) : any of a family of particles (as electrons, muons, and neutrinos) that have spin quantum number ¹/₂ and that experience no strong forces — **lep·ton·ic** \lep-'tä-nik\ *adj*

lep·to·some \'lep-tə-ˌsōm\ *adj* [G *Leptosom*, fr. Gk *leptos* + *sōma* body] (1931) : ECTOMORPHIC — **leptosome** n

lep·to·spire \-ˌspīr\ n [NL *Leptospira*, fr. L *spira* coil — more at SPIRE] (1952) : any of a genus (*Leptospira*) of slender aerobic spirochetes that are free-living or parasitic in mammals — **lep·to·spir·al** \ˌlep-tə-'spī-rəl\ *adj*

lep·to·spi·ro·sis \ˌlep-tə-spī-'rō-səs\ n, pl **-ro·ses** \-ˌsēz\ [NL] (ca. 1926) : any of several diseases of humans and domestic animals that are caused by infection with leptospires

lep·to·tene \'lep-tə-ˌtēn\ n [ISV] (1912) : a stage of meiotic prophase immediately preceding synapsis in which the chromosomes appear as fine discrete threads — **leptotene** *adj*

¹les·bi·an \'lez-bē-ən\ *adj*, *often cap* (1591) **1** : of or relating to Lesbos **2** [fr. the reputed homosexual band associated with Sappho of Lesbos] : of or relating to homosexuality between females

²lesbian n, *often cap* (ca. 1890) : a female homosexual

les·bi·an·ism \'lez-bē-ə-ˌni-zəm\ n (1870) : female homosexuality

lèse–ma·jes·té or **lese maj·es·ty** \ˌläz-'ma-jə-stē, ˌlez-, ˌlēz-\ n [MF *lese majesté*, fr. L *laesa majestas*, lit., injured majesty] (1536) **1** a : a crime (as treason) committed against a sovereign power **b** : an offense violating the dignity of a ruler as the representative of a sovereign power **2** : a detraction from or affront to dignity or importance

le·sion \'lē-zhən\ n [ME, fr. MF, fr. L *laesion-*, *laesio*, fr. *laedere* to injure] (15c) **1** : INJURY, HARM **2** : an abnormal change in structure of an organ or part due to injury or disease; *esp* : one that is circumscribed and well defined — **le·sioned** \-zhənd\ *adj*

les·pe·de·za \ˌles-pə-'dē-zə\ n [NL, irreg. fr. V. M. de *Zespedes* fl1785 Span. governor of East Florida] (1891) : any of a genus (*Lespedeza*) of herbaceous or shrubby leguminous plants including some widely used for forage, soil improvement, and esp. hay

¹less \'les\ *adj*, *comparative of* ¹LITTLE [ME, partly fr. OE *læs*, adv. & n.; partly fr. *læssa*, adj.; akin to OFris *lēs* less] (bef. 12c) **1** : constituting a more limited number ⟨~ than three⟩ **2** : of lower rank, degree, or importance ⟨no ~ a person than the president himself⟩ **3** a : of reduced size, extent, or degree **b** : more limited in quantity ⟨in ~ time⟩

usage The traditional view is that *less* applies to matters of degree, value, or amount and modifies collective nouns, mass nouns, or nouns denoting an abstract whole while *fewer* applies to matters of number and modifies plural nouns. *Less* has been used to modify plural nouns since the days of King Alfred and the usage, though roundly decried, appears to be increasing. *Less* is more likely than *fewer* to modify plural nouns when distances, sums of money, and a few fixed phrases

are involved ⟨*less* than 100 miles⟩ ⟨an investment of *less* than $2000⟩ ⟨in 25 words or *less*⟩ and as likely as *fewer* to modify periods of time ⟨in *less* (or *fewer*) than four hours⟩.

²less *adv*, *comparative of* ²LITTLE (bef. 12c) : to a lesser extent or degree — **less and less** : to a progressively smaller size or extent — **less than** : by no means : not at all ⟨*less than* honest in his replies⟩

³less n, pl **less** (bef. 12c) **1** : a smaller portion or quantity **2** : something of less importance

⁴less *prep* (15c) : diminished by : MINUS

-less *adj suffix* [ME *-les*, *-lesse*, fr. OE *-lēas*, fr. *lēas* devoid, false; akin to OHG *lōs* loose, OE *losian* to get lost — more at LOSE] **1** : destitute of : not having ⟨wit*less*⟩ ⟨child*less*⟩ **2** : unable to be acted on or to act (in a specified way) ⟨daunt*less*⟩ ⟨fade*less*⟩

les·see \le-'sē\ n [ME, fr. AF, fr. *lessé*, pp. of *lesser* to lease — more at LEASE] (15c) : one that holds real or personal property under a lease

less·en \'le-s°n\ vb **less·ened**; **less·en·ing** \'les-niŋ, 'le-s°n-iŋ\ vi (13c) : to shrink in size, number, or degree : DECREASE ~ vt **1** : to reduce in size, extent, or degree **2** a *archaic* : to represent as of little value **b** : to lower in status or dignity : DEGRADE *syn* see DECREASE

¹less·er \'le-sər\ *adj*, *comparative of* ¹LITTLE (13c) : of less size, quality, degree, or significance : of lower status

²lesser *adv* (1539) : LESS ⟨lesser-known⟩

lesser celandine n (ca. 1890) : a yellow-flowered Eurasian perennial herb (*Ranunculus ficaria*) of the buttercup family naturalized in No. America

lesser cornstalk borer n (ca. 1925) : a pyralid moth (*Elasmopalpus lignosellus*) having slender greenish larvae that burrow in the stalk esp. of Indian corn near ground level

lesser peach tree borer n (ca. 1924) : a moth (*Synanthedon pictipes* family Aegeriidae) whose larva is a borer in the forks and crotches of stone-fruit trees and esp. the peach

lesser yellowlegs n pl but sing or pl in constr (ca. 1903) : a common American marsh and shore bird (*Tringa flavipes*) that closely resembles the greater yellowlegs in color and markings but is smaller with a shorter more slender bill

¹les·son \'le-s°n\ n [ME, fr. OF *leçon*, fr. LL *lection-*, *lectio*, fr. L, act of reading, fr. *legere* to read — more at LEGEND] (13c) **1** : a passage from sacred writings read in a service of worship **2** a : a piece of instruction **b** : a reading or exercise to be studied by a pupil **c** : a division of a course of instruction **3** a : something learned by study or experience ⟨his years of travel had taught him valuable ~s⟩ **b** : an instructive example ⟨the ~s of history⟩ **c** : REPRIMAND

²lesson vt **les·soned**; **les·son·ing** \'le-sə-niŋ, 'les-niŋ\ (1555) **1** : to give a lesson to : INSTRUCT **2** : LECTURE, REBUKE

les·sor \'le-ˌsòr, le-'sòr\ n [ME *lessour*, fr. AF, fr. *lesser* to lease] (14c) : one that conveys property by lease

lest \'lest\ *conj* [ME *les the*, *leste*, fr. OE *thӯ læs the*, *thӯ* (instrumental of *thæt* that) + *læs* the, relative particle] (bef. 12c) : for fear that — used after an expression denoting fear or apprehension ⟨worried ~ she should be late⟩ ⟨hesitant to speak out ~ he be fired⟩

¹let \'let\ vt **let·ted**; **letted** or **let**; **let·ting** [ME *letten*, fr. OE *lettan* to delay, hinder; akin to OHG *lezzen* to delay, hurt, OE *læt* late] (bef. 12c) *archaic* : HINDER, PREVENT

²let n (12c) **1** : something that impedes : OBSTRUCTION **2** : a shot or point in racket games that does not count and must be replayed

³let vb **let**; **let·ting** [ME *leten*, fr. OE *lætan*; akin to OHG *lāzzan* to permit, and perh. to Lith *lénas* tranquil] vt (bef. 12c) **1** : to cause to : MAKE ⟨~ me know⟩ **2** a : to offer or grant for rent or lease ⟨~ rooms⟩ **b** : to assign esp. after bids ⟨~ a contract⟩ **3** a : to give opportunity to or fail to prevent ⟨live and ~ live⟩ ⟨a break in the clouds ~ us see the summit⟩ ⟨~ the opportunity slip⟩ **b** — used in the imperative to introduce a request or proposal ⟨~ us pray⟩ **c** — used as an auxiliary to express a warning ⟨~ him try⟩ **4** : to free from or as if from confinement ⟨~ out a scream⟩ ⟨~ blood⟩ **5** : to permit to enter, pass, or leave ⟨~ them through⟩ ⟨~ them off with a warning⟩ **6** : to make an adjustment to ⟨~ out the waist⟩ ~ vi **1** : to become rented or leased **2** : to become awarded to a contractor *syn* see HIRE — **let alone** : to leave undisturbed; *also* : to leave to oneself — **let fly** : to hurl an object — **let go** : to dismiss from employment ⟨the firm *let* him *go* at the end of the month⟩ — **let it all hang out** : to reveal one's true feelings : act without dissimulation — **let one have it** : to subject to vigorous assault — **let rip** **1** : to utter or release without restraint ⟨*let* 'er *rip*⟩ **2** : to do or utter something without restraint ⟨*let rip* at the press⟩ — **let the cat out of the bag** : to give away a secret

-let n suffix [ME, fr. MF *-elet*, fr. *-el*, dim. suffix (fr. L *-ellus*) + *-et*] **1** : small one ⟨book*let*⟩ **2** : article worn on ⟨wrist*let*⟩

let alone *conj* (1812) : to say nothing of : not to mention — used to add an example of narrower range by way of contrast esp. in negative contexts ⟨believed that he would never walk again *let alone* play golf — *Sports Illus.*⟩ ⟨great to read but bloody to speak, *let alone* sing —Robertson Davies⟩

letch \'lech\ n [back-formation fr. *letcher*, alter. of *lecher*] (ca. 1796) : CRAVING; *specif* : sexual desire

let·down \'let-ˌdaùn\ n (1768) **1** a : DISCOURAGEMENT, DISAPPOINTMENT **b** : a slackening of effort : RELAXATION **2** : the descent of an aircraft or spacecraft to the point at which a landing approach is begun

let down vt (12c) **1** : to allow to descend gradually **2** a : to fail to support ⟨felt her parents had *let her down*⟩ **b** : to fall short of the expectations of ⟨the plot *lets* you *down* at the end⟩

¹le·thal \'lē-thəl\ *adj* [L *letalis*, *lethalis*, fr. *letum* death] (1604) **1** a : of, relating to, or causing death ⟨death by ~ injection⟩ **b** : capable of causing death ⟨~ chemicals⟩ **2** : gravely damaging or destructive : DEVASTATING ⟨a ~ attack on his reputation⟩ *syn* see DEADLY — **le·thal·i·ty** \lē-'tha-lə-tē\ n — **le·thal·ly** \'lē-thə-lē\ *adv*

²lethal n (1917) **1** : an abnormality of genetic origin causing the death of the organism possessing it **2** : LETHAL GENE

\ə\ abut \ᵊ\ kitten, F table \ər\ further \a\ ash \ā\ ace \ä\ mop, mar \aù\ out \ch\ chin \e\ bet \ē\ easy \g\ go \i\ hit \ī\ ice \j\ job \ŋ\ sing \ō\ go \ò\ law \òi\ boy \th\ thin \t͟h\ the \ü\ loot \ù\ foot \y\ yet \zh\ vision \à, k̲, ⁿ, œ, œ̄, ue, ūe, ʸ\ *see* Guide to Pronunciation

lethal gene n (1939) : a gene that in some (as homozygous) conditions may prevent development or cause the death of an organism or its germ cells — called also *lethal factor, lethal mutant, lethal mutation*
le·thar·gic \la-'thär-jik, le-\ adj (14c) **1** : of, relating to, or characterized by lethargy : SLUGGISH **2** : INDIFFERENT, APATHETIC — **le·thar·gi·cal·ly** \-ji-k(a-)lē\ adv
leth·ar·gy \'le-thar-jē\ n [ME litargie, fr. ML litargia, fr. LL lethargia, fr. Gk lēthargia, fr. lēthargos forgetful, lethargic, irreg. fr. lēthē] (14c) **1** : abnormal drowsiness **2** : the quality or state of being lazy, sluggish, or indifferent
  syn LETHARGY, LANGUOR, LASSITUDE, STUPOR, TORPOR mean physical or mental inertness. LETHARGY implies such drowsiness or aversion to activity as is induced by disease, injury, or drugs ⟨months of *lethargy* followed my accident⟩. LANGUOR suggests inertia induced by an enervating climate or illness or love ⟨*languor* induced by a tropical vacation⟩. LASSITUDE stresses listlessness or indifference resulting from fatigue or poor health ⟨a depression marked by *lassitude*⟩. STUPOR implies a deadening of the mind and senses by shock, narcotics, or intoxicants ⟨lapsed into an alcoholic *stupor*⟩. TORPOR implies a state of suspended animation as of hibernating animals but may suggest merely extreme sluggishness ⟨a once alert mind now in a *torpor*⟩.
le·the \'lē-thē\ n [L, fr. Gk *Lēthē*, fr. *lēthē* forgetfulness; akin to Gk *lanthanein* to escape notice, *lanthanesthai* to forget — more at LATENT] **1** *cap* : a river in Hades whose waters cause drinkers to forget their past **2** : OBLIVION, FORGETFULNESS — **le·the·an** \'lē-thē-an, li-'thē-\ adj, often cap
let on vi (1725) **1** : to make acknowledgment : ADMIT ⟨knows more than he *lets on*⟩ **2** : to reveal a secret ⟨nobody *let on* about the surprise party⟩ **3** : PRETEND ⟨*let on* to being a stranger⟩
let out vi (1888) : to conclude a session or performance ⟨school *let out* in June⟩
let's \'lets, in rapid speech 'les\ (1573) : let us
Lett \'let\ n [G *Lette*, ultim. fr. Latvian *latvis*] (1589) : LATVIAN 2
¹**let·ter** \'le-tar\ n [ME, fr. OF *lettre*, fr. L *littera* letter of the alphabet, *litterae*, pl., epistle, literature] (13c) **1** : a symbol usu. written or printed representing a speech sound and constituting a unit of an alphabet **2 a** : a direct or personal written or printed message addressed to a person or organization **b** : a written communication containing a grant — usu. used in pl. **3** *pl but sing or pl in constr* **a** : LITERATURE, BELLES LETTRES **b** : LEARNING **4** : the strict or outward sense or significance ⟨the ~ of the law⟩ **5 a** : a single piece of type **b** : a style of type **6** : the initial of a school awarded to a student for achievement usu. in athletics
²**letter** vt (1668) **1** : to set down in letters : PRINT **2** : to mark with letters ~ vi : to win an athletic letter — **let·ter·er** \-tar-ar\ n
³**letter** \'le-tar\ n (1552) : one that rents or leases
let·ter·boxed \'le-tar-,bäkst\ adj [perh. fr. the resemblance of the picture on the TV screen or the bands above and below the picture to slots in a mailbox] (1989) *of a video recording* : formatted so as to display the full rectangular frame of a wide-screen motion picture — **let·ter·box·ing** \-,bäk-siŋ\ n
letter carrier n (ca. 1552) : a person who delivers mail
let·tered \'le-tard\ adj (14c) **1 a** : LEARNED, EDUCATED **b** : of, relating to, or characterized by learning : CULTURED **2** : inscribed with or as if with letters
let·ter·form \'le-tar-,fórm\ n (1908) : the shape of a letter of an alphabet esp. from the standpoint of design or development
let·ter·head \-,hed\ n (ca. 1887) **1** : a sheet of stationery printed or engraved usu. with the name and address of an organization **2** : the heading at the top of a letterhead
let·ter·ing \'le-ta-riŋ\ n (1811) : letters used in an inscription
let·ter·man \'le-tar-man\ n (1926) : an athlete who has earned a letter in a school sport
letter missive n, pl **letters missive** [ME, fr. MF *lettre missive* letter intended to be sent] (15c) : a letter from a superior authority conveying a command, recommendation, permission, or invitation
letter of credence (14c) : a formal document attesting to the power of a diplomatic agent to act for the issuing government — called also *letters of credence*
letter of credit (1645) **1** : a letter addressed by a banker to a correspondent certifying that a person named therein is entitled to draw on the writer's credit up to a certain sum **2** : a letter addressed by a banker to a person to whom credit is given authorizing drafts on the issuing bank or on a bank in the person's country up to a certain sum and guaranteeing to accept the drafts if duly made
letter of intent (ca. 1942) : a written statement of the intention to enter into a formal agreement
let·ter·per·fect \'le-tar-'par-fikt\ adj (1845) : correct to the smallest detail; esp : VERBATIM
let·ter·press \'le-tar-,pres\ n (ca. 1765) **1** : the process of printing from an inked raised surface esp. when the paper is impressed directly upon the surface **2** *chiefly Brit* : text (as of a book) distinct from pictorial illustrations
letters close \-'klōs\ n pl (1903) : letters issued by a government or sovereign to a private person in a private matter
letter sheet n (1851) : a sheet of stationery that can be folded and sealed with the message inside to form its own envelope
letters of administration (15c) : a letter evidencing the right of an administrator to administer the goods or estate of a deceased person
letters of marque \-'märk\ (15c) : written authority granted to a private person by a government to seize the subjects of a foreign state or their goods; *specif* : a license granted to a private person to fit out an armed ship to plunder the enemy
let·ter·spac·ing \'le-tar-,spā-siŋ\ n (1917) : insertion of space between the letters of a word
letters patent n pl (14c) : a writing (as from a sovereign) that confers on a designated person a grant in a form open for public inspection
¹**Lett·ish** \'le-tish\ adj (1831) : of or relating to the Latvians or their language
²**Lettish** n (1841) : LATVIAN 1
let·tre de ca·chet \'le-tra-da-,ka-'shā\ n, pl **lettres de cachet** \-tra(z)-\ [F, lit., letter with a seal] (1718) : a letter bearing an official seal and usu. authorizing imprisonment without trial of a named person

let·tuce \'le-tas\ n [ME *letuse*, fr. MF *laitues*, pl. of *laitue*, fr. L *lactuca*, fr. *lact-, lac* milk; fr. its milky juice — more at GALAXY] (14c) : any of a genus (*Lactuca*) of composite plants; *esp* : a common garden vegetable (*L. sativa*) whose succulent leaves are used esp. in salads
let-up \'let-,ap\ n (1837) : a lessening of effort or intensity
let up vi (1787) **1 a** : to diminish or slow down : SLACKEN **b** : CEASE, STOP **2** : to become less severe — used with *on*
leu \'leü\ n, pl **lei** \'lā\ [Rom, lit., lion, fr. L *leo* — more at LION] (1879) — see MONEY table
leuc- or **leuco-** chiefly Brit var of LEUK-
leu·cine \'lü-,sēn\ n [F, fr. *leuc-* leuk-] (1826) : a white crystalline essential amino acid $C_6H_{13}NO_2$ obtained by the hydrolysis of most dietary proteins
leu·cite \'lü-,sīt\ n [G *Leuzit*, fr. *leuz-* leuk-] (1799) : a white or gray mineral consisting of a silicate of potassium and aluminum and occurring in igneous rocks — **leu·cit·ic** \lü-'si-tik\ adj
leu·co·ci·din \,lü-kə-'sī-d'n\ n [ISV *leuc-* + *-cide* + ¹*-in*] (1894) : a bacterial substance that destroys white blood cells
leu·co·plast \'lü-kə-,plast\ n [ISV] (1886) : a colorless plastid esp. in the cytoplasm of interior plant tissues that is potentially capable of developing into a chloroplast
leuk- or **leuko-** comb form [NL *leuc-, leuco-*, fr. Gk *leuk-, leuko-*, fr. *leukos* — more at LIGHT] **1** : white : colorless : weakly colored ⟨*leukocyte*⟩ ⟨*leukorrhea*⟩ **2** : leukocyte ⟨*leukemia*⟩ **3** : white matter of the brain ⟨*leukotomy*⟩
leu·kae·mia chiefly Brit var of LEUKEMIA
leu·kae·mo·gen·e·sis chiefly Brit var of LEUKEMOGENESIS
leu·ke·mia \lü-'kē-mē-ə\ n [NL] (ca. 1855) : an acute or chronic disease in humans and other warm-blooded animals characterized by an abnormal increase in the number of white blood cells in the tissues and often in the blood — **leu·ke·mic** \-mik\ adj or n
leu·ke·mo·gen·e·sis \lü-,kē-mə-'je-nə-səs\ n (1942) : induction or production of leukemia — **leu·ke·mo·gen·ic** \-'je-nik\ adj
leu·ke·moid \-,móid\ adj (1926) : resembling leukemia but not involving the same changes in the blood-forming organs
leu·ko·cyte \'lü-kə-,sīt\ n [ISV] (1870) : WHITE BLOOD CELL — **leu·ko·cyt·ic** \,lü-kə-'si-tik\ adj
leu·ko·cy·to·sis \,lü-kə-sī-'tō-səs, -kə-sə-\ n [NL] (1866) : an increase in the number of white blood cells in the circulating blood
leu·ko·dys·tro·phy \,lü-kō-'dis-tra-fē\ n, pl **-phies** (1962) : any of several genetically determined diseases characterized by degeneration of the white matter of the brain
leu·ko·pe·nia \,lü-kə-'pē-nē-ə\ n [NL] (1898) : a condition in which the number of white blood cells circulating in the blood is abnormally low — **leu·ko·pe·nic** \-nik\ adj
leu·ko·pla·kia \,lü-kō-'plā-kē-ə\ n [NL, fr. *leuk-* + Gk *plak-, plax* flat surface — more at FLUKE] (ca. 1888) : an abnormal condition in which thickened white patches of epithelium occur on the mucous membranes (as of the mouth or vulva); *also* : a lesion or lesioned area of leukoplakia — **leu·ko·pla·kic** \-'plā-kik\ adj
leu·ko·poi·e·sis \-pói-'ē-səs\ n [NL] (ca. 1913) : the formation of white blood cells — **leu·ko·poi·et·ic** \-'e-tik\ adj
leu·kor·rhea \,lü-kə-'rē-ə\ n [NL] (ca. 1797) : a whitish viscid discharge from the vagina resulting from inflammation or congestion of the mucous membrane — **leu·kor·rhe·al** \-'rē-əl\ adj
leu·ko·sis \lü-'kō-səs\ n, pl **-ko·ses** \-,sēz\ [NL] (1922) : LEUKEMIA; *esp* : any of various leukemic diseases of poultry
leu·kot·o·my \lü-'kä-tə-mē\ n, pl **-mies** (1937) : LOBOTOMY
leu·ko·tri·ene \,lü-kō-'trī-,ēn\ n (1980) : any of a group of eicosanoids that participate in allergic responses
lev \'lef\ n, pl **le·va** \-lə-və\ [Bulg, lit., lion] (ca. 1900) — see MONEY table
lev- or **levo-** comb form [F *lévo-*, fr. L *laevus* left; akin to Gk *laios* left] **1** : levorotatory ⟨*levulose*⟩ **2** : to the left ⟨*levorotatory*⟩
Le·val·loi·si·an \lə-və-'lói-zē-ən, lə-,val-'wä-zē-\ adj [*Levallois*-Perret, suburb of Paris, France] (1932) : of or relating to a Middle Paleolithic culture characterized by a technique of manufacturing tools by striking flakes from a flint nodule
le·vant \lə-'vant\ vi [perh. fr. Sp *levantar* to break camp, ultim. fr. L *levare*] (1797) *chiefly Brit* : to run away from a debt
le·vant·er \lə-'van-tər\ n (1668) **1** *cap* : a native or inhabitant of the Levant **2** : a strong easterly Mediterranean wind
Le·vant storax \lə-'vant-\ n (1937) : STORAX 1a
le·va·tor \li-'vā-tər\ n, pl **le·va·to·res** \,le-və-'tōr-(,)ēz\ or **le·va·tors** \li-'vā-tərz\ [NL, fr. L *levare* to raise — more at LEVER] (1615) : a muscle that serves to raise a body part — compare DEPRESSOR
¹**le·vee** \'le-vē; lə-'vē, -'vā\ n [F *lever*, fr. MF, act of arising, fr. (se) *lever* to rise] (1672) **1** : a reception held by a person of distinction on rising from bed **2** : an afternoon assembly at which the British sovereign or his or her representative receives only men **3** : a reception usu. in honor of a particular person
²**le·vee** \'le-vē\ n [F *levée*, fr. OF, act of raising, fr. *lever* to raise — more at LEVER] (ca. 1720) **1 a** : an embankment for preventing flooding **b** : a river landing place : PIER **2** : a continuous dike or ridge (as of earth) for confining the irrigation areas of land to be flooded
³**le·vee** \'le-vē\ vt **lev·eed; lev·ee·ing** (1832) : to provide with a levee
¹**lev·el** \'le-vəl\ n [ME, plumb line, fr. MF *livel*, fr. (assumed) VL *libellum*, alter. of L *libella*, fr. dim. of *libra* weight, balance] (14c) **1** : a device for establishing a horizontal line or plane by means of a bubble in a liquid that shows adjustment to the horizontal by movement to the center of a slightly bowed glass tube **2** : a measurement of the difference of altitude of two points by means of a level **3** : horizontal condition; *esp* : equilibrium of a fluid marked by a horizontal surface of even altitude ⟨water seeks its own ~⟩ **4 a** : an approximately horizontal line or surface taken as an index of altitude **b** : a practically horizontal surface or area (as of land) **5** : a position in a scale or rank ⟨funded at the national ~⟩ **6 a** : a line or surface that cuts perpendicularly all plumb lines that it meets and hence would everywhere coincide with a surface of still water **b** : the plane of the horizon or a line in it **7** : a horizontal passage in a mine intended for regular working and transportation **8** : a concentration of a constituent esp. of a body fluid (as blood) **9** : the magnitude of a quantity considered in relation to an arbitrary reference value; *broadly* : MAGNITUDE, INTENSITY ⟨a high ~ of hostility⟩ — **on the level** : BONA FIDE, HONEST

²**level** *vb* **-eled** *or* **-elled; -el·ing** *or* **-el·ling** \'le-və-liŋ, 'lev-liŋ\ *vt* (15c) **1** : to make (a line or surface) horizontal : make flat or level ⟨~ a field⟩ ⟨~ off a house lot⟩ **2 a** : to bring to a horizontal aiming position **b** : AIM, DIRECT ⟨~ed a charge of fraud⟩ **3** : to bring to a common level or plane : EQUALIZE ⟨love ~s all ranks —W. S. Gilbert⟩ **4 a** : to lay level with or as if with the ground : RAZE **b** : to knock down ⟨~ed him with one punch⟩ **5** : to make (as color) even or uniform **6** : to find the heights of different points in (a piece of land) esp. with a surveyor's level ~ *vi* **1** : to attain or come to a level ⟨the plane ~ed off at 10,000 feet⟩ **2** : to aim a gun or other weapon horizontally **3** : to bring persons or things to a level **4** : to deal frankly and openly

³**level** *adj* (15c) **1 a** : having no part higher than another : conforming to the curvature of the liquid parts of the earth's surface **b** : parallel with the plane of the horizon : HORIZONTAL **2 a** : even or unvarying in height **b** : equal in advantage, progression, or standing **c** : proceeding monotonously or uneventfully **d** (1) : STEADY, UNWAVERING ⟨gave him a ~ look⟩ (2) : CALM, UNEXCITED ⟨spoke in ~ tones⟩ **3** : REASONABLE, BALANCED ⟨arrive at a justly proportional and ~ judgment on this affair —Sir Winston Churchill⟩ **4** : distributed evenly ⟨~ stress⟩ **5** : being a surface perpendicular to all lines of force in a field of force : EQUIPOTENTIAL **6** : suited to a particular rank or plane of ability or achievement ⟨top-*level* thinking⟩ **7** : of or relating to the spreading out of a cost or charge in even payments over a period of time — **lev·el·ly** \'le-və(l)-lē\ *adv* — **lev·el·ness** \-vəl-nəs\ *n* — **level best** : very best

syn LEVEL, FLAT, PLANE, EVEN, SMOOTH mean having a surface without bends, curves, or irregularities. LEVEL applies to a horizontal surface that lies on a line parallel with the horizon ⟨the vast prairies are nearly *level*⟩. FLAT applies to a surface devoid of noticeable curvatures, prominences, or depressions ⟨the work surface must be *flat*⟩. PLANE applies to any real or imaginary flat surface in which a straight line between any two points on it lies wholly within that surface ⟨the *plane* sides of a crystal⟩. EVEN applies to a surface that is noticeably flat or level or to a line that is observably straight ⟨trim the hedge so it is *even*⟩. SMOOTH applies esp. to a polished surface free of irregularities ⟨a *smooth* skating rink⟩.

level crossing *n* (ca. 1841) *Brit* : GRADE CROSSING

lev·el·er *or* **lev·el·ler** \'le-və-lər, 'lev-lər\ *n* (1598) **1** : one that levels **2 a** *cap* : one of a group of radicals arising during the English Civil War and advocating equality before the law and religious toleration **b** : one favoring the removal of political, social, or economic inequalities **c** : something that tends to reduce or eliminate differences among individuals

lev·el·head·ed \,le-vəl-'he-dəd\ *adj* (1879) : having sound judgment : SENSIBLE — **lev·el·head·ed·ness** *n*

leveling rod *n* (ca. 1889) : a graduated rod used in measuring the vertical distance between a point on the ground and the line of sight of a surveyor's level

level off *vi* (1919) : to approach or reach a steady rate, volume, or amount : STABILIZE ⟨expect prices to *level off*⟩

level of significance (1925) : the probability of rejecting the null hypothesis in a statistical test when it is true — called also *significance level*

¹**le·ver** \'le-vər, 'lē-\ *n* [ME, fr. MF *levier*, fr. *lever* to raise, fr. L *levare*, fr. *levis* light in weight — more at LIGHT] (14c) **1 a** : a bar used for prying or dislodging something **b** : an inducing or compelling force : TOOL ⟨use food as a political ~ —*Time*⟩ **2 a** : a rigid piece that transmits and modifies force or motion when forces are applied at two points and it turns about a third; *specif* : a rigid bar used to exert a pressure or sustain a weight at one point of its length by the application of a force at a second and turning at a third on a fulcrum **b** : a projecting piece by which a mechanism is operated or adjusted

²**lever** *vt* **le·vered; le·ver·ing** \'le-və-riŋ, 'lē-; 'lev-riŋ, 'lēv-riŋ, 'lēv-\ (1876) **1** : to pry, raise, or move with or as if with a lever **2** : to operate (a device) in the manner of a lever

¹**le·ver·age** \'le-və-rij, 'lē-; 'lev-rij, 'lēv-\ *n* (1830) **1** : the action of a lever or the mechanical advantage gained by it **2** : POWER, EFFECTIVENESS ⟨trying to gain more political ~⟩ **3** : the use of credit to enhance one's speculative capacity

²**leverage** *vt* **-aged; -ag·ing** (1937) : to provide (as a corporation) or supplement (as money) with leverage; *also* : to enhance as if by supplying with financial leverage

lev·er·aged \'le-və-rijd, 'lē-; 'lev-rijd, 'lēv-\ *adj* (1953) **1** : having a high proportion of debt relative to equity **2** *of the purchase of a company* : made with borrowed money that is secured by the assets of the company bought ⟨a ~ buyout⟩

lev·er·et \'le-və-rət, 'lev-rət\ *n* [ME, fr. (assumed) MF *levret*, fr. MF *levre* hare, fr. L *lepor-, lepus*] (15c) : a hare in its first year

Le·vi \'lē-,vī\ *n* [LL, from Heb *Lēwī*] : a son of Jacob and the traditional eponymous ancestor of the priestly tribe of Levi

levi·able \'le-vē-ə-bəl\ *adj* (15c) : capable of being levied or levied upon

le·vi·a·than \li-'vī-ə-thən\ *n* [ME, fr. LL, fr. Heb *liwyāthān*] **1 a** *often cap* : a sea monster defeated by Yahweh in various scriptural accounts **b** : a large sea animal **2** *cap* : the political state; *esp* : a totalitarian state having a vast bureaucracy **3** : something large or formidable — **leviathan** *adj*

levi·er \'le-vē-ər\ *n* (15c) : one that levies

lev·i·gate \'le-və-,gāt\ *vt* **-gat·ed; -gat·ing** [L *levigatus*, pp. of *levigare* to make smooth, fr. *levis* smooth (akin to Gk *leios* smooth and perh. to L *linere* to smear) + *-igare* (akin to *agere* to drive) — more at LIME, AGENT] (1612) **1** : POLISH, SMOOTH **2 a** : to grind to a fine smooth powder while in moist condition **b** : to separate (fine powder) from coarser material by suspending in a liquid — **lev·i·ga·tion** \,le-və-'gā-shən\ *n*

lev·in \'le-vən\ *n* [ME *levene*] (13c) *archaic* : LIGHTNING

le·vi·rate \'le-və-rət, 'lē-, -,rāt\ *n* [L *levir* husband's brother; akin to OE *tācor* husband's brother, Gk *daēr*] (1725) : the sometimes compulsory marriage of a widow to a brother of her deceased husband — **le·vi·rat·ic** \,le-və-'ra-tik, ,lē-\ *adj*

Le·vi's \'lē-,vīz\ *trademark* — used esp. for blue denim jeans

lev·i·tate \'le-və-,tāt\ *vb* **-tat·ed; -tat·ing** [*levity*] *vi* (1673) : to rise or float in the air esp. in seeming defiance of gravitation ~ *vt* : to cause to levitate

lev·i·ta·tion \,le-və-'tā-shən\ *n* (1668) : the act or process of levitating; *esp* : the rising or lifting of a person or thing by means held to be supernatural — **lev·i·ta·tion·al** \-shnəl, -shə-n°l\ *adj*

Le·vite \'lē-,vīt\ *n* (14c) : a member of the priestly Hebrew tribe of Levi; *specif* : a Levite of non-Aaronic descent assigned to lesser ceremonial offices under the Levitical priests of the family of Aaron

Le·vit·i·cal \li-'vi-ti-kəl\ *adj* [LL *Leviticus*] (1535) : of or relating to the Levites or to Leviticus

Le·vit·i·cus \-kəs\ *n* [LL, lit., of the Levites] : the third book of canonical Jewish and Christian Scripture consisting mainly of priestly legislation — see BIBLE table

lev·i·ty \'le-və-tē\ *n* [L *levitat-, levitas*, fr. *levis* light in weight — more at LIGHT] (1564) **1** : excessive or unseemly frivolity **2** : lack of steadiness : CHANGEABLENESS

le·vo \'lē-(,)vō\ *adj* (1938) : LEVOROTATORY

levo- — see LEV-

le·vo·do·pa \,le-və-'dō-pə\ *n* (1969) : L-DOPA

le·vo·ro·ta·to·ry \-'rō-tə-,tōr-ē, -,tōr-\ *or* **le·vo·ro·ta·ry** \-'rō-tə-rē\ *adj* (1873) : turning toward the left or counterclockwise; *esp* : rotating the plane of polarization of light to the left — compare DEXTROROTATORY

lev·u·lose \'lev-yə-,lōs, -,lōz\ *n* [ISV, irreg. fr. *lev-* + ²-*ose*] (1871) : FRUCTOSE 2

¹**levy** \'le-vē\ *n, pl* **lev·ies** [ME, fr. OF *levee*, act of raising — more at LEVEE] (13c) **1 a** : the imposition or collection of an assessment **b** : an amount levied **2 a** : the enlistment or conscription of men for military service **b** : troops raised by levy

²**levy** *vb* **lev·ied; levy·ing** *vt* (14c) **1 a** : to impose or collect by legal authority ⟨~ a tax⟩ **b** : to require by authority **2** : to enlist or conscript for military service **3** : to carry on (war) : WAGE ~ *vi* : to seize property

lewd \'lüd\ *adj* [ME *lewed* vulgar, fr. OE *lǣwede* laical, ignorant] (14c) **1** *obs* : EVIL, WICKED **2 a** : sexually unchaste or licentious **b** : OBSCENE, VULGAR — **lewd·ly** *adv* — **lewd·ness** *n*

lew·is \'lü-əs\ *n* [prob. fr. the name *Lewis*] (1743) : an iron dovetailed tenon that is made in sections, can be fitted into a dovetail mortise, and is used in hoisting large stones

Lew·is acid \'lü-əs-\ *n* [Gilbert N. *Lewis* †1946 Am. chemist] (1944) : a substance that is capable of accepting an unshared pair of electrons from a base to form a covalent bond

lew·is·ite \'lü-ə-,sīt\ *n* [Winford L. *Lewis* †1943 Am. chemist] (1919) : a colorless or brown vesicant liquid $C_2H_2AsCl_3$ developed as a poison gas for war use

lex \'leks\ *n, pl* **le·ges** \'lē-,jēz\ [L *leg-, lex*] (ca. 1775) : LAW

lex·eme \'lek-,sēm\ *n* [Gk *lexis* word, speech + E *-eme*] (1940) : a meaningful linguistic unit that is an item in the vocabulary of a language — **lex·em·ic** \lek-'sē-mik\ *adj*

lex·i·cal \'lek-si-kəl\ *adj* (1836) **1** : of or relating to words or the vocabulary of a language as distinguished from its grammar and construction **2** : of or relating to a lexicon or to lexicography — **lex·i·cal·i·ty** \,lek-sə-'ka-lə-tē\ *n* — **lex·i·cal·ly** \'lek-si-k(ə-)lē\ *adv*

lex·i·cal·i·sa·tion *Brit var of* LEXICALIZATION

lex·i·cal·i·za·tion \,lek-si-kə-lə-'zā-shən\ *n* (1949) **1** : the realization of a meaning in a single word or morpheme rather than in a grammatical construction **2** : the treatment of a formerly freely composed, grammatically regular, and semantically transparent phrase or inflected form as a formally or semantically idiomatic expression — **lex·i·cal·ize** \'lek-si-kə-,līz\ *vt*

lexical meaning *n* (1933) : the meaning of the base (as the word *play*) in a paradigm (as *plays, played, playing*) — compare GRAMMATICAL MEANING

lex·i·cog·ra·pher \,lek-sə-'kä-grə-fər\ *n* [LGk *lexikographos*, fr. *lexikon* + Gk *-graphos* writer, fr. *graphein* to write] (1658) : an author or editor of a dictionary

lex·i·cog·ra·phy \,lek-sə-'kä-grə-fē\ *n* (1680) **1** : the editing or making of a dictionary **2** : the principles and practices of dictionary making — **lex·i·co·graph·i·cal** \,lek-si-kō-'gra-fi-kəl\ *or* **lex·i·co·graph·ic** \-fik\ *adj* — **lex·i·co·graph·i·cal·ly** \-fi-k(ə-)lē\ *adv*

lex·i·col·o·gy \,lek-sə-'kä-lə-jē\ *n* [F *lexicologie*, fr. *lexico-* (fr. LGk *lexiko-*, fr. *lexikon*) + *-logie* -logy] (ca. 1828) : a branch of linguistics concerned with the signification and application of words — **lex·i·col·o·gist** \-jist\ *n*

lex·i·con \'lek-sə-,kän *also* -kən\ *n, pl* **lex·i·ca** \-kə\ *or* **lexicons** [LGk *lexikon*, fr. neut. of *lexikos* of words, fr. Gk *lexis* word, speech, fr. *legein* to say — more at LEGEND] (1603) **1** : a book containing an alphabetical arrangement of the words in a language and their definitions : DICTIONARY **2 a** : the vocabulary of a language, an individual speaker or group of speakers, or a subject **b** : the total stock of morphemes in a language **3** : REPERTOIRE, INVENTORY

lex·is \'lek-səs\ *n, pl* **lex·es** \-,sēz\ [Gk, speech, word] (1960) : LEXICON 2a

ley *var of* LEA

Ley·den jar \'lī-d°n-\ *n* [*Leiden, Leyden*, Netherlands] (1825) : an electrical capacitor consisting of a glass jar coated inside and outside with metal foil and having the inner coating connected to a conducting rod passed through the insulating stopper

L-form \'el-,fȯrm\ *n* [Lister Institute, London, where it was first isolated] (1948) : a variant bacterium formed esp. under stressful conditions and usu. lacking a cell wall

Lha·sa ap·so \'lä-sə-'äp-(,)sō, 'la-sə-'ap-\ *n, pl* **Lhasa apsos** *often cap* A [*Lhasa*, Tibet + Tibetan *apso*] (1935) : any of a Tibetan breed of small dogs that have a dense coat of long hard straight hair, a heavy fall over the

Lhasa apso

\ə\ abut \ᵊ\ kitten, F table \ər\ further \a\ ash \ā\ ace \ä\ mop, mar \aú\ out \ch\ chin \e\ bet \ē\ easy \g\ go \i\ hit \ī\ ice \j\ job \ŋ\ sing \ō\ go \ȯ\ law \ȯi\ boy \th\ thin \t̲h̲\ the \ü\ loot \ú\ foot \y\ yet \zh\ vision \à, k̲, ⁿ, œ, œ̄, ue, ūe, ᵉ\ *see* Guide to Pronunciation eyes, heavy whiskers and beard, and a well-feathered tail curled over the back — called also *Lhasa*

li·a·bil·i·ty \\,lī-ə-'bi-lə-tē\ *n, pl* **-ties** (ca. 1809) **1 a :** the quality or state of being liable **b :** PROBABILITY **2 :** something for which one is liable; *esp* : pecuniary obligation : DEBT — usu. used in pl. **3 :** one that acts as a disadvantage : DRAWBACK

li·a·ble \'lī-ə-bəl, *esp in sense 2 often* 'lī-bəl\ *adj* [ME *lyable*, fr. (assumed) AF, fr. OF *lier* to bind, fr. L *ligare* — more at LIGATURE] (15c) **1 a :** obligated according to law or equity : RESPONSIBLE **b :** subject to appropriation or attachment **2 a :** being in a position to incur — used with *to* \~ to a fine\ **b :** exposed or subject to some usu. adverse contingency or action \watch out or you're \~ to fall\
syn LIABLE, OPEN, EXPOSED, SUBJECT, PRONE, SUSCEPTIBLE, SENSITIVE mean being by nature or through circumstances likely to experience something adverse. LIABLE implies a possibility or probability of incurring something because of position, nature, or particular situation *liable* to get lost\. OPEN stresses a lack of barriers preventing incurrence \a claim *open* to question\. EXPOSED suggests lack of protection or powers of resistance against something actually present or threatening *exposed* to infection\. SUBJECT implies an openness for any reason to something that must be suffered or undergone \all reports are *subject* to review\. PRONE stresses natural tendency or propensity to incur something *prone* to procrastination\. SUSCEPTIBLE implies conditions existing in one's nature or individual constitution that make incurrence probable \very *susceptible* to flattery\. SENSITIVE implies a readiness to respond to or be influenced by forces or stimuli \unduly *sensitive* to criticism\.
usage Both *liable* and *apt* when followed by an infinitive are used nearly interchangeably with *likely*. Although conflicting advice has been given over the years, most current commentators accept *apt* when so used. They generally recommend limiting *liable* to situations having an undesirable outcome, and our evidence shows that in edited writing it is more often so used than not. **syn** see in addition RESPONSIBLE

li·aise \lē-'āz\ *vi* **li·aised; li·ais·ing** [back-formation fr. *liaison*] (1928) *chiefly Brit* **1 :** to establish liaison **2 :** to act as a liaison officer

li·ai·son \'lē-ə-,zän, lē-'ā-, ÷'lā-ə-\ *n* [F, fr. MF, fr. *lier*, fr. OF] (1759) **1 :** a binding or thickening agent used in cooking **2 a :** a close bond or connection : INTERRELATIONSHIP **b :** an illicit sexual relationship : AFFAIR 3a **3 a :** communication for establishing and maintaining mutual understanding and cooperation (as between parts of an armed force) **b :** one that establishes and maintains liaison **4 :** the pronunciation of an otherwise absent consonant sound at the end of the first of two consecutive words the second of which begins with a vowel sound and follows without pause

li·a·na \lē-'ä-nə, -'a-\ *also* **li·ane** \-'än, -'an\ *n* [F *liane*] (1796) : any of various usu. woody vines esp. of tropical rain forests that root in the ground

li·ar \'lī-(ə)r\ *n* [ME, fr. OE *lēogere*, fr. *lēogan* to lie — more at LIE] (bef. 12c) : one that tells lies

Li·as \'lī-əs\ *adj* [*Lias*, division of the European Jurassic, fr. F, fr. E, a limestone rock] (1813) *chiefly Brit* : LIASSIC

Li·as·sic \lī-'a-sik\ *adj* [modif. of F *liasique*, fr. *Lias*] (1833) : of, relating to, or being a subdivision of the European Jurassic

lib \'lib\ *n* (1970) : LIBERATION 2

li·ba·tion \lī-'bā-shən\ *n* [L *libation-, libatio*, fr. *libare* to pour as an offering; akin to Gk *leibein* to pour] (14c) **1 a :** an act of pouring a liquid as a sacrifice (as to a deity) **b :** a liquid (as wine) used in a libation **2 a :** an act or instance of drinking often ceremoniously **b :** BEVERAGE; *esp* : a drink containing alcohol — **li·ba·tion·ary** \-shə-,ner-ē\ *adj*

lib·ber \'li-bər\ *n* [*lib*] (1971) : a person who supports a liberation movement esp. for women — often used disparagingly

li·bec·cio \li-'be-chē-,ō, -'be-chō\ *or* **li·bec·chio** \-'be-kē-,ō\ *n* [It *libeccio*] (1667) : a southwest wind in Italy

¹li·bel \'lī-bəl\ *n* [ME, written declaration, fr. MF, fr. L *libellus*, dim. of *liber* book] (14c) **1 a :** a written statement in which a plaintiff in certain courts sets forth the cause of action or the relief sought **b** *archaic* : a handbill esp. attacking or defaming someone **2 a :** a written or oral defamatory statement or representation that conveys an unjustly unfavorable impression **b** (1) : a statement or representation published without just cause and tending to expose another to public contempt (2) : defamation of a person by written or representational means (3) : the publication of blasphemous, treasonable, seditious, or obscene writings or pictures (4) : the act, tort, or crime of publishing such a libel

²libel *vb* **-beled** *or* **-belled; -bel·ing** *or* **-bel·ling** *vi* (1570) : to make libelous statements \~ *vt* : to make or publish a libel against — **li·bel·er** \-bə-lər\ *n* — **li·bel·ist** \-bə-list\ *n*

li·bel·ant *or* **li·bel·lant** \'lī-bə-lənt\ *n* (1726) : one that institutes a suit by a libel

li·bel·ee *or* **li·bel·lee** \,lī-bə-'lē\ *n* (ca. 1856) : one against whom a libel has been filed in a court

li·bel·ous *or* **li·bel·lous** \'lī-b(ə-)ləs\ *adj* (1619) : constituting or including a libel : DEFAMATORY \a \~ statement\

Li·be·ra \'lē-bə-,rä, 'lē-brə\ *n* [L, lit., deliver, imper. of *liberare* to liberate; fr. the first word of the responsory] (ca. 1903) : a Roman Catholic funeral responsory

¹lib·er·al \'li-b(ə-)rəl\ *adj* [ME, fr. MF, fr. L *liberalis* suitable for a freeman, generous, fr. *liber* free; perh. akin to OE *lēodan* to grow, Gk *eleutheros* free] (14c) **1 a :** of, relating to, or based on the liberal arts \~ education\ **b** *archaic* : of or befitting a man of free birth **2 a :** marked by generosity : OPENHANDED \a \~ giver\ **b :** given or provided in a generous and openhanded way \a \~ meal\ **c :** AMPLE, FULL **3** *obs* : lacking moral restraint : LICENTIOUS **4 :** not literal or strict : LOOSE \a \~ translation\ **5 :** BROAD-MINDED; *esp* : not bound by authoritarianism, orthodoxy, or traditional forms **6 a :** of, favoring, or based upon the principles of liberalism **b** *cap* : of or constituting a political party advocating or associated with the principles of political liberalism; *esp* : of or constituting a political party in the United Kingdom associated with ideals of individual esp. economic freedom, greater individual participation in government, and constitutional, political, and administrative reforms designed to secure these objectives — **lib·er·al·ly** \-b(ə-)rə-lē\ *adv* — **lib·er·al·ness** *n*

syn LIBERAL, GENEROUS, BOUNTIFUL, MUNIFICENT mean giving or given freely and unstintingly. LIBERAL suggests openhandedness in the giver and largeness in the thing or amount given \a teacher *liberal* with her praise\. GENEROUS stresses warmhearted readiness to give more than size or importance of the gift \a *generous* offer of help\. BOUNTIFUL suggests lavish, unremitting giving or providing \children spoiled by *bountiful* presents\. MUNIFICENT suggests a scale of giving appropriate to lords or princes \a *munificent* foundation grant\.

²liberal *n* (1820) : a person who is liberal: as **a :** one who is open-minded or not strict in the observance of orthodox, traditional, or established forms or ways **b** *cap* : a member or supporter of a liberal political party **c :** an advocate or adherent of liberalism esp. in individual rights

liberal arts *n pl* (14c) **1 :** the medieval studies comprising the trivium and quadrivium **2 :** the studies (as language, philosophy, history, literature, abstract science) in a college or university intended to provide chiefly general knowledge and to develop the general intellectual capacities (as reason and judgment) as opposed to professional or vocational skills

lib·er·al·ism \'li-b(ə-)rə-,li-zəm\ *n* (1819) **1 :** the quality or state of being liberal **2 a** *often cap* : a movement in modern Protestantism emphasizing intellectual liberty and the spiritual and ethical content of Christianity **b :** a theory in economics emphasizing individual freedom from restraint and usu. based on free competition, the self-regulating market, and the gold standard **c :** a political philosophy based on belief in progress, the essential goodness of the human race, and the autonomy of the individual and standing for the protection of political and civil liberties **d** *cap* : the principles and policies of a Liberal party — **lib·er·al·ist** \-b(ə-)rə-list\ *n or adj* — **lib·er·al·is·tic** \,li-b(ə-)rə-'lis-tik\ *adj*

lib·er·al·ise *Brit var of* LIBERALIZE

lib·er·al·i·ty \,li-bə-'ra-lə-tē\ *n, pl* **-ties** (14c) : the quality or state of being liberal; *also* : an instance of this

lib·er·al·ize \'li-b(ə-)rə-,līz\ *vb* **-ized; -iz·ing** *vt* (1774) : to make liberal or more liberal \~ *vi* : to become liberal or more liberal — **lib·er·al·iza·tion** \,li-b(ə-)rə-lə-'zā-shən\ *n* — **lib·er·al·iz·er** \'li-b(ə-)rə-,lī-zər\ *n*

lib·er·ate \'li-bə-,rāt\ *vt* **-at·ed; -at·ing** [L *liberatus*, pp. of *liberare*, fr. *liber*] (ca. 1623) **1 :** to set at liberty : FREE; *specif* : to free (as a country) from domination by a foreign power **2 :** to free from combination \~ the gas by adding acid\ **3 :** to take or take over illegally or unjustly \material *liberated* from a nearby construction site —Thorne Dreyer\ **syn** see FREE — **lib·er·a·tor** \-,ā-tər\ *n*

liberated *adj* (1946) : freed from or opposed to traditional social and sexual attitudes or roles \a \~ woman\ \a \~ marriage\

lib·er·a·tion \,li-bə-'rā-shən\ *n* (15c) **1 :** the act of liberating : the state of being liberated **2 :** a movement seeking equal rights and status for a group \women's \~\ — **lib·er·a·tion·ist** \-sh(ə-)nist\ *n*

liberation theology *n* (1972) : a religious movement esp. among Roman Catholic clergy in Latin America that combines political philosophy usu. of a Marxist orientation with a theology of salvation as liberation from injustice — **liberation theologian** *n*

lib·er·tar·i·an \,li-bər-'ter-ē-ən\ *n* (1789) **1 :** an advocate of the doctrine of free will **2 a :** a person who upholds the principles of absolute and unrestricted liberty esp. of thought and action **b** *cap* : a member of a political party advocating libertarian principles — **libertarian** *adj* — **lib·er·tar·i·an·ism** \-ē-ə-,ni-zəm\ *n*

lib·er·tin·age \'li-bər-,tē-nij\ *n* (1611) : LIBERTINISM

lib·er·tine \'li-bər-,tēn\ *n* [ME *libertyn* freedman, fr. L *libertinus*, fr. *libertinus*, adj., of a freedman, fr. *libertus* freedman, fr. *liber*] (1577) **1 :** a freethinker esp. in religious matters — usu. used disparagingly **2 :** a person who is unrestrained by convention or morality; *specif* : one leading a dissolute life — **libertine** *adj*

lib·er·tin·ism \'li-bər-,tē-,ni-zəm, -tə-\ *n* (1611) : the quality or state of being libertine : the behavior of a libertine

lib·er·ty \'li-bər-tē\ *n, pl* **-ties** [ME, fr. MF *liberté*, fr. L *libertat-, libertas*, fr. *liber* free — more at LIBERAL] (14c) **1 :** the quality or state of being free: **a :** the power to do as one pleases **b :** freedom from physical restraint **c :** freedom from arbitrary or despotic control **d :** the positive enjoyment of various social, political, or economic rights and privileges **e :** the power of choice **2 a :** a right or immunity enjoyed by prescription or by grant : PRIVILEGE **b :** permission esp. to go freely within specified limits **3 :** an action going beyond normal limits: as **a :** a breach of etiquette or propriety : FAMILIARITY **b :** RISK, CHANCE \took foolish *liberties* with his health\ **c :** a violation of rules or a deviation from standard practice **d :** a distortion of fact **4 :** a short authorized absence from naval duty usu. for less than 48 hours **syn** see FREEDOM — **at liberty 1 :** FREE **2 :** at leisure : UNOCCUPIED

liberty cap *n* (1803) : a close-fitting conical cap used as a symbol of liberty by the French revolutionists and in the U.S. before 1800

liberty pole *n* (1770) : a tall flagstaff surmounted by a liberty cap or the flag of a republic and set up as a symbol of liberty

li·bid·i·nal \lə-'bi-d³n-əl, -'bid-n³l\ *adj* (1922) : of or relating to the libido — **li·bid·i·nal·ly** *adv*

li·bid·i·nous \-d³n-əs, -'bid-nəs\ *adj* [ME, fr. MF *libidineus*, fr. L *libidinosus*, fr. *libidin-, libido*] (15c) **1 :** having or marked by lustful desires : LASCIVIOUS **2 :** LIBIDINAL — **li·bid·i·nous·ly** *adv* — **li·bid·i·nous·ness** *n*

li·bi·do \lə-'bē-(,)dō *also* 'li-bə-,dō\ *n, pl* **-dos** [NL *libidin-, libido*, fr. L desire, lust, fr. *libēre* to please — more at LOVE] (1909) **1 :** emotional or psychic energy that in psychoanalytic theory is derived from primitive biological urges and that is usu. goal-directed **2 :** sexual drive

li·bra *for* 1 & 2a 'lē-brə, *sometimes* 'lī-brə, *for* 2b 'lē-brə *or* 'lēv-rə\ *n* [ME, fr. L (gen. *Librae*), lit., scales, pound] **1** *cap* **a :** a southern zodiacal constellation between Virgo and Scorpio represented by a pair of scales **b** (1) : the 7th sign of the zodiac in astrology — see ZODIAC table (2) : one born under the sign of Libra **2 a** *pl* **li·brae** \'lī-,brē, 'lē-,brī\ [L] : an ancient Roman unit of weight equal to 327.45 grams **b** [Sp & Pg, fr. L] : any of various Spanish, Portuguese, Colombian, or Venezuelan units of weight

Li·bran \'lē-brən, 'lī-\ *n* (1911) : LIBRA 1b(2)

li·brar·i·an \lī-'brer-ē-ən\ *n* (1703) : a specialist in the care or management of a library — **li·brar·i·an·ship** \-,ship\ *n*

li·brary \'lī-,brer-ē; *Brit usu & US sometimes* -brər-ē; *US sometimes*

-brē, ÷-,ber-ē\ *n, pl* **-brar·ies** [ME, fr. ML *librarium*, fr. L, neut. of *librarius* of books, fr. *libr-, liber* inner bark, rind, book] (14c) **1 a** : a place in which literary, musical, artistic, or reference materials (as books, manuscripts, recordings, or films) are kept for use but not for sale **b** : a collection of such materials **2 a** : a collection resembling or suggesting a library ⟨a ∼ of computer programs⟩ ⟨wine ∼⟩ **b** : MORGUE 2 **3 a** : a series of related books issued by a publisher **b** : a collection of publications on the same subject **4** : a collection of sequences of DNA and esp. recombinant DNA that are maintained in a suitable cellular environment and that represent the genetic material of a particular organism or tissue
    usage While the pronunciation \ˈlī-,brer-ē\ is the most frequent variant in the U.S., the other variants are not uncommon. The contraction \ˈlī-brē\ and the dissimilated form \ˈlī-,ber-ē\ result from the relative difficulty of repeating \r\ in successive syllables; our files contain citations for these variants from educated speakers, including college presidents and professors, as well as with somewhat greater frequency from less educated speakers.
library paste *n* (1953) : a thick white adhesive made from starch
library science *n* (ca. 1904) : the study or the principles and practices of library care and administration
li·bra·tion \lī-ˈbrā-shən\ *n* [L *libration-, libratio,* fr. *librare* to balance, fr. *libra* scales] (1669) : an oscillation in the apparent aspect of a secondary body (as a planet or a satellite) as seen from the primary object around which it revolves — **li·bra·tion·al** \-shnəl, -shə-nᵊl\ *adj* — **li·bra·to·ry** \ˈlī-brə-,tōr-ē, -,tòr-\ *adj*
libration point *n* (1962) : any of five positions in the plane of a celestial system consisting of one massive body orbiting another at which the gravitational influences of the two bodies are approximately equal
li·bret·tist \lə-ˈbre-tist\ *n* (1862) : the writer of a libretto
li·bret·to \lə-ˈbre-(,)tō\ *n, pl* **-tos** *or* **-ti** \-(,)tē\ [It, dim. of *libro* book, fr. L *libr-, liber*] (1742) **1** : the text of a work (as an opera) for the musical theater **2** : the book containing a libretto
li·bri·form \ˈlī-brə-,fȯrm\ *adj* [L *libr-, liber* + ISV *-iform*] (1877) : resembling phloem fibers
Lib·ri·um \ˈli-brē-əm\ *trademark* — used for a preparation of chlordiazepoxide
Lib·y·an \ˈli-bē-ən\ *n* (15c) **1** : a native or inhabitant of Libya **2** : a language of ancient No. Africa probably ancestral to Berber dialects — **Libyan** *adj*
lice *pl of* LOUSE
¹li·cense *or* **li·cence** \ˈlī-sᵊn(t)s\ *n* [ME, fr. MF *licence,* fr. L *licentia,* fr. *licent-, licens,* prp. of *licēre* to be permitted] (14c) **1 a** : permission to act **b** : freedom of action **2 a** : a permission granted by competent authority to engage in a business or occupation or in an activity otherwise unlawful **b** : a document, plate, or tag evidencing a license granted **3 a** : freedom that allows or is used with irresponsibility **b** : disregard for standards of personal conduct : LICENTIOUSNESS **c** : deviation from fact, form, or rule by an artist or writer for the sake of the effect gained *syn* see FREEDOM
²license *also* **licence** *vt* **li·censed; li·cens·ing** (15c) **1 a** : to issue a license to **b** : to permit or authorize esp. by formal license **2** : to give permission or consent to — **li·cens·able** \-sᵊn(t)-sə-bəl\ *adj* — **li·cens·er** \-sər\ *or* **li·cen·sor** \-sər, ,lī-sᵊn-ˈsȯr\ *n*
licensed practical nurse *n* (1951) : a person who has undergone training and obtained a license (as from a state) conferring authorization to provide routine care for the sick
li·cens·ee \,lī-sᵊn(t)-ˈsē\ *n* (ca. 1864) : one that is licensed
license plate *n* (1926) : a plate or tag (as of metal) attesting that a license has been secured and usu. bearing a registration number
li·cen·sure \ˈlī-sᵊn-shər, -,shùr\ *n* (ca. 1846) : the granting of licenses esp. to practice a profession; *also* : the state of being licensed
licente *pl of* SENTE
li·cen·ti·ate \lī-ˈsen(t)-shē-ət, *esp in sense* 2 li-\ *n* [ML *licentiatus,* fr. pp. of *licentiare* to allow, fr. L *licentia*] (1555) **1** : one who has a license granted esp. by a university to practice a profession **2** : an academic degree ranking below that of doctor given by some European universities
li·cen·tious \lī-ˈsen(t)-shəs\ *adj* [L *licentiosus,* fr. *licentia*] (1535) **1** : lacking legal or moral restraints; *esp* : disregarding sexual restraints **2** : marked by disregard for strict rules of correctness — **li·cen·tious·ly** *adv* — **li·cen·tious·ness** *n*
li·chee *var of* LITCHI
li·chen \ˈlī-kən, *Brit also* ˈli-chən\ *n* [L, fr. Gk *leichēn, lichēn,* fr. *leichein* to lick] (ca. 1657) **1** : any of several skin diseases characterized by a papular eruption **2** : any of numerous complex thallophytic plants made up of an alga and a fungus growing in symbiotic association on a solid surface (as a rock) — **li·chened** \-kənd\ *adj* — **li·chen·ous** \-kə-nəs\ *adj*
li·chen·ol·o·gy \,lī-kə-ˈnä-lə-jē\ *n* [ISV] (1855) : the study of lichens — **li·chen·o·log·i·cal** \,lī-kə-nə-ˈlä-ji-kəl\ *adj* — **li·chen·ol·o·gist** \,lī-kə-ˈnä-lə-jist\ *n*

lichen 2

lich-gate *var of* LYCH-GATE
licht \ˈlikt\ *Scot var of* LIGHT
lic·it \ˈli-sət\ *adj* [ME, fr. MF *licite,* fr. L *licitus,* fr. pp. of *licēre* to be permitted — more at LICENSE] (15c) : conforming to the requirements of the law : not forbidden by law : PERMISSIBLE *syn* see LAWFUL — **lic·it·ly** *adv*
¹lick \ˈlik\ *vb* [ME, fr. OE *liccian;* akin to OHG *leckōn* to lick, L *lingere,* Gk *leichein*] *vt* (bef. 12c) **1 a** (1) : to draw the tongue over ⟨∼ a stamp⟩ (2) : to flicker over like a tongue **b** : to take into the mouth with the tongue : LAP **2 a** : to strike repeatedly : THRASH **b** : to get the better of : OVERCOME, DEFEAT ⟨has ∼ed every problem⟩ ∼ *vi* **1** : to lap with or as if with the tongue **2** : to dart like a tongue ⟨flames ∼ing out of windows⟩ — **lick into shape** : to put into proper form or condition — **lick one's wounds** : to recover from defeat or disappointment
²lick *n* (1603) **1 a** : an act or instance of licking **b** : a small amount

: BIT ⟨couldn't swim a ∼⟩ **c** : a hasty careless effort **2 a** : a sharp hit : BLOW **b** : a directed effort : CRACK — usu. used in pl.; usu. used in the phrase *get in one's licks* **3 a** : a natural salt deposit (as a salt spring) that animals lick **b** : a block of often medicated saline preparation given to livestock to lick **4** : a musical figure; *specif* : an interpolated and usu. improvised figure or flourish **5** : a critical thrust : DIG, BARB — **lick and a promise** : a perfunctory performance of a task
lick·er·ish \ˈli-k(ə-)rish\ *adj* [alter. of *lickerous,* fr. ME *likerous,* fr. (assumed) ONF, fr. ONF *leckeur* lecher] (14c) **1** : GREEDY, DESIROUS **2** *obs* : tempting to the appetite **3** : LECHEROUS — **lick·er·ish·ly** *adv* — **lick·er·ish·ness** *n*
lick·e·ty-split \,li-kə-tē-ˈsplit\ *adv* [prob. irreg. fr. ¹*lick* + *split*] (ca. 1859) : at great speed
lick·ing *n* (1756) **1** : a sound thrashing : DRUBBING **2** : DEFEAT
lick·spit·tle \ˈlik-,spi-tᵊl\ *n* (1825) : a fawning subordinate : TOADY
lic·o·rice \ˈli-k(ə-)rish, -k(ə-)rəs\ *n* [ME *licorice,* fr. OF, fr. LL *liquiritia,* alter. of L *glycyrrhiza,* fr. Gk *glykyrrhiza,* fr. *glykys* sweet + *rhiza* root — more at DULCET, ROOT] (13c) **1 a** : the dried root of a European leguminous plant (*Glycyrrhiza glabra*) with pinnate leaves and spikes of blue flowers; *also* : an extract of this used esp. in medicine, liquors, and confectionery **b** : a candy flavored with licorice **2** : a plant yielding licorice
lic·tor \ˈlik-tər\ *n* [ME *littour,* fr. L *lictor*] (14c) : an ancient Roman officer who bore the fasces as the insignia of his office and whose duties included accompanying the chief magistrates in public appearances
¹lid \ˈlid\ *n* [ME, fr. OE *hlid;* akin to OHG *hlit* cover, and prob. to OE *hlinian* to lean — more at LEAN] (bef. 12c) **1** : a movable cover for the opening of a hollow container (as a vessel or box) **2** : EYELID **3** : the operculum in mosses **4** *slang* : HAT **5** : something that confines, limits, or suppresses : CHECK, RESTRAINT **6** : an ounce of marijuana
²lid *vt* **lid·ded; lid·ding** (13c) : to cover or supply with a lid
li·dar \ˈlī-,där\ *n* [*light* + *radar*] (1963) : a device that is similar in operation to radar but emits pulsed laser light instead of microwaves
lid·ded *adj* (bef. 12c) **1** : having or covered with a lid ⟨a ∼ tureen⟩ **2** : having lids esp. of a specified kind — usu. used in combination ⟨heavy-*lidded* eyes⟩
lid·less \ˈlid-ləs\ *adj* (14c) **1** : having no lid **2** *archaic* : WATCHFUL
li·do \ˈlē-(,)dō\ *n, pl* **lidos** [*Lido,* Italy] (1860) : a fashionable beach resort
li·do·caine \ˈlī-də-,kān\ *n* [acetan*ilid* + *-o-* + *-caine*] (ca. 1949) : a crystalline compound $C_{14}H_{22}N_2O$ that is used in the form of its hydrochloride as a local anesthetic and as an antiarrhythmic agent
¹lie \ˈlī\ *vi* **lay** \ˈlā\; **lain** \ˈlān\; **ly·ing** \ˈlī-iŋ\ [ME, fr. OE *licgan;* akin to OHG *ligen* to lie, L *lectus* bed, Gk *lechos*] (bef. 12c) **1 a** : to be or to stay at rest in a horizontal position : be prostrate : REST, RECLINE ⟨∼ motionless⟩ **b** : to assume a horizontal position — often used with *down* **c** *archaic* : to reside temporarily : stay for the night : LODGE **d** : to have sexual intercourse — used with *with* **e** : to remain inactive (as in concealment) ⟨∼ in wait⟩ **2** : to be in a helpless or defenseless state ⟨the town *lay* at the mercy of the invaders⟩ **3** *of an inanimate thing* : to be or remain in a flat or horizontal position upon a broad support ⟨books *lying* on the table⟩ **4** : to have direction : EXTEND ⟨the route *lay* to the west⟩ **5 a** : to occupy a certain relative place or position ⟨hills ∼ behind us⟩ **b** : to have a place in relation to something else ⟨the real reason ∼s deeper⟩ **c** : to have an effect through mere presence, weight, or relative position ⟨remorse *lay* heavily on him⟩ **d** : to be sustainable or admissible **6** : to remain at anchor or becalmed **7 a** : to have place : EXIST ⟨the choice *lay* between fighting or surrendering⟩ **b** : CONSIST, BELONG ⟨the success of the book ∼s in its direct style⟩ ⟨responsibility *lay* with the adults⟩ **8** : REMAIN; *esp* : to remain unused, unsought, or uncared for *usage* see LAY — **li·er** \ˈlī(-ə)r\ *n* — **lie low 1** : to lie prostrate, defeated, or disgraced **2** : to stay in hiding : strive to avoid notice **3** : to bide one's time : remain secretly ready for action
²lie *n* (1697) **1** *chiefly Brit* : LAY 6 **2** : the position or situation in which something lies ⟨a golf ball in a difficult ∼⟩ **3** : the haunt of an animal (as a fish) : COVERT **4** *Brit* : an act or instance of lying or resting
³lie *vb* **lied; ly·ing** \ˈlī-iŋ\ [ME, fr. OE *lēogan;* akin to OHG *liogan* to lie, OCS *lŭgati*] *vi* (bef. 12c) **1** : to make an untrue statement with intent to deceive **2** : to create a false or misleading impression ∼ *vt* : to bring about by telling lies ⟨*lied* his way out of trouble⟩
    syn LIE, PREVARICATE, EQUIVOCATE, PALTER, FIB mean to tell an untruth. LIE is the blunt term, imputing dishonesty ⟨*lied* about where he had been⟩. PREVARICATE softens the bluntness by implying quibbling or confusing the issue ⟨during the hearings the witness did his best to *prevaricate*⟩. EQUIVOCATE implies using words having more than one sense so as to seem to say one thing but intend another ⟨*equivocated* endlessly in an attempt to mislead their inquisitors⟩. PALTER implies making unreliable statements of fact or intention or insincere promises ⟨a swindler *paltering* with his investors⟩. FIB applies to a telling of a trivial untruth ⟨*fibbed* about the price of the new suit⟩.
⁴lie *n* [ME *lige, lie,* fr. OE *lyge;* akin to OHG *lugī,* OE *lēogan* to lie] (bef. 12c) **1 a** : an assertion of something known or believed by the speaker to be untrue with intent to deceive **b** : an untrue or inaccurate statement that may or may not be believed true by the speaker **2** : something that misleads or deceives **3** : a charge of lying
lieb·frau·milch \ˈlēp-,fraù-,milk, ˈleb-, -,milk̲, -,milsh\ *n* [G, alter. of *Liebfrauenmilch,* fr. *Liebfrauenstift,* religious foundation in Worms, Germany + *Milch* milk] (1833) : a fruity white Rhine wine
lie by *vi* (1613) : to remain inactive : REST
lied \ˈlēt, *n, pl* **lie·der** \ˈlē-dər\ [G, song, fr. OHG *liod*] (1852) : a German art song esp. of the 19th century
Lie·der·kranz \ˈlē-dər-,kran(t)s, -,krän(t)s\ *trademark* — used for a pungent surface-ripened cheese

---

\ə\ abut \ᵊ\ kitten, F table \ər\ further \a\ ash \ā\ ace \ä\ mop, mar \aù\ out \ch\ chin \e\ bet \ē\ easy \g\ go \i\ hit \ī\ ice \j\ job \ŋ\ sing \ō\ go \ò\ law \òi\ boy \th\ thin \t̲h̲\ the \ü\ loot \ù\ foot \y\ yet \zh\ vision \à, k̲, ⁿ, œ, œ̄, ue, u̇e, ᵊ\ *see* Guide to Pronunciation

lie detector *n* (1909) : an instrument for detecting physiological evidence of the tension that accompanies lying

lie down *vi* (1888) **1** : to submit meekly or abjectly to defeat, disappointment, or insult ⟨won't take that criticism *lying down*⟩ **2** : to fail to perform or to neglect one's part deliberately ⟨*lying down* on the job⟩

¹lief \'lēf, 'lēv\ *adj* [ME *lief, lef,* fr. OE *lēof;* akin to OE *lufu* love] (bef. 12c) **1** *archaic* : DEAR, BELOVED **2** *archaic* : WILLING, GLAD

²lief \'lēv, 'lēf\ *adv* (13c) : SOON, GLADLY ⟨I'd as ~ go as not⟩

¹liege \'lēj\ *adj* [ME, fr. OF, fr. LL *laeticus,* fr. *laetus* serf, of Gmc origin; akin to OFris *let* serf] (14c) **1 a** : having the right to feudal allegiance or service ⟨his ~ lord⟩ **b** : obligated to render feudal allegiance and service **2** : FAITHFUL, LOYAL

²liege *n* (14c) **1 a** : a vassal bound to feudal service and allegiance **b** : a loyal subject **2 a** : a feudal superior to whom allegiance and service are due

liege man *n* (14c) **1** : VASSAL **2** : a devoted follower

lie-in \'lī-,in\ *n* (1963) : an act of lying down (as in a public place) in organized protest or as a means of forcing compliance with demands

lien \'lēn, 'lē-ən\ *n* [MF, tie, band, fr. L *ligare* to bind — more at LIGATURE] (1531) : a charge upon real or personal property for the satisfaction of some debt or duty ordinarily arising by operation of law **2** : the security interest created by a mortgage

lie off *vi* (1573) **1** : to hold back in the early part of a race **2** : to keep a little away from the shore or another ship **3** : to cease work for a time

lie over *vi* (ca. 1847) : to await disposal or attention at a later time

li-erne \lē-'ərn, -'ern\ *n* [F, fr. MF, prob. fr. *lier* to bind, fr. L *ligare*] (1842) : a rib in Gothic vaulting that passes from one intersection of the principal ribs to another

lie to *vi* (1711) *of a ship* : to stay stationary with head to windward

lieu \'lü\ *n* [ME *liue,* fr. OF *lieu,* fr. L *locus* — more at STALL] (14c) *archaic* : PLACE, STEAD — **in lieu** : INSTEAD — **in lieu of** : in the place of : instead of

lie up *vi* (1699) **1** : to go into or remain in a dock **2** : to stay in bed or at rest

lieu-ten-an-cy \lü-'te-nən(t)-sē, *Brit* le(f)-'ten(t)-\ *n* (15c) : the office, rank, or commission of a lieutenant

lieu-ten-ant \-'te-nənt\ *n* [ME, fr. MF, fr. *lieu* + *tenant* holding, fr. *tenir* to hold, fr. L *tenēre* — more at THIN] (14c) **1 a** : an official empowered to act for a higher official **b** : an aide or representative of another in the performance of duty : ASSISTANT **2 a** (1) : FIRST LIEUTENANT (2) : SECOND LIEUTENANT **b** : a commissioned officer in the navy or coast guard ranking above a lieutenant junior grade and below a lieutenant commander **c** : a fire or police department officer ranking below a captain

lieutenant colonel *n* (1598) : a commissioned officer in the army, air force, or marine corps ranking above a major and below a colonel

lieutenant commander *n* (1839) : a commissioned officer in the navy or coast guard ranking above a lieutenant and below a commander

lieutenant general *n* (1589) : a commissioned officer in the army, air force, or marine corps who ranks above a major general and whose insignia is three stars

lieutenant governor *n* (1595) : a deputy or subordinate governor: as **a** : an elected official serving as deputy to the governor of an American state **b** : the formal head of the government of a Canadian province appointed by the federal government as the representative of the crown — **lieutenant governorship** *n*

lieutenant junior grade *n, pl* **lieutenants junior grade** (ca. 1909) : a commissioned officer in the navy or coast guard ranking above an ensign and below a lieutenant

¹life \'līf\ *n, pl* **lives** \'līvz\ [ME *lif,* fr. OE *līf;* akin to OE *libban* to live — more at LIVE] (bef. 12c) **1 a** : the quality that distinguishes a vital and functional being from a dead body **b** : a principle or force that is considered to underlie the distinctive quality of animate beings — compare VITALISM 1 **c** : an organismic state characterized by capacity for metabolism, growth, reaction to stimuli, and reproduction **2 a** : the sequence of physical and mental experiences that make up the existence of an individual **b** : one or more aspects of the process of living ⟨sex ~ of the frog⟩ **3** : BIOGRAPHY 1 **4** : spiritual existence transcending physical death **5 a** : the period from birth to death **b** : a specific phase of earthly existence ⟨adult ~⟩ **c** : the period from an event until death ⟨a judge appointed for ~⟩ **d** : a sentence of imprisonment for the remainder of a convict's life **6** : a way or manner of living **7** : LIVELIHOOD **8** : a vital or living being; *specif* : PERSON ⟨many *lives* were lost in the disaster⟩ **9** : an animating and shaping force or principle **10** : SPIRIT, ANIMATION ⟨there was no ~ in her dancing⟩ **11** : the form or pattern of something existing in reality ⟨painted from ~⟩ **12** : the period of duration, usefulness, or popularity of something ⟨the expected ~ of flashlight batteries⟩ **13** : the period of existence (as of a subatomic particle) — compare HALF-LIFE **14** : a property (as resilience or elasticity) of an inanimate substance or object resembling the animate quality of a living being **15** : living beings (as of a particular kind or environment) ⟨forest ~⟩ **16 a** : human activities **b** : animate activity and movement ⟨stirrings of ~⟩ **c** : the activities of a given sphere, area, or time ⟨the political ~ of the country⟩ **17** : one providing interest and vigor ⟨~ of the party⟩ **18** : an opportunity for continued viability ⟨gave the patient a new ~⟩ **19** *cap, Christian Science* : GOD 1b **20** : something resembling animate life ⟨a grant saved the project's ~⟩

²life *adj* (13c) **1** : of or relating to animate being **2** : LIFELONG ⟨a ~ member⟩ **3** : using a living model ⟨a ~ class⟩ **4** : of, relating to, or provided by life insurance ⟨a ~ policy⟩

life-and-death *also* **life-or-death** *adj* (1822) : involving or culminating in life or death : vitally important as if involving life or death

life belt *n* (ca. 1858) **1** *chiefly Brit* : a life preserver in the form of a buoyant belt **2** : SAFETY BELT

life-blood \'līf-,bləd, -,bləd\ *n* (1579) **1** : blood regarded as the seat of vitality **2** : a vital or life-giving force ⟨freedom of inquiry is the ~ of a university⟩

life-boat \-,bōt\ *n* (1801) : a sturdy buoyant boat (as one carried by a ship) for use in an emergency and esp. in saving lives at sea

life buoy *n* (1801) : a ring-shaped life preserver

life-care \'līf-,kar, -,ker\ *adj* (1980) : of, relating to, or being a residential complex for elderly people that provides an apartment, personal and social services, and health care for life

life cycle *n* (1873) **1** : the series of stages in form and functional activity through which an organism passes between successive recurrences of a specified primary stage **2** : LIFE HISTORY 2 **3** : a series of stages through which something (as an individual, culture, or manufactured product) passes during its lifetime

life expectancy *n* (1935) : the average life span of an individual

life force *n* (1896) : ÉLAN VITAL

life-form \'līf-,fȯrm, -,fȯrm\ *n* (1899) : the body form that characterizes a kind of organism (as a species) at maturity; *also* : a kind of organism

life-ful \'līf-fəl\ *adj* (13c) *archaic* : full of or giving vitality

life-giv-ing \-,gi-viŋ\ *adj* (1596) : giving or having power to give life and spirit : INVIGORATING

life-guard \'līf-,gärd\ *n* (1896) : a usu. expert swimmer employed (as at a beach or a pool) to safeguard other swimmers — **lifeguard** *vi*

life history *n* (1870) **1** : the history of an individual or thing **2** : a history of the changes through which an organism passes in its development from the primary stage to its natural death

life insurance *n* (1809) : insurance providing for payment of a stipulated sum to a designated beneficiary upon death of the insured

life jacket *n* (1883) : a life preserver in the form of a buoyant vest

life-less \'līf-ləs\ *adj* (bef. 12c) : having no life: **a** : DEAD **b** : INANIMATE **c** : lacking qualities expressive of life and vigor : INSIPID **d** : destitute of living beings — **life-less-ly** *adv* — **life-less-ness** *n*

life-like \'līf-,līk\ *adj* (14c) : accurately representing or imitating real life ⟨a ~ portrait⟩ — **life-like-ness** *n*

life-line \'līf-,līn\ *n* (1700) **1** : a line (as a rope) used for saving or preserving life: as **a** : a line along the outer edge of the deck of a boat or ship **b** : a line used to keep contact with a person (as a diver or astronaut) in a dangerous or potentially dangerous situation **2** : something regarded as indispensable for the maintaining or protection of life

life list *n* (1960) : a record kept of all birds sighted and identified by a birder

life-long \'līf-,lȯŋ\ *adj* (1855) **1** : lasting or continuing through life **2** : LONG-STANDING

life-man-ship \'līf-mən-,ship\ *n* (1949) : the skill or practice of achieving superiority or an appearance of superiority over others (as in conversation) by perplexing and demoralizing them

life net *n* (ca. 1904) : a strong net or sheet (as of canvas) used (as by firefighters) to catch a person jumping from a burning building

life of Ri-ley *also* **life of Reil-ly** \-'rī-lē\ [fr. the name *Riley* or *Reilly*] (1923) : a carefree comfortable way of living

life peer *n* (1869) : a British peer whose title is not hereditary — **life peerage** *n*

life preserver *n* (1804) **1** : a device (as a life jacket or life buoy) designed to save a person from drowning by providing buoyancy in water **2** *chiefly Brit* : BLACKJACK 3

lif-er \'lī-fər\ *n* (1827) **1** : a person sentenced to imprisonment for life **2** : a person who makes a career of one of the armed forces **3** : a person who has made a lifelong commitment (as to a way of life)

life raft *n* (1819) : a raft usu. made of wood or an inflatable material and designed for use by people forced into the water

life ring *n* (ca. 1909) : LIFE BUOY

life-sav-er \'līf-,sā-vər\ *n* (1887) **1** : one trained to save lives of drowning persons **2** : one that is at once timely and effective in time of distress or need

¹life-sav-ing \-,viŋ\ *adj* (1858) : designed for or used in saving lives ⟨~ drugs⟩

²lifesaving *n* (1919) : the skill or practice of saving or protecting the lives esp. of drowning persons

life science *n* (1941) : a branch of science (as biology, medicine, anthropology, or sociology) that deals with living organisms and life processes — usu. used in pl. — **life scientist** *n*

life-size \'līf-'sīz\ *or* **life-sized** \-'sīzd\ *adj* (1841) : of natural size : of the size of the original ⟨a ~ statue⟩

life span *n* (1918) **1** : the duration of existence of an individual **2** : the average length of life of a kind of organism or of a material object esp. in a particular environment or under specified circumstances

life-style \'līf-,stī(ə)l, -,stī(ə)l\ *n* (1939) : the typical way of life of an individual, group, or culture

life-support \-,sə-pȯrt, -pȯrt\ *adj* (1965) : providing support necessary to sustain life; *esp* : of or relating to a system providing such support ⟨~ equipment⟩

life support *n* (1975) : medical life-support equipment ⟨the patient was placed on ~⟩

life-support system *n* (1959) : an artificial or natural system that provides all or some of the items (as oxygen, food, water, control of temperature and pressure, disposition of carbon dioxide and body wastes) necessary for maintaining life or health

life table *n* (ca. 1859) : MORTALITY TABLE

¹life-time \'līf-,tīm\ *n* (13c) **1 a** : the duration of the existence of a living being or a thing (as a star or a subatomic particle) **b** : LIFE 12 **2** : an amount accumulated or experienced in a lifetime ⟨a ~ of regrets⟩

²lifetime *adj* (1904) **1** : LIFELONG **2** : measured or achieved over the span of a career ⟨a baseball player's ~ batting average⟩

life vest *n* (1939) : LIFE JACKET

life-way \-,wā\ *n* (1948) : LIFE 6

life-work \-'wərk\ *n* (1871) : the entire or principal work of one's lifetime; *also* : a work extending over a lifetime

life zone *n* (1901) : a region characterized by specific plants and animals

¹lift \'lift\ *n* [ME, fr. OE *lyft*] (bef. 12c) *chiefly Scot* : HEAVENS, SKY

²lift *vb* [ME, fr. ON *lypta;* akin to OE *lyft* air — more at LOFT] (14c) **1 a** : to raise from a lower to a higher position : ELEVATE **b** : to raise in rank or condition **c** : to raise in rate or amount **2** : to put an end to (a blockade or siege) by withdrawing or causing the withdrawal of investing forces **3** : REVOKE, RESCIND ⟨~ an embargo⟩ **4 a** : STEAL ⟨had her purse ~ed⟩ **b** : PLAGIARIZE **c** : to take out of normal setting ⟨~ a word out of context⟩ **5** : to take up (as a root crop or transplants) from the ground **6** : to pay off (an obligation) ⟨~ a mortgage⟩ **7** : to move from one place to another (as by aircraft) : TRANSPORT **8** : to take up (a fingerprint) from a surface ~ *vi* **1 a** : ASCEND, RISE ⟨the rocket ~ed off⟩ **b** : to appear elevated (as above surrounding objects) **2** *of inclement weather* : to dissipate and clear — **lift·able** \'lif-tə-bəl\ *adj* — **lift·er** *n*

syn LIFT, RAISE, REAR, ELEVATE, HOIST, HEAVE, BOOST mean to move from a lower to a higher place or position. LIFT usu. implies exerting effort to overcome resistance of weight ⟨*lift* the chair while I vacuum⟩. RAISE carries a stronger implication of bringing up to the vertical or to a high position ⟨scouts *raising* a flagpole⟩. REAR may add an element of suddenness to RAISE ⟨suddenly *reared* itself up on its hind legs⟩. ELEVATE may replace LIFT or RAISE esp. when exalting or enhancing is implied ⟨*elevated* the taste of the public⟩. HOIST implies lifting something heavy esp. by mechanical means ⟨*hoisted* the cargo on board⟩. HEAVE implies lifting and throwing with great effort or strain ⟨*heaved* the heavy crate inside⟩. BOOST suggests assisting to climb or advance by a push ⟨*boosted* his brother over the fence⟩.

³**lift** *n* (14c) **1** : the amount that may be lifted at one time : LOAD **2 a** : the action or an instance of lifting **b** : the action or an instance of rising **c** : elevated carriage (as of a body part) **d** : the lifting up (as of a dancer) usu. by a partner **3** : a device (as a handle or latch) for lifting **4** : an act of stealing : THEFT **5 a** : ASSISTANCE, HELP **b** : a ride esp. along one's way **6** : a layer in the heel of a shoe **7** : a rise or advance in position or condition **8** : a slight rise or elevation **9** : the distance or extent to which something rises **10** : an apparatus or machine used for hoisting: as **a** : a set of pumps used in a mine **b** *chiefly Brit* : ELEVATOR 1b **c** : an apparatus for raising an automobile (as for repair) **d** : SKI LIFT **11 a** : an elevating influence **b** : an elevation of the spirit **12 a** : the component of the total aerodynamic force acting on an airplane or airfoil that is perpendicular to the relative wind and that for an airplane constitutes the upward force that opposes the pull of gravity **b** : an updraft that can be used to increase altitude (as of a sailplane) **13** : an organized movement of people, equipment, or supplies by some form of transportation; *esp* : AIRLIFT

lift·gate \'lift-,gāt\ *n* (1953) : a rear panel (as on a station wagon) that opens upward

lift·man \-,man\ *n* (1883) *Brit* : an elevator operator

lift-off \-,óf\ *n* (ca. 1956) : a vertical takeoff by an aircraft or a rocket vehicle or missile

lift truck *n* (1926) : a small truck for lifting and transporting loads

lig·a·ment \'li-gə-mənt\ *n* [ME, fr. ML & L; ML *ligamentum*, fr. L, band, tie, fr. *ligare*] (14c) **1** : a tough band of tissue connecting the articular extremities of bones or supporting an organ in place **2** : a connecting or unifying bond ⟨the law of nations, the great ~ of mankind —Edmund Burke⟩ — **lig·a·men·tous** \-'men-təs\ *adj*

li·gand \'lī-gənd, 'li-\ *n* [L *ligandus*, gerundive of *ligare*] (1949) : a group, ion, or molecule coordinated to a central atom or molecule in a complex

li·gase \'lī-,gās, -,gāz\ *n* [ISV *lig-* (fr. L *ligare*) + *-ase*] (1961) : SYNTHETASE

li·gate \'lī-,gāt, lī-'\ *vt* **li·gat·ed; li·gat·ing** [L *ligatus*] (1599) : to tie with a ligature

li·ga·tion \lī-'gā-shən\ *n* (1597) **1** : an act of ligating **2** : something that binds : LIGATURE

lig·a·ture \'li-gə-,chùr, -chər, -,tùr, -,tyùr\ *n* [ME, fr. MF, fr. LL *ligatura*, fr. L *ligatus*, pp. of *ligare* to bind, tie; akin to MLG *lik* band, boltrope, Alb *lidh* I tie] (14c) **1 a** : something that is used to bind; *specif* : a filament (as a thread) used in surgery **b** : something that unites or connects : BOND **2** : the action of binding or tying **3** : a compound note in mensural notation indicating a group of musical notes to be sung to one syllable **4** : a printed or written character (as æ or *ff*) consisting of two or more letters or characters joined together

¹**light** \'līt\ *n* [ME, fr. OE *lēoht*; akin to OHG *lioht* light, L *luc-, lux* light, *lucēre* to shine, Gk *leukos* white] (bef. 12c) **1 a** : something that makes vision possible **b** : the sensation aroused by stimulation of the visual receptors **c** : an electromagnetic radiation in the wavelength range including infrared, visible, ultraviolet, and X rays and traveling in a vacuum with a speed of about 186,281 miles (300,000 kilometers) per second; *specif* : the part of this range that is visible to the human eye **2 a** : DAYLIGHT **b** : DAWN **3** : a source of light: as **a** : a celestial body **b** : CANDLE **c** : an electric light **4** *archaic* : SIGHT **4a 5 a** : spiritual illumination **b** : INNER LIGHT **c** : ENLIGHTENMENT **d** : TRUTH **6 a** : public knowledge ⟨facts brought to ~⟩ **b** : a particular aspect or appearance presented to view ⟨saw the matter in a different ~⟩ **7** : a particular illumination **8** : something that enlightens or informs ⟨shed some ~ on the problem⟩ **9** : a medium (as a window) through which light is admitted **10** *pl* : a set of principles, standards, or opinions ⟨worship according to one's ~s —Adrienne Koch⟩ **11** : a noteworthy person in a particular place or field **12** : a particular expression of the eye **13** *a* : LIGHTHOUSE, BEACON **b** : TRAFFIC LIGHT **14** : the representation of light in art **15** : a flame for lighting something — **in the light of 1** : from the point of view of **2** or **in light of** : in view of

²**light** *adj* (bef. 12c) **1** : having light : BRIGHT ⟨a ~ airy room⟩ **2 a** : not dark, intense, or swarthy in color or coloring : PALE **b** *of colors* : medium in saturation and high in lightness ⟨~ blue⟩ **3** *of coffee* : served with extra milk or cream

³**light** *vb* **lit** \'lit\ *or* **light·ed; light·ing** *vi* (bef. 12c) **1** : to become light : BRIGHTEN — usu. used with *up* ⟨her face *lit* up⟩ **2** : to take fire **3** : to ignite something (as a cigarette) — often used with *up* ~ *vt* **1** : to set fire to **2 a** : to conduct with a light : GUIDE **b** : ILLUMINATE ⟨rockets ~ up the sky⟩ **c** : ANIMATE, BRIGHTEN ⟨a smile *lit* up her face⟩

⁴**light** *adj* [ME, fr. OE *lēoht*; akin to OHG *lihti* light, L *levis*, Gk *elachys* small] (bef. 12c) **1 a** : having little weight : not heavy **b** : designed to carry a comparatively small load ⟨a ~ truck⟩ **c** : having relatively little weight in proportion to bulk ⟨aluminum is a ~ metal⟩ **d** : containing less than the legal, standard, or usual weight ⟨a ~ coin⟩ **2 a** : of little importance : TRIVIAL **b** : not abundant ⟨~ rain⟩ ⟨a ~ lunch⟩ **3 a** : easily disturbed ⟨a ~ sleeper⟩ **b** : exerting a minimum of force or pressure : GENTLE ⟨a ~ touch⟩ **c** : resulting from a very slight pressure : FAINT ⟨~ print⟩ **4 a** : easily endurable ⟨a ~ illness⟩ **b** : requiring little effort ⟨~ work⟩ **5** : capable of moving swiftly or nimbly ⟨~ on his feet⟩ **6 a** : FRIVOLOUS 1a ⟨~ conduct⟩ **b** : lacking

in stability : CHANGEABLE ⟨~ opinions⟩ **c** : sexually promiscuous **7** : free from care : CHEERFUL **8** : less powerful but usu. more mobile than usual for its kind ⟨~ cavalry⟩ **9 a** : made with a lower calorie content or with less of some ingredient (as salt, fat, or alcohol) than usual ⟨~ beer⟩ ⟨~ salad dressing⟩ **b** : having a relatively mild flavor **10 a** : easily digested ⟨a ~ soup⟩ **b** : well leavened ⟨a ~ crust⟩ **11** : coarse and sandy or easily pulverized ⟨~ soil⟩ **12 a** : DIZZY, GIDDY ⟨felt ~ in the head⟩ **13** : intended chiefly to entertain ⟨~ verse⟩ ⟨~ comedy⟩ **14 a** : carrying little or no cargo ⟨the ship returned ~⟩ **b** : producing goods for direct consumption by the consumer ⟨~ industry⟩ **15** : not bearing a stress or accent ⟨a ~ syllable⟩ **16** : having a clear soft quality ⟨a ~ voice⟩ **17** : being in debt to the pot in a poker game ⟨three chips ~⟩ **18** : SHORT 5d ⟨~ on experience⟩ **syn** see EASY — **light·ish** \'lī-tish\ *adj*

⁵**light** *adv* (bef. 12c) **1** : LIGHTLY **2** : with little baggage ⟨travel ~⟩

⁶**light** *vi* **lit** \'lit\ *or* **light·ed; light·ing** [ME, fr. OE *lihtan*; akin to OE *lēoht* light in weight] (bef. 12c) **1** : DISMOUNT **2** : SETTLE, ALIGHT ⟨a bird *lit* on the lawn⟩ **3** : to fall unexpectedly — usu. used with *on* or *upon* **4** : to arrive by chance : HAPPEN — usu. used with *on* or *upon* ⟨*lit* upon a solution⟩ — **light into** : to attack forcefully ⟨I *lit into* that food until I'd finished off the heel of the loaf —Helen Eustis⟩

light adaptation *n* (1900) : the process including contraction of the pupil and decrease in visual purple by which the eye adapts to conditions of increased illumination

light–adapt·ed \'lit-ə-,dap-təd\ *adj* (1900) : adjusted for vision in bright light : having undergone light adaptation

light air *n* (ca. 1881) : wind having a speed of 1 to 3 miles (1.6 to 4.8 kilometers) per hour — see BEAUFORT SCALE table

light bread \'lit-,bred\ *n* [²*light*] (1821) *chiefly Southern & Midland* : bread in loaves made from white flour leavened with yeast

light breeze *n* (ca. 1881) : wind having a speed of 4 to 7 miles (6.4 to 11 kilometers) per hour — see BEAUFORT SCALE table

light·bulb \'lit-,bəlb\ *n* (1884) : INCANDESCENT LAMP

light chain *n* (1964) : either of the two smaller of the four polypeptide chains comprising antibodies — compare HEAVY CHAIN

light curve *n* (1890) : a graph showing the variation in brightness of a celestial object (as a variable star) over a period of time

light–emitting diode *n* (1970) : LED

¹**light·en** \'lī-t³n\ *vb* **light·ened; light·en·ing** \'lit-niŋ, 'li-t³n-iŋ\ [ME *lightenen*, fr. *light*] *vt* (14c) **1** : to make light or clear : ILLUMINATE **2** *archaic* : ENLIGHTEN **3** : to make (as a color) lighter ~ *vi* **1 a** *archaic* : to shine brightly **b** : to grow lighter : BRIGHTEN **2** : to give out flashes of lightning — **light·en·er** \'lit-nər, 'li-t³n-ər\ *n*

²**light·en** *vb* **light·ened; light·en·ing** \'lit-niŋ, 'li-t³n-iŋ\ *vt* (14c) **1 a** : to relieve of a burden in whole or in part ⟨the news ~ed his mind⟩ **b** : to reduce in weight or quantity : LESSEN ⟨~ her duties⟩ **c** : to make less wearisome : ALLEVIATE ⟨~ our sorrow⟩ **2** : CHEER, GLADDEN ~ *vi* **1** : to become lighter or less burdensome **2** : to become more cheerful **syn** see RELIEVE — **light·en·er** \'lit-nər, 'li-t³n-ər\ *n*

lighten up *vi* (ca. 1968) : to take things less seriously

¹**light·er** \'lī-tər\ *n* [ME, fr. (assumed) MD *lichter*, fr. MD *lichten* to unload; akin to OE *lēoht* light in weight] (14c) : a large usu. flat≈ bottomed barge used esp. in unloading or loading ships

²**lighter** *vt* (1840) : to convey by a lighter

³**light·er** \'lī-tər\ *n* (1553) **1** : one that lights or sets a fire **2** : a device for lighting a fire; *esp* : a mechanical or electrical device used for lighting cigarettes, cigars, or pipes

light·er·age \'lī-tə-rij\ *n* (15c) **1** : the loading, unloading, or transportation of goods by means of a lighter **2** : a price paid for lightering

lighter–than–air *adj* (1903) : of less weight than the air displaced

light·face \'lit-,fās\ *n* (ca. 1871) : a typeface having comparatively light thin lines; *also* : printing in lightface — **light·faced** \-,fāst\ *adj*

light·fast \-,fast\ *adj* (1950) : resistant to light and esp. to sunlight; *esp* : colorfast to light — **light·fast·ness** \-,fas(t)-nəs\ *n*

light–fin·gered \-,fiŋ-gərd\ *adj* (1547) **1** : showing adroitness in stealing or a tendency to steal esp. by picking pockets or shoplifting **2** : having a light and dexterous touch : NIMBLE — **light–fin·gered·ness** *n*

light–foot·ed \-,fù-təd\ *also* **light–foot** \-,fùt\ *adj* (15c) **1** : having a light and springy step **2** : moving gracefully and nimbly

light guide *n* (1951) : an optical fiber used esp. for telecommunication

light–hand·ed \'lit-,han-dəd\ *adj* (15c) : having a light or delicate touch : FACILE — **light–hand·ed·ness** *n*

light–head·ed \-,he-dəd\ *adj* (1537) **1** : mentally disoriented : DIZZY **2** : lacking in maturity or seriousness : FRIVOLOUS — **light–head·ed·ly** *adv* — **light–head·ed·ness** *n*

light–heart·ed \-,här-təd\ *adj* (15c) **1** : free from care, anxiety, or seriousness : GAY **2** : cheerfully optimistic and hopeful : EASYGOING — **light–heart·ed·ly** *adv* — **light–heart·ed·ness** *n*

light heavyweight *n* (1903) : a boxer in a weight division having a maximum limit of 175 pounds for professionals and 178 pounds for amateurs — compare HEAVYWEIGHT, MIDDLEWEIGHT

light·house \'lit-,haùs\ *n* (1622) **1** : a structure (as a tower) with a powerful light that gives a continuous or intermittent signal to navigators **2** : BEACON 3

light housekeeping *n* (1904) **1** : domestic work restricted to the less laborious duties **2** : housekeeping in quarters with limited facilities for cooking

light·ing \'li-tiŋ\ *n* (bef. 12c) **1 a** : ILLUMINATION **b** : IGNITION **2** : an artificial supply of light or the apparatus providing it

light·less \'lit-ləs\ *adj* (14c) **1** : receiving no light : DARK **2** : giving no light

light·ly \'lit-lē\ *adv* (bef. 12c) : in a light manner: as **a** : with little weight or force : GENTLY **b** : with indifference or carelessness : UNCONCERNEDLY ⟨the problem should not be passed over —Shelly Halpern⟩ **c** : with little difficulty : EASILY **d** : GAILY, CHEERFULLY **e**

\ə\ abut \ʼ\ kitten, F table \ər\ further \a\ ash \ā\ ace \ä\ mop, mar
\aù\ out \ch\ chin \e\ bet \ē\ easy \g\ go \i\ hit \ī\ ice \j\ job
\ŋ\ sing \ō\ go \ò\ law \òi\ boy \th\ thin \t̲h̲\ the \ü\ loot \ù\ foot
\y\ yet \zh\ vision \ä, k̲, ⁿ, œ, œ̄, ᵫ, ᵫ̄, ʸ\ see Guide to Pronunciation

: in an agile manner : NIMBLY, SWIFTLY   f : in a small degree or amount ⟨~ salted food⟩

light meter n (1921) : a small and often portable device for measuring illumination; *esp* : EXPOSURE METER

light-mind·ed \'līt-ˌmīn-dəd\ adj (1611) : lacking in seriousness : FRIVOLOUS — **light-mind·ed·ly** adv — **light-mind·ed·ness** n

¹**light·ness** \-nəs\ n (bef. 12c) 1 : the quality or state of being illuminated : ILLUMINATION 2 : the attribute of object colors by which the object appears to reflect or transmit more or less of the incident light — compare BRIGHTNESS 2, HUE 2c, SATURATION 4

²**lightness** n (12c) 1 : the quality or state of being light esp. in weight 2 : lack of seriousness and stability of character often accompanied by casual heedlessness 3 a : the quality or state of being nimble b : an ease and gaiety of style or manner 4 : a lack of weightiness or force : DELICACY

¹**light·ning** \'līt-niŋ\ n [ME, fr. gerund of *lightenen* to lighten] (13c) 1 : the flashing of light produced by a discharge of atmospheric electricity; *also* : the discharge itself 2 : a sudden stroke of fortune

²**lightning** adj (1640) : having or moving with or as if with the speed and suddenness of lightning ⟨a ~ assault⟩

³**lightning** vi **light·ninged; lightning** (1903) : to discharge a flash of lightning

lightning arrester n (1860) : a device for protecting an electrical apparatus from damage by lightning

lightning bug n (1778) : FIREFLY

lightning rod n (1789) 1 : a grounded metallic rod set up on a structure (as a building) to protect it from lightning 2 : one that serves to divert attack from another or as a frequent target of criticism

light-o'-love \ˌlīt-ə-'ləv\ *also* **light-of-love** \-əv-'\ n, pl **light-o'-loves** *also* **lights-of-love** (1589) 1 : PROSTITUTE 2 : LOVER, PARAMOUR

light opera n (1882) : OPERETTA

light out vi [²*light*] (1866) 1 : to leave in a hurry ⟨*lit out* for home at once⟩ 2 : SET OFF

light pen n (1958) : a pen-shaped device for direct interaction with a computer through a cathode-ray tube display

light pipe n (1950) : an optical fiber or a solid transparent plastic rod for transmitting light lengthwise

light-plane \'līt-ˌplān\ n (1923) : a small and comparatively lightweight airplane; *esp* : a privately owned passenger airplane

light pollution n (1971) : artificial skylight (as from city lights) that interferes with astronomical observations

light quantum n (1925) : PHOTON; *esp* : one of luminous radiation

light-rail \'līt-ˌrā(ə)l\ n, often attrib (1975) : a means of urban railway transportation using trolley cars

light reaction n (ca. 1929) : the phase of photosynthesis that requires the presence of light and that involves photophosphorylation

lights \'līts\ n pl [ME *lightes*, fr. *light* light in weight] (12c) : the lungs esp. of a slaughtered animal

light-ship \'līt-ˌship\ n (1837) : a ship equipped with a brilliant light and moored at a place dangerous to navigation

light show n (1966) : a kaleidoscopic display of colored lights, slides, and film loops

¹**light-some** \'līt-səm\ adj (14c) 1 : free from care : LIGHTHEARTED 2 : AIRY, NIMBLE — **light·some·ly** adv — **light·some·ness** n

²**lightsome** adj (15c) 1 : well lighted : BRIGHT 2 : giving light

lights-out \'līts-'aút\ n (1868) 1 : a command or signal for putting out lights 2 : a prescribed bedtime for persons living under discipline

light table n (ca. 1948) : a device that projects even light through a flat translucent surface over which films or tracings may be spread out and viewed

light-tight \'līt-ˌtīt\ adj (1884) : LIGHTPROOF

light trap n (1906) 1 : a device that allows movement of a sliding part or passage of a person (as into a darkroom) but excludes light 2 : a device for collecting or destroying insects that consists of a bright light in association with a trapping or killing medium

light water n (1933) : WATER 1a — compare HEAVY WATER

¹**light·weight** \'līt-ˌwāt\ n (1773) 1 : one of less than average weight; *specif* : a boxer in a weight division having a maximum limit of 135 pounds for professionals and 132 pounds for amateurs 2 : one of little consequence or ability ⟨shows up its author as a ~ —C. J. Rolo⟩

²**lightweight** adj (1809) 1 : lacking in earnestness, ability, or profundity : INCONSEQUENTIAL 2 : having less than average weight 3 : of, relating to, or characteristic of a lightweight ⟨the ~ championship⟩

light-wood \'līt-ˌwúd, 'lī-təd\ n (1685) *chiefly Southern* : wood used for kindling; *esp* : coniferous wood abounding in pitch

light-year \'līt-ˌyir\ n (1888) 1 : a unit of length in astronomy equal to the distance that light travels in one year in a vacuum or about 5.88 trillion miles (9.46 trillion kilometers) 2 : an extremely large measure of comparison (as of distance, time, or quality) ⟨seems like *light-years* ago⟩ ⟨has *light-years* more talent⟩ ⟨two minutes and yet ~s away from the crowded village —Suzanne Patterson⟩

lign- or **ligni-** or **ligno-** *comb form* [L *lign-*, *ligni-*, fr. *lignum*] : wood ⟨*lignin*⟩ ⟨*lignocellulose*⟩

lig·ne·ous \'lig-nē-əs\ adj [L *ligneus*, fr. *lignum* wood, prob. fr. *legere* to gather — more at LEGEND] (1626) : of or resembling wood

lig·ni·fy \'lig-nə-ˌfī\ vb **-fied; -fy·ing** [F *lignifier*, fr. L *lignum*] vt (ca. 1828) : to convert into wood or woody tissue ~ vi : to become wood or woody — **lig·ni·fi·ca·tion** \ˌlig-nə-fə-'kā-shən\ n

lig·nin \'lig-nən\ n (1822) : an amorphous polymer related to cellulose that provides rigidity and together with cellulose forms the woody cell walls of plants and the cementing material between them

lig·nite \'lig-ˌnīt\ n [F, fr. L *lignum*] (ca. 1808) : a usu. brownish black coal intermediate between peat and bituminous coal; *esp* : one in which the texture of the original wood is distinct — called also *brown coal* — **lig·nit·ic** \lig-'ni-tik\ adj

lig·no·cel·lu·lose \ˌlig-nō-'sel-yə-ˌlōs, -ˌlōz\ n [ISV] (1900) : any of several closely related substances constituting the essential part of woody cell walls of plants and consisting of cellulose intimately associated with lignin — **lig·no·cel·lu·los·ic** \-ˌsel-yə-'lō-sik, -zik\ adj

lig·no·sul·fo·nate \-ˈsəl-fə-ˌnāt\ n (1908) : any of various compounds produced from the spent sulfite liquor in the pulping of softwood in papermaking and used esp. for binders and dispersing agents

lig·num vi·tae \ˌlig-nəm-'vī-tē\ n, pl **lignum vitaes** [NL, lit., wood of life] (1594) 1 : the very hard heavy wood of any of several tropical American guaiacums 2 : a tree yielding lignum vitae

lig·u·la \'li-gyə-lə\ n, pl **-lae** \-ˌlē, -ˌlī\ *also* **-las** [NL] (ca. 1760) 1 : LIGULE 2 : the distal lobed part of the labium of an insect

lig·u·late \'li-gyə-lət, -ˌlāt\ adj (1760) 1 : furnished with ligules, ligulae, or ligulate corollas 2 [L *ligula*] : shaped like a strap ⟨~ corolla of a ray flower⟩

lig·ule \'li-(ˌ)gyü(ə)l\ n [NL *ligula*, fr. L, small tongue, strap, fr. *lingere* to lick — more at LICK] (ca. 1847) : a scalelike projection esp. on a plant: as a : a thin appendage of a foliage leaf and esp. of the sheath of a blade of grass b : a ligulate corolla of a ray floret in a composite head

lig·ure \'li-ˌgyúr, -gyər\ n [ME *lygire*, fr. LL *ligurius*, fr. Gk *ligyrion*] (13c) : a traditional precious stone that is prob. the jacinth

lik·able or **like·able** \'lī-kə-bəl\ adj (1730) : having qualities that bring about a favorable regard : PLEASANT, AGREEABLE — **lik·abil·i·ty** \ˌlī-kə-'bi-lə-tē\ n — **lik·able·ness** n

¹**like** \'līk\ vb **liked; lik·ing** [ME, fr. OE *līcian*; akin to OE *gelīc* alike] vt (bef. 12c) 1 *chiefly dial* : to be suitable or agreeable to ⟨I like onions but they don't ~ me⟩ 2 a : to feel attraction toward or take pleasure in : ENJOY ⟨~s baseball⟩ b : to feel toward : REGARD ⟨how would you ~ a change⟩ 3 : to wish to have : WANT ⟨would ~ a drink⟩ 4 : to do well in ⟨this plant ~s dry soil⟩ ⟨my car does not ~ cold weather⟩ ~ vi 1 *dial* : APPROVE 2 : to feel inclined : CHOOSE, PREFER ⟨leave any time you ~⟩

²**like** n (1851) 1 : LIKING, PREFERENCE 2 : something that one likes

³**like** adj [ME, alter. of *ilich*, fr. OE *gelīc* like, alike, fr. *ge-*, associative prefix + *līc* body; akin to OHG *gilīh* like, alike, Lith *lygus* like — more at CO-] (13c) 1 a : the same or nearly the same (as in appearance, character, or quantity) ⟨suits of ~ design⟩ — formerly used with *as*, *unto*, *of* ⟨it behoved him to be made ~ unto his brethren —Heb 2:17(AV)⟩ b *chiefly Brit* : closely resembling the subject or original ⟨the portrait is very ~⟩ 2 : LIKELY ⟨the importance of statistics as the one discipline ~ to give accuracy of mind —H. J. Laski⟩

⁴**like** prep (13c) 1 a : having the characteristics of : similar to ⟨his house is ~ a barn⟩ ⟨it's ~ when we were kids⟩ b : typical of ⟨was ~ him to do that⟩ c : comparable to : APPROXIMATING ⟨costs something ~ fifty cents⟩ 2 : in the manner of : similarly to ⟨acts ~ a fool⟩ 3 : as though there would be ⟨looks ~ rain⟩ 4 : such as ⟨a subject ~ physics⟩ 5 — used to form intensive or ironic phrases ⟨fought ~ hell⟩ ⟨~ fun he did⟩ ⟨laughed ~ anything⟩

⁵**like** n (13c) 1 a : one that is similar : COUNTERPART, EQUAL ⟨have . . . never seen the ~ before —Sir Winston Churchill⟩ b : KIND 4a ⟨put him and his ~ to some job —J. R. R. Tolkien⟩ — used with *the* and often followed by *of* and a substantive, or with a preceding possessive 2 : one of many that are similar to each other — used chiefly in proverbial expressions ⟨~ breeds like⟩ — **and the like** 1 : ET CETERA — **the likes of** 1 : such people as : such things as ⟨reads *the likes of* Austen and Browning⟩ 2 : such a one as and perhaps others similar to — often used with a singular object and usu. with disparaging overtones ⟨have no use for *the likes of* you⟩

⁶**like** adv (14c) 1 *archaic* : EQUALLY 2 : LIKELY, PROBABLY ⟨you'll try it, some day, ~ enough —Mark Twain⟩ 3 a : to some extent : RATHER, ALTOGETHER ⟨saunter over nonchalantly ~ —Walter Karig⟩ b — used interjectionally in informal speech often to emphasize a word or phrase (as in "He was, like, gorgeous") or for an apologetic, vague, or unassertive effect (as in "I need to, like, borrow some money") 4 : NEARLY : APPROXIMATELY ⟨the actual interest is more ~ 18 percent⟩ — used interjectionally in informal speech with expressions of measurement ⟨it was, ~, five feet long⟩ ⟨goes there every day, ~⟩ — **as like as not** or **like as not** : PROBABLY

⁷**like** conj (14c) 1 a : AS IF ⟨middle-aged men who looked ~ they might be out for their one night of the year —Norman Mailer⟩ b — used in intensive phrases ⟨drove ~ mad⟩ ⟨hurts ~ crazy⟩ 2 : in the same way that : AS ⟨they raven down scenery ~ children do sweetmeats —John Keats⟩ 3 a : in the way or manner that ⟨the violin sounds ~ an old masterpiece should⟩ ⟨did it ~ you told me⟩ b — used interjectionally in informal speech often with the verb *be* to introduce a quotation, paraphrase, or thought expressed by or imputed to the subject of the verb, or with *it's* to report a generally held opinion ⟨so I'm ~, "Give me a break"⟩ ⟨it's ~, "Who cares what he thinks?"⟩ 4 : such as ⟨a bag ~ a doctor carries⟩ ⟨when your car has trouble — ~ when it won't start⟩ — used interjectionally in informal speech ⟨often stays up late, until ~ three in the morning⟩

   usage *Like* has been used as a conjunction since the 14th century. In the 14th, 15th, and 16th centuries it was used in serious literature, but not often; in the 17th and 18th centuries it grew more frequent but less literary. It became markedly more frequent in literary use again in the 19th century. By mid-century it was coming under critical fire, but not from grammarians, oddly enough, who were wrangling over whether it could be called a preposition or not. There is no doubt that, after 600 years of use, conjunctive *like* is firmly established. It has been used by many prestigious literary figures of the past, though perhaps not in their most elevated works; in modern use it may be found in literature, journalism, and scholarly writing. While the present objection to it is perhaps more heated than rational, someone writing in a formal prose style may well prefer to use *as*, *as if*, *such as*, or an entirely different construction instead.

⁸**like** or **liked** \'līkt\ *verbal auxiliary* (15c) *chiefly dial* : came near : was near ⟨just ~ to fell out of bed —Helen Eustis⟩

-like adj comb form : resembling or characteristic of ⟨bell-*like*⟩ ⟨lady-*like*⟩

like·li·hood \'lī-klē-ˌhúd\ n (14c) : PROBABILITY ⟨a strong ~ that he is correct —T. D. Anderson⟩

¹**like·ly** \'lī-klē\ adj **like·li·er; -est** [ME, fr. ON *glíkligr*, fr. *glíkr* like; akin to OE *gelīc*] (14c) 1 : having a high probability of occurring or being true : very probable ⟨rain is ~ today⟩ 2 : apparently qualified : SUITABLE ⟨a ~ place⟩ 3 : RELIABLE, CREDIBLE ⟨a ~ enough story⟩ 4 : PROMISING ⟨a ~ candidate⟩ 5 : ATTRACTIVE ⟨a ~ child⟩

²**likely** adv (14c) : in all probability : PROBABLY ⟨those who seek power will most ~ wind up exercising it —Halton Arp⟩

like–mind·ed \'līk-'mīn-dəd\ *adj* (1526) : having a like disposition or purpose : of the same mind or habit of thought — **like–mind·ed·ly** *adv* — **like–mind·ed·ness** *n*

lik·en \'lī-kən\ *vt* **lik·ened; lik·en·ing** \'lī-kə-niŋ, 'līk-niŋ\ (14c) : COMPARE

like·ness \'līk-nəs\ *n* (bef. 12c) **1** : COPY, PORTRAIT **2** : APPEARANCE, SEMBLANCE **3** : the quality or state of being like : RESEMBLANCE
syn LIKENESS, SIMILARITY, RESEMBLANCE, SIMILITUDE, ANALOGY mean agreement or correspondence in details. LIKENESS implies a closer correspondence than SIMILARITY which often implies that things are merely somewhat alike ⟨a remarkable *likeness* to his late father⟩ ⟨some *similarity* between the two cases⟩. RESEMBLANCE implies similarity chiefly in appearance or external qualities ⟨statements that bear little *resemblance* to the truth⟩. SIMILITUDE applies chiefly to correspondence between abstractions ⟨two schools of social thought showing points of *similitude*⟩. ANALOGY implies likeness or parallelism in relations rather than in appearance or qualities ⟨pointed out *analogies* to past wars⟩.

like·wise \'līk-,wīz\ *adv* (15c) **1** : in like manner : SIMILARLY ⟨go and do ~⟩ **2** : in addition **3** : similarly so with me ⟨answered "~" to "Pleased to meet you"⟩

lik·ing \'lī-kiŋ\ *n* (14c) : favorable regard : FONDNESS, TASTE ⟨had a greater ~ for law —E. M. Coulter⟩ ⟨took a ~ to the newcomer⟩

li·ku·ta \li-'kü-tə\ *n, pl* **ma·ku·ta** \mä-\ [of Bantu origin] (1967) — see *zaire* at MONEY table

li·lac \'lī-,läk, -,lak, -lək\ *n* [obs. F (now *lilas*), fr. Ar *līlak*, fr. Per *nīlak* bluish, fr. *nil* blue, fr. Skt *nīla* dark blue] (1625) **1 a** : a European shrub (*Syringa vulgaris*) of the olive family that is often an escape in No. America and has cordate ovate leaves and large panicles of fragrant pink-purple or white flowers **b** : a tree or shrub congeneric with the lilac **2** : a variable color averaging a moderate purple

lil·an·ge·ni \,li-lən-'ge-nē\ *n, pl* **em·a·lan·ge·ni** \,e-mə-lən-'ge-nē\ [Swazi] (ca. 1976) — see MONEY table

lil·ied \'li-lēd\ *adj* (1614) **1** *archaic* : resembling a lily in fairness **2** : full of or covered with lilies

Lil·ith \'li-ləth\ *n* [LHeb *lilīth*, fr. Heb, a female demon] **1** : a female figure who in rabbinic legend is Adam's first wife, is supplanted by Eve, and becomes an evil spirit **2** : a famous witch in medieval demonology

Lil·li·put \'li-li-(,)pət\ *n* : an island in Swift's *Gulliver's Travels* where the inhabitants are six inches tall

lil·li·pu·tian \,li-li-'pyü-shən\ *adj, often cap* (1726) **1** : of, relating to, or characteristic of the Lilliputians or the island of Lilliput **2 a** : SMALL, MINIATURE **b** : PETTY

Lilliputian *n* **1** : an inhabitant of Lilliput **2** *often not cap* : one resembling a Lilliputian; *esp* : an undersized individual

lilt \'lilt\ *n* (ca. 1680) **1** : a spirited and usu. cheerful song or tune **2** : a rhythmical swing, flow, or cadence **3** : a springy buoyant movement

²lilt *vb* [ME *lulten* to sound an alarm] *vt* (1722) : to sing or play in a lively cheerful manner ~ *vi* **1** : to sing or speak rhythmically and with fluctuating pitch **2** : to move in a lively springy manner

lilt·ing \'lil-tiŋ\ *adj* (1800) **1** : characterized by a rhythmical swing or cadence ⟨a ~ stride⟩ **2** : CHEERFUL, BUOYANT ⟨a ~ comedy⟩ — **lilt·ing·ly** \-lē\ *adv* — **lilt·ing·ness** *n*

lily \'li-lē\ *n, pl* **lil·ies** [ME *lilie*, fr. OE, fr. L *lilium*] (bef. 12c) **1** : any of a genus (*Lilium* of the family Liliaceae, the lily family) of erect perennial leafy-stemmed bulbous herbs that are native to the northern hemisphere and are widely cultivated for their showy flowers; *broadly* : any of various plants of the lily family or of the related amaryllis or iris families **2** : any of various plants with showy flowers: as **a** : a scarlet anemone (*Anemone coronaria*) of the Mediterranean region **b** : WATER LILY **c** : CALLA LILY **3** : FLEUR-DE-LIS 2

²lily *adj* (ca. 1553) : resembling a lily in fairness, purity, or fragility ⟨my lady's ~ hand —John Keats⟩

lily–liv·ered \'li-lē-'li-vərd\ *adj* (1605) : lacking courage : COWARDLY

lily of the valley (1563) : a low perennial herb (*Convallaria majalis*) of the lily family that has usu. two large oblong lanceolate leaves and a raceme of fragrant nodding bell-shaped white flowers

lily pad *n* (1814) : a floating leaf of a water lily

¹lily–white \'li-lē-'hwīt, -'wīt\ *adj* (14c) **1** : white as a lily **2** : characterized by or favoring the exclusion of blacks esp. from politics **3** : IRREPROACHABLE, PURE

²lily–white *n* (ca. 1903) : a member of a lily-white political organization

Li·ma \'lē-mə\ (ca. 1952) — a communications code word for the letter *l*

li·ma bean \'lī-mə-\ *n* [*Lima*, Peru] (1756) **1 a** : a bushy or tall-growing tropical American bean (*Phaseolus limensis*) that is widely cultivated for its flat edible usu. pale green or whitish seeds **b** : SIEVA BEAN **2** : the seed of a lima bean

li·ma·çon \,lē-mə-'sōⁿ\ *n* [F, lit., snail, fr. OF, dim. of *limaz* slug, snail, fr. L *limax*; akin to Russ *slimak* snail and prob. to OE *līm* birdlime — more at LIME] (1874) : a curve that is the locus of a variable point on a line as the line revolves about a fixed point of intersection with a circle while the variable point is always a fixed distance along the line from its second and variable point of intersection with the circle

¹limb \'lim\ *n* [ME *lim*, fr. OE; akin to ON *limr* limb and perh. to OE *lith* limb] (bef. 12c) **1 a** : one of the projecting paired appendages (as wings) of an animal body used esp. for movement and grasping but sometimes modified into sensory or sexual organs **b** : a leg or arm of a human being **2** : a large primary branch of a tree **3** : an active member or agent **4** : EXTENSION, BRANCH **5** : a mischievous child — **limb·less** \'lim-ləs\ *adj* — **limby** \'li-mē\ *adj* — **out on a limb** : in an exposed or dangerous position with little chance of retreat

²limb *vt* (1674) **1** : DISMEMBER **2** : to cut off the limbs of (a felled tree)

³limb *n* [L *limbus* border] (ca. 1677) **1** : the outer edge of the apparent disk of a celestial body : the expanded portion of an organ or structure; *esp* : the spreading upper portion of a gamopetalous corolla as distinguished from the lower tubular portion

lim·ba \'lim-bə\ *n* [origin unknown] (1943) **1** : a tall whitish-trunked West African tree (*Terminalia superba*) with straight-grained wood **2** : the wood of a limba

lim·beck \'lim-,bek\ *n* [ME *lembike*, fr. ML *alembicum*] (14c) : ALEMBIC

limbed \'limd\ *adj* (14c) : having limbs esp. of a specified kind or number — usu. used in combination ⟨strong-*limbed*⟩

¹lim·ber \'lim-bər\ *n* [ME *lymour*] (15c) : a two-wheeled vehicle to which a gun or caisson may be attached

²limber *adj* [origin unknown] (1565) **1** : capable of being shaped : FLEXIBLE **2** : having a supple and resilient quality (as of mind or body) : AGILE, NIMBLE — **lim·ber·ly** *adv* — **lim·ber·ness** *n*

³limber *vb* **lim·bered; lim·ber·ing** \-b(ə-)riŋ\ *vt* (1748) : to cause to become limber ⟨~ up his fingers⟩ ~ *vi* : to become limber ⟨~ up by running⟩

lim·bic \'lim-bik\ *adj* [NL *limbicus* of a border or margin, fr. L *limbus*] (1882) : of, relating to, or being the limbic system of the brain

limbic system *n* (1952) : a group of subcortical structures (as the hypothalamus, the hippocampus, and the amygdala) of the brain that are concerned esp. with emotion and motivation

¹lim·bo \'lim-(,)bō\ *n, pl* **limbos** [ME, fr. ML, abl. of *limbus* limbo, fr. L, border] (14c) **1** *often cap* : an abode of souls that are according to Roman Catholic theology barred from heaven because of not having received Christian baptism **2 a** : a place or state of restraint or confinement **b** : a place or state of neglect or oblivion ⟨proposals kept in ~⟩ **c** : an intermediate or transitional place or state **d** : a state of uncertainty

²limbo *n, pl* **limbos** [E of Trinidad & Barbados; akin to Jamaican E *limba* to bend, fr. E *³limber*] (ca. 1950) : a West Indian acrobatic dance orig. for men that involves bending over backwards and passing under a horizontal pole lowered slightly for each successive pass

Lim·burg·er \'lim-,bər-gər\ *n* [Flem, now from Limburg, fr. *Limburg*, Belgium] (1817) : a pungent semisoft surface-ripened cheese

lim·bus \'lim-bəs\ *n* [L, border] (1877) : the marginal region of the cornea of the eye by which it is continuous with the sclera

¹lime \'līm\ *n* [ME, fr. OE *līm*; akin to OHG *līm* birdlime, L *līmus* mud, slime, and perh. to L *linere* to smear] (bef. 12c) **1** : BIRDLIME **2 a** : a caustic highly infusible solid that consists of calcium oxide often together with magnesium oxide, that is obtained by calcining forms of calcium carbonate (as shells or limestone), and that is used in building (as in mortar and plaster) and in agriculture — called also quicklime **b** : a dry white powder consisting essentially of calcium hydroxide that is made by treating quicklime with water **c** : CALCIUM ⟨carbonate of ~⟩

²lime *vt* **limed; lim·ing** (13c) **1** : to smear with a sticky substance (as birdlime) **2** : to entangle with or as if with birdlime **3** : to treat or cover with lime ⟨~ the lawn in the spring⟩

³lime *adj* (15c) : of, relating to, or containing lime or limestone

⁴lime *n* [alter. of ME *lind*, fr. OE; akin to OHG *linta* linden] (1625) : LINDEN 1a

⁵lime *n* [F, fr. Sp *lima*, fr. Ar *līma, līm*] (1638) **1** : the small globose yellowish green fruit of a lime with an acid juicy pulp used as a flavoring agent and as a source of vitamin C **2** : a spiny tropical citrus tree (*Citrus aurantifolia*) with elliptical oblong narrowly winged leaves

lime·ade \,līm-'ād, 'lī-,mād\ *n* (1892) : a beverage of sweetened lime juice mixed with plain or carbonated water

lime glass *n* (ca. 1909) : glass containing a substantial proportion of lime

lime–juic·er \'līm-jü-sər\ *n* [fr. the use of lime juice on British ships as a beverage to prevent scurvy] (1859) **1** *slang* : ENGLISHMAN **2** *slang* **a** : a British ship **b** : a British sailor

lime–kiln \-,kil, -,kiln\ *n* (13c) : a kiln or furnace for reducing limestone or shells to lime by burning

¹lime·light \-,līt\ *n* (1826) **1 a** : a stage lighting instrument producing illumination by means of an oxyhydrogen flame directed on a cylinder of lime and usu. equipped with a lens to concentrate the light in a beam **b** : the white light produced by such an instrument **c** *Brit* : SPOTLIGHT **2** : the center of public attention

²limelight *vt* (1909) : to center attention on : SPOTLIGHT

li·men \'lī-mən\ *n* [L *limin-, limen* transverse beam in a door frame, threshold; prob. akin to L *limus* transverse] (1895) : THRESHOLD 3a

lim·er·ick \'li-mə-rik, 'lim-rik\ *n* [*Limerick*, Ireland] (1896) : a light or humorous verse form of 5 chiefly anapestic verses of which lines 1, 2, and 5 are of 3 feet and lines 3 and 4 are of 2 feet with a rhyme scheme of *aabba*

lime·stone \'līm-,stōn\ *n* (14c) : a rock that is formed chiefly by accumulation of organic remains (as shells or coral), consists mainly of calcium carbonate, is extensively used in building, and yields lime when burned

lime–twig \'līm-,twig\ *n* (15c) **1** : a twig covered with birdlime to catch birds **2** : SNARE

lime–wa·ter \-,wȯ-tər, -,wä-\ *n* (ca. 1500) : an alkaline water solution of calcium hydroxide used as an antacid

¹lim·ey \'lī-mē\ *n, pl* **limeys** *often cap* [*lime*-juicer + *⁴-y*] (1918) **1** *slang* : a British sailor **2** *slang* : ENGLISHMAN

²limey *var of* LIMY

lim·i·nal \'li-mə-n²l\ *adj* [L *limin-, limen* threshold] (1884) **1** : of or relating to a sensory threshold **2** : barely perceptible

¹lim·it \'li-mət\ *n* [ME, fr. MF *limite*, fr. L *limit-, limes* boundary] (14c) **1 a** : something that bounds, restrains, or confines **b** : the utmost extent **2 a** : a geographical or political boundary **b** *pl* : the place enclosed within a boundary : BOUNDS **3** : LIMITATION **4** : a determining feature or differentia in logic **5** : a prescribed maximum or minimum amount, quantity, or number: as **a** : the maximum quantity of game or fish that may be taken legally in a specified period **b** : a maximum established for a gambling bet, raise, or payoff **6 a** : a number whose numerical difference from a mathematical function is arbitrarily small for all values of the independent variables that are sufficiently close to but not equal to given prescribed numbers or that are sufficiently large positively or negatively **b** : a number that for an infinite sequence of numbers is such that ultimately each of the remaining

\ə\ abut \ᵊ\ kitten, F table \ər\ further \a\ ash \ā\ ace \ä\ mop, mar \au̇\ out \ch\ chin \e\ bet \ē\ easy \g\ go \i\ hit \ī\ ice \j\ job \ŋ\ sing \ō\ go \ȯ\ law \ȯi\ boy \th\ thin \t̷h\ the \ü\ loot \u̇\ foot \y\ yet \zh\ vision \à, k̲, ⁿ, œ, œ̄, ᵫ, ᵫ̄, ᵜ\ see Guide to Pronunciation terms of the sequence differs from this number by less than any given positive amount   **7** : something that is exasperating or intolerable — **lim·it·less** \-ləs\ *adj* — **lim·it·less·ly** *adv* — **lim·it·less·ness** *n*

²**limit** *vt* (14c)   **1 a** : to assign certain limits to : PRESCRIBE ⟨reserved the right to ~ use of the land⟩   **2 a** : to restrict the bounds or limits of ⟨the specialist can no longer ~ himself to his specialty⟩   **b** : to curtail or reduce in quantity or extent ⟨we must ~ the power of aggressors⟩ — **lim·it·able** \-mə-tə-bəl\ *adj* — **lim·it·er** *n*

syn LIMIT, RESTRICT, CIRCUMSCRIBE, CONFINE mean to set bounds for. LIMIT implies setting a point or line (as in time, space, speed, or degree) beyond which something cannot or is not permitted to go ⟨visits are *limited* to 30 minutes⟩. RESTRICT suggests a narrowing or tightening or restraining within or as if within an encircling boundary ⟨laws intended to *restrict* the freedom of the press⟩. CIRCUMSCRIBE stresses a restriction on all sides and by clearly defined boundaries ⟨the work of the investigating committee was carefully *circumscribed*⟩. CONFINE suggests severe restraint and a resulting cramping, fettering, or hampering ⟨our freedom of choice was *confined* by finances⟩.

lim·i·tary \'li-mə-ˌter-ē\ *adj* (1620)   **1** *archaic* : subject to limits   **2 a** *archaic* : of or relating to a boundary   **b** : LIMITING, ENCLOSING

lim·i·ta·tion \ˌli-mə-'tā-shən\ *n* (14c)   **1** : an act or instance of limiting   **2** : the quality or state of being limited   **3** : something that limits : RESTRAINT   **4** : a certain period limited by statute after which actions, suits, or prosecutions cannot be brought in the courts — **lim·i·ta·tion·al** \-shnəl, -shə-nᵊl\ *adj*

lim·i·ta·tive \'li-mə-ˌtā-tiv\ *adj* (1530) : LIMITING, RESTRICTIVE

lim·it·ed *adj* (1610)   **1 a** : confined within limits : RESTRICTED ⟨~ success⟩   **b** *of a train* : offering faster service esp. by making a limited number of stops   **2** : characterized by enforceable limitations prescribed (as by a constitution) upon the scope or exercise of powers ⟨a ~ monarchy⟩   **3** : lacking breadth and originality ⟨a bit ~; a bit thick in the head —Virginia Woolf⟩ — **lim·it·ed·ly** *adv* — **lim·it·ed·ness** *n*

limited–access *adj* (1944) *of a road* : having access restricted to a relatively small number of points

limited edition *n* (1903) : an issue of something collectible (as books, prints, or medals) that is advertised to be limited to a relatively small number of copies

limited liability *n* (1855) : liability (as of a stockholder or shipowner) limited by statute or treaty

limited partner *n* (1907) : a partner in a venture who has no management authority and whose liability is restricted to the amount of his investment — compare GENERAL PARTNER — **limited partnership** *n*

limited war *n* (1939) : a war whose objective is less than the total defeat of the enemy

lim·it·ing *adj* (1849)   **1 a** : functioning as a limit : RESTRICTIVE ⟨~ value⟩   **b** : being an environmental factor (as a nutrient) that limits the population size of an organism   **2** : serving to specify the application of the modified noun ⟨*this* in "this book" is a ~ word⟩ — **lim·it·ing·ly** *adv*

limit point *n* (1905) : a point that is related to a set of points in such a way that every neighborhood of the point no matter how small contains another point belonging to the set — called also *point of accumulation*

lim·i·trophe \'li-mə-ˌtrōf, -ˌtrȯf\ *adj* [F, fr. LL *limitrophus* bordering upon, lit., providing subsistence for frontier troops, irreg. fr. L *limit-, limes* boundary + Gk *trophos* feeder, fr. *trephein* to nourish] (1763) : situated on a border or frontier : ADJACENT

lim·mer \'li-mər\ *n* [ME (Sc)] (15c)   **1** *chiefly Scot* : SCOUNDREL   **2** *chiefly Scot* : PROSTITUTE

limn \'lim\ *vt* **limned; limn·ing** \'li-miŋ, 'lim-niŋ\ [ME *luminen, limnen* to illuminate (a manuscript), fr. MF *enluminer*, fr. L *illuminare* to illuminate] (1592)   **1** : to draw or paint on a surface   **2** : to outline in clear sharp detail : DELINEATE   **3** : DESCRIBE — **limn·er** \'li-mər, 'lim-nər\ *n*

lim·net·ic \lim-'ne-tik\ *adj* [ISV, fr. Gk *limnē* pool, marshy lake; perh. akin to L *limus* mud — more at LIME] (1899) : of, relating to, or inhabiting the open water of a body of fresh water ⟨~ environment⟩

lim·nol·o·gy \lim-'nä-lə-jē\ *n* [Gk *limnē* + ISV *-logy*] (ca. 1888) : the scientific study of bodies of fresh water (as lakes) — **lim·no·log·i·cal** \ˌlim-nə-'lä-ji-kəl\ *also* **lim·no·log·ic** \-'lä-jik\ *adj* — **lim·nol·o·gist** \lim-'nä-lə-jist\ *n*

limo \'li-(ˌ)mō\ *n, pl* **lim·os** (1968) : LIMOUSINE

Li·moges \li-'mōzh\ *n* [*Limoges*, France] : enamelware or porcelain made at Limoges

lim·o·nene \'li-mə-ˌnēn\ *n* [ISV, fr. F *limon* lemon, fr. MF] (1845) : a widely distributed terpene hydrocarbon $C_{10}H_{16}$ that occurs in essential oils (as of oranges or lemons) and has a lemon odor

li·mo·nite \'li-mə-ˌnīt\ *n* [G *Limonit*, fr. Gk *leimōn* wet meadow; akin to Gk *limnē* pool] (1823) : a native hydrous ferric oxide of variable composition that is a major ore of iron — **li·mo·nit·ic** \ˌli-mə-'ni-tik\ *adj*

Lim·ou·sin \li-'müü-sin, 'li-mə-ˌzēn, lē-mü-'zaⁿ\ *n* [*Limousin*, France] (1920) : any of a French breed of medium-sized yellow-red cattle bred esp. for meat

lim·ou·sine \'li-mə-ˌzēn, ˌli-mə-'\ *n* [F, lit., cloak, fr. *Limousin*, France] (1902)   **1** : a large luxurious often chauffeur-driven sedan that sometimes has a glass partition separating the driver's seat from the passenger compartment   **2** : a large vehicle for transporting passengers to and from an airport

limousine liberal *n* (1969) : a wealthy political liberal

¹**limp** \'limp\ *vi* [prob. fr. ME *lympen* to fall short; akin to OE *limpan* to happen, *lemphealt* lame] (ca. 1570)   **1 a** : to walk lamely; *esp* : to walk favoring one leg   **b** : to go unsteadily : FALTER   **2** : to proceed slowly or with difficulty ⟨the ship ~ed back to port⟩ — **limp·er** *n*

²**limp** *n* (1818) : a limping movement or gait

³**limp** *adj* [akin to ¹*limp*] (ca. 1706)   **1** : lacking firm texture, substance, or structure ⟨~ curtains⟩ ⟨her hair hung ~ about her shoulders⟩   **b** : not stiff or rigid ⟨a book in a ~ binding⟩   **2 a** : WEARY, EXHAUSTED ⟨~ with fatigue⟩   **b** : lacking in strength, vigor, or firmness : SPIRITLESS — **limp·ly** *adv* — **limp·ness** *n*

lim·pa \'lim-pə\ *n* [Sw] (1948) : rye bread made with molasses or brown sugar

lim·pet \'lim-pət\ *n* [ME *lempet*, fr. OE *lempedu*, fr. ML *lampreda* lamprey] (bef. 12c)   **1** : a marine gastropod mollusk (esp. families

Acmaeidae and Patellidae) that has a low conical shell broadly open beneath, browses over rocks or timbers in the littoral area, and clings very tightly when disturbed   **2** : one that clings tenaciously to someone or something   **3** : an explosive device designed to cling magnetically to a metallic surface (as the hull of a ship)

limpet 1

lim·pid \'lim-pəd\ *adj* [F or L; F *limpide*, fr. L *limpidus*, perh. fr. *lympha* water — more at LYMPH] (1613)   **1 a** : marked by transparency : PELLUCID ⟨~ streams⟩   **b** : clear and simple in style ⟨~ prose⟩   **2** : absolutely serene and untroubled   **syn** see CLEAR — **lim·pid·i·ty** \lim-'pi-də-tē\ *n* — **lim·pid·ly** \'lim-pəd-lē\ *adv* — **lim·pid·ness** *n*

limp·kin \'lim(p)-kən\ *n* [perh. fr. ¹*limp*] (1871) : a large brown wading bird (*Aramus guarauna*) of southern Georgia, Florida, and Central and So. America that resembles a bittern but has a longer slightly curved bill, longer neck and legs, and white stripes on head and neck

limp–wrist·ed \'limp-ˌris-təd\ *adj* (ca. 1960)   **1** : EFFEMINATE   **2** : WEAK

lim·u·lus \'lim-yə-ləs\ *n, pl* **-li** \-ˌlī, -ˌlē\ [NL, genus name, fr. L *limus* oblique, transverse — more at LIMEN] (1837) : HORSESHOE CRAB

limy \'lī-mē\ *adj* **lim·i·er; -est** (ca. 1552)   **1** : smeared with or consisting of lime : VISCOUS   **2** : containing lime or limestone   **3** : resembling or having the qualities of lime

lin·ac \'li-ˌnak\ *n* (1950) : LINEAR ACCELERATOR

lin·age \'lī-nij\ *n* (1884) : the number of lines of printed or written matter

lin·al·o·ol \lə-'na-lə-ˌwȯl, lī-, -ˌwȯl\ *n* [ISV, fr. MexSp *lináloe*, tree yielding perfume, fr. ML *lignum aloes*, lit., wood of the aloe] (1891) : a fragrant liquid alcohol $C_{10}H_{18}O$ that occurs both free and in the form of esters in many essential oils and is used in perfumes, soaps, and flavoring materials

linch·pin \'linch-ˌpin\ *n* [ME *lynspin*, fr. *lyns* linchpin (fr. OE *lynis*) + *pin*; akin to MHG *luns* linchpin] (13c)   **1** : a locking pin inserted crosswise (as through the end of an axle or shaft)   **2** : one that serves to hold together the elements of a complex ⟨the ~ in the defense's case⟩

Lin·coln \'liŋ-kən\ *n* [*Lincoln*shire, England] (1837) : any of an English breed of long-wooled mutton-type sheep

Lin·coln·i·a·na \(ˌ)liŋ-ˌkō-nē-'ä-nə, -'a-nə, -'ä-nə\ *n pl* (1921) : materials relating to Abraham Lincoln

Lincoln's Birthday \'liŋ-kənz-\ *n* (1898)   **1** : February 12 observed as a legal holiday in many states of the U.S.   **2** : the first Monday in February observed as a legal holiday by some states of the U.S.

lin·co·my·cin \ˌliŋ-kə-'mī-sᵊn\ *n* [NL *linco*lnensis (specific epithet of *Streptomyces lincolnensis*) + E *-mycin*] (1963) : an antibiotic obtained from an actinomycete (*Streptomyces lincolnensis*) and effective esp. against gram-positive bacteria

lin·dane \'lin-ˌdān\ *n* [T. van der *Linden*, 20th cent. Du. chemist] (ca. 1949) : an insecticide that consists chiefly of the gamma isomer of BHC and is biodegraded very slowly

lin·den \'lin-dən\ *n* [ME, made of linden wood, fr. OE, fr. *lind* linden tree; prob. akin to OE *līthe* gentle — more at LITHE] (1577)   **1** : any of a genus (*Tilia* of the family Tiliaceae, the linden family) of trees of temperate regions that are planted as shade trees and are distinguished by having cordate leaves and a winglike bract attached to the peduncle of the flower and fruit: as   **a** : a European tree (*T. europaea*) much used for ornamental planting   **b** : a tall forest tree (*T. americana*) chiefly of the central and eastern U.S. — called also *basswood, whitewood*   **2** : the light fine-grained white wood of a linden; *esp* : BASSWOOD 2

lin·dy \'lin-dē\ *n* [prob. fr. *Lindy*, nickname of Charles A. Lindbergh] (1931) : a jitterbug dance originating in Harlem and later developing many local variants

linden 1: branch with bract and fruit

¹**line** \'līn\ *n, often attrib* [ME; partly fr. OF *ligne*, fr. L *linea*, fr. fem. of *lineus* made of flax, fr. *linum* flax; partly fr. OE *line*; akin to OE *līn* flax — more at LINEN] (bef. 12c)   **1 a** : THREAD, STRING, CORD, ROPE: as   (1) : a comparatively strong slender cord   (2) : CLOTHESLINE   (3) : a rope used on shipboard   **b** (1) : a device for catching fish consisting of a cord with hooks and other fishing gear   (2) : scope for activity : ROPE   **c** : a length of material used in measuring and leveling   **d** : piping for conveying a fluid (as steam)   **e** (1) : a wire or pair of wires connecting one telegraph or telephone station with another or a whole system of such wires; *also* : any circuit in an electronic communication system   (2) : a telephone connection ⟨tried to get a ~⟩; *also* : an individual telephone extension ⟨a call on ~ 2⟩   (3) : the principal circuits of an electric power system   **2 a** (1) : a horizontal row of written or printed characters; *also* : a blank row in lieu of such characters   (2) : a unit in the rhythmic structure of verse formed by the grouping of a number of the smallest units of the rhythm (as metrical feet)   (3) : an often numbered section of a computer program containing a single command or a small number of commands   **b** : a short letter : NOTE   **c** *pl* : a certificate of marriage   **d** : the words making up a part in a drama — usu. used in pl.   **e** : any of the successive horizontal rows of picture elements on the screen of a cathode-ray tube (as a television screen)   **3 a** : something (as a ridge or seam) that is distinct, elongated, and narrow ⟨a ~ of cliffs⟩   **b** : a narrow crease (as on the face) : WRINKLE   **c** : the course or direction of something in motion : ROUTE   **d** (1) : a state of agreement or conformity : ACCORDANCE   (2) : a state of order, control, or obedience ⟨you're getting out of ~⟩   **e** : a boundary of an area ⟨the state ~⟩   **f** : the track and roadbed of a railway   **g** : an amount of cocaine that is arranged in a line to be inhaled through the nose   **4 a** : a course of conduct, action, or thought   **b** : a field of

activity or interest   c : a glib often persuasive way of talking 5 a : LIMIT, RESTRAINT b *archaic* : position in life : LOT 6 a (1) : FAMILY, LINEAGE (2) : a strain produced and maintained esp. by selective breeding or biological culture (3) : a chronological series b : dispositions made to cover extended military positions and presenting a front to the enemy — usu. used in pl. c : a military formation in which the different elements are abreast of each other d : naval ships arranged in a regular order e (1) : the combatant forces of an army distinguished from the staff corps and supply services (2) : the force of a regular navy f (1) : officers of the navy eligible for command at sea distinguished from officers of the staff (2) : officers of the army belonging to a combatant branch g : an arrangement or placement of persons or objects of one kind in an orderly series ⟨a ~ of trees⟩ ⟨stand on ~⟩ ⟨waiting in ~⟩; *also* : the persons or objects so positioned ⟨the ~ moved slowly at the bank⟩ h (1) : a group of public conveyances plying regularly under one management over a route (2) : a system of transportation together with its equipment, routes, and appurtenances; *also* : the company owning or operating it i : a succession of musical notes esp. considered in melodic phrases j (1) : an arrangement of operations in manufacturing permitting sequential occurrence on various stages of production (2) : the personnel of an organization that are responsible for its stated objective k (1) : the 7 players including center, 2 guards, 2 tackles, and 2 ends who in offensive football play line up on or within one foot of the line of scrimmage (2) : the players who in defensive play line up within one yard of the line of scrimmage 7 : a narrow elongated mark drawn or projected: as a (1) : a circle of latitude or longitude on a map (2) : EQUATOR b : a mark (as on a map) recording a boundary, division, or contour c : any of the horizontal parallel strokes on a music staff on or between which notes are placed — compare SPACE d : a mark (as by pencil) that forms part of the formal design of a picture distinguished from the shading or color e : a division on a bridge score dividing the score for bonuses from that for tricks f (1) : a demarcation of a limit with reference to which the playing of some game or sport is regulated — usu. used in combination (2) : a marked or imaginary line across a playing area (as a football field) parallel to the end line (3) : LINE OF SCRIMMAGE 8 : a straight or curved geometric element that is generated by a moving point and that has extension only along the path of the point : CURVE 9 a : a defining outline : CONTOUR b : a general plan : MODEL — usu. used in pl. 10 a *chiefly Brit* : PICA — used to indicate the size of large type b : the unit of fineness of halftones expressed as the number of screen lines to the linear inch 11 : merchandise or services of the same general class for sale or regularly available 12 a : a source of information : INSIGHT b : betting odds offered by a bookmaker esp. on a sporting event 13 : a complete game of 10 frames in bowling — called also *string* 14 : LINE DRIVE — **liny** *also* **lin•ey** \'lī-nē\ *adj* — **between the lines** 1 : by implication : in an indirect way 2 : by way of inference — **down the line** : all the way : FULLY — **in line for** : due or in a position to receive — **on line** : in or into operation — **on the line** 1 : in complete commitment and at great risk ⟨puts his future *on the line* by backing that policy⟩ 2 : on the border between two categories 3 : IMMEDIATELY ⟨paid cash *on the line*⟩

²**line** *vb* **lined; lin•ing** *vt* (1530) 1 : to mark or cover with a line or lines ⟨*lined* paper⟩ 2 : to depict with lines : DRAW 3 : to place or form a line along ⟨pedestrians ~ the walks⟩ 4 : to form into a line or lines : ALIGN ⟨~ up troops⟩ 5 : to hit (as a baseball) hard and in a usu. straight line ~ *vi* 1 : to hit a line drive in baseball 2 : to come into the correct relative position : ALIGN

³**line** *vt* **lined; lin•ing** [ME, fr. *line* flax, fr. OE *lin*] (14c) 1 : to cover the inner surface of ⟨~ a cloak with silk⟩ 2 : to put something in the inside of : FILL 3 : to serve as the lining of ⟨tapestries *lined* the walls⟩ 4 *obs* : FORTIFY — **line one's pockets** : to take money freely and esp. dishonestly

¹**lin•e•age** \'lin-ē-ij *also* 'li-nij\ *n* (14c) 1 a : descent in a line from a common progenitor b : DERIVATION 2 : a group of individuals tracing descent from a common ancestor; *esp* : such a group of persons whose common ancestor is regarded as its founder

²**line•age** \'lī-nij\ *var of* LINAGE

lin•e•al \'li-nē-əl\ *adj* (14c) 1 : LINEAR 2 : composed of or arranged in lines 3 a : consisting of or being in a direct male or female line of ancestry — compare COLLATERAL 2 b : relating to or derived from ancestors : HEREDITARY c : descended in a direct line 4 a : belonging to one lineage ⟨~ relatives⟩ b : of, relating to, or dealing with a lineage — **lin•e•al•i•ty** \,li-nē-'a-lə-tē\ *n* — **lin•e•al•ly** \'li-nē-ə-lē\ *adv*

lin•e•a•ment \'li-nē-ə-mənt\ *n* [ME, fr. L *lineamentum*, fr. *lineare* to draw a line, fr. *linea*] (15c) 1 a : an outline, feature, or contour of a body or figure and esp. of a face — usu. used in pl. b : a linear topographic feature (as of the earth or a planet) that reveals a characteristic (as a fault or the subsurface structure) 2 : a distinguishing or characteristic feature — usu. used in pl. — **lin•e•a•men•tal** \,li-nē-ə-'men-t²l\ *adj*

lin•e•ar \'li-nē-ər\ *adj* (ca. 1656) 1 a (1) : of, relating to, resembling, or having a graph that is a line and esp. a straight line : STRAIGHT (2) : involving a single dimension b (1) : of the first degree with respect to one or more variables (2) : of, relating to, based on, or being linear equations, linear differential equations, linear functions, linear transformations, or linear algebra c (1) : characterized by an emphasis on line ⟨~ art⟩ (2) : composed of simply drawn lines with little attempt at pictorial representation ⟨~ script⟩ d : consisting of a straight chain of atoms 2 : elongated with nearly parallel sides ⟨~ leaf⟩ — see LEAF illustration 3 : having or being a response or output that is directly proportional to the input 4 : of, relating to, or based or depending on sequential development ⟨~ thinking⟩ ⟨a ~ narrative⟩ — **lin•e•ar•i•ty** \,li-nē-'ar-ə-tē\ *n* — **lin•e•ar•ly** \'li-nē-ər-lē\ *adv*

Linear A \-'ā\ *n* (1948) : a linear form of writing used in Crete from the 18th to the 15th centuries B.C.

linear accelerator *n* (1945) : a device in which charged particles are accelerated in a straight line by successive impulses from a series of electric fields

linear algebra *n* (ca. 1884) : a branch of mathematics that is concerned with mathematical structures closed under the operations of addition and scalar multiplication and that includes the theory of systems of linear equations, matrices, determinants, vector spaces, and linear transformations

Linear B \-'bē\ *n* (1950) : a linear form of writing employing syllabic characters and used at Knossos on Crete and on the Greek mainland from the 15th to the 12th centuries B.C. for documents in the Mycenaean language

linear combination *n* (1960) : a mathematical entity (as $4x + 5y + 6z$) which is composed of sums and differences of elements (as variables, matrices, or functions) esp. when the coefficients are not all zero

linear dependence *n* (1955) : the property of one set (as of matrices or vectors) of having at least one linear combination of its elements equal to zero when the coefficients are taken from another given set and at least one of its coefficients is not equal to zero — **linearly dependent** *adj*

linear equation *n* (1816) : an equation of the first degree in any number of variables

linear function *n* (ca. 1889) 1 : a mathematical function in which the variables appear only in the first degree, are multiplied by constants, and are combined only by addition and subtraction 2 : LINEAR TRANSFORMATION

linear independence *n* (1967) : the property of a set (as of matrices or vectors) of having no linear combination of all its elements equal to zero when coefficients are taken from a given set unless the coefficient of each element is zero — **linearly independent** *adj*

lin•e•ar•ise *Brit var of* LINEARIZE

lin•e•ar•ize \'li-nē-ə-,rīz\ *vt* **-ized; -iz•ing** (1895) : to give a linear form to; *also* : to project in linear form — **lin•e•ar•i•za•tion** \,li-nē-ə-rə-'zā-shən\ *n*

linear measure *n* (ca. 1890) 1 : a measure of length 2 : a system of measures of length

linear motor *n* (1957) : a motor that produces thrust in a straight line by direct induction rather than with the use of gears — called also *linear induction motor*

linear perspective *n* (ca. 1656) : PERSPECTIVE 1a

linear programming *n* (1949) : a mathematical method of solving practical problems (as the allocation of resources) by means of linear functions where the variables involved are subject to constraints

linear space *n* (ca. 1889) : VECTOR SPACE

linear transformation *n* (ca. 1889) 1 : a transformation in which the new variables are linear functions of the old variables 2 : a function that maps the vectors of one vector space onto the vectors of the same or another vector space with the same field of scalars in such a way that the image of the sum of two vectors equals the sum of their images and the image of the product of a scalar and a vector equals the product of the scalar and the image of the vector

lin•e•a•tion \,li-nē-'ā-shən\ *n* [ME *lineacion* outline, fr. L *lineation-, lineatio*, fr. *lineare* to mark with lines, fr. *linea*] (14c) 1 a : the action of marking with lines : DELINEATION b : OUTLINE 2 : an arrangement of lines

line•back•er \'līn-,ba-kər\ *n* (1949) : a defensive football player who lines up immediately behind the line of scrimmage to make tackles on running plays through the line or defend against short passes

line•back•ing \-,ba-kiŋ\ *n* (1953) : the action or art of playing linebacker

line•breed•ing \-,brē-diŋ\ *n* (ca. 1879) : the interbreeding of individuals within a particular line of descent usu. to perpetuate desirable characters — **line•bred** \-,bred\ *adj*

line•cast•er \-,kas-tər\ *n* (1964) : a machine that casts metal type in lines — **line•cast•ing** \-tiŋ\ *n*

line•cut \'līn-,kət\ *n* (ca. 1909) : a photoengraving of a line drawing

line drawing *n* (1891) : a drawing made in solid lines

line drive *n* (1912) : a batted baseball hit in a nearly straight line usu. not far above the ground

line engraving *n* (1802) : an engraving cut by hand directly in the plate

line graph *n* (ca. 1924) : a graph in which points representing values of a variable for suitable values of an independent variable are connected by a broken line

line–haul \'līn-,hól\ *n* (ca. 1923) : the transporting of items or persons between terminals

line item *n* (1962) : an appropriation that is itemized on a separate line in a budget — **line–item** \'līn-'ī-təm\ *adj*

line judge *n* (1970) : a football linesman whose duties include keeping track of the official time for the game

line•man \'līn-mən\ *n* (1876) 1 : one who sets up or repairs electric wire communication or power lines — called also *linesman* 2 : a player in the forward line of a team; *specif* : a football player in the line

¹**lin•en** \'li-nən\ *adj* [ME, fr. OE *linen*, fr. *lin* flax, fr. L *linum* flax; akin to Gk *linon* flax, thread] (bef. 12c) 1 : made of flax 2 : made of or resembling linen

²**linen** *n* (14c) 1 a : cloth made of flax and noted for its strength, coolness, and luster b : thread or yarn spun from flax 2 : clothing or household articles made of linen cloth or similar fabric 3 : paper made from linen fibers or with a linen finish

line of credit (1917) : the maximum credit allowed a buyer or borrower

line of duty (ca. 1918) : all that is authorized, required, or normally associated with some field of responsibility

line officer *n* (1850) : a commissioned officer assigned to the line of the army or navy — compare STAFF OFFICER

line of force (1873) : a line in a field of force (as a magnetic or electric field) whose tangent at any point gives the direction of the field at that point

line of scrimmage (ca. 1909) : an imaginary line in football that is parallel to the goal lines and tangent to the nose of the ball laid on the ground and that marks the position of the ball at the start of each down

\ə\ abut \ᵊ\ kitten, F table \ər\ further \a\ ash \ā\ ace \ä\ mop, mar \aú\ out \ch\ chin \e\ bet \ē\ easy \g\ go \i\ hit \ī\ ice \j\ job \ŋ\ sing \ō\ go \ȯ\ law \ȯi\ boy \th\ thin \t̶h̶\ the \ü\ loot \ú\ foot \y\ yet \zh\ vision \á, k̲, ⁿ, œ, œ̄, ue, ūe, ʸ\ *see* Guide to Pronunciation

line of sight (1559)   **1** : a line from an observer's eye to a distant point   **2** : the straight path between a radio or television transmitting antenna and receiving antenna when unobstructed by the horizon

line out *vt* (1618)   **1** : to indicate with or as if with lines : OUTLINE ⟨*line out* a route⟩   **2** : to arrange in an extended line   **3** : BELT ⟨*line out* a song⟩ **~** *vi*   **1** : to move rapidly ⟨*lined out* for home⟩   **2** : to make an out by hitting a baseball in a line drive that is caught

line printer *n* (1955) : a high-speed printing device (as for a computer) that prints each line as a unit rather than character by character

¹lin·er \'li-nər\ *n* (15c)   **1** : one that makes, draws, or uses lines   **2   a** : a ship belonging to a regular line   **b** : an airplane belonging to an airline   **3** : LINE DRIVE   **4** : something with which lines are made

²liner *n* (1611)   **1** : one that lines or is used to line or back something   **2** : JACKET 3c(2) — **lin·er·less** \-ləs\ *adj*

li·ner·board \'li-nər-,bȯrd, -,bȯrd\ *n* (1948) : a thin paperboard used for the flat facings of corrugated containerboard

liner notes *n pl* (1955) : comments or explanatory notes about a recording printed on the jacket or an insert

line score *n* (1946) : a score of a baseball game giving the runs, hits, and errors made by each team — compare BOX SCORE

lines·man \'linz-mən\ *n* (1883)   **1** : LINEMAN 1   **2** : an official who assists a referee in various games (as football or hockey) esp. in determining if a ball, puck, or player is out-of-bounds or offside

line squall *n* (1887) : a squall or thunderstorm occurring along a cold front

line storm *n* (1850) : an equinoctial storm

line-up \'li-,nəp\ *n* (1889)   **1   a** : a list of players taking part in a game (as of baseball)   **b** : the players on such a list   **2   a** : an alignment (as in entertainment or politics) of persons or things having a common purpose, distinction, or bond ⟨the show's star-studded ~⟩   **b** : LINE 11   **c** : a television programming schedule   **3** : a line of persons arranged esp. for inspection or for identification by police

line up *vi* (1864)   **1** : to assume an orderly linear arrangement ⟨*line up* for inspection⟩   **2** : to align oneself ⟨he *lined up* with the liberals against the bill⟩ **~** *vt*   **1** : to put into alignment   **2** : to arrange for ⟨*line up* support for a candidate⟩

¹ling \'liŋ\ *n* [ME; akin to D *leng* ling, OE *lang* long] (13c)   **1** : any of various fishes (as a hake or burbot) of the cod family   **2** : LINGCOD

²ling *n* [ME, fr. ON *lyng*] (13c) : a heath plant; *esp* : a common Old World heather (*Calluna vulgaris*)

¹-ling *n suffix* [ME, fr. OE; akin to OE *-ing*]   **1** : one connected with or having the quality of ⟨hire*ling*⟩   **2** : young, small, or inferior one ⟨duck*ling*⟩

²-ling *or* **-lings** *adv suffix* [ME *-ling* (fr. OE), *-linges* (fr. *-ling* + *-es* -s); akin to OHG *-lingun* -ling, OE *lang* long] : in (such) a direction or manner ⟨side*ling*⟩ ⟨flat*ling*⟩

Lin·ga·la \liŋ-'gä-lə\ *n* (1922) : a Bantu language widely used in trade and public affairs in the Congo River area

lin·gam \'liŋ-gəm\ *or* **lin·ga** \-gə\ *n* [Skt *liṅga* (nom. *liṅgam*), lit., characteristic] (1719) : a stylized phallic symbol of the masculine cosmic principle and of the Hindu god Siva — compare YONI

Lin·ga·yat \liŋ-'gä-yət\ *n* [Kannada *lingāyata*] (1901) : a member of a Saiva sect of southern India marked by wearing of the lingam and characterized by denial of caste distinctions

ling·cod \'liŋ-,käd\ *n* (1940) : a large greenish-fleshed fish (*Ophiodon elongatus*) of the Pacific coast of No. America that is an important food and sport fish and belongs to the same family as the greenlings

lin·ger \'liŋ-gər\ *vb* **lin·gered; lin·ger·ing** \-g(ə-)riŋ\ [ME (northern dial.) *lengeren* to dwell, freq. of *lengen* to prolong, fr. *leng*; akin to OE *lang* long] *vi* (14c)   **1** : to be slow in parting or in quitting something : TARRY   **2   a** : to remain alive although gradually dying   **b** : to remain existent although often waning in strength, importance, or influence ⟨~*ing* doubts⟩   **3** : to be slow to act : PROCRASTINATE   **4** : to move slowly : SAUNTER **~** *vt*   **1** *obs* : DELAY   **2** : to pass (as a period of time) slowly — **lin·ger·er** \-gər-ər\ *n* — **lin·ger·ing·ly** \-g(ə-)riŋ-lē\ *adv*

lin·ge·rie \,län-jə-'rā, ,län-zhə-, -'rē; 'lan-zhə-(,)rē, 'län-jə-, 'län-zhə-, -,rā\ *n* [F, fr. MF, fr. *linge* linen, fr. L *lineus* made of linen — more at LINE] (1835)   **1** *archaic* : linen articles or garments   **2** : women's intimate apparel — **lingerie** *adj*

lin·go \'liŋ-(,)gō\ *n, pl* **lingoes** [prob. fr. Lingua Franca, language, tongue, fr. Prov., fr. L *lingua* — more at TONGUE] (1660) : strange or incomprehensible language or speech: as   **a** : a foreign language   **b** : the special vocabulary of a particular field of interest   **c** : language characteristic of an individual

ling·on·ber·ry \'liŋ-ən-,ber-ē\ *n* [Sw *lingon* mountain cranberry; akin to ON *lyng* ling] (1920) : the fruit of the mountain cranberry; *also* : MOUNTAIN CRANBERRY

lin·gua \'liŋ-gwə\ *n, pl* **lin·guae** \-,gwē, -,gwī\ [L — more at TONGUE] (ca. 1826) : a tongue or an organ resembling a tongue

lin·gua fran·ca \'liŋ-gwə-'fraŋ-kə\ *n, pl* **lingua francas** *or* **lin·guae fran·cae** \-,gwē-'fraŋ-(,)kē\ [It, lit., Frankish language] (1619)   **1** *often cap* : a common language consisting of Italian mixed with French, Spanish, Greek, and Arabic that was formerly spoken in Mediterranean ports   **2** : any of various languages used as common or commercial tongues among peoples of diverse speech   **3** : something resembling a common language

lin·gual \'liŋ-gwəl *also* 'liŋ-gyə-wəl\ *adj* [L *lingua*] (1650)   **1   a** : of, relating to, or resembling the tongue   **b** : lying near or next to the tongue; *esp* : relating to or being the surface of a tooth next to the tongue   **c** : produced by the tongue   **2** : LINGUISTIC — **lin·gual·ly** *adv*

lin·gui·ne *or* **lin·gui·ni** \liŋ-'gwē-nē\ *n* [It, pl. of *linguina*, dim. of *lingua* tongue, fr. L] (ca. 1948) : narrow flat pasta

lin·guist \'liŋ-gwist\ *n* [L *lingua* language, tongue] (1591)   **1** : a person accomplished in languages; *esp* : one who speaks several languages   **2** : a person who specializes in linguistics

lin·guis·tic \liŋ-'gwis-tik\ *also* **lin·guis·ti·cal** \-ti-kəl\ *adj* (1846) : of or relating to language or linguistics — **lin·guis·ti·cal·ly** \-ti-k(ə-)lē\ *adv*

linguistic atlas *n* (1923) : a publication containing a set of maps on which speech variations are recorded — called also *dialect atlas*

linguistic form *n* (1921) : a meaningful unit of speech (as a morpheme, word, or sentence) — called also *speech form*

linguistic geography *n* (1926) : local or regional variations of a language or dialect studied as a field of knowledge — called also *dialect geography* — **linguistic geographer** *n*

lin·guis·ti·cian \,liŋ-gwə-'sti-shən\ *n* (1895) : LINGUIST 2

lin·guis·tics \liŋ-'gwis-tiks\ *n pl but sing in constr* (ca. 1847) : the study of human speech including the units, nature, structure, and modification of language

lin·i·ment \'li-nə-mənt\ *n* [ME, fr. LL *linimentum*, fr. L *linere* to smear — more at LIME] (15c) : a liquid or semiliquid preparation that is applied to the skin as an anodyne or a counterirritant

lin·ing \'li-niŋ\ *n* (14c)   **1** : material that lines or that is used to line esp. the inner surface of something (as a garment)   **2** : the act or process of providing something with a lining

¹link \'liŋk\ *n* [ME, of Scand origin; akin to ON *hlekkr* chain; akin to OE *hlanc* lank] (15c)   **1** : a connecting structure: as   **a** (1) : a single ring or division of a chain   (2) : one of the standardized divisions of a surveyor's chain that is 7.92 inches (20.1 centimeters) long and serves as a measure of length   **b** : CUFF LINK   **c** : BOND 3c   **d** : an intermediate rod or piece for transmitting force or motion; *esp* : a short connecting rod with a hole or pin at each end   **e** : the fusible member of an electrical fuse   **2** : something analogous to a link of chain: as   **a** : a segment of sausage in a chain   **b** : a connecting element or factor ⟨found a ~ between smoking and cancer⟩   **c** : a unit in a communication system   **d** : an identifier attached to an element (as an index term) in a system in order to indicate or permit connection with other similarly identified elements

²link *vt* (15c) : to couple or connect by or as if by a link **~** *vi* : to become connected by or as if by a link   *syn* see JOIN — **link·er** *n*

³link *n* [perh. modif. of ML *linchinus* candle, alter. of L *lychnus*, fr. Gk *lychnos*; akin to Gk *leukos* white — more at LIGHT] (1526) : a torch formerly used to light a person's way through the streets

⁴link *vi* [origin unknown] (1715) *Scot* : to skip smartly along

link·age \'liŋ-kij\ *n* (1874)   **1** : the manner or style of being united: as   **a** : the manner in which atoms or radicals are linked in a molecule   **b** : BOND 3c   **2** : the quality or state of being linked; *esp* : the relationship between genes on the same chromosome that causes them to be inherited together — compare MENDEL'S LAW 2   **3** : a system of links; *esp* : a system of links or bars which are jointed together and more or less constrained by having a link or links fixed and by means of which straight or nearly straight lines or other point paths may be traced   **4** : LINK 2b

linkage group *n* (1921) : a set of linked genes at different loci on the same chromosome

link·boy \'liŋk-,bȯi\ *n* (1660) : an attendant formerly employed to bear a light for a person on the streets at night

linked \'liŋ(k)t\ *adj* (15c)   **1** : marked by linkage and esp. genetic linkage ⟨~ genes⟩   **2** : having or provided with links ⟨a ~ list⟩

linking verb *n* (1923) : a word or expression (as a form of *be, become, feel,* or *seem*) that links a subject with its predicate

link·man \'liŋk-mən\ *n* (1716)   **1** : LINKBOY   **2** *Brit* : a broadcasting moderator or anchorman

links \'liŋ(k)s\ *n pl* [ME, fr. OE *hlincas*, pl. of *hlinc* ridge; akin to OE *hlanc* lank] (15c)   **1** *Scot* : sand hills esp. along the seashore   **2** : GOLF COURSE

links·man \'liŋ(k)s-mən\ *n* (1937) : one who plays golf

link-up \'liŋk-,kəp\ *n* (1945)   **1** : establishment of contact : MEETING ⟨the ~ of two spacecraft⟩   **2   a** : something that serves as a linking device or factor   **b** : a functional whole resulting from the linking up of separate elements ⟨an instructional TV ~⟩

linn \'lin\ *n* [ScGael *linne* pool] (1513)   **1** *chiefly Scot* : WATERFALL   **2** *chiefly Scot* : PRECIPICE

Lin·nae·an *or* **Lin·ne·an** \lə-'nē-ən, -'nā-; 'li-nē-\ *adj* [Carolus *Linnaeus*] (1753) : of, relating to, or following the systematic methods of the Swedish botanist Linnaeus who established the system of binomial nomenclature

lin·net \'li-nət\ *n* [MF *linette*, fr. *lin* flax, fr. L *linum*; fr. its feeding on flax seeds] (ca. 1530) : a common small brownish Old World finch (*Acanthis cannabina*) of which the male has red on the breast and crown during breeding season

li·no \'li-(,)nō\ *n, pl* **linos** (1907) *chiefly Brit* : LINOLEUM

li·no·cut \'li-nō-,kət\ *n* (1907) : a print made from a design cut into a mounted piece of linoleum

li·no·le·ate \li-'nō-lē-,āt\ *n* (ca. 1865) : a salt or ester of linoleic acid

lin·o·le·ic acid \,li-nō-'lē-ik-, -'lā-\ *n* [Gk *linon* flax + ISV *oleic* (*acid*)] (1857) : a liquid unsaturated fatty acid $C_{18}H_{32}O_2$ found esp. in semi-drying oils (as peanut oil) and essential for the nutrition of some animals

lin·o·le·nic acid \-'lē-nik-, -'lā-\ *n* [ISV, irreg. fr. *linoleic*] (1887) : a liquid unsaturated fatty acid $C_{18}H_{30}O_2$ found esp. in drying oils (as linseed oil) and essential for the nutrition of some animals

li·no·leum \lə-'nō-lē-əm, -'nōl-yəm\ *n, often attrib* [L *linum* flax + *oleum* oil — more at OIL] (1878)   **1** : a floor covering made by laying on a burlap or canvas backing a mixture of solidified linseed oil with gums, cork dust or wood flour or both, and usu. pigments   **2** : a material similar to linoleum

Li·no·type \'li-nə-,tip\ *trademark* — used for a keyboard-operated typesetting machine that uses circulating matrices and produces each line of type in the form of a solid metal slug

lin·sang \'lin-,saŋ\ *n* [Jav *lingsang*] (1821) : either of two nocturnal chiefly forest-dwelling Asian mammals (*Prionodon pardicolor* and *P. linsang*) that resemble and are related to the mongooses, civets, and genets; *also* : a related mammal (*Poiana richardsoni*) of Africa

lin·seed \'lin-,sēd\ *n* [ME, fr. OE *linsǣd*, fr. *lin* flax + *sǣd* seed — more at LINEN] (bef. 12c) : FLAXSEED

linseed oil *n* (15c) : a yellowish drying oil obtained from flaxseed and used esp. in paint, varnish, printing ink, and linoleum

lin·sey–wool·sey \,lin-zē-'wul-zē\ *n* [ME *lynsy wolsye*] (15c) : a coarse sturdy fabric of wool and linen or cotton

lin·stock \'lin-,stäk\ *n* [D *lontstok*, fr. *lont* match + *stok* stick] (1575) : a staff having a pointed foot (as for sticking into the ground) and a forked tip and formerly used to hold a lighted match for firing cannon

lint \'lint\ *n* [ME] (14c)   **1   a** : a soft fleecy material made from linen usu. by scraping   **b** : fuzz consisting esp. of fine ravelings and short fibers of yarn and fabric **2** : a fibrous coat of thick convoluted hairs borne by cotton seeds that yields the cotton staple — **linty** \'lin-tē\ *adj*

lin·tel \'lin-t³l\ *n* [ME, fr. MF, fr. LL *limitaris* threshold, fr. L, constituting a boundary, fr. *limit-, limes* boundary] (14c) : a horizontal architectural member spanning and usu. carrying the load above an opening

1 lintel

lint·er \'lin-tər\ *n* (ca. 1889) **1** : a machine for removing linters **2** *pl* : the fuzz of short fibers that adheres to cottonseed after ginning

lint·white \'lint-,hwit, -,wit\ *n* [alter. of ME *lynk-whyt*, by folk etymology fr. OE *linetwige*] (1513) : LINNET

li·on \'lī-ən\ *n, pl* **lions** [ME, fr. OF, fr. L *leon-, leo,* fr. Gk *leōn*] (12c) **1** *a or pl* **lion** : a large heavily-built social cat (*Panthera leo* syn. *Leo leo*) of open or rocky areas chiefly of sub-Saharan Africa though once widely distributed throughout Africa and southern Asia that has a tawny body with a tufted tail and a shaggy blackish or dark brown mane in the male **b** : any of several large wildcats; *esp* : COUGAR **c** *cap* : LEO **2** **a** : a person felt to resemble a lion (as in courage or ferocity) **b** : a person of outstanding interest or importance **3** *cap* [*Lions (club)*] : a member of a major national and international service club — **li·on·like** \-,līk\ *adj*

li·on·ess \'lī-ə-nəs\ *n* (14c) : a female lion

li·on·fish \'lī-ən-,fish\ *n* (ca. 1907) : any of several scorpion fishes (genus *Pterois*) of the Indian Ocean and the tropical Pacific that are brilliantly striped and barred with elongated fins and venomous dorsal spines

li·on·heart·ed \'lī-ən-,här-təd\ *adj* (1708) : COURAGEOUS, BRAVE

li·on·ise *Brit var of* LIONIZE

li·on·ize \'lī-ə-,nīz\ *vt* **-ized; -iz·ing** (1809) **1** : to treat as an object of great interest or importance **2** *Brit* : to show the sights of a place to — **li·on·i·za·tion** \,lī-ə-nə-'zā-shən\ *n* — **li·on·iz·er** \'lī-ə-,nī-zər\ *n*

lion's share *n* (1790) : the largest portion (received the *lion's share* of the research money)

¹lip \'lip\ *n* [ME, fr. OE *lippa*; akin to OHG *leffur* lip and prob. to L *labium, labrum* lip] (bef. 12c) **1** : either of two fleshy folds that surround the mouth in humans and many other vertebrates and are the organs of human speech; *also* : the red or pinkish margin of the human lip **2** *slang* : BACK TALK **3** **a** : a fleshy edge or margin (as of a wound) **b** : LABIUM **c** : LABELLUM 1 **d** : a limb of a labiate corolla **4** **a** : the edge of a hollow vessel or cavity **b** : a projecting edge: as (1) : the beveled upper edge of the mouth of an organ flue pipe (2) : the sharp cutting edge on the end of a tool (as an auger) (3) : a short spout (as on a pitcher) **5** : EMBOUCHURE — **lip·less** \-ləs\ *adj* — **lip·like** \-,līk\ *adj*

²lip *adj* (1558) **1** : INSINCERE (~ praise) **2** : produced with the participation of the lips : LABIAL (~ consonants)

³lip *vt* **lipped; lip·ping** (1604) **1** : to touch with the lips; *esp* : KISS **2** : UTTER **3** : to lap against : LICK **4** : to hit (a putt) so that the ball hits the edge of the cup but fails to drop in

lip- *or* **lipo-** *comb form* [NL, fr. Gk, fr. *lipos* — more at LEAVE] : fat : fatty tissue : fatty (*lipoid*) (*lipoprotein*)

li·pase \'lī-,pās, -,pāz\ *n* [ISV] (1897) : an enzyme that hydrolyzes glycerides

lip·id \'li-pəd\ *also* **lip·ide** \-,pīd\ *n* [ISV] (1912) : any of various substances that are soluble in nonpolar organic solvents (as chloroform and ether), that with proteins and carbohydrates constitute the principal structural components of living cells, and that include fats, waxes, phosphatides, cerebrosides, and related and derived compounds — **lip·id·ic** \li-'pi-dik\ *adj*

Lip·iz·zan \'li-pət-'sän\ *or* **Lip·iz·zan·er** \-'sä-nər\ *also* **Lip·pi·zan** \-'sän\ *or* **Lip·pi·zan·er** \-'sä-nər\ *n* [G *Lipizzaner, Lipizzaner,* fr. *Lipizza, Lippiza,* former site of the Austrian Imperial Stud near Trieste, Italy] (1928) : any of a breed of spirited horses developed from Spanish, Italian, Danish, and Arab stock that are usu. born with a dark coat that lightens to white with age

li·po·gen·e·sis \,lī-pə-'je-nə-səs\ *n* [NL] (1882) : the formation of fatty acids from acetyl coenzyme A in the living body

li·po·ic acid \li-'pō-ik-, li-\ *n* [*lip-, lipo-*] (ca. 1951) : any of several microbial growth factors; *esp* : a crystalline compound $C_8H_{14}O_2S_2$ that is essential for the oxidation of alpha-keto acids (as pyruvic acid) in metabolism

¹li·poid \'lī-,pòid, 'li-\ *or* **li·poi·dal** \lī-'pòi-d³l, li-\ *adj* [ISV] (1876) : resembling fat

²lipoid *n* [ISV] (1906) : LIPID

li·pol·y·sis \lī-'pä-lə-səs, li-\ *n* [NL] (ca. 1903) : the hydrolysis of fat — **li·po·lyt·ic** \,lī-pə-'li-tik, ,li-\ *adj*

li·po·ma \li-'pō-mə, lī-\ *n, pl* **-mas** *or* **-ma·ta** \-mə-tə\ [NL] (1830) : a tumor of fatty tissue — **li·po·ma·tous** \-mə-təs\ *adj*

li·po·phil·ic \,lī-pə-'fi-lik, ,li-\ *adj* (1939) : having an affinity for lipids (as fats) (a ~ metabolite)

li·po·poly·sac·cha·ride \,lī-pō-,pä-li-'sa-kə-,rīd, ,li-\ *n* (1950) : a large molecule consisting of lipids and sugars joined by chemical bonds

li·po·pro·tein \-'prō-,tēn, -'prō-tē-ən\ *n* (1909) : a conjugated protein that is a complex of protein and lipid

li·po·some \'lī-pə-,sōm, 'li-\ *n* (1968) : a vesicle composed of one or more concentric phospholipid bilayers and usually used esp. to deliver a drug into the body — **li·po·so·mal** \,lī-pə-'sō-məl, ,li-\ *adj*

li·po·suc·tion \'lī-pə-,sək-shən, 'li-\ *n* (1986) : surgical removal of local fat deposits (as in the thighs) esp. for cosmetic purposes

li·po·tro·pic \,lī-pō-'trō-pik, ,li-, -'trä-\ *adj* [ISV] (1935) : promoting the physiological utilization of fat (~ dietary factors)

li·po·tro·pin \-'trō-pən\ *n* (1964) : either of two protein hormones of the pituitary gland that function in the mobilization of fat reserves

lipped \'lipt\ *adj* (14c) : having a lip or lips esp. of a specified kind or number — often used in combination (tight-*lipped*)

lip·pen \'li-pən\ *vb* [ME *lipnien*] *vi* (12c) *chiefly Scot* : TRUST, RELY ~ *vt, chiefly Scot* : ENTRUST

Lippes loop \'li-pəs-, -pēz-\ *n* [Jack *Lippes* b1924 Am. physician] (1964) : an S-shaped plastic intrauterine device

lip·ping \'li-piŋ\ *n* (1894) **1** : outgrowth of bone in liplike form at a joint margin **2** : a piece of wood set in an archer's bow where a flaw has been cut out **3** : EMBOUCHURE 1

lip·py \'li-pē\ *adj* **lip·pi·er; -est** (ca. 1875) : given to back talk

lip–read \'lip-,rēd\ *vb* **-read** \-,red\; **-read·ing** \-,rē-diŋ\ *vt* (1892) : to understand by lipreading ~ *vi* : to use lipreading — **lip–read·er** \-,rē-dər\ *n*

lipreading *n* (1874) : the interpreting of speech by watching the speaker's lip and facial movements without hearing the voice

lip service *n* (1644) : an avowal of advocacy, adherence, or allegiance expressed in words but not backed by deeds — usu. used with *pay*

lip·stick \'lip-,stik\ *n* (1880) : a waxy solid usu. colored cosmetic in stick form for the lips; *also* : a stick of such cosmetic with its case — **lip·sticked** *adj*

lip–synch *or* **lip–sync** \'lip-,siŋk\ *vt* (ca. 1961) : to pretend to sing or say in synchronization with recorded sound ~ *vi* : to lip-synch something — **lip sync** *n*

li·quate \'lī-,kwāt\ *vt* **li·quat·ed; li·quat·ing** [L *liquatus,* pp. of *liquare* to make liquid; akin to L *liquēre*] (ca. 1859) : to cause (a more fusible substance) to separate out of a combination or mixture by the application of heat (~ metallic lead from its ore) — **li·qua·tion** \lī-'kwā-shən\ *n*

liq·ue·fac·tion \,li-kwə-'fak-shən\ *n* [ME, fr. LL *liquefaction-, liquefactio,* fr. L *liquefacere, liquēre* to be fluid + *facere* to make — more at DO] (15c) **1** : the process of making or becoming liquid **2** : the state of being liquid

liquefied petroleum gas *n* (1925) : a compressed gas that consists of flammable hydrocarbons (as propane and butane) and is used esp. as fuel or as raw material for chemical synthesis

liq·ue·fy *also* **liq·ui·fy** \'li-kwə-,fī\ *vb* **-fied; -fy·ing** [ME *liquefien,* fr. MF *liquefier,* fr. L *liquefacere*] *vt* (15c) : to reduce to a liquid state ~ *vi* : to become liquid — **liq·ue·fi·er** \-,fī(-ə)r\ *n*

li·ques·cent \li-'kwe-s³nt\ *adj* [L *liquescent-, liquescens,* prp. of *liquescere* to become fluid, incho. of *liquēre*] (ca. 1727) : being or tending to become liquid : MELTING

li·queur \li-'kər, -'kúr, -'kyùr\ *n* [F, fr. OF *licour* liquid — more at LIQUOR] (1729) : a usu. sweetened alcoholic liquor (as brandy) flavored with fruit, spices, nuts, herbs, or seeds

¹liq·uid \'li-kwəd\ *adj* [ME, fr. MF *liquide,* fr. L *liquidus,* fr. *liquēre* to be fluid; akin to L *lixa* water, lye, and perh. to OIr *fliuch* damp] (14c) **1** : flowing freely like water **2** : having the properties of a liquid : being neither solid nor gaseous **3** **a** : shining and clear (large ~ eyes) **b** : being musical and free of harshness in sound **c** : smooth and unconstrained in movement **d** : articulated without friction and capable of being prolonged like a vowel (a ~ consonant) **4** : consisting of or capable of ready conversion into cash (~ assets) — **liq·uid·i·ty** \li-'kwi-də-tē\ *n* — **liq·uid·ly** \'li-kwəd-lē\ *adv* — **liq·uid·ness** *n*

²liquid *n* (1530) **1** : a liquid consonant **2** : a fluid (as water) that has no independent shape but has a definite volume and does not expand indefinitely and that is only slightly compressible

liq·uid·am·bar \,li-kwə-'dam-bər\ *n* [NL, fr. L *liquidus* + ML *ambar, ambra* amber] (ca. 1577) **1** : any of a genus (*Liquidambar*) of trees of the witch-hazel family with monoecious flowers and a globose fruit of many woody carpels **2** : STORAX 1b

liq·ui·date \'li-kwə-,dāt\ *vb* **-dat·ed; -dat·ing** [LL *liquidatus,* pp. of *liquidare* to melt, fr. L *liquidus*] *vt* (ca. 1575) **1** **a** (1) : to determine by agreement or by litigation the precise amount of (indebtedness, damages, or accounts) (2) : to determine the liabilities and apportion assets toward discharging the indebtedness of **b** : to settle (a debt) by payment or other settlement **2** *archaic* : to make clear **3** : to do away with **4** : to convert (assets) into cash ~ *vi* **1** : to liquidate debts, damages, or accounts **2** : to determine liabilities and apportion assets toward discharging indebtedness — **liq·ui·da·tion** \,li-kwə-'dā-shən\ *n*

liq·ui·da·tor \'li-kwə-,dā-tər\ *n* (ca. 1828) : one that liquidates; *esp* : an individual appointed by law to liquidate assets

liquid crystal *n* (1891) : an organic liquid whose physical properties resemble those of a crystal in the formation of loosely ordered molecular arrays similar to a regular crystalline lattice and the anisotropic refraction of light

liquid crystal display *n* (1968) : LCD

liq·uid·ize \'li-kwə-,dīz\ *vt* **-ized; -iz·ing** (1837) : to cause to be liquid

liquid measure *n* (ca. 1855) : a unit or series of units for measuring liquid capacity — see METRIC SYSTEM table, WEIGHT table

¹li·quor \'li-kər\ *n* [ME *licour,* fr. OF, fr. L *liquor,* fr. *liquēre*] (13c) : a liquid substance: as **a** : a usu. distilled rather than fermented alcoholic beverage **b** : a watery solution of a drug **c** : BATH 2b(1)

²liquor *vb* **li·quored; li·quor·ing** \'li-k(ə-)riŋ\ *vt* (1502) **1** : to dress (as leather) with oil or grease **2** : to make drunk with alcoholic liquor — usu. used with *up* ~ *vi* : to drink alcoholic liquor to excess — usu. used with *up*

li·quo·rice *chiefly Brit var of* LICORICE

¹li·ra \'lir-ə, 'lē-rə\ *n, pl* **li·re** \'lē-(,)rā\ *also* **liras** [It, fr. L *libra,* a unit of weight] (1617) — see MONEY table

²lira *n, pl* **liras** [Turk, fr. It] (1871) — see MONEY table

³lira *n, pl* **li·roth** *or* **li·rot** \'lē-,rōt, -,rōth\ [NHeb, fr. It] (ca. 1946) : the former Israeli pound

⁴lira *n, pl* **li·ri** \'lē-(,)rē\ [Maltese, fr. It] (ca. 1985) — see MONEY table

lir·i·pipe \'lir-ə-,pīp\ *n* [ML *liripipium*] (1614) : a pendent part of a tippet; *also* : TIPPET, SCARF

lisente *pl of* SENTE

lisle \'lī(ə)l\ *n, often attrib* [*Lisle* Lille, France] (1851) : a smooth tightly twisted thread usu. made of long-staple cotton

¹lisp \'lisp\ *vb* [ME, fr. OE *-wlyspian*; akin to OHG *lispen* to lisp] *vi* (bef. 12c) **1** : to pronounce the sibilants \s\ and \z\ imperfectly esp. by turning them into \th\ and \t̷h\ **2** : to speak falteringly, child-

---

\ə\ abut \³\ kitten, F table \ər\ further \a\ ash \ā\ ace \ä\ mop, mar \aú\ out \ch\ chin \e\ bet \ē\ easy \g\ go \i\ hit \ī\ ice \j\ job \ŋ\ sing \ō\ go \ò\ law \òi\ boy \th\ thin \t̷h\ the \ü\ loot \ú\ foot \y\ yet \zh\ vision \à, k̲, ⁿ, œ, œ̄, ᵫ, ūᴇ, ᴇ̄, ᵊ\ *see* Guide to Pronunciation ishly, or with a lisp ~ *vt* : to utter falteringly or with a lisp — **lisp·er** *n*

²**lisp** *n* (ca. 1625) **1** : a speech defect or affectation characterized by lisping **2** : a sound resembling a lisp

LISP \'lisp\ *n* [*list* processing] (1959) : a computer programming language that is designed for easy manipulation of data strings and is used extensively for work in artificial intelligence

lis·some *also* **lis·som** \'li-səm\ *adj* [alter. of *lithesome*] (ca. 1800) **1 a** : easily flexed **b** : LITHE 2 **2** : NIMBLE — **lis·some·ly** *adv* — **lis·some·ness** *n*

¹**list** \'list\ *vb* [ME *lysten,* fr. OE *lystan;* akin to OE *lust* desire, lust] *vt* (bef. 12c) *archaic* : PLEASE, SUIT ~ *vi, archaic* : WISH, CHOOSE

²**list** *n* [ME, prob. fr. *lysten*] (13c) *archaic* : INCLINATION, CRAVING

³**list** *vb* [ME, fr. OE *hlystan,* fr. *hlyst* hearing; akin to OE *hlysnan* to listen] *vt* (bef. 12c) *archaic* : LISTEN ~ *vt, archaic* : to listen to : HEAR

⁴**list** *n* [ME, fr. OE *liste;* akin to OHG *lista* edge, Alb *leth*] (bef. 12c) **1 a** : a band or strip of material: as **a** : LISTEL **b** : SELVAGE **c** : a narrow strip of wood cut from the edge of a board **2** *pl but sing or pl in constr* **a** : an arena for combat (as jousting) **b** : a field of competition or controversy **3** *obs* : LIMIT, BOUNDARY **4** : STRIPE

⁵**list** *vt* (1635) **1** : to cut away a narrow strip from the edge of **2** : to prepare or plant (land) in ridges and furrows with a lister

⁶**list** *n* [F *liste,* fr. It *lista,* of Gmc origin; akin to OHG *lista* edge] (1602) **1 a** : a simple series of words or numerals (as the names of persons or objects) ⟨a guest ~⟩ **b** : an official roster : ROLL **2** : CATALOG, CHECKLIST **3** : the total number to be considered or included ⟨a situation that heads their ~ of troubles⟩

⁷**list** *vt* (1614) **1 a** : to make a list of : ENUMERATE **b** : to include on a list : REGISTER **2** : to place (oneself) in a specified category ⟨~s himself as a political liberal⟩ **3** *archaic* : RECRUIT ~ *vi* **1** *archaic* : ENLIST **2** : to become entered in a catalog with a selling price ⟨a car that ~s for $12,000⟩ — **list·ee** \li-'stē\ *n*

⁸**list** *vb* [origin unknown] *vi* (1626) : to tilt to one side; *esp, of a boat or ship* : to tilt to one side in a state of equilibrium (as from an unbalanced load) — compare HEEL ~ *vt* : to cause to list

⁹**list** *n* (1633) : a deviation from the vertical : TILT; *also* : the extent of such a deviation

lis·tel \'lis-t²l, 'lis-tel\ *n* [F, fr. It *listello,* dim. of *lista* fillet, roster] (1598) : a narrow band in architecture : FILLET

¹**lis·ten** \'li-s²n\ *vb* **lis·tened; lis·ten·ing** \'lis-niŋ, 'li-s²n-iŋ\ [ME *listnen,* fr. OE *hlysnan;* akin to Skt *śroṣati* he hears, OE *hlūd* loud] *vt* (bef. 12c) *archaic* : to give ear to : HEAR ~ *vi* **1** : to pay attention to sound ⟨~ to music⟩ **2** : to hear something with thoughtful attention : give consideration ⟨~ to a plea⟩ **3** : to be alert to catch an expected sound ⟨~ for his step⟩ — **lis·ten·er** \'lis-nər, 'li-s²n-ər\ *n*

²**listen** *n* (1788) : an act of listening

lis·ten·able \'lis-nə-bəl, 'li-s²n-ə-\ *adj* (1942) : agreeable to listen to

lis·ten·er·ship \'lis-nər-,ship, 'li-s²n-ər-\ *n* (1943) : the audience for a radio program or recording; *also* : the number or kind of that audience

listen in *vi* (1905) **1** : to tune in to or monitor a broadcast **2** : to listen to a conversation without participating in it; *esp* : EAVESDROP — **lis·ten·er-in** \,lis-nər-'in, ,li-s²n-ər-\ *n*

listening post *n* (1942) : a center for monitoring electronic communications (as of an enemy)

¹**list·er** \'lis-tər\ *n* (1682) : one that lists or catalogs

²**lister** *n* [³*list*] (1887) : a double-moldboard plow often equipped with a subsoiling attachment and used mainly where rainfall is limited

lis·te·ri·o·sis \lis-,tir-ē-'ō-səs\ *n, pl* **-o·ses** \-,sēz\ [NL, fr. *Listeria,* fr. Joseph *Lister*] (1941) : a serious commonly fatal encephalitic disease of a great variety of wild and domestic mammals and birds and occas. humans that is caused by a bacterium (*Listeria monocytogenes*)

list·ing *n* (1659) **1** : an act or instance of making or including in a list **2** : something that is listed

list·less \'list-ləs\ *adj* [ME *listles,* fr. ²*list*] (15c) : characterized by lack of interest, energy, or spirit : LANGUID ⟨a ~ melancholy attitude⟩ — **list·less·ly** *adv* — **list·less·ness** *n*

list price *n* (1871) : the basic price of an item as published in a catalog, price list, or advertisement before any discounts are taken

¹**lit** \'lit\ *past and past part of* LIGHT

²**lit** *n* [by shortening] (1850) : LITERATURE

³**lit** *adj* [pp. of ³*light*] (1904) : affected by alcohol : DRUNK

lit·a·ny \'li-t²n-ē, 'lit-nē\ *n, pl* **-nies** [ME *letanie,* fr. OF & LL; OF, fr. LL *litania,* fr. LGk *litaneia,* fr. Gk, entreaty, fr. *litanos* suppliant] (13c) **1** : a prayer consisting of a series of invocations and supplications by the leader with alternate responses by the congregation **2 a** : a resonant or repetitive chant ⟨a ~ of cheering phrases —Herman Wouk⟩ **b** : a usu. lengthy recitation or enumeration ⟨a familiar ~ of complaints⟩

li·tchi \'lē-(,)chē, 'lī-\ *n* [Chin (Beijing) *lìzhī*] (1588) **1** : the oval fruit of a tree (*Litchi chinensis*) of the soapberry family having a hard scaly reddish outer covering and sweet whitish edible flesh that surrounds a single large seed — called also *litchi nut* **2** : a tree bearing litchis

lit crit \'lit-,krit\ *n* (1963) : literary criticism

lite \'lit\ *var of* ⁴LIGHT 9a

-lite *n comb form* [F, alter. of *-lithe,* fr. Gk *lithos* stone] : mineral ⟨rhodolite⟩ : rock ⟨aerolite⟩ : fossil ⟨stromatolite⟩

li·ter \'lē-tər\ *n* [F *litre,* fr. ML *litra,* a measure, fr. Gk, a weight] (1797) : a metric unit of capacity equal to one cubic decimeter — see METRIC SYSTEM table

lit·er·a·cy \'li-t(ə-)rə-sē\ *n* (1883) : the quality or state of being literate

¹**lit·er·al** \'li-t(ə-)rəl\ *adj* [ME, fr. MF, fr. ML *litteralis,* fr. L, of a letter, fr. *littera* letter] (14c) **1 a** : according with the letter of the scriptures **b** : adhering to fact or to the ordinary construction or primary meaning of a term or expression : ACTUAL ⟨liberty in the ~ sense is impossible —B. N. Cardozo⟩ **c** : free from exaggeration or embellishment ⟨the ~ truth⟩ **d** : characterized by a concern mainly with facts ⟨a very ~ man⟩ **2** : of, relating to, or expressed in letters **3** : reproduced word for word : EXACT, VERBATIM ⟨a ~ translation⟩ — **lit·er·al·i·ty** \,li-tə-'ra-lə-tē\ *n* — **lit·er·al·ness** \'li-t(ə-)rəl-nəs\ *n*

²**literal** *n* (1622) : a small error usu. of a single letter (as in writing)

lit·er·al·ism \'li-t(ə-)rə-,liz-əm\ *n* (1644) **1** : adherence to the explicit substance of an idea or expression ⟨biblical ~⟩ **2** : fidelity to observable fact : REALISM — **lit·er·al·ist** \-list\ *n* — **lit·er·al·is·tic** \,li-t(ə-)rə-'lis-tik\ *adj*

lit·er·al·ize \'li-t(ə-)rə-,līz\ *vt* **-ized; -iz·ing** (1826) : to make literal — **lit·er·al·i·za·tion** \,li-t(ə-)rə-lə-'zā-shən\ *n*

lit·er·al·ly \'li-tə-rə-lē, 'li-trə-lē, 'li-tər-lē\ *adv* (1533) **1** : in a literal sense or manner : ACTUALLY ⟨took the remark ~⟩ ⟨was ~ insane⟩ **2** : in effect : VIRTUALLY ⟨will ~ turn the world upside down to combat cruelty or injustice —Norman Cousins⟩

usage Since some people take sense 2 to be the opposite of sense 1, it has been frequently criticized as a misuse. Instead, the use is pure hyperbole intended to gain emphasis, but it often appears in contexts where no additional emphasis is necessary.

lit·er·ary \'li-tə-,rer-ē\ *adj* (1749) **1 a** : of, relating to, or having the characteristics of humane learning or literature **b** : BOOKISH 2 **c** : of or relating to books **2 a** : WELL-READ **b** : of or relating to authors or scholars or to their professions — **lit·er·ar·i·ly** \,li-tə-'rer-ə-lē\ *adv* — **lit·er·ar·i·ness** \'li-tə-,rer-ē-nəs\ *n*

literary executor *n* (1868) : a person entrusted with the management of the papers and unpublished works of a deceased author

¹**lit·er·ate** \'li-tə-rət *also* 'li-trət\ *adj* [ME *literat,* fr. L *litteratus* marked with letters, literate, fr. *litterae* letters, literature, fr. pl. of *littera*] (15c) **1 a** : EDUCATED, CULTURED **b** : able to read and write **2 a** : versed in literature or creative writing : LITERARY **b** : LUCID, POLISHED ⟨a ~ essay⟩ **c** : having knowledge or competence ⟨computer-*literate*⟩ ⟨politically ~⟩ — **lit·er·ate·ly** *adv* — **lit·er·ate·ness** *n*

²**literate** *n* (ca. 1550) **1** : an educated person **2** : a person who can read and write

li·te·ra·ti \,li-tə-'rä-(,)tē\ *n pl* [obs. It *litterati,* fr. L, pl. of *litteratus*] (1621) **1** : the educated class; *also* : INTELLIGENTSIA **2** : persons interested in literature or the arts

lit·er·a·tim \,li-tə-'rä-təm, -'rä-\ *adv or adj* [ML, fr. L *littera*] (1643) : letter for letter ⟨printed ~ from the manuscript —I. A. Gordon⟩

lit·er·a·tion \,li-tə-'rä-shən\ *n* [L *littera* + E *-ation*] (ca. 1889) : the representation of sound or words by letters

lit·er·a·tor \'li-tə-,rä-tər, ,li-tə-'rä-,tȯr\ *n* (1791) : LITTERATEUR

lit·er·a·ture \'li-tə-rə-,chu̇r, 'li-trə-,chu̇r, 'li-tə(r)-,chu̇r, -chər, -,tyu̇r, -,tu̇r\ *n* [ME, fr. L *litteratura* writing, grammar, learning, fr. *litteratus*] (14c) **1** *archaic* : literary culture **2** : the production of literary work esp. as an occupation **3 a** (1) : writings in prose or verse; *esp* : writings having excellence of form or expression and expressing ideas of permanent or universal interest (2) : an example of such writings ⟨what came out, though rarely ~, was always a roaring good story —*People*⟩ **b** : the body of written works produced in a particular language, country, or age **c** : the body of writings on a particular subject ⟨scientific ~⟩ **d** : printed matter (as leaflets or circulars) ⟨campaign ~⟩ **4** : the aggregate of a usu. specified type of musical compositions ⟨Brahms piano ~⟩

lit·er·a·tus \,li-tə-'rä-təs\ *n* [NL, back-formation fr. E *literati* (taken as L)] (1704) : a member of the literati

lith- *or* **litho-** *comb form* [L, fr. Gk, fr. *lithos*]: stone ⟨*litho*logy⟩

-lith *n comb form* [NL *-lithus* & F *-lithe,* fr. Gk *lithos*] **1** : structure or implement of stone ⟨mega*lith*⟩ ⟨eo*lith*⟩ **2** : calculus ⟨uro*lith*⟩ **3** : -LITE ⟨lacco*lith*⟩

li·tharge \'li-,thärj, li-'\ *n* [ME, fr. MF, fr. L *lithargyrus,* fr. Gk *lithargyros,* fr. *lithos* + *argyros* silver — more at ARGENT] (14c) : a fused lead monoxide; *broadly* : LEAD MONOXIDE

lithe \'līth, 'lith\ *adj* [ME, fr. OE *līthe* gentle; akin to OHG *lindi* gentle, L *lentus* slow] (14c) **1** : easily bent or flexed ⟨~ steel⟩ ⟨a ~ vine⟩ **2** : characterized by easy flexibility and grace ⟨a ~ dancer⟩ ⟨treading with a ~ silent step⟩; *also* : athletically slim ⟨the most ~ and graspable of waists —R. P. Warren⟩ — **lithe·ly** *adv* — **lithe·ness** *n*

lithe·some \'līth-səm, 'lith-\ *adj* (ca. 1774) : LISSOME

li·thi·a·sis \li-'thī-ə-səs\ *n, pl* **-a·ses** \-,sēz\ [NL, fr. Gk, fr. *lithos*] (ca. 1657) : the formation of stony concretions in the body (as in the gallbladder)

lith·ic \'li-thik\ *adj* [Gk *lithikos,* fr. *lithos*] (1797) **1** : STONY 1 **2** : of, relating to, or being a stone tool

-lithic *adj comb form* [*lithic*] : relating to or characteristic of a (specified) stage in humankind's use of stone as a cultural tool ⟨Neo*lithic*⟩

lith·i·fy \'li-thə-,fī\ *vb* **-fied; -fy·ing** *vt* (1877) : to change to stone : PETRIFY; *esp* : to convert (unconsolidated sediment) into solid rock ~ *vi* : to become changed into stone — **lith·i·fi·ca·tion** \,li-thə-fə-'kā-shən\ *n*

lith·i·um \'li-thē-əm\ *n* [NL, fr. *lithia* oxide of lithium, fr. Gk *lithos*] (1818) **1** : a soft silver-white element of the alkali metal group that is the lightest metal known and that is used in chemical synthesis and storage batteries — see ELEMENT table **2** : a salt of lithium (as lithium carbonate) used in psychiatric medicine

lithium carbonate *n* (1873) : a crystalline salt Li_2CO_3 used in the glass and ceramic industries and in medicine in the treatment of manic-depressive psychosis

lithium fluoride *n* (1944) : a crystalline salt LiF used esp. in making prisms and ceramics and as a flux

lithium ni·o·bate \-'nī-ə-,bāt\ *n* [*niobium* + ¹*-ate*] (1966) : a crystalline material $LiNbO_3$ whose physical properties change in response to pressure or the presence of an electric field and which is used in fiber optics and as a modulator

litho \'lī-(,)thō\ *n, pl* **lith·os** (ca. 1889) **1** : LITHOGRAPH **2** : LITHOGRAPHY 1

¹**lith·o·graph** \'li-thə-,graf\ *vt* (1825) : to produce, copy, or portray by lithography — **li·thog·ra·pher** \li-'thä-grə-fər, 'li-thə-,gra-fər\ *n*

²**lithograph** *n* (1828) : a print made by lithography — **lith·o·graph·ic** \,li-thə-'gra-fik\ *adj* — **lith·o·graph·i·cal·ly** \-fi-k(ə-)lē\ *adv*

li·thog·ra·phy \li-'thä-grə-fē\ *n* [G *Lithographie,* fr. *lith-* + *-graphie* -graphy] (1813) **1** : the process of printing from a plane surface (as a smooth stone or metal plate) on which the image to be printed is ink-receptive and the blank area ink-repellent **2** : the process of producing patterns on semiconductor crystals for use as integrated circuits

li·thol·o·gy \li-'thä-lə-jē\ *n, pl* **-gies** (1716) **1** : the study of rocks **2** : the character of a rock formation; *also* : a rock formation having a particular set of characteristics — **lith·o·log·ic** \,li-thə-'lä-jik\ *or* **lith·o·log·i·cal** \-ji-kəl\ *adj* — **lith·o·log·i·cal·ly** \-ji-k(ə-)lē\ *adv*

lith·o·phane \'li-thə-,fān\ *n* [prob. fr. G *Lithophan,* fr. Gk *lithos* + G *diaphan* diaphanous] (ca. 1889) : porcelain impressed with figures that are made distinct by transmitted light; *also* : an object of this material

lith·o·phyte \'li-thə-ˌfīt\ n [F, fr. *lith-* + *-phyte*] (1774) : a plant that grows on rock

lith·o·pone \'li-thə-ˌpōn\ n [ISV *lith-* + Gk *ponos* work] (ca. 1884) : a white pigment consisting essentially of zinc sulfide and barium sulfate

lith·o·sol \'li-thə-ˌsäl, -ˌsȯl\ n [*lith-* + L *solum* soil] (ca. 1938) : any of a group of shallow azonal soils consisting of imperfectly weathered rock fragments

lith·o·sphere \'li-thə-ˌsfir\ n [ISV] (1887) : the solid part of a celestial body (as the earth); *specif* : the outer part of the solid earth composed of rock essentially like that exposed at the surface and usu. considered to be about 50 miles (80 kilometers) in thickness — **lith·o·spher·ic** \ˌli-thə-'sfir-ik, -'sfer-\ *adj*

li·thot·o·my \li-'thä-tə-mē\ n, pl **-mies** [LL *lithotomia*, fr. Gk, fr. *lithotomein* to perform a lithotomy, fr. *lith-* + *temnein* to cut — more at TOME] (1721) : surgical incision of the urinary bladder for removal of a stone

lith·o·trip·sy \'li-thə-ˌtrip-sē\ n, pl **-sies** [*lith-* + Gk *tripsis* a rubbing, fr. *tribein* to rub — more at THROW] (1834) : the breaking of a stone (as by shock waves or crushing with a surgical instrument) in the urinary system into pieces small enough to be voided or washed out

lith·o·trip·ter also **lith·o·trip·tor** \'li-thə-ˌtrip-tər\ n [alter. of *lithontriptor*, fr. *lithontriptic* breaking up bladder stones, modif. of Gk (*pharmaka tōn*) *lithōn thryptika* (drugs) capable of pulverizing stones] (1825) : a device for performing lithotripsy; *esp* : a noninvasive device that pulverizes stones by focusing shock waves on a patient immersed in a water bath

Lith·u·a·nian \ˌli-thə-'wā-nē-ən, -nyən, *chiefly Brit* ˌlith-yü-\ n (1607) **1** : a native or inhabitant of Lithuania **2** : the Baltic language of the Lithuanian people — **Lithuanian** *adj*

lit·i·gant \'li-ti-gənt\ n (1659) : one engaged in a lawsuit — **litigant** *adj*

lit·i·gate \'li-tə-ˌgāt\ vb **-gat·ed; -gat·ing** [L *litigatus*, pp. of *litigare*, fr. *lit-, lis* lawsuit + *agere* to drive — more at AGENT] vi (1615) : to carry on a legal contest by judicial process ~ vt **1** *archaic* : DISPUTE **2** : to contest in law — **lit·i·ga·ble** \'li-ti-gə-bəl\ *adj* — **lit·i·ga·tion** \ˌli-tə-'gā-shən\ n — **lit·i·ga·tor** \'li-tə-ˌgā-tər\ n

li·ti·gious \lə-'ti-jəs, li-\ *adj* [ME, fr. MF *litigieux*, fr. L *litigiosus*, fr. *litigium* dispute, fr. *litigare*] (14c) **1 a** : DISPUTATIOUS, CONTENTIOUS **b** : prone to engage in lawsuits **2** : subject to litigation **3** : of, relating to, or marked by litigation — **li·ti·gious·ly** *adv* — **li·ti·gious·ness** n

lit·mus \'lit-məs\ n [ME *litmose*, of Scand origin; akin to ON *litmosi* herbs used in dyeing, fr. *litr* color (akin to OE *wlite* brightness) + *mosi* moss; akin to OE *mōs* moss] (14c) **1** : a coloring matter from lichens that turns red in acid solutions and blue in alkaline solutions and is used as an acid-base indicator **2** : the critical factor in a litmus test; *also* : LITMUS TEST

litmus paper n (1803) : unsized paper colored with litmus and used as an indicator

litmus test n (1952) : a test in which a single factor (as an attitude, event, or fact) is decisive

li·to·tes \'lī-tə-ˌtēz, lī-, li-'tō-ˌtēz\ n, pl **litotes** [Gk *litotēs*, fr. *litos* simple, perh. fr. *lit-, lis* linen cloth] (1589) : understatement in which an affirmative is expressed by the negative of the contrary (as in "not a bad singer" or "not unhappy")

li·tre \'lē-tər\ *var of* LITER

lit·ten \'li-t³n\ *adj* [alter. of *lit*, pp. of *light*] (ca. 1849) *archaic* : being lighted

¹**lit·ter** \'li-tər\ n [ME, fr. MF *litiere*, fr. *lit* bed, fr. L *lectus* — more at LIE] (14c) **1 a** : a covered and curtained couch provided with shafts and used for carrying a single passenger **b** : a device (as a stretcher) for carrying a sick or injured person **2 a** (1) : material used as bedding for animals (2) : material used to absorb the urine and feces of animals **b** : the uppermost slightly decayed layer of organic matter on the forest floor **3** : the offspring at one birth of a multiparous animal **4 a** : trash, wastepaper, or garbage lying scattered about 〈trying to clean up the roadside ~〉 **b** : an untidy accumulation of objects 〈a shabby writing-desk covered with a ~ of yellowish dusty documents —Joseph Conrad〉 — **lit·tery** \-tə-rē\ *adj*

²**litter** vt (14c) **1** : BED 1a **2** : to give birth to a litter of (young) **3 a** : to strew with scattered articles **b** : to scatter about in disorder **c** : to lie about in disorder 〈their upside-down hats ~ed the top of the bar —Michael Chabon〉 **d** : to mark with objects scattered at random 〈a book ~ed with misprints〉 ~ vi **1** : to give birth to a litter **2** : to strew litter

lit·te·rae hu·ma·ni·o·res \ˌli-tə-ˌrī-hü-ˌmä-nē-'ȯr-ˌās, -'ȯr-\ n pl [ML, lit., more humane letters] (1747) : HUMANITIES

lit·ter·a·teur or **lit·té·ra·teur** \ˌli-tə-rə-'tər, ˌli-trə-, -'tu̇r\ n [F *littérateur*, fr. L *litterator* critic, fr. *litterae* letters, literature] (1806) : a literary person; *esp* : a professional writer

lit·ter·bag \'li-tər-ˌbag\ n (1955) : a bag used (as in an automobile) for temporary refuse disposal

lit·ter·bug \-ˌbəg\ n (1947) : one who litters a public area

lit·ter·er \'li-tər-ər\ n (1928) : LITTERBUG

lit·ter·mate \'li-tər-ˌmāt\ n (1921) : one of the offspring in a litter in relation to the others

¹**lit·tle** \'li-t³l\ *adj* **lit·tler** \'li-t³l-ər, 'lit-lər\ or **less** \'les\ or **less·er** \'le-sər\; **lit·tlest** \'li-t³l-əst, 'lit-ləst\ or **least** \'lēst\ [ME *littel*, fr. OE *lȳtel*; akin to OHG *luzzil* little] (bef. 12c) **1** : not big: as **a** : small in size or extent : TINY 〈has ~ feet〉 **b** : YOUNG 〈was too ~ to remember〉 **c** *of a plant or animal* : small in comparison with related forms — used in vernacular names **d** : small in number **e** : small in condition, distinction, or scope 〈big business trampling on the ~ fellow〉 **f** : NARROW, MEAN 〈the pettiness of ~ minds〉 **g** : pleasingly small 〈a cute ~ thing〉 **h** — used as an intensive 〈why, you ~ devil!〉 **2** : not much: as **a** : existing only in a small amount or to a slight degree 〈has ~ money〉 **b** : short in duration : BRIEF **c** : existing to an appreciable though not extensive degree or amount — used with *a* 〈had a ~ money in the bank〉 **3** : small in importance or interest : TRIVIAL *syn* see SMALL — **lit·tle·ness** \'li-t³l-nəs\ n

²**little** *adv* **less** \'les\; **least** \'lēst\ (bef. 12c) **1 a** : in only a small quantity or degree : SLIGHTLY 〈facts that were ~ known at the time〉 **b** : not at all 〈cared ~ for their neighbors〉 **2** : RARELY, INFREQUENTLY

³**little** n (bef. 12c) **1** : a small amount, quantity, or degree; *also* : practically nothing 〈~ has changed〉 **2 a** : a short time **b** : a short distance — **a little** : SOMEWHAT, RATHER 〈found the play *a little* dull〉 — **in little** : on a small scale; *esp* : in miniature

Little Bear n : URSA MINOR

little bitty *adj* (1905) : SMALL, TINY

little bluestem n (ca. 1898) : a forage grass (*Schizachyrium scoparium* syn. *Andropogon scoparius*) of eastern and central No. America

little brown bat n (1842) : a small widely distributed insectivorous No. American bat (*Myotis lucifugus*) with brown fur

little by little *adv* (15c) : by small degrees or amounts : GRADUALLY

Little Dipper n : the seven principal stars in Ursa Minor

little finger n (bef. 12c) : the fourth and smallest finger of the hand counting the forefinger as the first

little guy n (1863) : LITTLE MAN

Little Hours n pl (ca. 1872) : the offices of prime, terce, sext, and none forming part of the canonical hours

little leaf n (1916) : a plant disorder characterized by small and often chlorotic and distorted foliage: as **a** : a zinc-deficiency disease of deciduous woody plants (as grape, peach, and pecan) **b** : a destructive disease of unknown cause that affects southern pines and esp. the shortleaf pine — called also *little-leaf disease*

Little League n (1952) : a commercially sponsored baseball league for boys and girls from 8 to 12 years old — **Little Leaguer** n

little magazine n (1900) : a literary usu. noncommercial magazine that features works esp. of writers who are not well-known

little man n (1933) : the ordinary individual

lit·tle·neck \'li-t³l-ˌnek\ n [*Littleneck* Bay, Long Island, N.Y.] (1883) : a young quahog suitable to be eaten raw — called also *littleneck clam*

Little Office n (ca. 1872) : an office in honor of the Virgin Mary like but shorter than the Divine Office

little people n pl (ca. 1731) **1** : tiny imaginary beings (as fairies, elves, and leprechauns) of folklore **2** : CHILDREN **3** : MIDGETS **4** : common people

little slam n (ca. 1897) : the winning of all tricks except one in bridge

little theater n (1812) : a small theater for low-cost dramatic productions designed for a relatively limited audience

little toe n (bef. 12c) : the outermost and smallest digit of the foot

little woman n (1795) : WIFE

¹**lit·to·ral** \'li-tə-rəl; ˌli-tə-'ral, -'räl\ *adj* [L *litoralis*, fr. *litor-, litus* seashore] (ca. 1656) : of, relating to, or situated or growing on or near a shore esp. of the sea

²**littoral** n (1828) : a coastal region; *esp* : the shore zone between high and low watermarks

lit up *adj* (ca. 1914) : DRUNK 1a

li·tur·gi·cal \lə-'tər-ji-kəl, li-\ *adj* (1641) **1** : of, relating to, or having the characteristics of liturgy **2** : using or favoring the use of liturgy 〈~ churches〉 — **li·tur·gi·cal·ly** \-k(ə-)lē\ *adv*

li·tur·gics \-jiks\ n pl but sing or pl in constr (ca. 1855) : the practice or study of formal public worship

li·tur·gi·ol·o·gist \-ˌtər-jē-'ä-lə-jist\ n (1866) : LITURGIST 2

li·tur·gi·ol·o·gy \-jē\ n (1863) : LITURGICS

lit·ur·gist \'li-tər-jist\ n (1649) **1** : one who adheres to, compiles, or leads a liturgy **2** : a specialist in liturgics

lit·ur·gy \'li-tər-jē\ n, pl **-gies** [LL *liturgia*, fr. Gk *leitourgia* public service, fr. Gk (Attic) *leitōn* public building (fr. Gk *laos* — Attic *leōs* — people) + *-ourgia* -urgy] (1560) **1** *often cap* : a eucharistic rite **2 a** : a rite or body of rites prescribed for public worship **3** : a customary repertoire of ideas, phrases, or observances

liv·abil·i·ty also **live·abil·i·ty** \ˌli-və-'bi-lə-tē\ n (1914) **1** : survival expectancy : VIABILITY — used esp. of poultry and livestock **2** : suitability for human living

liv·able also **live·able** \'li-və-bəl\ *adj* (1814) **1** : suitable for living in or with **2** : ENDURABLE — **liv·able·ness** n

¹**live** \'liv\ vb **lived; liv·ing** [ME, fr. OE *libban*; akin to OHG *lebēn* to live] vi (bef. 12c) **1** : to be alive : have the life of an animal or plant **2** : to continue alive **3** : to maintain oneself : SUBSIST **4** : to occupy a home : DWELL 〈*living* in a shabby room〉 〈they had always *lived* in the country〉 **5** : to attain eternal life 〈though he die, yet shall he ~ —Jn 11:25 (RSV)〉 **6** : to conduct or pass one's life 〈*lived* only for his work〉 **7** : to remain in human memory or record 〈the past ~s in us all —W. R. Inge〉 **8** : to have a life rich in experience **9** : COHABIT ~ vt **1** : to pass through or spend the duration of 〈*lived* their lives alone〉 **2** : ACT OUT, PRACTICE — often used with *out* 〈to ~ out their fantasies〉 **3** : to exhibit vigor, gusto, or enthusiasm in 〈*lived* life to the fullest〉 — **live it up** : to live with gusto and usu. fast and loose 〈*lived it up* with wine and song —*Newsweek*〉 — **live up to** : to act or be in accordance with 〈had no intention of *living up* to his promise〉

²**live** \'līv\ *adj* [short for *alive*] (1542) **1** : having life : LIVING **2** : exerting force or containing energy: as **a** : AFIRE, GLOWING 〈~ coals〉 **b** : connected to electric power **c** : charged with explosives and containing shot or a bullet 〈~ ammunition〉; *also* : armed but not exploded 〈a ~ bomb〉 **d** : imparting or driven by power 〈a ~ axle〉 : being in operation 〈a ~ microphone〉 **3** : abounding with life : VIVID **4** : being in a pure native state **5** : of bright vivid color **6** : of continuing or current interest 〈~ issues〉 **7 a** : not yet printed from or plated 〈~ type〉 **b** : not yet typeset 〈~ copy〉 **8 a** : of or involving a presentation (as a play or concert) in which both the performers and an audience are physically present 〈a ~ record album〉 〈a nightclub with ~ entertainment〉 **b** : broadcast directly at the time of production 〈a ~ radio program〉 **9** : being in play 〈a ~ ball〉

³**live** \'līv\ *adv* (1946) : at the actual time of occurrence : during, from, or at a live production 〈the programming originated ~ from New York City —*Current Biog.*〉

live–bear·er \'liv-ˌbar-ər, -ˌber-\ n (1934) : a fish that brings forth living young rather than eggs; *any* : of a family (Poeciliidae) of numerous small surface-feeding fishes

live–box \-ˌbäks\ n (1862) : a box or pen suspended in water to keep aquatic animals alive

\ə\ abut \ᵊ\ kitten, F table \ər\ further \a\ ash \ā\ ace \ä\ mop, mar \au̇\ out \ch\ chin \e\ bet \ē\ easy \g\ go \i\ hit \ī\ ice \j\ job \ŋ\ sing \ō\ go \ȯ\ law \ȯi\ boy \th\ thin \t͟h\ the \ü\ loot \u̇\ foot \y\ yet \zh\ vision \à, k̲, ⁿ, œ, ᴔ, ᵫ, ᴇ, ᵁ\ *see* Guide to Pronunciation

-lived \'līvd, 'livd\ *adj comb form* [ME, fr. *līf* life] : having a life of a specified kind or length ⟨long-*lived*⟩

lived–in \'liv-,din\ *adj* (1873) : of or suggesting long-term human habitation or use : COMFORTABLE

live down *vt* (1842) : to live so as to wipe out the memory or effects of ⟨made a mistake and couldn't *live* it *down*⟩

live–for·ev·er \'liv-fə-,re-vər\ *n* (1597) : SEDUM

live–in \'liv-,in\ *adj* (1953) **1** : living in one's place of employment ⟨a ~ maid⟩ **2** : involving or involved with cohabitation ⟨a ~ relationship⟩ ⟨a ~ partner⟩ — **live–in** *n*

live in *vi* (1890) : to live in one's place of employment : live in another's home

live·li·hood \'liv-lē-,hùd\ *n* [alter. of ME *livelode* course of life, fr. OE *līflād*, fr. *līf* + *lād* course — more at LODE] (15c) **1** : means of support or subsistence **2** : the quality or state of being lively

live load *n* (1866) : the load to which a structure is subjected in addition to its own weight

live·long \'liv-,lòŋ\ *adj* [ME *lef long*, fr. *lef* dear + *long* — more at LIEF] (15c) : WHOLE, ENTIRE ⟨the ~ day⟩

live·ly \'līv-lē\ *adj* **live·li·er; -est** [ME, fr. OE *līflīc*, fr. *līf* life] (bef. 12c) **1** *obs* : LIVING **2** : briskly alert and energetic : VIGOROUS, ANIMATED ⟨a ~ discussion⟩ ⟨~ children racing for home⟩ **3** : ACTIVE, INTENSE ⟨takes a ~ interest in politics⟩ **4** : BRILLIANT, FRESH ⟨a ~ wit⟩ **5** : imparting spirit or vivacity : STIMULATING ⟨many a peer of England brews *livelier* liquor than the Muse —A. E. Housman⟩ **6** : quick to rebound : RESILIENT **7** : responding readily to the helm ⟨a ~ boat⟩ **8** : full of life, movement, or incident ⟨~ streets at carnival time⟩ — **live·li·ly** \'līv-lə-lē\ *adv* — **live·li·ness** \'līv-lē-nəs\ *n* — **lively** *adv*
syn LIVELY, ANIMATED, VIVACIOUS, SPRIGHTLY, GAY mean keenly alive and spirited. LIVELY suggests briskness, alertness, or energy ⟨a *lively* debate on the issues⟩. ANIMATED applies to what is spirited and active ⟨an *animated* discussion of current events⟩. VIVACIOUS suggests an activeness of gesture and wit, often playful or alluring ⟨a *vivacious* party host⟩. SPRIGHTLY suggests lightness and spirited vigor of manner or wit ⟨a tuneful, *sprightly* musical⟩. GAY stresses complete freedom from care and overflowing spirits ⟨the *gay* spirit of Paris in the 1920s⟩.

liv·en \'lī-vən\ *vb* **liv·ened; liv·en·ing** \'lī-və-niŋ, 'līv-niŋ\ *vt* (1884) : ENLIVEN — often used with *up* ⟨he . . . ~*ed* up the editorial page — *Current Biog.*⟩ ~ *vi* : to become lively

live oak \'liv-\ *n* (1610) : any of several American evergreen oaks: as **a** : a medium-sized oak (*Quercus virginiana*) of southeastern No. America often cultivated as a shelter and shade tree and noted for its extremely hard tough durable wood **b** : any of several oaks of the western U.S. with evergreen foliage and hard durable wood

¹liv·er \'li-vər\ *n* [ME, fr. OE *lifer*; akin to OHG *lebra* liver] (bef. 12c) **1 a** : a large very vascular glandular organ of vertebrates that secretes bile and causes important changes in many of the substances contained in the blood (as by converting sugars into glycogen which it stores up until required and by forming urea) **b** : any of various large compound glands associated with the digestive tract of invertebrate animals and prob. concerned with the secretion of digestive enzymes **2** *archaic* : a determinant of the quality or temper of a man **3** : the liver of an animal (as a calf or chicken) eaten as food **4** : a grayish reddish brown — called also *liver brown, liver maroon*

²liv·er \'li-vər\ *n* (14c) **1** : one that lives esp. in a specified way ⟨a fast ~⟩ **2** : RESIDENT

-livered *adj comb form* : expressing vigor or courage considered suggestive of one with (such) a liver ⟨chicken-*livered*⟩ ⟨lily-*livered*⟩

liver fluke *n* (ca. 1798) : any of various trematode worms (as *Fasciola hepatica*) that invade the mammalian liver

liv·er·ied \'li-və-rēd, 'liv-rēd\ *adj* (1634) : wearing a livery ⟨a ~ chauffeur⟩

liv·er·ish \'li-və-rish, 'liv-rish\ *adj* (1740) **1** : resembling liver esp. in color **2 a** : suffering from liver disorder : BILIOUS **b** : PEEVISH, IRASCIBLE — **liv·er·ish·ness** *n*

liver sausage *n* (1855) : a sausage containing cooked ground liver and pork trimmings — called also *liver pudding*

liver spots *n pl* (ca. 1859) : spots of dark pigmentation on the skin (as from exposure to sun) occurring esp. among older people

liv·er·wort \'li-vər-,wərt, -,wört\ *n* (bef. 12c) **1** : any of a class (Hepaticae) of bryophytic plants characterized by a thalloid gametophyte or sometimes an upright leafy gametophyte that resembles a moss **2** : HEPATICA

liv·er·wurst \'li-və(r)-,wərst *also* -,vù(r)st; *sometimes* -,vùsht\ *n* [part trans. of G *Leberwurst*, fr. *Leber* liver + *Wurst* sausage] (1869) : LIVER SAUSAGE

¹liv·ery \'li-və-rē, 'liv-rē\ *n, pl* **-er·ies** [ME, fr. MF *livree*, lit., delivery, fr. *livrer* to deliver, fr. L *liberare* to free — more at LIBERATE] (14c) **1** *archaic* : the apportioning of provisions esp. to servants : ALLOWANCE **2 a** : the distinctive clothing or badge formerly worn by the retainers of a person of rank **b** : a servant's uniform **c** : distinctive dress : GARB **d** *chiefly Brit* : an identifying design (as on a vehicle) that designates ownership **3** *archaic* **a** : one's retainers or retinue **b** : the members of a British livery company **4** : the act of delivering legal possession of property **5 a** : the feeding, stabling, and care of horses for pay **b** : LIVERY STABLE **c** : a concern offering vehicles (as boats) for rent

²livery *adj* (1778) **1** : resembling liver **2** : suggesting liver disorder

livery company *n* (1766) : any of various London craft or trade associations that are descended from medieval guilds

liv·ery·man \'li-və-rē-mən, 'liv-rē-\ *n* (1682) **1** : a freeman of the City of London entitled to wear the livery of the company to which he belongs **2** *archaic* : a liveried retainer **3** : the keeper of a vehicle-rental service

livery stable *n* (1705) : a stable where horses and vehicles are kept for hire and where stabling is provided — called also *livery barn*

lives *pl of* LIFE

live steam *n* (ca. 1875) : steam direct from a boiler and under full pressure

live·stock \'līv-,stäk\ *n* (1742) : animals kept or raised for use or pleasure; *esp* : farm animals kept for use and profit

live–trap \-,trap\ *vt* (1944) : to capture (an animal) in a live trap

live trap *n* (ca. 1875) : a trap for catching an animal alive and uninjured

live wire *n* (1903) : an alert, active, or aggressive person

liv·id \'li-vəd\ *adj* [F *livide*, fr. L *lividus*, fr. *livēre* to be blue; akin to W *lliw* color and prob. to Russ *sliva* plum] (1622) **1** : discolored by bruising : BLACK-AND-BLUE ⟨the ~ traces of the sharp scourges —Abraham Cowley⟩ **2** : ASHEN, PALLID ⟨this cross, thy ~ face, thy pierced hands and feet —Walt Whitman⟩ **3** : REDDISH ⟨a fan of gladiolas blushed ~ under the electric letters —Truman Capote⟩ **4** : very angry : ENRAGED ⟨was ~ at his son's disobedience⟩ — **li·vid·i·ty** \li-'vi-də-tē\ *n* — **liv·id·ness** \'li-vəd-nəs\ *n*

¹liv·ing \'li-viŋ\ *adj* (bef. 12c) **1 a** : having life : ACTIVE, FUNCTIONING ⟨~ languages⟩ **2 a** : exhibiting the life or motion of nature : NATURAL ⟨the wilderness is a ~ museum . . . of natural history — *NEA Jour.*⟩ **b** : ²LIVE 2a **3 a** : full of life or vigor **b** : true to life : VIVID ⟨televised in ~ color⟩ **c** : suited for living ⟨the ~ area⟩ **4** : involving living persons **5** : VERY — used as an intensive ⟨scared the ~ daylights out of me⟩ — **liv·ing·ness** *n*

²living *n* (14c) **1** : the condition of being alive **2** : means of subsistence : LIVELIHOOD ⟨earning a ~⟩ **b** *archaic* : ESTATE, PROPERTY **c** *Brit* : BENEFICE 1 **3** : conduct or manner of life ⟨the collegiate way of ~ — J. B. Conant⟩

living death *n* (1671) : life emptied of joys and satisfactions

living fossil *n* (1922) : an organism (as a horseshoe crab or a ginkgo tree) that has remained essentially unchanged from earlier geologic times and whose close relatives are usu. extinct

liv·ing·ly \'li-viŋ-lē\ *adv* (15c) : in a vital manner : REALISTICALLY

living room *n* (1857) **1** : a room in a residence used for the common social activities of the occupants **2** : LEBENSRAUM — called also *living space*

living standard *n* (1944) : STANDARD OF LIVING

living unit *n* (ca. 1937) : an apartment or house for use by one family

living wage *n* (1888) **1** : a subsistence wage **2** : a wage sufficient to provide the necessities and comforts essential to an acceptable standard of living

living will *n* (1972) : a document in which the signer requests to be allowed to die rather than be kept alive by artificial means if disabled beyond a reasonable expectation of recovery

liv·re \'lēvrᵊ\ *n* [F, fr. L *libra*, a unit of weight] (1553) **1** : an old French monetary unit equal to 20 sols **2** : a coin representing one livre **3** : the pound of Lebanon

lix·iv·i·ate \lik-'si-vē-,āt\ *vt* **-at·ed; -at·ing** [L *lixivium* lye, fr. *lixivius* made of lye, fr. *lixa* lye — more at LIQUID] (1758) : to extract a soluble constituent from (a solid mixture) by washing or percolation — **lix·iv·i·a·tion** \(,)lik-,si-vē-'ā-shən\ *n*

liz·ard \'li-zərd\ *n* [ME *liserd*, fr. MF *laisarde*, fr. L *lacerta*] (14c) **1** : any of a suborder (Lacertilia) of reptiles distinguished from the snakes by a fused inseparable lower jaw, a single temporal opening, two pairs of well differentiated functional limbs which may be lacking in burrowing forms, external ears, and eyes with movable lids; *broadly* : any relatively long-bodied reptile (as a crocodile or dinosaur) with legs and tapering tail **2** : leather made from lizard skin

lizard's tail *n* (ca. 1753) : a perennial herb (*Saururus cernuus* of the family Saururaceae) of No. American wetlands having spikes of tiny white flowers

'll \l, əl, ᵊl\ *vb* (1578) : WILL ⟨you'll be late⟩

lla·ma \'lä-mə, 'yä-mə\ *n* [Sp, fr. Quechua] (1600) : any of a genus (*Lama*) of wild or domesticated So. American ruminants related to the camels but smaller and without a hump; *esp* : the domesticated guanaco used esp. in the Andes as a pack animal and a source of wool

lla·no \'lä-(,)nō, 'la-\ *n, pl* **llanos** [Sp, plain, fr. L *planum* — more at PLAIN] (1604) : an open grassy plain in Spanish America or the southwestern U.S.

lo \'lō\ *interj* [ME, fr. OE *lā*] (bef. 12c) — used to call attention or to express wonder or surprise ⟨~ these many years⟩

loach \'lōch\ *n* [ME *loche*, fr. MF] (14c) : any of a family (Cobitidae) of small Old World freshwater fishes related to the carps

¹load \'lōd\ *n* [ME *lod*, fr. OE *lād* support, carrying — more at LODE] (12c) **1 a** : the quantity that can be carried at one time by a specified means; *esp* : a measured quantity of a commodity fixed for each type of carrier — often used in combination ⟨a boat*load* of tourists⟩ **b** : whatever is put on a person or pack animal to be carried : PACK **c** : whatever is put in a ship or vehicle or airplane for conveyance : CARGO; *esp* : a quantity of material assembled or packed as a shipping unit **2 a** : a mass or weight supported by something ⟨branches bent low by their ~ of fruit⟩ **b** : the forces to which a structure is subjected due to superposed weight or to wind pressure on the vertical surfaces; *broadly* : the forces to which a given object is subjected **3 a** : something that weighs down the mind or spirits ⟨took a ~ off her mind⟩ **b** : a burdensome or laborious responsibility ⟨always carried his share of the ~⟩ **4** *slang* : an intoxicating amount of liquor drunk **5** : a large quantity : LOT — usu. used in pl. **6 a** : a charge for a firearm **b** : the quantity of material loaded into a device at one time **7** : external resistance overcome by a machine or prime mover **8 a** : power output (as of a power plant) or power consumption (as by a device) **b** : a device to which power is delivered **9 a** (1) : the amount of work that a person carries or is expected to carry (2) : the amount of authorized work to be performed by a machine, a group, a department, or a factory **b** : the demand on the operating resources of a system (as a telephone exchange or a refrigerating apparatus) **10** *slang* : EYEFUL — used in the phrase *get a load of* **11** : an amount added (as to the price of a security or the net premium in insurance) to represent selling expense and profit to the distributor **12** : the decrease in capacity for survival of the average individual in a population due to the presence of deleterious genes in the gene pool ⟨the mutational ~ is the genetic ~ caused by mutation⟩

²load *vt* (15c) **1 a** : to put a load in or on ⟨~ a truck⟩ **b** : to place in or on a means of conveyance ⟨~ freight⟩ **2 a** : to encumber or op-

llama

press with something heavy, laborious, or disheartening : BURDEN ⟨a company ∼ed down with debts⟩ **b** : to place as a burden or obligation ⟨∼ more work on him⟩ **3 a** : to increase the weight of by adding something heavy **b** : to add a conditioning substance (as a mineral salt) to for body **c** : to weight or shape (dice) to fall unfairly **d** : to pack with one-sided or prejudicial influences : BIAS **e** : to charge with multiple meanings (as emotional associations or hidden implications) **f** : to weight (as a test) with factors influencing validity or outcome **4 a** : to supply in abundance or excess : HEAP, PACK **b** : to put runners on (first, second, and third bases) in baseball **5 a** : to put a load or charge in (a device or piece of equipment) ⟨∼ a gun⟩ **b** : to place or insert esp. as a load in a device or piece of equipment ⟨∼ film in a camera⟩ ⟨∼ a program into a computer⟩ **6** : to alter (as an alcoholic drink) by adding an adulterant or drug **7 a** : to add a load to (an insurance premium) **b** : to add a sum to after profits and expenses are accounted for ⟨∼ed prices⟩ **∼** *vi* **1** : to receive a load **2** : to put a load on or in a carrier, device, or container; *esp* : to insert the charge or cartridge in the chamber of a firearm **3** : to go or go in as a load ⟨sightseers ∼*ing* onto a bus⟩ — **load·er** *n*
load·ed *adj* (1886) **1** *slang* : HIGH 12b **2** : having a large amount of money
load factor *n* (1943) : the percentage of available seats paid for and occupied in an aircraft
load·ing *n* (15c) **1** : a cargo, weight, or stress placed on something **2** : LOAD 11 **3** : material used to load something : FILLER
load line *n* (ca. 1859) : the line on a ship indicating the depth to which it sinks in the water when properly loaded — see PLIMSOLL MARK illustration
load·mas·ter \'lōd-,mas-tər\ *n* (1961) : a crew member of a transport aircraft who is in charge of the cargo
load·star *var of* LODESTAR
load·stone *var of* LODESTONE
¹**loaf** \'lōf\ *n, pl* **loaves** \'lōvz\ [ME *lof*, fr. OE *hlāf*; akin to OHG *hleib* loaf] (bef. 12c) **1** : a shaped or molded mass of bread **2** : a shaped or molded often symmetrical mass of food **3** *slang Brit* : HEAD, MIND
²**loaf** *vi* [prob. back-formation fr. *loafer*] (1835) : to spend time in idleness
loaf·er \'lō-fər\ *n* [perh. short for *landloafer*, fr. G *Landläufer* tramp, fr. *Land* + *Läufer* runner] (1830) : one that loafs : IDLER
Loafer *trademark* — used for a low step-in shoe
loam \'lōm, *chiefly Northern & Midland* 'lüm, *NewEng also* 'lùm\ *n* [ME *lom*, fr. OE *lām* clay, mud; akin to OE *līm* lime] (12c) **1 a** : a mixture (as for plastering) composed chiefly of moistened clay **b** : a coarse molding sand used in founding **2** : SOIL; *specif* : a soil consisting of a friable mixture of varying proportions of clay, silt, and sand — **loamy** \'lō-mē, 'lü-, 'lù-\ *adj*
¹**loan** \'lōn\ *n* [ME *lon*, fr. ON *lān*; akin to OE *lǣn* loan, *lēon* to lend, L *linquere* to leave, Gk *leipein*] (12c) **1 a** : money lent at interest **b** : something lent usu. for the borrower's temporary use **2 a** : the grant of temporary use **b** : the temporary duty of a person transferred to another job for a limited time **3** : LOANWORD
²**loan** *vt* (13c) : LEND — **loan·able** \'lō-nə-bəl\ *adj*
  usage The verb *loan* is one of the words English settlers brought to America and continued to use after it had died out in Britain. Its use was soon noticed by British visitors and somewhat later by the New England literati, who considered it a bit provincial. It was flatly declared wrong in 1870 by a popular commentator, who based his objection on etymology. A later scholar showed that the commentator was ignorant of Old English and thus unsound in his objection, but by then it was too late, as the condemnation had been picked up by many other commentators. Although a surprising number of critics still voice objections, *loan* is entirely standard as a verb. You should note that it is used only literally; *lend* is the verb used for figurative expressions, such as "lending a hand" or "lending enchantment."
lo and behold *interj* (1808) — used to express wonder or surprise
loan·er \'lō-nər\ *n* (1926) : one (as a car or a watch) that is lent esp. as a replacement for something being repaired
loan·ing \'lō-niŋ\ *n* [ME *loning*, fr. *lone*, alter. of *lane*] (14c) **1** *dial Brit* : LANE **2** *dial Brit* : a milking yard
loan shark *n* (1905) : one who lends money to individuals at exorbitant rates of interest
loan–shark·ing \-,shär-kiŋ\ *n* (1914) : the practice of lending money at exorbitant rates of interest
loan translation *n* (ca. 1933) : a compound, derivative, or phrase that is introduced into a language through translation of the constituents of a term in another language (as *superman* from German *Übermensch*)
loan·word \'lōn-,wərd\ *n* (1874) : a word taken from another language and at least partly naturalized
¹**loath** \'lōth, 'lōth\ *also* **loathe** \'lōth, 'lōth\ *adj* [ME *loth* loathsome, fr. OE *lāth*; akin to OHG *leid* loathsome, OIr *lius* loathing] (12c) : unwilling to do something contrary to one's ways of thinking : RELUCTANT *syn* see DISINCLINED — **loath·ness** *n*
loathe \'lōth\ *vt* **loathed; loath·ing** [ME *lothen*, fr. OE *lāthian* to dislike, be hateful, fr. *lāth*] (12c) : to dislike greatly and often with disgust or intolerance : DETEST *syn* see HATE — **loath·er** *n*
loathing *n* (14c) : extreme disgust : DETESTATION
¹**loath·ly** \'lōth-lē, 'lōth-\ *adj* (bef. 12c) : LOATHSOME, REPULSIVE
²**loath·ly** \'lōth-lē, 'lōth-\ *adv* (15c) : not willingly : RELUCTANTLY
loath·some \'lōth-səm, 'lōth-\ *adj* [ME *lothsum*, fr. *loth* evil, fr. OE *lāth*, *n. lāth*, adj.] (14c) : giving rise to loathing : DISGUSTING — **loath·some·ly** *adv* — **loath·some·ness** *n*
¹**lob** \'läb\ *n* [prob. of LG origin; akin to LG *lubbe* coarse person] (1508) *dial Brit* : a dull heavy person : LOUT
²**lob** *vb* **lobbed; lob·bing** [*lob* a loosely hanging object] *vt* (1599) **1** : to let hang heavily : DROOP **2** : to throw, hit, or propel easily or in a high arc **∼** *vi* **1 a** : to move slowly and heavily **b** : to move in an arc **2** : to hit a tennis ball easily in a high arc
³**lob** *n* (1851) : a soft high-arching shot, throw, or kick
lob- *or* **lobo-** *comb form* [*lobe*] : lobe ⟨*lobar*⟩ ⟨*lobotomy*⟩
lo·bar \'lō-bər, -,bär\ *adj* (ca. 1856) : of or relating to a lobe
lo·bate \'lō-,bāt\ *also* **lo·bat·ed** \-,bā-təd\ *adj* [NL *lobatus*, fr. LL *lobus*] (ca. 1760) **1** : LOBED **2** : resembling a lobe — **lo·ba·tion** \lō-'bā-shən\ *n*
¹**lob·by** \'lä-bē\ *n, pl* **lobbies** [ML *lobium* gallery, of Gmc origin; akin

to OHG *louba* porch] (1593) **1** : a corridor or hall connected with a larger room or series of rooms and used as a passageway or waiting room: **as a** : an anteroom of a legislative chamber; *esp* : one of two anterooms of a British parliamentary chamber to which members go to vote during a division **b** : a large hall serving as a foyer (as of a hotel or theater) **2** : a group of persons engaged in lobbying esp. as representatives of a particular interest group
²**lobby** *vb* **lob·bied; lob·by·ing** *vi* (1837) : to conduct activities aimed at influencing public officials and esp. members of a legislative body on legislation **∼** *vt* **1** : to promote (as a project) or secure the passage of (as legislation) by influencing public officials **2** : to attempt to influence or sway (as a public official) toward a desired action — **lob·by·er** *n* — **lob·by·ism** \-,i-zəm\ *n* — **lob·by·ist** \-ist\ *n*
lob·by·gow \'lä-bē-,gaù\ *n* [origin unknown] (1906) : an errand boy
lobe \'lōb\ *n* [MF, fr. LL *lobus*, fr. Gk *lobos*] (1541) : a curved or rounded projection or division; *specif* : a usu. somewhat rounded projection or division of a bodily organ or part
lo·bec·to·my \lō-'bek-tə-mē\ *n, pl* **-mies** [ISV] (ca. 1911) : surgical removal of a lobe of an organ (as a lung) or gland (as the thyroid)
lobed \'lōbd\ *adj* (1787) : having lobes ⟨palmately ∼ leaves⟩
lobe-fin \'lōb-,fin\ *n* (1941) : CROSSOPTERYGIAN — **lobe–finned** \-'find\ *adj*
lo·be·lia \lō-'bēl-yə, -'bē-lē-ə\ *n* [NL, fr. Matthias de *Lobel* †1616 Flem. botanist] (1739) **1** : any of a genus (*Lobelia* of the family Lobeliaceae, the lobelia family) of widely cultivated plants having terminal clusters of showy lipped flowers **2** : the leaves and tops of Indian tobacco
lo·be·line \'lō-bə-,lēn\ *n* [NL *Lobelia* + ²-*ine*] (1852) : a crystalline alkaloid $C_{22}H_{27}NO_2$ that is obtained from Indian tobacco and is used chiefly as a respiratory stimulant and as a smoking deterrent
lob·lol·ly \'läb-,lä-lē\ *n, pl* **-lies** [prob. fr. E dial. *lob* to boil + obs. E dial. *lolly* broth] (1597) **1** *dial* **a** : a thick gruel **b** : MIRE, MUDHOLE **2** *dial* : LOUT **3** : LOBLOLLY PINE
loblolly pine *n* (1760) : a pine (*Pinus taeda*) of the southeastern U.S. with flaky bark, long needles in groups of three, and cones having spine-tipped scales; *also* : its coarse-grained wood
lo·bo \'lō-(,)bō\ *n, pl* **lobos** [Sp, wolf, fr. L *lupus* — more at WOLF] (1839) : GRAY WOLF
lo·bot·o·mise *Brit var of* LOBOTOMIZE
lo·bot·o·mize \lō-'bä-tə-,mīz\ *vt* **-mized; -miz·ing** (1943) **1** : to perform a lobotomy on **2** : to deprive of sensitivity, intelligence, or vitality ⟨fear of prosecution was causing the press to ∼ itself —Tony Eprile⟩
lo·bot·o·my \lō-'bä-tə-mē\ *n, pl* **-mies** [ISV] (1936) : surgical severance of nerve fibers connecting the frontal lobes to the thalamus for the relief of some mental disorders
lob·scouse \'läb-,skaùs\ *n* [origin unknown] (1706) : a sailor's dish of stewed or baked meat with vegetables and hardtack
lob·ster \'läb-stər\ *n, often attrib* [ME, fr. OE *loppestre*, fr. *loppe* spider] (bef. 12c) **1** : any of a family (Nephropidae and esp. *Homarus americanus*) of large edible marine decapod crustaceans that have stalked eyes, a pair of large claws, and a long abdomen and that include species from coasts on both sides of the No. Atlantic and from the Cape of Good Hope **2** : SPINY LOBSTER — **lob·ster·like** \-,līk\ *adj*
lob·ster·ing \'läb-st(ə-)riŋ\ *n* (1881) : the activity or business of catching lobsters
lob·ster·man \-mən\ *n* (1881) : one whose business is lobstering
lobster pot *n* (1764) : an oblong case with slat sides and a funnel-shaped net used to trap lobsters — called also *lobster trap*
lobster shift *n* (ca. 1933) : a work shift (as on a newspaper) that covers the late evening and early morning hours — called also *lobster trick*

lobster pot

lobster ther·mi·dor \-'thər-mə-,dôr\ *n* [*thermidor*, fr. F, fr. *Thermidor*, drama (1891) by Victorien Sardou] (1930) : cooked lobster meat in a rich wine sauce stuffed into a lobster shell and browned
lob·u·lar \'lä-byə-lər\ *adj* (1826) : of, relating to, affecting, or resembling a lobule
lob·u·lat·ed \'lä-byə-,lā-təd\ *also* **lob·u·late** \-,lāt\ *adj* (1783) : made up of or having lobules ⟨the pancreas is a ∼ organ⟩ — **lob·u·la·tion** \,lä-byə-'lā-shən\ *n*
lob·ule \'lä-(,)byü(ə)l\ *n* (1682) : a small lobe; *also* : a subdivision of a lobe
¹**lo·cal** \'lō-kəl\ *adj* [ME *localle*, fr. MF *local*, fr. LL *localis*, fr. L *locus* place — more at STALL] (15c) **1** : characterized by or relating to position in space : having a definite spatial form or location **2 a** : of, relating to, or characteristic of a particular place : not general or widespread **b** : of, relating to, or applicable to part of a whole **3 a** : primarily serving the needs of a particular limited district **b** *of a public conveyance* : making all the stops on a route **4** : involving or affecting only a restricted part of the organism : TOPICAL **5** : of or relating to telephone communication within a specified area
²**local** *n* (ca. 1824) : a local person or thing: **as a** : a local public conveyance (as a train or an elevator) **b** : a local or particular branch, lodge, or chapter of an organization (as a labor union) **c** *Brit* : a nearby or neighborhood pub
local area network *n* (1981) : a network of personal computers in a small area (as an office) that are linked by cable, can communicate directly with other devices in the network, and can share resources
local color *n* (1884) : the presentation of the features and peculiarities of a particular locality and its inhabitants in writing

---

\ə\ abut \ᵊ\ kitten, F table \ər\ further \a\ ash \ā\ ace \ä\ mop, mar \aù\ out \ch\ chin \e\ bet \ē\ easy \g\ go \i\ hit \ī\ ice \j\ job \ŋ\ sing \ō\ go \ò\ law \òi\ boy \th\ thin \th\ the \ü\ loot \ù\ foot \y\ yet \zh\ vision \à, ḵ, ⁿ, œ, œ̄, ᵫ, ᵫ̄, ʸ\ *see* Guide to Pronunciation

lo·cale \lō-'kal\ *n* [modif. of F *local,* fr. *local, adj.*] (1772) **1** : a place or locality esp. when viewed in relation to a particular event or characteristic **2** : SITE, SCENE ⟨the ~ of a story⟩

local government *n* (1844) : the government of a specific local area constituting a major political unit (as a nation or state); *also* : the body of persons constituting such a government

lo·cal·ise *Brit var of* LOCALIZE

lo·cal·ism \'lō-kə-ˌli-zəm\ *n* (1823) **1 a** : a local peculiarity of speaking or acting **b** : a local idiom **2** : affection or partiality for a particular place : SECTIONALISM

lo·cal·ite \'lō-kə-ˌlīt\ *n* (1951) : a native or resident of the locality under consideration : LOCAL

lo·cal·i·ty \lō-'ka-lə-tē\ *n, pl* **-ties** (1628) **1** : the fact or condition of having a location in space or time **2** : a particular place, situation, or location

lo·cal·ize \'lō-kə-ˌlīz\ *vb* **-ized; -iz·ing** *vt* (1792) **1** : to make local : orient locally **2** : to assign to or keep within a definite locality ~ *vi* : to accumulate in or be restricted to a specific or limited area ⟨an infection that ~s in the ear⟩ — **lo·cal·iz·abil·i·ty** \ˌlō-kə-ˌlī-zə-'bi-lə-tē\ *n* — **lo·cal·iz·able** \'lō-kə-ˌlī-zə-bəl\ *adj* — **lo·cal·i·za·tion** \ˌlō-kə-lə-'zā-shən\ *n*

lo·cal·ly \'lō-k(ə-)lē\ *adv* (15c) **1** : with respect to a particular place or situation **2** : NEARBY **3** : in the region of origin

local option *n* (1878) : the power granted by a legislature to a political subdivision to determine by popular vote the local applicability of a law on a controversial issue (as the sale of liquor)

local time *n* (1833) : time based on the meridian through a particular place as contrasted with that of a time zone

lo·cate \'lō-ˌkāt, lō-'\ *vb* **lo·cat·ed; lo·cat·ing** [L *locatus,* pp. of *locare* to place, fr. *locus*] *vi* (1652) : to establish oneself or one's business : SETTLE ~ *vt* **1** : to determine or indicate the place, site, or limits of **2** : to set or establish in a particular spot : STATION **3** : to seek out and determine the location of **4** : to find or fix the place of esp. in a sequence : CLASSIFY — **lo·cat·able** \-ˌkā-tə-bəl, -'kā-\ *adj*

lo·ca·tion \lō-'kā-shən\ *n* (1597) **1 a** : a position or site occupied or available for occupancy or marked by some distinguishing feature : SITUATION **b** (1) : a tract of land designated for a purpose (2) *Austral* : FARM, STATION **c** : a place outside a motion-picture studio where a picture or part of it is filmed — usu. used in the phrase *on location* **2** : the act or process of locating — **lo·ca·tion·al** \-shnəl, -shə-n³l\ *adj* — **lo·ca·tion·al·ly** *adv*

¹loc·a·tive \'lä-kə-tiv\ *n* [L *locus* + E *-ative* (as in *vocative*)] (1804) : the locative case; *also* : a word in that case

²locative *adj* (1841) : of or being a grammatical case that denotes place or the place where or wherein

lo·ca·tor *also* **lo·cat·er** \'lō-ˌkā-tər, lō-'\ *n* (1784) : one that locates something (as a mining claim or the course of a road)

loch \'läk, 'läḵ\ *n* [ME (Sc) *louch,* fr. ScGael *loch;* akin to L *lacus* lake — more at LAKE] (14c) **1** *Scot* : LAKE **2** *Scot* : a bay or arm of the sea esp. when nearly landlocked

loch·an \'lä-kən\ *n* [ScGael, dim. of *loch*] (1670) *Scot* : a small lake

loci *pl of* LOCUS

¹lock \'läk\ *n* [ME *lok,* fr. OE *locc;* akin to OHG *loc* lock, Gk *lygos* withe, L *luxus* dislocated] (bef. 12c) **1 a** : a tuft, tress, or ringlet of hair **b** *pl* : the hair of the head **2** : a cohering bunch (as of wool, cotton, or flax) : TUFT

²lock *n* [ME *lok,* fr. OE *loc;* akin to OHG *loh* enclosure and perh. to OE *locc* lock of hair] (bef. 12c) **1 a** : a fastening (as for a door) operated by a key or a combination **b** : the mechanism for exploding the charge or cartridge of a firearm **2 a** : an enclosure (as in a canal) with gates at each end used in raising or lowering boats as they pass from level to level **b** : AIR LOCK **3 a** : a locking or fastening together **b** : an intricate mass of objects impeding each other (as in a traffic jam) **c** : a hold in wrestling secured on one part of the body; *broadly* : a controlling hold ⟨his paper . . . had a ~ on a large part of the state — John Corry⟩ **4** : one that is assured of success or favorable outcome

³lock *vt* (14c) **1 a** : to fasten the lock of **b** : to make fast with or as if with a lock ⟨~ up the house⟩ **2 a** : to fasten in or out or to make secure or inaccessible by or as if by means of locks ⟨~ed himself away from the curious world⟩ ⟨~ed her husband out⟩ **b** : to fix in a particular situation or method of operation ⟨a team firmly ~ed in last place⟩ **3 a** : to make fast, motionless, or inflexible esp. by the interlacing or interlocking of parts ⟨~ wheels⟩ ⟨~ a knee⟩ **b** : to hold in a close embrace **c** : to grapple in combat; *also* : to bind closely ⟨administration and students were ~ed in conflict⟩ **4** : to invest (capital) without assurance of easy convertibility into money **5** : to move or permit to pass (as a ship) by raising or lowering in a lock ~ *vi* **1** : to become locked **2** : to be capable of being locked **3** : to go or pass by means of a lock (as in a canal) — **lock·able** \'lä-kə-bəl\ *adj* — **lock horns** : to come into conflict — **lock on** *also* **lock onto** : to sight and follow (a target) automatically using a sensor (as radar)

lock·box \'läk-ˌbäks\ *n* (1872) : a box (as a post-office box, strongbox, or safe-deposit box) that locks

lock·down \-ˌdaun\ *n* (1977) : the confinement of prisoners to their cells for all or most of the day as a temporary security measure

locked–in \'läkt-'in\ *adj* (1952) **1** : not subject to adjustment : FIXED ⟨~ interest rates⟩ **2** : unable or unwilling to shift invested funds because of the tax effect of realizing capital gains

lock·er \'lä-kər\ *n* (14c) **1 a** : a drawer, cupboard, or compartment that may be closed with a lock; *esp* : one for individual storage use **b** : a chest or compartment on shipboard for compact stowage of articles **c** : a refrigerated compartment or room for the storage of fresh or frozen foods ⟨a meat ~⟩ **2** : one that locks

lock·er–room \'lä-kər(r)-ˌrüm\ *adj* (1946) : of, relating to, or suitable for use in a locker room; *esp* : of an earthy or sexual nature ⟨~ talk⟩

locker room *n* (ca. 1896) : a room for changing clothes and for storing clothing and equipment in lockers; *esp* : one for use by sports players

lock·et \'lä-kət\ *n* [MF *loquet* latch, fr. MD *loke;* akin to OE *loc*] (1679) : a small case usu. of precious metal that has space for a memento and that is worn typically suspended from a chain or necklace

lock·jaw \'läk-ˌjȯ\ *n* (1803) : an early symptom of tetanus characterized by spasm of the jaw muscles and inability to open the jaws; *also* : TETANUS

lock·keep·er \'läk-ˌkē-pər\ *n* (1794) : a person in charge of a lock (as on a canal)

lock·nut \-ˌnət\ *n* (ca. 1864) **1** : a nut screwed down hard on another to prevent it from slacking back **2** : a nut so constructed that it locks itself when screwed tight against another part

lock·out \-ˌaut\ *n* (1854) : the withholding of employment by an employer and the whole or partial closing of his business establishment in order to gain concessions from or resist demands of employees

lock out *vt* (1868) : to subject (a body of employees) to a lockout

lock·ram \'lä-krəm\ *n* [ME *lokerham,* fr. *Locronan,* town in Brittany] (14c) : a coarse plain-woven linen formerly used in England

lock·smith \'läk-ˌsmith\ *n* (13c) : a person who makes or repairs locks

lock·smith·ing \-ˌsmi-thiŋ\ *n* (ca. 1909) : the work or business of a locksmith

lock·step \'läk-ˌstep\ *n* (ca. 1802) **1** : a mode of marching in step by a body of men going one after another as closely as possible **2 a** : a standard method or procedure that is mindlessly adhered to or that minimizes individuality — **lockstep** *adj* — **in lockstep** : in perfect or rigid often mindless conformity or unison ⟨politicians marching *in lockstep* with the party line⟩

lock·stitch \'läk-ˌstich\ *n* (ca. 1859) : a sewing machine stitch formed by the looping together of two threads one on each side of the material being sewn — **lockstitch** *vb*

lock, stock, and barrel *adv* [fr. the principal parts of a flintlock] (1842) : WHOLLY, COMPLETELY ⟨the only thing which had not been sold *lock, stock, and barrel* with the . . . house was this piano —Marcia Davenport⟩

lock·up \'läk-ˌəp\ *n* (1839) **1** : JAIL; *esp* : a local jail where persons are detained prior to court hearing **2** : an act of locking : the state of being locked

¹lo·co \'lō-(ˌ)kō\ *adv or adj* [It dial., there, fr. L *in loco* in the place] (ca. 1801) : in the register as written — used as a direction in music

²loco *n, pl* **locos** *or* **locoes** [MexSp, fr. Sp, crazy] (1844) **1** : LOCOWEED **2** : LOCOISM

³loco *vt* (1884) **1** : to poison with locoweed **2** : to make frenzied or crazy

⁴loco *adj* [Sp] (1887) *slang* : mentally disordered : CRAZY, FRENZIED

Lo·co·fo·co \ˌlō-kə-'fō-(ˌ)kō\ *n, pl* **-focos** [*locofoco,* a kind of friction match, prob. fr. ¹*locomotive* + It *fuoco, foco* fire, fr. L *focus* hearth] (1835) **1** : a member of a radical group of New York Democrats organized in 1835 in opposition to the regular party organization **2** : DEMOCRAT 2

lo·co·ism \'lō-(ˌ)kō-ˌi-zəm\ *n* (1900) : a disease of horses, cattle, and sheep caused by chronic poisoning with locoweeds

lo·co·mote \'lō-kə-ˌmōt\ *vi* **-mot·ed; -mot·ing** [back-formation fr. *locomotion*] (1834) : to move about

lo·co·mo·tion \ˌlō-kə-'mō-shən\ *n* [L *locus* + E *motion*] (1646) **1** : an act or the power of moving from place to place **2** : TRAVEL ⟨interest in free ~ and choice of occupation —Zechariah Chafee Jr.⟩

¹lo·co·mo·tive \ˌlō-kə-'mō-tiv\ *adj* (1612) **1** : LOCOMOTORY **2** : of or relating to travel **3** : of, relating to, or being a machine that moves about by operation of its own mechanism

²locomotive *n* (1829) **1** : a self-propelled vehicle that runs on rails and is used for moving railroad cars **2** : a school or college cheer characterized by a slow beginning and a progressive increase in speed

lo·co·mo·tor \ˌlō-kə-'mō-tər\ *adj* (1870) **1** : of, relating to, or functioning in locomotion **2** : affecting or involving the locomotor organs

locomotor ataxia *n* (1878) : TABES DORSALIS

lo·co·mo·to·ry \ˌlō-kə-'mō-tə-rē\ *adj* (ca. 1836) **1** : LOCOMOTOR ⟨~ appendages⟩ **2** : capable of moving independently from place to place ⟨~ animals⟩

lo·co·weed \'lō-(ˌ)kō-ˌwēd\ *n* (1879) : any of several leguminous plants (genera *Astragalus* and *Oxytropis*) of western No. America that cause locoism in livestock

loc·u·lar \'lä-kyə-lər\ *adj* (1784) : having or composed of loculi — often used in combination ⟨unilocular⟩

loc·ule \'lä-(ˌ)kyü(ə)l\ *n* [F, fr. L *loculus*] (ca. 1888) : LOCULUS; *esp* : any of the cells of a compound ovary of a plant — **loc·uled** \-(ˌ)kyü(ə)ld\ *adj*

loc·u·li·ci·dal \ˌlä-kyə-lə-'sī-d³l\ *adj* [NL *loculus* + L *-cidere* to cut, fr. *caedere*] (ca. 1819) : dehiscing longitudinally so as to bisect each loculus ⟨~ fruit⟩

loc·u·lus \'lä-kyə-ləs\ *n, pl* **-li** \-ˌlī, -ˌlē\ [NL, fr. L, dim. of *locus*] (1858) : a small chamber or cavity esp. in a plant or animal body

lo·cum \'lō-kəm\ *n* (1901) *chiefly Brit* : LOCUM TENENS

locum te·nens \-'tē-ˌnenz, -'te-, -ˌnənz\ *n, pl* **locum te·nen·tes** \-ti-'nen-ˌtēz\ [ML, lit., (one) holding a place] (1641) : one filling an office for a time or temporarily taking the place of another — used esp. of a doctor or clergyman

lo·cus \'lō-kəs\ *n, pl* **lo·ci** \'lō-ˌsī, -ˌkī, -ˌkē\ [L — more at STALL] (1715) **1 a** : the place where something is situated or occurs : SITE, LOCATION ⟨was the culture of medicine in the beginning dispersed from a single focus or did it arise in several loci? —S. C. Harvey⟩ **b** : a center of activity, attention, or concentration ⟨in democracy the ~ of power is in the people —H. G. Rickover⟩ **2** : the set of all points whose location is determined by stated conditions **3** : the position in a chromosome of a particular gene or allele

locus clas·si·cus \ˌlō-kəs-'kla-si-kəs\ *n, pl* **loci clas·si·ci** \ˌlō-ˌkī-'kla-sə-ˌsī, -ˌkī, -ˌkē\ [NL] (1853) **1** : a passage that has become a standard for the elucidation of a word or subject **2** : a classic case or example

locus coe·ru·le·us *also* **locus ce·ru·le·us** \ˌsi-'rü-lē-əs\ *n* [NL, lit., dark blue place] (ca. 1889) : a blue area of the brain stem with many norepinephrine-containing neurons

lo·cust \'lō-kəst\ *n* [ME, fr. L *locusta*] (14c) **1** : SHORT-HORNED GRASSHOPPER; *esp* : a migratory grasshopper often traveling in vast swarms and stripping the areas passed of all vegetation **2** : CICADA **3 a** : any of various leguminous trees: as (1) : CAROB 1 (2) : BLACK LOCUST (3) : HONEY LOCUST **b** : the wood of a locust tree

locust bean *n* (1847) : CAROB

lo·cu·tion \lō-'kyü-shən\ *n* [ME *locucioun,* fr. L *locution-, locutio,* fr. *loqui* to speak] (15c) **1** : a particular form of expression or a peculiarity of phrasing; *esp* : a word or expression characteristic of a region, group, or cultural level **2** : style of discourse : PHRASEOLOGY

lode \'lōd\ *n* [ME, fr. OE *lād* course, support; akin to OE *lithan* to go — more at LEAD] (bef. 12c) **1** *dial Eng* : WATERWAY **2** : an ore deposit **3** : something that resembles a lode : an abundant store

lo·den \'lō-d⁵n\ *n* [G, fr. OHG *lodo* coarse cloth; akin to OE *lotha* mantle] (1911) **1** : a thick woolen cloth used for outer clothing **2** : a variable color averaging a dull grayish green

lode·star \'lōd-,stär\ *n* [ME *lode sterre*, fr. OE *lād*] (14c) **1** *archaic* : a star that leads or guides; *esp* : NORTH STAR **2** : one that serves as an inspiration, model, or guide

lode·stone \-,stōn\ *n* [obs. *lode* course, fr. ME] (ca. 1515) **1** : magnetite possessing polarity **2** : something that strongly attracts

¹lodge \'läj\ *vb* **lodged; lodg·ing** *vt* (13c) **1 a** (1) : to provide temporary quarters for (2) : to rent lodgings to **b** : to establish or settle in a place **2** : to serve as a receptacle for : CONTAIN **3** : to beat (as a crop) flat to the ground **4** : to bring to an intended or a fixed position (as by throwing or thrusting) **5** : to deposit for safeguard or preservation **6** : to place or vest esp. in a source, means, or agent **7** : to lay (as a complaint) before a proper authority : FILE ~ *vi* **1** : to occupy a place temporarily : SLEEP **b** (1) : to have a residence : DWELL (2) : to be a lodger **2** : to come to a rest **3** : to fall or lie down — used esp. of hay or grain crops

²lodge *n* [ME *loge*, fr. OF, of Gmc origin; akin to OHG *louba* porch] (13c) **1** *chiefly dial* : a rude shelter or abode **2 a** : a house set apart for residence in a particular season (as the hunting season) **b** : a resort hotel : INN **3 a** : a house on an estate orig. for the use of a gamekeeper, caretaker, or porter **b** : a shelter for an employee (as a gatekeeper) **4** : a den or lair esp. of gregarious animals **5 a** : the meeting place of a branch of an organization and esp. a fraternal organization **b** : the body of members of such a branch **6 a** : WIGWAM **b** : a family of No. American Indians

lodge·pole pine \'läj-,pōl-\ *n* (1859) : either of two pines of western No. America with needles in pairs and short ovoid usu. asymmetric cones: **a** : a scrubby chiefly coastal pine (*Pinus contorta*) with thick deeply furrowed bark and hard strong coarse-grained medium-light wood **b** : a tall straight pine (*P. contorta* var. *latifolia* syn. *P. murrayana*) with thin and little furrowed bark and soft weak fine-grained lightweight wood

lodg·er \'lä-jər\ *n* (1596) : ROOMER

lodging *n* (14c) **1 a** : a place to live : DWELLING **b** : LODGMENT 3b **2 a** : sleeping accommodations ⟨found ~ in the barn⟩ (2) : a temporary sleeping place to stay ⟨a ~ for the night⟩ **b** : a room in the house of another used as a residence — usu. used in pl. **3** : the act of lodging

lodging house *n* (1766) : ROOMING HOUSE

lodg·ment *or* **lodge·ment** \'läj-mənt\ *n* (1598) **1 a** : a lodging place : SHELTER **b** : ACCOMMODATIONS, LODGINGS ⟨found ~ in the city⟩ **2 a** : the act, fact, or manner of lodging ⟨a hut for temporary ~ of cattlemen⟩ **b** : a placing, depositing, or coming to rest **3 a** : an accumulation or collection deposited in a place or remaining at rest **b** : a place of rest or deposit

lod·i·cule \'lä-di-,kyü(ə)l\ *n* [L *lodicula*, dim. of *lodic-*, *lodix* cover] (1864) : one of usu. two delicate membranous hyaline scales at the base of the ovary of a grass that by their swelling assist in anthesis

loess \'les, 'ləs, 'lō-əs, 'lərs\ *n* [G *Löss*] (1833) : an unstratified usu. buff to yellowish brown loamy deposit found in No. America, Europe, and Asia and believed to be chiefly deposited by the wind — **loess·ial** \'le-sē-əl, 'ləs-, 'lō-'e-, 'lərs-\ *adj*

¹loft \'lȯft\ *n* [ME, fr. OE, air, sky, fr. ON *lopt;* akin to OHG *luft* air] (13c) **1** : an upper room or floor : ATTIC **2 a** : a gallery in a church or hall **b** : one of the upper floors of a warehouse or business building esp. when not partitioned ⟨living in a converted ~⟩ **c** : HAYLOFT **3 a** : the backward slant of the face of a golf-club head **b** : the act of lofting **4** : the thickness of a fabric or insulating material (as goose down) — **loft·like** \-,līk\ *adj*

²loft *vt* (1518) **1** : to place, house, or store in a loft **2** : to propel through the air or into space ⟨~*ed* a long hit to center⟩ ⟨instruments ~*ed* by a powerful rocket⟩ **3** : to lay out a full-sized working drawing of the lines and contours of (as a ship's hull) ~ *vi* **1** : to propel a ball high into the air **2** : to rise high

lofty \'lȯf-tē\ *adj* **loft·i·er; -est** (15c) **1 a** : elevated in character and spirit : NOBLE **b** : elevated in status : SUPERIOR **2** : having a haughty overbearing manner : SUPERCILIOUS **3 a** : rising to a great height : impressively high ⟨~ mountains⟩ **b** : REMOTE, ESOTERIC **syn** see HIGH — **loft·i·ly** \-tə-lē\ *adv* — **loft·i·ness** \-tē-nəs\ *n*

¹log \'lȯg, 'läg\ *n, often attrib* [ME *logge*, prob. of Scand origin; akin to ON *lāg* fallen tree; akin to OE *licgan* to lie — more at LIE] (14c) **1 a** : usu. bulky piece or length of unshaped timber; *esp* : a length of a tree trunk ready for sawing and over six feet (1.8 meters) long **2 a** : an apparatus for measuring the rate of a ship's motion through the water that consists of a block fastened to a line and run out from a reel **3 a** : the record of the rate of a ship's speed or of her daily progress; *also* : the full nautical record of a ship's voyage **b** : the full record of a flight by an aircraft **4** : a record of performance, events, or day-to-day activities ⟨a computer ~⟩

²log *vb* **logged; log·ging** *vt* (1699) **1 a** : to cut (trees) for lumber **b** : to clear (land) of trees in lumbering — often used with *off* **2** : to make a note or record of : enter details of or about in a log **3 a** : to move (an indicated distance) or attain (an indicated speed) as noted in a log **b** (1) : to sail a ship or fly an airplane for (an indicated distance or period of time) (2) : to have (an indicated record) to one's credit : ACHIEVE ~ *vi* : ³LUMBER 1

³log *n, often attrib* [by shortening] (1631) : LOGARITHM

log- *or* **logo-** *comb form* [Gk, fr. *logos* — more at LEGEND] : word : thought : speech : discourse ⟨*logogram*⟩ ⟨*logorrhea*⟩

-log — see -LOGUE

lo·gan·ber·ry \'lō-gən-,ber-ē\ *n* [James H. *Logan* †1928 Am. lawyer + E *berry*] (1893) : a red-fruited upright-growing dewberry regarded as a variety (*Rubus ursinus loganobaccus*) of a western dewberry or as a hybrid of a western dewberry and a red raspberry; *also* : its berry

log·a·oe·dic \,lä-gə-'ē-dik\ *adj* [LL *logaoedicus*, fr. LGk *logaoidikos*, fr. Gk *log-* + *aeidein* to sing; fr. the resemblance of such rhythm to prose — more at ODE] (1844) : marked by the mixture of several meters; *specif* : having a rhythm that uses both dactyls and trochees or anapests and iambs — **logaoedic** *n*

log·a·rithm \'lȯ-gə-,ri-thəm, 'lä-\ *n* [NL *logarithmus*, fr. *log-* + Gk *arithmos* number — more at ARITHMETIC] (ca. 1616) : the exponent that indicates the power to which a number is raised to produce a given number ⟨the ~ of 100 to the base 10 is 2⟩ — **log·a·rith·mic** \,lȯ-gə-'rith-mik, ,lä-\ *adj* — **log·a·rith·mi·cal·ly** \-mi-k(ə-)lē\ *adv*

logarithmic function *n* (1927) : a function (as $y = \log_a x$ or $y = \ln x$) that is the inverse of an exponential function (as $y = a^x$ or $y = e^x$) so that the independent variable appears in a logarithm

log·book \'lȯg-,bu̇k, 'läg-\ *n* (ca. 1679) : LOG 3, 4

loge \'lōzh\ *n* [F, fr. OF, a shelter — more at LODGE] (1749) **1 a** : a small compartment : BOOTH **b** : a box in a theater **2 a** : a small partitioned area **b** : a separate forward section of a theater mezzanine or balcony

logged \'lȯgd, 'lägd\ *adj* (ca. 1820) **1** : HEAVY, SLUGGISH **2** : sodden esp. with water

log·ger \'lȯ-gər, 'lä-\ *n* (1732) : one engaged in logging

log·ger·head \'lȯ-gər-,hed, 'lä-\ *n* [prob. fr. E dial. *logger* block of wood + E *head*] (1588) **1** *chiefly dial* : BLOCKHEAD **b** : HEAD; *esp* : a disproportionately large head **2 a** : a very large carnivorous sea turtle (*Caretta caretta*) of subtropical and temperate waters **b** : ALLIGATOR SNAPPER **3** : an iron tool consisting of a long handle terminating in a ball or bulb that is heated and used to melt tar or to heat liquids — **at loggerheads** : in or into a state of quarrelsome disagreement

log·gets *or* **log·gats** \'lȯ-gəts, 'lä-\ *n pl but sing or pl in constr* [prob. fr. ¹*log* + *-et*] (1581) : a game formerly played in England in which participants throw pieces of wood at a stake

log·gia \'lȯ-jē-ə, 'lō-(,)jä\ *n, pl* **loggias** \'lō-jē-əz, 'lō-(,)jäz\ *also* **log·gie** \'lō-(,)jä\ [It, fr. OF *loge* lodge] (1742) : a roofed open gallery esp. at an upper story overlooking an open court

1 loggia

log·ic \'lä-jik\ *n* [ME *logik*, fr. MF *logique*, fr. L *logica*, fr. Gk *logikē*, fr. fem. of *logikos* of reason, fr. *logos* reason — more at LEGEND] (12c) **1 a** (1) : a science that deals with the principles and criteria of validity of inference and demonstration : the science of the formal principles of reasoning (2) : a branch or variety of logic ⟨modal ~⟩ ⟨Boolean ~⟩ (3) : a branch of semiotic; *esp* : SYNTACTICS (4) : the formal principles of a branch of knowledge **b** (1) : a particular mode of reasoning viewed as valid or faulty (2) : RELEVANCE, PROPRIETY **c** : interrelation or sequence of facts or events when seen as inevitable or predictable **d** : the arrangement of circuit elements (as in a computer) needed for computation; *also* : the circuits themselves **2** : something that forces a decision apart from or in opposition to reason ⟨the ~ of war⟩ — **lo·gi·cian** \lō-'ji-shən\ *n*

log·i·cal \'lä-ji-kəl\ *adj* (15c) **1 a** (1) : of, relating to, involving, or being in accordance with logic (2) : skilled in logic **b** : formally true or valid : ANALYTIC, DEDUCTIVE **2** : capable of reasoning or of using reason in an orderly cogent fashion ⟨a ~ thinker⟩ — **log·i·cal·i·ty** \,lä-jə-'ka-lə-tē\ *n* — **log·i·cal·ly** \'lä-ji-k(ə-)lē\ *adv* — **log·i·cal·ness** \-kəl-nəs\ *n*

logical positivism *n* (1931) : a 20th century philosophical movement that holds characteristically that all meaningful statements are either analytic or conclusively verifiable or at least confirmable by observation and experiment and that metaphysical theories are therefore strictly meaningless — called also *logical empiricism* — **logical positivist** *n*

log in *vi* (1962) : LOG ON — **log–in** \'lȯg-,in, 'läg-\ *n*

lo·gi·on \'lō-gē-,än\ *n, pl* **lo·gia** \-ä\ *or* **logions** [Gk, dim. of *logos*] (1875) : SAYING; *esp* : a saying attributed to Jesus

¹lo·gis·tic \lō-'jis-tik, lə-\ *or* **lo·gis·ti·cal** \-ti-kəl\ *adj* (1628) **1 a** : of or relating to symbolic logic **b** : of or relating to the philosophical attempt to reduce mathematics to logic **2** : of or relating to logistics **3** *logistic* : of, represented by, or relating to a logistic curve ⟨a ~ process⟩ — **lo·gis·ti·cal·ly** \-ti-k(ə-)lē\ *adv*

²logistic *n* (1905) : SYMBOLIC LOGIC

logistic curve *n* (ca. 1903) : an S-shaped curve that represents an exponential function and is used in mathematical models of growth processes

lo·gis·ti·cian \,lō-jəs-'ti-shən\ *n* (1932) : a specialist in logistics

lo·gis·tics \lō-'jis-tiks, lə-\ *n pl but sing or pl in constr* [F *logistique* art of calculating, logistics, fr. Gk *logistikē* art of calculating, fr. fem. of *logistikos* of calculation, fr. *logizein* to calculate, fr. *logos* reason] (ca. 1861) **1** : the aspect of military science dealing with the procurement, maintenance, and transportation of military matériel, facilities, and personnel **2** : the handling of the details of an operation

log·jam \'lȯg-,jam, 'läg-\ *n* (1885) **1** : a jumble of logs jammed together in a watercourse **2 a** : DEADLOCK, IMPASSE ⟨trying to break the ~ in negotiations⟩ **b** : BLOCKAGE

log·nor·mal \,lȯg-'nȯr-məl, ,läg-\ *adj* (1945) : relating to or being a normal distribution that is the distribution of the logarithm of a random variable; *also* : relating to or being such a random variable — **log·nor·mal·i·ty** \-nȯr-'ma-lə-tē\ *n* — **log·nor·mal·ly** \-'nȯr-mə-lē\ *adv*

logo \'lō-(,)gō *also* 'lä-\ *n, pl* **log·os** \-(,)gōz\ (1937) **1** : LOGOTYPE **2** : an identifying statement : MOTTO

Lo·go \'lō-(,)gō\ *n* [modif. of Gk *logos* word] (1972) : a computer programming language that employs simple English commands and is used esp. for introducing school children to computers

logo- — see LOG-

logo·gram \'lȯ-gə-,gram, 'lä-\ *n* (1840) : a letter, symbol, or sign used to represent an entire word — **logo·gram·mat·ic** \,lȯ-gə-grə-'ma-tik, ,lä-\ *adj*

logo·graph \'lȯ-gə-,graf, 'lä-\ *n* (ca. 1888) : LOGOGRAM

\ə\ abut \ʼ\ kitten, F table \ər\ further \a\ ash \ā\ ace \ä\ mop, mar \aú\ out \ch\ chin \e\ bet \ē\ easy \g\ go \i\ hit \ī\ ice \j\ job \ŋ\ sing \ō\ go \ȯ\ law \ȯi\ boy \th\ thin \th\ the \ü\ loot \u̇\ foot \y\ yet \zh\ vision \á, k̲, ⁿ, œ, œ̄, ᵾe, ᵾē, ᵉ\ *see* Guide to Pronunciation

logo·graph·ic \,lȯ-gə-'gra-fik, ,lä-\ *adj* (1801) : of, relating to, or marked by the use of logographs : consisting of logographs — **logo·graph·i·cal·ly** \-fi-k(ə-)lē\ *adv*

logo·griph \'lȯ-gə-,grif, 'lä-\ *n* [*log-* + Gk *griphos* reed basket, riddle — more at CRIB] (ca. 1598) : a word puzzle (as an anagram)

lo·gom·a·chy \lō-'gä-mə-kē\ *n, pl* **-chies** [Gk *logomachia*, fr. *log-* + *machesthai* to fight] (1569) 1 : a dispute over or about words 2 : a controversy marked by verbiage

log on *vi* (1977) : to establish communication and initiate interaction with a time-shared computer or network — often used with *to* — **log-on** \'lȯg-,ȯn, 'läg-,än\ *n*

log·or·rhea \,lȯ-gə-'rē-ə, ,lä-\ *n* [NL] (ca. 1892) : excessive and often incoherent talkativeness or wordiness — **log·or·rhe·ic** \-'rē-ik\ *adj*

Lo·gos \'lō-,gäs, -,gōs\ *n, pl* **Lo·goi** \-,gȯi\ [Gk, speech, word, reason — more at LEGEND] (1587) 1 : the divine wisdom manifest in the creation, government, and redemption of the world and often identified with the second person of the Trinity 2 : reason that in ancient Greek philosophy is the controlling principle in the universe

logo·type \'lȯ-gə-,tīp, 'lä-\ *n* (ca. 1816) 1 : a single piece of type or a single plate faced with a term (as the name of a newspaper or a trade-mark) 2 : an identifying symbol (as for advertising)

log·roll \'lȯg-,rōl, 'läg-\ *vb* [back-formation fr. *logrolling*] *vi* (1835) : to take part in logrolling ~ *vt* : to promote passage of by logrolling — **log·roll·er** *n*

log·roll·ing \-,rō-liŋ\ *n* (1812) 1 [fr. a former American custom of neighbors assisting one another in rolling logs into a pile for burning] : the exchanging of assistance or favors; *specif* : the trading of votes by legislators to secure favorable action on projects of interest to each one 2 : the rolling of logs in water by treading; *also* : a sport in which contestants treading logs try to dislodge one another

-logue *or* **-log** *n comb form* [ME *-logue*, fr. OF, fr. L *-logus*, fr. Gk *-logos*, fr. *legein* to speak — more at LEGEND] 1 : discourse : talk ⟨duo*logue*⟩ 2 : student : specialist ⟨sino*logue*⟩

log·wood \'lȯg-,wu̇d, 'läg-\ *n* (1581) 1 a : a Mexican and West Indian leguminous tree (*Haematoxylon campechianum*) b : the very hard brown or brownish red heartwood of logwood 2 : a dye extracted from the heartwood of logwood — compare HEMATOXYLIN

lo·gy \'lō-gē\ *also* **log·gy** \'lō-gē, 'lä-\ *adj* **lo·gi·er; -est** [perh. fr. D *log* heavy; akin to MLG *luggich* lazy] (1847) : marked by sluggishness and lack of vitality : GROGGY

-logy *n comb form* [ME *-logie*, fr. OF, fr. L *-logia*, fr. Gk, fr. *logos* word] 1 : oral or written expression ⟨phrase*ology*⟩ 2 : doctrine : theory : science ⟨ethn*ology*⟩

Lo·hen·grin \'lō-ən-,grin\ *n* [G] : a son of Parsifal and knight of the Holy Grail in Germanic legend

loin \'lȯin\ *n* [ME *loyne*, fr. MF *loigne*, fr. (assumed) VL *lumbea*, fr. L *lumbus*; akin to OE *lendenu* loins, OCS *lędvije*] (14c) 1 a : the part of a human being or quadruped on each side of the spinal column between the hipbone and the false ribs b : a cut of meat comprising this part of one or both sides of a carcass with the adjoining half of the vertebrae included but without the flank 2 *pl* a : the upper and lower abdominal regions and the region about the hips b (1) : the pubic region (2) : the generative organs

loin·cloth \-,klȯth\ *n* (1859) : a cloth worn about the loins often as the sole article of clothing in warm climates

loi·ter \'lȯi-tər\ *vi* [ME] (14c) 1 : to delay an activity with aimless idle stops and pauses : DAWDLE 2 a : to remain in an area for no obvious reason : HANG AROUND b : to lag behind *syn* see DELAY — **loiter** *n* — **loi·ter·er** \-tər-ər\ *n*

Lo·ki \'lō-kē\ *n* [ON] : a Norse god who contrives evil and mischief for his fellow gods

Lo·li·ta \lō-'lē-tə\ *n* [fr. *Lolita*, character in the novel *Lolita* (1955) by Vladimir Nabokov] (1959) : a precociously seductive girl

¹**loll** \'läl\ *vb* [ME] *vi* (14c) 1 : to hang loosely or laxly : DROOP 2 : to act or move in a lax, lazy, or indolent manner : LOUNGE ~ *vt* : to let droop or dangle — **loll·er** \'lä-lər\ *n*

²**loll** *n* (1709) *archaic* : the act of lolling : a relaxed posture

Lol·lard \'lä-lərd\ *n* [ME, fr. MD *lollaert*, fr. *lollen* to mutter] (14c) : one of the followers of Wycliffe who traveled in the 14th and 15th centuries as lay preachers throughout England and Scotland — **Lol·lard·ism** \-diz-əm\ *n* — **Lol·lard·y** \-lər-dē\ *n*

lol·li·pop *or* **lol·ly·pop** \'lä-li-,päp\ *n* [perh. fr. E dial. *lolly* tongue + ²*pop*] (1784) 1 : a lump of hard candy on the end of a stick 2 *Brit* : a round stop sign on a pole used to stop traffic (as at a school crossing)

lol·lop \'lä-ləp\ *vi* [¹*loll* + *-op* (as in *gallop*)] (1745) 1 *dial Eng* : LOLL 2 : to proceed with a bounding or bobbing motion

lol·ly \'lä-lē\ *n, pl* **lollies** [short for *lollipop*] (1854) 1 *Brit* : a piece of candy; *esp* : HARD CANDY 2 *Brit* : MONEY

lol·ly·gag \'lä-lē-,gag\ *vi* **-gagged; -gag·ging** [origin unknown] (1868) : FOOL AROUND 1 : DAWDLE

Lom·bard \'läm-,bärd, -bərd\ *n* [ME *Lumbarde*, fr. MF *lombard*, fr. OIt *lombardo*, fr. L *Langobardus*] (14c) 1 a : a member of a Germanic people that invaded Italy in A.D. 568, settled in the Po valley, and established a kingdom b : a native or inhabitant of Lombardy 2 [fr. the prominence of Lombards as moneylenders] : BANKER, MONEY-LENDER — **Lom·bar·di·an** \läm-'bär-dē-ən\ *adj* — **Lom·bar·dic** \läm-'bär-dik\ *adj*

Lom·bar·dy poplar \'läm-,bär-dē-, -bər-\ *n* [Lombardy, Italy] (1766) : a poplar of a staminate variety (*Populus nigra italica*) of a European poplar having a columnar shape and strongly ascending branches

lo mein \'lō-'mān, ,lō-\ *n* [Chin (Guangdong) *lòu-mihn* stirred noodles] (1970) : a Chinese dish consisting of sliced vegetables, soft noodles, and usu. meat or shrimp in bite-size pieces stir-fried in a seasoned sauce

lo·ment \'lō-,ment, -mənt\ *n* [NL *lomentum*, fr. L, wash made fr. bean meal, fr. *lavere* to wash — more at LYE] (ca. 1830) : a dry indehiscent one-celled fruit that is produced from a single superior ovary and breaks transversely into numerous segments at maturity

Lon·don broil \'lən-dən-\ *n* [*London*, England] (1946) : a boneless cut of beef (as from the shoulder or flank) usu. served sliced diagonally across the grain

lone \'lōn\ *adj* [ME, short for *alone*] (14c) 1 a : having no company : SOLITARY b : preferring solitude : ONLY, SOLE 2 : situated by itself : ISOLATED *syn* see ALONE — **lone·ness** \'lōn-nəs\ *n*

lone·li·ness \'lōn-lē-nəs\ *n* (ca. 1586) : the quality or state of being lonely

lone·ly \'lōn-lē\ *adj* **lone·li·er; -est** (1607) 1 a : being without company : LONE b : cut off from others : SOLITARY 2 : not frequented by human beings : DESOLATE 3 : sad from being alone : LONESOME 4 : producing a feeling of bleakness or desolation *syn* see ALONE — **lone·li·ly** \-lə-lē\ *adv*

lonely hearts *adj* (1931) : of or relating to lonely persons who are seeking companions or spouses

lon·er \'lō-nər\ *n* (1947) : one that avoids others; *esp* : INDIVIDUALIST

lone ranger *n, often cap L&R* [*Lone Ranger*, hero of an Am. radio and television western] (1969) : one who acts alone and without consultation or the approval of others; *broadly* : LONER

¹**lone·some** \'lōn(t)-səm\ *adj* (1647) 1 a : sad or dejected as a result of lack of companionship or separation from others ⟨don't be ~ while we are gone⟩ b : causing a feeling of loneliness ⟨the empty house seemed so ~⟩ 2 a : REMOTE, UNFREQUENTED ⟨look down, look down that ~ road —Gene Austin⟩ b : LONE *syn* see ALONE — **lone·some·ly** *adv* — **lone·some·ness** *n*

²**lonesome** *n* (1899) : SELF ⟨sat all by his ~⟩

lone wolf *n* (1909) : a person who prefers to work, act, or live alone

¹**long** \'lȯŋ\ *adj* **lon·ger** \'lȯŋ-gər\ **lon·gest** \'lȯŋ-gəst *also* -əst\ [ME *long, lang*, fr. OE; akin to OHG *lang* long, L *longus*] (bef. 12c) 1 a : extending for a considerable distance b : having greater length than usual c : having greater height than usual : TALL d : having a greater length than breadth : ELONGATED e : having a greater length than desirable or necessary : FULL-LENGTH ⟨~ pants⟩ 2 a : having a specified length ⟨six feet ~⟩ b : forming the chief linear dimension ⟨the ~ side of the room⟩ 3 a : extending over a considerable time ⟨a ~ friendship⟩ b : having a specified duration ⟨two hours ~⟩ c : prolonged beyond the usual time ⟨a ~ look⟩ 4 a : containing many items in a series ⟨a ~ list⟩ b : having a specified number of units ⟨300 pages ~⟩ c : consisting of a greater number or amount than usual : LARGE 5 a *of a speech sound* : having a relatively long duration b : being the member of a pair of similarly spelled vowel or vowel-containing sounds that is descended from a vowel long in duration ⟨~ *a* in *fate*⟩ ⟨~ *i* in *sign*⟩ c *of a syllable in prosody* (1) : of relatively extended duration (2) : bearing a stress or accent 6 : having the capacity to reach, extend, or travel a considerable distance ⟨a ~ left jab⟩ ⟨tried to hit the ~ ball⟩ 7 : larger or longer than the standard ⟨a ~ count by the referee⟩ 8 a : extending far into the future ⟨the thoughts of youth are ~ thoughts —H. W. Longfellow⟩ b : extending beyond what is known ⟨a ~ guess⟩ c : payable after a considerable period ⟨a ~ note⟩ 9 : possessing a high degree or a great deal of something specified : STRONG ⟨~ on common sense⟩ 10 a : of an unusual degree of difference between the amounts wagered on each side ⟨~ odds⟩ b : of or relating to the larger amount wagered ⟨take the ~ end of the bet⟩ 11 : subject to great odds 12 : owning or accumulating securities or goods esp. in anticipation of an advance in prices ⟨they are now ~ on wheat⟩ ⟨take a ~ position in steel⟩ — **long·ness** \'lȯŋ-nəs\ *n* — **before long** : in a short time : SOON — **long in the tooth** : past one's best days : OLD — **not long for** : having little time left to do or enjoy something

²**long** *adv* (bef. 12c) 1 : for or during a long time ⟨~ a popular hangout⟩ 2 : at or to a long distance : FAR ⟨*long*-traveled⟩ 3 : for the duration of a specified period 4 : at a point of time far before or after a specified moment or event ⟨was excited ~ before the big day⟩ 5 : after or beyond a specified or implied time ⟨didn't stay ~*er* than midnight⟩ ⟨said it was no ~*er* possible⟩ 6 : for a considerable distance ⟨faded back and threw the ball ~⟩ 7 : in or into a long position (as on a market) — **so long** : GOOD-BYE

³**long** *n* (bef. 12c) 1 : a long period of time 2 : a long syllable 3 : one taking a long position esp. in a security or commodity market 4 a *pl* : long trousers b : a size in clothing for tall men — **the long and short** *or* **the long and the short** : GIST

⁴**long** *vi* **longed; long·ing** \'lȯŋ-iŋ\ [ME, fr. OE *langian*; akin to OHG *langēn* to long, OE *lang* long] (bef. 12c) : to feel a strong desire or craving esp. for something not likely to be attained ⟨they ~ for peace but are driven to war⟩ — **long·er** \'lȯŋ-ər\ *n*
syn LONG, YEARN, HANKER, PINE, HUNGER, THIRST mean to have a strong desire for something. LONG implies a wishing with one's whole heart and often a striving to attain ⟨*longed* for some rest⟩. YEARN suggests an eager, restless, or painful longing ⟨*yearned* for a stage career⟩. HANKER suggests the uneasy promptings of unsatisfied appetite or desire ⟨always *hankering* for money⟩. PINE implies a languishing or a fruitless longing for what is impossible ⟨*pined* for a lost love⟩. HUNGER and THIRST imply an insistent or impatient craving or a compelling need ⟨*hungered* for a business of his own⟩ ⟨*thirsted* for absolute power⟩.

⁵**long** *vi* [ME, fr. *along* (on) because (of)] (13c) *archaic* : to be suitable or fitting

long-ago \'lȯŋ-ə-'gō\ *adj* (ca. 1834) : of or relating to the past ⟨~ leaders⟩

long ago *n* (1851) : the distant past

lon·gan \'lȯŋ-gən, -ən\ *n* [Chin (Beijing) *lóngyǎn*, lit., dragon's eye] (1732) 1 : a pulpy fruit related to the litchi and produced by an Indian evergreen tree (*Euphoria longana*) 2 : a tree that bears the longan

lon·ga·nim·i·ty \,lȯŋ-gə-'ni-mə-tē\ *n* [ME *longanymyte*, fr. LL *longanimitat-, longanimitas*, fr. *longanimis* patient, fr. L *longus* long + *animus* soul — more at ANIMATE] (15c) : a disposition to bear injuries patiently : FORBEARANCE

long·boat \'lȯŋ-,bōt\ *n* (15c) : a large oared boat usu. carried by a merchant sailing ship

long bone *n* (ca. 1860) : any of the elongated bones supporting a vertebrate limb and consisting of an essentially cylindrical shaft that contains marrow and ends in enlarged heads for articulation with other bones

long·bow \'lȯŋ-,bō\ *n* (14c) : a hand-drawn wooden bow held vertically and used esp. by medieval English archers

long·bow·man \-mən\ *n* (1925) : an archer who uses a longbow

long-case clock \'lȯŋ-,kās-\ *n* (1892) : GRANDFATHER CLOCK

long-chain *adj* (1930) : having a relatively long chain of atoms and esp. carbon atoms in the molecule ⟨~ hydrocarbons⟩

long–day *adj* (1920) : responding to or relating to a long photoperiod — used esp. of a plant; compare DAY-NEUTRAL, SHORT-DAY

¹long–distance *adj* (1884) **1** : of or relating to telephone communication with a distant point **2 a** : situated a long distance away **b** : going or covering a long distance ⟨~ roads⟩ ⟨a ~ runner⟩ **c** : conducted or effective over long distance ⟨a ~ courtship⟩ ⟨~ listening devices⟩

²long–distance *adv* (ca. 1961) **1** : by long-distance telephone **2** : over or from a long distance

long distance *n* (1904) **1** : communication by long-distance telephone **2** : a telephone operator or exchange that gives long-distance connections

long division *n* (1827) : arithmetical division in which the several steps involved in the division are indicated in detail

long–drawn–out *or* **long–drawn** *adj* (1646) : extended to a great length

lon·ge·ron \'län-jə-ˌrän\ *n* [F] (1912) : a fore-and-aft framing member of an airplane fuselage

lon·gev·i·ty \län-'je-və-tē, lòn-\ *n* [LL *longaevitas*, fr. L *longaevus* long-lived, fr. *longus* long + *aevum* age — more at AYE] (1615) **1 a** : a long duration of individual life **b** : length of life ⟨a study of ~⟩ **2** : long continuance : PERMANENCE, DURABILITY

lon·ge·vous \-'je-vəs\ *adj* (1680) : LONG-LIVED

long face *n* (1786) : a facial expression of sadness or melancholy

long green *n* (ca. 1891) *slang* : MONEY

long·hair \'lòn-ˌhar, -ˌher\ *n* (1920) **1** : an impractical intellectual **2** : a person of artistic gifts or interests; *esp* : a lover of classical music **3** : a person with long hair; *esp* : a domestic cat having long outer fur — **long–haired** \-'hard, -'herd\ *or* **longhair** *adj*

long·hand \-ˌhand\ *n* (1666) : HANDWRITING: **a** : characters or words written out fully by hand **b** : cursive writing

long haul *n* (1936) **1** : a long distance **2** : a considerable period of time; *esp* : LONG RUN — **long–haul** *adj*

long·head \'lòn-ˌhed\ *n* (1650) : a dolichocephalic person

long·head·ed \-ˌhe-dəd\ *adj* (ca. 1700) **1** : having unusual foresight **2** : DOLICHOCEPHALIC — **long·head·ed·ness** *n*

long·horn \-ˌhòrn\ *n* (1834) **1 a** : any of the long-horned cattle of Spanish derivation formerly common in southwestern U.S. **b** : TEXAS LONGHORN 2 **2** : a firm-textured usu. mild cheese (as cheddar or Colby)

long–horned beetle \-ˌhòrn(d)-\ *n* (1840) : any of a family (Cerambycidae syn. Longicornia) of beetles usu. distinguished by their very long antennae — called also *longhorn beetle*

long–horned grasshopper *n* (1893) : any of various grasshoppers (family Tettigoniidae) distinguished by their very long antennae

long horse *n* (ca. 1934) : VAULTING HORSE

long·house \'lòn-ˌhaus, -'haus\ *n* (1643) : a long communal dwelling of some No. American Indians (as the Iroquois)

long hundredweight *n* (ca. 1934) *Brit* : HUNDREDWEIGHT 2

lon·gi·corn \'län-jə-ˌkòrn\ *adj* [ultim. fr. L *longus* long + *cornu* horn — more at HORN] (ca. 1848) **1** : of, relating to, or being long-horned beetles **2** : having long antennae — **longicorn** *n*

long·ing \'lòn-in\ *n* (bef. 12c) : a strong desire esp. for something unattainable : CRAVING — **long·ing·ly** \-in-lē\ *adv*

long·ish \'lòn-ish\ *adj* (1611) : somewhat long : moderately long

lon·gi·tude \'län-jə-ˌtüd, -ˌtyüd, *Brit also* 'län-gə-\ *n* [ME, fr. L *longitudin-, longitudo*, fr. *longus*] (14c) **1 a** : angular distance measured on a great circle of reference from the intersection of the adopted zero meridian with this reference circle to the similar intersection of the meridian passing through the object **b** : the arc or portion of the earth's equator intersected between the meridian of a given place and the prime meridian and expressed either in degrees or in time **2** *archaic* : long duration

lon·gi·tu·di·nal \ˌlän-jə-'tüd-nəl, -'tyüd-, -'t(y)üd-əⁿ-əl, *Brit also* ˌlän-gə-\ *adj* (15c) **1** : placed or running lengthwise **2** : of or relating to length or the lengthwise dimension **3** : involving the repeated observation or examination of a set of subjects over time with respect to one or more study variables — **lon·gi·tu·di·nal·ly** *adv*

longitude 1a: hemisphere marked with meridians of longitude

longitudinal wave *n* (ca. 1931) : a wave (as a sound wave) in which the particles of the medium vibrate in the direction of the line of advance of the wave

long johns \'lòn-ˌjänz\ *n pl* (1943) : long underwear

long jump *n* (1882) : a track-and-field event in which a jump for distance is made usu. from a running start — **long jumper** *n*

long·leaf pine \'lòn-ˌlēf-\ *n* (1796) : a tall pine (*Pinus palustris*) of the southeastern U.S. with long needles in bundles of three and long cones that is a major timber tree; *also* : its tough coarse-grained reddish orange wood

long–leaved pine \-ˌlēv(d)-\ *n* (1765) : LONGLEAF PINE

long·line \'lòn-ˌlin, -ˌlīn\ *n* (1876) : a heavy fishing line that may be several miles long and that has baited hooks in series

long–lin·er \-ˌli-nər\ *n* (1909) : one that fishes with a longline; *also* : a fishing vessel used in long-lining

long–lin·ing \-ˌli-nin\ *n* (1877) : fishing with a longline

long–lived \'lòn-'livd *also* -'livd\ *adj* (14c) **1** : having a long life : characterized by long life ⟨a ~ family⟩ **2** : lasting a long time : ENDURING

long meter *n* (1718) : a quatrain in iambic tetrameter in which the second and fourth lines and often the first and third lines rhyme — called also *long measure*

Lon·go·bard \'lòn-gə-ˌbärd, 'län-\ *n, pl* **Longobards** *also* **Lon·go·bar·di** \ˌlòn-gə-'bär-ˌdī, ˌlän-, -dē\ [ME *Longobardes*, pl., fr. L *Langobardi, Longobardi*] (14c) : LOMBARD 1a — **Lon·go·bar·dic** \ˌlòn-gə-'bär-dik, ˌlän-\ *adj*

long play *n* (1952) : a long-playing record

long–play·ing \'lòn-'plä-in\ *adj* (1929) : designed to be played at 33⅓ revolutions per minute — used of a microgroove record

long–range \-'ränj\ *adj* (1854) **1** : relating to or fit for long distances ⟨~ rockets⟩ **2** : involving or taking into account a long period of time ⟨~ planning⟩

long run *n* (1627) : a relatively long period of time — usu. used in the phrase *in the long run* — **long–run** \'lòn-'rən\ *adj*

long–shore·man \'lòn-ˌshòr-mən, -ˌshòr-, ˌlòn-\ *n* [*longshore*, short for *alongshore*] (1811) : a person who loads and unloads ships at a seaport

long–shor·ing \'lòn-ˌshòr-in, -ˌshòr-, ˌlòn-\ *n* (1926) : the act or occupation of working as a longshoreman

long shot \'lòn-ˌshät\ *n* (1867) **1** : a venture involving great risk but promising a great reward if successful; *also* : a venture unlikely to succeed **2** : an entry (as in a horse race) given little chance of winning **3** : a bet in which the chances of winning are slight but the possible winnings great — **by a long shot** : by a great deal

long·sight·ed \-ˌsī-təd\ *adj* (ca. 1790) : FARSIGHTED — **long·sight·ed·ness** *n*

long since *adv* (14c) **1** : long ago ⟨promises *long since* forgotten⟩ **2** : for a long time ⟨has *long since* been a devoted friend⟩

long·some \'lòn-səm\ *adj* (bef. 12c) : tediously long — **long·some·ly** *adv* — **long·some·ness** *n*

long·spur \'lòn-ˌspər\ *n* (1831) : any of several long-clawed finches (esp. genus *Calcarius*) of the arctic regions and the Great Plains of No. America

long–stand·ing \-'stan-din\ *adj* (1814) : of long duration

long–suf·fer·ing \-ˌsə-f(ə-)rin, -'sə-\ *n* (1526) : long and patient endurance of offense — **long–suffering** *adj* — **long–suf·fer·ing·ly** \-lē\ *adv*

long suit *n* (ca. 1876) **1** : a holding of more than the average number of cards in a suit **2** : the activity or quality in which one excels

long–term \'lòn-'tərm\ *adj* (1904) **1** : occurring over or involving a relatively long period of time **2 a** : of, relating to, or constituting a financial operation or obligation based on a considerable term and esp. one of more than 10 years ⟨~ bonds⟩ **b** : generated by assets held for longer than six months ⟨a ~ capital gain⟩

long–time \'lòn-ˌtim\ *adj* (1584) : having been so for a long time : LONG-STANDING ⟨a ~ friend⟩ ⟨a ~ friendship⟩

Long Tom \'lòn-'täm\ *n* [fr. the name *Tom*] (1832) **1** : a large land gun having a long range **2** : a trough for washing gold-bearing earth

long ton *n* (1829) — see WEIGHT table

lon·gueur \lòⁿ-'gœr\ *n, pl* **longueurs** \-'gœr(z)\ [F, lit., length] (1791) : a dull and tedious passage or section (as of a book)

long view *n* (1912) : an approach to a problem or situation that emphasizes long-range factors

long–wind·ed \ˌlòn-'win-dəd, 'lòn-ˌwin-\ *adj* (1589) **1** : tediously long in speaking or writing **2** : not easily subject to loss of breath — **long–wind·ed·ly** *adv* — **long–wind·ed·ness** *n*

¹loo \'lü\ *n* [short for obs. *E lanterloo*, fr. F *lanturelu* twaddle] (1675) **1** : an old card game in which the winner of each trick or a majority of tricks takes a portion of the pool while losing players are obligated to contribute to the next pool **2** : money staked at loo

²loo *vt* (1680) : to obligate to contribute to a new pool at loo for failing to win a trick

³loo *n* [origin unknown] (1940) *chiefly Brit* : TOILET 3

loo·by \'lü-bē\ *n, pl* **loobies** [ME *loby*] (14c) : an awkward clumsy fellow : LUBBER

loo·fah \'lü-fə\ *n* [NL *luffa*, fr. Ar *lūf*] (1887) **1** : any of a genus (*Luffa*) of Old World tropical plants of the gourd family with large fruits; *also* : its fruit **2** : a sponge consisting of the fibrous skeleton of the fruit of a loofah (esp. *Luffa aegyptiaca*)

¹look \'lùk\ *vb* [ME, fr. OE *lōcian*; akin to OS *lōcon* to look] *vt* (bef. 12c) **1** : to make sure or take care (that something is done) **2** : to ascertain by the use of one's eyes **3 a** : to exercise the power of vision upon : EXAMINE **b** *archaic* : to search for **4 a** : EXPECT, ANTICIPATE ⟨we ~ to have a good year⟩ **b** : to have in mind as an end ⟨~ing to win back some lost profits⟩ **5** *archaic* : to bring into a place or condition by the exercise of the power of vision **6** : to express by the eyes or facial expression **7** : to have an appearance that befits or accords with ~ *vi* **1 a** : to exercise the power of vision : SEE **b** : to direct one's attention ⟨~ upon the future with hope⟩ **c** : to direct the eyes **2** : to have the appearance or likelihood of being : SEEM ⟨it ~s unlikely⟩ ⟨~s to be hard work⟩ **3** : to have a specified outlook ⟨the house ~ed east⟩ **4** : to gaze in wonder or surprise : STARE **5** : to show a tendency ⟨the evidence ~s to acquittal⟩ *syn* see EXPECT — **look after** : to take care of — **look at** : CONSIDER 1 ⟨*looking at* the possibility of relocating⟩ — **look down one's nose** : to view something with arrogance, disdain, or disapproval — **look for** : to await with hope or anticipation — **look forward** : to anticipate with pleasure or satisfaction ⟨*looking forward* to your visit⟩ — **look into** : EXPLORE 1a — **look the other way** : to direct one's attention away from something unpleasant or troublesome — **look to 1** : to direct one's attention to ⟨*looking to the future*⟩ **2** : to rely upon ⟨*looks to* reading for relaxation⟩

²look *n* (13c) **1 a** : the act of looking **b** : GLANCE **2 a** : the expression of the countenance **b** : physical appearance; *esp* : attractive physical appearance — usu. used in pl. **c** : a combination of design features giving a unified appearance ⟨a new ~ in women's fashions⟩ **3** : the state or form in which something appears

look–alike \'lù-kə-ˌlik\ *n* (1947) : one that looks like another : DOUBLE — **look–alike** *adj*

look·down \'lùk-ˌdaun\ *n* (ca. 1882) : a silvery carangid fish (*Selene vomer*) chiefly of the Atlantic having a laterally compressed deep body and steeply sloping facial profile

look down *vi* (14c) **1** : to be in a position that affords a downward view **2** : to regard with contempt : DESPISE — used with *on* or *upon*

look·er \'lù-kər\ *n* (14c) **1** : one that looks **2 a** : one having an appearance of a specified kind **b** : one that has an attractive appearance : BEAUTY

look·er–on \ˌlù-kər-'ón, -'än\ *n, pl* **lookers–on** (1539) : ONLOOKER

\ə\ abut \ˈə\ kitten, F table \ər\ further \a\ ash \ā\ ace \ä\ mop, mar \au\ out \ch\ chin \e\ bet \ē\ easy \g\ go \i\ hit \ī\ ice \j\ job \ŋ\ sing \ō\ go \ò\ law \òi\ boy \th\ thin \th\ the \ü\ loot \ù\ foot \y\ yet \zh\ vision \ȧ, k̲, ⁿ, œ, œ̄, ᵫ, ᵫ̄, ʸ\ see Guide to Pronunciation

look–in \'lu̇k-,in\ n (1870) **1 :** a chance of success **2 :** a quick pass in football to a receiver running diagonally toward the center of the field

looking glass n (1562) **:** MIRROR

look–out \'lu̇k-,au̇t\ n (1699) **1 :** one engaged in keeping watch **:** WATCHMAN **2 :** an elevated place or structure affording a wide view for observation **3 :** a careful looking or watching ⟨on the ∼⟩ . **4 :** VIEW, OUTLOOK **5 :** a matter of care or concern

look out vi (1602) **:** to take care or concern oneself — used with for ⟨looking out for number one⟩

look over vt (14c) **:** to inspect or examine esp. in a cursory way

look–see \'lu̇k-'sē, -,sē\ n (1883) **:** a general survey **:** EVALUATION, INSPECTION

look–up \'lu̇k-,əp\ n (1936) **:** the process or an instance of looking something up; esp **:** the process of matching by computer the words of a text with material stored in memory

look up vi (14c) **1 :** to cheer up ⟨look up—things are not all bad⟩ **2 :** to improve in prospects or conditions ⟨business is looking up⟩ ∼ vt **1 :** to search for in or as if in a reference work ⟨look up a phone number⟩ **2 :** to seek out esp. for a brief visit

¹loom \'lüm\ n [ME lome tool, loom, fr. OE gelōma tool; akin to MD allame tool] (15c) **:** a frame or machine for interlacing at right angles two or more sets of threads or yarns to form a cloth

²loom vi [origin unknown] (ca. 1541) **1 :** to come into sight in enlarged or distorted and indistinct form often as a result of atmospheric conditions **2 a :** to appear in an impressively great or exaggerated form ⟨deficits ∼ed large⟩ **b :** to take shape as an impending occurrence

³loom n (1836) **:** the indistinct and exaggerated appearance of something seen on the horizon or through fog or darkness; also **:** a looming shadow or reflection

¹loon \'lün\ n [ME loun] (15c) **1 :** LOUT, IDLER **2** chiefly Scot **:** BOY **3 a :** a crazy person **b :** SIMPLETON

²loon n [of Scand origin; akin to ON lōmr loon] (1634) **:** any of several large birds (genus Gavia) of Holarctic regions that feed on fish by diving and have their legs placed far back under the body for optimal locomotion underwater

loo·ny also **loo·ney** \'lü-nē\ adj **loo·ni·er; -est** [by shortening & alter. fr. lunatic] (1872) **:** CRAZY, FOOLISH — **loo·ni·ness** n — **loony** n

loony bin n (1919) **:** an insane asylum **:** MADHOUSE

¹loop \'lüp\ n [ME loupe; perh. akin to MD lupen to watch, peer] (14c) archaic **:** LOOPHOLE 1a

²loop n [ME loupe, of unknown origin] (14c) **1 a :** a curving or doubling of a line so as to form a closed or partly open curve within itself through which another line can be passed or into which a hook may be hooked **b :** such a fold of cord or ribbon serving as an ornament **2 a :** something shaped like a loop **b :** a circular airplane maneuver executed in the vertical plane **3 :** a ring or curved piece used to form a fastening, handle, or catch **4 :** a closed electric circuit **5 :** a piece of film or magnetic tape whose ends are spliced together so as to project or play back the same material continuously **6 :** a series of instructions (as for a computer) that is repeated until a terminating condition is reached **7 :** a sports league **8 :** a select well-informed inner circle that is influential in decision making ⟨out of the policy ∼⟩ — **for a loop :** into a state of amazement, confusion, or distress

³loop vi (1832) **1 :** to make or form a loop **2 :** to execute a loop in an airplane **3 :** to move in loops or in an arc ∼ vt **1 a :** to make a loop in, on, or about **b :** to fasten with a loop **2 :** to join (two courses of loops) in knitting **3 :** to connect (electric conductors) so as to complete a loop **4 :** to cause to move in an arc

looped \'lüpd\ adj (1513) **1 :** having, formed in, or characterized by loops ⟨∼ fabrics⟩ **2 :** DRUNK 1a

loop·er \'lü-pər\ n (1731) **1 :** any of the usu. rather small hairless caterpillars that are mostly larvae of moths (families Geometridae and Noctuidae) and move with a looping movement in which the anterior legs and the posterior prolegs are alternately made fast and released — called also inchworm **2 :** one that loops

¹loop·hole \'lüp-,hōl\ n [¹loop] (1591) **1 a :** a small opening through which small arms may be fired **b :** a similar opening to admit light and air or to permit observation **2 :** a means of escape; esp **:** an ambiguity or omission in the text through which the intent of a statute, contract, or obligation may be evaded

²loophole vt (1664) **:** to make loopholes in

loop of Hen·le \-'hen-lē\ [F. G. J. Henle †1885 Ger. pathologist] (1890) **:** a U-shaped part of the nephron of birds and mammals that lies between and is continuous with the proximal and distal convoluted tubules and that functions in water resorption

loopy \'lü-pē\ adj **loop·i·er; -est** (1856) **1 :** having or characterized by loops **2 :** CRAZY, BIZARRE

¹loose \'lüs\ adj **loos·er; loos·est** [ME lous, fr. ON lauss; akin to OHG lōs loose — more at -LESS] (13c) **1 a :** not rigidly fastened or securely attached **b** (1) **:** having worked partly free from attachments ⟨a ∼ tooth⟩ (2) **:** having relative freedom of movement **c :** produced freely and accompanied by raising of mucus ⟨a ∼ cough⟩ **d :** not tight-fitting **2 a :** free from a state of confinement, restraint, or obligation ⟨a lion ∼ in the streets⟩ ⟨spend ∼ funds wisely⟩ **b :** not brought together in a bundle, container, or binding **c** archaic **:** DISCONNECTED, DETACHED **3 :** not dense, close, or compact in structure or arrangement **4 a :** lacking in restraint or power of restraint ⟨a ∼ tongue⟩ ⟨∼ bowels⟩ **b :** lacking moral restraint **:** UNCHASTE **5 a :** not tightly drawn or stretched **:** SLACK **b :** being flexible or relaxed ⟨stay ∼⟩ **6 a :** lacking in precision, exactness, or care ⟨∼ brushwork⟩ ⟨∼ usage⟩ **b :** permitting freedom of interpretation **7 :** not in the possession of either of two competing teams ⟨a ∼ ball⟩ ⟨a ∼ puck⟩ — **loose·ly** adv — **loose·ness** n

²loose vb **loosed; loos·ing** vt (13c) **1 a :** to let loose **:** RELEASE **b :** to free from tension **2 :** to make loose **:** UNTIE ⟨∼ a knot⟩ **3 :** to cast loose **:** DETACH **4 :** to let fly **:** DISCHARGE **5 :** to make less rigid, tight, or strict **:** RELAX ∼ vi **:** to let fly a missile (as an arrow) **:** FIRE

³loose adv (15c) **:** in a loose manner **:** LOOSELY

loose box n (1849) Brit **:** BOX STALL

loose cannon n (1981) **:** a dangerously uncontrollable person or thing

loose end n (1546) **1 :** something left hanging loose **2 :** a fragment of unfinished business — usu. used in pl.

loose–joint·ed \'lüs-'jȯin-təd\ adj (1859) **1 :** having joints apparently not closely articulated **2 :** characterized by unusually free movements — **loose–joint·ed·ness** n

loose–leaf \'lüs-'lēf\ adj (1902) **1 :** having leaves secured in book form in a cover whose backbone may be opened for adding, arranging, or removing leaves ⟨∼ notebook⟩ **2 :** of, relating to, or used with a loose-leaf binding ⟨∼ paper⟩

loos·en \'lü-sᵊn\ vb **loos·ened; loos·en·ing** \'lüs-niŋ, 'lü-sᵊn-iŋ\ vt (14c) **1 :** to release from restraint **2 :** to make looser **3 :** to relieve (the bowels) of constipation **4 :** to cause or permit to become less strict — often used with up ∼ vi **:** to become loose or looser

loosen up vi (1938) **:** to become less tense **:** RELAX

loose sentence n (ca. 1890) **:** a sentence in which the principal clause comes first and subordinate modifiers or trailing elements follow

loose smut n (1890) **:** a smut disease of grains in which the entire head is transformed into a dusty mass of spores

loose-strife \'lü(s)-,strīf\ n [intended as trans. of Gk lysimacheios loosestrife (as if fr. lysis act of loosing + machesthai to fight) — more at LYSIS] (1548) **1 :** any of a genus (Lysimachia) of plants of the primrose family with leafy stems and usu. yellow or white flowers **2 :** any of a genus (Lythrum, family Lythraceae, the loosestrife family) of herbs having entire leaves and including some with showy spikes of purple flowers; esp **:** PURPLE LOOSESTRIFE

loos·ey–goos·ey \,lü-sē-'gü-sē\ adj (1964) **:** notably loose or relaxed **:** not tense

¹loot \'lüt\ n [Hindi lūṭ; akin to Skt luṇṭati he plunders] (ca. 1788) **1 :** goods usu. of considerable value taken in war **:** SPOILS **2 :** something held to resemble goods of value seized in war **:** as **a :** something appropriated illegally often by force or violence **b :** illicit gains by public officials **c :** MONEY **3 :** the action of looting **syn** see SPOIL

²loot vt (1845) **1 a :** to plunder or sack in war **b :** to rob esp. on a large scale and usu. by violence or corruption **2 :** to seize and carry away by force esp. in war ∼ vi **:** to engage in robbing or plundering esp. in war — **loot·er** n

¹lop \'läp\ n [ME loppe] (14c) **:** material cut away from a tree; esp **:** parts discarded in lumbering

²lop vt **lopped; lop·ping** (1519) **1 a** (1) **:** to cut off branches or twigs from (2) **:** to sever from a woody plant **b** (1) archaic **:** to cut off the head or limbs of (2) **:** to cut from a person **2 a :** to remove superfluous parts from **b :** to eliminate as unnecessary or undesirable — usu. used with off — **lop·per** n

³lop vi **lopped; lop·ping** [perh. imit.] (1578) **:** to hang downward **:** DROOP

¹lope \'lōp\ n [ME loup, lope leap, fr. ON hlaup; akin to OE hlēapan to leap — more at LEAP] (1809) **1 :** an easy natural gait of a horse resembling a canter **2 :** an easy usu. bounding gait capable of being sustained for a long time

²lope vi **loped; lop·ing** (ca. 1825) **:** to move or ride at a lope — **lop·er** n

lop–eared \'läp-,ird\ adj (1687) **:** having ears that droop

loph·o·phore \'lä-fə-,fȯr, -,fȯr\ n [Gk lophos crest + E -phore] (1850) **:** a circular or horseshoe-shaped organ about the mouth esp. of a brachiopod or bryozoan that bears tentacles and functions esp. in food-getting

lop·sid·ed \'läp-,sī-dəd\ adj (1711) **1 :** leaning to one side **2 :** lacking in balance, symmetry, or proportion **:** disproportionately heavy on one side ⟨a ∼ vote of 99–1⟩ — **lop·sid·ed·ly** adv — **lop·sid·ed·ness** n

lo·qua·cious \lō-'kwā-shəs\ adj [L loquac-, loquax, fr. loqui to speak] (1667) **1 :** given to fluent or excessive talk **:** WORDY **syn** see TALKATIVE — **lo·qua·cious·ly** adv — **lo·qua·cious·ness** n

lo·quac·i·ty \-'kwa-sə-tē\ n (13c) **:** the quality or state of being very talkative

lo·quat \'lō-,kwät\ n [Chin (Guangdong) làuh-gwāt] (1820) **:** an Asian evergreen tree (Eriobotrya japonica) of the rose family often cultivated for its fruit; also **:** its small yellow edible fruit used esp. for preserves

lo·ran \'lȯr-,an, 'lōr-\ n [long-range navigation] (1932) **:** a system of long-range navigation in which pulsed signals sent out by two pairs of radio stations are used to determine the geographical position of a ship or an airplane

¹lord \'lȯrd\ n [ME loverd, lord, fr. OE hlāford, fr. hlāf loaf + weard keeper — more at LOAF, WARD] (bef. 12c) **1 :** one having power and authority over others **: a :** a ruler by hereditary right or preeminence to whom service and obedience are due **b :** one of whom a fee or estate is held in feudal tenure **c :** an owner of land or other real property **d** obs **:** the male head of a household **e :** HUSBAND **f :** one that has achieved mastery or that exercises leadership or great power in some area ⟨a drug ∼⟩ **2** cap **a :** GOD 1 **b :** JESUS **3 :** a man of rank or high position: as **a :** a feudal tenant whose right or title comes directly from the king **b :** a British nobleman: as (1) **:** BARON 2a (2) **:** an hereditary peer of the rank of marquess, earl, or viscount (3) **:** the son of a duke or a marquess or the eldest son of an earl (4) **:** a bishop of the Church of England **c** pl, cap **:** HOUSE OF LORDS **4 :** — used as a British title: as **a :** — used as part of an official title ⟨Lord Advocate⟩ **b :** — used informally in place of the full title for a marquess, earl, or viscount **c :** — used for a baron **d :** — used by courtesy before the name and surname of a younger son of a duke or a marquess **5 : a :** person chosen to preside over a festival

²lord vi (14c) **:** to act like a lord; esp **:** to put on airs — usu. used with it ⟨∼s it over his friends⟩

lord chancellor n, pl **lords chancellor** (15c) **:** a British officer of state who presides over the House of Lords in both its legislative and judicial capacities, serves as the head of the British judiciary, and is usu. a leading member of the cabinet

lord·ing \'lȯr-diŋ\ n (13c) **1** archaic **:** LORD **2** obs **:** LORDLING

lord·ling \'lȯrd-liŋ\ n (13c) **:** a little or insignificant lord

lord·ly \-lē\ adj **lord·li·er; -est** (bef. 12c) **1 a :** of, relating to, or having the characteristics of a lord **:** DIGNIFIED **b :** GRAND, NOBLE **2 :** exhibiting such pride and assurance as could only be felt as appropriate to one of the highest birth or rank **syn** see PROUD — **lord·li·ness** n — **lordly** adv

lord of misrule n (15c) **:** a master of Christmas revels in England esp. in the 15th and 16th centuries

lor·do·sis \lȯr-'dō-səs\ n [NL, fr. Gk lordōsis, fr. lordos curving for-

ward; akin to OE be*lyrtan* to deceive] (1704) **1** : abnormal curvature of the spine forward **2** : a mating posture of some sexually receptive female mammals (as rats) in which the head and rump are raised and the back is arched downward — **lor·dot·ic** \-'dä-tik\ *adj*

Lord Protector of the Commonwealth (ca. 1653) : PROTECTOR 2b

Lord's day *n, often cap D* (12c) : SUNDAY

lord·ship \'lord-,ship\ *n* (bef. 12c) **1 a** : the rank or dignity of a lord — used as a title **b** : the authority or power of a lord : DOMINION 2 : the territory under the jurisdiction of a lord : SEIGNIORY

Lord's Prayer *n* (ca. 1549) : the prayer with variant versions in Matthew and Luke that according to the Lucan account Christ taught his disciples

Lord's Supper *n* (14c) : COMMUNION 2a

Lord's table *n, often cap T* (1535) : ALTAR 2

Lordy \'lor-dē\ *interj* [¹lord (God) + ⁴-*y*] (1853) — used to express surprise or strength of feeling

¹lore \'lor, 'lor\ *n* [ME, fr. OE *lār;* akin to OHG *lēra* doctrine, OE *leornian* to learn] (bef. 12c) **1** *archaic* : something that is taught : LESSON **2** : something that is learned: **a** : knowledge gained through study or experience **b** : traditional knowledge or belief **3** : a particular body of knowledge or tradition

²lore *n* [NL *lorum,* fr. L, thong, rein; akin to Gk *eulēra* reins] (1828) : the space between the eye and bill in a bird or the corresponding region in a reptile or fish — **lo·re·al** \'lor-ē-əl, 'lor-\ *adj*

Lo·re·lei \'lor-ə-,lī, 'lor-\ *n* [G] : a siren of Germanic legend whose singing lures Rhine River boatmen to destruction on a reef

lor·gnette \lorn-'yet\ *n* [F, fr. *lorgner* to take a sidelong look at, fr. MF, fr. *lorgne* squinting] (1803) : a pair of eyeglasses or opera glasses with a handle

lor·gnon \lorn-'yōⁿ\ *n* [F, fr. *lorgner*] (1846) : LORGNETTE

lo·ri·ca \lə-'rī-kə\ *n, pl* **-cae** \-kē, -,sē\ [L] (ca. 1706) **1** : a Roman cuirass of leather or metal **2** [NL, fr. L] : a hard protective case or shell (as of a rotifer)

lor·i·keet \'lor-ə-,kēt, 'lär-\ *n* [*lory* + -*keet* (as in *parakeet*)] (1770) : any of numerous small arboreal chiefly Australasian parrots (family Loriidae) that usu. have long slender tongue papillae which form an organ resembling a brush

lo·ris \'lor-əs, 'lor-\ *n* [F, prob. fr. obs. D *loeris* simpleton] (1774) : any of several nocturnal slow-moving tailless arboreal primates (family Lorisidae): as **a** : a slim-bodied primate (*Loris tardigradus*) of southern India and Sri Lanka **b** : either of two larger related primates (*Nycticebus pygmaeus* or *N. coucang*) of southeastern Asia that are heavier limbed and slower moving

lorn \'lorn\ *adj* [ME, fr. *loren,* pp. of *lesen* to lose, fr. OE *lēosan* — more at LOSE] (14c) : DESOLATE, FORSAKEN — **lorn·ness** \'lorn-nəs\ *n*

Lor·raine cross \lə-'rān-, lo-\ *n* (1898) : CROSS OF LORRAINE

lor·ry \'lor-ē, 'lär-\ *n, pl* **lorries** [origin unknown] (1908) *chiefly Brit* : MOTORTRUCK

loris *a*

lo·ry \'lor-ē, 'lor-\ *n, pl* **lories** [D, fr. Malay *nuri, luri*] (1682) : any of numerous parrots (family Loriidae) of Australia, New Guinea, and adjacent islands related to the lorikeets and usu. having the tongue papillose at the tip and the mandibles less toothed than in other parrots

lose \'lüz\ *vb* **lost** \'lost\; **los·ing** \'lü-ziŋ\ [ME, fr. OE *losian* to perish, lose, fr. *los* destruction; akin to OE *lēosan* to lose; akin to ON *losa* to loosen, L *luere* to atone for, Gk *lyein* to loosen, dissolve, destroy] *vt* (bef. 12c) **1 a** : to bring to destruction — used chiefly in passive construction ⟨the ship was *lost* on the reef⟩ **b** : DAMN ⟨if he shall gain the whole world and ~ his own soul —Mt 16:26 (AV)⟩ **2 :** to miss from one's possession or from a customary or supposed place **3** : to suffer deprivation of : part with esp. in an unforeseen or accidental manner **4 a** : to suffer loss through the death or removal of or final separation from (a person) **b** : to fail to keep control of or allegiance of ⟨~ votes⟩ ⟨*lost* his temper⟩ **5 a** : to fail to use : let slip by : WASTE ⟨~ the tide⟩ **b** (1) : to fail to win, gain, or obtain ⟨~ a prize⟩ ⟨~ a contest⟩ (2) : to undergo defeat in ⟨*lost* every battle⟩ **c** : to fail to catch with the senses or the mind ⟨*lost* part of what she said⟩ **6** : to cause the loss of ⟨one careless statement *lost* him the election⟩ **7** : to fail to keep, sustain, or maintain ⟨*lost* my balance⟩ **8 a** : to cause to miss one's way or bearings ⟨*lost* himself in the maze of streets⟩ **b** : to make (oneself) withdrawn from immediate reality ⟨*lost* herself in daydreaming⟩ **9 a** : to wander or go astray from ⟨*lost* his way⟩ **b** : to draw away from : OUTSTRIP ⟨*lost* his pursuers⟩ **10** : to fail to keep in sight or in mind **11** : to free oneself from : get rid of ⟨dieting to ~ some weight⟩ ~ *vi* **1** : to undergo deprivation of something of value **2** : to undergo defeat ⟨~ with good grace⟩ **3** *of a timepiece* : to run slow — **los·able** \'lü-zə-bəl\ *adj* — **los·able·ness** *n* — **lose ground** : to suffer loss or disadvantage : fail to advance or improve — **lose one's heart** : to fall in love

lo·sel \'lō-zəl\ *n* [ME, fr. *losen* (pp. of *lesen* to lose), alter. of *loren* — more at LORN] (14c) : a worthless person

lose out *vi* (ca. 1858) : to fail to win in competition : fail to receive an expected reward or gain

los·er \'lü-zər\ *n* (1548) **1** : one that loses esp. consistently **2** : one who is incompetent or unable to succeed; *also* : something doomed to fail or disappoint

loss \'los\ *n* [ME *los,* prob. back-formation fr. *lost,* pp. of *losen* to lose] (13c) **1** : DESTRUCTION, RUIN **2 a** : the act of losing possession **b** : the harm or privation resulting from loss or separation **c** : an instance of losing **3** : a person or thing or an amount that is lost: as **a** *pl* : killed, wounded, or captured soldiers **b** : the power diminution of a circuit or circuit element corresponding to conversion of electrical energy into heat by resistance **4 a** : failure to gain, win, obtain, or utilize **b** : an amount by which the cost of an article or service exceeds the selling price **5** : decrease in amount, magnitude, or degree **6** : the amount of an insured's financial detriment by death or damage

that the insurer becomes liable for — **at a loss** : UNCERTAIN, PUZZLED — **for a loss** : into a state of distress

loss leader *n* (1917) : something (as merchandise) sold at a loss in order to draw customers — **loss–leader** *adj*

loss ratio *n* (1926) : the ratio between insurance losses incurred and premiums earned during a given period

lossy \'lo-sē\ *adj* (1946) : causing attenuation or dissipation of electrical energy ⟨a ~ transmission line⟩ ⟨a ~ dielectric⟩

lost \'lost\ *adj* [pp. of *lose*] (15c) **1** : not made use of, won, or claimed **2** : no longer possessed **b** : no longer known **3** : ruined or destroyed physically or morally : DESPERATE **4** : taken away or beyond reach or attainment : DENIED ⟨regions ~ to the faith⟩ **b** : INSENSIBLE, HARDENED ⟨~ to shame⟩ **5 a** : unable to find the way **b** : no longer visible **c** : lacking assurance or self-confidence : HELPLESS **6** : RAPT, ABSORBED ⟨~ in reverie⟩ **7** : not appreciated or understood : WASTED ⟨their jokes were ~ on me⟩ — **lost·ness** \'los(t)-nəs\ *n*

lost wax *n* (1909) : a process used in metal casting that consists of making a wax model, coating it with a refractory to form a mold, heating until the wax melts and runs out of the mold, and then pouring metal into the vacant mold

¹lot \'lät\ *n* [ME, fr. OE *hlot;* akin to OHG *hlōz*] (bef. 12c) **1** : an object used as a counter in determining a question by chance **2 a** : the use of lots as a means of deciding something **b** : the resulting choice **3 a** : something that comes to one upon whom a lot has fallen : SHARE **b** : one's way of life or worldly fate : FORTUNE **4 a** : a portion of land **b** : a measured parcel of land having fixed boundaries and designated on a plot or survey **c** : a motion-picture studio and its adjoining property **5 a** : a number of units of an article, a single article, or a parcel of articles offered as one item (as in an auction sale) **b** : all the members of a present group, kind, or quantity — used with *the* **6 a** : a number of associated persons : SET **b** : KIND, SORT **7 a** : a considerable quantity or extent ⟨a ~ of money⟩ ⟨~s of friends⟩ *syn* see FATE — **a lot 1** : to a considerable degree or extent ⟨this is *a lot* nicer⟩ **2** : OFTEN, FREQUENTLY ⟨runs *a lot* every day⟩ **3** : LOTS

²lot *vt* **lot·ted; lot·ting** (15c) **1** : ALLOT, APPORTION **2** : to form or divide into lots

Lot \'lät\ *n* [Heb *Lōṭ*] : a nephew of Abraham who according to the account in Genesis escaped from the doomed city of Sodom with his wife who turned into a pillar of salt when she looked back

lo·ta *also* **lo·tah** \'lō-tə\ *n* [Hindi *loṭā*] (1809) : a small usu. spherical water vessel of brass or copper used in India

loth \'lōth, 'lōth\ *var of* LOATH

lo·thar·io \lō-'thar-ē-,ō, -'ther-, -'thär-\ *n, pl* **-i·os** *often cap* [*Lothario,* seducer in the play *The Fair Penitent* (1703) by Nicholas Rowe] (1756) : a man whose chief interest is seducing women

lo·ti \'lō-tē\ *n, pl* **ma·lo·ti** \mə-'lō-tē\ [Sesotho] (1980) — see MONEY table

lo·tic \'lō-tik\ *adj* [L *lotus,* pp. of *lavere*] (1916) : of, relating to, or living in actively moving water ⟨a ~ habitat⟩ — compare LENTIC

lo·tion \'lō-shən\ *n* [ME *loscion,* fr. L *lotion-, lotio* act of washing, fr. *lavere* to wash — more at LYE] (14c) : a liquid preparation for cosmetic or external medicinal use

lots \'läts\ *adv* [pl. of ¹*lot*] (1891) : MUCH ⟨feeling ~ better⟩

lotte \'lät, 'lot\ *n* [F, fr. MF] (1977) : MONKFISH

lot·tery \'lä-tə-rē *also* 'lä-trē\ *n, pl* **-ter·ies** *often attrib* [MF *loterie,* fr. MD, fr. *lot* lot; akin to OE *hlot* lot] (1567) **1 a** : a drawing of lots in which prizes are distributed to the winners among persons buying a chance **b** : a drawing of lots used to decide something **2** : an event or affair whose outcome is or seems to be determined by chance

lot·to \'lä-(,)tō\ *n* [It, lottery, lotto, fr. F *lot* lot, of Gmc origin; akin to OE *hlot* lot] (1778) : a game of chance resembling bingo

lo·tus \'lō-təs\ *n* [L & Gk; L *lotus,* Gk *lōtos*] (ca. 1541) **1** *also* **lo·tos** \'lō-təs\ : a fruit eaten by the lotus-eaters and considered to cause indolence and dreamy contentment; *also* : a tree (as *Zizyphus lotus* of the buckthorn family) reputed to bear this fruit **2** : any of various water lilies including several represented in ancient Egyptian and Hindu art and religious symbolism **3** [NL, fr. L] : any of a genus (*Lotus*) of widely distributed upright leguminous herbs or subshrubs **b** : SWEET CLOVER

lotus 2

lo·tus–eat·er \-,ē-tər\ *n* (1832) **1** : any of a people in Homer's *Odyssey* subsisting on the lotus and living in the dreamy indolence it induces **2** : an indolent person

lo·tus·land \-,land\ *n* [fr. the Homeric land of lotus-eaters] (1842) **1** : a place inducing contentment esp. through offering an idyllic living situation **2** : a state or an ideal marked by contentment often achieved through self-indulgence

lotus position *n* [fr. the supposed resemblance of the position to a lotus blossom] (1953) : a cross-legged sitting position used in yoga in which the right foot is on the left thigh and the left foot is on the right thigh

louche \'lüsh\ *adj* [F, lit., cross-eyed, squint-eyed, fr. L *luscus* blind in one eye] (1819) : not reputable or decent

loud \'laúd\ *adj* [ME, fr. OE *hlūd;* akin to OHG *hlūt* loud, L in*clutus* famous, Gk *klytos,* Skt *śṛnoti* he hears] (bef. 12c) **1 a** : marked by intensity or volume of sound **b** : producing a loud sound **2** : CLAMOROUS, NOISY **3** : obtrusive or offensive in appearance or smell : OBNOXIOUS — **loud** *adv* — **loud·ly** *adv*

syn LOUD, STENTORIAN, EARSPLITTING, RAUCOUS, STRIDENT mean marked by intensity or volume of sound. LOUD applies to any volume above normal and may suggest undue vehemence or obtrusiveness ⟨*loud* shouts of protest⟩. STENTORIAN implies great power and range ⟨an

\ə\ abut \ᵊ\ kitten, F table \ər\ further \a\ ash \ā\ ace \ä\ mop, mar \aú\ out \ch\ chin \e\ bet \ē\ easy \g\ go \i\ hit \ī\ ice \j\ job \ŋ\ sing \ō\ go \ò\ law \òi\ boy \th\ thin \t̲h̲\ the \ü\ loot \ú\ foot \y\ yet \zh\ vision \á, k̲, ⁿ, œ, œ̄, ᵫ, ᵫ̄, ᵞ\ *see* Guide to Pronunciation actor with a *stentorian* voice). EARSPLITTING implies loudness that is physically discomforting ⟨the *earsplitting* sound of a siren⟩. RAUCOUS implies a loud harsh grating tone, esp. of voice, and may suggest rowdiness ⟨the *raucous* shouts of drunken revelers⟩. STRIDENT implies a rasping discordant but insistent quality, esp. of voice ⟨the *strident* voices of hecklers⟩.

loud·en \'laů-d°n\ *vb* **loud·ened; loud·en·ing** \'laůd-niṇ, 'laů-d°n-iṇ\ *vi* (ca. 1848) : to become loud ~ *vt* : to make loud

loud–hail·er \,laůd-'hā-lər\ *n* (1941) *chiefly Brit* : BULLHORN

loud·mouth \'laůd-,maůth\ *n* (1914) : a loudmouthed person

loud-mouthed \-,maůthd, -,maůtht\ *adj* (1628) : given to loud offensive talk

loud·ness *n* (bef. 12c) : the attribute of a sound that determines the magnitude of the auditory sensation produced and that primarily depends on the amplitude of the sound wave involved

loud·speak·er \'laůd-,spē-kər\ *n* (1920) : a device that changes electrical signals into sounds loud enough to be heard at a distance

Lou Geh·rig's disease \,lü-'ger-igz-, -'gar-\ *n* [*Lou Gehrig* †1941 Am. baseball player who suffered from the disease] (1958) : AMYOTROPHIC LATERAL SCLEROSIS

lough \'läk, 'läk\ *n* [ME, of Celt origin; akin to OIr *loch* lake; akin to L *lacus* lake — more at LAKE] (14c) **1** *chiefly Irish* : LAKE **2** *chiefly Irish* : a bay or inlet of the sea

lou·is d'or \,lü-ē-'dór\ *n, pl* **louis d'or** [F, fr. *Louis* XIII of France + *d'or* of gold] (1665) **1** : a French gold coin first struck in 1640 and issued up to the Revolution **2** : the French 20-franc gold piece issued after the Revolution

Lou·is Qua·torze \,lü-ē-kə-'tórz\ *adj* [F, *Louis* XIV] (1848) : of, relating to, or characteristic of the architecture or furniture of the reign of Louis XIV of France

Louis Quinze \-'kaⁿz\ *adj* [F, *Louis* XV] (1855) : of, relating to, or characteristic of the architecture or furniture of the reign of Louis XV of France

Louis Seize \-'sāz, -'sez\ *adj* [F, *Louis* XVI] (1882) : of, relating to, or characteristic of the architecture or furniture of the reign of Louis XVI of France

Louis Treize \-'trāz, -'trez\ *adj* [F, *Louis* XIII] (1883) : of, relating to, or characteristic of the architecture or furniture of the reign of Louis XIII of France

¹lounge \'laůnj\ *vb* **lounged; loung·ing** [origin unknown] *vi* (1508) : to act or move idly or lazily : LOAF ~ *vt* : to pass (time) idly

²lounge *n* (1775) **1** : a place for lounging: as **a** : a room in a private home or public building for leisure occupations : LIVING ROOM; *also* : LOBBY **b** : a room in a usu. public building or vehicle often combining lounging, smoking, and toilet facilities **2** : a long couch

lounge car *n* (1947) : CLUB CAR

lounge lizard *n* (1918) **1** : LADIES' MAN **2** : FOP **3** : a social parasite

loung·er \'laůn-jər\ *n* (1508) **1** : one that lounges; *esp* : IDLER **2** : an article of clothing or furniture designed for comfort and leisure use

lounge suit *n* (1901) *chiefly Brit* : BUSINESS SUIT

lounge·wear \'laůnj-,war, -,wer\ *n* (ca. 1957) : informal clothing usu. designed to be worn at home

loup \'laůp, 'lōp\ *vb* [ME, fr. ON *hlaupa*; akin to OE *hlēapan* to leap — more at LEAP] (14c) *chiefly Scot* : LEAP — **loup** *n*

loupe \'lüp\ *n* [F] (ca. 1775) : a small magnifier used esp. by jewelers and watchmakers

loup–ga·rou \,lü-gə-'rü\ *n, pl* **loups–garous** \,lü-gə-'rü(z)\ [MF, fr. OF *leu garoul*, fr. *leu* (fr. L *lupus*) wolf + *garoul* werewolf, of Gmc origin; akin to OHG *werwolf* werewolf] (ca. 1580) : WEREWOLF

lour \'laů(-ə)r\, **loury** \'laů(ə)r-ē\ *var of* LOWER, LOWERY

¹louse \'laůs\ *n* [ME *lous*, fr. OE *lūs*; akin to OHG *lūs* louse, W *llau* lice] (bef. 12c) **1** *pl* **lice** \'līs\ **a** : any of various small wingless usu. flattened insects (orders Anoplura and Mallophaga) parasitic on warm-blooded animals **b** : a small usu. sluggish arthropod that lives on other animals or on plants and sucks their blood or juices — usu. used in combination ⟨plant ~⟩ **c** : any of several small arthropods that are not parasitic — usu. used in combination ⟨book ~⟩ ⟨wood ~⟩ **2** *pl* **lous·es** \'laů-səz\ : a contemptible person

²louse \'laůs, 'laůz\ *vt* **loused; lous·ing** (14c) : to pick lice from : DELOUSE

louse up *vt* (1934) : FOUL UP, SNARL ~ *vi* : to make a mess

louse·wort \'laůs-,wort, -,wórt\ *n* (1597) : any of a genus (*Pedicularis*) of herbs of the snapdragon family typically having pinnatifid leaves and bilabiate flowers in terminal spikes

lousy \'laů-zē\ *adj* **lous·i·er; -est** (14c) **1** : infested with lice **2 a** : totally repulsive : CONTEMPTIBLE **b** : miserably poor or inferior ⟨got ~ grades⟩ ⟨felt ~ after dinner⟩ **c** : amply supplied : REPLETE ⟨~ with money⟩ **3** *of silk* : fuzzy and specked because of splitting of the fiber — **lous·i·ly** \-zə-lē\ *adv* — **lous·i·ness** \-zē-nəs\ *n*

¹lout \'laůt\ *vi* [ME, fr. OE *lūtan*; akin to ON *lūta* to bow down] (bef. 12c) **1** : to bow in respect **2** : SUBMIT, YIELD

²lout *n* [perh. fr. ON *lūtr* bent down, fr. *lūta*] (1542) : an awkward brutish person

³lout *vt* (ca. 1530) : to treat as a lout : SCORN

lout·ish \'laů-tish\ *adj* (1542) : resembling or befitting a lout *syn* see BOORISH — **lout·ish·ly** *adv* — **lout·ish·ness** *n*

lou·ver *or* **lou·vre** \'lü-vər\ *n* [ME *lover*, fr. MF *lovier*] (14c) **1** : a roof lantern or turret often with slatted apertures for escape of smoke or admission of light in a medieval building **2 a** : an opening provided with one or more slanted fixed or movable fins to allow flow of air but to exclude rain or sun or to provide privacy **b** : a finned or vaned device for controlling a flow of air or the radiation of light **c** : a fin or shutter of a louver — **lou·vered** *also* **lou·vred** \-vərd\ *adj*

lov·able *also* **love·able** \'lə-və-bəl\ *adj* (14c) : having qualities that attract affection — **lov·abil·i·ty** \,lə-və-'bi-lə-tē\ *n* — **lov·able·ness** *n* — **lov·ably** \-blē\ *adv*

lov·age \'lə-vij\ *n* [ME *lovache*, fr. AF, fr. LL *levisticum*, alter. of L *ligusticum*, fr. neut. of *ligusticus* Ligurian, fr. *Ligur-, Ligus*, n., Ligurian] (14c) : any of several aromatic perennial herbs of the carrot family; *esp* : a European herb (*Levisticum officinale*) sometimes cultivated as a domestic remedy, flavoring agent, or potherb

lov·a·stat·in \'lō-və-,sta-tən, 'lə-; ,lō-və-', ,lə-\ *n* [*lov-* (perh. fr. *mevinolin*, an earlier name) + connective *-a-* + *stat* + *-in*] (1987) : a drug $C_{24}H_{36}O_5$ used to lower cholesterol levels in the blood

lo·vat \'lə-vət\ *n* [prob. fr. T. A. Fraser, Lord *Lovat* †1875 Scot. nobleman who popularized muted tweeds] (1907) : a predominantly dusty color mixture (as of green) in fabrics

¹love \'ləv\ *n* [ME, fr. OE *lufu*; akin to OHG *luba* love, OE *lēof* dear, L *lubēre, libēre* to please] (bef. 12c) **1 a** (1) : strong affection for another arising out of kinship or personal ties ⟨maternal ~ for a child⟩ (2) : attraction based on sexual desire : affection and tenderness felt by lovers (3) : affection based on admiration, benevolence, or common interests ⟨~ for his old schoolmates⟩ **b** : an assurance of love ⟨give her my ~⟩ **2** : warm attachment, enthusiasm, or devotion ⟨~ of the sea⟩ **3 a** : the object of attachment, devotion, or admiration ⟨baseball was his first ~⟩ **b** (1) : a beloved person : DARLING — often used as a term of endearment ⟨*Brit* — used as an informal term of address⟩ **4 a** : unselfish loyal and benevolent concern for the good of another: as (1) : the fatherly concern of God for humankind (2) : brotherly concern for others **b** : a person's adoration of God **5 a** : god or personification of love **6** : an amorous episode : LOVE AFFAIR **7** : the sexual embrace : COPULATION **8** : a score of zero (as in tennis) **9** *cap, Christian Science* : GOD — **at love** : holding one's opponent scoreless in tennis — **in love** : inspired by affection

²love *vb* **loved; lov·ing** *vt* (bef. 12c) **1** : to hold dear : CHERISH **2 a** : to feel a lover's passion, devotion, or tenderness for **b** : CARESS (2) : to fondle amorously (3) : to copulate with **3** : to like or desire actively : take pleasure in ⟨*loved* to play the violin⟩ **4** : to thrive in ⟨the rose ~s sunlight⟩ ~ *vi* : to feel affection or experience desire

love affair *n* (1591) **1** : a romantic attachment or episode between lovers **2** : a lively enthusiasm ⟨America's love *affair* with baseball⟩

love apple *n* [prob. trans. of F *pomme d'amour*] (1578) : TOMATO

love beads *n pl* (1968) : beads worn as a symbol of love and peace

love·bird \'ləv-,bərd\ *n* (1595) : any of various small usu. gray or green parrots (esp. genus *Agapornis* of Africa) that show great affection for their mates

love·bug \-,bəg\ *n* [fr. the fact that it is usu. seen copulating] (ca. 1966) : a small black fly (*Plecia nearctica*) with a red thorax that swarms along highways in the Gulf states of the U.S.

love child *n* (1805) : an illegitimate child

love feast *n* (1580) **1** : a meal eaten in common by a Christian congregation in token of brotherly love **2** : a gathering held to promote reconciliation and good feeling or show someone affectionate honor

love grass *n* (1702) : any of a genus (*Eragrostis*) of grasses that resemble the bluegrasses but have flattened spikelets and deciduous lemmas

love handles *n pl* (1975) : fatty bulges along the sides at the waist

love–in \'ləv-,in\ *n* (1967) : a gathering of people esp. for the expression of their mutual love

love–in–a–mist \,ləv-ə-nə-,mist\ *n* (ca. 1760) : a European and African annual herb (*Nigella damascena*) of the buttercup family having whitish flowers enveloped in numerous finely dissected bracts

love knot *n* (14c) : a stylized knot sometimes used as an emblem of love

love·less \'ləv-ləs\ *adj* (14c) **1** : having no love **2** : not loved — **love·less·ly** *adv* — **love·less·ness** *n*

love·lock \-,läk\ *n* (1592) : a long lock of hair variously worn (as over the front of the shoulder) esp. by men in the 17th and 18th centuries

love·lorn \-,lórn\ *adj* (1634) : bereft of love or of a lover — **love·lorn·ness** \-,lórn-nəs\ *n*

¹love·ly \'ləv-lē\ *adj* **love·li·er; -est** (bef. 12c) **1** *obs* : LOVABLE **2** : delightful for beauty, harmony, or grace : ATTRACTIVE **3** : GRAND, SWELL **4** : eliciting love by moral or ideal worth *syn* see BEAUTIFUL — **love·li·ly** \'ləv-lə-lē\ *adv* — **love·li·ness** \'ləv-lē-nəs\ *n* — **lovely** *adv*

²lovely *n, pl* **lovelies** (1652) **1** : a beautiful woman **2** : a lovely object

love–mak·ing \'ləv-,mā-kiṇ\ *n* (15c) **1** : COURTSHIP **2** : sexual activity; *esp* : COPULATION

lov·er \'lə-vər\ *n* (13c) **1 a** : a person in love; *esp* : a man in love with a woman **b** *pl* : two persons in love with each other **2** : an affectionate or benevolent friend **3** : DEVOTEE **4 a** : PARAMOUR **b** : a person with whom one has sexual relations

lov·er·ly \-lē\ *adj* (1875) : resembling or befitting a lover

love seat *n* (1904) : a double chair, sofa, or settee for two persons

love·sick \'ləv-,sik\ *adj* (15c) **1** : languishing with love : YEARNING **2** : expressing a lover's longing — **love·sick·ness** *n*

love·some \-səm\ *adj* (bef. 12c) **1** : WINSOME, LOVELY **2** : AFFECTIONATE, AMOROUS

lovey–dovey \,ləv-ē-'də-vē\ *adj* (1886) : expressing much love or sentimentality; *also* : MUSHY — **lovey–dovey·ness** \-nəs\ *n*

lov·ing \'lə-viṇ\ *adj* (bef. 12c) **1** : AFFECTIONATE **2** : PAINSTAKING — **lov·ing·ly** \-viṇ-lē\ *adv* — **lov·ing·ness** *n*

loving cup *n* [fr. its former use in ceremonial drinking] (1812) **1** : a large ornamental drinking vessel with two or more handles **2** : a loving cup given as a token or trophy

lov·ing–kind·ness \,lə-viṇ-'kīn(d)-nəs\ *n* (1535) : tender and benevolent affection

¹low \'lō\ *vi* [ME *loowen*, fr. OE *hlōwan*; akin to OHG *hluoen* to moo, L *calare* to call, summon, Gk *kalein*] (bef. 12c) : MOO

²low *n* (1549) : the deep sustained sound characteristic esp. of a cow

³low *adj* **low·er** \'lō(-ə)r\; **low·est** \'lō-əst\ [ME *lah*, *low*, fr. ON *lāgr*; akin to MHG *læge* low, flat; prob. akin to OE *licgan* to lie] (12c) **1 a** : having a small upward extension or elevation ⟨a ~ wall⟩ **b** : situated or passing little above a reference line, point, or plane ⟨~ bridges⟩ **c** (1) : having a low-cut neckline (2) : not extending as high as the ankle ⟨~ oxfords⟩ **2 a** : situated or passing below the normal level, surface, or base of measurement, or the mean elevation ⟨~ ground⟩ **b** : marking a nadir or bottom ⟨the ~ point of his career⟩ **3** : DEAD — used as a predicate adjective **4 a** : not loud : SOFT **b** : FLAT 8a **c** : characterized by being toward the bottom of the range of pitch attainable (as by an instrument) **5 a** : being near the equator ⟨~ northern latitudes⟩ **b** : being near the horizon ⟨~ sun⟩ **6** : socially or economically humble in character or status ⟨~ birth⟩ **7 a** : lacking strength, health, or vitality : WEAK, PROSTRATE ⟨very ~ with pneumonia⟩ **b** : lacking spirit or vivacity : DEPRESSED ⟨a ~ frame of mind⟩ **8 a** : of lesser degree, size, or amount than average or ordinary ⟨~ energy⟩ **b** (1) : small in number or amount (2) : SUBSTANDARD, INADEQUATE ⟨a ~ level of employment⟩ ⟨a ~ income group⟩ (3) : CHEAP ⟨~

prices⟩ (4) : SHORT, DEPLETED ⟨oil is in ~ supply⟩ **c** : of lesser position, rank, or order **9** : falling short of some standard: as **a** : lacking dignity or elevation ⟨a ~ style of writing⟩ **b** : morally reprehensible : BASE ⟨a ~ trick⟩ **c** : COARSE, VULGAR ⟨~ language⟩ **10 a** : not advanced in complexity, development, or elaboration ⟨~ organisms⟩ **b** *often cap* : LOW CHURCH **11** : UNFAVORABLE, DISPARAGING ⟨had a ~ opinion of him⟩ **12** : designed for slow and usu. the slowest speed ⟨~ gear⟩ **13** : articulated with a wide opening between the relatively flat tongue and the palate : OPEN ⟨\ä\ is a ~ vowel⟩ **14** : intended to attract little attention ⟨kept a ~ profile⟩ *syn* see BASE — **low** *adv* — **low·ness** *n*

⁴**low** *n* (12c) **1** : something that is low: as **a** : DEPTH **b** : a region of low barometric pressure **2** : the transmission gear of an automotive vehicle giving the lowest ratio of driveshaft to crankshaft speed

⁵**low** *or* **lowe** \'lō\ *n* [ME, fr. ON *logi, log;* akin to OE *lēoht* light — more at LIGHT] (13c) *chiefly Scot* : FLAME, BLAZE

⁶**low** *or* **lowe** *vi* **lowed; low·ing** (14c) *Scot* : FLAME, BLAZE

low·ball \'lō-,bȯl\ *vt* (ca. 1961) : to give (a customer) a deceptively low price or cost estimate — **lowball** *n*

low beam *n* (ca. 1952) : the short-range focus of a vehicle headlight

low blood pressure *n* (1924) : HYPOTENSION

low blow *n* (1952) : an unprincipled attack ⟨gossip column that landed one *low blow* after another —James Fallows⟩

low-born \'lō-'bȯrn\ *adj* (13c) : born in a low condition or rank

low·boy \-,bȯi\ *n* (ca. 1891) : a chest or side table about three feet (one meter) high with drawers and usu. with cabriole legs

low·bred \-'bred\ *adj* (1757) : RUDE, VULGAR

low·brow \-,braů\ *n* (1906) : a person with little taste or intellectual interest — **lowbrow** *adj*

Low Church *adj* (1710) : tending esp. in Anglican worship to minimize emphasis on the priesthood, sacraments, and ceremonial in worship and often to emphasize evangelical principles

Low Churchman *n* (1702) : a person holding or advocating Low Church views

lowboy

low comedy *n* (1608) : comedy employing burlesque, horseplay, or the representation of low life — compare HIGH COMEDY

low country *n, often cap L&C* (15c) : a low-lying country or region; *esp* : the part of a southern state extending from the seacoast inland to the fall line — **low-country** *adj, often cap L&C*

low–density lipoprotein *n* (1951) : LDL

low–down \'lō-,daůn\ *n* (1915) : the inside facts : DOPE

low–down \'lō-,daůn\ *adj* (1850) **1** : CONTEMPTIBLE, BASE **2** : deeply emotional ⟨~ blues⟩

low earth orbit *n* (1963) : a usu. circular orbit from about 90 to 600 miles (144 to 960 kilometers) above the earth

low–end \'lō-,end\ *adj* (1926) : of, relating to, or being the lowest priced merchandise in a manufacturer's line

¹**low·er** \'laů(-ə)r, 'lō(-ə)r\ *vi* [ME *louren;* akin to MHG *lüren* to lie in wait] (13c) **1** : to look sullen : FROWN **2** : to be or become dark, gloomy, and threatening

²**lower** *n* (14c) : FROWN

³**low·er** \'lō(-ə)r\ *adj* [³*low*] (13c) **1** : relatively low in position, rank, or order **2** : SOUTHERN ⟨~ New York State⟩ **3** : less advanced in the scale of evolutionary development **4 a** : situated or held to be situated beneath the earth's surface **b** *cap* : being an earlier epoch or series of the period or series named ⟨*Lower* Cretaceous⟩ ⟨*Lower* Paleolithic⟩ **5** : constituting the popular and often the larger and more representative branch of a bicameral legislative body ⟨~ house⟩

⁴**low·er** \'lō(-ə)r\ *vi* (1606) : to move down : DROP; *also* : DIMINISH ~ *vt* **1 a** : to let descend : LET DOWN **b** : to depress as to direction ⟨~ your aim⟩ **c** : to reduce the height of **2 a** : to reduce in value, number, or amount **b** (1) : to bring down in quality or character : DEGRADE (2) : ABASE, HUMBLE **c** : to reduce the objective of

¹**low·er·case** \,lō(-ə)r-'kās\ *adj* [fr. the compositor's practice of keeping such types in the lower of a pair of type cases] (1683) *of a letter* : having as its typical form a f g or b n i rather than A F G or B N I — **lowercase** *n*

²**lowercase** *vt* **-cased; -cas·ing** (1908) : to print or set in lowercase letters

low·er–class \,lō(-ə)r-'klas\ *adj* (1892) **1** : of, relating to, or characteristic of the lower class **2** : being an inferior or low-ranking specimen of its kind

lower class *n* (1772) : a social class occupying a position below the middle class and having the lowest status in a society

lower criticism *n* (ca. 1889) : criticism concerned with the recovery of original texts esp. of Scripture through collation of extant manuscripts — compare HIGHER CRITICISM

lower fungus *n* (1900) : a fungus with hyphae absent or rudimentary and nonseptate

low·er·ing \'laů-(ə-)riŋ, 'lō-\ *adj* (15c) : dark and threatening : GLOOMY

low·er·most \'lō(-ə)r-,mōst\ *adj* (1547) : LOWEST

low·ery \'laů-(ə-)rē, 'lō-\ *adj* (15c) : GLOOMY, LOWERING

lowest common denominator *n* (1924) **1** : LEAST COMMON DENOMINATOR **2** : something of small intellectual content designed to appeal to a lowbrow audience; *also* : such an audience

lowest common multiple *n* (ca. 1924) : LEAST COMMON MULTIPLE

lowest terms *n pl* (1806) : the form of a fraction in which the numerator and denominator have no factor in common except 1 ⟨reduce a fraction to *lowest terms*⟩

low frequency *n* (ca. 1868) : a radio frequency between medium frequency and very low frequency — see RADIO FREQUENCY table

Low German *n* (1838) **1** : the German dialects of northern Germany esp. as used since the end of the medieval period : PLATTDEUTSCH **2** : the West Germanic languages other than High German

low–grade \'lō-'grād\ *adj* (1878) **1** : of inferior grade or quality **2** : being near that extreme of a specified range which is lowest, least intense, or least competent ⟨a ~ fever⟩ ⟨a ~ infection⟩

low–key \-'kē\ *also* **low–keyed** \-'kēd\ *adj* (1907) **1** : having or producing dark tones only with little contrast **2** : of low intensity

¹**low·land** \'lō-lənd, -,land\ *n* (15c) : low or level country

²**lowland** *adj* (1508) **1** *cap* : of or relating to the Lowlands of Scotland **2** : of or relating to a lowland

low·land·er \-lən-dər, -,lan-\ *n* (1692) **1** *cap* : an inhabitant of the Lowlands of Scotland **2** : a native or inhabitant of a lowland region

Low Latin *n* (1872) : postclassical Latin in its later stages

low–lev·el \'lō-'le-vəl\ *adj* (1881) **1** : occurring, done, or placed at a low level **2** : being of low importance or rank

low–life \'lō-,līf\ *n, pl* **low–lifes** \-,līfs\ *also* **low–lives** \-,līvz\ (1911) **1** : a person of low social status **2** : a person of low moral character — **low–life** *adj*

low–light \'lō-,līt\ *n* (1941) : a particularly bad or unpleasant event, detail, or part

low·li·head \'lō-lē-,hed\ *n* [ME *lowliheed*, fr. *lowly* + *-hed* -hood; akin to ME *-hod* -hood] (15c) *archaic* : lowly state

¹**low·ly** \'lō-lē\ *adv* (14c) **1** : in a humble or meek manner **2** : in a low position, manner, or degree **3** : not loudly

²**lowly** *adj* **low·li·er; -est** (14c) **1** : humble in manner or spirit : free from self-assertive pride **2** : not lofty or sublime : PROSAIC **3** : ranking low in some hierarchy **4** : of or relating to a low social or economic rank **5** : low in the scale of biological or cultural evolution — **low·li·ness** *n*

low–ly·ing \'lō-'lī-iŋ\ *adj* (1856) **1** : rising relatively little above the base of measurement ⟨~ hills⟩ **2** : lying below the normal level, surface, or the base of measurement or mean elevation ⟨~ clouds⟩

low mass *n, often cap L&M* (1568) : a mass that is recited without singing by the celebrant, without a deacon, subdeacon, or choir assisting the celebrant, and without the use of incense

low–mind·ed \'lō-'mīn-dəd\ *adj* (ca. 1746) : inclined to low or unworthy things — **low–mind·ed·ly** *adv* — **low–mind·ed·ness** *n*

lown \'laůn, 'lün\ *adj* (Sc) *lowne* (15c) *dial* : CALM, QUIET

low–pres·sure \'lō-'pre-shər\ *adj* (1827) **1** : having, exerting, or operating under a relatively small pressure **2** : EASYGOING

low relief *n* (1711) : BAS-RELIEF

low–rent \'lō-'rent\ *adj* (1957) : low in character, cost, or prestige ⟨~ thugs⟩ ⟨a ~ movie⟩ ⟨a ~ literary form⟩

low–rise \'lō-'rīz\ *adj* (1957) **1** : having few stories and not equipped with elevators ⟨a ~ classroom building⟩ **2** : of, relating to, or characterized by low-rise buildings ⟨a ~ housing development⟩

low–slung \'lō-'sləŋ\ *adj* (1943) : relatively low to the ground or floor ⟨a ~ convertible⟩ ⟨a ~ modern building⟩ ⟨a ~ sofa⟩

low–spir·it·ed \'lō-'spir-ə-təd\ *adj* (1693) : DEJECTED, DEPRESSED — **low–spir·it·ed·ly** *adv* — **low–spir·it·ed·ness** *n*

Low Sunday *n* (15c) : the Sunday following Easter

low–tech \'lō-'tek\ *adj* (1981) : technologically simple or unsophisticated ⟨~ industries⟩

low tide *n* (1843) : the farthest ebb of the tide

low water *n* (15c) : low stage of the water in a river or lake; *also* : LOW TIDE

¹**lox** \'läks\ *n* [*liquid oxygen*] (1923) : liquid oxygen

²**lox** *n, pl* **lox** *or* **lox·es** [Yiddish *laks*, fr. MHG *lahs* salmon, fr. OHG; akin to OE *leax* salmon] (1941) : smoked salmon

lox·o·drome \'läk-sə-,drōm\ *n* [back-formation fr. *loxodromic* of a rhumb line, fr. F *loxodromique*, fr. Gk *loxos* oblique + *dromos* course — more at DROMEDARY] (1880) : RHUMB LINE

loy·al \'lȯi(-ə)l\ *adj* [MF, fr. OF *leial, leel*, fr. L *legalis* legal] (1531) **1** : unswerving in allegiance: as **a** : faithful in allegiance to one's lawful sovereign or government **b** : faithful to a private person to whom fidelity is due **c** : faithful to a cause, ideal, custom, institution, or product **2** : showing loyalty **3** *obs* : LAWFUL, LEGITIMATE *syn* see FAITHFUL — **loy·al·ly** \'lȯi-ə-lē\ *adv*

loy·al·ist \'lȯi-ə-list\ *n* (1647) : one who is or remains loyal esp. to a political cause, party, government, or sovereign

loy·al·ty \'lȯi(-ə)l-tē\ *n, pl* **-ties** [ME *loyalte*, fr. MF *loialte*, fr. OF *leialté, leial*] (15c) : the quality or state or an instance of being loyal *syn* see FIDELITY

loz·enge \'lä-z°nj\ *also* **-s°nj**\ *n* [ME *losenge*, fr. MF *losange*] (14c) **1** : a figure with four equal sides and two acute and two obtuse angles : DIAMOND **2** : something shaped like a lozenge **3** : a small often medicated candy

LP \,el-'pē\ *n* [*long-playing*] (1948) : a microgroove phonograph record designed to be played at 33⅓ revolutions per minute

LPN \,el-(,)pē-'en\ *n* (1948) : LICENSED PRACTICAL NURSE

LSD \,el-(,)es-'dē\ *n* [G *Lysergsäure-Diäthylamid* lysergic acid diethylamide] (1950) : an organic compound $C_{20}H_{25}N_3O$ that induces psychotic symptoms similar to those of schizophrenia — called also *lysergic acid diethylamide*

lu·au \'lü-aů\ *n* [Hawaiian *lū'au*] (1853) : an Hawaiian feast

Lu·ba·vitch·er \'lü-bə-,vi-chər, lü-'bä-\ *n* [Yiddish *lyubavitsher*, fr. *Lyubavitsh*, town in Belarus] (1954) : a member of a Hasidic sect founded by Schneour Zalman of Lyady in the late 18th century — **Lubavitcher** *adj*

lub·ber \'lə-bər\ *n* [ME *lobre, lobur*] (14c) **1** : a big clumsy fellow **2** : a clumsy seaman — **lub·ber·li·ness** \-lē-nəs\ *n* — **lub·ber·ly** \-lē\ *adj or adv*

lubber line *n* (1889) : a fixed line on the compass of a ship or airplane that is aligned with the longitudinal axis of the vehicle

lubber's hole *n* (ca. 1784) : a hole in a square-rigger's top near the mast through which one may go farther aloft without going over the rim by the futtock shrouds

lube \'lüb\ *n* [short for *lubricating oil*] (1926) **1** : LUBRICANT **2** : an application of a lubricant : LUBRICATION

lu·bric \'lü-brik\ *adj* [MF *lubrique*, fr. ML *lubricus*] (15c) *archaic* : LUBRICIOUS — **lu·bri·cal** \-bri-kəl\ *adj*

lu·bri·cant \'lü-bri-kənt\ *n* (ca. 1828) **1** : a substance (as grease) capa-

\ə\ abut \ᵊ\ kitten, F table \ər\ further \a\ ash \ā\ ace \ä\ mop, mar
\aů\ out \ch\ chin \e\ bet \ē\ easy \g\ go \i\ hit \ī\ ice \j\ job
\ŋ\ sing \ō\ go \ȯ\ law \ȯi\ boy \th\ thin \t͟h\ the \ü\ loot \ů\ foot
\y\ yet \zh\ vision \á, k̟, ⁿ, œ, œ̄, ᵾ, ᵿᵉ, ᶄ\ see Guide to Pronunciation

ble of reducing friction, heat, and wear when introduced as a film between solid surfaces **2** : something that lessens or prevents friction or difficulty — **lubricant** *adj*

lu·bri·cate \'lü-brə-ˌkāt\ *vb* **-cat·ed; -cat·ing** [L *lubricatus*, pp. of *lubricare*, fr. *lubricus* slippery — more at SLEEVE] *vt* (ca. 1623) **1** : to make smooth or slippery **2** : to apply a lubricant to ~ *vi* : to act as a lubricant — **lu·bri·ca·tion** \ˌlü-brə-'kā-shən\ *n* — **lu·bri·ca·tive** \'lü-brə-ˌkā-tiv\ *adj* — **lu·bri·ca·tor** \-ˌkā-tər\ *n*

lu·bri·cious \lü-'bri-shəs\ *or* **lu·bri·cous** \'lü-bri-kəs\ *adj* [ML *lubricus*, fr. L, slippery, easily led astray] (1535) **1** : marked by wantonness : LECHEROUS; *also* : SALACIOUS **2** [L *lubricus*] : having a smooth or slippery quality 〈a ~ skin〉 — **lu·bri·cious·ly** *adv*

lu·bric·i·ty \lü-'bri-sə-tē\ *n, pl* **-ties** (15c) : the property or state of being lubricious; *also* : the capacity for reducing friction

Lu·can \'lü-kən\ *adj* [LL *lucanus*, fr. *Lucas* Luke, fr. Gk *Loukas*] (1890) : of or relating to Luke or the Gospel ascribed to him

lu·carne \lü-'kärn\ *n* [F] (ca. 1825) : DORMER

Lu·ca·yo \lü-'kī-(ˌ)ō\ *also* **Lu·ca·yan** \-'kī-ən\ *n* (1929) : a member of an Arawakan people of the Bahamas

lu·cen·cy \'lü-sᵊn(t)-sē\ *n* (1656) : the quality or state of being lucent

lu·cent \'lü-sᵊnt\ *adj* [ME, fr. L *lucent-, lucens*, prp. of *lucēre* to shine — more at LIGHT] (15c) **1** : glowing with light : LUMINOUS **2** : marked by clarity or translucence : CLEAR — **lu·cent·ly** *adv*

lu·cern *n* [prob. modif. of G *lüchsern* of a lynx, fr. *Luchs* lynx] (ca. 1533) *obs* : LYNX

lu·cerne *also* **lu·cern** \lü-'sərn\ *n* [F *luzerne*, fr. Prov *luserno*] (1626) *chiefly Brit* : ALFALFA

lu·cid \'lü-səd\ *adj* [L *lucidus*, fr. *lucēre*] (1591) **1 a** : suffused with light : LUMINOUS **b** : TRANSLUCENT **2** : having full use of one's faculties : SANE **3** : clear to the understanding : INTELLIGIBLE **syn** see CLEAR — **lu·cid·ly** *adv* — **lu·cid·ness** *n*

lu·cid·i·ty \lü-'si-də-tē\ *n* (1851) **1** : clearness of thought or style **2** : a presumed capacity to perceive the truth directly and instantaneously : CLAIRVOYANCE

Lu·ci·fer \'lü-sə-fər\ *n* [ME, the morning star, a fallen rebel archangel, the Devil, fr. OE, fr. L, the morning star, fr. *lucifer* light-bearing, fr. *luc-, lux* light + *-fer* -ferous — more at LIGHT] (bef. 12c) **1** — used as a name of the devil **2** : the planet Venus when appearing as the morning star **3** *not cap* : a friction match having as active substances antimony sulfide and potassium chlorate — **Lu·ci·fe·ri·an** \ˌlü-sə-'fir-ē-ən\ *adj*

lu·cif·er·ase \lü-'si-fə-ˌrās, -ˌrāz\ *n* [ISV, fr. *luciferin*] (1888) : an enzyme that catalyzes the oxidation of luciferin

lu·cif·er·in \-f(ə-)rən\ *n* [ISV, fr. L *lucifer* light-bearing] (1888) : any of various organic substances in luminescent organisms (as fireflies) that upon oxidation produce a virtually heatless light

lu·cif·er·ous \lü-'si-f(ə-)rəs\ *adj* [L *lucifer*] (1648) : bringing light or insight : ILLUMINATING

Lu·ci·na \lü-'sī-nə\ *n* [L, Roman goddess of childbirth] (1658) *archaic* : MIDWIFE

Lu·cite \'lü-ˌsīt\ *trademark* — used for an acrylic resin or plastic consisting essentially of polymerized methyl methacrylate

¹luck \'lək\ *n* [ME *lucke*, fr. MD *luc*; akin to MHG *gelücke* luck] (15c) **1 a** : a force that brings good fortune or adversity **b** : the events or circumstances that operate for or against an individual **2** : favoring chance; *also* : SUCCESS — **luck·less** \-ləs\ *adj*

²luck *vi* (ca. 1584) **1** : to prosper or succeed esp. through chance or good fortune — usu. used with *out* **2** : to come upon something desirable by chance — usu. used with *out, on, onto,* or *into*

luck·i·ly \'lə-kə-lē\ *adv* (1530) **1** : in a lucky manner **2** : FORTUNATELY **2** 〈~, we were on time〉 **usage** see HOPEFULLY

lucky \'lə-kē\ *adj* **luck·i·er; -est** (15c) **1** : having good luck **2** : happening by chance : FORTUITOUS **3** : producing or resulting in good by chance : FAVORABLE **4** : seeming to bring good luck 〈a ~ rabbit's foot〉 — **luck·i·ness** \'lə-kē-nəs\ *n*

syn LUCKY, FORTUNATE, HAPPY, PROVIDENTIAL mean meeting with unforeseen success. LUCKY stresses the agency of chance in bringing about a favorable result 〈was because of a *lucky* bounce〉. FORTUNATE suggests being rewarded beyond one's deserts 〈*fortunate* in my investments〉. HAPPY combines the implications of LUCKY and FORTUNATE with stress on being blessed 〈a series of *happy* accidents〉. PROVIDENTIAL more definitely implies the help or intervention of a higher power 〈a *providential* change in the weather〉.

lucky dip *n* (1925) *Brit* : GRAB BAG

lu·cra·tive \'lü-krə-tiv\ *adj* [ME *lucratif*, fr. MF, fr. L *lucrativus*, fr. *lucratus*, pp. of *lucrari* to gain, fr. *lucrum*] (15c) : producing wealth : PROFITABLE — **lu·cra·tive·ly** *adv* — **lu·cra·tive·ness** *n*

lu·cre \'lü-kər\ *n* [ME, fr. L *lucrum*; prob. akin to OE *lēan* reward, OHG *lōn*, Gk *apolauein* to enjoy] (14c) : monetary gain : PROFIT; *also* : MONEY

lu·cu·bra·tion \ˌlü-kyə-'brā-shən, ˌlü-kə-\ *n* [L *lucubration-, lucubratio* study by night, work produced at night, fr. *lucubrare* to work by lamplight; akin to L *luc-, lux*] (1595) : laborious or intensive study; *also* : the product of such study — usu. used in pl.

lu·cu·lent \'lü-kyə-lənt\ *adj* [L *luculentus*, fr. *luc-, lux* light] (ca. 1548) : clear in thought or expression : LUCID — **lu·cu·lent·ly** *adv*

Lu·cul·lan \lü-'kə-lən\ *also* **Lu·cul·li·an** \-'kə-lē-ən\ *adj* [L *Lucullanus* of Licinius *Lucullus*; fr. his reputation for luxurious banquets] (1861) : LAVISH, LUXURIOUS 〈a ~ feast〉

Lud·dite \'lə-ˌdīt\ *n* [perh. fr. Ned *Ludd*, 18th cent. Leicestershire workman who destroyed machinery] (1811) : one of a group of early 19th century English workmen destroying laborsaving machinery as a protest; *broadly* : one who is opposed to esp. technological change — **Luddite** *adj*

lu·dic \'lü-dik\ *adj* [F *ludique*, fr. L *ludus*] (1940) : of, relating to, or characterized by play : PLAYFUL 〈~ behavior〉 〈a ~ novel〉

lu·di·crous \'lü-də-krəs\ *adj* [L *ludicrus*, fr. *ludus* play, sport; perh. akin to Gk *loidoros* abusive] (1782) **1** : amusing or laughable through obvious absurdity, incongruity, exaggeration, or eccentricity **2** : meriting derisive laughter or scorn as absurdly inept, false, or foolish **syn** see LAUGHABLE — **lu·di·crous·ly** *adv* — **lu·di·crous·ness** *n*

lu·es \'lü-(ˌ)ēz\ *n, pl* **lues** [NL, fr. L, plague; akin to Gk *lyein* to loosen, destroy — more at LOSE] (1634) : SYPHILIS — **lu·et·ic** \lü-'e-tik\ *adj*

¹luff \'ləf\ *n* [ME, weather side of a ship, luff, fr. MF *lof* weather side of ship] (14c) **1** : the act of sailing a ship nearer to the wind **2** : the forward edge of a fore-and-aft sail

²luff *vi* (14c) : to turn the head of a ship toward the wind

luf·fa *var of* LOOFAH

luft·mensch \'lüft-ˌmen(t)sh\ *n, pl* **luft·mensch·en** \-ˌmen(t)-shən\ [Yiddish *luftmentsh*, fr. *luft* air + *mentsh* human being] (1907) : an impractical contemplative person having no definite business or income

¹lug \'ləg\ *vb* **lugged; lug·ging** [ME *luggen* to pull by the hair or ear, drag, prob. of Scand origin; akin to Norw *lugga* to pull by the hair] *vt* (14c) **1** : DRAG, PULL **2** : to carry laboriously **3** : to introduce in a forced manner 〈~s my name into the argument〉 ~ *vi* **1** : to pull with effort : TUG **2** : to move heavily or by jerks 〈the car ~s on hills〉 **3** *of a racehorse* : to swerve from the course toward or away from the inside rail

²lug *n* (1616) **1** *archaic* **a** : an act of lugging **b** : something that is lugged **c** : a shipping container for produce 〈LUGSAIL〉 **3** *pl* : superior airs or affectations 〈put on ~s〉 **4** *slang* : an exaction of money — used in the phrase *put the lug on*

³lug *n* [ME (Sc) *lugge*, perh. fr. ME *luggen*] (15c) **1** : something (as a handle) that projects like an ear: as **a** : a leather loop on a harness saddle through which the shaft passes **b** : a metal fitting to which electrical wires are soldered or connected **2** *chiefly Brit* : EAR **3** : a ridge (as on the bottom of a shoe) to increase traction **4** : a nut used to secure a wheel on an automotive vehicle — called also *lug nut* **5** : BLOCKHEAD, LOUT

Lu·gan·da \lü-'gän-də, -'gan-\ *n* (1889) : the Bantu language of the Ganda people

luge \'lüzh\ *n* [F] (1905) : a small sled that is ridden in a supine position and used esp. in competition; *also* : the competition itself — **luge** *vi* — **lug·er** \'lü-zhər\ *n*

lug·gage \'lə-gij\ *n* (1596) : something that is lugged; *esp* : suitcases for a traveler's belongings : BAGGAGE

lug·ger \'lə-gər\ *n* [*lugsail*] (1757) : a small fishing or coasting boat that carries one or more lugsails

lug·sail \'ləg-ˌsāl, -səl\ *n* [perh. fr. ³*lug*] (1677) : a 4-sided sail bent to an obliquely hanging yard that is hoisted and lowered with the sail

lu·gu·bri·ous \lü-'gü-brē-əs *also* -'gyü-\ *adj* [L *lugubris*, fr. *lugēre* to mourn; akin to Gk *lygros* mournful] (1601) **1** : MOURNFUL; *esp* : exaggeratedly or affectedly mournful 〈dark, dramatic and ~ brooding —V. S. Pritchett〉 **2** : DISMAL 〈a ~ landscape〉 — **lu·gu·bri·ous·ly** *adv* — **lu·gu·bri·ous·ness** *n*

lug·worm \'ləg-ˌwərm\ *n* [origin unknown] (1802) : any of a genus (*Arenicola*) of marine polychaete worms that have a row of tufted gills along each side of the back and are used for bait

Luk·an \'lü-kən\ *var of* LUCAN

Luke \'lük\ *n* [L *Lucas*, fr. Gk *Loukas*] **1** : a Gentile physician and companion of the apostle Paul traditionally identified as the author of the third Gospel in the New Testament and of the book of Acts **2** : the third Gospel in the New Testament — see BIBLE table

luke·warm \'lük-'wȯrm\ *adj* [ME, fr. *luke* lukewarm + *warm*; prob. akin to OHG *lāo* lukewarm — more at LEE] (14c) **1** : moderately warm : TEPID **2** : lacking conviction : HALFHEARTED — **luke·warm·ly** *adv* — **luke·warm·ness** *n*

¹lull \'ləl\ *vt* [ME; prob. of imit. origin] (14c) **1** : to cause to sleep or rest : SOOTHE **2** : to cause to relax vigilance

²lull *n* (1719) **1** *archaic* : something that lulls; *esp* : LULLABY **2** : a temporary pause or decline in activity 〈the early morning ~ in urban noise〉: as **a** : a temporary calm before or during a storm **b** : a temporary drop in business activity

lul·la·by \'lə-lə-ˌbī\ *n, pl* **-bies** [obs. E *lulla*, interj. used to lull a child (fr. ME) + *bye*, interj. used to lull a child, fr. ME *by*] (1588) : a soothing refrain; *specif* : a song to quiet children or lull them to sleep

lullaby *vt* **-bied; -by·ing** (1592) : to quiet with or as if with a lullaby

lu·lu \'lü-(ˌ)lü\ *n* [prob. fr. *Lulu*, nickname fr. *Louise*] (1886) *slang* : one that is remarkable or wonderful

lum \'ləm\ *n* [origin unknown] (ca. 1628) *chiefly Scot* : CHIMNEY

lum·ba·go \ˌləm-'bā-(ˌ)gō\ *n* [L, fr. *lumbus*] (ca. 1693) : usu. painful muscular rheumatism involving the lumbar region

lum·bar \'ləm-bər, -ˌbär\ *adj* [NL *lumbaris*, fr. L *lumbus* loin — more at LOIN] (ca. 1656) : of, relating to, or constituting the loins or the vertebrae between the thoracic vertebrae and sacrum 〈~ region〉

¹lum·ber \'ləm-bər\ *vi* **lum·bered; lum·ber·ing** \-b(ə-)riŋ\ [ME *lomeren*] (14c) **1** : to move ponderously **2** : RUMBLE

²lumber *n* [perh. fr. *Lombard*; fr. the use of pawnshops as storehouses of disused property] (1552) **1** : surplus or disused articles (as furniture) that are stored away **2 a** : timber or logs esp. when dressed for use **b** : any of various structural materials prepared in a form similar to lumber — **lumber** *adj*

³lumber *vb* **lum·bered; lum·ber·ing** \-b(ə-)riŋ\ *vt* (1642) **1** : to clutter with or as if with lumber: ENCUMBER **2** : to heap together in disorder **3** : to log and saw the timber of ~ *vi* **1** : to cut logs for lumber **2** : to saw logs into lumber for the market — **lum·ber·er** \-bər-ər\ *n*

lum·ber·jack \'ləm-bər-ˌjak\ *n* (1831) : LOGGER

lum·ber·man \-mən\ *n* (ca. 1817) : a person who is engaged in or oversees the business of cutting, processing, and marketing lumber

lumber room *n* (1741) : STOREROOM 1

lum·ber·yard \-ˌyärd\ *n* (1786) : a yard where a stock of lumber is kept for sale

lum·bo·sa·cral \ˌləm-bō-'sa-krəl, -'sā-\ *adj* (1840) : relating to the lumbar and sacral regions or parts

lu·men \'lü-mən\ *n, pl* **lumens** *also* **lu·mi·na** \-mə-nə\ [NL *lumin-, lumen*, fr. L, light, air shaft, opening] (1873) **1** : the cavity of a tubular organ 〈the ~ of a blood vessel〉 **2** : the bore of a tube (as of a hollow needle or catheter) **3** : a unit of luminous flux equal to the light emitted in a unit solid angle by a uniform point source of one candle intensity — **lu·mi·nal** *also* **lu·men·al** \-mə-nᵊl\ *adj*

lumin- *or* **lumini-** *comb form* [ME *lumin-*, fr. L *lumin-, lumen*] : light 〈*lumini*ferous〉

lu·mi·naire \ˌlü-mə-'nar, -'ner\ *n* [F, lamp, lighting] (1921) : a complete lighting unit

lu·mi·nance \'lü-mə-nən(t)s\ *n* (1880) **1** : the quality or state of being luminous **2** : the luminous intensity of a surface in a given direction per unit of projected area

lu·mi·nar·ia \,lü-mə-'ner-ē-ə\ *n, pl* **-nar·i·as** [Sp, decorative light, fr. LL] (1949) : a traditional Mexican Christmas lantern orig. consisting of a candle set in sand inside a paper bag

lu·mi·nary \'lü-mə-,ner-ē\ *n, pl* **-nar·ies** [ME *luminarye,* fr. MF & LL; MF *luminaire* lamp, fr. LL *luminaria,* pl. of *luminare* lamp, heavenly body, fr. L, window, fr. *lumin-, lumen* light; akin to L *lucēre* to shine — more at LIGHT] (15c) **1** : a person of prominence or brilliant achievement **2** : a body that gives light; *esp* : one of the celestial bodies — **luminary** *adj*

lu·mi·nesce \,lü-mə-'nes\ *vi* **-nesced; -nesc·ing** [back-formation fr. *luminescent*] (1896) : to exhibit luminescence

lu·mi·nes·cence \-'ne-s³n(t)s\ *n* (1889) : the low-temperature emission of light (as by a chemical or physiological process); *also* : light produced by luminescence — **lu·mi·nes·cent** \-s³nt\ *adj*

lu·mi·nif·er·ous \,lü-mə-'ni-f(ə-)rəs\ *adj* (1801) : transmitting, producing, or yielding light

lu·mi·nism \'lü-mə-,ni-zəm\ *n, often cap* (ca. 1974) : a theory or practice of realist landscape and seascape painting developed in the U.S. in the mid 19th century and concerned with the study and depiction of effects of light and atmosphere — **lu·mi·nist** \-nist\ *n, often cap*

lu·mi·nos·i·ty \,lü-mə-'nä-sə-tē\ *n, pl* **-ties** (1634) **1 a** : the quality or state of being luminous **b** : something luminous **2 a** : the relative quantity of light **b** : relative brightness of something **3** : the relative quantity of radiation emitted by a celestial source (as a star)

lu·mi·nous \'lü-mə-nəs\ *adj* [ME, fr. L *luminosus,* fr. *lumin-, lumen*] (15c) **1 a** : emitting or reflecting usu. steady, suffused, or glowing light **b** : of or relating to light or to luminous flux **2** : bathed in or exposed to steady light ⟨~ with sunlight⟩ **3** : CLEAR, ENLIGHTENING *syn* see BRIGHT — **lu·mi·nous·ly** *adv* — **lu·mi·nous·ness** *n*

luminous energy *n* (ca. 1931) : energy transferred in the form of visible radiation

luminous flux *n* (1925) : radiant flux in the visible-wavelength range usu. expressed in lumens instead of watts

luminous paint *n* (ca. 1889) : a paint containing a phosphor (as zinc sulfide activated with copper) and so able to glow in the dark

lum·mox \'lə-məks, -miks\ *n* [origin unknown] (ca. 1825) : a clumsy person

¹lump \'ləmp\ *n* [ME] (14c) **1** : a piece or mass of indefinite size and shape **2 a** : AGGREGATE, TOTALITY ⟨taken in the ~⟩ **b** : MAJORITY **3** : PROTUBERANCE; *esp* : an abnormal swelling **4** : a person who is heavy and awkward; *also* : one who is stupid or dull **5** *pl* **a** : BEATINGS, BRUISES ⟨had taken a lot of ~s growing up in the city⟩ **b** : DEFEAT, LOSS ⟨can cheerfully take his ~s on losers, because the payout is big on the winners —Martin Mayer⟩ — **lump in one's throat** : a constriction of the throat caused by emotion

²lump *vt* (1624) **1** : to group indiscriminately **2** : to make into lumps; *also* : to make lumps on or in **3** : to move noisily and clumsily ~ *vi* **1** : to become formed into lumps **2** : to move oneself noisily and clumsily

³lump *adj* (ca. 1700) : not divided into parts : ENTIRE ⟨~ sum⟩

⁴lump *vt* [origin unknown] (1791) : to put up with ⟨like it or ~ it

lump·ec·to·my \,ləm-'pek-tə-mē\ *n, pl* **-mies** (1972) : excision of a breast tumor with a limited amount of associated tissue

¹lum·pen \'lüm-pən, 'ləm-\ *adj* [G *Lumpenproletariat* degraded section of the proletariat, fr. *Lump* contemptible person (fr. *Lumpen* rags) + *Proletariat*] (1936) : of or relating to dispossessed and uprooted individuals cut off from the economic and social class with which they might normally be identified ⟨~ proletariat⟩ ⟨~ intellectuals⟩

²lumpen *n, pl* **lumpen** *also* **lumpens** (1941) : a member of the crude and uneducated lowest class of society

lump·er \'ləm-pər\ *n* (ca. 1785) **1** : a laborer employed to handle freight or cargo **2** : one who classifies organisms into large often variable taxonomic groups based on major characters — compare SPLITTER

lump·fish \'ləmp-,fish\ *n* [obs. E *lump* lumpfish (prob. fr. D *lomp* blenny, loach) + E *fish*] (ca. 1620) : a northern Atlantic usu. greenish fish (*Cyclopterus lumpus* of the family Cyclopteridae) having rows of nodules on the body and eggs used as a caviar

lump·ish \'ləm-pish\ *adj* (1528) **1** : DULL, SLUGGISH **2** *obs* : low in spirits **3** : HEAVY, AWKWARD **4** : LUMPY **1a 5** : tediously slow or dull : BORING; *also* : LUMPY **2** — **lump·ish·ly** *adv* — **lump·ish·ness** *n*

lumpy \'ləm-pē\ *adj* **lump·i·er; -est** (1707) **1 a** : filled or covered with lumps **b** : characterized by choppy waves **2** : having a heavy clumsy appearance **3** : uneven and often crude in style — **lump·i·ly** \-pə-lē\ *adv* — **lump·i·ness** \-pē-nəs\ *n*

lumpy jaw *n* (1890) : ACTINOMYCOSIS; *esp* : actinomycosis of the head in cattle

lu·na·cy \'lü-nə-sē\ *n, pl* **-cies** [*lunatic*] (1541) **1** : any of various forms of insanity: as **a** : intermittent insanity once believed to be related to phases of the moon **b** : insanity amounting to lack of capacity or of responsibility in the eyes of the law **2** : wild foolishness : extravagant folly **3** : a foolish act

luna moth *n* [NL *luna* (specific epithet of *Actias luna),* fr. L, moon] (1869) : a large mostly pale green American saturniid moth (*Actias luna*) with long tails on the hind wings

lu·nar \'lü-nər *also* -,när\ *adj* [ME, fr. L *lunaris,* fr. *luna* moon; akin to L *lucēre* to shine — more at LIGHT] (15c) **1** : CRESCENT, LUNATE **2 a** : of or relating to the moon **b** : designed for use on the moon ⟨~ vehicles⟩ **3** : measured by the moon's revolution ⟨~ month⟩

luna moth

lunar caustic *n* [obs. *luna* silver, fr. ML, fr. L, moon] (1771) : silver nitrate esp. when fused and molded into sticks for use as a caustic

lunar eclipse *n* (ca. 1737) : an eclipse in which the moon near the full phase passes partially or wholly through the umbra of the earth's shadow — see ECLIPSE illustration

lunar module *n* (1967) : a space vehicle module designed to carry astronauts from the command module to the surface of the moon and back — called also *lunar excursion module;* abbr. *LEM*

lu·nate \'lü-,nāt\ *adj* [L *lunatus,* pp. of *lunare* to bend in a crescent, fr. *luna*] (ca. 1777) : shaped like a crescent

lu·na·tic \'lü-nə-,tik\ *adj* [ME *lunatik,* fr. OF or LL; OF *lunatique,* fr. LL *lunaticus,* fr. L *luna;* fr. the belief that lunacy fluctuated with the phases of the moon] (14c) **1 a** : affected with lunacy : INSANE **b** : designed for the care of insane persons ⟨~ asylum⟩ **2** : wildly foolish — **lunatic** *n*

lunatic fringe *n* (1913) : the members of a usu. political or social movement espousing extreme, eccentric, or fanatical views

lu·na·tion \lü-'nā-shən\ *n* [ME *lunacioun,* fr. ML *lunation-, lunatio,* fr. L *luna*] (14c) : the period of time averaging 29 days, 12 hours, 44 minutes, and 2.8 seconds elapsing between two successive new moons

¹lunch \'lənch\ *n* [prob. short for *luncheon*] (1812) **1** : a usu. light meal; *esp* : one taken in the middle of the day **2** : the food prepared for a lunch — **out to lunch** *slang* : out of touch with reality

²lunch *vi* (1823) : to eat lunch ~ *vt* : to treat to lunch — **lunch·er** *n*

lunch counter *n* (1869) **1** : a long counter at which lunches are sold **2** : LUNCHEONETTE

lun·cheon \'lən-chən\ *n* [perh. alter. of *nuncheon* light snack] (ca. 1652) : LUNCH; *esp* : a formal usu. midday meal as part of a meeting or for entertaining a guest

lun·cheon·ette \,lən-chə-'net\ *n* (1924) : a small restaurant serving light lunches

lunch·room \'lənch-,rüm, -,rüm\ *n* (1830) **1** : LUNCHEONETTE **2** : a room (as in a school) where lunches supplied on the premises or brought from home may be eaten

lunch·time \-,tīm\ *n* (1859) : the time at which lunch is usu. eaten : NOON

lune \'lün\ *n* [L *luna* moon — more at LUNAR] (ca. 1704) : the part of a plane surface bounded by two intersecting arcs or of a spherical surface bounded by two great circles

lunes \'lünz\ *n pl* [F, pl. of *lune* crazy whim, fr. MF, moon, crazy whim, fr. L *luna*] (1602) : fits of lunacy

lu·nette \lü-'net\ *n* [F, fr. OF *lunete* small object shaped like the moon, fr. *lune* moon] (ca. 1673) **1** : something that has the shape of a crescent or half-moon: as **a** : an opening in a vault esp. for a window **b** : the surface at the upper part of a wall that is partly surrounded by a vault which the wall intersects and that is often filled by windows or by mural painting **c** : a low crescentic mound (as of sand) formed by the wind **2** : the figure or shape of a crescent moon

lung \'ləŋ\ *n* [ME *lunge,* fr. OE *lungen;* akin to OHG *lungun* lung, *lihti* light in weight — more at LIGHT] (bef. 12c) **1 a** : one of the usu. paired compound saccular thoracic organs that constitute the basic respiratory organ of air-breathing vertebrates **b** : any of various respiratory organs of invertebrates **2 a** : a device enabling individuals abandoning a submarine to rise to the surface **b** : a mechanical device for regularly introducing fresh air into and withdrawing stale air from the lung : RESPIRATOR — **lung·ful** \-,fùl\ *n*

¹lunge \'lənj\ *n* [modif. of F *allonge* extension, reach, fr. OF *alonge,* fr. *alongier* to lengthen, fr. (assumed) VL *allongare,* fr. L *ad-* ad- + LL *longare,* fr. L *longus* long] (1748) **1** : a quick thrust or jab (as of a sword) usu. made by leaning or striding forward **2** : a sudden forward rush or reach ⟨made a ~ to catch the ball⟩

²lunge *vb* **lunged; lung·ing** *vi* (1821) : to make a lunge : move with or as if with a lunge ~ *vt* : to thrust or propel (as a blow) in a lunge

lunged \'ləŋd\ *adj* (1693) **1** : having lungs : PULMONATE **2** : having a lung or lungs of a specified kind or number — used in combination ⟨one-*lunged*⟩

¹lung·er \'lən-jər\ *n* (1842) : one that lunges

²lung·er \'ləŋ-ər\ *n* (1893) : a person suffering from a chronic disease of the lungs; *esp* : one who is tubercular

lung·fish \'ləŋ-,fish\ *n* (1883) : any of a subclass (Dipneusti) of bony fishes that breathe by a modified swim bladder as well as gills

lung·worm \-,wərm\ *n* (1882) : any of various nematodes that infest the lungs and air passages of mammals

lung·wort \-,wərt, -,wòrt\ *n* (bef. 12c) : any of several plants (as a mullein) formerly used in the treatment of respiratory disorders; *esp* : a European herb (*Pulmonaria officinalis*) of the borage family with hispid leaves and usu. bluish flowers

lu·ni·so·lar \,lü-ni-'sō-lər *also* -,lär\ *adj* [L *luna* moon + E *-i-* + *solar*] (1691) : relating or attributed to the moon and the sun

lun·ker \'ləŋ-kər\ *n* [origin unknown] (1912) : something large of its kind — used esp. of a game fish

lunk·head \'ləŋk-,hed\ *n* [prob. alter. of *lump* + *head*] (1852) : a stupid person : DOLT — **lunk·head·ed** \-,he-dəd\ *adj*

lu·nule \'lü-(,)nyü(ə)l\ *n* [NL *lunula,* fr. L, crescent-shaped ornament, fr. dim. of *luna* moon] (1828) : a crescent-shaped body part or marking (as the whitish mark at the base of a fingernail)

lu·ny \'lü-nē\ *var of* LOONY

lu·pa·nar \lü-'pä-nər, -'pä-\ *n* [L, fr. *lupa* prostitute, lit., she-wolf, fem. of *lupus*] (1864) : BROTHEL

Lu·per·ca·lia \,lü-pər-'kä-lē-ə, -'käl-yə\ *n* [L, pl., fr. *Lupercus,* god of flocks] (1600) : an ancient Roman festival celebrated February 15 to ensure fertility for the people, fields, and flocks — **Lu·per·ca·lian** \-'kä-lē-ən, -'käl-yən\ *adj*

¹lu·pine *also* **lu·pin** \'lü-pən\ *n* [ME, fr. L *lupinus, lupinum,* fr. *lupinus,* adj.] (14c) : any of a genus (*Lupinus*) of leguminous herbs including some poisonous forms and others cultivated for their long showy racemes of usu. blue, purple, white, or yellow flowers or for green manure, fodder, or their edible seeds; *also* : an edible lupine seed

²lu·pine \-,pīn\ *adj* [L *lupinus,* fr. *lupus* wolf — more at WOLF] (1660) : WOLFISH

lu·pus \'lü-pəs\ *n* [ME, fr. ML, fr. L, wolf] (14c) : any of several diseases characterized by skin lesions; *esp* : SYSTEMIC LUPUS ERYTHEMATOSUS

lupus er·y·the·ma·to·sus \-,er-ə-,thē-mə-'tō-səs\ *n* [NL, lit., erythematous lupus] (1860) : a disorder characterized by skin inflammation; *esp* : SYSTEMIC LUPUS ERYTHEMATOSUS

\ə\ abut \³\ kitten, F table \ər\ further \a\ ash \ā\ ace \ä\ mop, mar
\aú\ out \ch\ chin \e\ bet \ē\ easy \g\ go \i\ hit \ī\ ice \j\ job
\ŋ\ sing \ō\ go \ò\ law \òi\ boy \th\ thin \t̠h\ the \ü\ loot \ù\ foot
\y\ yet \zh\ vision \ä, k̠, ⁿ, œ, œ̄, ᵫ, ᵫ̄, ʸ\ see Guide to Pronunciation

¹lurch \'lərch\ *vb* [ME *lorchen*, prob. alter. of *lurken* to lurk] *vi* (15c) *dial chiefly Eng* : to loiter about a place furtively : PROWL ~ *vt* **1** *obs* : STEAL **2** *archaic* : CHEAT
²lurch *n* [MF *lourche*, adj., defeated by a lurch, deceived] (1598) : a decisive defeat in which an opponent wins a game by more than double the defeated player's score esp. in cribbage — **in the lurch** : in a vulnerable and unsupported position
³lurch *vt* (ca. 1651) **1** *archaic* : to leave in the lurch **2** : to defeat by a lurch (as in cribbage)
⁴lurch *n* [origin unknown] (1819) **1** : a sudden roll of a ship to one side **2** : a jerking or swaying movement; *also* : STAGGER 3
⁵lurch *vi* (ca. 1828) : to roll or tip abruptly : PITCH; *also* : STAGGER
lurch•er \'lər-chər\ *n* [¹*lurch*] (1528) **1** *archaic* : a petty thief : PILFERER **2** *Brit* : a crossbred dog; *esp* : one that resembles a greyhound **3** *archaic* : one who lurks; *also* : SPY
lur•dane \'lər-dᵊn\ *n* [ME *lurdan*, fr. MF *lourdin* dullard, fr. *lourd* dull, stupid, fr. L *luridus* lurid] (14c) *archaic* : a lazy stupid person — **lurdane** *adj*
¹lure \'lu̇r\ *n* [ME, fr. MF *loire*, of Gmc origin; akin to MHG *luoder* bait; perh. akin to OE *lathian* to invite, OHG *ladōn*] (14c) **1** : an object usu. of leather or feathers attached to a long cord and used by a falconer to recall or exercise a hawk **2 a** : an inducement to pleasure or gain : ENTICEMENT **b** : APPEAL, ATTRACTION **3** : a decoy for attracting animals to capture: as **a** : artificial bait used for catching fish **b** : an often luminous structure on the head of pediculate fishes that is used to attract prey
²lure *vt* **lured; lur•ing** (14c) **1** : to recall or exercise (a hawk) by means of a lure **2** : to draw with a hint of pleasure or gain : attract actively and strongly
syn LURE, ENTICE, INVEIGLE, DECOY, TEMPT, SEDUCE mean to lead astray from one's true course. LURE implies a drawing into danger, evil, or difficulty through attracting and deceiving (*lured* naive investors with get-rich-quick schemes). ENTICE suggests drawing by artful or adroit means (advertising designed to *entice* new customers). INVEIGLE implies enticing by cajoling or flattering (fund-raisers *inveigling* wealthy alumni). DECOY implies a luring into entrapment by artifice (attempting to *decoy* the enemy into an ambush). TEMPT implies the presenting of an attraction so strong that it overcomes the restraints of conscience or better judgment (*tempted* by the offer of money). SEDUCE implies a leading astray by persuasion or false promises (*seduced* by assurances of assistance).
Lur•ex \'lu̇r-eks\ *trademark* — used for metallic yarn or thread
lu•rid \'lu̇r-əd\ *adj* [L *luridus* pale yellow, sallow] (ca. 1656) **1 a** : wan and ghastly pale in appearance **b** : of any of several light or medium grayish colors ranging in hue from yellow to orange **2** : shining with the red glow of fire seen through smoke or cloud **3** : causing horror or revulsion : GRUESOME **b** : MELODRAMATIC, SENSATIONAL; *also* : SHOCKING (paperbacks in the usual ~ covers —T. R. Fyvel) *syn* see GHASTLY — **lu•rid•ly** *adv* — **lu•rid•ness** *n*
lurk \'lərk\ *vi* [ME; akin to MHG *lüren* to lie in wait — more at LOWER] (14c) **1 a** : to lie in wait in a place of concealment esp. for an evil purpose **b** : to move furtively or inconspicuously **c** : to persist in staying **2 a** : to be concealed but capable of being discovered; *specif* : to constitute a latent threat **b** : to lie hidden — **lurk•er** *n*
syn LURK, SKULK, SLINK, SNEAK mean to behave so as to escape attention. LURK implies a lying in wait in a place of concealment and often suggests an evil intent (suspicious men *lurking* in alleyways). SKULK suggests more strongly cowardice or fear or sinister intent (something *skulking* in the shadows). SLINK implies moving stealthily often merely to escape attention (*slunk* around the corner). SNEAK may add an implication of entering or leaving a place or evading a difficulty by furtive, indirect, or underhanded methods (*sneaked* out early).
lus•cious \'lə-shəs\ *adj* [ME *lucius*, perh. alter. of *licius*, short for *delicious*] (15c) **1 a** : having a delicious taste or smell : SWEET **b** *archaic* : excessively sweet : CLOYING **c** : sexually attractive : SEDUCTIVE, SEXY **3 a** : richly luxurious or appealing to the senses **b** : excessively ornate — **lus•cious•ly** *adv* — **lus•cious•ness** *n*
¹lush \'ləsh\ *adj* [ME *lusch* soft, tender] (1610) **1 a** : growing vigorously esp. with luxuriant foliage (~ grass) **b** : lavishly productive: as **(1)** : FERTILE **(2)** : THRIVING **(3)** : characterized by abundance : PLENTIFUL **(4)** : PROSPEROUS, PROFITABLE **2 a** : SAVORY, DELICIOUS **b** : appealing to the senses (the ~ sounds of the orchestra) **c** : OPULENT, SUMPTUOUS *syn* see PROFUSE — **lush•ly** *adv* — **lush•ness** *n*
²lush *n* [origin unknown] (ca. 1790) **1** *slang* : intoxicating liquor : DRINK **2** : an habitual heavy drinker : DRUNKARD
³lush *vb* (ca. 1811) *slang* : DRINK
Lu•so- \'lü-(ˌ)sō\ *comb form* [Pg, fr. *lusitano* Portuguese, fr. L *Lusitanus* of Lusitania (ancient region corresponding approximately to modern Portugal)] : Portuguese and (*Luso-Brazilian*)
¹lust \'ləst\ *n* [ME, fr. OE; akin to OHG *lust* pleasure and perh. to L *lascivus* wanton] (bef. 12c) **1** *obs* **a** : PLEASURE, DELIGHT **b** : personal inclination : WISH **2** : usu. intense or unbridled sexual desire : LASCIVIOUSNESS **3 a** : an intense longing : CRAVING **b** : ENTHUSIASM, EAGERNESS
²lust *vi* (12c) : to have an intense desire or need : CRAVE; *specif* : to have a sexual urge
¹lus•ter *or* **lus•tre** \'ləs-tər\ *n* [ME *lustre*, fr. L *lustrum*] (14c) : a period of five years : LUSTRUM 2
²luster *or* **lustre** *n* [MF *lustre*, fr. OIt *lustro*, fr. *lustrare* to brighten, fr. L, to purify ceremonially, fr. *lustrum*] (ca. 1522) **1** : a glow of reflected light : SHEEN; *specif* : the appearance of the surface of a mineral dependent upon its reflecting qualities **2 a** : a glow of light from within : LUMINOSITY **b** : an inner beauty : RADIANCE **3** : a superficial attractiveness or appearance of excellence **4** : a glass pendant used esp. to ornament a candlestick or chandelier **b** : a decorative object (as a chandelier) hung with glass pendants **5** *chiefly Brit* : a fabric with cotton warp and a filling of wool, mohair, or alpaca **6** : LUSTERWARE — **lus•ter•less** \-tər-ləs\ *adj*
³luster *or* **lustre** *vb* **lus•tered** *or* **lus•tred; lus•ter•ing** *or* **lus•tring** \-t(ə-)riŋ\ *vi* (1582) : to have luster : GLEAM ~ *vt* **1** : to give luster or distinction to **2** : to coat or treat with a substance that imparts luster
lus•ter•ware \'ləs-tər-ˌwar, -ˌwer\ *n* (1825) : pottery with an iridescent metallic sheen in the glaze

lust•ful \'ləst-fəl\ *adj* (14c) : excited by lust : LECHEROUS — **lust•ful•ly** \-fə-lē\ *adv* — **lust•ful•ness** *n*
lust•i•hood \'ləs-tē-ˌhu̇d\ *n* (1599) **1** : vigor of body or spirit : ROBUSTNESS **2** : sexual inclination or capacity
lus•tral \'ləs-trəl\ *adj* [L *lustralis*, fr. *lustrum*] (1533) : PURIFICATORY
lus•trate \'ləs-ˌtrāt\ *vt* **lus•trat•ed; lus•trat•ing** [L *lustratus*, pp. of *lustrare*] (1653) : to purify ceremonially — **lus•tra•tion** \ˌləs-ˈtrā-shən\ *n*
¹lus•tring \'ləs-triŋ\ *n* [modif. of It *lustrino*] (1697) *archaic* : LUTESTRING
²lus•tring \'ləs-t(ə-)riŋ\ *n* [*lustring*, gerund of ³*luster*] (ca. 1889) : a finishing process (as calendering) for giving a gloss to yarns and cloth
lus•trous \'ləs-trəs\ *adj* (1601) **1** : reflecting light evenly and efficiently without glitter or sparkle (a ~ satin) (the ~ glow of an opal) **2** : radiant in character or reputation : ILLUSTRIOUS *syn* see BRIGHT — **lus•trous•ly** *adv* — **lus•trous•ness** *n*
lus•trum \'ləs-trəm\ *n, pl* **lustrums** *or* **lus•tra** \-trə\ [L] (1590) **1** : a period of five years **2 a** : a purification of the whole Roman people made in ancient times after the census every five years **b** : the Roman census
lusty \'ləs-tē\ *adj* **lust•i•er; -est** (13c) **1** *archaic* : MERRY, JOYOUS **2** : LUSTFUL (~ passion) **2 a** : full of strength and vitality : HEALTHY, VIGOROUS (a young, ~, growing country —Helen Harris) **b** : HEARTY, ROBUST (a ~ beef stew) **c** : ENTHUSIASTIC, ROUSING (a ~ rendition of the song) *syn* see VIGOROUS — **lust•i•ly** \-tə-lē\ *adv* — **lust•i•ness** \-tē-nəs\ *n*
¹lute \'lüt\ *n* [ME, fr. MF *lut*, fr. OProv *laut*, fr. Ar *al-'ūd*, lit., the wood] (13c) : a stringed instrument having a large pear-shaped body, a vaulted back, a fretted fingerboard, and a head with tuning pegs which is often angled backward from the neck
²lute *vt* **lut•ed; lut•ing** [ME, fr. L *lutare*, fr. *lutum* mud — more at POLLUTE] (14c) : to seal or cover (as a joint or surface) with lute
³lute *n* (15c) : a substance (as cement or clay) for packing a joint or coating a porous surface to make it impervious to gas or liquid
lute- *or* **luteo-** *comb form* [NL (*corpus*) *luteum*] : corpus luteum (*luteal*)
lu•te•al \'lü-tē-əl\ *adj* (1920) : of, relating to, characterized by, or involving the corpus luteum (the ~ phase of the menstrual cycle)
lute•fisk \'lüt-ˌfisk, 'lü-tə-\ *n* [Norw, fr. *lute* to wash in lye solution + *fisk* fish] (1924) : dried codfish that has been soaked in a water and lye solution before cooking
lu•tein \'lü-tē-ən, 'lü-ˌtēn\ *n* (1869) : an orange xanthophyll $C_{40}H_{56}O_2$ occurring in plants, animal fat, egg yolk, and the corpus luteum
lu•tein•i•za•tion \ˌlü-tē-ə-nə-ˈzā-shən, ˌlü-ˌtē-nə-\ *n* (1929) : the process of forming corpora lutea — **lu•tein•ize** \'lü-tē-ə-ˌnīz, 'lü-ˌtē-ˌnīz\ *vb*
luteinizing hormone *n* (1931) : a hormone from the anterior lobe of the pituitary gland that in the female stimulates esp. the development of corpora lutea and in the male the development of interstitial tissue in the testis
luteinizing hormone–releasing hormone *n* (1970) : a hormone secreted by the hypothalamus that stimulates the pituitary gland to release gonadotropins (as luteinizing hormone and follicle-stimulating hormone) — called also *luteinizing hormone-releasing factor*
lu•te•nist *or* **lu•ta•nist** \'lü-tᵊn-ist, 'lüt-nist\ *n* [ML *lutanista*, fr. *lutana* lute, prob. fr. MF *lut* lute] (1603) : a lute player
lu•teo•tro•pic \ˌlü-tē-ə-ˈtrō-pik, -ˈträ-\ *or* **lu•teo•tro•phic** \-ˈtrō-fik, -ˈträ-\ *adj* (1941) : acting on the corpora lutea
luteotropic hormone *or* **luteotrophic hormone** *n* (1949) : PROLACTIN
lu•teo•tro•pin \ˌlü-tē-ə-ˈtrō-pən\ *or* **lu•teo•tro•phin** \-fən\ *n* (1941) : PROLACTIN
lu•te•ous \'lü-tē-əs\ *adj* [L *luteus* yellow, fr. *lutum*, a plant (*Reseda luteola*) used for dyeing yellow] (1657) : yellow tinged with green or brown
lute•string \'lüt-ˌstriŋ\ *n* [by folk etymology fr. It *lustrino* glossy fabric, fr. *lustro* luster] (1661) : a plain glossy silk formerly much used for women's dresses and ribbons
lu•te•tium *also* **lu•te•cium** \lü-ˈtē-sh(ē-)əm\ *n* [NL, fr. L *Lutetia*, ancient name of Paris] (1907) : a metallic element of the rare-earth group — see ELEMENT table
¹Lu•ther•an \'lü-th(ə-)rən\ *n* (1521) : a member of a Lutheran church
²Lutheran *adj* (1530) **1** : of or relating to religious doctrines (as justification by faith alone) developed by Martin Luther or his followers **2** : of or relating to the Protestant churches adhering to Lutheran doctrines, liturgy, and polity — **Lu•ther•an•ism** \-rə-ˌni-zəm\ *n*
lu•thi•er \'lü-tē-ər, -thē-ər\ *n* [F, fr. *luth* lute (fr. MF *lut*)] (1879) : one who makes stringed musical instruments (as violins or guitars)
lutz \'ləts\ *n* [prob. irreg. fr. Gustave *Lussi* b1898 Swiss figure skater] (1938) : a figure-skating jump from the outer edge of one skate with a full turn in the air and a return to the outer edge of the other skate
Lu•wi•an \'lü-ē-ən\ *n* [*Luwi*, an Anatolian people of the southern coast of Asia Minor] (1924) : an Anatolian language of the Indo-European language family — see INDO-EUROPEAN LANGUAGES table — **Luwian** *adj*
lux \'ləks\ *n, pl* **lux** *or* **lux•es** [L, light — more at LIGHT] (1889) : a unit of illumination equal to the direct illumination on a surface that is everywhere one meter from a uniform point source of one candle intensity or equal to one lumen per square meter
lux•a•tion \ˌlək-ˈsā-shən\ *n* [LL *luxation-, luxatio*, fr. L *luxare* to dislocate, fr. *luxus* dislocated — more at LOCK] (1552) : dislocation of an anatomical part (as a bone at a joint or the lens of the eye)
luxe \'lu̇ks, 'ləks, 'lüks\ *n* [F, fr. L *luxus* — more at LUXURY] (1558) : LUXURY — **luxe** *adj*
lux•u•ri•ance \(ˌ)ləg-ˈzhu̇r-ē-ən(t)s, (ˌ)lək-ˈshu̇r-\ *n* (ca. 1746) : the quality or state of being luxuriant
lux•u•ri•ant \-ē-ənt\ *adj* (ca. 1540) **1 a** : yielding abundantly : FERTILE, FRUITFUL **b** : characterized by abundant growth : LUSH **2** : abundantly and often extravagantly rich and varied : PROLIFIC **3** : characterized by luxury : LUXURIOUS *syn* see PROFUSE — **lux•u•ri•ant•ly** *adv*

lute

lux·u·ri·ate \-ē-ˌāt\ vi **-at·ed; -at·ing** [L luxuriatus, pp. of luxuriare, fr. luxuria] (1621) **1 a :** to grow profusely **:** THRIVE **b :** to develop extensively **2 :** to indulge oneself luxuriously **:** REVEL
lux·u·ri·ous \(ˌ)ləg-'zhuṙ-ē-əs, (ˌ)lək-'shuṙ-\ adj (14c) **1 :** LECHEROUS **2 :** marked by or given to self-indulgence ⟨~ tastes⟩ ⟨~ feeling⟩ **3 :** of, relating to, or marked by luxury ⟨~ accommodations⟩ **4 :** of the finest and richest kind ⟨~ cashmeres⟩ ⟨a ~ chocolate sauce⟩ syn see SENSUOUS — **lux·u·ri·ous·ly** adv — **lux·u·ri·ous·ness** n
lux·u·ry \'lək-sh(ə-)rē, -zh(ə-)rē\ n, pl **-ries** [ME luxurie, fr. MF, fr. L luxuria rankness, luxury, excess; akin to L luxus luxury, excess] (14c) **1** archaic **:** LECHERY, LUST **2 :** a condition of abundance or great ease and comfort **:** sumptuous environment ⟨lived in ~⟩ **3 a :** something adding to pleasure or comfort but not absolutely necessary **b :** an indulgence in something that provides pleasure, satisfaction, or ease ⟨had the ~ of rejecting a handful of job offers . . . before accepting a choice assignment —Terri Minsky⟩ — **luxury** adj
lwei \lə-'wä\ n, pl **lwei** also **lweis** [prob. fr. Lwei (Lué), name of several rivers in Angola] (ca. 1979) — see kwanza at MONEY table
ly- or **lyo-** comb form [ISV, fr. Gk lyein to loosen, dissolve — more at LOSE] **1 :** degrading **:** reduction ⟨lyase⟩ **2 :** dispersed state **:** dispersion ⟨lyophilic⟩
¹-ly \lē; in some dialects, esp Brit, Southern, NewEng, often li but not shown at individual entries\ adj suffix [ME, fr. OE -līc, -lic; akin to OHG -lih, -lic, OE līc body — more at LIKE] **1 :** like in appearance, manner, or nature **:** having the characteristics of ⟨queenly⟩ ⟨fatherly⟩ **2 :** characterized by regular recurrence in (specified) units of time **:** every ⟨hourly⟩
²-ly adv suffix [ME, fr. OE -līce, -lice, fr. -līc, adj. suffix] **1 a :** in a (specified) manner ⟨slowly⟩ **b :** at a (specified) time interval ⟨annually⟩ **2 :** from a (specified) point of view ⟨eschatologically⟩ **3 :** with respect to ⟨partly⟩ **4 :** to a (specified) degree ⟨relatively⟩ **5 :** in a (specified) place in a series ⟨secondly⟩
ly·am·hound \'lī-əm-ˌhau̇nd\ or **lyme·hound** \'līm-ˌhau̇nd\ n [obs. lyam leash] (1527) archaic **:** BLOODHOUND
ly·art \'lī-ərt\ adj [ME, fr. MF liart] (14c) chiefly Scot **:** streaked with gray **:** GRAY
ly·ase \'lī-ˌās, -ˌāz\ n (1965) **:** an enzyme (as a decarboxylase) that forms double bonds by removing groups from a substrate other than by hydrolysis or that adds groups to double bonds
ly·can·thro·py \lī-'kan(t)-thrə-pē\ n [NL lycanthropia, fr. Gk lykanthrōpia, fr. lykanthrōpos werewolf, fr. lykos wolf + anthrōpos human being — more at WOLF] (1594) **1 :** a delusion that one has become a wolf **2 :** the assumption of the form and characteristics of a wolf held to be possible by witchcraft or magic
ly·cée \lē-'sā\ n [F, fr. MF, lyceum, fr. L Lyceum] (1865) **:** a French public secondary school that prepares students for the university
ly·ce·um \lī-'sē-əm, 'lī-sē-\ n [L, Lyceum, gymnasium near Athens where Aristotle taught, fr. Gk Lykeion, fr. neut. of lykeios, epithet of Apollo] (1786) **1 :** a hall for public lectures or discussions **2 :** an association providing public lectures, concerts, and entertainments **3 :** LYCÉE
ly·chee var of LITCHI
lych–gate \'lich-ˌgāt\ n [ME lycheyate, fr. lich body, corpse (fr. OE līc) + gate, yate gate] (15c) **:** a roofed gate in a churchyard under which a bier rests during the initial part of the burial service
lych·nis \'lik-nəs\ n [NL, fr. L, a red flower, fr. Gk; akin to Gk lychnos lamp, L lux light — more at LIGHT] (1601) **:** any of a genus (Lychnis) of herbs of the pink family with terminal cymes of showy mostly red or white flowers having 5 or rarely 4 styles
Ly·cian \'li-sh(ē-)ən\ n (1598) **1 :** a native or inhabitant of Lycia **2 :** an Anatolian language of the Indo-European language family — see INDO-EUROPEAN LANGUAGES table — **Lycian** adj
ly·co·pene \'lī-kə-ˌpēn\ n [ISV lycop- (fr. NL Lycopersicon, genus of herbs) + -ene] (ca. 1929) **:** a carotenoid pigment $C_{40}H_{56}$ that is the red coloring matter of the tomato
ly·co·pod \'lī-kə-ˌpäd\ n [NL Lycopodium] (1861) **:** LYCOPODIUM 1; broadly **:** CLUB MOSS
ly·co·po·di·um \ˌlī-kə-'pō-dē-əm\ n [NL, fr. Gk lykos wolf + podion, dim. of pod-, pous foot — more at FOOT] (ca. 1706) **1 :** any of a large genus (Lycopodium) of erect or creeping club mosses with reduced or scalelike evergreen leaves **2 :** a fine yellowish flammable powder composed of lycopodium spores and used esp. in pharmacy
Ly·cra \'lī-krə\ trademark — used for a spandex synthetic fiber
lyd·dite \'li-ˌdīt\ n [Lydd, England] (1888) **:** a high explosive composed chiefly of picric acid
Lyd·i·an \'li-dē-ən\ n (15c) **1 :** a native or inhabitant of Lydia **2 :** an Anatolian language of the Indo-European language family — see INDO-EUROPEAN LANGUAGES table — **Lydian** adj
lye \'lī\ n [ME, fr. OE lēag; akin to OHG louga lye, L lavare, lavere to wash, Gk louein] (bef. 12c) **1 :** a strong alkaline liquor rich in potassium carbonate leached from wood ashes and used esp. in making soap and washing; broadly **:** a strong alkaline solution (as of sodium hydroxide or potassium hydroxide) **2 :** a solid caustic (as sodium hydroxide)
ly·gus bug \'lī-gəs-\ n [NL Lygus] (1940) **:** any of various small sucking bugs (genus Lygus) including some pests of cultivated plants
¹ly·ing \'lī-iŋ\ pres part of LIE
²lying adj [ME leghynge, prp. of lien to lie] (14c) **:** marked by or containing falsehoods **:** FALSE ⟨a ~ account of the accident⟩
ly·ing–in \ˌlī-iŋ-'in\ n, pl **lyings–in** or **lying–ins** (15c) **:** the state attending and consequent to childbirth **:** CONFINEMENT
Lyme disease \'līm-\ n [Lyme, Connecticut, where it was first reported] (1980) **:** an acute inflammatory disease that is caused by a spirochete (Borrelia burgdorferi) transmitted by ticks (genus Ixodes and esp. I. dammini), that is often characterized initially by a spreading red annular skin lesion at the site of the infection, fever, and chills, and that may result in joint pain, arthritis, and cardiac and neurological disorders
lymph \'lim(p)f\ n [L lympha, water goddess, water, perh. modif. of Gk nymphē nymph — more at NUPTIAL] (ca. 1673) **1** archaic **:** the sap of plants **2** [NL lympha, fr. L, water] **:** a pale coagulable fluid that bathes the tissues, passes into lymphatic channels and ducts, is discharged into the blood by way of the thoracic duct, and consists of a

liquid portion resembling blood plasma and containing white blood cells but normally no red blood cells
lymph- or **lympho-** comb form [NL lympha] **:** lymph **:** lymphatic tissue ⟨lymphogranuloma⟩
lymph·ad·e·ni·tis \ˌlim-ˌfa-dᵊn-'ī-təs\ n [NL, fr. lymphaden lymph gland, fr. lymph- + Gk adēn gland — more at ADEN-] (1860) **:** inflammation of lymph nodes
lymph·ade·nop·a·thy \ˌlim-ˌfa-dᵊn-'ä-pə-thē\ n, pl **-thies** (1920) **:** abnormal enlargement of the lymph nodes
lymph·an·gi·og·ra·phy \ˌlim-ˌfan-jē-'ä-grə-fē\ n (ca. 1941) **:** X-ray depiction of lymph vessels and nodes after use of a radiopaque material — called also lymphography — **lymph·an·gio·gram** \ˌlim-'fan-jē-ə-ˌgram\ n — **lymph·an·gio·graph·ic** \ˌlim-ˌfan-jē-ə-'gra-fik\ adj
¹lym·phat·ic \lim-'fa-tik\ adj (1649) **1 a :** of, relating to, or produced by lymph, lymphoid tissue, or lymphocytes **b :** conveying lymph **2 :** lacking physical or mental energy **:** SLUGGISH — **lym·phat·i·cal·ly** \-ti-k(ə-)lē\ adv
²lymphatic n (1667) **:** a vessel that contains or conveys lymph — called also lymph vessel
lymph gland n (ca. 1858) **:** LYMPH NODE
lymph node n (1892) **:** any of the rounded masses of lymphoid tissue that are surrounded by a capsule of connective tissue, are distributed along the lymphatic vessels, and contain numerous lymphocytes which filter the flow of lymph
lym·pho·blast \'lim(p)-fə-ˌblast\ n [ISV] (ca. 1909) **:** a lymphocyte that has enlarged following stimulation by an antigen, has the capacity to recognize the stimulating antigen, and is undergoing proliferation and differentiation either to an effector state in which it functions to eliminate the antigen or to a memory state in which it functions to recognize the future reappearance of the antigen — **lym·pho·blas·tic** \ˌlim(p)-fə-'blas-tik\ adj
lym·pho·cyte \'lim(p)-fə-ˌsīt\ n [ISV] (1890) **:** any of the colorless weakly motile cells originating from stem cells and differentiating in lymphoid tissue (as of the thymus or bone marrow) that are the typical cellular elements of lymph, include the cellular mediators of immunity, and constitute 20 to 30 percent of the leukocytes of normal human blood — compare B CELL, T CELL — **lym·pho·cyt·ic** \ˌlim(p)-fə-'si-tik\ adj
lymphocytic cho·rio·men·in·gi·tis \-ˌkȯr-ē-ō-ˌme-nən-'jī-təs\ n [NL choriomeningitis cerebral meningitis, fr. chorio- of a membrane resembling the chorion] (1934) **:** an acute virus disease that is characterized by fever, nausea and vomiting, headache, stiff neck, and slow pulse, is marked by the presence of numerous lymphocytes in the cerebrospinal fluid, and is transmitted esp. by rodents and bloodsucking insects
lym·pho·cy·to·sis \ˌlim(p)-fə-ˌsī-'tō-səs, -fə-sə-\ n [NL, fr. ISV lymphocyte] (1896) **:** an increase in the number of lymphocytes in the blood usu. associated with chronic infections or inflammations
lym·pho·gran·u·lo·ma \'lim(p)-fō-ˌgran-yə-'lō-mə\ n, pl **-mas** or **-ma·ta** \-mə-tə\ [NL] (1924) **:** LYMPHOGRANULOMA VENEREUM
lymphogranuloma in·gui·na·le \-ˌiŋ-gwə-'nä-lē, -'na-, -'nä-\ n [NL, inguinal lymphogranuloma] (1932) **:** LYMPHOGRANULOMA VENEREUM
lym·pho·gran·u·lo·ma·to·sis \-ˌlō-mə-'tō-səs\ n, pl **-to·ses** \-ˌsēz\ [NL lymphogranulomat-, lymphogranuloma + -osis] (1911) **:** the development of benign or malignant nodular swellings of lymph nodes in various parts of the body; also **:** a condition characterized by these
lymphogranuloma ve·ne·re·um \-və-'nir-ē-əm\ n [NL, venereal lymphogranuloma] (1938) **:** a contagious venereal disease caused by various strains of a chlamydia (Chlamydia trachomatis) and marked by swelling and ulceration of lymphatic tissue in the iliac and inguinal regions
lym·phog·ra·phy \lim-'fä-grə-fē\ n (ca. 1935) **:** LYMPHANGIOGRAPHY — **lym·pho·gram** \'lim(p)-fə-ˌgram\ n — **lym·pho·graph·ic** \ˌlim-fə-'gra-fik\ adj
lym·phoid \'lim-ˌfȯid\ adj (1867) **1 :** of, relating to, or being tissue (as of the lymph nodes or thymus) containing lymphocytes **2 :** of, relating to, or resembling lymph
lym·pho·kine \'lim(p)-fə-ˌkīn\ n [lymph- + -kine, fr. Gk kinein to move about — more at -KINESIS] (1969) **:** any of various substances (as interleukin-2) of low molecular weight that are not immunoglobulins, are secreted by T cells in response to stimulation by antigens, and have a role (as the activation of macrophages or the enhancement or inhibition of antibody production) in cell-mediated immunity
lym·pho·ma \lim-'fō-mə\ n, pl **-mas** or **-ma·ta** \-mə-tə\ [NL] (1873) **:** a tumor of lymphoid tissue — **lym·pho·ma·tous** \-mə-təs\ adj
lym·pho·ma·to·sis \(ˌ)lim-ˌfō-mə-'tō-səs\ n, pl **-to·ses** \-ˌsēz\ [NL lymphomat-, lymphoma + -osis] (ca. 1900) **:** the presence of multiple lymphomas in the body
lym·pho·sar·co·ma \ˌlim(p)-fə-sär-'kō-mə\ n, pl **-mas** or **-ma·ta** \-mə-tə\ [NL] (1874) **:** a malignant lymphoma that tends to metastasize freely esp. along the regional lymphatic drainage
lynch \'linch\ vt [lynch law] (1836) **:** to put to death (as by hanging) by mob action without legal sanction — **lynch·er** n
lynch law n [William Lynch †1820 Am. vigilante] (1811) **:** the punishment of presumed crimes or offenses usu. by death without due process of law
lynch·pin var of LINCHPIN
lynx \'liŋ(k)s\ n, pl **lynx** or **lynx·es** [ME, fr. L, fr. Gk; akin to OE lox lynx and prob. to Gk leukos white — more at LIGHT] (14c) **:** any of several wildcats (genus Lynx) with relatively long legs, a short stubby tail, mottled coat, and often tufted ears: as **a :** a lynx (L. lynx) of northern Europe and Asia **b :** BOBCAT **c :** a No. American lynx (L. canadensis) distinguished from the bobcat by its larger size, longer tufted ears, and wholly black tail tip — called also Canadian lynx
lynx–eyed \'liŋ(k)s-ˌīd\ adj (1597) **:** SHARP-SIGHTED
lyo- — see LY-
ly·on·naise \ˌlī-ə-'nāz\ adj [F (à la) lyonnaise in the manner of Lyons, France] (1846) **:** prepared with onions ⟨~ potatoes⟩

\ə\ abut \ᵊ\ kitten, F table \ər\ further \a\ ash \ā\ ace \ä\ mop, mar \au̇\ out \ch\ chin \e\ bet \ē\ easy \g\ go \i\ hit \ī\ ice \j\ job \ŋ\ sing \ō\ go \ȯ\ law \ȯi\ boy \th\ thin \t͟h\ the \ü\ loot \u̇\ foot \y\ yet \zh\ vision \à, k̲, ⁿ, œ, œ̄, ᵫ, ᵫ̄, ᵜ\ see Guide to Pronunciation

Ly·on·nesse \ˌlī-ə-'nes\ n : a country that according to Arthurian legend was contiguous to Cornwall before sinking beneath the sea

lyo·phile \'lī-ə-ˌfil\ adj [ISV] (1934) **1** : of or relating to freeze-drying **2** or **lyo·philed** \-ˌfild\ : obtained by freeze-drying

lyo·phil·ic \ˌlī-ə-'fi-lik\ adj (1911) : marked by strong affinity between a dispersed phase and the liquid in which it is dispersed ⟨a ~ colloid⟩

ly·oph·i·lise Brit var of LYOPHILIZE

ly·oph·i·lize \lī-'ä-fə-ˌliz\ vt -**lized; -liz·ing** (1938) : FREEZE-DRY — **ly·oph·i·li·za·tion** \-ˌä-fə-lə-'zā-shən\ n — **ly·oph·i·liz·er** \-'ä-fə-ˌli-zər\ n

lyo·pho·bic \ˌlī-ə-'fō-bik\ adj (1911) : marked by lack of strong affinity between a dispersed phase and the liquid in which it is dispersed ⟨a ~ colloid⟩

Ly·ra \'lī-rə\ n [L (gen. Lyrae), lit., lyre] : a northern constellation representing the lyre of Orpheus or Mercury and containing Vega

ly·rate \'lī-ˌrāt\ adj (ca. 1760) : having or suggesting the shape of a lyre ⟨the ~ horns of the impala⟩

lyre \'līr\ n [ME lire, fr. OF, fr. L lyra, fr. Gk] (13c) **1** : a stringed instrument of the harp class used by the ancient Greeks esp. to accompany song and recitation **2** cap : LYRA

lyre·bird \-ˌbərd\ n (1834) : either of two Australian passerine birds (genus Menura) distinguished in the male by very long tail feathers displayed in the shape of a lyre during courtship

lyrebird

¹**lyr·ic** \'lir-ik\ n (1581) **1** : a lyric composition; specif : a lyric poem **2** : the words of a song — often used in pl.

²**lyric** adj [MF or L; MF lyrique, fr. L lyricus, fr. Gk lyrikos, fr. lyra] (1589) **1 a** : suitable for singing to the lyre or for being set to music and sung **b** : of, relating to, or being drama set to music; esp : OPERATIC ⟨~ stage⟩ **2 a** : expressing direct usu. intense personal emotion esp. in a manner suggestive of song ⟨~ poetry⟩ **b** : EXUBERANT, RHAPSODIC **3** of an opera singer : having a light voice and a melodic style — compare DRAMATIC

lyr·i·cal \'lir-i-kəl\ adj (1581) : LYRIC — **lyr·i·cal·ly** \-i-k(ə-)lē\ adv — **lyr·i·cal·ness** \-kəl-nəs\ n

lyr·i·cism \'lir-ə-ˌsi-zəm\ n (1760) **1** : the quality or state of being lyric : SONGFULNESS **2 a** : an intense personal quality expressive of feeling or emotion in an art (as poetry or music) **b** : EXUBERANCE ⟨the sort of author who inspires ~ or invective, not judicious interpretation —Time⟩

lyr·i·cist \-sist\ n (1881) : a writer of lyrics

lyr·ism \'lir-ˌi-zəm\ n (1859) : LYRICISM

lyr·ist n (ca. 1656) **1** \'lī-rist\ : a player on the lyre **2** \'lir-ist\ : LYRICIST

lys- or **lysi-** or **lyso-** comb form [NL, fr. Gk lys-, lysi- loosening, fr. lysis] : lysis ⟨lysin⟩

ly·sate \'lī-ˌsāt\ n (1922) : a product of lysis

lyse \'līs, 'līz\ vb **lysed; lys·ing** [back-formation fr. NL lysis] vt (1924) : to cause to undergo lysis ~ vi : to undergo lysis

-lyse chiefly Brit var of -LYZE

Ly·sen·ko·ism \lə-'sen-kō-ˌi-zəm\ n [Trofim Lysenko] (1948) : a biological doctrine asserting the fundamental influence of somatic and environmental factors on heredity in contradiction of orthodox genetics

ly·ser·gic acid \lə-'sər-jik-, (ˌ)lī-\ n [lys- + ergot] (1934) : a crystalline acid $C_{16}H_{16}N_2O_2$ from ergot alkaloids; also : LSD

lysergic acid di·eth·yl·am·ide \-ˌdī-ˌe-thə-'la-ˌmīd\ n (1944) : LSD

ly·sim·e·ter \lī-'si-mə-tər\ n (1879) : a device for measuring the percolation of water through soils and for determining the soluble constituents removed in the drainage — **ly·si·met·ric** \ˌlī-sə-'me-trik\ adj

ly·sin \'lī-sᵉn\ n (1900) : a substance (as an antibody) capable of causing lysis

ly·sine \'lī-ˌsēn\ n (1892) : a crystalline essential amino acid $C_6H_{14}N_2O_2$ obtained from the hydrolysis of various proteins

ly·sis \'lī-səs\ n, pl **ly·ses** \-ˌsēz\ [NL, fr. Gk, act of loosening, dissolution, remission of fever, fr. lyein to loosen — more at LOSE] (1543) **1** : the gradual decline of a disease process (as fever) **2** : a process of disintegration or dissolution (as of cells)

-lysis n comb form, pl **-lyses** [NL, fr. L & Gk; L, loosening, fr. Gk, fr. lysis] **1** : decomposition ⟨electrolysis⟩ **2** : disintegration : breaking down ⟨autolysis⟩

ly·so·gen \'lī-sə-jən\ n (ca. 1934) : a lysogenic bacterium or bacterial strain

ly·so·gen·ic \ˌlī-sə-'je-nik\ adj [fr. the capacity of the prophage to lyse other bacteria] (1899) **1** : harboring a prophage as hereditary material ⟨~ bacteria⟩ **2** : TEMPERATE **3** ⟨~ viruses⟩ — **ly·so·ge·nic·i·ty** \-jə-'ni-sə-tē\ n

ly·sog·e·nise Brit var of LYSOGENIZE

ly·sog·e·nize \lī-'sä-jə-ˌnīz\ vt **-nized; -niz·ing** (1953) : to render lysogenic — **ly·sog·e·ni·za·tion** \-ˌsä-jə-nə-'zā-shən\ n

ly·sog·e·ny \lī-'sä-jə-nē\ n (1956) : the state of being lysogenic

ly·so·lec·i·thin \ˌlī-sə-'le-sə-thən\ n (1923) : a hydrolytic substance formed by the enzymatic hydrolysis (as by some snake venoms) of a lecithin

ly·so·some \'lī-sə-ˌsōm\ n [ISV lys- + ³-some] (1955) : a saclike cellular organelle that contains various hydrolytic enzymes — see CELL illustration — **ly·so·som·al** \ˌlī-sə-'sō-məl\ adj

ly·so·zyme \'lī-sə-ˌzīm\ n (1922) : a basic bacteriolytic protein that hydrolyzes peptidoglycan and is present in egg white and in human tears and saliva

-lyte n comb form [Gk lytos that may be untied, soluble, fr. lyein] : substance capable of undergoing (such) decomposition ⟨electrolyte⟩

lyt·ic \'li-tik\ adj [Gk lytikos able to loose, fr. lyein] (1889) : of or relating to lysis or a lysin; also : productive of or effecting lysis (as of cells) — **ly·ti·cal·ly** \-ti-k(ə-)lē\ adv

-lytic adj suffix [Gk lytikos] : of, relating to, or effecting (such) decomposition ⟨hydrolytic⟩

-lyze vb comb form **-lyzed; -lyzing** [ISV, prob. irreg. fr. NL -lysis] : produce or undergo lytic disintegration or dissolution ⟨electrolyze⟩

---

m \'em\ n, pl **m's** or **ms** \'emz\ often cap, often attrib (bef. 12c) **1 a** : the 13th letter of the English alphabet **b** : a graphic representation of this letter **c** : a speech counterpart of orthographic m **2** : one thousand — see NUMBER table **3 a** : a graphic device for reproducing the letter m **4** : one designated m esp. as the 13th in order or class **5** : something shaped like the letter M **6 a** : EM 2 **b** : PICA 2

'm \m\ vb (ca. 1594) : AM ⟨I'm going⟩

ma \'mä, 'mȯ\ n [short for mama] (1829) : MOTHER

ma'am \'mam, after "yes" often əm\ n (1668) : MADAM

ma-and-pa \ˌmä-ən-'pä, ˌmȯ-ən-'pȯ\ adj (1965) : MOM-AND-POP

Mab \'mab\ n : a queen of fairies in English literature

mabe pearl \'mäb-\ n [origin unknown] (1952) : a cultured pearl essentially hemispherical in form — called also mabe

mac \'mak\ n (1901) Brit : MACKINTOSH

Mac \'mak\ n [Mac-, Mc-, patronymic prefix in Scottish and Irish surnames] (ca. 1937) : FELLOW — used informally to address a man whose name is not known

ma·ca·bre \mə-'käb; -'kä-brə, -bər; -'käbr\ adj [F, fr. (danse) macabre dance of death, fr. MF (danse de) Macabré] (1889) **1** : having death as a subject : comprising or including a personalized representation of death **2** : dwelling on the gruesome **3** : tending to produce horror in a beholder *syn* see GHASTLY

mac·ad·am \mə-'ka-dəm\ n [John L. McAdam †1836 Brit. engineer] (1824) : macadamized roadway or pavement esp. with a bituminous binder

mac·a·da·mia nut \ˌma-kə-'dā-mē-ə-\ n [NL Macadamia, fr. John Macadam †1865 Australian chemist] (1929) : a hard-shelled nut somewhat resembling a filbert and produced by an Australian evergreen tree (Macadamia integrifolia) of the protea family that is cultivated extensively in Hawaii — called also macadamia

mac·ad·am·ize \mə-'ka-də-ˌmīz\ vt **-ized; -iz·ing** (1826) : to construct or finish (a road) by compacting into a solid mass a layer of small broken stone on a convex well-drained roadbed and using a binder (as cement or asphalt) for the mass

ma·caque \mə-'kak, -'käk\ n [F, fr. Pg macaco] (1757) : any of a genus (Macaca) of chiefly Asian monkeys typically having a sturdy build and including some short-tailed or tailless forms; esp : RHESUS MONKEY

mac·a·ro·ni \ˌma-kə-'rō-nē\ n [It maccheroni, pl. of maccherone, fr. It dial. maccarone dumpling, macaroni] (1599) **1** : pasta made from semolina and shaped in the form of slender tubes **2** pl **macaronis** or **macaronies a** : a member of a class of traveled young Englishmen of the late 18th and early 19th centuries who affected foreign ways **b** : an affected young man : FOP

mac·a·ron·ic \ˌma-kə-'rä-nik\ adj [NL macaronicus, fr. It dial. maccarone macaroni] (1638) **1** : characterized by a mixture of vernacular words with Latin words or with non-Latin words having Latin endings **2** : characterized by a mixture of two languages — **macaronic** n

mac·a·roon \ˌma-kə-'rün\ n [F macaron, fr. It dial. maccarone] (ca. 1611) : a small cookie composed chiefly of egg whites, sugar, and ground almonds or coconut

ma·caw \mə-'kȯ\ n [Pg macau] (1668) : any of numerous parrots (esp. genus Ara) of South and Central America including some of the largest and showiest of parrots

Mac·beth \mək-'beth, mak-\ n : a Scottish general who is the protagonist of Shakespeare's tragedy Macbeth

Mac·ca·bees \'ma-kə-ˌbēz\ n pl [Gk Makkabaioi, fr. pl. of Makkabaios, surname of Judas Maccabaeus 2d cent. B.C. Jewish patriot] (1702) **1** : a priestly family leading a Jewish revolt begun in 168 B.C. against Hellenism and Syrian rule and reigning over Palestine from 142 B.C. to 63 B.C. **2** sing in constr : either of two narrative and historical books included in the Roman Catholic canon of the Old Testament and in the Protestant Apocrypha — see BIBLE table — **Mac·ca·be·an** \ˌma-kə-'bē-ən\ adj

¹mace \'mās\ n [ME, fr. MF macis, fr. L macir, an East Indian spice, fr. Gk makir] (13c) : an aromatic spice consisting of the dried external fibrous covering of a nutmeg

²mace n [ME, fr. OF, fr. (assumed) VL mattia; akin to L mateola mallet] (14c) **1 a** : a heavy often spiked staff or club used esp. in the Middle Ages for breaking armor **b** : a club used as a weapon **2 a** : an ornamental staff borne as a symbol of authority before a public official or a legislative body **b** : one who carries a mace

³mace vt maced; mac·ing (1968) : to attack with the liquid Mace

Mace \'mās\ trademark — used for a temporarily disabling liquid usu. used as a spray

ma·cé·doine \ˌma-sə-'dwän\ n [F, fr. Macédoine Macedonia; perh. fr. the mixture of ethnic groups in Macedonia] (1820) **1** : a confused mixture : MEDLEY **2** : a mixture of fruits or vegetables served as a salad or cocktail or in a jellied dessert or used in a sauce or as a garnish

Mac·e·do·nian \ˌma-sə-'dō-nyən, -nē-ən\ n (1582) **1** : a native or inhabitant of Macedonia **2** : the Slavic language of modern Macedonia **3** : the language of ancient Macedonia of uncertain affinity but generally assumed to be Indo-European

mace 1a

mac·er·ate \'ma-sə-ˌrāt\ vb **-at·ed; -at·ing** [L maceratus, pp. of macerare to soften, steep] vt (1547) **1** : to cause to waste away by or as if by excessive fasting **2** : to cause to become soft or separated into constituent elements by or as if by steeping in fluid; broadly : STEEP, SOAK ~ vi : to soften and wear away esp. as a result of being wetted or steeped — **mac·er·a·tion** \ˌma-sə-'rā-shən\ n — **mac·er·a·tor** \'ma-sə-ˌrā-tər\ n

Mach \'mäk\ n [Mach number] (1946) : a usu. high speed expressed by a Mach number ⟨an airplane flying at ~ 2⟩

Mach·a·bees \'ma-kə-ˌbēz\ n pl but sing in constr [ME, fr. LL Machabaei, modif. of Gk Makkabaioi] (14c) : MACCABEES

mâche \'mäsh\ n [F, perh. alter. of F dial. pomache, fr. (assumed) VL pomasca, fr. L pomum fruit] (1961) : CORN SALAD

ma·chete \mə-'she-tē, -'che-; -'shet\ n [Sp] (1598) : a large heavy knife used for cutting sugarcane and underbrush and as a weapon

Ma·chi·a·vel·lian \ˌma-kē-ə-'ve-lē-ən, -'vel-yən\ adj [Niccolo Machiavelli] (1579) **1** : of or relating to Machiavelli or Machiavellianism **2** : suggesting the principles of conduct laid down by Machiavelli; specif : marked by cunning, duplicity, or bad faith — **Machiavellian** n

Ma·chi·a·vel·lian·ism \-'ve-lē-ə-ˌni-zəm, -'vel-yə-ˌni-zəm\ n (1626) : the political theory of Machiavelli; esp : the view that politics is amoral and that any means however unscrupulous can justifiably be used in achieving political power

ma·chic·o·la·tion \mə-ˌchi-kə-'lā-shən\ n [ML machicolare to furnish with machicolations, fr. MF machicoller, fr. machicoleis machicolation, fr. macher to crush + col neck, fr. L collum — more at COLLAR] (1788) **1** : an opening between the corbels of a projecting parapet or in the floor of a gallery or roof of a portal for discharging missiles upon assailants below — see BATTLEMENT illustration **b** : a gallery or parapet containing such openings **2** : construction imitating medieval machicolation — **ma·chic·o·lat·ed** \mə-'chi-kə-ˌlā-təd\ adj

mach·i·nate \'ma-kə-ˌnāt, 'ma-shə-\ vb **-nat·ed; -nat·ing** [L machinatus, pp. of machinari, fr. machina machine, contrivance] vi (1600) : to plan or plot esp. to do evil ~ vt : to scheme or contrive to bring about : PLOT — **mach·i·na·tor** \-ˌnā-tər\ n

mach·i·na·tion \ˌma-kə-'nā-shən, ˌma-shə-\ n (15c) **1** : an act of machinating **2** : a scheming or crafty action or artful design intended to accomplish some usu. evil end ⟨backstage ~s and power plays that have dominated the film industry —Peter Bogdanovich⟩ syn see PLOT

¹ma·chine \mə-'shēn\ n, often attrib [MF, fr. L machina, fr. Gk mēchanē (Dor dial. machana), fr. mēchos means, expedient — more at MAY] (ca. 1545) **1 a** archaic : a constructed thing whether material or immaterial **b** : CONVEYANCE, VEHICLE; esp : AUTOMOBILE **c** archaic : a military engine **d** : any of various apparatuses formerly used to produce stage effects **e** (1) : an assemblage of parts that transmit forces, motion, and energy one to another in a predetermined manner (2) : an instrument (as a lever) designed to transmit or modify the application of power, force, or motion **f** : a mechanically, electrically, or electronically operated device for performing a task ⟨a calculating ~⟩ ⟨a card-sorting ~⟩ **g** : a coin-operated device ⟨a cigarette ~⟩ **h** : MACHINERY — used with the or in pl. **2 a** : a living organism or one of its functional systems **b** : a person or organization that resembles a machine (as in being methodical, tireless, or unemotional) **c** (1) : a combination of persons acting together for a common end along with the agencies they use (2) : a highly organized political group under the leadership of a boss or small clique **3** : a literary device or contrivance introduced for dramatic effect

²machine vt ma·chined; ma·chin·ing (ca. 1864) : to process by or as if by machine; esp : to reduce or finish by or as if by turning, shaping, planing, or milling by machine-operated tools — **ma·chin·abil·i·ty** \-ˌshē-nə-'bi-lə-tē\ n — **ma·chin·able** also **ma·chine·able** \-'shē-nə-bəl\ adj

ma·chine–gun \mə-'shēn-ˌgən\ adj (1906) : characterized by rapidity and sharpness : RAPID-FIRE ⟨a comic's ~ delivery⟩

machine gun n (1870) : a gun for sustained rapid fire that uses bullets; broadly : an automatic weapon — **machine–gun** vb — **machine gun·ner** n

machine language n (1949) **1** : the set of symbolic instruction codes usu. in binary form that is used to represent operations and data in a machine (as a computer) **2** : ASSEMBLY LANGUAGE

ma·chine·like \mə-'shēn-ˌlīk\ adj (ca. 1712) : resembling a machine esp. in regularity of action or stereotyped uniformity of product

machine pistol n (1940) : a usu. small submachine gun

machine–readable adj (1961) : directly usable by a computer ⟨~ text⟩

ma·chin·ery \mə-'shē-nə-rē, -'shēn-rē\ n, pl **-er·ies** (1687) **1 a** : machines in general or as a functioning unit **b** : the working parts of a machine **2** : the means or system by which something is kept in action

or a desired result is obtained ⟨the ~ of government⟩ ⟨genetic ~ of cells⟩

machine shop n (1827) : a workshop in which work is machined to size and assembled

machine tool n (1861) : a machine designed for shaping solid work

ma·chin·ist \mə-'shē-nist\ n (ca. 1706) **1 a** : a worker who fabricates, assembles, or repairs machinery **b** : a craftsman skilled in the use of machine tools **c** : one who operates a machine **2** archaic : a person in charge of the mechanical aspects of a theatrical production **3** : a warrant officer who supervises machinery and engine operation

ma·chis·mo \mä-'chēz-(ˌ)mō, mə-, -'kēz-, -'kiz-, -'chiz-\ n [Sp, fr. macho] (1948) **1** : a strong sense of masculine pride : an exaggerated masculinity **2** : an exaggerated or exhilarating sense of power or strength

Mach number \'mäk-\ n [Ernst Mach †1916 Austrian physicist] (1937) : a number representing the ratio of the speed of a body (as an aircraft) to the speed of sound in a surrounding medium (as air)

¹ma·cho \'mä-(ˌ)chō\ adj [Sp, lit., male, fr. L masculus — more at MASCULINE] (1928) : characterized by machismo : aggressively virile

²macho n, pl machos (1951) **1** : one who exhibits machismo **2** : MACHISMO

mack var of MAC

mack·er·el \'ma-k(ə-)rəl\ n, pl mackerel or mackerels [ME makerel, fr. MF] (14c) **1** : a scombroid bony fish (Scomber scombrus) of the No. Atlantic that is green above with dark blue bars and silvery below and is one of the most important food fishes **2** : any of a family (Scombridae) of fishes including the common mackerel; esp : a comparatively small member of this group as distinguished from a bonito or tuna

mackerel 1

mackerel shark n (1819) : any of a family (Lamnidae) of large pelagic sharks including the great white shark and mako sharks; esp : PORBEAGLE

mackerel sky n (1669) : a sky covered with rows of altocumulus or cirrocumulus clouds resembling the patterns on a mackerel's back

mack·i·naw \'ma-kə-ˌnò\ n [Mackinaw (Mackinac), trading post at site of Mackinaw City, Michigan] (1836) **1** : a heavy woolen blanket formerly distributed by the U.S. government to the Indians **2 a** : a heavy cloth of wool or wool and other fibers often with a plaid design and usu. heavily napped and felted **b** : a short coat of mackinaw or similar heavy fabric

Mackinaw trout n (1840) : a large dark No. American char (Salvelinus namaycush) that is an important commercial food fish in northern lakes

mack·in·tosh also **mac·in·tosh** \'ma-kən-ˌtäsh\ n [Charles Macintosh †1843 Scot. chemist & inventor] (1836) **1** chiefly Brit : RAINCOAT **2** : a lightweight waterproof fabric orig. of rubberized cotton

Mac·lau·rin's series \mə-'klòr-ən(z)-\ n [Colin Maclaurin †1746 Scot. mathematician] (ca. 1909) : a Taylor's series of the form

$$f(x) = f(0) + \frac{f'(0)}{1!}x + \frac{f''(0)}{2!}x^2 + \cdots + \frac{f^{(n)}(0)}{n!}x^n + \cdots$$

in which the expansion is about the reference point zero — called also Maclaurin series

ma·cle \'ma-kəl\ n [F, wide-meshed net, lozenge voided, macle, fr. OF, mesh, lozenge voided, of Gmc origin; akin to OHG masca mesh — more at MESH] (1801) **1** : a twin crystal **2** : any of a family of certain twin triangular diamond that is usu. a twin crystal — **ma·cled** \'ma-kəld\ adj

ma·con also **mâ·con** \mä-'kōⁿ\ n, often cap [F Mâcon, fr. Mâcon, France] (1863) : a dry red or white wine produced in the area around Mâcon, France

Mac·Pher·son strut \mək-'fir-s^ən-, -'fər-\ n [Earle S. MacPherson †1960 Am. engineer] (1975) : a component of an automobile suspension consisting of a shock absorber mounted within a coil spring

macr- or **macro-** comb form [F & L, fr. Gk makr-, makro- long, fr. makros — more at MEAGER] **1** : long ⟨macrobiotic⟩ **2** : large ⟨macromolecule⟩

mac·ra·mé also **mac·ra·me** \'ma-krə-ˌmā\ n [F or It; F macramé, fr. It macramè, fr. Turk makrama napkin, towel, fr. Ar miqramah coverlet] (1869) : a coarse lace or fringe made by knotting threads or cords in a geometrical pattern; also : the art of tying knots in patterns

¹mac·ro \'ma-(ˌ)krō\ adj [macr-] (1923) **1** : being large, thick, or exceptionally prominent **2 a** : of, involving, or intended for use with relatively large quantities or on a large scale **b** : of or relating to macroeconomics **3** : GROSS 1c

²macro n, pl macros [short for macroinstruction] (1959) : a single computer instruction that stands for a sequence of operations

mac·ro·ag·gre·gate \ˌma-krō-'a-gri-gət\ n (1926) : a relatively large particle (as of soil or a protein) — **mac·ro·ag·gre·gat·ed** \-ˌgā-təd\ adj

mac·ro·bi·ot·ic \-bī-'ä-tik, -bē-\ adj (1965) : of, relating to, or being an extremely restricted diet (as one containing chiefly whole grains) that is held by its advocates to promote health and well-being although it may actually be deficient in essential nutrients (as fats)

mac·ro·cosm \'ma-krə-ˌkä-zəm\ n [F macrocosme, fr. ML macrocosmos, fr. L macr- + Gk kosmos order, universe] (1600) **1** : the great

---

\ə\ abut \ᵊ\ kitten, F table \ər\ further \a\ ash \ā\ ace \ä\ mop, mar \aú\ out \ch\ chin \e\ bet \ē\ easy \g\ go \i\ hit \ī\ ice \j\ job \ŋ\ sing \ō\ go \ò\ law \òi\ boy \th\ thin \t̲h̲\ the \ü\ loot \ù\ foot \y\ yet \zh\ vision \à, k̲, ⁿ, œ, œ̄, ᵫ, ᵬ, ᵊ\ see Guide to Pronunciation world : UNIVERSE **2** : a complex that is a large-scale reproduction of one of its constituents — **mac·ro·cos·mic** \,ma-krə-'käz-mik\ adj — **mac·ro·cos·mi·cal·ly** \-mi-k(ə-)lē\ adv

mac·ro·cy·clic \,ma-krō-'si-klik, -'sī-\ adj (1936) : containing or being a chemical ring that consists usu. of 15 or more atoms

mac·ro·cyte \'ma-krə-,sīt\ n [ISV] (ca. 1889) : an exceptionally large red blood cell occurring chiefly in anemias — **mac·ro·cyt·ic** \,ma-krə-'si-tik\ adj

mac·ro·cy·to·sis \,ma-krə-si-'tō-səs, -krə-sə-\ n, pl **-to·ses** \-,sēz\ [NL] (ca. 1893) : the occurrence of macrocytes in the blood

mac·ro·eco·nom·ics \'ma-krō-,e-kə-'nä-miks, -,ē-kə-\ n pl but usu sing in constr (1948) : a study of economics in terms of whole systems esp. with reference to general levels of output and income and to the interrelations among sectors of the economy — compare MICROECONOMICS — **mac·ro·eco·nom·ic** \-mik\ adj

mac·ro·evo·lu·tion \,ma-krō-,e-və-'lü-shən also -,ē-və-\ n (1939) : evolution that results in relatively large and complex changes (as in species formation) — **mac·ro·evo·lu·tion·ary** \-shə-,ner-ē\ adj

mac·ro·fos·sil \'ma-krō-,fä-səl\ n (1937) : a fossil large enough to be observed by direct inspection

mac·ro·ga·mete \,ma-krō-'ga-,mēt also -gə-'mēt\ n [ISV] (1899) : the larger and usu. female gamete of a heterogamous organism

mac·ro·glob·u·lin \,ma-krō-'glä-byə-lən\ n [ISV] (1952) : a highly polymerized globulin (as IgM) of high molecular weight

mac·ro·glob·u·li·ne·mia \-,glä-byə-lə-'nē-mē-ə\ n [NL] (1949) : a disorder characterized by increased blood serum viscosity and the presence of macroglobulins in the serum — **mac·ro·glob·u·li·ne·mic** \-mik\ adj

mac·ro·in·struc·tion \,ma-krō-in-'strək-shən\ n (1959) : MACRO

macro lens n [macr-, fr. the fact that the focal length is greater than normal] (1961) : a camera lens designed to focus at very short distances with up to life-size magnification of the image

mac·ro·lep·i·dop·tera \'ma-krō-,le-pə-'däp-tə-rə\ n pl [NL] (1882) : lepidoptera (as butterflies, skippers, saturniids, noctuids, and geometrids) that include most of the large forms and none of the minute ones

mac·ro·mere \'ma-krə-,mir\ n (1877) : a large blastomere — see BLASTULA illustration

mac·ro·mol·e·cule \,ma-krō-'mä-li-,kyü(ə)l\ n [ISV] (ca. 1929) : a very large molecule (as of a protein or rubber) — **mac·ro·mo·lec·u·lar** \-mə-'le-kyə-lər\ adj

ma·cron \'mā-,krän, 'ma-, -krən\ n [Gk makron, neut. of makros long] (1851) : a mark ¯ placed over a vowel to indicate that the vowel is long or placed over a syllable or used alone to indicate a stressed or long syllable in a metrical foot

mac·ro·nu·cle·us \,ma-krō-'nü-klē-əs, -'nyü-\ n [NL] (1892) : a relatively large densely staining nucleus of most ciliate protozoans that is derived from micronuclei and controls various nonreproductive functions — **mac·ro·nu·cle·ar** \,mak-rō-'nü-klē-ər, -'nyü-, ÷-kyə-lər\ adj

mac·ro·nu·tri·ent \-'nü-trē-ənt, -'nyü-\ n (1942) : a chemical element (as nitrogen, phosphorus, or potassium) of which relatively large quantities are essential to the growth and health of a plant

mac·ro·phage \'ma-krə-,fāj\ n [ISV] (1890) : a phagocytic tissue cell of the reticuloendothelial system that may be fixed or freely motile, is derived from a monocyte, and functions in the protection of the body against infection and noxious substances — called also histiocyte — **mac·ro·phag·ic** \,ma-krə-'fa-jik\ adj

mac·ro·pho·tog·ra·phy \,ma-krō-fə-'tä-grə-fē\ n (1889) : the making of photographs in which the object is either unmagnified or slightly magnified up to a limit often of about 10 diameters — **mac·ro·pho·to·graph** \-'fō-tə-,graf\ n

mac·ro·phyte \'ma-krə-,fīt\ n (ca. 1909) : a member of the macroscopic plant life esp. of a body of water — **mac·ro·phyt·ic** \,ma-krə-'fi-tik\ adj

mac·rop·ter·ous \ma-'kräp-tə-rəs\ adj [Gk makropteros, fr. makr- + pteron wing — more at FEATHER] (ca. 1836) : having long or large wings

mac·ro·scale \'ma-krō-,skāl\ n (1931) : a large often macroscopic scale

mac·ro·scop·ic \,ma-krə-'skä-pik\ adj [ISV macr- + -scopic (as in microscopic)] (1872) **1** : large enough to be observed by the naked eye **2** : considered in terms of large units or elements — **mac·ro·scop·i·cal·ly** \-pi-k(ə-)lē\ adv

mac·ro·struc·ture \'ma-krō-,strək-chər\ n (ca. 1899) : the structure (as of metal, a body part, or the soil) revealed by visual examination with little or no magnification — **mac·ro·struc·tur·al** \,ma-krō-'strək-chə-rəl, 'strək-shə-rəl\ adj

mac·u·la \'ma-kyə-lə\ n, pl **-lae** \-,lē, -,lī\ also **-las** [ME, fr. L] (14c) **1** : SPOT, BLOTCH; esp : MACULE **2** : an anatomical structure (as the macula lutea) having the form of a spot differentiated from surrounding tissues — **mac·u·lar** \-lər\ adj

macula lu·tea \-'lü-tē-ə\ n, pl **maculae lu·te·ae** \-tē-,ē, -tē-,ī\ [NL, lit., yellow spot] (1848) : a small yellowish area lying slightly lateral to the center of the retina that constitutes the region of maximum visual acuity — called also yellow spot

mac·u·late \'ma-kyə-lət\ or **mac·u·lat·ed** \-,lā-təd\ adj [L maculatus, pp. of maculare to stain, fr. macula] (15c) **1** : marked with spots : BLOTCHED **2** : IMPURE, BESMIRCHED

mac·u·la·tion \,ma-kyə-'lā-shən\ n (15c) **1** archaic : the state of being spotted **2 a** : a blemish in the form of a discrete spot (acne scars and ~s) **b** : the arrangement of spots and markings on an animal or plant

mac·ule \'ma-(,)kyü(ə)l\ n [F, fr. L macula] (1863) : a patch of skin that is altered in color but usu. not elevated and that is a characteristic feature of various diseases (as smallpox)

ma·cum·ba \mə-'küm-bə\ n [BrazPg] (1939) : a polytheistic religion of African origin involving syncretistic elements and practiced mainly by Brazilian blacks in urban areas

¹mad \'mad\ adj **mad·der; mad·dest** [ME medd, madd, fr. OE gemæd, pp. of (assumed) gemædan to madden, fr. gemād silly, mad; akin to OHG gimeit foolish, crazy] (bef. 12c) **1** : disordered in mind : INSANE **2 a** : completely unrestrained by reason and judgment (driven ~ by the pain) **b** : incapable of being explained or accounted for (a ~ decision) **3** : carried away by intense anger : FURIOUS (~ at myself) (~ about the delay) **4** : carried away by enthusiasm or desire (~ about horses) (~ for the boy next door) **5** : affected with rabies : RABID **6** : marked by wild gaiety and merriment : HILARIOUS **7** : intensely

excited : FRANTIC (~ with jealousy) **8** : marked by intense and often chaotic activity : WILD (a ~ scramble) — **mad·dish** \'ma-dish\ adj

²mad vb **mad·ded; mad·ding** (14c) : MADDEN

³mad n (1834) **1** : a fit or mood of bad temper **2** : ANGER, FURY

Mad·a·gas·car periwinkle \,ma-də-'gas-kər-\ n [Madagascar, Africa] (1821) : ¹PERIWINKLE 1b

mad·am \'ma-dəm\ n, pl **madams** [ME, fr. MF ma dame, lit., my lady] (14c) **1** pl **mes·dames** \mā-'däm, -'dam\ : LADY — used without a name as a form of respectful or polite address to a woman **2** : MISTRESS — used as a title formerly with the given name but now with the surname or esp. with a designation of rank or office (Madam Chairman) (Madam President) **3** : the female head of a house of prostitution **4** : the female head of a household : WIFE

ma·dame \mə-'dam, ma-', before a surname also 'ma-dəm\ n [F, fr. OF ma dame] (1674) **1** pl **mes·dames** \mā-'däm, -'dam\ — used as a title equivalent to Mrs. for a married woman not of English-speaking nationality **2** pl **madames** : MADAM 3

mad–brained \'mad-'brānd\ adj (1562) : RASH, HOTHEADED

mad·cap \'mad-,kap\ adj (1588) : marked by capriciousness, recklessness, or foolishness — **madcap** n

mad·den \'ma-dⁿn\ vb **mad·dened; mad·den·ing** \'mad-niŋ, 'ma-dⁿn-iŋ\ vi (1735) : to become or act as if mad ~ vt **1** : to drive mad : CRAZE **2** : to make intensely angry : ENRAGE

maddening adj (1822) **1** : tending to craze **2 a** : tending to infuriate **b** : tending to vex : IRRITATING — **mad·den·ing·ly** \-lē\ adv

mad·der \'ma-dər\ n [ME, fr. OE mæddre; akin to OHG matara madder] (bef. 12c) **1** : a Eurasian herb (Rubia tinctorum of the family Rubiaceae, the madder family) with whorled leaves and small yellowish panicled flowers succeeded by berries; broadly : any of several related herbs (genus Rubia) **2 a** : the root of the Eurasian madder used formerly in dyeing; also : an alizarin dye prepared from it **b** : a moderate to strong red

mad·ding \'ma-diŋ\ adj (1579) : acting in a frenzied manner (the ~ crowd)

made \'mād\ adj [ME, fr. pp. of maken to make] (14c) **1 a** : FICTITIOUS, INVENTED (a ~ excuse) **b** : artificially produced (a ~ dish) **c** : put together of various ingredients (a ~ dish) **2** : assured of success (a ~ man) — usu. used in the phrase have it made

Ma·dei·ra \mə-'dir-ə, -'der-\ n [Pg, fr. Madeira Islands] (1596) : an amber-colored fortified wine from Madeira; also : a similar wine made elsewhere

mad·e·leine \'ma-dⁿl-ən, ,ma-dⁿl-'ān\ n [F, perh. fr. Madeleine Paumier, 19th cent. Fr. pastry cook] (1845) **1** : a small rich shell-shaped cake **2** : one that evokes a memory

ma·de·moi·selle \,mad-mwə-'zel, ,ma-də-, -mə-'zel, sometimes mam-'zel\ n, pl **ma·de·moi·selles** \-'zelz\ or **mes·de·moi·selles** \,mād-mwə-'zel, ,mä-də-, -mə-'zel\ [ME madamoiselle, fr. MF, fr. OF ma damoisele, lit., my (young) lady] (15c) **1** : an unmarried French girl or woman — used as a title equivalent to Miss for an unmarried woman not of English-speaking nationality **2** : a French governess **3** : SILVER PERCH a

made–to–order adj (ca. 1908) **1** : produced to supply a special or an individual demand : CUSTOM-MADE **2** : ideally suited (as to a particular purpose) (a ground ball ~ for a double play)

made–up \'mā-'dəp\ adj (1607) **1** : fancifully conceived or falsely devised **2** : fully manufactured **3** : marked by the use of makeup

mad·house \'mad-,haůs\ n (1687) **1** : a place where insane persons are detained and treated **2** : a place of uproar or confusion

Mad·i·son Avenue \'ma-də-sən-\ n [Madison Avenue, New York City, former center of the American advertising business] (1952) : the American advertising industry

mad·ly \'mad-lē\ adv (13c) **1** : in a mad manner **2** : to an extreme or excessive degree (~ in love)

mad·man \'mad-,man, -mən\ n (14c) : a man who is or acts as if insane

mad money n (1922) : money that a woman carries to pay her fare home in case a date ends in a quarrel; also : money set aside for an emergency or personal use

mad·ness \'mad-nəs\ n (14c) **1** : the quality or state of being mad: as **a** : RAGE **b** : INSANITY **c** : extreme folly **d** : ECSTASY, ENTHUSIASM **2** : any of several ailments of animals marked by frenzied behavior; specif : RABIES

Ma·don·na \mə-'dä-nə\ n [It, fr. OIt ma donna, lit., my lady] (1584) **1** archaic : LADY — used as a form of respectful address **2** obs : an Italian lady **3 a** : VIRGIN MARY **b** : an artistic depiction (as a painting or statue) of the Virgin Mary

Madonna lily n (1877) : a widely cultivated lily (Lilium candidum) with bell-shaped to broad funnel-shaped white flowers

ma·dras \'ma-drəs; mə-'dras, -'dras; -'dräs\ n [Madras, India] (ca. 1830) **1** : a large silk or cotton kerchief usu. of bright colors that is often worn as a turban **2 a** : a fine plain-woven shirting and dress fabric usu. of cotton with varied designs (as plaid) in bright colors or in white **b** : a light open usu. cotton fabric with a heavy design used for curtains

mad·re·pore \'ma-drə-,pōr, -,pȯr\ n [F madrépore, fr. It madrepora, fr. madre mother (fr. L mater) + poro pore (fr. L porus) — more at MOTHER] (1751) : any of various stony reef-building corals (order Madreporaria) of tropical seas that assume a variety of branching, encrusting, or massive forms — **mad·re·po·ri·an** \,ma-drə-'pōr-ē-ən, -'pȯr-\ adj or n — **mad·re·por·ic** \-'pȯr-ik, -'pȯr-\ adj

mad·re·por·ite \'ma-drə-,pōr-,īt, -,pȯr-\ n [ISV madrepore + ¹-ite (segment); fr. the resemblances of the perforations to those of a madrepore] (1877) : a perforated or porous body that is situated at the distal end of the stone canal in echinoderms

mad·ri·gal \'ma-dri-gəl\ n [It madrigale, prob. fr. ML matricale, fr. neut. of (assumed) matricalis simple, fr. LL, of the womb, fr. L matric-, matrix womb, fr. mater mother] (1588) **1** : a medieval short lyrical poem in a strict poetic form **2 a** : a complex polyphonic unaccompanied vocal piece on a secular text developed esp. in the 16th and 17th centuries **b** : PART-SONG; esp : GLEE — **mad·ri·gal·ian** \,ma-drə-'ga-lē-ən, -'gä-\ adj — **mad·ri·gal·ist** \'ma-dri-gə-list\ n

ma·dri·lene \,ma-drə-'len, -'lān\ n [F (consommé) madrilène, lit., Madrid consommé] (1907) : a consommé flavored with tomato

ma·dro·na or **ma·dro·ne** or **ma·dro·no** \mə-'drō-nə\ n [Sp madroño] (1841) : any of several evergreen trees (genus Arbutus) of the heath family; *esp* : one (*A. menziesii*) of the Pacific coast of No. America with smooth bark, thick shining leaves, and edible red berries

ma·du·ro \mə-'du̇r-(ˌ)ō\ *n, pl* **-ros** [Sp, fr. *maduro* ripe, fr. L *maturus* — more at MATURE] (1850) : a dark-colored relatively strong cigar

mad·wom·an \'mad-ˌwu̇-mən\ *n* (15c) : a woman who is or acts as if insane

mad·wort \-ˌwərt, -ˌwȯrt\ *n* (1597) **1** : ALYSSUM 1 **2** : a low hairy annual herb (*Asperugo procumbens*) of the borage family with blue flowers and a root used as a substitute for madder

Mae·ce·nas \mi-'sē-nəs\ *n* [L, fr. Gaius *Maecenas* †8 B.C. Roman statesman & patron of literature] (1542) : a generous patron esp. of literature or art

mael·strom \'mā(ə)l-strəm, -ˌsträm\ *n* [obs. D (now *maalstroom*), fr. *malen* to grind + *strom* stream] (1682) **1** : a powerful often violent whirlpool sucking in objects within a given radius **2** : something resembling a maelstrom in turbulence

mae·nad \'mē-ˌnad\ *n* [L *maenad-, maenas*, fr. Gk *mainad-, mainas*, fr. *mainesthai* to be mad; akin to Gk *menos* spirit — more at MIND] (1579) **1** : a woman participant in orgiastic Dionysian rites : BACCHANTE **2** : an unnaturally excited or distraught woman — **mae·nad·ic** \mē-'na-dik\ *adj*

mae·sto·so \mī-'stō-(ˌ)sō, -(ˌ)zō\ *adj or adv* [It, fr. L *majestosus*, fr. *majestas* majesty] (ca. 1724) : majestic and stately — used as a direction in music

mae·stro \'mī-(ˌ)strō\ *n, pl* **maestros** *or* **mae·stri** \-ˌstrē\ [It, lit., master, fr. L *magister* — more at MASTER] (1724) : a master usu. in an art; *esp* : an eminent composer, conductor, or teacher of music

Mae West \ˌmā-'west\ *n* [*Mae West* †1980 Am. actress noted for her full figure] (1940) : an inflatable life jacket in the form of a collar extending down the chest that was worn by fliers in World War II

maf·fick \'ma-fik\ *vi* [back-formation fr. *Mafeking Night*, English celebration of the lifting of the siege of Mafeking, So. Africa, May 17, 1900] (1900) : to celebrate with boisterous rejoicing and hilarious behavior

Ma·fia \'mä-fē-ə, 'ma-\ *n* [*Mafia, Maffia*, a Sicilian secret criminal society, fr. It dial. (Sicily)] (1875) **1 a** : a secret criminal society of Sicily or Italy **b** : a similarly conceived criminal organization in the U.S.; *also* : a similar organization elsewhere ⟨the Japanese ∼⟩ **c** : a criminal organization associated with a particular traffic ⟨the cocaine ∼⟩ **2** *often not cap* : a group of people likened to the Mafia; *esp* : a group of people of similar interests or backgrounds prominent in a particular field or enterprise : CLIQUE

maf·ic \'ma-fik\ *adj* [NL *magnesium* + L *ferrum* iron + E *-ic*] (1912) : of, relating to, or being a group of usu. dark-colored minerals rich in magnesium and iron

ma·fi·o·so \ˌmä-fē-'ō-(ˌ)sō, ˌma-, -(ˌ)zō\ *n, pl* **-si** \-(ˌ)sē, -(ˌ)zē\ [It, fr. *Mafia*] (1875) : a member of the Mafia or a mafia

mag \'mag\ *n* (1796) : MAGAZINE

mag·a·zine \'ma-gə-ˌzēn, ˌma-gə-'\ *n* [MF, fr. OProv. fr. Ar *makhāzin*, pl. of *makhzan* storehouse] (1583) **1** : a place where goods or supplies are stored : WAREHOUSE **2** : a room in which powder and other explosives are kept in a fort or a ship **3** : the contents of a magazine: as **a** : an accumulation of munitions of war **b** : a stock of provisions or goods **4 a** : a periodical containing miscellaneous pieces (as articles, stories, poems) often illustrated **b** : a similar section of a newspaper usu. appearing on Sunday **c** : a radio or television program presenting usu. several short segments on a variety of topics **5** : a supply chamber: as **a** : a holder in or on a gun for cartridges to be fed into the gun chamber **b** : a lightproof chamber for films or plates on a camera or for film on a motion-picture projector

mag·a·zin·ist \-ˌzē-nist, -'zē-\ *n* (1821) : a person who writes for or edits a magazine

mag·da·len \'mag-də-lən\ *n, often cap* [Mary *Magdalen* or *Magdalene* woman healed by Jesus of evil spirits (Lk 8:2), considered identical with a reformed prostitute (Lk 7:36–50)] (1697) **1** : a reformed prostitute **2** : a house of refuge or reformatory for prostitutes

Mag·da·le·ni·an \ˌmag-də-'lē-nē-ən\ *adj* [F *magdalénien*, fr. *La Madeleine*, rock shelter in southwest France] (1885) : of or relating to an Upper Paleolithic culture characterized by flint, bone, and ivory implements, carving, and paintings

mage \'māj\ *n* [ME, fr. L *magus*] (14c) : MAGUS

Mag·el·lan·ic Cloud \ˌma-jə-'la-nik-, *chiefly Brit* ˌma-gə-\ *n* [Ferdinand *Magellan*] (ca. 1686) : either of the two small galaxies that appear as conspicuous patches of light near the south celestial pole and are companions to the Milky Way galaxy

Ma·gen Da·vid \ˌmȯ-gən-'dȯ-vid, -'da-; 'mȯ-gən-'dä-vəd\ *n* [Heb *māghēn Dāwidh*, lit., shield of David] (ca. 1904) : a hexagram used as a symbol of Judaism

ma·gen·ta \mə-'jen-tə\ *n* [*Magenta*, Italy] (1860) **1** : FUCHSIN **2** : a deep purplish red

mag·got \'ma-gət\ *n* [ME *mathek, magotte*, of Scand origin; akin to ON *mathkr* maggot; akin to OE *matha* maggot] (14c) **1** : a soft-bodied legless grub that is the larva of a dipterous insect (as the housefly) **2** : a fantastic or eccentric idea : WHIM — **mag·goty** \-gə-tē\ *adj*

magi *pl of* MAGUS

¹Ma·gi·an \'mä-jē-ən\ *n* (1578) : MAGUS

²Ma·gi·an \-ən, -ji-\ *adj* (1716) : of or relating to the Magi — **Ma·gi·an·ism** \-ə-ˌni-zəm\ *n*

¹mag·ic \'ma-jik\ *n* [ME *magique*, fr. MF, fr. L *magice*, fr. Gk *magikē*, fem. of *magikos* Magian, magical, fr. *magos* sorcerer, magician, of Iranian origin; akin to OPer *maguš* sorcerer] (14c) **1 a** : the use of means (as charms or spells) believed to have supernatural power over natural forces **b** : magic rites or incantations **2 a** : an extraordinary power or influence seemingly from a supernatural source **b** : something that seems to cast a spell : ENCHANTMENT **3** : the art of producing illusions by sleight of hand

²magic *adj* (14c) **1** : of or relating to magic **2 a** : having seemingly supernatural qualities or powers **b** : giving a feeling of enchantment — **mag·i·cal** \'ma-ji-kəl\ *adj* — **mag·i·cal·ly** \-k(ə-)lē\ *adv*

³magic *vt* **mag·icked; mag·ick·ing** (1906) : to produce, remove, or influence by magic

magic bullet *n* (1940) : a substance or therapy capable of destroying pathogens (as bacteria or cancer cells) without undesirable side effects

ma·gi·cian \mə-'ji-shən\ *n* (14c) **1** : one skilled in magic; *esp* : SORCERER **2** : one who performs tricks of illusion and sleight of hand

magic lantern *n* (1696) : an early form of optical projector of still pictures using a transparent slide

Magic Marker *trademark* — used for a felt-tipped pen

magic realism *n* (1954) : painting in a meticulously realistic style of imaginary or fantastic scenes or images — **magic realist** *n*

magic square *n* (ca. 1704) : a square containing a number of integers arranged so that the sum of the numbers is the same in each row, column, and main diagonal and often in some or all of the other diagonals

magic squares

Ma·gi·not Line \'ma-zhə-ˌnō-, 'ma-jə-\ *n* [André *Maginot* †1932 Fr. minister of war] (1936) : a line of defensive fortifications built before World War II to protect the eastern border of France but easily outflanked by German invaders

mag·is·te·ri·al \ˌma-jə-'stir-ē-əl\ *adj* [LL *magisterialis* of authority, fr. *magisterium* office of a master, fr. *magister*] (1632) **1 a** (1) : of, relating to, or having the characteristics of a master or teacher : AUTHORITATIVE (2) : marked by an overbearingly dignified or assured manner or aspect **b** : of, relating to, or required for a master's degree **2** : of or relating to a magistrate or a magistrate's office or duties *syn* see DICTATORIAL — **mag·is·te·ri·al·ly** \-ē-ə-lē\ *adv*

mag·is·te·ri·um \ˌma-jə-'stir-ē-əm\ *n* [L] (1866) : teaching authority esp. of the Roman Catholic Church

mag·is·tra·cy \'ma-jə-strə-sē\ *n, pl* **-cies** (ca. 1585) **1** : the state of being a magistrate **2** : the office, power, or dignity of a magistrate **3** : a body of magistrates **4** : the district under a magistrate

mag·is·tral \'ma-jə-strəl, mə-'jis-trəl\ *adj* [LL *magistralis*, fr. L *magistr-, magister*] (1605) : MAGISTERIAL 1a — **ma·gis·tral·ly** \-ē\ *adv*

mag·is·trate \'ma-jə-ˌstrāt, -strət\ *n* [ME *magestrat*, fr. L *magistratus* magistracy, magistrate, fr. *magistr-, magister* master, political superior — more at MASTER] (14c) : an official entrusted with administration of the laws: as **a** : a principal official exercising governmental powers over a major political unit (as a nation) **b** : a local official exercising administrative and often judicial functions **c** : a local judiciary official having limited original jurisdiction esp. in criminal cases — **mag·is·trat·i·cal** \ˌma-jə-'stra-ti-kəl\ *adj* — **mag·is·trat·i·cal·ly** \-k(ə-)lē\ *adv*

magistrate's court *n* (1867) **1** : POLICE COURT **2** : a court that has minor civil and criminal jurisdiction

mag·is·tra·ture \'ma-jə-ˌstrā-chər, -strə-ˌchu̇r\ *n* (1672) : MAGISTRACY

mag·lev \'mag-lev\ *n, often attrib* [*magnetic levitation*] (1969) **1** : the use of the physical properties of magnetic fields generated by superconducting magnets to cause an object (as a vehicle) to float above a solid surface **2** : a train utilizing maglev technology

mag·ma \'mag-mə\ *n* [ME, fr. L *magmat-, magma*, fr. Gk, thick unguent, fr. *massein* to knead — more at MINGLE] (15c) **1** *archaic* : DREGS, SEDIMENT **2** : a thin pasty suspension (as of a precipitate in water) **3** : molten rock material within the earth from which igneous rock results by cooling — **mag·mat·ic** \mag-'ma-tik\ *adj*

Mag·na Car·ta *or* **Mag·na Char·ta** \'mag-nə-'kär-tə\ *n* [ME, fr. ML, lit., great charter] (15c) **1** : a charter of liberties to which the English barons forced King John to give his assent in June 1215 at Runnymede **2** : a document constituting a fundamental guarantee of rights and privileges

mag·na cum lau·de \ˌmäg-nə-(ˌ)ku̇m-'lau̇-də, -'lau̇-dē; 'mag-nə-ˌkəm-'lȯ-dē\ *adv or adj* [L] (1900) : with great distinction ⟨graduated *magna cum laude*⟩ — compare CUM LAUDE, SUMMA CUM LAUDE

mag·na·nim·i·ty \ˌmag-nə-'ni-mə-tē\ *n, pl* **-ties** (14c) **1** : the quality of being magnanimous : loftiness of spirit enabling one to bear trouble calmly, to disdain meanness and pettiness, and to display a noble generosity **2** : a magnanimous act

mag·nan·i·mous \mag-'na-nə-məs\ *adj* [L *magnanimus*, fr. *magnus* great + *animus* spirit — more at MUCH, ANIMATE] (1584) **1** : showing or suggesting a lofty and courageous spirit ⟨the irreproachable lives and ∼ sufferings of their followers —Joseph Addison⟩ **2** : showing or suggesting nobility of feeling and generosity of mind ⟨too sincere for dissimulation, too ∼ for resentment —Ellen Glasgow⟩ — **mag·nan·i·mous·ly** *adv* — **mag·nan·i·mous·ness** *n*

mag·nate \'mag-ˌnāt, -nət\ *n* [ME *magnates*, pl., fr. LL, fr. L *magnus*] (15c) : a person of rank, power, influence, or distinction often in a specified area

mag·ne·sia \mag-'nē-shə, -zhə\ *n* [NL, fr. *magnes carneus*, a white earth, lit., flesh magnet] (1755) : MAGNESIUM OXIDE — compare MILK OF MAGNESIA — **mag·ne·sian** \-shən, -zhən\ *adj*

mag·ne·site \'mag-nə-ˌsīt\ *n* (1815) : native magnesium carbonate used esp. in making refractories and magnesium oxide

mag·ne·sium \mag-'nē-zē-əm, -zhəm\ *n* [NL, fr. *magnesia*] (1812) : a silver-white light malleable ductile metallic element that occurs abundantly in nature and is used in metallurgical and chemical processes, in photography, signaling, and pyrotechnics because of the intense white light it produces on burning, and in construction esp. in the form of light alloys — see ELEMENT table

magnesium carbonate *n* (1903) : a carbonate of magnesium; *esp* : a white crystalline salt $MgCO_3$ that occurs naturally as dolomite and magnesite

magnesium chloride *n* (ca. 1910) : a bitter deliquescent salt $MgCl_2$ used esp. as a source of magnesium metal

magnesium hydroxide *n* (ca. 1909) : a slightly alkaline crystalline compound $Mg(OH)_2$ used esp. as a laxative and gastric antacid

---

\ə\ abut \ᵊ\ kitten, F table \ər\ further \a\ ash \ā\ ace \ä\ mop, mar
\au̇\ out \ch\ chin \e\ bet \ē\ easy \g\ go \i\ hit \ī\ ice \j\ job
\ŋ\ sing \ō\ go \ȯ\ law \ȯi\ boy \th\ thin \th̲\ the \ü\ loot \u̇\ foot
\y\ yet \zh\ vision \à, k̲, ⁿ, œ, œ̄, ue, ūe, ʸ\ *see* Guide to Pronunciation

magnesium oxide *n* (ca. 1909) : a white highly infusible compound MgO used esp. in refractories, cements, insulation, and fertilizers, in rubber manufacture, and in medicine as an antacid and mild laxative

magnesium sulfate *n* (ca. 1890) : a sulfate of magnesium: as **a** : a white salt MgSO₄ used in medicine and in industry   **b** : EPSOM SALTS

mag·net \'mag-nət\ *n* [ME *magnete*, fr. MF, fr. L *magnet-, magnes*, fr. Gk *magnēs* (*lithos*), lit., stone of Magnesia, ancient city in Asia Minor] (15c) **1 a** : LODESTONE   **b** : a body having the property of attracting iron and producing a magnetic field external to itself; *specif* : a mass of iron, steel, or alloy that has this property artificially imparted **2** : something that attracts ⟨a box-office ∼⟩

magnet- *or* **magneto-** *comb form* [L *magnet-, magnes*] **1** : magnetic force ⟨*magneto*meter⟩   **2** : magnetism : magnetic ⟨*magneto*electric⟩ ⟨*magneto*n⟩   **3** : magnetoelectric ⟨*magneto*resistance⟩   **4** : magnetosphere ⟨*magneto*pause⟩

¹mag·net·ic \mag-'ne-tik\ *adj* (1611) **1** : possessing an extraordinary power or ability to attract ⟨a ∼ personality⟩ **2 a** : of or relating to a magnet or to magnetism   **b** : of, relating to, or characterized by the earth's magnetism   **c** : magnetized or capable of being magnetized   **d** : actuated by magnetic attraction — **mag·net·i·cal·ly** \-ti-k(ə-)lē\ *adv*

²magnetic *n* (1654) : a magnetic substance

magnetic bubble *n* (1969) : a tiny movable magnetized cylindrical volume in a thin amorphous or crystalline magnetic material that along with other like volumes can be used to represent a bit of information (as in a computer)

magnetic disk *n* (ca. 1960) : DISK 4c

magnetic equator *n* (1832) : an imaginary line roughly parallel to the geographical equator and passing through those points where a magnetic needle has no dip

magnetic field *n* (1845) : the portion of space near a magnetic body or a current-carrying body in which the magnetic forces due to the body or current can be detected

magnetic flux *n* (1896) : lines of force used to represent magnetic induction

magnetic mirror *n* (1952) : a magnetic field that confines a plasma by reflecting ions of the plasma back toward the main plasma concentration

magnetic moment *n* (1865) : a vector quantity that is a measure of the torque exerted on a magnetic system (as a bar magnet or dipole) when placed in a magnetic field and that for a magnet is the product of the distance between its poles and the strength of either pole

magnetic north *n* (1812) : the northerly direction in the earth's magnetic field indicated by the north-seeking pole of a compass needle

magnetic pole *n* (1701) **1** : either of two small regions which are located respectively in the polar areas of the northern and southern hemispheres and toward which a compass needle points from any direction throughout adjacent regions; *also* : either of two comparable regions on a celestial body   **2** : either of the poles of a magnet

magnetic quantum number *n* (1923) : an integer that expresses the component of the quantized angular momentum of an electron, atom, or molecule in the direction of an externally applied magnetic field

magnetic recording *n* (1945) : the process of recording sound, data (as for a computer), or a television program by producing varying local magnetization of a moving tape or disc — **magnetic recorder** *n*

magnetic resonance *n* (1903) : the response of electrons, atoms, molecules, or nuclei to various discrete radiation frequencies as a result of space quantization in a magnetic field

magnetic resonance imaging *n* (1984) : a noninvasive diagnostic technique that produces computerized images of internal body tissues and is based on nuclear magnetic resonance of atoms within the body induced by the application of radio waves — *abbr* MRI

magnetic storm *n* (1860) : a marked temporary disturbance of the earth's magnetic field held to be related to sunspots

magnetic tape *n* (1937) : a thin ribbon (as of plastic) coated with a magnetic material on which information (as sound or television images) may be stored

mag·ne·tise *Brit var of* MAGNETIZE

mag·ne·tism \'mag-nə-ˌti-zəm\ *n* (1616) **1 a** : a class of physical phenomena that include the attraction for iron observed in lodestone and a magnet, are inseparably associated with moving electricity, are exhibited by both magnets and electric currents, and are characterized by fields of force   **b** : a science that deals with magnetic phenomena **2** : an ability to attract or charm

mag·ne·tite \'mag-nə-ˌtīt\ *n* (1851) : a black isometric mineral of the spinel group that is an oxide of iron and an important iron ore

mag·ne·ti·za·tion \ˌmag-nə-tə-'zā-shən\ *n* (1801) : an instance of magnetizing or the state of being magnetized; *also* : the degree to which a body is magnetized

mag·ne·tize \'mag-nə-ˌtīz\ *vt* **-tized; -tiz·ing** (1801) **1** : to induce magnetic properties in **2** : to attract like a magnet : CHARM — **mag·ne·tiz·able** \-ˌtī-zə-bəl\ *adj* — **mag·ne·tiz·er** *n*

mag·ne·to \mag-'nē-(ˌ)tō\ *n, pl* **-tos** (1882) : a magnetoelectric machine; *esp* : an alternator with permanent magnets used to generate current for the ignition in an internal-combustion engine

mag·ne·to·elec·tric \-ˌnē-tō-ə-'lek-trik, -ˌne-\ *adj* (1831) : relating to or characterized by electromotive forces developed by magnetic means

mag·ne·to·flu·id·dy·nam·ics \-ˌnē-tō-ˌflü-ə-dī-'na-miks, -ˌne-, -də-'-\ *n pl but sing or pl in constr* (1962) : the study of magnetohydrodynamic phenomena

mag·ne·to·graph \-ˌgraf\ *n* (1847) : an automatic instrument for recording measurements of a magnetic field (as of the earth or the sun)

mag·ne·to·hy·dro·dy·nam·ic \ˌmag-ˌnē-tō-ˌhī-drə-dī-'na-mik, -'ne-, -də-'-\ *adj* (1943) : of, relating to, or being phenomena arising from the motion of electrically conducting fluids (as plasmas) in the presence of electric and magnetic fields — **mag·ne·to·hy·dro·dy·nam·ics** \-miks\ *n pl but sing or pl in constr*

mag·ne·tom·e·ter \ˌmag-nə-'tä-mə-tər\ *n* (1827) : an instrument used to detect the presence of a metallic object or to measure the intensity of a magnetic field — **mag·ne·to·met·ric** \ˌmag-ˌnē-tə-'me-trik, -ˌne-\ *adj* — **mag·ne·tom·e·try** \ˌmag-nə-'tä-mə-trē\ *n*

mag·ne·to·mo·tive force \mag-ˌnē-tə-'mō-tiv-, -ˌne-\ *n* (1883) : a force that is the cause of a flux of magnetic induction

mag·ne·ton \'mag-nə-ˌtän\ *n* [ISV *magnet-* + ²-*on*] (1911) : a unit of the quantized magnetic moment of a particle (as an atom)

mag·ne·to·op·tic \ˌmag-ˌnē-tō-'äp-tik, -ˌne-\ *also* **mag·ne·to·op·ti·cal** \-ti-kəl\ *adj* (1848) : of or relating to the influence of a magnetic field upon light — **mag·ne·to·op·tics** \-tiks\ *n pl but sing or pl in constr*

mag·ne·to·pause \mag-'nē-tə-ˌpóz, -'ne-\ *n* (1962) : the outer boundary of a magnetosphere

mag·ne·to·re·sis·tance \-ˌnē-tō-ri-'zis-tən(t)s, -ˌne-\ *n* (1927) : a change in electrical resistance due to the presence of a magnetic field

mag·ne·to·sphere \mag-'nē-tə-ˌsfir, -'ne-\ *n* (1959) : a region of space surrounding a celestial object (as the earth or a star) that is dominated by the object's magnetic field so that charged particles are trapped in it — **mag·ne·to·spher·ic** \-ˌnē-tə-'sfir-ik, -'sfer-\ *adj*

mag·ne·to·stat·ic \mag-ˌnē-tō-'sta-tik, -ˌne-\ *adj* (1893) : of, relating to, or being a stationary magnetic field

mag·ne·to·stric·tion \-'strik-shən\ *n* [ISV *magnet-* + *-striction* (as in *constriction*)] (1896) : the change in the dimensions of a ferromagnetic body caused by a change in its state of magnetization — **mag·ne·to·stric·tive** \-'strik-tiv\ *adj* — **mag·ne·to·stric·tive·ly** *adv*

mag·ne·tron \'mag-nə-ˌträn\ *n* [blend of *magnet* and *-tron*] (1924) : a diode vacuum tube in which the flow of electrons is controlled by an externally applied magnetic field to generate power at microwave frequencies

magnet school *n* (1968) : a school with superior facilities and staff and specialized curricula designed to attract pupils from all segments of the community

mag·nif·ic \mag-'ni-fik\ *adj* [MF *magnifique*, fr. L *magnificus*] (15c) **1** : MAGNIFICENT 2   **2** : imposing in size or dignity **3 a** : SUBLIME, EXALTED   **b** : characterized by grandiloquence : POMPOUS ⟨commenced the conversation in the most ∼ style — S. T. Coleridge⟩ — **mag·nif·i·cal** \-fi-kəl\ *adj* — **mag·nif·i·cal·ly** \-k(ə-)lē\ *adv*

mag·nif·i·cat \mag-'ni-fi-ˌkat, -ˌkät; män-'yi-fi-ˌkät\ *n* [ME, fr. L, magnifies, fr. *magnificare* to magnify; fr. the first word of the canticle] (13c) **1** *cap* **a** : the canticle of the Virgin Mary in Luke 1:46–55   **b** : a musical setting for the Magnificat   **2** : an utterance of praise

mag·ni·fi·ca·tion \ˌmag-nə-fə-'kā-shən\ *n* (15c) **1** : the act of magnifying **2 a** : the state of being magnified   **b** : the apparent enlargement of an object by an optical instrument — called also *power*

mag·nif·i·cence \mag-'ni-fə-sən(t)s, məg-\ *n* [ME, fr. MF, fr. L *magnificentia*, fr. *magnificus* noble in character, magnificent, fr. *magnus* great — more at MUCH] (14c) **1** : the quality or state of being magnificent **2** : splendor of surroundings

mag·nif·i·cent \-sənt\ *adj* (15c) **1** : great in deed or exalted in place — used only of former famous rulers ⟨Lorenzo the M*a*gnificent⟩ **2** : marked by stately grandeur and lavishness ⟨a ∼ way of life⟩ **3** : sumptuous in structure and adornment ⟨a ∼ cathedral⟩; *broadly* : strikingly beautiful or impressive ⟨a ∼ physique⟩ **4** : impressive to the mind or spirit : SUBLIME ⟨∼ prose⟩ **5** : exceptionally fine ⟨a ∼ day⟩ *syn* see GRAND — **mag·nif·i·cent·ly** *adv*

mag·nif·i·co \mag-'ni-fi-ˌkō\ *n, pl* **-coes** *or* **-cos** [It, fr. *magnifico*, adj., magnificent, fr. L *magnificus*] (1573) **1** : a nobleman of Venice **2** : a person of high position

mag·ni·fi·er \'mag-nə-ˌfi(-ə)r\ *n* (1550) : one that magnifies; *esp* : a lens or combination of lenses that makes something appear larger

mag·ni·fy \'mag-nə-ˌfī\ *vb* **-fied; -fy·ing** [ME *magnifien*, fr. MF *magnifier*, fr. L *magnificare*, fr. *magnificus*] *vt* (14c) **1 a** : EXTOL, LAUD **b** : to cause to be held in greater esteem or respect **2 a** : to increase in significance : INTENSIFY   **b** : EXAGGERATE **3** : to enlarge in fact or in appearance ∼ *vi* : to have the power of causing objects to appear larger than they are

mag·nil·o·quence \mag-'ni-lə-kwən(t)s\ *n* [L *magniloquentia*, fr. *magniloquus* magniloquent, fr. *magnus* + *loqui* to speak] (ca. 1623) : the quality or state of being magniloquent

mag·nil·o·quent \-kwənt\ *adj* [back-formation fr. *magniloquence*] (ca. 1656) : speaking in or characterized by a high-flown often bombastic style or manner — **mag·nil·o·quent·ly** *adv*

mag·ni·tude \'mag-nə-ˌtüd, -ˌtyüd\ *n* [ME, fr. L *magnitudo*, fr. *magnus*] (15c) **1 a** : great size or extent   **b** (1) : spatial quality : SIZE (2) : QUANTITY, NUMBER **2** : the importance, quality, or caliber of something **3** : a number representing the intrinsic or apparent brightness of a celestial body on a logarithmic scale in which an increase of one unit corresponds to a reduction in the brightness of light by a factor of 2.512 **4** : a numerical quantitative measure expressed usu. as a multiple of a standard measure

mag·no·lia \mag-'nōl-yə\ *n* [NL, fr. Pierre *Magnol* †1715 Fr. botanist] (1748) : any of a genus (*Magnolia* of the family Magnoliaceae, the magnolia family) of American and Asian shrubs and trees with entire evergreen or deciduous leaves and usu. showy white, yellow, rose, or purple flowers usu. appearing in early spring

mag·num \'mag-nəm\ *n* [L, neut. of *magnus* great] (1788) : a large wine bottle holding about 1.5 liters

magnum opus \ˌmag-nəm-'ō-pəs\ *n* [L] (1791) : a. great work; *esp* : the greatest achievement of an artist or writer

¹mag·pie \'mag-ˌpī\ *n* [*Mag* (nickname for *Margaret*) + ¹*pie*] (1598) **1** : any of various birds (esp. *Pica pica*) related to the jays but having a long graduated tail and black-and-white or brightly colored plumage **2** : a person who chatters noisily **3** : one who collects indiscriminately

²magpie *adj* (1808) **1** : collected indiscriminately : MISCELLANEOUS ⟨∼ compilations of unrelated tidbits —Helen R. Cross⟩ **2** : given to indiscriminate collecting : ACQUISITIVE ⟨what possible ∼ instinct had impelled me to retain them —S. J. Perelman⟩

mag tape \'mag-\ *n* (1966) : MAGNETIC TAPE

ma·guey \mə-'gā\ *n* [Sp, fr. Taino] (1589) **1** : any of various fleshy-leaved agaves (as the century plant) **2** : any of several hard fibers derived from magueys; *esp* : CANTALA

ma·gus \'mä-gəs\ *n, pl* **ma·gi** \'mä-ˌjī\ [L, fr. Gk *magos* — more at MAGIC] (1621) **1 a** : a member of a hereditary priestly class among the ancient Medes and Persians   **b** *often cap* : one of the traditionally three wise men from the East paying homage to the infant Jesus **2** : MAGICIAN, SORCERER

Mag·yar \'mag-ˌyär, 'mäg-; 'mä-ˌjär\ *n* [Hung] (1797) **1** : a member of the dominant people of Hungary **2** : HUNGARIAN 2 — **Magyar** *adj*

ma·ha·ra·ja *or* **ma·ha·ra·jah** \ˌmä-hə-'rä-jə, -'rä-zhə\ *n* [Skt *mahārāja*, fr. *mahat* great + *rājan* raja; akin to L *rex* king — more at MUCH, ROYAL] (1698) : a Hindu prince ranking above a raja

ma·ha·ra·ni *or* **ma·ha·ra·nee** \,-'rä-nē\ *n* [Hindi *mahārānī*, fr. *mahā* great (fr. Skt *mahat*) + *rānī* rani] (ca. 1855) **1** : the wife of a maharaja **2** : a Hindu princess ranking above a rani

ma·ha·ri·shi \,mä-ə-'rē-shē, -hä-, -'ri-\ *n* [Skt *mahārṣi*, fr. *mahat* + *rṣi* sage and poet] (1785) : a Hindu teacher of mystical knowledge

ma·hat·ma \mə-'hät-mə, -'hat-\ *n* [Skt *mahātman*, fr. *mahātman* great=souled, fr. *mahat* + *ātman* soul — more at ATMAN] (1923) **1** : a person to be revered for high-mindedness, wisdom, and selflessness **2** : a person of great prestige in a field of endeavor

Ma·ha·ya·na \,mä-hə-'yä-nə\ *n* [Skt *mahāyāna*, lit., great vehicle] (1855) : a liberal and theistic branch of Buddhism comprising sects chiefly in China and Japan, recognizing a large body of scripture in addition to the Pali canon, and teaching social concern and universal salvation — compare THERAVADA — **Ma·ha·ya·nist** \-'yä-nist\ *n or adj* — **Ma·ha·ya·nis·tic** \-yä-'nis-tik\ *adj*

Mah·di \'mä-dē\ *n* [Ar *mahdīy*, lit., one rightly guided] (1800) **1** : the expected messiah of Muslim tradition **2** : a Muslim leader who assumes a messianic role — **Mah·dism** \'mä-,di-zəm\ *n* — **Mah·dist** \'mä-dist\ *n*

Ma·hi·can \mə-'hē-kən\ *n, pl* **Mahican** *or* **Mahicans** [Mahican] (ca. 1614) **1** : a member of an American Indian people of the upper Hudson River valley **2** : the extinct Algonquian language of the Mahican people

ma·hi·ma·hi \,mä-hē-'mä-(,)hē\ *n* [Hawaiian, Tahitian, & Marquesan] (1943) : the flesh of a dolphin (*Coryphaena hippurus*) used for food; *also* : the fish

mah-jongg *or* **mah-jong** \,mä-'zhäŋ, -'jäŋ, -'zhòŋ, -'jòŋ, 'mä-,\ *n* [fr. *Mah-Jongg*, a trademark] (1920) : a game of Chinese origin usu. played by four persons with 144 tiles that are drawn and discarded until one player secures a winning hand

mahl·stick \'mȯl-\ *var of* MAULSTICK

ma·hoe \mə-'hō, 'mä-,\ *n* [F *maho*, fr. Taino] (1666) : either of two tropical hibiscus trees (*Hibiscus elatus* and *H. tiliaceus*)

ma·hog·a·ny \mə-'hä-gə-nē\ *n, pl* **-nies** [origin unknown] (ca. 1660) **1** : the wood of any of various chiefly tropical trees (family Meliaceae, the mahogany family): **a** (1) : the durable yellowish brown to reddish brown usu. moderately hard and heavy wood of a West Indian tree (*Swietenia mahagoni*) that is widely used for cabinetwork and fine finish work (2) : a wood similar to mahogany from a congeneric tree (esp. *S. macrophylla*) **b** (1) : the rather hard heavy usu. odorless wood of any of several African trees (genus *Khaya*) (2) : the rather lightweight cedar-scented wood of any of several African trees (genus *Entandrophragma*) that varies in color from pinkish to deep reddish brown **2** : any of various woods resembling or substituted for mahogany obtained from trees of the mahogany family **3** : a tree that yields mahogany **4** : a moderate reddish brown

ma·ho·nia \mə-'hō-nē-ə\ *n* [NL, fr. Bernard McMahon †1816 Am. botanist] (1829) : any of a genus (*Mahonia*) of American and Asian shrubs (as the Oregon grape) of the barberry family

ma·hout \mə-'haȯt\ *n* [Hindi *mahāwat, mahāut*] (1662) : a keeper and driver of an elephant

Mah·rat·ta *var of* MARATHA

maid \'mād\ *n* [ME *maide*, short for *maiden*] (13c) **1** : an unmarried girl or woman esp. when young : VIRGIN **2 a** : MAIDSERVANT **b** : a woman or girl employed to do domestic work

¹maid·en \'mā-dᵊn\ *n* [ME, fr. OE *mægden, mæden*, dim. of *mægeth*; akin to OHG *magad* maiden, OIr *mug* serf] (bef. 12c) **1** : an unmarried girl or woman : MAID **2** : a former Scottish beheading device resembling the guillotine **3** : a horse that has never won a race

²maiden *adj* (14c) **1 a** (1) : not married ⟨~ aunt⟩ (2) : VIRGIN **b** *of a female animal* (1) : never yet mated (2) : never having borne young **2** : of, relating to, or befitting a maiden **3** : FIRST, EARLIEST ⟨~ voyage⟩ ⟨~ flight of a spacecraft⟩

maid·en·hair fern \-,har-, -,her-\ *n* (1833) : any of a genus (*Adiantum*) of ferns with delicate palmately branched fronds — called also *maidenhair*

maidenhair tree *n* (1773) : GINKGO

maid·en·head \'mā-dᵊn-,hed\ *n* [ME *maidenhed*, fr. *maiden* + *-hed* -hood; akin to ME *-hod* -hood] (13c) **1** : the quality or state of being a maiden : VIRGINITY **2** : HYMEN

maid·en·hood \-,hu̇d\ *n* (bef. 12c) : the quality, state, or time of being a maiden

maid·en·li·ness \-lē-nəs\ *n* (1555) : conduct or traits befitting a maiden

maid·en·ly \-lē\ *adj* (15c) : of, resembling, or suitable to a maiden

maiden name *n* (1689) : the surname of a woman before she marries

maid·hood \'mād-,hu̇d\ *n* (bef. 12c) : MAID-ENHOOD

maid–in–wait·ing \'mā-dᵊn-'wā-tiŋ\ *n, pl* **maids–in–wait·ing** \'mādz-\ (1953) : a young woman of a queen's or princess's household appointed to attend her

Maid Mar·i·an \-'mer-ē-ən, -'mar-\ *n* : a companion of Robin Hood in some forms of his legend

maid of honor (ca. 1586) **1** : an unmarried lady usu. of noble birth whose duty it is to attend a queen or a princess **2** : a bride's principal unmarried wedding attendant

maid·ser·vant \'mād-,sər-vənt\ *n* (14c) : a female servant

ma·ieu·tic \mā-'yü-tik, mī-\ *adj* [Gk *maieutikos* of midwifery] (1655) : relating to or resembling the Socratic method of eliciting new ideas from another

¹mail \'mā(ə)l\ *n* [ME *male, maille*, fr. OE *māl* agreement, pay, fr. ON *māl* speech, meeting; akin to OE *mǣl* speech] (bef. 12c) *chiefly Scot* : PAYMENT, RENT

²mail *n, often attrib* [ME *male*, fr. OF, of Gmc origin; akin to OHG *malaha* bag] (13c) **1** *chiefly Scot* : BAG, WALLET **2 a** : something sent or carried in the postal system **b** : a conveyance that transports mail **c** : messages sent electronically to an individual (as through a computer system) **3** : a nation's postal system — often used in pl.

³mail *vt* (1827) : to send by mail : POST — **mail·abil·i·ty** \,mā-lə-'bi-lə-tē\ *n* — **mail·able** \'mā-lə-bəl\ *adj*

⁴mail *n* [ME *maille*, fr. MF, fr. L *macula* spot, mesh] (14c) **1** : armor made of metal links or sometimes plates **2** : a hard enclosing covering of an animal (as a tortoise) — **mailed** \'mā(ə)ld\ *adj*

mail·bag \'mā(ə)l-,bag\ *n* (1812) **1** : a letter carrier's shoulder bag **2** : a pouch used in the shipment of mail

mail·box \-,bäks\ *n* (1872) **1** : a public box for deposit of outgoing mail **2** : a box at or near a dwelling for the occupant's mail **3** : a computer file in which electronic mail is collected

mail carrier *n* (1790) : LETTER CARRIER

mail drop *n* (1945) **1** : an address used in transmitting secret communications **2** : a receptacle or a slot for deposit of mail

mai·le \'mī-lē\ *n* [Hawaiian] (1903) : a Pacific island vine (*Alyxia olivaeformis*) of the dogbane family with fragrant leaves and bark that are used for decoration and in Hawaii for leis

mailed fist *n* (1897) : a threat of armed or overbearing force

mail·er \'mā-lər\ *n* (1884) **1** : one that mails **2** : a container for mailing something **3** : something (as an advertisement) sent by mail

Mail·gram \'māl-,gram\ *trademark* — used for a message sent by wire to a post office that delivers it to the addressee

mail·ing \'mā-liŋ\ *n* (1946) : the mail dispatched at one time by a sender

mail·lot \mī-'ō, mä-'yō\ *n* [F] (1888) **1** : tights for dancers or gymnasts **2** : JERSEY 2 **3** : a woman's one-piece bathing suit

mail·man \'mā(ə)l-,man\ *n* (1881) : a man who delivers mail — called also *postman*

mail order *n* (1867) : an order for goods that is received and filled by mail — **mail–or·der** \-,ȯr-dər\ *adj*

¹maim \'mām\ *vt* [ME *maynhen, maymen*, fr. OF *maynier* — more at MAYHEM] (14c) **1** : to commit the felony of mayhem upon **2** : to mutilate, disfigure, or wound seriously — **maim·er** *n*

syn MAIM, CRIPPLE, MUTILATE, BATTER, MANGLE mean to injure so severely as to cause lasting damage. MAIM implies the loss or injury of a bodily member through violence ⟨*maimed* by a shark⟩. CRIPPLE implies the loss or serious impairment of an arm or leg ⟨*crippled* for life in an accident⟩. MUTILATE implies the cutting off or removal of an essential part of a person or thing thereby impairing its completeness, beauty, or function ⟨a tree *mutilated* by inept pruning⟩. BATTER implies a series of blows that bruise deeply, deform, or mutilate ⟨an old ship *battered* by fierce storms⟩. MANGLE implies a tearing or crushing that leaves deep extensive wounds ⟨a soldier's leg *mangled* by shrapnel⟩.

²maim *n* (14c) **1** *obs* : serious physical injury; *esp* : loss of a member of the body **2** *obs* : a serious loss

¹main \'mān\ *n* [in sense 1, fr. ME, fr. OE *mægen* strength, OE *magan* to be able; in other senses, fr. ²main or by shortening — more at MAY] (bef. 12c) **1** : physical strength : FORCE — used in the phrase *with might and main* **2 a** : MAINLAND **b** : HIGH SEA **3** : the chief part : essential point (they are in the ~ well-trained) **4 a** : a pipe, duct, or circuit which carries the combined flow of tributary branches of a utility system **5 a** : MAINMAST **b** : MAINSAIL

²main *adj* [ME, fr. OE *mægen-*, fr. *mægen* strength] (15c) **1** : CHIEF, PRINCIPAL ⟨the ~ idea⟩ **2** : fully exerted : SHEER ⟨~ force⟩ ⟨by ~ strength⟩ **3** *obs* : of or relating to a broad expanse (as of sea) **4** : connected with or located near the mainmast or mainsail **5** : expressing the chief predication in a complex sentence ⟨the ~ clause⟩

main chance *n* (1584) : the best chance for personal or financial gain ⟨kept an eye on the *main chance*⟩

Maine coon *n* (1935) : any of a breed of large long-haired domestic cats that have a very full tapered tail — called also *coon cat, Maine cat*

main·frame \'mān-,frām\ *n* (ca. 1964) : a computer with its cabinet and internal circuits; *also* : a large fast computer that can handle multiple tasks concurrently

main·land \'mān-,land, -lənd\ *n* (14c) : a continent or the main part of a continent as distinguished from an offshore island or sometimes from a cape or peninsula — **main·land·er** \-,lan-dər, -lən-\ *n*

¹main·line \'mān-,līn\ *vt* (1938) *slang* : to take by or as if by injecting into a principal vein ~ *vi, slang* : to mainline a narcotic drug

Maine coon

²mainline *adj* (1941) : being part of an established group; *also* : being in the mainstream

main line *n* (1841) **1** : a principal highway or railroad line **2** *slang* : a principal vein of the circulatory system

main·ly \'mān-lē\ *adv* (13c) **1** *obs* : in a forceful manner **2** : for the most part : CHIEFLY

main man *n* (1967) **1** : best male friend **2** : a man whose character or work is most admired **3** : the most reliable or effective performer

main·mast \'mān-,mast, -məst\ *n* (15c) : a sailing ship's principal mast usu. second from the bow

mains \'mānz\ *adj* (ca. 1927) *Brit* : of or relating to utility distribution mains ⟨~ voltage⟩ ⟨~ water⟩

main·sail \'mān-,sāl, -,māl, -səl\ *n* (15c) : the principal sail on the mainmast — see SAIL illustration

main sequence *n* (1925) : the group of stars that on a graph of spectrum versus luminosity forms a band comprising 90% of stellar types and that includes stars believed to be representative of the stages a normal star passes through for the majority of its lifetime

main·sheet \'mān-,shēt\ *n* (15c) : a rope by which the mainsail is trimmed and secured

main·spring \'mān-,spriŋ\ *n* (1591) **1** : the chief spring in a mechanism esp. of a watch or clock **2** : the chief or most powerful motive, agent, or cause

\ə\ abut \ᵊ\ kitten, F table \ər\ further \a\ ash \ā\ ace \ä\ mop, mar \aù\ out \ch\ chin \e\ bet \ē\ easy \g\ go \i\ hit \ī\ ice \j\ job \ŋ\ sing \ō\ go \ò\ law \òi\ boy \th\ thin \t͟h\ the \ü\ loot \ù\ foot \y\ yet \zh\ vision \à, k̲, ⁿ, œ, œ̄, ᵫ, ūᴇ, ʸ\ see Guide to Pronunciation

main squeeze *n* (ca. 1968) *slang* : one's principal romantic partner
main·stay \'mān-ˌstā\ *n* (15c) **1 :** a ship's stay extending from the maintop forward usu. to the foot of the foremast **2 :** a chief support
main stem *n* (1832) : a main trunk or channel: as **a :** the main course of a river or stream **b :** the main street of a city or town
¹main·stream \'mān-ˌstrēm\ *n* (1831) : a prevailing current or direction of activity or influence — **mainstream** *adj*
²main·stream \'mān-ˌstrēm\ *vt* (1974) : to place (as a handicapped child) in regular school classes
Main Street *n* (ca. 1743) **1 :** the principal street of a small town **2 a :** the sections of a country centering about its small towns **b :** a place or environment characterized by materialistic self-complacent provincialism **c :** MIDDLE AMERICA **3 — Main Street·er** \'mān-ˌstrē-tər\ *n*
main·tain \mān-'tān, mən-\ *vt* [ME *mainteinen*, fr. OF *maintenir*, fr. ML *manutenēre*, fr. L *manu tenēre* to hold in the hand] (14c) **1 :** to keep in an existing state (as of repair, efficiency, or validity) : preserve from failure or decline ⟨~ machinery⟩ **2 :** to sustain against opposition or danger : uphold and defend ⟨~ a position⟩ **3 :** to continue or persevere in : CARRY ON, KEEP UP ⟨couldn't ~ his composure⟩ **4 a :** to support or provide for ⟨has a family to ~⟩ **b :** SUSTAIN ⟨enough food to ~ life⟩ **5 :** to affirm in or as if in argument : ASSERT ⟨~ed that the earth is flat⟩ — **main·tain·abil·i·ty** \-ˌtā-nə-'bi-lə-tē\ *n* — **main·tain·able** \-'tā-nə-bəl\ *adj* — **main·tain·er** *n*
syn MAINTAIN, ASSERT, DEFEND, VINDICATE, JUSTIFY mean to uphold as true, right, just, or reasonable. MAINTAIN stresses firmness of conviction ⟨steadfastly *maintained* his innocence⟩. ASSERT suggests determination to make others accept one's claim ⟨*asserted* her rights⟩. DEFEND implies maintaining in the face of attack or criticism ⟨*defended* his voting record⟩. VINDICATE implies successfully defending ⟨his success *vindicated* our faith in him⟩. JUSTIFY implies showing to be true, just, or valid by appeal to a standard or to a precedent ⟨the action was used to *justify* military intervention⟩.
main·te·nance \'mānt-nən(t)s, 'mān-t²n-ən(t)s\ *n* [ME, fr. MF, fr. OF, fr. *maintenir*] (14c) **1 :** the act of maintaining : the state of being maintained : SUPPORT **2 :** something that maintains **3 :** the upkeep of property or equipment **4 :** an officious or unlawful intermeddling in a legal suit by assisting either party with means to carry it on
main·top \'mān-ˌtäp\ *n* (15c) : a platform about the head of the mainmast of a square-rigged ship
main–top·mast \mān-'täp-ˌmast, -məst\ *n* (15c) : a mast next above the mainmast
main yard *n* (15c) : the yard of a mainsail
mair \'mār\ *chiefly Scot var of* MORE
mai·son·ette \ˌmā-z²n-'et, -s²n-\ *n* [F *maisonnette*, fr. OF, dim. of *maison* house, fr. L *mansion-, mansio* dwelling place — more at MANSION] (1793) **1 :** a small house **2 :** an apartment often on two floors
maî·tre d' *or* **mai·tre d'** \ˌmā-trə-'dē, ˌme-, -tər-\ *n*, *pl* **maître d's** *or* **maitre d's** \-'dēz\ (1950) : MAÎTRE D'HÔTEL
maî·tre d'hô·tel \ˌmā-trə-(ˌ)dō-'tel, ˌme-; ˌmāt-dō-, ˌmet-\ *n*, *pl* **maîtres d'hôtel** *same*\ [F, lit., master of house] (1538) **1 a :** MAJORDOMO **b :** HEADWAITER **2 :** a sauce of butter, parsley, salt, pepper, and lemon juice — called also *maître d'hôtel butter*
maize \'māz\ *n* [Sp *maíz*, fr. Taino *mahiz*] (1555) : INDIAN CORN
ma·jes·tic \mə-'jes-tik\ *adj* (1601) : having or exhibiting majesty : STATELY — **ma·jes·ti·cal·ly** \-ti-k(ə-)lē\ *adv*
maj·es·ty \'ma-jə-stē\ *n*, *pl* **-ties** [ME *maieste*, fr. MF *majesté*, fr. L *majestat-, majestas*; akin to L *major* greater] (14c) **1 :** sovereign power, authority, or dignity **2 —** used in addressing or referring to reigning sovereigns and their consorts ⟨Your *Majesty*⟩ ⟨Her *Majesty's* Government⟩ **3 a :** royal bearing or aspect : GRANDEUR **b :** greatness or splendor of quality or character
ma·jol·i·ca \mə-'jä-li-kə\ *also* **ma·iol·i·ca** \-'yä-\ *n* [It *maiolica*, fr. OIt *Maiolica, Maiorica* Majorca] (1555) **1 :** earthenware covered with an opaque tin glaze and decorated on the glaze before firing; *esp* : an Italian ware of this kind **2 :** a 19th century earthenware modeled in naturalistic shapes and glazed in lively colors
¹ma·jor \'mā-jər\ *adj* [ME *maiour*, fr. L *major*, compar. of *magnus* great, large — more at MUCH] (15c) **1 :** greater in dignity, rank, importance, or interest ⟨one of the ~ poets⟩ **2 :** greater in number, quantity, or extent ⟨the ~ part of his work⟩ **3 :** having attained majority **4 :** notable or conspicuous in effect or scope : CONSIDERABLE ⟨a ~ improvement⟩ **5 :** involving grave risk : SERIOUS ⟨a ~ illness⟩ **6 :** of or relating to a subject of academic study chosen as a field of specialization **7 a :** having half steps between the third and fourth and the seventh and eighth degrees ⟨~ scale⟩ **b :** based on a major scale ⟨~ key⟩ **c :** equivalent to the distance between the keynote and another tone (except the fourth and fifth) of a major scale ⟨~ third⟩ **d :** having a major third above the root ⟨~ triad⟩
²major *n* (1616) **1 :** a person who has attained majority **2 a :** one that is superior in rank, importance, size, or performance ⟨economic power of the oil ~s⟩ **b :** a major musical interval, scale, key, or mode **3 :** a commissioned officer in the army, air force, or marine corps ranking above a captain and below a lieutenant colonel **4 a :** an academic subject chosen as a field of specialization **b :** a student specializing in such a field ⟨a history ~⟩ **5** *pl* : major league baseball — used with *the*
³major *vi* (1913) : to pursue an academic major
major axis *n* (1854) : the axis passing through the foci of an ellipse
ma·jor·do·mo \ˌmā-jər-'dō-(ˌ)mō\ *n*, *pl* **-mos** [Sp *mayordomo* or obs. It *maiordomo*, fr. ML *major domus*, lit., chief of the house] (1589) **1 :** a head steward of a large household (as a palace) **2 :** BUTLER, STEWARD **3 :** a person who speaks, makes arrangements, or takes charge for another
ma·jor·ette \ˌmā-jə-'ret\ *n* (1940) : DRUM MAJORETTE 2
major general *n* [F *major général*, fr. *major*, n. + *général*, adj., general] (1642) : a commissioned officer in the army, air force, or marine corps who ranks above a brigadier general and whose insignia is two stars
major histocompatibility complex *n* (1975) : a group of genes in mammals that function esp. in determining the histocompatibility antigens found on cell surfaces
ma·jor·i·tar·i·an \mə-ˌjȯr-ə-'ter-ē-ən, -ˌjär-\ *n* (1942) : a person who believes in or advocates majoritarianism — **majoritarian** *adj*

ma·jor·i·tar·i·an·ism \-ē-ə-ˌni-zəm\ *n* (1942) : the philosophy or practice according to which decisions of an organized group should be made by a numerical majority of its members
ma·jor·i·ty \mə-'jȯr-ə-tē, -'jär-\ *n*, *pl* **-ties** (1552) **1** *obs* : the quality or state of being greater **2 a :** the age at which full civil rights are accorded **b :** the status of one who has attained this age **3 a :** a number greater than half of a total **b :** the excess of a majority over the remainder of the total : MARGIN **c :** the preponderant quantity or share **4 :** the group or political party whose votes preponderate **5 :** the military office, rank, or commission of a major — **majority** *adj*
majority leader *n* (1952) : a leader of the majority party in a legislative body (as the U.S. Senate)
majority rule *n* (1893) : a political principle providing that a majority usu. constituted by fifty percent plus one of an organized group will have the power to make decisions binding upon the whole
major league *n* (1906) **1 :** a league of highest classification in U.S. professional baseball; *broadly* : a league of major importance in any of various sports **2 :** BIG TIME 2 — **major–league** *adj*
ma·jor·ly \'mā-jər-lē\ *adv* (1956) : in a major way **a :** PRIMARILY 1 ⟨was ~ a poet⟩ **b :** EXTREMELY 1 ⟨was ~ annoyed⟩
major–medical *adj* (ca. 1955) : of, relating to, or being a form of insurance designed to pay all or part of the medical bills of major illnesses usu. after deduction of a fixed initial sum
major order *n* (ca. 1741) : one of the Roman Catholic or Eastern clerical orders that are sacramentally conferred and have a sacred character that implies major religious obligations (as clerical celibacy) — usu. used in pl.; compare MINOR ORDER
major party *n* (1950) : a political party having electoral strength sufficient to permit it to win control of a government usu. with comparative regularity and when defeated to constitute the principal opposition to the party in power
major penalty *n* (ca. 1936) : a 5-minute suspension of a player in ice hockey or lacrosse
major premise *n* (1860) : the premise of a syllogism containing the major term
major seminary *n* (1945) : a Roman Catholic seminary giving usu. the entire six years of senior college and theological training required for major orders
major suit *n* (1916) : either of the suits hearts or spades having superior scoring value in bridge
major term *n* (1847) : the term of a syllogism constituting the predicate of the conclusion
ma·jus·cule \'ma-jəs-ˌkyü(ə)l, mə-'jəs-\ *n* [F, fr. L *majusculus* rather large, dim. of *major*] (ca. 1825) : a large letter (as a capital) — **ma·jus·cu·lar** \mə-'jəs-kyə-lər\ *adj* — **majuscule** *adj*
mak·able *or* **make·able** \'mā-kə-bəl\ *adj* (15c) : capable of being made
mak·ar \'mä-kər, 'mā-\ *n* [ME *maker*] (14c) *chiefly Scot* : POET
¹make \'māk\ *vb* **made** \'mād\; **mak·ing** [ME, fr. OE *macian*; akin to OHG *mahhōn* to prepare, make, Gk *magēnai* to be kneaded, OCS *mazati* to anoint, smear] *vt* (bef. 12c) **1 a** *obs* : BEHAVE, ACT **b :** to seem to begin (an action) ⟨*made* to go⟩ **2 a :** to cause to happen to or be experienced by someone ⟨*made* trouble for us⟩ **b :** to cause to exist, occur, or appear : CREATE ⟨~ a disturbance⟩ **c :** to favor the growth or occurrence of ⟨haste ~s waste⟩ **d :** to fit, intend, or destine by or as if by creating ⟨was *made* to be an actor⟩ **3 a :** to bring into being by forming, shaping, or altering material : FASHION ⟨~ a dress⟩ **b :** COMPOSE, WRITE ⟨~ verses⟩ **c :** to lay out and construct ⟨~ a road⟩ **4 :** to frame or formulate in the mind ⟨~ plans⟩ **5 :** to put together from components : CONSTITUTE ⟨houses *made* of stone⟩ **6 a :** to compute or estimate to be **b :** to form and hold in the mind ⟨~ no doubt of it⟩ **7 a :** to assemble and set alight the materials for (a fire) : to set in order ⟨~ beds⟩ **c :** PREPARE, FIX ⟨~ dinner⟩ **d :** to shuffle (a deck of cards) in preparation for dealing **8 :** to prepare (hay) by cutting, drying, and storing **9 a :** to cause to be or become ⟨*made* them happy⟩ **b :** APPOINT ⟨*made* him bishop⟩ **10 a :** ENACT, ESTABLISH ⟨~ laws⟩ **b :** to execute in an appropriate manner ⟨~ a will⟩ **c :** SET, NAME ⟨~ a price⟩ **11 a** *chiefly dial* : SHUT ⟨the doors are *made* against you — Shak.⟩ **b :** to cause (an electric circuit) to be completed **12 a :** to conclude as to the nature or meaning of something ⟨what do you ~ of this development⟩ **b :** to regard as being ⟨not the fool some ~ him⟩ **13 a :** to carry out (an action indicated or implied by the object) ⟨~ war⟩ ⟨~ a speech⟩ **b :** to perform with a bodily movement ⟨~ a sweeping gesture⟩ **c :** to achieve by traversing ⟨~ a detour⟩ ⟨*making* the rounds⟩ **14 a :** to produce as a result of action, effort, or behavior with respect to something ⟨~ a mess of the job⟩ ⟨tried to ~ a thorough job of it⟩ **b** *archaic* : to turn into another language by translation **15 :** to cause to act in a certain way : COMPEL ⟨~ her give it back⟩ **16 :** to cause or assure the success or prosperity of ⟨can either ~ you or break you⟩ **17 a :** to amount to in significance ⟨~s a great difference⟩ **b :** to form the essential being of ⟨clothes ~ the man⟩ **c :** to form by an assembling of individuals ⟨~ a quorum⟩ **d :** to count as ⟨that ~s the third time you've said it⟩ **18 a :** to be or be capable of being changed or fashioned into ⟨rags ~ the best paper⟩ **b :** to develop into ⟨she will ~ a fine judge⟩ **c :** FORM 6b **19 a :** REACH, ATTAIN — often used with it ⟨you'll never ~ it that far⟩; *also* : SURVIVE ⟨half the cubs won't ~ it through their first year⟩ **b :** to gain the rank of ⟨~ major⟩ **c :** to gain a place on or in ⟨~ the team⟩ ⟨the story *made* the papers⟩ **20 :** to gain (as money) by working, trading, or dealing ⟨~ a living⟩ **21 a :** to act so as to win or acquire ⟨~s friends easily⟩ **b :** to score (points) in a game or sport **c :** to convert (a split) into a spare in bowling **22 a :** to fulfill (a contract) in a card game **b :** to win a trick with (a card) **23 a :** to include in a route or itinerary ⟨~ New York on the return trip⟩ ⟨~ it to the party⟩ **b :** CATCH 6b ⟨*made* the bus just in time⟩ **24 :** to persuade to consent to sexual intercourse : SEDUCE **25 :** to provide the most enjoyable or satisfying experience of ⟨meeting the star of the show really *made* our day⟩ ~ *vi* **1** *archaic* : to compose poetry **2 a :** BEHAVE, ACT **b :** to begin or seem to begin a certain action ⟨*made* as though to hand it to me⟩ **c :** to act so as to be or to seem to be ⟨~ merry⟩ **d** *slang* : to play a part — usu. used with *like* **3 :** SET OUT, HEAD ⟨*made* after the fox⟩ ⟨*made* straight for home⟩ **4 :** to increase in height or size ⟨the tide is *making* now⟩ **5 :** to reach or extend in a certain direction **6 :** to have considerable effect ⟨courtesy ~s for safer driving⟩ **7 :** to undergo manufac-

ture or processing ⟨the silk ∼s up beautifully⟩ — **make a face :** to distort one's features : GRIMACE — **make a mountain out of a molehill :** to treat a trifling matter as of great importance — **make away with 1 :** to carry off : STEAL **2 :** KILL — **make believe :** PRETEND, FEIGN — **make bold :** VENTURE, DARE — **make book :** to accept bets at calculated odds on all the entrants in a race or contest — **make common cause :** to unite to achieve a shared goal — **make do :** to get along or manage with the means at hand — **make ends meet :** to make one's means adequate to one's needs — **make eyes :** OGLE — **make fun of :** to make an object of amusement or laughter : RIDICULE, MOCK — **make good 1 :** to make valid or complete: as **a :** to make up for (a deficiency) **b :** INDEMNIFY ⟨*make good* the loss⟩ **c :** to carry out successfully ⟨*made good* his promise⟩ ⟨*made good* their escape⟩ **d :** PROVE ⟨*made good* a charge⟩ **2 :** to prove to be capable; *also* : SUCCEED — **make hay :** to make use of offered opportunity esp. in gaining an early advantage — **make head 1 :** to make progress esp. against resistance **2 :** to rise in armed revolt — **make it 1 :** to be successful ⟨trying to *make it* in the big time as a fashion photographer —Joe Kane⟩ ⟨the crème brûlée didn't quite *make it*⟩ **2 :** to have sexual intercourse — **make light of :** to treat as of little account — **make love 1 :** WOO, COURT **2 a :** NECK, PET **b :** to engage in sexual intercourse — **make much of 1 :** to treat as of importance **2 :** to treat with obvious affection or special consideration — **make no bones :** to be straightforward, unhesitating, or sure ⟨makes no bones about the seriousness of the matter⟩ — **make one's mark :** to achieve success or fame — **make public :** DISCLOSE — **make sail 1 :** to raise or spread sail **2 :** to set out on a voyage — **make shift :** to manage with difficulty — **make sport of :** RIDICULE, MOCK — **make the grade :** to measure up to some standard : be successful — **make the most of :** to show or use to the best advantage — **make the scene :** to be present at or participate in a usu. specified activity or event — **make time 1 :** to travel fast **2 :** to gain time **3 :** to make progress toward winning favor ⟨trying to *make time* with the waitress⟩ — **make tracks 1 :** to proceed at a walk or run **2 :** to go in a hurry : RUN AWAY, FLEE — **make use of :** to put to use : EMPLOY — **make water 1** *of a boat* : LEAK **2 :** URINATE — **make waves :** to create a stir or disturbance — **make way 1 :** to give room for passing, entering, or occupying **2 :** to make progress — **make with** *slang* : PRODUCE, PERFORM — usu. used with *the*

²**make** *n* (14c) **1 a :** the manner or style in which a thing is constructed **b :** BRAND 4a **2 :** the physical, mental, or moral constitution of a person ⟨men of his ∼ are rare⟩ **3 a :** the action of producing or manufacturing **b :** the actual yield or amount produced over a specified period : OUTPUT **4 :** the act of shuffling cards; *also* : turn to shuffle — **on the make 1 :** in the process of forming, growing, or improving **2 :** in quest of a higher social or financial status **3 :** in search of sexual adventure

make·bate \'māk-ˌbāt\ *n* (¹*make* + obs. *bate* strife] (1529) *archaic* : one that excites contention and quarrels

¹**make–be·lieve** \'māk-bə-ˌlēv\ *also* **make–be·lief** \-ˌlēf\ *n* (1811) : pretending to believe

²**make–believe** *adj* (1824) : IMAGINARY, PRETENDED

make–do \'māk-ˌdü\ *adj* (1923) : MAKESHIFT — **make–do** *n*

make·fast \-ˌfast\ *n* (1898) : something (as a post or buoy) to which a boat can be fastened

make off *vi* (1709) : to leave in haste — **make off with :** to take away; *esp* : GRAB, STEAL

make–or–break \'mā-kər-'brāk\ *adj* (1919) : allowing no middle ground between success and failure

make out *vt* (15c) **1 :** to complete (as a printed form) by supplying required information ⟨*make out* a check⟩ **2 :** to find or grasp the meaning of ⟨tried to *make out* what had really happened⟩ **3 :** to form an opinion or idea about : CONCLUDE ⟨how do you *make* that *out*⟩ **4 a :** to represent as being ⟨*made* them *out* to be losers⟩ **b :** to pretend to be true ⟨*made out* that he had never heard of me⟩ **5 :** to represent or delineate in detail **6 :** to see and identify with difficulty or effort : DISCERN ⟨*make out* a ship through the fog⟩ ∼ *vi* **1 :** GET ALONG, FARE ⟨how are you *making out* with the new job⟩ **2 a :** to engage in sexual intercourse **b :** NECK 1

make·over \'mā-ˌkō-vər\ *n* (1927) : an act or instance of making over; *esp* : a changing of a person's appearance (as by the use of cosmetics or a different hairdo)

make over (1546) **1 :** to transfer the title of (property) **2 :** REMAKE, REMODEL ⟨*made* the whole house *over*⟩

mak·er \'mā-kər\ *n* (14c) : one that makes: as **a** *cap* : GOD **1 b** *archaic* : POET **c :** a person who borrows money on a promissory note **d :** MANUFACTURER

make–ready \'māk-ˌre-dē\ *n, pl* **-readies** (1887) : final preparation (as of a form on a printing press) for running

make·shift \'māk-ˌshift\ *n* (ca. 1812) : a usu. crude and temporary expedient : SUBSTITUTE *syn* see RESOURCE — **makeshift** *adj*

make·up \'māk-ˌəp\ *n* (1821) **1 a :** the way in which the parts or ingredients of something are put together : COMPOSITION **b :** physical, mental, and moral constitution **2 a :** the operation of making up esp. pages for printing **b :** design or layout of printed matter **3 a** (1) : cosmetics used to color and beautify the face (2) : a cosmetic applied to other parts of the body **b :** materials (as wigs and cosmetics) used in making up or in special costuming (as for a play) **4 :** REPLACEMENT; *specif* : material added (as in a manufacturing process) to replace material that has been used up ⟨∼ water⟩ **5 :** a special examination in which a student may make up for absence or previous failure

make up *vt* (14c) **1 a :** to form by fitting together or assembling ⟨*make up* a train of cars⟩ **b :** to arrange typeset matter in (as pages) for printing **2 a :** to combine to produce (a sum or whole) **b :** CONSTITUTE, COMPOSE ⟨10 chapters *make up* this volume⟩ **3 :** to make good (a deficiency) **4 :** SETTLE, DECIDE ⟨*made up* my mind to depart⟩ **5 :** to wrap or fasten up ⟨*make* the books *up* into a parcel⟩ **6 a :** to prepare in physical appearance for a role **b :** to apply cosmetics to **7 a :** INVENT, IMPROVISE ⟨*make up* a story⟩ **b :** to set in order ⟨rooms are *made up* daily⟩ ∼ *vi* **1 :** to become reconciled ⟨quarreled but later *made up*⟩ **2 a :** to act ingratiatingly and flatteringly ⟨*made up* to his aunt for a new bicycle⟩ **b :** to make advances : COURT **3 :** COMPENSATE ⟨*make up* for lost time⟩ **4 a :** to put on costumes or makeup (as for a play) **b :** to apply cosmetics

make·weight \'māk-ˌwāt\ *n* (1695) **1 a :** something thrown into a scale to bring the weight to a desired value **b :** something of little independent value thrown in to fill a gap **2 :** COUNTERWEIGHT, COUNTERPOISE

make–work \'māk-ˌwərk\ *n* (1923) : work assigned or done chiefly to keep one busy

ma·ki·mo·no \ˌmä-ki-'mō-(ˌ)nō\ *n, pl* **-nos** [Jp, scroll, fr. *maki* roll + *mono* thing] (1882) : a horizontal Japanese ornamental pictorial or calligraphic scroll

mak·ing \'mā-kiŋ\ *n* [ME, fr. OE *macung*, fr. *macian* to make] (12c) **1 :** the act or process of forming, causing, doing, or coming into being ⟨spots problems in the ∼⟩ **2 :** a process or means of advancement or success **3 :** something made; *esp* : a quantity produced at one time : BATCH **4 a :** POTENTIALITY — often used in pl. ⟨had the ∼s of a great artist⟩ **b** *pl* : the material from which something is to be made; *esp* ⟨usu 'mā-kənz⟩ : paper and tobacco for rolling cigarettes by hand

ma·ko shark \'mä-(ˌ)kō-, 'mä-\ *n* [Maori *mako* mako shark] (1926) : either of two mackerel sharks (*Isurus paucus* and *I. oxyrinchus*) that are notable sport fish and are considered dangerous to humans — called also *mako*; see SHARK illustration

makuta *pl of* LIKUTA

mal- *comb form* [ME, fr. MF, fr. OF, fr. *mal* bad (fr. L *malus*) & *mal* badly, fr. L *male*, fr. *malus*] **1 a :** bad ⟨*mal*practice⟩ **b :** badly ⟨*mal*odorous⟩ **2 a :** abnormal ⟨*mal*formation⟩ **b :** abnormally ⟨*mal*formed⟩ **3 a :** inadequate ⟨*mal*adjustment⟩ **b :** inadequately ⟨*mal*nourished⟩

mal·ab·sorp·tion \ˌma-ləb-'sórp-shən, -'zórp-\ *n* (ca. 1929) : faulty absorption esp. of nutrient materials from the alimentary canal

ma·lac·ca \mə-'la-kə\ *adj* [*Malacca*, Malaya] (1844) : made or comprised of the cane of an Asian rattan palm (*Calamus rotang*) ⟨an umbrella with a ∼ handle⟩ — **malacca** *n*

Mal·a·chi \'ma-lə-ˌkī\ *n* [Heb *Mal'ākhī*] **1** — used as the conventional name for the unidentified 5th century B.C. writer of the book of Malachi **2 :** a prophetic book of canonical Jewish and Christian Scripture — see BIBLE table

Mal·a·chi·as \ˌma-lə-'kī-əs\ *n* [LL, fr. Gk, fr. Heb *Mal'ākhī*] : MALACHI

mal·a·chite \'ma-lə-ˌkīt\ *n* [alter. of ME *melochites*, fr. L *molochites*, fr. Gk *molochitēs*, fr. *molochē*, *malachē* mallow] (1656) : a mineral that is a green basic carbonate of copper used as an ore and for making ornamental objects

mal·a·col·o·gy \ˌma-lə-'kä-lə-jē\ *n* [F *malacologie*, contr. of *malacozoologie*, fr. NL *Malacozoa*, zoological group including soft= bodied animals (fr. Gk *malakos* soft + NL *-zoa*) + F *-logie* -logy] (1836) : a branch of zoology dealing with mollusks — **mal·a·co·log·i·cal** \ˌma-lə-kə-'lä-ji-kəl\ *adj* — **mal·a·col·o·gist** \ˌma-lə-'kä-lə-jist\ *n*

mal·a·cos·tra·can \ˌma-lə-'käs-tri-kən\ *n* [ultim. fr. Gk *malakostrakos* soft-shelled, fr. *malakos* soft + *ostrakon* shell — more at MOLLIFY, OYSTER] (1835) : any of a large subclass (Malacostraca) of crustaceans having a thorax consisting of eight segments usu. covered by a carapace and including the decapods and isopods — **malacostracan** *adj*

mal·ad·ap·ta·tion \ˌma-ˌla-ˌdap-'tā-shən\ *n* (1877) : poor or inadequate adaptation

mal·adapt·ed \ˌma-lə-'dap-təd\ *adj* (1943) : unsuited or poorly suited (as to a particular use, purpose, or situation)

mal·adap·tive \-tiv\ *adj* (1931) **1 :** marked by poor or inadequate adaptation **2 :** not conducive to adaptation

mal·ad·just·ed \ˌma-lə-'jəs-təd\ *adj* (1886) : poorly or inadequately adjusted; *specif* : lacking harmony with one's environment from failure to adjust one's desires to the conditions of one's life

mal·ad·jus·tive \-'jəs-tiv\ *adj* (1928) : not conducive to adjustment

mal·ad·just·ment \-'jəs(t)-mənt\ *n* (1833) : poor, faulty, or inadequate adjustment

mal·ad·min·is·tra·tion \ˌma-ləd-ˌmi-nə-'strā-shən\ *n* (1644) : administration that is corrupt or incompetent (as that of a public office) or incorrect (as that of a drug) — **mal·ad·min·is·ter** \-'mi-nə-stər\ *vt*

mal·adroit \ˌma-lə-'dróit\ *adj* [F, fr. MF, fr. *mal-* + *adroit*] (1685) : lacking adroitness : INEPT *syn* see AWKWARD — **mal·adroit·ly** *adv* — **mal·adroit·ness** *n*

mal·a·dy \'ma-lə-dē\ *n, pl* **-dies** [ME *maladie*, fr. OF, fr. *malade* sick, fr. L *male habitus* in bad condition] (13c) **1 :** a disease or disorder of the animal body **2 :** an unwholesome or disordered condition

ma·la fi·de \ˌma-lə-'fī-dē, -də\ *adv or adj* [LL] (1561) : with or in bad faith

Ma·la·ga \'ma-lə-gə\ *n* (1608) : a sweet brown fortified wine from *Málaga*, Spain; *also* : a similar wine made elsewhere

Mal·a·gasy \ˌma-lə-'ga-sē; ˌmä-lə-'gä-sē, -shē\ *n, pl* **Malagasy** *also* **Mal·a·gas·ies** (1839) **1 :** a member of a people of Indonesian and African origin who inhabit Madagascar **2 :** the Austronesian language of the Malagasy people — **Malagasy** *adj*

ma·la·gue·na \ˌma-lə-'gān-yə, ˌmä-\ *n* [Sp *malagueña*, fr. fem. of *malagueño* of Málaga, fr. *Málaga*] (ca. 1883) **1 :** a folk tune native to Málaga that is similar to a fandango **2 :** a Spanish dance for couples that is similar to a fandango

mal·aise \mə-'lāz, ma-, -'lez\ *n* [F *malaise*, fr. OF, fr. *mal-* + *aise* comfort — more at EASE] (ca. 1768) **1 :** an indefinite feeling of debility or lack of health often indicative of or accompanying the onset of an illness **2 :** a vague sense of mental or moral ill-being ⟨a ∼ of cynicism and despair —Malcolm Boyd⟩

mal·a·mute \'ma-lə-ˌmyüt, -ˌmüt\ *n* [*Malemute*, an Alaskan Eskimo people] (1898) : a sled dog of northern No. America; *esp* : ALASKAN MALAMUTE

mal·a·pert \ˌma-lə-'pərt\ *adj* [ME, fr. MF, unskillful, fr. *mal-* + *apert* skillful, lit., open — more at PERT] (14c) : impudently bold : SAUCY — **mal·a·pert·ly** *adv* — **mal·a·pert·ness** *n*

\ə\ abut \ᵊ\ kitten, F table \ər\ further \a\ ash \ā\ ace \ä\ mop, mar \aú\ out \ch\ chin \e\ bet \ē\ easy \g\ go \i\ hit \ī\ ice \j\ job \ŋ\ sing \ō\ go \ò\ law \òi\ boy \th\ thin \t̲h̲\ the \ü\ loot \ú\ foot \y\ yet \zh\ vision \à, k̲, ⁿ, œ, œ̄, ue, ūe, ʸ\ see Guide to Pronunciation

mal·ap·por·tioned \\,ma-lə-'pōr-shənd, -'pȯr-\ adj (1965) : characterized by an inequitable or unsuitable apportioning of representatives to a legislative body — **mal·ap·por·tion·ment** \-shən-mənt\ n

¹mal·a·prop \'ma-lə-,präp\ n [Mrs. Malaprop] (1823) : an example of malapropism ⟨was famed for ~s: he always said "polo bears" and "Remember Pearl Island" and "neon stockings" —Time⟩

²malaprop or **mal·a·prop·ian** \,ma-lə-'prä-pē-ən\ adj (1840) : using or marked by the use of malapropisms

mal·a·prop·ism \'ma-lə-,prä-,pi-zəm\ n [Mrs. Malaprop, character noted for her misuse of words in R. B. Sheridan's comedy The Rivals (1775)] (1849) 1 : the usu. unintentionally humorous misuse or distortion of a word or phrase; esp : the use of a word sounding somewhat like the one intended but ludicrously wrong in the context 2 : MALAPROP — **mal·a·prop·ist** \-,präp-ist\ n

mal·ap·ro·pos \,ma-,la-prə-'pō\ adv [F mal à propos] (1668) : in an inappropriate or inopportune way — **malapropos** adj

¹ma·lar \'mā-lər, -,lär\ adj [NL malaris, fr. L mala jawbone, cheek] (1782) : of or relating to the cheek or the side of the head

²malar n (ca. 1828) : ZYGOMATIC BONE — called also malar bone

ma·lar·ia \mə-'ler-ē-ə\ n [It, fr. mala aria bad air] (1740) 1 archaic : air infected with a noxious substance capable of causing disease; esp : MIASMA 2 a : a human disease that is caused by sporozoan parasites (genus Plasmodium) in the red blood cells, is transmitted by the bite of anopheline mosquitoes, and is characterized by periodic attacks of chills and fever b : any of various diseases of birds and mammals caused by blood protozoans — **ma·lar·i·al** \-əl\ adj — **ma·lar·i·ous** \-əs\ adj

ma·lar·i·ol·o·gy \-,ler-ē-'ä-lə-jē\ n (ca. 1923) : the scientific study of malaria — **ma·lar·i·ol·o·gist** \-jist\ n

ma·lar·key also **ma·lar·ky** \mə-'lär-kē\ n [origin unknown] (1929) : insincere or foolish talk : BUNKUM

ma·late \'ma-,lāt, 'mal-,āt\ n (1794) : a salt or ester of malic acid

mal·a·thi·on \,ma-lə-'thī-ən, -,än\ n [fr. Malathion, a trademark] (1953) : an insecticide $C_{10}H_{19}O_6PS_2$ with a lower mammalian toxicity than parathion

Ma·lay \mə-'lā, 'mā-,)lā\ n [obs. D Malayo (now Maleier), fr. Malay Mēlayu] (1598) 1 : a member of a people of the Malay Peninsula, eastern Sumatra, parts of Borneo, and some adjacent islands 2 : the Austronesian language of the Malays — **Malay** adj — **Ma·lay·an** \mə-'lā-ən, mā-; 'mā-,lā-\ n or adj

Mal·a·ya·lam \,ma-lə-'yä-ləm, ,mä-\ n (1837) : the Dravidian language of Kerala, southwest India, closely related to Tamil

¹mal·con·tent \,mal-kən-'tent\ n (1581) : a discontented person: **a** : one who bears a grudge from a sense of grievance or thwarted ambition **b** : one who is in active opposition to an established order or government : REBEL

²malcontent adj [MF, fr. OF, fr. mal- + content content] (1586) : dissatisfied with the existing state of affairs : DISCONTENTED

mal·con·tent·ed \-'ten-təd\ adj (1586) : MALCONTENT — **mal·con·tent·ed·ly** adv — **mal·con·tent·ed·ness** n

mal de mer \,mal-də-'mer\ n [F] (1778) : SEASICKNESS

mal·dis·tri·bu·tion \,mal-,dis-trə-'byü-shən\ n (1895) : bad or faulty distribution : undesirable inequality or unevenness of placement or apportionment (as of population, resources, or wealth) over an area or among members of a group

¹male \'mā(ə)l\ n [ME, fr. MF masle, male, adj. & n., fr. L masculus — more at MASCULINE] (14c) 1 **a** : a male person : a man or a boy **b** : an individual that produces small usu. motile gametes (as spermatozoa or spermatozoids) which fertilize the eggs of a female 2 : a staminate plant

²male adj (14c) 1 **a** (1) : of, relating to, or being the sex that produces gametes which fertilize the eggs of a female (2) : STAMINATE; esp : having only staminate flowers and not producing fruit or seeds ⟨a ~ holly⟩ **b** (1) : of, relating to, or characteristic of the male sex ⟨a deep ~ voice⟩ (2) : made up of usu. adult male individuals ⟨a ~ choir⟩ 2 : MASCULINE 3a 3 : designed for fitting into a corresponding female part ⟨~ hose coupling⟩ — **male·ness** \-nəs\ n

male alto n (ca. 1879) : COUNTERTENOR

ma·le·ate \'mā-lē-,āt, -lē-ət\ n (1853) : a salt or ester of maleic acid

¹mal·e·dict \,ma-lə-'dikt\ adj [LL maledictus] (ca. 1550) archaic : ACCURSED

²maledict vt (1623) : CURSE, EXECRATE

mal·e·dic·tion \,ma-lə-'dik-shən\ n [ME malediccioun, fr. LL malediction-, maledictio, fr. maledicere to curse, fr. L, to speak evil of, fr. male badly + dicere to speak, say — more at MAL-, DICTION] (14c) : CURSE, EXECRATION — **mal·e·dic·to·ry** \-'dik-t(ə-)rē\ adj

mal·e·fac·tion \,ma-lə-'fak-shən\ n (15c) : an evil deed : CRIME

mal·e·fac·tor \'ma-lə-,fak-tər\ n [ME malefactour, fr. L malefactor, fr. malefacere to do evil, fr. male + facere to do — more at DO] (15c) 1 : one who commits an offense against the law; esp : FELON 2 : one who does ill toward another

male fern n (1562) : a fern (Dryopteris filix-mas) producing an oleoresin used in expelling tapeworms

ma·lef·ic \mə-'le-fik\ adj [L maleficus wicked, mischievous, fr. male + -ficus -fic] (1652) 1 : having malignant influence : BALEFUL 2 : MALICIOUS

ma·lef·i·cence \mə-'le-fə-sən(t)s\ n [It maleficenza, fr. L maleficentia, fr. maleficus] (1598) 1 **a** : the act of committing harm or evil **b** : a harmful or evil act 2 : the quality or state of being maleficent

ma·lef·i·cent \-sənt\ adj [back-formation fr. maleficence] (1678) : working or productive of harm or evil : BALEFUL

ma·le·ic acid \mə-'lē-ik-, -'lā-\ n [F acide maléique, alter. of acide malique malic acid; fr. its formation by dehydration of malic acid] (1857) : a crystalline dicarboxylic acid $C_4H_4O_4$ that is isomeric with fumaric acid and is used esp. in organic synthesis

maleic anhydride n (1857) : a caustic crystalline cyclic anhydride $C_4H_2O_3$ used esp. in making resins

maleic hydrazide n (1949) : a crystalline cyclic hydrazide $C_4H_4N_2O_2$ used to retard plant growth

mal·e·mute var of MALAMUTE

male–ster·ile \'mā(ə)l-'ster-əl\ adj (1921) : having male gametes lacking or nonfunctional

ma·lev·o·lence \mə-'le-və-lən(t)s\ n (15c) 1 : the quality or state of being malevolent 2 : malevolent behavior **syn** see MALICE

ma·lev·o·lent \-lənt\ adj [L malevolent-, malevolens, fr. male badly + volent-, volens, prp. of velle to wish — more at MAL-, WILL] (1509) 1 : having, showing, or arising from intense often vicious ill will, spite, or hatred 2 : productive of harm or evil — **ma·lev·o·lent·ly** adv

mal·fea·sance \,mal-'fē-z²n(t)s\ n [mal- + obs. feasance doing, execution] (1696) : wrongdoing or misconduct esp. by a public official

mal·for·ma·tion \,mal-fȯr-'mā-shən, -fər-\ n (1800) : irregular, anomalous, abnormal, or faulty formation or structure

mal·formed \,mal-'fȯrmd\ adj (1817) : characterized by malformation : badly or imperfectly formed : MISSHAPEN

mal·func·tion \,mal-'fəŋ(k)-shən\ vi (1928) : to function imperfectly or badly : fail to operate normally — **malfunction** n

mal·gré \mal-'grā, 'mal-,\ prep [F, fr. OF maugré — more at MAUGRE] (1608) : DESPITE

ma·lic \'ma-lik, 'mā-\ adj (ca. 1909) : involved in and esp. catalyzing a reaction in which malic acid participates ⟨~ dehydrogenase⟩

malic acid n [F acide malique, ultim. fr. L malum apple, fr. Gk mēlon, malon] (1797) : a crystalline dicarboxylic acid $C_4H_6O_5$; esp : the optical isomer of malic acid that is found in various fruits (as apples) and is formed as an intermediate in the Krebs cycle

mal·ice \'ma-ləs\ n [ME, fr. MF, fr. L malitia, fr. malus bad] (14c) 1 : desire to cause pain, injury, or distress to another 2 : intent to commit an unlawful act or cause harm without legal justification or excuse

syn MALICE, MALEVOLENCE, ILL WILL, SPITE, MALIGNITY, SPLEEN, GRUDGE mean the desire to see another experience pain, injury, or distress. MALICE implies a deep-seated often unexplainable desire to see another suffer ⟨felt no malice toward their former enemies⟩. MALEVOLENCE suggests a bitter persistent hatred that is likely to be expressed in malicious conduct ⟨a look of dark malevolence⟩. ILL WILL implies a feeling of antipathy of limited duration ⟨ill will provoked by a careless remark⟩. SPITE implies petty feelings of envy and resentment that are often expressed in small harassments ⟨petty insults inspired by spite⟩. MALIGNITY implies deep passion and relentlessness ⟨a life consumed by motiveless malignity⟩. SPLEEN suggests the wrathful release of latent spite or persistent malice ⟨venting his spleen against politicians⟩. GRUDGE implies a harbored feeling of resentment or ill will that seeks satisfaction ⟨never one to harbor a grudge⟩.

ma·li·cious \mə-'li-shəs\ adj (13c) : given to, marked by, or arising from malice — **ma·li·cious·ly** adv — **ma·li·cious·ness** n

malicious mischief n (1769) : willful, wanton, or reckless damage to or destruction of another's property

¹ma·lign \mə-'līn\ adj [ME maligne, fr. MF, fr. L malignus, fr. male badly + gignere to beget — more at MAL-, KIN] (14c) 1 **a** : evil in nature, influence, or effect : INJURIOUS **b** : MALIGNANT, VIRULENT 2 : having or showing intense often vicious ill will : MALEVOLENT **syn** see SINISTER — **ma·lign·ly** adv

²malign vt [ME, fr. MF maligner to act maliciously, fr. LL malignari, fr. L malignus] (15c) : to utter injuriously misleading or false reports about : speak evil of

syn MALIGN, TRADUCE, ASPERSE, VILIFY, CALUMNIATE, DEFAME, SLANDER mean to injure by speaking ill of. MALIGN suggests specific and often subtle misrepresentation but may not always imply deliberate lying ⟨the most maligned monarch in British history⟩. TRADUCE stresses the resulting ignominy and distress to the victim ⟨so traduced the governor that he was driven from office⟩. ASPERSE implies continued attack on a reputation often by indirect or insinuated detraction ⟨both candidates aspersed the other's motives⟩. VILIFY implies attempting to destroy a reputation by open and direct abuse ⟨no criminal was more vilified in the press⟩. CALUMNIATE imputes malice to the speaker and falsity to the assertions ⟨falsely calumniated as a traitor⟩. DEFAME stresses the actual loss of or injury to one's good name ⟨sued them for defaming her reputation⟩. SLANDER stresses the suffering of the victim ⟨town gossips slandered their good name⟩.

ma·lig·nance \mə-'lig-nən(t)s\ n (ca. 1604) : MALIGNANCY

ma·lig·nan·cy \-nən(t)-sē\ n, pl -cies (1601) 1 : the quality or state of being malignant 2 **a** : exhibition (as by a tumor) of malignant qualities : VIRULENCE **b** : a malignant tumor

ma·lig·nant \mə-'lig-nənt\ adj [LL malignant-, malignans, prp. of malignari] (ca. 1545) 1 **a** obs : MALCONTENT, DISAFFECTED **b** : evil in nature, influence, or effect : INJURIOUS **c** : passionately and relentlessly malevolent : aggressively malicious 2 : tending to produce death or deterioration ⟨~ malaria⟩; esp : tending to infiltrate, metastasize, and terminate fatally ⟨~ tumor⟩ — **ma·lig·nant·ly** adv

ma·lig·ni·ty \mə-'lig-nə-tē\ n (14c) 1 : MALIGNANCY, MALEVOLENCE 2 : an instance of malignant or malicious behavior or nature **syn** see MALICE

ma·li·hi·ni \,mä-li-'hē-nē\ n [Hawaiian] (1914) : a newcomer or stranger among the people of Hawaii

ma·lines \mə-'lēn\ n, pl **ma·lines** \-'lēn(z)\ [F, fr. Malines (Mechelen), Belgium] (1833) 1 : MECHLIN 2 also **ma·line** : a fine stiff net with a hexagonal mesh that is usu. made of silk or rayon and is often used for veils

ma·lin·ger \mə-'liŋ-gər\ vi **ma·lin·gered**; **ma·lin·ger·ing** \-g(ə-)riŋ\ [F malingre sickly] (1820) : to pretend incapacity (as illness) so as to avoid duty or work — **ma·lin·ger·er** \-gər-ər\ n

Ma·lin·ke \mə-'liŋ-kē\ n, pl **Malinke** or **Malinkes** (1883) 1 : a member of a people of Mandingo affiliation widespread in the western part of Africa 2 : the language of the Malinke people

Ma·li·nois \,mal-ən-'wä\ n [F, one from Malines, fr. Malines (Mechelen), Belgium] (1929) : BELGIAN MALINOIS

mal·i·son \'ma-lə-sən, -zən\ n [ME, fr. OF maleïçon, fr. LL malediction-, maledictio] (13c) : CURSE, MALEDICTION

mal·kin \'mȯ(l)-kən, 'mal-\ n [ME malkyn servant woman, fr. Malkyn, dim. of the name Maud] (1586) 1 dial chiefly Brit : an untidy woman : SLATTERN 2 dial chiefly Brit : CAT **b** : HARE

¹mall \'mȯl\ var of MAUL

²mall \'mȯl, esp Brit & for 1 'mal\ n [short for obs. pall-mall mallet used in pall-mall] (1644) 1 : an alley used for pall-mall 2 [The Mall, promenade in London, orig. a pall-mall alley] **a** : a usu. public area often set with shade trees and designed as a promenade or as a pedestrian walk **b** : a usu. paved or grassy strip between two roadways 3 **a** : an urban shopping area featuring a variety of shops surrounding a usu. open-air concourse reserved for pedestrian traffic **b** : a usu. large suburban building or group of buildings containing various shops with associated passageways

mal·lard \'ma-lərd\ n, pl **mallard** or **mallards** [ME, fr. MF mallart] (14c) : a common and widely distributed wild duck (Anas platyrhynchos) of the northern hemisphere the males of which have a green head and white-ringed neck and which is the source of the domestic ducks

mal·lea·ble \'ma-lē-ə-bəl, 'mal-yə-bəl, 'ma-lə-bəl\ adj [ME malliable, fr. MF or ML; MF malleable, fr. ML malleabilis, fr. malleare to hammer, fr. L malleus hammer — more at MAUL] (14c) **1** : capable of being extended or shaped by beating with a hammer or by the pressure of rollers **2 a** : capable of being altered or controlled by outside forces or influences **b** : having a capacity for adaptive change **syn** see PLASTIC — **mal·lea·bil·i·ty** \,ma-lē-ə-'bi-lə-tē, ,mal-yə-, ,ma-lə-\ n

mal·lee \'ma-lē\ n \[Wuywurung (Australian aboriginal language of the Melbourne area, Victoria) mali\] (1845) **1** : any of various low-growing shrubby Australian eucalypts (as Eucalyptus dumosa and E. oleosa) **2** : a dense thicket or growth of mallees; also : land covered by such growth

mal·let \'ma-lət\ n [ME maillet, fr. MF, fr. OF, dim. of mail maul — more at MAUL] (15c) : a hammer with a typically barrel-shaped head: as **a** : a tool with a large head for driving another tool or for striking a surface without marring it **b** : a long-handled wooden implement used for striking a ball (as in polo or croquet) **c** : a light hammer with a small rounded or spherical usu. padded head used in playing certain musical instruments (as a vibraphone)

mal·le·us \'ma-lē-əs\ n, pl **mal·lei** \-lē-,ī, -lē-,ē\ [NL, fr. L, hammer] (1669) : the outermost of a chain of three small bones of the mammalian middle ear — see EAR illustration

mal·low \'ma-(,)lō\ n [ME malwe, fr. OE mealwe, fr. L malva] (bef. 12c) : any of a genus (Malva of the family Malvaceae, the mallow family) of herbs with palmately lobed or dissected leaves, usu. showy flowers, and a disk-shaped fruit

malm·sey \'mäm-zē, 'mälm-, NewEng also 'mám-\ n, often cap [ME malmesey, fr. ML Malmasia Monemvasia, village in Greece where a sweet wine was produced] (15c) : the sweetest variety of Madeira wine

mal·nour·ished \,mal-'nər-isht, -'nə-risht\ adj (1927) : UNDERNOURISHED

mal·nu·tri·tion \,mal-nù-'tri-shən, -nyü-\ n (1862) : faulty or inadequate nutrition

mal·oc·clu·sion \,ma-lə-'klü-zhən\ n (1888) : improper occlusion; esp : abnormality in the coming together of teeth

mal·odor \,mal-'ō-dər\ n (1825) : an offensive odor

mal·odor·ous \-'ō-də-rəs\ adj (1850) **1** : having a bad odor **2** : highly improper (~ practices and chicanery in high financial places —New Republic) — **mal·odor·ous·ly** adv — **mal·odor·ous·ness** n **syn** MALODOROUS, STINKING, FETID, NOISOME, PUTRID, RANK, FUSTY, MUSTY mean bad-smelling. MALODOROUS may range from the unpleasant to the strongly offensive (malodorous fertilizers). STINKING and FETID suggest the foul or disgusting (prisoners were held in stinking cells) (the fetid odor of skunk cabbage). NOISOME adds a suggestion of being harmful or unwholesome as well as offensive (a stagnant, noisome sewer). PUTRID implies particularly the sickening odor of decaying organic matter (the putrid smell of rotting fish). RANK suggests a strong unpleasant smell (rank cigar smoke). FUSTY and MUSTY suggest lack of fresh air and sunlight, FUSTY also implying prolonged uncleanliness, MUSTY stressing the effects of dampness, mildew, or age (a fusty attic) (the musty odor of a damp cellar).

ma·lo·lac·tic \,ma-lō-'lak-tik, ,mä-\ adj [malic + -o- + lactic] (1965) : relating to or involved in the bacterial conversion of malic acid to lactic acid in wine (~ fermentation)

maloti pl of LOTI

Mal·pi·ghi·an corpuscle \mal-'pi-gē-ən-, -'pē-\ n [Marcello Malpighi] (1848) : the part of a nephron that consists of a glomerulus and Bowman's capsule — called also Malpighian body

Malpighian layer n (1878) : the deeper part of the epidermis consisting of cells whose protoplasm has not yet changed into horny material

Malpighian tubule n (1877) : any of a group of long blind vessels opening into the posterior part of the alimentary canal in most insects and some other arthropods and functioning primarily as excretory organs — called also Malpighian tube

mal·po·si·tion \,mal-pə-'zi-shən\ n (ca. 1839) : wrong or faulty position

mal·prac·tice \,mal-'prak-təs\ n (1671) **1** : a dereliction from professional duty or a failure to exercise an accepted degree of professional skill or learning by one (as a physician) rendering professional services which results in injury, loss, or damage **2** : an injurious, negligent, or improper practice : MALFEASANCE

mal·prac·ti·tio·ner \,mal-prak-'ti-sh(ə-)nər\ n (1800) : one who engages in or commits malpractice

¹malt \'mölt\ n [ME, fr. OE mealt; akin to OHG malz malt, OE meltan to melt] (bef. 12c) **1** : grain (as barley) softened by steeping in water, allowed to germinate, and used esp. in brewing and distilling **2** : MALT LIQUOR **3** : MALTED MILK — **malty** \'mol-tē\ adj

²malt vt (15c) **1** : to convert into malt **2** : to make or treat with malt or malt extract ~ vi **1** : to become malt **2** : to make grain into malt

malt·ase \'mol-,tās, -,tāz\ n (1890) : an enzyme that catalyzes the hydrolysis of maltose to glucose

malted milk n (1887) **1** : a soluble powder prepared from dried milk and malted cereals **2** : a beverage made by dissolving malted milk in milk and usu. adding ice cream and flavoring — called also malted

Mal·tese \mol-'tēz, -'tēs\ n, pl **Maltese** (1615) **1** : a native or inhabitant of Malta **2** : the Semitic language of the Maltese people **3** : any of a breed of toy dogs with a long silky white coat, a black nose, and very dark eyes — **Maltese** adj

Maltese cross n (1877) **1 a** : a cross formée **b** : a cross that resembles the cross formée but has the outer face of each arm indented in a V — see CROSS illustration **2** : a Eurasian perennial (Lychnis chalcedonica) having scarlet or rarely white flowers in dense terminal heads

Mal·thu·sian \mal-'thü-zhən, mòl-, -'thyü-\ adj [Thomas R. Malthus] (1821) : of or relating to Malthus or to his theory that population tends to increase at a faster rate than its means of subsistence and that unless it is checked by moral restraint or disaster (as disease, famine, or war) widespread poverty and degradation inevitably result — **Malthusian** n — **Mal·thu·sian·ism** \-zhə-,ni-zəm\ n

malt liquor n (1693) : a fermented liquor (as beer) made with malt

malt·ose \'mòl-,tōs, -,tōz\ n [F, fr. E ¹malt] (1862) : a crystalline dextrorotatory fermentable sugar $C_{12}H_{22}O_{11}$ formed esp. from starch by amylase

mal·treat \,mal-'trēt\ vt [part. trans. of F maltraiter, fr. MF, fr. mal- + traiter to treat, fr. OF traitier — more at TREAT] (1708) : to treat cruelly or roughly : ABUSE — **mal·treat·er** \-'trē-tər\ n — **mal·treat·ment** \-'trēt-mənt\ n

malt·ster \'mólt-stər\ n (14c) : a maker of malt

malt sugar n (1862) : MALTOSE

malt whiskey n (ca. 1839) : SCOTCH 3

mal·ver·sa·tion \,mal-vər-'sā-shən\ n [MF, fr. malverser to be corrupt, fr. mal + verser to turn, handle, fr. L versare, freq. of vertere to turn — more at WORTH] (1549) **1** : misbehavior and esp. corruption in an office, trust, or commission **2** : corrupt administration

ma·ma or **mam·ma** \'mä-mə, chiefly Brit mə-'má\ n [baby talk] (1579) **1** : MOTHER **2** slang : WIFE, WOMAN

mama's boy n (1850) : a usu. polite or timid boy or man who is extremely or excessively close to and solicitous of his mother

mam·ba \'mäm-bə, 'mam-\ n [Zulu imamba] (1862) : any of several chiefly arboreal venomous green or black elapid snakes (genus Dendroaspis syn. Dendraspis) of sub-Saharan Africa

mam·bo \'mäm-(,)bō\ n, pl **mambos** [AmerSp] (1948) : a ballroom dance of Cuban origin that resembles the rumba and the cha-cha; also : the music for this dance — **mambo** vi

ma·mey \ma-'mē\ n [Sp, fr. Taino] (1604) : a tropical American tree (Mammea americana of the family Guttiferae) having an ovoid fruit with thick russet leathery rind and yellow or reddish juicy sweet flesh; also : the fruit

Mam·luk \'mam-,lük\ or **Mam·e·luke** \'ma-mə-,lük\ n [Ar mamlūk, lit., slave] (ca. 1506) **1** : a member of a politically powerful Egyptian military class occupying the sultanate from 1250 to 1517 **2** often not cap : a white or east Asian slave in Muslim countries

mam·ma \'ma-mə\ n, pl **mam·mae** \'ma-,mē, -,mī\ [L, mother, breast, of baby-talk origin] (ca. 1693) : a mammary gland and its accessory parts

mam·mal \'ma-məl\ n [NL Mammalia, fr. LL, neut. pl. of mammalis of the breast, fr. L mamma breast] (1826) : any of a class (Mammalia) of warm-blooded higher vertebrates (as placentals, marsupials, or monotremes) that nourish their young with milk secreted by mammary glands, have the skin usu. more or less covered with hair, and include humans — **mam·ma·li·an** \mə-'mā-lē-ən, ma-\ adj or n

mam·mal·o·gy \mə-'ma-lə-jē, ma-'ma-, -'mä-\ n [ISV, blend of mammal and -logy] (1835) : a branch of zoology dealing with mammals — **mam·mal·o·gist** \-jist\ n

mam·ma·ry \'ma-mə-rē\ adj (1682) : of, relating to, lying near, or affecting the mammae

mammary gland n (1831) : any of the large compound modified sebaceous glands that in female mammals are modified to secrete milk, are situated ventrally in pairs, and usu. terminate in a nipple

mam·mer vi [ME mameren to stammer, of imit. origin] (ca. 1555) obs : WAVER, HESITATE

mam·mil·la·ry \'ma-mə-,ler-ē, ma-'mi-lə-rē\ adj [L mammilla breast, nipple, dim. of mamma] (1669) **1** : of, relating to, or resembling the breasts **2** : studded with breast-shaped protuberances

mam·mil·lat·ed \'ma-mə-,lā-təd\ adj [LL mammillatus, fr. L mammilla] (1741) **1** : having nipples or small protuberances **2** : having the form of a bluntly rounded protuberance

¹mam·mock \'ma-mək\ n [origin unknown] (ca. 1529) chiefly dial : a broken piece : SCRAP

²mammock vt (1607) chiefly dial : to tear into fragments : MANGLE

mam·mo·gram \'ma-mə-,gram\ n [L mamma + E -o- + -gram] (1937) : a photograph of the breasts made by X rays

mam·mog·ra·phy \ma-'mä-grə-fē\ n (1937) : X-ray examination of the breasts (as for early detection of cancer) — **mam·mo·graph·ic** \,ma-mə-'gra-fik\ adj

mam·mon \'ma-mən\ n, often cap [LL mammona, fr. Gk mamōna, fr. Aram māmōnā riches] (15c) : material wealth or possessions esp. as having a debasing influence (you cannot serve God and ~ —Mt 6:24 (RSV)) — **mam·mon·ism** \-mə-,ni-zəm\ n

mam·mon·ist \-mə-nist\ n (1550) archaic : one devoted to the ideal or pursuit of wealth

¹mam·moth \'ma-məth\ n [Russ mamont, mamot] (1706) **1** : any of a genus (Mammuthus) of extinct Pleistocene elephants distinguished from recent elephants by highly ridged molars, usu. large size, very long tusks that curve upward, and well-developed body hair **2** : something immense of its kind : GIANT (a company that is a ~ of the industry)

²mammoth adj (1802) : of very great size **syn** see ENORMOUS

mam·my \'ma-mē\ n, pl **mammies** [alter. of mamma] (1523) **1** : MAMA **2** : a black woman serving as a nurse to white children esp. formerly in the southern U.S.

¹man \'man, in compounds ,man or mən\ n, pl **men** \'men, in compounds ,men or mən\ [ME, fr. OE man, mon human being, male human; akin to OHG man human being, Skt manu] (bef. 12c) **1 a** (1) : an individual human; esp : an adult male human (2) : a man belonging to a particular category (as by birth, residence, membership, or occupation) — usu. used in combination (councilman) (3) : HUSBAND (4) : LOVER **b** : the human race : MANKIND **c** : a bipedal primate mammal (Homo sapiens) that is anatomically related to the great apes but distinguished esp. by notable development of the brain with a resultant capacity for articulate speech and abstract reasoning, is usu. considered to form a variable number of freely interbreeding races, and is the sole representative of a natural family (Hominidae); broadly : any living or extinct member of this family **d** (1) : one possessing in high degree the qualities considered distinctive of manhood (2) obs : the quality or state of being manly : MANLINESS **e** : FELLOW, CHAP **f**

\ə\ abut \ʰ\ kitten, F table \ər\ further \a\ ash \ā\ ace \ä\ mop, mar \aù\ out \ch\ chin \e\ bet \ē\ easy \g\ go \i\ hit \ī\ ice \j\ job \ŋ\ sing \ō\ go \ò\ law \òi\ boy \th\ thin \ṯẖ\ the \ü\ loot \ù\ foot \y\ yet \zh\ vision \ä, k̲, ⁿ, œ, œ̄, ɷ, ūœ, ʸ\ see Guide to Pronunciation

— used interjectionally to express intensity of feeling ⟨~, what a game⟩ **2 a :** INDIVIDUAL, PERSON ⟨a ~ could get killed there⟩ **b :** the individual who can fulfill or who has been chosen to fulfill one's requirements ⟨she's your ~⟩ **3 a :** a feudal tenant **:** VASSAL **b :** an adult male servant **c** *pl* **:** the working force as distinguished from the employer and usu. the management **4 a :** one of the distinctive objects moved by each player in various board games **b :** one of the players on a team **5 :** an alumnus of or student at a college or university ⟨a Bowdoin ~⟩ **6** *Christian Science* **:** the compound idea of infinite Spirit **:** the spiritual image and likeness of God **:** the full representation of Mind **7** *often cap* **:** POLICE ⟨when I heard the siren, I knew it was the Man —*Amer. Speech*⟩ **8** *often cap* **:** the white establishment **:** white society ⟨surprise that any black . . . should take on so about The Man —Peter Goldman⟩ **9 :** one extremely fond of or devoted to something specified ⟨strictly a vanilla ice cream ~⟩ — **man·less** \'man-ləs\ *adj* — **man·like** \-‚līk\ *adj* — **as one man :** with the agreement and consent of all **:** UNANIMOUSLY — **one's own man :** free from interference or control **:** INDEPENDENT — **to a man :** without exception
²**man** *vt* **manned; man·ning** (12c) **1 a :** to supply with people (as for service) ⟨~ a fleet⟩ **b :** to station members of a ship's crew at ⟨~ the capstan⟩ **c :** to serve in the force or complement of ⟨we'll ~ the concession stand while you sell tickets⟩ **2 :** to accustom (as a hawk) to humans and the human environment **3 :** to furnish with strength or powers of resistance **:** BRACE
ma·na \'mä-nə\ *n* [of Polynesian origin; akin to Hawaiian & Maori *mana* mana] (ca. 1843) **1 :** the power of the elemental forces of nature embodied in an object or person **2 :** moral authority **:** PRESTIGE
man-about-town \‚man-ə-‚baùt-'taùn\ *n, pl* **men-about-town** \‚men-\ (1734) **:** a worldly and socially active man
¹**man·a·cle** \'ma-ni-kəl\ *n* [ME *manicle*, fr. MF, fr. L *manicula*, dim. of *manus* hand — more at MANUAL] (14c) **1 :** a shackle for the hand or wrist **:** HANDCUFF — usu. used in pl. **2 :** something used as a restraint
²**manacle** *vt* **man·a·cled; man·a·cling** \-k(ə-)liŋ\ (14c) **1 :** to confine (the hands) with manacles **2 :** to make fast or secure **:** BIND; *broadly* **:** to restrain from movement, progress, or action *syn* see HAMPER
¹**man·age** \'ma-nij\ *vb* **man·aged; man·ag·ing** [It *maneggiare*, fr. *mano* hand, fr. L *manus*] *vt* (1561) **1 :** to handle or direct with a degree of skill: as **a :** to make and keep compliant ⟨can't ~ her child⟩ **b :** to treat with care **:** HUSBAND ⟨*managed* his resources carefully⟩ **c :** to exercise executive, administrative, and supervisory direction of ⟨~ a business⟩ ⟨~ a bond issue⟩ ⟨~ a baseball team⟩ **2 :** to work upon or try to alter for a purpose ⟨~ the press⟩ ⟨~ stress⟩ **3 :** to succeed in accomplishing **:** CONTRIVE ⟨*managed* to escape from prison⟩ **4 :** to direct the professional career of ⟨an agency that ~s entertainers⟩ ~ *vi* **1 a :** to direct or carry on business or affairs; *also* **:** to direct a baseball team **b :** to admit of being carried on **2 :** to achieve one's purpose *syn* see CONDUCT
²**manage** *n* [It *maneggio* management, training of a horse, fr. *maneggiare*] (ca. 1587) **1 a** *archaic* **:** the action and paces of a trained riding horse **b :** the schooling or handling of a horse **c :** a riding school **2** *obs* **:** MANAGEMENT
man·age·able \'ma-ni-jə-bəl\ *adj* (1598) **:** capable of being managed — **man·age·abil·i·ty** \‚ma-ni-jə-'bi-lə-tē\ *n* — **man·age·able·ness** \'ma-ni-jə-bəl-nəs\ *n* — **man·age·ably** \-blē\ *adv*
man·age·ment \'ma-nij-mənt\ *n* (1598) **1 :** the act or art of managing **:** the conducting or supervising of something (as a business) **2 :** judicious use of means to accomplish an end **3 :** the collective body of those who manage or direct an enterprise — **man·age·men·tal** \‚ma-nij-'men-tᵊl\ *adj*
man·ag·er \'ma-ni-jər\ *n* (1588) **:** one that manages: as **a :** a person who conducts business or household affairs **b :** a person whose work or profession is management **c** (1) **:** a person who directs a team or athlete (2) **:** a student who in scholastic or collegiate sports supervises equipment and records under the direction of a coach — **man·a·ge·ri·al** \‚ma-nə-'jir-ē-əl\ *adj* — **man·a·ge·ri·al·ly** \-ē-ə-lē\ *adv* — **man·ag·er·ship** \'ma-ni-jər-‚ship\ *n*
man·ag·er·ess \'ma-ni-jə-rəs\ *n* (1797) **:** a woman who is a manager
managing editor *n* (1865) **:** an editor in executive and supervisory charge of all editorial activities of a publication (as a newspaper)
¹**ma·ña·na** \mən-'yä-nə\ *n* [Sp, lit., tomorrow, fr. (assumed) VL *maneana*, fr. fem. of *maneanus* early, fr. L *mane* early in the morning] (1845) **:** an indefinite time in the future
²**mañana** *adv* (1879) **:** at an indefinite time in the future
man ape *n* (ca. 1864) **1 :** GREAT APE **2 :** any of various fossil primates intermediate in characters between recent humans and the great apes
Ma·nas·seh \mə-'na-sə\ *n* [Heb *Mĕnashsheh*] **1 :** a son of Joseph and the traditional eponymous ancestor of one of the tribes of Israel **2 :** a king of Judah reigning in the 7th century B.C. and noted for his attempt to establish polytheism
man-at-arms \‚man-ət-'ärmz\ *n, pl* **men-at-arms** \‚men-\ (1581) **:** SOLDIER; *esp* **:** a heavily armed and usu. mounted soldier
man·a·tee \'ma-nə-‚tē\ *n* [Sp *manati*] (1555) **:** any of a genus (*Trichechus*) of chiefly tropical aquatic herbivorous mammals that differ from the related dugong esp. in having the tail rounded
Man·ches·ter terrier \'man-‚ches-tər-, -chə-stər-\ *n* [*Manchester*, England] (1891) **:** any of a breed of small short-haired black-and-tan terriers developed in England
man-child \'man-‚chīld\ *n, pl* **men-chil·dren** \'men-‚chil-drən, -dərn\ (14c) **:** a male child **:** SON
man·chi·neel \‚man-chə-'nē(ə)l\ *n* [F *mancenille*, fr. Sp *manzanilla*, fr. dim. of *manzana* apple] (1630) **:** a poisonous tropical American tree (*Hippomane mancinella*) of the spurge family having a blistering milky juice and apple-shaped fruit
Man·chu \'man-‚(‚)chü, man-'\ *n, pl* **Manchu** or **Manchus** (1697) **1 :** a member of an indigenous people of Manchuria who conquered China and established a dynasty there in 1644 **2 :** the Tungusic language of the Manchu people — **Manchu** *adj*

manatee

man·ci·ple \'man(t)-sə-pəl\ *n* [ME, fr. ML *mancipium* office of steward, fr. L, act of purchase, fr. *mancip-, manceps* purchaser — more at

EMANCIPATE] (13c) **:** a steward or purveyor esp. for a college or monastery
-mancy *n comb form* [ME *-mancie*, fr. OF, fr. L *-mantia*, fr. Gk *-manteia*, fr. *manteia*, fr. *mantis* diviner, prophet — more at MANTIS] **:** divination ⟨oneiro*mancy*⟩
Man·dae·an \man-'dē-ən\ *n* [Mandaean *mandayyā* having knowledge] (1875) **1 :** a member of a Gnostic sect of the lower Tigris and Euphrates regions **2 :** a form of Aramaic found in documents written by Mandaeans — **Mandaean** *adj*
man·da·la \'mən-də-lə\ *n* [Skt *mandala* circle] (1859) **1 :** a Hindu or Buddhist graphic symbol of the universe; *specif* **:** a circle enclosing a square with a deity on each side **2 :** a graphic and often symbolic pattern usu. in the form of a circle divided into four separate sections or bearing a multiple projection of an image — **man·dal·ic** \‚mən-'da-lik\ *adj*
man·da·mus \man-'dā-məs\ *n* [L, we enjoin, fr. *mandare*] (1535) **:** a writ issued by a superior court commanding the performance of a specified official act or duty
Man·dan \'man-‚dan, -dən\ *n, pl* **Mandan** or **Mandans** (1805) **1 :** a member of an American Indian people of the Missouri River Valley in No. Dakota **2 :** the Siouan language of the Mandans
¹**man·da·rin** \'man-d(ə-)rən\ *n* [Pg *mandarim*, fr. Malay *mĕntĕri*, fr. Skt *mantrin* counselor, fr. *mantra* counsel — more at MANTRA] (1589) **1 a :** a public official in the Chinese Empire of any of nine superior grades **b** (1) **:** a pedantic official (2) **:** BUREAUCRAT **c :** a person of position and influence often in intellectual or literary circles; *esp* **:** an elder and often traditionalize or reactionary member of such a circle **2** *cap* **a :** a form of spoken Chinese used by the court and the official classes of the Empire **b :** the group of closely related Chinese dialects that are spoken in about four fifths of the country and have a standard variety centering about Beijing **3** [F *mandarine*, fr. Sp *mandarina*, prob. fr. *mandarín* mandarin, fr. Pg *mandarim*; prob. fr. the color of a mandarin's robes] **a :** a small spiny orange tree (*Citrus reticulata*) of southeastern Asia with yellow to reddish orange loose-rinded fruits; *also* **:** a derivative of this tree developed in cultivation by artificial selection or hybridization **b :** the fruit of a mandarin — **man·da·rin·ic** \‚man-də-'ri-nik\ *adj* — **man·da·rin·ism** \'man-d(ə-)rə-‚ni-zəm\ *n*
²**mandarin** *adj* (1604) **1 :** of, relating to, or typical of a mandarin ⟨~ graces⟩ **2 :** marked by polished ornate complexity of language ⟨~ prose⟩
man·da·rin·ate \'man-d(ə-)rə-‚nāt\ *n* [prob. fr. F *mandarinat*, fr. *darin* mandarin, fr. Pg *mandarim*] (ca. 1741) **1 :** the office or status of a mandarin **2 :** a body of mandarins **3 :** rule by mandarins
mandarin collar *n* (1947) **:** a narrow stand-up collar usu. open in front
mandarin orange *n* (1771) **:** MANDARIN 3
man·da·tary \'man-də-‚ter-ē\ *n, pl* **-tar·ies** (15c) **:** MANDATORY
¹**man·date** \'man-‚dāt\ *n* [MF & L; MF *mandat*, fr. L *mandatum*, fr. neut. of *mandatus*, pp. of *mandare* to entrust, enjoin, prob. irreg. fr. *manus* hand + *-dere* to put — more at MANUAL, DO] (1501) **1 :** an authoritative command; *esp* **:** a formal order from a superior court or official to an inferior one **2 :** an authorization to act given to a representative ⟨accepted the ~ of the people⟩ **3 a :** an order or commission granted by the League of Nations to a member nation for the establishment of a responsible government over a former German colony or other conquered territory **b :** a mandated territory
²**mandate** *vt* **man·dat·ed; man·dat·ing** (1919) **1 :** to administer or assign (as a territory) under a mandate **2 :** to make mandatory **:** ORDER; *also* **:** DIRECT, REQUIRE
man·da·tor \'man-‚dā-tər\ *n* (1681) **:** one that gives a mandate
¹**man·da·to·ry** \'man-də-‚tōr-ē, -‚tor-\ *adj* (1576) **1 :** containing or constituting a command; *esp* **:** OBLIGATORY ⟨~ retirement age⟩ **2 :** of, by, relating to, or holding a League of Nations mandate — **man·da·tor·i·ly** \-‚tor-ə-lē, -‚tor-\ *adv*
²**mandatory** *n, pl* **-ries** (1661) **:** one given a mandate; *esp* **:** a nation holding a mandate from the League of Nations
man-day \'man-'dā\ *n* (1925) **:** a unit of one day's work by one person
Man·de \'män-‚dā, män-'\ *n* (1883) **1 :** MANDINGO **2 :** a branch of the Niger-Congo language family spoken primarily in Sierra Leone, Liberia, Guinea, Ivory Coast, Mali, and Burkina Faso
man·di·ble \'man-də-bəl\ *n* [MF, fr. LL *mandibula*, fr. L *mandere* to chew; prob. akin to Gk *masasthai* to chew] (15c) **1 a :** JAW 1a; *esp* **:** a lower jaw consisting of a single bone or of completely fused bones **b :** the lower jaw with its investing soft parts **c :** either the upper or lower segment of the bill of a bird **2 :** any of various invertebrate mouthparts serving to hold or bite food materials; *esp* **:** either member of the anterior pair of mouth appendages of an arthropod often forming strong biting jaws — **man·dib·u·lar** \man-'di-byə-lər\ *adj* — **man·dib·u·late** \-lət\ *adj*
Man·din·go \man-'diŋ-(‚)gō\ *n, pl* **Mandingo** or **Mandingoes** or **Mandingos** (1623) **1 :** a member of a people of western Africa centering in the area of the upper Niger valley **2 :** the language of the Mandingo people
Man·din·ka \man-'diŋ-kə\ *n, pl* **Mandinka** or **Mandinkas** (1939) **:** MALINKE
man·di·o·ca \‚man-dē-'ō-kə\ *var of* MANIOC
man·do·la \man-'dō-lə\ *n* [It, fr. F *mandore*, modif. of LL *pandura* 3-stringed lute — more at BANDORE] (1758) **:** a 16th and 17th century lute that is the ancestor of the smaller mandolin
man·do·lin \‚man-də-'lin, 'man-dᵊl-ən\ *also* **man·do·line** \‚man-də-'lēn, 'man-dᵊl-ən\ *n* [It *mandolino*, dim. of *mandola*] (1707) **1 :** a musical instrument of the lute family that has a usu. pear-shaped body and fretted neck and four to six pairs of strings **2** *usu* **mandoline** [F, fr. It *mandolino* mandolin] **:** a kitchen utensil with a blade for slicing and shredding — **man·do·lin·ist** \‚man-də-'li-nist\ *n*
man·drag·o·ra \man-'dra-gə-rə\ *n* [ME, fr. OE, fr. L *mandragoras*, fr. Gk] (bef. 12c) **:** MANDRAKE 1
man·drake \'man-‚drāk\ *n* [ME, prob. alter. of *mandragora*] (14c) **1 a :** a Mediterranean herb (*Mandragora officinarum*) of the nightshade family with ovate leaves, yellowish or purple flowers, and a large

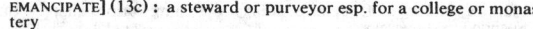
mandolin 1

forked root traditionally credited with human attributes **b** : the root of a mandrake formerly used esp. to promote conception, as a cathartic, or as a narcotic and soporific **2** : MAYAPPLE

man·drel also **man·dril** \'man-drəl\ n [prob. modif. of F mandrin] (1665) **1 a** : a usu. tapered or cylindrical axle, spindle, or arbor inserted into a hole in a piece of work to support it during machining **b** : a metal bar that serves as a core around which material (as metal) may be cast, molded, forged, bent, or otherwise shaped **2** : the shaft and bearings on which a tool (as a circular saw) is mounted

man·drill \'man-drəl\ n [prob. fr. ¹man + ³drill] (1744) : a large baboon (Papio sphinx syn. Mandrillus sphinx) of central Africa west of the Congo River with the male having a bright red and blue muzzle

mane \'mān\ n [ME, fr. OE manu; akin to OHG mana mane, L monile necklace] (bef. 12c) **1** : long and heavy hair growing about the neck and head of some mammals (as a horse or lion) **2** : long heavy hair on a person's head — **maned** \'mānd\ adj

man–eat·er \'man-ˌē-tər\ n (1600) : one that has or is thought to have an appetite for human flesh: as **a** : CANNIBAL **b** : MACKEREL SHARK; esp : GREAT WHITE SHARK — called also man-eater shark, man-eating shark **c** : a large feline (as a lion or tiger) that has acquired the habit of feeding on human flesh — **man–eat·ing** \-ˌē-tiŋ\ adj

maned wolf n (1903) : a yellowish red wild canid (Chrysocyon brachyurus) inhabiting So. American grasslands and having black coloration on the nape and lower legs

ma·nège also **ma·nege** \ma-'nezh, mə-, -'nāzh\ n [F manège, fr. It maneggio training of a horse — more at MANAGE] (1644) **1** : a school for teaching horsemanship and for training horses **2** : the art of horsemanship or of training horses **3** : the movements or paces of a trained horse

ma·nes \'mä-ˌnās, 'mā-ˌnēz\ n pl [L] **1** often cap : the deified spirits of the ancient Roman dead honored with graveside sacrifices **2** : the venerated or appeased spirit of a dead person

¹ma·neu·ver \mə-'nü-vər, -'nyü-\ n [F manœuvre, fr. OF maneuvre work done by hand, fr. ML manuopera, fr. L manu operare to work by hand] (1758) **1 a** : a military or naval movement **b** : an armed forces training exercise; esp : an extended and large-scale training exercise involving military and naval units separately or in combination — often used in pl. **2** : a procedure or method of working usu. involving expert physical movement **3 a** : evasive movement or shift of tactics **b** : an intended and controlled variation from a straight and level flight path in the operation of an airplane **4 a** : an action taken to gain a tactical end **b** : an adroit and clever management of affairs often using trickery and deception syn see TRICK

²maneuver vb **ma·neu·vered**; **ma·neu·ver·ing** \-'nü-və-riŋ, -'nyü-; -'n(y)üv-riŋ\ vi (1777) **1 a** : to perform a movement in military or naval tactics in order to secure an advantage **b** : to make a series of changes in direction and position for a specific purpose **2** : to use stratagems : SCHEME ~ vt **1** : to cause to execute tactical movements **2** : to manage into or out of a position or condition : MANIPULATE **3 a** : to guide with adroitness and design **b** : to bring about or secure as a result of skillful management — **ma·neu·ver·abil·i·ty** \-ˌnü-və-rə-'bi-lə-tē, -ˌnyü-; -ˌn(y)üv-rə-\ n — **ma·neu·ver·able** \-'nü-və-rə-bəl, -'nyü-; -'n(y)üv-rə-\ adj — **ma·neu·ver·er** \-'nü-vər-ər, -'nyü-\ n

man–for–man \ˌman-fər-'man\ adj (ca. 1949): MAN-TO-MAN 2

man Friday n [Friday, servant in Robinson Crusoe (1719), novel by Daniel Defoe] (1887) : an efficient and devoted aide or employee : a right-hand man

man·ful \'man-fəl\ adj (14c) : having or showing courage and resolution — **man·ful·ly** \-fə-lē\ adv — **man·ful·ness** n

man·ga·bey \'maŋ-gə-(ˌ)bē\ n, pl **-beys** [F, fr. Mangabey, region of Madagascar] (1774) : any of a genus (Cercocebus) of slender long-tailed African monkeys

mangan- comb form [G Mangan, fr. F manganèse] : manganese ⟨manganate⟩

man·ga·nate \'maŋ-gə-ˌnāt\ n (1839) **1** : a salt containing manganese in the anion MnO₄ : MANGANITE

man·ga·nese \'maŋ-gə-ˌnēz, -ˌnēs\ n [F manganèse, fr. It manganese manganese dioxide] (1783) : a grayish white usu. hard and brittle metallic element that resembles iron but is not magnetic — see ELEMENT table — **man·ga·ne·sian** \ˌmaŋ-gə-'nē-zhən, -shən\ adj

manganese dioxide n (1882) : a dark insoluble compound MnO₂ used esp. as an oxidizing agent, as a depolarizer of dry cells, and in making glass and ceramics

man·gan·ic \man-'ga-nik, maŋ-\ adj (ca. 1828) : of, relating to, or derived from manganese; esp : containing this element with a valence of three or six

man·ga·nite \'maŋ-gə-ˌnīt\ n (1827) **1** : an ore of manganese MnO(OH) that is a hydroxide of manganese usu. in brilliant gray crystals **2** : any of various unstable salts made by reaction of manganese dioxide with a base

man·ga·nous \-nəs\ adj (1842) : of, relating to, or derived from manganese; esp : containing this element with a valence of two

mange \'mānj\ n [alter. of ME manjewe, fr. MF mangene itching, fr. mangier to eat] (1540) : any of various persistent contagious skin diseases marked esp. by eczematous inflammation and loss of hair, affecting domestic animals or sometimes humans, and caused by a minute parasitic mite — compare SARCOPTIC MANGE

man·gel \'maŋ-gəl\ n [short for mangel-wurzel] (1877) : a large coarse yellow to reddish orange beet extensively grown as food for cattle

man·gel–wur·zel \-ˌwər-zəl\ n [G, alter. of Mangoldwurzel, fr. Mangold beet + Wurzel root] (1767) : MANGEL

man·ger \'mān-jər\ n [ME mangeour, manger, fr. MF maingeure, fr. mangier to eat, fr. L manducare to chew, devour, fr. manducus glutton, fr. mandere to chew — more at MANDIBLE] (14c) : a trough or open box in a stable designed to hold feed or fodder for livestock

¹man·gle \'maŋ-gəl\ vt **man·gled**; **man·gling** \-g(ə-)liŋ\ [ME, fr. AF mangler] (15c) **1** : to injure with deep disfiguring wounds by cutting, tearing, or crushing ⟨people . . . mangled by sharks —V. G. Heiser⟩ **2** : to spoil, injure, or make incoherent esp. through ineptitude ⟨a story mangled beyond recognition⟩ syn see MAIM — **man·gler** \-g(ə-)lər\ n

²mangle n [D mangel, fr. G, fr. MHG, dim. of mange mangonel, mangle, fr. L manganum] (1774) : a machine for ironing laundry by passing it between heated rollers

³mangle vt **man·gled**; **man·gling** \-g(ə-)liŋ\ (1775) : to press or smooth (as damp linen) with a mangle — **man·gler** \-g(ə-)lər\ n

man·go \'maŋ-(ˌ)gō\ n, pl **mangoes** also **mangos** [Pg manga, prob. fr. Malayalam māñña] (1582) **1** : a tropical fruit commonly with a firm yellowish red skin, hard central stone, and juicy aromatic pulp; also : an evergreen tree (Mangifera indica) of the cashew family that bears mangoes **2** : SWEET PEPPER

man·go·nel \'maŋ-gə-ˌnel\ n [ME, fr. OF, prob. fr. ML manganellus, dim. of LL manganum philter, mangonel, fr. Gk manganon] (13c) : a military engine formerly used to throw missiles

man·go·steen \'maŋ-gə-ˌstēn\ n [modif. of Malay manggisutan] (1598) : a dark reddish brown fruit of southeastern Asia with a thick rind and juicy flesh having a flavor suggestive of both peach and pineapple; also : a tree (Garcinia mangostana) of the Saint-John's-wort family that bears mangosteens

man·grove \'man-ˌgrōv, 'maŋ-\ n [prob. fr. Pg mangue mangrove (fr. Sp mangle, prob. fr. Taino) + E grove] (1613) **1** : any of a genus (Rhizophora, esp. R. mangle of the family Rhizophoraceae) of tropical maritime trees or shrubs that send out many prop roots and form dense masses important in coastal land building **2** : any of numerous trees (as of the genera Avicennia of the vervain family or Sonneratia of the family Sonneratiaceae) with growth habits like those of the true mangroves

mangy \'mān-jē\ adj **mang·i·er; -est** (1540) **1** : affected with or resulting from mange **2** : having many worn or bare spots : SEEDY, SHABBY — **man·gi·ness** \-jē-nəs\ n

man·han·dle \'man-ˌhan-d³l\ vt (ca. 1865) **1** : to handle roughly **2** : to move or manage by human force ⟨manhandled the posts into place⟩

man·hat·tan \man-'ha-t³n, mən-\ n, often cap [Manhattan, borough of New York City] (1890) : a cocktail consisting of vermouth, whiskey, and sometimes a dash of bitters

man·hole \'man-ˌhōl\ n (1793) : a hole through which one may go esp. to gain access to an underground or enclosed structure

man·hood \'man-ˌhùd\ n (13c) **1** : the condition of being a human being **2** : qualities associated with men **3** : the condition of being an adult male as distinguished from a child or female **4** : adult males : MEN

man–hour \'man-'aù(-ə)r\ n (1912) : a unit of one hour's work by one person that is used esp. as a basis for cost accounting and wages

man·hunt \'man-ˌhənt\ n (1846) : an organized and usu. intensive hunt for a person and esp. for one charged with a crime

ma·nia \'mā-nē-ə, -nyə\ n [ME, fr. LL, fr. Gk, fr. mainesthai to be mad; akin to Gk menos spirit — more at MIND] (14c) **1** : excitement manifested by mental and physical hyperactivity, disorganization of behavior, and elevation of mood; specif : the manic phase of manic-depressive psychosis **2** : excessive or unreasonable enthusiasm ⟨a ~ for saving things⟩; also : the object of such enthusiasm

ma·ni·ac \'mā-nē-ˌak\ n [LL maniacus maniacal, fr. Gk maniakos, fr. mania] (ca. 1763) **1** : MADMAN, LUNATIC **2** : a person characterized by an inordinate or ungovernable enthusiasm for something

ma·ni·a·cal \mə-'nī-ə-kəl\ also **ma·ni·ac** \'mā-nē-ˌak\ adj (1604) **1** : affected with or suggestive of madness **2** : characterized by ungovernable excitement or frenzy : FRANTIC — **ma·ni·a·cal·ly** \mə-'nī-ə-k(ə-)lē\ adv

man·ic \'ma-nik\ adj (1902) : affected with, relating to, or resembling mania — **manic** n — **man·i·cal·ly** \-ni-k(ə-)lē\ adv

man·ic–de·pres·sive \ˌma-nik-di-'pre-siv\ adj (1902) : characterized either by mania or by psychotic depression or by alternating mania and depression — **manic–depressive** n

Man·i·chae·an or **Man·i·che·an** \ˌma-nə-'kē-ən\ or **Man·i·chee** \'man-ə-ˌkē\ n [LL manichaeus, fr. LGk manichaios, fr. Manichaios Manes †ab 276 A.D. Pers. founder of the sect] (1556) **1** : a believer in a syncretistic religious dualism originating in Persia in the 3d century A.D. and teaching the release of the spirit from matter through asceticism **2** : a believer in religious or philosophical dualism — **Manichaean** adj — **Man·i·chae·an·ism** \ˌma-nə-'kē-ə-ˌni-zəm\ n — **Man·i·chae·ism** \ˌma-nə-'kē-ˌi-zəm\ n

man·i·cot·ti \ˌma-nə-'kä-tē\ n, pl **manicotti** [It, pl. of manicotto muff, fr. manica sleeve, fr. L, fr. manus hand] (1948) : tubular pasta shells that may be stuffed with ricotta or a meat mixture; also : a dish of stuffed manicotti usu. with tomato sauce

¹man·i·cure \'ma-nə-ˌkyùr\ n [F, fr. L manus hand + F -icure (as in pédicure pedicure) — more at MANUAL] (1880) **1** : MANICURIST **2** : a treatment for the care of the hands and fingernails

²manicure vt **-cured; -cur·ing** (ca. 1890) **1** : to do manicure work on; esp : to trim and polish the fingernails of **2 a** : to trim closely and evenly ⟨manicured lawns⟩ **b** : GROOM 2 ⟨manicured flower beds⟩

man·i·cur·ist \-ˌkyùr-ist\ n (1889) : a person who gives manicures

¹man·i·fest \'ma-nə-ˌfest\ adj [ME, fr. MF or L; MF manifeste, fr. L manifestus caught in the act, flagrant, obvious, perh. fr. manus + -festus (akin to L infestus hostile)] (14c) : readily perceived by the senses and esp. by the sight **1** : easily understood or recognized by the mind : OBVIOUS syn see EVIDENT — **man·i·fest·ly** adv

²manifest vt (14c) : to make evident or certain by showing or displaying syn see SHOW — **man·i·fest·er** n

³manifest n (1561) **1** : MANIFESTATION, INDICATION **2** : MANIFESTO **3** : a list of passengers or an invoice of cargo for a vehicle (as a ship or plane)

man·i·fes·tant \ˌma-nə-'fes-tənt\ n (1880) : one who makes or participates in a manifestation

man·i·fes·ta·tion \ˌma-nə-fə-'stā-shən, -ˌfe-'stā-\ n (15c) **1 a** : the act, process, or an instance of manifesting **b** : something that manifests or is manifest **c** : one of the forms in which an individual is manifested **d** : an occult phenomenon; specif : MATERIALIZATION **2** : a public demonstration of power and purpose

manifest destiny n, often cap M&D (1845) : a future event accepted as

---

\ə\ abut \ᵊ\ kitten, F table \ər\ further \a\ ash \ā\ ace \ä\ mop, mar \aù\ out \ch\ chin \e\ bet \ē\ easy \g\ go \i\ hit \ī\ ice \j\ job \ŋ\ sing \ō\ go \ò\ law \òi\ boy \th\ thin \t̲h̲\ the \ü\ loot \ù\ foot \y\ yet \zh\ vision \á, k̲, ⁿ, œ, œ̄, ue, ue̅, ʸ\ see Guide to Pronunciation inevitable ⟨in the mid-19th century expansion to the Pacific was regarded as the *Manifest Destiny* of the United States⟩; *broadly* : an ostensibly benevolent or necessary policy of imperialistic expansion

¹man·i·fes·to \ˌma-nə-'fes-(ˌ)tō\ *n, pl* **-tos** *or* **-toes** [It, denunciation, manifest, fr. *manifestare* to manifest, fr. L, fr. *manifestus*] (1647) : a written statement declaring publically the intentions, motives, or views of its issuer

²manifesto *vi* (1748) : to issue a manifesto

¹man·i·fold \'ma-nə-ˌfōld\ *adj* [ME, fr. OE *manigfeald*, fr. *manig* many + *-feald* -fold] (bef. 12c) **1 a** : marked by diversity or variety **b** : MANY **2** : comprehending or uniting various features : MULTIFARIOUS **3** : rightfully so-called for many reasons ⟨a ~ liar⟩ **4** : consisting of or operating many of one kind combined ⟨a ~ bellpull⟩ — **man·i·fold·ly** \-ˌfōl(d)-lē\ *adv* — **man·i·fold·ness** \-ˌfōl(d)-nəs\ *n*

²manifold *adv* (bef. 12c) : many times : a great deal ⟨will increase your blessings ~⟩

³manifold *vt* (bef. 12c) **1** : to make manifold : MULTIPLY **2** : to make several or many copies of ~ *vi* : to make several or many copies

⁴manifold *n* (1855) : something that is manifold: as **a** : a whole that unites or consists of many diverse elements ⟨the ~ of aspirations, passions, frustrations —Harry Slochower⟩ **b** : a pipe fitting with several lateral outlets for connecting one pipe with others; *also* : a fitting on an internal-combustion engine that directs a fuel and air mixture to or receives the exhaust gases from several cylinders **c** : SET 21 **d** : a topological space in which every point has a neighborhood that is homeomorphic to the interior of a sphere in Euclidean space of the same number of dimensions

man·i·kin *or* **man·ni·kin** \'ma-ni-kən\ *n* [D *mannekijn* little man, fr. MD, dim. of *man*; akin to OE *man*] (ca. 1536) **1** : MANNEQUIN **2** : a little man : DWARF, PYGMY

ma·nila *also* **ma·nil·la** \mə-'ni-lə\ *adj* (1834) **1** *cap* : made from Manila hemp **2** : made of manila paper — **manila** *n*

Manila hemp *n* [*Manila*, Philippine Islands] (ca. 1847) : ABACA

manila paper *n, often cap M* (1873) : a strong and durable paper of a brownish or buff color and smooth finish made orig. from Manila hemp

ma·nille \mə-'nil\ *n* [modif. of Sp *malilla*] (1674) : the second highest trump in various card games (as ombre)

man in the street (1831) : an average or ordinary person

man·i·oc \'ma-nē-ˌäk\ *n* [F *manioc* & Sp & Pg *mandioca*, fr. Tupi *manioca*] (1568) : CASSAVA

man·i·ple \'ma-nə-pəl\ *n* [ME, fr. ML *manipulus*, fr. L, handful, fr. *manus* hand + *-pulus* (perh. akin to L *plēre* to fill); fr. its having been orig. held in the hand — more at MANUAL, FULL] (15c) **1** : a long narrow strip of silk worn at mass over the left arm by clerics of or above the order of subdeacon **2** [L *manipulus*, fr. *manipulus* handful] : a subdivision of the Roman legion consisting of either 120 or 60 men

ma·nip·u·la·ble \mə-'ni-pyə-lə-bəl\ *adj* (1881) : capable of being manipulated — **ma·nip·u·la·bil·i·ty** \-ˌni-pyə-lə-'bi-lə-tē\ *n*

ma·nip·u·lar \mə-'ni-pyə-lər\ *adj* (1623) **1** : of or relating to the ancient Roman maniple **2** : of, relating to, or performed by manipulation : MANIPULATIVE

ma·nip·u·late \mə-'ni-pyə-ˌlāt\ *vt* **-lat·ed; -lat·ing** [back-formation fr. *manipulation*, fr. F, fr. *manipuler* to handle an apparatus in chemistry, ultim. fr. L *manipulus*] (1831) **1** : to treat or operate with the hands or by mechanical means esp. in a skillful manner **2 a** : to manage or utilize skillfully **b** : to control or play upon by artful, unfair, or insidious means esp. to one's own advantage **3** : to change by artful or unfair means so as to serve one's purpose : DOCTOR — **ma·nip·u·lat·able** \-ˌlā-tə-bəl\ *adj* — **ma·nip·u·la·tion** \-ˌni-pyə-'lā-shən\ *n* — **ma·nip·u·la·tive** \-'ni-pyə-ˌlā-tiv, -lə-\ *adj* — **ma·nip·u·la·tive·ly** *adv* — **ma·nip·u·la·tive·ness** *n* — **ma·nip·u·la·tor** \-ˌlā-tər\ *n* — **ma·nip·u·la·to·ry** \-lə-ˌtōr-ē, -ˌtór-\ *adj*

man·i·tou *or* **man·i·tu** \'ma-nə-ˌtü\ *also* **man·i·to** \-ˌtō\ *n* [Ojibwa *manito*] (1671) : a supernatural force that according to an Algonquian conception pervades the natural world

man jack \'man-'jak\ *n* (1840) : individual man ⟨every *man jack*⟩

man·kind *n sing but sing or pl in constr* (13c) **1** \'man-'kīnd, -ˌkīnd\ : the human race : the totality of human beings **2** \-ˌkīnd\ : men esp. as distinguished from women

¹man·ly \'man-lē\ *adv* (bef. 12c) : in a manly manner

²manly *adj* **man·li·er; -est** (13c) **1** : having qualities generally associated with a man : STRONG, VIRILE **2** : appropriate in character to a man ⟨~ sports⟩ — **man·li·ness** *n*

man–made \'man-'mād, -ˌmād\ *adj* (ca. 1718) : manufactured, created, or constructed by human beings; *specif* : SYNTHETIC ⟨~ fibers⟩

man·na \'ma-nə\ *n* [ME, fr. OE, fr. LL, fr. Gk, fr. Heb *mān*] (bef. 12c) **1 a** : food miraculously supplied to the Israelites in their journey through the wilderness **b** : divinely supplied spiritual nourishment **c** : a usu. sudden and unexpected source of gratification, pleasure, or gain **2 a** : the sweetish dried exudate of a European ash esp. *Fraxinus ornus*) that contains mannitol and has been used as a laxative and demulcent **b** : a similar product excreted by a scale insect (*Trabutina mannipara*) feeding on the tamarisk

manna grass *n* (1597) : any of a genus (*Glyceria*) of chiefly No. American perennial grasses of wetland or aquatic habitats

man·nan \'ma-ˌnan, -nən\ *n* [ISV *mannose* + ³-*an*] (1895) : any of several polysaccharides that are polymers of mannose and occur esp. in plant cell walls

manned \'mand\ *adj* (1617) : carrying or performed by a human being ⟨~ space-flight⟩

man·ne·quin \'ma-ni-kən\ *n* [F, fr. D *mannekijn* little man — more at MANIKIN] (1730) **1** : an artist's, tailor's, or dressmaker's lay figure; *also* : a form representing the human figure used esp. for displaying clothes **2** : one employed to model clothing

man·ner \'ma-nər\ *n* [ME *manere*, fr. OF *maniere* way of acting, fr. (assumed) VL *manuaria*, fr. L, fem. of *manuarius* of the hand, fr. *manus* hand — more at MANUAL] (12c) **1 a** : KIND, SORT ⟨what ~ of man is he⟩ **b** : KINDS, SORTS ⟨all ~ of problems⟩ **2 a** (1) : a characteristic or customary mode of acting : CUSTOM (2) : a mode of procedure or way of acting : FASHION (3) : method of artistic execution or mode of presentation : STYLE **b** *pl* : social conduct or rules of conduct as shown in the prevalent customs ⟨Victorian ~s⟩ **c** : characteristic or distinctive bearing, air, or deportment ⟨his poised gracious ~⟩ **d** *pl*

(1) : habitual conduct or deportment : BEHAVIOR ⟨mind your ~s⟩ (2) : good manners **e** : a distinguished or stylish air *syn* see BEARING, METHOD — **man·ner·less** \-ləs\ *adj*

man·nered \'ma-nərd\ *adj* (14c) **1** : having manners of a specified kind ⟨well-*mannered*⟩ **2 a** : having or displaying a particular manner **b** : having an artificial or stilted character ⟨passages . . . so ~ as to be unintelligible —R. G. G. Price⟩

man·ner·ism \'ma-nə-ˌri-zəm\ *n* (1803) **1 a** : exaggerated or affected adherence to a particular style or manner : ARTIFICIALITY, PRECIOSITY ⟨refined almost to the point of ~ —Winthrop Sargeant⟩ **b** *often cap* : an art style in late 16th century Europe characterized by spatial incongruity and excessive elongation of the human figures **2** : a characteristic and often unconscious mode or peculiarity of action, bearing, or treatment *syn* see POSE — **man·ner·ist** \-rist\ *n* — **man·ner·is·tic** \ˌma-nə-'ris-tik\ *adj*

man·ner·ly \'ma-nər-lē\ *adj* (ca. 1529) : showing good manners — **man·ner·li·ness** *n* — **mannerly** *adv*

man·nish \'ma-nish\ *adj* (14c) **1** : resembling or suggesting a man rather than a woman **2** : generally associated with or characteristic of a man rather than a woman ⟨her ~ clothes⟩ — **man·nish·ly** *adv* — **man·nish·ness** *n*

man·nite \'ma-ˌnīt\ *n* [F, fr. *manna*, fr. LL] (1830) : MANNITOL

man·ni·tol \'ma-nə-ˌtól, -ˌtōl\ *n* [ISV] (1879) : a slightly sweet crystalline alcohol $C_6H_{14}O_6$ found in many plants and used esp. as a diuretic and in testing kidney function

man·nose \'ma-ˌnōs, -ˌnōz\ *n* [ISV *mannite* + ²-*ose*] (1888) : an aldose $C_6H_{12}O_6$ whose dextrorotatory enantiomorph occurs esp. as a structural unit of mannans from which it can be recovered by hydrolysis

ma·no \'mä-(ˌ)nō\ *n, pl* **manos** [Sp, lit., hand, fr. L *manus* — more at MANUAL] (ca. 1892) : a stone used as the upper millstone for grinding foods (as Indian corn) by hand in a metate

ma·noeu·vre *chiefly Brit var of* MANEUVER

man of God (1748) : CLERGYMAN

man of letters (1645) **1** : SCHOLAR **2** : AUTHOR

man of straw (1624) : STRAW MAN

man of the house (ca. 1904) : the chief male in a household

man of the world (15c) : a practical or worldly-wise man of wide experience

man–of–war \ˌma-nə(v)-'wór\ *n, pl* **men–of–war** \ˌmen-\ (15c) : a combatant warship of a recognized navy

ma·nom·e·ter \mə-'nä-mə-tər\ *n* [F *manomètre*, fr. Gk *manos* sparse, loose, rare (akin to Arm *manr* small) + F *-mètre*] (ca. 1730) **1** : an instrument (as a pressure gauge) for measuring the pressure of gases and vapors **2** : SPHYGMOMANOMETER — **man·o·met·ric** \ˌma-nə-'me-trik\ *adj* — **man·o·met·ri·cal·ly** \-tri-k(ə-)lē\ *adv* — **ma·nom·e·try** \mə-'nä-mə-trē\ *n*

man on horseback (1860) **1** : a usu. military figure whose ambitions and popularity mark him as a potential dictator **2** : DICTATOR

man·or \'ma-nər\ *n* [ME *maner*, fr. OF *manoir*, fr. *manoir* to sojourn, dwell, fr. L *manēre* — more at MANSION] (14c) **1 a** : the house or hall of an estate : MANSION **b** : a landed estate **2 a** : a unit of English rural territorial organization; *esp* : such a unit in the Middle Ages consisting of an estate under a lord enjoying a variety of rights over land and tenants including the right to hold court **b** : a tract of land in No. America occupied by tenants who pay a fixed rent in money or kind to the proprietor — **ma·no·ri·al** \mə-'nōr-ē-əl, -'nór-\ *adj* — **ma·no·ri·al·ism** \-ə-ˌli-zəm\ *n*

manor house *n* (1575) : the house of the lord of a manor

man–o'–war bird \ˌma-nə-'wór-\ *n* (1707) : FRIGATE BIRD

man–pack \'man-ˌpak\ *adj* (1965) : designed to be carried by one person

man power *n* (1862) **1** : power available from or supplied by the physical effort of human beings **2** *usu* **man·pow·er** : the total supply of persons available and fitted for service

man·qué \mäⁿ-'kā\ *adj* [F, fr. pp. of *manquer* to lack, fail, fr. It *mancare*, fr. *manco* lacking, left-handed, fr. L, having a crippled hand, prob. fr. *manus*] (1778) : short of or frustrated in the fulfillment of one's aspirations or talents — used postpositively ⟨a poet ~⟩

man·rope \'man-ˌrōp\ *n* (1769) : a side rope (as to a ship's gangway or ladder) used as a handrail

man·sard \'man-ˌsärd, -sərd\ *n* [F *mansarde*, fr. François *Mansart* †1666 Fr. architect] (ca. 1734) : a roof having two slopes on all sides with the lower slope steeper than the upper one — see ROOF illustration — **man·sard·ed** \-ˌsär-dəd, -sər-\ *adj*

manse \'man(t)s\ *n* [ME *manss*, fr. ML *mansa, mansus, mansum*, fr. L *mansus* lodging, fr. *manēre*] (15c) **1** *archaic* : the dwelling of a householder **2** : the residence of a clergyman; *esp* : the house of a Presbyterian clergyman **3** : a large imposing residence

man·ser·vant \'man-ˌsər-vənt\ *n, pl* **men·ser·vants** \'men-ˌsər-vən(t)s\ (14c) : a male servant

-manship *n suffix* [*-man* + *-ship* (as in *horsemanship*)] **1** : art or practice of a competitive nature ⟨brink*manship*⟩ **2** : skilled engagement in a competitive activity ⟨grants*manship*⟩

man·sion \'man(t)-shən\ *n* [ME, fr. MF, fr. L *mansion-, mansio*, fr. *manēre* to remain, dwell; akin to Gk *menein* to remain] (14c) **1 a** *obs* : the act of remaining or dwelling : STAY **b** *archaic* : DWELLING, ABODE **2 a** (1) : the house of the lord of a manor (2) : a large imposing residence **b** : a separate apartment or lodging in a large structure **3 a** : HOUSE 3b **b** : one of the 28 parts into which the moon's monthly course through the heavens is divided

man–size \'man-ˌsīz\ *or* **man–sized** \-ˌsīzd\ *adj* (1913) **1** : suitable for or requiring a man ⟨a ~ job⟩ **2** : larger than others of its kind ⟨constructed a ~ map⟩

man·slaugh·ter \'man-ˌsló-tər\ *n* (15c) : the unlawful killing of a human being without express or implied malice

man·slay·er \-ˌslā-ər\ *n* (14c) : one who commits homicide

man's man *n* (1897) : a man noted or admired for traditionally masculine interests and activities

man·sue·tude \'man(t)-swi-ˌtüd, man-'sü-ə-, -ˌtyüd\ *n* [ME, fr. L *mansuetudo*, fr. *mansuescere* to tame, fr. *manus* hand + *suescere* to accustom; akin to Gk *ēthos* custom — more at MANUAL, SIB] (14c) : the quality or state of being gentle : MEEKNESS, TAMENESS

man·ta \'man-tə\ *n* [Sp, alter. of *manto* cloak, fr. LL *mantus*, prob. back-formation fr. L *mantellum* mantle] (1697) **1** : a square piece of cloth or blanket used in southwestern U.S. and Latin America usu. as a cloak or shawl **2** [AmerSp, fr. Sp; fr. its shape] : DEVILFISH 1

man–tai·lored \'man-ˌtā-lərd\ *adj* (1922) : made with the severe simplicity associated with men's coats and suits

manta ray *n* (1936) : DEVILFISH 1

man·teau \man-'tō, 'man-ˌ\ *n* [F, fr. OF *mantel*] (1671) : a loose cloak, coat, or robe

man·tel \'man-tᵊl\ *n* [ME, fr. MF, fr. OF, mantle] (15c) **1 a** : a beam, stone, or arch serving as a lintel to support the masonry above a fireplace **b** : the finish around a fireplace **2** : a shelf above a fireplace

man·tel·et \'mant-lət, 'man-tᵊl-ət, ˌmant-tᵊl-'et\ *n* [ME, fr. MF *mantlet*, dim. of *mantel*] (14c) **1** : a very short cape or cloak **2** *or* **mant·let** \'mant-lət\ : a movable shelter formerly used by besiegers as a protection when attacking

man·tel·piece \'man-tᵊl-ˌpēs\ *n* (1686) **1** : a mantel with its side elements **2** : MANTEL 2

man·tel·shelf \-ˌshelf\ *n* (ca. 1828) : MANTEL 2

man·tic \'man-tik\ *adj* [Gk *mantikos*, fr. *mantis*] (1850) : of or relating to the faculty of divination : PROPHETIC

man·ti·core \'man-ti-ˌkȯr, -ˌkȯr\ *n* [ME, fr. L *mantichora*, fr. Gk *mantichōras*] (14c) : a legendary animal with the head of a man, the body of a lion, and the tail of a dragon or scorpion

man·tid \'man-təd\ *n* [NL *Mantidae*, group name, fr. *Mantis*, genus name] (1895) : MANTIS

man·til·la \man-'tē-yə, -'ti-lə\ *n* [Sp, dim. of *manta*] (1717) **1** : a light scarf worn over the head and shoulders esp. by Spanish and Latin American women **2** : a short light cape or cloak

man·tis \'man-təs\ *n, pl* **man·tis·es** *or* **man·tes** \'man-ˌtēz\ [NL, fr. Gk, lit., diviner, prophet; akin to Gk *mainesthai* to be mad — more at MANIA] (1658) : any of an order or suborder (Mantodea and esp. family Mantidae) of large usu. green insects that feed on other insects and clasp their prey in forelimbs held up as if in prayer

man·tis·sa \man-'ti-sə\ *n* [L *mantisa, mantissa* makeweight, fr. Etruscan] (ca. 1847) : the part of a logarithm to the right of the decimal point

¹**man·tle** \'man-tᵊl\ *n* [ME *mantel*, fr. OF, fr. L *mantellum*] (13c) **1 a** : a loose sleeveless garment worn over other clothes : CLOAK **b** : a mantle regarded as a symbol of preeminence or authority ⟨invested his people with the ~ of universal champions of justice —Denis Goulet⟩ **2 a** : something that covers, enfolds, or envelops **b** : a fold or lobe or pair of lobes of the body wall of a mollusk or brachiopod that in shell-bearing forms lines the shell and bears shell-secreting glands — see CLAM illustration (2) : the soft external body wall that lines the test or shell of a tunicate or barnacle **c** : the outer wall and casing of a blast furnace above the hearth; *broadly* : an insulated support or casing in which something is heated **3** : the back, scapulars, and wings of a bird **4** : a lacy hood or sheath of some refractory material that gives light by incandescence when placed over a flame **5 a** : REGOLITH **b** : the part of the interior of a terrestrial planet and esp. the earth that lies beneath the lithosphere and above the central core **6** : MANTEL

²**mantle** *vb* **man·tled; man·tling** \'mant-liŋ, 'man-tᵊl-iŋ\ *vt* (13c) : to cover with or as if with a mantle : CLOAK ⟨the encroaching jungle growth that *mantled* the building —Sanka Knox⟩ ~ *vi* **1** : to become covered with a coating **2** : to spread over a surface **3** : BLUSH ⟨her rich face *mantling* with emotion —Benjamin Disraeli⟩

man–to–man \'man-tə-'man\ *adj* (1902) **1** : characterized by frankness and honesty ⟨a ~ talk⟩ **2** : of, relating to, or being a system of defense (as in football or basketball) in which each defensive player guards a specified opponent

Man·toux test \ˌman-'tü-, ˌmän-\ *n* [Charles *Mantoux* †1947 Fr. physician] (ca. 1923) : an intracutaneous test for hypersensitivity to tuberculin that indicates past or present infection with tubercle bacilli

man·tra \'män-trə *also* 'man- *or* 'mən-\ *n* [Skt, sacred counsel, formula, fr. *manyate* he thinks; akin to L *mens* mind — more at MIND] (1808) **1** : a mystical formula of invocation or incantation (as in Hinduism); *also* : WATCHWORD 2 — **man·tric** \-trik\ *adj*

man·trap \'man-ˌtrap\ *n* (1788) : a trap for catching humans : SNARE

man·tua \'man(t)-sh(ə-)wə, 'man-tə-wə\ *n* [modif. of F *manteau* mantle] (1678) : a usu. loose-fitting gown worn esp. in the 17th and 18th centuries

Manu \'ma-(ˌ)nü\ *n* [Skt] : the progenitor of the human race and giver of the religious laws of Manu according to Hindu mythology

¹**man·u·al** \'man-yə-wəl, -yəl\ *adj* [ME *manuel*, fr. MF, fr. L *manualis*, fr. *manus* hand; akin to OE *mund* hand and perh. to Gk *marē* hand] (15c) **1 a** : of, relating to, or involving the hands ⟨~ dexterity⟩ **b** : worked or done by hand and not by machine ⟨a ~ transmission⟩ ⟨~ computation⟩ ⟨~ indexing⟩ **2** : requiring or using physical skill and energy ⟨~ labor⟩ ⟨~ workers⟩ — **man·u·al·ly** *adv*

²**manual** *n* (15c) **1** : a book that is conveniently handled; *esp* : HANDBOOK **2** : the prescribed movements in the handling of a weapon or other military item during a drill or ceremony ⟨the ~ of arms⟩ **3 a** : a keyboard for the hands; *specif* : one of the several keyboards of an organ or harpsichord that controls a separate division of the instrument **b** : a device or apparatus intended for manual operation

manual alphabet *n* (ca. 1864) : an alphabet esp. for the deaf in which the letters are represented by finger positions

manual training *n* (1880) : a course of training to develop skill in using the hands and to teach practical arts (as woodworking and metalworking)

ma·nu·bri·um \mə-'nü-brē-əm, -'nyü-\ *n, pl* **-bria** \-brē-ə\ *also* **-briums** [NL, fr. L, handle, fr. *manus*] (ca. 1848) : an anatomical process or part shaped like a handle: as **a** : the cephalic segment of the sternum of humans and many other mammals **b** : the process that bears the mouth of a hydrozoan : HYPOSTOME

man·u·fac·to·ry \ˌman-yə-'fak-t(ə-)rē, ˌma-nə-\ *n* (1647) : FACTORY 2a

¹**man·u·fac·ture** \ˌman-yə-'fak-chər, ˌma-nə-\ *n* [MF, fr. ML *manufactura*, fr. L *manu factus*, lit., made by hand] (1567) **1** : something made from raw materials by hand or by machinery **2 a** : the process of making wares by hand or by machinery esp. when carried on systematically with division of labor **b** : a productive industry using mechanical power and machinery **3** : the act or process of producing something

²**manufacture** *vb* **-tured; -tur·ing** \-'fak-chə-riŋ, -'fak-shriŋ\ *vt* (1683) **1** : to make into a product suitable for use **2 a** : to make from raw

manual alphabet

materials by hand or by machinery **b** : to produce according to an organized plan and with division of labor **3** : INVENT, FABRICATE **4** : to produce as if by manufacturing : CREATE ⟨writers who ~ stories for television⟩ ~ *vi* : to engage in manufacture — **manufacturing** *n*

man·u·fac·tur·er \-'fak-chər-ər, -'fak-shrər\ *n* (1719) : one that manufactures; *esp* : an employer of workers in manufacturing

man·u·mis·sion \ˌman-yə-'mi-shən\ *n* [ME, fr. MF, fr. L *manumission-, manumissio*, fr. *manumittere*] (15c) : the act or process of manumitting; *esp* : formal emancipation from slavery

man·u·mit \ˌman-yə-'mit\ *vt* **-mit·ted; -mit·ting** [ME *manumitten*, fr. MF *manumitter*, fr. L *manumittere*, fr. *manus* hand + *mittere* to let go, send] (15c) : to release from slavery **syn** see FREE

¹**ma·nure** \mə-'nur, -'nyur\ *vt* **ma·nured; ma·nur·ing** [ME *manouren*, fr. MF *manouvrer*, lit., to do work by hand, fr. L *manu operare*] (15c) **1** *obs* : CULTIVATE **2** : to enrich (land) by the application of manure — **ma·nur·er** *n*

²**manure** *n* (1549) : material that fertilizes land; *esp* : refuse of stables and barnyards consisting of livestock excreta with or without litter — **ma·nu·ri·al** \-'n(y)ur-ē-əl\ *adj*

ma·nus \'mā-nəs, 'mä-\ *n, pl* **ma·nus** \-nəs, -ˌnüs\ [NL, fr. L, hand] (1826) : the distal segment of the vertebrate forelimb from carpus to terminus

¹**man·u·script** \'man-yə-ˌskript\ *adj* [L *manu scriptus*] (1597) : written by hand or typed ⟨~ letters⟩

²**manuscript** *n* (1600) **1** : a written or typewritten composition or document as distinguished from a printed copy; *also* : a document submitted for publication **2** : writing as opposed to print

¹**Manx** \'maŋ(k)s\ *adj* [alter. of *Maniske*, fr. (assumed) ON *manskr*, fr. *Mana* Isle of Man] (1630) : of, relating to, or characteristic of the Isle of Man, its people, or the Manx language

²**Manx** *n* (1672) **1** : the Celtic language of the Manx people almost completely displaced by English **2** *pl in constr* : the people of the Isle of Man **3** : MANX CAT

Manx cat *n* (1859) : any of a breed of shorthaired tailless domestic cats

¹**many** \'me-nē\ *adj* **more** \'mȯr, 'mȯr\; **most** \'mōst\ [ME, fr. OE *manig*; akin to OHG *manag* many, OCS *mŭnogŭ* much] (bef. 12c) **1** : consisting of or amounting to a large but indefinite number ⟨worked for ~ years⟩ **2** : being one of a large but indefinite number ⟨~ a man⟩ ⟨~ another student⟩ — **as many** : the same in number ⟨saw three plays in *as many days*⟩

²**many** *pron, pl in constr* (bef. 12c) : a large number of persons or things ⟨~ are called⟩

³**many** *n, pl in constr* (12c) **1** : a large but indefinite number ⟨a good ~ of them⟩ **2** : the great majority of people ⟨the ~⟩

man–year \'man-'yir\ *n* (1916) : a unit of the work done by one person in a year composed of a standard number of working days

many·fold \ˌme-nē-'fōld\ *adv* (14c) : by many times ⟨aid to research has increased ~⟩

many–sid·ed \ˌme-nē-'sī-dəd\ *adj* (1570) **1** : having many sides or aspects **2** : having many interests or aptitudes — **many–sid·ed·ness** *n*

many–val·ued \ˌme-nē-'val-(ˌ)yüd, -yəd\ *adj* (1934) **1** : possessing more than the customary two truth-values of truth and falsehood **2** : MULTIPLE-VALUED

Man·za·nil·la \ˌman-zə-'nē-yə, -'ni-lə\ *n* [Sp, dim. of *manzana* apple] (1843) : a pale very dry Spanish sherry

man·za·ni·ta \ˌman-zə-'nē-tə\ *n* [AmerSp, dim. of Sp *manzana* apple] (1846) : any of various western No. American evergreen shrubs (genus *Arctostaphylos*) of the heath family with alternate leaves

Mao·ism \'maù-ˌi-zəm\ *n* (1950) : the theory and practice of Marxism-Leninism developed in China chiefly by Mao Tse-tung — **Mao·ist** \-ist\ *n or adj*

Mao·ri \'maù(ə)r-ē\ *n, pl* **Maori** *or* **Maoris** (1843) **1** : a member of a Polynesian people native to New Zealand **2** : the Austronesian language of the Maori

\ə\ abut \ᵊ\ kitten, F table \ər\ further \a\ ash \ā\ ace \ä\ mop, mar \aú\ out \ch\ chin \e\ bet \ē\ easy \g\ go \i\ hit \ī\ ice \j\ job \ŋ\ sing \ō\ go \ȯ\ law \ȯi\ boy \th\ thin \t̲h̲\ the \ü\ loot \ù\ foot \y\ yet \zh\ vision \ä, ḵ, ⁿ, œ, œ̅, ue, ue̅, ᵜ\ see Guide to Pronunciation

mao-tai \'maủ-'tī, -'dĭ\ *n* [*Maotai*, town in China] (1943) : a strong Chinese liquor made from sorghum

¹map \'map\ *n* [ML *mappa*, fr. L, napkin, towel] (1527) **1 a** : a representation usu. on a flat surface of the whole or a part of an area **b** : a representation on a chromosome or a part of it **2** : something that represents with a clarity suggestive of a map **3** : the arrangement of genes on a chromosome — called also *genetic map* **4** : FUNCTION 5a — **map-like** \-,līk\ *adj* — **on the map** : in a position of prominence or fame ⟨had put the fledgling university *on the map* —Lon Tinkle⟩

²map *vb* **mapped; map-ping** *vt* (1586) **1 a** : to make a map of ⟨~ the surface of the moon⟩ **b** : to delineate as if on a map ⟨sorrow was *mapped* on her face⟩ **c** : to make a survey of for or as if for the purpose of making a map **d** : to assign (as a set or element) in a mathematical correspondence ⟨~ a set onto itself⟩ ⟨~ picture elements to video memory⟩ **2** : to plan in detail — often used with *out* ⟨~ out a program⟩ **3** : to locate (a gene) on a chromosome ~ *vi* : of a gene : to be located — **map-pa-ble** \'ma-pə-bəl\ *adj* — **map-per** *n*

ma-ple \'mā-pəl\ *n* [ME, fr. OE *mapul-*; akin to ON *mopurr* maple] (14c) : any of a genus (*Acer* of the family Aceraceae, the maple family) of chiefly deciduous trees or shrubs with opposite leaves and a fruit of two united samaras; *also* : the hard light-colored close-grained wood of a maple used esp. for flooring and furniture

maple sugar *n* (1720) : sugar made by boiling maple syrup

maple syrup *n* (1849) : syrup made by concentrating the sap of maple trees and esp. the sugar maple

map-mak-er \'map-,mā-kər\ *n* (1775) : CARTOGRAPHER — **map-mak-ing** \-,kiŋ\ *n*

map-ping \'ma-piŋ\ *n* (ca. 1775) **1** : the act or process of making a map **2** : FUNCTION 5a ⟨a one-to-one continuous ~⟩

ma-quette \ma-'ket\ *n* [F, fr. It *macchietta* sketch, dim. of *macchia*, ultim. fr. L *macula* spot] (1903) : a usu. small preliminary model (as of a sculpture or a building)

ma-qui-la-do-ra \mə,kē-lə-'dōr-ə, -'thŏr-\ *n* [MexSp (*planta*) *maquiladora*, fr. *maquilar* to process ore for a fee, fr. *maquila* processing fee, multure, fr. Sp, multure, fr. Ar. dial. *makīla* measure of grain] (1976) : a foreign-owned factory in Mexico at which imported parts are assembled by lower-paid workers into products for export

ma-quil-lage \,ma-kē-'yäzh\ *n* [F] (1892) : MAKEUP 3

ma-quis \ma-'kē, mä-\ *n, pl* **ma-quis** \-'kē(z)\ [F, fr. It *macchie*, pl. of *macchia* thicket, sketch, spot] (1858) **1** : thick scrubby underbrush of Mediterranean shores and esp. of the island of Corsica; *also* : an area of such underbrush **2** *often cap* **a** : a guerrilla fighter in the French underground during World War II **b** : a band of maquis

¹mar \'mär\ *vt* **marred; mar-ring** [ME *marren*, fr. OE *mierran* to obstruct, waste; akin to OHG *merren* to obstruct] (bef. 12c) **1** : to detract from the perfection or wholeness of : SPOIL **2** *archaic* **a** : to inflict serious bodily harm on **b** : DESTROY *syn* see INJURE

²mar *n* (1551) : something that mars : BLEMISH

mar-a-bou *also* **mar-a-bout** \'mar-ə-,bü\ *n* [F *marabout*, lit., marabout] (1823) **1 a** : a soft feathery fluffy material prepared from turkey feathers or the coverts of marabous and used esp. for trimming women's hats or clothes **b** *marabou* : a large dark gray African stork (*Leptoptilos crumeniferus*) that has a distensible pouch of pink skin at the front of the neck and feeds esp. on carrion — called also *marabou stork* **2 a** : a thrown silk usu. dyed in the gum **b** : a fabric made of this silk

mar-a-bout \'mar-ə-,bü\ *n, often cap* [F, fr. Pg *marabuto*, fr. Ar *murābiṭ*] (1621) : a dervish in Muslim Africa believed to have supernatural power

ma-ra-ca \mə-'rä-kə, -'ra-\ *n* [Pg *maracá*, fr. Tupi] (1824) : a rattle usu. made from a gourd that is used as a percussion instrument

marabou 1b

mar-ag-ing steel \'mär-,ā-jiŋ-\ *n* [*martensite* + *aging*] (1962) : a strong tough low-carbon martensitic steel which contains up to 25 percent nickel and in which hardening precipitates are formed by aging

mar-a-schi-no \,mar-ə-'skē-nō, -'shē-\ *n, pl* **-nos** *often cap* [It, fr. *marasca* bitter wild cherry, alter. of *amarasca*, fr. *amaro* bitter — more at AMARETTO] (ca. 1793) **1** : a sweet liqueur distilled from the fermented juice of a bitter wild cherry **2** : a usu. large cherry preserved in true or imitation maraschino

ma-ras-mus \mə-'raz-məs\ *n* [LL, fr. Gk *marasmos*, fr. *marainein* to waste away] (1656) : a condition of chronic undernourishment occurring esp. in children and usu. caused by a diet deficient in calories and proteins — **ma-ras-mic** \-'raz-mik\ *adj*

Ma-ra-tha \mə-'rä-tə\ *n* [Marathi *Marāṭhā* & Hindi *Marhaṭṭā*, fr. Skt *Mahārāṣṭra* Maharashtra] (1748) : a member of a people of the south central part of the subcontinent of India

Ma-ra-thi \mə-'rä-tē\ *n* [Marathi *marāṭhī*] (1698) : the chief Indo-Aryan language of the state of Maharashtra in India

mar-a-thon \'mar-ə-,thän\ *n, often attrib* [*Marathon*, Greece, site of a victory of Greeks over Persians in 490 B.C., the news of which was carried to Athens by a long-distance runner] (1896) **1 a** : a long-distance race: **a** : a footrace run on an open course usu. of 26 miles 385 yards (42.2 kilometers) **b** : a race other than a footrace marked esp. by great length **2 a** : an endurance contest **b** : something (as an event, activity, or session) characterized by great length or concentrated effort — **mar-a-thon-er** \-,thä-nər\ *n* (1923) : one (as a runner) who takes part in a marathon — **mar-a-thon-ing** \-niŋ\ *n*

ma-raud \mə-'rŏd\ *vb* [F *marauder*] *vi* (1711) : to roam about and raid in search of plunder ~ *vt* : RAID, PILLAGE — **ma-raud-er** *n*

¹mar-ble \'mär-bəl\ *n* [ME, fr. OF *marbre*, fr. L *marmor*, fr. Gk *marmaros*] (12c) **1 a** : a limestone that is more or less crystallized by metamorphism, that ranges from granular to compact in texture, that is capable of taking a high polish, and that is used esp. in architecture and sculpture **b** : something (as a piece of sculpture) composed of or made from marble **c** : something suggesting marble (as in hardness, coldness, or smoothness) ⟨a heart of ~⟩ **2 a** : a little ball made of a hard substance (as glass) and used in various games **b** *pl but sing in* constr : any of several games played with these little balls **3** : MARBLING **4** *pl* : elements of common sense; *esp* : SANITY ⟨persons who are born without all their ~s —Arthur Miller⟩ — **marble** *adj*

²marble *vt* **mar-bled; mar-bling** \-b(ə-)liŋ\ (1683) : to give a veined or mottled appearance to ⟨~ the edges of a book⟩

marble cake *n* (1871) : a cake made with light and dark batter so as to have a mottled appearance

mar-bled \'mär-bəld\ *adj* (1599) **1** [¹*marble*] **a** : made of or covered with marble or marbling **b** : marked by an extensive use of marble as an architectural or decorative feature ⟨ancient ~ cities⟩ **2** [²*marble*] : marked by an intermixture of fat and lean ⟨well-*marbled* beef⟩

mar-ble-ise *Brit var of* MARBLEIZE

mar-ble-ize \'mär-bə-,līz\ *vt* **-ized; -iz-ing** (ca. 1859) : MARBLE

marbling *n* (ca. 1752) **1** : the action or process of making like marble esp. in coloration **2** : coloration or markings resembling or suggestive of marble **3** : an intermixture of fat and lean esp. in a cut of meat when evenly distributed

mar-bly \-b(ə-)lē\ *adj* (15c) : resembling or suggestive of marble

marc \'märk\ *n* [F, fr. MF, fr. *marchier* to trample, march] (1601) **1** : the residue remaining after a fruit has been pressed; *broadly* : the organic residue from an extraction process ⟨the protein-rich cottonseed ~⟩ **2** : brandy made from the residue of wine grapes after pressing

mar-ca-site \'mär-kə-,sīt, -,zīt; ,mär-kə-'zēt\ *n* [ME *marchasite*, fr. ML *marcasita*] (15c) **1 a** : crystallized iron pyrites **b** : a mineral of the same composition and appearance as iron pyrites but of different crystalline organization and lower specific gravity **2** : a piece of marcasite used in jewelry

mar-ca-to \mär-'kä-(,)tō\ *adv or adj* [It, pp. of *marcare* to mark, accent, of Gmc origin; akin to OHG *marcōn* to mark] (ca. 1840) : with strong accentuation — used as a direction in music

¹mar-cel \mär-'sel\ *n* [*Marcel* Grateau †1936 Fr. hairdresser] (1895) : a deep soft wave made in the hair by the use of a heated curling iron

²marcel *vb* **mar-celled; mar-cel-ling** *vt* (1906) : to make a marcel in ~ *vi* : to make a marcel

¹march \'märch\ *n* [ME *marche*, fr. OF, of Gmc origin; akin to OHG *marha* boundary — more at MARK] (14c) **1** : a border region : FRONTIER; *esp* : a district orig. set up to defend a boundary — usu. used in pl.

²march *vi* (14c) : to have common borders or frontiers ⟨a region that ~es with Canada in the north and the Pacific in the west⟩

³march \'märch, imperatively often 'härch *in the military*\ *vb* [ME, fr. MF *marchier* to trample, march, fr. OF, to trample, prob. of Gmc origin; akin to OHG *marcōn* to mark] *vi* (15c) **1** : to move along steadily usu. with a rhythmic stride and in step with others **2 a** : to move in a direct purposeful manner : PROCEED **b** : to make steady progress : ADVANCE ⟨time ~es on⟩ **3** : to stand in orderly array suggestive of marching ~ *vt* : to cause to march ⟨~ed the children off to bed⟩ **2** : to cover by marching : TRAVERSE ⟨~ed 10 miles⟩

⁴march \'märch\ *n* (ca. 1572) **1** : a musical composition that is usu. in duple or quadruple time with a strongly accentuated beat and that is designed or suitable to accompany marching **2 a** (1) : the action of marching (2) : the distance covered within a specific period of time by marching (3) : a regular measured stride or rhythmic step used in marching **b** : forward movement : PROGRESS ⟨the ~ of a movie toward the climax⟩ **3** : an organized procession of demonstrators who are supporting or protesting something — **march-like** \-,līk\ *adj* — **on the march** : moving steadily : ADVANCING

March \'märch\ *n* [ME, fr. OF, fr. L *martius*, fr. *martius* of Mars, fr. *Mart-, Mars*] (13c) : the 3d month of the Gregorian calendar

mär-chen \'mer-kən\ *n, pl* **märchen** [G] (1871) : TALE; *esp* : FOLKTALE

¹march-er \'mär-chər\ *n* (14c) : one who inhabits a border region

²marcher *n* (1589) : one that marches; *esp* : one that marches for a specific cause ⟨a peace ~⟩

mar-che-sa \mär-'kā-zə\ *n, pl* **-se** \-(,)zā\ [It, fem. of *marchese*] (1797) : an Italian woman holding the rank of a marchese : MARCHIONESS

mar-che-se \-(,)zā\ *n, pl* **-si** \-(,)zē\ [It, fr. ML *marcensis*, fr. *marca* border region, of Gmc origin; akin to OHG *marha*] (1517) : an Italian nobleman next in rank above a count : MARQUIS

marching orders *n pl* (1780) : authoritative orders or instructions esp. to set out on or as if on a march

mar-chio-ness \'mär-sh(ə)-nəs\ *n* [ML *marchionissa*, fr. *marchion-, marchio* marquess, fr. *marca*] (ca. 1599) **1** : the wife or widow of a marquess **2** : a woman who holds the rank of marquess in her own right

march-pane \'märch-,pān\ *n* [MF *marcepain*, fr. It *marzapane*] (ca. 1556): MARZIPAN

march–past \'märch-,past\ *n* (ca. 1876) : a filing by : PROCESSION

Mar-cion-ism \'mär-shə-,ni-zəm, -sē-ə-, -shē-ə-\ *n* [*Marcion* 2d cent. A.D. Christian Gnostic] (1882) : the doctrinal system of a sect of the 2d and 3d centuries A.D. accepting some parts of the New Testament but denying Christ's corporality and humanity and condemning the Creator God of the Old Testament — **Mar-cion-ite** \-,nīt\ *n*

Mar-co-ni \mär-'kō-nē\ *adj* [prob. fr. the resemblance of the complex arrangement of stays and struts to that used to support the antennae used in wireless telegraphy, invented by Guglielmo *Marconi*] (1912) : of, having, or being a Bermuda rig

Mar-di Gras \'mär-dē-,grä, *in New Orleans commonly* -,grŏ\ *n* [F, lit., fat Tuesday] (1699) **1** : Shrove Tuesday often observed (as in New Orleans) with parades and festivities **b** : a carnival period climaxing on Shrove Tuesday **2** : a festive occasion resembling a pre-Lenten Mardi Gras

¹mare *n* [ME, fr. OE; akin to OHG *mara* incubus, Serbo-Croatian *mora* nightmare] (bef. 12c) *obs* : an evil preternatural being causing nightmare

²mare \'mar, 'mer\ *n* [ME, fr. OE *mere*; akin to OHG *merha* mare, OE *mearh* horse, W *march*] (bef. 12c) : a female horse or other equine animal esp. when fully mature or of breeding age

³ma-re \'mär-(,)ā\ *n, pl* **ma-ria** \'mär-ē-ə\ *also* **ma-res** \'mär-(,)āz\ [NL, fr. L, sea — more at MARINE] (1860) : any of several mostly flat dark areas of considerable extent on the surface of the moon or Mars

ma-re clau-sum \'mär-(,)ä-'klaủ-səm, -'klŏ-\ *n* [NL, lit., closed sea] (1652) : a navigable body of water (as a sea) that is under the jurisdiction of one nation and is closed to other nations

Mar-ek's disease \'mar-iks-, 'mer-\ *n* [József *Marek* †1952 Hung. veterinarian] (1947) : a highly contagious viral disease of poultry that is characterized esp. by proliferation of lymphoid cells and is caused by a herpesvirus

ma·re li·be·rum \'mär-(ˌ)ä-'lē-bə-ˌrúm\ *n* [NL, lit., free sea] (1652) **1** : a navigable body of water (as a sea) that is open to all nations **2** : FREEDOM OF THE SEAS

ma·ren·go \mə-'reŋ-(ˌ)gō\ *adj, often cap* [F, fr. *Marengo*, village in northwest Italy] (ca. 1924) : of, consisting of, or served with a sauce of mushrooms, tomatoes, olives, oil, and wine ⟨veal ~⟩

ma·re no·strum \'mär-(ˌ)ä-'nōs-trəm\ *n* [NL, lit., our sea] (1941) : a navigable body of water (as a sea) that belongs to a single nation or is mutually shared by two or more nations

mare's nest *n, pl* **mare's nests** *or* **mares' nests** (1576) **1** : a false discovery, illusion, or deliberate hoax **2** : a place, condition, or situation of great disorder or confusion ⟨a *mare's nest* of spurious ambiguities to bewilder the simpleminded —J. H. Sledd⟩

mare's tail *n, pl* **mare's tails** *or* **mares' tails** (ca. 1762) **1 a** : a common aquatic plant (*Hippuris vulgaris* of the family Hippuridaceae) with elongated shoots having dense whorls of narrow finely tapered leaves **b** : HORSEWEED 1 **2** : a cirrus cloud that has a long slender flowing appearance

Mar·fan's syndrome \'mär-ˌfanz-\ *n* [Antonin Bernard Jean *Marfan* †1942 Fr. pediatrician] (ca. 1923) : a hereditary disorder of connective tissue that is characterized by abnormal elongation of the bones and often by ocular and circulatory defects —called also *Marfan syndrome* \'mär-ˌfan-\

mar·ga·rine \'mär-jə-rən, -ˌrēn\ *n* [F, ultim. fr. Gk *margaron* pearl, prob. back-formation fr. *margarités*] (1873) : a food product made usu. from vegetable oils churned with ripened skim milk to a smooth emulsion and used like butter

mar·ga·ri·ta \ˌmär-gə-'rē-tə\ *n* [fr. the Sp feminine name *Margarita*] (1963) : a cocktail consisting of tequila, lime or lemon juice, and an orange-flavored liqueur

mar·ga·rite \'mär-gə-ˌrīt\ *n* [ME, fr. MF, fr. L *margarita*, fr. Gk *margarités*] (13c) *archaic* : PEARL

mar·gay \'mär-ˌgā, mär-'\ *n* [F, fr. Tupi *maracaja*] (1774) : a small American spotted cat (*Felis wiedii*) resembling the ocelot and ranging from southernmost Texas to Argentina

¹marge \'märj\ *n* [MF, fr. L *margo*] (1551) *archaic* : MARGIN

²marge *n* (1922) *Brit* : MARGARINE

mar·gent \'mär-jənt\ *n* (15c) *archaic* : MARGIN

margay

¹mar·gin \'mär-jən\ *n* [ME, fr. L *margin-, margo* border —more at MARK] (14c) **1** : the part of a page or sheet outside the main body of printed or written matter **2** : the outside limit and adjoining surface of something : EDGE ⟨at the ~ of the woods⟩ ⟨continental ~⟩ **3 a** : a spare amount or measure or degree allowed or given for contingencies or special situations ⟨left no ~ for error⟩ **b** (1) : a bare minimum below which or an extreme limit beyond which something becomes impossible or is no longer desirable ⟨on the ~ of good taste⟩ (2) : the limit below which economic activity cannot be continued under normal conditions **4 a** : the difference which exists between net sales and the cost of merchandise sold and from which expenses are usu. met or profit derived **b** : the excess market value of collateral over the face of a loan **c** (1) : cash or collateral that is deposited by a client with a commodity or securities broker to protect the broker from loss on a contract (2) : the client's equity in securities bought with the aid of credit obtained specif. (as from a broker) for that purpose **d** : a range about a specified figure within which a purchase is to be made **5** : measure or degree of difference ⟨the bill passed by a one-vote ~⟩ — **mar·gined** \-jənd\ *adj*

²margin *vt* (1715) **1 a** : to provide with an edging or border **b** : to form a margin to : BORDER **2 a** : to add margin to ⟨~ up an account⟩ **b** (1) : to use as margin ⟨~ bonds to buy stock⟩ (2) : to provide margin for ⟨~ a transaction⟩ **c** : to buy (securities) on margin

mar·gin·al \'märj-nəl, 'mär-jə-nᵊl\ *adj* [ML *marginalis*, fr. L *margin-, margo*] (1573) **1** : written or printed in the margin of a page or sheet ⟨~ notes⟩ **2 a** : of, relating to, or situated at a margin or border **b** : not of central importance ⟨regards violence as a ~ rather than a central problem⟩ **c** (1) : occupying the borderland of a relatively stable territorial or cultural area ⟨~ tribes⟩ (2) : characterized by the incorporation of habits and values from two divergent cultures and by incomplete assimilation in either ⟨the ~ cultural habits of new immigrant groups⟩ (3) : excluded from or existing outside the mainstream of society, a group, or a school of thought ⟨~ voters⟩ **3** : located at the fringe of consciousness ⟨~ sensations⟩ **4 a** : close to the lower limit of qualification, acceptability, or function : barely exceeding the minimum requirements ⟨a semiliterate person of ~ ability⟩ **b** (1) : having a character or capacity fitted to yield a supply of goods which when marketed at existing price levels will barely cover the cost of production ⟨~ land⟩ (2) : of, relating to, or derived from goods produced and marketed with such result ⟨~ profits⟩ **5** : relating to or being a function of a random variable that is obtained from a function of several random variables by integrating or summing over all possible values of the other variables ⟨a ~ probability function⟩ — **mar·gin·al·i·ty** \ˌmär-jə-'na-lə-tē\ *n* — **mar·gin·al·ly** \'märj-nə-lē, 'mär-jə-nᵊl-ē\ *adv*

mar·gi·na·lia \ˌmär-jə-'nä-lē-ə\ *n pl* [NL, fr. ML, neut. pl. of *marginalis*] (1832) **1** : marginal notes (as in a book) **2** : nonessential items ⟨the meat and ~ of American politics —*Saturday Rev.*⟩

mar·gin·al·ize \'märj-nə-ˌlīz, 'mär-jə-nᵊl-ˌīz\ *vt* **-ized; -iz·ing** (1970) : to relegate to a marginal position within a society or group — **mar·gin·al·i·za·tion** \ˌmärj-nə-lə-'zā-shən, ˌmär-jə-nᵊl-ə-\ *n*

marginal utility *n* (1890) : the amount of additional utility provided by an additional unit of an economic good or service

mar·gin·ate \'mär-jə-ˌnāt\ *vt* **-at·ed; -at·ing** (1623) **1** : MARGIN 1, 2a **2** : MARGINALIZE — **mar·gin·ation** \ˌmär-jə-'nä-shən\ *n*

mar·gin·at·ed \-ˌnä-təd\ *adj* (ca. 1727) : having a distinct margin

mar·gra·vate \'mär-grə-ˌvāt\ *or* **mar·gra·vi·ate** \mär-'grā-vē-ət, -ˌāt\ *n* (1802) : the territory of a margrave

mar·grave \'mär-ˌgrāv\ *n* [D *markgraaf*, fr. MD *marcgrave;* akin to OHG *marha* boundary and to OHG *grāvo* count —more at MARK] (1551) **1** : the military governor esp. of a German border province **2** : a member of the German nobility corresponding in rank to a British marquess — **mar·gra·vi·al** \mär-'grā-vē-əl\ *adj*

mar·gra·vine \'mär-grə-ˌvēn, ˌmär-grə-'\ *n* (1692) : the wife of a margrave

mar·gue·rite \ˌmär-gə-'rēt, -gyə-\ *n* [F, fr. MF *marguerite* pearl, daisy — more at MARGARITE] (ca. 1866) **1** : DAISY 1b **2** : any of various single-flowered chrysanthemums; *esp* : a chrysanthemum (*Chrysanthemum frutescens*) of the Canary Islands

maria *pl of* MARE

ma·ri·a·chi \ˌmär-ē-'ä-chē, ˌmar-\ *n* [MexSp, perh. modif. of F *mariage* marriage] (1927) **1** : a Mexican street band; *also* : a musician belonging to such a band **2** : the music performed by a mariachi

Mar·i·an \'mer-ē-ən, 'mar-ē-, 'mä-rē-\ *adj* (1608) **1** : of or relating to Mary Tudor or her reign **2** : of or relating to the Virgin Mary

Mar·i·an·ist \-ə-nist\ *n* (ca. 1899) : a member of the Roman Catholic Society of Mary of Paris founded by William Joseph Chaminade in France in 1817 and devoted esp. to education

Ma·ria The·re·sa dollar \mə-'rē-ə-tə-'rā-sə-, -'rā-zə-\ *n* (ca. 1883) : a 1780 silver trade coin used in the Middle East

mari·cul·ture \'mar-ə-ˌkəl-chər\ *n* [L *mare* sea + E *-culture* (as in *agriculture*)] (ca. 1909) : the cultivation of marine organisms in their natural environment — **mari·cul·tur·ist** \ˌmar-ə-'kəl-chə-rist, -'kəlch-rist\ *n*

mari·gold \'mar-ə-ˌgōld, 'mer-\ *n* [ME, fr. *Mary*, mother of Jesus + ME *gold*] (14c) **1** : POT MARIGOLD **2** : any of a genus (*Tagetes*) of composite herbs with showy yellow, orange, or maroon flower heads

mar·i·jua·na *also* **mar·i·hua·na** \ˌmar-ə-'wä-nə *also* -'hwä-\ *n* [MexSp *mariguana, marihuana*] (1894) **1** : HEMP 1a, c **2** : the dried leaves and flowering tops of the pistillate hemp plant that yield THC and are smoked in cigarettes for their intoxicating effect — compare BHANG, CANNABIS, HASHISH

ma·rim·ba \mə-'rim-bə\ *n* [of Bantu origin; akin to Kimbundu *marimba* xylophone] (1704) : a xylophone of southern Africa and Central America with resonators beneath each bar; *also* : a modern form of this instrument — **ma·rim·bist** \-bist\ *n*

ma·ri·na \mə-'rē-nə\ *n* [It & Sp, seashore, fr. fem. of *marino*, adj., marine, fr. L *marinus*] (1924) : a dock or basin providing secure moorings for pleasure boats and often offering supply, repair, and other facilities

¹mar·i·nade \ˌmar-ə-'nād\ *n* [F, fr. *mariner* to pickle, marinate, prob. fr. It *marinare*] (1725) : a savory usu. acidic sauce in which meat, fish, or a vegetable is soaked to enrich its flavor or to tenderize it

²marinade *vt* **-nad·ed; -nad·ing** (1727) : MARINATE

mar·i·na·ra \ˌmar-ə-'nar-ə, ˌmer-ə-'ner-, -'när-\ *adj* [It (*alla*) *marinara*, lit., in sailor style] (ca. 1948) : made with tomatoes, onions, garlic, and spices ⟨~ sauce⟩; *also* : served with marinara sauce ⟨spaghetti ~⟩

mar·i·nate \'mar-ə-ˌnāt\ *vb* **-nat·ed; -nat·ing** [prob. fr. It *marinato,* pp. of *marinare* to marinate, fr. *marino*] *vt* (ca. 1645) : to steep (meat, fish, or vegetables) in a marinade ~ *vi* : to become marinated — **mar·i·na·tion** \ˌmar-ə-'nä-shən\ *n*

¹ma·rine \mə-'rēn\ *adj* [ME, fr. L *marinus*, fr. *mare* sea; akin to OE *mere* sea, pool, OHG *meri* sea, OCS *morje*] (15c) **1 a** : of or relating to the sea ⟨~ life⟩ **b** : of or relating to the navigation of the sea : NAUTICAL ⟨a ~ chart⟩ **c** : of or relating to the commerce of the sea : MARITIME ⟨~ law⟩ **d** : depicting the sea, seashore, or ships ⟨a ~ painter⟩ **2** : of or relating to marines ⟨~ barracks⟩

²marine *n* (1669) **1 a** : the mercantile and naval shipping of a country **b** : seagoing ships esp. in relation to nationality or class **2** : one of a class of soldiers serving on shipboard or in close association with a naval force; *specif* : a member of the U.S. Marine Corps **3** : an executive department (as in France) having charge of naval affairs **4** : a marine picture : SEASCAPE

marine architect *n* (1949) : NAVAL ARCHITECT — **marine architecture** *n*

mar·i·ner \'mar-ə-nər\ *n* [ME, fr. AF *marinier*, fr. ML *marinarius*, fr. *marinus*] (14c) : a person who navigates or assists in navigating a ship : SEAMAN, SAILOR

mariner's compass *n* (1627) : a compass used in navigation that consists of parallel magnetic needles or bundles of needles permanently attached to a card marked to indicate direction and degrees of a circle

Mar·i·ol·a·try \ˌmer-ē-'ä-lə-trē, ˌmar-ē-, ˌmä-rē-\ *n* (1612) : excessive veneration of the Virgin Mary — **Mar·i·ol·a·ter** \-lə-tər\ *n*

Mar·i·ol·o·gy \-'ä-lə-jē\ *n* (1857) : study or doctrine relating to the Virgin Mary — **Mar·i·o·log·i·cal** \-ə-'lä-ji-kəl\ *adj*

mar·i·o·nette \ˌmar-ē-ə-'net, ˌmer-\ *n* [F *marionnette*, fr. MF *maryonete*, fr. *Marion*, dim. of *Marie* Mary] (ca. 1620) : a small-scale usu. wooden figure (as of a person) with jointed limbs that is moved from above by manipulation of the attached strings or wires

mar·i·po·sa lily \ˌmar-ə-'pō-zə-, -sə-\ *n* [prob. fr. AmerSp *mariposa,* fr. Sp, butterfly] (1882) : any of a genus (*Calochortus*) of western No. American plants of the lily family with showy flowers having three petals and three sepals —called also *mariposa tulip;* compare SEGO LILY

mar·ish \'mar-ish\ *n* (15c) *archaic* : MARSH

Mar·ist \'mar-ist, 'mer-\ *n* [F *mariste*, fr. *Marie* Mary] (ca. 1872) : a member of the Roman Catholic Society of Mary founded by Jean Claude Colin in France in 1816 and devoted to education

mar·i·tal \'mar-ə-tᵊl\ *adj* [L *maritalis*, fr. *maritus* married] (1603) **1** : of or relating to marriage or the married state ⟨~ vows⟩ **2** : of or relating to a husband and his role in marriage — **mar·i·tal·ly** \-tᵊl-ē\ *adv*

mar·i·time \'mar-ə-ˌtīm\ *adj* [L *maritimus*, fr. *mare*] (1550) **1** : of, relating to, or bordering on the sea ⟨a ~ province⟩ **2** : of or relating

\ə\ abut \ᵊ\ kitten, F table \ər\ further \a\ ash \ā\ ace \ä\ mop, mar \aú\ out \ch\ chin \e\ bet \ē\ easy \g\ go \i\ hit \ī\ ice \j\ job \ŋ\ sing \ō\ go \ò\ law \òi\ boy \th\ thin \t̲h̲\ the \ü\ loot \ú\ foot \y\ yet \zh\ vision \à, k̲, ⁿ, œ, œ̄, ūe, ūē, ʸ\ see Guide to Pronunciation to navigation or commerce on the sea **3** : having the characteristics of a mariner

mar·jo·ram \'mär-jə-rəm, 'märj-rəm\ *n* [alter. of ME *mageram, majorane*, fr. MF *majorane*, fr. ML *majorana*] (ca. 1550) : any of various usu. fragrant and aromatic Old World mints (genus *Origanum*) often used in cookery

¹mark \'märk\ *n* [ME, fr. OE *mearc* boundary, march, sign; akin to OHG *marha* boundary, L *margo*] (bef. 12c) **1 a** : a boundary land **2 a** (1) : a conspicuous object serving as a guide for travelers (2) : something (as a line, notch, or fixed object) designed to record position **b** : one of the bits of leather or colored bunting placed on a sounding line at intervals **c** : TARGET **d** : the starting line or position in a track event **e** (1) : GOAL, OBJECT (2) : an object of attack, ridicule, or abuse; *specif* : a victim or prospective victim of a swindle (3) : the point under discussion (4) : condition of being correct or accurate ⟨her observations are on the ~⟩ **f** : a standard of performance, quality, or condition : NORM ⟨not feeling up to the ~ lately⟩ **3 a** (1) : SIGN, INDICATION ⟨gave her the necklace as a ~ of his esteem⟩ (2) : an impression (as a scratch, scar, or stain) made on something (3) : a distinguishing trait or quality : CHARACTERISTIC ⟨the ~s of an educated person⟩ **b** : a symbol used for identification or indication of ownership **c** : a cross made in place of a signature **d** (1) : TRADEMARK **2** *cap* — used with a numeral to designate a particular model of a weapon or machine ⟨*Mark* II⟩ **e** : a written or printed symbol (as a comma or colon) **f** : POSTMARK **g** : a symbol used to represent a teacher's estimate of a student's work or conduct; *esp* : GRADE **h** : a figure registering a point or level reached or achieved ⟨the halfway ~ in the first period of play⟩; *esp* : RECORD **4 a** : ATTENTION, NOTICE ⟨nothing worthy of ~⟩ **b** : IMPORTANCE, DISTINCTION ⟨stands out as a person of ~⟩ **c** : a lasting or strong impression ⟨worked at several jobs but didn't make much of a ~⟩ **d** : an assessment of merits : RATING ⟨got high ~s for honesty⟩ **syn** see SIGN

²mark *vb* [ME, fr. OE *mearc*; akin to OHG *marcōn* to mark, determine the boundaries of, OE *mearc* boundary] *vt* (bef. 12c) **1 a** (1) : to fix or trace out the bounds or limits of (2) : to plot the course of : CHART **b** : to set apart by or as if by a line or boundary — usu. used with *off* **2 a** (1) : to designate as if by a mark ⟨~ed for greatness⟩ (2) : to make or leave a mark on (3) : to furnish with natural marks ⟨wings ~ed with white⟩ (4) : to label so as to indicate price or quality (5) : to make notations in or on **b** (1) : to make note of in writing : JOT ⟨~ing the date in his journal⟩ (2) : to indicate by a mark or symbol ⟨~ an accent⟩ (3) : REGISTER, RECORD (4) : to determine the value of by means of marks or symbols : GRADE ⟨~ term papers⟩ **c** (1) : CHARACTERIZE, DISTINGUISH ⟨the flamboyance that ~s her stage appearance⟩ (2) : SIGNALIZE ⟨this year ~s our 50th anniversary⟩ **3** : to take notice of : OBSERVE ⟨~ my words⟩ **4** : to pick up (one's golf ball) from a putting green and substitute a marker ~ *vi* : to take careful notice — **mark time 1** : to keep the time of a marching step by moving the feet alternately without advancing **2** : to maintain a static state of readiness ⟨the House was *marking time* while the Senate talked —F. L. Paxson⟩

³mark *n* [ME, fr. OE *marc*, prob. of Scand origin; akin to ON *mǫrk* mark; akin to OE *mearc* sign] (bef. 12c) **1** : any of various old European units of weight used esp. for gold and silver; *esp* : a unit equal to about 8 ounces (248 grams) **2** : a unit of value : **a** : an old English unit equal to 13s 4d **b** : any one of various old Scandinavian or German units of value; *specif* : a unit and corresponding silver coin of the 16th century worth ½ taler **c** (1) : DEUTSCHE MARK (2) : the basic monetary unit of East Germany replaced in 1990 by the West German deutsche mark **d** : MARKKA

Mark \'märk\ *n* [L *Marcus*] **1 a** : an early Jewish Christian traditionally identified as the writer of the Gospel of Mark — called also *John Mark* **b** : the second Gospel in the New Testament — see BIBLE table **2** : a king of Cornwall, uncle of Tristram, and husband of Isolde

mark·down \'märk-ˌdaun\ *n* (1880) **1** : a lowering of price **2** : the amount by which an original selling price is reduced

mark down *vt* (1859) : to put a lower price on

marked \'märkt\ *adj* (bef. 12c) **1** : having an identifying mark ⟨a ~ card⟩ **2** \or 'mär-kəd\ : having a distinctive or emphasized character : NOTICEABLE ⟨has a ~ drawl⟩ **3** : enjoying fame or notoriety ⟨being an object of attack, suspicion, or vengeance ⟨a ~ man⟩ **4** : overtly signaled by a linguistic feature ⟨with most English nouns the plural is the ~ number⟩ — **mark·ed·ly** \'mär-kəd-lē\ *adv* — **mark·ed·ness** \'mär-kəd-nəs\ *n*

mark·er \'mär-kər\ *n* (15c) **1** : one that marks **2** : something used for marking **3** : SCORE 7; *specif* : RUN **4** : PROMISSORY NOTE, IOU **5** : GENETIC MARKER

¹mar·ket \'mär-kət\ *n, often attrib* [ME, fr. ONF, fr. L *mercatus* trade, marketplace, fr. *mercari* to trade, fr. *merc-, merx* merchandise] (12c) **1 a** (1) : a meeting together of people for the purpose of trade by private purchase and sale and usu. not by auction (2) : the people assembled at such a meeting **b** (1) : a public place where a market is held; *esp* : a place where provisions are sold at wholesale ⟨a farmers' ~⟩ (2) : a retail establishment usu. of a specified kind ⟨a fish ~⟩ **2** *archaic* : the act or an instance of buying and selling **3** : the rate or price offered for a commodity or security **4 a** (1) : a geographical area of demand for commodities or services ⟨the foreign ~ for consulting firms⟩ (2) : a specified category of potential buyers ⟨the youth ~⟩ **b** : the course of commercial activity by which the exchange of commodities is effected : extent of demand ⟨the ~ is dull⟩ **c** (1) : an opportunity for selling ⟨a good ~ for used cars⟩ (2) : the available supply of or potential demand for specified goods or services ⟨the labor ~⟩ **d** : the area of economic activity in which buyers and sellers come together and the forces of supply and demand affect prices ⟨producing goods for ~ rather than for consumption⟩ — **in the market** : in the position of being a potential buyer ⟨*in the market* for a house⟩ — **on the market** : available for purchase; *also* : up for sale ⟨put their house *on the market*⟩

²market *vi* (1635) : to deal in a market ~ *vt* **1** : to expose for sale in a market **2** : SELL

mar·ket·able \'mär-kə-tə-bəl\ *adj* (1600) **1 a** : fit to be offered for sale in a market ⟨food that is not ~⟩ **b** : wanted by purchasers or employers : SALABLE ⟨~ securities⟩ ⟨~ skills⟩ **2** : of or relating to buying or selling — **mar·ket·abil·i·ty** \ˌmär-kə-tə-'bi-lə-tē\ *n*

market basket *n* (1943) : a variety of consumer goods and services used to calculate a consumer price index

mar·ke·teer \ˌmär-kə-'tir\ *n* (1832) : a specialist in promoting or selling a product or service

mar·ket·er \'mär-kə-tər\ *n* (1787) : one that deals in a market; *specif* : one that promotes or sells a product or service

market garden *n* (1811) *Brit* : TRUCK FARM — **market gardener** *n, Brit* — **market gardening** *n, Brit*

mar·ket·ing *n* (1561) **1 a** : the act or process of selling or purchasing in a market **b** : the process or technique of promoting, selling, and distributing a product or service **2** : an aggregate of functions involved in moving goods from producer to consumer

marketing research *n* (ca. 1937) : research into the means of promoting, selling, and distributing a product or service

market order *n* (ca. 1920) : an order to buy or sell securities or commodities immediately at the best price obtainable in the market

mar·ket·place \'mär-kət-ˌplās\ *n* (14c) **1 a** : an open square or place in a town where markets or public sales are held **b** : MARKET ⟨the ~ is the interpreter of supply and demand⟩ **2** : the world of trade or economic activity : the everyday world ⟨a conviction that religion belongs in the ~ —*Current Biog.*⟩ **3** : a sphere in which intangible values compete for acceptance ⟨the ~ of ideas⟩

market price *n* (15c) : a price actually given in current market dealings

market research *n* (1926) : research into the size, location, and makeup of a product market — **market researcher** *n*

market share *n* (1970) : the percentage of the market for a product or service that a company supplies

mark·ing *n* (14c) **1** : the act, process, or an instance of making or giving a mark **2 a** : a mark made **b** : arrangement, pattern, or disposition of marks

mark·ka \'mär-ˌkä\ *n, pl* **mark·kaa** \'mär-ˌkä\ *also* **mark·kas** \-ˌkäz\ [Finn, fr. Sw *mark*, a unit of value; akin to ON *mǫrk* mark] (ca. 1896) — see MONEY table

Markov chain *n* [A. A. *Markov* †1922 Russ. mathematician] (1942) : a usu. discrete stochastic process (as a random walk) in which the probabilities of occurrence of various future states depend only on the present state of the system or on the immediately preceding state and not on the path by which the present state was achieved — called also *Markoff chain*

Mar·kov·ian \mär-'kō-vē-ən, -'kò-\ *or* **Mar·kov** \'mär-ˌkòf, -ˌkòv\ *also* **Mar·koff** \'mär-ˌkòf\ *adj* (1950) : of, relating to, or resembling a Markov process or Markov chain esp. by having probabilities defined in terms of transition from the possible existing states to other states

Markov process *n* (1939) : a stochastic process (as Brownian motion) that resembles a Markov chain except that the states are continuous; *also* : MARKOV CHAIN — called also *Markoff process*

marks·man \'märks-mən\ *n* (1660) : a person skilled in shooting at a mark or target — **marks·man·ship** \-ˌship\ *n*

marks·wom·an \'märks-ˌwù-mən\ *n* (1802) : a woman skilled in shooting at a mark or target

mark·up \'mär-ˌkəp\ *n* (1916) **1** : an amount added to the cost price to determine the selling price; *broadly* : PROFIT **2** : a U.S. Congressional committee session at which a bill is put into final form before it is reported out

mark up *vt* (1869) : to put a markup on

marl \'mär(-ə)l\ *n* [ME, fr. MF *marle*, fr. ML *margila*, dim. of L *marga* marl, fr. Gaulish] (14c) : a loose or crumbling earthy deposit (as of sand, silt, or clay) that contains a substantial amount of calcium carbonate and is used esp. as a fertilizer for soils deficient in lime — **marly** \'mär-lē\ *adj*

mar·lin \'mär-lən\ *n* [short for *marlinspike*; fr. the appearance of its beak] (1917) : any of several large marine billfishes (genera *Makaira* and *Tetrapturus*) that are notable sport fishes

mar·line *also* **mar·lin** \'mär-lən\ *n* [ME *merlyn*, prob. fr. MLG *marlinc, merlinc*, fr. *mēren* to tie, moor] (15c) : a small usu. tarred line of two strands twisted loosely left-handed that is used esp. for seizing and as a covering for wire rope

mar·line·spike *also* **mar·lin·spike** \'mär-lən-ˌspīk\ *n* (1626) : a tool (as of wood or iron) that tapers to a point and is used to separate strands of rope or wire (as in splicing)

marl·stone \'mär(-ə)l-ˌstōn\ *n* (ca. 1839) : a rock that consists of a mixture of clay materials and calcium carbonate and often contains kerogen

mar·ma·lade \'mär-mə-ˌlād\ *n* [Pg *marmelada* quince conserve, fr. *marmelo* quince, fr. L *melimelum*, a sweet apple, fr. Gk *melimēlon*, fr. *meli* honey + *mēlon* apple — more at MELLIFLUOUS] (1524) : a clear sweetened jelly in which pieces of fruit and fruit rind are suspended

mar·mo·re·al \mär-'mòr-ē-əl, -'mòr-\ *also* **mar·mo·re·an** \-ē-ən\ *adj* [L *marmoreus*, fr. *marmor* marble] (1656) : of, relating to, or suggestive of marble or a marble statue esp. in coldness or aloofness — **mar·mo·re·al·ly** \-ē-ə-lē\ *adv*

mar·mo·set \'mär-mə-ˌset, -ˌzet\ *n* [ME *marmusette* kind of monkey, fr. MF *marmoset* grotesque figure, fr. *marmouser* to mumble, of imit. origin] (1679) : any of numerous small soft-furred So. and Central American monkeys (family Callithricidae) with claws instead of nails on all the digits except the great toe

mar·mot \'mär-mət\ *n* [F *marmotte*] (1607) : any of a genus (*Marmota*) of stout-bodied short-legged chiefly herbivorous burrowing rodents with coarse fur, a short bushy tail, and very small ears — compare WOODCHUCK

mar·o·cain \'mar-ə-ˌkān\ *n* [F (*crêpe*) *marocain*, lit., Moroccan crepe] (1922) : a ribbed crepe fabric used in women's clothing

Mar·o·nite \'mar-ə-ˌnīt\ *n* [ML *maronita*, fr. *Maron-, Maro* 5th cent. A.D. Syrian monk] (ca. 1511) : a member of a Uniate church chiefly in Lebanon having a Syriac liturgy and married clergy

marmot

¹ma·roon \mə-'rün\ *n* [F *maron, marron*, modif. of AmerSp *cimarrón*, fr. *cimarrón* wild, savage] (1666) **1** *cap*

: a fugitive black slave of the West Indies and Guiana in the 17th and 18th centuries; *also* : a descendant of such a slave **2** : a person who is marooned
²**maroon** *vt* (ca. 1709) **1** : to put ashore on a desolate island or coast and leave to one's fate **2** : to place or leave in isolation or without hope of ready escape
³**maroon** *n* [F *marron* Spanish chestnut] (1791) : a dark red
mar·plot \'mär-ˌplät\ *n* (1764) : one who frustrates or ruins a plan or undertaking by meddling
¹**marque** \'märk\ *n* [ME, fr. MF, fr. OProv *marca*, fr. *marcar* to mark, seize as pledge, of Gmc origin; akin to OHG *marcōn* to mark] (15c) **1** *obs* : REPRISAL, RETALIATION **2** : LETTERS OF MARQUE
²**marque** *n* [F, mark, brand, fr. MF, fr. *marquer* to mark, of Gmc origin; akin to OHG *marcōn* to mark] (1906) : a brand or make of a product (as a sports car)
mar·quee \mär-'kē\ *n* [modif. of F *marquise*, lit., marchioness] (1690) **1** *chiefly Brit* : a large tent set up for an outdoor party, reception, or exhibition **2** : a permanent canopy often of metal and glass projecting over an entrance (as of a hotel or theater) **3** : BOX OFFICE 2 ⟨~ value⟩
Mar·que·san \mär-'kā-z²n, -s²n\ *n* (1799) **1** : a native or inhabitant of the Marquesas Islands **2** : the Austronesian language of the Marquesans — **Marquesan** *adj*
mar·quess \'mär-kwəs\ *or* **mar·quis** \'mär-kwəs, mär-'kē\ *n, pl* **marquess·es** *or* **mar·quis·es** \-kwə-səz\ *or* **mar·quis** \-'kē(z)\ [ME *marquis, markis,* fr. MF *marquis,* alter. of *marchis,* fr. *marche* march] (14c) **1** : a nobleman of hereditary rank in Europe and Japan **2** : a member of the British peerage ranking below a duke and above an earl — **mar·quess·ate** \'mär-kwə-sət\ *or* **mar·quis·ate** \'mär-kwə-zət, -sət\ *n*
mar·que·try *also* **mar·que·terie** \'mär-kə-trē\ *n* [MF *marqueterie,* fr. *marqueter* to checker, inlay, fr. *marque* mark] (1563) : decorative work in which elaborate patterns are formed by the insertion of pieces of material (as wood, shell, or ivory) into a wood veneer that is then applied to a surface (as of a piece of furniture)
mar·quise \mär-'kēz\ *n, pl* **mar·quises** \-'kēz, -'kē-zəz\ [F, fem. of *marquis*] (1783) **1** : MARQUEE **2** : MARCHIONESS **3** : a gem or a ring setting or bezel usu. elliptical in shape but with pointed ends
mar·qui·sette \ˌmär-kwə-'zet, -kə-\ *n* [*marquise* + *-ette*] (1908) : a sheer meshed fabric used for clothing, curtains, and mosquito nets
mar·ram grass \'mar-əm-\ *n* [of Scand origin; akin to ON *maralmr,* a beach grass] (1834) : any of several beach grasses (genus *Ammophila* and esp. *A. arenaria*)
Mar·ra·no \mə-'rä-(ˌ)nō\ *n, pl* **-nos** [Sp, lit., pig] (1583) : a Christianized Jew of medieval Spain
mar·riage \'mar-ij *also* 'mer-\ *n* [ME *mariage,* fr. OF, fr. *marier* to marry] (14c) **1 a** : the state of being married **b** : the mutual relation of husband and wife : WEDLOCK **c** : the institution whereby men and women are joined in a special kind of social and legal dependence for the purpose of founding and maintaining a family **2** : an act of marrying or the rite by which the married status is effected; *esp* : the wedding ceremony and attendant festivities or formalities **3** : an intimate or close union ⟨the ~ of painting and poetry —J. T. Shawcross⟩ — **mar·riage·abil·i·ty** \ˌmar-i-jə-'bi-lə-tē *also* ˌmer-\ *n* — **mar·riage·able** \'mar-i-jə-bəl *also* 'mer-\ *adj*
marriage of convenience (1711) : a marriage contracted for social, political, or economic advantage rather than for mutual affection; *broadly* : a union or cooperation formed solely for pragmatic reasons
¹**mar·ried** \'mar-ēd *also* 'mer-\ *adj* (14c) **1 a** : being in the state of matrimony : WEDDED **b** : of or relating to marriage : CONNUBIAL **2** : UNITED, JOINED
²**married** *n, pl* **marrieds** *or* **married** (1890) : a married person ⟨young ~s are paid undue . . . attention —Paul Goodman⟩
mar·ron \ma-'rōⁿ\ *n* [F] (1594) **1** : a large Mediterranean chestnut (*Castanea sativa*) or its sweet edible nut — called also **Spanish chestnut 2 mar·rons** \-'rōⁿ(z)\ *pl* : chestnuts preserved in vanilla-flavored syrup
mar·rons gla·cés \ma-'rōⁿ-gla-'sā\ *n pl* [F, lit., glazed marrons] (1871) : MARRON 2
¹**mar·row** \'mar-(ˌ)ō\ *n* [ME *marowe,* fr. OE *mearg;* akin to OHG *marag* marrow, Skt *majjan*] (bef. 12c) **1 a** : a soft highly vascular modified connective tissue that occupies the cavities and cancellous part of most bones — compare RED MARROW **b** : the substance of the spinal cord **2 a** : the choicest of food **b** : the seat of animal vigor **c** : the inmost, best, or essential part : CORE ⟨personal liberty is the ~ of the American tradition —Clinton Rossiter⟩ **3** *chiefly Brit* : VEGETABLE MARROW — **mar·rowy** \'mar-ə-wē\ *adj*
²**marrow** *n* [ME *marwe, marrgh*] (1516) *chiefly Scot* : one of a pair
mar·row·bone \'mar-ə-ˌbōn, -ō-ˌbōn\ *n* (14c) **1** : a bone (as a shinbone) rich in marrow **2** *pl* : KNEES
mar·row·fat \-ə-ˌfat, -ō-ˌfat\ *n* (1733) : any of several wrinkled-seeded garden peas
¹**mar·ry** \'mar-ē *also* 'mer-\ *vb* **mar·ried; mar·ry·ing** [ME *marien,* fr. OF *marier,* fr. L *maritare,* fr. *maritus* married] *vt* (14c) **1 a** : to join as husband and wife according to law or custom **b** : to give in marriage ⟨*married* his daughter to his partner's son⟩ **c** : to take as spouse : WED ⟨*married* the girl next door⟩ **d** : to perform the ceremony of marriage for ⟨a priest will ~ them⟩ **e** : to obtain by marriage ⟨~ wealth⟩ **2** : to unite in close and usu. permanent relation ~ *vi* **1** : to take a spouse : WED **2** : COMBINE, UNITE ⟨seafood *marries* with other flavors⟩ — **marry into** : to become a member of by marriage ⟨*married into* a prominent family⟩
²**marry** *interj* [ME *marie,* fr. *Marie,* the Virgin Mary] (14c) *archaic* — used for emphasis and esp. to express amused or surprised agreement
Mars \'märz\ *n* [L *Mart-, Mars*] **1** : the Roman god of war — compare ARES **2** : the planet fourth in order from the sun and conspicuous for its red color — see PLANET table
mar·sa·la \mär-'sä-lə\ *n, often cap* [*Marsala,* town in Sicily] (1806) : a fortified Sicilian wine that varies from dry to sweet
marse \'märs\ *n* [by shortening & alter.] (1869) *Southern* : MASTER
Mar·seilles \mär-'sā(ə)lz\ *n* [*Marseilles,* France] (1762) : a firm cotton fabric that is similar to piqué
marsh \'märsh\ *n, often attrib* [ME *mersh,* fr. OE *merisc, mersc;* akin to MD *mersch* marsh, OE *mere* sea, pool — more at MARINE] (bef. 12c) : a tract of soft wet land usu. characterized by monocotyledons (as grasses or cattails)
¹**mar·shal** *also* **mar·shall** \'mär-shəl\ *n* [ME, fr. OF *mareschal,* of Gmc

origin; akin to OHG *marahscalc* marshal, fr. *marah* horse + *scalc* servant] (13c) **1 a** : a high official in the household of a medieval king, prince, or noble orig. having charge of the cavalry but later usu. in command of the military forces **b** : a person who arranges and directs the ceremonial aspects of a gathering **2 a** : FIELD MARSHAL **b** : a general officer of the highest military rank **3 a** : an officer having charge of prisoners **b** (1) : a ministerial officer appointed for a judicial district (as of the U.S.) to execute the process of the courts and perform various duties similar to those of a sheriff (2) : a city law officer entrusted with particular duties **c** : the administrative head of a city police department or fire department — **mar·shal·cy** \-sē\ *n* — **mar·shal·ship** \-ˌship\ *n*
²**marshal** *also* **marshall** *vb* **-shaled** *or* **-shalled; -shal·ing** *or* **-shalling** \'märsh-(ə-)liŋ\ *vt* (15c) **1** : to place in proper rank or position ⟨~ing the troops⟩ **2** : to bring together and order in an appropriate or effective way ⟨~ arguments⟩ **3** : to lead ceremoniously or solicitously : USHER ⟨~ing her little group of children down the street⟩ ~ *vi* : to take form or order ⟨ideas ~ing neatly⟩ *syn* see ORDER
marshal of the Royal Air Force (1947) : the highest ranking officer in the British air force
marsh elder *n* (ca. 1775) : any of a genus (*Iva*) of coarse shrubby composite plants of moist areas in eastern and central No. America
marsh gas *n* (1848) : METHANE
marsh hawk *n* (1772) : NORTHERN HARRIER
marsh hen *n* (1709) **1** : any of various American rails **2** : BITTERN
marsh·land \'märsh-ˌland\ *n* (12c) : a marshy tract or area : MARSH
marsh-mal·low \'märsh-ˌme-lō, -ˌma-\ *n* (bef. 12c) **1** : a pink-flowered European perennial herb (*Althaea officinalis*) of the mallow family that is naturalized in the eastern U.S. and has a mucilaginous root sometimes used in confectionery and in medicine **2** : a confection made from the root of the marshmallow or from corn syrup, sugar, albumen, and gelatin beaten to a light spongy consistency; *also* : a piece of partially dried marshmallow ⟨a bag of ~s⟩ — **marsh·mal·lowy** \-ˌme-lə-wē, -ˌma-\ *adj*
marsh marigold *n* (1578) : a swamp herb (*Caltha palustris*) of the buttercup family that occurs in No. America and has bright yellow flowers — called also *cowslip, kingcup*
marshy \'mär-shē\ *adj* **marsh·i·er; -est** (14c) **1** : resembling or constituting a marsh ⟨~ ground⟩ **2** : relating to or occurring in marshes ⟨~ vegetation⟩ — **marsh·i·ness** *n*
¹**mar·su·pi·al** \mär-'sü-pē-əl\ *adj* (1819) **1** : of, relating to, or being a marsupial **2** : of, relating to, or forming a marsupium
²**marsupial** *n* [NL *Marsupialia,* fr. *marsupium*] (ca. 1835) : any of an order (Marsupialia) of mammals comprising kangaroos, wombats, bandicoots, opossums, and related animals that do not develop a true placenta and that usu. have a pouch on the abdomen of the female which covers the teats and serves to carry the young
mar·su·pi·um \mär-'sü-pē-əm\ *n, pl* **-pia** \-pē-ə\ [NL, fr. L, purse, pouch, fr. Gk *marsypion*] (1698) **1** : an abdominal pouch that is formed of a fold of the skin and encloses the mammary glands of most marsupials **2** : any of several structures in various invertebrates (as a bryozoan or mollusk) for enclosing or carrying eggs or young
¹**mart** \'märt\ *n* [ME, fr. MD *marct, mart,* prob. fr. ONF *market*] (15c) **1** *archaic* : a coming together of people to buy and sell : ⁵FAIR 1 **2** *obs* : the activity of buying and selling; *also* : BARGAIN **3** : MARKET
²**mart** *vt* (1589) : to deal in : SELL
mar·tel·lo tower \mär-'te-lō-\ *n, often cap M* [*Cape Mortella,* Corsica] (1803) : a circular masonry fort or blockhouse
mar·ten \'mär-t²n\ *n, pl* **martens** *or* **martens** [ME *martryn,* fr. MF *martrine* marten fur, fr. OF, fr. *martre* marten, of Gmc origin; akin to OE *mearth* marten] (13c) **1** : any of several semiarboreal slender-bodied carnivorous mammals (genus *Martes*) chiefly of the northern hemisphere that are larger than the related weasels **2** : the fur or pelt of a marten
mar·tens·ite \'mär-t²n-ˌzīt\ *n* [Adolf *Martens* †1914 Ger. metallurgist] (1898) : the hard constituent that is the chief component of quenched steel — **mar·tens·it·ic** \ˌmar-t²n-'zi-tik, -'si-\ *adj* — **mar·tens·it·i·cal·ly** \-ti-k(ə-)lē\ *adv*
Mar·tha \'mär-thə\ *n* [LL, fr. Gk] : a sister of Lazarus and Mary and friend of Jesus
mar·tial \'mär-shəl\ *adj* [ME, fr. L *martialis* of Mars, fr. *Mart-, Mars*] (14c) **1** : of, relating to, or suited for war or a warrior **2** : relating to an army or to military life **3** : experienced in or inclined to war : WARLIKE — **mar·tial·ly** \-shə-lē\ *adv*
martial art *n* (1933) : any of several arts of combat and self-defense (as karate and judo) that are widely practiced as sport — **martial artist** *n*
martial law *n* (1568) **1** : the law applied in occupied territory by the military authority of the occupying power **2** : the law administered by military forces that is invoked by a government in an emergency when the civilian law enforcement agencies are unable to maintain public order and safety
mar·tian \'mär-shən\ *adj, often cap* (1880) : of or relating to the planet Mars or its hypothetical inhabitants — **martian** *n, often cap*
mar·tin \'mär-t²n\ *n* [prob. fr. St. *Martin*] (1589) **1** : a small Eurasian swallow (*Delichon urbica*) with a forked tail, bluish black head and back, and white rump and underparts **2** : any of various swallows and flycatchers other than the martin
mar·ti·net \ˌmär-t²n-'et\ *n* [Jean *Martinet,* 17th cent. Fr. army officer] (1779) **1** : a strict disciplinarian **2** : a person who stresses a rigid adherence to the details of forms and methods
mar·tin·gale \'mär-t²n-ˌgāl, -tiŋ-\ *n* [MF]

martingale 1

\ə\ abut \ᵊ\ kitten, F table \ər\ further \a\ ash \ā\ ace \ä\ mop, mar \au̇\ out \ch\ chin \e\ bet \ē\ easy \g\ go \i\ hit \ī\ ice \j\ job \ŋ\ sing \ō\ go \ȯ\ law \ȯi\ boy \th\ thin \t̲h̲\ the \ü\ loot \u̇\ foot \y\ yet \zh\ vision \ȧ, k̲, ⁿ, œ, œ̄, ue, ūe, ʸ\ see Guide to Pronunciation

(1589)   **1** : a device for steadying a horse's head or checking its upward movement that typically consists of a strap fastened to the girth, passing between the forelegs, and bifurcating to end in two rings through which the reins pass   **2 a** : a lower stay of rope or chain for the jibboom used to sustain the strain of the forestays and fastened to or rove through the dolphin striker   **b** : DOLPHIN STRIKER   **3** : any of several systems of betting in which a player increases the stake usu. by doubling each time a bet is lost

mar·ti·ni \mär-'tē-nē\ n [prob. alter. of *Martinez* (cocktail), fr. the name *Martinez*] (1894) : a cocktail made of gin and dry vermouth; *also* : VODKA MARTINI

Mar·tin Lu·ther King Day \'mär-t³n-'lü-thər-'kiŋ\ n (1977) : the third Monday in January observed as a legal holiday in some states of the U.S.

Mar·tin·mas \'mär-t³n-məs, -,mas\ n [ME *martinmasse,* fr. St. *Martin* + ME *masse* mass] (14c) : November 11 celebrated as the feast of Saint Martin

mart·let \'märt-lət\ n [alter. of *martinet,* fr. MF, prob. fr. St. *Martin*] (1538) : MARTIN 1

¹mar·tyr \'mär-tər\ n [ME, fr. OE, fr. LL, fr. Gk *martyr-, martys,* lit., witness] (bef. 12c)   **1** : a person who voluntarily suffers death as the penalty of witnessing to and refusing to renounce a religion   **2** : a person who sacrifices something of great value and esp. life itself for the sake of principle   **3** : VICTIM; *esp* : a great or constant sufferer ⟨a ∼ to asthma all his life —A. J. Cronin⟩ — **mar·tyr·i·za·tion** \,mär-tə-rə-'zä-shən\ n — **mar·tyr·ize** \'mär-tə-,rīz\ vt

²martyr vt (bef. 12c)   **1** : to put to death for adhering to a belief, faith, or profession   **2** : to inflict agonizing pain on : TORTURE

mar·tyr·dom \'mär-tər-dəm\ n (bef. 12c)   **1** : the suffering of death on account of adherence to a cause and esp. to one's religious faith   **2** : AFFLICTION, TORTURE

mar·tyr·ol·o·gist \,mär-tə-'rä-lə-jist\ n (1676) : a writer of or a specialist in martyrology

mar·tyr·ol·o·gy \-jē\ n (1599)   **1** : a catalog of Roman Catholic martyrs and saints arranged by the dates of their feasts   **2** : ecclesiastical history treating the lives and sufferings of martyrs

mar·tyry \'mär-tə-rē\ n, pl **-tyr·ies** [LL *martyrium,* fr. LGk *martyrion,* fr. Gk *martyr-, martys*] (ca. 1722) : a shrine erected in honor of a martyr

¹mar·vel \'mär-vəl\ n [ME *mervel,* fr. OF *merveille,* fr. LL *mirabilia* marvels, fr. L, neut. pl. of *mirabilis* wonderful, fr. *mirari* to wonder] (14c)   **1** : something that causes wonder or astonishment   **2** : intense surprise or interest : ASTONISHMENT

²marvel vb **mar·veled** or **mar·velled; mar·vel·ing** or **mar·vel·ling** \'märv-liŋ, 'mär-və-\ vi (14c) : to become filled with surprise, wonder, or amazed curiosity ⟨∼ed at the magician's skill⟩ ∼ vt : to feel astonishment or perplexity at or about ⟨∼ed that they had escaped⟩

mar·vel·ous or **mar·vel·lous** \'märv-(ə-)ləs\ adj (14c)   **1** : causing wonder : ASTONISHING   **2** : MIRACULOUS, SUPERNATURAL ⟨Gothic tales of the ∼ and the bizarre⟩   **3** : of the highest kind or quality : notably superior ⟨has a ∼ way with children⟩ — **mar·vel·ous·ly** adv — **mar·vel·ous·ness** n

Marx·ian \'märk-sē-ən\ adj (1887) : of, developed by, or influenced by the doctrines of Marx ⟨∼ socialism⟩

Marx·ism \'märk-,si-zəm\ n (1897) : the political, economic, and social principles and policies advocated by Marx; *esp* : a theory and practice of socialism including the labor theory of value, dialectical materialism, the class struggle, and dictatorship of the proletariat until the establishment of a classless society — **Marx·ist** \-sist\ n or adj

Marx·ism–Len·in·ism \'märk-,si-zəm-'le-nə-,ni-zəm\ n (1932) : a theory and practice of communism developed by Lenin from doctrines of Marx — **Marx·ist–Len·in·ist** \'märk-sist-'le-nə-nist\ n or adj

Mary \'mer-ē, 'mar-ē, 'mā-rē\ n [LL *Maria,* fr. Gk *Mariam, Maria,* fr. Heb *Miryām* Miriam]   **1** : the mother of Jesus   **2** : a sister of Lazarus and Martha and a friend of Jesus

Mary Jane \-'jān\ n [by folk etymology (influenced by Sp *Juana* Jane)] (1928) slang : MARIJUANA

Mary·knoll·er \-,nō-lər\ n (1943) : a member of the Catholic Foreign Mission Society of America founded by T. F. Price and J. A. Walsh at Maryknoll, N.Y. in 1911

Mary Mag·da·lene \-'mag-də-lən, -,lēn; -,mag-də-'lē-nē\ n [LL *Magdalene,* fr. Gk *Magdalēnē*] : a woman who was healed of evil spirits by Jesus and who saw the risen Christ near his sepulchre

mar·zi·pan \'märt-sə-,pän, -,pan; 'mär-zə-,pan\ n [G, fr. It *marzapane*] (1542) : a confection of crushed almonds or almond paste, sugar, and egg whites that is often shaped into various forms

Ma·sai \mä-'sī, 'mä-,\ n, pl **Masai** or **Masais** (1857)   **1** : a member of a pastoral and hunting people of Kenya and Tanzania   **2** : the Nilotic language of the Masai people

mas·cara \ma-'skar-ə\ n [prob. fr. It *maschera* mask] (1886) : a cosmetic esp. for coloring the eyelashes

mas·car·po·ne \,mas-kär-'pō-(,)nā\ n [It, fr. It dial. (Lombardy) *mascarpón,* aug. of *mascarpa* cream cheese] (1932) : an Italian cream cheese

mas·con \'mas-,kän\ n [²mass + concentration] (1968) : any of the high-density regions below the surface of lunar maria that are held to perturb the motion of spacecraft in lunar orbit

mas·cot \'mas-,kät also -kət\ n [F *mascotte,* fr. Prov *mascoto,* fr. *masco* witch, fr. ML *masca*] (1881) : a person, animal, or object adopted by a group as a symbolic figure esp. to bring them good luck ⟨the team had a mountain lion as their ∼⟩

¹mas·cu·line \'mas-kyə-lən\ adj [ME *masculin,* fr. MF, fr. L *masculinus,* fr. *masculus* n., male, dim. of *mas* male] (14c)   **1** : MALE b : having qualities appropriate to or usu. associated with a man   **2** : of, relating to, or constituting the gender that ordinarily includes most words or grammatical forms referring to males   **3 a** : having or occurring in a stressed final syllable ⟨∼ rhyme⟩   **b** : having the final chord occurring on a strong beat ⟨∼ cadence⟩   **4** : of or forming the formal, active, or generative principle of the cosmos — **mas·cu·line·ly** adv — **mas·cu·lin·i·ty** \,mas-kyə-'li-nə-tē\ n

²masculine n (14c)   **1** : the masculine gender   **2** : a noun, pronoun, adjective, or inflectional form or class of the masculine gender   **3** : a male person

mas·cu·lin·ise Brit var of MASCULINIZE

mas·cu·lin·ize \'mas-kyə-lə-,nīz\ vt **-ized; -iz·ing** (1912) : to give a chiefly masculine character to; *esp* : to cause (a female) to take on male characteristics — **mas·cu·lin·i·za·tion** \,mas-kyə-lə-nə-'zä-shən\ n

ma·ser \'mā-zər\ n [*m*icrowave *a*mplification by *s*timulated *e*mission of *r*adiation] (1955) : a device or object that emits coherent microwave radiation produced by the natural oscillations of atoms or molecules between energy levels

¹mash \'mash\ vt (13c)   **1 a** : to reduce to a soft pulpy state by beating or pressure   **b** : CRUSH, SMASH ⟨∼ a finger⟩   **2** : to subject (as crushed malt) to the action of water with heating and stirring in preparing wort

²mash n [ME *mash-,* fr. OE *māx-;* akin to MHG *meisch* mash] (1577)   **1** : a mixture of ground feeds for livestock   **2** : crushed malt or grain meal steeped and stirred in hot water to ferment (as for the production of beer or whiskey)   **3** : a soft pulpy mass   **4** Brit : mashed potatoes

³mash vt [origin unknown] (1879) : to flirt with or seek the affection of

⁴mash n (1880) : CRUSH 4

¹mash·er \'ma-shər\ n (ca. 1500) : one that mashes ⟨a potato ∼⟩

²masher n (1875) : a man who makes passes at women

¹mask \'mask\ n [MF *masque,* fr. OIt *maschera*] (1534)   **1 a** (1) : a cover or partial cover for the face used for disguise   (2) : a person wearing a mask : MASKER   **b** (1) : a figure of a head worn on the stage in antiquity to identify the character and project the voice   (2) : a grotesque false face worn at carnivals or in rituals   **c** : an often grotesque carved head or face used as an ornament (as on a keystone)   **d** : a sculptured face or a copy of a face made by means of a mold   **2 a** : something that serves to conceal or disguise : PRETENSE, CLOAK ⟨aware of the ∼s, facades and defenses people erect to protect themselves —Kenneth Keniston⟩   **b** : something that conceals from view   **c** : a translucent or opaque screen to cover part of the sensitive surface in taking or printing a photograph   **d** : a pattern of opaque material used to shield selected areas of a surface (as of a semiconductor) in deposition or etching (as in producing an integrated circuit)   **3 a** : a protective covering for the face   **b** : GAS MASK   **c** : a device covering the mouth and nose to facilitate inhalation   **d** : a comparable device to prevent exhalation of infective material   **e** : a cosmetic preparation for the skin of the face that produces a tightening effect as it dries   **4 a** : the head or face of an animal (as a fox or dog)   **b** : an area (as the one around the eyes) of an animal's face that is distinguished by usu. darker coloring

²mask vi (ca. 1562)   **1** : to take part in a masquerade   **2 a** : to assume a mask   **b** : to disguise one's true character or intentions ∼ vt   **1** : to provide or conceal with a mask: also   **2** : to conceal from view ⟨∼ a gun battery⟩   **b** : to make indistinct or imperceptible ⟨∼s undesirable flavors⟩   **c** : to cover up ⟨∼ed his real purpose⟩   **2** : to cover for protection   **3** : to modify the size or shape of (as a photograph) by means of an opaque border   *syn* see DISGUISE — **mask·like** \-,līk\ adj

masked \'maskt\ adj (1585)   **1** : marked by the use of masks ⟨a ∼ ball⟩   **2** : failing to present or produce the usual symptoms : LATENT ⟨∼ infection⟩ ⟨a ∼ virus⟩

mask·er \'mas-kər\ n (ca. 1548) : a person who wears a mask; *esp* : a participant in a masquerade

mask·ing tape \'mas-kiŋ-\ n (1936) : a tape with adhesive on one side that has a variety of uses (as to cover a surface when painting an adjacent surface)

mas·och·ism \'ma-sə-,ki-zəm, 'ma-zə- also 'mā-\ n [ISV, fr. Leopold von Sacher-*Masoch* †1895 Ger. novelist] (ca. 1893)   **1** : a sexual perversion characterized by pleasure in being subjected to pain or humiliation esp. by a love object — compare SADISM   **2** : pleasure in being abused or dominated : a taste for suffering — **mas·och·ist** \-kist\ n — **mas·och·is·tic** \,ma-sə-'kis-tik, ,ma-zə- also ,mā-\ adj — **mas·och·is·ti·cal·ly** \-'kis-ti-k(ə-)lē\ adv

ma·son \'mā-s³n\ n [ME, fr. OF *maçon,* of Gmc origin; akin to OE *macian* to make] (13c)   **1** : a skilled worker who builds by laying units of substantial material (as stone or brick)   **2** cap : FREEMASON

Ma·son·ic \mə-'sä-nik\ adj (1797) : of, relating to, or characteristic of Freemasons or Freemasonry

Ma·son·ite \'mā-s³n-,īt\ trademark — used for fiberboard made from steam-exploded wood fiber

ma·son jar \'mā-s³n-\ n, often cap M [John L. *Mason,* 19th cent. Am. inventor] (1888) : a widemouthed jar used esp. for home canning

ma·son·ry \'mā-s³n-rē\ n, pl **-ries** (13c)   **1 a** : something constructed of materials used by masons   **b** : the art, trade, or occupation of a mason   **c** : work done by a mason   **2** cap : FREEMASONRY

mason wasp n (1792) : any of various solitary wasps that construct nests of hardened mud

Ma·so·ra or **Ma·so·rah** \mə-'sör-ə, -'sör-\ n [NHeb *mĕsōrāh,* fr. LHeb *māsōreth* tradition, fr. Heb, bond] (1613) : a body of notes on the textual traditions of the Hebrew Old Testament compiled by scribes during the 1st millennium of the Christian era

Mas·o·rete or **Mas·so·rete** \'ma-sə-,rēt\ n [MF *massoreth,* fr. LHeb *māsōreth*] (1587) : one of the scribes who compiled the Masora — **Mas·o·ret·ic** \,ma-sə-'re-tik\ adj

masque also **mask** \'mask\ n [MF *masque* — more at MASK] (1514)   **1** : MASQUERADE   **2** : a short allegorical dramatic entertainment of the 16th and 17th centuries performed by masked actors

masqu·er \'mas-kər\ var of MASKER

¹mas·quer·ade \,mas-kə-'rād\ n [MF, fr. OIt dial. *mascarada,* fr. OIt *maschera* mask] (1587)   **1 a** : a social gathering of persons wearing masks and often fantastic costumes   **b** : a costume for wear at such a gathering   **2** : an action or appearance that is mere disguise or outward show

²masquerade vi **-ad·ed; -ad·ing** (1692)   **1 a** : to disguise oneself; *also* : to go about disguised   **b** : to take part in a masquerade   **2** : to assume the appearance of something one is not — **mas·quer·ad·er** n

¹mass \'mas\ n [ME, fr. OE *mæsse,* modif. of (assumed) VL *messa,* lit., dismissal at the end of a religious service, fr. LL *missa,* fr. L, fem. of *missus,* pp. of *mittere* to send] (bef. 12c)   **1** cap : the liturgy of the Eucharist esp. in accordance with the traditional Latin rite   **2** often cap : a celebration of the Eucharist ⟨Sunday ∼es held at three different hours⟩   **3** : a musical setting for the ordinary of the Mass

²mass n [ME *masse,* fr. MF, fr. L *massa,* fr. Gk *maza;* akin to Gk *massein* to knead — more at MINGLE] (15c)   **1 a** : a quantity or aggregate of matter usu. of considerable size   **b** (1) : EXPANSE, BULK   (2) : massive quality or effect ⟨impressed me with such ~ and such vividness — F. M. Ford⟩ (3) : the principal part or main body ⟨the great ~ of the continent is buried under an ice cap —Walter Sullivan⟩ (4) : AGGREGATE, WHOLE ⟨men in the ~⟩ **c** : the property of a body that is a measure of its inertia and that is commonly taken as a measure of the amount of material it contains and causes it to have weight in a gravitational field **2** : a large quantity, amount, or number ⟨a great ~ of material⟩ **3 a** : a large body of persons in a compact group : a body of persons regarded as an aggregate **b** : the great body of the people as contrasted with the elite — often used in pl. ⟨the underprivileged and disadvantaged ~es —C. A. Buss⟩ **syn** see BULK

³**mass** vt (14c) : to form or collect into a mass ~ vi : to assemble in a mass ⟨three thousand students had ~ed in the plaza —A. E. Neville⟩

⁴**mass** adj (1733) **1 a** : of or relating to the mass of the people ⟨~ market⟩ ⟨~ education⟩; also : being one of or at one with the mass : AVERAGE, COMMONPLACE ⟨~ man⟩ **b** : participated in by or affecting a large number of individuals ⟨~ destruction⟩ ⟨~ demonstrations⟩ **c** : having a large-scale character : WHOLESALE ⟨~ production⟩ **2** : viewed as a whole : TOTAL ⟨the ~ effect of a design⟩

mas·sa \'ma-sə\ n [by alter.] (1774) Southern : MASTER

Mas·sa·chu·set or **Mas·sa·chu·sett** \,ma-sə-'chü-sət, -zət also ,mas-'chü-\ n, pl **Massachusets** or **Massachuset** or **Massachusetts** or **Massachusett** [Massachuset, a locality, lit., at the big hill] (1616) **1** : a member of an American Indian people of Massachusetts **2** : the extinct Algonquian language of the Massachuset people

¹**mas·sa·cre** \'ma-si-kər\ n [MF] (ca. 1578) **1** : the act or an instance of killing a number of usu. helpless or unresisting human beings under circumstances of atrocity or cruelty **2** : a cruel or wanton murder **3** : a wholesale slaughter of animals **4** : an act of complete destruction ⟨the author's ~ of traditional federalist presuppositions —R. G. McCloskey⟩

²**massacre** vt **mas·sa·cred; mas·sa·cring** \-k(ə-)riŋ\ (1581) **1** : to kill by massacre : SLAUGHTER **2** : MANGLE 2 ⟨words were misspelled and syntax massacred —Bice Clemow⟩ — **mas·sa·crer** \-kər-ər, -krər\ n

¹**mas·sage** \mə-'säzh, -'säj\ n [F, fr. masser to massage, fr. Ar massa to stroke] (ca. 1860) : manipulation of tissues (as by rubbing, kneading, or tapping) with the hand or an instrument for therapeutic purposes

²**massage** vt **mas·saged; mas·sag·ing** (1887) **1** : to subject to massage **2 a** : to treat flatteringly : BLANDISH **b** : MANIPULATE 3, DOCTOR 2b ⟨researchers massaged the data to support their thesis⟩ — **mas·sag·er** n

massage parlor n (1913) : an establishment that provides massage treatments; also : one offering sexual services in addition to or in lieu of massage

mas·sa·sau·ga \,ma-sə-'sò-gə\ n [Missisauga River, Ontario, Canada] (1835) : a small No. American rattlesnake (Sistrurus catenatus)

mass card n (1948) : a card notifying the recipient (as a bereaved family) that a mass is to be offered for the repose of the soul of a specified deceased person

mass defect n (ca. 1923) : the difference between the mass of an isotope and its mass number

mass driver n (1977) : a large electromagnetic catapult designed to hurl material (as from an asteroid) into space

mas·sé \ma-'sā\ n [F, fr. pp. of masser to make a massé shot, fr. masse sledgehammer, fr. MF mace mace] (1873) : a shot in billiards or pool made by hitting the cue ball vertically or nearly vertically on the side to drive it around one ball in order to strike another

mas·se·ter \mə-'sē-tər, ma-\ n [NL, fr. Gk masetēr, fr. masasthai to chew — more at MANDIBLE] (1666) : a large muscle that raises the lower jaw and assists in mastication — **mas·se·ter·ic** \,ma-sə-'ter-ik\ adj

mas·seur \ma-'sər, mə-\ n [F, fr. masser] (1876) : a man who practices massage

mas·seuse \-'sə(r)z, -'süz\ n [F, fem. of masseur] (1876) : a woman who practices massage

mas·sif \ma-'sēf\ n [F, fr. massif, adj., fr. MF] (1885) **1** : a principal mountain mass **2** : a block of the earth's crust bounded by faults or flexures and displaced as a unit without internal change

mas·sive \'ma-siv\ adj [ME massiffe, fr. MF massif, fr. masse mass] (15c) **1** : forming or consisting of a large mass: **a** : BULKY **b** : WEIGHTY, HEAVY ⟨~ walls⟩ ⟨a ~ volume⟩ **c** : impressively large or ponderous **d** : having no regular form but not necessarily lacking crystalline structure ⟨~ sandstone⟩ **2 a** : large, solid, or heavy in structure ⟨~ jaw⟩ **b** : large in scope or degree ⟨the feeling of frustration, of being ineffectual, is ~ —David Halberstam⟩ **c** (1) : large in comparison to what is typical ⟨~ dose of penicillin⟩ (2) : being extensive and severe ⟨~ hemorrhage⟩ ⟨~ collapse of a lung⟩ (3) : imposing in excellence or grandeur : MONUMENTAL ⟨~ simplicity⟩ **3** : having mass ⟨a ~ boson⟩ — **mas·sive·ly** adv — **mas·sive·ness** n

mass·less \'mas-ləs\ adj (1879) : having no mass ⟨a ~ particle⟩

mass–mar·ket \'mas-'mär-kət\ adj (1952) : sold through such retail outlets as supermarkets and drugstores as well as through bookstores ⟨a ~ paperback⟩; also : of, relating to, or publishing mass-market materials

mass medium n, pl **mass media** (1923) : a medium of communication (as newspapers, radio, or television) that is designed to reach the mass of the people — usu. used in pl.

mass noun n (1933) : a noun (as sand or water) that characteristically denotes in many languages a homogeneous substance or a concept without subdivisions and that in English is preceded in indefinite singular constructions by some rather than a or an — compare COUNT NOUN

mass number n (1923) : an integer that approximates the mass of an isotope and designates the number of nucleons in the nucleus

mass–pro·duce \,mas-prə-'düs, -'dyüs\ vt [back-formation fr. mass production] (1923) : to produce in quantity usu. by machinery — **mass production** n

mass spectrograph n (1920) : an instrument used to separate and often to determine the masses of isotopes

mass spectrometry n (1943) : an instrumental method for identifying the chemical constitution of a substance by means of the separation of gaseous ions according to their differing mass and charge — called also

mass spectroscopy — **mass spectrometric** adj — **mass spectrometer** n

mass spectrum n (1920) : the spectrum of a stream of gaseous ions separated according to their mass and charge

massy \'ma-sē\ adj (14c) : MASSIVE

¹**mast** \'mast\ n [ME, fr. OE mæst; akin to OHG mast mast, L malus] (bef. 12c) **1** : a long pole or spar rising from the keel or deck of a ship and supporting the yards, booms, and rigging **2** : a slender vertical or nearly vertical structure (as an upright post in various cranes) **3** : a disciplinary proceeding at which the commanding officer of a naval unit hears and disposes of cases against enlisted men — called also captain's mast — **mast·ed** \'mas-təd\ adj — **before the mast 1** : forward of the foremast **2** : as a common sailor

²**mast** vt (1627) : to furnish with a mast

³**mast** n [ME, fr. OE mæst; akin to OHG mast food, mast, and prob. to OE mete food — more at MEAT] (bef. 12c) : nuts (as acorns) accumulated on the forest floor and eaten as food for animals (as hogs)

mas·ta·ba \'mas-tə-bə\ n [Ar mastabah stone bench] (1882) : an Egyptian tomb of the time of the Memphite dynasties that is oblong in shape with sloping sides and a flat roof

mast cell \'mast-\ n [part trans. of G Mastzelle, fr. Mast food, mast (fr. OHG) + Zelle cell] (ca. 1890) : a large cell that occurs esp. in connective tissue and has basophilic granules containing substances (as histamine and heparin) which mediate allergic reactions

mas·tec·to·my \ma-'stek-tə-mē\ n, pl **-mies** [Gk mastos breast + E -ectomy] (ca. 1923) : excision of the breast

¹**mas·ter** \'mas-tər\ n [ME, fr. OE magister & OF maistre, both fr. L magister; akin to L magnus large — more at MUCH] (bef. 12c) **1 a** (1) : a male teacher (2) : a person holding an academic degree higher than a bachelor's but lower than a doctor's **b** often cap : a revered religious leader **c** : a worker or artisan qualified to teach apprentices **d** (1) : an artist, performer, or player of consummate skill (2) : a great figure of the past (as in science or art) whose work serves as a model or ideal **2 a** : one having authority over another : RULER, GOVERNOR **b** : one that conquers or masters : VICTOR, SUPERIOR ⟨in this young, obscure challenger the champion found his ~⟩ **c** : a person licensed to command a merchant ship **d** (1) : one having control (2) : an owner esp. of a slave or animal **e** : the employer esp. of a servant **f** (1) dial : HUSBAND (2) : the male head of a household **3 a** (1) archaic : MR. (2) : a youth or boy too young to be called mister — used as a title **b** : the eldest son of a Scottish viscount or baron **4 a** : a presiding officer in an institution or society (as a college) **b** : any of several officers of court appointed to assist (as by hearing and reporting) a judge **5 a** : a master mechanism or device **b** : an original from which copies can be made; esp : a master phonograph record or magnetic tape — **mas·ter·ship** \-,ship\ n

²**master** adj (12c) : being or relating to a master: as **a** : having chief authority : DOMINANT **b** : SKILLED, PROFICIENT ⟨a prosperous ~ builder —Current Biog.⟩ **c** : PRINCIPAL, PREDOMINANT **d** : SUPERLATIVE — often used in combination ⟨a master-liar⟩ **e** : being a device or mechanism that controls the operation of another mechanism or that establishes a standard (as a dimension or weight) **f** : being or relating to a master from which duplicates are made

³**master** vt **mas·tered; mas·ter·ing** \-t(ə-)riŋ\ (13c) **1** : to become master of : OVERCOME **2 a** : to become skilled or proficient in the use of ⟨~ a foreign language⟩ **b** : to gain a thorough understanding of ⟨had ~ed every aspect of publishing —Current Biog.⟩ **3** : to produce a master phonograph record or magnetic tape of (as a musical rendition)

master–at–arms n, pl **masters–at–arms** (1748) : a petty officer charged with maintaining discipline aboard ship

master bedroom n (1925) : a large or principal bedroom

master chief petty officer n (1958) : an enlisted man in the navy or coast guard ranking above a senior chief petty officer

master chief petty officer of the coast guard (1966) : the ranking petty officer in the coast guard serving as adviser to the commandant

master chief petty officer of the navy (1966) : the ranking petty officer in the navy serving as adviser to the chief of naval operations

master class n (1952) : a seminar for advanced music students conducted by a master musician

mas·ter·ful \'mas-tər-fəl\ adj (15c) **1 a** : inclined and usu. competent to play the master **b** : suggestive of a domineering nature **2** : having or reflecting the power and skill of a master — **mas·ter·ful·ly** \-fə-lē\ adv — **mas·ter·ful·ness** n

syn MASTERFUL, DOMINEERING, IMPERIOUS, PEREMPTORY, IMPERATIVE mean tending to impose one's will on others. MASTERFUL implies a strong personality and ability to act authoritatively ⟨her masterful personality soon dominated the movement⟩. DOMINEERING suggests an overbearing or arbitrary manner and an obstinate determination to enforce one's will ⟨children controlled by domineering parents⟩. IMPERIOUS implies a commanding nature or manner and often suggests arrogant assurance ⟨an imperious executive used to getting his own way⟩. PEREMPTORY implies an abrupt dictatorial manner coupled with an unwillingness to brook disobedience or dissent ⟨given a peremptory dismissal⟩. IMPERATIVE implies peremptoriness arising more from the urgency of the situation than from an inherent will to dominate ⟨an imperative appeal for assistance⟩.

usage Some commentators insist that use of masterful should be limited to sense 1 in order to preserve a distinction between it and masterly. The distinction is a modern one, excogitated by a 20th century pundit in disregard of the history of the word. Both words developed in a parallel manner but the earlier sense of masterly, equivalent to masterful 1, dropped out of use. Since masterly had but one sense, the pundit opined that it would be tidy if masterful were likewise limited to one sense and he forthwith condemned use of masterful 2 as an error. Sense 2 of masterful, which is slightly older than the sense of

\ə\ abut \ᵊ\ kitten, F table \ər\ further \a\ ash \ā\ ace \ä\ mop, mar \aů\ out \ch\ chin \e\ bet \ē\ easy \g\ go \i\ hit \ī\ ice \j\ job \ŋ\ sing \ō\ go \ò\ law \òi\ boy \th\ thin \t̶h̶\ the \ü\ loot \ů\ foot \y\ yet \zh\ vision \á, k̲, ⁿ, œ, œ̄, ᵫ, ᵫ̄, ᵊ\ see Guide to Pronunciation

masterly intended to replace it, has continued in reputable use all along; it cannot rationally be called an error.

master gunnery sergeant *n* (1958) : a noncommissioned officer in the marine corps ranking above a master sergeant

master key *n* (1576) : a key designed to open several different locks

mas·ter·ly \'mas-tər-lē\ *adj* (15c) : suitable to or resembling that of a master; *esp* : indicating thorough knowledge or superior skill and power ⟨a ~ performance⟩ **usage** see MASTERFUL — **mas·ter·li·ness** *n* — **masterly** *adv*

¹mas·ter·mind \'mas-tər-ˌmīnd, ˌmas-tər-'-\ *n* (1720) : a person who supplies the directing or creative intelligence for a project

²mastermind *vt* (1940) : to be the mastermind of

master of arts *often cap M&A* (15c) 1 : the recipient of a master's degree that usu. signifies that the recipient has passed an integrated course of study in one or more of the humanities and sometimes has completed a thesis involving research or a creative project and that typically requires two years of work beyond a bachelor's degree 2 : the degree making one a master of arts — abbr. *M.A., A.M.*

master of ceremonies (1662) 1 : a person who determines the forms to be observed on a public occasion 2 : a person who acts as host at a formal event 3 : a person who acts as host for a program of entertainment (as on television)

master of science *often cap M&S* (ca. 1905) 1 : the recipient of a master's degree that usu. signifies that the recipient has passed an integrated course of study in one or more of the sciences and sometimes has completed a thesis involving research and that typically requires two years of work beyond a bachelor's degree 2 : the degree making one a master of science — abbr. *M.S., M.Sc.*

mas·ter·piece \'mas-tər-ˌpēs\ *n* (1605) 1 : a work done with extraordinary skill; *esp* : a supreme intellectual or artistic achievement 2 : a piece of work presented to a medieval guild as evidence of qualification for the rank of master

master plan *n* (ca. 1930) : a plan giving overall guidance

master race *n* (1937) : a people held to be racially preeminent and hence fitted to rule or enslave other peoples

master's *n* (1939) : a master's degree

master sergeant *n* (ca. 1934) : a noncommissioned officer ranking in the army above a sergeant first class and below a staff sergeant major, in the air force above a technical sergeant and below a senior master sergeant, and in the marine corps above a gunnery sergeant and below a master gunnery sergeant

mas·ter·sing·er \'mas-tər-ˌsin-ər\ *n* (1810) : MEISTERSINGER

mas·ter·stroke \-ˌstrōk\ *n* (1679) : a masterly performance or move

mas·ter·work \-ˌwərk\ *n* (1617) : MASTERPIECE

mas·tery \'mas-t(ə-)rē\ *n* [ME *maistrie*, fr. OF, fr. *maistre* master] (13c) 1 *a* : the authority of a master : DOMINION *b* : the upper hand in a contest or competition : SUPERIORITY, ASCENDANCY 2 *a* : possession or display of great skill or technique *b* : skill or knowledge that makes one master of a subject : COMMAND

mast·head \'mast-ˌhed\ *n* (1748) 1 : the top of a mast 2 *a* : the printed matter in a newspaper or periodical that gives the title and pertinent details of ownership, advertising rates, and subscription rates *b* : the name of a publication (as a newspaper) displayed on the top of the first page

mas·tic \'mas-tik\ *n* [ME *mastik*, fr. L *mastiche*, fr. Gk *mastichē*, prob. back-formation fr. *mastichan*] (14c) 1 : an aromatic resinous exudate from mastic trees used chiefly in varnishes 2 : any of various pasty materials used as protective coatings or cements

mas·ti·cate \'mas-tə-ˌkāt\ *vb* **-cat·ed; -cat·ing** [LL *masticatus*, pp. of *masticare*, fr. Gk *mastichan* to gnash the teeth; akin to Gk *masasthai* to chew — more at MANDIBLE] *vt* (1649) 1 : to grind or crush (food) with or as if with the teeth in preparation for swallowing : CHEW 2 : to soften or reduce to pulp by crushing or kneading ~ *vi* : CHEW — **mas·ti·ca·tion** \ˌmas-tə-'kā-shən\ *n* — **mas·ti·ca·tor** \'mas-tə-ˌkā-tər\ *n*

¹mas·ti·ca·to·ry \'mas-ti-kə-ˌtōr-ē, -ˌtōr-\ *adj* (1694) 1 : used for or adapted to chewing ⟨~ limbs of an arthropod⟩ 2 : of, relating to, or involving the organs of mastication ⟨~ paralysis⟩

²masticatory *n, pl* **-ries** (ca. 1611) : a substance chewed to increase saliva

mastic tree *n* (15c) : a small southern European evergreen tree (*Pistacia lentiscus*) of the cashew family that yields mastic

mas·tiff \'mas-təf\ *n* [ME *mastif*, modif. of MF *mastin*, fr. (assumed) VL *mansuetinus*, fr. L *mansuetus* tame — more at MANSUETUDE] (14c) : any of a breed of very large massive powerful smooth-coated dogs that are apricot, fawn, or brindle and are often used as guard dogs

mas·ti·goph·o·ran \ˌmas-tə-'gä-fə-rən\ *n* [ultim. fr Gk *mastig-, mastix* whip + *pherein* to carry — more at BEAR] (ca. 1911) : any of a subphylum (Mastigophora) of protozoans comprising forms with flagella and including many often treated as algae — **mastigophoran** *adj*

mas·ti·tis \ma-'stī-təs\ *n, pl* **-tit·i·des** \-'sti-tə-ˌdēz\ [NL, fr. Gk *mastos* breast] (ca. 1842) : inflammation of the breast or udder usu. caused by infection — **mas·tit·ic** \-'sti-tik\ *adj*

mas·to·don \'mas-tə-ˌdän, -dən\ *n* [NL *mastodont-, mastodon*, fr. Gk *mastos* + *odont-, odōn, odous* tooth — more at TOOTH] (1813) 1 : any of numerous extinct mammals (genus *Mastodon* syn. *Mammut*) that differ from the related mammoths and existing elephants chiefly in the form of the molar teeth 2 : one that is unusually large — **mas·to·don·ic** \ˌmas-tə-'dä-nik\ *adj* — **mas·to·dont** \'mas-tə-ˌdänt\ *adj or n*

¹mas·toid \'mas-ˌtȯid\ *adj* [NL *mastoides* resembling a nipple, mastoid, fr. Gk *mastoeidēs*, fr. *mastos* breast] (1732) 1 : being the process of the temporal bone behind the ear; *also* : being any of several bony elements that occupy a similar position in the skull of lower vertebrates 2 : of, relating to, or occurring in the region of the mastoid process

²mastoid *n* (1842) : a mastoid bone or process

mastoid cell *n* (1800) : one of the small cavities in the mastoid process that develop after birth and are filled with air

mas·toid·ec·to·my \ˌmas-ˌtȯi-'dek-tə-mē\ *n, pl* **-mies** [ISV] (1898) : surgical removal of part of the mastoid process of the temporal bone

mastiff

mas·toid·itis \ˌmas-ˌtȯi-'dī-təs\ *n* [NL] (ca. 1890) : inflammation of the mastoid and esp. of the mastoid cells

mas·tur·bate \'mas-tər-ˌbāt\ *vb* **-bat·ed; -bat·ing** [L *masturbatus*, pp. of *masturbari*] *vt* (1857) : to practice masturbation on ~ *vi* : to practice masturbation — **mas·tur·ba·tor** \-ˌbā-tər\ *n*

mas·tur·ba·tion \ˌmas-tər-'bā-shən\ *n* (1766) : erotic stimulation esp. of one's own genital organs commonly resulting in orgasm and achieved by manual or other bodily contact exclusive of sexual intercourse, by instrumental manipulation, occas. by sexual fantasies, or by various combinations of these agencies

mas·tur·ba·to·ry \'mas-tər-bə-ˌtōr-ē, -ˌtȯr-\ *adj* (1864) 1 : of, relating to, or involving masturbation ⟨~ fantasies⟩ 2 : excessively self-absorbed or self-indulgent ⟨write tedious, ~ books ... about themselves for people to read . . . with envy —D. R. Katz⟩

¹mat \'mat\ *n* [ME, fr. OE *meatte*, fr. LL *matta*, of Sem origin; akin to Heb *miṭṭāh* bed] (bef. 12c) 1 *a* (1) : a piece of coarse, woven, plaited, or felted fabric used esp. as a floor covering or a support (2) : a piece of material placed at a door for wiping soiled shoe soles *b* : a decorative piece of material used under a small item (as a dish) esp. for support or protection *c* : a large thick pad or cushion used as a surface for wrestling, tumbling, and gymnastics 2 : something made up of densely tangled or adhering strands esp. of organic matter ⟨algal ~⟩ ⟨a ~ of unkempt hair⟩ 3 : a large slab usu. of reinforced concrete used as the supporting base of a building

²mat *vb* **mat·ted; mat·ting** *vt* (1549) 1 : to provide with a mat or matting 2 *a* : to form into a tangled mass *b* : to pack down so as to form a dense mass ~ *vi* : to become matted

³mat \'mat\ *vt* **mat·ted; mat·ting** (1602) 1 : to make (as a metal, glass, or color) matte 2 : to provide (a picture) with a mat

⁴mat *var of* ²MATTE

⁵mat *n* [F *mat* dull color, unpolished surface, fr. *mat*, adj. — more at MATTE] (1845) : a border going around a picture between picture and frame or serving as the frame

⁶mat *n* (1904) : MATRIX 2a

mat·a·dor \'ma-tə-ˌdȯr\ *n* [Sp, fr. *matar* to kill] (1681) : a bullfighter who has the principal role and who kills the bull in a bullfight

¹match \'mach\ *n* [ME *macche*, equal; akin to OE *macian* to make — more at MAKE] (bef. 12c) 1 *a* : a person or thing equal or similar to another *b* : one able to cope with another *c* : an exact counterpart 2 *a* : a pair suitably associated ⟨carpet and curtains are a ~⟩ 3 *a* : a contest between two or more parties ⟨a golf ~⟩ ⟨a soccer ~⟩ ⟨a shouting ~⟩ *b* : a contest (as in tennis or volleyball) completed when one player or side wins a specified number of sets or games 4 *a* : a marriage union *b* : a prospective partner in marriage

²match *vt* (14c) 1 *a* : to encounter successfully as an antagonist *b* (1) : to set in competition or opposition (2) : to provide with a worthy competitor *c* : to set in comparison 2 : to join or give in marriage 3 *a* (1) : to put in a set possessing equal or harmonizing attributes (2) : to cause to correspond : SUIT *b* (1) : to be the counterpart of; *also* : to compare favorably with (2) : to harmonize with *c* : to provide with a counterpart *d* : to provide funds complementary to 4 : to fit together or make suitable for fitting together 5 *a* : to flip or toss (coins) and compare exposed faces *b* : to toss coins with ~ *vi* : to be a counterpart — **match·able** \'ma-chə-bəl\ *adj* — **match·er** *n*

³match *n* [ME *macche*, fr. MF *meiche*] (1549) 1 : a chemically prepared wick or cord formerly used in firing firearms or powder 2 : a short slender piece of flammable material (as wood) tipped with a combustible mixture that bursts into flame when slightly heated through friction (as by being scratched against a rough surface)

match·board \'mach-ˌbōrd, -ˌbȯrd\ *n* (ca. 1858) : a board with a groove cut along one edge and a tongue along the other so as to fit snugly with the edges of similarly cut boards

match·book \-ˌbu̇k\ *n* (1944) : a small folder containing rows of paper matches

match·box \-ˌbäks\ *n* (1786) : a box for matches

match·less \-ləs\ *adj* (ca. 1530) : having no equal : PEERLESS — **match·less·ly** *adv*

match·lock \-ˌläk\ *n* (1637) 1 : a slow-burning match lowered over a hole in the breech of a musket to ignite the charge 2 : a musket equipped with a matchlock

match·mak·er \-ˌmā-kər\ *n* (ca. 1639) : one that arranges a match; *esp* : one who tries to bring two unmarried individuals together in an attempt to promote a marriage — **match·mak·ing** \-ki\\ *n*

match play *n* (1893) : golf competition in which the winner is the person or team winning the greater number of holes — compare STROKE PLAY

match point *n* (1921) : a situation (as in tennis) in which one player or side will win the match by winning the next point; *also* : the point itself

match·stick \'mach-ˌstik\ *n* (1791) 1 : a slender piece esp. of wood from which a match is made 2 : something resembling a matchstick esp. in slenderness

match·up \-ˌəp\ *n* (1964) : ¹MATCH

match·wood \-ˌwu̇d\ *n* (1838) : small pieces of wood : SPLINTERS

¹mate \'māt\ *vt* **mat·ed; mat·ing** [ME, fr. MF *mater*, fr. OF *mat*, n., checkmate, fr. *mat* in *shah māt*] (14c) : CHECKMATE 2

²mate *n* (14c) : CHECKMATE 1

³mate *n* [ME, prob. fr. MLG *māt*; akin to OE *gemetta* guest at one's table, *mete* food — more at MEAT] (14c) 1 *a* (1) : ASSOCIATE, COMPANION (2) *chiefly Brit* : an assistant to a more skilled worker : HELPER (3) *chiefly Brit* : FRIEND, BUDDY — often used as a familiar form of address *b archaic* : MATCH, PEER 2 : a deck officer on a merchant ship ranking below the captain 3 : one of a pair: as *a* : either member of a couple and esp. a married couple *b* : either member of a breeding pair of animals *c* : either of two matched objects

⁴mate *vb* **mat·ed; mat·ing** *vt* (1509) 1 *archaic* : EQUAL, MATCH 2 : to join or fit together : COUPLE 3 *a* : to join together as mates *b* : to provide a mate for ~ *vi* 1 : to become mated ⟨gears that ~ well⟩ 2 : COPULATE

ma·té *or* **ma·te** \'mä-ˌtā\ *n* [F & AmerSp; F *maté*, fr. AmerSp *mate* maté, vessel for drinking it, fr. Quechua *mati* vessel] (1758) 1 : a tealike beverage drunk esp. in So. America 2 : a So. American shrub or tree (*Ilex paraguariensis*) of the holly family whose leaves and shoots are used in making maté; *also* : these leaves and shoots

mate·lot \'mat-,lō, 'ma-tə-\ n [F, fr. MF, fr. MD *mattenoot*, lit., bedmate] (1911) *Brit* : SAILOR

ma·te·lote \,ma-t²l-'ōt, mat-'lōt\ n [F, lit., sailor's wife, fr. *matelot*] (ca. 1736) : a stew made usu. of fish in a seasoned wine sauce

ma·ter \'mä-tər\ n [L — more at MOTHER] (ca. 1859) *chiefly Brit* : MOTHER

ma·ter·fa·mil·i·as \,mä-tər-fə-'mi-lē-əs, ,mä-\ n [L, fr. *mater* + *familias*, archaic gen. of *familia* household — more at FAMILY] (1756) : a woman who is head of a household

¹**ma·te·ri·al** \mə-'tir-ē-əl\ adj [ME *materiel*, fr. MF & LL; MF, fr. LL *materialis*, fr. L *materia* matter — more at MATTER] (14c) **1 a** (1) : relating to, derived from, or consisting of matter; *esp* : PHYSICAL ⟨the ∼ world⟩ (2) : BODILY ⟨∼ needs⟩ **b** (1) : of or relating to matter rather than form ⟨∼ cause⟩ (2) : of or relating to the subject matter of reasoning; *esp* : EMPIRICAL ⟨∼ knowledge⟩ **2** : having real importance or great consequences ⟨facts ∼ to the investigation⟩ **3 a** : being of a physical or worldly nature **b** : relating to or concerned with physical rather than spiritual or intellectual things ⟨∼ progress⟩ — **ma·te·ri·al·ly** \-ē-ə-lē\ adv — **ma·te·ri·al·ness** n

syn MATERIAL, PHYSICAL, CORPOREAL, PHENOMENAL, SENSIBLE, OBJECTIVE mean of or belonging to actuality. MATERIAL implies formation out of tangible matter; used in contrast with *spiritual* or *ideal* it may connote the mundane, crass, or grasping ⟨*material* values⟩. PHYSICAL applies to what is perceived directly by the senses and may contrast with *mental*, *spiritual*, or *imaginary* ⟨the *physical* benefits of exercise⟩. CORPOREAL implies having the tangible qualities of a body such as shape, size, or resistance to force ⟨artists have portrayed angels as *corporeal* beings⟩. PHENOMENAL applies to what is known or perceived through the senses rather than by intuition or rational deduction ⟨scientists concerned with the *phenomenal* world⟩. SENSIBLE stresses the capability of readily or forcibly impressing the senses ⟨the earth's rotation is not *sensible* to us⟩. OBJECTIVE may stress material or independent existence apart from a subject perceiving it ⟨no *objective* evidence of damage⟩. **syn** see in addition RELEVANT

²**material** n (1556) **1 a** (1) : the elements, constituents, or substances of which something is composed or can be made (2) : matter that has qualities which give it individuality and by which it may be categorized ⟨sticky ∼⟩ ⟨explosive ∼s⟩ **b** (1) : something (as data) that may be worked into a more finished form ⟨∼ for a biography⟩ (2) : something used for or made the object of study ⟨∼ for the next semester⟩ (3) : a performer's repertoire ⟨a comedian's ∼⟩ **c** : MATTER 3b **d** : CLOTH **e** : a person potentially suited to some pursuit ⟨varsity ∼⟩ ⟨leadership ∼⟩ **2 a** : apparatus necessary for doing or making something ⟨writing ∼s⟩ **b** : MATÉRIEL

ma·te·ri·al·ise *Brit var of* MATERIALIZE

ma·te·ri·al·ism \mə-'tir-ē-ə-,li-zəm\ n (1748) **1 a** : a theory that physical matter is the only or fundamental reality and that all being and processes and phenomena can be explained as manifestations or results of matter **b** : a doctrine that the only or the highest values or objectives lie in material well-being and in the furtherance of material progress **c** : a doctrine that economic or social change is materially caused — compare HISTORICAL MATERIALISM **2** : a preoccupation with or stress upon material rather than intellectual or spiritual things — **ma·te·ri·al·ist** \-list\ n or adj — **ma·te·ri·al·is·tic** \-,tir-ē-ə-'lis-tik\ adj — **ma·te·ri·al·is·ti·cal·ly** \-ti-k(ə-)lē\ adv

ma·te·ri·al·i·ty \mə-,tir-ē-'a-lə-tē\ n, pl -ties (1570) **1** : the quality or state of being material **2** : something that is material

ma·te·ri·al·i·za·tion \mə-,tir-ē-ə-lə-'zā-shən\ n (1843) **1** : the action of materializing or becoming materialized **2** : something that has been materialized; *esp* : APPARITION

ma·te·ri·al·ize \mə-'tir-ē-ə-,līz\ vb -ized; -iz·ing vt (1710) **1 a** : to make material : OBJECTIFY **b** : to cause to appear in bodily form ⟨∼ the spirits of the dead⟩ **2** : to cause to be materialistic ∼ vi **1** : to assume bodily form **2 a** : to appear esp. suddenly **b** : to come into existence — **ma·te·ri·al·iz·er** n

materials science n (1961) : the scientific study of the properties and applications of materials of construction or manufacture (as ceramics, metals, polymers, and composites) — **materials scientist** n

ma·te·ria med·i·ca \mə-'tir-ē-ə-'me-di-kə\ n [NL, lit., medical matter] (1699) **1** : substances used in the composition of medical remedies : DRUGS, MEDICINE **2 a** : a branch of medical science that deals with the sources, nature, properties, and preparation of drugs **b** : a treatise on materia medica

ma·té·ri·el *or* **ma·te·ri·el** \mə-,tir-ē-'el\ n [F *matériel*, fr. *matériel*, adj.] (1814) : equipment, apparatus, and supplies used by an organization or institution

ma·ter·nal \mə-'tər-n²l\ adj [ME, fr. MF *maternel*, fr. L *maternus*, fr. *mater* mother — more at MOTHER] (15c) **1** : of, relating to, belonging to, or characteristic of a mother : MOTHERLY **2 a** : related through a mother ⟨his ∼ aunt⟩ **b** : inherited or derived from the female parent ⟨∼ genes⟩ — **ma·ter·nal·ly** \-n²l-ē\ adv

¹**ma·ter·ni·ty** \mə-'tər-nə-tē\ n, pl -ties (1611) **1 a** : the quality or state of being a mother : MOTHERHOOD **b** : the qualities of a mother : MOTHERLINESS **2** : a hospital facility designed for the care of women before and during childbirth and for the care of newborn babies

²**maternity** adj (1893) **1** : designed for wear during pregnancy ⟨a ∼ dress⟩ **2** : effective for the period close to and including childbirth ⟨∼ leave⟩

mat·ey \'mä-tē\ adj (1915) *chiefly Brit* : COMPANIONABLE — **mat·ey·ness** \-nəs\ n, *chiefly Brit*

math \'math\ n (ca. 1878) : MATHEMATICS

math·e·mat·i·cal \,math-'ma-ti-kəl, ,ma-thə-\ *also* **math·e·mat·ic** \-tik\ adj [ME *mathematicalle*, fr. L *mathematicus*, fr. Gk *mathēmatikos*, fr. *mathēmat-*, *mathēma* learning, mathematics, fr. *manthanein* to learn; prob. akin to Goth *mundon* to pay attention] (15c) **1** : of, relating to, or according with mathematics **2 a** : rigorously exact : PRECISE **b** : CERTAIN **3** : possible but highly improbable ⟨only a ∼ chance⟩ — **math·e·mat·i·cal·ly** \-ti-k(ə-)lē\ adv

mathematical expectation n (1838) : EXPECTED VALUE

mathematical induction n (1838) : INDUCTION 2b

mathematical logic n (1858) : SYMBOLIC LOGIC

math·e·ma·ti·cian \,math-mə-'ti-shən, ,ma-thə-\ n (15c) : a specialist or expert in mathematics

math·e·mat·ics \,math-'ma-tiks, ,ma-thə-\ n pl but usu sing in constr

(1581) **1** : the science of numbers and their operations, interrelations, combinations, generalizations, and abstractions and of space configurations and their structure, measurement, transformations, and generalizations **2** : a branch of, operation in, or use of mathematics ⟨the ∼ of physical chemistry⟩

math·e·ma·ti·za·tion \,math-mə-tə-'zā-shən, ,ma-thə-\ n (1928) : reduction to mathematical form — **math·e·ma·tize** \'math-mə-,tiz, 'ma-thə-\ vb

maths \'maths\ n pl (1911) *chiefly Brit* : MATHEMATICS

mat·in \'ma-t²n\ adj [ME, fr. OF] (14c) : of or relating to matins or to early morning

mat·in·al \'ma-t²n-əl\ adj (1803) **1** : of or relating to matins **2** : EARLY

mat·i·nee *or* **mat·i·née** \,ma-t²n-'ā\ n [F *matinée*, lit., morning, fr. OF, fr. *matin* morning, fr. L *matutinum*, fr. neut. of *matutinus* of the morning, fr. *Matuta*, goddess of morning; akin to L *maturus* ripe — more at MATURE] (1858) : a musical or dramatic performance or social or public event held in the daytime and esp. the afternoon

matinee idol n (1902) : a handsome male performer

mat·ins \'ma-t²nz\ n pl but sing or pl in constr, often cap [ME *matines*, fr. OF, fr. LL *matutinae*, fr. L, fem. pl. of *matutinus*] (14c) **1** : the night office forming with lauds the first of the canonical hours **2** : MORNING PRAYER

matr- *or* **matri-** *or* **matro-** *comb form* [L *matr-*, *matri-*, fr. *matr-*, *mater*] : mother ⟨*matri*arch⟩ ⟨*matro*nymic⟩

ma·tri·arch \'mā-trē-,ärk\ n (1606) : a female who rules or dominates a family, group, or state; *specif* : a mother who is head and ruler of her family and descendants — **ma·tri·ar·chal** \,mā-trē-'är-kəl\ adj

ma·tri·ar·chate \'mā-trē-,är-kət, -,kät\ n (1885) : MATRIARCHY 1

ma·tri·ar·chy \'mā-trē-,är-kē\ n, pl -chies (1885) **1** : a family, group, or state governed by a matriarch **2** : a system of social organization in which descent and inheritance are traced through the female line

ma·tri·cide \'ma-trə-,sīd, 'mā-\ n (1594) **1** [L *matricidium*, fr. *matr-* + *-cidium* -cide] : murder of a mother by her son or daughter **2** [L *matricida*, fr. *matr-* + *-cida* -cide] : one that murders his or her mother — **ma·tri·cid·al** \,ma-trə-'sī-d²l, ,mā-\ adj

ma·tric·u·late \mə-'tri-kyə-,lāt\ vb -lat·ed; -lat·ing [ML *matriculatus*, pp. of *matriculare*, fr. LL *matricula* public roll, dim. of *matric-*, *matrix* list, fr. L, breeding female] vt (1577) : to enroll as a member of a body and esp. of a college or university ∼ vi : to become matriculated — **ma·tric·u·lant** \-lənt\ n — **ma·tric·u·la·tion** \-,tri-kyə-'lā-shən\ n

ma·tri·lin·eal \,ma-trə-'li-nē-əl, ,mā-\ adj (1904) : relating to, based on, or tracing descent through the maternal line ⟨∼ society⟩ — **ma·tri·lin·eal·ly** \-nē-ə-lē\ adv

mat·ri·mo·nial \,ma-trə-'mō-nē-əl, -nyəl\ adj (15c) : of or relating to marriage, the married state, or married persons — **mat·ri·mo·nial·ly** adv

mat·ri·mo·ny \'ma-trə-,mō-nē\ n [ME, fr. MF *matremoine*, fr. L *matrimonium*, fr. *matr-*, *mater* mother, matron — more at MOTHER] (14c) : the union of man and woman as husband and wife : MARRIAGE

matrimony vine n (ca. 1818) : a shrub or vine (genus *Lycium*) of the nightshade family with often showy flowers and usu. red berries

ma·trix \'mā-triks\ n, pl **ma·tri·ces** \'mā-trə-,sēz, 'ma-\ *or* **ma·trix·es** \'mā-trik-səz\ [L, female animal used for breeding, parent plant, fr. *matr-*, *mater*] (1555) **1** : something within or from which something else originates, develops, or takes form **2 a** : a mold from which a relief surface (as a piece of type) is made **b** : DIE 3a(1) **c** : an engraved or inscribed die or stamp **d** : an electroformed impression of a phonograph record used for mass-producing duplicates of the original **3 a** : the natural material (as soil or rock) in which something (as a fossil or crystal) is embedded **b** : material in which something is enclosed or embedded (as for protection or study) **4 a** : the intercellular substance in which tissue cells (as of connective tissue) are embedded **b** : the thickened epithelium at the base of a fingernail or toenail from which new nail substance develops **5 a** : a rectangular array of mathematical elements (as the coefficients of simultaneous linear equations) that can be combined to form sums and products with similar arrays having an appropriate number of rows and columns **b** : something resembling a mathematical matrix esp. in rectangular arrangement of elements into rows and columns **c** : an array of circuit elements (as diodes and transistors) for performing a specific function **6** : a main clause that contains a subordinate clause

ma·tron \'mā-trən\ n [ME *matrone*, fr. MF, fr. L *matrona*, fr. *matr-*, *mater*] (14c) **1 a** : a married woman usu. marked by dignified maturity or social distinction **b** : a woman who supervises women or children (as in a school or police station) **c** : the chief officer in a women's organization **2** : a female animal kept for breeding

ma·tron·ly \'mā-trən-lē\ adj (1656) : having the character of or suitable to a matron

matron of honor (1903) : a bride's principal married wedding attendant

mat·ro·nym·ic \,ma-trə-'ni-mik\ n [*matr-* + *-onymic* (as in *patronymic*)] (1794) : a name derived from that of the mother or a maternal ancestor

¹**matte** *or* **matt** \'mat\ *var of* ³MAT

²**matte** *also* **matt** \'mat\ adj [F *mat*, fr. OF, faded, defeated] (ca. 1648) : lacking or deprived of luster or gloss: as **a** : having a usu. smooth even surface free from shine or highlights ⟨∼ metals⟩ ⟨a ∼ finish⟩ **b** : having a rough or granular surface

³**matte** \'mat\ n [F, fr. MF, crude metal, curdled milk, fr. fem. of *mat* thick, dull, matte] (1839) **1** : a crude mixture of sulfides formed in smelting sulfide ores of metals (as copper, lead, or nickel) **2** : a motion-picture effect in which part of a scene is blocked out and later replaced by footage containing other material (as a background painting)

¹**mat·ter** \'ma-tər\ n [ME *matere*, fr. OF, fr. L *materia* matter, physical substance, fr. *mater*] (13c) **1 a** : a subject under consideration **b** : a

---

\ə\ abut \²\ kitten, F table \ər\ further \a\ ash \ā\ ace \ä\ mop, mar \aù\ out \ch\ chin \e\ bet \ē\ easy \g\ go \i\ hit \ī\ ice \j\ job \ŋ\ sing \ō\ go \o\ law \oi\ boy \th\ thin \t̲h̲\ the \ü\ loot \ù\ foot \y\ yet \zh\ vision \à, k̲, ⁿ, œ, œ̄, ᵫ, ᵫ̄, ʸ\ see Guide to Pronunciation

subject of disagreement or litigation **c** *pl* : the events or circumstances of a particular situation **d** : the subject or substance of a discourse or writing **e** : something of an indicated kind or having to do with an indicated field or situation ⟨this is a serious ∼⟩ ⟨as a ∼ of policy⟩ ⟨∼s of faith⟩ **f** : something to be proved in law **g** *obs* : sensible or serious material as distinguished from nonsense or drollery **h** (1) *obs* : REASON, CAUSE (2) : a source esp. of feeling or emotion **i** : PROBLEM, DIFFICULTY **2 a** : the substance of which a physical object is composed **b** : material substance that occupies space, has mass, and is composed predominantly of atoms consisting of protons, neutrons, and electrons, that constitutes the observable universe, and that is interconvertible with energy **c** : a material substance of a particular kind or for a particular purpose ⟨vegetable ∼⟩ **d** (1) : material (as feces or urine) discharged from the living body (2) : material discharged by suppuration : PUS **3 a** : the indeterminate subject of reality; *esp* : the element in the universe that undergoes formation and alteration **b** : the formless substratum of all things which exists only potentially and upon which form acts to produce realities **4** : a more or less definite amount or quantity ⟨cooks in a ∼ of minutes⟩ **5** : something written or printed **6** : MAIL **7** *Christian Science* : the illusion that the objects perceived by the physical senses have the reality of substance — **for that matter** : so far as that is concerned — **no matter** : without regard to : irrespective of ⟨points in the same direction *no matter* how it is tilted⟩ — **the matter** : WRONG ⟨nothing's *the matter* with me⟩
²matter *vi* (1530) **1** : to form or discharge pus : SUPPURATE ⟨∼*ing* wound⟩ **2** : to be of importance : SIGNIFY
matter of course (1739) : something that is to be expected as a natural or logical consequence
mat·ter-of-fact \ˌma-tə-rə(v)-ˈfakt\ *adj* (1712) : adhering to the unembellished facts; *also* : being plain, straightforward, or unemotional — **mat·ter-of-fact·ly** \-ˈfak(t)-lē\ *adv* — **mat·ter-of-fact·ness** \-ˈfak(t)-nəs\ *n*
mat·tery \ˈma-tə-rē\ *adj* (14c) : producing or containing pus or material resembling pus ⟨eyes all ∼⟩
Mat·the·an *or* **Mat·thae·an** \ma-ˈthē-ən, mə-\ *adj* [LL *Matthaeus*] (1897) : of, relating to, or characteristic of the evangelist Matthew or the gospel ascribed to him
Mat·thew \ˈma-(ˌ)thyü *also* -(ˌ)thü\ *n* [F *Mathieu*, fr. LL *Matthaeus*, fr. Gk *Matthaios*, fr. Heb *Mattithyāh*] **1** : an apostle traditionally identified as the author of the first Gospel in the New Testament **2** : the first Gospel in the New Testament — see BIBLE table
¹mat·ting \ˈma-tiŋ\ *n* (ca. 1847) **1** : material for mats **2** : MATS
²matting *n* [fr. gerund of **⁴mat**] (1854) : a dull lusterless surface (as on gilding, metalwork, or satin)
mat·tins *often cap, chiefly Brit var of* MATINS
mat·tock \ˈma-tək\ *n* [ME *mattok*, fr. OE *mattuc*] (bef. 12c) : a digging and grubbing tool with features of an adze and an ax or pick
mat·tress \ˈma-trəs\ *n* [ME *materas*, fr. OF, fr. Ar *maṭraḥ* place where something is thrown] (14c) **1 a** : a fabric case filled with resilient material (as cotton, hair, feathers, foam rubber, or an arrangement of coiled springs) used either alone as a bed or on a bedstead **b** : an inflatable airtight sack for use as a mattress **2** : a device (as of interwoven brush and poles) used to protect a shoreline, bank, or streambed from erosion
mat·u·rate \ˈma-chə-ˌrāt\ *vb* **-rat·ed; -rat·ing** (1622) : MATURE
mat·u·ra·tion \ˌma-chə-ˈrā-shən\ *n* (1541) **1 a** : the process of becoming mature **b** : the emergence of personal and behavioral characteristics through growth processes **c** : the final stages of differentiation of cells, tissues, or organs **2 a** : the entire process by which diploid gonocytes are transformed into haploid gametes that includes both meiosis and physiological and structural changes **b** : SPERMIOGENESIS — **mat·u·ra·tion·al** \-shnəl, -shə-nᵊl\ *adj*
¹ma·ture \mə-ˈtùr, -ˈtyùr *also* -ˈchùr\ *adj* **ma·tur·er; -est** [ME, fr. L *maturus* ripe; akin to L *mane* in the morning, *manus* good] (15c) **1** : based on slow careful consideration ⟨a ∼ judgment⟩ **2 a** (1) : having completed natural growth and development : RIPE (2) : having undergone maturation **b** : having attained a final or desired state ⟨∼ wine⟩ **c** : having achieved a low but stable growth rate ⟨paper is a ∼ industry⟩ **3 a** : of or relating to a condition of full development **b** : characteristic of or suitable to a mature individual ⟨∼ outlook⟩ **4** : due for payment ⟨a ∼ loan⟩ **5** : belonging to the middle portion of a cycle of erosion — **ma·ture·ly** *adv*
²mature *vb* **ma·tured; ma·tur·ing** *vt* (15c) : to bring to maturity or completion ∼ *vi* **1** : to become fully developed or ripe **2** : to become due
ma·tu·ri·ty \mə-ˈtùr-ə-tē, -ˈtyùr- *also* -ˈchùr-\ *n* (15c) **1** : the quality or state of being mature; *esp* : full development **2** : termination of the period that an obligation has to run
ma·tu·ti·nal \ˌma-chù-ˈti-nᵊl; mə-ˈtüt-nəl, -ˈtyüt-, -ˈtü-tᵊn-əl, -ˈtyü-\ *adj* [LL *matutinalis*, fr. L *matutinus* — more at MATINEE] (ca. 1656) : of, relating to, or occurring in the morning : EARLY — **ma·tu·ti·nal·ly** *adv*
mat·zo *or* **mat·zoh** \ˈmät-sə *also* -(ˌ)sō\ *n, pl* **mat·zoth** \-ˌsōt, -ˌsōth, -sōs\ *or* **mat·zos** *or* **mat·zohs** \-səz, -səs *also* -ˌsōz\ [Yiddish *matse*, fr. Heb *maṣṣāh*] (ca. 1846) **1** : unleavened bread eaten esp. at the Passover **2** : a wafer of matzo
matzo ball *n* (1952) : a small ball-shaped dumpling made from matzo meal
maud·lin \ˈmȯd-lən\ *adj* [alter. of Mary *Magdalene;* fr. her depiction as a weeping penitent] (1509) **1** : drunk enough to be emotionally silly **2** : weakly and effusively sentimental
mau·gre \ˈmȯ-gər\ *prep* [ME, fr. MF *maugré*, fr. *maugré* displeasure, fr. *mau, mal* evil + *gré* pleasure] (13c) *archaic* : in spite of
¹maul \ˈmȯl\ *n* [ME *malle* mace, maul, fr. OF *mail*, fr. L *malleus;* akin to OCS *mlatŭ* hammer, L *molere* to grind — more at MEAL] (13c) : a heavy often wooden-headed hammer used esp. for driving wedges; *also* : a tool like a sledgehammer with one wedge-shaped end that is used to split wood
²maul *vt* (13c) **1** : BEAT, BRUISE **2** : MANGLE 1 **3** : to handle roughly — **maul·er** *n*
maul·stick \ˈmȯl-stik\ *n* [part trans. of D *maalstok*, fr. obs. D *malen* to paint + D *stok* stick, stock] (ca. 1658) : a stick used by painters as a rest for the hand while working
mau-mau \ˈmaù-ˌmaù\ *vb* **mau–maued; mau–mau·ing** *often cap*

both *Ms* [*Mau Mau*, anti-European secret society in colonial Kenya] *vt* (1970) : to intimidate (as an official) by hostile confrontation or threats ∼ *vi* : to engage in mau-mauing someone
maun \ˈmȯn, ˈmän, mən\ *verbal auxiliary* [ME *man*, fr. ON, pres. of *munu* shall, will; akin to OE ge*mynd* mind — more at MIND] (13c) *chiefly Scot* : MUST
maun·der \ˈmȯn-dər, ˈmän-\ *vi* **maun·dered; maun·der·ing** \-d(ə-)riŋ\ [prob. imit.] (1621) **1** *dial Brit* : GRUMBLE **2** : to wander slowly and idly **3** : to speak indistinctly or disconnectedly — **maun·der·er** \-dər-ər\ *n*
Maun·dy Thursday \ˈmȯn-dē-, ˈmän-\ *n* [ME *maunde* ceremony of washing the feet of the poor on Maundy Thursday, fr. OF *mandé*, fr. L *mandatum* command; fr. Jesus' words in John 13:34 — more at MANDATE] (15c) : the Thursday before Easter observed in commemoration of the institution of the Eucharist
mau·so·le·um \ˌmȯ-sə-ˈlē-əm, ˌmȯ-zə-\ *n, pl* **-leums** *or* **-lea** \-ˈlē-ə\ [ME, fr. L, fr. Gk *mausōleion*, fr. *Mausōlos* Mausolus †ab 353 B.C., ruler of Caria] (15c) **1** : a large tomb; *esp* : a usu. stone building with places for entombment of the dead above ground **2** : a large gloomy building or room
mauve \ˈmōv, ˈmȯv\ *n* [F, mallow, fr. L *malva*] (1859) **1 a** : a moderate purple, violet, or lilac color **b** : a strong purple **2** : a dyestuff that produces a mauve color — **mauve** *adj*
ma·ven *or* **ma·vin** \ˈmā-vən\ *n* [Yiddish *meyvn*, fr. LHeb *mēbhīn*] (ca. 1952) : one who is experienced or knowledgeable : EXPERT; *also* : FREAK 4
¹mav·er·ick \ˈmav-rik, ˈma-və-\ *n* [perh. fr. Samuel A. *Maverick* †1870 Am. pioneer who did not brand his calves] (1867) **1** : an unbranded range animal; *esp* : a motherless calf **2** : an independent individual who does not go along with a group or party
²maverick *adj* (1886) : characteristic of, suggestive of, or inclined to be a maverick
ma·vis \ˈmā-vəs\ *n* [ME, fr. MF *mauvis*] (14c) : SONG THRUSH
ma·vour·neen \mə-ˈvùr-ˌnēn\ *n* [Ir *mo mhuirnín*] (1800) *Irish* : my darling
maw \ˈmȯ\ *n* [ME, fr. OE *maga;* akin to OHG *mago* stomach, Lith *makas* purse] (bef. 12c) **1** : the receptacle into which food is taken by swallowing: **a** : STOMACH **b** : CROP **2 a** : the throat, gullet, or jaws esp. of a voracious animal **b** : something suggestive of a gaping maw
mawk·ish \ˈmȯ-kish\ *adj* [ME *mawke* maggot, fr. ON *mathkr* — more at MAGGOT] (ca. 1697) **1** : having an insipid often unpleasant taste **2** : sickly or puerilely sentimental — **mawk·ish·ly** *adv* — **mawk·ish·ness** *n*
max \ˈmaks\ *n* (1968) : MAXIMUM 1, 2 — **to the max** : to the greatest extent possible
maxi \ˈmak-sē\ *n, pl* **max·is** [*maxi-*] (1967) : a long skirt, dress, or coat
maxi- *comb form* [*maximum*] **1** : extra long ⟨*maxi*skirt⟩ **2** : extra large ⟨*maxi*-problems⟩
max·il·la \mak-ˈsi-lə\ *n, pl* **max·il·lae** \-ˈsi-(ˌ)lē, -ˌlī\ *or* **maxillas** [L, dim. of *mala* jaw] (1676) **1 a** : JAW 1a **b** (1) : an upper jaw esp. of humans and other mammals in which the bony elements are closely fused (2) : either of the two bones that lie with one on each side of the upper jaw lateral to the premaxilla and that in higher vertebrates bear most of the teeth **2** : one of the first or second pair of mouthparts posterior to the mandibles in insects, myriapods, crustaceans, and closely related arthropods — **max·il·lary** \ˈmak-sə-ˌler-ē, *chiefly Brit* mak-ˈsi-lə-rē\ *adj or n*
max·il·li·ped \mak-ˈsi-lə-ˌped\ *n* [ISV *maxilli-* (fr. L *maxilla*) + *-ped*] (1846) : any of the crustacean appendages that comprise the first pair or first three pairs situated next behind the maxillae
max·il·lo·fa·cial \mak-ˌsi-(ˌ)lō-ˈfā-shəl, ˌmak-sə-(ˌ)lō-\ *adj* (ca. 1923) : of, relating to, or treating the maxilla and the face ⟨∼ surgeons⟩
max·im \ˈmak-səm\ *n* [ME *maxime*, fr. MF, fr. ML *maxima*, fr. L, fem. of *maximus*, superl. of *magnus* large — more at MUCH] (1567) **1** : a general truth, fundamental principle, or rule of conduct **2** : a saying of proverbial nature
max·i·mal \ˈmak-s(ə-)məl\ *adj* (1882) **1** : being an upper limit : HIGHEST **2** : most comprehensive : COMPLETE — **max·i·mal·ly** *adv*
max·i·mal·ist \-s(ə-)mə-list\ *n* (1907) : one who advocates immediate and direct action to secure the whole of a program or set of goals
maxi-min \ˈmak-sə-ˌmin\ *n* [*maximum* + *minimum*] (1951) : the maximum of a set of minima; *esp* : the largest of a set of minimum possible gains each of which occurs in the least advantageous outcome of a strategy followed by a participant in a situation governed by the theory of games — compare MINIMAX
max·i·mise *Brit var of* MAXIMIZE
max·i·mize \ˈmak-sə-ˌmīz\ *vt* **-mized; -miz·ing** (1802) **1** : to increase to a maximum **2** : to make the most of **3** : to find a maximum value of — **max·i·mi·za·tion** \ˌmak-sə-mə-ˈzā-shən\ *n* — **max·i·miz·er** \ˈmak-sə-ˌmī-zər\ *n*
max·i·mum \ˈmak-s(ə-)məm\ *n, pl* **max·i·ma** \-sə-mə\ *or* **maximums** \-s(ə-)məmz\ [L, neut. of *maximus*] (1740) **1 a** : the greatest quantity or value attainable or attained **b** : the period of highest, greatest, or utmost development **2** : an upper limit allowed (as by a legal authority) or allowable (as by the circumstances of a particular case) **3** : the largest of a set of numbers; *specif* : the largest value assumed by a real-valued continuous function defined on a closed interval — **maxi·mum** *adj*
maximum likelihood *n* (1959) : a statistical method for estimating population parameters (as the mean and variance) from sample data that selects as estimates those parameter values maximizing the probability of obtaining the observed data
ma·xixe \mə-ˈshēsh, -ˈshē-shə\ *n, pl* **ma·xi·xes** \-ˈshē-shəz\ [BrazPg] (1914) : a ballroom dance of Brazilian origin that resembles the two-step
max·well \ˈmaks-ˌwel, -wəl\ *n* [James Clerk *Maxwell*] (1900) : the centimeter-gram-second electromagnetic unit of magnetic flux equal to the flux per square centimeter of normal cross section in a region where the magnetic induction is one gauss : 10^{-8} weber
¹may \ˈmā\ *verbal auxiliary, past* **might** \ˈmīt\; *pres sing & pl* **may** [ME (1st & 3d sing. pres. indic.), fr. OE *mæg;* akin to OHG *mag* (1st & 3d sing. pres. indic.) have power, am able (infin. *magan*), and perh. to Gk *mēchos* means, expedient] (bef. 12c) **1 a** *archaic* : have the ability to

b : have permission to ⟨you ∼ go now⟩ : be free to ⟨a rug on which children ∼ sprawl —C. E. Silberman⟩ — used nearly interchangeably with *can* **c** — used to indicate possibility or probability ⟨you ∼ be right⟩ ⟨things you ∼ need⟩; sometimes used interchangeably with *can* ⟨one of those slipups that ∼ happen from time to time —Jessica Mitford⟩ ⟨copula ∼ optionally be deleted —J. D. McCawley⟩; sometimes used where *might* would be expected ⟨you ∼ think from a little distance that the country was solid woods —Robert Frost⟩ **2** — used in auxiliary function to express a wish or desire esp. in prayer, imprecation, or benediction ⟨long ∼ he reign⟩ **3** — used in auxiliary function expressing purpose or expectation ⟨I laugh that I ∼ not weep⟩ or contingency ⟨she'll do her duty come what ∼⟩ or concession ⟨he ∼ be slow but he is thorough⟩ or choice ⟨the angler ∼ catch them with a dip net, or he ∼ cast a large, bare treble hook —Nelson Bryant⟩ **4** : SHALL, MUST — used in law where the sense, purpose, or policy requires this interpretation *usage* see CAN

²may \'mā\ *n* [ME, fr. OE *mǣg* kinsman, kinswoman, maiden] (bef. 12c) *archaic* : MAIDEN

May \'mā\ *n* [ME, fr. OF & L; OF *mai*, fr. L *Maius*, fr. *Maia*, Roman goddess] (12c) **1** : the 5th month of the Gregorian calendar **2** *often not cap* : the early vigorous blooming part of human life : PRIME **3** : the festivities of May Day **4** *not cap* **a** : green or flowering branches used for May Day decorations **b** : a plant that yields may: as (1) : HAWTHORN (2) : a spring-flowering spirea

ma·ya \'mä-yə, 'mī-ə\ *n* [Skt *māyā*] (1788) : the sense-world of manifold phenomena held in Vedanta to conceal the unity of absolute being; *broadly* : ILLUSION

Ma·ya \'mī-ə\ *n, pl* **Maya** *or* **Mayas** [Sp] (1825) **1 a** : a Mayan language of the ancient Maya peoples recorded in inscriptions **b** : YUCATEC; *esp* : the older form of that language known from documents of the Spanish period **2** : a member of a group of Indian peoples chiefly of Yucatán, Belize, and Guatemala whose languages are Mayan

Ma·yan \'mī-ən\ *n* (1900) **1** : a member of the peoples speaking Mayan languages **2** : an extensive language family of Central America and Mexico — **Mayan** *adj*

Mayanist \'mī-ə-nist\ *n* (1950) : a specialist in Mayan culture and history

may·ap·ple \'mā-ˌa-pəl\ *n* [*May*] (ca. 1733) : a No. American herb (*Podophyllum peltatum*) of the barberry family with a poisonous rootstock, one or two large-lobed peltate leaves, and a single large white flower followed by a yellow egg-shaped edible fruit; *also* : its fruit

¹may·be \'mā-bē *also* 'me-\ *adv* (15c) : PERHAPS

²maybe *n* (ca. 1586) : UNCERTAINTY

May·day \'mā-ˌdā\ [F *m'aider* help me] (1927) — an international radio-telephone signal word used as a distress call

May Day \'mā-ˌdā\ *n* (13c) : May 1 celebrated as a springtime festival and in some countries as Labor Day

may·est *or* **mayst** \'mā-əst, 'māst\ *archaic pres 2d sing of* MAY

may·flow·er \'mā-ˌflau̇(-ə)r\ *n* (1594) : any of various spring-blooming plants; *esp* : ARBUTUS

may·fly \'mā-flī\ *n* (ca. 1653) : any of an order (Ephemeroptera) of insects with an aquatic nymph and a short-lived fragile adult having membranous wings and two or three long caudal styles — called *also ephemerid*

may·hap \'mā-ˌhap, mā-'\ *adv* [fr. the phrase *may hap*] (ca. 1531) : PERHAPS

may·hem \'mā-ˌhem, 'mā-əm\ *n* [ME *mayme*, fr. AF *mahaim*, fr. OF, fr. *maynier* to maim, prob. of Gmc origin; akin to MHG *meiden* gelding, ON *meitha* to injure] (15c) **1 a** : willful and permanent deprivation of a bodily member resulting in the impairment of a person's fighting ability **b** : willful and permanent crippling, mutilation, or disfigurement of any part of the body **2** : needless or willful damage or violence

mayfly

may·ing \'mā-iŋ\ *n, often cap* (14c) : the celebrating of May Day

mayn't \'mā-ənt, 'mānt\ (ca. 1631) : may not

mayo \'mā-(ˌ)ō\ *n* (ca. 1960) : MAYONNAISE

may·on·naise \'mā-ə-ˌnāz, ˌmā-ə-'\ *n* [F] (1841) : a dressing made of egg yolks, vegetable oils, and vinegar or lemon juice

may·or \'mā-ər, 'me(-ə)r, *esp before names* (ˌ)mer\ *n* [ME *maire*, fr. OF, fr. L *major* greater — more at MAJOR] (14c) : an official elected or appointed to act as chief executive or nominal head of a city, town, or borough — **may·or·al** \'mā-ə-rəl, 'me-ə-, 'mer-əl\ *adj*

may·or·al·ty \'mā-ə-rəl-tē, 'me-; 'mer-əl-\ *n* [ME *mairaltee*, fr. MF *mairalté*, fr. OF, fr. *maire*] (14c) : the office or term of office of a mayor

may·or·ess \'mā-ə-rəs, 'me-\ *n* (15c) *chiefly Brit* **1** : the wife or official hostess of a mayor **2** : a woman holding the office of mayor

may·pole \'mā-ˌpōl\ *n, often cap* (1554) : a tall flower-wreathed pole forming a center for May Day sports and dances

may·pop \'mā-ˌpäp\ *n* [alter. of *maracock*, perh. fr. Virginia Algonquian] (1851) : a climbing perennial passionflower (*Passiflora incarnata*) of the southern U.S. with a large ovoid yellow edible but insipid berry; *also* : its fruit

May·time \'mā-ˌtīm\ *n* (14c) : the month of May

maz·ard \'ma-zərd\ *n* [obs. E *mazard* mazer, alter. of E *mazer*] (1602) *chiefly dial* : HEAD, FACE

¹maze \'māz\ *vt* **mazed; maz·ing** [ME] (13c) **1** *chiefly dial* : STUPEFY, DAZE **2** : BEWILDER, PERPLEX

²maze *n* (14c) **1 a** : a confusing intricate network of passages **b** : something intricately or confusingly elaborate or complicated ⟨a ∼ of regulations⟩ **2** *chiefly dial* : a state of bewilderment — **maze·like** \-ˌlīk\ *adj*

ma·zer \'mā-zər\ *n* [ME, fr. MF *mazere*, of Gmc origin; akin to OHG *masar* gnarled excrescence on a tree] (14c) : a large drinking bowl orig. of a hard wood

ma·zur·ka \mə-'zər-kə, -'zür-\ *also* **ma·zour·ka** \-'zür-\ *n* [Russ, fr. Pol *mazurek*, fr. *Mazury* Masuria, region of NE Poland] (1818) **1** : a Polish folk dance in moderate triple measure **2** : music for the mazurka or its rhythm usu. in moderate ³/₄ or ³/₈ time

mazy \'mā-zē\ *adj* (1579) : resembling a maze

¹maz·zard \'ma-zərd\ *n* [origin unknown] (1578) : SWEET CHERRY; *esp* : wild or seedling sweet cherry used as a rootstock for grafting

²mazzard *var of* MAZARD

mbi·ra \em-'bir-ə\ *n* [Shona] (ca. 1911) : an African musical instrument that consists of a wooden or gourd resonator and a varying number of tuned metal or wooden strips that vibrate when plucked

MC \ˌem-'sē\ *n* (1790) : MASTER OF CEREMONIES

Mc·Car·thy·ism \mə-'kär-thē-ˌi-zəm *also* -'kär-tē-\ *n* [Joseph R. *McCarthy*] (1950) : a mid-20th century political attitude characterized chiefly by opposition to elements held to be subversive and by the use of tactics involving personal attacks on individuals by means of widely publicized indiscriminate allegations esp. on the basis of unsubstantiated charges — **Mc·Car·thy·ite** \-ˌīt\ *n or adj*

Mc·Coy \mə-'koi\ *n* [alter. of *Mackay* (in the phrase *the real Mackay*), of unknown origin] (1922) : something that is neither imitation nor substitute — often used in the phrase *the real McCoy*

Mc·In·tosh \'ma-kən-ˌtäsh\ *n* [John *McIntosh fl*1796 Canad. settler] (1878) : a juicy bright red eating apple with a thin skin, white flesh, and aromatic slightly tart flavor

M-day \'em-ˌdā\ *n* [*mobilization day*] (1924) : a day on which a military mobilization is to begin

me \'mē\ *pron, objective case of* I [ME, fr. OE *mē*; akin to OHG *mih* me, L *me*, Gk *me*, Skt *mā*]
usage *Me* is used in many constructions where strict grammarians prescribe *I*. This usage is not so much ungrammatical as indicative of the shrinking range of the nominative form: *me* began to replace *I* sometime around the 16th century largely because of the pressure of word order. *I* is now chiefly used as the subject of an immediately following verb. *Me* occurs in every other position: absolutely ⟨who, me?⟩, emphatically ⟨me too⟩, and after prepositions, conjunctions, and verbs, including *be* ⟨come with me⟩ ⟨you're as big as me⟩ ⟨it's me⟩. Almost all usage books recognize the legitimacy of *me* in these positions, esp. in speech; some recommend *I* in formal and esp. written contexts after *be* and after *as* and *than* when the first term of the comparison is the subject of a verb.

mea cul·pa \ˌmā-ə-'kul-pə, ˌmä-ä-, -'kul-(ˌ)pä\ *n* [L, through my fault] (1602) : a formal acknowledgment of personal fault or error

¹mead \'mēd\ *n* [ME *mede*, fr. OE *medu*; akin to OHG *metu* mead, Gk *methy* wine] (bef. 12c) : a fermented beverage made of water and honey, malt, and yeast

²mead *n* [ME *mede*, fr. OE *mǣd*] (bef. 12c) *archaic* : MEADOW

mead·ow \'me-(ˌ)dō\ *n, often attrib* [ME *medwe*, fr. OE *mǣdwe*, oblique case form of *mǣd*; akin to OE *māwan* to mow — more at MOW] (bef. 12c) : land in or predominantly in grass; *esp* : a tract of moist low-lying usu. level grassland — **mead·owy** \'me-də-wē\ *adj*

meadow beauty *n* (1840) : any of a genus (*Rhexia* of the family Melastomaceae, the meadow-beauty family) of low perennial American herbs with showy solitary or cymose flowers

meadow fescue *n* (1794) : a tall vigorous perennial European fescue grass (*Festuca pratensis*) with broad flat leaves widely cultivated for permanent pasture and hay

meadow grass *n* (13c) : any of various grasses (as of the genus *Poa*) that thrive in the presence of abundant moisture; *esp* : KENTUCKY BLUEGRASS

mead·ow·land \'me-dō-ˌland, -də-\ *n* (1530) : land that is or is used for meadow

mead·ow·lark \'me-dō-ˌlärk, -də-\ *n* (1611) : any of several American songbirds (genus *Sturnella*) that are streaked brown above and in northernmost forms have a yellow breast marked with a black crescent

meadow mouse *n* (1801) : any of various voles (esp. genus *Microtus*) that frequent open fields — called *also meadow vole*

meadow mushroom *n* (1884) : a common edible brown-spored agaric (*Agaricus campestris*) that occurs in moist open organically rich soil and is often cultivated

meadow nematode *n* (1946) : any of numerous plant-parasitic nematode worms (esp. genus *Pratylenchus*) that destructively invade the roots of plants

meadow rue *n* (1668) : any of a genus (*Thalictrum*) of widely distributed plants of the buttercup family with decompound or compound leaves

meadow saffron *n* (1578) : AUTUMN CROCUS

meadow spittlebug *n* (1942) : a No. American spittlebug (*Philaenus spumarius*) that does severe damage esp. to grasses

mead·ow·sweet \'me-dō-ˌswēt, -də-\ *n* (1530) **1** : SPIREA 1; *esp* : a No. American native or naturalized spirea (as *Spiraea alba* and *S. latifolia*) **2** : any of a genus (*Filipendula*) of herbs closely related to the spireas

mea·ger *or* **mea·gre** \'mē-gər\ *adj* [ME *megre*, fr. MF *maigre*, fr. L *macr-*, *macer* lean; akin to OE *mæger* lean, Gk *makros* long] (14c) **1** : having little flesh : THIN **2 a** : lacking desirable qualities (as richness or strength) ⟨leading a ∼ life⟩ **b** : deficient in quality or quantity ⟨a ∼ diet⟩ — **mea·ger·ly** *adv* — **mea·ger·ness** *n*
syn MEAGER, SCANTY, SCANT, SKIMPY, SPARE, SPARSE mean falling short of what is normal, necessary, or desirable. MEAGER implies the absence of elements, qualities, or numbers necessary to a thing's richness, substance, or potency ⟨a *meager* portion of meat⟩. SCANTY stresses insufficiency in amount, quantity, or extent ⟨supplies too *scanty* to last the winter⟩. SCANT suggests a falling short of what is desired or desirable rather than of what is essential ⟨in January the daylight hours are *scant*⟩. SKIMPY usu. suggests niggardliness or penury as the cause of the deficiency ⟨tacky housing developments on *skimpy* lots⟩. SPARE may suggest a slight falling short of adequacy or merely an absence of superfluity ⟨a *spare*, concise style of writing⟩. SPARSE implies a thin scattering of units ⟨a *sparse* population⟩.

¹meal \'mē(ə)l\ *n* [ME *mele* appointed time, meal, fr. OE *mǣl*; akin to OHG *māl* time, L *metiri* to measure — more at MEASURE] (bef. 12c) **1** : an act or the time of eating a portion of food to satisfy appetite **2** : the portion of food eaten at a meal

\ə\ abut \ˈ\ kitten, F table \ər\ further \a\ ash \ā\ ace \ä\ mop, mar \au̇\ out \ch\ chin \e\ bet \ē\ easy \g\ go \i\ hit \ī\ ice \j\ job \ŋ\ sing \ō\ go \ȯ\ law \ȯi\ boy \th\ thin \t͟h\ the \ü\ loot \u̇\ foot \y\ yet \zh\ vision \à, k̲, ⁿ, œ, œ̄, ᵫ, ᵬᴇ, � \ see Guide to Pronunciation

¹meal n [ME mele, fr. OE melu; akin to OHG melo meal, L molere to grind, Gk mylē mill] (bef. 12c) **1** : the usu. coarsely ground and un-bolted seeds of a cereal grass or pulse; esp : CORNMEAL **2** : a product resembling seed meal esp. in particle size or texture
-meal adv comb form [ME -mele, fr. OE -mǣlum, fr. mǣlum, dat. pl. of mǣl] : by a (specified) portion or measure at a time ⟨piecemeal⟩
mea·lie \'mē-lē\ n [Afrik mielie] (1855) SoAfr : INDIAN CORN; also : an ear of Indian corn
meals–on–wheels n pl but sing in constr (1961) : a service that delivers daily hot meals to the homes of elderly or disabled people
meal ticket n (ca. 1899) : one that serves as the ultimate source of one's income ⟨an advanced degree was his meal ticket⟩
meal·time \'mē(ə)l-,tīm\ n (12c) : the usual time for serving a meal
meal·worm \-,wərm\ n (1658) : the larva of various beetles (genus Tenebrio) that infests and pollutes grain products but is often raised as food for insectivorous animals, for laboratory use, or as fishing bait
mealy \'mē-lē\ adj **meal·i·er; -est** (1533) **1** : soft, dry, and friable **2** : containing meal : FARINACEOUS **3** : covered with meal or with fine granules **b** : flecked with another color ⟨a ~ complexion⟩ **d** : PALLID, BLANCHED ⟨a ~ complexion⟩ **4** : MEALYMOUTHED
mealy·bug \'mē-lē-,bəg\ n (1824) : any of a family (Pseudococcidae) of scale insects that have a white powdery covering and are destructive pests esp. of fruit trees
mealy·mouthed \'mē-lē-,maúthd, -,maútht\ adj (ca. 1572) : not plain and straightforward : DEVIOUS ⟨a ~ politician⟩
¹mean \'mēn\ vb **meant** \'ment\; **mean·ing** \'mē-nin\ [ME menen, fr. OE mǣnan; akin to OHG meinen to have in mind, OCS měniti to men-tion] vt (bef. 12c) **1** a : to have in the mind as a purpose : INTEND ⟨she ~s to win⟩ — sometimes used interjectionally with I, chiefly in informal speech for emphasis ⟨he throws, I ~, hard⟩ or to introduce a phrase restating the point of a preceding phrase ⟨we try to answer what we can, but I ~ we're not God —Bobbie Ann Mason⟩ **b** : to design for or destine to a specified purpose or future ⟨I was meant to teach⟩ **2** : to serve or intend to convey, show, or indicate : SIGNIFY ⟨a red sky ~s rain⟩ **3** : to have importance to the degree of ⟨health ~s every-thing⟩ **4** : to direct to a particular individual ~ vi : to have an in-tended purpose ⟨he ~s well⟩ — **mean·er** \'mē-nər\ n — **mean busi-ness** : to be in earnest
²mean \'mēn\ adj [ME mene, fr. imene common, shared, fr. OE gemǣne; akin to OHG gimeini common, L communis common, munus service, gift, Skt mayate he exchanges] (14c) **1** : lacking distinction or eminence : HUMBLE **2** : lacking in mental discrimination : DULL **3** a : of poor shabby inferior quality or status ⟨~ city streets⟩ **b** : worthy of little regard : CONTEMPTIBLE — often used in negative constructions as a term of praise ⟨no ~ feat⟩ **4** : lacking dignity or honor : BASE **5** a : PENURIOUS, STINGY **b** : characterized by petty selfishness or malice **c** : causing trouble or bother : VEXATIOUS **d** : EXCELLENT, EFFECTIVE ⟨plays a ~ trumpet⟩ ⟨a lean, ~ athlete⟩ **6** : ASHAMED 1b — **mean·ness** \'mēn-nəs\ n
syn MEAN, IGNOBLE, ABJECT, SORDID mean being below the normal stan-dards of human decency and dignity. MEAN suggests having such re-pellent characteristics as small-mindedness, ill temper, or cupidity ⟨mean and petty satire⟩. IGNOBLE suggests a loss or lack of some essen-tial high quality of mind or spirit ⟨an ignoble scramble after material possessions⟩. ABJECT may imply degradation, debasement, or servility ⟨abject poverty⟩. SORDID is stronger than all of these in stressing physi-cal or spiritual degradation and abjectness ⟨a sordid story of murder and revenge⟩.
³mean adj [ME mene, fr. MF meien, fr. L medianus — more at MEDIAN] (14c) **1** : occupying a middle position : intermediate in space, order, time, kind, or degree **2** : occupying a position about midway between extremes; esp : being the mean of a set of values : AVERAGE ⟨the ~ temperature⟩ **3** : serving as a means : INTERMEDIARY **syn** see AVER-AGE
⁴mean n (14c) **1** a (1) : something intervening or intermediate (2) : a middle point between extremes **b** : a value that lies within a range of values and is computed according to a prescribed law: as (1) : ARITHMETIC MEAN (2) : EXPECTED VALUE **c** : either of the middle two terms of a proportion **2** pl but sing or pl in constr : something useful or helpful to a desired end **3** pl : resources available for disposal; esp : material resources affording a secure life — **by all means** : most assuredly : CERTAINLY — **by means of** : through the use of — **by no means** : in no way : not at all
¹me·an·der \mē-'an-dər\ n [L maeander, fr. Gk maiandros, fr. Maian-dros (now Menderes), river in Asia Minor] (1576) **1** : a winding path or course; esp : LABYRINTH **2** : a turn or winding of a stream — **me-an·drous** \-drəs\ adj
²meander vi **-dered; -der·ing** \-d(ə-)rin\ (ca. 1612) **1** : to follow a winding or intricate course **2** : to wander aimlessly or casually with-out urgent destination : RAMBLE **syn** see WANDER
mean deviation n (1858) : the mean of the absolute values of the nu-merical differences between the numbers of a set (as statistical data) and their mean or median
mean distance n (ca. 1889) : the arithmetical mean of the maximum and minimum distances of an orbiting celestial object from its primary
mean free path n (1879) : the average distance traversed between collisions by particles (as molecules of a gas or free electrons in metal) in a system of agitated particles
mean·ie also **meany** \'mē-nē\ n, pl **meanies** (1910) : a mean or spite-ful person
mean·ing \'mē-nin\ n (14c) **1** a : the thing one intends to convey esp. by language : PURPORT **b** : the thing that is conveyed esp. by language : IMPORT **2** : something meant or intended : AIM ⟨a mischie-vous ~ was apparent⟩ **3** : significant quality; esp : implication of a hidden or special significance ⟨a glance full of ~⟩ **4** a : the logical connotation of a word or phrase **b** : the logical denotation or exten-sion of a word or phrase — **meaning** adj — **mean·ing·ly** \-nin-lē\ adv
mean·ing·ful \-fəl\ adj (1852) **1** a : having a meaning or purpose **b** : full of meaning : SIGNIFICANT ⟨a ~ life⟩ **2** : having an assigned func-tion in a language system ⟨~ propositions⟩ — **mean·ing·ful·ly** \-fə-lē\ adv — **mean·ing·ful·ness** n
mean·ing·less \'mē-nin-ləs\ adj (1797) **1** : having no meaning; esp : lacking any significance **2** : having no assigned function in a lan-guage system — **mean·ing·less·ly** adv — **mean·ing·less·ness** n

¹mean·ly \'mēn-lē\ adv (14c) obs : fairly well : MODERATELY
²meanly adv (15c) **1** : in a mean manner: as **a** : in a lowly manner : HUMBLY **b** : in an inferior manner : BADLY **c** : in a base or ungener-ous manner
mean proportional n (1571) : GEOMETRIC MEAN; esp : the square root (as x) of the product of two numbers (as a and b) when expressed as the means of a proportion (as a/x = x/b)
mean solar day n (1816) : the interval between successive transits of a given meridian by the mean sun
mean–spir·it·ed \'mēn-'spir-ə-təd, ,mēn-\ adj (1694) : exhibiting or characterized by meanness of spirit — **mean–spir·it·ed·ness** \-nəs\ n
mean square n (1845) : the mean of the squares of a set of values
mean square deviation n (1948) **1** : VARIANCE 5 **2** : STANDARD DEVIATION
means test \'mēnz-\ n (1930) : an examination into the financial state of a person to determine his eligibility for public assistance — **means-test·ed** \-,tes-təd\ adj
mean sun n (ca. 1890) : a fictitious sun used for timekeeping that moves uniformly along the celestial equator and maintains a constant rate of apparent motion equal to the average rate of apparent motion of the real sun
¹mean·time \'mēn-,tīm\ n (14c) : the intervening time
²meantime adv (1588) : MEANWHILE
mean time n (ca. 1864) : time that is based on the motion of the mean sun — called also mean solar time
mean value theorem n (1902) **1** : a theorem in differential calculus: if a function of one variable is continuous on a closed interval and dif-ferentiable on the interval minus its endpoints there is at least one point where the derivative of the function is equal to the slope of the line joining the endpoints of the curve representing the function on the interval **2** : a theorem in integral calculus: if a function of one variable is continuous on a closed interval and differentiable on the interval minus its endpoints, there is at least one point in the interval where the product of the value of the function and the length of the interval is equal to the integral of the function over the interval
¹mean·while \'mēn-,hwīl, -,wīl\ n (14c) : MEANTIME
²meanwhile adv (14c) **1** : during the intervening time **2** : at the same time
mea·sle \'mē-zəl\ n [sing. of measles] (1863) : a cysticercus tapeworm larva; specif : one found in the muscles of a domesticated mammal
mea·sles \'mē-zəlz\ n pl but sing or pl in constr [ME meseles, pl. of mesel measles, spot characteristic of measles; akin to MD masel spot charac-teristic of measles] (14c) **1** a : an acute contagious viral disease marked by an eruption of distinct red circular spots **b** : any of various eruptive diseases (as German measles) **2** [ME mesel infested with tapeworms, lit., leprous, fr. OF, fr. ML misellus leper, fr. L, wretch, fr. misellus, dim. of miser miserable] : infestation with or disease caused by larval tapeworms in the muscles and tissues
mea·sly \'mēz-lē, 'mē-zə-\ adj **mea·sli·er; -est** (1687) **1** : infected with measles **2** a : containing larval tapeworms **b** : infested with trichinae **3** : contemptibly small
¹mea·sure \'me-zhər, 'mā-\ n [ME mesure, fr. OF, fr. L mensura, fr. mensus, pp. of metiri to measure; akin to OE mǣth measure, Gk me-tron] (13c) **1** a (1) : an adequate or due portion (2) : a moderate degree; also : MODERATION, TEMPERANCE (3) : a fixed or suitable limit : BOUNDS ⟨rich beyond ~⟩ **b** : the dimensions, capacity, or amount of something ascertained by measuring **c** : an estimate of what is to be expected (as of a person or situation) **d** (1) : a measured quantity (2) : AMOUNT, DEGREE **2** a : an instrument or utensil for measuring **b** (1) : a standard or unit of measurement — see WEIGHT table (2) : a system of standard units of measure ⟨metric ~⟩ **3** : the act or process of measuring **4** a (1) : MELODY, TUNE (2) : DANCE; esp : a slow and stately dance **b** : rhythmic structure or movement : CADENCE: as (1) : poetic rhythm measured by temporal quantity or accent; specif : ME-TER (2) : musical time **c** (1) : a grouping of a specified number of musical beats located between two consecutive vertical lines on a staff (2) : a metrical unit : FOOT **5** : an exact divisor of a number **6** : a basis or standard of comparison ⟨wealth is not a ~ of happiness⟩ **7** : a step planned or taken as a means to an end; specif : a proposed legislative act — **for good measure** : in addition to the minimum required : as an extra
²measure vb **mea·sured; mea·sur·ing** \'me-zhə-rin, 'mā-; 'mezh-rin, 'māzh-\ vt (14c) **1** a : to choose or control with cautious restraint : REGULATE ⟨~ his acts⟩ **b** : to regulate by a standard : GOVERN **2** : to allot or apportion in measured amounts ⟨~ out 3 cups⟩ **3** : to lay off by making measurements **4** : to ascertain the measurements of **5** : to estimate or appraise by a criterion ⟨~s his skill against his rival⟩ **6** archaic : to travel over : TRAVERSE **7** : to serve as a means of mea-suring ⟨a thermometer ~s temperature⟩ ~ vi **1** : to take or make a measurement **2** : to have a specified measurement — **mea·sur·abil·i·ty** \,me-zhə-rə-'bi-lə-tē, ,mā-; ,mezh-rə-, ,māzh-\ n — **mea·sur·able** \'me-zhə-rə-bəl, 'mā-; 'mezh-rə-, 'māzh-\ adj — **mea·sur·ably** \-blē\ adv — **mea·sur·er** \-zhər-ər\ n
mea·sured \'me-zhərd, 'mā-\ adj (14c) **1** : marked by due proportion **2** a : marked by rhythm : regularly recurrent ⟨a ~ gait⟩ **b** : METRI-CAL **3** : DELIBERATE, CALCULATED ⟨a ~ response⟩ — **mea·sured·ly** adv
mea·sure·less \-zhər-ləs\ adj (14c) **1** : having no observable limit : IMMEASURABLE ⟨the ~ universe⟩ **2** : very great ⟨had ~ energy⟩
mea·sure·ment \'me-zhər-mənt, 'mā-\ n (1751) **1** : the act or process of measuring **2** : a figure, extent, or amount obtained by measuring : DIMENSION **3** : MEASURE 2b
measurement ton n (ca. 1934) : TON 1c
measure up vi (1910) **1** : to have necessary or fitting qualifications — often used with to **2** : to be the equal (as in ability) — used with to
measuring worm n (1843) : LOOPER 1
meat \'mēt\ n [ME mete, fr. OE; akin to OHG maz food] (bef. 12c) **1** a : FOOD; esp : solid food as distinguished from drink **b** : the edible part of something as distinguished from its covering (as a husk or shell) **2** : animal tissue considered esp. as food: **a** : FLESH 2b **b** : FLESH 1a; specif : flesh of domesticated animals **3** archaic : MEAL 1; esp : DIN-NER **4** a : the core of something : HEART **b** : PITH 2b ⟨a novel with ~⟩ **5** : favorite pursuit or interest — **meat·ed** \'mē-təd\ adj — **meat-less** adj
meat–and–potatoes adj (1949) **1** : of fundamental importance : BA-

SIC; *also* : concerned with or emphasizing the basic aspects of something   **2** : PRACTICAL; *also* : EVERYDAY   **3** : providing or preferring simple food (as meat and potatoes)

meat and potatoes *n pl but sing or pl in constr* (1951) : the most interesting or fundamental part : MEAT 4

meat-ax \'mēt-ˌaks\ *n* (1834)   **1** : CLEAVER 1   **2** : an extreme or heavy-handed method of cutting or altering something

meat-ball \-ˌbȯl\ *n* (ca. 1838) : a small ball of chopped or ground meat often mixed with bread crumbs and spices

meat-head \-ˌhed\ *n* (1945) : a stupid or bungling person

meat loaf *n* (1899) : a dish of ground meat seasoned and baked in the form of a loaf

meat market *n* (1896) : a depersonalizing environment in which people are treated as sexual or economic resources

meat-pack-ing \'mēt-ˌpa-kiŋ\ *n* (1873) : the wholesale meat industry

me-a-tus \mē-'ā-təs\ *n*, *pl* **me-a-tus-es** \-tə-səz\ *or* **me-a-tus** \-'ā-təs, -ˌtüs\ [LL, fr. L, going, passage, fr. *meatus*, pp. of *meare* to go — more at PERMEATE] (1665) : a natural body passage

meaty \'mē-tē\ *adj* **meat-i-er; -est** (ca. 1787)   **1 a** : full of meat   **b** : having the character of meat   **2** : rich esp. in matter for thought : SUBSTANTIAL ⟨actors looking for ∼ roles⟩ — **meat-i-ness** *n*

mec-a-myl-amine \ˌme-kə-'mi-lə-ˌmēn\ *n* [fr. *Mecamylamine*, a trademark] (1955) : a drug that in the hydrochloride $C_{11}H_{21}N \cdot HCl$ is used orally as a ganglionic blocking agent to effect a rapid lowering of severely elevated blood pressure

mec-ca \'me-kə\ *n*, *often cap* [*Mecca*, Saudi Arabia, a destination of pilgrims in the Islamic world] (1850) : a center of activity sought as a goal by people sharing a common interest

mechan- *or* **mechano-** *comb form* [Gk, fr. *mēchanē* machine — more at MACHINE] : mechanical ⟨*mechano*receptor⟩

¹me-chan-ic \mi-'ka-nik\ *adj* [ME, prob. fr. MF *mechanique*, adj. & n., fr. L *mechanicus*, fr. Gk *mēchanikos*, fr. *mēchanē*] (14c)   **1** : of or relating to manual work or skill   **2** : MECHANICAL 3a

²mechanic *n* (1562)   **1** : a manual worker : ARTISAN   **2** : MACHINIST; *esp* : one who repairs machines

¹me-chan-i-cal \mi-'ka-ni-kəl\ *adj* (15c)   **1 a** (1) : of or relating to machinery or tools ⟨∼ applications of science⟩ ⟨a ∼ genius⟩ ⟨∼ aptitude⟩   (2) : produced or operated by a machine or tool ⟨∼ power⟩ ⟨a ∼ refrigerator⟩ ⟨a ∼ saw⟩   **b** : of or relating to manual operations   **2** : of or relating to artisans or machinists ⟨the ∼ trades⟩   **3 a** : done as if by machine : seemingly uninfluenced by the mind or emotions : AUTOMATIC ⟨her singing was cold and ∼⟩   **b** : of or relating to technicalities or petty matters   **4 a** : relating to, governed by, or in accordance with the principles of mechanics ⟨∼ work⟩ ⟨∼ energy⟩   **b** : relating to the quantitative relations of force and matter ⟨∼ pressure of wind on a tower⟩   **5** : caused by, resulting from, or relating to a process that involves a purely physical as opposed to a chemical change ⟨∼ erosion of rock⟩   *syn* see SPONTANEOUS — **me-chan-i-cal-ly** \-ni-k(ə-)lē\ *adv*

²mechanical *n* (1590)   **1** *obs* : MECHANIC 1   **2** : a piece of finished copy consisting typically of type proofs and artwork positioned and mounted for photomechanical reproduction

mechanical advantage *n* (1894) : the advantage gained by the use of a mechanism in transmitting force; *specif* : the ratio of the force that performs the useful work of a machine to the force that is applied to the machine

mechanical drawing *n* (ca. 1890)   **1** : drawing done with the aid of instruments   **2** : a drawing made with instruments

mechanical engineering *n* (ca. 1890) : a branch of engineering concerned primarily with the industrial application of mechanics and with the production of tools, machinery, and their products

mech-a-ni-cian \ˌme-kə-'ni-shən\ *n* (1570) : MECHANIC, MACHINIST

me-chan-ics \mi-'ka-niks\ *n pl but sing or pl in constr* (1648)   **1** : a branch of physical science that deals with energy and forces and their effect on bodies   **2** : the practical application of mechanics to the design, construction, or operation of machines or tools   **3** : mechanical or functional details or procedure

mech-a-nist \-nist\ *n* (1606)   **1** *archaic* : MECHANIC   **2** : an adherent of the doctrine of mechanism

mech-a-nis-tic \ˌme-kə-'nis-tik\ *adj* (1884)   **1** : mechanically determined ⟨∼ universe⟩   **2** : of or relating to a mechanism or the doctrine of mechanism   **3** : MECHANICAL — **mech-a-nis-ti-cal-ly** \-ti-k(ə-)lē\ *adv*

mech-a-nize \'me-kə-ˌnīz\ *vt* **-nized; -niz-ing** (1678)   **1** : to make mechanical; *esp* : to make automatic or routine   **2 a** : to equip with machinery   **b** : to replace human or animal labor   **b** : to equip with armed and armored motor vehicles   **c** : to provide with mechanical power   **3** : to produce by or as if by machine — **mech-a-niz-able** \-ˌnī-zə-bəl\ *adj* — **mech-a-ni-za-tion** \ˌme-kə-nə-'zā-shən\ *n* — **mech-a-niz-er** \'me-kə-ˌnī-zər\ *n*

mech-a-no-chem-is-try \ˌme-kə-nō-'ke-mə-strē\ *n* (1928) : chemistry that deals with the conversion of chemical energy into mechanical work (as in the contraction of a muscle) — **mech-a-no-chem-i-cal** \-'ke-mi-kəl\ *adj*

mech-a-no-re-cep-tor \-ri-'sep-tər\ *n* (1927) : a neural end organ (as a tactile receptor) that responds to a mechanical stimulus (as a change in pressure) — **mech-a-no-re-cep-tion** \-'sep-shən\ *n* — **mech-a-no-re-cep-tive** \-'sep-tiv\ *adj*

Mech-lin \'me-klən\ *n* [*Mechlin*, Belgium] (1699) : a delicate bobbin lace used for dresses and millinery

mec-li-zine \'me-klə-ˌzēn\ *n* [*methyl* + *chlor-* + *-izine* (alter. of *azine*)] (1954) : a drug $C_{25}H_{27}ClN_2$ used usu. in the form of its hydrochloride to treat nausea and vertigo

me-co-ni-um \mi-'kō-nē-əm\ *n* [L, lit., poppy juice, fr. Gk *mēkōnion*, fr. *mēkōn* poppy; akin to OHG *mago* poppy] (1706) : a dark greenish mass that accumulates in the bowel during fetal life and is discharged shortly after birth

med \'med\ *adj* (1891) : MEDICAL ⟨∼ school⟩

me-da-ka \mə-'dä-kə\ *n* [Jp] (1933) : a small Japanese freshwater fish (*Oryzias latipes*) usu. silvery brown in the wild but from pale yellow to deep red in aquarium strains

med-al \'me-d³l\ *n* [MF *medaille*, fr. OIt *medaglia* coin worth half a denarius, medal, fr. (assumed) VL *medalis* half, alter. of LL *medialis* middle, fr. L *medius* — more at MID] (ca. 1578)   **1** : a small usu. metal object bearing a religious emblem or picture   **2** : a piece of metal often resembling a coin and having a stamped design that is issued to commemorate a person or event or awarded for excellence or achievement

Medal for Merit (1942) : a U.S. decoration awarded to civilians for exceptionally meritorious conduct in the performance of outstanding services

med-al-ist *or* **med-al-list** \'me-d³l-ist\ *n* (ca. 1757)   **1** : a designer, engraver, or maker of medals   **2** : a recipient of a medal as an award

me-dal-lic \mə-'da-lik\ *adj* (1702) : of, relating to, or shown on a medal

me-dal-lion \mə-'dal-yən\ *n* [F *médaillon*, fr. It *medaglione*, aug. of *medaglia*] (1658)   **1** : a large medal   **2** : something resembling a large medal; *esp* : a tablet or panel in a wall or window bearing a figure in relief, a portrait, or an ornament   **3** *also* **me-dail-lon** \mā-dä-yōⁿ\ : a small round or oval serving (as of meat)

Medal of Freedom (1945) : a U.S. decoration awarded to civilians for meritorious achievement in any of various fields

Medal of Honor (1898) : a U.S. military decoration awarded in the name of the Congress for conspicuous intrepidity at the risk of life in action with an enemy

medal play *n* (1899) : STROKE PLAY

med-dle \'me-d³l\ *vi* **med-dled; med-dling** \'med-liŋ, 'me-d³l-iŋ\ [ME *medlen*, fr. MF *mesler, medler*, fr. (assumed) VL *misculare*, fr. L *miscēre* to mix — more at MIX] (14c) : to interest oneself in what is not one's concern : interfere without right or propriety — **med-dler** \'med-lər, 'me-d³l-ər\ *n*

med-dle-some \'me-d³l-səm\ *adj* (1615) : given to meddling   *syn* see IMPERTINENT — **med-dle-some-ness** *n*

Mede \'mēd\ *n* [ME, fr. L *Medus*, fr. Gk *Mēdos*] (14c) : a native or inhabitant of ancient Media in Persia

Me-dea \mə-'dē-ə\ *n* [L, fr. Gk *Mēdeia*] : an enchantress noted in Greek mythology for helping Jason gain the Golden Fleece and for repeatedly resorting to murder to gain her ends

med-e-vac \'me-də-ˌvak, -dē-\ *n* [*medical evacuation*] (1966)   **1** : emergency evacuation of the sick or wounded (as from a combat area)   **2** : a helicopter used for medevac

med-fly \'med-ˌflī\ *n*, *often cap* (1935) : MEDITERRANEAN FRUIT FLY

¹me-dia \'mē-dē-ə\ *n*, *pl* **me-di-ae** \-dē-ˌē\ (1841)   **1** [LL, fr. L, fem. of *medius*; fr. the voiced stops' being regarded as intermediate between the tenues and the aspirates]: a voiced stop   **2** [NL, fr. L]: the middle coat of the wall of a blood or lymph vessel consisting chiefly of circular muscle fibers

²media *n*, *pl* **me-di-as** *often attrib* [pl. of *medium*] (1923)   **1** : a medium of cultivation, conveyance, or expression; *esp* : MEDIUM 2b   **2 a** *sing or pl in constr* : MASS MEDIA   **b** *pl* : members of the mass media

usage The singular *media* and its plural *medias* seem to have originated in the field of advertising over 50 years ago; they are apparently still so used without stigma in that specialized field. In most other applications *media* is used as a plural of *medium*. The great popularity of the word in references to the agencies of mass communication is leading to the formation of a mass noun, construed as a singular ⟨there's no basis for it. You know, the news *media* gets on to something —Edwin Meese 3d⟩ ⟨the *media* is less interested in the party's policies —James Lewis, *Guardian Weekly*⟩. This use is not as well established as the mass-noun use of *data* and is likely to incur criticism esp. in writing.

me-di-ad \'mē-dē-ˌad\ *adv* (1878) : toward the median line or plane of a body or part

media event *n* (1972) : a publicity event staged for coverage by the news media

me-dia-gen-ic \ˌmē-dē-ə-'je-nik\ *adj* (1971) : attractive or well-suited to the communications media

me-di-al \'mē-dē-əl\ *adj* [LL *medialis*, fr. L *medius*] (1570)   **1** : MEAN, AVERAGE   **2 a** : being or occurring in the middle   **b** : extending toward the middle   **3** : situated between the extremes of initial and final in a word or morpheme — **medial** *n* — **me-di-al-ly** \-ə-lē\ *adv*

¹me-di-an \'mē-dē-ən\ *n* (15c)   **1** : a medial part (as a vein or nerve)   **2 a** : a value in an ordered set of values below and above which there is an equal number of values or which is the arithmetic mean of the two middle values if there is no one middle number   **b** : a vertical line that divides the histogram of a frequency distribution into two parts of equal area   **c** : a value of a random variable for which all greater values make the distribution function greater than one half and all lesser values make it less than one half   **3 a** : a line from a vertex of a triangle to the midpoint of the opposite side   **b** : a line joining the midpoints of the nonparallel sides of a trapezoid   **4** : MEDIAN STRIP   *syn* see AVERAGE

²median *adj* [MF or L; MF, fr. L *medianus*, fr. *medius* middle — more at MID] (1645)   **1** : being in the middle or in an intermediate position : MEDIAL   **2** : lying in the plane dividing a bilateral animal into right and left halves   **3** : relating to or constituting a statistical median   **4** : produced without occlusion along the lengthwise middle line of the tongue — **me-di-an-ly** *adv*

median strip *n* (1948) : a paved or planted strip dividing a highway into lanes according to direction of travel

me-di-ant \'mē-dē-ənt\ *n* [It *mediante*, fr. LL *mediant-, medians*, prp. of *mediare* to be in the middle] (ca. 1741) : the third tone of a diatonic scale

me-di-as-ti-num \ˌmē-dē-ə-'stī-nəm\ *n*, *pl* **-na** \-nə\ [NL, fr. ML, neut. of *mediastinus* medial, fr. L *medius*] (1541) : the space in the chest between the pleural sacs of the lungs that contains all the viscera of the

---

\ə\ abut   \³\ kitten, F table   \ər\ further   \a\ ash   \ā\ ace   \ä\ mop, mar
\au̇\ out   \ch\ chin   \e\ bet   \ē\ easy   \g\ go   \i\ hit   \ī\ ice   \j\ job
\ŋ\ sing   \ō\ go   \ȯ\ law   \ȯi\ boy   \th\ thin   \t̲h̲\ the   \ü\ loot   \u̇\ foot
\y\ yet   \zh\ vision   \à, k̲, ⁿ, œ, œ̄, ᵫ, ᵿ, ᵊ\ *see* Guide to Pronunciation

chest except the lungs and pleurae; *also* : this space with its contents — **me·di·as·ti·nal** \-'stī-n²l\ *adj*

¹me·di·ate \'mē-dē-ət\ *adj* [ME, fr. LL *mediatus* intermediate, fr. pp. of *mediare*] (15c) **1** : occupying a middle position **2 a** : acting through an intervening agency **b** : exhibiting indirect causation, connection, or relation — **me·di·a·cy** \-dē-ə-sē\ *n* — **me·di·ate·ly** *adv*

²me·di·ate \-,āt\ *vb* **-at·ed; -at·ing** [ML *mediatus*, pp. of *mediare*, fr. LL, to be in the middle, fr. L *medius* middle] *vt* (1568) **1 a** : to effect by action as an intermediary **b** : to bring accord out of by action as an intermediary **2 a** : to act as intermediary agent in bringing, effecting, or communicating : CONVEY **b** : to transmit as intermediate mechanism or agency ~ *vi* **1** : to interpose between parties in order to reconcile them **2** : to reconcile differences *syn* see INTERPOSE — **me·di·a·tive** \-,ā-tiv\ *adj* — **me·di·a·to·ry** \-ə-,tōr-ē, -,tȯr-\ *adj*

me·di·a·tion \,mē-dē-'ā-shən\ *n* (14c) : the act or process of mediating; *esp* : intervention between conflicting parties to promote reconciliation, settlement, or compromise — **me·di·a·tion·al** \-shnəl, -shə-n²l\ *adj*

me·di·a·tor \'mē-dē-,ā-tər\ *n* [ME, fr. LL, fr. *mediare*] (14c) **1** : one that mediates; *esp* : one that mediates between parties at variance **2** : a mediating agent in a physical, chemical, or biological process

me·di·a·trix \-'ā-triks\ *n* [ME, fr. LL, fem. of *mediator*] (15c) : a woman who is a mediator

¹med·ic \'me-dik\ *n* [ME *medike*, fr. L *medica*, fr. Gk *mēdikē*, fr. fem. of *mēdikos* of Media, fr. *Mēdia* Media] (15c) : any of a genus (*Medicago*) of leguminous herbs (as alfalfa)

²medic *n* [L *medicus*] (1659) : one engaged in medical work or study; *esp* : CORPSMAN

med·i·ca·ble \'me-di-kə-bəl\ *adj* (ca. 1616) : CURABLE, REMEDIABLE

med·ic·aid \'me-di-,kād\ *n, often cap* [*medical aid*] (1966) : a program of medical aid designed for those unable to afford regular medical service and financed by the state and federal governments

med·i·cal \'me-di-kəl\ *adj* [F or LL; F *médical*, fr. LL *medicalis*, fr. L *medicus* physician, fr. *mederi* to remedy, heal; akin to Av vi-*mad*-healer, Gk *medesthai* to be mindful of — more at METE] (1646) **1** : of, relating to, or concerned with physicians or the practice of medicine **2** : requiring or devoted to medical treatment — **med·i·cal·ly** \-k(ə-)lē\ *adv*

medical examiner *n* (1877) : a public officer who conducts autopsies of bodies to find the cause of death

me·di·ca·ment \mi-'di-kə-mənt, 'me-di-kə-\ *n* [MF, fr. L *medicamentum*, fr. *medicare*] (1541) : a substance used in therapy — **me·di·ca·men·tous** \mi-,di-kə-men-təs, ,me-di-kə-\ *adj*

medi·care \'me-di-,ker, -,kar\ *n, often cap* [blend of *medical* and *care*] (1955) : a government program of medical care esp. for the aged

med·i·cate \'me-də-,kāt\ *vt* **-cat·ed; -cat·ing** [L *medicatus*, pp. of *medicare* to heal, fr. *medicus*] (ca. 1623) **1** : to treat medicinally **2** : to impregnate with a medicinal substance ⟨*medicated* soap⟩

med·i·ca·tion \,me-də-'kā-shən\ *n* (15c) **1** : the act or process of medicating **2** : a medicinal substance : MEDICAMENT

me·dic·i·na·ble \mi-'dis-nə-bəl, -'di-s²n-ə-; *in Shak* 'med-sə-nə-\ *adj* (14c) : MEDICINAL

me·dic·i·nal \mə-'dis-nəl, -'di-s²n-əl; *in Shak & Milton* ,me-di-'sī-n²l & 'med-sə-nəl\ *adj* (14c) **1** : tending or used to cure disease or relieve pain **2** : SALUTARY — **medicinal** *n* — **me·dic·i·nal·ly** *adv*

medicinal leech *n* (ca. 1890) : a large European freshwater leech (*Hirudo medicinalis*) formerly used by physicians for bleeding patients

med·i·cine \'me-də-sən, *Brit usu* 'med-sən\ *n* [ME, fr. OF, fr. L *medicina*, fr. fem. of *medicinus* of a physician, fr. *medicus*] (13c) **1 a** : a substance or preparation used in treating disease **b** : something that affects well-being **2 a** : the science and art dealing with the maintenance of health and the prevention, alleviation, or cure of disease **b** : the branch of medicine concerned with the nonsurgical treatment of disease **3** : a substance (as a drug or potion) used to treat something other than disease **4** : an object held in traditional American Indian belief to give control over natural or magical forces; *also* : magical power or a magical rite — **medicine** *vt*

medicine ball *n* (1895) : a heavy stuffed leather-covered ball used for conditioning exercises

medicine dropper *n* (1898) : DROPPER 2

medicine man *n* (1801) : a priestly healer or sorcerer esp. among the American Indians : SHAMAN

medicine show *n* (ca. 1906) : a traveling show using entertainers to attract a crowd among which remedies or nostrums are sold

med·i·co \'me-di-,kō\ *n, pl* **-cos** [It *medico* or Sp *médico*, both fr. L *medicus*] (1689) : a medical practitioner : PHYSICIAN; *also* : a medical student

med·i·co·le·gal \,me-di-kō-'lē-gəl\ *adj* [NL *medicolegalis*, fr. L *medicus* medical + -*o*- + *legalis* legal] (1835) : of or relating to both medicine and law

¹me·di·e·val *or* **me·di·ae·val** \mē-'dē-vəl, mi-, me-, -dē-'ē-vəl\ *adj* [NL *medium aevum* Middle Ages] (1827) **1** : of, relating to, or characteristic of the Middle Ages **2** : extremely outmoded or antiquated — **me·di·e·val·ly** *adv*

²medieval *or* **mediaeval** *n* (1856) : a person of the Middle Ages

me·di·e·val·ism \-və-,li-zəm\ *n* (1853) **1** : medieval quality, character, or state **2** : devotion to the institutions, arts, and practices of the Middle Ages

me·di·e·val·ist \-'dēv-list, -'dē-və-, -dē-ēv-, -dē-'ē-və-\ *n* (ca. 1859) **1** : a specialist in medieval history and culture **2** : a connoisseur or devotee of medieval arts and culture

Medieval Latin *n* (ca. 1889) : the Latin used esp. for liturgical and literary purposes from the 7th to the 15th centuries inclusive

me·di·na \mə-'dē-nə\ *n* [Ar *madina* city] (1906) : the non-European part of a northern African city

me·di·o·cre \,mē-dē-'ō-kər\ *adj* [ME, fr. MF, fr. L *mediocris*, fr. *medius* middle + OL *ocris* stony mountain; akin to L *acer* sharp — more at EDGE] (ca. 1586) : of moderate or low quality, value, ability, or performance : ORDINARY, SO-SO

me·di·oc·ri·ty \,mē-dē-'ä-krə-tē\ *n, pl* **-ties** (1531) **1 a** : the quality or state of being mediocre **b** : moderate ability or value **2** : a mediocre person

med·i·tate \'me-də-,tāt\ *vb* **-tat·ed; -tat·ing** [L *meditatus*, pp. of

meditari, freq. of *mederi* to remedy — more at MEDICAL] *vi* (1560) : to engage in contemplation or reflection ~ *vt* **1** : to focus one's thoughts on : reflect on or ponder over **2** : to plan or project in the mind : INTEND, PURPOSE *syn* see PONDER — **med·i·ta·tor** \-,tā-tər\ *n*

med·i·ta·tion \,me-də-'tā-shən\ *n* (13c) **1** : a discourse intended to express its author's reflections or to guide others in contemplation **2** : the act or process of meditating

med·i·ta·tive \'me-də-,tā-tiv\ *adj* (ca. 1656) **1** : disposed or given to meditation **2** : marked by or conducive to meditation — **med·i·ta·tive·ly** *adv* — **med·i·ta·tive·ness** *n*

Med·i·ter·ra·nean \,me-də-tə-'rā-nē-ən, -nyən\ *adj* (15c) **1 a** : of, relating to, or characteristic of the Mediterranean Sea **b** : of, relating to, or characteristic of the peoples, lands, or cultures bordering the Mediterranean Sea **2** *not cap* [L *mediterraneus*, fr. *medius* middle + *terra* land — more at TERRACE] : enclosed or nearly enclosed with land **3** : of or relating to a group or physical type of the Caucasian race characterized by medium or short stature, slender build, dolichocephaly, and dark complexion

Mediterranean flour moth *n* (1895) : a small largely gray and black nearly cosmopolitan pyralid moth (*Anagasta kuehniella*) whose larva destroys processed grain products

Mediterranean fruit fly *n* (1907) : a small widely distributed dipteran fly (*Ceratitis capitata*) with black-and-white markings whose larva lives and feeds in ripening fruit

¹me·di·um \'mē-dē-əm\ *n, pl* **mediums** *or* **me·dia** \-dē-ə\ [L, fr. neuter of *medius* middle — more at MID] (1593) **1** : something in a middle position **b** : a middle condition or degree : MEAN **2** : a means of effecting or conveying something: as **a** (1) : a substance regarded as the means of transmission of a force or effect (2) : a surrounding or enveloping substance (3) : the tenuous material (as gas and dust) in space that exists outside large agglomerations of matter (as stars) ⟨interstellar ~⟩ **b** *pl usu* **media** (1) : a channel or system of communication, information, or entertainment — compare MASS MEDIUM (2) : a publication or broadcast that carries advertising (3) : a mode of artistic expression or communication (4) : something (as a magnetic disk) on which information may be stored **c** : GO-BETWEEN, INTERMEDIARY **d** *pl* **mediums** : an individual held to be a channel of communication between the earthly world and a world of spirits **e** : material or technical means of artistic expression **3 a** : a condition or environment in which something may function or flourish **b** *pl* **media** (1) : a nutrient system for the artificial cultivation of cells or organisms and esp. bacteria (2) : a fluid or solid in which organic structures are placed (as for preservation or mounting) **c** : a liquid with which pigment is mixed by a painter *usage* see MEDIA

²medium *adj* (1711) : intermediate in quantity, quality, position, size, or degree

medium frequency *n* (1920) : a radio frequency between high frequency and low frequency — see RADIO FREQUENCY table

me·di·um·is·tic \,mē-dē-ə-'mis-tik\ *adj* (1868) : of, relating to, or having the qualities of a spiritualistic medium

medium of exchange (1714) : something commonly accepted in exchange for goods and services and recognized as representing a standard of value

me·di·um·ship \'mē-dē-əm-,ship\ *n* (1868) : the capacity, function, or profession of a spiritualistic medium

med·lar \'med-lər\ *n* [ME *medeler*, fr. MF *medlier*, fr. *medle* medlar fruit, fr. L *mespilum*, fr. Gk *mespilon*] (14c) : a small Eurasian tree (*Mespilus germanica*) of the rose family whose fruit resembles a crab apple and is used in preserves; *also* : its fruit

¹med·ley \'med-lē\ *n, pl* **medleys** [ME *medle*, fr. MF *medlee*, fr. fem. of *medlé*, pp. of *medler* to mix — more at MEDDLE] (14c) **1** *archaic* : MELEE **2** : a diverse assortment or mixture; *esp* : HODGEPODGE **3** : a musical composition made up of a series of songs or short musical pieces

²medley *adj* (14c) : MIXED, MOTLEY

medley relay *n* (1949) : a relay race in swimming in which each member of a team uses a different stroke

me·dul·la \mə-'dəl-lə\ *n, pl* **-las** *or* **-lae** \-(,)lē, -,lī\ [ME, fr. L] (15c) **1** *pl* **medullae** **a** : MARROW 1 **b** : MEDULLA OBLONGATA **2 a** : the inner or deep part of an animal or plant structure ⟨the adrenal ~⟩ **b** : MYELIN SHEATH

medulla ob·lon·ga·ta \-,ä-,blȯŋ-'gä-tə\ *n, pl* **medulla oblongatas** *or* **medullae ob·lon·ga·tae** \-'gä-tē, -,tī\ [NL, lit., oblong medulla] (1676) : the part of the vertebrate brain that is continuous posteriorly with the spinal cord and that contains the centers controlling involuntary vital functions — see BRAIN illustration

med·ul·lary \'me-d²l-,er-ē, 'me-jə-,ler-; mə-'dəl-ə-rē\ *adj* (1620) **1** : of or relating to the pith of a plant **2** : of or relating to a medulla and esp. the medulla oblongata

medullary ray *n* (1830) **1** : a primary tissue composed of radiating bands of parenchyma cells extending between the vascular bundles of herbaceous dicotyledonous stems and connecting the pith with the cortex **2** : VASCULAR RAY

medullary sheath *n* (ca. 1846) : MYELIN SHEATH

med·ul·lat·ed \'me-d²l-,ā-təd, 'me-jə-,lā-\ *adj* (1867) **1** : MYELINATED **2** : having a medulla — used of fibers other than nerve fibers

me·dul·lo·blas·to·ma \mə-,də-lō-,blas-'tō-mə\ *n, pl* **-tomas** *also* **-to·ma·ta** \-'tō-mə-tə\ [NL, fr. *medulla* + -*o*- + *blast*- + -*oma*] (1925) : a malignant tumor of the central nervous system arising in the cerebellum esp. in children

me·du·sa \mi-'dü-sə, -'dyü-, -zə\ *n* **1** *cap* [L, fr. Gk *Medousa*] : a mortal Gorgon who is slain when decapitated by Perseus **2** *pl* **me·du·sae** \-,sē, -,zē, -,sī, -,zī\ [NL, fr. L] : JELLYFISH 1a — **me·du·san** \-s²n, -z²n\ *adj or n* — **me·du·soid** \-,sȯid, -,zȯid\ *adj or n*

meed \'mēd\ *n* [ME, fr. OE *mēd*; akin to OHG *miata* reward, Gk *misthos*] (bef. 12c) **1** *archaic* : an earned reward or wage **2** : a fitting return or recompense

meek \'mēk\ *adj* [ME, of Scand origin; akin to ON *mjūkr* gentle; akin to W *mwyth* soft] (13c) **1** : enduring injury with patience and without resentment : MILD **2** : deficient in spirit and courage : SUBMISSIVE **3** : not violent or strong : MODERATE — **meek·ly** *adv* — **meek·ness** *n*

meer·kat \'mir-,kat\ *n* [Afrik, fr. D, a kind of monkey, fr. MD *meercatte* monkey, fr. *meer* sea + *catte* cat] (1801) : any of several African mongooses; *esp* : a burrowing highly social mammal (*Suricata suri-*

catta) of southern Africa that is chiefly grayish with inconspicuous black markings

meer·schaum \'mir-shəm, -,shȯm\ *n* [G, fr. *Meer* sea + *Schaum* foam] (1784) **1 :** a fine light white clayey mineral that is a hydrous magnesium silicate found chiefly in Asia Minor and is used esp. for tobacco pipes **2 :** a tobacco pipe of meerschaum

¹meet \'mēt\ *vb* **met** \'met\; **meet·ing** [ME *meten*, fr. OE *mētan*; akin to OE *gemōt* assembly — more at MOOT] *vt* (bef. 12c) **1 a :** to come into the presence of **:** FIND **b :** to come together with esp. at a particular time or place ⟨I'll ∼ you at the station⟩ **c :** to come into contact or conjunction with **:** JOIN **d :** to appear to the perception of **2 :** to encounter as antagonist or foe **:** OPPOSE **3 :** to enter into conference, argument, or personal dealings with **4 :** to conform to esp. with exactitude and precision ⟨a concept to ∼ all requirements⟩ **5 :** to pay fully **:** SETTLE **6 :** to cope with ⟨was able to ∼ every social situation⟩ **7 :** to provide for ⟨enough money to ∼ our needs⟩ **8 :** to become acquainted with **9 :** ENCOUNTER, EXPERIENCE **10 :** to receive or greet in an official capacity ∼ *vi* **1 a :** to come face-to-face **b :** to come together for a common purpose **:** ASSEMBLE **c :** to come together as contestants, opponents, or enemies **2 :** to form a junction or confluence ⟨the lines ∼ in a point⟩ **3 :** to occur together — **meet·er** *n* — **meet halfway :** to compromise with — **meet with :** to be subjected to **:** ENCOUNTER ⟨the proposal met with opposition⟩

²meet *n* (ca. 1834) **1 :** the act of assembling for a hunt or for competitive sports **2 :** a competition in which individuals (as athletes) match skills

³meet *adj* [ME *mete*, fr. OE *gemǣte*; akin to OE *metan* to mete] (14c) **:** precisely adapted to a particular situation, need, or circumstance **:** very proper *syn* see FIT — **meet·ly** *adv*

meet·ing \'mē-tiŋ\ *n* (14c) **1 :** an act or process of coming together: as **a :** an assembly for a common purpose (as worship) **b :** a session of horse or dog racing **2 :** a permanent organizational unit of the Society of Friends **3 :** INTERSECTION, JUNCTION

meet·ing·house \-,haȯs\ *n* (1632) **:** a building used for public assembly and esp. for Protestant worship

meeting of minds (1939) **:** AGREEMENT, CONCORD

mef·e·nam·ic acid \,me-fə-'na-mik-\ *n* [*dimethyl*- + *fen*- (by shortening & alter. fr. *phenyl*) + *aminobenzoic acid*] (ca. 1964) **:** a drug $C_{15}H_{15}NO_2$ used as an anti-inflammatory

mega- *or* **meg-** *comb form* [Gk, fr. *megas* — more at MUCH] **1 a :** great **:** large ⟨*megaspore*⟩ **b :** greatly surpassing others of its kind ⟨*megahit*⟩ **2 :** million **:** multiplied by one million ⟨*megohm*⟩ ⟨*megacycle*⟩

mega·bar \'me-gə-,bär\ *n* [ISV] (1903) **:** a unit of pressure equal to one million bars

mega·bit \-,bit\ *n* (1956) **:** one million bits

mega·buck \-,bək\ *n* (1946) **:** one million dollars; *also* **:** an indeterminately large sum of money — usu. used in pl.

mega·byte \-,bīt\ *n* [fr. the fact that 1,048,576 (2^{20}) is the power of 2 closest to one million] (1970) **:** a unit of computer information storage capacity equal to 1,048,576 bytes

mega·city \-,si-tē\ *n* (1968) **:** MEGALOPOLIS 1

mega·cor·po·ra·tion \,me-gə-,kȯr-pə-'rā-shən\ *n* (1973) **:** a huge and powerful corporation

mega·cy·cle \'me-gə-,sī-kəl\ *n* (1926) **:** one million cycles; *esp* **:** MEGAHERTZ

mega·deal \-,dēl\ *n* (1981) **:** a business deal involving a lot of money

mega·death \-,deth\ *n* (1953) **:** one million deaths — usu. used as a unit in reference to nuclear warfare

mega·dose \-,dōs\ *n* (1973) **:** a large dose (as of a vitamin)

mega·fau·na \-,fȯ-nə, -,fä-\ *n* (1935) **:** fauna consisting of individuals large enough to be visible to the naked eye — **mega·fau·nal** \-n⁷l\ *adj*

mega·ga·mete \,me-gə-'ga-,mēt *also* -gə-'mēt\ *n* (1891) **:** MACROGAMETE

mega·ga·me·to·phyte \-gə-'mē-tə-,fīt\ *n* (1933) **:** the female gametophyte produced by a megaspore

mega·hertz \'me-gə-,hərts, -,herts\ *n* [ISV] (1941) **:** a unit of frequency equal to one million hertz — abbr. *MHz*

mega·hit \-,hit\ *n* (1982) **:** something (as a motion picture) that is extremely successful

mega·kar·yo·cyte \,me-gə-'kar-ē-ō-,sīt\ *n* (1890) **:** a large cell that has a lobulated nucleus, is found esp. in the bone marrow, and is the source of blood platelets — **mega·kar·yo·cyt·ic** \-,kar-ē-ō-'si-tik\ *adj*

megal- *or* **megalo-** *comb form* [NL, fr. Gk, fr. *megal-*, *megas* — more at MUCH] **1 :** large **:** of giant size ⟨*megalopolis*⟩ **:** grandiose ⟨*megalomania*⟩

mega·lith \'me-gə-,lith\ *n* (1853) **:** a very large usu. rough stone used in prehistoric cultures as a monument or building block — **mega·lith·ic** \,me-gə-'li-thik\ *adj*

meg·a·lo·blast \'me-gə-lō-,blast\ *n* (1899) **:** a large erythroblast that appears in the blood esp. in pernicious anemia — **meg·a·lo·blas·tic** \,me-gə-lō-'blas-tik\ *adj*

meg·a·lo·ma·nia \,me-gə-lō-'mā-nē-ə, -nyə\ *n* [NL] (ca. 1890) **1 :** a mania for great or grandiose performance **2 :** a delusional mental disorder that is marked by infantile feelings of personal omnipotence and grandeur — **meg·a·lo·ma·ni·ac** \-'mā-nē-,ak\ *adj or n* — **meg·a·lo·ma·ni·a·cal** \-mə-'nī-ə-kəl\ *also* **meg·a·lo·man·ic** \-'ma-nik\ *adj* — **meg·a·lo·ma·ni·a·cal·ly** \-mə-'nī-ə-k(ə-)lē\ *adv*

meg·a·lop·o·lis \,me-gə-'lä-pə-ləs\ *n* (ca. 1828) **1 :** a very large city **2 :** a thickly populated region centering in a metropolis or embracing several metropolises — **meg·a·lo·pol·i·tan** \-,lä-'pä-lə-t⁷n\ *n or adj*

-megaly *n comb form* [NL *-megalia*, fr. Gk *megal-*, *megas*] **:** abnormal enlargement ⟨*hepatomegaly*⟩

mega·par·sec \,me-gə-'pär-,sek\ *n* [ISV] (1933) **:** a unit of measure for distances in intergalactic space equal to one million parsecs

¹mega·phone \'me-gə-,fōn\ *n* (1878) **:** a cone-shaped device used to intensify or direct the voice — **mega·phon·ic** \,me-gə-'fä-nik\ *adj*

²megaphone *vt* (1901) **:** to transmit or address through or as if through a megaphone ∼ *vi* **:** to speak through or as if through a megaphone

mega·proj·ect \-,prä-,jekt, -,jikt *also* -,prō-\ *n* (1982) **:** a major project or undertaking (as in business or construction)

Me·gar·i·an \mə-'gar-ē-ən, me-\ *adj* (1603) **:** of or relating to a Socratic school of philosophy founded by Euclid of Megara and noted for its subtle attention to logic — **Megarian** *n*

Me·gar·ic \-'gar-ik\ *adj* (1656) **:** MEGARIAN — **Megaric** *n*

mega·scop·ic \,me-gə-'skä-pik\ *adj* [*mega*- + *-scopic* (as in *microscopic*)] (1879) **1 :** MACROSCOPIC 1 ⟨∼ features of leaves⟩ **2 :** based on or relating to observations made with the unaided eye — **mega·scop·i·cal·ly** \-pi-k(ə-)lē\ *adv*

mega·spo·ran·gi·um \,me-gə-spə-'ran-jē-əm\ *n* [NL] (1886) **:** a sporangium that develops only megaspores

mega·spore \'me-gə-,spȯr, -,spȯr\ *n* [ISV] (1858) **:** a spore in heterosporous plants that gives rise to female gametophytes and is generally larger than a microspore — **mega·spor·ic** \,me-gə-'spȯr-ik, -'spȯr-\ *adj*

mega·spo·ro·gen·e·sis \,me-gə-,spȯr-ə-'je-nə-səs, -,spȯr-\ *n* [NL] (ca. 1928) **:** the formation and maturation of a megaspore

mega·spo·ro·phyll \-'spȯr-ə-,fil, -'spȯr-\ *n* (ca. 1899) **:** a sporophyll that develops only megasporangia

mega·star \'me-gə-,stär\ *n* (1975) **:** SUPERSTAR

mega·ton \'me-gə-,tən\ *n* (1952) **:** an explosive force equivalent to that of one million tons of TNT

mega·ton·nage \-,tə-nij\ *n* (1955) **:** the destructive capability expressed in megatons esp. of a collection of nuclear weapons

mega·vi·ta·min \,me-gə-'vī-tə-mən, *Brit usu* -'vi-\ *adj* (1970) **:** relating to or consisting of very large doses of vitamins ⟨∼ therapy⟩

mega·vi·ta·mins \-mənz\ *n pl* (1974) **:** a large quantity of vitamins

mega·watt \'me-gə-,wät\ *n* [ISV] (ca. 1900) **:** one million watts

me·gil·lah \mə-'gi-lə\ *n* [Yiddish *megile*, fr. Heb *mĕgillāh* scroll, volume (used esp. of the Book of Esther, read aloud at the Purim celebration)] (ca. 1952) *slang* **:** a long involved story or account ⟨the whole ∼⟩

me·gilp \mə-'gilp\ *n* [origin unknown] (1768) **:** a gelatinous preparation commonly of linseed oil and mastic varnish that is used by artists as a vehicle for oil colors

meg·ohm \'meg-,ōm\ *n* [ISV] (ca. 1868) **:** one million ohms

me·grim \'mē-grəm\ *n* [ME *migreime*, fr. MF *migraine* — more at MIGRAINE] (14c) **1 a :** MIGRAINE **b :** VERTIGO, DIZZINESS **2 a :** FANCY, WHIM **b** *pl* **:** low spirits

Mei·ji \'mā-(,)jē\ *n* [Jp, lit., enlightened rule] (1873) **:** the period of the reign (1868–1912) of Emperor Mutsuhito of Japan

mei·kle \'mē-kəl\ *var of* MICKLE

mei·ny *n, pl* **meinies** [ME *meynie* — more at MENIAL] (13c) **1** \'mā-nē\ *archaic* **:** RETINUE, COMPANY **2** \'men-yē\ *chiefly Scot* **:** MULTITUDE

mei·o·sis \mī-'ō-səs\ *n* [NL, fr. Gk *meiōsis* diminution, fr. *meioun* to diminish, fr. *meiōn* less; akin to Skt *miyate* he diminishes] (1550) **1 :** the presentation of a thing with underemphasis esp. in order to achieve a greater effect **:** UNDERSTATEMENT **2 :** the cellular process that results in the number of chromosomes in gamete-producing cells being reduced to one half and that involves a reduction division in which one of each pair of homologous chromosomes passes to each daughter cell and a mitotic division — compare MITOSIS — **mei·ot·ic** \mī-'ä-tik\ *adj* — **mei·ot·i·cal·ly** \-ti-k(ə-)lē\ *adv*

Meis·sen \'mī-s⁷n\ *n* [*Meissen*, Saxony, Germany] (1863) **:** a ceramic ware made at Meissen near Dresden; *esp* **:** a European porcelain developed under the patronage of the king of Saxony about 1715 and used for both ornamental and table wares — called also *Meissen china*, *Meissen ware*

Mei·ster·sing·er \'mīs-tər-,siŋ-ər, -,ziŋ-\ *n, pl* **Meistersinger** *or* **Meistersingers** [G, fr. MHG, fr. *meister* master + *singer* singer] (1845) **:** a member of any of various German guilds formed chiefly in the 15th and 16th centuries by workingmen and craftsmen for the cultivation of poetry and music

mel·a·mine \'me-lə-,mēn\ *n* [G *Melamin*] (ca. 1835) **1 :** a white crystalline organic base $C_3H_6N_6$ with a high melting point that is used esp. in melamine resins **2 :** a melamine resin or a plastic made from such a resin

melamine resin *n* (1939) **:** a thermosetting resin made from melamine and an aldehyde and used esp. in molded or laminated products, adhesives, and coatings

melan- *or* **melano-** *comb form* [ME, fr. MF, fr. LL, fr. Gk, fr. *melan-*, *melas*; perh. akin to Lith *mélynas* blue, Skt *malina* dirty] **1 :** black **:** dark ⟨*melanic*⟩ ⟨*melanin*⟩ **2 :** melanin ⟨*melanophore*⟩

mel·an·cho·lia \,me-lən-'kō-lē-ə\ *n* [NL, fr. LL, melancholy] (ca. 1693) **:** a mental condition characterized by extreme depression, bodily complaints, and often hallucinations and delusions; *esp* **:** a manic-depressive psychosis — **mel·an·cho·li·ac** \-lē-,ak\ *n*

mel·an·chol·ic \,me-lən-'kä-lik\ *adj* (14c) **1 :** of, relating to, or subject to melancholy **:** DEPRESSED **2 :** of or relating to melancholia **3 :** tending to depress the spirits **:** SADDENING — **melancholic** *n*

¹mel·an·choly \'me-lən-,kä-lē\ *n, pl* **-chol·ies** [ME *malencolie*, fr. MF *melancolie*, fr. LL *melancholia*, fr. Gk, fr. *melan-* + *cholē* bile — more at GALL] (14c) **1 a :** an abnormal state attributed to an excess of black bile and characterized by irascibility or depression **b :** BLACK BILE **c :** MELANCHOLIA **2 a :** depression of spirits **:** DEJECTION **b :** a pensive mood

²melancholy *adj* (14c) **1 a :** suggestive or expressive of melancholy ⟨sang in a ∼ voice⟩ **b :** causing or tending to cause sadness or depression of mind or spirit **:** DISMAL ⟨a ∼ thought⟩ **2 a :** depressed in spirits **:** DEJECTED, SAD **b :** PENSIVE

Mel·a·ne·sian \,me-lə-'nē-zhən, -shən\ *n* (1849) **1 :** a language group consisting of the Austronesian languages of Melanesia **2 :** a member of the dominant native group of Melanesia — **Melanesian** *adj*

mé·lange \mā-'läⁿzh, -'läⁿj\ *n* [F, fr. MF, fr. *mesler*, *meler* to mix — more at MEDDLE] (1653) **:** a mixture often of incongruous elements

¹me·lan·ic \mə-'la-nik\ *adj* (1826) **1 :** MELANOTIC **2 :** affected with or characterized by melanism

²melanic *n* (1952) **:** a melanic individual

mel·a·nin \'me-lə-nən\ *n* (1843) **:** a dark brown or black animal or plant pigment

mel·a·nism \'me-lə-,ni-zəm\ *n* (1843) **1 :** an increased amount of black or nearly black pigmentation (as of skin, feathers, or hair) of an

---

\ə\ abut \ᵊ\ kitten, F table \ər\ further \a\ ash \ā\ ace \ä\ mop, mar \aȯ\ out \ch\ chin \e\ bet \ē\ easy \g\ go \i\ hit \ī\ ice \j\ job \ŋ\ sing \ō\ go \ȯ\ law \ȯi\ boy \th\ thin \t̲h̲\ the \ü\ loot \u̇\ foot \y\ yet \zh\ vision \à, k̲, ⁿ, œ, œ̄, ᵫ, ᵿ\ *see* Guide to Pronunciation individual or kind of organism **2** : intense human pigmentation of the skin, eyes, and hair — **mel·a·nis·tic** \,me-lə-'nis-tik\ *adj*

mel·a·nite \'me-lə-,nīt\ *n* [G *Melanit*, fr. *melan-*] (ca. 1807) : a black andradite garnet — **mel·a·nit·ic** \,me-lə-'ni-tik\ *adj*

mel·a·nize \'me-lə-,nīz\ *vt* **-nized; -niz·ing** (1885) **1** : to convert into or infiltrate with melanin **2** : to make dark or black — **mel·a·ni·za·tion** \,me-lə-nə-'zā-shən\ *n*

me·la·no·blast \mə-'la-nə-,blast, 'me-lə-nō-\ *n* [ISV] (1901) : a cell that is a precursor to a melanocyte or melanophore

me·la·no·cyte \mə-'la-nə-,sīt, 'me-lə-nō-\ *n* [ISV] (ca. 1890) : an epidermal cell that produces melanin

melanocyte–stimulating hormone *n* (1953) : either of two vertebrate hormones of the pituitary gland esp. of reptiles and amphibians that darken the skin by stimulating melanin dispersion in pigment‑containing cells — called also *melanophore-stimulating hormone*

me·la·no·gen·e·sis \mə-,la-nə-'je-nə-səs, ,me-lə-nō-\ *n* [NL] (ca. 1928) : the formation of melanin

mel·a·no·ma \,me-lə-'nō-mə\ *n, pl* **-mas** *also* **-ma·ta** \-mə-tə\ [NL] (1830) : a usu. malignant tumor containing dark pigment

me·la·no·phore \mə-'la-nə-,fōr, 'me-lə-nō-, -,fȯr\ *n* (1903) : a melanin‑containing cell esp. of fishes, amphibians, and reptiles

me·la·no·some \-,sōm\ *n* (1940) : a melanin-producing granule in a melanocyte

mel·a·not·ic \,me-lə-'nä-tik\ *adj* (1829) : having or characterized by black pigmentation

mel·a·to·nin \,me-lə-'tō-nən\ *n* [Gk *melas* black + *-tonin* (as in *serotonin*)] (1958) : a vertebrate hormone of the pineal gland that produces lightening of the skin by causing concentration of melanin in pigment‑containing cells

mel·ba toast \'mel-bə-\ *n* [Nellie *Melba*] (1925) : very thin crisp toast

Mel·chite *or* **Mel·kite** \'mel-,kīt\ *n* [ML *Melchita*, fr. MGk *Melchitēs*, lit., royalist, fr. Syriac *malkā* king] (1619) **1** : an Eastern Christian chiefly of Syria and Egypt adhering to Chalcedonian orthodoxy in preference to Monophysitism **2** : a member of a Uniate body derived from the Melchites

¹Mel·chiz·e·dek \mel-'ki-zə-,dek\ *n* [Gk *Melchisedek*, fr. Heb *Malkīsedheq*] : a priest-king of Jerusalem who prepared a ritual meal for Abraham and received tithes from him

²Melchizedek *adj* (1842) : of or relating to the higher order of the Mormon priesthood

¹meld \'meld\ *vb* [G *melden* to announce, fr. OHG *meldōn*; akin to OE *meldian* to announce, Lith *malda* prayer] *vt* (1897) : to declare or announce (a card or combination of cards) for a score in a card game esp. by placing face up on the table ~ *vi* : to declare a card or combination of cards as a meld

²meld *n* (1897) : a card or combination of cards that is or can be melded in a card game

³meld *vb* [blend of *melt* and *weld*] (1936) : MERGE, BLEND

⁴meld *n* (1954) : BLEND, MIXTURE

me·lee *also* **mê·lée** \'mā-,lā, mā-'\ *n* [F *mêlée*, fr. OF *meslee*, fr. *mesler* to mix — more at MEDDLE] (ca. 1648) : a confused struggle; *esp* : a hand-to-hand fight among several people

mel·ic \'me-lik\ *adj* [L *melicus*, fr. Gk *melikos*, fr. *melos* song — more at MELODY] (1699) : of or relating to song : LYRIC; *esp* : of or relating to Greek lyric poetry of the 7th and 6th centuries B.C.

mel·i·lot \'me-lə-,lät\ *n* [ME *mellilot*, fr. OF *melilot*, fr. L *melilotos*, fr. Gk *melilōtos*, fr. *meli* honey + *lōtos* clover, lotus — more at MELLIFLUOUS] (14c) : SWEET CLOVER; *esp* : a yellow-flowered sweet clover (*Melilotus officinalis*)

me·lio·rate \'mēl-yə-,rāt, 'mē-lē-ə-\ *vb* **-rat·ed; -rat·ing** [LL *melioratus*, pp. of *meliorare*, fr. L *melior* better; akin to L *multus* much, Gk *mala* very] (1542) : AMELIORATE — **me·lio·ra·tion** \,mēl-yə-'rā-shən, ,mē-lē-ə-\ *n* — **me·lio·ra·tive** \'mēl-yə-,rā-tiv, 'mē-lē-ə-\ *adj* — **me·lio·ra·tor** \-,rā-tər\ *n*

me·lio·rism \'mēl-yə-,ri-zəm, 'mē-lē-ə-\ *n* (1877) : the belief that the world tends to become better and that humans can aid its betterment — **me·lio·rist** \-rist\ *adj or n* — **me·lio·ris·tic** \,mēl-yə-'ris-tik, ,mē-lē-ə-\ *adj*

me·lis·ma \mi-'liz-mə\ *n, pl* **-ma·ta** \-mə-tə\ [NL, fr. Gk, song, melody, fr. *melizein* to sing, fr. *melos* song] (ca. 1880) **1** : a group of notes or tones sung on one syllable in plainsong **2** : melodic embellishment or ornamentation **3** : CADENZA — **mel·is·mat·ic** \,me-ləz-'ma-tik\ *adj*

mell \'mel\ *vb* [ME, fr. MF *mesler*] (14c) : MIX

mel·lif·lu·ent \me-'li-flə-wənt\ *adj* [LL *mellifluent-, mellifluens*, fr. L *mell-, mel* + *fluent-, fluens*, prp. of *fluere*] (1601) : MELLIFLUOUS — **mel·lif·lu·ent·ly** *adv*

mel·lif·lu·ous \me-'li-flə-wəs, mə-\ *adj* [ME *mellyfluous*, fr. LL *mellifluus*, fr. L *mell-, mel* honey + *fluere* to flow; akin to Goth *milith* honey, Gk *melit-, meli*] (15c) **1** : having a smooth rich flow ⟨a ~ voice⟩ **2** : filled with something (as honey) that sweetens — **mel·lif·lu·ous·ly** *adv* — **mel·lif·lu·ous·ness** *n*

mel·lo·phone \'me-lə-,fōn\ *n* [¹*mellow* + *-phone*] (1926) : a valved brass instrument similar in form and range to the French horn

mel·lo·tron \'me-lə-,trän\ *n* [fr. *Mellotron*, a trademark] (1967) : an electronic keyboard instrument programmed to produce the tape‑recorded sounds usu. of orchestral instruments

¹mel·low \'me-(,)lō\ *adj* [ME *melowe*] (15c) **1** **a** *of a fruit* : tender and sweet because of ripeness **b** *of a wine* : well aged and pleasingly mild **2** **a** : made gentle by age or experience **b** : rich and full but free from garishness or stridency **c** : warmed and relaxed by or as if by liquor **d** : PLEASANT, AGREEABLE **e** : LAID-BACK **3** *of soil* : having a soft and loamy consistency — **mel·low·ly** *adv* — **mel·low·ness** *n*

²mellow *vt* (1572) : to make mellow ~ *vi* : to become mellow

me·lo·de·on \mə-'lō-dē-ən\ *n* [G *Melodion*, fr. *Melodie* melody, fr. OF] (1847) : a small reed organ in which a suction bellows draws air inward through the reeds

me·lod·ic \mə-'lä-dik\ *adj* (1823) : of or relating to melody : MELODIOUS — **me·lod·i·cal·ly** \-di-k(ə-)lē\ *adv*

me·lo·di·ous \mə-'lō-dē-əs\ *adj* (14c) **1** : having a pleasing melody **2** : of, relating to, or producing melody — **me·lo·di·ous·ly** *adv* — **me·lo·di·ous·ness** *n*

mel·o·dist \'me-lə-dist\ *n* (1789) **1** : SINGER **2** : a composer of melodies

mel·o·dize \'me-lə-,dīz\ *vb* **-dized; -diz·ing** *vi* (1662) : to compose a melody ~ *vt* : to make melodious : set to melody — **mel·o·diz·er** *n*

melo·dra·ma \'me-lə-,drä-mə, -,dra-\ *n* [modif. of F *mélodrame*, fr. Gk *melos* song + F *drame* drama, fr. LL *drama*] (1809) **1** **a** : a work (as a movie or play) characterized by extravagant theatricality and by the predominance of plot and physical action over characterization **b** : the genre of dramatic literature constituted by such works **2** : something resembling a melodrama or having a melodramatic quality — **melo·dra·ma·tist** \,me-lə-'dra-mə-tist, -'drä-\ *n*

melo·dra·mat·ic \,me-lə-drə-'ma-tik\ *adj* (1816) **1** : of, relating to, or characteristic of melodrama **2** : appealing to the emotions : SENSATIONAL *syn* see DRAMATIC — **melo·dra·mat·i·cal·ly** \-ti-k(ə-)lē\ *adv*

melo·dra·mat·ics \-tiks\ *n pl but sing or pl in constr* (1915) : melodramatic conduct or writing

melo·dra·ma·tise *Brit var of* MELODRAMATIZE

melo·dra·ma·tize \,me-lə-'dra-mə-,tīz, -'drä-\ *vt* (1820) **1** : to make melodramatic ⟨~ a situation⟩ **2** : to make a melodrama of (as a novel) — **melo·dra·ma·ti·za·tion** \,dra-mə-tə-'zā-shən, -,drä-\ *n*

mel·o·dy \'me-lə-dē\ *n, pl* **-dies** [ME *melodie*, fr. OF, fr. LL *melodia*, fr. Gk *melōidia* chanting, music, fr. *melos* limb, musical phrase, song (prob. akin to Bret *mell* joint) + *aeidein* to sing — more at ODE] (13c) **1** : a sweet or agreeable succession or arrangement of sounds : TUNEFULNESS **2** : a rhythmic succession of single tones organized as an aesthetic whole

mel·on \'me-lən\ *n, often attrib* [ME, fr. MF, fr. LL *melon-, melo*, short for L *melopepon-, melopepo*, fr. Gk *mēlopepōn*, fr. *mēlon* apple + *pepōn*, an edible gourd — more at PUMPKIN] (14c) **1** : any of various gourds (as a muskmelon or watermelon) usu. eaten raw as fruits **2** : something rounded like a melon: as **a** : the rounded organ in the front of the head of some cetaceans **b** *pl, slang* : large breasts **3** **a** : a surplus of profits available for distribution to stockholders **b** : a financial windfall

mel·pha·lan \'mel-fə-,lan\ *n* [prob. fr. *methanol* + *phenylalanine*] (ca. 1964) : an antineoplastic drug $C_{13}H_{18}Cl_2N_2O_2$

Mel·pom·e·ne \mel-'pä-mə-(,)nē\ *n* [L, fr. Gk *Melpomenē*] : the Greek Muse of tragedy

¹melt \'melt\ *vb* [ME, fr. OE *meltan*; akin to ON *melta* to digest, Gk *meldein* to melt] *vi* (bef. 12c) **1** : to become altered from a solid to a liquid state usu. by heat **2** **a** : DISSOLVE, DISINTEGRATE ⟨the sugar ~ed in the coffee⟩ **b** : to disappear as if by dissolving ⟨her anger ~ed at his kind words⟩ **3** *obs* : to become subdued or crushed (as by sorrow) **4** : to become mild, tender, or gentle **5** : to lose outline or distinctness : BLEND ~ *vt* **1** : to reduce from a solid to a liquid state usu. by heat **2** : to cause to disappear or disperse **3** : to make tender or gentle : SOFTEN — **melt·abil·i·ty** \,mel-tə-'bi-lə-tē\ *n* — **melt·able** \'mel-tə-bəl\ *adj* — **melt·er** *n*

²melt *n* (1854) **1** **a** : material in the molten state **b** : the mass melted at a single operation or the quantity melted during a specified period **2** **a** : the action or process of melting or the period during which it occurs ⟨the spring ~⟩ **b** : the condition of being melted **3** : a sandwich with melted cheese ⟨a tuna ~⟩

³melt *n* [ME *milte*, fr. OE; akin to OHG *miltzi* spleen] (bef. 12c) : SPLEEN; *esp* : spleen of slaughtered animals for use as feed or food

melt·down \'melt-,daȯn\ *n* (1963) **1** : the accidental melting of the core of a nuclear reactor **2** : a rapid or disastrous decline or collapse

melt·ing \'mel-tiŋ\ *adj* (1565) : TENDER, DELICATE ⟨a love song's ~ lyric⟩ — **melt·ing·ly** *adv*

melting point *n* (1823) : the temperature at which a solid melts

melting pot *n* (1912) **1** **a** : a place where racial amalgamation and social and cultural assimilation are going on ⟨long cherished the myth of the public school as the *melting pot* —M. R. Berube⟩ **b** : the population of such a place **2** : a process of blending that often results in invigoration or novelty

mel·ton \'mel-tⁿn\ *n* [*Melton* Mowbray, town in England] (1823) : a heavy smooth woolen fabric with short nap

melt·wa·ter \'melt-,wȯ-tər, -,wä-\ *n* (1923) : water derived from the melting of ice and snow

mem \'mem\ *n* [Heb *mēm*, lit., water] (ca. 1823) : the 13th letter of the Hebrew alphabet — see ALPHABET table

mem·ber \'mem-bər\ *n, often attrib* [ME *membre*, fr. OF, fr. L *membrum*; akin to Goth *mimz* flesh, Gk *mēros* thigh] (14c) **1** : a body part or organ: as **a** : LIMB **b** : PENIS : a unit of structure in a plant body **2** : one of the individuals composing a group **3** : a person baptized or enrolled in a church **4** : a constituent part of a whole: as **a** : a syntactic or rhythmic unit of a sentence : CLAUSE **b** : one of the propositions of a syllogism **c** : one of the elements of a set or class **d** : either of the equated elements in a mathematical equation *syn* see PART

mem·bered \'mem-bərd\ *adj* (14c) : made up of or divided into members

mem·ber·ship \'mem-bər-,ship\ *n* (1647) **1** : the state or status of being a member **2** : the body of members ⟨an organization with a large ~⟩ **3** : the relation between an element of a set or class and the set or class — compare INCLUSION 3

mem·brane \'mem-,brān\ *n* [ME, fr. L *membrana* skin, parchment, fr. *membrum*] (15c) **1** : a thin soft pliable sheet or layer esp. of animal or plant origin **2** : a piece of parchment forming part of a roll — **mem·braned** \'mem-,brānd\ *adj*

mem·bra·nous \'mem-brə-nəs\ *adj* (1597) **1** : of, relating to, or resembling membrane **2** : thin, pliable, and often somewhat transparent ⟨~ leaves⟩ **3** : characterized or accompanied by the formation of a usu. abnormal membrane or membranous layer ⟨~ croup⟩ — **mem·bra·nous·ly** *adv*

membranous labyrinth *n* (1840) : the sensory structures of the inner ear

me·men·to \mə-'men-(,)tō, ÷mō-\ *n, pl* **-tos** *or* **-toes** [ME, fr. L, remember, imper. of *meminisse* to remember; akin to L *ment-, mens* mind — more at MIND] (1580) : something that serves to warn or remind; *also* : SOUVENIR

me·men·to mo·ri \mə-'men-tō-'mȯr-ē, -'mȯr-ē\ *n, pl* memento mori [L, remember that you must die] (1596) : a reminder of mortality; *esp* : DEATH'S-HEAD

Mem·non \'mem-,nän\ *n* [Gk *Memnōn*] : an Ethiopian king slain by Achilles at a late stage of the Trojan War

memo \'me-(,)mō\ *n, pl* **mem·os** (1889) : MEMORANDUM

mem·oir \'mem-ˌwär, -ˌwȯr\ *n* [MF *memoire*, fr. *memoire* memory, fr. L *memoria*] (1567) **1** : an official note or report : MEMORANDUM **2 a** : a narrative composed from personal experience **b** : AUTOBIOGRAPHY — usu. used in pl. **c** : BIOGRAPHY **3 a** : an account of something noteworthy : REPORT **b** *pl* : the record of the proceedings of a learned society — **mem·oir·ist** \-ist\ *n*

mem·o·ra·bil·ia \ˌme-mə-rə-'bil-ē-ə, -'bē-lē-ə, -'bil-yə\ *n pl* [L, fr. neut. pl. of *memorabilis*] (ca. 1807) : things that are remarkable and worthy of remembrance; *also* : things that stir recollection : MEMENTOS

mem·o·ra·bil·i·ty \-'bi-lə-tē\ *n* (ca. 1661) : the quality or state of being easy to remember or worth remembering

mem·o·ra·ble \'mem-rə-bəl, 'mə-mə-rə-, 'me-mər-\ *adj* [ME, fr. L *memorabilis*, fr. *memorare* to remind, mention, fr. *memor* mindful] (15c) : worth remembering : NOTABLE — **mem·o·ra·ble·ness** *n* — **mem·o·ra·bly** \-blē\ *adv*

mem·o·ran·dum \ˌme-mə-'ran-dəm\ *n, pl* **-dums** *or* **-da** \-də\ [ME, to be remembered, fr. L, neut. of *memorandus*, gerundive of *memorare*] (ca. 1543) **1** : an informal record; *also* : a written reminder **2** : an informal written note of a transaction or proposed instrument **3 a** : an informal diplomatic communication **b** : a usu. brief communication written for interoffice circulation **c** : a communication that contains directive, advisory, or informative matter

usage Although some commentators warn against the use of *memoranda* as a singular and condemn the plural *memorandas*, our evidence indicates that these forms are rarely encountered in print. We have a little evidence of the confusion of forms, including use of *memorandum* as a plural, in speech (as at congressional hearings). As plurals *memoranda* and *memorandums* are about equally frequent.

¹me·mo·ri·al \mə-'mȯr-ē-əl, -'mȯr-\ *adj* [ME, fr. L *memorialis*, fr. *memoria* memory] (14c) **1** : serving to preserve remembrance : COMMEMORATIVE **2** : of or relating to memory — **me·mo·ri·al·ly** \-ə-lē\ *adv*

²memorial *n* (14c) **1** : something that keeps remembrance alive: as **a** : MONUMENT **b** : something (as a speech or ceremony) that commemorates **c** : KEEPSAKE, MEMENTO **2 a** : RECORD, MEMOIR ⟨language and literature . . . the ∼s of another age —J. H. Fisher⟩ **b** : MEMORANDUM, NOTE; *specif* : a legal abstract **c** : a statement of facts addressed to a government and often accompanied by a petition or remonstrance

Memorial Day *n* (1869) **1** : May 30 formerly observed as a legal holiday in most states of the U.S. in remembrance of war dead **2** : the last Monday in May observed as a legal holiday in most states of the U.S. **3** : CONFEDERATE MEMORIAL DAY

me·mo·ri·al·ise *Brit var of* MEMORIALIZE

me·mo·ri·al·ist \mə-'mȯr-ē-ə-list, -'mȯr-\ *n* (1706) **1** : a person who writes or signs a memorial **2** : a person who writes a memoir

me·mo·ri·al·ize \-ˌliz\ *vt* **-ized; -iz·ing** (1798) **1** : to address or petition by a memorial **2** : COMMEMORATE

memorial park *n* (ca. 1928) : CEMETERY

me·mo·ri·ter \mə-'mȯr-ə-ˌter, -'mär-\ *adj* [L, adv., by memory, fr. *memor*] (ca. 1742) : marked by emphasis on memorization

mem·o·rise *Brit var of* MEMORIZE

mem·o·rize \'me-mə-ˌriz\ *vt* **-rized; -riz·ing** (1838) : to commit to memory : learn by heart — **mem·o·riz·able** \ˌme-mə-'rī-zə-bəl\ *adj* — **mem·o·ri·za·tion** \ˌme-mə-rə-'zā-shən, ˌme-mə-(ˌ)rī-, ˌmem-rə-\ *n* — **mem·o·riz·er** *n*

mem·o·ry \'mem-rē, 'me-mə-\ *n, pl* **-ries** [ME *memorie*, fr. MF *memoire*, fr. L *memoria*, fr. *memor* mindful; akin to OE *gemimor* well-known, Gk *mermēra* care, Skt *smarati* he remembers] (14c) **1 a** : the power or process of reproducing or recalling what has been learned and retained esp. through associative mechanisms **b** : the store of things learned and retained from an organism's activity or experience as evidenced by modification of structure or behavior or by recall and recognition **2 a** : commemorative remembrance ⟨erected a statue in ∼ of the hero⟩ **b** : the fact or condition of being remembered ⟨days of recent ∼⟩ **3 a** : a particular act of recall or recollection **b** : an image or impression of one that is remembered ⟨fond *memories* of her youth⟩ **c** : the time within which past events can be or are remembered ⟨within the ∼ of living men⟩ **4 a** : a device or a component of a device in which information esp. for a computer can be inserted and stored and from which it may be extracted when wanted **b** : capacity for storing information ⟨four megabytes of ∼⟩ **5** : a capacity for showing effects as the result of past treatment or for returning to a former condition — used esp. of a material (as metal or plastic)

syn MEMORY, REMEMBRANCE, RECOLLECTION, REMINISCENCE mean the capacity for or the act of remembering, or the thing remembered. MEMORY applies both to the power of remembering and to what is remembered ⟨gifted with a remarkable *memory*⟩ ⟨that incident was now just a distant *memory*⟩. REMEMBRANCE applies to the act of remembering or the fact of being remembered ⟨any *remembrance* of his deceased wife was painful⟩. RECOLLECTION adds an implication of consciously bringing back to mind often with some effort ⟨after a moment's *recollection* he produced the name⟩. REMINISCENCE suggests the recalling of usu. pleasant incidents, experiences, or feelings from a remote past ⟨recorded my grandmother's *reminiscences* of her Iowa girlhood⟩.

memory lane *n* (1954) : an imaginary path through the nostalgically remembered past — usu. used in such phrases as *a walk down memory lane*

memory trace *n* (1923) : ENGRAM

mem·sa·hib \'mem-ˌsä-(ˌh)ib, -ˌsäb\ *n* [Hindi, fr. E *ma'am* + Hindi *sahib* sahib] (1857) : a white foreign woman of high social status living in India; *esp* : the wife of a British official

men *pl of* MAN

men- *or* **meno-** *comb form* [NL, fr. Gk *mēn* month — more at MOON] : menstruation ⟨*menorrhagia*⟩

¹men·ace \'me-nəs\ *n* [ME, fr. MF, fr. L *minacia*, fr. *minac-, minax* threatening, fr. *minari* to threaten — more at MOUNT] (14c) **1** : a show of intention to inflict harm : THREAT **2 a** : one that represents a threat : DANGER **b** : a person who causes annoyance

²menace *vb* **men·aced; men·ac·ing** *vt* (14c) **1** : to make a show of intention to harm **2** : to represent or pose a threat to : ENDANGER ∼ *vi* : to act in a threatening manner — **men·ac·ing·ly** \-nə-siŋ-lē\ *adv*

me·nad *var of* MAENAD

men·a·di·one \ˌme-nə-'dī-ˌōn, -dī-'\ *n* [*methyl* + *naphthalene* + *di-* + *ketone*] (1941) : a yellow crystalline compound $C_{11}H_8O_2$ with the biological activity of natural vitamin K

mé·nage \mā-'näzh\ *n* [F, fr. OF *mesnage* dwelling, fr. (assumed) VL *mansionaticum*, fr. L *mansion-, mansio* mansion] (1698) : a domestic establishment : HOUSEHOLD; *also* : HOUSEKEEPING

mé·nage à trois \-ä-'trwä\ *n* [F, lit., household for three] (1891) : an arrangement in which three persons (as a married pair and the lover of one of the pair) share sexual relations esp. while living together

me·nag·er·ie \mə-'naj-rē, -'na-jə- *also* -'nazh-rē, -'na-zhə-\ *n* [F *ménagerie*, fr. MF, management of a household or farm, fr. *menage*] (1676) **1 a** : a place where animals are kept and trained esp. for exhibition **b** : a collection of wild or foreign animals kept esp. for exhibition **2** : a varied mixture ⟨a wonderful ∼ of royal hangers-on —V. S. Pritchett⟩

men·ar·che \'me-ˌnär-kē\ *n* [NL, fr. *men-* + Gk *archē* beginning] (1900) : the beginning of the menstrual function; *esp* : the first menstrual period of an individual — **men·ar·che·al** \me-'när-'kē-əl\ *adj*

¹mend \'mend\ *vb* [ME, short for *amenden* — more at AMEND] *vt* (13c) **1** : to free from faults or defects: as **a** : to improve in manners or morals : REFORM **b** : to set right : CORRECT **c** : to put into good shape or working order again : patch up : REPAIR **d** : to improve or strengthen (as a relationship) by negotiation or conciliation — used chiefly in the phrase *mend fences* ⟨spends the weekend ∼*ing* political fences —E. O. Hauser⟩ **e** : to restore to health : CURE **2** : to make amends or atonement for ⟨least said, soonest ∼*ed*⟩ ∼ *vi* **1** : to improve morally : REFORM **2** : to become corrected or improved **3** : to improve in health; *also* : HEAL — **mend·able** \'men-də-bəl\ *adj* — **mend·er** *n*

syn MEND, REPAIR, PATCH, REBUILD mean to put into good order something that has been injured, damaged, or defective. MEND implies making whole or sound something broken, torn, or injured ⟨*mended* the torn dress⟩. REPAIR applies to the fixing of more extensive damage or dilapidation ⟨*repaired* the back steps⟩. PATCH implies an often temporary fixing of a hole or break with new material ⟨*patch* worn jeans⟩. REBUILD suggests making like new without completely replacing ⟨a *rebuilt* automobile engine⟩.

²mend *n* (14c) **1** : an act of mending : REPAIR **2** : a mended place — **on the mend** : getting better : IMPROVING

men·da·cious \men-'dā-shəs\ *adj* [L *mendac-, mendax* — more at AMEND] (1616) : given to or characterized by deception or falsehood or divergence from absolute truth ⟨∼ tales of his adventures⟩ *syn* see DISHONEST — **men·da·cious·ly** *adv* — **men·da·cious·ness** *n*

men·dac·i·ty \men-'da-sə-tē\ *n, pl* **-ties** (1646) **1** : the quality or state of being mendacious **2** : LIE

Men·de \'men-dē, -dā\ *n, pl* **Mende** *or* **Mendes** (1732) **1** : a Mande language of southern Sierra Leone and eastern Liberia **2** : a member of a people speaking Mende

men·de·le·vi·um \ˌmen-də-'lē-vē-əm, -'lā-\ *n* [NL, fr. Dmitry *Mendeleyev*] (1955) : a radioactive element that is artificially produced — see ELEMENT table

Men·de·lian \men-'dē-lē-ən, -'dēl-yən\ *adj* (1901) : of, relating to, or according with Mendel's laws or Mendelism — **Mendelian** *n*

Mendelian factor *n* (1927) : GENE

Mendelian inheritance *n* (ca. 1923) : PARTICULATE INHERITANCE

Men·del·ism \'men-d²l-ˌi-zəm\ *n* (1903) : the principles or the operations of Mendel's laws; *also* : PARTICULATE INHERITANCE — **Men·del·ist** \-d²l-ist\ *adj or n*

Men·del's law \'men-d²lz-\ *n* [Gregor *Mendel*] (1903) **1** : a principle in genetics: hereditary units occur in pairs that separate during gamete formation so that every gamete receives but one member of a pair — called also *law of segregation* **2** : a principle in genetics limited and modified by the subsequent discovery of the phenomenon of linkage: the different pairs of hereditary units are distributed to the gametes independently of each other, the gametes combine at random, and the various combinations of hereditary pairs occur in the zygotes according to the laws of chance — called also *law of independent assortment* **3** : a principle in genetics proved subsequently to be subject to many limitations: because one of each pair of hereditary units dominates the other in expression, characters are inherited alternatively on an all-or-nothing basis — called also *law of dominance*

men·di·can·cy \'men-di-kən(t)-sē\ *n* (1790) **1** : the condition of being a beggar **2** : the practice of begging

men·di·cant \'men-di-kənt\ *n* [ME, fr. L *mendicant-, mendicans*, prp. of *mendicare* to beg, fr. *mendicus* beggar — more at AMEND] (14c) **1** : BEGGAR 1 **2** *often cap* : a member of a religious order (as the Franciscans) combining monastic life and outside religious activity and orig. owning neither personal nor community property : FRIAR — **mendicant** *adj*

men·dic·i·ty \men-'di-sə-tē\ *n* [ME *mendicite*, fr. MF *mendicité*, fr. L *mendicitat-, mendicitas*, fr. *mendicus*] (15c) : MENDICANCY

Men·e·la·us \ˌme-nə-³l-'ā-əs\ *n* [L, fr. Gk *Menelaos*] : a king of Sparta, brother of Agamemnon, and husband of the abducted Helen of Troy

men·folk \'men-ˌfōk\ *or* **men·folks** \-ˌfōks\ *n pl* (1802) **1** : men in general **2** : the men of a family or community

men·ha·den \men-'hā-d²n, mən-\ *n, pl* **-den** *also* **-dens** [of Algonquian origin; akin to Narraganset *munnawhatteaûg* menhaden] (1792) : a marine fish (*Brevoortia tyrannus*) of the herring family abundant along the Atlantic coast of the U.S. where it is used for bait or converted into oil and fertilizer; *also* : any of several congeneric fishes

men·hir \'men-ˌhir\ *n* [F, fr. Bret. *men* stone + *hir* long] (1840) : a single upright rude monolith usu. of prehistoric origin

¹me·nial \'mē-nē-əl, -nyəl\ *n* (14c) : a person doing menial work; *specif* : a domestic servant or retainer

²menial *adj* [ME *meynial*, fr. *meynie* household, retinue, fr. OF *mesnie*, fr. (assumed) VL *mansionata*, fr. L *mansion-, mansio* dwelling — more at MANSION] (15c) **1** : of or relating to servants : LOWLY **2 a** : ap-

\ə\ abut \ᵊ\ kitten, F table \ər\ further \a\ ash \ā\ ace \ä\ mop, mar
\aù\ out \ch\ chin \e\ bet \ē\ easy \g\ go \i\ hit \ī\ ice \j\ job
\ŋ\ sing \ō\ go \ȯ\ law \ȯi\ boy \th\ thin \t̷h\ the \ü\ loot \ù\ foot
\y\ yet \zh\ vision \ä, k̲, ⁿ, œ, œ̄, ue, ūe, ᵝ\ see Guide to Pronunciation

propriate to a servant : HUMBLE, SERVILE ⟨answered in ∼ tones⟩ **b** : lacking interest or dignity ⟨a ∼ task⟩ — **me·nial·ly** *adv*

Mé·nière's disease \mən-'yerz-, 'men-yərz-\ *n* [Prosper *Ménière* †1862 Fr. physician] (1876) : a disorder of the membranous labyrinth of the inner ear that is marked by recurrent attacks of dizziness, tinnitus, and deafness — called also *Ménière's syndrome*

mening- *or* **meningo-** *also* **meningi-** *comb form* [NL, fr. *mening-, meninx*] **1** : meninges ⟨*meningo*coccus⟩ ⟨*mening*itis⟩ **2** : meninges and ⟨*meningo*encephalitis⟩

men·in·ge·al \,me-nən-'jē-əl\ *adj* (1829) : of, relating to, or affecting the meninges

meninges *pl of* MENINX

me·nin·gi·o·ma \mə-,nin-jē-'ō-mə\ *n, pl* **-mas** *or* **-ma·ta** \-'ō-mə-tə\ [NL] (1922) : a slow-growing encapsulated tumor arising from the meninges and often causing damage by pressing upon the brain and adjacent parts

men·in·gi·tis \,me-nən-'jī-təs\ *n, pl* **-git·i·des** \-'ji-tə-,dēz\ [NL] (1828) **1** : inflammation of the meninges and esp. of the pia mater and the arachnoid **2** : a usu. bacterial disease in which inflammation of the meninges occurs — **men·in·git·ic** \-'ji-tik\ *adj*

me·nin·go·coc·cus \mə-,nin-gə-'kä-kəs, -,nin-jə-\ *n, pl* **-coc·ci** \-'käk-,sī, -,sē; -'kä-,kī, -,kē\ [NL] (ca. 1893) : the bacterium (*Neisseria meningitidis*) that causes cerebrospinal meningitis — **me·nin·go·coc·cal** \-'käk-səl\ *also* **me·nin·go·coc·cic** \-'käk-sik, -'kä-kik\ *adj*

me·nin·go·en·ceph·a·li·tis \-gō-ən,se-fə-'li-təs, -jō-\ *n, pl* **-lit·i·des** \-'li-tə-,dēz\ [NL] (ca. 1860) : inflammation of the brain and meninges — **me·nin·go·en·ceph·a·lit·ic** \-'li-tik\ *adj*

me·ninx \'mē-niŋ(k)s, 'me-\ *n, pl* **me·nin·ges** \mə-'nin-(,)jēz\ [NL, fr. Gk *mēning-, mēninx* membrane] (1543) : any of the three membranes that envelop the brain and spinal cord

me·nis·cus \mə-'nis-kəs\ *n, pl* **me·nis·ci** \-'ni-,skī, -,skē, -,sī\ *also* **me·nis·cus·es** [NL, fr. Gk *mēniskos*, fr. dim. of *mēnē* moon, crescent — more at MOON] (1693) **1** : a concavo-convex lens **2** : a crescent or crescent-shaped body **3** : the curved upper surface of a column of liquid **4** : a fibrous cartilage within a joint esp. of the knee

Men·no·nite \'me-nə-,nīt\ *n* [G *Mennonit*, fr. *Menno* Simons] (1565) : a member of any of various Protestant groups derived from the Anabaptist movement in Holland and characterized by congregational autonomy and rejection of military service

meno- — see MEN-

me·no mos·so \,mā-nō-'mò(s)-(,)sō\ *adv* [It] (ca. 1854) : less rapid — used as a direction in music

men·o·pause \'me-nə-,pòz, 'mē-\ *n* [F *ménopause*, fr. *méno-* men- + *pause* stop, pause] (1872) : the period of natural cessation of menstruation occurring usu. between the ages of 45 and 50 — **men·o·paus·al** \,me-nə-'pò-zəl, ,mē-\ *adj*

me·no·rah \mə-'nòr-ə, -'nòr-\ *n* [Heb *mĕnōrāh* candlestick] (1888) : a candelabrum with seven or nine candles that is used in Jewish worship

men·or·rha·gia \,me-nə-'rä-j(ē-)ə, -'rä-zhə; -'rä-jə, -zhə\ *n* [NL] (ca. 1784) : abnormally profuse menstrual flow

men·sal \'men(t)-səl\ *adj* [ME, fr. LL *mensalis*, fr. L *mensa* table] (15c) : of, relating to, or done at the table

mensch \'men(t)sh\ *n* [Yiddish *mentsh* human being, fr. MHG *mensch*, fr. OHG *mennisco*; akin to OE *man* human being, man] (1953) : a person of integrity and honor

¹mense \'men(t)s\ *n* [ME *menske* honor, fr. ON *mennska* humanity; akin to OE *man* man] (1500) *chiefly Scot* : PROPRIETY — **mense·ful** \-fəl\ *adj* — **mense·less** \-ləs\ *adj*

²mense *vt* **mensed; mens·ing** (1540) *chiefly Scot* : to do honor to : GRACE

men·ses \'men-,sēz\ *n pl but sing or pl in constr* [L, lit., months, pl. of *mensis* month — more at MOON] (1597) : the menstrual flow

Men·she·vik \'men(t)-shə-,vik, -,vēk\ *n, pl* **Mensheviks** *or* **Men·she·vi·ki** \,men(t)-shə-'vi-kē, -'vē-kē\ [Russ *men'shevik*, fr. *men'she* less; fr. their forming the minority group of the party] (1907) : a member of a wing of the Russian Social Democratic party before and during the Russian Revolution believing in the gradual achievement of socialism by parliamentary methods in opposition to the Bolsheviks — **Men·she·vism** \'men(t)-shə-,vi-zəm\ *n* — **Men·she·vist** \-vist\ *n or adj*

mens rea \'menz-'rē-ə\ *n* [NL, lit., guilty mind] (1861) : criminal intent

men's room *n* (1929) : a room equipped with one or more sinks, toilets, and usu. urinals for the use of men and boys

men·stru·al \'men(t)-strü-əl, -strəl\ *adj* (14c) : of or relating to menstruation

men·stru·ate \'men(t)-strü-,wāt, 'men-,strāt\ *vi* **-at·ed; -at·ing** [LL *menstruatus*, pp. of *menstruari*, fr. L *menstrua* menses, fr. neut. pl. of *menstruus* monthly, fr. *mensis*] (1800) : to undergo menstruation

men·stru·a·tion \,men(t)-strü-'wā-shən, men-'strä-\ *n* (ca. 1784) : a discharging of blood, secretions, and tissue debris from the uterus that recurs in nonpregnant breeding-age primate females at approximately monthly intervals and that is considered to represent a readjustment of the uterus to the nonpregnant state following proliferative changes accompanying the preceding ovulation; *also* : PERIOD 6c

men·stru·um \'men(t)-strü-əm, -strəm\ *n, pl* **-stru·ums** *or* **-strua** \-strü-ə, -strə\ [ML, lit., menses, alter. of L *menstrua*] (1612) : a substance that dissolves a solid or holds it in suspension : SOLVENT

men·su·ra·ble \'men(t)s-rə-bəl, 'men(t)sh-; 'men(t)-sə-rə-, -shə-\ *adj* [LL *mensurabilis*, fr. *mensurare* to measure, fr. L *mensura* measure — more at MEASURE] (1604) **1** : capable of being measured : MEASURABLE **2** : MENSURAL 1 — **men·sur·abil·i·ty** \,men(t)s-rə-'bi-lə-tē, ,men(t)sh-; ,men(t)-sə-rə-, -shə-\ *n*

men·su·ral \'men(t)s-rəl, 'men(t)sh-; 'men(t)-sə-rəl, -shə-\ *adj* [LL *mensuralis* measurable, fr. L *mensura*] (1609) **1** : of, relating to, or being polyphonic music originating in the 13th century with each note having a definite and exact time value **2** : of or relating to measure

men·su·ra·tion \,men(t)-sə-'rā-shən, -shə-\ *n* (1571) **1** : the act of measuring : MEASUREMENT **2** : geometry applied to the computation of lengths, areas, or volumes from given dimensions or angles

mens·wear \'menz-,war, -,wer\ *n* (1908) : clothing for men

-ment \mənt; *in verbs derived by functional shift* (*as* ²ORNAMENT) ,ment *also* mənt\ *n suffix* [ME, fr. OF, fr. L *-mentum*; akin to L *-men*, suffix denoting concrete result, Gk *-mat-, -ma*] **1 a** : concrete result, object, or agent of a (specified) action ⟨embank*ment*⟩ ⟨entangle*ment*⟩ **b** : concrete means or instrument of a (specified) action ⟨entertain*ment*⟩ **2 a** : action : process ⟨encircle*ment*⟩ ⟨develop*ment*⟩ **b** : place of a (specified) action ⟨encamp*ment*⟩ **3** : state or condition resulting from (a specified action) ⟨involve*ment*⟩

¹men·tal \'men-t³l\ *adj* [ME, fr. MF, fr. LL *mentalis*, fr. L *ment-, mens* mind — more at MIND] (15c) **1 a** : of or relating to the mind; *specif* : of or relating to the total emotional and intellectual response of an individual to external reality ⟨∼ health⟩ **b** : of or relating to intellectual as contrasted with emotional activity **c** : of, relating to, or being intellectual as contrasted with overt physical activity **d** : occurring or experienced in the mind : INNER ⟨∼ anguish⟩ **e** : relating to the mind, its activity, or its products as an object of study : IDEOLOGICAL **f** : relating to spirit or idea as opposed to matter **2 a** (1) : of, relating to, or affected by a psychiatric disorder ⟨a ∼ patient⟩ ⟨∼ illness⟩ (2) : mentally disordered : MAD, CRAZY **b** : intended for the care or treatment of persons affected by psychiatric disorders ⟨∼ hospitals⟩ **3** : of or relating to telepathic or mind-reading powers — **men·tal·ly** \-t³l-ē\ *adv*

²mental *adj* [L *mentum* chin — more at MOUTH] (ca. 1727) : of or relating to the chin : GENIAL

mental age *n* (1912) : a measure used in psychological testing that expresses an individual's mental attainment in terms of the number of years it takes an average child to reach the same level

mental deficiency *n* (1856) : MENTAL RETARDATION

men·tal·ist \'men-t³l-ist\ *n* (1930) : MIND READER

men·tal·is·tic \,men-t³l-'is-tik\ *adj* (1882) **1** : of or relating to any school of psychology or psychiatry that in contrast to behaviorism values subjective data (as those gained by introspection) in the study and explanation of behavior **2** : of or relating to mental phenomena — **men·tal·ism** \'men-t³l-,i-zəm\ *n*

men·tal·i·ty \men-'ta-lə-tē\ *n, pl* **-ties** (1691) **1** : mental power or capacity : INTELLIGENCE **2** : mode or way of thought : OUTLOOK

mental retardation *n* (1914) : subaverage intellectual ability that is equivalent to or less than an IQ of 70, is present from birth or infancy, and is manifested esp. by abnormal development, by learning difficulties, and by problems in social adjustment

men·ta·tion \men-'tā-shən\ *n* [L *ment-, mens* + E *-ation*] (1850) : mental activity

men·thol \'men-,thòl, -,thōl\ *n* [G, ultim. fr. L *mentha* mint] (1876) : a crystalline alcohol $C_{10}H_{20}O$ that occurs esp. in mint oils and has the odor and cooling properties of peppermint

men·tho·lat·ed \'men(t)-thə-,lā-təd\ *adj* (1922) : containing or impregnated with menthol ⟨a ∼ salve⟩

¹men·tion \'men(t)-shən\ *n* [ME *mencioun*, fr. MF *mention*, fr. L *mention-, mentio;* akin to L *meminisse* to remember, *ment-, mens* mind] (14c) **1** : the act or an instance of citing or calling attention to someone or something esp. in a casual or incidental manner **2** : formal citation for outstanding achievement

²mention *vt* **men·tioned; men·tion·ing** \'men(t)-sh(ə-)niŋ\ (1530) : to make mention of : refer to; *also* : to cite for outstanding achievement — **men·tion·able** \'men(t)-sh(ə-)nə-bəl\ *adj* — **men·tion·er** \-sh(ə-)nər\ *n* — **not to mention** : to say nothing of

¹men·tor \'men-,tòr, -tər\ *n* [L, fr. Gk *Mentōr*] **1** *cap* : a friend of Odysseus entrusted with the education of Odysseus' son Telemachus **2 a** : a trusted counselor or guide **b** : TUTOR, COACH — **men·tor·ship** \-,ship\ *n*

²mentor *vt* (1983) : to serve as a mentor for

men·tum \'men-təm\ *n, pl* **men·ta** \-tə\ [L, chin — more at MOUTH] (1826) : a median plate of the labium of an insect

menu \'men-(,)yü, 'mān-\ *n, pl* **menus** [F, fr. *menu* small, detailed, fr. OF — more at MINUET] (1837) **1 a** : a list of the dishes that may be ordered (as in a restaurant) or that are to be served (as at a banquet) **b** (1) : a comparable list or assortment of offerings ⟨a ∼ of television programs⟩ (2) : a list shown on the display of a computer from which a user can select the operation the computer is to perform **2** : the dishes available for or served at a meal; *also* : the meal itself

menu–driv·en \-,dri-vən\ *adj* (1977) : relating to or being a computer program in which options are offered to the user via menus

me·ow \mē-'aủ\ *n* [imit.] (1600) **1** : the cry of a cat **2** : a spiteful or malicious remark — **meow** *vi*

me·per·i·dine \mə-'per-ə-,dēn\ *n* [*methyl* + *piperidine*] (1947) : a synthetic narcotic drug $C_{15}H_{21}NO_2$ used in the form of its hydrochloride as an analgesic, sedative, and antispasmodic

Meph·is·toph·e·les \,me-fə-'stä-fə-,lēz\ *n* [G] : a chief devil in the Faust legend — **Me·phis·to·phe·lian** \,mef-ə-stə-'fēl-yən, mə-,fis-tə-\ *or* **Me·phis·to·phe·lean** \,same, *or* ,me-fə-,stä-fə-'lē-ən\ *adj*

me·phit·ic \mə-'fi-tik\ *adj* (ca. 1623) : of, relating to, or resembling mephitis : foul-smelling

me·phi·tis \mə-'fī-təs\ *n* [L] (ca. 1706) : a noxious, pestilential, or foul exhalation from the earth; *also* : STENCH

mep·ro·bam·ate \,me-prō-'ba-,māt\ *n* [*methyl* + *propyl* + *dicarbamate*] (1955) : a bitter carbamate $C_9H_{18}N_2O_4$ used as a tranquilizer

-mer *n comb form* [ISV, fr. Gk *meros* part — more at MERIT] : member of a (specified) class ⟨mono*mer*⟩

mer·bro·min \,mər-'brō-mən\ *n* [*mercuric* + *brom-* + *fluorescein*] (1945) : a green crystalline mercurial compound $C_{20}H_8Br_2HgNa_2O_6$ used as a topical antiseptic and germicide in the form of its red solution

Mer·cal·li scale \mer-'kä-lē-, (,)mər-\ *n* [Giuseppe *Mercalli* †1914 Ital. priest and geologist] (1921) : a scale of earthquake intensity ranging from I for an earthquake detected only by seismographs to XII for one causing total destruction of all buildings

mer·can·tile \'mər-kən-,tēl, -,til\ *adj* [F, fr. It, fr. *mercante* merchant, fr. L *mercant-, mercans*, fr. prp. of *mercari* to trade — more at MARKET] (1642) **1** : of or relating to merchants or trading **2** : of, relating to, or having the characteristics of mercantilism ⟨∼ system⟩

mer·can·til·ism \-,tē-,li-zəm, -,tī-, -tə-\ *n* (1873) **1** : the theory or

menorah

practice of mercantile pursuits : COMMERCIALISM **2** : an economic system developing during the decay of feudalism to unify and increase the power and esp. the monetary wealth of a nation by a strict governmental regulation of the entire national economy usu. through policies designed to secure an accumulation of bullion, a favorable balance of trade, the development of agriculture and manufactures, and the establishment of foreign trading monopolies — **mer·can·til·ist** \-list\ *n or adj* — **mer·can·til·is·tic** \‚mər-kən-‚tē-'lis-tik, -‚tī-, -tə-\ *adj*

mer·cap·tan \(‚)mər-'kap-‚tan\ *n* [G, fr. Dan, fr. ML *mercurium captans*, lit., seizing mercury] (1835) : any of various compounds that contain a thiol functional group : THIOL 1

mer·cap·to·pu·rine \(‚)mər-‚kap-tə-'pyür-‚ēn\ *n* [*mercapt*an + -*o*- + *purine*] (ca. 1952) : an antimetabolite $C_5H_4N_4S$ that interferes esp. with the metabolism of purine bases and the biosynthesis of nucleic acids and that is sometimes useful in the treatment of acute leukemia

Mer·ca·tor \(‚)mər-'kā-tər\ *adj* (ca. 1876) : of, relating to, or drawn on the Mercator projection

Mercator projection *n* [Gerardus *Mercator*] (ca. 1881) : a conformal map projection in the usual case of which the meridians are drawn parallel to each other and the parallels of latitude are straight lines whose distance from each other increases with their distance from the equator

Mercator projection

¹**mer·ce·nary** \'mər-s²n-‚er-ē\ *n*, *pl* **-nar·ies** [ME, fr. L *mercenarius*, irreg. fr. *merced-*, *merces* wages — more at MERCY] (14c) : one that serves merely for wages; *esp* : a soldier hired into foreign service

²**mercenary** *adj* (1532) **1** : serving merely for pay or sordid advantage : VENAL; *also* : GREEDY **2** : hired for service in the army of a foreign country — **mer·ce·nar·i·ly** \‚mər-s²n-'er-ə-lē\ *adv* — **mer·ce·nar·i·ness** \'mər-s²n-‚er-ē-nəs\ *n*

mer·cer \'mər-sər\ *n* [ME, fr. OF *mercier* merchant, fr. *mers* merchandise, fr. L *merc-*, *merx*] (13c) *Brit* : a dealer in usu. expensive fabrics

mer·cer·ise *Brit var of* MERCERIZE

mer·cer·ize \'mər-sə-‚rīz\ *vt* **-ized; -iz·ing** [John *Mercer* †1866 Eng. calico printer] (1859) : to give (as cotton yarn) luster, strength, and receptiveness to dyes by treatment under tension with caustic soda — **mer·cer·i·za·tion** \‚mərs-rə-'zā-shən, ‚mər-sə-\ *n*

mer·cery \'mərs-rē, 'mər-sə-\ *n*, *pl* **-cer·ies** (14c) *Brit* : a mercer's wares, shop, or occupation

¹**mer·chan·dise** \'mər-chən-‚dīz, -‚dīs\ *n* [ME *marchaundise*, fr. OF *marcheandise*, fr. *marcheant*] (13c) **1** *archaic* : the occupation of a merchant : TRADE **2** : the commodities or goods that are bought and sold in business : WARES

²**mer·chan·dise** *also* **mer·chan·dize** \-‚dīz\ *vb* **-dised** *also* **-dized; -dis·ing** *also* **diz·ing** *vi* (14c) *archaic* : to carry on commerce : TRADE ~ *vt* **1** : to buy and sell in business **2** : to promote for or as if for sale ⟨~ a movie star⟩ — **mer·chan·dis·er** *n*

mer·chan·dis·ing *also* **mer·chan·diz·ing** \-‚dī-ziŋ\ *n* (1932) : sales promotion as a comprehensive function including market research, development of new products, coordination of manufacture and marketing, and effective advertising and selling

¹**mer·chant** \'mər-chənt\ *n* [ME *marchant*, fr. OF *marcheant*, fr. (assumed) VL *mercatant-*, *mercatans*, fr. prp. of *mercatare* to trade, freq. of L *mercari* — more at MARKET] (13c) **1** : a buyer and seller of commodities for profit : TRADER **2** : the operator of a retail business : STOREKEEPER **3** : one that is noted for a particular quality or activity : SPECIALIST ⟨a speed ~ on the base paths⟩ — **merchant** *adj*

²**merchant** *vi* (14c) *archaic* : to deal or trade as a merchant ~ *vt* : to deal or trade in

mer·chant·able \'mər-chən-tə-bəl\ *adj* (15c) : of commercially acceptable quality : SALABLE — **mer·chant·abil·i·ty** \‚mər-chən-tə-'bi-lə-tē\ *n*

merchant bank *n* (1930) *chiefly Brit* : a bank that specializes in bankers' acceptances and in underwriting or syndicating equity or bond issues — **merchant banker** *n* — **merchant banking** *n*

mer·chant·man \'mər-chənt-mən\ *n* (15c) **1** *archaic* : MERCHANT 2 : a ship used in commerce

merchant marine *n* (1855) **1** : the privately or publicly owned commercial ships of a nation **2** : the personnel of a merchant marine

merchant ship *n* (15c) : MERCHANTMAN 2

Mer·cian \'mər-sh(ē-)ən\ *n* (1513) **1** : a native or inhabitant of Mercia **2** : the Old English dialect of Mercia — **Mercian** *adj*

mer·ci·ful \'mər-si-fəl\ *adj* (14c) : full of mercy : COMPASSIONATE; *also* : providing relief — **mer·ci·ful·ness** \-fəl-nəs\ *n*

mer·ci·ful·ly \-f(ə-)lē\ *adv* (14c) **1** : in a merciful manner **2** : FORTUNATELY 2 ⟨~ we didn't have to attend the meeting⟩

mer·ci·less \'mər-si-ləs\ *adj* (14c) : having or showing no mercy : PITILESS — **mer·ci·less·ly** *adv* — **mer·ci·less·ness** *n*

mer·cu·rate \'mər-kyə-‚rāt\ *vt* **-rat·ed; -rat·ing** (1923) : to combine or treat with mercury or a mercury salt — **mer·cu·ra·tion** \‚mər-kyə-'rā-shən\ *n*

¹**mer·cu·ri·al** \(‚)mər-'kyür-ē-əl\ *adj* (14c) **1** : of, relating to, or born under the planet Mercury **2** : having qualities of eloquence, ingenuity, or thievishness attributed to the god Mercury or to the influence of the planet Mercury **3** : characterized by rapid and unpredictable changeableness of mood **4** : of, relating to, containing, or caused by mercury — *syn* see INCONSTANT — **mer·cu·ri·al·ly** \-ē-ə-lē\ *adv* — **mer·cu·ri·al·ness** *n*

²**mercurial** *n* (1676) : a pharmaceutical or chemical containing mercury

mer·cu·ric \(‚)mər-'kyür-ik\ *adj* (ca. 1828) : of, relating to, or containing mercury; *esp* : containing mercury with a valence of two

mercuric chloride *n* (1874) : a heavy crystalline poisonous compound $HgCl_2$ used as a disinfectant and fungicide and in photography

Mer·cu·ro·chrome \(‚)mər-'kyür-ə-‚krōm\ *trademark* — used for merbromin

mer·cu·rous \(‚)mər-'kyür-əs, 'mər-kyə-rəs\ *adj* (ca. 1865) : of, relating to, or containing mercury; *esp* : containing mercury with a valence of one

mercurous chloride *n* (ca. 1885) : CALOMEL

mer·cu·ry \'mər-kyə-rē, -k(ə-)rē\ *n*, *pl* **-ries** [L *Mercurius*, Roman god and the planet] **1 a** *cap* : a Roman god of commerce, eloquence, travel, cunning, and theft who serves as messenger to the other gods — compare HERMES **b** *often cap, archaic* : a bearer of messages or news or a conductor of travelers **2** [ME *mercurie*, fr. ML *mercurius*, fr. L, the god] **a** : a heavy silver-white poisonous metallic element that is liquid at ordinary temperatures and is used esp. in scientific instruments — called also *quicksilver*; see ELEMENT table **b** : the mercury in a thermometer or barometer **3** *cap* : the planet nearest the sun — see PLANET table

mercury chloride *n* (ca. 1885) : a chloride of mercury: as **a** : CALOMEL **b** : MERCURIC CHLORIDE

mercury–vapor lamp *n* (1904) : an electric lamp in which the discharge takes place through mercury vapor — called also *mercury lamp*

mer·cy \'mər-sē\ *n*, *pl* **mercies** [ME, fr. OF *merci*, fr. ML *merced-*, *merces*, fr. L, price paid, wages, fr. *merc-*, *merx* merchandise] (13c) **1 a** : compassion or forbearance shown esp. to an offender or to one subject to one's power; *also* : lenient or compassionate treatment ⟨begged for ~⟩ **b** : imprisonment rather than death imposed as penalty for first-degree murder **2 a** : a blessing that is an act of divine favor or compassion **b** : a fortunate circumstance ⟨it was a ~ they found her before she froze⟩ **3** : compassionate treatment of those in distress ⟨works of ~ among the poor⟩ — **mercy** *adj* — **at the mercy of** : wholly in the power of : with no way to protect oneself against

syn MERCY, CHARITY, CLEMENCY, GRACE, LENIENCY mean a disposition to show kindness or compassion. MERCY implies compassion that forbears punishing even when justice demands it ⟨threw himself on the *mercy* of the court⟩. CHARITY stresses benevolence and goodwill shown in broad understanding and tolerance of others ⟨show a little *charity* for the less fortunate⟩. CLEMENCY implies a mild or merciful disposition in one having the power or duty of punishing ⟨the judge refused to show *clemency*⟩. GRACE implies a benign attitude and a willingness to grant favors or make concessions ⟨by the *grace* of God⟩. LENIENCY implies lack of severity in punishing ⟨criticized the courts for excessive *leniency*⟩.

mercy killing *n* (1935) : EUTHANASIA

merde \'merd, 'mard\ *n* [F, fr. OF, fr. L *merda*; perh. akin to Lith *smirdėti* to stink] (1920) : ²CRAP 1a, 2 — sometimes considered vulgar

¹**mere** \'mir\ *n* [ME, fr. OE — more at MARINE] (bef. 12c) *chiefly Brit* : an expanse of standing water : LAKE, POOL

²**mere** [ME, fr. OE *mære*; akin to ON *landamæri* borderland] (bef. 12c) : BOUNDARY; *also* : LANDMARK

³**mere** \'mir\ *adj*, *superlative* **mer·est** [ME, fr. L *merus*; akin to OE *āmerian* to purify and perh. to Gk *marmairein* to sparkle — more at MORN] (1536) **1** : having no admixture : PURE **2** *obs* : being nothing less than : ABSOLUTE **3** : being nothing more than ⟨a ~ mortal⟩ — **mere·ly** *adv*

-mere *n comb form* [F *-mère*, fr. Gk *meros* part — more at MERIT] : part : segment ⟨metamere⟩

me·ren·gue \mə-'reŋ-‚)gä\ *n* [AmerSp *merengue* & Haitian Creole *méringue*] (1936) : a ballroom dance of Dominican and Haitian origin in which one foot is dragged on every step; *also* : the music for a merengue

mer·e·tri·cious \‚mer-ə-'tri-shəs\ *adj* [L *meretricius*, fr. *meretric-*, *meretrix* prostitute, fr. *merēre* to earn — more at MERIT] (ca. 1626) **1** : of or relating to a prostitute : having the nature of prostitution ⟨~ relationship⟩ **2 a** : tawdrily and falsely attractive ⟨the paradise they found was a piece of ~ trash —Carolyn See⟩ **b** : superficially significant : PRETENTIOUS ⟨scholarly names to provide fig-leaves of respectability for ~ but stylish books —*Times Lit. Supp.*⟩ *syn* see GAUDY — **mer·e·tri·cious·ly** *adv* — **mer·e·tri·cious·ness** *n*

mer·gan·ser \(‚)mər-'gan(t)-sər\ *n* [NL, fr. L *mergus*, a waterfowl (fr. *mergere*) + *anser* goose — more at GOOSE] (1752) : any of various fish-eating diving ducks (esp. genus *Mergus*) with a slender bill hooked at the end and serrated along the margins and usu. a crested head

merganser

merge \'mərj\ *vb* **merged; merg·ing** [L *mergere*; akin to Skt *majjati* he dives] *vt* (1636) **1** *archaic* : to plunge or engulf in something : IMMERSE **2** : to cause to combine, unite, or coalesce **3** : to blend gradually by stages that blur distinctions ~ *vi* **1** : to become combined into one **2** : to blend or come together without abrupt change ⟨merging traffic⟩ *syn* see MIX — **mer·gence** \'mər-jən(t)s\ *n*

merg·er \'mər-jər\ *n* [*merge* + *-er* (as in *waiver*)] (1728) **1** *law* : the

\a\ abut \²\ kitten, F table \ər\ further \a\ ash \ā\ ace \ä\ mop, mar \aů\ out \ch\ chin \e\ bet \ē\ easy \g\ go \i\ hit \ī\ ice \j\ job \ŋ\ sing \ō\ go \ò\ law \òi\ boy \th\ thin \th\ the \ü\ loot \ů\ foot \y\ yet \zh\ vision \á, k̲, ⁿ, œ, œ̄, ᵫ, ᵫ̄, ʸ\ *see* Guide to Pronunciation absorption of an estate, a contract, or an interest in another, of a minor offense in a greater, or of an obligation into a judgment   **2   a** : the act or process of merging   **b** : absorption by a corporation of one or more others; *also* : any of various methods of combining two or more organizations (as business concerns)

me·rid·i·an \mə-'ri-dē-ən\ *n* [ME, fr. MF *meridien*, fr. *meridien* of noon, fr. L *meridianus*, fr. *meridies* noon, south, irreg. fr. *medius* mid + *dies* day — more at MID, DEITY] (14c)   **1** *archaic* : the hour of noon : MIDDAY   **2** : a great circle of the celestial sphere passing through its poles and the zenith of a given place   **3** : a high point   **4   a** (1) : a great circle on the surface of the earth passing through the poles   (2) : the half of such a circle included between the poles   **b** : a representation of such a circle or half circle numbered for longitude on a map or globe — see LONGITUDE illustration — **meridian** *adj*

¹me·rid·i·o·nal \mə-'ri-dē-ə-n⁾l\ *adj* [ME, fr. MF *meridionel*, fr. LL *meridionalis*, fr. L *meridies*] (14c)   **1** : of, relating to, or situated in the south : SOUTHERN   **2** : of, relating to, or characteristic of people living in the south esp. of France   **3** : of, relating to, or situated on or along a meridian — **me·rid·i·o·nal·ly** \-n⁾l-ē\ *adv*

²meridional *n* (1591) : a native or inhabitant of southern Europe and esp. southern France

me·ringue \mə-'raŋ\ *n* [F] (1706)   **1** : a dessert topping baked from a mixture of stiffly beaten egg whites and sugar   **2** : a shell made of meringue and filled with fruit or ice cream

me·ri·no \mə-'rē-(,)nō\ *n, pl* **-nos** [Sp] (1810)   **1** : any of a breed of fine-wooled white sheep originating in Spain and producing a heavy fleece of exceptional quality   **2** : a soft wool or wool and cotton clothing fabric resembling cashmere   **3** : a fine wool and cotton yarn used for hosiery and knitwear — **merino** *adj*

-merism *n comb form* [ISV, fr. Gk *meros* part — more at MERIT] : possession of (such) an arrangement of or relation among constituent chemical units ⟨tauto*merism*⟩

mer·i·stem \'mer-ə-,stem\ *n* [Gk *meristos* divided (fr. *merizein* to divide, fr. *meros*) + E *-em* (as in *system*)] (1874) : a formative plant tissue usu. made up of small cells capable of dividing indefinitely and giving rise to similar cells or to cells that differentiate to produce the definitive tissues and organs — **mer·i·ste·mat·ic** \,mer-əs-tə-'ma-tik\ *adj* — **mer·i·ste·mat·i·cal·ly** \-ti-k(ə-)lē\ *adv*

me·ris·tic \mə-'ris-tik\ *adj* [Gk *meristos*] (1894)   **1** : SEGMENTAL   **2** : involving modification in number or in geometrical relation of body parts ⟨~ variation in flower petals⟩ — **me·ris·ti·cal·ly** \-ti-k(ə-)lē\ *adv*

¹mer·it \'mer-ət\ *n* [ME, fr. MF *merite*, fr. L *meritum*, fr. neut. of *meritus*, pp. of *merēre* to deserve, earn; akin to Gk *meiresthai* to receive as one's portion, *meros* part] (14c)   **1   a** *obs* : reward or punishment due   **b** : the qualities or actions that constitute the basis of one's deserts   **c** : a praiseworthy quality : VIRTUE   **d** : character or conduct deserving reward, honor, or esteem; *also* : ACHIEVEMENT   **2** : spiritual credit held to be earned by performance of righteous acts and to ensure future benefits   **3   a** *pl* : the intrinsic nature of a legal case apart from considerations of circumstance, jurisdiction, or procedure   **b** : individual significance or justification

²merit *vt* (1526) : to be worthy of or entitled or liable to : EARN   ~ *vi*   **1** *obs* : to be entitled to reward or honor   **2** : DESERVE

mer·i·toc·ra·cy \,mer-ə-'tä-krə-sē\ *n, pl* **-cies** ['*merit* + *-o-* + *-cracy*] (1958)   **1** : a system in which the talented are chosen and moved ahead on the basis of their achievement   **2** : leadership selected on the basis of intellectual criteria — **mer·it·o·crat·ic** \,mer-ə-tə-'kra-tik\ *adj*

mer·it·o·crat \'mer-ə-tə-,krat\ *n* (1960) *chiefly Brit* : a person who advances through a meritocratic system

mer·i·to·ri·ous \,mer-ə-'tōr-ē-əs, -'tȯr-\ *adj* (15c) : deserving of honor or esteem — **mer·i·to·ri·ous·ly** *adv* — **mer·i·to·ri·ous·ness** *n*

merit system *n* (1879) : a system by which appointments and promotions in the civil service are based on competence rather than political favoritism

¹merle *also* **merl** \'mər(-ə)l\ *n* [ME, fr. MF, fr. L *merulus*; akin to OE *ōsle* blackbird, OHG *amsla*] (15c) : BLACKBIRD 1a

²merle *n* [origin unknown] (1905) : a bluish or reddish gray mixed with splotches of black that is the color of the coats of some dogs

mer·lin \'mər-lən\ *n* [ME *merlioun*, fr. AF *merilun*, fr. OF *esmerillon*, aug. of *esmeril*, of Gmc origin; akin to OHG *smiril* merlin] (14c) : a small compact Holarctic falcon (*Falco columbarius*) which has a broad dark terminal band on the tail and of which the upperparts are slate blue in males and dark brown in females — compare PIGEON HAWK 1

Mer·lin \'mər-lən\ *n* [ML *Merlinus*, fr. MW *Myrddin*] : a prophet and magician in Arthurian legend

mer·lon \'mər-lən\ *n* [F, fr. It *merlone*, aug. of *merlo* battlement, fr. ML *merulus*, fr. L, merle] (ca. 1704) : any of the solid intervals between crenellations of a battlement — see BATTLEMENT illustration

mer·lot \mer-'lō\ *n, often cap* [F] (ca. 1941) : a dry red wine made from a widely grown grape orig. used in the Bordeaux region of France for blending

mer·maid \'mər-,mād\ *n* [ME *mermayde*, fr. *mere* sea (fr. OE) + *mayde* maid — more at MARINE] (14c) : a fabled marine creature with the head and upper body of a woman and the tail of a fish

mer·man \-,man, -mən\ *n* (1601) : a fabled marine creature with the head and upper body of a man and the tail of a fish

mero- *comb form* [ISV, fr. Gk, fr. *meros* part — more at MERIT] : part : partial ⟨*mero*blastic⟩

mer·o·blas·tic \,mer-ə-'blas-tik\ *adj* [ISV] (1870) : characterized by incomplete cleavage as a result of the presence of a mass of yolk material — compare HOLOBLASTIC — **mer·o·blas·ti·cal·ly** \-ti-k(ə-)lē\ *adv*

mer·o·crine \'mer-ə-krən, -,krīn, -,krēn\ *adj* [ISV, fr *mero-* + Gk *krinein* to separate — more at CERTAIN] (ca. 1905) : producing a secretion that is discharged without major damage to the secretory cells; *also* : produced by a merocrine gland

mer·o·mor·phic \,mer-ə-'mȯr-fik\ *adj* (ca. 1890) : relating to or being a function of a complex variable that is analytic everywhere in a region except for singularities at each of which infinity is the limit and each of which is contained in a neighborhood where the function is analytic except for the singular point itself

mer·o·my·o·sin \,mer-ə-'mī-ə-sən\ *n* (1952) : either of two structural subunits of myosin that are obtained esp. by tryptic digestion

-merous *adj comb form* [NL *-merus*, fr. Gk *-merēs*, fr. *meros* — more at MERIT] : having (such or so many) parts ⟨dimerous⟩

Mer·o·vin·gian \,mer-ə-'vin-j(ē-)ən\ *adj* [F *mérovingien*, fr. ML *Merovingi* Merovingians, fr. *Merovaeus* Merowig †458 Frankish founder of the dynasty] (ca. 1694) : of or relating to the first Frankish dynasty reigning from about A.D. 500 to 751 — **Merovingian** *n*

mer·o·zo·ite \,mer-ə-'zō-,īt\ *n* [ISV, fr. *mero-* + *zo-* + *-ite*] (1900) : a sporozoan trophozoite produced by schizogony that is capable of initiating a new sexual or asexual cycle of development

mer·ri·ment \'mer-i-mənt\ *n* (1576)   **1** : lighthearted gaiety or funmaking : HILARITY   **2** : a lively celebration or party : FESTIVITY

mer·ry \'mer-ē\ *adj* **mer·ri·er; -est** [ME *mery*, fr. OE *myrge, merge*; akin to OHG *murg* short — more at BRIEF] (bef. 12c)   **1** *archaic* : giving pleasure : DELIGHTFUL   **2** : full of gaiety or high spirits : MIRTHFUL   **3** : marked by festivity or gaiety   **4** : QUICK, BRISK ⟨at a ~ pace⟩ — **mer·ri·ly** \'mer-ə-lē\ *adv* — **mer·ri·ness** \'mer-ē-nəs\ *n*

syn MERRY, BLITHE, JOCUND, JOVIAL, JOLLY mean showing high spirits or lightheartedness. MERRY suggests cheerful, joyous, uninhibited enjoyment of frolic or festivity ⟨a *merry* group of revelers⟩. BLITHE suggests carefree, innocent, or even heedless gaiety ⟨arrived late in his usual *blithe* way⟩. JOCUND stresses elation and exhilaration of spirits ⟨singing, dancing, and *jocund* feasting⟩. JOVIAL suggests the stimulation of conviviality and good fellowship ⟨dinner put them in a *jovial* mood⟩. JOLLY suggests high spirits expressed in laughing, bantering, and jesting ⟨our *jolly* host enlivened the party⟩.

mer·ry–an·drew \,mer-ē-'an-(,)drü\ *n, often cap M&A* [*merry* + *Andrew*, proper name] (1673) : a person who clowns publicly

mer·ry–go–round \'mer-ē-gō-,raůnd, -gə-\ *n* (1729)   **1** : an amusement park ride with seats often in the form of animals (as horses) revolving about a fixed center   **2** : a cycle of activity that is complex, fast-paced, or hard to break out of ⟨the corporate ~⟩

mer·ry·mak·er \'mer-ē-,mā-kər\ *n* (1827) : REVELER

mer·ry·mak·ing \-,kiŋ\ *n* (1714)   **1** : gay or festive activity : CONVIVIALITY   **2** : a convivial occasion : FESTIVITY

mer·ry·thought \'mer-ē-,thȯt\ *n* (1607) *chiefly Brit* : WISHBONE

merry widow *n, often cap M&W* [*The Merry Widow*, operetta (1905) by Franz Lehár] (1964) : a strapless corset or bustier usu. having garters attached

Mer·thi·o·late \(,)mər-'thī-ə-,lāt, -lət\ *trademark* — used for thimerosal

mes- *or* **meso-** *comb form* [L, fr. Gk, fr. *mesos* — more at MID]   **1** : mid : in the middle ⟨*meso*carp⟩   **2** : intermediate (as in size or type) ⟨*meso*morph⟩ ⟨*meson*⟩

me·sa \'mā-sə\ *n* [Sp, lit., table, fr. L *mensa*] (1759) : an isolated relatively flat-topped natural elevation usu. more extensive than a butte and less extensive than a plateau; *also* : a broad terrace with an abrupt slope on one side : BENCH

més·al·liance \,mā-,zal-'yäⁿs, ,mā-zə-'li-ən(t)s\ *n, pl* **mésalliances** \-'yäⁿs(-əz), -'li-ən(t)-səz\ [F, fr. *més- mis-* + *alliance*] (1782) : a marriage with a person of inferior social position

mes·arch \'me-,zärk, 'mē-, -,särk\ *adj* (1891) : having metaxylem developed both internal and external to the protoxylem

mes·cal \me-'skal, mə-\ *n* [AmerSp *mezcal*, *mescal*, fr. Nahuatl *mexcalli* mescal liquor] (1702)   **1   a** : a small cactus (*Lophophora williamsii*) with rounded stems covered with jointed tubercles that are used as a stimulant and antispasmodic esp. among the Mexican Indians   **2   a** : a usu. colorless Mexican liquor distilled esp. from the central leaves of maguey plants   **b** : a plant from which mescal is produced; *esp* : MAGUEY

mescal button *n* (1888) : one of the dried discoid tops of the mescal

Mes·ca·le·ro \,mes-kə-'ler-(,)ō\ *n, pl* **Mescalero** *or* **Mescaleros** [AmerSp, fr. *mescal*, *mescal* maguey, mescal liquor] (1844) : a member of an Apache people of Texas and New Mexico

mes·ca·line \'mes-kə-lən, -,lēn\ *n* (1896) : a hallucinatory crystalline alkaloid $C_{11}H_{17}NO_3$ that is the chief active principle in mescal buttons

mesdames *pl of* MADAM *or of* MADAME *or of* MRS.

mesdemoiselles *pl of* MADEMOISELLE

me·seems \mi-'sēmz\ *vb impersonal, past* **me·seemed** \-'sēmd\ (15c) *archaic* : it seems to me

me·sem·bry·an·the·mum \mə-,zem-brē-'an(t)-thə-məm\ *n* [NL, irreg. fr. Gk *mesēmbria* midday (fr. *mes-* + *hēmera* day) + *anthemon* flower, fr. *anthos* — more at ANTHOLOGY] (1753) : any of a genus (*Mesembryanthemum*) of chiefly southern African fleshy-leaved herbs or subshrubs of the carpetweed family

mes·en·ceph·a·lon \,me-,zen-'se-fə-,län, ,mē-, -z⁾n-, -sen-, -s⁾n-, -lən\ *n* [NL] (1846) : MIDBRAIN — **mes·en·ce·phal·ic** \-,zen(t)-sə-'fa-lik, -z⁾n(t)-, -,sen(t)-, -s⁾n(t)-\ *adj*

mes·en·chy·mal \mə-'zeŋ-kə-məl, -'sen-; ,me-z⁾ən-'kī-məl, ,mē-, -s⁾n-\ *adj* [ISV] (1886) : of, resembling, or being mesenchyme

mes·en·chyme \'me-z⁾n-,kim, 'mē-, -s⁾n-\ *n* [G *Mesenchym*, fr. *mes-* + NL *-enchyma*] (1888) : loosely organized undifferentiated mostly mesodermal cells that give rise to such structures as connective tissues, blood, lymphatics, bone, and cartilage

mes·en·ter·on \(,)me-'zen-tə-,rän, ,mē-, -'sen-, -rən\ *n, pl* **-tera** \-tə-rə\ [NL] (1877) : the part of the alimentary canal that is developed from the archenteron and is lined with hypoblast

mes·en·tery \'me-z⁾n-,ter-ē, -s⁾n-\ *n, pl* **-ter·ies** [ME *mesenterie*, fr. MF & ML; MF *mesentere*, fr. ML *mesenterion*, fr. Gk, fr. *mes-* + *enteron* intestine — more at INTER.] (15c)   **1   a** : one or more vertebrate membranes that consist of a double fold of the peritoneum and invest the intestines and their appendages and connect them with the dorsal wall of the abdominal cavity   **b** : a fold of membrane comparable to a mesentery and supporting a viscus (as the heart) that is not a part of the digestive tract   **2** : a support or partition in an invertebrate like the vertebrate mesentery — **mes·en·ter·ic** \,me-z⁾n-'ter-ik, -s⁾n-\ *adj*

¹mesh \'mesh\ *n* [ME, prob. fr. MD *maesche*; akin to OHG *masca* mesh, Lith *mazgos* knot] (14c)   **1** : one of the openings between the threads or cords of a net; *also* : one of the similar spaces in a network — often used to designate screen size as the number of openings per

mescal 1

linear inch **2 a :** the fabric of a net **b :** a woven, knit, or knotted material of open texture with evenly spaced holes **c :** an arrangement of interlocking metal links used esp. for jewelry **3 a :** an interlocking or intertwining arrangement or construction : NETWORK **b :** WEB, SNARE — usu. used in pl. **4 :** working contact (as of the teeth of gears) ⟨in ~⟩ — **meshed** \'mesht\ *adj*

²**mesh** *vt* (ca. 1547) **1 a :** to catch in the openings of a net **b :** ENMESH, ENTANGLE **2 :** to cause to resemble network **3 a :** to cause (as gears) to engage **b :** to coordinate closely : INTERLOCK ~ *vi* **1 :** to become entangled in or as if in meshes **2 :** to be in or come into mesh — used esp. of gears **3 :** to fit or work together properly : COORDINATE

me·shuga *or* **me·shug·ge** *also* **me·shug·ah** *or* **me·shug·gah** \mə-'shùgə\ *adj* [Yiddish *meshuge*, fr. Heb *měshuggā'*] (1892) : CRAZY, FOOLISH

me·shug·gen·er \-'shù-gə-nər\ *n* [Yiddish *meshugener*, fr. *meshuge*] (1900) : a foolish or crazy person

mesh·work \'mesh-,wərk\ *n* (1830) : NETWORK ⟨a vascular ~⟩

me·si·al \'mē-zē-əl, -sē-\ *adj* (1803) **1 :** MIDDLE, MEDIAN **2 :** of, relating to, or being the surface of a tooth that is next to the tooth in front of it or that is closest to the middle of the front of the jaw — compare DISTAL 2 — **me·si·al·ly** \-ə-lē\ *adv*

¹**me·sic** \'me-zik, 'mē-, -sik\ *adj* [*mes-* + *-ic*] (1926) : characterized by, relating to, or requiring a moderate amount of moisture ⟨a ~ habitat⟩ ⟨a ~ plant⟩ — compare HYDRIC, XERIC

²**mesic** *adj* [*meson* + *-ic*] (1939) : of or relating to a meson

mes·mer·ic \mez-'mer-ik *also* mes-\ *adj* (1829) **1 :** of, relating to, or induced by mesmerism **2 :** FASCINATING, IRRESISTIBLE — **mes·mer·i·cal·ly** \-i-k(ə-)lē\ *adv*

mes·mer·ise *Brit var of* MESMERIZE

mes·mer·ism \'mez-mə,ri-zəm *also* 'mes-\ *n* [F. A. *Mesmer*] (1784) **1 :** hypnotic induction held to involve animal magnetism ; *broadly* : HYPNOTISM **2 :** hypnotic appeal — **mes·mer·ist** \-rist\ *n*

mes·mer·ize \-,rīz\ *vt* **-ized; -iz·ing** (1829) **1 :** to subject to mesmerism; *also* : HYPNOTIZE **2 :** SPELLBIND, FASCINATE — **mes·mer·iz·er** *n*

mesne \'mēn\ *adj* [AF, alter. of MF *meien* — more at MEAN] (1548) : INTERMEDIATE, INTERVENING — used in law

mesne lord *n* (1614) : a feudal lord who holds land as tenant of a superior (as a king) but who is lord to his own tenant

meso- — see MES-

me·so·carp \'me-zə,kärp, 'mē-, -sə-\ *n* (1849) : the middle layer of a pericarp — see ENDOCARP illustration

me·so·cy·clone \,me-zə-'sī-,klōn, ,mē-, -sə-'sī-\ *n* (1975) : a rapidly rotating air mass within a thunderstorm that often gives rise to a tornado

me·so·derm \'me-zə-,dərm, 'mē-, -sə-\ *n* [ISV] (1873) : the middle of the three primary germ layers of an embryo that is the source of many bodily tissues and structures (as bone, muscle, connective tissue, and dermis); *broadly* : tissue derived from this germ layer — **me·so·der·mal** \,me-zə-'dər-məl, ,mē-, -sə-\ *adj*

me·so·glea *or* **me·so·gloea** \,me-zə-'glē-ə, ,mē-, -sə-\ *n* [NL, fr. *mes-* + LGk *gloia, glia* glue — more at CLAY] (1886) : a gelatinous substance between the endoderm and ectoderm of sponges or coelenterates

Me·so·lith·ic \,me-zə-'li-thik\ *adj* [ISV] (1866) : of, relating to, or being a transitional period of the Stone Age between the Paleolithic and the Neolithic

me·so·mere \'me-zə-,mir, 'mē-, -sə-\ *n* (ca. 1900) : a blastomere of medium size; *also* : an intermediate part of the mesoderm

me·so·morph \'me-zə-,mòrf, 'mē-, -sə-\ *n* [*mesoderm* + *-morph*] (1940) : a mesomorphic body or person

me·so·mor·phic \,me-zə-'mòr-fik, ,mē-, -sə-\ *adj* [*mesoderm* + *-morphic*; fr. the predominance in such types of structures developed from the mesoderm] (1940) **1 :** of or relating to the component in W. H. Sheldon's classification of body types that measures esp. the degree of muscularity and bone development **2 :** having a husky muscular body built — **me·so·mor·phy** \'me-zə-,mòr-fē, -sə-\ *n*

me·son \'me-,zän, 'mā-, 'mē-, -,sän\ *n* [ISV *mes-* + ²*-on*] (1939) : any of a group of fundamental particles (as the pion and kaon) made up of a quark and an antiquark that are subject to the strong force and have zero or an integer number of quantum units of spin — **me·son·ic** \me-'zä-nik, mā-, mē-, -'sä-\ *adj*

me·so·neph·ros \,me-zə-'ne-frəs, ,mē-, -sə-, -,fräs\ *n, pl* **-neph·roi** \-,fròi\ [NL, fr. *mes-* + Gk *nephros* kidney — more at NEPHRITIS] (1887) : either member of the second and midmost of the three paired vertebrate renal organs that functions in adult fishes and amphibians but functions only in the embryo of reptiles, birds, and mammals in which it is replaced by a metanephros in the adult — compare META-NEPHROS, PRONEPHROS — **me·so·neph·ric** \-frik\ *adj*

me·so·pause \'me-zə-,pòz, 'mē-, -sə-\ *n* [*mesosphere* + *pause*] (1950) : the upper boundary of the mesosphere where the temperature of the atmosphere reaches its lowest point

me·so·pe·lag·ic \,me-zə-,pə-'la-jik, ,mē-, -sə-\ *adj* (1947) : of or relating to oceanic depths from about 600 feet to 3000 feet (200 to 1000 meters)

me·so·phyll \'me-zə-,fil, 'mē-, -sə-\ *n* [NL *mesophyllum*, fr. *mes-* + Gk *phyllon* leaf — more at BLADE] (1839) : the parenchyma between the epidermal layers of a foliage leaf — **me·so·phyl·lic** \,me-zə-'fi-lik, ,mē-, -sə-\ *or* **me·so·phyl·lous** \-ləs\ *adj*

me·so·phyte \'me-zə-,fīt, 'mē-, -sə-\ *n* [ISV] (1899) : a plant that grows under medium conditions of moisture — **me·so·phyt·ic** \,me-zə-'fi-tik, ,mē-, -sə-\ *adj*

me·so·scale \'me-zə-,skāl, 'mē-, -sə-\ *adj* (1956) : of intermediate size; *esp* : of or relating to a meteorological phenomenon approximately 10 to 1000 kilometers in horizontal extent ⟨~ cloud pattern⟩

me·so·some \-,sōm\ *n* (1960) : an organelle of bacteria that appears as an invagination of the plasma membrane and functions either in DNA replication and cell division or excretion of exoenzymes

me·so·sphere \-,sfir\ *n* (1950) : the part of the earth's atmosphere between the stratosphere and the thermosphere in which temperature decreases with altitude to the atmosphere's absolute minimum of about −112°F (−80°C) — **me·so·spher·ic** \,me-zə-'sfir-ik, ,mē-, -sə-, -'sfer-\ *adj*

me·so·the·li·o·ma \,me-zə-,thē-lē-'ō-mə, ,mē-, -sə-\ *n, pl* **-mas** *or* **-ma·ta** \-mə-tə\ [NL] (ca. 1899) : a tumor derived from mesothelial tissue (as that lining the peritoneum or pleura)

me·so·the·li·um \-'thē-lē-əm\ *n, pl* **-lia** \-lē-ə\ [NL, fr. *mes-* + *epithelium*] (1886) : epithelium derived from mesoderm that lines the body cavity of a vertebrate embryo and gives rise to epithelia (as of the peritoneum, pericardium, and pleurae), striated muscle, heart muscle, and several minor structures — **me·so·the·li·al** \-lē-əl\ *adj*

me·so·tho·rac·ic \-thə-'ra-sik\ *adj* (1839) : of or relating to the mesothorax

me·so·tho·rax \-'thòr-,aks, -'thòr-\ *n* [NL] (ca. 1826) : the middle of the three segments of the thorax of an insect — see INSECT illustration

me·so·tro·phic \,me-zə-'trō-fik, ,mē-, -sə-, 'trä-fik\ *adj* (1940) *of a body of water* : having a moderate amount of dissolved nutrients — compare EUTROPHIC, OLIGOTROPHIC

Me·so·zo·ic \-'zō-ik\ *adj* (1840) : of, relating to, or being an era of geological history comprising the interval between the Permian and the Tertiary or the corresponding system of rocks that was marked by the presence of dinosaurs, marine and flying reptiles, ammonites, ferns, and gymnosperms and the appearance of angiosperms, mammals, and birds — see GEOLOGIC TIME table — **Mesozoic** *n*

mes·quite \mə-'skēt, me-\ *n* [AmerSp, fr. Nahuatl *mizquitl*] (1759) : any of several spiny leguminous trees or shrubs (genus *Prosopis* and esp. *P. glandulosa*) chiefly of the southwestern U.S. that often form extensive thickets and have sweet pods eaten by livestock; *also* : the wood of the mesquite used esp. in grilling food

¹**mess** \'mes\ *n* [ME *mes*, fr. OF, fr. LL *missus* course at a meal, fr. *missus*, pp. of *mittere* to put, fr. L, to send — more at SMITE] (14c) **1 :** a quantity of food: **a** *archaic* : food set on a table at one time **b :** a prepared dish of soft food; *also* : a mixture of ingredients cooked or eaten together **c :** enough food of a specified kind for a dish or a meal ⟨picked a ~ of peas for dinner⟩ **2 a :** a group of persons who regularly take their meals together; *also* : a meal so taken **b :** a place where meals are regularly served to a group : MESS HALL **3 a :** a disordered, untidy, offensive, or unpleasant state or condition ⟨your room is in a ~⟩ **b :** one that is disordered, untidy, offensive, or unpleasant usu. because of blundering, laxity, or misconduct ⟨the movie⟩ is a ~, as sloppy in concept as it is in execution —Judith Crist⟩ ⟨made a ~ of his life⟩

²**mess** *vt* (14c) **1 :** to provide with meals at a mess **2 a :** to make dirty or untidy : DISARRANGE ⟨warned not to ~ up your room⟩ **b :** to mix up : BUNGLE ⟨really ~ed up my life⟩ **3 :** to interfere with ⟨magnetic storms that ~ up communications —*Time*⟩ **4 :** to rough up : MANHANDLE ⟨~ him up good so he won't double-cross us again⟩ ~ *vi* **1 :** to take meals with a mess **2 :** to make a mess **3 a :** PUTTER, TRIFLE ⟨small boys and girls who like to ~ around with paints⟩ **b :** to handle or play with something esp. carelessly ⟨don't ~ with my camera⟩ — often used with *around* **c :** to take an active interest in something or someone ⟨~ing around with new video techniques⟩; *also* : INTERFERE, MEDDLE ⟨~ing in other people's affairs⟩ ⟨you'd better not ~ with me⟩ **4 :** to become confused or make an error — usu. used with *up* ⟨got another chance and didn't want to ~ up again⟩

¹**mes·sage** \'me-sij\ *n* [ME, fr. OF, fr. ML *missaticum*, fr. L *missus*, pp. of *mittere*] (14c) **1 :** a communication in writing, in speech, or by signals **2 :** a messenger's errand or function **3 :** an underlying theme or idea

²**message** *vb* **mes·saged; mes·sag·ing** (1583) **1 :** to send as a message by messenger **2 :** to send a message to ~ *vi* : to communicate by message

mes·sa·line \,me-sə-'lēn\ *n* [F] (ca. 1890) : a soft lightweight silk dress fabric with a satin weave

mes·san \'me-sᵊn\ *n* [ScGael *measan*] (15c) *chiefly Scot* : LAPDOG 1

mess around *vi* (ca. 1932) **1 :** to waste time : DAWDLE, IDLE **2 a :** ASSOCIATE ⟨don't *mess around* with admirals much —K. M. Dodson⟩ **b :** FLIRT, PHILANDER ⟨caught him *messing around* with my wife⟩

messeigneurs *pl of* MONSEIGNEUR

mes·sen·ger \'me-sᵊn-jər\ *n* [ME *messangere*, fr. OF *messagier*, fr. *message*] (14c) **1 :** one who bears a message or does an errand: as **a** *archaic* : FORERUNNER, HERALD **b :** a dispatch bearer in government or military service **c :** an employee who carries messages **2 :** a light line used in hauling a heavier line (as between ships) **3 :** a substance (as a hormone) that mediates a biological effect **4 :** MESSENGER RNA

messenger RNA *n* (1961) : an RNA produced by transcription that carries the code for a particular protein from the nuclear DNA to a ribosome in the cytoplasm and acts as a template for the formation of that protein — compare TRANSFER RNA

mess hall *n* (1862) : a hall or building (as on an army post) in which mess is served

mes·si·ah \mə-'sī-ə\ *n* [Heb *māshiah* & Aram *měshiḥā*, lit., anointed] **1** *cap* **a :** the expected king and deliverer of the Jews **b :** JESUS 1 **2 :** a professed or accepted leader of some hope or cause — **mes·si·ah·ship** \-,ship\ *n*

mes·si·an·ic \,me-sē-'a-nik\ *adj* [prob. fr. F *messianique*, fr. *messianisme*] (ca. 1834) **1 :** of or relating to a messiah **2 :** marked by idealism and an aggressive crusading spirit ⟨a ~ sense of historic mission —Edmond Taylor⟩

mes·si·a·nism \'me-sē-ə-,ni-zəm; mə-'sī-ə-, me-\ *n* [F *messianisme*, fr. *messie* messiah + *-anisme* (as in *christianisme* Christianity)] (1876) **1 :** belief in a messiah as the savior of mankind **2 :** religious devotion to an ideal or cause

Mes·si·as \mə-'sī-əs\ *n* [ME, fr. LL, fr. Gk, fr. Aram *měshiḥā*] : MESSIAH 1

messieurs *pl of* MONSIEUR

mess jacket *n* (1891) : a fitted waist-length man's jacket worn esp. as part of a dress uniform

mess kit *n* (ca. 1877) : a compact kit of nested cooking and eating utensils for use by soldiers and campers

mess·mate \'mes-,māt\ *n* (1746) : a person with whom one regularly takes mess at a mess

mess over *vt* (1965) *slang* : to treat harshly or unfairly : ABUSE

\ə\ abut \ᵊ\ kitten, F table \ər\ further \a\ ash \ā\ ace \ä\ mop, mar
\aù\ out \ch\ chin \e\ bet \ē\ easy \g\ go \i\ hit \ī\ ice \j\ job
\ŋ\ sing \ō\ go \ò\ law \òi\ boy \th\ thin \t̲h̲\ the \ü\ loot \ù\ foot
\y\ yet \zh\ vision \à, k̲, ⁿ, œ, œ̄, ᵫ, ūē, ᵜ\ see Guide to Pronunciation

Messrs. \'me-sərz\ *pl of* MR. ⟨∼ Jones, Brown, and Robinson⟩

mes·suage \'mes-wij\ *n* [ME, fr. AF, prob. alter. of OF *mesnage* — more at MÉNAGE] (14c) : PREMISE 3b

messy \'me-sē\ *adj* **mess·i·er; -est** (1843) **1** : marked by confusion, disorder, or dirt : UNTIDY ⟨a ∼ room⟩ **2** : lacking neatness or precision : CARELESS, SLOVENLY ⟨∼ thinking⟩ **3** : extremely unpleasant or trying ⟨∼ lawsuits⟩ — **mess·i·ly** \'me-sə-lē\ *adv* — **mess·i·ness** \'me-sē-nəs\ *n*

mes·ti·za \me-'stē-zə\ *n* [Sp, fem. of *mestizo*] (ca. 1582) : a woman who is a mestizo

mes·ti·zo \-(,)zō\ *n, pl* **-zos** [Sp, fr. *mestizo*, adj., mixed, fr. LL *mixticius*, fr. L *mixtus*, pp. of *miscēre* to mix — more at MIX] (1582) : a person of mixed blood; *specif* : a person of mixed European and American Indian ancestry

mes·tra·nol \'mes-trə-,nól, -,nōl\ *n* [*meth-* + *estrogen* + *pregnane* ($C_{21}H_{36}$) + ^{1}-*ol*] (1962) : a synthetic estrogen $C_{21}H_{26}O_2$ used in oral contraceptives

met *past and past part of* MEET

meta- *or* **met-** *prefix* [NL & ML, fr. L or Gk; L, fr. Gk, among, with, after, fr. *meta* among, with, after; akin to OE *mid, mith* with, OHG *mit*] **1 a** : occurring later than or in succession to : after ⟨*metestrus*⟩ **b** : situated behind or beyond ⟨*met*encephalon⟩ ⟨*meta*carpus⟩ **c** : later or more highly organized or specialized form of ⟨*meta*xylem⟩ **2** : change : transformation **3** [*metaphysics*] : more comprehensive : transcending ⟨*meta*psychology⟩ — used with the name of a discipline to designate a new but related discipline designed to deal critically with the original one ⟨*meta*mathematics⟩ **4 a** : involving substitution at or characterized by two positions in the benzene ring that are separated by one carbon atom ⟨*meta*-xylene⟩ **b** : derived from by loss of water ⟨*meta*phosphoric acid⟩

met·a·bol·ic \,me-tə-'bä-lik\ *adj* (1845) : of, relating to, or based on metabolism — **met·a·bol·i·cal·ly** \-li-k(ə-)lē\ *adv*

me·tab·o·lism \mə-'ta-bə-,li-zəm\ *n* [ISV, fr. Gk *metabolē* change, fr. *metaballein* to change, fr. *meta-* + *ballein* to throw — more at DEVIL] (1872) **1 a** : the sum of the processes in the buildup and destruction of protoplasm; *specif* : the chemical changes in living cells by which energy is provided for vital processes and activities and new material is assimilated **b** : the sum of the processes by which a particular substance is handled in the living body ⟨the ∼ of a lake⟩ **2** : METAMORPHOSIS 2 — usu. used in combination ⟨holo*metabolism*⟩

me·tab·o·lite \-,līt\ *n* (1884) **1** : a product of metabolism **2** : a substance essential to the metabolism of a particular organism or to a particular metabolic process

me·tab·o·lize \-,līz\ *vb* **-lized; -liz·ing** *vt* (1887) : to subject to metabolism — *vi* : to perform metabolism — **me·tab·o·liz·able** \mə-,ta-bə-'lī-zə-bəl\ *adj*

^{1}**meta·car·pal** \,me-tə-'kär-pəl\ *adj* (1739) : of, relating to, or being the metacarpus or a metacarpal

^{2}**metacarpal** *n* (1854) : a bone of the part of the hand or forefoot between the carpus and the phalanges that typically contains five more or less elongated bones when all the digits are present

meta·car·pus \,me-tə-'kär-pəs\ *n* [NL] (1676) : the part of the hand or forefoot that contains the metacarpals

meta·cen·ter \'me-tə-,sen-tər\ *n* [F *métacentre*, fr. *méta-* meta- + *centre* center] (1794) : the point of intersection of the vertical through the center of buoyancy of a floating body with the vertical through the new center of buoyancy when the body is displaced

meta·cen·tric \,me-tə-'sen-trik\ *adj* (1798) **1** : of or relating to a metacenter **2** : having the centromere medially situated so that the two chromosomal arms are of roughly equal length — **metacentric** *n*

metacenter: *1* center of gravity, *2* center of buoyancy, *3* new center of buoyancy when floating body is displaced, *4* point of intersection

meta·cer·car·ia \,me-tə-(,)sər-'kar-ē-ə, -'ker-\ *n, pl* **-i·ae** \-ē-,ī\ (1928) : a tailless encysted late larva of a digenetic trematode that is usu. the form which is infective for the definitive host — **meta·cer·car·i·al** \-ē-əl\ *adj*

meta·chro·mat·ic \,me-tə-krō-'ma-tik\ *adj* (1876) **1** : staining or characterized by staining in a different color or shade from what is typical ⟨∼ granules in a bacterium⟩ **2** : having the capacity to stain different elements of a cell or tissue in different colors or shades ⟨∼ stains⟩

meta·eth·ics \-'e-thiks\ *n pl but usu sing in constr* (1949) : the study of the meanings of ethical terms, the nature of ethical judgments, and the types of ethical arguments — **meta·eth·i·cal** \-thi-kəl\ *adj*

meta·fic·tion \-'fik-shən\ *n* (1978) : fiction which refers to or takes as its subject fictional writing and its conventions — **meta·fic·tion·al** \-shnəl, -shə-nəl\ *adj* — **meta·fic·tion·ist** \-shə-nist\ *n*

meta·gal·axy \-'ga-lək-sē\ *n* [ISV] (1930) : the entire system of galaxies : UNIVERSE — **meta·ga·lac·tic** \,me-tə-gə-'lak-tik\ *adj*

meta·gen·e·sis \'je-nə-səs\ *n* [NL] (ca. 1864) : alternation of generations in animals; *esp* : regular alteration of a sexual and an asexual generation — **meta·ge·net·ic** \-jə-'ne-tik\ *adj*

^{1}**met·al** \'me-t^{3}l\ *n, often attrib* [ME, fr. OF, fr. L *metallum* mine, metal, fr. Gk *metallon*] (14c) **1** : any of various opaque, fusible, ductile, and typically lustrous substances that are good conductors of electricity and heat, form cations by loss of electrons, and yield basic oxides and hydroxides; *esp* : one that is a chemical element as distinguished from an alloy **2 a** : METTLE 1a **b** : the material or substance out of which a person or thing is made **3** : glass in its molten state **4 a** : printing type metal **b** : matter set in metal type **5** : ROAD METAL **6** : HEAVY METAL

^{2}**metal** *vt* **-aled** *or* **-alled; -al·ing** *or* **-al·ling** (1610) : to cover or furnish with metal

meta·lan·guage \'me-tə-,laŋ-gwij\ *n* (1936) : a language used to talk about language

meta·lin·guis·tic \'me-tə-liŋ-,gwis-tik\ *adj* (1944) : of or relating to a metalanguage or to metalinguistics

meta·lin·guis·tics \-tiks\ *n pl but usu sing in constr* (1949) : a branch of linguistics that deals with the relation between language and other cultural factors in a society

metall- *or* **metallo-** *comb form* [NL, fr. L *metallum*] : metal ⟨*metallo*phone⟩

^{1}**me·tal·lic** \mə-'ta-lik\ *adj* (15c) **1 a** : of, relating to, or being a metal **b** : made of or containing a metal **c** : having properties of a metal **2** : yielding metal **3** : resembling metal: as **a** : having iridescent and reflective properties ⟨∼ blond hair⟩ **b** : having an acrid quality like that of metal ⟨the tea has a ∼ taste⟩ **4 a** : having a harsh resonance : GRATING ⟨a ∼ voice⟩ **b** : having an impersonal or mechanical quality ⟨a ∼ smile⟩ — **me·tal·li·cal·ly** \-li-k(ə-)lē\ *adv*

^{2}**metallic** *n* (1952) : a fiber or yarn made of or coated with metal; *also* : a fabric made with this

met·al·lif·er·ous \,me-t^{3}l-'i-f(ə-)rəs\ *adj* [L *metallifer*, fr. *metallum* + *-fer* -ferous] (ca. 1656) : yielding or containing metal

met·al·lize *also* **met·al·ize** \'me-t^{3}l-,īz\ *vt* **met·al·lized** *also* **met·al·ized; met·al·liz·ing** *also* **met·al·iz·ing** (1594) : to coat, treat, or combine with a metal — **met·al·li·za·tion** \,me-t^{3}l-ə-'zā-shən\ *n*

met·al·log·ra·phy \,me-t^{3}l-'ä-grə-fē\ *n* [ISV] (ca. 1864) : a study of the structure of metals esp. with the microscope — **met·al·log·ra·pher** \,me-t^{3}l-'ä-grə-fər\ *n* — **met·al·lo·graph·ic** \mə-,ta-lə-'gra-fik\ *adj* — **met·al·lo·graph·i·cal·ly** \-'gra-fi-k(ə-)lē\ *adv*

^{1}**met·al·loid** \'me-t^{3}l-,óid\ *n* (1832) **1** : a nonmetal that can combine with a metal to form an alloy **2** : an element intermediate in properties between the typical metals and nonmetals

^{2}**metalloid** *also* **met·al·loi·dal** \,me-t^{3}l-'ói-d^{3}l\ *adj* (ca. 1850) **1** : resembling a metal **2** : of, relating to, or being a metalloid

me·tal·lo·phone \mə-'ta-lə-,fōn\ *n* (ca. 1883) : a percussion musical instrument consisting of a series of metal bars of varying pitch struck with hammers

met·al·lur·gy \'me-t^{3}l-,ər-jē, *esp Brit* mə-'ta-lər-\ *n* [NL *metallurgia*, fr. *metall-* + *-urgia* -urgy] (ca. 1704) : the science and technology of metals — **met·al·lur·gi·cal** \,me-t^{3}l-'ər-ji-kəl\ *also* **met·al·lur·gic** \-jik\ *adj* — **met·al·lur·gi·cal·ly** \-k(ə-)lē\ *adv* — **met·al·lur·gist** \'me-t^{3}l-,ər-jist, *esp Brit* mə-'ta-lər-\ *n*

met·al·mark \'me-t^{3}l-,märk\ *n* (ca. 1909) : any of a family (Riodinidae) of small or medium-sized usu. brightly colored chiefly tropical butterflies that often have metallic coloration on the wings

met·al·smith \-,smith\ *n* (14c) : a person skilled in metalworking

met·al·ware \-,war, -,wer\ *n* (1896) : ware made of metal; *esp* : metal utensils for household use

met·al·work \-,wərk\ *n* (ca. 1850) : the product of metalworking; *esp* : a metal object of artistic merit — **met·al·work·er** \-,wər-kər\ *n*

met·al·work·ing \-,wər-kiŋ\ *n* (1882) : the act or process of shaping things out of metal

meta·math·e·mat·ics \'me-tə-,math-'ma-tiks, -ma-thə-\ *n pl but usu sing in constr* (ca. 1890) : a field of study concerned with the formal structure and properties (as the consistency and completeness of axioms) of mathematical systems — **meta·math·e·mat·i·cal** \-ti-kəl\ *adj*

meta·mere \'me-tə-,mir\ *n* [ISV] (1877) : any of a linear series of primitively similar segments into which the body of a higher invertebrate or vertebrate is divisible — **meta·mer·ic** \,me-tə-'mer-ik, -'mir-\ *adj* — **meta·mer·i·cal·ly** \-i-k(ə-)lē\ *adv*

me·tam·er·ism \mə-'ta-mə-,ri-zəm\ *n* (1877) : the condition of having or the stage of evolutionary development characterized by a body made up of metameres

meta·mor·phic \,me-tə-'mór-fik\ *adj* (1816) **1** : of or relating to metamorphosis **2** *of a rock* : of, relating to, or produced by metamorphism — **meta·mor·phi·cal·ly** \-fi-k(ə-)lē\ *adv*

meta·mor·phism \-'mór-,fi-zəm\ *n* (1845) : a change in the constitution of rock; *specif* : a pronounced change effected by pressure, heat, and water that results in a more compact and more highly crystalline condition

meta·mor·phose \-,fōz, -,fōs\ *vb* **-phosed; -phos·ing** [prob. fr. MF *metamorphoser*, fr. *metamorphose* metamorphosis, fr. L *metamorphosis*] *vt* (1576) **1 a** : to change into a different physical form esp. by supernatural means **b** : to change strikingly the appearance or character of : TRANSFORM ⟨you are so *metamorphosed* I can hardly think you my master —Shak.⟩ **2 a** : to cause (rock) to undergo metamorphism ∼ *vi* **1** : to undergo metamorphosis **2** : to become transformed *syn* see TRANSFORM

meta·mor·pho·sis \,me-tə-'mór-fə-səs\ *n, pl* **-pho·ses** \-,sēz\ [L, fr. Gk *metamorphōsis*, fr. *metamorphoun* to transform, fr. *meta-* + *morphē* form] (1533) **1 a** : change of physical form, structure, or substance esp. by supernatural means **b** : a striking alteration in appearance, character, or circumstances **2** : a marked and more or less abrupt developmental change in the form or structure of an animal (as a butterfly or a frog) occurring subsequent to birth or hatching

met·anal·y·sis \,me-tə-'na-lə-səs\ *n* (1914) : a reanalysis of the division between sounds or words resulting in different constituents (as in the development of *an apron* from *a napron*)

meta·neph·ros \-'ne-frəs, -,fräs\ *n, pl* **-roi** \-,fròi\ [NL, fr. *meta-* + Gk *nephros* kidney — more at NEPHRITIS] (1884) : either member of the final and most caudal pair of the three successive pairs of vertebrate renal organs that functions as a permanent adult kidney in reptiles, birds, and mammals but is not present at all in lower forms — compare MESONEPHROS, PRONEPHROS — **meta·neph·ric** \-frik\ *adj*

meta·phase \'me-tə-,fāz\ *n* [ISV] (1887) : the stage of mitosis and meiosis in which the chromosomes become arranged in the equatorial plane of the spindle

metaphase plate *n* (1939) : a section in the equatorial plane of the metaphase spindle having the chromosomes oriented upon it

met·a·phor \'me-tə-,fór *also* -fər\ *n* [MF or L; MF *metaphore*, fr. L *metaphora*, fr. Gk, fr. *metapherein* to transfer, fr. *meta-* + *pherein* to bear — more at BEAR] (1533) **1** : a figure of speech in which a word or phrase literally denoting one kind of object or idea is used in place of another to suggest a likeness or analogy between them (as in *drowning in money*); *broadly* : figurative language — compare SIMILE **2** : an object, activity, or idea treated as a metaphor : SYMBOL **2** — **met·a·phor·ic** \,me-tə-'fór-ik, -'fär-\ *or* **met·a·phor·i·cal** \-i-kəl\ *adj* — **met·a·phor·i·cal·ly** \-i-k(ə-)lē\ *adv*

meta·phos·phate \,me-tə-'fäs-,fāt\ *n* [ISV] (1833) : a salt or ester of a metaphosphoric acid

meta·phos·pho·ric acid \-,fäs-'fór-ik-, -'fär-; -'fäs-f(ə-)rik-\ *n* (1833) : a glassy solid acid HPO_3 or $(HPO_3)_n$ formed by heating orthophosphoric acid

meta·phrase \'me-tə-,frāz\ *n* (1640) : a literal translation

meta·phys·ic \,me-tə-'fi-zik\ *n* [ME *metaphesyk*, fr. ML *metaphysica*] (14c) **1 a :** METAPHYSICS **b :** a particular system of metaphysics **2 :** the system of principles underlying a particular study or subject **:** PHILOSOPHY 3b — **metaphysic** *adj*

meta·phys·i·cal \-'fi-zi-kəl\ *adj* (15c) **1 :** of or relating to metaphysics **2 a :** of or relating to the transcendent or to a reality beyond what is perceptible to the senses **b :** SUPERNATURAL **3 :** highly abstract or abstruse; *also* **:** THEORETICAL **4** *often cap* **:** of or relating to poetry esp. of the early 17th century that is highly intellectual and philosophical and marked by unconventional imagery — **meta·phys·i·cal·ly** \-k(ə-)lē\ *adv*

Metaphysical *n* (1898) **:** a metaphysical poet of the 17th century

meta·phy·si·cian \,me-tə-fə-'zi-shən\ *n* (15c) **:** a student of or specialist in metaphysics

meta·phys·ics \-'fi-ziks\ *n pl but sing in constr* [ML *Metaphysica*, title of Aristotle's treatise on the subject, fr. Gk (*ta*) *meta* (*ta*) *physika*, lit., the (works) after the physical (works); fr. its position in his collected works] (1569) **1 a** (1) **:** a division of philosophy that is concerned with the fundamental nature of reality and being and that includes ontology, cosmology, and often epistemology (2) **:** ONTOLOGY **2 b :** abstract philosophical studies **:** a study of what is outside objective experience **2 :** METAPHYSIC 2

meta·pla·sia \-'plā-zh(ē-)ə\ *n* [NL] (1890) **1 :** transformation of one tissue into another **2 :** abnormal replacement of cells of one type by cells of another — **meta·plas·tic** \-'plas-tik\ *adj*

meta·psy·chol·o·gy \-si-'kä-lə-jē\ *n* [ISV] (ca. 1909) **:** speculative psychology concerned with postulating the structure (as the ego and id) and processes (as cathexis) of the mind which usu. cannot be demonstrated objectively — **meta·psy·cho·log·i·cal** \-,si-kə-'lä-ji-kəl\ *adj*

meta·se·quoia \-si-'kwói-ə\ *n* [NL] (1948) **:** any of a genus (*Metasequoia*) of fossil and living deciduous coniferous trees of the bald cypress family that have leaves, buds, and branches arranged oppositely and flat leaves resembling needles

meta·so·ma·tism \-'sō-mə-,ti-zəm\ *n* (1886) **:** metamorphism that involves changes in the chemical composition as well as in the texture of rock — **meta·so·mat·ic** \-sō-'ma-tik\ *adj*

meta·sta·ble \-'stā-bəl\ *adj* [ISV] (1897) **:** having or characterized by only a slight margin of stability (a ~ compound) — **meta·sta·bil·i·ty** \-stə-'bi-lə-tē\ *n* — **meta·sta·bly** \-'stā-b(ə-)lē\ *adv*

me·tas·ta·sis \mə-'tas-tə-səs\ *n, pl* **-ta·ses** \-,sēz\ [NL, fr. LL, transition, fr. Gk, fr. *methistanai* to change, fr. *meta-* + *histanai* to set — more at STAND] (1663) **:** change of position, state, or form: as **a :** transfer of a disease-producing agency from the site of disease to another part of the body **b :** a secondary metastatic growth of a malignant tumor — **met·a·stat·ic** \,me-tə-'sta-tik\ *adj* — **met·a·stat·i·cal·ly** \-ti-k(ə-)lē\ *adv*

me·tas·ta·size \mə-'tas-tə-,sīz\ *vi* **-sized; -siz·ing** (1907) **:** to spread by or as if by metastasis

¹meta·tar·sal \,me-tə-'tär-səl\ *adj* (1739) **:** of, relating to, or being the part of the human foot or of the hind foot in quadrupeds between the tarsus and the phalanges

²metatarsal *n* (1854) **:** a metatarsal bone

meta·tar·sus \,me-tə-'tär-səs\ *n* [NL] (1676) **:** the metatarsal part of a human foot or of a hind foot in quadrupeds

me·ta·te \mə-'tä-tē\ *n* [Sp, fr. Nahuatl *metatl*] (1834) **:** a stone with a concave upper surface used as the lower millstone for grinding grains and esp. maize

me·tath·e·sis \mə-'ta-thə-səs\ *n, pl* **-e·ses** \-,sēz\ [LL, fr. Gk, fr. *metatithenai* to transpose, fr. *meta-* + *tithenai* to place — more at DO] (1577) **:** a change of place or condition: as **a :** transposition of two phonemes in a word (as in the development of *crud* from *curd* or the pronunciation \'pûr-tē\ for *pretty*) **b :** a chemical reaction in which different kinds of molecules exchange parts to form other kinds of molecules — **met·a·thet·i·cal** \,me-tə-'the-ti-kəl\ *or* **met·a·thet·ic** \-tik\ *adj* — **met·a·thet·i·cal·ly** \-ti-k(ə-)lē\ *adv*

meta·tho·rac·ic \,me-tə-thə-'ra-sik\ *adj* (ca. 1839) **:** of, relating to, or situated in or on the metathorax (~ legs)

meta·tho·rax \-'thōr-,aks, -'thôr-\ *n* [NL] (1816) **:** the posterior segment of the thorax of an insect — see INSECT illustration

meta·xy·lem \-'zī-ləm, -,lem\ *n* (1902) **:** the part of the primary xylem that differentiates after the protoxylem and that is distinguished typically by broader tracheids and vessels with pitted or reticulate walls

meta·zo·al \-'zō-əl\ *adj* [NL *Metazoa*] (1928) **:** of or relating to the metazoans

meta·zo·an \-'zō-ən\ *n* [NL *Metazoa*, fr. *meta-* + *-zoa*] (1884) **:** any of a group (*Metazoa*) that comprises all animals having the body composed of cells differentiated into tissues and organs and usu. a digestive cavity lined with specialized cells — **metazoan** *adj*

¹mete \'mēt\ *vt* **met·ed; met·ing** [ME, fr. OE *metan;* akin to OHG *mezzan* to measure, L *modus* measure, Gk *medesthai* to be mindful of] (bef. 12c) **1** *archaic* **:** MEASURE **2 :** to give out by measure **:** DOLE — usu. used with *out* (~ out punishment)

²mete *n* [ME, fr. AF, fr. L *meta*] (15c) **:** BOUNDARY (~s and bounds)

me·tem·psy·cho·sis \mə-,tem(p)-si-'kō-səs, ,me-təm-,si-\ *n* [LL, fr. Gk *metempsychōsis*, fr. *metempsychousthai* to undergo metempsychosis, fr. *meta-* + *empsychos* animate, fr. *en-* + *psychē* soul — more at PSYCH] (1591) **:** the passing of the soul at death into another body either human or animal

met·en·ceph·a·lon \,met-,en-'se-fə-,län, -lən\ *n* [NL] (ca. 1871) **:** the anterior segment of the developing vertebrate hindbrain or the corresponding part of the adult brain composed of the cerebellum and pons — **met·en·ce·phal·ic** \-,en(t)-sə-'fa-lik\ *adj*

me·te·or \'mē-tē-ər, -,ôr\ *n* [ME, fr. MF *meteore*, fr. ML *meteorum*, fr. Gk *meteōron*, fr. neut. of *meteōros* high in air, fr. *meta-* + *-eōros*, fr. *aeirein* to lift] (15c) **1 :** an atmospheric phenomenon (as lightning or a snowfall) **2 a :** any of the small particles of matter in the solar system that are directly observable only by their incandescence from frictional heating on entry into the atmosphere **b :** the streak of light produced by the passage of a meteor

me·te·or·ic \,mē-tē-'ôr-ik, -'är-\ *adj* (1789) **1 :** of, relating to, or derived from the earth's atmosphere (~ water) **2 a :** of or relating to a meteor **b :** resembling a meteor in speed or in sudden and temporary brilliance (a ~ rise to fame) — **me·te·or·i·cal·ly** \-i-k(ə-)lē\ *adv*

me·te·or·ite \'mē-tē-ə-,rīt\ *n* (1824) **:** a meteor that reaches the surface of the earth without being completely vaporized — **me·te·or·it·ic** \,mē-tē-ə-'ri-tik\ *also* **me·te·or·it·i·cal** \-ti-kəl\ *adj*

me·te·or·it·ics \,mē-tē-ə-'ri-tiks\ *n pl but sing in constr* (ca. 1930) **:** a science that deals with meteors — **me·te·or·it·i·cist** \-'ri-tə-sist\ *n*

me·te·or·oid \'mē-tē-ə-,rôid\ *n* (1865) **1 :** a meteor particle itself without relation to the phenomena it produces when entering the earth's atmosphere **2 :** a meteor in orbit around the sun — **me·te·or·oi·dal** \,mē-tē-ə-'rôi-d²l\ *adj*

me·te·o·rol·o·gy \,mē-tē-ə-'rä-lə-jē\ *n* [F *or* Gk; F *météorologie*, fr. MF, fr. Gk *meteōrologia*, fr. *meteōron* + *-logia* -logy] (1620) **1 :** a science that deals with the atmosphere and its phenomena and esp. with weather and weather forecasting **2 :** the atmospheric phenomena and weather of a region — **me·te·o·ro·log·ic** \-rə-'lä-jik\ *or* **me·te·o·ro·log·i·cal** \-ji-kəl\ *adj* — **me·te·o·ro·log·i·cal·ly** \-ji-k(ə-)lē\ *adv* — **me·te·o·rol·o·gist** \-'rä-lə-jist\ *n*

¹me·ter \'mē-tər\ *n* [ME, fr. OE & MF; OE *mēter*, fr. L *metrum*, fr. Gk *metron* measure, meter; MF *metre*, fr. OF, fr. L *metrum* — more at MEASURE] (bef. 12c) **1 a :** systematically arranged and measured rhythm in verse: (1) **:** rhythm that continuously repeats a single basic pattern (iambic ~) (2) **:** rhythm characterized by regular recurrence of a systematic arrangement of basic patterns in larger figures (ballad ~) **b :** a measure or unit of metrical verse — usu. used in combination (pentameter); compare FOOT 4 **c :** a fixed metrical pattern : verse form **2 :** the basic recurrent rhythmical pattern of note values, accents, and beats per measure in music

²me·ter *n* [ME, fr. *meten* to mete] (14c) **:** one that measures; *esp* **:** an official measurer of commodities

³me·ter *n* [F *mètre*, fr. Gk *metron* measure] (1797) **:** the base unit of length in the International System of Units that is equal to the distance traveled by light in a vacuum in ¹⁄₂₉₉,₇₉₂,₄₅₈ second or to about 39.37 inches — see METRIC SYSTEM table

⁴me·ter *n* [*-meter*] (1815) **1 :** an instrument for measuring and sometimes recording the time or amount of something (a parking ~) (a gas ~) **2 :** POSTAGE METER; *also* **:** a postal marking printed by a postage meter

⁵me·ter *vt* (1884) **1 :** to measure by means of a meter **2 :** to supply in a measured or regulated amount **3 :** to print postal indicia on by means of a postage meter

-meter *n comb form* [F *-mètre*, fr. Gk *metron* measure] **:** instrument or means for measuring (barometer)

meter–kilogram–second *adj* (ca. 1940) **:** of, relating to, or being a system of units using the meter, kilogram, and second as its base units — abbr. **mks**

meter maid *n* (1957) **:** a woman assigned by a police or traffic department to write tickets for parking violations

me·ter·stick \'mē-tər-,stik\ *n* (1931) **:** a measuring stick one meter long that is marked off in centimeters and usu. millimeters

met·es·trus \,met-'es-trəs\ *n* [NL] (1900) **:** the period of regression that follows estrus

meth- *or* **metho-** *comb form* [ISV, fr. *methyl*] **:** methyl (methacrylic)

meth·ac·ry·late \,me-'tha-krə-,lāt\ *n* [ISV] (1865) **:** a salt or ester of methacrylic acid **2 :** an acrylic resin or plastic made from a derivative of methacrylic acid

meth·acryl·ic acid \,me-thə-'kri-lik-\ *n* [ISV] (1865) **:** an acid $C_4H_6O_2$ used esp. in making acrylic resins or plastics

meth·a·done \'me-thə-,dōn\ *also* **meth·a·don** \-,dän\ *n* [*methyl* + *amino* + *diphenyl* + *-one*] (1947) **:** a synthetic addictive narcotic drug $C_{21}H_{27}NO$ used esp. in the form of its hydrochloride for the relief of pain and as a substitute narcotic in the treatment of heroin addiction

meth·am·phet·amine \,me-tham-'fe-tə-,mēn, -thəm-, -mən\ *n* (1949) **:** an amine $C_{10}H_{15}N$ used medically in the form of its crystalline hydrochloride esp. in the treatment of obesity and often used illicitly as a stimulant — called also *methedrine*

meth·a·na·tion \,me-thə-'nā-shən\ *n* (1926) **:** the production of methane esp. from carbon monoxide and hydrogen

meth·ane \'me-,thān, Brit usu 'mē-\ *n* [ISV] (ca. 1868) **:** a colorless odorless flammable gaseous hydrocarbon CH_4 that is a product of decomposition of organic matter and of the carbonization of coal, is used as a fuel and as a starting material in chemical synthesis, and is the simplest of the alkanes

meth·a·nol \'me-thə-,nōl, -,nōl\ *n* [ISV] (1894) **:** a light volatile flammable poisonous liquid alcohol CH_3OH used esp. as a solvent, antifreeze, or denaturant for ethyl alcohol and in the synthesis of other chemicals

meth·aqua·lone \me-'tha-kwə-,lōn\ *n* [*meth-* + *-a-* (of unknown origin) + *quinoline* + *azole* + *-one*] (1961) **:** a sedative and hypnotic nonbarbiturate drug $C_{16}H_{14}N_2O$ that is habit-forming — compare QUAALUDE

meth·e·drine \'me-thə-,drēn, -drən\ *n* [fr. *Methedrine*, a trademark] (1939) **:** METHAMPHETAMINE

me·theg·lin \mə-'the-glən\ *n* [W *meddyglyn*] (1533) **:** ¹MEAD

met·he·mo·glo·bin \,met-'hē-mə-,glō-bən\ *n* [ISV] (1870) **:** a soluble brown crystalline basic blood pigment that differs from hemoglobin in containing ferric iron and in being unable to combine reversibly with molecular oxygen

met·he·mo·glo·bi·ne·mia \,met-,hē-mə-,glō-bə-'nē-mē-ə\ *n* [NL] (1888) **:** the presence of methemoglobin in the blood

me·the·na·mine \mə-'thē-nə-,mēn, -mən\ *n* [*methene* (methylene) + *amine*] (1926) **:** hexamethylenetetramine esp. when used as a urinary antiseptic

meth·i·cil·lin \,me-thə-'si-lən\ *n* [*meth-* + *penicillin*] (1961) **:** a semisynthetic penicillin $C_{17}H_{19}N_2O_6NaS$ that is esp. effective against penicillinase-producing staphylococci

me·thinks \mi-'thiŋ(k)s\ *vb impersonal, past* **me·thought** \-'thôt\ [ME *me thinketh*, fr. OE *mē thincth*, fr. *mē* (dat. of *ic* I) + *thincth* seems, fr. *thyncan* to seem — more at I, THINK] (bef. 12c) *archaic* **:** it seems to me

\ə\ abut \ˀ\ kitten, F table \ər\ further \a\ ash \ā\ ace \ä\ mop, mar \aů\ out \ch\ chin \e\ bet \ē\ easy \g\ go \i\ hit \ī\ ice \j\ job \ŋ\ sing \ō\ go \ô\ law \ôi\ boy \th\ thin \t̲h̲\ the \ü\ loot \ů\ foot \y\ yet \zh\ vision \á, k̲, ⁿ, œ, œ̄, ᵫ, ᵫ̄, ᵊ\ *see* Guide to Pronunciation me·thi·o·nine \mə-'thī-ə-ˌnēn\ n [ISV, fr. methyl + thion- + ²-ine] (1928) : a crystalline sulfur-containing essential amino acid $C_5H_{11}NO_2S$

meth·od \'me-thəd\ n [MF or L; MF methode, fr. L methodus, fr. Gk methodos, fr. meta- + hodos way] (1541) 1 : a procedure or process for attaining an object: as a (1) : a systematic procedure, technique, or mode of inquiry employed by or proper to a particular discipline or art (2) : a systematic plan followed in presenting material for instruction b (1) : a way, technique, or process of or for doing something (2) : a body of skills or techniques 2 : a discipline that deals with the principles and techniques of scientific inquiry 3 a : orderly arrangement, development, or classification : PLAN b : the habitual practice of orderliness and regularity 4 cap : a dramatic technique by which an actor seeks to gain complete identification with the inner personality of the character being portrayed

syn METHOD, MODE, MANNER, WAY, FASHION, SYSTEM mean the means taken or procedure followed in achieving an end. METHOD implies an orderly logical effective arrangement usu. in steps ⟨effective teaching methods⟩. MODE implies an order or course followed by custom, tradition, or personal preference ⟨the preferred mode of transportation⟩. MANNER is close to MODE but may imply a procedure or method that is individual or distinctive ⟨an odd manner of conducting⟩. WAY is very general and may be used for any of the preceding words ⟨has her own way of doing things⟩. FASHION may suggest a peculiar or characteristic way of doing something ⟨rushing about in his typical fashion⟩. SYSTEM suggests a fully developed or carefully formulated method often emphasizing the idea of rational orderliness ⟨a filing system⟩.

me·thod·i·cal \mə-'thä-di-kəl\ also me·thod·ic \-dik\ adj (1570) 1 : arranged, characterized by, or performed with method or order ⟨a ~ treatment of the subject⟩ 2 : habitually proceeding according to method ⟨~ in his daily routine⟩ — me·thod·i·cal·ly \-di-k(ə-)lē\ adv — me·thod·i·cal·ness \-di-kəl-nəs\ n

meth·od·ise Brit var of METHODIZE

meth·od·ism \'me-thə-ˌdi-zəm\ n (1739) 1 cap a : the doctrines and practice of Methodists b : the Methodist churches 2 : methodical procedure

meth·od·ist \-dist\ n (1593) 1 : a person devoted to or laying great stress on method 2 cap : a member of one of the denominations deriving from the Wesleyan revival in the Church of England, having Arminian doctrine and in the U.S. modified episcopal polity, and stressing personal and social morality — methodist adj, often cap — meth·od·is·tic \ˌme-thə-'dis-tik\ adj

meth·od·ize \'me-thə-ˌdīz\ vt -ized; -iz·ing (1589) : to reduce to method : SYSTEMATIZE syn see ORDER

method of fluxions (ca. 1719) : DIFFERENTIAL CALCULUS

meth·od·o·log·i·cal \ˌme-thə-də-'lä-ji-kəl\ adj (1849) : of or relating to method or methodology — meth·od·o·log·i·cal·ly \-k(ə-)lē\ adv

meth·od·ol·o·gist \-thə-'dä-lə-jist\ n (1865) : a student of methodology

meth·od·ol·o·gy \ˌme-thə-'dä-lə-jē\ n, pl -gies [NL methodologia, fr. L methodus + -logia -logy] (1800) 1 : a body of methods, rules, and postulates employed by a discipline : a particular procedure or set of procedures 2 : the analysis of the principles or procedures of inquiry in a particular field

meth·o·trex·ate \ˌme-thə-'trek-ˌsāt\ n [meth- + -trexate, of unknown origin] (1955) : a toxic anticancer drug $C_{20}H_{22}N_8O_5$ that is an analogue of folic acid and an antimetabolite

me·thoxy·chlor \me-'thäk-si-ˌklȯr, -ˌklȯr\ n [meth- + oxy- + chlor-] (1947) : a chlorinated hydrocarbon insecticide $C_{16}H_{15}Cl_3O_2$

me·thoxy·flu·rane \me-ˌthäk-sē-'flur-ˌān\ n [meth- + oxy- + fluor- + ethane] (1962) : a potent nonexplosive inhalational general anesthetic $C_3H_4Cl_2F_2O$ administered as a vapor

Me·thu·se·lah \mə-'thü-zə-lə, -'thyü-; -'th(y)üz-lə\ n [Heb Mĕthūselah] 1 : an ancestor of Noah held to have lived 969 years 2 : an oversize wine bottle holding about 6 liters

meth·yl \'me-thəl\ n [ISV, back-formation fr. methylene] (ca. 1844) : an alkyl group CH_3 derived from methane by removal of one hydrogen atom — meth·yl·ic \-'thi-lik\ adj

methyl acetate n (1885) : a flammable fragrant liquid $C_3H_6O_2$ used as a solvent and paint remover and in organic synthesis

methyl alcohol n (ca. 1847) : METHANOL

meth·yl·amine \ˌme-thə-lə-'mēn, -'la-mən; me-'thi-lə-ˌmēn\ n [ISV] (ca. 1850) : a flammable explosive gas CH_3NH_2 with a strong ammoniacal odor used esp. in organic synthesis (as of dyes and insecticides)

meth·yl·ase \'me-thə-ˌlās, -ˌlāz\ n (ca. 1952) : an enzyme that catalyzes methylation (as of RNA or DNA)

meth·yl·ate \'me-thə-ˌlāt\ vt -at·ed; -at·ing (1861) : to introduce the methyl group into — meth·yl·a·tion \ˌme-thə-'lā-shən\ n — meth·yl·a·tor \'me-thə-ˌlā-tər\ n

methyl bromide n (ca. 1897) : a poisonous gaseous compound CH_3Br used chiefly as a fumigant against rodents, worms, and insects

meth·yl·cel·lu·lose \ˌme-thəl-'sel-yə-ˌlōs, -ˌlōz\ n (1921) : any of various gummy products of cellulose methylation that swell in water and are used esp. as emulsifiers, adhesives, thickeners, and bulk laxatives

meth·yl·cho·lan·threne \-kə-'lan-ˌthrēn\ n [methyl + cholic acid + anthracene] (1937) : a potent carcinogenic hydrocarbon $C_{21}H_{16}$

meth·yl·do·pa \ˌme-thəl-'dō-pə\ n (1954) : a drug $C_{10}H_{13}NO_4$ used to lower blood pressure

meth·y·lene \'me-thə-ˌlēn, -lən\ n [F méthylène, fr. Gk methy wine + hylē wood — more at MEAD] (1835) : a bivalent hydrocarbon group CH_2 derived from methane by removal of two hydrogen atoms

methylene blue n (ca. 1890) : a basic thiazine dye $C_{16}H_{18}ClN_3S·3H_2O$ used esp. as a biological stain, an antidote in cyanide poisoning, and an oxidation-reduction indicator

methylene chloride n (1880) : a nonflammable liquid CH_2Cl_2 used esp. as a solvent, paint remover, and aerosol propellant

methyl ethyl ketone n (1876) : a flammable liquid compound C_4H_8O similar to acetone and used chiefly as a solvent — abbr. MEK

methyl isocyanate n (ca. 1894) : an extremely toxic chemical CH_3NCO used esp. in the manufacture of pesticides — abbr. MIC

meth·yl·mer·cury \ˌme-thəl-'mər-kyə-rē, -'mər-k(ə-)rē\ n (1919) : any of various toxic compounds of mercury containing the complex CH_3Hg— that often occur as pollutants which accumulate in living organisms (as fish) esp. in higher levels of a food chain

methyl methacrylate n (1933) : a volatile flammable liquid $C_5H_8O_2$ that polymerizes readily and is used esp. as a monomer for resins

meth·yl·naph·tha·lene \ˌme-thəl-'naf-thə-ˌlēn, -'nap-\ n (ca. 1885) : either of two isomeric hydrocarbons $C_{11}H_{10}$; esp : an oily liquid used in determining cetane numbers

methyl orange n (1881) : an alkaline dye used as a chemical indicator that in dilute solution is yellow when neutral and pink when acid

methyl parathion n (1957) : a potent synthetic organophosphate insecticide $C_8H_{10}NO_5PS$ that is more toxic than parathion

meth·yl·phe·ni·date \ˌme-thəl-'fe-nə-ˌdāt, -'fē-\ n [methyl + phenyl + piperidine + acetate] (1958) : a mild stimulant $C_{14}H_{19}NO_2$ of the central nervous system used in the form of its hydrochloride to treat narcolepsy and hyperkinetic behavior disorders in children

meth·yl·pred·nis·o·lone \-pred-'ni-sə-ˌlōn\ n (1957) : a glucocorticoid $C_{22}H_{30}O_5$ that is a derivative of prednisolone and is used as an antiinflammatory agent; also : any of several of its salts (as an acetate) used similarly

meth·yl·xan·thine \-'zan-ˌthēn\ n (1949) : a methylated xanthine derivative (as caffeine, theobromine, or theophylline)

meth·y·ser·gide \ˌme-thə-'sər-ˌjīd\ n [methyl + lysergic acid + amide] (1962) : a serotonin antagonist $C_{21}H_{27}N_3O_2$ used in the form of its maleate esp. in the treatment and prevention of migraine headaches

met·i·cal \'me-ti-kəl\ n, pl met·i·cais \-(ˌ)kī\ also meticals [Pg, fr. Ar mithqāl] (1981) — see MONEY table

me·tic·u·lous \mə-'ti-kyə-ləs\ adj [L meticulosus fearful, irreg. fr. metus fear] (1827) : marked by extreme or excessive care in the consideration or treatment of details syn see CAREFUL — me·tic·u·los·i·ty \-ˌti-kyə-'lä-sə-tē\ n — me·tic·u·lous·ly \-'ti-kyə-ləs-lē\ adv — me·tic·u·lous·ness \-nəs\ n

mé·tier also me·tier \'me-ˌtyā, me-'\ n [F, fr. (assumed) VL misterium, alter. of L ministerium work, ministry] (1792) 1 : VOCATION, TRADE 2 : an area of activity in which one excels : FORTE syn see WORK

mé·tis \mā-'tē(s), -'tēs\ n, pl mé·tis \-'tē(s), -'tēz\ [F, fr. LL mixticius mixed — more at MESTIZO] (1816) : one of mixed blood; esp, often cap : the offspring of an American Indian and a person of European ancestry

met·o·nym \'me-tə-ˌnim\ n [back-formation fr. metonymy] (1862) : a word used in metonymy

me·ton·y·my \mə-'tä-nə-mē\ n, pl -mies [L metonymia, fr. Gk metōnymia, fr. meta- + -ōnymon -onym] (1547) : a figure of speech consisting of the use of the name of one thing for that of another of which it is an attribute or with which it is associated (as "crown" in "lands belonging to the crown") — met·o·nym·ic \ˌme-tə-'ni-mik\ or met·o·nym·i·cal \-mi-kəl\ adj

me-too \'mē-'tü\ adj (1926) 1 : marked by similarity to or by adoption of successful or persuasive policies or practices used or promoted by someone else 2 : similar or identical to an established product (as a drug) with no significant advantage over it — me-too·er \-ər\ n — me-too·ism \-ˌi-zəm\ n

met·o·pe \'me-tə-(ˌ)pē\ n [Gk metopē, fr. meta- + opē opening; akin to Gk ōps eye, face — more at EYE] (1563) : the space between two triglyphs of a Doric frieze often adorned with carved work

met·o·pon \'me-tə-ˌpän\ n [meth- + hydro- + morphine + -one] (1941) : a narcotic drug $C_{18}H_{21}NO_3$ that is derived from morphine and is used in the form of the hydrochloride to relieve pain

me·tre \'mē-tər\ chiefly Brit var of METER

¹met·ric \'me-trik\ n [Gk metrikē, fr. fem. of metrikos in meter, by measure, fr. metron measure — more at MEASURE] (1760) 1 pl : a part of prosody that deals with metrical structure 2 : a standard of measurement ⟨no ~ exists that can be applied directly to happiness —Scientific Monthly⟩ 3 : a mathematical function that associates with each pair of elements of a set a real nonnegative number with the general properties of distance such that the number is zero only if the two elements are identical, the number is the same regardless of the order in which the two elements are taken, and the number associated with one pair of elements plus that associated with a second pair that has one element in common is equal to or greater than the number associated with the other member of the pair and the third element

²metric adj [F métrique, fr. mètre meter] (1864) : of, relating to, or using the metric system ⟨a ~ study⟩ — met·ri·cal·ly \-tri-k(ə-)lē\ adv

-metric or -metrical adj comb form 1 : of, employing, or obtained by (such) a meter ⟨galvanometric⟩ 2 : of or relating to (such) an art, process, or science of measuring ⟨geometrical⟩

met·ri·cal \'me-tri-kəl\ or met·ric \-trik\ adj (15c) 1 : of, relating to, or composed in meter 2 : of or relating to measurement — met·ri·cal·ly \-tri-k(ə-)lē\ adv

met·ri·ca·tion \ˌme-tri-'kā-shən\ n (1965) : the act or process of metricizing; specif : conversion of an existent system of units into the metric system

met·ri·cize \'me-trə-ˌsīz\ vt -cized; -ciz·ing (1873) : to change into or express in the metric system

metric space n (1927) : a mathematical set for which a metric is defined for any pair of elements

metric system n (1864) : a decimal system of weights and measures based on the meter and on the kilogram

metric ton n (ca. 1890) — see METRIC SYSTEM table

me·trist \'me-trist, 'mē-\ n (1535) 1 : a maker of verses 2 : one skillful in handling meter 3 : a student of meter or metrics

¹met·ro \'me-(ˌ)trō, in French context also mā-'\ n, pl metros [F métro, short for (chemin de fer) métropolitain metropolitan railroad] (1904) : SUBWAY b

²met·ro \'me-(ˌ)trō\ adj (1953) : METROPOLITAN 2

me·trol·o·gy \me-'trä-lə-jē\ n [F métrologie, fr. Gk metrologia theory of ratios, fr. metron measure — more at MEASURE] (1816) 1 : the science of weights and measures or of measurement 2 : a system of weights and measures — met·ro·log·i·cal \ˌme-trə-'lä-ji-kəl\ adj — met·rol·o·gist \me-'trä-lə-jist\ n

met·ro·ni·da·zole \ˌme-trə-'nī-də-ˌzōl\ n [methyl + -tron- (prob. alter. of nitro-) + imide + azole] (1962) : a drug $C_6H_9N_3O_3$ used esp. in treating vaginal trichomoniasis

met·ro·nome \'me-trə-ˌnōm\ n [Gk metron + -nomos controlling, fr. nomos law — more at NIMBLE]

metronome

METRIC SYSTEM[1]

LENGTH

Unit	Abbreviation	Number of Meters	Approximate U.S. Equivalent
kilometer	km	1,000	0.62 mile
hectometer	hm	100	328.08 feet
dekameter	dam	10	32.81 feet
meter	m	1	39.37 inches
decimeter	dm	0.1	3.94 inches
centimeter	cm	0.01	0.39 inch
millimeter	mm	0.001	0.039 inch
micrometer	μm	0.000001	0.000039 inch

AREA

Unit	Abbreviation	Number of Square Meters	Approximate U.S. Equivalent
square kilometer	sq km or km²	1,000,000	0.3861 square miles
hectare	ha	10,000	2.47 acres
are	a	100	119.60 square yards
square centimeter	sq cm or cm²	0.0001	0.155 square inch

VOLUME

Unit	Abbreviation	Number of Cubic Meters	Approximate U.S. Equivalent
cubic meter	m³	1	1.307 cubic yards
cubic decimeter	dm³	0.001	61.023 cubic inches
cubic centimeter	cu cm or cm³ also cc	0.000001	0.061 cubic inch

CAPACITY

Unit	Abbreviation	Number of Liters	Approximate U.S. Equivalent		
			cubic	dry	liquid
kiloliter	kl	1,000	1.31 cubic yards		
hectoliter	hl	100	3.53 cubic feet	2.84 bushels	
dekaliter	dal	10	0.35 cubic foot	1.14 pecks	2.64 gallons
liter	l	1	61.02 cubic inches	0.908 quart	1.057 quarts
cubic decimeter	dm³	1	61.02 cubic inches	0.908 quart	1.057 quarts
deciliter	dl	0.10	6.1 cubic inches	0.18 pint	0.21 pint
centiliter	cl	0.01	0.61 cubic inch		0.338 fluid ounce
milliliter	ml	0.001	0.061 cubic inch		0.27 fluid dram
microliter	μl	0.000001	0.000061 cubic inch		0.00027 fluid dram

MASS AND WEIGHT

Unit	Abbreviation	Number of Grams	Approximate U.S. Equivalent
metric ton	t	1,000,000	1.102 short tons
kilogram	kg	1,000	2.2046 pounds
hectogram	hg	100	3.527 ounces
dekagram	dag	10	0.353 ounce
gram	g	1	0.035 ounce
decigram	dg	0.10	1.543 grains
centigram	cg	0.01	0.154 grain
milligram	mg	0.001	0.015 grain
microgram	μg	0.000001	0.000015 grain

[1]For metric equivalents of U.S. units, see Weights and Measures table

(1816) : an instrument designed to mark exact time by a regularly repeated tick

met·ro·nom·ic \,me-trə-'nä-mik\ *also* **met·ro·nom·i·cal** \-mi-kəl\ *adj* (1866) : mechanically regular (as in action or tempo) — **met·ro·nom·i·cal·ly** \-mi-k(ə-)lē\ *adv*

me·trop·o·lis \mə-'trä-p(ə-)ləs\ *n* [ME, fr. LL, fr. Gk *mētropolis*, fr. *mētr-*, *mētēr* mother + *polis* city — more at MOTHER, POLICE] (14c) 1 : the chief or capital city of a country, state, or region 2 : the city or state of origin of a colony (as of ancient Greece) 3 **a** : a city regarded as a center of a specified activity ⟨a great business ∼⟩ **b** : a large important city ⟨the world's great ∼*es* —P. E. James⟩

¹met·ro·pol·i·tan \,me-trə-'pä-lə-t²n\ *n* (14c) 1 : the primate of an ecclesiastical province 2 : one who lives in a metropolis or displays metropolitan manners or customs

²metropolitan *adj* [ME, fr. LL *metropolitanus* of the see of a metropolitan, fr. *metropolita*, n., metropolitan, fr. LGk *metropolitēs*, fr. *mētropolis* see of a metropolitan, fr. Gk, capital] (15c) 1 : of or constituting a metropolitan or his see 2 : of, relating to, or characteristic of a metropolis and sometimes including its suburbs 3 : of, relating to, or constituting a mother country as distinguished from a colony

me·tror·rha·gia \,mē-trə-'rä-j(ē-)ə, -'rä-zhə; -'rä-jə, -zhə\ *n* [NL, fr. *metro-* womb (fr. Gk *mētra*, fr. *mētr-*, *mētēr* mother) + *-rrhagia* — more at MOTHER] (1879) : profuse uterine bleeding esp. between menstrual periods

-metry *n comb form* [ME *-metrie*, fr. MF, fr. L *-metria*, fr. Gk, fr. *metrein* to measure, fr. *metron* — more at MEASURE] : art, process, or science of measuring ⟨chronometry⟩ ⟨photometry⟩

met·tle \'me-t²l\ *n* [alter. of *metal*] (1581) 1 **a** : vigor and strength of spirit or temperament ⟨suspected to have more tongue in his head than ∼ in his bosom —Sir Walter Scott⟩ **b** : staying quality : STAMINA ⟨trucks had proved their ∼ in army transport —*Pioneer & Pacemaker*⟩ 2 : quality of temperament or disposition ⟨gentlemen of brave ∼ — Shak.⟩ *syn* see COURAGE — **met·tled** \-t²ld\ *adj* — **on one's mettle** : aroused to do one's best

met·tle·some \'me-t²l-səm\ *adj* (1662) : full of mettle : SPIRITED

meu·nière \,(,)mə(r)n-'yer, mœn-\ *adj* [F (à la) meunière, lit., in the manner of a miller's wife] (1903) : rolled lightly in flour and sautéed in butter ⟨sole ∼⟩

Meur·sault \mə(r)-'sō, mœ-\ *n* [F, fr. *Meursault*, commune in France] (1833) : a dry white burgundy wine

¹mew \'myü\ *n* [ME, fr. OE *mǣw*; akin to ON *mār* gull] (bef. 12c) : GULL; *esp* : the common European gull (*Larus canus*)

²mew *vb* [ME *mewen*, of imit. origin] *vi* (14c) : to utter a mew or similar sound ⟨gulls ∼*ed* over the bay⟩ ∼ *vt* : to utter by mewing : MEOW

³mew *n* (1596) : MEOW

⁴mew *n* [ME *mewe*, fr. MF *mue*, fr. *muer* to molt, fr. L *mutare* to change — more at MUTABLE] (14c) 1 : an enclosure for trained hawks — usu. used in pl. 2 : a place for hiding or retirement 3 *pl but sing or pl in constr, chiefly Brit* **a** (1) : stables usu. with living quarters built around a court (2) : living quarters adapted from such stables **b** : back street : ALLEY

⁵mew *vt* (15c) : to shut up : CONFINE — often used with *up*

mewl \'myü(ə)l\ *vi* [imit.] (1600) : to cry weakly : WHIMPER

Mex·i·can \'mek-si-kən\ *n* (1604) 1 **a** : a native or inhabitant of Mexico **b** : a person of Mexican descent **c** *Southwest* : a person of mixed Spanish and Indian descent 2 : NAHUATL — **Mexican** *adj*

Mexican bean beetle *n* (1921) : a spotted ladybug (*Epilachna varivestis*) that feeds on the leaves of beans

Mexican jumping bean *n* (ca. 1929) : JUMPING BEAN

Mexican Spanish *n* (1945) : the Spanish used in Mexico

Mexican standoff *n* (1891) : a situation in which no one emerges a clear winner; *also* : DEADLOCK

me·ze \'me-'zä, 'mä-(,)zä\ *n, pl* **mezes** *also* **meze** [NGk & Turk; NGk *mezes*, fr. Turk *meze*, perh. fr. Ar dial. *mazza*, *māzza*] (1926) : an appetizer in Greek or Middle Eastern cuisine often served with an aperitif

me·ze·re·on \mə-'zir-ē-ən\ *n* [ME *mizerion*, fr. ML *mezereon*, fr. Ar *māzariyūn*, fr. Per] (15c) : a small European shrub (*Daphne mezereum* of the family Thymelaeaceae, the mezereon family) with fragrant lilac purple flowers and poisonous emetic leaves, fruit, and bark

me·zu·zah *or* **me·zu·za** \mə-'zü-zə\ *n, pl* **-zahs** *or* **-zas** *or* **-zot** \-'zù-,zôt\ [Heb *mĕzūzāh* doorpost] (1650) : a small parchment scroll inscribed with Deut 6:4–9 and 11:13–21 and the name Shaddai and placed in a case fixed to the doorpost by some Jewish families as a sign and reminder of their faith

mez·za·nine \'me-z²n-,ēn, ,me-z²n-'\ *n* [F, fr. It *mezzanino*, fr. *mezzano* middle, fr. L *medianus* middle, median] (1711) 1 : a low-ceilinged story between two main stories of a building; *esp* : an intermediate story that projects in the form of a balcony 2 **a** : the lowest balcony in a theater **b** : the first few rows of such a balcony

\ə\ abut \²\ kitten, F table \ər\ further \a\ ash \ā\ ace \ä\ mop, mar
\aù\ out \ch\ chin \e\ bet \ē\ easy \g\ go \i\ hit \ī\ ice \j\ job
\ŋ\ sing \ō\ go \ò\ law \òi\ boy \th\ thin \t̲h̲\ the \ü\ loot \ù\ foot
\y\ yet \zh\ vision \å, ḵ, ⁿ, œ, œ̄, ᵫ, ᵫ̄, ʸ\ see Guide to Pronunciation

mez·za vo·ce \,met-sä-'vō-(,)chä, ,med-zä-\ *adv or adj* [It, half voice] (1775) : with medium or half volume — used as a direction in music

mez·zo \'met-(,)sō, 'med-(,)zō\ *n, pl* **mezzos** [It, lit., middle, moderate, half, fr. L *medius* — more at MID] (1832) : MEZZO-SOPRANO

mez·zo for·te \,met-(,)sō-'fôr-,tä, ,med-(,)zō-, -'fôr-tē\ *adj or adv* [It] (1811) : moderately loud — used as a direction in music

mez·zo pia·no \-pē-'ä-(,)nō\ *adj or adv* [It] (1811) : moderately soft — used as a direction in music

mez·zo-re·lie·vo *or* **mez·zo-ri·lie·vo** \-ri-'lē-(,)vō, -rēl-'yä-(,)vō\ *n, pl* **-vos** [It *mezzorilievo*, fr. *mezzo* + *rilievo* relief] (1598) : sculptural relief intermediate between bas-relief and high relief

mez·zo-so·pra·no \-sə-'pra-(,)nō, -'prä-\ *n* [It *mezzosoprano*, fr. *mezzo* + *soprano* soprano] (ca. 1753) 1 : a woman's voice with a range between that of the soprano and contralto 2 : a singer having a mezzo-soprano voice

mez·zo·tint \'met-sō-,tint, 'med-zō-\ *n* [modif. of It *mezzatinta*, fr. *mezza* (fem. of *mezzo*) + *tinta* tint] (1738) 1 : a manner of engraving on copper or steel by scraping or burnishing a roughened surface to produce light and shade 2 : an engraving produced by mezzotint

mho \'mō\ *n, pl* **mhos** [backward spelling of *ohm*] (1883) : a unit of conductance equal to the reciprocal of the ohm : SIEMENS

mi \'mē\ *n* [ML, fr. the syllable sung to this note in a medieval hymn to St. John the Baptist] (15c) : the 3d tone of the diatonic scale in solmization

MIA \,em-(,)ī-'ā\ *n* [*missing in action*] (1944) : a member of the armed forces whose whereabouts following a combat mission are unknown and whose death cannot be established beyond reasonable doubt

Mi·ami \mī-'a-mē, -mə\ *n, pl* **Mi·ami** *or* **Mi·am·is** (1722) : a member of an American Indian people orig. of Wisconsin and Indiana

mi·aow \mē-'aů\ *var of* MEOW

mi·as·ma \mī-'az-mə, mē-\ *n, pl* **-mas** *also* **-ma·ta** \-mə-tə\ [NL, fr. Gk, defilement, fr. *miainein* to pollute] (1665) 1 : a vaporous exhalation formerly believed to cause disease; *also* : a heavy vaporous emanation or atmosphere ⟨a ∼ of tobacco smoke⟩ 2 : an influence or atmosphere that tends to deplete or corrupt ⟨freed from the ∼ of poverty — Sir Arthur Bryant⟩; *also* : an atmosphere that obscures : FOG ⟨retreated into an asexual mental ∼ —*Times Lit. Supp.*⟩ — **mi·as·mal** \-məl\ *adj* — **mi·as·mat·ic** \,mī-əz-'ma-tik\ *adj* — **mi·as·mic** \mī-'az-mik, mē-\ *adj* — **mi·as·mi·cal·ly** \-mi-k(ə-)lē\ *adv*

mi·ca \'mī-kə\ *n* [NL, fr. L, grain, crumb; perh. akin to Gk *mikros* small] (1777) : any of various colored or transparent mineral silicates crystallizing in monoclinic forms that readily separate into very thin leaves — **mi·ca·ceous** \mī-'kā-shəs\ *adj*

Mi·cah \'mī-kə\ *n* [Heb *Mīkhāh*, short for *Mikhāyāh*] 1 : a Hebrew prophet of the 8th century B.C. 2 : a prophetic book of canonical Jewish and Christian Scripture — see BIBLE table

Mi·caw·ber \mi-'kô-bər, -'kä-\ *n* [Wilkins *Micawber*, character in the novel *David Copperfield* (1849–50) by Charles Dickens] (1852) : one who is poor but lives in optimistic expectation of better fortune — **Mi·caw·ber·ish** \-bə-rish\ *adj*

mice *pl of* MOUSE

mi·celle \mī-'sel\ *n* [NL *micella*, fr. L *mica*] (1881) : a unit of structure built up from polymeric molecules or ions: as a : an ordered region in a fiber (as of cellulose or rayon) b : a molecular aggregate that constitutes a colloidal particle — **mi·cel·lar** \-'se-lər\ *adj*

Mi·chael \'mī-kəl\ *n* [Heb *Mikhā'ēl*] : one of the four archangels named in Hebrew tradition

Mi·chae·lis constant \mi-'kā-ləs-, mə-\ *n* [Leonor *Michaelis* †1949 Am. biochemist] (1949) : a constant that is a measure of the kinetics of an enzyme reaction and that is equivalent to the concentration of substrate at which the reaction takes place at one half its maximum rate

Mich·ael·mas \'mi-kəl-məs\ *n* [ME *mychelmesse*, fr. OE *Michaeles mæsse* Michael's mass] (bef. 12c) : September 29 celebrated as the feast of St. Michael the Archangel

Michaelmas daisy *n* (1785) : a wild aster; *esp* : one blooming about Michaelmas

Mi·che·as \'mī-kē-əs, mi-\ *n* [LL *Michaeas*, fr. Gk *Michaias*, fr. Heb *Mikhāyāh*] : MICAH

mick \'mik\ *n, often cap* [*Mick*, nickname for *Michael*, common Irish given name] (1856) : IRISHMAN — often taken to be offensive

Mick·ey Finn \,mi-kē-'fin\ *n* [prob. fr. the name Mickey *Finn*] (1928) : a drink of liquor doctored with a purgative or a drug

Mickey Mouse \'mi-kē-'maůs\ *adj* [*Mickey Mouse*, cartoon character created by Walt Disney] (1936) 1 *often not cap* : being or performing insipid or corny popular music 2 : lacking importance : INSIGNIFICANT ⟨*Mickey Mouse* courses, where you don't work too hard —Willie Cager⟩ 3 : annoyingly petty ⟨*Mickey Mouse* regulations⟩

mick·le \'mi-kəl\ *adj* [ME *mikel*, fr. OE *micel* — more at MUCH] (bef. 12c) *chiefly Scot* : GREAT, MUCH — **mickle** *adv, chiefly Scot*

Mic·mac \'mik-,mak\ *n, pl* **Micmac** *or* **Micmacs** [Micmac *mi'kəmaw*] (1830) 1 : a member of an American Indian people of eastern Canada 2 : the Algonquian language of the Micmac people

micr- *or* **micro-** *comb form* [ME *micro-*, fr. L, fr. Gk *mikr-*, *mikro-*, fr. *mikros*, *smikros* small, short; perh. akin to OE *smēalīc* careful, exquisite] 1 a : small : minute ⟨*microcapsule*⟩ b : used for or involving minute quantities or variations ⟨*microbarograph*⟩ 2 : one millionth part of a (specified) unit ⟨*microgram*⟩ 3 a : using microscopy ⟨*microdissection*⟩ : used in microscopy b : revealed by or having the structure discernible only by microscopic examination ⟨*microorganism*⟩ 4 : abnormally small ⟨*microcyte*⟩ 5 : of or relating to a small area ⟨*microclimate*⟩ 6 : employed in or connected with microphotographing or microfilming ⟨*microcopy*⟩

¹**mi·cro** \'mī-(,)krō\ *adj* [*micr-*] (1923) 1 : very small; *esp* : MICROSCOPIC 2 : involving minute quantities or variations

²**micro** *n, pl* **micros** (1971) 1 : MICROCOMPUTER 2 : MICROPROCESSOR

mi·cro·am·pere \,mī-krō-'am-,pir\ *n* (ca. 1890) : a unit of current equal to one millionth of an ampere

mi·cro·anal·y·sis \-ə-'na-lə-səs\ *n* (1856) : chemical analysis on a small or minute scale that usu. requires special, very sensitive, or small-scale apparatus — **mi·cro·an·a·lyst** \-'a-nᵊl-ist\ *n* — **mi·cro·an·a·lyt·i·cal** \-ᵊl-ti-kəl\ *also* **mi·cro·an·a·lyt·ic** \-,a-nᵊl-'i-tik\ *adj*

mi·cro·anat·o·my \-ə-'na-tə-mē\ *n* (ca. 1899) : HISTOLOGY — **mi·cro·an·a·tom·i·cal** \-,a-nə-'tä-mi-kəl\ *adj*

mi·cro·bal·ance \'mī-krō-,ba-lən(t)s\ *n* (1903) : a balance designed to measure very small weights

mi·cro·baro·graph \,mī-krō-'bar-ə-,graf\ *n* [ISV] (1904) : a barograph for recording small and rapid changes

mi·crobe \'mī-,krōb\ *n* [ISV *micr-* + Gk *bios* life — more at QUICK] (1881) : MICROORGANISM, GERM — **mi·cro·bi·al** \mī-'krō-bē-əl\ *also* **mi·cro·bic** \-bik\ *adj*

mi·cro·beam \'mī-krō-,bēm\ *n* (1950) : a beam of radiation of small cross section ⟨a focused laser ∼⟩ ⟨a ∼ of electrons⟩

mi·cro·bi·ol·o·gy \,mī-krō-bī-'ä-lə-jē\ *n* [ISV] (1888) : a branch of biology dealing esp. with microscopic forms of life — **mi·cro·bi·o·log·i·cal** \-bī-ə-'lä-ji-kəl\ *also* **mi·cro·bi·o·log·ic** \-'lä-jik\ *adj* — **mi·cro·bi·o·log·i·cal·ly** \-ji-k(ə-)lē\ *adv* — **mi·cro·bi·ol·o·gist** \-bī-'ä-lə-jist\ *n*

mi·cro·brew \'mī-krō-,brü\ *n* (1987) : a beer produced by a microbrewery

mi·cro·brew·ery \,mī-krō-'brü-ə-rē, -'brü(-ə)r-ē\ *n* (1984) : a small brewery making specialty beer in limited quantities — **mi·cro·brew·er** \'mī-krō-,brü-ər, -,brü(-ə)r\ *n* — **mi·cro·brew·ing** \-,brü-iŋ\ *n*

mi·cro·burst \'mī-krō-,bərst\ *n* (1982) : a violent short-lived localized downdraft that creates extreme wind shears at low altitudes and is usu. associated with thunderstorms

mi·cro·bus \-,bəs\ *n* (1945) : a station wagon shaped like a bus

mi·cro·cal·o·rim·e·ter \,mī-krō-,ka-lə-'ri-mə-tər\ *n* (1911) : an instrument for measuring very small quantities of heat — **mi·cro·ca·lo·ri·met·ric** \-,ka-lə-rə-'me-trik; -ka-,lôr-ə-, -,lör-ə-, -,lär-\ *adj* — **mi·cro·cal·o·rim·e·try** \-,ka-lə-'ri-mə-trē\ *n*

mi·cro·cap·sule \'mī-krō-,kap-səl, -(,)sül *also* -,syü(ə)l\ *n* (1961) : a tiny capsule containing material (as an adhesive or a medicine) that is released when the capsule is broken, melted, or dissolved

mi·cro·cas·sette \,mī-krō-kə-'set, -ka-\ *n* (1979) : a small cassette of magnetic tape that is used esp. for dictation

¹**mi·cro·ce·phal·ic** \-sə-'fa-lik\ *adj* (ca. 1856) : having an abnormally small head; *specif* : having an abnormally small head

²**microcephalic** *n* (ca. 1873) : one that is microcephalic

mi·cro·ceph·a·ly \-'se-fə-lē\ *n* [NL *microcephalia*, fr. *microcephalus* microcephalic, fr. *micr-* + Gk *kephalē* head — more at CEPHALIC] (1863) : a condition of abnormal smallness of the head usu. associated with mental defects

mi·cro·chip \'mī-krō-,chip\ *n* (1969) : INTEGRATED CIRCUIT

mi·cro·cir·cuit \-,sər-kət\ *n* (1959) : a compact electronic circuit : INTEGRATED CIRCUIT — **mi·cro·cir·cuit·ry** \,mī-krō-'sər-kə-trē\ *n*

mi·cro·cir·cu·la·tion \,mī-krō-,sər-kyə-'lā-shən\ *n* (1959) : blood circulation in the microvascular system; *also* : the microvascular system itself — **mi·cro·cir·cu·la·to·ry** \-'sər-kyə-lə-,tōr-ē, -,tôr-\ *adj*

mi·cro·cli·mate \'mī-krō-,klī-mət\ *n* [ISV] (1925) : the essentially uniform local climate of a usu. small site or habitat — **mi·cro·cli·mat·ic** \,mī-krō-klī-'ma-tik\ *adj*

mi·cro·cline \'mī-krō-,klīn\ *n* [G *Mikroklin*, fr. *mikr-* micr- + Gk *klinein* to lean — more at LEAN] (1849) : a triclinic mineral of the feldspar group that is like orthoclase in composition

mi·cro·coc·cus \,mī-krō-'kä-kəs\ *n, pl* **-coc·ci** \-'käk-(,)sī, -(,)sē; -(,)kī, -(,)kē\ [NL] (1870) : a small spherical bacterium; *esp* : any of a genus (*Micrococcus*) of gram-positive chiefly harmless bacteria that typically occur in irregular clusters — **mi·cro·coc·cal** \-'kä-kəl\ *adj*

mi·cro·code \'mī-krō-,kōd\ *n* (ca. 1962) : the microinstructions esp. of a microprocessor

mi·cro·com·put·er \'mī-krō-kəm-,pyü-tər\ *n* (1971) 1 : a very small computer that uses a microprocessor to handle information 2 : MICROPROCESSOR

mi·cro·copy \'mī-krō-,kä-pē\ *n* [ISV] (1935) : a photographic copy in which graphic matter is reduced in size (as on microfilm)

mi·cro·cosm \'mī-krə-,käzm\ *n* [ME, fr. ML *microcosmus*, modif. of Gk *mikros kosmos*] (15c) 1 : a little world; *esp* : the human race or human nature seen as an epitome of the world or the universe 2 : a community or other unity that is an epitome of a larger unity — **mi·cro·cos·mic** \,mī-krə-'käz-mik\ *adj* — **mi·cro·cos·mi·cal·ly** \-mi-k(ə-)lē\ *adv* — **in microcosm** : in a greatly diminished size, form, or scale

microcosmic salt *n* (1783) : a white crystalline salt $NaNH_4PO_4·4H_2O$ used as a flux in testing for metallic oxides and salts

mi·cro·cos·mos \'mī-krə-,käz-məs, -,mōs, -,mäs\ *n* [ME *mycrocossmos*, fr. ML *microcosmus*] (13c) 1 : MICROCOSM 2 : the microscopic or submicroscopic world

mi·cro·crys·tal \'mī-krō-,kris-tᵊl\ *n* (1886) : a crystal visible only under the microscope — **mi·cro·crys·tal·line** \,mī-krō-'kris-tə-lən *also* -,lēn *or* -,lən\ *adj* — **mi·cro·crys·tal·lin·i·ty** \-,kris-tə-'li-nə-tē\ *n*

mi·cro·cul·ture \'mī-krō-,kəl-chər\ *n* (1892) 1 : a microscopic culture of cells or organisms 2 : the culture of a small group of human beings with limited perspective — **mi·cro·cul·tur·al** \,mī-krō-'kəlch-rəl, -'kəl-chə-\ *adj*

mi·cro·cu·rie \'mī-krō-,kyůr-ē, ,mī-krō-kyů-'rē\ *n* (1911) : a unit of quantity or of radioactivity equal to one millionth of a curie

mi·cro·cyte \'mī-krə-,sīt\ *n* [ISV] (1876) : a small red blood cell present esp. in some anemias — **mi·cro·cyt·ic** \,mī-krə-'si-tik\ *adj*

mi·cro·den·si·tom·e·ter \'mī-krō-,den(t)-sə-'tä-mə-tər\ *n* (1935) : a densitometer for measuring the densities of very small areas of a photographic film or plate — **mi·cro·den·si·to·met·ric** \-sə-tə-'me-trik\ *adj* — **mi·cro·den·si·tom·e·try** \-sə-'tä-mə-trē\ *n*

mi·cro·dis·sec·tion \,mī-krō-di-'sek-shən, -dī-\ *n* (1915) : dissection under the microscope; *specif* : dissection of cells and tissues by means of fine needles that are precisely manipulated by levers

mi·cro·dot \'mī-krə-,dät, -krō-\ *n* (1946) : a photographic reproduction of printed matter reduced to the size of a dot for ease or security of transmittal

mi·cro·earth·quake \,mī-krō-'ərth-,kwāk\ *n* (1965) : an earthquake of low intensity

mi·cro·eco·nom·ics \-,e-kə-'nä-miks, -,ē-kə-\ *n pl but usu sing in constr* (1947) : a study of economics in terms of individual areas of activity (as a firm, household, or prices) — compare MACROECONOMICS — **mi·cro·eco·nom·ic** \-'nä-mik\ *adj*

mi·cro·elec·trode \,mī-krō-i-'lek-,trōd\ *n* (1917) : a minute electrode; *esp* : one that is inserted in a living biological cell or tissue in studying its electrical characteristics

mi·cro·elec·tron·ics \-i-ˌlek-ˈträ-niks\ *n pl* (1958) **1** *sing in constr* : a branch of electronics that deals with the miniaturization of electronic circuits and components **2** : devices, equipment, or circuits produced using the methods of microelectronics — **mi·cro·elec·tron·ic** \-nik\ *adj* — **mi·cro·elec·tron·i·cal·ly** \-ni-k(ə-)lē\ *adv*

mi·cro·elec·tro·pho·re·sis \-i-ˌlek-trə-fə-ˈrē-səs\ *n* [NL] (1936) : electrophoresis in which the movement of single particles is observed in a microscope; *also* : electrophoresis in which micromethods are used — **mi·cro·elec·tro·pho·ret·ic** \-ˈre-tik\ *adj* — **mi·cro·elec·tro·pho·ret·i·cal·ly** \-ti-k(ə-)lē\ *adv*

mi·cro·el·e·ment \-ˈe-lə-mənt\ *n* (1936) : TRACE ELEMENT

mi·cro·en·cap·su·late \-in-ˈkap-sə-ˌlāt\ *vt* (1963) : to enclose in a microcapsule ⟨*microencapsulated* aspirin⟩ — **mi·cro·en·cap·su·la·tion** \-in-ˌkap-sə-ˈlā-shən\ *n*

mi·cro·en·vi·ron·ment \-in-ˈvi-rən-mənt, -ˈvī(-ə)rn-\ *n* (1938) : a small or relatively small usu. distinctly specialized and effectively isolated habitat (as a forest canopy) or environment (as of a nerve cell) — **mi·cro·en·vi·ron·men·tal** \-ˌvī-rən-ˈmen-tᵊl\ *adj*

mi·cro·evo·lu·tion \-ˌe-və-ˈlü-shən *also* -ˌē-və-\ *n* (1940) : comparatively minor evolutionary change involving the accumulation of variations in populations usu. below the species level — **mi·cro·evo·lu·tion·ary** \-shə-ˌner-ē\ *adj*

mi·cro·far·ad \ˈmī-krō-ˌfar-ˌad, -ˌfar-əd\ *n* (1873) : a unit of capacitance equal to one millionth of a farad

mi·cro·fau·na \ˌmī-krō-ˈfȯ-nə, -ˈfä-\ *n* [NL] (1902) **1** : minute animals; *esp* : those invisible to the naked eye ⟨the soil ∼⟩ **2** : a small or strictly localized fauna (as of a microenvironment) — **mi·cro·fau·nal** \-ˈfȯ-nᵊl, -ˈfä-\ *adj*

mi·cro·fi·bril \-ˈfī-brəl, -ˈfi-\ *n* (1938) : a fine fibril; *esp* : one of the submicroscopic elongated bundles of cellulose of a plant cell wall — **mi·cro·fi·bril·lar** \-brə-lər\ *adj*

mi·cro·fiche \ˈmī-krō-ˌfēsh, -ˌfish\ *n, pl* **-fiche** *or* **-fiches** \-ˌfē-shəz, -ˌfēsh, -ˌfi-shəz, -ˌfish\ [F, fr. *micr-* micr- + *fiche* fiche] (1950) : a sheet of microfilm containing rows of microimages of pages of printed matter

mi·cro·fil·a·ment \ˌmī-krō-ˈfi-lə-mənt\ *n* (1963) : any of the minute actin-containing protein filaments of eukaryotic cytoplasm that function in maintaining structure and in intracellular movement

mi·cro·fi·lar·ia \-fə-ˈlar-ē-ə, -ˈler-\ *n* [NL] (1878) : a minute larval filaria — **mi·cro·fi·lar·i·al** \-ē-əl\ *adj*

¹mi·cro·film \ˈmī-krə-ˌfilm\ *n* [ISV] (1927) : a film bearing a photographic record on a reduced scale of printed or other graphic matter

²microfilm *vt* (1937) : to reproduce on microfilm ∼ *vi* : to make microfilms — **mi·cro·film·able** \ˌmī-krə-ˈfil-mə-bəl\ *adj* — **mi·cro·film·er** \ˈmī-krə-ˌfil-mər\ *n*

mi·cro·flo·ra \ˌmī-krə-ˈflōr-ə, -ˈflȯr-\ *n* [NL] (1904) **1** : minute plants; *esp* : those invisible to the naked eye **2** : a small or strictly localized flora (as of a microenvironment) — **mi·cro·flo·ral** \-əl\ *adj*

mi·cro·form \ˈmī-krə-ˌfȯrm\ *n* (1958) **1** : a process for reproducing printed matter in a much reduced size ⟨documents in ∼⟩ **2 a** : matter reproduced by microform **b** : MICROCOPY

mi·cro·fos·sil \ˌmī-krō-ˈfä-səl\ *n* (1924) : a fossil that can be studied only microscopically and that may be either a fragment of a larger organism or an entire minute organism

mi·cro·fun·gus \-ˈfən-gəs\ *n* [NL] (1874) : a fungus (as a mold) with a microscopic fruiting body

mi·cro·ga·mete \-ˈga-ˌmēt *also* -gə-ˈmēt\ *n* [ISV] (ca. 1891) : the smaller and usu. male gamete of a heterogamous organism

mi·cro·ga·me·to·cyte \-gə-ˈmē-tə-ˌsīt\ *n* [ISV] (1902) : a gametocyte producing microgametes

mi·cro·gram \ˈmī-krə-ˌgram\ *n* [ISV] (ca. 1890) : one millionth of a gram — see METRIC SYSTEM table

mi·cro·graph \-ˌgraf\ *n* [ISV] (1904) : a graphic reproduction of the image of an object formed by a microscope — **micrograph** *vt*

mi·cro·graph·ics \ˌmī-krə-ˈgra-fiks\ *n pl but sing in constr* (1969) : the industry concerned with the manufacture and sale of graphic material in microform; *also* : the production of such material — **mi·cro·graph·ic** \-fik\ *adj* — **mi·cro·graph·i·cal·ly** \-fi-k(ə-)lē\ *adv*

mi·cro·grav·i·ty \-ˈgra-və-tē\ *n* (1974) : a condition in space in which only minuscule forces are experienced : virtual absence of gravity; *broadly* : a condition of weightlessness

mi·cro·groove \ˈmī-krō-ˌgrüv\ *n* (1948) : a narrow continuous V≠shaped spiral track that has closely spaced turns and that is used on long-playing records

mi·cro·hab·i·tat \ˌmī-krō-ˈha-bə-ˌtat\ *n* (1933) : the microenvironment in which an organism lives ⟨decaying wood creates a ∼ for insects⟩

mi·cro·im·age \-ˈi-mij\ *n* (1950) : an image (as on a microfilm) that is greatly reduced in size

mi·cro·inch \-ˈinch\ *n* (1941) : one millionth of an inch

mi·cro·in·jec·tion \ˌmī-krō-in-ˈjek-shən\ *n* (1921) : injection under the microscope; *specif* : injection into tissues by means of a fine mechanically controlled capillary tube — **mi·cro·in·ject** \-ˈjekt\ *vt*

mi·cro·in·struc·tion \-ˈstrək-shən\ *n* (1959) : a computer instruction that activates the circuits necessary to perform a single machine operation usu. as part of the execution of a machine-language instruction

mi·cro·lep·i·dop·tera \ˌmī-krō-ˌle-pə-ˈdäp-tə-rə\ *n pl* [NL] (1852) : lepidopterous insects (as tortricids) that belong to families of minute or medium-sized moths — **mi·cro·lep·i·dop·ter·ous** \-tə-rəs\ *adj*

mi·cro·li·ter \ˈmī-krō-ˌlē-tər\ *n* [ISV] (ca. 1894) : a unit of capacity equal to one millionth of a liter — see METRIC SYSTEM table

mi·cro·lith \ˈmī-krə-ˌlith\ *n* [ISV] (1908) : a tiny blade tool esp. of the Mesolithic usu. in a geometric shape (as that of a triangle) and often set in a bone or wooden haft — **mi·cro·lith·ic** \ˌmī-krə-ˈli-thik\ *adj*

mi·cro·man·age \ˌmī-krō-ˈma-nij\ *vt* (1979) : to manage with great or excessive control or attention to details — **mi·cro·man·age·ment** \-mənt\ *n* — **mi·cro·man·ag·er** \-ˈma-ni-jər\ *n*

mi·cro·ma·nip·u·la·tion \ˌmī-krō-mə-ˌni-pyə-ˈlā-shən\ *n* (1921) : the technique or practice of microdissection and microinjection

mi·cro·ma·nip·u·la·tor \-ˈni-pyə-ˌlā-tər\ *n* (1921) : an instrument for micromanipulation

mi·cro·mere \ˈmī-krō-ˌmir\ *n* [ISV] (1877) : a small blastomere — see BLASTULA illustration

mi·cro·me·te·or·ite \ˌmī-krō-ˈmē-tē-ə-ˌrīt\ *n* (1949) **1** : a meteorite so small that it can pass through the earth's atmosphere without becom-

ing intensely heated **2** : a very small particle in interplanetary space — **mi·cro·me·te·or·it·ic** \-ˌmē-tē-ə-ˈri-tik\ *adj*

mi·cro·me·te·or·oid \-ˈmē-tē-ə-ˌrȯid\ *n* (1954) : MICROMETEORITE 2

mi·cro·me·te·o·rol·o·gy \-ˌmē-tē-ə-ˈrä-lə-jē\ *n* (1930) : meteorology that deals with small-scale weather systems ranging up to several kilometers in diameter and confined to the lower troposphere — **mi·cro·me·te·o·ro·log·i·cal** \-ˌmē-tē-ˌȯr-ə-ˈlä-ji-kəl, -ˌär-ə-, -ə-rə-\ *adj* — **mi·cro·me·te·o·rol·o·gist** \-ˌmē-tē-ə-ˈrä-lə-jist\ *n*

¹mi·crom·e·ter \mī-ˈkrä-mə-tər\ *n* [F *micromètre*, fr. *micr-* + *-mètre* -meter] (1670) **1** : an instrument used with a telescope or microscope for measuring minute distances **2** : a caliper for making precise measurements that has a spindle moved by a finely threaded screw

²mi·cro·me·ter \ˈmī-krō-ˌmē-tər\ *n* [ISV *micr-* + ³*meter*] (1880) : a unit of length equal to one millionth of a meter — called also *micron*; see METRIC SYSTEM table

micrometer 2

mi·cro·meth·od \ˈmī-krō-ˌme-thəd\ *n* (1919) : a method (as of microanalysis) that requires only very small quantities of material or that involves the use of the microscope

mi·cro·mini \ˌmī-krō-ˈmi-nē\ *n* (1966) : a very short miniskirt

mi·cro·min·i·a·ture \-ˈmi-nē-ə-ˌchủr, -ˈmi-ni-ˌchủr, -ˈmin-yə-, -chər, -ˌtyủr, -ˌtủr\ *adj* (1958) **1** : MICROMINIATURIZED **2** : suitable for use with microminiaturized parts

mi·cro·min·i·a·tur·iza·tion \-ˌmi-nē-ə-ˌchủr-ə-ˈzā-shən, -ˌmi-ni-ˌchủr-, -ˌmin-yə-ˌchủr-, -chər-, -ˌtyủr-, -ˌtủr-\ *n* (1955) : the process of producing microminiaturized things

mi·cro·min·i·a·tur·ized \-ˈmi-nē-ə-chə-ˌrīzd, -ˈmi-ni-chə-, -ˈmin-yə-chə-, -ˌtyủ-, -ˌtủ-\ *adj* (1959) : reduced to or produced in a very small size and esp. in a size smaller than one considered miniature

mi·cro·mole \ˈmī-krə-ˌmōl\ *n* [ISV] (1936) : one millionth of a mole — **mi·cro·mo·lar** \-ˈmō-lər\ *adj*

mi·cro·mor·phol·o·gy \ˌmī-krō-mȯr-ˈfä-lə-jē\ *n* (1945) : MICROSTRUCTURE — **mi·cro·mor·pho·log·i·cal** \-fə-lä-ji-kəl\ *adj*

mi·cron \ˈmī-ˌkrän\ *n* [NL, fr. Gk *mikron*, neut. of *mikros* small — more at MICR-] (1885) : ²MICROMETER

Mi·cro·ne·sian \ˌmī-krə-ˈnē-zhən, -shən\ *n* (1847) **1** : a native or inhabitant of Micronesia **2** : a group of Austronesian languages spoken in the Micronesian islands — **Micronesian** *adj*

mi·cron·ize \ˈmī-krə-ˌnīz\ *vt* **-ized; -iz·ing** [*micron*] (1940) : to pulverize esp. into particles a few micrometers in diameter

mi·cro·nu·cle·us \ˌmī-krō-ˈnü-klē-əs, -ˈnyü-\ *n* [NL] (1892) : a minute nucleus; *specif* : one that is primarily concerned with reproductive and genetic functions in most ciliated protozoans

mi·cro·nu·tri·ent \-ˈnü-trē-ənt, -ˈnyü-\ *n* (1939) **1** : TRACE ELEMENT **2** : an organic compound (as a vitamin) essential in minute amounts to the growth and health of an animal

mi·cro·or·gan·ism \-ˈȯr-gə-ˌni-zəm\ *n* [ISV] (1880) : an organism of microscopic or ultramicroscopic size

mi·cro·pa·le·on·tol·o·gy \-ˌpā-lē-ˌän-ˈtä-lə-jē, -lē-ən-, *esp Brit* -ˌpa-\ *n* [ISV] (1883) : the study of microscopic fossils — **mi·cro·pa·le·on·to·log·i·cal** \-ˌän-tᵊl-ˈä-ji-kəl\ *also* **mi·cro·pa·le·on·to·log·ic** \-jik\ *adj* — **mi·cro·pa·le·on·tol·o·gist** \-ˌän-ˈtä-lə-jist, -ən-\ *n*

mi·cro·par·ti·cle \-ˈpär-ti-kəl\ *n* (1929) : a very small particle; *esp* : one that is microscopic in size

mi·cro·phage \ˈmī-krə-ˌfāj *also* -ˌfäzh\ *n* [ISV] (1890) : a small phagocyte

mi·cro·phone \ˈmī-krə-ˌfōn\ *n* [ISV] (1878) : an instrument whereby sound waves are caused to generate or modulate an electric current usu. for the purpose of transmitting or recording sound (as speech or music) — **mi·cro·phon·ic** \ˌmī-krə-ˈfä-nik\ *adj*

mi·cro·phon·ics \ˌmī-krə-ˈfä-niks\ *n pl* (1929) : noises in a loudspeaker caused by mechanical shock or vibration of the electronic components

mi·cro·pho·to·graph \-ˈfō-tə-ˌgraf\ *n* [ISV] (1858) **1** : a small photograph that is normally magnified for viewing : MICROCOPY **2** : PHOTOMICROGRAPH — **microphotograph** *vt* — **mi·cro·pho·tog·ra·pher** \-fə-ˈtä-grə-fər\ *n* — **mi·cro·pho·to·graph·ic** \-ˌfō-tə-ˈgra-fik\ *adj* — **mi·cro·pho·tog·ra·phy** \-fə-ˈtä-grə-fē\ *n*

mi·cro·pho·tom·e·ter \-fō-ˈtä-mə-tər\ *n* [ISV] (1899) : an instrument for measuring the amount of light transmitted or reflected by small areas or for measuring the relative densities of spectral lines on a photographic film or plate — **mi·cro·pho·to·met·ric** \-ˌfō-tə-ˈme-trik\ *adj* — **mi·cro·pho·to·met·ri·cal·ly** \-tri-k(ə-)lē\ *adv* — **mi·cro·pho·tom·e·try** \-fō-ˈtä-mə-trē\ *n*

mi·cro·phyll \ˈmī-krə-ˌfil\ *n* [ISV] (1935) **1** : a small leaf **2** : a leaf (as of a club moss) with single unbranched veins and no demonstrable gap around the leaf trace — **mi·cro·phyl·lous** \ˌmī-krə-ˈfi-ləs\ *adj*

mi·cro·phys·ics \ˌmī-krō-ˈfi-ziks\ *n* (1885) : the physics of molecules, atoms, and elementary particles — **mi·cro·phys·i·cal** \-ˈfi-zi-kəl\ *adj* — **mi·cro·phys·i·cal·ly** \-k(ə-)lē\ *adv*

mi·cro·pi·pette *or* **mi·cro·pi·pet** \-pī-ˈpet\ *n* (1918) **1** : a pipette for the measurement of minute volumes **2** : a small and extremely fine≠pointed pipette used in making microinjections

mi·cro·plank·ton \-ˈplaŋ(k)-tən, -ˌtän\ *n* [ISV] (1903) : microscopic plankton

mi·cro·pore \ˈmī-krə-ˌpōr, -ˌpȯr\ *n* (1884) : a very fine pore — **mi·cro·po·ros·i·ty** \ˌmī-krə-pə-ˈrä-sə-tē, -pȯ-\ *n* — **mi·cro·po·rous** \ˌmī-krə-ˈpōr-əs, -ˈpȯr-\ *adj*

mi·cro·prism \ˈmī-krə-ˌpri-zəm\ *n* (1966) : a usu. circular area on the focusing screen of a camera that is made up of tiny prisms and that causes the image in the viewfinder to blur if the subject is not in focus

mi·cro·probe \-ˌprōb\ *n* (1944) : a device for microanalysis that operates by exciting radiation in a minute area of material so that the composition may be determined from the emission spectrum

---

\ə\ abut \ᵊ\ kitten, F table \ər\ further \a\ ash \ā\ ace \ä\ mop, mar \aủ\ out \ch\ chin \e\ bet \ē\ easy \g\ go \i\ hit \ī\ ice \j\ job \ŋ\ sing \ō\ go \ȯ\ law \ȯi\ boy \th\ thin \t͟h\ the \ü\ loot \ủ\ foot \y\ yet \zh\ vision \à, k̟, ⁿ, œ, œ̄, ɶ, ῡ, ᵜ\ see Guide to Pronunciation

mi·cro·pro·ces·sor \‚mī-krō-'prä-‚se-sər, -'prō-\ *n* (1970) : a computer processor contained on an integrated-circuit chip; *also* : such a processor with memory and associated circuits

mi·cro·pro·gram \-'prō‚gram, -grəm\ *n* (1953) : a routine composed of microinstructions used in microprogramming

mi·cro·pro·gram·ming \-‚gra-miŋ\ *n* (1953) : the use of routines stored in memory rather than specialized circuits to control a device (as a computer)

mi·cro·pro·jec·tor \-prə-'jek-tər\ *n* (1927) : a projector utilizing a compound microscope for projecting on a screen a greatly enlarged image of a microscopic object — **mi·cro·pro·jec·tion** \-'jek-shən\ *n*

mi·cro·pub·lish·ing \-‚pə-bli-shiŋ\ *n* (1966) : publishing in microform — **mi·cro·pub·lish·er** \-bli-shər\ *n*

mi·cro·pul·sa·tion \-‚pəl-'sā-shən\ *n* (1949) : a pulsation having a short period ⟨a ~ of the earth's magnetic field with a period in the range from a fraction of a second to several hundred seconds⟩

mi·cro·punc·ture \-'pəŋ(k)-chər\ *n* (1948) : an extremely small puncture (as of a nephron); *also* : an act of making a micropuncture

mi·cro·pyle \'mī-krə-‚pīl\ *n* [F, fr. *micr-* + Gk *pylē* gate] (1821) **1** : a minute opening in the integument of an ovule of a seed plant **2** : a differentiated area of surface in an egg through which a sperm enters — **mi·cro·py·lar** \‚mī-krə-'pī-lər\ *adj*

mi·cro·quake \'mī-krō-‚kwāk\ *n* (1967) : MICROEARTHQUAKE

mi·cro·ra·di·og·ra·phy \‚mī-krō-‚rā-dē-'ä-grə-fē\ *n* (1913) : radiography in which an X-ray photograph is prepared showing minute internal structure — **mi·cro·ra·dio·graph** \-'rā-dē-ə-‚graf\ *n* — **mi·cro·ra·dio·graph·ic** \-‚rā-dē-ə-'gra-fik\ *adj*

mi·cro·read·er \'mī-krō-‚rē-dər\ *n* (1949) : an apparatus that gives an enlarged image of a microphotograph esp. for reading

mi·cro·re·pro·duc·tion \‚mī-krō-‚rē-prə-'dək-shən\ *n* (1938) : the reproduction of written or printed matter in microform; *also* : an item so reproduced

mi·cro·scale \'mī-krō-‚skāl\ *n* (1931) : a very small scale

mi·cro·scope \'mī-krə-‚skōp\ *n* [NL *microscopium*, fr. *micr-* + *-scopium* -scope] (1654) **1** : an optical instrument consisting of a lens or combination of lenses for making enlarged images of minute objects; *esp* : COMPOUND MICROSCOPE **2** : an instrument using radiations other than light or using vibrations for making enlarged images of minute objects ⟨acoustic ~⟩

mi·cro·scop·ic \‚mī-krə-'skä-pik\ *or* **mi·cro·scop·i·cal** \-pi-kəl\ *adj* (1732) **1** : resembling a microscope esp. in perception **2 a** : invisible or indistinguishable without the use of a microscope **b** : very small or fine or precise **3** : of, relating to, or conducted with the microscope or microscopy — **mi·cro·scop·i·cal·ly** \-pi-k(ə-)lē\ *adv*

mi·cros·co·py \mī-'kräs-kə-pē\ *n* (ca. 1665) : the use of or investigation with the microscope — **mi·cros·co·pist** \-pist\ *n*

mi·cro·sec·ond \'mī-krō-‚se-kənd, -kənt\ *n* [ISV] (1906) : one millionth of a second

mi·cro·seism \'mī-krə-‚sī-zəm\ *n* [ISV *micr-* + Gk *seismos* earthquake — more at SEISMIC] (1887) : a feeble rhythmically and persistently recurring earth tremor — **mi·cro·seis·mic** \‚mī-krə-'sīz-mik, -'sīs-\ *adj* — **mi·cro·seis·mic·i·ty** \-‚sīz-'mi-sə-tē, -sīs-\ *n*

mi·cro·some \'mī-krə-‚sōm\ *n* [G *Mikrosom*, fr. *mikr-* micr- + *-som* -some] (1885) **1** : any of various minute cellular structures (as a ribosome) **2** : a particle in a particulate fraction that is obtained by heavy centrifugation of broken cells and consists of various amounts of ribosomes, fragmented endoplasmic reticulum, and mitochondrial cristae — **mi·cro·som·al** \‚mī-krə-'sō-məl\ *adj*

mi·cro·spec·tro·pho·tom·e·ter \‚mī-krə-‚spek-trə-fō-'tä-mə-tər\ *n* (1949) : a spectrophotometer adapted to the examination of light transmitted by a very small specimen (as a single organic cell) — **mi·cro·spec·tro·pho·to·met·ric** \-‚fō-tə-'me-trik\ *adj* — **mi·cro·spec·tro·pho·tom·e·try** \-fō-'tä-mə-trē\ *n*

mi·cro·sphere \'mī-krə-‚sfir\ *n* (1894) : a minute sphere — **mi·cro·spher·i·cal** \‚mī-krə-'sfir-i-kəl, -'sfer-\ *adj*

mi·cro·spo·ran·gi·um \‚mī-krō-spə-'ran-jē-əm\ *n* [NL] (1881) : a sporangium that develops only microspores — **mi·cro·spo·ran·gi·ate** \-jē-ət\ *adj*

mi·cro·spore \'mī-krə-‚spōr, -‚spȯr\ *n* [ISV] (1858) : any of the spores in heterosporous plants that give rise to male gametophytes and are generally smaller than the megaspore — **mi·cro·spo·rous** \‚mī-krə-'spōr-əs, -'spȯr-; mī-'kräs-pə-rəs\ *adj*

mi·cro·spo·ro·cyte \-'spōr-ə-‚sīt, -'spȯr-\ *n* (1940) : a microspore mother cell

mi·cro·spo·ro·gen·e·sis \‚mī-krə-‚spȯr-ə-'je-nə-səs, -‚spȯr-\ *n* [NL] (1921) : the formation and maturation of microspores

mi·cro·spo·ro·phyll \-‚fil\ *n* (ca. 1890) : a sporophyll that develops only microsporangia

mi·cro·state \'mī-krō-‚stāt\ *n* (1962) : a nation that is extremely small in area and population

mi·cro·struc·ture \'mī-krō-‚strək-chər\ *n* [ISV] (1885) : the microscopic structure of a material (as a mineral or a biological cell) — **mi·cro·struc·tur·al** \‚mī-krō-'strək-chə-rəl, -'strək-shrəl\ *adj*

mi·cro·sur·gery \‚mī-krō-'sərj-rē, -'sər-jə-\ *n* (1926) : minute dissection or manipulation (as by a micromanipulator or laser beam) of living structures or tissue — **mi·cro·sur·gi·cal** \-'sər-ji-kəl\ *adj*

mi·cro·switch \-‚swich\ *n* (1940) : a very small switch that is sensitive to minute motions and is used esp. in automatic devices

mi·cro·tech·nique \‚mī-krō-tek-'nēk\ *also* **mi·cro·tech·nic** \-'tek-nik, -tek-'nēk\ *n* [ISV] (1892) : any of various methods of handling and preparing material for microscopic observation and study

mi·cro·tome \'mī-krə-‚tōm\ *n* [ISV] (1856) : an instrument for cutting sections (as of organic tissues) for microscopic examination

mi·cro·tone \'mī-krə-‚tōn\ *n* (1920) : a musical interval smaller than a halftone — **mi·cro·ton·al** \‚mī-krō-'tōn-ᵊl\ *adj* — **mi·cro·to·nal·i·ty** \-tō-'na-lə-tē\ *n* — **mi·cro·ton·al·ly** \-'tōn-ᵊl-ē\ *adv*

mi·cro·tu·bule \‚mī-krō-'tü-(‚)byü(ə)l, -'tyü-\ *n* (1961) : any of the minute tubules in eukaryotic cytoplasm that are composed of the protein tubulin and form an important component of the cytoskeleton, mitotic spindle, cilia, and flagella — **mi·cro·tu·bu·lar** \-byə-lər\ *adj*

mi·cro·vas·cu·lar \-'vas-kyə-lər\ *adj* (1959) : of, relating to, or constituting the part of the circulatory system made up of minute vessels (as venules or capillaries) that average less than 0.3 millimeters in diameter — **mi·cro·vas·cu·la·ture** \-lə-‚chur, -‚tyur, -‚tur\ *n*

mi·cro·vil·lus \-'vi-ləs\ *n* [NL] (1953) : a microscopic projection of a tissue, cell, or cell organelle; *esp* : any of the fingerlike outward projections of some cell surfaces — **mi·cro·vil·lar** \-'vi-lər\ *adj* — **mi·cro·vil·lous** \-'vi-ləs\ *adj*

mi·cro·volt \'mī-krə-‚vōlt\ *n* (1868) : one millionth of a volt

mi·cro·watt \-‚wät\ *n* (ca. 1909) : one millionth of a watt

¹**mi·cro·wave** \-‚wāv\ *n, often attrib* (1931) **1** : a comparatively short electromagnetic wave; *esp* : between about 1 millimeter and 1 meter in wavelength **2** : MICROWAVE OVEN

²**microwave** *vt* (1973) : to cook or heat in a microwave oven — **mi·cro·wav·able** *or* **mi·cro·wave·able** \‚mī-krə-'wā-və-bəl\ *adj*

microwave oven *n* (1963) : an oven in which food is cooked by the heat produced by the absorption of microwave energy by water molecules in the food

mi·cro·world \-‚wər(-ə)ld\ *n* (1955) : a small universe; *specif* : the natural universe observed at the microscopic or submicroscopic level

mic·tu·rate \'mik-chə-‚rāt, 'mik-tə-\ *vi* **-rat·ed; -rat·ing** [L *micturire* to desire to urinate, fr. *meiere* to urinate; akin to OE *mīgan* to urinate, Gk *omeichein*] (1842) : URINATE — **mic·tu·ri·tion** \‚mik-chə-'ri-shən, ‚mik-tə-\ *n*

¹**mid** \'mid\ *adj* [ME, fr. OE *midde*; akin to OHG *mitti* middle, L *medius*, Gk *mesos*] (bef. 12c) **1** : being the part in the middle or midst ⟨in ~ ocean⟩ — often used in combination ⟨*mid*-August⟩ **2** : occupying a middle position ⟨the ~ finger⟩ **3** *of a vowel* : articulated with the arch of the tongue midway between its highest and its lowest elevation — **mid** *adv*

²**mid** *prep* (1808) : AMID

mid·air \'mid-‚ar, -‚er\ *n* (1667) : a point or region in the air not immediately adjacent to the ground ⟨planes collided in ~⟩

Mi·das \'mī-dəs\ *n* [L, fr. Gk] : a legendary Phrygian king who is given the power of turning everything he touches to gold

Midas touch *n* (1883) : an uncanny ability for making money in every venture

mid·brain \'mid-‚brān\ *n* (1875) : the middle of the three primary divisions of the developing vertebrate brain or the corresponding part of the adult brain — called also *mesencephalon*; see BRAIN illustration

mid·course \-'kȯrs, -‚kȯrs\ *adj* (ca. 1956) : being or occurring in the middle part of a course (as of a spacecraft) ⟨a ~ correction⟩

mid·day \'mid-‚dā, -'dā\ *n, often attrib* (bef. 12c) : the middle of the day

mid·den \'mi-dᵊn\ *n* [ME *midding*, of Scand origin; akin to ON *myki* dung & ON *dyngja* manure pile — more at DUNG] (14c) **1** : DUNGHILL **2 a** : a refuse heap; *esp* : KITCHEN MIDDEN **b** : a small pile (as of seeds, bones, or leaves) gathered by a rodent (as a pack rat)

¹**mid·dle** \'mi-dᵊl\ *adj* [ME *middel*, fr. OE; akin to OE *midde*] (bef. 12c) **1** : equally distant from the extremes : MEDIAL, CENTRAL ⟨the ~ house in the row⟩ **2** : being at neither extreme : INTERMEDIATE **3** *cap* **a** : constituting a division intermediate between those prior and later or upper and lower ⟨*Middle* Paleozoic⟩ **b** : constituting a period of a language or literature intermediate between one called *Old* and one called *New* or *Modern* ⟨*Middle* Dutch⟩ **4** *of a verb form or voice* : typically asserting that a person or thing both performs and is affected by the action represented

²**middle** *n* (bef. 12c) **1** : a middle part, point, or position **2** : the central portion of the human body : WAIST **3** : the position of being among or in the midst of something **4** : something intermediate between extremes : MEAN **5** : the center of an offensive or defensive formation; *esp* : the area between the second baseman and the shortstop

middle age *n* (14c) : the period of life from about 40 to about 60 — **mid·dle-aged** \‚mi-dᵊl-'ājd\ *adj* — **mid·dle-ag·er** \-'ā-jər\ *n*

Middle Ages *n pl* (1616) : the period of European history from about A.D. 500 to about 1500

Middle America *n* (1898) **1** : the region of the western hemisphere including Mexico, Central America, often the West Indies, and sometimes Colombia and Venezuela **2** : the midwestern section of the U.S. **3** : the middle-class segment of the U.S. population; *esp* : the traditional or conservative element of the middle class — **middle-American** — **Middle American** *n*

mid·dle·brow \'mi-dᵊl-‚brau̇\ *n* (1925) : a person who is moderately but not highly cultivated — **middlebrow** *adj*

middle C *n* (1840) : the note designated by the first ledger line below the treble staff and the first above the bass staff

mid·dle–class \‚mi-dᵊl-'klas\ *adj* (1836) : of or relating to the middle class; *esp* : characterized by a high material standard of living, sexual morality, and respect for property — **mid·dle–class·ness** \-nəs\ *n*

middle class *n* (1766) : a class occupying a position between the upper class and the lower class; *esp* : a fluid heterogeneous socioeconomic grouping composed principally of business and professional people, bureaucrats, and some farmers and skilled workers sharing common social characteristics and values

middle distance *n* (1813) **1** : a part of a pictorial representation or scene between the foreground and the background **2** : any footrace distance usu. from 800 to 1500 meters or from 880 yards to one mile

Middle Dutch *n* (ca. 1959) : the Dutch language in use from about 1100 to about 1500 — see INDO-EUROPEAN LANGUAGES table

middle ear *n* (1852) : a small bony-lined cavity that is separated from the outer ear by the eardrum and that transmits sound waves from the eardrum to the partition between the middle and inner ears through a chain of tiny bones

Middle English *n* (1830) : the English in use from the 12th to 15th centuries — see INDO-EUROPEAN LANGUAGES table

middle finger *n* (bef. 12c) : the midmost of the five digits of the hand

Middle French *n* (1889) : the French in use from the 14th to 16th centuries — see INDO-EUROPEAN LANGUAGES table

middle game *n* (1894) : the middle phase of a board game; *specif* : the part of a chess game after the pieces have been developed when players attempt to gain and exploit positional and material superiority — compare ENDGAME, OPENING

Middle Greek *n* (1889) : the Greek language used in the 7th to 15th centuries

middle ground *n* (1801) **1** : a standpoint midway between extremes **2** : MIDDLE DISTANCE 1

Middle High German *n* (1889) : the High German in use from about 1100 to 1500 — see INDO-EUROPEAN LANGUAGES table

Middle Irish *n* (1952) : the Irish in use between the 10th and 13th centuries — see INDO-EUROPEAN LANGUAGES table

middle lamella *n* (ca. 1886) : a layer of pectinaceous intercellular material lying between the walls of adjacent plant cells — see CELL illustration

Middle Low German *n* (ca. 1889) : the Low German in use from about 1100 to 1500 — see INDO-EUROPEAN LANGUAGES table

mid·dle·man \'mi-d³l-,man\ *n* (1795) : an intermediary or agent between two parties; *esp* : a dealer or agent intermediate between the producer of goods and the retailer or consumer

middle management *n* (ca. 1948) : management personnel intermediate between operational supervisors and policy-making administrators — **middle manager** *n*

middle name *n* (1835) : a name between one's first name and surname

middle-of-the-road *adj* (1894) : standing for or following a course of action midway between extremes; *esp* : being neither liberal nor conservative in politics — **middle-of-the-road·er** \-'rō-dər\ *n* — **middle-of-the-road·ism** \-'rō-,di-zəm\ *n*

middle of the road (1918) : a course of action or a standpoint midway between extremes

Middle Persian *n* (1930) : any of the varieties of Persian in use from about 200 B.C. to about A.D. 1000

mid·dler \'mid-lər, 'mi-d³l-ər\ *n* (1882) : one belonging to an intermediate group, division, or class: as **a** : a student in the second-year class of a three-year program (as at a seminary or law school) **b** : a student in the second- or third-year class in some private secondary schools having a four-year course **c** : a student in a division in some private schools that corresponds approximately to junior high school

middle school *n* (1945) : a school usu. including grades 5 to 8 or 6 to 8 — **middle school·er** \-,skü-lər\ *n*

Middle Scots *n* (ca. 1903) : the Scots language in use between the latter half of the 15th and the early decades of the 17th centuries

middle term *n* (1685) : the term of a syllogism that occurs in both premises

mid·dle·weight \'mi-d³l-,wāt\ *n* (1889) : one of average weight; *specif* : a boxer in a weight division having a maximum limit of 160 pounds for professionals and 165 pounds for amateurs — compare LIGHT HEAVYWEIGHT, WELTERWEIGHT

Middle Welsh *n* (ca. 1922) : the Welsh in use from about 1150 to 1500 — see INDO-EUROPEAN LANGUAGES table

¹**mid·dling** \'mid-liŋ, -lən\ *n* (1543) **1** : any of various commodities of intermediate size, quality, or position **2** *pl but sing or pl in constr* : a granular product of grain milling; *esp* : a wheat milling by-product used in animal feeds

²**middling** *adj* (1550) **1** : of middle, medium, or moderate size, degree, or quality **2** : MEDIOCRE, SECOND-RATE — **middling** *adv* — **mid·dling·ly** \-lē\ *adv*

mid·dor·sal \'mid-'dòr-səl\ *adj* (1879) : of, relating to, or situated in the middle part or median line of the back

mid·dy \'mi-dē\ *n, pl* **middies** [by shortening & alter.] (1818) **1** : MIDSHIPMAN **2** : a loosely fitting blouse with a sailor collar worn by women and children

mid·field \'mid-,fēld, ,mid-'\ *n* (15c) **1** : the middle portion of a field; *esp* : the portion of a playing field (as in football) that is midway between goals **2** : the players on a team (as in lacrosse or soccer) that normally play in the midfield

mid·field·er \-,fēl-dər, -'fēl-\ *n* (1938) : a member of a midfield

Mid·gard \'mid-,gärd\ *n* [ON *mithgarthr*] : the abode of human beings in Norse mythology

midge \'mij\ *n* [ME *migge*, fr. OE *mycg*; akin to OHG *mucka* midge, Gk *myia* fly, L *musca*] (bef. 12c) : a tiny dipteran fly (as a chironomid)

midg·et \'mi-jət\ *n, often attrib* [*midge*] (1865) **1** : a very small person; *specif* : a person of unusually small size who is physically well-proportioned **2** : something (as an animal) much smaller than usual **3** : a front-engine, single-seat, open-wheel racing car smaller and of less engine displacement than standard cars of the type

mid·gut \'mid-,gət\ *n* (1875) : the middle part of an alimentary canal

midi \'mi-dē\ *n* [¹*mid* + *-i* (as in *mini*)] (1967) : a dress, skirt, or coat that usu. extends to the mid-calf

Mid·i·an·ite \'mi-dē-ə-,nīt\ *n* [*Midian*, son of Abraham] (1560) : a member of an ancient northern Arabian people

mid·land \'mid-lənd, -,land\ *n* (1555) **1** : the interior or central region of a country **2** *cap* **a** : the dialect of English spoken in the midland counties of England **b** : the dialect of English spoken in an area of the east central U.S. often divided into north Midland extending westward from an area including southern New Jersey; northern Delaware and Maryland; central and southern Pennsylvania; and central Ohio, Indiana, and Illinois and south Midland extending westward and southwestward from an area including the Appalachian regions of Virginia, No. Carolina, So. Carolina, and Georgia; Tennessee, Kentucky, West Virginia; and southern Ohio, Indiana, and Illinois — **midland** *adj, often cap* — **Mid·land·er** \-lən-dər, -,lan-\ *n*

mid·lat·i·tudes \'mid-'la-tə-,tüdz, ,mid-, -,tyüdz\ *n pl* (1925) : latitudes of the temperate zones or from about 30 to 60 degrees north or south of the equator — **mid·lat·i·tude** \-,tüd, -,tyüd\ *adj*

mid·life \'mid-'līf\ *n* (1898) : MIDDLE AGE

midlife crisis *n* (1965) : a period of emotional turmoil in middle age characterized esp. by a strong desire for change

mid·line \'mid-,līn, -'līn\ *n* (ca. 1859) : a median line; *esp* : the median line or median plane of the body or some part of the body

mid·most \-,mōst\ *adj* (bef. 12c) **1** : being in or near the exact middle **2** : most intimate : INNERMOST — **midmost** *adv or n*

mid·night \'mid-,nīt\ *n* (bef. 12c) **1** : the middle of the night; *specif* : 12 o'clock at night **2** : deep or extended darkness or gloom — **midnight** *adj* — **mid·night·ly** *adv or adj*

midnight blue *n* (1916) : a deep blackish blue

midnight sun *n* (1857) : the sun above the horizon at midnight in the arctic or antarctic summer

mid·point \'mid-,pòint, -'pòint\ *n* (14c) : a point at or near the center or middle

mid·rash \'mi-,dräsh\ *n, pl* **mid·rash·im** \mi-'drä-shəm\ [Heb *midhrāsh* exposition, explanation] (1613) **1** : a haggadic or halakic exposition of the underlying significance of a Bible text **2** : a collec-

tion of midrashim **3** *cap* : the midrashic literature written during the first Christian millennium — **mid·rash·ic** \mi-'drä-shik\ *adj, often cap*

mid·rib \'mid-,rib\ *n* (1794) : the central vein of a leaf

mid·riff \'mi-,drif\ *n* [ME *midrif*, fr. OE *midhrif*, fr. *midde* mid + *hrif* belly; akin to OHG *href* body, and prob. to L *corpus* body] (bef. 12c) **1** : DIAPHRAGM **1 2** : the mid-region of the human torso **3 a** : a section of a woman's garment that covers the midriff **b** : a woman's garment that exposes the midriff

mid·rise \'mid-,rīz, -'rīz\ *adj* (1967) : being approximately 5 to 10 stories high ⟨~ condominiums⟩

mid·sag·it·tal \'mid-'sa-jə-t³l\ *adj* (1947) : median and sagittal

mid·sec·tion \-,sek-shən\ *n* (1936) : a section midway between the extremes; *esp* : MIDRIFF 2

mid·ship·man \'mid-,ship-mən, ,mid-'\ *n* (1685) : a person in training for a naval commission; *esp* : a student in a naval academy

mid·ships \'mid-,ships\ *adv* (ca. 1828) : AMIDSHIPS

mid·size \-,sīz\ *also* **mid·sized** \-,sīzd\ *adj* (1970) : of intermediate size ⟨~ car⟩

mid·sole \-,sōl\ *n* (1926) : a layer (as of leather or rubber) between the insole and the outsole of a shoe

midst \'midst, 'mitst\ *n* [ME *middest*, alter. of *middes*, short for *amiddes* amid] (15c) **1** : the interior or central part or point : MIDDLE ⟨in the ~ of the forest⟩ **2** : a position of proximity to the members of a group ⟨a traitor in our ~⟩ **3** : the condition of being surrounded or beset ⟨in the ~ of his troubles⟩ **4** : a period of time about the middle of a continuing act or condition ⟨in the ~ of a meal⟩ — **midst** *prep*

mid·stream \'mid-'strēm, -,strēm\ *n* (1669) **1** : the middle of a stream **2** : an intermediate stage in an act or process ⟨the tone changes in ~⟩

mid·sum·mer \-'sə-mər, -,səm-\ *n* (bef. 12c) **1** : the middle of summer **2** : the summer solstice — **midsummer** *adj*

Midsummer Day *n* (bef. 12c) : June 24 celebrated as the feast of the nativity of John the Baptist

mid·term \'mid-,tərm (*usual for 1b*), -'tərm\ *n* (1906) **1 a** : the middle of an academic term **b** : an examination at midterm **2** : the approximate middle of a term of office

mid·town \'mid-,taùn, -'taùn\ *n* (1926) : a central section of a city; *esp* : one situated between sections conventionally called *downtown* and *uptown* — **midtown** *adj*

¹**mid·way** \'mid-,wā, -'wā\ *adv* (13c) : in the middle of the way or distance : HALFWAY

²**mid·way** \-,wā\ *n* [*Midway* (*Plaisance*), Chicago, site of the amusement section of the Columbian Exposition 1893] (1893) : an avenue at a fair, carnival, or amusement park for concessions and amusements

mid·week \-,wēk\ *n* (1707) : the middle of the week — **midweek** *adj or adv* — **mid·week·ly** \-,wē-klē, -'wē-\ *adj or adv*

¹**mid·wife** \'mid-,wīf\ *n* [ME *midwif*, fr. *mid* with (fr. OE) + *wif* woman] (14c) **1** : a person who assists women in childbirth **2** : one that helps to produce or bring forth something

²**midwife** *vt* **mid·wifed** \-,wīft\ *or* **mid·wived** \-,wīvd\; **mid·wif·ing** \-,wī-fiŋ\ *or* **mid·wiv·ing** \-,wī-viŋ\ (1638) : to assist in producing, bringing forth, or bringing about

mid·wife·ry \,mid-'wi-f(ə-)rē, -'wī-; 'mid-,wī-\ *n* (15c) **1** : the art or act of assisting at childbirth; *also* : OBSTETRICS **2** : the art, act, or process of producing, bringing forth, or bringing about

mid·win·ter \'mid-'win-tər, -,win-\ *n* (bef. 12c) **1** : the winter solstice **2** : the middle of winter — **midwinter** *adj*

mid·year \-,yir\ *n* (1896) **1 a** : an examination at the middle of an academic year **b** *pl* : the set of examinations at the middle of an academic year; *also* : the period of such examinations **2 a** : the middle or middle portion of a calendar year **b** : the middle of an academic year — **midyear** *adj*

mien \'mēn\ *n* [by shortening & alter. fr. ¹*demean*] (1513) **1** : air or bearing esp. as expressive of attitude or personality : DEMEANOR ⟨of aristocratic ~⟩ **2** : APPEARANCE, ASPECT ⟨the inherent dangers of government encroachment . . . presented such a distasteful ~ —H. W. Baldwin⟩ *syn* see BEARING

¹**miff** \'mif\ *n* [origin unknown] (1623) **1** : a fit of ill humor **2** : a trivial quarrel

²**miff** *vt* (1811) : to put into an ill humor : OFFEND

¹**might** \'mīt\ [ME, fr. OE *meahte, mihte*; akin to OHG *mahta, mohta* could] *past of* MAY (bef. 12c) — used in auxiliary function to express permission, liberty, probability, possibility in the past ⟨the president ~ do nothing without the board's consent⟩ or a present condition contrary to fact ⟨if you were older you ~ understand⟩ or less probability or possibility than *may* ⟨~ get there before it rains⟩ or as a polite alternative to *may* ⟨~ I ask who is calling⟩ or to *ought* or *should* ⟨you ~ at least apologize⟩

²**might** *n* [ME, fr. OE *miht*; akin to OHG *maht* might, *magan* to be able — more at MAY] (bef. 12c) **1 a** : the power, authority, or resources wielded (as by an individual or group) ⟨the ~ of the armed forces⟩ **b** (1) : bodily strength (2) : the power, energy, or intensity of which one is capable ⟨striving with ~ and main⟩ **2** *dial* : a great deal *syn* see POWER

might·i·ly \'mī-t³l-ē\ *adv* (bef. 12c) **1** : in a mighty manner : VIGOROUSLY ⟨applauded ~⟩ **2** : very much ⟨depressed me ~⟩

might·i·ness \'mī-tē-nəs\ *n* (14c) : the quality or state of being mighty

mightn't \'mī-t³nt\ (1889) : might not

¹**mighty** \'mī-tē\ *adj* **might·i·er; -est** (bef. 12c) **1** : possessing might : POWERFUL **2** : accomplished or characterized by might ⟨a ~ thrust⟩ **3** : great or imposing in size or extent : EXTRAORDINARY

²**mighty** *adv* (14c) : EXTREMELY, VERY ⟨a ~ handy gadget⟩

usage The use of *mighty* as an intensive usu. conveys a folksy down-home feeling ⟨plain and simple fare . . . but *mighty* filling and *mighty* satisfying —*Asheville (N.C.) Citizen-Times*⟩. It is used esp. to create a chatty style ⟨turnip greens, corn bread and biscuits. That sounds *mighty* good to me —Julia Child⟩ or to stress a rural atmosphere ⟨a man must be *mighty* serious about his squirrel hunting —Stuart Wil-

---

\ə\ abut \³\ kitten, F table \ər\ further \a\ ash \ā\ ace \ä\ mop, mar
\aù\ out \ch\ chin \e\ bet \ē\ easy \g\ go \i\ hit \ī\ ice \j\ job
\ŋ\ sing \ō\ go \ò\ law \òi\ boy \th\ thin \t̲h̲\ the \ü\ loot \ù\ foot
\y\ yet \zh\ vision \ä, k̲, ⁿ, œ, œ̄, ue, ū̄, ᵉ\ *see* Guide to Pronunciation

liams, *Field & Stream*⟩. In a more formal context, *mighty* is used to create additional emphasis by drawing attention to itself ⟨the chairman made sure that there were *mighty* few of them —Mollie Panter= Downes⟩.

mi·gnon \mēn-'yōⁿ, min-'yòn\ *n* (ca. 1919) : FILET MIGNON

mi·gnon·ette \,min-yə-'net\ *n* [F *mignonnette*, fr. obs. F, fem. of *mignonnet* dainty, fr. MF, fr. *mignon* darling] (1798) : any of a genus (*Reseda* of the family Resedaceae, the mignonette family) of herbs; *esp* : a garden annual (*R. odorata*) bearing racemes of fragrant whitish flowers

mi·graine \'mī-grãn, *Brit often* 'mē-\ *n* [F, modif. of LL *hemicrania* pain in one side of the head, fr. Gk *hēmikrania*, fr. *hēmi-* hemi- + *kranion* cranium] (15c) 1 : a condition marked by recurrent severe headache often with nausea and vomiting 2 : an episode or attack of migraine — **mi·grain·ous** \-,grã-nəs\ *adj*

mi·grant \'mī-grənt\ *n* [L *migrant-, migrans*, prp. of *migrare*] (1760) : one that migrates: as a : a person who moves regularly in order to find work esp. in harvesting crops b : an animal that shifts from one habitat to another — **migrant** *adj*

mi·grate \'mī-,grãt, mī-'\ *vi* **mi·grat·ed; mi·grat·ing** [L *migratus*, pp. of *migrare*; perh. akin to Gk *ameibein* to change] (1697) 1 : to move from one country, place, or locality to another 2 : to pass usu. periodically from one region or climate to another for feeding or breeding 3 : to change position in an organism or substance ⟨filarial worms ~ within the human body⟩ — **mi·gra·tion** \mī-'grã-shən\ *n* — **mi·gra·tion·al** \-shnəl, -shə-nᵊl\ *adj* — **mi·gra·tor** \'mī-,grã-tər, mī-'\ *n*

mi·gra·to·ry \'mī-grə-,tōr-ē, -,tòr-\ *adj* (1753) 1 : of, relating to, or characterized by migration 2 : WANDERING, ROVING

mih·rab \'mē-,rəb\ *n* [Ar *miḥrāb*] (1816) : a niche or chamber in a mosque indicating the direction of Mecca

mi·ka·do \mə-'kä-(,)dō\ *n, pl* **-dos** [Jp] (1727) : an emperor of Japan

¹mike \'mīk\ *n* [by shortening & alter.] (1924) : MICROPHONE

²mike *vt* **miked; mik·ing** (1939) : to supply with a microphone

Mike \'mīk\ (1942) — a communications code word for the letter *m*

¹mil \'mil\ *n* [L *mille* thousand] (1721) 1 : THOUSAND ⟨found a salinity of 38.4 per ~⟩ 2 : a monetary unit formerly used in Cyprus equal to 1/1000 pound 3 : a unit of length equal to 1/1000 inch used esp. in measuring thickness (as of plastic films) 4 : a unit of angular measurement equal to 1/6400 of 360 degrees and used esp. in artillery

²mil *n, pl* **mil** [short for *million*] (ca. 1955) *slang* : a million dollars

mi·la·dy \mi-'lā-dē, *US also* mi-\ *n* [F, fr. E *my lady*] (1839) 1 : an Englishwoman of noble or gentle birth 2 : a woman of fashion

milch \'milk, 'milch, 'milks\ *adj* [ME *milche*, fr. OE *-milce*; akin to OE *melcan* to milk — more at EMULSION] (14c) : MILK

mil·chig \'mil-,kik\ *adj* [Yiddish *milkhik*, fr. *milkh* milk, fr. MHG, fr. OHG *miluh* — more at MILK] (ca. 1928) : made of or derived from milk or dairy products — compare FLEISHIG, PAREVE

mild \'mī(ə)ld\ *adj* [ME, fr. OE *milde*; akin to Gk *malthakos* soft, L *mollis* — more at MELT] (bef. 12c) 1 : gentle in nature or behavior ⟨has a ~ disposition⟩ 2 a (1) : moderate in action or effect ⟨a ~ cigar⟩ (2) : not sharp or bitter ⟨~ cheese⟩ ⟨~ ale⟩ b : not being or involving what is extreme ⟨an analysis under ~ conditions⟩ ⟨a ~ slope⟩ 3 : not severe : TEMPERATE ⟨a ~ climate⟩ ⟨~ symptoms of disease⟩ — **mild·ly** \'mī(ə)l(d)-lē\ *adv* — **mild·ness** \'mī(ə)l(d)-nəs\ *n*

¹mil·dew \'mil-,dü, -,dyü\ *n* [ME, fr. OE *meledēaw* honeydew; akin to OHG *militou* honeydew] (14c) 1 a : a superficial usu. whitish growth produced esp. on organic matter or living plants by fungi (as of the families Erysiphaceae and Peronosporaceae) b : a fungus producing mildew 2 : a discoloration caused by fungi — **mil·dewy** \-ē-\ *adj*

²mildew *vt* (ca. 1552) : to affect with or as if with mildew ~ *vi* : to become affected with mildew

mild steel *n* (1868) : a low-carbon structural steel that is easily worked

mile \'mī(ə)l\ *n* [ME, fr. OE *mil*, fr. L *milia* miles, fr. *milia passuum*, lit., thousands of paces, fr. *milia*, pl. of *mille* thousand] (bef. 12c) 1 : any of various units of distance: as a : a unit equal to 5280 feet — see WEIGHT table b : NAUTICAL MILE 2 : a race of a mile 3 : a relatively great distance or interval — used chiefly adverbially in pl. ⟨was ~s too small⟩

mile·age \'mī-lij\ *n* (1754) 1 : an allowance for traveling expenses at a certain rate per mile 2 : aggregate length or distance in miles: as a : the total miles traveled esp. in a given period of time b : the amount of service that something will yield esp. as expressed in terms of miles of travel c : the average number of miles a car will travel on a gallon of gasoline that is used as a measure of fuel economy ⟨gets good ~⟩ 3 a : USEFULNESS ⟨got a lot of ~ left in her⟩ b : benefit derived from something ⟨got good political ~ from the debates⟩

mile·post \'mī(ə)l-,pōst\ *n* (1768) 1 : a post indicating the distance in miles from or to a given point; *also* : a post placed a mile from a similar post 2 : MILESTONE 2

mil·er \'mī-lər\ *n* (1889) 1 : one that competes in mile races — often qualified in combination ⟨a quarter-*miler*⟩ 2 : one that is a specified number of miles in length — used in combination ⟨a 15-*miler*⟩

mi·les glo·ri·o·sus \,mē-,lās-,glōr-ə-'ō-səs, -,glòr-\ *n, pl* **mi·li·tes glo·ri·o·si** \'mē-lə-,tās-,glōr-ē-'ō-(,)sē, -,glòr-\ [L] (1917) : a boastful soldier; *esp* : a stock character of this type in comedy

mile·stone \'mī(ə)l-,stōn\ *n* (ca. 1746) 1 : a stone serving as a milepost 2 : a significant point in development

mil·foil \'mil-,fòil\ *n* [ME, fr. OF, fr. L *millefolium*, fr. *mille* + *folium* leaf — more at BLADE] (13c) 1 : YARROW 2 : WATER MILFOIL

mil·i·ar·ia \,mi-lē-'ar-ē-ə, -'er-\ *n* [NL, fr. L, fem. of *miliarius*] (1807) : an inflammatory disorder of the skin characterized by redness, eruption, burning or itching, and the release of sweat in abnormal ways (as by the eruption of vesicles) due to blockage of the ducts of the sweat glands; *esp* : PRICKLY HEAT — **mil·i·ar·i·al** \-əl\ *adj*

mil·i·ary \'mil-ē-,er-ē\ *adj* [L *miliarius* of millet, fr. *milium* millet — more at MILLET] (1685) : having or made up of many small projections or lesions ⟨~ tubercles⟩

mi·lieu \mēl-'yə(r), -'yü; 'mēl-,yü, mē-lyœ\ *n, pl* **milieus** *or* **mi·lieux** \-'yə(r)(z), -'yüz; -,yü(z), -lyœ(z)\ [F, fr. OF, midst, fr. *mi* middle (fr. L *medius*) + *lieu* place, fr. L *locus* — more at MID, STALL] (1854) : the physical or social setting in which something occurs or develops : ENVIRONMENT *syn* see BACKGROUND

mil·i·tance \'mi-lə-tən(t)s\ *n* (ca. 1947) : MILITANCY

mil·i·tan·cy \-tən(t)-sē\ *n* (1648) : the quality or state of being militant

mil·i·tant \-tənt\ *adj* (15c) 1 : engaged in warfare or combat : FIGHT-

ING 2 : aggressively active (as in a cause) : COMBATIVE ⟨~ conservationists⟩ ⟨a ~ attitude⟩ *syn* see AGGRESSIVE — **militant** *n* — **mil·i·tant·ly** *adv* — **mil·i·tant·ness** *n*

mil·i·tar·ia \,mi-lə-'ter-ē-ə\ *n pl* (1964) : military objects (as firearms and uniforms) of historical value or interest

mil·i·tar·i·ly \,mi-lə-'ter-ə-lē\ *adv* (1660) 1 : in a military manner 2 : from a military standpoint

mil·i·ta·rise *Brit var of* MILITARIZE

mil·i·ta·rism \'mi-lə-tə-,ri-zəm\ *n* (1864) 1 a : predominance of the military class or its ideals b : exaltation of military virtues and ideals 2 : a policy of aggressive military preparedness — **mil·i·ta·rist** \-rist\ *n or adj* — **mil·i·ta·ris·tic** \,mi-lə-tə-'ris-tik\ *adj* — **mil·i·ta·ris·ti·cal·ly** \-ti-k(ə-)lē\ *adv*

mil·i·ta·rize \'mi-lə-tə-,rīz\ *vt* **-rized; -riz·ing** (1880) 1 : to equip with military forces and defenses 2 : to give a military character to 3 : to adapt for military use — **mil·i·ta·ri·za·tion** \,mi-lə-r(ə-)rə-'zā-shən\ *n*

¹mil·i·tary \'mi-lə-,ter-ē\ *adj* [ME, fr. MF *militaire*, fr. L *militaris*, fr. *milit-, miles* soldier] (15c) 1 a : of or relating to soldiers, arms, or war b : of or relating to armed forces; *esp* : of or relating to ground or sometimes ground and air forces as opposed to naval forces 2 a : performed or made by armed forces b : supported by armed force 3 : of or relating to the army

²military *n, pl* **military** *also* **mil·i·tar·ies** (1736) 1 : military persons; *esp* : army officers 2 : ARMED FORCES

military-industrial complex *n* (1961) : an informal alliance of the military and related government departments with defense industries that is held to influence military policy

military police *n* (1827) : a branch of an army that exercises guard and police functions

military press *n* (1939) : ¹PRESS 9

military science *n* (ca. 1830) : the principles of military conflict

military time *n* (1955) : time measured in hours numbered to twenty-four (as 0100 or 2300) from one midnight to the next

mil·i·tate \'mi-lə-,tāt\ *vi* **-tat·ed; -tat·ing** [L *militatus*, pp. of *militare* to engage in warfare, fr. *milit-, miles*] (1642) : to have weight or effect ⟨his boyish appearance *militated* against his getting an early promotion⟩ *usage* see MITIGATE

mi·li·tia \mə-'li-shə\ *n* [L, military service, fr. *milit-, miles*] (ca. 1660) 1 a : a part of the organized armed forces of a country liable to call only in emergency b : a body of citizens organized for military service 2 : the whole body of able-bodied male citizens declared by law as being subject to call to military service

mi·li·tia·man \-mən\ *n* (1780) : a member of a militia

mil·i·um \'mi-lē-əm\ *n, pl* **mil·ia** \-lē-ə\ [NL, fr. L, millet — more at MILLET] (1856) : a small whitish lump in the skin due to retention of keratin in an oil gland duct — called also *whitehead*

¹milk \'milk\ *n* [ME, fr. OE *meolc, milc;* akin to OHG *miluh* milk, OE *melcan* to milk — more at EMULSION] (bef. 12c) 1 a : a fluid secreted by the mammary glands of females for the nourishment of their young; *esp* : cow's milk used as a food by humans b : LACTATION ⟨cows in ~⟩ 2 : a liquid resembling milk in appearance: as a : the latex of a plant b : the juice of a coconut c : the contents of an unripe kernel of grain

²milk *vt* (bef. 12c) 1 a (1) : to draw milk from the breasts or udder of (2) *obs* : SUCKLE 2 b : to draw (milk) from the breast or udder c : SUCKLE 1 — used of lower mammals 2 : to draw something from as if by milking: as a : to induce (a snake) to eject venom b : to draw or coerce profit or advantage from illicitly or to an extreme degree : EXPLOIT ~ *vi* : to draw or yield milk

³milk *adj* (14c) : giving milk; *specif* : bred or suitable primarily for milk production ⟨~ cows⟩

milk-and-water *adj* (1783) : WEAK, INSIPID

milk chocolate *n* (1904) : chocolate made with milk solids

milk·er \'mil-kər\ *n* (15c) 1 : one that milks an animal 2 : one that yields milk

milk fever *n* (1758) 1 : a febrile disorder following parturition 2 : a disease of fresh cows, sheep, or goats that is caused by excessive drain on the body mineral reserves during the establishment of the milk flow

milk·fish \'milk-,fish\ *n* (ca. 1890) : a large fork-tailed silvery herbivorous food fish (*Chanos chanos*) of warm parts of the Pacific and Indian oceans that is the sole living representative of its family (Chanidae)

milk glass *n* (1874) : an opaque and typically milky white glass used esp. for novelty and ornamental objects

milk house *n* (1589) : a building for the cooling, handling, or bottling of milk

milk leg *n* (ca. 1860) : a painful swelling of the leg caused by inflammation and clotting in the veins and affecting some postpartum women

milk-liv·ered \'milk-,li-vərd\ *adj* (1605) *archaic* : COWARDLY, TIMOROUS

milk·maid \-,mād\ *n* (1552) : DAIRYMAID

milk·man \-,man, -mən\ *n* (1589) : one who sells or delivers milk or milk products

milk of magnesia *n* (1880) : a milky white suspension of magnesium hydroxide in water used as an antacid and laxative

milk punch *n* (1704) : a mixed drink of alcoholic liquor, milk, and sugar

milk run *n* [fr. the resemblance in regularity and uneventfulness to the morning delivery of milk] (1925) : a short, routine, or uneventful flight

milk shake *n* (1889) : a thoroughly shaken or blended drink made of milk, a flavoring syrup, and often ice cream

milk sickness *n* (1823) 1 : an acute disease characterized by weakness, vomiting, and constipation and caused by eating dairy products or meat from cattle poisoned by various plants 2 : TREMBLE 2

milk snake *n* (1800) : a common harmless grayish or tan American colubrid snake (*Lampropeltis triangulum*) having an arrow-shaped occipital marking and brown blotches on the body bordered with black or rings usu. of black, red, and yellow; *broadly* : KING SNAKE

milk·sop \'milk-,säp\ *n* [ME, lit., bread soaked in milk] (14c) : an unmanly man : MOLLYCODDLE

milk sugar *n* (1846) : LACTOSE

milk tooth *n* (ca. 1752) : a deciduous tooth of a young mammal; *esp* : one of the human dentition including four incisors, two canines, and four molars in each jaw

milk vein *n* (1844) : a large subcutaneous vein that extends along the lower side of the abdomen of a cow and returns blood from the udder — see COW illustration

milk vetch *n* [fr. the popular belief that it increases the milk yield of goats] (1597) : any of a genus (*Astragalus*) of leguminous herbs; *esp* : an Old World perennial (*A. glycyphyllos*) that has sulfur yellow flowers in dense spikes

milk·weed \'milk-ˌwēd\ *n* (ca. 1598) : any of various plants that secrete latex; *esp* : any of a genus (*Asclepias* of the family Asclepiadaceae, the milkweed family) of erect chiefly perennial herbs with milky juice and umbellate flowers

milkweed bug *n* (1905) : a large black red-marked bug (*Oncopeltus fasciatus*) cultured as a research organism

milkweed butterfly *n* (1880) : any of a family (Danaidae) or nymphalid subfamily (Danainae) of large butterflies feeding on plants of the milkweed family as larvae; *esp* : MONARCH BUTTERFLY

milk·wort \'milk-ˌwərt, -ˌwȯrt\ *n* (1578) : any of a genus (*Polygala* of the family Polygalaceae, the milkwort family) of plants typically having showy flowers with three sometimes crested petals united below into a tube and an irregular calyx with two petaloid sepals

milky \'mil-kē\ *adj* **milk·i·er; -est** (14c) **1** : resembling milk in color or consistency **2** : MILD, TIMOROUS **3 a** : consisting of, containing, or abounding in milk **b** : yielding milk; *specif* : having the characteristics of a good milk producer — **milk·i·ness** *n*

milky disease *n* (ca. 1940) : a destructive bacterial disease of scarab beetle grubs and esp. Japanese beetle larvae

Milky Way *n* **1** : a broad luminous irregular band of light that stretches completely around the celestial sphere and is caused by the light of myriads of faint stars **2** : MILKY WAY GALAXY

Milky Way galaxy *n* : the galaxy of which the sun and the solar system are a part and which contains the myriads of stars that comprise the Milky Way

¹mill \'mil\ *n* [ME *mille*, fr. OE *mylen*, fr. LL *molina, molinum*, fr. fem. and neut. of *molinus* of a mill, of a millstone, fr. L *mola* mill, millstone; akin to L *molere* to grind — more at MEAL] (bef. 12c) **1** : a building provided with machinery for grinding grain into flour **2 a** : a machine or apparatus (as a quern) for grinding grain **b** : a machine for crushing or comminuting **3** : a machine that manufactures by the continuous repetition of some simple action **4** : a building or collection of buildings with machinery for manufacturing **5 a** : a machine formerly used for stamping coins **b** : a machine for expelling juice from vegetable tissues by pressure or grinding **6** : MILLING MACHINE, MILLING CUTTER **7 a** : a slow, laborious, or mechanical process or routine **b** : one that produces or processes people or things mechanically or in large numbers ⟨a diploma ∼⟩ ⟨a rumor ∼⟩ **8** : a difficult and often educational experience — used in the phrase *through the mill* **9** *slang* : the engine of an automobile or boat

²mill *vt* (1552) **1** : to subject to an operation or process in a mill: as **a** : to grind into flour, meal, or powder **b** : to shape or dress by means of a rotary cutter **c** : to mix and condition (as rubber) by passing between rotating rolls **2** : to give a raised rim or a ridged or corrugated edge to (a coin) **3** : to cut grooves in the metal surface of (as a knob) ∼ *vi* **1** : to hit out with the fists **2** : to move in a circle or in an eddying mass; *also* : WANDER **3** : to undergo milling

³mill *n* [L *mille* thousand] (1786) : a money of account equal to ¹/₁₀ cent

⁴mill *var of* ²MIL

mill·age \'mi-lij\ *n* (1891) : a rate (as of taxation) expressed in mills per dollar

mill·dam \'mil-ˌdam\ *n* (12c) : a dam to make a millpond; *also* : MILLPOND

mille \'mil\ *n* [L] (1894) : THOUSAND

mille–feuille \mēl-'fwē\ *n* [F, fr. *mille feuilles* a thousand leaves] (1895) : a dish composed of puff pastry layered with a filling (as salmon or cream)

mil·le·fi·o·ri \ˌmi-lə-fē-'ȯr-ē, -'ȯr-\ *n* [It, fr. *mille fiori* a thousand flowers] (1849) : ornamental glass produced by cutting cross sections of fused bundles of glass rods of various colors and sizes

mille·fleur *or* **mille–fleurs** \(ˌ)mēl-'flər, -'flʉr\ *adj* [F *mille-fleurs*, fr. *mille fleurs* a thousand flowers] (1908) : having an allover pattern of small flowers and plants ⟨∼ tapestry⟩

¹mil·le·nar·i·an \ˌmi-lə-'ner-ē-ən\ *adj* (1631) **1 a** : of or relating to belief in a millennium **b** : APOCALYPTIC 2 **2** : of or relating to 1000 years

²millenarian *n* (ca. 1674) : one that believes in a millennium

mil·le·nar·i·an·ism \-ē-ə-ˌni-zəm\ *n* (ca. 1847) **1** : belief in the millennium of Christian prophecy **2** : belief in a coming ideal society and esp. one created by revolutionary action

¹mil·le·na·ry \'mi-lə-ˌner-ē, mə-'le-nə-rē\ *n, pl* **-ries** [LL *millenarium*, fr. neut. of *millenarius* of a thousand, fr. L *milleni* one thousand each, fr. *mille*] (1550) **1 a** : a group of 1000 units or things **b** : 1000 years : MILLENNIUM **2** : MILLENARIAN

²millenary *adj* [L *millenarius*] (ca. 1641) **1** : relating to or consisting of 1000 **2** : suggesting a millennium

mil·len·ni·al \mə-'le-nē-əl\ *adj* (1664) : of or relating to a millennium

mil·len·ni·al·ism \-ē-ə-ˌli-zəm\ *n* (1906) : MILLENARIANISM

mil·len·ni·al·ist \-ist\ *n* (ca. 1841) : MILLENARIAN

mil·len·ni·um \mə-'le-nē-əm\ *n, pl* **-nia** \-nē-ə\ *or* **-niums** [NL, fr. L *mille* thousand + NL *-ennium* (as in *biennium*)] (ca. 1638) **1 a** : the thousand years mentioned in Revelation 20 during which holiness is to prevail and Christ is to reign on earth **b** : a period of great happiness or human perfection **2 a** : a period of 1000 years **b** : a 1000th anniversary or its celebration

mill·er \'mi-lər\ *n* (14c) **1** : one that operates a mill; *specif* : one that grinds grain into flour **2** : any of various moths having powdery wings **3 a** : MILLING MACHINE **b** : a tool for use in a milling machine

mil·ler·ite \'mi-lə-ˌrīt\ *n* [G *Millerit*, fr. William H. *Miller* †1880 Eng. mineralogist] (1854) : sulfide of nickel NiS usu. occurring as a mineral in capillary yellow crystals

miller's–thumb \ˌmi-lərz-'thəm\ *n* (15c) : any of several small freshwater spiny-finned sculpins (genus *Cottus*) of Europe and No. America

mil·les·i·mal \mə-'le-sə-məl\ *n* [L *millesimus*, adj., thousandth, fr. *mille*] (1719) : the quotient of a unit divided by 1000 : one of 1000 equal parts — **millesimal** *adj* — **mil·les·i·mal·ly** \-mə-lē\ *adv*

mil·let \'mi-lət\ *n* [ME *milet*, fr. MF, dim. of *mil*, fr. L *milium*; akin to

Gk *melinē* millet] (15c) **1** : any of various small-seeded annual cereal and forage grasses: **a** : a grass (*Panicum miliaceum*) cultivated for its grain which is used for food **b** : any of several grasses related to common millet **2** : the seed of a millet

milli- *comb form* [F, fr. L *milli-* thousand, fr. *mille*] : thousandth ⟨*milliampere*⟩

mil·li·am·pere \ˌmi-lē-'am-ˌpir\ *n* [ISV] (1885) : one thousandth of an ampere

mil·liard \'mil-ˌyärd, 'mi-lē-ˌärd\ *n* [F, fr. MF *miliart*, fr. *mili-* (fr. *million* million)] (1793) *Brit* : a thousand millions — see NUMBER table

mil·li·ary \'mi-lē-ˌer-ē\ *adj* [L *milliarius, miliarius* consisting of a thousand, one mile long, fr. *mille* thousand, mile] (1644) : marking the distance of a Roman mile

mil·li·bar \'mi-lə-ˌbär\ *n* [ISV] (1910) : a unit of atmospheric pressure equal to ¹/₁₀₀₀ bar or 1000 dynes per square centimeter

mil·li·cu·rie \ˌmi-lə-'kyu̇r-(ˌ)ē, -kyu̇-'rē\ *n* [ISV] (1910) : one thousandth of a curie

mil·li·de·gree \-di-'grē\ *n* (1942) : one thousandth of a degree

mil·lieme \mēl-'yem\ *n, pl* **milliemes** \-'yem(z)\ [F *millième* thousandth, fr. MF, fr. *mille* thousand, fr. L] (1902) : a unit of value of Egypt and Sudan equal to ¹/₁₀₀₀ pound

mil·li·gal \'mi-lə-ˌgal\ *n* [ISV] (1914) : a unit of acceleration equivalent to ¹/₁₀₀₀ gal

mil·li·gram \-ˌgram\ *n* [F *milligramme*, fr. *milli-* + *gramme* gram] (ca. 1810) — see METRIC SYSTEM table

mil·li·hen·ry \-ˌhen-rē\ *n* [ISV] (1897) : one thousandth of a henry

mil·li·lam·bert \-ˌlam-bərt\ *n* (1916) : one thousandth of a lambert

mil·li·li·ter \'mi-lə-ˌlē-tər\ *n* [F *millilitre*, fr. *milli-* + *litre* liter] (ca. 1810) — see METRIC SYSTEM table

mil·lime \mə-'lēm\ *n* [modif. of Ar *mallim*, fr. F *millième*] (ca. 1919) — see *dinar* at MONEY table

mil·li·me·ter \'mi-lə-ˌmē-tər\ *n* [F *millimètre*, fr. *milli-* + *mètre* meter] (1807) — see METRIC SYSTEM table

mil·li·mi·cron \ˌmi-lə-'mī-ˌkrän\ *n* [ISV] (1904) : NANOMETER

mil·li·mole \'mi-lə-ˌmōl\ *n* [ISV *milli-* + ⁵*mole*] (ca. 1904) : one thousandth of a mole (as of a substance) — **mil·li·mo·lar** \-ˌmō-lər\ *adj*

mil·li·ner \'mi-lə-nər\ *n* [irreg. fr. *Milan*, Italy; fr. the importation of women's finery from Italy in the 16th century] (1530) : a person who designs, makes, trims, or sells women's hats

mil·li·nery \'mi-lə-ˌner-ē\ *n* (ca. 1688) **1** : women's apparel for the head **2** : the business or work of a milliner

mill·ing \'mi-liŋ\ *n* (1817) : a corrugated edge on a coin

milling cutter *n* (1884) : a rotary tool-steel cutter used in a milling machine for shaping and dressing metal surfaces

milling machine *n* (1876) : a machine tool on which work usu. of metal secured to a carriage is shaped by rotating milling cutters

mil·lion \'mil(l)-yən\ *n, pl* **millions** *or* **million** [ME *milioun*, fr. MF *milion*, fr. OIt *milione*, aug. of *mille* thousand, fr. L] (14c) **1** — see NUMBER table **2** : a very large number ⟨∼s of cars on the road⟩ **3** : the mass of common people (someone who writes for the ∼s —Bergen Evans) — **million** *adj* — **mil·lion·fold** \-ˌfōld\ *adv or adj* — **mil·lionth** \'mil(l)-yən(t)th\ *adj or n*

mil·lion·aire \ˌmil(l)-yə-'nar, -'ner, 'mil(l)-yə-ˌ\ *n* [F *millionnaire*, fr. *million*, fr. MF *million*] (1826) : a person whose wealth is estimated at a million or more (as of dollars or pounds)

mil·lion·air·ess \-'ar-əs, -'er-, -ˌar-, -ˌer-\ *n* (1881) **1** : a woman who is a millionaire **2** : the wife of a millionaire

mil·li·os·mol \ˌmi-lē-'äz-ˌmōl, -'äs-\ *n* (1939) : one thousandth of an osmol

mil·li·pede \'mi-lə-ˌpēd\ *n* [L *millepeda*, a small crawling animal, fr. *mille* thousand + *ped-, pes* foot — more at FOOT] (1601) : any of a class (Diplopoda) of myriapod arthropods having usu. a cylindrical segmented body covered with hard integument, two pairs of legs on most apparent segments, and unlike centipedes no poison fangs

mil·li·ra·di·an \ˌmi-lə-'rā-dē-ən\ *n* [ISV] (1954) : one thousandth of a radian

mil·li·rem \'mi-lə-ˌrem\ *n* (1947) : one thousandth of a rem

mil·li·roent·gen \ˌmi-lə-'rent-gən, -'rənt-, -jən, -shən\ *n* [ISV] (1947) : one thousandth of a roentgen

mil·li·sec·ond \'mi-lə-ˌse-kənd, -kənt\ *n* [ISV] (1909) : one thousandth of a second

mil·li·volt \-ˌvōlt\ *n* [ISV] (1861) : one thousandth of a volt

mil·li·watt \-ˌwät\ *n* [ISV] (ca. 1914) : one thousandth of a watt

mill·pond \'mil-ˌpänd\ *n* (14c) : a pond created by damming a stream to produce a head of water for operating a mill

mill·race \-ˌrās\ *n* (15c) : a canal in which water flows to and from a mill wheel; *also* : the current that drives the wheel

mill·stone \'mil-ˌstōn\ *n* (bef. 12c) **1** : either of two circular stones used for grinding (as grain) **2** : something that grinds or crushes **b** : a heavy burden

mill·stream \-ˌstrēm\ *n* (bef. 12c) **1** : a stream whose flow is utilized to run a mill **2** : MILLRACE

mill wheel *n* (bef. 12c) : a waterwheel that drives a mill

mill·work \'mil-ˌwərk\ *n* (1899) : woodwork (as doors, sashes, or trim) manufactured at a mill

mill·wright \-ˌrīt\ *n* (14c) **1** : one whose occupation is planning and building mills or setting up their machinery **2** : one who maintains and cares for mechanical equipment (as of a mill or factory)

mi·lo \'mī-(ˌ)lō\ *n, pl* **milos** [perh. fr. Sesotho *maili*] (1882) : a small usu. early and drought-resistant grain sorghum with compact bearded heads of large yellow or whitish seeds

mi·lord \mi-'lȯr(d)\ *n* [F, fr. E *my lord*] (1596) : an Englishman of noble or gentle birth

mil·pa \'mil-pə\ *n* [MexSp, fr. Nahuatl *milpan*] (1844) **1 a** : a small field in Mexico or Central America that is cleared from the forest, cropped for a few seasons, and abandoned for a fresh clearing **b** : a maize field in Mexico or Central America **2** : the maize plant

---

\ə\ abut \ᵊ\ kitten, F table \ər\ further \a\ ash \ā\ ace \ä\ mop, mar \au̇\ out \ch\ chin \e\ bet \ē\ easy \g\ go \i\ hit \ī\ ice \j\ job \ŋ\ sing \ō\ go \ȯ\ law \ȯi\ boy \th\ thin \t͟h\ the \ü\ loot \u̇\ foot \y\ yet \zh\ vision \à, k̇, ⁿ, œ, œ̄, ᴜ, ᵫ, ʸ\ see Guide to Pronunciation

Milque·toast \'milk-ˌtōst\ n [Caspar *Milquetoast*, comic strip character created by H. T. Webster †1952 Am. cartoonist] (1935) : a timid, meek, or unassertive person

mil·reis \mil-'rāsh, -'rās\ n, pl **mil·reis** \same or -'rāz, -'rāzh\ [Pg *milréis*] (1589) **1** : a Portuguese unit of value equal before 1911 to 1000 reis **2** : the basic monetary unit of Brazil until 1942 **3** : a coin representing one milreis

milt \'milt\ n [prob. fr. MD *milte* milt of fish, spleen; akin to OE *milte* spleen — more at MELT] (15c) : the sperm-containing fluid of a male fish

mim \'mim\ adj [imit. of the act of pursing the lips] (1641) dial : affectedly shy or modest

¹mime \'mīm also 'mēm\ n [L *mimus*, fr. Gk *mimos*] (1603) **1** : an ancient dramatic entertainment representing scenes from life usu. in a ridiculous manner **2 a** : an actor in a mime **b** : one that practices mime **3** : MIMIC 2 **4** : PANTOMIME 3a,b

²mime vb **mimed; mim·ing** vi (1616) **1** : to act a part with mimic gesture and action usu. without words ~ vt **1** : MIMIC **2** : to act out in the manner of a mime — **mim·er** n

mim·eo·graph \'mi-mē-ə-ˌgraf\ n [fr. *Mimeograph*, a trademark] (1889) : a duplicator for making many copies that utilizes a stencil through which ink is pressed — **mimeograph** vt

mi·me·sis \mə-'mē-səs, mī-\ n [LL, fr. Gk *mimēsis*, fr. *mimeisthai*] (1550) : IMITATION, MIMICRY

mi·met·ic \-'me-tik\ adj [LL *mimeticus*, fr. Gk *mimētikos*, fr. *mimeisthai* to imitate, fr. *mimos* mime] (1637) **1** : IMITATIVE **2** : relating to, characterized by, or exhibiting mimicry ⟨~ coloring of a butterfly⟩ — **mi·met·i·cal·ly** \-ti-k(ə-)lē\ adv

¹mim·ic \'mi-mik\ n (1590) **1** : MIME 2 **2** : one that mimics

²mimic adj [L *mimicus*, fr. Gk *mimikos*, fr. *mimos* mime] (1598) **1 a** : IMITATIVE **b** : IMITATION, MOCK ⟨a ~ battle⟩ **2** : of or relating to mime or mimicry

³mimic vt **mim·icked** \-mikt\; **mim·ick·ing** (1687) **1** : to imitate closely : APE **2** : to ridicule by imitation **3** : SIMULATE **4** : to resemble by biological mimicry **syn** see COPY

mim·ic·ry \'mi-mi-krē\ n, pl **-ries** (1687) **1 a** : an instance of mimicking **b** : the action, practice, or art of mimicking **2** : a superficial resemblance of one organism to another or to natural objects among which it lives that secures it a selective advantage (as protection from predation)

mi·mo·sa \mə-'mō-sə, mī-, -zə\ n [NL, fr. L *mimus* mime] (1751) **1** : any of a genus (*Mimosa*) of leguminous trees, shrubs, and herbs of tropical and warm regions with usu. bipinnate often prickly leaves and globular heads of small white or pink flowers **2** : SILK TREE **3** : a mixed drink consisting of champagne and orange juice

mi·na \'mi-nə\ n [L, fr. Gk *mna*, of Sem origin; akin to Heb *māneh* mina] (ca. 1580) : an ancient unit of weight and value equal to ¹/₆₀ talent

min·able or **mine·able** \'mī-nə-bəl\ adj (ca. 1570) : capable of being mined

min·a·ret \ˌmi-nə-'ret, 'mi-nə-ˌ\ n [F, fr. Turk *minare*, fr. Ar *manārah* lighthouse] (1682) : a tall slender tower of a mosque having one or more balconies from which the summons to prayer is cried by the muezzin

mi·na·to·ry \'mi-nə-ˌtōr-ē, 'mī-, -ˌtȯr-\ adj [LL *minatorius*, fr. L *minari* to threaten — more at MOUNT] (1532) : having a menacing quality : THREATENING

min·au·dière \ˌmē-nōd-'yer\ n [F, fem. of *minaudier* affected, coquettish, fr. *minauder* to mince] (1940) : a small decorative case for carrying small articles (as cosmetics or jewelry)

¹mince \'min(t)s\ vb **minced; minc·ing** [ME, fr. MF *mincer*, fr. (assumed) VL *minutiare*, fr. L *minutia* smallness — more at MINUTIA] vt (14c) **1 a** : to cut or chop into very small pieces **b** : to subdivide minutely; *esp* : to damage by cutting up **2** : to utter or pronounce with affectation **3** a archaic : MINIMIZE **b** : to restrain (words) within the bounds of decorum ~ vi : to walk with short steps in a prim affected manner — **minc·er** n

²mince n (1600) **1** : small chopped bits (as of food); specif : MINCEMEAT **2** Brit : HAMBURGER 1a

mince·meat \'min(t)s-ˌmēt\ n (1663) **1** : minced meat **2** : a finely chopped mixture (as of raisins, apples, and spices) sometimes with meat that is often used as pie filling **3** : a state of destruction or annihilation — used in the phrase *make mincemeat of*

minc·ing \'min(t)-siŋ\ adj (1530) : affectedly dainty or delicate — **minc·ing·ly** \-siŋ-lē\ adv

¹mind \'mīnd\ n [ME, fr. OE *gemynd*; akin to OHG *gimunt* memory, L *ment-, mens* mind, *monēre* to remind, warn, Gk *menos* spirit, *mnasthai, mimnēskesthai* to remember] (bef. 12c) **1** : RECOLLECTION, MEMORY ⟨keep that in ~⟩ ⟨time out of ~⟩ **2 a** : the element or complex of elements in an individual that feels, perceives, thinks, wills, and esp. reasons **b** : the conscious mental events and capabilities in an organism **c** : the organized conscious and unconscious adaptive mental activity of an organism **3** : INTENTION, DESIRE ⟨I changed my ~⟩ **4** : the normal or healthy condition of the mental faculties **5** : OPINION, VIEW **6** : DISPOSITION, MOOD **7 a** : a person or group embodying mental qualities ⟨the public ~⟩ **b** : intellectual ability **8** cap, Christian Science : GOD 1b **9** : a conscious substratum or factor in the universe

²mind vt (14c) **1** chiefly dial : REMIND **2** chiefly dial : REMEMBER **3** : to attend to closely **4** (1) : to become aware of : NOTICE (2) : to regard with attention : consider important — often used in the imperative with following *you* for emphasis ⟨I'm not against inspiration, ~ you; I simply refuse to sit and stare at a blank page waiting for it —Dennis Whitcomb⟩ **b** chiefly dial : INTEND, PURPOSE **5 a** : to give heed to attentively in order to obey **b** : to follow the orders or instructions of **6 a** : to be concerned about **b** : DISLIKE ⟨I don't ~ going⟩ **7 a** : to be careful : SEE ⟨~ you finish it⟩ **b** : to be cautious about ⟨~ the broken rung⟩ **8** : to give protective care to : TEND ~ vi

minaret

1 : to be attentive or wary **2** : to become concerned : CARE **3** : to pay obedient heed or attention — **mind·er** n

mind–bend·ing \'mīn(d)-ˌben-diŋ\ adj (1965) : MIND-BLOWING

mind–blow·ing \-ˌblō-iŋ\ adj (1967) **1** : PSYCHEDELIC 1a **2** : MIND-BOGGLING — **mind–blow·er** \-ˌblō(-ə)r\ n

mind–bog·gling \-ˌbä-g(ə-)liŋ\ adj (1964) : mentally or emotionally exciting or overwhelming — **mind–bog·gling·ly** \-lē\ adv

mind·ed \'mīn-dəd\ adj (15c) **1** : INCLINED, DISPOSED **2** : having a mind esp. of a specified kind or concerned with a specified thing — usu. used in combination ⟨narrow-*minded*⟩ ⟨health-*minded*⟩ — **mind·ed·ness** \-dəd-nəs\ n

mind–ex·pand·ing \'mīnd-ik-ˌspan-diŋ\ adj (1963) : PSYCHEDELIC 1a

mind·ful \'mīn(d)-fəl\ adj (14c) **1** : bearing in mind : AWARE **2** : inclined to be aware — **mind·ful·ly** \-fə-lē\ adv — **mind·ful·ness** n

mind·less \-ləs\ adj (bef. 12c) **1 a** : marked by a lack of mind or consciousness ⟨a ~ sleep⟩ **b** (1) : marked by or displaying no use of the powers of the intellect ⟨~ violence⟩ (2) : requiring little attention or thought; *esp* : not intellectually challenging or stimulating ⟨~ work⟩ ⟨a ~ movie⟩ **2** : not mindful : HEEDLESS ⟨~ of the consequences⟩ — **mind·less·ly** adv — **mind·less·ness** n

mind reader n (1887) : one that professes or is held to be able to perceive another's thought without normal means of communication — **mind reading** n

mind–set \'mīn(d)-ˌset\ n (1926) **1** : a mental attitude or inclination **2** : a fixed state of mind

mind's eye n (15c) : the mental faculty of conceiving imaginary or recollected scenes; also : the mental picture so conceived ⟨in the *mind's eye* one sees dinosaurs, mammoths, and sabertoothed tigers —F. P. Brooks Jr.⟩

¹mine \'mīn\ adj [ME *min*, fr. OE *mīn* — more at MY] (bef. 12c) : MY — used before a word beginning with a vowel or h ⟨this treasure is ~ arms —Shak.⟩ or sometimes as a modifier of a preceding noun; archaic except in an elevated style

²mine pron, sing or pl in constr (bef. 12c) : that which belongs to me — used without a following noun as a pronoun equivalent in meaning to the adjective my

³mine n [ME, fr. MF, fr. (assumed) VL *mina*, prob. of Celt origin; akin to W *mwyn* ore] (14c) **1 a** : a pit or excavation in the earth from which mineral substances are taken **b** : an ore deposit **2** : a subterranean passage under an enemy position **3** : an encased explosive that is placed in the ground or in water and set to explode when disturbed **4** : a rich source of supply

⁴mine vb **mined; min·ing** vt (14c) **1 a** : to dig under to gain access or cause the collapse of (an enemy position) **b** : UNDERMINE **2 a** : to get (as ore) from the earth **b** : to extract from a source ⟨information *mined* from the files⟩ **3** : to burrow beneath the surface of ⟨larva that ~s leaves⟩ **4** : to place military mines in, on, or under ⟨~ a harbor⟩ **5 a** : to dig into for ore or metal **b** : to process for obtaining a natural constituent ⟨~ the air for nitrogen⟩ **c** : to seek valuable material in ~ vi : to dig a mine — **min·er** n

mine·field \'mīn-ˌfēld\ n (1886) **1** : an area (as of water or land) set with mines **2** : something resembling a minefield esp. in having many dangers or requiring extreme caution

mine·lay·er \-ˌlā-ər, -ˌle(-ə)r\ n (1909) : a naval vessel for laying underwater mines

¹min·er·al \'min-rəl, 'mi-nə-\ n [ME, fr. ML *minerale*, fr. neut. of *mineralis*] (15c) **1** : ORE **2** : an inorganic substance (as in the ash of calcined tissue) **3** obs : MINE **4** : something neither animal nor vegetable **5 a** : a solid homogeneous crystalline chemical element or compound that results from the inorganic processes of nature; *broadly* : any of various naturally occurring homogeneous substances (as stone, coal, salt, sulfur, sand, petroleum, water, or natural gas) obtained usu. from the ground **b** : a synthetic substance having the chemical composition and crystalline form and properties of a naturally occurring mineral **6** pl, Brit : MINERAL WATER

²mineral adj [ME, fr. ML *mineralis*, fr. *minera* mine, ore, fr. OF *miniere*, fr. *mine*] (15c) **1** : of or relating to minerals; *also* : INORGANIC **2** : impregnated with mineral substances

min·er·al·ise Brit var of MINERALIZE

min·er·al·ize \'min-rə-ˌlīz, 'mi-nə-\ vt **-ized; -iz·ing** (1655) **1** : to transform (a metal) into an ore **2 a** : to impregnate or supply with minerals or an inorganic compound **b** : to convert into mineral or inorganic form **3** : PETRIFY — **min·er·al·iz·able** \ˌmin-rə-'lī-zə-bəl, ˌmi-nə-\ adj — **min·er·al·i·za·tion** \-rə-lə-'zā-shən\ n — **min·er·al·iz·er** \'min-rə-ˌlī-zər, 'mi-nə-\ n

mineral kingdom n (ca. 1691) : a basic group of natural objects that includes inorganic objects — compare ANIMAL KINGDOM, PLANT KINGDOM

min·er·al·o·cor·ti·coid \ˌmin-rə-lō-'kȯr-tə-ˌkȯid, ˌmi-nə-\ n (1946) : a corticosteroid (as aldosterone) that affects chiefly the electrolyte and fluid balance in the body — compare GLUCOCORTICOID

min·er·al·o·gy \ˌmin-nə-'rä-lə-jē, -'ra-\ n [prob. fr. (assumed) NL *mineralogia*, irreg. fr. ML *minerale* + L *-logia* -logy] (1690) **1** : a science dealing with minerals, their crystallography, properties, classification, and the ways of distinguishing them **2** : the minerological characteristics of an area, a rock, or a rock formation — **min·er·al·og·i·cal** \ˌmi-nə-rə-'lä-ji-kəl, ˌmin-rə-\ also **min·er·al·og·ic** \-'lä-jik\ adj — **min·er·al·og·i·cal·ly** \-'lä-ji-k(ə-)lē\ adv — **min·er·al·o·gist** \ˌmi-nə-'rä-lə-jist, -'ra-\ n

mineral oil n (1805) : an oil of mineral origin; *esp* : a refined petroleum oil used esp. as a laxative

mineral spirits n pl but sing or pl in constr (1927) : a petroleum distillate that is used esp. as a paint or varnish thinner

mineral water n (1562) : water naturally or artificially infused with mineral salts or gases (as carbon dioxide)

mineral wax n (ca. 1864) : a wax of mineral origin; *esp* : OZOKERITE

mineral wool n (ca. 1881) : any of various lightweight vitreous fibrous materials used esp. in heat and sound insulation

Mi·ner·va \mə-'nər-və\ n [L] : the Roman goddess of wisdom — compare ATHENA

min·e·stro·ne \ˌmi-nə-'strō-nē, -'strōn\ n [It, aug. of *minestra*, fr. *minestrare* to serve, dish up, fr. L *ministrare*, fr. *minister* servant — more at MINISTER] (1891) : a rich thick vegetable soup usu. with dried beans and pasta (as macaroni or vermicelli)

mine·sweep·er \'mīn-‚swē-pər\ n (1905) : a warship designed for removing or neutralizing mines by dragging — **mine·sweep·ing** \-piŋ\ n

Ming \'miŋ\ n [Chin (Beijing) *míng* luminous] (1795) : a Chinese dynasty dated 1368–1644 and marked by restoration of earlier traditions and in the arts by perfection of established techniques

min·gle \'miŋ-gəl\ vb **min·gled; min·gling** \-g(ə-)liŋ\ [ME *menglen,* freq. of *mengen* to mix, fr. OE *mengan;* akin to MHG *mengen* to mix, Gk *massein* to knead] vt (15c) **1 :** to bring or mix together or with something else usu. without fundamental loss of identity : INTERMIX **2** *archaic* **:** to prepare by mixing : CONCOCT ～ vi **1 :** to become mingled **2 a :** to come into contact : ASSOCIATE **b :** to move about (as in a group) ⟨*mingled* with the guests⟩ *syn* see MIX

ming tree n [perh. fr. *Ming*] (1948) : a dwarfed evergreen conifer grown as bonsai; *also* : an artificial plant resembling this

min·gy \'min-jē\ adj **min·gi·er; -est** [perh. blend of ¹*mean* and *stingy*] (1912) : MEAN, STINGY

¹mini \'mi-nē\ adj [*mini-*] (1954) **1 :** small in relation to others of the same kind **2 :** of short length or duration : BRIEF

²mini n, pl **min·is** (1961) : something small of its kind: as **a :** MINICAR **b :** MINISKIRT **c :** MINICOMPUTER

mini- comb form [*miniature*] : smaller or briefer than usual, normal, or standard ⟨*minicourse*⟩ ⟨*minibus*⟩

¹min·i·a·ture \'mi-nē-ə-‚chùr, 'mi-ni-‚chùr, 'min-yə-, -chər, -‚tyùr, -‚tùr\ n [It *miniatura* art of illuminating a manuscript, fr. ML, fr. L *miniatus,* pp. of *miniare* to color with minium, fr. *minium* red lead] (ca. 1586) **1 a :** a copy on a much reduced scale **b :** something small of its kind **2 :** a painting in an illuminated book or manuscript **3 :** the art of painting miniatures **4 :** a very small portrait or other painting (as on ivory or metal) — **min·i·a·tur·ist** \-‚chùr-ist, -chər-, -‚tyùr-, -‚tùr\ n — **min·i·a·tur·is·tic** \‚mi-nē-ə-chə-'ris-tik, ‚mi-ni-, ‚min-yə-, -‚tyù-, -‚tù-\ adj — **in miniature :** in a greatly diminished size, form, or scale

²miniature adj (1714) : being or represented on a small scale *syn* see SMALL

miniature golf n (1915) : a novelty golf game played with a putter on a miniature course usu. having tunnels, bridges, sharp corners, and obstacles

miniature pin·scher \-'pin(t)-shər\ n (1929) : any of a breed of toy dogs that suggest a small Doberman pinscher and are 10 to 12½ inches (25 to 32 centimeters) in height at the withers

miniature schnauzer n (ca. 1929) : any of a breed of schnauzers that are 12 to 14 inches (30 to 36 centimeters) in height at the withers and are classified as terriers

min·i·a·tur·ize \'mi-nē-ə-chə-‚rīz, 'mi-ni-chə-, 'min-yə-chə-, -‚tyù-, -‚tù-\ vt **-ized; -iz·ing** (1946) : to design or construct in small size — **min·i·a·tur·i·za·tion** \‚mi-nē-ə-‚chùr-ə-'zā-shən, ‚mi-ni-, ‚min-yə-, -chər-, -‚tyùr-, -‚tùr-\ n

mini·bike \'mi-nē-‚bik\ n (1962) : a small one-passenger motorcycle with a low frame and raised handlebars — **mini·bik·er** n

mini·bus \-‚bəs\ n (1958) : a small bus or van

Mini·cam \-‚kam\ trademark — used for a portable television camera

mini·camp \-‚kamp\ n (1979) : a special abbreviated training camp for football players held esp. in the spring or early summer

mini·car \-‚kär\ n (1949) : a very small automobile; *esp* : SUBCOMPACT

mini·com·put·er \‚mi-nē-kəm-'pyü-tər\ n (1968) : a small computer that is intermediate between a microcomputer and a mainframe in size, speed, and capacity, that can support time-sharing, and that is often dedicated to a single application

mini·course \'mi-nē-‚kórs, -‚kòrs\ n (1970) : a brief course of study usu. lasting less than a semester

min·ié ball \'mi-nē-, ‚mi-nē-'ā-\ n [Claude Étienne *Minié* †1879 Fr. army officer] (1859) : a rifle bullet with a conical head used in muzzle-loading firearms

min·i·fy \'mi-nə-‚fī\ vt **-fied; -fy·ing** [L *minus* less + E *-ify*] (1676) : LESSEN

min·i·kin \'mi-ni-kən\ n [obs. D *minneken* darling, ultim. fr. MD *minne* love, beloved; akin to OE *gemynd* mind, memory — more at MIND] (1761) *archaic* : a small or dainty creature — **minikin** adj

mini·lab \'mi-nē-‚lab\ n (1982) : a retail outlet offering rapid on-site film development and printing

min·im \'mi-nəm\ n [L *minimus* least] (15c) **1 :** HALF NOTE **2 :** something very minute **3** — see WEIGHT table — **minim** adj

min·i·mal \'mi-nə-məl\ adj (1666) **1 :** relating to or being a minimum: as **a :** the least possible ⟨a victory won with ～ loss of life⟩ **b :** barely adequate ⟨a ～ standard of living⟩ **c :** very small or slight ⟨a ～ interest in art⟩ **2** often cap **:** of, relating to, or being minimal art or minimalism — **min·i·mal·ly** \-mə-lē\ adv

minimal art n (1965) : abstract art consisting primarily of simple geometric forms executed in an impersonal style

minimal brain dysfunction n (1972) : ATTENTION DEFICIT DISORDER

min·i·mal·ism \'mi-nə-mə-‚li-zəm\ n (1969) **1 :** MINIMAL ART **2 :** a style or technique (as in music, literature, or design) that is characterized by extreme spareness and simplicity

¹min·i·mal·ist \-list\ n (1907) **1 :** one who favors restricting the functions and powers of a political organization or the achievement of a set of goals to a minimum **2 a :** a minimal artist **b :** an adherent of minimalism

²minimalist adj (1967) : of, relating to, or done in the style of minimalism

minimal pair n (1942) : two linguistic units that differ in a single distinctive feature or constituent (as voice in the initial consonants of *bat* and *pat*)

mini·max \'mi-ni-‚maks\ n [*mini*mum + *max*imum] (1918) : the minimum of a set of maxima; *esp* : the smallest of a set of maximum possible losses each of which occurs in the most unfavorable outcome of a strategy followed by a participant in a situation governed by the theory of games — compare MAXIMIN

mini·mill \'mi-nē-‚mil\ n (1969) : a relatively small-scale steel mill that uses scrap metal as starting material

min·i·mise Brit var of MINIMIZE

min·i·mize \'mi-nə-‚mīz\ vt **-mized; -miz·ing** (1802) **1 :** to reduce or keep to a minimum **2 :** to underestimate intentionally : play down : SOFT-PEDAL ⟨*minimizing* losses in our own forces while maximizing those of the enemy⟩ — **min·i·mi·za·tion** \‚mi-nə-mə-'zā-shən\ n — **min·i·miz·er** \'mi-nə-‚mī-zər\ n

min·i·mum \'mi-nə-məm\ n, pl **-i·ma** \-nə-mə\ or **-i·mums** [L, neut. of *minimus* smallest; akin to L *minor* smaller — more at MINOR] (1674) **1 :** the least quantity assignable, admissible, or possible **2 :** the least of a set of numbers; *specif* : the smallest value assumed by a continuous function defined on a closed interval **3 a :** the lowest degree or amount of variation (as of temperature) reached or recorded **b :** the lowest speed allowed on a highway — **minimum** adj

minimum wage n (1860) **1 :** LIVING WAGE **2 :** the lowest wage paid or permitted to be paid; *specif* : a wage fixed by legal authority or by contract as the least that may be paid either to employed persons generally or to a particular category of employed persons

min·ing \'mī-niŋ\ n (1523) : the process or business of working mines

min·ion \'min-yən\ n [MF *mignon* darling] (1501) **1 :** a servile dependent, follower, or underling **2 :** one highly favored : IDOL **3 :** a subordinate or petty official

mini·park \'mi-nē-‚pärk\ n (1967) : a small city park

mini·school \-‚skül\ n (1968) : an experimental school offering specialized or individual instruction to its students

min·is·cule \'mi-nəs-‚kyü(ə)l\ var of MINUSCULE

mini·se·ries \'mi-nē-‚sir-(‚)ēz\ n (1973) : a television production of a story presented in sequential episodes

mini·skirt \'mi-nē-‚skərt\ n (1965) : a woman's short skirt with the hemline several inches above the knee — **mini·skirt·ed** adj

mini·state \-‚stāt\ n (1966) : a small independent nation

¹min·is·ter \'mi-nə-stər\ n [ME *ministre,* fr. OF, fr. L *minister* servant; akin to L *minor* smaller] (14c) **1 :** AGENT **2 a :** one officiating or assisting the officiant in church worship **b :** a clergyman esp. of a Protestant communion **3 a :** the superior of one of several religious orders — called also *minister-general* **b :** the assistant to the rector or the bursar of a Jesuit house **4 :** a high officer of state entrusted with the management of a division of governmental activities **5 a :** a diplomatic representative (as an ambassador) accredited to the court or seat of government of a foreign state **b :** a diplomatic representative ranking below an ambassador

²minister vi **-tered; -ter·ing** \-st(ə-)riŋ\ (14c) **1 :** to perform the functions of a minister of religion **2 :** to give aid or service ⟨～ to a sick⟩

min·is·te·ri·al \‚mi-nə-'stir-ē-əl\ adj (1561) **1 :** of, relating to, or characteristic of a minister or the ministry **2 a :** being or having the characteristics of an act or duty prescribed by law as part of the duties of an administrative office **b :** relating to or being an act done after ascertaining the existence of a specified state of facts in obedience to a legal order without exercise of personal judgment or discretion **3 :** acting or active as an agent : INSTRUMENTAL — **min·is·te·ri·al·ly** \-ē-ə-lē\ adv

minister plenipotentiary n, pl **ministers plenipotentiary** (1796) : a diplomatic agent ranking below an ambassador but possessing full power and authority

minister resident n, pl **ministers resident** (1848) : a diplomatic agent resident at a foreign court or seat of government and ranking below a minister plenipotentiary

¹min·is·trant \'mi-nə-strənt\ adj (1667) *archaic* : performing service in attendance on someone

²ministrant n (1818) : one that ministers

min·is·tra·tion \‚mi-nə-'strā-shən\ n (14c) : the act or process of ministering

min·is·try \'mi-nə-strē\ n, pl **-tries** (14c) **1 :** MINISTRATION **2 :** the office, duties, or functions of a minister **3 :** the body of ministers of religion : CLERGY **4 :** AGENCY 2, INSTRUMENTALITY **5 :** the period of service or office of a minister or ministry **6** often cap **a :** the body of ministers governing a nation or state from which a smaller cabinet is sometimes selected **b :** the group of ministers constituting a cabinet **7 a :** a government department presided over by a minister **b :** the building in which the business of a ministry is transacted

mini·van \'mi-nē-‚van\ n (1960) : a small van

min·i·ver \'mi-nə-vər\ n [ME *meniver,* fr. MF *menu vair* small vair] (13c) : a white fur worn orig. by medieval nobles and used chiefly for robes of state

mink \'miŋk\ n, pl **mink** or **minks** [ME] (15c) **1 :** soft fur or pelt of the mink varying in color from white to dark brown **2 :** either of two slender-bodied semiaquatic carnivorous mammals (*Mustela vison* of No. America and *M. lutreola* of Eurasia) that resemble the related weasels and have partially webbed feet, a rather short bushy tail, and a soft thick coat

mink 2

min·ke whale \'miŋ-kə-\ n [part trans. of Norw *minkehval,* fr. *minke-* (perh. fr. *Meincke,* a crewman of Svend Foyn †1894 Norw. whaler) + *hval* whale] (1939) : a small grayish baleen whale (*Balaenoptera acutorostrata*) with a whitish underside — called also *minke*

min·ne·sing·er \'mi-nə-‚siŋ-ər, -‚ziŋ-\ n [G, fr. MHG, fr. *minne* love + *singer* singer] (1825) : any of a class of German poets and musicians of the 12th to the 14th centuries

Min·ne·so·ta Multiphasic Personality Inventory \‚mi-nə-'sō-tə-‚məl-ti-'fā-zik-, -‚məl-‚tī-\ n [University of *Minnesota*] (1943) : a test of personal and social adjustment based on a complex scaling of the answers to an elaborate true or false test

min·now \'mi-(‚)nō\ n, pl **minnows** also **minnow** [ME *menawe;* akin to OE *myne* minnow, OHG *munewa,* a kind of fish] (15c) **1 a :** a small cyprinid, killifish, or topminnow **b :** any of various small fish that are less than a designated size and are not game fish **2 :** a live or artificial minnow used as bait

¹Mi·no·an \mə-'nō-ən, mī-\ adj [L *minous* of Minos, fr. Gk *minōios,* fr. *Minōs* Minos] (1894) : of or relating to a Bronze Age culture of Crete (3000 B.C.–1100 B.C.)

\ə\ abut \ʾ\ kitten, F table \ər\ further \a\ ash \ā\ ace \ä\ mop, mar \aú\ out \ch\ chin \e\ bet \ē\ easy \g\ go \i\ hit \ī\ ice \j\ job \ŋ\ sing \ō\ go \ò\ law \òi\ boy \th\ thin \t̲h̲\ the \ü\ loot \ú\ foot \y\ yet \zh\ vision \á, k̲, ⁿ, œ, œ̄, ᵫ, ūe, ᵬ\ see Guide to Pronunciation

²**Minoan** *n* (1902) : a native or inhabitant of ancient Crete
¹**mi·nor** \'mī-nər\ *adj* [L, smaller, inferior; akin to OHG *minniro* smaller, L *minuere* to lessen] (1526) **1** : inferior in importance, size, or degree : comparatively unimportant **2** : not having reached majority **3 a** : having half steps between the second and third, the fifth and sixth, and sometimes the seventh and eighth degrees ⟨~ scale⟩ **b** : based on a minor scale ⟨~ key⟩ **c** : less by a semitone than the corresponding major interval ⟨~ third⟩ **d** : having a minor third above the root ⟨~ triad⟩ **4** : not serious or involving risk to life ⟨~ illness⟩ **5** : of or relating to an academic subject requiring fewer courses than a major
²**minor** *n* (1612) **1** : a person who has not attained majority **2** : a minor musical interval, scale, key, or mode **3 a** : a minor academic subject **b** : a student taking a specified minor **4** : a determinant or matrix obtained from a given determinant or matrix by eliminating the row and column in which a given element lies **5** *pl* : minor league baseball — used with *the*
³**minor** *vi* (1926) : to take courses in a minor subject
minor axis *n* (1862) : the chord of an ellipse passing through the center and perpendicular to the major axis
minor element *n* (ca. 1945) : TRACE ELEMENT
Mi·nor·ite \'mī-nə-ˌrīt\ *n* [fr. *Friar Minor* Franciscan] (ca. 1587) : FRANCISCAN
mi·nor·i·ty \mə-'nȯr-ə-tē, mī-, -'när-\ *n, pl* **-ties** *often attrib* (1547) **1 a** : the period before attainment of majority **b** : the state of being a legal minor **2** : the smaller in number of two groups constituting a whole; *specif* : a group having less than the number of votes necessary for control **3 a** : a part of a population differing from others in some characteristics and often subjected to differential treatment **b** : a member of a minority group ⟨an effort to hire more *minorities*⟩
minority leader *n* (1949) : the leader of the minority party in a legislative body
minor league *n* (1889) : a league of professional clubs in a sport other than the recognized major leagues
minor order *n* (1844) : one of the Roman Catholic or Eastern clerical orders that are lower in rank and less sacred in character than major orders — usu. used in pl.
minor party *n* (1949) : a political party whose electoral strength is so small as to prevent its gaining control of a government except in rare and exceptional circumstances
minor penalty *n* (1936) : a two-minute suspension of a player in ice hockey with no substitute allowed
minor planet *n* (1861) : ASTEROID
minor premise *n* (ca. 1741) : the premise of a syllogism that contains the minor term
minor seminary *n* (ca. 1948) : a Roman Catholic seminary giving all or part of high school and junior college training with emphasis on preparing candidates for a major seminary
minor suit *n* (1916) : either of the suits diamonds or clubs having inferior scoring value in bridge
minor term *n* (1843) : the term of a syllogism that forms the subject of the conclusion
Mi·nos \'mī-nəs\ *n* [L, fr. Gk *Minōs*] : a son of Zeus and Europa and king of Crete who for his just rule is made supreme judge in the underworld after his death
Mi·no·taur \'mi-nə-ˌtȯr, 'mī-\ *n* [ME, fr. MF, fr. L *Minotaurus*, fr. Gk *Minōtauros*, fr. *Minōs* + *tauros* bull] : a monster shaped half like a man and half like a bull, confined in the labyrinth built by Daedalus for Minos, and given a periodic tribute of youths and maidens as food until slain by Theseus
mi·nox·i·dil \mə-'näk-sə-ˌdil\ *n* [perh. fr. a*min*o + *oxi*- (alter. of *oxy*-) + *pi*peri*dine* + -*yl*] (1972) : a peripheral vasodilator $C_9H_{15}N_5O$ used orally to treat hypertension and topically in a propylene glycol solution to promote hair regrowth in some forms of baldness
min·ster \'min(t)-stər\ *n* [ME, monastery, church attached to a monastery, fr. OE *mynster*, fr. LL *monasterium* monastery] (bef. 12c) : a large or important church often having cathedral status
min·strel \'min(t)-strəl\ *n* [ME *menestrel*, fr. MF, official, servant, minstrel, fr. LL *ministerialis* imperial household officer, fr. L *ministerium* service, fr. *minister* servant — more at MINISTER] (14c) **1** : one of a class of medieval musical entertainers; *esp* : a singer of verses to the accompaniment of a harp **2 a** : MUSICIAN **b** : POET **3 a** : any of a troupe of performers typically giving a program of black American melodies, jokes, and impersonations and usu. wearing blackface in a performance by a troupe of minstrels
min·strel·sy \-sē\ *n* [ME *menstralcie*, fr. MF *menestralsie*, fr. *menestrel*] (14c) **1** : the singing and playing of a minstrel **2** : a body of minstrels **3** : a group of songs or verse
¹**mint** \'mint\ *n* [ME *minte*, fr. OE, fr. L *mentha, menta*; akin to Gk *minthē* mint] (bef. 12c) **1** : any of a family (Labiatae, the mint family) of aromatic plants with a square stem and a 4-lobed ovary which produces four one-seeded nutlets in fruit; *esp* : any of a genus (*Mentha*) of mints that have white, purple, or pink verticillate flowers with a nearly regular corolla and four equal stamens and that include some used in flavoring and cookery **2** : a confection flavored with mint — **minty** \'min-tē\ *adj*
²**mint** *n* [ME *mynt* coin, money, fr. OE *mynet*, fr. L *moneta* mint, coin, fr. *Moneta*, epithet of Juno; fr. the fact that the Romans coined money in the temple of Juno Moneta] (15c) **1** : a place where coins, medals, or tokens are made **2** : a place where something is manufactured **3** : a vast sum or amount
³**mint** *vt* (1546) **1** : to make (as coins) out of metal : COIN **2** : CREATE, PRODUCE — **mint·er** *n*
⁴**mint** *adj* (1902) : unmarred as if fresh from a mint ⟨in ~ condition⟩
mint·age \'min-tij\ *n* (ca. 1570) **1** : the action or process of minting coins **2** : an impression placed upon a coin **3** : coins produced by minting or in a single period of minting
mint julep *n* (1809) : JULEP 2
min·u·end \'min-yə-ˌwend\ *n* [L *minuendum*, neut. of *minuendus*, gerundive of *minuere* to lessen — more at MINOR] (1706) : a number from which the subtrahend is to be subtracted
min·u·et \ˌmin-yə-'wet\ *n* [F *menuet*, fr. obs. F, tiny, fr. OF, fr. *menu* small, fr. L *minutus*] (1673) **1** : a slow graceful dance in ¾ time char-

acterized by forward balancing, bowing, and toe pointing **2** : music for or in the rhythm of a minuet
¹**mi·nus** \'mī-nəs\ *prep* [ME, fr. L *minus*, adv., less, fr. neut. of *minor* smaller — more at MINOR] (15c) **1** : diminished by : LESS ⟨seven ~ four is three⟩ **2** : deprived of : WITHOUT ⟨~ his hat⟩
²**minus** *n* (1654) **1** : a negative quantity **2** : DEFICIENCY, DEFECT
³**minus** *adj* (1800) **1** : algebraically negative ⟨a ~ quantity⟩ **2** : having negative qualities **3** : relating to or being a particular one of the two mating types that are required for successful fertilization in sexual reproduction in some lower plants (as a fungus) **4** : falling low in a specified range ⟨B ~⟩
¹**mi·nus·cule** \'mi-nəs-ˌkyü(ə)l *also* mi-'nəs-\ *n* [F, fr. L *minusculus* rather small, dim. of *minor* smaller] (1705) **1** : one of several ancient and medieval writing styles developed from cursive and having simplified and small forms **b** : a letter in this style **2** : a lowercase letter
²**minuscule** *adj* (ca. 1741) **1** : written in or in the size or style of minuscules **2** : very small
minus sign *n* (1668) : a sign — used in mathematics to indicate subtraction (as in $8 - 6 = 2$) or a negative quantity (as in $-10°$)
¹**min·ute** \'mi-nət\ *n* [ME, fr. MF, fr. LL *minuta*, fr. L *minutus* small, fr. pp. of *minuere* to lessen — more at MINOR] (14c) **1** : a 60th part of an hour of time or of a degree : 60 seconds **2** : the distance one can traverse in a minute **3** : a short space of time : MOMENT **4 a** : a brief note (as of summary or recommendation) **b** : MEMORANDUM, DRAFT **c** *pl* : the official record of the proceedings of a meeting
²**minute** *vt* **min·ut·ed; min·ut·ing** (ca. 1648) : to make notes or a brief summary of
³**mi·nute** \mī-'nüt, mə-, -'nyüt\ *adj* **mi·nut·er; -est** [L *minutus*] (ca. 1626) **1** : very small : INFINITESIMAL **2** : of small importance : TRIFLING **3** : marked by close attention to details *syn* see SMALL, CIRCUMSTANTIAL — **mi·nute·ness** *n*
minute hand *n* (1726) : the long hand that marks the minutes on the face of a watch or clock
¹**mi·nute·ly** \mī-'nüt-lē, mə-, -'nyüt-\ *adv* (1599) **1** : into very small pieces **2** : in a minute manner or degree
²**min·ute·ly** \'mi-nət-lē\ *adj* (1605) *archaic* : minute by minute
min·ute·man \'mi-nət-ˌman\ *n* (1774) : a member of a group of armed men pledged to take the field at a minute's notice during and immediately before the American Revolution
minute steak \'mi-nət-\ *n* (1921) : a small thin steak that can be quickly cooked
mi·nu·tia \mə-'nü-sh(ē-)ə, mī-, -'nyü-\ *n, pl* **-ti·ae** \-shē-ˌē, -ˌī\ [L *minutiae* trifles, details, fr. pl. of *minutia* smallness, fr. *minutus*] (1751) : a minute or minor detail — usu. used in pl.
minx \'miŋ(k)s\ *n* [origin unknown] (1592) **1** : a pert girl **2** *obs* : a wanton woman
min·yan \'min-yən\ *n, pl* **-ya·nim** \ˌmin-yə-'nēm\ *or* **-yans** [Heb *minyān*, lit., number, count] (1753) : the quorum of 10 adult Jews required for communal worship
Mio·cene \'mī-ə-ˌsēn\ *adj* [*mio*- (fr. Gk *meiōn* less) + -*cene* — more at MEIOSIS] (1831) : of, relating to, or being an epoch of the Tertiary between the Pliocene and the Oligocene or the corresponding system of rocks — see GEOLOGIC TIME table — **Miocene** *n*
mi·o·sis \mī-'ō-səs, mē-\ *n, pl* **mi·o·ses** \-ˌsēz\ [NL, fr. Gk *myein* to be closed (of the eyes) + NL -*osis*] (1819) : excessive smallness or contraction of the pupil of the eye
¹**mi·ot·ic** \-'ä-tik\ *n* (1864) : an agent that causes miosis
²**miotic** *adj* (1864) : relating to or characterized by miosis
mi·que·let \ˌmi-kə-'let, -mē-\ *n* [Sp *miquelete*] (1827) : a Spanish or French irregular soldier during the Peninsular War
mir \'mir\ *n* [Russ] (1877) : a village community in czarist Russia in which land was owned jointly but cultivated by individual families
mi·ra·bi·le dic·tu \mə-ˌrä-bə-lē-'dik-(ˌ)tü\ [L] (1831) : wonderful to relate
mi·ra·cid·i·um \ˌmir-ə-'si-dē-əm, ˌmī-rə-\ *n, pl* **-cid·ia** \-dē-ə\ [NL, fr. Gk *meirak-, meirax* youth, stripling + NL -*idium*] (1898) : the free-swimming ciliated first larva of a digenetic trematode that seeks out and penetrates a suitable snail intermediate host in which it develops into a sporocyst — **mi·ra·cid·i·al** \-dē-əl\ *adj*
mir·a·cle \'mir-i-kəl\ *n* [ME, fr. OF, fr. LL *miraculum*, fr. L, a wonder, marvel, fr. *mirari* to wonder at] (12c) **1** : an extraordinary event manifesting divine intervention in human affairs **2** : an extremely outstanding or unusual event, thing, or accomplishment **3** *Christian Science* : a divinely natural phenomenon experienced humanly as the fulfillment of spiritual law
miracle drug *n* (1950) : a drug usu. newly discovered that elicits a dramatic response in a patient's condition — called also *wonder drug*
miracle fruit *n* (1964) : a tropical African shrub (*Synsepalum dulcificum*) of the sapodilla family whose fruit contains a glycoprotein that when applied to the tongue causes sour substances to taste sweet; *also* : its fruit
miracle play *n* (ca. 1852) **1** : a medieval drama based on episodes from the life of a saint or martyr **2** : MYSTERY PLAY
mi·rac·u·lous \mə-'ra-kyə-ləs\ *adj* [ME, fr. MF *miraculeux*, fr. ML *miraculosus*, fr. L *miraculum*] (15c) **1** : of the nature of a miracle : SUPERNATURAL ⟨a ~ event⟩ **2** : suggesting a miracle : MARVELOUS ⟨gave proof of a ~ memory —*Time*⟩ **3** : working or able to work miracles ⟨~ power⟩ — **mi·rac·u·lous·ly** *adv* — **mi·rac·u·lous·ness** *n*
mir·a·dor \'mir-ə-ˌdȯr, ˌmir-ə-'\ *n* [Sp, fr. Catal, fr. *mirar* to look at, fr. L *mirarī*] (1797) : a turret, window, or balcony designed to command an extensive outlook
mi·rage \mə-'räzh\ *n* [F, fr. *mirer* to look at, fr. L *mirarī*] (1803) **1** : an optical effect that is sometimes seen at sea, in the desert, or over a hot pavement, that may have the appearance of a pool of water or a mirror in which distant objects are seen inverted, and that is caused by the bending or reflection of rays of light by a layer of heated air of varying density **2** : something illusory and unattainable like a mirage
Mi·ran·da \mə-'ran-də\ *adj* [fr. *Miranda v. Arizona*, the U.S. Supreme Court ruling establishing such rights] (1972) : of, relating to, or being the legal rights of an arrested person to have an attorney and to remain silent so as to avoid self-incrimination ⟨~ warnings⟩
¹**mire** \'mir\ *n* [ME, fr. ON *mȳrr*; akin to OE *mōs* marsh — more at MOSS] (14c) **1** : wet spongy earth (as of a bog or marsh) **2** : heavy

often deep mud or slush **3** : a troublesome or intractable situation ⟨found themselves in a ~ of debt⟩ — **miry** \'mīr-ē\ *adj*
²**mire** *vb* **mired; mir·ing** *vt* (15c) **1 a** : to cause to stick fast in or as if in mire **b** : to hamper or hold back as if by mire : ENTANGLE **2** : to cover or soil with mire ~ *vi* : to stick or sink in mire

mi·rex \'mī-ˌreks\ *n* [origin unknown] (1962) : an organochlorine insecticide $C_{10}Cl_{12}$ used esp. against ants

mirk, mirky *var of* MURK, MURKY

mir·li·ton \ˌmir-lə-'tōⁿ\ *n* [F] (ca. 1909) : CHAYOTE

¹**mir·ror** \'mir-ər\ *n* [ME *mirour*, fr. OF, fr. *mirer* to look at, fr. L *mirari* to wonder at] (13c) **1** : a polished or smooth surface (as of glass) that forms images by reflection **2 a** : something that gives a true representation **b** : an exemplary model — **mir·rored** \-ə(r)d\ *adj* — **mir·ror·like** \-ˌlīk\ *adj*
²**mirror** *vt* (1593) : to reflect in or as if in a mirror

mirror image *n* (1885) : something that has its parts reversely arranged in comparison with another similar thing or that is reversed with reference to an intervening axis or plane

mirth \'mərth\ *n* [ME, fr. OE *myrgth*, fr. *myrge* merry — more at MERRY] (bef. 12c) : gladness or gaiety as shown by or accompanied with laughter — **mirth·ful** \-fəl\ *adj* — **mirth·ful·ly** \-fə-lē\ *adv* — **mirth·ful·ness** *n* — **mirth·less** \-ləs\ *adj* — **mirth·less·ly** \-lē\ *adv*

¹**MIRV** \'mərv\ *n* [*multiple independently targeted reentry vehicle*] (1967) : a missile with two or more warheads designed to strike separate enemy targets; *also* : any of the warheads of such a missile
²**MIRV** *vb* **MIRVed; MIRV·ing** *vt* (1969) : to equip with MIRV warheads ~ *vi* : to arm one's forces with MIRVs

mis- *prefix* [partly fr. ME, fr. OE; partly fr. ME *mes-*, *mis-*, fr. OF *mes-*, of Gmc origin; akin to OE *mis-*; akin to OE *missan* to miss] **1 a** : badly : wrongly ⟨*misjudge*⟩ **b** : unfavorably ⟨*misesteem*⟩ **c** : in a suspicious manner ⟨*misdoubt*⟩ **2** : bad : wrong ⟨*misdeed*⟩ **3** : opposite or lack of ⟨*mistrust*⟩ **4** : not ⟨*misknow*⟩

mis·act	mis·con·strue	mis·mark
mis·ad·dress	mis·copy	mis·mar·riage
mis·ad·just	mis·cor·re·la·tion	mis·match
mis·ad·min·is·tra·tion	mis·cre·ate	mis·mate
mis·ad·vise	mis·cre·a·tion	mis·or·der
mis·aim	mis·cut	mis·ori·ent
mis·align	mis·date	mis·ori·en·ta·tion
mis·align·ment	mis·deem	mis·pack·age
mis·al·lo·cate	mis·de·fine	mis·per·ceive
mis·al·lo·ca·tion	mis·de·scribe	mis·per·cep·tion
mis·anal·y·sis	mis·de·scrip·tion	mis·plan
mis·ap·pli·ca·tion	mis·de·vel·op	mis·po·si·tion
mis·ap·ply	mis·di·ag·nose	mis·print
mis·ap·prais·al	mis·di·ag·no·sis	mis·pro·gram
mis·ar·tic·u·late	mis·dial	mis·quo·ta·tion
mis·as·sem·ble	mis·dis·tri·bu·tion	mis·quote
mis·as·sump·tion	mis·di·vi·sion	mis·rec·ol·lec·tion
mis·at·trib·ute	mis·draw	mis·re·cord
mis·at·tri·bu·tion	mis·ed·u·cate	mis·ref·er·ence
mis·bal·ance	mis·ed·u·ca·tion	mis·reg·is·ter
mis·be·have	mis·em·pha·sis	mis·reg·is·tra·tion
mis·be·hav·er	mis·em·pha·size	mis·re·late
mis·be·hav·ior	mis·em·ploy	mis·re·mem·ber
mis·bound	mis·em·ploy·ment	mis·ren·der
mis·but·ton	mis·es·ti·mate	mis·re·port
mis·cal·cu·late	mis·es·ti·ma·tion	mis·route
mis·cal·cu·la·tion	mis·eval·u·ate	mis·set
mis·cap·tion	mis·eval·u·a·tion	mis·shape
mis·cat·a·log	mis·field	mis·shap·en
mis·chan·nel	mis·file	mis·shap·en·ly
mis·char·ac·ter·i·za·tion	mis·fo·cus	mis·sort
mis·char·ac·ter·ize	mis·func·tion	mis·strike
mis·charge	mis·gauge	mis·throw
mis·choice	mis·gov·ern	mis·time
mis·ci·ta·tion	mis·gov·ern·ment	mis·ti·tle
mis·clas·si·fi·ca·tion	mis·grade	mis·train
mis·clas·si·fy	mis·iden·ti·fi·ca·tion	mis·tran·scribe
mis·code	mis·iden·ti·fy	mis·tran·scrip·tion
mis·com·pre·hen·sion	mis·in·form	mis·trans·late
mis·com·pu·ta·tion	mis·in·for·ma·tion	mis·trans·la·tion
mis·com·pute	mis·kick	mis·truth
mis·con·ceive	mis·la·bel	mis·tune
mis·con·ceiv·er	mis·learn	mis·type
mis·con·cep·tion	mis·lo·cate	mis·uti·li·za·tion
mis·con·nect	mis·lo·ca·tion	mis·vo·cal·i·za·tion
mis·con·nec·tion	mis·man·age	mis·write
mis·con·struc·tion	mis·man·age·ment	

mis·ad·ven·ture \ˌmi-səd-'ven-chər\ *n* [ME *mesaventure*, fr. OF, fr. *mesavenir* to chance badly, fr. *mes-* mis- + *avenir* to chance, happen, fr. L *advenire* — more at ADVENTURE] (14c) : MISFORTUNE, MISHAP
mis·al·li·ance \ˌmi-sə-'lī-ən(t)s\ *n* [modif. of F *mésalliance*] (1738) **1** : an improper alliance **2 a** : MÉSALLIANCE **b** : a marriage between persons unsuited to each other
mis·an·thrope \'mi-s°n-ˌthrōp\ *n* [Gk *misanthrōpos* hating mankind, fr. *misein* to hate + *anthrōpos* human being] (1683) : a person who hates or distrusts mankind
mis·an·throp·ic \ˌmi-s°n-'thrä-pik\ *adj* (1762) **1** : of, relating to, or characteristic of a misanthrope **2** : marked by a hatred or contempt for mankind *syn see* CYNICAL — **mis·an·throp·i·cal·ly** \-pi-k(ə-)lē\ *adv*
mis·an·thro·py \mi-'san(t)-thrə-pē\ *n* (ca. 1656) : a hatred or distrust of mankind
mis·ap·pre·hend \(ˌ)mis-ˌa-pri-'hend\ *vt* (ca. 1629) : to apprehend wrongly : MISUNDERSTAND — **mis·ap·pre·hen·sion** \-'hen(t)-shən\ *n*
mis·ap·pro·pri·ate \ˌmi-sə-'prō-prē-ˌāt\ *vt* (1857) : to appropriate wrongly (as by theft or embezzlement) — **mis·ap·pro·pri·a·tion** \-ˌprō-prē-'ā-shən\ *n*
mis·be·come \ˌmis-bi-'kəm\ *vt* **-came** \-'kām\; **-come; -com·ing** (1530) : to be inappropriate or unbecoming to
mis·be·got·ten \-bi-'gä-t°n\ *adj* (1554) **1** : unlawfully conceived : IL-

LEGITIMATE ⟨a ~ child⟩ **2 a** : having a disreputable or improper origin : ill-conceived ⟨antiquated and ~ tax laws —R. M. Blough⟩ **b** : CONTEMPTIBLE, DEFORMED ⟨a ~ scoundrel⟩
mis·be·lief \ˌmis-bə-'lēf\ *n* (13c) : erroneous or false belief
mis·be·lieve \-'lēv\ *vi* (14c) *obs* : to hold a false or unorthodox belief
mis·be·liev·er \-'lē-vər\ *n* (15c) : HERETIC, INFIDEL
mis·brand \ˌmis-'brand\ *vt* (ca. 1930) : to brand falsely or in a misleading way; *specif* : to label in violation of statutory requirements
mis·call \ˌmis-'kȯl\ *vt* (14c) : to call by a wrong name : MISNAME
mis·car·riage \ˌmis-'kar-ij, 'mis-ˌ\ *n* (ca. 1652) **1** : corrupt or incompetent management; *esp* : a failure in the administration of justice **2** : spontaneous expulsion of a human fetus before it is viable and esp. between the 12th and 28th weeks of gestation
mis·car·ry \ˌmis-'kar-ē, 'mis-ˌkar-ē\ *vi* (14c) **1** *obs* : to come to harm **2** : to suffer miscarriage of a fetus **3** : to fail to achieve the intended purpose : go wrong or amiss ⟨the plan *miscarried*⟩
mis·cast \ˌmis-'kast\ *vt* **-cast; -cast·ing** (1925) : to cast in an unsuitable role ⟨life had ~ her in the role of wife and mother —Edna Ferber⟩
mis·ce·ge·na·tion \(ˌ)mi-ˌse-jə-'nā-shən, ˌmi-si-jə-'nā-\ *n* [irreg. fr. L *miscēre* to mix + *genus* race — more at MIX, KIN] (1864) : a mixture of races; *esp* : marriage or cohabitation between a white person and a member of another race — **mis·ce·ge·na·tion·al** \-shnəl, -shə-n°l\ *adj*
mis·cel·la·nea \ˌmi-sə-'lā-nē-ə, -nyə\ *n pl* [L, fr. neut. pl. of *miscellaneus*] (1571) : a collection of miscellaneous objects or writings
mis·cel·la·neous \ˌmi-sə-'lā-nē-əs, -nyəs\ *adj* [L *miscellaneus*, fr. *miscellus* mixed] (1637) **1** : consisting of diverse things or members : HETEROGENEOUS **2 a** : having various traits **b** : dealing with or interested in diverse subjects ⟨as a writer I was too ~ —George Santayana⟩ — **mis·cel·la·neous·ly** *adv* — **mis·cel·la·neous·ness** *n*
mis·cel·la·nist \'mi-sə-ˌlā-nist, chiefly Brit mi-'se-lə-nist\ *n* (1810) : a writer of miscellanies
mis·cel·la·ny \-nē\ *n, pl* **-nies** [prob. modif. of F *miscellanées*, pl., fr. L *miscellanea*] (1615) **1 a** *pl* : separate writings collected in one volume **b** : a collection of writings on various subjects **2** : a mixture of various things
mis·chance \ˌmis-'chan(t)s\ *n* [ME *mischaunce*, fr. OF *meschance*, fr. *mes-* mis- + *chance* chance] (14c) **1** : bad luck **2** : a piece of bad luck : MISHAP *syn see* MISFORTUNE
mis·chief \'mis-chəf, 'mish-\ *n* [ME *meschief*, fr. OF, calamity, fr. *mes-* + *chief* head, end — more at CHIEF] (14c) **1** : a specific injury or damage attributed to a particular agent **2** : a cause or source of harm, evil, or irritation; *esp* : a person who causes mischief **3 a** : action that annoys or irritates **b** : the quality or state of being mischievous : MISCHIEVOUSNESS ⟨had ~ in his eyes⟩
mis·chie·vous \'mis-chə-vəs, 'mish-; ÷mis-'chē-vē-əs, mish-\ *adj* (14c) **1** : HARMFUL, INJURIOUS ⟨~ gossip⟩ **2 a** : able or tending to cause annoyance, trouble, or minor injury **b** : irresponsibly playful ⟨~ behavior⟩ — **mis·chie·vous·ly** *adv* — **mis·chie·vous·ness** *n*
usage A pronunciation \mis-'chē-vē-əs\ and a consequent spelling *mischievious* are of long standing: evidence for the spelling goes back to the 16th century. Our pronunciation files contain modern attestations ranging from dialect speakers to Herbert Hoover. But both the pronunciation and the spelling are still considered nonstandard.
misch metal \'mish-\ *n* [G *Mischmetall*, fr. *mischen* to mix + *Metall* metal] (1916) : a complex alloy of rare earth metals used esp. in tracer bullets and as a flint in lighters
mis·ci·ble \'mi-sə-bəl\ *adj* [ML *miscibilis*, fr. L *miscēre* to mix — more at MIX] (1570) : capable of being mixed; *specif* : capable of mixing in any ratio without separation of two phases ⟨~ liquids⟩ — **mis·ci·bil·i·ty** \ˌmi-sə-'bi-lə-tē\ *n*
mis·com·mu·ni·ca·tion \ˌmis-kə-ˌmyü-nə-'kā-shən\ *n* (1964) : failure to communicate clearly
mis·con·duct \-'kän-(ˌ)dəkt\ *n* (1710) **1** : mismanagement esp. of governmental or military responsibilities **2** : intentional wrongdoing; *specif* : deliberate violation of a law or standard esp. by a government official : MALFEASANCE **3 a** : improper behavior **b** : ADULTERY — **mis·con·duct** \-kən-'dəkt\ *vt*
mis·count \-'kaunt\ *vb* [ME *misconten*, fr. MF *mesconter*, fr. *mes-* + *conter* to count] *vi* (14c) : to make a wrong count ~ *vt* : to count wrongly : MISCALCULATE — **miscount** \-'kaunt, mis-\ *n*
¹**mis·cre·ant** \'mis-krē-ənt\ *adj* [ME *miscreant*, fr. MF *mescreant*, prp. of *mescroire* to disbelieve, fr. *mes-* + *croire* to believe, fr. L *credere* — more at CREED] (14c) **1** : UNBELIEVING, HERETICAL **2** : DEPRAVED, VILLAINOUS
²**miscreant** *n* (14c) **1** : INFIDEL, HERETIC **2** : one who behaves criminally or viciously
¹**mis·cue** \ˌmis-'kyü, 'mis-ˌkyü\ *n* (1873) **1** : a faulty stroke in billiards in which the cue slips **2** : MISTAKE, SLIP
²**miscue** *vi* (1894) : to make a miscue
mis·deal \ˌmis-'dē(ə)l\ *vb* **-dealt** \-'delt\; **-deal·ing** *vi* (1850) : to deal cards incorrectly ~ *vt* : to deal incorrectly — **misdeal** *n*
mis·deed \'dēd\ *n* (bef. 12c) : a wrong deed : OFFENSE
mis·de·mean·ant \ˌmis-di-'mē-nənt\ *n* (1819) : a person convicted of a misdemeanor
mis·de·mean·or \-di-'mē-nər\ *n* (15c) **1** : a crime less serious than a felony **2** : MISDEED
mis·di·rect \ˌmis-də-'rekt, -(ˌ)dī-\ *vt* (1603) **1** : to give a wrong direction to **2** : to direct wrongly ⟨~ed their energies⟩
mis·di·rec·tion \-'rek-shən\ *n* (1768) **1 a** : the act or an instance of misdirecting **b** : the state of being misdirected **2** : a wrong direction
mis·do \ˌmis-'dü\ *vb* **-did** \-'did\; **-done** \-'dən\; **-do·ing** \-'dü-iŋ\; **-does** \-'dəz\ *vi* (bef. 12c) *obs* : to act wrongly : transgress the laws of God ⟨the erring soul not wilfully ~*ing* —John Milton⟩ ~ *vt* : to do (something) incorrectly or poorly — **mis·do·er** \-'dü-ər\ *n*
misdoing *n* (15c) : the act or an instance of misbehaving : MISCONDUCT
mis·doubt \ˌmis-'daut\ *vt* (ca. 1540) **1** : DOUBT **2** : SUSPECT, FEAR — **misdoubt** *n*

\ə\ abut \ᵊ\ kitten, F table \ər\ further \a\ ash \ā\ ace \ä\ mop, mar \aú\ out \ch\ chin \e\ bet \ē\ easy \g\ go \i\ hit \ī\ ice \j\ job \ŋ\ sing \ō\ go \ȯ\ law \ȯi\ boy \th\ thin \th\ the \ü\ loot \ú\ foot \y\ yet \zh\ vision \à, k̟, ⁿ, œ, œ̄, ᵫ, ᵫ̄, ᵞ\ *see* Guide to Pronunciation

mise-en-scène \ˌmē-ˌzän-ˈsen, -ˈsän\ n, pl **mise-en-scènes** \-ˈsen(z), -ˈsän(z)\ [F mise en scène] (1833) **1 a :** the arrangement of actors and scenery on a stage for a theatrical production : CONTEXT **b :** ENVIRONMENT, MILIEU **syn** see BACKGROUND

mi·ser \ˈmī-zər\ n [L miser miserable] (ca. 1560) : a mean grasping person; esp : one who is extremely stingy with money

mis·er·a·ble \ˈmi-zər-bəl, ˈmiz-rə-, ˈmi-zə-rə-\ adj [ME, fr. MF, fr. L miserabilis wretched, pitiable, fr. miserari to pity, fr. miser] (15c) **1 :** being in a pitiable state of distress or unhappiness (as from want or shame) ⟨~ refugees⟩ **2 a :** wretchedly inadequate or meager ⟨a ~ hovel⟩ **b :** causing extreme discomfort or unhappiness ⟨a ~ situation⟩ **3 :** being likely to discredit or shame ⟨his ~ neglect of his wife⟩ ⟨it was ~ of you to make fun of him⟩ — **miserable** n — **mis·er·a·ble·ness** n — **mis·er·a·bly** \-blē\ adv

mis·e·re·re \ˌmi-zə-ˈrir-ē, -ˈrer-; ˌmē-zə-ˈrā-(ˌ)rä\ n [ME, fr. L, be merciful, fr. miserere to be merciful, fr. miser wretched; fr. the first word of the Psalm] (13c) **1** cap : the 50th Psalm in the Vulgate **2 :** MISERICORD **3 :** a vocal complaint or lament

mis·er·i·cord also **mis·er·i·corde** \mə-ˈzer-ə-ˌkȯrd, -ˈser-\ n [ML misericordia seat in church, fr. L, mercy, fr. misericord-, misericors merciful, fr. misereri + cord-, cor heart — more at HEART] (ca. 1515) : a small projection on the bottom of a hinged church seat that gives support to a standing worshiper when the seat is turned up

mi·ser·ly \ˈmī-zər-lē\ adj (1593) : of, relating to, or characteristic of a miser; esp : marked by grasping meanness and penuriousness **syn** see STINGY — **mis·er·li·ness** n

mis·ery \ˈmi-zə-rē, ˈmiz-rē\ n, pl **-er·ies** (14c) **1 :** a state of suffering and want that is the result of poverty or affliction **2 :** a circumstance, thing, or place that causes suffering or discomfort **3 :** a state of great unhappiness and emotional distress **syn** see DISTRESS

mis·es·teem \ˌmi-sə-ˈstēm\ vt (1611) : to esteem wrongly; esp : to hold in too little regard

mis·fea·sance \mis-ˈfē-zᵊn(t)s\ n [MF mesfaisance, fr. mesfaire to do wrong, fr. mes- mis- + faire to make, do, fr. L facere — more at DO] (1596) : TRESPASS; specif : the performance of a lawful action in an illegal or improper manner — **mis·fea·sor** \-ˈfē-zər, -ˌzȯr\ n

¹mis·fire \mis-ˈfīr\ vi (1752) **1 :** to have the explosive or propulsive charge fail to ignite at the proper time ⟨the engine misfired⟩ **2 :** to fail to fire ⟨the gun misfired⟩ **3 :** to miss an intended effect or objective

²mis·fire \mis-ˈfīr, ˈmis-\ n (1839) : a failure (as of a cartridge or firearm) to fire **2 :** something that misfires

mis·fit \ˈmis-ˌfit also ˌmis-ˈfit\ n (ca. 1823) **1 :** something that fits badly **2 :** one who is poorly adapted to a situation or environment ⟨social ~s⟩

mis·for·tune \mis-ˈfȯr-chən\ n (15c) **1 a :** an event or conjunction of events that causes an unfortunate or distressing result : bad luck ⟨by ~ he fell into bad company⟩ ⟨had the ~ to break his leg⟩ **b :** an unhappy situation ⟨always ready to help people in ~⟩ **2 :** a distressing or unfortunate incident or event ⟨~s never come singly⟩

syn MISFORTUNE, MISCHANCE, ADVERSITY, MISHAP mean adverse fortune or an instance of this. MISFORTUNE may apply to either the incident or conjunction of events that is the cause of an unhappy change of fortune or to the ensuing state of distress ⟨never lost hope even in the depths of misfortune⟩. MISCHANCE applies esp. to a situation involving no more than slight inconvenience or minor annoyance ⟨took the wrong road by mischance⟩. ADVERSITY applies to a state of grave or persistent misfortune ⟨had never experienced great adversity⟩. MISHAP applies to an often trivial instance of bad luck ⟨the usual mishaps of a family vacation⟩.

mis·give \mis-ˈgiv\ vb **-gave** \-ˈgāv\; **-giv·en** \-ˈgi-vən\; **-giv·ing** vt (1513) : to suggest doubt or fear to ~ vi : to be fearful or apprehensive

mis·giv·ing \-ˈgi-viŋ\ n (1601) : a feeling of doubt or suspicion esp. concerning a future event

mis·guid·ance \ˌmis-ˈgī-dᵊn(t)s\ n (1640) : MISDIRECTION

mis·guide \-ˈgīd\ vt (14c) : to lead astray : MISDIRECT ⟨prejudice ~s our minds⟩ — **mis·guid·er** n

mis·guid·ed \(ˌ)mis-ˈgī-dəd\ adj (1659) : led or prompted by wrong or inappropriate motives or ideals ⟨well-meaning but ~ do-gooders⟩ — **mis·guid·ed·ly** \-lē\ adv — **mis·guid·ed·ness** \-nəs\ n

mis·han·dle \-ˈhan-dᵊl\ vt (1530) **1 :** to treat roughly : MALTREAT **2 :** to deal with or manage wrongly or ignorantly

mi·shan·ter \mi-ˈshän-tər\ n [ME misaunter, alter. of mesaventure] (1742) chiefly Scot : MISADVENTURE

mis·hap \ˈmis-ˌhap, mis-ˈ\ n (14c) **1 :** an unfortunate accident **2 :** bad luck **syn** see MISFORTUNE

mis·hear \ˌmis-ˈhir\ vb **-heard** \-ˈhərd\; **-hear·ing** \-ˈhir-iŋ\ vt (bef. 12c) : to hear wrongly ~ vi : to misunderstand what is heard

mis·hit \ˌmis-ˈhit\ vt **-hit; -hit·ting** (1904) : to hit in a faulty manner — **mis·hit** \ˈmis-ˌhit, ˈmis-\ n

mish·mash \ˈmish-ˌmash, -ˌmäsh\ n [ME & Yiddish; ME mysse masche, perh. redupl. of mash mash; Yiddish mish-mash, perh. redupl. of mishn to mix] (15c) : HODGEPODGE, JUMBLE

Mish·nah or **Mish·na** \ˈmish-nə\ n [Heb mishnāh instruction, oral law] (1610) : the collection of mostly halakic Jewish traditions compiled about A.D. 200 and made the basic part of the Talmud — **Mish·na·ic** \mish-ˈnā-ik\ adj

mis·im·pres·sion \ˌmi-sim-ˈpre-shən\ n (1670) : a mistaken impression

mis·in·ter·pret \ˌmi-sᵊn-ˈtər-prət, -pət\ vt (1547) **1 :** to explain wrongly **2 :** to understand wrongly — **mis·in·ter·pre·ta·tion** \-ˌtər-prə-ˈtā-shən, -pə-\ n

mis·join·der \mis-ˈjȯin-dər\ n (ca. 1847) : an improper union of parties or of causes of action in a single legal proceeding

mis·judge \ˌmis-ˈjəj\ vi (15c) **1 :** to be mistaken in judgment ~ vt **1 :** to estimate wrongly **2 :** to have an unjust opinion of — **mis·judg·ment** \-ˈjəj-mənt\ n

Mi·ski·to \mis-ˈkē-(ˌ)tō\ n, pl **Miskito** or **Miskitos** (1789) **1 :** a member of an American Indian people of the Atlantic coast of Nicaragua and Honduras **2 :** the language of the Miskito people

mis·know \mis-ˈnō\ vt **-knew** \-ˈnü, -ˈnyü\; **-known** \-ˈnōn\; **-know·ing** (1535) : MISUNDERSTAND — **mis·knowl·edge** \-ˈnä-lij\ n

mis·lay \ˌmis-ˈlā\ vt **-laid** \-ˈlād\; **-lay·ing** (1614) : to put in an unremembered place : LOSE

mis·lead \ˌmis-ˈlēd\ vb **-led** \-ˈled\; **-lead·ing** vt (bef. 12c) : to lead in a wrong direction or into a mistaken action or belief often by deliberate deceit ~ vi : to lead astray **syn** see DECEIVE — **mis·lead·er** n — **mis·lead·ing·ly** \-ˈlē-diŋ-lē\ adv

mis·leared \-ˈlird, -ˈlerd\ adj [¹mis- + lear to learn] (1560) chiefly Scot : UNMANNERLY, ILL-BRED

mis·like \-ˈlīk\ vt (bef. 12c) **1** archaic : DISPLEASE **2 :** DISLIKE — **mislike** n

mis·name \-ˈnām\ vt (1537) : to name incorrectly : MISCALL

mis·no·mer \mis-ˈnō-mər\ n [ME misnoumer, fr. MF mesnommer to misname, fr. mes- mis- + nommer to name, fr. L nominare — more at NOMINATE] (15c) **1 :** the misnaming of a person in a legal instrument **2 a :** a use of a wrong name **b :** a wrong name or designation — **mis·no·mered** \-mərd\ adj

mi·so \ˈmē-(ˌ)sō\ n [Jp] (1727) : a high-protein food paste consisting chiefly of soybeans, salt, and usu. fermented grain (as barley or rice) and ranging in taste from very salty to very sweet

mi·sog·a·my \mi-ˈsä-gə-mē, mī-\ n [Gk misein to hate + E -gamy] (ca. 1656) : a hatred of marriage — **mi·sog·a·mist** \-mist\ n

mi·sog·y·ny \mə-ˈsä-jə-nē\ n [Gk misogynia, fr. misein to hate + gynē woman — more at QUEEN] (ca. 1656) : a hatred of women — **mi·sog·y·nic** \ˌmi-sə-ˈji-nik, -ˈgī-\ adj — **mi·sog·y·nist** \mə-ˈsä-jə-nist\ n or adj — **mi·sog·y·nis·tic** \mə-ˌsä-jə-ˈnis-tik\ adj

mi·sol·o·gy \mi-ˈsä-lə-jē\ n [Gk misologia, fr. misein + -logia -logy] (1833) : a hatred of argument, reasoning, or enlightenment

mi·so·ne·ism \ˌmi-sə-ˈnē-ˌi-zəm\ n [It misoneismo, fr. Gk misein + neos new + It -ismo -ism — more at NEW] (1886) : a hatred, fear, or intolerance of innovation or change

mis·place \mis-ˈplās\ vt (1594) **1 a :** to put in a wrong or inappropriate place ⟨~ a comma⟩ **b :** MISLAY ⟨misplaced the keys⟩ **2 :** to set on a wrong object or eventuality ⟨his trust had been misplaced⟩ — **mis·place·ment** \-ˈplās-mənt\ n

mis·play \mis-ˈplā\ n (1867) : a wrong or unskillful play : ERROR — **mis·play** \ˌmis-ˈplā, ˈmis-\ vt

¹mis·pri·sion \(ˌ)mis-ˈpri-zhən\ n [ME, fr. MF mesprison error, wrongdoing, fr. OF, fr. mesprendre to make a mistake, fr. mes- mis- + prendre to take, fr. L prehendere to seize — more at GET] (15c) **1 a :** neglect or wrong performance of official duty **b :** concealment of treason or felony by one who is not a participant in the treason or felony **c :** seditious conduct against the government or the courts **2 :** MISUNDERSTANDING, MISINTERPRETATION

²misprision n [misprize] (1586) : CONTEMPT, SCORN

mis·prize \mis-ˈprīz\ vt [MF mespriser, fr. mes- mis- + prisier to appraise — more at PRIZE] (14c) **1 :** to hold in contempt : DESPISE **2 :** UNDERVALUE

mis·pro·nounce \ˌmis-prə-ˈnaün(t)s\ vt (1593) : to pronounce incorrectly or in a way regarded as incorrect

mis·pro·nun·ci·a·tion \-ˌnən(t)-sē-ˈā-shən also -ˌnaün(t)-\ n (1530) : the act or an instance of mispronouncing

mis·read \ˌmis-ˈrēd\ vt **-read** \-ˈred\; **-read·ing** \-ˈrē-diŋ\ (1809) **1 :** to read incorrectly **2 :** to misinterpret in or as if in reading ⟨totally ~ the lesson of history —Christopher Hollis⟩

mis·reck·on \ˈre-kən\ vb (ca. 1525) : MISCOUNT, MISCALCULATE

mis·rep·re·sent \(ˌ)mis-ˌre-pri-ˈzent\ vt (1647) **1 :** to give a false or misleading representation of usu. with an intent to deceive or be unfair ⟨~ed the facts⟩ **2 :** to serve badly or improperly as a representative of — **mis·rep·re·sen·ta·tion** \(ˌ)mis-ˌre-pri-ˌzen-ˈtā-shən, -zən-\ n — **mis·rep·re·sen·ta·tive** \-ˈzen-tə-tiv\ adj

¹mis·rule \ˌmis-ˈrül\ vt (14c) : to rule incompetently : MISGOVERN

²misrule n (14c) **1 :** the action of misruling : the condition of being misruled **2 :** DISORDER, ANARCHY

¹miss \ˈmis\ vb [ME, fr. OE missan; akin to OHG missan to miss] vt (bef. 12c) **1 :** to fail to hit, reach, or contact **2 :** to discover or feel the absence of **3 :** to fail to obtain **4 :** ESCAPE, AVOID ⟨just ~ed hitting the other car⟩ **5 :** to leave out : OMIT **6 :** to fail to comprehend, sense, or experience ⟨~ed the point of the speech⟩ **7 :** to fail to perform or attend ⟨had to ~ school for a week⟩ ~ vi **1** archaic : to fail to get, reach, or do something ⟨fail to hit something **3 a :** to be unsuccessful **b :** MISFIRE ⟨the engine ~ed⟩ — **miss·able** \ˈmi-sə-bəl\ adj — **miss a beat :** to deviate from regular smooth performance ⟨the company changed ownership without missing a beat⟩ — **miss out on :** to lose a good opportunity for ⟨missed out on a better job⟩ — **miss the boat :** to fail to take advantage of an opportunity

²miss n (12c) **1** chiefly dial : disadvantage or regret resulting from loss ⟨we know the ~ of you, and even hunger . . . to see you —Samuel Richardson⟩ **2 a :** a failure to hit **b :** a failure to attain a desired result **3 :** MISFIRE

³miss n [short for mistress] (ca. 1667) **1** cap **a** — used as a title prefixed to the name of an unmarried woman or girl **b** — used before the name of a place or of a line of activity or before some epithet to form a title for a usu. young unmarried female who is representative of the thing indicated ⟨Miss America⟩ **2 :** young lady — used without a name as a conventional term of address to a young woman **3 :** a young unmarried woman or girl

mis·sa can·ta·ta \ˌmi-sə-kən-ˈtä-tə\ n [NL, sung mass] (ca. 1903) : HIGH MASS

mis·sal \ˈmi-səl\ n [ME messel, fr. MF & ML; MF, fr. ML missale, fr. neut. of missalis of the mass, fr. LL missa mass — more at MASS] (14c) : a book containing all that is said or sung at mass during the entire year

mis·send \mis-ˈsend\ vt **-sent** \-ˈsent\; **-send·ing** (15c) : to send incorrectly ⟨missent mail⟩

mis·sense \ˈmis-ˌsen(t)s\ n [¹mis- + -sense (as in nonsense)] (1961) : genetic mutation involving alteration of one or more codons so that different amino acids are determined — compare ANTISENSE, NONSENSE

¹mis·sile \ˈmi-səl, chiefly Brit -ˌsīl\ adj [L missilis, fr. mittere to throw, send] (1611) **1 :** capable of being thrown or projected to strike a distant object **2 :** adapted for throwing or hurling missiles

²missile n (ca. 1656) : an object (as a weapon) thrown or projected usu. so as to strike something at a distance ⟨stones, artillery shells, bullets, and rockets are ~s⟩: as **a :** GUIDED MISSILE **b :** BALLISTIC MISSILE

mis·sil·eer \ˌmi-sə-ˈlir\ n (1958) : MISSILEMAN

mis·sile·man \ˈmi-səl-mən\ n (1951) : one engaged in designing, building, or operating guided missiles

mis·sile·ry \\'mi-səl-rē\ n (1880) : MISSILES; esp : GUIDED MISSILES
miss·ing \\'mi-siŋ\ adj (ca. 1530) : ABSENT; also : LOST ⟨~ in action⟩
missing link n (1851) 1 : an absent member needed to complete a series or resolve a problem 2 : a hypothetical intermediate form between humans and their presumed simian progenitors
mis·si·ol·o·gy \,mi-sē-'ä-lə-jē\ n [mission + -logy] (1924) : the study of the church's mission esp. with respect to missionary activity
¹mis·sion \\'mi-shən\ n [NL, ML, & L; NL mission-, missio religious mission, fr. ML, task assigned, fr. L, act of sending,\fr. mittere to send] (1606) 1 obs : the act or an instance of sending 2 a : a ministry commissioned by a religious organization to propagate its faith or carry on humanitarian work b : assignment to or work in a field of missionary enterprise c (1) : a mission establishment (2) : a local church or parish dependent on a larger religious organization for direction or financial support d pl : organized missionary work e : a course of sermons and services given to convert the unchurched or quicken Christian faith 3 : a body of persons sent to perform a service or carry on an activity: as a : a group sent to a foreign country to conduct diplomatic or political negotiations b : a permanent embassy or legation c : a team of specialists or cultural leaders sent to a foreign country 4 a : a specific task with which a person or a group is charged b (1) : a definite military, naval, or aerospace task ⟨a bombing ~⟩ ⟨a space ~⟩ (2) : a flight operation of an aircraft or spacecraft in the performance of a mission ⟨a ~ to Mars⟩ 5 : CALLING, VOCATION
²mission vt **mis·sioned; mis·sion·ing** \\'mi-sh(ə-)niŋ\ (1692) 1 : to send on or entrust with a mission 2 : to carry on a religious mission among or in
³mission adj (1904) 1 : of or relating to a style used in the early Spanish missions of the southwestern U.S. ⟨~ architecture⟩ 2 : of, relating to, of having the characteristics of a style of plain heavy usu. oak furniture originating in the U.S. in the early part of the 20th century
¹mis·sion·ary \\'mi-shə-,ner-ē\ adj (1644) 1 : relating to, engaged in, or devoted to missions 2 : characteristic of a missionary
²missionary n, pl **-ar·ies** (ca. 1656) : a person undertaking a mission and esp. a religious mission
missionary position n [perh. fr. the notion that missionaries insisted that this coital position is the only acceptable one] (1948) : a coital position in which the female lies on her back with the male on top and with his face opposite hers
mis·sion·er \\'mi-shə-)nər\ n (1654) : MISSIONARY
mis·sion·ize \\'mi-shə-,nīz\ vb **-ized; -iz·ing** vi (1826) : to carry on missionary work ~ vt : to do missionary work among — **mis·sion·i·za·tion** \,mi-shə-nə-'zā-shən\ n — **mis·sion·iz·er** \\'mi-shə-,nī-zər\ n
Mis·sis·sip·pi·an \,mi-sə-'si-pē-ən, (,)mis-'si-\ adj [Mississippi River] (1835) 1 : of or relating to Mississippi, its people, or the Mississippi River 2 : of, relating to, or being the period of the Paleozoic era in No. America following the Devonian and preceding the Pennsylvanian or the corresponding system of rocks — see GEOLOGIC TIME table — **Mississippian** n
mis·sive \\'mi-siv\ n [MF lettre missive, lit., letter intended to be sent] (1501) : a written communication : LETTER
miss·out \\'mis-,aút\ n (1945) : a throw of dice that loses the main bet
miss out vt (1870) Brit : to leave out : OMIT
mis·speak \,mis-'spēk\ vb **-spoke** \-'spōk\; **-spo·ken** \-'spō-kən\; **-speak·ing** vt (14c) 1 : to speak (as a word) incorrectly 2 : to express (oneself) imperfectly or incorrectly ⟨claims now that he misspoke himself⟩ ~ vi : to speak incorrectly : misspeak oneself
mis·spell \,mis-'spel\ vt (1655) : to spell incorrectly
mis·spell·ing \-'spe-liŋ\ n (ca. 1696) : an incorrect spelling
mis·spend \,mis-'spend\ vt **-spent** \-'spent\; **-spend·ing** (14c) : to spend wrongly : SQUANDER ⟨a misspent life⟩
mis·state \,mis-'stāt\ vt (1650) : to state incorrectly : give a false account of — **mis·state·ment** \-mənt\ n
mis·step \-'step\ n (ca. 1800) 1 : a mistake in judgment or action : BLUNDER 2 : a wrong step
mis·sus or **mis·sis** \\'mi-səz, -səs, esp Southern -zəz\ n [alter. of mistress] (1790) 1 dial : MISTRESS 1a 2 : WIFE ⟨men spend money on themselves, but argue over every dime the ~ wants —W. A. Lydgate⟩
missy \\'mi-sē\ n (1676) : a young girl : MISS
¹mist \\'mist\ n [ME, fr. OE; akin to MD mist mist, Gk omichlē] (bef. 12c) 1 : water in the form of particles floating or falling in the atmosphere at or near the surface of the earth and approaching the form of rain 2 : something that obscures understanding ⟨~s of antiquity⟩ 3 : a film before the eyes 4 a : a cloud of small particles or objects suggestive of a mist b : a suspension of a finely divided liquid in a gas c : a fine spray 5 : a drink of liquor served over cracked ice
²mist vi (bef. 12c) 1 : to be or become misty 2 : to become moist or blurred ~ vt : to cover or spray with or convert to mist
mis·tak·able \mə-'stā-kə-bəl\ adj (1646) : capable of being misunderstood or mistaken
¹mis·take \mə-'stāk\ vb **mis·took** \-'stúk\; **mis·tak·en** \-'stā-kən\; **mis·tak·ing** [ME, fr. ON mistaka to take by mistake, fr. mis- + taka to take — more at TAKE] vt (14c) 1 : to blunder in the choice of ⟨mistook her way in the dark⟩ 2 a : to misunderstand the meaning or intention of : MISINTERPRET ⟨don't ~ me, I mean exactly what I said⟩ b : to make a wrong judgment of the character or ability of 3 : to identify wrongly : confuse with another ⟨I mistook him for his brother⟩ ~ vi : to be wrong ⟨you mistook when you thought I laughed at you — Thomas Hardy⟩ — **mis·tak·en·ly** adv — **mis·tak·er** n
²mistake n (1638) 1 : a misunderstanding of the meaning or implication of something 2 : a wrong action or statement proceeding from faulty judgment, inadequate knowledge, or inattention syn see ERROR
¹mis·ter \\'mis-tər, for 1 ,mis-tər or in rapid speech (,)mis(t)\ n [alter. of ¹master] (1551) 1 cap : MR. — used sometimes in writing instead of Mr. 2 : SIR — used without a name as a generalized term of direct address of a man who is a stranger ⟨hey, ~, do you want to buy a paper⟩ 3 : a man not entitled to a title of rank or an honorific or professional title ⟨though he was only a ~, he was a greater scholar in his field than any PhD⟩ 4 : HUSBAND
²mist·er \\'mis-tər\ n [²mist + ²-er] (1973) : a device for spraying a mist
mis·think \,mis-'thiŋk\ vb **-thought** \-'thót\; **-think·ing** vi (ca. 1530) archaic : to think mistakenly or unfavorably ~ vt, archaic : to think badly or unfavorably of

mis·tle·toe \\'mi-səl-,tō, chiefly Brit 'mi-zəl-\ n [ME mistilto, fr. OE misteltān, fr. mistel mistletoe + tān twig; akin to OHG & OS mistil mistletoe and to OHG zein twig] (bef. 12c) : a European semiparasitic green shrub (Viscum album of the family Loranthaceae, the mistletoe family) with thick leaves, small yellowish flowers, and waxy-white glutinous berries; broadly : any of various plants of the mistletoe family (as of an American genus Phoradendron) resembling the true mistletoe
mis·tral \\'mis-trəl, mi-'sträl\ n [F, fr. Prov. fr. mistral masterful, fr. LL magistralis of a teacher — more at MAGISTRAL] (1604) : a strong cold dry northerly wind of southern France
mis·treat \mis-'trēt\ vt [ME mistreten, prob. fr. MF mestraitier, fr. OF, fr. mes- mis- + traitier to treat — more at TREAT] (15c) : to treat badly : ABUSE — **mis·treat·ment** \-mənt\ n
mis·tress \\'mis-trəs\ n [ME maistresse, fr. MF, fr. OF, fem. of maistre master — more at MASTER] (15c) 1 : a woman who has power, authority, or ownership: as a : the female head of a household b : a woman who employs or supervises servants c : a woman who is in charge of a school or other establishment d : a woman of the Scottish nobility having a status comparable to that of a master 2 a chiefly Brit : a female teacher or tutor b : a woman who has achieved mastery in some field 3 : something personified as female that rules, directs, or dominates ⟨when Rome was ~ of the world⟩ 4 a : a woman other than his wife with whom a married man has a continuing sexual relationship b archaic : SWEETHEART 5 — used archaically as a title prefixed to the name of a married or unmarried woman b chiefly Southern & Midland : MRS. 1a
mistress of ceremonies (1952) : a woman who presides at a public ceremony or who acts as hostess of a stage, radio, or television show
mis·tri·al \\'mis-,trī(ə)l\ n (1628) : a trial that has no legal effect by reason of some error or serious prejudicial misconduct in the proceedings
¹mis·trust \,mis-'trəst\ n (14c) : a lack of confidence : DISTRUST syn see UNCERTAINTY — **mis·trust·ful** \-fəl\ adj — **mis·trust·ful·ly** \-fə-lē\ adv — **mis·trust·ful·ness** n
²mistrust vt (14c) 1 : to have no trust or confidence in : SUSPECT ⟨~ed his neighbors⟩ 2 : to doubt the truth, validity, or effectiveness of ⟨~ed his own judgment⟩ 3 : SURMISE ⟨your mind ~ed there was something wrong —Robert Frost⟩ ~ vi : to be suspicious
misty \\'mis-tē\ adj **mist·i·er; -est** (bef. 12c) 1 a : obscured by mist b : consisting of or marked by mist 2 a : INDISTINCT ⟨a ~ recollection of the event⟩ b : VAGUE, CONFUSED ⟨avoided the large, vague, ~ issues —Reuben Abel⟩ 3 : TEARFUL — **mist·i·ly** \-tə-lē\ adv — **mist·i·ness** \-tē-nəs\ n
misty-eyed \\'mis-tē-,īd\ adj (1928) 1 : having tearful eyes 2 : DREAMY, SENTIMENTAL ⟨~ recollections⟩
mis·un·der·stand \(,)mi-,sən-dər-'stand\ vt **-stood** \-'stúd\; **-stand·ing** (13c) 1 : to fail to understand 2 : to interpret incorrectly
mis·un·der·stand·ing n (15c) 1 : a failure to understand : MISINTERPRETATION 2 : QUARREL, DISAGREEMENT
mis·us·age \,mis-'yü-sij, ,mish-, -zij\ n [MF mesusage, fr. mes- mis- + usage usage] (1532) 1 : bad treatment : ABUSE 2 : wrong or improper use (as of words)
¹mis·use \-'yüz\ vt [ME, partly fr. mis- + usen to use; partly fr. MF mesuser to abuse, fr. OF, fr. mes- + user to use] (14c) 1 : to use incorrectly : MISAPPLY ⟨misused his talents⟩ 2 : ABUSE, MISTREAT ⟨misused his servants⟩ — **mis·us·er** n
²mis·use \-'yüs\ n (14c) : incorrect or improper use : MISAPPLICATION
¹mite \\'mīt\ n [ME, fr. OE mite; akin to MD mīte mite, small copper coin and perh. to OHG meizan to cut] (bef. 12c) : any of numerous small acarid arachnids that often infest animals, plants, and stored foods and include important disease vectors
²mite n [ME, fr. MF or MD; MF, small Flemish copper coin, fr. MD] (14c) 1 : a small coin or sum of money 2 a : a very little : BIT b : a very small object or creature — **a mite** : SOMEWHAT, RATHER ⟨could be that I am a mite prejudiced —John Fischer⟩
¹mi·ter or **mi·tre** \\'mī-tər\ n [ME mitre, fr. MF, fr. L mitra headband, turban, fr. Gk] (14c) 1 a : a liturgical headdress worn by bishops and abbots 2 a : a surface forming the beveled end or edge of a piece where a joint is made by cutting two pieces at an angle and fitting them together b : MITER JOINT

miter 2a: 1 plain, 2 milled, 3 rabbeted

²miter or **mitre** vt **mi·tered** or **mi·tred; mi·ter·ing** or **mi·tring** \\'mī-tə-riŋ\ (14c) 1 : to confer a miter on 2 a : to match or fit together in a miter joint b : to bevel the ends of for making a miter joint — **mi·ter·er** \\'mī-tər-ər\ n
miter box n (1678) : a device for guiding a handsaw at the proper angle in making a miter joint in wood
miter joint n (1688) : a joint made by fastening together usu. perpendicularly parts with the ends cut at an angle
miter square n (1678) : a bevel with an immovable arm at an angle of 45 degrees for striking marking lines; also : a square with an arm adjustable to any angle
Mith·ra·ic \mi-'thrā-ik\ adj [LGk mithraikos of Mithras, fr. Gk Mithras, fr. OPer Mithra] (1678) : of or relating to an oriental mystery cult for men flourishing in the late Roman empire — **Mith·ra·ism** \\'mith-rə-,i-zəm, -(,)rā-\ n — **Mith·ra·ist** \mi-'thrā-ist\ n or adj
mith·ri·date \\'mith-rə-,dāt\ n [ML mithridatum, fr. LL mithridatium, fr. L, dogtooth violet (used as an antidote), fr. Gk mithridation, fr. Mithridatēs Mithridates VI] (1528) : an antidote against poison; esp : an electuary held to be effective against poison

---

\ə\ abut \ʾ\ kitten, F table \ər\ further \a\ ash \ā\ ace \ä\ mop, mar
\aú\ out \ch\ chin \e\ bet \ē\ easy \g\ go \i\ hit \ī\ ice \j\ job
\ŋ\ sing \ō\ go \ó\ law \ói\ boy \th\ thin \th\ the \ü\ loot \ú\ foot
\y\ yet \zh\ vision \ä, k̲, ⁿ, œ, œ̄, ᵫ, ᵫ̄, ʸ\ see Guide to Pronunciation

mi·ti·cide \'mī-tə-ˌsīd\ *n* [*mite*] (ca. 1946) : an agent used to kill mites — **mi·ti·cid·al** \ˌmī-tə-'sī-d²l\ *adj*

mit·i·gate \'mi-tə-ˌgāt\ *vt* **-gat·ed; -gat·ing** [ME, fr. L *mitigatus,* pp. of *mitigare* to soften, fr. *mitis* soft + *-igare* (akin to L *agere* to drive); akin to OIr *moith* soft — more at AGENT] (15c) **1 :** to cause to become less harsh or hostile : MOLLIFY ⟨aggressiveness may be *mitigated* or . . . channeled —Ashley Montagu⟩ **2 a :** to make less severe or painful : ALLEVIATE **b :** EXTENUATE *syn* see RELIEVE — **mit·i·ga·tion** \ˌmi-tə-'gā-shən\ *n* — **mit·i·ga·tive** \'mi-tə-ˌgā-tiv\ *adj* — **mit·i·ga·tor** \-ˌgā-tər\ *n* — **mit·i·ga·to·ry** \'mi-ti-gə-ˌtōr-ē, -ˌtȯr-\ *adj*
usage Mitigate is sometimes used as an intransitive (followed by *against*) where *militate* might be expected. Even though Faulkner used it ⟨some intangible and invisible social force that *mitigates* against him —William Faulkner⟩ and one critic thinks it should be called an American idiom, it is usu. considered a mistake.

mi·to·chon·dri·on \ˌmī-tə-'kän-drē-ən\ *n, pl* **-dria** \-drē-ə\ [NL, fr. Gk *mitos* thread + *chondrion,* dim. of *chondros* grain] (1901) : any of various round or long cellular organelles of most eukaryotes that are found outside the nucleus, produce energy for the cell through cellular respiration, and are rich in fats, proteins, and enzymes — see CELL illustration — **mi·to·chon·dri·al** \-drē-əl\ *adj*

mi·to·gen \'mī-tə-jən\ *n* [*mitosis* + *-gen*] (ca. 1951) : a substance that induces mitosis — **mi·to·gen·ic** \ˌmī-tə-'je-nik\ *adj* — **mi·to·gen·ic·i·ty** \-jə-'ni-sə-tē\ *n*

mi·to·my·cin \ˌmī-tə-'mī-s²n\ *n* [ISV *mito-* (prob. fr. NL *mitosis*) + *-mycin*] (1956) : a complex of antibiotic substances which is produced by a Japanese streptomyces (*Streptomyces caespitosus*) and one form of which acts directly on DNA and shows promise as an anticancer agent

mi·to·sis \mī-'tō-səs\ *n, pl* **-to·ses** \-ˌsēz\ [NL, fr. Gk *mitos* thread] (1887) **1 :** a process that takes place in the nucleus of a dividing cell, involves typically a series of steps consisting of prophase, metaphase, anaphase, and telophase, and results in the formation of two new nuclei each having the same number of chromosomes as the parent nucleus — compare MEIOSIS **2 :** cell division in which mitosis occurs — **mi·tot·ic** \-'tä-tik\ *adj* — **mi·tot·i·cal·ly** \-ti-k(ə-)lē\ *adv*

mi·tral \'mī-trəl\ *adj* (1610) **1 :** resembling a miter **2 :** of, relating to, being, or adjoining a mitral valve or orifice

mitral valve *n* (1705) : BICUSPID VALVE

mi·tre·wort *also* **mi·ter·wort** \'mī-tər-ˌwərt, -ˌwȯrt\ *n* (ca. 1818) : any of a genus (*Mitella*) of rhizomatous perennial herbs of the saxifrage family that bear a capsule resembling a bishop's miter

mitt \'mit\ *n* [short for *mitten*] (1765) **1 :** a woman's glove that leaves the fingers uncovered **b :** MITTEN 1 **c :** a baseball catcher's or first baseman's glove made in the style of a mitten **2** *slang* : HAND

mit·ten \'mi-t²n\ *n* [ME *mitain,* fr. MF *mitaine,* fr. OF, fr. *mite* mitten] (14c) **1 :** a covering for the hand and wrist having a separate section for the thumb only **2 :** MITT 1a

mit·ti·mus \'mi-tə-məs\ *n* [L, we send, fr. *mittere* to send] (ca. 1591) : a warrant of commitment to prison

mitz·vah \'mits-və\ *n, pl* **mitz·voth** \-ˌvōt, -ˌvōth, -ˌvōs *or* **mitz·vahs** [Heb *miṣwāh*] (1650) **1 :** a commandment of the Jewish law **2 :** a meritorious or charitable act

¹mix \'miks\ *vb* [ME, back-formation fr. *mixte* mixed, fr. MF, fr. L *mixtus,* pp. of *miscēre* to mix; akin to Gk *mignynai* to mix] *vt* (15c) **1 a** (1) **:** to combine or blend into one mass (2) **:** to combine with another **b :** to bring into close association ⟨~ business with pleasure⟩ **2 a :** to form by mixing components ⟨~ a drink at the bar⟩ **b :** to produce (a sound recording) by electronically combining or adjusting sounds from more than one source **3 :** CONFUSE — often used with *up* ⟨~es things up in his eagerness to speak out —Irving Howe⟩ ~ *vi* **1 a :** to become mixed **b :** to be capable of mixing **2 :** to enter into relations : ASSOCIATE **3 :** CROSSBREED **4 :** to become involved : PARTICIPATE ⟨decided not to ~ in politics⟩ — **mix·able** \'mik-sə-bəl\ *adj* — **mix it up :** to engage in a fight, contest, or dispute
syn MIX, MINGLE, COMMINGLE, BLEND, MERGE, COALESCE, AMALGAMATE, FUSE mean to combine into a more or less uniform whole. MIX may or may not imply loss of each element's identity ⟨*mix* the salad greens⟩ ⟨*mix* a drink⟩. MINGLE usu. suggests that the elements are still somewhat distinguishable or separately active ⟨fear *mingled* with anticipation in my mind⟩. COMMINGLE implies a closer or more thorough mingling ⟨a sense of duty *commingled* with a fierce pride drove her⟩. BLEND implies that the elements as such disappear in the resulting mixture ⟨*blended* several teas to create a balanced flavor⟩. MERGE suggests a combining in which one or more elements are lost in the whole ⟨in his mind reality and fantasy *merged*⟩. COALESCE implies an affinity in the merging elements and usu. a resulting organic unity ⟨telling details that *coalesce* into a striking portrait⟩. AMALGAMATE implies the forming of a close union without complete loss of individual identities ⟨refugees who were readily *amalgamated* into the community⟩. FUSE stresses oneness and indissolubility of the resulting product ⟨a building in which modernism and classicism are *fused*⟩.

²mix *n* (ca. 1586) **1 :** an act or process of mixing **2 :** a product of mixing: as **a :** a commercially prepared mixture of food ingredients ⟨a cake ~⟩ **b :** a combination of different kinds ⟨the right ~ of jobs, people and amenities —*London Times*⟩ **3 :** MIXER 2b

mixed \'mikst\ *adj* [ME *mixte*] (15c) **1 :** combining characteristics of more than one kind; *specif* : combining features of two or more systems of government ⟨a ~ constitution⟩ **2 :** made up of or involving individuals or items of more than one kind: as **a :** made up of or involving persons differing in race, national origin, religion, or class **b** : made up of or involving individuals of both sexes ⟨~ company⟩ ⟨a ~ school⟩ **3 :** including or accompanied by inconsistent, incompatible, or contrary elements ⟨~ emotions⟩ ⟨received ~ reviews⟩ ⟨a ~ blessing⟩ **4 :** deriving from two or more races or breeds ⟨a stallion of ~ blood⟩

mixed alphabet *n* (1931) : an alphabet (as in a cryptographic system) that has been rearranged or disordered systematically or randomly

mixed bag *n* (1926) : a miscellaneous collection : ASSORTMENT

mixed bud *n* (1900) : a bud that produces a branch and leaves as well as flowers

mixed drink *n* (1943) : an alcoholic beverage prepared from two or more ingredients

mixed farming *n* (1872) : the growing of food or cash crops, feed crops, and livestock on the same farm

mixed grill *n* (1913) : meats (as lamb chop, kidney, and bacon) and vegetables broiled together and served on one plate

mixed marriage *n* (1829) : a marriage between persons of different races or religions

mixed-media *n* (1962) : MULTIMEDIA

mixed metaphor *n* (1800) : a figure of speech combining inconsistent or incongruous metaphors

mixed nerve *n* (1878) : a nerve containing both sensory and motor fibers

mixed number *n* (1542) : a number (as 5⅔) composed of an integer and a fraction

mixed-up \'mikst-'əp\ *adj* (1862) : marked by bewilderment, perplexity, or disorder : CONFUSED

mix·er \'mik-sər\ *n* (ca. 1611) **1 :** one that mixes: as **a** (1) **:** one whose work is mixing the ingredients of a product (2) **:** one who balances and controls the dialogue, music, and sound effects to be recorded for or with a motion picture or television **b :** a container, device, or machine for mixing **c :** a game, stunt, or dance used at a get-together to give members of the group an opportunity to meet one another in a friendly and informal atmosphere **2 :** one that mixes with others: as **a :** a person considered in regard to casual sociability ⟨was shy and a poor ~⟩ **b :** a nonalcoholic beverage (as ginger ale) used in a mixed drink

mix·ol·o·gy \mik-'sä-lə-jē\ *n* (1948) : the art or skill of preparing mixed drinks — **mix·ol·o·gist** \-jist\ *n*

Mix·tec \mēs-'tek, mis-, mēsh-, mish-\ *n, pl* **Mixtec** *or* **Mixtecs** [AmerSp *mixteco*] (1850) **1 :** the language of the Mixtec people **2 :** a member of an American Indian people of the state of Oaxaca, Mexico

mix·ture \'miks-chər\ *n* [ME, fr. MF, fr. OF *misture,* fr. L *mixtura,* fr. *mixtus*] (15c) **1 a :** the act, the process, or an instance of mixing **b** (1) **:** the state of being mixed (2) **:** the relative proportions of constituents; *esp* : the proportion of fuel to air produced in a carburetor **2 :** a product of mixing : COMBINATION: as **a :** a portion of matter consisting of two or more components in varying proportions that retain their own properties **b :** a fabric woven of variously colored threads **c :** a combination of several different kinds

mix-up \'miks-ˌəp\ *n* (1841) **1 :** a state or instance of confusion **2** : MIXTURE **3 :** CONFLICT, FIGHT

¹miz·zen *also* **miz·en** \'mi-z²n\ *n* [ME *meson,* fr. MF *misaine* foremast sail, prob. ultim. fr. L *medianus* of the middle — more at MEDIAN] (15c) **1 :** a fore-and-aft sail set on the mizzenmast **2 :** MIZZENMAST

²mizzen *also* **mizen** *adj* (15c) : of or relating to the mizzenmast

miz·zen·mast \-ˌmast, -məst\ *n* (15c) : the mast aft or next aft of the mainmast in a ship

¹miz·zle \'mi-zəl\ *vi* **miz·zled; miz·zling** \'mi-zə-liŋ, 'miz-liŋ\ [ME *misellen;* akin to Flem *mizzelen* to drizzle, MD *mist* fog, mist] (15c) : to rain in very fine drops : DRIZZLE — **mizzle** *n* — **miz·zly** \'mi-zə-lē, 'miz-lē\ *adj*

²mizzle *vi* **miz·zled; miz·zling** \'mi-zə-liŋ, 'miz-liŋ\ [origin unknown] (1781) *chiefly Brit* : to depart suddenly

¹mne·mon·ic \ni-'mä-nik\ *adj* [Gk *mnēmonikos,* fr. *mnēmōn* mindful, fr. *mimnēskesthai* to remember — more at MIND] (1753) **1 :** assisting or intended to assist memory; *also* : of or relating to mnemonics **2** : of or relating to memory — **mne·mon·i·cal·ly** \-ni-k(ə-)lē\ *adv*

²mnemonic *n* (1858) : a mnemonic device or code

mne·mon·ics \ni-'mä-niks\ *n pl but sing in constr* (ca. 1721) : a technique of improving the memory

Mne·mos·y·ne \ni-'mä-s²n-ē, -z²n-\ *n* [L, fr. Gk *Mnēmosynē*] : the Greek goddess of memory and mother of the Muses by Zeus

-mo *n suffix* [*duodecimo*] — after numerals or their names to indicate the number of leaves made by folding a sheet of paper ⟨sixteen*mo*⟩ ⟨16*mo*⟩

moa \'mō-ə\ *n* [Maori] (1842) : any of various usu. very large extinct flightless birds of New Zealand of a ratite family (Dinornithidae) including one (*Dinornis giganteus*) about 12 feet (3.7 meters) in height

Mo·ab·ite \'mō-ə-ˌbīt\ *n* [ME, fr. LL *Moabita, Moabites,* fr. Gk *Mōabītēs,* fr. *Mōab* Moab, ancient kingdom in Syria] (14c) : a member of an ancient Semitic people related to the Hebrews — **Moabite** *or* **Mo·ab·it·ish** \-ˌbī-tish\ *adj*

¹moan \'mōn\ *n* [ME *mone,* fr. (assumed) OE *mān*] (13c) **1 :** LAMENTATION, COMPLAINT **2 :** a low prolonged sound of pain or of grief

²moan *vt* (14c) **1 :** to bewail audibly : LAMENT **2 :** to utter with moans ~ *vi* **1 :** LAMENT, COMPLAIN **2 a :** to make a moan : GROAN **b :** to emit a sound resembling a moan ⟨the wind ~ed in the trees⟩ — **moan·er** \'mō-nər\ *n*

moat \'mōt\ *n* [ME *mote,* prob. fr. MF *motte* hill, mound] (14c) **1 :** a deep and wide trench around the rampart of a fortified place (as a castle) that is usu. filled with water **2 :** a channel resembling a moat (as about a seamount or for confinement of animals in a zoo) — **moat·ed** \'mō-təd\ *adj* — **moat·like** \-ˌlīk\ *adj*

¹mob \'mäb\ *n* [L *mobile vulgus* vacillating crowd] (1688) **1 :** a large or disorderly crowd; *esp* : one bent on riotous or destructive action **2** : the lower classes of a community : MASSES, RABBLE **3** *chiefly Austral* : a flock, drove, or herd of animals **4 :** a criminal set : GANG; *esp, often cap* : MAFIA 1 **5** *chiefly Brit* : a group of people : CROWD. *syn* see CROWD — **mob·bish** \'mä-bish\ *adj*

²mob *vt* **mobbed; mob·bing** (1709) **1 :** to crowd about and attack or annoy ⟨*mobbed* by autograph hunters⟩ ⟨a crow *mobbed* by songbirds⟩ **2 :** to crowd into or around ⟨customers ~ the stores on sale days⟩

mob-cap \'mäb-ˌkap\ *n* [*mob* woman's cap + *cap*] (1795) : a woman's fancy indoor cap made with a high full crown and often tied under the chin

mo·be pearl *or* **mo·bé pearl** \'mō-ˌbā-, ˌmō-'\ *n, often cap M* [origin unknown] (1955) : MABE

¹mo·bile \'mō-bəl, -ˌbil *also* -ˌbēl\ *adj* [ME *mobyll,* fr. MF *mobile,* fr. L *mobilis,* fr. *movēre* to move] (15c) **1 :** capable of moving or being moved : MOVABLE ⟨a ~ missile launcher⟩ **2 a :** changeable in appearance, mood, or purpose ⟨~ face⟩ **b :** ADAPTABLE, VERSATILE **3 :** MIGRATORY **4 a :** characterized by the mixing of social groups **b :** having the opportunity for or undergoing a shift in status within the hierarchical social levels of a society ⟨socially ~ workers⟩ **5 :** marked by the use of vehicles for transportation ⟨~ warfare⟩ **6 :** of or relating to a mobile — **mo·bil·i·ty** \mō-'bi-lə-tē\ *n*

²mo·bile \'mō-ˌbēl\ *n* (1936) : a construction or sculpture frequently of wire and sheet metal shapes with parts that can be set in motion by air currents; *also* : a similar structure (as of paper or plastic) suspended so that it moves in a current of air

-mobile *comb form* [auto*mobile*] **1** : motorized vehicle ⟨snow*mobile*⟩ **2** : automotive vehicle bringing services to the public ⟨blood*mobile*⟩ ⟨book*mobile*⟩

mobile home *n* (1949) : a dwelling structure built on a steel chassis and fitted with wheels that is intended to be hauled to a usu. permanent site — compare MOTOR HOME

mo·bi·lise *chiefly Brit var of* MOBILIZE

mo·bi·li·za·tion \ˌmō-bə-lə-'zā-shən\ *n* (1799) **1** : the act of mobilizing **2** : the state of being mobilized

mo·bi·lize \'mō-bə-ˌlīz\ *vb* -**lized**; -**liz·ing** *vt* (1838) **1 a** : to put into movement or circulation ⟨~ financial assets⟩ **b** : to release (something stored in the organism) for bodily use **2 a** : to assemble and make ready for war duty **b** : to marshal (as resources) for action ⟨~ support for a proposal⟩ ~ *vi* : to undergo mobilization

Mö·bi·us strip \'mœ-bē-əs-, 'mə(r)-, 'mō-\ *n* [August F. *Möbius* †1868 Ger. mathematician] (1904) : a one-sided surface that is constructed from a rectangle by holding one end fixed, rotating the opposite end through 180 degrees, and joining it to the first end

mo·bled \'mä-bəld\ *adj* [pp. of *moble* to muffle, prob. freq. of *mob* to muffle, of unknown origin] (1603) : being wrapped or muffled in or as if in a hood

mob·oc·ra·cy \mä-'bä-krə-sē\ *n* (1754) **1** : rule by the mob **2** : the mob as a ruling class — **mob·o·crat** \'mä-bə-ˌkrat\ *n* — **mob·o·crat·ic** \ˌmä-bə-'kra-tik\ *adj*

Möbius strip

mob·ster \'mäb-stər\ *n* (1917) : a member of a criminal gang

moc \'mäk\ *n* (1948) : MOCCASIN 1

moc·ca·sin \'mä-kə-sən\ *n* [Virginia Algonquian *mockasin*] (ca. 1612) **1 a** : a soft leather heelless shoe or boot with the sole brought up the sides of the foot and over the toes where it is joined with a puckered seam to a U-shaped piece lying on top of the foot **b** : a regular shoe having a seam on the forepart of the vamp imitating the seam of a moccasin **2 a** : WATER MOCCASIN **b** : a snake (as of the genus *Natrix*) resembling a water moccasin

moccasin flower *n* (1680) : any of several lady's slippers (genus *Cypripedium*; *esp* : a once common woodland orchid (*C. acaule*) of eastern No. America with pink or white moccasin-shaped flowers

mo·cha \'mō-kə\ *n* [*Mocha*, Yemen] (1773) **1 a** (1) : a superior Arabian coffee consisting of small green or yellowish beans (2) : a coffee of superior quality **b** : a flavoring made of a strong coffee infusion or of a mixture of cocoa or chocolate with coffee **2** : a pliable suede-finished glove leather from African sheepskins **3** : a dark chocolate-brown color

¹mock \'mäk, 'mȯk\ *vb* [ME, fr. MF *mocquer*] *vt* (15c) **1** : to treat with contempt or ridicule : DERIDE **2** : to disappoint the hopes of **3** : DEFY, CHALLENGE **4 a** : to imitate (as a mannerism) closely : MIMIC **b** : to mimic in sport or derision ~ *vi* : JEER, SCOFF *syn* see RIDICULE, COPY — **mock·er** *n* — **mock·ing·ly** \'mä-kiŋ-lē, 'mȯ-\ *adv*

²mock *n* (15c) **1** : an act of ridicule or derision : JEER **2** : one that is an object of derision or scorn **3** : MOCKERY **4 a** : an act of imitation **b** : something made as an imitation

³mock *adj* (1548) : of, relating to, or having the character of an imitation : SIMULATED, FEIGNED ⟨the ~ solemnity of the parody⟩

⁴mock *adv* (ca. 1619) : in an insincere or counterfeit manner — usu. used in combination ⟨*mock*-serious⟩

mock·ery \'mä-k(ə-)rē, 'mȯ-\ *n, pl* -**er·ies** (15c) **1** : insulting or contemptuous action or speech : DERISION **2** : a subject of laughter, derision, or sport **3 a** : a counterfeit appearance : IMITATION **b** : an insincere, contemptible, or impertinent imitation ⟨makes a ~ of justice⟩ **4** : something ridiculously or impudently unsuitable

¹mock-he·ro·ic \ˌmäk-hi-'rō-ik, ˌmȯk-\ *adj* (ca. 1712) : ridiculing or burlesquing heroic style, character, or action ⟨a ~ poem⟩ — **mock-he·ro·i·cal·ly** \-i-k(ə-)lē\ *adv*

²mock-heroic *n* (1728) : a mock-heroic composition — called also *mock-epic*

mock·ing·bird \'mä-kiŋ-ˌbərd, 'mȯ-\ *n* (1676) : a common grayish bird (*Mimus polyglottos*) esp. of the southern U.S. that is remarkable for its exact imitations of the notes of other birds

mock orange *n* (1731) **1** : any of a genus (*Philadelphus*) of ornamental shrubs of the saxifrage family of which several are widely grown for their showy white flowers — called also *philadelphus, syringa* **2** : any of several usu. shrubby plants considered to resemble the orange

mock turtle soup *n* (1783) : a soup made of meat (as calf's head or veal), wine, and spices in imitation of green turtle soup

mock-up \'mäk-ˌəp, 'mȯk-\ *n* (1920) : a full-sized structural model built accurately to scale chiefly for study, testing, or display

¹mod \'mäd\ *n* [prob. fr. ²*mod*] (1960) : one who wears mod clothes

²mod *adj* [short for *modern*] (1964) **1** : of, relating to, or being the characteristic style of 1960s British youth culture **2** : HIP, TRENDY

mod·acryl·ic fiber \ˌmä-də-ˌkri-lik-\ *n* [*mod*ified *acrylic*] (1960) : any of various synthetic textile fibers that are long-chain polymers composed of 35 to 85 percent by weight of acrylonitrile units

mod·al \'mō-dᵊl\ *adj* [ML *modalis*, fr. L *modus*] (1569) **1** : of or relating to modality in logic **2** : containing provisions as to the mode of procedure or the manner of taking effect — used of a contract or legacy **3** : of or relating to a musical mode **4** : of or relating to structure as opposed to substance **5** : of, relating to, or constituting a grammatical form or category characteristically indicating predication of an action or state in some manner other than as a simple fact **6** : of or relating to a statistical mode — **mod·al·ly** \-dᵊl-ē\ *adv*

modal auxiliary *n* (ca. 1904) : an auxiliary verb (as *can, must, might, may*) that is characteristically used with a verb of predication and expresses a modal modification and that in English differs formally from other verbs in lacking -*s* and -*ing* forms

mo·dal·i·ty \mō-'da-lə-tē\ *n, pl* -**ties** (ca. 1617) **1 a** : the quality or state of being modal **b** : a modal quality or attribute : FORM **2** : the classification of logical propositions according to their asserting or denying the possibility, impossibility, contingency, or necessity of their

content **3** : one of the main avenues of sensation (as vision) **4** : a usu. physical therapeutic agency

mod con \ˌmäd-'kän\ *n* [fr. *mod. con.*, abbr. for *modern convenience*] (1934) *chiefly Brit* : a modern convenience — usu. used in pl.

¹mode \'mōd\ *n* [ME *moede*, fr. L *modus* measure, manner, musical mode — more at METE] (14c) **1 a** : an arrangement of the eight diatonic notes or tones of an octave according to one of several fixed schemes of their intervals **b** : a rhythmical scheme (as in 13th and 14th century music) **2** : ²MOOD 2 **3** [LL *modus*, fr. L] **a** : ²MOOD 1 **b** : the modal form of the assertion or denial of a logical proposition **4 a** : a particular form or variety of something **b** : a form or manner of expression : STYLE **5** : a possible, customary, or preferred way of doing something ⟨explained in the usual solemn ~⟩ **6 a** : a manifestation, form, or arrangement of being; *specif* : a particular form or manifestation of an underlying substance **b** : a particular functioning arrangement or condition : STATUS ⟨a spacecraft in reentry ~⟩ ⟨a computer operating in parallel ~⟩ **7 a** : the most frequent value of a set of data **b** : a value of a random variable for which a function of probabilities defined on it achieves a relative maximum **8** : any of various stationary vibration patterns of which an elastic body or oscillatory system is capable ⟨the vibration ~ of an airplane propeller blade⟩ ⟨the vibrational ~s of a molecule⟩ *syn* see METHOD

²mode *n* [F, fr. L *modus*] (ca. 1645) : a prevailing fashion or style (as of dress or behavior) *syn* see FASHION

¹mod·el \'mä-dᵊl\ *n* [MF *modelle*, fr. OIt *modello*, fr. (assumed) VL *modellus*, fr. L *modulus* small measure, fr. *modus*] (1575) **1** *obs* : a set of plans for a building **2** *dial Brit* : COPY, IMAGE **3** : structural design ⟨a home on the ~ of an old farmhouse⟩ **4** : a usu. miniature representation of something; *also* : a pattern of something to be made **5** : an example for imitation or emulation **6** : a person or thing that serves as a pattern for an artist; *esp* : one who poses for an artist **7** : ARCHETYPE **8** : an organism whose appearance a mimic imitates **9** : one who is employed to display clothes or other merchandise : MANNEQUIN **10 a** : a type or design of clothing **b** : a type or design of product (as a car) **11** : a description or analogy used to help visualize something (as an atom) that cannot be directly observed **12** : a system of postulates, data, and inferences presented as a mathematical description of an entity or state of affairs **13** : VERSION

syn MODEL, EXAMPLE, PATTERN, EXEMPLAR, IDEAL mean someone or something set before one for guidance or imitation. MODEL applies to something taken or proposed as worthy of imitation ⟨a decor that is a *model* of good taste⟩. EXAMPLE applies to a person to be imitated or in some contexts on no account to be imitated but to be regarded as a warning ⟨children tend to follow the *example* of their parents⟩. PATTERN suggests a clear and detailed archetype or prototype ⟨American industry set a *pattern* for others to follow⟩. EXEMPLAR suggests either a faultless example to be emulated or a perfect typification ⟨cited Joan of Arc as the *exemplar* of courage⟩. IDEAL implies the best possible exemplification either in reality or in conception ⟨never found a job that matched his *ideal*⟩.

²model *vb* **mod·eled** *or* **mod·elled**; **mod·el·ing** *or* **mod·el·ling** \'mäd-liŋ, 'mä-dᵊl-iŋ\ *vt* (1625) **1** : to plan or form after a pattern : SHAPE **2** *archaic* : to make into an organization (as an army, government, or parish) **3 a** : to shape or fashion in a plastic material **b** : to produce a representation or simulation of ⟨using a computer to ~ a problem⟩ **4** : to construct or fashion in imitation of a particular model ⟨~ed its constitution on that of the U.S.⟩ **5** : to display by wearing, using, or posing with ⟨~ed gowns⟩ ~ *vi* **1** : to design or imitate forms : make a pattern ⟨enjoys ~ing in clay⟩ **2** : to work or act as a fashion model — **mod·el·er** \'mäd-lər, 'mä-dᵊl-ər\ *n*

³model *adj* (1844) **1** : serving as or capable of serving as a pattern ⟨a ~ student⟩ **2** : being a usu. miniature representation of something ⟨a ~ airplane⟩

mo·dem \'mō-ˌdəm, -ˌdem\ *n* [*modulator + demodulator*] (ca. 1952) : a device that converts signals produced by one type of device (as a computer) to a form compatible with another (as a telephone)

¹mod·er·ate \'mä-d(ə-)rət\ *adj* [ME, fr. L *moderatus*, fr. pp. of *moderare* to moderate; akin to L *modus* measure] (15c) **1 a** : avoiding extremes of behavior or expression : observing reasonable limits ⟨a ~ drinker⟩ **b** : CALM, TEMPERATE **2 a** : tending toward the mean or average amount or dimension **b** : having average or less than average quality : MEDIOCRE **3** : professing or characterized by political or social beliefs that are not extreme **4** : limited in scope or effect **5** : not expensive : reasonable or low in price **6** *of a color* : of medium lightness and medium chroma — **mod·er·ate·ly** *adv* — **mod·er·ate·ness** *n*

²mod·er·ate \'mä-də-ˌrāt\ *vb* -**at·ed**; -**at·ing** *vt* (15c) **1** : to lessen the intensity or extremeness of ⟨the sun *moderated* the chill⟩ **2** : to preside over or act as chairman of ~ *vi* **1** : to act as a moderator **2** : to become less violent, severe, or intense — **mod·er·a·tion** \ˌmä-də-'rā-shən\ *n*

³mod·er·ate \'mä-d(ə-)rət\ *n* (1794) : one who holds moderate views or who belongs to a group favoring a moderate course or program

moderate breeze *n* (1881) : wind having a speed of 13 to 18 miles (21 to 29 kilometers) per hour — see BEAUFORT SCALE table

moderate gale *n* (1704) : wind having a speed of 32 to 38 miles (51 to 61 kilometers) per hour — see BEAUFORT SCALE table

mo·der·a·to \ˌmä-də-'rä-(ˌ)tō\ *adv or adj* [It, fr. L *moderatus*] (ca. 1724) : MODERATE — used as a direction in music to indicate tempo

mod·er·a·tor \'mä-də-ˌrā-tər\ *n* (ca. 1560) **1** : one who arbitrates : MEDIATOR **2** : one who presides over an assembly, meeting, or discussion: as **a** : the presiding officer of a Presbyterian governing body **b** : the nonpartisan presiding officer of a town meeting **c** : the chairman of a discussion group **3** : a substance (as graphite) used for slowing down neutrons in a nuclear reactor — **mod·er·a·tor·ship** \-ˌship\ *n*

¹mod·ern \'mä-dərn, ÷'mä-d(ə-)rən\ *adj* [LL *modernus*, fr. L *modo*

\ə\ abut \ᵊ\ kitten, F table \ər\ further \a\ ash \ā\ ace \ä\ mop, mar \au̇\ out \ch\ chin \e\ bet \ē\ easy \g\ go \i\ hit \ī\ ice \j\ job \ŋ\ sing \ō\ go \ȯ\ law \ȯi\ boy \th\ thin \t͟h\ the \ü\ loot \u̇\ foot \y\ yet \zh\ vision \a̱, k̲, ⁿ, œ, œ̄, ᵫ, ᵫ̄, �\ see Guide to Pronunciation

just now, fr. *modus* measure — more at METE] (1585) **1 a :** of, relating to, or characteristic of the present or the immediate past : CONTEMPORARY **b :** of, relating to, or characteristic of a period extending from a relevant remote past to the present time **2 :** involving recent techniques, methods, or ideas : UP-TO-DATE **3** *cap* : of, relating to, or having the characteristics of the present or most recent period of development of a language **4 :** of or relating to modernism : MODERNIST — **mo·der·ni·ty** \mə-'dər-nə-tē, mä- *also* -'der-\ *n* — **mod·ern·ly** \'mä-dərn-lē\ *adv* — **mod·ern·ness** \-dərn-nəs\ *n*
²**modern** *n* (1585) **1 a :** a person of modern times or views **b :** an adherent of modernism : MODERNIST **2 :** a style of printing type distinguished by regularity of shape, precise curves, straight hairline serifs, and heavy downstrokes
mo·derne \mō-'dern, mə-\ *n, often cap* [F, modern] (1955) : ART DECO
Modern Hebrew *n* (1949) : NEW HEBREW
mod·ern·i·sa·tion, mod·ern·ise *Brit var of* MODERNIZATION, MODERNIZE
mod·ern·ism \'mä-dər-,ni-zəm\ *n* (1737) **1 :** a practice, usage, or expression peculiar to modern times **2** *often cap* : a tendency in theology to accommodate traditional religious teaching to contemporary thought and esp. to devalue supernatural elements **3 :** modern artistic or literary philosophy and practice; *esp* : a self-conscious break with the past and a search for new forms of expression — **mod·ern·ist** \-nist\ *n or adj* — **mod·ern·is·tic** \,mä-dər-'nis-tik\ *adj*
mod·ern·i·za·tion \,mä-dər-nə-'zā-shən\ *n* (1770) **1 :** the act of modernizing : the state of being modernized **2 :** something modernized : a modernized version
mod·ern·ize \'mä-dər-,nīz\ *vb* **-ized; -iz·ing** *vt* (1748) : to make modern (as in taste, style, or usage) ~ *vi* : to adopt modern ways — **mod·ern·iz·er** *n*
modern pentathlon *n* (ca. 1912) : a composite contest in which all contestants compete in a 300-meter freestyle swim, a 4000-meter cross-country run, a 5000-meter 30-jump equestrian steeplechase, épée fencing, and target shooting at 25 meters
mod·est \'mä-dəst\ *adj* [L *modestus* moderate; akin to L *modus* measure] (1565) **1 a :** placing a moderate estimate on one's abilities or worth **b :** neither bold nor self-assertive : tending toward diffidence **2 :** arising from or characteristic of a modest nature **3 :** observing the proprieties of dress and behavior : DECENT **4 a :** limited in size, amount, or scope **b :** UNPRETENTIOUS ⟨a ~ cottage⟩ *syn* see SHY, CHASTE — **mod·est·ly** *adv*
mod·es·ty \'mä-də-stē\ *n* (1531) **1 :** freedom from conceit or vanity **2 :** propriety in dress, speech, or conduct
mo·di·cum \'mä-di-kəm *also* 'mō-\ *n* [ME, fr. L, neut. of *modicus* moderate, fr. *modus* measure] (15c) : a small portion : a limited quantity
mod·i·fi·ca·tion \,mä-də-fə-'kā-shən\ *n* (1603) **1 :** the limiting of a statement : QUALIFICATION **2 :** ¹MODE 6a **3 a :** the making of a limited change in something; *also* : the result of such a change **b :** a change in an organism caused by environmental factors **4 :** a limitation or qualification of the meaning of a word by another word, by an affix, or by internal change
mod·i·fi·er \'mä-də-,fī(-ə)r\ *n* (1583) **1 :** one that modifies **2 :** a word or phrase that makes specific the meaning of another word or phrase **3 :** a gene that modifies the effect of another
mod·i·fy \'mä-də-,fī\ *vb* **-fied; -fy·ing** [ME *modifien*, fr. MF *modifier*, fr. L *modificare* to measure, moderate, fr. *modus*] *vt* (14c) **1 :** to make less extreme : MODERATE **2 a :** to limit or restrict the meaning of esp. in a grammatical construction **b :** to change (a vowel) by umlaut **3 a :** to make minor changes in **b :** to make basic or fundamental changes in often to give a new orientation to or to serve a new end ⟨the wing of a bird is an arm *modified* for flying⟩ ~ *vi* : to undergo change *syn* see CHANGE — **mod·i·fi·abil·i·ty** \,mä-də-,fī-ə-'bi-lə-tē\ *n* — **mod·i·fi·able** \'mä-də-,fī-ə-bəl\ *adj*
mo·dil·lion \mō-'dil-yən\ *n* [It *modiglione*] (1563) : an ornamental block or bracket under the corona of the cornice (as in the Corinthian order)
mod·ish \'mō-dish\ *adj* (1660) : FASHIONABLE, STYLISH ⟨a ~ hat⟩ ⟨a ~ writer⟩ — **mod·ish·ly** *adv* — **mod·ish·ness** *n*
mo·diste \mō-'dēst\ *n* [F, fr. *mode* style, mode] (ca. 1840) : one who makes and sells fashionable dresses and hats for women
Mo·dred \'mō-dred\ *n* : a knight of the Round Table and nephew of King Arthur
mod·u·la·bil·i·ty \,mä-jə-lə-'bi-lə-tē\ *n* (1928) : the capability of being modulated
mod·u·lar \'mä-jə-lər\ *adj* (1798) **1 :** of, relating to, or based on a module or a modulus **2 :** constructed with standardized units or dimensions for flexibility and variety in use — **mod·u·lar·i·ty** \,mä-jə-'lar-ə-tē\ *n* — **mod·u·lar·ly** \'mä-jə-lər-lē\ *adv*
modular arithmetic *n* (1959) : arithmetic that deals with whole numbers where the numbers are replaced by their remainders after division by a fixed number ⟨in a *modular arithmetic* with modulus 5, 3 multiplied by 4 is 2⟩
mod·u·lar·ized \'mä-jə-lə-,rīzd\ *adj* (1959) **1 :** containing or consisting of modules **2 :** produced in the form of modules
mod·u·late \'mä-jə-,lāt\ *vb* **-lat·ed; -lat·ing** [L *modulatus*, pp. of *modulari* to play, sing, fr. *modulus* small measure, rhythm, dim. of *modus* measure — more at METE] *vt* (1615) **1 :** to tune to a key or pitch **2 :** to adjust to or keep in proper measure or proportion : TEMPER **3 :** to vary the amplitude, frequency, or phase of (a carrier wave or a light wave) for the transmission of intelligence (as by radio); *also* : to vary the velocity of electrons in an electron beam ~ *vi* **1 :** to play or sing with modulation **2 :** to pass from one musical key into another by means of intermediary chords or notes that have some relation to both keys **3 :** to pass gradually from one state to another — **mod·u·la·tor** \-,lā-tər\ *n* — **mod·u·la·to·ry** \-lə-,tōr-ē, -,tȯr-\ *adj*
mod·u·la·tion \,mä-jə-'lā-shən\ *n* (1531) **1 :** a regulating according to measure or proportion : TEMPERING **2 :** an inflection of the tone or pitch of the voice; *specif* : the use of stress or pitch to convey meaning **3 :** a change from one musical key to another by modulating **4 :** the process of modulating a carrier or signal (as in radio); *also* : the result of this process
mod·ule \'mä-(,)jü(ə)l\ *n* [L *modulus*] (ca. 1628) **1 :** a standard or unit of measurement **2 :** the size of some one part taken as a unit of measure by which the proportions of an architectural composition are

regulated **3 a :** any in a series of standardized units for use together: as **(1) :** a unit of furniture or architecture **(2) :** an educational unit which covers a single subject or topic **b :** a usu. packaged functional assembly of electronic components for use with other such assemblies **4 :** an independently-operable unit that is a part of the total structure of a space vehicle **5 a :** a subset of an additive group that is also a group under addition **b :** a mathematical set that is a commutative group under addition and that is closed under multiplication which is distributive from the left or right or both by elements of a ring and for which $a(bx) = (ab)x$ or $(xb)a = x(ba)$ or both where *a* and *b* are elements of the ring and *x* belongs to the set
mod·u·lo \'mä-jə-,lō\ *prep* [NL, abl. of *modulus*] (1897) : with respect to a modulus of ⟨19 and 54 are congruent ~ 7⟩
mod·u·lus \'mä-jə-ləs\ *n, pl* **-li** \-,lī, -,lē\ [NL, fr. L, small measure] (1753) **1 a :** the factor by which a logarithm of a number to one base is multiplied to obtain the logarithm of the number to a new base **b :** ABSOLUTE VALUE 2 **c (1) :** the number (as a positive integer) or other mathematical entity (as a polynomial) in a congruence that divides the difference of the two congruent members without leaving a remainder — compare RESIDUE b **(2) :** the number of different numbers used in a system of modular arithmetic **2 :** a constant or coefficient that expresses usu. numerically the degree to which a body or substance possesses a particular property (as elasticity)
mo·dus ope·ran·di \,mō-dəs-,ä-pə-'ran-dē, -,dī\ *n, pl* **mo·di operandi** \'mō-,dē-, 'mō-,dī-\ [NL] (1654) : a method of procedure
mo·dus vi·ven·di \,mō-dəs-vi-'ven-dē, -,dī\ *n, pl* **mo·di vivendi** \'mō-,dē-, 'mō-,dī-\ [NL, manner of living] (ca. 1879) **1 :** a feasible arrangement or practical compromise; *esp* : one that bypasses difficulties **2 :** a manner of living : a way of life
Mogen David *var of* MAGEN DAVID
mog·gy *also* **mog·gie** \'mä-gē\ *n, pl* **mog·gies** [prob. fr. *Moggy*, fr. *Mog*, nickname fr. the name *Margaret*] (ca. 1911) *Brit* : CAT
¹**mo·gul** \'mō-(,)gəl\ *n* [Per *Mughul*, fr. Mongolian *mongyol* Mongol] (1588) **1** *or* **mo·ghul** *cap* : an Indian Muslim of or descended from one of several conquering groups of Mongol, Turkish, and Persian origin; *esp* : GREAT MOGUL **2 :** a great personage : MAGNATE — **mogul** *adj, often cap*
²**mo·gul** \'mō-gəl\ *n* [G dial.; akin to G dial. (Viennese) *mugl* small hill] (1959) : a bump in a ski run
mo·hair \'mō-,har, -,her\ *n* [modif. of obs. It *mocaiarro*, fr. Ar *mukhayyar*, lit., choice] (1619) : a fabric or yarn made wholly or in part of the long silky hair of the Angora goat; *also* : this hair
Mo·ham·med·an *var of* MUHAMMADAN
Mo·hawk \'mō-,hȯk\ *n, pl* **Mohawk** *or* **Mohawks** [of Algonquian origin; akin to Narraganset or Massachuset *Mohowawog* Mohawk, lit., cannibal] (1634) **1 :** a member of an American Indian people of the Mohawk River valley, New York **2 :** the Iroquoian language of the Mohawk people **3 :** a hairstyle with a narrow center strip of upright hair and the sides shaved
Mo·he·gan \mō-'hē-gən, mə-\ *or* **Mo·hi·can** \-'hē-kən\ *n, pl* **Mohegan** *or* **Mohegans** *or* **Mohican** *or* **Mohicans** (1660) : a member of an American Indian people of southeastern Connecticut
Mo·hi·can \mō-'hē-kən, mə-\ *var of* MAHICAN
Mo·ho \'mō-,hō\ *n* [short for *Mohorovicic discontinuity*] (1960) : the boundary layer between the earth's crust and mantle whose depth varies from about 3 miles (5 kilometers) beneath the ocean floor to about 25 miles (40 kilometers) beneath the continents
Mo·hock \'mō-,häk\ *n* [alter. of *Mohawk*] (ca. 1712) : one of a gang of aristocratic ruffians who assaulted and otherwise maltreated people in London streets in the early 18th century — **Mo·hock·ism** \-,hä-,ki-zəm\ *n*
Mo·ho·ro·vi·cic discontinuity \,mō-hə-'rō-və-,chich-\ *n* (1936) : MOHO
Mohs' scale \'mōz-, 'mōs-, 'mō-səz-\ *n* [Friedrich *Mohs* †1839 Ger. mineralogist] (1879) : a scale of hardness for minerals that ranges from a value of 1 for talc to 10 for diamond
mo·hur \'mō-,hər\ *n* [Hindi *muhr* gold coin, seal, fr. Per, fr. MPer; akin to Skt *mudrā* seal] (1690) : a former gold coin of India and Persia equal to 15 rupees
moi·e·ty \'mȯi-ə-tē\ *n, pl* **-ties** [ME *moite*, fr. MF *moité*, fr. LL *medietat-, medietas*, fr. L *medius* middle — more at MID] (15c) **1 a :** one of two equal parts : HALF **b :** one of two approximately equal parts **2 :** one of the portions into which something is divided : COMPONENT, PART **3 :** one of two basic complementary tribal subdivisions
¹**moil** \'mȯi(ə)l\ *vb* [ME *moillen*, fr. MF *moillier*, fr. (assumed) VL *molliare*, fr. L *mollis* soft — more at MOLLIFY] *vt* (15c) *chiefly dial* : to make wet or dirty ~ *vi* **1 :** to work hard : DRUDGE **2 :** to be in continuous agitation : CHURN, SWIRL — **moil·er** *n*
²**moil** *n* (1612) **1 :** hard work : DRUDGERY **2 :** CONFUSION, TURMOIL
moil·ing \'mȯi-liŋ\ *adj* (1603) **1 a :** requiring hard work **b :** INDUSTRIOUS ⟨~ workers⟩ **2 :** violently agitated : TURBULENT — **moil·ing·ly** \-lē\ *adv*
Moi·rai \'mȯi-,rī\ *n pl* [Gk, fr. pl. of *moira* lot, fate; akin to Gk *meros* part — more at MERIT] : FATE 4
moire \'mȯi-(ə)r, 'mȯr, 'mwär\ *n* [F, fr. E *mohair*] (1660) *archaic* : a watered mohair
moi·ré \mȯ-'rā, mwä-\ *or* **moire** *same as* 'mȯi-(ə)r, 'mȯr, 'mwär\ *n* [F *moiré*, fr. *moire* like moire, fr. *moire*] (1818) **1 a :** an irregular wavy finish on a fabric **b :** a ripple pattern on a stamp **2 :** a fabric having a wavy watered appearance **3 :** an independent usu. shimmering pattern seen when two geometrically regular patterns (as two sets of parallel lines or two halftone screens) are superimposed esp. at an acute angle — **moiré** *or* **moire** *adj*
moist \'mȯist\ *adj* [ME *moiste*, fr. MF, perh. fr. (assumed) VL *muscidus*, alter. of L *mucidus* slimy, fr. *mucus* nasal mucus] (14c) **1 :** slightly or moderately wet : DAMP **2 :** TEARFUL **3 :** characterized by high humidity *syn* see WET — **moist·ly** *adv* — **moist·ness** \'mȯis(t)-nəs\ *n*
moist·en \'mȯi-s³n\ *vb* **moist·ened; moist·en·ing** \'mȯis-niŋ, 'mȯi-s³n-iŋ\ *vt* (1580) : to make moist ~ *vi* : to become moist — **moist·en·er** \'mȯis-nər, 'mȯi-s³n-ər\ *n*
mois·ture \'mȯis-chər, 'mȯish-\ *n* [ME, modif. of MF *moistour*, fr. *moiste*] (14c) : liquid diffused or condensed in relatively small quantity

mois·tur·ise *Brit var of* MOISTURIZE
mois·tur·ize \-chə-ˌrīz\ *vt* **-ized; -iz·ing** (1945) : to add moisture to ⟨~ the air⟩ — **mois·tur·iz·er** *n*
mo·jo \ˈmō-(ˌ)jō\ *n, pl* **mojoes** *or* **mojos** [prob. of African origin; akin to Fulani *moco'o* medicine man] (1926) : a magic spell, hex, or charm; *broadly* : magical power
moke \ˈmōk\ *n* [origin unknown] (1848) **1** *slang Brit* : DONKEY **2** *slang Austral* : ¹NAG
mol·al \ˈmō-ləl\ *adj* [⁵*mole*] (1905) : of, relating to, or containing a mole of solute per 1000 grams of solvent — **mo·lal·i·ty** \mō-ˈla-lə-tē\ *n*
¹**mo·lar** \ˈmō-lər\ *n* [ME *molares,* pl., fr. L *molaris,* fr. *molaris* of a mill, fr. *mola* millstone — more at MILL] (14c) : a tooth with a rounded or flattened surface adapted for grinding; *specif* : one of the cheek teeth in mammals behind the incisors and canines — see TOOTH illustration
²**molar** *adj* (1626) **1** : pulverizing by friction : GRINDING **2** : of, relating to, or located near the molar teeth
³**molar** *adj* [⁵*mole*] (1902) **1** : of or relating to a mole of a substance ⟨the ~ volume of a gas⟩ **2** : containing one mole of solute in one liter of solution — **mo·lar·i·ty** \mō-ˈlar-ə-tē\ *n*
mo·las·ses \mə-ˈla-səz\ *n* [modif. of Pg *melaço,* fr. LL *mellaceum* grape juice, fr. L *mell-, mel* honey — more at MELLIFLUOUS] (1582) **1** : the thick dark to light brown syrup that is separated from raw sugar in sugar manufacture **2** : a syrup made from boiling down sweet vegetable or fruit juice ⟨citrus ~⟩
¹**mold** \ˈmōld\ *n* [ME, fr. OE *molde;* akin to OHG *molta* soil, L *molere* to grind — more at MEAL] (bef. 12c) **1** : crumbling soft friable earth suited to plant growth : SOIL; *esp* : soil rich in humus — compare LEAF MOLD **2** *dial Brit* **a** : the surface of the earth : GROUND **b** : the earth of the burying ground **3** *archaic* : earth that is the substance of the human body ⟨be merciful great Duke to men of ~ —Shak.⟩
²**mold** *n* [ME, modif. of OF *modle,* fr. L *modulus,* dim. of *modus* measure — more at METE] (13c) **1** : distinctive nature or character : TYPE **2** : the frame on or around which an object is constructed **3 a** : a cavity in which a substance is shaped: as (1) : a matrix for casting metal (2) : a form in which food is given a decorative shape **b** : a molded object **4** : MOLDING **5 a** *obs* : an example to be followed **b** : PROTOTYPE **c** : a fixed pattern : DESIGN
³**mold** *vt* (14c) **1** *archaic* : to knead (dough) into a desired consistency or shape **2** : to give shape to ⟨the wind ~s the waves⟩ **3** : to form in a mold ⟨~ candles⟩ **4** : to determine or influence the quality or nature of ⟨~ public opinion⟩ **5** : to fit the contours of **6** : to ornament with molding or carving ⟨~ed picture frames⟩ — **mold·able** \ˈmōl-də-bəl\ *adj* — **mold·er** *n*
⁴**mold** *n* [ME *mowlde,* perh. alter. of *mowle,* fr. *moulen* to grow moldy, of Scand origin; akin to ON *mygla* to grow moldy] (14c) **1** : a superficial often woolly growth produced esp. on damp or decaying organic matter or on living organisms **2** : a fungus (as of the order Mucorales) that produces mold
⁵**mold** *vi* (1530) : to become moldy
mold·board \ˈmōl(d)-ˌbōrd, -ˌbȯrd\ *n* (1508) **1** : a curved iron plate attached above a plowshare to lift and turn the soil **2** : the flat or curved blade (as of a bulldozer) that pushes material to one side as the machine advances
mold·er \ˈmōl-dər\ *vi* **mold·ered; mold·er·ing** \-d(ə-)riŋ\ [freq. of ⁵*mold*] (1531) : to crumble into particles : DISINTEGRATE, DECAY
mold·ing \ˈmōl-diŋ\ *n* (14c) **1 a** : the art or occupation of a molder **b** : an object produced by molding **2 a** : a decorative recessed or relieved surface **b** : a decorative plane or curved strip used for ornamentation or finishing
moldy \ˈmōl-dē\ *adj* **mold·i·er; -est** (14c) **1** : of, resembling, or covered with a mold-producing fungus **2 a** : being old and moldering : CRUMBLING **b** : ANTIQUATED, FUSTY ⟨~ tradition⟩ — **mold·i·ness** *n*

¹**mole** \ˈmōl\ *n* [ME, fr. OE *māl;* akin to OHG *meil* spot] (14c) : a pigmented spot, mark, or small permanent protuberance on the human body; *esp* : NEVUS

molding 2a: *1* fillet and fascia, *2* torus, *3* reeding, *4* cavetto, *5* scotia, *6* congé, *7* beak

²**mole** *n* [ME; akin to MLG *mol*] (14c) **1** : any of numerous burrowing insectivores (esp. family Talpidae) with tiny eyes, concealed ears, and soft fur **2** : one who works in the dark **3** : a machine for tunneling **4** : a spy (as a double agent) who establishes a cover long before beginning espionage
³**mole** *n* [ME, fr. L *mola* mole, lit., mill, millstone — more at MILL] (15c) : an abnormal mass in the uterus esp. when containing fetal tissues
⁴**mole** *n* [MF, fr. OIt *molo,* fr. LGk *mōlos,* fr. L *moles,* lit., mass, exertion; akin to Gk *mōlos* exertion] (ca. 1548) **1** : a massive work formed of masonry and large stones or earth laid in the sea as a pier or breakwater **2** : the harbor formed by a mole
⁵**mole** *also* **mol** \ˈmōl\ *n* [G *Mol,* short for *Molekulargewicht* molecular weight, fr. *molekular* molecular + *Gewicht* weight] (1902) : the base unit of amount of pure substance in the International System of Units that contains the same number of elementary entities as there are atoms in exactly 12 grams of the isotope carbon 12
⁶**mo·le** \ˈmō-lā\ *n* [MexSp, fr. Nahuatl *mōlli* sauce] (1927) : a spicy sauce made with chilies and usu. chocolate and served with meat
mo·lec·u·lar \mə-ˈle-kyə-lər\ *adj* (1823) **1** : of, relating to, or produced by molecules ⟨~ oxygen⟩ **2** : of or relating to simple or elementary organization — **mo·lec·u·lar·ly** \-lē\ *adv*
molecular biology *n* (1938) : a branch of biology dealing with the ultimate physicochemical organization of living matter and esp. with the molecular basis of inheritance and protein synthesis — **molecular biologist** *n*
molecular formula *n* (ca. 1903) : a chemical formula that is based on both analysis and molecular weight and gives the total number of atoms of each element in a molecule — compare STRUCTURAL FORMULA

molecular mass *n* (1970) : the mass of a molecule that is equal to the sum of the masses of all the atoms contained in the molecule
molecular orbital *n* (1932) : a solution of the Schrödinger equation that describes the probable location of an electron relative to the nuclei in a molecule and so indicates the nature of any bond in which the electron is involved
molecular sieve *n* (1926) : a crystalline substance (as a zeolite) characterized by uniformly sized pores of molecular dimension that can adsorb small molecules and is used esp. in separations
molecular weight *n* (1880) : the average mass of a molecule of a compound compared to $\frac{1}{12}$ the mass of carbon 12 and calculated as the sum of the atomic weights of the constituent atoms
mol·e·cule \ˈmä-li-ˌkyü(ə)l\ *n* [F *molécule,* fr. NL *molecula,* dim. of L *moles* mass] (1794) **1** : the smallest particle of a substance that retains all the properties of the substance and is composed of one or more atoms **2** : a tiny bit : PARTICLE
mole·hill \ˈmōl-ˌhil\ *n* (15c) : a little mound or ridge of earth pushed up by a mole
mole·skin \-ˌskin\ *n* (1668) **1** : the skin of the mole used as fur **2 a** : a heavy durable cotton fabric with a short thick velvety nap on one side **b** : a garment made of moleskin — usu. used in pl.
mo·lest \mə-ˈlest\ *vt* [ME, fr. MF *molester,* fr. L *molestare,* fr. *molestus* burdensome, annoying; akin to L *moles* mass] (14c) **1** : to annoy, disturb, or persecute esp. with hostile intent or injurious effect **2** : to make annoying sexual advances to; *esp* : to force physical and usu. sexual contact on — **mo·les·ta·tion** \ˌmō-ˌles-ˈtā-shən, ˌmä-, -ləs-\ *n* — **mo·lest·er** \mə-ˈles-tər\ *n*
mo·line \mə-ˈlēn, -ˈlīn\ *adj* [(assumed) AF *moliné,* fr. OF *molin* mill, fr. LL *molinum* — more at MILL] (1562) *of a heraldic cross* : having the end of each arm forked and recurved — see CROSS illustration
moll \ˈmäl, ˈmȯl\ *n* [prob. fr. *Moll,* nickname for *Mary*] (1604) **1** : PROSTITUTE **2 a** : DOLL **2 b** : a gangster's girlfriend
mol·li·fy \ˈmä-lə-ˌfī\ *vb* **-fied; -fy·ing** [ME *mollifien,* fr. MF *mollifier,* fr. LL *mollificare,* fr. L *mollis* soft; akin to Gk *amaldynein* to soften, Skt *mṛdu* soft, and prob. to Gk *malakos* soft, *amblys* dull, OE *meltan* to melt] *vt* (15c) **1** : to soothe in temper or disposition : APPEASE ⟨*mollified* the staff with a raise⟩ **2** : to reduce the rigidity of : SOFTEN **3** : to reduce in intensity : ASSUAGE, TEMPER ~ *vi, archaic* : SOFTEN, RELENT *syn* see PACIFY — **mol·li·fi·ca·tion** \ˌmä-lə-fə-ˈkā-shən\ *n*
mol·lus·ci·cide \mə-ˈləs-kə-ˌsīd, -ˈläs-kə-\ *n* [NL *Mollusca* + E -*i-* + -*cide*] (ca. 1947) : an agent for destroying mollusks (as snails) — **mol·lus·ci·cid·al** \-ˌləs-kə-ˈsī-dᵊl, -ˌlə-sə-\ *adj*
mol·lusk *or* **mol·lusc** \ˈmä-ləsk\ *n* [F *mollusque,* fr. NL *Mollusca,* fr. L, neut. pl. of *molluscus* thin-shelled (of a nut), fr. *mollis*] (1783) : any of a large phylum (Mollusca) of invertebrate animals (as snails, clams, or squids) with a soft unsegmented body usu. enclosed in a calcareous shell; *broadly* : SHELLFISH — **mol·lus·can** *also* **mol·lus·kan** \mə-ˈləs-kən, mä-\ *adj*
mol·ly *also* **mol·lie** \ˈmä-lē\ *n, pl* **mollies** [by shortening fr. NL *Mollienisia,* former genus name, fr. Comte François N. *Mollien* †1850 Fr. statesman] (ca. 1933) : any of several brightly colored live-bearers (genus *Poecilia* of the family Poeciliidae) highly valued as aquarium fishes
¹**mol·ly·cod·dle** \ˈmä-lē-ˌkä-dᵊl\ *n* [*Molly,* nickname for *Mary*] (1833) : a pampered or effeminate man or boy
²**mollycoddle** *vt* **-cod·dled; -cod·dling** \-ˌkäd-liŋ, -ˌkä-dᵊl-iŋ\ (1864) : to surround with an excessive or absurd degree of indulgence and attention *syn* see INDULGE — **mol·ly·cod·dler** \-ˌkäd-lər, -ˌkä-dᵊl-ər\ *n*
Mo·loch \ˈmä-lək, ˈmō-ˌläk\ *n* [LL, fr. Gk, fr. Heb *Mōlekh*] : a Semitic god to whom children were sacrificed
Mo·lo·tov cocktail \ˈmä-lə-ˌtȯf-, ˈmō-, ˈmȯ-, -ˌtȯv-\ *n* [Vyacheslav M. *Molotov*] (1939) : a crude bomb made of a bottle filled with a flammable liquid (as gasoline) and usu. fitted with a wick (as a saturated rag) that is ignited just before the bottle is hurled
¹**molt** \ˈmōlt\ *vb* [alter. of ME *mouten,* fr. OE *-mūtian* to change, fr. L *mutare* — more at MUTABLE] *vi* (1591) : to shed hair, feathers, shell, horns, or an outer layer periodically ~ *vt* : to cast off (an outer covering) periodically; *specif* : to throw off (the old cuticle) — used of arthropods — **molt·er** *n*
²**molt** *n* (1815) : the act or process of molting; *specif* : ECDYSIS
mol·ten \ˈmōl-tᵊn\ *adj* [ME, fr. pp. of *melten* to melt] (14c) **1** *obs* : made by melting and casting **2** : fused or liquefied by heat : MELTED ⟨~ lava⟩ **3** : having warmth or brilliance : GLOWING ⟨the ~ sunlight of warm skies —T. B. Costain⟩
mol·to \ˈmōl-(ˌ)tō, ˈmȯl-\ *adv* [It, fr. L *multum,* fr. neut. of *multus* much] (ca. 1801) : MUCH, VERY — used in music directions ⟨~ vivace⟩
mo·ly \ˈmō-lē\ *n* [L, fr. Gk *mōly*] : a mythical herb with a black root, white blossoms, and magical powers
mo·lyb·date \mə-ˈlib-ˌdāt\ *n* (1794) : a salt of molybdenum containing the group MoO_4 or Mo_2O_7
mo·lyb·de·nite \mə-ˈlib-də-ˌnīt\ *n* [NL *molybdena*] (1796) : a blue usu. foliated mineral consisting of molybdenum disulfide that is a source of molybdenum
mo·lyb·de·num \-nəm\ *n* [NL, fr. *molybdena,* a lead ore, molybdenite, molybdenum, fr. L *molybdaena* galena, fr. Gk *molybdaina,* fr. *molybdos* lead] (1816) : a metallic element that resembles chromium and tungsten in many properties, is used esp. in strengthening and hardening steel, and is a trace element in plant and animal metabolism — see ELEMENT table
molybdenum disulfide *n* (ca. 1931) : a compound MoS_2 used esp. as a lubricant in grease
mom \ˈmäm, ˈmȯm\ *n* [short for *momma*] (ca. 1894) : MOTHER
mom–and–pop \ˈmäm-ən(d)-ˈpäp\ *adj* (1951) : being a small owner-operated business
mome \ˈmōm\ *n* [origin unknown] (1553) *archaic* : BLOCKHEAD, FOOL
mo·ment \ˈmō-mənt\ *n* [ME, fr. MF, fr. L *momentum* movement,

\ə\ abut \ᵊ\ kitten, F table \ər\ further \a\ ash \ā\ ace \ä\ mop, mar \aů\ out \ch\ chin \e\ bet \ē\ easy \g\ go \i\ hit \ī\ ice \j\ job \ŋ\ sing \ō\ go \ȯ\ law \ȯi\ boy \th\ thin \t̲h̲\ the \ü\ loot \ů\ foot \y\ yet \zh\ vision \à, k̲, ⁿ, œ, œ̄, ᵫ, ᵫ̄, ᵞ\ *see* Guide to Pronunciation

particle sufficient to turn the scales, moment, fr. *movēre* to move] (14c)
1 a : a minute portion or point of time : INSTANT **b :** a comparatively brief period of time **2 a :** present time ⟨at the ~ she is working on a novel⟩ **b :** a time of excellence or conspicuousness ⟨he has his ~s⟩ **3** : importance in influence or effect ⟨a matter of great ~⟩ **4** *obs* **:** a cause or motive of action **5 :** a stage in historical or logical development **6 a :** tendency or measure of tendency to produce motion esp. about a point or axis **b :** the product of quantity (as a force) and the distance to a particular axis or point **7 a :** the mean of the *n*th powers of the deviations of the observed values in a set of statistical data from a fixed value **b :** the expected value of a power of the deviation of a random variable from a fixed value *syn* see IMPORTANCE
mo·men·tar·i·ly \ˌmō-mən-ˈter-ə-lē\ *adv* (ca. 1666) **1 :** for a moment **2** *archaic* **:** INSTANTLY **3 :** at any moment : in a moment
mo·men·tary \ˈmō-mən-ˌter-ē\ *adj* (15c) **1 a :** continuing only a moment : FLEETING **b :** having a very brief life **2 :** operative or recurring at every moment *syn* see TRANSIENT — **mo·men·tar·i·ness** *n*
mo·ment·ly \ˈmō-mənt-lē\ *adv* (1676) **1 :** from moment to moment **2 :** at any moment **3 :** for a moment
mo·men·to *var of* MEMENTO
moment of inertia (1830) **:** a measure of the resistance of a body to angular acceleration about a given axis that is equal to the sum of the products of each element of mass in the body and the square of the element's distance from the axis
moment of truth (1932) **1 :** the final sword thrust in a bullfight **2** : a moment of crisis on whose outcome much or everything depends
mo·men·tous \mō-ˈmen-təs, mə-\ *adj* (1652) : IMPORTANT, CONSEQUENTIAL — **mo·men·tous·ly** *adv* — **mo·men·tous·ness** *n*
mo·men·tum \mō-ˈmen-təm, mə-\ *n, pl* **mo·men·ta** \-ˈmen-tə\ *or* **momentums** [NL, fr. L, movement] (1610) **1 :** a property of a moving body that the body has by virtue of its mass and motion and that is equal to the product of the body's mass and velocity; *broadly* : a property of a moving body that determines the length of time required to bring it to rest when under the action of a constant force or moment **2** : strength or force gained by motion or through the development of events : IMPETUS ⟨the campaign gained ~⟩
mom·ma \ˈmä-mə\ *var of* MAMA
mom·my \ˈmä-mē, ˈmə-mə\ *n, pl* **mom·mies** [alter. of *mammy*] (1899) : MOTHER
mommy track *n* (1989) : a career path that allows a mother flexible or reduced work hours but tends to slow or block advancement
Mo·mus \ˈmō-məs\ *n* [L, fr. Gk *Mōmos*] : the Greek god of censure and mockery
mon \ˈmän\ *dial chiefly Brit var of* MAN
Mon \ˈmōn\ *n, pl* **Mon** *or* **Mons** (1798) **1 :** a member of the dominant native people of Pegu division, Myanmar (Burma) **2 :** the Mon-Khmer language of the Mon people
mon- *or* **mono-** *comb form* [ME, fr. MF & L; MF, fr. L, fr. Gk, fr. *monos* alone, single — more at MONK] **1 :** one : single : alone ⟨*monoplane*⟩ ⟨*monodrama*⟩ **2 a :** containing one (usu. specified) atom, radical, or group ⟨*monohydroxy*⟩ **b :** monomolecular ⟨*monolayer*⟩
mon·a·chal \ˈmä-ni-kəl\ *adj* [MF or LL; MF, fr. LL *monachalis*, fr. *monachus* monk — more at MONK] (1587) : MONASTIC — **mon·a·chism** \ˈmä-nə-ˌki-zəm\ *n*
mo·nad \ˈmō-ˌnad\ *n* [LL *monad-, monas*, fr. Gk, fr. *monos*] (1615) **1 a :** UNIT, ONE **b :** ATOM 1 **c :** an elementary individual substance which reflects the order of the world and from which material properties are derived **2 :** a flagellated protozoan (as of the genus *Monas*) — **mo·nad·ic** \mō-ˈna-dik, mə-\ *adj* — **mo·nad·ism** \ˈmō-ˌna-ˌdi-zəm\ *n*
mon·adel·phous \ˌmä-nə-ˈdel-fəs\ *adj* (1806) *of stamens* : united by the filaments into one group usu. forming a tube around the pistil
mo·nad·nock \mə-ˈnad-ˌnäk\ *n* [Mt. *Monadnock*, N.H.] (1893) : INSELBERG
mon·an·dry \ˈmä-ˌnan-drē\ *n, pl* **-dries** [*mon-* + *-andry* (as in *polyandry*)] (1855) : a marriage form or custom in which a woman has only one husband at a time
mon·arch \ˈmä-nərk, -ˌnärk\ *n* [LL *monarcha*, fr. Gk *monarchos*, fr. *mon-* + *-archos* -arch] (15c) **1 :** a person who reigns over a kingdom or empire: as **a :** a sovereign ruler **b :** a constitutional king or queen **2 :** one that holds preeminent position or power **3 :** MONARCH BUTTERFLY] — **mo·nar·chal** \mə-ˈnär-kəl, mä-\ *or* **mo·nar·chi·al** \-kē-əl\ *adj*
monarch butterfly *n* (1890) : a large migratory American butterfly (*Danaus plexippus*) that has orange-brown wings with black veins and borders and a larva that feeds on milkweed
Mo·nar·chi·an \mə-ˈnär-kē-ən, mä-\ *n* (1765) : an adherent of one of two anti-Trinitarian groups of the 2d and 3d centuries A.D. teaching that God is one person as well as one being — **Mo·nar·chi·an·ism** \-kē-ə-ˌni-zəm\ *n*
mo·nar·chi·cal \mə-ˈnär-ki-kəl, mä-\ *also* **mo·nar·chic** \-kik\ *adj* (1576) : of, relating to, suggestive of, or characteristic of a monarch or monarchy — **mo·nar·chi·cal·ly** \-ki-k(ə-)lē\ *adv*
mon·ar·chism \ˈmä-nər-ˌki-zəm, -ˌnär-\ *n* (1838) : monarchical government or principles — **mon·ar·chist** \-kist\ *n or adj*
mon·ar·chy \ˈmä-nər-kē *also* -ˌnär-\ *n, pl* **-chies** (14c) **1 :** undivided rule or absolute sovereignty by a single person **2 :** a nation or state having a monarchical government **3 :** a government having an hereditary chief of state with life tenure and powers varying from nominal to absolute
mo·nar·da \mə-ˈnär-də\ *n* [NL, fr. Nicolás *Monardes* †1588 Span. botanist] (1712) : any of a genus (*Monarda*) of coarse No. American mints with a tubular many-nerved calyx and whorls of showy flowers
mon·as·tery \ˈmä-nə-ˌster-ē\ *n, pl* **-ter·ies** [ME *monasterie*, fr. LL *monasterium*, fr. LGk *monastērion*, fr. Gk, hermit's cell, fr. *monazein* to live alone, fr. *monos* single — more at MONK] (15c) : a house for persons under religious vows; *esp* : an establishment for monks
mo·nas·tic \mə-ˈnas-tik\ *adj* (ca. 1563) **1 :** of or relating to monasteries or to monks or nuns **2 :** resembling (as in seclusion or ascetic simplicity) life in a monastery — **monastic** *n* — **mo·nas·ti·cal·ly** \-ti-k(ə-)lē\ *adv* — **mo·nas·ti·cism** \-tə-ˌsi-zəm\ *n*
mon·atom·ic \ˌmä-nə-ˈtä-mik\ *adj* (1848) : consisting of one atom; *esp* : having but one atom in the molecule
mon·au·ral \(ˌ)mä-ˈnȯr-əl\ *adj* (1931) : MONOPHONIC 2 — **mon·au·ral·ly** \-ə-lē\ *adv*
mon·a·zite \ˈmä-nə-ˌzīt\ *n* [G *Monazit*, fr. Gk *monazein*] (1836) : a mineral that is a yellow, red, or brown phosphate of cerium and other rare earth elements and thorium and is found often in sand and gravel deposits
Mon·day \ˈmən-dē, -(ˌ)dā\ *n* [ME, fr. OE *mōnandæg*; akin to OHG *mānatag* Monday; akin to OE *mōna* moon and to OE *dæg* day] (bef. 12c) : the second day of the week — **Mon·days** \-dēz\ *adv*
Monday–morning quarterback *n* [fr. a fan's usu. critical rehashing of the weekend football game strategy] (1941) : one who second-guesses — **Monday–morning quarterbacking** *n*
mon·e·cious *var of* MONOECIOUS
mo·ner·an \mō-ˈnir-ən, mə-\ *n* [NL *Monera*, kingdom comprising prokaryotes, ultim. fr. Gk *monērēs* single] (1869) : PROKARYOTE — **moneran** *adj*
M1 rifle \ˈem-ˈwən-\ *n* (1938) : a .30 caliber gas-operated clip-fed semiautomatic rifle used by U.S. troops in World War II
mon·es·trous \(ˌ)mä-ˈnes-trəs\ *adj* (1900) : experiencing estrus once each year or breeding season
mon·e·tar·ism \ˈmä-nə-tə-ˌri-zəm *also* ˈmən-\ *n* (1969) : a theory in economics that stable economic growth can be assured only by control of the rate of increase of the money supply to match the capacity for growth of real production — **mon·e·tar·ist** \-rist *n or adj*
mon·e·tary \ˈmä-nə-ˌter-ē *also* ˈmə-\ *adj* [LL *monetarius* of a mint, of money, fr. L *moneta*] (ca. 1812) : of or relating to money or to the mechanisms by which it is supplied to and circulates in the economy — **mon·e·tar·i·ly** \ˌmä-nə-ˈter-ə-lē *also* ˌmə-\ *adv*
monetary aggregate *n* (1979) : one of the formal categories of money (as cash and demand deposits or bank credits) in a national economy that is used as a measure in predictions of economic growth
monetary unit *n* (ca. 1864) : the standard unit of value of a currency
mon·e·tize \ˈmä-nə-ˌtīz *also* ˈmə-\ *vt* **-tized; -tiz·ing** [L *moneta*] (ca. 1879) **1 :** to coin into money; *also* : to establish as legal tender **2 :** to purchase (public or private debt) and thereby free for other uses moneys that would have been devoted to debt service — **mon·e·ti·za·tion** \ˌmä-nə-tə-ˈzā-shən *also* ˌmə-\ *n*
¹mon·ey \ˈmə-nē\ *n, pl* **moneys** *or* **mon·ies** \ˈmə-nēz\ *often attrib* [ME *moneye*, fr. MF *moneie*, fr. L *moneta* mint, money — more at MINT] (14c) **1 :** something generally accepted as a medium of exchange, a measure of value, or a means of payment: as **a :** officially coined or stamped metal currency **b :** MONEY OF ACCOUNT **c :** PAPER MONEY **2 a :** wealth reckoned in terms of money **b :** an amount of money *c pl* : sums of money : FUNDS **3 :** a form or denomination of coin or paper money **4 a :** the first, second, and third place winners (as in a horse or dog race) — usu. used in the phrases *in the money* or *out of the money* **b :** prize money ⟨his horse took third ~⟩ **5 a :** persons or interests possessing or controlling great wealth **b :** a position of wealth ⟨born into ~⟩ — **for one's money** : according to one's preference or opinion — **on the money** : exactly right or accurate
²money *adj* (1935) : involving or reliable in a crucial situation ⟨a ~ player⟩ ⟨a ~ pitch⟩
mon·ey–back \-ˈbak\ *adj* (1922) : providing that the consumer is entitled to a refund if the purchased product is unsatisfactory ⟨a ~ guarantee⟩
mon·ey·bags \ˈmə-nē-ˌbagz\ *n pl but sing or pl in constr* (1596) **1** : WEALTH **2 :** a wealthy person
money changer *n* (15c) **1 :** one whose business is the exchanging of kinds or denominations of currency **2 :** a device for holding and dispensing sorted change
mon·eyed *also* **mon·ied** \ˈmə-nēd\ *adj* (15c) **1 :** having money : WEALTHY **2 :** consisting in or derived from money
mon·ey·er \ˈmə-nē-ər\ *n* [ME, fr. OF *monier*, fr. LL *monetarius* master of a mint, coiner, fr. *monetarius* of a mint — more at MONETARY] (15c) : an authorized coiner of money : MINTER
mon·ey–grub·ber \ˈmə-nē-ˌgrə-bər\ *n* (1840) : a person bent on accumulating money — **mon·ey–grub·bing** \-biŋ\ *adj or n*
mon·ey–lend·er \-ˌlen-dər\ *n* (ca. 1780) : one whose business is lending money; *specif* : PAWNBROKER
mon·ey–mak·er \-ˌmā-kər\ *n* (1834) **1 :** one that accumulates wealth **2 :** one that produces profit — **mon·ey–mak·ing** \-kiŋ\ *adj or n*
mon·ey–man \-ˌman\ *n* (ca. 1585) : FINANCIER
money market *n* (1950) : the trade in short-term negotiable instruments (as certificates of deposit or U.S. Treasury securities)
money of account (1691) : a denominator of value or basis of exchange which is used in keeping accounts and for which there may or may not be an equivalent coin or denomination of paper money
money order *n* (1802) : an order issued by a post office, bank, or telegraph office for payment of a specified sum of money usu. at any branch of the organization
mon·ey–spin·ner \ˈmə-nē-ˌspi-nər\ *n* (1859) *chiefly Brit* : MONEY-MAKER — **mon·ey–spin·ning** \-niŋ\ *adj or n, chiefly Brit*
mon·ey·wort \-ˌwərt, -ˌwȯrt\ *n* (1578) : a trailing perennial herb (*Lysimachia nummularia*) of the primrose family with rounded opposite leaves and solitary yellow flowers in their axils
¹mon·ger \ˈməŋ-gər, ˈmäŋ-\ *n* [ME *mongere*, fr. OE *mangere*, fr. L *mangon-, mango*, of Gk origin; akin to Gk *manganon* charm, philter] (bef. 12c) **1 :** BROKER, DEALER — usu. used in combination ⟨*alemonger*⟩ **2** : a person who attempts to stir up or spread something that is usu. petty or discreditable — usu. used in combination ⟨*warmonger*⟩
²monger *vt* **mon·gered; mon·ger·ing** \-g(ə-)riŋ\ (ca. 1864) : PEDDLE
mon·go \ˈmäŋ-(ˌ)gō\ *n, pl* **mongo** [Mongolian *möngö*] (1935) — see *tugrik* at MONEY table
Mon·gol \ˈmäŋ-gəl; ˈmän-ˌgōl, ˈmäŋ-\ *n* [Mongolian *mongyol*] (1698) **1 :** a member of any of a group of traditionally pastoral peoples of Mongolia **2 :** MONGOLIAN 1 **3 :** a person of Mongoloid racial stock **4** *often not cap* : one affected with Down's syndrome — **Mongol** *adj*
¹Mon·go·lian \män-ˈgōl-yən, mäŋ-, -ˈgō-lē-ən\ *adj* (1706) **1 :** of, relating to, or constituting Mongolia, the Mongolian People's Republic, the Mongols, or Mongolian **2 :** MONGOLOID 2

MONEY

NAME	SYMBOL	SUBDIVISION	COUNTRY
afghani	Af	100 puls	Afghanistan
baht *or* tical	B	100 satang	Thailand
balboa		100 centesimos	Panama
birr		100 cents	Ethiopia
bolivar	B	100 centimos	Venezuela
boliviano	$b	100 centavos	Bolivia
cedi	¢	100 pesewas	Ghana
colón	C *or* ₡	100 centimos	Costa Rica
colón	₡	100 centavos	El Salvador
cordoba	C$	100 centavos	Nicaragua
dalasi		100 bututs	Gambia
deutsche mark	DM	100 pfennig	Germany
dinar	DA	100 centimes	Algeria
dinar	BD	1000 fils	Bahrain
dinar	ID	1000 fils	Iraq
dinar	JD	1000 fils	Jordan
dinar	KD	1000 fils	Kuwait
dinar	LD	1000 dirhams	Libya
dinar	D	1000 millimes	Tunisia
dinar[1]	£	1000 fils	Yemen
dinar		100 paras	Yugoslavia
dirham	DH	100 centimes	Morocco
dirham		100 fils	United Arab Emirates
dobra	Db	100 centimos	Sao Tome and Principe
dollar	EC$[2] *or* $	100 cents	Antigua and Barbuda, Dominica, Grenada, St. Kitts-Nevis, St. Lucia, St. Vincent and the Grenadines
dollar	$A *or* $	100 cents	Australia
dollar	$ *or* B$	100 cents	Bahamas
dollar	$ *or* Bds$	100 cents	Barbados
dollar	$	100 cents	Belize
dollar	$	100 cents	Bermuda
dollar	B$	100 sen *or* cents	Brunei
dollar		100 cents	Canada
dollar *or* yuan	NT$	100 cents	China (Taiwan)
dollar	$ *or* F$	100 cents	Fiji
dollar	$ *or* G$	100 cents	Guyana
dollar	$ *or* HK$	100 cents	Hong Kong
dollar	$ *or* J$	100 cents	Jamaica
dollar	L$	100 cents	Liberia
dollar	NZ$	100 cents	New Zealand
dollar	$ *or* S$	100 cents	Singapore
dollar	$ *or* TT$	100 cents	Trinidad and Tobago
dollar	$	100 cents	United States
dollar	$ *or* Z$	100 cents	Zimbabwe
dollar—see RINGGIT, below			
dong		100 xu	Vietnam
drachma	Dr	100 lepta	Greece
escudo		100 centavos	Cape Verde
escudo	$ *or* Esc	100 centavos	Portugal
florin—see GULDEN, below			
forint	Ft	100 filler	Hungary
franc	BF *or* F *or* FR	100 centimes	Belgium
franc	Fr *or* FR *or* F *or* CFA[3]	100 centimes	Benin, Burkina Faso, Cameroon, Central African Republic, Chad, Congo, Equatorial Guinea, Gabon, Ivory Coast, Mali, Niger, Senegal, Togo
franc	F *or* FBu	100 centimes	Burundi
franc	Fr *or* F	100 centimes	Djibouti
franc	Fr *or* F	100 centimes	France
franc	GF	100 centimes	Guinea
franc	F *or* Flux	100 centimes	Luxembourg
franc	FMG	100 centimes	Madagascar
franc	FR *or* RF	100 centimes	Rwanda
franc	Fr *or* FR	100 centimes *or* rappen	Switzerland
gourde	G	100 centimes	Haiti
guarani	G *or* ₲	100 centimos	Paraguay
gulden *or* guilder *or* florin	f *or* Fl *or* G	100 cents	Netherlands
gulden *or* guilder *or* florin	Sf	100 cents	Suriname
kina	K	100 toea	Papua New Guinea
kip	K	100 at	Laos
koruna	Kčs	100 haleru	Czech Republic
koruna	Kčs	100 haleru	Slovakia
krona	KR	100 aurar (*sing* eyrir)	Iceland
krona	SKr *or* KR	100 ore	Sweden
krone	DKr	100 ore	Denmark
krone	KR *or* Nkr	100 ore	Norway
kwacha	K	100 tambala	Malawi
kwacha	K	100 ngwee	Zambia
kwanza		100 lwei	Angola

NAME	SYMBOL	SUBDIVISION	COUNTRY
kyat	K	100 pyas	Myanmar
lat			Latvia
lek		100 qindarka	Albania
lempira	L	100 centavos	Honduras
leone	Le	100 cents	Sierra Leone
leu		100 bani (*sing* ban)	Romania
lev		100 stotinki	Bulgaria
lilangeni (*pl* emalangeni)	E	100 cents	Swaziland
lira	L *or* Lit	100 centesimi[4]	Italy
lira *or* pound	£ *or* £M *or* Lm	100 cents	Malta
lira	TL	100 kurus	Turkey
livre—see POUND, below			
loti (*pl* maloti)		100 licente *or* lisente (*sing* sente)	Lesotho
mark—see DEUTSCHE MARK, above			
markka	Fmk	100 pennia	Finland
metical		100 centavos	Mozambique
naira	₦	100 kobo	Nigeria
ngultrum	Nu	100 chetrums	Bhutan
ouguiya		5 khoums	Mauritania
pa'anga	T$	100 seniti	Tonga
pataca		100 avos	Macao
peseta	PTA	100 centimos[4]	Spain
peso			Argentina
peso		100 centavos	Chile
peso		100 centavos	Colombia
peso		100 centavos	Cuba
peso	RD$	100 centavos	Dominican Republic
peso		100 centavos	Guinea-Bissau
peso	$	100 centavos	Mexico
peso *or* piso	P	100 sentimos *or* centavos	Philippines
peso	$	100 centesimos	Uruguay
pound	£	100 cents	Cyprus
pound	£E	100 piastres	Egypt
pound	£	100 pence (*sing* penny)	Ireland
pound *or* livre	L	100 piastres	Lebanon
pound	£S	100 piastres	Sudan
pound		100 piastres	Syria
pound	£	100 pence (*sing* penny)	United Kingdom
pound—see LIRA, above			
pula	P	100 thebe	Botswana
quetzal	Q	100 centavos	Guatemala
rand	R	100 cents	South Africa
real		100 centavos	Brazil
rial	R *or* Rl	100 dinars	Iran
rial	RO	1000 baiza	Oman
rial[1] *also* riyal	YR *or* R	100 fils	Yemen
rial—see RIYAL, below			
riel		100 sen	Cambodia
ringgit *or* dollar	$ *or* M$	100 sen	Malaysia
riyal	QR	100 dirhams	Qatar
riyal *also* rial		100 halala	Saudi Arabia
riyal—see RIAL, above			
ruble		100 kopecks	Russia
rufiyaa	Rf	100 laari	Maldives
rupee	Re (*pl* Rs)	100 paise	India
rupee	Re (*pl* Rs)	100 cents	Mauritius
rupee	Re (*pl* Rs)	100 paisa	Nepal
rupee	Re (*pl* Rs)	100 paisa	Pakistan
rupee	SR	100 cents	Seychelles
rupee	Re (*pl* Rs)	100 cents	Sri Lanka
rupiah	Rp	100 sen	Indonesia
schilling	S *or* Sch	100 groschen	Austria
shekel *or* sheqel	IS	100 agorot	Israel
shilling	S *or* KSh	100 cents	Kenya
shilling		100 cents	Somalia
shilling	TSh	100 cents	Tanzania
shilling		100 cents	Uganda
sol		100 centavos	Peru
sucre		100 centavos	Ecuador
taka	Tk	100 paisa *or* poisha	Bangladesh
tala	$	100 sene	Western Samoa
tical—see BAHT, above			
tugrik		100 mongo	Mongolia
vatu			Vanuatu
won		100 chon	North Korea
won		100 chon	South Korea
yen	¥	100 sen	Japan
yuan		100 fen	China (mainland)
yuan—see DOLLAR, above			
zaire	Z	100 makuta (*sing* likuta)	Zaire
zloty	Zl	100 groszy	Poland

[1] The currencies of the formerly separate countries of Southern Yemen and the Yemen Arab Republic are both legal in unified Yemen.

[2] Dollars issued by the *E*astern *C*aribbean Central Bank, established to promote economic cooperation among the member nations.

[3] Francs issued by the African Financial Community (Communauté *F*inancière *A*fricaine), established to promote economic cooperation among the member nations.

[4] Now a subdivision in name only.

²**Mongolian** *n* (1846) **1 a :** the language of the Mongol people **b :** a family of Altaic languages that includes the languages of the Mongols and the Kalmucks **2 a :** MONGOL 1 **b :** a person of Mongoloid racial stock **c :** a native or inhabitant of Mongolia

Mongolian gerbil *n* (1948) **:** a gerbil (*Meriones unguiculatus*) of Mongolia and northern China that has an external resemblance to a rat, has a high capacity for temperature regulation, and is used as an experimental laboratory animal

Mon·gol·ic \män-ˈgä-lik, män-\ *adj* (1834) **:** MONGOLOID 1

mon·gol·ism \ˈmäŋ-gə-ˌli-zəm\ *n* (1900) **:** DOWN'S SYNDROME

Mon·gol·oid \ˈmäŋ-gə-ˌlȯid\ *adj* (1868) **1 :** of, constituting, or characteristic of a major racial stock native to Asia as classified according to physical features (as the presence of an epicanthic fold) that includes peoples of northern and eastern Asia, Malaysians, Eskimos, and often American Indians **2** *often not cap* **:** of, relating to, or affected with Down's syndrome — **Mongoloid** *n*

mon·goose \ˈmän-ˌgüs, ˈmäŋ-\ *n, pl* **mon·goos·es** *also* **mon·geese** \-ˌgēs\ [Hindi & Marathi *magūs*, fr. Prakrit *maṃgūsa*] (1698) **:** any of the viverrid mammals that comprise two subfamilies (Herpestinae and Galidiinae) often grouped in a separate family (Herpestidae), that include agile ferret-sized mammals sometimes with bands or stripes, and that feed on small animals and fruits

mongoose

mon·grel \ˈmäŋ-grəl, ˈmäŋ-\ *n* [ME, prob. fr. *mong* mixture, short for *ymong*, fr. OE *gemong* crowd — more at AMONG] (15c) **1 :** an individual resulting from the interbreeding of diverse breeds or strains; *esp* **:** one of unknown ancestry **2 :** a cross between types of persons or things — **mongrel** *adj* — **mon·grel·i·za·tion** \ˌmäŋ-grə-lə-ˈzā-shən, ˌmäŋ-\ *n* — **mon·grel·ize** \ˈmäŋ-grə-ˌlīz, ˈmäŋ-\ *vt*

monies *pl of* MONEY

mon·i·ker *also* **mon·ick·er** \ˈmä-ni-kər\ *n* [prob. fr. Shelta (language of Irish itinerants) *münnik*, modif. of Ir *ainm*] (1851) **:** NAME, NICKNAME

mo·ni·li·a·sis \ˌmō-nə-ˈlī-ə-səs, ˌmä-\ *n, pl* **-a·ses** \-ˌsēz\ [NL, fr. *Monilia*, genus of fungi, fr. L *monile* necklace] (1920) **:** CANDIDIASIS

mo·nil·i·form \mə-ˈni-lə-ˌfȯrm\ *adj* [L *monile* necklace — more at MANE] (ca. 1803) **:** jointed or constricted at regular intervals so as to resemble a string of beads ⟨a ~ root⟩ ⟨~ insect antennae⟩

mon·ish \ˈmä-nish\ *vt* [ME *monesen*, alter. of *monesten*, fr. OF *monester*, fr. (assumed) VL *monestare*, fr. L *monēre* to warn] (14c) **:** WARN

mo·nism \ˈmō-ˌni-zəm, ˈmä-\ *n* [G *Monismus*, fr. *mon-* + *-ismus* -ism] (1862) **1 a :** a view that there is only one kind of ultimate substance **b :** the view that reality is one unitary organic whole with no independent parts **2 :** MONOGENESIS **3 :** a viewpoint or theory that reduces all phenomena to one principle — **mo·nist** \ˈmō-nist, ˈmä-\ *n* — **mo·nis·tic** \mō-ˈnis-tik, mä-\ *adj*

mo·ni·tion \mō-ˈni-shən, mə-\ *n* [ME *monicioun*, fr. MF *monition*, fr. L *monition-, monitio*, fr. *monēre*] (14c) **1 :** WARNING, CAUTION **2 :** an intimation of danger

¹**mon·i·tor** \ˈmä-nə-tər\ *n* [L, one that warns, overseer, fr. *monēre* to warn — more at MIND] (1546) **1 a :** a student appointed to assist a teacher **b :** one that warns or instructs **c :** one that monitors or is used in monitoring: as (1) **:** a cathode-ray tube used for display (as of television pictures or computer information) (2) **:** a device for observing a biological condition or function ⟨a heart ~⟩ **2 :** any of various large tropical Old World lizards (genus *Varanus* of the family Varanidae) closely related to the iguanas **3** [*Monitor*, first ship of the type] **a :** a heavily armored warship formerly used in coastal operations having a very low freeboard and one or more revolving gun turrets **b :** a small modern warship with shallow draft for coastal bombardment **4 :** a raised central portion of a roof having low windows or louvers for providing light and air — **mon·i·to·ri·al** \ˌmä-nə-ˈtȯr-ē-əl, -ˈtȯr-\ *adj* — **mon·i·tor·ship** \ˈmä-nə-tər-ˌship\ *n*

²**monitor** *vt* **mon·i·tored; mon·i·tor·ing** \ˈmä-nə-t(ə-)riŋ\ (1924) **:** to watch, keep track of, or check usu. for a special purpose

¹**mon·i·to·ry** \ˈmä-nə-ˌtȯr-ē, -ˌtȯr-\ *adj* [ME, fr. L *monitorius*, fr. *monēre*] (15c) **:** giving admonition **:** WARNING

²**monitory** *n, pl* **-ries** (15c) **:** a letter containing an admonition or warning

¹**monk** \ˈməŋk\ *n* [ME, fr. OE *munuc*, fr. LL *monachus*, fr. LGk *monachos*, fr. Gk, adj., single, fr. *monos* single, alone] (bef. 12c) **:** a man who is a member of a religious order and lives in a monastery; *also* **:** FRIAR

²**monk** *n* (1843) **:** MONKEY

monk·ery \ˈməŋ-kə-rē\ *n, pl* **-er·ies** (1536) **1 :** monastic life or practice **:** MONASTICISM **2 :** a monastic house **:** MONASTERY

¹**mon·key** \ˈməŋ-kē\ *n, pl* **monkeys** [prob. of LG origin; akin to *Moneke*, name of an ape, prob. of Romance origin; akin to OSp *mona* monkey] (ca. 1530) **1 :** a nonhuman primate mammal with the exception usu. of the lemurs and tarsiers; *esp* **:** any of the smaller longer-tailed primates as contrasted with the apes **2 a :** a person resembling a monkey **b :** a ludicrous figure **:** DUPE **3 :** any of various machines, implements, or vessels; *esp* **:** the falling weight of a pile driver **4 :** a desperate desire for or addiction to drugs — often used in the phrase *monkey on one's back; broadly* **:** a persistent or annoying encumbrance or problem

²**monkey** *vb* **mon·keyed; mon·key·ing** *vt* (1859) **:** MIMIC, MOCK ~ *vi* **1 :** to act in a grotesque or mischievous manner **2 a :** FOOL, TRIFLE — often used with *around* **b :** TAMPER — usu. used with *with*

monkey bars *n pl* (1955) **:** a three-dimensional framework of horizontal and vertical bars from which children can hang and swing

monkey business *n* (1883) **:** SHENANIGAN 2

monkey jacket *n* (1830) **:** MESS JACKET

mon·key·pod \ˈməŋ-kē-ˌpäd\ *n* (1888) **1 :** an ornamental tropical leguminous tree (*Samanea saman* syn. *Pithecolobium saman*) that has bipinnate leaves, globose clusters of flowers with crimson stamens, sweet-pulp pods eaten by cattle, and wood used in carving — called also *rain tree* **2 :** the wood of a monkeypod

monkey puzzle *n* (1866) **:** a tall araucaria (*Araucaria araucana*) that is native to Chile and western Argentina but widely grown elsewhere — called also *monkey puzzle tree*

mon·key·shine \ˈməŋ-kē-ˌshīn\ *n* (ca. 1832) **:** PRANK — usu. used in pl.

monkey wrench *n* (ca. 1858) **1 :** a wrench with one fixed and one adjustable jaw at right angles to a straight handle **2 :** something that disrupts ⟨threw a *monkey wrench* into the peace negotiations⟩

monk·fish \ˈməŋk-ˌfish\ *n* (1666) **:** either of two goosefishes (*Lophius americanus* of America and *L. piscatorius* of Europe) used for food

Mon–Khmer \ˌmōn-kə-ˈmer\ *n* (1887) **:** a language family containing Mon, Khmer, and a number of other languages of southeast Asia

monk·hood \ˈməŋk-ˌhu̇d\ *n* (bef. 12c) **1 :** the character, condition, or profession of a monk **:** MONASTICISM **2 :** monks as a class

monk·ish \ˈməŋ-kish\ *adj* (1546) **1 :** of, relating to, or resembling a monk; *also* **:** resembling that of a monk **2 :** inclined to disciplinary self-denial

monk's cloth *n* (ca. 1847) **:** a coarse heavy fabric in basket weave made orig. of worsted and used for monk's habits but now chiefly of cotton or linen and used for draperies

monk seal *n* (1841) **:** any of a genus (*Monachus*) of hair seals of Hawaii, the Mediterranean Sea, and formerly the Caribbean Sea

monks·hood \ˈməŋ(k)s-ˌhu̇d\ *n* (1578) **:** any of a genus (*Aconitum*) of usu. bluish flowered poisonous herbs of the buttercup family; *esp* **:** a poisonous Eurasian herb (*A. napellus*) often cultivated for its showy terminal racemes of white or purplish flowers — compare WOLFSBANE

¹**mono** \ˈmä-(ˌ)nō\ *n, pl* **mon·os** [²*mono*] (1959) **:** monophonic reproduction

²**mono** *adj* (1961) **:** MONOPHONIC 2

³**mono** *n* (1962) **:** INFECTIOUS MONONUCLEOSIS

mono- — see MON-

mono·ac·id \ˌmä-nō-ˈa-səd\ *n* (1863) **:** an acid having only one acid hydrogen atom

mono·acid·ic \-ə-ˈsi-dik\ *adj* (ca. 1929) **:** able to react with one molecule of a monobasic acid to form a salt or ester — used esp. of bases

mono·amine \ˌmä-nō-ə-ˈmēn\ *n* [ISV] (1951) **:** an amine RNH_2 that has one organic substituent attached to the nitrogen atom; *esp* **:** one (as serotonin) that is functionally important in neural transmission

monoamine oxidase *n* (1951) **:** an enzyme that deaminates monoamines oxidatively and that functions in the nervous system by breaking down monoamine neurotransmitters oxidatively

mono·am·in·er·gic \ˌmä-nō-ˌa-mə-ˈnər-jik\ *adj* (1966) **:** liberating or involving monoamines (as serotonin or norepinephrine) in neural transmission ⟨~ neurons⟩ ⟨~ mechanisms⟩

mono·ba·sic \ˌmä-nō-ˈbā-sik\ *adj* [ISV] (1842) *of an acid* **:** having only one replaceable hydrogen atom

mono·car·box·yl·ic \-ˌkär-(ˌ)bäk-ˈsi-lik\ *adj* (ca. 1909) **:** containing one carboxyl group ⟨acetic acid is a ~ acid⟩

mono·car·pic \-ˈkär-pik\ *adj* [prob. fr. (assumed) NL *monocarpicus*, fr. NL *mon-* + *-carpicus* -carpic] (1849) **:** bearing fruit but once and then dying

mono·cha·si·um \-ˈkä-zē-əm, -zhē-\ *n, pl* **-sia** \-zē-ə, -zhē-\ [NL, fr. *mon-* + *-chasium* (as in *dichasium*)] (ca. 1890) **:** a cymose inflorescence that produces only one main axis — **mono·cha·sial** \-zē-əl, -zhē-\ *adj*

mono·chord \ˈmä-nə-ˌkȯrd\ *n* [ME *monocorde*, fr. MF, fr. ML *monochordum*, fr. Gk *monochordon*, fr. *mon-* + *chordē* string — more at YARN] (15c) **:** an instrument of ancient origin for measuring and demonstrating the mathematical relations of musical tones and that consists of a single string stretched over a sound box and a movable bridge set on a graduated scale

mono·chro·mat \ˈmä-nə-krō-ˌmat, ˌmä-nə-ˈ\ *n* [*mon-* + Gk *chrōmat-, chrōma*] (1902) **:** a completely color-blind individual

mono·chro·mat·ic \ˌmä-nə-krō-ˈma-tik\ *adj* [L *monochromatos*, fr. Gk *monochrōmatos*, fr. *mon-* + *chrōmat-, chrōma* color] (1822) **1 a :** having or consisting of one color or hue **b :** MONOCHROME 2 **2 :** consisting of radiation of a single wavelength or of a very small range of wavelengths **3 :** of, relating to, or exhibiting monochromatism — **mono·chro·mat·i·cal·ly** \-ti-k(ə-)lē\ *adv* — **mono·chro·ma·tic·i·ty** \-ˌkrō-mə-ˈti-sə-tē\ *n*

mono·chro·ma·tism \-ˈkrō-mə-ˌti-zəm\ *n* (ca. 1930) **:** complete color blindness in which all colors appear as shades of gray

mono·chro·ma·tor \ˌmä-nə-ˈkrō-ˌmā-tər\ *n* [*monochro*matic + *illuminator*] (1909) **:** a device for isolating a narrow portion of a spectrum

¹**mono·chrome** \ˈmä-nə-ˌkrōm\ *n* [ML *monochroma*, fr. L, fem. of *monochromos* of one color, fr. Gk *monochrōmos*, fr. *mon-* + *-chrōmos* -chrome] (1662) **:** a painting, drawing, or photograph in a single hue — **mono·chro·mic** \ˌmä-nə-ˈkrō-mik\ *adj* — **mono·chrom·ist** \ˈmä-nə-ˌkrō-mist\ *n*

²**monochrome** *adj* (1849) **1 :** of, relating to, or made with a single color or hue **2 :** involving or producing visual images in a single color or in varying tones of a single color (as gray) ⟨~ film⟩ ⟨~ television monitor⟩

mon·o·cle \ˈmä-ni-kəl\ *n* [F, fr. LL *monoculus* having one eye, fr. L *mon-* + *oculus* eye — more at EYE] (ca. 1858) **:** an eyeglass for one eye — **mon·o·cled** \-kəld\ *adj*

mono·cline \ˈmä-nə-ˌklīn\ *n* (1879) **:** an oblique geologic fold

mono·clin·ic \ˌmä-nə-ˈkli-nik\ *adj* [ISV] (ca. 1864) **:** having one oblique intersection of the crystallographic axes

monoclinic system *n* (1869) **:** a crystal system characterized by three unequal axes with one oblique intersection

mono·clo·nal \ˌmä-nə-ˈklō-n³l\ *adj* (1914) **:** produced by, being, or composed of cells derived from a single cell ⟨~ antibodies⟩ ⟨a ~ tumor⟩ — **monoclonal** *n*

monocle

mono·coque \ˈmä-nə-ˌkōk, -ˌkäk\ *n* [F, fr. *mon-* + *coque* shell, prob. fr. L *coccum* kermes — more at COCOON] (1913) **1 :** a type of construction (as of a fuselage) in which the outer skin carries all or a major part of the stresses **2 :** a type of vehicle construction (as of an automobile) in which the body is integral with the chassis

mono·cot \-ˌkät\ *n* (1890) **:** MONOCOTYLEDON

mono·cot·y·le·don \ˌmä-nə-ˌkä-t³l-ˈē-d³n\ *n* [ultim. fr. NL *mon-* + *cotyledon* cotyledon] (ca. 1727) **:** any of a class or subclass (Liliopsida or Monocotyledoneae) of chiefly herbaceous seedplants having an embryo with a single cotyledon, usu. parallel-veined leaves, and floral organs arranged in cycles of three — compare DICOTYLEDON — **mono-cot·y·le·don·ous** \-d⁰n-əs\ *adj*

mo·noc·ra·cy \mä-'nä-krə-sē, mə-\ *n* (1651) : government by a single person — **mono-crat** \'mä-nə-,krat\ *n* — **mono-crat·ic** \,mä-nə-'kra-tik\ *adj*

mono·crys·tal \'mä-nə-,kris-t⁰l\ *n* (1926) : a single crystal — **mono-crystal** *adj* — **mono·crys·tal·line** \,mä-nə-'kris-tə-lən *also* -,līn, -,lēn\ *adj*

¹**mon·oc·u·lar** \mä-'nä-kyə-lər, mə-\ *adj* [LL *monoculus* having one eye] (1640) **1** : of, involving, or affecting a single eye **2** : suitable for use with only one eye — **mon·oc·u·lar·ly** *adv*

²**monocular** *n* (1936) : a monocular device

mono·cul·ture \'mä-nə-,kəl-chər\ *n* (1915) **1** : the cultivation or growth of a single crop or organism esp. on agricultural or forest land **2** : a crop or a population of a single kind of organism grown on land in monoculture — **mono·cul·tur·al** \,mä-nə-'kəlch-rəl, -'kəl-chə-\ *adj*

mono·cy·clic \,mä-nə-'sī-klik, -'si-\ *adj* [ISV] (1910) : containing one ring in the molecular structure

mono·cyte \'mä-nə-,sīt\ *n* [ISV] (ca. 1913) : a large white blood cell with finely granulated chromatin dispersed throughout the nucleus that is formed in the bone marrow, enters the blood, and migrates into the connective tissue where it differentiates into a macrophage — **mono·cyt·ic** \,mä-nə-'si-tik\ *adj*

mono·dis·perse \,mä-nō-dis-'pərs\ *adj* [*mon-* + *disperse*, adj., fr. *disperse*, v.] (1925) : characterized by particles of uniform size in a dispersed phase

mon·o·dist \'mä-nə-dist\ *n* (1751) : a writer, singer, or composer of monody

mono·dra·ma \'mä-nə-,drä-mə, -,dra-\ *n* (1793) : a drama acted or designed to be acted by a single person — **mono·dra·mat·ic** \,mä-nə-drə-'ma-tik\ *adj*

mon·o·dy \'mä-nə-dē\ *n, pl* **-dies** [ML *monodia*, fr. Gk *monōidia*, fr. *monōidos* singing alone, fr. *mon-* + *aeidein* to sing — more at ODE] (ca. 1623) **1** : an ode sung by one voice (as in a Greek tragedy) **2** : an elegy or dirge performed by one person **3 a** : a monophonic vocal piece **b** : the monophonic style of 17th century opera — **mo·nod·ic** \mə-'nä-dik\ *or* **mo·nod·i·cal** \-di-kəl\ *adj* — **mo·nod·i·cal·ly** \-di-k(ə-)lē\ *adv*

mon·oe·cious \mə-'nē-shəs, mä-\ *adj* [ultim. fr. Gk *mon-* + *oikos* house — more at VICINITY] (1753) **1** : having pistillate and staminate flowers on the same plant **2** : having male and female sex organs in the same individual : HERMAPHRODITIC

mon·oe·cism \-'nē-,si-zəm\ *n* (1875) : the condition of being monoecious

mono·es·ter \'mä-nō-,es-tər\ *n* (1927) : an ester (as of a dibasic acid) that contains only one ester group

mono·fil·a·ment \,mä-nə-'fi-lə-mənt\ *n* (1940) : a single untwisted synthetic filament (as of nylon)

mo·nog·a·mist \mə-'nä-gə-mist\ *n* (1651) : one who practices or upholds monogamy

mo·nog·a·my \-mē\ *n* [F *monogamie*, fr. LL *monogamia*, fr. Gk, fr. *monogamos* monogamous, fr. *mon-* + *gamos* marriage, fr. *gamein* to marry] (1612) **1** *archaic* : the practice of marrying only once during a lifetime **2** : the state or custom of being married to one person at a time **3** : the condition or practice of having a single mate during a period of time ⟨∼ is common among birds⟩ — **mo·nog·a·mous** \mə-'nä-gə-məs\ *also* **mono·gam·ic** \,mä-nə-'ga-mik\ *adj* — **mo·nog·a·mous·ly** *adv*

mono·gas·tric \,mä-nə-'gas-trik\ *adj* (1814) : having a stomach with only a single compartment ⟨swine, chicks, and human beings are ∼⟩

mono·ge·ne·an \-'jē-nē-ən\ *n* [NL *Monogenea*, group name] (1899) : a monogenetic trematode — **monogenean** *adj*

mono·gen·e·sis \-'je-nə-səs\ *n* [NL] (ca. 1859) : origin of diverse individuals or kinds (as of language) by descent from a single ancestral individual or kind

mono·ge·net·ic \-jə-'ne-tik\ *adj* (1873) **1** : relating to or involving monogenesis **2** : of, relating to, or being any of a subclass (Monogenea) of trematode worms that ordinarily live as ectoparasites on a single host (as a fish or amphibian) throughout their entire life cycle

mono·gen·ic \-'je-nik\ *adj* [ISV] (1939) : of, relating to, or controlled by a single gene and esp. by either of an allelic pair — **mono·gen·i·cal·ly** \-ni-k(ə-)lē\ *adv*

mono·germ \'mä-nə-,jərm\ *adj* [*mon-* + *germinate*] (1950) : producing or being a fruit that gives rise to a single plant ⟨a ∼ sugar beet⟩

mono·glot \-,glät\ *adj* [*mono-* + *-glot* (as in *polyglot*)] (1830) : MONOLINGUAL — **monoglot** *n*

mono·glyc·er·ide \,mä-nə-'gli-sə-,rīd\ *n* (1860) : any of various esters of glycerol in which only one of the three hydroxyl groups is esterified and which are often used as emulsifiers

¹**mono·gram** \'mä-nə-,gram\ *n* [LL *monogramma*, fr. Gk *mon-* + *gramma* letter — more at GRAM] (ca. 1696) : a sign of identity usu. formed of the combined initials of a name — **mono·gram·mat·ic** \,mä-nə-grə-'ma-tik\ *adj*

²**monogram** *vt* **-grammed; -gram·ming** (1868) : to mark with a monogram — **mono·gram·mer** \-,gra-mər\ *n*

¹**mono·graph** \'mä-nə-,graf\ *n* (1821) : a learned treatise on a small area of learning; *also* : a written account of a single thing — **mono·graph·ic** \,mä-nə-'gra-fik\ *adj*

²**monograph** *vt* (1876) : to write a monograph on

mo·nog·y·nous \mə-'nä-jə-nəs, mä-\ *adj* (ca. 1890) : of, relating to, or living in monogyny

mo·nog·y·ny \-nē\ *n* [ISV] (1876) : the state or custom of having only one wife at a time

mono·hull \'mä-nə-,həl\ *n* (1967) : a vessel (as a sailboat) with a single hull — compare MULTIHULL

mono·hy·brid \'mä-nə-'hī-brəd\ *n* (1903) : an individual or strain heterozygous for one specified gene — **monohybrid** *adj*

mono·hy·dric \-'hī-drik\ *adj* (1880) : MONOHYDROXY

mono·hy·droxy \-(,)hī-'dräk-sē\ *adj* [ISV *monohydroxy-*, fr. *mon-* + *hydroxy-*] (ca. 1934) : containing one hydroxyl group in the molecule

mono·lay·er \'mä-nō-,lā-ər, -,le-(ə)r\ *n* (1926) : a single continuous layer or film that is one cell or molecule in thickness

mono·lin·gual \,mä-nə-'liŋ-gwəl, ,mō-, -'liŋ-gyə-wəl\ *adj* (1926) : knowing or using only one language — **monolingual** *n*

mono·lith \'mä-n⁰l-,ith\ *n* [F *monolithe*, fr. *monolithe* consisting of a single stone, fr. L *monolithus*, fr. Gk *monolithos*, fr. *mon-* + *lithos* stone] (1848) **1** : a single great stone often in the form of an obelisk or column **2** : a massive structure **3** : an organized whole that acts as a single unified powerful or influential force

mono·lith·ic \,mä-n⁰l-'i-thik\ *adj* (1825) **1 a** : of, relating to, or resembling a monolith : HUGE, MASSIVE **b** (1) : formed from a single crystal ⟨a ∼ silicon chip⟩ (2) : produced in or on a monolithic chip ⟨a ∼ circuit⟩ **2 a** : cast as a single piece ⟨a ∼ concrete wall⟩ **b** : formed or composed of material without joints or seams ⟨a ∼ floor covering⟩ ⟨a ∼ furnace lining⟩ **c** : consisting of or constituting a single unit **3 a** : constituting a massive undifferentiated and often rigid whole ⟨a ∼ society⟩ **b** : exhibiting or characterized by often rigidly fixed uniformity ⟨∼ party unity⟩ — **mono·lith·i·cal·ly** \-thi-k(ə-)lē\ *adv*

mono·logue *also* **mono·log** \'mä-n⁰l-,óg, -,äg\ *n* [MF *monologue*, fr. *mon-* + *-logue*] (1549) **1 a** : SOLILOQUY **2 b** : a dramatic sketch performed by one actor **c** : the routine of a stand-up comic **2** : a literary composition written in the form of a soliloquy **3** : a long speech monopolizing conversation — **mono·logu·ist** \-,ò-gist, -,ä-\ *or* **mo·no·lo·gist** *same or* mə-'nä-lə-jist, -gist\ *n*

mono·ma·nia \,mä-nə-'mä-nē-ə, -nyə\ *n* [NL] (1823) **1** : mental illness esp. when limited in expression to one idea or area of thought **2** : excessive concentration on a single object or idea — **mono·ma·ni·ac** \-nē-,ak\ *n or adj* — **mono·ma·ni·a·cal** \-mə-'nī-ə-kəl\ *adj* — **mono·ma·ni·a·cal·ly** \-k(ə-)lē\ *adv*

mono·mer \'mä-nə-mər\ *n* [ISV] (1914) : a chemical compound that can undergo polymerization — **mo·no·mer·ic** \,mä-nə-'mer-ik, ,mō-\ *adj*

mono·me·tal·lic \,mä-nō-mə-'ta-lik\ *adj* (1877) **1** : of or relating to monometallism **2** : consisting of or employing one metal

mono·met·al·lism \-'me-t⁰l-,i-zəm\ *n* [ISV *mon-* + *-metallism* (as in *bimetallism*)] (1879) : the adoption of one metal only in a currency — **mono·met·al·list** \-'t⁰l-ist\ *n*

mo·nom·e·ter \mə-'nä-mə-tər, mä-\ *n* [LL, fr. Gk *monometros*, fr. *mon-* + *metron* measure — more at MEASURE] (ca. 1846) : a line of verse consisting of a single metrical foot or dipody

mo·no·mi·al \mä-'nō-mē-əl, mə-\ *n* [blend of *mon-* and *-nomial* (as in *binomial*)] (ca. 1706) **1** : a mathematical expression consisting of a single term **2** : a taxonomic name consisting of a single word or term — **monomial** *adj*

mono·mo·lec·u·lar \,mä-nə-mə-'le-kyə-lər\ *adj* (1917) : being only one molecule thick ⟨a ∼ film⟩ — **mono·mo·lec·u·lar·ly** *adv*

mono·phe·mic \-mōr-'fē-mik\ *adj* (1936) : consisting of only one morpheme ⟨the word *talk* is ∼ but *talked* is not⟩

mono·mor·phic \-'mòr-fik\ *adj* (ca. 1879) : having but a single form, structural pattern, or genotype ⟨a ∼ species of insect⟩ — **mono·mor·phism** \-,fi-zəm\ *n*

mono·nu·cle·ar \-'nü-klē-ər, -'nyü-, -÷-kyə-lər\ *adj* [ISV] (1886) : having only one nucleus ⟨a ∼ cell⟩ — **mononuclear** *n*

mono·nu·cle·at·ed \-'nü-klē-,ā-təd, -'nyü-\ *also* **mono·nu·cle·ate** \-klē-ət, -,ät\ *adj* (1890) : MONONUCLEAR

mono·nu·cle·o·sis \-,nü-klē-'ō-səs, -,nyü-\ *n* [NL, fr. ISV *mononuclear* + NL *-osis*] (1920) : an abnormal increase of mononuclear white blood cells in the blood; *specif* : INFECTIOUS MONONUCLEOSIS

mono·nu·cle·o·tide \-'nü-klē-ə-,tīd, -'nyü-\ *n* (1908) : a nucleotide that is derived from one molecule each of a nitrogenous base, a sugar, and a phosphoric acid

mo·noph·a·gous \mə-'nä-fə-gəs, mä-\ *adj* (ca. 1868) : feeding on or utilizing a single kind of food; *esp* : feeding on a single kind of plant or animal — **mo·noph·a·gy** \-fə-jē\ *n*

mono·pho·nic \,mä-nə-'fä-nik, -'fō-\ *adj* (ca. 1864) **1** : having a single unaccompanied melodic line **2** : of or relating to sound transmission, recording, or reproduction involving a single transmission path — **mono·pho·ni·cal·ly** \-ni-k(ə-)lē\ *adv*

mo·noph·o·ny \mə-'nä-fə-nē, mä-\ *n* (ca. 1890) : monophonic music

mon·oph·thong \'mä-nə(f)-,thòŋ\ *n* [LGk *monophthongos* single vowel, fr. Gk *mon-* + *phthongos* sound] (1616) : a vowel sound that throughout its duration has a single constant articulatory position — **mon·oph·thon·gal** \,mä-nə(f)-'thòŋ-(g)əl\ *adj*

mono·phy·let·ic \,mä-nō-fī-'le-tik\ *adj* [ISV] (1874) : of or relating to a single stock; *specif* : developed from a single common ancestral form — **mono·phy·ly** \'mä-nə-,fī-lē\ *n*

Mo·noph·y·site \mə-'nä-fə-,sīt\ *n* [ML *Monophysita*, fr. MGk *Monophysitēs*, fr. Gk *mon-* + *physis* nature — more at PHYSICS] (1698) : one holding the doctrine that Christ's nature remains altogether divine and not human even though he has taken on an earthly and human body with its cycle of birth, life, and death — **Monophysite** *or* **Mo·noph·y·sit·ic** \-,nä-fə-'si-tik\ *adj* — **Mo·noph·y·sit·ism** \-'nä-fə-,si-,ti-zəm\ *n*

mono·plane \'mä-nə-,plān\ *n* (1907) : an airplane with only one main supporting surface

¹**mono·ploid** \'mä-nə-,plòid\ *adj* (1928) **1** : HAPLOID **2** : having or being the basic haploid number of chromosomes in a polyploid series of organisms

²**monoploid** *n* [ISV] (1944) : a monoploid individual or organism

mono·po·di·al \,mä-nə-'pō-dē-əl\ *adj* [NL *monopodium* main axis, fr. *mon-* + *-podium*] (1876) : having or involving the formation of offshoots from a main axis — **mono·po·di·al·ly** \-dē-ə-lē\ *adv*

mono·pole \'mä-nə-,pōl\ *n* (1937) **1** : a single positive or negative electrical charge; *also* : a hypothetical north or south magnetic pole existing alone **2** : a radio antenna consisting of a single often straight element

mo·nop·o·lise *Brit var of* MONOPOLIZE

\ə\ abut \ə⁰\ kitten, F table \ər\ further \a\ ash \ā\ ace \ä\ mop, mar \au̇\ out \ch\ chin \e\ bet \ē\ easy \g\ go \i\ hit \ī\ ice \j\ job \ŋ\ sing \ō\ go \ò\ law \òi\ boy \th\ thin \th̶\ the \ü\ loot \u̇\ foot \y\ yet \zh\ vision \ä, ḵ, ⁿ, œ, œ̄, ue, ūe, ʸ\ *see* Guide to Pronunciation

mo·nop·o·list \mə-'nä-pə-list\ *n* (1601) : one who monopolizes — **mo·nop·o·lis·tic** \-,nä-pə-'lis-tik\ *adj* — **mo·nop·o·lis·ti·cal·ly** \-ti-k(ə-)lē\ *adv*

mo·nop·o·lize \mə-'nä-pə-,līz\ *vt* **-lized; -liz·ing** (1611) : to get a monopoly of : assume complete possession or control of 〈~ a conversation〉 — **mo·nop·o·li·za·tion** \-,nä-pə-lə-'zā-shən\ *n* — **mo·nop·o·liz·er** \-'nä-pə-,lī-zər\ *n*

mo·nop·o·ly \mə-'nä-p(ə-)lē\ *n, pl* **-lies** [L *monopolium,* fr. Gk *monopōlion,* fr. *mon-* + *pōlein* to sell] (1534) **1** : exclusive ownership through legal privilege, command of supply, or concerted action **2** : exclusive possession or control **3** : a commodity controlled by one party **4** : one that has a monopoly

mono·pro·pel·lant \,mä-nō-prə-'pe-lənt\ *n* (ca. 1945) : a rocket propellant containing both the fuel and the oxidizer in a single substance

mo·nop·so·ny \mə-'näp-sə-nē\ *n, pl* **-nies** [*mon-* + *-opsony* (as in *oligopsony*)] (1933) : an oligopsony limited to one buyer — **mo·nop·so·nis·tic** \-,näp-sə-'nis-tik\ *adj*

mono·rail \'mä-nə-,rāl\ *n* (1897) : a single rail serving as a track for a wheeled vehicle; *also* : a vehicle traveling on such a track

mon·or·chid \mä-'nȯr-kəd\ *n* [irreg. fr. Gk *monorchis,* fr. *mon-* + *orchis* testicle — more at ORCHIS] (1874) : an individual who has only one testis or only one descended into the scrotum — **monorchid** *adj* — **mon·or·chi·dism** \-kə-,di-zəm\ *n*

mono·rhyme \'mä-nə-,rīm\ *n* (1731) : a strophe or poem in which all the lines have the same end rhyme — **mono·rhymed** \-,rīmd\ *adj*

mono·sac·cha·ride \,mä-nə-'sa-kə-,rīd\ *n* [ISV] (1896) : a sugar not decomposable to simpler sugars by hydrolysis

mono·so·di·um glu·ta·mate \,mä-nə-,sō-dē-əm-'glü-tə-,māt\ *n* (1929) : a crystalline salt $C_5H_8O_4NaN$ used to enhance the flavor of food — abbr. *MSG*

mono·some \'mä-nə-,sōm\ *n* (ca. 1909) **1** : a chromosome lacking a synaptic mate; *esp* : an unpaired X chromosome **2** : a single ribosome

mono·so·mic \,mä-nə-'sō-mik\ *adj* (1926) : having one less than the diploid number of chromosomes — **monosomic** *n* — **mono·so·my** \'mä-nə-,sō-mē\ *n*

mono·spe·cif·ic \,mä-nō-spə-'si-fik\ *adj* (1947) : specific for a single antigen or receptor site on an antigen — **mono·spec·i·fic·i·ty** \-,spe-sə-'fi-sə-tē\ *n*

mono·stele \'mä-nə-,stēl, ,mä-nə-'stē-lē\ *n* (ca. 1900) : PROTOSTELE — **mono·ste·lic** \,mä-nə-'stē-lik\ *adj* — **mono·ste·ly** \'mä-nə-,stē-lē\ *n*

mono·syl·lab·ic \,mä-nə-sə-'la-bik\ *adj* [prob. fr. F *monosyllabe,* fr. *monosyllabe*] (1768) **1** : consisting of one syllable or of monosyllables **2** : using or speaking only monosyllables **3** : conspicuously brief in answering or commenting : TERSE — **mono·syl·lab·i·cal·ly** \-bi-k(ə-)lē\ *adv* — **mono·syl·la·bic·i·ty** \-,si-lə-'bi-sə-tē\ *n*

mono·syl·la·ble \'mä-nə-,si-lə-bəl, ,mä-nə-'-\ *n* [modif. of MF or LL; MF *monosyllabe,* fr. LL *monosyllabon,* fr. Gk, fr. neut. of *monosyllabos* having one syllable, fr. *mon-* + *syllabē* syllable] (1533) : a word of one syllable

mono·syn·ap·tic \,mä-nō-sə-'nap-tik\ *adj* (1942) : having or involving a single neural synapse — **mono·syn·ap·ti·cal·ly** \-ti-k(ə-)lē\ *adv*

mono·ter·pene \,mä-nə-'tər-,pēn\ *n* (ca. 1959) : any of a class of terpenes $C_{10}H_{16}$ containing two isoprene units per molecule; *also* : a derivative of a monoterpene

mono·the·ism \'mä-nə-(,)thē-,i-zəm\ *n* (1660) : the doctrine or belief that there is but one God — **mono·the·ist** \-,thē-ist\ *n* — **mono·the·is·tic** \,mä-nə-thē-'is-tik\ *also* **mono·the·is·ti·cal** \-ti-kəl\ *adj* — **mono·the·is·ti·cal·ly** \-ti-k(ə-)lē\ *adv*

¹mono·tone \'mä-nə-,tōn\ *n* [Gk *monotonos* monotonous] (1644) **1** : a succession of syllables, words, or sentences in one unvaried key or pitch **2** : a single unvaried musical tone **3** : a tedious sameness or reiteration **4** : a person unable to produce or to distinguish between musical intervals

²monotone *adj* (1769) **1** : MONOTONIC **2** : having a uniform color

mono·ton·ic \,mä-nə-'tä-nik\ *adj* (1797) **1** : characterized by the use of or uttered in a monotone **2** : having the property either of never increasing or of never decreasing as the values of the independent variable or the subscripts of the terms increase 〈~ functions〉 〈a ~ sequence〉 — **mono·ton·i·cal·ly** \-ni-k(ə-)lē\ *adv* — **mono·to·nic·i·ty** \,mä-nə-tō-'ni-sə-tē\ *n*

mo·not·o·nous \mə-'nä-t²n-əs, -'nät-nəs\ *adj* [Gk *monotonos,* fr. *mon-* + *tonos* tone] (1778) **1** : uttered or sounded in one unvarying tone : marked by a sameness of pitch and intensity **2** : tediously uniform or unvarying — **mo·not·o·nous·ly** *adv* — **mo·not·o·nous·ness** *n*

mo·not·o·ny \mə-'nä-t²n-ē, -'nät-nē\ *n* (1706) **1** : tedious sameness **2** : sameness of tone or sound

mono·treme \'mä-nə-,trēm\ *n* [NL *Monotremata,* fr. Gk *mon-* + *trēmat-, trēma* hole — more at TREMATODE] (1835) : any of an order (Monotremata) of egg-laying mammals comprising the platypuses and echidnas

mono·type \'mä-nə-,tīp\ *n* (1882) : an impression on paper of a design painted usu. with the finger or a brush on a surface (as glass)

Monotype *trademark* — used for a keyboard typesetting machine that casts and sets type in separate characters

mono·typ·ic \,mä-nə-'ti-pik\ *adj* [*mon-* + *type* + *-ic*] (ca. 1859) : including a single representative — used esp. of a genus with only one species

mono·un·sat·u·rat·ed \,mä-nō-,ən-'sa-chə-,rā-təd\ *adj* (ca. 1939) : containing one double or triple bond per molecule — used esp. of an oil or fatty acid; compare POLYUNSATURATED — **mono·un·sat·u·rate** \-,rət\ *n*

mono·va·lent \,mä-nə-'vā-lənt\ *adj* [ISV] (1869) **1** : having a valence of one **2** : containing antibodies specific for or antigens of a single strain of a microorganism 〈a ~ vaccine〉

mon·ovu·lar \(,)mä-'nä-vyə-lər, -'nōv-\ *adj* (1929) : MONOZYGOTIC

mon·ox·ide \mə-'näk-,sīd\ *n* [ISV] (1869) : an oxide containing one atom of oxygen in a molecule

mono·zy·got·ic \,mä-nə-zī-'gä-tik\ *adj* (1916) : derived from a single egg 〈~ twins〉

Mon·roe Doctrine \mən-'rō- *also* 'mən- *or* 'män-\ *n* [James *Monroe*] (1853) : a statement of U.S. foreign policy expressing opposition to extension of European control or influence in the western hemisphere

mon·sei·gneur \,mōⁿ-,sān-'yər\ *n, pl* **mes·sei·gneurs** \,mā-,sān-'yər(z)\ [F, lit., my lord] (1602) : a French dignitary (as a prince or prelate) — used as a title preceding a title of office or rank

mon·sieur \məs-'yə(r), məsh-; mə-'sir\ *n, pl* **mes·sieurs** \məs-'yə(r)(z), məsh-, mäs-; mə-'sir(z)\ [MF, lit., my lord] (1512) : a Frenchman of high rank or station — used as a title equivalent to *Mister* and prefixed to the name of a Frenchman

mon·si·gnor \män-'sē-nyər, mən-\ *n, pl* **monsignors** *or* **mon·si·gno·ri** \,män-,sēn-'yȯr-ē, -'yȯr-\ [It *monsignore,* fr. F *monseigneur*] (1641) : a Roman Catholic prelate having a dignity or titular distinction (as of domestic prelate or protonotary apostolic) usu. conferred by the pope — used as a title prefixed to the surname or to the given name and surname — **mon·si·gno·ri·al** \,män-,sēn-'yȯr-ē-əl, -'yȯr-\ *adj*

mon·soon \män-'sün, 'män-,\ *n* [obs. D *monssoen,* fr. Pg *monção,* fr. Ar *mawsim* time, season] (1584) **1** : a periodic wind esp. in the Indian Ocean and southern Asia **2** : the season of the southwest monsoon in India and adjacent areas that is characterized by very heavy rainfall **3** : rainfall that is associated with the monsoon — **mon·soon·al** \-'sü-n²l, -,sü-\ *adj*

mons pu·bis \'mänz-'pyü-bəs\ *n, pl* **mon·tes pubis** \'män-tēz-\ [NL, pubic eminence] (ca. 1903) : a rounded eminence of fatty tissue upon the pubic symphysis esp. of the human female

¹mon·ster \'män(t)-stər\ *n* [ME *monstre,* fr. MF, fr. L *monstrum* omen, monster, fr. *monēre* to warn — more at MIND] (14c) **1** a : an animal or plant of abnormal form or structure **b** : one who deviates from normal or acceptable behavior or character **2** : a threatening force **3** a : an animal of strange or terrifying shape **b** : one unusually large for its kind **4** : something monstrous; *esp* : a person of unnatural or extreme ugliness, deformity, wickedness, or cruelty **5** : one that is highly successful

²monster *adj* (1837) : enormous or impressive in size, extent, or numbers

mon·strance \'män(t)-strən(t)s\ *n* [ME *monstrans,* fr. MF *monstrance,* fr. ML *monstrantia,* fr. L *monstrant-, monstrans,* prp. of *monstrare* to show, fr. *monstrum*] (15c) : a vessel in which the consecrated Host is exposed for the adoration of the faithful

mon·stros·i·ty \män-'strä-sə-tē\ *n, pl* **-ties** (15c) **1** a : a malformation of a plant or animal **b** : something deviating from the normal : FREAK **2** : the quality or state of being monstrous **3** a : an object of great and often frightening size, force, or complexity **b** : an excessively bad or shocking example

mon·strous \'män(t)-strəs\ *adj* (15c) **1** *obs* : STRANGE, UNNATURAL **2** : having extraordinary often overwhelming size : GIGANTIC **3** a : having the qualities or appearance of a monster **b** *obs* : teeming with monsters **4** a : extraordinarily ugly or vicious : HORRIBLE **b** : shockingly wrong or ridiculous **5** : deviating greatly from the natural form or character : ABNORMAL **6** : very great — used as an intensive — **mon·strous·ly** *adv* — **mon·strous·ness** *n*

syn MONSTROUS, PRODIGIOUS, TREMENDOUS, STUPENDOUS mean extremely impressive. MONSTROUS implies a departure from the normal (as in size, form, or character) and often carries suggestions of deformity, ugliness, or fabulousness 〈the *monstrous* waste of the project〉. PRODIGIOUS suggests a marvelousness exceeding belief, usu. in something felt as going far beyond a previous maximum (as of goodness, greatness, intensity, or size) 〈made a *prodigious* effort and rolled the stone aside〉. TREMENDOUS may imply a power to terrify or inspire awe 〈the *tremendous* roar of the cataract〉. STUPENDOUS implies a power to stun or astound, usu. because of size, numbers, complexity, or greatness beyond description 〈a *stupendous* volcanic eruption〉.

mons ve·ne·ris \'mänz-'ve-nə-rəs\ *n, pl* **mon·tes veneris** \'män-,tēz-\ [NL, lit., eminence of Venus or of venery] (1621) : the mons pubis of the human female

mon·ta·dale \'män-tə-,dāl\ *n* [*Montana* state + *dale*] (1949) : any of an American breed of white-faced hornless sheep noted for heavy fleece and good meat conformation

¹mon·tage \män-'täzh, mōⁿ(n)-, -'täzh\ *n* [F, fr. *monter* to mount] (1929) **1** : the production of a rapid succession of images in a motion picture to illustrate an association of ideas **2** a : a literary, musical, or artistic composite of juxtaposed more or less heterogeneous elements **b** : a composite picture made by combining several separate pictures **3** : a heterogeneous mixture : JUMBLE 〈a ~ of emotions〉

²montage *vt* **mon·taged; mon·tag·ing** (1944) : to combine into or depict in a montage

mon·ta·gnard \,mōⁿ-,tän-'yär(d)\ *n, often cap* [F, mountaineer, fr. *montagne* mountain, fr. OF *montaigne*] (1842) : a member of any of various peoples inhabiting the highlands of central and southern Vietnam — **montagnard** *adj, often cap*

Mon·ta·gue \'män-tə-,gyü\ *n* : the family of Romeo in Shakespeare's *Romeo and Juliet*

mon·tane \,män-'tän, 'män-,\ *adj* [L *montanus* of a mountain — more at MOUNTAIN] (1863) **1** : of, relating to, growing in, or being the biogeographic zone of relatively moist cool upland slopes below timberline dominated by large coniferous trees **2** : of, relating to, or made up of montane plants or animals

Mon·ta·nist \'män-t²n-ist\ *n* [*Montanus,* 2d cent. A.D. Phrygian schismatic] (1577) : an adherent of a Christian sect arising in the late second century and stressing apocalyptic expectations, the continuing prophetic gifts of the Spirit, and strict ascetic discipline — **Mon·ta·nism** \-t²n-,i-zəm\ *n*

mon·tan wax \'män-t²n-\ *n* [L *montanus* of a mountain] (1908) : a hard brittle mineral wax obtained usu. from lignites by extraction and used esp. in polishes, carbon paper, and insulating compositions

mon·te \'män-tē\ *n* [Sp, bank, mountain, heap, fr. It, fr. L *mont-, mons* mountain] (1824) **1** : a card game in which players select any two of four cards turned face up in a layout and bet that one of them will be matched before the other as cards are dealt one at a time from the pack — called also *monte bank* **2** : THREE-CARD MONTE

Mon·te Car·lo \,män-ti-'kär-(,)lō\ *adj* [*Monte Carlo,* Monaco, famous for its gambling casino] (1949) : of, relating to, or involving the use of random sampling techniques and often the use of computer simulation to obtain approximate solutions to mathematical or physical problems esp. in terms of a range of values each of which has a calculated probability of being the solution ⟨*Monte Carlo* calculations⟩

mon·teith \män-'tēth\ *n* [*Monteith*, 17th cent. Scot. eccentric who wore a cloak with a scalloped hem] (1683) : a large silver punch bowl with scalloped rim

Mon·te·rey cypress \'män-tə-,rā-\ *n* [*Monterey*, California] (1873) : a California cypress (*Cupressus macrocarpa*) that is endemic to the Monterey and Carmel seacoast and is often planted for ornament or in a windbreak

Monterey Jack *n* (ca. 1947) : a semisoft whole-milk cheese with high moisture content

Monterey pine *n* (1834) : a pine (*Pinus radiata*) native to coastal California that is widely grown esp. in the southern hemisphere for its wood

mon·te·ro \män-'ter-(,)ō\ *n, pl* **-ros** [Sp, hunter, fr. *monte* mountain] (1622) : a round hunter's cap with ear flaps

Mon·te·zu·ma's revenge \,män-tə-'zü-məz-\ *n* [*Montezuma* II] (1962) : diarrhea contracted in Mexico esp. by tourists

month \'mən(t)th\ *n, pl* **months** \'mən(t)s, 'mən(t)ths\ [ME, fr. OE *mōnath*; akin to OHG *mānōd* month, OE *mōna* moon] (bef. 12c) 1 : a measure of time corresponding nearly to the period of the moon's revolution and amounting to approximately 4 weeks or 30 days or 1/12 of a year 2 *pl* : an indefinite usu. extended period of time ⟨he has been gone for ~*s*⟩ 3 : one ninth of the typical duration of human pregnancy ⟨she was in her eighth ~⟩

month-long \'mən(t)th-'lȯŋ\ *adj* (1843) : lasting a month

1**month·ly** \-lē\ *adv* (ca. 1534) : once a month : by the month

2**monthly** *adj* (1572) 1 a : of or relating to a month b : payable or reckoned by the month 2 : lasting a month 3 : occurring or appearing every month

3**monthly** *n, pl* **monthlies** (1833) 1 : a monthly periodical 2 *pl* : a menstrual period

Monthly Meeting *n* (ca. 1772) : a district unit of an organization of Friends

month's mind *n* (15c) : a Roman Catholic requiem mass held a month after a person's death

Mont·mo·ren·cy \,mänt-mə-'ren(t)-sē\ *n* [F, fr. *Montmorency*, France] (1924) : a cherry that is grown commercially for its bright red sour fruit; *also* : the fruit

mont·mo·ril·lon·ite \,mänt-mə-'ri-lə-,nīt, -'rē-ə-,nīt\ *n* [F, fr. *Montmorillon*, commune in western France] (1854) : a soft clayey mineral that is a hydrous aluminum silicate with considerable capacity for exchanging part of the aluminum for magnesium and bases — **mont·mo·ril·lon·it·ic** \-,ri-lə-'ni-tik, -,rē-ə-'ni-tik\ *adj*

Mon·tra·chet \,mōn-trä-'she\ *n* [F, fr. *Montrachet*, vineyard in Burgundy, France] (1833) : a dry white burgundy wine

mon·u·ment \'män-yə-mənt\ *n* [ME, fr. L *monumentum*, lit., memorial, fr. *monēre* to remind — more at MIND] (13c) 1 *obs* : a burial vault : SEPULCHRE 2 : a written legal document or record : TREATISE 3 a (1) : a lasting evidence, reminder, or example of someone or something notable or great (2) : a distinguished person b : a memorial stone or a building erected in remembrance of a person or event 4 *archaic* : an identifying mark : EVIDENCE; *also* : PORTENT, SIGN 5 *obs* : a carved statue : EFFIGY 6 : a boundary or position marker (as a stone) 7 : NATIONAL MONUMENT 8 : a written tribute

mon·u·men·tal \,män-yə-'men-t³l\ *adj* (1604) 1 : of or relating to a monument 2 : serving as or resembling a monument : MASSIVE; *also* : highly significant : OUTSTANDING 3 : very great — **mon·u·men·tal·i·ty** \-mən-'ta-lə-tē, -,men-\ *n* — **mon·u·men·tal·ly** \-t³l-ē\ *adv*

mon·u·men·tal·ize \-'men-t³l-,īz\ *vt* **-ized; -iz·ing** (1857) : to record or memorialize lastingly by a monument

mon·u·ron \'män-yə-,rän\ *n* [*mon*- + *urea* + 1-*on*] (ca. 1957) : a persistent herbicide C₉H₁₁ClN₂O used esp. to control broad-leaved weeds

mon·zo·nite \'män-'zō-,nīt, 'män-zə-\ *n* [F, fr. Mt. *Monzoni*, Italy] (1895) : a granular igneous rock composed of plagioclase and orthoclase in about equal quantities together with augite and a little biotite

moo \'mü\ *vi* [imit.] (1549) : to make the throat noise of a cow — **moo** *n*

mooch \'müch\ *vb* [prob. fr. F dial. *muchier* to hide, lurk] *vi* (1851) 1 : to wander aimlessly : AMBLE; *also* : SNEAK 2 : SPONGE, CADGE ~ *vt* 1 : to take surreptitiously : STEAL 2 : BEG, CADGE — **mooch·er** *n*

1**mood** \'müd\ *n* [ME, fr. OE *mōd*; akin to OHG *muot* mood] (bef. 12c) 1 : a conscious state of mind or predominant emotion : FEELING; *also* : the expression of mood esp. in art or literature 2 *archaic* : a fit of anger : RAGE 3 a : a prevailing attitude : DISPOSITION b : a receptive state of mind predisposing to action c : a distinctive atmosphere or context : AURA

2**mood** *n* [alter. of 1*mode*] (1569) 1 : the form of a syllogism as determined by the quantity and quality of its constituent propositions 2 : distinction of form or a particular set of inflectional forms of a verb to express whether the action or state it denotes is conceived as fact or in some other manner (as command, possibility, or wish) 3 : MODE 1b

moody \'mü-dē\ *adj* **mood·i·er; -est** (1593) 1 : subject to depression : GLOOMY 2 : subject to moods : TEMPERAMENTAL 3 : expressive of a mood — **mood·i·ly** \'mü-d³l-ē\ *adv* — **mood·i·ness** \'mü-dē-nəs\ *n*

moo·la *or* **moo·lah** \'mü-(,)lä, -lə\ *n* [origin unknown] (1939) *slang* : MONEY

1**moon** \'mün\ *n* [ME *mone*, fr. OE *mōna*; akin to OHG *māno* moon, L *mensis* month, Gk *mēn* month, *mēnē* moon] (bef. 12c) 1 *a often cap* : the earth's natural satellite that shines by the sun's reflected light, revolves about the earth from west to east in about 29½ days with reference to the sun or about 27⅓ days with reference to the stars, and has a diameter of 2160 miles (3475 kilometers), a mean distance from the earth of about 238,900 miles (384,400 kilometers), and a mass about one eightieth that of the earth — usu. used with *the* b : one complete moon cycle consisting of four phases c : SATELLITE 2; *specif* : a natural satellite of a planet 2 : an indefinite usu. extended period of time ⟨a labor of many ~*s*⟩ 3 : MOONLIGHT 4 : something that resembles a moon: as a : a highly translucent spot on old porcelain b : LUNULE c *slang* : naked buttocks 5 : something impossible or inaccessible ⟨reach for the ~⟩ — **moon·like** \-,līk\ *adj* — **over the moon** : very pleased : in high spirits

2**moon** *vt* (1836) 1 : to spend in idle reverie : DREAM — used with *away* 2 *slang* : to expose one's naked buttocks to ~ *vi* : to spend time in idle reverie : behave abstractedly

moon·beam \'mün-,bēm\ *n* (1590) : a ray of light from the moon

moon blindness *n* (ca. 1720) : a recurrent inflammation of the eye of the horse

moon·calf \'mün-,kaf, -,kȧf\ *n* (1614) : a foolish or absentminded person : SIMPLETON

moon·dust \-,dəst\ *n* (ca. 1959) : fine dry particles of the moon's soil

moon·eye \-,ī\ *n* (1842) : any of a genus (*Hiodon*) of silvery No. American freshwater fishes that resemble shad

moon·eyed \-'īd\ *adj* (1699) : having the eyes wide open

moon·faced \-,fāst\ *adj* (1855) : having a round face

moon·fish \-,fish\ *n, pl* **moonfish** *or* **moon·fish·es** (1646) : any of various compressed often short deep-bodied silvery or yellowish marine fishes: as a : OPAH b : PLATY

moon·flow·er \-,flaü(-ə)r\ *n* (ca. 1909) : a tropical American morning glory (*Calonyction aculeatum* syn. *Ipomoea alba*) with fragrant flowers; *also* : any of several related plants

Moon·ie \'mü-nē\ *n* [Sun Myung *Moon* b1920 Korean evangelist] (1974) : a member of the Unification Church founded by Sun Myung Moon

moon·ish \'mü-nish\ *adj* (15c) : influenced by the moon; *also* : CAPRICIOUS — **moon·ish·ly** *adv*

moon·less \'mün-ləs\ *adj* (1508) : lacking the light of the moon

moon·let \-lət\ *n* (1832) : a small natural or artificial satellite

1**moonlight** \-,līt\ *n* (14c) : the light of the moon

2**moonlight** *vi* **moon·light·ed; moon·light·ing** [back-formation fr. *moonlighter*] (1957) : to hold a second job in addition to a regular one — **moon·light·er** *n*

moon·lit \-,lit\ *adj* (ca. 1827) : lighted by the moon

moon·quake \-,kwāk\ *n* (1946) : a seismic event on the moon

MONTHS OF THE PRINCIPAL CALENDARS

GREGORIAN[1]			JEWISH			ISLAMIC		
Name		Days	Name		Days	Name		Days
January begins 10 days after the winter solstice		31	Tishri in year 5753 began Sept. 28, 1992		30	Muharram[4] in A.H. 1413 began July 2, 1992		30
February in leap years		28 29	Heshvan		29 *or* 30	Safar		29
March		31	Kislev		29 *or* 30	Rabi I		30
April		30	Tebet		29	Rabi II		29
May		31	Shebat		30	Jumada I		30
June		30	Adar[2]		29 *or* 30	Jumada II		29
July		31	Nisan[3]		30	Rajab		30
August		31	Iyar		29	Sha'ban		29
September		30	Sivan		30	Ramadan		30
October		31	Tammuz		29	Shawwal		29
November		30	Ab		30	Dhu'l-Qa'dah		30
December		31	Elul		29	Dhu'l-Hijja in leap years		29 30

[1] The equinoxes occur about March 21 and September 23, the solstices about June 22 and December 22.

[2] In leap years an intercalary month of 30 days takes the place of Adar, and is sometimes called Adar I. Adar then becomes the 29-day Veadar or Adar Sheni (sometimes called Adar II), and retains the usual festivals and holidays of Adar.

[3] The first month of the ecclesiastical year; anciently called Abib.

[4] Retrogresses through the seasons; the Islamic year is lunar and each month begins at the approximate new moon; the year 1 A.H. began on Friday, July 16, A.D. 622.

moon·rise \-,rīz\ *n* (1728) **1** : the rising of the moon above the horizon **2** : the time of the moon's rising

moon·scape \-,skāp\ *n* (1916) : the surface of the moon as seen or as depicted; *also* : a landscape resembling this surface

moon·seed \-,sēd\ *n* (1739) : a twining plant (*Menispermum canadense* of the family Menispermaceae, the moonseed family) of eastern No. America that has crescent-shaped seeds and black fruits

moon·set \-,set\ *n* (1845) **1** : the descent of the moon below the horizon **2** : the time of the moon's setting

moon shell *n* (1936) : any of a cosmopolitan family (Naticidae) of carnivorous marine snails having smooth globose shells

moon shell

moon·shine \'mün-,shīn\ *n* (15c) **1** : MOONLIGHT **2** : empty talk : NONSENSE **3** : intoxicating liquor; *esp* : illegally distilled corn whiskey

moon·shin·er \-,shī-nər\ *n* (1860) : a maker or seller of illicit whiskey

moon shot *n* (1958) : a spacecraft mission to the moon

moon·stone \-,stōn\ *n* (1632) : a transparent or translucent feldspar of pearly or opaline luster used as a gem

moon·struck \-,strək\ *adj* (1674) : affected by or as if by the moon: as **a** : mentally unbalanced **b** : romantically sentimental **c** : lost in fantasy or reverie

moon·ward \-wərd\ *adv* (1855) : toward the moon

moony \'mü-nē\ *adj* (ca. 1586) **1** : of or relating to the moon **2 a** : crescent-shaped **b** : resembling the full moon : ROUND **3** : MOONLIT **4** : DREAMY, MOONSTRUCK

¹moor \'mur\ *n* [ME *mor*, fr. OE *mōr*; akin to OHG *muor* moor] (bef. 12c) **1** *chiefly Brit* : an expanse of open rolling infertile land **2** : a boggy area; *esp* : one that is peaty and dominated by grasses and sedges

²moor *vb* [ME *moren*; akin to MD *meren, maren* to tie, moor] *vt* (15c) : to make fast with or as if with cables, lines, or anchors ~ *vi* **1** : to secure a boat by mooring : ANCHOR **2** : to be made fast

Moor \'mur\ *n* [ME *More*, fr. MF, fr. L *Maurus* inhabitant of Mauretania] (14c) **1** : one of the Arab and Berber conquerors of Spain **2** : BERBER — **Moor·ish** \-ish\ *adj*

moor·age \'mur-ij\ *n* (1648) **1** : an act of mooring **2** : a place to moor

moor·hen \'mur-,hen\ *n* (14c) : the common gallinule (*Gallinula chloropus*) of the New World, Eurasia, and Africa

moor·ing \-iŋ\ *n* (15c) **1** : an act of making fast a boat or aircraft with lines or anchors **2 a** : a place where or an object to which something (as a craft) can be moored **b** : a device (as a line or chain) by which an object is secured in place **3** : an established practice or stabilizing influence : ANCHORAGE 2 — usu. used in pl.

moor·land \-lənd, -,land\ *n* (bef. 12c) : land consisting of moors : a stretch of moor

moose \'müs\ *n, pl* **moose** [of Algonquian origin; akin to Massachuset *moos* moose] (1603) **1** : a ruminant mammal (*Alces alces*) with humped shoulders, long legs, and broadly palmated antlers that is the largest existing member of the deer family and inhabits forested areas of Canada, the northern U.S., Europe, and Asia **2** *cap* [Loyal Order of *Moose*] : a member of a major benevolent and fraternal order

¹moot \'müt\ *n* [ME, fr. OE *mōt, gemōt*; akin to MHG *muoze* meeting] (bef. 12c) **1** : a deliberative assembly primarily for the administration of justice; *esp* : one held by the freemen of an Anglo-Saxon community **2** *obs* : ARGUMENT, DISCUSSION

²moot *vt* (bef. 12c) **1** *archaic* : to discuss from a legal standpoint : ARGUE **2 a** : to bring up for discussion : BROACH **b** : DEBATE

³moot *adj* (ca. 1587) **1 a** : open to question : DEBATABLE **b** : subjected to discussion : DISPUTED **2** : deprived of practical significance : made abstract or purely academic

moot court *n* (1788) : a mock court in which law students argue hypothetical cases for practice

¹mop \'mäp\ *n* [ME *mappe*] (15c) **1** : an implement made of absorbent material fastened to a handle and used esp. for cleaning floors **2** : something that resembles a mop; *esp* : a thick mass of hair

²mop *vb* **mopped; mop·ping** *vt* (1709) : to use a mop on: as **a** : to clean or clear away by mopping (~ the floors) — often used with *up* (~ up the spillage) **b** : to wipe as if with a mop (*mopped* his brow with a handkerchief) ~ *vi* : to clean a surface (as a floor) with a mop — **mop·per** *n*

mop·board \'mäp-,bōrd, -,bȯrd\ *n* (1853) : BASEBOARD

¹mope \'mōp\ *vi* **moped; mop·ing** [prob. fr. obs. *mop, mope* fool] (1568) **1** *archaic* : to act in a dazed or stupid manner **2** : to give oneself up to brooding : become listless or dejected **3** : to move slowly or aimlessly : DAWDLE — **mop·er** *n* — **mop·ey** \'mō-pē\ *adj*

²mope *n* (1693) **1** : one that mopes **2** *pl* : BLUES 1

mo·ped \'mō-,ped\ *n* [Sw, fr. *motor* motor + *pedal* pedal] (1955) : a lightweight low-powered motorbike that can be pedaled

mop·pet \'mä-pət\ *n* [obs. E *mop* fool, child] (1601) **1** *archaic* : BABY, DARLING **2** : CHILD

mop–up \'mäp-,əp\ *n* (1900) : a concluding action

mop up *vt* (ca. 1811) **1** *Brit* : to consume eagerly **2** : to gather as if by absorbing : GARNER (*mopped up* all the awards) **3** : to overcome decisively : TROUNCE **4** : to clear (an area) of remaining pockets of resistance in the wake of a military offensive ~ *vi* : to complete a project or transaction

mo·quette \mō-'ket\ *n* [F] (1762) : a carpet or upholstery fabric having a velvety pile

mor \'mȯr\ *n* [Dan, lit., humus] (1931) : forest humus that forms a layer of largely organic matter abruptly distinct from the mineral soil beneath

mo·ra \'mȯr-ə, 'mōr-\ *n, pl* **mo·rae** \'mȯr-(,)ē, 'mōr-, -,ī\ *or* **mo·ras** [L, delay; akin to OIr *maraid* it lasts] (1832) : the minimal unit of measure in quantitative verse equivalent to the time of an average short syllable

mo·raine \mə-'rān\ *n* [F, fr. F dial. (Savoy) *morēna*] (1789) : an accumulation of earth and stones carried and finally deposited by a glacier — **mo·rain·al** \-'rā-n°l\ *adj* — **mo·rain·ic** \-'rā-nik\ *adj*

¹mor·al \'mȯr-əl, 'mär-\ *adj* [ME, fr. MF, fr. L *moralis*, fr. *mor-, mos*

custom] (14c) **1 a** : of or relating to principles of right and wrong in behavior : ETHICAL (~ judgments) **b** : expressing or teaching a conception of right behavior (a ~ poem) **c** : conforming to a standard of right behavior **d** : sanctioned by or operative on one's conscience or ethical judgment (a ~ obligation) **e** : capable of right and wrong action (a ~ agent) **2** : probable though not proved : VIRTUAL (a ~ certainty) **3** : having the effects of such on the mind, confidence, or will (a ~ victory) (~ support) — **mor·al·ly** \-ə-lē\ *adv*

syn MORAL, ETHICAL, VIRTUOUS, RIGHTEOUS, NOBLE mean conforming to a standard of what is right and good. MORAL implies conformity to established sanctioned codes or accepted notions of right and wrong (the basic *moral* values of a community). ETHICAL may suggest the involvement of more difficult or subtle questions of rightness, fairness, or equity (committed to the highest *ethical* principles). VIRTUOUS implies the possession or manifestation of moral excellence in character (not a religious person, but *virtuous* nevertheless). RIGHTEOUS stresses guiltlessness or blamelessness and often suggests the sanctimonious (wished to be *righteous* before God and the world). NOBLE implies moral eminence and freedom from anything petty, mean, or dubious in conduct and character (had the *noblest* of reasons for seeking office).

²mor·al \'mȯr-əl, 'mär-; *3 is* mə-'ral\ *n* (15c) **1 a** : the moral significance or practical lesson (as of a story) **b** : a passage pointing out usu. in conclusion the lesson to be drawn from a story **2** *pl* **a** : moral practices or teachings : modes of conduct **b** : ETHICS **3** : MORALE

mo·rale \mə-'ral\ *n* [in sense 1, fr. F. fr. fem. of *moral*, adj.; in other senses, modif. of F *moral* morale, fr. *moral*, adj.] (1752) **1** : moral principles, teachings, or conduct **2 a** : the mental and emotional condition (as of enthusiasm, confidence, or loyalty) of an individual or group with regard to the function or tasks at hand **b** : a sense of common purpose with respect to a group : ESPRIT DE CORPS **3** : the level of individual psychological well-being based on such factors as a sense of purpose and confidence in the future

moral hazard *n* (ca. 1917) : the possibility of loss to an insurance company arising from the character or circumstances of the insured

mor·al·ise *Brit var of* MORALIZE

mor·al·ism \'mȯr-ə-,li-zəm, 'mär-\ *n* (1828) **1 a** : the habit or practice of moralizing **b** : a conventional moral attitude or saying **2** : an often exaggerated emphasis on morality (as in politics)

mor·al·ist \-list\ *n* (1621) **1** : one who leads a moral life **2** : a philosopher or writer concerned with moral principles and problems **3** : one concerned with regulating the morals of others

mor·al·is·tic \,mȯr-ə-'lis-tik, ,mär-\ *adj* (1865) **1** : characterized by or expressive of a concern with morality **2** : characterized by or expressive of a narrow and conventional moral attitude — **mor·al·is·ti·cal·ly** \-ti-k(ə-)lē\ *adv*

mo·ral·i·ty \mə-'ra-lə-tē, mȯ-\ *n, pl* **-ties** (14c) **1 a** : a moral discourse, statement, or lesson **b** : a literary or other imaginative work teaching a moral lesson **2 a** : a doctrine or system of moral conduct **b** *pl* : particular moral principles or rules of conduct **3** : conformity to ideals of right human conduct **4** : moral conduct : VIRTUE

morality play *n* (1929) **1** : an allegorical play popular esp. in the 15th and 16th centuries in which the characters personify abstract qualities or concepts (as virtues, vices, or death) **2** : something which involves a direct conflict between right and wrong or good and evil and from which a moral lesson may be drawn

mor·al·ize \'mȯr-ə-,līz, 'mär-\ *vb* **-ized; -iz·ing** *vt* (15c) **1** : to explain or interpret morally **2 a** : to give a moral quality or direction to **b** : to improve the morals of ~ *vi* : to make moral reflections — **mor·al·i·za·tion** \,mȯr-ə-lə-'zā-shən, ,mär-\ *n* — **mor·al·iz·er** \'mȯr-ə-,lī-zər, 'mär-\ *n*

moral philosophy *n* (1606) : ETHICS; *also* : the study of human conduct and values

mo·rass \mə-'ras, mȯ-\ *n* [D *moeras*, modif. of OF *maresc*, of Gmc origin; akin to OE *mersc* marsh — more at MARSH] (1655) **1** : MARSH, SWAMP **2** : something that traps, confuses, or impedes (a ~ of troubles) — **mo·rassy** \-'ra-sē\ *adj*

mor·a·to·ri·um \,mȯr-ə-'tōr-ē-əm, ,mär-, -'tȯr-\ *n, pl* **-riums** *or* **-ria** \-ē-ə\ [NL, fr. LL, neut. of *moratorius* dilatory, fr. L *morari* to delay, fr. *mora* delay] (1875) **1 a** : a legally authorized period of delay in the performance of a legal obligation or the payment of a debt **b** : a waiting period set by an authority **2** : a suspension of activity

Mo·ra·vi·an \mə-'rā-vē-ən\ *n* (1555) **1 a** : a native or inhabitant of Moravia **b** : the group of Czech dialects spoken in Moravia **2** : a member of a Protestant denomination arising from a 15th century religious reform movement in Bohemia and Moravia — **Moravian** *adj*

mo·ray eel \mə-'rā-, 'mȯr-(,)ā\ *n* [Pg *moréia*, fr. L *muraena*, fr. Gk *myraina*] (1926) : any of numerous often brightly colored eels (family Muraenidae) that have sharp teeth capable of inflicting a severe bite, that occur in warm seas, and that include a chiefly Mediterranean eel (*Muraena helena*) sometimes used for food — called also *moray*

mor·bid \'mȯr-bəd\ *adj* [L *morbidus* diseased, fr. *morbus* disease] (1656) **1 a** : of, relating to, or characteristic of disease (~ anatomy) **b** : affected with or induced by disease (a ~ condition) **c** : productive of disease (~ substances) **2** : abnormally susceptible to or characterized by gloomy or unwholesome feelings **3** : GRISLY, GRUESOME (~ details) (~ curiosity) — **mor·bid·ly** *adv* — **mor·bid·ness** *n*

mor·bid·i·ty \mȯr-'bi-də-tē\ *n* (ca. 1721) **1** : the quality or state of being morbid **2** : the relative incidence of disease

mor·ceau \mȯr-'sō\ *n, pl* **mor·ceaux** \-'sō(z)\ [F, fr. OF *morsel* morsel] (1751) : a short literary or musical piece

mor·dan·cy \'mȯr-d°n(t)-sē\ *n* (ca. 1656) **1** : a biting and caustic quality of style : INCISIVENESS **2** : a sharply critical or bitter quality of thought or feeling : HARSHNESS

¹mor·dant \'mȯr-d°nt\ *adj* [ME, fr. MF, prp. of *mordre* to bite, fr. L *mordēre*; perh. akin to Skt *mrdnāti* he presses, rubs] (15c) **1** : biting and caustic in thought, manner, or style : INCISIVE (a ~ wit) **2** : acting as a mordant **3** : BURNING, PUNGENT **syn** see CAUSTIC — **mor·dant·ly** *adv*

²mordant *n* (1791) **1** : a chemical that fixes a dye in or on a substance by combining with the dye to form an insoluble compound **2** : a corroding substance used in etching

³mordant *vt* (1836) : to treat with a mordant

Mor·de·cai \'mȯr-di-ˌkī\ *n* [Heb *Mordēkhai*] : a relative of Esther who gives advice on saving the Jews from the destruction planned by Haman

mor·dent \'mȯr-dᵊnt, mȯr-'dent\ *n* [It *mordente*, fr. L *mordent-*, *mordens*, prp. of *mordēre*] (1806) : a musical ornament made by a quick alternation of a principal tone with the tone immediately below it

¹**more** \'mōr, 'mȯr\ *adj* [ME, fr. OE *māra*; akin to OE *mā*, adv., more, OHG *mēr*, OIr *mó* more] (bef. 12c) **1** : GREATER ⟨something ~ than she expected⟩ **2** : ADDITIONAL, FURTHER ⟨~ guests arrived⟩

²**more** *adv* (bef. 12c) **1 a** : in addition ⟨a couple of times ~⟩ **b** : MOREOVER **2** : to a greater or higher degree — often used with an adjective or adverb to form the comparative ⟨~ evenly matched⟩

³**more** *n* (bef. 12c) **1** : a greater quantity, number, or amount ⟨liked the idea better the ~ I thought about it⟩ **2** : something additional : an additional amount **3** *obs* : persons of higher rank

⁴**more** *pron, sing or pl in constr* (13c) : additional persons or things or a greater amount ⟨~ were found as the search continued⟩ ⟨~ was spilled⟩

more and more *adv* (13c) : to a progressively increasing extent

mo·reen \mə-'rēn, mȯ-\ *n* [prob. irreg. fr. *moire*] (ca. 1691) : a strong fabric of wool, wool and cotton, or cotton with a plain glossy or moiré finish

mo·rel \mə-'rel, mȯ-\ *n* [F *morille*, prob. fr. (assumed) VL *mauricula*, fr. *maurus* brown, fr. L *Maurus* inhabitant of Mauretania] (1672) : any of several edible fungi (genus *Morchella*, esp. *M. esculenta*) having a cap with a highly pitted surface

mo·rel·lo \mə-'re-(ˌ)lō\ *n, pl* **-los** [prob. modif. of Flem *amarelle*, *marelle*, fr. ML *amarellum*, a sour cherry, fr. L *amarus* bitter, sour] (1598) : a cultivated sour cherry (as the Montmorency) having a dark-colored skin and juice

more or less *adv* (13c) **1** : to a varying or undetermined extent or degree : SOMEWHAT ⟨they were *more or less* willing to help⟩ **2** : with small variations : APPROXIMATELY ⟨contains 16 acres *more or less*⟩

more·over \mōr-'ō-vər, mȯr-, 'mōr-ˌ, 'mȯr-ˌ\ *adv* (14c) : in addition to what has been said : BESIDES

mo·res \'mȯr-ˌāz, 'mōr- *also* -(ˌ)ēz\ *n pl* [L, pl. of *mor-*, *mos* custom] (ca. 1899) **1** : the fixed morally binding customs of a particular group **2** : moral attitudes **3** : HABITS, MANNERS

¹**mo·resque** \mȯ-'resk, mə-\ *adj, often cap* [F, fr. Sp *morisco*, fr. *moro* Moor, fr. L *Maurus*] (ca. 1611) : having the characteristics of Moorish art or architecture

²**moresque** *n, often cap* (ca. 1752) : an ornament or decorative motif in Moorish style

mor·gan \'mȯr-gən\ *n* [Thomas Hunt *Morgan*] (1919) **1** : a unit of inferred distance between genes on a chromosome that is used in constructing genetic maps and is equal to the distance for which the frequency of crossing over between specific pairs of genes is 100 percent **2** : CENTIMORGAN

Mor·gan \'mȯr-gən\ *n* [Justin *Morgan* †1798 Am. teacher] (1841) : any of an American breed of light strong horses originated in Vermont from the progeny of one prepotent stallion of uncertain ancestry

mor·ga·nat·ic \ˌmȯr-gə-'na-tik\ *adj* [NL *matrimonium ad morganaticam*, lit., marriage with morning gift] (ca. 1741) : of, relating to, or being a marriage between a member of a royal or noble family and a person of inferior rank in which the rank of the inferior partner remains unchanged and the children of the marriage do not succeed to the titles, fiefs, or entailed property of the parent of higher rank — **mor·ga·nat·i·cal·ly** \-ti-k(ə-)lē\ *adv*

mor·gan·ite \'mȯr-gə-ˌnīt\ *n* [J. P. *Morgan* †1913] (1911) : a rose-colored gem variety of beryl

Morgan le Fay \-lə-'fā\ *n* [OF *Morgain la fee* Morgan the fairy] : a sorceress and sister of King Arthur

mor·gen \'mȯr-gə(n)\ *n, pl* **morgen** [D, lit., morning] (1626) : a Dutch and southern African unit of land area equal to 2.116 acres (0.856 hectare)

morgue \'mȯrg\ *n* [F] (1821) **1** : a place where the bodies of persons found dead are kept until identified and claimed by relatives or are released for burial **2** : a collection of reference works and files of reference material in a newspaper or news periodical office

mor·i·bund \'mȯr-ə-(ˌ)bənd, 'mär-\ *adj* [L *moribundus*, fr. *mori* to die — more at MURDER] (ca. 1721) **1** : being in the state of dying : approaching death **2** : being in a state of inactivity or obsolescence — **mor·i·bund·i·ty** \ˌmȯr-ə-'bən-də-tē, ˌmär-\ *n*

¹**mo·ri·on** \'mȯr-ē-ˌän, 'mōr-\ *n* [MF] (1563) : a high-crested helmet with no visor

²**morion** *n* [modif. of L *mormorion*] (1748) : a nearly black variety of smoky quartz

Mo·ris·co \mə-'ris-(ˌ)kō, mȯ-\ *n, pl* **-cos** *or* **-coes** [Sp, fr. *morisco*, adj., fr. *moro* Moor] (1629) : MOOR; *esp* : a Spanish Moor — **Morisco** *adj*

Mor·mon \'mȯr-mən\ *n* **1** : the ancient redactor and compiler of the Book of Mormon presented as divine revelation by Joseph Smith **2** : LATTER-DAY SAINT; *esp* : a member of the Church of Jesus Christ of Latter-day Saints — **Mor·mon·ism** \-mə-ˌni-zəm\ *n*

Mormon cricket *n* (1896) : a large dark wingless katydid (*Anabrus simplex*) that resembles a cricket and is found in the arid parts of the western U.S. where it is occas. an abundant pest of crops

morn \'mȯrn\ *n* [ME, fr. OE *morgen*; akin to OHG *morgan* morning and perh. to Gk *marmairein* to sparkle] (bef. 12c) **1** : DAWN **2** : MORNING

Mor·nay sauce \mȯr-'nā-\ *n* [Philippe de *Mornay*] (ca. 1924) : a cheese-flavored cream sauce

morn·ing \'mȯr-niŋ\ *n* [ME, fr. *morn* + *-ing* (as in *evening*)] (13c) **1 a** : DAWN **b** : the time from sunrise to noon **c** : the time from midnight to noon **2** : a period of first development : BEGINNING

morn·ing-after pill \ˌmȯr-niŋ-'af-tər-\ *n* [fr. its being taken after rather than before intercourse] (1966) : an oral drug that interferes with pregnancy by blocking implantation of a fertilized egg in the human uterus

morning glory *n* (1814) : any of various usu. twining plants (genus *Ipomoea* of the family Convolvulaceae, the morning-glory family) with showy trumpet-shaped flowers; *broadly* : a plant of the morning-glory family including herbs, shrubs, or trees with alternate leaves and regular pentamerous flowers

morning line *n* (ca. 1935) : a bookmaker's list of entries for a race meet and the probable odds on each that is printed or posted before the betting begins

Morning Prayer *n* (1552) : a service of liturgical prayer used for regular morning worship in churches of the Anglican communion

morn·ings \'mȯr-niŋz\ *adv* (1652) : in the morning repeatedly : on any morning

morning sickness *n* (1879) : nausea and vomiting that occur on rising in the morning esp. during the earlier months of pregnancy

morning star *n* (1535) : a bright planet (as Venus) seen in the eastern sky before or at sunrise

Mo·ro \'mȯr-(ˌ)ō, 'mōr-\ *n, pl* **Moros** [Sp, lit., Moor, fr. L *Maurus*] (1886) **1** : a member of any of several Muslim peoples of the southern Philippines **2** : any of the Austronesian languages of the Moro peoples

mo·roc·co \mə-'rä-(ˌ)kō\ *n* [*Morocco*, Africa] (1634) : a fine leather from goatskin tanned with sumac

mo·ron \'mȯr-ˌän, 'mōr-\ *n* [irreg. fr. Gk *mōros* foolish, stupid] (1910) **1** : a mentally retarded person who has a potential mental age of between 8 and 12 years and is capable of doing routine work under supervision **2** : a very stupid person — **mo·ron·ic** \mə-'rä-nik, mō-\ *adj* — **mo·ron·i·cal·ly** \-ni-k(ə-)lē\ *adv* — **mo·ron·ism** \'mȯr-ˌä-ˌni-zəm, 'mōr-\ *n* — **mo·ron·i·ty** \mə-'rä-nə-tē, mō-\ *n*

mo·rose \mə-'rōs, mō-\ *adj* [L *morosus*, lit., capricious, fr. *mor-*, *mos* will] (1565) **1** : having a sullen and gloomy disposition **2** : marked by or expressive of gloom *syn* see SULLEN — **mo·rose·ly** *adv* — **mo·rose·ness** *n* — **mo·ros·i·ty** \-'rä-sə-tē\ *n*

morph \'mȯrf\ *n* [back-formation fr. *morpheme*] (1947) **1 a** : ALLOMORPH **b** : a distinctive collocation of phones (as a portmanteau form) that serves as the realization of more than one morpheme in a context (as the French *du* for the sequence of *de* and *le*) **2 a** : a local population of a species that consists of interbreeding organisms and is distinguishable from other populations by morphology or behavior though capable of interbreeding with them **b** : a phenotypic variant of a species

morph- *or* **morpho-** *comb form* [G, fr. Gk, fr. *morphē*] **1** : form ⟨*mor*phogenesis⟩ **2** : morpheme ⟨*morpho*phonemics⟩

-morph *n comb form* [ISV, fr. *-morphous*] : one having (such) a form ⟨iso*morph*⟩

mor·phac·tin \mȯr-'fak-tən\ *n* [prob. fr. *morph-* + *active* + ¹*-in*] (1966) : any of several synthetic fluorine-containing compounds that tend to produce morphological changes and suppress growth in plants

mor·phal·lax·is \ˌmȯr-fə-'lak-səs\ *n, pl* **-lax·es** \-ˌsēz\ [NL, fr. *morph-* + Gk *allaxis* exchange, fr. *allassein* to change, exchange, fr. *allos* other — more at ELSE] (1901) : regeneration of a part or organism from a fragment by reorganization without cell proliferation

mor·pheme \'mȯr-ˌfēm\ *n* [F *morphème*, fr. Gk *morphē* form] (1926) : a distinctive collocation of phonemes (as the free form *pin* or the bound form *-s* of *pins*) that contains no smaller meaningful parts — **mor·phe·mic** \mȯr-'fē-mik\ *adj* — **mor·phe·mi·cal·ly** \-mi-k(ə-)lē\ *adv*

mor·phe·mics \mȯr-'fē-miks\ *n pl but sing in constr* (1947) **1** : a branch of linguistic analysis that consists of the study of morphemes **2** : the structure of a language in terms of morphemes

Mor·pheus \'mȯr-fē-əs, -ˌfyüs, -ˌfüs\ *n* [L, fr. Gk] : the Greek god of dreams

mor·phia \'mȯr-fē-ə\ *n* [NL, fr. *Morpheus*] (1818) : MORPHINE

-morphic *adj comb form* [prob. fr. F *-morphique*, fr. Gk *morphē*] : having (such) a form ⟨endo*morphic*⟩

mor·phine \'mȯr-ˌfēn\ *n* [F, fr. *Morpheus*] (1828) : a bitter crystalline addictive narcotic base $C_{17}H_{19}NO_3$ that is the principal alkaloid of opium and is used in the form of a soluble salt (as a hydrochloride or a sulfate) as an analgesic and sedative

mor·phin·ism \'mȯr-ˌfē-ˌni-zəm, -fə-\ *n* (1882) : a disordered condition of health produced by habitual use of morphine

-morphism *n comb form* [LL *-morphus* -morphous, fr. Gk *-morphos*] : quality or state of having (such) a form ⟨hetero*morphism*⟩

mor·pho \'mȯr-(ˌ)fō\ *n, pl* **morphos** [NL, fr. Gk *Morphō*, epithet of Aphrodite] (1853) : any of a genus (*Morpho* of the family Morphoidae) of large showy tropical American butterflies that typically have a brilliant blue metallic luster on the upper surface of the wings

mor·pho·gen \'mȯr-fə-jən, -ˌjen\ *n* (1950) : a diffusible chemical substance that exerts control over morphogenesis esp. by forming a gradient in concentration

mor·pho·gen·e·sis \ˌmȯr-fə-'je-nə-səs\ *n* [NL] (ca. 1890) : the formation and differentiation of tissues and organs — compare ORGANOGENESIS

mor·pho·ge·net·ic \-jə-'ne-tik\ *adj* (1884) : relating to or concerned with the development of normal organic form ⟨~ movements of early embryonic cells⟩ — **mor·pho·ge·net·i·cal·ly** \-ti-k(ə-)lē\ *adv*

mor·pho·gen·ic \-'je-nik\ *adj* (ca. 1890) : MORPHOGENETIC

mor·phol·o·gy \mȯr-'fä-lə-jē\ *n* [G *Morphologie*, fr. *morph-* + *-logie* -logy] (1830) **1 a** : a branch of biology that deals with the form and structure of animals and plants **b** : the form and structure of an organism or any of its parts **2 a** : a study and description of word formation (as inflection, derivation, and compounding) in language **b** : the system of word-forming elements and processes in a language **3 a** : a study of structure or form **b** : STRUCTURE, FORM **4** : the external structure of rocks in relation to the development of erosional forms or topographic features — **mor·pho·log·i·cal** \ˌmȯr-fə-'lä-ji-kəl\ *also* **mor·pho·log·ic** \-'lä-jik\ *adj* — **mor·pho·log·i·cal·ly** \-k(ə-)lē\ *adv* — **mor·phol·o·gist** \mȯr-'fä-lə-jist\ *n*

mor·phom·e·try \mȯr-'fä-mə-trē\ *n* (ca. 1856) : measurement of external form — **mor·pho·met·ric** \ˌmȯr-fə-'me-trik\ *adj* — **mor·pho·met·ri·cal·ly** \-tri-k(ə-)lē\ *adv*

mor·pho·pho·ne·mics \ˌmȯr-fō-fə-'nē-miks\ *n pl but sing in constr* (1939) **1** : a study of the phonemic differences between allomorphs of

the same morpheme **2** : the distribution of allomorphs in one morpheme **3** : the structure of a language in terms of morphophonemics
-morphous *adj comb form* [Gk -morphos, fr. morphē] : having (such) a form ⟨iso*morphous*⟩
-morphy *n comb form* [ISV, fr. -morphous] : quality or state of having (such) a form ⟨endo*morphy*⟩
mor·ris \'mȯr-əs, 'mär-\ *n* [ME moreys daunce, fr. moreys Moorish (fr. More Moor) + daunce dance] (1512) : a vigorous English dance traditionally performed by men wearing costumes and bells
morris chair *n* [William Morris] (1900) : an easy chair with adjustable back and removable cushions
mor·row \'mär-(,)ō, 'mȯr-\ *n* [ME morn, morwen morn] (13c) **1** *archaic* : MORNING **2** : the next day **3** : the time immediately after a specified event
Morse code \'mȯrs-\ *n* [Samuel F. B. Morse] (1867) : either of two codes consisting of variously spaced dots and dashes or long and short sounds used for transmitting messages by audible or visual signals

INTERNATIONAL MORSE CODE

a	·—	n	—·	á	·——·—	8	———··
b	—···	o	———	ä	·—·—	9	————·
c	—·—·	p	·——·	é	··—··	0	—————
d	—··	q	——·—	ñ	——·——	,	——··—— (comma)
e	·	r	·—·	ö	———·		
f	··—·	s	···	ü	··——	?	··——··
g	——·	t	—	1	·————	;	—·—·—
h	····	u	··—	2	··———	:	———···
i	··	v	···—	3	···——	'	·————· (apostrophe)
j	·———	w	·——	4	····—	-	—····— (hyphen)
k	—·—	x	—··—	5	·····	/	—··—·
l	·—··	y	—·——	6	—····	(	—·——· (left parenthesis)
m	——	z	——··	7	——···	)	—·——·— (right parenthesis)

¹mor·sel \'mȯr-səl\ *n* [ME, fr. OF, dim. of mors bite, fr. L morsus, fr. mordēre to bite — more at MORDANT] (14c) **1** : a small piece of food : BITE **2** : a small quantity : FRAGMENT **3 a** : a tasty dish **b** : something delectable and pleasing **4** : a negligible person
²morsel *vt* **-seled** *or* **-selled**; **-sel·ing** *or* **-sel·ling** (1598) : to divide into or distribute in small pieces
¹mort \'mȯrt\ *n* [prob. alter. of ME mot horn note, fr. MF, word, horn note — more at MOT] (ca. 1500) **1** : a note sounded on a hunting horn when a deer is killed **2** : KILLING 1
²mort *n* [perh. back-formation fr. ¹mortal] (1694) : a great quantity or number
mor·ta·del·la \,mȯr-tə-'de-lə\ *n* [It, fr. L murtatum sausage seasoned with myrtle berries, fr. murtus myrtle] (1613) : a large smoked sausage made of beef, pork, and pork fat and seasoned with pepper and garlic
¹mor·tal \'mȯr-t²l\ *adj* [ME, fr. MF, fr. L mortalis, fr. mort-, mors death — more at MURDER] (14c) **1** : causing or having caused death : FATAL ⟨a ~ injury⟩ **2 a** : subject to death ⟨~ man⟩ **b** : POSSIBLE, CONCEIVABLE ⟨have done every ~ thing⟩ **c** : DEADLY 3 ⟨waited three ~ hours⟩ **3** : marked by unrelenting hostility : IMPLACABLE ⟨a ~ enemy⟩ **4** : marked by great intensity or severity : EXTREME ⟨~ fear⟩ ⟨a ~ shame⟩ **5** : HUMAN ⟨~ limitations⟩ **6** : of, relating to, or connected with death ⟨~ agony⟩ *syn* see DEADLY
²mortal *adv* (15c) *chiefly dial* : MORTALLY
³mortal *n* (1567) : a human being
mor·tal·i·ty \mȯr-'ta-lə-tē\ *n* (14c) **1** : the quality or state of being mortal **2** : the death of large numbers (as of people or animals) **3** *archaic* : DEATH **4** : the human race **5 a** : the number of deaths in a given time or place **b** : the proportion of deaths to population **c** : the number lost or the rate of loss or failure
mortality table *n* (1880) : an actuarial table based on mortality statistics over a number of years
mor·tal·ly \'mȯr-t²l-ē\ *adv* (14c) **1** : in a deadly or fatal manner : to death ⟨~ wounded⟩ **2** : to an extreme degree : INTENSELY ⟨~ afraid⟩
mortal mind *n* (1875) *Christian Science* : a belief that life, substance, and intelligence are in and of matter : ILLUSION
mortal sin *n* (15c) : a sin (as murder) that is deliberately committed and is of such serious consequence according to Thomist theology that it deprives the soul of sanctifying grace — compare VENIAL SIN
¹mor·tar \'mȯr-tər\ *n* [ME morter, fr. OE mortere & MF mortier, fr. L mortarium] (bef. 12c) **1** : a strong vessel in which material is pounded or rubbed with a pestle **2** [MF mortier] **a** : a muzzle-loading cannon having a tube short in relation to its caliber that is used to throw projectiles with low muzzle velocities at high angles **b** : any of several similar firing devices
²mortar *n* [ME morter, fr. OF mortier, fr. L mortarium] (14c) : a plastic building material (as a mixture of cement, lime, or gypsum plaster with sand and water) that hardens and is used in masonry or plastering — **mor·tar·less** *adj*
³mortar *vt* (14c) : to plaster or make fast with mortar
mor·tar·board \'mȯr-tər-,bȯrd, -,bȯrd\ *n* (1854) **1 a** : HAWK 2 **b** : a board or platform about three feet (one meter) square for holding mortar **2** : an academic cap consisting of a closely fitting headpiece with a broad flat projecting square top
¹mort·gage \'mȯr-gij\ *n* [ME morgage, fr. MF, fr. OF, fr. mort dead (fr. L mortuus) + gage gage — more at MURDER] (15c) **1** : a conveyance of or lien against property that is defeated upon payment or performance according to stipulated terms **2 a** : the instrument evidencing the mortgage **b** : the state of the property so mortgaged **c** : the interest of the mortgagee in such property

mortarboard 2

²mortgage *vt* **mort·gaged**; **mort·gag·ing** (15c) **1** : to grant or convey by a mortgage **2** : to subject to a claim or obligation : PLEDGE
mort·gag·ee \,mȯr-gi-'jē\ *n* (1584) : a person to whom property is mortgaged
mort·gag·or \,mȯr-gi-'jȯr\ *also* **mort·gag·er** \'mȯr-gi-jər\ *n* (1584) : a person who mortgages property
mor·ti·cian \mȯr-'ti-shən\ *n* [L mort-, mors death] (1895) : UNDERTAKER 2
mor·ti·fi·ca·tion \,mȯr-tə-fə-'kā-shən\ *n* (14c) **1** : the subjection and denial of bodily passions and appetites by abstinence or self-inflicted pain or discomfort **2** : NECROSIS, GANGRENE **3 a** : a sense of humiliation and shame caused by something that wounds one's pride or self-respect **b** : the cause of such humiliation or shame
mor·ti·fy \'mȯr-tə-,fī\ *vb* **-fied**; **-fy·ing** [ME mortifien, fr. MF mortifier, fr. LL mortificare, fr. L mort-, mors] *vt* (14c) **1** *obs* : to destroy the strength, vitality, or functioning of **2** : to subdue or deaden (as the body or bodily appetites) esp. by abstinence or self-inflicted pain or discomfort **3** : to subject to severe and vexing embarrassment : SHAME ~ *vi* **1** : to practice mortification **2** : to become necrotic or gangrenous
¹mor·tise *also* **mor·tice** \'mȯr-təs\ *n* [ME mortays, fr. MF mortaise] (15c) : a hole, groove, or slot into or through which some other part of an arrangement of parts fits or passes; *esp* : a cavity cut into a piece of material (as timber) to receive a tenon — see DOVETAIL illustration
²mortise *also* **mortice** *vt* **mor·tised** *also* **mor·ticed**; **mor·tis·ing** *also* **mor·tic·ing** (15c) **1** : to join or fasten securely; *specif* : to join or fasten by a tenon and mortise **2** : to cut or make a mortise in
mort·main \'mȯrt-,mān\ *n* [ME morte-mayne, fr. MF mortemain, fr. OF, fr. morte (fem. of mort dead) + main hand, fr. L manus — more at MANUAL] (15c) **1 a** : an inalienable possession of lands or buildings by an ecclesiastical or other corporation **b** : the condition of property or other gifts left to a corporation in perpetuity esp. for religious, charitable, or public purposes **2** : the influence of the past regarded as controlling the present
¹mor·tu·ary \'mȯr-chə-,wer-ē\ *adj* [L mortuarius of the dead, fr. mortuus dead] (1514) **1** : of or relating to the burial of the dead **2** : of, relating to, or characteristic of death
²mortuary *n, pl* **-ar·ies** (1865) : a place in which dead bodies are kept until burial; *esp* : FUNERAL HOME
mor·u·la \'mȯr-(y)ə-lə, 'mär-\ *n, pl* **-lae** \-,lē, -,lī\ [NL, fr. L morum mulberry, fr. Gk moron] (1874) : a globular solid mass of blastomeres formed by cleavage of a zygote that typically precedes the blastula — **mor·u·lar** \-lər\ *adj* — **mor·u·la·tion** \,mȯr-(y)ə-'lā-shən, ,mär-\ *n*
¹mo·sa·ic \mō-'zā-ik\ *n* [ME musycke, fr. MF mosaique, fr. OIt mosaico, fr. ML musaicum, alter. of LL musivum, fr. L museum, musaeum] (15c) **1** : a surface decoration made by inlaying small pieces of variously colored material to form pictures or patterns; *also* : the process of making it **2** : a picture or design made in mosaic **3** : something resembling a mosaic ⟨a ~ of visions and daydreams and memories —Lawrence Shainberg⟩ **4** : an organism or one of its parts composed of cells of more than one genotype : CHIMERA 3 **5** : a virus disease of plants characterized by diffuse light and dark green or yellow and green mottling of the foliage **6** : a composite map made of photographs taken by an aircraft or spacecraft **7** : the part of a television camera tube consisting of many minute photoelectric particles that convert light to an electric charge — **mo·sa·ic·like** \-'zā-ik-,līk\ *adj*
²mosaic *adj* (1585) **1** : of, relating to, produced by, or resembling a mosaic **2** : exhibiting mosaicism **3** : DETERMINATE 5 — **mo·sa·i·cal·ly** \-'zā-ə-k(ə-)lē\ *adv*
³mosaic *vt* **-icked**; **-ick·ing** (1839) **1** : to decorate with mosaics **2** : to form into a mosaic
Mo·sa·ic \mō-'zā-ik\ *adj* [NL Mosaicus, fr. Moses Moses] (1662) : of or relating to Moses or the institutions or writings attributed to him
mo·sa·i·cism \mō-'zā-ə-,si-zəm\ *n* (1926) : the condition of possessing cells of two or more different genetic constitutions
mo·sa·i·cist \-sist\ *n* (1847) **1 a** : a designer of mosaics **b** : a worker who makes mosaics **2** : a dealer in mosaics
mo·sa·saur \'mō-zə-,sȯr\ *n* [NL Mosasaurus, fr. L Mosa the river Meuse + Gk sauros lizard] (1841) : any of a family (Mosasauridae) of very large extinct marine fish-eating lizards of the Upper Cretaceous with limbs modified into paddles that are related to the recent monitor lizards
Mo·selle \mō-'zel\ *n* [G Moselwein, fr. Mosel Moselle, river in Germany + G Wein wine] (1693) : a white wine from the Moselle valley
Mo·ses \'mō-zəz *also* -zəs\ *n* [L, fr. Gk Mōsēs, fr. Heb Mōsheh] : a Hebrew prophet who led the Israelites out of Egyptian slavery and at Mt. Sinai delivered to them the Law establishing God's covenant with them
mo·sey \'mō-zē\ *vi* **mo·seyed**; **mo·sey·ing** [origin unknown] (1829) **1** : to hurry away **2** : to move in a leisurely or aimless manner : SAUNTER ⟨~ed around the general store, testing the cheese straight off the round —Eric Sevareid⟩
mo·shav \mō-'shäv\ *n, pl* **mo·sha·vim** \,mō-shə-'vēm\ [NHeb mōshābh, fr. Heb, dwelling] (1931) : a cooperative settlement of small individual farms in Israel — compare KIBBUTZ
Mos·lem \'mäz-ləm *also* 'mäs-\ *var of* MUSLIM
Mo·so·tho \mō-'sō-(,)tō, -'sü-(,)tü\ *n, pl* **Ba·so·tho** \bä-\ (1952) : a member of the Basotho people
mosque \'mäsk\ *n* [MF mosquee, fr. OIt moschea, fr. OSp mezquita, fr. Ar masjid temple, fr. sajada to prostrate oneself, worship] (1711) : a building used for public worship by Muslims
mos·qui·to \mə-'skē-(,)tō\ *n, pl* **-toes** *also* **-tos** [Sp, dim. of mosca fly, fr. L musca — more at MIDGE] (ca. 1583) : any of a family (Culicidae) of dipteran flies with females that have a set of slender organs in the proboscis adapted to puncture the skin of animals and to suck their blood and that are in some cases vectors of serious diseases — **mos·qui·to·ey** \-'skē-tə-wē\ *adj*
mosquito fish *n* (1928) : either of two No. American live-bearers (Gambusia affinis and Heterandria formosa of the family Poeciliidae) used esp. to exterminate mosquito larvae
mosquito hawk *n* (1737) : DRAGONFLY
mosquito net *n* (1745) : a net or screen for keeping out mosquitoes
¹moss \'mȯs\ *n* [ME, fr. OE mos; akin to OHG mos moss, L muscus] (bef. 12c) **1** *chiefly Scot* : BOG, SWAMP; *esp* : a peat bog **2 a** : any of a

class (Musci) of bryophytic plants having a small leafy often tufted stem bearing sex organs at its tip; *also* : a clump or sward of these plants   **b** : any of various plants resembling moss in appearance or habit of growth : a mossy covering — **moss-like** \-,līk\ *adj*
²**moss** *vt* (15c) : to cover or overgrow with moss
moss agate *n* (1798) : an agate mineral containing brown, black, or green mosslike or dendritic markings
moss animal *n* (1881) : BRYOZOAN
moss-back \'mòs-,bak\ *n* (1872)   **1** : a large sluggish fish (as a largemouth bass)   **2** : an extremely old-fashioned or reactionary person : FOGY — **moss-backed** \-,bakt\ *adj*
moss green *n* (1884) : a variable color averaging a moderate yellow= green
moss-grown \'mòs-,grōn\ *adj* (14c)   **1** : overgrown with moss   **2** : ANTIQUATED
moss pink *n* (ca. 1856) : a low-growing perennial phlox (*Phlox subulata*) widely cultivated for its abundant usu. pink or white flowers
moss rose *n* (1776) : an old-fashioned garden rose (*Rosa centifolia mucosa*) that has a glandular mossy calyx and flower stalk
moss-troop-er \'mòs-,trü-pər\ *n* (1645)   **1** : one of a class of 17th century raiders in the marshy border country between England and Scotland   **2** : PIRATE — **moss-troop-ing** \-,pin\ *adj*
mossy \'mò-sē\ *adj* **moss-i-er; -est** (15c)   **1** : resembling moss   **2** : covered with moss or something like moss   **3** : ANTIQUATED ⟨the ~ precepts of the . . . prescriptive grammarians —Thomas Pyles⟩
mossy zinc *n* (1910) : a granulated form of zinc made by pouring melted zinc into water
¹**most** \'mōst\ *adj* [ME, fr. OE *mǣst*; akin to OHG *meist* most, OE *māra* more — more at MORE] (bef. 12c)   **1** : greatest in quantity, extent, or degree ⟨the ~ ability⟩   **2** : the majority of ⟨~ people⟩
²**most** *adv* (bef. 12c)   **1** : to the greatest or highest degree — often used with an adjective or adverb to form the superlative ⟨the ~ challenging job he ever had⟩   **2** : to a very great degree ⟨was ~ persuasive⟩
³**most** *n* (12c) : the greatest amount ⟨it's the ~ I can do⟩ — **at most** or **at the most** : as an extreme limit ⟨took him an hour *at most*⟩
⁴**most** *pron, sing or pl in constr* (13c) : the greatest number or part ⟨~ become discouraged and quit⟩
⁵**most** *adv* [by shortening] (ca. 1584) : ALMOST ⟨we'll be crossing the river ~ any time now —Hamilton Basso⟩
usage Although considered by some to be unacceptable in all cases, *most* is often used to mean "almost" in both spoken and, to a lesser extent, written English to modify the adjectives *all, every,* and *any;* the pronouns *all, everyone, everything, everybody, anyone, anything,* and *anybody;* and the adverbs *everywhere, anywhere,* and *always.* Other uses of this sense of *most* are dialectal.
-most *adj suffix* [ME, alter. of *-mest* (as in *formest* foremost)] : most ⟨*inner*most⟩ : most toward ⟨*head*most⟩
most-ly \'mōst-lē\ *adv* (1594) : for the greatest part : MAINLY
Most Reverend (15c) — used as a title for an archbishop or a Roman Catholic bishop
mot \'mō\ *n, pl* **mots** \'mō(z)\ [F, word, saying, fr. LL *muttum* grunt — more at MOTTO] (1631) : a pithy or witty saying
¹**mote** \'mōt\ *verbal auxiliary* [ME, fr. OE *mōtan* to be allowed to — more at MUST] (bef. 12c) *archaic* : MAY, MIGHT
²**mote** \'mōt\ *n* [ME *mot,* fr. OE; akin to MD & Fris *mot* sand] (bef. 12c) : a small particle : SPECK
mo-tel \mō-'tel\ *n* [blend of *motor* and *hotel*] (1925) : an establishment which provides lodging and parking and in which the rooms are usu. accessible from an outdoor parking area
mo-tet \mō-'tet\ *n* [ME, fr. MF, dim. of *mot*] (14c) : a polyphonic choral composition on a sacred text usu. without instrumental accompaniment
moth \'mòth\ *n, pl* **moths** \'mòthz, 'mòths\ [ME *mothe,* fr. OE *moth-the;* akin to MHG *motte* moth] (bef. 12c)   **1** : CLOTHES MOTH   **2** : any of various usu. nocturnal lepidopteran insects with antennae that are often feathery, with a stouter body, duller coloring, and proportionately smaller wings than the butterflies, and with larvae that are plant= eating caterpillars — **moth-like** \-,līk\ *adj* — **mothy** \'mò-thē\ *adj*
¹**moth-ball** \'mòth-,bòl\ *n* (1906)   **1** : a ball made formerly of camphor but now often of naphthalene and used to keep moths from clothing   **2** *pl* : a condition of protective storage ⟨put the ships in ~s after the war⟩; *also* : a state of having been rejected for further use or dismissed from further consideration ⟨put that idea in ~s⟩
²**mothball** *vt* (1943)   **1** : to deactivate (as a ship) and prevent deterioration chiefly by dehumidification   **2** : to withdraw from use or service and keep in reserve
moth bean *n* [prob. by folk etymology fr. Marathi *math* moth bean] (1884) : a bean (*Phaseolus aconitifolius*) that is cultivated esp. in India for its cylindrical pods and small yellowish brown seeds
moth-eat-en \'mòth-,ē-t³n\ *adj* (14c)   **1** : eaten into by moth larvae ⟨~ clothes⟩   **2 a** : DILAPIDATED   **b** : ANTIQUATED, OUTMODED
¹**moth-er** \'mə-thər\ *n* [ME *moder,* fr. OE *mōdor;* akin to OHG *muoter* mother, L *mater,* Gk *mētēr,* Skt *mātṛ*] (bef. 12c)   **1 a** : a female parent   **b** (1) : a woman in authority; *specif* : the superior of a religious community of women   (2) : an old or elderly woman   **2** : SOURCE, ORIGIN ⟨necessity is the ~ of invention⟩   **3** : maternal tenderness or affection   **4** [short for *motherfucker*] : one that is particularly impressive or contemptible — sometimes considered vulgar — **moth-er-hood** \-,hùd\ *n* — **moth-er-less** \-ləs\ *adj* — **moth-er-less-ness** *n*
²**mother** *adj* (13c)   **1 a** : of, relating to, or being a mother   **b** : bearing the relation of a mother   **2** : derived from or as if from one's mother   **3** : acting as or providing parental stock — used without reference to sex
³**mother** *vt* **moth-ered; moth-er-ing** \'mə-thə-rin, 'məth-rin\ (1548)   **1 a** : to give birth to   **b** : to give rise to : PRODUCE   **2** : to care for or protect like a mother
⁴**mother** *n* [archaic *mother* dregs, lees; akin to MD *moeder* dregs] (ca. 1828) : MOTHER OF VINEGAR
moth-er-board \-,bȯrd, -,bōrd\ *n* (1972) : the main circuit board esp. of a microcomputer
Mother Car-ey's chicken \-'kar-ēz-, -'ker-\ *n* [origin unknown] (1767) : STORM PETREL
mother cell *n* (1845) : a cell that gives rise to other cells usu. of a different sort

mother country *n* (1587)   **1** : the country from which the people of a colony or former colony derive their origin   **2** : the country of one's parents or ancestors; *also* : FATHERLAND   **3** : a country that is the origin of something
moth-er-fuck-er \'mə-thər-,fə-kər\ *n* (1959) : one that is formidable, contemptible, or offensive — usu. considered obscene; usu. used as a generalized term of abuse — **moth-er-fuck-ing** \-kin\ *adj*
Mother Goose *n* : the legendary author of a collection of nursery rhymes first published in London about 1760
mother hen *n* (1954) : a person who assumes an overly protective maternal attitude
moth-er-house \-,haùs\ *n* (1661)   **1** : the convent in which the superior of a religious community resides   **2** : the original convent of a religious community
Mother Hub-bard \-'hə-bərd\ *n* [prob. fr. *Mother Hubbard,* character in a nursery rhyme] (1884) : a loose usu. shapeless dress
moth-er-in-law \'mə-thər-ən-,lȯ, 'məth-rən-, 'mə-thərn-\ *n, pl* **moth-ers-in-law** \'mə-thər-zən-\ (14c)   **1** : the mother of one's spouse   **2** *archaic* : STEPMOTHER
moth-er-land \'mə-thər-,land\ *n* (1711)   **1** : a country regarded as a place of origin (as of an idea or a movement)   **2** : MOTHER COUNTRY 2
mother lode *n* (1874)   **1** : the principal vein or lode of a region   **2** : a principal source or supply
moth-er-ly \-lē\ *adj* (bef. 12c)   **1** : of, relating to, or characteristic of a mother ⟨~ advice⟩   **2** : resembling a mother : MATERNAL — **moth-er-li-ness** *n*
moth-er-na-ked \,mə-thər-'nā-kəd, *esp Southern* -'ne-kəd\ *adj* (14c) : stark naked
Mother Nature *n* (1601) : nature personified as a woman considered as the source and guiding force of creation
moth-er-of-pearl \,mə-thə-rə(v)-'pər(-ə)l\ *n* (ca. 1510) : the hard pearly iridescent substance forming the inner layer of a mollusk shell
mother of vinegar (1601) : a slimy membrane composed of yeast and bacterial cells that develops on the surface of alcoholic liquids undergoing acetous fermentation and is added to wine or cider to produce vinegar — called also *mother*
Mother's Day *n* (1908) : the 2d Sunday in May appointed for the honoring of mothers
mother tongue *n* (14c)   **1** : one's native language   **2** : a language from which another language derives
mother wit *n* (15c) : natural wit or intelligence
¹**moth-proof** \'mòth-,prüf\ *adj* (1893) : impervious to penetration by moths ⟨~ wool⟩
²**mothproof** *vt* (1925) : to make mothproof — **moth-proof-er** *n*
mo-tif \mō-'tēf\ *n* [F, motive, motif, fr. MF — more at MOTIVE] (1848)   **1** : a usu. recurring salient thematic element (as in the arts); *esp* : a dominant idea or central theme   **2** : a single or repeated design or color — **mo-tif-ic** \-'tē-fik, -'ti-\ *adj*
¹**mo-tile** \'mō-t³l, -,tīl\ *adj* [L *motus,* pp. of *movēre*] (ca. 1859) : exhibiting or capable of movement — **mo-til-i-ty** \mō-'ti-lə-tē\ *n*
²**motile** *n* (1886) : a person whose prevailing mental imagery takes the form of inner feelings of action
¹**mo-tion** \'mō-shən\ *n* [ME *mocioun,* fr. MF *motion,* fr. L *motion-, motio* movement, fr. *movēre* to move] (14c)   **1 a** : an act, process, or instance of changing place : MOVEMENT   **b** : an active or functioning state or condition ⟨set the divorce proceedings in ~⟩   **2** : an impulse or inclination of the mind or will   **3 a** : a proposal for action; *esp* : a formal proposal made in a deliberative assembly   **b** : an application made to a court or judge to obtain an order, ruling, or direction   **4** *obs* **a** : a puppet show   **b** : PUPPET   **5** : MECHANISM   **6 a** : an act or instance of moving the body or its parts : GESTURE   **b** *pl* : ACTIVITIES, MOVEMENTS   **7** : melodic change of pitch — **mo-tion-al** \'mō-shnəl, -shə-n³l\ *adj* — **mo-tion-less** \'mō-shən-ləs\ *adj* — **mo-tion-less-ly** *adv* — **mo-tion-less-ness** *n* — **in motion** *of an offensive football player* : running parallel to the line of scrimmage before the snap
²**motion** *vb* **mo-tioned; mo-tion-ing** \'mō-sh(ə-)nin\ *vi* (1747) : to signal by a movement or gesture ⟨the pitcher ~ed to the catcher⟩ ~ *vt* : to direct by a motion ⟨~ed me to the seat⟩
motion picture *n* (1896)   **1** : a series of pictures projected on a screen in rapid succession with objects shown in successive positions slightly changed so as to produce the optical effect of a continuous picture in which the objects move   **2** : a representation (as of a story) by means of motion pictures : MOVIE
motion sickness *n* (1942) : sickness induced by motion (as in travel by air, car, or ship) and characterized by nausea
mo-ti-vate \'mō-tə-,vāt\ *vt* **-vat-ed; -vat-ing** (1885) : to provide with a motive : IMPEL ⟨questions that excite and ~ youth⟩ — **mo-ti-va-tive** \-,vā-tiv\ *adj* — **mo-ti-va-tor** \-,vā-tər\ *n*
mo-ti-va-tion \,mō-tə-'vā-shən\ *n* (1873)   **1 a** : the act or process of motivating   **b** : the condition of being motivated   **2** : a motivating force, stimulus, or influence : INCENTIVE, DRIVE — **mo-ti-va-tion-al** \-shnəl, -shə-n³l\ *adj* — **mo-ti-va-tion-al-ly** *adv*
¹**mo-tive** \'mō-tiv, 2 *is also* mō-'tēv\ *n* [ME, fr. MF *motif,* fr. *motif,* adj., moving, fr. ML *motivus,* fr. L *motus,* pp. of *movēre* to move] (15c)   **1** : something (as a need or desire) that causes a person to act   **2** : a recurrent phrase or figure that is developed through the course of a musical composition — **mo-tive-less** \-ləs\ *adj* — **mo-tive-less-ly** *adv* — **mo-ti-vic** \mō-'tē-vik\ *adj*
syn MOTIVE, IMPULSE, INCENTIVE, INDUCEMENT, SPUR, GOAD mean a stimulus to action. MOTIVE implies an emotion or desire operating on the will and causing it to act ⟨a *motive* for the crime⟩. IMPULSE suggests a driving power arising from personal temperament or constitution ⟨buying on *impulse*⟩. INCENTIVE applies to an external influence (as an expected reward) inciting to action ⟨a bonus was offered as an *incentive*⟩. INDUCEMENT suggests a motive prompted by the deliberate enticements or allurements of another ⟨offered a watch as an *inducement* to subscribe⟩. SPUR applies to a motive that stimulates the facul-

\ə\ abut \³\ kitten, F table \ər\ further \a\ ash \ā\ ace \ä\ mop, mar \aù\ out \ch\ chin \e\ bet \ē\ easy \g\ go \i\ hit \ī\ ice \j\ job \ŋ\ sing \ō\ go \ò\ law \òi\ boy \th\ thin \t̷h\ the \ü\ loot \ù\ foot \y\ yet \zh\ vision \ä, k̲, ⁿ, œ, œ̅, ue, ue̅, ³\ see Guide to Pronunciation ties or increases energy or ardor ⟨fear was a *spur* to action⟩. GOAD suggests a motive that keeps one going against one's will or desire ⟨thought insecurity a *goad* to worker efficiency⟩

²**mo·tive** \'mō-tiv\ *adj* [MF or ML; MF *motif*, fr. ML *motivus*] (1502) **1 :** moving or tending to move to action **2 :** of or relating to motion or the causing of motion ⟨∼ energy⟩

³**mo·tive** \'mō-tiv\ *vt* **mo·tived; mo·tiv·ing** (ca. 1650) **:** MOTIVATE

motive power *n* (1889) **1 :** an agency (as water or steam) used to impart motion esp. to machinery **2 :** something (as a locomotive or a motor) that provides motive power to a system

mo·tiv·i·ty \mō-'ti-və-tē\ *n* (ca. 1687) **:** the power of moving or producing motion

mot juste \mō-zhüst\ *n, pl* **mots justes** *same*\ [F] (1912) **:** the exactly right word or phrasing

¹**mot·ley** \'mät-lē\ *adj* [ME, perh. fr. *mot* mote, speck] (14c) **1 :** variegated in color ⟨a ∼ coat⟩ **2 :** composed of diverse often incongruous elements ⟨a ∼ crowd⟩

²**motley** *n* [ME, prob. fr. ¹*motley*] (14c) **1 :** a woolen fabric of mixed colors made in England between the 14th and 17th centuries **2 :** a garment made of motley; *esp* **:** the characteristic dress of the professional fool **3 :** JESTER, FOOL **4 :** a mixture esp. of incongruous elements

mot·mot \'mät-,mät\ *n* [NL *momot, motmot*] (1837) **:** any of a family (Momotidae) of long-tailed mostly green nonpasserine birds of Central and So. American tropical forests

mo·to·cross \'mō-tə-,krós\ *n* [F, fr. *moto* motorcycle (short for *motocyclette*) + *cross*-country, fr. E] (1951) **:** a closed-course motorcycle race over natural or simulated rough terrain (as with steep inclines, hairpin turns, and mud); *also* **:** the sport of engaging in motocross races

mo·to·neu·ron \,mō-tə-'nü-,rän, -'nyü-; -'nur-,än, -'nyur-\ *n* [*motor* + *neuron*] (1908) **:** a neuron that passes from the central nervous system or a ganglion toward a muscle and conducts an impulse that causes movement — called also *motor neuron* — **mo·to·neu·ro·nal** \-'nür-ə-n³l, -'nyur-; -nü-'rō-n³l, -nyü-\ *adj*

¹**mo·tor** \'mō-tər\ *n* [L, fr. *movēre* to move] (1586) **1 :** one that imparts motion; *specif* **:** PRIME MOVER **2 :** any of various power units that develop energy or impart motion: as **a :** a small compact engine **b :** INTERNAL COMBUSTION ENGINE; *esp* **:** a gasoline engine **c :** a rotating machine that transforms electrical energy into mechanical energy **3 :** MOTOR VEHICLE; *esp* **:** AUTOMOBILE — **mo·tor·dom** \-dəm\ *n* — **mo·tor·less** \-ləs\ *adj*

²**motor** *adj* (1840) **1 a :** causing or imparting motion **b :** of, relating to, or being a motoneuron or a nerve containing motoneurons ⟨∼ fiber⟩ **c :** of, relating to, concerned with, or involving muscular movement ⟨∼ areas of the brain⟩ **2 a :** equipped with or driven by a motor **b :** of, relating to, or involving an automobile **c :** designed for motor vehicles or motorists

³**motor** *vi* (1896) **1 :** to travel by automobile **:** DRIVE **2 :** to move or proceed at a vigorous steady pace ⟨∼ed down the field for a touchdown⟩ ∼ *vt* **:** to transport by automobile

mo·tor·bike \'mō-tər-,bīk\ *n* (1903) **:** a small usu. lightweight motorcycle — **motorbike** *vi*

mo·tor·boat \-,bōt\ *n* (1902) **:** a boat propelled usu. by an internal combustion engine — **mo·tor·boat·er** \-,bō-tər\ *n* — **mo·tor·boat·ing** \-tiŋ\ *n*

motor bus *n* (1901) **:** BUS 1a — called also *motor coach*

mo·tor·cade \'mō-tər-,kād\ *n* (1913) **:** a procession of motor vehicles — **motorcade** *vi*

mo·tor·car \-,kär\ *n* (ca. 1890) **1 :** AUTOMOBILE **2** *usu* **motor car : a** railroad car containing motors for propulsion

motor court *n* (1936) **:** MOTEL

mo·tor·cy·cle \'mō-tər-,sī-kəl\ *n* [*motor* bi*cycle*] (1896) **:** a 2-wheeled automotive vehicle having one or two saddles — **motorcycle** *vi* — **mo·tor·cy·clist** \-k(ə-)list\ *n*

motor home *n* (1965) **:** a large motor vehicle equipped as living quarters — compare MOBILE HOME

mo·tor·ic \mō-'tor-ik, -'tär-\ *adj* (1930) **:** MOTOR 1c — **mo·tor·i·cal·ly** \-i-k(ə-)lē\ *adv*

motor inn *n* (1951) **:** MOTEL; *esp* **:** a large multistory motel — called also *motor hotel*

mo·tor·ise *Brit var of* MOTORIZE

mo·tor·ist \'mō-tə-rist\ *n* (1896) **:** a person who travels by automobile

mo·tor·ize \'mō-tə-,rīz\ *vt* **-ized; -iz·ing** (ca. 1913) **1 :** to equip with a motor **2 :** to equip with automobiles — **mo·tor·i·za·tion** \,mō-tə-rə-'zā-shən\ *n*

motor lodge *n* (1949) **:** MOTEL

mo·tor·man \'mō-tər-mən\ *n* (1890) **:** an operator of a motor-driven vehicle (as a streetcar or subway train)

mo·tor·mouth \-,maúth\ *n* (1971) **:** a person who talks excessively

motor pool *n* (1942) **:** a group of motor vehicles centrally controlled (as by a governmental agency) and dispatched for use as needed

motor sailer *n* (1923) **:** a motorboat with sailing equipment

motor scooter *n* (1919) **:** a low 2- or 3-wheeled automotive vehicle resembling a child's scooter and having a seat so that the rider does not straddle the engine

motor ship *n* (1915) **:** a seagoing ship propelled by an internal combustion engine

motor torpedo boat *n* (1940) **:** PT BOAT

mo·tor·truck \'mō-tər-,trək\ *n* (1930) **:** an automotive truck used esp. for transporting freight

motor unit *n* (1925) **:** a motoneuron together with the muscle fibers on which it acts

motor vehicle *n* (1890) **:** an automotive vehicle not operated on rails; *esp* **:** one with rubber tires for use on highways

mo·tor·way \'mō-tər-,wā\ *n* (1903) *chiefly Brit* **:** SUPERHIGHWAY

motte \'mät\ *n* [ME *mote*, fr. OF *mote, motte*] (13c) **:** MOUND, HILL; *esp* **:** a hill serving as a site for a Norman castle in Britain

motte and bailey *n* (1900) **:** a medieval Norman castle consisting of two connecting ditched stockaded mounds with the higher mound surmounted by the keep and the lower one containing barracks and other buildings

¹**mot·tle** \'mä-t³l\ *n* [prob. back-formation fr. *motley*] (1676) **1 : a** colored spot **2 a :** a surface having colored spots or blotches **b**

: the arrangement of such spots or blotches on a surface **3 :** MOSAIC 5 — **mot·tled** \-t³ld\ *adj*

²**mottle** *vt* **mot·tled; mot·tling** \'mät-liŋ, 'mä-t³l-iŋ\ (1676) **:** to mark with spots or blotches of different color or shades of color as if stained — **mot·tler** \'mät-lər, 'mä-t³l-ər\ *n*

mottled enamel *n* (1928) **:** spotted tooth enamel caused by drinking water containing excessive fluorides during the time the teeth are calcifying

mot·to \'mä-(,)tō\ *n, pl* **mottoes** *also* **mottos** [It, fr. LL *muttum* grunt, fr. L *muttire* to mutter] (1588) **1 :** a sentence, phrase, or word inscribed on something as appropriate to or indicative of its character or use **2 :** a short expression of a guiding principle

moue \'mü\ *n* [F, fr. MF — more at MOW] (1850) **:** a little grimace **:** POUT

mou·flon *also* **mouf·flon** \'mü-,flän\ *n* [F *mouflon*, fr. It dial. *muvrone*, fr. LL *mufron-, mufro*] (1774) **:** either of two wild sheep (*Ovis orientalis* and *O. musimon*) of the mountains of Sardinia, Corsica and western Asia that have large curling horns in the males and are sometimes included in a single species

mou·jik \mü-'zhēk, -'zhik\ *var of* MUZHIK

mou·lage \mü-'läzh\ *n* [F, molding, fr. MF, fr. *mouler* to mold, fr. OF *modle* mold — more at MOLD] (1902) **1 :** an impression or cast made for use esp. as evidence in a criminal investigation **2 :** the taking of an impression for use as evidence in a criminal investigation

mould \'mōld\ *var of* MOLD

mould·ing \'mōl-diŋ\ *var of* MOLDING

moult \'mōlt\ *var of* MOLT

¹**mound** \'maúnd\ *vt* [origin unknown] (1515) **1** *archaic* **:** to enclose or fortify with a fence or wall **2 :** to form into a mound

²**mound** *n, often attrib* [origin unknown] (1551) **1** *archaic* **:** HEDGE, FENCE **2 a** (1) **:** an artificial bank or hill of earth or stones; *esp* **:** one constructed over a burial or ceremonial site (2) **:** the slightly elevated ground on which a baseball pitcher stands **b :** a rounded hill or natural formation **3 a :** HEAP, PILE ⟨∼s of work⟩ **b :** a small rounded mass ⟨a ∼ of mashed potatoes⟩

Mound Builder *n* (1838) **:** a member of a prehistoric American Indian people whose extensive earthworks are found from the Great Lakes down the Mississippi valley to the Gulf of Mexico

¹**mount** \'maúnt\ *n* [ME, fr. OE *munt* & OF *mont*, both fr. L *mont-, mons*; akin to W *mynydd* mountain, L *minari* to project, threaten] (bef. 12c) **1 :** a high hill **:** MOUNTAIN — used esp. before an identifying name ⟨*Mount* Everest⟩ **2** *archaic* **:** EARTHWORK 1 **3 :** MOUND 2a(1)

²**mount** *vb* [ME, fr. MF *monter*, fr. (assumed) VL *montare*, fr. L *mont-, mons*] *vi* (14c) **1 :** RISE, ASCEND **2 :** to increase in amount or extent ⟨expenses began to ∼⟩ **3 :** to get up on something above the level of the ground; *esp* **:** to seat oneself (as on a horse) for riding ∼ *vt* **1 a :** to go up **:** CLIMB **b** (1) **:** to seat or place oneself on (2) **:** COVER 6a **2 a :** to lift up **:** RAISE **b** (1) **:** to put or have (as artillery) in position (2) **:** to have as equipment **c** (1) **:** to organize and equip (an attacking force) ⟨∼ an army⟩ (2) **:** to launch and carry out (as an assault or a campaign) **3 :** to set on something that elevates **4 a :** to cause to get on a means of conveyance **b :** to furnish with animals for riding **5 :** to post or set up for defense or observation ⟨∼ed some guards⟩ **6 a :** to attach to a support **b :** to arrange or assemble for use or display **7 a :** to prepare (as a specimen) for examination or display **b :** to prepare and supply with materials needed for performance or execution ⟨∼ an opera⟩ — **mount·able** \'maún-tə-bəl\ *adj* — **mount·er** *n*

³**mount** *n* (15c) **1 :** an act or instance of mounting; *specif* **:** an opportunity to ride a horse in a race **2 :** FRAME, SUPPORT: as **a :** the material (as cardboard) on which a picture is mounted **b :** a jewelry setting **c** (1) **:** an undercarriage or part on which a device (as a motor or an artillery piece) rests in service (2) **:** an attachment for an accessory **d : a** hinge, card, or acetate envelope for mounting a stamp **e :** a glass slide with its accessories on which objects are placed for examination with a microscope **3 :** a means of conveyance; *esp* **:** SADDLE HORSE

moun·tain \'maún-t³n\ *n, often attrib* [ME, fr. OF *montaigne*, fr. (assumed) VL *montanea*, fr. fem. of *montaneus* of a mountain, alter. of L *montanus*, fr. *mont-, mons*] (13c) **1 a :** a landmass that projects conspicuously above its surroundings and is higher than a hill **b :** an elongated ridge **2 a :** a great mass **b :** a vast number or quantity

mountain ash *n* (1597) **:** any of various trees or shrubs (genus *Sorbus*) of the rose family with pinnate leaves and red or orange-red fruits

mountain bike *n* (1984) **:** an all-terrain bicycle with wide knobby tires, straight handlebars, and typically 18 or 21 gears — **mountain biker** *n* — **mountain biking** *n*

mountain bluebird *n* (1860) **:** a bluebird (*Sialia currucoides*) of western No. America having a blue-breasted rather than red-breasted male

mountain cranberry *n* (1848) **:** a low evergreen shrub (*Vaccinium vitis-idaea minus*) of north temperate uplands with red edible berries — called also *lingonberry*

mountain dew *n* (1827) **:** MOONSHINE 3

moun·tain·eer \,maún-t³n-'ir\ *n* (1610) **1 :** a native or inhabitant of a mountainous region **2 :** a person who climbs mountains for sport

moun·tain·eer·ing *n* (1803) **:** the sport or technique of scaling mountains

mountain goat *n* (1833) **:** a ruminant mammal (*Oreamnos americanus*) of mountainous northwestern No. America that has a thick white coat and slightly curved horns and resembles a goat

mountain gorilla *n* (1939) **:** a gorilla (*Gorilla gorilla beringei*) inhabiting the Virunga mountain range

mountain laurel *n* (1759) **:** a No. American evergreen shrub or small tree (*Kalmia latifolia*) of the heath family with glossy leaves and umbels of rose-colored or white flowers

mountain lion *n* (1859) **:** COUGAR

mountain mahogany *n* (1810) **:** any of a genus (*Cercocarpus*) of western No. American evergreen shrubs or small trees of the rose family

mountain man *n* (1839) **:** an American frontiersman (as a trapper) at home in the wilderness

mountain goat

moun·tain·ous \'maún-t³n-əs, 'maúnt-nəs\ *adj* (14c) **1** : containing many mountains **2** : resembling a mountain : HUGE — **moun·tain·ous·ly** *adv* — **moun·tain·ous·ness** *n*

mountain sheep *n* (1802) : any of various wild sheep (as bighorn, argali, or Dall sheep) inhabiting high mountains

mountain sickness *n* (1848) : altitude sickness experienced esp. above 10,000 feet (3000 meters) and caused by insufficient oxygen in the air

moun·tain-side \'maún-t³n-,sid\ *n* (14c) : the side of a mountain

mountain time *n, often cap M* (1883) : the time of the 7th time zone west of Greenwich that includes the Rocky mountain states of the U.S. — see TIME ZONE illustration

moun·tain-top \'maún-t³n-,täp\ *n* (1593) : the summit of a mountain

moun·tainy \'maún-t³n-ē, 'maúnt-nē\ *adj* (1613) **1** : MOUNTAINOUS **2** : of, relating to, or living in mountains

¹moun·te·bank \'maún-ti-,baŋk\ *n* [It *montimbanco*, fr. *montare* to mount (fr.—assumed—VL) + *in* in, on (fr. L) + *banco, banca* bench — more at BANK] (1577) **1** : a person who sells quack medicines from a platform **2** : a boastful unscrupulous pretender : CHARLATAN — **moun·te·bank·ery** \-,baŋ-k(ə-)rē\ *n*

²mountebank *vt* (1607) *obs* : to beguile or transform by trickery ⟨I'll ~ their loves —Shak.⟩ ~ *vi* : to play the mountebank

Mount·ie \'maún-tē\ *n* [*mounted* policeman] (1914) : a member of the Royal Canadian Mounted Police

mount·ing \'maún-tiŋ\ *n* (1563) : ³MOUNT 2

mourn \'mōrn, 'mórn\ *vb* [ME, fr. OE *murnan*; akin to OHG *mornēn* to mourn, Gk *mermēra* care — more at MEMORY] *vi* (bef. 12c) **1** : to feel or express grief or sorrow **2** : to show the customary signs of grief for a death; *esp* : to wear mourning **3** : to murmur mournfully — used esp. of doves ~ *vt* **1** : to feel or express grief or sorrow for **2** : to utter mournfully — **mourn·er** *n* — **mourn·ing·ly** \'mōr-niŋ-lē, 'mór-\ *adv*

mourn·ful \'mōrn-fəl, 'mórn-\ *adj* (15c) **1** : expressing sorrow : SORROWFUL **2** : full of sorrow : SAD **3** : causing sorrow or melancholy : GLOOMY — **mourn·ful·ly** \-fə-lē\ *adv* — **mourn·ful·ness** *n*

mourn·ing \'mōr-niŋ, 'mór-\ *n* (13c) **1** : the act of sorrowing **2** : an outward sign (as black clothes or an armband) of grief for a person's death **b** : a period of time during which signs of grief are shown

mourning cloak *n* (1898) : a blackish brown nymphalid butterfly (*Nymphalis antiopa*) with a broad yellow border on the wings found in temperate parts of Europe, Asia, and No. America

mourning dove *n* (1833) : a wild American dove (*Zenaida macroura*) with a pointed tail and a plaintive coo

¹mouse \'maús\ *n, pl* **mice** \'mis\ [ME, fr. OE *mūs*; akin to OHG *mūs* mouse, L *mus*, Gk *mys* mouse, muscle] (bef. 12c) **1** : any of numerous small rodents (as of the genus *Mus*) with pointed snout, rather small ears, elongated body, and slender tail **2** : a timid person **3** : a dark-colored swelling caused by a blow; *specif* : BLACK EYE **4** : a small mobile manual device that controls movement of the cursor and selection of functions on a computer display

²mouse \'maúz\ *vb* **moused; mous·ing** *vi* (13c) **1** : to hunt for mice **2** : to search or move stealthily or slowly ~ *vt* **1** *obs* **a** : BITE, GNAW **b** : to toy with roughly **2** : to search for carefully — usu. used with *out*

mouse-ear \'maús-,ir\ *n* (13c) **1** : a Eurasian hawkweed (*Hieracium pilosella*) that has soft hairy leaves and has been introduced into No. America **2** : any of several plants other than mouse-ear that have soft hairy leaves

mouse-ear chickweed *n* (1731) : any of several hairy chickweeds (genus *Cerastium* and esp. *C. vulgatum*)

mous·er \'maú-sər, *US also & chiefly Brit* -zər\ *n* (15c) : a catcher of mice and rats; *esp* : a cat proficient at mousing

¹mouse-trap \'maús-,trap\ *n* (15c) **1** : a trap for mice **2** : a stratagem that lures one to defeat or destruction : TRAP 2b

²mousetrap *vt* (ca. 1864) : to snare in or as if in a mousetrap

Mous·que·taire \,mü-skə-'tar, -'ter\ *n* [F — more at MUSKETEER] (1705) : a French musketeer; *esp* : one of the royal musketeers of the 17th and 18th centuries conspicuous for their daring and their dandified dress

mous·sa·ka \,mü-sə-'kä\ *n* [NGk *mousakas*, fr. Turk *musakka*] (1931) : a Middle Eastern dish of ground meat (as lamb or beef) and sliced eggplant often topped with a seasoned sauce

¹mousse \'müs\ *n* [F, lit., froth, moss, of Gmc origin; akin to OHG *mos* moss — more at MOSS] (1892) **1** : a light spongy food usu. containing cream or gelatin **2** : a molded chilled dessert made with sweetened and flavored whipped cream or egg whites and gelatin ⟨chocolate ~⟩ **3** : a foamy preparation used in styling hair

²mousse *vt* **moussed; mouss·ing** (1984) : to style (hair) with mousse

mous·se·line \,mü-sə-'lēn, ,müs-'lēn\ *n* [F, lit., muslin — more at MUSLIN] (1696) **1** : a fine sheer fabric (as of rayon) that resembles muslin **2 a** : a sauce (as hollandaise) to which whipped cream or beaten egg whites have been added **b** : MOUSSE 1 ⟨salmon ~⟩

mousseline de soie \-də-'swä\ *n, pl* **mousselines de soie** *same*\ [F, lit., silk muslin] (1850) : a silk muslin having a crisp finish

mous·tache *var of* MUSTACHE

mous·ta·chio *var of* MUSTACHIO

Mous·te·ri·an \mü-'stir-ē-ən\ *adj* [F *moustérien*, fr. Le Moustier, cave in Dordogne, France] (1890) : of or relating to a Middle Paleolithic culture that is characterized by well-made flake tools often considered the work of Neanderthal man

mousy *or* **mous·ey** \'maú-sē, -zē\ *adj* **mous·i·er; -est** (1853) : of, relating to, or resembling a mouse: as **a** : QUIET, STEALTHY **b** : TIMID, RETIRING **c** : grayish brown — **mous·i·ly** \-sə-lē, -zə-\ *adv* — **mous·i·ness** \-sē-nəs, -zē-\ *n*

¹mouth \'maúth\ *n, pl* **mouths** \'maúthz *also* 'maúz, 'maúths; *in synecdochic compounds like* "blabbermouths" ths *more frequently*\ *often attrib* [ME, fr. OE *mūth*; akin to OHG *mund* mouth and perh. to L *mentum* chin] (bef. 12c) **1 a** : the natural opening through which food passes into the body of an animal and which in vertebrates is typically bounded externally by the lips and internally by the pharynx and encloses the tongue, gums, and teeth **b** : GRIMACE ⟨made a ~⟩ **c** : an individual requiring food ⟨had too many ~s to feed⟩ **2 a** : VOICE, SPEECH ⟨finally gave ~ to her feelings⟩ **b** : MOUTHPIECE 3a **c** (1) : a tendency to excessive talk (2) : saucy or disrespectful language : IMPUDENCE **3** : something that resembles a mouth esp. in affording entrance or exit: as **a** : the place where a stream enters a larger body of water **b** : the surface opening of an underground cavity **c** : the opening of a container **d** : an opening in the side of an organ flue pipe — **mouth-like** \'maúth-,lik\ *adj* — **down in the mouth** : DEJECTED, SULKY

²mouth \'maúth *also* 'maúth\ *vt* (14c) **1 a** : SPEAK, PRONOUNCE **b** : to utter bombastically : DECLAIM **c** : to repeat without comprehension or sincerity ⟨always ~*ing* platitudes⟩ **d** : to form soundlessly with the lips ⟨the librarian ~*ed* the word "quiet"⟩ **e** : to utter indistinctly : MUMBLE ⟨~*ed* his words⟩ **2** : to take into the mouth; *esp* : EAT ~ *vi* **1 a** : to talk pompously : RANT — often used with *off* **b** : to talk insolently or impudently — usu. used with *off* **2** : to move the mouth esp. so as to make faces — **mouth·er** *n*

mouth·breed·er \'maúth-,brē-dər\ *n* (1927) : any of several fishes that carry their eggs and young in the mouth; *esp* : a No. African cichlid fish (*Haplochromis multicolor*) often kept in aquariums

mouthed \'maúthd, 'maúth\ *adj* (14c) : having a mouth esp. of a specified kind — often used in combination ⟨a soft-*mouthed* fish⟩

mouth·ful \'maúth-,fúl\ *n* (15c) **1 a** : as much as a mouth will hold **b** : the quantity usu. taken into the mouth at one time **2 a** : a small quantity **3 a** : a very long word or phrase **b** : a comment or a statement rich in meaning or substance

mouth hook *n* (1937) : one of a pair of hooked larval mouthparts of some dipteran flies that function as jaws

mouth organ *n* (1866) : HARMONICA 2

mouth·part \'maúth-,pärt\ *n* (1799) : a structure or appendage near the mouth (as of an insect) esp. when adapted for use in gathering or eating food

mouth·piece \-,pēs\ *n* (1683) **1** : something placed at or forming a mouth **2** : a part (as of an instrument) that goes in the mouth or to which the mouth is applied **3 a** : one that expresses or interprets another's views : SPOKESMAN **b** *slang* : a criminal lawyer

mouth-to-mouth *adj* (1941) : of, relating to, or being a method of artificial respiration in which the rescuer's mouth is placed tightly over the victim's mouth in order to force air into the victim's lungs by blowing forcefully enough every few seconds to inflate them

mouth·wash \'maúth-,wósh, -,wäsh\ *n* (1840) : a usu. antiseptic liquid preparation for cleaning the mouth and teeth or freshening the breath

mouth·wa·ter·ing \-,wó-tə-riŋ, -,wä-\ *adj* (1900) : arousing the appetite : tantalizingly delicious or appealing ⟨a ~ aroma⟩ — **mouth·wa·ter·ing·ly** \-lē\ *adv*

mouthy \'maú-thē, -thē\ *adj* **mouth·i·er; -est** (1589) **1** : excessively talkative : GARRULOUS **2** : marked by bombast or loud talk

mou·ton \'mü-,tän, mü-'\ *n* [F, sheep, sheepskin, fr. MF, ram — more at MUTTON] (1944) : processed sheepskin that has been sheared and dyed to resemble beaver or seal

¹mov·able *or* **move·able** \'mü-və-bəl\ *adj* (14c) **1** : capable of being moved **2** : changing date from year to year ⟨~ holidays⟩ — **mov·abil·i·ty** \,mü-və-'bi-lə-tē\ *n* — **mov·able·ness** \'mü-və-bəl-nəs\ *n* — **mov·ably** \-blē\ *adv*

²movable *or* **moveable** *n* (15c) : something (as an article of furniture) that can be removed or displaced

¹move \'müv\ *vb* **moved; mov·ing** [ME, fr. MF *movoir*, fr. L *movēre*; prob. akin to Skt *mivati* he moves, pushes] *vi* (13c) **1 a** (1) : to go or pass to another place or in a certain direction with a continuous motion ⟨*moved* into the shade⟩ (2) : to proceed toward a certain state or condition ⟨*moving* up the executive ladder⟩ ⟨*moved* into second place in the tournament⟩ (3) : to become transferred during play ⟨checkers ~ along diagonally adjacent squares⟩ (4) : to keep pace ⟨*moving* with the times⟩ **b** : to start away from some point or place : DEPART **c** : to change one's residence or location **2** : to carry on one's life or activities in a specified environment ⟨~s in the best circles⟩ **3** : to change position or posture : STIR ⟨told him to be quiet and not to ~⟩ **4** : to take action : ACT **5 a** : to begin operating or functioning or working in a usual way **b** : to show marked activity ⟨after a brief lull things really began to ~⟩ **c** : to move a piece (as in chess or checkers) during one's turn **6** : to make a formal request, application, or appeal **7** : to change hands by being sold or rented ⟨goods that were *moving* slowly⟩ **8** *of the bowels* : EVACUATE ~ *vt* **1 a** (1) : to change the place or position of (2) : to dislodge or displace from a fixed position : BUDGE **b** : to transfer (as a piece in chess) from one position to another **2 a** (1) : to cause to go or pass from one place to another with a continuous motion ⟨*moved* the flag slowly up and down⟩ (2) : to cause to advance **b** : to cause to operate or function : ACTUATE ⟨this button ~s the whole machine⟩ **c** : to put into activity or rouse up from inactivity **3** : to cause to change position or posture **4** : to prompt or rouse to the doing of something : PERSUADE ⟨the report *moved* the faculty to take action⟩ **5 a** : to stir the emotions, feelings, or passions of ⟨was deeply *moved* by such kindness⟩ **b** : to affect in such a way as to lead to an indicated show of emotion ⟨the story *moved* her to tears⟩ **6 a** *obs* : BEG **b** : to make a formal application to **7** : to propose formally in a deliberative assembly ⟨*moved* adjournment⟩ **8** : to cause (the bowels) to void **9** : to cause to change hands through sale or rent

syn MOVE, ACTUATE, DRIVE, IMPEL mean to set or keep in motion. MOVE is very general and implies no more than the fact of changing position ⟨*moved* the furniture⟩. ACTUATE stresses transmission of power so as to work or set in motion ⟨turbines *actuated* by waterpower⟩. DRIVE implies imparting forward and continuous motion and often stresses the effect rather than the impetus ⟨a ship *driven* aground by hurricane winds⟩. IMPEL is usu. figurative and suggests a great motivating impetus ⟨a candidate *impelled* by ambition⟩.

²move *n* (1656) **1 a** : the act of moving a piece (as in chess) **b** : the turn of a player to move **2 a** : a step taken so as to gain an objective : MANEUVER ⟨a ~ to end the dispute⟩ **b** : the action of moving from a motionless position **c** : a change of residence or location **d** : an agile or deceptive action esp. in sports — **on the move** **1** : in a state of moving about from place to place ⟨a salesman is constantly *on the*

\ə\ abut \ᵊ\ kitten, F table \ər\ further \a\ ash \ā\ ace \ä\ mop, mar \aú\ out \ch\ chin \e\ bet \ē\ easy \g\ go \i\ hit \ī\ ice \j\ job \ŋ\ sing \ō\ go \ó\ law \ói\ boy \th\ thin \th\ the \ü\ loot \ú\ foot \y\ yet \zh\ vision \à, k̲, ⁿ, œ, œ̄, ue, ūe, ʸ\ *see* Guide to Pronunciation *move*⟩ **2 :** in a state of moving ahead or making progress ⟨said that civilization is always *on the move*⟩

move in *vi* (1898) **:** to occupy a dwelling or place of work — **move in on :** to make advances or aggressive movements toward

move·less \'müv-ləs\ *adj* (1578) **:** being without movement **:** FIXED, IMMOBILE — **move·less·ly** *adv* — **move·less·ness** *n*

move·ment \'müv-mənt\ *n* (14c) **1 a** (1) **:** the act or process of moving; *esp* **:** change of place or position or posture (2) **:** a particular instance or manner of moving **b** (1) **:** a tactical or strategic shifting of a military unit **:** MANEUVER (2) **:** the advance of a military unit **c :** ACTION, ACTIVITY — usu. used in pl. **2 a :** TENDENCY, TREND ⟨detected a ~ toward fairer pricing⟩ **b :** a series of organized activities working toward an objective; *also* **:** an organized effort to promote or attain an end ⟨the civil rights ~⟩ **3 :** the moving parts of a mechanism that transmit a definite motion **4 a :** MOTION **7 b :** the rhythmic character or quality of a musical composition **c :** a distinct structural unit or division having its own key, rhythmic structure, and themes and forming part of an extended musical composition **d :** particular rhythmic flow of language **:** CADENCE **5 a :** the quality (as in a painting or sculpture) of representing or suggesting motion **b :** the vibrant quality in literature that comes from elements that constantly hold a reader's interest (as a quickly moving action-filled plot) **6 a :** an act of voiding the bowels **b :** matter expelled from the bowels at one passage

mov·er \'mü-vər\ *n* (14c) **:** one that moves or sets something in motion; *esp* **:** one whose business or occupation is the moving of household goods from one residence to another

mover and shaker *n*, *pl* **movers and shakers** (1951) **:** a person who is active or influential in some field of endeavor

mov·ie \'mü-vē\ *n* [*moving picture*] (1912) **1 :** MOTION PICTURE **2** *pl* **:** a showing of a motion picture **3** *pl* **:** the motion-picture medium or industry

mov·ie·dom \'mü-vē-dəm\ *n* (1916) **:** FILMDOM

mov·ie·go·er \-,gō(-ə)r\ *n* (1923) **:** FILMGOER — **mov·ie·going** \-,gō-iŋ, -,gō(-)iŋ\ *n*

mov·ie·mak·er \-,mā-kər\ *n* (1915) **:** one who makes movies — **mov·ie·mak·ing** \-,mā-kiŋ\ *n*

mov·ing *adj* (14c) **1 a :** marked by or capable of movement **b :** of or relating to a change of residence ⟨~ expenses⟩ **c :** used for transferring furnishings from one residence to another ⟨a ~ van⟩ **d :** involving a motor vehicle that is in motion ⟨a ~ violation⟩ **2 a :** producing or transferring motion or action **b :** stirring deeply in a way that evokes a strong emotional response ⟨a ~ story of a faithful dog⟩ — **mov·ing·ly** \'mü-viŋ-lē\ *adv*

syn MOVING, IMPRESSIVE, POIGNANT, AFFECTING, TOUCHING, PATHETIC mean having the power to produce deep emotion. MOVING may apply to any strong emotional effect including thrilling, agitating, saddening, or calling forth pity or sympathy ⟨a *moving* appeal for contributions⟩. IMPRESSIVE implies compelling attention, admiration, wonder, or conviction ⟨an *impressive* list of achievements⟩. POIGNANT applies to what keenly or sharply affects one's sensitivities ⟨a *poignant* documentary on the homeless⟩. AFFECTING is close to MOVING but most often suggests pathos ⟨an *affecting* deathbed reunion⟩. TOUCHING implies arousing tenderness or compassion ⟨the *touching* innocence in a child's eyes⟩. PATHETIC implies moving to pity or sometimes contempt ⟨*pathetic* attempts to justify misconduct⟩.

moving picture *n* (1896) **:** MOTION PICTURE

Mov·i·ola \,mü-vē-'ō-lə\ *trademark* — used for a device for editing motion-picture film and synchronizing the sound

¹mow \'maů\ *n* [ME, heap, stack, fr. OE *mūga*; akin to ON *mūgi* heap] (bef. 12c) **1 :** a piled-up stack (as of hay or fodder); *also* **:** a pile of hay or grain in a barn **2 :** the part of a barn where hay or straw is stored

²mow \'mō\ *vb* **mowed; mowed** *or* **mown** \'mōn\; **mow·ing** [ME, fr. OE *māwan*; akin to OHG *māen* to mow, L *metere* to reap, mow, Gk *aman*] *vt* (bef. 12c) **1 a :** to cut down with a scythe or sickle or machine **b :** to cut the standing herbage (as grass) of **2 a** (1) **:** to kill or destroy in great numbers or mercilessly ⟨machine guns ~ed down the enemy⟩ (2) **:** to cause to fall **:** KNOCK DOWN **b :** to overcome swiftly and decisively **:** ROUT ⟨~ed down the opposing team⟩ ~ *vi* **:** to cut down standing herbage (as grass) — **mow·er** \'mō(-ə)r\ *n*

³mow \'maů, 'mō\ *n* [ME *mowe*, fr. MF *moue*, of Gmc origin; akin to MD *mouwe* protruding lip] (14c) **:** GRIMACE

⁴mow \'maů, 'mō\ *vi* (15c) **:** to make grimaces

mox·ie \'mäk-sē\ *n* [fr. *Moxie*, a trademark for a soft drink] (1930) **1 :** ENERGY, PEP **2 :** COURAGE, DETERMINATION **3 :** KNOW-HOW, EXPERTISE

moyen–âge \mwä-ye-näzh\ *adj* [F *moyen âge* Middle Ages] (1849) **:** of or relating to medieval times

moz·za·rel·la \,mät-sə-'re-lə\ *n* [It, dim. of *mozza*, a kind of cheese, fr. *mozzare* to cut off, fr. *mozzo* cut off, docked, fr. (assumed) VL *mutius*, alter. of L *mutilus*] (1911) **:** a moist white unsalted unripened cheese of mild flavor and a smooth rubbery texture

moz·zet·ta \mōt-'se-tə\ *n* [It, prob. fr. *mozzo* cut off] (1774) **:** a short cape with a small ornamental hood worn over the rochet by Roman Catholic prelates

M phase *n* [*mitosis*] (1945) **:** the period in the cell cycle during which cell division takes place — compare G₁ PHASE, G₂ PHASE, S PHASE

Mr. \'mis-tər, *in rapid speech esp in sense 2* (,)mis(t)\ *n*, *pl* **Messrs.** \'me-sərz\ [Mr. fr. ME, abbr. of *maister* master; Messrs. abbr. of *Messieurs*, fr. F, pl. of *Monsieur*] (15c) **1** — used as a conventional title of courtesy except when usage requires the substitution of a title of rank or an honorific or professional title before a man's surname ⟨spoke to *Mr.* Doe⟩ **2** — used in direct address as a conventional title of respect before a man's title of office ⟨may I ask one more question, *Mr.* President⟩ **3** — used before the name of a place (as a country or city) or of a profession or activity (as a sport) or before some epithet (as *clever*) to form a title applied to a male viewed or recognized as representative of the thing indicated ⟨*Mr.* Baseball⟩

Mr. Charlie \-'chär-lē\ *n* [*Charlie*, fr. *Charles*, proper name] (ca. 1941) **:** a white man **:** white people — usu. used disparagingly

mri·dan·ga \mri-'däŋ-gə, ,mər-i-\ *or* **mri·dan·gam** \-gəm\ *n* [Skt *mṛdaṅga*] (1921) **:** a drum of India that is shaped like an elongated barrel and has tuned heads of different diameters

Mrs. \'mi-səz, -səs, *esp Southern* 'mi-zəz, -zəs, *or in rapid speech in sense 1* (,)miz, *or before given names* (,)mis\ *n*, *pl* **Mes·dames** \mā-'däm,

-'dam\ [Mrs. abbr. of *mistress; Mesdames* fr. F, pl. of *Madame*] (1615) **1 a** — used as a conventional title of courtesy except when usage requires the substitution of a title of rank or an honorific or professional title before a married woman's surname ⟨spoke to *Mrs.* Doe⟩ **b** — used before the name of a place (as a country or city) or of a profession or activity (as a sport) or before some epithet (as *clever*) to form a title applied to a married woman viewed or recognized as representative of the thing indicated ⟨*Mrs.* Golf⟩ **2 :** WIFE ⟨took the *Mrs.* to dinner⟩

Mrs. Grun·dy \-'grən-dē\ *n* [fr. a character alluded to in Thomas Morton's *Speed the Plough* (1798)] (1813) **:** one marked by prudish conventionality in personal conduct

Ms. \'miz\ *n*, *pl* **Mss.** *or* **Mses.** \'mi-zəz\ [prob. blend of *Miss* and *Mrs.*] (1949) — used instead of *Miss* or *Mrs.* (as when the marital status of a woman is unknown or irrelevant) ⟨*Ms.* Mary Smith⟩

M16 \,em-(,)sik-'stēn\ *n* [*model 16*] (1968) **:** a .223 caliber (5.56 mm.) gas-operated magazine-fed rifle for semiautomatic or automatic operation used by U.S. troops since the mid 1960s — called also *M16 rifle*

mu \'myü, 'mü\ *n* [Gk *my*] (1823) **:** the 12th letter of the Greek alphabet — see ALPHABET table

muc- *or* **muci-** *or* **muco-** *comb form* [L *muc-*, fr. *mucus*] **1 :** mucus ⟨*muco*protein⟩ **2 :** mucous and ⟨*muco*cutaneous⟩

¹much \'məch\ *adj* **more** \'mōr, 'mór\; **most** \'mōst\ [ME *muche* large, much, fr. *michel, muchel,* fr. OE *micel, mycel;* akin to OHG *mihhil* great, large, L *magnus,* Gk *megas,* Skt *mahat*] (13c) **1 :** great in quantity, amount, extent, or degree ⟨there is ~ truth in what you say⟩ ⟨taken too ~ time⟩ **2** *obs* **:** many in number **3 :** more than is expected or acceptable **:** more than enough ⟨eighty bedrooms, a bit ~ for a family of seven —Peter Dragadze⟩ — **too much 1 :** WONDERFUL, EXCITING **2 :** TERRIBLE, AWFUL

²much *adv* **more; most** (13c) **1 a** (1) **:** to a great degree or extent **:** CONSIDERABLY ⟨~ happier⟩ (2) **:** VERY **b** (1) **:** FREQUENTLY, OFTEN (2) **:** by or for a long time ⟨didn't get to work ~ before noon⟩ **c :** by far ⟨was ~ the brightest student⟩ **2 :** NEARLY, APPROXIMATELY ⟨looks ~ the way his father did⟩ — **as much :** the same in quantity

³much *n* (13c) **1 :** a great quantity, amount, extent, or degree ⟨gave away ~⟩ **2 :** something considerable or impressive ⟨was not ~ to look at⟩

mu·cha·cho \mü-'chä-(,)chō\ *n*, *pl* **-chos** [Sp, prob. fr. *mocho* cropped, shorn] (1591) **1** *chiefly Southwest* **:** a male servant **2** *chiefly Southwest* **:** a young man

much as *conj* (ca. 1699) **:** however much **:** even though

much less *conj* (1710) **:** to say nothing of — used esp. in negative contexts to add to one item another denoting something less likely ⟨can hardly grow, *much less* ripen, till the stock is in the earth —Jonathan Swift⟩ ⟨he is never going to get out of the eighth grade, *much less* ever make it to college —Thomas Meehan⟩

much·ness \'məch-nəs\ *n* (14c) **:** the quality or state of being great **:** GREATNESS — **much of a muchness :** very much the same

mu·ci·lage \'myü-s(ə-)lij\ *n* [ME *muscilage*, fr. LL *mucilago* mucus, musty juice, fr. L *mucus*] (15c) **1 :** a gelatinous substance of various plants (as legumes or seaweeds) that contains protein and polysaccharides and is similar to plant gums **2 :** an aqueous usu. viscid solution (as of a gum) used esp. as an adhesive

mu·ci·lag·i·nous \,myü-sə-'la-jə-nəs\ *adj* [ME *musciliaginous*, fr. LL *mucilaginosus,* fr. *mucilagin-, mucilago*] (15c) **1 :** STICKY, VISCID **2 :** of, relating to, full of, or secreting mucilage — **mu·ci·lag·i·nous·ly** *adv*

mu·cin \'myü-sᵊn\ *n* [ISV *muc-*] (1846) **:** any of various mucoproteins that occur esp. in secretions of mucous membranes — **mu·cin·ous** \-sᵊn-əs, 'myüs-nəs\ *adj*

¹muck \'mək\ *n* [ME *muk*, perh. fr. OE *-moc;* akin to ON *myki* dung] (13c) **1 :** soft moist farmyard manure **2 :** slimy dirt or filth **3 :** defamatory remarks or writings **4 a** (1) **:** dark highly organic soil (2) **:** MIRE, MUD **b :** something resembling muck **:** GUNK **5 :** material removed in the process of excavating or mining — **mucky** \'mə-kē\ *adj*

²muck *vt* (14c) **1 a :** to clean up; *esp* **:** to clear of manure or filth — usu. used with *out* **b :** to clear of muck **2 :** to dress (as soil) with muck **3 :** to dirty with or as if with muck **:** SOIL ~ *vi* **1 :** to move or load muck (as in a mine) **2 :** to engage in aimless activity — usu. used with *about* or *around* — **muck·er** *n*

muck–a–muck \'mə-kə-,mək\ *or* **muck·ety–muck** \'mə-kə-tē-\ *n* (1912) **:** HIGH-MUCK-A-MUCK

muck-luck *var of* MUKLUK

muck·rake \'mək-,rāk\ *vi* [obs. *muckrake*, n., rake for dung] (1910) **:** to search out and publicly expose real or apparent misconduct of a prominent individual or business — **muck·rak·er** *n*

muck up *vt* (1896) **:** to make a mess of **:** BUNGLE, SPOIL

mu·co·cu·ta·ne·ous \,myü-kō-kyü-'tā-nē-əs\ *adj* (1898) **:** made up of or involving both typical skin and mucous membrane

¹mu·coid \'myü-,kóid\ *adj* [ISV *muc-*] (1849) **:** resembling mucus

²mucoid *n* [ISV] (1900) **:** MUCOPROTEIN

mu·co·lyt·ic \,myü-kə-'li-tik\ *adj* (ca. 1923) **:** hydrolyzing mucopolysaccharides **:** tending to break down or lower the viscosity of mucin-containing body secretions or components ⟨~ enzymes⟩

mu·co·pep·tide \,myü-kō-'pep-,tīd\ *n* (1956) **:** PEPTIDOGLYCAN

mu·co·poly·sac·cha·ride \'myü-kō-,pä-li-'sa-kə-,rīd\ *n* [ISV] (1938) **:** GLYCOSAMINOGLYCAN

mu·co·pro·tein \,myü-kə-'prō-,tēn *also* -'prō-tē-ən\ *n* (1925) **:** any of various complex conjugated proteins (as mucins) that contain polysaccharides and occur in body fluids and tissues

mu·co·sa \myü-'kō-zə\ *n*, *pl* **-sae** \-(,)zē, -,zi\ *or* **-sas** [NL, fr. L, fem. of *mucosus* mucous] (1880) **:** MUCOUS MEMBRANE — **mu·co·sal** \-zəl\ *adj*

mu·cous \'myü-kəs\ *adj* [L *mucosus,* fr. *mucus*] (1646) **1 :** of, relating to, or resembling mucus **2 :** secreting or containing mucus **3 :** covered with or as if with mucus **:** SLIMY

mucous membrane *n* (1812) **:** a membrane rich in mucous glands; *specif* **:** one that lines body passages and cavities which communicate directly or indirectly with the exterior

mu·cro \'myü-,krō\ *n*, *pl* **mu·cro·nes** \myü-'krō-(,)nēz\ [NL *mucron-, mucro,* fr. L, point, edge] (1646) **:** an abrupt sharp terminal point or tip or process (as of a leaf) — **mu·cro·nate** \'myü-krə-,nāt\ *adj*

mu·cus \'myü-kəs\ n [L, nasal mucus; akin to Gk *myxa* mucus] (1661) : a viscid slippery secretion that is usu. rich in mucins and is produced by mucous membranes which it moistens and protects

¹**mud** \'məd\ n [ME *mudde*, prob. fr. MLG] (14c) **1** : a slimy sticky mixture of solid material with a liquid and esp. water; *esp* : soft wet earth **2** : abusive and malicious remarks or charges ⟨political campaigners arguing ~ at each other⟩ **3** : ANATHEMA 1b — usu. used in the phrase *one's name is mud*

²**mud** vt **mud·ded; mud·ding** (1593) **1** : to make muddy or turbid **2** : to treat or plaster with mud

mud dauber n (1856) : any of various wasps (esp. family Sphecidae) that construct mud cells in which the female places an egg with spiders or insects paralyzed by a sting to serve as food for the larva

¹**mud·dle** \'mə-d²l\ vb **mud·dled; mud·dling** \'məd-liŋ, 'mə-d²l-iŋ\ [prob. fr. obs. D *moddelen*, fr. MD, fr. *modde* mud; akin to MLG *mudde*] vt (1676) **1** : to make turbid or muddy **2** : to befog or stupefy esp. with liquor **3** : to mix confusedly **4** : to make a mess of : BUNGLE ~ vi : to think or act in a confused aimless way — **mud·dler** \'məd-lər, 'mə-d²l-ər\ n

²**muddle** n (ca. 1818) **1** : a state of esp. mental confusion **2** : a confused mess — **mud·dly** \'məd-lē, 'mə-d²l-ē\ adj

mud·dle·head·ed \ˌmə-d²l-'he-dəd\ adj (1759) **1** : mentally confused **2** : INEPT, BUNGLING — **mud·dle·head·ed·ly** adv — **mud·dle·head·ed·ness** n

muddle through vi (ca. 1864) : to achieve a degree of success without much planning or effort

¹**mud·dy** \'mə-dē\ adj **mud·di·er; -est** (15c) **1** : morally impure : BASE **2 a** : full of or covered with mud **b** : characteristic or suggestive of mud ⟨a ~ flavor⟩ ⟨~ colors⟩ **c** : turbid with sediment **3 a** : lacking in clarity or brightness : CLOUDY, DULL ⟨a ~ recording⟩ ⟨eyes ~ with sleep⟩ **b** : obscure in meaning : MUDDLED, CONFUSED ⟨~ thinking⟩ ⟨a ~ style⟩ — **mud·di·ly** \'mə-d²l-ē\ adv — **mud·di·ness** \'mə-dē-nəs\ n

²**muddy** vt **mud·died; mud·dy·ing** (1601) **1** : to soil or stain with or as if with mud **2** : to make turbid **3** : to make cloudy or dull **4** : CONFUSE

Mu·de·jar \mü-'the-ˌhär, -ˌkär\ n, pl **-ja·res** \-'the-hä-ˌräs, -kä-\ [Sp *mudéjar*, fr. Ar *mudajjan*, lit., allowed to remain] (1893) : a Muslim living under a Christian king esp. during the 8th to 11th centuries — **Mudejar** adj

mud·flat \'məd-ˌflat\ n (1813) : a level tract lying at little depth below the surface of water or alternately covered and left bare by the tide

mud·flow \-ˌflō\ n (ca. 1900) : a moving mass of soil made fluid by rain or melting snow

mud·guard \-ˌgärd\ n (1886) **1 a** : FENDER d **b** : SPLASH GUARD **2** : a strip of material applied to a shoe upper just above the sole for protection against dampness or as an ornament

mud puppy n (1882) : a large American salamander (*Necturus maculosus*) that has external gills and is gray to rusty brown usu. with bluish black spots

mu·dra \mə-'drä\ n [Skt *mudrā*] (1811) : one of the symbolic hand gestures used in religious ceremonies and dances of India

mud·room \'məd-ˌrüm, -ˌrùm\ n (ca. 1950) : a room in a house designed esp. for the shedding of dirty or wet footwear and clothing and located typically off the kitchen or in the basement

mud puppy

mud·sill \-ˌsil\ n (1685) **1** : a supporting sill (as of a building or bridge) resting directly on a base and esp. the earth **2** : a person of the lowest social level

mud·skip·per \-ˌski-pər\ n (1860) : any of several Asian and Polynesian gobies (genera *Periophthalmus* and *Boleophthalmus*) that are able to skip about actively over wet mud and sand

mud·sling·er \-ˌsliŋ-ər\ n (ca. 1890) : one that uses offensive epithets and invective esp. against a political opponent — **mud·sling·ing** \-ˌsliŋ-iŋ\ n

mud·stone \-ˌstōn\ n (ca. 1736) : an indurated shale produced by the consolidation of mud

mud turtle n (1785) : any of a genus (*Kinosternon*) of bottom-dwelling freshwater turtles with two transverse hinges on the plastron

Muen·ster \'mən(t)-stər, 'mün(t)-, 'mùn(t)-, 'min(t)-\ n [*Münster*, *Munster*, France] (1902) : a semisoft cheese that may be bland or sharp in flavor

mues·li \'myüs-lē, 'myüz-\ n [G dial. (Swiss) *Müsli*, dim. of G *Mus* soft food, mush, fr. OHG *muos*; akin to OE *mōs* food and prob. to OE *mete* food — more at MEAT] (1939) : a breakfast cereal of Swiss origin consisting of rolled oats, nuts, and fruit

mu·ez·zin \mü-'e-z²n, myü-; 'mwe-z²n\ n [Ar *mu'adhdhin*] (1585) : a Muslim crier who calls the hour of daily prayers

¹**muff** \'məf\ n [D *mof*, fr. MF *moufle* mitten, fr. ML *muffula*] (1599) **1** : a warm tubular covering for the hands **2** : a cluster of feathers on the side of the face of some domestic fowls

²**muff** vb [prob. fr. ¹*muff*] vt (1827) **1** : to handle awkwardly : BUNGLE **2** : to fail to hold (a ball) when attempting a catch ~ vi **1** : to act or do something stupidly or clumsily **2** : to muff a ball — compare FUMBLE

³**muff** n (1871) **1** : a bungling performance **2** : a failure to hold a ball in attempting a catch

muf·fin \'mə-fən\ n [prob. fr. LG *muffen*, pl. of *muffe* cake] (1703) : a quick bread made of batter containing egg and baked in a muffin pan

muf·fle \'mə-fəl\ vt **muf·fled; muf·fling** \'mə-f(ə-)liŋ\ [ME *muflen*] (15c) **1** : to wrap up so as to conceal or protect : ENVELOP **2** obs : BLINDFOLD **3 a** : to wrap or pad with something to dull the sound ⟨~ the oarlocks⟩ **b** : to deaden the sound of **4** : KEEP DOWN, SUPPRESS

muf·fler \'mə-flər\ n (ca. 1536) **1 a** : a scarf worn around the neck **b** : something that hides or disguises **2** : a device to deaden noise; *esp* : one forming part of the exhaust system of an automotive vehicle — **muf·flered** adj

¹**muf·ti** \'mə-fē, 'mùf-\ n [Ar *mufti*] (1586) : a professional jurist who interprets Muslim law

²**muf·ti** \'məf-tē\ n [prob. fr. ¹*mufti*] (1816) : ordinary dress as distinguished from that denoting an occupation or station ⟨a priest in ~⟩; *esp* : civilian clothes when worn by a person in the armed forces

¹**mug** \'məg\ n [origin unknown] (1664) **1** : a cylindrical drinking cup **2 a** : the face or mouth of a person **b** : GRIMACE **c** : MUG SHOT **3 a** *chiefly Brit* (1) : FOOL, BLOCKHEAD (2) : a person easily deceived **b** : PUNK, THUG — **mug·ful** n

²**mug** vb **mugged; mug·ging** vi (1855) : to pose or make faces esp. to attract attention or for a camera ~ vt : PHOTOGRAPH

³**mug** vt **mugged; mug·ging** [prob. fr. earlier *mug* to strike in the face, perh. fr. ¹*mug*] (ca. 1864) : to assault usu. with intent to rob — **mug·gee** \ˌmə-'gē\ n

¹**mug·ger** \'mə-gər\ n [Hindi *magar*, fr. Skt *makara* water monster] (1844) : a common usu. harmless freshwater crocodile (*Crocodylus palustris*) of southeastern Asia

²**mugger** n [³*mug*] (1863) : one who attacks with intent to rob

²**mugger** n [²*mug*] (1892) : one that grimaces esp. before an audience

mug·gy \'mə-gē\ adj **mug·gi·er; -est** [E dial. *mug* drizzle] (1746) : being warm, damp, and close — **mug·gi·ness** \'mə-gē-nəs\ n

Mu·ghal var of MOGUL

mu·gho pine \'mü-(ˌ)gō-, 'myü-\ n [prob. fr. F *mugho* mugho pine, fr. It *mugo*] (ca. 1756) : a shrubby spreading pine (*Pinus mugo mughus*) widely cultivated as an ornamental — called also *mugo pine*

mug's game \ˈməgz-\ n (1910) : a profitless or futile activity

mug shot n (1950) : a photograph of usu. a person's head and esp. face; *specif* : a police photograph of a suspect's face or profile

mug up vi (ca. 1860) *Brit* : to study intensively (as for an examination) ~ vt : to work up by study

mug·wump \'məg-ˌwəmp\ n [obs. slang *mugwump* kingpin, fr. Massachuset *mugguomp*, *muggumquomp* war leader] (1884) **1** : a bolter from the Republican party in 1884 **2** : an independent in politics

Mu·ham·mad·an \mō-'ha-mə-dən, -'hä- *also* mü-\ adj (1681) : of or relating to Muhammad or Islam — **Muhammadan** n — **Mu·ham·mad·an·ism** \-də-ˌni-zəm\ n

Muhammadan calendar n (ca. 1889) : ISLAMIC CALENDAR

Muhammadan era n (ca. 1889) : ISLAMIC ERA

Mu·har·ram \mü-'har-əm\ n [Ar *Muḥarram*] (ca. 1615) **1** : the 1st month of the Islamic year — see MONTH table **2** : a Muslim festival held during Muharram

mu·ja·hid·een *or* **mu·ja·hed·in** *also* **mu·ja·hed·een** \mü-ˌja-hi-'dēn, mü-, -jä-\ n pl [Ar *mujahidin*, pl. of *mujāhid*, lit., person who wages jihad] (1922) : Islamic guerrilla fighters esp. in the Middle East

mu·jik \mü-'zhēk, -'zhik\ var of MUZHIK

muk·luk \'mək-ˌlək\ n [Yupik *maklak* bearded seal] (1868) **1** : a sealskin or reindeer-skin boot worn by Eskimos **2** : a boot often of duck with a soft leather sole and worn over several pairs of socks

muk·tuk \'mək-ˌtək\ n [Inuit *maktak*] (1835) : whale skin used for food

mu·lat·to \mə-'la-(ˌ)tō, mù-, myù-, -'lä-\ n, pl **-toes** *or* **-tos** [Sp *mulato*, fr. *mulo* mule, fr. L *mulus*] (1593) **1** : the first-generation offspring of a black person and a white person **2** : a person of mixed white and black ancestry

mul·ber·ry \'məl-ˌber-ē, -b(ə-)rē\ n [ME *murberie, mulberie*, fr. MF *moure* mulberry (fr. L *morum*, fr. Gk *moron*) + ME *berie* berry] (14c) **1** : any of a genus (*Morus* of the family Moraceae, the mulberry family) of trees with an edible usu. purple multiple fruit that is an aggregate of juicy one-seeded drupes; *also* : the fruit **2** : a dark purple or purplish black

mulch \'məlch\ n [perh. irreg. fr. E dial. *melch* soft, mild] (1657) : a protective covering (as of sawdust, compost, or paper) spread or left on the ground to reduce evaporation, maintain even soil temperature, prevent erosion, control weeds, enrich the soil, or keep fruit (as strawberries) clean — **mulch** vt

¹**mulct** \'məlkt\ n [L *multa, mulcta*] (1598) : FINE, PENALTY

²**mulct** vt (1611) **1** : to punish by a fine **2 a** : to defraud esp. of money : SWINDLE **b** : to obtain by fraud, duress, or theft

¹**mule** \'myü(ə)l\ n [ME, fr. OF *mul*, fr. L *mulus*] (13c) **1 a** : a hybrid between a horse and a donkey; *esp* : the offspring of a male donkey and a mare **b** : a self-sterile plant whether hybrid or not **c** : a usu. sterile hybrid **2** : a very stubborn person **3** : a machine for simultaneously drawing and twisting fiber into yarn or thread and winding it into cops **4** *slang* : a person who smuggles or delivers illicit drugs

²**mule** n [MF, a kind of slipper, fr. L *mulleus* shoe worn by magistrates] (1562) : a shoe or slipper without quarter or heel strap — compare SCUFF

mule deer n (1805) : a long-eared deer (*Odocoileus hemionus*) of western No. America that is larger and more heavily built than the common whitetail

mule skinner n (1870) : MULETEER

mu·le·ta \mü-'lā-tə, myü-\ n [Sp, crutch, muleta, dim. of *mula* she-mule, fr. L, fem. of *mulus* mule] (1838) : a small cloth attached to a short tapered stick and used by a matador in place of the large cape during the final stage of a bullfight

mu·le·teer \ˌmyü-lə-'tir\ n [F *muletier*, fr. *mulet*, fr. OF, dim. of *mul* mule] (1538) : one who drives mules

mu·ley \'myü-lē, 'mù-, 'mü\ adj [of Celtic origin; akin to Ir & ScGael *maol* bald, hornless, W *moel*] (1840) : POLLED, HORNLESS; *esp* : naturally hornless

mu·li·eb·ri·ty \ˌmyü-lē-'e-brə-tē\ n [LL *muliebritat-, muliebritas*, fr. L *muliebris* of a woman, fr. *mulier* woman] (1592) : FEMININITY

mul·ish \'myü-lish\ adj [¹*mule*] (1751) : unreasonably and inflexibly obstinate *syn* see OBSTINATE — **mul·ish·ly** adv — **mul·ish·ness** n

¹**mull** \'məl\ vb [ME, fr. *mul, mol* dust, prob. fr. MD; akin to OE *melu* meal — more at MEAL] vt (15c) **1** : to grind or mix thoroughly : PULVERIZE **2** : to consider at length : PONDER — often used with *over* ~ vi : MEDITATE, PONDER

\ə\ abut \ᵊ\ kitten, F table \ər\ further \a\ ash \ā\ ace \ä\ mop, mar \aù\ out \ch\ chin \e\ bet \ē\ easy \g\ go \i\ hit \ī\ ice \j\ job \ŋ\ sing \ō\ go \ò\ law \òi\ boy \th\ thin \th̶\ the \ü\ loot \ù\ foot \y\ yet \zh\ vision \á, k̲, ⁿ, œ, œ̄, ᵫ, ᵫ̄, ᵞ\ see Guide to Pronunciation

²**mull** *vt* [origin unknown] (1618) : to heat, sweeten, and flavor (as wine or cider) with spices

³**mull** *n* [by shortening & alter. fr. *mulmul* muslin, fr. Hindi *malmal*] (1798) : a soft fine sheer fabric of cotton, silk, or rayon

⁴**mull** *n* [G, fr. Dan *muld*, fr. ON *mold* dust, soil; akin to OHG *molta* dust, soil — more at MOLD] (1928) **1** : friable forest humus that forms a layer of mixed organic matter and mineral soil and merges gradually into the mineral soil beneath **2** : a finely powdered solid esp. in a suspension

mul·lah \'mə-lə, 'mü-\ *n* [Turk *molla* & Per & Hindi *mulla*, fr. Ar *mawlā*] (1613) : an educated Muslim trained in traditional religious law and doctrine and usu. holding an official post — **mul·lah·ism** \-lə-ˌi-zəm\ *n*

mul·lein *also* **mul·len** \'mə-lən\ *n* [ME *moleyne*, fr. AF *moleine*] (14c) : any of a genus (*Verbascum*) of usu. woolly-leaved Eurasian herbs of the snapdragon family including some that are naturalized in No. America

mullein pink *n* (ca. 1850) : an Old World herb (*Lychnis coronaria*) of the pink family cultivated chiefly for its woolly herbage and crimson flowers

mull·er \'mə-lər\ *n* [alter. of ME *molour*, prob. fr. *mullen* to grind] (1612) : a stone or piece of wood, metal, or glass used as a pestle for pounding or grinding

Mül·le·ri·an \myü-'lir-ē-ən, mi-, ˌmə-\ *adj* [Fritz *Müller* †1897 Ger. zoologist] (1899) : of, relating to, or being mimicry that exists between two or more inedible or dangerous species (as of butterflies) and that is considered in evolutionary theory to be a mechanism reducing loss to predation by simplification of the recognition process

mul·let \'mə-lət\ *n, pl* **mullet** *or* **mullets** [ME *molet*, fr. MF *mulet*, fr. L *mullus* red mullet, fr. Gk *myllos*] (14c) : any of a family (Mugilidae) of valuable chiefly marine food fishes with an elongate rather stout body

mul·li·gan \'mə-li-gən\ *n* [prob. fr. the name *Mulligan*] (ca. 1949) : a free shot sometimes given a golfer in informal play when the previous shot was poorly played

mulligan stew *n* [prob. fr. the name *Mulligan*] (1904) : a stew made from whatever ingredients are available

mul·li·ga·taw·ny \ˌmə-li-gə-'tȯ-nē, -'tä-\ *n* [Tamil *miḷakutanni*, fr. *miḷaku* pepper + *taṇṇi* water] (1784) : a rich soup usu. of chicken stock seasoned with curry

mul·lion \'mə-lyən\ *n* [prob. alter. of *monial* mullion] (1567) : a slender vertical member that forms a division between units of a window, door, or screen or is used decoratively — **mullion** *vt*

mull·ite \'mə-ˌlīt\ *n* [*Mull*, island of the Inner Hebrides] (1924) : a mineral that is an orthorhombic silicate of aluminum which is resistant to corrosion and heat and is used as a refractory

multi- *comb form* [ME, fr. MF or L; MF, fr. L, fr. *multus* much, many — more at MELIORATE] **1 a** : many : multiple : much (*multivalent*) **b** : more than two (*multilateral*) **c** : more than one (*multiparous*) **2** : many times over (*multimillionaire*)

mul·ti·age	mul·ti·em·ploy·er	mul·ti·phasic
mul·ti·agen·cy	mul·ti·en·gine	mul·ti·pho·ton
mul·ti·armed	mul·ti·eth·nic	mul·ti·pic·ture
mul·ti·at·om	mul·ti·fac·et·ed	mul·ti·piece
mul·ti·au·thor	mul·ti·fam·i·ly	mul·ti·pi·on
mul·ti·ax·i·al	mul·ti·fil·a·ment	mul·ti·pis·ton
mul·ti·band	mul·ti·flash	mul·ti·plant
mul·ti·bank	mul·ti·fo·cal	mul·ti·play·er
mul·ti·bar·rei	mul·ti·fre·quen·cy	mul·ti·pole
mul·ti·bar·reled	mul·ti·func·tion	mul·ti·pow·er
mul·ti·bil·lion	mul·ti·func·tion·al	mul·ti·prob·lem
mul·ti·bil·lion·aire	mul·ti·gen·er·a·tion·al	mul·ti·prod·uct
mul·ti·blad·ed	mul·ti·gen·ic	mul·ti·pur·pose
mul·ti·branched	mul·ti·grade	mul·ti·range
mul·ti·build·ing	mul·ti·grain	mul·ti·re·gion·al
mul·ti·cam·pus	mul·ti·grid	mul·ti·re·li·gious
mul·ti·car	mul·ti·group	mul·ti·room
mul·ti·car·bon	mul·ti·hand·i·capped	mul·ti·screen
mul·ti·caus·al	mul·ti·head·ed	mul·ti·ser·vice
mul·ti·cell	mul·ti·hos·pi·tal	mul·ti·sid·ed
mul·ti·celled	mul·ti·hued	mul·ti·site
mul·ti·cel·lu·lar	mul·ti·in·dus·try	mul·ti·size
mul·ti·cel·lu·lar·i·ty	mul·ti·in·sti·tu·tion·al	mul·ti·skilled
mul·ti·cen·ter	mul·ti·lane	mul·ti·source
mul·ti·chain	mul·ti·lev·el	mul·ti·spe·cies
mul·ti·cham·bered	mul·ti·lev·eled	mul·ti·speed
mul·ti·chan·nel	mul·ti·line	mul·ti·sport
mul·ti·char·ac·ter	mul·ti·lobed	mul·ti·stemmed
mul·ti·city	mul·ti·manned	mul·ti·step
mul·ti·cli·ent	mul·ti·mega·ton	mul·ti·sto·ried
mul·ti·coat·ed	mul·ti·mega·watt	mul·ti·sto·ry
mul·ti·col·or	mul·ti·mem·ber	mul·ti·strand·ed
mul·ti·col·ored	mul·ti·met·al·lic	mul·ti·syl·lab·ic
mul·ti·col·umn	mul·ti·mil·len·ni·al	mul·ti·sys·tem
mul·ti·com·po·nent	mul·ti·mil·lion	mul·ti·tal·ent·ed
mul·ti·con·duc·tor	mul·ti·mil·lion·aire	mul·ti·ter·mi·nal
mul·ti·copy	mul·ti·mode	mul·ti·tiered
mul·ti·coun·ty	mul·ti·mo·lec·u·lar	mul·ti·ton
mul·ti·course	mul·ti·na·tion	mul·ti·tone
mul·ti·cu·rie	mul·ti·nu·cle·ar	mul·ti·tow·ered
mul·ti·cur·ren·cy	mul·ti·nu·cle·ate	mul·ti·track
mul·ti·di·a·lec·tal	mul·ti·nu·cle·at·ed	mul·ti·tril·lion
mul·ti·di·men·sion·al	mul·ti·or·gas·mic	mul·ti·union
mul·ti·di·men·sion·al·i·ty	mul·ti·page	mul·ti·unit
mul·ti·di·rec·tion·al	mul·ti·paned	mul·ti·use
mul·ti·dis·ci·plin·ary	mul·ti·pa·ram·e·ter	mul·ti·vi·ta·min
mul·ti·dis·ci·pline	mul·ti·part	mul·ti·vol·ume
mul·ti·di·vi·sion·al	mul·ti·par·ti·cle	mul·ti·wall
mul·ti·do·main	mul·ti·par·ty	mul·ti·war·head
mul·ti·drug	mul·ti·path	mul·ti·wave·length
mul·ti·elec·trode	mul·ti·phase	mul·ti·year
mul·ti·el·e·ment		

mul·ti·cul·tur·al \ˌməl-tē-'kəlch-rəl, -ˌtī-, -'kəl-chə-\ *adj* (1941) : of, relating to, reflecting, or adapted to diverse cultures (a ~ society) (~ education) (a ~ menu) — **mul·ti·cul·tur·al·ism** \-rə-ˌli-zəm\ *n*

mul·ti·en·zyme \-'en-ˌzīm\ *adj* (1961) : composed of or involving two or more enzymes that function in a biosynthetic pathway (~ complex)

mul·ti·fac·to·ri·al \-fak-'tȯr-ē-əl, -'tȯr-\ *adj* (1920) **1** : having characters or a mode of inheritance dependent on a number of genes at different loci **2** *or* **mul·ti·fac·tor** \-'fak-tər\ : having, involving, or produced by a variety of elements or causes — **mul·ti·fac·to·ri·al·ly** \-fak-'tȯr-ē-ə-lē, -'tȯr-\ *adv*

mul·ti·far·i·ous \ˌməl-tə-'far-ē-əs, -'fer-\ *adj* [ML *multifarius*, fr. L *multifariam* in many places] (1593) : having or occurring in great variety : DIVERSE — **mul·ti·far·i·ous·ness** *n*

mul·ti·flo·ra rose \ˌməl-tə-'flȯr-ə-, -'flȯr-\ *n* [NL *multiflora*, specific epithet, lit., having many flowers] (1829) : a vigorous thorny rose (*Rosa multiflora*) with clusters of small flowers

mul·ti·fold \'məl-ti-ˌfōld\ *adj* (1806) : MANY, NUMEROUS

mul·ti·form \'məl-ti-ˌfȯrm\ *adj* [F *multiforme*, fr. L *multiformis*, fr. *multi-* + *-formis* -form] (1603) : having many forms or appearances — **mul·ti·for·mi·ty** \ˌməl-ti-'fȯr-mə-tē\ *n*

mul·ti·germ \'məl-ti-'jərm, -ˌti-\ *adj* [prob. fr. *multi-* + *germinate*] (1950) : producing or being a fruit cluster capable of giving rise to several plants (a ~ variety of sugar beet)

mul·ti·hull \'məl-ti-ˌhəl, -'həl\ *n* (1960) : a vessel (as a catamaran or trimaran) with multiple side-by-side hulls — compare MONOHULL

mul·ti·lat·er·al \ˌməl-ti-'la-t(ə-)rəl, -ˌti-\ *adj* (1696) **1** : having many sides **2** : involving or participated in by more than two nations or parties (~ agreements) — **mul·ti·lat·er·al·ism** \-'la-t(ə-)rə-ˌli-zəm\ *n* — **mul·ti·lat·er·al·ist** \-list\ *n* — **mul·ti·lat·er·al·ly** *adv*

mul·ti·lay·ered \-'lā-ərd, -'le(-ə)rd\ *or* **mul·ti·lay·er** \-'lā-ər, -'le(-ə)r\ *adj* (1923) : having or involving several distinct layers, strata, or levels

mul·ti·lin·gual \-'liŋ-gwəl, -'liŋ-gyə-wəl\ *adj* (1838) **1** : of, containing, or expressed in several languages (a ~ sign) (~ dictionaries) **2** : using or able to use several languages (~ translators) — **mul·ti·lin·gual·ism** \-gwə-ˌli-zəm, -gyə-wə-\ *n* — **mul·ti·lin·gual·ly** \-gwə-lē, -gyə-wə-lē\ *adv*

mul·ti·me·dia \-'mē-dē-ə\ *adj* (1962) : using, involving, or encompassing several media (a ~ approach to learning) — **multimedia** *n*

mul·ti·mod·al \-'mō-d²l\ *adj* (1902) : having or involving several modes, modalities, or maxima (~ distributions) (~ responses)

mul·ti·na·tion·al \-'nash-nəl, -'na-shə-n²l\ *adj* (1926) **1** : of or relating to more than two nationalities (a ~ society) **2 a** : of, relating to, or involving more than two nations (a ~ alliance) **b** : having divisions in more than two countries (a ~ corporation) — **multinational** *n*

mul·ti·no·mi·al \-'nō-mē-əl\ *n* [*multi-* + *-nomial* (as in *binomial*)] (1674) : a mathematical expression that consists of the sum of several terms : POLYNOMIAL — **multinomial** *adj*

mul·tip·a·rous \ˌməl-'ti-pə-rəs\ *adj* [NL *multiparus*, fr. *multi-* + L *-parus* -parous] (1646) **1** : producing many or more than one at a birth **2** : having experienced one or more previous parturitions

mul·ti·par·tite \ˌməl-ti-'pär-ˌtīt\ *adj* [L *multipartitus*, fr. *multi-* + *partitus*, pp. of *partire* to divide, fr. *part-*, *pars* part] (ca. 1721) **1** : divided into several or many parts **2** : having numerous members or signatories (a ~ treaty)

¹**mul·ti·ple** \'məl-tə-pəl\ *adj* [F, fr. L *multiplex*, fr. *multi-* + *-plex* -fold — more at -FOLD] (1647) **1** : consisting of, including, or involving more than one (~ births) **2** : MANY, MANIFOLD (~ achievements) **3** : shared by many (~ ownership) **4** : having numerous aspects or functions : VARIOUS **5** : being a group of terminals which make a circuit available at a number of points **6** : formed by coalescence of the ripening ovaries of several flowers (a ~ fruit)

²**multiple** *n* (1685) **1 a** : the product of a quantity by an integer (35 is a ~ of 7) **b** : something in units of more than one or two **2** : PARALLEL 4b **3** *chiefly Brit* : CHAIN STORE

multiple allele *n* (1938) : an allele of a genetic locus having more than two allelic forms within a population

multiple–choice *adj* (1926) **1** : having several answers from which one is to be chosen (a ~ question) **2** : composed of multiple-choice questions (a ~ test)

multiple factor *n* (1915) : one of a group of nonallelic genes that according to the multiple-factor hypothesis control various quantitative hereditary characters

multiple myeloma *n* (1897) : a disease of bone marrow that is characterized by the presence of numerous myelomas in various bones of the body

multiple personality *n* (1901) : an hysterical neurosis in which the personality becomes dissociated into two or more distinct but complex and socially and behaviorally integrated parts each of which becomes dominant and controls behavior from time to time to the exclusion of the others — compare SCHIZOPHRENIA, SPLIT PERSONALITY

multiple regression *n* (1924) : regression in which one variable is estimated by the use of more than one other variable

multiple sclerosis *n* (1885) : a demyelinating disease marked by patches of hardened tissue in the brain or the spinal cord and associated esp. with partial or complete paralysis and jerking muscle tremor

multiple star *n* (1850) : several stars in close proximity that appear to form a single system

multiple store *n* (1929) *chiefly Brit* : CHAIN STORE

mul·ti·plet \'məl-tə-plət\ *n* (1922) **1** : a spectrum line having several components **2** : a group of elementary particles that are different in charge but similar in other properties (as mass)

multiple–valued *adj* (1882) : having at least one and sometimes more of the values of the range associated with each value of the domain (a ~ function) — compare SINGLE-VALUED

¹**mul·ti·plex** \'məl-tə-ˌpleks\ *adj* [L] (1557) **1** : MANY, MULTIPLE **2** : being or relating to a system of transmitting several messages or signals simultaneously on the same circuit or channel

²**multiplex** *vt* (1907) : to send (messages or signals) by a multiplex system ~ *vi* : to multiplex messages or signals — **mul·ti·plex·er** *also* **mul·ti·plex·or** \-ˌplek-sər\ *n*

³**multiplex** *n* (1985) : a complex that houses several movie theaters

mul·ti·pli·cand \ˌməl-tə-plə-'kand\ *n* [L *multiplicandus*, gerundive of *multiplicare*] (1594) : the number that is to be multiplied by another

mul·ti·pli·ca·tion \,məl-tə-plə-'kā-shən\ n [ME *multiplicacioun*, fr. MF *multiplication*, fr. L *multiplication-, multiplicatio*, fr. *multiplicare* to multiply] (14c) **1** : the act or process of multiplying : the state of being multiplied **2 a** : a mathematical operation that at its simplest is an abbreviated process of adding an integer to itself a specified number of times and that is extended to other numbers in accordance with laws that are valid for integers **b** : any of various mathematical operations that are analogous in some way to multiplication of the real numbers but are defined for other or larger sets of elements (as complex numbers, vectors, matrices, or functions)

multiplication sign n (1907) : a symbol used to indicate multiplication: as TIMES SIGN **b** : DOT 2b

mul·ti·pli·ca·tive \,məl-tə-'pli-kə-tiv, 'məl-tə-plə-,kā-tiv\ adj (1653) **1** : tending or having the power to multiply **2** : of, relating to, or associated with a mathematical operation of multiplication ⟨the ~ property of 0 requires that a·0 = 0 and 0·a = 0⟩ — **mul·ti·pli·ca·tive·ly** adv

multiplicative identity n (1958) : an identity element (as 1 in the group of rational numbers without 0) that in a given mathematical system leaves unchanged any element by which it is multiplied

multiplicative inverse n (1958) : an element of a mathematical set that when multiplied by a given element yields the identity element — called also *reciprocal*

mul·ti·plic·i·ty \,məl-tə-'pli-sə-tē\ n, pl **-ties** [ME, fr. MF *multiplicité*, fr. LL *multiplicitat-, multiplicitas*, fr. L *multiplic-, multiplex*] (15c) **1 a** : the quality or state of being multiple or various **b** : the number of components in a system (as a multiplet or a group of energy levels) **2** : a great number **3** : the number of times a root of an equation or zero of a function occurs when there is more than one root or zero ⟨the ~ of x = 2 for the equation $(x - 2)^3 = 0$ is 3⟩

mul·ti·pli·er \'məl-tə-,plī(-ə)r\ n (15c) : one that multiplies: as **a** : a number by which another number is multiplied **b** : an instrument or device for multiplying or intensifying some effect **c** : a machine, mechanism, or circuit that multiplies figures

¹**mul·ti·ply** \'məl-tə-,plī\ vb **-plied; -ply·ing** [ME *multiplien*, fr. OF *multiplier*, fr. L *multiplicare*, fr. *multiplic-, multiplex* multiple] vt (13c) **1** : to increase in number esp. greatly or in multiples : AUGMENT **2** : to find the product of by multiplication ⟨~ 7 and 8⟩ **b** : to use as a multiplicand in multiplication with another number ⟨~ 7 by 8⟩ ~ vi **1 a** : to become greater in number : SPREAD **b** : BREED, PROPAGATE **2** : to perform multiplication *syn* see INCREASE

²**mul·ti·ply** \-plē\ adv (1881) : in a multiple manner : in several ways ⟨~ handicapped children⟩

mul·ti·ply \,məl-ti-'plī, -,tī-\ adj (1926) : composed of several plies

mul·ti·po·lar \-'pō-lər\ adj [ISV] (1859) **1** : having several poles ⟨a ~ generator⟩ ⟨~ mitoses⟩ **2** : having several dendrites ⟨~ nerve cells⟩ **3** : characterized by more than two centers of power or interest ⟨a ~ world⟩ — **mul·ti·po·lar·i·ty** \-pō-'lar-ə-tē\ n

mul·ti·po·ten·tial \-pə-'ten(t)-shəl\ adj (1913) : having the potential of becoming any of several mature cell types ⟨~ stem cell⟩

mul·ti·pro·cess·ing \-'prä-,se-siŋ, -'prō-, -sə-siŋ\ n (1961) : the processing of several computer programs at the same time esp. by a computer system with two or more processors sharing a single memory — **mul·ti·pro·ces·sor** \-sər\ n

mul·ti·pro·gram·ming \-'prō-,gra-miŋ, -grə-\ n (1959) : the technique of utilizing several interleaved programs concurrently in a single computer system

mul·ti·pronged \-'prȯŋd\ adj (1957) **1** : having several prongs ⟨~ fishing spears⟩ **2** : having several distinct aspects or elements ⟨a ~ attack on the problem⟩

mul·ti·ra·cial \-'rā-shəl\ adj (1923) : composed of, involving, or representing various races — **mul·ti·ra·cial·ism** \-shə-,li-zəm\ n

mul·ti·sense \'məl-ti-,sen(t)s\ adj (1957) : having several meanings ⟨~ words⟩

mul·ti·sen·so·ry \,məl-ti-'sen(t)-sə-rē, -'sen(t)s-rē\ adj (1949) : relating to or involving several physiological senses ⟨~ teaching methods⟩ ⟨~ experience⟩

mul·ti·spec·tral \-'spek-trəl\ adj (1965) : of or relating to two or more ranges of frequencies or wavelengths in the electromagnetic spectrum

mul·ti·stage \'məl-ti-,stāj, -,tī-\ adj (1904) **1** : having successive operating stages; *esp* : having propulsion units that operate in turn ⟨~ rockets⟩ **2** : conducted by or occurring in stages ⟨a ~ investigation⟩

mul·ti·state \-,stāt\ adj (1944) **1** : having divisions in several states ⟨~ enterprises⟩ **2** : of, relating to, or involving several states ⟨a ~ attack on environmental pollution⟩

mul·ti·task·ing \-,tas-kiŋ\ n, *often attrib* (1966) : the concurrent performance of several jobs by a computer

mul·ti·tude \'məl-tə-,tüd, -,tyüd\ n [ME, fr. MF or L; MF, fr. L *multitudin-, multitudo*, fr. *multus* much — more at MELIORATE] (14c) **1** : the state of being many **2** : a great number : HOST **3** : a great number of people **4** : POPULACE, PUBLIC

mul·ti·tu·di·nous \,məl-tə-'tüd-nəs, -'tyüd-; -'tü-dᵊn-əs, -'tyü-\ adj (1604) **1** : including a multitude of individuals : POPULOUS ⟨the ~ city⟩ **2** : existing in a great multitude ⟨~ opportunities⟩ **3** : existing in or consisting of innumerable elements or aspects ⟨~ applause⟩ — **mul·ti·tu·di·nous·ly** adv — **mul·ti·tu·di·nous·ness** n

mul·ti·us·er \,məl-ti-'yü-zər, -tē-, -ti-\ adj (1964) : able to be used by more than one person simultaneously

mul·tiv·a·lence \,məl-'ti-və-lən(t)s\ n (ca. 1881) : the quality or state of having many values, meanings, or appeals

mul·ti·va·lent \,məl-ti-'vā-lənt, -,tī-, *esp in sense 3* ,məl-'ti-və-\ adj [ISV] (1874) **1** : POLYVALENT **2** : represented more than twice in the somatic chromosome number ⟨~ chromosomes⟩ **3** : having many values, meanings, or appeals — **multivalent** n

mul·ti·var·i·able \,məl-ti-'ver-ē-ə-bəl, -,tī-, -'var-\ adj (1963) : MULTIVARIATE

mul·ti·var·i·ate \-'ver-ē-ət, -,āt\ adj [multi- + variable + ³-ate] (1951) : having or involving a number of independent mathematical or statistical variables ⟨~ calculus⟩ ⟨~ data analysis⟩

mul·ti·ver·si·ty \-'vər-sə-tē, -stē-\ n, pl **-ties** [multi- + -versity (as in university)] (1963) : a very large university with many component schools, colleges, or divisions and widely diverse functions

mul·ti·vol·tine \-'vōl-,tēn, -'vȯl-\ adj [multi- + -voltine having a given number of broods (fr. F, fr. It *volta* time, turn) — more at VOLT] (1874) : having several broods in a season ⟨~ insects⟩

mul·ture \'məl-chər, *Scot usu* 'mü-tər\ n [ME *multyr*, fr. MF *molture*, lit., grinding, fr. (assumed) VL *molitura*, fr. L *molitus*, pp. of *molere* to grind — more at MEAL] (14c) *chiefly Scot* : a fee for grinding grain at a mill

¹**mum** \'məm\ adj [prob. imit. of a sound made with closed lips] (14c) : SILENT ⟨keep ~⟩

²**mum** vi **mummed; mum·ming** [ME *mommen*, fr. MF *momer* to go masked] (1530) **1** : to perform in a pantomime **2** : to go about merrymaking in disguise during festivals

³**mum** n [G *Mumme*] (1640) : a strong ale or beer

⁴**mum** *chiefly Brit var of* MOM

⁵**mum** n (1917): CHRYSANTHEMUM

mum·ble \'məm-bəl\ vb **mum·bled; mum·bling** \-b(ə-)liŋ\ [ME *momelen*, of imit. origin] vi (14c) **1** : to utter words in a low confused indistinct manner : MUTTER ~ vt **1** : to utter with a low inarticulate voice **2** : to chew or bite with or as if with toothless gums — **mumble** n — **mum·bler** \-b(ə-)lər\ n — **mum·bly** \-b(ə-)lē\ adj

mum·ble·ty–peg \'məm-bəl-(tē-)peg, -blē-,peg\ *also* **mum·ble–the–peg** \-bəl-(thə-),peg, -blē-,peg\ *or* **mumble peg** \-bəl-,peg, -blē-\ n [fr. the phrase *mumble the peg*; fr. the loser's orig. having to pull out with his teeth a peg driven into the ground] (1627) : a game in which the players try to flip a knife from various positions so that the blade will stick into the ground

mum·bo jum·bo \,məm-bō-'jəm-(,)bō\ n [*Mumbo Jumbo*, a masked figure among Mandingo peoples of western Africa] (1738) **1** : an object of superstitious homage and fear **2 a** : a complicated often ritualistic observance with elaborate trappings **b** : complicated activity usu. intended to obscure and confuse **3** : unnecessarily involved and incomprehensible language: GIBBERISH

mum·mer \'mə-mər\ n [MF *momeur*, fr. *momer* to go masked] (1502) **1** : a performer in a pantomime; *broadly* : ACTOR **2** : one who goes merrymaking in disguise during festivals

mum·mery \'mə-mə-rē\ n, pl **-mer·ies** (ca. 1530) **1** : a performance by mummers **2** : a ridiculous, hypocritical, or pretentious ceremony or performance

mum·mi·chog \'mə-mi-,chȯg, -,chäg\ n [Narraganset *moamitteaúg*] (1787) : a common American killifish (*Fundulus heteroclitus* of the family Cyprinodontidae)

mum·mi·fy \'mə-mi-,fī\ vb **-fied; -fy·ing** vt (1628) **1** : to embalm and dry as or as if a mummy **2 a** : to make into or like a mummy **b** : to cause to dry up and shrivel ~ vi : to dry up and shrivel like a mummy — **mum·mi·fi·ca·tion** \,mə-mi-fə-'kā-shən\ n

¹**mum·my** \'mə-mē\ n, pl **mummies** [ME *mummie* powdered parts of a mummified body used as a drug, fr. MF *momie*, fr. ML *mumia* mummy, powdered mummy, fr. Ar *mūmiyah* bitumen, mummy, fr. Per *mūm* wax] (1615) **1 a** : a body embalmed or treated for burial with preservatives in the manner of the ancient Egyptians **b** : a body unusually well preserved **2** : one resembling a mummy

²**mummy** *chiefly Brit var of* MOMMY

mumps \'məmps\ n pl but sing or pl in constr [fr. pl. of obs. *mump* grimace] (1598) : an acute contagious virus disease marked by fever and by swelling esp. of the parotid gland

munch \'mənch\ vb [ME *monchen*, prob. of imit. origin] vt (14c) : to eat with a chewing action ⟨many a mouthful is ~ed in private —Washington Irving⟩; *also* : to snack on ⟨drank coffee and ~ed homemade cookies —Lady Bird Johnson⟩ ~ vi : to eat or chew something; *also* : SNACK — usu. used with *on* — **munch·er** n

Mun·chau·sen syndrome \'mən-,chaú-zən-, ,mən-'chaú-\ n [Baron K. F. H. von *Münchausen* †1797 Ger. soldier and proverbial teller of exaggerated tales] (1951) : a condition characterized by the feigning of the symptoms of a disease or injury in order to undergo diagnostic tests, hospitalization, or medical or surgical treatment — called also *Munchausen's syndrome*

munch·ies \'mən-chēz\ n pl (ca. 1971) **1** : hunger pangs **2** : light snack foods

munch·kin \'mənch-,kin\ n [the *Munchkins*, diminutive creatures in *The Wonderful Wizard of Oz* (1900) by L. Frank Baum] (1972) : a person who is notably small and often endearing

Mun·da \'mùn-də\ n (1901) : a branch of the Austroasiatic language family spoken by tribal peoples of central and eastern India

mun·dane \,mən-'dān, 'mən-,\ adj [ME *mondeyne*, fr. MF *mondain*, fr. LL *mundanus*, fr. L *mundus* world] (15c) **1** : of, relating to, or characteristic of the world **2** : characterized by the practical, transitory, and ordinary : COMMONPLACE ⟨the ~ concerns of day-to-day life⟩ *syn* see EARTHLY — **mun·dane·ly** adv — **mun·dane·ness** \-'dān-nəs, -,dān-\ n — **mun·dan·i·ty** \,mən-'dā-nə-tē\ n

mun·dun·gus \,mən-'dəŋ-gəs\ n [modif. of Sp *mondongo* tripe] (1641) *archaic* : foul-smelling tobacco

mung bean \'məŋ-\ n [Hindi *mūg*, fr. Skt *mudga*] (1910) : an erect bushy annual bean (*Phaseolus aureus*) that is widely cultivated in warm regions for its edible usu. green or yellow seeds, for forage, and as the chief source of bean sprouts; *also* : the seed of the mung bean

mun·go \'məŋ-(,)gō\ n, pl **mungos** [origin unknown] (1857) : reclaimed wool of poor quality and very short staple

mu·ni \'myü-nē\ n (1973) : MUNICIPAL

¹**mu·nic·i·pal** \myù-'ni-s(ə-)pəl *also* myə-, mə-, -'ni-sə-bəl, ÷,myü-nə-'si-pəl\ adj [L *municipalis* of a municipality, fr. *municip-, municeps* inhabitant of a municipality, fr. *munus* duty, service + *capere* to take — more at MEAN, HEAVE] (ca. 1540) **1** : of or relating to the internal affairs of a major political unit (as a nation) **2 a** : of, relating to, or characteristic of a municipality **b** : having local self-government **3** : restricted to one locality

²**municipal** n (1925) : a security issued by a state or local government or by an authority set up by such a government — usu. used in pl.

municipal court n (1828) **1** : a court that sits in some cities and larger towns and that usu. has civil and criminal jurisdiction over cases arising within the municipality **2** : POLICE COURT

\ə\ abut \ᵊ\ kitten, F table \ər\ further \a\ ash \ā\ ace \ä\ mop, mar \aú\ out \ch\ chin \e\ bet \ē\ easy \g\ go \i\ hit \ī\ ice \j\ job \ŋ\ sing \ō\ go \ȯ\ law \ȯi\ boy \th\ thin \t̲h̲\ the \ü\ loot \ú\ foot \y\ yet \zh\ vision \ä, k̲, ⁿ, œ, œ̄, ɶ, ᵫ̄, ʸ\ see Guide to Pronunciation

mu·nic·i·pal·i·ty \myu̇-ˌni-sə-'pa-lə-tē\ n, pl **-ties** (1790) **1** : a primarily urban political unit having corporate status and usu. powers of self-government **2** : the governing body of a municipality

mu·nic·i·pal·ize \myu̇-'ni-sə-pə-ˌlīz\ vt **-ized; -iz·ing** (1880) : to bring under municipal ownership or supervision — **mu·nic·i·pal·i·za·tion** \-ˌni-s(ə-)pə-lə-'zā-shən\ n

mu·nic·i·pal·ly \myu̇-'ni-fə-sənt\ adv (ca. 1842) : by or in terms of a municipality

mu·nif·i·cent \myu̇-'ni-fə-sənt\ adj [back-formation fr. munificence, fr. L munificentia, fr. munificus generous, fr. munus service, gift — more at MEAN] (1583) **1** : very liberal in giving or bestowing : LAVISH **2** : characterized by great liberality or generosity syn see LIBERAL — **mu·nif·i·cence** \-sən(t)s\ n — **mu·nif·i·cent·ly** adv

mu·ni·ment \'myü-nə-mənt\ n [ME, fr. AF, fr. MF, defense, fr. L munimentum, fr. munire to fortify] (15c) **1** : the evidence (as documents) that enables one to defend the title to an estate or a claim to rights and privileges — usu. used in pl. **2** archaic : a means of defense

mu·ni·tion \myu̇-'ni-shən\ n [MF, fr. L munition-, munitio, fr. munire to fortify, fr. moenia walls; akin to L murus wall and perh. to Skt minoti he builds, fastens] (1508) **1** archaic : RAMPART, DEFENSE **2** : ARMAMENT, AMMUNITION — **munition** vt

Mun·ster var of MUENSTER

mun·tin \'mən-tᵊn\ n [alter. of montant vertical dividing bar, fr. F, fr. prp. of monter to rise — more at MOUNT] (1774) : a strip separating panes of glass in a sash

munt·jac \'mən(t)-ˌjak, 'mən-ˌchak\ n [Sundanese (Austronesian language of western Java) monyčak] (ca. 1798) : any of a genus (Muntiacus) of small deer of southeastern Asia and the East Indies — called also barking deer

mu·on \'myü-ˌän\ n [contr. of earlier mu-meson, fr. mu] (1952) : an unstable lepton that is common in the cosmic radiation near the earth's surface, has a mass about 207 times the mass of the electron, and exists in negative and positive forms — **mu·on·ic** \myü-'ä-nik\ adj

mu·on·ium \myü-'ō-nē-əm, -'ä-\ n [NL] (1957) : a short-lived quasi-atom consisting of an electron and a positive muon

muntjac

¹**mu·ral** \'myu̇r-əl\ adj [L muralis, fr. murus wall — more at MUNITION] (1586) **1** : of, relating to, or resembling a wall **2** : applied to and made integral with a wall or ceiling surface

²**mural** n (1916) : a mural work of art (as a painting) — **mu·ral·ist** \-ə-list\ n

mu·ram·ic acid \myü-'ra-mik-\ n [L murus wall + E + glucosamine + ¹-ic] (1957) : an amino sugar $C_9H_{17}NO_7$ that is a lactic acid derivative of glucosamine and is found esp. in bacterial cell walls and in blue-green algae

¹**mur·der** \'mər-dər\ n [partly fr. ME murther, fr. OE morthor; partly fr. ME murdre, fr. OF, of Gmc origin; akin to OE morthor; akin to OHG mord murder, L mort-, mors death, mori to die, mortuus dead, Gk brotos mortal] (bef. 12c) **1** : the crime of unlawfully killing a person esp. with malice aforethought **2 a** : something very difficult or dangerous ⟨the traffic was ∼⟩ **b** : something outrageous or blameworthy ⟨getting away with ∼⟩

²**murder** vb **mur·dered; mur·der·ing** \'mər-d(ə-)riŋ\ vt (13c) **1** : to kill (a human being) unlawfully and with premeditated malice **2** : to slaughter wantonly : SLAY **3 a** : to put an end to **b** : TEASE, TORMENT **c** : MUTILATE, MANGLE ⟨∼s French⟩ **d** : to defeat badly ∼ vi : to commit murder syn see KILL

mur·der·ee \ˌmər-də-'rē\ n (1920) : an actual or potential victim of a murder

mur·der·er \'mər-dər-ər\ n (14c) : one who murders; esp : one who commits the crime of murder

mur·der·ess \'mər-də-rəs\ n (14c) : a woman who murders

mur·der·ous \'mər-d(ə-)rəs\ adj (1535) **1 a** : having the purpose or capability of murder **b** : characterized by or causing murder or bloodshed **2** : having the ability or power to overwhelm : DEVASTATING ⟨∼ heat⟩ — **mur·der·ous·ly** adv — **mur·der·ous·ness** n

mu·rein \'myu̇r-ē-ən, 'myu̇r-ˌēn\ n [muramic acid + -ein, alter. of ²-ine] (1964) : PEPTIDOGLYCAN

mu·rex \'myu̇r-ˌeks\ n, pl **mu·ri·ces** \'myu̇r-ə-ˌsēz\ or **mu·rex·es** [NL, fr. L mollusk yielding a purple dye; akin to Gk myak-, myax mussel] (1589) : any of a genus (Murex) of marine gastropod mollusks having a rough and often spinose shell, abounding in tropical seas, and yielding a purple dye

mu·ri·ate \'myu̇r-ē-ˌāt\ n [F, back-formation fr. (acide) muriatique muriatic acid] (1790) : CHLORIDE

mu·ri·at·ic acid \ˌmyu̇r-ē-'a-tik-\ n [F muriatique, fr. L muriaticus pickled in brine, fr. muria brine] (1790) : HYDROCHLORIC ACID

mu·rid \'myu̇r-əd\ adj [ultim. fr. L mur-, mus mouse — more at MOUSE] (ca. 1909) : of or relating to a family (Muridae) comprising the typical mice and rats — **murid** n

mu·rine \'myu̇r-ˌīn\ adj [ultim. fr. L mur-, mus] (1607) : of or relating to a murid genus (Mus) or its subfamily (Murinae) which includes the common household rats and mice; also : of, relating to, or involving these rodents and esp. the house mouse — **murine** n

murine typhus n (1933) : a mild febrile disease that is marked by headache and rash, is caused by a rickettsia (Rickettsia mooseri), is widespread in nature in rodents, and is transmitted to humans by a flea

murk \'mərk\ n [ME mirke, fr. OE mirce; akin to ON myrkr darkness] (bef. 12c) : GLOOM, DARKNESS; also : FOG — **murk** adj, archaic

murky \'mər-kē\ adj **murk·i·er; -est** (14c) **1** : characterized by a heavy dimness or obscurity caused by or like that caused by overhanging fog or smoke **2** : characterized by thickness and heaviness of air : FOGGY, MISTY **3** : darkly vague or obscure ⟨∼ official rhetoric⟩ — **murk·i·ly** \-kə-lē\ adv — **murk·i·ness** \-kē-nəs\ n

¹**mur·mur** \'mər-mər\ n [ME murmure, fr. MF, fr. L murmur murmur, roar, of imit. origin] (14c) **1** : a half-suppressed or muttered complaint : GRUMBLING **2 a** : a low indistinct but often continuous sound **b** : a soft or gentle utterance **3** : an atypical sound of the heart indicating a functional or structural abnormality

²**murmur** vi (14c) **1** : to make a murmur ⟨the breeze ∼ed in the pines⟩ **2** : COMPLAIN, GRUMBLE ∼ vt : to say in a murmur — **mur·mur·er** n

mur·mur·ous \'mər-mə-rəs, 'mərm-rəs\ adj (1582) : filled with or characterized by murmurs : low and indistinct — **mur·mur·ous·ly** adv

Mur·phy \'mər-fē\ n [Miss Murphy, nonexistent prostitute used to lure victims] (1959) : any of various confidence games; esp : one in which the victim believes he is paying for sex

Murphy bed n [William L. Murphy †1959 Am. inventor] (1925) : a bed that may be folded or swung into a closet

Murphy's Law n [Edward A. Murphy b1917 Am. engineer] (1958) : an observation: anything that can go wrong will go wrong

mur·rain \'mər-ən, 'mə-rən\ n [ME moreyne, fr. MF morine, fr. morir to die, fr. L mori — more at MURDER] (14c) : a pestilence or plague esp. affecting domestic animals

murre \'mər\ n [origin unknown] (1602) : any of a genus (Uria) of seabirds; esp : a common bird (U. aalge) of northern seas

mur·rey \'mər-ē, 'mə-rē\ n [ME, fr. MF moré, fr. ML moratum, fr. neut. of moratus mulberry colored, fr. L morum mulberry — more at MULBERRY] (15c) : a purplish black : MULBERRY

mur·ther \'mər-thər\ chiefly dial var of MURDER

mus·ca·det \ˌməs-kə-'dā, -'de\ n, often cap [F, fr. Prov, muscadet grape, fr. musc musk] (ca. 1899) : a dry white wine from the Loire valley of France

mus·ca·dine \'məs-kə-ˌdin\ n [prob. alter. of muscatel] (ca. 1785) : a grape (Vitis rotundifolia) of the southern U.S. with musky fruits borne in small clusters; also : the fruit

mus·cae vo·li·tan·tes \'məs-ˌkē-ˌvä-lə-'tan-ˌtēz, 'mə-ˌsē-\ n pl [NL, lit., flying flies] (1797) : spots before the eyes due to cells and cell fragments in the vitreous humor and lens

mus·ca·rine \'məs-kə-ˌrēn\ n [G Muskarin, fr. NL (Amanita) muscaria fly agaric] (1872) : a toxic ammonium base $[C_9H_{20}NO_2]^+$ that is biochemically related to acetylcholine, is found esp. in fly agaric, and acts directly on smooth muscle

mus·ca·rin·ic \ˌməs-kə-'ri-nik\ adj (1936) : relating to, resembling, producing, or mediating the parasympathetic effects (as a slowed heart rate and increased activity of smooth muscle) produced by muscarine ⟨∼ receptors⟩ — compare NICOTINIC

mus·cat \'məs-ˌkat, -kət\ n [MF, fr. OProv, fr. muscat musky, fr. musc musk, fr. LL muscus — more at MUSK] (1548) **1** : MUSCATEL **2** : any of several cultivated grapes used in making wine and raisins

mus·ca·tel \ˌməs-kə-'tel\ n [ME muskadelle, fr. MF muscadel, fr. OProv, fr. muscadel resembling musk, fr. muscat] (15c) **1** : a sweet fortified wine from muscat grapes **2** : a raisin from muscat grapes

¹**mus·cle** \'mə-səl\ n, often attrib [ME, fr. MF, fr. L musculus, fr. dim. of mus mouse — more at MOUSE] (14c) **1 a** : a body tissue consisting of long cells that contract when stimulated and produce motion **b** : an organ that essentially a mass of muscle tissue attached at either end to a fixed point and that by contracting moves or checks the movement of a body part **2 a** : muscular strength : BRAWN **b** : effective strength : POWER ⟨political ∼⟩

²**muscle** vb **mus·cled; mus·cling** \'mə-s(ə-)liŋ\ vt (1913) : to move or force by or as if by muscular effort ⟨muscled him out of office⟩ ∼ vi : to make one's way by brute strength or by force

mus·cle-bound \'mə-səl-ˌbau̇nd\ adj (1879) **1** : having some of the muscles tense and enlarged and of impaired elasticity sometimes as a result of excessive exercise **2** : lacking in flexibility : RIGID

muscle car \-ˌkär\ n (1969) : any of a group of American-made 2-door sports coupes with powerful engines designed for high-performance driving

mus·cled \'mə-səld\ adj (1644) : having muscles esp. of a specified kind — often used in combination ⟨hard-muscled arms⟩

muscle spindle n (1894) : a sensory end organ in a muscle that is sensitive to stretch in the muscle, consists of small striated muscle fibers richly supplied with nerve fibers, and is enclosed in a connective tissue sheath — called also stretch receptor

mus·co·vite \'məs-kə-ˌvīt\ n [ML or NL Muscovia, Moscovia Moscow] (1535) **1** cap **a** : a native or resident of the ancient principality of Moscow or of the city of Moscow **b** : RUSSIAN **2** [muscovy (glass)] : a mineral that is a colorless to pale brown potassium mica — **Muscovite** adj

Mus·co·vy duck \'məs-ˌkō-vē-\ n [Muscovy, principality of Moscow, Russia] (1657) : a large dark crested duck (Cairina moschata) of Central and So. America that is widely kept in domestication

muscul- or **musculo-** comb form [LL musculi-, fr. L musculus] **1** : muscle ⟨muscular⟩ **2** : muscular and ⟨musculoskeletal⟩

mus·cu·lar \'məs-kyə-lər\ adj (1681) **1 a** : of, relating to, or constituting muscle **b** : of, relating to, or performed by the muscles **2** : having well-developed musculature **3 a** : of or relating to physical strength : BRAWNY **b** : having strength of expression or character : VIGOROUS ⟨∼ prose⟩ — **mus·cu·lar·i·ty** \ˌməs-kyə-'lar-ə-tē\ n — **mus·cu·lar·ly** \'məs-kyə-lər-lē\ adv

muscular dystrophy n (1886) : any of a group of hereditary diseases characterized by progressive wasting of muscles

mus·cu·la·ture \'məs-kyə-lə-ˌchu̇r, -chər, -ˌtyu̇r, -ˌtu̇r\ n [F, fr. L musculus] (1875) : the muscles of all or a part of the animal body

mus·cu·lo·skel·e·tal \ˌməs-kyə-lō-'ske-lə-tᵊl\ adj (ca. 1944) : of, relating to, or involving both musculature and skeleton

¹**muse** \'myüz\ vb **mused; mus·ing** [ME, fr. MF muser to gape, idle, muse, fr. muse mouth of an animal, fr. ML musus] vi (14c) **1** : to become absorbed in thought; esp : to turn something over in the mind meditatively and often inconclusively **2** archaic : WONDER, MARVEL ∼ vt : to think or say reflectively syn see PONDER — **mus·er** n

²**muse** n (15c) : a state of deep thought or dreamy abstraction

³**muse** n [ME, fr. MF, fr. L Musa, fr. Gk Mousa] (14c) **1** cap : any of the nine sister goddesses in Greek mythology presiding over song and poetry and the arts and sciences **2** : a source of inspiration; esp : a guiding genius **3** : POET

mu·se·ol·o·gy \ˌmyü-zē-'ä-lə-jē\ n [museum + -logy] (1885) : the science or profession of museum organization and management — **mu·seo·log·i·cal** \-ə-'lä-ji-kəl\ adj — **mu·se·ol·o·gist** \-ē-'ä-lə-jist\ n

mu·sette \myu̇-'zet\ n [ME, fr. MF, dim. of muse bagpipe, fr. muser to muse, play the bagpipe] (14c) **1** : a bellows-blown bagpipe popular in France in the 17th and 18th centuries **2** : a small knapsack; *also* : a similar bag with one shoulder strap — called also *musette bag*

mu·se·um \myü-'zē-əm\ n [L *Museum* place for learned occupation, fr. Gk *Mouseion*, fr. neut. of *Mouseios* of the Muses, fr. *Mousa*] (1672) : an institution devoted to the procurement, care, study, and display of objects of lasting interest or value; *also* : a place where objects are exhibited

museum piece n (1901) **1** : something preserved in or suitable for a museum **2** : one that is out-of-date : a thing of the past

¹mush \'məsh, esp 3 also 'mu̇sh\ n [prob. alter. of *mash*] (1671) **1** : a thick porridge made with cornmeal boiled in water or milk **2** : something soft and spongy or shapeless **3 a** : weak sentimentality : DRIVEL **b** : mawkish amorousness

²mush vt (ca. 1781) *chiefly dial* : to reduce to a crumbly mass ∼ vi, *of an airplane* : to fly in a partly or nearly stalled condition — **mush·er** n

³mush vi [prob. fr. F *marchons*, 1st pl. imper. of *marcher* to move, march, fr. MF *marchier* — more at MARCH] (1897) : to travel esp. over snow with a sled drawn by dogs — often used as a command to a dog team — **mush·er** n

⁴mush n (1902) : a trip esp. across snow with a dog team

¹mush·room \'məsh-,rüm, -,ru̇m; *chiefly Northern & Midland* -,rün; *dial* 'mə-shə-,rüm, -,ru̇m, -,rün\ n [alter. of ME *musseroun*, fr. MF *mousseron*, fr. LL *mussirion-, mussirio*] (1533) **1 a** : an enlarged complex aboveground fleshy fruiting body of a fungus (as a basidiomycete) that consists typically of a stem bearing a pileus; *esp* : one that is edible **b** : FUNGUS **2** : UPSTART **3** : something resembling a mushroom

²mushroom vi (1894) **1** : to collect wild mushrooms **2 a** : to well up and spread out laterally from a central source **b** : to become enlarged or extended : GROW **3** : to spring up suddenly or multiply rapidly

mushroom cloud n (ca. 1909) : a mushroom-shaped cloud; *specif* : one caused by the explosion of a nuclear weapon

mushy \'mə-shē, esp 2 also 'mu̇-\ adj **mush·i·er; -est** (1839) **1 a** : having the consistency of mush : SOFT **b** : lacking in definition or precision **2** : excessively tender or emotional; *esp* : mawkishly amorous — **mush·i·ly** \'mə-shə-lē, 'mu̇-\ adv — **mush·i·ness** \'mə-shē-nəs, 'mu̇-\ n

mu·sic \'myü-zik\ n, often attrib [ME *musik*, fr. OF *musique*, fr. L *musica*, fr. Gk *mousikē* any art presided over by the Muses, esp. music, fr. fem. of *mousikos* of the Muses, fr. *Mousa* Muse] (13c) **1 a** : the science or art of ordering tones or sounds in succession, in combination, and in temporal relationships to produce a composition having unity and continuity **b** : vocal, instrumental, or mechanical sounds having rhythm, melody, or harmony **2 a** : an agreeable sound : EUPHONY 〈her voice was ∼ to my ears〉 **b** : musical quality 〈the ∼ of verse〉 **3** : a musical accompaniment 〈a play set to ∼〉 **4** : the score of a musical composition set down on paper **5** : a distinctive type or category of music 〈there is a ∼ for everybody —Eric Salzman〉

¹mu·si·cal \'myü-zi-kəl\ adj [ME, fr. MF, fr. ML *musicalis*, fr. *musica*] (15c) **1 a** : of or relating to music **b** : having the pleasing harmonious qualities of music : MELODIOUS **2** : having an interest in or talent for music **3** : set to or accompanied by music **4** : of or relating to musicians or music lovers — **mu·si·cal·ly** \-k(ə-)lē\ adv

²musical n (1823) **1** *archaic* : MUSICALE **2** : a film or theatrical production typically of a sentimental or humorous nature that consists of musical numbers and dialogue based on a unifying plot

musical box n (1829) *chiefly Brit* : MUSIC BOX

musical chairs n pl but sing in constr (1877) : a game in which players march to music around a row of chairs numbering one less than the players and scramble for seats when the music stops; *also* : a situation or series of events suggesting the game of musical chairs (as in rapid change or confusing activity)

musical comedy n (1765) : MUSICAL 2

mu·si·cale \,myü-zi-'kal\ n [F *soirée musicale*, lit., musical evening] (1872) : a social entertainment with music as the leading feature

mu·si·cal·ise Brit var of MUSICALIZE

mu·si·cal·i·ty \,myü-zi-'ka-lə-tē\ n (1853) **1** : sensitivity to, knowledge of, or talent for music **2** : the quality or state of being musical : MELODIOUSNESS

mu·si·cal·ize \'myü-zi-kə-,līz\ vt *-ized; -iz·ing* (1919) : to set to music — **mu·si·cal·i·za·tion** \,myü-zi-kə-lə-'zā-shən\ n

musical saw n (1927) : a handsaw made to produce melody by bending the blade while sounding it with a hammer or violin bow

music box n (1844) : a container enclosing an apparatus that reproduces music mechanically when activated by a clockwork

music drama n (1877) : an opera in which the action is not interrupted by formal song divisions (as recitatives or arias) and the music is determined solely by dramatic appropriateness

music hall n (1842) : a vaudeville theater; *also* : VAUDEVILLE

mu·si·cian \myü-'zi-shən\ n (14c) : a composer, conductor, or performer of music; *esp* : INSTRUMENTALIST — **mu·si·cian·ly** \-lē\ adj — **mu·si·cian·ship** \-,ship\ n

music of the spheres (1609) : an ethereal harmony thought by the Pythagoreans to be produced by the vibration of the celestial spheres

mu·si·col·o·gy \,myü-zi-'kä-lə-jē\ n [It *musicologia*, fr. L *musica* music + *-logia* -logy] (1909) : a study of music as a branch of knowledge or field of research as distinct from composition or performance — **mu·si·co·log·i·cal** \-kə-'lä-ji-kəl\ adj — **mu·si·col·o·gist** \-'kä-lə-jist\ n

¹mus·ing \'myü-ziŋ\ n (14c) : MEDITATION

²musing adj (15c) : thoughtfully abstracted : MEDITATIVE — **mus·ing·ly** \-lē\ adv

mu·sique con·crète \myü-'zēk-kōⁿ-'kret, mü̇ē-\ n [F, lit., concrete music] (1952) : a recorded montage of natural sounds often electronically modified and presented as a musical composition

musk \'məsk\ n [ME *muske*, fr. MF *musc*, fr. LL *muscus*, fr. LGk *moschos*, fr. (assumed) MPer *mušk*-, fr. Skt *muṣka* testicle, fr. dim. of *mūṣ* mouse; akin to OE *mūs* mouse] (14c) **1 a** : a substance with a penetrating persistent odor obtained from a sac beneath the abdominal skin of the male musk deer and used as a perfume fixative; *also* : a similar substance from another animal or a synthetic substitute **b** : the odor of musk; *also* : an odor resembling musk esp. in heaviness or persistence **2** : any of various plants with musky odors; *esp* : MUSK PLANT

musk deer n (1681) : any of a genus (*Moschus*) of small heavy-limbed hornless deer of central Asian uplands with tusked musk-producing males

mus·keg \'məs-,keg, -,käg\ n [Cree *maske·k*] (1806) **1** : BOG; *esp* : a sphagnum bog of northern No. America often with tussocks **2** : a usu. thick deposit of partially decayed vegetable matter of wet boreal regions

mus·kel·lunge \'məs-kə-,lənj\ n, pl **muskellunge** [alter. of CanF *maskinongé*, fr. Ojibwa *maʼskinoʼše*] (1789) : a large No. American pike (*Esox masquinongy*) that has dark markings, may weigh over 60 pounds (27 kilograms), and is a valuable sport fish

mus·ket \'məs-kət\ n [MF *mousquet*, fr. OIt *moschetto* arrow for a crossbow, musket, fr. dim. of *mosca* fly, fr. L *musca* — more at MIDGE] (ca. 1587) **1 a** : a heavy large-caliber muzzle-loading usu. smoothbore shoulder firearm; *broadly* : a shoulder gun carried by infantry

mus·ke·teer \,məs-kə-'tir\ n [modif. of MF *mousquetaire*, fr. *mousquet*] (1590) **1** : a soldier armed with a musket **2** [fr. the musketeers' friendship in the novel *Les Trois Mousquetaires* (1844) by Alexandre Dumas] : a good friend : BUDDY

mus·ket·ry \'məs-kə-trē\ n (1646) **1** : MUSKETS **2** : MUSKETEERS **3 a** : musket fire **b** : the art or science of using small arms esp. in battle

mus·kie or **mus·ky** \'məs-kē\ n, pl **muskies** (1894) : MUSKELLUNGE

musk·mel·on \'məsk-,me-lən\ n (1573) : a usu. sweet musky-odored edible melon that is the fruit of a trailing or climbing Asian herbaceous vine (*Cucumis melo*): as **a** : any of various melons of small or moderate size with netted skin that include most of the muskmelons cultivated in No. America **b** : CANTALOUPE 1 **c** : WINTER MELON

Mus·ko·ge·an or **Mus·kho·ge·an** \(,)məs-'kō-gē-ən\ n (1891) : a language family of southeastern U.S. that includes Muskogee

Mus·ko·gee \mə-'skō-gē\ n, pl **Muskogee** or **Muskogees** (1775) **1** : a member of an American Indian people of Georgia and eastern Alabama constituting the nucleus of the Creek confederacy **2** : the language of the Muskogees and of some of the Seminoles

musk ox n (1744) : a heavyset shaggy-coated wild ox (*Ovibos moschatus*) now confined to Greenland and the barren northern lands of No. America

musk plant n (1852) : a yellow-flowered No. American herb (*Mimulus moschatus*) of the snapdragon family that has hairy foliage and sometimes a musky odor

musk·rat \'məs-,krat\ n, pl **muskrat** or **muskrats** [prob. by folk etymology fr. a word of Algonquian origin; akin to Massachuset *musquash* muskrat] (1607) : an aquatic rodent (*Ondatra zibethica*) of the U.S. and Canada with a long scaly laterally compressed tail, webbed hind feet, and dark glossy brown fur; *also* : its fur or pelt

musk rose n (1577) : a rose (*Rosa moschata*) of the Mediterranean region with white flowers having a musky odor

musk thistle n (1731) : a Eurasian thistle (*Carduus nutans*) that has nodding musky flower heads and is naturalized in eastern No. America

musk turtle n (1868) : any of various small American freshwater turtles (genera *Sternotherus* and *Kinosternon*) that have musk glands; *esp* : a dark turtle (*S. odoratus*) having a strong musky odor

musky \'məs-kē\ adj **musk·i·er; -est** (1613) : having an odor of or resembling musk — **musk·i·ness** n

Mus·lim \'məz-ləm, 'mu̇s-, 'mu̇z-\ n [Ar *muslim*, lit., one who surrenders (to God)] (1615) **1** : an adherent of Islam **2** : BLACK MUSLIM — **Muslim** adj

Muslim era n (1948) : ISLAMIC ERA

mus·lin \'məz-lən\ n [F *mousseline*, fr. It *mussolina*, fr. Ar *mawṣiliy* of Mosul, fr. al-*Mawṣil* Mosul, Iraq] (1609) : a plain-woven sheer to coarse cotton fabric

mus·quash \'məs-,kwäsh, -,kwȯsh\ n [Massachuset] (1633) : MUSKRAT

¹muss \'məs\ n [origin unknown] (1591) **1 a** : a game in which players scramble for small objects thrown to the ground **b** : SCRAMBLE **2** *slang* : a confused conflict : ROW **3** : a state of disorder : MESS

²muss vt (1837) : to make untidy : DISARRANGE

mus·sel \'mə-səl\ n [ME *muscle*, fr. OE *muscle*, fr. (assumed) VL *muscula*, fr. L *musculus* muscle, mussel] (bef. 12c) **1** : a marine bivalve mollusk (esp. genus *Mytilus*) usu. having a dark elongated shell **2** : a freshwater bivalve mollusk (as of *Unio, Anodonta*, or related genera) that is esp. abundant in rivers of the central U.S. and has a shell with a lustrous nacreous lining

Mus·sul·man also **Mus·sal·man** \'mə-səl-mən\ n, pl **Mus·sul·men** \-mən\ or **Mussulmans** [Turk *müslüman* & Per *musulmān*, modif. of Ar *muslim*] (ca. 1583) : MUSLIM

mussy \'mə-sē\ adj **muss·i·er; -est** (ca. 1859) : characterized by clutter or muss : MESSY — **muss·i·ly** \'mə-sə-lē\ adv — **muss·i·ness** \'mə-sē-nəs\ n

¹must \məs(t), 'məst\ vb, pres & past all persons **must** [ME *moste*, fr. OE *mōste*, past indic. & subj. of *mōtan* to be allowed to, have to; akin to OHG *muozan* to be allowed to, have to] (bef. 12c) *verbal auxiliary* **1 a** : be commanded or requested to 〈you ∼ stop〉 **b** : be urged to : ought by all means to 〈you ∼ read that book〉 **2** : be compelled by physical necessity to 〈man ∼ eat to live〉 : be required by immediate or future need or purpose to 〈we ∼ hurry to catch the bus〉 **3 a** : be obliged to : be compelled by social considerations to 〈I ∼ say you're looking well〉 **b** : be required by law, custom, or moral conscience to 〈we ∼ obey the rules〉 **c** : be determined to 〈if you ∼ go at least wait for me〉 **d** : be unreasonably or perversely compelled to 〈why ∼ you be so stubborn〉 **4** : be logically inferred or supposed to 〈it ∼ be time〉 **5** : be compelled by fate or by natural law to 〈what ∼ be will be〉 **6** : was or were presumably certain to : was or were bound to 〈if he really was there I ∼ have seen him〉 **7** *dial* : MAY, SHALL — used chiefly in questions ∼ vi, *archaic* : to be obliged to go 〈I ∼ to Coventry —Shak.〉

²must \'məst\ n (1616) **1** : an imperative need or duty : REQUIREMENT **2** : an indispensable item : ESSENTIAL 〈exercise is a ∼〉

\ə\ abut \ʾ\ kitten, F table \ər\ further \a\ ash \ā\ ace \ä\ mop, mar \au̇\ out \ch\ chin \e\ bet \ē\ easy \g\ go \i\ hit \ī\ ice \j\ job \ŋ\ sing \ō\ go \ȯ\ law \ȯi\ boy \th\ thin \t̲h̲\ the \ü\ loot \u̇\ foot \y\ yet \zh\ vision \ä, k̲, ⁿ, œ, œ̄, ᵫ, ᵫ̄, ᶢ\ *see* Guide to Pronunciation

³**must** *n* [ME, fr. OE, fr. L *mustum*] (bef. 12c) : the expressed juice of fruit and esp. grapes before and during fermentation; *also* : the pulp and skins of the crushed grapes

⁴**must** *n* [ME (Sc) *moist,* fr. MF *must,* alter. of *musc* musk] (15c) **1** : MUSK **2** : MOLD, MUSTINESS

mus·tache \'məs-,tash, (,)mə-'stash\ *n* [MF *moustache,* fr. OIt *mustaccio,* fr. MGk *moustaki,* dim. of Gk *mystak-, mystax* upper lip, mustache] (1585) **1** : the hair growing on the human upper lip; *esp* : such hair grown and often trimmed in a particular style **2** : hair or bristles about the mouth of a mammal — **mus·tached** *adj*

mus·ta·chio \(,)mə-'sta-shē-,ō, -'stä-, -shō\ *n, pl* **-chios** [Sp & It; Sp *mostacho,* fr. It *mustaccio,* fr. OIt] (1588) : MUSTACHE; *esp* : a large mustache — **mus·ta·chioed** \-shē-,ōd, -shōd\ *adj*

mus·tang \'məs-,taŋ\ *n* [MexSp *mestengo,* fr. Sp, stray, fr. *mesteño* strayed, fr. *mesta* annual roundup of cattle that disposed of strays, fr. ML (*animalia*) *mixta* mixed animals] (1808) **1** : the small hardy naturalized horse of the western plains directly descended from horses brought in by the Spaniards; *also* : BRONC **2** *slang* : a commissioned officer (as in the U.S. Navy) who has risen from the ranks

mus·tard \'məs-tərd\ *n* [ME, fr. OF *mostarde,* fr. *moust* must, fr. L *mustum*] (13c) **1 a** : a pungent yellow powder of the seeds of any of several common mustards (*Brassica hirta, B. nigra,* or *B. juncea*) used as a condiment or in medicine as a stimulant and diuretic, an emetic, or a counterirritant **b** *slang* : ZEST **2** : any of several herbs (genus *Brassica* of the family Cruciferae, the mustard family) with lobed leaves, yellow flowers, and linear beaked pods **3** : a dark to moderate yellow — **mus·tardy** \-tər-dē\ *adj*

mustard gas *n* (1917) : an irritant vesicant oily liquid $C_4H_8Cl_2S$ used esp. as a chemical weapon

mustard plaster *n* (1810) : a counterirritant and rubefacient plaster containing powdered mustard

¹**mus·ter** \'məs-tər\ *n* [ME *mustre,* fr. MF *mostre, monstre,* fr. *monstrer*] (14c) **1** : a representative specimen : SAMPLE **2 a** : an act of assembling; *specif* : formal military inspection **b** : critical examination **c** : an assembled group : COLLECTION **d** : INVENTORY

²**muster** *vb* **mus·tered; mus·ter·ing** \-t(ə-)riŋ\ [ME *mustren* to show, muster, fr. MF *monstrer,* fr. L *monstrare* to show, fr. *monstrum* evil omen, monster — more at MONSTER] *vt* (15c) **1 a** : to cause to gather : CONVENE **b** : to enroll formally — usu. used with *in* or *into* ⟨was *~ed* into the army⟩ **c** : to call the roll of **2 a** : to bring together : COLLECT **b** : to call forth : ROUSE **3** : to amount to : COMPRISE *~ vi* : to come together : CONGREGATE *syn* see SUMMON

muster out *vt* (1834) : to discharge from service

muster roll *n* (1605) : INVENTORY, ROSTER; *specif* : a register of the officers and men in a military unit or ship's company

musth *also* **must** \'məst\ *n* [Hindi *mast* intoxicated, fr. Per] (1878) : a periodic state of the bull elephant characterized esp. by aggressive behavior and usu. connected with the rutting season

mustn't \'mə-sᵊnt\ (1741) : must not

must-see \'məst-'sē\ *n* (1946) : something (as a film) that must or should be seen — **must-see** *adj*

musty \'məs-tē\ *adj* **must·i·er; -est** (1530) **1 a** : impaired by damp or mildew : MOLDY **b** : tasting of mold **c** : smelling of damp and decay : FUSTY **2 a** : TRITE, STALE **b** (1) : ANTIQUATED (2) : SUPER-ANNUATED *syn* see MALODOROUS — **must·i·ly** \'məs-tə-lē\ *adv* — **must·i·ness** \-tē-nəs\ *n*

mu·ta·ble \'myü-tə-bəl\ *adj* [ME, fr. L *mutabilis,* fr. *mutare* to change; akin to OE *mīthan* to conceal, Skt *mināti* he exchanges, deceives] (14c) **1** : prone to change : INCONSTANT **2 a** : capable of change or of being changed **b** : capable of or liable to mutation — **mu·ta·bil·i·ty** \,myü-tə-'bi-lə-tē\ *n* — **mu·ta·bly** \'myü-tə-blē\ *adv*

mu·ta·gen \'myü-tə-jən\ *n* [ISV *mutation* + *-gen*] (1933) : an agent (as mustard gas or various radiations) that tends to increase the frequency or extent of mutation — **mu·ta·gen·ic** \,myü-tə-'je-nik\ *adj* — **mu·ta·gen·i·cal·ly** \-ni-k(ə-)lē\ *adv*

mu·ta·gen·e·sis \,myü-tə-'je-nə-səs\ *n* [NL] (1948) : the occurrence or induction of mutation

mu·ta·ge·nic·i·ty \-jə-'ni-sə-tē\ *n* (1956) : the capacity to induce mutations

mu·tant \'myü-tᵊnt\ *adj* [L *mutant-, mutans,* prp. of *mutare*] (1903) : of, relating to, or produced by mutation — **mutant** *n*

mu·tase \'myü-,tās, -,tāz\ *n* [ISV *mut-* (fr. L *mutare*) + *-ase*] (1938) : any of various enzymes that catalyze molecular rearrangements and esp. those involving the transfer of phosphate from one hydroxyl group to another in the same molecule

mu·tate \'myü-,tāt, myü-'\ *vb* **mu·tat·ed; mu·tat·ing** [L *mutatus,* pp. of *mutare*] *vi* (1818) : to undergo mutation *~ vt* : to cause to undergo mutation — **mu·ta·tive** \'myü-,tā-tiv, -tə-tiv\ *adj*

mu·ta·tion \myü-'tā-shən\ *n* (14c) **1** : a significant and basic alteration : CHANGE **2** : UMLAUT **3 a** : a relatively permanent change in hereditary material involving either a physical change in chromosome relations or a biochemical change in the codons that make up genes; *also* : the process of producing a mutation **b** : an individual strain or trait resulting from mutation — **mu·ta·tion·al** \-shnəl, -shə-nᵊl\ *adj* — **mu·ta·tion·al·ly** *adv*

mu·ta·tis mu·tan·dis \m(y)ü-'tä-təs-m(y)ü-'tän-dəs, -'tä-təs-, -'tan-\ *adv* [ME, fr. ML] (15c) **1** : with the necessary changes having been made **2** : with the respective differences having been considered

mutch·kin \'məch-kən\ *n* [ME (Sc) *muchekyn*] (15c) : a Scottish unit of liquid capacity equal to 0.90 pint (0.42 liter)

¹**mute** \'myüt\ *adj* **mut·er; mut·est** [alter. of ME *muet,* fr. MF, fr. OF *mu,* fr. L *mutus,* prob. fr. *mu,* representation of a muttered sound] (1513) **1** : unable to speak : DUMB **2** : characterized by absence of speech: as **a** : felt or experienced but not expressed ⟨touched her hand in *~* sympathy⟩ **b** : refusing to plead directly or stand trial ⟨the prisoner stands *~*⟩ **3** : remaining silent, undiscovered, or unrecognized **4 a** : contributing nothing to the pronunciation of a word ⟨the *b* in *plumb* is *~*⟩ **b** : contributing to the pronunciation of a word but not representing the nucleus of a syllable ⟨the *e* in *mate* is *~*⟩ — **mute·ly** *adv* — **mute·ness** *n*

²**mute** *n* (1530) **1** : STOP 9 **2** : a person who cannot or does not speak **3** : a device attached to a musical instrument to reduce, soften, or muffle its tone

³**mute** *vt* **mut·ed; mut·ing** (1883) **1** : to muffle, reduce, or eliminate the sound of **2** : to tone down : SOFTEN, SUBDUE ⟨*~* a color⟩

⁴**mute** *vi* **mut·ed; mut·ing** [ME *meutir,* short for *esmeutir,* fr. OF *esmeltir,* of Gmc origin; akin to MD *smelten* to melt, defecate (used of birds)] (15c) *of a bird* : to evacuate the cloaca

mut·ed \'myü-təd\ *adj* (1861) **1** : provided with or produced or modified by the use of a mute **2 a** : being mute : SILENT **b** : toned down : LOW-KEY, SUBDUED — **mut·ed·ly** *adv*

mute swan *n* (1785) : a common white swan (*Cygnus olor*) that produces no loud notes, is native to Europe and western Asia, and has been introduced into parts of the U.S.

mu·ti·late \'myü-tᵊl-,āt\ *vt* **-lat·ed; -lat·ing** [L *mutilatus,* pp. of *mutilare,* fr. *mutilus* truncated, maimed] (1534) **1** : to cut up or alter radically so as to make imperfect ⟨the child *mutilated* the book with his scissors⟩ **2** : to cut off or permanently destroy a limb or essential part of : CRIPPLE *syn* see MAIM — **mu·ti·la·tion** \,myü-tᵊl-'ā-shən\ *n* — **mu·ti·la·tor** \'myü-tᵊl-,ā-tər\ *n*

mu·tine \'myü-tᵊn\ *vi* **mu·tined; mu·tin·ing** [MF (*se*) *mutiner*] (1555) *obs* : REBEL, MUTINY

mu·ti·neer \,myü-tᵊn-'ir\ *n* (1610) : one that mutinies

mu·ti·nous \'myü-tᵊn-əs, 'myüt-nəs\ *adj* (1578) **1 a** : disposed to or in a state of mutiny : REBELLIOUS **b** : TURBULENT, UNRULY **2** : of, relating to, or constituting mutiny — **mu·ti·nous·ly** *adv* — **mu·ti·nous·ness** *n*

mu·ti·ny \'myü-tᵊn-ē, 'myüt-nē\ *n, pl* **-nies** [*mutine* to rebel, fr. MF (*se*) *mutiner,* fr. *mutin* mutinous, fr. *meute* revolt, fr. (assumed) VL *movita,* fr. fem. of *movitus,* alter. of L *motus,* pp. of *movēre* to move] (1567) **1** *obs* : TUMULT, STRIFE **2** : forcible or passive resistance to lawful authority; *esp* : concerted revolt (as of a naval crew) against discipline or a superior officer *syn* see REBELLION — **mutiny** *vi*

mut·ism \'myü-,ti-zəm\ *n* [F *mutisme,* fr. L *mutus* mute] (1824) : the condition of being mute

mutt \'mət\ *n* [short for *muttonhead* dull-witted person] (1901) **1** : a stupid or insignificant person : FOOL **2** : a mongrel dog : CUR

mut·ter \'mə-tər\ *vb* [ME *muteren,* of imit. origin] *vi* (14c) **1** : to utter sounds or words indistinctly or with a low voice and with the lips partly closed **2** : to murmur complainingly or angrily : GRUMBLE *~ vt* : to utter esp. in a low or imperfectly articulated manner — **mutter** *n* — **mut·ter·er** \-tər-ər\ *n*

mut·ton \'mə-tᵊn\ *n* [ME *motoun,* fr. OF *moton* ram, wether, of Celt origin; akin to OIr *molt* wether] (13c) : the flesh of a mature sheep used for food — **mut·tony** \'mə-tᵊn-ē, 'mət-nē\ *adj*

mut·ton-chops \'mə-tᵊn-,chäps\ *n pl* (1865) : side-whiskers that are narrow at the temple and broad and round by the lower jaws — called also *muttonchop whiskers*

mut·ton·fish \-,fish\ *n* [fr. its flavor] (1735) : a common snapper (*Lutjanus analis*) of the warmer parts of the western Atlantic that is usu. olive green and sometimes nearly white or tinged with rosy red and that is a commercially important food and sport fish — called also *mutton snapper*

mu·tu·al \'myü-chə-wəl, -chəl; 'myüch-wəl\ *adj* [ME, fr. MF *mutuel,* fr. L *mutuus* lent, borrowed, mutual, fr. *mutare* to change — more at MUTABLE] (15c) **1 a** : directed by each toward the other or the others ⟨*~* affection⟩ **b** : having the same feelings one for the other ⟨they had long been *~* enemies⟩ **c** : shared in common ⟨enjoying their *~* hobby⟩ **d** : JOINT **2** : characterized by intimacy **3** : of or relating to a plan whereby the members of an organization share in the profits and expenses; *specif* : of, relating to, or taking the form of an insurance method in which the policyholders constitute the members of the insuring company — **mu·tu·al·ly** *adv*

mutual fund *n* (1934) : an open-end investment company that invests money of its shareholders in a usu. diversified group of securities of other corporations

mu·tu·al·ism \'myü-chə-wə-,li-zəm, 'myü-chə-,li-, 'myüch-wə-,li-\ *n* (1849) **1** : the doctrine or practice of mutual dependence as the condition of individual and social welfare **2** : mutually beneficial association between different kinds of organisms — **mu·tu·al·ist** \-list\ *n* — **mu·tu·al·is·tic** \,myü-chə-wə-'lis-tik, ,myü-chə-'lis-, ,myüch-wə-'lis-\ *adj*

mu·tu·al·i·ty \,myü-chə-'wa-lə-tē\ *n* (ca. 1586) **1** : the quality or state of being mutual **2** : a sharing of sentiments : INTIMACY

mu·tu·al·ize \'myü-chə-wə-,līz, 'myü-chə-,līz, 'myüch-wə-,līz\ *vt* **-ized; -iz·ing** (1812) : to make mutual — **mu·tu·al·i·za·tion** \,myü-chə-wə-lə-'zā-shən, ,myü-chə-lə-, ,myüch-wə-lə-\ *n*

mutually exclusive *adj* (1874) : being related such that each excludes or precludes the other ⟨*mutually exclusive* events⟩; *also* : INCOMPATIBLE ⟨their outlooks were not *mutually exclusive*⟩

mutuel *n* (1908) : PARI-MUTUEL

muu-muu \'mü-,mü\ *n* [Hawaiian *mu'umu'u,* fr. *mu'umu'u* cut off] (1923) : a loose often long dress having bright colors and patterns and adapted from the dresses orig. distributed by missionaries to the native women of Hawaii

Mu·zak \'myü-,zak\ *trademark* — used for recorded background music transmitted by wire to the loudspeaker of a subscriber (as in an office)

mu·zhik \mü-'zhek, -'zhik\ *n* [Russ] (1568) : a Russian peasant

¹**muz·zle** \'mə-zəl\ *n* [ME *musell,* fr. MF *musel,* fr. dim. of *muse* mouth of an animal, fr. ML *musus*] (15c) **1** : the projecting jaws and nose of an animal : SNOUT **2 a** : a fastening or covering for the mouth of an animal used to prevent eating or biting **b** : something (as censorship) that restrains normal expression **3** : the open end of an implement; *esp* : the discharging end of a weapon

²**muzzle** *vt* **muz·zled; muz·zling** \'məz-liŋ, 'mə-zə-\ (15c) **1** : to fit with a muzzle **2** : to restrain from expression : GAG — **muz·zler** \-lər\ *n*

muzzle 2a

muz·zy \'mə-zē\ *adj* **muz·zi·er; -est** [perh. blend of *muddled* and *fuzzy*] (ca. 1728) **1 a** : deficient in brightness : DULL, GLOOMY ⟨a *~* day⟩ **b** : lacking in clarity and precision ⟨his conclusions can be *~* and naive —*Times Lit. Supp.*⟩ **2** : muddled or confused in mind — **muz·zi·ly** \'mə-zə-lē\ *adv* — **muz·zi·ness** \'mə-zē-nəs\ *n*

MX \,em-'eks\ *n* [*m*issile, e*x*perimental] (1976) : a mobile ICBM having up to 10 independently targeted nuclear warheads

my \'mī, mə\ *adj* [ME, fr. OE *mīn*, fr. *min*, suppletive gen. of *ic* I; akin to OE *mē* me] (12c) **1** : of or relating to me or myself esp. as possessor, agent, or object of an action ⟨~ car⟩ ⟨~ promise⟩ ⟨~ injuries⟩ **2** — used interjectionally to express surprise and sometimes reduplicated ⟨~ oh ~⟩; used also interjectionally with names of various parts of the body to express doubt or disapproval ⟨~ foot⟩

my- or **myo-** *comb form* [NL, fr. Gk, fr. *mys* mouse, muscle — more at MOUSE] : muscle ⟨*myo*globin⟩ : muscle and ⟨*myo*neural⟩

my·al·gia \mī-'al-j(ē-)ə\ *n* [NL] (1860) : pain in one or more muscles — **my·al·gic** \-jik\ *adj*

my·as·the·nia \,mī-əs-'thē-nē-ə\ *n* [NL] (ca. 1856) : muscular debility — **my·as·then·ic** \-'the-nik\ *adj or n*

myasthenia gra·vis \-'gra-vəs, -'grä-\ *n* [NL, lit., grave myasthenia] (1900) : a disease characterized by progressive weakness and exhaustibility of voluntary muscles without atrophy or sensory disturbance and caused by an autoimmune attack on acetylcholine receptors at the neuromuscular junction

myc- or **myco-** *comb form* [NL, fr. Gk *mykēt-, mykēs* fungus; akin to Gk *myxa* nasal mucus] : fungus ⟨*myco*logy⟩ ⟨*myco*sis⟩

my·ce·li·um \mī-'sē-lē-əm\ *n, pl* **-lia** \-lē-ə\ [NL, fr. *myc-* + Gk *hēlos* nail, wart, callus] (1836) : the mass of interwoven filamentous hyphae that forms esp. the vegetative portion of the thallus of a fungus and is often submerged in another body (as of soil or organic matter or the tissues of a host); *also* : a similar mass of filaments formed by some bacteria (as streptomyces) — **my·ce·li·al** \-əl\ *adj*

My·ce·nae·an \,mī-sə-'nē-ən\ *also* **My·ce·ni·an** \mī-'sē-nē-ən\ *adj* (1598) **1** : of, relating to, or characteristic of Mycenae, its people, or the period (1400 to 1100 B.C.) of Mycenae's political ascendancy **2** : characteristic of the Bronze Age Mycenaean culture of the eastern Mediterranean area — **Mycenaean** *n*

my·ce·to·ma \,mī-sə-'tō-mə\ *n, pl* **-mas** *or* **-ma·ta** \-mə-tə\ [NL, fr. Gk *mykēt-, mykēs*] (1874) : a condition marked by invasion of the deep subcutaneous tissues with fungi or actinomycetes; *also* : a tumorous mass occurring in such a condition — **my·ce·to·ma·tous** \-mə-təs\ *adj*

my·ce·toph·a·gous \,mī-sə-'tä-fə-gəs\ *adj* [Gk *mykēt-, mykēs* + E *-phagous*] (ca. 1890) : feeding on fungi

my·ce·to·zo·an \mī-,sē-tə-'zō-ən\ *n* [NL *Mycetozoa*, order of protozoans, fr. Gk *mykēt-, mykēs* + NL *-zoa*] (1881) : SLIME MOLD — **mycetozoan** *adj*

-mycin *n comb form* [*streptomycin*] : substance obtained from a funguslike bacterium ⟨erythro*mycin*⟩

my·co·bac·te·ri·um \,mī-kō-bak-'tir-ē-əm\ *n* [NL] (1909) : any of a genus (*Mycobacterium*) of nonmotile aerobic acid-fast bacteria that include numerous saprophytes and the pathogens causing tuberculosis and leprosy — **my·co·bac·te·ri·al** \-ē-əl\ *adj*

my·co·flo·ra \mi-kə-'flōr-ə, -'flor-\ *n* [NL] (1945) : the fungi characteristic of a region or special environment

my·col·o·gy \mī-'kä-lə-jē\ *n* [NL *mycologia*, fr. *myc-* + L *-logia* -logy] (1836) **1** : a branch of biology dealing with fungi **2** : fungal life — **my·co·log·i·cal** \,mī-kə-'lä-ji-kəl\ *adj* — **my·co·log·i·cal·ly** \,mī-kə-'lä-ji-k(ə-)lē\ *adv* — **my·col·o·gist** \mī-'kä-lə-jist\ *n*

my·coph·a·gist \mī-'kä-fə-jist\ *n* [*mycophagy*, fr. *myc-* + *-phagy*] (1861) : one that eats fungi (as mushrooms) — **my·coph·a·gy** \-jē\ *n*

my·coph·a·gous \-gəs\ *adj* (ca. 1909) : feeding on fungi

my·co·phile \'mī-kō-,fīl\ *n* (1953) : a person whose hobby is hunting wild edible mushrooms

my·co·plas·ma \,mī-kō-'plaz-mə\ *n, pl* **-mas** *or* **-ma·ta** \-mə-tə\ [NL] (1955) : any of a genus (*Mycoplasma*) of minute pleomorphic gramnegative chiefly nonmotile microorganisms without cell walls that are intermediate in some respects between viruses and bacteria, are mostly parasitic usu. in mammals — called also *pleuropneumonia-like organism* — **my·co·plas·mal** \-məl\ *adj*

mycoplasma–like organism *n* (1968) : any of a group of prokaryotic organisms that resemble mycoplasmas, cause disease in plants, are transmitted by insect vectors, and have proved extremely difficult to grow in artificial media

my·cor·rhi·za \,mī-kə-'rī-zə\ *n, pl* **-zae** \-,zē\ *or* **-zas** [NL, fr. *myc-* + Gk *rhiza* root — more at ROOT] (1895) : the symbiotic association of the mycelium of a fungus with the roots of a seed plant — **my·cor·rhi·zal** \-zəl\ *adj*

my·co·sis \mī-'kō-səs\ *n, pl* **my·co·ses** \-,sēz\ [NL] (1876) : infection with or disease caused by a fungus — **my·cot·ic** \-'kä-tik\ *adj*

my·co·tox·in \,mī-kə-'täk-sən\ *n* (1962) : a toxic substance produced by a fungus and esp. a mold

my·dri·a·sis \mə-'drī-ə-səs\ *n* [L, fr. Gk] (ca. 1775) : a long-continued or excessive dilatation of the pupil of the eye — **myd·ri·at·ic** \,mi-drē-'a-tik\ *adj or n*

myel- or **myelo-** *comb form* [NL, fr. Gk, fr. *myelos*, prob. fr. *myōn* cluster of muscles, fr. *mys* mouse, muscle — more at MOUSE] : marrow : spinal cord ⟨*myel*encephalon⟩

my·el·en·ceph·a·lon \,mī-ə-len-'se-fə-,län, -lən\ *n* [NL] (1871) : the posterior part of the developing vertebrate hindbrain or the corresponding part of the adult brain composed of the medulla oblongata — **my·el·en·ce·phal·ic** \-,len(t)-sə-'fa-lik\ *adj*

my·e·lin \'mī-ə-lən\ *n* [ISV] (1873) : a soft white somewhat fatty material that forms a thick myelin sheath about the protoplasmic core of a myelinated nerve fiber — **my·e·lin·ic** \,mī-ə-'li-nik\ *adj*

my·e·lin·at·ed \'mī-ə-lə-,nā-təd\ *adj* (1899) : having a myelin sheath ⟨~ nerve fibers⟩

myelin sheath *n* (1896) : a layer of myelin surrounding some nerve fibers — called also *medullary sheath*

my·e·li·tis \,mī-ə-'lī-təs\ *n, pl* **-lit·i·des** \-'li-tə-,dēz\ [NL] (1835) : inflammation of the spinal cord or of the bone marrow

my·e·lo·blast \'mī-ə-lə-,blast\ *n* [ISV] (ca. 1904) : a large mononuclear nongranular bone-marrow cell; *esp* : one that is a precursor of a myelocyte — **my·e·lo·blas·tic** \,mī-ə-lə-'blas-tik\ *adj*

my·e·lo·cyte \'mī-ə-lə-,sīt\ *n* [ISV] (1891) : a bone-marrow cell; *esp* : a motile cell with cytoplasmic granules that gives rise to the granulocytes of the blood and occurs abnormally in the circulating blood — **my·e·lo·cyt·ic** \,mī-ə-lə-'si-tik\ *adj*

my·e·lo·fi·bro·sis \,mī-ə-lō-fī-'brō-səs\ *n* [NL] (1947) : an anemic condition in which bone marrow becomes fibrotic and the liver and spleen usu. exhibit a development of blood-cell precursors — **my·e·lo·fi·brot·ic** \-'brä-tik\ *adj*

my·e·log·e·nous \,mī-ə-'lä-jə-nəs\ *adj* [ISV] (1876) : of, relating to, originating in, or produced by the bone marrow ⟨~ sarcoma⟩

myelogenous leukemia *n* (1904) : leukemia characterized by proliferation of myeloid tissue (as of the bone marrow and spleen) and an abnormal increase in the number of granulocytes, myelocytes, and myeloblasts in the circulating blood — called also *myelocytic leukemia, myeloid leukemia*

my·e·loid \'mī-ə-,lȯid\ *adj* [ISV] (1857) : of, relating to, or resembling bone marrow

my·e·lo·ma \,mī-ə-'lō-mə\ *n* [NL] (ca. 1857) : a primary tumor of the bone marrow — **my·e·lo·ma·tous** \-mə-təs\ *adj*

my·e·lop·a·thy \,mī-ə-'lä-pə-thē\ *n* [ISV] (ca. 1891) : a disease or disorder of the spinal cord or bone marrow — **my·e·lo·path·ic** \,mī-ə-lō-'pa-thik\ *adj*

my·e·lo·pro·lif·er·a·tive \'mī-ə-lō-prə-'li-f(ə-)rə-tiv, -fə-,rā-\ *adj* (1951) : of, relating to, or being a disorder (as leukemia) marked by excessive proliferation of bone marrow elements and esp. blood cell precursors

my·i·a·sis \mī-'ī-ə-səs, mē-\ *n, pl* **my·i·a·ses** \-,sēz\ [NL, fr. Gk *myia* fly — more at MIDGE] (1837) : infestation with fly maggots

My·lar \'mī-,lär\ *trademark* — used for a polyester film

my·nah *or* **my·na** \'mī-nə\ *n* [Hindi *mainā* hill mynah fr. Skt *madana*, a kind of bird] (1769) : any of various Asian starlings (esp. genera *Acridotheres, Gracula,* and *Sturnus*); *esp* : a dark brown slightly crested bird (*A. tristis*) of southeastern Asia with a white tail tip and wing markings and bright yellow bill and feet — compare HILL MYNAH

myn·heer \mə-'ner\ *n* [D *mijnheer*, fr. *mijn* my + *heer* master, sir] (1652) : a male Netherlander — used as a title equivalent to *Mr.*

myo- — see MY-

myo·blast \'mī-ə-,blast\ *n* [ISV] (1884) : an undifferentiated cell capable of giving rise to muscle cells

myo·car·di·tis \,mī-ə-(,)kär-'dī-təs\ *n* [NL] (1866) : inflammation of the myocardium

myo·car·di·um \,mī-ə-'kär-dē-əm\ *n* [NL, fr. *my-* + Gk *kardia* heart — more at HEART] (1879) : the middle muscular layer of the heart wall — **myo·car·di·al** \-dē-əl\ *adj*

my·oc·lo·nus \mī-'ä-klə-nəs\ *n* [NL] (1883) : irregular involuntary contraction of a muscle usu. resulting from functional disorder of controlling motoneurons; *also* : a condition characterized by myoclonus — **myo·clon·ic** \,mī-ə-'klä-nik\ *adj*

myo·elec·tric \,mī-ō-i-'lek-trik\ *also* **myo·elec·tri·cal** \-tri-kəl\ *adj* (ca. 1919) : of, relating to, or utilizing electricity generated by muscle

myo·fi·bril \,mī-ə-'fī-brəl, -'fi-\ *n* [NL *myofibrilla*, fr. *my-* + *fibrilla* fibril] (1898) : any of the longitudinal parallel contractile elements of a muscle cell that are composed of myosin and actin — **myo·fi·bril·lar** \-brə-lər\ *adj*

myo·fil·a·ment \-'fi-lə-mənt\ *n* (1949) : one of the individual filaments of actin or myosin that make up a myofibril

myo·gen·ic \-'je-nik\ *adj* [ISV] (1904) : taking place or functioning in ordered rhythmic fashion because of the inherent properties of cardiac muscle rather than specific neural stimuli ⟨a ~ heartbeat⟩

myo·glo·bin \-'glō-bən, 'mī-ə-,\ *n* [ISV] (1925) : a red iron-containing protein pigment in muscles that is similar to hemoglobin

myo·ino·si·tol \,mī-ō-i-'nō-sə-,tȯl, -,tōl\ *n* (1951) : a biologically active inositol that is a component of the vitamin B complex and a lipotropic agent

my·ol·o·gy \mī-'ä-lə-jē\ *n* [F or NL; F *myologie*, fr. NL *myologia*, fr. *my-* + L *-logia* -logy] (1649) : a scientific study of muscles

my·o·ma \mī-'ō-mə\ *n, pl* **-mas** *or* **-ma·ta** \-mə-tə\ [NL] (1875) : a tumor consisting of muscle tissue — **my·o·ma·tous** \-mə-təs\ *adj*

myo·neu·ral \,mī-ə-'nu̇r-əl, -'nyu̇r-\ *adj* (1905) : of, relating to, or connecting muscles and nerves ⟨~ junctions⟩

my·op·a·thy \mī-'ä-pə-thē\ *n* (ca. 1849) : a disorder of muscle tissue or muscles — **myo·path·ic** \,mī-ə-'pa-thik\ *adj*

my·ope \'mī-,ōp\ *n* [F, fr. LL *myops* myopic, fr. Gk *myōps*, fr. *myein* to be closed + *ōps* eye, face — more at EYE] (1728) : a myopic person

my·o·pia \mī-'ō-pē-ə\ *n* [NL, fr. Gk *myōpia*, fr. *myōp-, myōps*] (ca. 1752) **1** : a condition in which the visual images come to a focus in front of the retina of the eye resulting esp. in defective vision of distant objects **2** : a lack of foresight or discernment : a narrow view of something — **my·o·pic** \-'ō-pik, -'ä-\ *adj* — **my·o·pi·cal·ly** \-pi-k(ə-)lē\ *adv*

my·o·sin \'mī-ə-sən\ *n* [ISV *my-* + *2-ose* + *1-in*] (1942) : a fibrous globulin of muscle that can split ATP and that reacts with actin to form actomyosin

my·o·sis, my·ot·ic *var of* MIOSIS, MIOTIC

myo·si·tis \,mī-ə-'sī-təs\ *n* [NL, irreg. fr. Gk *mys* muscle, mouse] (ca. 1819) : muscle soreness

myo·tome \'mī-ə-,tōm\ *n* [ISV] (1894) : the portion of an embryonic somite from which skeletal musculature is produced

myo·to·nia \,mī-ə-'tō-nē-ə\ *n* [NL] (ca. 1896) : tonic spasm of one or more muscles; *also* : a condition characterized by such spasms — **myo·ton·ic** \-'tä-nik\ *adj*

¹myr·i·ad \'mir-ē-əd\ *n* [Gk *myriad-, myrias,* fr. *myrioi* countless, ten thousand] (1555) **1** : ten thousand **2** : a great number ⟨a ~ of ideas⟩

²myriad *adj* (1791) **1** : INNUMERABLE ⟨those ~ problems⟩ **2** : having innumerable aspects or elements ⟨the ~ activity of the new land — Meridel Le Sueur⟩

myr·ia·pod *also* **myr·io·pod** \'mir-ē-ə-,päd\ *n* [ultim. fr. Gk *myrioi* + *pod-, pous* foot — more at FOOT] (1826) : any of a group (Myriapoda) of arthropods having the body made up of numerous similar segments nearly all of which bear true jointed legs and including the millipedes and centipedes — **myriapod** *also* **myriopod** *adj*

\ə\ abut \ᵊ\ kitten, F table \ər\ further \a\ ash \ā\ ace \ä\ mop, mar \au̇\ out \ch\ chin \e\ bet \ē\ easy \g\ go \i\ hit \ī\ ice \j\ job \ŋ\ sing \ō\ go \ȯ\ law \ȯi\ boy \th\ thin \t̷h\ the \ü\ loot \u̇\ foot \y\ yet \zh\ vision \á, k̲, ⁿ, œ, œ̄, ᴜᴇ, ᵿᴇ, ᵞ\ see Guide to Pronunciation

my·ris·tic acid \mə-'ris-tik-, mī-\ n [ISV, fr. NL *Myristica*, genus of trees] (1848) : a crystalline fatty acid C₁₄H₂₈O₂ occurring esp. in the form of glycerides in most fats

myrmeco- *comb form* [Gk *myrmēko-*, fr. *myrmēk-*, *myrmēx* — more at PISMIRE] : ant ⟨*myrmecophilous*⟩

myr·me·col·o·gy \,mər-mə-'kä-lə-jē\ n [ISV] (ca. 1902) : the scientific study of ants — **myr·me·co·log·i·cal** \-kə-'lä-ji-kəl\ *adj* — **myr·me·col·o·gist** \-'kä-lə-jist\ n

myr·me·co·phile \'mər-mi-kə-,fīl\ n [ISV] (1898) : an organism that habitually shares an ant nest

myr·me·coph·i·lous \,mər-mə-'kä-fə-ləs\ *adj* (1866) : fond of, associated with, or benefited by ants

myr·mi·don \'mər-mə-,dän, -dən\ n [ME *Mirmydon*, L *Myrmidon-*, *Myrmido*, fr. Gk *Myrmidōn*] (15c) **1** *cap* : a member of a legendary Thessalian people who accompanied their king Achilles in the Trojan War **2** : a loyal follower; *esp* : a subordinate who executes orders unquestioningly or unscrupulously

my·rob·a·lan \mī-'rä-bə-lən, mə-\ n [MF *mirobolan*, fr. L *myrobalanus*, fr. Gk *myrobalanos*, fr. *myron* unguent + *balanos* acorn — more at GLAND] (ca. 1530) : the dried astringent fruit of an East Indian tree (genus *Terminalia* of the family Combretaceae) used chiefly in tanning and in inks

myrrh \'mər\ n [ME *myrre*, fr. OE, fr. L *myrrha*, fr. Gk, of Sem origin; akin to Ar *murr* myrrh] (bef. 12c) : a yellowish brown to reddish brown aromatic gum resin with a bitter slightly pungent taste obtained from a tree (esp. *Commiphora abyssinica* of the family Burseraceae) of eastern Africa and Arabia; *also* : a mixture of myrrh and labdanum

myr·tle \'mər-t⁸l\ n, *often attrib* [ME *mirtille*, fr. MF, fr. ML *myrtillus*, fr. L *myrtus*, fr. Gk *myrtos*] (1562) **1 a** : a common evergreen bushy shrub (*Myrtus communis*) of southern Europe with oval to lance-shaped shiny leaves, fragrant white or rosy flowers, and black berries **b** : any of a family (Myrtaceae, the myrtle family) of chiefly tropical shrubs or trees to which the common myrtle belongs **2 a** : ¹PERIWINKLE 1a **b** : CALIFORNIA LAUREL

myrtle 1a

my·self \mī-'self, mə-, *Southern also* -'sef\ *pron* (bef. 12c) **1** : that identical one that is I — used reflexively ⟨I'm going to get ~ a new suit⟩, for emphasis ⟨I ~ will go⟩, or in absolute constructions ⟨~ a tourist, I nevertheless avoided other tourists⟩ **2** : my normal, healthy, or sane condition ⟨didn't feel ~ yesterday⟩

usage Myself is often used where *I* or *me* might be expected: as subject ⟨to wonder what *myself* will say —Emily Dickinson⟩ ⟨others and *myself* continued to press for the legislation⟩, after *as, than*, or *like* ⟨an aversion to paying such people as *myself* to tutor⟩ ⟨was enough to make a better man than *myself* quail⟩ ⟨old-timers like *myself*⟩, and as object ⟨now here you see *myself* with the diver⟩ ⟨for my wife and *myself* it was a happy time⟩. Such uses almost always occur when the speaker or writer is referring to himself or herself as an object of discourse rather than as a participant in the discourse. The other reflexive personal pronouns are similarly but less frequently used in the same circumstances. Critics have frowned on these uses since about the turn of the century, prob. unaware that they serve a definite purpose. Users themselves are as unaware as the critics—they simply follow their instincts. These uses are standard.

mys·ta·gogue \'mis-tə-,gäg\ n [L *mystagogus*, fr. Gk *mystagōgos*, fr. *mystēs* initiate (perh. akin to Gk *myein* to be closed) + *agein* to lead — more at AGENT] (ca. 1550) **1** : one who initiates another into a mystery cult **2** : one who understands or teaches mystical doctrines — **mys·ta·go·gy** \-,gä-jē, -,gō-\ n

mys·te·ri·ous \mis-'tir-ē-əs\ *adj* (1600) **1 a** : of, relating to, or constituting mystery ⟨the ~ ways of God⟩ **b** : exciting wonder, curiosity, or surprise while baffling efforts to comprehend or identify : MYSTIFYING ⟨heard a ~ noise⟩ ⟨a ~ stranger⟩ **2** : stirred by or attracted to the inexplicable — **mys·te·ri·ous·ly** *adv* — **mys·te·ri·ous·ness** n

¹mys·tery \'mis-t(ə-)rē\ n, *pl* **-ter·ies** [ME *mysterie*, fr. L *mysterium*, fr. Gk *mystērion*, fr. *mystēs* initiate] (14c) **1 a** : a religious truth that one can know only by revelation and cannot fully understand **b** (1) : any of the 15 events (as the Nativity, the Crucifixion, or the Assumption) serving as a subject for meditation during the saying of the rosary (2) *cap* : a Christian sacrament; *specif* : EUCHARIST **c** (1) : a secret religious rite believed (as in Eleusinian and Mithraic cults) to impart enduring bliss to the initiate (2) : a cult devoted to such rites **2 a** : something not understood or beyond understanding : ENIGMA **b** *obs* : a private secret **c** : the secret or specialized practices or ritual peculiar to an occupation or a body of people ⟨the *mysteries* of the tailor's craft⟩ **d** : a piece of fiction dealing usu. with the solution of a mysterious crime **3** : profound, inexplicable, or secretive quality or character ⟨the ~ of her smile⟩

syn MYSTERY, PROBLEM, ENIGMA, RIDDLE, PUZZLE mean something which baffles or perplexes. MYSTERY applies to what cannot be fully understood by human reason or less strictly to whatever resists or defies explanation ⟨the *mystery* of the stone monoliths⟩. PROBLEM applies to any question or difficulty calling for a solution or causing concern ⟨the *problems* created by high technology⟩. ENIGMA applies to utterance or behavior that is very difficult to interpret ⟨his suicide was an *enigma* his family never understood⟩. RIDDLE suggests an enigma or problem involving paradox or apparent contradiction ⟨the *riddle* of the reclusive pop star⟩. PUZZLE applies to an enigma or problem that challenges ingenuity for its solution ⟨the mechanisms of heredity were long a *puzzle* for scientists⟩.

²mystery n, *pl* **-ter·ies** [ME, fr. LL *misterium*, *mysterium*, alter. of *ministerium* service, occupation, fr. *minister* servant — more at MINISTER] (14c) **1** *archaic* : TRADE, CRAFT **2** *archaic* : a body of persons engaged in a particular trade, business, or profession : GUILD **3** : MYSTERY PLAY

mystery play n [²*mystery*] (1852) : a medieval drama based on scriptural incidents (as the creation of the world, the Flood, or the life, death, and resurrection of Christ) — compare MIRACLE PLAY

¹mys·tic \'mis-tik\ *adj* [ME *mistik*, fr. L *mysticus* of mysteries, fr. Gk *mystikos*, fr. *mystēs* initiate] (14c) **1** : MYSTICAL 1a **2** : of or relating to mysteries or esoteric rites : OCCULT **3** : of or relating to mysticism or mystics **4 a** : MYSTERIOUS **b** : OBSCURE, ENIGMATIC **c** : inducing a feeling of awe or wonder **d** : having magical properties

²mystic n (1679) **1** : a follower of a mystical way of life **2** : an advocate of a theory of mysticism

mys·ti·cal \'mis-ti-kəl\ *adj* (15c) **1 a** : having a spiritual meaning or reality that is neither apparent to the senses nor obvious to the intelligence ⟨the ~ food of the sacrament⟩ **b** : involving or having the nature of an individual's direct subjective communion with God or ultimate reality ⟨the ~ experience of the Inner Light⟩ **2** : MYSTERIOUS, UNINTELLIGIBLE **3** : MYSTIC 2, 3 — **mys·ti·cal·ly** \-k(ə-)lē\ *adv*

mys·ti·cism \'mis-tə-,si-zəm\ n (1736) **1** : the experience of mystical union or direct communion with ultimate reality reported by mystics **2** : the belief that direct knowledge of God, spiritual truth, or ultimate reality can be attained through subjective experience (as intuition or insight) **3 a** : vague speculation : a belief without sound basis **b** : a theory postulating the possibility of direct and intuitive acquisition of ineffable knowledge or power

mys·ti·fi·ca·tion \,mis-tə-fə-'kā-shən\ n (1815) **1** : an act or instance of mystifying **2** : the quality or state of being mystified **3** : something designed to mystify

mys·ti·fy \'mis-tə-,fī\ *vt* **-fied; -fy·ing** [F *mistifier*, fr. *mystère* mystery, fr. L *mysterium*] (ca. 1734) **1** : to perplex the mind of : BEWILDER **2** : to make mysterious or obscure ⟨~ an interpretation of a prophecy⟩ — **mys·ti·fi·er** \-,fī(-ə)r\ n — **mys·ti·fy·ing·ly** \-,fī-iŋ-lē\ *adv*

mys·tique \mi-'stēk\ n [F, fr. *mystique*, adj., mystic, fr. L *mysticus*] (1891) **1** : an air or attitude of mystery and reverence developing around something or someone **2** : the special esoteric skill essential in a calling or activity

myth \'mith\ n [Gk *mythos*] (1830) **1 a** : a usu. traditional story of ostensibly historical events that serves to unfold part of the world view of a people or explain a practice, belief, or natural phenomenon **b** : PARABLE, ALLEGORY **2 a** : a popular belief or tradition that has grown up around something or someone; *esp* : one embodying the ideals and institutions of a society or segment of society ⟨seduced by the American ~ of individualism —Orde Coombs⟩ **b** : an unfounded or false notion **3** : a person or thing having only an imaginary or unverifiable existence **4** : the whole body of myths

myth·i·cal \'mith-i-kəl\ *or* **myth·ic** \-ik\ *adj* (1669) **1** : based on or described in a myth esp. as contrasted with history **2** *usu mythical* : existing only in the imagination : FICTITIOUS, IMAGINARY ⟨sportswriters picked a ~ all-star team⟩ **3** *usu mythic* : having qualities suitable to myth : LEGENDARY ⟨the twilight of a *mythic* professional career — Clayton Riley⟩ *syn* see FICTITIOUS — **myth·i·cal·ly** \-thi-k(ə-)lē\ *adv*

myth·i·cize \'mi-thə-,sīz\ *vt* **-cized; -ciz·ing** (1840) **1** : to turn into or envelop in myth **2** : to treat as myth — **myth·i·ciz·er** n

myth·mak·er \'mith-,mā-kər\ n (1871) : a creator of myths or of mythical situations or lore — **myth·mak·ing** \-kiŋ\ n

my·thog·ra·phy \mi-'thä-grə-fē\ n [Gk *mythographia*, fr. *mythos* + *-graphia* -graphy] (1851) **1** : the representation of mythical subjects in art **2** : a critical compilation of myths — **my·thog·ra·pher** \-fər\ n

myth·o·log·i·cal \,mi-thə-'lä-ji-kəl\ *also* **myth·o·log·ic** \-jik\ *adj* (1614) **1** : of or relating to mythology or myths : dealt with in mythology **2** : lacking factual basis or historical validity : MYTHICAL, FABULOUS — **myth·o·log·i·cal·ly** \-ji-k(ə-)lē\ *adv*

my·thol·o·gize \mi-'thä-lə-,jīz\ *vb* **-gized; -giz·ing** *vt* (1603) **1** *obs* : to explain the mythological significance of **2** : to build a myth around : MYTHICIZE — *vi* **1** : to relate, classify, and explain myths **2** : to create or perpetuate myths — **my·thol·o·giz·er** n

my·thol·o·gy \mi-'thä-lə-jē\ n, *pl* **-gies** [F or LL; F *mythologie*, fr. LL *mythologia* interpretation of myths, fr. Gk, legend, myth, fr. *mythologein* to relate myths, fr. *mythos* + *logos* speech — more at LEGEND] (1603) **1** : an allegorical narrative **2** : a body of myths: as **a** : the myths dealing with the gods, demigods, and legendary heroes of a particular people **b** : MYTHOS 2 ⟨cold war ~⟩ **3** : a branch of knowledge that deals with myth **4** : a popular belief or assumption that has grown up around someone or something ⟨defective *mythologies* that ignore masculine depth of feeling —Robert Bly⟩ — **my·thol·o·ger** \-jər\ n — **my·thol·o·gist** \-jist\ n

mytho·ma·nia \,mi-thə-'mā-nē-ə, -nyə\ n [NL, fr. Gk *mythos* + L *mania* mania] (ca. 1909) : an excessive or abnormal propensity for lying and exaggerating — **mytho·ma·ni·ac** \-nē-,ak\ n *or adj*

mytho·poe·ia \,mi-thə-'pē-ə\ n [LL, fr. Gk *mythopoiia*, fr. *mythopoiein* to make a myth, fr. *mythos* + *poiein* to make — more at POET] (1846) : a creating of myth : a giving rise to myths — **mytho·poe·ic** \-'pē-ik\ *adj also* **mytho·po·et·ic** \-pō-'e-tik\ *or* **mytho·po·et·i·cal** \-ti-kəl\ *adj*

my·thos \'mi-,thōs, -,thäs\ n, *pl* **my·thoi** \-,thòi\ [Gk] (1753) **1 a** : MYTH 1a **b** : MYTHOLOGY 2a **2** : a pattern of beliefs expressing often symbolically the characteristic or prevalent attitudes in a group or culture **3** : THEME, PLOT

mythy \'mi-thē\ *adj* (1931) : resembling, concerned with, or of a subject for myth ⟨a ~ theme⟩

my word *interj* (1841) — used to express surprise or astonishment

myx·ede·ma \,mik-sə-'dē-mə\ n [NL, fr. Gk *myxa* lamp wick, nasal mucus + NL *edema* edema — more at MUCUS] (1877) : severe hypothyroidism characterized by firm inelastic edema, dry skin and hair, and loss of mental and physical vigor — **myx·ede·ma·tous** \-'de-mə-təs, -'dē-\ *adj*

myx·o·ma \mik-'sō-mə\ n, *pl* **-mas** *or* **-ma·ta** \-mə-tə\ [NL, fr. Gk *myxa*] (1870) : a soft tumor made up of gelatinous connective tissue like that of the umbilical cord — **myx·o·ma·tous** \-mə-təs\ *adj*

myx·o·ma·to·sis \mik-,sō-mə-'tō-səs\ n [NL, fr. *myxomat-*, *myxoma*] (1927) : a condition characterized by the presence of myxomas in the body; *specif* : a severe virus disease of rabbits that is caused by a poxvirus transmitted by mosquitoes and that has been used in the biological control of rabbits in plague areas

myxo·my·cete \,mik-sō-'mī-,sēt, ,mik-sō-(,)mī-'\ n [ultim. fr. Gk *myxa* + *mykēt-*, *mykēs* fungus — more at MYC-] (1877) : SLIME MOLD

myxo·vi·rus \'mik-sə-,vī-rəs\ n [NL, fr. Gk *myxa* + NL *virus* virus; fr. its affinity for certain mucins] (1955) : any of a group of rather large RNA-containing viruses that includes the influenza viruses — **myxo·vi·ral** \,mik-sə-'vī-rəl\ *adj*

n \'en\ *n, pl* **n's** *or* **ns** \'enz\ *often cap, often attrib* (bef. 12c) **1 a** : the 14th letter of the English alphabet **b** : a graphic representation of this letter **c** : a speech counterpart of orthographic *n* **2** : a graphic device for reproducing the letter *n* **3 a** : one designated *n* esp. as the 14th in order or class **b** : an indefinite number; *esp* : a constant integer or a variable taking on integral values **4** : something shaped like the letter N **5** : the haploid or gametic number of chromosomes **6** : EN 2
-n — see -EN

'n \ən, ᵊn\ *conj* [by shortening] : THAN

'n' *also* **'n** \ən, ᵊn\ *conj* [by shortening] : AND ⟨fish 'n' chips⟩

naan *var of* NAN

nab \'nab\ *vt* **nabbed; nab·bing** [perh. alter. of E dial. *nap*] (1686) **1** : to catch or seize in arrest : APPREHEND **2** : to seize suddenly

nabe \'nāb\ *n* [by shortening & alter. fr. *neighborhood*] (1935) : a neighborhood theater — usu. used in pl. with the

na·bob \'nā-,bäb\ *n* [Urdu *nawwāb*, fr. Ar *nuwwāb*, pl. of *nā'ib* governor] (1612) **1** : a provincial governor of the Mogul empire in India **2** : a person of great wealth or prominence

Na·both \'nā-,bäth\ *n* [Heb *Nābhōth*] : the owner of a vineyard coveted and seized by Ahab king of Israel

na·celle \nə-'sel\ *n* [F, lit., small boat, fr. LL *navicella*, dim. of L *navis* ship — more at NAVE] (1904) : a streamlined enclosure (as for an engine) on an aircraft

na·cho \'nä-(,)chō\ *n, pl* **nachos** [AmerSp, perh. fr. Sp *nacho* flat-nosed] (1969) : a tortilla chip topped with melted cheese and often additional savory toppings (as hot peppers or refried beans)

na·cre \'nā-kər\ *n* [MF, fr. OIt *naccara* drum, nacre, fr. Ar *naqqārah* drum] (1718) : MOTHER-OF-PEARL — **na·cre·ous** \-krē-əs, -k(ə-)rəs\ *adj*

NAD \,en-(,)ā-'dē\ *n* [nicotinamide adenine dinucleotide] (ca. 1962) : a coenzyme $C_{21}H_{27}N_7O_{14}P_2$ of numerous dehydrogenases that occurs in most cells and plays an important role in all phases of intermediary metabolism as an oxidizing agent or when in the reduced form as a reducing agent for various metabolites — called also *nicotinamide adenine dinucleotide, diphosphopyridine nucleotide, DPN*

na·da \'nä-də\ *n* [Sp, fr. L (*res*) *nata* situation, circumstance, lit., a thing come into being] (1914) : NOTHING

Na–dene *also* **Na–dé·né** \nä-'dā-(,)nä, -'de-, -nē\ *n, often cap D* [*na-* (fr. Haida *na* to dwell & Tlingit *na* people) + *Déné*] (1915) : a hypothetically related group of American Indian languages that includes the Athabascan family, Tlingit, and Haida

NADH \,en-(,)ā-(,)dē-'āch\ *n* [*NAD* + *H*, symbol for hydrogen] (1965) : the reduced form of NAD

na·dir \'nā-,dir, 'nā-dər\ *n* [ME, fr. MF, fr. Ar *nazīr* opposite] (15c) **1** : the point of the celestial sphere that is directly opposite the zenith and vertically downward from the observer **2** : the lowest point

NADP \,en-(,)ā-(,)dē-'pē\ *n* [nicotinamide adenine dinucleotide phosphate] (ca. 1962) : a coenzyme $C_{21}H_{28}N_7O_{17}P_3$ of numerous dehydrogenases (as that acting on glucose-6-phosphate) that occurs esp. in red blood cells and plays a role in intermediary metabolism similar to NAD but acting often on different metabolites — called also *nicotinamide adenine dinucleotide phosphate, TPN, triphosphopyridine nucleotide*

NADPH \,en-(,)ā-(,)dē-(,)pē-'āch\ *n* [*NADP* + *H*, symbol for hydrogen] (ca. 1966) : the reduced form of NADP

¹nag \'nag\ *n* [ME *nagge*; akin to D *negge* small horse] (15c) : HORSE; *esp* : one that is old or in poor condition

²nag *vb* **nagged; nag·ging** [prob. of Scand origin; akin to ON *gnaga* to gnaw; akin to OE *gnagan* to gnaw] *vi* (ca. 1828) **1** : to find fault incessantly : COMPLAIN **2** : to be a persistent source of annoyance or distraction ~ *vt* **1** : to irritate by constant scolding or urging **2** : BADGER, WORRY — **nag·ger** *n* — **nagging** *adj* — **nag·ging·ly** \'na-giŋ-lē\ *adv*

³nag *n* (1925) : one who nags habitually

na·ga·na \nə-'gä-nə\ *n* [Zulu *unakane, ulunakane*] (1895) : trypanosomiasis esp. when caused by *Trypanosoma brucei* of domestic animals

nah \'nä, 'nä\ *adv* of NO

Na·huatl \'nä-,wä-t'l\ *n* [Sp *náhuatl*, fr. Nahuatl *Nāhuatl*] (1822) : a group of closely related Uto-Aztecan languages that includes the speech of several peoples (as the Aztecs) of central and southern Mexico and Central America — **Na·huat·lan** \'nä-'wät-lən\ *adj or n*

Na·hum \'nä-əm, -həm\ *n* [Heb *Nahūm*] **1** : a Hebrew prophet of the 7th century B.C. **2** : a prophetic book of canonical Jewish and Christian Scripture — see BIBLE table

na·iad \'nā-əd, 'nī-, -,ad\ *n, pl* **na·iads** *or* **na·ia·des** \-ə-,dēz\ [ME, fr. MF or L; MF *naïade*, fr. L *naiad-, naias*, fr. Gk, fr. *nan* to flow — more at NOURISH] (14c) **1** : any of the nymphs in classical mythology living in and giving life to lakes, rivers, springs, and fountains **2** : any of the aquatic young of a mayfly, dragonfly, damselfly, or stone fly — compare NYMPH 3 **3** : any of a genus (*Najas* of the family Najadaceae) of submerged aquatic plants

¹na·if *or* **naif** \nä-'ēf\ *adj* [F] (1598) : NAIVE

²naïf *or* **naif** *n* (1893) : a naive person

¹nail \'nā(ə)l\ *n* [ME, fr. OE *nægl*; akin to OHG *nagal* nail, fingernail, L *unguis* fingernail, toenail, claw, Gk *onyx*] (bef. 12c) **1 a** : a horny sheath protecting the upper end of each finger and toe of humans and most other primates **b** : a structure (as a claw) that terminates a digit and corresponds to a nail **2** : a slender usu. pointed and headed fastener designed to be pounded in

²nail *vt* (bef. 12c) **1** : to fasten with or as if with a nail **2** : to fix in steady attention ⟨~ed his eye on the crack⟩ **3 a** : CATCH, TRAP **b** : to detect and expose usu. so as to discredit **4 a** : STRIKE, HIT **b** : to put out (a runner) in baseball **5** : to perform or complete perfectly or impressively ⟨~ed a jump shot⟩ — **nail·er** *n*

nail–bit·er \'nā(ə)l-,bī-tər\ *n* (1971) : something (as a close contest) that induces tension or anxiety ⟨lost a tough, 14-inning ~ —Steve Pate⟩

nail·brush \-,brəsh\ *n* (1802) : a small firm-bristled brush for cleaning the hands and esp. the fingernails

nail down *vt* (1615) **1** : to gain or win decisively ⟨*nail down* his consent⟩ **2** : to settle or establish clearly and unmistakably

nail file *n* (1875) : a small narrow instrument (as of metal or cardboard) with a rough or emery surface that is used for shaping fingernails

nain·sook \'nän-,suk\ *n* [Hindi *nainsukh*, fr. *nain* eye + *sukh* delight] (1790) : a soft lightweight muslin

nai·ra \'nī-rə\ *n* [alter. of *Nigeria*] (1972) — see MONEY table

na·ive *or* **na·ïve** \nä-'ēv\ *adj* **na·iv·er; -est** [F *naïve*, fem. of *naïf*, fr. OF, inborn, natural, fr. L *nativus* native] (1654) **1** : marked by unaffected simplicity : ARTLESS, INGENUOUS **2 a** : deficient in worldly wisdom or informed judgment; *esp* : CREDULOUS **b** : not previously subjected to experimentation or a particular experimental situation ⟨made the test with ~ rats⟩; *also* : not having previously used a particular drug (as marijuana) **3** : SELF-TAUGHT, PRIMITIVE *syn* see NATURAL — **na·ive·ly** *or* **na·ïve·ly** *adv* — **na·ive·ness** *n*

na·ive·té *also* **na·ive·te** \(,)nä-,ēv-'tā, -,ē-və-; nä-'ēv-,tā, -'ē-və-\ *n* [F *naïveté*, fr. OF, inborn character, fr. *naïf*] (1673) **1** : a naive remark or action **2** : the quality or state of being naive

na·ive·ty *also* **na·ïve·ty** \nä-'ēv-tē, -'ēv-tē\ *n, pl* **-ties** (1708) *chiefly Brit* : NAÏVETÉ

na·ked \'nā-kəd, *esp Southern* 'ne-kəd\ *adj* [ME, fr. OE *nacod*; akin to OHG *nackot* naked, L *nudus*, Gk *gymnos*] (bef. 12c) **1** : not covered by clothing : NUDE **2** : devoid of customary or natural covering **a** : BARE: *as* **a** : not enclosed in a sheath or scabbard **b** : not provided with a shade **c** *of a plant or one of its parts* : lacking pubescence or enveloping or subtending parts **d** : lacking foliage or vegetation **e** *of an animal or one of its parts* : lacking an external covering (as of hair, feathers, or shell) **3 a** : scantily supplied or furnished **b** : lacking embellishment : UNADORNED **4** : UNARMED, DEFENSELESS **5** : lacking confirmation or support **6** : devoid of concealment or disguise **7** : unaided by any optical device or instrument (visible to the ~ eye) **8** : not backed by the writer's ownership of the commodity contract or security *syn* see BARE — **na·ked·ly** *adv* — **na·ked·ness** *n*

na·led \'nā-,led\ *n* [origin unknown] (ca. 1962) : a short-lived insecticide $C_4H_7Br_2Cl_2O_4P$ of relatively low toxicity to warm-blooded animals that is used esp. to control crop pests and mosquitoes

na·li·dix·ic acid \,nä-lə-'dik-sik-\ *n* [perh. fr. *naphthyridine* ($C_8H_6N_2$ — fr. *naphth-* + *pyridine*) + *carboxylic acid*] (1964) : an antibacterial agent $C_{12}H_{12}N_2O_3$ that is used esp. in the treatment of genitourinary infections

na·lor·phine \na-'lor-,fēn\ *n* [*N-allyl* + *morphine*] (ca. 1953) : a white crystalline compound $C_{19}H_{21}NO_3$ that is derived from morphine and is used in the form of its hydrochloride as a respiratory stimulant to counteract poisoning by morphine and similar narcotic drugs

nal·ox·one \na-'läk-,sōn\ *n* [*N-allyl* + *hydroxy-* + *-one*] (1964) : a potent antagonist $C_{19}H_{21}NO_4$ of narcotic drugs and esp. morphine that is administered esp. as the hydrochloride

nal·trex·one \nal-'trek-,sōn\ *n* [*N-allyl* + *trex-* (as in *methotrexate*) + *-one*] (1973) : a narcotic antagonist $C_{20}H_{23}NO_4$

nam·by–pam·by \,nam-bē-'pam-bē\ *adj* [*Namby Pamby*, nickname given to Ambrose Philips] (1745) **1** : lacking in character or substance : INSIPID **2** : WEAK, INDECISIVE — **namby–pamby** *n*

¹name \'nām\ *n* [ME, fr. OE *nama*; akin to OHG *namo* name, L *nomen*, Gk *onoma, onyma*] (bef. 12c) **1 a** : a word or phrase that constitutes the distinctive designation of a person or thing **b** : a word or symbol used in logic to designate an entity **2** : a descriptive often disparaging epithet ⟨called him ~s⟩ **3 a** : REPUTATION ⟨gave the town a bad ~⟩ **b** : an illustrious record : FAME ⟨made a ~ for himself in golf⟩ **c** : a person or thing with a reputation **4** : FAMILY, CLAN **5** : appearance as opposed to reality ⟨a friend in ~ only⟩ **6** : one referred to by a name ⟨praise his holy ~⟩ — **in the name of 1** : by authority of ⟨open *in the name of* the law⟩ **2** : for the reason of : using the excuse of ⟨called for reforms *in the name of* progress⟩

²name *vt* **named; nam·ing** (bef. 12c) **1** : to give a name to : CALL **2 a** : to mention or identify by name **b** : to accuse by name **3** : to nominate for office : APPOINT **4** : to decide on : CHOOSE ⟨~ the day for the wedding⟩ **5** : to mention explicitly : SPECIFY ⟨unwilling to ~ a price⟩ — **nam·er** *n*

³name *adj* (1598) **1** : of, relating to, or bearing a name ⟨~ tags⟩ **2** : appearing in the name of a literary or theatrical production **3 a** : having an established reputation **b** : featuring celebrities

name·able *also* **nam·able** \'nā-mə-bəl\ *adj* (1780) **1** : worthy of being named : MEMORABLE **2** : capable of being named : IDENTIFIABLE

name–call·ing \'nām-,kȯ-liŋ\ *n* (1853) : the use of offensive names esp. to win an argument or to induce rejection or condemnation (as of a person or project) without objective consideration of the facts

name day *n* (1721) : the church feast day of the saint after whom one is named

name–drop·ping \-,drä-piŋ\ *n* (1950) : the practice of seeking to impress others by studied but apparently casual mention of prominent persons as associates — **name–drop·per** \-pər\ *n*

name·less \'nām-ləs\ *adj* (14c) **1** : OBSCURE, UNDISTINGUISHED **2** : not known by name : ANONYMOUS **3** : having no legal right to a name : ILLEGITIMATE **4** : not having been given a name : UNNAMED **5** : not marked with a name ⟨a ~ grave⟩ **6** : incapable of precise description : INDEFINABLE **b** : too repulsive or distressing to describe — **name·less·ly** *adv* — **name·less·ness** *n*

name·ly \'nām-lē\ *adv* (14c) : that is to say : TO WIT

name of the game (1966) **1** : the essential quality or matter ⟨patience is the *name of the game* in coastal duck hunting —Dick Beals⟩ **2** : the fundamental goal of an activity

name·plate \-,plāt\ *n* (ca. 1859) : something (as a plate or plaque) bearing a name (as of a resident or manufacturer)

name·sake \-,sāk\ *n* [prob. fr. *name's sake*] (1646) : one that has the same name as another; *esp* : one who is named after another or for whom another is named

nan \'nän, 'nan\ *n* [Hindi & Per; Hindi *nān*, fr. Per] (1948) : a round flat leavened bread esp. of the Indian subcontinent

---

\ə\ abut \ᵊ\ kitten, F table \ər\ further \a\ ash \ā\ ace \ä\ mop, mar \au̇\ out \ch\ chin \e\ bet \ē\ easy \g\ go \i\ hit \ī\ ice \j\ job \ŋ\ sing \ō\ go \ȯ\ law \ȯi\ boy \th\ thin \th\ the \ü\ loot \u̇\ foot \y\ yet \zh\ vision \à, k̲, ⁿ, œ, ōe, ue, ūe, ᴵ\ see Guide to Pronunciation

nana \'na-nə\ *n* [prob. of baby-talk origin] (ca. 1844) : GRANDMOTHER

nance \'nan(t)s\ *n* [short for *nancy*, fr. the name *Nancy*] (1920) **1** : an effeminate male — often used disparagingly **2** : HOMOSEXUAL — often used disparagingly

NAND \'nand\ *n* [*not AND*] (1958) : a computer logic circuit that produces an output which is the inverse of that of an AND circuit

nan·di·na \nan-'dī-nə, -'dē-\ *n* [NL, fr. Jp *nanten*] (ca. 1890) : a widely cultivated Asian evergreen shrub (*Nandina domestica*) of the barberry family

nan·keen \,nan-'kēn\ *n* [*Nanking* (Nanjing), China] (1755) **1** : a durable brownish yellow cotton fabric orig. loomed by hand in China **2** *pl* : trousers made of nankeen

Nan·kin \'nan-'kin, 'nän-\ *or* **Nan·king** \-'kiŋ\ *n* [*Nanking* (Nanjing), China] (1781) : Chinese porcelain decorated in blue and on a white ground

nan·no·plank·ton \,na-nō-'plaŋ(k)-tən, -,tän\ *n* [NL, fr. Gk *nanos, nannos* dwarf + NL *plankton* plankton] (1912) : the smallest plankton that consists of those organisms (as bacteria) passing through nets of very fine mesh silk cloth

nan·ny *also* **nan·nie** \'na-nē\ *n, pl* **nannies** [prob. of baby-talk origin] (1795) : a child's nurse : NURSEMAID

nanny goat *n* [*Nanny*, nickname for *Anne*] (1788) : a female domestic goat

nano- *comb form* [ISV, fr. Gk *nanos* dwarf] : one billionth (10^{-9}) part of 〈*nanosecond*〉

nano·gram \'na-nə-,gram\ *n* [ISV] (1951) : one billionth of a gram

nano·me·ter \'na-nō-,mē-tər\ *n* [ISV] (1963) : one billionth of a meter

nano·sec·ond \-,se-kənd, -kənt\ *n* [ISV] (1959) : one billionth of a second

nano·tech·nol·o·gy \,na-nō-tek-'nä-lə-jē\ *n* (1987) : the art of manipulating materials on an atomic or molecular scale esp. to build microscopic devices (as robots)

nano·tes·la \'na-nō-,tes-lə\ *n* (1968) : a unit of magnetic flux density equal to 10^{-9} tesla

Nan·tua sauce \nän(n)-'twä-\ *n* [*Nantua*, France] (ca. 1961) : a cream sauce flavored with shellfish (as lobster)

Na·o·mi \nā-'ō-mē\ *n* [Heb *Nā'ŏmī*] : the mother-in-law of the Old Testament heroine Ruth

¹nap \'nap\ *vi* **napped; nap·ping** [ME *nappen*, fr. OE *hnappian*; akin to OHG *hnaffezen* to doze] (bef. 12c) **1** : to sleep briefly esp. during the day : DOZE **2** : to be off guard

²nap *n* (14c) : a short sleep esp. during the day : SNOOZE

³nap *n* [ME *noppe*, fr. MD, flock of wool, nap] (15c) : a hairy or downy surface (as on a fabric) — **nap·less** \-ləs\ *adj* — **napped** \'napt\ *adj*

⁴nap *vt* **napped; nap·ping** (1620) : to raise a nap on (fabric or leather)

⁵nap *n* [fr. to go *nap* (to make all the points in the card game Napoleon)] (1895) *Brit* : a pick or recommendation as a good bet to win a contest (as a horse race); *also* : one named in a nap

⁶nap *vt* **napped; nap·ping** (1927) *Brit* : to pick or single out in a nap

napa cabbage \'na-pə-\ *n* [perh. fr. Jp dial. *nappa* greens] (1980) : CHINESE CABBAGE b

napa leather *n* [*Napa*, California] (1897) : a glove leather made by tawing sheepskins with a soap-and-oil mixture; *also* : a similarly soft leather

¹na·palm \'nā-,päm *also* -,pälm *also* 'na- *also* nə-'pä(l)m\ *n* [*naphthene* + *palm*itate] (1942) **1** : a thickener consisting of a mixture of aluminum soaps used in jelling gasoline (as for incendiary bombs) **2** : fuel jelled with napalm

²napalm *vt* (1950) : to assault with napalm

nape \'nāp, 'nap\ *n* [ME] (14c) : the back of the neck

na·pery \'nā-p(ə-)rē\ *n* [ME, fr. MF *naperie*, fr. *nappe, nape* tablecloth — more at NAPKIN] (14c) : household linen; *esp* : TABLE LINEN

Naph·ta·li \'naf-tə-,lī\ *n* [Heb *Naphtālī*] : a son of Jacob and the traditional eponymous ancestor of one of the tribes of Israel

naph·tha \'naf-thə, ÷'nap-\ *n* [L, fr. Gk, of Iranian origin; akin to Per *neft* naphtha] (1572) **1** : any of various volatile often flammable liquid hydrocarbon mixtures used chiefly as solvents and diluents **2** : PETROLEUM

naph·tha·lene \-,lēn\ *n* [alter. of earlier *naphthaline*, irreg. fr. *naphtha*] (1821) : a crystalline aromatic hydrocarbon $C_{10}H_8$ usu. obtained by distillation of coal tar and used esp. in organic synthesis

naph·thene \'naf-,thēn, ÷'nap-\ *n* (1884) : CYCLOPARAFFIN — **naph·then·ic** \naf-'thē-nik, ÷,nap-, -'the-\ *adj*

naph·thol \'naf-,thól, ÷'nap-, -,thōl\ *n* [ISV] (1849) **1** : either of two isomeric derivatives $C_{10}H_8O$ of naphthalene used as antiseptics and in the manufacture of dyes **2** : any of various hydroxy derivatives of naphthalene that resemble the simpler phenols

naph·thyl·amine \naf-'thi-lə-,mēn, ÷'nap-\ *n* [ISV] (1857) : either of two isomeric crystalline bases $C_{10}H_9N$ used esp. as dye intermediates

na·pi·er grass \'nā-pē-ər-\ *n* [*Napier*, town in So. Africa] (1914) : a tall stout African perennial grass (*Pennisetum purpureum*) that resembles sugarcane and is widely grown for forage — called also *elephant grass*

Na·pier·ian logarithm \nə-'pir-ē-ən-, nā-\ *n* [John *Napier*] (1816) : NATURAL LOGARITHM

Na·pi·er's bones \'nā-pē-ərz-\ *n* (ca. 1658) : a set of graduated rods (as of wood or bone) invented by John Napier and used for multiplication and division based on the principles of logarithms

na·pi·form \'nā-pə-,fórm\ *adj* [L *napus* turnip (perh. fr. Gk *napy, sinapy* mustard) + ISV *-iform*] (ca. 1846) : globular at the top and tapering off abruptly — used esp. of roots

nap·kin \'nap-kən\ *n* [ME *nappekin*, fr. *nappe* tablecloth, fr. MF, fr. L *mappa* napkin] (14c) **1** : a piece of material (as cloth or paper) used at table to wipe the lips or fingers and protect the clothes **2** : a small cloth or towel: as **a** *dial Brit* : HANDKERCHIEF **b** *chiefly Scot* : KERCHIEF **c** *chiefly Brit* : DIAPER 3 **3** : SANITARY NAPKIN

na·po·leon \nə-'pōl-yən, -'pō-lē-ən\ *n* [F *napoléon*, fr. *Napoléon* Napoleon I] (1814) **1** : a former French 20-franc gold coin **2** : an oblong pastry with a filling of cream, custard, or jelly **3** *cap* : one like Napoleon I (as in ambition)

nappe \'nap\ *n* [F, tablecloth, sheet, nappe — more at NAPKIN] (1904) **1** : SHEET 6 **2** : a large mass thrust over other rocks **3** : one of the two sheets that lie on opposite sides of the vertex and together make up a cone

¹nap·py \'na-pē\ *n* [obs. *nappy*, adj., foaming] (1700) *chiefly Scot* : LIQUOR; *specif* : ALE

²nappy *n, pl* **nappies** [E dial. *nap* bowl, fr. ME, fr. OE *hnæpp*; akin to OHG *hnapf* bowl] (1864) : a rimless shallow open serving dish

³nappy *n, pl* **nappies** [*napkin* + -y] (1927) *chiefly Brit* : DIAPER 3

⁴nappy *adj* **nap·pi·er; -est** [³*nap*] (1928) : KINKY 1

na·prap·a·thy \nə-'pra-pə-thē\ *n* [Czech *naprava* correction + E *-pathy*] (1909) : a system of treatment by manipulation of connective tissue and adjoining structures (as ligaments, joints, and muscles) and by dietary measures that is held to facilitate the recuperative and regenerative processes of the body

narc \'närk\ *n* [short for *narcotics agent*] (1967) *slang* : a person (as a government agent) who investigates narcotics violations

nar·cis·sism \'när-sə-,si-zəm\ *n* [G *Narzissismus*, fr. *Narziss* Narcissus, fr. L *Narcissus*] (1822) **1** : EGOISM, EGOCENTRISM **2** : love of or sexual desire for one's own body — **nar·cis·sist** \'när-sə-sist\ *n or adj* — **nar·cis·sis·tic** \,när-sə-'sis-tik\ *adj*

nar·cis·sus \när-'si-səs\ *n* [L, fr. Gk *Narkissos*] **1** *cap* : a beautiful youth in Greek mythology who pines away for love of his own reflection and is then turned into the narcissus flower **2** *pl* **nar·cis·si** \-'si-,sī, -(,)sē\ *or* **nar·cis·sus·es** *or* **narcissus** [NL, genus name, fr. L, narcissus, fr. Gk *narkissos*] : DAFFODIL; *esp* : one whose flowers have a short corona and are usu. borne separately

nar·co \'när-(,)kō\ *n, pl* **narcos** (1955) *slang* : NARC

nar·co·lep·sy \'när-kə-,lep-sē\ *n, pl* **-sies** [ISV, fr. Gk *narkē*] (1880) : a condition characterized by brief attacks of deep sleep — **nar·co·lep·tic** \,när-kə-'lep-tik\ *adj*

nar·co·lep·tic \,när-kə-'lep-tik\ *n* (1928) : a person who is subject to attacks of narcolepsy

nar·co·sis \när-'kō-səs\ *n, pl* **-co·ses** \-,sēz\ [NL, fr. Gk *narkōsis*, action of benumbing, fr. *narkoun*] (ca. 1693) : a state of stupor, unconsciousness, or arrested activity produced by the influence of narcotics or other chemicals

¹nar·cot·ic \när-'kä-tik\ *n* [ME *narkotik*, fr. MF *narcotique*, fr. *narcotique*, adj., fr. ML *narcoticus*, fr. Gk *narkōtikos*, fr. *narkoun* to benumb, fr. *narkē* numbness — more at SNARE] (14c) **1 a** : a drug (as opium) that in moderate doses dulls the senses, relieves pain, and induces profound sleep but in excessive doses causes stupor, coma, or convulsions **b** : a drug (as marijuana or LSD) subject to restriction similar to that of addictive narcotics whether physiologically addictive and narcotic or not **2** : something that soothes, relieves, or lulls

²narcotic *adj* (1526) **1 a** : having the properties of or yielding a narcotic **b** : inducing mental lethargy : SOPORIFEROUS **2** : of, induced by, or concerned with narcotics **3** : of, involving, or intended for narcotic addicts — **nar·cot·i·cal·ly** \-ti-k(ə-)lē\ *adv*

nar·co·tize \'när-kə-,tīz\ *vb* **-tized; -tiz·ing** [ISV] *vt* (1526) **1 a** : to treat with or subject to a narcotic **b** : to put into a state of narcosis **2** : to soothe to unconsciousness or unawareness ~ *vi* : to act as a narcotizing agent

nard \'närd\ *n* [ME *narde*, fr. OE, fr. L *nardus*, fr. Gk *nardos*, of Sem origin; akin to Heb *nērd* nard] (bef. 12c) : SPIKENARD 1b

na·res \'nar-(,)ēz, 'ner-\ *n pl* [L, pl. of *naris*; akin to L *nasus* nose — more at NOSE] (14c) : the pair of openings of the nose or nasal cavity of a vertebrate

nar·ghi·le \'när-gə-lē\ *or* **nar·gi·leh** \-,lē\ *n* [Per *nārgīla*, fr. *nārgīl* coconut, of Indo-Aryan origin; akin to Skt *nārikela* coconut; fr. the original material used in making its bowl] (1758) : a water pipe that originated in the Near East

¹nark \'närk\ *n* [perh. fr. Romany *nak* nose] (ca. 1860) *Brit* : STOOL PIGEON

²nark *var of* NARC

³nark *vt* [origin unknown] (1888) *Brit* : IRRITATE, ANNOY

Nar·ra·gan·set *or* **Nar·ra·gan·sett** \,nar-ə-'gan(t)-sət\ *n, pl* **Narraganset** *or* **Narragansets** *or* **Narragansett** *or* **Narragansetts** (1622) **1** : a member of an American Indian people of Rhode Island **2** : the Algonquian language of the Narraganset people

nar·rate \'nar-,āt, na-'rāt\ *vt* **nar·rat·ed; nar·rat·ing** [L *narratus*, pp. of *narrare*, fr. L *gnarus* knowing; akin to L *gnoscere, noscere* to know — more at KNOW] (1656) : to tell (as a story) in detail; *also* : to provide spoken commentary for (as a movie or television show) — **nar·ra·tor** \'nar-,ā-tər; na-'rāt-\ *n*

nar·ra·tion \na-'rā-shən, nə-\ *n* (15c) **1** : the act or process or an instance of narrating **2** : STORY, NARRATIVE — **nar·ra·tion·al** \-shnəl, -shə-nᵊl\ *adj*

nar·ra·tive \'nar-ə-tiv\ *n* (1566) **1** : something that is narrated : STORY **2** : The art or practice of narration **3** : the representation in art of an event or story; *also* : an example of such a representation — **narrative** *adj* — **nar·ra·tive·ly** *adv*

nar·ra·tol·o·gy \,nar-ə-'tä-lə-jē\ *n* (1976) : the study of structure in narratives — **nar·ra·to·log·i·cal** \-tə-'lä-ji-kəl\ *adj* — **nar·ra·tol·o·gist** \-'tä-lə-jist\ *n*

¹nar·row \'nar-(,)ō\ *adj* [ME *narowe*, fr. OE *nearu*; akin to OHG *narwa* scar] (bef. 12c) **1 a** : of slender width **b** : of less than standard width **c** *of a textile* : woven in widths less than 18 inches (46 centimeters) **2** : limited in size or scope **3 a** : illiberal in views or disposition : PREJUDICED **b** *chiefly dial* : STINGY, NIGGARDLY **4 a** : barely sufficient : CLOSE **b** : barely successful **5** : minutely precise : METICULOUS **6** *of a ration* : relatively rich in protein as compared with carbohydrate and fat **7** : TENSE 3 — **nar·row·ly** *adv* — **nar·row·ness** *n*

²narrow *vt* (bef. 12c) **1** : to decrease the breadth or extent of : CONTRACT — often used with *down* **2** : to decrease the scope or sphere of : LIMIT — often used with *down* ~ *vi* : to lessen in width or extent : CONTRACT — often used with *down*

³narrow *n* (13c) : a narrow part or passage; *specif* : a strait connecting two bodies of water — usu. used in pl. but sing. or pl. in constr.

nar·row·band \'nar-ō-,band, 'nar-ə-\ *adj* (1950) : operating at, responsive to, or including a narrow range of frequencies

narrow boat *n* (1949) *Brit* : a barge with a beam of less than seven feet (2.1 meters)

nar·row·cast·ing \'nar-ō-,kas-tiŋ, 'nar-ə-\ *n* (1928) : radio or television transmission aimed at a narrowly defined area or audience (as paying subscribers or night workers)

nar·row–mind·ed \,nar-ō-'mīn-dəd, ,nar-ə-\ *adj* (1625) : lacking in tolerance or breadth of vision : PETTY — **nar·row–mind·ed·ly** *adv* — **nar·row–mind·ed·ness** *n*

nar·thex \'när-,theks\ *n* [LGk *narthēx*, fr. Gk, giant fennel, cane, casket] (ca. 1673) **1** : the portico of an ancient church **2** : a vestibule leading to the nave of a church

nar·whal \'när-,wäl, -,hwäl, -wəl\ *also* **nar·whale** \-,wäl, -,hwäl\ *n* [Norw & Dan *narhval* & Sw *narval*, prob. modif. of Icel *nárhvalur*, fr. ON *náhvalr*, fr. *nār* corpse + *hvalr* whale; fr. its color] (1646) : an arctic cetacean (*Monodon monoceros*) about 20 feet (6 meters) long with the male having a long twisted ivory tusk

narwhal

nary \'nar-ē, 'ner-\ *adj* [alter. of *ne'er a*] (1746) : not any ⟨~ a person wanted to go⟩

¹na·sal \'nā-zəl\ *n* [ME, fr. MF, fr. OF, fr. *nes* nose, fr. L *nasus* — more at NOSE] (14c) **1** : the nosepiece of a helmet **2** : a nasal part **3** : a nasal consonant

²nasal *adj* (1656) **1** : of or relating to the nose **2 a** : uttered with the soft palate lowered and with passage of air through the nose (as with \m\, \n\, \ŋ\, \ōⁿ\, or \aⁿ\) **b** : characterized by resonance produced through the nose **3** *of a musical tone* : SHARP, PENETRATING — **na·sal·i·ty** \nā-'za-lə-tē\ *n* — **na·sal·ly** \'nā-zə-lē, 'näz-lē\ *adv*

na·sal·ize \'nā-zə-,līz\ *vb* **-ized; -iz·ing** *vt* (1817) : to make nasal or pronounce as a nasal sound — **na·sal·i·za·tion** \,nā-zə-lə-'zā-shən\ *n*

na·scence \'na-s^ən(t)s, 'nā-\ *n* (1570) : NASCENCY

na·scen·cy \-s^ən(t)-sē\ *n, pl* **-cies** (1682) : BIRTH, ORIGIN

na·scent \'na-s^ənt, 'nā-\ *adj* [L *nascent-, nascens*, prp. of *nasci* to be born] (ca. 1624) : coming or having recently come into existence

naso- *comb form* [L *nasus* nose] **1** : nose and ⟨*nasopharynx*⟩ **2** : nasal ⟨*nasogastric*⟩

na·so·gas·tric \,nā-zō-'gas-trik\ *adj* (1942) : being or performed by intubation of the stomach through the nasal passages ⟨~ tube⟩ ⟨~ suction⟩

na·so·pha·ryn·geal \-fə-'rin-j(ē-)əl, -,far-ən-'jē-əl\ *adj* (1872) : of, relating to, or affecting the nose and pharynx or the nasopharynx

na·so·phar·ynx \-'far-in(k)s\ *n* [NL] (1877) : the upper part of the pharynx continuous with the nasal passages

nas·tic \'nas-tik\ *adj* [Gk *nastos* close-pressed, fr. *nassein* to press] (1908) : of, relating to, or constituting a movement of a plant part caused by disproportionate growth or increase of turgor in one surface

nas·tur·tium \nə-'stər-shəm, na-\ *n* [L, a cress] (1704) : any of a genus (*Tropaeolum* of the family Tropaeolaceae, the nasturtium family) of herbs of Central and So. America with showy spurred flowers and pungent seeds; *esp* : either of two widely cultivated ornamentals (*T. majus* and *T. minus*)

nasturtium

nas·ty \'nas-tē\ *adj* **nas·ti·er; -est** [ME] (14c) **1 a** : disgustingly filthy **b** : physically repugnant **2** : INDECENT, OBSCENE **3** : MEAN, TAWDRY **4 a** : extremely hazardous or harmful ⟨had a ~ climb to reach the summit⟩ **b** : causing severe pain or suffering ⟨a ~ wound⟩ **c** : sharply unpleasant : DISAGREEABLE ⟨~ weather⟩ **5 a** : difficult to understand or deal with : VEXATIOUS ⟨a ~ problem⟩ **b** : psychologically unsettling : TRYING ⟨a ~ fear that she was lost⟩ **6** : lacking in courtesy or sportsmanship ⟨a ~ trick⟩ *syn* see DIRTY — **nas·ti·ly** \-tə-lē\ *adv* — **nas·ti·ness** \-tē-nəs\ *n* — **nasty** *n*

na·tal \'nā-t^əl\ *adj* [ME, fr. L *natalis*, fr. *natus*, pp. of *nasci* to be born — more at NATION] (15c) **1** : NATIVE **2** : of, relating to, or present at birth; *esp* : associated with one's birth ⟨a ~ star⟩

na·tal·i·ty \nā-'ta-lə-tē, nə-\ *n, pl* **-ties** (1888) : BIRTHRATE

na·tant \'nā-t^ənt\ *adj* [ME *natand*, fr. L *natant-, natans*, prp. of *natare* to swim; akin to L *nare* to swim; akin to Gk *nein*, *nēchein* to swim, Skt *snāti* he bathes] (15c) : swimming or floating in water ⟨~ decapods⟩

na·ta·tion \nā-'tā-shən, na-\ *n* (1542) : the action or art of swimming

na·ta·to·ri·al \,nā-nə-'tōr-ē-əl, ,na-, -'tȯr-\ *or* **na·ta·to·ry** \'nā-tə-,tōr-ē, 'na-, -,tȯr-\ *adj* (1816) **1** : of or relating to swimming **2** : adapted to or characterized by swimming ⟨a ~ leg of an aquatic insect⟩

na·ta·to·ri·um \,nā-tə-'tōr-ē-əm, ,na-, -'tȯr-\ *n* [LL, fr. L *natare*] (ca. 1890) : an indoor swimming pool

natch \'nach\ *adv* [by shortening & alter. fr. *naturally*] (ca. 1945) *slang* : of course : NATURALLY

Natch·ez \'na-chəz\ *n, pl* **Natchez** (1845) **1** : a member of an American Indian people of southwestern Mississippi **2** : the language of the Natchez people

na·tes \'nā-,tēz\ *n pl* [L, pl. of *natis* buttock] (ca. 1706) : BUTTOCKS

nathe·less \'nāth-ləs\ *or* **nath·less** \'nath-\ *adv* [ME, fr. OE *nā thē lǣs* not the less] (bef. 12c) *archaic* : NEVERTHELESS, NOTWITHSTANDING

na·tion \'nā-shən\ *n* [ME *nacioun*, fr. MF *nation*, fr. L *nation-, natio* birth, race, nation, fr. *nasci* to be born; akin to L *gignere* to beget — more at KIN] (14c) **1 a** (1) : NATIONALITY 5a (2) : a politically organized nationality (3) : a non-Jewish nationality ⟨why do the ~s conspire —Ps 2:1 (RSV)⟩ **b** : a community of people composed of one or more nationalities and possessing a more or less defined territory and government **c** : a territorial division containing a body of people of one or more nationalities and usu. characterized by relatively large size and independent status **2** *archaic* : GROUP, AGGREGATION **3** : a tribe or federation of tribes (as of American Indians)

¹na·tion·al \'nash-nəl, 'na-shə-n^əl\ *adj* (1597) **1** : of or relating to a nation **2** : NATIONALIST **3** : comprising or characteristic of a national-

ity **4** : belonging to or maintained by the federal government **5** : of, relating to, or being a coalition government formed by most or all major political parties usu. in a crisis — **na·tion·al·ly** *adv*

²national *n* (1887) **1** : one that owes allegiance to or is under the protection of a nation without regard to the more formal status of citizen or subject **2** : a competition that is national in scope — usu. used in pl. *syn* see CITIZEN

national bank *n* (1790) **1** : CENTRAL BANK **2** : a bank operating under federal charter and supervision

national forest *n* (ca. 1905) : a usu. forested area of considerable extent that is preserved by government decree from private exploitation and is harvested only under supervision

National Guard *n* (1847) **1** : a militia force recruited by each state of the U.S., equipped by the federal government, and jointly maintained subject to the call of either **2** *often not cap* : a military establishment serving as a national constabulary and defense force

national income *n* (1878) : the aggregate of earnings from a nation's current production including compensation of employees, interest, rental income, and profits of business after taxes

na·tion·al·ise *chiefly Brit var of* NATIONALIZE

na·tion·al·ism \'nash-nə-,li-zəm, 'na-shə-n^əl-,i-zəm\ *n* (1844) : loyalty and devotion to a nation; *esp* : a sense of national consciousness exalting one nation above all others and placing primary emphasis on promotion of its culture and interests as opposed to those of other nations or supranational groups

¹na·tion·al·ist \-list, -ist\ *n* (1715) **1** : an advocate of or believer in nationalism **2** *cap* : a member of a political party or group advocating national independence or strong national government

²nationalist *adj* (1889) **1** : of, relating to, or advocating nationalism **2** *cap* : of, relating to, or being a political group advocating or associated with nationalism

na·tion·al·is·tic \,nash-nə-'lis-tik, ,na-shə-n^əl-'is-tik\ *adj* (1866) **1** : of, favoring, or characterized by nationalism ⟨~ election speeches⟩ **2** : NATIONAL 1 — **na·tion·al·is·ti·cal·ly** \-ti-k(ə-)lē\ *adv*

na·tion·al·i·ty \,na-shə-'na-lə-tē, ,nash-'na-\ *n, pl* **-ties** (1691) **1** : national character **2** : NATIONALISM **3** : national status; *specif* : a legal relationship involving allegiance on the part of an individual and usu. protection on the part of the state **b** : membership in a particular nation **4** : political independence or existence as a separate nation **5 a** : a people having a common origin, tradition, and language and capable of forming or actually constituting a nation-state **b** : an ethnic group constituting one element of a larger unit (as a nation)

na·tion·al·ize \'nash-nə-,līz, 'na-shə-n^əl-,īz\ *vt* **-ized; -iz·ing** (1800) **1** : to give a national character to **2** : to invest control or ownership of in the national government — **na·tion·al·i·za·tion** \,nash-nə-lə-'zā-shən, ,na-shə-n^əl-ə-\ *n* — **na·tion·al·iz·er** \'nash-nə-,lī-zər, ,na-shə-n^əl-,ī-zər\ *n*

national monument *n* (1916) : a place of historic, scenic, or scientific interest set aside for preservation usu. by presidential proclamation

national park *n* (1868) : an area of special scenic, historical, or scientific importance set aside and maintained by a national government and in the U.S. by an act of Congress

national seashore *n* (1962) : a recreational area adjacent to a seacoast and maintained by the federal government

national socialism *n, often cap N&S* (1931) : NAZISM — **national socialist** *adj, often cap N&S*

na·tion·hood \'nā-shən-,hu̇d\ *n* (1850) : NATIONALITY 1, 3a, 4

na·tion–state \'nā-shən-'stāt, -,stāt\ *n* (1918) : a form of political organization under which a relatively homogeneous people inhabits a sovereign state; *esp* : a state containing one as opposed to several nationalities

¹na·tion·wide \,nā-shən-'wīd\ *adj* (1912) : extending throughout a nation

²nationwide *adv* (1926) : throughout the nation

¹na·tive \'nā-tiv\ *adj* [ME *natif*, fr. MF, fr. L *nativus*, fr. *natus*, pp. of *nasci* to be born — more at NATION] (14c) **1** : INBORN, INNATE ⟨~ talents⟩ **2** : belonging to a particular place by birth ⟨~ to Wisconsin⟩ **3** *archaic* : closely related **4** : belonging to or associated with one by birth **5** : NATURAL, NORMAL **6 a** : grown, produced, or originating in a particular place or in the vicinity : LOCAL **b** : living or growing naturally in a particular region : INDIGENOUS **7** : SIMPLE, UNAFFECTED **8 a** : constituting the original substance or source **b** : found in nature esp. in an unadulterated form ⟨mining ~ silver⟩ **9** *chiefly Austral* : having a usu. superficial resemblance to a specified English plant or animal — **na·tive·ly** *adv* — **na·tive·ness** *n*

syn NATIVE, INDIGENOUS, ENDEMIC, ABORIGINAL mean belonging to a locality. NATIVE implies birth or origin in a place or region and may suggest compatibility with it ⟨*native* tribal customs⟩. INDIGENOUS applies to species or races and adds to NATIVE the implication of not having been introduced from elsewhere ⟨maize is *indigenous* to America⟩. ENDEMIC implies being peculiar to a region ⟨edelweiss is *endemic* in the Alps⟩. ABORIGINAL implies having no known race preceding in occupancy of the region ⟨the *aboriginal* peoples of Australia⟩.

²native *n* (1535) **1** : one born or reared in a particular place **2 a** : an original or indigenous inhabitant **b** : something indigenous to a particular locality **3** : a local resident; *esp* : a person who has always lived in a place as distinguished from a visitor or a temporary resident

Native American *n* (1925) : AMERICAN INDIAN — **Native American** *adj*

na·tiv·ism \'nā-ti-,vi-zəm\ *n* (1844) **1** : a policy of favoring native inhabitants as opposed to immigrants **2** : the revival or perpetuation of an indigenous culture esp. in opposition to acculturation — **na·tiv·ist** \-vist\ *n or adj* — **na·tiv·is·tic** \,nā-ti-'vis-tik\ *adj*

na·tiv·i·ty \nə-'ti-və-tē, nā-\ *n, pl* **-ties** [ME *nativite*, fr. MF *nativité*, fr. ML *nativitat-, nativitas*, fr. LL, fr. L *nativus*] (14c) **1** : the process or circumstances of being born : BIRTH; *esp, cap* : the birth of Jesus **2** : a horoscope at or of the time of one's birth **3** : the place of origin

---

\ə\ abut \^ə\ kitten, F table \ər\ further \a\ ash \ā\ ace \ä\ mop, mar
\au̇\ out \ch\ chin \e\ bet \ē\ easy \g\ go \i\ hit \ī\ ice \j\ job
\ŋ\ sing \ō\ go \ȯ\ law \ȯi\ boy \th\ thin \t̲h̲\ the \ü\ loot \u̇\ foot
\y\ yet \zh\ vision \à, k̲, ⁿ, œ, œ̄, ᵫ, ᵫ̄, ʸ\ see Guide to Pronunciation

na·tri·ure·sis \ˌnā-trē-yù-ˈrē-səs\ n [NL, fr. *natrium* sodium (fr. ISV *natron*) + *uresis* urination, fr. Gk *ourēsis*, fr. *ourein* to urinate — more at URINE] (1957) : excessive loss of sodium in the urine — **na·tri·uret·ic** \-ˈre-tik\ adj or n
na·tro·lite \ˈnā-trə-ˌlīt\ n [G *Natrolith*, fr. *Natron* (fr. F) + *-lith* -lite] (ca. 1805) : a hydrous silicate of sodium and aluminum that is related to zeolite
na·tron \ˈnā-ˌträn, -trən\ n [F, fr. Sp *natrón*, fr. Ar *naṭrūn*, fr. Gk *nitron*] (1684) : a hydrous native sodium carbonate used in ancient times in embalming, in ceramic pastes, and as a cleansing agent
¹**nat·ter** \ˈna-tər\ vi [prob. imit.] (1942) : CHATTER 2
²**natter** n (1943) *chiefly Brit* : idle talk or conversation : CHAT
nat·ty \ˈna-tē\ adj **nat·ti·er; -est** [perh. alter. of earlier *netty*, fr. obs. *net* neat, clean] (1557) : trimly neat and tidy : SMART — **nat·ti·ly** \ˈna-tᵊl-ē\ adv — **nat·ti·ness** \ˈna-tē-nəs\ n
¹**nat·u·ral** \ˈna-chə-rəl, ˈnach-rəl\ adj [ME, fr. MF, fr. L *naturalis* of nature, fr. *natura* nature] (14c) **1 :** based on an inherent sense of right and wrong ⟨~ justice⟩ **2 a :** being in accordance with or determined by nature **b :** having or constituting a classification based on features existing in nature **3 a** (1) **:** begotten as distinguished from adopted; *also* : LEGITIMATE (2) **:** being a relation by actual consanguinity as distinguished from adoption ⟨~ parents⟩ **b :** ILLEGITIMATE ⟨a ~ child⟩ **4 :** having an essential relation with someone or something : following from the nature of the one in question ⟨his guilt is a ~ deduction from the evidence⟩ **5 :** implanted or being as if implanted by nature : seemingly inborn ⟨a ~ talent for art⟩ **6 :** of or relating to nature as an object of study and research **7 :** having a specified character by nature ⟨a ~ athlete⟩ **8 a :** occurring in conformity with the ordinary course of nature : not marvelous or supernatural ⟨~ causes⟩ **b :** formulated by human reason alone rather than revelation ⟨~ religion⟩ ⟨~ rights⟩ **c :** having a normal or usual character ⟨events followed their ~ course⟩ **9 :** possessing or exhibiting the higher qualities (as kindliness and affection) of human nature ⟨a noble . . . brother . . . ever most kind and ~ —Shak.⟩ **10 a :** growing without human care; *also* : not cultivated ⟨~ prairie unbroken by the plow⟩ **b :** existing in or produced by nature : not artificial ⟨~ turf⟩ ⟨~ curiosities⟩ **c :** relating to or being natural food **11 a :** being in a state of nature without spiritual enlightenment : UNREGENERATE ⟨~ man⟩ **b :** living in or as if in a state of nature untouched by the influences of civilization and society **12 a :** having a physical or real existence as contrasted with one that is spiritual, intellectual, or fictitious ⟨a corporation is a legal but not a ~ person⟩ **b :** of, relating to, or operating in the physical as opposed to the spiritual world ⟨~ laws describe phenomena of the physical universe⟩ **13 a :** closely resembling an original : true to nature **b :** marked by easy simplicity and freedom from artificiality, affectation, or constraint **c :** having a form or appearance found in nature **14 a :** having neither flats nor sharps ⟨the ~ scale of C major⟩ **b :** being neither sharp nor flat **c :** having the pitch modified by the natural sign **15 :** of an off-white or beige color — **nat·u·ral·ness** \-nəs\ n
syn NATURAL, INGENUOUS, NAIVE, UNSOPHISTICATED, ARTLESS mean free from pretension or calculation. NATURAL implies lacking artificiality and self-consciousness and having a spontaneousness suggesting the natural rather than the man-made world ⟨her unaffected, *natural* manner⟩. INGENUOUS implies inability to disguise or conceal one's feelings or intentions ⟨the *ingenuous* enthusiasm of children⟩. NAIVE suggests lack of worldly wisdom often connoting credulousness and unchecked innocence ⟨politically *naive*⟩. UNSOPHISTICATED implies a lack of experience and training necessary for social ease and adroitness ⟨*unsophisticated* adolescents⟩. ARTLESS suggests a naturalness resulting from unawareness of the effect one is producing on others ⟨*artless* charm⟩. **syn** see in addition REGULAR
²**natural** n (1533) **1 :** one born without the usual powers of reason and understanding **2 a :** a sign ♮ placed on any degree of the musical staff to nullify the effect of a preceding sharp or flat **b :** a note or tone affected by the natural sign **3 a :** a result or combination that immediately wins the stake in a game; *specif* : a throw of 7 or 11 on the first cast in craps **4 a :** one having natural skills, talents, or abilities **b :** something that is likely to become an immediate success **c :** one that is obviously suitable for a specific purpose **5 :** AFRO
natural childbirth n (1933) **:** a system of managing childbirth in which the mother receives preparatory education in order to remain conscious during and assist in delivery with minimal or no use of drugs or anesthetics
natural family planning n (1975) **:** a method of birth control that involves abstention from sexual intercourse during the period of ovulation which is determined through observation and measurement of bodily symptoms
natural food n (1917) **:** food that has undergone minimal processing and contains no preservatives or artificial additives
natural gas n (1825) **1 :** gas issuing from the earth's crust through natural openings or bored wells; *esp* : a combustible mixture of methane and higher hydrocarbons used chiefly as a fuel and raw material **2 :** gas manufactured from organic matter (as coal)
natural history n (1567) **1 :** a treatise on some aspect of nature **2 :** the natural development of something (as an organism or disease) over a period of time **3 :** the study of natural objects esp. in the field from an amateur or popular point of view
nat·u·ral·ise *Brit var of* NATURALIZE
nat·u·ral·ism \ˈna-chə-rə-ˌli-zəm, ˈnach-rə-\ n (ca. 1641) **1 :** action, inclination, or thought based only on natural desires and instincts **2 :** a theory denying that an event or object has a supernatural significance; *specif* : the doctrine that scientific laws are adequate to account for all phenomena **3 :** realism in art or literature; *specif* : a theory in literature emphasizing scientific observation of life without idealization or the avoidance of the ugly
nat·u·ral·ist \-list\ n (1587) **1 :** one that advocates or practices naturalism **2 :** a student of natural history; *esp* : a field biologist
nat·u·ral·is·tic \ˌna-chə-rə-ˈlis-tik, ˌnach-rə-\ *also* **nat·u·ral·ist** \ˈna-chə-rə-list, ˈnach-rə-\ adj (1838) **:** of, characterized by, or according with naturalism — **nat·u·ral·is·ti·cal·ly** \ˌna-chə-rə-ˈlis-ti-k(ə-)lē, ˌnach-rə-\ adv
nat·u·ral·ize \ˈna-chə-rə-ˌlīz, ˈnach-rə-\ vb **-ized; -iz·ing** vt (1593) **1 :** to introduce into common use or into the vernacular **2 :** to bring

into conformity with nature **3 :** to confer the rights of a national on; *esp* : to admit to citizenship **4 :** to cause (as a plant) to become established if native **~** vi **:** to become established as if native — **nat·u·ral·i·za·tion** \ˌna-chə-rə-lə-ˈzā-shən, ˌnach-rə-\ n
natural killer cell n (1975) **:** a large granular lymphocyte capable of killing a tumor or microbial cell without prior exposure to the target cell and without having it presented with or marked by a histocompatibility antigen
natural law n (15c) **:** a body of law or a specific principle held to be derived from nature and binding upon human society in the absence of or in addition to positive law
natural logarithm n (1816) **:** a logarithm with *e* as a base
nat·u·ral·ly \ˈna-chər-ə-lē, ˈnach-rə-, ˈna-chər-\ adv (14c) **1 :** by nature : by natural character or ability ⟨~ timid⟩ **2 :** according to the usual course of things : as might be expected ⟨we ~ dislike being hurt⟩ **3 a :** without artificial aid ⟨hair that curls ~⟩ **b :** without affectation ⟨speak ~⟩ **4 :** with truth to nature : REALISTICALLY
natural number n (1763) **:** the number 1 or any number (as 3, 12, 432) obtained by adding 1 to it one or more times : a positive integer
natural philosophy n (14c) **:** NATURAL SCIENCE; *esp* : PHYSICAL SCIENCE — **natural philosopher** n
natural resource n (1870) **1** *pl* **:** industrial materials and capacities (as mineral deposits and waterpower) supplied by nature **2 :** RESOURCE 1b
natural science n (14c) **:** any of the sciences (as physics, chemistry, or biology) that deal with matter, energy, and their interrelations and transformations or with objectively measurable phenomena — **natural scientist** n
natural selection n (1857) **:** a natural process that results in the survival and reproductive success of individuals or groups best adjusted to their environment and that leads to the perpetuation of genetic qualities best suited to that particular environment
natural theology n (1677) **:** theology deriving its knowledge of God from the study of nature independent of special revelation
na·ture \ˈnā-chər\ n [ME, fr. MF, fr. L *natura*, fr. *natus*, pp. of *nasci* to be born — more at NATION] (14c) **1 a :** the inherent character or basic constitution of a person or thing : ESSENCE **b :** DISPOSITION, TEMPERAMENT **2 a :** a creative and controlling force in the universe **b :** an inner force or the sum of such forces in an individual **3 :** a kind or class usu. distinguished by fundamental or essential characteristics ⟨documents of a confidential ~⟩ ⟨acts of a ceremonial ~⟩ **4 :** the physical constitution or drives of an organism; *esp* : an excretory organ or function — used in phrases like *the call of nature* **5 :** a spontaneous attitude (as of generosity) **6 :** the external world in its entirety **7 a :** humankind's original or natural condition **b :** a simplified mode of life resembling this condition **8 :** the genetically controlled qualities of an organism **9 :** natural scenery **syn** see TYPE
na·tur·ism \ˈnā-chə-ˌri-zəm\ n (1847) **1 :** NATURALISM 1, 2 **2 :** the worship of the forces of nature **3 :** NUDISM — **na·tur·ist** \-rist\ n
na·tu·rop·a·thy \ˌnā-chə-ˈrä-pə-thē\ n (1901) **:** a system of treatment of disease that avoids drugs and surgery and emphasizes the use of natural agents (as air, water, and sunshine) and physical means (as manipulation and electrical treatment) — **na·tu·ro·path** \ˈnā-chər-ə-ˌpath, ˈna-\ n — **na·tu·ro·path·ic** \ˌnā-chər-ə-ˈpa-thik, ˌna-; nə-ˌtyùr-ə-, -ˌtùr-\ adj
Nau·ga·hyde \ˈnȯ-gə-ˌhīd, ˈnä-\ *trademark* — used for vinyl-coated fabrics
¹**naught** \ˈnȯt, ˈnät\ pron [ME *nought*, fr. OE *nāwiht*, fr. *nā* no + *wiht* creature, thing — more at NO, WIGHT] (bef. 12c) **:** NOTHING ⟨efforts came to ~⟩
²**naught** n (bef. 12c) **1 :** NOTHINGNESS, NONEXISTENCE **2 :** the arithmetical symbol 0 : ZERO, CIPHER
naugh·ty \ˈnȯ-tē, ˈnä-\ adj **naugh·ti·er; -est** [ME *noughti*, fr. *nought*] (14c) **1 a** *archaic* **:** vicious in moral character : WICKED **b :** guilty of disobedience or misbehavior **2 :** lacking in taste or propriety — **naugh·ti·ly** \ˈnȯ-tᵊl-ē, ˈnä-\ adv — **naugh·ti·ness** \ˈnȯ-tē-nəs, ˈnä-\ n
nau·ma·chia \nȯ-ˈmā-kē-ə, -ˈma-\ n, pl **-chi·ae** \-kē-ˌē, -kē-ˌī\ *or* **-chias** [L, fr. Gk, naval battle, fr. *naus* ship + *machesthai* to fight — more at NAVE] (1596) **1 :** an ancient Roman spectacle representing a naval battle **2 :** a place for naumachiae
nau·pli·us \ˈnȯ-plē-əs\ n, pl **-plii** \-plē-ˌī, -ˌē\ [NL, fr. L, a shellfish, fr. Gk *nauplios*] (1836) **:** a crustacean larva in usu. the first stage after leaving the egg and with three pairs of appendages, a median eye, and little or no segmentation
nau·sea \ˈnȯ-zē-ə, -sē-ə; ˈnȯ-zhə, -shə\ n [L, seasickness, nausea, fr. Gk *nautia, nausia*, fr. *nautēs* sailor] (1569) **1 :** a stomach distress with distaste for food and an urge to vomit **2 :** extreme disgust — **nau·se·ant** \-zhē-ənt, -shē-, -zē-, -sē-\ n or adj
nau·se·ate \ˈnȯ-zhē-ˌāt, -shē-, -zē-, -sē-\ vb **-at·ed; -at·ing** vi (1640) **1 :** to become affected with nausea **2 :** to feel disgust **~** vt **:** to affect with nausea or disgust
nauseating adj (1645) **:** causing nausea or esp. disgust **usage** see NAUSEOUS — **nau·se·at·ing·ly** adv
nau·seous \ˈnȯ-shəs, ˈnȯ-zē-əs\ adj (1612) **1 :** causing nausea or disgust : NAUSEATING **2 :** affected with nausea or disgust — **nau·seous·ly** adv — **nau·seous·ness** n
usage Those who insist that *nauseous* can properly be used only in sense 1 and that in sense 2 it is an error for *nauseated* are mistaken. Current evidence shows these facts: *nauseous* is most frequently used to mean physically affected with nausea, usu. after a linking verb such as *feel* or *become*; figurative use is quite a bit less frequent. Use of *nauseous* in sense 1 is much more often figurative than literal, and this use appears to be losing ground to *nauseating*. *Nauseated*, while not rare, is less common than *nauseous* in sense 2.
nautch \ˈnȯch\ n [Hindi *nāc*, fr. Skt *nṛtya*, fr. *nṛtyati* he dances] (1809) **:** an entertainment in India consisting chiefly of dancing by professional dancing girls
nau·ti·cal \ˈnȯ-ti-kəl, ˈnä-\ adj [L *nauticus*, fr. Gk *nautikos*, fr. *nautēs* sailor, fr. *naus* ship — more at NAVE] (1552) **:** of, relating to, or associated with seamen, navigation, or ships — **nau·ti·cal·ly** \-k(ə-)lē\ adv
nautical mile n (1834) **:** any of various units of distance used for sea and air navigation based on the length of a minute of arc of a great circle of the earth and differing because the earth is not a perfect sphere: as **a :** a British unit equal to 6080 feet (1853.2 meters) **b :** an

international unit equal to 6076.115 feet (1852 meters) used officially in the U.S. since July 1, 1959

nau·ti·loid \'no̊-t²l-,o̊id, 'nä-\ *n* (ca. 1847) : any of a subclass (Nautiloidea) of shell-bearing cephalopods that were abundant in the Ordovician and esp. the Silurian but are represented in the recent fauna only by the nautiluses — **nautiloid** *adj*

nau·ti·lus \'no̊-t²l-əs, 'nä-\ *n, pl* **-lus·es** *or* **-li** \-t²l-,ī, -,ē\ [NL, fr. L, paper nautilus, fr. Gk *nautilos*, lit., sailor, fr. *naus* ship] (1601) 1 : any of a genus (*Nautilus*) of cephalopod mollusks of the So. Pacific and Indian Oceans with a spiral chambered shell that is pearly on the inside — called also *chambered nautilus* 2 : PAPER NAUTILUS

nautilus

nav·aid \'na-,vād\ *n* [*nav*igation *aid*] (1956) : a device or system (as a radar beacon) that provides a navigator with navigational data

Na·va·jo *also* **Na·va·ho** \'na-və-,hō, 'nä-\ *n, pl* **-jo** *or* **-jos** *also* **-ho** *or* **-hos** [Sp (*Apache de*) *Navajó*, lit., Apache of Navajó, fr. *Navajó*, area occupied by Navajos, prob. fr. Tewa (Pueblo Indian language of northern New Mexico) *navahu̇*, lit., arroyo with planted fields] (1780) 1 : a member of an American Indian people of northern New Mexico and Arizona 2 : the language of the Navajo people

na·val \'nā-vəl\ *adj* [ME, fr. L *navalis*, fr. *navis* ship] (15c) 1 *obs* : or relating to ships or shipping 2 **a** : of or relating to a navy **b** : consisting of or involving warships

naval architect *n* (ca. 1885) : one who designs ships

naval stores *n pl* [fr. their former use in the construction and maintenance of wooden sailing vessels] (1678) : products (as turpentine, pitch, and rosin) obtained from resinous conifers and esp. pines

¹nave \'nāv\ *n* [ME, fr. OE *nafu*; akin to OE *nafela* navel] (bef. 12c) : the hub of a wheel

²nave *n* [ML *navis*, fr. L, ship; akin to OE *nōwend* sailor, Gk *naus* ship, Skt *nau*] (1673) : the main part of the interior of a church; *esp* : the long narrow central hall in a cruciform church that rises higher than the aisles flanking it to form a clerestory

na·vel \'nā-vəl\ *n* [ME, fr. OE *nafela*; akin to OHG *nabalo* navel, L *umbilicus*, Gk *omphalos*] (bef. 12c) 1 : a depression in the middle of the abdomen that marks the point of former attachment of the umbilical cord or yolk stalk 2 : the central point : MIDDLE

navel orange *n* (1888) : a seedless orange having a pit at the apex where the fruit encloses a small secondary fruit — called also *navel*

¹na·vic·u·lar \nə-'vi-kyə-lər\ *adj* [ME *naviculare*, fr. L *navicula* boat, dim. of *navis*] (15c) 1 : shaped like a boat ⟨a ~ bone⟩ 2 : of, relating to, or involving a navicular bone ⟨~ disease⟩

²navicular *n* [NL (*os*) *naviculare* navicular bone] (1816) : a navicular bone; *esp* : one situated on the big-toe side of the tarsus

nav·i·ga·ble \'na-vi-gə-bəl\ *adj* (15c) 1 : deep enough and wide enough to afford passage to ships 2 : capable of being steered — **nav·i·ga·bil·i·ty** \,na-vi-gə-'bi-lə-tē\ *n* — **nav·i·ga·bly** \'na-vi-gə-blē\ *adv*

nav·i·gate \'na-və-,gāt\ *vb* **-gat·ed; -gat·ing** [L *navigatus*, pp. of *navigare*, fr. *navis* ship + *-igare* (fr. *agere* to drive) — more at AGENT] *vi* (1588) 1 : to travel by water : SAIL 2 : to steer a course through a medium; *specif* : to operate an airplane 3 : GET AROUND, MOVE ~ *vt* 1 **a** : to sail over, on, or through **b** : to make one's way over or through : TRAVERSE 2 **a** : to steer or manage (a boat) in sailing **b** : to operate or control the course of (as an airplane)

nav·i·ga·tion \,na-və-'gā-shən\ *n* (1547) 1 : the act or practice of navigating 2 : the science of getting ships, aircraft, or spacecraft from place to place; *esp* : the method of determining position, course, and distance traveled 3 : ship traffic or commerce — **nav·i·ga·tion·al** \-shnəl, -shə-n²l\ *adj* — **nav·i·ga·tion·al·ly** *adv*

nav·i·ga·tor \'na-və-,gā-tər\ *n* (1590) : one that navigates or is qualified to navigate

nav·vy \'na-vē\ *n, pl* **navvies** [by shortening & alter. fr. *navigator* construction worker on a canal] (ca. 1834) *chiefly Brit* : an unskilled laborer

na·vy \'nā-vē\ *n, pl* **navies** [ME *navie*, fr. MF, fr. L *navigia* ships, fr. *navigare*] (14c) 1 : a group of ships : FLEET 2 : a nation's ships of war and of logistic support 3 *often cap* : the complete naval establishment of a nation including yards, stations, ships, and personnel 4 : a dark grayish purplish blue

navy bean *n* (1856) : a white-seeded kidney bean grown esp. for its nutritious seeds

Navy Cross *n* (1919) : a U.S. Navy decoration awarded for extraordinary heroism in operations against an armed enemy

navy yard *n* (1771) : a yard where naval vessels are built or repaired

na·wab \nə-'wäb\ *n* [Urdu *nawwāb*] (1758) : NABOB

¹nay \'nā\ *adv* [ME, fr. ON *nei*, fr. *ne* not + *ei* ever — more at NO, AYE] (13c) : NO

²nay *n* (14c) 1 : DENIAL, REFUSAL 2 **a** : a negative reply or vote **b** : one who votes no

³nay *conj* (1560) : not merely this but also : not only so but ⟨the letter made him happy, ~, ecstatic⟩

nay·say·er \'nā-,sā-ər, -,se(-ə)r\ *n* (1721) : one who denies, refuses, opposes, or is skeptical or cynical about something — **nay–say·ing** \-,sā-iŋ\ *n*

Naz·a·rene \,na-zə-'rēn\ *n* [ME *Nazaren*, fr. LL *Nazarenus*, fr. Gk *Nazarēnos*, fr. *Nazareth* Nazareth, Palestine] (13c) 1 : a native or resident of Nazareth 2 **a** : CHRISTIAN 1a **b** : a member of the Church of the Nazarene that is a Protestant denomination deriving from the merging of three holiness groups, stressing sanctification, and following Methodist polity

Na·zi \'nät-sē, 'nat-\ *n* [G, by shortening & alter. fr. *Nationalsozialist*, fr. *national* national + *Sozialist* socialist] (1930) 1 : a member of a German fascist party controlling Germany from 1933 to 1945 under Adolf Hitler 2 *often not cap* : one who resembles a German Nazi — **nazi** *adj, often cap* — **na·zi·fi·ca·tion** \,nät-si-fə-'kā-shən, ,nat-\ *n, often cap* — **na·zi·fy** \'nät-si-,fī, 'nat-\ *vt, often cap*

Naz·i·rite *or* **Naz·a·rite** \'na-zə-,rīt\ *n* [LL *nazaraeus*, fr. Gk *nazaraios*,

nazaraios, fr. Heb *nāzīr*, lit., consecrated] (1560) : a Jew of biblical times consecrated to God by a vow to avoid drinking wine, cutting the hair, and being defiled by the presence of a corpse — **Naz·i·rit·ism** \-,rī-,ti-zəm\ *n*

Na·zism \'nät-,si-zəm, 'nat-\ *or* **Na·zi·ism** \-sē-,i-zəm\ *n* [*Nazi* + *-ism*] (1934) : the body of political and economic doctrines held and put into effect by the National Socialist German Workers' party in the Third German Reich including the totalitarian principle of government, state control of all industry, predominance of groups assumed to be racially superior, and supremacy of the führer

NCO \,en-(,)sē-'ō\ *n* (ca. 1810) : NONCOMMISSIONED OFFICER

NC-17 \'en-,sē-,se-vən-'tēn\ *certification mark* — used to certify that a motion picture is of such a nature that no one under the age of 17 can be admitted; compare G, PG, PG-13, R

-nd *symbol* — used after the figure 2 to indicate the ordinal number second ⟨2nd⟩ ⟨72nd⟩

né \'nā\ *adj* [F, lit., born — more at NÉE] (1905) 1 — used to indicate the original, former, or legal name of a man ⟨Robert Roe, ~ John Doe⟩ 2 : originally or formerly called

ne- *or* **neo-** *comb form* [Gk, fr. *neos* new — more at NEW] 1 **a** : new : recent ⟨*Neo*gene⟩ **b** : new and different period or form of ⟨*Neo*platonism⟩ : in a new and different form or manner ⟨*Neo*platonic⟩ **c** : New World ⟨*Neo*tropical⟩ **d** : new and abnormal ⟨*neo*plasm⟩ 2 : new chemical compound isomeric with or otherwise related to (such) a compound ⟨*neo*stigmine⟩

Ne·an·der·thal \nē-'an-dər-,tȯl, -,thȯl; nā-'än-dər-,täl\ *adj* (1861) 1 *also* **Ne·an·der·tal** \-,tȯl, -,täl\ : being, relating to, or resembling Neanderthal man 2 : suggesting a caveman in appearance, mentality, or behavior — **Neanderthal** *n*

Neanderthal man *n* [*Neanderthal*, valley in western Germany] (1863) : a Middle Paleolithic hominid (*Homo sapiens neanderthalensis*) known from skeletal remains in Europe, northern Africa, and western Asia — **Ne·an·der·thal·oid** \-,tȯ-,lȯid, -,thȯ-, -,tä-\ *adj or n*

¹neap \'nēp\ *adj* [ME *neep*, fr. OE *nēp* being at the stage of neap tide] (bef. 12c) : of, relating to, or constituting a neap tide

²neap *n* (1584) : NEAP TIDE

Ne·a·pol·i·tan \,nē-ə-'pä-lə-t²n\ *n* [ME, fr. L *neapolitanus* of Naples, fr. Gk *neapolitēs* citizen of Naples, fr. *Neapolis* Naples] (15c) : a native or inhabitant of Naples, Italy — **Neapolitan** *adj*

Neapolitan ice cream *n* (1895) : a brick of from two to four layers of ice cream of different flavors

neap tide *n* (ca. 1548) : a tide of minimum range occurring at the first and the third quarters of the moon

¹near \'nir\ *adv* [ME *ner*, partly fr. *ner* nearer, fr. OE *nēar*, comparative of *nēah* nigh; partly fr. ON *nær* nearer, compar. of *nā-* nigh — more at NIGH] (13c) 1 **a** : at, within, or to a short distance or time 2 : ALMOST, NEARLY ⟨~ dead⟩ 3 : in a close or intimate manner : CLOSELY ⟨~ related⟩ 4 *archaic* : in a frugal manner

²near *prep* (13c) : close to

³near *adj* (14c) 1 **a** : not far distant in time, place, or degree ⟨in the ~ future⟩ **b** : almost happening : narrowly missed or avoided ⟨a ~ win in the primary⟩ ⟨a ~ midair collision⟩ **c** : nearly not happening ⟨a ~ escape⟩ 2 : closely related or intimately associated 3 **a** : being the closer of two ⟨the ~ side⟩ **b** : being the left-hand one of a pair ⟨the ~ wheel of a cart⟩ 4 : DIRECT, SHORT ⟨the ~*est* road⟩ 5 : STINGY, CLOSEFISTED 6 **a** : closely resembling the standard or typical ⟨a ~ desert⟩ **b** : approximating the genuine ⟨~ silk⟩ — **near·ness** *n*

⁴near *vb* (1513) : APPROACH

near beer *n* (1909) : any of various malt liquors considered nonalcoholic because they contain less than a specified percentage of alcohol

near·by \nir-'bī, 'nir-,\ *adv or adj* (14c) : close at hand

Ne·arc·tic \nē-'ärk-tik, -'är-tik\ *adj* (1858) : of, relating to, or being the biogeographic subregion that includes Greenland and No. America north of tropical Mexico

near gale *n* (ca. 1975) : MODERATE GALE — see BEAUFORT SCALE table

near–in·fra·red \,nir-,in-frə-'red, -(,)frä-\ *adj* (1950) : of or relating to the shorter wavelengths of radiation in the infrared spectrum and esp. to those between 0.7 and 2.5 micrometers

near·ly \'nir-lē\ *adv* (1561) 1 : in a close manner or relationship ⟨~ related⟩ 2 **a** : almost but not quite ⟨~ identical⟩ ⟨~ a year later⟩ **b** : to the least extent ⟨not ~ as good as we expected⟩

near miss *n* (1940) 1 **a** : a miss (as with a bomb) close enough to cause damage **b** : something that falls just short of success 2 **a** : a near collision (as between aircraft) **b** : CLOSE CALL

near money *n* (1942) : assets (as savings accounts or government bonds) quickly and easily converted to cash

near point *n* (1876) : the point nearest the eye at which an object is accurately focused on the retina at full accommodation

near·shore \'nir-,shōr, -'shȯr, 'nir-,\ *adj* (1896) : extending outward an indefinite but usu. short distance from shore ⟨~ sediments⟩

near·side \-,sīd\ *adj* (ca. 1840) *Brit* : LEFT-HAND 1 — **nearside** *n*

near·sight·ed \-,sī-təd\ *adj* (1686) : able to see near things more clearly than distant ones : MYOPIC — **near·sight·ed·ly** *adv* — **near·sight·ed·ness** *n*

near–ul·tra·vi·o·let \,nir-,əl-trə-'vi-(ə-)lət\ *adj* (1951) : of, relating to, or being the longest wavelengths of radiation esp. between 300 and 400 nanometers

¹neat \'nēt\ *n, pl* **neat** *or* **neats** [ME *neet*, fr. OE *nēat*; akin to OHG *nōz* head of cattle, OE *nēotan* to make use of, Lith *nauda* use] (bef. 12c) : the common domestic bovine (*Bos taurus*)

²neat *adj* [MF *net*, fr. L *nitidus* bright, neat, fr. *nitēre* to shine; prob. akin to MIr *níam* luster] (1542) 1 : free from dirt and disorder ; habitually clean and orderly 2 **a** : free from admixture or dilution : STRAIGHT ⟨~ brandy⟩ ⟨~ cement⟩ **b** : free from irregularity : SMOOTH ⟨~ silk⟩ 3 : marked by tasteful simplicity ⟨a ~ outfit⟩ 4 **a** : PRECISE, SYSTEMATIC **b** : marked by skill or ingenuity : ADROIT 5 : NET ⟨~ profit⟩ 6 : FINE, ADMIRABLE — **neat·ly** *adv* — **neat·ness** *n*

\ə\ abut \ˌ⁹\ kitten, F table \ər\ further \a\ ash \ā\ ace \ä\ mop, mar \au̇\ out \ch\ chin \e\ bet \ē\ easy \g\ go \i\ hit \ī\ ice \j\ job \ŋ\ sing \ō\ go \ȯ\ law \ȯi\ boy \th\ thin \t͟h\ the \ü\ loot \u̇\ foot \y\ yet \zh\ vision \ä, ḵ, ⁿ, œ, œ̄, ue, ᵫ, ᵊ\ *see* Guide to Pronunciation

³neat *adv* (1649) : without admixture or dilution : STRAIGHT

neat·en \'nē-t⁸n\ *vt* **neat·ened; neat·en·ing** \'nēt-niŋ, 'nē-t⁸n-iŋ\ (1898) **1** : to set in order : make neat **2** : to finish (as a piece of sewing) carefully

neath \'nēth\ *prep* (1787) *dial* : BENEATH

neat·herd \'nēt-,hərd\ *n* (14c) : HERDSMAN

neat's–foot oil \'nēts-,fût\ *n* (1787) : a pale yellow fatty oil made esp. from the bones of cattle and used chiefly as a leather dressing

neb \'neb\ *n* [ME, fr. OE; akin to ON *nef* beak] (bef. 12c) **1 a** : the beak of a bird or tortoise : BILL **b** *chiefly dial* : a person's mouth **c** : NOSE 1, SNOUT **2** : NIB, TIP

neb·bish \'ne-bish\ *n* [Yiddish *nebekh* poor, unfortunate, fr. Czech *nebohý*] (1951) : a timid, meek, or ineffectual person — **neb·bishy** \-bi-shē\ *adj*

ne·ben·kern \'nā-bən-,kərn, -,kern\ *n* [G, lit., subsidiary nucleus] (1898) : a 2-stranded helical structure of the proximal tail region of a spermatozoon that is derived from mitochondria

neb·u·la \'ne-byə-lə\ *n, pl* **-lae** \-,lē, -,lī\ *also* **-las** [NL, fr. L, mist, cloud; akin to OHG *nebul* fog, Gk *nephelē, nephos* cloud] (ca. 1738) **1** : any of numerous clouds of gas or dust in interstellar space **2** : GALAXY; *esp* : a galaxy other than the Milky Way galaxy — not used technically — **neb·u·lar** \-lər\ *adj*

nebular hypothesis *n* (1837) : a hypothesis in astronomy: the solar system has evolved from a hot gaseous nebula

neb·u·lize \'ne-byə-,līz\ *vt* **-lized; -liz·ing** [L *nebula*] (1872) : to reduce to a fine spray — **neb·u·li·za·tion** \,ne-byə-lə-'zā-shən\ *n* — **neb·u·liz·er** \'ne-byə-,lī-zər\ *n*

neb·u·los·i·ty \,ne-byə-'lä-sə-tē\ *n, pl* **-ties** (1761) **1** : the quality or state of being nebulous **2** : nebulous matter; *also* : NEBULA 1

neb·u·lous \'ne-byə-ləs\ *adj* [L *nebulosus* misty, fr. *nebula*] (1784) **1** : of, relating to, or resembling a nebula : NEBULAR **2** : INDISTINCT, VAGUE — **neb·u·lous·ly** *adv* — **neb·u·lous·ness** *n*

nec·es·sar·i·ly \,ne-sə-'ser-ə-lē\ *adv* (15c) **1** : of necessity : UNAVOIDABLY **2** : as a logical result or consequence

¹nec·es·sary \'ne-sə-,ser-ē\ *adj* [ME *necessarie*, fr. L *necessarius*, fr. *necesse* necessary, prob. fr. *ne-* not + *cedere* to withdraw — more at NO] (14c) **1 a** : of an inevitable nature : INESCAPABLE **b** (1) : logically unavoidable (2) : that cannot be denied without contradiction **c** : determined or produced by the previous condition of things **d** : COMPULSORY **2** : absolutely needed : REQUIRED

²necessary *n, pl* **-sar·ies** (14c) : an indispensable item : ESSENTIAL

necessary condition *n* (1817) **1** : a proposition whose falsity assures the falsity of another **2** : a state of affairs that must prevail if another is to occur : PREREQUISITE

ne·ces·si·tar·i·an·ism \ni-,se-sə-'ter-ē-ə-,ni-zəm\ *n* (1854) : the theory that results follow by invariable sequence from causes — **ne·ces·si·tar·i·an** \-'ter-ē-ən\ *adj or n*

ne·ces·si·tate \ni-'se-sə-,tāt\ *vt* **-tat·ed; -tat·ing** (1628) **1** : to make necessary : REQUIRE **2** : FORCE, COMPEL — **ne·ces·si·ta·tion** \-,se-sə-'tā-shən\ *n*

ne·ces·si·tous \ni-'se-sə-təs\ *adj* (1611) **1** : NEEDY, IMPOVERISHED **2** : URGENT, PRESSING **3** : NECESSARY — **ne·ces·si·tous·ly** *adv* — **ne·ces·si·tous·ness** *n*

ne·ces·si·ty \ni-'se-sə-tē, -'ses-tē\ *n, pl* **-ties** [ME *necessite*, fr. MF *necessité*, fr. L *necessitat-, necessitas*, fr. *necesse*] (14c) **1** : the quality or state of being necessary **2 a** : pressure of circumstance **b** : physical or moral compulsion **c** : impossibility of a contrary order or condition **3** : the quality or state of being in need; *esp* : POVERTY **4 a** : something that is necessary : REQUIREMENT **b** : an urgent need or desire — **of necessity** : in such a way that it cannot be otherwise; *also* : as a necessary consequence

¹neck \'nek\ *n* [ME *nekke*, fr. OE *hnecca*; akin to OHG *hnac* nape] (bef. 12c) **1 a** (1) : the part of an animal that connects the head with the body (2) : the siphon of a bivalve mollusk (as a clam) **b** : the part of a garment that covers or is next to the neck **2 a** (1) : a relatively narrow part suggestive of a neck: as **a** (1) : the constricted end of a bottle (2) : the slender proximal end of a fruit **b** : CERVIX **2 c** : the part of a stringed musical instrument extending from the body and supporting the fingerboard and strings **d** : a narrow stretch of land **e** : STRAIT 1b **f** : the part of a tooth between the crown and the root — see TOOTH illustration **g** : a column of solidified magma of a volcanic pipe or laccolith **3** : a narrow margin ⟨won by a ∼⟩ **4** : REGION, PART ⟨my ∼ of the woods⟩

²neck *vt* (1842) **1** : to kiss and caress amorously **2** : to reduce in diameter ∼ *vi* **1** : to engage in amorous kissing and caressing **2** : to become constricted : NARROW

neck and neck *adv or adj* (1799) : very close (as in a race)

necked \'nekt\ *adj* (14c) : having a neck esp. of a specified kind — often used in combination ⟨long-*necked*⟩

neck·er·chief \'ne-kər-chəf, -(,)chif, -,chēf\ *n, pl* **-chiefs** *also* **-chieves** *see* HANDKERCHIEF *pl*\ [ME *nekkerchef*, fr. *nekke* + *kerchef* kerchief] (14c) : a kerchief for the neck

neck·ing \'ne-kiŋ\ *n* (1804) **1** : a narrow molding near the top of a column or pilaster **2** : the act or practice of kissing and caressing amorously

neck·lace \'ne-kləs\ *n* (ca. 1590) : an ornament worn around the neck

neck·line \'nek-,līn\ *n* (1904) : the line of the neck opening of a garment

neck–rein \-,rān\ *vi* (1940) *of a saddle horse* : to respond to the pressure of a rein on one side of the neck by turning in the opposite direction ∼ *vt* : to direct (a horse) by pressures of the rein on the neck

neck·tie \-,tī\ *n* (1838) : a narrow length of material worn about the neck and tied in front; *esp* : FOUR-IN-HAND

neck·wear \-,war, -,wer\ *n* (ca. 1879) : articles of clothing (as ties and scarves) worn about the neck

necr- *or* **necro-** *comb form* [LL, fr. Gk *nekr-, nekro-*, fr. *nekros* dead body — more at NOXIOUS] **1** : those that are dead ⟨*necro*philia⟩ **2** : one that is dead ⟨*necro*psy⟩

ne·crol·o·gy \nə-'krä-lə-jē, ne-\ *n, pl* **-gies** [NL *necrologium*, fr. *necr-* + *-logium* (as in ML *eulogium* eulogy)] (1799) **1** : OBITUARY **2** : a list of the recently dead — **ne·cro·log·i·cal** \,ne-krə-'lä-ji-kəl\ *adj* — **ne·crol·o·gist** \nə-'krä-lə-jist, ne-\ *n*

nec·ro·man·cy \'ne-krə-,man(t)-sē\ *n* [alter. of ME *nigromancie*, fr. MF, fr. ML *nigromantia*, by folk etymology fr. LL *necromantia*, fr.

LGk *nekromanteia*, fr. Gk *nekr-* + *-manteia* -mancy] (1522) **1** : conjuration of the spirits of the dead for purposes of magically revealing the future or influencing the course of events **2** : MAGIC, SORCERY — **nec·ro·man·cer** \-sər\ *n* — **nec·ro·man·tic** \,ne-krə-'man-tik\ *adj* — **nec·ro·man·ti·cal·ly** \-ti-k(ə-)lē\ *adv*

ne·croph·a·gous \nə-'krä-fə-gəs, ne-\ *adj* (1835) : feeding on corpses or carrion ⟨∼ insects⟩

nec·ro·phil·ia \,ne-krə-'fi-lē-ə\ *n* [NL] (1892) : obsession with and esu. erotic interest in or stimulation by corpses — **nec·ro·phil·i·ac** \-'fi-lē-,ak\ *adj or n* — **nec·ro·phil·ic** \-'fi-lik\ *adj*

nec·roph·i·lism \nə-'krä-fə-,li-zəm, ne-\ *n* (1864) : NECROPHILIA

ne·crop·o·lis \nə-'krä-pə-ləs, ne-\ *n, pl* **-lis·es** *or* **-les** \-,lēz\ *or* **-leis** \-,läs\ *or* **-li, -,lī, -,lē** [LL, city of the dead, fr. Gk *nekropolis*, fr. *nekr-* + *-polis* -polis] (1819) : CEMETERY; *esp* : a large elaborate cemetery of an ancient city

¹nec·rop·sy \'ne-,kräp-sē\ *n, pl* **-sies** (1856) : AUTOPSY 1

²necropsy *vt* **-sied; -sy·ing** (1927) : to perform an autopsy on

ne·cro·sis \nə-'krō-səs, ne-\ *n, pl* **ne·cro·ses** \-,sēz\ [LL, fr. Gk *nekrōsis*, fr. *nekroun* to make dead, fr. *nekros* dead body] (1665) : usu. localized death of living tissue — **ne·crot·ic** \-'krä-tik\ *adj*

nec·ro·tiz·ing \'ne-krə-,tī-ziŋ\ *adj* [Gk *nekrōtikos* necrotic, fr. *nekroun*] (1899) : causing, associated with, or undergoing necrosis ⟨∼ infections⟩ ⟨∼ tissue⟩

nec·tar \'nek-tər\ *n* [L, fr. Gk *nektar*] **1 a** : the drink of the Greek and Roman gods **b** : something delicious to drink **c** : a beverage of fruit juice and pulp ⟨apricot ∼⟩ **2** : a sweet liquid that is secreted by the nectaries of a plant and is the chief raw material of honey — **nec·tar·ous** \-t(ə-)rəs\ *adj*

nec·tar·ine \,nek-tə-'rēn\ *n* [obs. *nectarine*, adj., like nectar] (1611) : a peach with a smooth-skinned fruit that is a frequent somatic mutation of the normal peach; *also* : its fruit

nec·tary \'nek-t(ə-)rē\ *n, pl* **-tar·ies** [NL *nectarium*, irreg. fr. L *nectar* + *-arium* -ary] (1759) : a plant gland that secretes nectar

née *or* **nee** \'nā\ *adj* [F *née*, fem. of *né*, lit., born, pp. of *naître* to be born, fr. L *nasci* — more at NATION] (1758) **1** — used to identify a woman by her maiden family name **2** : originally or formerly called ⟨the Brewers ∼ Pilots who also are in their third year —Fred Ciampa⟩

¹need \'nēd\ *n* [ME *ned*, fr. OE *nied, nēd*; akin to OHG *nōt* distress, need, OPruss *nautin* need] (bef. 12c) **1** : necessary duty : OBLIGATION **2 a** : a lack of something requisite, desirable, or useful **b** : a physiological or psychological requirement for the well-being of an organism **3** : a condition requiring supply or relief **4** : lack of the means of subsistence : POVERTY

²need *vb* **need·ed; need·ing; needs** *or* (*auxiliary*) **need** *vi* (bef. 12c) **1** : to be needful or necessary **2** : to be in want ∼ *vt* : to be in need of : REQUIRE ∼ *verbal auxiliary* : be under necessity or obligation to ⟨you ∼ not answer⟩

¹need·ful \'nēd-fəl\ *adj* (12c) **1** : being in need **2** : NECESSARY, REQUISITE — **need·ful·ly** \-fə-lē\ *adv* — **need·ful·ness** *n*

²needful *n* (1709) **1** : something needed or requisite **2** : MONEY

¹nee·dle \'nē-d⁸l\ *n* [ME *nedle*, fr. OE *nǣdl*; akin to OHG *nādala* needle, *nājan* to sew, L *nēre* to spin, Gk *nēn*] (bef. 12c) **1 a** : a small slender usu. steel instrument that has an eye for thread or surgical sutures at one end and that is used for sewing **b** : any of various devices for carrying thread and making stitches (as in crocheting or knitting) **c** (1) : a slender hollow instrument for introducing material into or removing material from the body parenterally (2) : any of various slender hollow devices used to introduce matter (as air) into or remove it from an object (as a ball) **2 a** : a slender bar of magnetized steel that when allowed to turn freely (as in a compass) indicates the direction of a magnetic field (as of the earth) **b** : a slender usu. sharp-pointed indicator on a dial **3 a** : a slender pointed object resembling a needle: as (1) : a pointed crystal (2) : a sharp rock (3) : OBELISK **b** : a needle-shaped leaf (as of a conifer) **c** : a slender rod (as of jewel or steel) with a rounded tip used in a phonograph to transmit vibrations from a record : STYLUS **d** : a slender pointed rod controlling a fine inlet or outlet (as in a valve) **4** : a teasing or gibing remark — **nee·dle·like** \-,dⁱlīk\ *adj*

²needle *vb* **nee·dled; nee·dling** \'nēd-liŋ, 'nē-d⁸l-iŋ\ *vt* (ca. 1715) **1** : to sew or pierce with or as if with a needle **2 a** : TEASE, TORMENT **b** : to incite to action by repeated gibes ⟨*needled* the boy into a fight⟩ ∼ *vi* : SEW, EMBROIDER — **nee·dler** \'nēd-lər, 'nē-d⁸l-ər\ *n*

nee·dle·fish \'nē-d⁸l-,fish\ *n* (1601) **1** : any of a family (Belonidae) of elongate green and silvery chiefly marine bony fishes with long slender jaws **2** : PIPEFISH

nee·dle·point \-,point\ *n* (1865) **1** : lace worked with a needle over a paper pattern **2** : embroidery done on canvas usu. in simple even stitches across counted threads — **needlepoint** *adj*

needlefish 1

need·less \'nēd-ləs\ *adj* (14c) : not needed : UNNECESSARY ⟨∼ to say⟩ — **need·less·ly** *adv* — **need·less·ness** *n*

nee·dle·wom·an \'nē-d⁸l-,wú-mən\ *n* (1535) : a woman who does needlework; *esp* : SEAMSTRESS

nee·dle·work \-,wərk\ *n* (14c) **1** : work done with a needle; *esp* : work (as embroidery) other than plain sewing **2** : the occupation of one who does needlework — **nee·dle·work·er** \-,wər-kər\ *n*

needn't \'nē-d⁸nt\ (1865) : need not

needs \'nēdz\ *adv* [ME *nedes*, fr. OE *nēdes*, fr. gen. of *nēd* need] (bef. 12c) : of necessity : NECESSARILY ⟨must ∼ be recognized⟩

needy \'nē-dē\ *adj* **need·i·er; -est** (12c) : being in want : POVERTY-STRICKEN ⟨∼ families⟩ — **need·i·ness** *n*

neem \'nēm\ *n* [Hindi *nim*, fr. Skt *nimba*] (1813) : a large East Indian tree (*Azadirachta indica* of the family Meliaceae) whose trunk exudes a tenacious gum and whose bitter bark used as a tonic and whose fruit and seeds yield a medicinal aromatic oil

neep \'nēp\ *n* [ME *nepe*, fr. OE *nǣp*, fr. L *napus* — more at NAPIFORM] (bef. 12c) *chiefly Scot* : TURNIP

ne'er \'nar\ *adv* (13c) : NEVER

ne'er–do–well \-,dü-,wel\ *n* (1736) : an idle worthless person — **ne'er–do–well** *adj*

ne·far·i·ous \ni-'far-ē-əs, -'fer-\ *adj* [L *nefarius,* fr. *nefas* crime, fr. *ne-* not + *fas* right, divine law; perh. akin to Gk *themis* law, *tithenai* to place — more at DO] (ca. 1609) : flagrantly wicked or impious : EVIL *syn* see VICIOUS — **ne·far·i·ous·ly** *adv*

ne·gate \ni-'gāt\ *vt* **ne·gat·ed; ne·gat·ing** [L *negatus,* pp. of *negare* to say no, deny, fr. *neg-* no, not (akin to *ne-* not) — more at NO] (ca. 1623) **1** : to deny the existence or truth of **2** : to cause to be ineffective or invalid *syn* see NULLIFY — **negate** *n* — **ne·ga·tor** \-'gā-tər\ *n*

ne·ga·tion \ni-'gā-shən\ *n* (15c) **1 a** : the action or logical operation of negating or making negative **b** : a negative statement, judgment, or doctrine; *esp* : a logical proposition formed by asserting the falsity of a given proposition **2 a** : something that is the absence of something actual : NONENTITY **b** : something considered the opposite of something regarded as positive — **ne·ga·tion·al** \-shnəl, -shə-n⁹l\ *adj*

¹neg·a·tive \'ne-gə-tiv\ *adj* (15c) **1 a** : marked by denial, prohibition, or refusal ⟨received a ~ answer⟩; *also* : marked by absence, withholding, or removal of something positive ⟨the ~ motivation of shame — Garrett Hardin⟩ **b** (1) : denying a predicate of a subject or a part of a subject ⟨"no A is B" is a ~ proposition⟩ (2) : denoting the absence or the contradictory of something ⟨nontoxic is a ~ term⟩ (3) : expressing negation ⟨~ particles such as *no* and *not*⟩ **c** : ADVERSE, UNFAVORABLE ⟨the reviews were mostly ~⟩ **2 a** : lacking positive qualities; *esp* : DISAGREEABLE **b** : marked by features of hostility, withdrawal, or pessimism that hinder or oppose constructive treatment or development ⟨a ~ outlook⟩ ⟨~ criticism⟩ **3 a** (1) : less than zero and opposite in sign to a positive number that when added to the given number yields zero ⟨−2 is a ~ number⟩ (2) : having more outgo than income : constituting a loss ⟨~ cash flow⟩ ⟨~ worth⟩ **b** : extending or generated in a direction opposite to an arbitrarily chosen regular direction or position ⟨~ angle⟩ **4 a** : being, relating to, or charged with electricity of which the electron is the elementary unit **b** : having more electrons than protons ⟨a ~ ion⟩ **c** (1) : having lower electric potential and constituting the part toward which the current flows from the external circuit ⟨the ~ pole⟩ (2) : being the electron-emitting electrode of an electron tube **5 a** : not affirming the presence of the organism or condition in question ⟨a ~ TB test⟩ **b** : directed or moving away from a source of stimulation ⟨~ tropism⟩ **c** : less than the pressure of the atmosphere ⟨~ pressure⟩ **6** : having the light and dark parts in approximately inverse order to those of the original photographic subject **7** *of a lens* : diverging light rays and forming a virtual inverted image — **neg·a·tive·ly** *adv* — **neg·a·tive·ness** *n* — **neg·a·tiv·i·ty** \,ne-gə-'ti-və-tē\ *n*

²negative *n* (1571) **1 a** (1) : a reply that indicates the withholding of assent : REFUSAL (2) *archaic* : a right of veto (3) *obs* : an adverse vote : VETO **b** : a proposition which denies or contradicts another; *esp* : the one of a pair of propositions in which negation is expressed **2 a** : something that is the opposite or negation of something else **b** : DRAWBACK, LIABILITY **3 a** : an expression (as the word *no*) of negation or denial **b** : a negative number **4** : the side that upholds the contradictory proposition in a debate **5** : a negative photographic image on transparent material used for printing positive pictures; *also* : the material that carries such an image **6** : a reverse impression taken from a piece of sculpture or ceramics

³negative *vt* **-tived; -tiv·ing** (1706) **1 a** : to refuse assent to **b** : to reject by or as if by a vote **2** : to demonstrate the falsity of **3** : to deny the truth, reality, or validity of **4** : NEUTRALIZE, COUNTERACT

negative feedback *n* (1934) : feedback that tends to stabilize a process by reducing its rate or output when its effects are too great

negative income tax *n* (1966) : a system of federal subsidy payments to families with incomes below a stipulated level

negative transfer *n* (1921) : the impeding of learning or performance in a situation by the carry-over of learned responses from another situation

neg·a·tiv·ism \'ne-gə-ti,vi-zəm\ *n* (1824) **1** : an attitude of mind marked by skepticism esp. about nearly everything affirmed by others **2** : a tendency to refuse to do, to do the opposite of, or to do something at variance with what is asked — **neg·a·tiv·ist** \-vist\ *n or adj* — **neg·a·tiv·is·tic** \,ne-gə-ti-'vis-tik\ *adj*

¹ne·glect \ni-'glekt\ *vt* [L *neglectus,* pp. of *neglegere, neclegere,* fr. *nec-* not (akin to *ne-* not) + *legere* to gather — more at NO, LEGEND] (1529) **1** : to give little attention or respect to : DISREGARD **2** : to leave undone or unattended to esp. through carelessness — **ne·glect·er** *n* *syn* NEGLECT, DISREGARD, IGNORE, OVERLOOK, SLIGHT, FORGET mean to pass over without giving due attention. NEGLECT implies giving insufficient attention to something that has a claim to one's attention ⟨habitually *neglected* his studies⟩. DISREGARD suggests voluntary inattention ⟨*disregarded* the wishes of other members⟩. IGNORE implies a failure to regard something obvious ⟨*ignored* the snide remark⟩. OVERLOOK suggests disregarding or ignoring through haste or lack of care ⟨in my rush I *overlooked* a key example⟩. SLIGHT implies contemptuous or disdainful disregarding or omitting ⟨*slighted* several major authors in her survey⟩. FORGET may suggest either a willful ignoring or a failure to impress something on one's mind ⟨*forget* what others say and listen to me⟩.

²neglect *n* (1588) **1** : an act or instance of neglecting something **2** : the condition of being neglected

ne·glect·ful \ni-'glek(t)-fəl\ *adj* (1644) : given to neglecting : CARELESS, HEEDLESS *syn* see NEGLIGENT — **ne·glect·ful·ly** \-fə-lē\ *adv* — **ne·glect·ful·ness** *n*

neg·li·gee *also* **neg·li·gé** \,ne-glə-'zhā, 'ne-glə-,\ *n* [F *négligé,* fr. pp. of *négliger* to neglect, fr. L *neglegere*] (1756) **1** : a woman's long flowing usu. sheer dressing gown **2** : carelessly informal or incomplete attire

neg·li·gence \'ne-gli-jən(t)s\ *n* (14c) **1 a** : the quality or state of being negligent **b** : failure to exercise the care that a prudent person usu. exercises **2** : an act or instance of being negligent

neg·li·gent \-jənt\ *adj* [ME, fr. MF & L; MF, fr. L *negligent-, negligens,* prp. of *neglegere*] (14c) **1** : marked by or given to neglect esp. habitually or culpably : not taking prudent care **2** : marked by a carelessly easy manner — **neg·li·gent·ly** *adv* *syn* NEGLIGENT, NEGLECTFUL, LAX, SLACK, REMISS mean culpably careless or indicative of such carelessness. NEGLIGENT implies inattention to one's duty or business ⟨*negligent* about writing a note of thanks⟩. NEGLECTFUL adds a more disapproving implication of laziness or deliberate inattention ⟨a society callously *neglectful* of the poor⟩. LAX im-

plies a blameworthy lack of strictness, severity, or precision ⟨a reporter *lax* about accurate quotation⟩. SLACK implies want of due or necessary diligence or care ⟨*slack* workmanship and slipshod construction⟩. REMISS implies blameworthy carelessness shown in slackness, forgetfulness, or neglect ⟨had been *remiss* in her familial duties⟩.

neg·li·gi·ble \'ne-gli-jə-bəl\ *adj* [L *neglegere, negligere*] (1829) : so small or unimportant or of so little consequence as to warrant little or no attention : TRIFLING — **neg·li·gi·bil·i·ty** \,ne-gli-jə-'bi-lə-tē\ *n* — **neg·li·gi·bly** \'ne-gli-jə-blē\ *adv*

ne·go·tia·ble \ni-'gō-sh(ē-)ə-bəl\ *adj* (1758) : capable of being negotiated: as **a** : transferable from one person to another by being delivered with or without endorsement so that the title passes to the transferee ⟨~ securities⟩ **b** : capable of being traversed, dealt with, or accomplished ⟨a difficult but ~ road⟩ ⟨~ demands⟩ **c** : open to discussion or dispute — **ne·go·tia·bil·i·ty** \-,gō-sh(ē-)ə-'bi-lə-tē\ *n*

ne·go·ti·ant \-'gō-sh(ē-)ənt\ *n* (ca. 1611) : one that negotiates

ne·go·ti·ate \ni-'gō-shē-,āt, -̇-sē-\ *vb* **-at·ed; -at·ing** [L *negotiatus,* pp. of *negotiari* to carry on business, fr. *negotium* business, fr. *neg-* not + *otium* leisure — more at NEGATE] *vi* (1599) : to confer with another so as to arrive at the settlement of some matter ⟨~ vt **1 a** : to deal with ⟨some matter or affair that requires ability for its successful handling⟩ : MANAGE **b** : to arrange for or bring about through conference, discussion, and compromise ⟨~ a treaty⟩ **2 a** : to transfer (as a bill of exchange) to another by delivery or endorsement **b** : to convert into cash or the equivalent value ⟨~ a check⟩ **3 a** : to successfully travel along or over ⟨~ a turn⟩ **b** : COMPLETE, ACCOMPLISH ⟨~ the trip in two hours⟩ — **ne·go·ti·a·tor** \-,ā-tər\ *n* — **ne·go·ti·a·to·ry** \-sh(ē-)ə-,tōr-ē, -̇-sē-, -,tȯr-\ *adj*

ne·go·ti·a·tion \ni-,gō-shē-'ā-shən, -̇-sē-\ *n* (15c) : the action or process of negotiating or being negotiated — often used in pl.

Ne·gress \'nē-grəs\ *n* (1786) : a black woman or girl — sometimes taken to be offensive

Ne·gril·lo \ni-'gri-(,)lō, -'grē-(,)yō\ *n, pl* **-los** *or* **-loes** [Sp, dim. of *negro*] (1853) : a member of a people (as Pygmies) belonging to a group of dark-skinned peoples of small stature that live in Africa

Ne·gri·to \nə-'grē-(,)tō\ *n, pl* **-tos** *or* **-toes** [Sp, dim. of *negro*] (1812) : a member of a people (as the Andamanese) belonging to a group of dark-skinned peoples of small stature that live in Oceania and the southeastern part of Asia

ne·gri·tude \'ne-grə-,tüd, 'nē-, -,tyüd\ *n* [F *négritude,* fr. *nègre* Negro + *-i- + -tude*] (1950) **1** : a consciousness of and pride in the cultural and physical aspects of the African heritage **2** : the state or condition of being black

Ne·gro \'nē-(,)grō\ *n, pl* **Negroes** [Sp or Pg, fr. *negro* black, fr. L *nigr-, niger*] (1555) **1** : a member of the black race distinguished from members of other races by usu. inherited physical and physiological characteristics without regard to language or culture; *esp* : a member of a people belonging to the African branch of the black race — sometimes taken to be offensive **2** : a person of Negro descent — sometimes taken to be offensive — **Negro** *adj* — **Ne·gro·ness** \-grō-nəs\ *n*

ne·groid \'nē-,grȯid\ *adj, often cap* (1859) : of, resembling, related to, or characteristic of the Negro race — **negroid** *n, often cap*

ne·gro·phobe \'nē-grə-,fōb\ *n, often cap* (1900) : one who strongly dislikes or fears black people — **ne·gro·pho·bia** \,nē-grə-'fō-bē-ə\ *n, often cap*

¹ne·gus \'nē-gəs, ni-'güs\ *n* [Amharic *nəgus,* fr. Ge'ez *nĕgŭša nagašt* king of kings] (1594) : KING — used as a title of the sovereign of Ethiopia

²ne·gus \'nē-gəs\ *n* [Francis *Negus* †1732 Eng. colonel] (1743) : a beverage of wine, hot water, sugar, lemon juice, and spices

Ne·he·mi·ah \,nē-(h)ə-'mī-ə\ *n* [Heb *Nĕhemyāh*] **1** : a Jewish leader of the 5th century B.C. who supervised the rebuilding of the Jerusalem city walls and instituted religious reforms in the city **2** : a narrative and historical book of canonical Jewish and Christian Scripture — see BIBLE table

Ne·he·mi·as \-'mī-əs\ *n* [LL, fr. Heb *Nĕhemyāh*] : NEHEMIAH

neigh \'nā\ *vi* [ME *neyen,* fr. OE *hnǣgan;* akin to MHG *nēgen* to neigh] (bef. 12c) : to make the prolonged cry of a horse — **neigh** *n*

¹neigh·bor \'nā-bər\ *n* [ME, fr. OE *nēahgebūr* (akin to OHG *nāhgibūr*); akin to OE *nēah* near and OE *gebūr* dweller — more at NIGH, BOOR] (bef. 12c) **1** : one living or located near another **2** : FELLOWMAN

²neighbor *adj* (1530) : being immediately adjoining or relatively near

³neighbor *vb* **neigh·bored; neigh·bor·ing** \-b(ə-)riŋ\ *vt* (ca. 1586) : to adjoin immediately or lie relatively near to ⟨~ *vi* **1** : to live or be located as a neighbor **2** : to associate in a neighborly way

neigh·bor·hood \'nā-bər-,húd\ *n* (15c) **1** : neighborly relationship **2** : the quality or state of being neighbors : PROXIMITY **3** : a place or region near : VICINITY **b** : an approximate amount, extent, or degree ⟨cost in the ~ of $10⟩ **4 a** : the people living near one another **b** : a section lived in by neighbors and usu. having distinguishing characteristics **5** : the set of all points belonging to a given set whose distances from a given point are less than a given positive number; *broadly* : a set that contains a neighborhood

neigh·bor·ly \-lē\ *adj* (1558) : of, relating to, or characteristic of congenial neighbors; *esp* : FRIENDLY *syn* see AMICABLE — **neigh·bor·li·ness** *n*

neigh·bour \-bər\ *chiefly Brit var of* NEIGHBOR

¹nei·ther \'nē-thər *also* 'nī-\ *conj* [ME, alter. (influenced by *either*) of *nauther, nother,* fr. OE *nāhwæther, nōther,* fr. *nā, nō* not + *hwæther* which of two, whether] (12c) **1** : not either ⟨~ black nor white⟩ **2** : also not ⟨~ did I⟩

usage Although use with *or* is sometimes archaic nor wrong, *neither* is usu. followed by *nor.* A few commentators think that *neither* must be limited in reference to two, but reference to more than two has been quite common since the 17th century ⟨rigid enforcement of antique decorum will help *neither* language, literature, nor literati —James Sledd⟩.

\ə\ abut \ᵊ\ kitten, F table \ər\ further \a\ ash \ā\ ace \ä\ mop, mar \aú\ out \ch\ chin \e\ bet \ē\ easy \g\ go \i\ hit \ī\ ice \j\ job \ŋ\ sing \ō\ go \ȯ\ law \ȯi\ boy \th\ thin \t̷h\ the \ü\ loot \ú\ foot \y\ yet \zh\ vision \à, k̲, ⁿ, œ, œ̄, ɏ, ŭē, ᵒ\ *see* Guide to Pronunciation

²**neither** *pron* (13c) : not the one or the other of two or more
  usage Some commentators insist that *neither* must be used with a singular verb. It generally is, but esp. when a prepositional phrase intervenes between it and the verb, a plural verb is quite common ⟨*neither* of those ideal solutions are in sight —C. P. Snow⟩.
³**neither** *adj* (14c) : not either ⟨~ hand⟩
⁴**neither** *adv* (1551)   **1** *chiefly dial* : EITHER ⟨are not to be understood ~ —Earl of Chesterfield⟩   **2** : similarly not : also not ⟨just as the serf was not permitted to leave the land, so ~ was his offspring —G. G. Coulton⟩
nek·ton \'nek-tən, -ˌtän\ *n* [G *Nekton*, fr. Gk *nēkton*, neut. of *nēktos* swimming, fr. *nēchein* to swim — more at NATANT] (1893) : free-swimming aquatic animals essentially independent of wave and current action — **nek·ton·ic** \nek-'tä-nik\ *adj*
nel·son \'nel-sən\ *n* [prob. fr. the name *Nelson*] (1889) : a wrestling hold marked by the application of leverage against an opponent's arm, neck, and head — compare FULL NELSON, HALF NELSON
nemat- *or* **nemato-** *comb form* [NL, fr. Gk *nēmat-*, fr. *nēmat-*, *nēma*, fr. *nēn* to spin — more at NEEDLE]   **1** : thread ⟨*nematocyst*⟩   **2** : nematode ⟨*nematology*⟩
ne·mat·ic \ni-'ma-tik\ *adj* [ISV *nemat-* + ¹-*ic*] (1923) : of, relating to, or being the phase of a liquid crystal characterized by arrangement of the long axes of the molecules in parallel lines but not layers — compare CHOLESTERIC, SMECTIC
nem·a·to·cide *or* **nem·a·ti·cide** \'ne-mə-tə-ˌsīd, ni-'ma-tə-\ *n* (1898) : a substance or preparation used to destroy nematodes — **nem·a·to·ci·dal** *also* **nem·a·ti·ci·dal** \ˌne-mə-tə-'sī-dᵊl, ni-ˌma-tə-\ *adj*
nem·a·to·cyst \-ˌsist\ *n* [ISV] (1875) : one of the stinging organelles of coelenterates used in catching prey
nem·a·tode \'ne-mə-ˌtōd\ *n* [ultim. fr. Gk *nēmat-*, *nēma*] (1865) : any of a phylum (Nematoda or Nemata) of elongated cylindrical worms parasitic in animals or plants or free-living in soil or water
nem·a·tol·o·gy \ˌne-mə-'tä-lə-jē\ *n* (ca. 1916) : a branch of zoology that deals with nematodes — **nem·a·to·log·i·cal** \ne-mə-tᵊl-'ä-ji-kəl\ *adj* — **nem·a·tol·o·gist** \ˌne-mə-'tä-lə-jist\ *n*
Nem·bu·tal \'nem-byə-ˌtȯl\ *trademark* — used for the sodium salt of pentobarbital
ne·mer·te·an \ni-'mər-tē-ən\ *n* [ultim. fr. Gk *Nēmertēs* Nemertes, one of the Nereids] (1861) : any of a phylum (Nemertea syn. Rhynchocoela) of often vividly colored marine worms most of which burrow in the mud or sand along seacoasts — called also *ribbon worm* — **nem·er·tine** \'ne-mər-ˌtīn\ *adj or n*
nem·e·sis \'ne-mə-səs\ *n* [L, fr. Gk]   **1** *cap* : the Greek goddess of retributive justice   **2** *pl* -**e·ses** \-ˌsēz\   **a** : one that inflicts retribution or vengeance   **b** : a formidable and usu. victorious rival or opponent   **3** *pl* -**eses**   **a** : an act or effect of retribution   **b** : BANE 2
ne·moph·i·la \ni-'mä-fə-lə\ *n* [NL, fr. Gk *nemos* wooded pasture + *philos* loving] (1838) : any of a genus (*Nemophila*) of American annual herbs of the waterleaf family cultivated for their showy blue or white sometimes spotted flowers
ne·ne \'nā-(ˌ)nā\ *n* [Hawaiian *nēnē*] (1902) : an endangered goose (*Branta sandvicensis* syn. *Nesochen sandvicensis*) of the Hawaiian Islands that usu. inhabits waterless uplands and feeds on berries and vegetation
neo- — see NE-
neo·clas·sic \ˌnē-ō-'kla-sik\ *or* **neo·clas·si·cal** \-si-kəl\ *adj* (1877) : of, relating to, or constituting a revival or adaptation of the classical esp. in literature, music, art, or architecture — **neo·clas·si·cism** \-'kla-sə-ˌsi-zəm\ *n* — **neo·clas·si·cist** \-sist\ *n or adj*
neo·co·lo·nial·ism \ˌnē-ō-kə-'lōn-yə-ˌli-zəm, -'lō-nē-ə-ˌli-\ *n* (1961) : the economic and political policies by which a great power indirectly maintains or extends its influence over other areas or people — **neo·co·lo·nial** \-'lōn-yəl, -'lō-nē-əl\ *adj* — **neo·co·lo·nial·ist** \-yə-list, -ə-list\ *n or adj*
neo·con·ser·va·tive \-kən-'sər-və-tiv\ *n* (1955) : a former liberal espousing political conservatism — **neo·con·ser·va·tism** \-və-ˌti-zəm\ *n* — **neoconservative** *adj*
neo·cor·tex \ˌnē-ō-'kȯr-ˌteks\ *n* [NL; fr. its being the cortex of the phylogenetically most recently developed part of the brain] (1909) : the dorsal region of the cerebral cortex that is unique to mammals **neo·cor·ti·cal** \-'kȯr-ti-kəl\ *adj* (1909) : of or relating to the neocortex
neo–Dar·win·ian \-där-'wi-nē-ən\ *adj, often cap N* (1895) : of or relating to neo-Darwinism
neo–Dar·win·ism \-'där-wə-ˌni-zəm\ *n, often cap N* (ca. 1900) : a theory of evolution that is a synthesis of Darwin's theory in terms of natural selection and modern population genetics — **neo–Dar·win·ist** \-'där-wə-nist\ *n, often cap N*
neo·dym·i·um \ˌnē-ō-'di-mē-əm\ *n* [NL, fr. *ne-* + -*dymium* (fr. *didymium*)] (1885) : a yellow metallic element of the rare-earth group that is used in magnets and lasers — see ELEMENT table
neo–Ex·pres·sion·ism \-ik-'spre-shə-ˌni-zəm\ *n, often cap N* (1961) : a revival of expressionism in art characterized by intense colors, dramatic usu. figural forms, and emotive subject matter — **neo–Ex·pres·sion·ist** \-nist\ *n or adj, often cap N*
neo–Freud·ian \-'frȯi-dē-ən\ *adj, often cap N* (1945) : of or relating to a school of psychoanalysis that differs from Freudian orthodoxy in emphasizing the importance of social and cultural factors in the development of an individual's personality — **neo–Freudian** *n, often cap N*
Neo·gene \'nē-ə-ˌjēn\ *adj* [ISV *ne-* + -*gene* (fr. Gk -*genēs* born) — more at -GEN] (1878) : of, relating to, or being the later portion of the Tertiary including the Miocene and Pliocene or the corresponding system of rocks — **Neogene** *n*
neo–Goth·ic \ˌnē-ō-'gä-thik\ *adj* (1892) : of, relating to, or constituting a revival or adaptation of the Gothic esp. in literature or architecture
neo–im·pres·sion·ism \ˌnē-ō-im-'pre-shə-ˌni-zəm\ *n, often cap N&I* [F *néo-impressionisme*, fr. *né-* *ne-* + *impressionisme* impressionism] (1892) : a late 19th century French art theory and practice characterized by

an attempt to make impressionism more precise in form and the use of a pointillist painting technique — **neo·im·pres·sion·ist** \-'pre-sh(ə-)nist\ *adj or n, often cap N&I*
Neo–Lat·in \-'la-tᵊn\ *n* [ISV] (1850)   **1** : NEW LATIN   **2** : ROMANCE 5
neo·lib·er·al \-'li-b(ə-)rəl\ *n* (1945) : a liberal who de-emphasizes traditional liberal doctrines in order to seek progress by more pragmatic methods — **neoliberal** *adj* — **neo·lib·er·al·ism** \-b(ə-)rə-ˌli-zəm\ *n*
neo·lith \'nē-ə-ˌlith\ *n* [back-formation fr. *neolithic*] (1882) : a Neolithic stone implement
neo·lith·ic \ˌnē-ə-'li-thik\ *adj* (1865)   **1** *cap* : of or relating to the latest period of the Stone Age characterized by polished stone implements   **2** : belonging to an earlier age and now outmoded
ne·ol·o·gism \nē-'ä-lə-ˌji-zəm\ *n* [F *néologisme*, fr. *ne-* + *log-* + -*isme* -ism] (1800)   **1** : a new word, usage, or expression   **2** : a meaningless word coined by a psychotic — **ne·ol·o·gis·tic** \-ˌä-lə-'jis-tik\ *adj*
neo–Mal·thu·sian \ˌnē-ō-mal-'thü-zhən, -mȯl-, -'thyü-\ *adj* (1896) : advocating control of population growth (as by contraception) — **neo–Malthusian** *n* — **neo–Mal·thu·sian·ism** \-zhə-ˌni-zəm\ *n*
neo·my·cin \ˌnē-ə-'mī-sᵊn\ *n* (1949) : a broad-spectrum highly toxic antibiotic or mixture of antibiotics produced by a streptomyces (*Streptomyces fradiae*) and used medically esp. to treat local infections
¹**ne·on** \'nē-ˌän\ *n* [Gk, neut. of *neos* new — more at NEW] (1898)   **1** : a colorless odorless mostly inert gaseous element that is found in minute amounts in air and is used in electric lamps — see ELEMENT table   **2** **a** : a discharge lamp in which the gas contains a large proportion of neon   **b** : a sign composed of such lamps   **c** : the illumination provided by such lamps or signs — **ne·oned** \-ˌänd\ *adj*
²**neon** *adj* (1904)   **1** : of, relating to, or using neon   **2** : extremely bright : FLUORESCENT ⟨~ yellow⟩
neo·na·tal \ˌnē-ō-'nā-tᵊl\ *adj* (1902) : of, relating to, or affecting the newborn and esp. the human infant during the first month after birth ⟨~ mortality⟩ — **neo·na·tal·ly** \-tᵊl-ē\ *adv*
ne·o·nate \'nē-ə-ˌnāt\ *n* [NL *neonatus*, fr. *ne-* + L *natus*, pp. of *nasci* to be born — more at NATION] (1932) : a newborn child; *esp* : a child less than a month old
neo·na·tol·o·gy \ˌnē-ō-nā-'tä-lə-jē\ *n* (1960) : a branch of medicine concerned with the care, development, and diseases of newborn infants — **neo·na·tol·o·gist** \-jist\ *n*
neo–Na·zi \ˌnē-ō-'nät-sē, -'nat-\ *n* (1938) : a member of a group espousing the programs and policies of Hitler's Nazis — **neo–Nazi** *adj* — **neo–Na·zism** \-'nät-ˌsi-zəm, -'nat-\ *n*
neo·or·tho·dox \ˌnē-ō-'ȯr-thə-ˌdäks\ *adj* (1946) : of or relating to a 20th century movement in Protestant theology characterized by a reaction against liberalism and emphasis on various scripturally based Reformation doctrines — **neo·or·tho·doxy** \-ˌdäk-sē\ *n*
neo·phil·ia \ˌnē-ə-'fi-lē-ə\ *n* (ca. 1947) : love of or enthusiasm for what is new or novel — **neo·phil·i·ac** \-lē-ˌak\ *n*
neo·phyte \'nē-ə-ˌfīt\ *n* [ME, fr. LL *neophytus*, fr. Gk *neophytos*, fr. *neophytos* newly planted, newly converted, fr. *ne-* + *phyein* to bring forth — more at BE] (14c)   **1** : a new convert : PROSELYTE   **2** : NOVICE 1   **3** : TYRO, BEGINNER
neo·pla·sia \ˌnē-ə-'plā-zh(ē-)ə\ *n* [NL] (1890)   **1** : the formation of tumors   **2** : a tumorous condition
neo·plasm \'nē-ə-ˌpla-zəm\ *n* [ISV] (1864) : a new growth of tissue serving no physiological function : TUMOR
neo·plas·tic \ˌnē-ə-'plas-tik\ *adj* [ISV] (ca. 1890)   **1** : of, relating to, or constituting a neoplasm or neoplasia   **2** : of or relating to neoplasticism
neo·plas·ti·cism \-tə-ˌsi-zəm\ *n* [F *néo-plasticisme*, fr. *ne-* + *plastique* plastic + -*isme* -ism] (1933) : DE STIJL — **neo·plas·ti·cist** \-sist\ *n*
Neo·pla·to·nism \ˌnē-ō-'plā-tᵊn-ˌi-zəm\ *n* (1845)   **1** : Platonism modified in later antiquity to accord with Aristotelian, post-Aristotelian, and oriental conceptions that conceives of the world as an emanation from an ultimate indivisible being with whom the soul is capable of being reunited in trance or ecstasy   **2** : a doctrine similar to ancient Neoplatonism — **Neo·pla·ton·ic** \-plə-'tä-nik, -plä-\ *adj* — **Neo·pla·to·nist** \-'plä-tᵊn-ist\ *n*
neo·prene \'nē-ə-ˌprēn\ *n* [*ne-* + chloroprene] (1937) : a synthetic rubber made by the polymerization of chloroprene, characterized by superior resistance (as to oils), and used esp. for special-purpose clothing (as gloves and wet suits)
neo·re·al·ism \ˌnē-ō-'rē-ə-ˌli-zəm, -'ri-ə-\ *n* (1950) : a movement esp. in Italian filmmaking characterized by the simple direct depiction of lower-class life — **neo·re·al·ist** \-list\ *n or adj* — **neo·re·al·is·tic** \-ˌrē-ə-'lis-tik, -ˌri-ə-\ *adj*
Neo·ri·can \nē-ō-'rē-kən\ *n* [AmerSp *neorriqueño* Puerto Rican living in New York City, blend of Sp *neoyorquino* New Yorker and *puertorriqueño* Puerto Rican] (1970) : a Puerto Rican who lives on the U.S. mainland or has lived there but has returned to Puerto Rico
neo·scho·las·ti·cism \ˌnē-ō-skə-'las-tə-ˌsi-zəm\ *n* (ca. 1909) : a movement among Catholic scholars aiming to restate medieval Scholasticism in a manner suited to present intellectual needs
neo·stig·mine \ˌnē-ō-'stig-ˌmēn\ *n* [*ne-* + -*stigmine* (as in *physostigmine*)] (1941) : a cholinergic drug used in the form of its bromide $C_{12}H_{19}BrN_2O_2$ or a methyl sulfate derivative $C_{13}H_{22}N_2O_6S$ esp. in the treatment of some ophthalmic conditions and in the diagnosis and treatment of myasthenia gravis
ne·o·te·ny \nē-'ä-tᵊn-ē\ *n* [NL *neotenia*, fr. *ne-* + Gk *teinein* to stretch — more at THIN] (1901)   **1** : retention of some larval or immature characters in adulthood   **2** : attainment of sexual maturity during the larval stage — **ne·o·ten·ic** \ˌnē-ə-'te-nik\ *adj*
ne·o·ter·ic \ˌnē-ə-'ter-ik\ *adj* [LL *neotericus*, fr. LGk *neōterikos*, fr. Gk, youthful, fr. *neōteros*, compar. of *neos* new, young — more at NEW] (1596) : recent in origin : MODERN
Neo·trop·i·cal \ˌnē-ō-'trä-pi-kəl\ *also* **Neo·trop·ic** \-pik\ *adj* [ISV] (1858) : of, relating to, or constituting the biogeographic region that extends south, east, and west from the central plateau of Mexico
neo·trop·ics \-'trä-piks\ *n pl* (1923) : the Neotropical region
neo·type \'nē-ə-ˌtīp\ *n* (1905) : a type specimen that is selected subsequent to the description of a species to replace a preexisting type that has been lost or destroyed
Ne·pali \nə-'pȯ-lē, -'pä-, -'pa-\ *n, pl* **Nepali** *also* **Ne·pal·is** [Hindi *naipāli* of Nepal, fr. Skt *naipālīya*, fr. *Nepāla* Nepal] (ca. 1885)   **1** : a

native or inhabitant of Nepal **2** : an Indo-Aryan language spoken in Nepal — **Nepali** *adj*

ne·pen·the \nə-'pen(t)-thē\ *n* [L *nepenthes*, fr. Gk *nēpenthes*, neut. of *nēpenthēs* banishing pain and sorrow, fr. *nē*- not + *penthos* grief, sorrow; akin to Gk *pathos* suffering — more at NO, PATHOS] (1580) **1** : a potion used by the ancients to induce forgetfulness of pain or sorrow **2** : something capable of causing oblivion of grief or suffering — **ne·pen·the·an** \-thē-ən\ *adj*

neph·e·line \'ne-fə-ˌlēn\ *also* **neph·e·lite** \-ˌlīt\ *n* [F *néphéline*, fr. Gk *nephelē* cloud — more at NEBULA] (ca. 1814) : a hexagonal mineral that is a usu. glassy crystalline silicate of sodium, potassium, and aluminum common in igneous rocks — **neph·e·lin·ic** \ˌne-fə-'li-nik\ *adj*

neph·e·lin·ite \'ne-fə-lə-ˌnīt\ *n* [ISV] (ca. 1863) : a silica-deficient igneous rock having nepheline as the predominant mineral — **neph·e·lin·it·ic** \ˌne-fə-lə-'ni-tik\ *adj*

neph·e·lom·e·ter \ˌne-fə-'lä-mə-tər\ *n* [Gk *nephelē* cloud + ISV *-meter*] (1884) **1** : an instrument for measuring the extent or degree of cloudiness **2** : an instrument for determining the concentration or particle size of suspensions by means of transmitted or reflected light — **neph·e·lo·met·ric** \ˌne-fə-lō-'me-trik\ *adj* — **neph·e·lo·met·ri·cal·ly** \-tri-k(ə-)lē\ *adv* — **neph·e·lom·e·try** \-'lä-mə-trē\ *n*

neph·ew \'ne-(ˌ)fyü, *chiefly Brit* -(ˌ)vyü\ *n* [ME *nevew*, fr. OF *neveu*, fr. L *nepot-*, *nepos* grandson, nephew; akin to OE *nefa* grandson, nephew, Skt *napāt* grandson] (14c) **1 a** : a son of one's brother or sister or of one's brother-in-law or sister-in-law **b** : an illegitimate son of an ecclesiastic **2** *obs* : a lineal descendant; *esp* : GRANDSON

nepho·scope \'ne-fə-ˌskōp\ *n* [Gk *nephos* cloud + ISV *-scope* — more at NEBULA] (1881) : an instrument for observing the direction and velocity of clouds

nephr- *or* **nephro-** *comb form* [NL, fr. Gk, fr. *nephros* — more at NEPHRITIS] : kidney ⟨*nephric*⟩ ⟨*nephrology*⟩

ne·phrec·to·my \ni-'frek-tə-mē\ *n, pl* **-mies** [ISV] (1880) : the surgical removal of a kidney — **ne·phrec·to·mize** \-ˌmīz\ *vt*

neph·ric \'ne-frik\ *adj* (1887) : RENAL

ne·phrid·i·um \ni-'fri-dē-əm\ *n, pl* **-ia** \-dē-ə\ [NL] (1877) : a tubular glandular excretory organ characteristic of various invertebrates — **ne·phrid·i·al** \-dē-əl\ *adj*

neph·rite \'ne-ˌfrīt\ *n* [G *Nephrit*, fr. Gk *nephros*; fr. its formerly being worn as a remedy for kidney diseases] (1794) : a compact tremolite or actinolite that is the commoner and less valuable kind of jade and that varies in color from white to dark green or black

ne·phrit·ic \ni-'fri-tik\ *adj* (1580) **1** : RENAL **2** : of, relating to, or affected with nephritis

ne·phri·tis \ni-'frī-təs\ *n, pl* **ne·phrit·i·des** \-'fri-tə-ˌdēz\ [LL, fr. Gk, fr. *nephros* kidney; prob. akin to ME *nere* kidney] (1580) : acute or chronic inflammation of the kidney caused by infection, degenerative process, or vascular disease

ne·phrol·o·gy \ni-'frä-lə-jē\ *n* (ca. 1842) : a branch of medicine concerned with the kidneys — **ne·phrol·o·gist** \-jist\ *n*

neph·ron \'ne-ˌfrän\ *n* [G, fr. Gk *nephros*] (1932) : a single excretory unit of the vertebrate kidney

ne·phrop·a·thy \ni-'frä-pə-thē\ *n, pl* **-thies** [ISV] (ca. 1900) : an abnormal state of the kidney; *esp* : one associated with or secondary to some other pathological process — **neph·ro·path·ic** \ˌne-frə-'pa-thik\ *adj*

ne·phro·sis \ni-'frō-səs\ *n* [NL] (1916) : a noninflammatory disease of the kidneys chiefly affecting function of the nephrons; *also* : NEPHROTIC SYNDROME — **ne·phrot·ic** \-'frä-tik\ *adj or n*

neph·ro·stome \'ne-frə-ˌstōm\ *n* [NL *nephrostoma*, fr. *nephr-* + *stoma*] (1888) : the ciliated funnel-shaped coelomic opening of a typical nephridium

nephrotic syndrome *n* (1939) : an abnormal condition that is marked by deficiency of albumin in the blood and its excretion in the urine due to altered permeability of the glomerular basement membranes

neph·ro·tox·ic \ˌne-frə-'täk-sik\ *adj* (1902) : poisonous to the kidney ⟨~ drugs⟩; *also* : resulting from or marked by poisoning of the kidney ⟨~ effects⟩ — **neph·ro·tox·i·ci·ty** \-ˌtäk-'si-sə-tē\ *n*

ne plus ul·tra \ˌnā-ˌpləs-'əl-trə, ˌnē-\ *n* [NL, (go) no more beyond] (1638) **1** : the highest point capable of being attained : ACME **2** : the most profound degree of a quality or state

nep·o·tism \'ne-pə-ˌti-zəm\ *n* [F *népotisme*, fr. It *nepotismo*, fr. *nepote* nephew, fr. L *nepot-*, *nepos* grandson, nephew — more at NEPHEW] (1670) : favoritism (as in appointment to a job) based on kinship — **nep·o·tis·tic** \ˌne-pə-'tis-tik\ *adj*

Nep·tune \'nep-ˌtün, -ˌtyün\ *n* [L *Neptunus*] **1 a** : the Roman god of the sea — compare POSEIDON **b** : OCEAN **2** : the planet 8th in order from the sun — see PLANET table — **Nep·tu·ni·an** \nep-'tü-nē-ən, -'tyü-\ *adj*

nep·tu·ni·um \nep-'tü-nē-əm, -'tyü-\ *n* [NL, fr. ISV *Neptune*] (1941) : a radioactive metallic element that is chemically similar to uranium and is obtained in nuclear reactors as a by-product in the production of plutonium — see ELEMENT table

nerd \'nərd\ *n* [perh. fr. *nerd*, a creature in the children's book *If I Ran the Zoo* (1950) by Dr. Seuss (Theodor Geisel)] (1951) : an unstylish, unattractive, or socially inept person; *esp* : one slavishly devoted to intellectual or academic pursuits (computer ~s) — **nerd·ish** \'nər-dish\ *adj* — **nerdy** \-dē\ *adj*

ne·re·id \'nir-ē-əd\ *n* [NL *Nereidae*, fr. *Nereis*, a genus, fr. L, Nereid] (1840) : any of a family (Nereidae) of polychaete worms; *esp* : any of a genus (*Nereis*) of usu. large often dimorphic and greenish mostly marine worms — **nereid** *adj*

Ne·re·id \'nir-ē-əd\ *n* [L *Nereid-*, *Nereis*, fr. Gk *Nērēid-*, *Nēreis*, fr. *Nēreus* Nereus] (1680) : any of the sea nymphs fathered by Nereus

Ne·re·us \'nir-ē-əs\ *n* [L, fr. Gk *Nēreus*] : a sea-god in Greek mythology

ne·rit·ic \nə-'ri-tik\ *adj* [ISV, perh. fr. NL *Nerita*, genus of marine snails] (1891) : of, relating to, inhabiting, or constituting the belt or region of shallow water adjoining the seacoast

ne·rol \'ner-ˌōl, 'nir-\ *n* [ISV *ner-* (fr. *neroli oil*) + ¹*-ol*] (1869) : a liquid alcohol $C_{10}H_{18}O$ that has a rose scent and is used in perfumery

ner·o·li oil \'ner-ə-lē-\ *n* [F *néroli*, fr. It *neroli*, fr. Anna Maria de La Trémoille, princess of *Nerola* fl1670] (1849) : a fragrant pale yellow essential oil obtained from orange flowers and used esp. in cologne and as a flavoring

nerts \'nərts\ *n pl* [alter. of *nuts*] (ca. 1932) *slang* : NONSENSE, NUTS — often used interjectionally

ner·va·tion \ˌnər-'vā-shən\ *n* (1849) : an arrangement or system of nerves; *also* : VENATION

¹**nerve** \'nərv\ *n* [L *nervus* sinew, nerve; akin to Gk *neuron* sinew, nerve, *nēn* to spin — more at NEEDLE] (14c) **1** : SINEW, TENDON ⟨strain every ~⟩ **2** : any of the filamentous bands of nervous tissue that connect parts of the nervous system with the other organs, conduct nervous impulses, and are made up of axons and dendrites together with protective and supportive structures **3 a** : power of endurance or control : FORTITUDE, STRENGTH **b** : ASSURANCE, BOLDNESS; *also* : presumptuous audacity : GALL **4 a** : a sore or sensitive point **b** *pl* : nervous disorganization or collapse : NERVOUSNESS **5** : VEIN 3 **6** : the sensitive pulp of a tooth *syn* see TEMERITY

²**nerve** *vt* **nerved; nerv·ing** (ca. 1749) : to give strength or courage to : supply with physical or moral force

nerve cell *n* (1858) : NEURON; *also* : CELL BODY

nerve center *n* (1868) **1** : CENTER 2c **2** : a source of leadership, organization, control, or energy ⟨the financial *nerve center* of the nation⟩

nerve cord *n* (1877) **1** : the pair of closely united ventral longitudinal nerves with their segmental ganglia that is characteristic of many elongate invertebrates (as earthworms) **2** : the dorsal tubular cord of nervous tissue above the notochord of a chordate that comprises or develops into the central nervous system

nerved \'nərvd\ *adj* (1800) **1 a** : VEINED ⟨a ~ wing⟩ **b** : having veins or nerves esp. of a specified kind or number — used in combination ⟨fan-*nerved* leaves⟩ **2** : showing courage or strength

nerve ending *n* (ca. 1890) : a structure forming the distal end of a nerve axon

nerve fiber *n* (ca. 1847) : any of the processes (as axons or dendrites) of a neuron

nerve gas *n* (1940) : an organophosphate chemical weapon that interferes with normal nerve transmission and induces intense bronchial spasm with resulting inhibition of respiration

nerve growth factor *n* (1962) : a protein that promotes development of the sensory and sympathetic nervous systems and is required for maintenance of sympathetic neurons

nerve impulse *n* (1900) : the progressive physicochemical change in the membrane of a nerve fiber that follows stimulation and serves to transmit a record of sensation from a receptor or an instruction to act to an effector — called also *nervous impulse*

nerve·less \'nərv-ləs\ *adj* (1742) **1** : lacking strength or courage : FEEBLE **2** : exhibiting control or balance : POISED, COOL — **nerve·less·ly** *adv* — **nerve·less·ness** *n*

nerve net *n* (1904) : a network of nerve cells apparently continuous with one another and conducting impulses in all directions; *also* : a primitive nervous system (as in a jellyfish) consisting of such a network

nerve–rack·ing *or* **nerve–wrack·ing** \'nərv-ˌra-kiŋ\ *adj* (1812) : extremely trying on the nerves ⟨a ~ ordeal⟩

nerve trunk *n* (1851) : a bundle of nerve fibers enclosed in a connective tissue sheath

ner·vos·i·ty \ˌnər-'vä-sə-tē\ *n* (1787) : the quality or state of being nervous

ner·vous \'nər-vəs\ *adj* (14c) **1** *archaic* : SINEWY, STRONG **2** : marked by strength of thought, feeling, or style : SPIRITED ⟨a vibrant tight-packed ~ style of writing⟩ **3** : of, relating to, or composed of neurons **4 a** : of or relating to the nerves; *also* : originating in or affected by the nerves ⟨~ energy⟩ **b** : easily excited or irritated : JUMPY **c** : TIMID, APPREHENSIVE ⟨a ~ smile⟩ **5 a** : tending to produce nervousness or agitation : UNEASY ⟨a ~ situation⟩ **b** : appearing or acting unsteady, erratic, or irregular — used of inanimate things *syn* see VIGOROUS — **ner·vous·ly** *adv* — **ner·vous·ness** *n*

nervous breakdown *n* (1905) : an attack of mental or emotional disorder esp. when of sufficient severity to require hospitalization

nervous Nel·lie *or* **nervous Nel·ly** \-'ne-lē\ *n, pl* **nervous Nellies** *often cap 1st N* [fr. the name *Nellie*] (1926) : a timid or worrisome person

nervous system *n* (1740) : the bodily system that in vertebrates is made up of the brain and spinal cord, nerves, ganglia, and parts of the receptor organs and that receives and interprets stimuli and transmits impulses to the effector organs — compare CENTRAL NERVOUS SYSTEM; AUTONOMIC NERVOUS SYSTEM, PERIPHERAL NERVOUS SYSTEM

ner·vure \'nər-vyər\ *n* [F, fr. *nerf* sinew, fr. L *nervus*] (1816) : VEIN 3

nervy \'nər-vē\ *adj* **nerv·i·er; -est** (1607) **1** *archaic* : SINEWY, STRONG **2 a** : showing calm courage : BOLD **b** : marked by effrontery or presumption : BRASH **3** : EXCITABLE, NERVOUS — **nerv·i·ly** \-və-lē\ *adv* — **nerv·i·ness** \-vē-nəs\ *n*

ne·science \'ne-sh(ē-)ən(t)s, 'nē-, -sē-ən(t)s\ *n* [LL *nescientia*, fr. L *nescient-*, *nesciens*, prp. of *nescire* not to know, fr. *ne-* not + *scire* to know — more at NO, SCIENCE] (1612) : lack of knowledge or awareness : IGNORANCE — **ne·scient** \-sh(ē-)ənt, -sē-ənt\ *adj*

ness \'nes\ *n* [ME *nasse*, fr. OE *næss*; akin to OE *nasu* nose — more at NOSE] (bef. 12c) : CAPE, PROMONTORY

-ness \nəs\ *n suffix* [ME *-nes*, fr. OE; akin to OHG *-nissa* -ness] : state : condition : quality : degree ⟨good*ness*⟩

Nes·sel·rode \'ne-səl-ˌrōd\ *n* [Count Karl R. *Nesselrode* †1862 Russ. statesman] (1845) : a mixture of candied fruits, nuts, and maraschino used in puddings, pies, and ice cream

Nes·sus \'ne-səs\ *n* [L, fr. Gk *Nessos*] : a centaur slain by Hercules for trying to carry away Hercules' wife but avenged by means of a poisoned garment that causes Hercules to die in torment

¹**nest** \'nest\ *n* [ME, fr. OE; akin to OHG *nest* nest, L *nidus*] (bef. 12c) **1 a** : a bed or receptacle prepared by an animal and esp. a bird for its eggs and young **b** : a place or specially modified structure serving as an abode of animals and esp. of their immature stages ⟨an ants' ~⟩ **c** : a receptacle resembling a bird's nest **2 a** : a place of rest, retreat, or lodging : HOME ⟨grown children who have left the ~⟩ **b** : DEN,

---

\ə\ abut \ᵊ\ kitten, F table \ər\ further \a\ ash \ā\ ace \ä\ mop, mar \aú\ out \ch\ chin \e\ bet \ē\ easy \g\ go \i\ hit \ī\ ice \j\ job \ŋ\ sing \ō\ go \ó\ law \ói\ boy \th\ thin \t̲h̲\ the \ü\ loot \ú\ foot \y\ yet \zh\ vision \ä, k̸, ⁿ, œ, œ̄, ᵫ, ᵫ̄, �803\ *see* Guide to Pronunciation

HANGOUT **3** : the occupants or frequenters of a nest **4 a** : a group of similar things : AGGREGATION ⟨a ~ of giant mountains —Helen Mac-Innes⟩ **b** : HOTBED 2 ⟨a ~ of rebellion⟩ **5** : a group of objects made to fit close together or one within another **6** : an emplaced group of weapons

²**nest** vi (13c) **1** : to build or occupy a nest : settle in or as if in a nest **2** : to fit compactly together or within one another : EMBED ~ vt **1** : to form a nest for **2** : to pack compactly together **3** : to form a hierarchy, series, or sequence of with each member, element, or set contained in or containing the next ⟨~ed subroutines in a computer program⟩

nest egg n (14c) **1** : a natural or artificial egg left in a nest to induce a fowl to continue to lay there **2** : a fund of money accumulated as a reserve

nest·er \'nes-tər\ n (1880) **1** West : a homesteader or squatter who takes up land on open range for a farm **2** : one that nests

nes·tle \'ne-səl\ vb **nes·tled; nes·tling** \-s(ə-)liŋ\ [ME, fr. OE nestlian, fr. nest] vi (bef. 12c) **1** archaic : NEST 1 **2** : to settle snugly or comfortably **3** : to lie in an inconspicuous or sheltered manner ~ vt **1** : to settle, shelter, or house in or as if in a nest ⟨the children were nestled all snug in their beds —Clement Moore⟩ **2** : to press closely and affectionately ⟨~s a kitten in her arms⟩ — **nes·tler** \-s(ə-)lər\ n

nest·ling \'nest-liŋ\ n (14c) : a young bird that has not abandoned the nest

Nes·tor \'nes-tər, -,tȯr\ n [L, fr. Gk Nestōr] **1** : a king of Pylos who serves in his old age as a counselor to the Greeks at Troy **2** often not cap : one who is a patriarch or leader in a field

Nes·to·ri·an \ne-'stȯr-ē-ən, -'stȯr-\ adj (1565) **1** : of or relating to the doctrine ascribed to Nestorius and ecclesiastically condemned in 431 that divine and human persons remained separate in the incarnate Christ **2** : of or relating to a church separating from Byzantine Christianity after 431, centering in Persia, and surviving chiefly in Asia Minor — **Nestorian** n — **Nes·to·ri·an·ism** \-ə-,ni-zəm\ n

¹**net** \'net\ n [ME nett, fr. OE; akin to OHG nezzi net] (bef. 12c) **1 a** : an open-meshed fabric twisted, knotted, or woven together at regular intervals **b** : something made of net: as (1) : a device for catching fish, birds, or insects (2) : a fabric barricade which divides a court in half (as in tennis or volleyball) and over which a ball or shuttlecock must be hit to be in play (3) : the fabric that encloses the sides and back of the goal in various games (as soccer or hockey) **2** : an entrapping device or situation ⟨caught in the ~ of suspicious circumstances⟩ **3** : something resembling a net in reticulation ⟨as of lines, fibers, or figures⟩ **4 a** : a group of communications stations operating under unified control **b** : NETWORK 4 — **net·less** \-ləs\ adj — **net·like** \-,līk\ adj — **net·ty** \'ne-tē\ adj

²**net** vt **net·ted; net·ting** (1593) **1** : to cover or enclose with or as if with a net **2** : to catch in or as if in a net **3** : to cover with or as if with a network **4 a** : to hit (a ball) into the net for the loss of a point in a racket game **b** : to hit (a ball or puck) into the goal for a score (as in hockey or soccer) — **net·ter** n

³**net** adj [ME, clean, bright, fr. MF — more at NEAT] (15c) **1** : free from all charges or deductions: as **a** : remaining after the deduction of all charges, outlay, or loss ⟨~ earnings⟩ ⟨~ worth⟩ — compare GROSS **b** : excluding all tare ⟨~ weight⟩ **2** : excluding all nonessential considerations : BASIC, FINAL ⟨the ~ result⟩ ⟨~ effect⟩

⁴**net** vt **net·ted; net·ting** (1758) **1 a** : to receive by way of profit : CLEAR **b** : to produce by way of profit : YIELD **2** : to get possession of : GAIN

⁵**net** n (ca. 1904) **1** : a net amount, profit, weight, or price **2** : the score of a golfer in a handicap match after deducting his handicap from his gross **3** : FINESSE, GIST

neth·er \'ne-thər\ adj [ME, fr. OE nithera, fr. nither down; akin to OHG nidar down, Skt nī] (bef. 12c) **1** : situated down or below : LOWER ⟨the ~ side⟩ **2** : situated or believed to be situated beneath the earth's surface ⟨the ~ regions⟩

neth·er·most \-,mōst\ adj (14c) : farthest down : LOWEST

neth·er·world \-,wərld\ n (1638) **1** : the world of the dead **2** : UNDERWORLD 4 ⟨the ~ of deceit, subversion, and espionage —R. M. Nixon⟩

net·mind·er \'net-,mīn-dər\ n (1937) : GOALKEEPER

net·su·ke \'nets-(,)kā, -kē, -ke also 'net-sü-\ n, pl **netsuke** or **netsukes** [Jp] (1876) : a small and often intricately carved toggle (as of wood, ivory, or metal) used to fasten a small container to a kimono sash

nett Brit var of NET

net·ting \'ne-tiŋ\ n (1567) **1** : NETWORK 1 **2** : the act or process of making a net or network **3** : the act, process, or right of fishing with a net

¹**net·tle** \'ne-t°l\ n [ME, fr. OE netel; akin to OHG nazza nettle, Gk adikē] (bef. 12c) **1** : any of a genus (Urtica of the family Urticaceae, the nettle family) of chiefly coarse herbs armed with stinging hairs **2** : any of various prickly or stinging plants other than the true nettles (genus Urtica)

²**nettle** vt **net·tled; net·tling** \'net-liŋ, 'ne-t°l-iŋ\ (15c) **1** : to strike or sting with or as if with nettles **2** : to arouse to sharp but transitory annoyance or anger **syn** see IRRITATE

nettle rash n (1740) : URTICARIA

net·tle·some \'ne-t°l-səm\ adj (1766) : causing vexation : IRRITATING

net-veined \'net-,vānd\ adj (1861) : having veins arranged in a fine network ⟨a ~ leaf⟩ — compare PARALLEL-VEINED; see VENATION illustration — **net venation** n

net-winged \-,wiŋd\ adj (ca. 1890) : having wings with a fine network of veins

¹**net·work** \'net-,wərk\ n (1560) **1** : a fabric or structure of cords or wires that cross at regular intervals and are knotted or secured at the crossings **2** : a system of lines or channels resembling a network **3 a** : an interconnected or interrelated chain, group, or system ⟨a ~ of hotels⟩ **b** : a system of computers, terminals, and databases connected by communications lines **4 a** : a group of radio or television stations linked by wire or radio relay **b** : a radio or television company that produces programs for broadcast over such a network

²**network** vt (1887) **1** : to cover with or as if with a network ⟨a continent . . . so ~ed with navigable rivers and canals —Lamp⟩ **2** chiefly Brit : to distribute for broadcast on a television network; also : BROAD-

CAST 3 **3** : to join (as computers) in a network ~ vi : to engage in networking

net·work·ing n (1966) **1** : the exchange of information or services among individuals, groups, or institutions **2** : the establishment or use of a computer network

Neuf·châ·tel \,nü-shä-'tel, ,nyü-, ,nə(r)-\ n [F, fr. Neufchâtel, France] (ca. 1865) : a soft unripened cheese similar to cream cheese but containing less fat and more moisture

neume \'nüm, 'nyüm\ n [ME, fr. ML pneuma, neuma, fr. Gk pneuma breath — more at PNEUMATIC] (14c) : any of various symbols used in the notation of Gregorian chant — **neu·mat·ic** \nü-'ma-tik, nyü-\ adj

neur- or **neuro-** comb form [NL, fr. Gk, nerve, sinew, fr. neuron — more at NERVE] **1** : nerve ⟨neural⟩ ⟨neurology⟩ **2** : neural : neural and ⟨neuromuscular⟩

neu·ral \'nùr-əl, 'nyùr-\ adj (ca. 1847) **1** : of, relating to, or affecting a nerve or the nervous system **2** : situated in the region of or on the same side of the body as the brain and spinal cord : DORSAL — **neu·ral·ly** \-ə-lē\ adv

neural arch n (ca. 1860) : the cartilaginous or bony arch enclosing the spinal cord on the dorsal side of a vertebra

neural crest n (ca. 1885) : the ridge of one of the folds forming the neural tube that gives rise to the spinal ganglia and various structures of the autonomic nervous system

neu·ral·gia \nù-'ral-jə, nyù-\ n [NL] (ca. 1834) : acute paroxysmal pain radiating along the course of one or more nerves usu. without demonstrable changes in the nerve structure — **neu·ral·gic** \-jik\ adj

neural net n (1949) : a computer architecture in which a number of processors are interconnected in a manner suggestive of the connections between neurons in a human brain and which is able to learn by a process of trial and error — called also neural network

neural plate n (1888) : a thickened plate of ectoderm along the dorsal midline of the early vertebrate embryo that gives rise to the neural tube and crests

neural tube n (1888) : the hollow longitudinal dorsal tube formed by infolding and subsequent fusion of the opposite ectodermal folds in the vertebrate embryo that gives rise to the brain and spinal cord

neur·amin·i·dase \,nùr-ə-'mi-nə-,dās, ,nyùr-, -,dāz\ n [neuraminic acid, an amino acid + -ide + -ase] (1956) : a glycosidase that splits mucoproteins by breaking a glucoside link and occurs esp. in influenza viruses as an antigen

neur·as·the·nia \,nùr-əs-'thē-nē-ə, ,nyùr-\ n [NL] (1856) : an emotional and psychic disorder that is characterized esp. by easy fatigability and often by lack of motivation, feelings of inadequacy, and psychosomatic symptoms — **neur·as·then·ic** \-'the-nik, -'thē-\ adj or n — **neur·as·then·i·cal·ly** \-ni-k(ə-)lē\ adv

neu·ri·lem·ma \,nùr-ə-'le-mə, ,nyùr-\ n [NL, fr. neur- + Gk eilēma covering, coil, fr. eilein to wind; akin to Gk eilyein to wrap — more at VOLUBLE] (1852) : the plasma membrane surrounding a Schwann cell of a myelinated nerve fiber and separating layers of myelin — **neu·ri·lem·mal** \-'le-məl\ adj

neu·ri·tis \nù-'rī-təs, nyù-\ n, pl **-rit·i·des** \-'ri-tə-,dēz\ or **-ri·tis·es** [NL] (1840) : an inflammatory or degenerative lesion of a nerve marked esp. by pain, sensory disturbances, and impaired or lost reflexes — **neu·rit·ic** \-'ri-tik\ adj or n

neu·ro·ac·tive \,nùr-ō-'ak-tiv, ,nyùr-\ adj (1961) : stimulating neural tissue

neu·ro·anat·o·my \-ə-'na-tə-mē\ n (ca. 1899) : the anatomy of nervous tissue and the nervous system — **neu·ro·an·a·tom·i·cal** \-,a-nə-'tä-mi-kəl\ also **neu·ro·an·a·tom·ic** \-mik\ adj — **neu·ro·anat·o·mist** \-ə-'na-tə-mist\ n

neu·ro·bi·ol·o·gy \-bī-'ä-lə-jē\ n (1906) : a branch of the life sciences that deals with the anatomy, physiology, and pathology of the nervous system — **neu·ro·bi·o·log·i·cal** \-,bī-ə-'lä-ji-kəl\ adj — **neu·ro·bi·ol·o·gist** \-bī-'ä-lə-jist\ n

neu·ro·blas·to·ma \-blas-'tō-mə\ n, pl **-mas** or **-ma·ta** \-mə-tə\ [NL, fr. ISV neuroblast embryonic ganglion cell, fr. neur- + -blast -blast] (1910) : a malignant tumor formed of embryonic ganglion cells

neu·ro·chem·is·try \-'ke-mə-strē\ n (1924) **1** : the study of the chemical makeup and activities of nervous tissue **2** : chemical processes and phenomena related to the nervous system — **neu·ro·chem·i·cal** \-'ke-mi-kəl\ adj or n — **neu·ro·chem·ist** \-'ke-mist\ n

neu·ro·de·gen·er·a·tive \-di-'je-nə-rə-tiv, -'jen-rə-; -'je-nə-,rā-; -dē-\ adj (1907) : relating to or characterized by degeneration of nervous tissue

neu·ro·en·do·crine \-'en-də-krən, -,krīn, -,krēn\ adj (1922) **1** : of, relating to, or being a hormonal substance that influences the activity of nerves **2** : of, relating to, or functioning in neurosecretion

neu·ro·en·do·cri·nol·o·gy \-,en-də-kri-'nä-lə-jē, -(,)krī-\ n (1922) : a branch of the life sciences dealing with neurosecretion and the physiological interaction between the central nervous system and the endocrine system — **neu·ro·en·do·cri·no·log·i·cal** \-,kri-n°l-'ä-ji-kəl, -,krī-, -,krē-\ adj — **neu·ro·en·do·cri·nol·o·gist** \-kri-'nä-lə-jist, -,krī-\ n

neu·ro·fi·bril \-'fī-brəl, -'fi-\ n [NL neurofibrilla, fr. neur- + fibrilla fibril] (1898) : a fine proteinaceous fibril that is found in cytoplasm (as of a neuron or a paramecium) and is capable of conducting excitation — **neu·ro·fi·bril·lary** \-brə-,ler-ē\ adj

neu·ro·fi·bro·ma \-fī-'brō-mə\ n (1892) : a fibroma composed of nervous and connective tissue and produced by proliferation of Schwann cells

neu·ro·fi·bro·ma·to·sis \-(,)fī-,brō-mə-'tō-səs\ n [NL, fr. neurofibromat-, neurofibroma] (1896) : a disorder inherited as an autosomal dominant and characterized esp. by brown spots on the skin, neurofibromas of peripheral nerves, and deformities of subcutaneous tissue and bone

neu·ro·gen·ic \,nùr-ə-'je-nik, ,nyùr-\ adj (1901) **1** : originating in or controlled by nervous tissue ⟨~ heartbeat⟩ **2** : induced or modified by nervous factors; esp : disordered because of abnormally altered neural relations — **neu·ro·gen·i·cal·ly** \-ni-k(ə-)lē\ adv

neu·ro·glia \nù-'rō-glē-ə, nyù-, -'rä-; ,n(y)ùr-ə-'glē-ə, -'gli-\ n [NL, fr. neur- + MGk glia glue — more at CLAY] (1873) : supporting tissue intermingled with the essential elements of nervous tissue esp. in the brain, spinal cord, and ganglia — **neu·ro·gli·al** \-əl\ adj

neu·ro·hor·mon·al \,nŭr-ō-hŏr-'mō-n°l, ,nyŭr-\ *adj* (ca. 1935) **1** : involving both neural and hormonal mechanisms **2** : of, relating to, or being a neurohormone

neu·ro·hor·mone \-'hŏr-,mōn\ *n* [ISV] (1935) : a hormone (as acetylcholine or norepinephrine) produced by or acting on nervous tissue

neu·ro·hu·mor \-'hyü-mər, -'yü-\ *n* (1932) : NEUROHORMONE; *esp* : NEUROTRANSMITTER — **neu·ro·hu·mor·al** \-mə-rəl\ *adj*

neu·ro·hy·poph·y·sis \-hī-'pä-fə-səs\ *n* [NL] (1912) : the portion of the pituitary gland that is composed of the infundibulum and posterior lobe and is concerned with the secretion of various hormones — **neu·ro·hy·po·phys·e·al** *or* **neu·ro·hy·po·phys·i·al** \-(,)hī-,pä-fə-'sē-əl, -,hī-pə-fə-, -'zē-, -,hī-pə-fə-'sē-əl\ *adj*

neu·ro·lep·tic \,nŭr-ə-'lep-tik, ,nyŭr-\ *n* [F *neuroleptique*, fr. *neur-* + *-leptique* affecting, fr. Gk *lēptikos* seizing, fr. *lambanein* to take, seize — more at LATCH] (1958) : any of the powerful tranquilizers (as the phenothiazines) used esp. to treat psychosis and believed to act by blocking dopamine nervous receptors — called also *antipsychotic* — **neuroleptic** *adj*

neu·rol·o·gist \nŭ-'rä-lə-jist, nyŭ-\ *n* (1832) : one specializing in neurology; *esp* : a physician skilled in the diagnosis and treatment of disease of the nervous system

neu·rol·o·gy \-jē\ *n* [NL *neurologia*, fr. *neur-* + *-logia* -logy] (ca. 1681) : the scientific study of the nervous system esp. in respect to its structure, functions, and abnormalities — **neu·ro·log·i·cal** \,nŭr-ə-'lä-ji-kəl, ,nyŭr-\ *or* **neu·ro·log·ic** \-jik\ *adj* — **neu·ro·log·i·cal·ly** \-ji-k(ə-)lē\ *adv*

neu·ro·ma \nŭ-'rō-mə, nyŭ-\ *n, pl* **-mas** *or* **-ma·ta** \-mə-tə\ [NL] (ca. 1847) : a tumor or mass growing from a nerve and usu. consisting of nerve fibers

neu·ro·mus·cu·lar \,nŭr-ō-'məs-kyə-lər, ,nyŭr-\ *adj* [ISV] (1864) : of or relating to nerves and muscles; *esp* : jointly involving nervous and muscular elements ⟨a ~ junction⟩

neu·ron \'nü-,rän, 'nyü-; 'nŭr-,än, 'nyŭr-\ *also* **neu·rone** \-,rōn, -,ōn\ *n* [NL *neuron*, fr. Gk, nerve, sinew — more at NERVE] (1891) : a grayish or reddish granular cell with specialized processes that is the fundamental functional unit of nervous tissue — **neu·ro·nal** \'nŭr-ə-n°l, 'nyŭr-; nŭ-'rō-n°l, nyŭ-\ *also* **neu·ron·ic** \nŭ-'rä-nik, nyŭ-\ *adj*

neuron: *1* cell body, *2* dendrite, *3* axon, *4* nerve ending

neu·ro·pa·thol·o·gy \,nŭr-ō-pə-'thä-lə-jē, ,nyŭr-, -pa-\ *n* [ISV] (1853) : pathology of the nervous system — **neu·ro·path·o·log·ic** \-,pa-thə-'lä-jik\ *or* **neu·ro·path·o·log·i·cal** \-ji-kəl\ *adj* — **neu·ro·pa·thol·o·gist** \-pə-'thä-lə-jist, -pa-\ *n*

neu·rop·a·thy \nŭ-'rä-pə-thē, nyŭ-\ *n, pl* **-thies** [ISV] (1857) : an abnormal and usu. degenerative state of the nervous system or nerves; *also* : a systemic condition that stems from a neuropathy — **neu·ro·path·ic** \,nŭr-ə-'pa-thik, nyŭr-\ *adj* — **neu·ro·path·i·cal·ly** \-thi-k(ə-)lē\ *adv*

neu·ro·pep·tide \,nŭr-ə-'pep-,tīd, ,nyŭr-\ *n* (1975) : an endogenous peptide that influences neural activity or functioning

neu·ro·phar·ma·col·o·gy \,nŭr-ō-,fär-mə-'kä-lə-jē, ,nyŭr-\ *n* (1950) **1** : a branch of medical science dealing with the action of drugs on and in the nervous system **2** : the properties and reactions of a drug on and in the nervous system — **neu·ro·phar·ma·co·log·i·cal** \-kə-'lä-ji-kəl\ *also* **neu·ro·phar·ma·co·log·ic** \-jik\ *adj* — **neu·ro·phar·ma·col·o·gist** \-'kä-lə-jist\ *n*

neu·ro·phys·i·ol·o·gy \-,fi-zē-'ä-lə-jē\ *n* (1868) : physiology of the nervous system — **neu·ro·phys·i·o·log·i·cal** \-ə-'lä-ji-kəl\ *also* **neu·ro·phys·i·o·log·ic** \-jik\ *adj* — **neu·ro·phys·i·ol·o·gist** \-'ä-lə-jist\ *n*

neu·ro·psy·chi·a·try \-sə-'kī-ə-trē, -sī-\ *n* (1918) : a branch of medicine concerned with both neurology and psychiatry — **neu·ro·psy·chi·at·ric** \-,sī-kē-'a-trik\ *adj* — **neu·ro·psy·chi·at·ri·cal·ly** \-tri-k(ə-)lē\ *adv* — **neu·ro·psy·chi·a·trist** \-sə-'kī-ə-trist, -sī-\ *n*

neu·ro·psy·chol·o·gy \-sī-'kä-lə-jē\ *n* (ca. 1893) : a science concerned with the integration of psychological observations on behavior and the mind with neurological observations on the brain and nervous system — **neu·ro·psy·cho·log·i·cal** \-,sī-kə-'lä-ji-kəl\ *adj* — **neu·ro·psy·chol·o·gist** \-sī-'kä-lə-jist\ *n*

neu·rop·ter·an \nŭ-'räp-tə-rən, nyŭ-\ *n* [ultim. fr. Gk *neur-* + *pteron* wing — more at FEATHER] (ca. 1842) : any of an order (Neuroptera) of usu. net-winged insects that include the lacewings and ant lions — **neuropteran** *adj* — **neu·rop·ter·ous** \-rəs\ *adj*

neu·ro·ra·di·ol·o·gy \,nŭr-ō-,rä-dē-'ä-lə-jē, ,nyŭr-\ *n* (1938) : radiology of the nervous system — **neu·ro·ra·di·o·log·i·cal** \-ə-'lä-ji-kəl\ *adj* — **neu·ro·ra·di·ol·o·gist** \-'ä-lə-jist\ *n*

neu·ro·sci·ence \-'sī-ən(t)s\ *n* (1963) : a branch (as neurophysiology) of the life sciences that deals with the anatomy, physiology, biochemistry, or molecular biology of nerves and nervous tissue and esp. with their relation to behavior and learning — **neu·ro·sci·en·tif·ic** \-,sī-ən-'ti-fik\ *adj* — **neu·ro·sci·en·tist** \-'sī-ən-tist\ *n*

neu·ro·se·cre·tion \-si-'krē-shən\ *n* (1941) **1** : the process of producing a secretion by nerve cells **2** : a secretion produced by neurosecretion — **neu·ro·se·cre·to·ry** \-'krē-tə-rē\ *adj*

neu·ro·sen·so·ry \-'sen(t)-sə-rē, -'sen(t)s-rē\ *adj* (1929) : of or relating to afferent nerves

neu·ro·sis \nŭ-'rō-səs, nyŭ-\ *n, pl* **-ro·ses** \-,sēz\ [NL] (ca. 1784) : a mental and emotional disorder that affects only part of the personality, is accompanied by a less distorted perception of reality than in a psychosis, does not result in disturbance of the use of language, and is accompanied by various physical, physiological, and mental disturbances (as visceral symptoms, anxieties, or phobias)

neu·ros·po·ra \nŭ-'räs-pə-(,)rə, nyŭ-\ *n* [NL, fr. *neur-* + *spora* spore] (1928) : any of a genus (*Neurospora* of the family Sordariaceae) of ascomycetous fungi which are used extensively in genetic research and have black perithecia and persistent asci and some of which have salmonpink or orange spore masses and are severe pests in bakeries

neu·ro·sur·gery \-'sər-jə-rē, -'sərj-rē\ *n* (1904) : surgery of nervous structures (as nerves, the brain, or the spinal cord) — **neu·ro·sur·geon** \-'sər-jən\ *n* — **neu·ro·sur·gi·cal** \-'sər-ji-kəl\ *adj*

¹neu·rot·ic \nŭ-'rä-tik\ *adj* (1873) : of, relating to, constituting, or affected with neurosis — **neu·rot·i·cal·ly** \-ti-k(ə-)lē\ *adv*

²neurotic *n* (1896) **1** : one affected with a neurosis **2** : an emotionally unstable individual

neu·rot·i·cism \nŭ-'rä-tə-,si-zəm, nyŭ-\ *n* (1900) : a neurotic character, condition, or trait

neu·ro·tox·ic \,nŭr-ō-'täk-sik, ,nyŭr-\ *adj* (ca. 1903) : toxic to the nerves or nervous tissue — **neu·ro·tox·ic·i·ty** \-,täk-'si-sə-tē\ *n*

neu·ro·tox·in \-'täk-sən\ *n* [ISV] (1902) : a poisonous complex esp. of protein that acts on the nervous system

neu·ro·trans·mis·sion \-tran(t)s-'mi-shən, -tranz-\ *n* (1961) : the transmission of nerve impulses across a synapse

neu·ro·trans·mit·ter \-tran(t)s-'mi-tər, -tranz-\ *n* (1961) : a substance (as norepinephrine or acetylcholine) that transmits nerve impulses across a synapse

neu·ro·trop·ic \-'trä-pik\ *adj* [ISV] (1903) : having an affinity for or localizing selectively in nerve tissue ⟨a ~ virus⟩

neu·ru·la \'nŭr-ə-lə, 'nyŭr-, -yə-lə\ *n, pl* **-lae** \-,lē\ *or* **-las** [NL, fr. *neur-* + L *-ula* -ule] (ca. 1890) : an early vertebrate embryo which follows the gastrula and in which nervous tissue begins to differentiate and the basic pattern of the vertebrate begins to emerge — **neu·ru·la·tion** \,nŭr-ə-'lā-shən, ,nyŭr-, -yə-\ *n*

neus·ton \'nü-,stän, nyü-\ *n* [G, fr. Gk, neut. of *neustos* swimming, fr. *nein* to swim — more at NATANT] (1928) : minute organisms that float in the surface film of water

¹neu·ter \'nü-tər, 'nyü-\ *adj* [ME *neutre*, fr. MF & L; MF *neutre*, fr. L *neuter*, lit., neither, fr. *ne-* not + *uter* which of two — more at NO, WHETHER] (14c) **1 a** : of, relating to, or constituting the gender that ordinarily includes most words or grammatical forms referring to things classed as neither masculine nor feminine **b** : neither active nor passive : INTRANSITIVE **2** : taking no side : NEUTRAL **3** : lacking or having imperfectly developed or nonfunctional generative organs ⟨the worker bee is ~⟩

²neuter *n* (15c) **1 a** : a noun, pronoun, adjective, or inflectional form or class of the neuter gender **b** : the neuter gender **2** : one that is neutral **3 a** : WORKER **2 b** : a spayed or castrated animal

³neuter *vt* (1903) : CASTRATE, ALTER

¹neu·tral \'nü-trəl, 'nyü-\ *n* (15c) **1** : one that is neutral **2** : a neutral color **3** : a position of disengagement (as of gears)

²neutral *adj* [MF, fr. (assumed) ML *neutralis*, fr. L, of neuter gender, fr. *neutr-, neuter*] (1549) **1** : not engaged on either side; *specif* : not aligned with a political or ideological grouping ⟨a ~ nation⟩ **2** : of or relating to a neutral state or power ⟨~ territory⟩ **3 a** : not decided or pronounced as to characteristics : INDIFFERENT **b** (1) : ACHROMATIC (2) : nearly achromatic **c** (1) : NEUTER **3** (2) : lacking stamens or pistils **d** : neither acid nor basic **e** : not electrically charged **4** : produced with the tongue in the position it has when at rest ⟨the ~ vowels of \ə-'bəv\ *above*⟩ — **neu·tral·ly** \-trə-lē\ *adv* — **neu·tral·ness** *n*

neu·tral·ise *Brit var of* NEUTRALIZE

neu·tral·ism \'nü-trə-,li-zəm, 'nyü-\ *n* (1579) **1** : NEUTRALITY **2** : a policy or the advocacy of neutrality esp. in international affairs — **neu·tral·ist** \-list\ *n* — **neu·tral·is·tic** \,nü-trə-'lis-tik, ,nyü-\ *adj*

neu·tral·i·ty \nü-'tra-lə-tē, nyü-\ *n* (15c) : the quality or state of being neutral; *esp* : refusal to take part in a war between other powers

neu·tral·i·za·tion \,nü-trə-lə-'zā-shən, ,nyü-\ *n* (1808) **1** : an act or process of neutralizing **2** : the quality or state of being neutralized

neu·tral·ize \'nü-trə-,līz, 'nyü-\ *vb* **-ized; -iz·ing** *vt* (1759) **1** : to make chemically neutral **2 a** : to counteract the activity or effect of : make ineffective ⟨propaganda that is difficult to ~⟩ **b** : KILL, DESTROY **3** : to make electrically inert by combining equal positive and negative quantities **4** : to invest (as a territory or a nation) with conventional or obligatory neutrality conferring inviolability during a war **5** : to make neutral by blending with the complementary color **6** : to give (as a pair of phonemes) a nondistinctive form or pronunciation ⟨\t\ and \d\ are *neutralized* when pronounced as flaps⟩ ~ *vi* : to undergo neutralization — **neu·tral·iz·er** *n*

neutral red *n* (1890) : a basic dye used chiefly as a biological stain and acid-base indicator

neutral spirits *n pl but sing or pl in constr* (1919) : ethyl alcohol of 190 or higher proof used esp. for blending other alcoholic liquors

neu·tri·no \nü-'trē-(,)nō, nyü-\ *n, pl* **-nos** [It, fr. *neutro* neutral, neuter, fr. L *neutr-, neuter*] (1934) : an uncharged elementary particle that is believed to be massless or to have a very small mass, that has any of three forms, and that interacts only rarely with other particles — **neu·tri·no·less** \-ləs\ *adj*

neu·tron \'nü-,trän, 'nyü-\ *n* [prob. fr. *neutral*] (1932) : an uncharged elementary particle that has a mass nearly equal to that of the proton and is present in all known atomic nuclei except the hydrogen nucleus — **neu·tron·ic** \nü-'trä-nik, nyü-\ *adj*

neutron activation analysis *n* (1951) : an analytical method used to determine the chemical elements comprising a material by bombarding it with neutrons to produce radioactive atoms whose radiations are indicative of the elements present — called also *neutron activation*

neutron bomb *n* (1959) : a nuclear bomb designed to produce lethal neutrons but less blast and fire damage than other nuclear bombs

neutron star *n* (1934) : a hypothetical dense celestial object that consists primarily of closely packed neutrons and that results from the collapse of a much larger stellar body

¹neu·tro·phil \'nü-trə-,fil, 'nyü-\ *or* **neu·tro·phil·ic** \,nü-trə-'fi-lik, ,nyü-\ *adj* [ISV *neutro-* (fr. L *neutr-, neuter* neither) + *-phil*] (ca. 1890) : staining to the same degree with acid or basic dyes ⟨~ granulocytes⟩

²neutrophil *n* (1897) : a granulocyte that is the chief phagocytic white blood cell of the blood

---

\ə\ abut \ᵊ\ kitten, F table \ər\ further \a\ ash \ā\ ace \ä\ mop, mar
\aú\ out \ch\ chin \e\ bet \ē\ easy \g\ go \i\ hit \ī\ ice \j\ job
\ŋ\ sing \ō\ go \ó\ law \ói\ boy \th\ thin \t͟h\ the \ü\ loot \ú\ foot
\y\ yet \zh\ vision \á, k̲, ⁿ, œ, œ̄, ᵫ, ūᵉ, ᵊ\ see Guide to Pronunciation

né·vé \nā-'vā\ *n* [F dial. (Swiss), fr. (assumed) VL *nivatum*, fr. L *niv-, nix* snow — more at SNOW] (1843) : the partially compacted granular snow that forms the surface part of the upper end of a glacier; *broadly* : a field of granular snow

nev·er \'ne-vər\ *adv* [ME, fr. OE *næfre*, fr. *ne* not + *æfre* ever — more at NO] (bef. 12c) **1** : not ever : at no time 〈~ saw her before〉 **2** : not in any degree : not under any condition 〈~ the wiser for his experience〉

never mind *conj* (1954) : MUCH LESS, LET ALONE — used esp. in negative contexts to add to one term another denoting something less likely 〈with this knee I can hardly walk, *never mind* run〉

nev·er·more \,ne-vər-'mōr, -'mȯr\ *adv* (12c) : never again

nev·er–nev·er land \,ne-vər-'ne-vər-\ *n* (1907) : an ideal or imaginary place

nev·er·the·less \,ne-vər-thə-'les\ *adv* (14c) : in spite of that : HOWEVER 〈her childish but ~ real delight —Richard Corbin〉

ne·vus \'nē-vəs\ *n, pl* **ne·vi** \-,vi\ [NL, fr. L *naevus*] (ca. 1836) : a congenital pigmented area on the skin : BIRTHMARK

¹new \'nü, *chiefly Brit* 'nyü\ *in place names usu* (,)nü *or* nə *or* (,)ni\ *adj* [ME, fr. OE *niwe*; akin to OHG *niuwi* new, L *novus*, Gk *neos*] (bef. 12c) **1** : having existed or having been made but a short time : RECENT, MODERN **2 a** (1) : having been seen, used, or known for a short time : NOVEL 〈rice was a ~ crop for the area〉 (2) : UNFAMILIAR 〈visit ~ places〉 **b** : being other than the former or old 〈a steady flow of ~ money〉 **3** : having been in a relationship or condition but a short time 〈~ to the job〉 **4 a** : beginning as the resumption or repetition of a previous act or thing 〈a ~ day〉 〈the ~ edition〉 **b** : made or become fresh 〈awoke a ~ person〉 **5** : different from one of the same category that has existed previously 〈~ realism〉 **6** : of dissimilar origin and usu. of superior quality 〈introducing ~ blood〉 **7** *cap* : MODERN 3; *esp* : having been in use after medieval times — **new·ish** \'nü-ish, 'nyü-\ *adj* — **new·ness** *n*

syn NEW, NOVEL, ORIGINAL, FRESH mean having recently come into existence or use. NEW may apply to what is freshly made and unused 〈*new* brick〉 or has not been known before 〈*new* designs〉 or not experienced before 〈starts the *new* job〉. NOVEL applies to what is not only new but strange or unprecedented 〈a *novel* approach to the problem〉. ORIGINAL applies to what is the first of its kind to exist 〈a man without one *original* idea〉. FRESH applies to what has not lost its qualities of newness such as liveliness, energy, brightness 〈*fresh* towels〉 〈a *fresh* start〉.

²new *adv* (bef. 12c) : NEWLY, RECENTLY — usu. used in combination

New Age *adj* (1956) **1** : of, relating to, or being a late 20th century social movement drawing on ancient concepts esp. from Eastern and American Indian traditions and incorporating such themes as holism, concern for nature, spirituality, and metaphysics **2** : of, relating to, or being a soft soothing form of instrumental music often used to promote relaxation

¹new·born \-,bȯrn\ *adj* (14c) **1** : recently born **2** : born anew

²newborn *n, pl* **newborn** *or* **newborns** (1879) : a newborn individual

New·burg *or* **New·burgh** \'nü-,bərg, 'nyü-\ *adj* [origin unknown] (1902) : served with a sauce made of cream, butter, sherry, and egg yolks 〈lobster ~〉 〈shrimp ~〉

New·cas·tle disease \'nü-,ka-səl-, 'nyü-; n(y)ü-'\ *n* [*Newcastle* upon Tyne, England] (1927) : a destructive virus disease of birds and esp. domestic fowl that involves respiratory and nervous symptoms

new·com·er \'nü-,kə-mər, 'nyü-\ *n* (15c) **1** : one recently arrived **2** : BEGINNER

New Criticism *n* (1941) : an analytic literary criticism that is marked by concentration on the language, imagery, and emotional or intellectual tensions in literary works — **New Critic** *n* — **New Critical** *adj*

New Deal *n* [fr. the supposed resemblance to the situation of freshness and equality of opportunity afforded by a fresh deal in a card game] (1932) : the legislative and administrative program of President F. D. Roosevelt designed to promote economic recovery and social reform during the 1930s; *also* : the period of this program — **New Dealer** *n* — **New Deal·ish** \-'dē-lish\ *adj* — **New Deal·ism** \-'dē(ə)-,li-zəm\ *n*

new drug *n* (ca. 1951) : a drug that has not been declared safe and effective by qualified experts under the conditions prescribed, recommended, or suggested in the label and that may be a new chemical formula or an established drug prescribed for use in a new way

new economics *n pl but usu sing in constr* (1928) : an economic concept that is a logical extension of Keynesianism and that holds that appropriate fiscal and monetary maneuvering can maintain healthy economic growth and prosperity indefinitely

new·el \'nü-əl, 'nyü-\ *n* [ME *nowell*, fr. MF *nouel* stone of a fruit, fr. LL *nucalis* like a nut, fr. L *nuc-, nux* nut — more at NUT] (14c) **1** : an upright post about which the steps of a circular staircase wind **2** : a post at the foot of a straight stairway or one at a landing

New English Bible *n* (1957) : a translation of the Bible by a British interdenominational committee first published in its entirety in 1970

new·fan·gled \'nü-'faŋ-gəld\ *adj* [ME, fr. *newefangel*, fr. *new* + (assumed) OE *-fangol*, fr. OE *fōn* (pp. *fangen*) to take, seize — more at PACT] (14c) **1** : attracted to novelty **2** : of the newest style or kind 〈had many ~ gadgets in the kitchen〉 — **new·fan·gled·ness** *n*

new–fash·ioned \-'fa-shənd\ *adj* (1592) **1** : made in a new fashion or form **2** : UP-TO-DATE

new·found \-'faůnd\ *adj* (15c) : newly found 〈a ~ friend〉

New·found·land \'nü-fən(d)-lənd, 'nyü-, -,land; n(y)ü-'faůnd-lənd\ [*Newfoundland*, Canada] (1773) : any of a breed of very large heavy highly intelligent, black, black and white, or bronze dogs developed in Newfoundland

New·gate \'nü-,gāt, 'nyü-, -gət\ *n* (14c) : a London prison razed in 1902

New Greek *n* (ca. 1958) : Greek as used by the Greeks since the end of the medieval period

New Hebrew *n* (ca. 1959) : the Hebrew language in use in present-day Israel

new·ie \'nü-ē, 'nyü-\ *n* (ca. 1945) : something new

New Jer·sey tea \,nü-'jər-zē-, nyü-\ *n* [*New Jersey*, state of U.S.; fr. the use of its leaves as a substitute for tea during the American Revolution] (1759) : a low deciduous shrub (*Ceanothus americanus*) of the buckthorn family that is found in the eastern U.S. and has dull green leaves and small white flowers borne in large terminal panicles

New Je·ru·sa·lem \-jə-'rü-s(ə-)ləm, -zə-ləm; -'rüz-ləm\ *n* [fr. the phrase "the holy city, *New Jerusalem*" (Rev. 21:2)] (1535) **1** : the final abode of souls redeemed by Christ **2** : an ideal earthly community

New Journalism *n* (1967) : journalism that features the author's subjective responses to people and events and that often includes fictional elements meant to illuminate and dramatize those responses

New Latin *n* (ca. 1889) : Latin as used since the end of the medieval period esp. in scientific description and classification

New Left *n* (1960) : a political movement originating esp. among students in the 1960s, favoring confrontational tactics, often breaking with traditional leftist ideologies, and associated esp. with antiwar, antinuclear, feminist, and ecological issues — **new leftist** *n, often cap* N&L

new·ly \'nü-lē, 'nyü-\ *adv* (bef. 12c) **1** : LATELY, RECENTLY 〈a ~ married couple〉 **2** : ANEW, AFRESH

new·ly·wed \-,wed\ *n* (1918) : a person recently married

new·mar·ket \'nü-,mär-kət, 'nyü-\ *n* [*Newmarket*, England] (1837) : a long close-fitting coat worn in the 19th century

new math *n* (1964) : basic mathematics taught with emphasis on abstraction and the principles of set theory — called also *new mathematics*

new moon *n* (bef. 12c) **1** : the moon's phase when it is in conjunction with the sun so that its dark side is toward the earth; *also* : the thin crescent moon seen shortly after sunset for a few days after the actual occurrence of the new moon phase **2** : the first day of each Jewish month marked by a special liturgy

New Right *n* (1966) : a political movement made up esp. of Protestants, opposed esp. to secular humanism, and concerned with issues esp. of church and state, patriotism, laissez-faire economics, pornography, and abortion

news \'nüz, 'nyüz\ *n pl but sing in constr, often attrib* (15c) **1 a** : a report of recent events **b** : previously unknown information 〈I've got ~ for you〉 **2 a** : material reported in a newspaper or news periodical or on a newscast **b** : matter that is newsworthy **3** : NEWSCAST — **news·less** \-ləs\ *adj*

news agency *n* (1873) : an organization that supplies news to subscribing newspapers, periodicals, and newscasters

news·agent \'nüz-,ā-jənt, 'nyüz-\ *n* (1851) *chiefly Brit* : NEWSDEALER

news·boy \-,bȯi\ *n* (1764) : one who delivers or sells newspapers

news·break \-,brāk\ *n* (1944) : a newsworthy event

news·cast \-,kast\ *n* [*news* + broad*cast*] (ca. 1939) : a radio or television broadcast of news — **news·cast·er** \-,kas-tər\ *n*

news conference *n* (1946) : PRESS CONFERENCE

news·deal·er \-,dē-lər\ *n* (1861) : a dealer in newspapers, magazines, and often paperback books

news·hound \-,haůnd\ *n* (1918) : an aggressive journalist

news·let·ter \-,le-tər\ *n* (1903) : a small publication (as a leaflet or newspaper) containing news of interest chiefly to a special group

news·mag·a·zine \-,ma-gə-,zēn, -,zēn\ *n* (1923) **1** : a usu. weekly magazine devoted chiefly to summarizing and analyzing news **2** : MAGAZINE 4c

news·man \-mən, -,man\ *n* (1596) : one who gathers, reports, or comments on the news : REPORTER, CORRESPONDENT

news·mon·ger \-,məŋ-gər, -,mäŋ-\ *n* (1592) : one who is active in gathering and repeating news; *esp* : GOSSIP

¹news·pa·per \'nüz-,pā-pər, 'nyüz-, -,n(y)üs-\ *n* (1670) **1** : a paper that is printed and distributed usu. daily or weekly and that contains news, articles of opinion, features, and advertising **2** : an organization that publishes a newspaper **3** : the paper of a newspaper : NEWSPRINT

²newspaper *vi* (1943) : to do newspaper work

news·pa·per·man \-,man\ *n* (1806) : one who owns or is employed by a newspaper

news·pa·per·wom·an \-,wu-mən\ *n* (1881) : a woman who owns or is employed by a newspaper

new·speak \'nü-,spēk, 'nyü-\ *n, often cap* [*Newspeak*, a language "designed to diminish the range of thought," in the novel *1984* (1949) by George Orwell] (1950) : propagandistic language marked by euphemism, circumlocution, and the inversion of customary meanings : DOUBLE-TALK 2

news·peo·ple \'nüz-,pē-pəl, 'nyüz-\ *n pl* (1972) : REPORTERS

news·per·son \-,pər-s⁸n\ *n* (1973) : REPORTER

news·print \-,print\ *n* (1909) : paper made chiefly from groundwood pulp and used mostly for newspapers

news·read·er \-,rē-dər\ *n* (1925) *chiefly Brit* : one who broadcasts the news

news·reel \-,rēl\ *n* (1916) : a short movie dealing with current events

news·room \-,rüm, -,rům\ *n* (1929) **1** : a place (as an office) where news is prepared for publication or broadcast **2** : NEWSSTAND

news·stand \-,stand\ *n* (1872) : a place (as an outdoor stall) where newspapers and periodicals are sold

New Style *adj* (1615) : using or according to the Gregorian calendar

news·week·ly \-,wē-klē\ *n* (1947) : a weekly newspaper or newsmagazine

news·wom·an \-,wu-mən\ *n* (1928) : a woman who is a reporter

news·wor·thy \-,wər-thē\ *adj* (1932) : sufficiently interesting to the general public to warrant reporting (as in a newspaper) — **news·wor·thi·ness** \-thē-nəs\ *n*

news·writ·ing \-,ri-tiŋ\ *n* (1916) : JOURNALISM 1a

newsy \'nü-zē, 'nyü-\ *adj* **news·i·er; -est** (1832) **1** : containing or filled with news 〈~ letters〉 **2** : NEWSWORTHY — **news·i·ness** *n*

newt \'nüt, 'nyüt\ *n* [ME, alter. (resulting from misdivision of *an ewte*) of *ewte* — more at EFT] (15c) : any of various small semiaquatic salamanders (as of the genus *Triturus*)

newt

New Testament *n* (14c) : the second part of the Christian Bible comprising the canonical Gospels and Epistles and also the book of Acts and the book of Revelation — see BIBLE table

new·ton \'nü-t⁸n, 'nyü-\ *n* [Sir Isaac *Newton*] (1904) : the unit of force in the meter-kilogram-second system equal to the force required to impart an acceleration of one meter per second per second to a mass of one kilogram

new town n (1918) : an urban development comprising a small to medium-sized city with a broad range of housing and planned industrial, commercial, and recreational facilities

new wave n, often cap N&W (1960) **1 :** a cinematic movement that is characterized by improvisation, abstraction, and subjective symbolism and that often makes use of experimental photographic techniques **2 :** a new movement in a particular field **3 :** rock music characterized by cohesive ensemble playing and usu. lyrics which express anger and social discontent **4 :** DERNIER CRI; esp : fashion that is strikingly outrageous — **new-wave** \'nü-'wāv, 'nyü-, -,wāv\ adj — **new wav·er** \-'wā-vər\ n

New World n (1555) : WESTERN HEMISPHERE; esp : the continental landmass of No. and So. America

New Year n (13c) **1 :** the calendar year about to start or recently started **2 a :** NEW YEAR'S DAY **b :** the first days of a calendar year **3 :** ROSH HASHANAH

New Year's Day n (13c) : the first day of the calendar year observed as a legal holiday in many countries

¹**next** \'nekst\ adj [ME, fr. OE nīehst, superl. of nēah nigh — more at NIGH] (bef. 12c) **1 :** immediately adjacent (as in place, rank, or time) **2 :** any other considered hypothetically ⟨knew it as well as the ∼ man⟩

²**next** prep (bef. 12c) : nearest or adjacent to

³**next** adv (14c) **1 :** in the time, place, or order nearest or immediately succeeding ⟨∼ we drove home⟩ ⟨the ∼ closest school⟩ **2 :** on the first occasion ⟨come ⟨when ∼ we meet⟩

next–door \'neks(t)-'dōr, -'dȯr\ adj (1749) : located or living in the next building, house, apartment, or room; broadly : NEARBY, ADJACENT

next door adv (1579) : in or to the next building, house, apartment, or room ⟨lives next door⟩; broadly : in or at an adjacent place — **next door to :** NEXT TO

next friend n (1579) : a person admitted to or appointed by a court to act for the benefit of a person (as an infant) lacking full legal capacity

next of kin (1766) : one or more persons in the nearest degree of relationship to another person

¹**next to** prep (1633) **1 :** immediately following or adjacent to **2 :** in comparison to ⟨next to you I'm wealthy⟩

²**next to** adv (1667) : very nearly : ALMOST ⟨it was next to impossible to see in the fog⟩

nex·us \'nek-səs\ n, pl **nex·us·es** \-sə-səz\ or **nex·us** \-səs, -,süs\ [L, fr. nectere to bind] (1663) **1 :** CONNECTION, LINK; also : a causal link **2 :** a connected group or series **3 :** CENTER, FOCUS

Nez Percé or **Nez Perce** \'nez-'pərs, 'nes-'pers, -̇'nā-per-'sā\ n, pl **Nez Percé** or **Nez Perce** or **Nez Per·cés** \same or -'pər-səz, -'per-; -̇-per-'sā(z)\ or **Nez Perce** or **Nez Per·ces** \same or -'pər-səz, -'per-\ [F, lit., pierced nose] (1812) **1 :** a member of an American Indian people of Idaho, Washington, and Oregon **2 :** the language of the Nez Percé people

ngul·trum \eŋ-'gùl-trəm, en-\ n [Tibetan] (1973) — see MONEY table

ngwee \eŋ-'gwē, en-\ n, pl **ngwee** [Bemba, lit., bright] (1966) — see kwacha at MONEY table

ni·a·cin \'nī-ə-sən\ n [nicotinic acid + ¹-in] (1942) : NICOTINIC ACID; also : NICOTINAMIDE

ni·a·cin·amide \,nī-ə-'si-nə-,mīd\ n (1942) : NICOTINAMIDE

Ni·ag·a·ra \nī-'a-g(ə-)rə\ n [Niagara Falls] (1841) : an overwhelming flood : TORRENT ⟨a ∼ of protests⟩

ni·al·amide \nī-'a-lə-,mīd\ n [nicotinic acid + amyl + amide] (1959) : a synthetic antidepressant drug $C_{16}H_{18}N_4O_2$ that is an inhibitor of monoamine oxidase

nib \'nib\ n [prob. alter. of neb] (1585) **1 :** BILL, BEAK **2 a :** the sharpened point of a quill pen **b :** PEN POINT; also : each of the two divisions of a pen point **3 :** a small pointed or projecting part

¹**nib·ble** \'ni-bəl\ vb **nib·bled; nib·bling** \-b(ə-)liŋ\ [origin unknown] vt (ca. 1512) **1 a :** to bite gently **b :** to eat or chew in small bits **2 :** to take away bit by bit ⟨waves nibbling the shore⟩ ∼ vi **1 :** to take gentle, small, or cautious bites; also : SNACK **2 :** to deal with something as if by nibbling — **nib·bler** \-b(ə-)lər\ n

²**nibble** n (1658) **1 :** an act of nibbling **2 :** a very small quantity or portion (as of food); also : SNACK **3 :** a tentative expression of interest

Ni·be·lung \'nē-bə-,lùŋ\ n, pl **-lungs** also **-lung·en** \-,lùŋ-ən\ [G] (1861) **1 :** a member of a race of dwarfs in Germanic legend **2 :** any of the followers of Siegfried **3 :** any of the Burgundian kings in the medieval German Nibelungenlied

nibs \'nibz\ n pl but sing in constr [origin unknown] (ca. 1821) : an important or self-important person — usu. used in the phrases his nibs or her nibs as if a title of honor

ni·cad \'nī-,kad\ n [¹nickel + cadmium] (1965) : a rechargeable dry cell that has a nickel cathode and a cadmium anode

nic·co·lite \'ni-kə-,līt\ n [NL niccolum nickel, prob. fr. Sw nickel] (1868) : a pale copper-red usu. massive mineral of metallic luster that is essentially a nickel arsenide

nice \'nīs\ adj **nic·er; nic·est** [ME, foolish, wanton, fr. OF, fr. L nescius ignorant, fr. nescire not to know — more at NESCIENCE] (14c) **1** obs **a :** WANTON, DISSOLUTE **b :** COY, RETICENT **2 a :** showing fastidious or finicky tastes : PARTICULAR **b :** exacting in requirements or standards : PUNCTILIOUS **3 :** possessing, marked by, or demanding great or excessive precision and delicacy **4** obs : TRIVIAL **5 a :** PLEASING, AGREEABLE ⟨a ∼ time⟩ ⟨a ∼ person⟩ **b :** well-executed ⟨∼ shot⟩ **c :** APPROPRIATE, FITTING **6 a :** socially acceptable : WELL-BRED **b :** VIRTUOUS, RESPECTABLE **7 :** POLITE, KIND ⟨that's ∼ of you to say⟩ syn see CORRECT — **nice** adv — **nice·ly** adv — **nice·ness** n

Ni·cene \'nī-,sēn, nī-'\ adj [ME, fr. LL Nicaenus, fr. L Nicaea Nicaea, fr. Gk Nikaia] (14c) **1 :** of or relating to Nicaea or the Nicaeans **2 :** of or relating to the ecumenical church council held in Nicaea in A.D. 325 or to the Nicene Creed

Nicene Creed n (ca. 1569) : a Christian creed expanded from a creed issued by the first Nicene Council, beginning "I believe in one God," and used in liturgical worship

nice–nel·ly \'nis-'ne-lē\ adj, often cap 2d N [fr. the name Nelly] (1925) **1 :** marked by euphemism **2 :** PRUDISH — **nice nelly** n, often cap 2d N — **nice–nel·ly·ism** \-,i-zəm\ n, often cap 2d N

nice·ty \'nī-sə-tē, -stē\ n, pl **-ties** [ME nicete, fr. MF niceté foolishness, fr. nice, adj.] (14c) **1 :** the quality or state of being nice **2 :** an elegant, delicate, or civilized feature ⟨enjoy the niceties of life⟩ **3 :** a fine point or distinction : SUBTLETY ⟨the niceties of table manners⟩ **4**

: careful attention to details : delicate exactness : PRECISION **5 :** delicacy of taste or feeling : FASTIDIOUSNESS

¹**niche** \'nich, ÷'nēsh\ n [F, fr. MF, fr. nicher to nest, fr. (assumed) VL nidicare, fr. L nidus nest — more at NEST] (1611) **1 a :** a recess in a wall esp. for a statue **b :** something that resembles a niche **2 a :** a place, employment, status, or activity for which a person or thing is best fitted **b :** a habitat supplying the factors necessary for the existence of an organism or species **c :** the ecological role of an organism in a community esp. in regard to food consumption **d :** a specialized market

²**niche** vt **niched; nich·ing** (1752) : to place in or as if in a niche

Ni·chrome \'nī-,krōm\ trademark — used for an alloy of nickel, chromium, and iron that is commonly used in the heating elements of electrical appliances

¹**nick** \'nik\ n [ME nyke, prob. alter. of nocke nock] (15c) **1 a :** a small notch or groove **b :** a break in one strand of two-stranded DNA caused by a missing phosphodiester bond **c :** a small cut incurred in shaving **2 :** a final critical moment ⟨in the ∼ of time⟩ **3** slang Brit : PRISON; also : POLICE STATION **4** Brit : CONDITION ⟨in good ∼⟩

²**nick** vt (1523) **1 :** to jot down : RECORD **2 a :** to make a nick in : NOTCH, CHIP **b :** to cut into or wound slightly ⟨a bullet ∼ed his leg⟩ **3 :** to cut short ⟨cold weather, which ∼ed steel and automobile output —Time⟩ **4 :** to catch at the right point or time **5 :** CHEAT, OVERCHARGE **6 a** slang Brit : ARREST **b** slang Brit : STEAL ∼ vi **1 :** to make petty attacks : SNIPE **2 :** to complement one another genetically and produce superior offspring

nick·el also **nick·le** \'ni-kəl\ n [prob. fr. Sw nickel, fr. G Kupfernickel niccolite, prob. fr. Kupfer copper + Nickel goblin; fr. the deceptive copper color of niccolite] (1755) **1 :** a silver-white hard malleable ductile metallic element capable of a high polish and resistant to corrosion that is used chiefly in alloys and as a catalyst — see ELEMENT table **2 a** (1) **:** the U.S. 5-cent piece regularly containing 25 percent nickel and 75 percent copper (2) **:** the Canadian 5-cent piece **b :** five cents **3 :** a pass defense in football that employs five defensive backs

¹**nick·el–and–dime** \,ni-kəl-ən-'dīm\ adj (1950) **1 :** involving or offering only a small amount of money **2 :** SMALL-TIME

²**nickel–and–dime** vt **nick·eled–and–dimed** \,ni-kəld-ən-'dīmd\ or **nick·el–and–dimed** \-ən-'dīmd\; **nick·el·ing–and–dim·ing** \-'dī-miŋ\ or **nickel–and–diming** (1961) **:** to impair, weaken, or defeat gradually (as through a series of small incursions or excessive attention to detail)

nick·el·if·er·ous \,ni-kə-'li-f(ə-)rəs\ adj (1821) : containing nickel

nick·el·ode·on \,ni-kə-'lō-dē-ən\ n [prob. fr. nickel + -odeon (as in melodeon music hall)] (1907) **1 :** an early movie theater to which admission usu. cost five cents **2 :** JUKEBOX

nickel silver n (1860) : GERMAN SILVER

¹**nick·er** \'ni-kər\ vi **nick·ered; nick·er·ing** \-k(ə-)riŋ\ [perh. alter. of neigh] (1641) **:** NEIGH, WHINNY — **nicker** n

²**nicker** n [perh. fr. nick to nick] (1910) slang Brit : ¹POUND 2a

nick·nack var of KNICKKNACK

¹**nick·name** \'nik-,nām\ n [ME nekename additional name, alter. (resulting from misdivision of an ekename) of ekename, fr. eke eke, also + name name] (15c) **1 :** a usu. descriptive name given instead of or in addition to the one belonging to a person, place, or thing **2 :** a familiar form of a proper name (as of a person or a city)

²**nickname** vt (1536) **1 :** MISNAME, MISCALL **2 :** to give a nickname to — **nick·nam·er** n

ni·co·ti·a·na \ni-,kō-shē-'a-nə, -'ā-nə, -'ä-nə\ n [NL, fr. herba nicotiana, lit., Nicot's herb, fr. Jean Nicot †1600 Fr. diplomat and scholar] (1600) **:** any of several tobaccos (as Nicotiana alata) grown for their showy flowers

nic·o·tin·amide \,ni-kə-'tē-nə-,mīd, -'ti-\ n [ISV] (1895) : a compound $C_6H_6N_2O$ of the vitamin B complex found esp. as a constituent of coenzymes and used similarly to nicotinic acid

nicotinamide adenine dinucleotide n (1961): NAD

nicotinamide adenine dinucleotide phosphate n (1962): NADP

nic·o·tine \'ni-kə-,tēn\ n [F, fr. NL nicotiana] (1819) **:** a poisonous alkaloid $C_{10}H_{14}N_2$ that is the chief active principle of tobacco and is used as an insecticide

nic·o·tin·ic \,ni-kə-'tē-nik, -'ti-\ adj [ISV] (1873) **:** relating to, resembling, producing, or mediating the effects produced by nicotine on nerve fibers at autonomic ganglia and at the neuromuscular junctions of voluntary muscle which increases activity in small doses and inhibits it in larger doses ⟨∼ receptors⟩ — compare MUSCARINIC

nicotinic acid n (1873) **:** an acid $C_6H_5NO_2$ of the vitamin B complex found widely in animals and plants and used esp. against pellagra — called also niacin

nic·ti·tate \'nik-tə-,tāt\ vi **-tat·ed; -tat·ing** [alter. of nictate to wink, fr. L nictatus, pp. of nictare — more at CONNIVE] (ca. 1834) **:** WINK

nictitating membrane n (1713) **:** a thin membrane found in many vertebrates at the inner angle or beneath the lower lid of the eye and capable of extending across the eyeball

ni·dic·o·lous \nī-'di-kə-ləs\ adj [L nidus nest + E -colous — more at NEST] (ca. 1902) **1 :** reared for a time in a nest **2 :** sharing the nest of another kind of animal

ni·di·fi·ca·tion \,ni-də-fə-'kā-shən, ,nī-\ n [ML nidification-, nidificatio, fr. L nidificare to build a nest, fr. nidus nest] (1658) **:** the act, process, or technique of building a nest

ni·dif·u·gous \nī-'di-fyə-gəs\ adj [L nidus nest + fugere to flee — more at FUGITIVE] (1896) : leaving the nest soon after hatching

ni·dus \'nī-dəs\ n, pl **ni·di** \'nī-,dī\ or **ni·dus·es** [NL, fr. L] (1742) **1 :** a nest or breeding place; esp : a place or substance in an animal or plant where bacteria or other organisms lodge and multiply **2 :** a place where something originates, develops, or is located

niece \'nēs\ n [ME nece granddaughter, niece, fr. OF niece, fr. LL neptia, fr. L neptis; akin to L nepot-, nepos grandson, nephew — more at

---

\ə\ abut \ᵊ\ kitten, F table \ər\ further \a\ ash \ā\ ace \ä\ mop, mar
\aù\ out \ch\ chin \e\ bet \ē\ easy \g\ go \i\ hit \ī\ ice \j\ job
\ŋ\ sing \ō\ go \ȯ\ law \ȯi\ boy \th\ thin \t̲h̲\ the \ü\ loot \ù\ foot
\y\ yet \zh\ vision \å, k̲, ⁿ, œ, œ̄, ᵫ, ᵾ̄, ʸ\ see Guide to Pronunciation

NEPHEW] (14c) **1** : a daughter of one's brother, sister, brother-in-law, or sister-in-law **2** : an illegitimate daughter of an ecclesiastic

¹ni·el·lo \nē-'e-(,)lō\ *n, pl* **ni·el·li** \-(,)lē\ *or* **niellos** [It., fr. ML *nigellum*, fr. neut. of L *nigellus* blackish, dim. of *niger* black] (1816) **1** : any of several black enamel-like alloys usu. of sulfur with silver, copper, and lead **2** : the art or process of decorating metal with incised designs filled with niello **3** : a piece of metal or an object decorated with niello

²niello *vt* (1866) : to inlay or ornament with niello

ni·fed·i·pine \nə-'fe-də-,pēn, -pən\ *n* [prob. nitr- + -fe- (fr. *phenyl*) + -*dipine* (by alter. & shortening fr. *pyridine*)] (1974) : a calcium channel blocker $C_{17}H_{18}N_2O_6$ that is a coronary vasodilator used esp. in the treatment of angina pectoris

Nifl·heim \'ni-vəl-,häm\ *n* [ON *Niflheimr*] : the abode of the dead in Norse mythology

¹nif·ty \'nif-tē\ *adj* **nif·ti·er; -est** [origin unknown] (1865) : very good : very attractive : FINE ⟨~ clothes⟩ — **nif·ti·ly** \'nif-tə-lē\ *adv*

²nifty *n, pl* **nifties** (1923) : something that is nifty; *esp* : a clever or neatly turned phrase or joke

Ni·ger–Con·go \,nī-jər-'kän-(,)gō\ *n* [*Niger* (river) + *Congo* (river)] (ca. 1950) : a language family that includes the Mande and Kwa branches and that is spoken by most of the indigenous peoples of west, central, and south Africa

nig·gard \'ni-gərd\ *n* [ME, of Scand origin; akin to ON *hnøggr* niggardly; akin to OE *hnēaw* niggardly] (14c) : a meanly covetous and stingy person : MISER — **niggard** *adj*

²niggard *vi* (ca. 1600) *obs* : to act niggardly ~ *vt, obs* : to treat in a niggardly manner

nig·gard·ly \-lē\ *adj* (1571) **1** : grudgingly mean about spending or granting : BEGRUDGING **2** : provided in meanly limited supply *syn* see STINGY — **nig·gard·li·ness** *n* — **niggardly** *adv*

nig·ger \'ni-gər\ *n* [alter. of earlier *neger*, fr. MF *negre*, fr. Sp or Pg *negro*, fr. *negro* black, fr. L *niger*] (1700) **1** : a black person — usu. taken to be offensive **2** : a member of any dark-skinned race — usu. taken to be offensive **3** : a member of a socially disadvantaged class of persons ⟨it's time for somebody to lead all of America's ~s . . . all the people who feel left out of the political process —Ron Dellums⟩ *usage Nigger* in senses 1 and 2 can be found in the works of such writers of the past as Joseph Conrad, Mark Twain, and Charles Dickens, but it now ranks as perhaps the most offensive and inflammatory racial slur in English. Its use by and among blacks is not always intended or taken as offensive, but, except in sense 3, it is otherwise a word expressive of racial hatred and bigotry.

¹nig·gle \'ni-gəl\ *vb* **nig·gled; nig·gling** \-g(ə-)liŋ\ [origin unknown] *vi* (ca. 1616) **1 a** : TRIFLE **b** : to spend too much effort on minor details **2** : to find fault constantly in a petty way : CARP ⟨she haggles, she ~s, she wears out our patience —Virginia Woolf⟩ **3** : GNAW ~ *vt* : to give stingily or in tiny portions — **nig·gler** \-g(ə-)lər\ *n*

²niggle *n* (1886) *chiefly Brit* : a trifling doubt, objection, or complaint

nig·gling \'ni-g(ə-)liŋ\ *adj* (1599) : PETTY; *also* : bothersome or persistent esp. in a petty or tiresome way ⟨~ injuries⟩ — **niggling** *n* — **nig·gling·ly** \-lē\ *adv*

¹nigh \'nī\ *adv* [ME, fr. OE *nēah*; akin to OHG *nāh*, adv., nigh, prep., nigh, after, ON *nā-* nigh] (bef. 12c) **1** : near in place, time, or relationship — often used with *on*, *onto*, or *unto* **2** : NEARLY, ALMOST

²nigh *adj* (bef. 12c) **1** : CLOSE, NEAR **2** *chiefly dial* : DIRECT, SHORT **3** : being on the left side ⟨the ~ horse⟩

³nigh *prep* (bef. 12c) : NEAR

⁴nigh *vt* (13c) : to draw or come near to : APPROACH ~ *vi* : to draw near

¹night \'nīt\ *n* [ME, fr. OE *niht*; akin to OHG *naht* night, L *noct-, nox*, Gk *nykt-, nyx*] (bef. 12c) **1** : the time from dusk to dawn when no sunlight is visible **2 a** : an evening or night taken as an occasion or point of time ⟨the opening ~⟩ **b** : an evening set aside for a particular purpose **3 a** : the quality or state of being dark **b** : a condition or period felt to resemble the darkness of night: as **(1)** : a period of dreary inactivity or affliction **(2)** : absence of moral values **c** : the beginning of darkness : NIGHTFALL — **night·less** \-ləs\ *adj*

²night *adj* (bef. 12c) **1** : of, relating to, or associated with the night ⟨~ air⟩ **2** : intended for use at night ⟨a ~ lamp⟩ **3** : existing, occurring, or functioning at night ⟨~ baseball⟩ ⟨a ~ nurse⟩ **b** : active or functioning then at night ⟨~ people⟩

night and day *adv* (bef. 12c) : all the time : CONTINUALLY

night blindness *n* (1754) : reduced visual capacity in faint light (as at night) — **night–blind** \'nīt-,blīnd\ *adj*

night–blooming cereus *n* (1832) : any of several night-blooming cacti; *esp* : a slender sprawling or climbing cactus (*Selenicereus grandiflorus*) often cultivated for its large showy fragrant white flowers

night·cap \'nīt-,kap\ *n* (14c) **1** : a cloth cap worn with nightclothes **2** : a usu. alcoholic drink taken at the end of the day **3** : the final race or contest of a day's sports; *esp* : the second game of a baseball doubleheader

night·clothes \-,klō(th)z\ *n pl* (1602) : garments for wear in bed

¹night·club \-,kləb\ *n* (1894) : a place of entertainment open at night usu. serving food and liquor, having a floor show, and providing music and space for dancing

²nightclub *vi* (1936) : to patronize nightclubs — **night·club·ber** *n*

night court *n* (1934) : a criminal court in a large city that sits at night (as for the summary disposition of criminal charges and the granting of bail)

night crawler *n* (1924) : EARTHWORM; *esp* : a large earthworm found on the soil surface at night

night·dress \'nīt-,dres\ *n* (ca. 1714) **1** : NIGHTGOWN **2** : NIGHTCLOTHES

night·fall \'nīt-,fȯl\ *n* (1700) : the close of the day : DUSK

night·glow \-,glō\ *n* (1951) : airglow seen during the night

night·gown \-,gaȯn\ *n* (14c) **1** *archaic* : DRESSING GOWN **2** : a loose garment for wear in bed

night·hawk \-,hȯk\ *n* (1611) **1 a** : any of a genus (*Chordeiles*) of American nightjars related to the whippoorwill **b** : a common European nightjar (*Caprimulgus europaeus*) **2** : a person who habitually is active late at night

night heron *n* (1784) : any of various widely distributed nocturnal or crepuscular herons (esp. genus *Nycticorax*)

night·ie \'nī-tē\ *or* **nighty** *n, pl* **night·ies** [*night*gown + -*ie*] (1871) : a nightgown for a woman or child

night·in·gale \'nī-t²n-,gāl, -tiŋ-\ *n* [ME, alter. of OE *nihtegale*, fr. *niht* + *galan* to sing — more at YELL] (13c) : any of several Old World thrushes (genus *Erithacus* and esp. *E. megarhynchos*) noted for the sweet usu. nocturnal song of the male; *also* : any of various other birds that sing at night

night·jar \'nīt-,jär\ *n* [fr. its harsh sound] (1630) : any of a family (Caprimulgidae) of medium-sized long-winged crepuscular or nocturnal birds (as the whippoorwills and nighthawks) having a short bill, short legs, and soft mottled plumage and feeding on insects which they catch on the wing — called also goatsucker

night latch *n* (1854) : a door lock having a spring bolt operated from the outside by a key and from the inside by a knob

night letter *n* (1910) : a telegram sent at night at a reduced rate for delivery the following morning

night·life \'nīt-,līf\ *n* (1852) : the activity of or entertainment provided for pleasure-seekers at night (as in nightclubs); *also* : establishments providing nightlife

night·light \-,līt\ *n* (1839) : a light kept burning throughout the night

¹night·long \-,lȯŋ\ *adj* (1850) : lasting the whole night ⟨~ festivities⟩

²night·long \-'lȯŋ\ *adv* (1870) : through the whole night

¹night·ly \-lē\ *adj* (bef. 12c) **1** : happening, done, or used by night or every night **2** : of or relating to the night or every night

²nightly *adv* (15c) : every night; *also* : at or by night

night·mare \'nīt-,mar, -,mer\ *n* [ME, fr. ¹night + ¹mare] (14c) **1** : an evil spirit formerly thought to oppress people during sleep **2** : a frightening dream that usu. awakens the sleeper **3** : something (as an experience, situation, or object) having the monstrous character of a nightmare or producing a feeling of anxiety or terror — **nightmare** *adj* — **night·mar·ish** \-,mar-ish, -,mer-\ *adj* — **night·mar·ish·ly** *adv*

night owl *n* (ca. 1846) : a person who keeps late hours at night

night rail *n* \-,rāl\ *n* [*night* + *rail*, a woman's loose garment] (1554) *archaic* : NIGHTGOWN

night raven *n* (bef. 12c) : a bird that cries at night

night rider *n* (1877) : a member of a secret band who ride masked at night doing acts of violence for the purpose of punishing or terrorizing

nights \'nīts\ *adv* (bef. 12c) : in the nighttime repeatedly : on any night ⟨works ~⟩

night·scope \'nīt-,skōp\ *n* (1972) : an optical device usu. using infrared radiation that enables a person to see objects in the dark better

night·shade \-,shād\ *n* (bef. 12c) **1** : any of a genus (*Solanum* of the family Solanaceae, the nightshade family) of herbs, shrubs, and trees having alternate leaves, cymose flowers, and fruits that are berries and including some poisonous weeds, various ornamentals, and important crop plants (as the potato and eggplant) **2** : BELLADONNA 1

night·shirt \-,shərt\ *n* (1857) : a nightgown resembling a shirt

night·side \-,sīd\ *n* (1848) : the side of a celestial body (as the earth, the moon, or a planet) not in daylight

night soil *n* (ca. 1774) : human excrement used esp. for fertilizing the soil

night·spot \'nīt-,spät\ *n* (1936) : NIGHTCLUB

night·stand \-,stand\ *n* (1892) : NIGHT TABLE

night·stick \-,stik\ *n* (1887) : a police officer's club

night table *n* (1788) : a small bedside table or stand

night·time \-,tīm\ *n, often attrib* (14c) : the time from dusk to dawn

night·walk·er \-,wȯ-kər\ *n* (15c) **1** : a person who roams about at night esp. with criminal intent **2** : PROSTITUTE, STREETWALKER

ni·hil·ism \'nī-(h)ə-,li-zəm, 'nē-\ *n* [G *Nihilismus*, fr. L *nihil* nothing — more at NIL] (ca. 1817) **1 a** : a viewpoint that traditional values and beliefs are unfounded and that existence is senseless and useless **b** : a doctrine that denies any objective ground of truth and esp. of moral truths **2 a (1)** : a doctrine or belief that conditions in the social organization are so bad as to make destruction desirable for its own sake independent of any constructive program or possibility **(2)** *cap* : the program of a 19th century Russian party advocating revolutionary reform and using terrorism and assassination **b** : TERRORISM — **ni·hil·ist** \-list\ *n or adj* — **ni·hil·is·tic** \,nī-(h)ə-'lis-tik, ,nē-\ *adj*

-nik *n suffix* [Yiddish, fr. Pol & Ukrainian] : one connected with or characterized by being ⟨beat*nik*⟩

Ni·ke \'nī-kē\ *n* [Gk *Nikē*] : the Greek goddess of victory

nil \'nil\ *n* [L, nothing, contr. of *nihil*, fr. OL *nihilum*, fr. *ne-* not + *hilum* trifle — more at NO] (1833) : NOTHING, ZERO — **nil** *adj*

nile green *n, often cap N* [*Nile* River, Africa] (1871) : a pale yellow green

Nile perch *n* (1926) : a large predaceous food fish (*Lates niloticus*) of the rivers and lakes of northern and central Africa that may exceed 200 pounds (91 kilograms) in weight

nill \'nil\ *vb* [ME *nilen*, fr. OE *nyllan*, fr. *ne* not + *wyllan* to wish — more at NO, WILL] *vi* (bef. 12c) *archaic* : to be unwilling : will not ⟨will you — you, I will marry you —Shak.⟩ ~ *vt, archaic* : REFUSE

Ni·lot·ic \nī-'lä-tik\ *adj* [L *Niloticus*, fr. Gk *Neilōtēs*, fr. *Neilos* Nile] (1653) **1** : of or relating to the Nile or the peoples of the Nile basin **2** : of, relating to, or being the languages of the Nilotic people

nil·po·tent \'nil-,pō-t²nt\ *adj* [L *nil* nothing + *potent-, potens* having power — more at POTENT] (1870) : equal to zero when raised to some power ⟨~ matrices⟩

¹nim \'nim\ *vb* **nimmed; nim·ming** [earlier *nim* to take, fr. ME *nimen*, fr. OE *niman*] *vt* (12c) *archaic* : STEAL, FILCH ~ *vi, archaic* : THIEVE

²nim *n* [prob. fr. ¹*nim*] (1901) : any of various games in which counters are laid out in one or more piles and each player in turn draws one or more counters with the object of taking the last counter, forcing the opponent to take it, or taking the most or fewest counters

nim·ble \'nim-bəl\ *adj* **nim·bler** \-b(ə-)lər\; **nim·blest** \-b(ə-)ləst\ [ME *nimel*, fr. OE *numol* holding much, fr. *niman* to take; akin to OHG *neman* to take, Gk *nemein* to distribute, manage, *nomos* pasture, *nomos* usage, custom, law] (14c) **1** : quick and light in motion : AGILE ⟨~ fingers⟩ **2** : marked by quick, alert, clever conception, comprehension, or resourcefulness ⟨a ~ mind⟩ **b** : RESPONSIVE, SENSITIVE ⟨a ~ listener⟩ — **nim·ble·ness** \-bəl-nəs\ *n* — **nim·bly** \-blē\ *adv*

nim·bo·stra·tus \,nim-bō-'strā-təs, -'stra-\ *n* [NL, fr. L *nimbus* + NL *stratus* stratus] (ca. 1909) : a low dark gray rainy cloud layer — see CLOUD illustration

nim·bus \'nim-bəs\ *n, pl* **nim·bi** \-,bī, -,bē\ *or* **nim·bus·es** [L, rainstorm, cloud; prob. akin to L *nebula* cloud — more at NEBULA] (1616) **1 a :** a luminous vapor, cloud, or atmosphere about a god or goddess when on earth **b :** a cloud or atmosphere (as of romance) about a person or thing **2 :** an indication (as a circle) of radiant light or glory about the head of a drawn or sculptured divinity, saint, or sovereign **3 a :** a rain cloud **b :** THUNDERHEAD; *also :* CUMULUS 2

ni·mi·e·ty \ni-'mī-ə-tē\ *n, pl* **-ties** [LL *nimietas,* fr. L *nimius* too much, adj., fr. *nimis,* adv.] (ca. 1564) : EXCESS, REDUNDANCY

nim·i·ny–pim·i·ny \,ni-mə-nē-'pi-mə-nē\ *adj* [prob. alter. of *namby-pamby*] (1786) : affectedly refined : FINICKY

nimbus 2

Nim·rod \'nim-,räd\ *n* [Heb *Nimrōdh*] **1 :** a descendant of Ham represented in Genesis as a mighty hunter and a king of Shinar **2** *not cap* : HUNTER

nin·com·poop \'nin-kəm-,püp, 'niŋ-\ *n* [origin unknown] (1676) : FOOL, SIMPLETON — **nin·com·poop·ery** \-,pü-pə-rē\ *n*

nine \'nīn\ *n* [ME, fr. *nyne,* adj., fr. OE *nigon;* akin to OHG *niun* nine, L *novem,* Gk *ennea*] (bef. 12c) **1** — see NUMBER table **2 :** the ninth in a set or series ⟨wears a ~⟩ **3 :** something having nine units or members: as **a** *cap* : the nine Muses **b :** a baseball team **c :** the first or last nine holes of an 18-hole golf course — **nine** *adj* — **nine** *pron, pl in constr* — **to the nines 1 :** to perfection **2 :** in a highly elaborate or showy manner ⟨dressed *to the nines*⟩

nine days' wonder *n* (1594) : something or someone that creates a short-lived sensation — called also *nine day wonder*

nine·fold \'nīn-,fōld, -'fōld\ *adj* (bef. 12c) **1 :** being nine times as great or as many **2 :** having nine units or members — **nine·fold** \-'fōld\ *adv*

nine·pin \-,pin\ *n* (1580) **1** *pl but sing in constr* **:** a bowling game resembling tenpins played without the headpin **2 :** a pin used in ninepins

nine·teen \nīn-'tēn, 'nīn-,\ *n* [ME *nynetene,* adj., fr. OE *nigontēne,* fr. *nigon* + *-tiene* (akin to OE *tien* ten) — more at TEN] (bef. 12c) — see NUMBER table — **nineteen** *adj* — **nineteen** *pron, pl in constr* — **nineteenth** \-'tēn(t)th, -,tēn(t)th\ *adj or n*

nine·ty \'nīn-tē\ *n, pl* **nineties** [ME *ninety,* adj., fr. OE *nigontig,* short for *hundnigontig,* fr. *hundnigontig,* n., group of 90, fr. *hund-,* lit., hundred + *nigon* nine + *-tig* group of 10; akin to OE *tien* ten] (bef. 12c) **1** — see NUMBER table **2** *pl* **:** the numbers 90 to 99; *specif* : the years 90 to 99 in a lifetime or century — **nine·ti·eth** \-tē-əth\ *adj or n* — **ninety** *adj* — **ninety** *pron, pl in constr*

nin·hy·drin \nin-'hī-drən\ *n* [fr. *Ninhydrin,* a trademark] (1913) : a poisonous crystalline oxidizing agent $C_9H_6O_4$ used esp. as an analytical reagent

nin·ja \'nin-jə, -(,)jä\ *n, pl* **ninja** *also* **ninjas** [Jp, fr. *nin-* persevere + *-ja* person] (1975) : a person trained in ancient Japanese martial arts and employed esp. for espionage and assassinations

nin·ny \'ni-nē\ *n, pl* **ninnies** [perh. by shortening & alter. fr. *an innocent*] (1593) : FOOL, SIMPLETON

nin·ny·ham·mer \'ni-nē-,ha-mər\ *n* (1592) : NINNY

ni·non \'nē-,nän\ *n* [prob. fr. F *Ninon,* nickname for *Anne*] (1911) : a smooth sheer fabric

ninth \'nīn(t)th\ *n, pl* **ninths** \'nīn(t)s, 'nīn(t)ths\ (13c) **1** — see NUMBER table **2 a :** a musical interval embracing an octave and a second **b :** the tone at this interval **c :** a chord containing a ninth — **ninth** *adj or adv*

ninth cranial nerve *n* (ca. 1961) : GLOSSOPHARYNGEAL NERVE

ni·o·bate \'nī-ə-,bāt\ *n* [NL *niobium* + E 1*-ate*] (1845) : a salt containing an anionic grouping of niobium and oxygen

Ni·o·be \'nī-ə-bē\ *n* [L, fr. Gk *Niobē*] : a daughter of Tantalus and wife of Amphion who while weeping for her slain children is turned into a stone from which her tears continue to flow

ni·o·bi·um \nī-'ō-bē-əm\ *n* [NL, fr. L *Niobe;* fr. its occurrence in tantalite] (1845) : a lustrous light gray ductile metallic element that resembles tantalum chemically and is used in alloys — see ELEMENT table

1nip \'nip\ *vb* **nipped; nip·ping** [ME *nippen;* akin to ON *hnippa* to prod] *vt* (14c) **1 a :** to catch hold of and squeeze tightly between two surfaces, edges, or points : PINCH, BITE ⟨the dog *nipped* his ankle⟩ **b :** to pinch in (as a garment) ⟨a dress *nipped* at the waist⟩ **2 a :** to sever by or as if by pinching sharply **b :** to destroy the growth, progress, or fulfillment of ⟨*nipped* in the bud⟩ **3 :** to injure or make numb with cold : CHILL **4 :** SNATCH, STEAL **5 :** to defeat by a small margin ~ *vi* **1 :** to move briskly, nimbly, or quickly **2** *chiefly Brit* : to make a quick trip

2nip *n* (1549) **1 :** something that nips: as **a** *archaic* : a sharp biting comment **b :** a sharp stinging cold ⟨a ~ in the air⟩ **c :** a biting or pungent flavor : TANG ⟨cheese with a ~⟩ **2 :** the act of nipping : PINCH, BITE **3 :** the region of a squeezing or crushing device (as a calender) where the rolls or jaws are closest together **4 :** a small portion

3nip *n* [prob. fr. *nipperkin,* a liquor container] (ca. 1796) : a small quantity of liquor : SIP; *also :* a very small bottle of liquor

4nip *vi* **nipped; nip·ping** (1887) : to take liquor in nips : TIPPLE

ni·pa \'nē-pə\ *n* [prob. fr. It, fr. Malay *nipah* nipa palm] (1779) : thatch made of leaves of the nipa palm

nip and tuck \,nip-ən(d)-'tək\ *adj or adv* (1832) : being so close that the lead or advantage shifts rapidly from one opponent to another

nipa palm *n* (1882) : a semiaquatic creeping palm (*Nipa fruticans*) found chiefly from India to Melanesia

nip·per \'ni-pər\ *n* (1541) **1 :** any of various devices (as pincers) for nipping — usu. used in pl. **2 a** *chiefly Brit* : a boy employed as a helper (as of a carter or hawker) **b :** CHILD; *esp* : a small boy

nipa palm

nip·ping \'ni-piŋ\ *adj* (1547) : SHARP, CHILLING — **nip·ping·ly** \-lē\ *adv*

nip·ple \'ni-pəl\ *n* [earlier *neble, nible,* prob. dim. of *neb, nib*] (1530) **1 :** the protuberance of a mammary gland upon which in the female the lactiferous ducts open and from which milk is drawn **2 a :** an artificial teat through which a bottle-fed infant nurses **b :** a device with an orifice through which the discharge of a liquid can be regulated **3 a :** a protuberance resembling or suggesting the nipple of a breast **b :** a small projection through which oil or grease is injected into machinery **4 :** a pipe coupling consisting of a short piece of threaded tubing — **nip·pled** \-pəld\ *adj*

Nip·pon·ese \,ni-pə-'nēz, -'nēs\ *adj* [*Nippon,* Japan] (1859) : JAPANESE — **Nipponese** *n*

nip·py \'ni-pē\ *adj* **nip·pi·er; -est** (1575) **1 :** marked by a tendency to nip ⟨a ~ dog⟩ **2 :** brisk, quick, or nimble in movement : SNAPPY **3 :** PUNGENT, SHARP **4 :** CHILLY, CHILLING ⟨a ~ day⟩ — **nip·pi·ly** \'ni-pə-lē\ *adv* — **nip·pi·ness** \'ni-pē-nəs\ *n*

nip–up \'nip-,əp\ *n* (1938) : a spring from a supine position to a standing position

nir·va·na \nir-'vä-nə, (,)nər-\ *n, often cap* [Skt *nirvāṇa,* lit., act of extinguishing, fr. *nis-* out + *vāti* it blows — more at WIND] (1801) **1 :** the final beatitude that transcends suffering, karma, and samsara and is sought esp. in Buddhism through the extinction of desire and individual consciousness **2 a :** a place or state of oblivion to care, pain, or external reality; *also :* BLISS, HEAVEN **b :** a goal hoped for but apparently unattainable : DREAM — **nir·van·ic** \-'vä-nik, -'va-\ *adj*

Ni·san \'ni-s⁰n, nē-'sän\ *n* [Heb *Nīsān*] (14c) : the 7th month of the civil year or the 1st month of the ecclesiastical year in the Jewish calendar — see MONTH table

ni·sei \nē-'sā, 'nē-,\ *n, pl* **nisei** *often cap* [Jp, lit., second generation, fr. *ni* second + *sei* generation] (1929) : a son or daughter of Japanese immigrants who is born and educated in America and esp. in the U.S.

ni·si \'nī-,sī\ *adj* [L, unless, fr. *ne-* not + *si* if] (1836) : taking effect at a specified time unless previously modified or avoided by cause shown, further proceedings, or a condition fulfilled ⟨a decree ~⟩

Nis·sen hut \'ni-s⁰n-\ *n* [Peter N. *Nissen* †1930 Brit. mining engineer] (1932) : a prefabricated shelter with a semicircular arching roof of corrugated iron sheeting and a concrete floor

ni·sus \'nī-səs\ *n, pl* **ni·sus** \-səs, -,süs\ [L, fr. *niti* to lean, rely, strive; akin to L *nictare* to wink — more at CONNIVE] (1699) : a mental or physical effort to attain an end : a perfective urge or endeavor

1nit \'nit\ *n* [ME *nite,* fr. OE *hnitu;* akin to OHG *hniz* nit, Gk *konid-, konis*] (bef. 12c) : the egg of a louse or other parasitic insect; *also :* the insect itself when young

2nit *n* (ca. 1941) *chiefly Brit* : NITWIT

nite *var of* NIGHT

ni·ter \'nī-tər\ *n* [ME *nitre* natron, fr. MF, fr. L *nitrum,* fr. Gk *nitron,* fr. Egypt *ntry*] (1684) **1 :** POTASSIUM NITRATE **2** *archaic* : CHILE SALTPETER

nit·ery *also* **nit·er·ie** \'nī-tə-rē\ *n, pl* **ni·ter·ies** [*nite* + *-ery* (as in *eatery*); *niterie* fr. *nite* + F *-erie* -ery] (ca. 1934) : NIGHTCLUB

nit·id \'ni-təd\ *adj* [L *nitidus* — more at NEAT] (ca. 1656) : BRIGHT, LUSTROUS

ni·ti·nol \'nī-t⁰n-,ōl, -,ōl\ *n* [*nickel* + *titanium* + *-nol* (fr. Naval Ordnance *Laboratory,* where it was created)] (1968) : a nonmagnetic alloy of titanium and nickel that after being deformed returns to its original shape upon being reheated

nit·pick \'nit-,pik\ *vb* [back-formation fr. *nit-picking*] *vi* (1966) : to engage in nit-picking ~ *vt* : to criticize by nit-picking — **nitpick** *n* — **nit·pick·er** *n* — **nit·picky** \-,pi-kē\ *adj*

nit–pick·ing \'nit-,pi-kiŋ\ *n* [1*nit*] (1956) : minute and usu. unjustified criticism

nitr- *or* **nitro-** *comb form* [*niter*] **1 :** nitrogen ⟨*nitride*⟩ **2** *usu nitro-* : containing the univalent group NO_2 composed of one nitrogen and two oxygen atoms ⟨*nitrobenzene*⟩

ni·trate \'nī-,trāt, -trət\ *n* [F, fr. *nitrique*] (1794) **1 :** a salt or ester of nitric acid **2 :** sodium nitrate or potassium nitrate used as a fertilizer

nitrate of soda (1843) : sodium nitrate used as a fertilizer

ni·tra·tion \nī-'trā-shən\ *n* (1887) : the process of adding a nitro group to an organic compound — **ni·trate** \'nī-,trāt\ *vt* — **ni·tra·tor** \-,trā-tər\ *n*

ni·tre *chiefly Brit var of* NITER

ni·tric acid \'nī-trik-\ *n* [F *nitrique,* fr. *nitre* niter, fr. MF] (1794) : a corrosive liquid inorganic acid HNO_3 used esp. as an oxidizing agent, in nitrations, and in making organic compounds (as fertilizers, explosives, and dyes)

nitric oxide *n* (1807) : a colorless poisonous gas NO formed by oxidation of nitrogen or ammonia

1ni·tride \'nī-,trīd\ *n* [ISV] (1850) : a binary compound of nitrogen with a more electropositive element

2nitride *vt* **ni·trid·ed; ni·trid·ing** (1928) : to case-harden (as steel) by causing the surface to absorb nitrogen

ni·tri·fi·ca·tion \,nī-trə-fə-'kā-shən\ *n* (1827) : the oxidation (as by bacteria) of ammonium salts to nitrites and the further oxidation of nitrites to nitrates

ni·tri·fi·er \'nī-trə-,fī-(ə-)r\ *n* (1903) : any of the nitrifying bacteria

ni·tri·fy·ing \'nī-trə-,fī-iŋ\ *adj* [F *nitrifier* to convert into nitrite, fr. *nitr-*] (1827) : active in or relating to nitrification ⟨~ organisms⟩ ⟨~ activities⟩

nitrifying bacteria *n pl* (1925) : bacteria of a family (Nitrobacteraceae) comprising gram-negative bacteria commonly found in the soil and obtaining energy through the process of nitrification

ni·trile \'nī-trəl, -,trīl\ *n* [ISV *nitr-* + *-il, -ile* (fr. L *-ilis* 1*-ile*)] (1848) : an organic cyanide containing the group CN which on hydrolysis yields an acid with elimination of ammonia

ni·trite \'nī-,trīt\ *n* (1800) : a salt or ester of nitrous acid

1ni·tro \'nī-(,)trō\ *adj* [*nitr-*] (1892) : containing or being the univalent group NO_2 united through nitrogen

\ə\ abut \³\ kitten, F table \ər\ further \a\ ash \ā\ ace \ä\ mop, mar \aů\ out \ch\ chin \e\ bet \ē\ easy \g\ go \i\ hit \ī\ ice \j\ job \ŋ\ sing \ō\ go \ò\ law \òi\ boy \th\ thin \t̲h\ the \ü\ loot \ů\ foot \y\ yet \zh\ vision \ȧ, k̲, ⁿ, œ, œ̄, ᵫ, ᵫ̄, ᵛ\ see Guide to Pronunciation

²**nitro** *n, pl* **nitros** (1903) : any of various nitrated products; *specif* : NITROGLYCERIN

ni·tro·ben·zene \,nī-trō-'ben-,zēn, -ben-'\ *n* [ISV] (1868) : a poisonous yellow insoluble oil $C_6H_5NO_2$ with an almond odor that is used esp. as a solvent, as a mild oxidizing agent, and in making aniline

ni·tro·cel·lu·lose \-'sel-yə-,lōs, -,lōz\ *n* [ISV] (1882) : any of several nitric-acid esters of cellulose used esp. for making explosives, plastics, and varnishes

ni·tro·fu·ran \,nī-trō-'fyúr-,an, -fyù-'ran\ *n* (1930) : any of several nitro derivatives of furan used as bacteria-inhibiting agents

ni·tro·gen \'nī-trə-jən\ *n, often attrib* [F *nitrogène,* fr. *nitre* niter + *-gène* -gen] (1794) : a colorless tasteless odorless element that as a diatomic gas is relatively inert and constitutes 78 percent of the atmosphere by volume and that occurs as a constituent of all living tissues — see ELEMENT table — **ni·trog·e·nous** \nī-'trä-jə-nəs\ *adj*

ni·tro·ge·nase \nī-'trä-jə-,nās, 'nī-trə-jə-, -,nāz\ *n* (1934) : an enzyme of various nitrogen-fixing bacteria that catalyzes the reduction of molecular nitrogen to ammonia

nitrogen balance *n* (1944) : the difference between nitrogen intake and nitrogen loss in the body or the soil

nitrogen cycle *n* (1908) : a continuous series of natural processes by which nitrogen passes successively from air to soil to organisms and back to air or soil involving principally nitrogen fixation, nitrification, decay, and denitrification

nitrogen dioxide *n* (1885) : a toxic reddish brown gas NO_2 that is a strong oxidizing agent, is produced by combustion (as of fossil fuels), and is an atmospheric pollutant

nitrogen fixation *n* (1895) : the metabolic assimilation of atmospheric nitrogen into ammonia by soil microorganisms and esp. rhizobia

nitrogen–fixer *n* (1912) : any of various soil microorganisms that are involved in nitrogen fixation

nitrogen–fixing *adj* (1899) : capable of nitrogen fixation ⟨~ bacteria⟩

nitrogen mustard *n* (1943) : any of various toxic blistering compounds analogous to mustard gas but containing nitrogen instead of sulfur

nitrogen narcosis *n* (1937) : a state of euphoria and exhilaration that occurs when nitrogen in normal air enters the bloodstream at approximately seven times atmospheric pressure (as in deep-water diving) — called also *rapture of the deep*

nitrogen oxide *n* (ca. 1934) : any of several oxides of nitrogen most of which are produced in combustion and are considered to be atmospheric pollutants: as **a** : NITRIC OXIDE **b** : NITROGEN DIOXIDE **c** : NITROUS OXIDE

nitrogen tetroxide *n* (1885) : a colorless toxic gas N_2O_4 that is a dimer of nitrogen dioxide and that in liquid form is used as an oxidizer in rocket engines

ni·tro·glyc·er·in *or* **ni·tro·glyc·er·ine** \,nī-trə-'glis-rən, -'gli-sə-\ *n* [ISV] (1857) : a heavy oily explosive poisonous liquid $C_3H_5N_3O_9$ used chiefly in making dynamites and in medicine as a vasodilator

ni·tro·meth·ane \,nī-trō-'me-,thān, *Brit usu* -'mē-\ *n* (1872) : a liquid nitroparaffin CH_3NO_2 that is used as an industrial solvent, in chemical synthesis, and as a fuel for rockets and high-performance engines

ni·tro·par·af·fin \-'par-ə-fən\ *n* [ISV] (1892) : any of various nitro derivatives of alkanes

nitros- *or* **nitroso-** *comb form* [NL *nitrosus* nitrous] : containing the group NO ⟨*nitrosamine*⟩

ni·tro·sa·mine \nī-'trō-sə-,mēn\ *n* (1878) : any of various organic compounds which are characterized by the grouping NNO and some of which are powerful carcinogens

ni·trous \'nī-trəs\ *adj* [NL *nitrosus,* fr. L, full of natron, fr. *nitrum* natron — more at NITER] (1601) *archaic* : of, relating to, or containing niter

nitrous acid *n* (1676) : an unstable acid HNO_2 known only in solution or in the form of its salts

nitrous oxide *n* (1800) : a colorless gas N_2O that when inhaled produces loss of sensibility to pain preceded by exhilaration and sometimes laughter and is used esp. as an anesthetic in dentistry and that is an atmospheric pollutant produced by combustion and a suspected contributor to greenhouse warming — called also *laughing gas*

nit·ty–grit·ty \'ni-tē-,gri-tē, ,ni-tē-'\ *n* [origin unknown] (1963) : what is essential and basic : specific practical details ⟨get down to the ~ of the problem⟩ — **nitty–gritty** *adj*

nit·wit \'nit-,wit\ *n* [prob. fr. G dial. *nit* not + E *wit*] (ca. 1922) : a scatterbrained or stupid person

¹**nix** \'niks\ *n* [G *nichts* nothing] (1789) : NOTHING

²**nix** *vt* (ca. 1934) : VETO, REJECT ⟨the court ~ed the merger⟩

³**nix** *adv* (ca. 1909) : NO — used to express disagreement or the withholding of permission; often used with *on* ⟨they said ~ on our plan⟩

⁴**nix** *n* [G, fr. OHG *nihhus*; akin to OE *nicor* water monster and perh. to Gk *nizein* to wash] (1833) : a water sprite of Germanic folklore

¹**nix·ie** \'nik-sē\ *n* [G *Nixe* female nix, fr. OHG *nichessa,* fem. of *nihhus* nix] (1816) : ⁴NIX

²**nixie** *also* **nixy** \'nik-sē\ *n, pl* **nix·ies** [¹*nix* + *-ie*] (ca. 1890) : a piece of mail that is undeliverable because illegibly or incorrectly addressed

Nix·ie \'nik-sē\ *trademark* — used for an electronic indicator tube

ni·zam \ni-'zäm, 'ni-,zam, nī-'\ *n* [Hindi *niẓām* order, governor, fr. Ar *niẓām*] (1768) : one of a line of sovereigns of Hyderabad, India, reigning from 1713 to 1950 — **ni·zam·ate** \ni-'zä-,māt, nī-'za-\ *n*

¹**no** \'nō\ *adv* [ME, fr. OE *nā,* fr. *ne* not + *ā* always; akin to ON & OHG *ne* not, L *ne-,* Gk *nē-* — more at AYE] (bef. 12c) **1 a** *chiefly Scot* : NOT **b** — used as a function word to express the negative of an alternative choice or possibility ⟨shall we go out to dinner or ~⟩ **2 :** in no respect or degree — used in comparisons ⟨is no better⟩ **3 :** not so — used to express negation, dissent, denial, or refusal ⟨~, I'm not going⟩ **4** — used with a following adjective to imply a meaning expressed by the opposite positive statement ⟨in ~ uncertain terms⟩ **5** — used as a function word to emphasize a following negative or to introduce a more emphatic, explicit, or comprehensive statement **6** — used as an interjection to express surprise, doubt, or incredulity **7** — used in combination with a verb to form a compound adjective ⟨*no*-bake pie⟩

²**no** *adj* (12c) **1 a :** not any ⟨~ parking⟩ ⟨~ disputing the decision⟩ **b :** hardly any : very little ⟨finished in ~ time⟩ **2 :** not a : quite other than a ⟨he's ~ expert⟩ **3** — used in combination with a noun to form a compound adjective ⟨a *no*-nonsense realist⟩

³**no** \'nō\ *n, pl* **noes** *or* **nos** \'nōz\ (1588) **1 :** an act or instance of refusing or denying by the use of the word *no* : DENIAL **2 a :** a negative vote or decision **b** *pl* : persons voting in the negative

No *or* **Noh** \'nō\ *n, pl* **No** *or* **Noh** [Jp *nō,* lit., talent] (1871) : classic Japanese dance-drama having a heroic theme, a chorus, and highly stylized action, costuming, and scenery

no–account *adj* (1845) : of no account : TRIFLING ⟨her ~ relatives⟩

No·a·chi·an \nō-'ā-kē-ən\ *adj* [Heb *Nōaḥ* Noah] (1678) **1 :** of or relating to the patriarch Noah or his time **2 :** ANCIENT, ANTIQUATED

No·ah \'nō-ə\ *n* [Heb *Nōaḥ*] : an Old Testament patriarch who built the ark in which he, his family, and living creatures of every kind survived the Flood

¹**nob** \'näb\ *n* [prob. alter. of *knob*] (ca. 1700) **1 :** HEAD 1 **2 :** a jack of the same suit as the starter in cribbage that scores one point for the holder — usu. used in the phrases *his nob* or *his nobs*

²**nob** *n* [perh. fr. ¹*nob*] (1703) *chiefly Brit* : one in a superior position in life

nob·ble \'nä-bəl\ *vt* **nob·bled; nob·bling** \-b(ə-)liŋ\ [perh. irreg. freq. of *nab*] (1847) **1** *Brit* **a :** to incapacitate (a racehorse) esp. by drugging **2** *slang Brit* **a :** to win over to one's side **b :** STEAL **c :** SWINDLE, CHEAT **d :** to get hold of : CATCH — **nob·bler** \-b(ə-)lər\ *n*

nob·by \'nä-bē\ *adj* **nob·bi·er; -est** (1788) : CHIC, SMART

No·bel·ist \nō-'be-list\ *n* (1938) : a winner of a Nobel prize

no·bel·i·um \nō-'be-lē-əm\ *n* [NL, fr. Alfred B. *Nobel*] (1957) : a radioactive element produced artificially — see ELEMENT table

No·bel prize \nō-'bel-, 'nō-,bel-\ *n* (1900) : any of various annual prizes (as in peace, literature, medicine) established by the will of Alfred Nobel for the encouragement of persons who work for the interests of humanity

no·bil·i·ty \nō-'bi-lə-tē\ *n* [ME *nobilite,* fr. MF *nobilité,* fr. L *nobilitat-, nobilitas,* fr. *nobilis*] (14c) **1 :** the quality or state of being noble in character, quality, or rank **2 :** the body of persons forming the noble class in a country or state : ARISTOCRACY

¹**no·ble** \'nō-bəl\ *adj* **no·bler** \-b(ə-)lər\; **no·blest** \-b(ə-)ləst\ [ME, fr. OF, fr. L *nobilis* well-known, noble, fr. *noscere* to come to know — more at KNOW] (13c) **1 a :** possessing outstanding qualities : ILLUSTRIOUS **b :** FAMOUS, NOTABLE ⟨~ deeds⟩ **2 :** of high birth or exalted rank : ARISTOCRATIC **3 a :** possessing very high or excellent qualities or properties ⟨~ wine⟩ **b :** very good or excellent **4 :** grand or impressive esp. in appearance ⟨~ edifice⟩ **5 :** possessing, characterized by, or arising from superiority of mind or character or of ideals or morals : LOFTY ⟨~ ambition⟩ **6 :** chemically inert or inactive esp. toward oxygen ⟨a ~ metal such as platinum⟩ — compare BASE 6a *syn* see MORAL — **no·ble·ness** \-bəl-nəs\ *n* — **no·bly** \-blē *also* -bə-lē\ *adv*

²**noble** *n* (14c) **1 :** a person of noble rank or birth **2 :** an old English gold coin equivalent to 6s 8d

noble gas *n* (1902) : any of a group of rare gases that include helium, neon, argon, krypton, xenon, and sometimes radon and that exhibit great stability and extremely low reaction rates — called also *inert gas*

no·ble·man \'nō-bəl-mən\ *n* (14c) : a man of noble rank : PEER

noble savage *n* (1672) : a mythic conception of people belonging to non-European cultures as having innate natural simplicity and virtue uncorrupted by European civilization; *also* : a person exemplifying this conception

no·blesse \nō-'bles\ *n* [ME, fr. OF *noblesce,* fr. *noble*] (13c) **1 :** noble birth or condition **2 :** the members esp. of the French nobility

no·blesse oblige \nō-'bles-ə-'blēzh\ *n* [F, lit., nobility obligates] (1837) : the obligation of honorable, generous, and responsible behavior associated with high rank or birth

no·ble·wom·an \'nō-bəl-,wù-mən\ *n* (13c) : a woman of noble rank : PEERESS

¹**no·body** \'nō-bə-dē, -,bä-dē\ *pron* (14c) : no person : not anybody

²**nobody** *n, pl* **no·bod·ies** (1581) : a person of no influence or consequence

no–brain·er \'nō-'brā-nər\ *n* (1973) : something that requires a minimum of thought

no·cent \'nō-s°nt\ *adj* [ME, fr. L *nocent-, nocens,* fr. prp. of *nocēre* to harm, hurt — more at NOXIOUS] (15c) : HARMFUL

no·ci·cep·tive \,nō-si-'sep-tiv\ *adj* [L *nocēre* + E *-i-* + *receptive*] (1904) **1** *of a stimulus* : PAINFUL, INJURIOUS **2 :** of, induced by, or responding to a nociceptive stimulus — used esp. of receptors or protective reflexes

¹**nock** \'näk\ *n* [ME *nocke* notched tip on the end of a bow; akin to MD *nocke* summit] (14c) **1 :** one of the notches cut in either of two tips of horn fastened on the ends of a bow or in the bow itself for holding the string **2 a :** the part of an arrow having a notch for the bowstring **b :** the notch itself

²**nock** *vt* (14c) **1 :** to make a nock in (a bow or arrow) **2 :** to fit (an arrow) against the bowstring

no contest *n* (1952) : NOLO CONTENDERE

noct·am·bu·list \näk-'tam-byə-list\ *n* [L *noct-, nox* night + *-ambulist* (as in *somnambulist*)] — more at NIGHT] (ca. 1731) : SLEEPWALKER

noc·ti·lu·cent cloud \,näk-tə-'lü-s°nt-\ *n* [*noctilucent* ultim. fr. L *noct- + lucent-, lucens* lucent] (1910) : a luminous thin usu. colored cloud seen esp. at twilight at a height of about 50 miles (80 kilometers)

noc·tu·id \'näk-chə-wəd, 'näk-tə-\ *n* [NL *Noctuidae,* fr. *Noctua,* genus of moths, fr. L, the little owl (*Athene noctua*); akin to L *nox* night] (1894) : any of a large family (Noctuidae) of medium-sized often dull-colored moths with larvae (as cutworms and armyworms) that are often destructive agricultural pests — **noctuid** *adj*

noc·turn \'näk-,tərn\ *n* [ME *nocturne,* fr. MF, fr. ML *nocturna,* fr. L, fem. of *nocturnus*] (14c) : a principal division of the office of matins

noc·tur·nal \näk-'tər-n°l\ *adj* [ME, fr. MF or LL; MF, fr. LL *nocturnalis,* fr. L *nocturnus* of night, nocturnal, fr. *noct-, nox* night] (15c) **1 :** of, relating to, or occurring in the night ⟨a ~ journey⟩ **2 :** active at night ⟨a ~ predator⟩ — **noc·tur·nal·ly** \-n°l-ē\ *adv*

noc·turne \'näk-,tərn\ *n* [F, adj., nocturnal, fr. L *nocturnus*] (1862) : a work of art dealing with evening or night; *esp* : a dreamy pensive composition for the piano — compare AUBADE 3

noc·u·ous \'nä-kyə-wəs\ *adj* [L *nocuus,* fr. *nocēre* to harm — more at NOXIOUS] (1635) : HARMFUL — **noc·u·ous·ly** *adv*

¹**nod** \'näd\ *vb* **nod·ded; nod·ding** [ME *nodden;* perh. akin to OHG *hnotōn* to shake] *vi* (14c) **1 :** to make a quick downward motion of the head whether deliberately (as in expressing assent, salutation, or command) or involuntarily (as from drowsiness) **2 :** to incline or sway

from the vertical as though ready to fall **3 :** to bend or sway the upper part gently downward or forward **:** bob gently **4 :** to make a slip or error in a moment of abstraction ~ *vt* **·1 :** to incline (as the head) downward or forward **2 :** to bring, invite, or send by a nod ⟨*nodded* them into the room⟩ **3 :** to signify by a nod ⟨*nodded* their approval⟩ — **nod·der** *n*

²**nod** *n* (ca. 1541) **1 :** the act or an instance of nodding ⟨gave a ~ of greeting⟩ **2 :** an indication esp. of approval or recognition ⟨received the party's ~ as candidate for governor⟩

nod·al \'nō-d⁹l\ *adj* (1831) **:** being, relating to, or located at or near a node — **no·dal·i·ty** \nō-'da-lə-tē\ *n* — **nod·al·ly** \'nō-d⁹l-ē\ *adv*

nodding *adj* (1590) **1 :** bending downward or forward **:** PENDULOUS, DROOPING ⟨a plant with ~ flowers⟩ **2 :** SLIGHT, SUPERFICIAL ⟨a ~ acquaintance⟩

nod·dle \'nä-d⁹l\ *n* [ME *nodle* back of the head or neck] (1579) **:** HEAD, PATE

nod·dy \'nä-dē\ *n, pl* **noddies** [prob. short for obs. *noddypoll*, alter. of *hoddypoll* fumbling inept person] (ca. 1530) **1 :** a stupid person **2 :** any of several stout-bodied terns (esp. genus *Anous*) of warm seas

node \'nōd\ *n* [ME, fr. L *nodus* knot, node; akin to MIr *naidm* bond] (15c) **1 a :** a pathological swelling or enlargement (as of a rheumatic joint) **b :** a discrete mass of one kind of tissue enclosed in tissue of a different kind **2 :** an entangling complication (as in a drama) **:** PREDICAMENT **3 :** either of the two points where the orbit of a planet or comet intersects the ecliptic; *also* **:** either of the points at which the orbit of an earth satellite crosses the plane of the equator **4 a :** a point, line, or surface of a vibrating body or system that is free or relatively free from vibratory motion **b :** a point at which a wave has an amplitude of zero **5 a :** a point at which subsidiary parts originate or center **b :** a point on a stem at which a leaf or leaves are inserted **c :** a point at which a curve intersects itself in such a manner that the branches have different tangents **d :** VERTEX 1b

node of Ran·vier \-'räⁿ-vē-ˌā\ [Louis A. *Ranvier* †1922 Fr. histologist] (ca. 1885) **:** a constriction in the myelin sheath of a myelinated nerve fiber

nod off *vi* (1914) **:** to fall asleep

no·dose \'nō-ˌdōs\ *adj* [L *nodosus*, fr. *nodus*] (ca. 1721) **:** having numerous or conspicuous protuberances — **no·dos·i·ty** \nō-'dä-sə-tē\ *n*

nod·u·lar \'nä-jə-lər\ *adj* (1794) **:** of, relating to, characterized by, or occurring in the form of nodules ⟨~ lesions⟩

nod·u·la·tion \ˌnä-jə-'lā-shən\ *n* (1872) **1 :** the process of forming nodules and esp. root nodules containing symbiotic bacteria **2 :** NODULE

nod·ule \'nä-(ˌ)jü(ə)l\ *n* [ME, fr. L *nodulus*, dim. of *nodus*] (15c) **:** a small mass of rounded or irregular shape: as **a :** a small rounded lump of a mineral or mineral aggregate **b :** a swelling on a leguminous root that contains symbiotic bacteria **c :** a small abnormal knobby bodily protuberance (as a tumorous growth or a calcification near an arthritic joint)

no·dus \'nō-dəs\ *n, pl* **no·di** \'nō-ˌdī, -ˌdē\ [L, knot, node] (ca. 1738) **:** COMPLICATION, DIFFICULTY

no·el \nō-'el\ *n* [F *noël* Christmas, carol, fr. L *natalis* birthday, fr. *natalis* natal] (1811) **1 :** a Christmas song, carol **2** *cap* **:** CHRISTMAS

noes *pl of* NO

no·et·ic \nō-'e-tik\ *adj* [Gk *noētikos* intellectual, fr. *noein* to think, fr. *nous* mind] (1653) **:** of, relating to, or based on the intellect

no–fault *adj* (1967) **1 :** of, relating to, or being a motor vehicle insurance plan under which someone involved in an accident is compensated usu. up to a stipulated limit for actual losses (as for property damage, medical bills, and lost wages) by that person's own insurance company regardless of who is responsible for the accident **2 :** of, relating to, or being a divorce law under which neither party is held responsible for the breakup of the marriage **3 :** characterized by the absence of a prevailing sense of individual responsibility (as for behavior) ⟨a ~ society⟩

no–frills \'nō-'frilz\ *adj* (1960) **:** offering or providing only the essentials **:** not fancy, elaborate, or luxurious

nog \'näg\ *n* [origin unknown] (1693) **1 :** a strong ale formerly brewed in Norfolk, England **2** [by shortening] **:** EGGNOG

nog·gin \'nä-gən\ *n* [origin unknown] (1630) **1 :** a small mug or cup **2 :** a small quantity (as a gill) of drink **3 :** a person's head

nog·ging \'nä-gən, -giŋ\ *n* [*nog* wooden block the size of a brick] (1825) **:** rough brick masonry used to fill in the open spaces of a wooden frame

¹**no–good** \'nō-'gủd\ *adj* (1908) **:** having no worth, virtue, use, or chance of success

²**no–good** \'nō-ˌgủd\ *n* (1924) **:** a no-good person or thing

Noh *var of* NO

no–hit *adj* (1916) **:** of, relating to, or being a baseball game or a part of a game in which a pitcher allows the opposition no base hits

no–hit·ter \ˌnō-'hi-tər\ *n* (1947) **:** a no-hit game in baseball

no–holds–barred \ˌnō-ˌhōl(d)z-'bärd\ *adj* (1942) **:** free of restrictions or hampering conventions ⟨a ~ contest⟩

no–hop·er \'nō-ˌhō-pər\ *n* (ca. 1943) *chiefly Brit* **:** one that has no chance of success

no·how \'nō-ˌhaủ\ *adv* (1775) **1 :** in no manner or way **:** not at all ⟨was ~ equal to the task⟩ **2** *dial* **:** ANYHOW

noil \'nói(ə)l\ *n* [origin unknown] (ca. 1624) **:** short fiber removed during the combing of a textile fiber and often separately spun into yarn

noir \'nwär\ *n* [short for *film noir*] (1980) **1 :** crime fiction featuring hard-boiled cynical characters and bleak sleazy settings **2 :** FILM NOIR — **noir·ish** \-ish\ *adj*

¹**noise** \'nóiz\ *n* [ME, fr. OF, strife, quarrel, noise, fr. L *nausea* nausea] (13c) **1 :** loud, confused, or senseless shouting or outcry **2 a :** SOUND; *esp* **:** one that lacks agreeable musical quality or is noticeably unpleasant **b :** any sound that is undesired or interferes with one's hearing of something **c :** an unwanted signal or a disturbance (as static or a variation of voltage) in an electronic device or instrument (as radio or television); *broadly* **:** a disturbance interfering with the operation of a usu. mechanical device or system **d :** electromagnetic radiation (as light or radio waves) that is composed of several frequencies and that involves random changes in frequency or amplitude **e :** irrelevant or meaningless data or output occurring along with desired infor-

mation **3 :** common talk **:** RUMOR; *esp* **:** SLANDER **4 :** something that attracts attention ⟨the play ... will make little ~ in the world —Brendan Gill⟩ **5 :** something spoken or uttered — **noise·less** \-ləs\ *adj* — **noise·less·ly** *adv*

²**noise** *vb* **noised; nois·ing** *vi* (14c) **1 :** to talk much or loudly **2 :** to make a noise ~ *vt* **:** to spread by rumor or report — usu. used with *about* or *abroad* ⟨the scandal was quickly *noised* about⟩

noise·mak·er \'nóiz-ˌmā-kər\ *n* (1574) **:** one that makes noise; *esp* **:** a device (as a horn or rattle) used to make noise at parties — **noise·mak·ing** \-kiŋ\ *n or adj*

noise pollution *n* (1966) **:** annoying or harmful noise (as of automobiles or jet airplanes) in an environment

noi·sette \nwä-'zet, nwä-\ *n* [F, dim. of *nois* choice cut of meat, lit., nut, fr. OF, fr. L *nux* — more at NUT] (1891) **:** a small piece of lean meat

noi·some \'nói-səm\ *adj* [ME *noysome*, fr. *noy* annoyance, fr. OF *enui*, *anoi* — more at ENNUI] (14c) **1 a :** NOXIOUS, HARMFUL **2 a :** offensive to the senses and esp. to the sense of smell **b :** highly obnoxious or objectionable *syn* see MALODOROUS — **noi·some·ly** *adv* — **noi·some·ness** *n*

noisy \'nói-zē\ *adj* **nois·i·er; -est** (1693) **1 :** making noise **2 :** full of or characterized by noise or clamor **3 :** noticeably showy, gaudy, or bright **:** CONSPICUOUS — **nois·i·ly** \'nói-zə-lē\ *adv* — **nois·i·ness** \-zē-nəs\ *n*

no·li me tan·ge·re \ˌnō-lē-(ˌ)mē-'tan-jə-rē, -ˌlī-, -(ˌ)mā-\ *n* [L, do not touch me; fr. Jesus' words to Mary Magdalene (Jn 20:17)] (1591) **:** a warning against touching or interference

nol·le pro·se·qui \ˌnä-lē-'prä-sə-ˌkwī\ *n* [L, to be unwilling to pursue] (1681) **:** an entry on the record of a legal action denoting that the prosecutor or plaintiff will proceed no further in an action or suit either as a whole or as to some count or as to one or more of several defendants

no·lo \'nō-(ˌ)lō\ *n* (1914) **:** NOLO CONTENDERE

no–load \'nō-'lōd\ *adj* (1963) **:** charging no sales commission ⟨a ~ mutual fund⟩ — **no–load** \'nō-ˌlōd\ *n*

no·lo con·ten·de·re \'nō-(ˌ)lō-kən-'ten-də-rē\ *n* [L, I do not wish to contend] (1872) **:** a plea in a criminal prosecution that without admitting guilt subjects the defendant to conviction but does not preclude denying the truth of the charges in a collateral proceeding

nol–pros \'näl-'präs\ *vt* **nol–prossed; nol–pros·sing** [*nolle prosequi*] (ca. 1878) **:** to discontinue by entering a nolle prosequi

no·ma \'nō-mə\ *n* [NL, fr. Gk *nomē*, fr. *nemein* to spread (of an ulcer), lit., to graze, pasture — more at NIMBLE] (1834) **:** a spreading invasive gangrene chiefly of the lining of the cheek and lips that is usu. fatal and occurs most often in persons severely debilitated by disease or profound nutritional deficiency

no·mad \'nō-ˌmad, *Brit also* 'nä-\ *n* [L *nomad-, nomas* member of a wandering pastoral people, fr. Gk, fr. *nemein*] (1579) **1 :** a member of a people who have no fixed residence but move from place to place usu. seasonally and within a well-defined territory **2 :** an individual who roams about aimlessly — **nomad** *adj* — **no·mad·ism** \'nō-ˌma-ˌdi-zəm\ *n*

no·mad·ic \nō-'ma-dik\ *adj* (ca. 1818) **1 :** of, relating to, or characteristic of nomads ⟨a ~ tribe⟩ **2 :** roaming about from place to place aimlessly, frequently, or without a fixed pattern of movement

no–man's–land \'nō-ˌmanz-ˌland\ *n* (14c) **1 a :** an area of unowned, unclaimed, or uninhabited land **b :** an unoccupied area between opposing armies **2 :** an anomalous, ambiguous, or indefinite area esp. of operation, application, or jurisdiction ⟨the ~ between art and science⟩

nom·bril \'näm-brəl\ *n* [MF, lit., navel, ultim. fr. L *umbilicus*] (1562) **:** the center point of the lower half of an armorial escutcheon

nom de guerre \ˌnäm-di-'ger\ *n, pl* **noms de guerre** \ˌnäm(z)-di-\ [F, lit., war name] (1679) **:** PSEUDONYM

nom de plume \-'plüm\ *n, pl* **noms de plume** \ˌnäm(z)-di-\ [F, pen name; prob. coined in E] (1823) **:** PSEUDONYM, PEN NAME

nome \'nōm\ *n* [Gk *nomos* pasture, district — more at NIMBLE] (ca. 1727) **:** a province of ancient Egypt

no·men \'nō-mən\ *n, pl* **no·mi·na** \'nä-mə-nə, 'nō-\ [L *nomin-, nomen* name — more at NAME] (ca. 1890) **:** the second of the three usual names of an ancient Roman male

no·men·cla·tor \'nō-mən-ˌklā-tər\ *n* [L, slave whose duty was to announce the names of persons met during a political campaign, fr. *nomen* + *calare* to call — more at LOW] (1585) **1 :** a book containing collections or lists of words **2** *archaic* **:** one who announces the names of guests or of persons generally **3 :** one who gives names to or invents names for things

no·men·cla·to·ri·al \ˌnō-mən-klə-'tōr-ē-əl, -'tòr-\ *adj* (1885) **:** relating to or connected with nomenclature

no·men·cla·ture \'nō-mən-ˌklā-chər *also* nō-'men-klə-ˌchủr, -'meŋ-, -chər, -ˌtyủr, -ˌtủr\ *n* [L *nomenclatura* assigning of names, fr. *nomen* + *calatus*, pp. of *calare*] (1610) **1 :** NAME, DESIGNATION **2 :** the act or process or an instance of naming **3 a :** a system or set of terms or symbols esp. in a particular science, discipline, or art **b :** an international system of standardized New Latin names used in biology for kinds and groups of kinds of animals and plants — **no·men·cla·tur·al** \ˌnō-mən-'kläch-rəl, -'klā-chə-\ *adj*

no·men con·ser·van·dum \'nō-mən-ˌkän(t)-sər-'van-dəm\ *n, pl* **no·mi·na con·ser·van·da** \'nä-mə-nə-ˌkän(t)-sər-'van-də, 'nō-\ [NL, name to be kept] (ca. 1925) **:** a biological taxonomic name that is preserved by special sanction in exception to the usual rules

nomen du·bi·um \-'dü-bē-əm, -'dyü-\ *n, pl* **nomina du·bia** \-bē-ə\ [NL, doubtful name] (1937) **:** a taxonomic name that cannot be assigned with certainty to any taxonomic group because the description is insufficient for identification and the original specimens no longer exist

nomen nu·dum \-'nü-dəm, -'nyü-\ *n, pl* **nomina nu·da** \-də\ [NL, bare name] (1900) **:** a proposed taxonomic name that is invalid because the group designated is not described or illustrated sufficiently for

---

\ə\ abut \ᵊ\ kitten, F table \ər\ further \a\ ash \ā\ ace \ä\ mop, mar \aủ\ out \ch\ chin \e\ bet \ē\ easy \g\ go \i\ hit \ī\ ice \j\ job \ŋ\ sing \ō\ go \ò\ law \òi\ boy \th\ thin \t̲h̲\ the \ü\ loot \ủ\ foot \y\ yet \zh\ vision \à, k̲, ⁿ, œ, œ̄, ụe, ụ̄e, ᵞ\ *see* Guide to Pronunciation recognition, that has no nomenclatural status, and that consequently can be used as though never previously proposed

¹nom·i·nal \'nä-mə-n²l, 'näm-nəl\ *adj* [ME *nominalle*, fr. ML *nominalis*, fr. L, of a name, fr. *nomin-, nomen* name — more at NAME] (15c) **1** : of, relating to, or being a noun or a word or expression taking a noun construction **2 a** : of, relating to, or constituting a name **b** : bearing the name of a person **3 a** : existing or being something in name or form only ⟨~ head of his party⟩ **b** : of, being, or relating to a designated or theoretical size that may vary from the actual : APPROXIMATE **c** : TRIFLING, INSIGNIFICANT **4** *of a rate of interest* **a** : equal to the annual rate of simple interest that would obtain if interest were not compounded when in fact it is compounded and paid for periods of less than a year **b** : equal to the percentage by which a repaid loan exceeds the principal borrowed with no adjustment made for inflation **5** : being according to plan : SATISFACTORY ⟨everything was ~ during the spacecraft launch⟩ — **nom·i·nal·ly** *adv*

²nominal *n* (1904) : a word or word group functioning as a noun

nom·i·nal·ism \'nä-mə-n²l-,i-zəm, 'näm-nə-,li-zəm\ *n* (1844) **1** : a theory that there are no universal essences in reality and that the mind can frame no single concept or image corresponding to any universal or general term **2** : the theory that only individuals and no abstract entities (as essences, classes, or propositions) exist — compare ESSENTIALISM, REALISM — **nom·i·nal·ist** \-ist, -list\ *n* — **nominalist** or **nom·i·nal·is·tic** \,nä-mə-n²l-'is-tik, ,näm-nə-'lis-\ *adj*

nominal value *n* (ca. 1901) : PAR 1b

nominal wages *n pl* (1898) : wages measured in money as distinct from actual purchasing power

nom·i·nate \'nä-mə-,nāt\ *vt* **-nat·ed; -nat·ing** [L *nominatus*, pp. of *nominare*, fr. *nomin-, nomen* name — more at NAME] (1545) **1** : DESIGNATE, NAME **2 a** : to appoint or propose for appointment to an office or place **b** : to propose as a candidate for election to office **c** : to propose for an honor ⟨~ her for player of the year⟩ **3** : to enter (a horse) in a race — **nom·i·na·tor** \-,nā-tər\ *n*

nom·i·na·tion \,nä-mə-'nā-shən\ *n* (15c) **1** : the act, process, or an instance of nominating **2** : the state of being nominated

nom·i·na·tive \'näm-nə-tiv, 'nä-mə-; *2 & 3 are also* 'nä-mə-,nä-\ *adj* [ME *nominatyf*, fr. MF or L; MF *nominatif*, fr. L (*casus*) *nominativus* nominative case, fr. *nominare*; fr. the traditional use of the nominative form in naming a noun] (14c) **1 a** : marking typically the subject of a verb esp. in languages that have relatively full inflection ⟨~ case⟩ **b** : of or relating to the nominative case ⟨a ~ ending⟩ **2** : nominated or appointed by nomination **3** : bearing a person's name — **nominative** *n*

nom·i·nee \,nä-mə-'nē\ *n* [*nominate*] (1688) : a person who has been nominated

no·mo·gram \'nä-mə-,gram, 'nō-\ *n* [Gk *nomos* law + ISV *-gram* — more at NIMBLE] (1908) : a graphic representation that consists of several lines marked off to scale and arranged in such a way that by using a straightedge to connect known values on two lines an unknown value can be read at the point of intersection with another line

no·mo·graph \-,graf\ *n* (ca. 1909) : NOMOGRAM — **no·mo·graph·ic** \,nä-mə-'gra-fik, ,nō-\ *adj* — **no·mog·ra·phy** \nō-'mä-grə-fē\ *n*

no·mo·log·i·cal \,nä-mə-'lä-ji-kəl, ,nō-\ *adj* [*nomology* science of physical and logical laws, fr. Gk *nomos* + E *-logy*] (1845) : relating to or expressing basic physical laws or rules of reasoning ⟨~ universals⟩

no·mo·thet·ic \,nä-'the-tik\ *adj* [Gk *nomothetikos* of legislation, fr. *nomothetēs* lawgiver, fr. *nomos* law + *-thetēs* one who establishes, fr. *tithenai* to put — more at DO] (1658) : relating to, involving, or dealing with abstract, general, or universal statements or laws

-nomy *n comb form* [ME *-nomie*, fr. OF, fr. L *-nomia*, fr. Gk, fr. *nomos*] : system of laws governing or sum of knowledge regarding a (specified) field ⟨agronomy⟩

non- \(')nän *also* ,nən *or* 'nən *before* '-stressed *syllable,* ,nän *also* ,nən *before* ,-stressed *or unstressed syllable; the variant with* ə *is also to be understood at pronounced entries, though not shown*\ *prefix* [ME, fr. MF, fr. L *non* not, fr. OL *noenum,* fr. *ne-* not + *oinom,* neut. of *oinos* one — more at NO, ONE] **1** : not : other than : reverse of : absence of **2** : of little or no consequence : unimportant : worthless ⟨*non*issues⟩ ⟨*non*system⟩ **3** : lacking the usual esp. positive characteristics of the thing specified ⟨*non*celebration⟩ ⟨*non*art⟩

non-abra·sive	non-al·co·hol·ic	non-as·so·ci·at·ed
non-ab·sorb·able	non-al·ler·gen·ic	non-as·tro·nom·i·cal
non-ab·sor·bent	non-al·ler·gic	non·ath·lete
non-ab·sorp·tive	non-al·pha·bet·ic	non·ath·let·ic
non-ab·stract	non-alu·mi·num	non·atom·ic
non-ac·a·dem·ic	non-am·big·u·ous	non·at·tached
non-ac·cep·tance	non–Amer·i·can	non·at·tach·ment
non-ac·count·able	non-an·a·lyt·ic	non·at·ten·dance
non-ac·cred·it·ed	non-an·a·tom·ic	non·at·tend·er
non-ac·cru·al	non-an·i·mal	non·au·di·to·ry
non-achieve·ment	non-an·swer	non·au·thor
non-ac·id	non-an·tag·o·nis·tic	non·au·thor·i·tar·i·an
non-acid·ic	non-an·thro·po·log·i·cal	non·au·to·mat·ed
non-ac·quis·i·tive	non-an·thro·pol·o·gist	non·au·to·mat·ic
non-act·ing	non-an·ti·bi·ot·ic	non·au·to·mo·tive
non-ac·tion	non-an·ti·gen·ic	non·au·ton·o·mous
non-ac·ti·vat·ed	non-ap·pear·ance	non·avail·abil·i·ty
non-ac·tor	non·aquat·ic	non·bac·te·ri·al
non-adap·tive	non·aque·ous	non·bar·bi·tu·rate
non-ad·dict	non·ar·a·ble	non·ba·sic
non-ad·dic·tive	non·ar·bi·trar·i·ness	non·bear·ing
non-ad·he·sive	non·ar·bi·trary	non·be·hav·ior·al
non-adi·a·bat·ic	non·ar·chi·tect	non·be·ing
non-ad·ja·cent	non·ar·chi·tec·ture	non·be·lief
non-ad·mir·er	non·ar·gu·ment	non·be·liev·er
non-ad·mis·sion	non·aris·to·crat·ic	non·bel·lig·er·en·cy
non-aes·thet·ic	non·ar·o·mat·ic	non·bel·lig·er·ent
non-af·fil·i·at·ed	non·art	non·bet·ting
non·af·flu·ent	non·art·ist	non·bib·lio·graph·ic
non–Af·ri·can	non·ar·tis·tic	non·bi·na·ry
non·ag·gres·sion	non·as·cet·ic	non·bind·ing
non·ag·gres·sive	non·as·pi·rin	non·bio·de·grad·able
non·ag·ri·cul·tur·al	non·as·ser·tive	non·bio·graph·i·cal

non·bi·o·log·i·cal	non·com·press·ible	non·de·pressed
non·bi·o·log·i·cal·ly	non·com·put·er	non·de·riv·a·tive
non·bi·ol·o·gist	non·com·put·er·ized	non·de·scrip·tive
non·bit·ing	non·con·cep·tu·al	non·de·sert
non·black	non·con·cern	non·de·tach·able
non·body	non·con·clu·sion	non·de·ter·min·is·tic
non·bond·ed	non·con·cur·rent	non·de·vel·op·ment
non·bot·a·nist	non·con·dens·able	non·de·vi·ant
non·brand	non·con·di·tioned	non·di·a·bet·ic
non·break·able	non·con·duct·ing	non·di·a·lyz·able
non·breath·ing	non·con·duc·tion	non·di·dac·tic
non·breed·er	non·con·duc·tive	non·dif·fus·ible
non·breed·ing	non·con·fer·ence	non·di·men·sion·al
non·broad·cast	non·con·fi·dence	non·dip·lo·mat·ic
non·build·ing	non·con·fi·den·tial	non·di·rect·ed
non·burn·able	non·con·flict·ing	non·di·rec·tion·al
non·buy·ing	non·con·fron·ta·tion	non·dis·clo·sure
non·cab·i·net	non·con·fron·ta·tion·al	non·dis·cre·tion·ary
non·cak·ing	non·con·gru·ent	non·dis·crim·i·na·tion
non·call·able	non·con·ju·gat·ed	non·dis·crim·i·na·to·ry
non·cam·pus	non·con·nec·tion	non·dis·cur·sive
non·can·cel·able	non·con·scious	non·dis·per·sive
non·can·cer·ous	non·con·sec·u·tive	non·dis·rup·tive
non·can·ni·bal·is·tic	non·con·sen·su·al	non·di·ver·si·fied
non·cap·i·tal	non·con·ser·va·tion	non·doc·tor
non·cap·i·tal·ist	non·con·ser·va·tive	non·doc·tri·naire
non·car·cin·o·gen	non·con·sol·i·dat·ed	non·doc·u·men·ta·ry
non·car·ci·no·gen·ic	non·con·stant	non·dog·mat·ic
non·car·di·ac	non·con·sti·tu·tion·al	non·dol·lar
non·ca·reer	non·con·struc·tion	non·do·mes·tic
non·car·ri·er	non·con·struc·tive	non·dom·i·nant
non·cash	non·con·sum·er	non·dra·mat·ic
non·ca·su·al	non·con·sum·ing	non·driv·er
non–Cath·o·lic	non·con·sump·tion	non·drug
non·caus·al	non·con·sump·tive	non·du·ra·ble
non·cel·e·bra·tion	non·con·tact	non·earn·ing
non·ce·leb·ri·ty	non·con·ta·gious	non·ec·cle·si·as·ti·cal
non·cel·lu·lar	non·con·tem·po·rary	non·econ·o·mist
non·cel·lu·los·ic	non·con·tig·u·ous	non·ed·i·ble
non–Celt·ic	non·con·tin·gent	non·ed·i·to·ri·al
non·cen·tral	non·con·tin·u·ous	non·ed·u·ca·tion
non·cer·tif·i·cat·ed	non·con·tract	non·ed·u·ca·tion·al
non·cer·ti·fied	non·con·trac·tu·al	non·ef·fec·tive
non·char·ac·ter	non·con·tra·dic·tion	non·elas·tic
non·char·is·mat·ic	non·con·tra·dic·to·ry	non·elect·ed
non·chau·vin·ist	non·con·trib·u·to·ry	non·elec·tion
non·chem·i·cal	non·con·trol·la·ble	non·elec·tive
non·chro·no·log·i·cal	non·con·trol·ling	non·elec·tric
non·church	non·con·tro·ver·sial	non·elec·tri·cal
non·church·go·er	non·con·ven·tion·al	non·elec·tron·ic
non·cir·cu·lar	non·con·vert·ible	non·el·e·men·ta·ry
non·cir·cu·lat·ing	non·co·pla·nar	non·elite
non·cit·i·zen	non·cor·po·rate	non·emer·gen·cy
non·clan·des·tine	non·cor·re·la·tion	non·emo·tion·al
non·class	non·cor·rod·ible	non·em·phat·ic
non·clas·si·cal	non·cor·rod·ing	non·em·pir·i·cal
non·clas·si·fied	non·cor·ro·sive	non·em·ploy·ee
non·class·room	non·coun·try	non·em·ploy·ment
non·cler·i·cal	non·coun·ty	non·emp·ty
non·cling	non·cov·er·age	non·en·cap·su·lat·ed
non·clin·i·cal	non·cre·a·tive	non·end·ing
non·clog·ging	non·cre·a·tiv·i·ty	non·en·er·gy
non·co·er·cive	non·cre·den·tialed	non·en·force·abil·i·ty
non·cog·ni·tive	non·crime	non·en·force·ment
non·co·her·ent	non·crim·i·nal	non·en·gage·ment
non·co·in·ci·dence	non·cri·sis	non·en·gi·neer·ing
non·co·i·tal	non·crit·i·cal	non·en·ter·tain·ment
non·cok·ing	non·crush·able	non·en·zy·mat·ic
non·co·la	non·crys·tal·line	non·en·zy·mic
non·col·lec·tor	non·cu·li·nary	non·equi·lib·ri·um
non·col·lege	non·cul·ti·vat·ed	non·equiv·a·lence
non·col·le·giate	non·cul·ti·va·tion	non·equiv·a·lent
non·col·lin·ear	non·cul·tur·al	non·erot·ic
non·col·or	non·cu·mu·la·tive	non·es·tab·lished
non·col·or·fast	non·cur·rent	non·es·tab·lish·ment
non·col·ored	non·cus·tom·er	non·es·ter·i·fied
non·com·bat	non·cy·clic	non·eth·i·cal
non·com·bat·ive	non·cy·cli·cal	non·eth·nic
non·com·bus·ti·ble	non·dance	non–Eu·ro·pe·an
non·com·mer·cial	non·danc·er	non·eval·u·a·tive
non·com·mit·ment	non–Dar·win·ian	non·ev·i·dence
non·com·mit·ted	non·de·cep·tive	non·ex·clu·sive
non·com·mu·ni·cat·ing	non·de·ci·sion	non·ex·ec·u·tive
non·com·mu·ni·ca·tion	non·de·creas·ing	non·ex·empt
non·com·mu·ni·ca·tive	non·de·duc·tive	non·ex·is·ten·tial
non·com·mu·nist	non·de·fer·ra·ble	non·ex·ot·ic
non·com·mu·ni·ty	non·de·form·ing	non·ex·pend·able
non·com·mu·ta·tive	non·de·gen·er·ate	non·ex·per·i·men·tal
non·com·mu·ta·tiv·i·ty	non·de·grad·able	non·ex·pert
non·com·pa·ra·bil·i·ty	non·de·gree	non·ex·plan·a·to·ry
non·com·pa·ra·ble	non·del·e·gate	non·ex·ploi·ta·tion
non·com·pat·i·ble	non·de·lib·er·ate	non·ex·ploi·ta·tive
non·com·pe·ti·tion	non·de·lin·quent	non·ex·ploi·ta·tive
non·com·pet·i·tor	non·de·liv·ery	non·ex·ploi·ta·tive
non·com·ple·men·ta·ry	non·de·mand·ing	non·ex·plo·sive
non·com·plex	non·dem·o·crat·ic	non·ex·posed
non·com·pli·ance	non·de·nom·i·na·tion·al	non·ex·tant
non·com·pli·cat·ed	non·de·nom·i·na·tion·al·ism	non·fact
non·com·ply·ing	non·de·part·men·tal	non·fac·tor
non·com·pos·er	non·de·pen·dent	non·fac·tu·al
non·com·pound	non·de·plet·able	non·fac·ul·ty
non·com·pre·hen·sion	non·de·plet·ing	non·fad·ing
	non·de·po·si·tion	non·fa·mil·ial

non·fam·i·ly	non·in·flam·ma·ble	non·met·ro	non·preg·nant	non–Rus·sian	non·syn·chro·nous
non·fan	non·in·flam·ma·to·ry	non·met·ro·pol·i·tan	non·print	non·sal·able	non·sys·tem·at·ic
non·farm	non·in·fla·tion·ary	non·mi·cro·bi·al	non·prob·lem	non·sa·line	non·sys·tem·ic
non·farm·er	non·in·flec·tion·al	non·mi·grant	non·pro·duc·ing	non·sa·pon·i·fi·able	non·tar·iff
non·fa·tal	non·in·flu·ence	non·mi·gra·to·ry	non·pro·fes·sion·al	non·schizo·phren·ic	non·tax·able
non·fat·ten·ing	non·in·for·ma·tion	non·mil·i·tant	non·pro·fes·sion·al·ly	non·school	non·teach·ing
non·fat·ty	non·ini·tial	non·mil·i·tary	non·pro·fes·so·ri·al	non·sci·en·tif·ic	non·tech·ni·cal
non·fed·er·al	non·ini·ti·ate	non·mi·met·ic	non·pro·gram	non·sci·en·tist	non·tem·po·ral
non·fed·er·at·ed	non·in·ju·ry	non·mi·nor·i·ty	non·pro·gram·mer	non·sea·son·al	non·ten·ured
non·fem·i·nist	non·in·sect	non·mo·bile	non·pro·pri·etary	non·sec·re·tory	non·ter·mi·nal
non·fil·a·men·tous	non·in·sec·ti·cid·al	non·mo·lec·u·lar	non·psy·chi·at·ric	non·se·cure	non·the·at·ri·cal
non·fil·ter·able	non·in·stall·ment	non·mon·e·tar·ist	non·psy·chi·a·trist	non·sed·i·ment·able	non·the·ist
non·fi·nal	non·in·sti·tu·tion·al	non·mon·e·tary	non·psy·cho·log·i·cal	non·seg·re·gat·ed	non·the·is·tic
non·fi·nan·cial	non·in·sti·tu·tion·al·ized	non·mon·ey	non·psy·chot·ic	non·seg·re·ga·tion	non·theo·log·i·cal
non·fi·nite	non·in·struc·tion·al	non·mo·nog·a·mous	non·pub·lic	non·se·lect·ed	non·the·o·ret·i·cal
non·fis·sion·able	non·in·stru·men·tal	non·mo·tile	non·pu·ni·tive	non·se·lec·tive	non·ther·a·peu·tic
non·flu·o·res·cent	non·in·sur·ance	non·mo·til·i·ty	non·pur·po·sive	non·self–gov·ern·ing	non·think·ing
non·fly·ing	non·in·sured	non·mo·tor·ized	non·quan·ti·fi·able	non·sen·sa·tion·al	non·threat·en·ing
non·food	non·in·te·gral	non·mov·ing	non·quan·ti·ta·tive	non·sen·si·tive	non·tid·al
non·for·feit·able	non·in·te·grat·ed	non·mu·nic·i·pal	non·ra·cial	non·sen·su·ous	non·to·bac·co
non·for·fei·ture	non·in·tel·lec·tu·al	non·mu·sic	non·ra·cial·ly	non·sen·tence	non·ton·al
non·for·mal	non·in·ter·act·ing	non·mu·si·cal	non·ra·dio·ac·tive	non·sep·tate	non·to·tal·i·tar·i·an
non·fos·sil	non·in·ter·ac·tive	non·mu·si·cian	non·rail·road	non·se·quen·tial	non·tox·ic
non·frat·er·ni·za·tion	non·in·ter·change·able	non·mu·tant	non·ran·dom	non·se·ri·ous	non·tra·di·tion·al
non·freez·ing	non·in·ter·course	non·my·e·lin·at·ed	non·ran·dom·ness	non·sex·ist	non·trans·fer·able
non·friv·o·lous	non·in·ter·est	non·mys·ti·cal	non·rat·ed	non·sex·u·al	non·treat·ment
non·fro·zen	non·in·ter·fer·ence	non·nar·ra·tive	non·ra·tio·nal	non·shrink	non·triv·i·al
non·fuel	non·in·ter·sect·ing	non·na·tion·al	non·re·ac·tive	non·shrink·able	non·trop·i·cal
non·ful·fill·ment	non·in·tim·i·dat·ing	non·na·tive	non·re·ac·tor	non·sign·er	non·tur·bu·lent
non·func·tion·al	non·in·tox·i·cant	non·nat·u·ral	non·re·al·is·tic	non·si·mul·ta·neous	non·typ·i·cal
non·func·tion·ing	non·in·tox·i·cat·ing	non·ne·ces·si·ty	non·re·ap·point·ment	non·sink·able	non·unan·i·mous
non·game	non·in·tru·sive	non·neg·li·gent	non·re·ceipt	non·skat·er	non·uni·form
non·gas·eous	non·in·tu·i·tive	non·ne·go·tia·ble	non·re·cip·ro·cal	non·skel·e·tal	non·uni·for·mi·ty
non·gay	non·ion·iz·ing	non·net·work	non·rec·og·ni·tion	non·ski·er	non·union·ized
non·ge·net·ic	non·ir·ra·di·at·ed	non·news	non·re·cy·cla·ble	non·smok·er	non·unique
non·gen·i·tal	non·ir·ri·gat·ed	non·ni·trog·e·nous	non·re·duc·ing	non·smok·ing	non·unique·ness
non·geo·met·ri·cal	non·ir·ri·tant	non·nor·ma·tive	non·re·dun·dant	non·so·cial·ist	non·uni·ver·sal
non·ghet·to	non·ir·ri·tat·ing	non·nov·el	non·re·fill·able	non·so·lar	non·uni·ver·si·ty
non·glam·or·ous	non·is·sue	non·nu·cle·at·ed	non·re·flect·ing	non·so·lu·tion	non·ur·ban
non·glare	non–Jap·a·nese	non·nu·mer·i·cal	non·reg·u·lat·ed	non·spa·tial	non·ur·gent
non·golf·er	non–Jew	non·nu·tri·tious	non·reg·u·la·tion	non·speak·er	non·util·i·tar·i·an
non·gov·ern·ment	non–Jew·ish	non·nu·tri·tive	non·rel·a·tive	non·speak·ing	non·util·i·ty
non·gov·ern·men·tal	non·join·er	non·ob·scene	non·rel·e·vant	non·spe·cial·ist	non·uto·pi·an
non·grad·ed	non·ju·di·cial	non·ob·ser·vance	non·re·li·gious	non·spe·cif·ic	non·val·id
non·grad·u·ate	non·ju·ry	non·ob·ser·vant	non·re·new·able	non·spe·cif·i·cal·ly	non·va·lid·i·ty
non·gram·mat·i·cal	non·jus·ti·cia·ble	non·ob·vi·ous	non·re·new·al	non·spec·tac·u·lar	non·vas·cu·lar
non·gran·u·lar	non·ko·sher	non·oc·cu·pa·tion·al	non·re·pay·able	non·spec·u·la·tive	non·veg·e·tar·i·an
non·grav·i·ta·tion·al	non·la·bor	non·oc·cur·rence	non·rep·re·sen·ta·tive	non·speech	non·ven·om·ous
non·greasy	non·land·own·er	non·of·fi·cial	non·re·pro·duc·tive	non·spher·i·cal	non·vet·er·an
non·gre·gar·i·ous	non·lan·guage	non·ohm·ic	non·res·i·den·tial	non·sta·tion·ary	non·vi·a·ble
non·grow·ing	non·law·yer	non·oily	non·res·o·nant	non·sta·tis·ti·cal	non·view·er
non·growth	non·lead·ed	non·op·er·at·ic	non·re·spon·dent	non·steady	non·vi·ral
non·guest	non·league	non·op·er·at·ing	non·re·spond·er	non·sto·ry	non·vir·gin
non·ha·lo·ge·nat·ed	non·le·gal	non·op·er·a·tion·al	non·re·sponse	non·stra·te·gic	non·vis·cous
non·hand·i·capped	non·le·gume	non·op·er·a·tive	non·re·spon·sive	non·struc·tur·al	non·vi·su·al
non·hap·pen·ing	non·le·gu·mi·nous	non·op·ti·mal	non·re·strict·ed	non·struc·tured	non·vo·cal
non·har·dy	non·le·thal	non·or·gan·ic	non·re·trac·tile	non·stu·dent	non·vo·ca·tion·al
non·har·mon·ic	non·lex·i·cal	non·or·tho·dox	non·ret·ro·ac·tive	non·style	non·vol·ca·nic
non·haz·ard·ous	non·li·brar·i·an	non·over·lap·ping	non·re·us·able	non·sub·ject	non·vol·un·tary
non·heme	non·li·brary	non·own·er	non·re·vers·ible	non·sub·jec·tive	non·vot·er
non·he·mo·lyt·ic	non·life	non·ox·i·diz·ing	non·rev·o·lu·tion·ary	non·sub·si·dized	non·vot·ing
non·he·red·i·tary	non·lin·e·al	non·paid	non·ri·ot·er	non·suc·cess	non·war
non·hi·er·ar·chi·cal	non·lin·e·ar	non·par·al·lel	non·ri·ot·ing	non·sug·ar	non·win·ning
non–His·pan·ic	non·lin·e·ar·i·ty	non·par·a·sit·ic	non·ro·tat·ing	non·su·per·im·pos·able	non·woody
non·his·tor·i·cal	non·lin·guis·tic	non·par·tic·i·pant	non·rou·tine	non·su·per·vi·so·ry	non·work
non·home	non·liq·uid	non·par·tic·i·pat·ing	non·roy·al	non·sur·gi·cal	non·work·er
non·ho·mo·ge·neous	non·lit·er·al	non·par·tic·i·pa·tion	non·rub·ber	non·swim·mer	non·work·ing
non·ho·mol·o·gous	non·lit·er·ary	non·par·tic·i·pa·to·ry	non·rul·ing	non·sym·bol·ic	non·writ·er
non·ho·mo·sex·u·al	non·liv·ing	non·par·ty	non·ru·mi·nant	non·sym·met·ric	non·yel·low·ing
non·hor·mon·al	non·lo·cal	non·pas·sive		non·sym·met·ri·cal	
non·hos·pi·tal	non·lu·mi·nous	non·past			
non·hos·pi·tal·ized	non·mag·net·ic	non·pay·ing			
non·hos·tile	non·main·stream	non·pay·ment			
non·hous·ing	non·ma·jor	non·per·for·mance			
non·hu·man	non·ma·lig·nant	non·per·form·er			
non·hunt·er	non·mal·lea·ble	non·per·ish·able			
non·hunt·ing	non·man·age·ment	non·per·mis·sive			
non·hy·gro·scop·ic	non·man·a·ge·ri·al	non·per·son·al			
non·hys·ter·i·cal	non·man·u·al	non·pe·tro·leum			
non·ide·al	non·man·u·fac·tur·ing	non·phi·los·o·pher			
non·iden·ti·ty	non·mar·i·tal	non·phil·o·soph·i·cal			
non·ideo·log·i·cal	non·mar·ket	non·pho·ne·mic			
non·im·age	non–Marx·ist	non·pho·net·ic			
non·im·i·ta·tive	non·ma·te·ri·al	non·phos·phate			
non·im·mi·grant	non·ma·te·ri·al·is·tic	non·pho·to·graph·ic			
non·im·mune	non·math·e·mat·i·cal	non·phys·i·cal			
non·im·pact	non·math·e·ma·ti·cian	non·phy·si·cian			
non·im·pli·ca·tion	non·ma·tric·u·lat·ed	non·pla·nar			
non·im·por·ta·tion	non·mean·ing·ful	non·plas·tic			
non·in·clu·sion	non·mea·sur·able	non·play			
non·in·creas·ing	non·meat	non·play·ing			
non·in·cum·bent	non·me·chan·i·cal	non·po·et·ic			
non·in·de·pen·dence	non·mech·a·nis·tic	non·poi·son·ous			
non–In·di·an	non·med·i·cal	non·po·lar·iz·able			
non·in·dig·e·nous	non·meet·ing	non·po·lice			
non·in·di·vid·u·al	non·mem·ber	non·po·lit·i·cal			
non–In·do–Eu·ro·pe·an	non·mem·ber·ship	non·po·lit·i·cal·ly			
non·in·dus·tri·al	non·men·tal	non·pol·i·ti·cian			
non·in·dus·tri·al·ized	non·mer·cu·ri·al	non·pol·lut·ing			
non·in·dus·try	non·meta·mer·ic	non·poor			
non·in·fect·ed	non·met·a·phor·i·cal	non·po·rous			
non·in·fec·tious	non·met·ric	non·pos·ses·sion			
non·in·fec·tive	non·met·ri·cal	non·prac·ti·cal			
non·in·fest·ed		non·prac·tic·ing			

non·ad·di·tive \ˌnän-ˈa-də-tiv\ *adj* (1926) **1** : not having a numerical value equal to the sum of values for the component parts **2** : of, relating to, or being a genic effect that is not additive — **non·ad·di·tiv·i·ty** \ˌnän-ˌa-də-ˈti-və-tē\ *n*

non·age \ˈnä-nij, ˈnō-\ *n* [ME, fr. MF, fr. *non-* + *age* age] (15c) **1** : MINORITY 1 **2 a** : a period of youth **b** : lack of maturity

no·na·ge·nar·i·an \ˌnō-nə-jə-ˈner-ē-ən, ˌnä-\ *n* [L *nonagenarius* containing ninety, fr. *nonageni* ninety each, fr. *nonaginta* ninety, fr. *nona-* (akin to *novem* nine) + *-ginta* (akin to *viginti* twenty) — more at NINE, VIGESIMAL] (1804) : a person whose age is in the nineties — **nonagenarian** *adj*

no·na·gon \ˈnō-nə-ˌgän\ *n* [L *nonus* ninth + E *-gon* — more at NOON] (ca. 1639) : a polygon of nine angles and nine sides

non·aligned \ˌnän-ə-ˈlīnd\ *adj* (1960) : not allied with other nations and esp. with either the Communist or the non-Communist blocs — **non·align·ment** \-mənt\ *n*

non·al·le·lic \ˌnän-ə-ˈlē-lik, -ˈle-\ *adj* (1945) : not behaving as alleles toward one another ⟨∼ genes⟩

non–A, non–B hepatitis \ˈnän-ˈā-ˈnän-ˈbē-\ *n* (1976) : hepatitis clinically and immunologically similar to hepatitis A and hepatitis B but caused by different viruses

non·bank \ˈnän-ˈbaŋk\ *n, often attrib* (1939) : a business that is not an officially established bank but offers many similar services — **non·bank·ing** \-ˈbaŋ-kiŋ\ *adj*

\ə\ abut \ˈ, ˌ\ kitten, F table \ər\ further \a\ ash \ā\ ace \ä\ mop, mar
\aù\ out \ch\ chin \e\ bet \ē\ easy \g\ go \i\ hit \ī\ ice \j\ job
\ŋ\ sing \ō\ go \ò\ law \òi\ boy \th\ thin \t͟h\ the \ü\ loot \ù\ foot
\y\ yet \zh\ vision \à, k̲, ⁿ, œ, œ̄, ᵫ, ᵫ̄, ᵊ\ *see* Guide to Pronunciation

non·bond·ing \-'bän-diŋ\ adj (1952) : being or occupied by electrons esp. of an atom's valence shell that are not involved in a chemical bond ⟨a ~ atomic orbital⟩

¹non·book \-'bûk\ adj (1949) : being something other than a book; esp : being a library holding (as a microfilm) that is not a book

²non·book \-,bûk\ n (1960) : a book of little literary merit which is often a compilation (as of pictures, press clippings, or speeches)

non·busi·ness \-'biz-nəs, -nəz\ adj (1927) : not related to business; esp : not related to one's primary business

non·ca·lo·ric \,nän-kə-'lȯr-ik, -'lör-\ adj (1950) : free from or very low in calories

non·can·di·date \'nän-'kan-də-,dāt, -'ka-nə-, -dət\ n (1944) : a person who is not a candidate; esp : one who has refused to be a candidate for a particular political office — **non·can·di·da·cy** \-də-sē\ n

¹nonce \'nän(t)s\ n [ME nanes, alter. (fr. misdivision of then anes in such phrases as to then anes for the one purpose) of anes one purpose, irreg. fr. an, one one — more at ONE] (13c) 1 : the one, particular, or present occasion, purpose, or use ⟨for the ~⟩ 2 : the time being

²nonce adj (1884) : occurring, used, or made only once or for a special occasion ⟨a ~ word⟩

non·cha·lance \,nän-shə-'län(t)s; 'nän-shə-,län(t)s, -lən(t)s\ n (1678) : the quality or state of being nonchalant

non·cha·lant \-'länt, -,länt, -lənt\ adj [F, fr. OF, fr. prp. of nonchaloir to disregard, fr. non- + chaloir to concern, fr. L calēre to be warm — more at LEE] (ca. 1734) : having an air of easy unconcern or indifference **syn** see COOL — **non·cha·lant·ly** adv

non·chro·mo·som·al \,nän-,krō-mə-'sō-məl\ adj (1960) 1 : not situated on a chromosome 2 : not involving chromosomes

non·com \'nän-,käm\ n (1883) : NONCOMMISSIONED OFFICER

non·com·bat·ant \,nän-kəm-'ba-t²nt also 'nän-'käm-bə-tənt\ n (1811) : one that does not engage in combat: as **a** : a member (as a chaplain) of the armed forces whose duties do not include fighting **b** : CIVILIAN — **noncombatant** adj

non·com·mis·sioned officer \,nän-kə-'mi-shənd-\ n (1703) : a subordinate officer (as a sergeant) in the army, air force, or marine corps appointed from among enlisted personnel

non·com·mit·tal \-kə-'mi-t²l\ adj (1829) 1 : giving no clear indication of attitude or feeling 2 : having no clear or distinctive character — **non·com·mit·tal·ly** \-t²l-ē\ adv

non com·pos men·tis \,nän-,käm-pəs-'men-təs, ,nȯn-\ adj [L, lit., not having mastery of one's mind] (1607) : not of sound mind

non·con·cur \,nän-kən-'kər\ vi (ca. 1847) : to refuse or fail to concur — **non·con·cur·rence** \-'kər-ən(t)s, -'kə-rən(t)s\ n

non·con·duc·tor \-kən-'dək-tər\ n (1751) : a substance that conducts heat, electricity, or sound only in very small degree

non·con·form \-kən-'fȯrm\ vi [back-formation fr. nonconformist] (1681) : to fail to conform — **non·con·form·er** n

non·con·for·mance \-'fȯr-mən(t)s\ n (1843) : failure to conform

non·con·form·ism \-'fȯr-,mi-zəm\ n (1844) : NONCONFORMITY

non·con·form·ist \-'fȯr-mist\ n (1619) 1 often cap : a person who does not conform to an established church; esp : one who does not conform to the Church of England 2 : a person who does not conform to a generally accepted pattern of thought or action — **nonconformist** adj, often cap

non·con·for·mi·ty \-'fȯr-mə-tē\ n (1618) 1 **a** : failure or refusal to conform to an established church **b** often cap : the movement or principles of English Protestant dissent **c** often cap : the body of English Nonconformists 2 : refusal to conform to an established or conventional creed, rule, or practice 3 : absence of agreement or correspondence

non·co·op·er·a·tion \,nän-kō-,ä-pə-'rā-shən\ n (1795) : failure or refusal to cooperate; specif : refusal through civil disobedience of a people to cooperate with the government of a country — **non·co·op·er·a·tion·ist** \-sh(ə-)nist\ n — **non·co·op·er·a·tor** \-'ä-pə-,rā-tər\ n

non·co·op·er·a·tive \-'ä-p(ə-)rə-tiv, -pə-,rā-\ adj (1922) : of, relating to, or characterized by noncooperation

non·cred·it \'nän-'kre-dət\ adj (1965) : not offering credit toward a degree ⟨~ courses⟩

non·cross·over \-'krȯ-,sō-vər\ adj (1919) : having or being chromosomes that have not participated in genetic crossing-over ⟨~ offspring⟩

non·cus·to·di·al \-kə-'stō-dē-əl\ adj (1973) : of or being a parent who does not have legal custody of a child

non·dairy \-'der-ē, -'dar-; 'nän-,\ adj (1968) : containing no milk or milk products ⟨~ whipped topping⟩

non·de·duct·ible \,nän-di-'dək-tə-bəl\ adj (1943) : not deductible; esp : not deductible for income tax purposes — **non·de·duct·ibil·i·ty** \-,dək-tə-'bi-lə-tē\ n

non·de·fense \,nän-di-'fen(t)s\ adj (1961) : not used or intended for or associated with the military ⟨~ spending⟩

non·de·script \,nän-di-'skript\ adj [non- + L descriptus, pp. of describere to describe] (ca. 1807) 1 : belonging or appearing to belong to no particular class or kind : not easily described 2 : lacking distinctive or interesting qualities : DULL, DRAB — **nondescript** n

non·de·struc·tive \-di-'strək-tiv\ adj (1926) : not destructive; specif : not causing destruction of material being investigated or treated ⟨~ testing of metal⟩ — **non·de·struc·tive·ly** adv — **non·de·struc·tive·ness** n

non·dia·paus·ing \,nän-,dī-ə-'pȯ-ziŋ\ adj (1963) 1 : not having a diapause 2 : not being in a state of diapause

non·di·rec·tive \,nän-də-'rek-tiv, -(,)dī-\ adj (1931) : of, relating to, or being psychotherapy, counseling, or interviewing in which the counselor refrains from interpretation or explanation but encourages the client (as by repeating phrases) to talk freely

non·dis·junc·tion \,nän-dis-'jəŋ(k)-shən\ n [ISV] (1913) : failure of homologous chromosomes or sister chromatids to separate subsequent to metaphase in meiosis or mitosis so that one daughter cell has both and the other neither of the chromosomes — **non·dis·junc·tion·al** \-shnəl, -shə-n²l\ adj

non·dis·tinc·tive \-di-'stiŋ(k)-tiv\ adj (1916) of a speech sound : having no signaling value

non·di·vid·ing \,nän-də-'vī-diŋ\ adj (1945) : not undergoing cell division

non·dor·mant \'nän-'dȯr-mənt\ adj (1940) 1 : being in such a condition that germination is possible ⟨~ seeds⟩ 2 : being in active vegetative growth ⟨~ plants⟩

non·drink·er \-'driŋ-kər\ n (1899) : a person who abstains from alcoholic beverages — **non·drink·ing** \-kiŋ\ adj

non·dry·ing oil \'nän-'drī-iŋ-\ n (1905) : a highly saturated oil (as olive oil) that is unable to solidify when exposed in a thin film to air

¹none \'nən\ pron [ME, fr. OE nān, fr. ne not + ān one — more at NO, ONE] (bef. 12c) 1 : not any 2 : not one : NOBODY 3 : not any such thing or person 4 : no part : NOTHING

²none adj (bef. 12c) archaic : not any : NO

³none adv (1651) 1 : by no means : not at all ⟨~ too soon to begin⟩ 2 : in no way : to no extent ⟨~ the worse for wear⟩

⁴none \'nōn\ n, often cap [LL nona, fr. L, 9th hour of the day from sunrise — more at NOON] (1845) : the fifth of the canonical hours

non·eco·nom·ic \,nän-,e-kə-'nä-mik, -,ē-kə-\ adj (1920) : not economic; esp : having no economic importance or implication

non·elec·tro·lyte \,nän-ə-'lek-trə-,līt\ n (1891) : a substance that does not readily ionize when dissolved or melted and is a poor conductor of electricity

non·en·ti·ty \-'en-tə-tē, -'e-nə-\ n (ca. 1600) 1 : something that does not exist or exists only in the imagination 2 : NONEXISTENCE 3 : a person of little consequence or significance

nones \'nōnz\ n pl but sing or pl in constr [ME nonys, fr. L nonae, fr. fem. pl. of nonus ninth] (14c) 1 : the ninth day before the ides according to ancient Roman reckoning 2 often cap : ⁴NONE

non·es·sen·tial \,nän-i-'sen(t)-shəl\ adj (1751) 1 : not essential 2 : synthesized by the body in sufficient quantity to satisfy dietary needs ⟨~ amino acids⟩ — **nonessential** n

none·such \'nən-,səch\ n (1590) : a person or thing without an equal — **nonesuch** adj

no·net \nō-'net\ n [It nonetto, fr. nono ninth, fr. L nonus — more at NOON] (1865) : a combination of nine instruments or voices; also : a musical composition for such a combination

none·the·less \,nən-thə-'les\ adv (1847) : NEVERTHELESS

non–eu·clid·e·an \,nän-yü-'kli-dē-ən\ adj, often cap E (ca. 1864) : not assuming or in accordance with all the postulates of Euclid's Elements ⟨~ geometry⟩

non·event \'nän-i-,vent, ,nän-i-'\ n (1962) 1 **a** : an expected event that fails to take place or to satisfy expectations **b** : an often highly publicized event of little intrinsic interest or significance 2 : an occurrence that is officially ignored

non·ex·is·tence \,nän-ig-'zis-tən(t)s\ n (1646) : absence of existence : the negation of being — **non·ex·is·tent** \-tənt\ adj

non·fat \'nän-'fat\ adj (1926) : lacking fat solids : having fat solids removed ⟨~ milk⟩

non·fea·sance \'nän-'fē-z²n(t)s\ n [non- + obs. E feasance doing, execution] (1596) : failure to act; esp : failure to do what ought to be done

non·fer·rous \-'fer-əs\ adj (1887) 1 : not containing, including, or relating to iron 2 : of or relating to metals other than iron

non·fic·tion \'nän-'fik-shən\ n (1909) : literature that is not fictional — **non·fic·tion·al** \,nän-'fik-shnəl, -shə-n²l\ adj

non·fig·u·ra·tive \'nän-'fi-gyə-rə-tiv, -'fi-gə-\ adj (1927) : NONOBJECTIVE 2

non·flam·ma·ble \-'fla-mə-bəl\ adj (1915) : not flammable; specif : not easily ignited and not burning rapidly if ignited — **non·flam·ma·bil·i·ty** \,nän-,fla-mə-'bi-lə-tē\ n

non·flow·er·ing \'nän-'flaů(-ə)r-iŋ\ adj (ca. 1934) : producing no flowers; specif : lacking a flowering stage in the life cycle

non·flu·en·cy \-'flü-ən(t)-sē\ n, pl -cies (ca. 1945) 1 : lack of fluency 2 : an instance of nonfluency

non·gon·o·coc·cal \,nän-,gä-nə-'kä-kəl\ adj (1961) : not caused by a gonococcus ⟨~ urethritis⟩

non gra·ta \,nän-'gra-tə, -'grä-\ adj [persona non grata] (1925) : not approved : UNWELCOME

non·green \'nän-'grēn\ adj (1897) : not green; specif : containing no chlorophyll ⟨~ saprophytes⟩

non·he·ro \'nän-'hē-(,)rō, -'hir-(,)ō\ n (1940) : ANTI-HERO

non·his·tone \-'his-,tōn\ adj (ca. 1966) : relating to or being any of the eukaryotic proteins (as DNA polymerase) that bind to nuclear DNA but are not histones

non–Hodg·kin's lymphoma \'nän-'häj-kənz-\ n (1976) : any of the numerous malignant lymphomas (as Burkitt's lymphoma) that are not classified as Hodgkin's disease

non·iden·ti·cal \,nä-(,)ī-'den-ti-kəl, -ə-'den-\ adj (1890) 1 : DIFFERENT 2 : FRATERNAL 2

no·nil·lion \nō-'nil-yən\ n, often attrib [F, fr. L nonus ninth + F -illion (as in million) — more at NOON] (1690) — see NUMBER table

non·in·duc·tive \,nän-in-'dək-tiv\ adj (1896) : not inductive; esp : having negligible inductance

non·in·ter·ven·tion \-,in-tər-'ven(t)-shən\ n (1831) : the state or policy of not intervening ⟨~ in the affairs of other countries⟩ — **non·in·ter·ven·tion·ist** \-'ven(t)-sh(ə-)nist\ n or adj

non·in·va·sive \-in-'vā-siv, -'vā-ziv\ adj (1971) : not involving penetration (as by surgery or hypodermic needle) of the skin of the intact organism ⟨~ diagnostic techniques⟩

non·in·volve·ment \-in-'välv-mənt, -'vȯlv- also -'väv-, -'vȯv-\ n (1936) : absence of involvement or emotional attachment — **non·in·volved** \-'vä(l)vd, -'vȯ(l)vd\ adj

non·ion·ic \-(,)ī-'ä-nik\ adj (1929) : not ionic; esp : not dependent on a surface-active anion for effect ⟨~ surfactants⟩

non·join·der \'nän-'jȯin-dər\ n (1833) : failure to include a necessary party to a suit at law

non·judg·men·tal \,nän-jəj-'men-t²l\ adj (1952) : avoiding judgments based on one's personal and esp. moral standards

non·jur·ing \'nän-'jùr-iŋ\ adj [non- + L jurare to swear — more at JURY] (1691) : not swearing allegiance — used esp. of a member of a party in Great Britain that would not swear allegiance to William and Mary or to their successors

non·ju·ror \-'jùr-ər, -'jùr-,ȯr\ n (1691) : a person refusing to take an oath esp. of allegiance, supremacy, or abjuration; specif : one of the beneficed clergy in England and Scotland refusing to take an oath of allegiance to William and Mary or to their successors after the revolution of 1688

non·lit·er·ate \-'li-t(ə-)rət\ *adj* (1947) **1** : not literate **2** : having no written language — **nonliterate** *n*

non·met·al \-'me-t²l\ *n* (ca. 1864) : a chemical element (as boron, carbon, or nitrogen) that lacks the characteristics of a metal

non·me·tal·lic \,nän-mə-'ta-lik\ *adj* (1815) **1** : not metallic **2** : of, relating to, or being a nonmetal

non·mor·al \'nän-'mór-əl, -'mär-\ *adj* (ca. 1866) : not falling into or existing in the sphere of morals or ethics

non·neg·a·tive \-'ne-gə-tiv\ *adj* (1885) : not negative: as **a** : being either positive or zero **b** : taking on nonnegative values ⟨a ∼ function⟩

non·nu·cle·ar \-'nü-klē-ər, 'nyü-, ÷-kyə-lər\ *adj* (1953) **1** : not nuclear: as **a** : being a weapon whose destructive power is not derived from a nuclear reaction **b** : not operated by, using, or produced by nuclear energy **c** : not using or involving nuclear weapons **2** : not having nuclear weapons ⟨a ∼ country⟩

no–no \'nō-,nō\ *n, pl* **no–no's** *or* **no–nos** (ca. 1942) : something unacceptable or forbidden

non·ob·jec·tive \,nän-əb-'jek-tiv\ *adj* (1905) **1** : not objective **2** : representing or intended to represent no natural or actual object, figure, or scene ⟨∼ art⟩ — **non·ob·jec·tiv·ism** \-ti-,vi-zəm\ *n* — **non·ob·jec·tiv·ist** \-vist\ *n* — **non·ob·jec·tiv·i·ty** \-,äb-jek-'ti-və-tē, -əb-\ *n*

non ob·stan·te \,nän-äb-'stan-tē, ,nōn-\ *prep* [ME, fr. ML] (15c) : NOTWITHSTANDING

non–oil \'nän-'ói(ə)l\ *adj* (1979) **1** : not relating to, containing, or derived from oil **2** : being a net importer of petroleum or petroleum products ⟨∼ nations⟩

no–nonsense *adj* (1928) : tolerating no nonsense : SERIOUS, BUSINESSLIKE

non·or·gas·mic \,nän-ór-'gaz-mik\ *adj* (1973) : not capable of experiencing orgasm

no·nox·y·nol-9 \nä-'näk-si-,nól-'nīn, nə-, -,nōl-\ *n* [nonyl (the radical C_9H_{19}) + oxy- + phenol + 9 (fr. the fact that the compounds it contains have an average of nine ethylene oxide groups per molecule)] (1980) : a spermicide used in contraceptive products

non·para·met·ric \-,par-ə-'me-trik\ *adj* (1942) : not involving the estimation of parameters of a statistical function ⟨∼ statistical tests⟩

¹non·pa·reil \,nän-pə-'rel\ *adj* [ME *nonparaille*, fr. MF *nonpareil*, fr. *non-* + *pareil* equal, fr. (assumed) VL *pariculus*, fr. L *par* equal] (15c) : having no equal

²nonpareil *n* (1593) **1** : an individual of unequaled excellence : PARAGON **2 a** : a small flat disk of chocolate covered with white sugar pellets **b** : sugar in small pellets of various colors

non·par·ti·san \,nän-'pär-tə-zən, -sən\ *adj* (1885) : not partisan; *esp* : free from party affiliation, bias, or designation ⟨∼ ballot⟩ ⟨a ∼ board⟩ — **non·par·ti·san·ship** \-,ship\ *n*

non·pas·ser·ine \-'pa-sə-,rīn\ *adj* (ca. 1909) : not passerine; *esp* : of or relating to an order (Coraciiformes) of arboreal birds including the rollers, kingfishers, and hornbills

non·patho·gen·ic \,nän-,pa-thə-'je-nik\ *adj* (1884) : not capable of inducing disease — compare AVIRULENT

non·peak \'nän-'pēk\ *adj* (ca. 1914) : OFF-PEAK

non·per·form·ing \,nän-pə(r)-'fór-miŋ\ *adj* (1979) : not bringing in the expected return ⟨∼ loans⟩ ⟨∼ assets⟩

non·per·sis·tent \-pər-'sis-tənt, -'zis-\ *adj* (1900) : not persistent: as **a** : decomposed rapidly by environmental action ⟨∼ insecticides⟩ **b** : capable of being transmitted by a vector for only a relatively short time ⟨∼ viruses⟩

non·per·son \'nän-'pər-s²n\ *n* (ca. 1909) : a person who is regarded as nonexistent: as **a** : UNPERSON **b** : one having no social or legal status

non pla·cet \'nän-'plä-sət, 'nōn-\ *n* [L, it does not please] (1589) : a negative vote

¹non·plus \,nän-'pləs\ *n* [L *non plus* no more] (1582) : a state of bafflement or perplexity : QUANDARY

²nonplus *vt* **-plussed** *also* **-plused** \-'pləst\; **-plus·sing** *also* **-plus·ing** \-'plə-siŋ\ (1591) : to cause to be at a loss as to what to say, think, or do; PERPLEX *syn* see PUZZLE

non·point \'nän-'póint\ *adj* (1977) : not occurring at a single well-defined site; *specif* : being pollution that cannot be traced to a single location

non·po·lar \,nän-'pō-lər\ *adj* (1892) : not polar; *esp* : consisting of molecules not having a dipole ⟨a ∼ solvent⟩

non pos·su·mus \'nän-'pä-sə-məs, 'nōn-\ *n* [L, we cannot] (1883) : a statement expressing inability to do something

non·pre·scrip·tion \,nän-pri-'skrip-shən\ *adj* (1958) : capable of being bought without a doctor's prescription ⟨∼ drugs⟩

non·pro·duc·tive \-prə-'dək-tiv\ *adj* (1901) : not productive: as **a** : failing to produce or yield : UNPRODUCTIVE ⟨a ∼ oil well⟩ **b** : not directly concerned with production ⟨the ∼ labor of clerks and inspectors⟩ **c** *of a cough* : DRY — **non·pro·duc·tive·ness** *n*

non·prof·it \'nän-'prä-fət\ *adj* (1903) : not conducted or maintained for the purpose of making a profit ⟨a ∼ organization⟩ — **nonprofit** *n*

non·pro·lif·er·a·tion \,nän-prə-,li-fə-'rä-shən\ *adj* (1964) : providing for the stoppage of proliferation (as of nuclear arms) ⟨∼ treaty⟩ — **nonproliferation** *n*

non·pros \'nän-'präs\ *vt* **non·prossed**; **non·pros·sing** [non prosequitur] (1755) : to enter a non prosequitur against

non pro·se·qui·tur \,nän-prə-'se-kwə-tər, ,nōn-\ *n* [LL, he does not prosecute] (1768) : a judgment entered against the plaintiff in a suit in which that party does not appear to prosecute

non·pro·tein \,nän-'prō-,tēn, -'prō-tē-ən\ *adj* (1926) : not being or derived from protein ⟨the ∼ part of an enzyme⟩ ⟨∼ nitrogen⟩

non·read·er \-'rē-dər\ *n* (1924) **1** : one who does not or cannot read **2** : a child who is very slow in learning to read — **non·read·ing** \-diŋ\ *adj*

non·re·com·bi·nant \,nän-(,)rē-'käm-bə-nənt\ *adj* (1962) : not exhibiting the results of genetic recombination — **nonrecombinant** *n*

non·re·course \'nän-'rē-,kórs, -,kórs, -ri-'\ *adj* (1926) : being or based on an agreement in which the lender has no right of recourse to the borrower's assets beyond stated limits ⟨a ∼ note⟩ ⟨a ∼ loan⟩

non·re·cur·rent \,nän-ri-'kər-ənt, -'kə-rənt\ *adj* (ca. 1864) : not recurring

non·re·cur·ring \-ri-'kər-iŋ, -'kə-riŋ\ *adj* (ca. 1864) : NONRECURRENT; *specif* : unlikely to happen again — used of financial transactions that affect a profit and loss statement abnormally

non·re·fund·able \-ri-'fən-də-bəl\ *adj* (1963) : not subject to refunding or being refunded ⟨a ∼ fee⟩

non·rel·a·tiv·is·tic \,re-lə-ti-'vis-tik\ *adj* (1930) **1** : not based on or involving the theory of relativity ⟨∼ equations⟩ ⟨∼ kinematics⟩ **2** : of, relating to, or being a body moving at less than a relativistic velocity — **non·rel·a·tiv·is·ti·cal·ly** \-'vis-ti-k(ə-)lē\ *adv*

non·rep·re·sen·ta·tion·al \,nän-,re-pri-,zen-'tä-shnəl, -zən-, -shə-n²l\ *adj* (1923) : NONOBJECTIVE 2 — **non·rep·re·sen·ta·tion·al·ism** \-shnə-,li-zəm, -shə-n²l-,i-zəm\ *n*

non·res·i·dence \'nän-'re-zə-dən(t)s, -'rez-dən(t)s, -,den(t)s\ *n* (1585) : the state or fact of being nonresident

non·res·i·den·cy \-'re-zə-dən(t)-sē, -'rez-dən(t)-, -,den(t)-\ *n* (1584) : NONRESIDENCE

non·res·i·dent \-'re-zə-dənt, -'rez-dənt, -,dent\ *adj* (1540) : not residing in a particular place — **nonresident** *n*

non·re·sis·tance \,nän-ri-'zis-tən(t)s\ *n* (1643) : the principles or practice of passive submission to constituted authority even when unjust or oppressive; *also* : the principle or practice of not resisting violence by force

non·re·sis·tant \-'tənt\ *adj* (1702) : not resistant; *specif* : susceptible to the effects of a deleterious agent (as an insecticide, a pathogen, or an extreme environmental condition) — **nonresistant** *n*

non·re·stric·tive \-ri-'strik-tiv\ *adj* (1916) : not restrictive; *specif* : not limiting the reference of a modified word or phrase

nonrestrictive clause *n* (1916) : a descriptive clause that is not essential to the definiteness of the meaning of the word it modifies (as *who is retired* in "my father, who is retired, does volunteer work")

non·re·turn·able \-ri-'tər-nə-bəl\ *adj* (1903) : not returnable; *specif* : not returnable to a dealer in exchange for a deposit ⟨∼ bottles⟩ — **nonreturnable** *n*

non·rig·id \'nän-'ri-jəd\ *adj* (1909) : not rigid; *esp* : maintaining form by pressure of contained gas ⟨a ∼ airship⟩

non·sched·uled \-'ske-(,)jü(ə)ld, -jəld\ *adj* (1947) : licensed to transport by air without a regular schedule ⟨∼ airlines⟩

¹non·sci·ence \-'sī-ən(t)s\ *n* (1855) : something (as a discipline) that is not a science

²nonscience *adj* (1944) : of or relating to fields other than science

non·se·cre·tor \,nän-si-'krē-tər\ *n* (1944) : an individual of blood group A, B, or AB who does not secrete the antigens characteristic of these blood groups in bodily fluids (as saliva)

non·sec·tar·i·an \,nän-(,)sek-'ter-ē-ən\ *adj* (1831) : not having a sectarian character : not affiliated with or restricted to a particular religious group

non·self \'nän-'self, *Southern also* -'sef\ *n* (1963) : material that is foreign to the body of an organism

¹non·sense \'nän-,sen(t)s, 'nän(t)-sən(t)s\ *n* (1614) **1 a** : words or language having no meaning or conveying no intelligible ideas **b** (1) : language, conduct, or an idea that is absurd or contrary to good sense (2) : an instance of absurd action **2 a** : things of no importance or value : TRIFLES **b** : affected or impudent conduct ⟨took no ∼ from subordinates⟩ **3** : genetic information consisting of one or more codons that do not code for any amino acid and usu. cause termination of the molecular chain in protein synthesis — compare ANTISENSE, MISSENSE — **non·sen·si·cal** \,nän-'sen(t)-si-kəl\ *adj* — **non·sen·si·cal·ly** \-k(ə-)lē\ *adv* — **non·sen·si·cal·ness** \-kəl-nəs\ *n*

²nonsense *adj* (1778) **1** : consisting of an arbitrary grouping of speech sounds or symbols ⟨'shròg-,thī-əmpth\ is a ∼ word⟩ ⟨a ∼ syllable⟩ **2** : consisting of one or more codons that are genetic nonsense

nonsense verse *n* (1799) : humorous or whimsical verse that features absurd characters and actions and often contains evocative but meaningless nonce words

non se·qui·tur \'nän-'se-kwə-tər *also* -,túr\ *n* [L, it does not follow] (1540) **1** : an inference that does not follow from the premises; *specif* : a fallacy resulting from a simple conversion of a universal affirmative proposition or from the transposition of a condition and its consequent **2** : a statement (as a response) that does not follow logically from anything previously said

non·sig·nif·i·cant \,nän-sig-'ni-fi-kənt\ *adj* (1902) : not significant: as **a** : INSIGNIFICANT **b** : MEANINGLESS **c** : having or yielding a value lying within limits between which variation is attributed to chance ⟨a ∼ statistical test⟩ — **non·sig·nif·i·cant·ly** *adv*

non·sked \'nän-'sked\ *n* [by shortening & alter. fr. *nonscheduled*] (1949) : a nonscheduled transport plane or airline

non·skid \-'skid\ *adj* (1904) : designed or equipped to prevent skidding

non·slip \-'slip\ *adj* (1903) : designed to reduce or prevent slipping

non·so·cial \-'sō-shəl\ *adj* (1902) : not socially oriented : lacking a social component

non·sport·ing \-'spór-tiŋ, -'spòr-\ *adj* (1852) : lacking the qualities characteristic of a hunting dog

non·stan·dard \-'stan-dərd\ *adj* (1923) **1** : not standard **2** : not conforming in pronunciation, grammatical construction, idiom, or word choice to the usage generally characteristic of educated native speakers of a language — compare SUBSTANDARD

non·start·er \-'stär-tər\ *n* (1902) **1** : one that does not start **2** : someone or something that is not productive or effective ⟨his son has been, in politics a ∼ —Anthony Lejeune⟩

non·ste·roi·dal \,nän-stə-'rói-d²l\ *also* **-'ster-** *adj* (1964) : of, relating to, or being a compound and esp. a drug that is not a steroid — **nonsteroid** *n*

non·stick \'nän-'stik\ *adj* [³stick] (1958) : allowing of easy removal of cooked food particles ⟨a ∼ coating in a frying pan⟩

non·stop \'nän-'stäp\ *adj* (1902) : done, made, or held without a stop : not easing or letting up — **nonstop** *adv*

\ə\ abut \²\ kitten, F table \ər\ further \a\ ash \ā\ ace \ä\ mop, mar \aú\ out \ch\ chin \e\ bet \ē\ easy \g\ go \i\ hit \ī\ ice \j\ job \ŋ\ sing \ō\ go \ò\ law \ói\ boy \th\ thin \t̷h\ the \ü\ loot \ú\ foot \y\ yet \zh\ vision \ä, k̲, ⁿ, œ, œ̄, ᵫ, ūᵉ, ᵍ\ *see* Guide to Pronunciation

non·such \'nən-ˌsəch *also* 'nän-\ *var of* NONESUCH

non·suit \'nän-ˌsüt\ *n* [ME, fr. AF *nounsuyte*, fr. *noun-* non- + OF *siute* following, pursuit — more at SUIT] (14c) : a judgment against a plaintiff for failure to prosecute a case or inability to establish a prima facie case — **nonsuit** *vt*

non·sup·port \ˌnän-sə-'pōrt, -'pȯrt\ *n* (1909) : failure to support; *specif* : failure (as of a parent) to honor a statutory or contractual obligation to provide maintenance

non·syl·lab·ic \-sə-'la-bik\ *adj* (ca. 1909) : not constituting a syllable or the nucleus of a syllable ⟨the second vowel of a falling diphthong is ~ ⟨as \i\ in \ȯi\⟩⟩

non·sys·tem \'nän-'sis-təm\ *n* (1964) : a system that lacks effective organization

non·tar·get \-'tär-gət\ *adj* (1945) : not being the intended object of action by a particular agent ⟨effect of insecticides on ~ organisms⟩

non·ter·mi·nat·ing \-'tər-mə-ˌnā-tiŋ\ *adj* (ca. 1908) : not terminating or ending; *esp* : being a decimal for which there is no place to the right of the decimal point such that all places farther to the right contain the entry 0 ⟨1/3 gives the ~ decimal .33333 . . .⟩

non·ther·mal \-'thər-məl\ *adj* (ca. 1964) : not produced by heat; *specif* : of, relating to, or being radiation having a spectrum that is not the spectrum of a blackbody

non·ti·tle \-'tī-tᵊl\ *adj* (1968) : of, relating to, or being an athletic contest in which a title is not at stake

non trop·po \'nän-'trȯ-(ˌ)pō, 'nȯn-\ *adv or adj* [It, lit., not too much] (ca. 1854) : without excess — used to qualify a direction in music

non–U \'nän-'yü\ *adj* (1954) : not characteristic of the upper classes

non·union \-'yün-yən\ *adj* (1863) 1 : not belonging to or connected with a trade union ⟨~ carpenters⟩ 2 : not recognizing or favoring trade unions or their members 3 : not produced or worked on by members of a trade union ⟨~ lettuce⟩

non·use \'nän-'yüs\ *n* (1542) 1 : failure to use ⟨~ of available material⟩ 2 : the fact or condition of not being used

non·us·er \-'yü-zər\ *n* (1926) : one who does not make use of something (as an available public facility or a harmful drug)

non·van·ish·ing \-'va-ni-shiŋ\ *adj* (1907) : not zero or becoming zero

non·vec·tor \-'vek-tər\ *n* (1956) : an organism (as an insect) that does not transmit a particular pathogen (as a virus)

non·ver·bal \-'vər-bəl\ *adj* (1924) : not verbal: as **a** : being other than verbal ⟨~ factors⟩ **b** : involving minimal use of language ⟨~ tests⟩ **c** : ranking low in verbal skill — **non·ver·bal·ly** \-bə-lē\ *adv*

non·vin·tage \-'vin-tij\ *adj* (1924) : undated and usu. blended to approximate a standard ⟨a ~ wine⟩

non·vi·o·lence \-'vī-ə-lən(t)s\ *n* (1920) 1 : abstention from violence as a matter of principle; *also* : the principle of such abstention 2 **a** : the quality or state of being nonviolent : avoidance of violence **b** : nonviolent demonstrations for the purpose of securing political ends ⟨studied the history and techniques of ~⟩

non·vi·o·lent \-lənt\ *adj* (1920) : abstaining or free from violence — **non·vi·o·lent·ly** *adv*

non·vol·a·tile \-'vä-lə-tᵊl\ *adj* (1866) : not volatile: as **a** : not vaporizing readily ⟨a ~ solvent⟩ **b** *of a computer memory* : retaining data when power is shut off

non–West·ern \-'wes-tərn\ *adj* (1902) 1 : not being part of the western tradition ⟨~ countries⟩ 2 : of or relating to non-Western societies ⟨~ values⟩

non·white \-'hwīt, -'wīt\ *n* (1927) : a person whose features and esp. whose skin color are distinctively different from those of peoples of northwestern Europe; *esp* : one who has African ancestors of the black race — **nonwhite** *adj*

non·word \-'wərd\ *n* (1961) : a word that has no meaning, is not known to exist, or is disapproved

non·wo·ven \-'wō-vən\ *adj* (1945) 1 : made of fibers held together by interlocking or bonding (as by chemical or thermal means) : not woven, knitted, or felted ⟨~ fabric⟩ 2 : made of nonwoven fabric ⟨a ~ dress⟩ — **nonwoven** *n*

non·ze·ro \-'zē-(ˌ)rō, -'zir-(ˌ)ō\ *adj* (1905) 1 : being, having, or involving a value other than zero 2 : having phonetic content ⟨~ affixes⟩

¹noo·dle \'nü-dᵊl\ *n* [perh. alter. of *noddle*] (1753) 1 : a stupid person : SIMPLETON 2 : HEAD, NOGGIN

²noodle *n* [G *Nudel*] (1779) : a food paste made with egg and shaped typically in ribbon form

³noodle *vi* **noo·dled; noo·dling** \'nüd-liŋ, 'nü-dᵊl-iŋ\ [imit.] (ca. 1937) : to improvise on an instrument in an informal or desultory manner

nook \'nu̇k\ *n* [ME *noke, nok*] (14c) 1 *chiefly Scot* : a right-angled corner 2 **a** : an interior angle formed by two meeting walls : RECESS **b** : a secluded or sheltered place or part ⟨searched every ~ and cranny⟩

nooky \'nu̇-kē\ *n* [perh. fr. *nook* + ⁴-*y*] (1928) 1 : SEXUAL INTERCOURSE — often considered vulgar 2 : the female partner in sexual intercourse — often considered vulgar

noon \'nün\ *n* [ME, fr. OE *nōn* ninth hour from sunrise, fr. L *nona*, fr. fem. of *nonus* ninth; akin to L *novem* nine — more at NINE] (13c) 1 : MIDDAY; *specif* : 12 o'clock at midday 2 *archaic* : MIDNIGHT — used chiefly in the phrase *noon of night* 3 : the highest point

noon·day \-ˌdā\ *n* (1535) : MIDDAY

no one *pron* (bef. 12c) : no person : NOBODY

noon·ing \'nü-niŋ, -nən\ *n* (ca. 1652) 1 *chiefly dial* : a meal eaten at noon 2 *chiefly dial* : a period at noon for eating or resting

noon·tide \'nün-ˌtīd\ *n* (12c) 1 : NOONTIME 2 : the culminating point

noon·time \-ˌtīm\ *n* (14c) : the time of noon : MIDDAY

¹noose \'nüs, *Brit also* 'nüz\ *n* [ME *nose*, perh. of Prov origin; akin to Prov *nous* knot, fr. L *nodus* — more at NODE] (15c) 1 : a loop with a running knot that binds closer the more it is drawn 2 : something that snares like a noose

²noose *vt* **noosed; noos·ing** (1600) 1 : to secure by a noose 2 : to make a noose in or of

noo·sphere \'nō-ō-ˌsfir\ *n* [ISV *noo-* mind (fr. Gk *noos, nous*) + *sphere* sphere] (1945) : the sphere of human consciousness and mental activity esp. in regard to its influence on the biosphere and in relation to evolution

Noot·ka \'nu̇t-kə\ *n, pl* **Nootka** *or* **Nootkas** (1841) 1 : a member of a Wakashan people inhabiting the West Coast of Vancouver Island 2 : the language of the Nootka people

no·pal \nō-'päl, -'pal; 'nō-pəl\ *n* [Sp, fr. Nahuatl *nohpalli*] (1730) : any of a genus (*Nopalea*) of cacti of Mexico and Central America that differ from the prickly pears in having erect petals and scarlet flowers with the stamens much longer than the petals; *broadly* : PRICKLY PEAR

no–par *or* **no–par–value** *adj* (1922) : having no nominal value ⟨~ stocks⟩

nope \'nōp, *or with glottal stop instead of* p\ *adv* [by alter.] (1888) : NO

¹nor \nər, 'nȯr, *Southern also* 'när\ *conj* [ME, contr. of *nother* neither, nor, fr. *nother*, pron. & adj., neither — more at NEITHER] (14c) 1 — used as a function word to introduce the second or last member or the second and each following member of a series of items each of which is negated ⟨neither here ~ there⟩ ⟨not done by you ~ me ~ anyone⟩ 2 — used as a function word to introduce and negate a following clause or phrase 3 *chiefly Brit* : NEITHER

²nor *conj* [ME, perh. fr. ¹*nor*] (15c) *dial* : THAN

nor- *comb form* [normal] : homologue containing one less methyl group ⟨*nor*epinephrine⟩

NOR \'nȯr\ *n* [*not* OR] (1957) : a computer logic circuit that produces an output that is the inverse of that of an OR circuit

nor·adren·a·line *also* **nor·adren·a·lin** \ˌnȯr-ə-'dre-nᵊl-ən\ *n* (1932) : NOREPINEPHRINE

nor·ad·ren·er·gic \ˌnȯr-ˌa-drə-'nər-jik\ *adj* [*noradren*aline + -*ergic*] (1963) : liberating, activated by, or involving norepinephrine in the transmission of nerve impulses ⟨~ nerve endings⟩ ⟨~ nerve fibers⟩

¹Nor·dic \'nȯr-dik\ *adj* [F *nordique*, fr. *nord* north, fr. OE *north*] (1898) 1 : of or relating to the Germanic peoples of northern Europe and esp. of Scandinavia 2 : of or relating to a group or physical type of the Caucasian race characterized by tall stature, long head, light skin and hair, and blue eyes 3 **a** : of or relating to competitive ski events involving cross-country racing, ski jumping, or biathlon — compare ALPINE **b** : of, relating to, or being cross-country skiing

²Nordic *n* (1901) 1 : a native of northern Europe 2 : a person of Nordic physical type 3 : a member of the peoples of Scandinavia

nor·epi·neph·rine \ˌnȯr-ˌe-pə-'ne-frən\ *n* (1945) : a catecholamine $C_8H_{11}NO_3$ that is the chemical means of transmission across synapses in postganglionic neurons of the sympathetic nervous system and in some parts of the central nervous system, is a vasopressor hormone of the adrenal medulla, and is a precursor of epinephrine in its major biosynthetic pathway

nor·eth·in·drone \ˌnȯ-'re-thən-ˌdrōn\ *n* [*nor-* + *eth*inyl + *hydr-* + -*one* (as in *progesterone*)] (1958) : a synthetic progestational hormone $C_{20}H_{26}O_2$ used in oral contraceptives often in the form of its acetate

Nor·folk jacket \'nȯr-fək-, -ˌfȯk-\ *n* [*Norfolk*, England] (1866) : a loose-fitting belted single-breasted jacket with box pleats

Norfolk terrier *n* (1964) : any of a breed of dogs developed in England and resembling the Norwich terrier but having folded-over ears

no·ri \'nō-rē, 'nȯr-ē\ *n* [Jp] (1892) : dried laver seaweed pressed into thin sheets and used esp. as a seasoning or as a wrapper for sushi

nor·land \'nȯr-lənd\ *n* (ca. 1578) *chiefly dial* : NORTHLAND

norm \'nȯrm\ *n* [L *norma*, lit., carpenter's square] (1674) 1 : an authoritative standard : MODEL 2 : a principle of right action binding upon the members of a group and serving to guide, control, or regulate proper and acceptable behavior 3 : AVERAGE: as **a** : a set standard of development or achievement usu. derived from the average or median achievement of a large group **b** : a pattern or trait taken to be typical in the behavior of a social group **c** : a widespread practice, procedure, or custom : RULE ⟨standing ovations became the ~⟩ 4 **a** : a real-valued nonnegative function defined on a vector space and satisfying the conditions that the function is zero if and only if the vector is zero, the function of the product of a scalar and a vector is equal to the product of the absolute value of the scalar and the function of the vector, and the function of the sum of two vectors is less than or equal to the sum of the functions of the two vectors; *specif* : the square root of the sum of the squares of the absolute values of the elements of a matrix or of the components of a vector **b** : the greatest distance between two successive points of a set of points that partition an interval into smaller intervals *syn* see AVERAGE

¹nor·mal \'nȯr-məl\ *adj* [L *normalis*, fr. *norma*] (ca. 1696) 1 : PERPENDICULAR; *esp* : perpendicular to a tangent at a point of tangency 2 **a** : according with, constituting, or not deviating from a norm, rule, or principle **b** : conforming to a type, standard, or regular pattern 3 : occurring naturally ⟨~ immunity⟩ 4 **a** : of, relating to, or characterized by average intelligence or development **b** : free from mental disorder : SANE 5 *of a solution* : having a concentration of one gram equivalent of solute per liter **b** : containing neither basic hydroxyl nor acid hydrogen ⟨~ silver phosphate⟩ **c** : not associated ⟨~ molecules⟩ **d** : having a straight-chain structure ⟨~ pentane⟩ ⟨~ butyl alcohol⟩ 6 *of a subgroup* : having the property that every coset produced by operating on the left by a given element is equal to the coset produced by operating on the right by the same element 7 : relating to, involving, or being a normal curve or normal distribution ⟨~ approximation to the binomial distribution⟩ 8 *of a matrix* : having the property of commutativity under multiplication by the transpose of the matrix each of whose elements is a conjugate complex number with respect to the corresponding element of the given matrix *syn* see REGULAR — **nor·mal·i·ty** \nȯr-'ma-lə-tē\ *n* — **nor·mal·ly** \'nȯr-mə-lē\ *adv*

²normal *n* (ca. 1738) 1 **a** : a normal line **b** : the portion of a normal line to a plane curve between the curve and the x-axis 2 : one that is normal 3 : a form or state regarded as the norm : STANDARD

normal curve *n* (1894) : the symmetrical bell-shaped curve of a normal distribution

nor·mal·cy \'nȯr-məl-sē\ *n* (1857) : the state or fact of being normal

normal distribution *n* (1897) : a probability density function that approximates the distribution of many random variables (as the proportion of outcomes of a particular sort in a large number of independent repetitions of an experiment in which the probabilities remain constant from trial to trial) and that has the form

$$f(x) = \frac{1}{\sigma\sqrt{2\pi}}\, e^{-\frac{1}{2}\left(\frac{x-\mu}{\sigma}\right)^2}$$

where μ is the mean and σ is the standard deviation — compare NORMAL CURVE

nor·mal·ise *Brit var of* NORMALIZE

nor·mal·ize \'nȯr-mə-ˌlīz\ vt **-ized; -iz·ing** (1865) **1** : to make conform to or reduce to a norm or standard **2** : to make normal (as by a transformation of variables) **3** : to bring or restore (as relations between countries) to a normal condition — **nor·mal·iz·able** \-ˌlī-zə-bəl\ adj — **nor·mal·i·za·tion** \ˌnȯr-mə-lə-'zā-shən\ n

nor·mal·iz·er \'nȯr-mə-ˌlī-zər\ n (1926) **1** : one that normalizes **2 a** : a subgroup consisting of those elements of a group for which the group operation with regard to a given element is commutative **b** : the set of elements of a group for which the group operation with regard to every element of a given subgroup is commutative

normal school n [trans. of F école normale; fr. the fact that the first French school so named was intended to serve as a model] (1839) : a usu. 2-year school for training chiefly elementary teachers

Nor·man \'nȯr-mən\ n [ME, fr. OF Normant, fr. ON Northmann-, Northmathr Norseman, fr. northr north + mann-, mathr man; akin to OE north north and to OE man man] (13c) **1** : a native or inhabitant of Normandy: **a** : one of the Scandinavian conquerors of Normandy in the 10th century **b** : one of the Norman-French conquerors of England in 1066 **2** : NORMAN-FRENCH — **Norman** adj

Norman architecture n (1797) : a Romanesque style first appearing in and near Normandy about A.D. 950; also : architecture resembling or imitating this style

nor·mande \nȯr-'mand\ adj [F, fr. fem. of normand Norman, fr. Normandy, France] (ca. 1929) : prepared with any of several foods traditionally associated with Normandy (as cream, apples, cider, or calvados) ⟨veal ~⟩

Norman–French n (1605) **1** : the French language of the medieval Normans **2** : the modern dialect of Normandy

nor·ma·tive \'nȯr-mə-tiv\ adj [F normatif, fr. norme norm, fr. L norma] (1878) **1** : of, relating to, or determining norms or standards ⟨~ tests⟩ **2** : conforming to or based on norms ⟨~ behavior⟩ ⟨~ judgments⟩ **3** : prescribing norms ⟨~ rules of ethics⟩ ⟨~ grammar⟩ — **nor·ma·tive·ly** adv — **nor·ma·tive·ness** n

normed \'nȯrmd\ adj (1935) : being a mathematical entity upon which a norm is defined ⟨a ~ vector space⟩

nor·mo·ten·sive \ˌnȯr-mō-'ten(t)-siv\ adj [normal + -o- + -tensive (as in hypotensive)] (ca. 1941) : having blood pressure typical of the group to which one belongs — **normotensive** n

nor·mo·ther·mia \-'thər-mē-ə\ n [NL, fr. normalis normal + -o- + -thermia -thermy] (1960) : normal body temperature — **nor·mo·ther·mic** \-mik\ adj

Norn \'nȯrn\ n [ON] : any of the three Norse goddesses of fate

¹Norse \'nȯrs\ n, pl **Norse** [prob. fr. obs. D noorsch, adj., Norwegian, Scandinavian, alter. of obs. D noordsch northern, fr. D noord north; akin to OE north north] (ca. 1688) **1 a** : NORWEGIAN 2 **b** : any of the western Scandinavian dialects or languages **c** : the Scandinavian group of Germanic languages **2** pl **a** : SCANDINAVIANS **b** : NORWEGIANS

²Norse adj (1768) **1** : of or relating to ancient Scandinavia or the language of its inhabitants **2** : NORWEGIAN

Norse·man \'nȯrs-mən\ n (1817) : any of the ancient Scandinavians

¹north \'nȯrth\ adv [ME, fr. OE; akin to OHG nord north and perh. to Gk nerteros lower, infernal] (bef. 12c) : to, toward, or in the north

²north adj (bef. 12c) **1** : situated toward or at the north ⟨the ~ entrance⟩ **2** : coming from the north ⟨a ~ wind⟩

³north n (13c) **1 a** : the direction of the north terrestrial pole : the direction to the left of one facing east **b** : the compass point directly opposite to south **2** cap **a** : regions or countries lying to the north of a specified or implied point of orientation **b** : the industrially and economically developed nations of the world — compare SOUTH 3 often cap **a** : the one of four positions at 90-degree intervals that lies to the north or at the top of a diagram **b** : a person occupying this position in the course of a specified activity (as the game of bridge)

north·bound \'nȯrth-ˌbau̇nd\ adj (1903) : traveling or headed north

north by east (1725) : a compass point that is one point east of due north : N11°15′E

north by west (ca. 1771) : a compass point that is one point west of due north : N11°15′W

¹north·east \nȯr-'thēst, naut nȯ-'rēst\ adv (bef. 12c) : to, toward, or in the northeast

²northeast adj (bef. 12c) **1** : coming from the northeast ⟨a ~ wind⟩ **2** : situated toward or at the northeast ⟨the ~ corner⟩

³northeast n (12c) **1 a** : the general direction between north and east **b** : the point midway between the north and east compass points **2** cap : regions or countries lying to the northeast of a specified or implied point of orientation

northeast by east (ca. 1771) : a compass point that is one point east of due northeast : N56°15′E

northeast by north (ca. 1771) : a compass point that is one point north of due northeast : N33°45′E

north·east·er \nȯr-'thē-stər, nȯ-'rē-\ n (1774) **1** : a strong northeast wind **2** : a storm with northeast winds

north·east·er·ly \nȯr-'thē-stər-lē\ adv or adj (1739) **1** : from the northeast **2** : toward the northeast

north·east·ern \-stərn\ adj (14c) **1** often cap : of, relating to, or characteristic of a region conventionally designated Northeast **2** : lying toward or coming from the northeast — **north·east·ern·most** \-stərn-ˌmōst\ adj

North·east·ern·er \-stə(r)-nər\ n (1961) : a native or inhabitant of a northeastern region (as of the U.S.)

¹north·east·ward \nȯr-'thēs-twərd, nȯ-'rēs-\ adv or adj (1553) : toward the northeast — **north·east·wards** \-twərdz\ adv

²northeastward n (1892) : NORTHEAST

north·er \'nȯr-thər\ n (1820) **1** : a strong north wind **2** : a storm with north winds

¹north·er·ly \-lē\ adj or adv [³north + -erly (as in easterly)] (1551) **1** : situated toward or belonging to the north ⟨the ~ border⟩ **2** : coming from the north ⟨a ~ wind⟩

²northerly n, pl **-lies** (1955) : a wind from the north

¹north·ern \'nȯr-thə(r)n\ adj [ME northerne, fr. OE; akin to OHG nordrōni northern, OE north north] (bef. 12c) **1** cap **a** : of, relating to, or characteristic of a region conventionally designated North **b** : of, relating to, or constituting the northern dialect **2 a** : lying toward the north **b** : coming from the north ⟨a ~ storm⟩ — **north·ern·most** \-ˌmōst\ adj

²northern n (1950) **1** cap : the dialect of English spoken in the part of the U.S. north of a line running northwest through central New Jersey, below the northern tier of counties in Pennsylvania, through northern Ohio, Indiana, and Illinois, across central Iowa, and through the northwest corner of So. Dakota **2** : ³PIKE 1a

northern corn rootworm n (1952) : a corn rootworm (Diabrotica barberi syn. D. longicornis) often destructive to Indian corn in the northern parts of the central and eastern U.S.

Northern Cross n : a cross formed by six stars in Cygnus

North·ern·er \'nȯr-thə(r)-nər\ n (1599) : a native or inhabitant of the North; esp : a native or resident of the northern part of the U.S.

northern harrier n (1980) : a widely distributed brown or grayish hawk (Circus cyaneus) that inhabits open and marshy regions and has a conspicuous white patch on the rump — called also marsh hawk

northern hemisphere n, often cap N&H (ca. 1771) : the half of the earth that lies north of the equator

northern lights n pl (14c) : AURORA BOREALIS

northern oriole n (1974) : an American oriole (Icterus galbula) that is characterized by the black and orange plumage of the male and that includes the Baltimore oriole of the eastern U.S. and a more western form (I. g. bullockii) with a black and orange head

northern pike n (1856) : ³PIKE 1a

northern white cedar n (1926) : an arborvitae (Thuja occidentalis) of eastern No. America that has branchlets in horizontal planes; also : its wood — called also white cedar

North Germanic n (ca. 1930) : a subdivision of the Germanic languages including Icelandic, Norwegian, Swedish, and Danish — see INDO-EUROPEAN LANGUAGES table

north·ing \'nȯr-thiŋ, -thiŋ\ n (1669) **1** : difference in latitude to the north from the last preceding point of reckoning **2** : northerly progress

north·land \'nȯrth-ˌland, -lənd\ n, often cap (bef. 12c) : land in the north : the north of a country

North·man \'nȯrth-mən\ n (bef. 12c) : NORSEMAN

north–north·east \'nȯrth-ˌnȯr-'thēst, -ˌnȯ-'rēst\ n (14c) : a compass point that is two points east of due north : N22°30′E

north–north·west \'nȯrth-ˌnȯr(th)-'west\ n (14c) : a compass point that is two points west of due north : N22°30′W

north pole n (14c) **1** often cap N&P : the northernmost point of the earth; broadly : the corresponding point of a celestial body (as a planet) **a** : the zenith of the heavens as viewed from the north terrestrial pole **2** of a magnet : the pole that points toward the north when the magnet is freely suspended

north–seeking pole n (ca. 1920) : NORTH POLE 2

North Star n : the star of the northern hemisphere toward which the axis of the earth points — called also polestar

¹North·um·bri·an \nȯr-'thəm-brē-ən\ adj (1622) **1** : of, relating to, or characteristic of ancient Northumbria, its people, or its language **2** : of, relating to, or characteristic of Northumberland, its people, or its language

²Northumbrian n (1752) **1** : a native or inhabitant of ancient Northumbria **2** : a native or inhabitant of Northumberland **3 a** : the Old English dialect of Northumbria **b** : the Modern English dialect of Northumberland

¹north·ward \'nȯrth-wərd\ adv or adj (bef. 12c) : toward the north — **north·wards** \-wərdz\ adv

²northward n (14c) : northward direction or part ⟨sail to the ~⟩

¹north·west \nȯrth-'west, naut nȯr-'west\ adv (bef. 12c) : to, toward, or in the northwest

²northwest adj (bef. 12c) **1** : coming from the northwest ⟨a ~ wind⟩ **2** : situated toward or at the northwest ⟨the ~ corner⟩

³northwest n (12c) **1 a** : the general direction between north and west **b** : the point midway between the north and west compass points **2** cap : regions or countries lying to the northwest of a specified or implied point of orientation

northwest by north (ca. 1771) : a compass point that is one point north of due northwest : N33°45′W

northwest by west (ca. 1771) : a compass point that is one point west of due northwest : N56°15′W

north·west·er \nȯr(th)-'wes-tər\ n (1737) : a strong northwest wind

north·west·er·ly \-lē\ adv or adj (ca. 1611) **1** : from the northwest **2** : toward the northwest

north·west·ern \-'wes-tərn\ adj (1612) **1** often cap : of, relating to, or characteristic of a region conventionally designated Northwest **2** : lying toward or coming from the northwest — **north·west·ern·most** \-ˌmōst\ adj

North·west·ern·er \-'wes-tə(r)-nər\ n (1955) : a native or inhabitant of the Northwest and esp. the northwestern part of the U.S.

¹north·west·ward \-'wes-twərd\ adv or adj (14c) : toward the northwest — **north·west·wards** \-twərdz\ adv

²northwestward n (1796) : NORTHWEST

nor·trip·ty·line \nȯr-'trip-tə-ˌlēn\ n [nor- + -tript- (perh. fr. tricyclic + hepta-) + -yl + ²-ine] (1964) : a tricyclic antidepressant $C_{19}H_{21}N$

Nor·way maple \'nȯr-ˌwā-\ n (1797) : a European maple (Acer platanoides) with dark green or often reddish or red veined leaves that is much planted for shade in the U.S.

Norway rat n (ca. 1759) : BROWN RAT

Norway spruce n (1797) : a widely cultivated spruce (Picea abies) that is native to northern Europe and has a pyramidal shape, spreading branches and pendulous branchlets, dark foliage, and long pendulous cones

Nor·we·gian \nȯr-'wē-jən\ n [ML Norwegia Norway] (1605) **1 a** : a native or inhabitant of Norway **b** : a person of Norwegian descent **2** : the Germanic language of the Norwegian people — **Norwegian** adj

\ə\ abut \ᵊ\ kitten, F table \ər\ further \a\ ash \ā\ ace \ä\ mop, mar \au̇\ out \ch\ chin \e\ bet \ē\ easy \g\ go \i\ hit \ī\ ice \j\ job \ŋ\ sing \ō\ go \ȯ\ law \ȯi\ boy \th\ thin \t͟h\ the \ü\ loot \u̇\ foot \y\ yet \zh\ vision \à, ᵏ, ⁿ, œ, œ̄, ᵫ, ᵫ̄, ᶌ\ see Guide to Pronunciation

Norwegian elkhound *n* (1930) : any of a Norwegian breed of short-bodied medium-sized dogs with erect ears and a very heavy coat of gray hairs with black tips

Nor·wich terrier \'nȯr-(ͺ)wich-, *Brit* 'när-ich- *or* 'när-ij-\ *n* [*Norwich*, England] (1931) : any of an English breed of small active low-set terriers that have a long straight wiry coat and erect ears

Norwegian elkhound

¹**nose** \'nōz\ *n* [ME, fr. OE *nosu*; akin to OHG *nasa* nose, L *nasus*] (bef. 12c) **1 a** : the part of the face that bears the nostrils and covers the anterior part of the nasal cavity; *broadly* : this part together with the nasal cavity **b** : the anterior part of the head at the top or end of the muzzle : SNOUT, PROBOSCIS **2 a** : the sense of smell : OLFACTION **b** : AROMA, BOUQUET **3** : the vertebrate olfactory organ **4 a** : the forward end or projection of something **b** : the projecting or working end of a tool **5** : the stem of a boat or its protective metal covering **6 a** : the nose as a symbol of prying or meddling curiosity or interference **b** : a knack for discovery or understanding ⟨a keen ~ for absurdity⟩ — **on the nose 1 a** : at or to a target point ⟨the bombs landed right *on the nose*⟩ **b** (1) : on target : ACCURATE (2) : ACCURATELY **2** : to win — used of horse or dog racing bets

²**nose** *vb* **nosed; nos·ing** *vt* (ca. 1587) **1** : to detect by or as if by smell : SCENT **2 a** : to push or move with the nose **b** : to move (as a vehicle) ahead slowly or cautiously ⟨*nosed* my car into the parking space⟩ **3** : to touch or rub with the nose : NUZZLE ~ *vi* **1** : to use the nose in examining, smelling, or showing affection **2** : to search impertinently : PRY **3** : to move ahead slowly or cautiously ⟨the boat *nosed* around the bend⟩

nose·band \'nōz-ͺband\ *n* (1611) : the part of a headstall that passes over a horse's nose

nose·bleed \-ͺblēd\ *n* (1848) : an attack of bleeding from the nose

nose cone *n* (1949) : a protective cone constituting the forward end of an aerospace vehicle

nosed \'nōzd\ *adj* (1505) : having a nose esp. of a specified kind — usu. used in combination ⟨snub-*nosed*⟩

nose-dive \'nōz-ͺdīv\ *n* (1912) **1** : a downward nose-first plunge of a flying object (as an airplane) **2** : a sudden extreme drop ⟨stock prices took a ~⟩ — **nose-dive** *vi*

no-see-um \nō-'sē-əm\ *n* [fr. the words (as supposedly spoken by American Indians) *no see um* you don't see them] (1848) : BITING MIDGE

nose·gay \'nōz-ͺgā\ *n* [ME, fr. *nose* nose + *gay* ornament, lit., something gay, fr. *gay*] (15c) : a small bunch of flowers : POSY

nose·guard \-ͺgärd\ *n* (1950) : a defensive lineman in football who plays opposite the offensive center

nose job *n* (1963) : RHINOPLASTY

nose out *vt* (ca. 1630) **1** : to discover often by prying **2** : to defeat by a narrow margin

nose·piece \-ͺpēs\ *n* (1611) **1** : a piece of armor for protecting the nose **2** : the end piece of a microscope body to which an objective is attached **3** : the bridge of a pair of eyeglasses

nose tackle *n* (1977) : NOSEGUARD

nose·wheel \-ͺhwēl, -ͺwēl\ *n* (1934) : a landing-gear wheel under the nose of an airplane

nos·ey par·ker \ͺnō-zē-'pär-kər\ *n, often cap N&P* [prob. fr. the name *Parker*] (1907) *chiefly Brit* : BUSYBODY

¹**nosh** \'näsh\ *n* (1952) : a light meal : SNACK

²**nosh** *vb* [Yiddish *nashn*, fr. MHG *naschen* to eat on the sly] *vi* (1956) : to eat a snack ~ *vt* : CHEW, MUNCH — **nosh·er** *n*

no-show \'nō-ͺshō, -'shō\ *n* (1941) **1** : a person who reserves space (as on an airplane) but neither uses nor cancels the reservation **2** : a person who buys a ticket (as to a sporting event) but does not attend; *broadly* : a person who is expected but who does not show up **3** : failure to show up

nos·ing \'nō-ziŋ\ *n* (ca. 1775) : the usu. rounded edge of a stair tread that projects over the riser; *also* : a similar rounded projection

nos·o·co·mi·al \ͺnä-sə-'kō-mē-əl\ *adj* [LL *nosocomium* hospital, fr. LGk *nosokomeion*, fr. Gk *nosokomos* one who tends the sick, fr. *nosos* disease + *-komos*; akin to Gk *kamnein* to suffer, toil, Skt *śamyati* he tires] (ca. 1843) : originating or taking place in a hospital ⟨~ infection⟩

no·sol·o·gy \nō-'sä-lə-jē, -'zä-\ *n* [prob. fr. NL *nosologia*, fr. Gk *nosos* disease + NL *-logia* -logy] (ca. 1721) **1** : a classification or list of diseases **2** : a branch of medical science that deals with classification of diseases — **no·so·log·i·cal** \ͺnō-sə-'lä-ji-kəl\ *or* **no·so·log·ic** \-jik\ *adj* — **no·so·log·i·cal·ly** \-ji-k(ə-)lē\ *adv*

nos·tal·gia \nä-'stal-jə, nə- *also* nö-, nó-; nə-'stäl-\ *n* [NL, fr. Gk *nostos* return home + NL *-algia*; akin to Gk *neisthai* to return, OE *genesan* to survive, Skt *nasate* he approaches] (1770) **1** : the state of being homesick : HOMESICKNESS **2** : a wistful or excessively sentimental yearning for return to or of some past period or irrecoverable condition; *also* : something that evokes nostalgia — **nos·tal·gic** \-jik\ *adj or n* — **nos·tal·gi·cal·ly** \-ji-k(ə-)lē\ *adv*

nos·tal·gist \-jist\ *n* (1953) : a person given to nostalgia for the past

nos·toc \'näs-ͺtäk\ *n* [NL] (1650) : any of a genus (*Nostoc*) of blue-green algae that fix nitrogen

nos·tril \'näs-trəl\ *n* [ME *nosethirl*, fr. OE *nosthyrl*, fr. *nosu* nose + *thyrel* hole; akin to OE *thurh* through] (bef. 12c) **1** : either of the external nares; *broadly* : either of the nares with the adjoining passage on the same side of the septum **2** : either fleshy lateral wall of the nose

nos·trum \'näs-trəm\ *n* [L, neut. of *noster* our, ours, fr. *nos* we — more at US] (1602) **1** : a medicine of secret composition recommended by its preparer but usu. without scientific proof of its effectiveness **2** : a usu. questionable remedy or scheme : PANACEA

nosy *or* **nos·ey** \'nō-zē\ *adj* **nos·i·er; -est** [¹*nose*] (1882) : of prying or inquisitive disposition or quality : INTRUSIVE — **nos·i·ly** \'nō-zə-lē\ *adv* — **nos·i·ness** \-zē-nəs\ *n*

not \'nät\ *adv* [ME, alter. of *nought*, fr. *nought*, pron. — more at NAUGHT] (13c) **1** — used as a function word to make negative a group of words or a word **2** — used as a function word to stand for the negative of a preceding group of words ⟨is sometimes hard to see and sometimes ~⟩

NOT \'nät\ *n* [*not*] (1947) : a logical operator that produces a statement that is the inverse of an input statement

nota *pl of* NOTUM

no·ta be·ne \ͺnō-tə-'bē-nē, -'be-\ [L, mark well] (ca. 1721) — used to call attention to something important

no·ta·bil·i·ty \ͺnō-tə-'bi-lə-tē\ *n, pl* **-ties** (1832) : a notable or prominent person

¹**no·ta·ble** \'nō-tə-bəl, *for 2 also* 'nä-\ *adj* (14c) **1 a** : worthy of note : REMARKABLE **b** : DISTINGUISHED, PROMINENT **2** *archaic* : efficient or capable in performance of housewifely duties — **no·ta·ble·ness** *n*

²**no·ta·ble** \'nō-tə-bəl\ *n* (1815) **1** : a person of note : NOTABILITY **2** *pl, often cap* : a group of persons summoned esp. in monarchical France to act as a deliberative body

no·ta·bly \'nō-tə-blē\ *adv* (14c) **1** : in a notable manner **2** : ESPECIALLY, PARTICULARLY ⟨other powers, ~ Britain and the United States —C. A. Fisher⟩

no·tar·i·al \nō-'ter-ē-əl\ *adj* (15c) **1** : of, relating to, or characteristic of a notary public **2** : done or executed by a notary public — **no·tar·i·al·ly** \-ə-lē\ *adv*

no·ta·ri·za·tion \ͺnō-tə-rə-'zā-shən\ *n* (1940) **1** : the act, process, or an instance of notarizing **2** : the notarial certificate appended to a document

no·ta·rize \'nō-tə-ͺrīz\ *vt* **-rized; -riz·ing** (1926) : to acknowledge or attest as a notary public

no·ta·ry public \'nō-tə-rē-\ *n, pl* **notaries public** *or* **notary publics** [ME *notary* clerk, notary public, fr. L *notarius* clerk, secretary, fr. *notarius* of shorthand, fr. *nota* note, shorthand character] (15c) : a public officer who attests or certifies writings (as a deed) to make them authentic and takes affidavits, depositions, and protests of negotiable paper — called also *notary*

no·tate \'nō-ͺtāt\ *vt* **no·tat·ed; no·tat·ing** [back-formation fr. *notation*] (1903) : to put into notation

no·ta·tion \nō-'tā-shən\ *n* [L *notation-, notatio*, fr. *notare* to note] (1584) **1** : ANNOTATION, NOTE **2 a** : the act, process, method, or an instance of representing by a system or set of marks, signs, figures, or characters **b** : a system of characters, symbols, or abbreviated expressions used in an art or science or in mathematics or logic to express technical facts or quantities — **no·ta·tion·al** \-shnəl, -shə-n²l\ *adj*

¹**notch** \'näch\ *n* [perh. alter. (fr. misdivision of *an otch*) of (assumed) *otch*, fr. MF *oche*] (1577) **1 a** : a V-shaped indentation **b** : a slit made to serve as a record **c** : a rounded indentation cut into the pages of a book on the edge opposite the spine **2** : a deep close pass : GAP **3** : DEGREE, STEP — **notched** \'nächt\ *adj*

²**notch** *vt* (1600) **1** : to cut or make a notch in **2 a** : to mark or record by a notch **b** : SCORE, ACHIEVE — sometimes used with *up*

notch·back \'näch-ͺbak\ *n* (1965) : an automobile with a trunk whose lid forms a distinct deck; *also* : the back of such an automobile

¹**note** \'nōt\ *vt* **not·ed; not·ing** [ME, fr. OF *noter*, fr. L *notare* to mark, note, fr. *nota*] (13c) **1 a** : to notice or observe with care **b** : to record or preserve in writing **2** : to make special mention of : REMARK **b** : INDICATE, SHOW — **not·er** *n*

²**note** *n* [ME, fr. OF, fr. L *nota* mark, character, written note] (13c) **1 a** (1) *obs* : MELODY, SONG (2) : TONE 2a (3) : CALL, SOUND; *esp* : the musical call of a bird **b** : a written symbol used to indicate duration and pitch of a tone by its shape and position on the staff **2 a** : a characteristic feature (as of odor or flavor) **b** : something (as an emotion or disposition) like a note in tone or resonance ⟨a ~ of sadness⟩ ⟨end on a high ~⟩ **3 a** (1) : MEMORANDUM (2) : a condensed or informal record **b** (1) : a brief comment or explanation (2) : a printed comment or reference set apart from the text **c** (1) : a written promise to pay a debt (2) : a piece of paper money **d** (1) : a short informal letter (2) : a formal diplomatic communication **e** : a scholarly or technical essay shorter than an article and restricted in scope **f** : a sheet of notepaper **4** : DISTINCTION, REPUTATION ⟨a figure of international ~⟩ **b** : OBSERVATION, NOTICE ⟨took full ~ of the proceedings⟩ **c** : KNOWLEDGE, INFORMATION *syn* see SIGN

	whole
	half
	quarter
	eighth
	sixteenth
	thirty-second
	sixty-fourth

²note 1b

note·book \'nōt-ͺbu̇k\ *n* (1579) **1** : a book for notes or memoranda **2** : a small portable microcomputer about the size of an ordinary loose-leaf binder

note·case \-ͺkās\ *n* (1838) *Brit* : WALLET 2a

not·ed \'nō-təd\ *adj* (14c) : well-known by reputation : EMINENT, CELEBRATED — *syn* see FAMOUS — **not·ed·ly** *adv* — **not·ed·ness** *n*

note·less \'nōt-ləs\ *adj* (ca. 1616) : not noticed : UNDISTINGUISHED

note of hand (ca. 1738) : PROMISSORY NOTE

note·pad \'nōt-ͺpad\ *n* (1922) : PAD 4

note·pa·per \-ͺpā-pər\ *n* (1849) : writing paper suitable for notes

note·wor·thy \-ͺwər-thē\ *adj* (1552) : worthy of or attracting attention esp. because of some special excellence — **note·wor·thi·ly** \-thə-lē\ *adv* — **note·wor·thi·ness** \-thē-nəs\ *n*

not-for-profit *adj* (ca. 1973) : NONPROFIT

noth·er *or* **'noth·er** \'nə-thər\ *adj* [alter. (fr. misdivision of *another*) of *other*, adj.] (1956) : OTHER — used esp. in the phrase *a whole nother*, used chiefly in speech or informal prose

¹**noth·ing** \'nə-thiŋ\ *pron* [ME, fr. OE *nān* thing, *nāthing*, fr. *nān* no + *thing* thing — more at NONE] (bef. 12c) **1** : not any thing : no thing ⟨leaves ~ to the imagination⟩ **2** : no part **3** : one of no interest, value, or consequence ⟨they mean ~ to me⟩ — **nothing doing** : by no means : definitely no — **nothing for it** : no alternative ⟨*nothing for it* but to start over⟩

²**nothing** *adv* (12c) : not at all : in no degree — **nothing like** : not nearly ⟨it's *nothing like* thorough enough⟩

³nothing n (1535)   **1 a :** something that does not exist   **b :** the absence of all magnitude or quantity; *also* **:** ZERO 1a   **c :** NOTHINGNESS 3b   **2 :** someone or something of no or slight value or size
⁴nothing adj (1611) **:** of no account **:** WORTHLESS
noth·ing·ness \-nəs\ n (ca. 1631)   **1 :** the quality or state of being nothing: as   **a :** NONEXISTENCE   **b :** utter insignificance   **c :** DEATH   **2 :** something insignificant or valueless   **3 a :** VOID, EMPTINESS   **b :** a metaphysical entity opposed to and devoid of being and regarded by some existentialists as the ground of anxiety
¹no·tice \'nō-təs\ n [ME, fr. MF, acquaintance, fr. L *notitia* knowledge, acquaintance, fr. *notus* known, fr. pp. of *noscere* to come to know — more at KNOW] (15c)   **1 a** (1) **:** warning or intimation of something **:** ANNOUNCEMENT   (2) **:** notification by one of the parties to an agreement or relation of intention of terminating it at a specified time   (3) **:** the condition of being warned or notified — usu. used in the phrase *on notice*   **b :** INFORMATION, INTELLIGENCE   **2 a :** ATTENTION, HEED   **b :** polite or favorable attention **:** CIVILITY   **3 :** a written or printed announcement   **4 :** a short critical account or examination
²notice vt **no·ticed; no·tic·ing** (15c)   **1 :** to give notice of   **2 a :** to comment upon   **b :** REVIEW   **3 a :** to treat with attention or civility   **b :** to take notice of **:** MARK   **4 :** to give a formal notice to — **no·tic·er** n
no·tice·able \'nō-tə-sə-bəl\ adj (1796)   **1 :** worthy of notice   **2 :** capable of being noticed — **no·tice·ably** \-blē\ adv
syn NOTICEABLE, REMARKABLE, PROMINENT, OUTSTANDING, CONSPICUOUS, SALIENT, STRIKING mean attracting notice or attention. NOTICEABLE applies to something unlikely to escape observation ⟨a piano recital with no *noticeable* errors⟩. REMARKABLE applies to something so extraordinary or exceptional as to invite comment ⟨a film of *remarkable* intelligence and wit⟩. PROMINENT applies to something commanding notice by standing out from its surroundings or background ⟨a doctor who occupies a *prominent* position in the town⟩. OUTSTANDING applies to something that rises above and excels others of the same kind ⟨honored for her *outstanding* contributions to science⟩. CONSPICUOUS applies to something that is obvious and unavoidable to the sight or mind ⟨*conspicuous* bureaucratic waste⟩. SALIENT applies to something of significance that merits the attention given it ⟨the *salient* points of the speech⟩. STRIKING applies to something that impresses itself powerfully and deeply upon the observer's mind or vision ⟨the region's *striking* poverty⟩.
notice board n (1854) *chiefly Brit* **:** a board bearing a notice or on which notices may be posted; *esp* **:** BULLETIN BOARD
no·ti·fi·able \'nō-tə-,fī-ə-bəl, ,nō-tə-'-\ adj (1889) **:** required by law to be reported to official health authorities ⟨a ~ disease⟩
no·ti·fi·ca·tion \,nō-tə-fə-'kā-shən\ n (14c)   **1 :** the act or an instance of notifying   **2 :** a written or printed matter that gives notice
no·ti·fy \'nō-tə-,fī\ vt **-fied; -fy·ing** [ME *notifien*, fr. MF *notifier* to make known, fr. LL *notificare*, fr. L *notus* known] (14c)   **1** obs **:** to point out   **2 :** to give notice of or report the occurrence of ⟨he *notified* his intention to sue⟩   **3 :** to give formal notice to ⟨~ a family of the death of a relation⟩   **syn** see INFORM — **no·ti·fi·er** \-,fī(-ə)r\ n
no·till \'nō-'til\ n (1968) **:** NO-TILLAGE
no·till·age \-'ti-lij\ n (1968) **:** a system of farming that consists of planting a narrow slit trench without tillage and with the use of herbicides to suppress weeds
no·tion \'nō-shən\ n [L *notion-, notio*, fr. *noscere*] (1537)   **1 a** (1) **:** an individual's conception or impression of something known, experienced, or imagined   (2) **:** an inclusive general concept   (3) **:** a theory or belief held by a person or group   **b :** a personal inclination **:** WHIM   **2** obs **:** MIND, INTELLECT   **3** pl **:** small useful items **:** SUNDRIES   **syn** see IDEA
no·tion·al \'nō-shnəl, -shə-nᵊl\ adj (1597)   **1 :** THEORETICAL, SPECULATIVE   **2 :** existing in the mind only **:** IMAGINARY   **3 :** given to foolish or fanciful moods or ideas   **4 :** of, relating to, or being a notion or idea **:** CONCEPTUAL   **b** (1) **:** presenting an idea of a thing, action, or quality ⟨*has* is ~ in *he has luck*, relational in *he has gone*⟩   (2) **:** of or representing what exists or occurs in the world of things as distinguished from syntactic categories — **no·tion·al·i·ty** \,nō-shə-'na-lə-tē\ n — **no·tion·al·ly** \'nō-shnə-lē, -shə-nᵊl-ē\ adv
no·to·chord \'nō-tə-,kȯrd\ n [Gk *nōton, nōtos* back + L *chorda* cord — more at CORD] (1848) **:** a longitudinal flexible rod of cells that in the lowest chordates (as a lancelet or a lamprey) and in the embryos of the higher vertebrates forms the supporting axis of the body — **no·to·chord·al** \,nō-tə-'kȯr-dᵊl\ adj
no·to·ri·e·ty \,nō-tə-'rī-ə-tē\ n, pl **-ties** [MF or ML; MF *notorieté*, ML *notorietat-, notorietas*, fr. *notorius*] (ca. 1650)   **1 :** the quality or state of being notorious   **2 :** a notorious person
no·to·ri·ous \nō-'tȯr-ē-əs, nə-, -'tȯr-\ adj [ML *notorius*, fr. LL *notorium* information, indictment, fr. L *noscere* to come to know — more at KNOW] (1534) **:** generally known and talked of; *esp* **:** widely and unfavorably known   **syn** see FAMOUS
no·to·ri·ous·ly \-lē\ adv (1512)   **1 :** in a notorious manner   **2 :** it is notorious **:** as is very well known
no–trump n (1899) **:** being a bid, contract, or hand suitable to play without any suit being trumps — **no–trump** n
no·tum \'nō-təm\ n, pl **no·ta** \'nō-tə\ [NL, fr. Gk *nōton* back] (1877) **:** the dorsal surface of a thoracic segment of an insect
¹not·with·stand·ing \,nät-with-'stan-diŋ, -with-\ prep [ME *notwithstonding*, fr. *not* + withstonding, prp. of *withstonden* to withstand] (14c) **:** DESPITE ⟨~ their lack of experience, they were an immediate success⟩ — often used after its object ⟨the motion passed, our objection ~⟩
²notwithstanding adv (15c) **:** NEVERTHELESS, HOWEVER
³notwithstanding conj (15c) **:** ALTHOUGH
nou·gat \'nü-gət, *esp Brit* -,gä\ n [F, fr. Prov. fr. OProv *nogat*, fr. *noga* nut, fr. (assumed) VL *nuca*, fr. L *nuc-, nux* — more at NUT] (1827) **:** a confection of nuts or fruit pieces in a sugar paste
nought \'nȯt, 'nät\ *var of* NAUGHT
nou·me·non \'nü-mə-,nän\ n, pl **-na** \-nə, -,nä\ [G, fr. Gk *nooumenon* that which is apprehended by thought, fr. neut. of pres. pass. part. of *noein* to think, conceive, fr. *nous* mind] (1796) **:** a posited object or event as it appears in itself independent of perception by the senses — **nou·men·al** \-mə-nᵊl\ adj
noun \'naun\ n [ME *nowne*, fr. AF *noun* name, noun, fr. OF *nom*, fr. L *nomen* — more at NAME] (14c) **:** any member of a class of words that typically can be combined with determiners to serve as the subject of a

verb, can be interpreted as singular or plural, can be replaced with a pronoun, and refer to an entity, quality, state, action, or concept
noun phrase n, *often cap* N&P (1923) **:** a phrase formed by a noun and all its modifiers and determiners; *broadly* **:** any syntactic element (as a clause, clitic, pronoun, or zero element) with a noun's function (as the subject of a verb or the object of a verb or preposition) — abbr. *NP*
nour·ish \'nər-ish, 'nə-rish\ vt [ME *nurishen*, fr. OF *nuriss-*, stem of *norrir*, fr. L *nutrire* to suckle, nourish; akin to Gk *nan* to flow, *noteros* damp, Skt *snauti* it drips] (14c)   **1 :** NURTURE, REAR   **2 :** to promote the growth of ⟨no occasions to exercise the feelings nor ~ passion —L. O. Coxe⟩   **3 a :** to furnish or sustain with nutriment **:** FEED   **b :** MAINTAIN, SUPPORT ⟨their profits . . . ~ other criminal activities —Beverly Smith⟩ — **nour·ish·er** n
nour·ish·ing adj (14c) **:** giving nourishment **:** NUTRITIOUS
nour·ish·ment \'nər-ish-mənt, 'nə-rish-\ n (15c)   **1 a :** FOOD, NUTRIMENT   **b :** SUSTENANCE 3 ⟨books for intellectual ~⟩   **2 :** the act of nourishing **:** the state of being nourished
nous n [Gk *noos, nous* mind] (1678)   **1** \'nüs *also* 'naùs\ **:** MIND, REASON: as   **a :** an intelligent purposive principle of the world   **b :** the divine reason regarded in Neoplatonism as the first emanation of God   **2** \'naùs\ *chiefly Brit* **:** COMMON SENSE, ALERTNESS
nou·veau \nü-'vō\ adj [F, fr. MF *novel*] (1828) **:** newly arrived or developed
nou·veau riche \,nü-,vō-'rēsh\ n, pl **nou·veaux riches** \same\ [F, lit., new rich] (1813) **:** a person newly rich **:** PARVENU
nou·velle \nü-'vel\ adj [*nouvelle* cuisine] (1976) **:** of or relating to nouvelle cuisine ⟨a ~ restaurant⟩
nouvelle cuisine n [F, lit., new cuisine] (1975) **:** a form of French cuisine that uses little flour or fat and stresses light sauces and the use of fresh seasonal produce; *also* **:** any national cuisine that stresses lightness and freshness in preparation ⟨American *nouvelle cuisine*⟩
nouvelle vague \-'väg, -'väg\ n [F] (1959) **:** NEW WAVE 1, 2
no·va \'nō-və\ n, pl **novas** or **no·vae** \-(,)vē, -,vī\ [NL, fem. of L *novus* new] (1927) **:** a star that suddenly increases its light output tremendously and then fades away to its former obscurity in a few months or years — **no·va·like** \-və-,līk\ adj
no·vac·u·lite \nō-'va-kyə-,līt\ n [L *novacula* razor] (1796) **:** a very hard fine-grained siliceous rock used for whetstones and possibly of sedimentary origin
no·va·tion \nō-'vā-shən\ n [LL *novation-, novatio* renewal, legal novation, fr. L *novare* to make new, fr. *novus*] (1682) **:** the substitution of a new legal obligation for an old one
¹nov·el \'nä-vəl\ adj [ME, fr. MF, new, fr. L *novellus*, fr. dim. of *novus* new — more at NEW] (15c)   **1 :** new and not resembling something formerly known or used   **2 :** original or striking esp. in conception or style ⟨a ~ scheme to collect money⟩   **syn** see NEW
²novel n [It *novella*] (1639)   **1 :** an invented prose narrative that is usu. long and complex and deals esp. with human experience through a usu. connected sequence of events   **2 :** the literary genre consisting of novels — **nov·el·is·tic** \,nä-və-'lis-tik\ adj — **nov·el·is·ti·cal·ly** \-ti-k(ə-)lē\ adv
nov·el·ette \,nä-və-'let\ n (1814) **:** NOVELLA 2
nov·el·ett·ish \-'le-tish\ adj (1904) **:** of, relating to, or characteristic of a novelette; *esp* **:** SENTIMENTAL
nov·el·ist \'näv-list, 'nä-və-\ n (1728) **:** a writer of novels
nov·el·ize \'nä-və-,līz\ vt **-ized; -iz·ing** (1828) **:** to convert into the form of a novel ⟨~ a play⟩ — **nov·el·iza·tion** \,nä-və-lə-'zā-shən\ n
no·vel·la \nō-'ve-lə\ n, pl **novellas** or **no·vel·le** \-'ve-lē\ [It, fr. fem. of *novello* new, fr. L *novellus*] (1898)   **1** pl **novelle :** a story with a compact and pointed plot   **2** pl usu **novellas :** a work of fiction intermediate in length and complexity between a short story and a novel
nov·el·ty \'nä-vəl-tē\ n, pl **-ties** [ME *novelte*, fr. MF *noveleté*, fr. *novel*] (14c)   **1 :** something new or unusual   **2 :** the quality or state of being novel **:** NEWNESS   **3 :** a small manufactured article intended mainly for personal or household adornment — usu. used in pl.
¹No·vem·ber \nō-'vem-bər, nə-\ n [ME *Novembre*, fr. OF, fr. L *November*, ninth month of the early Roman calendar, fr. *novem* nine — more at NINE] (13c) **:** the 11th month of the Gregorian calendar
²November (1956) — a communications code word for the letter *n*
no·vem·de·cil·lion \,nō-,vem-di-'sil-yən\ n, *often attrib* [L *novemdecim* nineteen (fr. *novem* + *decem* ten) + E *-illion* (as in *million*) — more at TEN] (ca. 1934) — see NUMBER table
no·ve·na \nō-'vē-nə\ n [ML, fr. L, fem. of *novenus* nine each, fr. *novem*] (1853) **:** a Roman Catholic period of prayer lasting nine consecutive days
nov·ice \'nä-vəs\ n [ME, fr. MF, fr. ML *novicius*, fr. L, newly imported, fr. *novus* — more at NEW] (14c)   **1 :** a person admitted to probationary membership in a religious community   **2 :** BEGINNER, TYRO
no·vi·tiate \nō-'vi-shət, nə-\ n [F *noviciat*, fr. ML *noviciatus*, fr. *novicius*] (1600)   **1 :** the period or state of being a novice   **2 :** a house where novices are trained   **3 :** NOVICE
no·vo·bi·o·cin \,nō-və-'bī-ə-sən\ n [*novo-* (perh. modif. of L *niveus* snowy, specific epithet of the bacterium *Streptomyces niveus*) + *bi-* + *-mycin*] (1956) **:** a weak dibasic acid $C_{31}H_{36}N_2O_{11}$ that is highly toxic to humans and is used as an antimicrobial drug in some serious cases of staphylococcic and urinary tract infection
No·vo·cain \'nō-və-,kān\ *trademark* — used for a preparation containing the hydrochloride of procaine
no·vo·caine \-,kān\ n [ISV *novo-* (fr. L *novus* new) + *cocaine*] (1910) **:** PROCAINE; *also* **:** its hydrochloride
¹now \'naù\ adv [ME, fr. OE *nū*; akin to OHG *nū* now, L *nunc*, Gk *nyn*] (bef. 12c)   **1 a :** at the present time or moment   **b :** in the time immediately before the present ⟨thought of them just ~⟩   **c :** in the time immediately to follow **:** FORTHWITH ⟨come in ~⟩   **2** — used with the sense of present time weakened or lost to express command, request, or admonition ⟨~ hear this⟩ ⟨~ you be sure to write⟩   **3** — used with the sense of present time weakened or lost to introduce an impor-

---

\ə\ abut   \ᵊ\ kitten, F table   \ər\ further   \a\ ash   \ā\ ace   \ä\ mop, mar   \aù\ out   \ch\ chin   \e\ bet   \ē\ easy   \g\ go   \i\ hit   \ī\ ice   \j\ job   \ŋ\ sing   \ō\ go   \ȯ\ law   \ȯi\ boy   \th\ thin   \t͟h\ the   \ü\ loot   \ù\ foot   \y\ yet   \zh\ vision   \à, k̟, ⁿ, œ, œ̄, ᵫ, ᵫ̄, ᵊ\ see Guide to Pronunciation tant point or indicate a transition (as of ideas) **4** : SOMETIMES ⟨~ one and — another⟩ **5** : under the present circumstances **6** : at the time referred to ⟨~ the trouble began⟩

²**now** *conj* (bef. 12c) : in view of the fact that : SINCE — often followed by *that* ⟨~ that we are here⟩

³**now** *n* (12c) : the present time or moment ⟨been ill up to ~⟩

⁴**now** *adj* (14c) **1** : of or relating to the present time : EXISTING ⟨the ~ president⟩ **2 a** : excitingly new ⟨~ clothes⟩ **b** : constantly aware of what is new ⟨the ~ people⟩ ⟨the ~ generation⟩

NOW account \ˈnau̇-\ *n* [negotiable order of withdrawal] (1974) : a savings account on which checks may be drawn

now·a·days \ˈnau̇-(ə-)ˌdāz\ *adv* [ME *now a dayes,* fr. ¹*now* + *a dayes* during the day] (14c) : at the present time

now and then *adv* (15c) : from time to time : OCCASIONALLY ⟨*now and then* we go off to the country⟩

no·way *adv* (13c) **1** \ˈnō-ˌwā\ or **no·ways** \-ˌwāz\ : NOWISE **2** *usu* **no way** \-ˈwā\ : NO — used emphatically

¹**no·where** \ˈnō-ˌhwer, -ˌhwar, or without h\ *adv* (bef. 12c) **1** : not in or at any place **2** : to no place

²**nowhere** *n* (1831) **1** : a nonexistent place **2** : an unknown, distant, or obscure place or state ⟨rose to fame out of ~⟩ — **miles from no·where** : in an extremely remote place

nowhere near *adv* (15c) : not nearly

no·wheres \ˈnō-ˌhwerz, -ˌhwarz, -ˌhwərz or without h\ *adv* (ca. 1866) *chiefly dial* : NOWHERE

no·whith·er \ˈnō-ˌhwi-thər, -ˌwi-thər; ˌnō-ˈ\ *adv* (bef. 12c) : to or toward no place

no-win \ˈnō-ˈwin, -ˌwin\ *adj* (1962) : not likely to give victory, success, or satisfaction : that cannot be won ⟨a ~ situation⟩ ⟨a ~ war⟩

no·wise \ˈnō-ˌwīz\ *adv* (14c) : not at all

now·ness \ˈnau̇-nəs\ *n* (1674) : the quality or state of existing or occurring in or belonging to the present time

nowt \ˈnau̇t *also* ˈnōt\ *dial Eng var of* NOUGHT

nox·ious \ˈnäk-shəs\ *adj* [ME *noxius,* fr. L, fr. *noxa* harm; akin to L *nocēre* to harm, *nec-, nex* violent death, Gk *nekros* dead body] (15c) **1 a** : physically harmful or destructive to living beings ⟨~ wastes that poison our streams⟩ **b** : constituting a harmful influence on mind or behavior : morally corrupting ⟨~ doctrines⟩ **2** : DISTASTEFUL, OBNOXIOUS *syn* see PERNICIOUS — **nox·ious·ly** *adv* — **nox·ious·ness** *n*

noz·zle \ˈnä-zəl\ *n* [dim. of *nose*] (1683) **1 a** : a projecting vent of something **b** : a short tube with a taper or constriction used (as on a hose) to speed up or direct a flow of fluid **c** : a part in a rocket engine that accelerates the exhaust gases from the combustion chamber to a high velocity **2** *slang* : NOSE

NSAID \ˈen-ˌsed *also* -ˌsäd\ *n* [*nonsteroidal anti-inflammatory drug*] (1985) : a nonsteroidal anti-inflammatory drug (as ibuprofen)

-n't *vb comb form* : not ⟨isn't⟩

nth \ˈen(t)th\ *adj* [*n* (indefinite number) + *-th*] (1852) **1** : numbered with an unspecified or indefinitely large ordinal number ⟨for the ~ time⟩ **2** : EXTREME, UTMOST ⟨to the ~ degree⟩

n–type \ˈen-ˌtīp\ *adj* [*negative* + *type*] (1946) : relating to or being a semiconductor in which charge is carried by electrons — compare P-TYPE

nu \ˈnü, ˈnyü\ *n* [Gk *ny,* of Sem origin; akin to Heb *nūn* nun] (ca. 1823) : the 13th letter of the Greek alphabet — see ALPHABET table

nu·ance \ˈnü-ˌän(t)s, ˈnyü-, -ˌäⁿs; nü-ˈ, nyü-ˈ\ *n* [F, fr. MF, shade of color, fr. *nuer* to make shades of color, fr. *nue* cloud, fr. L *nubes*; perh. akin to W *nudd* mist] (1781) **1** : a subtle distinction or variation **2** : a subtle quality : NICETY **3** : sensibility to, awareness of, or ability to express delicate shadings (as of meaning, feeling, or value) — **nu·anced** \-ˌän(t)st, -ˌäⁿ(t)st\ *adj*

nub \ˈnəb\ *n* [alter. of E dial. *knub,* prob. fr. LG *knubbe*] (1727) **1** : KNOB, LUMP **2** : NUBBIN **3** : GIST, POINT

nub·bin \ˈnə-bən\ *n* [perh. dim. of *nub*] (1692) **1** : something (as an ear of Indian corn) that is small for its kind, stunted, undeveloped, or imperfect **2** : a small usu. projecting part or bit **3** : NUB 3

nub·ble \ˈnə-bəl\ *n* [dim. of *nub*] (1818) : a small knob or lump — **nub·bly** \-b(ə-)lē\ *adj*

nub·by \ˈnə-bē\ *adj* **nub·bi·er; -est** [*nub* + ¹*-y*] (ca. 1876) **1** : having or being like nubbles **2** : having nubs ⟨a ~ knit fabric⟩

Nu·bi·an \ˈnü-bē-ən, ˈnyü-\ *n* (15c) **1 a** : a native or inhabitant of Nubia **b** : a member of one of the group of dark-skinned peoples that formed a powerful empire between Egypt and Ethiopia from the 6th to the 14th centuries **2** : any of several languages spoken in central and northern Sudan — **Nubian** *adj*

nu·bile \ˈnü-ˌbīl, ˈnyü-, -bəl\ *adj* [F, fr. L *nubilis,* fr. *nubere* to marry — more at NUPTIAL] (ca. 1642) **1** : of marriageable condition or age **2** : sexually attractive — used of a young woman — **nu·bil·i·ty** \nü-ˈbi-lə-tē, nyü-\ *n*

nu·cel·lus \nü-ˈse-ləs, nyü-\ *n, pl* **nu·cel·li** \-ˈse-ˌlī\ [NL, fr. L *nucella* small nut, fr. *nuc-, nux* nut — more at NUT] (1882) : the central and chief part of a plant ovule that encloses the female gametophyte — **nu·cel·lar** \-ˈse-lər\ *adj*

nu·chal \ˈnü-kəl, ˈnyü-\ *adj* [ML *nucha* nape, fr. Ar *nukhāˈ* spinal marrow] (1835) : of, relating to, or lying in the region of the nape

nucle- or nucleo- *comb form* [F *nuclé-, nucléo-,* fr. NL *nucleus*] **1** : nucleus ⟨*nucleoplasm*⟩ **2** : nucleic acid ⟨*nucleoprotein*⟩

nu·cle·ar \ˈnü-klē-ər, ˈnyü-, ÷-kyə-lər\ *adj* (1846) **1** : of, relating to, or constituting a nucleus **2 a** : of or relating to the atomic nucleus ⟨~ reaction⟩ ⟨~ physics⟩ **b** : used in or produced by a nuclear reaction (as fission) ⟨~ fuel⟩ ⟨~ waste⟩ ⟨~ energy⟩ **c** (1) : being a weapon whose destructive power derives from an uncontrolled nuclear reaction (2) : of, produced by, or involving nuclear weapons ⟨the ~ age⟩ ⟨~ war⟩ (3) : armed with nuclear weapons ⟨~ powers⟩ **d** : of, relating to, or powered by nuclear energy ⟨a ~ submarine⟩ ⟨the ~ debate⟩ ⟨a ~ plant⟩

usage Though disapproved of by many, pronunciations ending in \-kyə-lər\ have been found in widespread use among educated speakers including scientists, lawyers, professors, congressmen, U.S. cabinet members, and at least one U.S. president and one vice president. While most common in the U.S., these pronunciations have also been heard from British and Canadian speakers.

nuclear family *n* (1947) : a family group that consists only of father, mother, and children

nuclear magnetic resonance *n* (1942) : the magnetic resonance of an atomic nucleus

nuclear medicine *n* (1952) : a branch of medicine dealing with the use of radioactive materials in the diagnosis and treatment of disease

nuclear membrane *n* (1888) : a double membrane enclosing a cell nucleus and having its outer part continuous with the endoplasmic reticulum — see CELL illustration

nuclear–powered *adj* (1948) : powered by nuclear energy

nuclear resonance *n* (1940) : the resonance absorption of a gamma ray by a nucleus identical to the nucleus that emitted the gamma ray

nuclear sap *n* (1877) : the clear homogeneous ground substance of a cell nucleus — called also *karyolymph*

nuclear winter *n* (1983) : the chilling of climate that is hypothesized to be a consequence of nuclear war and to result from the prolonged blockage of sunlight by high-altitude dust clouds produced by nuclear explosions

nu·cle·ase \ˈnü-klē-ˌās, ˈnyü-, -ˌāz\ *n* (1902) : any of various enzymes that promote hydrolysis of nucleic acids

nu·cle·ate \ˈnü-klē-ˌāt, ˈnyü-\ *vb* **-at·ed; -at·ing** [LL *nucleatus,* pp. of *nucleare* to become stony, fr. L *nucleus*] *vt* (ca. 1864) **1** : to form into a nucleus : CLUSTER **2** : to act as a nucleus for **3** : to supply nuclei to ~ *vi* **1** : to form a nucleus **2** : to act as a nucleus **3** : to begin to form — **nu·cle·ation** \ˌnü-klē-ˈā-shən, ˌnyü-\ *n* — **nu·cle·a·tor** \ˈnü-klē-ˌā-tər, ˈnyü-\ *n*

nu·cle·at·ed \ˈnü-klē-ˌā-təd, ˈnyü-\ *or* **nu·cle·ate** \-klē-ət\ *adj* [L *nucleatus,* fr. *nucleus* kernel] (1845) **1** : having a nucleus or nuclei ⟨~ cells⟩ **2** *usu* **nucleate** : originating or occurring at nuclei ⟨*nucleate* boiling⟩

nu·cle·ic acid \nü-ˈklē-ik-, -ˈklā-, nyü-\ *n* [fr. their occurrence in cell nuclei] (1892) : any of various acids (as DNA or RNA) that are composed of nucleotide chains

nu·cle·in \ˈnü-klē-ən, ˈnyü-\ *n* (1878) **1** : NUCLEOPROTEIN **2** : NUCLEIC ACID

nu·cle·o·cap·sid \ˌnü-klē-ō-ˈkap-səd, ˌnyü-\ *n* (1963) : the nucleic acid and surrounding protein coat in a virus

nu·cle·oid \ˈnü-klē-ˌoid, ˈnyü-\ *n* (1938) : the DNA-containing area of a prokaryotic cell (as a bacterium)

nu·cle·o·lus \nü-ˈklē-ə-ləs, nyü-\ *n, pl* **-li** \-ˌlī\ [NL, fr. L, dim. of *nucleus*] (1845) : a spherical body of the nucleus of most eukaryotes that becomes enlarged during protein synthesis, is associated with a nucleolus organizer, and contains the DNA templates for ribosomal RNA — see CELL illustration — **nu·cle·o·lar** \-lər\ *adj*

nucleolus organizer *n* (1939) : the specific part of a chromosome with which a nucleolus is associated esp. during its reorganization after nuclear division — called also *nucleolar organizer*

nu·cle·on \ˈnü-klē-ˌän, ˈnyü-\ *n* [ISV] (1923) **1** : a nuclear particle: **a** : PROTON **b** : NEUTRON **2** : a hypothetical single entity with one-half unit of isospin that can manifest itself as either a proton or a neutron — **nu·cle·on·ic** \ˌnü-klē-ˈä-nik, ˌnyü-\ *adj*

nu·cle·on·ics \ˌnü-klē-ˈä-niks, ˌnyü-\ *n pl but sing or pl in constr* (1937) : a branch of physical science that deals with nucleons or with all phenomena of the atomic nucleus

nu·cle·o·phile \ˈnü-klē-ə-ˌfīl, ˈnyü-\ *n* (1943) : a nucleophilic substance (as an electron-donating reagent)

nu·cle·o·phil·ic \ˌnü-klē-ə-ˈfi-lik, ˌnyü-\ *adj* (1933) **1** *of an atom, ion, or molecule* : having an affinity for atomic nuclei : being an electron donor **2** : involving a nucleophilic species ⟨a ~ reaction⟩ — compare ELECTROPHILIC — **nu·cle·o·phil·i·cal·ly** \-i-k(ə-)lē\ *adv* — **nu·cle·o·phi·lic·i·ty** \-klē-ō-fi-ˈli-sə-tē\ *n*

nu·cle·o·plasm \ˈnü-klē-ə-ˌpla-zəm, ˈnyü-\ *n* [ISV] (1888) : the protoplasm of a nucleus; *esp* : NUCLEAR SAP — **nu·cle·o·plas·mic** \ˌnü-klē-ə-ˈplaz-mik\ *adj*

nu·cle·o·pro·tein \ˌnü-klē-ō-ˈprō-ˌtēn, ˌnyü-, -ˈprō-tē-ən\ *n* [ISV] (1907) : a compound that consists of a protein (as a histone) conjugated with a nucleic acid (as a DNA) and that is the principal constituent of the hereditary material in chromosomes

nu·cle·o·side \ˈnü-klē-ə-ˌsid, ˈnyü-\ *n* [ISV *nucle-* + ²*-ose* + *-ide*] (1911) : a compound (as guanosine or adenosine) that consists of a purine or pyrimidine base combined with deoxyribose or ribose and is found esp. in DNA or RNA

nu·cle·o·some \-ˌsōm\ *n* (1962) : any of the repeating globular subunits of chromatin that consist of a complex of DNA and histone — **nu·cle·o·so·mal** \ˌnü-klē-ə-ˈsō-məl, ˌnyü-\ *adj*

nu·cle·o·syn·the·sis \ˌnü-klē-ō-ˈsin(t)-thə-səs, ˌnyü-\ *n* [NL] (1960) : the production of a chemical element from simpler nuclei (as of hydrogen) esp. in a star — **nu·cle·o·syn·thet·ic** \-sin-ˈthe-tik\ *adj*

nu·cle·o·tid·ase \ˌnü-klē-ə-ˈtī-ˌdās, ˌnyü-, -ˌdāz\ *n* (1911) : a phosphatase that promotes hydrolysis of a nucleotide (as into a nucleoside and phosphoric acid)

nu·cle·o·tide \ˈnü-klē-ə-ˌtīd, ˈnyü-\ *n* [ISV, irreg. fr. *nucle-* + *-ide*] (1908) : any of several compounds that consist of a ribose or deoxyribose sugar joined to a purine or pyrimidine base and to a phosphate group and that are the basic structural units of nucleic acids (as RNA and DNA) — compare NUCLEOSIDE

nu·cle·us \ˈnü-klē-əs, ˈnyü-\ *n, pl* **nu·clei** \-klē-ˌī\ *also* **nu·cle·us·es** [NL, fr. L, kernel, dim. of *nuc-, nux* nut — more at NUT] (1704) **1** : the small brighter and denser portion of a galaxy or of the head of a comet **2** : a central point, group, or mass about which gathering, concentration, or accretion takes place: as **a** : a cellular organelle of eukaryotes that is essential to cell functions (as reproduction and protein synthesis), is composed of nuclear sap and a nucleoprotein-rich network from which chromosomes and nucleoli arise, and is enclosed in a definite membrane — see CELL illustration **b** : a mass of gray matter or group of nerve cells in the central nervous system **c** : a characteristic and stable complex of atoms or groups in a molecule; *esp* : RING ⟨the naphthalene ~⟩ **d** : the positively charged central portion of an atom that comprises nearly all of the atomic mass and that consists of protons and neutrons except in hydrogen which consists of one proton only **3** : the peak of sonority in the utterance of a syllable

nu·clide \ˈnü-ˌklīd, ˈnyü-\ *n* [*nucleus* + Gk *eidos* form, species — more at IDOL] (1947) : a species of atom characterized by the constitution of its nucleus and hence by the number of protons, the number of neutrons, and the energy content — **nu·clid·ic** \nü-ˈkli-dik, nyü-\ *adj*

¹**nude** \ˈnüd, ˈnyüd\ *adj* **nud·er; nud·est** [L *nudus* naked — more at

NAKED](1531) **1** : lacking something essential esp. to legal validity 〈a ~ contract〉 **2 a** : devoid of a natural or conventional covering; *esp* : not covered by clothing or a drape **b** (1) : of the color of a white person's flesh (2) : giving the appearance of nudity 〈a ~ dress〉 **c** : featuring nudes 〈a ~ movie〉 **d** : frequented by naked people 〈a ~ beach〉 **syn** see BARE — **nude** *adv* — **nude·ly** *adv* — **nude·ness** *n* — **nu·di·ty** \'nü-də-tē, 'nyü-\ *n*

²**nude** *n* (1708) **1 a** : a representation of a nude human figure **b** : a nude person **2** : the condition of being nude 〈in the ~〉

nudge \'nəj\ *vb* **nudged; nudg·ing** [origin unknown] *vt* (1675) **1** : to touch or push gently; *esp* : to seek the attention of by a push of the elbow **2** : to prod lightly : urge into action **3** : APPROACH 〈its circulation is *nudging* the four million mark —Bennett Cerf〉 ~ *vi* : to give a nudge — **nudge** *n* — **nudg·er** *n*

nu·di·branch \'nü-də-,braŋk, 'nyü-\ *n, pl* **-branchs** [NL *Nudibranchia*, fr. L *nudus* + Gk *branchia* gills] (1847) : any of an order (Nudibranchia) of marine gastropod mollusks without a shell in the adult state and without true gills — **nudibranch** *adj*

nud·ism \'nü-,di-zəm, 'nyü-\ *n* (1929) : the practice of going nude esp. in sexually mixed groups and during periods of time spent at specially secluded places — **nud·ist** \'nü-dist, 'nyü-\ *adj or n*

nud·nick *or* **nud·nik** \'nüd-nik\ *n* [Yiddish *nudnik*, fr. *nudyen* to bore, fr. Pol *nudzić*, fr. *nuda* boredom] (1947) : a person who is a bore or nuisance

nu·ga·to·ry \'nü-gə-,tōr-ē, 'nyü-, -,tòr-\ *adj* [L *nugatorius*, fr. *nugari* to trifle, fr. *nugae* trifles] (1603) **1** : of little or no consequence : TRIFLING, INCONSEQUENTIAL **2** : having no force : INOPERATIVE **syn** see VAIN

nug·get \'nə-gət\ *n* [origin unknown] (1852) **1** : a solid lump; *esp* : a native lump of precious metal **2** : TIDBIT 2 〈~s of wisdom〉 **3** : a small usu. rounded piece of food 〈chicken ~s〉

nui·sance \'nü-s^ən(t)s, 'nyü-\ *n* [ME *nusaunce*, fr. AF, fr. OF *nuire* to harm, fr. L *nocēre* — more at NOXIOUS] (15c) **1** : HARM, INJURY **2** : one that is annoying, unpleasant, or obnoxious : PEST

nuisance tax *n* (1924) : an excise tax collected in small amounts on a wide range of commodities directly from the consumer

¹**nuke** \'nük, 'nyük\ *n* [by shortening & alter. fr. *nuclear*] (1959) **1** : a nuclear weapon **2** : a nuclear-powered electric generating station

²**nuke** *vt* **nuked; nuk·ing** (1967) **1** : to attack or destroy with or as if with nuclear bombs **2** : MICROWAVE

¹**null** \'nəl\ *adj* [MF *nul*, lit., not any, fr. L *nullus*, fr. *ne-* not + *ullus* any; akin to L *unus* one — more at NO, ONE] (ca. 1567) **1** : having no legal or binding force : INVALID **2** : amounting to nothing : NIL **3** : having no value : INSIGNIFICANT **4 a** : having no elements 〈~ set〉 **b** : having zero as a limit 〈~ sequence〉 **c** *of a matrix* : having all elements equal to zero **5 a** : indicating usu. by a zero reading on a scale when a given quantity (as current or voltage) is zero or when two quantities are equal — used of an instrument **b** : being or relating to a method of measurement in which an unknown quantity (as of electric current) is compared with a known quantity of the same kind and found equal by a null detector **6** : of, being, or relating to zero **7** : ZERO 1c

²**null** *n* (1605) **1** : ZERO 3a(1) **2 a** : a condition of a radio receiver when minimum or zero signal is received **b** : minimum or zero value of an electric current or of a radio signal

³**null** *vt* (1643) : to make null

nul·lah \'nə-lə\ *n* [Hindi *nālā*] (1776) : GULLY, RAVINE

null and void *adj* (1669) : having no force, binding power, or validity

null hypothesis *n* (1935) : a statistical hypothesis to be tested and accepted or rejected in favor of an alternative; *specif* : the hypothesis that an observed difference (as between the means of two samples) is due to chance alone and not due to a real cause

nul·li·fi·ca·tion \,nə-lə-fə-'kā-shən\ *n* (1798) **1** : the act of nullifying : the state of being nullified **2** : the action of a state impeding or attempting to prevent the operation and enforcement within its territory of a law of the U.S. — **nul·li·fi·ca·tion·ist** \-sh(ə-)nist\ *n*

nul·li·fi·er \'nə-lə-,fī(-ə)r\ *n* (1832) : one that nullifies; *specif* : one maintaining the right of nullification against the U.S. government

nul·li·fy \'nə-lə-,fī\ *vt* **-fied; -fy·ing** [LL *nullificare*, fr. L *nullus*] (1535) **1** : to make null; *esp* : to make legally null and void **2** : to make of no value or consequence

syn NULLIFY, NEGATE, ANNUL, ABROGATE, INVALIDATE mean to deprive of effective or continued existence. NULLIFY implies counteracting completely the force, effectiveness, or value of something 〈a penalty *nullified* the touchdown〉. NEGATE implies the destruction or canceling out of each of two things by the other 〈the arguments *negate* each other〉. ANNUL suggests making ineffective or nonexistent often by legal or official action 〈the treaty *annuls* all previous agreements〉. ABROGATE is like ANNUL but more definitely implies a legal or official purposeful act 〈a law to *abrogate* trading privileges〉. INVALIDATE implies making something powerless or unacceptable by declaration of its logical or moral or legal unsoundness 〈the court *invalidated* the statute〉.

nul·lip·a·rous \,nə-'li-pə-rəs\ *adj* [NL *nullipara* one who has never borne an offspring, fr. L *nullus* not any + *-para* -para] (1859) : of, relating to, or being a female that has not borne offspring

nul·li·ty \'nə-lə-tē\ *n, pl* **-ties** (1570) **1 a** : the quality or state of being null; *esp* : legal invalidity **b** (1) : NOTHINGNESS; *also* : INSIGNIFICANCE (2) : a mere nothing : NONENTITY **2** : one that is null; *specif* : an act void of legal effect **3** : the number of elements in a basis of a null-space

null–space \'nəl-,spās\ *n* (1884) : a subspace of a vector space consisting of vectors that under a given linear transformation are mapped onto zero

numb \'nəm\ *adj* [ME *nomen*, fr. pp. of *nimen* to take — more at NIM] (14c) **1** : devoid of sensation esp. as a result of cold or anesthesia **2** : devoid of emotion : INDIFFERENT — **numb** *vt* — **numb·ing·ly** \'nə-miŋ-lē\ *adv* — **numb·ly** \'nəm-lē\ *adv* — **numb·ness** *n*

¹**num·ber** \'nəm-bər\ *n* [ME *nombre*, fr. OF, fr. L *numerus*] (14c) **1 a** (1) : a sum of units : TOTAL (2) : COMPLEMENT 1b (3) : an indefinite usu. large total 〈a ~ of members were absent〉 〈the ~ of elderly is rising〉 (4) *pl* : a numerous group : MANY (5) : a numerical preponderance **b** (1) : the characteristic of an individual by which it is treated as a unit or a collection by which it is treated in terms of units (2)

: an ascertainable total 〈bugs beyond ~〉 **c** (1) : a unit belonging to an abstract mathematical system and subject to specified laws of succession, addition, and multiplication; *esp* : NATURAL NUMBER (2) : an element (as π) of any of many mathematical systems obtained by extension of or analogy with the natural number system (3) *pl* : ARITHMETIC **2** : a distinction of word form to denote reference to one or more than one; *also* : a form or group of forms so distinguished **3** *pl* **a** (1) : metrical structure : METER (2) : metrical lines : VERSES **b** *archaic* : musical sounds : NOTES **4 a** : a word, symbol, letter, or combination of symbols representing a number **b** : a numeral or combination of numerals or other symbols used to identify or designate 〈dialed the wrong ~〉 **c** (1) : a member of a sequence or collection designated by esp. consecutive numbers (as an issue of a periodical) (2) : a position in a numbered sequence **d** : a group of one kind 〈not of their ~〉 **5** : one singled out from a group : INDIVIDUAL: as **a** : GIRL, WOMAN 〈met an attractive ~ at the dance〉 **b** (1) : a musical, theatrical, or literary selection or production (2) : ROUTINE, ACT **c** : an item of merchandise and esp. clothing **6** : insight into a person's ability or character 〈had my ~〉 **7** *pl but sing or pl in constr* **a** : a form of lottery in which an individual wagers on the appearance of a certain combination of digits (as in regularly published numbers) — called also **numbers game b** : POLICY 2a **8** *pl* **a** : figures representing amounts of money usu. in dollars spent, earned, or involved **b** (1) : STATISTICS 2; *esp* : individual statistics (as of an athlete) (2) : RATING 3c **9** : a person represented by a number or considered without regard to individuality 〈at the university I was just a ~〉 **usage** see AMOUNT — **by the numbers 1** : in unison to a specific count or cadence **2** : in a systematic, routine, or mechanical manner

☞ The Table of Numbers is on the following page.

²**number** *vb* **num·bered; num·ber·ing** \-b(ə-)riŋ\ *vt* (14c) **1** : COUNT, ENUMERATE **2** : to claim as part of a total : INCLUDE **3** : to restrict to a definite number 〈your days are ~ed〉 **4** : to assign a number to **5** : to amount to in number : TOTAL 〈the crew ~s 100〉 ~ *vi* **1** : to reach a total number **2** : to call off numbers in sequence — **num·ber·able** \-b(ə-)rə-bəl\ *adj* — **num·ber·er** \-bər-ər\ *n*

number cruncher *n* (1966) **1** : a computer that performs fast numerical calculations esp. on large amounts of data **2** : a person concerned with complex numerical data (as statistics) — **number crunching** *n*

num·ber·less \'nəm-bər-ləs\ *adj* (1573) : INNUMERABLE, COUNTLESS

number line *n* (1960) : a line of infinite extent whose points correspond to the real numbers according to their distance in a positive or negative direction from a point arbitrarily taken as zero

¹**number one** *n* (ca. 1705) **1** : one's own interests or welfare : ONESELF 〈looking out for *number one*〉 — often written *No. 1* **2** : one that is first in rank, importance, or influence — often written *No. 1*

²**number one** *adj* (1839) **1** : first in rank, importance, or influence : FOREMOST 〈cancer is the country's *number one* killer〉 — often written *No. 1* **2** : of highest or of high quality

Num·bers \'nəm-bərz\ *n pl but sing in constr* : the mainly narrative fourth book of canonical Jewish and Christian Scripture — see BIBLE table

number theory *n* (1912) : the study of the properties of integers — **number theoretic** *adj* — **number theorist** *n*

numb·skull \'nəm-,skəl\ *var of* NUMSKULL

nu·men \'nü-mən, 'nyü-\ *n, pl* **nu·mi·na** \-mə-nə\ [L, nod, divine will, numen; akin to L *nutare* to nod, Gk *neuein*] (1628) : a spiritual force or influence often identified with a natural object, phenomenon, or place

nu·mer·a·ble \'nüm-rə-bəl, 'nü-mə-; 'nyüm-, 'nyü-mə-\ *adj* [L *numerabilis*, fr. *numerare* to count] (1570) : capable of being counted

¹**nu·mer·al** \'nüm-rəl, 'nü-mə-; 'nyüm-, 'nyü-mə-\ *adj* [ME, fr. MF, fr. LL *numeralis*, fr. L *numerus*] (14c) **1** : of, relating to, or expressing numbers **2** : consisting of numbers or numerals — **nu·mer·al·ly** *adv*

²**numeral** *n* (1686) **1** : a conventional symbol that represents a number **2** *pl* : numbers that designate by year a school or college class and that are awarded for distinction in an extracurricular activity

¹**nu·mer·ate** \'nü-mə-,rāt, 'nyü-\ *vt* **-at·ed; -at·ing** [L *numeratus*, pp. of *numerare* to count, fr. *numerus*] (ca. 1721) : ENUMERATE

²**nu·mer·ate** \'nüm-rət, 'nü-mə-; 'nyüm-, 'nyü-mə-\ *adj* [L *numerus* number + E *-ate* (as in *literate*)] (1959) : marked by the capacity for quantitative thought and expression — **nu·mer·a·cy** \'n(y)üm-rə-sē, 'n(y)ü-mə-\ *n*

nu·mer·a·tion \,nü-mə-'rā-shən, ,nyü-\ *n* (15c) **1 a** : the act or process or an instance of counting or numbering; *also* : a system of counting or numbering **b** : an act or instance of designating by a number **2** : the art of reading in words numbers expressed by numerals

nu·mer·a·tor \'nü-mə-,rā-tər, 'nyü-\ *n* (1575) **1** : the part of a fraction that is above the line and signifies the number of parts of the denominator taken **2** : one that numbers

¹**nu·mer·ic** \nü-'mer-ik, nyü-\ *adj* (ca. 1828) : NUMERICAL; *esp* : denoting a number or a system of numbers 〈~ code〉 〈a ~ sign〉

²**nu·mer·ic** *n* (1879) : NUMBER, NUMERAL

nu·mer·i·cal \nü-'mer-i-kəl, nyü-\ *adj* [L *numerus*] (1628) **1** : of or relating to numbers 〈the ~ superiority of the enemy〉 **2** : expressed in or involving numbers or a number system 〈~ standing in a class〉 〈a ~ code〉 — **nu·mer·i·cal·ly** \-k(ə-)lē\ *adv*

numerical analysis *n* (1946) : the study of quantitative approximations to the solutions of mathematical problems including consideration of the errors and bounds to the errors involved

numerical taxonomy *n* (1963) : taxonomy in which many quantitatively measured characters are given equal weight in the determination of taxa and the construction of diagrams indicating systematic relationships — **numerical taxonomic** *adj* — **numerical taxonomist** *n*

nu·mer·ol·o·gy \,nü-mə-'rä-lə-jē, ,nyü-\ *n* [L *numerus* + E *-o-* + *-logy*] (1911) : the study of the occult significance of numbers — **nu·mer·o·log·i·cal** \-mə-rə-'lä-ji-kəl\ *adj* — **nu·mer·ol·o·gist** \-mə-'rä-lə-jist\ *n*

nu·me·ro uno \'nü-mə-rō-'ü-(,)nō, 'nyü-\ *n or adj* [It *numero uno* or Sp *número uno*] (1968) : NUMBER ONE

\ə\ abut \'^\ kitten, F table \ər\ further \a\ ash \ā\ ace \ä\ mop, mar \aů\ out \ch\ chin \e\ bet \ē\ easy \g\ go \i\ hit \ī\ ice \j\ job \ŋ\ sing \ō\ go \ò\ law \òi\ boy \th\ thin \ṯẖ\ the \ü\ loot \ů\ foot \y\ yet \zh\ vision \ā, k̩, ^n, œ, œ̄, ue, ūe, ^y\ see Guide to Pronunciation

TABLE OF NUMBERS

CARDINAL NUMBERS[1]

NAME[2]	SYMBOL Hindu-Arabic	SYMBOL Roman[3]
zero or naught or cipher	0	
one	1	I
two	2	II
three	3	III
four	4	IV
five	5	V
six	6	VI
seven	7	VII
eight	8	VIII
nine	9	IX
ten	10	X
eleven	11	XI
twelve	12	XII
thirteen	13	XIII
fourteen	14	XIV
fifteen	15	XV
sixteen	16	XVI
seventeen	17	XVII
eighteen	18	XVIII
nineteen	19	XIX
twenty	20	XX
twenty-one	21	XXI
twenty-two	22	XXII
twenty-three	23	XXIII
twenty-four	24	XXIV
twenty-five	25	XXV
twenty-six	26	XXVI
twenty-seven	27	XXVII
twenty-eight	28	XXVIII
twenty-nine	29	XXIX
thirty	30	XXX
thirty-one	31	XXXI
thirty-two etc	32	XXXII
forty	40	XL
forty-one etc	41	XLI
fifty	50	L
sixty	60	LX
seventy	70	LXX
eighty	80	LXXX
ninety	90	XC
one hundred	100	C
one hundred and one or one hundred one	101	CI
one hundred and two etc	102	CII
two hundred	200	CC
three hundred	300	CCC
four hundred	400	CD
five hundred	500	D
six hundred	600	DC
seven hundred	700	DCC
eight hundred	800	DCCC
nine hundred	900	CM
one thousand or ten hundred etc	1,000	M
two thousand etc	2,000	MM
five thousand	5,000	V
ten thousand	10,000	X
one hundred thousand	100,000	C
one million	1,000,000	M

ORDINAL NUMBERS[4]

NAME[5]	SYMBOL[6]
first	1st
second	2d or 2nd
third	3d or 3rd
fourth	4th
fifth	5th
sixth	6th
seventh	7th
eighth	8th
ninth	9th
tenth	10th
eleventh	11th
twelfth	12th
thirteenth	13th
fourteenth	14th
fifteenth	15th
sixteenth	16th
seventeenth	17th
eighteenth	18th
nineteenth	19th
twentieth	20th
twenty-first	21st
twenty-second	22d or 22nd
twenty-third	23d or 23rd
twenty-fourth	24th
twenty-fifth	25th
twenty-sixth	26th
twenty-seventh	27th
twenty-eighth	28th
twenty-ninth	29th
thirtieth	30th
thirty-first	31st
thirty-second etc	32d or 32nd
fortieth	40th
forty-first	41st
forty-second etc	42d or 42nd
fiftieth	50th
sixtieth	60th
seventieth	70th
eightieth	80th
ninetieth	90th
hundredth or one hundredth	100th
hundred and first or one hundred and first	101st
hundred and second etc	102d or 102nd
two hundredth	200th
three hundredth	300th
four hundredth	400th
five hundredth	500th
six hundredth	600th
seven hundredth	700th
eight hundredth	800th
nine hundredth	900th
thousandth or one thousandth	1,000th
two thousandth etc	2,000th
ten thousandth	10,000th
hundred thousandth or one hundred thousandth	100,000th
millionth or one millionth	1,000,000th

[1] The cardinal numbers are used in simple counting or in answer to "how many?" The words for these numbers may be used as nouns (he counted to *twelve*), as pronouns (*twelve* were found), or as adjectives (*twelve* boys).

[2] In formal contexts the numbers one to one hundred and in less formal contexts the numbers one to nine are commonly written out, while larger numbers are given in numerals. In nearly all contexts a number occurring at the beginning of a sentence is usually written out. Except in very formal contexts numerals are invariably used for dates. Hindu-Arabic numbers from 1,000 to 9,999 are often written without commas or spaces (1000, 9999). Year numbers are always written without commas (1783).

[3] The Roman numerals are written either in capitals or in lowercase letters.

[4] The ordinal numbers are used to show the order of succession in which such items as names, objects, and periods of time are considered (the *twelfth* month; the *fourth* row of seats; the *18th* century).

[5] Each of the terms for the ordinal numbers excepting *first* and *second* is used in designating one of a number of parts into which a whole may be divided (a *fourth*; a *sixth*; a *tenth*) and as the denominator in fractions designating the number of such parts constituting a certain portion of a whole (*one fourth*; *three fifths*). When used as nouns the fractions are usually written as two words, although they are regularly hyphenated as adjectives (a *two-thirds* majority). When fractions are written in numerals, the cardinal symbols are used ($^1/_4$, $^3/_5$, $^5/_6$).

[6] The Hindu-Arabic symbols for the cardinal numbers may be read as ordinals in certain contexts (January 1 = January first; 2 Samuel = Second Samuel). The Roman numerals are sometimes read as ordinals (Henry IV = Henry the Fourth); sometimes they are written with the ordinal suffixes (XIXth Dynasty).

DENOMINATIONS ABOVE ONE MILLION

American system[1] NAME	VALUE IN POWERS OF TEN	NUMBER OF ZEROS[2]	NUMBER OF GROUPS OF THREE 0'S AFTER 1,000	British system[1] NAME	VALUE IN POWERS OF TEN	NUMBER OF ZEROS[2]	POWERS OF 1,000,000
billion	10^9	9	2	milliard	10^9	9	—
trillion	10^{12}	12	3	billion	10^{12}	12	2
quadrillion	10^{15}	15	4	trillion	10^{18}	18	3
quintillion	10^{18}	18	5	quadrillion	10^{24}	24	4
sextillion	10^{21}	21	6	quintillion	10^{30}	30	5
septillion	10^{24}	24	7	sextillion	10^{36}	36	6
octillion	10^{27}	27	8	septillion	10^{42}	42	7
nonillion	10^{30}	30	9	octillion	10^{48}	48	8
decillion	10^{33}	33	10	nonillion	10^{54}	54	9
undecillion	10^{36}	36	11	decillion	10^{60}	60	10
duodecillion	10^{39}	39	12	undecillion	10^{66}	66	11
tredecillion	10^{42}	42	13	duodecillion	10^{72}	72	12
quattuordecillion	10^{45}	45	14	tredecillion	10^{78}	78	13
quindecillion	10^{48}	48	15	quattuordecillion	10^{84}	84	14
sexdecillion	10^{51}	51	16	quindecillion	10^{90}	90	15
septendecillion	10^{54}	54	17	sexdecillion	10^{96}	96	16
octodecillion	10^{57}	57	18	septendecillion	10^{102}	102	17
novemdecillion	10^{60}	60	19	octodecillion	10^{108}	108	18
vigintillion	10^{63}	63	20	novemdecillion	10^{114}	114	19
centillion	10^{303}	303	100	vigintillion	10^{120}	120	20
				centillion	10^{600}	600	100

[1] The American system of numeration for denominations above one million was modeled on the French system but more recently the French system has been changed to correspond to the German and British systems. In the American system each of the denominations above 1,000 millions (the American *billion*) is 1,000 times the preceding one (one trillion = 1,000 billions; one quadrillion = 1,000 trillions). In the British system the first denomination above 1,000 millions (the British *milliard*) is 1,000 times the preceding one, but each of the denominations above 1,000 milliards (the British *billion*) is 1,000,000 times the preceding one (one trillion = 1,000,000 billions; one quadrillion = 1,000,000 trillions).

[2] For convenience in reading large numerals, the thousands, millions, etc., are usually separated by commas (21,530; 1,155,465) or esp. in technical contexts by spaces (1 155 465). Serial numbers (as a social security number) are often written with hyphens (042-24-4705).

nu·mer·ous \'nüm-rəs, 'nü-mə-; 'nyüm-, 'nyü-mə-\ *adj* [ME, fr. MF *numereux*, fr. L *numerosus*, fr. *numerus*] (15c) : consisting of great numbers of units or individuals ⟨born into a ~ family⟩; *also* : MANY ⟨received ~ complaints⟩ — **nu·mer·ous·ly** *adv* — **nu·mer·ous·ness** *n*

nu·mi·nous \'nü-mə-nəs, 'nyü-\ *adj* [L *numin-, numen* numen] (1647) **1** : SUPERNATURAL, MYSTERIOUS **2** : filled with a sense of the presence of divinity : HOLY **3** : appealing to the higher emotions or to the aesthetic sense : SPIRITUAL — **nu·mi·nous·ness** \-nəs\ *n*

nu·mis·mat·ic \,nü-məz-'ma-tik, -məs-, ,nyü-\ *adj* [F *numismatique*, fr. L *nomismat-, nomisma* coin, fr. Gk, current coin, fr. *nomizein* to use, fr. *nomos* custom, law — more at NIMBLE] (1792) **1** : of or relating to numismatics **2** : of or relating to currency : MONETARY — **nu·mis·mat·i·cal·ly** \-ti-k(ə-)lē\ *adv*

nu·mis·mat·ics \-tiks\ *n pl but sing in constr* (ca. 1828) : the study or collection of coins, tokens, and paper money and sometimes related objects (as medals) — **nu·mis·ma·tist** \nü-'miz-mə-tist, nyü-\ *n*

num·mu·lar \'nəm-yə-lər\ *adj* [F *nummulaire*, fr. L *nummulus*, dim. of *nummus* coin, prob. fr. Gk *nomimos* customary, fr. *nomos*] (1846) : characterized by circular or oval lesions or drops ⟨~ dermatitis⟩

num·mu·lit·ic limestone \,nəm-yə-'li-tik-\ *n* [NL *Nummulites*, genus of foraminifers, fr. L *nummulus*] (1833) : the most widely distributed and distinctive formation of the Eocene in Europe, Asia, and northern Africa

num·skull \'nəm-,skəl\ *n* [*numb + skull*] (1717) **1** : a thick or muddled head **2** : a dull or stupid person : DUNCE

¹nun \'nən\ *n* [ME, fr. OE *nunne*, fr. LL *nonna*] (bef. 12c) : a woman belonging to a religious order; *esp* : one under solemn vows of poverty, chastity, and obedience — **nun·like** \-,līk\ *adj*

²nun \'nün\ *n* [Heb *nūn*] (ca. 1823) : the 14th letter of the Hebrew alphabet — see ALPHABET table

nun·a·tak \'nə-nə-,tak\ *n* [Inuit (Greenland) *nunataq*] (1877) : a hill or mountain completely surrounded by glacial ice

Nunc Di·mit·tis \,nunk-də-'mi-təs, ,nunk-\ *n* [L, now lettest thou depart; fr. the first words of the canticle] (1552) : the prayer of Simeon in Luke 2:29–32 used as a canticle

nun·cha·ku \nən-,chək, nən-'chä-kü\ *n* [Jp dial. (Okinawa)] (1970) : a weapon that consists of two hardwood sticks joined at their ends by a short length of rawhide, cord, or chain

nun·ci·a·ture \'nən(t)-sē-ə-,chùr, 'nùn(t)-, -chər, -,tyùr, -,tùr\ *n* [It *nunciatura*, fr. *nuncio*] (1652) **1** : a papal diplomatic mission headed by a nuncio **2** : the office or period of office of a nuncio

nun·cio \'nən(t)-sē-,ō, 'nùn(t)-\ *n, pl* **-ci·os** [It, fr. L *nuntius* messenger, message] (1528) : a papal legate of the highest rank permanently accredited to a civil government

nun·cle \'nəŋ-kəl\ *n* [by alter. (fr. misdivision of *an uncle*)] (ca. 1589) *chiefly dial* : UNCLE

nun·cu·pa·tive \'nən-kyù-,pā-tiv, 'nəŋ-; ,nən-'kyü-pə-\ *adj* [ML *nuncupativus*, fr. LL, so-called, fr. L *nuncupatus*, pp. of *nuncupare* to name, prob. ultim. fr. *nomen* name + *capere* to take — more at NAME, HEAVE] (1546) : not written : ORAL ⟨a ~ will⟩

nun·nery \'nən-rē, 'nə-nə-\ *n, pl* **-ner·ies** (14c) : a convent of nuns

Nu·pe \'nü-(,)pā\ *n, pl* **Nupe** *or* **Nupes** (1883) **1** : the language of the Nupe people **2** : a member of a people of west central Nigeria

¹nup·tial \'nəp-shəl, -chəl, ÷-shə-wəl, ÷-chə-wəl\ *adj* [L *nuptialis*, fr. *nuptiae*, pl., wedding, fr. *nubere* to marry; perh. akin to Gk *nymphē* bride, nymph] (15c) **1** : of or relating to marriage or the marriage ceremony **2** : characteristic of or occurring in the breeding season ⟨~ flight⟩

²nuptial *n* (ca. 1555) : MARRIAGE, WEDDING — usu. used in pl.

nup·tial·i·ty \,nəp-shē-'a-lə-tē, -chē-\ *n, pl* **-ties** (1899) : the marriage rate

Nur·i·stani \,nùr-ə-'stä-nē, ,nyùr-\ *n* [*Nuristan*, Afghanistan] (1957) : KAFIRI

¹nurse \'nərs\ *n* [ME, fr. OF *nurice*, fr. LL *nutricia*, fr. L, fem. of *nutricius* nourishing — more at NUTRITIOUS] (13c) **1 a** : a woman who suckles an infant not her own : WET NURSE **b** : a woman who takes care of a young child : DRY NURSE **2** : one that looks after, fosters, or advises **3** : a person who is skilled or trained in caring for the sick or infirm esp. under the supervision of a physician **4 a** : a member of an insect society that belongs to the worker caste and cares for the young **b** : a female mammal used to suckle the young of another

²nurse *vb* **nursed; nurs·ing** [ME *nurshen* to suckle, nourish, contr. of *nurishen*] *vt* (14c) **1 a** : to nourish at the breast : SUCKLE **b** : to take nourishment from the breast of **2** : REAR, EDUCATE **3 a** : to promote the development or progress of **b** : to manage with care or economy ⟨*nursed* the business through hard times⟩ **c** : to take charge of and watch over **4 a** : to care for and wait on (as a sick person) **b** : to attempt to cure by care and treatment **5** : to hold in one's memory or consideration ⟨~ a grievance⟩ **6 a** : to use, handle, or operate carefully so as to conserve energy or avoid injury or pain ⟨~ a sprained ankle⟩ **b** : to use sparingly **c** : to consume slowly or over a long period ⟨~ a cup of coffee⟩ ~ *vi* **1 a** : to feed an offspring from the breast **b** : to feed at the breast : SUCK **2** : to act or serve as a nurse — **nurs·er** *n*

nurse·maid \'nərs-,mād\ *n* (1657) : a girl or woman who is regularly employed to look after children

nurse–mid·wife \-'mid-,wīf\ *n* (1952) : a registered nurse with additional training as a midwife who delivers infants and provides antepartum and postpartum care — **nurse–mid·wife·ry** \-,mid-'wi-f(ə-)rē, -'wī-; -'mid-,wi-\ *n*

nurse–prac·ti·tion·er \-prak-'ti-sh(ə-)nər\ *n* (1969) : a registered nurse who is qualified through advanced training to assume some of the duties and responsibilities formerly assumed only by a physician

nurs·ery \'nərs-rē, 'nər-sə-\ *n, pl* **-er·ies** (14c) **1** *obs* : attentive care : FOSTERAGE **2 a** : a child's bedroom **b** : a place where children are temporarily cared for in their parents' absence **c** : DAY NURSERY **3 a** : something that fosters, develops, or promotes **b** : a place in which persons are trained or educated **4** : an area where plants are grown for transplanting, for use as stocks for budding and grafting, or for sale **5** : a place where young animals grow or are cared for

nurs·ery·man \-mən\ *n* (1672) : one whose occupation is the cultivation of plants (as trees and shrubs) esp. for sale

nursery rhyme *n* (1832) : a short rhyme for children that often tells a story

nursery school *n* (1835) : a school for children usu. under five years

nurse's aide *n* (1943) : a worker who assists trained nurses in a hospital by performing unspecialized services (as giving baths)

nurse shark *n* [alter. of ME *nusse*] (1851) : any of various sharks of a widely distributed family (Orectolobidae); *esp* : a shark (*Ginglymostoma cirratum*) of the warmer parts of the Atlantic Ocean

nurs·ing *n* (1860) **1** : the profession of a nurse ⟨schools of ~⟩ **2** : the duties of a nurse ⟨proper ~ is difficult work⟩

nursing home *n* (1896) : a privately operated establishment providing maintenance and personal or nursing care for persons (as the aged or the chronically ill) who are unable to care for themselves properly

nurs·ling \'nərs-liŋ\ *n* (1557) **1** : one that is solicitously cared for **2** : a nursing child

nur·tur·ance \'nər-chə-rən(t)s\ *n* (ca. 1938) : affectionate care and attention — **nur·tur·ant** \-rənt\ *adj*

¹nur·ture \'nər-chər\ *n* [ME, fr. MF *norriture*, fr. LL *nutritura* act of nursing, fr. L *nutritus*, pp. of *nutrire* to suckle, nourish — more at NOURISH] (14c) **1** : TRAINING, UPBRINGING **2** : something that nourishes : FOOD **3** : the sum of the influences modifying the expression of the genetic potentialities of an organism

²nurture *vt* **nur·tured; nur·tur·ing** \'nərch-riŋ, 'nər-chə-\ (15c) **1** : to supply with nourishment **2** : EDUCATE **3** : to further the development of : FOSTER — **nur·tur·er** \'nər-chər-ər\ *n*

¹nut \'nət\ *n* [ME *nute, note*, fr. OE *hnutu*; akin to OHG *nuz* nut and perh. to L *nux* nut] (bef. 12c) **1 a** (1) : a hard-shelled dry fruit or seed with a separable rind or shell and interior kernel (2) : the kernel of a nut **b** : a dry indehiscent one-seeded fruit with a woody pericarp **2 a** : a hard problem or undertaking **b** : CORE, HEART **3** : a perforated block usu. of metal that has an internal screw thread and is used on a bolt or screw for tightening or holding something **4** : the ridge in a stringed instrument (as a violin) over which the strings pass on the upper end of the fingerboard **5** : a small lump (as of butter) **6 a** : a foolish, eccentric, or crazy person **b** : ENTHUSIAST ⟨a movie ~⟩ **7** *pl* : NONSENSE — often used interjectionally **8** *slang* : a person's head **9** : TESTIS — usu. considered vulgar **10** : the amount of money that must be earned in order to break even **11** : EN 1 — **nut·like** \-,līk\ *adj*

²nut *vi* **nut·ted; nut·ting** (1604) : to gather or seek nuts

nu·tate \'nü-,tāt, 'nyü-\ *vi* **nu·tat·ed; nu·tat·ing** (1880) : to exhibit or undergo nutation

nu·ta·tion \nü-'tā-shən, nyü-\ *n* [L *nutation-, nutatio*, fr. *nutare* to nod, rock — more at NUMEN] (1612) **1** *archaic* : the act of nodding the head **2** : oscillatory movement of the axis of a rotating body (as the earth) : WOBBLE **3** : a spontaneous usu. spiral movement of a growing plant part — **nu·ta·tion·al** \-shnəl, -shə-n°l\ *adj*

nut–brown \'nət-'braùn\ *adj* (14c) : of the color of a brown nut

nut·case \-,kās\ *n* (1959) : NUT 6a

nut·crack·er \-,kra-kər\ *n* (ca. 1548) : an implement for cracking nuts

nut·gall \-,gòl\ *n* (15c) : a gall that resembles a nut; *esp* : a gall produced on oak

nut grass *n* (1775) : a perennial sedge (*Cyperus rotundus*) of wide distribution that has slender rootstocks bearing small edible tubers resembling nuts; *also* : a related sedge (*C. esculentus*)

nut·hatch \'nət-,hach\ *n* [ME *notehache*, fr. *note* nut + *-hache*; akin to OE to*haccian* to hack — more at HACK] (14c) : any of various small tree-climbing chiefly insectivorous birds (family Sittidae and esp. genus *Sitta*) that have a compact body, a narrow bill, a short tail, and sometimes a black cap

nut·house \'nət-,haùs\ *n* (1900) *slang* : an insane asylum

nut·let \'nət-lət\ *n* (1856) **1 a** : a small nut **b** : a small fruit similar to a nut **2** : the stone of a drupelet

nut·meg \'nət-,meg, -,mäg\ *n* [ME *notemigge, notemuge*, ultim. fr. OProv *noz muscada*, fr. *noz* nut (fr. L *nuc-, nux*) + *muscada*, fem. of *muscat* musky — more at MUSCAT] (15c) : an aromatic seed that is used as a spice and is produced by an evergreen tree (*Myristica fragrans*) of the family Myristicaceae, the nutmeg family) native to the Moluccas; *also* : a tree yielding nutmeg

nut·pick \'nət-,pik\ *n* (ca. 1889) : a small sharp-pointed implement for extracting the kernels from nuts

nu·tria \'nü-trē-ə, 'nyü-\ *n* [AmerSp, fr. Sp, otter, modif. of L *lutra*; prob. akin to OE *oter* otter] (1820) **1** : the durable usu. light brown fur of a nutria **2** : a large So. American semiaquatic rodent (*Myocastor coypus*) with webbed hind feet that has been introduced into parts of Europe, Asia, and No. America

¹nu·tri·ent \'nü-trē-ənt, 'nyü-\ *adj* [L *nutrient-, nutriens*, prp. of *nutrire* to nourish — more at NOURISH] (1650) : furnishing nourishment

²nutrient *n* (ca. 1828) : a nutritive substance or ingredient

nu·tri·ment \'nü-trə-mənt, 'nyü-\ *n* [ME, fr. L *nutrimentum*, fr. *nutrire*] (15c) : something that nourishes or promotes growth and repairs the natural wastage of organic life

nu·tri·tion \nü-'tri-shən, nyü-\ *n* [ME *nutricioun*, fr. MF *nutrition*, fr. LL *nutrition-, nutritio*, fr. L *nutrire*] (15c) : the act or process of nourishing or being nourished; *specif* : the sum of the processes by which an animal or plant takes in and utilizes food substances — **nu·tri·tion·al** \-'trish-nəl, -'tri-shə-n°l\ *adj* — **nu·tri·tion·al·ly** *adv*

nu·tri·tion·ist \-'tri-sh(ə-)nist\ *n* (1926) : a specialist in the study of nutrition

nu·tri·tious \nù-'tri-shəs, nyù-\ *adj* [L *nutricius*, fr. *nutric-, nutrix* nurse, fr. *nutrire* to nourish — more at NOURISH] (1665) : NOURISHING — **nu·tri·tious·ly** *adv* — **nu·tri·tious·ness** *n*

nu·tri·tive \'nü-trə-tiv, 'nyü-\ *adj* (14c) **1** : of or relating to nutrition **2** : NOURISHING — **nu·tri·tive·ly** *adv*

nutritive ratio *n* (1897) : the ratio of digestible protein to other nutrients in a foodstuff or ration

nuts \'nəts\ *adj* (1785) **1** : ENTHUSIASTIC, KEEN ⟨everyone seems ~ about it —Lois Long⟩ **2** : INSANE, CRAZY ⟨said that it was a novel and all the people who said otherwise were ~ —Flannery O'Connor⟩

\ə\ abut \ᵊ\ kitten, F table \ər\ further \a\ ash \ā\ ace \ä\ mop, mar \aù\ out \ch\ chin \e\ bet \ē\ easy \g\ go \i\ hit \ī\ ice \j\ job \ŋ\ sing \ō\ go \ò\ law \òi\ boy \th\ thin \t̲h̲\ the \ü\ loot \ù\ foot \y\ yet \zh\ vision \à, k̲, ⁿ, œ, œ̄, ᴜe, ūe, ᵞ\ see Guide to Pronunciation

nuts and bolts n (1967)   **1** : the working parts or elements   **2** : the practical workings of a machine or enterprise as opposed to theoretical considerations or speculative possibilities — **nuts–and–bolts** adj

nut-sedge \'nət-,sej\ n (ca. 1909) : NUT GRASS

nut-shell \'nət-,shel\ n (13c)   **1** : the hard external covering in which the kernel of a nut is enclosed   **2** : something of small size, amount, or scope — **in a nutshell** : in a very brief statement

nut-ter \'nə-tər\ n (1958) slang Brit : NUT 6a

nut-ty \'nə-tē\ adj **nut-ti-er; -est** (15c)   **1** : having or producing nuts   **2** : having a flavor like that of nuts   **3** : ECCENTRIC, SILLY; also : mentally unbalanced — **nut-ti-ly** \-tə-lē\ adv — **nut-ti-ness** n

nux vom-i-ca \'nəks-'vä-mi-kə\ n, pl **nux vomica** [NL, lit., emetic nut] (14c)   **1** : the poisonous seed of an Asian tree (Strychnos nux-vomica of the family Loganiaceae) that contains several alkaloids and esp. strychnine and brucine; also : the tree yielding nux vomica   **2** : a drug containing nux vomica

nuz-zle \'nə-zəl\ vb **nuz-zled; nuz-zling** \'nəz-liŋ, 'nə-zə-\ [ME noselen to bring the nose toward the ground, fr. nose] vi (1530)   **1** : to work with or as if with the nose; esp : to root, rub, or snuff something   **2** : to lie close or snug : NESTLE ~ vt   **1** : to root, rub, or touch with or as if with the nose : NUDGE   **2** : to rub or push gently (as one's face) against something ⟨nuzzled her face into the pillow⟩

ny-a-la \nē-'ä-lə\ n, pl **nyalas** or **ny-ala** [of Bantu origin; akin to Venda dzi-nyàlà nyala buck] (1894) : an antelope (Tragelaphus angasi) of southeastern Africa with vertical white stripes on the sides of the body and with shaggy black hair along the male underside; also : a related antelope (T. buxtoni) of Ethiopia

nyc-ta-lo-pia \,nik-tə-'lō-pē-ə\ n [NL, fr. L nyctalops suffering from night blindness, fr. Gk nyktalops, fr. nykt-, nyx night + alaos blind + ōp-, ōps eye — more at NIGHT, EYE] (1684) : NIGHT BLINDNESS

ny-lon \'nī-,län\ n [coined word] (1938)   **1** : any of numerous strong tough elastic synthetic polyamide materials that are fashioned into

nyala

fibers, filaments, bristles, or sheets and used esp. in textiles and plastics   **2** pl : stockings made of nylon

nymph \'nim(p)f\ n [ME nimphe, fr. MF, fr. L nympha bride, nymph, fr. Gk nymphē— more at NUPTIAL] (14c)   **1** : any of the minor divinities of nature in classical mythology represented as beautiful maidens dwelling in the mountains, forests, trees, and waters   **2** : GIRL   **3** : any of various immature insects; esp : a larva of an insect (as a grasshopper, true bug, or mayfly) with incomplete metamorphosis that differs from the imago esp. in size and in its incompletely developed wings and genitalia — compare NAIAD 2 — **nymph-al** \'nim(p)-fəl\ adj

nym-pha-lid \nim-'fa-ləd, 'nim-fə-ləd\ n [NL Nymphalidae, ultim. fr. L nympha nymph] (1897) : any of a family (Nymphalidae) of butterflies (as a mourning cloak or fritillary) with the first pair of legs reduced in size in both sexes and useless for walking — **nymphalid** adj

nym-phet also **nym-phette** \nim-'fet, 'nim(p)-fət\ n (1955) : a sexually precocious girl barely in her teens

nym-pho \'nim(p)-(,)fō\ n, pl **nymphos** [short for nymphomaniac] (ca. 1910) : a person affected by nymphomania : NYMPHOMANIAC

nym-pho-lep-sy \'nim(p)-fə-,lep-sē\ n [nympholept, fr. Gk nympholēptos frenzied, lit., caught by nymphs, fr. nymphē + lambanein to seize — more at LATCH] (1775)   **1** : a demoniac enthusiasm held by the ancients to seize one bewitched by a nymph   **2** : a frenzy of emotion — **nym-pho-lept** \-,lept\ n — **nym-pho-lep-tic** \,nim(p)-fə-'lep-tik\ adj

nym-pho-ma-nia \,nim(p)-fə-'mā-nē-ə, -nyə\ n [NL, fr. nymphae inner lips of the vulva (fr. L, pl. of nympha) + LL mania mania] (1775) : excessive sexual desire by a female — **nym-pho-ma-ni-ac** \-nē-,ak\ n or adj — **nym-pho-ma-ni-a-cal** \-mə-'nī-ə-kəl\ adj

Ny-norsk \nü-'nòrsk, nyü-, nūē-\ n [Norw, lit., new Norwegian] (1931) : a literary form of Norwegian based on the spoken dialects of Norway — compare BOKMÅL

nys-tag-mus \nis-'tag-məs\ n [NL, fr. Gk nystagmos drowsiness, fr. nystazein to doze; prob. akin to Lith snusti to doze] (1822) : a rapid involuntary oscillation of the eyeballs (as from dizziness) — **nys-tag-mic** \-mik\ adj

nys-ta-tin \'nis-tə-tən\ n [New York State (where it was developed) + ¹-in] (1952) : an antibiotic that is derived from a soil actinomycete (Streptomyces noursei) and is used esp. in the treatment of candidiasis

o \'ō\ n, pl **o's** or **os** \'ōz\ often cap, often attrib (bef. 12c)   **1 a** : the 15th letter of the English alphabet   **b** : a graphic representation of this letter   **c** : a speech counterpart of orthographic o   **2** : a graphic device for reproducing the letter o   **3** : one designated o esp. as the 15th in order or class   **4** : something shaped like the letter O; esp : ZERO

O \'ō\ var of OH

o- or **oo-** comb form [Gk ōi-, ōio-, fr. ōion — more at EGG] : egg ⟨oology⟩; specif : ovum ⟨oogonium⟩
-o- [ME, fr. OF, fr. L, fr. Gk, thematic vowel of many nouns and adjectives in combination] — used as a connective vowel orig. to join word elements of Greek origin and now also to join word elements of Latin or other origin ⟨speedometer⟩ ⟨elastomer⟩

¹-o n suffix [perh. fr. ¹oh] : one that is, has the qualities of, or is associated with ⟨bucko⟩

²-o interj suffix [prob. fr. ¹oh] — in interjections formed from other parts of speech ⟨cheerio⟩ ⟨righto⟩

o' also **o** \ə, ō\ prep [ME o, o-, contr. of on & of] (13c)   **1** chiefly dial : ON   **2** : OF ⟨one o'clock⟩

oaf \'ōf\ n, pl **oafs** [of Scand origin; akin to ON alfr elf — more at ELF] (1625)   **1** : a stupid person : BOOB   **2** : a big clumsy slow-witted person — **oaf-ish** \'ō-fish\ adj — **oaf-ish-ly** adv — **oaf-ish-ness** n

oak \'ōk\ n, pl **oaks** or **oak** often attrib [ME ook, fr. OE āc; akin to OHG eih oak and perh. to Gk aigilōps, a kind of oak] (bef. 12c)   **1 a** : any of a genus (Quercus) of trees or shrubs of the beech family that produce acorns; also : any of various plants related to or resembling the oaks   **b** : the tough hard durable wood of an oak tree   **2** : the leaves of an oak used as decoration — **oak-en** \'ō-kən\ adj

oak apple n (15c) : a large round gall produced on oak leaves and twigs by a gall wasp (esp. Amphibolips concluenta or Andricus quercus-californicus)

oak–leaf cluster n (1918) : a bronze or silver cluster of oak leaves and acorns added to various military decorations to signify a second or subsequent award of the basic decoration

oak-moss \'ōk-,mòs\ n (1921) : any of several lichens (as Evernia prunastri) that grow on oak trees and yield a resin used in perfumery

oa-kum \'ō-kəm\ n [ME okum, fr. OE ācumba tow, fr. ā- (separative & perfective prefix) + -cumba (akin to OE camb comb) — more at ABIDE] (15c) : loosely twisted hemp or jute fiber impregnated with tar or a tar derivative and used in caulking seams and packing joints

oak wilt n (1942) : a destructive disease of oak trees that is caused by a fungus (Ceratocystis fagacearum) and is characterized by wilting, discoloration, and defoliation

¹oar \'ōr, 'òr\ n [ME oor, fr. OE ār; akin to ON ār oar] (bef. 12c)   **1 a** : a long pole with a broad blade at one end used for propelling or steering a boat   **2** : OARSMAN — **oared** \'ōrd, 'òrd\ adj

²oar vt (1610) : to propel with or as if with oars : ROW ~ vi : to progress by or as if by using oars

oar-fish \'ōr-,fish, 'òr-\ n (1860) : any of several sea fishes (genus Regalecus and esp. R. glesne) with narrow soft bodies from 20 to 30 feet (6 to 9 meters) long, a red dorsal fin running the entire length of the body, and red-tipped anterior rays rising above the head

oar-lock \-,läk\ n (bef. 12c) : a usu. U-shaped device for holding an oar in place

oars-man \'ōrz-mən, 'òrz-\ n (1701) : one who rows esp. in a racing crew — **oars-man-ship** \-,ship\ n

oars-wom-an \-,wu̇-mən\ n (1882) : a woman who rows esp. in a racing crew

oa-sis \ō-'ā-səs\ n, pl **oa-ses** \-,sēz\ [LL, fr. Gk] (1613)   **1** : a fertile or green area in an arid region (as a desert)   **2** : something that provides refuge, relief, or pleasant contrast

oast \'ōst\ n [ME ost, fr. OE āst; akin to MD eest kiln, L aestus heat, aestas summer — more at EDIFY] (bef. 12c) : a usu. conical kiln used for drying hops, malt, or tobacco — called also oast-house \-,hȧu̇s\

oat \'ōt\ n, often attrib [ME ote, fr. OE āte] (bef. 12c)   **1 a** : any of several grasses (genus Avena); esp : a widely cultivated cereal grass (A. sativa)   **b** : a crop or plot of the oat; also : oat seed — usu. used in pl. but sing. or pl. in constr.   **2** archaic : a reed instrument made of an oat straw

oat-cake \'ōt-,kāk\ n (14c) : a thin flat oatmeal cake

oat–cell \-,sel\ adj (1903) : of, relating to, or being a highly malignant form of cancer esp. of the lungs that is characterized by rapid proliferation of small anaplastic cells ⟨~ carcinomas⟩

oat-en \'ō-t²n\ adj (14c) : of or relating to oats, oat straw, or oatmeal

oat-er \'ō-tər\ n (1946) : WESTERN 2

oat grass n (1578) : WILD OAT 1a; broadly : one of several grasses resembling the oat

oath \'ōth\ n, pl **oaths** \'ōthz, 'ōths\ [ME ooth, fr. OE āth; akin to OHG eid oath, MIr oeth] (bef. 12c)   **1 a** (1) : a solemn usu. formal calling upon God or a god to witness to the truth of what one says or to witness that one sincerely intends to do what one says   (2) : a solemn attestation of the truth or inviolability of one's words   **b** : something (as a promise) corroborated by an oath   **2** : an irreverent or careless use of a sacred name; broadly : SWEARWORD

oat-meal \'ōt-,mēl, ōt-'mē(ə)l\ n (14c)   **1 a** : meal made from oats   **b** : rolled oats   **2** : porridge made from ground or rolled oats

ob- prefix [NL, fr. L, in the way, against, toward, fr. ob in the way of, on account of; akin to OCS o, ob on, around] : inversely ⟨obovate⟩

Oba·di·ah \ˌō-bə-ˈdī-ə\ n [Heb *Ōbhadhyāh*] **1** : a Hebrew prophet **2** : a prophetic book of canonical Jewish and Christian Scripture — see BIBLE table

¹ob·bli·ga·to \ˌä-blə-ˈgä-(ˌ)tō\ adj [It, obligatory, fr. pp. of *obbligare* to oblige, fr. L *obligare* — more at OBLIGE] (1794) : not to be omitted : OBLIGATORY — used as a direction in music; compare AD LIBITUM

²obbligato n, pl **-tos** also **-ti** \-ˈgä-tē\ (1845) **1** : an elaborate esp. melodic part accompanying a solo or principal melody and usu. played by a single instrument ⟨a song with violin ~⟩ **2** : ACCOMPANIMENT 2b; esp : an attendant background sound

ob·cor·date \ˌäb-ˈkȯr-ˌdāt\ adj (1775) : heart-shaped with the notch apical ⟨~ leaf⟩

ob·du·ra·cy \ˈäb-də-rə-sē, -dyə-; äb-ˈdu̇r-ə-, əb-, -ˈdyu̇r-\ n, pl **-cies** (1597) : the quality or state of being obdurate

ob·du·rate \ˈäb-də-rət, -dyə-; äb-ˈdu̇r-ət, əb-, -ˈdyu̇r-\ adj [ME, fr. L *obduratus*, pp. of *obdurare* to harden, fr. *ob-* against + *durus* hard — more at DURING] (15c) **1 a** : stubbornly persistent in wrongdoing **b** : hardened in feelings **2** : resistant to persuasion or softening influences *syn* see INFLEXIBLE — **ob·du·rate·ly** adv — **ob·du·rate·ness** n

obe·ah \ˈō-bē-ə\ also **obi** \ˈō-bē\ n, often cap [of African origin; akin to Twi *ɔ-bayifó* sorcerer, Ibo *díbìà* folk healer] (1760) : a system of belief among blacks chiefly of the British West Indies, the Guianas, and the southeastern U.S. that is characterized by the use of sorcery and magic ritual

obe·di·ence \ō-ˈbē-dē-ən(t)s, ə-\ n (13c) **1 a** : an act or instance of obeying **b** : the quality or state of being obedient **2** : a sphere of jurisdiction; esp : an ecclesiastical or sometimes secular dominion

obe·di·ent \-ənt\ adj [ME, fr. OF, fr. L *oboedient-, oboediens*, fr. prp. of *oboedire* to obey] (13c) : submissive to the restraint or command of authority : willing to obey — **obe·di·ent·ly** adv
syn OBEDIENT, DOCILE, TRACTABLE, AMENABLE mean submissive to the will of another. OBEDIENT implies compliance with the demands or requests of one in authority ⟨*obedient* to the government⟩. DOCILE implies a predisposition to submit readily to control or guidance ⟨a *docile* child⟩. TRACTABLE suggests having a character that permits easy handling or managing ⟨*tractable* beasts of burden⟩. AMENABLE suggests a willingness to yield or to cooperate either because of a desire to be agreeable or because of a natural open-mindedness ⟨*amenable* to new ideas⟩.

obei·sance \ō-ˈbē-s²n(t)s, ə-, -ˈbā-\ n [ME *obeisaunce* obedience, obeisance, fr. MF *obeissance*, fr. *obeissant*, prp. of *obeir* to obey] (14c) **1** : a movement of the body made in token of respect or submission : BOW **2** : DEFERENCE, HOMAGE — **obei·sant** \-s²nt\ adj — **obei·sant·ly** adv

obe·lia \ō-ˈbēl-yə\ n [NL] (1868) : any of a genus (*Obelia*) of small colonial marine hydroids with colonies branched like trees

obe·lisk \ˈä-bə-ˌlisk also \ˈō-\ n [MF *obelisque*, fr. L *obeliscus*, fr. Gk *obeliskos*, fr. dim. of *obelos*] (1569) **1** : an upright 4-sided usu. monolithic pillar that gradually tapers as it rises and terminates in a pyramid **2 a** : OBELUS **b** : DAGGER 2b

obe·lize \-ˌlīz\ vt **-lized; -liz·ing** (ca. 1656) : to designate or annotate with an obelus

obe·lus \-ləs\ n, pl **obe·li** \-ˌlī, -ˌlē\ [ME, fr. LL, fr. Gk *obelos* spit, pointed pillar, obelus] (14c) **1** : a symbol — or ÷ used in ancient manuscripts to mark a questionable passage **2** : the symbol ÷

Ober·on \ˈō-bə-ˌrän, -rən\ n [F, fr. OF *Auberon*] : the king of the fairies in medieval folklore

obese \ō-ˈbēs\ adj [L *obesus*, fr. *ob-* against + *esus*, pp. of *edere* to eat — more at OB-, EAT] (1651) : excessively fat

obe·si·ty \ō-ˈbē-sə-tē\ n (1611) : a condition characterized by excessive bodily fat

obey \ō-ˈbā, ə-\ vb **obeyed; obey·ing** [ME *obeien*, fr. OF *obeir*, fr. L *oboedire*, fr. *ob-* toward + *-oedire* (akin to *audire* to hear) — more at OB-, AUDIBLE] vt (14c) **1** : to follow the commands or guidance of **2** : to conform to or comply with ⟨~ an order⟩ ⟨falling objects ~ the laws of physics⟩ ~ vi : to behave obediently — **obey·er** n

ob·fus·cate \ˈäb-fə-ˌskāt; äb-ˈfəs-ˌkāt, əb-\ vt **-cat·ed; -cat·ing** [LL *obfuscatus*, pp. of *obfuscare*, fr. L *ob-* in the way + *fuscus* dark brown — more at OB-, DUSK] (1577) **1 a** : DARKEN **b** : to make obscure **2** : CONFUSE — **ob·fus·ca·tion** \ˌäb-(ˌ)fəs-ˈkā-shən\ n — **ob·fus·ca·to·ry** \äb-ˈfəs-kə-ˌtōr-ē, əb-, -ˌtȯr-\ adj

obi \ˈō-bē\ n [Jp] (1876) : a broad sash worn esp. with a Japanese kimono

Obie \ˈō-bē\ n [*O.B.*, abbr. for *off Broadway*] (1965) : an award presented annually by a professional organization for notable achievement in plays presented off-Broadway

obit \ō-ˈbit, ˈō-bət, esp Brit ˈä-bit\ n [ME, fr. MF, fr. L *obitus* death, fr. *obire* to go to meet, die, fr. *ob-* in the way + *ire* to go — more at ISSUE] (15c) : OBITUARY

obi·ter dic·tum \ˌō-bə-tər-ˈdik-təm, ˌä-\ n, pl **obiter dic·ta** \-tə\ [LL, lit., something said in passing] (1812) **1** : an incidental and collateral opinion that is uttered by a judge but is not binding **2** : an incidental remark or observation

obit·u·ary \ə-ˈbi-chə-ˌwer-ē, ō-, -ˈbi-chə-rē\ n, pl **-ar·ies** [ML *obituarium*, fr. L *obitus* death] (1738) : a notice of a person's death usu. with a short biographical account — **obit·u·ar·ist** \-ˈbi-chə-ˌwər-ist, -ˈbi-chə-rist\ n — **obituary** adj

¹ob·ject \ˈäb-jikt, -(ˌ)jekt\ n [ME, fr. ML *objectum*, fr. L, neut. of *objectus*, pp. of *obicere* to throw in the way, present, hinder, fr. *ob-* in the way + *jacere* to throw — more at OB-, JET] (14c) **1 a** : something material that may be perceived by the senses ⟨I see an ~ in the distance⟩ **b** : something that when viewed stirs a particular emotion ⟨as pity⟩ ⟨look to the tragic loading of this bed . . . the ~ poisons sight; let it be hid —Shak.⟩ **2** : something mental or physical toward which thought, feeling, or action is directed ⟨an ~ for study⟩ ⟨the ~ of my affection⟩ ⟨delicately carved art ~s⟩ **3 a** : the goal or end of an effort or activity : PURPOSE, OBJECTIVE ⟨their ~ is to investigate the matter thoroughly⟩ **b** : a cause for attention or concern ⟨money is no ~⟩ **4** : a thing that forms an element of or constitutes the subject matter of an investigation or science **5 a** : a noun or noun equivalent (as a pronoun, gerund, or clause) denoting the goal or result of the action of a verb **b** : a noun or noun equivalent in a prepositional phrase *syn* see INTENTION — **ob·ject·less** \-ləs\ adj — **ob·ject·less·ness** n

²ob·ject \əb-ˈjekt\ vb [ME, fr. L *objectus*, pp. of *obicere* to throw in the way, about] vt (15c) : to put forth in opposition or as an objection ⟨~ed that the statement was misleading⟩ ~ vi **1** : to oppose something firmly and usu. with words or arguments **2** : to feel distaste for something — **ob·jec·tor** \-ˈjek-tər\ n

ob·ject ball \ˈäb-jikt(t)-, -(ˌ)jekt(t)-\ n (1856) : the ball first struck by the cue ball in pool or billiards; also : a ball hit by the cue ball

ob·jec·ti·fy \əb-ˈjek-tə-ˌfī\ vt **-fied; -fy·ing** (ca. 1837) **1** : to treat as an object or cause to have objective reality **2** : to give expression to (as an abstract notion, feeling, or ideal) in a form that can be experienced by others ⟨it is the essence of the fairy tale to ~ differing facets of the child's emotional experience —John Updike⟩ — **ob·jec·ti·fi·ca·tion** \-ˌjek-tə-fə-ˈkā-shən\ n

ob·jec·tion \əb-ˈjek-shən\ n (14c) **1** : an act or instance of objecting **2 a** : a reason or argument presented in opposition **b** : a feeling or expression of disapproval

ob·jec·tion·able \-sh(ə-)nə-bəl\ adj (1781) : UNDESIRABLE, OFFENSIVE — **ob·jec·tion·able·ness** n — **ob·jec·tion·ably** \-blē\ adv

¹ob·jec·tive \əb-ˈjek-tiv, äb-\ adj (1620) **1 a** : relating to or existing as an object of thought without consideration of independent existence — used chiefly in medieval philosophy **b** : of, relating to, or being an object, phenomenon, or condition in the realm of sensible experience independent of individual thought and perceptible by all observers : having reality independent of the mind ⟨~ reality⟩ ⟨our reveries . . . are significantly and repeatedly shaped by our transactions with the ~ world —Marvin Reznikoff⟩ — compare SUBJECTIVE 3a **c** *of a symptom of disease* : perceptible to persons other than the affected individual — compare SUBJECTIVE 4c **d** : involving or deriving from sense perception or experience with actual objects, conditions, or phenomena ⟨~ awareness⟩ ⟨~ data⟩ **2** : relating to, characteristic of, or constituting the case of words that follow prepositions or transitive verbs **3 a** : expressing or dealing with facts or conditions as perceived without distortion by personal feelings, prejudices, or interpretations ⟨~ art⟩ ⟨an ~ history of the war⟩ ⟨an ~ judgment⟩ **b** *of a test* : limited to choices of fixed alternatives and reducing subjective factors to a minimum *syn* see MATERIAL, FAIR — **ob·jec·tive·ly** adv — **ob·jec·tive·ness** n — **ob·jec·tiv·i·ty** \ˌäb-ˌjek-ˈti-və-tē, əb-\ n

²objective n (1835) **1** : a lens or system of lenses that forms an image of an object **2 a** : something toward which effort is directed : an aim, goal, or end of action **b** : a strategic position to be attained or a purpose to be achieved by a military operation *syn* see INTENTION

objective complement n (1870) : a noun, adjective, or pronoun used in the predicate as complement to a verb and as qualifier of its direct object (as *chairman* in "we elected him chairman")

objective correlative n (1919) : something (as a situation or chain of events) that symbolizes or objectifies a particular emotion and that may be used in creative writing to evoke a desired emotional response in the reader

ob·jec·tiv·ism \əb-ˈjek-ti-ˌvi-zəm, äb-\ n (1854) **1** : any of various theories asserting the validity of objective phenomena over subjective experience; esp : REALISM 2a **2** : an ethical theory that moral good is objectively real or that moral precepts are objectively valid **3** : a 20th century movement in poetry growing out of imagism and putting stress on form — **ob·jec·tiv·ist** \-vist\ adj or n — **ob·jec·tiv·is·tic** \-ˌjek-ti-ˈvis-tik\ adj

ob·ject language \ˈäb-jikt-, -(ˌ)jekt-\ n (1935) : TARGET LANGUAGE

ob·ject lesson \ˈäb-jikt-, -(ˌ)jekt-\ n (1831) : something that serves as a practical example of a principle or abstract idea

ob·jet d'art \ˌȯb-ˌzhā-ˈdär\ n, pl **ob·jets d'art** *same*\ [F, lit., art object] (1865) **1** : an article of some artistic value **2** : CURIO — called also *objet*

ob·jet trou·vé \ˈȯb-ˌzhā-trü-ˈvā\ n, pl **objets trouvés** *same*\ [F, lit., found object] (1937) : a natural object (as a piece of driftwood) found by chance and held to have aesthetic value esp. through the working of natural forces on it; also : an artifact not orig. intended as art but held to have aesthetic value esp. when displayed as a work of art

ob·jur·ga·tion \ˌäb-jər-ˈgā-shən\ n [ME *objurgacyon*, fr. MF or L; MF *objurgation*, fr. L *objurgation-, objurgatio*, fr. *objurgare* to scold, blame, fr. *ob-* against + *jurgare* to quarrel, lit., to take to law, fr. *jur-, jus* law + *-igare* (fr. *agere* to lead) — more at OB-, JUST, AGENT] (15c) : a harsh rebuke — **ob·jur·gate** \ˈäb-jər-ˌgāt\ vt — **ob·jur·ga·to·ry** \əb-ˈjər-gə-ˌtōr-ē, -ˌtȯr-\ adj

ob·lan·ceo·late \(ˌ)äb-ˈlan(t)-sē-ə-ˌlāt\ adj (1850) : inversely lanceolate ⟨an ~ leaf⟩ — see LEAF illustration

ob·last \ˈä-ˌblast, ˈȯ-bləst\ n, pl **oblasts** also **ob·las·ti** \-ˌblas-tē, -bləs-\ [Russ *oblast*] (ca. 1886) : a political subdivision of Imperial Russia or of a republic in the U.S.S.R.

¹ob·late \ˈä-ˌblāt, ˈä-, -ˌ\ adj [prob. fr. NL *oblatus*, fr. *ob-* + *-latus* (as in *prolatus* prolate)] (1705) : flattened or depressed at the poles ⟨an ~ spheroid⟩ — **ob·late·ness** n

²oblate \-ˌblāt\ n [ML *oblatus*, lit., one offered up, fr. L, pp. of *offerre* — more at OFFER] (1864) **1** : a layman living in a monastery under a modified rule and without vows **2** : a member of one of several Roman Catholic communities of men or women

ob·la·tion \ə-ˈblā-shən, ō-\ n [ME *oblacioun*, fr. MF *oblation*, fr. LL *oblation-, oblatio*, fr. L *offerre*] (15c) **1** : the act of making a religious offering; specif, cap : the act of offering the eucharistic elements to God **2** : something offered in worship or devotion : a holy gift offered usu. at an altar or shrine

¹ob·li·gate \ˈä-blə-ˌgāt\ vt **-gat·ed; -gat·ing** [L *obligatus*, pp. of *obligare*] (1533) **1** : to bind legally or morally : CONSTRAIN **2** : to commit (as funds) to meet an obligation

obelisk

\ə\ abut \ˌ²\ kitten, F table \ər\ further \a\ ash \ā\ ace \ä\ mop, mar \au̇\ out \ch\ chin \e\ bet \ē\ easy \g\ go \i\ hit \ī\ ice \j\ job \ŋ\ sing \ō\ go \ȯ\ law \ȯi\ boy \th\ thin \th\ the \ü\ loot \u̇\ foot \y\ yet \zh\ vision \ä, ḵ, ⁿ, œ, œ̄, ue, ūe, ᵒ\ see Guide to Pronunciation

²**ob·li·gate** \'ä-bli-gət, -blə-ˌgāt\ *adj* (1887) **1 :** restricted to one particularly characteristic mode of life ⟨an ~ parasite⟩ **2 :** biologically essential for survival ⟨~ mutualism⟩ — **ob·li·gate·ly** *adv*

ob·li·ga·tion \ˌä-blə-'gā-shən\ *n* (14c) **1 :** the action of obligating oneself to a course of action (as by a promise or vow) **2 a :** something (as a formal contract, a promise, or the demands of conscience or custom) that obligates one to a course of action **b :** a debt security (as a mortgage or corporate bond) **c :** a commitment (as by a government) to pay a particular sum of money; *also :* an amount owed under such an obligation ⟨unable to meet its ~s, the company went into bankruptcy⟩ **3 a :** a condition or feeling of being obligated **b :** a debt of gratitude **4 :** something one is bound to do : DUTY, RESPONSIBILITY

oblig·a·to·ry \ə-'bli-gə-ˌtōr-ē, ä-, -ˌtȯr- *also* 'ä-bli-gə-\ *adj* (15c) **1 :** binding in law or conscience **2 :** relating to or enforcing an obligation ⟨a writ ~⟩ **3 :** MANDATORY, REQUIRED ⟨~ military service⟩; *also :* so commonplace as to be a convention, fashion, or cliché ⟨the ~ death scene in opera⟩ **4 :** OBLIGATE 1 — **oblig·a·to·ri·ly** \ə-ˌbli-gə-'tȯr-ə-lē, ä-, -ˌtȯr- *also* ˌä-bli-gə-\ *adv*

oblige \ə-'blīj\ *vb* **obliged; oblig·ing** [ME, fr. OF *obliger*, fr. L *obligare*, lit., to bind to, fr. *ob*- toward + *ligare* to bind — more at LIGATURE] *vt* (14c) **1 :** to constrain by physical, moral, or legal force or by the exigencies of circumstance ⟨*obliged* to find a job⟩ **2 a :** to put in one's debt by a favor or service ⟨we are much *obliged* for your help⟩ **b :** to do a favor for ⟨always ready to ~ a friend⟩ ~ *vi :* to do something as or as if a favor *syn* see FORCE — **oblig·er** *n*

ob·li·gee \ˌä-blə-'jē\ *n* (1574) **:** one to whom another is obligated (as by a contract); *specif :* one who is protected by a surety bond

oblig·ing \ə-'blī-jiŋ\ *adj* (1632) **:** willing to do favors : ACCOMMODATING *syn* see AMIABLE — **oblig·ing·ly** \-jiŋ-lē\ *adv* — **oblig·ing·ness** *n*

ob·li·gor \ˌä-blə-'gȯr, -'jȯr\ *n* (1541) **:** one who is bound by a legal obligation

¹**oblique** \ō-'blēk, ə-, -'blik; *military usu* ī\ *adj* [ME *oblike*, fr. L *obliquus*] (15c) **1 a :** neither perpendicular nor parallel : INCLINED **b :** having the axis not perpendicular to the base ⟨an ~ cone⟩ **c :** having no right angle ⟨an ~ triangle⟩ **2 a :** not straightforward : INDIRECT; *also :* OBSCURE **b :** DEVIOUS, UNDERHANDED **3 :** situated obliquely and having one end not inserted on bone ⟨~ muscles⟩ **4 :** taken from an airplane with the camera directed horizontally or diagonally downward ⟨an ~ photograph⟩ — **oblique·ly** *adv* — **oblique·ness** *n*

²**oblique** *n* (ca. 1608) **1 :** something (as a line) that is oblique **2 :** any of several oblique muscles; *esp :* any of the thin flat muscles forming the middle and outer layers of the lateral walls of the abdomen

³**oblique** *adv* (1667) **:** at a 45 degree angle ⟨to the right ~, march⟩

oblique angle *n* (1695) **:** an acute or obtuse angle

oblique case *n* (1530) **:** a grammatical case other than the nominative or vocative

obliq·ui·ty \ō-'bli-kwə-tē, ə-\ *n, pl* **-ties** (15c) **1 :** deviation from moral rectitude or sound thinking **2 a :** deviation from parallelism or perpendicularity; *also :* the amount of such deviation **b :** the angle between the planes of the earth's equator and orbit having a value of about 23°27' ⟨~ of the ecliptic⟩ **3 a :** indirectness or deliberate obscurity of speech or conduct **b :** an obscure or confusing statement

oblit·er·ate \ə-'bli-tə-ˌrāt, ō-\ *vt* **-at·ed; -at·ing** [L *oblitteratus*, pp. of *oblitterare*, fr. *ob*- ob- + *littera* letter] (1609) **1 :** to make undecipherable or imperceptible by obscuring or wearing away **2 a :** to remove utterly from recognition or memory **b :** to remove from existence : destroy utterly all trace, indication, or significance of **c :** to cause to disappear (as a bodily part or a scar) or collapse (as a duct conveying body fluid) : REMOVE 4 ⟨a blood vessel *obliterated* by inflammation⟩ **3 :** CANCEL 4 — **oblit·er·a·tion** \-ˌbli-tə-'rā-shən\ *n* — **oblit·er·a·tor** \-'bli-tə-ˌrā-tər\ *n*

oblit·er·a·tive \ə-'bli-tə-ˌrā-tiv, ō-, -rə-tiv\ *adj* (ca. 1812) **:** inducing or characterized by obliteration: as **a :** causing or accompanied by closure or collapse of a lumen ⟨~ arterial disease⟩ **b :** tending to make inconspicuous ⟨~ behavior⟩

obliv·i·on \ə-'bli-vē-ən, ō-, ä-\ *n* [ME, fr. MF, fr. L *oblivion-, oblivio*, fr. *oblivisci* to forget, perh. fr. *ob*- in the way + *levis* smooth — more at OB-, LEVIGATE] (14c) **1 :** the fact or condition of forgetting or having forgotten; *esp :* the condition of being oblivious **2 :** the condition or state of being forgotten or unknown

obliv·i·ous \-vē-əs\ *adj* (15c) **1 :** lacking remembrance, memory, or mindful attention **2 :** lacking active conscious knowledge or awareness — usu. used with *of* or *to* — **obliv·i·ous·ly** *adv* — **obliv·i·ous·ness** *n*

ob·long \'ä-ˌblȯŋ\ *adj* [ME, fr. L *oblongus*, fr. *ob*- toward + *longus* long — more at LONG] (15c) **:** deviating from a square, circular, or spherical form by elongation in one dimension ⟨an ~ piece of paper⟩ ⟨an ~ melon⟩ — **oblong** *n*

ob·lo·quy \'ä-blə-kwē\ *n, pl* **-quies** [ME, fr. LL *obloquium*, fr. *obloqui* to speak against, fr. *ob*- against + *loqui* to speak] (15c) **1 :** a strongly condemnatory utterance : abusive language **2 :** the condition of one that is discredited : bad repute *syn* see ABUSE

ob·nox·ious \äb-'näk-shəs, əb-\ *adj* [L *obnoxius*, fr. *ob* in the way of, exposed to + *noxa* harm — more at NOXIOUS] (1597) **1** *archaic :* exposed to something unpleasant or harmful — used with *to* **2** *archaic :* deserving of censure **3 :** odiously or disgustingly objectionable : highly offensive — **ob·nox·ious·ly** *adv* — **ob·nox·ious·ness** *n*

ob·nu·bi·late \äb-'nü-bə-ˌlāt, -'nyü-\ *vt* **-lat·ed; -lat·ing** [L *obnubilatus*, pp. of *obnubilare*, fr. *ob*- in the way + *nubilare* to be cloudy, fr. *nubilus* cloudy, fr. *nubes* cloud — more at OB-, NUANCE] (1583) **:** BECLOUD, OBSCURE — **ob·nu·bi·la·tion** \-ˌnü-bə-'lā-shən, -ˌnyü-\ *n*

oboe \'ō-(ˌ)bō\ *n* [It, fr. F *hautbois* — more at HAUTBOIS] (1794) **:** a double-reed woodwind instrument having a conical tube, a brilliant penetrating tone, and a usual range from B flat below middle C upward for over 2½ octaves

obo·ist \'ō-(ˌ)bō-ist\ *n*

oboe

obol \'ä-bəl, 'ō-\ *n* [L *obolus*, fr. Gk *obolos, obelos*, lit., spit] (1579) **:** an ancient Greek coin or weight equal to ⅙ drachma

ob·ovate \(ˌ)äb-'ō-ˌvāt\ *adj* (1785) **:** ovate with the narrower end basal ⟨~ leaves⟩ — see LEAF illustration

ob·ovoid \-ˌvȯid\ *adj* (1819) **:** ovoid with the broad end toward the apex ⟨an ~ fruit⟩

ob·scene \äb-'sēn, əb-\ *adj* [MF, fr. L *obscenus, obscaenus*] (1593) **1 :** disgusting to the senses : REPULSIVE **2 a :** abhorrent to morality or virtue; *specif :* designed to incite to lust or depravity **b :** containing or being language regarded as taboo in polite usage ⟨~ lyrics⟩ **c :** repulsive by reason of crass disregard of moral or ethical principles ⟨an ~ misuse of power⟩ **d :** so excessive as to be offensive ⟨~ wealth⟩ ⟨~ waste⟩ *syn* see COARSE — **ob·scene·ly** *adv*

ob·scen·i·ty \-'se-nə-tē *also* -'sē-\ *n, pl* **-ties** (1589) **1 :** the quality or state of being obscene **2 :** something (as an utterance or act) that is obscene

ob·scur·ant \äb-'skyu̇r-ənt, əb-\ *or* **ob·scu·ran·tic** \ˌäb-skyə-'ran-tik\ *adj* (1878) **:** tending to make obscure — **obscurant** *n*

ob·scu·ran·tism \äb-'skyu̇r-ən-ˌti-zəm, əb-; ˌäb-skyu̇-'ran-\ *n* (1834) **1 :** opposition to the spread of knowledge : a policy of withholding knowledge from the general public **2 a :** a style (as in literature or art) characterized by deliberate vagueness or abstruseness **b :** an act or instance of obscurantism — **ob·scu·ran·tist** \-ən-tist, -'ran-tist\ *n or adj*

¹**ob·scure** \äb-'skyu̇r, əb-\ *adj* [ME, fr. MF *obscur*, fr. L *obscurus*] (15c) **1 a :** DARK, DIM **b :** shrouded in or hidden by darkness **c :** not clearly seen or easily distinguished : FAINT **2 :** not readily understood or clearly expressed; *also :* MYSTERIOUS **3 :** relatively unknown: as **a :** REMOTE, SECLUDED **b :** not prominent or famous ⟨an ~ poet⟩ **4 :** constituting the unstressed vowel \ə\ or having unstressed \ə\ as its value — **ob·scure·ly** *adv* — **ob·scure·ness** *n*

syn OBSCURE, DARK, VAGUE, ENIGMATIC, CRYPTIC, AMBIGUOUS, EQUIVOCAL mean not clearly understandable. OBSCURE implies a hiding or veiling of meaning through some inadequacy of expression or withholding of full knowledge ⟨*obscure* poems⟩. DARK implies an imperfect or clouded revelation often with ominous or sinister suggestion ⟨muttered *dark* hints of revenge⟩. VAGUE implies a lack of clear formulation due to inadequate conception or consideration ⟨a *vague* sense of obligation⟩. ENIGMATIC stresses a puzzling, mystifying quality ⟨*enigmatic* occult writings⟩. CRYPTIC implies a purposely concealed meaning ⟨*cryptic* hints of hidden treasure⟩. AMBIGUOUS applies to language capable of more than one interpretation ⟨an *ambiguous* directive⟩. EQUIVOCAL applies to language left open to differing interpretations with the intention of deceiving or evading ⟨moral precepts with *equivocal* phrasing⟩.

²**obscure** *vt* **ob·scured; ob·scur·ing** (15c) **1 :** to make dark, dim, or indistinct **2 :** to conceal or hide by or as if by covering **3 :** to reduce (a vowel) to the value \ə\ — **ob·scu·ra·tion** \ˌäb-skyu̇-'rā-shən\ *n*

³**obscure** *n* (1667) **:** OBSCURITY

ob·scu·ri·ty \äb-'skyu̇r-ə-tē, əb-\ *n, pl* **-ties** (14c) **1 :** one that is obscure **2 :** the quality or state of being obscure

ob·se·qui·ous \əb-'sē-kwē-əs, äb-\ *adj* [ME, compliant, fr. L *obsequiosus*, fr. *obsequium* compliance, fr. *obsequi* to comply, fr. *ob*- toward + *sequi* to follow — more at OB., SUE] (15c) **:** marked by or exhibiting a fawning attentiveness *syn* see SUBSERVIENT — **ob·se·qui·ous·ly** *adv* — **ob·se·qui·ous·ness** *n*

ob·se·quy \'äb-sə-kwē\ *n, pl* **-quies** [ME *obsequie*, fr. MF, fr. ML *obsequiae* (pl.), alter. of L *exsequiae*, fr. *exsequi* to follow out, execute — more at EXECUTION] (15c) **:** a funeral or burial rite — usu. used in pl.

ob·serv·able \əb-'zər-və-bəl\ *adj* (1609) **1 :** NOTEWORTHY **2 :** capable of being observed : DISCERNIBLE — **ob·serv·abil·i·ty** \-ˌzər-və-'bi-lə-tē\ *n* — **observable** *n* — **ob·serv·ably** \-'zər-və-blē\ *adv*

ob·ser·vance \əb-'zər-vən(t)s\ *n* (13c) **1 a :** a customary practice, rite, or ceremony ⟨Sabbath ~s⟩ **b :** a rule governing members of a religious order **2 :** an act or instance of following a custom, rule, or law ⟨~ of the speed limits⟩ **3 :** an act or instance of watching

¹**ob·ser·vant** \-vənt\ *adj* (1602) **1 :** paying strict attention : WATCHFUL ⟨an ~ spectator⟩ **b :** KEEN, PERCEPTIVE **2 :** careful in observing (as rites, laws, or customs) : MINDFUL ⟨pious and religiously ~ families —Sidney Hook⟩ ⟨always ~ of the amenities⟩ — **ob·ser·vant·ly** *adv*

²**observant** *n* (1605) *obs :* an assiduous or obsequious servant or attendant

ob·ser·va·tion \ˌäb-sər-'vā-shən, -zər-\ *n* [MF, fr. L *observation-, observatio*, fr. *observare*] (1535) **1 :** an act or instance of observing a custom, rule, or law : OBSERVANCE **2 a :** an act of recognizing and noting a fact or occurrence often involving measurement with instruments ⟨weather ~s⟩ **b :** a record or description so obtained **3 :** a judgment on or inference from what one has observed; *broadly :* REMARK, STATEMENT **4** *obs :* attentive care : HEED **5 :** the condition of one that is observed ⟨under ~ at the hospital⟩ — **ob·ser·va·tion·al** \-shnəl, -shə-n²l\ *adj* — **ob·ser·va·tion·al·ly** *adv*

ob·ser·va·to·ry \əb-'zər-və-ˌtōr-ē, -ˌtȯr-\ *n, pl* **-ries** [prob. fr. NL *observatorium*, fr. L *observare*] (1676) **1 :** a building or place given over to or equipped for observation of natural phenomena (as in astronomy); *also :* an institution whose primary purpose is making such observations **2 :** a situation or structure commanding a wide view

ob·serve \əb-'zərv\ *vb* **ob·served; ob·serv·ing** [ME, fr. MF *observer*, fr. L *observare* to guard, watch, observe, fr. *ob*- in the way, toward + *servare* to keep — more at CONSERVE] *vt* (14c) **1 :** to conform one's action or practice to (as a law, rite, or condition) : comply with **2 :** to inspect or take note of as an augury, omen, or presage **3 :** to celebrate or solemnize (as a ceremony or festival) in a customary or accepted way **4 a :** to watch carefully esp. with attention to details or behavior for the purpose of arriving at a judgment **b :** to make a scientific observation on or of **5 :** to come to realize or know esp. through consideration of noted facts **6 :** to utter as a remark ~ *vi* **1 a :** to take notice **b :** to make observations : WATCH **2 :** REMARK, COMMENT *syn* see KEEP — **ob·serv·ing·ly** \-'zər-viŋ-lē\ *adv*

ob·serv·er \əb-'zər-vər\ *n* (ca. 1550) **:** one that observes: as **a :** a representative sent to observe but not participate officially in an activity (as a meeting or war) **b :** an expert analyst and commentator in a particular field ⟨political ~s⟩

ob·sess \əb-'ses, äb-\ *vb* [L *obsessus*, pp. of *obsidēre* to frequent, besiege, fr. *ob-* against + *sedēre* to sit — more at OB-, SIT] *vt* (1531) : to haunt or excessively preoccupy the mind of ⟨was ∼ed with the idea⟩ ∼ *vi* : to engage in obsessive thinking : become obsessed with an idea

ob·ses·sion \äb-'se-shən, əb-\ *n* (1680) **1** : a persistent disturbing preoccupation with an often unreasonable idea or feeling; *broadly* : compelling motivation ⟨an ∼ with profits⟩ **2** : something that causes an obsession — **ob·ses·sion·al** \-'sesh-nəl, -'se-shə-nᵊl\ *adj* — **ob·ses·sion·al·ly** *adv*

ob·ses·sive \äb-'se-siv, əb-\ *adj* (1901) **1 a** : tending to cause obsession **b** : excessive often to an unreasonable degree **2** : of, relating to, or characterized by obsession : deriving from obsession — **obsessive** *n* — **ob·ses·sive·ly** *adv* — **ob·ses·sive·ness** *n*

obsessive–compulsive *adj* (1927) : relating to or characterized by recurring obsessions and compulsions esp. as symptoms of a neurotic state — **obsessive–compulsive** *n*

ob·sid·i·an \əb-'si-dē-ən\ *n* [NL *obsidianus,* fr. L *obsidianus lapis,* false MS reading for *obsianus lapis,* lit., stone of Obsius, fr. *Obsius,* its supposed discoverer] (1796) : a dark natural glass formed by the cooling of molten lava

ob·so·lesce \äb-sə-'les\ *vb* **-lesced; -lesc·ing** [L *obsolescere*] *vi* (1873) : to be or become obsolescent ∼ *vt* : to make obsolescent

ob·so·les·cence \-'le-sᵊn(t)s\ *n* (ca. 1841) : the process of becoming obsolete or the condition of being nearly obsolete ⟨the gradual ∼ of machinery⟩ ⟨reduced to ∼⟩

ob·so·les·cent \-sᵊnt\ *adj* (1755) : going out of use : becoming obsolete — **ob·so·les·cent·ly** *adv*

¹ob·so·lete \äb-sə-'lēt, 'äb-sə-,\ *adj* [L *obsoletus,* fr. pp. of *obsolescere* to grow old, become disused, perh. fr. *ob-* toward + *solēre* to be accustomed] (1579) **1 a** : no longer in use or no longer useful **b** : of a kind or style no longer current : OLD-FASHIONED **2** *of a plant or animal part* : indistinct or imperfect as compared with a corresponding part in related organisms : VESTIGIAL **syn** see OLD — **ob·so·lete·ly** *adv* — **ob·so·lete·ness** *n*

²obsolete *vt* **-let·ed; -let·ing** (1640) : to make obsolete

ob·sta·cle \'äb-sti-kəl, -,sti-\ *n* [ME, fr. MF, fr. L *obstaculum,* fr. *obstare* to stand in front of, fr. *ob-* in the way + *stare* to stand — more at OB-, STAND] (14c) : something that impedes progress or achievement

obstacle course *n* (1943) : a military training course filled with obstacles (as hurdles, fences, walls, and ditches) that must be negotiated; *broadly* : a series of obstacles that must be overcome

ob·stet·ric \əb-'ste-trik, äb-\ *or* **ob·stet·ri·cal** \-tri-kəl\ *adj* [modif. of L *obstetricius,* fr. *obstetric-, obstetrix* midwife, fr. *obstare*] (1742) : of, relating to, or associated with childbirth or obstetrics — **ob·stet·ri·cal·ly** \-tri-k(ə-)lē\ *adv*

ob·ste·tri·cian \,äb-stə-'tri-shən\ *n* (ca. 1828) : a physician specializing in obstetrics

ob·stet·rics \əb-'ste-triks, äb-\ *n pl but sing or pl in constr* (ca. 1819) : a branch of medical science that deals with birth and with its antecedents and sequels

ob·sti·na·cy \'äb-stə-nə-sē\ *n, pl* **-cies** (14c) **1 a** : the quality or state of being obstinate : STUBBORNNESS **b** : the quality or state of being difficult to remedy, relieve, or subdue ⟨the ∼ of tuberculosis⟩ **2** : an instance of being obstinate

ob·sti·nate \'äb-stə-nət\ *adj* [ME, fr. L *obstinatus,* pp. of *obstinare* to be resolved, fr. *ob-* in the way + *-stinare* (akin to *stare* to stand)] (14c) **1** : perversely adhering to an opinion, purpose, or course in spite of reason, arguments, or persuasion **2** : not easily subdued, remedied, or removed ⟨∼ fever⟩ — **ob·sti·nate·ly** *adv* — **ob·sti·nate·ness** *n*
syn see DOGGED, STUBBORN, PERTINACIOUS, MULISH mean fixed and unyielding in course or purpose. OBSTINATE implies usu. an unreasonable persistence ⟨an *obstinate* proponent of conspiracy theories⟩. DOGGED suggests an admirable often tenacious and unwavering persistence ⟨pursued the story with *dogged* perseverance⟩. STUBBORN implies sturdiness in resisting change which may or may not be admirable ⟨a person too *stubborn* to admit error⟩. PERTINACIOUS suggests an annoying or irksome persistence ⟨a *pertinacious* salesclerk refusing to take no for an answer⟩. MULISH implies a thoroughly unreasonable obstinacy ⟨a *mulish* determination to have his own way⟩.

ob·strep·er·ous \əb-'stre-p(ə-)rəs, äb-\ *adj* [L *obstreperus,* fr. *obstrepere* to clamor against, fr. *ob-* against + *strepere* to make a noise] (ca. 1600) **1** : marked by unruly or aggressive noisiness : CLAMOROUS ⟨∼ merriment⟩ **2** : stubbornly resistant to control : UNRULY **syn** see VOCIFEROUS — **ob·strep·er·ous·ly** *adv* — **ob·strep·er·ous·ness** *n*

ob·struct \əb-'strəkt, äb-\ *vt* [L *obstructus,* pp. of *obstruere,* fr. *ob-* in the way + *struere* to build, heap up — more at OB-, STREW] (1590) **1** : to block or close up by an obstacle **2** : to hinder from passage, action, or operation : IMPEDE **3** : to cut off from sight ⟨a wall ∼s the view⟩ **syn** see HINDER — **ob·struc·tive** \-'strək-tiv\ *adj or n* — **ob·struc·tive·ness** *n* — **ob·struc·tor** \-tər\ *n*

ob·struc·tion \əb-'strək-shən, äb-\ *n* (1533) **1 a** : an act of obstructing **b** : the state of being obstructed; *esp* : a condition of being clogged or blocked **2** : something that obstructs

ob·struc·tion·ism \-shə,ni-zəm\ *n* (1879) : deliberate interference with the progress or business esp. of a legislative body — **ob·struc·tion·ist** \-sh(ə-)nist\ *n or adj* — **ob·struc·tion·is·tic** \-,strək-shə-'nis-tik\ *adj*

ob·tain \əb-'tān, äb-\ *vb* [ME *obteinen,* fr. MF & L; MF *obtenir,* fr. L *obtinēre* to hold on to, possess, obtain, fr. *ob-* in the way + *tenēre* to hold — more at THIN] *vt* (15c) : to gain or attain usu. by planned action or effort ∼ *vi* **1** *archaic* : SUCCEED **2** : to be generally recognized or established : PREVAIL — **ob·tain·abil·i·ty** \-,tā-nə-'bi-lə-tē\ *n* — **ob·tain·able** \-'tā-nə-bəl\ *adj* — **ob·tain·er** *n* — **ob·tain·ment** \-'tān-mənt\ *n*

ob·tect \äb-'tekt, äb-\ *also* **ob·tect·ed** \-'tek-təd\ *adj* [L *obtectus,* pp. of *obtegere* to cover over, fr. *ob-* in the way + *tegere* to cover — more at THATCH, ca. 1902) : enclosed in or characterized by enclosure in a firm chitinous case or covering ⟨an ∼ pupa⟩

ob·trude \əb-'trüd, äb-\ *vb* **ob·trud·ed; ob·trud·ing** [L *obtrudere* to thrust at, fr. *ob-* in the way + *trudere* to thrust — more at OB-, THREAT] *vt* (ca. 1609) **1** : to thrust out : EXTRUDE **2** : to force or impose (as oneself or one's ideas) without warrant or request ∼ *vi* : to become unduly prominent or interfering : INTRUDE — **ob·trud·er** *n*

ob·tru·sion \-'trü-zhən\ *n* [LL *obtrusion-, obtrusio,* fr. L *obtrudere*] (1579) **1** : an act of obtruding **2** : something that is obtruded

ob·tru·sive \-'trü-siv, -ziv\ *adj* (1667) **1 a** : forward in manner or conduct ⟨∼ behavior⟩ **b** : undesirably prominent **2** : thrust out : PROTRUDING **syn** see IMPERTINENT — **ob·tru·sive·ly** *adv* — **ob·tru·sive·ness** *n*

ob·tund \äb-'tənd\ *vt* [ME, fr. L *obtundere*] (14c) : to reduce the edge or violence of : DULL ⟨∼ed reflexes⟩

ob·tu·ra·tion \,äb-tyə-'rā-shən, -tə-\ *n* [L *obturation-, obturatio,* fr. *obturare* to obstruct] (1610) : OBSTRUCTION, CLOSURE — **ob·tu·rate** \'äb-tyə-,rāt, -tə-\ *vt*

ob·tu·ra·tor \'äb-tyə-,rā-tər, -tə-\ *n* [NL, fr. L *obturare*] (ca. 1741) : one that closes: as **a** : one (as a prosthetic device) that closes or blocks up an opening (as a fissure in the palate) **b** : a hooded swelling of the placenta that fits over the nucellus in some plants

ob·tuse \äb-'tüs, əb-, -'tyüs\ *adj* **ob·tus·er; -est** [ME, fr. L *obtusus* blunt, dull, fr. pp. of *obtundere* to beat against, blunt, fr. *ob-* against + *tundere* to beat — more at OB-, CONTUSION] (15c) **1 a** : not pointed or acute : BLUNT **b** (1) *of an angle* : exceeding 90 degrees but less than 180 degrees (2) : having an obtuse angle ⟨an ∼ triangle⟩ — see TRIANGLE illustration **c** *of a leaf* : rounded at the free end **2 a** : lacking sharpness or quickness of sensibility or intellect : INSENSITIVE, STUPID **b** : difficult to comprehend : not clear or precise in thought or expression **syn** see DULL — **ob·tuse·ly** *adv* — **ob·tuse·ness** *n*

¹ob·verse \äb-'vərs, əb-, 'äb-,\ *adj* [L *obversus,* fr. pp. of *obvertere* to turn toward, fr. *ob-* toward + *vertere* to turn — more at OB-, WORTH] (ca. 1656) **1** : facing the observer or opponent **2** : having the base narrower than the top ⟨an ∼ leaf⟩ **3** : constituting the obverse of something : OPPOSITE — **ob·verse·ly** *adv*

²ob·verse \'äb-,vərs, äb-'; əb-'\ *n* (1658) **1** : the side of a coin or currency note bearing the chief device and lettering; *broadly* : a front or principal surface **2** : a counterpart having the opposite orientation or force ⟨their rise was merely the ∼ of the Empire's fall —A. J. Toynbee⟩; *also* : OPPOSITE 1 ⟨joy and its ∼, sorrow⟩ **3** : a proposition inferred immediately from another by denying the opposite of what the given proposition affirms ⟨the ∼ of "all *A* is *B*" is "no *A* is not *B*"⟩

ob·vi·ate \'äb-vē-,āt\ *vt* **-at·ed; -at·ing** [LL *obviatus,* pp. of *obviare* to meet, withstand, fr. L *obviam*] (1598) : to anticipate and prevent (as a situation) or make unnecessary (as an action) — **ob·vi·a·tion** \,äb-vē-'ā-shən\ *n*

ob·vi·ous \'äb-vē-əs\ *adj* [L *obvius,* fr. *obviam* in the way, fr. *ob* in the way of + *viam,* acc. of *via* way — more at OB-, VIA] (1603) **1** *archaic* : being in the way or in front **2** : easily discovered, seen, or understood **syn** see EVIDENT — **ob·vi·ous·ness** *n*

ob·vi·ous·ly \-lē\ *adv* (1638) **1** : in an obvious manner ⟨showed his anger ∼⟩ **2** : as is plainly evident ⟨∼, something is wrong⟩

oca \'ō-kə\ *n* [Sp, fr. Quechua *oqa*] (1604) : either of two So. American wood sorrels (*Oxalis crenata* and *O. tuberosa*) cultivated for their edible tubers; *also* : the tuber of an oca

oc·a·ri·na \,ä-kə-'rē-nə\ *n* [It, fr. It dial., dim. of *oca* goose, fr. LL *auca,* fr. L *avis* bird — more at AVIARY] (1877) : a simple wind instrument typically having an oval body with finger holes and a projecting mouthpiece

ocarina

Oc·cam's razor \'ä-kəmz-\ *n* [William of *Occam*] (ca. 1837) : a scientific and philosophic rule that entities should not be multiplied unnecessarily which is interpreted as requiring that the simplest of competing theories be preferred to the more complex or that explanations of unknown phenomena be sought first in terms of known quantities

¹oc·ca·sion \ə-'kā-zhən\ *n* [ME, fr. MF or L; MF, fr. L *occasion-, occasio,* fr. *occidere* to fall, fall down, fr. *ob-* toward + *cadere* to fall — more at OB-, CHANCE] (14c) **1** : a favorable opportunity or circumstance ⟨did not have ∼ to talk with them⟩ **2 a** : a state of affairs that provides a ground or reason ⟨the ∼ of the discord was their mutual intolerance⟩ **b** : an occurrence or condition that brings something about; *esp* : the immediate inciting circumstance as distinguished from the fundamental cause ⟨his insulting remark was the ∼ of a bitter quarrel⟩ **3** : HAPPENING, INCIDENT **b** : a time at which something happens : INSTANCE **4 a** : a need arising from a particular circumstance **b** *archaic* : a personal want or need — usu. used in pl. **5** *pl* : AFFAIRS, BUSINESS **6** : a special event or ceremony : CELEBRATION — **on occasion** : from time to time

²occasion *vt* **-sioned; -sion·ing** \-'käzh-niŋ, -'kā-zhə-\ (15c) : BRING ABOUT, CAUSE

oc·ca·sion·al \-'käzh-nəl, -'kā-zhə-nᵊl\ *adj* (ca. 1631) **1 a** : of or relating to a particular occasion ⟨a budget able to meet ∼ demands as well as regular ones⟩ **b** : created for a particular occasion ⟨∼ verse⟩ **2** : acting as the occasion or contributing cause of something **3** : encountered, occurring, appearing, or taken at irregular or infrequent intervals ⟨∼ visitors⟩ ⟨an ∼ vacation⟩ **4** : acting in a specified capacity from time to time ⟨an ∼ lecturer⟩ **5** : designed or constructed to be used as the occasion demands ⟨∼ furniture⟩

oc·ca·sion·al·ly \-'käzh-nə-lē, -'kä-zhə-nᵊl-ē\ *adv* (1630) : on occasion : NOW AND THEN

Oc·ci·dent \'äk-sə-dənt, -,dent\ *n* [ME, fr. MF, fr. L *occident-, occidens,* fr. prp. of *occidere* to fall, set (of the sun)] (14c) : WEST 2a

oc·ci·den·tal \,äk-sə-'den-tᵊl\ *adj, often cap* (14c) **1** : of, relating to, or situated in the Occident : WESTERN **2** : of or relating to Occidentals — **oc·ci·den·tal·ly** *adv*

Occidental *n* (1857) : a member of one of the occidental peoples; *esp* : a person of European ancestry

Oc·ci·den·tal·ism \,äk-sə-'den-tᵊl-,i-zəm\ *n* (1839) : the characteristic features of occidental peoples or culture

---

\ə\ abut \ᵊ\ kitten, F table \ər\ further \a\ ash \ā\ ace \ä\ mop, mar \au̇\ out \ch\ chin \e\ bet \ē\ easy \g\ go \i\ hit \ī\ ice \j\ job \ŋ\ sing \ō\ go \ȯ\ law \ȯi\ boy \th\ thin \t̲h̲\ the \ü\ loot \u̇\ foot \y\ yet \zh\ vision \á, k̲, ⁿ, œ, œ̄, ᴜᴇ, ᵫ, ᵞ\ see Guide to Pronunciation

oc·ci·den·tal·ize \-t²l-ˌīz\ *vt* **-ized; -iz·ing** *often cap* (1870) : to make occidental (as in culture)
oc·cip·i·tal \äk-'si-pə-t²l\ *adj* (1541) : of, relating to, or located within or near the occiput or the occipital bone — **occipital** *n* — **oc·cip·i·tal·ly** *adv*
occipital bone *n* (1679) : a compound bone that forms the posterior part of the skull and bears a condyle by which the skull articulates with the atlas
occipital condyle *n* (ca. 1860) : an articular surface on the occipital bone by which the skull articulates with the atlas
occipital lobe *n* (ca. 1890) : the posterior lobe of each cerebral hemisphere that bears the visual areas and has the form of a 3-sided pyramid
oc·ci·put \'äk-sə-(ˌ)pət\ *n, pl* **occiputs** *or* **oc·cip·i·ta** \äk-'si-pə-tə\ [ME, fr. L *occiput, occiput,* fr. *ob-* against + *capit, caput* head — more at OB-, HEAD] (14c) : the back part of the head or skull
Oc·ci·tan \'äk-sə-ˌtan\ *n* [F, fr. ML *occitanus,* fr. OProv *oc* yes (contrasted with OF *oïl* yes) + ML *-itanus* (perh. as in *aquitanus* of Aquitaine)] (1958) : PROVENÇAL 2 — **Occitan** *adj*
oc·clude \ə-'klüd, ä-\ *vb* **oc·clud·ed; oc·clud·ing** [L *occludere,* fr. *ob-* in the way + *claudere* to shut, close — more at CLOSE] *vt* (1597) **1 :** to close up or block off : OBSTRUCT ⟨a thrombus *occluding* a coronary artery⟩; *also* : CONCEAL **2 :** SORB ~ *vi* **1 :** to come into contact with cusps of the opposing teeth fitting together ⟨his teeth do not ~ properly⟩ **2 :** to become occluded
occluded front *n* (ca. 1938) : OCCLUSION 2
oc·clu·sal \ə-'klü-səl, ä-, -zəl\ *adj* (1897) : of or relating to the grinding or biting surface of a tooth or to occlusion of the teeth
oc·clu·sion \ə-'klü-zhən\ *n* [L *occludere*] (ca. 1645) **1 :** the act of occluding : the state of being occluded: as **a :** the complete obstruction of the breath passage in the articulation of a speech sound **b :** the bringing of the opposing surfaces of the teeth of the two jaws into contact; *also* : the relation between the surfaces when in contact **c :** the inclusion or sorption of gas trapped during solidification of a material **2 :** the front formed by a cold front overtaking a warm front and lifting the warm air above the earth's surface
oc·clu·sive \-siv, -ziv\ *adj* [L *occlusus,* pp. of *occludere*] (1888) **1 :** serving to occlude **2 :** characterized by occlusion
¹oc·cult \ə-'kəlt, ä-\ *vt* [L *occultare,* freq. of *occulere*] (1500) : to shut off from view or exposure : COVER, ECLIPSE — **oc·cult·er** *n*
²oc·cult \ə-'kəlt, ä-; 'ä-ˌkəlt\ *adj* [L *occultus,* fr. pp. of *occulere* to cover up, fr. *ob-* in the way + *-culere* (akin to *celare* to conceal) — more at OB-, HELL] (1567) **1 :** not revealed : SECRET **2 :** not easily apprehended or understood : ABSTRUSE, MYSTERIOUS **3 :** hidden from view : CONCEALED **4 :** of or relating to the occult **5 :** not manifest or detectable by clinical methods alone ⟨~ carcinoma⟩; *also* : not present in macroscopic amounts ⟨~ blood in a stool⟩ — **oc·cult·ly** *adv*
³occult *same as* ²\ *n* (1923) : matters regarded as involving the action or influence of supernatural or supernormal powers or some secret knowledge of them — used with *the*
oc·cul·ta·tion \ˌä-(ˌ)kəl-'tā-shən\ *n* (15c) **1 :** the state of being hidden from view or lost to notice **2 :** the interruption of the light from a celestial body or of the signals from a spacecraft by the intervention of a celestial body; *esp* : an eclipse of a star or planet by the moon
oc·cult·ism \ə-'kəl-ˌti-zəm, ä-; 'ä-ˌkəl-\ *n* (1881) : occult theory or practice : belief in or study of the action or influence of supernatural or supernormal powers — **oc·cult·ist** \-tist\ *n*
oc·cu·pan·cy \'ä-kyə-pən(t)-sē\ *n, pl* **-cies** (1596) **1 :** the fact or condition of holding, possessing, or residing in or on something ⟨~ of the estate⟩ **2 :** the act or fact of taking or having possession (as of unowned land) to acquire ownership **3 :** the fact or condition of being occupied ⟨~ by more than 400 persons is unlawful⟩ **4 :** the use to which a property is put ⟨industrial ~⟩ **5 :** a building or part of a building intended to be occupied (as by a tenant) ⟨multiple ~ buildings⟩
oc·cu·pant \-pənt\ *n* (1596) **1 :** one who occupies a particular place; *esp* : RESIDENT **2 :** one who acquires title by occupancy
oc·cu·pa·tion \ˌä-kyə-'pā-shən\ *n* [ME *occupacioun,* fr. MF *occupation,* fr. L *occupation-, occupatio,* fr. *occupare*] (14c) **1 a :** an activity in which one engages ⟨in the first three grades learning to read is perhaps the major ~ of the pupil —J. B. Conant⟩ **b :** the principal business of one's life : VOCATION **2 a :** the possession, use, or settlement of land : OCCUPANCY **b :** the holding of an office or position **3 a :** the act or process of taking possession of a place or area : SEIZURE **b :** the holding and control of an area by a foreign military force **c :** the military force occupying a country or the policies carried out by it **syn** see WORK — **oc·cu·pa·tion·al** \-shnəl, -shə-n²l\ *adj* — **oc·cu·pa·tion·al·ly** *adv*
occupational therapy *n* (1915) : therapy by means of activity; *esp* : creative activity prescribed for its effect in promoting recovery or rehabilitation — **occupational therapist** *n*
oc·cu·py \'ä-kyə-ˌpī\ *vt* **-pied; -py·ing** [ME *occupien* to take possession of, occupy, modif. of MF *occuper,* fr. L *occupare,* fr. *ob-* toward + *-cupare* (akin to *capere* to seize) — more at OB-, HEAVE] (14c) **1 :** to engage the attention or energies of **2 a :** to take up (a place or extent in space) ⟨this chair is *occupied*⟩ ⟨the fireplace will ~ this corner of the room⟩ **b :** to take or fill (an extent in time) ⟨the hobby *occupies* all of my free time⟩ **3 a :** to take or hold possession or control of ⟨enemy troops *occupied* the ridge⟩ **b :** to fill or perform the functions of (an office or position) **4 :** to reside in as an owner or tenant — **oc·cu·pi·er** \-ˌpī(-ə)r\ *n*
oc·cur \ə-'kər\ *vi* **oc·curred; oc·cur·ring** \-'kər-iŋ, -'kə-riŋ\ [L *occurrere,* fr. *ob-* in the way + *currere* to run — more at OB-, CAR] (1534) **1 :** to be found or met with : APPEAR **2 :** to come into existence : HAPPEN **3 :** to come to mind
oc·cur·rence \ə-'kər-ən(t)s, -'kə-rən(t)s\ *n* (1539) **1 :** something that occurs ⟨a startling ~⟩ **2 :** the action or instance of occurring ⟨the repeated ~ of petty theft in the locker room⟩
syn OCCURRENCE, EVENT, INCIDENT, EPISODE, CIRCUMSTANCE mean something that happens or takes place. OCCURRENCE may apply to a happening without intent, volition, or plan ⟨an encounter that was a chance *occurrence*⟩. EVENT usu. implies an occurrence of some importance and frequently one having antecedent cause ⟨the *events* following the assassination⟩. INCIDENT suggests an occurrence of brief dura-

tion or secondary importance ⟨a minor wartime *incident*⟩. EPISODE stresses the distinctiveness or apartness of an incident ⟨a brief romantic *episode* in a life devoted to work⟩. CIRCUMSTANCE implies a specific detail attending an action or event as part of its setting or background ⟨couldn't recall the exact *circumstances*⟩.
¹oc·cur·rent \ə-'kər-ənt, -'kə-rənt\ *adj* [ME, fr. MF, fr. L *occurrent-, occurrens,* prp. of *occurrere*] (15c) **1 :** occurring at a particular time or place : CURRENT **2 :** INCIDENTAL
²occurrent *n* (1535) : something that occurs as distinguished from something that continues to exist
ocean \'ō-shən\ *n, often attrib* [ME *occean,* fr. L *oceanus,* fr. Gk *Ōkeanos,* a river thought of as encircling the earth, ocean] (14c) **1 a :** the whole body of salt water that covers nearly three fourths of the surface of the globe **b :** any of the large bodies of water (as the Atlantic Ocean) into which the great ocean is divided **2 :** a very large or unlimited space or quantity
ocean·ar·i·um \ˌō-shə-'nar-ē-əm, -'ner-\ *n, pl* **-iums** *or* **-ia** \-ē-ə\ (1938) : a large marine aquarium
ocean·front \'ō-shən-ˌfrənt\ *n* (1919) : a shore area on the ocean
ocean·go·ing \-ˌgō-iŋ\ *adj* (1885) : of, relating to, or designed for travel on the ocean
oce·an·ic \ˌō-shē-'a-nik\ *adj* (1656) **1 a :** of or relating to the ocean **b :** occurring in or frequenting the ocean and esp. the open sea as distinguished from littoral or neritic waters **2 :** VAST, GREAT
Oce·an·id \ō-'sē-ə-nəd\ *n* [Gk *ōkeanid-, ōkeanis,* fr. *Ōkeanos* Oceanus] : any of the ocean nymphs that are daughters of Oceanus and Tethys in Greek mythology
ocean·og·ra·phy \ˌō-shə-'nä-grə-fē\ *n* [ISV] (1859) : a science that deals with the oceans and includes the delimitation of their extent and depth, the physics and chemistry of their waters, marine biology, and the exploitation of their resources — **ocean·og·ra·pher** \-fər\ *n* — **ocean·o·graph·ic** \-nə-'gra-fik\ *also* **ocean·o·graph·i·cal** \-fi-kəl\ *adj* — **ocean·o·graph·i·cal·ly** \-fi-k(ə-)lē\ *adv*
ocean·ol·o·gy \ˌō-shə-'nä-lə-jē\ *n* (ca. 1864) : OCEANOGRAPHY; *specif* : the science of marine resources and technology — **ocean·ol·o·gist** \-'nä-lə-jist\ *n*
ocean perch *n* (1943) : any of several marine scorpaenid food fishes (genus *Sebastes*): **a :** REDFISH a; *also* : a related food fish (*S. fasciatus*) **b :** one (*S. alutus*) abundant in the northeastern Pacific from Japan to the Bering Sea to southern California
ocean sunfish *n* (1629) : a large bony fish (*Mola mola* of the order Tetraodontiformes) having high dorsal and anal fins and a body nearly oval in outline and attaining a length of 10 feet (3 meters) and a weight in excess of 2 tons (1.8 metric tons)
Oce·anus \ō-'sē-ə-nəs\ *n* [L, fr. Gk *Ōkeanos*] : a Titan who rules over a great river encircling the earth in Greek mythology
ocel·lus \ō-'se-ləs\ *n, pl* **ocel·li** \-'se-ˌlī, -(ˌ)lē\ [NL, fr. L, dim. of *oculus* eye — more at EYE] (1819) **1 :** a minute simple eye or eyespot of an invertebrate **2 :** an eyelike colored spot (as on a peacock feather or the wings of some butterflies) — **ocel·lar** \ō-'se-lər\ *adj*
oce·lot \'ä-sə-ˌlät, 'ō-\ *n* [F, fr. Nahuatl *ōcēlōtl* jaguar] (1774) : a medium-sized American wildcat (*Felis pardalis*) that ranges from Texas to northern Argentina and has a tawny yellow or grayish coat dotted and striped with black
ocher *or* **ochre** \'ō-kər\ *n* [ME *oker,* fr. MF *ocre,* fr. L *ochra,* fr. Gk *ōchra,* fr. fem. of *ōchros* yellow] (14c) **1 :** an earthy usu. red or yellow and often impure iron ore used as a pigment **2 :** the color of ocher; *esp* : the color of yellow ocher — **ocher·ous** \'ō-k(ə-)rəs\ *or* **ochre·ous** \'ō-k(ə-)rəs, -krē-əs\ *adj*
och·loc·ra·cy \ä-'klä-krə-sē\ *n* [Gk & MF; MF *ochlocratie,* fr. Gk *ochlokratia,* fr. *ochlos* mob + *-kratia* -cracy] (1584) : government by the mob : mob rule — **och·lo·crat** \'ä-klə-ˌkrat\ *n* — **och·lo·crat·ic** \ˌä-klə-'kra-tik\ *or* **och·lo·crat·i·cal** \-ti-kəl\ *adj*
-ock *n suffix* [ME *-oc,* fr. OE] : small one ⟨*hillock*⟩
Ock·ham's razor \'ä-kəmz-\ *var of* OCCAM'S RAZOR
o'·clock \ə-'kläk, ō-\ *adv* [contr. *of of the clock*] (ca. 1601) **1 :** according to the clock ⟨the time is three ~⟩ **2 :** — used for indicating position or direction as if on a clock dial that is oriented vertically or horizontally ⟨an airplane approaching at six ~⟩
oco·ti·llo \ˌō-kə-'tē-(ˌ)yō\ *n, pl* **-llos** [MexSp] (1856) : a thorny scarlet-flowered candlewood (*Fouquieria splendens* of the family Fouquieriaceae) of the southwestern U.S. and Mexico
octa- *or* **octo-** *also* **oct-** *comb form* [Gk *okta-, oktō-, okt-* (fr. *oktō*) & L *octo-, oct-,* fr. *octo* — more at EIGHT] : eight ⟨*octane*⟩ ⟨*octoroon*⟩
oc·ta·gon \'äk-tə-ˌgän\ *n* [L *octagonum,* fr. Gk *oktagōnon,* fr. *okta-* + *-gōnon* -gon] (1639) : a polygon of eight angles and eight sides — **oc·tag·o·nal** \äk-'ta-gə-n²l\ *adj* — **oc·tag·o·nal·ly** \-n²l-ē\ *adv*
oc·ta·he·dral \ˌäk-tə-'hē-drəl\ *adj* (1758) **1 :** having eight plane faces **2 :** of, relating to, or formed in octahedrons — **oc·ta·he·dral·ly** \-drə-lē\ *adv*
oc·ta·he·dron \-drən\ *n, pl* **-drons** *or* **-dra** \-drə\ [Gk *oktaedron,* fr. *okta-* + *-edron* -hedron] (1570) : a solid bounded by eight plane faces

ocotillo

oc·tal \'äk-t²l\ *adj* (1948) : of, relating to, or being a number system with a base of eight
oc·tam·e·ter \äk-'ta-mə-tər\ *n* [LL, having eight feet, fr. LGk *oktametros,* fr. *okta-* + *metron* measure — more at MEASURE] (1889) : a line of verse consisting of eight metrical feet
oc·tane \'äk-ˌtän\ *n* [ISV] (ca. 1872) **1 :** any of several isomeric liquid alkanes C_8H_{18} **2 :** OCTANE NUMBER
octane number *n* (1931) : a number that is used to measure the antiknock properties of a liquid motor fuel (as gasoline) with a higher number indicating a smaller likelihood of knocking — called also *octane rating*; compare CETANE NUMBER
oc·tant \'äk-tənt\ *n* [L *octant-, octans* eighth of a circle, fr. *octo*] (1731) **1 :** an instrument for observing altitudes of a celestial body from a moving ship or aircraft **2 :** any of the eight parts into which a space is divided by three coordinate planes

oc·ta·pep·tide \,äk-tə-'pep-,tīd\ *n* (1961) : a protein fragment or molecule (as oxytocin or vasopressin) that consists of eight amino acids linked in a polypeptide chain

oc·tave \'äk-tiv, -təv, -,tāv\ *n* [ME, fr. ML *octava*, fr. L, fem. of *octavus* eighth, fr. *octo* eight — more at EIGHT] (14c) **1 a :** an 8-day period of observances beginning with a festival day **2 a :** a stanza of eight lines : OTTAVA RIMA **b :** the first eight lines of an Italian sonnet **3 a :** a musical interval embracing eight diatonic degrees **b :** a tone or note at this interval **c :** the harmonic combination of two tones an octave apart **d :** the whole series of notes, tones, or digitals comprised within this interval and forming the unit of the modern scale **e :** an organ stop giving tones an octave above those corresponding to the digitals **4 :** the interval between two frequencies (as in an electromagnetic spectrum) having a ratio of 2 to 1 **5 :** a group of eight

oc·ta·vo \äk-'tā-(,)vō, -'tä-\ *n, pl* **-vos** [L, abl. of *octavus* eighth] (1582) : the size of a piece of paper cut eight from a sheet; *also* : a book, a page, or paper of this size

oc·tet \äk-'tet\ *n* (1879) **1 :** a group or set of eight: as **a :** OCTAVE 2b **b :** the performers of an octet **2 :** a musical composition for eight instruments or voices

oc·til·lion \äk-'til-yən\ *n* [F, fr. MF, fr. *oct-* octa- + *-illion* (as in *million*)] (1690) — see NUMBER table

Oc·to·ber \äk-'tō-bər\ *n* [ME *Octobre*, fr. OE & OF; OE *October*, fr. L, 8th month of the early Roman calendar, fr. *octo;* OF, fr. L *October*] (bef. 12c) : the 10th month of the Gregorian calendar

oc·to·de·cil·lion \,äk-tō-di-'sil-yən\ *n* [L *octodecim* eighteen + E *-illion* (as in *million*)] (1939) — see NUMBER table

oc·to·ge·nar·i·an \,äk-tə-jə-'ner-ē-ən\ *n* [L *octogenarius* containing eighty, fr. *octogeni* eighty each, fr. *octoginta* eighty, fr. *octo* eight + *-ginta* (akin to *viginti* twenty) — more at VIGESIMAL] (1815) : a person whose age is in the eighties — **octogenarian** *adj*

oc·to·ploid \'äk-tə-,plȯid\ *adj* [ISV] (1925) : having a chromosome number eight times the basic haploid chromosome number — **octoploid** *n*

oc·to·pod \'äk-tə-,päd\ *n* [ultim. fr. Gk *oktōpod-, oktōpous* scorpion, fr. *oktō-* octa- + *pod-, pous* foot — more at FOOT] (ca. 1836) : any of an order (Octopoda) of cephalopod mollusks (as an octopus or argonaut) that have eight arms bearing sessile suckers — **octopod** *adj*

oc·to·pus \'äk-tə-pəs, -,pùs\ *n, pl* **-pus·es** or **-pi** \-,pī\ [NL *Octopod-, Octopus*, fr. Gk *oktō-pous*] (1758) **1 :** any of a genus (*Octopus*) of cephalopod mollusks that have eight muscular arms equipped with two rows of suckers; *broadly* : any octopod excepting the paper nautilus **2 :** something that resembles an octopus esp. in having many centrally directed branches

octopus 1

oc·to·roon \,äk-tə-'rün\ *n* [*octa-* + *-roon* (as in *quadroon*)] (1861) : a person of one-eighth black ancestry

oc·to·syl·lab·ic \,äk-tə-sə-'la-bik\ *adj* [LL *octosyllabus*, fr. Gk *oktasyllabos*, fr. *okta-* octa- + *syllabē* syllable] (ca. 1771) **1 :** consisting of eight syllables **2 :** composed of verses of eight syllables — **octosyllabic** *n*

oc·to·syl·la·ble \'äk-tə-,si-lə-bəl, ,äk-tə-'\ *n* (ca. 1846) : a word or line of eight syllables

oc·to·thorp \'äk-tə-,thȯrp, -tō-\ *n* [*octo-* + *thorp*, of unknown origin; fr. the eight points on its circumference] (1971) : the symbol #

¹oc·u·lar \'ä-kyə-lər\ *adj* [LL *ocularis* of eyes, fr. L *oculus* eye] (ca. 1575) **1 a :** done or perceived by the eye ⟨~ inspection⟩ **b :** based on what has been seen ⟨~ testimony⟩ **2 a :** of or relating to the eye ⟨~ muscles⟩ **b :** resembling an eye in form or function

²ocular *n* (1835) : EYEPIECE

oc·u·lar·ist \'ä-kyə-lə-rist\ *n* (1866) : a person who makes and fits artificial eyes

oc·u·list \'ä-kyə-list\ *n* [F *oculiste*, fr. L *oculus*] (1615) **1 :** OPHTHALMOLOGIST **2 :** OPTOMETRIST

oc·u·lo·mo·tor \,ä-kyə-lə-'mō-tər\ *adj* [L *oculus* eye + E *-o-* + *motor*] (ca. 1890) **1 :** moving or tending to move the eyeball **2 :** of or relating to the oculomotor nerve

oculomotor nerve *n* (1881) : either of the pair of chiefly motor nerves that comprise the 3d pair of cranial nerves, arise from the midbrain, and supply four muscles of the eye

oc·u·lus \'ä-kyə-ləs\ *n, pl* **oc·u·li** \-,lī, -,lē\ [L, lit., eye — more at EYE] (1848) **1 :** a circular or oval window **2 :** a circular opening at the top of a dome

od *or* **odd** \'äd\ *interj, often cap* [euphemism for *God*] (1695) *archaic* — used as a mild oath

¹OD \,ō-'dē\ *n* [*overdose*] (ca. 1960) **1 :** an overdose of a narcotic **2** : one who has taken an OD

²OD *vi* **OD'd** *or* **ODed; OD'·ing; OD's** (1966) **1 :** to become ill or die of an OD **2 :** to have or experience too much of something — used with *on* ⟨~ on television⟩

oda·lisque \'ō-də-l,isk\ *n* [F, fr. Turk *odalık*, fr. *oda* room] (ca. 1681) **1** : a female slave **2 :** a concubine in a harem

odd \'äd\ *adj* [ME *odde*, fr. ON *oddi* point of land, triangle, odd number; akin to OE *ord* point of a weapon] (14c) **1 a :** being without a corresponding mate ⟨an ~ shoe⟩ **b** (1) **:** left over after others are paired or grouped **(2) :** separated from a set or series **2 a :** somewhat more than the indicated approximate quantity, extent, or degree — usu. used in combination ⟨300-*odd* pages⟩ **b** (1) **:** left over as a remainder ⟨had a few ~ dollars for entertainment after paying his bills⟩ **(2) :** constituting a small amount ⟨had some ~ change in her pocket⟩ **3 a :** being any of the integers (as −3, −1, +1, and +3) that are not exactly divisible by two **b :** marked by an odd number of units **c :** being a function such that $f(-x) = -f(x)$ where the sign is reversed but the absolute value remains the same if the sign of the independent variable is reversed **4 a :** not regular, expected, or planned ⟨worked at ~ jobs⟩ **b :** encountered or experienced from time to time : OCCASIONAL **5 :** having an out-of-the-way location : REMOTE **6 :** differing markedly from the usual or ordinary or accepted : PECULIAR *syn* see STRANGE — **odd·ness** *n*

odd·ball \'äd-,bȯl\ *n* (1948) : one that is eccentric — **oddball** *adj*

Odd Fellow *n* [Independent Order of *Odd Fellows*] (1795) : a member of a major benevolent and fraternal order

odd·i·ty \'ä-də-tē\ *n, pl* **-ties** (1713) **1 :** an odd person, thing, event, or trait **2 :** the quality or state of being odd

odd lot *n* (1897) : a number or quantity other than the usual unit in transactions; *esp* : a quantity of less than 100 shares of stock

odd·ly \'äd-lē\ *adv* (1610) **1 :** in an odd manner **2 :** it is odd that ⟨was quite happy, ~ enough⟩

odd man out *n* (1923) : a person who differs from the other members of a group

odd·ment \'äd-mənt\ *n* (1796) **1 a :** something left over : REMNANT **b** *pl* **:** ODDS AND ENDS **2 :** something odd : ODDITY

odd permutation *n* (1929) : a permutation that is produced by the successive application of an odd number of interchanges of pairs of elements

odd–pin·nate \'äd-'pi-,nāt\ *adj* (ca. 1890) : having leaflets on each side of the petiole and having a single leaflet at the tip of the petiole — **odd–pin·nate·ly** *adv*

odds \'ädz\ *n but sing or pl in constr* (ca. 1520) **1 a** *archaic* : INEQUALITIES **b** *obs* : degree of unlikeness **2 a :** an amount by which one thing exceeds or falls short of another ⟨won the election by considerable ~⟩ **b** (1) **:** a difference favoring one of two opposed things ⟨overwhelming ~⟩ **(2) :** a difference in terms of advantage or disadvantage ⟨what's the ~, if thinking so makes them happy —Flora Thompson⟩ **c** (1) **:** the probability that one thing is so or will happen rather than another : CHANCES ⟨the ~ are against it⟩ **(2) :** the ratio of the probability of one event to that of an alternative event **3** : DISAGREEMENT, VARIANCE — usu. used with *at* ⟨faculty and administration often are at ~ on everything —W. E. Brock b1930⟩ **4 a** : special favor : PARTIALITY **b :** an allowance granted by one making a bet to one accepting the bet and designed to equalize the chances favoring one of the bettors **c :** the ratio between the amount to be paid off for a winning bet and the amount of the bet — **by all odds :** in every way : without question ⟨by all odds the best book of the year⟩

odds and ends *n pl* (ca. 1746) **1 a :** miscellaneous articles **b :** miscellaneous small matters (as of business) to be attended to **2 :** miscellaneous remnants or leftovers ⟨odds and ends of food⟩

odds-maker \'ädz-,mā-kər\ *n* (ca. 1949) : one who figures odds

odds–on \'ädz-'ȯn, -'än\ *adj* (1890) **1 :** having or viewed as having a better than even chance to win ⟨the ~ favorite⟩ **2 :** not involving much risk : pretty sure ⟨an ~ bet⟩

odd trick *n* (1897) : each trick in excess of six won by declarer's side at bridge — compare BOOK 9

ode \'ōd\ *n* [MF or LL; MF, fr. LL, fr. Gk *ōidē*, lit., song, fr. *aeidein, aidein* to sing; akin to Gk *audē* voice] (1588) : a lyric poem usu. marked by exaltation of feeling and style, varying length of line, and complexity of stanza forms — **od·ist** \-ist\ *n*

-ode *n comb form* [Gk *-odos*, fr. *hodos*] **1 :** way : path ⟨electrode⟩ **2** : electrode ⟨diode⟩

ode·um \ō-'dē-əm, 'ō-dē-\ *n, pl* **odea** \-ə\ [L & Gk; L, fr. Gk *ōideion*, fr. *ōidē* song] (1616) **1 :** a small roofed theater of ancient Greece and Rome used chiefly for competitions in music and poetry **2 :** a theater or concert hall

od·ic \'ō-dik\ *adj* (1863) : of, relating to, or forming an ode

Odin \'ō-d⁵n\ *n* [Dan, fr. ON *Ōthinn*] : the supreme god and creator in Norse mythology

odi·ous \'ō-dē-əs\ *adj* [ME, fr. MF *odieus*, fr. L *odiosus*, fr. *odium*] (14c) : exciting or deserving hatred or repugnance ⟨~ associates⟩ ⟨an ~ business⟩ — **odi·ous·ly** *adv* — **odi·ous·ness** *n*

odi·um \'ō-dē-əm\ *n* [L, hatred, fr. *odisse* to hate; akin to OE *atol* terrible, Gk *odyssasthai* to be angry] (1602) **1 :** the state or fact of being subjected to hatred and contempt as a result of a despicable act or blameworthy circumstance **2 :** hatred and condemnation accompanied by loathing or contempt : DETESTATION **3 :** disrepute or infamy attached to something : OPPROBRIUM

odom·e·ter \ō-'dä-mə-tər\ *n* [F *odomètre*, fr. Gk *hodometron*, fr. *hodos* way, road + *metron* measure — more at MEASURE] (1791) : an instrument for measuring the distance traveled (as by a vehicle)

odo·nate \'ō-dⁿ-,āt, ō-'dä-(,)nāt\ *n* [irreg. fr. Gk *odous, odōn* tooth] (1947) : any of an order (Odonata) of predaceous insects comprising the dragonflies and damselflies — **odonate** *adj*

odont- *or* **odonto-** *comb form* [F, fr. Gk, *odont-, odous* — more at TOOTH] : tooth ⟨odontoblast⟩

-odont *adj comb form* [Gk *odont-, odous* tooth] : having teeth of a (specified) nature ⟨acrodont⟩

-odontia *n comb form* [NL, fr. Gk *odont-, odous*] : form, condition, or mode of treatment of the teeth ⟨orthodontia⟩

odon·to·blast \ō-'dän-tə-,blast\ *n* [ISV] (1878) : any of the elongated radially arranged cells on the surface of the dental pulp that secrete dentin — **odon·to·blas·tic** \-,dän-tə-'blas-tik\ *adj*

odon·to·glos·sum \ō-,dän-tə-'glä-səm\ *n* [NL, fr. Gk *odont-* + *glōssa* tongue — more at GLOSS] (1880) : any of a genus (*Odontoglossum*) of widely cultivated tropical American orchids

odon·toid process \ō-'dän-,tȯid-\ *n* (ca. 1819) : a toothlike process projecting from the anterior end of the centrum of the axis vertebra on which the atlas vertebra rotates

odor \'ō-dər\ *n* [ME *odour*, fr. MF, fr. L *odor;* akin to L *olēre* to smell, Gk *ozein* to smell, *osmē* smell, odor] (13c) **1 a :** a quality of something that stimulates the olfactory organ : SCENT **b :** a sensation resulting from adequate stimulation of the olfactory organ : SMELL **2 a** : a characteristic or predominant quality : FLAVOR ⟨the ~ of sanctity⟩ **b :** REPUTE, ESTIMATION ⟨in bad ~⟩ **3** *archaic* : something that emits a sweet or pleasing scent : PERFUME *syn* see SMELL — **odored** \'ō-dərd\ *adj* — **odor·less** \-dər-ləs\ *adj*

odor·ant \'ō-də-rənt\ *n* (1935) : an odorous substance; *esp* : one added to a dangerous odorless substance to warn of its presence

---

\ə\ abut \ᵊ\ kitten, F table \ər\ further \a\ ash \ā\ ace \ä\ mop, mar
\aù\ out \ch\ chin \e\ bet \ē\ easy \g\ go \i\ hit \ī\ ice \j\ job
\ŋ\ sing \ō\ go \ȯ\ law \ȯi\ boy \th\ thin \t̲h̲\ the \ü\ loot \ù\ foot
\y\ yet \zh\ vision \ȧ, k̲, ⁿ, œ, œ̄, ᵫ, ᵫ̄, ᵊ\ see Guide to Pronunciation

odor·if·er·ous \ˌō-də-'ri-f(ə-)rəs\ *adj* (15c) **1** : yielding an odor : ODOROUS **2** : morally offensive — **odor·if·er·ous·ly** *adv* — **odor·if·er·ous·ness** *n*

odor·ize \'ō-də-ˌrīz\ *vt* **-ized; -iz·ing** (1884) : to make odorous : SCENT

odor·ous \'ō-də-rəs\ *adj* (15c) : having an odor: as **a** : FRAGRANT **b** : MALODOROUS — **odor·ous·ly** *adv* — **odor·ous·ness** *n*
syn ODOROUS, FRAGRANT, REDOLENT, AROMATIC mean emitting and diffusing scent. ODOROUS applies to whatever has a strong distinctive smell whether pleasant or unpleasant ⟨*odorous* cheeses should be tightly wrapped⟩. FRAGRANT applies to things (as flowers or spices) with sweet or agreeable odors ⟨a *fragrant* rose⟩. REDOLENT applies usu. to a place or thing impregnated with odors ⟨the kitchen was *redolent* of garlic and tomatoes⟩. AROMATIC applies to things emitting pungent often fresh odors ⟨an *aromatic* blend of tobaccos⟩.

odour *chiefly Brit var of* ODOR

Odys·se·an \ˌä-də-'sē-ən ("*Odysseus*"), ˌä-də-'sē-ən ("*journey*")\ *adj* (ca. 1711) : of, relating to, or characteristic of Odysseus or his journey

Odys·seus \ō-'di-sē-əs, -'dis-yəs, -'di-shəs, -'di-ˌshüs\ *n* [Gk] : a king of Ithaca and Greek leader in the Trojan War who after the war wanders 10 years before reaching home

od·ys·sey \'ä-də-sē\ *n, pl* **-seys** [the *Odyssey*, epic poem attributed to Homer recounting the long wanderings of Odysseus] (1889) **1** : a long wandering or voyage usu. marked by many changes of fortune **2** : an intellectual or spiritual wandering or quest

oe·cu·men·i·cal *esp Brit* ˌē-\ *var of* ECUMENICAL

oe·de·ma *chiefly Brit var of* EDEMA

oe·di·pal \'e-də-pəl, 'ē-\ *adj, often cap* (1939) : of, relating to, or resulting from the Oedipus complex — **oe·di·pal·ly** \-pə-lē\ *adv, often cap*

¹Oe·di·pus \-pəs\ *n* [L, fr. Gk *Oidipous*] : the son of Laius and Jocasta who in fulfillment of an oracle unknowingly kills his father and marries his mother

²Oedipus *adj* (1910) : OEDIPAL

Oedipus complex *n* (1910) : the positive libidinal feelings of a child toward the parent of the opposite sex and hostile or jealous feelings toward the parent of the same sex that may be a source of adult personality disorder when unresolved

oeil–de–boeuf \ˌə(r)-də-'bəf, ˌəi-\ *n, pl* **oeils–de–boeuf** *same*\ [F *œil-de-bœuf*, lit., ox's eye] (1849) : OCULUS 1

oeil·lade \ˌə(r)-'yäd, œ-yäd\ *n* [MF *œillade*, fr. *oeil* eye, fr. L *oculus* — more at EYE] (1592) : a glance of the eye; *esp* : OGLE

OEM \ˌō-(ˌ)ē-'em\ *n* [original equipment manufacturer] (1968) : one that produces complex equipment (as a computer system) from components usu. bought from other manufacturers

oe·nol·o·gy *var of* ENOLOGY

Oe·no·ne \ē-'nō-nē\ *n* [L, fr. Gk *Oinōnē*] : a nymph who is abandoned by her husband Paris for Helen of Troy

oe·no·phile \'ē-nə-ˌfil\ *n* [F *œnophile*, fr. *œno-* (fr. Gk *oinos* wine) + *-phile* -phile — more at WINE] (1930) : a lover or connoisseur of wine

¹o'er \'ȯr, 'ȯ(ə)r\ *adv* (1592) : OVER

²o'er *prep* (1593) : OVER

oer·sted \'ər-stəd\ *n* [Hans Christian *Oersted*] (1930) : the unit of magnetic field strength in the centimeter-gram-second system

oe·soph·a·gus *chiefly Brit var of* ESOPHAGUS

oestr- or **oestro-** *chiefly Brit var of* ESTR-

oeu·vre \'œvr'\ *n, pl* **oeuvres** *same*\ [F *œuvre*, lit., work, fr. L *opera* — more at OPERA] (1875) : a substantial body of work constituting the lifework of a writer, an artist, or a composer

¹of \əv, *before consonants* əv; 'əv, 'äv\ *prep* [ME, off, of, fr. OE, adv. & prep.; akin to OHG *aba* off, away, L *ab* from, away, Gk *apo*] (bef. 12c) **1** — used as a function word to indicate a point of reckoning ⟨north ~ the lake⟩ **2** — used as a function word to indicate origin or derivation ⟨a man ~ noble birth⟩ **b** — used as a function word to indicate the cause, motive, or reason ⟨died ~ flu⟩ **c** : BY ⟨plays ~ Shakespeare⟩ **d** : on the part of ⟨very kind ~ you⟩ **3** — used as a function word to indicate the component material, parts, or elements or the contents ⟨throne ~ gold⟩ ⟨cup ~ water⟩ **4 a** — used as a function word to indicate the whole that includes the part denoted by the preceding word ⟨most ~ the army⟩ **b** — used as a function word to indicate a whole or quantity from which a part is removed or expended ⟨gave ~ his time⟩ **5 a** : relating to : ABOUT ⟨stories ~ her travels⟩ **b** : in respect to ⟨slow ~ speech⟩ **6 a** — used as a function word to indicate belonging or a possessive relationship ⟨king ~ England⟩ **b** — used as a function word to indicate relationship between a result determined by a function or operation and a basic entity (as an independent variable) ⟨a function ~ x⟩ ⟨the product ~ two numbers⟩ **7** — used as a function word to indicate something from which a person or thing is delivered ⟨eased ~ her pain⟩ or with respect to which someone or something is made destitute ⟨robbed ~ all their belongings⟩ **8 a** — used as a function word to indicate a particular example belonging to the class denoted by the preceding noun ⟨the city ~ Rome⟩ **b** — used as a function word to indicate apposition ⟨that fool ~ a husband⟩ **9 a** — used as a function word to indicate the object of an action denoted or implied by the preceding noun ⟨love ~ nature⟩ **b** — used as a function word to indicate the application of a verb ⟨cheats him ~ a dollar⟩ or of an adjective ⟨fond ~ candy⟩ **10** — used as a function word to indicate a characteristic or distinctive quality or possession ⟨a woman ~ courage⟩ **11** — used as a function word to indicate the position in time of an action or occurrence ⟨died ~ a Monday⟩ **b** : BEFORE ⟨quarter ~ ten⟩ **12** *archaic* : ON ⟨a plague ~ all cowards —Shak.⟩

²of \əv, *before consonants also* ə\ *verbal auxiliary* [by alter.] (1837) *nonstand* : HAVE — used in place of the contraction *'ve* often in representations of uneducated speech ⟨I could ~ beat them easy —Ring Lardner⟩

ofay \'ō-ˌfā, ō-'\ *n* [origin unknown] (1925) : a white person — usu. used disparagingly

¹off \'ȯf\ *adv* [ME *of*, fr. OE — more at OF] (bef. 12c) **1 a** (1) : away from a place or position ⟨march ~⟩; *specif* : away from land ⟨ship stood ~ to sea⟩ (2) : at a distance in space or time ⟨stood 10 paces ~⟩ ⟨a long way ~⟩ **b** : from a course : ASIDE ⟨turned ~ into a bypath⟩; *specif* : away from the wind **c** : into an unconscious state ⟨dozed ~⟩ **2 a** : so as to be separated from support ⟨rolled to the edge of the table and ~⟩ or close contact ⟨blew the lid ~⟩ ⟨the handle came ~⟩ **b** : so as to

be divided ⟨surface marked ~ into squares⟩ **3 a** : to a state of discontinuance or suspension ⟨shut ~ an engine⟩ **b** — used as an intensifier ⟨drink ~ a glass⟩ ⟨finish it ~⟩ **4** : in absence from or suspension of regular work or service ⟨take time ~ for lunch⟩ **5** : OFFSTAGE

²off *prep* (bef. 12c) **1 a** — used as a function word to indicate physical separation or distance from a position of rest, attachment, or union ⟨take it ~ the table⟩ ⟨a path ~ the main walk⟩ ⟨a shop just ~ the main street⟩ **b** : to seaward of ⟨two miles ~ shore⟩ **2** — used as a function word to indicate the object of an action ⟨borrowed a dollar ~ him⟩ ⟨dined ~ oysters⟩ **3 a** — used as a function word to indicate the suspension of an occupation or activity ⟨~ duty⟩ ⟨~ liquor⟩ **b** : below the usual standard or level of ⟨~ his game⟩

³off *adj* (1666) **1 a** : more removed or distant ⟨the ~ side of the building⟩ **b** : SEAWARD **c** : RIGHT **2 a** : started on the way ⟨~ on a spree⟩ **b** : not taking place or staying in effect : CANCELED ⟨the deal was ~⟩ **c** : not operating **d** : not placed so as to permit operation **3 a** : not corresponding to fact : INCORRECT ⟨~ in his reckoning⟩ **b** : POOR, SUBNORMAL **c** : not entirely sane : ECCENTRIC **d** : REMOTE, SLIGHT ⟨~ a chance⟩ **4 a** : spent off duty ⟨reading on his ~ days⟩ **b** : SLACK ⟨~ season⟩ **5 a** : OFF-COLOR **b** : INFERIOR ⟨~ grade of oil⟩; *also* : affected with putrefaction **c** : DOWN ⟨stocks were ~⟩ **6** : CIRCUMSTANCED ⟨worse ~⟩

⁴off *vi* (1717) : to go away : DEPART — used chiefly as an imperative ⟨~, or I'll shoot⟩ ~ *vt, slang* : KILL, MURDER

of·fal \'ȯ-fəl, 'ä-\ *n* [ME, fr. *of* off + *fall*] (14c) **1** : the waste or by-product of a process: as **a** : trimmings of a hide **b** : the by-products of milling used esp. for stock feeds **c** : the viscera and trimmings of a butchered animal removed in dressing **2** : RUBBISH

off and on *adv* (1535) : with periodic cessation : INTERMITTENTLY ⟨rained *off and on* all day⟩

¹off·beat \'ȯf-ˌbēt\ *n* (ca. 1928) : the unaccented beat of a musical measure

²off·beat \-'bēt\ *adj* (1938) : ECCENTRIC, UNCONVENTIONAL

off Broadway *n, often cap O* [fr. its usu. being produced in smaller theaters outside of the Broadway theatrical district] (1954) : a part of the New York professional theater stressing fundamental and artistic values and formerly engaging in experimentation — **off–Broadway** *adj or adv, often cap O*

off-cast \'ȯf-ˌkast\ *adj* (1571) : cast off : DISCARDED — **offcast** *n*

off–col·or \'ȯf-'kə-lər\ *or* **off–col·ored** \-lərd\ *adj* (1860) **1 a** : not having the right or standard color **b** : being out of sorts **2 a** : of doubtful propriety : DUBIOUS **b** : verging on the indecent

off-cut \'ȯf-ˌkət\ *n* (ca. 1664) *chiefly Brit* : something that is cut off (as a waste piece of lumber)

of·fend \ə-'fend\ *vb* [ME, fr. MF *offendre*, fr. L *offendere* to strike against, offend, fr. *ob-* against + *-fendere* to strike — more at OB-, DEFEND] *vi* (14c) **1 a** : to transgress the moral or divine law : SIN ⟨if it be a sin to covet honor, I am the most ~*ing* soul alive —Shak.⟩ **b** : to violate a law or rule : do wrong ⟨~ against the law⟩ **2 a** : to cause difficulty, discomfort, or injury ⟨took off his shoe and removed the ~*ing* pebble⟩ **b** : to cause dislike, anger, or vexation ⟨thoughtless words that ~ needlessly⟩ ~ *vt* **1 a** : VIOLATE, TRANSGRESS **b** : to cause pain to : HURT **2** *obs* : to cause to sin or fall **3** : to cause to feel vexation or resentment usu. by violation of what is proper or fitting ⟨was ~*ed* by their language⟩ — **of·fend·er** *n*
syn OFFEND, OUTRAGE, AFFRONT, INSULT mean to cause hurt feelings or deep resentment. OFFEND need not imply an intentional hurting but it may indicate merely a violation of the victim's sense of what is proper or fitting ⟨hoped that my remarks had not *offended* her⟩. OUTRAGE implies offending beyond endurance and calling forth extreme feelings ⟨*outraged* by their accusations⟩. AFFRONT implies treating with deliberate rudeness or contemptuous indifference to courtesy ⟨deeply *affronted* by his callousness⟩. INSULT suggests deliberately causing humiliation, hurt pride, or shame ⟨managed to *insult* every guest at the party⟩.

of·fense *or* **of·fence** \ə-'fen(t)s, *esp for 3* 'ä-ˌfen(t)s, 'ȯ-\ *n* [ME, fr. MF, fr. L *offensa*, fr. fem. of *offensus*, pp. of *offendere*] (14c) **1 a** *obs* : an act of stumbling **b** *archaic* : a cause or occasion of sin : STUMBLING BLOCK **2** : something that outrages the moral or physical senses **3 a** : the act of attacking : ASSAULT **b** : the means or method of attacking or of attempting to score **c** : the offensive team or members of a team playing offensive positions **d** : scoring ability **4 a** : the act of displeasing or affronting **b** : the state of being insulted or morally outraged ⟨takes ~ at the slightest criticism⟩ **5 a** : a breach of a moral or social code : SIN, MISDEED **b** : an infraction of law; *esp* : MISDEMEANOR — **of·fense·less** \-ləs\ *adj*
syn OFFENSE, RESENTMENT, UMBRAGE, PIQUE, DUDGEON, HUFF mean an emotional response to or an emotional state resulting from a slight or indignity. OFFENSE implies hurt displeasure ⟨takes deep *offense* at racial slurs⟩. RESENTMENT suggests a longer lasting indignation or smoldering ill will ⟨harbored a lifelong *resentment* of his brother⟩. UMBRAGE may suggest hurt pride, resentment, or suspicion of another's motives ⟨took *umbrage* at the offer of advice⟩. PIQUE applies to a transient feeling of wounded vanity ⟨in a *pique* I foolishly declined the invitation⟩. DUDGEON suggests an angry fit of indignation ⟨stormed out of the meeting in high *dudgeon*⟩. HUFF implies a peevish short-lived spell of anger usu. at a petty cause ⟨in a *huff* he slammed the door⟩.
syn OFFENSE, SIN, VICE, CRIME, SCANDAL mean a transgression of law. OFFENSE applies to the infraction of any law, rule, or code ⟨at that school no *offense* went unpunished⟩. SIN implies an offense against moral or religious law ⟨the *sin* of blasphemy⟩. VICE applies to a habit or practice that degrades or corrupts ⟨regarded gambling as a *vice*⟩. CRIME implies a serious offense punishable by the law of the state ⟨the *crime* of murder⟩. SCANDAL applies to an offense that outrages the public conscience ⟨a career ruined by a sex *scandal*⟩.

¹of·fen·sive \ə-'fen(t)-siv, *esp for 1* 'ä-ˌfen(t)-, 'ȯ-\ *adj* (ca. 1548) **1 a** : making attack : AGGRESSIVE **b** : of, relating to, or designed for attack ⟨~ weapons⟩ **c** : of or relating to an attempt to score in a game or contest; *also* : of or relating to a team in possession of the ball or puck **2** : giving painful or unpleasant sensations : NAUSEOUS, OBNOXIOUS ⟨~ odor of garbage⟩ **3** : causing displeasure or resentment — **of·fen·sive·ly** *adv* — **of·fen·sive·ness** *n*

²offensive *n* (1720) **1** : the act of an attacking party **2** : ATTACK

¹of·fer \'ȯ-fər, 'ä-\ *vb* **of·fered; of·fer·ing** \-f(ə-)riŋ\ [ME *offren*, in sense 1, fr. OE *offrian*, fr. LL *offerre*, fr. L, to present, tender, fr. *ob*- toward + *ferre* to carry; in other senses, fr. OF *offrir*, fr. L *offerre* — more at BEAR] *vt* (bef. 12c) **1 a :** to present as an act of worship or devotion : SACRIFICE **b :** to utter (as a prayer) in devotion **2 a :** to present for acceptance or rejection : TENDER ⟨was *~ed* a job⟩ **b :** to present in order to satisfy a requirement ⟨candidates for degrees may *~* French as one of their foreign languages⟩ **3 a :** PROPOSE, SUGGEST ⟨*~* a solution to a problem⟩ **b :** to declare one's readiness or willingness ⟨*~ed* to help me⟩ **4 a :** to try or begin to exert : PUT UP ⟨*~ed* stubborn resistance⟩ **b :** THREATEN ⟨*~ed* to strike him with his cane⟩ **5 :** to make available : AFFORD; *esp :* to place (merchandise) on sale **6 :** to present in performance or exhibition **7 :** to propose as payment : BID *~ vi* **1 :** to present something as an act of worship or devotion : SACRIFICE **2** *archaic :* to make an attempt **3 :** to present itself **4 :** to make a proposal (as of marriage)

²**offer** *n* (15c) **1 a :** a presenting of something for acceptance ⟨considering job *~s* from several firms⟩ ⟨an *~* of marriage⟩ **b :** an undertaking to do an act or give something on condition that the party to whom the proposal is made do some specified act or make a return promise **2** *obs :* OFFERING **3 :** a price named by one proposing to buy : BID **4 :** ATTEMPT, TRY **b :** an action or movement indicating a purpose or intention — **on offer** *chiefly Brit :* being offered esp. for sale

of·fer·ing \'ò-f(ə-)riŋ, 'ä-\ *n* (bef. 12c) **1 a :** the act of one who offers **b :** something offered; *esp :* a sacrifice ceremonially offered as a part of worship **c :** a contribution to the support of a church **2 :** something offered for sale or patronage ⟨latest *~s* of the leading novelists⟩ **3 :** a course of instruction or study

of·fer·to·ry \'ò-fə(r)-,tör-ē, ä-, -,tòr-\ *n, pl* **-ries** [ML *offertorium*, fr. LL *offerre*] (1539) **1** *often cap* **a :** the eucharistic offering of bread and wine to God before they are consecrated at Communion **b :** a verse from a Psalm said or sung at the beginning of the offertory **2 a :** the period of collection and presentation of the offerings of the congregation at public worship **b :** a musical composition played or sung during an offertory

¹**off·hand** \'òf-'hand, -,hand\ *adv* (1694) **:** without premeditation or preparation : EXTEMPORE ⟨couldn't give the figures *~*⟩

²**offhand** *adj* (1708) **1 :** CASUAL, INFORMAL ⟨a relaxed, *~* manner⟩ **2 :** done or made offhand ⟨*~* excuses⟩

off·hand·ed \-'han-dəd, -,han-\ *adj* (1835) **:** OFFHAND — **off·hand·ed·ly** *adv* — **off·hand·ed·ness** *n*

off–hour \'òf-,aü(-ə)r\ *n* (1932) **1 :** a period of time other than a rush hour **2 :** a period of time other than regular business hours

of·fice \'ä-fəs, 'ò-\ *n* [ME, fr. MF, fr. L *officium* service, duty, office, fr. *opus* work + *facere* to make, do — more at OPERATE, DO] (13c) **1 a :** a special duty, charge, or position conferred by an exercise of governmental authority and for a public purpose : a position of authority to exercise a public function and to receive whatever emoluments may belong to it **b :** a postion of responsibility or some degree of executive authority **2** [ME, fr. OF, fr. LL *officium*, fr. L] **:** a prescribed form or service of worship; *specif, cap :* DIVINE OFFICE **3 :** a religious or social ceremonial observance : RITE **4 :** something that one ought to do or must do : an assigned or assumed duty, task, or role **b :** the proper or customary action of something : FUNCTION **c :** something done for another : SERVICE **5 :** a place where a particular kind of business is transacted or a service is supplied: as **a :** a place in which the functions of a public officer are performed **b :** the directing headquarters of an enterprise or organization **c :** the place in which a professional person conducts business **6** *pl, chiefly Brit :* the apartments, attached buildings, or outhouses in which the activities attached to the service of a house are carried on **7 a :** a major administrative unit in some governments ⟨British Foreign *Office*⟩ **b :** a subdivision of some government departments ⟨Patent *Office*⟩ *syn* see FUNCTION

office boy *n* (1846) **:** a boy or man employed for odd jobs in a business office

of·fice·hold·er \-,hōl-dər\ *n* (1818) **:** one holding a public office

¹**of·fi·cer** \'ä-fə-sər, 'ò-\ *n* [ME, fr. MF *officier*, fr. ML *officiarius*, fr. L *officium*] (14c) **1 a** *obs :* AGENT **b :** one charged with police duties **2 :** one who holds an office of trust, authority, or command ⟨the *~s* of the bank⟩ **3 :** one who holds a position of authority or command in the armed forces; *specif :* COMMISSIONED OFFICER **b :** the master or any of the mates of a merchant or passenger ship

²**officer** *vt* (1670) **1 :** to furnish with officers **2 :** to command or direct as an officer

officer of arms (ca. 1500) **:** any of the officers (as king of arms, herald, or pursuivant) of a monarch or government responsible for devising and granting armorial bearings

¹**of·fi·cial** \ə-'fi-shəl *also* ō-\ *n* (14c) **1 :** one who holds or is invested with an office : OFFICER ⟨government *~s*⟩ **2 :** one who administers the rules of a game or sport esp. as a referee or umpire

²**official** *adj* (ca. 1604) **1 :** of or relating to an office, position, or trust ⟨*~* duties⟩ **2 :** holding an office **3 a :** AUTHORITATIVE, AUTHORIZED ⟨*~* statement⟩ **b :** prescribed or recognized as authorized ⟨an *~* language⟩ **c :** described by the U.S. Pharmacopeia or the National Formulary **4 :** befitting or characteristic of a person in office ⟨extended an *~* greeting⟩ — **of·fi·cial·ly** \-'fi-sh(ə-)lē\ *adv*

of·fi·cial·dom \ə-'fi-shəl-dəm\ *n* (1863) **:** officials as a class

of·fi·cial·ese \-,fi-shə-'lēz, -'lēs\ *n* (1884) **:** the characteristic language of official statements : wordy, pompous, or obscure language

of·fi·cial·ism \-'fi-shə-,li-zəm\ *n* (1857) **:** lack of flexibility and initiative combined with excessive adherence to regulations in the behavior of usu. government officials

of·fi·ci·ant \ə-'fi-shē-ənt\ *n* (1844) **:** one (as a priest) that officiates at a religious rite

¹**of·fi·ci·ary** \ə-'fi-shē-,er-ē, ò-, ä-\ *n, pl* **-ar·ies** [ML *officiarius*] (1611) **1 :** OFFICER, OFFICIAL **2 :** a body of officers or officials

²**officiary** *adj* (1612) **:** connected with, derived from, or having a title or rank by virtue of holding an office ⟨*~* earl⟩

of·fi·ci·ate \ə-'fi-shē-,āt\ *vb* **-at·ed; -at·ing** *vi* (1631) **1 :** to carry out (an official duty or function) **2 :** to serve as a leader or celebrant of (a ceremony) **3 :** to administer the rules of (a game or sport) esp. as a referee or umpire *~ vi* **1 :** to perform a ceremony, function, or duty ⟨*~* at a wedding⟩ **2 :** to act in an official capacity : act as an official (as at a sports contest) — **of·fi·ci·a·tion** \-,fi-shē-'ā-shən\ *n*

of·fi·ci·nal \ə-'fi-s²n-əl, ò-, ä-; ,ò-fə-'sī-n²l, ,ä-\ *adj* [ML *officinalis* of a

storeroom, fr. *officina* storeroom, fr. L, workshop, fr. *opific-, opifex* workman, fr. *opus* work + *facere* to do] (ca. 1720) **:** MEDICINAL ⟨a monograph on *~* flora⟩

of·fi·cious \ə-'fi-shəs\ *adj* [L *officiosus*, fr. *officium* service, office] (1565) **1** *archaic* **a :** KIND, OBLIGING **b :** DUTIFUL **2 :** volunteering one's services where they are neither asked nor needed : MEDDLESOME **3 :** INFORMAL, UNOFFICIAL *syn* see IMPERTINENT — **of·fi·cious·ly** *adv* — **of·fi·cious·ness** *n*

off·ing \'ò-fiŋ, 'ä-\ *n* [¹*off*] (1627) **1 :** the part of the deep sea seen from the shore **2 :** the near or foreseeable future ⟨in the *~*⟩

off·ish \'ò-fish\ *adj* [¹*off*] (1831) **:** STANDOFFISH — **off·ish·ness** *n*

off–key \'ò-'kē\ *adj or adv* (1927) **1 :** varying in pitch from the proper tone of a melody **2 :** IRREGULAR, ANOMALOUS

off–kil·ter \-'kil-tər\ *adj* (ca. 1944) **:** not in perfect balance : a bit askew

off–lim·its \'òf-'li-məts\ *adj* (1945) **:** not to be entered or patronized by a designated class (as military personnel); *also :* not to be interfered with, considered, or spoken of ⟨the subject of sex was *~* in her family⟩

off–line \-'līn\ *adj* (1950) **:** not connected to or served by a system and esp. a computer or telecommunications system; *also :* done independently of a system ⟨*~* computer storage⟩ — **off–line** *adv*

off·load \(,)òf-'lōd, 'òf-,\ *vb* (1850) **:** UNLOAD

off of *prep* (1593) **:** OFF

usage The *of* is often criticized as superfluous, a comment that is irrelevant because *off of* is an idiom. It is much more common in speech than in edited writing and is more common in American English than in British.

off–off–Broadway *n, often cap both Os* [fr. its relation to off Broadway being analogous to the relation of off Broadway to Broadway] (1965) **:** an avant-garde theatrical movement in New York — **off–off–Broadway** *adj or adv, often cap both Os*

off–peak \'òf-'pēk\ *adj* (1920) **:** not being in the period of maximum use or business : not peak ⟨telephone rates during *~* hours⟩

off–price \'òf-'prīs\ *adj* (1952) **:** of, relating to, selling, or being discounted merchandise ⟨an *~* store⟩ ⟨*~* apparel⟩

off·print \'òf-,print\ *n* (1885) **:** a separately printed excerpt (as a magazine article) — **offprint** *vt*

off–put·ting \-,pu̇-tiŋ\ *adj* (1828) **:** that puts one off : REPELLENT, DISCONCERTING — **off–put·ting·ly** \-lē\ *adv*

off–ramp \-,ramp\ *n* (1954) **:** a ramp by which one leaves a limited⁻access highway

off–road \'òf-'rōd\ *adj* (1968) **:** of, relating to, done with, or being a vehicle designed esp. to operate away from public roads

off·scour·ing \-,skaü(-ə)r-iŋ\ *n* (1526) **1 :** someone rejected by society : OUTCAST **2 :** something that is scoured off : REFUSE

off–screen \'òf-'skrēn\ *adv or adj* (1935) **1 :** out of sight of the motion picture or television viewer **2 :** in private life

off–sea·son \'òf-,sē-z²n\ *n* (1848) **:** a time of suspended or reduced activity; *esp :* the time during which an athlete is not training or competing

¹**off·set** \'òf-,set\ *n* (ca. 1555) **1 a** *archaic :* OUTSET, START **b :** CESSATION **2 a** (1) **:** a short prostrate lateral shoot arising from the base of a plant (2) **:** a small bulb arising from the base of another bulb **b :** a lateral or collateral branch (as of a family or race) : OFFSHOOT **c :** a spur from a range of hills **3 a :** a horizontal ledge on the face of a wall formed by a diminution of its thickness above **b :** DISPLACEMENT **c :** an abrupt change in the dimension or profile of an object or the part set off by such change **4 :** something that sets off to advantage or embellishes something else : FOIL **5 :** an abrupt bend in an object by which one part is turned aside out of line **6 :** something that serves to counterbalance or to compensate for something else; *esp :* either of two balancing ledger items **7 a :** unintentional transfer of ink (as from a freshly printed sheet) **b :** a printing process in which an inked impression from a plate is first made on a rubber-blanketed cylinder and then transferred to the paper being printed — **offset** *adj or adv*

²**off·set** \'òf-,set, *vt senses are also* òf-'\ *vb* **-set; -set·ting** *vt* (1792) **1 a :** to place over against something : BALANCE ⟨credits *~* debits⟩ **b :** to serve as a counterbalance for : COMPENSATE ⟨his speed *~* his opponent's greater weight⟩ *~ vi :* to form an offset in ⟨*~* a wall⟩ *~ vi :* to become marked by offset

off·shoot \'òf-,shüt\ *n* (1710) **1 a :** a collateral or derived branch, descendant, or member : OUTGROWTH **b :** a lateral branch (as of a mountain range) **2 :** a branch of a main stem esp. of a plant

¹**off·shore** \'òf-'shòr, -'shòr\ *adv* (1720) **1 :** from the shore : SEAWARD; *also :* at a distance from the shore **2 :** outside the country : ABROAD

²**off·shore** \'òf-,\ *adj* (1845) **1 :** coming or moving away from the shore toward the water ⟨an *~* breeze⟩ **2 a :** situated off the shore but within waters under a country's control ⟨*~* fisheries⟩ **b :** distant from the shore — compare INSHORE **3 :** situated or operating in a foreign country ⟨*~* mutual funds⟩ ⟨*~* banking⟩

³**off·shore** \'òf-,\ *prep* (1965) **:** off the shore of

off·side \'òf-'sīd\ *adv or adj* (1867) **:** illegally in advance of the ball or puck

off–site \-'sīt\ *adj or adv* (1946) **:** not located or occurring at the site of a particular activity

off–speed \-'spēd\ *adj* (1965) **:** being slower than usual or expected ⟨throwing *~* pitches⟩

off·spring \'òf-,spriŋ\ *n, pl* **offspring** *also* **offsprings** [ME *ofspring*, fr. OE, fr. *of* off + *springan* to spring] (bef. 12c) **1 a :** the progeny of an animal or plant : YOUNG **b :** CHILD **2 a :** PRODUCT, RESULT ⟨scholarly manuscripts—the labored *~s* of PhDs —Donna Martin⟩ **b :** OFFSHOOT 1a

off·stage \'òf-'stāj, -,stāj\ *adv or adj* (1921) **1 :** on a part of the stage not visible to the audience **2 :** in private life ⟨known *~* as a kindly person⟩ **3 :** behind the scenes ⟨much of the public view ⟨much of the important work of the conference was done *~*⟩

\ə\ abut \ᵊ\ kitten, F table \ər\ further \a\ ash \ā\ ace \ä\ mop, mar \aü\ out \ch\ chin \e\ bet \ē\ easy \g\ go \i\ hit \ī\ ice \j\ job \ŋ\ sing \ō\ go \ò\ law \òi\ boy \th\ thin \t͟h\ the \ü\ loot \u̇\ foot \y\ yet \zh\ vision \à, k̟, ⁿ, œ, œ̅, ᵫ, ᵫ̅, ᵊ\ *see* Guide to Pronunciation

off–the–books *adj* (1980) : not reported or recorded ⟨∼ transactions⟩ ⟨∼ covert operations⟩ — **off the books** *adv*

off–the–cuff *adj* (1938) : not prepared in advance : SPONTANEOUS, INFORMAL ⟨∼ remarks⟩ — **off–the–cuff** *adv*

off–the–peg *adj* (1959) *chiefly Brit* : READY-MADE 1

off–the–rack *adj* (1965) : READY-MADE 1 ⟨∼ suits⟩

off–the–record *adj* (1933) : given or made in confidence and not for publication ⟨∼ comments⟩

off–the–shelf *adj* (1950) : available as a stock item : not specially designed or custom-made ⟨made of ∼ components⟩

off–the–wall *adj* (ca. 1966) : highly unusual : BIZARRE ⟨an ∼ sense of humor⟩

off–track \'òf-'trak\ *adv or adj* (1944) : away from a racetrack ⟨betting ∼⟩ ⟨∼ bookies⟩

off–white \'òf-'hwīt, -'wit\ *n* (1927) : a yellowish or grayish white

off year *n* (1873) **1** : a year in which no major election is held **2** : a year of diminished activity or production ⟨an *off year* for auto sales⟩

oft \'òft\ *adv* [ME, fr. OE; akin to OHG *ofto* often] (bef. 12c) : OFTEN

of·ten \'ò-fən, -ˌòf-tən\ *adv* [ME, alter. of *oft*] (14c) : many times : FREQUENTLY

of·ten·times \-ˌtīmz\ *or* **oft·times** \'òf(t)-ˌtīmz\ *adv* (14c) : OFTEN, REPEATEDLY

ogee *also* **OG** \'ō-ˌjē\ *n* [obs. E *ogee* ogive; fr. the use of such moldings in ogives] (1677) **1** : a molding with an S-shaped profile **2** : a pointed arch having on each side a reversed curve near the apex — see ARCH illustration

ogham *or* **ogam** \'ä-gəm, 'ò-; 'ō(-ə)m\ *n* [Ir *ogham*, fr. MIr *ogom, ogum*] (1729) : the alphabetic system of 5th and 6th century Irish in which an alphabet of 20 letters is represented by notches for vowels and lines for consonants and which is known principally from inscriptions cut on the edges of rough standing tombstones — **ogham·ic** \ä-'gä-mik, ō-; 'ō-(ə-)mik\ *adj* — **ogham·ist** \'ä-gə-mist, 'ō-; 'ō-(ə-)mist\ *n*

ogi·val \ō-'jī-vəl\ *adj* (1841) : of, relating to, or having the form of an ogive or an ogee

ogive \'ō-ˌjīv\ *n* [ME *oggif* stone comprising an arch, fr. MF *augive* diagonal arch] (1611) **1 a** : a diagonal arch or rib across a Gothic vault **b** : a pointed arch **2** : a graph of a distribution function or a cumulative frequency distribution **3** : OGEE 1

¹ogle \'ō-gəl *also* 'ä-\ *vb* **ogled; ogling** \-g(ə-)liŋ\ [prob. fr. LG *oegeln*, fr. *oog* eye; akin to OHG *ouga* eye — more at EYE] *vi* (1682) : to glance with amorous invitation or challenge ∼ *vt* **1** : to eye amorously or provocatively **2** : to look at esp. with greedy or interested attention — **ogler** \-g(ə-)lər\ *n*

²ogle *n* (1711) : an amorous or coquettish glance

ogre \'ō-gər\ *n* [F, prob. ultim. fr. L *Orcus*, god of the underworld] (1713) **1** : a hideous giant of fairy tales and folklore that feeds on human beings : MONSTER **2** : a dreaded person or object — **ogre·ish** \'ō-g(ə-)rish\ *adj*

ogress \'ō-g(ə-)rəs\ *n* (1713) : a female ogre

¹oh \(')ō\ *interj* [ME *o*] (13c) **1** — used to express an emotion (as surprise or desire) or in response to physical stimuli **2** — used in direct address ⟨∼, waiter! Will you come here, please?⟩ **3** — used to express acknowledgment or understanding of a statement **4** — used to introduce an example or approximation

²oh \'ō\ *n* [o; fr. the similarity of the symbol for zero (0) to the letter *O*] (1936) : ZERO

ohia \ō-'hē-ə\ *n* [Hawaiian *ōhi'a*] (1824) : LEHUA

ohia lehua *n* [Hawaiian *ōhi'a-lehua*] (1888) : LEHUA

ohm \'ōm\ *n* [Georg Simon *Ohm*] (1867) : the practical meter–kilogram-second unit of electric resistance equal to the resistance of a circuit in which a potential difference of one volt produces a current of one ampere — **ohm·ic** \'ō-mik\ *adj* — **ohm·i·cal·ly** \-mi-k(ə-)lē\ *adv*

ohm·me·ter \'ō(m)-ˌmē-tər\ *n* [ISV] (ca. 1890) : an instrument for indicating resistance in ohms directly

Ohm's law \'ōmz-\ *n* (1863) : a law in electricity: the strength of a direct current is directly proportional to the potential difference and inversely proportional to the resistance of the circuit

-oic *adj suffix* [F *-oïque* (as in *acide caproïque* caproic acid)] : containing carboxyl or a derivative ⟨benz*oic* acid⟩

¹-oid *n suffix* : something resembling a (specified) object or having a (specified) quality ⟨glob*oid*⟩

²-oid *adj suffix* [MF & L; MF *-oïde*, fr. L *-oïdes*, fr. Gk *-oeidēs*, fr. *-o-* + *eidos* appearance, form — more at WISE] : resembling : having the form or appearance of ⟨petal*oid*⟩

oid·i·um \ō-'i-dē-əm\ *n, pl* **-ia** \-dē-ə\ [NL, fr. *o-* + *-idium*] (1857) **1 a** : any of a genus (*Oidium* of the family Moniliaceae) of imperfect fungi many of which are now considered to be conidial stages of various powdery mildews **b** : one of the small conidia borne in chains by various fungi (as an oidium) — called also *arthrospore* **2** : a powdery mildew caused by an oidium esp. in the grape

¹oil \'òi(ə)l\ *n, often attrib* [ME *oile*, fr. OF, fr. L *oleum* olive oil, fr. Gk *elaion*, fr. *elaia* olive] (13c) **1 a** : any of numerous unctuous combustible substances that are liquid or can be liquefied easily on warming, are soluble in ether but not in water, and leave a greasy stain on paper or cloth **b** (1) : PETROLEUM (2) : the petroleum industry **2 a** : a substance (as a cosmetic preparation) of oily consistency ⟨bath ∼⟩ **3 a** : an oil color used by an artist **b** : a painting done in oil colors **4** : unctuous or flattering speech

²oil *vt* (15c) : to smear, rub over, furnish, or lubricate with oil ∼ *vi* : to take on fuel oil — **oil the hand** *or* **oil the palm** : BRIBE, TIP

oil beetle *n* (1658) : any of various blister beetles (genus *Meloe* or a related genus) that emit a yellowish liquid from the leg joints when disturbed

oil·bird \'òi(ə)l-ˌbərd\ *n* (ca. 1890) : a nocturnal bird (*Steatornis caripensis*) of northern So. America and Trinidad that is related to the nightjars, feeds chiefly on the fatty fruits of various palms, and has fatty young from which oil is extracted for use instead of butter — called also *guacharo*

oil cake *n* (1743) : the solid residue after extracting the oil from seeds (as of cotton)

oil·can \'òi(ə)l-ˌkan\ *n* (1839) : a can for oil; *esp* : a spouted can designed to release oil drop by drop (as for lubricating machinery)

oil·cloth \-ˌklòth\ *n* (1796) : cloth treated with oil or paint and used for table and shelf coverings

oil color *n* (1539) **1** : a pigment used for oil paint **2** : OIL PAINT

oiled \'òi(ə)ld\ *adj* (1535) **1** : lubricated, treated, or covered with or as if with oil ⟨∼ paper⟩ **2** *slang* : DRUNK 1a

oil·er \'òi-lər\ *n* (ca. 1846) **1** : one (as a workman) that oils something **2** : a receptacle or device for applying oil **3** *pl* : OILSKIN 3 **4** : an auxiliary naval vessel used for refueling at sea

oil field *n* (1894) : a region rich in petroleum deposits; *esp* : one that has been brought into production

oil gland *n* (ca. 1836) : a gland (as of the skin) that produces an oily secretion; *specif* : UROPYGIAL GLAND

oil·man \'òi(ə)l-mən, -ˌman\ *n* (1865) **1** : an oil company executive **2** : an oil field worker

oil of vitriol (1580) : concentrated sulfuric acid

oil of wintergreen (1866) : the methyl ester of salicylic acid that is used as a flavoring and as a counterirritant

oil paint *n* (1790) : paint in which a drying oil is the vehicle

oil painting *n* (1782) **1 a** : the act or art of painting in oil colors **b** : a picture painted in oils **2** : painting that uses pigments orig. ground in oil

oil palm *n* (ca. 1864) : an African pinnate-leaved palm (*Elaeis guineensis*) cultivated for its clustered fruit whose flesh and seeds yield oil

oil pan *n* (1908) : the lower section of the crankcase used as a lubricating-oil reservoir on an internal combustion engine

oil patch *n* (ca. 1952) **1** : OIL FIELD **2** : the petroleum industry

oil·seed \'òi(ə)l-ˌsēd\ *n* (1562) : a seed or crop (as flaxseed) grown mainly for oil

oil shale *n* (1873) : a rock (as shale) from which oil can be recovered by distillation

oil·skin \'òi(ə)l-ˌskin\ *n* (1812) **1** : an oiled waterproof cloth used for coverings and garments **2** : an oilskin raincoat **3** *pl* : an oilskin suit of coat and trousers

oil slick *n* (1889) : a film of oil floating on water

oil·stone \'òi(ə)l-ˌstōn\ *n* (1585) : a whetstone for use with oil

oil well *n* (1847) : a well from which petroleum is obtained

oily \'òi-lē\ *adj* **oil·i·er; -est** (14c) **1** : of, relating to, or consisting of oil **2 a** : covered or impregnated with oil ⟨∼ rags⟩ **b** : relatively high in naturally secreted oils ⟨∼ skin⟩ ⟨∼ hair⟩ **3** : excessively smooth or suave in manner — **oil·i·ly** \'òi-lə-lē\ *adv* — **oil·i·ness** \-lē-nəs\ *n*

oink \'òiŋk\ *n* [imit.] (1941) : the natural noise of a hog — **oink** *vi*

oint·ment \'òint-mənt\ *n* [ME, alter. of *oignement*, fr. OF, ultim. fr. L *unguentum*, fr. *unguere* to anoint; akin to OHG *ancho* butter, Skt *anakti* he salves] (14c) : a salve or unguent for application to the skin

oi·ti·ci·ca \ˌòi-tə-'sē-kə\ *n* [Pg, fr. Tupi] (1901) : any of several So. American trees; *esp* : a Brazilian tree (*Licania rigida*) with seeds that yield a drying oil similar to tung oil

Ojib·wa *or* **Ojib·way** \ō-'jib-(ˌ)wä\ *n, pl* **Ojibwa** *or* **Ojibwas** *or* **Ojibway** *or* **Ojibways** [Ojibwa *ocïpwe*, an Ojibwa band] (1700) **1** : a member of an American Indian people of the region around Lake Superior and westward **2** : an Algonquian language of the Ojibwa people

¹OK *or* **okay** \ō-'kā, in *assenting or agreeing also* 'ō-ˌkā\ *adv or adj* [abbr. of *oll korrect*, facetious alter. of *all correct*] (1839) : ALL RIGHT

²OK *or* **okay** \ō-'kā\ *n* (1841) : APPROVAL, ENDORSEMENT

³OK *or* **okay** \ō-'kā\ *vt* **OK'd** *or* **okayed; OK'·ing** *or* **okay·ing** (1888) : APPROVE, AUTHORIZE

oka *var of* OCA

oka·pi \ō-'kä-pē\ *n* [Mvu'ba (language of northeast Zaire)] (1900) : an ungulate mammal (*Okapia johnstoni*) of Zaire that is closely related to the giraffe but has a relatively short neck, a coat typically of solid reddish chestnut on the trunk, yellowish white on the cheeks, and purplish black and cream rings on the upper parts of the legs

okey-doke \ˌō-kē-'dōk\ *or* **okey-do·key** \-'dō-kē\ *adv or adj* [redupl. of *OK*] (ca. 1932) — used to express assent

Okie \'ō-kē\ *n* [*Oklahoma* + *-ie*] (1938) : a migrant agricultural worker; *esp* : one from Oklahoma in the 1930s — sometimes used disparagingly

okapi

okra \'ō-krə, *Southern also* -krē\ *n* [of African origin; akin to Ibo *ókùrù* okra] (1679) **1** : a tall annual (*Abelmoschus esculentus*) of the mallow family that is cultivated for its mucilaginous green pods used esp. in soups or stews; *also* : the pods of this plant **2** : ¹GUMBO 1

¹-ol *n suffix* [ISV, fr. *alcohol*] : chemical compound (as an alcohol or phenol) containing hydroxyl ⟨glycer*ol*⟩ ⟨cres*ol*⟩

²-ol — see -OLE

³-ol *n comb form* [ISV, fr. L *oleum* oil — more at OIL] : hydrocarbon chemically related to benzene ⟨xyl*ol*⟩

¹old \'ōld; *for sense* 9 *usu* 'ōl\ *adj* [ME, fr. OE *eald*; akin to OHG *alt* old, L *alere* to nourish, *alescere* to grow, *altus* high, deep] (bef. 12c) **1 a** : dating from the remote past : ANCIENT ⟨∼ traditions⟩ **b** : persisting from an earlier time ⟨an ∼ ailment⟩ ⟨they brought up the same ∼ argument⟩ **c** : of long standing ⟨an ∼ friend⟩ **2 a** : distinguished from an object of the same kind by being of an earlier date ⟨many still used the ∼ name⟩ **b** *cap* : belonging to an early period in the development of a language or literature ⟨*Old* Persian⟩ **3** : having existed for a specified period of time ⟨a girl three years ∼⟩ **4** : of, relating to, or originating in a past era ⟨∼ chronicles record the event⟩ **5 a** : advanced in years or age ⟨an ∼ man⟩ **b** : showing the characteristics of age ⟨looked ∼ at 20⟩ **6** : EXPERIENCED ⟨an ∼ trooper speaking of the last war⟩ **7** : FORMER ⟨his ∼ students⟩ **8 a** : showing the effects of time or use : WORN, AGED ⟨∼ shoes⟩ **b** : well advanced toward reduction by running water to the lowest level possible — used of topographic features **c** : no longer in use : DISCARDED ⟨∼ rags⟩ **d** : of a grayish or dusty color ⟨∼ mauve⟩ **e** : TIRESOME ⟨gets ∼ fast⟩ **9 a** : long familiar ⟨same ∼ story⟩ ⟨good ∼ Joe⟩ **b** — used as an intensive ⟨a high ∼ time⟩ **c** — used to express an attitude of affection or amusement ⟨a big ∼ dog⟩ ⟨flex the ∼ biceps⟩ ⟨any ∼ time⟩

syn OLD, ANCIENT, VENERABLE, ANTIQUE, ANTIQUATED, ARCHAIC, OBSO-

LETE mean having come into existence or use in the more or less distant past. OLD may apply to either actual or merely relative length of existence ⟨*old* houses⟩ ⟨an *old* sweater of mine⟩. ANCIENT applies to occurrence, existence, or use in or survival from the distant past ⟨*ancient* accounts of dragons⟩. VENERABLE stresses the impressiveness and dignity of great age ⟨the family's *venerable* patriarch⟩. ANTIQUE applies to what has come down from a former or ancient time ⟨collected *antique* Chippendale furniture⟩. ANTIQUATED implies being discredited or outmoded or otherwise inappropriate to the present time ⟨*antiquated* teaching methods⟩. ARCHAIC implies having the character or characteristics of a much earlier time ⟨the play used *archaic* language to convey a sense of period⟩. OBSOLETE may apply to something regarded as no longer acceptable or useful even though it is still in existence ⟨a computer that makes earlier models *obsolete*⟩.

²**old** n (13c) **1** : one of a specified age — usu. used in combination ⟨a 3-year-*old*⟩ **2** : old or earlier time — used in the phrase *of old* ⟨mighty men of ~⟩

old boy n (1868) **1** *often cap O&B, Brit* : an alumnus esp. of a boys' school **2** : a man who is a member of a long-standing and usu. influential clique esp. in a professional, business, or social sphere

Old Bulgarian n (1861) : OLD CHURCH SLAVONIC

Old Catholic n (1871) : a member of one of various hierarchical and liturgical churches separating from the Roman Catholic Church at various times since the 18th century

Old Christmas n (1863) *chiefly Midland* : EPIPHANY 1

Old Church Slavonic n (ca. 1929) : the Slavic language used in the liturgical and Biblical translations of Cyril and Methodius as attested in manuscripts of the 10th and 11th centuries — called also *Old Church Slavic;* compare INDO-EUROPEAN LANGUAGES table

old country n, *often cap O&C* (1782) : an emigrant's country of origin; *esp* : one in Europe — usu. used with *the*

old·en \'ōl-dən\ adj (14c) : of or relating to a bygone era

Old English n (13c) **1 a** : the language of the English people from the time of the earliest documents in the 7th century to about 1100 — see INDO-EUROPEAN LANGUAGES table **b** : English of any period before Modern English **2** : BLACK LETTER

Old English sheepdog n (1891) : any of a breed of tailless dogs developed in England and having a profuse blue-gray and white coat

old–fan·gled \'ōl(d)-'faŋ-gəld\ adj [*old* + *-fangled* (as in *newfangled*)] (1842) : OLD-FASHIONED

¹**old–fash·ioned** \-'fa-shənd\ adj (1596) **1 a** : of, relating to, or characteristic of a past era ⟨wears an ~ black bow tie —Green Peyton⟩ **b** : adhering to customs of a past era **2** : OUTMODED — **old–fash·ioned·ly** \-shən(d)-lē\ adv — **old–fash·ioned·ness** \-nəs\ n

²**old–fashioned** n (1901) : a cocktail usu. made with whiskey, bitters, sugar, a twist of lemon peel, and a small amount of water or soda

Old French n (1708) : the French language from the 9th to the 16th century; *esp* : French from the 9th to the 13th century — see INDO-EUROPEAN LANGUAGES table

Old Glory n (1862) : the flag of the U.S.

old gold n (1879) : a dark yellow

old guard n, *often cap O&G* (1850) **1** : a group of established prestige and influence **2** : the conservative members of an organization (as a political party)

old hand n (ca. 1785) : HAND 10e

old hat adj (1911) **1** : OLD-FASHIONED **2** : lacking in freshness : TRITE

Old High German n (ca. 1884) : High German exemplified in documents prior to the 12th century — see INDO-EUROPEAN LANGUAGES table

old·ie \'ōl-dē\ n (1874) : one that is old; *esp* : a popular song of an earlier day

Old Ionic n (ca. 1889) : the Greek dialect of the Homeric epics

Old Iranian n (1939) : any Iranian language in use in the period B.C.

Old Irish n (ca. 1884) : the Irish in use from the 7th century to about 950 — see INDO-EUROPEAN LANGUAGES table

old·ish \'ōl-dish\ adj (ca. 1669) : somewhat old or elderly

old lady n (1836) **1** : WIFE **2** : MOTHER **3** : GIRLFRIEND; *esp* : one with whom a man cohabits

Old Latin n (ca. 1889) : Latin used in the early inscriptions and in literature prior to the classical period

old–line \'ōl(d)-'līn\ adj (1856) **1 a** : having a reputation or authority based on length or proven quality of service ⟨an ~ firm⟩ **b** : of established prestige and influence ⟨~ families⟩ **2** : adhering to traditional policies or practices : CONSERVATIVE

old maid n (ca. 1530) **1** : SPINSTER 3 **2** : a prim fussy person ⟨he was a real *old maid* about burning rubbish —R. C. Ruark⟩ **3** : a simple card game in which cards are matched in pairs and the player holding the unmatched card at the end loses — **old–maid·ish** \'ōl(d)-'mā-dish\ adj — **old–maid·ish·ness** \-nəs\ n

old man n (1768) **1 a** : HUSBAND **b** : FATHER **2** *cap* : one in authority; *esp* : COMMANDING OFFICER **3** : BOYFRIEND; *esp* : one with whom a woman cohabits

old–man's–beard \'ōl(d)-'manz-\ n (1742) **1** : any of several clematises (esp. *Clematis vitalba*) having plumose styles **2** : a greenish gray pendulous lichen (*Usnea barbata*) growing on trees

old master n (1824) : a work of art by an established master and esp. by any of the distinguished painters of the 16th, 17th, or early 18th century; *also* : such an artist

Old Nick \'ōl(d)-'nik\ n (1668) — used as a name of the devil

Old Norse n (1844) : the North Germanic language of the Scandinavian peoples prior to about 1350 — see INDO-EUROPEAN LANGUAGES table

Old North French n (ca. 1930) : the northern dialects of Old French including esp. those of Normandy and Picardy

Old Persian n (ca. 1909) : an ancient Iranian language known from cuneiform inscriptions from the 5th and 6th centuries B.C. — see INDO-EUROPEAN LANGUAGES table

Old Prussian n (1872) : a Baltic language used in East Prussia until the 17th century — see INDO-EUROPEAN LANGUAGES table

old rose n (1893) : a variable color averaging a grayish red

Old Saxon n (1841) : the language of the Saxons of northwest Germany until about the 12th century — see INDO-EUROPEAN LANGUAGES table

old school n (1749) : adherents of traditional policies and practices

old school tie n (1932) **1 a** : an attitude of conservatism, aplomb,

and upper-class solidarity associated with English public school graduates **b** : a necktie displaying the colors of an English public school **2** : clannishness among members of an established clique

old–shoe \'ōl(d)-'shü\ adj (1944) : characterized by familiarity or freedom from restraint : COMFORTABLE, UNPRETENTIOUS

old sledge n (1830) : SEVEN-UP

old–squaw \'ōl(d)-'skwȯ\ n (1838) : a common sea duck (*Clangula hyemalis*) of the more northern parts of the northern hemisphere

old·ster \'ōl(d)-stər\ n (1848) : an old or elderly person

old style n (1617) **1** *cap O&S* : a style of reckoning time used before the adoption of the Gregorian calendar **2** : a style of type distinguished by graceful irregularity among individual letters, bracketed serifs, and but slight contrast between light and heavy strokes

Old Style adj (1678) : using or according to the Julian calendar

Old Swedish n (ca. 1909) : the Swedish language as exemplified in documents prior to about 1350

Old Testament n (14c) : the first part of the Christian Bible containing the books of the Jewish canon of Scripture — see BIBLE table

old–time \'ōl(d)-'tīm\ adj (1824) **1** : of, relating to, or characteristic of an earlier period ⟨~ songs⟩ **2** : of long standing ⟨~ residents⟩

old–tim·er \-'tī-mər, -,tī-mər\ n (1879) **1 a** : VETERAN **b** : OLDSTER **2** : something that is old-fashioned : ANTIQUE

old–timey \'ōl(d)-'tī-mē\ adj (1850) : of a kind or style prevalent in or reminiscent of an earlier time ⟨~ music⟩

Old Welsh n (1882) : the Welsh language exemplified in documents prior to about 1150 — see INDO-EUROPEAN LANGUAGES table

old·wife \'ōl(d)-,wīf\ n (1588) **1** : any of several marine fishes (as an alewife, menhaden, or triggerfish) **2** : OLD-SQUAW

old wives' tale n (1656) : an often traditional belief that is not based on fact : SUPERSTITION

old–world \'ōl(d)-'wər(-ə)ld\ adj (1712) : of, relating to, or characteristic of the Old World; *esp* : having the charm or picturesque qualities of the Old World ⟨narrow ~ streets⟩

Old World n (ca. 1596) : the eastern hemisphere exclusive of Australia; *specif* : Europe

ole \'ōl\ adj [by alter.] (1844) : OLD

ole- *or* **oleo-** *comb form* [F *olé*, *oléo-*, fr. L *ole-*, fr. *oleum* — more at OIL] : oil ⟨*oleo*graph⟩

-ole *also* **-ol** *n comb form* [ISV, fr. L *oleum*] **1** : chemical compound containing a 5-membered usu. heterocyclic ring ⟨pyr*role*⟩ **2** : chemical compound not containing hydroxyl ⟨eucalypt*ol*⟩ — esp. in names of ethers ⟨safr*ole*⟩

olé \ō-'lā\ n [Sp] (1922) : ²BRAVO

ole·ag·i·nous \,ō-lē-'a-jə-nəs\ adj [ME, fr. MF *oleagineux*, fr. L *oleagineus* or an olive tree, fr. *olea* olive tree, fr. Gk *elaia*] (15c) **1** : resembling or having the properties of oil : OILY; *also* : containing or producing oil **2** : marked by an offensively ingratiating manner or quality — **ole·ag·i·nous·ly** adv — **ole·ag·i·nous·ness** n

ole·an·der \'ō-lē-,an-dər, ,ō-lē-'\ n [ML, alter. of *arodandrum*, *lorandrum*, perh. alter. of L *rhododendron* — more at RHODODENDRON] (1548) : a poisonous evergreen shrub (*Nerium oleander*) of the dogbane family with fragrant white to red flowers

ole·an·do·my·cin \,ō-lē-,an-də-'mī-sⁿn\ n [*oleander*ose, a sugar derived from oleandrin (a glycoside contained in oleander leaves) + *-o-* + *-mycin*] (1956) : an antibiotic $C_{35}H_{61}NO_{12}$ produced by a streptomyces (*Streptomyces antibioticus*)

ole·as·ter \'ō-lē-,as-tər, ,ō-lē-'\ n [ME, fr. L, fr. *olea*] (14c) : any of several plants (genus *Elaeagnus* of the family Elaeagnaceae, the oleaster family) having alternate leaves and perfect flowers with four stamens; *esp* : RUSSIAN OLIVE

ole·ate \'ō-lē-,āt\ n (ca. 1823) : a salt or ester of oleic acid

olec·ra·non \ō-'le-krə-,nän\ n [NL, fr. Gk *ōlekranon*, fr. *ōlenē* elbow + *kranion* skull — more at ELL, CRANIUM] (ca. 1741) : the process of the ulna projecting behind the elbow joint

ole·fin \'ō-lə-fən\ n [ISV, fr. F (gaz) *oléfiant* ethylene, fr. L *oleum*] (1860) **1** : ALKENE **2** : a synthetic fiber (as polypropylene) derived from an alkene — **ole·fin·ic** \,ō-lə-'fi-nik\ adj

oleic acid n (1819) : a monounsaturated fatty acid $C_{18}H_{34}O_2$ found in natural fats and oils

ole·in \'ō-lē-ən\ n [F *oléine*, fr. L *oleum*] (1838) **1** : an ester of glycerol and oleic acid **2** : the liquid portion of a fat

oleo \'ō-lē-,ō\ n [short for *oleomargarine*] (1884) : MARGARINE

oleo·graph \'ō-lē-ə-,graf\ n [ISV] (1873) : a chromolithograph printed on cloth to imitate an oil painting

oleo·mar·ga·rine \,ō-lē-ō-'mär-jə-rən, -,rēn; -'märj-rən\ n [F *oléomargarine*, fr. *olé-* + *margarine* margarine] (1873) : MARGARINE

oleo·res·in \,ō-lē-ō-'re-zⁿn\ n [ISV] (ca. 1846) **1** : a natural plant product (as copaiba) containing chiefly essential oil and resin; *esp* : TURPENTINE 1b **2** : a preparation consisting essentially of oil holding resin in solution — **oleo·res·in·ous** \-'re-zⁿn-əs, -'rez-nəs\ adj

ole·um \'ō-lē-əm\ n [L, fr. L, olive oil — more at OIL] (ca. 1823) *1 pl* **olea** \-lē-ə\ : OIL *2 pl* **oleums** : a heavy oily strongly corrosive solution of sulfur trioxide in anhydrous sulfuric acid

O level n (1949) : the lowest of three levels of standardized British examinations in a secondary school subject; *also* : successful completion of an O-level examination in a particular subject — called also *Ordinary level;* compare A LEVEL, S LEVEL **a** : the level of education required to pass an O-level examination **b** : a course leading to an O-level examination

ol·fac·tion \äl-'fak-shən, ōl-\ n (ca. 1846) **1** : the sense of smell **2** : the act or process of smelling

ol·fac·tom·e·ter \,äl-,fak-'tä-mə-tər, ,ōl-\ n (1889) : an instrument for measuring the sensitivity of the sense of smell

ol·fac·to·ry \äl-'fak-t(ə-)rē, ōl-\ adj [L *olfactorius*, fr. *olfacere* to smell, fr. *olēre* to smell + *facere* to do — more at ODOR, DO] (ca. 1658) : of, relating to, or connected with the sense of smell

---

\ə\ abut \ᵊ\ kitten, F table \ər\ further \a\ ash \ā\ ace \ä\ mop, mar \aù\ out \ch\ chin \e\ bet \ē\ easy \g\ go \i\ hit \ī\ ice \j\ job \ŋ\ sing \ō\ go \ȯ\ law \ȯi\ boy \th\ thin \th\ the \ü\ loot \ù\ foot \y\ yet \zh\ vision \á, k̲, ⁿ, œ, œ̄, ɯ, ɯ̄, ᵜ\ see Guide to Pronunciation

olfactory bulb *n* (ca. 1860) : a bulbous anterior projection of the olfactory lobe that is the place of termination of the olfactory nerves and is esp. well developed in lower vertebrates (as fishes)

olfactory lobe *n* (ca. 1860) : an anterior projection of each cerebral hemisphere that is continuous anteriorly with the olfactory nerve

olfactory nerve *n* (1670) : either of the pair of nerves that are the first cranial nerves and that arise in the olfactory neurosensory cells of the nasal mucous membrane and pass to the anterior part of the cerebrum 〈olfact scant〉: few 〈oligophagous〉

olig- *or* **oligo-** *comb form* [ML, fr. Gk, fr. *oligos;* perh. akin to Arm *ałkat* scant]

ol·i·garch \'ä-lə-gärk, 'ō-\ *n* [Gk *oligarchēs,* fr. *olig-* + *-archēs* -arch] (ca. 1610) : a member or supporter of an oligarchy

ol·i·gar·chic \,ä-lə-'gär-kik, ,ō-\ *or* **ol·i·gar·chi·cal** \-ki-kəl\ *adj* (1586) : of, relating to, or based on an oligarchy

ol·i·gar·chy \'ä-lə-,gär-kē, 'ō-\ *n, pl* **-chies** (1542) **1** : government by the few **2** : a government in which a small group exercises control esp. for corrupt and selfish purposes; *also* : a group exercising such control **3** : an organization under oligarchic control

Ol·i·go·cene \'ä-li-gō-,sēn, 'ō-; ə-'li-gə-\ *adj* [ISV] (ca. 1859) : of, relating to, or being an epoch of the Tertiary between the Eocene and Miocene or the corresponding system of rocks — see GEOLOGIC TIME table — **Oligocene** *n*

ol·i·go·chaete \-,kēt\ *n* [NL *Oligochaeta,* ultim. fr. Gk *olig-* + *chaitē* long hair] (1896) : any of a class or order (Oligochaeta) of hermaphroditic terrestrial or aquatic annelids (as an earthworm) that lack a specialized head — **oligochaete** *adj*

ol·i·go·clase \'ä-li-gō-,klās, 'ō-, -,klāz; ə-'li-gə-\ *n* [G *Oligoklas,* fr. *olig-* olig- + Gk *klasis* breaking, fr. *klan* to break — more at CLAST] (1832) : a mineral of the plagioclase series

ol·i·go·den·dro·cyte \'ä-li-gō-'den-drə-,sīt, 'ō-; ə-,li-gə-\ *n* [ISV, fr. *olig-* + *dendr-* + *-cyte*] (1932) : a neuroglial cell resembling an astrocyte but smaller with few and slender processes having few branches

ol·i·go·den·dro·glia \-den-'drä-glē-ə, -'drō-\ *n* [NL, fr. *oligodendrocyte* + *-glia* (form of neuroglia)] (1924) : neuroglia made up of oligodendrocytes that is held to function in myelin formation in the central nervous system — **ol·i·go·den·dro·gli·al** \-glē-əl\ *adj*

olig·o·mer \ə-'li-gə-mər\ *n* (1952) : a polymer or polymer intermediate containing relatively few structural units — **olig·o·mer·ic** \-,li-gə-'mer-ik\ *adj* — **olig·o·mer·i·za·tion** \-mə-rə-'zā-shən\ *n*

ol·i·go·nu·cle·o·tide \-'nü-klē-ə-,tīd, -'nyü-\ *n* (1942) : a chain of usu. up to 20 nucleotides

ol·i·goph·a·gous \,ä-lə-'gä-fə-gəs, ,ō-\ *adj* (1920) : eating only a few specific kinds of food — **ol·i·goph·a·gy** \-'gä-fə-jē\ *n*

ol·i·gop·o·ly \-'gä-pə-lē\ *n* [*olig-* + *-poly* (as in *monopoly*)] (1895) : a market situation in which each of a few producers affects but does not control the market — **ol·i·gop·o·lis·tic** \-,gä-pə-'lis-tik\ *adj*

ol·i·gop·so·ny \-'gäp-sə-nē\ *n* [*olig-* + Gk *opsōnia* purchase of victuals, fr. *opsōnein* to purchase victuals, fr. *opson* food + *ōneisthai* to buy — more at VENAL] (1942) : a market situation in which each of a few buyers exerts a disproportionate influence on the market — **ol·i·gop·so·nis·tic** \-,gäp-sə-'nis-tik\ *adj*

ol·i·go·sac·cha·ride \,ä-li-gō-'sa-kə-,rīd, ,ō-; ə-'li-gə-\ *n* [ISV] (1930) : a saccharide (as a disaccharide) that contains a known small number of monosaccharide units

ol·i·go·tro·phic \-'trō-fik\ *adj* [ISV] (1928) : deficient in plant nutrients 〈~ boggy acid soils〉; *esp* : having abundant dissolved oxygen 〈an ~ body of water〉 — compare EUTROPHIC, MESOTROPHIC

olio \'ō-lē-,ō\ *n, pl* **oli·os** [modif. of Sp *olla*] (ca. 1643) **1** : OLLA PODRIDA 1 **2 a** : a miscellaneous mixture : HODGEPODGE **b** : a miscellaneous collection (as of literary or musical selections)

ol·i·va·ceous \,ä-lə-'vā-shəs\ *adj* (1776) : OLIVE 1

¹ol·ive \'ä-liv, -ləv\ *n* [ME, fr. OF, fr. L *oliva,* fr. Gk *elaia*] (13c) **1 a** : a Mediterranean evergreen tree (*Olea europaea* of the family Oleaceae, the olive family) cultivated for its drupaceous fruit that is an important food and source of oil; *also* : the fruit **b** : any of various shrubs and trees resembling the olive **2** : any of several colors resembling that of the unripe fruit of the olive tree that are yellowish green **3** : an oval eminence on each ventrolateral aspect of the medulla oblongata

²olive *adj* (1657) **1** : of the color olive or olive green **2** : approaching olive in color or complexion

olive branch *n* (14c) **1** : a branch of the olive tree esp. when used as a symbol of peace **2** : an offer or gesture of conciliation or goodwill

olive drab *n* (1897) **1** : a grayish olive **2 a** : a wool or cotton fabric of an olive drab color **b** : a uniform of this fabric

olive green *n* (ca. 1757) : a greenish olive

oliv·en·ite \ō-'li-və-,nīt\ *n* [G *Olivenit,* fr. *oliven-, olive* olive] (1820) : a mineral that is a basic arsenate of copper

Ol·i·ver \'ä-lə-vər\ *n* [F *Olivier*] : the close friend of Roland in the Charlemagne legends

ol·i·vine \'ä-lə-,vēn\ *n* [G *Olivin,* fr. L *oliva*] (1794) : a usu. greenish mineral that is a complex silicate of magnesium and iron used in refractories — compare PERIDOT — **ol·iv·in·ic** \,ä-lə-'vi-nik\ *or* **ol·iv·in·it·ic** \-və-'ni-tik\ *adj*

ol·la \'ä-lə, 'öi-ə\ *n* [Sp, fr. L *olla, aulla* pot; akin to Skt *ukhā* pot and prob. to Goth *auhns* oven] (1622) : a large bulging widemouthed earthenware vessel sometimes with looped handles used (as by Pueblo Indians) for storage, cooking, or as a container for water

ol·la po·dri·da \-pə-'drē-də\ *n, pl* **olla podridas** \-'drē-dəz\ *also* **ollas podridas** [Sp, lit., rotten pot] (1599) **1** : a rich highly seasoned stew of meat and vegetables usu. including sausage and chick-peas that is slowly simmered and is a traditional Spanish and Latin= American dish **2** : HODGEPODGE

olo·liu·qui \,ō-lō-lē-'ü-kē\ *n* [Sp *ololiuque,* fr. Nahuatl *ololiuhqui,* lit., something rolled into a ball] (1915) : a woody stemmed Mexican vine (*Rivea corymbosa*) of the morning glory family having small fleshy fruits with single seeds that are used esp. by the Indians for medicinal, narcotic, and religious purposes

olla

olo·ro·so \,ō-lə-'rō-(,)sō\ *n, pl* **-sos** [Sp, fr. *oloroso* fragrant, fr. *olor* odor, fr. L, fr. *olēre* to smell — more at ODOR] (1876) : a dry full-bodied Spanish sherry

olym·pi·ad \ə-'lim-pē-,ad, ō-\ *n, often cap* [ME, fr. MF *Olympiade,* fr. L *Olympiad-, Olympias,* fr. Gk, fr. *Olympia,* site of ancient Olympic Games] (14c) **1** : one of the 4-year intervals between Olympic Games by which time was reckoned in ancient Greece **2** : a quadrennial celebration of the modern Olympic Games

¹Olym·pi·an \-pē-ən\ *adj* (15c) **1** : of or relating to Mount Olympus in Thessaly **2** : befitting or characteristic of an Olympian; *esp* : LOFTY 〈his . . . formula of glib simplicity and ~ arrogance —Richard Pollak〉

²Olympian (1593) **1** : of or relating to the ancient Greek region of Olympia **2** : of, relating to, or constituting the Olympic Games

³Olympian *n* (1606) : a participant in Olympic Games

⁴Olympian *n* (1843) **1** : one of the ancient Greek deities dwelling on Olympus **2** : a being of lofty detachment or superior attainments

Olympian Games *n pl* (1593) : OLYMPIC GAMES 1

Olym·pia oyster \ə-'lim-pē-ə-, ō-\ *n* [*Olympia,* Washington] (1908) : a small flavorful native oyster (*Ostrea lurida*) of the Puget Sound area of the Pacific coast of No. America — called also *Olympia*

Olym·pic \ə-'lim-pik, ō-\ *adj* (1590) **1** : ¹OLYMPIAN **2** : of or relating to the Olympic Games

Olympic Games *n pl* (ca. 1610) **1** : an ancient Panhellenic festival held every fourth year and made up of contests of sports, music, and literature with the victor's prize a crown of wild olive **2** : a modified revival of the ancient Olympic Games consisting of international athletic contests that are held at separate winter and summer gatherings at four year intervals — called also *Olympics*

Olym·pus \ə-'lim-pəs, ō-\ *n* [L, fr. Gk *Olympos*] (1580) : a mountain in Thessaly that in Greek mythology is the abode of the gods

om \'ōm\ *n* [Skt] (1788) : a mantra consisting of the sound \'ōm\ used in contemplation of ultimate reality

-oma *n suffix, pl* **-omas** *or* **-omata** [L *omat-, -oma,* fr. Gk *-ōmat-, -ōma,* fr. *-ō-* (stem vowel of causative verbs in *-oun*) + *-mat-, -ma,* suffix denoting result — more at -MENT]: tumor 〈adeno*ma*〉 〈fibro*ma*〉

Oma·ha \'ō-mə-,hö, -,hä\ *n, pl* **Omaha** *or* **Omahas** (1804) : a member of an American Indian people of northeastern Nebraska

oma·sum \ō-'mä-səm\ *n, pl* **oma·sa** \-sə\ [NL, fr. L, tripe of a bullock] (ca. 1706) : the third chamber of the ruminant stomach that is situated between the reticulum and the abomasum — compare RUMEN

om·bre \'äm-brē, 'äm-brē, 'əm-, -(,)brā\ *n* [F *or* Sp; F *hombre,* fr. Sp, lit., man — more at HOMBRE] (1661) : an old three-handed card game popular in Europe esp. in the 17th and 18th centuries

om·bré \'äm-,brā\ *adj* [F, pp. of *ombrer* to shade, fr. It *ombrare,* fr. *ombra* shade, fr. L *umbra* — more at UMBRAGE] (ca. 1896) : having colors or tones that shade into each other — used esp. of fabrics in which the color is graduated from light to dark — **ombré** *n*

om·buds·man \'äm-,büdz-mən, 'öm-, -,bədz-, -,mən; äm-'büdz-, öm-\ *n, pl* **-men** \-mən\ [Sw, lit., representative, fr. ON *umbothsmathr,* fr. *umboth* commission + *mathr* man] (1959) **1** : a government official (as in Sweden or New Zealand) appointed to receive and investigate complaints made by individuals against abuses or capricious acts of public officials **2** : one that investigates reported complaints (as from students or consumers), reports findings, and helps to achieve equitable settlements — **om·buds·man·ship** \-,ship\ *n*

-ome *n suffix* [NL *-oma,* fr. L, -oma]: mass 〈phyllo*me*〉

ome·ga \ō-'mä-gə, -'mē-, -'me-\ *n* [ME, fr. MF, fr. Gk *ō mega,* lit., large o] (15c) **1** : the 24th and last letter of the Greek alphabet — see ALPHABET table **2** : LAST, ENDING **3 a** : a negatively charged elementary particle that has a mass 3270 times the mass of an electron — called also *omega minus* **b** : a very short-lived unstable meson with mass 1532 times the mass of an electron — called also *omega meson*

ome·ga-3 \-'thrē\ *adj* (1980) : being or composed of polyunsaturated fatty acids that have the final double bond in the hydrocarbon chain between the third and fourth carbon atoms from one end of the molecule and that are found esp. in fish, fish oils, vegetable oils, and green leafy vegetables

om·e·lette *or* **om·e·let** \'äm-lət, 'ä-mə-\ *n* [F *omelette,* alter. of MF *alumelle,* lit., knife blade, modif. of L *lamella,* dim. of *lamina* thin plate] (ca. 1611) : beaten eggs cooked without stirring until set and served folded in half

omen \'ō-mən\ *n* [L *omin-, omen*] (1582) : an occurrence or phenomenon believed to portend a future event : AUGURY

omen·tum \ō-'men-təm\ *n, pl* **-ta** \-tə\ *or* **-tums** [L; perh. akin to L *induere* to put on, *exuere* to take off — more at EXUVIAE] (1547) : a fold of peritoneum connecting or supporting abdominal structures (as the viscera); *also* : a fold of peritoneum free at one end — **omen·tal** \-'men-t³l\ *adj*

omer \'ō-mər\ *n* [Heb *'ōmer*] (ca. 1608) **1** : an ancient Hebrew unit of dry capacity equal to ¹/₁₀ ephah **2** *often cap* : the sheaf of barley traditionally offered in Jewish Temple worship on the second day of the Passover **b** *cap* : a 7-week liturgical period of expectancy between the second day of the Passover and Shabuoth

om·i·cron \'ä-mə-,krän, 'ō-, *Brit* ō-'mī-(,)krän\ *n* [ME, fr. MF, fr. Gk *o mikron,* lit., small o] (15c) : the 15th letter of the Greek alphabet — see ALPHABET table

om·i·nous \'ä-mə-nəs\ *adj* (1587) : being or exhibiting an omen : PORTENTOUS; *esp* : foreboding or foreshowing evil : INAUSPICIOUS — **om·i·nous·ly** *adv* — **om·i·nous·ness** *n*
    syn OMINOUS, PORTENTOUS, FATEFUL mean having a menacing or threatening aspect. OMINOUS implies having a menacing, alarming character foreshadowing evil or disaster 〈*ominous* rumblings from a once-dormant volcano〉. PORTENTOUS suggests being frighteningly big or impressive but now seldom definitely connotes forwarning of calamity 〈an eerie and *portentous* stillness〉. FATEFUL suggests being of momentous or decisive importance 〈the *fateful* conference that led to war〉.

omis·si·ble \ō-'mi-sə-bəl\ *adj* (1816) : that may be omitted

omis·sion \ō-'mi-shən, ə-\ *n* [ME *omissioun,* fr. LL *omission-, omissio,* fr. L *omittere*] (14c) **1 a** : something neglected or left undone **b** : apathy toward or neglect of duty **2** : the act of omitting : the state of being omitted

omit \ō-'mit, ə-\ *vt* **omit·ted; omit·ting** [ME *omitten,* fr. L *omittere,* fr. *ob-* toward + *mittere* to let go, send — more at OB-] (15c) **1** : to leave out or leave unmentioned **2 :** to fail to perform or make use of **:** FOR-BEAR **3** *obs* **:** DISREGARD **4** *obs* **:** GIVE UP

om·ma·tid·i·um \,ä-mə-'ti-dē-əm\ *n, pl* **-tid·ia** \-dē-ə\ [NL, fr. Gk *ommat-, omma* eye; akin to Gk *ōps* eye — more at EYE] (1884) **:** one of the elements corresponding to a small simple eye that make up the compound eye of an arthropod — **om·ma·tid·i·al** \-dē-əl\ *adj*

omni- *comb form* [L, fr. *omnis*] **:** all **:** universally ⟨*omni*directional⟩

¹om·ni·bus \'äm-ni-(,)bəs\ *n* [F, fr. L, for all, dat. pl. of *omnis*] (1829) **1 :** a usu. automotive public vehicle designed to carry a large number of passengers **:** BUS **2 :** a book containing reprints of a number of works

²omnibus *adj* (1842) **1 :** of, relating to, or providing for many things at once **2 :** containing or including many items

om·ni·com·pe·tent \,äm-ni-'käm-pə-tənt\ *adj* (1827) **:** able to handle any situation; *esp* **:** having the authority or legal capacity to act in all matters — **om·ni·com·pe·tence** \-tən(t)s\ *n*

om·ni·di·rec·tion·al \,äm-ni-də-'rek-shnəl, -nī-, -(,)dī-, -shə-n²l\ *adj* (1927) **:** being in or involving all directions; *esp* **:** receiving or sending radio waves equally well in all directions ⟨~ antenna⟩

om·ni·far·i·ous \,äm-nə-'far-ē-əs, -'fer-\ *adj* [LL *omnifarius,* fr. L *omni-* + *-farius* (as in *multifarius* diverse) — more at MULTIFARIOUS] (1653) **:** of all varieties, forms, or kinds

om·nif·i·cent \äm-'ni-fə-sənt\ *adj* [L *omni-* + E *-ficent* (as in *magnificent*)] (1677) **:** unlimited in creative power

om·nip·o·tence \äm-'ni-pə-tən(t)s\ *n* (15c) **1 :** the quality or state of being omnipotent **2 :** an agency or force of unlimited power

¹om·nip·o·tent \-tənt\ *adj* [ME, fr. MF, fr. L *omnipotent-, omnipotens,* fr. *omni-* + *potent-, potens* potent] (14c) **1** *often cap* **:** ALMIGHTY 1 **2 :** having virtually unlimited authority or influence **3** *obs* **:** ARRANT — **om·nip·o·tent·ly** *adv*

²omnipotent *n* (1600) **1 :** one who is omnipotent **2** *cap* **:** GOD 1

om·ni·pres·ence \,äm-ni-'pre-z²n(t)s\ *n* (1601) **:** the quality or state of being omnipresent **:** UBIQUITY

om·ni·pres·ent \-z²nt\ *adj* (1609) **:** present in all places at all times

om·ni·range \'äm-ni-,rānj\ *n* (1946) **:** a system of radio navigation in which any bearing relative to a special radio transmitter on the ground may be chosen and flown by an airplane pilot — called also *omnidirectional range*

om·ni·science \äm-'ni-shən(t)s\ *n* [ML *omniscientia,* fr. L *omni-* + *scientia* knowledge — more at SCIENCE] (1612) **:** the quality or state of being omniscient

om·ni·scient \-shənt\ *adj* [NL *omniscient-, omnisciens,* back-formation fr. ML *omniscientia*] (1604) **1 :** having infinite awareness, understanding, and insight **2 :** possessed of universal or complete knowledge — **om·ni·scient·ly** *adv*

om·ni·um-gath·er·um \,äm-nē-əm-'ga-thə-rəm\ *n, pl* **omnium-gatherums** [L *omnium* (gen. pl. of *omnis*) + E *gather* + L *-um,* noun ending] (1530) **:** a miscellaneous collection (as of things or persons)

om·ni·vore \'äm-ni-,vōr, -,vȯr\ *n* [NL *omnivora,* neut. pl. of *omnivorus,* fr. L] (1890) **:** one that is omnivorous

om·niv·o·rous \äm-'niv-rəs, -'ni-və-\ *adj* [L *omnivorus,* fr. *omni-* + *-vorus* -vorous] (ca. 1656) **1 :** feeding on both animal and vegetable substances **2 :** avidly taking in everything as if devouring or consuming — **om·niv·o·rous·ly** *adv*

om·pha·los \'äm(p)-fə-,läs, -ləs\ *n* [Gk, navel — more at NAVEL] (1855) **:** a central point **:** HUB 2 , FOCAL POINT

om·pha·lo·skep·sis \,äm(p)-fə-lō-'skep-səs\ *n* [NL, fr. Gk *omphalos* + *skepsis* examination — more at SPY] (1925) **:** contemplation of one's navel as an aid to meditation; also **:** INERTIA 2

¹on \'ȯn, 'än\ *prep* [ME *an, on,* prep. & adv., fr. OE; akin to OHG *ana* on, Gk *ana* up, on] (bef. 12c) **1 a** — used as a function word to indicate position in contact with and supported by the top surface of ⟨the book is lying ~ the table⟩ **b** — used as a function word to indicate position in or in contact with an outer surface ⟨the fly landed ~ the ceiling⟩ ⟨I have a cut ~ my finger⟩ ⟨paint ~ the wall⟩ **c** — used as a function word to indicate position in close proximity with ⟨a village ~ the sea⟩ ⟨stay ~ your opponent⟩ **d** — used as a function word to indicate direction or location with respect to something ⟨~ the south⟩ ⟨the garden is ~ the side of the house⟩ **2 a** — used as a function word to indicate a source of attachment or support ⟨~ a string⟩ ⟨stand ~ one foot⟩ ⟨hang it ~ a nail⟩ **b** — used as a function word to indicate a source of dependence ⟨you can rely ~ me⟩ ⟨feeds ~ insects⟩ ⟨lives ~ a pension⟩ **c** — used as a function word to indicate means of conveyance ⟨~ the bus⟩ or presence within the confines or in possession of ⟨had a knife ~ him⟩ **3** — used as a function word to indicate a time frame during which something takes place ⟨a parade ~ Sunday⟩ or an instant, action, or occurrence when something begins or is done ⟨~ cue⟩ ⟨~ arriving home, I found your letter⟩ ⟨news ~ the hour⟩ ⟨cash ~ delivery⟩ **4** *archaic* **:** OF **5 a** — used as a function word to indicate manner of doing something; often used with *the* ⟨~ the sly⟩ ⟨keep everything ~ the up-and-up⟩ **b** — used as a function word to indicate means or agency ⟨cut myself ~ a knife⟩ ⟨talk ~ the telephone⟩ **c** — used as a function word to indicate a medium of expression; used orig. to refer to physical position ⟨best show ~ television⟩ **6 a** (1) — used as a function word to indicate active involvement in a condition or status ⟨~ fire⟩ ⟨~ the increase⟩ ⟨~ the lookout⟩ (2) **:** regularly using or showing the effects of using ⟨~ drugs⟩ **b** — used as a function word to indicate involvement with the activity, work, or function of ⟨~ tour⟩ ⟨~ the jury⟩ ⟨~ duty⟩ **c** — used as a function word to indicate position or status in proper relationship with a standard or objective ⟨~ schedule⟩ **7** — used as a function word to indicate reason, ground, or basis (as for an action, opinion, or computation) ⟨I have it ~ good authority⟩ ⟨~ one condition⟩ ⟨the interest will be 10 cents ~ the dollar⟩ **b** — used as a function word to indicate the cause or source ⟨profited ~ the sale of stock⟩ **c** — used as a function word to indicate the focus of obligation or responsibility ⟨drinks are ~ the house⟩ ⟨put the blame ~ my actions⟩ **8 a** — used as a function word to indicate the object of collision, opposition, or hostile action ⟨bumped my head ~ a limb⟩ ⟨an attack ~ religion⟩ ⟨pulled a gun ~ me⟩ **b** — used as a function word to indicate the object with respect to some disadvantage, handicap, or detriment ⟨has three inches in height ~ me⟩ ⟨a 3-game lead ~ the second-place team⟩ ⟨the joke's ~ me⟩ **9 a** — used as a function word to indicate destination or the focus of some action, movement, or directed effort ⟨crept up ~ him⟩ ⟨feast your

eyes ~ this⟩ ⟨working ~ my skiing⟩ ⟨made a payment ~ the loan⟩ **b** — used as a function word to indicate the focus of feelings, determination, or will ⟨have pity ~ me⟩ ⟨keen ~ sports⟩ ⟨a curse ~ you⟩ **c** — used as a function word to indicate the object with respect to some misfortune or disadvantageous event ⟨the crops died ~ them⟩ **d** — used as a function word to indicate the subject of study, discussion, or consideration ⟨a book ~ insects⟩ ⟨reflect ~ that a moment⟩ ⟨agree ~ price⟩ **10** — used as a function word to indicate reduplication or succession in a series ⟨loss ~ loss⟩

²on *adv* (bef. 12c) **1 a :** in or into a position of contact with an upper surface *esp.* so as to be positioned for use or operation ⟨put the plates ~⟩ **b :** in or into a position of being attached to or covering a surface; *esp* **:** in or into the condition of being worn ⟨put his new shoes ~⟩ **2 a :** forward or at a more advanced point in space or time ⟨went ~ home⟩ ⟨later ~⟩ **b :** in continuance or succession ⟨rambled ~⟩ ⟨and so ~⟩ **3 :** into operation or a position permitting operation ⟨switched the light ~⟩

³on *adj* (ca. 1541) **1 :** engaged in an activity or function (as a dramatic role) **2 a** (1) **:** being in operation ⟨the radio is ~⟩ (2) **:** placed so as to permit operation ⟨the switch is ~⟩ **b :** taking place ⟨the game is ~⟩ **3 :** aware of something — usu. used with *to* ⟨my boss was ~ to me⟩ **4 :** INTENDED, PLANNED ⟨has nothing ~ for tonight⟩ **5** *Brit* **:** talking or harping incessantly — used with *about* **6** *chiefly Brit* **:** regarded as possible or feasible — usu. used in negative constructions **7 a :** engaged in or as if in a performance ⟨the comedian was always ~⟩ **b :** being at a high level of performance

¹-on *n suffix* [ISV, alter. of *-one*] **:** chemical compound not a ketone or other oxo compound ⟨parathi*on*⟩

²-on *n suffix* [fr. *-on* (in *ion*)] **1 :** subatomic particle ⟨nucle*on*⟩ **2 a :** unit **:** quantum ⟨phot*on*⟩ ⟨magnet*on*⟩ **b :** basic hereditary component ⟨cistr*on*⟩ ⟨oper*on*⟩

³-on *n suffix* [NL, fr. *-on* (in *argon*)] **:** noble gas ⟨rad*on*⟩

on–again, off–again *adj* (1948) **:** existing briefly and then disappearing in an intermittent unpredictable way ⟨*on-again, off-again* fads⟩

on·a·ger \'ä-ni-jər\ *n* [ME, wild ass, fr. L, fr. Gk *onagros,* fr. *onos* ass + *agros* field — more at ACRE] (14c) **1 :** an Asian wild ass (*Equus hemionus onager* syn. *E. onager*) that usu. has a broad dorsal stripe and is related to the kiang **2** [LL, fr. L] **:** a heavy catapult used in ancient and medieval times

on and off *adv* (1855) **:** OFF AND ON — **on–and–off** *adj*

onan·ism \'ō-nə-,ni-zəm\ *n* [prob. fr. NL *onanismus,* fr. *Onan,* son of Judah (Gen 38:9)] (ca. 1741) **1 :** MASTURBATION **2 :** COITUS INTERRUPTUS **3 :** SELF-GRATIFICATION — **onan·is·tic** \,ō-nə-'nis-tik\ *adj*

on·board \'ȯn-'bȯrd, 'än-, -'bȯrd\ *adj* (1960) **:** carried within or occurring aboard a vehicle (as a satellite or spacecraft) ⟨an ~ computer⟩

¹once \'wən(t)s\ *adv* [ME *ones,* fr. gen. of *on* one] (12c) **1 :** one time and no more **2 :** at any one time **:** under any circumstances **:** EVER **3 :** at some indefinite time in the past **:** FORMERLY **4 :** by one degree of relationship — **once and for all 1 :** with finality **:** DEFINITIVELY **2 :** for the last time

²once *n* (13c) **:** one single time **:** one time at least — **at once 1 :** at the same time **:** SIMULTANEOUSLY **2 :** IMMEDIATELY **3 :** ²BOTH

³once *adj* (1691) **:** that once was **:** FORMER

⁴once *conj* (1761) **:** at the moment when **:** AS SOON AS

once–over \,wən(t)s-'ō-vər, 'wən(t)s-,\ *n* (1914) **:** a swift examination or survey; *esp* **:** a swift comprehensive appraising glance

once that *conj* (1874) **:** ONCE

on·cho·cer·ci·a·sis \,äŋ-kō-,sər-'kī-ə-səs\ *n, pl* **-a·ses** \-,sēz\ [NL, fr. *Onchocerca,* genus of worms] (1911) **:** infestation with or disease caused by filarial worms (genus *Onchocerca*); *esp* **:** a human disease caused by a worm (*O. volvulus*) that is native to Africa but now present in parts of tropical America and is transmitted by several blackflies

on·cid·i·um \än-'si-dē-əm, äŋ-'ki-\ *n* [NL, fr. Gk *onkos* barbed hook — more at ANGLE] (ca. 1868) **:** any of a genus (*Oncidium*) of showy tropical American chiefly epiphytic orchids

onco- *comb form* [NL, fr. Gk *onkos* bulk, mass; akin to Gk *enenkein* to carry — more at ENOUGH] **:** tumor ⟨*onco*logy⟩

on·co·gene \'äŋ-kō-,jēn\ *n* (1969) **:** a gene having the potential to cause a normal cell to become cancerous

on·co·gen·e·sis \,äŋ-kō-'je-nə-səs\ *n* [NL] (ca. 1932) **:** the induction or formation of tumors

on·co·gen·ic \-'je-nik\ *adj* (1936) **1 :** relating to tumor formation **2 :** tending to cause tumors — **on·co·ge·nic·i·ty** \-jə-'ni-sə-tē\ *n* (1944) **:** the capacity to induce or form tumors

on·col·o·gy \än-'kä-lə-jē, äŋ-\ *n* (ca. 1857) **:** the study of tumors — **on·co·log·i·cal** \,än-kō-'lä-ji-kəl\ *also* **on·co·log·ic** \-jik\ *adj* — **on·col·o·gist** \än-'kä-lə-jist, äŋ-\ *n*

on·com·ing \'ȯn-,kə-miŋ, 'än-\ *adj* (1844) **1 a :** coming nearer in time or space ⟨the ~ year⟩ ⟨an ~ car⟩ **b :** FUTURE ⟨looked forward to his ~ visit⟩ **2 :** EMERGENT, RISING ⟨the ~ generation⟩

on·cor·na·vi·rus \,äŋ-,kȯr-nə-'vī-rəs\ *n* [*onco-* + *RNA* + *virus*] (1970) **:** any of a group of RNA-containing viruses that produce tumors

¹one \'wən\ *adj* [ME *on, an,* fr. OE *ān*; akin to OHG *ein* one, L *unus* (OL *oinos,* Skt *eka*] (bef. 12c) **1 :** being a single unit or thing ⟨~ day at a time⟩ **2 a :** being one in particular ⟨early ~ morning⟩ **b :** being preeminently what is indicated ⟨~ fine person⟩ **3 a :** being the same in kind or quality ⟨both of ~ species⟩ **b :** constituting a unified entity of two or more components ⟨the combined elements form ~ substance⟩ (2) **:** being in agreement or union ⟨am ~ with you on this⟩ **4 a :** SOME 1 ⟨will see you again ~ day⟩ **b :** being a certain individual

onager 2

\ə\ abut \ᵊ\ kitten, F table \ər\ further \a\ ash \ā\ ace \ä\ mop, mar \aú\ out \ch\ chin \e\ bet \ē\ easy \g\ go \i\ hit \ī\ ice \j\ job \ŋ\ sing \ō\ go \ȯ\ law \ȯi\ boy \th\ thin \t̲h̲\ the \ü\ loot \ú\ foot \y\ yet \zh\ vision \à, k̲, ⁿ, œ, œ̄, ᵫ, ᵫ̄, �\ *see* Guide to Pronunciation

specified by name ⟨∼ John Doe made a speech⟩ **5** : ONLY 2 ⟨the ∼ person she wanted to marry⟩
²one *n* (bef. 12c) **1** — see NUMBER table **2** : the number denoting unity **3 a** : the first in a set or series — often used with an attributive noun ⟨day ∼⟩ **b** : an article of clothing of a size designated *one* ⟨wears a ∼⟩ **4** : a single person or thing ⟨has the ∼ but needs the other⟩ **5** : a one-dollar bill — **at one** : at harmony : in a state of agreement — **for one** : as one example ⟨I *for one* disagree⟩
³one *pron* (13c) **1** : a certain indefinitely indicated person or thing ⟨saw ∼ of his friends⟩ **2 a** : an individual of a vaguely indicated group : anyone at all ⟨∼ never knows⟩ **b** — used as a third person substitute for a first person pronoun ⟨I'd like to read more but ∼ doesn't have the time⟩ **3** : a single instance of a specified action ⟨felt like belting him ∼ —John Casey⟩
   usage Sense 2a is usu. a sign of a formal style. A formal style excludes the participation of the reader or hearer; thus *one* is used where a less formal style might address the reader directly ⟨for the consequences of such choices, *one* has only oneself to thank —Walker Gibson⟩. This generic *one* has never been common in informal use in either British or American English, and people who start sentences with *one* often shift to another pronoun more natural to casual discourse ⟨when *one* is learning the river, he is not allowed to do or think about anything else —Mark Twain⟩. Use of *one* to replace a first-person pronoun—sense 2b—has occas. been criticized. It is more common in British English than in American ⟨I'm watching this pretty carefully and I hope that the issue will come up in the Lords and *one* may be able to speak about it —Donald Coggan, Archbishop of Canterbury⟩.
-one *n suffix* [ISV, alter. of *-ene*] : ketone or related or analogous compound or class of compounds ⟨*lactone*⟩ ⟨*quinone*⟩
one another *pron* (1526) : EACH OTHER *usage* see EACH OTHER
one–armed bandit \'wən-'ärm(d)-\ *also* **one–arm bandit** *n* (1934) : SLOT MACHINE 2
one–bag·ger \-'ba-gər\ *n* (1952) : SINGLE 2
one–di·men·sion·al (1883) **1** : having one dimension **2** : lacking depth : SUPERFICIAL ⟨∼ characters⟩ — **one–di·men·sion·al·i·ty** *n*
one·fold \'wən-,fōld, -'fōld\ *adj* (bef. 12c) : constituting a single undivided whole
one–hand·ed \-'han-dəd\ *adj* (15c) **1** : having or using only one hand ⟨could beat him up ∼⟩ **2 a** : designed for or requiring the use of only one hand **b** : effected by the use of only one hand
one–horse \-'hors\ *adj* (1750) **1** : drawn or operated by one horse **2** : SMALL, SMALL-TIME ⟨a ∼ town⟩
Onei·da \ō-'nī-də\ *n, pl* **Oneida** *or* **Oneidas** [Oneida *onʸóte?*, lit., standing rock] (1666) **1** : a member of an American Indian people orig. of New York **2** : the Iroquoian language of the Oneida people
onei·ric \ō-'nī-rik\ *adj* [Gk *oneiros* dream; akin to Arm *anurj* dream] (1859) : of or relating to dreams : DREAMY — **onei·ri·cal·ly** \-ri-k(ə-)lē\ *adv*
onei·ro·man·cy \ō-'nī-rə-,man(t)-sē\ *n* [Gk *oneiros* + E *-mancy*] (1652) : divination by means of dreams
one–line octave *n* (1931) : the musical octave that begins on middle C — see PITCH illustration
one–lin·er \,wən-'lī-nər\ *n* (1967) : a very succinct joke or witticism
one–man *adj* (1842) : of or relating to just one individual: as **a** : consisting of only one individual ⟨a ∼ committee⟩ **b** (1) : done, presented, or produced by only one individual ⟨a ∼ stage play⟩ (2) : featuring the work of a single artist ⟨a ∼ show of oils⟩ **c** : designed for or limited to one individual
one·ness \'wən-nəs\ *n* (1594) : the quality or state or fact of being one: as **a** : SINGLENESS **b** : INTEGRITY, WHOLENESS **c** : HARMONY **d** : SAMENESS, IDENTITY **e** : UNITY, UNION
one–night·er \,wən-'nī-tər\ *n* (ca. 1937) : ONE-NIGHT STAND
one–night stand *n* (1880) **1** : a performance (as of a play or concert) given (as by a traveling group of actors or musicians) only once in each of a series of localities **2 a** : a locality used for one-night stands **b** : a stopover for a one-night stand **3** : a sexual encounter limited to a single occasion; *also* : a partner in such an encounter
one–note \'wən-,nōt\ *adj* (1973) : unvarying in tone or emphasis : MONOTONOUS
one–off \,wən-'ȯf\ *adj* (1934) *Brit* : limited to a single time, occasion, or instance : ONE-SHOT, UNIQUE — **one–off** *n*
one–on–one \,wən-ȯn-'wən, ,wən-än-\ *adj or adv* (1967) **1** : playing directly against a single opposing player **2** : involving a direct encounter between one person and another
one–piece *adj* (1880) : consisting of or made in a single undivided piece ⟨a ∼ bathing suit⟩ — **one–piec·er** \'wən-'pē-sər\ *n*
oner·ous \'ä-nə-rəs, 'ō-\ *adj* [ME, fr. MF *onereus*, fr. L *onerosus*, fr. *oner-, onus* burden; akin to Skt *anas* cart] (14c) **1** : involving, imposing, or constituting a burden : TROUBLESOME ⟨an ∼ task⟩ **2** : having legal obligations that outweigh the advantages ⟨∼ contract⟩ — **oner·ous·ly** *adv* — **oner·ous·ness** *n*
   syn ONEROUS, BURDENSOME, OPPRESSIVE, EXACTING mean imposing hardship. ONEROUS stresses being laborious and heavy esp. because distasteful ⟨the *onerous* task of cleaning up the mess⟩. BURDENSOME suggests causing mental as well as physical strain ⟨*burdensome* responsibilities⟩. OPPRESSIVE implies extreme harshness or severity in what is imposed ⟨the *oppressive* tyranny of a police state⟩. EXACTING implies rigor or sternness rather than tyranny or injustice in the demands made or in the one demanding ⟨an *exacting* employer⟩.
one·self \(,)wən-'self, Southern *also* -'sef\ *also* **one's self** \(,)wən-, ,wənz-\ *pron* (1548) **1** : a person's self : one's own self — used reflexively as object of a preposition or verb or for emphasis in various constructions **2** : one's normal, healthy, or sane condition or self — **be oneself** : to conduct oneself in a usual or fitting manner
one–shot \'wən-shät\ *adj* (1927) **1** : that is complete or effective through being done or used or applied only once ⟨there is no easy ∼ answer to the problem⟩ **2** : that is not followed by something else of the same kind ⟨a ∼ tax cut⟩ — **one–shot** *n*
one–sid·ed \'wən-'sī-dəd\ *adj* (1813) **1 a** (1) : having one side prominent : LOPSIDED (2) : having or occurring on one side only **b** : limited to one side : PARTIAL ⟨a ∼ interpretation⟩ **2** : UNILATERAL ⟨a ∼ decision⟩ — **one–sid·ed·ly** *adv* — **one–sid·ed·ness** *n*
ones place *n* (1976) : UNITS PLACE

one–step \'wən-,step\ *n* (1911) **1** : a ballroom dance in ²/₄ time marked by quick walking steps backward and forward **2** : music used for the one-step — **one–step** *vi*
one–stop \-'stäp\ *adj* (1934) : being or relating to a business that provides a complete range of goods or services of a particular kind
one–tailed \'wən-'tāl(d)\ *also* **one–tail** \-'tāl\ *adj* (1947) : being a statistical test for which the critical region consists of all values of the test statistic greater than a given value or less than a given value but not both — compare TWO-TAILED
¹one–time \'wən-'tīm\ *adj* (1840) **1** : FORMER, SOMETIME ⟨a ∼ actor⟩ **2** : occurring only once : ONE-SHOT
²onetime *adv* (1886) : FORMERLY
one–to–one \,wən-tə-'wən, -də-\ *adj* (1873) **1** : pairing each element of a set uniquely with an element of another set **2** : ONE-ON-ONE 2
one–track *adj* (1926) : marked by often narrowly restricted attention to or absorption in just one thing ⟨a ∼ mind⟩
one–two \'wən-'tü, -,tü\ *n* (1809) **1** : a combination of two quick blows in rapid succession in boxing; *esp* : a left jab followed at once by a hard blow with the right hand **2** *or* **one–two punch** : a combination of two forces acting against something
one–up \,wən-'əp, 'wən-\ *vt* [back-formation fr. *one-upmanship*] (1963) : to practice one-upmanship on
one up *adj* (1919) : being in a position of advantage — usu. used with **on**
one–up·man·ship \,wən-'əp-mən-,ship\ *also* **one–ups·man·ship** \-'əps-mən-\ *n* (1952) : the art or practice of outdoing or keeping one jump ahead of a friend or competitor ⟨engaged in a round of verbal ∼⟩
one–way *adj* (1824) **1** : that moves in or allows movement in only one direction ⟨∼ street⟩ **2** : ONE-SIDED, UNILATERAL ⟨a ∼ conversation⟩ **3** : that functions in only one of two or more ways
on·go·ing \'ȯn-,gō-iŋ, 'än-, -,gȯ(-)iŋ\ *adj* (1877) **1 a** : being actually in process **b** : CONTINUING **2** : continuously moving forward : GROWING — **on·go·ing·ness** \-nəs\ *n*
on·ion \'ən-yən\ *n* [ME, fr. MF *oignon*, fr. L *union-, unio*] (14c) **1** : a widely cultivated Asian herb (*Allium cepa*) of the lily family with pungent edible bulbs; *also* : its bulb **2** : any of various plants of the same genus as the onion — **on·iony** \-yə-nē\ *adj*
onion dome *n* (1941) : a dome (as of a church) having the general shape of an onion — **onion–domed** *adj*
onion ring *n* (1946) : a ring of sliced onion coated with batter or crumbs and fried
on·ion·skin \-,skin\ *n* (1879) : a thin strong translucent paper of very light weight
oni·um \'ō-nē-əm\ *adj* [*-onium*] (1905) : being or characterized by a usu. complex cation
-onium *n suffix* [NL, fr. *ammonium*] : an ion having a positive charge ⟨hydr*onium*⟩ — compare -IUM 1b
on–line *adj or adv* (1950) : connected to, served by, or available through a system and esp. a computer or telecommunications system ⟨an ∼ database⟩; *also* : done while connected to a system ⟨∼ computer storage⟩
on·look·er \'ȯn-,lu̇-kər, 'än-\ *n* (1606) : one that looks on; *esp* : a passive spectator — **on·look·ing** \-kiŋ\ *adj*
¹on·ly \'ōn-lē\ *adj* [ME, fr. OE *ānlic*, fr. *ān* one — more at ONE] (bef. 12c) **1** : unquestionably the best : PEERLESS **2** : alone in its class or kind : SOLE ⟨an ∼ child⟩
²only *adv* (14c) **1 a** : as a single fact or instance and nothing more or different : MERELY ⟨has ∼ lost one election —George Orwell⟩ **b** : SOLELY, EXCLUSIVELY ⟨known ∼ to him⟩ **2** : at the very least ⟨it was ∼ too true⟩ **3 a** : in the final outcome ⟨will ∼ make you sick⟩ **b** : with nevertheless the final result ⟨won the battles, ∼ to lose the war⟩ **4 a** : as recently as ⟨∼ last week⟩ **b** : in the immediate past ⟨∼ just talked to her⟩
   usage The placement of *only* in a sentence has been a source of studious commentary since the 18th century, most of it intended to prove by force of argument that prevailing standard usage is wrong. After 200 years of preachment the following observations may be made: the position of *only* in standard spoken English is not fixed, since ambiguity is avoided through sentence stress; in casual prose that keeps close to the rhythms of speech *only* is often placed where it would be in speech; and in edited and more formal prose *only* tends to be placed immediately before the word or words it modifies.
³only *conj* (14c) **1 a** : with the restriction that : BUT ⟨you may go, ∼ come back early⟩ **b** : and yet : HOWEVER ⟨they look very nice, ∼ we can't use them⟩ **2** : were it not that : EXCEPT ⟨I'd introduce you to her, ∼ you'd win her —Jack London⟩
on·o·mas·tic \,ä-nə-'mas-tik\ *adj* [Gk *onomastikos*, fr. *onomazein* to name, fr. *onoma* name — more at NAME] (1716) : of, relating to, or consisting of a name or names — **on·o·mas·ti·cal·ly** \-ti-k(ə-)lē\ *adv*
on·o·mas·tics \-tiks\ *n pl but sing or pl in constr* (1930) **1 a** : the science or study of the origins and forms of words esp. as used in a specialized field **b** : the science or study of the origin and forms of proper names of persons or places **2** : the system underlying the formation and use of words esp. for proper names or of words used in a specialized field — **on·o·mas·ti·cian** \,ä-nə-mas-'ti-shən\ *n*
on·o·ma·tol·o·gy \,ä-nə-mə-'tä-lə-jē\ *n* [F *onomatologie*, fr. Gk *onomat-, onoma* name + F *-logie* *-logy*] (ca. 1847) : ONOMASTICS — **on·o·ma·tol·o·gist** \-jist\ *n*
on·o·mato·poe·ia \,ä-nə-,mä-tə-'pē-ə, -,ma-\ *n* [LL, fr. Gk *onomatopoiia*, fr. *onomat-, onoma* name + *poiein* to make — more at POET] (ca. 1577) **1** : the naming of a thing or action by a vocal imitation of the sound associated with it (as *buzz*, *hiss*) **2** : the use of words whose sound suggests the sense — **on·o·mato·po·et·ic** \-pō-'e-tik\ *or* **on·o·mato·po·et·ic** \-pō-'e-tik\ *adj* — **on·o·mato·poe·i·cal·ly** \-'pē-ə-k(ə-)lē\ *adv* — **on·o·mato·po·et·i·cal·ly** \-pō-'e-ti-k(ə-)lē\ *adv*
On·on·da·ga \,ä-nə(n)-'dȯ-gə, -'dä-, -'dä-\ *n, pl* **-ga** *or* **-gas** [Onondaga *onǫtá?ke*, the chief Onondaga town] (1684) **1** : a member of an American Indian people of New York and Canada **2** : the Iroquoian language of the Onondaga people
on–ramp \'ȯn-,ramp, 'än-\ *n* (1958) : a ramp by which one enters a limited-access highway
on·rush \-,rəsh\ *n* (1844) **1** : a rushing forward or onward **2** : ONSET — **on·rush·ing** \-,rə-shiŋ\ *adj*

on–screen \'ȯn-'skrēn, 'än-\ *adv or adj* (1955) : in a motion picture or a television program

on-set \-ˌset\ *n* (1535) **1** : ATTACK, ASSAULT ⟨withstand the ~ of the army⟩ **2** : BEGINNING, COMMENCEMENT ⟨the ~ of winter⟩

on-shore \'ȯn-ˌshȯr, 'än-, -ˌshȯr\ *adj* (1875) **1** : coming or moving from the water toward or onto the shore ⟨an ~ wind⟩ **2 a** : situated on or near the shore as distinguished from being in deep or open water **b** : situated on land **3** : DOMESTIC 2 ⟨~ markets⟩ — **on-shore** \'ȯn-', 'än-\ *adv*

on-side \-'sīd\ *adv or adj* (1871) : not offside : in a position legally to play or receive the ball or puck

onside kick *n* (1926) : a kickoff in football in which the ball travels just far enough to be legally recoverable by the kicking team

on–site \-'sīt\ *adj or adv* (1946) : carried out or located at the place connected with a particular activity ⟨~ training in construction skills⟩

on-slaught \'än-ˌslȯt, 'ȯn-\ *n* [modif. of D *aanslag* act of striking; akin to OE *an* on and to OE *slēan* to strike — more at SLAY] (ca. 1625) : an esp. fierce attack; *also* : something resembling such an attack ⟨an ~ of technological changes⟩

on-stage \'ȯn-ˌstāj, 'än-, -ˌstāj\ *adv or adj* (1925) : on a part of the stage visible to the audience

on-stream \'ȯn-'strēm, 'än-\ *adv or adj* (1930) : in or into production ⟨plants scheduled to come ~⟩

ont- *or* **onto-** *comb form* [NL, fr. LGk, fr. Gk *ont-, ōn,* prp. of *einai* to be — more at IS] **1** : being : existence ⟨*ont*ology⟩ **2** : organism ⟨*on*togeny⟩

-ont *n comb form* [Gk *ont-, ōn,* prp.] : cell : organism ⟨dipl*ont*⟩

on–the–job *adj* (1946) : of, relating to, or being something (as training or experience) learned, gained, or done while working at a job and often under supervision

on-tic \'än-tik\ *adj* (1942) : of, relating to, or having real being — **on-ti-cal-ly** \-ti-k(ə-)lē\ *adv*

¹on-to \'ȯn-(ˌ)tü, 'än-\ *prep* (1581) **1** : to a position on **2** : in or into a state of awareness about ⟨put me ~ your methods⟩ **3** — used as a function word to indicate a set each element of which is the image of at least one element of another set ⟨a function mapping the set *S* ~ the set *T*⟩

²onto *adj* (1942) : mapping elements in such a way that every element in one set is the image of at least one element in another set ⟨a function that is one-to-one and ~⟩

on-to-gen-e-sis \ˌän-tə-'je-nə-səs\ *n* [NL] (1875) : ONTOGENY

on-to-ge-net-ic \-jə-'ne-tik\ *adj* [ISV] (1878) **1** : of, relating to, or appearing in the course of ontogeny **2** : based on visible morphological characters — **on-to-ge-net-i-cal-ly** \-ti-k(ə-)lē\ *adv*

on-tog-e-ny \än-'tä-jə-nē\ *n* [ISV] (1872) : the development or course of development esp. of an individual organism

on-to-log-i-cal \ˌän-tᵊl-'ä-ji-kəl\ *adj* (1782) **1** : of or relating to ontology **2** : relating to or based upon being or existence — **on-to-log-i-cal-ly** \-k(ə-)lē\ *adv*

ontological argument *n* (1877) : an argument for the existence of God based upon the meaning of the term *God*

on-tol-o-gy \än-'täl-ə-jē\ *n* [NL *ontologia,* fr. *ont-* + *-logia* -logy] (ca. 1721) **1** : a branch of metaphysics concerned with the nature and relations of being **2** : a particular theory about the nature of being or the kinds of existents — **on-tol-o-gist** \-jist\ *n*

onus \'ō-nəs\ *n* (ca. 1640) **1** [L — more at ONEROUS] **a** : BURDEN **b** : a disagreeable necessity : OBLIGATION **c** : BLAME **d** : STIGMA **2** [NL *onus (probandi),* lit., burden of proving] : BURDEN OF PROOF

¹on-ward \'ȯn-wərd, 'än-\ *also* **on-wards** \-wərdz\ *adv* (1532) : toward or at a point lying ahead in space or time — FORWARD

²onward *adj* (1660) : directed or moving onward : FORWARD

on-y-choph-o-ran \ˌä-ni-'kä-fə-rən\ *n* [NL *Onychophora,* group name, fr. Gk *onych-, onyx* claw + *-phoros* -phore] (ca. 1890) : PERIPATUS — **onychophoran** *adj*

-onym *n comb form* [ME, fr. L *-onymum,* fr. Gk *-ōnymon,* fr. *onyma* — more at NAME] : name : word ⟨anton*ym*⟩

on-yx \'ä-niks\ *n* [ME *onix,* fr. MF & L; MF, fr. L *onych-, onyx,* fr. Gk, lit., claw, nail — more at NAIL] (14c) : a translucent chalcedony in parallel layers of different colors

oo- — see O-

oo-cyst \'ō-ə-ˌsist\ *n* [ISV] (1875) : ZYGOTE; *specif* : a sporozoan zygote undergoing sporogenous development

oo-cyte \'ō-ə-ˌsīt\ *n* [ISV] (1895) : an egg before maturation : a female gametocyte

oo-dles \'ü-dᵊlz\ *n pl but sing or pl in constr* [origin unknown] (1869) : a great quantity : LOT

oog-a-mous \ō-'ä-gə-məs\ *adj* (1888) : having or involving a small motile male gamete and a large immobile female gamete — **oog-a-my** \-mē\ *n*

oo-gen-e-sis \ˌō-ə-'je-nə-səs\ *n* [NL] (ca. 1879) : formation and maturation of the egg — **oo-ge-net-ic** \-jə-'ne-tik\ *adj*

oo-go-ni-um \ˌō-ə-'gō-nē-əm\ *n, pl* **-nia** \-nē-ə\ [NL] (1867) **1** : a female sexual organ in various algae and fungi that corresponds to the archegonium of ferns and mosses **2** : a descendant of a primordial germ cell that gives rise to oocytes — **oo-go-ni-al** \-nē-əl\ *adj*

¹ooh \'ü\ *interj* (1939) — used to express amazement, joy, or surprise

²ooh *vi* (1951) : to exclaim in amazement, joy, or surprise ⟨~ing and aahing over the new automobiles⟩ — **ooh** *n*

oo-lite \'ō-ə-ˌlīt\ *n* [prob. fr. F *oolithe,* fr. *oo-* + *-lithe* -lite] (1785) : a rock consisting of small round grains usu. of calcium carbonate cemented together — **oo-lit-ic** \ˌō-ə-'li-tik\ *adj*

ool-o-gist \ō-'ä-lə-jist\ *n* (1863) **1** : a person specializing in the study of birds' eggs **2** : a collector of birds' eggs — **ool-o-gy** \-jē\ *n*

oo-long \'ü-ˌlȯŋ\ *n* [Chin (Beijing) *wūlóng,* lit., black dragon] (1850) : tea made from leaves that have been partially fermented before firing

oom-pah \'üm-(ˌ)pä, 'üm-\ *also* **oom-pah-pah** \-(ˌ)pä-'pä, ˌüm-\ *n* [imit.] (1877) : a repeated rhythmic bass accompaniment esp. in a band — **oompah** *vb*

oomph \'üm(p)f\ *n* [imit. of a sound made under exertion] (1936) **1** : personal charm or magnetism : GLAMOUR **2** : SEX APPEAL **3** : PUNCH, VITALITY

oo-pho-rec-to-my \ˌō-ə-fə-'rek-tə-mē\ *n, pl* **-mies** [NL *oophoron* ovary (fr. *o-* + Gk *-phoron,* neut. of *-phoros* -phore) + E *-ectomy*] (1872) : OVARIECTOMY

oops \'(w)ü(ə)ps\ *interj* (1933) — used typically to express mild apology, surprise, or dismay

Oort cloud \'ȯrt-, 'ȯrt-\ *n* [Jan *Oort* †1992 Dutch astronomer] (1968) : a spherical shell of small frozen bodies believed to surround the sun far beyond the orbit of Pluto and from which some are dislodged when perturbed (as by a passing star) to fall toward the sun as comets

oo-spore \'ō-ə-ˌspȯr, -ˌspȯr\ *n* [ISV] (1865) : ZYGOTE; *esp* : a spore produced by heterogamous fertilization that yields a sporophyte

oo-the-ca \ˌō-ə-'thē-kə\ *n, pl* **oo-the-cae** \-'thē-(ˌ)kē, -(ˌ)sē\ [NL] (ca. 1856) : a firm-walled and distinctive egg case (as of a cockroach) — **oo-the-cal** \-'thē-kəl\ *adj*

oo-tid \'ō-ə-ˌtid\ *n* [irreg. fr. *o-* + *-id*] (1904) : an egg cell after meiosis

¹ooze \'üz\ *n* [ME *wose,* fr. OE *wāse* mire; akin to ON *veisa* stagnant water] (bef. 12c) **1** : a soft deposit (as of mud, slime, or shells) on the bottom of a body of water **2** : a piece of soft wet plastic ground

²ooze *vb* **oozed; ooz-ing** [ME *wosen,* fr. *wose* sap] *vi* (14c) **1** : to pass or flow slowly through or as if through small openings or interstices **2** : to move slowly or imperceptibly ⟨the crowd began to ~ forward — Bruce Marshall⟩ **3 a** : to exude moisture **b** : to exude something often in a faintly repellent manner ⟨~ with sympathy⟩ ~ *vt* **1** : to emit slowly **2** : EXUDE 2 ⟨~ confidence⟩

³ooze *n* [ME *wose* sap, juice, fr. OE *wōs;* akin to OHG *waso* damp] (ca. 1581) **1** : a decoction of vegetable material used for tanning leather **2** : the act of oozing **3** : something that oozes

oozy \'ü-zē\ *adj* **ooz-i-er; -est** (14c) **1** : containing or composed of ooze : resembling ooze **2** : exuding moisture : SLIMY

op \'äp\ *n* (1964) : OPTICAL ART

opac-i-ty \ō-'pa-sə-tē\ *n, pl* **-ties** [F *opacité* shadiness, fr. L *opacitat-, opacitas,* fr. *opacus* shaded, dark] (ca. 1611) **1** : the quality or state of a body that makes it impervious to the rays of light; *broadly* : the relative capacity of matter to obstruct the transmission of radiant energy **2 a** : obscurity of sense : UNINTELLIGIBLENESS **b** : the quality or state of being mentally obtuse : DULLNESS **3** : an opaque spot in a normally transparent structure (as the lens of the eye)

opah \'ō-pə, -ˌpä\ *n* [perh. fr. Ibo *úbà*] (1750) : a large elliptical marine bony fish (*Lampris guttatus* of the family Lampridae) with brilliant colors

opal \'ō-pəl\ *n* [L *opalus,* fr. Gk *opallios,* fr. Skt *upala* stone, jewel] (1591) : a mineral that is a hydrated amorphous silica softer and less dense than quartz and typically with definite and often marked iridescent play of colors

opal-es-cent \ˌō-pə-'le-sᵊnt\ *adj* (ca. 1813) : reflecting an iridescent light — **opal-es-cence** \-ᵊn(t)s\ *n* — **opal-es-cent-ly** \-sᵊnt-lē\ *adv*

opal-ine \'ō-pə-ˌlīn, -ˌlēn\ *adj* (1784) : resembling opal

opah

opaque \ō-'pāk\ *adj* [L *opacus*] (1641) **1** : exhibiting opacity : blocking the passage of radiant energy and esp. light **2 a** : hard to understand or explain ⟨~ prose⟩ **b** : OBTUSE, THICKHEADED — **opaque** *n* — **opaque-ly** *adv* — **opaque-ness** *n*

opaque projector *n* (1951) : a projector using reflected light for projecting an image of an opaque object or matter on an opaque support (as a photograph)

op art \'äp-\ *n* (1964) : OPTICAL ART — **op artist** *n*

ope \'ōp\ *vb* **oped; op-ing** (15c) *archaic* : OPEN

op-ed \'äp-'ed\ *n, often cap O&E, often attrib* [short for *opposite editorial*] (1970) : a page of special features usu. opposite the editorial page of a newspaper

¹open \'ō-pən, -p³m\ *adj* **open-er** \'ōp-nər, 'ō-pə-\; **open-est** \'ōp-nəst, 'ō-pə-\ [ME, fr. OE; akin to OHG *offan* open, OE *ūp* up] (bef. 12c) **1** : having no enclosing or confining barrier : accessible on all or nearly all sides ⟨cattle grazing on an ~ range⟩ **2 a** (1) : being in a position or adjustment to permit passage : not shut or locked ⟨an ~ door⟩ (2) : having a barrier (as a door) so adjusted as to allow passage ⟨the house was ~⟩ **b** : having the lips parted ⟨stood there with his mouth wide ~⟩ **c** : not buttoned or zipped ⟨an ~ shirt⟩ **3 a** : completely free from concealment : exposed to general view or knowledge ⟨their hostilities eventually erupted with ~ war⟩ **b** : exposed or vulnerable to attack or question : SUBJECT ⟨~ to doubt⟩ **4 a** : not covered with a top, roof, or lid ⟨an ~ car⟩ ⟨her eyes were ~⟩ **b** : having no protective covering ⟨~ wiring⟩ ⟨an ~ wound⟩ **5** : not restricted to a particular group or category of participants ⟨~ to the public⟩ ⟨~ housing⟩: as **a** : enterable by both amateur and professional contestants ⟨an ~ tournament⟩ **b** : enterable by a registered voter regardless of political affiliation ⟨an ~ primary⟩ **6** : fit to be traveled over : presenting no obstacle to passage or view ⟨the ~ road⟩ ⟨~ country⟩ **7** : having the parts or surfaces laid out in an expanded position : spread out ⟨an UN-FOLDED ⟨an ~ book⟩ **8 a** (1) : LOW 13 (2) : formed with the tongue in a lower position ⟨Italian has an ~ and a close *e*⟩ **b** (1) : having clarity and resonance unimpaired by undue tension or constriction of the throat ⟨an ~ vocal tone⟩ (2) *of a tone* : produced by an open string or on a wind instrument by the lip without the use of slides, valves, or keys **9 a** : available to follow or make use of ⟨the only course ~ to us⟩ **b** : not taken up with duties or engagements ⟨keep an hour ~ on Friday⟩ **c** : not finally decided : subject to further consideration ⟨the salary is ~⟩ ⟨an ~ question⟩ **d** : available for a qualified applicant : VACANT ⟨the job is still ~⟩ **e** : remaining available for use or filling until canceled ⟨an ~ order for more items⟩ **f** : available for future purchase ⟨these items are in ~ stock⟩ **10 a** : characterized by ready accessibility and usu. generous attitude: as (1) : generous in giving (2) : willing to hear and consider or to accept and deal with : RESPONSIVE (3) : free from reserve or pretense : FRANK

\ə\ abut \ᵊ\ kitten, F table \ər\ further \a\ ash \ā\ ace \ä\ mop, mar \aú\ out \ch\ chin \e\ bet \ē\ easy \g\ go \i\ hit \ī\ ice \j\ job \ŋ\ sing \ō\ go \ȯ\ law \ȯi\ boy \th\ thin \t͟h\ the \ü\ loot \ú\ foot \y\ yet \zh\ vision \à, ᵏ, ⁿ, œ, œ̄, ᵫ, �ᵉ, ᵞ\ *see* Guide to Pronunciation

b : accessible to the influx of new factors (as foreign goods) ⟨an ~ market⟩ **11 a** : having openings, interruptions, or spaces: as (1) : being porous and friable ⟨~ soil⟩ (2) : sparsely distributed : SCATTERED ⟨~ population⟩ (3) *of a compound* : having components separated by a space in writing or printing (as *opaque projector*) **b** : not made up of a continuous closed circuit of channels ⟨the insect circulatory system is ~⟩ **12 a** *of an organ pipe* : not stopped at the top **b** *of a string on a musical instrument* : not stopped by the finger **13** : being in operation ⟨an ~ microphone⟩; *esp* : ready for business, patronage, or use ⟨the store is ~ from 9 to 5⟩ ⟨the new highway will be ~ next week⟩ **14 a** (1) : characterized by lack of effective regulation of various commercial enterprises ⟨an ~ town⟩ (2) : not repressed by legal controls ⟨~ gambling⟩ **b** : free from checking or hampering restraints ⟨an ~ economy⟩ **c** : relatively unguarded by opponents ⟨passed to an ~ teammate⟩ **15** : having been opened by a first ante, bet, or bid ⟨the bidding is ~⟩ **16** *of punctuation* : characterized by sparing use esp. of the comma **17 a** : containing none of its endpoints ⟨an ~ interval⟩ **b** : being a set or composed of sets each point of which has a neighborhood all of whose points are contained in the set ⟨the interior of a sphere is an ~ set⟩ **18 a** : being an incomplete electrical circuit **b** : not allowing the flow of electricity ⟨an ~ switch⟩ *syn* see FRANK, LIABLE — **open** *adv* — **open·ly** \'ō-pən-lē\ *adv* — **open·ness** \-pə(n)-nəs\ *n*

²**open** *vb* **opened** \'ō-pənd, 'ō-p²md\; **open·ing** \'ōp-niŋ, 'ō-pə-\ *vt* (bef. 12c) **1 a** : to move (as a door) from a closed position **b** : to make available for entry or passage by turning back (as a barrier) or removing (as a cover or an obstruction) **2 a** : to make available for or active in a regular function ⟨~ a new store⟩ **b** : to make accessible for a particular purpose ⟨~ed new land for settlement⟩ ⟨~ the way for changes⟩ **c** : to initiate access to (a computer file) prior to use **3 a** : to disclose or expose to view : REVEAL **b** : to make more discerning or responsive : ENLIGHTEN ⟨must ~ our minds to the problems⟩ **c** : to bring into view or come in sight of by changing position **4 a** : to make an opening in ⟨~ed the boil⟩ **b** : to loosen and make less compact ⟨~ the soil⟩ **5** : to spread out : UNFOLD ⟨~ed the book⟩ **6 a** : to enter upon : BEGIN ⟨~ed the meeting⟩ **b** : to commence action in a card game by making (a first bid), putting a first bet in (the pot), or playing (a card or suit) as first lead **7** : to restore or recall (as an order) from a finally determined state to a state in which the parties are free to prosecute or oppose ~ *vi* **1** : to become open ⟨the office ~ed early⟩ **2 a** : to spread out : EXPAND ⟨the wound ~ed under the strain⟩ **b** : to become disclosed ⟨a beautiful vista ~ed before us⟩ **3** : to become enlightened or responsive **4** : to give access ⟨the rooms ~ onto a hall⟩ **5** : SPEAK OUT **2** ⟨finally he ~ed freely on the subject⟩ **6 a** : to begin a course or activity ⟨the play ~s on Tuesday⟩ **b** : to make a bet, bid, or lead in commencing a round or hand of a card game — **open·abil·i·ty** \ˌōp-nə-'bil-ə-tē, ˌō-pə-\ *n* — **open·able** \'ōp-nə-bəl, 'ō-pə-\ *adj*

³**open** *n* (13c) **1** : OPENING **2** : open and unobstructed space: as **a** : OPEN AIR **b** : open water **3** : an open contest, competition, or tournament **4** : a public or unconcealed state or position

open admission *n* (1969) : OPEN ENROLLMENT 2

open-air *adj* (1830) : OUTDOOR

open air *n* (15c) : the space where air is unconfined; *esp* : OUTDOORS

open-and-shut *adj* (1841) **1** : perfectly simple : OBVIOUS **2** : easily settled ⟨an ~ case⟩

open bar *n* (1973) : a bar (as at a wedding reception) at which drinks are served free — compare CASH BAR

open·cast \'ō-pən-ˌkast\ *adj* (ca. 1890) *chiefly Brit* : worked from a surface open to the air ⟨an ~ mine⟩ ⟨~ mining⟩

open chain *n* (1884) : an arrangement of atoms represented in a structural formula by a chain whose ends are not joined so as to form a ring

open city *n* (1914) : a city that is not occupied or defended by military forces and that is not allowed to be bombed under international law

open dating *n* (1971) : the marking of perishable food products with a clearly readable date indicating when the food was packaged or the last date on which it should be sold or used

open door *n* (1526) **1** : a recognized right of admittance : freedom of access **2** : a policy allowing opportunity for commercial relations with a country to all nations on equal terms — **open-door** *adj*

open-end *adj* (1917) **1** : organized to allow for contingencies: as **a** : permitting additional debt to be incurred under the original indenture subject to specified conditions ⟨an ~ mortgage⟩ **b** : having a fluctuating capitalization of shares that are issued or redeemed at the current net asset value or at a figure in fixed ratio to this ⟨an ~ investment company⟩ — compare CLOSED-END

open-end·ed \ˌō-pən-'en-dəd\ *adj* (1825) : not rigorously fixed: as **a** : adaptable to the developing needs of a situation **b** : permitting or designed to permit spontaneous and unguided responses — **open-end·ed·ness** *n*

open enrollment *n* (1964) **1** : the voluntary enrollment of a student in a public school other than the one assigned on the basis of residence **2** : enrollment on demand as a student in an institution of higher learning irrespective of formal qualifications

open·er \'ōp-nər, 'ō-pə-\ *n* (15c) : one that opens ⟨a bottle ~⟩: as **a** *pl* : cards of sufficient value for a player to open the betting in a poker game **b** : the first item, contest, or event of a series — **for openers** : to begin with

open-eyed \ˌō-pən-'īd\ *adj* (1601) **1** : having the eyes open **2** : carefully observant : DISCERNING

open·hand·ed \-'han-dəd\ *adj* (1593) : GENEROUS, MUNIFICENT — **open·hand·ed·ly** *adv* — **open·hand·ed·ness** *n*

open-heart *adj* (1960) : of, relating to, or performed on a heart temporarily relieved of circulatory function and surgically opened for inspection and treatment ⟨~ surgery⟩

open·heart·ed \ˌō-pən-'här-təd\ *adj* (1611) **1** : candidly straightforward : FRANK **2** : responsive to emotional appeal — **open·heart·ed·ly** *adv* — **open·heart·ed·ness** *n*

open-hearth *adj* (1885) : of, relating to, involving, or produced in the open-hearth process ⟨~ steel⟩

open-hearth process *n* (1882) : a process of making steel from pig iron in a furnace of the regenerative reverberatory type

open house *n* (15c) **1** : ready and usu. informal hospitality or entertainment for all comers **2** : a house or apartment open for inspection esp. by prospective buyers or tenants

open·ing \'ōp-niŋ, 'ō-pə-\ *n* (13c) **1 a** : an act or instance of making or becoming open **b** : an act or instance of beginning : COMMENCEMENT; *esp* : a formal and usu. public event by which something new is put officially into operation **2** : something that is open: as **a** (1) : BREACH, APERTURE (2) : an open width : SPAN **b** : an area without trees or with scattered usu. mature trees that occurs as a break in a forest **c** : two pages that face one another in a book **3** : something that constitutes a beginning: as **a** : a planned series of moves made at the beginning of a game of chess or checkers — compare ENDGAME, MIDDLE GAME **b** : a first performance **4 a** : OCCASION, CHANCE **b** : an opportunity for employment

open letter *n* (1878) : a published letter of protest or appeal usu. addressed to an individual but intended for the general public

open loop *n* (1947) : a control system for an operation or process in which there is no self-correcting action as there is in a closed loop

open marriage *n* (1971) : a marriage in which the partners agree to let each other have sexual partners outside the marriage

open-mind·ed *adj* (1828) : receptive to arguments or ideas — **open-mind·ed·ly** *adv* — **open-mind·ed·ness** *n*

open-mouthed \ˌō-pən-'maůthd, -'maůtht\ *adj* (15c) **1** : CLAMOROUS, VOCIFEROUS **2** : having the mouth wide open **3** : struck with amazement or wonder — **open-mouth·ed·ly** \-'maů-thəd-lē, -thəd-\ *adv* — **open-mouth·ed·ness** \-'maů-thəd-nəs, -thəd-\ *n*

open-pol·li·nat·ed \ˌō-pən-'pä-lə-ˌnā-təd\ *adj* (1925) : pollinated by natural agencies without human intervention

open season *n* (ca. 1890) **1** : a period when it is legal to kill or catch game or fish protected at other times by law **2** : a time during which someone or something is the object of sustained attack or criticism

open secret *n* (1828) : a supposedly secret but generally known matter

open sentence *n* (1937) : a statement (as in mathematics) that contains at least one blank or unknown and that becomes true or false when the blank is filled or a quantity is substituted for the unknown

open ses·a·me \-'se-sə-mē\ *n* [fr. *open sesame*, the magical command used by Ali Baba to open the door of the robbers' den in *Ali Baba and the Forty Thieves*] (ca. 1837) : something that unfailingly brings about a desired end

open shop *n* (1903) : an establishment in which eligibility for employment and retention on the payroll are not determined by membership or nonmembership in a labor union though there may be an agreement by which a union is recognized as sole bargaining agent

open sight *n* (1591) : a firearm rear sight having an open notch

open stance *n* (1948) : a stance (as in golf) in which the forward foot is farther from the line of play than the back foot — compare CLOSED STANCE

open syllable *n* (1891) : a syllable ended by a vowel or diphthong

open up *vt* (1582) **1** : to make available **2** : to make plain or visible : DISCLOSE **3** : to open by cutting into ~ *vi* **1** : to spread out or come into view ⟨the road *opens up* ahead⟩ **2** : to commence firing **3** : to become communicative ⟨tried to get the patient to *open up*⟩

open·work \'ō-pən-ˌwərk\ *n, often attrib* (1598) : work constructed so as to show openings through its substance : work that is perforated or pierced ⟨wrought-iron ~⟩ — **open-worked** \-ˌwərkt\ *adj*

¹**opera** *pl of* OPUS

²**op·era** \'ä-p(ə-)rə, *Southern also* 'ä-prē\ *n* [It, work, opera, fr. L, work, pains; akin to L *oper-, opus* — more at OPERATE] (1644) **1** : a drama set to music and made up of vocal pieces with orchestral accompaniment and orchestral overtures and interludes; *specif* : GRAND OPERA **2** : the score of a musical drama **3** : the performance of an opera; *also* : a house where operas are performed

op·er·a·ble \'ä-p(ə-)rə-bəl\ *adj* (1646) **1** : fit, possible, or desirable to use : PRACTICABLE **2** : likely to result in a favorable outcome upon surgical treatment ⟨an ~ cancer⟩ — **op·er·a·bil·i·ty** \ˌä-p(ə-)rə-'bi-lə-tē\ *n* — **op·er·a·bly** \'ä-p(ə-)rə-blē\ *adv*

op·éra bouffe \ˌō-pä-rä-'büf, 'ä-p(ə-)rə-\ *n* [F, fr. It *opera buffa*] (1870) : satirical comic opera

opera buf·fa \-'bü-fə\ *n* [It, lit., comic opera] (1802) : an 18th century farcical comic opera with dialogue in recitative

opéra co·mique \-kä-'mēk, -kō-\ *n* [F, lit., comic opera] (1744) : an opera characterized by spoken dialogue interspersed between the arias and ensemble numbers — compare GRAND OPERA

opera glass *n* (1738) : a small low-power binocular without prisms for use at the opera or theater — often used in pl.

op·era·go·er \'ä-p(ə-)rə-ˌgō(-ə)r\ *n* (1850) : a person who frequently goes to operas — **op·era·go·ing** \-ˌgō-iŋ, -ˌgó(-)iŋ\ *n*

opera hat *n* (1810) : a man's collapsible top hat

opera house *n* (1720) : a theater devoted principally to the performance of operas; *broadly* : THEATER

op·er·and \'ä-pə-ˌrand\ *n* [L *operandum*, neut. of gerundive of *operari*] (1886) : something (as a quantity or data) that is operated on (as in a mathematical operation); *also* : the address in a computer instruction of data to be operated on

¹**op·er·ant** \'ä-pə-rənt\ *adj* (15c) **1** : functioning or tending to produce effects : EFFECTIVE ⟨an ~ conscience⟩ **2** : of or relating to the observable or measurable **3** : of, relating to, or being an operant or operant conditioning ⟨~ behavior⟩ — **op·er·ant·ly** *adv*

²**operant** *n* (1937) : behavior (as bar pressing by a rat to obtain food) that operates on the environment to produce rewarding and reinforcing effects

operant conditioning *n* (1941) : conditioning in which the desired behavior or increasingly closer approximations to it are followed by a rewarding or reinforcing stimulus — compare CLASSICAL CONDITIONING

opera se·ria \'ser-ē-ə, -'sir-\ *n* [It, lit., serious opera] (ca. 1854) : an 18th century opera with a heroic or legendary subject

op·er·ate \'ä-pə-ˌrāt, -ˌprāt\ *vb* **-at·ed; -at·ing** [L *operatus*, pp. of *operari* to work, fr. *oper-, opus* work; akin to OE *efnan* to perform, Skt *apas* work] *vi* (1588) **1** : to perform a function : exert power or influence ⟨factors operating against our success⟩ **2** : to produce an appropriate effect ⟨the drug *operated* quickly⟩ **3 a** : to perform an operation or a series of operations **b** : to perform surgery **c** : to carry on a military or naval action or mission **4** : to follow a course of conduct that is often irregular ⟨crooked gamblers *operating* in the club⟩ ~ *vt*

1 : BRING ABOUT, EFFECT 2 a : to cause to function : WORK b : to put or keep in operation 3 : to perform an operation on; *esp* : to perform surgery on

op·er·at·ic \ˌä-pə-'ra-tik\ *adj* (1749) 1 : of or relating to opera 2 : grand, dramatic, or romantic in style or effect — **op·er·at·i·cal·ly** \-ti-k(ə-)lē\ *adv*

operating *adj* (1808) : of, relating to, or used for or in operations ⟨~ expenses⟩ ⟨a hospital ~ room⟩

operating system *n* (1961) : software that controls the operation of a computer and directs the processing of programs (as by assigning storage space in memory and controlling input and output functions)

op·er·a·tion \ˌä-pə-'rā-shən\ *n* [ME *operacioun*, fr. MF *operation*, fr. L *operation-, operatio*, fr. *operari*] (14c) 1 : performance of a practical work or of something involving the practical application of principles or processes 2 a : an exertion of power or influence ⟨the ~ of a drug⟩ b : the quality or state of being functional or operative ⟨the plant is now in ~⟩ c : a method or manner of functioning ⟨a machine of very simple ~⟩ 3 : EFFICACY, POTENCY — archaic except in legal usage 4 : a procedure carried out on a living body usu. with instruments esp. for the repair of damage or the restoration of health 5 : any of various mathematical or logical processes (as addition) of deriving one entity from others according to a rule 6 a : a usu. military action, mission, or maneuver including its planning and execution b *pl* : the office on the flight line of an airfield where pilots file clearance for flights and where flying from the field is controlled c *pl* : the agency of an organization charged with carrying on the principal planning and operating functions of a headquarters and its subordinate units 7 : a business transaction esp. when speculative 8 : a single step performed by a computer in the execution of a program

op·er·a·tion·al \-shnəl, -shə-nᵊl\ *adj* (ca. 1909) 1 : of or relating to operation or to an operation ⟨the ~ gap between planning and production⟩ 2 : of, relating to, or based on operations 3 a : of, engaged in, or connected with execution of military or naval operations in campaign or battle b : ready for or in condition to undertake a destined function — **op·er·a·tion·al·ly** *adv*

op·er·a·tion·al·ism \-shnə-ˌli-zəm, -shə-nᵊl-ˌi-zəm\ *n* (1931) : a view that the concepts or terms used in nonanalytic scientific statements must be definable in terms of identifiable and repeatable operations — **op·er·a·tion·al·ist** \-list, -ist\ *n* — **op·er·a·tion·al·is·tic** \-ˌrä-shnə-ᵊlis-tik, -shə-nᵊl-'is-tik\ *adj*

op·er·a·tion·ism \ˌä-pə-'rä-shə-ˌni-zəm\ *n* (1935) : OPERATIONALISM — **op·er·a·tion·ist** \-sh(ə-)nist\ *n*

operations research *n* (1945) : the application of scientific and esp. mathematical methods to the study and analysis of problems involving complex systems — called also *operational research*

¹op·er·a·tive \'ä-p(ə-)rə-tiv, 'ä-pə-ˌrā-\ *adj* (15c) 1 : producing an appropriate effect : EFFICACIOUS 2 : exerting force or influence : OPERATING 3 a : having to do with physical operations (as of machines) b : WORKING ⟨an ~ craftsman⟩ 4 : based on or consisting of an operation ⟨~ dentistry⟩ — **op·er·a·tive·ly** *adv* — **op·er·a·tive·ness** *n*

²operative *n* (ca. 1810) : OPERATOR: as a : ARTISAN, MECHANIC b : a secret agent c : PRIVATE DETECTIVE

op·er·a·tor \'ä-pə-ˌrā-tər, 'ä-ˌprā-\ *n* (1611) 1 : one that operates: as a : one that operates a machine or device b : one that operates a business c : one that performs surgical operations d : one that deals in stocks or commodities 2 a : MOUNTEBANK, FRAUD b : a shrewd and skillful person who knows how to circumvent restrictions or difficulties 3 a : something used and esp. a symbol that denotes or performs a mathematical or logical operation b : a mathematical function 4 : a binding site in a DNA chain at which a genetic repressor binds to inhibit the initiation of transcription of messenger RNA by one or more nearby structural genes — called also *operator gene*; compare OPERON — **op·er·a·tor·less** *adj*

¹oper·cu·lar \ō-'pər-kyə-lər\ *adj* (1830) : of, relating to, or constituting an operculum

²opercular *n* (ca. 1890) : an opercular part (as a bone or scale)

oper·cu·late \ō-'pər-kyə-lət\ *also* **oper·cu·lat·ed** \-ˌlā-təd\ *adj* (ca. 1775) : having an operculum

oper·cu·lum \ō-'pər-kyə-ləm\ *n, pl* **-la** \-lə\ *also* **-lums** [NL, fr. L, cover, fr. *operire* to shut, cover] (1752) 1 : a body process or part that suggests a lid: as a : a horny or shelly plate on the posterior dorsal surface of the foot in many gastropod mollusks that closes the shell when the animal is retracted b : the covering of the gills of a fish — see FISH illustration 2 : a lid or covering flap (as of a moss capsule or a pyxidium in a seed plant)

op·er·et·ta \ˌä-pə-'re-tə\ *n* [It, dim. of *opera*] (1770) : a usu. romantic comic opera that includes songs and dancing — **op·er·et·tist** \-'re-tist\ *n*

op·er·on \'ä-pə-ˌrän\ *n* [F *opéron*, fr. *opérer* to bring about, effect (fr. L *operari*) + *-on* ²-on] (1961) : a group of closely linked genes that produces a single messenger RNA molecule in transcription and that consists of structural genes and regulating elements (as an operator and promoter)

op·er·ose \'ä-pə-ˌrōs\ *adj* [L *operosus*, fr. *oper-, opus* work — more at OPERATE] (1678) : TEDIOUS, WEARISOME — **op·er·ose·ly** *adv* — **op·er·ose·ness** *n*

Ophe·lia \ō-'fēl-yə\ *n* : the daughter of Polonius in Shakespeare's *Hamlet*

ophid·i·an \ō-'fi-dē-ən\ *adj* [ultim. fr. Gk *ophis*] (1883) : of, relating to, or resembling snakes — **ophidian** *n*

Ophir \'ō-fər\ *n* [Heb *Ōphīr*] : a biblical land of uncertain location but reputedly rich in gold

ophit·ic \ä-'fi-tik, ō-\ *adj* [ophite serpentine (stone), fr. L *ophites*, fr. Gk *ophitēs* (*lithos*), fr. *ophitēs* snakelike, fr. *ophis* snake; akin to Skt *ahi* snake and prob. to L *anguis* snake, *anguilla* eel, Gk *enchelys* eel, *echidna* viper, *echinos* hedgehog, OE *igil*] (1875) : having or being a rock fabric in which lath-shaped plagioclase crystals are enclosed in later formed augite

ophi·u·roid \ˌō-fē-'yur-ˌóid, ä-\ *n* [NL *Ophiuroidea*, group name, fr. *Ophiura*, genus name, fr. Gk *ophis* + *oura* tail — more at ASS] (ca. 1879) : BRITTLE STAR — **ophiuroid** *adj*

ophthalm- *or* **ophthalmo-** *comb form* [Gk, fr. *ophthalmos*] : eye ⟨*oph*thalmology⟩

oph·thal·mia \äf-'thal-mē-ə, äp-\ *n* [ME *obtalmia*, fr. LL *ophthalmia*, fr. Gk, fr. *ophthalmos* eye; akin to Gk *ōps* eye — more at EYE] (14c) : inflammation of the conjunctiva or the eyeball

oph·thal·mic \-mik\ *adj* (ca. 1741) 1 : of, relating to, or situated near the eye 2 : supplying or draining the eye or structures in the region of the eye ⟨~ artery⟩

oph·thal·mol·o·gist \ˌäf-thə(l)-'mä-lə-jist, ˌäp-, -ˌthal-\ *n* (1834) : a physician that specializes in ophthalmology — compare OPTICIAN, OPTOMETRIST

oph·thal·mol·o·gy \-'mä-lə-jē\ *n* (ca. 1842) : a branch of medical science dealing with the structure, functions, and diseases of the eye — **oph·thal·mo·log·ic** \-mə-'lä-jik\ *or* **oph·thal·mo·log·i·cal** \-ji-kəl\ *adj* — **oph·thal·mo·log·i·cal·ly** \-ji-k(ə-)lē\ *adv*

oph·thal·mo·scope \äf-'thal-mə-ˌskōp, äp-\ *n* [ISV] (ca. 1857) : an instrument for use in viewing the interior of the eye and esp. the retina — **oph·thal·mo·scop·ic** \(ˌ)äf-ˌthal-mə-'skä-pik, (ˌ)äp-\ *adj* — **oph·thal·mos·co·py** \ˌäf-thal-'mäs-kə-pē, äp-, -ˌthal-\ *n*

-opia *n comb form* [NL, fr. Gk *-ōpia*, fr. *ōps*] 1 : condition of having (such) vision ⟨diplopia⟩ 2 : condition of having (such) a visual defect ⟨hyperopia⟩

¹opi·ate \'ō-pē-ət, -ˌāt\ *n* (15c) 1 : a preparation or derivative of opium; *broadly* : a narcotic or opioid peptide 2 : something that induces rest or inaction or quiets uneasiness

²opiate *adj* (1543) 1 : containing or mixed with opium b : of, relating to, binding, or being an opiate ⟨~ receptors⟩ 2 a : inducing sleep : NARCOTIC b : causing dullness or inaction

opine \ō-'pīn\ *vb* **opined; opin·ing** [ME, fr. MF *opiner*, fr. L *opinari* to have an opinion] *vi* (15c) : to express opinions ~ *vt* : to state as an opinion

opin·ion \ə-'pin-yən\ *n* [ME, fr. MF, fr. L *opinion-, opinio*, fr. *opinari*] (14c) 1 a : a view, judgment, or appraisal formed in the mind about a particular matter b : APPROVAL, ESTEEM 2 a : belief stronger than impression and less strong than positive knowledge b : a generally held view 3 a : a formal expression of judgment or advice by an expert b : the formal expression (as by a judge, court, or referee) of the legal reasons and principles upon which a legal decision is based — **opin·ioned** \-yənd\ *adj*

syn OPINION, VIEW, BELIEF, CONVICTION, PERSUASION, SENTIMENT mean a judgment one holds as true. OPINION implies a conclusion thought out yet open to dispute ⟨each expert seemed to have a different *opinion*⟩. VIEW suggests a subjective opinion ⟨very assertive in stating his *views*⟩. BELIEF implies often deliberate acceptance and intellectual assent ⟨a firm *belief* in her party's platform⟩. CONVICTION applies to a firmly and seriously held belief ⟨the *conviction* that animal life is as sacred as human⟩. PERSUASION suggests a belief grounded on assurance (as by evidence) of its truth ⟨was of the *persuasion* that everything changes⟩. SENTIMENT suggests a settled opinion reflective of one's feelings ⟨her feminist *sentiments* are well-known⟩.

opin·ion·at·ed \-yə-ˌnā-təd\ *adj* (1601) : unduly adhering to one's own opinion or to preconceived notions — **opin·ion·at·ed·ly** *adv* — **opin·ion·at·ed·ness** *n*

opin·ion·a·tive \-ˌnā-tiv\ *adj* (1536) 1 : of, relating to, or consisting of opinion : DOCTRINAL 2 : OPINIONATED — **opin·ion·a·tive·ly** *adv* — **opin·ion·a·tive·ness** *n*

opi·oid \'ō-pē-ˌóid\ *adj* (1957) 1 : possessing some properties characteristic of opiate narcotics but not derived from opium 2 : of, involving, or induced by an opioid substance or an opioid peptide

opioid peptide *n* (1976) : any of a group of endogenous neural polypeptides (as an endorphin or enkephalin) that bind esp. to opiate receptors and mimic some of the pharmacological properties of opiate drugs — called also *opioid*

opis·tho·branch \ə-'pis-thə-ˌbraŋk\ *n, pl* **-branchs** [NL *Opisthobranchia*, fr. Gk *opisthen* behind (akin to Gk *epi* on) + *branchia* gills — more at EPI-] (ca. 1856) : any of a subclass (Opisthobranchia) of marine gastropod mollusks that have the gills when present posterior to the heart and often lack a shell — **opisthobranch** *adj*

opi·um \'ō-pē-əm\ *n* [ME, fr. L, fr. Gk *opion*, fr. dim. of *opos* sap] (14c) 1 : a bitter brownish addictive narcotic drug that consists of the dried juice of the opium poppy 2 : something having an effect like that of opium

opium poppy *n* (1863) : an annual Eurasian poppy (*Papaver somniferum*) cultivated since antiquity as the source of opium, for its edible oily seeds, or for its showy flowers

opos·sum \(ə-)'pä-səm\ *n, pl* **opossums** *also* **opossum** [Virginia Algonquian, lit., white animal] (1610) 1 : any of a family (Didelphidae) of American marsupials that usu. have a pointed snout and prehensile tail; *esp* : a common omnivorous largely nocturnal and arboreal mammal (*Didelphis virginiana*) of No. America having grayish to blackish fur with white on the cheeks 2 : any of several Australian phalangers

opossum 1

¹op·po·nent \ə-'pō-nənt\ *n* [L *opponent-, opponens*, prp. of *opponere*] (1588) 1 : one that takes an opposite position (as in a debate, contest, or conflict) 2 : a muscle that opposes or counteracts and limits the action of another

²opponent *adj* (1647) 1 : ANTAGONISTIC, OPPOSING 2 : situated in front

op·por·tune \ˌä-pər-'tün, -'tyün\ *adj* [ME, fr. MF *opportun*, fr. L *opportunus*, fr. *ob-* toward + *portus* port, harbor — more at OB-, FORD] (15c) 1 : suitable or convenient for a particular occurrence ⟨an ~ moment⟩ 2 : occurring at an appropriate time ⟨an ~ offer of assistance⟩ — **op·por·tune·ly** *adv* — **op·por·tune·ness** \-'t(y)ün-nəs\ *n*

op·por·tun·ism \-'tü-ˌni-zəm, -'tyü-\ *n* (1870) : the art, policy, or prac-

\ə\ abut \ᵊ\ kitten, F table \ər\ further \a\ ash \ā\ ace \ä\ mop, mar \aú\ out \ch\ chin \e\ bet \ē\ easy \g\ go \i\ hit \ī\ ice \j\ job \ŋ\ sing \ō\ go \ó\ law \ói\ boy \th\ thin \th̲\ the \ü\ loot \ú\ foot \y\ yet \zh\ vision \ə̄, k̲, ⁿ, œ, œ̄, ue, üe, ᵊ\ *see* Guide to Pronunciation tice of taking advantage of opportunities or circumstances often with little regard for principles or consequences — **op·por·tun·ist** \-'tü-nist, -'tyü-\ *n or adj*

op·por·tu·nis·tic \-tü-'nis-tik, -tyü-\ *adj* (1892) : taking advantage of opportunities as they arise: as **a** : exploiting opportunities with little regard to principle or consequences ⟨a politician considered ∼⟩ **b** : feeding on whatever food is available ⟨∼ feeders⟩ **c** : being or caused by a usu. harmless microorganism that can become pathogenic when the host's resistance is impaired ⟨∼ infections⟩ — **op·por·tu·nis·ti·cal·ly** \-ti-k(ə-)lē\ *adv*

op·por·tu·ni·ty \ˌä-pər-'tü-nə-tē, -'tyü-\ *n, pl* **-ties** (14c) **1** : a favorable juncture of circumstances ⟨the halt provided an ∼ for rest and refreshment⟩ **2** : a good chance for advancement or progress

opportunity cost *n* (1911) : the cost of making an investment that is the difference between the return on one investment and the return on an alternative

op·pos·able \ə-'pō-zə-bəl\ *adj* (1667) **1** : capable of being opposed or resisted **2** : capable of being placed against one or more of the remaining digits of a hand or foot ⟨the ∼ human thumb⟩ — **op·pos·abil·i·ty** \-ˌpō-zə-'bi-lə-tē\ *n*

op·pose \ə-'pōz\ *vt* **op·posed; op·pos·ing** [F *opposer*, fr. L *opponere* (perf. indic. *opposui*), fr. *ob-* against + *ponere* to place — more at OB-, POSITION] (1579) **1** : to place opposite or against something **2** : to place over against something so as to provide resistance, counterbalance, or contrast **3** : to offer resistance to — **op·pos·er** *n*

syn OPPOSE, COMBAT, RESIST, WITHSTAND mean to set oneself against someone or something. OPPOSE can apply to any conflict, from mere objection to bitter hostility or warfare ⟨*opposed* the plan⟩. COMBAT stresses the forceful or urgent countering of something ⟨*combat* disease⟩. RESIST implies an overt recognition of a hostile or threatening force and a positive effort to counteract or repel it ⟨*resisting* temptation⟩. WITHSTAND suggests a more passive resistance ⟨trying to *withstand* peer pressure⟩.

op·posed \ə-'pōzd\ *adj* (1596) : set or placed in opposition : CONTRARY ⟨with politicians, as ∼ to soap, you cannot return what you have bought —Felix G. Rohatyn⟩

op·pose·less \ə-'pōz-ləs\ *adj* (1605) *archaic* : IRRESISTIBLE

¹op·po·site \'ä-pə-zət, 'äp-sət\ *adj* [ME, fr. MF, fr. L *oppositus*, pp. of *opponere*] (14c) **1 a** : set over against something that is at the other end or side of an intervening line or space ⟨∼ interior angles⟩ ⟨∼ ends of a diameter⟩ **b** : situated in pairs on an axis with each member being separated from the other by half the circumference of the axis ⟨∼ leaves⟩ — compare ALTERNATE **2 a** : occupying an opposing and often antagonistic position ⟨∼ sides of the question⟩ **b** : diametrically different (as in nature or character) ⟨∼ meanings⟩ **3** : contrary to one another or to a thing specified : REVERSE ⟨gave them ∼ directions⟩ **4** : being the other of a pair that are corresponding or complementary in position, function, or nature ⟨members of the ∼ sex⟩ **5** : of, relating to, or being the side of a baseball field that is near the first base line for a right-handed batter and near the third base line for a left-handed batter — **op·po·site·ly** *adv* — **op·po·site·ness** *n*

syn OPPOSITE, CONTRADICTORY, CONTRARY, ANTITHETICAL mean being so far apart as to be or seem irreconcilable. OPPOSITE applies to things in sharp contrast or in conflict ⟨*opposite* views on foreign aid⟩. CONTRADICTORY applies to two things that completely negate each other so that if one is true or valid the other must be untrue or invalid ⟨made *contradictory* predictions about whether the market would rise or fall⟩. CONTRARY implies extreme divergence or diametrical opposition ⟨*contrary* assessments of the war situation⟩. ANTITHETICAL stresses clear and unequivocal diametrical opposition ⟨a law that is *antithetical* to the very idea of democracy⟩.

²opposite *n* (15c) **1** : something that is opposed to some other often specified thing **2** : ANTONYM **3** : ADDITIVE INVERSE; *esp* : the additive inverse of a real number

³opposite *adv* (1667) : on or to an opposite side

⁴opposite *prep* (1758) **1** : across from and usu. facing or on the same level with ⟨sat ∼ each other⟩ **2** : in a role complementary to ⟨played ∼ the leading man in the comedy⟩

opposite number *n* (1906) : a member of a system or class who holds relatively the same position as a particular member in a corresponding system or class : COUNTERPART

op·po·si·tion \ˌä-pə-'zi-shən\ *n* (14c) **1** : a configuration in which one celestial body is opposite another in the sky or in which the elongation is near or equal to 180 degrees **2** : the relation between two propositions having the same subject and predicate but differing in quantity or quality or both **3** : an act of setting opposite or over against : the condition of being so set **4** : hostile or contrary action or condition **5 a** : something that opposes; *specif* : a body of persons opposing something **b** *often cap* : a political party opposing and prepared to replace the party in power — **op·po·si·tion·al** \-'zish-nəl, -'zi-shə-nᵊl\ *adj*

op·po·si·tion·ist \-'zi-sh(ə-)nist\ *n* (1773) : a member of an opposition — **oppositionist** *adj*

op·press \ə-'pres\ *vt* [ME, fr. MF *oppresser*, fr. L *oppressus*, pp. of *op-primere*, fr. *ob-* against + *premere* to press — more at OB-, PRESS] (14c) **1 a** *archaic* : SUPPRESS **b** : to crush or burden by abuse of power or authority **2** : to burden spiritually or mentally : weigh heavily upon — **syn** see WRONG — **op·pres·sor** \-'pre-sər\ *n*

op·pres·sion \ə-'pre-shən\ *n* (14c) **1 a** : unjust or cruel exercise of authority or power **b** : something that oppresses esp. in being an unjust or excessive exercise of power **2** : a sense of being weighed down in body or mind : DEPRESSION

op·pres·sive \ə-'pre-siv\ *adj* (ca. 1677) **1** : unreasonably burdensome or severe ⟨∼ legislation⟩ **2** : TYRANNICAL **3** : overwhelming or depressing to the spirit or senses ⟨an ∼ climate⟩ **syn** see ONEROUS — **op·pres·sive·ly** *adv* — **op·pres·sive·ness** *n*

op·pro·bri·ous \ə-'prō-brē-əs\ *adj* (14c) **1** : expressive of opprobrium : SCURRILOUS ⟨∼ language⟩ **2** : deserving of opprobrium : INFAMOUS — **op·pro·bri·ous·ly** *adv* — **op·pro·bri·ous·ness** *n*

op·pro·bri·um \-brē-əm\ *n* [L, fr. *opprobrare* to reproach, fr. *ob* in the way of + *probrum* reproach; akin to L *pro* forward and to L *ferre* to carry, bring — more at OB-, FOR, BEAR] (1656) **1** : something that brings disgrace **2 a** : public disgrace or ill fame that follows from conduct considered grossly wrong or vicious **b** : CONTEMPT, REPROACH

op·pugn \ə-'pyün, ä-\ *vt* [ME, fr. L *oppugnare*, fr. *ob-* against + *pugnare* to fight — more at OB-, PUNGENT] (15c) **1** : to fight against **2** : to call in question — **op·pugn·er** *n*

Ops \'äps\ *n* [L] : the Roman goddess of abundance and the wife of Saturn

op·sin \'äp-sən\ *n* [prob. fr. *rhodopsin*] (1951) : any of various colorless proteins that in combination with retinal or a related prosthetic group form a visual pigment (as rhodopsin) in a reaction which is reversed by light

-opsis *n comb form, pl* **-opses** or **-opsides** [NL, fr. Gk, fr. *opsis* appearance, vision] : structure resembling a (specified) thing ⟨cary*opsis*⟩

op·son·ic \äp-'sä-nik\ *adj* (1903) : of, relating to, or involving opsonin

op·so·nin \'äp-sə-nən\ *n* [L *opsonare* to buy provisions, cater (fr. Gk *opsōnein*) + E ¹-*in* — more at OLIGOPSONY] (1903) : an antibody of blood serum that makes foreign cells more susceptible to the action of the phagocytes

-opsy *n comb form* [Gk -*opsia*, fr. *opsis*] : examination ⟨necr*opsy*⟩

opt \'äpt\ *vi* [F *opter*, fr. L *optare*] (1877) : to make a choice; *esp* : to decide in favor of something ⟨∼*ed* for a tax increase —Tom Wicker⟩

op·ta·tive \'äp-tə-tiv\ *adj* (15c) **1 a** : of, relating to, or constituting a verbal mood that is expressive of wish or desire **b** : of, relating to, or constituting a sentence that is expressive of wish or hope **2** : expressing desire or wish — **optative** *n* — **op·ta·tive·ly** *adv*

¹op·tic \'äp-tik\ *adj* [ME, fr. MF *optique*, fr. ML *opticus*, fr. Gk *optikos*, fr. *opsesthai* to be going to see; akin to Gk *opsis* appearance, *ōps* eye — more at EYE] (14c) **1** : of or relating to vision or the eye

²optic *n* (1600) **1** : EYE **2 a** : any of the elements (as lenses, mirrors, or light guides) of an optical instrument or system — usu. used in pl. **b** : an optical instrument

op·ti·cal \'äp-ti-kəl\ *adj* (1570) **1** : of or relating to the science of optics **2 a** : of or relating to vision : VISUAL **b** : VISIBLE 1 ⟨∼ wavelength⟩ **c** : of, relating to, or being objects that emit light in the visible range of frequencies ⟨an ∼ galaxy⟩ **d** : using the properties of light to aid vision ⟨an ∼ instrument⟩ **3 a** : of, relating to, or utilizing light esp. instead of other forms of energy ⟨∼ microscopy⟩ **b** : involving the use of light-sensitive devices to acquire information for a computer ⟨∼ character recognition⟩ **4** : of or relating to optical art — **op·ti·cal·ly** \-k(ə-)lē\ *adv*

optical activity *n* (1877) : ability of a chemical substance to rotate the plane of vibration of polarized light to the right or left

optical art *n* (1964) : nonobjective art characterized by the use of straight or curved lines or geometric patterns often for an illusory effect (as of motion)

optical bench *n* (1883) : an apparatus that is fitted for the convenient location and adjustment of light sources and optical devices and that is used for the observation and measurement of optical phenomena

optical disk *n* (1980) : a disk with a plastic coating on which information (as music or visual images) is recorded digitally (as in the form of tiny pits) and which is read by using a laser

optical fiber *n* (1962) : a single fiber-optic strand

optical glass *n* (1840) : flint or crown glass of well-defined characteristics used esp. for making lenses

optical illusion *n* (1794) : ILLUSION 2a(1)

optically active *adj* (1885) : capable of rotating the plane of polarization of light to the right or left — used of compounds, molecules, or atoms

optical rotation *n* (1895) : the angle through which the plane of vibration of polarized light that traverses an optically active substance is rotated

optic axis *n* (1664) : a line in a doubly refracting medium that is parallel to the direction in which all components of plane-polarized light travel with the same speed

optic chiasma *n* (1872) : the X-shaped partial decussation on the undersurface of the hypothalamus through which the optic nerves are continuous with the brain — called also *optic chiasm*

optic cup *n* (ca. 1885) : the optic vesicle after invaginating to form a 2-layered cup from which the retina and pigmented layer of the eye will develop — called also *eyecup*

optic disk *n* (ca. 1890) : BLIND SPOT 1a

op·ti·cian \äp-'ti-shən\ *n* (1687) **1** : a maker of or dealer in optical items and instruments **2** : a person who reads prescriptions for visual correction, orders lenses, and dispenses spectacles and contact lenses — compare OPHTHALMOLOGIST, OPTOMETRIST

optic lobe *n* (1854) : either of two prominences of the midbrain concerned with vision

optic nerve *n* (1615) : either of the pair of nerves that comprise the 2d pair of cranial nerves, arise from the ventral part of the diencephalon, supply the retina, and conduct visual stimuli to the brain — see EYE illustration

op·tics \'äp-tiks\ *n pl but sing in constr* (1579) : a science that deals with the genesis and propagation of light, the changes that it undergoes and produces, and other phenomena closely associated with it

optic vesicle *n* (ca. 1885) : an evagination of each lateral wall of the embryonic vertebrate forebrain from which the nervous structures of the eye develop

op·ti·mal \'äp-tə-məl\ *adj* (1890) : most desirable or satisfactory : OPTIMUM — **op·ti·mal·i·ty** \ˌäp-tə-'ma-lə-tē\ *n* — **op·ti·mal·ly** \-mə-lē\ *adv*

op·ti·mi·sa·tion, op·ti·mise *Brit var of* OPTIMIZATION, OPTIMIZE

op·ti·mism \'äp-tə-ˌmi-zəm\ *n* [F *optimisme*, fr. L *optimum*, n., best, fr. neut. of *optimus* best; akin to L *ops* power — more at OPULENT] (1759) **1** : a doctrine that this world is the best possible world **2** : an inclination to put the most favorable construction upon actions and events or to anticipate the best possible outcome — **op·ti·mist** \-mist\ *n* — **op·ti·mis·tic** \ˌäp-tə-'mis-tik\ *adj* — **op·ti·mis·ti·cal·ly** \-ti-k(ə-)lē\ *adv*

Op·ti·mist \'äp-tə-mist\ *n* [*Optimist (Club)*] (1911) : a member of a major international service club

op·ti·mi·za·tion \ˌäp-tə-mə-'zā-shən\ *n* (1857) : an act, process, or methodology of making something (as a design, system, or decision) as fully perfect, functional, or effective as possible; *specif* : the mathematical procedures (as finding the maximum of a function) involved in this

op·ti·mize \'äp-tə-ˌmīz\ *vt* **-mized; -miz·ing** (1857) : to make as perfect, effective, or functional as possible — **op·ti·miz·er** \-ˌmī-zər\ *n*

op·ti·mum \'äp-tə-məm\ *n, pl* **-ma** \-mə\ *also* **-mums** [L] (1879) **1**

: the amount or degree of something that is most favorable to some end; *esp* : the most favorable condition for the growth and reproduction of an organism **2** : greatest degree attained or attainable under implied or specified conditions — **optimum** *adj*

¹op·tion \'äp-shən\ *n* [F, fr. L *option-, optio* free choice; akin to L *optare* to choose] (ca. 1604) **1** : an act of choosing **2 a** : the power or right to choose **b** : freedom of choice **b** : a privilege of demanding fulfillment of a contract on any day within a specified time **c** : a contract conveying a right to buy or sell designated securities, commodities, or property interest at a specified price during a stipulated period; *also* : the right conveyed by an option **d** : a right of an insured person to choose the form in which payments due on a policy shall be made or applied **3** : something that may be chosen: as **a** : an alternative course of action ⟨didn't have many ~s open⟩ **b** : an item that is offered in addition to or in place of standard equipment **4** : an offensive football play in which a back may choose whether to pass or run with the ball — called also **option play** *syn* see CHOICE

²option *vt* (1926) : to grant or take an option on

op·tion·al \'äp-shnəl, -shə-nᵊl\ *adj* (1792) : involving an option : not compulsory — **op·tion·al·i·ty** \,äp-shə-'na-lə-tē\ *n* — **op·tion·al·ly** *adv*

opto- *comb form* [Gk *optos,* verbal of *opsesthai* — more at OPTIC] **1** : vision ⟨optometry⟩ **2** : optic and ⟨optoelectronics⟩

op·to·elec·tron·ics \,äp-(,)tō-i-lek-'trä-niks, -ē-lek-\ *n pl but sing in constr* (1959) : a branch of electronics that deals with electronic devices for emitting, modulating, transmitting, and sensing light — **op·to·elec·tron·ic** \-nik\ *adj*

op·to·ki·net·ic \,äp-tō-kə-'ne-tik, -kī-\ *adj* (1925) : of, relating to, or involving movements of the eyes

op·tom·e·trist \äp-'tä-mə-trist\ *n* (1903) : a specialist licensed to practice optometry — compare OPHTHALMOLOGIST, OPTICIAN

op·tom·e·try \-trē\ *n* [ISV] (1886) : the art or profession of examining the eye for defects and faults of refraction and prescribing correctional lenses or exercises — **op·to·met·ric** \,äp-tə-'me-trik\ *adj*

opt out *vi* (1951) : to choose not to participate in something — often used with of ⟨opted out of the project⟩

op·u·lence \'ä-pyə-lən(t)s\ *n* (ca. 1510) **1** : WEALTH, AFFLUENCE **2** : ABUNDANCE, PROFUSION

op·u·lent \-lənt\ *adj* [L *opulentus,* fr. *ops* power, help; akin to L *opus* work] (1601) : exhibiting or characterized by opulence: as **a** : having a large estate or property : WEALTHY ⟨hoping to marry an ~ widow⟩ **b** : amply or plentifully provided or fashioned often to the point of ostentation ⟨living in ~ comfort⟩ *syn* see RICH — **op·u·lent·ly** *adv*

opun·tia \ō-'pən(t)-sh(ē-)ə\ *n* [L, a plant, fr. fem. of *opuntius* of Opus, fr. *Opunt-, Opus* Opus, ancient city in Greece] (1601) : any of a large genus (*Opuntia*) of cacti with usu. yellow flowers and flat or terete joints usu. studded with tubercles bearing spines or prickly hairs — compare CHOLLA, PRICKLY PEAR

opus \'ō-pəs\ *n, pl* **op·era** \'ō-pə-rə, 'ä-\ *also* **opus·es** \'ō-pə-səz\ [L *oper-, opus* — more at OPERATE] (1809) : WORK; *esp* : a musical composition or set of compositions usu. numbered in the order of its issue

opus·cule \ō-'pəs-(,)kyü(ə)l\ *n* [F, fr. L *opusculum,* dim. of *opus*] (ca. 1656) : a small or petty work : OPUSCULUM

opus·cu·lum \ō-'pəs-kyə-ləm\ *n, pl* **-la** \-lə\ [L] (1654) : a minor work (as of literature) — usu. used in pl.

¹or \ər, 'ôr, *Southern also* 'är\ *conj* [ME, alter. of *other,* alter. of OE *oththe;* akin to OHG *eddo* etc] (12c) **1** — used as a function word to indicate an alternative ⟨coffee ~ tea⟩ ⟨sink ~ swim⟩, the equivalent or substitutive character of two words or phrases ⟨lessen ~ abate⟩, or approximation or uncertainty ⟨in five ~ six days⟩ **2** *archaic* : EITHER **3** *archaic* : WHETHER **4** — used in logic as a sentential connective that forms a complex sentence which is true when at least one of its constituent sentences is true; compare DISJUNCTION

²or *prep* [ME, fr. *or,* adv., early, before, fr. ON *ār;* akin to OE *ǣr* early — more at ERE] (13c) *archaic* : BEFORE

³or *conj* (13c) *archaic* : BEFORE

⁴or \'ôr\ *n* [ME, fr. MF, gold, fr. L *aurum* — more at AUREUS] (15c) : the heraldic color gold or yellow

OR \'ôr\ *n* ['or] (1947) : a logical operator that requires either of two inputs to be present or conditions to be met for an output to be made or a statement to be executed ⟨~ gate in a computer⟩

¹-or *n suffix* [ME, fr. OF *-eur, -eor* & L *-or;* OF *-eur,* fr. L *-or;* OF *-eor,* fr. L *-ator,* fr. *-a-,* v. stem + *-tor,* agent suffix; akin to Gk *-tōr,* agent suffix, Skt *-tā*] : one that does a (specified) thing ⟨grant*or*⟩

²-or *n suffix* [ME, fr. OF *-eur,* fr. L *-or*] : condition : activity ⟨demeanor⟩

ora *pl of* OS

or·ache *or* **or·ach** \'ôr-ich, 'är-\ *n* [ME *orage, arage,* fr. MF *arrache,* fr. (assumed) VL *atrapic-, atrapex,* fr. Gk *atraphaxys*] (13c) : any of various herbs (genus *Atriplex*) of the goosefoot family that include some (as *A. hortensis*) used as potherbs

or·a·cle \'ôr-ə-kəl, 'är-\ *n* [ME, fr. MF, fr. L *oraculum,* fr. *orare* to speak — more at ORATION] (14c) **1 a** : a person (as a priestess of ancient Greece) through whom a deity is believed to speak **b** : a shrine in which a deity reveals hidden knowledge or the divine purpose through such a person **c** : an answer or decision given by an oracle **2 a** : a person giving wise or authoritative decisions or opinions **b** : an authoritative or wise expression or answer

orac·u·lar \ò-'ra-kyə-lər, ə-\ *adj* [L *oraculum*] (1678) **1** : of, relating to, or being an oracle **2** : resembling an oracle (as in solemnity of delivery) *syn* see DICTATORIAL — **orac·u·lar·i·ty** \-,ra-kyə-'lar-ə-tē\ *n* — **orac·u·lar·ly** \-'ra-kyə-lər-lē\ *adv*

¹oral \'ôr-əl, 'ôr-, 'är-\ *adj* [L *or-, os* mouth; akin to ON *ōss* mouth of a river, Skt *ās* mouth] (1628) **1 a** : uttered by the mouth or in words : SPOKEN **b** : using speech or the lips esp. in teaching the deaf **2 a** : of, given through, or involving the mouth **b** : being on or relating to the same surface as the mouth **3 a** : of, relating to, or characterized by the first stage of psychosexual development in psychoanalytic theory during which libidinal gratification is derived from intake (as of food), by sucking, and later by biting **b** : of, relating to, or characterized by personality traits of passive dependency and aggressiveness — **oral·i·ty** \ò-'ra-lə-tē, ō-\ *n* — **oral·ly** \'ôr-ə-lē, 'ôr-, 'är-\ *adv*

²oral *n* (1876) : an oral examination — usu. used in pl.

oral history *n* (1955) **1** : tape-recorded historical information obtained in interviews concerning personal experiences and recollections; *also* : the study of such information **2** : a written work based on oral history — **oral historian** *n*

oral·ism \'ôr-ə-,li-zəm, 'ôr-, 'är-\ *n* (1883) : advocacy or use of the oral method of teaching the deaf — **oral·ist** \-list\ *n*

orang \ə-'raŋ\ *n* [by shortening] (1778) : ORANGUTAN

¹or·ange \'är-inj, 'är-(ə)nj; *chiefly Northern & Midland* 'ôr-inj, 'ôr-(ə)nj\ *n* [ME, fr. MF, fr. OProv *auranja,* fr. Ar *nāranj,* fr. Per *nārang,* fr. Skt *nāraṅga* orange tree] (14c) **1 a** : a globose berry with a yellowish to reddish orange rind and a sweet edible pulp **b** : any of various rather small evergreen trees (genus *Citrus*) with ovate unifoliolate leaves, hard yellow wood, fragrant white flowers, and fruits that are oranges **2** : any of several trees or fruits resembling the orange **3** : any of a group of colors that lie midway between red and yellow in hue

²orange *adj* (1542) **1** : of or relating to the orange **2** : of the color orange

Orange *adj* (1795) : of, relating to, or sympathizing with Orangemen — **Or·ange·ism** \'är-in-,ji-zəm, 'är(ə)n-, 'ôr-in-, 'ôr(ə)n-\ *n*

or·ange·ade \,är-in-'jād, ,är-(ə)n-, ,ôr-in-, ,ôr(ə)n-\ *n* [F, fr. *orange* + *-ade*] (1706) : a beverage of sweetened orange juice mixed with water

orange chromide *n* [*chromide,* ultim. fr. Gk *chromis,* a sea fish] (1933) : a brilliant orange or yellow red-spotted fish (*Etroplus maculatus*) often kept in tropical aquariums

orange hawkweed *n* (ca. 1900) : a European hawkweed (*Hieracium aurantiacum*) that has flower heads with bright orange-red rays and is a troublesome weed esp. in northeastern No. America

Or·ange·man \'är-inj-mən, 'är-(ə)nj-, 'ôr-inj-, 'ôr(ə)nj-\ *n* [William III of England, prince of *Orange*] (1796) **1** : a member of a secret society organized in the north of Ireland in 1795 to defend the British sovereign and to support the Protestant religion **2** : a Protestant Irishman esp. of Ulster

orange peel *n* (ca. 1909) : a rough surface (as on porcelain) like that of an orange

orange pekoe *n* (ca. 1877) : tea made from the smallest and youngest leaves of the shoot

or·ange·ry *also* **or·ange·rie** \'är-inj-rē, 'är-(ə)nj-, 'ôr-inj-, 'ôr(ə)nj-\ *n, pl* **-ries** (1664) : a protected place and esp. a greenhouse for raising oranges in cool climates

or·ange·wood \'är-inj-,wùd, 'är-(ə)nj-, 'ôr-inj-, 'ôr(ə)nj-\ *n* (1884) : the wood of the orange tree used esp. in turnery and carving

or·ang·ish \'är-in-jish, 'är-(ə)n-, 'ôr-in-, 'ôr(ə)n-\ *adj* (1967) : somewhat orange

orang·u·tan \ə-'raŋ-ə-,taŋ, -'raŋ-gə-, -,tan\ *n* [Bazaar Malay (Malay-based pidgin), fr. Malay *orang* man + *hutan* forest] (1691) : a largely herbivorous arboreal anthropoid ape (*Pongo pygmaeus*) of Borneo and Sumatra that is about two thirds as large as the gorilla and has brown skin, long sparse reddish brown hair, and very long arms

or·angy *or* **or·ang·ey** \'är-in-jē, 'är(-ə)n-, 'ôr-in-, 'ôr(-ə)n-\ *adj* (1778) : resembling or suggestive of an orange (as in flavor or color)

orate \ò-'rāt, ō-; 'ôr-,āt, 'ôr-\ *vi* (ca. 1600) : to speak in an elevated and often pompous manner

ora·tion \ə-'rā-shən, ò-\ *n* [L *oration-, oratio* speech, oration, fr. *orare* to plead, speak, pray; akin to Hitt *ariya-* to consult an oracle and perh. to Gk *ara* prayer] (1502) : an elaborate discourse delivered in a formal and dignified manner

or·a·tor \'ôr-ə-tər, 'är-\ *n* (15c) **1** : one who delivers an oration **2** : one distinguished for skill and power as a public speaker

Or·a·to·ri·an \,ôr-ə-'tōr-ē-ən, ,är-, -'tòr-\ *n* (ca. 1656) : a member of the Congregation of the Oratory of St. Philip Neri founded in Rome in 1575 and comprising independent communities of secular priests under obedience but without vows — **Oratorian** *adj*

or·a·tor·i·cal \,ôr-ə-'tôr-i-kəl, ,är-ə-'tär-\ *adj* (1589) : of, relating to, or characteristic of an orator or oratory — **or·a·tor·i·cal·ly** \-k(ə-)lē\ *adv*

or·a·to·rio \,ôr-ə-'tôr-ē-,ō, ,är-, -'tòr-\ *n, pl* **-ri·os** [It, fr. the *Oratorio di San Filippo Neri* (Oratory of St. Philip Neri) in Rome] (ca. 1738) : a lengthy choral work usu. of a religious nature consisting chiefly of recitatives, arias, and choruses without action or scenery

¹or·a·to·ry \'ôr-ə-,tôr-ē, 'är-, -,tòr-\ *n, pl* **-ries** [ME *oratorie,* fr. LL *oratorium,* fr. L *orare*] (14c) **1** : a place of prayer; *esp* : a private or institutional chapel **2** *cap* : an Oratorian congregation, house, or church

²oratory *n* [L *oratoria,* fr. fem. of *oratorius* oratorical, fr. *orare*] (1593) **1** : the art of speaking in public eloquently or effectively **2 a** : public speaking that employs oratory **b** : public speaking that is characterized by the use of stock phrases and that appeals chiefly to the emotions

orb \'ôrb\ *n* [ME, fr. MF *orbe,* fr. L *orbis* circle, disk, orb] (14c) **1** : any of the concentric spheres in old astronomy surrounding the earth and carrying the celestial bodies in their revolutions **2** *archaic* : something circular : CIRCLE, ORBIT **3** : a spherical body; *esp* : a spherical celestial object **4** : EYE **5** : a sphere surmounted by a cross symbolizing kingly power and justice

²orb *vt* (1600) **1** : to form into a disk or circle **2** *archaic* : ENCIRCLE, SURROUND, ENCLOSE ~ *vi, archaic* : to move in an orbit

or·bic·u·lar \ôr-'bi-kyə-lər\ *adj* [ME *orbiculer,* fr. MF or LL; MF *orbiculaire,* fr. LL *orbicularis,* fr. L *orbiculus,* dim. of *orbis*] (15c) : SPHERICAL, CIRCULAR — **or·bic·u·lar·ly** \-'bi-kyə-lər-lē\ *adv*

or·bic·u·late \ôr-'bi-kyə-lət\ *adj* (ca. 1760) : circular or nearly circular in outline ⟨an ~ leaf⟩ — see LEAF illustration

¹or·bit \'ôr-bət\ *n* [ME, fr. ML *orbita,* fr. L, rut, track, prob. fr. *orbis*] (15c): the bony socket of the eye — **or·bit·al** \-bə-ᵊl\ *adj*

²orbit *n* [L *orbita* path, rut, orbit] (1696) **1 a** : a path described by one body in its revolution about another (as by the earth about the sun or by an electron about an atomic nucleus); *also* : one complete revolution of a body describing such a path **b** : a circular path **2** : a range or sphere of activity or influence *syn* see RANGE — **or·bit·al** \-t ᵊl\ *adj*

\ə\ abut \ᵊ\ kitten, F table \ər\ further \a\ ash \ā\ ace \ä\ mop, mar \aù\ out \ch\ chin \e\ bet \ē\ easy \g\ go \i\ hit \ī\ ice \j\ job \ŋ\ sing \ō\ go \ò\ law \òi\ boy \th\ thin \t̲h̲\ the \ü\ loot \ù\ foot \y\ yet \zh\ vision \à, k̲, ⁿ, œ, œ̄, ue̽, ūe̽, ᵒ\ see Guide to Pronunciation

³**orbit** *vt* (1943) **1** : to revolve in an orbit around : CIRCLE **2** : to send up and make revolve in an orbit ⟨~ a satellite⟩ ~ *vi* : to travel in circles

or·bit·al \'ȯr-bə-t²l\ *n* [*orbital,* adj.] (1932) : a subdivision of a nuclear shell containing zero, one, or two electrons

or·bit·er \-bə-tər\ *n* (1951) : one that orbits: as **a** : a spacecraft designed to orbit a celestial body without landing on its surface **b** : SPACE SHUTTLE

orb weaver *n* (1889) : any of a family (Araneidae) of No. American spiders that have eight similar eyes and typically spin a large elaborate web

or·ca \'ȯr-kə\ *n* [NL *Orca,* genus name, fr. L, a whale, prob. modif. of Gk *oryg-, oryx* — more at ORYX] (1866) : KILLER WHALE

Or·ca·di·an \ȯr-'kā-dē-ən\ *n* [L *Orcades* Orkney Islands] (1661) : a native or inhabitant of the Orkney Islands — **Orcadian** *adj*

or·chard \'ȯr-chərd\ *n* [ME, fr. OE *ortgeard,* fr. *ort-* (fr. L *hortus* garden) + *geard* yard — more at YARD] (bef. 12c) : a planting of fruit trees, nut trees, or sugar maples; *also* : the trees of such a planting

orchard grass *n* (1765) : a widely grown tall stout hay and pasture grass (*Dactylis glomerata*) that grows in tufts and has loose open panicles

or·chard·ist \'ȯr-chər-dist\ *n* (1794) : an owner or supervisor of orchards

or·ches·tra \'ȯr-kəs-trə, -,kes-\ *n* [L, fr. Gk *orchēstra,* fr. *orcheisthai* to dance; perh. akin to Skt *rghāyati* he trembles, he rages] (1606) **1 a** : the circular space used by the chorus in front of the proscenium in an ancient Greek theater **b** : a corresponding semicircular space in a Roman theater used for seating important persons **2 a** : the space in front of the stage in a modern theater that is used by an orchestra **b** : the forward section of seats on the main floor of a theater **c** : the main floor of a theater **3** : a group of musicians including esp. string players organized to perform ensemble music — compare BAND

or·ches·tral \ȯr-'kes-trəl\ *adj* (ca. 1811) **1** : of, relating to, or composed for an orchestra **2** : suggestive of an orchestra or its musical qualities — **or·ches·tral·ly** \-trə-lē\ *adv*

or·ches·trate \'ȯr-kə-,strāt\ *vt* **-trat·ed; -trat·ing** (1880) **1 a** : to compose or arrange (music) for an orchestra **b** : to provide with orchestration ⟨~ a ballet⟩ **2** : to arrange or combine so as to achieve a desired or maximum effect ⟨*orchestrated* preparations for the banquet⟩ — **or·ches·tra·tor** *also* **or·ches·trat·er** \-,strā-tər\ *n*

or·ches·tra·tion \,ȯr-kə-'strā-shən\ *n* (ca. 1859) **1** : the arrangement of a musical composition for performance by an orchestra; *also* : orchestral treatment of a musical composition **2** : harmonious organization ⟨develop a world community through ~ of cultural diversities — L. K. Frank⟩ — **or·ches·tra·tion·al** \-shnəl, -shə-n²l\ *adj*

or·chid \'ȯr-kəd\ *n* [irreg. fr. NL *Orchis*] (1845) **1** : any of a large family (Orchidaceae, the orchid family) of perennial epiphytic or terrestrial monocotyledonous plants that usu. have showy 3-petaled flowers with the middle petal enlarged into a lip and differing from the others in shape and color **2** : a light purple — **or·chid-like** \-,līk\ *adj*

or·chi·da·ceous \,ȯr-kə-'dā-shəs\ *adj* [NL *Orchidaceae,* family name, fr. *Orchis*] (1838) **1** : of, relating to, or resembling the orchids **2** : SHOWY, OSTENTATIOUS

or·chis \'ȯr-kəs\ *n* [NL, fr. L, orchid, fr. Gk, testicle, orchid; akin to MIr *uirgge* testicle] (1562) : ORCHID; *esp* : any of a genus (*Orchis*) with fleshy roots and a spurred lip

or·dain \ȯr-'dān\ *vb* [ME *ordeinen,* fr. OF *ordener,* fr. LL *ordinare,* fr. L, to put in order, appoint, fr. *ordin-, ordo* order] *vt* (14c) **1** : to invest officially (as by the laying on of hands) with ministerial or priestly authority **2 a** : to establish or order by appointment, decree, or law : ENACT **b** : DESTINE, FOREORDAIN ~ *vi* : to issue an order — **or·dain·er** *n* — **or·dain·ment** \-'dān-mənt\ *n*

or·deal \ȯr-'dē(-ə)l, 'ȯr-\ *n* [ME *ordal,* fr. OE *ordāl;* akin to OHG *urteil* judgment, OE *dāl* division — more at DEAL] (bef. 12c) **1** : a primitive means used to determine guilt or innocence by submitting the accused to dangerous or painful tests believed to be under supernatural control ⟨~ by fire⟩ **2** : a severe trial or experience

¹**order** \'ȯr-dər\ *vb* **or·dered; or·der·ing** \'ȯr-d(ə-)riŋ\ [ME, fr. *ordre,* n.] *vt* (13c) **1** : to put in order : ARRANGE **2** : to give an order to : COMMAND **b** : DESTINE, ORDAIN **c** : to command to go or come to a specified place **d** : to give an order for ⟨~ a meal⟩ ~ *vi* **1** : to bring about order : REGULATE **2 a** : to issue orders : COMMAND **b** : to give or place an order — **or·der·able** \-ə-bəl\ *adj* — **or·der·er** \-dər-ər\ *n*

syn ORDER, ARRANGE, MARSHAL, ORGANIZE, SYSTEMATIZE, METHODIZE mean to put persons or things into their proper places in relation to each other. ORDER suggests a straightening out so as to eliminate confusion ⟨*ordered* her business affairs⟩. ARRANGE implies a setting in sequence, relationship, or adjustment ⟨*arranged* the files numerically⟩. MARSHAL suggests gathering and arranging in preparation for a particular operation or effective use ⟨*marshaling* the facts for argument⟩. ORGANIZE implies arranging so that the whole aggregate works as a unit with each element having a proper function ⟨*organized* the volunteers into teams⟩. SYSTEMATIZE implies arranging according to a predetermined scheme ⟨*systematized* billing procedures⟩. METHODIZE suggests imposing an orderly procedure rather than a fixed scheme ⟨*methodizes* every aspect of daily living⟩.

syn see in addition COMMAND

²**order** *n* [ME, fr. MF *ordre,* fr. ML & L; ML *ordin-, ordo* ecclesiastical order, fr. L, arrangement, group, class; akin to L *ordiri* to lay the warp, begin] (14c) **1 a** : a group of people united in a formal way: as (1) : a fraternal society ⟨the Masonic *Order*⟩ (2) : a community under a religious rule; *esp* : one requiring members to take solemn vows **b** : a badge or medal of such a society; *also* : a military decoration **2 a** : any of the several grades of the Christian ministry **b** *pl*

order 8b: *1* Corinthian, *2* Doric, *3* Ionic

: the office of a person in the Christian ministry **c** *pl* : ORDINATION **3 a** : a rank, class, or special group in a community or society **b** : a class of persons or things grouped according to quality, value, or natural characteristics: as (1) : a category of taxonomic classification ranking above the family and below the class (2) : the broadest category in soil classification **4 a** (1) : RANK, LEVEL ⟨a statesman of the first ~⟩ (2) : CATEGORY, CLASS ⟨in emergencies of this ~ —R. B. Westerfield⟩ **b** (1) : the arrangement or sequence of objects or of events in time ⟨listed the items in ~ of importance⟩ (2) : a sequential arrangement of mathematical elements **c** : DEGREE 12a, b **d** (1) : the number of times differentiation is applied successively ⟨derivatives of higher ~⟩ (2) *of a differential equation* : the order of the derivative of highest order **e** : the number of columns or rows or columns and rows in a magic square, determinant, or matrix ⟨the ~ of a matrix with 2 rows and 3 columns is 2 by 3⟩ **f** : the number of elements in a finite mathematical group **5 a** (1) : a sociopolitical system ⟨was opposed to changes in the established ~⟩ (2) : a particular sphere or aspect of a sociopolitical system ⟨the present economic ~⟩ **b** : a regular or harmonious arrangement ⟨the ~ of nature⟩ **6 a** : a prescribed form of a religious service : RITE **b** : the customary mode of procedure esp. in debate ⟨point of ~⟩ **7 a** : the state of peace, freedom from confused or unruly behavior, and respect for law or proper authority ⟨promised to restore law and ~⟩ **b** : a specific rule, regulation, or authoritative direction : COMMAND **8 a** : a style of building **b** : a type of column and entablature forming the unit of a style **9 a** : state or condition esp. with regard to functioning or repair ⟨things were in terrible ~⟩ **b** : a proper, orderly, or functioning condition ⟨their passports were in ~⟩ ⟨the phone is out of ~⟩ **10 a** : a written direction to pay money to someone **b** : a commission to purchase, sell, or supply goods or to perform work **c** : goods or items bought or sold **d** : an assigned or requested undertaking ⟨landing men on the moon was a large ~⟩ **11** : ORDER OF THE DAY ⟨flat roofs were the ~ in the small villages⟩ — **or·der·less** \-ləs\ *adj* — **in order** : APPROPRIATE, DESIRABLE ⟨an apology is *in order*⟩ — **in order to** : for the purpose of — **on order** : in the process of being ordered — **on the order of 1** : after the fashion of : LIKE ⟨much *on the order of* Great Lakes bulk carriers —*Ships and the Sea*⟩ **2** : ABOUT, APPROXIMATELY ⟨spent *on the order of* two million dollars⟩ — **to order** : according to the specifications of an order ⟨shoes made *to order*⟩

order arms *n* [fr. the command *order arms!*] (1844) **1** : a position in the manual of arms in which the rifle is held vertically beside the right leg with the butt resting on the ground **2** : a command to return the rifle to order arms from present arms or to drop the hand from a hand salute

or·dered \'ȯr-dərd\ *adj* (1579) : characterized by order: as **a** : marked by regularity or discipline ⟨led an ~ life⟩ **b** : marked by regular or harmonious arrangement or disposition ⟨an ~ landscape⟩ ⟨the ~ crystal structure⟩ **c** : having elements arranged or identified according to a rule: as (1) : having the property that every pair of different elements is related by a transitive relationship that is not symmetric (2) : having elements labeled by ordinal numbers ⟨an ~ triple has a first, second, and third element⟩

or·der·li·ness \'ȯrd-ər-lē-nəs\ *n* (1571) : the quality or state of being orderly

¹**or·der·ly** \-lē\ *adj* (ca. 1577) **1 a** (1) : arranged or disposed in some order or pattern : REGULAR ⟨~ rows of houses⟩ (2) : not marked by disorder : TIDY ⟨keeps an ~ desk⟩ **b** : governed by law : REGULATED ⟨an ~ universe⟩ **c** : METHODICAL ⟨an ~ mind⟩ **2** : well behaved : PEACEFUL ⟨an ~ crowd⟩ — **orderly** *adv*

²**orderly** *n, pl* **-lies** (1781) **1** : a soldier assigned to perform various services (as carrying messages) for a superior officer **2** : a hospital attendant who does routine or heavy work (as cleaning, carrying supplies, or moving patients)

order of business [*order of business* (predetermined sequence of matters to be dealt with by an assembly)] (ca. 1890) : a matter which must be dealt with : TASK ⟨the discipline problem was the first *order of business* at the meeting of the school board⟩

order of magnitude (1875) : a range of magnitude extending from some value to ten times that value

order of the day (1698) **1** : the business or tasks appointed for an assembly for a given day **2** : the characteristic or dominant feature or activity ⟨growth and change are the *order of the day* in every field — Ruth G. Strickland⟩

¹**or·di·nal** \'ȯrd-nəl, 'ȯr-d²n-əl\ *n* (14c) **1** *cap* [ME, fr. ML *ordinale,* fr. LL, neut. of *ordinalis*] : a book of rites for the ordination of deacons, priests, and bishops **2** [LL *ordinalis,* fr. *ordinalis,* adj.] : ORDINAL NUMBER

²**ordinal** *adj* [LL *ordinalis,* fr. L *ordin-, ordo*] (1599) **1** : of a specified order or rank in a series **2** : of or relating to a taxonomic order

ordinal number (1607) **1** : a number designating the place (as first, second, or third) occupied by an item in an ordered sequence — see NUMBER table **2** : a number assigned to an ordered set that designates both the order of its elements and its cardinal number

or·di·nance \'ȯrd-nən(t)s, 'ȯr-d²n-ən(t)s\ *n* [ME, fr. MF & ML; MF *ordenance,* lit., act of arranging, fr. ML *ordinantia,* fr. L *ordinant-, ordinans,* prp. of *ordinare* to put in order — more at ORDAIN] (14c) **1 a** : an authoritative decree or direction : ORDER **b** : a law set forth by a governmental authority; *specif* : a municipal regulation **2** : something ordained or decreed by fate or a deity **3** : a prescribed usage, practice, or ceremony **syn** see LAW

or·di·nand \,ȯr-d²n-'and\ *n* [LL *ordinandus,* gerundive of *ordinare* to ordain] (ca. 1842) : a candidate for ordination

¹**or·di·nary** \'ȯr-d²n-,er-ē\ *n, pl* **-nar·ies** [ME *ordinarie,* fr. AF & ML; AF, fr. ML *ordinarius,* fr. L *ordinarius,* adj.] (14c) **1 a** (1) : a prelate exercising original jurisdiction over a specified territory or group (2) : a clergyman appointed formerly in England to attend condemned criminals **b** : a judge of probate in some states of the U.S. **2** *often cap* : the parts of the Mass that do not vary from day to day **3** : the regular or customary condition or course of things — usu. used in the phrase *out of the ordinary* **4 a** *Brit* : a meal served to all comers at a fixed price **b** *chiefly Brit* : a tavern or eating house serving regular meals **5** : a common heraldic charge (as the bend) of simple form

²**ordinary** *adj* [ME *ordinarie,* fr. L *ordinarius,* fr. *ordin-, ordo* order] (15c) **1** : of a kind to be expected in the normal order of events : ROU-

TINE, USUAL **2 :** having or constituting immediate or original jurisdiction; *also* : belonging to such jurisdiction **3 a :** of common quality, rank, or ability **b :** deficient in quality : POOR, INFERIOR *syn* see COMMON — **or·di·nar·i·ly** \ˌȯr-dᵊn-'er-ə-lē\ *adv* — **or·di·nar·i·ness** \'ȯr-dᵊn-ˌer-ē-nəs\ *n*

ordinary–language philosophy *n* (1957) : a trend in philosophical analysis that seeks to resolve philosophical perplexity by revealing sources of puzzlement in the misunderstanding of ordinary language

Ordinary level *n* (1947) : O LEVEL

ordinary seaman *n* (1702) : a seaman of some experience but not as skilled as an able seaman

ordinary share *n* (1891) *Brit* : a share of common stock

or·di·nate \'ȯrd-nət, 'ȯr-dᵊn-ət, -dᵊn-ˌāt\ *n* [NL (*linea*) *ordinate* (*applicata*), lit., line applied in an orderly manner] (1676) : the Cartesian coordinate obtained by measuring parallel to the y-axis — compare ABSCISSA

or·di·na·tion \ˌȯr-dᵊn-'ā-shən\ *n* (14c) : the act or an instance of ordaining : the state of being ordained

ord·nance \'ȯrd-nən(t)s\ *n* [ME *ordinaunce*, fr. MF *ordenance*, lit., act of arranging] (14c) **1 a :** military supplies including weapons, ammunition, combat vehicles, and maintenance tools and equipment **b :** a service of the army charged with the procuring, distributing, and safekeeping of ordnance **2 :** CANNON, ARTILLERY

or·do \'ȯr-(ˌ)dō\ *n, pl* **ordos** *or* **or·di·nes** \'ȯr-dᵊn-ˌēz\ [ML, fr. L, order] (1849) : a list of offices and feasts of the Roman Catholic Church for each day of the year

or·don·nance \ˌȯr-dᵊn-'äⁿs\ *n* [F, alter. of MF *ordenance*] (1644) : disposition of the parts (as of a literary composition) with regard to one another and the whole : ARRANGEMENT

Or·do·vi·cian \ˌȯr-də-'vi-shən\ *adj* [L *Ordovices*, ancient people in northern Wales] (1879) : of, relating to, or being the period between the Cambrian and the Silurian or the corresponding system of rocks — see GEOLOGIC TIME table — **Ordovician** *n*

or·dure \'ȯr-jər\ *n* [ME, fr. MF, fr. *ord* filthy, fr. L *horridus* horrid] (14c) **1 :** EXCREMENT **2 :** something that is morally degrading

¹ore \'ȯr, 'ȯr\ *n, often attrib* [ME *or, oor,* partly fr. OE *ōra* ore; partly fr. OE *ār* brass; akin to OHG *ēr* bronze, L *aes* copper, bronze] (bef. 12c) **1 :** a mineral containing a valuable constituent (as metal) for which it is mined and worked **2 :** a source from which valuable matter is extracted

²ore \'ər-ə\ *n, pl* **ore** [Sw *öre* & Dan & Norw *øre*] (1716) — see *krona, krone* at MONEY table

ore·ad \'ȯr-ē-ˌad, 'ȯr-, -ē-əd\ *n* [ME *oreades,* pl., fr. L *oread-, oreas,* fr. Gk *oreiad-, oreias,* fr. *oreios* of a mountain, fr. *oros* mountain — more at ORIENT] (14c) : any of the nymphs of mountains and hills in Greek mythology

ore dressing *n* (1862) : mechanical preparation (as by crushing) and concentration (as by flotation) of ore

oreg·a·no \ə-'re-gə-ˌnō\ *n* [AmerSp *orégano,* fr. Sp, wild marjoram, fr. L *origanum* — more at ORIGANUM] (1771) **1 :** a bushy perennial mint (*Origanum vulgare*) that is used as a seasoning and a source of aromatic oil — called also *origanum, wild marjoram* **2 :** any of several plants (genera *Lippia* and *Coleus*) other than oregano of the vervain or mint families

Or·e·gon grape \'ȯr-i-gən-, 'är-, -ˌgän-\ *n* [*Oregon,* state of the U.S.] (1869) : an evergreen shrub (*Mahonia aquifolium*) of the barberry family that has yellow flowers, bears edible bluish black berries, and is native to western No. America

Oregon grape

Or·eo \'ȯr-ē-(ˌ)ō, 'ȯr-, 'är-\ *n* [fr. *Oreo,* trademark for a chocolate cookie with a white cream filling] (1969) : a black person who adopts the characteristic mentality and behavior of white middle-class society — usu. used disparagingly

Ores·tes \ə-'res-(ˌ)tēz, ȯ-\ *n* [L, fr. Gk *Orestēs*] : the son of Agamemnon and Clytemnestra who with his sister Electra avenges his father by killing his mother and her lover Aegisthus

or·gan \'ȯr-gən\ *n* [ME, partly fr. OE *organa,* fr. L *organum,* fr. Gk *organon,* lit., tool, instrument; partly fr. OF *organe,* fr. L *organum;* akin to Gk *ergon* work — more at WORK] (bef. 12c) **1 a** *archaic* : any of various musical instruments; *esp* : WIND INSTRUMENT **b** (1) : a wind instrument consisting of sets of pipes made to sound by compressed air and controlled by keyboards and producing a variety of musical effects — called also *pipe organ* (2) : REED ORGAN (3) : an instrument in which the sound and resources of the pipe organ are approximated by means of electronic devices (4) : any of various similar cruder instruments **2 a :** a differentiated structure (as a heart, kidney, leaf, or stem) consisting of cells and tissues and performing some specific function in an organism **b :** bodily parts performing a function or cooperating in an activity ⟨the eyes and related structures that make up the visual ∼s⟩ **3 :** a subordinate group or organization that performs specialized functions ⟨the various ∼s of government⟩ **4 :** PERIODICAL

organ- *or* **organo-** *comb form* [ME, fr. ML, fr. L *organum*] **1 :** organ ⟨*organogenesis*⟩ **2 :** organic ⟨*organomercurial*⟩

or·gan·dy *also* **or·gan·die** \'ȯr-gən-dē\ *n, pl* **-dies** [F *organdi*] (1835) : a very fine transparent muslin with a stiff finish

or·gan·elle \ˌȯr-gə-'nel\ *n* [NL *organella,* fr. L *organum*] (1920) : a specialized cellular part (as a mitochondrion, lysosome, or ribosome) that is analogous to an organ

or·gan–grind·er \'ȯr-gən-ˌgrīn-dər\ *n* (ca. 1807) : one that cranks a hand organ; *esp* : a street musician who operates a barrel organ

¹or·gan·ic \ȯr-'ga-nik\ *adj* (1517) **1** *archaic* : INSTRUMENTAL **2 a :** of, relating to, or arising in a bodily organ **b :** affecting the structure of the organism **3 a** (1) : of, relating to, or derived from living organisms (2) : of, relating to, yielding, or involving the use of food produced with the use of feed or fertilizer of plant or animal origin without employment of chemically formulated fertilizers, growth stimulants, antibiotics, or pesticides ⟨∼ farming⟩ ⟨∼ produce⟩ **b** (1) : of, relating to, or containing carbon compounds (2) : relating to, being, or dealt with by a branch of chemistry concerned with the carbon com-

pounds of living beings and most other carbon compounds **4 a :** forming an integral element of a whole : FUNDAMENTAL ⟨incidental music rather than ∼ parts of the action —Francis Fergusson⟩ **b :** having systematic coordination of parts : ORGANIZED ⟨an ∼ whole⟩ **c :** having the characteristics of an organism : developing in the manner of a living plant or animal ⟨society is ∼⟩ **5 :** of, relating to, or constituting the law by which a government or organization exists — **or·gan·i·cal·ly** \-ni-k(ə-)lē\ *adv* — **or·ga·nic·i·ty** \ˌȯr-gə-'ni-sə-tē\ *n*

²organic *n* (1942) : an organic substance: as **a :** a fertilizer of plant or animal origin **b :** a pesticide whose active component is an organic compound or a mixture of organic compounds

or·gan·i·cism \ȯr-'ga-nə-ˌsi-zəm\ *n* [ISV] (1883) **1 a :** the explanation of life and living processes in terms of the levels of organization of living systems rather than in terms of the properties of their smallest components **b :** VITALISM **2 :** any of various theories that attribute to society or the universe as a whole an existence or characteristics analogous to those of a biological organism — **or·gan·i·cist** \-sist\ *n or adj*

or·ga·ni·sa·tion, or·ga·nise, or·ga·nis·er *Brit var of* ORGANIZATION, ORGANIZE, ORGANIZER

or·gan·ism \'ȯr-gə-ˌni-zəm\ *n* (ca. 1774) **1 :** a complex structure of interdependent and subordinate elements whose relations and properties are largely determined by their function in the whole **2 :** an individual constituted to carry on the activities of life by means of organs separate in function but mutually dependent : a living being — **or·gan·is·mic** \ˌȯr-gə-'niz-mik\ *also* **or·gan·is·mal** \-məl\ *adj* — **or·gan·is·mi·cal·ly** \-mi-k(ə-)lē\ *adv*

or·gan·ist \'ȯr-gə-nist\ *n* (1591) : a person who plays the organ

¹or·ga·ni·za·tion \ˌȯr-gə-nə-'zā-shən, ˌȯrg-nə-\ *n* (15c) **1 a :** the act or process of organizing or of being organized **b :** the condition or manner of being organized **2 a :** ASSOCIATION, SOCIETY ⟨charitable ∼s⟩ **b :** an administrative and functional structure (as a business or a political party); *also* : the personnel of such a structure

²organization *adj* (1949) : characterized by complete conformity to the standards and requirements of an organization ⟨an ∼ man⟩

or·ga·ni·za·tion·al \-shnəl, -shə-nᵊl\ *adj* (1881) **1 :** of or relating to organization : involving organization ⟨the ∼ state of a crystal⟩ **2 :** ORGANIZATION — **or·ga·ni·za·tion·al·ly** *adv*

or·ga·nize \'ȯr-gə-ˌnīz\ *vb* **-nized; -niz·ing** *vt* (15c) **1 :** to cause to develop an organic structure **2 :** to form into a coherent unity or functioning whole : INTEGRATE ⟨trying to ∼ her thoughts⟩ **3 a :** to set up an administrative structure for **b :** to persuade to associate in an organization; *esp* : UNIONIZE **4 :** to arrange by systematic planning and united effort ∼ *vi* **1 :** to undergo physical or organic organization **2 :** to arrange elements into a whole of interdependent parts **3 :** to form an organization; *specif* : to form or persuade workers to join a union *syn* see ORDER — **or·gan·iz·able** \ˌȯr-gə-'nī-zə-bəl\ *adj*

organized *adj* (1817) **1 :** having a formal organization to coordinate and carry out activities ⟨∼ baseball⟩ ⟨∼ crime⟩ **2 :** affiliated by membership in an organization (as a union) ⟨∼ steelworkers⟩

or·ga·niz·er \'ȯr-gə-ˌnī-zər\ *n* (1849) **1 :** one that organizes **2 :** a region of a developing embryo or a substance produced by such a region that is capable of inducing a specific type of development in undifferentiated tissue — called also *inductor*

or·gan·o·chlo·rine \ˌȯr-gə-nō-'klȯr-ˌēn, ȯr-ˌga-nō-, -'klȯr-, -ən\ *adj* (1961) : of, relating to, or belonging to the chlorinated hydrocarbon pesticides (as aldrin, DDT, or dieldrin) — **organochlorine** *n*

organ of Cor·ti \-'kȯr-tē\ [Alfonso *Corti* †1876 Ital. anatomist] (1882) : a complex epithelial structure in the cochlea that rests on the internal surface of the basilar membrane and in mammals is the chief part of the ear by which sound is directly perceived

or·gan·o·gen·e·sis \ˌȯr-gə-nō-'je-nə-səs, ȯr-ˌga-nə-\ *n* [NL] (ca. 1860) : the origin and development of bodily organs — compare MORPHOGENESIS — **or·gan·o·ge·net·ic** \-jə-'ne-tik\ *adj*

or·gan·o·lep·tic \ˌȯr-gə-nō-'lep-tik, ȯr-ˌga-nə-\ *adj* [F *organoleptique,* fr. *organ-* + Gk *lēptikos* disposed to take, fr. *lambanein* to take — more at LATCH] (1852) **1 :** being, affecting, or relating to qualities (as taste, color, odor, and feel) of a substance (as a food or drug) that stimulate the sense organs **2 :** involving use of the sense organs ⟨∼ evaluation of foods⟩ — **or·gan·o·lep·ti·cal·ly** \-ti-k(ə-)lē\ *adv*

or·ga·nol·o·gy \ˌȯr-gə-'nä-lə-jē\ *n* [ISV] (ca. 1842) : the study of the organs of plants and animals

or·gan·o·mer·cu·ri·al \ˌȯr-gə-nō-(ˌ)mər-'kyúr-ē-əl, ȯr-ˌga-nə-\ *n* (1938) : an organic compound or a pharmaceutical preparation containing mercury

or·gan·o·me·tal·lic \-mə-'ta-lik\ *adj* [ISV] (1852) : of, relating to, or being an organic compound that contains a metal or metalloid bonded directly to carbon — **organometallic** *n*

or·ga·non \'ȯr-gə-ˌnän\ *n* [Gk, lit., tool — more at ORGAN] (1610) : an instrument for acquiring knowledge; *specif* : a body of principles of scientific or philosophic investigation

or·gan·o·phos·phate \ˌȯr-gə-nō-'fäs-ˌfāt, ȯr-ˌga-nō-\ *n* (1949) : an organophosphorus compound (as a pesticide) — **organophosphate** *adj*

or·gan·o·phos·pho·rus \-'fäs-f(ə-)rəs\ *also* **or·gan·o·phos·pho·rous** \-fäs-'fōr-əs, -'fȯr-\ *adj* (1950) : of, relating to, or being a phosphorus-containing organic compound and esp. a pesticide (as malathion) that acts by inhibiting cholinesterase — **organophosphorus** *n*

organ–pipe cactus *n* (1908) : any of several tall upright cacti (as *Lemaireocereus thurberi* or *L. marginatus*) of the southwestern U.S. and adjacent Mexico that usu. branch at the base to form several upright stems

or·ga·num \'ȯr-gə-nəm\ *n* [ML, fr. L, organ] (1614) **1 :** ORGANON 2 **2 :** early polyphony of the late Middle Ages that consists of one or more voice parts accompanying the cantus firmus in parallel motion usu. at a fourth, fifth, or octave above or below; *also* : a composition in this style

---

\ə\ abut \ᵊ\ kitten, F table \ər\ further \a\ ash \ā\ ace \ä\ mop, mar \au̇\ out \ch\ chin \e\ bet \ē\ easy \g\ go \i\ hit \ī\ ice \j\ job \ŋ\ sing \ō\ go \ȯ\ law \ȯi\ boy \th\ thin \t͟h\ the \ü\ loot \u̇\ foot \y\ yet \zh\ vision \à, k̲, ⁿ, œ, œ̄, ᵫ, ᵫ̄, ᵊ\ *see* Guide to Pronunciation

or·gan·za \òr-'gan-zə\ *n* [prob. alter. of *Lorganza*, a trademark] (1820) : a sheer dress fabric (as of silk or nylon) resembling organdy

or·gan·zine \'òr-gən-ˌzēn\ *n* [F or It; F *organsin*, fr. It *organzino*] (1699) : a raw silk yarn used for warp threads in fine fabrics

or·gasm \'òr-ˌga-zəm\ *n* [NL *orgasmus*, fr. Gk *orgasmos*, fr. *organ* to grow ripe, be lustful; prob. akin to Skt *ūrjā* sap, strength] (ca. 1763) : intense or paroxysmal excitement; *esp* : the climax of sexual excitement that is usu. accompanied by the ejaculation of semen in the male and vaginal contractions in the female — **or·gas·mic** \òr-'gaz-mik\ *also* **or·gas·tic** \-'gas-tik\ *adj*

or·geat \'òr-ˌzhä(t)\ *n* [F, fr. MF, fr. *orge* barley, fr. L *hordeum;* akin to OHG *gersta* barley] (1754) : a sweet almond-flavored nonalcoholic syrup used as a cocktail ingredient or food flavoring

or·gi·as·tic \ˌòr-jē-'as-tik\ *adj* [Gk *orgiastikos*, fr. *orgiazein* to celebrate orgies, fr. *orgia*] (1698) 1 : of, relating to, or marked by orgies 2 : characterized by unrestrained emotion : FRENZIED — **or·gi·as·ti·cal·ly** \-ti-k(ə-)lē\ *adv*

or·gone \'òr-ˌgōn\ *n* [prob. fr. *orgasm* + *-one* (as in *hormone*)] (1942) : a vital energy held to pervade nature and be a factor in health in the theories of Wilhelm Reich

or·gu·lous \'òr-gyə-ləs, -gə-\ *adj* [ME, fr. OF *orgueilleus*, fr. *orgueil* pride, of Gmc origin; akin to OHG *urguol* distinguished] (13c) : PROUD

or·gy \'òr-jē\ *n, pl* **orgies** [MF *orgie*, fr. L *orgia*, pl., fr. Gk; akin to Gk *ergon* work — more at WORK] (ca. 1561) 1 : secret ceremonial rites held in honor of an ancient Greek or Roman deity and usu. characterized by ecstatic singing and dancing 2 a : drunken revelry b : a sexual encounter involving many people; *also* : an excessive sexual indulgence 3 : something that resembles an orgy in lack of control or moderation ⟨an ∼ of destruction⟩

-oria *pl of* -ORIUM

-orial *adj suffix* [ME, fr. L *-orius* -ory + ME *-al*] : of, belonging to, or connected with ⟨combinat*orial*⟩

orib·a·tid \ò-'ri-bə-təd, òr-ə-'ba-təd\ *n* [NL *Oribatidae* (coextensive with *Oribatoidea*), fr. *Oribata*, genus name, fr. Gk *oribatēs* walking the mountains, fr. *oros* mountain + *-batēs*, fr. *bainein* to go — more at ORIENT, COME] (1875) : any of a superfamily (Oribatoidea) of small oval eyeless nonparasitic mites having a heavily sclerotized integument with a leathery appearance — **oribatid** *adj*

ori·el \'òr-ē-əl, 'òr-\ *n* [ME, porch, oriel, fr. MF *oriol* porch] (14c) : a large bay window projecting from a wall and supported by a corbel or bracket

¹ori·ent \'òr-ē-ənt, 'òr-, -ē-ˌent\ *n* [ME, fr. MF, fr. L *orient-, oriens*, fr. prp. of *oriri* to rise; akin to Skt *r̥noti* he moves, arises, Gk *ornynai* to rouse, *oros* mountain] (14c) 1 *archaic* : EAST 1b 2 *cap* : EAST 2 3 a : a pearl of great luster b : the luster of a pearl

²orient *adj* (15c) 1 *archaic* : ORIENTAL 1 2 a : LUSTROUS, SPARKLING ⟨∼ gems⟩ b *archaic* : RADIANT, GLOWING 3 *archaic* : rising in the sky

³ori·ent \'òr-ē-ˌent, 'òr-\ *vt* [F *orienter*, fr. MF, fr. *orient*] (ca. 1741) 1 a : to cause to face or point toward the east; *specif* : to build (a church or temple) with the longitudinal axis pointing eastward and the chief altar at the eastern end b : to set or arrange in any determinate position esp. in relation to the points of the compass c : to ascertain the bearings of 2 a : to set right by adjusting to facts or principles b : to acquaint with the existing situation or environment 3 : to direct (as a book or film) toward the interests of a particular group 4 : to cause the axes of the molecules of to assume the same direction

ori·en·tal \ˌòr-ē-'en-t⁹l, ˌòr-\ *adj* (14c) 1 *often cap* : of, relating to, or situated in the Orient 2 a : of superior grade, luster, or value b : being corundum or sapphire but simulating another gem in color 3 *often cap* : of, relating to, or having the characteristics of Orientals 4 *cap* : of, relating to, or constituting the biogeographic region that includes Asia south and southeast of the Himalayas and the Malay Archipelago west of Wallace's line — **ori·en·tal·ly** \-t⁹l-ē\ *adv*

Oriental *n* (15c) : a member of one of the indigenous peoples of the Orient

oriental fruit moth *n* (1921) : a small nearly cosmopolitan moth (*Grapholita molesta*) prob. of Japanese origin whose larva is injurious to the twigs and fruit of orchard trees and esp. the peach — called also *oriental peach moth*

Ori·en·ta·lia \ˌòr-ē-ən-'tāl-yə, ˌòr-, -ˌen-, -'tä-lē-ə\ *n pl* [NL] (1903) : materials concerning or characteristic of the Orient

ori·en·tal·ism \ˌòr-ē-'en-t⁹l-ˌi-zəm\ *n, often cap* (1769) 1 : a trait, custom, or habit of expression characteristic of oriental peoples 2 : scholarship or learning in oriental subjects — **ori·en·tal·ist** \-t⁹l-ist\ *n, often cap*

ori·en·tal·ize \-t⁹l-ˌīz\ *vb* **-ized; -iz·ing** *vt* (1823) *often cap* : to make oriental ∼ *vi, often cap* : to become oriental

Oriental poppy *n* (1731) : an Asian perennial poppy (*Papaver orientale*) that is commonly cultivated for its large showy flowers

Oriental rug *n* (1881) : a handwoven or hand-knotted one-piece rug or carpet made in the Orient — called also *Oriental carpet*

ori·en·tate \'òr-ē-ən-ˌtāt, 'òr-, -ˌen-\ *vb* **-tat·ed; -tat·ing** *vt* (1849) : ORIENT ∼ *vi* : to face or turn to the east

ori·en·ta·tion \ˌòr-ē-ən-'tā-shən, ˌòr-, -ˌen-\ *n* (1839) 1 a : the act or process of orienting or of being oriented b : the state of being oriented; *broadly* : ARRANGEMENT, ALIGNMENT 2 : a usu. general or lasting direction of thought, inclination, or interest 3 : change of position by gonads, organelles, or organisms in response to external stimulus — **ori·en·ta·tion·al** \-shnəl, -shə-n⁹l\ *adj* — **ori·en·ta·tion·al·ly** *adv*

ori·ent·ed \'òr-ē-ˌen-təd, 'òr-\ *adj* (1944) : intellectually, emotionally, or functionally directed ⟨humanistically ∼ scholars⟩

ori·en·teer \ˌòr-ē-ən-'tir, ˌòr-, -ˌen-\ *n* [back-formation fr. *orienteering*] (1965) : one who engages in orienteering

ori·en·teer·ing \ˌòr-ē-ən-'tir-iŋ, ˌòr-, -ˌen-\ *n* [modif. of Sw *orientering*, fr. *orientera* to orient] (1948) : a cross-country race in which each participant uses a map and compass to navigate between checkpoints along an unfamiliar course

or·i·fice \'òr-ə-fəs, 'är-\ *n* [ME, fr. MF, fr. LL *orificium*, fr. L *or-, os* mouth + *facere* to make, do — more at ORAL, DO] (15c) : an opening (as a vent, mouth, or hole) through which something may pass — **or·i·fi·cial** \ˌòr-ə-'fi-shəl, ˌär-\ *adj*

ori·flamme \'òr-ə-ˌflam, 'är-\ *n* [ME *oriflamble*, the banner of St. Denis, fr. MF, fr. ML *aurea flamma*, lit., golden flame] (1600) : a banner, symbol, or ideal inspiring devotion or courage

ori·ga·mi \ˌòr-ə-'gä-mē\ *n* [Jp, fr. *ori* fold + *kami* paper] (1956) : the Japanese art or process of folding squares of paper into representational shapes

orig·a·num \ə-'ri-gə-nəm\ *n* [ME, fr. L, wild marjoram, fr. Gk *origanon*] (14c) : any of several aromatic mints (esp. genus *Origanum*) used as seasonings; *esp* : OREGANO 1

or·i·gin \'òr-ə-jən, 'är-\ *n* [ME *origine*, prob. fr. MF, fr. L *origin-, origo*, fr. *oriri* to rise — more at ORIENT] (15c) 1 : ANCESTRY, PARENTAGE 2 a : rise, beginning, or derivation from a source b : the point at which something begins or rises or from which it derives ⟨the ∼ of the custom is forgotten⟩; *also* : something that creates, causes, or gives rise to another ⟨this spring is the ∼ of the brook⟩ 3 : the more fixed, central, or larger attachment of a muscle 4 : the intersection of coordinate axes

syn ORIGIN, SOURCE, INCEPTION, ROOT mean the point at which something begins its course or existence. ORIGIN applies to the things or persons from which something is ultimately derived and often to the causes operating before the thing itself comes into being ⟨an investigation into the *origin* of baseball⟩. SOURCE applies more often to the point where something springs into being ⟨the *source* of the Nile⟩ ⟨the *source* of recurrent trouble⟩. INCEPTION stresses the beginning of something without implying causes ⟨the business has been a success since its *inception*⟩. ROOT suggests a first, ultimate, or fundamental source often not easily discerned ⟨the real *root* of the violence⟩.

¹orig·i·nal \ə-'rij-ə-n⁹l, -'rij-nəl\ *n* (14c) 1 *archaic* : the source or cause from which something arises; *specif* : ORIGINATOR 2 a : that from which a copy, reproduction, or translation is made b : a work composed firsthand 3 a : a person of fresh initiative or inventive capacity b : a unique or eccentric person

²original *adj* (14c) 1 : of, relating to, or constituting an origin or beginning : INITIAL ⟨the ∼ part of the house⟩ 2 a : not secondary, derivative, or imitative b : being the first instance or source from which a copy, reproduction, or translation is or can be made 3 : independent and creative in thought or action : INVENTIVE *syn* see NEW

orig·i·nal·i·ty \ə-ˌri-jə-'na-lə-tē\ *n* (1742) 1 : the quality or state of being original 2 : freshness of aspect, design, or style 3 : the power of independent thought or constructive imagination

orig·i·nal·ly \ə-'ri-jə-n⁹l-ē; -'rij-nə-lē, -'ri-jən-\ *adv* (14c) 1 *archaic* : by origin or derivation : INHERENTLY 2 : in the beginning : in the first place : INITIALLY 3 : in a fresh or original manner

original sin *n* (14c) : the state of sin that according to Christian theology characterizes all human beings as a result of Adam's fall

orig·i·nate \ə-'ri-jə-ˌnāt\ *vb* **-nat·ed; -nat·ing** *vt* (1667) : to give rise to : INITIATE ∼ *vi* : to take or have origin : BEGIN *syn* see SPRING — **orig·i·na·tion** \-ˌri-jə-'nā-shən\ *n* — **orig·i·na·tor** \-'ri-jə-ˌnā-tər\ *n*

orig·i·na·tive \ə-'ri-jə-ˌnā-tiv, -nə-\ *adj* (1827) : having ability to originate : CREATIVE — **orig·i·na·tive·ly** *adv*

O-ring \'ō-ˌriŋ\ *n* (1946) : a ring (as of synthetic rubber) used as a gasket

ori·ole \'òr-ē-ˌōl, 'òr-, -ē-əl\ *n* [F *oriol*, fr. L *aureolus*, dim. of *aureus* golden — more at AUREUS] (1776) 1 : any of various usu. brightly colored Old World passerine birds (family Oriolidae and esp. genus *Oriolus*) 2 : any of various New World passerine birds (family Icteridae and esp. genus *Icterus*) of which the males are usu. black and yellow or black and orange

Ori·on \ə-'rī-ən, ò-\ *n* [L, fr. Gk *Ōriōn*] 1 : a giant hunter slain by Artemis in Greek mythology 2 [L (gen. *Orionis*)] : a constellation on the equator east of Taurus represented on charts by the figure of a hunter with belt and sword

or·is·mol·o·gy \ˌòr-əz-'mä-lə-jē, ˌär-\ *n* [Gk *horismos* definition (fr. *horizein* to define) + E *-logy* — more at HORIZON] (1816) : the science of defining technical terms — **or·is·mo·log·i·cal** \ˌòr-əz-mə-'lä-ji-kəl, ˌär-; ò-ˌriz-\ *adj*

or·i·son \'òr-ə-sən, 'är-, -zən\ *n* [ME, fr. OF, fr. LL *oration-, oratio*, fr. L, oration] (13c) : PRAYER

-orium *n suffix, pl* **-oriums** *or* **-oria** [L, fr. neut. of *-orius -ory*] : ¹-ORY ⟨haust*orium*⟩

Ori·ya \ò-'rē-ə\ *n* (1801) : the Indo-Aryan language of Orissa, India

Or·lean·ist \'òr-lē-ə-nist, òr-'lē-(ə-)nist\ *n* (1834) : a supporter of the Orleans family in its claim to the throne of France by descent from a younger brother of Louis XIV

Or·lon \'òr-ˌlän\ *trademark* — used for an acrylic fiber

or·lop deck \'òr-ˌläp-\ *n* [ME *overlop* deck of a single decker, fr. MLG *overlōp*, lit., something that overleaps] (1758) : the lowest deck in a ship having four or more decks

Or·mazd \'òr-(ˌ)məzd, -ˌmazd\ *n* [Per *Urmazd*, fr. MPer, fr. Av *Ahura-mazdāh-*] (1603) : AHURA MAZDA

or·mo·lu \'òr-mə-ˌlü\ *n, often attrib* [F *or moulu*, lit., ground gold] (1765) : golden or gilded brass or bronze used for decorative purposes (as in mounts for furniture)

¹or·na·ment \'òr-nə-mənt\ *n* [ME, fr. OF *ornement*, fr. L *ornamentum*, fr. *ornare*] (13c) 1 *archaic* : a useful accessory 2 a : something that lends grace or beauty b : a manner or quality that adorns 3 : one whose virtues or graces add luster to a place or society 4 : the act of adorning or being adorned 5 : an embellishing note not belonging to the essential harmony or melody — called also *embellishment, fioritura*

²or·na·ment \-ˌment\ *vt* (1720) : to provide with ornament : EMBELLISH *syn* see ADORN

¹or·na·men·tal \ˌòr-nə-'men-t⁹l\ *adj* (1646) : of, relating to, or serving as ornament; *specif* : grown as an ornamental — **or·na·men·tal·ly** \-t⁹l-ē\ *adv*

²ornamental *n* (1650) : a decorative object; *esp* : a plant cultivated for its beauty rather than for use

or·na·men·ta·tion \ˌòr-nə-mən-'tā-shən, -ˌmen-\ *n* (1851) 1 : something that ornaments : EMBELLISHMENT 2 : the act or process of ornamenting : the state of being ornamented

or·nate \òr-'nāt\ *adj* [ME *ornat*, fr. L *ornatus*, pp. of *ornare* to furnish, embellish; akin to L *ordo* order — more at ORDER] (15c) 1 : marked by elaborate rhetoric or florid style 2 : elaborately or excessively decorated — **or·nate·ly** *adv* — **or·nate·ness** *n*

or·nery \'òr-nə-rē, 'är-\ *adj* [alter. of *ordinary*] (1816) : having an irritable disposition : CANTANKEROUS — **or·neri·ness** *n*

ornith- *or* **ornitho-** *comb form* [L, fr. Gk, fr. *ornith-, ornis* — more at ERNE] : bird ⟨*ornith*ology⟩

or·nith·ic \òr-'ni-thik\ *adj* [Gk *ornithikos*, fr. *ornith-, ornis*] (1854) : of, relating to, or characteristic of birds

or·ni·thine \'òr-nə-ˌthēn\ *n* [ISV *ornithuric* acid (a compound of which ornithine is a component, found in the urine of birds) + [2]-*ine*] (1881) : a crystalline amino acid $C_5H_{12}N_2O_2$ that functions esp. in urea production as a carrier by undergoing conversion to citrulline and then arginine in reaction with ammonia and carbon dioxide followed by recovery along with urea by enzymatic hydrolysis of arginine

or·nith·is·chi·an \ˌòr-nə-'this-kē-ən\ *n* [NL *Ornithischia*, fr. *ornith-* + *ischium*] (1933) : any of an order (Ornithischia) of herbivorous dinosaurs (as a stegosaurus) that have the pubis of the pelvis rotated backward to a position parallel and close to the ischium — compare SAURISCHIAN — **ornithischian** *adj*

or·ni·thol·o·gy \ˌòr-nə-'thä-lə-jē\ *n, pl* **-gies** [NL *ornithologia*, fr. *ornith-* + *-logia* -logy] (1678) 1 : a branch of zoology dealing with birds 2 : a treatise on ornithology — **or·ni·tho·log·i·cal** \-thə-'lä-ji-kəl\ *also* **or·ni·tho·log·ic** \-jik\ *adj* — **or·ni·tho·log·i·cal·ly** \-ji-k(ə-)lē\ *adv* — **or·ni·thol·o·gist** \-'thä-lə-jist\ *n*

or·nith·o·pod \òr-'ni-thə-ˌpäd, 'òr-ni-thə-\ *n* [ultim. fr. Gk *ornith-* + *pod-, pous* foot — more at FOOT] (ca. 1890) : any of a suborder (Ornithopoda) of bipedal ornithischian dinosaurs (as a hadrosaur) with digitigrade walking limbs usu. having only three functional toes

or·ni·thop·ter \'òr-nə-ˌthäp-tər\ *n* [ISV *ornith-* + *-pter* (as in *helicopter*)] (1908) : an aircraft designed to derive its chief support and propulsion from flapping wings

or·ni·tho·sis \ˌòr-nə-'thō-səs\ *n, pl* **-tho·ses** \-ˌsēz\ [NL] (1939) : PSITTACOSIS

[1]**oro-** *comb form* [Gk *oros* — more at ORIENT] : mountain ⟨*orography*⟩

[2]**oro-** *comb form* [L *or-, os* — more at ORAL] : mouth ⟨*oropharynx*⟩

oro·gen·e·sis \ˌòr-ə-'je-nə-səs, ˌór-\ *n* [NL] (1886) : OROGENY — **oro·ge·net·ic** \-jə-'ne-tik\ *adj*

orog·e·ny \ò-'rä-jə-nē\ *n* [ISV] (1890) : the process of mountain formation esp. by folding of the earth's crust — **oro·gen·ic** \ˌòr-ə-'je-nik, ˌór-\ *adj*

oro·graph·ic \ˌòr-ə-'gra-fik, ór-\ *also* **oro·graph·i·cal** \-fi-kəl\ *adj* (ca. 1803) : of or relating to mountains; *esp* : associated with or induced by the presence of mountains ⟨∼ rainfall⟩

orog·ra·phy \ò-'rä-grə-fē\ *n* [ISV] (ca. 1846) : a branch of physical geography that deals with mountains

Oro·mo \ò-'rō-(ˌ)mō, ō-\ *n, pl* **Oromos** *or* **Oromo** (1893) 1 : a member of a Cushitic-speaking people of southern Ethiopia and adjacent parts of Kenya 2 : the Cushitic language of the Oromo

oro·pha·ryn·geal \ˌòr-ə-ˌfar-ən-'jē-əl, ór-, -fə-'rin-j(ē-)əl\ *adj* (1885) 1 : of or relating to the oropharynx 2 : of or relating to the mouth and pharynx

oro·phar·ynx \-'far-iŋ(k)s\ *n* (1887) : the part of the pharynx that is below the soft palate and above the epiglottis and is continuous with the mouth

oro·tund \'òr-ə-ˌtənd, 'är-\ *adj* [modif. of L *ore rotundo*, lit., with round mouth] (ca. 1799) 1 : marked by fullness, strength, and clarity of sound : SONOROUS 2 : POMPOUS, BOMBASTIC — **oro·tun·di·ty** \ˌòr-ə-'tən-də-tē, ˌär-, ór-\ *n*

[1]**or·phan** \'òr-fən\ *n* [ME, fr. LL *orphanus*, fr. Gk *orphanos*; akin to OHG *erbi* inheritance, L *orbus* orphaned] (15c) 1 : a child deprived by death of one or usu. both parents 2 : a young animal that has lost its mother 3 : one deprived of some protection or advantage ⟨∼s of the storm⟩ — **orphan** *adj* — **or·phan·hood** \-ˌhùd\ *n*

[2]**orphan** *vt* **or·phaned; or·phan·ing** \-fə-niŋ, 'órf-niŋ\ (1814) : to cause to become an orphan

or·phan·age \'òr-fə-nij, 'órf-nij\ *n* (ca. 1580) 1 : the state of being an orphan 2 : an institution for the care of orphans

orphan drug *n* (1981) : a drug that is not developed or marketed because its extremely limited use makes it unprofitable

orphan's court *n* (1713) : a probate court which in some states has jurisdiction over the affairs of minors and the administration of estates

Or·phe·us \'òr-fyüs, -fē-əs\ *n* [L, fr. Gk] : a poet and musician in Greek mythology who almost rescues his wife Eurydice from Hades by charming Pluto and Persephone with his music

or·phic \'òr-fik\ *adj* (1678) 1 *cap* : of or relating to Orpheus or the rites or doctrines ascribed to him 2 : MYSTIC, ORACULAR 3 : FASCINATING, ENTRANCING — **or·phi·cal·ly** \-fi-k(ə-)lē\ *adv*

Or·phism \'òr-ˌfi-zəm\ *n* [*Orpheus*, its reputed founder] (1880) : a mystic Greek religion offering initiates purification of the soul from innate evil and release through the cycle of reincarnation

or·phrey \'òr-frē\ *n, pl* **orphreys** [ME *orfrey*, fr. MF *orfreis*, fr. ML *aurifrigium*, fr. L *aurum* gold + *Phrygius* Phrygian — more at AUREUS] (13c) 1 a : elaborate embroidery b : a piece of such embroidery 2 : an ornamental border or band esp. on an ecclesiastical vestment

or·pi·ment \'òr-pə-mənt\ *n* [ME, fr. MF, fr. L *auripigmentum*, fr. *aurum* + *pigmentum* pigment] (14c) : native orange to lemon-yellow arsenic trisulfide

or·pine \'òr-pən\ *n* [ME *orpin*, fr. MF, fr. *orpiment*] (14c) : an herb (*Sedum telephium* of the family Crassulaceae, the orpine family) that has fleshy leaves and pink or purple flowers and was formerly used in folk medicine; *broadly* : SEDUM

Or·ping·ton \'òr-piŋ-tən\ *n* [*Orpington*, England] (1897) : any of an English breed of large deep-chested domestic fowls

or·rery \'òr-ər-ē, 'är-\ *n, pl* **or·rer·ies** [Charles Boyle †1731 4th Earl of *Orrery*] (1713) : an apparatus showing the relative positions and motions of bodies in the solar system by balls moved by a clockwork

or·ris \'òr-əs, 'är-\ *n* [prob. alter. of ME *ireos*, fr. ML, alter. of L *iris* iris] (1545) : ORRISROOT

or·ris·root \-ˌrüt, -ˌrùt\ *n* (1598) : the fragrant rootstock of any of three European irises (*Iris florentina, I. germanica,* and *I. pallida*) used esp. in perfumery

ort \'òrt\ *n* [ME, fr. MLG *orte*] (15c) : a morsel left at a meal : SCRAP

orth- *or* **ortho-** *comb form* [ME, fr. MF, straight, right, true, fr. L, fr. Gk, fr. *orthos*; akin to Skt *ūrdhva*

orrery

high, upright] 1 : straight : upright : vertical ⟨*orthograde*⟩ 2 : perpendicular ⟨*orthorhombic*⟩ 3 : correct : corrective ⟨*orthodontia*⟩ 4 a : hydrated or hydroxylated to the highest degree ⟨*orthophosphoric acid*⟩ b : involving substitution at or characterized by or having the relationship of two neighboring positions in the benzene ring ⟨*orthoxylene*⟩

or·thi·con \'òr-thi-ˌkän\ *n* [ISV *orth-* + *iconoscope*] (1939) : a camera tube similar to but more sensitive than an iconoscope in which the charges are scanned by a low-velocity beam

or·tho \'òr-(ˌ)thō\ *adj* (1904) : ORTHOCHROMATIC

or·tho·cen·ter \'òr-thə-ˌsen-tər\ *n* [ISV] (1869) : the common intersection of the three altitudes of a triangle or their extensions or of the several altitudes of a polyhedron provided these latter exist and meet in a point

or·tho·chro·mat·ic \ˌòr-thə-krō-'ma-tik\ *adj* [ISV] (1887) 1 : of, relating to, or producing tone values of light and shade in a photograph that correspond to the tones in nature 2 : sensitive to all colors except red

or·tho·clase \'òr-thə-ˌklās, -ˌklāz\ *n* [G *Orthoklas*, fr. *orth-* + Gk *klasis* breaking, fr. *klan* to break — more at CLAST] (1849) : a mineral consisting of a monoclinic form of feldspar

or·tho·don·tia \ˌòr-thə-'dän(t)-sh(ē-)ə\ *n* [NL] (ca. 1849) : ORTHODONTICS

or·tho·don·tics \-'dän-tiks\ *n pl but sing in constr* (1909) : a branch of dentistry dealing with irregularities of the teeth and their correction (as by means of braces) — **or·tho·don·tic** \-tik\ *adj* — **or·tho·don·ti·cal·ly** \-ti-k(ə-)lē\ *adv* — **or·tho·don·tist** \-'dän-tist\ *n*

[1]**or·tho·dox** \'òr-thə-ˌdäks\ *adj* [ME *orthodoxe*, fr. MF or LL; MF *orthodoxe*, fr. LL *orthodoxus*, fr. LGk *orthodoxos*, fr. Gk *orth-* + *doxa* opinion — more at DOXOLOGY] (15c) 1 a : conforming to established doctrine esp. in religion b : CONVENTIONAL 2 *cap* : of, relating to, or constituting any of various conservative religious or political groups: as a : EASTERN ORTHODOX b : of or relating to Orthodox Judaism — **or·tho·dox·ly** *adv*

[2]**orthodox** *n, pl* **orthodox** *also* **or·tho·dox·es** (1587) 1 : one that is orthodox 2 *cap* : a member of an Eastern Orthodox church

Orthodox Judaism *n* (1904) : Judaism that adheres to the Torah and Talmud as interpreted in an authoritative rabbinic law code and applies their principles and regulations to modern living — compare CONSERVATIVE JUDAISM, REFORM JUDAISM

or·tho·doxy \'òr-thə-ˌdäk-sē\ *n, pl* **-dox·ies** (1630) 1 : the quality or state of being orthodox 2 : an orthodox belief or practice 3 *cap* a : Eastern Orthodox Christianity b : ORTHODOX JUDAISM

or·tho·epy \'òr-thə-ˌwe-pē, òr-'thō-ə-pē\ *n* [NL *orthoepia*, fr. Gk *orthoepeia*, fr. *orth-* + *epos* word — more at VOICE] (1668) 1 : the customary pronunciation of a language 2 : the study of the pronunciation of a language — **or·tho·ep·ic** \ˌòr-thə-'we-pik\ *adj* — **or·tho·ep·i·cal·ly** \-pi-k(ə-)lē\ *adv* — **or·tho·epist** \'òr-thə-ˌwe-pist, òr-'thō-ə-pist\ *n*

or·tho·gen·e·sis \ˌòr-thə-'je-nə-səs\ *n* [NL] (1895) : variation of organisms in successive generations that in some evolutionary theories takes place in some predestined direction and results in progressive evolutionary trends independent of external factors — **or·tho·ge·net·ic** \-jə-'ne-tik\ *adj* — **or·tho·ge·net·i·cal·ly** \-ti-k(ə-)lē\ *adv*

or·thog·o·nal \òr-'thä-gə-n°l\ *adj* [MF, fr. L *orthogonius*, fr. Gk *orthogōnios*, fr. *orth-* + *gōnia* angle — more at -GON] (1612) 1 a : intersecting or lying at right angles b : having perpendicular slopes or tangents at the point of intersection ⟨∼ curves⟩ 2 : having a sum of products or an integral that is zero or sometimes one under specified conditions: as a *of real-valued functions* : having the integral of the product of each pair of functions over a specific interval equal to zero b *of vectors* : having the scalar product equal to zero c *of a square matrix* : having the sum of products of corresponding elements in any two rows or any two columns equal to one if the rows or columns are the same and equal to zero otherwise ; having a transpose with which the product equals the identity matrix 3 *of a linear transformation* : having a matrix that is orthogonal : preserving length and distance 4 : composed of mutually orthogonal elements ⟨an ∼ basis of a vector space⟩ 5 : statistically independent — **or·thog·o·nal·i·ty** \-ˌthä-gə-'na-lə-tē\ *n* — **or·thog·o·nal·ly** \-'thä-gə-n°l-ē\ *adv*

or·thog·o·nal·ize \òr-'thä-gə-n°l-ˌīz\ *vt* **-ized; -iz·ing** (1930) : to make orthogonal — **or·thog·o·nal·i·za·tion** \-ˌthä-gə-n°l-ə-'zä-shən\ *n*

or·tho·grade \'òr-thə-ˌgrād\ *adj* (1902) : walking with the body upright or vertical

or·tho·graph·ic \ˌòr-thə-'gra-fik\ *also* **or·tho·graph·i·cal** \-fi-kəl\ *adj* (1706) 1 : of, relating to, being, or prepared by orthographic projection ⟨an ∼ map⟩ 2 a : of or relating to orthography b : correct in spelling — **or·tho·graph·i·cal·ly** \-fi-k(ə-)lē\ *adv*

orthographic projection *n* (1668) 1 : projection of a single view of an object (as a view of the front) onto a drawing surface in which the lines of projection are perpendicular to the drawing surface 2 : the representation of related views of an object as if they were all in the same plane and projected by orthographic projection

or·thog·ra·phy \òr-'thä-grə-fē\ *n* [ME *ortografie*, fr. MF, fr. L *orthographia*, fr. Gk, fr. *orth-* + *graphein* to write — more at CARVE] (15c) 1 a : the art of writing words with the proper letters according to standard usage b : the representation of the sounds of a language by written or printed symbols 2 : a part of language study that deals with letters and spelling

TOP

↓

RIGHT SIDE

TOP VIEW

FRONT

FRONT VIEW   RIGHT VIEW

A

object A with top view, front view, and right view in orthographic projection

\ə\ abut \\ kitten, F table \ər\ further \a\ ash \ā\ ace \ä\ mop, mar \aù\ out \ch\ chin \e\ bet \ē\ easy \g\ go \i\ hit \ī\ ice \j\ job \ŋ\ sing \ō\ go \ò\ law \òi\ boy \th\ thin \ṯẖ\ the \ü\ loot \ù\ foot \y\ yet \zh\ vision \ä, k̲, ⁿ, œ, œ̄, ᵫ, ᵫ̄, ᵊ\ *see* Guide to Pronunciation

or·tho·mo·lec·u·lar \ˌȯr-thə-mə-'le-kyə-lər\ *adj* (1968) : relating to, based on, using, or being a theory according to which disease and esp. mental illness may be cured by restoring the optimum amounts of substances normally present in the body ⟨~ therapy⟩ ⟨an ~ psychiatrist⟩

or·tho·nor·mal \ˌȯr-thə-'nȯr-məl\ *adj* (1932) **1** *of real-valued functions* : orthogonal with the integral of the square of each function over a specified interval equal to one **2** : being or composed of orthogonal elements of unit length ⟨~ basis of a vector space⟩

or·tho·pe·dic *also* **or·tho·pae·dic** \ˌȯr-thə-'pē-dik\ *adj* [F *orthopédique*, fr. *orthopédie* orthopedics, fr. *orth-* + Gk *paid-, pais* child — more at FEW] (1840) **1** : of, relating to, or employed in orthopedics **2** : marked by deformities or crippling — **or·tho·pe·di·cal·ly** \-'pē-di-k(ə-)lē\ *adv*

or·tho·pe·dics *also* **or·tho·pae·dics** \-'pē-diks\ *n pl but sing or pl in constr* (ca. 1853) : a branch of medicine concerned with the correction or prevention of skeletal deformities — **or·tho·pe·dist** \-'pē-dist\ *n*

or·tho·phos·phate \ˌȯr-thə-'fäs-ˌfāt\ *n* (1859) : a salt or ester of orthophosphoric acid

or·tho·phos·pho·ric acid \ˌȯr-thə-ˌfäs-'fȯr-ik-, -'fär-; -'fäs-f(ə-)rik-\ *n* [ISV] (1885) : PHOSPHORIC ACID 1

or·tho·psy·chi·a·try \-sə-'kī-ə-trē, -ˌ(ˌ)sī-\ *n* (ca. 1927) : prophylactic psychiatry concerned esp. with incipient mental and behavioral disorders in youth — **or·tho·psy·chi·at·ric** \-ˌsī-kē-'a-trik\ *adj* — **or·tho·psy·chi·a·trist** \-sə-'kī-ə-trist, -ˌ(ˌ)sī-\ *n*

or·thop·tera \ȯr-'thäp-tə-rə\ *n pl* [NL, order name, fr. *orth-* + Gk *pteron* wing — more at FEATHER] (1828) : insects that are orthopterans

or·thop·ter·an \ȯr-'thäp-tə-rən\ *n* [NL *Orthoptera*] (ca. 1842) : any of an order (Orthoptera) of insects (as crickets, grasshoppers, and sometimes mantises) that are characterized by biting mouthparts, two pairs of wings or none, and an incomplete metamorphosis — **orthopteran** *adj* — **or·thop·ter·ist** \-rist\ *n* — **or·thop·ter·oid** \-ˌrȯid\ *n or adj*

or·tho·rhom·bic \ˌȯr-thə-'räm-bik\ *adj* [ISV] (ca. 1859) : of, relating to, or constituting a system of crystallization characterized by three unequal axes at right angles to each other

or·tho·scop·ic \-'skä-pik\ *adj* [ISV *orth-* + *-scopic* (as in *microscopic*)] (1853) : giving an image in correct and normal proportions

or·tho·sis \ȯr-'thō-səs\ *n, pl* **or·tho·ses** \-ˌsēz\ [NL, fr. Gk *orthōsis* straightening, fr. *orthoun* to straighten, fr. *orthos*] (1958) : ORTHOTIC

or·tho·stat·ic \ˌȯr-thə-'sta-tik\ *adj* (1902) : of, relating to, or caused by erect posture ⟨~ hypotension⟩

or·thot·ic \ȯr-'thä-tik\ *n* [NL *orthosis*] (1955) : a support or brace for weak or ineffective joints or muscles

or·thot·ics \-tiks\ *n pl but sing in constr* (1957) : a branch of mechanical and medical science that deals with the support and bracing of weak or ineffective joints or muscles — **or·thot·ic** \-tik\ *adj* — **or·tho·tist** \ȯr-'thä-tist, 'ȯr-thə-tist\ *n*

or·thot·ro·pous \ȯr-'thä-trə-pəs\ *adj* [ISV] (1830) : having the ovule straight so that the chalaza, hilum, and micropyle are in the same axial line

or·to·lan \'ȯr-t²l-ən\ *n* [F or It; F, fr. It *ortolano*, lit., gardener, fr. L *hortulanus*, fr. *hortulus*, dim. of *hortus* garden — more at YARD] (1656) : an Old World bunting (*Emberiza hortulana*) having a greenish gray head and breast, streaky brown back and wings, and a yellow throat

Or·vie·to \ȯr-'vyä-(ˌ)tō\ *n* [*Orvieto*, city in central Italy] (1846) : a usu. dry Italian white wine

¹**o·ry** *n suffix* [ME *-orie*, fr. L *-orium*, fr. neut. of *-orius*, adj. suffix] **1** : place of or for ⟨*observatory*⟩ **2** : something that serves for ⟨*crematory*⟩

²**o·ry** *adj suffix* [ME *-orie*, fr. MF & L; MF, fr. L *-orius*] **1** : of, relating to, or characterized by ⟨*gustatory*⟩ **2** : serving for, producing, or maintaining ⟨*justificatory*⟩

oryx \'ȯr-iks, 'ȯr-, 'är-\ *n, pl* **oryx** *or* **oryx·es** [NL, fr. L, a gazelle, fr. Gk, pickax, antelope, kind of whale, fr. *oryssein* to dig; akin to L *runcare* to grub up, weed, Skt *luñcati* he plucks] (1535) : any of a small genus (*Oryx*) of large heavily-built African and Arabian antelopes that have a light-colored coat with dark conspicuous markings esp. on the face

or·zo \'ȯrd-(ˌ)zō\ *n* [It, lit., barley, fr. L *hordeum* — more at ORGEAT] (ca. 1929) : rice-shaped pasta

¹**os** \'äs\ *n, pl* **ossa** \'ä-sə\ [L *oss-, os* — more at OSSEOUS] (15c) : BONE

²**os** \'ōs\ *n, pl* **ora** \'ōr-ə, 'ȯr-ə\ [L *or-, os* — more at ORAL] (1737) : MOUTH, ORIFICE

Osage \ō-'säj, 'ō-ˌ\ *n, pl* **Osag·es** *or* **Osage** (1698) **1** : a member of an American Indian people orig. of Missouri **2** : the Siouan language of the Osage people

Osage orange *n* (1817) : an ornamental usu. thorny American tree (*Maclura pomifera*) of the mulberry family with shiny ovate leaves and hard bright orange wood; *also* : its yellowish globose fruit

Os·can \'äs-kən\ *n* [L *Oscus*] (1753) **1** : a member of a people of ancient Italy occupying Campania **2** : the language of the Oscan people — see INDO-EUROPEAN LANGUAGES table

¹**Os·car** \'äs-kər\ *trademark* — used esp. for any of a number of golden statuettes awarded annually by a professional organization for notable achievement in motion pictures

²**Oscar** (1952) — a communications code word for the letter *o*

os·cil·late \'ä-sə-ˌlāt\ *vi* **-lat·ed; -lat·ing** [L *oscillatus*, pp. of *oscillare* to swing, fr. *oscillum* swing] (1726) **1 a** : to swing backward and forward like a pendulum **b** : to move or travel back and forth between two points **2** : to vary between opposing beliefs, feelings, or theories **3** : to vary above and below a mean value *syn* see SWING — **os·cil·la·to·ry** \'ä-sə-lə-ˌtōr-ē, -ˌtȯr-\ *adj*

os·cil·la·tion \ˌä-sə-'lā-shən\ *n* (1658) **1** : the action or state of oscillating **2** : VARIATION, FLUCTUATION **3** : a flow of electricity changing periodically from a maximum to a minimum; *esp* : a flow periodically changing direction **4** : a single swing (as of an oscillating body) from one extreme limit to the other — **os·cil·la·tion·al** \-shnəl, -shə-n²l\ *adj*

os·cil·la·tor \'ä-sə-ˌlā-tər\ *n* (1835) **1** : one that oscillates **2** : a device for producing alternating current; *esp* : a radio-frequency or audio-frequency generator

oscillo- *comb form* [ISV, fr. L *oscillare*] : wave : oscillation ⟨*oscilloscope*⟩

os·cil·lo·gram \ä-'si-lə-ˌgram, ə-\ *n* [ISV] (1903) : a record made by an oscillograph or oscilloscope

os·cil·lo·graph \-ˌgraf\ *n* [ISV] (1893) : an instrument for recording alternating current wave forms or other electrical oscillations — **os·cil·lo·graph·ic** \ä-ˌsi-lə-'gra-fik, ˌä-sə-lə-\ *adj* — **os·cil·lo·graph·i·cal·ly** \-fi-k(ə-)lē\ *adv* — **os·cil·log·ra·phy** \ˌä-sə-'lä-grə-fē\ *n*

os·cil·lo·scope \ä-'si-lə-ˌskōp, ə-\ *n* [ISV] (1906) : an instrument in which the variations in a fluctuating electrical quantity appear temporarily as a visible wave form on the fluorescent screen of a cathode-ray tube — **os·cil·lo·scop·ic** \ä-ˌsi-lə-'skä-pik, ˌä-sə-lə-\ *adj*

os·cine \'ä-ˌsīn\ *adj* [NL *Oscines*, suborder name, fr. L, pl. of *oscin-, oscen* songbird, bird giving omens by its cry, fr. *obs-, ob-* in front of, in the way + *canere* to sing — more at OB-, CHANT] (1883) : of or relating to a large suborder (Oscines) of passerine birds (as larks, shrikes, finches, orioles, and crows) characterized by a vocal apparatus highly specialized for singing — **oscine** *n*

Os·co-Um·bri·an \ˌäs-kō-'əm-brē-ən\ *n* [L *Oscus* + E *Umbrian*] (1894) : a subdivision of the Italic branch of the Indo-European language family containing Oscan and Umbrian

os·cu·late \'äs-kyə-ˌlāt\ *vt* **-lat·ed; -lat·ing** [L *osculatus*, pp. of *osculari*, fr. *osculum* kiss, fr. dim. of *os* mouth — more at ORAL] (ca. 1656) : KISS

os·cu·la·tion \ˌäs-kyə-'lā-shən\ *n* (ca. 1658) : the act of kissing; *also* : KISS — **os·cu·la·to·ry** \'äs-kyə-lə-ˌtōr-ē, -ˌtȯr-\ *adj*

os·cu·lum \'äs-kyə-ləm\ *n* [NL, fr. L, dim. of *os* mouth] (1887) : an excurrent opening of a sponge

¹**-ose** *adj suffix* [ME, fr. L *-osus*] : full of : having : possessing the qualities of ⟨*cymose*⟩

²**-ose** *n suffix* [F, fr. *glucose*] **1** : carbohydrate ⟨*amylose*⟩; *esp* : sugar ⟨*pentose*⟩ **2** : primary hydrolysis product ⟨*proteose*⟩

Osee \'ō-ˌzē, ō-'zā-ə\ *n* [LL, fr. Heb *Hōshēa*] : HOSEA

osier \'ō-zhər\ *n* [ME, fr. MF, fr. ML *auseria* osier bed] (14c) **1** : any of various willows (esp. *Salix viminalis*) whose pliable twigs are used for furniture and basketry **2** : a willow rod used in basketry **3** : any of several American dogwoods

Osi·ris \ō-'sī-rəs\ *n* [L, fr. Gk, fr. Egypt *Ws'r*] : the Egyptian god of the underworld and husband and brother of Isis

-osis *n suffix, pl* **-oses** *or* **-osises** [ME, fr. L, fr. Gk *-ōsis*, fr. *-ō-* (stem of causative verbs in *-oun*) + *-sis*] **1 a** : action : process : condition ⟨*hypnosis*⟩ **b** : abnormal or diseased condition ⟨*leukosis*⟩ **2** : increase : formation ⟨*leukocytosis*⟩

Os·man·li \äz-'man-lē\ *n* [Turk *osmanlı*, fr. *Osman*, founder of the Ottoman Empire] (1813) **1** : OTTOMAN 1 **2** : TURKISH

os·me·te·ri·um \ˌäz-mə-'tir-ē-əm\ *n, pl* **-ria** \-ē-ə\ [NL, irreg. fr. Gk *osmē* odor] (1816) : a protrusible forked glandular process that emits a disagreeable odor, is borne on the first thoracic segment of the larvae of many swallowtails and related butterflies, and is a defensive organ

osmic acid *n* (1842) : OSMIUM TETROXIDE

os·mi·rid·i·um \ˌäz-mə-'ri-dē-əm\ *n* [Gk *osmē* + NL *iridium*] (1880) : IRIDOSMINE

os·mi·um \'äz-mē-əm\ *n* [NL, fr. Gk *osmē* odor] (1804) : a hard brittle blue-gray or blue-black polyvalent metallic element of the platinum group with a high melting point that is the heaviest metal known and is used esp. as a catalyst and in hard alloys — see ELEMENT table

osmium tetroxide *n* (1876) : a crystalline compound OsO_4 that is an oxide of osmium, has a poisonous irritating vapor, and is used as a catalyst, oxidizing agent, and biological fixative and stain

os·mol *or* **os·mole** \'äz-ˌmōl, 'äs-\ *n* [blend of *osmosis* and *mol* (⁵mole)] (1942) : a standard unit of osmotic pressure based on a one molal concentration of an ion in a solution

os·mo·lal·i·ty \ˌäz-mō-'la-lə-tē, ˌäs-\ *n, pl* **-ties** [*osmol* + ¹*-al* + *-ity*] (ca. 1944) : the concentration of an osmotic solution esp. when measured in osmols or milliosmols per 1000 grams of solvent — **os·mo·lal** \äz-'mō-ləl, äs-\ *adj*

os·mo·lar·i·ty \ˌäz-mō-'lar-ə-tē, ˌäs-\ *n, pl* **-ties** [*osmol* + *-ar* + *-ity*] (1948) : the concentration of an osmotic solution esp. when measured in osmols or milliosmols per liter of solution — **os·mo·lar** \äz-'mō-lər, äs-\ *adj*

os·mom·e·ter \äz-'mä-mə-tər, äs-\ *n* [*osmosis* + *-meter*] (1854) : an apparatus for measuring osmotic pressure — **os·mo·met·ric** \ˌäz-mə-'me-trik, ˌäs-\ *adj* — **os·mom·e·try** \äz-'mä-mə-trē\ *n*

os·mo·reg·u·la·tion \'äz-mō-ˌre-gyə-'lā-shən, ˌäs-\ *n* [*osmosis* + *regulation*] (1927) : regulation of osmotic pressure esp. in the body of a living organism

os·mo·reg·u·la·to·ry \-'re-gyə-lə-ˌtōr-ē, -ˌtȯr-\ *adj* (ca. 1911) : of, relating to, or concerned with the maintenance of constant osmotic pressure

os·mo·sis \äz-'mō-səs, äs-\ *n* [NL, short for *endosmosis*] (1867) **1** : movement of a solvent through a semipermeable membrane (as of a living cell) into a solution of higher solute concentration that tends to equalize the concentrations of solute on the two sides of the membrane **2** : a process of absorption or diffusion suggestive of the flow of osmotic action; *esp* : a usu. effortless often unconscious assimilation ⟨learned a number of languages by ~ —Roger Kimball⟩

os·mot·ic \-'mä-tik\ *adj* (1854) : of, relating to, or having the properties of osmosis — **os·mot·i·cal·ly** \-ti-k(ə-)lē\ *adv*

osmotic pressure *n* (1888) : the pressure produced by or associated with osmosis and dependent on molar concentration and absolute temperature: as **a** : the maximum pressure that develops in a solution separated from a solvent by a membrane permeable only to the solvent **b** : the pressure that must be applied to a solution to just prevent osmosis

osmotic shock *n* (1950) : a rapid change in the osmotic pressure (as by transfer to a medium of different concentration) affecting a living system

os·mun·da \äz-'mən-də\ *n* [NL, fr. ML, fr. OF *osmonde*] (1789) : any of a genus (*Osmunda*) of rather large ferns (as the cinnamon fern) with pinnate or bipinnate fronds and fibrous creeping rhizomes

os·prey \'äs-prē, -ˌprā\ *n, pl* **ospreys** [ME *ospray*, fr. (assumed) MF *osfraie*, fr. L *ossifraga*, a bird of prey] (15c) **1** : a large fish-eating hawk (*Pandion haliaetus*)

osprey 1

that is a dark brown color above and mostly pure white below 2 : a feather trimming used for millinery

ossa *pl of* OS

os·se·in \'ä-sē-ən\ *n* [ISV, fr. L *oss-, os*] (1857) : the collagen of bones

os·se·ous \'ä-sē-əs\ *adj* [L *osseus*, fr. *oss-, os* bone; akin to Gk *osteon* bone, Skt *asthi*] (1682) : BONY 1

Os·sete \'ä-,sēt\ *also* **Os·set** \'ä-sət, -,set\ *n* [Russ *osetin*, fr. *Osetiya* Ossetia, fr. Georgian *Oseti*, fr. *osi* Ossete] (1814) : a member of a people of the central Caucasus — **Os·se·tian** \ä-'sē-shən\ *adj or n*

Os·set·ic \ä-'se-tik\ *n* (ca. 1890) : the Iranian language of the Ossetes

Os·si·an·ic \,ä-sē-'a-nik, -shē-\ *adj* (1808) : of, relating to, or resembling the legendary Irish bard Ossian, the poems ascribed to him, or the rhythmic prose style used by James Macpherson in the poems he claimed to have translated from Ossian

os·si·cle \'ä-si-kəl\ *n* [L *ossiculum*, dim. of *oss-, os*] (1578) : a small bone or bony structure (as the malleus, incus, or stapes) — **os·sic·u·lar** \ä-'si-kyə-lər\ *adj*

os·si·fi·ca·tion \,ä-sə-fə-'kā-shən\ *n* (1697) **1 a** : the natural process of bone formation **b** : the hardening (as of muscular tissue) into a bony substance **2** : a mass or particle of ossified tissue **3** : a tendency toward or state of being molded into a rigid, conventional, sterile, or unimaginative condition

os·si·frage \'ä-sə-frij, -,frāj\ *n* [L *ossifraga*, a bird of prey, fr. fem. of *ossifragus* bone-breaking, fr. *oss-, os* + *frangere* to break — more at BREAK] (1601) : LAMMERGEIER

os·si·fy \'ä-sə-,fī\ *vb* **-fied; -fy·ing** [L *oss-, os* + E -*ify*] *vi* (1713) **1** : to change into bone **2** : to become hardened or conventional and opposed to change ~ *vt* : to change (as cartilage) into bone **2** : to make rigidly conventional and opposed to change

os·so bu·co *also* **os·so buc·co** \,ō-sō-'bü-(,)kō, ,ó-sō-\ *n* [It *ossobuco* veal shank, lit., pierced bone] (1935) : braised veal shanks

os·su·ary \'ä-shə-,wer-ē, -syə-, -sə-\ *n, pl* **-ar·ies** [LL *ossuarium*, fr. L, neut. of *ossuarius* of bones, fr. OL *ossua*, pl. of *oss-, os*] (1658) : a depository for the bones of the dead

oste- *or* **osteo-** *comb form* [NL, fr. Gk, fr. *osteon* — more at OSSEOUS] : bone ⟨*osteal*⟩ ⟨*osteo*myelitis⟩

os·te·al \'äs-tē-əl\ *adj* [ISV] (1877) : of, relating to, or resembling bone; *also* : affecting or involving bone or the skeleton

os·te·i·tis \,äs-tē-'ī-təs\ *n* [NL] (ca. 1847) : inflammation of bone

os·ten·si·ble \ä-'sten(t)-sə-bəl, ə-\ *adj* [F, fr. L *ostensus*, pp. of *ostendere* to show, fr. *obs-, ob-* in the way + *tendere* to stretch — more at OB-, THIN] (ca. 1771) **1** : intended for display : open to view **2** : being such in appearance : plausible rather than demonstrably true or real ⟨the ~ purpose for the trip⟩ *syn* see APPARENT

os·ten·si·bly \-blē\ *adv* (1765) **1** : in an ostensible manner **2** : to all outward appearances

os·ten·sive \ä-'sten(t)-siv\ *adj* (1782) **1** : OSTENSIBLE 2 **2** : of, relating to, or constituting definition by exemplifying the thing or quality being defined — **os·ten·sive·ly** *adv*

os·ten·so·ri·um \,äs-tən-'sōr-ē-əm, -,ten-, -'sór-\ *n, pl* **-ria** \-ē-ə\ [ML, fr. L *ostendere*] (ca. 1772) : MONSTRANCE

os·ten·ta·tion \,äs-tən-'tā-shən\ *n* [ME *ostentacion*, fr. MF *ostentation*, fr. L *ostentation-, ostentatio*, fr. *ostentare* to display, freq. of *ostendere*] (15c) **1** : excessive display : PRETENTIOUSNESS **2** *archaic* : an act of displaying

os·ten·ta·tious \-shəs\ *adj* (1673) : marked by or fond of conspicuous or vainglorious and sometimes pretentious display *syn* see SHOWY — **os·ten·ta·tious·ly** *adv* — **os·ten·ta·tious·ness** *n*

os·te·o·ar·thri·tis \,äs-tē-ō-är-'thrī-təs\ *n* [NL] (1878) : arthritis marked by degeneration of the cartilage and bone of joints — **os·te·o·ar·thrit·ic** \-'thri-tik\ *adj*

os·te·o·blast \'äs-tē-ə-,blast\ *n* [ISV] (1875) : a bone-forming cell — **os·te·o·blas·tic** \,äs-tē-ə-'blas-tik\ *adj*

os·te·o·clast \'äs-tē-ə-,klast\ *n* [ISV *oste-* + Gk *klastos* broken — more at CLAST] (1872) : any of the large multinucleate cells closely associated with areas of bone resorption — **os·te·o·clas·tic** \,äs-tē-ə-'klas-tik\ *adj*

os·te·o·cyte \'äs-tē-ə-,sīt\ *n* (1942) : a cell that is characteristic of adult bone and is isolated in a lacuna of the bone substance

os·te·o·gen·e·sis \,äs-tē-ə-'je-nə-səs\ *n* [NL] (1830) : development and formation of bone

osteogenesis im·per·fec·ta \-,im-(,)pər-'fek-tə\ *n* [NL, imperfect osteogenesis] (ca. 1901) : a hereditary disease marked esp. by extreme brittleness of the long bones

os·te·o·gen·ic \,äs-tē-ə-'je-nik\ *adj* (1867) **1** : producing bone **2** : originating in bone

osteogenic sarcoma *n* (ca. 1923) : OSTEOSARCOMA

¹os·te·oid \'äs-tē-,óid\ *adj* [ISV] (1840) : resembling bone

²osteoid *n* (1934) : uncalcified bone matrix

os·te·ol·o·gy \,äs-tē-'ä-lə-jē\ *n* [NL *osteologia*, fr. Gk, description of bones, fr. *oste-* + -*logia* -logy] (1670) **1** : a branch of anatomy dealing with the bones **2** : the bony structure of an organism — **os·te·o·log·i·cal** \-tē-ə-'lä-ji-kəl\ *adj* — **os·te·ol·o·gist** \-tē-'ä-lə-jist\ *n*

os·te·o·ma \,äs-tē-'ō-mə\ *n, pl* **-mas** *or* **-ma·ta** \-mə-tə\ [NL] (ca. 1849) : a benign tumor composed of bone tissue

os·te·o·ma·la·cia \,äs-tē-ō-mə-'lā-sh(ē-)ə\ *n* [NL, fr. *oste-* + Gk *malakia* softness, fr. *malakos* soft — more at MOLLIFY] (ca. 1834) : a disease of adults that is characterized by softening of the bones and is analogous to rickets in the immature

os·te·o·my·e·li·tis \,äs-tē-ō-,mī-ə-'lī-təs\ *n* [NL] (1854) : an infectious inflammatory disease of bone often of bacterial origin that is marked by local death and separation of tissue

os·te·o·path \'äs-tē-ə-,path\ *n* (1897) : a practitioner of osteopathy

os·te·op·a·thy \,äs-tē-'ä-pə-thē\ *n* [NL *osteopathia*, fr. *oste-* + L -*pathia* -pathy] (1899) : a system of medical practice based on a theory that diseases are due chiefly to loss of structural integrity which can be restored by manipulation of the parts supplemented by therapeutic measures (as use of medicine or surgery) — **os·te·o·path·ic** \,äs-tē-ə-'pa-thik\ *adj* — **os·te·o·path·i·cal·ly** \-thi-k(ə-)lē\ *adv*

os·te·o·plas·ty \'äs-tē-ə-,plas-tē\ *n* (ca. 1860) : plastic surgery on bone; *esp* : replacement of lost bone tissue or reconstruction of defective bony parts — **os·te·o·plas·tic** \,äs-tē-ə-'plas-tik\ *adj*

os·te·o·po·ro·sis \,äs-tē-ō-pə-'rō-səs\ *n, pl* **-ro·ses** \-,sēz\ [NL, fr. *oste-* + *porosis* rarefaction, fr. *porus* pore + -*osis*] (1846) : a condition that affects esp. older women and is characterized by decrease in bone mass

with decreased density and enlargement of bone spaces producing porosity and fragility — **os·te·o·po·rot·ic** \-'rä-tik\ *adj*

os·te·o·sar·co·ma \-sär-'kō-mə\ *n, pl* **-mas** *or* **-ma·ta** \-mə-tə\ [NL] (ca. 1826) : a sarcoma derived from bone or containing bone tissue

os·ti·na·to \,äs-tə-'nä-(,)tō, ,ós-\ *n, pl* **-tos** *also* **-ti** \-tē\ [It, obstinate, fr. L *obstinatus*] (ca. 1876) : a musical figure repeated persistently at the same pitch throughout a composition — compare IMITATION, SEQUENCE

os·ti·ole \'äs-tē-,ōl\ *n* [NL *ostiolum*, fr. L, dim. of *ostium*] (ca. 1857) : a small bodily aperture, orifice, or pore

os·ti·um \'äs-tē-əm\ *n, pl* **os·tia** \-tē-ə\ [NL, fr. L, door, mouth of a river; akin to L *os* mouth — more at ORAL] (1828) : a mouthlike opening in a bodily organ

os·tler *var of* HOSTLER

ost·mark \'ōst-,märk, 'óst-\ *n* [G, lit., East mark] (1948) : the former East German mark

os·to·my \'äs-tə-mē\ *n, pl* **-mies** [*colostomy*] (1957) : an operation (as a colostomy) to create an artificial passage for bodily elimination

-ostosis *n comb form, pl* **-ostoses** *or* **-ostosises** [NL, fr. Gk -*ostōsis*, fr. *osteon* bone — more at OSSEOUS] : ossification of a (specified) part or to a (specified) degree ⟨hyper*ostosis*⟩

os·tra·cise *Brit var of* OSTRACIZE

os·tra·cism \'äs-trə-,si-zəm\ *n* (1588) **1** : a method of temporary banishment by popular vote without trial or special accusation practiced in ancient Greece **2** : exclusion by general consent from common privileges or social acceptance

os·tra·cize \-,sīz\ *vt* **-cized; -ciz·ing** [Gk *ostrakizein* to banish by voting with potsherds, fr. *ostrakon* shell, potsherd — more at OYSTER] (1649) **1** : to exile by ostracism **2** : to exclude from a group by common consent

os·tra·cod \'äs-trə-,käd\ *also* **os·tra·code** \-,kōd\ *n* [ultim. fr. Gk *ostrakon*] (1865) : any of a subclass (Ostracoda) of very small active mostly freshwater crustaceans that have the body enclosed in a bivalve carapace, the body segmentation obscured, the abdomen rudimentary, and only seven pairs of appendages

os·tra·co·derm \'äs-trə-kō-,dərm, äs-'tra-kə-\ *n* [ultim. fr. Gk *ostrakon* + *derma* skin — more at DERM-] (1891) : any of the early fossil jawless fishes of the Lower Paleozoic usu. having a bony covering of plates or scales

os·tra·con \'äs-trə-,kän\ *n, pl* **-tra·ca** \-trə-kə\ [Gk *ostrakon* potsherd, shell — more at OYSTER] (1883) : a fragment (as of pottery) containing an inscription — usu. used in pl.

os·trich \'äs-trich, 'ós- *also* -trij\ *n* [ME, fr. OF *ostrusce*, fr. (assumed) VL *avis struthio*, fr. L *avis* bird + LL *struthio* ostrich — more at STRU-THIOUS] (13c) **1 a** : a swift-footed 2-toed flightless ratite bird (*Struthio camelus*) of Africa that is the largest of existing birds and often weighs 300 pounds (140 kilograms) **b** : RHEA **c** : leather made from ostrich skin **2** [fr. the belief that the ostrich when pursued hides its head in the sand and believes itself to be unseen] : one who attempts to avoid danger or difficulty by refusing to face it — **os·trich-like** \-,līk\ *adj*

Os·tro·goth \'äs-trə-,gäth\ *n* [ME, fr. LL *Ostrogothi*, pl.] (14c) : a member of the eastern division of the Goths — **Os·tro·goth·ic** \,äs-trə-'gä-thik\ *adj*

Os·we·go tea \ä-'swē-gō-\ *n* [*Oswego* River, N. Y.] (1752) : a No. American mint (*Monarda didyma*) with showy scarlet irregular flowers

ot- *or* **oto-** *comb form* [Gk *ōt-, ōto-*, fr. *ōt-, ous* — more at EAR] : ear ⟨*otitis*⟩ : ear and ⟨*oto*laryngology⟩

Othel·lo \ə-'the-(,)lō, ō-\ *n* : a Moor in the military service of Venice, husband of Desdemona, and protagonist of Shakespeare's tragedy *Othello*

¹oth·er \'ə-thər\ *adj* [ME, fr. OE *ōther*; akin to OHG *andar* other, Skt *antara*] (bef. 12c) **1 a** : being the one (as of two or more) remaining or not included ⟨held on with one hand and waved with the ~ one⟩ **b** : being the one or ones distinct from that or those first mentioned or implied ⟨taller than the ~ boys⟩ **c** : SECOND ⟨every ~ day⟩ **2** : not the same : DIFFERENT ⟨any ~ color would have been better⟩ ⟨something ~ than it seems to be⟩ **3** : ADDITIONAL ⟨sold in the U.S. and 14 ~ countries⟩ **4 a** : recently past ⟨the ~ evening⟩ **b** : FORMER ⟨in ~ times⟩

²other *n* (bef. 12c) **1 a** : one that remains of two or more **b** : a thing opposite to or excluded by something else ⟨went from one side to the ~⟩ **2** : a different or additional one ⟨the ~s came later⟩

³other *pron, sometimes pl in constr* (bef. 12c) **1 obs a** : one of two that remains **b** : each preceding one **2** : a different or additional one ⟨something or ~⟩

⁴other *adv* (13c) : OTHERWISE — used with *than* ⟨was unable to see them ~ than by going to their home⟩

oth·er–di·rect·ed \,ə-thər-də-'rek-təd, -dī-\ *adj* (1950) : directed in thought and action primarily by external norms rather than by one's own scale of values — **oth·er–di·rect·ed·ness** *n*

oth·er·guess \'ə-thər-,ges\ *adj* [alter. of E dial. *othergates*] (1632) *archaic* : DIFFERENT

oth·er·ness \'ə-thər-nəs\ *n* (1587) **1** : the quality or state of being other or different **2** : something that is other or different

other than *prep* (1679) : with the exception of : EXCEPT FOR, BESIDES ⟨*other than* that, nothing happened⟩

oth·er·where \-,hwer, -,hwar, -,wer, -,war\ *adv* (14c) : ELSEWHERE

oth·er·while \-,hwīl, -,wīl\ *also* **oth·er·whiles** \-,hwīlz, -,wilz\ *adv* (13c) *chiefly dial* : at another time

¹oth·er·wise \-,wīz\ *pron* [ME, fr. OE (on) *ōthre wīsan* in another manner] (bef. 12c) : something or anything else : something to the contrary ⟨do very little to enforce competition—and have never intended ~ —Milton Viorst⟩

²otherwise *adv* (13c) **1** : in a different way or manner ⟨glossed over or ~ handled —*Playboy*⟩ **2** : in different circumstances ⟨might ~ have left⟩ **3** : in other respects ⟨an ~ flimsy farce —*Current Biog.*⟩ **4** : if not ⟨do what I tell you, ~ you'll be sorry⟩ **5** : NOT — paired with an

---

\ə\ abut \ᵊ\ kitten, F table \ər\ further \a\ ash \ā\ ace \ä\ mop, mar
\aú\ out \ch\ chin \e\ bet \ē\ easy \g\ go \i\ hit \ī\ ice \j\ job
\ŋ\ sing \ō\ go \ó\ law \ói\ boy \th\ thin \t͟h\ the \ü\ loot \ú\ foot
\y\ yet \zh\ vision \ȧ, k̶, ⁿ, œ, œ̄, ᵫ, ᵫ̄, ᵊ\ *see* Guide to Pronunciation

adjective, adverb, noun, or verb to indicate its contrary or to suggest an indefinite alternative ⟨people whose deeds, admirable or ~ —John Fischer⟩ ⟨almost thirty thousand women, Irish and ~ —J. M. Burns⟩ ⟨his opinion as to the success or ~ of it —*Austral. Dict. of Biog.*⟩

³**otherwise** *adj* (14c) : DIFFERENT ⟨if conditions were ~⟩

other woman *n* (1855) : a woman with whom a married man has an affair — usu. used with *the*

oth·er·world \'ə-thər-,wǝrld\ *n* (13c) : a world beyond death or beyond present reality

oth·er·world·ly \,ə-thǝr-'wǝrl(d)-lē\ *adj* (1879) **1 a** : of, relating to, or resembling that of a world other than the actual world **b** : devoted to preparing for a world to come **2** : devoted to intellectual or imaginative pursuits — **oth·er·world·li·ness** *n*

¹**-otic** *adj suffix* [Gk -ōtikos, fr. -ōtos, ending of verbals, fr. -o- (stem of causative verbs in -*oun*) + -*tos*, suffix forming verbals — more at -ED] : of, relating to, or characterized by a (specified) action, process, or condition ⟨symbiotic⟩

²**-otic** *adj comb form* [Gk ōtikos of the ear, fr. ōt-, ous ear] : having (such) a relationship to the ear ⟨dichotic⟩

oti·ose \'ō-shē-,ōs, 'ō-tē-\ *adj* [L otiosus, fr. otium leisure] (1794) **1** : producing no useful result : FUTILE **2** : being at leisure : IDLE **3** : lacking use or effect : FUNCTIONLESS   *syn* see VAIN — **oti·ose·ly** *adv* — **oti·ose·ness** *n* — **oti·os·i·ty** \,ō-shē-'ä-sǝ-tē, ,ō-tē-\ *n*

oti·tis \ō-'tī-tǝs\ *n* [NL] (ca. 1799) : inflammation of the ear

otitis me·dia \-'mē-dē-ǝ\ *n* [NL] (1874) : inflammation of the middle ear marked by pain, fever, dizziness, and abnormalities of hearing

oto·cyst \'ō-tǝ-,sist\ *n* [ISV; fr. its probable auditory function] (1877) : a fluid-containing organ of many invertebrates that contains an otolith : STATOCYST — **oto·cys·tic** \,ō-tǝ-'sis-tik\ *adj*

oto·lar·yn·gol·o·gy \,ō-tō-,lar-ǝn-'gä-lǝ-jē\ *n* (1897) : a medical specialty concerned esp. with the ear, nose, and throat — **oto·lar·yn·go·log·i·cal** \-gǝ-'lä-ji-kǝl\ *adj* — **oto·lar·yn·gol·o·gist** \-'gä-lǝ-jist\ *n*

oto·lith \'ō-t ⁱl-,ith\ *n* [F otolithe, fr. ot- + -lithe -lith] (ca. 1836) : a calcareous concretion in the inner ear of a vertebrate or in the otocyst of an invertebrate — **oto·lith·ic** \,ō-t ⁱl-'i-thik\ *adj*

oto·rhi·no·lar·yn·gol·o·gy \,ō-tō-,rī-nō-,lar-ǝn-'gä-lǝ-jē\ *n* (ca. 1900) : OTOLARYNGOLOGY — **oto·rhi·no·lar·yn·go·log·i·cal** \-gǝ-'lä-ji-kǝl\ *adj* — **oto·rhi·no·lar·yn·gol·o·gist** \-'gä-lǝ-jist\ *n*

oto·scle·ro·sis \,ō-tō-sklǝ-'rō-sǝs\ *n* [NL] (1901) : growth of spongy bone in the inner ear that causes progressively increasing deafness

oto·tox·ic \,ō-tǝ-'täk-sik\ *adj* (1951) : producing, involving, or being adverse effects on organs or nerves involved in hearing or balance — **oto·tox·ic·i·ty** \-täk-'si-sǝ-tē\ *n*

ot·ta·va \ō-'tä-vǝ\ *adv or adj* [It, octave, fr. ML octava] (1848) : at an octave higher or lower than written — used as a direction in music

ottava ri·ma \-'rē-mǝ\ *n, pl* **ottava rimas** [It, lit., eighth rhyme] (1820) : a stanza of eight lines of heroic verse with a rhyme scheme of *abababcc*

Ot·ta·wa \'ä-tǝ-wǝ, -,wä, -,wȯ\ *n, pl* **-was** *or* **-wa** (1687) : a member of an American Indian people of Michigan and southern Ontario

ot·ter \'ä-tǝr\ *n, pl* **otters** *also* **ot·ter** [ME oter, fr. OE otor; akin to OHG ottar otter, Gk hydōr water — more at WATER] (bef. 12c) **1** : any of various largely aquatic carnivorous mammals (as genus *Lutra* or *Enhydra*) that are related to the weasels and minks and usu. have webbed and clawed feet and dark brown fur **2** : the fur or pelt of an otter

otter 1

otter hound *n* [fr. its use in hunting otters] (1607) : any of a British breed of large hounds that have a wiry water-resistant coat and a keen scent

ot·to \'ä-(,)tō\ *var of* ATTAR

ot·to·man \'ä-tǝ-mǝn\ *n* (1605) **1** *cap* **a** : a member of a Turkish dynasty founded by Osman I that ruled the Ottoman Empire **b** : a citizen or functionary of the Ottoman Empire **2** [F ottomane, fr. fem. of ottoman, adj.] **a** : an upholstered often overstuffed seat or couch usu. without a back **b** : an overstuffed footstool **3** : a heavy clothing fabric characterized by pronounced crosswise ribs

Ot·to·man \'ä-tǝ-mǝn\ *adj* [F, adj. & n., prob. fr. It ottomano, fr. Ar 'othmānī, fr. 'Othmān Osman I, founder of the Ottoman Empire] (1603) : of or relating to the Ottoman Empire, its rulers, or its citizens or functionaries

oua·bain \wä-'bä-ǝn, 'wä-,bäⁱn\ *n* [ISV, fr. F ouabaïo, an African tree, fr. Somali waabayyo arrow poison] (1893) : a poisonous glycoside $C_{29}H_{44}O_{12}$ obtained from several African shrubs or trees (genera *Strophanthus* and *Acokanthera*) of the dogbane family and used medically like digitalis and in Africa as an arrow poison

ou·bli·ette \,ü-blē-'et\ *n* [F, fr. MF, fr. oublier to forget, fr. (assumed) VL oblitare, freq. of L oblivisci to forget — more at OBLIVION] (1819) : a dungeon with an opening only at the top

¹**ouch** \'auch\ *n* [ME, alter. (fr. misdivision of *a nouche*) of *nouche*, fr. MF, fr. Gmc origin; akin to OHG nusca clasp] (14c) **1** *obs* : CLASP, BROOCH **2 a** : a setting for a precious stone **b** : JEWEL, ORNAMENT; *esp* : a buckle or brooch set with precious stones

²**ouch** *interj* [origin unknown] (1838) — used esp. to express sudden pain

oud \'üd\ *n* [Ar 'ūd, lit., wood] (1738) : a musical instrument of the lute family used in southwest Asia and northern Africa

¹**ought** \'ȯt\ *verbal auxiliary* [ME oughte (1st & 3d sing. pres. indic.), fr. oughte, 1st & 3d sing. past indic. & subj. of owen to own, owe — more at OWE] (12c) — used to express obligation ⟨~ to pay our debts⟩, advisability ⟨~ to take care of yourself⟩, natural expectation ⟨~ to be here by now⟩, or logical consequence ⟨the result ~ to be infinity⟩

²**ought** \'ȯ(k)t\ *vt* [ME oughte, 1st & 3d sing. past indic. of owen] (13c) **1** *chiefly Scot* : POSSESS **2** *chiefly Scot* : OWE

³**ought** \'ȯt\ *n* (1678) : moral obligation : DUTY

⁴**ought** \'ȯt, 'ät\ *var of* AUGHT

oughtn't \'ȯ-t ⁱnt\ (1884) : ought not

ou·gui·ya \ü-'gwē-ǝ, -'gē-ǝ\ *n, pl* **ouguiya** [Ar dial. ūgīyah, fr. Ar ūqīyah, lit., ounce] (1973) — see MONEY table

Oui·ja \'wē-jǝ, -jē\ *trademark* — used for a board with the alphabet and other signs on it that is used with a planchette to seek spiritualistic or telepathic messages

¹**ounce** \'aun(t)s\ *n* [ME, fr. MF unce, fr. L uncia 12th part, ounce, fr. unus one — more at ONE] (14c) **1 a** : a unit of weight equal to $\frac{1}{12}$ troy pound — see WEIGHT table **b** : a unit of weight equal to $\frac{1}{16}$ avoirdupois pound **c** : a small amount ⟨an ~ of common sense⟩ **2** : FLUIDOUNCE

²**ounce** *n* [ME once lynx, fr. MF, alter. (by misdivision, as if *l'once* ounce) of *lonce*, fr. (assumed) VL lyncea, fr. L lync-, lynx] (1774) : SNOW LEOPARD

our \är, 'au(-ǝ)r\ *adj* [ME oure, fr. OE ūre; akin to OHG unsēr our, OE ūs us] (bef. 12c) : of or relating to us or ourselves or ourself esp. as possessors or possessor, agents or agent, or objects or object of an action ⟨~ throne⟩ ⟨~ actions⟩ ⟨~ being chosen⟩

Our Father *n* [fr. the opening words] (1882) : LORD'S PRAYER

ours \'au(-ǝ)rz, ärz\ *pron, sing or pl in constr* (14c) : that which belongs to us — used without a following noun as a pronoun equivalent in meaning to the adjective *our*

our·self \är-'self, au(-ǝ)r-\ *pron* (14c) : MYSELF — used to refer to the single-person subject when *we* is used instead of *I* (as by a sovereign) ⟨will keep ~ till supper time alone —Shak.⟩

our·selves \-'selvz\ *pron pl* (15c) **1** : those identical ones that are we — compare WE 1; used reflexively ⟨we're doing it solely for ~⟩, for emphasis ⟨we ~ will never go⟩, or in absolute constructions ⟨~ no longer young, we can sympathize with those who are old⟩ **2** : our normal, healthy, or sane condition ⟨just not ~ today⟩

-ous *adj suffix* [ME, fr. OF -ous, -eus, -eux, fr. L -osus] **1** : full of : abounding in : having : possessing the qualities of ⟨clamorous⟩ ⟨poisonous⟩ **2** : having a valence lower than in compounds or ions named with an adjectival ending in -ic ⟨mercurous⟩

ou·sel \'ü-zǝl\ *var of* OUZEL

Ou·shak \ü-'shäk\ *n, often attrib* [fr. Oushak, Ushak (Uşak), town in Turkey] (1901) : a heavy wool Oriental rug characterized esp. by bright primary colors and an elaborate medallion pattern

oust \'aust\ *vt* [ME, fr. AF ouster, fr. OF oster, fr. LL obstare to ward off, fr. L, to stand in the way, fr. ob- in the way + stare to stand — more at OB-, STAND] (15c) **1 a** : to remove from or dispossess of property or position by legal action, by force, or by the compulsion of necessity **b** : to take away (as a right or authority) : BAR, REMOVE **2** : to take the place of : SUPPLANT   *syn* see EJECT

oust·er \'aus-tǝr\ *n* [AF, to oust] (1531) **1 a** : a wrongful dispossession **b** : a judgment removing an officer or depriving a corporation of a franchise **2** : EXPULSION

¹**out** \'aut\ *adv* [ME, fr. OE ūt; akin to OHG ūz out, Gk hysteros later, Skt ud up, out] (bef. 12c) **1 a** (1) : in a direction away from the inside or center ⟨went ~ into the garden⟩ (2) : OUTSIDE ⟨it's raining ~⟩ **b** : from among others **c** : away from the shore **d** : away from home or work ⟨~ to lunch⟩ **e** : away from a particular place **2 a** : so as to be missing or displaced from the usual or proper place ⟨left a word ~⟩ ⟨threw his shoulder ~⟩ **b** : into the possession or control of another ⟨lend ~ money⟩ **c** : into a state of loss or defeat ⟨was voted ~⟩ **d** : into a state of vexation ⟨they do not mark me, and that brings me ~ —Shak.⟩ **e** : into groups or shares ⟨sorted ~ her notes⟩ ⟨parceled ~ the farm⟩ **3 a** : to the point of depletion, extinction, or exhaustion ⟨the food ran ~⟩ ⟨turn the light ~⟩ ⟨all tuckered ~⟩ **b** : to completion or satisfaction ⟨hear me ~⟩ ⟨work the problem ~⟩ **c** : to the full or a great extent or degree ⟨all decked ~⟩ ⟨stretched ~ on the floor⟩ **4 a** : in or into the open ⟨the sun came ~⟩ **b** : OUT LOUD ⟨cried ~⟩ **c** : in or into public circulation ⟨the evening paper isn't ~ yet⟩ ⟨hand ~ pamphlets⟩ ⟨the library book is still ~⟩ **5 a** : at an end ⟨before the day is ~⟩ **b** : in or into an insensible or unconscious state ⟨she was ~ cold⟩ **c** : in or into a useless state ⟨landed the plane with one engine ~⟩ **d** : so as to put a player or side out or to be put out in baseball **6** — used on a two-way radio circuit to indicate that a message is complete and no reply is expected

²**out** *vt* (bef. 12c) : EJECT, OUST ~ *vi* : to become publicly known ⟨the truth will ~⟩

³**out** *prep* (13c) — used as a function word to indicate an outward movement ⟨ran ~ the door⟩ ⟨looked ~ the window⟩

⁴**out** *adj* (13c) **1 a** : situated outside : EXTERNAL **b** : OUT-OF-BOUNDS **2** : situated at a distance : OUTLYING ⟨the ~ islands⟩ **3** : not being in power **4** : ABSENT **5** : put out while at bat or baserunning in baseball **6** : directed outward or serving to direct something outward ⟨the ~ basket⟩ **7** : not being in vogue or fashion **8** : not to be considered : out of the question **9** : DETERMINED 1 ⟨was ~ to get revenge⟩

⁵**out** *n* (1717) **1** : OUTSIDE **2** : one who is out of office or power or on the outside ⟨a matter of ~s versus ins⟩ **3 a** : an act or instance of putting a player out or of being put out in baseball **b** : a player that is put out **c** : a way of escaping from an embarrassing or difficult situation — **on the outs** : on unfriendly terms : at variance

out- *prefix* [¹*out*] : in a manner that exceeds or surpasses and sometimes overpowers or defeats ⟨outmaneuver⟩

out·achieve	out·de·sign	out·in·trigue
out·act	out·dress	out·jump
out·bar·gain	out·dress	out·kick
out·bid	out·drink	out·kill
out·bitch	out·drive	out·last
out·bluff	out·du·el	out·leap
out·box	out·earn	out·learn
out·brag	out·eat	out·man
out·brawl	out·fight	out·ma·neu·ver
out·bulk	out·fig·ure	out·ma·nip·u·late
out·buy	out·fish	out·march
out·catch	out·fly	out·mus·cle
out·charge	out·fum·ble	out·or·ga·nize
out·climb	out·gain	out·pass
out·coach	out·glit·ter	out·per·form
out·com·pete	out·gross	out·pitch
out·dance	out·hit	out·play
out·daz·zle	out·ho·mer	out·plot
out·de·bate	out·hunt	out·pol·i·tick
out·de·liv·er	out·hus·tle	out·poll

out·pop·u·late	out·sail	out·swim
out·pow·er	out·scheme	out·talk
out·pray	out·scoop	out·think
out·preach	out·score	out·throw
out·price	out·shout	out·trade
out·pro·duce	out·sing	out·vie
out·prom·ise	out·sit	out·vote
out·punch	out·skate	out·wait
out·rate	out·soar	out·walk
out·re·bound	out·spar·kle	out·watch
out·re·pro·duce	out·speed	out·wres·tle
out·ri·val	out·sprint	out·write
out·roar	out·stride	out·yell
out·row	out·swear	out·yield
out·rush		

out·age \'aů-tij\ *n* (1899) **1** : a quantity or bulk of something lost in transportation or storage **2 a** : a failure or interruption in use or functioning **b** : a period of interruption esp. of electric current

out–and–out \,aůt-ᵊn(d)-'aůt\ *adj* (1813) : being such completely at all times, in every way, or from every point of view ⟨an ~ fraud⟩

out–and–out·er \-'aů-tər\ *n* (ca. 1812) : one who goes to extremes

out·back \'aůt-,bak, -,bak\ *n* (1893) : isolated rural country esp. of Australia

out·bal·ance \,aůt-'ba-lən(t)s\ *vt* (1644) : OUTWEIGH

¹out·board \'aůt-,bôrd, -,bôrd\ *adj* (ca. 1823) **1** : situated outboard **2** : having, using, or limited to the use of an outboard motor

²outboard *adv* (ca. 1848) **1** : outside a ship's bulwarks : in a lateral direction from the hull **2** : in a position closer or closest to either of the wingtips of an airplane or to the sides of an automobile

³outboard *n* (1935) **1** : OUTBOARD MOTOR **2** : a boat with an outboard motor

outboard motor *n* (1909) : a small internal combustion engine with propeller integrally attached for mounting at the stern of a small boat

out·bound \'aůt-,baůnd\ *adj* (1598) : outward bound ⟨~ traffic⟩

out·brave \,aůt-'brāv\ *vt* (1589) **1** : to face or resist defiantly **2** : to exceed in courage

out·break \'aůt-,brāk\ *n* (1602) **1 a** : a sudden or violent increase in activity or currency ⟨the ~ of war⟩ **b** : a sudden rise in the incidence of a disease ⟨an ~ of measles⟩ **c** : a sudden increase in numbers of a harmful organism and esp. an insect within a particular area ⟨an ~ of locusts⟩ **2** : INSURRECTION, REVOLT

out·breed *vt* **-bred** \-,bred, -'bred\; **-breed·ing** (ca. 1909) **1** \'aůt-,brēd\ : to subject to outbreeding **2** \aůt-'\ : to breed faster than

out·breed·ing \'aůt-,brē-diŋ\ *n* (1901) : the interbreeding of individuals or stocks that are relatively unrelated

out·build·ing \'aůt-,bil-diŋ\ *n* (1626) : a building (as a stable or a woodshed) separate from but accessory to a main house

out·burst \-,bərst\ *n* (1657) **1** : a violent expression of feeling ⟨an ~ of anger⟩ **2** : a surge of activity or growth ⟨new ~s of creative power —C. E. Montague⟩ **3** : ERUPTION ⟨volcanic ~s⟩

out·bye *or* **out·by** \üt-'bī\ *adv* [ME (Sc) *out-by*, fr. *out* + *by*] (15c) *chiefly Scot* : a short distance away; *also* : OUTDOORS

out·cast \'aůt-,kast\ *n* (14c) **1** : one that is cast out or refused acceptance (as by society) : PARIAH **2** [Sc *cast out* to quarrel] *Scot* : QUARREL — **outcast** *adj*

out·caste \-,kast\ *n* (1876) **1** : a Hindu who has been ejected from his caste for violation of its customs or rules **2** : one who has no caste

out·class \,aůt-'klas\ *vt* (1870) : to excel or surpass so decisively as to be or appear to be of a higher class

out·come \'aůt-,kəm\ *n* (1788) : something that follows as a result or consequence

¹out·crop \'aůt-,kräp\ *n* (1805) **1** : a coming out of bedrock or of an unconsolidated deposit to the surface of the ground **2** : the part of a rock formation that appears at the surface of the ground

²out·crop \'aůt-,kräp, ,aůt-'\ *vi* (ca. 1847) **1** : to project from the surrounding soil ⟨ledges *outcropping* from the eroded slope⟩ **2** : to come to the surface : APPEAR

out·crop·ping \'aůt-,krä-piŋ\ *n* (1872) : OUTCROP

¹out·cross \'aůt-,krös\ *n* (1890) **1** : a cross between relatively unrelated individuals **2** : the progeny of an outcross

²outcross *vt* (1918) : to cross with a relatively unrelated individual or strain

out·cry \'aůt-,krī\ *n* (14c) **1 a** : a loud cry : CLAMOR **b** : a vehement protest **2** : AUCTION

out·dat·ed \,aůt-'dā-təd\ *adj* (1616) : no longer current : OUTMODED — **out·dat·ed·ly** *adv* — **out·dat·ed·ness** *n*

out·dis·tance \,aůt-'dis-tən(t)s\ *vt* (1857) : to go far ahead of (as in a race) : OUTSTRIP

out·do \-'dü\ *vt* **-did** \-'did\; **-done** \-'dən\; **-do·ing** \-'dü-iŋ\; **-does** \-'dəz\ (1607) **1** : to go beyond in action or performance : DEFEAT, OVERCOME *syn* see EXCEED

out·door \'aůt-,dōr, -,dôr; 'aůt-'\ *also* **out·doors** \-,dōrz, -,dôrz; 'aůt-'\ *adj* [*out* (of) *door*, *out* (of) *doors*] (1748) **1** : of or relating to the outdoors **2 a** : performed outdoors ⟨~ sports⟩ **b** : OUTDOORSY ⟨an ~ couple⟩ **3** : not enclosed : having no roof ⟨an ~ restaurant⟩

¹out·doors \'aůt-'dōrz, -'dôrz; 'aůt-'\ *adv* (1817) : outside a building : in or into the open air

²outdoors *n pl but sing in constr* (1844) **1** : a place or location away from the confines of a building **2** : the world away from human habitations

out·doors·man \-mən\ *n* (1918) : one who spends much time in the outdoors or in outdoor activities — **out·doors·man·ship** \-,ship\ *n*

out·doorsy \,aůt-'dōr-zē, -'dôr-\ *adj* (1936) : relating to, characteristic of, or appropriate for the outdoors ⟨~ clothing⟩ **2** : fond of outdoor activities ⟨sounded rugged and ~ —*N.Y. Times*⟩

out·draw \aůt-'drö\ *vt* **-drew** \-'drü\; **-drawn** \-'drön\; **-draw·ing** (ca. 1909) **1** : to attract a larger audience or following than **2** : to draw a handgun more quickly than

out·er \'aů-tər\ *adj* [ME, fr. ¹*out* + ¹*-er*] (13c) **1** : existing independent of mind : OBJECTIVE **2** : situated farther out ⟨the ~ limits⟩ **b** : being away from a center **c** : situated at or belonging on the outside ⟨the ~ covering⟩

out·er·coat \'aů-tər-,kōt\ *n* (1948) : COAT 1a

outer ear *n* (1935) : the outer visible portion of the ear that collects and directs sound waves toward the eardrum by way of a canal which extends inward through the temporal bone

out·er·most \'aů-tər-,mōst\ *adj* (14c) : farthest out

outer planet *n* (1941) : any of the planets Jupiter, Saturn, Uranus, Neptune, and Pluto whose orbits lie beyond the asteroid belt

outer space *n* (1901) : space immediately outside the earth's atmosphere; *broadly* : interplanetary or interstellar space

out·er·wear \'aů-tər-,war, -,wer\ *n* (1921) : clothing for outdoor wear

out·face \aůt-'fās\ *vt* (ca. 1529) **1** : to cause to waver or submit by or as if by staring **2** : to confront unflinchingly : DEFY

out·fall \'aůt-,föl\ *n* (1629) **1** : the outlet of a body of water (as a river or lake); *esp* : the mouth of a drain or sewer

out·field \-,fēld\ *n* (1868) **1** : the part of a baseball field beyond the infield and between the foul lines **2** : the baseball defensive positions comprising right field, center field, and left field; *also* : the players who occupy these positions — **out·field·er** \-,fēl-dər\ *n*

¹out·fit \'aůt-,fit\ *n* (ca. 1769) **1** : the act of fitting out or equipping (as for a voyage or expedition) **2 a** : the tools or equipment for the practice of a trade **b** : wearing apparel with accessories usu. for a special occasion or activity **c** : physical, mental, or moral endowments or resources **3** : a group that works as a team : ORGANIZATION; *esp* : a military unit

²outfit *vb* **out·fit·ted; out·fit·ting** *vt* (1847) **1** : to furnish with an outfit **2** : SUPPLY ⟨*outfitting* every family with shoes —*Amer. Guide Series: Vt.*⟩ ~ *vi* : to acquire an outfit *syn* see FURNISH

out·fit·ter \-,fi-tər\ *n* (1846) : one that outfits: as **a** : HABERDASHER **b** : a business providing equipment, supplies, and often trained guides (as for hunting trips); *also* : a guide working for such an outfitter

out·flank \,aůt-'flaŋk\ *vt* (1765) **1** : to get around the flank of (an opposing force) **2** : GET AROUND, CIRCUMVENT

¹out·flow \'aůt-,flō, aůt-'\ *vi* (ca. 1580) : to flow out

²out·flow \'aůt-,flō\ *n* (ca. 1864) **1** : a flowing out ⟨the ~ of dollars⟩ **2** : something that flows out ⟨~ of a sewage treatment plant⟩

out·foot \aůt-'füt\ *vt* (1737) : to outdo in speed : OUTSTRIP

out·fox \-'fäks\ *vt* (1924) : OUTSMART

out–front \-'frənt\ *adj* (1968) : FRANK, OPEN

out·gas \'aůt-,gas, aůt-'\ *vt* (1925) **1** : to remove occluded gases from usu. by heating; *broadly* : to remove gases from **2** : to remove (gases) from a material or a space ~ *vi* : to lose gases

out·gen·er·al \,aůt-'jen-rəl, -'je-nə-\ *vt* (1767) : to surpass in generalship : OUTMANEUVER

¹out·giv·ing \'aůt-,gi-viŋ\ *n* (1663) : something that is given out; *esp* : a public statement or utterance

²outgiving *adj* (1942) : socially responsive and demonstrative

¹out·go \'aůt-,gō\ *vt* (1530) : to go beyond : OUTDO

²out·go \'aůt-,gō\ *n, pl* **outgoes** (ca. 1640) **1** : something that goes out; *specif* : EXPENDITURE **2 a** : the act of going out **b** : DEPARTURE **3** : OUTLET 1a

out·go·ing \'aůt-,gō-iŋ, -,gó(-)iŋ\ *adj* (1633) **1 a** : going away : DEPARTING ⟨an ~ ship⟩ **b** : retiring or withdrawing from a place or position ⟨the ~ president⟩ **c** : directed to an intended recipient ⟨~ mail⟩ **2** : openly friendly and responsive : EXTROVERTED — **out·go·ing·ness** *n*

out·go·ings \-,gō-iŋz, -,gó(-)iŋz\ *n pl* (1765) *Brit* : costs incurred : EXPENSES

out·group \'aůt-,grüp\ *n* (ca. 1907) : a group that is distinct from one's own and so usu. an object of hostility or dislike — compare INGROUP 1

out·grow \,aůt-'grō\ *vt* **-grew** \-'grü\; **-grown** \-'grōn\; **-grow·ing** (1594) **1** : to grow or increase faster than ⟨mankind is ~*ing* food supplies —R. C. Murphy⟩ **2** : to grow too large or too mature for ⟨*outgrew* his best suit⟩ ⟨the need to ~ the habit of war —Norman Cousins⟩

out·growth \'aůt-,grōth\ *n* (1837) **1** : a process or product of growing out ⟨an ~ of hair⟩ **2** : CONSEQUENCE, BY-PRODUCT ⟨crime is often an ~ of poverty⟩

out·guess \aůt-'ges\ *vt* (1911) : to anticipate the expectations, intentions, or actions of : OUTWIT

out·gun \-'gən\ *vt* (1691) **1** : to surpass in firepower; *broadly* : to OUTDO

out·haul \'aůt-,höl\ *n* (1840) : a rope used to haul a sail taut along a spar

out–Her·od \,aůt-'her-əd\ *vt* [*out-* + *Herod* the Great, depicted in medieval mystery plays as a blustering tyrant] (1602) : to exceed in violence or extravagance — usu. used in the phrase *out-Herod Herod*

out·house \'aůt-,haůs\ *n* (14c) : OUTBUILDING; *esp* : PRIVY 1a

out·ing \'aů-tiŋ\ *n* (1821) **1** : a brief usu. outdoor pleasure trip **2** : an athletic competition or race; *also* : an appearance therein **3** : a usu. public presentation or appearance (as in a particular role) ⟨her first ~ as a novelist⟩ **4** : the public disclosure of the covert homosexuality of a prominent person by homosexual activists

outing flannel *n* (1890) : a flannelette sometimes having an admixture of wool

out·land \'aůt-,land, -lənd\ *n* (bef. 12c) **1** : a foreign land **2** *pl* : the outlying regions of a country : PROVINCES — **outland** *adj*

out·land·er \-,lan-dər, -lən-\ *n* (1598) : a person who belongs to another region, culture, or group : FOREIGNER, STRANGER

out·land·ish \,aůt-'lan-dish\ *adj* (bef. 12c) **1** : of or relating to another country : FOREIGN **2 a** : strikingly out of the ordinary : BIZARRE ⟨an ~ costume⟩ **b** : exceeding proper or reasonable limits or standards **3** : remote from civilization *syn* see STRANGE — **out·land·ish·ly** *adv* — **out·land·ish·ness** *n*

¹out·law \'aůt-,lö\ *n* [ME *outlawe*, fr. OE *ūtlaga*, fr. ON *ūtlagi*, fr. *ūt* out (akin to OE *ūt* out) + *lag-*, *lǫg* law] (bef. 12c) **1** : a person excluded from the benefit or protection of the law **2 a** : a lawless person or a fugitive from the law **b** : a person or organization under a ban or restriction **c** : one that is unconventional or rebel-

\ə\ abut \ᵊ\ kitten, F table \ər\ further \a\ ash \ā\ ace \ä\ mop, mar \aů\ out \ch\ chin \e\ bet \ē\ easy \g\ go \i\ hit \ī\ ice \j\ job \ŋ\ sing \ō\ go \ó\ law \ói\ boy \th\ thin \th\ the \ü\ loot \ů\ foot \y\ yet \zh\ vision \à, k̟, ⁿ, œ, œ̄, ɵ, ɵ̄, ʸ\ see Guide to Pronunciation lious **3** : an animal (as a horse) that is wild and unmanageable — **outlaw** adj

²**outlaw** vt (bef. 12c) **1 a** : to deprive of the benefit and protection of law : declare to be an outlaw **b** : to make illegal ⟨~ed dueling⟩ **2** : to place under a ban or restriction **3** : to remove from legal jurisdiction or enforcement — **out·law·ry** \'aút-,lör-ē\ n

¹**out·lay** \'aút-,lā, ,aút-'\ vt -laid \-,lād, -'lād\; -lay·ing (1555) : to lay out (money) : EXPEND

²**out·lay** \'aút-,lā\ n (1798) **1** : the act of expending **2** : EXPENDITURE, PAYMENT ⟨~s for national defense⟩

out·let \'aút-,let, -lət\ n [ME ut-lete, fr. ut out + -lete watercourse, fr. OE gelæt, fr. lætan to let] (13c) **1 a** : a place or opening through which something is let out : EXIT, VENT **b** : a means of release or satisfaction for an emotion or impulse ⟨sexual ~s⟩ **c** : a medium of expression or publication **2** : a stream flowing out of a lake or pond **3 a** : a market for a commodity **b** : an agency (as a store or dealer) through which a product is marketed ⟨retail ~s⟩ **4** : a receptacle for the plug of an electrical device

outlet pass n (ca. 1975) : a pass made in basketball by the player taking a defensive rebound to a teammate to start a fast break

out·li·er \-,lī(-ə)r\ n (1676) **1** : a person whose residence and place of business are at a distance **2** : something (as a geological feature) that is situated away from or classed differently from a main or related body

¹**out·line** \'aút-,līn\ n (1662) **1 a** : a line that marks the outer limits of an object or figure : BOUNDARY **b** : SHAPE **2 a** : a style of drawing in which contours are marked without shading **b** : a sketch in outline **3 a** : a condensed treatment of a particular subject ⟨an ~ of world history⟩ **b** : a summary of a written work : SYNOPSIS **4** : a preliminary account of a project : PLAN **5** : a fishing line set out overnight : TROTLINE
syn OUTLINE, CONTOUR, PROFILE, SILHOUETTE mean the line that bounds and gives form to something. OUTLINE applies to a line marking the outer limits or edges of a body or mass ⟨traced the *outline* of his hand⟩. CONTOUR stresses the quality of an outline or a bounding surface as being smooth, jagged, curving, or sharply angled ⟨a car with flowing *contours*⟩. PROFILE suggests a varied and sharply defined outline against a lighter background ⟨a portrait of her face in *profile*⟩. SILHOUETTE suggests a shape esp. of a head or figure with all detail blacked out in shadow leaving only the outline clearly defined ⟨photograph in *silhouette* against a bright sky⟩.

²**outline** vt (ca. 1790) **1** : to draw the outline of **2** : to indicate the principal features or different parts of ⟨*outlined* their responsibilities⟩

out·live \,aút-'liv\ vt (15c) **1** : to live beyond or longer than ⟨*outlived* most of his friends⟩ ⟨~ its usefulness⟩ **2** : to survive the effects of ⟨universities ... ~ many political and social changes —J. B. Conant⟩

out·look \'aút-,lúk\ n (1667) **1 a** : a place offering a view **b** : a view from a particular place **2** : POINT OF VIEW ⟨a positive ~ on life⟩ **3** : the act of looking out **4** : the prospect for the future ⟨the ~ for steel demand in the U.S. —*Wall Street Jour.*⟩ **syn** see PROSPECT

out loud adv (1821) : loudly enough to be heard : ALOUD

out·ly·ing \'aút-,lī-iŋ\ adj (ca. 1690) : remote from a center or main body ⟨~ areas⟩

out·match \,aút-'mach\ vt (1603) : to prove superior to : OUTDO

out—mi·grant \'aút-,mī-grənt\ n (1945) : one that out-migrates

out—mi·grate \-'grāt\ vi (1953) : to leave one region or community in order to settle in another esp. as part of a large-scale and continuing movement of population — compare IN-MIGRATE — **out—mi·gra·tion** \,aút-mī-'grā-shən\ n

out·mode \,aút-'mōd\ vt **out·mod·ed; out·mod·ing** [out (of) mode] (1906) : to make unfashionable or obsolete

out·mod·ed \-'mō-dəd\ adj (1903) **1** : not being in style **2** : no longer acceptable, current, or usable ⟨~ customs⟩

out·most \'aút-,mōst\ adj (12c) : farthest out : OUTERMOST

out·num·ber \,aút-'nəm-bər\ vt (1670) : to exceed in number

out of prep (bef. 12c) **1 a** (1) — used as a function word to indicate direction or movement from within to the outside of ⟨walked *out of* the room⟩ (2) — used as a function word to indicate a change in quality, state, or form ⟨woke up *out of* a deep sleep⟩ **b** (1) — used as a function word to indicate a position or situation beyond the range, limits, or sphere of ⟨*out of* control⟩ (2) — used as a function word to indicate a position or state away from the usual or expected ⟨*out of* practice⟩ **2** — used as a function word to indicate origin, source, or cause ⟨a remarkable colt *out of* an ordinary mare⟩ ⟨built *out of* old lumber⟩ ⟨came *out of* fear⟩ **3** — used as a function word to indicate exclusion from or deprivation of ⟨cheated him *out of* his savings⟩ ⟨*out of* breath⟩ **4** — used as a function word to indicate choice or selection from a group ⟨one *out of* four survived⟩ — **out of it 1** : not part of a group, activity, or fashion **2** : in a dazed or confused state

out—of—body adj (1970) : relating to or involving a feeling of separation from one's body and of being able to view oneself and others from an external perspective ⟨an ~ experience⟩

out—of—bounds \,aút-ə(v)-'baún(d)z\ adv or adj (1857) : outside the prescribed boundaries or limits

out—of—date \-'dāt\ adj (1628) : OUTMODED, OBSOLETE

out—of—door \-'dōr, -'dòr\ or **out—of—doors** \-'dōrz, -'dòrz\ adj (1800) : OUTDOOR

out—of—doors n pl but sing in constr (1819) : OUTDOORS

out—of—pock·et \-'pä-kət\ adj (1885) : requiring an outlay of cash ⟨~ expenses⟩

out—of—sight \,aút-ə-'sīt\ adj (1893) slang : WONDERFUL

out—of—the—way \,aút-ə(v)-thə-'wā\ adj (1704) **1** : UNUSUAL ⟨~ information⟩ **2** : being off the beaten track ⟨an ~ restaurant⟩

out·pace \,aút-'pās\ vt (1611) **1** : to surpass in speed **2** : OUTDO

out·pa·tient \'aút-,pā-shənt\ n (1715) : a patient who is not hospitalized overnight but who visits a hospital, clinic, or associated facility for diagnosis or treatment — compare INPATIENT

out·place·ment \,aút-'plās-mənt, 'aút-,\ n (1970) : the process of easing unwanted or unneeded executives out of a company by providing company-paid assistance in finding them new jobs

out·point \,aút-'póint\ vt (1883) **1** : to sail closer to the wind than **2** : to win more points than (as in a boxing match)

out·port \'aút-,pōrt, -,pòrt\ n (1642) **1** chiefly Brit : a port other than the main port of a country **2** : a small fishing village esp. in Newfoundland

out·post \'aút-,pōst\ n (1757) **1 a** : a security detachment dispatched by a main body of troops to protect it from enemy surprise **b** : a military base established by treaty or agreement in another country **2 a** : an outlying or frontier settlement **b** : an outlying branch or position of a main organization or group

¹**out·pour** \,aút-'pōr, -'pòr, 'aút-,\ vt (1671) : to pour out

²**out·pour** \'aút-,pōr, -,pòr\ n (1864) : OUTPOURING

out·pour·ing \'aút-,pōr-iŋ, -,pòr-\ n (15c) **1** : the act of pouring out **2** : something that pours out or is poured out : OUTFLOW

out·pull \,aút-'púl\ vt (1926) : OUTDRAW 1

¹**out·put** \'aút-,pút\ n (ca. 1858) **1** : something produced: as **a** : mineral, agricultural, or industrial production ⟨steel ~⟩ **b** : mental or artistic production ⟨literary ~⟩ **c** : the amount produced by a person in a given time **d** : power or energy produced or delivered by a machine or system (as for storage or for conversion in kind or in characteristics) ⟨solar X-ray ~⟩ **e** : the information produced by a computer **2** : the act, process, or an instance of producing **3** : the terminal for the output on an electrical device

²**output** vt **out·put·ted** or **output; out·put·ting** (1858) : to produce as output

out·race \,aút-'rās\ vt (1657) : OUTPACE

¹**out·rage** \'aút-,rāj\ n [ME, fr. MF, excess, outrage, fr. *outre* beyond, in excess, fr. L *ultra* — more at ULTRA] (14c) **1** : an act of violence or brutality **2 a** : INJURY, INSULT ⟨do no ~s on silly women or poor passengers —Shak.⟩ **b** : an act that violates accepted standards of behavior or taste ⟨an ~ alike against decency and dignity —John Buchan⟩ **3** : the anger and resentment aroused by injury or insult

²**outrage** vt **out·raged; out·rag·ing** (1590) **1 a** : RAPE **b** : to violate the standards or principles of ⟨he has *outraged* respectability past endurance —John Braine⟩ **2** : to arouse anger or resentment in usu. by some grave offense **syn** see OFFEND

out·ra·geous \(,)aút-'rā-jəs\ adj (14c) **1** : exceeding the limits of what is usual **b** : not conventional or matter-of-fact : FANTASTIC **2** : VIOLENT, UNRESTRAINED **3 a** : going beyond all standards of what is right or decent ⟨an ~ disregard of human rights⟩ **b** : deficient in propriety or good taste ⟨~ language⟩ ⟨~ manners⟩ — **out·ra·geous·ly** adv — **out·ra·geous·ness** n

ou·trance \ü-'träⁿs\ n [ME, fr. MF, fr. *outrer* to pass beyond, carry to excess, fr. *outre*] (15c) : the last extremity

out·range \,aút-'rānj\ vt (1858) : to surpass in range

out·rank \-'raŋk\ vt (1842) **1** : to rank higher than **2** : to exceed in importance

ou·tré \ü-'trā\ adj [F, fr. pp. of *outrer* to carry to excess] (1722) : violating convention or propriety : BIZARRE

¹**out·reach** \,aút-'rēch\ vt (ca. 1568) **1 a** : to surpass in reach **b** : EXCEED ⟨the demand ~es the supply⟩ **2** : to get the better of by trickery ~ vi **1** : to go too far **2** : to reach out

²**out·reach** \'aút-,rēch\ n (1870) **1** : the act of reaching out **2** : the extent or limit of reach ⟨the ~ of the Ohio floods —Clifton Johnson⟩ **3** : the extending of services or assistance beyond current or usual limits ⟨an ~ program⟩; also : the extent of such services or assistance

¹**out·ride** \,aút-'rīd\ vt -rode \-'rōd\; -rid·den \-'ri-dᵊn\; -rid·ing \-'rī-diŋ\ (1530) **1** : to ride better, faster, or farther than : OUTSTRIP **2** : to ride out (a storm)

²**out·ride** \'aút-,rīd\ n (1880) : an unstressed syllable or group of syllables added to a foot in sprung rhythm but not counted in the scansion

out·rid·er \-,rī-dər\ n (1530) **1** : a mounted attendant **2** : one who escorts or clears the way for a vehicle or person **3** : FORERUNNER, HARBINGER

out·rig·ger \'aút-,ri-gər\ n (1748) **1 a** : a projecting spar with a shaped log at the end attached to a canoe to prevent upsetting **b** : a spar or projecting beam run out from a ship's side to help secure the masts or from a mast to extend a rope or sail **c** : a projecting support for an oarlock; also : a boat equipped with these supports **2** : a projecting member run out from a main structure to provide additional stability or to support something; esp : a projecting frame to support the elevator or tailplanes of an airplane or the rotor of a helicopter

¹**out·right** \,aút-'rīt\ adv (14c) **1** archaic : straight ahead : DIRECTLY **2** : in entirety : COMPLETELY ⟨rejected the proposal ~⟩ **3** : without restraint or reservation ⟨laughed ~⟩ **4** : on the spot : INSTANTANEOUSLY ⟨was killed ~⟩ **5** : without lien or encumbrance ⟨purchased the property ~ for cash⟩

²**out·right** \'aút-,rīt\ adj (1532) **1 a** : being completely or exactly what is stated ⟨an ~ lie⟩ **b** : given without reservation ⟨~ grants for research⟩ **c** : made without encumbrance or lien ⟨~ sale⟩ **2** archaic : proceeding directly onward — **out·right·ly** adv

out·run \,aút-'rən\ vt **-ran** \-'ran\; **-run; -run·ning** (1526) **1** : to run faster than **2** : EXCEED, SURPASS ⟨his ambitions ~ his abilities⟩

out·sell \-'sel\ vt **-sold** \-'sōld\; **-sell·ing** (1609) **1** archaic : to exceed in value **2** : to exceed in number of items sold **3** : to surpass in selling or salesmanship

out·set \'aút-,set\ n (1759) : BEGINNING, START

out·shine \,aút-'shīn\ vb **-shone** \-'shōn, esp Brit -'shän\ or **-shined**; **-shin·ing** vt (1596) **1 a** : to shine brighter than **b** : to excel in splendor or showiness **2** : OUTDO, SURPASS ⟨*outshone* most of the other films in quality —Kathleen Karr⟩ ~ vi : to shine out

out·shoot \,aút-'shüt\ vt **-shot** \-'shät\; **-shoot·ing** (1530) **1** : to surpass in shooting or making shots **2** : to shoot or go beyond

¹**out·side** \,aút-'sīd, 'aút-,\ n (1505) **1 a** : a place or region beyond an enclosure or boundary: as (1) : the world beyond the confines of an institution (as a prison) (2) often cap, Alaska : the world beyond the territory or state of Alaska; esp : the 48 contiguous states **b** : the area farthest from a specified point of reference: as (1) : the side of home plate farthest from the batter (2) : the part of a playing area toward the sidelines (3) : the part of a playing area away from the goal **2** : an outer side or surface **3** : an outer manifestation : APPEARANCE **4** : the extreme limit of a guess : MAXIMUM ⟨the crowd numbered 10,000 at the ~⟩

²**outside** adj (1634) **1 a** : of, relating to, or being on or toward the outer side or surface ⟨the ~ edge⟩ **b** : of, relating to, or being on or toward the outer side of a curve or turn **c** : of, relating to, or being on or near the outside ⟨an ~ pitch⟩ **2 a** : situated or performed outside a particular place **b** : connected with or giving access to the outside ⟨~ telephone line⟩ **3** : MAXIMUM **4 a** : not included or originating in

a particular group or organization ⟨blamed the riot on ~ agitators⟩ **b** : not belonging to one's regular occupation or duties ⟨~ interests⟩ **5** : barely possible : REMOTE ⟨an ~ chance⟩ **6** : made or done from the outside ⟨borrowed a basketball and practiced his ~ shot⟩

³out·side *adv* (1813) **1** : on or to the outside **2** : OUTDOORS

⁴out·side *prep* (1826) **1** — used as a function word to indicate movement to or position on the outer side of **2** : beyond the limits of ⟨~ the scope of this report⟩ ⟨~ the law⟩ **3** : EXCEPT

outside of *prep* (ca. 1840) **1** : OUTSIDE **2** : ASIDE FROM

out·sid·er \ˌaut-ˈsī-dər, ˈaut-ˌ\ *n* (1800) **1** : a person who does not belong to a particular group **2** *chiefly Brit* : a contender not expected to win — **out·sid·er·ness** *n*

out·sight \ˈaut-ˌsīt\ *n* (1605) : the power or act of perceiving external things ⟨the clear-eyed insight and ~ of the born writer —*New Yorker*⟩

¹out·size \ˈaut-ˌsīz\ *n* (1845) : an unusual size; *esp* : a size larger than the standard

²outsize *also* **out·sized** \-ˌsīzd\ *adj* (1880) **1** : unusually large or heavy **2** : exaggerated or extravagant in size or degree

out·skirt \ˈaut-ˌskərt\ *n* (1596) : a part remote from the center : BORDER — usu. used in pl. ⟨on the ~s of town⟩

out·slick \ˌaut-ˈslik\ *vt* (1926) : to get the better of esp. by trickery or cunning

out·smart \ˌaut-ˈsmärt\ *vt* (1924) : to get the better of; *esp* : OUTWIT

out·sole \ˈaut-ˌsōl\ *n* (1884) : the outside sole of a boot or shoe

out·sourc·ing \-ˌsōr-siŋ, -ˌsȯr-\ *n* (1982) : the practice of subcontracting manufacturing work to outside and esp. foreign or nonunion companies

out·speak \ˌaut-ˈspēk\ *vt* **-spoke** \-ˈspōk\; **-spo·ken** \-ˈspō-kən\; **-speak·ing** (1603) **1** : to excel in speaking **2** : to declare openly or boldly

out·spend \-ˈspend\ *vt* (1586) **1** : to exceed the limits of in spending ⟨~s his income⟩ **2** : to spend more than ⟨outspent the other candidates⟩

out·spent \-ˈspent\ *adj* (1652) : completely worn out : EXHAUSTED ⟨spurred him, like an ~ horse, to death —P. B. Shelley⟩

out·spo·ken \ˌaut-ˈspō-kən\ *adj* (ca. 1808) **1** : direct and open in speech or expression : FRANK ⟨~ in his criticism —*Current Biog.*⟩ **2** : spoken or expressed without reserve ⟨his ~ advocacy of gun control⟩ — **out·spo·ken·ly** *adv* — **out·spo·ken·ness** \-kən-nəs\ *n*

out·spread \ˌaut-ˈspred\ *vt* **-spread; -spread·ing** (14c) : to spread out

out·stand \ˌaut-ˈstand\ *vb* **-stood; -stand·ing** *vt* (1571) : to endure beyond ⟨I have *outstood* my time —Shak.⟩ ~ *vi* : STAND OUT

out·stand·ing \ˌaut-ˈstan-diŋ, ˈaut-ˌ\ *adj* (1611) **1** : standing out : PROJECTING **2 a** : UNPAID ⟨left several bills ~⟩ **b** : continuing to exist : UNRESOLVED ⟨a long ~ problem in astronomy⟩ **c** *of securities* : publicly issued and sold **3 a** : standing out from a group : CONSPICUOUS **b** : marked by eminence and distinction *syn* see NOTICEABLE — **out·stand·ing·ly** \-diŋ-lē\ *adv*

out·stare \ˌaut-ˈstar, -ˈster\ *vt* (1596) : OUTFACE 1

out·sta·tion \ˈaut-ˌstā-shən\ *n* (1844) : a remote or outlying station

out·stay \ˌaut-ˈstā\ *vt* (1600) **1** : OVERSTAY 1 ⟨~ed their welcome⟩ **2** : to surpass in staying power ⟨~ed his competitors⟩

out·stretch \ˌaut-ˈstrech\ *vt* (15c) : to stretch out : EXTEND

out·strip \ˌaut-ˈstrip\ *vt* [*out-* + obs. *strip* to move fast] (1580) **1** : to go faster or farther than **2** : to get ahead of : leave behind ⟨has civilization *outstripped* the ability of its users to use it? —Margaret Mead⟩ *syn* see EXCEED

out·take \ˈaut-ˌtāk\ *n* (1902) **1** : a passage outward : FLUE, VENT **2** : something that is taken out: as **a** : a take that is not used in an edited version of a film or video tape **b** : a recorded musical selection not included in a record album

out·turn \ˈaut-ˌtərn\ *n* (1800) : a quantity produced : OUTPUT

¹out·ward \ˈaut-wərd\ *adj* (bef. 12c) **1** : moving, directed, or turned toward the outside or away from a center ⟨an ~ flow⟩ **2** : situated on the outside : EXTERIOR **3** : of or relating to the body or to appearances rather than to the mind or the inner life ⟨~ beauty⟩ **4** : EXTERNAL

²outward *or* **out·wards** \-wərdz\ *adv* (bef. 12c) **1** : toward the outside **2** *obs* : on the outside : EXTERNALLY

³outward *n* (1606) : external form, appearance, or reality

out·ward–bound \ˌaut-wərd-ˈbaund\ *adj* (1602) : bound in an outward direction or to foreign parts ⟨an ~ ship⟩

out·ward·ly \ˈaut-wərd-lē\ *adv* (14c) **1 a** : on the outside : EXTERNALLY **b** : toward the outside **2** : in outward state, behavior, or appearance ⟨was ~ friendly⟩

out·ward·ness \-nəs\ *n* (1650) **1** : the quality or state of being external **2** : concern with or responsiveness to outward things

out·wash \ˈaut-ˌwȯsh, -ˌwäsh\ *n* (1894) : detritus chiefly consisting of gravel and sand carried by running water from the melting ice of a glacier and laid down in stratified deposits

out·wear \ˌaut-ˈwar, -ˈwer\ *vt* **-wore** \-ˈwōr, -ˈwȯr\; **-worn** \-ˈwōrn, -ˈwȯrn\; **-wear·ing** (ca. 1541) **1** : WEAR OUT, EXHAUST **2** : to last longer than ⟨a fabric that ~s others⟩

out·weigh \-ˈwā\ *vt* (1597) : to exceed in weight, value, or importance ⟨the advantages ~ the disadvantages⟩

out·wit \aut-ˈwit\ *vt* **-wit·ted; -wit·ting** (1652) **1** : to get the better of by superior cleverness : OUTSMART **2** *archaic* : to surpass in wisdom

¹out·work \ˌaut-ˈwərk\ *vt* (13c) **1** : WORK OUT, COMPLETE **2** : to work harder, faster, or better than

²out·work \ˈaut-ˌwərk\ *n* (ca. 1615) : a minor defensive position constructed outside a fortified area

out·work·er \-ˌwər-kər\ *n* (1813) *chiefly Brit* : a person who works at home for a business firm

out·worn \ˌaut-ˈwōrn, -ˈwȯrn\ *adj* (1565) : no longer useful or acceptable : OUTMODED ⟨an ~ social system⟩

out–year \ˈaut-ˌyir\ *n* (1981) : the year beyond a current fiscal year — usu. used in pl. except when attrib.

ou·zel \ˈü-zəl\ *n* [ME *ousel*, fr. OE *ōsle* — more at MERLE] (bef. 12c) **1** : BLACKBIRD 1a; *also* : a related bird (*Turdus torquatus*) **2** : DIPPER 1

ou·zo \ˈü-(ˌ)zō, -(ˌ)zȯ\ *n* [NGk] (1898) : a colorless anise-flavored unsweetened Greek liqueur

ov- *or* **ovi-** *or* **ovo-** *comb form* [L *ov-, ovi-*, fr. *ovum* — more at EGG] : egg ⟨*ovicide*⟩ : ovum ⟨*oviduct*⟩

ova *pl of* OVUM

¹oval \ˈō-vəl\ *n* (1570) **1** : an oval figure or object **2** : a racetrack in the shape of an oval or a rectangle having rounded corners

²oval *adj* [ML *ovalis*, fr. LL, of an egg, fr. L *ovum*] (1577) : having the shape of an egg; *also* : broadly elliptical — **oval·i·ty** \ō-ˈva-lə-tē\ *n* — **oval·ly** \-və-lē\ *adv* — **oval·ness** *n*

ov·al·bu·min \ˌä-val-ˈbyü-mən, ˌō-\ *n* (ca. 1836) **1** : the principal albumin of white of egg; *esp* : the crystalline part of egg albumins **2** : dried whites of eggs

Oval Office *n* [fr. the *Oval Office*, the U.S. president's office in the west wing of the White House] (1962) : the seat of the executive department of the U.S. government

oval window *n* (1683) : FENESTRA 1a

Ovam·bo \ō-ˈvam-(ˌ)bō, -ˈväm-\ *n, pl* **Ovambo** *or* **Ovambos** (1853) **1** : a member of a Bantu people of northern Namibia **2** : the Bantu language of the Ovambo people

ovar·i·an \ō-ˈvar-ē-ən, -ˈver-\ *also* **ovar·i·al** \-ē-əl\ *adj* (ca. 1834) : of, relating to, or involving an ovary

ovari·ec·to·my \ō-ˌvar-ē-ˈek-tə-mē, -ˌver-\ *n, pl* **-mies** (1889) : the surgical removal of an ovary — **ovari·ec·to·mized** \-ˌmīzd\ *adj*

ovar·i·ole \ō-ˈvar-ē-ˌōl, -ˈver-\ *n* [(assumed) NL *ovariolum*, dim. of *ovarium*] (1877) : one of the tubes of which the ovaries of most insects are composed

ovar·i·ot·o·my \ō-ˌvar-ē-ˈä-tə-mē, -ˌver-\ *n, pl* **-mies** (1844) **1** : surgical incision of an ovary **2** : OVARIECTOMY

ova·ry \ˈō-və-rē, ˈōv-rē\ *n, pl* **-ries** [NL *ovarium*, fr. L *ovum* egg] (1658) **1** : one of the typically paired essential female reproductive organs that produce eggs and in vertebrates female sex hormones **2** : the enlarged rounded usu. basal portion of the pistil or gynoecium of an angiospermous plant that bears the ovules and consists of one or more carpels — see FLOWER illustration

ovate \ˈō-ˌvāt\ *adj* (1760) **1** : shaped like an egg **2** : having an outline like a longitudinal section of an egg with the basal end broader ⟨~ leaves⟩ — see LEAF illustration

ova·tion \ō-ˈvā-shən\ *n* [L *ovation-, ovatio*, fr. *ovare* to exult; akin to Gk *euoi*, interjection used in bacchic revels] (1533) **1** : a ceremony attending the entering of Rome by a general who had won a victory of less importance than that for which a triumph was granted **2** : an expression or demonstration of popular acclaim esp. by enthusiastic applause ⟨received a standing ~⟩

ov·en \ˈə-vən\ *n* [ME, fr. OE *ofen*; akin to OHG *ofan* oven and perh. to Gk *ipnos* oven] (bef. 12c) : a chamber used for baking, heating, or drying

ov·en·bird \-ˌbərd\ *n* [fr. the shape of its nest] (ca. 1825) **1** : any of various So. American small brown passerine birds (genus *Furnarius*) **2** : an American warbler (*Seiurus aurocapillus*) that builds a dome-shaped nest on the ground

ovenbird 2

ov·en·proof \-ˌprüf\ *adj* (ca. 1940) : capable of withstanding the temperature range of a kitchen oven ⟨~ dishes⟩

¹over \ˈō-vər\ *adv* [ME, adv. & prep., fr. OE *ofer*; akin to OHG *ubar* (prep.) above, beyond, over, L *super*, Gk *hyper*] (bef. 12c) **1 a** : across a barrier or intervening space; *esp* : across the goal line in football **b** : forward beyond an edge or brink and often down ⟨wandered too near the cliff and fell ~⟩ **c** : across the brim ⟨soup boiled ~⟩ **d** : so as to bring the underside up ⟨turned his cards ~⟩ **e** : from a vertical to a prone or inclined position ⟨knocked the lamp ~⟩ **f** : from one person or side to another ⟨hand it ~⟩ **g** : ACROSS ⟨got his point ~⟩ **h** : to one's home ⟨invite some friends ~⟩ **i** : on the other side of an intervening space ⟨the next town ~⟩ **j** : to agreement or concord ⟨won them ~⟩ **2 a** (1) : beyond some quantity, limit, or norm often by a specified amount or to a specified degree ⟨show ran a minute ~⟩ (2) : in an excessive manner : INORDINATELY **b** : till a later time (as the next day) : OVERNIGHT ⟨stay ~⟩ ⟨sleep ~⟩ **3 a** : ABOVE **b** : so as to cover the whole surface ⟨windows boarded ~⟩ **4** — used on a two-way radio circuit to indicate that a message is complete and a reply is expected **5 a** : THROUGH ⟨read it ~⟩; *also* : in an intensive or comprehensive manner **b** : once more : AGAIN ⟨do it ~⟩

²over *prep* (bef. 12c) **1** — used as a function word to indicate motion or situation in a position higher than or above another ⟨towered ~ his mother⟩ ⟨flew ~ the lake⟩ ⟨rode ~ the old Roman road⟩ **2 a** — used as a function word to indicate the possession of authority, power, or jurisdiction in regard to some thing or person ⟨respected those ~ him⟩ **b** — used as a function word to indicate superiority, advantage, or preference ⟨a big lead ~ the others⟩ **c** — used as a function word to indicate one that is overcome, circumvented, or disregarded ⟨passed ~ the governor's veto⟩ **3 a** : more than ⟨cost ~ $5⟩ **b** : ABOVE 4 **4 a** — used as a function word to indicate position upon or movement down upon ⟨laid a blanket ~ the child⟩ ⟨hit him ~ the head⟩ **b** (1) : all through or throughout ⟨showed me ~ the house⟩ ⟨went ~ his notes⟩ (2) — used as a function word connecting one mathematical set and another whose elements are coefficients or values of parameters used to form elements of the first set ⟨polynomials ~ the field of real numbers⟩ **c** — used as a function word to indicate a particular medium or channel of communication ⟨~ the radio⟩ **5** — used as a function word to indicate position on or motion to the other side or beyond ⟨lives ~ the way⟩ ⟨fell ~ the edge⟩ **6 a** : THROUGHOUT, DURING ⟨~ the past 25 years⟩ **b** : until the end of ⟨stay ~ Sunday⟩ **7 a** — used

---

\ə\ abut \ʰ\ kitten, F table \ər\ further \a\ ash \ā\ ace \ä\ mop, mar \au̇\ out \ch\ chin \e\ bet \ē\ easy \g\ go \i\ hit \ī\ ice \j\ job \ŋ\ sing \ō\ go \ȯ\ law \ȯi\ boy \th\ thin \t͟h\ the \ü\ loot \u̇\ foot \y\ yet \zh\ vision \à, ⱪ, ⁿ, œ, œ̄, ᴜ, ᵫ, ᵊ\ see Guide to Pronunciation as a function word to indicate an object of solicitude, interest, consideration, or reference ⟨the Lord watches ~ his own⟩   **b** — used as a function word to indicate the object of an expressed or implied occupation, activity, or concern ⟨trouble ~ money⟩ ⟨met with advisers ~ lunch⟩

³**over** *adj* (bef. 12c)   **1 a** : UPPER, HIGHER   **b** : OUTER, COVERING   **c** : EXCESSIVE ⟨~ imagination⟩   **2 a** : not used up : REMAINING ⟨something ~ to provide for unusual requirements —J. A. Todd⟩   **b** : having or showing an excess or surplus   **3** : being at an end ⟨the day is ~⟩   **4** : fried on both sides ⟨ordered two eggs ~⟩ — **over easy** : fried on one side then turned and fried lightly on the other side ⟨eggs *over easy*⟩

⁴**over** *vt* **overed; over·ing** \'ō-və-riŋ, 'ōv-riŋ\ (1837) : to leap over

over- *prefix*   **1** : so as to exceed or surpass ⟨*over*achieve⟩   **2** : EXCESSIVE ⟨*over*stimulation⟩   **3** : to an excessive degree ⟨*over*thin⟩

over·ab·stract
over·abun·dance
over·abun·dant
over·ac·cen·tu·ate
over·ad·just·ment
over·ad·ver·tise
over·ag·gres·sive
over·alert
over·am·bi·tious
over·am·bi·tious·ness
over·am·pli·fied
over·anal·y·sis
over·an·a·lyt·i·cal
over·an·a·lyze
over·anx·i·ety
over·anx·ious
over·ap·pli·ca·tion
over·arous·al
over·ar·range
over·ar·tic·u·late
over·as·sert
over·as·ser·tion
over·as·ser·tive
over·as·sess·ment
over·at·ten·tion
over·bake
over·beat
over·be·jew·eled
over·bill
over·bleach
over·boil
over·bold
over·bor·row
over·breath·ing
over·brief
over·bright
over·broad
over·browse
over·bru·tal
over·burn
over·busy
over·care·ful
over·cau·tion
over·cau·tious
over·cen·tral·i·za·tion
over·cen·tral·ize
over·chill
over·civ·i·lized
over·claim
over·clas·si·fi·ca·tion
over·clas·si·fy
over·clean
over·clear
over·coach
over·com·mer·cial·i·za·tion
over·com·mer·cial·ize
over·com·mu·ni·cate
over·com·mu·ni·ca·tion
over·com·plex
over·com·pli·ance
over·com·pli·cate
over·com·pli·cat·ed
over·com·press
over·con·cen·tra·tion
over·con·cern
over·con·cerned
over·con·fi·dence
over·con·fi·dent
over·con·fi·dent·ly
over·con·sci·en·tious
over·con·scious
over·con·ser·va·tive
over·con·struct
over·con·sume
over·con·sump·tion
over·con·trol
over·cook
over·cool
over·cor·rect
over·count
over·cred·u·lous
over·crit·i·cal
over·cul·ti·va·tion
over·cure
over·dec·o·rate
over·dec·o·ra·tion
over·de·mand·ing
over·de·pen·dence
over·de·pen·dent

over·de·sign
over·dif·fer·en·ti·a·tion
over·di·rect
over·dis·count
over·di·ver·si·ty
over·doc·u·ment
over·dra·mat·ic
over·dra·ma·tize
over·drink
over·dry
over·ea·ger
over·ea·ger·ness
over·ear·nest
over·ed·it
over·ed·u·cate
over·ed·u·cat·ed
over·ed·u·ca·tion
over·elab·o·rate
over·elab·o·ra·tion
over·em·bel·lish
over·emote
over·emo·tion·al
over·em·pha·sis
over·em·pha·size
over·em·phat·ic
over·en·am·ored
over·en·cour·age
over·en·er·get·ic
over·en·gi·neer
over·en·rolled
over·en·ter·tained
over·en·thu·si·asm
over·en·thu·si·as·tic
over·equipped
over·es·ti·mate
over·es·ti·ma·tion
over·eval·u·a·tion
over·ex·ag·ger·ate
over·ex·ag·ger·a·tion
over·ex·cite
over·ex·cit·ed
over·ex·er·cise
over·ex·ert
over·ex·er·tion
over·ex·pand
over·ex·pan·sion
over·ex·pec·ta·tion
over·ex·plain
over·ex·plic·it
over·ex·ploit
over·ex·ploi·ta·tion
over·ex·trac·tion
over·ex·trap·o·la·tion
over·ex·trav·a·gant
over·fac·ile
over·fa·mil·iar
over·fa·mil·iar·i·ty
over·fas·tid·i·ous
over·fat
over·fa·vor
over·fer·til·i·za·tion
over·fer·til·ize
over·fo·cus
over·fond
over·ful·fill
over·fund
over·fussy
over·gen·er·al·i·za·tion
over·gen·er·al·ize
over·gen·er·os·i·ty
over·gen·er·ous
over·gen·er·ous·ly
over·glam·or·ize
over·gov·ern
over·han·dle
over·har·vest
over·hasty
over·ho·mog·e·nize
over·hunt
over·hunt·ing
over·ide·al·ize
over·iden·ti·fi·ca·tion
over·iden·ti·fy
over·imag·i·na·tive
over·im·press
over·in·debt·ed·ness
over·in·dulge

over·in·dul·gence
over·in·dul·gent
over·in·dus·tri·al·ize
over·in·flate
over·in·flat·ed
over·in·fla·tion
over·in·form
over·in·formed
over·in·ge·nious
over·in·ge·nu·ity
over·in·sis·tent
over·in·tel·lec·tu·al·i·za·tion
over·in·tel·lec·tu·al·ize
over·in·tense
over·in·ten·si·ty
over·in·ter·pre·ta·tion
over·in·vest·ment
over·la·bor
over·la·bored
over·lad·en
over·large
over·lav·ish
over·lend
over·length
over·length·en
over·light
over·lit·er·al
over·lit·er·ary
over·load
over·long
over·loud
over·lush
over·man·age
over·man·nered
over·ma·ture
over·ma·tu·ri·ty
over·med·i·cate
over·med·i·ca·tion
over·mighty
over·milk
over·mine
over·mix
over·mod·est
over·mod·est·ly
over·mus·cled
over·nice
over·nour·ish
over·nu·tri·tion
over·ob·vi·ous
over·op·er·ate
over·opin·ion·at·ed
over·op·ti·mism
over·op·ti·mist
over·op·ti·mis·tic
over·op·ti·mis·ti·cal·ly
over·or·ches·trate
over·or·ga·nize
over·or·ga·nized
over·or·na·ment
over·pack·age
over·par·tic·u·lar
over·pay
over·pay·ment
over·ped·al
over·peo·ple
over·plan
over·plant
over·plot
over·po·tent
over·praise
over·pre·cise
over·pre·scribe
over·pre·scrip·tion
over·priv·i·leged
over·prize
over·pro·cess
over·pro·duce
over·pro·duc·tion
over·pro·gram
over·prom·ise
over·pro·mote
over·pro·tect
over·pro·tec·tion
over·pro·tec·tive
over·pro·tec·tive·ness
over·pump
over·rate
over·re·act
over·re·ac·tion

over·re·fined
over·re·fine·ment
over·reg·u·late
over·reg·u·la·tion
over·re·li·ance
over·re·port
over·re·spond
over·rich
over·rig·id
over·salt
over·san·guine
over·sat·u·rate
over·sat·u·ra·tion
over·sauce
over·scru·pu·lous
over·se·cre·tion
over·sen·si·tive
over·sen·si·tive·ness
over·sen·si·tiv·i·ty
over·se·ri·ous
over·se·ri·ous·ly
over·ser·vice
over·sim·plis·tic
over·smoke

over·so·lic·i·tous
over·so·phis·ti·cat·ed
over·spe·cial·i·za·tion
over·spe·cial·ize
over·spec·u·late
over·spec·u·la·tion
over·sta·bil·i·ty
over·staff
over·stim·u·late
over·stim·u·la·tion
over·stock
over·strain
over·stress
over·stretch
over·struc·tured
over·sub·tle
over·suds
over·sup·ply
over·sus·pi·cious
over·sweet
over·sweet·en
over·sweet·ness
over·swing

over·talk
over·talk·a·tive
over·tax
over·tax·a·tion
over·thin
over·think
over·tight·en
over·tip
over·tired
over·train
over·treat
over·treat·ment
over·use
over·uti·li·za·tion
over·uti·lize
over·vi·o·lent
over·viv·id
over·wa·ter
over·wea·ry
over·wind
over·with·hold
over·zeal·ous
over·zeal·ous·ness

over·achiev·er \,ō-və-rə-'chē-vər\ *n* (1952) : one who achieves success over and above the standard or expected level esp. at an early age — **over·achieve** \-'chēv\ *vi* — **over·achieve·ment** \-mənt\ *n*

over·act \,ō-vər-'akt\ *vi* (1611)   **1** : to act more than is necessary   **2** : to overact a part   ~ *vt* : to exaggerate in acting — **over·ac·tion** \-'ak-shən\ *n*

over·ac·tive \-'ak-tiv\ *adj* (1854) : excessively or abnormally active — **over·ac·tiv·i·ty** \-ak-'ti-və-tē\ *n*

over against *prep* (1517) : as opposed to : in contrast with

¹**over·age** \,ō-vər-'āj\ *also* **over·aged** \-'ājd\ *adj* [²*over* + *age*] (15c)   **1** : too old to be useful   **2** : older than is normal for one's position, function, or grade

²**over·age** \'ō-və-rij, 'ōv-rij\ *n* [³*over* + *-age*] (1909) : SURPLUS, EXCESS

¹**over·all** \'ō-vər-'ȯl\ *adv* (13c)   **1** : ALL OVER 1 ⟨the pattern used ~⟩   **2** : from one end to the other ⟨600 feet long ~⟩   **3 a** : in view of all the circumstances or conditions ⟨~, the sale was a success⟩   **b** : as a whole : GENERALLY ⟨doesn't do as well ~⟩   **c** : with everyone or everything taken into account ⟨was third ~ in earnings⟩ ⟨got 31 miles to the gallon ~⟩

²**over·all** \'ō-vər-,ȯl\ *n* (1815)   **1** *pl* **a** *archaic* : loose protective trousers worn over regular clothes   **b** : trousers of strong material usu. with a bib and shoulder straps   **2** *chiefly Brit* : a loose-fitting protective smock worn over regular clothing

³**over·all** \,ō-vər-'ȯl, 'ō-vər-,\ *adj* (1894)   **1** : including everything   **2** : viewed as a whole : GENERAL

over·alled \'ō-vər-,ȯld\ *adj* (1908) : wearing overalls

over and above *prep* (15c) : in addition to : BESIDES

over and over *adv* (15c) : REPEATEDLY

over·arch·ing \,ō-vər-'är-chiŋ\ *adj* (1720)   **1** : forming an arch overhead   **2** : dominating or embracing all else ⟨~ goals⟩

over·arm \'ō-vər-,ärm\ *adj* (1864)   **1** : OVERHAND   **2** *of a swimming stroke* : made with the arm lifted out of the water and stretched forward over the shoulder to begin the stroke

over·awe \,ō-vər-'ȯ\ *vt* (1579) : to restrain or subdue by awe

¹**over·bal·ance** \,ō-vər-'ba-lən(t)s\ *vt* (1608)   **1** : OUTWEIGH   **2** : to cause to lose balance

²**over·bal·ance** \'ō-vər-,\ *n* (1659) : something more than an equivalent

over·bear \,ō-vər-'bar, -'ber\ *vt* **-bore** \-'bōr, -'bȯr\; **-borne** \-'bōrn, -'bȯrn\ *also* **-born** \-'bȯrn\; **-bear·ing** (1535)   **1** : to bring down by superior weight or force : OVERWHELM   **2 a** : to domineer over   **b** : to surpass in importance or cogency : OUTWEIGH

overbearing *adj* (ca. 1677)   **1 a** : tending to overwhelm : OVERPOWERING   **b** : decisively important : DOMINANT   **2** : harshly and haughtily arrogant   *syn* see PROUD — **over·bear·ing·ly** \-iŋ-lē\ *adv*

over·bid \,ō-vər-'bid\ *vb* **-bid; -bid·ding** *vi* (ca. 1616)   **1** : to bid in excess of value   **2 a** : to bid more than the scoring capacity of a hand at cards   **b.** *Brit* : to make a higher bid than the preceding one   ~ *vt* : to bid beyond or in excess of; *esp* : to bid more than the value of (one's hand at cards) — **over·bid** \'ō-vər-,bid\ *n*

over·bite \'ō-vər-,bīt\ *n* (1887) : the projection of the upper anterior teeth over the lower in the normal occlusal position of the jaws

over·blouse \-,blaús, -,blaúz\ *n* (1921) : a usu. fitted or belted blouse worn untucked

¹**over·blown** \,ō-vər-'blōn\ *adj* [³*blow*] (1616) : past the prime of bloom ⟨~ roses⟩

²**overblown** *adj* [¹*blow*] (1864)   **1** : excessively large in girth : PORTLY   **2** : INFLATED ⟨~ claims⟩ ⟨~ rhetoric⟩; *also* : PRETENTIOUS

over·board \'ō-vər-,bȯrd, -,bȯrd\ *adv* (bef. 12c)   **1** : over the side of a ship or boat into the water   **2** : to extremes of enthusiasm   **3** : into discard : ASIDE

over·book \,ō-vər-'búk\ *vt* (1903) : to issue reservations for (as an airplane flight) in excess of the space available   ~ *vi* : to issue reservations in excess of the space available

over·bought \-'bȯt\ *adj* (1929) : not likely to show an immediate rise in price because of prior heavy buying and accompanying price rises ⟨an ~ market⟩

over·build \-'bild\ *vb* **-built** \-'bilt\; **-build·ing** *vt* (1601) : to build beyond the actual demand of   ~ *vi* : to build houses or commercial developments in excess of demand

¹**over·bur·den** \-'bər-d°n\ *vt* (1532) : to place an excessive burden on

²**over·bur·den** \'ō-vər-,bər-d°n\ *n* (1855) : material overlying a deposit of useful geological materials or bedrock

over·buy \,ō-vər-'bī\ *vb* **-bought** \-'bȯt\; **-buy·ing** *vt* (1745) : to buy in excess of needs or demand   ~ *vi* : to make purchases beyond one's needs or in excess of one's ability to pay

over·call \-'kȯl\ *vt* (ca. 1903) : to make a higher bid than (the previous bid or bidder) in a card game   ~ *vi* : to bid over an opponent's bid in bridge when one's partner has not bid or doubled — **over·call** \'ō-vər-,kȯl\ *n*

over·ca·pac·i·ty \ˌō-vər-kə-'pa-sə-tē, -'pas-tē\ n (1928) : excessive capacity for production or services in relation to demand

over·cap·i·tal·ize \-'ka-pə-tᵊl-ˌīz, -'kap-tᵊl-\ vt (1890) **1** : to put a nominal value on the capital of (a corporation) higher than actual cost or fair market value **2** : to capitalize beyond what the business or the profit-making prospects warrant — **over·cap·i·tal·i·za·tion** \-ˌka-pə-tᵊl-ə-'zā-shən, -ˌkap-tᵊl-\ n

¹over·cast vt **-cast; -cast·ing** (14c) **1** \ˌō-vər-'kast, 'ō-vər-ˌ\ : DARKEN, OVERSHADOW **2** \'ō-vər-ˌ\ : to sew (raw edges of a seam) with long slanting widely spaced stitches to prevent raveling

²over·cast \'ō-vər-ˌkast, ˌō-vər-'\ adj (1536) : clouded over ⟨an ~ day⟩

³over·cast \'ō-vər-ˌkast\ n (1686) : COVERING; esp : a covering of clouds over the sky

over·cast·ing \'ō-vər-ˌkas-tiŋ\ n (1885) : the act of stitching raw edges of fabric to prevent raveling; also : the stitching so done

overcast stitch n (1891) : a small close embroidery stitch sometimes done over a foundation thread and used to form outlines

over·charge \ˌō-vər-'chärj\ vt (14c) **1** : to charge too much or too fully **2** : to fill too full **3** : EXAGGERATE, OVERDRAW ~ vi : to make an excessive charge — **over·charge** \'ō-vər-ˌ\ n

over·cloud \ˌō-vər-'klaůd\ vt (1592) : to overspread with or as if with clouds

over·coat \'ō-vər-ˌkōt\ n (1802) **1** : a warm coat worn over indoor clothing **2** : a protective coating (as of paint)

overcast stitch

over·come \ˌō-vər-'kəm\ vb **-came** \-'kām\; **-come; -com·ing** [ME, fr. OE ofercuman, fr. ofer over + cuman to come] vt (bef. 12c) **1** : to get the better of : SURMOUNT ⟨~ difficulties⟩ **2** : OVERWHELM ~ vi : to gain the superiority : WIN syn see CONQUER — **over·com·er** n

over·com·mit \-kə-'mit\ vt (1951) : to commit excessively: as **a** : to obligate (as oneself) beyond the ability for fulfillment **b** : to allocate (resources) in excess of the capacity for replenishment — **over·com·mit·ment** \-mənt\ n

over·com·pen·sa·tion \-ˌkäm-pən-'sā-shən, -ˌpen-\ n (1912) : excessive compensation; specif : excessive reaction to a feeling of inferiority, guilt, or inadequacy leading to an exaggerated attempt to overcome the feeling — **over·com·pen·sate** \-'käm-pən-ˌsāt\ vb — **over·com·pen·sa·to·ry** \-kəm-'pen(t)-sə-ˌtōr-ē, -ˌtȯr-\ adj

over·crowd \ˌō-vər-'kraůd\ vt (1766) : to cause to be too crowded ~ vi : to crowd together too much

over·cut \-'kət\ vt (1906) : to cut excessively; specif : to cut timber from (a forest) in excess of annual growth or an allotted annual amount

over·de·ter·mined \-di-'tər-mənd\ adj (1915) **1** : excessively determined **2** : having more than one determining psychological factor

over·de·vel·op \-di-'ve-ləp\ vt (1869) : to develop excessively; esp : to subject (exposed photographic material) to a developing solution for excessive time or at excessive temperature, agitation, or concentration — **over·de·vel·op·ment** \-mənt\ n

over·do \ˌō-vər-'dü\ vb **-did** \-'did\; **-done** \-'dən\; **-do·ing** \-'dü-iŋ\; **-does** \-'dəz\ vt (bef. 12c) **1** a : to do in excess **b** : to use to excess **c** : EXAGGERATE **2** : to cook too long **3** : EXHAUST ~ vi : to go to extremes

over·dog \'ō-vər-ˌdȯg\ n [³over + underdog] (1938) : one that is dominant or victorious

over·dom·i·nance \ˌō-vər-'dä-mə-nən(t)s, -'däm-nən(t)s\ n (1947) : the condition wherein a heterozygote produces a phenotype more extreme or better adapted than that of the homozygote — **over·dom·i·nant** \-nənt\ adj

¹over·dose \'ō-vər-ˌdōs\ n (1700) **1** : too great a dose (as of a therapeutic agent); also : a lethal or toxic amount (as of a drug) **2** : an excessive quantity or amount ⟨an ~ of sports⟩ — **over·dos·age** \ˌō-vər-'dō-sij\ n

²over·dose \ˌō-vər-'dōs\ vt (1727) : to give an overdose or too many doses to ~ vi : to take or experience an overdose — usu. used with on

over·draft \'ō-vər-ˌdraft\ n (1878) **1** : an act of overdrawing at a bank : the state of being overdrawn; also : the sum overdrawn **2** : LINE OF CREDIT

over·draw \ˌō-vər-'drȯ\ vb **-drew** \-'drü\; **-drawn** \-'drȯn\; **-draw·ing** vt (1734) **1** : to draw checks on (a bank account) for more than the balance ⟨the account was overdrawn⟩ **2** : EXAGGERATE, OVERSTATE ~ vi : to make an overdraft

over·drawn adj (1866) : having an overdrawn account

¹over·dress \ˌō-vər-'dres\ vt (1706) : to dress or adorn to excess ~ vi : to dress oneself to excess

²over·dress \'ō-vər-ˌdres\ n (1812) : a dress worn over another

over·drive \'ō-vər-ˌdrīv\ n (1926) **1** : an automotive transmission gear that transmits to the drive shaft a speed greater than engine speed **2** : a state of heightened activity ⟨going into rhetorical ~⟩

¹over·dub \'ō-vər-ˌdəb\ n (ca. 1965) : an or an instance of overdubbing **2** : recorded sound that is overdubbed ⟨vocal ~s⟩

²over·dub \ˌō-vər-'dəb\ vt (1967) : to transfer (recorded sound) onto a recording that bears sound recorded earlier in order to produce a combined effect

over·due \-'dü, -'dyü\ adj (1845) **1** a : unpaid when due **b** : delayed beyond an appointed time **2** : past due : EXCESSIVE **3** : more than ready

over·eat \ˌō-vər-'ēt\ vi **over·ate** \-'āt\; **over·eat·en** \-'ē-tᵊn\; **over·eat·ing** (1599) : to eat to excess — **over·eat·er** \ˌō-vər-'ē-tər, 'ō-vər-ˌ\ n

over·ex·pose \ˌō-vər-ik-'spōz\ vt (1869) : to expose excessively; esp : to expose (as film) to excessive radiation (as light) — **over·ex·po·sure** \-'spō-zhər\ n

over·ex·tend \ˌō-vər-ik-'stend\ vt (1937) : to extend or expand beyond a safe or reasonable point; esp : to commit (oneself) financially beyond what can be paid — **over·ex·ten·sion** \-'sten(t)-shən\ n

over·fa·tigue \ˌō-vər-fə-'tēg\ n (1711) : excessive fatigue esp. when carried beyond the recuperative capacity of the individual — **over·fa·tigued** \-'tēgd\ adj

over·feed \ˌō-vər-'fēd\ vb **-fed** \-'fed\; **-feed·ing** vt (1608) : to feed to excess ~ vi : to eat to excess

over·fill \-'fil\ vt (13c) : to fill to overflowing ~ vi : to become full to overflowing

over·fish \-'fish\ vt (1867) : to fish to the detriment of (a fishing ground) or to the depletion of (a kind of organism)

over·flight \'ō-vər-ˌflīt\ n (1950) : a passage over an area in an airplane

¹over·flow \ˌō-vər-'flō\ vt (bef. 12c) **1** : to cover with or as if with water : INUNDATE **2** : to flow over the brim of **3** : to cause to overflow ~ vi **1** : to flow over bounds **2** : to fill a space to capacity and spread beyond its limits ⟨the crowd ~ed into the street⟩

²over·flow \'ō-vər-ˌflō\ n (1589) **1** : a flowing over : INUNDATION **2** : something that flows over : SURPLUS **3** : an outlet or receptacle for surplus liquid

over·fly \ˌō-vər-'flī\ vt **-flew** \-'flü\; **-flown** \-'flōn\; **-fly·ing** (14c) : to fly over; esp : to pass over in an airplane or spacecraft

over·gar·ment \'ō-vər-ˌgär-mənt\ n (15c) : an outer garment

over·glaze \-ˌglāz\ adj (1879) : applied or suitable for applying on top of a fired glaze ⟨~ enamels⟩ — **overglaze** n

over·graze \ˌō-vər-'grāz\ vt (1919) : to allow animals to graze (as a pasture) to the point of damaging vegetational cover

over·grow \ˌō-vər-'grō\ vb **-grew** \-'grü\; **-grown** \-'grōn\; **-grow·ing** vt (14c) **1** : to grow over so as to cover with herbage **2** : to grow beyond or rise above : OUTGROW ~ vi **1** : to grow excessively **2** : to become grown over — **over·growth** \'ō-vər-ˌgrōth\ n

overgrown adj (1604) : grown abnormally or excessively large ⟨dismissed him as an ~ adolescent⟩

¹over·hand \'ō-vər-ˌhand\ n (1656) : made with the hand brought forward and down from above shoulder level — **overhand** adv — **over·hand·ed** \ˌō-vər-'han-dəd\ adv or adj

²overhand vt (1871) : to sew with short vertical stitches

³overhand n (ca. 1934) : an overhand stroke (as in handball)

overhand knot n (1840) : a small knot often used to prevent the end of a cord from fraying — see KNOT illustration

¹over·hang \ˌō-vər-'haŋ, ˌō-vər-ˌ\ vb **-hung** \-ˌhəŋ, -'həŋ\; **-hang·ing** vt (1592) **1** : to project over **2** : to impend over : THREATEN ~ vi : to project so as to be over something

²over·hang \'ō-vər-ˌhaŋ\ n (1864) **1** : the part of the bow or stern of a ship that projects over the water above the waterline **2** : something that overhangs; also : the extent of the overhanging **3** : a projection of the roof or upper story of a building beyond the wall of the lower part **4** : an excess supply of a commodity that cannot be readily converted, sold, or disposed of ⟨dollar ~⟩ ⟨inventory ~⟩

over·haul \ˌō-vər-'hȯl\ vt (1705) **1** a : to examine thoroughly **b** (1) : REPAIR (2) : to renovate, revise, or renew thoroughly **2** : to haul or drag over **3** : OVERTAKE — **over·haul** \'ō-vər-ˌhȯl\ n

¹over·head \ˌō-vər-'hed\ adv (15c) : above one's head : ALOFT

²over·head \'ō-vər-ˌhed\ adj (1874) **1** a : operating, lying, or coming from above **b** : having the driving part above the part driven ⟨valves operated by an ~ camshaft⟩ **2** : of or relating to overhead ⟨~ costs⟩

³over·head \'ō-vər-ˌhed\ n (1914) **1** : business expenses (as rent, insurance, or heating) not chargeable to a particular part of the work or product **2** : CEILING; esp : the ceiling of a ship's compartment **3** : a stroke in a racket game made above head height : SMASH

overhead projector n (1951) : a projector for projecting onto a vertical screen magnified images of graphic material on a horizontal transparency illuminated from below — called also overhead

over·hear \ˌō-vər-'hir\ vb **-heard** \-'hərd\; **-hear·ing** \-'hir-iŋ\ vt (1549) : to hear without the speaker's knowledge or intention ~ vi : to overhear something

over·heat \-'hēt\ vt (14c) **1** : to heat to excess **2** : to stimulate or agitate unduly ~ vi : to become heated beyond a safe or desirable point

over·heat·ed \-'hē-təd\ adj (1953) : PERFERVID

over·is·sue \ˌō-vər-'i-(ˌ)shü\ n (1803) : an issue exceeding the limit of capital, credit, or authority — **over·is·su·ance** \-'i-shə-wən(t)s\ n — **overissue** vt

over·joyed \-'jȯid\ adj (1594) : feeling great joy

¹over·kill \ˌō-vər-'kil\ vt (1957) : to obliterate (a target) with more nuclear force than required

²over·kill \'ō-vər-ˌkil\ n (1958) **1** : a destructive capacity greatly exceeding that required for a given target **2** : an excess of something (as a quantity or an action) beyond what is required or suitable for a particular purpose ⟨a propaganda ~⟩ ⟨an ~ in weaponry⟩ **3** : killing in excess of what is intended or required

¹over·land \'ō-vər-ˌland, -lənd\ adv (12c) : by, on, or across land

²overland adj (1800) : going or accomplished over the land instead of by sea ⟨~ emigrants⟩ ⟨an ~ route⟩

over·lap \ˌō-vər-'lap\ vt (1726) **1** : to extend over or past and cover a part of **2** : to have something in common with ~ vi **1** : to occupy the same area in part : lap over **2** : to have something in common — **over·lap** \'ō-vər-ˌlap\ n

¹over·lay \ˌō-vər-'lā\ vt **-laid** \-'lād\; **-lay·ing** (14c) **1** a : to lay or spread over or across : SUPERIMPOSE **b** : to prepare an overlay for **2** : OVERLIE 2

²over·lay \'ō-vər-ˌlā\ n (1794) : a covering either permanent or temporary: as **a** : an ornamental veneer **b** : a decorative and contrasting design or article placed on top of a plain one **c** : a transparent sheet containing graphic matter to be superimposed on another sheet

over·leaf \'ō-vər-ˌlēf, -'lēf\ adv (1843) : on the other side of a leaf (as of a book)

over·leap \ˌō-vər-'lēp\ vt **-leaped** or **-leapt** \-'lēpt also -'lept\; **-leap·ing** \-'lē-piŋ\ (bef. 12c) **1** : to leap over or across **2** : to defeat (oneself) by going too far

over·learn \-'lərn\ vt (1874) : to continue to study or practice after attaining proficiency

over·lie \-'lī\ vt **-lay** \-'lā\; **-lain** \-'lān\; **-ly·ing** \-'lī-iŋ\ (13c) **1** : to lie over or upon **2** : to cause the death of by lying upon

¹over·look \-'lůk\ vt (14c) **1** : to look over : INSPECT **2** a : to look

\ə\ abut \ᵊ\ kitten, F table \ər\ further \a\ ash \ā\ ace \ä\ mop, mar \aů\ out \ch\ chin \e\ bet \ē\ easy \g\ go \i\ hit \ī\ ice \j\ job \ŋ\ sing \ō\ go \ȯ\ law \ȯi\ boy \th\ thin \t͟h\ the \ü\ loot \ů\ foot \y\ yet \zh\ vision \ä, k̲, ⁿ, œ, œ̄, ue, ūe, ᵜ\ see Guide to Pronunciation

down upon from above **b** : to rise above or afford a view of **3 a** : to look past : MISS **b** : IGNORE 1 **c** : EXCUSE 2 **4** : SUPERINTEND, OVERSEE **5** : to look on with the evil eye : BEWITCH *syn* see NEGLECT
²**over·look** \'ō-vər-ˌlúk\ *n* (1861) : a place from which one may look down on a scene below ⟨plenty of ~s and trails —Thelma H. Bell⟩
over·lord \'ō-vər-ˌlórd\ *n* (13c) **1** : a lord over other lords : a lord paramount **2 a** : an absolute or supreme ruler **b** : one having great power or authority ⟨a corporate ~⟩ — **over·lord·ship** \-ˌship, ˌō-vər-'\ *n*
over·ly \'ō-vər-lē\ *adv* (1821) : to an excessive degree
¹**over·man** \-mən, -ˌman\ *n* (13c) **1** : a man in authority over others; *specif* : FOREMAN **2** \-ˌman\ [trans. of G *Übermensch*] : SUPERMAN 1
²**over·man** \ˌō-vər-'man\ *vt* (ca. 1637) : to have or get too many personnel for the needs of ⟨~ a ship⟩
over·man·tel \'ō-vər-ˌman-t²l\ *n* (1882) : an ornamental structure (as a painting) above a mantelpiece — **overmantel** *adj*
over·mas·ter \ˌō-vər-'mas-tər\ *vt* (14c) : OVERPOWER, SUBDUE
over·mas·ter·ing \-'mas-tə-riŋ\ *adj* (1645) : DOMINANT ⟨~ behavior⟩ ⟨the ~ question⟩
over·match \-'mach\ *vt* (14c) **1** : to be more than a match for : DEFEAT **2** : to match with a superior opponent
¹**over·much** \-'məch\ *adj* (13c) : too much
²**overmuch** *adv* (14c) : to too great a degree
³**over·much** \ˌō-vər-ˌməch, ˌō-vər-'\ *n* (14c) : too great an amount
¹**over·night** \ˌō-vər-'nīt\ *adv* (14c) **1 a** : on the evening before **b** : during the night ⟨stayed away ~⟩ **2** : very quickly or suddenly ⟨became famous ~⟩
²**overnight** *adj* (1824) **1** : of, lasting, or staying the night **2** : SUDDEN, RAPID ⟨an ~ sensation⟩
³**overnight** \ˌō-vər-ˌnīt, ˌō-vər-'\ *vi* (1891) : to stay overnight
⁴**over·night** \'ō-vər-ˌnīt\ *n* (1959) : an overnight stay
overnight bag *n* (1925) : a suitcase of a size to carry clothing and personal articles for an overnight trip — called also *overnight case*
over·night·er \ˌō-vər-'nī-tər\ *n* (1949) : OVERNIGHT BAG
¹**over·pass** \ˌō-vər-'pas\ *vt* (14c) **1** : to pass across, over, or beyond : CROSS; *also* : SURPASS **2** : TRANSGRESS **3** : DISREGARD, IGNORE
²**over·pass** \'ō-vər-ˌpas\ *n* (1929) : a crossing of two highways or of a highway and pedestrian path or railroad at different levels where clearance to traffic on the lower level is obtained by elevating the higher level; *also* : the upper level of such a crossing
over·per·suade \ˌō-vər-pər-'swād\ *vt* (1624) : to persuade to act contrary to one's conviction or preference — **over·per·sua·sion** \-'swā-zhən\ *n*
over·plaid \'ō-vər-ˌplad\ *n* (1926) : a textile design consisting of a plaid pattern superimposed on another plaid or on a textured ground; *also* : a fabric with such a design — **over·plaid·ed** *adj*
over·play \ˌō-vər-'plā\ *vt* (1819) **1 a** : to present (as a dramatic role) extravagantly : EXAGGERATE **b** : to place too much emphasis on **2** : to rely too much on the strength of — usu. used in the phrase *overplay one's hand* **3** : to strike a golf ball beyond (a putting green) ~ *vi* : to exaggerate a part or effect
over·plus \'ō-vər-ˌpləs\ *n* [ME, part trans. of MF *surplus*] (14c) : SURPLUS
over·pop·u·late \ˌō-vər-'päp-yə-ˌlāt\ *vt* (1868) : to furnish or provide with more than the environment or market will bear ~ *vi* : to become overly populous
over·pop·u·la·tion \ˌō-vər-ˌpä-pyə-'lā-shən\ *n* (1823) : the condition of having a population so dense as to cause environmental deterioration, an impaired quality of life, or a population crash
over·pow·er \ˌō-vər-'paú(-ə)r\ *vt* (1593) **1** : to overcome by superior force : SUBDUE **2** : to affect with overwhelming intensity ⟨the stench ~ed us⟩ **3** : to provide with more power than is needed or desirable ⟨a dangerously ~ed car⟩ — **over·pow·er·ing·ly** \-'paú(-ə)r-iŋ-lē\ *adv*
over·pres·sure \'ō-vər-ˌpre-shər\ *n* (1644) : pressure significantly above what is usual or normal
over·price \ˌō-vər-'prīs\ *vt* (1605) : to price too high
¹**over·print** \ˌō-vər-'print\ *vt* (1863) : to print over with something additional
²**over·print** \'ō-vər-ˌ\ *n* (1876) : something added by or as if by overprinting; *esp* : a printed marking added to a postage or revenue stamp esp. to alter the original or to commemorate a special event
over·proof \ˌō-vər-'prüf\ *adj* (1807) : containing more alcohol than proof spirit
over·pro·por·tion \ˌō-vər-'pōr-shən, -'pór-\ *vt* (1642) : to make disproportionately large — **overproportion** *n* — **over·pro·por·tion·ate** \-sh(ə-)nət\ *adj* — **over·pro·por·tion·ate·ly** *adv*
over·qual·i·fied \ˌō-vər-'kwä-lə-ˌfīd\ *adj* (1954) : having more education, training, or experience than a job calls for
over·reach \ˌō-vər-'rēch\ *vt* (14c) **1** : to reach above or beyond : OVERTOP **2** : to defeat (oneself) by seeking to do or gain too much **3** : to get the better of esp. in dealing and bargaining and typically by unscrupulous or crafty methods ~ *vi* **1** *of a horse* : to strike the forefoot with the front end of the hind foot **2 a** : to go to excess **b** : EXAGGERATE **3** : to overreach oneself — **over·reach** \'ō-vər-ˌrēch, ˌō-vər-'\ *n* — **over·reach·er** \-ˌrē-chər, -'rē-chər\ *n*
over·rep·re·sent·ed \ˌō-və(r)-ˌre-pri-'zen-təd\ *adj* (1900) : represented excessively; *esp* : having representatives in a proportion higher than the average — **over·rep·re·sen·ta·tion** \-ˌre-pri-ˌzen-'tā-shən, -zən-\ *n*
¹**over·ride** \'ō-vər-ˌrīd\ *vt* -rode \-'rōd\; -rid·den \-'ri-d²n\; -rid·ing \-'rī-diŋ\ (bef. 12c) **1** : to ride over or across : TRAMPLE **2** : to ride (as a horse) too much or too hard **3 a** : to prevail over : DOMINATE **b** : to set aside : ANNUL ⟨~ a veto⟩ **c** : to neutralize the action of (as an automatic control) **4** : to extend or pass over; *esp* : OVERLAP
²**over·ride** \'ō-və(r)-ˌrīd\ *n* (1931) **1** : a commission paid to managerial personnel on sales made by subordinates **2** : ROYALTY 5a **3** : a device or system used to override a control **4** : an act or an instance of overriding
over·ripe \ˌō-və(r)-'rīp\ *adj* (1671) **1** : passed beyond maturity or ripeness toward decay **2 a** : DECADENT **b** : lacking originality or vigor — **over·ripe·ness** \-nəs\ *n*
over·rule \-'rül\ *vt* (1576) **1** : to rule over : GOVERN **2** : to prevail over : OVERCOME **3** : to rule against **b** : to set aside : REVERSE
¹**over·run** \-'rən\ *vt* -ran \-'ran\; -run; -run·ning (bef. 12c) **1 a** (1) : to defeat decisively and occupy the positions of (2) : to invade and

occupy or ravage **b** : to spread or swarm over : INFEST **2 a** : to run or go beyond or past ⟨the plane *overran* the runway⟩ **b** : EXCEED **c** : to readjust (set type) by shifting letters or words from one line into another **3** : to flow over
²**over·run** \'ō-və(r)-ˌrən\ *n* (1898) **1** : an act or instance of overrunning; *esp* : an exceeding of the costs estimated in a contract for development and manufacture of new equipment **2** : the amount by which something overruns **3** : a run in excess of the quantity ordered by a customer
over·scale \'ō-vər-ˌskāl\ or **over·scaled** \-ˌskāld\ *adj* (1953) : OVERSIZE ⟨an ~ coat⟩ ⟨an ~ sofa⟩
over·sea \ˌō-vər-'sē, 'ō-vər-ˌ\ *adj or adv* (12c) *chiefly Brit* : OVERSEAS
¹**over·seas** \ˌō-vər-'sēz\ *adv* (1533) : beyond or across the sea ⟨lived ~ for a time⟩
²**over·seas** \ˌō-vər-ˌsēz\ *adj* (1892) **1** : of or relating to movement, transport, or communication over the sea ⟨an ~ liner⟩ **2** : situated, originating in, or relating to lands beyond the sea ⟨~ installations⟩ ⟨~ immigrants⟩
over·see \ˌō-vər-'sē\ *vt* -saw \-'só\; -seen \-'sēn\; -see·ing (bef. 12c) **1** : SURVEY, WATCH **2 a** : INSPECT, EXAMINE **b** : SUPERVISE
over·seer \'ō-və(r)-ˌsir, -ˌsē-ər, ˌō-və(r)-'\ *n* (1523) : SUPERVISOR, SUPERINTENDENT
over·sell \ˌō-vər-'sel\ *vt* -sold \-'sōld\; -sell·ing (ca. 1879) **1 a** : to sell too much or too many to **b** : to sell too much or too many of **2** : to make excessive claims for — **over·sell** \'ō-vər-ˌsel\ *n*
over·set \-'set\ *vt* -set; -set·ting (1583) **1 a** : to disturb mentally or physically : UPSET **b** : to turn or tip over : OVERTURN **2** : to set too much type matter for — **over·set** \'ō-vər-ˌset\ *n*
over·sexed \ˌō-vər-'sekst\ *adj* (1898) : exhibiting an excessive sexual drive or interest
over·shad·ow \-'sha-(ˌ)dō\ *vt* (bef. 12c) **1** : to cast a shadow over **2** : to exceed in importance : OUTWEIGH
over·shirt \'ō-vər-ˌshərt\ *n* (1805) : a shirt usu. worn over another shirt without being tucked in
over·shoe \-ˌshü\ *n* (1823) : an outer shoe; *esp* : GALOSH
over·shoot \ˌō-vər-'shüt\ *vt* -shot \-'shät\; -shoot·ing (14c) **1** : to pass swiftly beyond **2** : to shoot or pass over or beyond so as to miss **3** : to excel in shooting — **over·shoot** \'ō-vər-ˌshüt\ *n*
¹**over·shot** \'ō-vər-ˌshät\ *adj* (ca. 1535) **1** : actuated by the weight of water passing over and flowing from above ⟨an ~ waterwheel⟩ **2 a** : having the upper jaw extending beyond the lower **b** : projecting beyond the lower jaw
²**overshot** *n* (1945) : a pattern or weave featuring filling threads which pass two or more warp yarns before reentering the fabric
over·sight \'ō-vər-ˌsīt\ *n* (15c) **1 a** : watchful and responsible care **b** : regulatory supervision ⟨congressional ~⟩ **2** : an inadvertent omission or error
over·sim·ple \ˌō-vər-'sim-pəl\ *adj* (15c) : too simple : not thoroughgoing or exhaustive ⟨~ theories⟩ — **over·sim·ply** \-plē\ *adv*
over·sim·pli·fy \-'sim-plə-ˌfī\ *vt* (1923) : to simplify to such an extent as to bring about distortion, misunderstanding, or error ~ *vi* : to engage in undue or extreme simplification — **over·sim·pli·fi·ca·tion** \-ˌsim-plə-fə-'kā-shən\ *n*
over·size \ˌō-vər-'sīz\ *or* **over·sized** \-'sīzd\ *adj* (1853) : being of more than standard or ordinary size ⟨~ pillows⟩ ⟨an ~ shirt⟩
over·skirt \'ō-vər-ˌskərt\ *n* (1870) : a skirt worn over another skirt
over·slaugh \ˌō-vər-'sló\ *vt* [D *overslaan* to pass over, omit, fr. MD *overslaun*, fr. *over-* over- + *slaen* to strike] (1846) : to pass over for appointment or promotion in favor of another
over·sleep \ˌō-vər-'slēp\ *vb* -slept \-'slept\; -sleep·ing *vi* (14c) : to sleep beyond the time for waking ~ *vt* : to allow (oneself) to oversleep
over·slip \-'slip\ *vt* (15c) *obs* : ESCAPE
over·sold \ˌō-vər-'sōld\ *adj* (1926) : likely to show a rise in price because of prior heavy selling and accompanying decline in price ⟨an ~ stock⟩
over·soul \'ō-vər-ˌsōl\ *n* (ca. 1844) : the absolute reality and basis of all existences conceived as a spiritual being in which the ideal nature imperfectly manifested in human beings is perfectly realized
over·spend \ˌō-vər-'spend\ *vb* -spent \-'spent\; -spend·ing *vt* (ca. 1618) **1** : to spend or use to excess : EXHAUST **2** : to exceed in expenditure ~ *vi* : to spend beyond one's means — **over·spend·er** *n*
over·spill \'ō-vər-ˌspil\ *n* (1884) **1** : the act or an instance of spilling over **2** *chiefly Brit* : the movement of excess urban population into less crowded areas
over·spread \ˌō-vər-'spred\ *vt* -spread; -spread·ing (bef. 12c) : to spread over or above — **over·spread** \'ō-vər-ˌspred\ *n*
over·state \-'stāt\ *vt* (1803) : to state in too strong terms : EXAGGERATE — **over·state·ment** \-mənt\ *n*
over·stay \-'stā\ *vt* (1646) : to stay beyond the time or the limits of
over·steer \'ō-vər-ˌstir\ *n* (1951) : the tendency of an automobile to steer into a sharper turn than the driver intends sometimes with a thrusting of the rear to the outside; *also* : the action or an instance of oversteer
over·step \ˌō-vər-'step\ *vt* (bef. 12c) : EXCEED, TRANSGRESS
over·sto·ry \'ō-vər-ˌstōr-ē, -ˌstór-\ *n* (1925) **1** : the layer of foliage in a forest canopy **2** : the trees contributing to an overstory
over·strew \ˌō-vər-'strü\ *vt* -strewed; -strewed *or* -strewn \-'strün\; -strew·ing (ca. 1570) **1** : to strew or scatter about **2** : to cover here and there
over·stride \-'strīd\ *vt* -strode \-'strōd\; -strid·den \-'stri-d²n\; -strid·ing \-'strī-diŋ\ (13c) **1 a** : to stride over, across, or beyond **b** : BESTRIDE **2** : to stride faster than or beyond
over·strung \-'strəŋ\ *adj* (1810) : too highly strung : too sensitive
over·stuff \-'stəf\ *vt* (1904) **1** : to stuff too full **2** : to cover (as a chair or sofa) completely and deeply with upholstery
over·sub·scribe \-səb-'skrīb\ *vt* (1891) : to subscribe for more of than is available — **over·sub·scrip·tion** \-'skrip-shən\ *n*
overt \ō-'vərt, 'ō-(ˌ)vərt\ *adj* [ME, fr. MF *ouvert, overt*, fr. pp. of *ouvrir* to open, fr. (assumed) VL *operire*, alter. of L *aperire*] (14c) : open to view : MANIFEST — **overt·ly** *adv* — **overt·ness** *n*
over·take \ˌō-vər-'tāk\ *vt* -took \-'túk\; -tak·en \-'tā-kən\; -tak·ing [ME, fr. ¹*over* + *taken* to take] (13c) **1 a** : to catch up with **b** : to catch up with and pass by **2** : to come upon suddenly

over–the–counter *adj* (1921) **1** : not traded or effected on an organized securities exchange 〈~ transactions〉 〈~ securities〉 **2** : sold lawfully without prescription 〈~ drugs〉

over–the–hill *adj* (1946) **1** : past one's prime **2** : advanced in age

over–the–top *adj* (1985) : extremely or excessively flamboyant or outrageous 〈an ~ performance〉

over–the–transom *adj* (ca. 1952) : offered without prior arrangement esp. for publication : UNSOLICITED 〈an ~ manuscript〉

over·throw \ˌō-vər-'thrō\ *vt* **-threw** \-'thrü\; **-thrown** \-'thrōn\; **-throw·ing** (14c) **1** : OVERTURN, UPSET **2** : to cause the downfall of : BRING DOWN, DEFEAT **3** : to throw a ball over or past (as a base or a receiver) — **over·throw** \'ō-vər-ˌthrō\ *n*

over·time \'ō-vər-ˌtīm\ *n* (1536) **1** : time in excess of a set limit: as **a** : working time in excess of a standard day or week **b** : an extra period of play in a contest **2** : the wage paid for overtime — **overtime** *adv*

over·tone \-ˌtōn\ *n* (1867) **1 a** : one of the higher tones produced simultaneously with the fundamental and that with the fundamental comprise a complex musical tone : HARMONIC 1a **b** : HARMONIC 2 **2** : the color of the light reflected (as by a paint) **3** : a secondary effect, quality, or meaning : SUGGESTION 3, CONNOTATION

over·top \ˌō-vər-'täp\ *vt* (ca. 1594) **1** : to rise above the top of **2** : to be superior to **3** : SURPASS

over·trade \-'trād\ *vi* (1734) : to trade beyond one's capital

over·trick \'ō-vər-ˌtrik\ *n* (1903) : a card trick won in excess of the number bid

over·trump \ˌō-vər-'trəmp\ *vt* (1746) : to trump with a higher trump card than the highest previously played on the same trick ~ *vi* : to play a higher trump card than the highest previously played on the same trick

¹over·ture \'ō-və(r)-ˌchùr, -chər, -ˌtyùr, -ˌtùr\ *n* [ME, lit., opening, fr. MF, fr. (assumed) VL *opertura*, alter. of L *apertura* — more at APERTURE] (15c) **1 a** : an initiative toward agreement or action : PROPOSAL **b** : something introductory : PRELUDE **2 a** : the orchestral introduction to a musical dramatic work **b** : an orchestral concert piece written esp. as a single movement in sonata form

²overture *vt* **-tured; -tur·ing** (ca. 1650) **1** : to put forward as an overture **2** : to make or present an overture to

¹over·turn \ˌō-vər-'tərn\ *vt* (13c) **1** : to cause to turn over : UPSET **2** : INVALIDATE, DESTROY ~ *vi* : UPSET, TURN OVER

²over·turn \'ō-vər-ˌtərn\ *n* (ca. 1592) **1** : the act of overturning : the state of being overturned **2** : the sinking of surface water and rise of bottom water in a lake or sea that results from changes in temperature that commonly occur in spring and fall

over·val·ue \ˌō-vər-'val-(ˌ)yü\ *vt* (1597) : to assign an excessive or fictitious value to — **over·valu·a·tion** \-ˌval-yə-'wā-shən\ *n*

over·view \'ō-vər-ˌvyü\ *n* (1588) : a general survey : SUMMARY

over·volt·age \ˌō-vər-'vōl-tij\ *n* (1907) **1** : the excess potential required for the discharge of an ion at an electrode over and above the equilibrium potential of the electrode **2** : voltage in excess of the normal operating voltage of a device or circuit

over·wear \-'war, -'wer\ *vt* **-wore** \-'wōr, -'wòr\; **-worn** \-'wōrn, -'wòrn\; **-wear·ing** (1578) : WEAR OUT, EXHAUST

over·ween·ing \ˌō-vər-'wē-niŋ\ *adj* [ME *overwening*, prp. of *overwenen* to be arrogant, fr. *over* + *wenen* to ween] (14c) **1** : ARROGANT, PRESUMPTUOUS **2** : IMMODERATE, EXAGGERATED — **over·ween·ing·ly** *adv*

over·weigh \-'wā\ *vt* (13c) **1** : to exceed in weight **2** : OPPRESS 2

¹over·weight \'ō-vər-ˌwāt, *2 is usu* ˌō-vər-'\ *n* (1552) **1** : weight over and above what is required or allowed **2** : excessive or burdensome weight

²over·weight \ˌō-vər-'wāt\ *vt* (1603) **1** : to give too much weight or consideration to **2** : to weight excessively

³over·weight \ˌō-vər-'wāt\ *adj* (1638) : exceeding expected, normal, or proper weight; *esp* : exceeding the bodily weight normal for one's age, height, and build

over·whelm \ˌō-vər-'hwelm, -'welm\ *vt* [ME, fr. ¹over + *whelmen* to turn over, cover up] (14c) **1** : UPSET, OVERTHROW **2 a** : to cover over completely : SUBMERGE **b** : to overcome by superior force or numbers **c** : to overpower in thought or feeling

over·whelm·ing *adj* (1742) : tending or serving to overwhelm 〈an ~ majority〉; *also* : EXTREME, GREAT 〈~ indifference〉 — **over·whelm·ing·ly** *adv*

¹over·win·ter \ˌō-vər-'win-tər\ *vi* (bef. 12c) : to survive the winter

²overwinter *adj* (1900) : occurring during the period spanning the winter

over with *adj* (1915) : being at an end : FINISHED, COMPLETED

over·work \ˌō-vər-'wərk\ *vt* (1818) **1** : to cause to work too hard, too long, or to exhaustion **2** : to decorate all over **3 a** : to work too much on : OVERDO **b** : to make excessive use of ~ *vi* : to work too much or too long : OVERDO — **overwork** *n*

over·write \ˌō-və(r)-'rīt\ *vb* **-wrote** \-'rōt\; **-writ·ten** \-'ri-tᵊn\; **-writ·ing** \-'rī-tiŋ\ *vt* (1699) **1** : to write over the surface of **2** : to write in inflated or overly elaborate style ~ *vi* : to write too much or in an overly elaborate style

over·wrought \-'ròt\ *adj* [pp. of *overwork*] (1670) **1** : extremely excited : AGITATED **2** : elaborated to excess : OVERDONE

ovi- *or* **ovo-** — see OV-

ovi·cide \'ō-və-ˌsīd\ *n* [ISV] (1913) : an agent that kills eggs; *esp* : an insecticide effective against the egg stage — **ovi·cid·al** \ˌō-və-'sī-dᵊl\ *adj*

ovi·duct \'ō-və-ˌdəkt\ *n* [NL *oviductus*, fr. *ov-* + *ductus* duct] (1672) : a tube that serves exclusively or esp. for the passage of eggs from an ovary — **ovi·duc·tal** \ˌō-və-'dək-tᵊl\ *adj*

ovine \'ō-ˌvīn\ *adj* [LL *ovinus*, fr. L *ovis* sheep — more at EWE] (ca. 1828) : of, relating to, or resembling sheep — **ovine** *n*

ovip·a·rous \ō-'vi-p(ə-)rəs\ *adj* [L *oviparus*, fr. *ov-* + *-parus* -parous] (1646) : producing eggs that develop and hatch outside the maternal body; *also* : involving the production of such eggs

ovi·pos·it \'ō-və-ˌpä-zət, ˌō-və-'\ *vi* [prob. back-formation fr. *ovipositor*] (1816) : to lay eggs — used esp. of insects — **ovi·po·si·tion** \ˌō-və-pə-'zi-shən\ *n* — **ovi·po·si·tion·al** \-'zish-nəl, -ˌzi-shə-nᵊl\ *adj*

ovi·pos·i·tor \'ō-və-ˌpä-zə-tər, ˌō-və-'\ *n* [NL, fr. L *ov-* + *positor* one that places, fr. *ponere* to place — more at POSITION] (1816) : a specialized organ (as of an insect) for depositing eggs — see INSECT illustration

ovoid \'ō-ˌvòid\ *also* **ovoi·dal** \ō-'vòi-dᵊl\ *adj* [F *ovoïde*, fr. L *ovum* egg — more at EGG] (ca. 1828) : resembling an egg in shape : OVATE — **ovoid** *n*

ovo·lo \'ō-və-ˌlō\ *n, pl* **-los** [It, dim. of *uovo, ovo* egg, fr. L *ovum*] (1663) : a rounded convex molding

Ovon·ics \ō-'vä-niks\ *n pl but usu sing in constr* [Stanford R. *Ov*shinsky *b*1923 Am. inventor + electr*onics*] (1968) : a branch of electronics that deals with applications of the change from an electrically nonconducting state to a semiconducting state shown by glasses of special composition upon application of a certain minimum voltage — **ovon·ic** \-nik\ *adj*

ovo·tes·tis \ˌō-vō-'tes-təs\ *n* [NL] (1877) : a hermaphrodite gonad (as in some scale insects)

ovo·vi·vip·a·rous \ˌō-vō-ˌvī-'vi-p(ə-)rəs\ *adj* (1801) : producing eggs that develop within the maternal body (as of various fishes or reptiles) and hatch within or immediately after extrusion from the parent — **ovo·vi·vip·a·rous·ly** *adv* — **ovo·vi·vip·a·rous·ness** *n*

ovu·late \'äv-yə-ˌlāt, 'ōv-, -lət\ *adj* (1861) : bearing an ovule

ovu·la·tion \ˌäv-yə-'lā-shən, ˌōv-\ *n* (1848) : the discharge of a mature ovum from the ovary — **ovu·late** \'äv-yə-ˌlāt, 'ōv-\ *vb*

ovu·la·to·ry \'äv-yə-lə-ˌtòr-ē, 'ōv-, -ˌtòr-\ *adj* (1931) : of, relating to, or involving ovulation

ovule \'äv-(ˌ)yü(ə)l, 'ōv-\ *n* [NL *ovulum*, dim. of L *ovum*] (1830) **1** : an outgrowth of the ovary of a seed plant that is a megasporangium and encloses an embryo sac within a nucellus **2** : a small egg; *esp* : one in an early stage of growth

ovum \'ō-vəm\ *n, pl* **ova** \-və\ [NL, fr. L, egg — more at EGG] (ca. 1706) : a female gamete : MACROGAMETE

ow \'aú, 'ü\ *interj* [fr. *ou*, interj. expressing surprise, fr. ME] (ca. 1911) — used esp. to express sudden pain

owe \'ō\ *vb* **owed; ow·ing** [ME, to possess, own, owe, fr. OE *āgan*; akin to OHG *eigun* (1st & 3d pl. pres. indic.) possess, Skt *īśe* he possesses] *vt* (bef. 12c) **1 a** *archaic* : POSSESS, OWN **b** : to have or bear (an emotion or attitude) to someone or something 〈~s the boss a grudge〉 **2 a** (1) : to be under obligation to pay or repay in return for something received : be indebted in the sum of 〈~s me $5〉 (2) : to be under obligation to render (as duty or service) 〈I ~ you a favor〉 **b** : to be indebted to 〈~s the grocer for supplies〉 **3** : to be indebted for 〈*owed* his wealth to his father〉 〈~s much to good luck〉 ~ *vi* **1** : to be in debt 〈~s for his house〉 **2** : to be attributable 〈an idea that ~s to Greek philosophy〉

owing *adj* (15c) : due to be paid 〈has bills ~〉

owing to *prep* (1695) : BECAUSE OF 〈delayed *owing* to a crash〉

owl \'aú(ə)l\ *n* [ME *owle*, fr. OE *ūle*; akin to OHG *uwila* owl] (bef. 12c) : any of an order (Strigiformes) of chiefly nocturnal birds of prey with a large head and eyes, short hooked bill, strong talons, and soft fluffy often mottled brown plumage

owl·et \'aú-lət\ *n* (1542) : a small or young owl

owl·ish \'aú-lish\ *adj* (1611) : resembling or suggesting an owl — **owl·ish·ly** *adv* — **owl·ish·ness** *n*

¹own \'ōn\ *adj* [ME *owen*, fr. OE *āgen*; akin to OHG *eigan* own, ON *eiginn*, OE *āgan* to possess — more at OWE] (bef. 12c) **1** : belonging to oneself or itself — usu. used following a possessive case or possessive adjective 〈cooked my ~ dinner〉 **2** — used to express immediate or direct kinship 〈an ~ son〉 〈an ~ sister〉

²own *vt* (bef. 12c) **1 a** : to have or hold as property : POSSESS **b** : to have power over : CONTROL 〈wanted to ~ his own life〉 **2** : to acknowledge to be true, valid, or as claimed : ADMIT 〈~ a debt〉 ~ *vi* : to acknowledge something to be true, valid, or as claimed — used with *to* or *up* *syn* see ACKNOWLEDGE — **own·er** \'ō-nər\ *n*

³own *pron, sing or pl in constr* (bef. 12c) : one or ones belonging to oneself — used after a possessive and without a following noun 〈gave out books so that each of us had our ~〉 〈a room of your ~〉 — **on one's own** : for or by oneself : independently of assistance or control

own·er·ship \'ō-nər-ˌship\ *n* (1583) **1** : the state, relation, or fact of being an owner **2** : a group or organization of owners

ox \'äks\ *n, pl* **ox·en** \'äk-sən\ *also* **ox** [ME, fr. OE *oxa*; akin to OHG *ohso* ox, Skt *ukṣā* bull, and perh. to Skt *ukṣati* he moistens, Gk *hygros* wet — more at HUMOR] (bef. 12c) **1** : a domestic bovine mammal (*Bos taurus*); *broadly* : a bovine mammal **2** : an adult castrated male domestic ox

ox- *or* **oxo-** *comb form* [F, fr. *oxygène*] : oxygen 〈*oxacillin*〉

ox·a·cil·lin \ˌäk-sə-'si-lən\ *n* [*ox-* + *azole* + penic*illin*] (1962) : a semisynthetic penicillin that is esp. effective in the control of infections caused by penicillin-resistant staphylococci

ox·a·late \'äk-sə-ˌlāt\ *n* (1791) : a salt or ester of oxalic acid

ox·al·ic acid \(ˌ)äk-'sa-lik-\ *n* [F (*acide*) *oxalique*, fr. L *oxalis*] (1791) : a poisonous strong acid (COOH)₂ or H₂C₂O₄ that occurs in various plants as oxalates and is used esp. as a bleaching or cleaning agent and as a chemical intermediate

ox·al·is \äk-'sa-ləs\ *n* [NL, genus name, fr. L, wood sorrel, fr. Gk, fr. *oxys* sharp — more at OXYGEN] (ca. 1706) : WOOD SORREL

ox·a·lo·ac·e·tate \ˌäk-sə-lō-'a-sə-ˌtāt\ *also* **ox·al·ac·e·tate** \ˌäk-sə-'la-\ *n* (1891) : a salt or ester of oxaloacetic acid

ox·a·lo·ace·tic acid \ˌäk-sə-lō-ə-ˌsē-tik-\ *also* **ox·al·ace·tic acid** \ˌäk-sə-lə-'sē-tik-\ *n* [*oxalic* + *acetic acid*] (1896) : a crystalline acid C₄H₄O₅ that is formed by reversible oxidation of malic acid (as in carbohydrate metabolism via the Krebs cycle) and in reversible transamination reactions (as from aspartic acid)

ox·a·lo·suc·cin·ic acid \'äk-sə-lō-sək-ˌsi-nik-, äk-'sa-lō-\ *n* [*oxalic* + *succinic acid*] (1925) : a tricarboxylic acid C₆H₆O₇ that is formed as an intermediate in the Krebs cycle

ox·az·e·pam \äk-'sa-zə-ˌpam\ *n* [hydroxy- + di*azepam*] (1964) : a tranquilizing drug C₁₅H₁₁ClN₂O₂

ox·blood \'äks-ˌbləd\ *n* (1705) : a moderate reddish brown

\ə\ abut \ᵊ\ kitten, F table \ər\ further \a\ ash \ā\ ace \ä\ mop, mar \aú\ out \ch\ chin \e\ bet \ē\ easy \g\ go \i\ hit \ī\ ice \j\ job \ŋ\ sing \ō\ go \ò\ law \òi\ boy \th\ thin \th\ the \ü\ loot \ù\ foot \y\ yet \zh\ vision \à, k̲, ⁿ, œ, œ̄, ᵫ, ᵫ̄, ʸ\ *see* Guide to Pronunciation

ox·bow \'äks-ˌbō\ n (14c) **1** : a U‑shaped frame forming a collar about an ox's neck and supporting the yoke **2** : something (as a bend in a river) resembling an oxbow — oxbow adj

oxbow 1

Ox·bridge \'äks-ˌbrij\ adj [Oxford + Cambridge] (1960) : of, relating to, or characteristic of Oxford and Cambridge Universities — compare PLATEGLASS, REDBRICK 2

ox·cart \-ˌkärt\ n (1749) : a cart drawn by oxen

ox·eye \-ˌī\ n (15c) : any of several composite plants (as of the genera Chrysanthemum or Heliopsis) having heads with both disk and ray flowers; esp : DAISY 1b

oxeye daisy n (ca. 1763) : DAISY 1b

ox·ford \'äks-fərd\ n [Oxford, England] (ca. 1890) **1** : a low shoe laced or tied over the instep **2** : a soft durable cotton or synthetic fabric made in plain or basket weaves — called also oxford cloth

Oxford down n, often cap D [Oxfordshire, England] (1859) : any of a Down breed of large hornless sheep developed by crossing Cotswolds and Hampshires — called also Oxford

Oxford movement n (1841) : a High Church movement within the Church of England begun at Oxford in 1833

ox·heart \'äks-ˌhärt\ n (1870) : any of various large sweet cherries

ox·i·dant \'äk-sə-dənt\ n (1884) : OXIDIZING AGENT — oxidant adj

ox·i·dase \'äk-sə-ˌdās, -ˌdāz\ n [ISV] (1896) : any of various enzymes that catalyze oxidations; esp : one able to react directly with molecular oxygen — ox·i·da·sic \ˌäk-sə-'dā-sik, -zik\ adj

ox·i·da·tion \ˌäk-sə-'dā-shən\ n [F, fr. oxider, oxyder to oxidize, fr. oxide] (1791) **1** : the act or process of oxidizing **2** : the state or result of being oxidized — ox·i·da·tive \'äk-sə-ˌdā-tiv\ adj — ox·i·da·tive·ly adv

oxidation number n (1926) : a positive or negative number that represents the effective charge of an atom or element and that indicates the extent or possibility of its oxidation ⟨the usual oxidation number of sodium is +1 and of oxygen −2⟩ — called also oxidation state

oxidation–reduction n (1909) : a chemical reaction in which one or more electrons are transferred from one atom or molecule to another

oxidative phosphorylation n (1954) : the synthesis of ATP by phosphorylation of ADP for which energy is obtained by electron transport and which takes place in the mitochondria during aerobic respiration

ox·ide \'äk-ˌsīd\ n [F oxide, oxyde, fr. ox- (fr. oxygène oxygen) + -ide (fr. acide acid)] (1790) : a binary compound of oxygen with a more electropositive element or group — ox·id·ic \äk-'si-dik\ adj

ox·i·dize \'äk-sə-ˌdīz\ vb -dized; -diz·ing vt (1806) **1** : to combine with oxygen **2** : to dehydrogenate esp. by the action of oxygen **3** : to change (a compound) by increasing the proportion of the electronegative part or change (an element or ion) from a lower to a higher positive valence : remove one or more electrons from (an atom, ion, or molecule) ~ vi : to become oxidized — ox·i·diz·able \ˌäk-sə-'dī-zə-bəl\ adj

ox·i·diz·er \-ˌdī-zər\ n (1875) : OXIDIZING AGENT; esp : one used to support the combustion of a rocket propellant

oxidizing agent n (1903) : a substance that oxidizes something esp. chemically (as by accepting electrons)

ox·i·do·re·duc·tase \ˈäk-sə-dō-ri-'dək-ˌtās, -ˌtāz\ n [oxidation + -o- + reduction + -ase] (1922) : an enzyme that catalyzes an oxidation‑reduction reaction

ox·ime \'äk-ˌsēm\ n [ISV ox- + -ime (fr. imide)] (ca. 1890) : any of various compounds obtained chiefly by the action of hydroxylamine on aldehydes and ketones and characterized by the bivalent grouping C=NOH

ox·lip \'äk-ˌslip\ n [(assumed) ME oxeslippe, fr. OE oxanslyppe, lit., ox dung, fr. oxa ox + slypa, slyppe paste — more at SLIP] (bef. 12c) : a Eurasian primula (Primula elatior) having usu. yellow flowers

oxo \'äk-(ˌ)sō\ adj [ox-] (ca. 1926) : containing oxygen

oxo- — see OX-

Ox·o·ni·an \äk-'sō-nē-ən\ n [ML Oxonia Oxford] (ca. 1540) : a student or graduate of Oxford University — Oxonian adj

ox·tail \'äks-ˌtāl\ n (15c) : the tail of a beef animal; esp : the skinned tail used for food (as in soup)

ox·ter \'äk-stər\ n [ME Sc), alter. of OE ōxta; akin to OE eax axis, axle — more at AXIS] (15c) **1** chiefly Scot & Irish : ARMPIT 1 **2** chiefly Scot & Irish : ARM

ox·tongue \'äks-ˌtəŋ\ n (14c) : a European hawkweed (Picris echioides) that has yellow flowers and is now naturalized in the eastern U.S.

oxy \'äk-sē\ adj [F, fr. oxygène oxygen] (1910) : containing oxygen or additional oxygen — often used in combination ⟨oxyhemoglobin⟩

oxy·acet·y·lene \ˌäk-sē-ə-'se-tᵊl-ən, -t'l-ˌēn\ adj [ISV] (1909) : of, relating to, or utilizing a mixture of oxygen and acetylene ⟨an ~ torch⟩

oxy·ac·id \ˌäk-sē-ˌa-səd\ n (ca. 1841) : an acid (as sulfuric acid) that contains oxygen — called also oxygen acid

ox·y·gen \'äk-si-jən\ n, often attrib [F oxygène, fr. Gk oxys, adj., acidic, lit., sharp + F -gène -gen; akin to L acer sharp — more at EDGE] (1790) : a colorless tasteless odorless gaseous element that constitutes 21 percent of the atmosphere and is found in water, in most rocks and minerals, and in numerous organic compounds, that is capable of combining with all elements except the inert gases, that is active in physiological processes, and that is involved esp. in combustion — see ELEMENT table — ox·y·gen·ic \ˌäk-si-'je-nik\ adj — ox·y·gen·less \'äk-si-jən-ləs\ adj

ox·y·gen·ate \'äk-si-jə-ˌnāt, äk-'si-jə-\ vt -at·ed; -at·ing (1790) : to impregnate, combine, or supply (as blood) with oxygen — ox·y·gen·a·tion \ˌäk-si-jə-'nā-shən, äk-ˌsi-jə-\ n

ox·y·gen·a·tor \'äk-si-jə-ˌnā-tər, äk-'si-jə-\ n (ca. 1864) : one that oxygenates; specif : an apparatus that oxygenates the blood extracorporeally (as during open-heart surgery)

oxygen cycle n (1935) : the cycle whereby atmospheric oxygen is converted to carbon dioxide in animal respiration and regenerated by green plants in photosynthesis

oxygen debt n (1923) : a cumulative deficit of oxygen available for oxidative metabolism that develops during periods of intense bodily activity and must be made good when the body returns to rest

oxygen demand n (1950) : BIOCHEMICAL OXYGEN DEMAND

oxygen mask n (1920) : a device worn over the nose and mouth (as by pilots at high altitudes) through which oxygen is supplied from a storage tank

oxygen tent n (1925) : a canopy which can be placed over a bedridden person and within which a flow of oxygen can be maintained

oxy·he·mo·glo·bin \ˌäk-si-'hē-mə-ˌglō-bən\ n [ISV] (1873) : hemoglobin loosely combined with oxygen that it releases to the tissues

oxy·hy·dro·gen \-'hī-drə-jən\ adj (1827) : of, relating to, or utilizing a mixture of oxygen and hydrogen ⟨~ torch⟩

ox·y·mo·ron \ˌäk-si-'mōr-ˌän, -'mòr-\ n, pl -mo·ra \-'mōr-ə, -'mòr-\ [LGk oxymōron, fr. neut. of oxymōros pointedly foolish, fr. Gk oxys sharp, keen + mōros foolish] (1657) : a combination of contradictory or incongruous words (as cruel kindness) — ox·y·mo·ron·ic \-mə-'rä-nik, -mò-\ adj — ox·y·mo·ron·i·cal·ly \-ni-k(ə-)lē\ adv

oxy·phen·bu·ta·zone \ˌäk-sē-ˌfen-'byü-tə-ˌzōn\ n [oxy + phenylbutazone] (1961) : a phenylbutazone derivative $C_{19}H_{20}N_2O_3$ used for its anti-inflammatory, analgesic, and antipyretic effects

oxy·phil·ic \ˌäk-si-'fi-lik\ adj [Gk oxys acidic + E -phil — more at OXYGEN] (1901) : ACIDOPHILIC

oxy·tet·ra·cy·cline \-ˌte-trə-'sī-ˌklēn\ n (1953) : a yellow crystalline broad-spectrum antibiotic $C_{22}H_{24}N_2O_9$ produced by a soil actinomycete (Streptomyces rimosus)

oxy·to·cic \ˌäk-si-'tō-sik\ adj [ISV, fr. Gk oxys sharp, quick + tokos childbirth, fr. tiktein to bear — more at THANE] (1873) : hastening parturition; also : inducing contraction of uterine smooth muscle — oxytocic n

oxy·to·cin \-'tō-sᵊn\ n [ISV, fr. oxytocic] (1928) : a pituitary octapeptide hormone $C_{43}H_{66}N_{12}O_{12}S_2$ that stimulates esp. the contraction of uterine muscle and the secretion of milk

oxy·uri·a·sis \ˌäk-si-yü-'rī-ə-səs\ n [NL, fr. Oxyuris, genus of worms] (ca. 1909) : infestation with or disease caused by pinworms (family Oxyuridae)

oy·er and ter·mi·ner \ˌòi-ər-ən(d)-'tər-mə-nər\ n [ME, part trans. of AF oyer et terminer, lit., to hear and determine] (15c) **1** : a commission authorizing a British judge to hear and determine a criminal case at the assizes **2** : a high criminal court in some U.S. states

¹oyez \ō-'yez, -'yā, -'yes, 'ō-ˌ\ vb imper [ME, fr. AF, hear ye, imper. pl. of oir to hear, fr. L audire — more at AUDIBLE] (15c) — used by a court or public crier to gain attention before a proclamation

²oyez n, pl oyes·ses \-'ye-səz, -ˌye-səz\ (15c) : a cry of oyez

oys·ter \'òis-tər\ n, often attrib [ME oistre, fr. MF, fr. L ostrea, fr. Gk ostreon; akin to Gk ostrakon shell, osteon bone — more at OSSEOUS] (13c) **1 a** : any of various marine bivalve mollusks (family Ostreidae) that have a rough irregular shell closed by a single adductor muscle and include commercially important shellfish **b** : any of various mollusks resembling or related to the oysters **2** : something that is or can be readily made to serve one's personal ends ⟨the world was her ~⟩ **3** : a small mass of muscle contained in a concavity of the pelvic bone on each side of the back of a fowl **4** : an extremely taciturn person **5** : a grayish-white color

oyster bed n (1591) : a place where oysters grow or are cultivated

oys·ter·catch·er \-ˌka-chər, -ˌke-\ n (1731) : any of a genus (Haematopus) of wading birds that have stout legs, a heavy wedge-shaped bill, and often black-and-white plumage

oyster crab n (1756) : a tiny crab (Pinnotheres ostreum) that lives as a commensal in the gill cavity of the oyster

oyster cracker n (1873) : a small salted usu. round cracker

oyster drill n (1925) : DRILL 4a

oys·ter·ing \'òis-t(ə-)riŋ\ n (1662) : the act or business of taking oysters for the market or for food

oys·ter·man \'òis-tər-mən\ n (1552) : one who gathers, opens, breeds, or sells oysters

oyster mushroom n (1875) : an edible mushroom (Pleurotus ostreatus) that grows esp. on deciduous trees and dead wood

oyster plant n (1821) : SALSIFY

oysters Rocke·fel·ler \-'rä-ki-ˌfe-lər\ n pl [prob. fr. John D. Rockefeller †1937] (1939) : a dish of oysters on the half shell cooked with various savory toppings typically including chopped spinach and a seasoned sauce

ozo·ke·rite \ˌō-zō-'kir-ˌīt\ also ozo·ce·rite \-'sir-\ n [G Ozokerit, fr. Gk ozein to smell + kēros wax — more at CERUMEN] (ca. 1837) : a waxy mineral mixture of hydrocarbons that is colorless or white when pure and often of unpleasant odor and is used esp. in making candles and in electrotyping

ozon·a·tion \ˌō-(ˌ)zō-'nā-shən\ n (1854) : the treatment or combination of a substance or compound with ozone — ozon·ate \'ō-(ˌ)zō-ˌnāt, -zə-\ vt

ozone \'ō-ˌzōn\ n [G Ozon, fr. Gk ozōn, prp. of ozein to smell — more at ODOR] (ca. 1840) **1** : a triatomic very reactive form of oxygen that is a bluish irritating gas of pungent odor, that is formed naturally in the atmosphere by a photochemical reaction and is a major air pollutant in the lower atmosphere but a beneficial component of the upper atmosphere, and that is used for oxidizing, bleaching, disinfecting, and deodorizing **2** : pure and refreshing air — ozon·ic \ō-'zō-nik, -'zä-\ adj

ozone hole n (1986) : an area of the ozone layer (as near the south pole) that is seasonally depleted of ozone

ozone layer n (1929) : an atmospheric layer at heights of about 20 to 30 miles (32 to 48 kilometers) that is normally characterized by high ozone content which blocks most solar ultraviolet radiation from entry into the lower atmosphere

ozon·ide \'ō-(ˌ)zə-ˌnīd\ n (1867) : a compound of ozone; specif : a compound formed by the addition of ozone to the double or triple bond of an unsaturated organic compound

ozon·ize \-ˌnīz\ vt -ized; -iz·ing (1850) : to treat, impregnate, or combine with ozone — ozon·i·za·tion \ˌō-zō-nə-'zā-shən\ n — ozon·iz·er \'ō-(ˌ)zō-ˌnī-zər\ n

ozo·no·sphere \ō-'zō-nə-ˌsfir\ n (1933) : OZONE LAYER

p \'pē\ *n, pl* **p's** *or* **ps** \'pēz\ *often cap, often attrib* (bef. 12c) **1 a** : the 16th letter of the English alphabet **b** : a graphic representation of this letter **c** : a speech counterpart of orthographic *p* **2** : a graphic device for reproducing the letter *p* **3** : one designated *p* esp. as the 16th in order or class **4** [abbr. for *pass*] **a** : a grade rating a student's work as passing **b** : one graded or rated with a P **5** : something shaped like the letter P

pa \'pä, 'pȯ\ *n* [short for *papa*] (1811) : FATHER

PA \(,)pē-'ā\ *n* (1970) : PHYSICIAN'S ASSISTANT

pa·'an·ga \pä-'äŋ-ɡə, -'äŋ-ə\ *n* [Tongan, lit., seed from a species of vine] (1966) — see MONEY table

PABA \'pa-bə, 'pä-; ˌpē-(ˌ)ä-'bē-(ˌ)ä\ *n* [*para-aminobenzoic acid*] (1943) : PARA-AMINOBENZOIC ACID

pab·lum \'pa-bləm\ *n* [fr. *Pablum*, a trademark for an infant cereal] (1948) : PABULUM 3

pab·u·lum \'pa-byə-ləm\ *n* [L, food, fodder; akin to L *pascere* to feed — more at FOOD] (1733) **1** : FOOD: esp : a suspension or solution of nutrients in a state suitable for absorption **2** : intellectual sustenance **3** : something (as writing or speech) that is insipid, simplistic, or bland

pa·ca \'pä-kə, 'pa-\ *n* [Pg & Sp, fr. Tupi *páka*] (1657) : either of two large chiefly Central and So. American rodents that constitute a genus (*Agouti* syn. *Cuniculus*) and typically have a white-spotted brownish coat

¹**pace** \'pās\ *n* [ME *pas*, fr. OF, step, fr. L *passus*, fr. *pandere* to spread — more at FATHOM] (14c) **1 a** : rate of movement; *esp* : an established rate of locomotion **b** : rate of progress; *specif* : parallel rate of growth or development ⟨supplies kept ~ with demand⟩ **c** : an example to be emulated; *specif* : first place in a competition ⟨three strokes off the ~ —*Time*⟩ **d** (1) : rate of performance or delivery : TEMPO; *esp* : SPEED ⟨serves with great ~⟩ ⟨a ~ bowler in cricket⟩ (2) : rhythmic animation : FLUENCY ⟨writes with color, with zest, and with ~ —Amy Loveman⟩ **2** : a manner of walking : TREAD **3 a** : STEP 2a(1) **b** : any of various units of distance based on the length of a human step **4 a** *pl* : an exhibition or test of skills or capacities ⟨the trainer put the tiger through its ~s⟩ **b** : GAIT: *esp* : a fast 2-beat gait (as of the horse) in which the legs move in lateral pairs and support the animal alternately on the right and left legs

²**pace** *vb* **paced; pac·ing** *vi* (1513) **1 a** : to walk with often slow or measured tread **b** : to move along : PROCEED **2** : to go at a pace — used esp. of a horse ~ *vt* **1 a** : to measure by pacing — often used with *off* ⟨*paced* off a 10-yard penalty⟩ **b** : to cover at a walk ⟨could hear him *pacing* the floor⟩ **2** : to cover (a course) by pacing — used of a horse **3 a** : to set or regulate the pace of ⟨taught them how to ~ their solos for . . . impact —Richard Goldstein⟩; *also* : to establish a moderate or steady pace for (oneself) **b** (1) : to go before : PRECEDE (2) : to set an example for : LEAD **c** : to keep pace with

³**pa·ce** \'pä-(ˌ)sē; 'pä-(ˌ)chä, -(ˌ)kä\ *prep* [L, abl. of *pac-, pax* peace, permission — more at PACT] (1863) : contrary to the opinion of — usu. used as an expression of deference to someone's contrary opinion; usu. ital. ⟨easiness is a virtue in grammar, ~ old-fashioned grammarians —Philip Howard⟩

pace car *n* (1965) : an automobile that leads the field of competitors through a pace lap but does not participate in the race

pace lap *n* (1971) : a lap of an auto racecourse by the entire field of competitors before the start of a race to allow the engines to warm up and to permit a flying start

pace·mak·er \'pās-ˌmā-kər\ *n* (1884) **1** : one that sets the pace for another **b** : one that takes the lead or sets an example **2 a** : a body part (as the sinoatrial node of the heart) that serves to establish and maintain a rhythmic activity **b** : an electrical device for stimulating or steadying the heartbeat or reestablishing the rhythm of an arrested heart — **pace·mak·ing** \-kiŋ\ *n*

pac·er \'pā-sər\ *n* (ca. 1661) **1** : one that paces; *specif* : a horse whose predominant gait is the pace **2** : PACEMAKER

pace·set·ter \'pās-ˌse-tər\ *n* (1895) : PACEMAKER 1 — **pace·set·ting** \-tiŋ\ *adj*

pa·chi·si \pə-'chē-zē\ *n* [Hindi *pacīsī*, fr. *pacīs* twenty-five] (1867) : an ancient board game played with dice and counters on a cruciform board in which players attempt to be the first to reach the home square

pa·chu·co \pə-'chü-(ˌ)kō\ *n, pl* **-cos** [AmerSp] (1943) : a young Mexican-American having a taste for flashy clothes and a special jargon and usu. belonging to a neighborhood gang

pachy·derm \'pa-ki-ˌdərm\ *n* [F *pachyderme*, fr. Gk *pachydermos* thick-skinned, fr. *pachys* thick + *derma* skin; akin to Skt *bahu* dense, much — more at DERM-] (1838) : any of various nonruminant hoofed mammals (as an elephant, a rhinoceros, or a pig) most of which have a thick skin

pachy·der·ma·tous \ˌpa-ki-'dər-mə-təs\ *adj* [ultim. fr. Gk *pachys* *dermat-, derma* skin] (1823) **1** : of or relating to the pachyderms **2 a** : THICK, THICKENED ⟨~ skin⟩ **b** : CALLOUS, INSENSITIVE

pach·y·san·dra \ˌpa-ki-'san-drə\ *n* [NL, irreg. fr. Gk *pachys* + NL *-andrus* -androus] (1813) : any of a genus (*Pachysandra*) of shrubby evergreen plants of the box family often used as a ground cover

pachy·tene \'pa-ki-ˌtēn\ *n* [ISV *pachy-* (fr. Gk *pachys*) + *-tene*] (1912) : the stage of meiotic prophase that immediately follows the zygotene and that is characterized by paired chromosomes thickened and visibly divided into chromatids and by the occurrence of crossing-over — **pachytene** *adj*

pa·cif·ic \pə-'si-fik\ *adj* [ME *pacifique*, fr. L *pacificus*, fr. *pac-, pax* peace + *-i-* + *-ficus* -fic — more at PACT] (ca. 1548) **1 a** : tending to lessen conflict : CONCILIATORY **b** : rejecting the use of force as an instrument of policy **2 a** : having a soothing appearance or effect ⟨mild ~ breezes⟩ **b** : mild of temper : PEACEABLE **3** *cap* : of, relating to, bordering on, or situated near the Pacific Ocean — **pa·cif·i·cal·ly** \-fi-k(ə-)lē\ *adv*

pac·i·fi·ca·tion \ˌpa-sə-fə-'kā-shən\ *n* (15c) **1 a** : the act or process of pacifying **b** : the state of being pacified **2** : the act of forcibly suppressing or eliminating a population considered to be hostile **2** : a treaty of peace

pa·cif·i·ca·tor \pə-'si-fə-ˌkā-tər\ *n* (1539) : PACIFIER 1

pa·cif·i·cism \pə-'si-fə-ˌsi-zəm\ *n* (1910) : PACIFISM — **pa·cif·i·cist** \-sist\ *n*

Pacific salmon *n* (1888) : any of several anadromous salmonid fishes (genus *Oncorhynchus*) chiefly of the northern Pacific including the sockeye, coho, chum salmon, and chinook salmon

Pacific time *n* [*Pacific Ocean*] (1883) : the time of the 8th time zone west of Greenwich that includes the Pacific coastal region of the U.S. — see TIME ZONE illustration

pac·i·fi·er \'pa-sə-ˌfī(-ə)r\ *n* (1533) **1** : one that pacifies **2** : a usu. nipple-shaped device for babies to suck or bite on

pac·i·fism \'pa-sə-ˌfi-zəm\ *n* [F *pacifisme*, fr. *pacifique* pacific] (1902) **1** : opposition to war or violence as a means of settling disputes; *specif* : refusal to bear arms on moral or religious grounds **2** : an attitude or policy of nonresistance — **pac·i·fist** \-fist\ *n*

pac·i·fist \'pa-sə-fist\ *or* **pac·i·fis·tic** \ˌpa-sə-'fis-tik\ *adj* (1908) **1** : of, relating to, or characteristic of pacifism or pacifists **2** : strongly and actively opposed to conflict and esp. war — **pac·i·fis·ti·cal·ly** \ˌpa-sə-'fis-ti-k(ə-)lē\ *adv*

pac·i·fy \'pa-sə-ˌfī\ *vt* **-fied; -fy·ing** [ME *pacifien*, fr. L *pacificare*, fr. *pac-, pax* peace] (15c) **1 a** : to allay the anger or agitation of : SOOTHE ⟨~ a crying child⟩ **b** : APPEASE, PROPITIATE **2 a** : to restore to a tranquil state ⟨made an attempt to ~ the commotion⟩ **b** : to reduce to a submissive state : SUBDUE ⟨forces moved in to ~ the country⟩ — **pac·i·fi·able** \ˌpa-sə-'fī-ə-bəl\ *adj*
syn PACIFY, APPEASE, PLACATE, MOLLIFY, PROPITIATE, CONCILIATE mean to ease the anger or disturbance of. PACIFY suggests a soothing or calming ⟨*pacified* by a sincere apology⟩. APPEASE implies quieting insistent demands by making concessions ⟨*appease* their territorial ambitions⟩. PLACATE suggests changing resentment or bitterness to goodwill ⟨a move to *placate* local opposition⟩. MOLLIFY implies soothing hurt feelings or rising anger ⟨a speech that *mollified* the demonstrators⟩. PROPITIATE implies averting anger or malevolence esp. of a superior being ⟨*propitiated* his parents by dressing up⟩. CONCILIATE suggests ending an estrangement by persuasion, concession, or settling of differences ⟨*conciliating* the belligerent nations⟩.

Pa·cin·i·an corpuscle \pə-'si-nē-ən-\ *n* [Filippo *Pacini* †1883 Ital. anatomist] (ca. 1860) : an oval capsule that terminates some sensory nerve fibers esp. in the skin of the hands and feet

¹**pack** \'pak\ *n, often attrib* [ME, of LG or D origin; akin to MLG & MD *pak* pack] (13c) **1 a** : a bundle arranged for convenience in carrying esp. on the back **b** : a group or pile of related objects **c** (1) : a number of individual components packaged as a unit ⟨a ~ of cigarettes⟩ (2) : CONTAINER (3) : a compact unitized assembly to perform a specific function (4) : a stack of magnetic disks in a container for use as a storage device **2 a** : the contents of a bundle **b** : a large amount or number : HEAP ⟨a ~ of lies⟩ **c** : a full set of playing cards **3 a** : an act or instance of packing **b** : a method of packing **4 a** : a set of persons with a common interest : CLIQUE **b** : an organized troop (as of Cub Scouts) **5 a** (1) : a group of domesticated animals trained to hunt or run together (2) : a group of often predatory animals of the same kind ⟨a wolf ~⟩ (3) : a large group of individuals massed together (as in a race) **b** : WOLF PACK **6** : a concentrated or compacted mass (as of snow or ice) **7** : wet absorbent material for therapeutic application to the body **8 a** : a cosmetic paste for the face **b** : an application or treatment of oils or creams for conditioning the scalp and hair **9** : material used in packing

²**pack** *vt* (14c) **1 a** : to make into a compact bundle **b** : to fill completely ⟨fans ~ed the stadium⟩ **c** : to fill with packing ⟨~ a joint in a pipe⟩ **d** : to load with a pack ⟨~ a mule⟩ **e** : to put in a protective container ⟨goods ~ed for shipment⟩ **2 a** : to crowd together **b** : to increase the density of : COMPRESS **3 a** : to cause or command to go without ceremony ⟨~ed him off to school⟩ **b** : to bring to an end : GIVE UP — used with *up* or *in* ⟨might ~ up the assignment⟩; used esp. in the phrase *pack it in* **4** : to gather into tight formation : make a pack of (as hounds) **5** : to cover or surround with a pack **6 a** : to transport on foot or on the back of an animal ⟨~ a canoe overland⟩ **b** : to wear or carry as equipment ⟨~ a gun⟩ **c** : to be supplied or equipped with : POSSESS ⟨a storm ~ing hurricane winds⟩ **d** : to cause or be capable of making (an impact) ⟨a book that ~s a man-sized punch —C. J. Rolo⟩ ~ *vi* **1 a** : to go away without ceremony : DEPART ⟨simply ~ed up and left⟩ **b** : QUIT, STOP — used with *up* or *in* ⟨why don't you ~ in, before you kill yourself —Millard Lampell⟩ **2 a** : to stow goods and equipment for transportation **b** : to be suitable for packing ⟨a knit dress ~s well⟩ **3 a** : to assemble in a group : CONGREGATE **b** : to crowd together **4** : to become built up or compacted in a layer or mass ⟨the ore ~ed into a stony mass⟩ **5 a** : to carry goods or equipment **b** : to travel with one's baggage (as by horse) — **pack·abil·i·ty** \ˌpa-kə-'bi-lə-tē\ *n* — **pack·able** \'pa-kə-bəl\ *adj*

³**pack** *vt* [obs. *pack* to make a secret agreement] (1587) **1** : to influence the composition of (as a political agency) so as to bring about a desired result ⟨~ a jury⟩ **2** *archaic* : to arrange (the cards in a pack) so as to cheat

⁴**pack** *adj* [perh. fr. obs. *pack* to make a secret agreement] (1701) *chiefly Scot* : INTIMATE

¹**pack·age** \'pa-kij\ *n* (1611) **1** *archaic* : the act or process of packing **2 a** : a small or moderate-sized pack : PARCEL **b** : a commodity or a unit of a product uniformly wrapped or sealed **c** : a preassembled unit **3** : a covering wrapper or container **4** : something that suggests a package: as **a** : PACKAGE DEAL **b** : a radio or television series offered for sale at a lump sum **c** : contract benefits gained through collective bargaining **d** : a ready-made computer program or collection of related software **e** : a travel arrangement contract that offers for a fixed price transportation, accommodations, and often sightseeing and entertainment **f** : a collection of related items; *esp* : one to be considered or acted on together ⟨presented his tax ~ to the nation⟩

²**package** *vt* **pack·aged; pack·ag·ing** (1921) **1 a** : to make into a

\ə\ abut \ᵊ\ kitten, F table \ər\ further \a\ ash \ā\ ace \ä\ mop, mar \aᵿ\ out \ch\ chin \e\ bet \ē\ easy \g\ go \i\ hit \ī\ ice \j\ job \ŋ\ sing \ō\ go \ȯ\ law \ȯi\ boy \th\ thin \t̲h̲\ the \ü\ loot \ᵿ\ foot \y\ yet \zh\ vision \ä, k̲, ⁿ, œ, œ̄, ᵫ, ᵬ, ʸ\ see Guide to Pronunciation

package; *esp* : to produce as an entertainment package **b** : to present (as a product) in such a way as to heighten its appeal to the public **2** : to enclose in a package or covering — **pack·ag·er** *n*
package deal *n* (ca. 1948) **1** : an offer or agreement involving a number of related items or one making acceptance of one item dependent on the acceptance of another **2** : the items offered in a package deal
package store *n* (ca. 1918) : a store that sells bottled or canned alcoholic beverages for consumption off the premises
pack animal *n* (1847) : an animal used for carrying packs
pack·board \'pak-,bōrd, -,bȯrd\ *n* (1939) : a usu. canvas-covered light wood or metal frame with shoulder straps used for carrying goods and equipment
packed \'pakt\ *adj* (1777) **1 a** : COMPRESSED ⟨hard-*packed* snow⟩ **b** : that is crowded or stuffed — often used in combination ⟨an action-*packed* story⟩ **2** : filled to capacity ⟨played to a ~ house⟩
pack·er \'pa-kər\ *n* (14c) **1** : one that packs: as **a** : one engaged in processing food (as meat) and distributing it to retailers **b** : an automotive vehicle with a closed body and a compressing device (as for compacting rubbish) in the rear **2** : PORTER 1 **3** : one that conveys goods by means of a pack
pack·et \'pa-kət\ *n* [ME, fr. MF *pacquet*, of Gmc origin; akin to MD *pak* back] (15c) **1 a** : a small bundle or parcel **b** : a small thin package **c** *Brit* (1) : PAY ENVELOPE (2) : SALARY, PAYCHECK **d** *chiefly Brit* : a considerable amount ⟨that trip will cost you a ~⟩ **2 a** : a number of letters dispatched at one time **b** : a small group, cluster, or mass **3** : a passenger boat usu. carrying mail and cargo **4** *Brit* : a pack of cigarettes **5** : a short fixed-length section of data that is transmitted as a unit in an electronic communications network
pack·horse \'pak-,hȯrs\ *n* (ca. 1500) : a horse used as a pack animal
pack ice *n* (1850) : sea ice formed into a mass by the crushing together of pans, floes, and brash
pack·ing \'pa-kiŋ\ *n* (14c) **1 a** : the action or process of packing something; *also* : a method of packing **b** : the processing of food and esp. meat for future sale **2** : material (as a covering or stuffing) used to protect packed goods (as for shipping); *also* : material used for making airtight or watertight ⟨~ for a faucet⟩
pack·ing·house \-,haus\ *n* (1834) : an establishment for slaughtering livestock and processing and packing meat, meat products, and by-products; *also* : one for processing and packing other foodstuffs — called also *packing plant*
pack·man \'pak-mən\ *n* (ca. 1625) : PEDDLER
pack rat *n* (1885) **1** : WOOD RAT; *esp* : a bushy-tailed rodent (*Neotoma cinerea*) of the Rocky Mountain area that has well-developed cheek pouches and hoards food and miscellaneous objects **2** : one who collects or hoards esp. unneeded items
pack·sack \'pak-,sak\ *n* (1851) : a case (as of canvas) held on the back by shoulder straps and used to carry gear when traveling on foot
pack·sad·dle \-,sa-d'l\ *n* (14c) : a saddle designed to support loads on the backs of pack animals
pack·thread \-,thred\ *n* (14c) : strong thread or small twine used for sewing or tying packs or parcels
pact \'pakt\ *n* [ME, fr. MF, fr. L *pactum*, fr. neut. of *pactus*, pp. of *pacisci* to agree, contract; akin to OE *fōn* to seize, L *pax* peace, *pangere* to fix, fasten, Gk *pēgnynai*] (15c) : ⁴COMPACT; *esp* : an international treaty
¹pad \'pad\ *vb* **pad·ded; pad·ding** [perh. fr. MD *paden* to follow a path, fr. *pad* path] *vt* (1553) : to traverse on foot ~ *vi* : to go on foot : WALK; *esp* : to walk with or as if with padded feet ⟨the dog *padded* along beside him⟩ ⟨*padding* around in bedroom slippers⟩
²pad *n* [MD *pad*] (1567) **1** *dial Brit* : PATH **2** : a horse that moves along at an easy pace **3** *archaic* : FOOTPAD
³pad *n* [origin unknown] (1570) **1 a** : a thin flat mat or cushion: as (1) : a piece of soft stuffed material used as or under a saddle (2) : padding used to shape an article of clothing (3) : a guard worn to shield body parts against impact (4) : a piece of usu. folded absorbent material (as gauze) used as a surgical dressing or protective covering (5) : frictional material that presses against the disks in a disk brake **b** : a piece of material saturated with ink for inking the surface of a rubber stamp **2 a** : the foot of an animal **b** : the cushioned thickening of the underside of the toes of an animal **3** : a floating leaf of a water plant **4** : a collection of sheets of paper glued together at one end **5 a** (1) : a section of an airstrip used for warm-ups or turnarounds (2) : an area used for helicopter takeoffs and landings **b** : LAUNCHPAD **c** : a horizontal concrete surface (as for parking a mobile home) **6 a** : BED **b** : living quarters
⁴pad *vt* **pad·ded; pad·ding** (1827) **1 a** : to furnish with a pad or padding **b** : MUTE, MUFFLE **2** : to expand or increase esp. with needless, misleading, or fraudulent matter ⟨~ an expense account⟩ — often used with *out* ⟨they ~ out their bibliographies —J. P. Kenyon⟩
⁵pad *n* [imit.] (1594) : a soft muffled or slapping sound
pad·ding \'pa-diŋ\ *n* (1828) : material with which something is padded
¹pad·dle \'pa-d'l\ *vi* **pad·dled; pad·dling** \'pad-liŋ, 'pa-d'l-iŋ\ [origin unknown] (1530) **1** : to move the hands or feet about in shallow water **2** *archaic* : to use the fingers or hands in toying or caressing **3** : TODDLE — **pad·dler** \'pad-lər, 'pa-d'l-ər\ *n*
²paddle *n* [ME *padell* spade-shaped tool for cleaning a plow] (1624) **1 a** : a usu. wooden implement that has a long handle and a broad flattened blade and that is used to propel and steer a small craft (as a canoe) **b** : an implement often with a short handle and a broad flat blade that is used for stirring, mixing, or hitting; *esp* : one used to hit a ball in any of various games (as table tennis) **2 a** : any of the broad boards at the circumference of a paddle wheel or waterwheel **b** : any of the broad blades attached to a shaft (as in an ice cream machine) and used for stirring **3** : a computer input device with a dial used to control linear movement of a cursor on a computer display
³paddle *vb* **pad·dled; pad·dling** \'pad-liŋ, 'pa-d'l-iŋ\ *vi* (1677) : to go on or through water by or as if by means of a paddle or paddle wheel ~ *vt* **1 a** : to propel by a paddle **b** : to transport in a paddled craft ⟨*paddled* us to shore in his canoe⟩ **2 a** : to beat or stir with or as if with a paddle (as in washing or dyeing) **b** : to punish by or as if by beating with a paddle — **pad·dler** \'pad-lər, 'pa-d'l-ər\ *n*
pad·dle·ball \'pa-d'l-,bȯl\ *n* (1935) : a game like handball played by hitting the ball with a paddle; *also* : the ball used in this game

pad·dle·board \-,bōrd, -,bȯrd\ *n* (1938) : a long narrow buoyant board used for riding the surf or in rescuing swimmers
pad·dle·boat \-,bōt\ *n* (1874) : a boat propelled by a paddle wheel
pad·dle·fish \-,fish\ *n* (1807) : any of a family (Polyodontidae) of ganoid fishes; *esp* : a large fish (*Polyodon spathula*) of the Mississippi valley that has a long paddle-shaped snout

paddlefish

paddle tennis *n* (1925) : a game like tennis that is played with a paddle and rubber ball on a small court
paddle wheel *n* (1685) : a wheel with paddles around its circumference used to propel a boat
paddle wheeler *n* (1924) : a steamer propelled by a paddle wheel
pad·dock \'pa-dək, -dik\ *n* [alter. of ME *parrok*, fr. OE *pearroc*, fr. ML *parricus*] (1622) **1 a** : a usu. enclosed area used esp. for pasturing or exercising animals; *esp* : an enclosure where racehorses are saddled and paraded before a race **b** *Austral & NewZeal* : an often enclosed field **2** : an area at an automobile racecourse where racing cars are parked
pad·dy *also* **padi** \'pa-dē\ *n, pl* **paddies** *also* **pad·is** [Malay *padi*] (1623) **1** : RICE; *esp* : threshed unmilled rice **2** : wet land in which rice is grown
Pad·dy \'pa-dē\ *n, pl* **Paddies** [fr. *Paddy*, Hiberno-English nickname for *Patrick*] (1780) : IRISHMAN — often taken to be offensive
paddy wagon *n* \'pa-dē-\ [prob. fr. *Paddy*] (1930) : an enclosed motortruck used by police to carry prisoners — called also *Black Maria, patrol wagon*
pad·lock \'pad-,läk\ *n* [ME *padlok*, fr. *pad-* (of unknown origin) + *lok* lock] (15c) : a removable lock with a shackle that can be passed through a staple or link and then secured — **padlock** *vt*
pa·dre \'pä-(,)drā, -drē\ *n* [Sp or It or Pg, lit., father, fr. L *pater* — more at FATHER] (1584) **1** : a Christian clergyman; *esp* : PRIEST **2** : a military chaplain
pa·dro·ne \pə-'drō-nē\ *n, pl* **-nes** *or* **-ni** \-nē\ [It, protector, owner, fr. L *patronus* patron] (1670) **1 a** : MASTER **b** : an Italian innkeeper **2** : one that secures employment esp. for Italian immigrants
pad·u·a·soy \'pa-jə-wə-,sȯi, 'paj-wə-\ *n* [alter. of earlier *poudesoy*, fr. F *pou-de-soie*] (1663) : a corded silk fabric; *also* : a garment made of it
pae·an \'pē-ən\ *n* [L, hymn of thanksgiving esp. addressed to Apollo, fr. Gk *paian, paiōn*, fr. *Paian, Paiōn*, epithet of Apollo in the hymn] (1589) : a joyous song or hymn of praise, tribute, thanksgiving, or triumph; *broadly* : ENCOMIUM, TRIBUTE
paed- *or* **paedo-** — see PED-
pae·di·at·ric, pae·di·a·tri·cian, pae·di·at·rics *chiefly Brit var of* PEDIATRIC, PEDIATRICIAN, PEDIATRICS
pae·do·gen·e·sis \,pē-dō-'je-nə-səs\ *n* [NL] (ca. 1871) : reproduction by young or larval animals : NEOTENY — **pae·do·ge·net·ic** \-jə-'ne-tik\ *or* **pae·do·gen·ic** \-'je-nik\ *adj* — **pae·do·ge·net·i·cal·ly** \-jə-'ne-ti-k(ə-)lē\ *adv*
pae·do·mor·phic \,pē-də-'mȯr-fik\ *adj* (1891) : of, relating to, or involving paedomorphosis or paedomorphism
pae·do·mor·phism \-'mȯr-,fi-zəm\ *n* (ca. 1891) : retention in the adult of infantile or juvenile characters
pae·do·mor·pho·sis \-'mȯr-fə-səs\ *n* [NL, fr. *paed-* + Gk *morphōsis* formation, fr. *morphoun* to form, fr. *morphē* form] (1922) : phylogenetic change that involves retention of juvenile characters by the adult
pa·el·la \pä-'e-lə, -ä-; -'äl-yə, -'ā-yə\ *n* [Catal, lit., pot, pan, fr. MF *paelle*, fr. L *patella* small pan — more at PATELLA] (ca. 1892) : a saffron-flavored dish containing rice, meat, seafood, and vegetables
pae·on \'pē-ən, -,än\ *n* [L, fr. Gk *paiōn, paian, paiōn* paean] (1603) : a metrical foot of four syllables with one long and three short syllables (as in classical prosody) or with one stressed and three unstressed syllables (as in English prosody)
pa·gan \'pā-gən\ *n* [ME, fr. LL *paganus*, fr. L, country dweller, fr. *pagus* country district; akin to L *pangere* to fix — more at PACT] (14c) **1** : HEATHEN **2** : one who has little or no religion and who delights in sensual pleasures and material goods : an irreligious or hedonistic person — **pagan** *adj* — **pa·gan·ish** \-gə-nish\ *adj*
pa·gan·ism \'pā-gə-,ni-zəm\ *n* (15c) **1 a** : pagan beliefs or practices **b** : a pagan religion **2** : the quality or state of being a pagan
pa·gan·ize \-,nīz\ *vb* **-ized; -iz·ing** *vt* (1615) : to make pagan ~ *vi* : to become pagan — **pa·gan·iz·er** *n*
¹page \'pāj\ *n* [ME, fr. MF, fr. OF] (14c) **1 a** (1) : a youth being trained for the medieval rank of knight and in the personal service of a knight (2) : a youth attendant on a person of rank esp. in the medieval period **b** : a boy serving as an honorary attendant at a formal function (as a wedding) **2** : one employed to deliver messages, assist patrons, serve as a guide, or attend to similar duties **3** : an act or instance of paging ⟨a ~ came over the loudspeaker⟩
²page *vt* **paged; pag·ing** (15c) **1** : to wait on or serve in the capacity of a page **2** : to summon by repeatedly calling out the name of
³page *n* [MF, fr. L *pagina*; akin to L *pangere* to fix, fasten — more at PACT] (1589) **1 a** : one of the leaves of a publication or manuscript; *also* : a single side of one of these leaves **b** : the material printed or written on a page **2 a** : a written record **b** : a noteworthy event or period ⟨one of the brightest ~s of my life⟩ **3** : a sizable subdivision of computer memory; *also* : a block of information that fills a page and can be transferred as a unit between the internal and external storage of a computer
⁴page *vb* **paged; pag·ing** (1628) **1** : to number or mark the pages of ~ *vi* : to turn the pages (as of a book or magazine) esp. in a steady or haphazard manner — usu. used with *through*
pag·eant \'pa-jənt\ *n* [ME *pagyn, pageant*, lit., scene of a play, fr. ML *pagina*, perh. fr. L, page] (14c) **1 a** : a mere show : PRETENSE **b** : an

ostentatious display   **2** : SHOW. EXHIBITION: *esp* : an elaborate colorful exhibition or spectacle often with music that consists of a series of tableaux, of a loosely unified drama, or of a procession usu. with floats   **3** : PAGEANTRY 1

pag·eant·ry \'pa-jən-trē\ *n* (1608)   **1** : pageants and the presentation of pageants   **2** : colorful, rich, or splendid display : SPECTACLE   **3** : mere show : empty display

page boy *n* (1874)   **1** : a boy serving as a page   **2** *usu* **pageboy** : an often shoulder-length hairdo with the ends of the hair turned under in a smooth roll

pag·er \'pā-jər\ *n* (1901) : one that pages: *esp* : BEEPER

Pag·et's disease \'pa-jəts-\ *n* [Sir James *Paget* †1899 Eng. surgeon] (1889)   **1** : an eczematous inflammatory precancerous condition esp. of the nipple and areola   **2** : a chronic disease in which the bones become enlarged, weak, and deformed

page–turn·er \'pāj-,tər-nər\ *n* (1972) : an engrossing book or story

pag·i·nate \'pa-jə-,nāt\ *vt* **-nat·ed; -nat·ing** [L *pagina* page] (1884) : 4PAGE

pag·i·na·tion \,pa-jə-'nā-shən\ *n* (1841)   **1** : the action of paging : the condition of being paged   **2 a** : the numbers or marks used to indicate the sequence of pages (as of a book)   **b** : the number and arrangement of pages or an indication of these

pa·go·da \pə-'gō-də\ *n* [Pg *pagode* oriental idol, temple] (1588)   **1** : a Far Eastern tower usu. with roofs curving upward at the division of each of several stories and erected as a temple or memorial

Pah·la·vi \'pa-lə-(,)vē, 'pä-\ *n* [Per *pahlawi*, fr. *Pahlav* Parthia, fr. OPer *Parthava-*] (1773)   **1** : the Iranian language of Sassanian Persia — see INDO-EUROPEAN LANGUAGES table   **2** : a script used for writing Pahlavi

1paid \'pād\ *past and past part of* PAY

2paid *adj* (1817)   **1** : marked by the receipt of pay ⟨~ vacation time⟩   **2** : being or having been paid or paid for ⟨a ~ official⟩ ⟨a ~ political announcement⟩

pail \'pā(ə)l\ *n* [ME *payle, paille*] (14c)   **1** : a usu. cylindrical container with a handle : BUCKET   **2** : the quantity that a pail contains — **pail·ful** \-,fúl\ *n*

pail·lard \pī-'yär, pā-'yär\ *n* [F *paillarde*, fr. *Paillard*, late 19th cent. Fr. restaurateur] (1972) : a piece of beef or veal usu. pounded thin and grilled

pail·lette \pī-'yet, pā-'yet, pə-'let\ *n* [F, fr. *paille* straw — more at PALLET] (ca. 1890)   **1** : a small shiny object (as a spangle) applied in clusters as a decorative trimming (as on women's clothing)   **2** : a trimming made of paillettes

1pain \'pān\ *n* [ME, fr. OF *peine*, fr. L *poena*, fr. Gk *poinē* payment, penalty; akin to Gk *tinein* to pay, *tinesthai* to punish, Av *kaēnā* revenge, Skt *cayate* he revenges] (14c)   **1** : PUNISHMENT   **2** a : usu. localized physical suffering associated with bodily disorder (as a disease or an injury); *also* : a basic bodily sensation induced by a noxious stimulus, received by naked nerve endings, characterized by physical discomfort (as pricking, throbbing, or aching), and typically leading to evasive action   **b** : acute mental or emotional distress or suffering : GRIEF   **3** *pl* : the throes of childbirth   **4** *pl* : trouble, care, or effort taken for the accomplishment of something ⟨was at ~s to reassure us⟩   **5** : one that irks or annoys or is otherwise troublesome — often used in such phrases as *pain in the neck* — **pain·less** \-ləs\ *adj* — **pain·less·ly** *adv* — **pain·less·ness** *n* — **on pain of** *or* **under pain of** : subject to penalty or punishment of ⟨ordered not to leave the country *on pain of death*⟩

2pain *vt* (14c)   **1** : to make suffer or cause distress to : HURT   **2** *archaic* : to put (oneself) to trouble or exertion ~ *vi* **1** *archaic* : SUFFER   **2** : to give or have a sensation of pain

pained \'pānd\ *adj* (14c)   **1** : feeling pain : HURT   **2** : expressing or involving pain ⟨a ~ expression⟩ ⟨with ~ surprise⟩

pain·ful \'pān-fəl\ *adj* **pain·ful·ler** \-fə-lər\; **pain·ful·lest** (14c)   **1 a** : feeling or giving pain   **b** : IRKSOME, ANNOYING   **2** : requiring effort or exertion ⟨a long ~ trip⟩   **3** *archaic* : CAREFUL, DILIGENT — **pain·ful·ly** \-f(ə-)lē\ *adv* — **pain·ful·ness** \-fəl-nəs\ *n*

pain·kill·er \-,ki-lər\ *n* (1853) : something (as a drug) that relieves pain — **pain·kill·ing** \-liŋ\ *adj*

1pains·tak·ing \'pān-,stā-kiŋ\ *n* (1538) : the action of taking pains : diligent care and effort

2painstaking *adj* (1696) : taking pains : expending, showing, or involving diligent care and effort — **pains·tak·ing·ly** \-kiŋ-lē\ *adv*

1paint \'pānt\ *vb* [ME, fr. OF *peint*, pp. of *peindre*, fr. L *pingere* to tattoo, embroider, paint; akin to OE *fāh* variegated, Gk *poikilos* variegated, *pikros* sharp, bitter] *vt* (13c)   **1 a** (1) : to apply color, pigment, or paint to   (2) : to color with a cosmetic   **b** (1) : to apply with a movement resembling that used in painting   (2) : to treat with a liquid by brushing or swabbing ⟨~ the wound with iodine⟩   **2 a** (1) : to produce in lines and colors on a surface by applying pigments   (2) : to depict by such lines and colors   **b** : to decorate, adorn, or variegate by applying lines and colors   **c** : to produce or evoke as if by painting ⟨~s glowing pictures of the farm⟩   **3** : to touch up or cover over by or as if by painting   **4** : to depict as having specified or implied characteristics ⟨~s them whiter than the evidence justifies —Oliver La Farge⟩ ~ *vi*   **1** : to practice the art of painting   **2** : to use cosmetics

2paint *n* (1602)   **1** : the action of painting : something produced by painting   **2** : MAKEUP: *esp* : a cosmetic to add color   **3 a** (1) : a mixture of a pigment and a suitable liquid to form a closely adherent coating when spread on a surface in a thin coat   (2) : the pigment used in this mixture esp. when in the form of a cake ⟨a box of ~s⟩   **b** : an applied coating of paint   **4** : PINTO   **5** : FREE THROW LANE

paint·brush \'pānt-,brəsh\ *n* (1827)   **1** : a brush for applying paint   **2 a** : INDIAN PAINTBRUSH 1   **b** : ORANGE HAWKWEED

painted bunting *n* (ca. 1811) : a brightly colored finch (*Passerina ciris*) that is found from the southern U.S. to Panama

painted cup *n* (1787) : INDIAN PAINTBRUSH 1

painted lady *n* (1753)   **1** : a migratory nymphalid butterfly (*Vanessa cardui*) with wings mottled in brown, orange, black, and white   **2** : PROSTITUTE 1a

painted trillium *n* (1855) : a trillium (*Trillium undulatum*) of northeastern No. America that has a solitary flower with white petals streaked with purple

painted turtle *n* (1876) : a No. American turtle (*Chrysemys picta*) having a greenish to black carapace with yellow, red, or olive bordered scutes and a yellow plastron

1paint·er \'pān-tər\ *n* (14c) : one that paints: as   **a** : an artist who paints   **b** : one who applies paint esp. as an occupation

2pain·ter \'pān-tər\ *n* [ME *paynter*, prob. fr. MF *pendoir, pentoir* clothesline, fr. *pendre* to hang — more at PENDANT] (14c) : a line used for securing or towing a boat

3pain·ter *alter.* of *panther*] (ca. 1764) : COUGAR

paint·er·ly \'pān-tər-lē\ *adj* (1586) : of, relating to, or typical of a painter : ARTISTIC — **paint·er·li·ness** *n*

painter's colic *n* (ca. 1834) : intestinal colic associated with obstinate constipation due to chronic lead poisoning

paint·ing \'pān-tiŋ\ *n* (13c)   **1** : a product of painting; *esp* : a work produced through the art of painting   **2** : the art or occupation of painting

paint·work \'pānt-,wərk\ *n* (1888) *chiefly Brit*   **1** : work with paint   **2** : PAINT 3b

1pair \'par, 'per\ *n, pl* **pairs** *or* **pair** [ME *paire*, fr. OF, fr. L *paria* equal things, fr. neut. pl. of *par* equal] (14c)   **1 a** (1) : two corresponding things designed for use together ⟨a ~ of shoes⟩   (2) : two corresponding bodily parts or members ⟨a ~ of hands⟩   **b** : something made up of two corresponding pieces ⟨a ~ of trousers⟩   **2 a** : two similar or associated things: as   (1) : two mated animals   (2) : a couple in love, engaged, or married ⟨were a devoted ~⟩   (3) : two playing cards of the same value or denomination and esp. of the same rank   (4) : two horses harnessed side by side   (5) : two members of a deliberative body that agree not to vote on a specific issue during a time agreed on; *also* : an agreement not to vote made by the two members   **b** : a partnership esp. of two players in a contest against another partnership   **3** *chiefly dial* : a set or series of small objects (as beads)

2pair *vt* (1606)   **1 a** : to make a pair of — often used with *off* or *up* ⟨~ed off the animals⟩   **b** : to cause to be a member of a pair   **c** : to arrange a voting pair between   **2** : to arrange in pairs ~ *vi*   **1** : to constitute a member of a pair ⟨a sock that didn't ~⟩   **2 a** : to become associated with another — often used with *off* or *up* ⟨~ed up with an old friend⟩   **b** : to become grouped or separated into pairs — often used with *off* ⟨~ed off for the next dance⟩

pair–bond \-,bänd\ *n* (1940) : a monogamous relationship — **pair–bond·ing** *n*

paired–associate learning *n* (1966) : the learning of syllables, digits, or words in pairs (as in the study of a foreign language) so that one member of the pair evokes recall of the other

pair of compasses (1563) : COMPASS 3c

pair of virginals (1542) : VIRGINAL

pair production *n* (1934) : the transformation of a quantum of radiant energy simultaneously into an electron and a positron when the quantum interacts with the intense electric field near a nucleus

pai·sa \pī-'sä\ *n* [ultim. fr. Hindi *paisā*, a quarter-anna coin] (1956)   **1** *pl* **paisa** — see *rupee, taka* at MONEY table   **2** *pl* **pai·se** \-'sä\ — see *rupee* at MONEY table

pais·ley \'pāz-lē\ *adj, often cap* [*Paisley*, Scotland] (1824)   **1** : made typically of soft wool and woven or printed with colorful curved abstract figures   **2** : marked by designs, patterns, or figures typically used in paisley fabrics ⟨a ~ print⟩ — **paisley** *n*

Pai·ute \'pī-,yüt\ *n* (1827)   **1** : a member of an American Indian people orig. of Utah, Arizona, Nevada, and California   **2** : either of the two Uto-Aztecan languages of the Paiute people

pa·ja·ma \pə-'jä-mə, -'ja-\ *n* [Hindi *pājāma*, fr. Per *pā* leg + *jāma* garment] (1883) : PAJAMAS — **pa·ja·maed** \-məd\ *adj*

pa·ja·mas \-məz\ *n pl* [pl. of *pajama*] (1800)   **1** : loose lightweight trousers formerly much worn in the Near East   **2** : a loose usu. two-piece lightweight suit designed esp. for sleeping or lounging

pak choi \'päk-'choi, 'pak-\ *var of* BOK CHOY

pa·ke·ha \'päk-ə-,hä, 'päk-ə-\ *n, pl* **pakeha** *or* **pakehas** *often cap* [Maori] (1832) *chiefly NewZeal* : a person who is not of Maori descent; *esp* : a white person

Paki \'pa-kē, 'pä-\ *n* [short for *Pakistani*] (1964) *chiefly Brit* : a Pakistani immigrant — usu. used disparagingly

1pal \'pal\ *n* [Romany *phral, phal* brother, friend, fr. Skt *bhrātṛ* brother; akin to OE *brōthor* brother] (ca. 1682) : a close friend — **pal·ship** \-,ship\ *n*

2pal *vi* **palled; pal·ling** (1879) : to be or become pals : associate as pals ⟨they've *palled* around for years⟩

1pal·ace \'pa-ləs\ *n* [ME *palais*, fr. OF, fr. L *palatium*, fr. *Palatium*, the Palatine Hill in Rome where the emperors' residences were built] (13c)   **1 a** : the official residence of a chief of state (as a monarch or a president)   **b** *chiefly Brit* : the official residence of an archbishop or bishop   **2 a** : a large stately house   **b** : a large public building ⟨a ~ ⟩ highly decorated place for public amusement or refreshment ⟨a movie ~⟩

2palace *adj* (14c)   **1** : of or relating to a palace   **2** : of, relating to, or involving the intimates of a chief executive ⟨a ~ revolution⟩ ⟨~ politics⟩   **3** : LUXURIOUS, DELUXE

pal·a·din \'pa-lə-dən\ *n* [F, fr. It *paladino*, fr. ML *palatinus* courtier, fr. LL, imperial official — more at PALATINE] (1592)   **1** : a trusted military leader (as for a medieval prince)   **2** : a leading champion of a cause

palae- *or* **palaeo-** *chiefly Brit var of* PALE-

pa·laes·tra \pə-'les-trə\ *n, pl* **-trae** \-(,)trē\ [ME *palestre* arena, fr. L *palaestra* place for wrestling, fr. Gk *palaistra*, fr. *palaiein* to wrestle] (1580)   **1** : a school in ancient Greece or Rome for sports (as wrestling)   **2** : GYMNASIUM

pa·lan·quin \,pa-lən-'kēn, -'kwin, -'kin, 'pa-lən-,; pə-'laŋ-kwən\ *n* [Pg *palanquim*, fr. Malay or Jav *pelangki*, of Indo-Aryan origin; akin to

---

\ə\ abut \'ə\ kitten, F table \ər\ further \a\ ash \ā\ ace \ä\ mop, mar \aú\ out \ch\ chin \e\ bet \ē\ easy \g\ go \i\ hit \ī\ ice \j\ job \ŋ\ sing \ō\ go \ò\ law \òi\ boy \th\ thin \th\ the \ü\ loot \ú\ foot \y\ yet \zh\ vision \ä, k̟, ⁿ, œ, œ̄, ue, ūe, ᵞ\ *see* Guide to Pronunciation

Bengali *pālaṅka* bed] (1588) : a conveyance formerly used esp. in eastern Asia usu. for one person that consists of an enclosed litter borne on the shoulders of men by means of poles

pal·at·able \'pa-lə-tə-bəl\ *adj* (1669) **1** : agreeable to the palate or taste **2** : agreeable or acceptable to the mind — **pal·at·abil·i·ty** \,pa-lə-tə-'bi-lə-tē\ *n* — **pal·at·able·ness** *n* — **pal·at·ably** \'pa-lə-tə-blē\ *adv*

syn PALATABLE, APPETIZING, SAVORY, TASTY, TOOTHSOME mean agreeable or pleasant esp. to the sense of taste. PALATABLE often applies to something that is found to be merely agreeable ⟨butterflies that birds find *palatable*⟩. APPETIZING suggests a whetting of the appetite and applies to aroma and appearance as well as taste ⟨*appetizing* hors d'oeuvres⟩. SAVORY applies to both taste and aroma and suggests piquancy and often spiciness ⟨dumplings with *savory* fillings⟩. TASTY implies a pronounced taste ⟨a tart and *tasty* pie⟩. TOOTHSOME stresses the notion of agreeableness and sometimes implies tenderness or daintiness ⟨an enticing array of *toothsome* desserts⟩.

pal·a·tal \'pa-lə-tᵊl\ *adj* (1728) **1 a** : formed with some part of the tongue near or touching the hard palate posterior to the teethridge ⟨the \sh\ and \y\ in English and the \k\ of *ich* \ik\ in German are examples of ~ consonants⟩ **b** *of a vowel* : FRONT 2 **2** : of, relating to, forming, or affecting the palate — **palatal** *n* — **pal·a·tal·ly** \-tᵊl-ē\ *adv*

pal·a·tal·i·za·tion \,pa-lə-tᵊl-ə-'zā-shən\ *n* (1863) **1** : the quality or state of being palatalized **2** : an act or instance of palatalizing an utterance ⟨in rapid speech the \t\ in *got* undergoes ~ before *you* to yield 'gächə\⟩

pal·a·tal·ize \'pa-lə-tᵊl-,īz\ *vt* **-ized; -iz·ing** (1867) : to pronounce as or change into a palatal sound

pal·ate \'pa-lət\ *n* [ME, fr. L *palatum*] (14c) **1** : the roof of the mouth separating the mouth from the nasal cavity **2 a** : a usu. intellectual taste or liking **b** : the sense of taste

pa·la·tial \pə-'lā-shəl\ *adj* [L *palatium* palace] (1754) **1** : of, relating to, or being a palace **2** : suitable to a palace : MAGNIFICENT — **pa·la·tial·ly** \-shə-lē\ *adv* — **pa·la·tial·ness** *n*

pal·a·ti·nate \pə-'la-tᵊn-ət\ *n* (ca. 1580) : the territory of a palatine

¹pal·a·tine \'pa-lə-,tīn\ *adj* [ME, fr. L *palatinus* imperial, fr. *palatium*] (15c) **1 a** : possessing royal privileges **b** : of or relating to a palatine or a palatinate **2 a** : of or relating to a palace esp. of a Roman or Holy Roman emperor **b** : PALATIAL

²palatine \-,tin, *3 is also* -tēn\ *n* [LL *palatinus* imperial official, fr. L *palatinus,* adj.] (1591) **1 a** : a feudal lord having sovereign power within his domains **b** : a high officer of an imperial palace **2** *cap* : a native or inhabitant of the Palatinate **3** [F, fr. Elisabeth Charlotte of Bavaria †1722 Princess *Palatine*] : a fur cape or stole covering the neck and shoulders

³palatine \-,tin\ *adj* [F *palatin,* fr. L *palatum* palate] (ca. 1656) : of, relating to, or lying near the palate

⁴palatine \-,tin\ *n* (1854) : either of a pair of bones that are situated behind and between the maxillae and in humans are of extremely irregular form

¹pa·lav·er \pə-'la-vər, -'lä-\ *n* [Pg *palavra* word, speech, fr. LL *parabola* parable, speech] (1735) **1 a** : a long parley usu. between persons of different cultures or levels of sophistication **b** : CONFERENCE, DISCUSSION **2** : idle talk **b** : misleading or beguiling speech

²palaver *vb* **pa·lav·ered; pa·lav·er·ing** \pə-'la-və-riŋ, -'lä-; -'lav-riŋ, -'läv-\ *vi* (1773) **1** : to talk profusely or idly **2** : PARLEY ~ *vt* : to use palaver to : CAJOLE

pa·laz·zo \pə-'lät-(,)sō\ *n, pl* **pa·laz·zi** \-(,)sē\ [It, fr. L *palatium* palace] (ca. 1666) : a large imposing building (as a museum or a place of residence) esp. in Italy

¹pale \'pā(ə)l\ *n* [ME, fr. MF *pal* stake, fr. L *palus* — more at POLE] (12c) **1** *archaic* : PALISADE, PALING **2 a** : one of the stakes of a palisade **b** : PICKET **3 a** : a space or field having bounds : ENCLOSURE **b** : a territory or district within certain bounds or under a particular jurisdiction **4** : an area or the limits within which one is privileged or protected (as from censure) ⟨conduct that was beyond the ~⟩ **5** : a perpendicular stripe on a heraldic shield

²pale *vt* **paled; pal·ing** (14c) : to enclose with pales : FENCE

³pale *adj* **pal·er; pal·est** [ME, fr. MF, fr. L *pallidus,* fr. *pallēre* to be pale — more at FALLOW] (14c) **1** : deficient in color or intensity of color : PALLID ⟨a ~ complexion⟩ **2** : not bright or brilliant : DIM ⟨a ~ sun shining through the fog⟩ **3** : FEEBLE, FAINT ⟨a ~ imitation⟩ **4** : deficient in chroma ⟨a ~ pink⟩ — **pale·ly** \'pā(ə)l-lē\ *adv* — **pale·ness** \-nəs\ *n* — **pal·ish** \'pā-lish\ *adj*

⁴pale *vb* **paled; pal·ing** *vi* (14c) : to become pale ~ *vt* : to make pale

pale- *or* **paleo-** *comb form* [Gk *palai-, palaio-* ancient, fr. *palaios,* fr. *palai* long ago; prob. akin to Gk *tēle* far off, Skt *carama* last] **1** : involving or dealing with ancient forms or conditions ⟨*paleobotany*⟩ **2** : early : primitive : archaic ⟨*Paleolithic*⟩

pa·lea \'pā-lē-ə\ *n, pl* **pa·le·ae** \-lē-,ē\ [NL, fr. L, chaff — more at PALLET] (1753) **1** : one of the chaffy scales on the receptacle of many composite plants **2** : the upper bract that with the lemma encloses the flower in grasses — **pa·le·al** \-lē-əl\ *adj*

Pa·le·arc·tic \,pā-lē-'ärk-tik, -'är-tik\ *adj* (1858) : of, relating to, or being a biogeographic region or subregion that includes Europe, Asia north of the Himalayas, northern Arabia, and Africa north of the Sahara

pale dry *adj* (1953) : dry and light colored ⟨*pale dry* ginger ale⟩

pale·face \'pā(ə)l-,fās\ *n* (1822) : a white person

pa·leo·an·thro·pol·o·gy \,pā-lē-ō-,an(t)-thrə-'pä-lə-jē, *esp Brit* ,pa-\ *n* (1916) : a branch of anthropology dealing with fossil hominids — **pa·leo·an·thro·po·log·i·cal** \-pə-'lä-ji-kəl\ *adj* — **pa·leo·an·thro·pol·o·gist** \-'pä-lə-jist\ *n*

pa·leo·bi·ol·o·gy \-bī-'ä-lə-jē\ *n* (1893) : a branch of paleontology concerned with the biology of fossil organisms — **pa·leo·bi·o·log·i·cal** \-bī-ə-'lä-ji-kəl\ *also* **pa·leo·bi·o·log·ic** \-'lä-jik\ *adj* — **pa·leo·bi·ol·o·gist** \-bī-'ä-lə-jist\ *n*

pa·leo·bot·a·ny \,pā-lē-ō-\ *n* [ISV] (1872) : a branch of botany dealing with fossil plants — **pa·leo·bo·tan·i·cal** \-bə-'ta-ni-kəl\ *or* **pa·leo·bo·tan·ic** \-'ta-nik\ *adj* — **pa·leo·bo·tan·i·cal·ly** \-ni-k(ə-)lē\ *adv* — **pa·leo·bot·a·nist** \-'bä-tᵊn-ist, -'bät-nist\ *n*

Pa·leo·cene \'pā-lē-ə-,sēn, *esp Brit* 'pa-\ *adj* [ISV] (1877) : of, relating to, or being the earliest epoch of the Tertiary or the corresponding system of rocks — see GEOLOGIC TIME table — **Paleocene** *n*

pa·leo·cli·ma·tol·o·gy \,pā-lē-ō-,klī-mə-'tä-lə-jē, *esp Brit* ,pa-\ *n* [ISV] (ca. 1909) : a science dealing with the climate of past ages — **pa·leo·cli·ma·tol·o·gist** \-jist\ *n*

pa·leo·ecol·o·gy \-i-'kä-lə-jē, -e-'kä-\ *n* (1898) : a branch of ecology that is concerned with the characteristics of ancient environments and with their relationships to ancient plants and animals — **pa·leo·eco·log·i·cal** \-,ē-kə-'lä-ji-kəl, -,e-kə-\ *also* **pa·leo·eco·log·ic** \-jik\ *adj* — **pa·leo·ecol·o·gist** \-i-'kä-lə-jist, -e-'kä-\ *n*

Pa·leo·gene \'pā-lē-ə-,jēn, *esp Brit* 'pa-\ *adj* [G *Paläogen,* fr. *palä-* pale- + *-gen* (fr. Gk *-genēs* born) — more at GEN] (1882) : of, relating to, or being the earlier part of the Tertiary including the Paleocene, Eocene, and Oligocene or the corresponding system of rocks — **Paleogene** *n*

pa·leo·ge·og·ra·phy \,pā-lē-ō-jē-'ä-grə-fē, *esp Brit* ,pa-\ *n* [ISV] (1881) : the geography of ancient times or of a particular past geological epoch — **pa·leo·geo·graph·ic** \-,jē-ə-'gra-fik\ *or* **pa·leo·geo·graph·i·cal** \-fi-kəl\ *adj* — **pa·leo·geo·graph·i·cal·ly** \-fi-k(ə-)lē\ *adv*

pa·leo·graph·ic \-ə-'gra-fik\ *or* **pa·leo·graph·i·cal** \-fi-kəl\ *adj* (ca. 1842) : relating to writings of former times — **pa·leo·graph·i·cal·ly** \-fi-k(ə-)lē\ *adv*

pa·le·og·ra·phy \,pā-lē-'ä-grə-fē, *esp Brit* ,pa-\ *n* [NL *palaeographia,* fr. Gk *palai-* pale- + *-graphia* -graphy] (ca. 1818) **1** : the study of ancient writings and inscriptions **2 a** : an ancient manner of writing **b** : ancient writings — **pa·le·og·ra·pher** \-fər\ *n*

Pa·leo–In·di·an \,pā-lē-ō-'in-dē-ən, *esp Brit* ,pa-\ *n* (1940) : one of the early American hunting people of Asian origin extant in the late Pleistocene — **Paleo–Indian** *adj*

Pa·leo·lith·ic \,pā-lē-ə-'li-thik, *esp Brit* ,pa-\ *adj* [ISV] (1865) : of or relating to the earliest period of the Stone Age characterized by rough or chipped stone implements

pa·leo·mag·ne·tism \,pā-lē-ō-'mag-nə-,ti-zəm, *esp Brit* ,pa-\ *n* (1854) **1** : the intensity and direction of residual magnetization in ancient rocks **2** : a science that deals with paleomagnetism — **pa·leo·mag·net·ic** \-mag-'ne-tik\ *adj* — **pa·leo·mag·net·i·cal·ly** \-ti-k(ə-)lē\ *adv* — **pa·leo·mag·ne·tist** \-'mag-nə-tist\ *n*

pa·le·on·tol·o·gy \,pā-lē-,än-'tä-lə-jē, -ən-, *esp Brit* ,pa-\ *n* [F *paléontologie,* fr. *palé-* pale- + *onta* existing things (fr. neut. pl. of *ont-, ōn,* prp. of *einai* to be) + F *-logie* -logy — more at IS] (1838) : a science dealing with the life of past geological periods as known from fossil remains — **pa·le·on·to·log·i·cal** \-,än-tᵊl-'ä-ji-kəl\ *or* **pa·le·on·to·log·ic** \-jik\ *also* **pa·le·on·tol·o·gist** \-,än-'tä-lə-jist, -ən-\ *n*

pa·leo·pa·thol·o·gy \,pā-lē-ō-pə-'thä-lə-jē, -pa-'thä-, *esp Brit* ,pa-lē-\ *n* (1893) : a branch of pathology concerned with diseases of former times as evidenced esp. in fossil or other remains — **pa·leo·patho·log·i·cal** \-,pa-thə-'lä-ji-kəl\ *adj* — **pa·leo·pa·thol·o·gist** \-pə-'thä-lə-jist, -pa-\ *n*

Pa·leo·zo·ic \,pā-lē-ə-'zō-ik, *esp Brit* ,pa-\ *adj* (1838) : of, relating to, originating in, or being an era of geological history that extends from the beginning of the Cambrian to the close of the Permian and is marked by the culmination of nearly all classes of invertebrates except the insects and in the later epochs by the appearance of terrestrial plants, amphibians, and reptiles; *also* : relating to the corresponding system of rocks — see GEOLOGIC TIME table — **Paleozoic** *n*

pa·leo·zo·ol·o·gy \-zō-'ä-lə-jē, -zə-'wä-\ *n* [ISV] (1857) : a branch of paleontology dealing with ancient and fossil animals — **pa·leo·zoo·log·i·cal** \-,zō-ə-'lä-ji-kəl\ *adj* — **pa·leo·zo·ol·o·gist** \-jist\ *n*

pal·et \pā-'let, 'pa-lət\ *n* [*pale* palea + ¹*-et*] (ca. 1880) : PALEA

pal·ette \'pa-lət\ *n* [F, fr. MF, dim. of *pale* spade, fr. L *pala;* prob. akin to L *pangere* to fix — more at PACT] (1622) **1** : a thin oval or rectangular board or tablet that a painter holds and mixes pigments on **2 a** : the set of colors put on the palette **b** (1) : a particular range, quality, or use of color (2) : a comparable range, quality, or use of available elements esp. in another art (as music)

palette knife *n* (1759) : a knife with usu. a flexible steel blade and no cutting edge used to mix colors or to apply colors (as to a painting)

pal·frey \'pȯl-frē\ *n, pl* **palfreys** [ME, fr. OF *palefrei,* fr. ML *palafredus,* fr. LL *paraveredus* post-horse for secondary roads, fr. Gk *para-* beside, subsidiary + LL *veredus* post-horse, fr. a Gaulish word akin to W *gorwydd* horse; akin to OIr *rēidid* he rides — more at PARA-, RIDE] (13c) *archaic* : a saddle horse other than a warhorse; *esp* : a lady's light easy-gaited horse

Pa·li \'pä-lē\ *n* [Skt *pāli* row, series of Buddhist sacred texts] (1800) : an Indo-Aryan language used as the liturgical and scholarly language of Theravada Buddhism — see INDO-EUROPEAN LANGUAGES table

pal·i·mo·ny \'pa-lə-,mō-nē\ *n* [blend of *pal* and *alimony*] (1979) : a court-ordered allowance paid by one member of a couple formerly living together out of wedlock to the other

pa·limp·sest \'pa-ləm(p)-,sest, pə-'lim(p)-\ *n* [L *palimpsestus,* fr. Gk *palimpsēstos* scraped again, fr. *palin* + *psēn* to rub, scrape; akin to Skt *psāti, babhasti* he chews] (1825) **1** : writing material (as a parchment or tablet) used one or more times after earlier writing has been erased **2** : something having usu. diverse layers or aspects apparent beneath the surface

pal·in·drome \'pa-lən-,drōm\ *n* [Gk *palindromos* running back again, fr. *palin* back, again + *dramein* to run; akin to Gk *polos* axis, pole — more at POLE, DROMEDARY] (ca. 1629) : a word, verse, or sentence (as "Able was I ere I saw Elba") or a number (as 1881) that reads the same backward or forward — **pal·in·drom·ic** \,pa-lən-'drō-mik, -'drä-\ *adj* — **pal·in·drom·ist** \'pa-lən-,drō-mist\ *n*

pal·ing \'pā-liŋ\ *n* (15c) **1** : a fence of pales or pickets **2** : wood for making pales **3** : a pale or picket for a fence

pal·in·gen·e·sis \,pa-lən-'je-nə-səs\ *n* [NL, fr. Gk *palin* again + L *genesis* genesis] (1818) : METEMPSYCHOSIS

pal·in·ge·net·ic \-jə-'ne-tik\ *adj* (1833) : of or relating to palingenesis

pal·in·ode \'pa-lə-,nōd\ *n* [Gk *palinōidia,* fr. *palin* + *aeidein* to sing — more at ODE] (1599) **1** : an ode or song recanting or retracting something in an earlier poem **2** : a formal retraction

¹pal·i·sade \,pa-lə-'sād\ *n* [F *palissade,* ultim. fr. L *palus* stake — more at POLE] (1600) **1 a** : a fence of stakes esp. for defense **b** : a long strong stake pointed at the top and set close with others as a defense **2** : a line of bold cliffs

²palisade *vt* **pal·i·sad·ed; -sad·ing** (1632) : to fortify with palisades

palisade cell *n* (1875) : a cell of the palisade layer

palisade layer *n* (1914) : a layer of columnar cells rich in chloroplasts found beneath the upper epidermis of foliage leaves — called also *pali-*

sade mesophyll, palisade parenchyma, palisade tissue; compare SPONGY PARENCHYMA

¹pall \'pȯl\ *vb* [ME, short for *appallen* to become pale — more at APPALL] *vi* (14c) **1** : to lose strength or effectiveness **2** : to lose in interest or attraction ⟨his humor began to ~ on us⟩ **3** : to become tired of something ~ *vt* **1** : to cause to become insipid **2** : to deprive of pleasure in something by satiating *syn* see SATIATE

²pall *n* [ME, cloak, mantle, fr. OE *pæll*, fr. L *pallium*] (14c) **1** : PALLIUM 1a **2 a** : a square of linen usu. stiffened with cardboard that is used to cover the chalice **b** (1) : a heavy cloth draped over a coffin (2) : a coffin esp. when holding a body **3** : something that covers or conceals; *esp* : an overspreading element that produces an effect of gloom ⟨a ~ of thick black smoke⟩

³pall *vt* (15c) : to cover with a pall : DRAPE

Pal·la·di·an \pə-'lā-dē-ən, -'lä-\ *adj* (1731) : of or relating to a revived classical style in architecture based on the works of Andrea Palladio — **Pal·la·di·an·ism** \-ə-,ni-zəm\ *n*

¹pal·la·di·um \pə-'lā-dē-əm\ *n* [ME, fr. L, fr. Gk *palladion*, fr. *Pallad-, Pallas*] **1** *cap* : a statue of Pallas whose preservation was believed to ensure the safety of Troy **2** *pl* **pal·la·dia** \-dē-ə\ : SAFEGUARD

²palladium *n* [NL, fr. *Pallad-, Pallas*, an asteroid] (1803) : a silverwhite ductile malleable metallic element of the platinum group that is used esp. in electrical contacts, as a catalyst, and in alloys — see ELEMENT table — **pal·la·dous** \pə-'lā-dəs\ *adj*

Pal·las \'pa-ləs\ *n* [L *Pallad-, Pallas*, fr. Gk] : ATHENA

pall·bear·er \'pȯl-,bar-ər, -,ber-\ *n* [²pall] (1707) : a person who helps to carry the coffin at a funeral; *also* : a member of the escort or honor guard of the coffin who does not actually help to carry it

¹pal·let \'pa-lət\ *n* [ME *pailet*, fr. (assumed) MF *paillet*, fr. *paille* straw, fr. L *palea* chaff, straw; akin to Skt *palāva* chaff] (14c) **1** : a strawfilled tick or mattress **2** : a small, hard, or temporary bed

²pallet *n* [ME *palette*, lit., small shovel, fr. MF — more at PALETTE] (1558) **1** : a wooden flat-bladed instrument **2** : a lever or surface in a timepiece that receives an impulse from the escapement wheel and imparts motion to a balance or pendulum **3** : a portable platform for handling, storing, or moving materials and packages (as in warehouses, factories, or vehicles)

pal·let·ise *Brit var of* PALLETIZE

pal·let·ize \'pa-lə-,tīz\ *vt* **-ized; -iz·ing** (1944) : to place on, transport, or store by means of pallets — **pal·let·i·za·tion** \,pa-lə-tə-'zā-shən\ *n*

pal·lette \pa-'let\ *n* [alter. of *pallet*] (1834) : one of the plates at the armpits of a suit of armor — see ARMOR illustration

pal·li·al \'pa-lē-əl\ *adj* [NL *pallium*] (1836) **1** : of, relating to, or produced by a mantle of a mollusk **2** : of or relating to the cerebral cortex

pal·liasse \pal-'yas\ *n* [modif. of F *paillasse*, fr. *paille* straw] (1763) : a thin straw mattress used as a pallet

pal·li·ate \'pa-lē-,āt\ *vt* **-at·ed; -at·ing** [ME, fr. LL *palliatus*, pp. of *palliare* to cloak, conceal, fr. L *pallium* cloak] (15c) **1** : to reduce the violence of (a disease) : ABATE **2** : to cover by excuses and apologies **3** : to moderate the intensity of ⟨trying to ~ the boredom⟩ — **pal·li·a·tion** \,pa-lē-'ā-shən\ *n* — **pal·li·a·tor** \'pa-lē-,ā-tər\ *n*

¹pal·li·a·tive \'pa-lē-,ā-tiv, 'pal-yə-\ *adj* (15c) : serving to palliate ⟨~ surgery⟩ — **pal·lia·tive·ly** *adv*

²palliative *n* (1724) : something that palliates

pal·lid \'pa-ləd\ *adj* [L *pallidus* — more at PALE] (1590) **1** : deficient in color : WAN ⟨a ~ countenance⟩ **2** : lacking sparkle or liveliness : DULL ⟨a ~ entertainment⟩ — **pal·lid·ly** *adv* — **pal·lid·ness** *n*

pal·li·um \'pa-lē-əm\ *n, pl* **-lia** \-lē-ə\ *or* **-li·ums** [ME, fr. L] (12c) **1 a** : a white woolen band with pendants in front and back worn over the chasuble by a pope or archbishop as a symbol of full episcopal authority **b** : a draped rectangular cloth worn as a cloak by men of ancient Greece and Rome **2** [NL, fr. L, cloak] **a** : CEREBRAL CORTEX **b** : the mantle of a mollusk, brachiopod, or bird

pall–mall \'pel-'mel, ,pal-'mal, *US often* ,pȯl-'mȯl\ *n* [MF *pallemaille*, fr. It *pallamaglio*, fr. *palla* ball (of Gmc origin; akin to OHG *balla* ball) + *maglio* mallet, fr. L *malleus* — more at BALL, MAUL] (1598) : a 17th century game in which each player attempts to drive a wooden ball with a mallet down an alley and through a raised ring in as few strokes as possible; *also* : the alley in which it is played

pal·lor \'pa-lər\ *n* [ME, fr. L, fr. *pallēre* to be pale — more at FALLOW] (15c) : deficiency of color esp. of the face : PALENESS

pal·ly \'pa-lē\ *adj* (1895) : sharing the relationship of pals : INTIMATE

¹palm \'päm, 'pälm, 'pȯm, 'pȯlm, *NewEng also* 'pam\ *n* [ME, fr. OE, fr. L *palma* palm of the hand, palm tree; fr. the resemblance of the tree's leaves to the outstretched hand; akin to Gk *palamē* palm of the hand, OE *folm*, OIr *lám* hand] (bef. 12c) **1** : any of a family (Palmae, the palm family) of mostly tropical or subtropical monocotyledonous trees, shrubs, or vines with usu. a simple stem and a terminal crown of large pinnate or fan-shaped leaves **2** : a leaf of the palm as a symbol of victory or rejoicing; *also* : a branch (as of laurel) similarly used **3** : a symbol of triumph; *also* : VICTORY, TRIUMPH **4** : an addition to a military decoration in the form of a palm frond esp. to indicate a second award of the basic decoration — **palm·like** \-,līk\ *adj*

²palm *n* [ME *paume*, fr. MF, fr. L *palma*] (14c) **1** : the somewhat concave part of the human hand between the bases of the fingers and the wrist or the corresponding part of the forefoot of a lower mammal **2** : a flat expanded part esp. at the end of a base or stalk (as of an anchor) **3** [L *palmus*, fr. *palma*] : a unit of length based on the breadth or length of the hand **4** : something (as a part of a glove) that covers the palm of the hand **5** : an act of palming (as of cards)

³palm *vt* (1673) **1 a** : to conceal in or with the hand ⟨~ a card⟩ **b** : to pick up stealthily **2** : to impose by fraud ⟨a second imposter to be ~ed upon you —Sir Walter Scott⟩ **3** : to touch with the palm: as **a** : to stroke with the palm or hand **b** : to shake hands with **c** : to allow (a basketball) to come to rest momentarily in the hand while dribbling thus committing a violation

pal·mar \'pal-mər, 'pä-, 'päl-, 'pȯ-, 'pȯl-\ *adj* (1656) : of, relating to, or involving the palm of the hand

pal·ma·ry \'pal-mə-rē, 'pä-, 'päl-, 'pȯ-, 'pȯl-\ *adj* [L *palmarius* deserving the palm, fr. *palma*] (1657) : OUTSTANDING, BEST

pal·mate \'pal-,māt, 'pä-, 'päl-, 'pȯ-, 'pȯl- *also* **pal·mat·ed** \-,mā-təd\ *adj* (ca. 1760) : resembling a hand with the fingers spread: as **a** : having lobes radiating from a common point ⟨a ~ leaf⟩ — see LEAF illustration **b** : having the distal portion broad, flat, and lobed ⟨a ~ antler⟩ — **pal·mate·ly** *adv* — **pal·ma·tion** \pal-'mā-shən, pä-, 'päl-, 'pȯ-, 'pȯl-\ *n*

palmed \'pämd, 'pälmd, 'pȯmd, 'pȯlmd, *NewEng also* 'pamd\ *adj* (15c) : having a palm of a specified kind — used in combination ⟨leather-*palmed* gloves⟩

palm·er \'pä-mər, 'päl-, 'pȯ-, 'pȯl-\ *n* (13c) : a person wearing two crossed palm leaves as a sign of a pilgrimage made to the Holy Land

palm·er·worm \-,wərm\ *n* (1560) : a caterpillar that suddenly appears in great numbers devouring herbage

pal·mette \,pal-'met\ *n* [F, fr. *palme* palm, fr. L *palma*] (1850) : a decorative motif suggestive of a palm

palmetto 1

pal·met·to \pal-'me-(,)tō *also* pä-, päl-, pȯ-, pȯl-\ *n, pl* **-tos** *or* **-toes** [modif. of Sp *palmito*, fr. *palma* palm, fr. L] (ca. 1746) **1** : any of several usu. low-growing fan-leaved palms; *esp* : CABBAGE PALMETTO **2** : strips of the leaf blade of a palmetto used in weaving

palm·ist \'pä-mist, 'päl-, 'pȯ-, 'pȯl-\ *n* [prob. back-formation fr. *palmistry*] (1886) : one who practices palmistry

palm·ist·ry \'pä-mə-strē, 'päl-, 'pȯ-, 'pȯl-\ *n* [ME *pawmestry*, prob. fr. *paume* palm + *maistrie* mastery] (15c) : the art or practice of reading a person's character or future from the lines on the palms

pal·mi·tate \'pal-mə-,tāt, 'pä-, 'päl-, 'pȯ-, 'pȯl-\ *n* (1873) : a salt or ester of palmitic acid

pal·mit·ic acid \(,)pal-'mi-tik-, (,)pä-, (,)päl-, (,)pȯ-, (,)pȯl-\ *n* [ISV, fr. *palmitin*] (1857) : a waxy crystalline saturated fatty acid $C_{16}H_{32}O_2$ occurring free or in the form of esters (as glycerides) in most fats and fatty oils and in several essential oils and waxes

pal·mi·tin \'pal-mə-tən, 'pä-, 'päl-, 'pȯ-, 'pȯl-\ *n* [F *palmitine*, prob. fr. *palmite* pith of the palm tree, fr. Sp *palmito*] (1857) : an ester of glycerol and palmitic acid; *esp* : a solid ester found in animal fats

palm off *vt* (1822) **1** : to dispose of usu. by trickery or guile **2** : PASS OFF 2

palm oil *n* (1705) : an edible fat obtained from the flesh of the fruit of several palms and used esp. in soap and lubricating greases

Palm Sunday *n* [fr. the palm branches strewn in Christ's way] (bef. 12c) : the Sunday before Easter celebrated in commemoration of Christ's triumphal entry into Jerusalem

palmy \'pä-mē, 'päl-, 'pȯ-, 'pȯl- *NewEng also* 'pa-mē\ *adj* **palm·i·er; -est** (1602) **1** : marked by prosperity : FLOURISHING **2** : abounding in or bearing palms

pal·my·ra \pal-'mī-rə\ *n* [Pg *palmeira*, fr. *palma* palm, fr. L] (1698) : a tall fan-leaved palm (*Borassus flabellifer*) of India cultivated for its hard resistant wood, fiber, and sugar-rich sap — called also *palmyra palm*

pal·o·mi·no \,pa-lə-'mē-(,)nō\ *n, pl* **-nos** [AmerSp, fr. Sp, like a dove, fr. L *palumbinus*, fr. *palumbes* ringdove; akin to Gk *peleia* dove, L *pallēre* to be pale — more at FALLOW] (1914) : a horse that is pale cream to gold in color and has a flaxen or white mane and tail

pa·loo·ka \pə-'lü-kə\ *n* [origin unknown] (1925) **1** : an inexperienced or incompetent boxer **2** : OAF, LOUT

pal·o·ver·de \,pa-lō-'ver-(,)dā, ,pä-, -'vər-\ *n* [MexSp, lit., green tree] (1854) **1** : any of several small spiny leguminous trees or shrubs (genus *Cercidium*) that have greenish branches and are found chiefly in dry regions of the southwestern U.S. and Mexico **2** : JERUSALEM THORN

palp \'palp\ *n* [NL *palpus*] (1842) : PALPUS

pal·pa·ble \'pal-pə-bəl\ *adj* [ME, fr. LL *palpabilis*, fr. L *palpare* to stroke, caress — more at FEEL] (14c) **1** : capable of being touched or felt : TANGIBLE **2** : easily perceptible : NOTICEABLE **3** : easily perceptible by the mind : MANIFEST *syn* see PERCEPTIBLE — **pal·pa·bil·i·ty** \,pal-pə-'bi-lə-tē\ *n* — **pal·pa·bly** \'pal-pə-blē\ *adv*

pal·pate \'pal-,pāt\ *vt* **pal·pat·ed; pal·pat·ing** [prob. back-formation fr. *palpation*, fr. L *palpation-, palpatio*, fr. *palpare*] (ca. 1852) : to examine by touch esp. medically — **pal·pa·tion** \pal-'pā-shən\ *n*

pal·pe·bral \pal-'pē-brəl\ *adj* [LL *palpebralis*, fr. L *palpebra* eyelid; akin to L *palpare*] (1840) : of, relating to, or located on or near the eyelids

pal·pi·tant \'pal-pə-tənt\ *adj* (1837) : marked by trembling or throbbing

pal·pi·tate \'pal-pə-,tāt\ *vi* **-tat·ed; -tat·ing** [L *palpitatus*, pp. of *palpitare*, freq. of *palpare* to stroke] (ca. 1623) : to beat rapidly and strongly : THROB — **pal·pi·ta·tion** \,pal-pə-'tā-shən\ *n*

pal·pus \'pal-pəs\ *n, pl* **pal·pi** \-,pī, -(,)pē\ [NL, fr. L, caress, soft palm of the hand, fr. *palpare*] (1813) : a segmented usu. tactile or gustatory process on an arthropod mouthpart — see INSECT illustration

pals·grave \'pȯlz-,grāv\ *n* [D *paltsgrave*] (1539) : COUNT PALATINE 1a

pal·sied \'pȯl-zēd\ *adj* (1550) : affected with or as if with palsy

¹pal·sy \'pȯl-zē\ *n, pl* **palsies** [ME *parlesie*, fr. MF *paralisie*, fr. L *paralysis*] (14c) **1** : PARALYSIS **2** : a condition marked by uncontrollable tremor of the body or a part

²palsy *vt* **pal·sied; pal·sy·ing** (1615) : to affect with or as if with palsy

³palsy \'pal-zē\ *adj* (1951) : PALSY-WALSY

palsy–walsy \,pal-zē-'wal-zē\ *adj* [redupl. of *palsy*] (1943) *slang* : being or appearing to be very intimate

pal·ter \'pȯl-tər\ *vi* **pal·tered; pal·ter·ing** \-t(ə-)riŋ\ [origin unknown] (1601) **1** : to act insincerely or deceitfully : EQUIVOCATE **2** : HAGGLE, CHAFFER *syn* see LIE — **pal·ter·er** \-tər-ər\ *n*

pal·try \'pȯl-trē\ *adj* **pal·tri·er; -est** [obs. *paltry* trash, fr. dial. *palt, pelt* piece of coarse cloth, trash; akin to MLG *palte* rag] (1570) **1** : IN-

FERIOR, TRASHY **2** : MEAN, DESPICABLE **3** : TRIVIAL **4** : MEAGER, MEA-SLY ⟨made a ∼ donation⟩ — **pal·tri·ness** *n*

pa·lu·dal \pə-'lü-d°l, 'pal-yə-d°l\ *adj* [L *palud-, palus* marsh; akin to Skt *palvala* pond] (ca. 1820) : of or relating to marshes or fens : MARSHY

paly \'pā-lē\ *adj* (1560) *archaic* : somewhat pale : PALLID

pal·y·nol·o·gy \,pa-lə-'nä-lə-jē\ *n* [Gk *palynein* to sprinkle, fr. *palē* fine meal] (1944) : a branch of science dealing with pollen and spores — **pal·y·no·log·i·cal** \-nə-'lä-ji-kəl\ *also* **pal·y·no·log·ic** \-jik\ *adj* — **pal·y·no·log·i·cal·ly** \-ji-k(ə-)lē\ *adv* — **pal·y·nol·o·gist** \-'nä-lə-jist\ *n*

pam·pa \'pam-pə, 'päm-\ *n, pl* **pam·pas** \-pəz, -pəs\ [AmerSp, fr. Quechua] (1704) : an extensive generally grass-covered plain of temperate So. America east of the Andes — PRAIRIE

pam·pas grass \-pəz, -pəs-\ *n* (ca. 1851) : a So. American grass (*Cortaderia selloana*) often grown for ornament that has showy white panicles borne on tall stems

pam·pe·an \'pam-pē-ən, pam-', päm-', päm-\ *adj* (1839) : of or relating to the pampas of So. America or their Indian inhabitants

pam·per \'pam-pər\ *vt* **pam·pered; pam·per·ing** \-p(ə-)riŋ\ [ME, prob. of D origin; akin to Flem *pamperen* to pamper] (14c) **1** *archaic* : to cram with rich food : GLUT **2 a** : to treat with extreme or excessive care and attention ⟨∼ed their guests⟩ **b** : GRATIFY, HUMOR ⟨enabled him to ∼ his wanderlust —*New Yorker*⟩ **syn** see INDULGE — **pam·per·er** \-pər-ər\ *n*

pam·pe·ro \pam-'per-(,)ō, päm-\ *n, pl* **-ros** [AmerSp, fr. *pampa*] (1818) : a strong cold wind from the west or southwest that sweeps over the pampas

pam·phlet \'pam(p)-flət\ *n* [ME *pamflet* unbound booklet, fr. *Pamphilus seu De Amore* Pamphilus or On Love, popular Latin love poem of the 12th cent.] (14c) : an unbound printed publication with no cover or with a paper cover

¹**pam·phle·teer** \,pam(p)-flə-'tir\ *n* (1642) : a writer of pamphlets attacking something or urging a cause

²**pamphleteer** *vi* (1698) **1** : to write and publish pamphlets **2** : to engage in partisan arguments indirectly in writings

¹**pan** \'pan\ *n* [ME *panne*, fr. OE (akin to OHG *phanna* pan), fr. L *patina*, fr. Gk *patanē*] (bef. 12c) **1 a** : a usu. broad, shallow, and open container for domestic use (as for warming, baking, or frying) **b** : any of various similar usu. metal receptacles: as (1) : the hollow part of the lock in a firelock or flintlock gun that receives the priming (2) : either of the receptacles in a pair of scales (3) : a round shallow metal container for separating metal (as gold) from waste by washing **2 a** (1) : a natural basin or depression in land (2) : a similar artificial basin (as for evaporating brine) **b** : a drifting fragment of the flat thin ice that forms in bays or along the shore **3** : HARDPAN 1 **4** *slang* : FACE **5** : a harsh criticism

²**pan** *vb* **panned; pan·ning** *vt* (1839) **1 a** : to wash in a pan for the purpose of separating heavy particles **b** : to separate (as gold) by panning **c** : to place in a pan **2** : to criticize severely ⟨the show was *panned*⟩ ∼ *vi* **1** : to wash material (as earth or gravel) in a pan in search of metal (as gold) **2** : to yield precious metal in the process of panning — usu. used with *out*

³**pan** \'pän\ *n* [Hindi *pān*, fr. Skt *parṇa* wing, leaf — more at FERN] (1616) **1** : a betel leaf **2** : a masticatory of betel nut, mineral lime, and pan

⁴**pan** \'pan\ *n* [short for *panorama*] (ca. 1922) **1** : the process of panning a motion-picture or video camera **2** : a shot in which the camera is panned

⁵**pan** \'pan\ *vb* **panned; pan·ning** *vt* (1930) : to rotate (as a motion‑picture camera) so as to keep an object in the picture or secure a panoramic effect ∼ *vi* **1** : to pan a motion‑picture or video camera **2** *of a camera* : to undergo panning

Pan \'pan\ *n* [L, fr. Gk] : a Greek god of pastures, flocks, and shepherds usu. represented as having the legs, horns, and ears of a goat

pan- *comb form* [Gk, fr. *pan*, neut. of *pant-, pas* all, every; akin to Toch B *pont-* all] **1** : all : completely ⟨*panchromatic*⟩ **2 a** : involving all of a (specified) group ⟨*Pan-American*⟩ **b** : advocating or involving the union of a (specified) group ⟨*Pan-Slavism*⟩ **3** : whole : general ⟨*panleukopenia*⟩

pan·a·cea \,pa-nə-'sē-ə\ *n* [L, fr. Gk *panakeia*, fr. *panakēs* all‑healing, fr. *pan-* + *akos* remedy] (1548) : a remedy for all ills or difficulties : CURE‑ALL — **pan·a·ce·an** \-'sē-ən\ *adj*

pa·nache \pə-'nash, -'näsh\ *n* [MF *pennache*, fr. OIt *pennacchio*, fr. LL *pinnaculum* small wing — more at PINNACLE] (1553) **1** : an ornamental tuft (as of feathers) esp. on a helmet **2** : dash or flamboyance in style and action : VERVE

pa·na·da \pə-'nä-də\ *n* [Sp, fr. *pan* bread, fr. L *panis* — more at FOOD] (ca. 1598) : a paste of flour or bread crumbs and water or stock used as a base for sauce or a binder for forcemeat or stuffing

pan·a·ma \'pa-nə-,mä, -,mȯ\ *n, often cap* [AmerSp *panamá*, fr. *Panama*, Central America] (1848) : a lightweight hat of natural‑colored straw hand‑plaited of narrow strips from the young leaves of the jipijapa; *also* : a machine‑made imitation of this

Panama Red *n* (1967) : marijuana of a reddish tint that is of Panamanian origin and is held to be very potent

Pan–Amer·i·can \,pa-nə-'mer-ə-kən\ *adj* (1889) : of, relating to, or involving the independent republics of No. and So. America

Pan–Amer·i·can·ism \-kə-,ni-zəm\ *n* (1901) : a movement for greater cooperation among the Pan‑American nations

pan·a·tela \,pa-nə-'te-lə\ *n* [Sp, AmerSp, a long thin biscuit, ultim. fr. L *panis* bread] (1847) : a long slender straight‑sided cigar

¹**pan·cake** \'pan-,kāk\ *n* (14c) : a flat cake made of thin batter and cooked (as on a griddle) on both sides

²**pancake** *vb* **pan·caked; pan·cak·ing** *vi* (1911) : to make a pancake landing ∼ *vt* : to cause to pancake

Pan–Cake \'pan-,kāk\ *trademark* — used for a cosmetic in semimoist cake form

pancake landing *n* (1928) : a landing in which the airplane is stalled usu. unintentionally above the landing surface causing it to drop abruptly in an approximately horizontal position with little forward motion

pan·cet·ta \(,)pan-'che-tə\ *n* [It, fr. dim. of *pancia* belly, paunch, fr. L *pantic-, pantex*] (1974) : unsmoked bacon used esp. in Italian cuisine

pan·chax \'pan-,kaks\ *n* [NL] (1961) : any of various small brilliantly colored Old World killifishes (genus *Aplocheilus*) often kept in the tropical aquarium

Pan·chen Lama \'pän-chən-\ *n* [*Panchen* fr. Chin (Beijing) *bānchán*] (1794) : the lama who is the chief spiritual adviser of the Dalai Lama

pan·chro·mat·ic \,pan-krō-'ma-tik\ *adj* [ISV] (1903) : sensitive to light of all colors in the visible spectrum ⟨∼ film⟩

pan·cra·ti·um \pan-'krā-shē-əm\ *n* [L, fr. Gk *pankration*, fr. *pan-* + *kratos* strength — more at HARD] (1603) : an ancient Greek athletic contest involving both boxing and wrestling

pan·cre·as \'paŋ-krē-əs, 'pan-\ *n* [NL, fr. Gk *pankreas* sweetbread, fr. *pan-* + *kreas* flesh, meat — more at RAW] (1578) : a large lobulated gland of vertebrates that secretes digestive enzymes and the hormones insulin and glucagon — **pan·cre·at·ic** \,paŋ-krē-'a-tik, ,pan-\ *adj*

pancreat- *comb form* [NL, fr. Gk *pankreat-, pancreas*] : pancreas ⟨*pancreatic*⟩

pan·cre·a·tec·to·my \,paŋ-krē-ə-'tek-tə-mē, ,pan-\ *n* (ca. 1900) : surgical removal of all or part of the pancreas — **pan·cre·a·tec·to·mized** \-,mīzd\ *adj*

pancreatic duct *n* (ca. 1860) : a duct leading from the pancreas and opening into the duodenum

pancreatic juice *n* (ca. 1666) : a clear alkaline secretion of pancreatic enzymes (as trypsin and lipase) that flows into the duodenum and acts on food already acted on by the gastric juice and saliva

pan·cre·a·tin \pan-'krē-ə-tən; 'paŋ-krē-, 'pan-\ *n* (ca. 1860) : a mixture of enzymes from the pancreatic juice; *also* : a preparation containing such a mixture

pan·cre·a·ti·tis \,paŋ-krē-ə-'tī-təs, ,pan-\ *n, pl* **-tit·i·des** \-'ti-tə-,dēz\ [NL] (ca. 1842) : inflammation of the pancreas

pan·cre·o·zy·min \-krē-ō-'zī-mən\ *n* [*pancreas* + *-o-* + *zym-* + ¹*-in*] (1943) : CHOLECYSTOKININ

pan·cy·to·pe·nia \,pan-,sī-tə-'pē-nē-ə\ *n* [NL, fr. *pan-* + *cyt-* + *-penia*] (ca. 1941) : an abnormal reduction in the number of erythrocytes, white blood cells, and blood platelets in the blood; *also* : a disorder (as aplastic anemia) characterized by such a reduction

pan·da \'pan-də\ *n* [F, fr. a language of the southeast Himalayas] (1835) **1** : a long‑tailed largely herbivorous mammal (*Ailurus fulgens*) that is related to and resembles the American raccoon, has long rusty or chestnut fur, and is found from the Himalayas to China **2** : GIANT PANDA

A panda 1, *B* giant panda

panda car *n* [fr. its black and white coloration] (1967) *Brit* : a police patrol car

pan·da·nus \pan-'dā-nəs, -'da-\ *n, pl* **-ni** \-nī\ [NL, genus name, fr. Malay *pandan* screw pine] (1830) : SCREW PINE; *also* : a fiber made from screw‑pine leaves and used for woven products (as mats)

Pan·da·rus \'pan-də-rəs\ *n* [L, fr. Gk *Pandaros*] : a Lycian archer in the Trojan War who in medieval legend procures Cressida for Troilus

pan·dect \'pan-,dekt\ *n* [LL *Pandectae*, the Pandects, digest of Roman civil law (6th cent. A.D.), fr. L, pl. of *pandectes* encyclopedic work, fr. Gk *pandektēs* all‑receiving, fr. *pan-* + *dechesthai* to receive; akin to Gk *dokein* to seem, seem good — more at DECENT] (1533) **1** : a complete code of the laws of a country or system of law **2** : a treatise covering an entire subject

¹**pan·dem·ic** \pan-'de-mik\ *adj* [LL *pandemus*, fr. Gk *pandēmos* of all the people, fr. *pan-* + *dēmos* people — more at DEMAGOGUE] (1666) : occurring over a wide geographic area and affecting an exceptionally high proportion of the population ⟨∼ malaria⟩

²**pandemic** *n* (ca. 1853) : a pandemic outbreak of a disease

Pan·de·mo·ni·um \,pan-də-'mō-nē-əm\ *n* [NL, fr. Gk *pan-* + *daimōn* evil spirit — more at DEMON] **1** : the capital of Hell in Milton's *Paradise Lost* **2** : the infernal regions : HELL **3** *not cap* : a wild uproar : TUMULT

¹**pan·der** \'pan-dər\ *n* [ME *Pandare* Pandarus, fr. L *Pandarus*] (1530) **1 a** : a go‑between in love intrigues **b** : PIMP **2** : someone who caters to or exploits the weaknesses of others

²**pander** *vi* **pan·dered; pan·der·ing** \-d(ə-)riŋ\ (1602) : to act as a pander; *esp* : to provide gratification for others' desires ⟨films that ∼ to the basest emotions⟩ — **pan·der·er** \-dər-ər\ *n*

pan·dit \'pən-dət, 'pən-\ *n* [Hindi *paṇḍit*, fr. Skt *paṇḍita*] (ca. 1828) : a wise or learned man in India — often used as an honorary title

pan·do·ra \pan-'dȯr-ə, -'dȯr-\ *n* [It, fr. LL *pandura* 3‑stringed lute, fr. Gk *pandoura*] (1597) : BANDORE

Pan·do·ra's box \pan-'dȯr-əz-, -'dȯr-\ *n* [fr. the box, sent by the gods to Pandora, which she was forbidden to open and which loosed a swarm of evils upon mankind when she opened it out of curiosity] (1579) : a prolific source of troubles

pan-dow-dy \pan-'daù-dē\ *n, pl* **-dies** [origin unknown] (1805) : a deep-dish spiced apple dessert sweetened with sugar, molasses, or maple syrup and covered with a rich crust

pan-dy \'pan-dē\ *vt* **pan-died; pan-dy-ing** [prob. fr. L *pande,* imper. sing. of *pandere* to spread out (the hand); command of the schoolmaster to the boy — more at FATHOM] (1863) *Brit* : to punish (a schoolboy) with a blow on the palm of the hand esp. with a ferule

pane \'pān\ *n* [ME *pan, pane* strip of cloth, pane, fr. MF *pan,* fr. L *pannus* cloth, rag — more at VANE] (14c) : a piece, section, or side of something: as **a** : a framed sheet of glass in a window or door **b** : one of the sections into which a sheet of postage stamps is cut for distribution — **paned** \'pānd\ *adj*

pan-e-gy-ric \,pa-nə-'jir-ik, -'ji-rik\ *n* [L *panegyricus,* fr. Gk *panēgyrikos,* fr. *panēgyrikos* of or for a festival assembly, fr. *panēgyris* festival assembly, fr. *pan-* + *agyris* assembly; akin to Gk *ageirein* to gather] (1603) : a eulogistic oration or writing; *also* : formal or elaborate praise *syn* see ENCOMIUM — **pan-e-gy-ri-cal** \-'jir-i-kəl, -'ji-ri-\ *adj* — **pan-e-gy-ri-cal-ly** \-k(ə-)lē\ *adv*

pan-e-gy-rist \,pa-nə-'jir-ist, -'ji-rist\ *n* (1605) : EULOGIST

¹pan-el \'pa-n³l\ *n* [ME, piece of cloth, slip of parchment, jury schedule, fr. MF, piece of cloth, piece, fr. (assumed) VL *pannellus,* dim. of L *pannus*] (14c) **1 a** (1) : a schedule containing names of persons summoned as jurors (2) : the group of persons so summoned (3) : JURY 1 **b** (1) : a group of persons selected for some service (as in investigation or arbitration) ⟨a ~ of experts⟩ (2) : a group of persons who discuss before an audience a topic of public interest; *also* : PANEL DISCUSSION (3) : a group of entertainers or guests engaged as players in a quiz or guessing game on a radio or television program **2 a** : a separate or distinct part of a surface: as **a** : a fence section : HURDLE **b** (1) : a thin usu. rectangular board set in a frame (as in a door) (2) : a usu. sunken or raised section of a surface set off by a margin (3) : a flat usu. rectangular piece of construction material (as plywood or precast masonry) made to form part of a surface **c** : a vertical section of fabric (as a gore) **d** : COMIC STRIP; *also* : a frame of a comic strip **e** : any of several units of construction of an airplane wing surface **3 a** : a thin flat piece of wood on which a picture is painted; *also* : a painting on such a surface **4 a** : a section of a switchboard **b** : a flat often insulating support (as for computer hardware or parts of an electrical device) usu. with control handles on one face **c** : a usu. vertical mount for controls or dials (as of instruments of measurement)

²panel *vt* **-eled** *or* **-elled; -el-ing** *or* **-el-ling** (15c) : to furnish or decorate with panels ⟨*paneled* the living room⟩

panel discussion *n* (ca. 1938) : a formal discussion by a panel

pan-el-ing *also* **panelling** *n* (1824) : panels joined in a continuous surface; *esp* : decorative wood panels so joined

pan-el-ist \'pa-n³l-ist\ *n* (1951) : a member of a discussion or advisory panel or of a radio or television panel

panel truck *n* (1937) : a small motortruck with a fully enclosed body

pan-e-tela *var of* PANATELA

pan-et-to-ne \,pä-nə-'tō-nē, ,pa-\ *n* [It, fr. *panetto* small loaf, dim. of *pane* bread, fr. L *panis* — more at FOOD] (1922) : a usu. yeast-leavened bread containing raisins and candied fruit

pan-fish \'pan-,fish\ *n* (1805) : a small food fish (as a sunfish) usu. taken with hook and line and not available on the market

pan-fry \'pan-,frī, pan-'frī\ *vt* (ca. 1929) : to cook in a frying pan with a small amount of fat

pan-ful \'pan-,fùl\ *n* (ca. 1864) : as much or as many as a pan will hold

¹pang \'paŋ\ *n* [origin unknown] (15c) **1** : a brief piercing spasm of pain **2** : a sharp attack of mental anguish ⟨~s of remorse⟩ ⟨a ~ of jealousy struck me —Graham Greene⟩

²pang *vt* (1502) : to cause to have pangs : TORMENT

pan-ga \'pän-gə\ *n* [Swahili] (1925) : MACHETE

pan-gen-e-sis \,pan-'je-nə-səs\ *n* [NL] (1868) : a disproven hypothetical mechanism of heredity in which the cells throw off particles that collect in the reproductive products or in buds so that the egg or bud contains particles from all parts of the parent — **pan-ge-net-ic** \-jə-'ne-tik\ *adj*

Pan-gloss-ian \pan-'glä-sē-ən, paŋ-, -'glō-\ *adj* [*Pangloss,* optimistic tutor in Voltaire's *Candide* (1759)] (1831) : marked by the view that all is for the best in this best of possible worlds : excessively optimistic

pan-go-la grass \pan-'gō-lə-, paŋ-\ *n* [alter. of *Pongola grass,* fr. the *Pongola* River, So. Africa] (1948) : a rapid-growing perennial grass (*Digitaria decumbens*) of southern Africa that has been introduced into the southern U.S. as a pasture grass

pan-go-lin \'paŋ-gə-lən, 'pan-\ *n* [Malay dial. *pēngguling*] (1774) : any of a family (Manidae) of Asian and African edentate mammals having the body covered with large imbricated horny scales

¹pan-han-dle \'pan-,han-d³l\ *n* (1856) : a narrow projection of a larger territory (as a state) ⟨the Texas ~⟩

²panhandle *vb* **pan-han-dled; pan-han-dling** \-,han(d)-liŋ, -,han-d³l-iŋ\ [back-formation fr. *panhandler,* prob. fr. *panhandle,* n.; fr. the extended forearm] *vi* (1903) : to stop people on the street and ask for food or money : BEG ~ *vt* **1** : to accost on the street and beg from **2** : to get by panhandling — **pan-han-dler** \-,han(d)-lər, -,han-d³l-ər\ *n*

Pan-hel-len-ic \,pan-hə-'le-nik\ *adj* (1847) **1** : of or relating to all Greece or all the Greeks **2** : of or relating to the Greek-letter sororities or fraternities in American colleges and universities or to an association representing them

pan-hu-man \pan-'hyü-mən, -'yü-\ *adj* (ca. 1909) : of or relating to all humanity ⟨the ~ problem of evil —R. K. Merton⟩

¹pan-ic \'pa-nik\ *adj* [F *panique,* fr. Gk *panikos,* lit., of Pan, fr. *Pan*] (1603) **1** : of, relating to, or resembling the mental or emotional state believed induced by the god Pan ⟨~ fear⟩ **2** : of, relating to, or arising from a panic ⟨a wave of ~ buying⟩ **3** : of or relating to the god Pan

²panic *n* (1708) **1** : a sudden overpowering fright; *esp* : a sudden unreasoning terror often accompanied by mass flight **2** : a sudden widespread fright concerning financial affairs that results in a depression of values caused by extreme measures for protection of property (as securities) **3** *slang* : one that is very funny *syn* see FEAR — **pan-icky** \'pa-ni-kē\ *adj*

³panic *vb* **pan-icked** \-nikt\; **pan-ick-ing** *vt* (1827) **1** : to affect with panic **2** : to produce demonstrative appreciation on the part of ⟨~ an audience with a gag⟩ ~ *vi* : to be affected with panic

panic button *n* (ca. 1950) : something setting off a precipitous emergency response ⟨there was no pushing of *panic buttons* at the White House, no rushing of troops —J. C. Harsch⟩

pan-ic grass \'pa-nik-\ *n* [ME *panik,* fr. MF or L; MF *panic* foxtail millet, fr. L *panicum,* fr. *panus* stalk of a panicle] (1597) : any of various grasses (*Panicum* and related genera) including some important forage and cereal grasses

pan-i-cle \'pa-ni-kəl\ *n* [L *panicula,* dim. of *panus*] (1597) **1** : a compound racemose inflorescence — see INFLORESCENCE illustration **2** : a pyramidal loosely branched flower cluster — **pan-i-cled** \-kəld\ *adj* — **pa-nic-u-late** \-'ni-kyə-lət, pə-\ *adj*

pan-ic-strick-en \'pa-nik-,stri-kən\ *adj* (1804) : overcome with panic

pan-i-cum \'pa-ni-kəm\ *n* [NL, fr. L, foxtail millet] (ca. 1864) : any of a large and widely distributed genus (*Panicum*) of grasses that have a very diverse habit and 1- to 2-flowered spikelets arranged in a panicle

Pan-ja-bi \,pən-'jä-bē, -'ja-\ *n* [Hindi *pañjābī,* fr. *pañjābi* of Punjab] (1854) **1** : an Indo-Aryan language of the Punjab **2** : PUNJABI 2

pan-jan-drum \pan-'jan-drəm\ *n, pl* **-drums** *also* **-dra** \-drə\ [*Grand Panjandrum,* burlesque title of an imaginary personage in some nonsense lines by Samuel Foote] (1755) : a powerful personage or pretentious official

pan-leu-ko-pe-nia \,pan-,lü-kə-'pē-nē-ə\ *n* [NL] (1940) : an acute usu. fatal viral epizootic disease esp. of cats characterized by fever, diarrhea and dehydration, and extensive destruction of white blood cells

pan-mic-tic \,pan-'mik-tik\ *adj* [*pan-* + Gk *miktos,* verbal of *mignynai* to mix] (1943) : of, relating to, or exhibiting panmixia

pan-mix-ia \-'mik-sē-ə\ *n* [NL, fr. *pan-* + Gk *mixis* act of mingling, mating, fr. *mignynai* to mix — more at MIX] (ca. 1889) : random mating within a breeding population

panne \'pan\ *n* [F, fr. OF *penne, panne* fur used for lining, fr. L *pinna* feather, wing — more at PEN] (ca. 1794) **1** : a silk or rayon velvet with lustrous pile flattened in one direction — called also *panne velvet* **2** : a heavy silk or rayon satin with high luster and waxy smoothness

pan-nier *also* **pan-ier** \'pan-yər, 'pa-nē-ər\ *n* [ME *panier,* fr. MF, fr. L *panarium,* fr. *panis* bread — more at FOOD] (13c) **1** : a large container: as **a** : a basket often carried on the back of an animal or the shoulders of a person **b** : one of a pair of packs or baskets hung over the rear wheel of a vehicle (as a bicycle) **2 a** : one of a pair of hoops formerly used to expand women's skirts at the sides **b** : an overskirt draped at the sides of a skirt for an effect of fullness

pannier 2b

pan-ni-kin \'pa-ni-kən\ *n* [¹*pan* + *-nikin* (as in *cannikin*)] (1823) *Brit* : a small pan or cup

pa-no-cha \pə-'nō-chə\ *or* **pa-no-che** \-chē\ *var of* PENUCHE

pan-o-plied \'pa-nə-plēd\ *adj* (1832) : dressed in or having a panoply

pan-op-tic \,pa-'näp-tik\ *adj* [Gk *panoptēs* all-seeing, fr. *pan-* + *opsesthai* to be going to see — more at OPTIC] (1826) : being or presenting a comprehensive or panoramic view

pan-o-ply \'pa-nə-plē\ *n, pl* **-plies** [Gk *panoplia,* fr. *pan-* + *hopla* arms, armor, pl. of *hoplon* tool, weapon — more at HOPLITE] (1632) **1 a** : a full suit of armor **b** : ceremonial attire **2** : something forming a protective covering **3 a** : a magnificent or impressive array ⟨the full ~ of a military funeral⟩ **b** : a display of all appropriate appurtenances ⟨has the ~ of science fiction . . . but it is not true science fiction —Isaac Asimov⟩

pan-o-rama \,pa-nə-'ra-mə, -'rä-mə\ *n* [*pan-* + Gk *horama* sight, fr. *horan* to see — more at WARY] (1796) **1 a** : CYCLORAMA 1 **b** : a picture exhibited a part at a time by being unrolled before the spectator **2 a** : an unobstructed or complete view of an area in every direction **b** : a comprehensive presentation of a subject ⟨a ~ of American history⟩ **c** : RANGE **3** : a mental picture of a series of images or events — **pan-o-ram-ic** \-'ra-mik\ *adj* — **pan-o-ram-i-cal-ly** \-mi-k(ə-)lē\ *adv*

pan out *vi* [²*pan*] (ca. 1868) : TURN OUT: SUCCEED ⟨the signs revealed that the experiment wasn't *panning out* —Ronald Reagan⟩

pan-pipe \'pan-,pīp\ *n* [*Pan,* its traditional inventor] (1820) : a primitive wind instrument consisting of a series of short vertical pipes of graduated length bound together with the mouthpieces in an even row — often used in pl.

pan-sex-u-al \,pan-'sek-sh(ə-)wəl, -shəl\ *adj* (1926) : exhibiting or implying many forms of sexual expression — **pan-sex-u-al-i-ty** \,pan-,sek-shə-'wa-lə-tē\ *n*

Pan–Slav-ism \,pan-'slä-,vi-zəm, -'sla-\ *n* (1850) : a political and cultural movement orig. emphasizing the cultural ties between the Slavic peoples but later associated with Russian expansionism — **Pan–Slav-ic** \-'slä-vik, -'slä-\ *adj* — **Pan–Slav-ist** \-'slä-vist, -'sla-\ *n*

¹pan-sy \'pan-zē\ *n, pl* **pansies** [ME *pensee,* fr. MF *pensée,* fr. *pensée* thought, fr. fem. of *pensé,* pp. of *penser* to think, fr. L *pensare* to ponder — more at PENSIVE] (15c) **1** : a garden plant (*Viola wittrockiana*) derived chiefly from the wild pansy (*Viola tricolor*) and distinguished by the latter with other wild violets; *also* : its flower **2 a** : an effeminate man or boy — usu. used disparagingly **b** : a male homosexual — usu. used disparagingly

²pansy *adj* (1929) : EFFEMINATE 1; *also* : HOMOSEXUAL — usu. used disparagingly

¹pant \'pant\ *vb* [ME, modif. of MF *pantaisier,* fr. (assumed) VL *phantasiare* to have hallucinations, fr. Gk *phantasioun,* fr. *phantasia* appearance, imagination — more at FANCY] *vi* (14c) **1 a** : to breathe quickly, spasmodically, or in a labored manner **b** : to run panting ⟨~ing along beside the bicycle⟩ **c** : to move with or make a throbbing

\ə\ abut \'\ kitten, F table \ər\ further \a\ ash \ā\ ace \ä\ mop, mar \aù\ out \ch\ chin \e\ bet \ē\ easy \g\ go \i\ hit \ī\ ice \j\ job \ŋ\ sing \ō\ go \ò\ law \òi\ boy \th\ thin \t̲h̲\ the \ü\ loot \ù\ foot \y\ yet \zh\ vision \ȧ, k̲, ⁿ, œ, œ̄, ue, ūe, ᵼ\ see Guide to Pronunciation or puffing sound **2 :** to long eagerly **:** YEARN **3 :** THROB, PULSATE ~ *vt* **:** to utter with panting **:** GASP

²pant *n* (1513) **1 a :** a panting breath **b :** the visible movement of the chest accompanying such a breath **2 :** a throbbing or puffing sound

³pant *n* [short for *pantaloons*] (1840) **1 :** an outer garment covering each leg separately and usu. extending from the waist to the ankle — usu. used in pl. **2** *pl, chiefly Brit* **:** men's underpants **3** *pl* **:** PANTIE — **with one's pants down :** in an embarrassing position (as of being unprepared to act)

⁴pant *adj* (1899) **:** of or relating to pants ⟨a ~ leg⟩

pant- *or* **panto-** *comb form* [MF, fr. L, fr. Gk, fr. *pant-*, *pas* — more at PAN·] **:** all ⟨*pant*isocracy⟩

Pan·ta·gru·el \,pan-tə-'grü-əl; pan-'ta-grə-wəl, -,wel\ *n* [F] **:** the huge son of Gargantua in Rabelais's *Pantagruel* — **Pan·ta·gru·el·ian** \,pan-tə-grü-'e-lē-ən, (,)pan-,ta-grə-'we-\ *adj* — **Pan·ta·gru·el·ism** \,pan-tə-grü-ə,li-zəm; pan-'ta-grə-wə-,li-zəm, -,we-\ *n* — **Pan·ta·gru·el·ist** \-list\ *n*

pan·ta·lets *or* **pan·ta·lettes** \,pan-tə-'lets\ *n pl* [*pantaloons*] (1834) **:** long drawers with a ruffle at the bottom of each leg worn esp. by women and children in the first half of the 19th century

pan·ta·loon \,pan-tə-'lün\ *n* [MF & OIt; MF *Pantalon*, fr. OIt *Pantaleone*, *Pantalone*] (ca. 1590) **1 a** *or* **pan·ta·lo·ne** \-tə-'lō-nē\ *cap* **:** a character in the commedia dell'arte that is usu. a skinny old dotard who wears spectacles, slippers, and a tight-fitting combination of trousers and stockings **b :** a buffoon in pantomimes **2** *pl* **a :** wide breeches worn esp. in England during the reign of Charles II **b :** close-fitting trousers usu. having straps passing under the instep and worn esp. in the 19th century **3** *pl* **:** loose-fitting usu. shorter than ankle-length trousers

pant-dress \'pant-,dres\ *n* (1964) **:** a dress having a divided skirt

pan·tech·ni·con \pan-'tek-ni-kən\ *n* [short for *pantechnicon van*, fr. *pantechnicon* storage warehouse] (1891) *Brit* **:** ³VAN 1

pan·the·ism \'pan(t)-thē-,i-zəm\ *n* [F *panthéisme*, fr. *panthéiste* pantheist, fr. E pantheist, fr. *pan-* + Gk *theos* god] (1732) **1 :** a doctrine that equates God with the forces and laws of the universe **2 :** the worship of all gods of different creeds, cults, or peoples indifferently; *also* **:** toleration of worship of all gods (as at certain periods of the Roman empire) — **pan·the·ist** \-thē-ist\ *n* — **pan·the·is·tic** \,pan(t)-thē-'is-tik\ *also* **pan·the·is·ti·cal** \-ti-kəl\ *adj* — **pan·the·is·ti·cal·ly** \-ti-k(ə-)lē\ *adv*

pan·the·on \'pan(t)-thē-,än, -ən\ *n* [ME *Panteon*, a temple at Rome, fr. L *Pantheon*, fr. Gk *pantheion* temple of all the gods, fr. neut. of *pantheios* of all gods, fr. *pan-* + *theos* god] (14c) **1 :** a temple dedicated to all the gods **2 :** a building serving as the burial place of or containing memorials to the famous dead of a nation **3 :** the gods of a people; *esp* **:** the officially recognized gods **4 :** a group of illustrious persons

pan·ther \'pan(t)-thər\ *n, pl* **panthers** *also* **panther** [ME *pantere*, fr. OF, fr. L *panthera*, fr. Gk *panthēr*] (13c) **1 :** LEOPARD: as **a :** a leopard of a hypothetical exceptionally large fierce variety **b :** a leopard of the black color phase **2 :** COUGAR **3 :** JAGUAR

pant·ie *or* **panty** \'pan-tē\ *n, pl* **pant·ies** [³*pant*] (1908) **:** a woman's or child's undergarment covering the lower trunk and made with closed crotch — usu. used in pl.

pantie girdle *n* (1941) **:** a woman's girdle having a sewed-in or detachable crotch and made with or without garters and bones

pan·tile \'pan-,tīl\ *n* [¹*pan*] (1640) **1 :** a roofing tile whose cross section is an ogee curve **2 :** a roofing tile of which the cross section is an arc of a circle and which is laid with alternate convex and concave surfaces uppermost — **pan·tiled** \-,tīld\ *adj*

pant·i·soc·ra·cy \,pant-ī-'sä-krə-sē, ,pant-ə-\ *n, pl* **-cies** [*pant-* + *isocracy* equal rule, fr. Gk *isokratia*, fr. *is-* + *-kratia* -cracy] (1794) **:** a utopian community in which all rule equally — **pant·i·so·crat·ic** \,pan-,ti-sə-'kra-tik\ *or* **pant·i·so·crat·i·cal** \-'kra-ti-kəl\ *adj* — **pant·i·soc·ra·tist** \,pan-tə-'sä-krə-tist, ,pan-,ti-\ *n*

pan·to \'pan-(,)tō\ *n, pl* **pantos** (1852) *Brit* **:** PANTOMIME 2c

pan·to·fle \'pan-'tō-fəl, -'tä-, -'tü-; 'pan-tō-fəl\ *n* [ME *pantufle*, fr. MF *pantoufle*] (15c) **:** SLIPPER

pan·to·graph \'pan-tə-,graf\ *n* [F *pantographe*, fr. *pant-* + *-graphe* -graph] (1723) **1 :** an instrument for copying (as a map) on a predetermined scale consisting of four light rigid bars jointed in parallelogram form; *also* **:** any of various extensible devices of similar construction (as for use as brackets or gates) **2 :** an electrical trolley carried by a collapsible and adjustable frame — **pan·to·graph·ic** \,pan-tə-'gra-fik\ *adj*

pantograph 1

¹pan·to·mime \'pan-tə-,mīm\ *n* [L *pantomimus*, fr. *pant-* + *mimus* mime] (1589) **1 :** PANTOMIMIST **2 a :** an ancient Roman dramatic performance featuring a solo dancer and a narrative chorus **b :** any of various dramatic or dancing performances in which a story is told by expressive bodily or facial movements of the performers **c :** a British theatrical entertainment of the Christmas season based on a nursery tale and featuring topical songs, tableaux, and dances **3 a :** conveyance of a story by bodily or facial movements esp. in drama or dance **b :** the art or genre of conveying a story by bodily movements only — **pan·to·mim·ic** \,pan-tə-'mi-mik\ *adj*

²pantomime *vb* **-mimed; -mim·ing** *vi* (1768) **:** to engage in pantomime ~ *vt* **:** to represent by pantomime

pan·to·mim·ist \'pan-tə-,mim-ist, -,mi-mist, -,mi-\ *n* (1838) **1 :** an actor or dancer in pantomimes **2 :** a composer of pantomimes

pan·to·the·nate \,pan-tə-'the-,nāt, pan-'tä-thə-,nāt\ *n* (ca. 1934) **:** a salt or ester of pantothenic acid

pan·to·then·ic acid \,pan-tə-'the-nik-, -'thē-\ *n* [Gk *pantothen* from all sides, fr. *pant-*, *pas* all — more at PAN·] (1933) **:** a viscous oily acid $C_9H_{17}NO_5$ of the vitamin B complex found in all living tissues

pan·trop·i·cal \,pan-'trä-pi-kəl\ *also* **pan·trop·ic** \-'pik\ *adj* (1936) **:** occurring or distributed throughout the tropical regions of the earth

pan·try \'pan-trē\ *n, pl* **pantries** [ME *paneterie*, fr. OF, fr. *panetier* servant in charge of the pantry, fr. *pan* bread, fr. L *panis* — more at FOOD] (14c) **1 :** a room or closet used for storing (as

---

provisions) or from which food is brought to the table **2 :** a room (as in a hotel or hospital) for preparation of foods on order

pan·try·man \-mən\ *n* (ca. 1567) **:** a man in charge of or working in a pantry (as in a hotel or hospital)

pants suit *n* (1964) **:** PANTSUIT

pant·suit \'pant-,süt\ *n* (1964) **:** a woman's ensemble consisting usu. of a long jacket and tailored pants of the same material — **pant·suit·ed** *adj*

panty hose *n* (1963) **:** a one-piece undergarment for women that consists of hosiery made with a panty-style top — usu. pl. in constr.

panty raid *n* (ca. 1952) **:** a raid on a women's dormitory by college men usu. to obtain panties as trophies

panty·waist \'pan-tē-,wāst\ *n* (ca. 1936) **:** SISSY — **pantywaist** *adj*

Pan·urge \'pa-,nərj, pa-'nürzh\ *n* [F] **:** a witty rascal and companion of Pantagruel in Rabelais's *Pantagruel*

pan·zer \'pan-zər, 'pän(t)-sər\ *n* [G *Panzer* tank, armor, coat of mail, fr. MHG *panzier*, fr. OF *pancière*, fr. *pance*, *panche* belly — more at PAUNCH] (ca. 1939) **:** TANK 3; *specif* **:** a German tank of World War II

panzer division *n* (ca. 1939) **:** a German armored division

¹pap \'pap\ *n* [ME *pappe*; of imit. origin] (13c) **1** *chiefly dial* **:** NIPPLE, TEAT **2 :** something shaped like a nipple

²pap *n* [ME] (15c) **1 :** a soft food for infants or invalids **2 :** political patronage **3 :** something lacking solid value or substance

pa·pa \'pä-pə, *chiefly Brit* pə-'pä, -'pä\ *n* [F (baby talk)] (1681) **:** FATHER

Pa·pa \pə-'pä, 'pä-pə\ (1952) — a communications code word for the letter *p*

pa·pa·cy \'pā-pə-sē\ *n, pl* **-cies** [ME *papacie*, fr. ML *papatia*, fr. LL *papa* pope — more at POPE] (14c) **1 :** the office of pope **2 :** a succession or line of popes **3 :** the term of a pope's reign **4** *cap* **:** the system of government of the Roman Catholic Church of which the pope is the supreme head

Pa·pa·go \'pä-pə-,gō, 'pa-\ *n, pl* **Papago** *or* **Papagos** (1839) **1 :** a member of an American Indian people of southwestern Arizona and northwestern Mexico **2 :** the Uto-Aztecan language of the Papago people

pa·pa·in \pə-'pā-ən, -'pī-ən\ *n* [ISV, fr. *papaya*] (ca. 1890) **:** a protease in the juice of unripe papaya that is used esp. as a tenderizer for meat and in medicine

pa·pal \'pā-pəl\ *adj* [ME, fr. MF, fr. ML *papalis*, fr. LL *papa*] (14c) **:** of or relating to a pope or to the Roman Catholic Church; *also* **:** resembling a pope or that of a pope — **pa·pal·ly** \-pə-lē\ *adv*

papal cross *n* (ca. 1889) **:** a figure of a cross having a long upright shaft and three crossbars with the longest at or somewhat above its middle and the two other successively shorter crossbars above the longest one — see CROSS illustration

papal infallibility *n* (1870) **:** the Roman Catholic doctrine that the pope cannot err when speaking ex cathedra in defining a doctrine of Christian faith or morals

Pa·pa·ni·co·laou smear \,pä-pə-'nē-kə-,laü-, ,pa-pə-'ni-\ *n* [George N. *Papanicolaou* †1962 Am. medical scientist] (1950) **:** PAP SMEAR

Papanicolaou test *n* (1946) **:** PAP SMEAR

pa·pa·raz·zo \,pä-pə-'rät-(,)sō\ *n, pl* **-raz·zi** \-(,)sē\ [It] (1966) **:** a free-lance photographer who aggressively pursues celebrities for the purpose of taking candid photographs

pa·pav·er·ine \pə-'pa-və-,rēn; -'pav-rən, -'pa-və-\ *n* [ISV, fr. L *papaver* poppy] (1857) **:** a crystalline alkaloid $C_{20}H_{21}NO_4$ that is found in opium and is used chiefly as an antispasmodic for its ability to relax smooth muscle

pa·paw *n* [prob. modif. of Sp *papaya*] (1624) **1** \pə-'pò\ **:** PAPAYA **2** \'pä-(,)pò, 'pò-\ **:** a No. American tree (*Asimina triloba*) of the custard-apple family with purple flowers and an edible fruit; *also* **:** its fruit

pa·pa·ya \pə-'pī-ə\ *n* [Sp, of AmerInd origin; akin to Arawak *papáia*] (1598) **:** a tropical American tree (*Carica papaya* of the family Caricaceae, the papaya family) with an oblong to globose yellow edible fruit; *also* **:** its fruit

¹pa·per \'pā-pər\ *n* [ME *papir*, fr. MF *papier*, fr. L *papyrus* papyrus, paper, fr. Gk *papyros* papyrus] (14c) **1 a** (1) **:** a felted sheet of usu. vegetable fibers laid down on a fine screen from a water suspension (2) **:** a similar sheet of other material (as plastic) **b :** a piece of paper **2 a :** a piece of paper containing a written or printed statement **:** DOCUMENT ⟨pedigree ~s⟩ **b :** a piece of paper containing writing or print **c :** a formal written composition often designed for publication and often intended to be read aloud ⟨presented a scholarly ~ at the meeting⟩ **d :** a piece of written schoolwork **3 :** a paper container or wrapper **4 :** NEWSPAPER **5 :** the negotiable notes or instruments of commerce **6 :** WALLPAPER **7 :** TICKETS; *esp* **:** free passes **8 :** PAPER-BACK — **on paper 1 :** in writing ⟨wants these promises *on paper*⟩ **2 :** in theory ⟨the plan looks good *on paper*⟩ **3 :** figured at face value ⟨*on paper* the stock was worth nearly a million dollars⟩

²paper *vb* **pa·pered; pa·per·ing** \'pā-p(ə-)riŋ\ *vt* (1594) **1** *archaic* **:** to put down or describe in writing **2 :** to fold or enclose in paper **3 :** to cover or line with paper; *esp* **:** to apply wallpaper to **4 :** to fill by giving out free passes ⟨~ the theater for opening night⟩ **5 :** to cover (an area) with advertising bills, circulars, or posters ~ *vi* **:** to hang wallpaper — **pa·per·er** \-pər-ər\ *n*

³paper *adj* (1594) **1 a :** made of paper, paperboard, or papier-mâché ⟨a ~ bag⟩ **:** PAPERY **2 :** of or relating to clerical work or written communication **3 :** existing only in theory **:** NOMINAL ⟨a ~ blockade⟩ **4 :** admitted by free passes ⟨a ~ audience⟩ **5 :** finished with a crisp smooth surface similar to that of paper ⟨~ taffeta⟩

pa·per·back \'pā-pər-,bak\ *n* (1899) **:** a book with a flexible paper binding — **paperback** *also* **pa·per·backed** \-,bakt\ *adj*

paper birch *n* (1810) **:** a No. American birch (*Betula papyrifera*) with peeling white bark and toothed ovate leaves

pa·per·board \'pä-pər-,bòrd, -,bòrd\ *n* (1549) **:** a material made from cellulose fiber (as wood pulp) like paper but usu. thicker

pa·per·bound \-,baùnd\ *adj* (1950) **:** PAPERBACK — **paperbound** *adj*

pa·per·boy \-,bòi\ *n* (1876) **:** a boy who delivers newspapers **:** NEWS-BOY

paper chromatography *n* (1948) **:** chromatography that uses paper strips or sheets as the adsorbent stationary phase through which a solution flows and that is used esp. to separate amino acids

paper clip n (1919) : a length of wire bent into flat loops that is used to hold papers together

paper cutter n (ca. 1828) **1** : PAPER KNIFE **2** : a machine or device for cutting or trimming sheets of paper to required dimensions

pa·per·hang·er \'pā-pər-ˌhaŋ-ər\ n (1796) **1** : one that applies wallpaper **2** slang : one who passes worthless checks

pa·per·hang·ing \-ˌhaŋ-iŋ\ n (1873) : the act of applying wallpaper

paper knife n (ca. 1807) **1** : a knife for slitting envelopes or uncut pages **2** : the knife of a paper cutter

pa·per·less \'pā-pər-ləs\ adj (1969) : recording or relaying information by electronic media rather than on paper ⟨∼ offices⟩

pa·per·mak·er \'pā-pər-ˌmā-kər\ n (ca. 1580) : one that makes paper — **pa·per·mak·ing** \-kiŋ\ n

paper money n (1691) **1** : money consisting of government notes and banknotes **2** : BANK MONEY

paper mulberry n (1777) : an Asian tree (Broussonetia papyrifera) of the mulberry family that is widely grown as a shade tree

paper nautilus n (1835) : a pelagic cephalopod (genus Argonauta) of which the female has a delicate papery shell

paper over vt (1955) **1** : to gloss over, explain away, or patch up (as major differences or disparities) esp. in order to maintain a semblance of unity or agreement **2** : HIDE, CONCEAL

paper profit n (1893) : a profit that can be realized only by selling something (as a security) that has appreciated in market value

paper–thin adj (1928) : extremely thin ⟨∼ partitions⟩

paper tiger n (1850) : one that is outwardly powerful or dangerous but inwardly weak or ineffectual

paper trail n (1965) : documents (as financial records or published materials) from which a person's actions may be traced or opinions learned

pa·per–train \'pā-pər-ˌtrān\ vt (1971) : to train (as a dog) to defecate and urinate on paper indoors

pa·per·weight \-ˌwāt\ n (ca. 1858) : a usu. small heavy object used to hold down loose papers (as on a desk)

pa·per·work \-ˌwərk\ n (1889) : routine clerical or record-keeping work often incidental to a more important task

pa·pery \'pā-p(ə-)rē\ adj (1627) : resembling paper in thinness or consistency ⟨∼ leaves⟩ ⟨∼ silk⟩ — **pa·per·i·ness** n

pa·pe·terie \'pa-pə-trē, ˌpa-pə-'\ n [F] (ca. 1847) : packaged fancy stationery

¹Pa·phi·an \'pā-fē-ən\ n [L paphius, fr. Gk paphios, fr. Paphos, ancient city of Cyprus that was the center of worship of Aphrodite] (1598) **1** often not cap : PROSTITUTE **2** : a native or inhabitant of Paphos

²Paphian adj (1605) **1** : of or relating to illicit love : WANTON **2** : of or relating to Paphos or its people

Pa·pia·men·to \ˌpä-pyə-'men-(ˌ)tō\ also **Pa·pia·men·tu** \-(ˌ)tü\ n [Sp, fr. Papiamento papya talk + -mentu -ment] (1923) : a Spanish-based creole language of Netherlands Antilles

pa·pier col·lé \ˌpä-ˌpyä-(ˌ)kō-'lā, ˌpa-\ n, pl **papiers collés** \-ˌpyä-(ˌ)kō-'lā(z)\ [F, glued paper] (1935) : COLLAGE

¹pa·pier–mâ·ché \ˌpā-pər-mə-'shā, ˌpa-ˌpyä-mə-, -(ˌ)ma-\ n [F, lit., chewed paper] (1753) : a light strong molding material of wastepaper pulped with glue and other additives

²papier–mâché adj (1753) **1** : formed of papier-mâché **2** : UNREAL, ARTIFICIAL

pa·pil·io·na·ceous \pə-ˌpi-lē-ə-'nā-shəs\ adj [L papilion-, papilio butterfly — more at PAVILION] (1668) : having a corolla (as in the bean or pea) with usu. five petals that include a large standard enclosing two lateral wings and a lower carina

pa·pil·la \pə-'pi-lə\ n, pl **pa·pil·lae** \-'pi-(ˌ)lē, -ˌlī\ [L, nipple, fr. dim. of papula pimple; akin to Lith papas nipple] (1713) : a small projecting body part similar to a nipple in form: **a** : a vascular process of connective tissue extending into and nourishing the root of a hair, feather, or developing tooth **b** : any of the vascular protuberances of the dermal layer of the skin extending into the epidermal layer and often containing tactile corpuscles **c** : any of the small protuberances on the upper surface of the tongue — **pap·il·lary** \'pa-pə-ˌler-ē, esp Brit pə-'pi-lə-rē\ adj — **pap·il·late** \'pa-pə-ˌlāt, pə-'pi-lət\ adj — **pa·pil·lose** \'pa-pə-ˌlōs, pə-'pi-ˌlōs\ adj

pap·il·lo·ma \ˌpa-pə-'lō-mə\ n, pl **-mas** or **-ma·ta** \-mə-tə\ [NL] (1866) **1** : a benign tumor (as a wart) due to overgrowth of epithelial tissue on papillae of vascular connective tissue (as of the skin) **2** : an epithelial tumor caused by a virus — **pap·il·lo·ma·tous** \-'lō-mə-təs\ adj

pap·il·lo·ma·vi·rus \-ˌvī-rəs\ n [NL] (1960) : any of a group of papovaviruses that cause papillomas

pa·pil·lon \ˌpä-pē-'yōⁿ, ˌpa-\ n [F, lit., butterfly, fr. L papilion-, papilio] (1907) : any of a breed of small slender toy spaniels having large erect heavily fringed ears

pa·pil·lote \ˌpä-pē-'yōt, ˌpa-\ n [F, fr. papillon butterfly] (1818) : a greased usu. paper wrapper in which food (as meat or fish) is cooked

pa·pist \'pā-pist\ n, often cap [MF or NL; MF papiste, fr. papa pope; NL papista, fr. LL papa pope] (1534) : ROMAN CATHOLIC — usu. used disparagingly — **papist** adj

pa·pist·ry \'pā-pə-strē\ n (1535) : the Roman Catholic religion — usu. used disparagingly

pa·poose \pa-'püs, pə-\ n [Narraganset papoòs] (1634) : a young child of American Indian parents

pa·po·va·vi·rus \pə-'pō-və-ˌvī-rəs\ n [papilloma + polyoma + vacuolating + virus] (1962) : any of a group of viruses that have a capsid composed of 72 subunits and that are associated with or responsible for various neoplasms (as some warts) of mammals

pap·pose \'pa-ˌpōs\ adj (1691) : having or being a pappus

pap·pus \'pa-pəs\ n, pl **pap·pi** \'pa-ˌpī, -ˌpē\ [L, fr. Gk pappos] (ca. 1704) : an appendage or tuft of appendages that crowns the ovary or fruit in various seed plants and functions in dispersal of the fruit

pap·py \'pa-pē\ n (1763) chiefly Southern & Midland : PAPA

pa·pri·ka \pə-'prē-kə, pa-\ n [Hung, fr. Serbo-Croation, fr. papar ground pepper, ultim. fr. L piper — more at PEPPER] (ca. 1896) : a usu. mild red condiment consisting of the dried finely ground pods of various cultivated sweet peppers; also : a sweet pepper used for making paprika

Pap smear \'pap-\ n [George N. Papanicolaou †1962 Am. medical scientist] (1952) : a method for the early detection of uterine cancer that involves the staining of exfoliated cells using a special technique which differentiates diseased tissue — called also Papanicolaou smear, Papanicolaou test, Pap test

Pap·u·an \'pa-pyə-wən, -pə-\ n (1814) **1** : a native or inhabitant of Papua **2** : a member of any of the native peoples of New Guinea and adjacent areas of Melanesia **3** : any of a heterogeneous group of languages spoken in New Guinea, New Britain, and the Solomon islands — **Papuan** adj

pap·u·lar \'pa-pyə-lər\ adj (ca. 1820) : consisting of or characterized by papules

pap·ule \'pa-(ˌ)pyü(ə)l\ n [L papula] (1864) : a small solid usu. conical elevation of the skin

pap·y·rol·o·gy \ˌpa-pə-'rä-lə-jē\ n [ISV] (1898) : the study of papyrus manuscripts — **pap·y·rol·o·gist** \-jist\ n

pa·py·rus \pə-'pī-rəs\ n, pl **pa·py·ri** \-'pī-(ˌ)rē, -ˌrī\ or **pa·py·rus·es** [ME, fr. L — more at PAPER] (14c) **1** : a tall sedge (Cyperus papyrus) of the Nile valley **2** : the pith of the papyrus plant esp. when cut in strips and pressed into a material to write on **3 a** : a writing on papyrus **b** : a written scroll made of papyrus

¹par \'pär\ n [L, one that is equal, fr. par equal] (1622) **1 a** : the established value of the monetary unit of one country expressed in terms of the monetary unit of another country using the same metal as the standard of value **b** : the face amount of an instrument of value (as a check or note): as (1) : the monetary value assigned to each share of stock in the charter of a corporation (2) : the principal of a bond **2** : common level : EQUALITY — usu. used with on ⟨judged the recording to be on a ∼ with previous ones⟩ **3 a** : an amount taken as an average or norm **b** : an accepted standard; specif : a usual standard of physical condition or health **4** : the score standard for each hole of a golf course; also : a score equal to par — **par** adj — **par for the course** : not unusual : NORMAL

²par vt **parred; par·ring** (1950) : to score par on (a hole)

pa·ra \'pär-ə\ n, pl **paras** or **para** [Turk, fr. Per pārah, lit., piece] (1687) **1 a** : any of several monetary units of the Turkish Empire **b** : a coin representing one para **2** [Serbo-Croatian, fr. Turk] — see dinar at MONEY table

¹para- or par- prefix [ME, fr. MF, fr. L, fr. Gk, fr. para; akin to Gk pro before — more at FOR] **1** : beside : alongside of : beyond : aside from ⟨parathyroid⟩ ⟨parenteral⟩ **2 a** : closely related to ⟨paraldehyde⟩ **b** : involving substitution at or characterized by two opposite positions in the benzene ring that are separated by two carbon atoms ⟨paradichlorobenzene⟩ **3 a** : faulty : abnormal ⟨paresthesia⟩ **b** : associated in a subsidiary or accessory capacity ⟨paramedical⟩ **c** : closely resembling : almost ⟨paratyphoid⟩

²para- comb form [parachute] : parachute ⟨paratrooper⟩

-para n comb form, pl **-paras** or **-parae** [L, fr. parere to give birth to — more at PARE] : woman delivered of (so many) children ⟨primipara⟩

para–ami·no·ben·zo·ic acid \ˌpar-ə-ə-ˌmē-nō-ˌben-'zō-ik-, ˌpar-ə-ˌmə-(ˌ)nō-\ n [ISV] (1906) : a colorless para-substituted aminobenzoic acid that is a growth factor of the vitamin B complex — called also PABA

para–ami·no·sal·i·cyl·ic acid \-ˌsa-lə-'si-lik-\ n (1946) : the white crystalline para-substituted isomer of aminosalicylic acid that is made synthetically and is used in the treatment of tuberculosis

para·bi·o·sis \ˌpar-ə-(ˌ)bī-'ō-səs, -bē-\ n [NL] (1903) **1** : reversible suspension of obvious vital activities **2** : anatomical and physiological union of two organisms — **para·bi·ot·ic** \-'ä-tik\ adj — **para·bi·ot·i·cal·ly** \-ti-k(ə-)lē\ adv

par·a·ble \'par-ə-bəl\ n [ME, fr. MF, fr. LL parabola, fr. Gk parabolē comparison, fr. paraballein to compare, fr. para- + ballein to throw — more at DEVIL] (14c) : EXAMPLE; specif : a usu. short fictitious story that illustrates a moral attitude or a religious principle

pa·rab·o·la \pə-'ra-bə-lə\ n [NL, fr. Gk parabolē, lit., comparison] (1579) : a plane curve generated by a point moving so that its distance from a fixed point is equal to its distance from a fixed line : the intersection of a right circular cone with a plane parallel to an element of the cone **2** : something bowl-shaped (as an antenna or microphone reflector)

par·a·bol·ic \ˌpar-ə-'bä-lik\ adj [in sense 1, fr. LL parabola parable; in sense 2, fr. NL parabola] (1669) **1** : expressed by or being a parable : ALLEGORICAL **2** : of, having the form of, or relating to a parabola ⟨motion in a ∼ curve⟩ — **par·a·bol·i·cal·ly** \-li-k(ə-)lē\ adv

pa·rab·o·loid \pə-'ra-bə-ˌlȯid\ n (ca. 1702) : a surface all of whose intersections by planes are either parabolas and ellipses or parabolas and hyperbolas \-ˌra-bə-'lȯi-d'l\ adj

papyrus 1

C
P
y
x
A
B
F
D
p'
parabola 1: F fixed point; CD fixed line; x moving point; AB axis; xy distance from x to CD; pp' parabola

¹para·chute \'par-ə-ˌshüt\ n [F, fr. para- (as in parasol) + chute fall — more at CHUTE] (1785) **1** : a device for slowing the descent of a person or object through the air that consists of a usu. hemispherical fabric canopy beneath which the person or object is suspended **2** : PATAGIUM **3** : a device or structure suggestive of a parachute in form, use, or operation — **para·chut·ic** \ˌpar-ə-'shü-tik\ adj

²parachute vb **-chut·ed; -chut·ing** vt (1809) : to convey by means of a parachute ∼ vi : to descend by means of a parachute

para·chut·ist \'par-ə-ˌshü-tist\ n (1888) : one that parachutes: as **a** : PARATROOPER **b** : a person who parachutes as a sport

\ə\ abut \ᵊ\ kitten, F table \ər\ further \a\ ash \ā\ ace \ä\ mop, mar \aů\ out \ch\ chin \e\ bet \ē\ easy \g\ go \i\ hit \ī\ ice \j\ job \ŋ\ sing \ō\ go \ȯ\ law \ȯi\ boy \th\ thin \th\ the \ü\ loot \ů\ foot \y\ yet \zh\ vision \a̱, k̲, ⁿ, œ, œ̄, ɶ, ɣ, ᵊ\ see Guide to Pronunciation

Par·a·clete \'par-ə-,klēt\ n [ME Paraclyte, fr. LL Paracletus, Paraclitus, fr. Gk Paraklētos, lit., advocate, intercessor, fr. parakalein to invoke, fr. para- + kalein to call — more at LOW] (15c) : HOLY SPIRIT

¹**pa·rade** \pə-'rād\ n [F, fr. MF, fr. parer to prepare — more at PARE] (ca. 1656) **1 a** : a pompous show : EXHIBITION **2 a** : the ceremonial formation of a body of troops before a superior officer **b** : a place where troops assemble regularly for parade **3 a** : an informal procession **b** : a public procession **c** : a showy array or succession ⟨a ∼ of tycoons' castles —Gail Sheehy⟩ **4 a** : a place for strolling **b** : those who promenade

²**parade** vb **pa·rad·ed; pa·rad·ing** vt (1686) **1** : to cause to maneuver or march : MARSHAL **2** : PROMENADE **3** : to exhibit ostentatiously ∼ vi **1** : to march in or as if in a procession **2** : PROMENADE **3 a** : SHOW OFF **b** : MASQUERADE ⟨myths which ∼ as modern science —M. R. Cohen⟩ syn see SHOW — **pa·rad·er** n

para·di·chlo·ro·ben·zene \,par-ə-,dī-,klōr-ə-'ben-,zēn, -,klȯr-, -,ben-'\ n [ISV] (1876) : a white crystalline compound $C_6H_4Cl_2$ made by chlorinating benzene and used chiefly as a fumigant against clothes moths

par·a·did·dle \'par-ə-,did-ᵊl\ n [origin unknown] (1927) : a quick succession of drumbeats slower than a roll and alternating left- and right-hand strokes in a typical L-R-L-L, R-L-R-R pattern

par·a·digm \'par-ə-,dīm also -,dim\ n [LL paradigma, fr. Gk paradeigma, fr. paradeiknynai to show side by side, fr. para- + deiknynai to show — more at DICTION] (15c) **1** : EXAMPLE, PATTERN; esp : an outstandingly clear or typical example or archetype **2** : an example of a conjugation or declension showing a word in all its inflectional forms **3** : a philosophical and theoretical framework of a scientific school or discipline within which theories, laws, and generalizations and the experiments performed in support of them are formulated — **par·a·dig·mat·ic** \,par-ə-dig-'ma-tik\ adj — **par·a·dig·mat·i·cal·ly** \-ti-k(ə-)lē\ adv

par·a·di·sa·ic \,par-ə-,dī-'sā-ik, -'zā-\ adj [paradise + -aic (as in Hebraic)] (1754) : PARADISIACAL — **par·a·di·sa·i·cal** \-'sā-ə-kəl, -'zā-\ adj — **par·a·di·sa·i·cal·ly** \-ə-k(ə-)lē\ adv

par·a·dis·al \,par-ə-'dī-səl, -zəl\ adj (1560) : PARADISIACAL

par·a·dise \'par-ə-,dīs, -,dīz\ n [ME paradis, fr. OF, fr. LL paradisus, fr. Gk paradeisos, lit., enclosed park, of Iranian origin; akin to Av pairidaēza- enclosure; akin to Gk peri around and to Gk teichos wall — more at PERI-, DOUGH] (12c) **1 a** : EDEN 2 **b** : an intermediate place or state where the righteous departed await resurrection and judgment **c** : HEAVEN **2** : a place or state of bliss, felicity, or delight — **par·a·dis·i·al** \,par-ə-'dī-sē-əl, -zē-\ also **par·a·dis·i·cal** \-si-kəl, -zi-\ adj

par·a·di·si·a·cal \,par-ə-də-'sī-ə-kəl, -,dī-, -'zī-\ or **par·a·dis·i·ac** \-'dī-zē-,ak, -sē-\ adj [LL paradisiacus, fr. paradisus] (1649) : of, relating to, or resembling paradise — **par·a·di·si·a·cal·ly** \-də-'sī-ə-k(ə-)lē, -,di-, -'zi-\ adv

pa·ra·dor \,pä-rä-'thȯr\ n [Sp, inn, fr. parar to stop, lodge for the night, fr. L parare to prepare — more at PARE] (1845) : a usu. government-operated hostelry found esp. in Spain

par·a·dox \'par-ə-,däks\ n [L paradoxum, fr. Gk paradoxon, fr. neut. of paradoxos contrary to expectation, fr. para- + dokein to think, seem — more at DECENT] (1540) **1** : a tenet contrary to received opinion **2 a** : a statement that is seemingly contradictory or opposed to common sense and yet is perhaps true **b** : a self-contradictory statement that at first seems true **c** : an argument that apparently derives self-contradictory conclusions by valid deduction from acceptable premises **3** : something or someone with seemingly contradictory qualities or phases

par·a·dox·i·cal \,par-ə-'däk-si-kəl\ adj (1581) **1 a** : of the nature of a paradox **b** : inclined to paradoxes **2** : not being the normal or usual kind ⟨∼ pulse⟩ — **par·a·dox·i·cal·i·ty** \-,däk-si-'ka-lə-tē\ n — **par·a·dox·i·cal·ly** \-'däk-si-k(ə-)lē\ adv — **par·a·dox·i·cal·ness** \-kəl-nəs\ n

paradoxical sleep n (1964) : REM SLEEP

par·aes·the·sia var of PARESTHESIA

par·af·fin \'par-ə-fən\ n [G, fr. L parum too little (akin to Gk pauros little, paid-, pais child) + affinis bordering on — more at FEW, AFFINITY] (1838) **1 a** : a waxy crystalline flammable substance obtained esp. from distillates of wood, coal, petroleum, or shale oil that is a complex mixture of hydrocarbons and is used chiefly in coating and sealing, in candles, in rubber compounding, and in pharmaceuticals and cosmetics **b** : any of various mixtures of similar hydrocarbons including mixtures that are semisolid or oily **2** : ALKANE **3** chiefly Brit : KEROSENE — **par·af·fin·ic** \,par-ə-'fi-nik\ adj

par·a·for·mal·de·hyde \,par-ə-fȯr-'mal-də-,hīd, -fər-\ n (1894) : a white powder (CH_2O) that consists of a polymer of formaldehyde and is used esp. as a fungicide

par·a·gen·e·sis \,par-ə-'je-nə-səs\ n [NL] (1853) : the formation of minerals in contact in such a manner as to affect one another's development — **par·a·ge·net·ic** \-jə-'ne-tik\ adj — **par·a·ge·net·i·cal·ly** \-ti-k(ə-)lē\ adv

¹**par·a·gon** \'par-ə-,gän, -gən\ n [MF, fr. OIt paragone, lit., touchstone, fr. paragonare to test on a touchstone, fr. Gk parakonan to sharpen, fr. para- + akonē whetstone, fr. akē point; akin to Gk akmē point — more at EDGE] (ca. 1548) : a model of excellence or perfection

²**paragon** vt (ca. 1586) **1** : to compare with : PARALLEL **2** : to put in rivalry : MATCH **3** obs : SURPASS

¹**par·a·graph** \'par-ə-,graf\ n [MF & ML; MF paragraphe, fr. ML paragraphus sign marking a paragraph, fr. Gk paragraphos line used to mark change of persons in a dialogue, fr. paragraphein to write alongside, fr. para- + graphein to write — more at CARVE] (1525) **1 a** : a subdivision of a written composition that consists of one or more sentences, deals with one point or gives the words of one speaker, and begins on a new usu. indented line **b** : a short composition or note that is complete in one paragraph **2** : a character (as ¶) used to indicate the beginning of a paragraph and as a reference mark — **par·a·graph·ic** \,par-ə-'gra-fik\ adj

²**paragraph** vt (1764) **1** : to write paragraphs about **2** : to divide into paragraphs ∼ vi : to write paragraphs

par·a·graph·er \'par-ə-,gra-fər\ n (1822) : a writer of paragraphs esp. for the editorial page of a newspaper

para·in·flu·en·za virus \,par-ə-,in-flü-'en-zə-\ n (1959) : any of several paramyxoviruses that are associated with or responsible for some respiratory infections esp. in children — called also parainfluenza

para·jour·nal·ism \,par-ə-'jər-nᵊl-,i-zəm\ n (1965) : journalism that is heavily colored by the opinions of the reporter

par·a·keet \'par-ə-,kēt\ n [Sp & MF; Sp periquito, fr. MF perroquet parrot] (1581) : any of numerous usu. small slender parrots with a long graduated tail

para·lan·guage \'par-ə-,laŋ-gwij\ n (ca. 1958) : optional vocal effects (as tone of voice) that accompany or modify the phonemes of an utterance and that may communicate meaning

par·al·de·hyde \pa-'ral-də-,hīd, pə-\ n (1857) : a colorless liquid polymeric modification $C_6H_{12}O_3$ of acetaldehyde used as a hypnotic

para·le·gal \,par-ə-'lē-gəl\ adj (1971) : of, relating to, or being a paraprofessional who assists a lawyer — **para·le·gal** \'par-ə-,lē-gəl\ n

para·lin·guis·tics \,par-ə-liŋ-'gwis-tiks\ n (ca. 1958) : the study of paralanguage — **para·lin·guis·tic** \-tik\ adj

Par·a·li·pom·e·non \,par-ə-lə-'pä-mə-,nän, -li-\ n [LL, fr. Gk Paraleipomenōn, gen. of Paraleipomena, lit., things left out, fr. neut. pl. of passive prp. of paraleipein to leave out, fr. para- + leipein to leave; fr. its forming a supplement to Samuel and Kings — more at LOAN] : CHRONICLES

par·al·lac·tic \,par-ə-'lak-tik\ adj [NL parallacticus, fr. Gk parallaktikos, fr. parallaxis] (1630) : of, relating to, or due to parallax

par·al·lax \'par-ə-,laks\ n [MF parallaxe, fr. Gk parallaxis, fr. parallassein to change, fr. para- + allassein to change, fr. allos other] (1580) : the apparent displacement or the difference in apparent direction of an object as seen from two different points not on a straight line with the object; esp : the angular difference in direction of a celestial body as measured from two points on the earth's orbit

¹**par·al·lel** \'par-ə-,lel, -ləl\ adj [L parallelus, fr. Gk parallēlos, fr. para beside + allēlon of one another, fr. allos... allos one... another, fr. allos other — more at ELSE] (1549) **1 a** : extending in the same direction, everywhere equidistant, and not meeting ⟨∼ rows of trees⟩ **b** : everywhere equally distant ⟨concentric spheres are ∼⟩ **2 a** : having parallel sides ⟨a ∼ reamer⟩ **b** : being or relating to an electrical circuit having a number of conductors in parallel **c** : arranged in parallel ⟨a ∼ processor⟩ **d** : relating to or being a connection in a computer system in which the bits of a byte are transmitted over separate channels at the same time — compare SERIAL 3 **a** : similar, analogous, or interdependent in tendency or development **b** : readily compared : COMPANION **c** : having identical syntactical elements in corresponding positions; also : being such an element **d** (1) : having the same tonic — used of major and minor keys and scales (2) : keeping the same distance apart in musical pitch **4** : performed while keeping one's skis parallel ⟨∼ turns⟩ syn see SIMILAR

²**parallel** n (1551) **1 a** : a parallel line, curve, or surface **b** : one of the imaginary circles on the surface of the earth paralleling the equator and marking the latitude; also : the corresponding line on a globe or map — see LATITUDE illustration **c** : a character ‖ used in printing esp. as a reference mark **2 a** : something equal or similar in all essential particulars : COUNTERPART **b** : SIMILARITY, ANALOGUE **3** : a comparison to show resemblance : a tracing of similarities **4 a** : the state of being physically parallel : PARALLELISM **b** : an arrangement of electrical devices in a circuit in which the same potential difference is applied to two or more resistances with each resistance being on a different branch of the circuit — compare SERIES **c** : an arrangement or state that permits several operations or tasks to be performed simultaneously rather than consecutively

³**parallel** vt (1598) **1** : to indicate analogy of : COMPARE **2 a** : to show something equal to : MATCH **b** : to correspond to **3** : to place so as to be parallel in direction with something **4** : to extend, run, or move in a direction parallel to

⁴**parallel** adv (1787) : in a parallel manner

parallel bars n pl (1868) **1** : a pair of wooden bars supported horizontally above the floor at the same height or at different heights usu. by a common base and used in gymnastics **2** : an event in gymnastics competition in which even or uneven parallel bars are used

par·al·lel·e·pi·ped \,par-ə-,le-lə-'pi-pəd also -,le-'le-pə-,ped\ n [Gk parallēlepipedon, fr. parallēlos + epipedon plane surface, fr. neut. of epipedos flat, fr. epi- epi- + pedon ground; akin to L ped-, pes foot — more at FOOT] (1570) : a 6-faced polyhedron all of whose faces are parallelograms lying in pairs of parallel planes

par·al·lel·ism \'par-ə-,le-,li-zəm, -lə-,li-\ n (1610) **1** : the quality or state of being parallel **2** : RESEMBLANCE, CORRESPONDENCE **3** : repeated syntactical similarities introduced for rhetorical effect **4** : a theory that mind and matter accompany one another but are not causally related **5** : the development of similar new characters by two or more related organisms in response to similarity of environment — called also parallel evolution

par·al·lel·o·gram \,par-ə-'le-lə-,gram\ n [LL or Gk; LL parallelogrammum, fr. Gk parallēlogrammon, fr. neut. of parallēlogrammos bounded by parallel lines, fr. parallēlos + grammē line, fr. graphein to write — more at CARVE] (1570) : a quadrilateral with opposite sides parallel and equal

par·al·lel–veined \,par-ə-,lel-'vānd, -ləl-\ adj (1861) of a leaf : having veins arranged nearly parallel to one another — compare NET-VEINED

pa·ral·o·gism \pə-'ra-lə-,ji-zəm\ n [MF paralogisme, fr. LL paralogismus, fr. Gk paralogismos, fr. paralogos unreasonable, fr. para- + logos speech, reason — more at LEGEND] (1565) : a fallacious argument

par·a·lyse Brit var of PARALYZE

pa·ral·y·sis \pə-'ra-lə-səs\ n, pl **-y·ses** \-,sēz\ [L, fr. Gk, fr. paralyein to loosen, disable, fr. para- + lyein to loosen — more at LOSE] (1525) **1** : complete or partial loss of function esp. when involving the motion or sensation in a part of the body **2** : loss of the ability to move **3** : a state of powerlessness or incapacity to act

paralysis agi·tans \-'a-jə-,tanz\ n [NL, lit., shaking palsy] (1817) : PARKINSON'S DISEASE

¹**par·a·lyt·ic** \,par-ə-'li-tik\ adj [ME paralytyk, fr. MF paralitike, fr. L paralyticus, fr. Gk paralytikos, fr. paralyein] (14c) **1** : affected with or characterized by paralysis **2** : of, relating to, or resembling paralysis — **par·a·lyt·i·cal·ly** \-ti-k(ə-)lē\ adv

²**paralytic** n (14c) : one affected with paralysis

par·a·lyze \'par-ə-,līz\ vt **-lyzed; -lyz·ing** [F paralyser, back-formation fr. paralysie paralysis, fr. L paralysis] (1804) **1** : to affect with paralysis **2** : to make powerless or ineffective **3** : UNNERVE **4** : STUN, STUPEFY **5** : to bring to an end : PREVENT, DESTROY — **par·a·ly-**

za·tion \,par-ə-lə-'zā-shən\ *n* — **par·a·lyz·er** \'par-ə-‚lī-zər\ *n* — **par·a·lyz·ing·ly** \-‚lī-ziŋ-lē\ *adv*

para·mag·net \'par-ə-‚mag-nət\ *n* [back-formation fr. *paramagnetic*] (ca. 1900) : a paramagnetic substance

para·mag·net·ic \,par-ə-mag-'ne-tik\ *adj* [ISV] (ca. 1850) : being or relating to a magnetizable substance (as aluminum) that has small but positive susceptibility which varies little with magnetizing force — **para·mag·net·i·cal·ly** \-ti-k(ə-)lē\ *adv* — **para·mag·ne·tism** \-'mag-nə-‚ti-zəm\ *n*

par·a·me·cium \,par-ə-'mē-sh(ē-)əm, -sē-əm\ *n, pl* -**cia** \-sh(ē-)ə, -sē-ə\ *also* -**ciums** [NL, fr. Gk *paramēkēs* oblong, fr. *para-* + *mēkos* length; akin to Gk *makros* long — more at MEAGER] (1752) : any of a genus (*Paramecium*) of ciliate protozoans that have an elongate body rounded at the anterior end and an oblique funnel-shaped buccal groove bearing the mouth at the extremity

para·med·ic \,par-ə-'me-dik\ *also* **para·med·i·cal** \-di-kəl\ *n* (1967) **1** : a person who works in a health field in an auxiliary capacity to a physician (as by giving injections and taking X rays) **2** : a specially trained medical technician licensed to provide a wide range of emergency services (as defibrillation and the intravenous administration of drugs) before or during transportation to a hospital — compare EMT

para·med·i·cal \,par-ə-'me-di-kəl\ *also* **para·med·ic** \-dik\ *adj* (1921) : concerned with supplementing the work of highly trained medical professionals 〈~ aides and technicians〉

par·a·ment \'par-ə-mənt\ *n* [ME, fr. ML *paramentum*, fr. *parare* to adorn, fr. L to prepare — more at PARE] (15c) : an ornamental ecclesiastical hanging or vestment

pa·ram·e·ter \pə-'ram-ə-tər\ *n* [NL, fr. *para-* + Gk *metron* measure — more at MEASURE] (1656) **1 a** : an arbitrary constant whose value characterizes a member of a system (as a family of curves); *also* : a quantity (as a mean or variance) that describes a statistical population **b** : an independent variable used to express the coordinates of a variable point and functions of them — compare PARAMETRIC EQUATION **2** : any of a set of physical properties whose values determine the characteristics or behavior of something 〈~s of the atmosphere such as temperature, pressure, and density〉 **3** : something represented by a parameter : a characteristic element; *broadly* : CHARACTERISTIC, ELEMENT, FACTOR 〈political dissent as a ~ of modern life〉 **4** : LIMIT, BOUNDARY — usu. used in pl. 〈the ~s of science fiction〉 — **para·met·ric** \,par-ə-'me-trik\ *adj* — **para·met·ri·cal·ly** \-tri-k(ə-)lē\ *adv*

pa·ram·e·ter·ize \pə-'ra-mə-tə-‚rīz, -mə-‚triz\ *or* **pa·ram·e·trize** \-'ra-mə-‚triz\ *vt* **-ized** *or* **-trized;** **-er·iz·ing** *or* **-triz·ing** (1940) : to express in terms of parameters — **pa·ram·e·ter·i·za·tion** \-‚ra-mə-tə-rə-'zā-shən, -mə-trə-\ *or* **pa·ram·e·tri·za·tion** \-mə-trə-\ *n*

parametric equation *n* (1909) : any of a set of equations that express the coordinates of the points of a curve as functions of one parameter or that express the coordinates of the points of a surface as functions of two parameters

para·mil·i·tary \,par-ə-'mi-lə-‚ter-ē\ *adj* (1935) : of, relating to, being, or characteristic of a force formed on a military pattern esp. as a potential auxiliary military force 〈a ~ border patrol〉 〈~ training〉

par·am·ne·sia \,par-‚am-'nē-zhə, -əm-\ *n* [NL, fr. *para-* + *-mnesia* (as in *amnesia*)] (1888) : a disorder of memory; *esp* : DÉJÀ VU 1

¹par·a·mount \'par-ə-‚maunt\ *adj* [AF *paramont*, fr. OF *par* by (fr. L *per*) + *amont* above, fr. *a* to (fr. L *ad*) + *mont* mountain — more at FOR, AT, MOUNT] (1579) : superior to all others : SUPREME *syn* see DOMINANT — **par·a·mount·cy** \-‚maun(t)-sē\ *n* — **par·a·mount·ly** \-‚maunt-lē\ *adv*

²paramount *n* (1616) : a supreme ruler

par·amour \'par-ə-‚mur\ *n* [ME, fr. *par amour* by way of love, fr. MF] (14c) : an illicit lover

par·am·y·lum \pa-'ra-mə-ləm\ *n* [NL, fr. *para-* + L *amylum* starch — more at AMYL] (1897) : a reserve carbohydrate that is found in various protozoans and algae and resembles starch

para·myxo·vi·rus \,par-ə-'mik-sə-‚vī-rəs\ *n* [NL] (1962) : any of a group of RNA-containing viruses (as the mumps, measles, and parainfluenza viruses)

pa·rang \'pär-‚aŋ\ *n* [Malay] (1839) : a short sword, cleaver, or machete common in Malaysia and Indonesia

para·noia \,par-ə-'nói-ə\ *n* [NL, fr. Gk, madness, fr. *paranous* demented, fr. *para-* + *nous* mind] (ca. 1811) **1** : a psychosis characterized by systematized delusions of persecution or grandeur usu. without hallucinations **2** : a tendency on the part of an individual or group toward excessive or irrational suspiciousness and distrustfulness of others — **para·noi·ac** \-'nói-‚ak, -'nói-ik\ *also* **para·noic** \-'nói(-i)k, -'nō-ik\ *adj or n* — **para·noi·cal·ly** \-'nói(-i)-k(ə-)lē, -'nō-i-k(ə-)lē\ *adv*

para·noid \'par-ə-‚nóid\ *also* **para·noi·dal** \,par-ə-'nói-d²l\ *adj* (1904) **1** : characterized by or resembling paranoia **2** : characterized by suspiciousness, persecutory trends, or megalomania **3** : extremely fearful — **paranoid** *n*

paranoid schizophrenia *n* (1940) : schizophrenia characterized esp. by persecutory or grandiose delusions or hallucinations or by delusional jealousy

para·nor·mal \,par-ə-'nór-məl, 'par-ə-‚\ *adj* (ca. 1920) : not scientifically explainable : SUPERNATURAL — **paranormal** *n* — **para·nor·mal·i·ty** \,par-ə-‚nór-'ma-lə-tē\ *n* — **para·nor·mal·ly** \-'nór-mə-lē\ *adv*

para·nymph \'par-ə-‚nim(p)f\ *n* [LL *paranymphus*, fr. Gk *paranymphos*, fr. *para-* + *nymphē* bride — more at NUPTIAL] (1600) **1** : a friend going with a bridegroom to fetch home the bride in ancient Greece; *also* : the bridesmaid conducting the bride to the bridegroom **2 a** : BEST MAN **b** : BRIDESMAID

par·a·pet \'par-ə-pət, -‚pet\ *n* [It *parapetto*, fr. *parare* to shield (fr. L, to prepare) + *petto* chest, fr. L *pectus* — more at PARE, PECTORAL] (1590) **1** : a wall, rampart, or elevation of earth or stone to protect soldiers : BREASTWORK **2** : a low wall or railing to protect the edge of a platform, roof, or bridge — called also *parapet wall* — **par·a·pet·ed** \-‚pe-təd\ *adj*

pa·raph \'par-əf, pə-'raf\ *n* [MF, fr. L *paragraphus* paragraph] (1584) : a flourish at the end of a signature

par·a·pher·na·lia \,par-ə-fə(r)-'nāl-yə\ *n pl but sing or pl in constr* [ML, ultim. fr. Gk *parapherna* bride's property beyond her dowry, fr. *para-* + *phernē* dowry, fr. *pherein* to bear — more at BEAR] (1651) **1** : the separate real or personal property of a married woman that she can

dispose of by will and sometimes according to common law during her life **2** : personal belongings **3 a** : articles of equipment : FURNISHINGS **b** : accessory items : APPURTENANCES

¹para·phrase \'par-ə-‚frāz\ *n* [MF, fr. L *paraphrasis*, fr. Gk, fr. *paraphrazein* to paraphrase, fr. *para-* + *phrazein* to point out] (1548) **1** : a restatement of a text, passage, or work giving the meaning in another form **2** : the use or process of paraphrasing in studying or teaching composition

²paraphrase *vb* **-phrased; -phras·ing** *vi* (1596) : to make a paraphrase ~ *vt* : to make a paraphrase of — **para·phras·able** \,par-ə-'frā-zə-bəl\ *adj* — **para·phras·er** *n*

para·phras·tic \,par-ə-'fras-tik\ *adj* [F *paraphrastique*, fr. Gk *paraphrastikos*, fr. *paraphrazein*] (ca. 1623) : having the nature of or being a paraphrase — **para·phras·ti·cal·ly** \-ti-k(ə-)lē\ *adv*

pa·raph·y·sis \pə-'ra-fə-səs\ *n, pl* -**y·ses** \-‚sēz\ [NL, fr. Gk, sucker, offshoot, fr. *paraphyein* to produce at the side, fr. *para-* + *phyein* to bring forth — more at BE] (1857) : one of the slender sterile filaments borne among the sporogenous or gametogenous organs in cryptogamic plants

para·ple·gia \,par-ə-'plē-j(ē-)ə\ *n* [NL, fr. Gk *paraplēgiē* hemiplegia, fr. *para-* + *-plēgia* -plegia] (ca. 1657) : paralysis of the lower half of the body with involvement of both legs — **para·ple·gic** \-jik\ *adj or n*

para·po·di·um \-'pō-dē-əm\ *n, pl* -**dia** \-dē-ə\ [NL] (1877) **1** : either of a pair of fleshy lateral processes borne by most segments of a polychaete worm **2** : a lateral expansion on each side of the foot usu. forming a broad swimming organ in some gastropods — **para·po·di·al** \-dē-əl\ *adj*

para·pro·fes·sion·al \-prə-'fesh-nəl, -'fe-shə-n²l\ *n* (1965) : a trained aide who assists a professional person (as a teacher or doctor) — **paraprofessional** *adj*

para·psy·chol·o·gy \,par-ə-(‚)sī-'kä-lə-jē\ *n* [ISV] (1925) : a field of study concerned with the investigation of evidence for paranormal psychological phenomena (as telepathy, clairvoyance, and psychokinesis) — **para·psy·cho·log·i·cal** \-‚sī-kə-'lä-ji-kəl\ *adj* — **para·psy·chol·o·gist** \-(‚)sī-'kä-lə-jist\ *n*

para·quat \'par-ə-‚kwät\ *n* [*para-* + *quaternary*] (ca. 1961) : a highly toxic contact herbicide containing a salt of a cation $[C_{12}H_{14}N_2]^{2+}$

para·ros·an·i·line \,par-ə-‚rō-'za-n²l-ən\ *n* [ISV] (ca. 1879) : a white crystalline base $C_{19}H_{19}N_3O$ that is the parent compound of many dyes; *also* : its red chloride used esp. as a biological stain

Pa·ra rubber \'par-ə-, pə-'rä-\ *n* [*Pará*, Brazil] (1857) : native rubber from So. American rubber trees (genus *Hevea* and esp. *H. brasiliensis*)

Para rubber tree *n* (1930) : a So. American rubber tree (*Hevea brasiliensis*)

para·sail·ing \'par-ə-‚sā-liŋ\ *n* (1967) : the recreational sport of soaring in a parachute while being towed usu. by a motorboat

par·a·sang \'par-ə-‚saŋ\ *n* [L *parasanga*, fr. Gk *parasangēs*, of Iranian origin; akin to Per *farsang* parasang] (1594) : any of various Persian units of distance; *esp* : an ancient unit of about four miles (six kilometers)

para·sex·u·al \-'sek-sh(ə-)wəl, -shəl\ *adj* (1954) : relating to or being reproduction that results in recombination of genes from different individuals but does not involve meiosis and formation of a zygote by fertilization as in sexual reproduction 〈the ~ cycle in some fungi〉 — **para·sex·u·al·i·ty** \-‚sek-shə-'wa-lə-tē\ *n*

pa·ra·shah \'pär-ə-‚shä\ *n* [Heb *pārāshāh*, lit., explanation] (1624) : a passage in Jewish Scripture dealing with a single topic; *specif* : a section of the Torah assigned for weekly reading in synagogue worship

par·a·site \'par-ə-‚sīt\ *n* [MF, fr. L *parasitus*, fr. Gk *parasitos*, fr. *para-* + *sitos* grain, food] (1539) **1** : a person who exploits the hospitality of the rich and earns welcome by flattery **2** : an organism living in, with, or on another organism in parasitism **3** : something that resembles a biological parasite in dependence on something else for existence or support without making a useful or adequate return — **par·a·sit·ic** \,par-ə-'si-tik\ *also* **par·a·sit·i·cal** \-ti-kəl\ *adj* — **par·a·sit·i·cal·ly** \-ti-k(ə-)lē\ *adv*

syn PARASITE, SYCOPHANT, TOADY, LEECH, SPONGE mean a usu. obsequious flatterer or self-seeker. PARASITE applies to one who clings to a person of wealth, power, or influence or is useless to society 〈a jet-setter with an entourage of *parasites*〉. SYCOPHANT adds to this a strong suggestion of fawning, flattery, or adulation 〈a powerful prince surrounded by *sycophants*〉. TOADY emphasizes the servility and snobbery of the self-seeker 〈cultivated leaders of society and became their *toady*〉. LEECH stresses persistence in clinging to or bleeding another for one's own advantage 〈a *leech* living off his family and friends〉. SPONGE stresses the parasitic laziness, dependence, and opportunism of the cadger 〈a shiftless *sponge*, always looking for a handout〉.

par·a·sit·i·cid·al \,par-ə-‚si-tə-'sī-d²l\ *adj* (1892) : destructive to parasites — **par·a·sit·i·cide** \-'si-tə-‚sīd\ *n*

par·a·sit·ise *Brit var of* PARASITIZE

par·a·sit·ism \'par-ə-sə-‚ti-zəm, -‚sī-\ *n* (1611) **1** : the behavior of a parasite **2** : an intimate association between organisms of two or more kinds; *esp* : one in which a parasite obtains benefits from a host which it usu. injures **3** : PARASITOSIS

par·a·sit·ize \-sə-‚tīz, -‚sī-\ *vt* **-ized; -iz·ing** (1890) : to infest or live on or with as a parasite — **par·a·sit·i·za·tion** \,par-ə-sə-tə-'zā-shən, -‚sī-\ *n*

par·a·sit·oid \'par-ə-sə-‚tóid, -‚sī-\ *n* (1922) : an insect and esp. a wasp that completes its larval development within the body of another insect eventually killing it and is free-living as an adult — **parasitoid** *adj*

par·a·si·tol·o·gy \,par-ə-sə-'tä-lə-jē, -‚sī-\ *n* [L *parasitus* + ISV *-logy*] (1882) : a branch of biology dealing with parasites and parasitism esp. among animals — **par·a·si·to·log·i·cal** \-‚si-t²l-'ä-ji-kəl, -‚sī-\ *also* **par·a·si·to·log·ic** \-jik\ *adj* — **par·a·si·to·log·i·cal·ly** \-ji-k(ə-)lē\ *adv* — **par·a·si·tol·o·gist** \-sə-'tä-lə-jist, -‚sī-\ *n*

par·a·sit·o·sis \-sə-'tō-səs, -‚sī-\ *n, pl* -**o·ses** \-‚sēz\ [NL] (ca. 1899) : infestation with or disease caused by parasites

---

\ə\ abut \'ᵊ\ kitten, F table \ər\ further \a\ ash \ā\ ace \ä\ mop, mar \au̇\ out \ch\ chin \e\ bet \ē\ easy \g\ go \i\ hit \ī\ ice \j\ job \ŋ\ sing \ō\ go \ȯ\ law \ȯi\ boy \th\ thin \th̲\ the \ü\ loot \u̇\ foot \y\ yet \zh\ vision \á, k̲, ⁿ, œ, œ̄, ᵫ, ᵫ̄, ᐟ\ *see* Guide to Pronunciation

par·a·sol \'par-ə-ˌsȯl, -ˌsäl\ *n* [F, fr. OIt *parasole*, fr. *parare* to shield + *sole* sun, fr. L *sol* — more at PARAPET, SOLAR] (1660) : a lightweight umbrella used as a sunshade esp. by women

¹para·sym·pa·thet·ic \ˌpar-ə-ˌsim-pə-'the-tik\ *adj* [ISV] (1905) : of, relating to, being, or acting on the parasympathetic nervous system

²parasympathetic *n* (1925) **1** : a parasympathetic nerve **2** : PARA-SYMPATHETIC NERVOUS SYSTEM

parasympathetic nervous system *n* (ca. 1934) : the part of the autonomic nervous system that contains chiefly cholinergic fibers, that tends to induce secretion, to increase the tone and contractility of smooth muscle, and to slow heart rate, and that consists of a cranial and a sacral part — compare SYMPATHETIC NERVOUS SYSTEM

para·sym·pa·tho·mi·met·ic \ˌpar-ə-ˌsim-pə-(ˌ)thō-mī-'me-tik, -mə-\ *adj* [ISV] (1942) : simulating parasympathetic nervous action in physiological effect

para·syn·the·sis \ˌpar-ə-'sin(t)-thə-səs\ *n* [NL] (1862) : the formation of words by adding a derivative ending and prefixing a particle (as in *denationalize*) — **para·syn·thet·ic** \-sin-'the-tik\ *adj*

para·tac·tic \ˌpar-ə-'tak-tik\ *also* **para·tac·ti·cal** \-ti-kəl\ *adj* (1871) : of or relating to parataxis — **para·tac·ti·cal·ly** \-ti-k(ə-)lē\ *adv*

para·tax·is \ˌpar-ə-'tak-səs\ *n* [NL, fr. Gk, act of placing side by side, fr. *paratassein* to place side by side, fr. *para-* + *tassein* to arrange] (ca. 1842) : the placing of clauses or phrases one after another without coordinating or subordinating connectives

para·thi·on \ˌpar-ə-'thī-ˌän, -ˌän\ *n* [*para-* + *thiophosphate* + ¹-*on*] (1947) : an extremely toxic insecticide $C_{10}H_{14}NO_5PS$

par·a·thor·mone \ˌpar-ə-'thȯr-ˌmōn\ *n* [fr. *Parathormone*, a trademark] (1925) : PARATHYROID HORMONE

¹para·thy·roid \-'thī-ˌrȯid\ *n* (1897) : PARATHYROID GLAND

²parathyroid *adj* [ISV] (1902) : of, relating to, or produced by the parathyroid glands

para·thy·roid·ec·to·my \-ˌrȯi-'dek-tə-mē\ *n, pl* **-mies** (1903) : partial or complete excision of the parathyroid glands — **para·thy·roid·ec·to·mized** \-ˌmīzd\ *adj*

parathyroid gland *n* [ISV] (ca. 1903) : any of usu. four small endocrine glands that are adjacent to or embedded in the thyroid gland and produce parathyroid hormone

parathyroid hormone *n* (1953) : a hormone of the parathyroid gland that regulates the metabolism of calcium and phosphorus in the body

para·troop·er \'par-ə-ˌtrü-pər\ *n* (1927) : a member of the paratroops

para·troops \-ˌtrüps\ *n pl* [²*para-*] (1940) : troops trained and equipped to parachute from an airplane — **para·troop** \-ˌtrüp\ *adj*

¹para·ty·phoid \ˌpar-ə-'tī-ˌfȯid, -(ˌ)tī-\ *adj* [ISV] (1902) **1** : resembling typhoid fever **2** : of or relating to paratyphoid or its causative organisms ⟨~ infection⟩

²paratyphoid *n* (1903) : a salmonellosis that resembles typhoid fever and is commonly contracted by eating contaminated food — called also *paratyphoid fever*

para·vane \'par-ə-ˌvān\ *n* [prob. fr. F *para-* warding off (as in *parachute*) + E *vane*] (1919) : a torpedo-shaped protective device with serrate teeth in its forward end used underwater by a ship in mined areas to sever the moorings of mines

par·boil \'pär-ˌbȯil\ *vt* [ME, fr. *parboilen* to boil thoroughly, fr. MF *parboillir*, fr. LL *perbullire*, fr. L *per-* thoroughly (fr. *per* through) + *bullire* to boil, fr. *bulla* bubble — more at FOR] (14c) : to boil briefly as a preliminary or incomplete cooking procedure

par·buck·le \'pär-ˌbə-kəl\ *n* [origin unknown] (1626) **1** : a purchase for hoisting or lowering a cylindrical object by making fast the middle of a long rope aloft and looping both ends around the object which rests in the loops and rolls in them as the ends are hauled up or paid out; *also* : a single line made fast at one end and passed around an object that is used similarly — **parbuckle** *vt*

Par·cae \'pär-ˌkī, -ˌsē\ *n pl* [L] : FATE 4

parbuckle

¹par·cel \'pär-səl\ *n* [ME, fr. MF, fr. (assumed) VL *particella*, fr. L *particula* small part — more at PARTICLE] (14c) **1 a** : FRAGMENT, PORTION **b** : a volume of a fluid (as air) considered as a single entity within a greater volume of the same fluid **2** : a tract or plot of land **3** : a company, collection, or group of persons, animals, or things : LOT ⟨the whole story was a ~ of lies⟩ **4 a** : a wrapped bundle : PACKAGE **b** : a unit of salable merchandise

²parcel *adv* (15c) *archaic* : PARTLY

³parcel *adj* (15c) : PART-TIME, PARTIAL

⁴parcel *vt* **-celed** *or* **-celled; -cel·ing** *or* **-cel·ling** \'pär-s(ə-)liŋ\ (15c) **1** : to divide into parts : DISTRIBUTE — often used with *out* **2** : to make up into a parcel : WRAP **3** : to cover (as a rope) with strips of canvas or tape

parcel post *n* (1837) **1** : a mail service handling parcels **2** : packages handled by parcel post

par·ce·nary \'pär-s°n-ˌer-ē\ *n* [AF *parcenarie*, fr. OF *parçonerie*, fr. *parçon* portion, fr. L *partition-, partitio* partition] (1544) : COPARCENARY 1

par·ce·ner \'pärs-nər, 'pär-s°n-ər\ *n* [AF, fr. OF *parçonier*, fr. *parçon*] (1574) : COPARCENER

parch \'pärch\ *vb* [ME] *vt* (14c) **1** : to toast under dry heat **2** : to shrivel with heat **3** : to dry or shrivel with cold ~ *vi* : to become dry or scorched

parched \'pärcht\ *adj* (ca. 1552) : deprived of natural moisture; *also* : THIRSTY

Par·chee·si \pär-'chē-zē, pər-, *esp Brit* -sē\ *trademark* — used for a board game adapted from pachisi

parch·ment \'pärch-mənt\ *n* [ME *parchemin*, fr. MF, modif. of L *pergamena*, fr. Gk *pergamēnē*, fr. fem. of *Pergamēnos* of Pergamum, fr. *Pergamon* Pergamum] (14c) **1** : the skin of a sheep or goat prepared for writing on **2** : strong, tough, and often somewhat translucent paper made to resemble parchment **3** : a parchment manuscript; *also* : an academic diploma

¹pard \'pärd\ *n* [ME *parde*, fr. MF, fr. L *pardus*, fr. Gk *pardos*] (14c) : LEOPARD

²pard *n* [short for *pardner*] (1850) *chiefly dial* : PARTNER, CHUM

par·die *or* **par·di** *or* **par·dy** \pər-'dē, pär-\ *interj* [ME *pardee*, fr. OF *par Dé* by God] (14c) *archaic* — used as a mild oath

pard·ner \'pärd-nər\ *n* [alter. of *partner*] (1795) *chiefly dial* : PARTNER, CHUM

¹par·don \'pärd-ᵊn\ *n* [ME, fr. MF, fr. *pardoner*] (14c) **1** : INDULGENCE 1 **2** : the excusing of an offense without exacting a penalty **3 a** : a release from the legal penalties of an offense **b** : an official warrant of remission of penalty **4** : excuse or forgiveness for a fault, offense, or discourtesy ⟨I beg your ~⟩

²pardon *vt* **par·doned; par·don·ing** \'pärd-niŋ, 'pär-d°n-iŋ\ [ME, MF *pardoner*, fr. LL *perdonare* to grant freely, fr. L *per-* thoroughly + *donare* to give — more at PARBOIL, DONATION] (15c) **1 a** : to absolve from the consequences of a fault or crime **b** : to allow (an offense) to pass without punishment : FORGIVE **c** : to relieve of a penalty improperly assessed **2** : TOLERATE *syn* see EXCUSE

par·don·able \'pärd-nə-bəl, 'pär-d°n-ə-bəl\ *adj* (15c) : admitting of being pardoned : EXCUSABLE ⟨~ offenses⟩ — **par·don·able·ness** *n* — **par·don·ably** \-blē\ *adv*

par·don·er \'pärd-nər, 'pär-d°n-ər\ *n* (14c) **1** : a medieval preacher delegated to raise money for religious works by soliciting offerings and granting indulgences **2** : one that pardons

pare \'par, 'per\ *vt* **pared; par·ing** [ME, fr. MF *parer* to prepare, trim, fr. L *parare* to prepare, acquire; akin to L *parere* to give birth to, produce, Lith *peréti* to hatch] (14c) **1** : to trim off an outside, excess, or irregular part of ⟨~ apples⟩ ⟨*paring* his nails⟩ **2** : to diminish or reduce by or as if by paring ⟨~ expenses⟩ ⟨the novel was *pared* down to 200 pages⟩ — **par·er** *n*

par·e·gor·ic \ˌpar-ə-'gȯr-ik, -'gȯr-, -'gär-\ *n* [F *parégorique* mitigating pain, fr. LL *paregoricus*, fr. Gk *parēgorikos*, fr. *parēgorein* to talk over, soothe, fr. *para-* + *agora* assembly, fr. *ageirein* to gather] (ca. 1847) : camphorated tincture of opium used esp. to relieve pain

pa·ren·chy·ma \pə-'reŋ-kə-mə\ *n* [NL, fr. Gk, visceral flesh, fr. *parenchein* to pour in beside, fr. *para-* + *en-* en- + *chein* to pour — more at FOUND] (1651) **1** : a tissue of higher plants that consists of thin-walled living photosynthetic or storage cells capable of division even when mature and that makes up much of the substance of leaves and roots, the pulp of fruits, and parts of stems and supporting structures **2** : the essential and distinctive tissue of an organ or an abnormal growth as distinguished from its supportive framework — **par·en·chy·ma·tous** \ˌpar-ən-'kī-mə-təs, -'ki-\ *or* **pa·ren·chy·mal** \pə-'reŋ-kə-məl, ˌpar-ən-'kī-\ *adj*

¹par·ent \'par-ənt, 'per-\ *n* [ME, fr. MF, fr. L *parent-, parens;* akin to L *parere* to give birth to] (15c) **1 a** : one that begets or brings forth offspring **b** : a person who brings up and cares for another **2 a** : an animal or plant that is regarded in relation to its offspring **b** : the material or source from which something is derived **c** : a group from which another arises and to which it usu. remains subsidiary ⟨a ~ company⟩ — **parent** *adj* — **pa·ren·tal** \pə-'ren-t°l\ *adj* — **pa·ren·tal·ly** \-t°l-ē\ *adv* — **par·ent·less** \'par-ənt-ləs, 'per-\ *adj*

²parent *vt* (1663) : to be or act as the parent of : ORIGINATE, PRODUCE

par·ent·age \'par-ən-tij, 'per-\ *n* [ME, fr. MF, fr. *parent*] (15c) **1 a** : descent from parents or ancestors : LINEAGE ⟨a person of noble ~⟩ **b** : DERIVATION, ORIGIN ⟨a tradition of uncertain ~⟩ **2** : PARENTHOOD

par·en·ter·al \pə-'ren-tə-rəl\ *adj* [ISV *para-* + *enteral*] (ca. 1910) : situated or occurring outside the intestine; *esp* : introduced otherwise than by way of the intestines — **par·en·ter·al·ly** \-rə-lē\ *adv*

pa·ren·the·sis \pə-'ren(t)-thə-səs\ *n, pl* **-the·ses** \-ˌsēz\ [LL, fr. Gk, lit., act of inserting, fr. *parentithenai* to insert, fr. *para-* + *en-* en- + *tithenai* to place — more at DO] (ca. 1550) **1 a** : an amplifying or explanatory word, phrase, or sentence inserted in a passage from which it is usu. set off by punctuation **b** : a remark or passage that departs from the theme of a discourse : DIGRESSION **2** : INTERLUDE, INTERVAL **3** : one or both of the curved marks ( ) used in writing and printing to enclose a parenthetical expression or to group a symbolic unit in a logical or mathematical expression — **par·en·thet·i·cal** \ˌpar-ən-'the-ti-kəl\ *also* **par·en·thet·ic** \-tik\ *adj* — **par·en·thet·i·cal·ly** \-ti-k(ə-)lē\ *adv*

pa·ren·the·size \pə-'ren(t)-thə-ˌsīz\ *vt* **-sized; -siz·ing** (1837) **1** : to make a parenthesis of : enclose within parentheses

par·ent·hood \'par-ənt-ˌhud, 'per-\ *n* (1856) : the state of being a parent; *specif* : the position, function, or standing of a parent

par·ent·ing \'par-ən-tiŋ, 'per-\ *n* (1958) **1** : the raising of a child by its parents **2** : the act or process of becoming a parent **3** : the act of caring for someone in the manner of a parent

parent–teacher association *n, often cap* P&T&A (1915) : an organization of local groups of teachers and the parents of their pupils that works for the improvement of the schools and the benefit of the pupils

pa·re·sis \pə-'rē-səs, 'par-ə-\ *n, pl* **pa·re·ses** \-ˌsēz\ [NL, fr. Gk, fr. *parienai* to let fall, fr. *para-* + *hienai* to let go, send — more at JET] (1693) **1** : slight or partial paralysis **2** : GENERAL PARESIS — **pa·ret·ic** \pə-'re-tik\ *adj or n*

par·es·the·sia \ˌpar-əs-'thē-zhə\ *n* [NL, fr. *para-* + *-esthesia* (as in *anesthesia*)] (ca. 1860) : a sensation of pricking, tingling, or creeping on the skin that has no objective cause — **par·es·thet·ic** \-'the-tik\ *adj*

pa·reu *or* **pa·reo** \'pär-ā-(ˌ)ü\ *n* [Tahitian] (1860) : a wraparound skirt usu. made from a rectangular piece of printed cloth and worn by men and women throughout Polynesia

pa·re·ve \'pär-(ə-)və\ *adj* [Yiddish *parev*] (1941) : made without milk, meat, or their derivatives ⟨~ margarine⟩ — compare FLEISHIG, MILCHIG

par ex·cel·lence \'pär-ˌek-sə-'läns\ *adj* [F, lit., by excellence] (1695) : being the best of a kind : PREEMINENT ⟨a salesman *par excellence*⟩

par·fait \pär-'fā\ *n* [F, lit., something perfect, fr. *parfait* perfect, fr. L *perfectus*] (1894) **1** : a flavored custard containing whipped cream and syrup frozen without stirring **2** : a cold dessert made of layers of fruit, syrup, ice cream, and whipped cream

parfait glass *n* (ca. 1951) : a tall narrow glass with a short stem

par·fleche \'pär-ˌflesh\ *n* [CanF *parflèche*, fr. F *parer* to ward off + *flèche* arrow] (1827) **1** : a raw hide soaked in lye to remove the hair and dried **2** : an article (as a bag or case) made of parfleche

par·fo·cal \ˌpär-'fō-kəl\ *adj* [L *par* equal + E *focal*] (1886) : being or having lenses or lens sets (as eyepieces) with the corresponding focal

points all in the same plane — **par·fo·cal·i·ty** \‚pär-fō-'ka-lə-tē\ *n* —
par·fo·cal·ize \‚pär-'fō-kə-‚līz\ *vt*
parge \'pärj\ *vt* **parged; parg·ing** (1701) : PARGET
¹par·get \'pär-jət\ *vt* **-get·ed** *or* **-get·ted; -get·ing** *or* **-get·ting** [ME
pargetten, fr. MF *parjeter* to throw on top of, fr. *par-* thoroughly (fr. L
per-) + *jeter* to throw — more at JET] (14c) : to coat with plaster; *esp*
: to apply ornamental or waterproofing plaster to
²parget *n* (14c) **1** : plaster, whitewash, or roughcast for coating a wall
2 : plasterwork esp. in raised ornamental figures on walls
par·gy·line \'pär-jə-‚lēn\ *n* [*propargyl* (an alcohol) + ²-*ine*] (1961) : a
monoamine oxidase inhibitor $C_{11}H_{13}N$ that is used in the hydrochloride esp. as an antihypertensive agent
parhelic circle *n* (1890) : a luminous circle or halo parallel to the
horizon at the altitude of the sun — called also *parhelic ring*
par·he·lion \pär-'hēl-yən\ *n, pl* **-lia** \-yə\ [L *parelion*, fr. Gk *parēlion*,
fr. *para-* + *hēlios* sun — more at SOLAR] (1647) : any of several bright
spots often tinged with color that often appear on the parhelic circle —
par·he·lic \-'hē-lik\ *adj*
pa·ri·ah \pə-'rī-ə\ *n* [Tamil *paraiyan*, lit., drummer] (1613) **1** : a member of a low caste of southern India **2** : OUTCAST I
par·i·an \'par-ē-ən, 'per-\ *n* [*Parian*, adj.; fr. its suitability for making
statuettes] (1850) : a porcelain composed essentially of kaolin and
feldspar and usu. used unglazed in ornamental articles
Par·i·an \'par-ē-ən, 'per-\ *adj* (1611) : of or relating to the island of
Paros noted for its marble used extensively for sculpture in ancient
times
Parian ware *n* (1894) **1** : PARIAN **2** : articles made of parian
¹pa·ri·e·tal \pə-'rī-ə-t°l\ *adj* [MF, fr. NL *pariet-, paries* wall of a cavity
or hollow organ, fr. L wall] (15c) **1 a** : of or relating to the walls of
a part or cavity **b** : of, relating to, or forming the upper posterior wall
of the head **2** : attached to the main wall rather than the axis or a
cross wall of a plant ovary — used of an ovule or a placenta **3** : of or
relating to college living or its regulation; *esp* : of or relating to pari-
etals
²parietal *n* (15c) **1** : a parietal part (as a bone, scale, or plate) **2** *pl*
: the regulations governing the visiting privileges of members of the
opposite sex in campus dormitories
parietal bone *n* (15c) : either of a pair of bones of the roof of the skull
between the frontal bones and the occipital bones
parietal cell *n* (1875) : any of the large oval cells of the gastric mucous
membrane that secrete hydrochloric acid
parietal lobe *n* (ca. 1889) : the middle division of each cerebral hemisphere that contains an area concerned with bodily sensations
pari–mu·tu·el \‚par-i-'myü-chə-wəl, -chəl; -'myüch-wəl\ *n* [F *pari
mutuel*, lit., mutual stake] (1888) **1** : a betting pool in which those
who bet on competitors finishing in the first three places share the total
amount bet minus a percentage for the management **2** : a machine for
registering the bets and computing the payoffs in pari-mutuel betting
par·ing \'par-iŋ, 'per-\ *n* (14c) **1** : the act of cutting away an edge or
surface **2** : something pared off ⟨apple ~s⟩
paring knife *n* (1591) : a small short-bladed knife (as for paring fruit)
pa·ri pas·su \'par-i-'pa-(‚)sü\ *adv or adj* [L, with equal step] (1567) : at
an equal rate or pace
Par·is \'par-əs\ *n* [L, fr. Gk] : a son of Priam whose abduction of
Helen leads to the Trojan War
Paris green \'par-əs-\ *n* [*Paris*, France] (1868) **1** : a very poisonous
copper-based bright green powder that is used as an insecticide and
pigment **2** : a brilliant yellowish green
par·ish \'par-ish\ *n* [ME *parisshe*, fr. MF *paroche*, fr. LL *parochia*, fr.
LGk *paroikia*, fr. *paroikos* Christian, fr. Gk, stranger, fr. *para-* + *oikos*
house — more at VICINITY] (14c) **1 a** (1) : the ecclesiastical unit of
area committed to one pastor (2) : the residents of such an area **b**
Brit : a subdivision of a county often coinciding with an original ecclesiastical parish and constituting the unit of local government **2** : a
local church community composed of the members or constituents of a
Protestant church **3** : a civil division of the state of Louisiana corresponding to a county in other states
pa·rish·ion·er \pə-'ri-sh(ə-)nər\ *n* [ME *parisshoner*, prob. modif. of MF
parrochien, fr. *parroche*] (15c) : a member or inhabitant of a parish
¹par·i·ty \'par-ə-tē\ *n, pl* **-ties** [L *paritas*, fr. *par* equal] (ca. 1609) **1**
: the quality or state of being equal or equivalent **2 a** : equivalence
of a commodity price expressed in one currency to its price expressed in
another **b** : equality of purchasing power established by law between
different kinds of money at a given ratio **3** : an equivalence between
farmers' current purchasing power and their purchasing power at a
selected base period maintained by government support of agricultural
commodity prices **4 a** : the property of an integer with respect to
being odd or even ⟨3 and 7 have the same ~⟩ **b** (1) : the state of
being odd or even used as the basis of a method of detecting errors in
binary-coded data (2) : PARITY BIT **5** : the property of oddness or
evenness of a quantum mechanical function **6** : the symmetry of behavior in an interaction of a physical entity (as a subatomic particle)
with that of its mirror image
²parity *n* [-*parous*] (1878) : the state or fact of having borne offspring;
also : the number of children previously borne
parity bit *n* (1957) : a bit added to an array of bits (as on magnetic
tape) to provide parity
¹park \'pärk\ *n* [ME, fr. OF *parc* enclosure, fr. ML *parricus*] (13c) **1**
a : an enclosed piece of ground stocked with game and held by royal
prescription or grant **b** : a tract of land that often includes lawns,
woodland, and pasture attached to a country house and is used as a
game preserve and for recreation **2 a** : a piece of ground in or near a
city or town kept for ornament and recreation **b** : an area maintained
in its natural state as a public property **3 a** *West* : a level valley between mountain ranges **b** : an open space and esp. a grassland that is
often all or partly surrounded by woodland and is suitable for cultivation or grazing **4 a** : a space occupied by military animals, vehicles,
or materials **b** : PARKING LOT **5** : an enclosed arena or stadium used
esp. for ball games **6** : an area designed for a specified industrial,
commercial, or residential use ⟨amusement ~⟩ ⟨industrial ~⟩ ⟨mobile
home ~⟩ — **park·like** \'pärk-‚līk\ *adj*
²park *vt* (1526) **1** : to enclose in a park **2 a** (1) : to bring (a vehicle) to a stop and keep standing at the edge of a public way (2) : to
leave temporarily on a public way or in a parking lot or garage **b** : to

land and leave (as an airplane) **c** : to establish (as a satellite) in orbit
3 a : to set and leave temporarily ⟨~ed his hat on the chair⟩ **b** : to
place, settle, or establish esp. for a considerable time ⟨kids ~ed in front
of the TV⟩ ⟨~ed her money in a savings account⟩ **4** : to assemble (as
equipment or stores) in a military dump or park ~ *vi* : to park a vehicle — **park·er** *n*
par·ka \'pär-kə\ *n* [Aleut, fr. Russ dial., ultim. fr. Nenets (Samoyedic
language of northern Russia)] (1780) **1** : a hooded fur pullover garment for arctic wear **2** : a usu. lined fabric outerwear pullover or
jacket
parking lot *n* (1924) : an area used for the parking of motor vehicles
parking meter *n* (1936) : a coin-operated device which registers the
purchase of parking time for a motor vehicle
par·kin·so·nian \‚pär-kən-'sō-nē-ən, -nyən\ *adj* (1906) **1** : of or similar to that of parkinsonism **2** : affected with parkinsonism and esp.
Parkinson's disease
par·kin·son·ism \'pär-kən-sə-‚ni-zəm\ *n* (ca. 1923) **1** : PARKINSON'S
DISEASE **2** : a nervous disorder that resembles Parkinson's disease
Par·kin·son's disease \'pär-kən-sənz-\ *n* [James *Parkinson* †1824
Eng. physician] (1877) : a chronic progressive nervous disease chiefly
of later life that is linked to decreased dopamine production in the
substantia nigra and is marked by tremor and weakness of resting muscles and by a shuffling gait — called also *paralysis agitans, Parkinson's,
Parkinson's syndrome*
Parkinson's Law *n* [C. Northcote *Parkinson* b1909 Eng. historian]
(1955) **1** : an observation in office organization: the number of subordinates increases at a fixed rate regardless of the amount of work produced **2** : an observation in office organization: work expands so as to
fill the time available for its completion
park·land \'pärk-‚land\ *n* (1907) : land with clumps of trees and
shrubs in cultivated condition used as or suitable for use as a park
park·way \'pärk-‚wā\ *n* (1887) : a broad landscaped thoroughfare
par·lance \'pär-lən(t)s\ *n* [MF, fr. OF, fr. *parler*] (ca. 1580) **1**
: SPEECH; *esp* : formal debate or parley **2** : manner or mode of speech
: IDIOM
par·lan·do \pär-'län-(‚)dō\ *or* **par·lan·te** \-(‚)tā\ *adj* [*parlando* fr. It,
verbal of *parlare* to speak, fr. ML *parabolare; parlante* fr. It, prp. of
parlare] (ca. 1854) : delivered or performed in a style suggestive of
speech — used as a direction in music
¹par·lay \'pär-‚lā, -lē\ *vt* [*paroli*, n., parlay, fr. It dial., pl. of *parolo*,
perh. fr. *paro* equal, fr. L *par*] (1828) **1** : to bet in a parlay **2** : to
exploit successfully **b** : to increase or otherwise transform into something of much greater value
²parlay *n* (1904) : a series of two or more bets so set up in advance that
the original stake plus its winnings are risked on the successive wagers;
broadly : the fresh risking of an original stake together with its winnings
parle \'pär(-ə)l\ *vi* **parled; parl·ing** [ME, to parley, fr. MF *parler*]
(14c) *archaic* : PARLEY — **parle** *n, archaic*
¹par·ley \'pär-lē\ *n, pl* **parleys** [ME *parlai* speech, prob. fr. MF *parlee*,
fr. fem. of *parlé*, pp. of *parler* to speak, fr. ML *parabolare*, fr. LL *parabola* speech, parable — more at PARABLE] (1581) **1 a** : a conference
for discussion of points in dispute **b** : a conference with an enemy **2**
: DISCUSSION
²par·ley *vi* **par·leyed; par·ley·ing** (1591) : to speak with another
: CONFER; *specif* : to discuss terms with an enemy
par·lia·ment \'pär-lə-mənt *also* 'pärl-yə-\ *n* [ME, fr. OF *parlement*, fr.
parler] (13c) **1** : a formal conference for the discussion of public affairs; *specif* : a council of state in early medieval England **2 a** : an
assemblage of the nobility, clergy, and commons called together by the
British sovereign as the supreme legislative body in the United Kingdom **b** : a similar assemblage in another nation or state **3 a** : the
supreme legislative body of a usu. major political unit that is a continuing institution comprising a series of individual assemblages **b** : the
British House of Commons **4** : one of several principal courts of justice existing in France before the revolution of 1789
par·lia·men·tar·i·an \‚pär-lə-‚men-'ter-ē-ən, -mən- *also* ‚pärl-yə-\ *n*
(1644) **1** *often cap* : an adherent of the parliament in opposition to the
king during the English Civil War **2** : an expert in the rules and usages of a deliberative assembly (as a parliament) **3** : a member of a
parliament
par·lia·men·ta·ry \-'men-t(ə-)rē\ *adj* (1616) **1 a** : of or relating to a
parliament **b** : enacted, done, or ratified by a parliament **2** : of or
adhering to the parliament as opposed to the king during the English
Civil War **3** : of, based on, or having the characteristics of parliamentary government **4** : of or relating to members of a parliament **5** : of
or according to parliamentary law ⟨~ procedure⟩
parliamentary government *n* (1858) : a system of government having the real executive power vested in a cabinet composed of members
of the legislature who are individually and collectively responsible to
the legislature
parliamentary law *n* (1893) : the rules and precedents governing the
proceedings of deliberative assemblies and other organizations
¹par·lor \'pär-lər\ *n* [ME *parlour*, fr. OF, fr. *parler*] (13c) **1** : a room
used primarily for conversation or the reception of guests: as **a** : a
room in a private dwelling for the entertainment of guests **b** : a conference chamber or private reception room **c** : a room in an inn, hotel,
or club for conversation or semiprivate uses **2** : any of various business places ⟨a funeral ~⟩ ⟨a beauty ~⟩
²parlor *adj* (1552) **1** : used in or suitable for a parlor ⟨~ furniture⟩ **2**
a : fostered or advocated in comfortable seclusion without consequent
action or application to affairs ⟨~ bolshevism⟩ **b** : given to or characterized by fostering or advocating something (as a doctrine) in such a
manner ⟨~ socialist⟩
parlor car *n* (1868) : an extra-fare railroad passenger car for day travel
equipped with individual chairs
parlor game *n* (1872) : a game suitable for playing indoors

\ə\ abut \ʳ\ kitten, F table \ər\ further \a\ ash \ā\ ace \ä\ mop, mar
\aú\ out \ch\ chin \e\ bet \ē\ easy \g\ go \i\ hit \ī\ ice \j\ job
\ŋ\ sing \ō\ go \ó\ law \ói\ boy \th\ thin \t̷h\ the \ü\ loot \ú\ foot
\y\ yet \zh\ vision \à, k̲, ⁿ, œ, œ̄, ᴜᴇ, ᵫ, ʸ\ see Guide to Pronunciation

parlor grand n (1856) : a grand piano intermediate in length between a concert grand and a baby grand

par·lour \'pär-lər\ chiefly Brit var of PARLOR

par·lous \'pär-ləs\ adj [ME, alter. of perilous] (14c) **1** obs : dangerously shrewd or cunning **2** : full of danger or risk : HAZARDOUS — **par·lous·ly** adv

Par·me·san \'pär-mə-ˌzän, -ˌzhän, -zən, ˌ-zan\ n [Parmesan of Parma, fr. MF parmesan, fr. OIt parmigiano] (1538) : a very hard dry sharply flavored cheese that is sold grated or in wedges

par·mi·gia·na \ˌpär-mi-'jä-nə, -'zhän; 'pär-mi-ˌzhän, -ˌzän\ or **par·mi·gia·no** \-'jä-(ˌ)nō\ adj [It parmigiana, fem. of parmigiano of Parma, fr. Parma] (1943) : made or covered with Parmesan cheese ⟨veal ∼⟩

Par·nas·si·an \pär-'na-sē-ən\ adj (ca. 1644) **1** [L parnassius of Parnassus, fr. Gk parnasios, fr. Parnasos Parnassus, mountain in Greece sacred to Apollo and the Muses]: of or relating to poetry **2** [F parnassien, fr. Parnasse Parnassus; fr. Le Parnasse contemporain (1866), an anthology of poetry]: of or relating to a school of French poets of the second half of the 19th century emphasizing metrical form rather than emotion — **Parnassian** n

pa·ro·chi·al \pə-'rō-kē-əl\ adj [ME parochiall, fr. MF parochial, fr. LL parochialis, fr. parochia parish — more at PARISH] (14c) **1** : of or relating to a church parish **2** : of or relating to a parish as a unit of local government **3** : confined or restricted as if within the borders of a parish : limited in range or scope (as to a narrow area or region) : PROVINCIAL, NARROW — **pa·ro·chi·al·ly** \-kē-ə-lē\ adv

pa·ro·chi·al·ism \-kē-ə-ˌli-zəm\ n (1847) : the quality or state of being parochial; esp : selfish pettiness or narrowness (as of interests, opinions, or views)

parochial school n (1755) : a private school maintained by a religious body usu. for elementary and secondary instruction

par·o·dist \'par-ə-dist\ n (1742) : a writer of parodies

¹par·o·dy \'par-ə-dē\ n, pl **-dies** [L parodia, fr. Gk parōidia, fr. para- + aidein to sing — more at ODE] (1598) **1** : a literary or musical work in which the style of an author or work is closely imitated for comic effect or in ridicule **2** : a feeble or ridiculous imitation syn see CARICATURE — **pa·rod·ic** \pə-'rä-dik, pa-\ adj — **par·o·dis·tic** \ˌpar-ə-'dis-tik\ adj

²parody vt **-died; -dy·ing** (ca. 1745) **1** : to compose a parody on ⟨∼ a poem⟩ **2** : to imitate in the manner of a parody

par·ol \'par-əl\ n [MF parole] (1590) : WORD OF MOUTH — **parol** adj

¹pa·role \pə-'rōl\ n [F, speech, parole, fr. MF, fr. LL parabola speech — more at PARABLE] (ca. 1616) **1** : a promise made with or confirmed by a pledge of one's honor; esp : the promise of a prisoner of war to fulfill stated conditions in consideration of his release **2** : a watchword given only to officers of the guard and of the day **3** : a conditional release of a prisoner serving an indeterminate or unexpired sentence **4 a** : language viewed as a specific individual usage : PERFORMANCE **b** : a linguistic act — compare LANGUE — **parole** adj

²parole vt **pa·roled; pa·rol·ing** (1790) : to release (a prisoner) on parole

pa·rol·ee \pə-ˌrō-'lē, -'rō-(ˌ); ˌpar-ə-'lē\ n (1903) : one released on parole

par·o·no·ma·sia \ˌpar-ə-nō-'mā-zh(ē-)ə, ˌpar-ˌä-nə-'mā-\ n [L, fr. Gk, fr. paronomazein to call with a slight change of name, fr. para- + onoma name — more at NAME] (1577) : a play on words : PUN — **par·o·no·mas·tic** \-'mas-tik\ adj

par·o·nym \'par-ə-ˌnim\ n [LL paronymon, fr. Gk parōnymon, neut. of parōnymos] (ca. 1846) : a paronymous word

par·on·y·mous \pə-'rä-nə-məs, pa-\ adj [Gk parōnymos, fr. para- + -ōnymos (as in homōnymos homonymous)] (ca. 1661) **1** : CONJUGATE 4 **2 a** : formed from a word in another language **b** : having a form similar to that of a cognate foreign word

pa·rot·id \pə-'rä-təd\ adj [NL parotid-, parotis parotid gland, fr. L, tumor near the ear, fr. Gk parōtid-, parōtis, fr. para- + ōt-, ous ear — more at EAR] (1687) : of or relating to the parotid gland

parotid gland n (ca. 1771) : either of a pair of large serous salivary glands situated below and in front of the ear

par·o·ti·tis \ˌpar-ə-'tī-təs\ n (1822) : inflammation of the parotid glands; also : MUMPS

par·ous \'par-əs, 'per-\ adj [-parous] (ca. 1889) : having produced offspring

-parous adj comb form [L -parus, fr. parere to give birth to, produce — more at PARE]: giving birth to : producing ⟨multiparous⟩

Par·ou·sia \ˌpär-ü-'sē-ə, pə-'rü-zē-ə\ n [Gk, lit., presence, fr. paront-, parōn, prp. of pareinai to be present, fr. para- + einai to be — more at IS] (1875) : SECOND COMING

par·ox·ysm \'par-ək-ˌsi-zəm also pə-'räk-\ n [F & ML; F paroxysme, fr. ML paroxysmus, fr. Gk paroxysmos, fr. paroxynein to stimulate, fr. para- + oxynein to provoke, fr. oxys sharp — more at OXYGEN] (15c) **1** : a fit, attack, or sudden increase or recurrence of symptoms (as of a disease) : CONVULSION ⟨a ∼ of coughing⟩ **2** : a sudden violent emotion or action : OUTBURST ⟨a ∼ of rage⟩ — **par·ox·ys·mal** \ˌpar-ək-'siz-məl pə-ˌräk-\ adj

¹par·quet \pär-'kā\ vt **par·queted** \-'kād\; **par·quet·ing** \-'kā-iŋ\ (1678) **1** : to furnish with a floor of parquet **2** : to make of parquetry

²parquet \'pär-ˌkā, pär-'\ n [F, fr. MF, small enclosure, fr. parc park] (1816) **1 a** : a patterned wood surface (as flooring or paneling); esp : one made of parquetry **b** : PARQUETRY **2** : the main floor of a theater; specif : the part from the front of the stage to the parquet circle

parquet circle n (1854) : the part of the main floor of a theater that is beneath the galleries

par·que·try \'pär-kə-trē\ n, pl **-tries** (ca. 1842) : work in the form of usu. geometrically patterned wood laid or inlaid esp. for floors

parr \'pär\ n, pl **parr** also **parrs** [origin unknown] (ca. 1722) : a young salmon actively feeding in freshwater

par·ra·keet var of PARAKEET

par·rel or **par·ral** \'par-əl\ n [ME perell, fr. alter. of parail apparel, short for parail MF apareil, fr. apareillier to prepare — more at APPAREL] (15c) : a rope loop or sliding collar by which a yard or spar is held to a mast in such a way that it may be hoisted or lowered

par·ri·cid·al \ˌpar-ə-'sī-d'l\ adj (1627) : of, relating to, or guilty of parricide

par·ri·cide \'par-ə-ˌsīd\ n (1554) **1** [L parricida killer of a close relative, fr. parri- (perh. akin to Gk pēos kinsman by marriage) + -cida

-cide]: one that murders his or her father, mother, or a close relative **2** [L parricidium murder of a close relative, fr. parri- + -cidium -cide] : the act of a parricide

¹par·rot \'par-ət\ n [prob. irreg. fr. MF perroquet] (ca. 1525) **1** : any of numerous widely distributed tropical zygodactyl birds (order Psittaciformes and esp. family Psittacidae) that have a distinctive stout curved hooked bill, are often crested and brightly variegated, and include some excellent mimics **2** : a person who sedulously echoes another's words — **parrot** adj

²parrot vt (1596) : to repeat by rote

parrot fever n (1930) : PSITTACOSIS

parrot fish n (1712) : any of a family (Scaridae) of usu. brightly colored chiefly tropical marine fishes that have the teeth in each jaw fused into a cutting plate like a beak

par·ry \'par-ē\ vb **par·ried; par·ry·ing** [prob. fr. F parez, imper. of parer to parry, fr. OProv parar, fr. L parare to prepare — more at PARE] vi (1672) **1** : to ward off a weapon or blow **2** : to evade or turn aside something ∼ vt **1** : to ward off (as a blow) **2** : to evade esp. by an adroit answer ⟨∼ an embarrassing question⟩ — **parry** n

¹parse \'pärs, chiefly Brit 'pärz\ vb **parsed; pars·ing** [L pars orationis part of speech] vt (1553) **1 a** : to resolve (as a sentence) into component parts of speech and describe them grammatically **b** : to describe grammatically by stating the part of speech and explaining the inflection and syntactical relationships **2** : to examine in a minute way : analyze critically ⟨∼s appellate court opinions⟩ ∼ vi **1** : to give a grammatical description of a word or a group of words **2** : to admit of being parsed

²parse n (1963) : a product or an instance of parsing

par·sec \'pär-ˌsek\ n [parallax + second] (1913) : a unit of measure for interstellar space equal to the distance to an object having a parallax of one second or to 3.26 light-years

pars·er \'pär-sər\ n (ca. 1864) : one that parses; specif : a computer program that breaks down text into recognized strings of characters for further analysis

Par·si also **Par·see** \'pär-(ˌ)sē\ n [Per pārsī, fr. Pārs Persia] (1615) **1** : a Zoroastrian descended from Persian refugees settled principally at Bombay **2** : the Iranian dialect of the Parsi religious literature — **Par·si·ism** \-ˌi-zəm\ n

par·si·mo·ni·ous \ˌpär-sə-'mō-nē-əs\ adj (1598) : exhibiting or marked by parsimony; esp : frugal to the point of stinginess syn see STINGY — **par·si·mo·ni·ous·ly** adv

par·si·mo·ny \'pär-sə-ˌmō-nē\ n [ME parcimony, fr. L parsimonia, fr. parsus, pp. of parcere to spare] (15c) **1 a** : the quality of being careful with money or resources : THRIFT **b** : the quality or state of being stingy **2** : economy in the use of means to an end; esp : economy of explanation in conformity with Occam's razor

pars·ley \'pär-slē\ n [ME persely, fr. OE petersilie, fr. (assumed) VL petrosilium, alter. of L petroselinum, fr. Gk petroselinon, fr. petros stone + selinon celery] (bef. 12c) : a European biennial herb (Petroselinum crispum) of the carrot family that is widely cultivated for its leaves which are used as a culinary herb or garnish

pars·leyed also **pars·lied** \-slēd\ adj (1952) : garnished or flavored with parsley ⟨∼ potatoes⟩

pars·nip \'pär-snəp\ n [ME pasnepe, modif. of MF pasnaie, fr. L pastinaca, fr. pastinum 2-pronged dibble] (14c) : a Eurasian biennial herb (Pastinaca sativa) of the carrot family with large pinnate leaves and yellow flowers that is cultivated for its long tapered edible root; also : the root

par·son \'pär-s'n\ n [ME persone, fr. OF, fr. ML persona, lit., person, fr. L] (13c) **1** : RECTOR **2** : CLERGYMAN; esp : a Protestant pastor

par·son·age \'pär-s(ə-)nij, 'pär-s'n-ij\ n (15c) : the house provided by a church for its pastor

Par·sons ta·ble \'pär-s'nz-\ n [Parsons School of Design, New York City] (1967) : a usu. rectangular table having straight legs that are flush with the edge of the top

¹part \'pärt\ n [ME, fr. OF & OE, both fr. L part-, pars; perh. akin to L parare to prepare — more at PARE] (bef. 12c) **1 a** (1) : one of the often indefinite or unequal subdivisions into which something is or is regarded as divided and which together constitute the whole (2) : an essential portion or integral element **b** : one of several or many equal units of which something is composed or into which it is divisible : an amount equal to another amount ⟨mix one ∼ of the powder with three ∼s of water⟩ **c** (1) : an exact divisor of a quantity : ALIQUOT (2) : PARTIAL FRACTION **d** : one of the constituent elements of a plant or animal body: as (1) : ORGAN, MEMBER (2) pl : PRIVATE PARTS **e** : a division of a literary work **f** (1) : a vocal or instrumental line or melody in concerted music or in harmony (2) : a particular voice or instrument in concerted music; also : the score for it **g** : a constituent member of a machine or other apparatus; also : a spare part **2** : something falling to one in a division or apportionment : SHARE **3** : one's share or allotted task (as in an action) ⟨one must do one's ∼⟩ **4** : one of the opposing sides in a conflict or dispute **5** : a general area of indefinite boundaries — usu. used in pl. ⟨you're not from around these ∼s⟩ ⟨took off for ∼s unknown⟩ **6** : a function or course of action performed **7 a** : an actor's lines in a play **b** : the role of a character in a play **8** : a constituent of character or capacity : TALENT ⟨a man of many ∼s⟩ **9** : the line where the hair is parted — **for the most part** : in general : on the whole ⟨for the most part the crowd was orderly⟩ — **in part** : in some degree : PARTIALLY — **on the part of** : with regard to the one specified

syn PART, PORTION, PIECE, MEMBER, DIVISION, SECTION, SEGMENT, FRAGMENT mean something less than the whole. PART is a general term appropriate when indefiniteness is required ⟨they ran only part of the way⟩. PORTION implies an assigned or allotted part ⟨cut the pie into six portions⟩. PIECE applies to a separate or detached part of a whole ⟨a puzzle with 500 pieces⟩. MEMBER suggests one of the functional units composing a body ⟨a structural member⟩. DIVISION applies to a large or diversified part ⟨the manufacturing division of the company⟩. SECTION applies to a relatively small or uniform part ⟨the entertainment section of the newspaper⟩. SEGMENT applies to a part separated or marked out by or as if by natural lines of cleavage ⟨the retired segment of the population⟩. FRAGMENT applies to a part produced by or as if by breaking off or shattering ⟨only a fragment of the play still exists⟩.

²part vb [ME, fr. OF partir, fr. L partire to divide, fr. part-, pars] vi (13c)

1 a : to separate from or take leave of someone **b :** to take leave of one another **2 :** to become separated into parts **3 a :** to go away **:** DEPART **b :** DIE **4 :** to become separated, detached, or broken **5 :** to relinquish possession or control ⟨hated to ~ with that money⟩ ~ *vt* **1 a :** to divide into parts **b :** to separate by combing on each side of a line ⟨ ~ the hair⟩ **c :** to break or suffer the breaking of ⟨as a rope or anchor chain⟩ **2 :** to divide into shares and distribute **:** APPORTION **3 a :** to remove from contact or association ⟨if aught but death ~ thee and me —Ruth 1:17(AV)⟩ **b :** to keep separate ⟨the narrow channel that ~s England from France⟩ **c :** to hold (as brawlers) apart **d :** to separate by a process of extraction, elimination, or secretion **4 a** *archaic* **:** LEAVE, QUIT **b** *dial Brit* **:** RELINQUISH, GIVE UP *syn* see SEPARATE

³**part** *adv* (1513) **:** PARTLY

⁴**part** *adj* (1818) **:** PARTIAL 1

par·take \pär-ˈtāk, pər-\ *vb* **-took** \-ˈtuk\; **-tak·en** \-ˈtā-kən\; **-tak·ing** [back-formation fr. *partaker*, alter. of *part taker*] *vi* (ca. 1585) **1 :** to take part in or experience something along with others ⟨ ~ in the revelry⟩ ⟨ ~ of the good life⟩ **2 :** to have a portion (as of food or drink) **3 :** to possess or share a certain nature or attribute ⟨the experience ~s of a mystical quality⟩ ~ *vt* **:** to take part in *syn* see SHARE — **par·tak·er** *n*

part and parcel *n* (15c) **:** an essential or integral component ⟨stress was *part and parcel* of the job⟩

part·ed \ˈpär-təd\ *adj* (1590) **1 a :** divided into parts **b :** cleft so that the divisions reach nearly but not quite to the base — usu. used in combination ⟨a 3-*parted* corolla⟩ **2** *archaic* **:** DEAD

par·terre \pär-ˈter\ *n* [F, fr. MF, fr. *par terre* on the ground] (ca. 1639) **1 :** an ornamental garden with paths between the beds **2 :** the part of the main floor of a theater that is behind the orchestra; *esp* **:** PARQUET CIRCLE

par·the·no·car·py \ˈpär-thə-nō-ˌkär-pē\ *n* [ISV, fr. Gk *parthenos* virgin + *karpos* fruit — more at HARVEST] (1911) **:** the production of fruits without fertilization ⟨bananas set fruit by ~ and without pollination⟩ — **par·the·no·car·pic** \ˌpär-thə-nō-ˈkär-pik\ *adj*

par·the·no·gen·e·sis \ˌpär-thə-nō-ˈje-nə-səs\ *n* [NL, fr. Gk *parthenos* + L *genesis* genesis] (1849) **:** reproduction by development of an unfertilized usu. female gamete that occurs esp. among lower plants and invertebrate animals

par·the·no·ge·net·ic \-jə-ˈne-tik\ *adj* (1872) **:** of, characterized by, or produced by parthenogenesis — **par·the·no·ge·net·i·cal·ly** \-ˈti-k(ə-)lē\ *adv*

Par·the·non \ˈpär-thə-ˌnän\ *n* [L, fr. Gk *Parthenōn*] (ca. 1841) **:** a Doric temple of Athena built on the acropolis at Athens in the 5th century B.C.

Par·thi·an \ˈpär-thē-ən\ *adj* (1579) **1 :** of, relating to, or characteristic of ancient Parthia or its people **2 :** relating to, being, or having the effect of a shot fired while in real or feigned retreat — **Parthian** *n*

¹**par·tial** \ˈpär-shəl\ *adj* [ME *parcial*, fr. MF *partial*, fr. ML *partialis*, fr. LL, of a part, fr. L *part-*, *pars* part] (14c) **1 :** of or relating to a part rather than the whole **:** not general or total ⟨a ~ solution⟩ **2 :** inclined to favor one party more than the other **:** BIASED **3 :** markedly fond of someone or something — used with *to* ⟨ ~ to pizza⟩

²**partial** *n* (1880) **:** OVERTONE 1a

partial denture *n* (1860) **:** a usu. removable artificial replacement of one or more teeth

partial derivative *n* (1889) **:** the derivative of a function of several variables with respect to one of them and with the remaining variables treated as constants

partial differential equation *n* (1889) **:** a differential equation containing at least one partial derivative

partial differentiation *n* (ca. 1890) **:** the process of finding a partial derivative

partial fraction *n* (1816) **:** one of the simpler fractions into the sum of which the quotient of two polynomials may be decomposed

par·tial·i·ty \ˌpär-shē-ˈa-lə-tē, pär-ˈsha-lə-tē\ *n*, *pl* **-ties** (15c) **1 :** the quality or state of being partial **2 :** a special taste or liking

par·tial·ly \ˈpär-sh(ə-)lē\ *adv* (15c) **1** *archaic* **:** in a biased manner **:** with partiality **2 :** to some extent **:** in some degree

partially ordered *adj* (1941) **:** having some or all elements connected by a relation that is reflexive, transitive, and antisymmetric

partial pressure *n* (1857) **:** the pressure exerted by a (specified) component in a mixture of gases

partial product *n* (ca. 1924) **:** a product obtained by multiplying a multiplicand by one digit of a multiplier having more than one digit

par·ti·ble \ˈpär-tə-bəl\ *adj* (14c) **:** capable of being parted **:** DIVISIBLE ⟨a ~ inheritance⟩ — **par·ti·bil·i·ty** \ˌpär-tə-ˈbi-lə-tē\ *n*

par·tic·i·pant \pär-ˈti-sə-pənt, pər-\ *n* (1562) **:** one that participates — **participant** *adj*

par·tic·i·pate \pär-ˈti-sə-ˌpāt, pər-\ *vb* **-pat·ed; -pat·ing** [L *participatus*, pp. of *participare*, fr. *particip-, participes* participant, fr. *part-, pars* part + *capere* to take — more at HEAVE] *vt* (1531) *archaic* **:** PARTAKE ~ *vi* **1 :** to possess some of the attributes of a person, thing, or quality **2 :** to take part ⟨always tried to ~ in class discussions⟩ **b :** to have a part or share in something *syn* see SHARE — **par·tic·i·pa·tor** \-ˌpā-tər\ *n*

par·tic·i·pa·tion \(ˌ)pär-ˌti-sə-ˈpā-shən, pər-\ *n* (14c) **:** the act of participating **:** the state of being related to a larger whole

par·tic·i·pa·tion·al \-ˈpā-shnəl, -ˈpā-shə-n³l\ *adj* (1959) **:** PARTICIPATORY

par·tic·i·pa·tive \pär-ˈti-sə-pə-tiv, pər-, -ˌpā-tiv\ *adj* (1951) **:** relating to or involving participation; *esp* **:** of, relating to, or being a style of management in which subordinates participate in decision making

par·tic·i·pa·to·ry \pär-ˈti-sə-pə-ˌtōr-ē, pər-, -ˌtōr-\ *adj* (1881) **:** characterized by or involving participation; *esp* **:** providing the opportunity for individual participation ⟨ ~ democracy⟩

par·ti·cip·i·al \ˌpär-tə-ˈsi-pē-əl\ *adj* [L *participialis*, fr. *participium*] (1591) **:** of, relating to, or formed with or from a participle — **par·ti·cip·i·al·ly** \-pē-ə-lē\ *adv*

par·ti·ci·ple \ˈpär-tə-ˌsi-pəl\ *n* [ME, fr. MF, modif. of L *participium*, fr. *particip-, participes*] (14c) **:** a word having the characteristics of both verb and adjective; *esp* **:** an English verbal form that has the function of an adjective and at the same time shows such verbal features as tense and voice and capacity to take an object

par·ti·cle \ˈpär-ti-kəl\ *n* [ME, fr. L *particula*, fr. dim. of *part-, pars*]

(14c) **1 a :** a minute quantity or fragment **b :** a relatively small or the smallest discrete portion or amount of something **2** *archaic* **:** a clause or article of a composition or document **3 :** any of the basic units of matter and energy (as a molecule, atom, proton, electron, or photon) **4 :** a unit of speech expressing some general aspect of meaning or some connective or limiting relation and including the articles, most prepositions and conjunctions, and some interjections and adverbs ⟨the ~ *up* has a perfective meaning in phrases such as *beat up* and *cut up*⟩ **5 :** a small eucharistic wafer distributed to a Roman Catholic layman at Communion

particle accelerator *n* (1946) **:** ACCELERATOR d

par·ti·cle·board \-ˌbōrd, -ˌbȯrd\ *n* (ca. 1957) **:** a composition board made of very small pieces of wood bonded together

particle physics *n* (1946) **:** a branch of physics dealing with the constitution, properties, and interactions of elementary particles esp. as revealed in experiments using particle accelerators — called also *high-energy physics* — **particle physicist** *n*

par·ti·col·or \ˈpär-tē-ˌkə-lər\ *or* **par·ti-col·ored** \-lərd\ *adj* [obs. E *party* parti-color, fr. ME *parti*, fr. MF, striped, fr. pp. of *partir* to divide] (1535) **:** showing different colors or tints; *esp* **:** having a predominant color broken by patches of one or more other colors ⟨ ~ setters⟩ — **parti-color** *n*

¹**par·tic·u·lar** \pə(r)-ˈti-kyə-lər, -k(ə-)lər\ *adj* [ME *particuler*, fr. MF, fr. LL *particularis*, fr. L *particula* small part] (14c) **1 :** of, relating to, or being a single person or thing ⟨the ~ person I had in mind⟩ **2** *obs* **:** PARTIAL **3 :** of, relating to, or concerned with details ⟨gave us a very ~ account of the trip⟩ **4 a :** distinctive among other examples or cases of the same general category **:** notably unusual ⟨suffered from measles of ~ severity⟩ **b :** being one unit or element among others ⟨~ incidents in a story⟩ **5 a :** denoting an individual member or subclass in logic **b :** affirming or denying a predicate to a part of the subject — used of a proposition in logic ⟨"some men are wise" is a ~ affirmative⟩ **6 a :** concerned over or attentive to details **:** METICULOUS ⟨a very ~ gardener⟩ **b :** nice in taste **:** FASTIDIOUS **c :** hard to please **:** EXACTING *syn* see CIRCUMSTANTIAL, SPECIAL

²**particular** *n* (15c) **1** *archaic* **:** a separate part of a whole **2 a :** an individual fact, point, circumstance, or detail **b :** a specific item or detail of information or news ⟨bill of ~s⟩ **3 a :** an individual or a specific subclass (as in logic) falling under some general concept or term **b :** a particular proposition in logic *syn* see ITEM — **in particular :** in distinction from others **:** SPECIFICALLY

par·tic·u·lar·ise *Brit var of* PARTICULARIZE

par·tic·u·lar·ism \pə(r)-ˈti-k(yə-)lə-ˌri-zəm *also* pär-\ *n* (1824) **1 :** exclusive or special devotion to a particular interest **2 :** a political theory that each political group has a right to promote its own interests and esp. independence without regard to the interests of larger groups **3 :** a tendency to explain complex social phenomena in terms of a single causative factor — **par·tic·u·lar·ist** \-rist\ *n or adj* — **par·tic·u·lar·is·tic** \-ˌti-k(yə-)lə-ˈris-tik\ *adj*

par·tic·u·lar·i·ty \pə(r)-ˌti-kyə-ˈlar-ə-tē *also* (ˌ)pär-\ *n*, *pl* **-ties** (1528) **1 a :** a minute detail **:** PARTICULAR **b :** an individual characteristic **:** PECULIARITY; *also* **:** SINGULARITY **2 :** the quality or state of being particular as distinguished from universal **3 a :** attentiveness to detail **:** EXACTNESS **b :** the quality or state of being fastidious in behavior or expression

par·tic·u·lar·i·za·tion \-ˌti-k(yə-)lə-rə-ˈzā-shən\ *n* (1657) **:** the act of particularizing **:** the condition of being particularized

par·tic·u·lar·ize \pə(r)-ˈti-k(yə-)lə-ˌrīz *also* pär-\ *vb* **-ized; -iz·ing** *vt* (1593) **:** to state in detail **:** SPECIFY ~ *vi* **:** to go into details

par·tic·u·lar·ly \pə(r)-ˈti-k(yə-)lər-)lē, -kyə-lə-lē; pə(r)-ˈti-k(ə-)lē; *also* pär-\ *adv* (14c) **1 :** in a particular manner **:** in detail **2 :** to an unusual degree **3 :** in particular **:** SPECIFICALLY

¹**par·tic·u·late** \pär-ˈti-kyə-lət *also* -ˌlāt\ *adj* [L *particula*] (1871) **:** of or relating to minute separate particles

²**particulate** *n* (1942) **:** a particulate substance

particulate inheritance *n* (1889) **:** inheritance of characters specif. transmitted by genes in accord with Mendel's laws

¹**part·ing** \ˈpär-tiŋ\ *n* (15c) **:** a place or point where a division or separation occurs — **parting of the ways 1 :** a point of separation or divergence **2 :** a place or time at which a choice must be made

²**parting** *adj* (ca. 1577) **:** given, taken, or performed at parting ⟨a ~ kiss⟩

par·ti pris \ˈpär-ˌtē-ˈprē\ *n*, *pl* **partis pris** \-ˌtē-ˈprē(z)\ [F, lit., side taken] (1860) **:** a preconceived opinion **:** PREJUDICE — **parti pris** *adj*

¹**par·ti·san** *also* **par·ti·zan** \ˈpär-tə-zən, -sən, -ˌzan, *chiefly Brit* ˌpär-tə-ˈzan\ *n* [MF *partisan*, fr. OIt *partigiano*, fr. *parte* part, party, fr. L *part-, pars* part] (1555) **1 :** a firm adherent to a party, faction, cause, or person; *esp* **:** one exhibiting blind, prejudiced, and unreasoning allegiance **2 a :** a member of a body of detached light troops making forays and harassing an enemy **b :** a member of a guerrilla band operating within enemy lines *syn* see FOLLOWER — **partisan** *adj* — **par·ti·san·ly** \-lē\ *adv* — **par·ti·san·ship** \-ˌship\ *n*

²**par·ti·san** *or* **par·ti·zan** \ˈpär-tə-zən, -sən\ *n* [MF *partisane*, fem. of *partigiano*] (1556) **:** a weapon of the 16th and 17th centuries with long shaft and broad blade

par·ti·ta \pär-ˈtē-tə\ *n* [It, fr. *partire* to divide, fr. L — more at PART] (1880) **1 :** VARIATION 4 **2 :** SUITE 2b(1)

par·tite \ˈpär-ˌtīt\ *adj* [L *partitus*, fr. pp. of *partire*] (ca. 1570) **1 :** divided into a usu. specified number of parts **2 :** PARTED 1b ⟨a ~ leaf⟩

¹**par·ti·tion** \pär-ˈti-shən, pər-\ *n* (15c) **1 :** the action of parting **:** the state of being parted **:** DIVISION **2 :** something that divides; *esp* **:** an interior dividing wall **3 :** one of the parts or sections of a whole

²**partition** *vt* (1741) **1 a :** to divide into parts or shares **b :** to divide (as a country) into two or more territorial units having separate political status **2 :** to separate or divide by a partition (as a wall) — often used with *off* — **par·ti·tion·er** \-ˈti-sh(ə-)nər\ *n*

\ə\ abut \ᵊ\ kitten, F table \ər\ further \a\ ash \ā\ ace \ä\ mop, mar \au̇\ out \ch\ chin \e\ bet \ē\ easy \g\ go \i\ hit \ī\ ice \j\ job \ŋ\ sing \ō\ go \ȯ\ law \ȯi\ boy \th\ thin \t͟h\ the \ü\ loot \u̇\ foot \y\ yet \zh\ vision \à, k̲, ⁿ, œ, œ̄, ᵫ, ᵬ, ᵶ, �\ see Guide to Pronunciation

par·ti·tion·ist \-'ti-sh(ə-)nist\ *n* (ca. 1900) : an advocate of political partition

par·ti·tive \'pär-tə-tiv\ *adj* (14c) **1** : serving to part or divide into parts **2 a** : of, relating to, or denoting a part ⟨a ~ construction⟩ **b** : serving to indicate the whole of which a part is specified ⟨~ genitive⟩ — **par·ti·tive·ly** *adv*

part·let \'pärt-lət\ *n* [ME (Sc) *patelet*, fr. MF *patelette*, fr. dim. of *patte* paw] (1519) : a 16th century chemisette with a band or collar

part·ly \'pärt-lē\ *adv* (1523) : in some measure or degree : PARTIALLY

¹part·ner \'pärt-nər *also* 'pärd-\ *n* [ME *partener*, alter. of *parcener*, fr. AF, coparcener — more at PARCENER] (14c) **1** *archaic* : one that shares : PARTAKER **2** : one associated with another esp. in an action : ASSOCIATE, COLLEAGUE **b** : either of two persons who dance together **c** : one of two or more persons who play together in a game against an opposing side **d** : either of two people living together; *esp* : SPOUSE **3** : a member of a partnership; *also* : such membership **4** : one of the heavy timbers that strengthen a ship's deck to support a mast — usu. used in pl. — **part·ner·less** \-ləs\ *adj*

²partner *vt* (1611) **1** : to join or associate with another as partner **2** : to provide with a partner ~ *vi* : to act as a partner

partners desk *n* (1946) : a large desk with an open kneehole which allows use of the desk by two people seated opposite each other

part·ner·ship \-,ship\ *n* (1576) **1** : the state of being a partner : PARTICIPATION **2 a** : a legal relation existing between two or more persons contractually associated as joint principals in a business **b** : the persons joined together in a partnership **3** : a relationship resembling a legal partnership and usu. involving close cooperation between parties having specified and joint rights and responsibilities

part of speech (1509) : a traditional class of words distinguished according to the kind of idea denoted and the function performed in a sentence

par·ton \'pär-,tän\ *n* [*particle* + *²-on*] (1969) : a hypothetical particle (as a quark or gluon) that is held to be a constituent of hadrons

par·tridge \'pär-trij\ *dial* 'pa-trij\ *n, pl* **partridge** *or* **par·tridg·es** [ME *partrich*, modif. of OF *perdris*, modif. of L *perdic-*, *perdix*, fr. Gk *perdik-*, *perdix*] (14c) **1** : any of various typically medium-sized stout-bodied Old World gallinaceous game birds (*Perdix*, *Alectoris*, and related genera) with variegated plumage **2** : any of numerous gallinaceous birds (as the American ruffed grouse or bobwhite) somewhat like the Old World partridges in size, habits, or value as game

par·tridge·ber·ry \-,ber-ē\ *n* (1714) : an American trailing evergreen plant (*Mitchella repens*) of the madder family with insipid scarlet berries; *also* : its fruit

part–song \'pärt-,sȯŋ\ *n* (1850) : a usu. unaccompanied song consisting of two or more voice parts with one part carrying the melody

partridge 1

part–time \'pärt-'tim\ *adj* (1891) : involving or working less than customary or standard hours ⟨a ~ job⟩ ⟨~ students⟩ — **part–time** *adv* — **part–tim·er** \-,ti-mər, -'ti-\ *n*

¹par·tu·ri·ent \pär-'tur-ē-ənt, -'tyur-\ *adj* [L *parturient-*, *parturiens*, prp. of *parturire* to be in labor, fr. *parere* to give birth to — more at PARE] (1592) **1** : bringing forth or about to bring forth young **2** : of or relating to parturition

²parturient *n* (1947) : a parturient individual

par·tu·ri·tion \,pär-chə-'ri-shən, ,pär-tyü-, ,pär-tə-\ *n* [LL *parturition-*, *parturitio*, fr. L *parturire*] (1646) : the action or process of giving birth to offspring

part·way \'pärt-'wā\ *adv* (1859) **1** : to some extent : PARTIALLY, PARTLY **2** : at a point in the way or distance ⟨~ through the trip they met some friends⟩

¹par·ty \'pär-tē\ *n, pl* **parties** [ME *partie* part, party, fr. OF, fr. *partir* to divide — more at PART] (14c) **1** : a person or group taking one side of a question, dispute, or contest **2** : a group of persons organized for the purpose of directing the policies of a government **3** : a person or group participating in an action or affair ⟨mountain-climbing ~⟩ ⟨a ~ to the transaction⟩ **4** : a particular individual : PERSON ⟨an old ~ approaching 80⟩ **5** : a detail of soldiers **6** : a social gathering; *also* : the entertainment provided for it — **party** *adj*

²party *vi* **par·tied; par·ty·ing** (1919) : to attend or give parties; *broadly* : REVEL I — **par·ty·er** \-tē-ər\ *n*

party line *n* (1834) **1** : the policy or practice of a political party **2** : a single telephone circuit connecting two or more subscribers with the exchange — called also *party wire* **3** : the principles or policies of an individual or organization; *also* : the explanation or interpretation usu. put forth ⟨the *party line* that her mother was a saint —Leslie Bennetts⟩ — **par·ty·lin·er** \,pär-tē-'li-nər\ *n*

party poop·er \-'pü-pər\ *n* [*³poop* + *-er*] (1954) : one who refuses to join in the fun of a party; *broadly* : one who refuses to go along with everyone else

party wall *n* (ca. 1798) : a wall which divides two adjoining properties and in which each of the owners shares the rights

pa·rure \pə-'rùr\ *n* [F, lit., adornment, fr. OF *pareure*, fr. *parer* to prepare, adorn — more at PARE] (1818) : a matched set of ornaments (as jewelry)

par value *n* (1807) : PAR 1b(1)

par·ve \'pär-və\ *var of* PAREVE

par·ve·nu \'pär-və-,nü, -,nyü\ *n, pl* **-nus** \-,n(y)üz\ [F, fr. pp. of *parvenir* to arrive, fr. L *pervenire*, fr. *per* through + *venire* to come — more at FOR, COME] (1802) : one that has recently or suddenly risen to an unaccustomed position of wealth or power and has not yet gained the prestige, dignity, or manner associated with it — **parvenu** *adj*

par·ve·nue \-,nü, -,nyü\ *n* [F, fr. *parvenue*, fem. of *parvenum*, pp.] (1826) : a woman who is a parvenu — **parvenue** *adj*

par·vis *also* **par·vise** \'pär-vəs\ *n* [ME *parvis*, fr. MF, modif. of LL *paradisus* enclosed park — more at PARADISE] (14c) **1** : a court or enclosed space before a building (as a church) **2** : a single portico or colonnade before a church

---

par·vo \'pär-(,)vō\ *n* (1980) : PARVOVIRUS 2

par·vo·vi·rus \'pär-vō-,vi-rəs\ *n* [NL, fr. L *parvus* small (akin to Gk *pauros* small, *paid-*, *pais* child) + NL *-o-* + *virus* — more at FEW] (1965) **1** : any of a group of small single-stranded DNA viruses pathogenic for vertebrates **2** : a highly contagious febrile disease of dogs that is caused by a parvovirus and marked by loss of appetite, lethargy, often bloody diarrhea and vomiting, and sometimes death

pas \'pä\ *n, pl* **pas** \'pä(z)\ [F, fr. L *passus* step — more at PACE] (1707) **1** : the right of precedence **2** : a dance step or combination of steps

pas·cal \pas-'kal, päs-'käl\ *n* [Blaise *Pascal*] (1956) **1** : a unit of pressure in the meter-kilogram-second system equivalent to one newton per square meter **2** *usu cap P or all cap* : a structured computer programming language developed from Algol and designed to process both numerical and textual data

Pas·cal's triangle \pas-'kalz-, päs-'kälz-\ *n* (1886) : a system of numbers triangularly arranged in rows that consist of the coefficients in the expansion of $(a + b)^n$ for $n = 0, 1, 2, 3, \ldots$

Pasch \'pask\ *also* **Pas·cha** \'päs-kə\ *n* [ME *pasche* Passover, Easter, fr. OF, fr. LL *pascha*, fr. LGk, fr. Gk, Passover, fr. Heb *pesaḥ*] (12c) **1** : EASTER **2** : PASSOVER — **pas·chal** \'pas-kəl\ *adj*

paschal full moon *n* (1892) : the 14th day of a lunar month occurring on or next after March 21 according to a fixed set of ecclesiastical calendar rules and without regard to the real moon

Paschal Lamb *n* (15c) : AGNUS DEI 2

pas de bour·rée \,pä-də-bù-'rā\ *n, pl* **pas de bourrée** *same*\ *or* **pas de bour·rées** \-'rā(z)\ [F, lit., bourrée step] (1897) : a walking or running ballet step usu. executed on the points of the toes

pas de chat \-'sha\ *n, pl* **pas de chat** *same*\ [F, lit., cat's step] (1914) : a forward leap in ballet

pas de deux \-'də(r), -'dü\ *n, pl* **pas de deux** \-'dər(z), -'də(z), -'dü(z)\ [F, lit., step for two] (ca. 1762) **1** : a dance or figure for two performers **2** : an intricate relationship or activity involving two parties or things

pas de qua·tre \-'kat, -'ka-trə, -'kätr\ *n, pl* **pas de quatre** *same*\ [F, lit., step for four] (1884) : a dance or figure for four performers

pas de trois \-'trwä, -'twä\ *n, pl* **pas de trois** \-'trwä(z), -'twä(z)\ [F, lit., step for three] (ca. 1762) : a dance or figure for three performers

pa·se \'pä-(,)sä\ *n* [Sp, lit., feint, fr. *pase* let him pass, fr. *pasar* to pass, fr. (assumed) VL *passare*] (1937) : a movement of a cape by a matador in drawing a bull and taking his charge

pa·seo \pə-'sä-(,)ō, pä-\ *n, pl* **pa·se·os** [Sp, fr. *pasear* to take a stroll, fr. *paso* passage, pace, fr. L *passus*] (1832) **1 a** : a leisurely stroll : PROMENADE **b** : a public walk or boulevard **2** : a formal entrance march of bullfighters into an arena

¹pash \'pash\ *vt* [ME *passhen*] (14c) *dial Eng* : SMASH

²pash *n* [origin unknown] (1611) *dial Eng* : HEAD

pa·sha \'pä-shə, 'pa-; pə-'shä, -'shȯ\ *n* [Turk *paşa*] (1646) : a man of high rank or office (as in Turkey or northern Africa)

Pash·to \'pȯsh-(,)tō\ *n* [Pashto *pašto*] (1784) : the Iranian language of the Pashtuns

Pash·tun \,pȯsh-'tün\ *n, pl* **Pashtuns** *or* **Pashtun** (1815) : a member of a people of eastern and southern Afghanistan and adjacent parts of Pakistan

Pa·siph·a·ë \pə-'si-fə-,ē\ *n* [L, fr. Gk *Pasiphaē*] : the wife of Minos and mother of the Minotaur by a white bull

pasque·flow·er \'pask-,flau̇(-ə)r\ *n* [modif. of MF *passefleur*, fr. *passer* to pass (fr. OF) + *fleur* flower, fr. L *flor-*, *flos* — more at BLOW] (1597) : any of several low perennial herbs (genus *Anemone*) of the buttercup family with palmately compound leaves and large usu. white or purple early spring flowers

pas·qui·nade \,pas-kwə-'nād\ *n* [MF, fr. It *pasquinata*, fr. *Pasquino*, name given to a statue in Rome on which lampoons were posted] (1658) **1** : a lampoon posted in a public place **2** : satirical writing : SATIRE — **pasquinade** *vt*

¹pass \'pas\ *vb* [ME, fr. OF *passer*, fr. (assumed) VL *passare*, fr. L *passus* step — more at PACE] *vi* (13c) **1** : MOVE, PROCEED, GO **2 a** : to go away : DEPART **b** : DIE — often used with *on* **3 a** : to move in a path so as to approach and continue beyond something : move past; *esp* : to move past another vehicle going in the same direction **b** : to run the normal course — used of time or a period of time ⟨the hours ~ quickly⟩ **4 a** : to go or make one's way through ⟨allow no one to ~⟩ **b** : to go uncensured, unchallenged, or seemingly unnoticed ⟨let the remark ~⟩ **5** : to go from one quality, state, or form to another ⟨~es from a liquid to a gaseous state⟩ **6 a** : to sit in inquest or judgment **b** (1) : to render a decision, verdict, or opinion ⟨the court ~ed on the legality of wiretapping⟩ (2) : to become legally rendered ⟨judgment ~ed for the plaintiff⟩ **7** : to go from the control, ownership, or possession of one person or group to that of another ⟨the throne ~ed to the king's son⟩ ⟨title ~es to the buyer upon payment in full⟩ **8 a** : HAPPEN, OCCUR **b** : to take place or be exchanged as or in a social, personal, or business interaction ⟨words ~ed⟩ **9 a** : to become approved by a legislature or body empowered to sanction or reject ⟨the proposal ~ed⟩ **b** : to undergo an inspection, test, or course of study successfully **10 a** : to serve as a medium of exchange **b** : to be accepted or regarded ⟨drivel that ~es for literature⟩ **c** : to identify oneself or be identified as something one isn't ⟨tried to ~ as an adult⟩ ⟨Mom could ~ as my sister⟩ **11 a** *obs* : to make a pass in fencing **b** : to throw or hit a ball or puck to a teammate — often used with *off* **12 a** : to decline to bid, double, or redouble in a card game **b** : to withdraw from the current poker pot ~ *vt* **1** : to go beyond: as **a** : SURPASS, EXCEED ⟨~es all expectations⟩ **b** : to advance or develop beyond **c** : to go past (one moving in the same direction) **2** : to omit a regularly scheduled declaration and payment of (a dividend) **3 a** : to go across, over, or through : CROSS **b** : to live through (as an experience or peril) : UNDERGO **c** : to go through (as a test) successfully **4 a** : to secure the approval of ⟨the bill ~ed the Senate⟩ **b** : to cause or permit to win approval or legal or official sanction ⟨~ a law⟩ **c** : to give approval or a passing grade to ⟨~ the students⟩ **5 a** : to let (as time or a period of time) go by esp. while involved in a leisure activity ⟨I'll read to ~ the time⟩ **b** : to let go unnoticed : OVERLOOK, DISREGARD **6 a** : PLEDGE **b** : to transfer the right to or property in ⟨~ title to a house⟩ **7 a** : to put in circulation ⟨~ bad checks⟩ **b** (1) : to transfer or transmit from one to another (2) : to relay or communicate (as information) to another **c** : to cause or enable to go

: TRANSPORT **d** : to throw or hit (a ball or puck) esp. to a teammate **8 a** : to pronounce (as a sentence or opinion) esp. judicially **b** : UTTER ⟨~ed a cutting remark⟩ **9 a** : to cause or permit to go past or through a barrier **b** : to move or cause to move in a particular manner or direction ⟨~ed my hand over my face⟩ ⟨~ the rope through the loop⟩ **c** : to cause to march or go by in order ⟨~ the troops in review⟩ **10** : to emit or discharge from a bodily part and esp. the bowels **11 a** : to give a base on balls to **b** : to hit a ball past (an opponent) in a game (as tennis) — **pass·er** *n* — **pass muster** : to gain approval or acceptance — **pass the buck** : to shift a responsibility to someone else — **pass the hat** : to take up a collection for money — **pass the time of day** : to exchange greetings or engage in pleasant conversation

²**pass** *n* [ME, fr. MF *pas*, fr. L *passus*] (14c) **1** : a means (as an opening, road, or channel) by which a barrier may be passed or access to a place may be gained; *esp* : a low place in a mountain range **2** : a position to be held usu. against odds

³**pass** *n* [¹*pass*] (1523) **1** : REALIZATION ⟨brought his dream to ~⟩ **2** : the act or an instance of passing : PASSAGE **3** : a usu. distressing or bad state of affairs ⟨what has brought you to such a ~?⟩ **4 a** : a written permission to move about freely in a place or to leave or enter it **b** : a written leave of absence from a military post or station for a brief period **c** : a permit or ticket allowing free transportation or free admission **5** *archaic* : a thrust or lunge in fencing **6 a** : a transference of objects by sleight of hand or other deceptive means **b** : a moving of the hands over or along something **7** *archaic* : an ingenious sally (as of wit) **8** : the passing of an examination or course of study; *also* : the mark or certification of such passing **9** : a single complete mechanical operation; *also* : a single complete cycle of operations (as for processing, manufacturing, or printing) **10 a** (1) : a transfer of a ball or a puck from one player to another on the same team (2) : a ball or puck so transferred **b** : PASSING SHOT **11** : BASE ON BALLS **12** : an election not to bid, bet, or draw an additional card in a card game **13** : a throw of dice in the game of craps that wins the bet for the shooter — compare ³CRAP 2, MISSOUT **14** : a single passage or movement (as of an airplane) over a place or toward a target **15 a** : EFFORT, TRY **b** : a sexually inviting gesture or approach **16** : PASE

pass·able \'pa-sə-bəl\ *adj* (15c) **1 a** : capable of being passed, crossed, or traveled on ⟨~ roads⟩ **b** : capable of being freely circulated **2** : good enough : ADEQUATE — **pass·ably** \-blē\ *adv*

pas·sa·ca·glia \ˌpä-sə-ˈkäl-yə, ˌpa-sə-ˈkal-yə\ *n* [modif. of Sp *pasacalle*, fr. *pasar* to pass + *calle* street, fr. L *callis* path — more at PASE] (1659) **1** : an old Italian or Spanish dance tune **b** : an instrumental musical composition consisting of variations usu. on a ground bass in moderately slow triple time **2** : an old dance performed to a passacaglia

pas·sa·do \pə-ˈsä-(ˌ)dō\ *n, pl* **-dos** *or* **-does** [modif. of F *passade* (fr. It *passata*) or It *passata*, fr. *passare* to pass, fr. (assumed) VL] (1588) *archaic* : a thrust in fencing with one foot advanced

¹**pas·sage** \'pa-sij\ *n* (13c) **1 a** : a way of exit or entrance : a road, path, channel, or course by which something passes **b** : a corridor or lobby giving access to the different rooms or parts of a building or apartment **2 a** : the action or process of passing from one place, condition, or stage to another **b** : DEATH 1 **c** : a continuous movement or flow ⟨the ~ of time⟩ **3 a** (1) : a specific act of traveling or passing esp. by sea or air (2) : a privilege of conveyance as a passenger : ACCOMMODATIONS **b** : the passing of a legislative measure or law : ENACTMENT **4** : a right, liberty, or permission to pass **5 a** : something that happens or is done : INCIDENT **b** : something that takes place between two persons mutually **6 a** : a usu. brief portion of a written work or speech that is relevant to a point under discussion or noteworthy for content or style **b** : a phrase or short section of a musical composition **c** : a detail of a work of art (as a painting) **7** : the act or action of passing something or undergoing a passing **8** : incubation of a pathogen (as a virus) in culture, a living organism, or a developing egg

²**passage** *vb* **pas·saged; pas·sag·ing** *vi* (1824) : to go past or across : CROSS ~ *vt* : to subject to passage ⟨passaged a virus⟩

pas·sage·way \-ˌwā\ *n* (1649) : a way that allows passage

pas·sage·work \-ˌwərk\ *n* (1865) : a section of a musical composition characteristically unimportant thematically and consisting esp. of ornamental figures

pas·sant \'pa-sⁿnt\ *adj* [ME *passaunt*, fr. MF *passant*, fr. prp. of *passer* to pass] (15c) : walking with the farther forepaw raised — used of a heraldic animal

pass away *vi* (13c) **1** : to go out of existence **2** : DIE 1

pass·band \'pas-ˌband\ *n* (1922) : a band of frequencies (as in a radio circuit or a light filter) that is transmitted with maximum efficiency

pass·book \-ˌbuk\ *n* (1828) : BANKBOOK

pass degree *n* (1868) : a bachelor's degree without honors that is taken at a British university

pas·sé \pa-ˈsā\ *adj* [F, fr. pp. of *passer*] (1775) **1** : past one's prime **2 a** : OUTMODED **b** : behind the times

passed ball *n* (1861) : a baseball pitch not hit by the batter that passes the catcher when it should have been caught and allows a base runner to advance — compare WILD PITCH

passed pawn *n* (1797) : a chess pawn that has no enemy pawn in front of it on its own or an adjacent file

pas·sel \'pa-səl\ *n* [alter. of *parcel*] (1835) : a large number or amount

passe·men·terie \pas-ˈmen-t(ə-)rē\ *n* [F, fr. *passement* ornamental braid, fr. *passer*] (1794) : a fancy edging or trimming made of braid, cord, gimp, beading, or metallic thread

pas·sen·ger \'pa-sⁿ-jər\ *n, often attrib* [ME *passager*, fr. MF, fr. *passager*, adj., passing, fr. *passage* act of passing, fr. OF, fr. *passer*] (14c) **1** : WAYFARER **2** : a traveler in a public or private conveyance

passenger pigeon *n* (1802) : an extinct but formerly abundant No. American migratory pigeon (*Ectopistes migratorius*)

passe–par·tout \ˌpas-pər-ˈtü, -ˌpär-\ *n* [F, fr. *passe partout* pass everywhere] (1675) **1** : MASTER KEY **2 a** : ⁵MAT **b** : a method of framing in which a picture, a mat, a glass, and a back (as of cardboard) are held together by strips of paper or cloth pasted over the edges **3** : a strong paper gummed on one side and used esp. for mounting pictures

pass·er–by \ˌpa-sər-ˈbī, 'pa-sər-ˌ\ *n, pl* **pass·ers·by** \-sərz-\ (1568) : one who passes by

pas·ser·ine \'pa-sə-ˌrīn\ *adj* [L *passerinus* of sparrows, fr. *passer* spar-

row] (1776) : of or relating to the largest order (Passeriformes) of birds which includes more than half of all living birds and consists chiefly of altricial songbirds of perching habits — compare OSCINE — **passerine** *n*

pas seul \ˌpä-ˈsəl, -ˈsər(-ə)l\ *n* [F, lit., solo step] (1813) : a solo dance or dance figure

pass–fail \'pas-ˈfā(ə)l\ *adj* (1959) : being a system of grading whereby the grades "pass" and "fail" replace the traditional letter grades — **pass–fail** *n*

pas·si·ble \'pa-sə-bəl\ *adj* [ME, fr. MF, fr. LL *passibilis*, fr. L *passus*, pp. of *pati* to suffer — more at PATIENT] (14c) : capable of feeling or suffering

pas·sim \'pa-səm; 'pa-ˌsim, 'pä-\ *adv* [L, fr. *passus* scattered, fr. pp. of *pandere* to spread — more at FATHOM] (1803) : HERE AND THERE

¹**pass·ing** \'pa-siŋ\ *n* (14c) : the act of one that passes or causes to pass; *esp* : DEATH 1 — **in passing** : by the way : INCIDENTALLY

²**passing** *adj* (14c) **1** : going by or past ⟨a ~ pedestrian⟩ **2** : having a brief duration ⟨a ~ whim⟩ **3** *obs* : SURPASSING **4** : SUPERFICIAL ⟨a ~ acquaintance⟩ ⟨a ~ resemblance⟩ **5 a** : of, relating to, or used in or for the act or process of passing ⟨~ lanes⟩ **b** : given on satisfactory completion of an examination or course of study ⟨a ~ grade⟩

³**passing** *adv* (14c) : to a surpassing degree : EXCEEDINGLY ⟨~ strange⟩

passing note *n* (1730) : a nonharmonic tone interposed between essential harmonic tones of adjacent chords — called also *passing tone*

passing shot *n* (ca. 1949) : a stroke (as in tennis) that drives the ball to one side and beyond the reach of an opponent

pas·sion \'pa-shən\ *n* [ME, fr. OF, fr. LL *passion-, passio* suffering, being acted upon, fr. L *pati* to suffer — more at PATIENT] (13c) **1** *often cap* **a** : the sufferings of Christ between the night of the Last Supper and his death **b** : an oratorio based on a gospel narrative of the Passion **2** *obs* : SUFFERING **3** : the state or capacity of being acted on by external agents or forces **4 a** (1) : EMOTION ⟨his ruling ~ is greed⟩ (2) *pl* : the emotions as distinguished from reason **b** : intense, driving, or overmastering feeling or conviction **c** : an outbreak of anger **5 a** : ardent affection : LOVE **b** : a strong liking or desire for or devotion to some activity, object, or concept **c** : sexual desire **d** : an object of desire or deep interest — **pas·sion·less** \-ləs\ *adj*

syn PASSION, FERVOR, ARDOR, ENTHUSIASM, ZEAL mean intense emotion compelling action. PASSION applies to an emotion that is deeply stirring or ungovernable ⟨was a slave to his *passions*⟩. FERVOR implies a warm and steady emotion ⟨read the poem aloud with great *fervor*⟩. ARDOR suggests warm and excited feeling likely to be fitful or short-lived ⟨the *ardor* of their honeymoon soon faded⟩. ENTHUSIASM applies to lively or eager interest in or admiration for a proposal, cause, or activity ⟨never showed much *enthusiasm* for sports⟩. ZEAL implies energetic and unflagging pursuit of an aim or devotion to a cause ⟨preaches with the *zeal* of the converted⟩. *syn* see in addition FEELING

pas·sion·al \'pa-shə-nᵊl, 'pash-nəl\ *adj* (15c) : of, relating to, or marked by passion

pas·sion·ate \'pa-sh(ə-)nət\ *adj* (15c) **1 a** : easily aroused to anger **b** : filled with anger : ANGRY **2 a** : capable of, affected by, or expressing intense feeling **b** : ENTHUSIASTIC, ARDENT **3** : swayed by or affected with sexual desire *syn* see IMPASSIONED — **pas·sion·ate·ly** *adv* — **pas·sion·ate·ness** *n*

pas·sion·flow·er \'pa-shən-ˌflau̇(-ə)r\ *n* [fr. the fancied resemblance of parts of the flower to the instruments of Christ's crucifixion] (1633) : any of a genus (*Passiflora* of the family Passifloraceae, the passionflower family) of chiefly tropical woody tendrilled climbing vines or erect herbs with usu. showy flowers and pulpy often edible berries

passion fruit *n* (1752) : the edible fruit of a passionflower

Pas·sion·ist \'pa-sh(ə-)nist\ *n* [It *passionista*, fr. *passione* passion, fr. LL *passion-, passio*] (1832) : a member of a Roman Catholic mendicant order founded by St. Paul of the Cross in Italy in 1720 and devoted chiefly to missionary work and retreats

passionflower

passion play *n, often cap 1st P* (1870) : a dramatic representation of the scenes connected with the passion and crucifixion of Christ

Passion Sunday *n* (14c) : the fifth Sunday in Lent

Pas·sion·tide \'pa-shən-ˌtīd\ *n* (1847) : the last two weeks of Lent

Passion Week *n* (15c) **1** : HOLY WEEK **2** : the week between Passion Sunday and Palm Sunday

pas·siv·ate \'pa-si-ˌvāt\ *vt* **-at·ed; -at·ing** (1913) **1** : to make inactive or less reactive ⟨~ the surface of steel by chemical treatment⟩ **2** : to protect (as a solid-state device) against contamination by coating or surface treatment — **pas·siv·ation** \ˌpa-si-ˈvā-shən\ *n*

¹**pas·sive** \'pa-siv\ *adj* [ME, fr. L *passivus*, fr. *passus*, pp.] (14c) **1 a** (1) : acted upon by an external agency (2) : receptive to outside impressions or influences **b** (1) : asserting that the grammatical subject of a verb is subjected to or affected by the action represented by that verb (2) : containing or yielding a passive verb form **c** (1) : lacking in energy or will : LETHARGIC (2) : tending not to take an active or dominant part **d** : induced by an outside agency ⟨~ exercise of a paralyzed leg⟩ **2 a** : not active or operating : INERT **b** : of, relating to, or making direct use of the sun's heat usu. without the intervention of mechanical devices ⟨~ technique⟩ ⟨~ solar house⟩ **c** : LATENT **d** (1) : of, relating to, or characterized by a state of chemical inactivity; *esp* : resistant to corrosion (2) : not involving expenditure of chemical energy ⟨~ transport across a cell membrane⟩ **e** *of an electronic element* : exhibiting no gain or control **f** : operating solely by means

\ə\ abut \ᵊ\ kitten, F table \ər\ further \a\ ash \ā\ ace \ä\ mop, mar \au̇\ out \ch\ chin \e\ bet \ē\ easy \g\ go \i\ hit \ī\ ice \j\ job \ŋ\ sing \ō\ go \ȯ\ law \ȯi\ boy \th\ thin \th\ the \ü\ loot \u̇\ foot \y\ yet \zh\ vision \à, ḵ, ⁿ, œ, œ̄, ᵫ, ᵫ̄, ᵊ\ *see* Guide to Pronunciation of the power of an input signal ⟨a ~ communication satellite that reflects television signals⟩ **g** : relating to the detection of an object through its emission of energy **3 a** : receiving or enduring without resistance : SUBMISSIVE **b** : existing or occurring without being active, open, or direct ⟨~ support⟩ **4** : of, relating to, or being business activity in which the investor does not have immediate control over income **syn** see INACTIVE — **pas·sive·ly** *adv* — **pas·sive·ness** *n* — **pas·siv·i·ty** \pa-'si-və-tē\ *n*

²**passive** *n* (1530) **1** : a passive verb form **2** : the passive voice of a language

passive immunity *n* (1895) : immunity acquired by transfer of antibodies (as by injection of serum from an individual with active immunity) — **passive immunization** *n*

passive resistance *n* (1819) : resistance esp. to a government or an occupying power characterized mainly by noncooperation

passive restraint *n* (1970) : a restraint (as a self-locking seat belt) that acts automatically to protect an automobile rider during a crash

passive smoking *n* (1971) : the involuntary inhalation of tobacco smoke (as from another's cigarette) esp. by a nonsmoker

passive transfer *n* (1935) : a local transfer of skin sensitivity from an allergic to a normal person by injection of serum from the former that is used esp. for identifying specific allergens when a high degree of allergic sensitivity is suspected

pas·siv·ism \'pa-si-ˌvi-zəm\ *n* (1872) : a passive attitude, behavior, or way of life — **pas·siv·ist** \-vist\ *n*

pass·key \'pas-ˌkē\ *n* (ca. 1817) **1** : MASTER KEY : SKELETON KEY

pass off *vt* (1799) **1** : to make public or offer for sale with intent to deceive **2** : to give a false identity or character to

pass out *vi* (1899) **1** : DIE **I 2** : to lose consciousness ~ *vt* : to reject (a deal in bridge) as unplayable because everyone has passed on the first round of bidding

Pass·over \'pas-ˌō-vər\ *n* [fr. the exemption of the Israelites from the slaughter of the firstborn in Egypt (Exod 12:23–27)] (1530) : a Jewish holiday beginning on the 14th of Nisan and commemorating the Hebrews' liberation from slavery in Egypt

pass over *vt* (14c) **1** : to ignore in passing **2** : to pay no attention to the claims of : DISREGARD

pass·port \'pas-ˌpōrt, -ˌpȯrt\ *n* [ME (Sc) *pasport*, fr. MF *passeport*, fr. *passer* to pass + *port* port, fr. L *portus* — more at FORD] (15c) **1 a** : a formal document issued by an authorized official of a country to one of its citizens that is usu. necessary for exit from and reentry into the country, that allows the citizen to travel in a foreign country in accordance with visa requirements, and that requests protection for the citizen while abroad **b** : a license issued by a country permitting a foreign citizen to pass or take goods through its territory : SAFE-CONDUCT **c** : a document of identification required by law to be carried by persons residing or traveling within a country **2 a** : a permission or authorization to go somewhere **b** : something that secures admission, acceptance, or attainment ⟨education as a ~ to success⟩

pass–through *n* (1951) **1** : the act, action, or process of offsetting increased costs by raising prices **2** : an opening in a wall between two rooms through which something (as dishes) may be passed

pass up *vt* (1896) : to let go by without accepting or taking advantage of ⟨*pass up* a chance for promotion⟩; *also* : DECLINE, REJECT

pass·word \'pas-ˌwərd\ *n* (ca. 1817) **1** : something that enables one to pass or gain admission: as **a** : a spoken word or phrase required to pass by a guard **b** : a sequence of characters required for access to a computer system **2** : WATCHWORD

¹**past** \'past\ *adj* [ME, fr. pp. of *passen* to pass] (14c) **1 a** : AGO ⟨12 years ~⟩ **b** : just gone or elapsed ⟨for the ~ few months⟩ **2** : having existed or taken place in a period before the present : BYGONE **3** : of, relating to, or constituting a verb tense that is expressive of elapsed time and that in English is usu. formed by internal vowel change (as in *sang*) or by the addition of a suffix (as in *laughed*) **4** : having served as a specified officer in an organization ⟨~ president⟩

²**past** *prep* (14c) **1 a** : beyond the age for or of ⟨~ playing with dolls⟩ **b** : AFTER ⟨half ~ two⟩ **2 a** : at the farther side of : BEYOND **b** : in a course or direction going close to and then beyond ⟨drove ~ the house⟩ **3** *obs* : more than **4** : beyond the capacity, range, or sphere of ⟨~ belief⟩

³**past** *n* (1590) **1 a** : time gone by **b** : something that happened or was done in the past ⟨regret the ~⟩ **2 a** : the past tense of a language **b** : a verb form in the past tense **3** : a past life, history, or course of action; *esp* : one that is kept secret — **past·less** \'pas(t)-ləs\ *adj*

⁴**past** *adv* (1784) : so as to reach and go beyond a point near at hand

pas·ta \'päs-tə *also* 'pas-\ *n* [It, fr. LL] (1874) **1** : paste in processed form (as spaghetti) or in the form of fresh dough (as ravioli) **2** : a dish of cooked pasta

¹**paste** \'pāst\ *n* [ME, fr. MF, fr. LL *pasta* dough, paste] (14c) **1 a** : a dough that contains a considerable proportion of fat and is used for pastry crust or fancy rolls **b** : a confection made by evaporating fruit with sugar or by flavoring a gelatin, starch, or gum arabic preparation **c** : a smooth food product made by evaporation or grinding ⟨tomato ~⟩ ⟨almond ~⟩ **d** : a shaped dough (as spaghetti or ravioli) prepared from semolina, farina, or wheat flour **2** : a soft plastic mixture or composition: as **a** : a preparation usu. of flour or starch and water used as an adhesive or a vehicle for mordant or color **b** : clay or a clay mixture used in making pottery or porcelain **3** : a brilliant glass of high lead content used for the manufacture of artificial gems

²**paste** *vt* **past·ed; past·ing** (1561) **1** : to cause to adhere by or as if by paste : STICK **2** : to cover with something pasted on

³**paste** *vt* **past·ed; past·ing** [alter. of *baste*] (1846) **1** : to strike hard at **2** : to beat or defeat soundly

¹**paste·board** \'pāst-ˌbȯrd, -ˌbörd\ *n* (1562) **1** : a solid paperboard with a paper facing; *broadly* : PAPERBOARD **2** : TICKET

²**pasteboard** *adj* (1599) **1** : made of pasteboard **2** : SHAM, UNSUBSTANTIAL ⟨prefabricated plots and ~ heroes —Peter Andrews⟩

paste·down \-ˌdaůn\ *n* (ca. 1888) : the outer leaf of an endpaper that is pasted down to the inside of the front or back cover of a book

¹**pas·tel** \pa-'stel\ *n* [F, fr. It *pastello*, fr. LL *pastellus* woad, fr. dim. of *pasta*] (1662) **1** : a paste made of powdered pigment ranging from pale to deep colors and used for making crayons; *also* : a crayon made of such paste **2 a** : a drawing in pastel **b** : the process or art of

drawing with pastels **3** : a light literary sketch **4** : any of various pale or light colors

²**pastel** *adj* (1884) **1 a** : of or relating to a pastel **b** : made with pastels **2** : pale and light in color **3** : lacking in body or vigor

pas·tel·ist *or* **pas·tel·list** \-'ste-list\ *n* (1881) : an artist who works with pastels

pas·tern \'pas-tərn\ *n* [MF *pasturon*, fr. *pasture* tether attached to a horse's foot, alter. of (assumed) OF *pastoire*, fr. ML *pastoria*, fr. L, fem. of *pastorius* of a herdsman, fr. *pastor* herdsman — more at PASTOR] (ca. 1530) **1** : a part of the foot of an equine extending from the fetlock to the top of the hoof — see HORSE illustration **2** : a part of the leg of an animal other than an equine that corresponds to the pastern

paste·up \'pāst-ˌəp\ *n* (ca. 1930) : MECHANICAL; *also* : the process of making mechanicals

pas·teur·ise *Brit var of* PASTEURIZE

pas·teur·i·za·tion \ˌpas-chə-rə-'zā-shən, ˌpas-tyə-, -tə-\ *n* (1886) **1** : partial sterilization of a substance and esp. a liquid (as milk) at a temperature and for a period of exposure that destroys objectionable organisms without major chemical alteration of the substance **2** : partial sterilization of perishable food products (as fruit or fish) with radiation (as gamma rays)

pas·teur·ize \'pas-chə-ˌrīz, 'pas-tyə-, -tə-\ *vt* **-ized; -iz·ing** [Louis *Pasteur*] (1881) : to subject to pasteurization — **pas·teur·iz·er** *n*

Pasteur treatment *n* (1926) : a method of aborting rabies by stimulating production of antibodies through successive inoculations with attenuated virus of gradually increasing strength

pas·tic·cio \pa-'stē-ch(ē-)ō, pä-\ *n, pl* **-ci** \-(ˌ)chē\ *or* **-cios** [It, lit., pasty, fr. (assumed) VL *pasticium*, fr. LL *pasta*] (1752) : PASTICHE

pas·tiche \pa-'stēsh, pä-\ *n* [F, fr. It *pasticcio*] (1878) **1** : a literary, artistic, musical, or architectural work that imitates the style of previous work; *also* : such stylistic imitation **2 a** : a musical, literary, or artistic composition made up of selections from different works : POTPOURRI **b** : HODGEPODGE — **pas·ti·cheur** \ˌpas-tē-'shər, ˌpäs-\ *n*

past·ies \'pās-tēz\ *n pl* [²*paste*] (ca. 1954) : small round coverings for a woman's nipples worn esp. by a stripteaser

pas·tille \pas-'tē(ə)l\ *also* **pas·til** \'pas-t²l\ *n* [F *pastille*, fr. L *pastillus* small loaf, lozenge; akin to L *panis* bread — more at FOOD] (1658) **1** : a small mass of aromatic paste for fumigating or scenting the air of a room **2** : an aromatic or medicated lozenge : TROCHE

pas·time \'pas-ˌtīm\ *n* (15c) : something that amuses and serves to make time pass agreeably : DIVERSION

pas·ti·na \'päs-tē-nə\ *n* [It, dim. of *pasta* pasta] (ca. 1948) : very small bits of pasta used in soup or broth

pas·tis \päs-'tēs\ *n* [F, fr. F dial. (Marseilles), lit., jumble, kind of pastry, fr. Prov, fr. OProv *pastitz* cake, fr. (assumed) VL *pasticium*] (1926) : a French liqueur flavored with aniseed

past master *n* (1762) **1** : one who has held the office of worshipful master in a lodge of Freemasons or of master in a guild, club, or society **2** [alter. of *passed master*] : one who is expert : ADEPT

past·ness \'pas(t)-nəs\ *n* (1829) **1** : the quality or state of being past **2** : the subjective quality of something being remembered rather than immediately experienced

¹**pas·tor** \'pas-tər\ *n* [ME *pastour*, fr. MF, fr. L *pastor* herdsman, fr. *pascere* to feed — more at FOOD] (14c) : a spiritual overseer; *esp* : a clergyman serving a local church or parish — **pas·tor·ship** \-ˌship\ *n*

²**pastor** *vt* **pas·tored; pas·tor·ing** \-t(ə-)riŋ\ (1623) : to serve as pastor of (as a church)

³**pas·tor** \päs-'tȯr\ *n* [Sp, fr. L] (1849) *chiefly Southwest* : HERDSMAN

¹**pas·to·ral** \'pas-t(ə-)rəl\ *adj* [ME, fr. L *pastoralis*, fr. *pastor* herdsman] (15c) **1 a** (1) : of, relating to, or composed of shepherds or herdsmen (2) : devoted to or based on livestock raising **b** : of or relating to the countryside : not urban **c** : portraying or expressive of the life of shepherds or country people esp. in an idealized and conventionalized manner ⟨~ poetry⟩ **d** : pleasingly peaceful and innocent : IDYLLIC **2 a** : of or relating to spiritual care or guidance esp. of a congregation **b** : of or relating to the pastor of a church — **pas·to·ral·ly** \-t(ə-)rə-lē\ *adv* — **pas·to·ral·ness** *n*

²**pastoral** \'pas-t(ə-)rəl; *1d is often* ˌpas-tə-'räl, -'ral\ *n* (1584) **1 a** : a literary work (as a poem or play) dealing with shepherds or rural life in a usu. artificial manner and typically drawing a contrast between the innocence and serenity of the simple life and the misery and corruption of city and esp. court life **b** : pastoral poetry or drama **c** : a rural picture or scene **d** : PASTORALE 1b **2** : CROSIER 1 **3** : a letter of a pastor to his charge: as **a** : a letter addressed by a bishop to his diocese **b** : a letter of the house of bishops of the Protestant Episcopal Church to be read in each parish

pas·to·rale \ˌpas-tə-'räl, -'ral *also* -'rä-lē\ *n* [It, fr. *pastorale* of herdsmen, fr. L *pastoralis*] (1724) **1 a** : an opera of the 16th or 17th centuries having a pastoral plot **b** : an instrumental or vocal composition having a pastoral theme **2** : PASTORAL 1a

Pastoral Epistle *n* (1836) : one of three New Testament letters including two addressed to Timothy and one to Titus that give advice on matters of church government and discipline

pas·to·ral·ism \'pas-t(ə-)rə-ˌli-zəm\ *n* (1854) **1** : the quality or style characteristic of pastoral writing **2 a** : livestock raising **b** : social organization based on livestock raising as the primary economic activity — **pas·to·ral·ist** \-list\ *n or adj*

pas·tor·ate \'pas-t(ə-)rət\ *n* (1795) **1** : the office, state, jurisdiction, or tenure of office of a pastor **2** : a body of pastors

past participle *n* (1798) : a participle that typically expresses completed action, that is traditionally one of the principal parts of the verb, and that is traditionally used in English in the formation of perfect tenses in the active voice and of all tenses in the passive voice

past perfect *adj* (1889) : of, relating to, or constituting a verb tense that is traditionally formed in English with *had* and denotes an action or state as completed at or before a past time spoken of — **past perfect** *n*

pas·tra·mi *also* **pas·tromi** \pə-'strä-mē\ *n* [Yiddish *pastrame*, fr. Rom *pastramă* pressed and cured meat] (1936) : a highly seasoned smoked beef prepared esp. from shoulder cuts

pas·try \'pās-trē\ *n, pl* **pastries** [¹*paste*] (ca. 1538) **1 a** : PASTE 1a **b** : sweet baked goods made of dough having a high fat content **2 a** : a piece of pastry

past tense *n* (1813) : a verb tense expressing action or state in or as if in the past: **a** : a verb tense expressive of elapsed time (as *wrote* in "on arriving I wrote a letter") **b** : a verb tense expressing action or state in progress or continuance or habitually done or customarily occurring at a past time (as *was writing* in "I was writing while he dictated" or *loved* in "their sons loved fishing")

pas·tur·age \'pas-chə-rij\ *n* (ca. 1533) : PASTURE

¹**pas·ture** \'pas-chər\ *n* [ME, fr. MF, fr. LL *pastura*, fr. L *pastus*, pp. of *pascere* to feed — more at FOOD] (14c) **1** : plants (as grass) grown for the feeding esp. of grazing animals **2** : land or a plot of land used for grazing **3** : the feeding of livestock : GRAZING

²**pasture** *vb* **pas·tured; pas·tur·ing** *vi* (14c) : GRAZE, BROWSE ~ *vt* **1** : to feed (as cattle) on pasture **2** : to use as pasture

pas·ture·land \'pas-chər-,land\ *n* (1591) : PASTURE 2

¹**pas·ty** \'pas-tē\ *n, pl* **pasties** [ME *pastee*, fr. MF *pasté*, fr. *paste* dough, paste] (13c) **1** : ²PIE 1, 2; *esp* : a meat pie **2** : TURNOVER 5

²**pasty** \'pās-tē\ *adj* **past·i·er; -est** (1659) : resembling paste; *esp* : pallid and unhealthy in appearance — **past·i·ness** \-nəs\ *n*

PA system \,pē-'ā-\ *n* (ca. 1936) : PUBLIC-ADDRESS SYSTEM

¹**pat** \'pat\ *n* [ME *patte*, prob. of imit. origin] (15c) **1** : a light blow esp. with the hand or a flat instrument **2** : a light tapping often rhythmical sound **3** : something (as butter) shaped into a small cake usu. square individual portion — **pat on the back** : an expression of approval

²**pat** *adv* (1578) : in a pat manner : APTLY, PERFECTLY

³**pat** *vb* **pat·ted; pat·ting** *vt* (1591) **1** : to strike lightly with a flat instrument **2** : to flatten, smooth, or put into place or shape with light blows **3** : to tap or stroke gently with the hand to soothe, caress, or show approval ~ *vi* : to strike or beat gently

⁴**pat** *adj* (1646) **1 a** : exactly suited to the purpose or occasion : APT **b** : suspiciously appropriate : CONTRIVED **2** : learned, mastered, or memorized exactly **3** : FIRM, UNYIELDING **4** : reduced to a simple or mechanical form : STANDARD, TRITE

pa·ta·ca \pə-'tä-kə\ *n* [Pg] (1830) — see MONEY table

pat–a–cake \'pa-də-,kāk, 'pat-ə-\ *var of* PATTY-CAKE

pa·ta·gi·um \pə-'tā-jē-əm\ *n, pl* **-gia** \-jē-ə\ [NL, fr. L, gold edging on a tunic] (1826) **1** : the fold of skin connecting the forelimbs and hind limbs of some tetrapods (as flying squirrels) **2** : the fold of skin in front of the main segments of a bird's wing

¹**patch** \'pach\ *n* [ME *pacche*] (14c) **1** : a piece of material used to mend or cover a hole or a weak spot **2** : a tiny piece of black silk or court plaster worn on the face or neck esp. by women to hide a blemish or to heighten beauty **3 a** : a piece of material (as adhesive plaster) used medically usu. to cover a wound or repair a defect **b** : a shield worn over the socket of an injured or missing eye **4 a** : a small piece : SCRAP **b** : a part or area distinct from that about it ⟨cabbage ~⟩ **c** : a period of time : SPELL ⟨was going through a rough ~⟩ **5** : a piece of cloth sewed on a garment as an ornament or insignia; *esp* : SHOULDER PATCH **6** : a temporary connection in a communication system (as a telephone hookup) **7** : a minor usu. temporary correction or modification in a computer program

²**patch** *vt* (15c) **1** : to mend, cover, or fill up a hole or weak spot in **2** : to provide with a patch **3 a** : to make of patches or fragments **b** : to mend or put together esp. in hasty or shabby fashion — usu. used with *up* **c** : to make a patch in (a computer program) **4** : to connect (as circuits) by a patch cord *syn* see MEND

³**patch** *n* [perh. by folk etymology fr. It dial. *paccio*] (1549) : FOOL, DOLT

patch·board \'pach-,bōrd, -,bȯrd\ *n* (1934) : a switchboard in which circuits are interconnected by patch cords

patch cord *n* (1926) : a wire with a plug at each end that is used to connect electrical devices

patch·ou·li *also* **patch·ou·ly** \'pa-chə-lē, pə-'chü-lē\ *n* [Tamil *paccuḷi*] (1845) : a heavy perfume made from a fragrant essential oil from an East Indian shrubby mint (*Pogostemon cablin*); *also* : the plant itself

patch pocket *n* (1895) : a flat pocket applied to the outside of a garment

patch test *n* (1933) : a test for determining allergic sensitivity that is made by applying to the unbroken skin small pads soaked with the allergen to be tested

patch·work \'pach-,wərk\ *n, often attrib* (1692) **1** : something composed of miscellaneous or incongruous parts : HODGEPODGE **2** : pieces of cloth of various colors and shapes sewn together to form a covering

patchwork quilt *n* (1840) **1** : a quilt made of patchwork **2** : PATCHWORK 1

patchy \'pa-chē\ *adj* **patch·i·er; -est** (1798) **1** : marked by, consisting of, or diversified with patches **2** : irregular in appearance, makeup, or quality — **patch·i·ly** \'pa-chə-lē\ *adv* — **patch·i·ness** \'pa-chē-nəs\ *n*

pate \'pāt\ *n* [ME] (14c) **1** : HEAD **2** : the crown of the head **3** : BRAIN — used chiefly disparagingly — **pat·ed** \'pā-təd\ *adj*

pâte \'pät\ *n* [F, lit., paste, fr. OF *paste*] (1838) : PASTE 2b

pâ·té *also* **pate** \pä-'tā, pa-\ *n* [F, fr. MF *pasté* — more at PASTY] (1706) **1** : a meat or fish pie or patty **2** : a spread of finely chopped or pureed seasoned meat ⟨chicken liver ~⟩

pâ·té de foie gras \,(,)pä-,tā-də-,fwä-'grä, (,)pa-,tā-\ *n, pl* **pâ·tés de foie gras** \-,tā(z)-\ [F, lit., pâté of fat liver] (1827) : a pâté of fat goose liver and usu. truffles sometimes with added fat pork

pa·tel·la \pə-'te-lə\ *n, pl* **-lae** \-'te-(,)lē, -,lī\ *or* **-las** [L, fr. dim. of *patina* shallow dish] (1693) : a thick flat triangular movable bone that forms the anterior point of the knee and protects the front of the joint — called also *kneecap* — **pa·tel·lar** \-'te-lər\ *adj*

pa·tel·li·form \pə-'te-lə-,fȯrm\ *adj* [NL *Patella*, genus including the limpet, fr. L, small shallow dish] (1819) **1** : resembling a limpet or limpet shell **2** : disk-shaped with a narrow rim

pat·en \'pa-tᵊn\ *n* [ME, fr. MF *patene*, fr. ML & L; ML *patina*, fr. L, shallow dish, fr. Gk *patanē*] (14c) **1** : a plate usu. made of precious metal and used to carry the bread at the Eucharist **2 a** : PLATE **b** : something (as a metal disk) resembling a plate

pa·ten·cy \'pa-tᵊn(t)-sē, 'pā-\ *n* (1656) : the quality or state of being patent

¹**pat·ent** \1–3 *are* 'pa-tᵊnt, *chiefly Brit* 'pā-; 4 'pā-; 5 'pā-, 'pa-; 6–7 'pa-, 'pā-, *Brit usu* 'pā-\ *adj* [ME, fr. MF, fr. L *patent-, patens*, fr. prp. of *patēre* to be open — more at FATHOM] (14c) **1** : open to public inspection — used chiefly in the phrase *letters patent* **b** (1) : secured by letters patent or by a patent to the exclusive control and possession

of a particular individual or party (2) : protected by a patent : made under a patent ⟨~ locks⟩ **c** : protected by a trademark or a trade name so as to establish proprietary rights analogous to those conveyed by letters patent or a patent : PROPRIETARY ⟨~ drugs⟩ **2** : of, relating to, or concerned with the granting of patents esp. for inventions ⟨a ~ lawyer⟩ **3** : making exclusive or proprietary claims or pretensions **4** : affording free passage : UNOBSTRUCTED ⟨a ~ opening⟩ **5** : PATULOUS, SPREADING ⟨a ~ calyx⟩ **6** *archaic* : ACCESSIBLE, EXPOSED **7** : readily visible or intelligible : OBVIOUS *syn* see EVIDENT — **pat·ent·ly** *adv*

²**pat·ent** \'pa-tᵊnt, *Brit also* 'pā-\ *n* (14c) **1** : an official document conferring a right or privilege : LETTERS PATENT **2 a** : a writing securing to an inventor for a term of years the exclusive right to make, use, or sell an invention **b** : the monopoly or right so granted **c** : a patented invention **3** : PRIVILEGE, LICENSE **4** : an instrument making a conveyance of public land; *also* : the land so conveyed **5** : PATENT LEATHER

³**pat·ent** *vt* (1675) **1** : to obtain or grant a patent right to **2** : to grant a privilege, right, or license to by patent **3** : to obtain or secure by patent; *esp* : to secure by letters patent exclusive right to make, use, or sell — **pat·ent·abil·i·ty** \,pa-tᵊn-tə-'bi-lə-tē, *Brit also* ,pā-\ *n* — **pat·ent·able** \'pa-tᵊn-tə-bəl, *Brit also* 'pā-\ *adj*

pat·ent·ed \'pa-tᵊn-təd, *Brit also* 'pā-\ *adj* (1951) : originated by or peculiar to one person or group : INDIVIDUALIZED

pat·en·tee \,pa-tᵊn-'tē, *Brit also* ,pā-\ *n* (15c) : one to whom a grant is made or a privilege secured by patent

patent flour \'pa-tᵊn(t)-, *Brit also* 'pā-\ *n* (1886) : a high-grade wheat flour that consists solely of endosperm

patent leather \'pa-tᵊn(t)-, *Brit usu* 'pā-\ *n* (1829) : a leather with a hard smooth glossy surface

patent medicine *n* (1770) : a packaged nonprescription drug which is protected by a trademark and whose contents are incompletely disclosed; *also* : any drug that is a proprietary

patent office *n* (1696) : a government office for examining claims to patents and granting patents

pat·en·tor \'pa-tᵊn-tər, ,pa-tᵊn-'tȯr, *Brit also* 'pā-, ,pā-\ *n* (ca. 1890) : one that grants a patent

patent right *n* (1805) : a right granted by letters patent; *esp* : the exclusive right to an invention

pa·ter *n* (14c) **1** \'pä-,ter\ *often cap* : PATERNOSTER **2** \'pā-tər\ [L] : *chiefly Brit* : FATHER

pa·ter·fa·mil·i·as \,pa-tər-fə-'mi-lē-əs, ,pä-, ,pā-\ *n, pl* **pa·tres·fa·mil·i·as** \,pä-,trēz-, ,pä-,träs-\ [ME, fr. L, fr. *pater* father + *familias*, archaic gen. of *familia* household — more at FATHER, FAMILY] (15c) **1** : the male head of a household **2** : the father of a family

pa·ter·nal \pə-'tər-nᵊl\ *adj* [ME, fr. L *paternalis*, fr. L *paternus* paternal, fr. *pater*] (15c) **1 a** : of or relating to a father **b** : like that of a father ⟨~ benevolence⟩ **2** : received or inherited from one's male parent **3** : related through one's father ⟨~ grandfather⟩ — **pa·ter·nal·ly** \-ē\ *adv*

pa·ter·nal·ism \pə-'tər-nᵊl-,i-zəm\ *n* (1881) **1** : a system under which an authority undertakes to supply needs or regulate conduct of those under its control in matters affecting them as individuals as well as in their relations to authority and to each other **2** : a policy or practice based on or characteristic of paternalism — **pa·ter·nal·ist** \-nᵊl-ist\ *n or adj* — **pa·ter·nal·is·tic** \-,tər-nᵊl-'is-tik\ *adj* — **pa·ter·nal·is·ti·cal·ly** \-ti-k(ə-)lē\ *adv*

pa·ter·ni·ty \pə-'tər-nə-tē\ *n* (1582) **1** : the quality or state of being a father **2** : origin or descent from a father

paternity test *n* (1926) : a test esp. of DNA or genetic traits to determine whether a given man could be the biological father of a given child

pa·ter·nos·ter \,pä-tər-'näs-tər, 'pa-tər-,, 'pä-,ter-, -'näs-,ter\ *n* [ME, fr. OE, fr. ML, fr. L *pater noster* our father, fr. the opening words] (bef. 12c) **1** *often cap* : LORD'S PRAYER **2** : a word formula repeated as a prayer or magical charm

path \'path, 'path\ *n, pl* **paths** \'pathz, 'pa<u>th</u>z, 'pȧthz, 'pȧths\ [ME, fr. OE *pæth*; akin to OHG *pfad* path] (bef. 12c) **1** : a trodden way **2** : a track specially constructed for a particular use **3 a** : COURSE, ROUTE **b** : a way of life, conduct, or thought **4 a** : the continuous series of positions or configurations that can be assumed in any motion or process of change by a moving or varying system **b** : a sequence of arcs in a network that can be traced continuously without retracing any arc **5** : PATHWAY 2

path- *or* **patho-** *comb form* [NL, fr. Gk, fr. *pathos*, lit., suffering — more at PATHOS] : pathological state : disease ⟨*pathogen*⟩

-path *n comb form* [G, back-formation fr. *-pathie* -pathy] **1** : practitioner of a (specified) system of medicine that emphasizes one aspect of disease or its treatment ⟨*naturopath*⟩ **2** [ISV, fr. Gk *-pathēs*, adj., suffering, fr. *pathos*] **a** : one suffering from a disorder (of such a part or system) ⟨*psychopath*⟩ **b** : one perceiving ⟨*telepath*⟩

Pa·than \pə-'tän, ,pä-\ *n* [Hindi *Pathān*, fr. Pashto (eastern dial.) *Pakhtana*, pl. of *Pakhtun*] (1658) : PASHTUN

path·break·ing \'path-,brā-kiŋ\ *adj* (1914) : TRAILBLAZING

pa·thet·ic \pə-'the-tik\ *adj* [MF *or* LL; MF *pathetique*, fr. LL *patheticus*, fr. Gk *pathētikos* capable of feeling, pathetic, fr. *paschein* (aor. *pathein*) to experience, suffer — more at PATHOS] (1598) **1** : having a capacity to move one to either compassionate or contemptuous pity **2** : marked by sorrow or melancholy : SAD *syn* see MOVING — **pa·thet·i·cal** \-ti-kəl\ *adj* — **pa·thet·i·cal·ly** \-ti-k(ə-)lē\ *adv*

pathetic fallacy *n* (1856) : the ascription of human traits or feelings to inanimate nature (as in *cruel sea*)

path·find·er \'path-,fin-dər, 'pȧth-\ *n* (1840) : one that discovers a way; *esp* : one that explores untraversed regions to mark out a new route — **path·find·ing** \-diŋ\ *n or adj*

path·less \-ləs\ *adj* (1591) : UNTRODDEN, TRACKLESS — **path·less·ness** *n*

patho·bi·ol·o·gy \,pa-thō-bī-'ä-lə-jē\ *n* (ca. 1909) : PATHOLOGY

\ə\ abut \ᵊ\ kitten, F table \ər\ further \a\ ash \ā\ ace \ä\ mop, mar \aů\ out \ch\ chin \e\ bet \ē\ easy \g\ go \i\ hit \ī\ ice \j\ job \ŋ\ sing \ō\ go \ȯ\ law \ȯi\ boy \th\ thin \<u>th</u>\ the \ü\ loot \ů\ foot \y\ yet \zh\ vision \a, ᶄ, ⁿ, œ, œ̄, ǔ, ū̃, ᵊ\ *see* Guide to Pronunciation

path·o·gen \'pa-thə-jən\ *n* [ISV] (1880) : a specific causative agent (as a bacterium or virus) of disease

path·o·gen·e·sis \,pa-thə-'je-nə-səs\ *n* [NL] (1876) : the origination and development of a disease

path·o·ge·net·ic \-jə-'ne-tik\ *adj* [ISV] (1838)   **1** : of or relating to pathogenesis   **2** : PATHOGENIC 2

path·o·gen·ic \-'je-nik\ *adj* [ISV] (1852)   **1** : PATHOGENETIC 1   **2** : causing or capable of causing disease — **path·o·ge·nic·i·ty** \-jə-'ni-sə-tē\ *n*

pa·tho·gno·mon·ic \,pa-thə(g)-nō-'mä-nik\ *adj* [Gk *pathognōmonikos,* fr. *path-* + *gnōmonikos* fit to judge, fr. *gnōmōn* interpreter; akin to Gk *gignōskein* to know — more at KNOW] (1625) : distinctively characteristic of a particular disease

path·o·log·i·cal \,pa-thə-'lä-ji-kəl\ *also* **path·o·log·ic** \-jik\ *adj* (1688)   **1** : of or relating to pathology   **2** : altered or caused by disease — **path·o·log·i·cal·ly** \-ji-k(ə-)lē\ *adv*

pa·thol·o·gist \pə-'thä-lə-jist, pa-\ *n* (1650) : a specialist in pathology; *specif* : one who interprets and diagnoses the changes caused by disease in tissues and body fluids

pa·thol·o·gy \-jē\ *n, pl* **-gies** [NL *pathologia* & MF *pathologie,* fr. Gk *pathologia* study of the emotions, fr. *path-* + *-logia* -logy] (1611)   **1** : the study of the essential nature of diseases and esp. of the structural and functional changes produced by them   **2** : something abnormal: **a** : the structural and functional deviations from the normal that constitute disease or characterize a particular disease   **b** : deviation from propriety or from an assumed normal state of something nonliving or nonmaterial

path·o·phys·i·ol·o·gy \'pa-thō-,fi-zē-'ä-lə-jē\ *n* (1947) : the physiology of abnormal states; *specif* : the functional changes that accompany a particular syndrome or disease — **path·o·phys·i·o·log·i·cal** \-zē-ə-'lä-ji-kəl\ *also* **path·o·phys·i·o·log·ic** \-jik\ *adj*

pa·thos \'pā-,thäs, -,thȯs, -,thōs *also* 'pa-\ *n* [Gk, suffering, experience, emotion, fr. *paschein* (aor. *pathein*) to experience, suffer; perh. akin to Lith *kęsti* to suffer] (1591)   **1** : an element in experience or in artistic representation evoking pity or compassion   **2** : an emotion of sympathetic pity

path·way \'path-,wā, 'päth-\ *n* (15c)   **1** : PATH, COURSE   **2** : a line of communication over interconnecting neurons extending from one organ or center to another   **3** : the sequence of enzyme catalyzed reactions by which an energy-yielding substance is utilized by protoplasm ⟨metabolic ∼s⟩

-pathy *n comb form* [L *-pathia,* fr. Gk *-patheia,* fr. *-pathēs* suffering, fr. *pathos*]   **1** : feeling : suffering ⟨empathy⟩ : perception ⟨telepathy⟩   **2** : disorder of (such) a part or kind ⟨neuropathy⟩   **3** : system of medicine based on (such) a factor ⟨osteopathy⟩

pa·tience \'pā-shən(t)s\ *n* (13c)   **1** : the capacity, habit, or fact of being patient   **2** *chiefly Brit* : SOLITAIRE 2

¹pa·tient \'pā-shənt\ *adj* [ME *pacient,* fr. MF, fr. L *patient-, patiens,* fr. prp. of *pati* to suffer; perh. akin to Gk *pēma* suffering] (14c)   **1** : bearing pains or trials calmly or without complaint   **2** : manifesting forbearance under provocation or strain   **3** : not hasty or impetuous   **4** : steadfast despite opposition, difficulty, or adversity   **5** : able or willing to bear — used with *of* : SUSCEPTIBLE, ADMITTING ⟨∼ of one interpretation⟩ — **pa·tient·ly** *adv*

²patient *n* (14c)   **1 a** : an individual awaiting or under medical care and treatment   **b** : the recipient of any of various personal services   **2** : one that is acted upon

pa·ti·na \pə-'tē-nə, 'pa-tə-nə\ *n, pl* **pa·ti·nas** \-nəz\ *or* **pa·ti·nae** \-,nē, -,nī\ [It, fr. L, shallow dish — more at PATEN] (1748)   **1 a** : a usu. green film formed naturally on copper and bronze by long exposure or artificially (as by acids) and often valued aesthetically for its color   **b** : a surface appearance of something grown beautiful esp. with age or use   **2** : an appearance or aura that is derived from association, habit, or established character   **3** : a superficial covering or exterior

pat·i·nate \'pa-tə-,nāt\ *vb* **-nat·ed; -nat·ing** *vt* (1880) : to give a patina to ∼ *vi* : to take on a patina — usu. used in the past participle ⟨*patinated* bronze⟩ — **pat·i·na·tion** \,pa-tə-'nā-shən\ *n*

¹pa·tine \pa-'tēn\ *n* [F, fr. It *patina*] (1883) : PATINA

²patine *vt* **pa·tined; pa·tin·ing** (1896) : to cover with a patina

pa·tio \'pa-tē-,ō *also* 'pä-\ *n, pl* **pa·ti·os** [Sp] (1828)   **1** : COURTYARD; *esp* : an inner court open to the sky   **2** : a recreation area that adjoins a dwelling, is often paved, and is adapted esp. to outdoor dining

pa·tis·se·rie *or* **pâ·tis·se·rie** \pə-'ti-sə-rē, pä-\ *n* [F *pâtisserie,* fr. MF *pastiserie,* fr. *pasticier* to make pastry, fr. (assumed) OF *pastitz* cake, fr. (assumed) VL *pasticium,* fr. LL *pasta* dough] (1784)   **1** : PASTRY   **2** : a pastry shop

pâ·tis·sier *or* **pa·tis·sier** \pä-tis-'yā\ *n* [F *pâtissier,* fr. OF *pasticier,* fr. (assumed) OF *pastitz* cake] (ca. 1905) : a pastry chef

pa·tois \'pa-,twä, 'pä-\ *n, pl* **pa·tois** \-,twäz\ [F] (1643)   **1 a** : a dialect other than the standard or literary dialect   **b** : uneducated or provincial speech   **2** : the characteristic special language of an occupational or social group : JARGON

patr- *or* **patri-** *or* **patro-** *comb form* [*patr-, patri-* fr. L, fr. *patr-, pater; patr-, patro-* fr. Gk, fr. *patr-, patēr* — more at FATHER] : father ⟨*patris*tic⟩

pa·tri·arch \'pā-trē-,ärk\ *n* [ME *patriarche,* fr. OF, fr. LL *patriarcha,* fr. Gk *patriarchēs,* fr. *patria* lineage (fr. *patr-, patēr* father) + *-archēs* -arch — more at FATHER] (13c)   **1 a** : one of the scriptural fathers of the human race or of the Hebrew people   **b** : a man who is father or founder   **c** (1) : the oldest member or representative of a group   (2) : a venerable old man   **d** : a man who is head of a patriarchy   **2 a** : any of the bishops of the ancient or Eastern Orthodox sees of Constantinople, Alexandria, Antioch, and Jerusalem or the ancient and Western see of Rome with authority over other bishops   **b** : the head of any of various Eastern churches   **c** : a Roman Catholic bishop next in rank to the pope with purely titular or with metropolitan jurisdiction   **3** : a Mormon of the Melchizedek priesthood empowered to perform the ordinances of the church and pronounce blessings within a stake or prescribed jurisdiction

pa·tri·ar·chal \,pā-trē-'är-kəl\ (15c) : of, relating to, or being a patriarch or patriarchy

patriarchal cross *n* (ca. 1727) : a chiefly heraldic cross denoting a cardinal's or archbishop's rank and having two crossbars of which the

lower is the longer and intersects the upright above or at its center — see CROSS illustration

pa·tri·arch·ate \'pā-trē-,är-kət, -,kät\ *n* (1617)   **1 a** : the office, jurisdiction, or time in office of a patriarch   **b** : the residence or headquarters of a patriarch   **2** : PATRIARCHY

pa·tri·ar·chy \-,är-kē\ *n, pl* **-chies** (1632)   **1** : social organization marked by the supremacy of the father in the clan or family, the legal dependence of wives and children, and the reckoning of descent and inheritance in the male line; *broadly* : control by men of a disproportionately large share of power   **2** : a society or institution organized according to the principles or practices of patriarchy

pa·tri·cian \pə-'tri-shən\ *n* [ME *patricion,* fr. MF *patricien,* fr. L *patricius,* fr. *patres* senators, fr. pl. of *pater* father — more at FATHER] (15c)   **1** : a member of one of the original citizen families of ancient Rome   **2 a** : a person of high birth : ARISTOCRAT   **b** : a person of breeding and cultivation — **patrician** *adj*

pa·tri·ci·ate \-'tri-shē-ət, -,āt\ *n* (ca. 1656)   **1** : the position or dignity of a patrician   **2** : a patrician class

pat·ri·cide \'pa-trə-,sīd\ *n* (1593)   **1** [L *patricida,* fr. *patr-* + *-cida* -cide] : one who murders his or her own father   **2** [LL *patricidium,* fr. L *patr-* + *-cidium* -cide] : the murder of one's own father — **pat·ri·cid·al** \,pa-trə-'sī-dᵊl\ *adj*

pat·ri·lin·eal \,pa-trə-'li-nē-əl\ *adj* (1904) : relating to, based on, or tracing descent through the paternal line ⟨∼ society⟩

pat·ri·mo·ny \'pa-trə-,mō-nē\ *n* [ME *patrimonie,* fr. MF, fr. L *patrimonium,* fr. *patr-, pater* father] (14c)   **1 a** : an estate inherited from one's father or ancestor   **b** : anything derived from one's father or ancestors : HERITAGE   **2** : an estate or endowment belonging by ancient right to a church — **pat·ri·mo·ni·al** \,pa-trə-'mō-nē-əl\ *adj*

pa·tri·ot \'pā-trē-ət, -,ät, *chiefly Brit* 'pa-trē-ət\ *n* [MF *patriote* compatriot, fr. LL *patriota,* fr. Gk *patriōtēs,* fr. *patria* lineage, fr. *patr-, patēr* father] (1605) : one who loves his or her country and supports its authority and interests

pa·tri·ot·ic \,pā-trē-'ä-tik, *chiefly Brit* ,pa-\ (1757)   **1** : inspired by patriotism   **2** : befitting or characteristic of a patriot — **pa·tri·ot·i·cal·ly** \-ti-k(ə-)lē\ *adv*

pa·tri·ot·ism \'pā-trē-ə-,ti-zəm, *chiefly Brit* 'pa-\ *n* (ca. 1726) : love for or devotion to one's country

Patriots' Day *n* (1897) : the third Monday in April observed as a legal holiday in Maine and Massachusetts in commemoration of the battles of Lexington and Concord in 1775

pa·tris·tic \pə-'tris-tik\ *adj* (ca. 1828) : of or relating to the church fathers or their writings — **pa·tris·ti·cal** \-ti-kəl\ *adj*

pa·tris·tics \-tiks\ *n pl but sing in constr* (1847) : the study of the writings and background of the church fathers

Pa·tro·clus \pə-'trō-kləs, -'trä-\ *n* [L, fr. Gk *Patroklos*] : a Greek hero and friend of Achilles slain by Hector at Troy

¹pa·trol \pə-'trōl\ *n* (1664)   **1 a** : the action of traversing a district or beat or of going the rounds along a chain of guards for observation or the maintenance of security   **b** : the person performing such an action   **c** : a unit of persons or vehicles employed for reconnaissance, security, or combat   **2** : a subdivision of a Boy Scout troop or Girl Scout troop

²patrol *vb* **pa·trolled; pa·trol·ling** [F *patrouiller,* fr. MF, to tramp around in the mud, fr. *patte* paw — more at PATTEN] (1691) : to carry out a patrol ∼ *vt* : to carry out a patrol of — **pa·trol·ler** *n*

pa·trol·man \pə-'trōl-mən\ *n* (1867) : one who patrols; *esp* : a police officer assigned to a beat

patrol wagon *n* (1887) : PADDY WAGON

pa·tron \'pā-trən, *for 6 also* pa-'trōⁿ\ *n* [ME, fr. MF, fr. ML & L; ML *patronus* patron saint, patron of a benefice, pattern, fr. L, defender, fr. *patr-, pater*] (14c)   **1 a** : a person chosen, named, or honored as a special guardian, protector, or supporter   **b** : a wealthy or influential supporter of an artist or writer   **c** : a social or financial sponsor of a social function (as a ball or concert)   **2** : one that uses wealth or influence to help an individual, an institution, or a cause   **3** : one who buys the goods or uses the services offered esp. by an establishment   **4** : the holder of the right of presentation to an English ecclesiastical benefice   **5** : a master in ancient times who freed his slave but retained some rights over him   **6** [F, fr. MF] : the proprietor of an establishment (as an inn) esp. in France   **7** : the chief male officer in some fraternal lodges having both men and women members — **pa·tron·al** \'pā-trə-nᵊl; *Brit* pə-'trō-nᵊl, pa-\ *adj*

pa·tron·age \'pa-trə-nij, 'pā-\ *n* (14c)   **1** : ADVOWSON   **2** : the support or influence of a patron   **3** : kindness done with an air of superiority   **4** : business or activity provided by patrons ⟨the new branch library is expected to have a heavy ∼⟩   **5 a** : the power to make appointments to government jobs esp. for political advantage   **b** : the distribution of jobs on the basis of patronage   **c** : jobs distributed by patronage

pa·tron·ess \'pā-trə-nəs\ *n* (15c) : a woman who is a patron

pa·tron·ise *Brit var of* PATRONIZE

pa·tron·ize \'pā-trə-,nīz, 'pa-\ *vt* **-ized; -iz·ing** (1589)   **1** : to act as patron of : provide aid or support for   **2** : to adopt an air of condescension toward : treat haughtily or coolly   **3** : to be a frequent or regular customer or client of — **pa·tron·i·za·tion** \,pā-trə-nə-'zā-shən, pa-\ *n* — **pa·tron·iz·ing·ly** \'pā-trə-,nī-ziŋ-lē, 'pa-\ *adv*

patron saint *n* (1717)   **1** : a saint to whose protection and intercession a person, a society, a church, or a place is dedicated   **2** : an original leader or prime exemplar

pat·ro·nym·ic \,pa-trə-'ni-mik\ *n* [LL *patronymicum,* fr. neut. of *patronymicus* of a patronymic, fr. Gk *patronymikos,* fr. *patronymia* patronymic, fr. *patr-* + *onyma* name — more at NAME] (1612) : a name derived from that of the father or a paternal ancestor usu. by the addition of an affix — **patronymic** *adj*

pa·troon \pə-'trün\ *n* [F *patron* & Sp *patrón,* fr. ML *patronus,* fr. L, patron] (1743)   **1** *archaic* : the captain or officer commanding a ship   **2** [D, fr. F *patron*] : the proprietor of a manorial estate esp. in New York orig. granted under Dutch rule but in some cases existing until the mid-19th century

pat·sy \'pat-sē\ *n, pl* **pat·sies** [perh. fr. It *pazzo* fool] (1903) : a person who is easily manipulated or victimized : SUCKER

pat·ten \'pa-tᵊn\ *n* [ME *patin,* fr. MF, fr. *patte* paw, hoof, fr. (assumed) VL *patta,* of imit. origin] (14c) : a clog, sandal, or overshoe often with a wooden sole or metal device to elevate the foot and increase the wearer's height or aid in walking in mud

¹pat·ter \'pa-tər\ *vb* [ME *patren*, fr. *paternoster*] *vt* (14c) : to say or speak in a rapid or mechanical manner ~ *vi* **1** : to recite prayers (as paternosters) rapidly or mechanically **2** : to talk glibly and volubly **3** : to speak or sing rapid-fire words in a theatrical performance — **pat·ter·er** \-tər-ər\ *n*

²patter *n* (1758) **1** : a specialized lingo : CANT; *esp* : the jargon of criminals (as thieves) **2** : the spiel of a street hawker or of a circus barker **3** : empty chattering talk **4 a** (1) : the rapid-fire talk of a comedian (2) : the talk with which an entertainer accompanies a routine **b** : the words of a comic song or of a rapidly spoken usu. humorous monologue introduced into such a song

³patter *vb* [freq. of ³*pat*] *vi* (1611) **1** : to strike or pat rapidly and repeatedly **2** : to run with quick light-sounding steps ~ *vt* : to cause to patter

⁴patter *n* (1844) : a quick succession of light sounds or pats

¹pat·tern \'pa-tərn\ *n* [ME *patron*, fr. MF, fr. ML *patronus*] (14c) **1** : a form or model proposed for imitation : EXEMPLAR **2** : something designed or used as a model for making things ⟨a dressmaker's ~⟩ **3** : a model for making a mold into which molten metal is poured to form a casting **4** : an artistic, musical, literary, or mechanical design or form **5** : a natural or chance configuration ⟨frost ~⟩ ⟨the ~ of events⟩ **6** : a length of fabric sufficient for an article (as of clothing) **7 a** : the distribution of shrapnel, bombs on a target, or shot from a shotgun **b** : the grouping made on a target by bullets **8** : a reliable sample of traits, acts, tendencies, or other observable characteristics of a person, group, or institution ⟨behavior ~⟩ ⟨spending ~⟩ **9 a** : the flight path prescribed for an airplane that is coming in for a landing **b** : a prescribed route to be followed by a pass receiver in football **10** : TEST PATTERN **11** : a discernible coherent system based on the intended interrelationship of component parts ⟨foreign policy ~s⟩ **12** : frequent or widespread incidence ⟨a ~ of dissent⟩ *syn* see MODEL — **pat·terned** \-tərnd\ *adj* — **pat·tern·less** *adj*

²pattern *vt* (ca. 1586) **1** *dial chiefly Eng* **a** : MATCH **b** : IMITATE **2** : to make, adapt, or fashion according to a pattern **3** : to furnish, adorn, or mark with a design ~ *vi* : to form a pattern

pat·tern·ing \'pa-tər-niŋ\ *n* (1862) **1** : decoration, composition, or configuration according to a pattern **2** : physiotherapy that is designed to improve malfunctioning nervous control by means of feedback from muscular activity imposed by an outside source or induced by other muscles

pat·ty *also* **pat·tie** \'pa-tē\ *n, pl* **patties** [F *pâté* pâté] (1710) **1** : a little pie **2 a** : a small flat cake of chopped food ⟨a hamburger ~⟩ **b** : a small flat candy ⟨a peppermint ~⟩ **3** : PATTY SHELL

pat·ty–cake \-ˌkāk\ *n* [alter. of *pat-a-cake*, fr. the opening words of the rhyme] (1889) : a game in which two participants (as mother and child) clap their hands together to the rhythm of an accompanying nursery rhyme

pat·ty·pan \-ˌpan\ *n* [pattypan pan for baking patties] (1900) : a summer squash having a scalloped edge — called also *cymling*

patty shell *n* (1909) : a shell of puff pastry made to hold a creamed meat, fish, or vegetable filling

pat·u·lous \'pa-chə-ləs\ *adj* [L *patulus*, fr. *patēre* to be open — more at FATHOM] (1616) : spreading widely from a center ⟨a tree with ~ branches⟩

pat·zer \'pät-sər, 'pat-\ *n* [prob. fr. G *Patzer* bungler, fr. *patzen* to blunder] (1959) : an inept chess player

pau·ci·ty \'pȯ-sə-tē\ *n* [ME *paucite*, fr. MF or L; MF *paucité*, fr. L *paucitat-, paucitas*, fr. *paucus* little — more at FEW] (15c) **1** : smallness of number : FEWNESS **2** : smallness of quantity : DEARTH

Paul \'pȯl\ *n* [L *Paulus*, fr. Gk *Paulos*] : an early Christian apostle and missionary and author of several New Testament epistles

Paul Bun·yan \-ˈbən-yən\ *n* : a giant lumberjack of American folklore

Pau·li exclusion principle \'pau̇-lē-\ *n* [Wolfgang *Pauli*] (1926) : EXCLUSION PRINCIPLE — called also *Pauli principle*

Pau·line \'pȯ-ˌlīn\ *adj* (1817) : of or relating to the apostle Paul, his epistles, or the doctrine or theology implicit in his epistles

Paul·ist \'pȯ-list\ *n* (ca. 1883) : a member of the Roman Catholic Congregation of the Missionary Priests of St. Paul the Apostle founded by I. T. Hecker in the U.S. in 1858

pau·low·nia \pȯ-ˈlō-nē-ə\ *n* [NL, fr. Anna *Pavlovna* †1865 Russ. princess] (1843) : any of a genus (*Paulownia*) of Chinese trees of the snapdragon family; *esp* : one (*P. tomentosa*) widely cultivated for its panicles of fragrant violet flowers

paunch \'pȯnch, 'pänch\ *n* [ME, fr. MF *panche*, fr. L *pantic-, pantex*] (14c) **1 a** : the belly and its contents **b** : POTBELLY **2** : RUMEN

paunchy \'pȯn-chē, 'pän-\ *adj* **paunch·i·er; -est** (1598) : having a potbelly — **paunch·i·ness** *n*

pau·per \'pȯ-pər\ *n* [L, poor — more at POOR] (1516) **1** : a person destitute of means except such as are derived from charity; *specif* : one who receives aid from funds designated for the poor **2** : a very poor person — **pau·per·ism** \-pə-ˌri-zəm\ *n*

pau·per·ize \'pȯ-pə-ˌrīz\ *vt* **-ized; -iz·ing** (1834) : to reduce to poverty

pau·piette \pȯ-ˈpyet\ *n* [F *paupiette*, fr. It *polpetta* meat croquette, dim. of *polpa* pulp, flesh, fr. L *pulpa*] (1889) : a thin slice of meat or fish wrapped around a forcemeat filling

¹pause \'pȯz\ *n* [ME, fr. L *pausa*, fr. Gk *pausis*, fr. *pauein* to stop] (15c) **1** : a temporary stop **2 a** : a break in a verse **b** : a brief suspension of the voice to indicate the limits and relations of sentences and their parts **3** : temporary inaction esp. as caused by uncertainty : HESITATION **4 a** : the sign denoting a fermata **b** : a mark (as a period or comma) used in writing or printing to indicate or correspond to a pause of voice **5** : a reason or cause for pausing (as to reconsider) ⟨a thought that should give one ~⟩

²pause *vb* **paused; paus·ing** *vi* (15c) **1** : to stop temporarily **2** : to linger for a time ~ *vt* : to cause to pause : STOP

pa·vane \pə-ˈvän, -ˈvan\ *also* **pa·van** \'pa-vən, *same or* 'pa-vən\ *n* [MF *pavane*, fr. It dial. *pavana*, fr. fem. of *pavano* of Padua, fr. *Pava* (Tuscan *Padova*) Padua] (1535) **1** : a stately court dance by couples that was introduced from southern Europe into England in the 16th century **2** : music for the pavane; *also* : music having the slow duple rhythm of a pavane

pave \'pāv\ *vt* **paved; pav·ing** [ME, fr. MF *paver*, fr. L *pavire* to strike, pound; perh. akin to Gk *paiein* to strike] (14c) **1** : to lay or cover with material (as asphalt or concrete) that forms a firm level surface for

travel **2** : to cover firmly and solidly as if with paving material **3** : to serve as a covering or pavement of — **pav·er** *n* — **pave the way** : to prepare a smooth easy way : facilitate development

pa·vé \pa-ˈvā\ *also* **pa·véed** *or* **pa·véd** \pa-ˈvād\ *or* **pa·ve** \pa-ˈvā\ *adj* [*pavé* fr. F, fr. pp. of *paver* to pave] (1903) *of jewels* : set as close together as possible to conceal a metal base

pave·ment \'pāv-mənt\ *n* [ME, fr. OF, fr. L *pavimentum*, fr. *pavire*] (13c) **1** : a paved surface **2** : the artificially covered surface of a public thoroughfare **b** *chiefly Brit* : SIDEWALK **2** : the material with which something is paved **3** : something that suggests a pavement (as in flatness, hardness, and extent of surface)

pav·id \'pa-vəd\ *adj* [L *pavidus*, fr. *pavēre* to be frightened; akin to L *pavire*] (ca. 1656) : TIMID

¹pa·vil·ion \pə-ˈvil-yən\ *n* [ME *pavilon*, fr. OF *paveillon*, fr. L *papilion-, papilio* butterfly, perh. akin to OHG *fifaltra* butterfly] (13c) **1 a** : a large often sumptuous tent **b** : something resembling a canopy or tent ⟨tree ferns spread their delicate ~s —Blanche E. Baughan⟩ **2 a** : a part of a building projecting from the rest **b** : one of several detached or semidetached units into which a building is sometimes divided **3 a** : a light sometimes ornamental structure in a garden, park, or place of recreation that is used for entertainment or shelter **b** : a temporary structure erected at an exposition by an individual exhibitor **4** : the lower faceted part of a brilliant below the girdle — see BRILLIANT illustration

²pavilion *vt* (14c) : to furnish or cover with or put in a pavilion

pav·ing \'pā-viŋ\ *n* (15c) : PAVEMENT

pav·ior *or* **pav·iour** \'pāv-yər\ *n* [ME *pavier*, fr. *paven* to pave] (15c) *Brit* : one that paves

pav·lo·va \'pav-lə-və, pav-ˈlō-\ *n, often cap* [Anna *Pavlova*] (1926) : a dessert of Australian and New Zealand origin consisting of a meringue shell topped with whipped cream and usu. fruit

Pav·lov·i·an \pav-ˈlȯ-vē-ən, -ˈlȯ-; -ˈlȯ-fē-\ *adj* (1926) **1** : of or relating to Ivan Pavlov or to his work and theories ⟨~ conditioning⟩ **2** : being or expressing a conditioned or predictable reaction : AUTOMATIC ⟨the candidates gave ~ answers⟩

¹paw \'pȯ\ *n* [ME, fr. MF *poue*] (14c) **1** : the foot of a quadruped (as a lion or dog) that has claws; *broadly* : the foot of an animal **2** : a human hand esp. when large or clumsy

²paw *vt* (15c) **1** : to touch or strike at with a paw **2** : to feel or touch clumsily, rudely, or sexually **3** : to scrape or beat with or as if with a hoof **4** : to flail at or grab for wildly ~ *vi* **1** : to beat or scrape something with or as if with a hoof **2** : to touch or strike with a paw **3** : to feel or touch someone or something clumsily, rudely, or sexually **4** : to flail or grab wildly

paw·ky \'pȯ-kē\ *adj* [obs. E dial. *pawk* trick] (1676) *chiefly Brit* : artfully shrewd : CANNY

pawl \'pȯl\ *n* [perh. modif. of D *pal* pawl] (1626) : a pivoted tongue or sliding bolt on one part of a machine that is adapted to fall into notches or interdental spaces on another part (as a ratchet wheel) so as to permit motion in only one direction — see RATCHET WHEEL illustration

¹pawn \'pȯn, 'pän\ *n* [ME *pown*, fr. MF *poon*, fr. ML *pedon-, pedo* foot soldier, fr. LL, one with broad feet, fr. L *ped-, pes* foot — more at FOOT] (14c) **1** : one of the chessmen of least value having the power to move only forward ordinarily one square at a time, to capture only diagonally forward, and to be promoted to any piece except a king upon reaching the eighth rank **2** : one that can be used to further the purposes of another

²pawn *n* [ME *paun*, modif. of MF *pan*] (15c) **1 a** : something delivered to or deposited with another as security for a loan **b** : HOSTAGE **2** : the state of being pledged **3** : something used as a pledge : GUARANTY **4** : the act of pawning

³pawn *vt* (1570) : to deposit in pledge or as security — **pawn·er** \'pȯ-nər, 'pä-\ *or* **paw·nor** *same or* pȯ-'nȯr, pä-\ *n*

pawn·bro·ker \'pȯn-ˌbrō-kər, 'pän-\ *n* (1687) : one who lends money on the security of personal property pledged in his keeping — **pawn·bro·king** \-kiŋ\ *n*

Paw·nee \pȯ-ˈnē, pä-\ *n, pl* **Pawnee** *or* **Pawnees** (1770) : a member of an American Indian people orig. of Kansas and Nebraska

pawn off *vt* (1832) : to get rid of or pass off usu. by deception : PALM OFF

pawn·shop \'pȯn-ˌshäp, 'pän-\ *n* (1849) : a pawnbroker's shop

paw–paw *var of* PAPAW

pax \'paks, 'päks\ *n* [ME, fr. ML, fr. L, peace — more at PEACE] (14c) **1** : a tablet decorated with a sacred figure (as of Christ) and sometimes ceremonially kissed by participants at mass **2** : the kiss of peace in the Mass **3** : PEACE; *esp, cap* : a period of general stability in international affairs under the influence of a dominant military power — usu. used in combination with a latinized name ⟨Pax Americana⟩

¹pay \'pā\ *vb* **paid** \'pād\ *also in sense 7* **payed; pay·ing** [ME, fr. OF *paier*, fr. L *pacare* to pacify, fr. *pac-, pax* peace] *vt* (13c) **1 a** : to make due return to for services rendered or property delivered **b** : to engage for money : HIRE ⟨you couldn't ~ me to do that⟩ **2 a** : to give in return for goods or service ⟨~ wages⟩ **b** : to discharge indebtedness for : SETTLE ⟨~ a bill⟩ **c** : to make a disposal or transfer of (money) **3** : to give or forfeit in expiation or retribution ⟨~ the penalty⟩ **4 a** : to make compensation for **b** : to requite according to what is deserved ⟨~ them back⟩ **5** : to give, offer, or make freely or as fitting ⟨~ attention⟩ ⟨~ your respects⟩ **6 a** : to return value or profit to ⟨it ~s you to stay open⟩ **b** : to bring in as a return ⟨an investment ~ing five percent⟩ **7** : to slacken (as a rope) and allow to run out — used with *out* ~ *vi* **1** : to discharge a debt or obligation **2** : to be worth the expense or effort ⟨crime doesn't ~⟩ **3** : to suffer the consequences of an act — **pay one's dues** **1** : to earn a right or position through experience, suffering, or hard work **2** *also* **pay dues** : PAY *vi* 3 — **pay one's way** *or* **pay one's own way** : to pay one's share of expenses — **pay the piper** : to bear the cost of something — **pay through the nose** : to pay exorbitantly or dearly

\ə\ abut \ᵊ\ kitten, F table \ər\ further \a\ ash \ā\ ace \ä\ mop, mar \au̇\ out \ch\ chin \e\ bet \ē\ easy \g\ go \i\ hit \ī\ ice \j\ job \ŋ\ sing \ō\ go \o\ law \oi\ boy \th\ thin \t͟h\ the \ü\ loot \u̇\ foot \y\ yet \zh\ vision \ȧ, k̟, ⁿ, œ, œ̄, ᵫ, ᵫ̄, ᵻ, ᷥ\ see Guide to Pronunciation

syn PAY, COMPENSATE, REMUNERATE, SATISFY, REIMBURSE, INDEMNIFY, REPAY, RECOMPENSE mean to give money or its equivalent in return for something. PAY implies the discharge of an obligation incurred ⟨*paid* their bills on time⟩. COMPENSATE implies a making up for services rendered or help given ⟨an attorney well *compensated* for her services⟩. REMUNERATE more clearly suggests paying for services rendered and may extend to payment that is generous or not contracted for ⟨promised to *remunerate* the searchers handsomely⟩. SATISFY implies paying a person what is demanded or required by law ⟨all creditors will be *satisfied* in full⟩. REIMBURSE implies a return of money that has been expended for another's benefit ⟨*reimbursed* emplⱼyees for expenses⟩. INDEMNIFY implies making good a loss suffered through accident, disaster, warfare ⟨*indemnified* the families of the killed miners⟩. REPAY stresses paying back an equivalent in kind or amount ⟨*repay* a favor with a favor⟩. RECOMPENSE suggests due return in amends, friendly repayment, or reward ⟨hotel guests were *recompensed* for the inconvenience⟩.

²pay *n* (14c) **1** : something paid for a purpose and esp. as a salary or wage : REMUNERATION **2 a** : the act or fact of paying or being paid **b** : the status of being paid by an employer : EMPLOY **3** : a person viewed with respect to reliability or promptness in paying debts or bills **4 a** : ore or a natural situation that yields metal and esp. gold in profitable amounts **b** : an oil-yielding stratum or zone *syn* see WAGE

³pay *adj* (1856) **1** : containing or leading to something precious or valuable **2** : equipped with a coin slot for receiving a fee for use ⟨~ telephone⟩ **3** : requiring payment

⁴pay *vt* **payed** *also* **paid; pay·ing** [obs. F *peier*, fr. L *picare*, fr. *pic-*, *pix* pitch — more at PITCH] (1627) : to coat with a waterproof composition

pay·able \'pā-ə-bəl\ *adj* (14c) **1** : that may, can, or must be paid **2** : PROFITABLE

pay–as–you–go *adj* (1840) : of or relating to a system or policy of paying bills when due or of paying for goods and services when purchased

pay·back \'pā-,bak\ *n* (1955) **1** : a return on an investment equal to the original capital outlay; *also* : the period of time elapsed before an investment is recouped **2** : REQUITAL

pay–cable *n* (1975) : pay-TV utilizing a cable television system

pay·check \'pā-,chek\ *n* (1899) **1** : a check in payment of wages or salary **2** : WAGES, SALARY

pay·day \-,dā\ *n* (1529) : a regular day on which wages are paid

pay dirt *n* (1856) **1** : earth or ore that yields a profit to a miner **2** : a useful or remunerative discovery or object

pay·ee \(,)pā-'ē\ *n* (1758) : one to whom money is or is to be paid

pay envelope *n* (1901) : an envelope containing one's wages; *also* : WAGES

pay·er \'pā-ər\ *also* **pay·or** \'pā-ər, (,)pā-'òr\ *n* (14c) : one that pays; *esp* : the person by whom a bill or note has been or should be paid

pay·load \'pā-,lōd\ *n* (ca. 1922) **1** : the load carried by a vehicle exclusive of what is necessary for its operation; *esp* : the load carried by an aircraft or spacecraft consisting of things (as passengers or instruments) necessary to the purpose of the flight **2** : the weight of a payload

pay·mas·ter \-,mas-tər\ *n* (1550) : an officer or agent whose duty it is to pay salaries or wages

pay·ment \'pā-mənt\ *n* (14c) **1** : the act of paying **2** : something that is paid : PAY **3** : REQUITAL

pay·nim \'pā-nəm\ *n* [ME *painim*, fr. OF *paienime* heathendom, fr. LL *paganismus*, fr. *paganus* pagan] (13c) *archaic*: *esp* : MUSLIM

¹pay·off \'pā-,òf\ *n* (1905) **1 a** : PROFIT, REWARD **b** : RETRIBUTION **2** : the act or occasion of receiving money or material gain esp. as compensation or as a bribe **3** : the climax of an incident or enterprise; *specif* : the denouement of a narrative **4** : a decisive fact or factor resolving a situation or bringing about a definitive conclusion

²payoff *adj* (1934) : yielding results in the final test : DECISIVE

pay off *vt* (1710) **1 a** : to give all due wages to; *esp* : to pay in full and discharge (an employee) **b** : to pay (a debt or a creditor) in full **c** : BRIBE **2** : to inflict retribution on **3** : to allow (a thread or rope) to run off a spool or drum ~ *vi* : to yield returns

pay·o·la \pā-'ō-lə\ *n* [¹*pay* + *-ola* (as in *Pianola*, trademark for a player piano)] (1938) : undercover or indirect payment (as to a disc jockey) for a commercial favor (as for promoting a particular record)

pay·out \'pā-,aut\ *n* (1943) : the act of paying out : PAYOFF

pay–per–view *n* (1980) : a cable television service by which customers can order access to a single program for a fee

pay phone *n* (1936) : a usu. coin-operated public telephone

pay·roll \'pā-,rōl\ *n* (1740) **1** : a paymaster's or employer's list of those entitled to pay and of the amounts due to each **2** : the sum necessary for distribution to those on a payroll; *also* : the money to be distributed

pay station *n* (1919) : PAY PHONE

pay–TV *n* (ca. 1956) : a service providing noncommercial television programming (as recent movies and entertainment specials) by means of a scrambled signal to subscribers who are provided with a decoder — called also *pay television*; compare PAY-CABLE, SUBSCRIPTION TV

pay up *vi* (15c) : to pay what is due ~ *vt* : to pay in full

PBB \,pē-(,)bē-'bē\ *n* (ca. 1975) : POLYBROMINATED BIPHENYL

PBX \,pē-(,)bē-'eks\ *n* [*private branch exchange*] (ca. 1961) : a private telephone switchboard

PC \,pē-'sē\ *n, pl* **PCs** *or* **PC's** (1978) : PERSONAL COMPUTER

PCB \,pē-(,)sē-'bē\ *n* (1966) : POLYCHLORINATED BIPHENYL

PCP \,pē-(,)sē-'pē\ *n* [*phenyl* + *cycl-* + *piperidine*] (ca. 1970) : PHEN-CYCLIDINE

PDQ \,pē-(,)dē-'kyü\ *adv, often not cap* [abbr. of *pretty damned quick*] (1875) : IMMEDIATELY

pe \'pā\ *n* [Heb *pē*] (1823) : the 17th letter of the Hebrew alphabet — see ALPHABET table

pea \'pē\ *n, pl* **peas** *also* **pease** \'pēz\ *often attrib* [back-formation fr. ME *pease* (taken as a pl.), fr. OE *pise*, fr. L *pisa*, pl. of *pisum*, fr. Gk *pison*] (1611) **1 a** : a variable annual leguminous Eurasian vine (*Pisum sativum*) that is cultivated esp. for its rounded smooth or wrinkled edible protein-rich seeds **b** : the seed of the pea **c** *pl* : the immature pods of the pea with their included seeds **2** : any of various leguminous plants related to or resembling the pea — usu. used in combination or with a qualifying term ⟨chick*pea*⟩ ⟨black-eyed ~⟩; *also*

: the seed of such a plant **3** : something resembling a pea (as in size or shape)

pea aphid *n* (1925) : a widely distributed aphid (*Acyrthosiphon pisum*) that is a serious pest on legumes (as alfalfa, pea, and clover)

pea bean *n* (ca. 1887) : any of various kidney beans cultivated for their small white seeds which are used dried (as for baking)

¹peace \'pēs\ *n* [ME *pees*, fr. OF *pais*, fr. L *pac-*, *pax*; akin to L *pacisci* to agree — more at PACT] (12c) **1** : a state of tranquillity or quiet: as **a** : freedom from civil disturbance **b** : a state of security or order within a community provided for by law or custom ⟨a breach of the ~⟩ **2** : freedom from disquieting or oppressive thoughts or emotions **3** : harmony in personal relations **4 a** : a state or period of mutual concord between governments **b** : a pact or agreement to end hostilities between those who have been at war or in a state of enmity **5** — used interjectionally to ask for silence or calm or as a greeting or farewell — **at peace** : in a state of concord or tranquillity

²peace *vi* (14c) *obs* : to be, become, or keep silent or quiet

peace·able \'pē-sə-bəl\ *adj* (14c) **1 a** : disposed to peace : not contentious or quarrelsome **b** : quietly behaved **2** : marked by freedom from strife or disorder — **peace·able·ness** *n* — **peace·ably** \-blē\ *adv*

peace corps *n* (1960) : a body of trained personnel sent as volunteers esp. to assist underdeveloped nations

peace·ful \'pēs-fəl\ *adj* (14c) **1** : PEACEABLE 1 **2** : untroubled by conflict, agitation, or commotion : QUIET, TRANQUIL **3** : of or relating to a state or time of peace **4** : devoid of violence or force *syn* see CALM — **peace·ful·ly** \-fə-lē\ *adv* — **peace·ful·ness** *n*

peace·keep·ing \'pēs-,kē-piŋ\ *n* (1945) : the preserving of peace; *esp* : international enforcement and supervision of a truce between hostile states or communities — **peace·keep·er** \-pər\ *n*

peace·mak·er \-,mā-kər\ *n* (15c) : one who makes peace esp. by reconciling parties at variance — **peace·mak·ing** \-kiŋ\ *n or adj*

peace·nik \-,nik\ *n* (1965) : an opponent of the Vietnam War; *broadly* : PACIFIST

peace offering *n* (ca. 1530) : a gift or service for the purpose of procuring peace or reconciliation

peace officer *n* (1714) : a civil officer (as a police officer) whose duty it is to preserve the public peace

peace pipe *n* (1760) : CALUMET

peace sign *n* (1969) **1** : a sign made by holding the palm outward and forming a V with the index and middle fingers and used to indicate the desire for peace **2** : PEACE SYMBOL

peace symbol *n* (1970) : the symbol ☮ used to signify peace

peace·time \'pēs-,tīm\ *n* (1551) : a time when a nation is not at war

¹peach \'pēch\ *n* [ME *peche*, fr. MF (the fruit), fr. LL *persica*, fr. L (*malum*) *persicum*, lit., Persian fruit] (14c) **1 a** : a low spreading freely branching Chinese tree (*Prunus persica*) of the rose family that is widely cultivated in temperate areas and has lanceolate leaves, sessile usu. pink flowers borne on the naked twigs in early spring, and a fruit which is a single-seeded drupe with a hard endocarp, a pulpy white or yellow mesocarp, and a thin downy epicarp **b** : the edible fruit of the peach **2** : a moderate yellowish pink **3** : one resembling a peach (as in sweetness, beauty, or excellence)

²peach *vb* [ME *pechen*, short for *apechen* to accuse, fr. (assumed) AF *apecher*, fr. LL *impedicare* to entangle — more at IMPEACH] *vt* (1570) : to inform against : BETRAY ~ *vi* : to turn informer : BLAB

peach leaf curl *n* (1888) : leaf curl of the peach that is caused by a fungus (*Taphrina deformans*)

peach tree borer *n* (1850) : a blue-black orange-marked clearwing moth (*Synanthedon exitiosa* syn. *Sanninoidea exitiosa*) whose white brown-headed larva bores in the wood of stone fruit trees (as the peach)

peachy \'pē-chē\ *adj* **peach·i·er; -est** (1599) **1** : resembling a peach **2** : unusually fine : DANDY

¹pea·cock \'pē-,käk\ *n* [ME *pecok*, fr. *pe-* (fr. OE *pēa* peafowl, fr. L *pavon-*, *pavo* peacock) + *cok* cock] (14c) **1** : a male peafowl distinguished by a crest of upright plumules and by greatly elongated loosely webbed upper tail coverts which are mostly tipped with ocellated spots and can be erected and spread at will in a fan shimmering with iridescent color; *broadly* : PEAFOWL **2** : one making a proud display of himself : SHOW-OFF — **pea·cock·ish** \-,kä-kish\ *adj* — **pea·cocky** \-kē\ *adj*

²peacock *vi* (1586) : SHOW-OFF

peacock blue *n* (1881) : a moderate greenish blue

peacock flower *n* (1884) : ROYAL POINCIANA

pea·fowl \'pē-,faul\ *n* [*pea-* (as in *peacock*) + *fowl*] (1804) : either of two very large terrestrial pheasants (*Pavo cristatus* and *P. muticus* of southeastern Asia and the East Indies often reared as ornamental fowls

pea green *n* (1752) : a moderate yellow-green

pea·hen \'pē-,hen\ *n* [ME *pehenne*, fr. *pe-* + *henne* hen] (15c) : a female peafowl

pea jacket \'pē-\ *n* [by folk etymology fr. D *pijjekker*, fr. *pij*, a kind of cloth + *jekker* jacket] (1721) : a heavy woolen double-breasted jacket orig. worn by sailors — called also *pea-coat* \'pē-,kōt\

¹peak \'pēk\ *n* [perh. alter. of *pike*] (1530) **1** : a pointed or projecting part of a garment; *esp* : the visor of a cap or hat **2** : PROMONTORY **3** : a sharp or pointed end **4 a** (1) : the top of a hill or mountain ending in a point (2) : a prominent mountain usu. having a well-defined summit **b** : something resembling a mountain peak **5 a** : the upper aftermost corner of a fore-and-aft sail **b** : the narrow part of a ship's bow or stern or the part of the hold in it **6 a** : the highest level or greatest degree **b** : a high point in a course of development esp. as represented on a graph **7** : a point formed by the hair on the forehead *syn* see SUMMIT

peafowl: *A* female; *B* male

²**peak** *vi* (1577) : to reach a maximum (as of capacity, value, or activity) — often used with *out* ~ *vt* : to cause to come to a peak, point, or maximum

³**peak** *adj* (1903) : being at or reaching the maximum

⁴**peak** *vi* [origin unknown] (1605) **1** : to grow thin or sickly **2** : to dwindle away

⁵**peak** *vt* [fr. *apeak* held vertically] (1626) **1** : to set (as a gaff) nearer the perpendicular **2** : to hold (oars) with blades well raised

¹**peaked** \'pēkt *also* 'pē-kəd\ *adj* (15c) : having a peak : POINTED — **peaked·ness** \'pēk(t)-nəs, 'pē-kəd-nəs\ *n*

²**peak·ed** \'pē-kəd *also* 'pi-kəd\ *adj* (1835) : being pale and wan or emaciated : SICKLY

peaky \'pē-kē\ *adj* (1821) : ²PEAKED

¹**peal** \'pē(ə)l\ *n* [ME, appeal, summons to church, short for *appel* appeal, fr. *appelen* to appeal] (14c) **1 a** : the loud ringing of bells **b** : a complete set of changes on a given number of bells **c** : a set of bells tuned to the tones of the major scale for change ringing **2** : a loud sound or succession of sounds ⟨~s of laughter⟩

²**peal** *vi* (1632) : to give out peals ~ *vt* : to utter or give forth loudly

pea-like \'pē-,līk\ *adj* (1774) **1** : resembling a garden pea esp. in size, firmness, and shape ⟨a ~ lump under the skin⟩ **2** *of a flower* : being showy and papilionaceous

¹**pea·nut** \'pē-(,)nət\ *n* (1802) **1** : a low-branching widely cultivated leguminous annual herb (*Arachis hypogaea*) with showy yellow flowers having a peduncle which elongates and bends into the soil where the ovary ripens into a pod containing one to three oily edible seeds; *also* : its seed or seed-containing pod **2** : an insignificant or tiny person **3** *pl* : a trifling amount

²**peanut** *adj* (1836) : INSIGNIFICANT, PETTY ⟨~ politics⟩

peanut oil *n* (1882) : a colorless to yellow fatty nondrying oil that is obtained from peanuts and is used chiefly as a salad oil, in margarine, in soap, and as a vehicle in pharmaceutical preparations and cosmetics

pear \'par, 'per\ *n* [ME *pere*, fr. OE *peru*, fr. (assumed) VL *pira*, fr. L, pl. of *pirum*\ (bef. 12c) **1** : a fleshy pome fruit that is borne by a tree (genus *Pyrus*, esp. *P. communis*) of the rose family and is usu. larger at the apical end **2** : a tree bearing pears

¹**pearl** \'pər(-ə)l\ *n* [ME *perle*, fr. MF, prob. fr. (assumed) VL *pernula*, dim. of L *perna* upper leg, kind of sea mussel; akin to OE *fiersn* heel, Gk *pternē*] (14c) **1 a** : a dense variously colored and usu. lustrous concretion formed of concentric layers of nacre as an abnormal growth within the shell of some mollusks and used as a gem **b** : MOTHER-OF-PEARL **2** : one that is very choice or precious **3** : something resembling a pearl intrinsically or physically **4** : a nearly neutral slightly bluish medium gray

²**pearl** *vt* (14c) **1** : to set or adorn with pearls **2** : to sprinkle or bead with pearly drops **3** : to form into small round grains **4** : to give a pearly color or luster to ~ *vi* **1** : to form drops or beads like pearls **2** : to fish or search for pearls — **pearl·er** \'pər-lər\ *n*

³**pearl** *adj* (1610) **1 a** : of, relating to, or resembling pearl **b** : made of or adorned with pearls **2** : having medium-sized grains

⁴**pearl** *n or vt* [alter. of *purl*] (1824) *Brit* : PICOT

pearl·es·cent \,pər-'le-sᵊnt\ *adj* (1936) : having a pearly luster ⟨a ~ lacquer⟩ — **pearl·es·cence** \-sᵊn(t)s\ *n*

pearl essence *n* (ca. 1909) : a translucent substance that occurs in the silvery scales of various fish (as herring) and is used in making artificial pearls, lacquers, and plastics

pearl gray *n* (1796) **1** : a yellowish to light gray **2** : a pale blue

Pearl Harbor *n* [*Pearl Harbor*, Oahu, Hawaii, Am. naval station attacked without warning by the Japanese on December 7, 1941] (1942) : a sneak attack often with devastating effect

pearl·ite \'pər-(,)līt\ *n* [F *perlite*, fr. *perle* pearl] (1888) : the lamellar mixture of ferrite and cementite in slowly cooled iron-carbon alloys occurring normally as a principal constituent of both steel and cast iron — **pearl·it·ic** \,pər-'li-tik\ *adj*

pearl·ized \'pər(-ə)-,līzd\ *adj* (1937) : given a pearlescent surface or finish

pearl millet *n* (ca. 1890) : a tall cereal grass (*Pennisetum glaucum* syn. *P. americanum*) that has large leaves and dense round spikes and is widely grown for its seeds and for forage

pearl onion *n* (ca. 1890) : a very small usu. pickled onion used esp. in appetizers and as a garnish

pearly \'pər-lē\ *adj* **pearl·i·er; -est** (15c) **1** : resembling, containing, or adorned with pearls or mother-of-pearl **2** : highly precious

pearly everlasting *n* (1857) : an everlasting (*Anaphalis margaritacea*) that has herbage covered with white woolly hairs and corymbose heads with white scarious involucres

pearly nautilus *n* (1822) : NAUTILUS 1

pear psylla *n* (1904) : a yellowish or greenish jumping plant louse (*Psylla pyricola*) that is often destructive to the pear

pear–shaped \'par-,shäpt, 'per-\ *adj* (1758) **1** : having an oval shape markedly tapering at one end **2** *of a vocal tone* : free from harshness, thinness, or nasality

peart \'pirt\ *adj* [alter. of *pert*] (1578) *chiefly Southern & Midland* : being in good spirits : LIVELY — **peart·ly** *adv*

peas·ant \'pe-zᵊnt\ *n* [ME *paissaunt*, fr. MF *paisant*, fr. OF, fr. *païs* country, fr. LL *pagensis* inhabitant of a district, fr. L *pagus* district] (15c) **1** : a member of a European class of persons tilling the soil as small landowners or as laborers; *also* : a member of a similar class elsewhere **2** : a usu. uneducated person of low social status

peas·ant·ry \-zᵊn-trē\ *n* (ca. 1553) **1** : PEASANTS **2** : the position, rank, or behavior of a peasant

pease·cod *or* **peas·cod** \'pēz-,käd\ *n* [ME *pesecod*, fr. *pese* + *cod* bag, husk — more at CODPIECE] (14c) : a pea pod

pea-shoot·er \'pē-,shü-tər\ *n* (1803) : a toy blowgun that uses peas for projectiles

pea soup *n* (1711) **1** : a thick purée made of dried peas **2** : a thick fog

¹**peat** \'pēt\ *n, often attrib* [ME *pete*, fr. ML *peta*] (14c) **1** : TURF 2b **2** : partially carbonized vegetable tissue formed by partial decomposition in water of various plants (as mosses of the genus *Sphagnum*) — **peaty** \'pē-tē\ *adj*

²**peat** *n* [origin unknown] (1599) : a bold lively woman

peat moss *n* (1880) : SPHAGNUM

pea·vey *or* **pea·vy** \'pē-vē\ *n, pl* **peaveys** *or* **peavies** [prob. fr. the name *Peavey*] (1870) : a lumberman's lever that has a pivoting hooked arm and metal spike at one end — called also *cant dog*; compare CANT HOOK

¹**peb·ble** \'pe-bəl\ *n* [ME *pobble*, fr. OE *papolstān*, fr. *papol-* (of unknown origin) + *stān* stone] (14c) **1** : a small usu. rounded stone esp. when worn by the action of water **2** : transparent and colorless quartz : ROCK CRYSTAL **3** : an irregular, crinkled, or grainy surface — **peb·bly** \-b(ə-)lē\ *adj*

peavey

²**pebble** *vt* **peb·bled; peb·bling** \-b(ə-)liŋ\ (1605) **1** : to pelt with pebbles **2** : to pave or cover with pebbles or something resembling pebbles **3** : to grain (as leather) so as to produce a rough and irregularly indented surface

pec \'pek\ *n* (1966) : PECTORAL MUSCLE

pe·can \pi-'kän, -'kan; 'pē-,kan\ *n* [AmerF *pacane*, of Algonquian origin; akin to Ojibwa *pakan*, a hard-shelled nut] (1712) **1** : a large hickory (*Carya illinoensis*) that has roughish bark and hard but brittle wood and is widely grown in the warmer parts of the U.S. and in Mexico for its edible nut **2** : the wood of the pecan tree **3** : the smooth oblong thin-shelled nut of the pecan tree

pec·ca·dil·lo \,pe-kə-'di-(,)lō\ *n, pl* **-loes** *or* **-los** [Sp *pecadillo*, dim. of *pecado* sin, fr. L *peccatum*, fr. neut. of *peccatus*, pp. of *peccare*] (1591) : a slight offense

pec·cant \'pe-kənt\ *adj* [L *peccant-, peccans*, prp. of *peccare* to stumble, sin] (ca. 1604) **1** : guilty of a moral offense : SINNING **2** : violating a principle or rule : FAULTY — **pec·cant·ly** *adv*

pec·ca·ry \'pe-kə-rē\ *n, pl* **-ries** [perh. modif. of Carib *baquira*] (1613) : any of several largely nocturnal gregarious American mammals resembling the related pigs: as **a** : a grizzled animal (*Tayassu tajacu*) with an indistinct white collar **b** : a blackish animal (*Tayassu pecari*) with a whitish mouth region

pec·ca·vi \pe-'kä-(,)wē, -(,)vē; -'kä-,vī\ *n* [L, I have sinned, fr. *peccare*] (1553) : an acknowledgment of sin

¹**peck** \'pek\ *n* [ME *pek*, fr. MF] (13c) **1** — see WEIGHT table **2** : a large quantity or number

²**peck** *vb* [ME, perh. fr. MLG *pekken*] *vt* (14c) **1 a** : to strike or pierce esp. repeatedly with the bill or a pointed tool **b** : to make by pecking ⟨~ a hole⟩ **2** : to pick up with the bill ~ *vi* **1** : to strike, pierce, or pick up something with or as if with the bill **b** : CARP, NAG **2** : to eat reluctantly and in small bites ⟨~ at food⟩

³**peck** *n* (ca. 1591) **1** : an impression or hole made by pecking **2** : a quick sharp stroke

peck·er \'pe-kər\ *n* (1587) **1** : one that pecks **2** *chiefly Brit* : COURAGE **3** : PENIS — often considered vulgar

peck·er·wood \'pe-kər-,wud\ *n* [prob. inversion of *woodpecker*] (1904) : a rural white Southerner — often used disparagingly

pecking order *also* **peck order** *n* (1928) **1** : the basic pattern of social organization within a flock of poultry in which each bird pecks another lower in the scale without fear of retaliation and submits to pecking by one of higher rank; *broadly* : a dominance hierarchy in a group of social animals **2** : a social hierarchy

peck·ish \'pe-kish\ *adj* [²*peck*] (1785) **1** *chiefly Brit* : HUNGRY **2** : CROTCHETY

Peck·sniff·ian \pek-'sni-fē-ən\ *adj* [Seth *Pecksniff*, character in *Martin Chuzzlewit* (1843–44) by Charles Dickens] (1851) : unctuously hypocritical : PHARISAICAL

pecky \'pe-kē\ *adj* [³*peck*] (1848) **1** : marked by lenticular or finger-shaped pockets of decay caused by fungi ⟨~ cypress⟩ **2** : containing discolored or shriveled grains ⟨~ rice⟩

pec·o·ri·no \,pe-kə-'rē-(,)nō\ *n, often cap* [It, fr. *pecorino* of sheep, fr. *pecora* sheep, ewe, fr. L, domestic animals, fr. pl. of *pecus* cattle — more at FEE] (1912) : any of various cheeses of Italian origin made from sheep's milk

pec·ten \'pek-tən\ *n, pl* **pectens** [NL *pectin-, pecten*, fr. L, comb, scallop] (1682) **1** : SCALLOP 1a **2** *pl usu* **pec·ti·nes** \-tə-,nēz\ : a body part that resembles a comb; *esp* : a folded vascular pigmented membrane projecting into the vitreous humor in the eye of a bird or reptile

pec·tic \'pek-tik\ *adj* [F *pectique*, fr. Gk *pēktikos* coagulating, fr. *pēgnynai* to fix, coagulate — more at PACT] (1831) : of, relating to, or derived from pectin

pectic acid *n* (1831) : any of various water-insoluble substances formed by hydrolyzing the methyl ester groups of pectins

pec·tin \'pek-tən\ *n* [F *pectine*, fr. *pectique*] (1838) : any of various water-soluble substances that bind adjacent cell walls in plant tissues and yield a gel which is the basis of fruit jellies; *also* : a commercial product rich in pectins

pec·ti·na·ceous \,pek-tə-'nā-shəs\ *adj* (ca. 1844) : of, relating to, or containing pectin

pec·ti·nate \'pek-tə-,nāt\ *adj* [L *pectinatus*, fr. *pectin-, pecten* comb; akin to Gk *kten-, kteis* comb] (1793) : having narrow parallel projections or divisions suggestive of the teeth of a comb ⟨~ antennae⟩ — **pec·ti·na·tion** \,pek-tə-'nā-shən\ *n*

pec·tin·es·ter·ase \,pek-tə-'nes-tə-,rās, -,rāz\ *n* (1945) : an enzyme that catalyzes the hydrolysis of pectins into pectic acids and methanol

¹**pec·to·ral** \'pek-t(ə-)rəl\ *n* (15c) : something worn on the breast

²**pectoral** *adj* [MF or L; MF, fr. L *pectoralis*, fr. *pector-, pectus* breast; akin to Toch A *pässäm* breasts, OIr *ucht* breast] (1578) **1** : of, situated in or on, or worn on the chest **2** : coming from the breast or heart as the seat of emotion

pectoral cross *n* (ca. 1735) : a cross worn on the breast esp. by a prelate

pectoral fin *n* (1769) : either of the fins of a fish that correspond to the forelimbs of a quadruped

pectoral girdle *n* (ca. 1890) : the bony or cartilaginous arch that supports the forelimbs of a vertebrate

\ə\ abut \ᵊ\ kitten, F table \ər\ further \a\ ash \ā\ ace \ä\ mop, mar \aú\ out \ch\ chin \e\ bet \ē\ easy \g\ go \i\ hit \ī\ ice \j\ job \ŋ\ sing \ō\ go \ò\ law \òi\ boy \th\ thin \t͟h\ the \ü\ loot \ù\ foot \y\ yet \zh\ vision \à, k̲, ⁿ, œ, œ̄, ᵫ, ᵫ̄, ʸ\ see Guide to Pronunciation

pectoral muscle *n* (1615) : any of the muscles which connect the ventral walls of the chest with the bones of the upper arm and shoulder and of which there are two on each side of the human body

pec·u·late \'pe-kyə-ˌlāt\ *vt* **-lat·ed; -lat·ing** [L *peculatus*, pp. of *peculari*, fr. *peculium*] (1802) : EMBEZZLE — **pec·u·la·tion** \ˌpe-kyə-'lā-shən\ *n* — **pec·u·la·tor** \'pe-kyə-ˌlā-tər\ *n*

¹pe·cu·liar \pi-'kyül-yər\ *adj* [ME *peculier*, fr. L *peculiaris* of private property, special, fr. *peculium* private property, fr. *pecu* cattle; akin to L *pecus* cattle — more at FEE] (15c) **1** : characteristic of only one person, group, or thing : DISTINCTIVE **2** : different from the usual or normal: **a** : SPECIAL, PARTICULAR **b** : ODD, CURIOUS **c** : ECCENTRIC, QUEER *syn* see CHARACTERISTIC, STRANGE — **pe·cu·liar·ly** *adv*

²peculiar *n* (1562) : something exempt from ordinary jurisdiction; *esp* : a church or parish exempt from the jurisdiction of the ordinary in whose territory it lies

pe·cu·liar·i·ty \pi-ˌkyül-'yar-ə-tē, -ˌkyü-lē-'ar-\ *n, pl* **-ties** (1646) **1** : the quality or state of being peculiar **2** : a distinguishing characteristic **3** : ODDITY, QUIRK

pe·cu·ni·ary \pi-'kyü-nē-ˌer-ē\ *adj* [L *pecuniarius*, fr. *pecunia* money — more at FEE] (1502) **1** : consisting of or measured in money **2** : of or relating to money : MONETARY — **pe·cu·ni·ar·i·ly** \-ˌkyü-nē-'er-ə-lē\ *adv*

ped \'ped\ *n* [Gk *pedon* ground; akin to L *ped-, pes* foot — more at FOOT] (1951) : a natural soil aggregate

ped- *or* **pedo-** *or* **paed-** *or* **paedo-** *comb form* [Gk *paid-, paido-*, fr. *paid-, pais* child, boy — more at FEW] : child ⟨*pediatric*⟩ : childhood ⟨*paedogenesis*⟩

-ped *or* **-pede** *n comb form* [L *ped-, pes*]: foot ⟨maxilli*ped*⟩

ped·a·gog·i·cal \ˌpe-də-'gä-ji-kəl, -'gō-\ *also* **ped·a·gog·ic** \-jik\ *adj* (1619) : of, relating to, or befitting a teacher or education — **ped·a·gog·i·cal·ly** \-ji-k(ə-)lē\ *adv*

ped·a·gog·ics \-jiks\ *n pl but sing in constr* (ca. 1859) : PEDAGOGY

ped·a·gogue *also* **ped·a·gog** \'pe-də-ˌgäg\ *n* [ME *pedagoge*, fr. MF, fr. L *paedagogus*, fr. Gk *paidagōgos*, slave who escorted children to school, fr. *paid-* ped- + *agōgos* leader, fr. *agein* to lead — more at AGENT] (14c) : TEACHER, SCHOOLMASTER; *esp* : a dull, formal, or pedantic teacher

ped·a·go·gy \'pe-də-ˌgō-jē *also* -ˌgä-, *esp Brit* -ˌgä-gē\ *n* (1583) : the art, science, or profession of teaching; *esp* : EDUCATION 2

¹ped·al \'pe-d³l\ *n* [MF *pedale*, fr. It, fr. L *pedalis*, adj.] (1611) **1** : a lever pressed by the foot in the playing of a musical instrument (as an organ or piano) **2** : a foot lever or treadle by which a part is activated in a mechanism

²ped·al *adj* [L *pedalis*, fr. *ped-, pes*] (1625) **1** \'pe-d³l *also* 'pē-\ : of or relating to the foot **2** \'pe-\ : of, relating to, or involving a pedal

³ped·al \'pe-d³l\ *vb* **ped·aled** *also* **ped·alled; ped·al·ing** *also* **ped·al·ling** \'pe-d³l-iŋ, 'ped-liŋ\ *vi* (1888) **1** : to ride a bicycle **2** : to use or work a pedal ~ *vt* : to work the pedals of

pedal bone *n* (1881) : COFFIN BONE

ped·al·fer \pə-'dal-fər, -ˌfer\ *n* [Gk *pedon* ground + E *alumen* + L *ferrum* iron] (1928) : a soil that lacks a hardened layer of accumulated carbonates

ped·al–note \'pe-d³l-ˌnōt\ *n* [fr. the playing of the lowest notes on the organ by means of pedals] (ca. 1828) **1** : PEDAL POINT **2** : one of the lowest tones that can be sounded on a brass instrument being an octave below the normal usable range and representing the fundamental of the harmonic series

ped·alo \'pe-də-(ˌ)lō\ *n, pl* **-los** [F *pédalo*, fr. *pédale* pedal + -*o* (perh. as in *meccano* children's construction set)] (1945) *chiefly Brit* : a small recreational paddleboat powered by pedals

pedal point *n* (1852) : a single tone usu. the tonic or dominant that is normally sustained in the bass and sounds against changing harmonies in the other parts

pedal pushers *n pl* (1944) : women's and girls' calf-length trousers

pedal steel *n* (1969) : a box-shaped musical instrument with legs that has usu. 10 strings which can be altered in pitch by the use of pedals and which are plucked while being pressed with a movable steel bar — called also *pedal steel guitar*

ped·ant \'pe-d³nt\ *n* [MF, fr. It *pedante*] (1588) **1** *obs* : a male schoolteacher **2 a** : one who makes a show of knowledge **b** : one who is unimaginative or who unduly emphasizes minutiae in the presentation or use of knowledge **c** : a formalist or precisionist in teaching

pe·dan·tic \pi-'dan-tik\ *adj* (ca. 1600) **1** : of, relating to, or being a pedant **2** : narrowly, stodgily, and often ostentatiously learned **3** : UNIMAGINATIVE, PEDESTRIAN — **pe·dan·ti·cal·ly** \-'dan-ti-k(ə-)lē\ *adv*

ped·ant·ry \'pe-d³n-trē\ *n, pl* **-ries** (1612) **1** : pedantic presentation or application of knowledge or learning **2** : an instance of pedantry

ped·dle \'pe-d³l\ *vb* **ped·dled; ped·dling** \'ped-liŋ, 'pe-d³l-iŋ\ [back-formation fr. *peddler*, fr. ME *pedlere*] *vi* (1532) **1** : to travel about with wares for sale; *broadly* : SELL **2** : to be busy with trifles : PIDDLE ~ *vt* **1** : to sell or offer for sale from place to place : HAWK; *broadly* : SELL **2** : to deal out or seek to disseminate

ped·dler *also* **ped·lar** \'ped-lər\ *n* (14c) : one who peddles: as **a** : one who offers merchandise (as fresh produce) for sale along the street or from door to door **b** : one who deals in or promotes something intangible (as a personal asset or an idea) ⟨influence ~s⟩

ped·er·ast \'pe-də-ˌrast\ *n* [Gk *paiderastēs*, lit., lover of boys, fr. *paid-* ped- + *erastēs* lover, fr. *erasthai* to love — more at EROS] (ca. 1736) : one that practices anal intercourse esp. with a boy — **ped·er·as·tic** \ˌpe-də-'ras-tik\ *adj* — **ped·er·as·ty** \'pe-də-ˌras-tē\ *n*

¹ped·es·tal \'pe-dəs-t³l\ *n* [MF *piedestal*, fr. OIt *piedestallo*, fr. *pie di stallo* foot of a stall] (1563) **1 a** : the support or foot of a late classic or neoclassic column — see COLUMN illustration **b** : the base of an upright structure **2** : BASE, FOUNDATION **3** : a position of esteem

²pedestal *vt* **-taled** *or* **-talled; -tal·ing** *or* **-tal·ling** (1648) : to place on or furnish with a pedestal

¹pe·des·tri·an \pə-'des-trē-ən\ *adj* [L *pedestr-, pedester*, lit., going on foot, fr. *ped-, pes* foot — more at FOOT] (1716) **1** : COMMONPLACE, UNIMAGINATIVE **2** **a** : going or performed on foot **b** : of, relating to, or designed for walking ⟨a ~ mall⟩

²pedestrian *n* (1793) : a person going on foot : WALKER

pe·des·tri·an·ism \-ə-ˌni-zəm\ *n* (1809) **1 a** : the practice of walking **b** : fondness for walking for exercise or recreation **2** : the quality or state of being unimaginative or commonplace

pe·di·at·ric \ˌpē-dē-'a-trik\ *adj* (1880) : of or relating to pediatrics

pe·di·a·tri·cian \ˌpē-dē-ə-'tri-shən\ *or* **pe·di·a·trist** \ˌpē-dē-'a-trist, pē-'dī-ə-\ *n* (ca. 1903) : a specialist in pediatrics

pe·di·at·rics \ˌpē-dē-'a-triks\ *n pl but sing or pl in constr* (1884) : a branch of medicine dealing with the development, care, and diseases of children

pedi·cab \'pe-di-ˌkab\ *n* [L *ped-, pes* + E *cab*] (1945) : a tricycle with a 2-seat passenger compartment covered by a usu. folding top and a separate seat for a driver who pedals

ped·i·cel \'pe-də-ˌsel\ *n* [NL *pedicellus*, dim. of L *pediculus*] (1676) : a slender basal part of an organism or one of its parts: as **a** : a plant stalk that supports a fruiting or spore-bearing organ **b** : a narrow basal attachment (as of the abdomen of an ant) of an animal organ or part — **ped·i·cel·late** \ˌpe-də-'se-lət\ *adj*

ped·i·cle \'pe-di-kəl\ *n* [L *pediculus*, fr. dim. of *ped-, pes*] (1626) **1** : PEDICEL **b** : the part of a skin or tissue graft left attached to the original site during the preliminary stages of union — **ped·i·cled** \-kəld\ *adj*

pe·dic·u·late \pi-'di-kyə-lət\ *adj* [ultim. fr. L *pediculus* little foot, pedicel] (ca. 1890) : of or relating to an order (Lophiiformes syn. Pediculati) of marine bony fishes with pectoral fins at the end of an armlike process and part of the dorsal fin modified into a lure — **pe·dic·u·late** *n*

pe·dic·u·lo·sis \pi-ˌdi-kyə-'lō-səs\ *n* [NL, fr. L *pediculus* louse, dim. of *pedis* louse] (ca. 1890) : infestation with lice

pe·dic·u·lous \pi-'di-kyə-ləs\ *adj* [L *pediculosus*, fr. *pediculus*] (ca. 1550) : infested with lice : LOUSY

ped·i·cure \'pe-di-ˌkyùr\ *n* [F *pédicure*, fr. L *ped-, pes* foot + *curare* to take care, fr. *cura* care] (ca. 1842) **1** : one who practices chiropody **2 a** : care of the feet, toes, and nails **b** : a single treatment of these parts — **ped·i·cur·ist** \-ˌkyùr-ist\ *n*

ped·i·gree \'pe-də-ˌgrē\ *n* [ME *pedegru*, fr. MF *pie de grue* crane's foot; fr. the shape made by the lines of a genealogical chart] (15c) **1** : a register recording a line of ancestors **2 a** : an ancestral line : LINEAGE **b** : the origin and the history of something **3 a** : a distinguished ancestry **b** : the recorded purity of breed of an individual or strain — **ped·i·greed** \-ˌgrēd\ *or* **pedigree** *adj*

ped·i·ment \'pe-də-mənt\ *n* [alter. of obs. E *periment*, prob. alter. of E *pyramid*] (1592) **1** : a triangular space that forms the gable of a low-pitched roof and that is usu. filled with relief sculpture in classical architecture; *also* : a similar form used as a decoration **2** : a broad gently sloping bedrock surface with low relief that is situated at the base of a steeper slope and is usu. thinly covered with alluvial gravel and sand — **ped·i·men·tal** \ˌpe-də-'men-t³l\ *adj* — **ped·i·ment·ed** \'pe-də-ˌmen-təd\ *adj*

ped·i·palp \'pe-də-ˌpalp\ *n* [NL *pedipalpus*, fr. *ped-, pes* foot + *palpus* palpus] (1826) : either of the second pair of appendages of an arachnid (as a spider) that are borne near the mouth and are often modified for a special (as sensory) function

pedo- — see PED-

ped·o·cal \'pe-də-ˌkal\ *n* [Gk *pedon* earth + L *calc-, calx* lime — more at PED, CHALK] (1928) : a soil that includes a definite hardened layer of accumulated carbonates — **ped·o·cal·ic** \ˌpe-də-'ka-lik\ *adj*

¹pe·do·gen·e·sis \ˌpē-də-'je-nə-səs\ *var of* PAEDOGENESIS

²ped·o·gen·e·sis \ˌpe-də-'je-nə-səs\ *n* [NL, fr. Gk *pedon* + L *genesis*] (1936) : the formation and development of soil — **ped·o·gen·ic** \-'je-nik\ *also* **ped·o·ge·net·ic** \-jə-'ne-tik\ *adj*

pe·dol·o·gy \pi-'dä-lə-jē, pe-\ *n* [Gk *pedon* + ISV -*logy*] (1912) : SOIL SCIENCE — **ped·o·log·i·cal** \ˌpe-d³l-'ä-ji-kəl\ *also* **ped·o·log·ic** \-jik\ *adj* — **pe·dol·o·gist** \pi-'dä-lə-jist, pe-\ *n*

pe·dom·e·ter \pi-'dä-mə-tər\ *n* [F *pédomètre*, fr. L *ped-, pes* foot + F -*mètre* -meter — more at FOOT] (1723) : an instrument usu. in watch form that records the distance a person covers on foot by responding to the body motion at each step

pe·do·phile \'pē-də-ˌfīl\ *n* (1951) : one affected with pedophilia

pe·do·phil·ia \ˌpe-də-'fi-lē-ə\ *n* [NL] (1906) : sexual perversion in which children are the preferred sexual object — **pe·do·phil·i·ac** \-'fi-lē-ˌak\ *or* **pe·do·phil·ic** \-'fi-lik\ *adj*

pe·dun·cle \'pē-ˌdəŋ-kəl, pi-'\ *n* [NL *pedunculus*, dim. of L *ped-, pes*] (ca. 1753) **1** : a stalk bearing a flower or flower cluster or a fructification **2** : a narrow part by which some larger part or the whole body of an organism is attached : STALK, PEDICEL **3** : a narrow stalk by which a tumor or polyp is attached — **pe·dun·cled** \-kəld\ *adj* — **pe·dun·cu·lar** \pi-'dəŋ-kyə-lər\ *adj*

pe·dun·cu·lat·ed \pi-'dəŋ-kyə-ˌlā-təd\ *also* **pe·dun·cu·late** \-lət\ *adj* [NL *pedunculus*] (1752) : having, growing on, or being attached by a peduncle ⟨a ~ tumor⟩

¹pee \'pē\ *n* (1612) **1** : the letter *p* **2** *pl* **pee** *Brit* : PENNY

²pee *vi* **peed; pee·ing** [euphemism fr. the initial letter of *piss*] (ca. 1880) : URINATE — sometimes considered vulgar

³pee *n* (1946) **1** : URINE — sometimes considered vulgar **2** : an act of urination — sometimes considered vulgar

¹peek \'pēk\ *vi* [ME *piken*] (14c) **1 a** : to look furtively **b** : to peer through a crack or hole or from a place of concealment — often used with *in* or *out* **2** : to take a brief look : GLANCE

²peek *n* (1843) **1** : a surreptitious look **2** : a brief look : GLANCE

¹peek·a·boo \'pē-kə-ˌbü\ *n* [*peek* + *boo*] (1599) : a game for amusing a baby by repeatedly hiding one's face or body and popping back into view exclaiming "Peekaboo!"

²peekaboo *adj* (1895) **1** : trimmed with eyelet embroidery ⟨a ~ blouse⟩ **2** : made of a sheer or transparent fabric **3** : offering only limited display or disclosure esp. of a teasing sort ⟨~ publicity⟩

¹peel \'pē(ə)l\ *vb* [ME *pelen*, fr. MF *peler*, fr. L *pilare* to remove the hair from, fr. *pilus* hair] *vt* (13c) **1** : to strip off an outer layer of ⟨~ an orange⟩ **2** : to remove by stripping ⟨~ the label off the can⟩ ~ *vi* **1 a** : to come off in sheets or scales **b** : to lose an outer layer (as of skin) ⟨his face is ~ing⟩ **2** : to take off one's clothes **3** : to break away from a group or formation — often used with *off* — **peel·able** \'pē-lə-bəl\ *adj*

²peel *n* (14c) **1** : the skin or rind of a fruit **2** : a thin layer of organic material that is embedded in a film of collodion and stripped from the surface of an object (as a plant fossil) for microscopic study

³peel *n* [ME *pele*, fr. MF, fr. L *pala*] (14c) : a usu. long-handled spade-shaped instrument that is used chiefly by bakers for getting something (as bread or pies) into or out of the oven

⁴peel *n* [ME *pel* stockade, stake, fr. AF, stockade & MF, stake, fr. L *palus* stake — more at POLE] (1726) : a medieval small massive fortified tower along the Scottish-English border — called also *peel tower*

¹peel·er \'pē-lər\ *n* (1597) **1** : one that peels **2** : a crab that is about to shed its shell **3** : a log of wood (as Douglas fir) suitable for cutting into rotary veneer — called also *peeler log*

²peeler *n* [Sir Robert *Peel*] (1817) *Brit* : POLICE OFFICER

peel·ing \'pē-liŋ\ *n* (1597) : a peeled-off piece or strip

peel off *vi* (1941) **1** : to veer away from an airplane formation esp. for diving or landing **2** : DEPART, LEAVE

¹peen \'pēn\ *vt* (1513) : to draw, bend, or flatten by or as if by hammering with a peen

²peen *n* [prob. of Scand origin; akin to Norw *penn* peen] (1683) : a usu. hemispherical or wedge-shaped end of the head of a hammer that is opposite the face and is used esp. for bending, shaping, or cutting the material struck

¹peep \'pēp\ *vi* [ME *pepen*, of imit. origin] (15c) **1** : to utter a feeble shrill sound as of a bird newly hatched : CHEEP **2** : to utter the slightest sound

²peep *n* (15c) **1** : a feeble shrill sound : CHEEP **2** : a slight utterance esp. of complaint or protest ⟨don't let me hear another ∼ out of you⟩ **3** : any of several small sandpipers

³peep *vb* [ME *pepen*, perh. alter. of *piken* to peek] *vi* (15c) **1 a** : to peer through or as if through a crevice **b** : to look cautiously or slyly **2** : to begin to emerge from or as if from concealment : show slightly ∼ *vt* : to put forth or cause to protrude slightly

⁴peep *n* (1530) **1 a** : a first glimpse or faint appearance ⟨at the ∼ of dawn⟩ **2 a** : a brief look : GLANCE **b** : a furtive look

¹peep·er \'pē-pər\ *n* (1591) **1** : one that makes a peeping sound **2** : any of various tree frogs that peep shrilly; *esp* : SPRING PEEPER

²peeper *n* (1652) **1** : one that peeps; *specif* : VOYEUR **2** : EYE

peep·hole \'pēp-,hōl\ *n* (1681) : a hole or crevice to peep through

Peeping Tom \-'täm\ *n* [*Peeping Tom*, legendary citizen of Coventry who watched Lady Godiva riding naked] (ca. 1796) : a pruriently prying person : VOYEUR — **Peeping Tom·ism** \-'tä-,mi-zəm\ *n*

peep show *n* (1851) : an entertainment (as a film) or object (as a small picture) that is viewed through a small opening or a magnifying glass and is usu. sexually explicit

peep sight *n* (1881) : a rear sight for a gun having an adjustable metal piece pierced with a small hole to peep through in aiming

¹peer \'pir\ *n* [ME, fr. MF *per*, fr. *per*, adj., equal, fr. L *par*] (13c) **1** : one that is of equal standing with another : EQUAL; *esp* : one belonging to the same societal group esp. based on age, grade, or status **2** *archaic* : COMPANION **3 a** : a member of one of the five ranks (as duke, marquess, earl, viscount, or baron) of the British peerage **b** : NOBLE l — **peer** *adj*

²peer *vi* (14c) *archaic* : RIVAL, MATCH

³peer *vi* [perh. by shortening & alter. fr. *appear*] (1591) **1** : to look narrowly or curiously; *esp* : to look searchingly at something difficult to discern **2** : to come slightly into view : emerge partly

peer·age \'pir-ij\ *n* (15c) **1** : the body of peers **2** : the rank or dignity of a peer **3** : a book containing a list of peers with their genealogy, history, and titles

peer·ess \'pir-əs\ *n* (1689) **1** : the wife or widow of a peer **2** : a woman who holds in her own right the rank of a peer

peer·less \'pir-ləs\ *adj* (14c) : MATCHLESS, INCOMPARABLE

¹peeve \'pēv\ *vt* **peeved; peev·ing** [back-formation fr. *peevish*] (1908) : to make peevish or resentful : ANNOY *syn* see IRRITATE

²peeve *n* (1911) **1** : a feeling or mood of resentment **2** : a particular grievance or source of aggravation

pee·vish \'pē-vish\ *adj* [ME *pevish* spiteful] (ca. 1530) **1** : querulous in temperament or mood : FRETFUL **2** : perversely obstinate **3** : marked by ill temper — **pee·vish·ly** *adv* — **pee·vish·ness** *n*

pee·wee \'pē-(,)wē\ *n* [imit.] (1806) **1** : PEWEE **2** : one that is diminutive or small; *esp* : a small person — **peewee** *adj*

pee·wit \'pē-,wit, 'pyü-ət\ *n* [imit.] (ca. 1529) : any of several birds; *esp* : LAPWING

¹peg \'peg\ *n* [ME *pegge*, prob. fr. MD] (15c) **1 a** : a small usu. cylindrical pointed or tapered piece (as of wood) used to pin down or fasten things or to fit into or close holes : PIN, PLUG **b** *Brit* : CLOTHESPIN **c** : a predetermined level at which something (as a price) is fixed **2 a** : a projecting piece used as a support or boundary marker **b** : something (as a fact or opinion) used as a support, pretext, or reason **3 a** : one of the movable wooden pegs set in the head of a stringed instrument (as a violin) that are turned to regulate the pitch of the strings — see VIOLIN illustration **b** : a step or degree esp. in estimation **4** : a pointed prong or claw for catching or tearing **5** *Brit* : DRINK ⟨poured himself out a stiff ∼ —Dorothy Sayers⟩ **6** : something (as a leg) resembling a peg **7** : THROW; *esp* : a hard throw in baseball made in an attempt to put out a base runner

²peg *vb* **pegged; peg·ging** *vt* (1543) **1 a** : to put a peg into **b** *Brit* : to pin (laundry) on a clothesline **2 a** : to attach or fix as if with a peg: as **a** : to pin down : RESTRICT **b** : to fix or hold (as prices or wage increases) at a predetermined level or rate **c** : to place in a definite category : IDENTIFY **3** : to mark by pegs **4** : THROW ∼ *vi* **1** : to work steadily and diligently — often used with *away* **2** : to move along vigorously or hastily : HUSTLE

³peg \'peg\ *or* **pegged** \'pegd\ *adj* (1681) : wide at the top and narrow at the bottom ⟨∼ pants⟩

Peg·a·sus \'pe-gə-səs\ *n* [L (gen. *Pegasi*), fr. Gk *Pēgasos*] **1** : a winged horse that causes the stream Hippocrene to spring from Mount Helicon with a blow of his hoof **2** : poetic inspiration **3** : a northern constellation near the vernal equinoctial point

Peg–Board \'peg-,bȯrd, -,bȯrd\ *trademark* — used for material (as fiberboard) with regularly spaced perforations into which hooks may be inserted for the storage or display of articles

peg leg *n* [³*peg*] (1769) : an artificial leg; *esp* : one fitted at the knee

peg·ma·tite \'peg-mə-,tīt\ *n* [F, fr. Gk *pēgmat-, pēgma* something fastened together, fr. *pēgnynai* to fasten together — more at PACT] (ca. 1828) : a coarse variety of granite occurring in dikes or veins — **peg·ma·tit·ic** \,peg-mə-'ti-tik\ *adj*

peg–top \'peg-,täp\ *or* **peg–topped** \-'täpt\ *adj* (1858) : PEG

peg top *n* (1788) **1** \'peg-'täp\ : a pear-shaped top that is made to spin on the sharp metal peg in its base by the unwinding of a string wound round its center **2** *pl* \-,täps\ : peg trousers

pei·gnoir \pān-'wär, pen-\ *n* [F, lit., garment worn while combing the hair, fr. MF, fr. *peigner* to comb the hair, fr. L *pectinare*, fr. *pectin-, pecten* comb — more at PECTINATE] (1835) : a woman's loose negligee or dressing gown

pein *var of* PEEN

¹pe·jo·ra·tive \pi-'jȯr-ə-tiv, -'jär- *also* 'pe-jə-rə-tiv *or* 'pē- *or* -,rä- *or* 'pej-rə- *or* 'pēj-\ (1882) : a pejorative word or phrase

²pejorative *adj* [LL *pejoratus*, pp. of *pejorare* to make or become worse, fr. L *pejor*; akin to Skt *padyate* he falls, L *ped-, pes* foot — more at FOOT] (ca. 1888) : having negative connotations; *esp* : tending to disparage or belittle : DEPRECIATORY — **pe·jo·ra·tive·ly** *adv*

peke \'pēk\ *n*, *often cap* (1915) : PEKINGESE 2

Pe·kin \pi-'kin, 'pē-\ *n* [*Pekin, Peking* (Beijing), China] (1885) : any of a breed of large white ducks of Chinese origin used for meat production

Pe·king duck \'pē-,kiŋ-\ *n* (1955) : a Chinese dish consisting of roasted duck meat and strips of crispy duck skin topped with scallions and sauce and wrapped in thin pancakes

Pe·king·ese *or* **Pe·kin·ese** \,pē-kə-'nēz, -'nēs; -,kiŋ-'ēz, -'ēs\ *n, pl* **Pe·kingese** *or* **Pekinese** (1849) **1 a** : the Chinese dialect of Beijing **b** : a native or resident of Beijing **2** : any of a Chinese breed of small short-legged dogs with a broad flat face and a profuse long soft coat

Peking man *n* (1926) : an extinct Pleistocene hominid that is known from skeletal and cultural remains in cave deposits at Cho-k'ou-tien, China and is now classified with the pithecanthropines

pe·koe \'pē-(,)kō *also* 'pe-\ *n* [Chin (Xiamen) *pek-ho*] (1712) : a tea made from young leaves that are slightly larger than those of orange pekoe

pel·age \'pe-lij\ *n* [F, fr. MF, fr. *poil* hair, fr. L *pilus*] (ca. 1828) : the hairy covering of a mammal

¹Pe·la·gian \pə-'lā-j(ē-)ən\ *n* (15c) : one agreeing with Pelagius in denying original sin and consequently in holding that mankind has perfect freedom to do either right or wrong

²Pelagian *adj* (15c) : of or relating to Pelagians or Pelagianism

Pe·la·gian·ism \-j(ē-)ə-,ni-zəm\ *n* (1583) : the teaching of Pelagius or Pelagians

pe·lag·ic \pə-'la-jik\ *adj* [L *pelagicus*, fr. Gk *pelagikos*, fr. *pelagos* sea — more at PLAGAL] (ca. 1656) : of, relating to, or living or occurring in the open sea : OCEANIC ⟨∼ sediment⟩ ⟨∼ birds⟩

pel·ar·go·ni·um \,pe·lär-'gō-nē-əm, -lər-\ *n* [NL, fr. Gk *pelargos* stork (akin to Gk *pelios* livid, *polios* gray) + NL *-nium* (as in *Geranium*) — more at FALLOW] (ca. 1819) : any of a genus (*Pelargonium*) of southern African herbs (as a garden geranium) of the geranium family with showy flowers of various shades of red, pink, or white distinguished by a spurred calyx and irregular corolla

Pe·las·gian \pə-'laz-j(ē-)ən, -'laz-gē-ən\ *n* [Gk *pelasgios*, adj., Pelasgian, fr. *Pelasgoi* Pelasgians] (15c) : a member of an ancient people mentioned by classical writers as early inhabitants of Greece and the eastern islands of the Mediterranean — **Pelasgian** *adj* — **Pe·las·gic** \-jik, -gik\ *adj*

pe·lec·y·pod \pə-'le-sə-,päd\ *n* [NL *Pelecypoda*, group name, fr. Gk *pelekys* ax (akin to Skt *paraśu* ax) + *pod-, pous* foot — more at FOOT] (ca. 1890) : LAMELLIBRANCH

pel·er·ine \,pe-lə-'rēn, 'pe-lə-rən\ *n* [obs. F, neckerchief, fr. F *pèlerine*, fem. of *pèlerin* pilgrim, fr. LL *pelegrinus* — more at PILGRIM] (1744) : a woman's narrow cape made of fabric or fur and usu. with long ends hanging down in front

Pe·leus \'pēl-,yüs, 'pē-lē-əs\ *n* [L, fr. Gk *Pēleus*] : a son of Aeacus who becomes by the goddess Thetis the father of Achilles

pelf \'pelf\ *n* [ME, fr. MF *pelfre* booty] (14c) : MONEY, RICHES

pel·i·can \'pe-li-kən\ *n* [ME, fr. OE *pellican*, fr. LL *pelecanus*, fr. Gk *pelekan*] (bef. 12c) : any of a genus (*Pelecanus*) of large web-footed fish-eating birds with a very large bill and distensible gular pouch

pe·lisse \pə-'lēs, pe-\ *n* [F, fr. LL *pellicia*, fr. fem. of *pellicius* made of skin, fr. L *pellis* skin — more at FELL] (1717) **1** : a long cloak or coat made of fur or lined or trimmed with fur **2** : a woman's loose lightweight cloak with wide collar and fur trimming

pel·la·gra \pə-'la-grə, -'lā-, -'lä-\ *n* [It, fr. *pelle* skin (fr. L *pellis*) + *-agra* (as in *podagra*, fr. L *podagra*, L)] (ca. 1811) : a disease marked by dermatitis, gastrointestinal disorders, and central nervous symptoms and associated with a diet deficient in niacin — **pel·la·grous** \-grəs\ *adj*

pel·la·grin \-grən\ *n* [irreg. fr. *pellagra*] (1865) : a person who is affected with pellagra

¹pel·let \'pe-lət\ *n* [ME *pelote*, fr. MF, fr. (assumed) VL *pilota*, dim. of L *pila* ball] (14c) **1** : a usu. small rounded, spherical, or cylindrical body (as of food or medicine) **2** : any of various projectiles fired from a weapon (as an air rifle) — **pel·let·al** \-lə-t⁸l\ *adj*

²pellet *vt* (1597) **1** : PELLETIZE **2** : to strike with pellets

pellet gun *n* (1952) : AIR GUN 1

pel·let·ise *Brit var of* PELLETIZE

pel·let·ize \'pe-lə-,tīz\ *vt* **-ized; -iz·ing** (1942) : to form or compact into pellets ⟨∼ ore⟩ — **pel·let·i·za·tion** \,pe-lə-tə-'zā-shən\ *n* — **pel·let·iz·er** \'pe-lə-,tī-zər\ *n*

pel·li·cle \'pe-li-kəl\ *n* [MF *pellicule*, fr. ML *pellicula*, fr. L, dim. of *pellis*] (1541) : a thin skin or film: as **a** : an outer membrane of some protozoans (as euglenoids or paramecia) **b** : a film that reflects a part of the light falling upon it and transmits the rest and that is used for dividing a beam of light (as in a photographic device)

¹pel·li·to·ry \'pe-lə-,tȯr-ē, -,tȯr-\ *n, pl* **-ries** [ME *peletre*, fr. MF *piretre*, fr. L *pyrethrum* — more at PYRETHRUM] (1533) : a southern European composite plant (*Anacyclus pyrethrum*) resembling yarrow — called also *pellitory-of-Spain*

²pellitory *n* [ME *paritorie*, fr. MF *paritaire*, fr. LL *parietaria*, fr. fem. of *parietarius* of a wall, fr. L *pariet-, paries* wall] (1548) : any of a genus

\ə\ abut \ᵊ\ kitten, F table \ər\ further \a\ ash \ā\ ace \ä\ mop, mar \aú\ out \ch\ chin \e\ bet \ē\ easy \g\ go \i\ hit \ī\ ice \j\ job \ŋ\ sir̲, g \ō\ go \ò\ law \òi\ boy \th\ thin \t̲h̲\ the \ü\ loot \ú\ foot \y\ yet \zh\ vision \ā, k̲, ⁿ, œ, œ̄, ᵫ, ūᵉ, ᵊ\ see Guide to Pronunciation

(*Parietaria*) of herbs of the nettle family with alternate leaves and inconspicuous flowers — called also *pellitory-of-the-wall*

pell-mell \‚pel-'mel\ *adv* [MF *pelemele*] (1596)　**1 :** in mingled confusion or disorder　**2 :** in confused haste — **pell-mell** *adj or n*

pel-lu-cid \pə-'lü-səd\ *adj* [L *pellucidus*, fr. *per* through + *lucidus* lucid — more at FOR] (1619)　**1 :** admitting maximum passage of light without diffusion or distortion　**2 :** reflecting light evenly from all surfaces　**3 :** easy to understand — **pel-lu-cid-ly** \pə-'lü-səd-lē\ *adv*

pel-met \'pel-mət\ *n* [prob. modif. of F *palmette* palmette] (1821) : a short valance or small cornice for concealing curtain fixtures

Pe-lops \'pē-,läps, 'pe-\ *n* [L, fr. Gk] : a son of Tantalus served by his father to the gods for food but later restored to life by them

pe-lo-rus \pə-'lōr-əs, -'lȯr-\ *n* [origin unknown] (1854) : a navigational instrument resembling a mariner's compass without magnetic needles and having two sight vanes by which bearings are taken

pe-lo-ta \pə-'lō-tə\ *n* [Sp, fr. OF *pelote* little ball — more at PELLET] (1844)　**1 :** a court game related to jai alai　**2 :** the ball used in jai alai

¹pelt \'pelt\ *n* [ME, perh. back-formation fr. *peltry*] (15c)　**1 :** a usu. undressed skin with its hair, wool, or fur　**2 :** a skin stripped of hair or wool for tanning

²pelt *vt* (1596) : to strip off the skin or pelt of (an animal)

³pelt *vb* [ME] *vt* (15c)　**1 a :** to strike with a succession of blows or missiles 〈~ed him with stones〉　**b :** to assail vigorously or persistently 〈~ed her with accusations〉　**2 :** HURL, THROW 〈~ed snowballs at them〉　**3 :** to beat or dash repeatedly against 〈hailstones ~ing the roof〉 ~ *vi*　**1 :** to deliver a succession of blows or missiles 〈~ed incessantly〉　**3 :** to move rapidly and vigorously : HURRY — **pelt-er** *n*

⁴pelt *n* (1513) : BLOW, WHACK

pel-tate \'pel-,tāt\ *adj* [L *pelta* small shield, fr. Gk *peltē*] (ca. 1760) : shaped like a shield; *specif* : having the stem or support attached to the lower surface instead of at the base or margin — see LEAF illustration

pelt-ing \'pel-tiŋ\ *adj* [prob. fr. E dial. *pelt* piece of trash] (1540) *archaic* : PALTRY, INSIGNIFICANT

pelt-ry \'pel-trē\ *n, pl* **peltries** [ME, fr. AF *pelterie*] (15c) : PELTS, FURS; *esp* : raw undressed skins — often used in pl.

pel-vic \'pel-vik\ *adj* (1830) : of, relating to, or located in or near the pelvis — **pelvic** *n*

pelvic fin *n* (ca. 1909) : one of the paired fins of a fish that are homologous with the hind limbs of a quadruped

pelvic girdle *n* (1883) : a bony or cartilaginous arch that supports the hind limbs of a vertebrate

pelvic inflammatory disease *n* (1974) : inflammation of the female reproductive tract and esp. the fallopian tubes that is caused esp. by sexually transmitted disease, occurs more often in women using IUDs, and is a leading cause of female sterility

pel-vis \'pel-vəs\ *n, pl* **pel-vis-es** \-və-səz\ *or* **pel-ves** \-,vēz\ [NL, fr. L, basin; perh. akin to OE & ON *full* cup] (1615)　**1 :** a basin-shaped structure in the skeleton of many vertebrates that is formed by the pelvic girdle and adjoining bones of the spine　**2 :** the cavity of the pelvis　**3 :** the funnel-shaped cavity of the kidney into which urine is discharged

pel-y-co-saur \'pe-li-kə-,sȯr\ *n* [ultim. fr. Gk *pelyc-, pelyx* bowl + *sauros* lizard] (1904) : any of an order (Pelycosauria) of primitive Permian quadruped reptiles that resemble mammals and often have extreme development of the dorsal vertebral processes

Pem-broke table \'pem-,brȯk-, -,brük-\ *n* [*Pembroke*, Wales] (1778) : a small 4-legged table originating in the Georgian period and having two drop leaves and a drawer

Pembroke Welsh corgi *n* (1938) : any of a breed of Welsh corgis with pointed ears, straight forelegs, and a short tail — called also *Pembroke;* see WELSH CORGI illustration

pem-mi-can *also* **pem-i-can** \'pe-mi-kən\ *n* [Cree *pimihkaⁿ*] (1791) : a concentrated food used by No. American Indians and consisting of lean meat dried, pounded fine, and mixed with melted fat; *also* : a similar preparation (as of dried beef, flour, molasses, suet) used for emergency rations

pem-o-line \'pe-mə-,lēn\ *n* [origin unknown] (1961) : a synthetic organic drug $C_9H_8N_2O_2$ that is a mild stimulant of the central nervous system

pem-phi-gus \'pem(p)-fi-gəs, pem-'fī-\ *n* [NL, fr. Gk *pemphig-, pemphix* pustule] (ca. 1779) : a disease characterized by large blisters on skin and mucous membranes and often by itching or burning

¹pen \'pen\ *vt* **penned; pen-ning** [ME *pennen*, fr. OE *-pennian*] (13c) : to shut in or as if in a pen

²pen *n* [ME, perh. fr. *pennen*] (14c)　**1 a :** a small enclosure for animals　**b :** the animals in a pen 〈a ~ of sheep〉　**2 :** a small place of confinement or storage　**3 :** a protected dock or slip for a submarine　**4 :** BULL PEN 2

³pen *n* [ME *penne*, fr. MF, feather, pen, fr. L *penna, pinna* feather; akin to Gk *pteron* wing — more at FEATHER] (14c)　**1 :** an implement for writing or drawing with ink or a similar fluid: as　**a :** QUILL　**b :** PEN POINT　**c :** a penholder containing a pen point　**d :** FOUNTAIN PEN　**e :** BALLPOINT　**2 a :** a writing instrument regarded as a means of expression 〈enlisted the ~s of the best writers —F. H. Chase〉　**b :** WRITER　**3 :** the internal horny feather-shaped shell of a squid

⁴pen *vt* **penned; pen-ning** (15c) : WRITE, INDITE 〈~ a letter〉

⁵pen *n* [origin unknown] (1550) : a female swan

⁶pen *n* (1884) : PENITENTIARY

pe-nal \'pē-n°l\ *adj* [ME, fr. MF, fr. L *poenalis*, fr. *poena* punishment — more at PAIN] (15c)　**1 :** of, relating to, or involving punishment, penalties, or punitive institutions　**2 :** liable to punishment 〈a ~ offense〉　**3 :** used as a place of confinement and punishment 〈a ~ colony〉 — **pe-nal-ly** \-n°l-ē\ *adv*

penal code *n* (1845) : a code of laws concerning crimes and offenses and their punishment

pe-nal-ise *Brit var of* PENALIZE

pe-nal-ize \'pē-n°l-,īz, 'pe-\ *vt* **-ized; -iz-ing** (1868)　**1 :** to inflict a penalty on　**2 :** to put at a serious disadvantage — **pe-nal-i-za-tion** \-n°l-ə-'zā-shən\ *n*

pen-al-ty \'pe-n°l-tē\ *n, pl* **-ties** [ML *poenalitas*, fr. L *poenalis*] (15c)　**1 :** the suffering in person, rights, or property that is annexed by law or judicial decision to the commission of a crime or public offense　**2 :** the suffering or the sum to be forfeited to which a person agrees to be sub-

jected in case of nonfulfillment of stipulations　**3 a :** disadvantage, loss, or hardship due to some action　**b :** a disadvantage (as loss of yardage, time, or possession of the ball or an addition to or subtraction from the score) imposed on a team or competitor for violation of the rules of a sport　**4 :** points scored in bridge by the side that defeats the opposing contract — usu. used in pl. — **penalty** *adj*

penalty box *n* (1931) : an area alongside an ice hockey rink to which penalized players are confined for the duration of their penalty

penalty kick (1889)　**1 :** a free kick in rugby　**2 :** a free kick at the goal in soccer made from a point 12 yards in front of the goal and allowed for certain violations within a designated area around the goal

penalty shot *n* (ca. 1948) : an unhindered shot at the goal in ice hockey awarded to an individual for certain violations by an opponent

¹pen-ance \'pe-nən(t)s\ *n* [ME, fr. OF, fr. ML *poenitentia* penitence] (14c)　**1 :** an act of self-abasement, mortification, or devotion performed to show sorrow or repentance for sin　**2 :** a sacramental rite that is practiced in Roman, Eastern, and some Anglican churches and that consists of private confession, absolution, and a penance directed by the confessor　**3 :** something (as a hardship or penalty) resembling an act of penance (as in compensating for an offense)

²penance *vt* **pen-anced; pen-anc-ing** (1600) : to impose penance on

Pe-na-tes \pə-'nä-tēz, -'nā-\ *n pl* [L, fr. *penus* food, provisions] : the Roman gods of the household worshiped in close connection with Vesta and with the Lares

pence \'pen(t)s\ *pl of* PENNY

pen-cel *or* **pen-cil** \'pen(t)-səl\ *n* [ME *pencel*, modif. of OF *penoncel*] (13c) : PENNONCEL

pen-chant \'pen-chənt, *esp Brit* 'pä^n-,shä^n\ [F, fr. prp. of *pencher* to incline, fr. (assumed) VL *pendicare*, fr. L *pendere* to weigh] (1672) : a strong and continued inclination; *broadly* : LIKING　**syn** see LEANING

¹pen-cil \'pen(t)-səl\ *n* [ME *pensel*, fr. MF *pincel*, fr. (assumed) VL *penicellus*, alter. of L *penicillus*, dim. of *peniculus* brush, fr. dim. of *penis* tail, penis] (14c)　**1 :** an artist's brush　**2 :** an artist's individual skill or style　**3 a :** an implement for writing, drawing, or marking consisting of or containing a slender cylinder or strip of a solid marking substance　**b :** a small medicated or cosmetic roll or stick for local applications　**4 :** a set of geometric objects each pair of which has a common property 〈the lines in a plane through a point comprise a ~ of lines〉　**5 :** something (as a beam of radiation) long and thin like a pencil

²pencil *vt* **-ciled** *or* **-cilled; -cil-ing** *or* **-cil-ling** \-s(ə-)liŋ\ (ca. 1532) : to paint, draw, write, or mark with a pencil

pen-cil-ing *or* **pen-cil-ling** *n* (1706) : the work of the pencil or brush; *also* : a product of this

pencil pusher *n* (1881) : a person who does predominantly paperwork

pen-dant *also* **pen-dent** \'pen-dənt; *3 & 4 are also* 'pe-nənt, *5 is also* pä^n-dä^n\ *n* [ME *pendaunt*, fr. MF *pendant*, fr. prp. of *pendre* to hang, fr. (assumed) VL *pendere*, fr. L *pendēre* to weigh; akin to L *pendere* to weigh, estimate, pay, *pondus* weight] (14c)　**1 :** something suspended: as　**a :** an ornament (as on a necklace) allowed to hang free　**b :** an electrical fixture suspended from the ceiling　**2 :** a hanging ornament of roofs or ceilings much used in the later styles of Gothic architecture　**3 :** a length of line usu. used as a connector on a boat or ship; *esp* : a short rope hanging from a spar and having at its free end a block or spliced thimble　**4** *chiefly Brit* : PENNANT 1a　**5 a :** COMPANION PIECE　**b** : something secondary or supplementary

pen-den-cy \'pen-dən(t)-sē\ *n* (1637) : the state of being pending

pen-dent *or* **pen-dant** \'pen-dənt\ *adj* [ME *pendaunt*] (14c)　**1 :** jutting or leaning over : OVERHANGING 〈a ~ cliff〉　**2 :** supported from above : SUSPENDED 〈icicles ~ from the eaves〉　**3 :** remaining undetermined : PENDING

pen-den-tive \pen-'den-tiv\ *n* [F *pendentif*, fr. L *pendent-, pendens*, prp. of *pendēre*] (ca. 1741) : one of the concave triangular members that supports a dome over a square space

1 pendentive

¹pend-ing \'pen-diŋ\ *prep* [F *pendant*, fr. prp. of *pendre*] (1642)　**1 :** DURING　**2 :** while awaiting

²pending *adj* (1797)　**1 :** not yet decided : being in continuance　**2 :** IMMINENT, IMPENDING

pen-du-lar \'pen-jə-lər, 'pen-dyə-, -də-\ *adj* (1878) : being or resembling the movement of a pendulum

pen-du-lous \-ləs\ *adj* [L *pendulus*, fr. *pendēre* to hang] (ca. 1605)　**1** *archaic* : poised without visible support　**2 a :** suspended so as to swing freely 〈branches hung with ~ vines〉　**b :** inclined or hanging downward 〈~ jowls〉　**3 :** marked by vacillation, indecision, or uncertainty — **pen-du-lous-ness** *n*

pen-du-lum \-ləm\ *n* [NL, fr. L, neut. of *pendulus*] (1660)　**1 :** a body suspended from a fixed point so as to swing freely to and fro under the action of gravity and commonly used to regulate movements (as of clockwork)　**2 :** something (as a state of affairs) that alternates between opposites

Pe-nel-o-pe \pə-'ne-lə-pē\ *n* [L, fr. Gk *Pēnelopē*] : the wife of Odysseus who waits faithfully for him during his 20 years' absence

pe-ne-plain *also* **pe-ne-plane** \'pē-ni-,plān, 'pe-\ *n* [L *paene, pene* almost + E *plain* or *plane*] (1889) : a land surface of considerable area and slight relief shaped by erosion

pen-e-tra-ble \'pe-nə-trə-bəl\ *adj* (1538) : capable of being penetrated — **pen-e-tra-bil-i-ty** \,pe-nə-trə-'bi-lə-tē\ *n*

pen-e-tra-lia \,pe-nə-'trā-lē-ə\ *n pl* [L, neut. pl. of *penetralis* inner, fr. *penetrare* to penetrate] (1668) : the innermost or most private parts

pen-e-trance \'pe-nə-trən(t)s\ *n* [ISV, fr. L *penetrare*] (1934) : the proportion of individuals of a particular genotype that express its phenotypic effect in a given environment

¹pen-e-trant \-trənt\ *adj* (1543) : PENETRATING

²penetrant *n* (ca. 1734) : one that penetrates or is capable of penetrating

pen-e-trate \'pe-nə-,trāt\ *vb* **-trat-ed; -trat-ing** [L *penetratus*, pp. of *penetrare*, fr. *penitus* deep within, far; akin to L *penus* provisions] *vt* (ca. 1530)　**1 a :** to pass into or through　**b :** to enter by overcoming resistance : PIERCE **c :** to gain entrance to **2 a :** to see into or through **b :** to discover the inner contents or meaning of **3 :** to affect profoundly with feeling ~ *vi* **1 a :** to diffuse through or into ~ *vi* **1 a :** to pass, extend, pierce, or diffuse into or through something **b :** to pierce something with the eye or mind **2 :** to affect deeply the senses or feelings *syn* see ENTER

pen·e·trat·ing *adj* (1593) **1 :** having the power of entering, piercing, or pervading (a ~ shriek) **2 :** ACUTE, DISCERNING (~ insights into life) — **pen·e·trat·ing·ly** \-,trā-tiŋ-lē\ *adv*

pen·e·tra·tion \,pe-nə-'trā-shən\ *n* (1605) **1 a :** the power to penetrate; *esp* : the ability to discern deeply and acutely **b :** the depth to which something penetrates **c :** the extent to which a commercial product or agency is familiar or sells in a market **2 :** the act or process of penetrating: as **a :** the act of entering a country so that actual establishment of influence is accomplished **b :** an attack that penetrates the enemy's front or territory *syn* see DISCERNMENT

pen·e·tra·tive \'pe-nə-,trā-tiv\ *adj* (15c) **1 :** tending to penetrate : PIERCING **2 :** ACUTE (~ observations) **3 :** IMPRESSIVE (a ~ speaker)

pen·e·trom·e·ter \,pe-nə-'trä-mə-tər\ *n* [L *penetrare* + ISV *-meter*] (1905) : an instrument for measuring firmness or consistency (as of soil)

pen·gö \'peŋ-,gə(r), -,gœ\ *n, pl* **pengö** *or* **pengös** [Hung *pengő*, lit., jingling] (1925) : the basic monetary unit of Hungary from 1925 to 1946

pen·guin \'peŋ-gwən, 'peŋ-\ *n* [obs. E *penguin* great auk, perh. fr. W *pen gwyn* white head (applied to the bird in winter plumage)] (1588) : any of various erect short-legged flightless aquatic birds (family Spheniscidae) of the southern hemisphere

pen·hold·er \'pen-,hōl-dər\ *n* (1815) : a holder or handle for a pen point

-penia *comb form* [NL, fr. Gk *penia*] : deficiency (leuko*penia*)

pen·i·cil·la·mine \,pe-nə-'si-lə-,mēn\ *n* [*penicillin* + *amine*] (1943) : an amino acid $C_5H_{11}NO_2S$ that is obtained from penicillins and is used esp. in the treatment of poisoning by metals (as copper or lead) and of cystinuria

pen·i·cil·late \,pe-nə-'si-lət, -,lāt\ *adj* [L *penicillus* brush — more at PENCIL] (1819) : furnished with a tuft of fine filaments (a ~ stigma)

pen·i·cil·lin \,pe-nə-'si-lən\ *n* [NL *Penicillium*] (1929) **1 :** any of several relatively nontoxic antibiotic acids of the general constitution $C_9H_{11}N_2O_4SR$ that are produced by molds (genus *Penicillium* as *P. notatum* or *P. chrysogenum*) or synthetically and are used esp. against cocci; *also* : a mixture of such acids **2 :** a salt or ester of a penicillin or a mixture of such salts or esters

pen·i·cil·lin·ase \-'si-lə-,nās, -,nāz\ *n* (1940) : an enzyme found esp. in staphylococcal bacteria that inactivates the penicillins by hydrolyzing them

pen·i·cil·li·um \-'si-lē-əm\ *n, pl* **-lia** \-lē-ə\ [NL, fr. L *penicillus*] (1867) : any of a genus (*Penicillium* of the family Moniliaceae) of fungi (as a blue mold) that are found chiefly on moist nonliving organic matter

pe·nile \'pē-,nil\ *adj* (ca. 1861) : of, relating to, or affecting the penis

pen·in·su·la \pə-'nin(t)-s(ə-)lə, -shə-lə\ *n* [L *paeninsula*, fr. *paene* almost + *insula* island] (1538) : a portion of land nearly surrounded by water and connected with a larger body by an isthmus; *also* : a piece of land jutting out into the water whether with or without a well-defined isthmus — **pen·in·su·lar** \-s(ə-)lər, -shə-lər\ *adj*

pe·nis \'pē-nəs\ *n, pl* **pe·nes** \'pē-(,)nēz\ *or* **pe·nis·es** [L, penis, tail; akin to OHG *fasel* penis, Gk *peos*] (1676) : a male organ of copulation that in male mammals including humans usu. functions as the channel by which urine leaves the body

penis envy *n* (1924) : the supposed coveting of the penis by a young human female which is held in Freudian psychoanalytic theory to lead to feelings of inferiority and defensive or compensatory behavior

pen·i·tence \'pe-nə-tən(t)s\ *n* [ME, fr. OF, fr. ML *paenitentia*, alter. of L *paenitentia* regret, fr. *paenitent-, paenitens*, prp.] (13c) : the quality or state of being penitent : sorrow for sins or faults

syn PENITENCE. REPENTANCE. CONTRITION. COMPUNCTION. REMORSE mean regret for sin or wrongdoing. PENITENCE implies sad and humble realization of and regret for one's misdeeds (absolution is dependent upon sincere *penitence*). REPENTANCE adds the implication of a resolve to change (*repentance* accompanied by a complete change of character). CONTRITION stresses the sorrowful regret that constitutes true penitence (tearful expressions of *contrition*). COMPUNCTION implies a painful sting of conscience esp. for contemplated wrongdoing (had no *compunctions* about taking back what is mine). REMORSE suggests prolonged and insistent self-reproach and mental anguish for past wrongs and esp. for those whose consequences cannot be remedied (thieves untroubled by feelings of *remorse*).

¹**pen·i·tent** \-tənt\ *adj* [ME, fr. MF, fr. L *paenitent-, paenitens*, fr. prp. of *paenitēre* to cause regret, feel regret, perh. fr. *paene* almost] (14c) : feeling or expressing humble or regretful pain or sorrow for sins or offenses : REPENTANT — **pen·i·tent·ly** *adv*

²**penitent** *n* (14c) **1 :** a person who repents of sin **2 :** a person under church censure but admitted to penance or reconciliation esp. under the direction of a confessor

pen·i·ten·tial \,pe-nə-'ten(t)-shəl\ *adj* (1508) : of or relating to penitence or penance — **pen·i·ten·tial·ly** \-'ten(t)-sh(ə-)lē\ *adv*

¹**pen·i·ten·tia·ry** \,pe-nə-'ten(t)-sh(ə-)rē\ *n, pl* **-ries** [ME *penitenciary*, fr. ML *poenitentiarius*, fr. *poenitentia*] (15c) **1 a :** an officer in some Roman Catholic dioceses vested with power from the bishop to deal with cases of a nature normally handled only by the bishop **b** *cap* : a cardinal presiding over a tribunal of the Roman curia concerned with dispensations and indulgences **2 :** a public institution in which offenders against the law are confined for detention or punishment; *specif* : a state or federal prison in the U.S.

²**pen·i·ten·tia·ry** \,pe-nə-'ten(t)-sh(ə-)rē, *l* also -'ten(t)-shē-,er-ē\ *adj* (1577) **1 :** PENITENTIAL **2 :** of, relating to, or incurring confinement in a penitentiary

pen·knife \'pen-,nif\ *n* [ME; fr. its original use for mending quill pens] (15c) : a small pocketknife usu. with only one blade

pen·light *also* **pen·lite** \-,līt\ *n* (1945) : a small flashlight resembling a fountain pen in size or shape

pen·man \-mən\ *n* (1539) **1 a :** CALLIGRAPHER **b :** COPYIST. SCRIBE **c** : a person with a specified quality or kind of handwriting (a poor ~) **2 :** AUTHOR

pen·man·ship \-,ship\ *n* (1695) **1 :** the art or practice of writing with the pen **2 :** quality or style of handwriting

pen name *n* (ca. 1864) : an author's pseudonym

pen·nant \'pe-nənt\ *n* [alter. of *pendant*] (1698) **1 a :** any of various nautical flags tapering usu. to a point or swallowtail and used for identification or signaling **b :** a flag or banner longer in the fly than in the hoist; *esp* : one that tapers to a point **2 :** a flag emblematic of championship (as in a professional baseball league); *also* : the championship itself

pen·nate \'pe-,nāt\ *adj* [irreg. fr. NL *Pennales*] (1938) : of, relating to, or being diatoms of an order (Pennales) usu. characterized by a raphe or a structure resembling a raphe and by ornamentation of the valves that is bilaterally symmetrical

pen·ne \'pe(n)-(,)nā\ *n, pl* **penne** [It, pl. of *penna*, lit., quill, feather, pen, fr. L *pinna* feather & *penna* wing — more at PEN] (1974) : short thick diagonally cut tubular pasta

pen·ni \'pe-nē\ *n, pl* **pen·nia** \-nē-ə\ *also* **penni** *or* **pen·nis** -nēz\ [Finn] (ca. 1893) — see *markka* at MONEY table

pen·ni·less \'pe-ni-ləs, 'pe-n⁹l-əs\ *adj* (14c) : destitute of money

pen·non \'pe-nən\ *n* [ME, fr. MF *penon*, dim. of *penne* quill, wing feather — more at PEN] (14c) **1 a :** a long usu. triangular or swallowtailed streamer typically attached to the head of a lance as an ensign **b** : PENNANT 1a **2 :** WING, PINION

pen·non·cel *or* **pen·on·cel** \'pe-nən-,sel\ *n* [ME *penoncell*, fr. MF *penoncel*, dim. of *penon*] (14c) : a small pennon used in late medieval or Renaissance times

Penn·syl·va·nia Dutch \,pen(t)-səl-'vā-nyə-, -nē-ə-\ *n* (ca. 1824) **1** : a people living mostly in eastern Pennsylvania whose characteristic cultural traditions go back to the German migrations of the 18th century **2 :** a dialect of High German spoken in parts of Pennsylvania and Maryland — **Pennsylvania Dutchman** *n*

Pennsylvania German *n* (1869) : PENNSYLVANIA DUTCH

Penn·syl·va·nian \-'vā-nyən, -nē-ən\ *adj* (1698) **1 :** of or relating to Pennsylvania or its people **2 :** of, relating to, or being the period of the Paleozoic era in No. America between the Mississippian and Permian or the corresponding system of rocks — see GEOLOGIC TIME table — **Pennsylvanian** *n*

pen·ny \'pe-nē\ *n, pl* **pennies** \-nēz\ *or* **pence** \'pen(t)s\ *often attrib* [ME, fr. OE *penning, penig*; akin to OHG *pfenning*, a coin] (bef. 12c) **1 a :** a monetary unit of the United Kingdom formerly equal to $1/240$ pound but now equal to $1/100$ pound **b :** a similar monetary unit of any of various other countries in or formerly in the Commonwealth — see *pound* at MONEY table **c :** a coin representing one penny **2 :** DENARIUS **3** *pl* **pennies :** CENT **4 :** a trivial amount **5 :** a piece or sum of money (that will cost a pretty ~)

-penny *adj comb form* [*penny*; perh. fr. the original price per hundred] : being a (designated) nail size (an eight*penny* nail)

pen·ny-an·te \'pe-nē-'an-tē\ *adj* (1868) : SMALL-TIME. TWO-BIT

penny ante *n* (1855) : poker played for very low stakes

penny arcade *n* (1908) : an amusement center having coin-operated devices for entertainment

pen·ny·cress \'pe-nē-,kres\ *n* (1713) : a Eurasian herb (*Thlaspi arvense*) with round flat pods that is widely naturalized in the New World

penny dreadful *n* (ca. 1873) : a novel of violent adventure or crime

pen·ny-pinch·ing \-,pin-chiŋ\ *n* (1935) : FRUGALITY. PARSIMONY — **pen·ny-pinch·er** \-chər\ *n* — **penny-pinching** *adj*

pen·ny·roy·al \,pen-ē-'rȯi(-ə)l, 'pe-ni-,ril\ *n* [prob. by folk etymology fr. MF *poullieul*, modif. of L *pulegium* fleabane, pennyroyal] (1530) **1** : a European perennial mint (*Mentha pulegium*) with small aromatic leaves **2 :** an aromatic No. American mint (*Hedeoma pulegioides*) that has blue or violet flowers borne in axillary tufts and yields an oil used in folk medicine or to drive away mosquitoes

penny stock *n* (ca. 1920) : a usu. unlisted highly speculative stock selling for a dollar or less

pen·ny·weight \'pe-nē-,wāt\ *n* (14c) — see WEIGHT table

pen·ny·whistle \-,hwi-səl, -,wi-\ *n* (1818) **1 :** a small fipple flute **2** : a toy whistle

pen·ny·wise \-,wiz\ *adj* [fr. the phrase *penny-wise and pound-foolish*] (1607) : wise or prudent only in dealing with small sums or matters

pen·ny·wort \-,wərt, -,wȯrt\ *n* (14c) : any of several usu. round-leaved plants (as of the genus *Hydrocotyle* of the carrot family)

pen·ny·worth \'pe-nē-, *Brit often* 'pe-nərth\ *n, pl* **pennyworth** *or* **pennyworths** (bef. 12c) **1 :** a penny's worth **2 :** value for the money spent : BARGAIN **3 :** a small quantity : MODICUM

Pe·nob·scot \pə-'näb-,skät, -skət\ *n, pl* **-scot** *or* **-scots** (1624) : a member of an American Indian people of the Penobscot river valley and Penobscot Bay region of Maine

pe·no·che \pə-'nō-chē\ *var of* PENUCHE

pe·nol·o·gy \pi-'nä-lə-jē\ *n* [Gk *poinē* penalty + E *-logy* — more at PAIN] (1838) : a branch of criminology dealing with prison management and the treatment of offenders — **pe·no·log·i·cal** \,pē-nə-'lä-ji-kəl\ *adj* — **pe·nol·o·gist** \pi-'nä-lə-jist\ *n*

pen pal *n* (1938) : a friend made and kept through correspondence

pen point *n* (ca. 1864) : a small thin convex metal device that tapers to a split point, fits into a holder, and is used for writing or drawing

pen pusher *n* (ca. 1905) : PENCIL PUSHER

¹**pen·sion** \'pen(t)-shən\ *n* [ME, fr. MF, fr. L *pension-, pensio*, fr. *pendere* to pay — more at PENDANT] (14c) **1** \'pen(t)-shən\ **:** a fixed sum paid regularly to a person : *archaic* : WAGE **b :** a gratuity granted (as by a government) as a favor or reward **c :** one paid under given conditions to a person following retirement from service or to surviving dependents **2** \päⁿs-yōⁿ\ [F, fr. MF] **a :** accommodations esp. at a continental European hotel or boardinghouse : ROOM AND BOARD **b** *also* **pen·sio·ne** \pen(t)-'syō-(,)nä\ [*pensione*, fr. It] : a hotel or boardinghouse esp. in continental Europe — **pen·sion·less** \'pen(t)-shən-ləs\ *adj*

\ə\ abut \⁹\ kitten, F table \ər\ further \a\ ash \ā\ ace \ä\ mop, mar \au̇\ out \ch\ chin \e\ bet \ē\ easy \g\ go \i\ hit \ī\ ice \j\ job \ŋ\ sing \ō\ go \ȯ\ law \ȯi\ boy \th\ thin \t͟h\ the \ü\ loot \u̇\ foot \y\ yet \zh\ vision \ä, k̲, ⁿ, œ, œ̄, ue, ūe, ᵊ\ *see* Guide to Pronunciation

²**pension** *vt* **pen·sioned; pen·sion·ing** \'pen(t)-sh(ə-)niŋ\ (1702)   1
: to grant or pay a pension to   2 : to dismiss or retire from service
with a pension ⟨∼*ed* off his faithful old servant⟩
pen·sion·able \'pen(t)-sh(ə-)nə-bəl\ *adj* (1882) *chiefly Brit* : of, relating
to, qualified for, or qualifying for a pension ⟨∼ employees⟩ ⟨a ∼ post⟩
pen·sion·ary \'pen(t)-shə-,ner-ē\ *n, pl* **-ar·ies** (1536) : PENSIONER: *esp*
: HIRELING — **pensionary** *adj*
pen·sion·er \'pen(t)-sh(ə-)nər\ *n* (15c)   1 : a person who receives or
lives on a pension   2 *obs* a : GENTLEMAN-AT-ARMS b : RETAINER c
: MERCENARY. HIRELING
pen·sive \'pen(t)-siv\ *adj* [ME *pensif*, fr. MF, fr. *penser* to think, fr. L
pensare to ponder, freq. of *pendere* to weigh — more at PENDANT] (14c)
1 : musingly or dreamily thoughtful   2 : suggestive of sad thoughtful-
ness — **pen·sive·ly** *adv* — **pen·sive·ness** *n*
pen·ste·mon \pen-'stē-mən, 'pen(t)-stə-\ *n* [NL, fr. *penta-* + Gk
stēmōn warp, thread — more at STAMEN] (1760) : any of a genus (*Penstemon*) of chiefly American herbs of the snapdragon family with
showy tubular flowers
pen·stock \'pen-,stäk\ *n* (ca. 1607)   1 : a sluice or gate for regulating a
flow (as of water)   2 : a conduit or pipe for conducting water
pent \'pent\ *adj* [prob. fr. pp. of obs. E *pend* to confine] (1550) : shut
up : CONFINED. REPRESSED ⟨a ∼ crowd⟩ ⟨*pent*-up feelings⟩
penta- *or* **pent-** *comb form* [ME, fr. Gk, fr. *pente* — more at FIVE]   1
: five ⟨*pentahedron*⟩   2 : containing five atoms or groups ⟨*pentane*⟩
pen·ta·chlo·ro·phe·nol \,pen-tə-,klōr-ə-'fē-,nōl, -,klȯr-, -fi-'\ *n* (1879)
: a crystalline compound C_6Cl_5OH used esp. as a wood preservative
and fungicide and a disinfectant
pen·ta·cle \'pen-ti-kəl\ *n* [(assumed) ML *pentaculum*, prob. fr. Gk
pente] (1594) : PENTAGRAM
pen·tad \'pen-,tad\ *n* [Gk *pentad-, pentas*, fr. *pente*] (1653) : a group of
five
pen·ta·gon \'pen-tə-,gän\ *n* [Gk *pentagōnon*, fr. neut. of *pentagōnos*
pentagonal, fr. *penta-* + *gōnia* angle — more at -GON] (1571) : a polygon of five angles and five sides
Pentagon *n* [the *Pentagon* building, headquarters of the Department of
Defense] (1941) : the U.S. military leadership
pen·tag·o·nal \pen-'ta-gə-n³l\ *adj* (1571)   1 : having five sides and five
angles   2 : having a pentagon as a cross section or as a base ⟨a ∼
pyramid⟩ — **pen·tag·o·nal·ly** \-n³l-ē\ *adv*
Pen·ta·gon·ese \,pen-tə-,gä-'nēz, -'nēs\ *n* (1951) : military jargon
pen·ta·gram \'pen-tə-,gram\ *n* [Gk *pentagrammon*, fr. *penta-* +
-grammon (akin to *gramma* letter) — more at GRAM] (1833) : a figure
of a 5-pointed star usu. made with alternate points connected by a
continuous line and used as a magic or occult symbol; *also* : a similar
6-pointed star ⟨a Solomon's seal⟩
pen·ta·he·dron \,pen-tə-'hē-drən\ *n* [NL] (ca. 1775) : a solid bounded
by five faces — **pen·ta·he·dral** \-drəl\ *adj*
pen·tam·er·ous \pen-'ta-mə-rəs\ *adj* [NL *pentamerus*, fr. *penta-* (fr.
Gk) + *-merus* -merous] (1826) : divided into or consisting of five
parts; *specif* : having each floral whorl consisting of five or a multiple
of five members
pen·tam·e·ter \pen-'ta-mə-tər\ *n* [L, fr. Gk *pentametros* having five
metrical feet, fr. *penta-* + *metron* measure — more at MEASURE] (1589)
: a line of verse consisting of five metrical feet
pent·am·i·dine \pen-'ta-mə-,dēn, -dən\ *n* (1941) : a drug $C_{19}H_{24}N_4O_2$
used esp. to treat protozoal infections (as leishmaniasis) and to prevent
AIDS-related pneumonia
pen·tane \'pen-,tān\ *n* [ISV] (1877) : any of three isomeric alkanes
C_5H_{12} that occur esp. in petroleum
pen·tan·gle \'pen-,aŋ-gəl, 'pen-,taŋ-\ *n* (14c) : PENTAGRAM
pen·ta·pep·tide \,pen-tə-'pep-,tīd\ *n* (1907) : a polypeptide that contains five amino acid residues
pen·ta·ploid \'pen-tə-,plȯid\ *adj* (1921) : having or being a chromosome number that is five times the basic number — **pentaploid** *n* —
pen·ta·ploi·dy \-,plȯi-dē\ *n*
pen·tar·chy \'pen-,tär-kē\ *n* [Gk *pentarchia*, fr. *penta-* + *-archia*
-archy] (1587) : a group of five countries or districts each under its
own ruler or government
Pen·ta·teuch \'pen-tə-,tük, -,tyük\ *n* [ME *Penteteuke*, fr. LL *Pentateu-
chus*, fr. Gk *Pentateuchos*, fr. *penta-* + *teuchos* tool, vessel, book, fr.
teuchein to make — more at DOUGHTY] (15c) : the first five books of
Jewish and Christian Scriptures
pen·tath·lete \pen-'tath-,lēt\ *n* (1828) : an athlete participating in a
pentathlon
pen·tath·lon \pen-'tath-lən, -,län\ *n* [Gk, fr. *penta-* + *athlon* contest]
(1603) : an athletic contest involving participation by each contestant
in five different events; *esp* : MODERN PENTATHLON
pen·ta·ton·ic \,pen-tə-'tä-nik\ *adj* (1864) : consisting of five tones;
specif : being or relating to a scale in which the tones are arranged like
a major scale with the fourth and seventh tones omitted
pen·ta·va·lent \,pen-tə-'vā-lənt\ *adj* (1871) : having a valence of five
pen·taz·o·cine \pen-'ta-zə-,sēn\ *n* [prob. fr. *penta-* + *az-* + *octa-* +
²-*ine*] (1963) : an analgesic drug $C_{19}H_{27}NO$ that is less addictive than
morphine
Pen·te·cost \'pen-ti-,kȯst, -,käst\ *n* [ME, fr. OE *pentecosten*, fr. LL
pentecoste, fr. Gk *pentēkostē*, lit., fiftieth day, fr. *pentēkostos* fiftieth, fr.
pentēkonta fifty, fr. *penta-* + *-konta* (akin to L *viginti* twenty) — more
at VIGESIMAL] (bef. 12c)   1 : SHABUOTH   2 : a Christian feast on the
seventh Sunday after Easter commemorating the descent of the Holy
Spirit on the apostles — called also *Whitsunday*
¹**Pen·te·cos·tal** \,pen-ti-'käs-t³l, -'kȯs-\ *adj* (1663)   1 : of, relating to,
or suggesting Pentecost   2 : of, relating to, or constituting any of various Christian religious bodies that emphasize individual experiences of
grace, spiritual gifts (as glossolalia and faith healing), expressive worship, and evangelism — **Pen·te·cos·tal·ism** \-tə-,li-zəm\ *n* — **Pen·te-
cos·tal·ist** \-tə-list\ *n or adj*
²**Pentecostal** *n* (1904) : a member of a Pentecostal religious body
pent·house \'pent-,haůs\ *n* [alter. of ME *apentiz*, fr. MF *apentis*, fr.
apent, pp. of *apendre, appendre* to attach, hang against — more at AP-
PEND] (1530)   1 a : a shed or roof attached to and sloping from a wall
or building b : a smaller structure joined to a building : ANNEX   2 : a
structure or dwelling built on the roof of a building

pent·land·ite \'pent-lən-,dīt\ *n* [F, fr. Joseph *Pentland* †1873 Irish
scientist] (ca. 1858) : a bronzy yellow mineral that is an isometric
nickel iron sulfide and the principal ore of nickel
pen·to·bar·bi·tal \,pen-tə-'bär-bə-,tȯl\ *n* [*penta-* + *-o-* + *barbital*]
(1931) : a granular barbiturate $C_{11}H_{18}N_2O_3$ used esp. in the form of its
sodium or calcium salt as a sedative, hypnotic, and antispasmodic
pen·to·bar·bi·tone \-,tōn\ *n* [*penta-* + *-o-* + *barbitone*] (1938) *Brit*
: PENTOBARBITAL
pen·to·san \'pen-tə-,san\ *n* [ISV] (1892) : any of various polysaccharides that yield only pentoses on hydrolysis and occur widely in plants
pen·tose \'pen-,tōs, -,tōz\ *n* [ISV] (1890) : a monosaccharide $C_5H_{10}O_5$
(as ribose) that contains five carbon atoms in the molecule
Pen·to·thal \'pen-tə-,thȯl\ *trademark* — used for thiopental
pent·ox·ide \pent-'äk-,sīd\ *n* [ISV] (ca. 1872) : an oxide containing five
atoms of oxygen in the molecule
pent·ste·mon *var of* PENSTEMON
pen·tyl·ene·tet·ra·zol \,pen-t³l-,ēn-'te-trə-,zȯl, -,zōl\ *n* [*penta-* + *methylene* + *tetrazole* (CH_2N_4)] (1949) : an analeptic drug $C_6H_{10}N_4$
pe·nu·che \pə-'nü-chē\ *n* [MexSp *panocha* raw sugar, fr. Sp, ear of
maize, ultim. fr. L *panicula* panicle — more at PANICLE] (1871) : fudge
made usu. of brown sugar, butter, cream or milk, and nuts
pe·nult \'pē-,nəlt, pi-'\ *n* [L *paenultima* penult, fr. fem. of *paenultimus*
almost last, fr. *paene* almost + *ultimus* last — more at ULTIMATE]
(1537) : the next to the last member of a series; *esp* : the next to the
last syllable of a word
pen·ul·ti·ma \pi-'nəl-tə-mə\ *n* [L] (1589) : PENULT
pen·ul·ti·mate \pi-'nəl-tə-mət\ *adj* (1677)   1 : next to the last (the ∼
chapter of a book)   2 : of or relating to a penult ⟨a ∼ accent⟩ — **pen-
ul·ti·mate·ly** *adv*
pen·um·bra \pə-'nəm-brə\ *n, pl* **-brae** \-(,)brē, -,brī\ *or* **-bras** [NL, fr.
L *paene* almost + *umbra* shadow — more at UMBRAGE] (1666)   1 a
: a space of partial illumination (as in an eclipse) between the perfect
shadow on all sides and the full light b : a shaded region surrounding
the dark central portion of a sunspot   2 : a surrounding or adjoining
region in which something exists in a lesser degree : FRINGE   3 : a body
of rights held to be guaranteed by implication in a civil constitution —
pen·um·bral \-brəl\ *adj*
pe·nu·ri·ous \pə-'nür-ē-əs, -'nyùr-\ *adj* (1590)   1 : marked by or suffering from penury   2 : given to or marked by extreme stinting frugality   *syn* see STINGY — **pe·nu·ri·ous·ly** *adv* — **pe·nu·ri·ous·ness** *n*
pen·u·ry \'pen-yə-rē\ *n* [ME, fr. L *penuria, paenuria* want; perh. akin to
L *paene* almost] (14c)   1 : a cramping and oppressive lack of resources
(as money); *esp* : severe poverty   2 : extreme and often niggardly frugality   *syn* see POVERTY
pe·on \'pē-,än, -ən *also* pā-'ōn *for* 2, *Brit also* 'pyün *for* 1\ *n, pl* **peons** *or*
pe·o·nes \pā-'ō-nēz\ [Pg *peão* & F *pion*, fr. ML *pedon-, pedo* foot soldier — more at PAWN] (1826)   1 : any of various workers in India, Sri
Lanka, or Malaysia: as a : INFANTRYMAN b : ORDERLY   2 [Sp *peón*,
fr. L *pedon-, pedo*] : a member of the landless laboring class in Spanish
America   3 *pl peons* a : a person held in compulsory servitude to a
master for the working out of an indebtedness b : DRUDGE, MENIAL
pe·on·age \'pē-ə-nij\ *n* (1844)   1 a : the use of laborers bound in
servitude because of debt b : a system of convict labor by which convicts are leased to contractors   2 : the condition of a peon
pe·o·ny \'pē-ə-nē\ *n, pl* **-nies** [ME *piony*, fr. MF *pioine*, fr. L *paeonia*, fr.
Gk *paiōnia*, fr. *Paiōn* Paeon, physician of the gods] (14c) : any of a
genus (*Paeonia* of the family Paeoniaceae) of chiefly Eurasian plants
with large often double flowers
¹**peo·ple** \'pē-pəl\ *n, pl* **people** [ME *peple*, fr. OF *peuple*, fr. L *populus*]
(13c)   1 *pl* : human beings making up a group or assembly or linked
by a common interest   2 *pl* : HUMAN BEINGS. PERSONS — often used in
compounds instead of *persons* ⟨sales*people*⟩   3 *pl* : the members of a
family or kinship   4 *pl* : the mass of a community as distinguished
from a special class ⟨disputes between the ∼ and the nobles⟩ — often
used by Communists to distinguish Communists from other people   5
pl **peoples** : a body of persons that are united by a common culture,
tradition, or sense of kinship, that typically have common language,
institutions, and beliefs, and that often constitute a politically organized group   6 : lower animals usu. of a specified kind or situation ∼
: the body of enfranchised citizens of a state — **peo·ple·less** \-pəl-
ləs\ *adj*
²**people** *vt* **peo·pled; peo·pling** \-p(ə-)liŋ\ [MF *peupler*, fr. OF, fr.
peuple] (15c)   1 : to supply or fill with people   2 : to dwell in : IN-
HABIT
peo·ple·hood \'pē-pəl-,hůd\ *n* (ca. 1899)   1 : the quality or state of
constituting a people   2 : the awareness of the underlying unity that
makes the individual a part of a people
people mover *n* (1968) : any of various rapid-transit systems (as of
moving sidewalks or automated driverless cars) for shuttling people
¹**pep** \'pep\ *n* [short for *pepper*] (1912) : brisk energy or initiative and
high spirits
²**pep** *vt* **pepped; pep·ping** (1925) : to inject pep into ⟨∼ him up⟩
pep·er·o·mia \,pe-pə-'rō-mē-ə\ *n* [NL, fr. Gk *peperi* pepper + *homoios*
like, similar — more at HOMEO.] (1882) : any of a genus (*Peperomia*) of
fleshy tropical herbs of the pepper family often cultivated for their
showy foliage
pep·los \'pe-pləs, -,pläs\ *also* **pep·lus** \-pləs\ *n* [L *peplus*, fr. Gk *peplos*]
(1776) : a garment worn like a shawl by women of
ancient Greece
pep·lum \-pləm\ *n* [L, fr. Gk *peplon* peplos] (1866)
: a short section attached to the waistline of a blouse,
jacket, or dress — **pep·lumed** \-pləmd\ *adj*
pe·po \'pē-(,)pō\ *n, pl* **pepos** [L, a melon — more at
PUMPKIN] (ca. 1859) : an indehiscent fleshy 1-celled
or falsely 3-celled many-seeded berry (as a pumpkin,
squash, melon, or cucumber) that has a hard rind and
is the characteristic fruit of the gourd family
¹**pep·per** \'pe-pər\ *n* [ME *peper*, fr. OE *pipor*, fr. L
piper, fr. Gk *peperi*] (bef. 12c)   1 a : either of two
pungent products from the fruit of an East Indian
plant that are used as a condiment, carminative, or
stimulant: (1) : BLACK PEPPER (2) : WHITE PEPPER b
: any of a genus (*Piper* of the family Piperaceae, the
pepper family) of tropical mostly jointed climbing

peplum

shrubs with aromatic leaves; *esp* : a woody vine (*P. nigrum*) with spicate flowers that is widely cultivated in the tropics for its red berries from which black pepper and white pepper are prepared **2 a** : any of several products similar to pepper that are obtained from close relatives of the pepper plant **b** : any of various pungent condiments obtained from plants of other genera than that of the pepper **3 a** : CAPSICUM 1; *esp* : a New World capsicum (*Capsicum annuum*) whose fruits are hot peppers or sweet peppers **b** : the fruit of a pepper that is usu. red or yellow when ripe — **pepper** *adj*

²**pepper** *vt* **pep·pered; pep·per·ing** \'pe-p(ə-)riŋ\ (1538) **1 a** : to sprinkle, season, or cover with or as if with pepper **b** : to shower with or as if with shot or other missiles **2** : to hit with rapid repeated blows **3** : to sprinkle as if with pepper ⟨~ed the report with statistics⟩ — **pep·per·er** \-pər-ər\ *n*

pep·per-and—salt \,pe-pər-(-ə)n(d)-'sȯlt\ *adj* (1774) : SALT-AND-PEPPER

pep·per·box \'pe-pər-,bäks\ *n* (1546) **1** : a small usu. cylindrical box or bottle with a perforated top used for sprinkling ground pepper on food **2** : a pistol of the late 18th century with five or six revolving barrels

pep·per·corn \-,kȯrn\ *n* (bef. 12c) : a dried berry of the black pepper

peppered moth *n* (ca. 1832) : a European geometrid moth (*Biston betularia*) that typically has white wings with small black specks but also occurs as a solid black form esp. in areas where the air is heavily polluted by industry

pep·per·grass \'pe-pər-,gras\ *n* (15c) : any of a genus (*Lepidium*) of cresses; *esp* : GARDEN CRESS

pepper mill *n* (ca. 1858) : a hand mill for grinding peppercorns

pep·per·mint \-,mint, -mənt, *in rapid speech* 'pep-mənt *or* -'m-ənt\ *n* (1696) **1 a** : a pungent and aromatic mint (*Mentha piperita*) with dark green lanceolate leaves and whorls of small pink flowers in spikes **b** : any of several mints (as *M. arvensis*) that are related to the peppermint **2** : candy flavored with peppermint — **pep·per·minty** \'pe-pər-,min-tē\ *adj*

pep·per·o·ni \,pe-pə-'rō-nē\ *n* [It *peperoni* cayenne peppers, pl. of *peperone*, aug. of *pepe* pepper, fr. L *piper* — more at PEPPER] (1921) : a highly seasoned beef and pork sausage

pepper pot *n* (1679) **1** *Brit* : PEPPERBOX 1 **2 a** : a highly seasoned West Indian stew of vegetables and meat or fish **b** : a thick soup of tripe, meat, dumplings, and vegetables highly seasoned esp. with crushed peppercorns — called also *Philadelphia pepper pot*

pepper shaker *n* (1895) : a container with a perforated top for sprinkling pepper

pep·per·tree \'pe-pər-,trē\ *n* (ca. 1692) : a Peruvian evergreen tree (*Schinus molle*) of the cashew family grown as a shade tree in mild regions

pep·pery \'pe-p(ə-)rē\ *adj* (1699) **1** : of, relating to, or having the qualities of pepper : HOT, PUNGENT ⟨a ~ taste⟩ **2** : having a hot temper : TOUCHY ⟨a ~ boss⟩ **3** : FIERY, STINGING ⟨a ~ satire⟩ — **pep·per·i·ness** \-nəs\ *n*

pep pill *n* (1937) : any of various stimulant drugs in pill or tablet form

pep·py \'pe-pē\ *adj* **pep·pi·er; -est** (ca. 1918) : full of pep — **pep·pi·ness** *n*

pep·sin \'pep-sən\ *n* [G, fr. Gk *pepsis* digestion, fr. *pessein*] (ca. 1844) **1** : a protease of the stomach that breaks down most proteins to polypeptides **2** : a preparation containing pepsin that is obtained from the stomach esp. of the hog and is used esp. as a digestive

pep·sin·o·gen \pep-'si-nə-jən\ *n* [ISV] (1878) : a granular zymogen of the gastric glands that is readily converted into pepsin in a slightly acid medium

pep talk *n* (1925) : a usu. brief, intense, and emotional talk designed to influence or encourage an audience

pep·tic \'pep-tik\ *adj* [L *pepticus*, fr. Gk *peptikos*, fr. *peptos* cooked, fr. *peptein, pessein* to cook, digest — more at COOK] (1651) **1** : relating to or promoting digestion : DIGESTIVE **2** : of, relating to, producing, or caused by pepsin ⟨~ digestion⟩ **3** : connected with or resulting from the action of digestive juices ⟨a ~ ulcer⟩

pep·ti·dase \'pep-tə-,dās, -,dāz\ *n* (1918) : an enzyme that hydrolyzes simple peptides or their derivatives

pep·tide \'pep-,tīd\ *n* [ISV, fr. *peptone*] (1906) : any of various amides that are derived from two or more amino acids by combination of the amino group of one acid with the carboxyl group of another and are usu. obtained by partial hydrolysis of proteins — **pep·tid·ic** \pep-'ti-dik\ *adj*

peptide bond *n* (1935) : the chemical bond between carbon and nitrogen in a peptide linkage

peptide linkage *n* (1925) : the bivalent group CONH that unites the amino acid residues in a peptide

pep·ti·do·gly·can \,pep-tə-dō-'glī-,kan\ *n* (1966) : a polymer that is composed of polysaccharide and peptide chains and is found esp. in bacterial cell walls — called also *mucopeptide, murein*

pep·tone \'pep-,tōn\ *n* [G *Pepton*, fr. Gk, neut. of *peptos* cooked] (1860) : any of various water-soluble products of partial hydrolysis of proteins

Pe·quot \'pē-,kwät\ *n* [Narraganset *Pequttôog*] (1631) : a member of an American Indian people of what is now eastern Connecticut

¹**per** \'pər\ *prep* [L, through, by means of, by — more at FOR] (14c) **1** : by the means or agency of : THROUGH ⟨~ bearer⟩ **2** : with respect to every member of a specified group : for each **3** : according to — often used with *as* ⟨~ instructions⟩ ⟨as ~ usual⟩

usage *Per* occurs most frequently in business contexts; its use outside such contexts is often criticized but is quite widespread, esp. in sense 2. Its most common and natural nonbusiness uses always involve figures, usu. in relation to price ⟨$150 *per* performance⟩, automobiles ⟨32 miles *per* gallon⟩ ⟨55 miles *per* hour⟩, or sports ⟨averages 15 points and 9 rebounds *per* game⟩.

²**per** *adv* (1899) : for each : APIECE ⟨a bargain at $3.50 ~⟩

per- *prefix* [L, through, throughout, thoroughly, detrimental to, fr. *per*] **1** : throughout : thoroughly ⟨*peruse*⟩ **2 a** : containing the largest possible or a relatively large proportion of a (specified) chemical element ⟨*perchloroethylene*⟩ **b** : containing an element in its highest or a high oxidation state ⟨*perchloric acid*⟩

¹**per·ad·ven·ture** \'pər-əd-,ven-chər, 'per-; ,pər-əd-'\ *adv* [ME *per aventure*, fr. OF, by chance] (14c) *archaic* : PERHAPS, POSSIBLY

²**peradventure** *n* (1627) **1** : DOUBT ⟨a fact established beyond ~⟩ **2** : CHANCE 4a ⟨beyond ~ of doubt⟩

per·am·bu·late \pə-'ram-byə-,lāt\ *vb* **-lat·ed; -lat·ing** [L *perambulatus*, pp. of *perambulare*, fr. *per-* through + *ambulare* to walk] *vt* (1568) **1** : to travel over or through esp. on foot : TRAVERSE **2** : to make an official inspection of (a boundary) on foot ~ *vi* : STROLL — **per·am·bu·la·tion** \-,ram-byə-'lā-shən\ *n* — **per·am·bu·la·to·ry** \-'ram-byə-lə-,tōr-ē, -,tȯr-\ *adj*

per·am·bu·la·tor \pə-'ram-byə-,lā-tər, *for 2 also* 'pram-\ *n* (1611) **1** : one that perambulates **2** *chiefly Brit* : a baby carriage

per an·num \(,)pər-'a-nəm\ *adv* [ML] (1536) : in or for each year

per·bo·rate \(,)pər-'bōr-,āt, -'bȯr-\ *n* [ISV] (1881) : a salt that is a compound of a borate with hydrogen peroxide

per·cale \(,)pər-'kā(ə)l, 'pər-,; (,)pər-'kal\ *n* [Per *pargālah*] (1840) : a fine closely woven cotton cloth variously finished for clothing, sheeting, and industrial uses

per·ca·line \,pər-kə-'lēn\ *n* [F, fr. *percale*] (ca. 1858) : a lightweight cotton fabric; *esp* : a glossy fabric used for bookbindings

per cap·i·ta \(,)pər-'ka-pə-tə\ *adv or adj* [ML, by heads] (1682) **1** : equally to each individual **2** : per unit of population : by or for each person ⟨the highest income *per capita* of any state in the union⟩

per·ceive \pər-'sēv\ *vt* **per·ceived; per·ceiv·ing** [ME, fr. MF *perceivre*, fr. L *percipere*, fr. *per-* thoroughly + *capere* to take — more at HEAVE] (14c) **1 a** : to attain awareness or understanding of **b** : to regard as being such ⟨*perceived* threats⟩ ⟨was *perceived* as a loser⟩ **2** : to become aware of through the senses; *esp* : SEE, OBSERVE — **per·ceiv·able** \-'sē-və-bəl\ *adj* — **per·ceiv·ably** \-blē\ *adv* — **per·ceiv·er** *n*

¹**per·cent** \pər-'sent\ *adv* [earlier *per cent*, fr. *per* + L *centum* hundred — more at HUNDRED] (1568) : in the hundred : of each hundred

²**percent** *n, pl* **percent** *or* **percents** (1667) **1** *pl* **percent** : one part in a hundred : PERCENTAGE ⟨a large ~ of his income⟩ **2** **percents** *pl, Brit* : securities bearing a specified rate of interest

³**percent** *adj* (1888) **1** : reckoned on the basis of a whole divided into one hundred parts **2** : paying interest at a specified percent

per·cent·age \pər-'sen-tij\ *n* (ca. 1789) **1 a** : a part of a whole expressed in hundredths **b** : the result obtained by multiplying a number by a percent **2 a** : a share of winnings or profits **b** : ADVANTAGE, PROFIT ⟨no ~ in going around looking like an old sack of laundry —Wallace Stegner⟩ **3** : an indeterminate part : PROPORTION **4 a** : PROBABILITY **b** : favorable odds

per·cen·tile \pər-'sen-,tīl\ *n* (1885) : a value on a scale of one hundred that indicates the percent of a distribution that is equal to or below it ⟨a score in the 95th ~⟩

per cen·tum \pər-'sen-təm\ *n* [*per* + L *centum*] (ca. 1565) : PERCENT

per·cept \'pər-,sept\ *n* [back-formation fr. *perception*] (1837) : an impression of an object obtained by use of the senses : SENSE-DATUM

per·cep·ti·ble \pər-'sep-tə-bəl\ *adj* (1603) : capable of being perceived esp. by the senses ⟨a ~ change in her tone⟩ ⟨the light became increasingly ~⟩ — **per·cep·ti·bil·i·ty** \-,sep-tə-'bi-lə-tē\ *n* — **per·cep·ti·bly** \-blē\ *adv*

syn PERCEPTIBLE, SENSIBLE, PALPABLE, TANGIBLE, APPRECIABLE, PONDERABLE mean apprehensible as real or existent. PERCEPTIBLE applies to what can be discerned by the senses often to a minimal extent ⟨a *perceptible* difference in sound to a careful listener⟩. SENSIBLE applies to whatever is clearly apprehended through the senses or impresses itself strongly on the mind ⟨an abrupt, *sensible* drop in temperature⟩. PALPABLE applies either to what has physical substance or to what is obvious and unmistakable ⟨the tension in the air was almost *palpable*⟩. TANGIBLE suggests what is capable of being handled or grasped both physically and mentally ⟨no *tangible* evidence of UFOs⟩. APPRECIABLE applies to what is distinctly discernible by the senses or definitely measurable ⟨an *appreciable* increase in income⟩. PONDERABLE suggests having definitely measurable weight or importance ⟨exerted a *ponderable* influence on world events⟩.

per·cep·tion \pər-'sep-shən\ *n* [L *perception-, perceptio* act of perceiving, fr. *percipere*] (14c) **1 a** : a result of perceiving : OBSERVATION **b** : a mental image : CONCEPT **2** *obs* : CONSCIOUSNESS **3 a** : awareness of the elements of environment through physical sensation ⟨color ~⟩ **b** : physical sensation interpreted in the light of experience **4 a** : a quick, acute, and intuitive cognition : APPRECIATION **b** : capacity for comprehension **syn** see DISCERNMENT — **per·cep·tion·al** \-shnəl, -shə-n³l\ *adj*

per·cep·tive \pər-'sep-tiv\ *adj* (1656) **1** : responsive to sensory stimuli : DISCERNING ⟨a ~ eye⟩ **2 a** : capable of or exhibiting keen perception : OBSERVANT ⟨a ~ scholar⟩ **b** : characterized by sympathetic understanding or insight ⟨a ~ critic⟩ — **per·cep·tive·ly** *adv* — **per·cep·tive·ness** *n* — **per·cep·tiv·i·ty** \(,)pər-,sep-'ti-və-tē\ *n*

per·cep·tu·al \(,)pər-'sep-chə-wəl, -chəl, -shwəl\ *adj* [*percept* + *-ual* (as in *conceptual*)] (1878) : of, relating to, or involving perception esp. in relation to immediate sensory experience — **per·cep·tu·al·ly** *adv*

Per·ce·val \'pər-sə-vəl\ *n* [OF] : a knight of King Arthur who wins a sight of the Holy Grail

¹**perch** \'pərch\ *n* [ME *perche*, fr. MF, fr. L *pertica* pole] (14c) **1 a** : a bar or peg on which something is hung **2 a** : a roost for a bird **b** : a resting place or vantage point : SEAT **c** : a prominent position ⟨his new ~ as president⟩ **3** *chiefly Brit* : ROD 2

²**perch** *vi* (14c) : to alight, settle, or rest on a perch, a height, or a precarious spot ~ *vt* : to place on a perch, a height, or a precarious spot

³**perch** *n, pl* **perch** *or* **perch·es** [ME *perche*, fr. MF, fr. L *perca*, fr. Gk *perkē*; akin to OHG *faro* colored, L *porcus*, a spiny fish] (14c) **1 a** : a small European freshwater bony fish (*Perca fluviatilis* of the family Percidae, the perch family) **b** : YELLOW PERCH **2** : any of numerous bony fishes (as of the families Percidae, Centrarchidae, and Serranidae)

per·chance \pər-'chan(t)s\ *adv* [ME *per chance*, fr. MF, by chance] (14c) : PERHAPS, POSSIBLY

\ə\ abut \ᵊ\ kitten, F table \ər\ further \a\ ash \ā\ ace \ä\ mop, mar \au̇\ out \ch\ chin \e\ bet \ē\ easy \g\ go \i\ hit \ī\ ice \j\ job \ŋ\ sing \ō\ go \ȯ\ law \ȯi\ boy \th\ thin \t͟h\ the \ü\ loot \u̇\ foot \y\ yet \zh\ vision \ä, k̶, ⁿ, œ, œ̄, ᵫ, ᵫ̄, ᵊ\ *see* Guide to Pronunciation

Per·che·ron \'pər-chə-ˌrän, -shə-\ n [F] (1875) : any of a breed of powerful rugged draft horses that originated in the Perche region of France

per·chlo·rate \(ˌ)pər-'klōr-ˌāt, -'klȯr-, -ət\ n [ISV] (1826) : a salt or ester of perchloric acid

per·chlo·ric acid \(ˌ)pər-'klōr-ik-, -'klȯr-\ n (1818) : a fuming corrosive strong acid HClO₄ that is the most highly oxidized acid of chlorine and a powerful oxidizing agent when heated

per·chlo·ro·eth·y·lene \(ˌ)pər-ˌklȯr-ō-'e-thə-ˌlēn, -ˌklȯr-\ n (1873) : a colorless nonflammable liquid C₂Cl₄ used often as a solvent in dry cleaning and for removal of grease from metals

Percheron

per·cip·i·ence \pər-'si-pē-ən(t)s\ n (ca. 1774) : PERCEPTION 4

¹per·cip·i·ent \-ənt\ n [L percipient-, percipiens, prp. of percipere to perceive] (1662) **1** : one that perceives **2** : a person on whose mind a telepathic impulse or message is held to fall

²percipient adj (1692) : capable of or characterized by perception : DISCERNING — **per·cip·i·ent·ly** adv

per·co·late \'pər-kə-ˌlāt, ÷-kyə-\ vb **-lat·ed; -lat·ing** [L percolatus, pp. of percolare, fr. per- through + colare to sieve — more at PER-, COLANDER] vt (1626) **1 a** : to cause (a solvent) to pass through a permeable substance (as a powdered drug) esp. for extracting a soluble constituent **b** : to prepare (coffee) in a percolator **2** : to be diffused through : PENETRATE ∼ vi **1** : to ooze or trickle through a permeable substance : SEEP **2 a** : to become percolated **b** : to become lively or effervescent **3** : to spread gradually ⟨allow the sunlight to ∼ into our rooms —Norman Douglas⟩ **4** : SIMMER 2a — **per·co·la·tion** \ˌpər-kə-'lā-shən\ n

per·co·la·tor \'pər-kə-ˌlā-tər, ÷-kyə-\ n (ca. 1842) : one that percolates; specif : a coffeepot in which boiling water rising through a tube is repeatedly deflected downward through a perforated basket containing ground coffee beans to extract their essence

per con·tra \(ˌ)per-'kän-trə\ adv [It, by the opposite side (of the ledger)] (1554) **1 a** : on the contrary **b** : by way of contrast **2** : as an offset

per cu·ri·am decision \(ˌ)pər-'kyür-ē-ˌäm-, -'kür-\ n [ML per curiam, lit., by the court] (1927) : a very brief usu. unanimous decision of a court rendered without elaborate discussion

per·cuss \pər-'kəs\ vt [L percussus, pp. of percutere] (1560) : to tap sharply; esp : to practice percussion on

per·cus·sion \pər-'kə-shən\ n [ME, fr. L percussion-, percussio, fr. percutere to beat, fr. per- thoroughly + quatere to shake] (15c) **1** : the act of percussing: as **a** : the striking of a percussion cap so as to set off the charge in a firearm **b** : the beating or striking of a musical instrument **c** : the act or technique of tapping the surface of a body part to learn the condition of the parts beneath by the resultant sound **2** : the striking of sound on the ear **3** : percussion instruments that form a section of a band or orchestra — **percussion** adj

percussion cap n (1823) : CAP 5

percussion instrument n (1872) : a musical instrument (as a drum, xylophone, or maraca) sounded by striking, shaking, or scraping

per·cus·sion·ist \pər-'kə-sh(ə-)nist\ n (1939) : one skilled in the playing of percussion instruments

per·cus·sive \pər-'kə-siv\ adj (1793) **1** : of or relating to percussion; esp : operative or operated by striking **2** : having powerful impact — **per·cus·sive·ly** adv — **per·cus·sive·ness** n

per·cu·ta·ne·ous \ˌpər-kyü-'tā-nē-əs\ adj (1887) : effected or performed through the skin — **per·cu·ta·ne·ous·ly** adv

per·die \(ˌ)pər-'dē, per-\ var of PARDIE

¹per di·em \(ˌ)pər-'dē-əm, -'dī-\ adv [ML] (1520) : by the day : for each day

²per diem adj (1809) **1** : based on use or service by the day : DAILY **2** : paid by the day

³per diem n, pl **per diems** (1812) **1** : a daily allowance **2** : a daily fee

per·di·tion \pər-'di-shən\ n [ME perdicion, fr. LL perdition-, perditio, fr. L perdere to destroy, fr. per- through + dare to give — more at PER-, DATE] (14c) **1** archaic : utter destruction **b** obs : LOSS **2 a** : eternal damnation **b** : HELL

¹per·du or **per·due** \'pər-(ˌ)dü, -(ˌ)dyü; (ˌ)pər-'\ n [F sentinelle perdue, lit., lost sentinel] (1605) obs : a soldier assigned to extremely hazardous duty

²per·du or **per·due** \per-dǖ\ adj [F perdu, masc., & perdue, fem., fr. pp. of perdre to lose, fr. L perdere] (1624) : remaining out of sight

per·du·ra·ble \(ˌ)pər-'dür-ə-bəl, -'dyür-; 'pər-jə-rə-\ adj [ME, fr. MF, fr. LL perdurabilis, fr. L perdurare to endure, fr. per- throughout + durare to last — more at DURING] (14c) : very durable — **per·du·ra·bil·i·ty** \(ˌ)pər-ˌdür-ə-'bil-ət-ē, -ˌdyür-; ˌpər-jə-rə-\ n — **per·du·ra·bly** \(ˌ)pər-'dür-ə-blē, -'dyür-; 'pər-jə-rə-\ adv

per·dure \(ˌ)pər-'dür, -'dyür\ vi **per·dured; per·dur·ing** [ME, fr. L perdurare] (15c) : to continue to exist : LAST

per·e·gri·nate \'per-ə-grə-ˌnāt\ vb **-nat·ed; -nat·ing** vi (1593) : to travel esp. on foot : WALK ∼ vt : to walk or travel over : TRAVERSE — **per·e·gri·na·tion** \ˌper-ə-grə-'nā-shən\ n

¹per·e·grine \'per-ə-grən, -ˌgrēn\ adj [ME, fr. ML peregrinus, fr. L, foreign — more at PILGRIM] (14c) : having a tendency to wander

²peregrine n (1555) : a swift nearly cosmopolitan falcon (Falco peregrinus) that is much used in falconry — called also peregrine falcon

pe·re·i·on \pə-'rī-ən\ or **pe·re·on** \-'rē-\ n [NL, fr. Gk peraiōn, prp. of peraioun to transport, fr. peraios situated beyond, fr. pera beyond; akin to Gk poros passage — more at FARE] (1855) : the thorax or the seven metameres comprising the thorax of some crustaceans (as a decapod)

pe·re·io·pod \pə-'rī-ə-ˌpäd\ or **pe·reo·pod** \-'rē-\ n [NL perion + E -pod] (1893) : an appendage of the pereion

pe·remp·to·ry \pə-'rem(p)-t(ə-)rē\ adj [LL & L; LL peremptorius, fr. L, destructive, fr. perimere to take entirely, destroy, fr. per- thoroughly + emere to take — more at REDEEM] (15c) **1 a** : putting an end to or

precluding a right of action, debate, or delay ⟨a ∼ mandamus⟩ **b** : admitting of no contradiction ⟨a ∼ conclusion based on absolute evidence⟩ **2** : expressive of urgency or command ⟨a ∼ call⟩ **3 a** : characterized by often imperious or arrogant self-assurance ⟨how insolent of late he is become, how proud, how ∼ —Shak.⟩ **b** : indicative of a peremptory attitude or nature : HAUGHTY ⟨a ∼ tone⟩ ⟨∼ disregard of an objection⟩ **syn** see MASTERFUL — **pe·remp·to·ri·ly** \-'rem(p)-t(ə-)rə-lē; -ˌrem(p)-'tōr-ə-lē, -'tȯr-\ adv — **pe·remp·to·ri·ness** \-'rem(p)-t(ə-)rē-nəs\ n

peremptory challenge n (ca. 1531) : a challenge (as of a juror) made as of right without assigning any cause

pe·ren·nate \'per-ə-ˌnāt, pə-'re-ˌnāt\ vi **-nat·ed; -nat·ing** [L perennatus, pp. of perennare, fr. perennis] (ca. 1623) : to live over from season to season ⟨a perennating rhizome⟩ — **per·en·na·tion** \ˌper-ə-'nā-shən\ n

pe·ren·ni·al \pə-'re-nē-əl\ adj [L perennis, fr. per- throughout + annus year — more at PER-, ANNUAL] (1644) **1** : present at all seasons of the year **2** : persisting for several years usu. with new herbaceous growth from a perennating part ⟨∼ asters⟩ **3 a** : PERSISTENT, ENDURING ⟨∼ traditions⟩ **b** : continuing without interruption : CONSTANT, PERPETUAL ⟨the ∼ quest for certainty⟩ ⟨a ∼ student⟩ **c** : regularly repeated or renewed : RECURRENT ⟨death is a ∼ literary theme⟩ **syn** see CONTINUAL — **perennial** n — **pe·ren·ni·al·ly** \-nē-ə-lē\ adv

per·e·stroi·ka \ˌper-ə-'strȯi-kə\ n [Russ perestroĭka, lit., restructuring] (1986) : the policy of economic and governmental reform instituted by Mikhail Gorbachev in the Soviet Union during the mid-1980s

¹per·fect \'pər-fikt\ adj [ME parfit, fr. OF, fr. L perfectus, fr. pp. of perficere to carry out, perfect, fr. per- thoroughly + facere to make, do — more at DO] (14c) **1 a** : being entirely without fault or defect : FLAWLESS ⟨a ∼ diamond⟩ **b** : satisfying all requirements : ACCURATE **c** : corresponding to an ideal standard or abstract concept ⟨a ∼ gentleman⟩ **d** : faithfully reproducing the original; specif : LETTER-PERFECT **e** : legally valid **2** : EXPERT, PROFICIENT ⟨practice makes ∼⟩ **3 a** : PURE, TOTAL **b** : lacking in no essential detail : COMPLETE **c** obs : SANE **d** : ABSOLUTE, UNEQUIVOCAL ⟨enjoys ∼ happiness⟩ **e** : of an extreme kind : UNMITIGATED ⟨a ∼ brat⟩ ⟨an act of ∼ foolishness⟩ **4** obs : MATURE **5** : of, relating to, or constituting a verb form or verbal that expresses an action or state completed at the time of speaking or at a time spoken of **6** obs : CERTAIN, SURE **b** : CONTENTED, SATISFIED **7** of a musical interval : belonging to the consonances unison, fourth, fifth, and octave which retain their character when inverted and when raised or lowered by a half step become augmented or diminished **8 a** : sexually mature and fully differentiated ⟨a ∼ insect⟩ **b** : having both stamens and pistils in the same flower ⟨a ∼ flower⟩ — **per·fect·ness** \-fik(t)-nəs\ n

syn PERFECT, WHOLE, ENTIRE, INTACT mean not lacking or faulty in any particular. PERFECT implies the soundness and the excellence of every part, element, or quality of a thing frequently as an unattainable or theoretical state ⟨a perfect set of teeth⟩. WHOLE suggests a completeness or perfection that can be sought, gained, or regained ⟨felt like a whole person again after vacation⟩. ENTIRE implies perfection deriving from integrity, soundness, or completeness of a thing ⟨the entire Beethoven corpus⟩. INTACT implies retention of perfection of a thing in its natural or original state ⟨the boat survived the storm intact⟩.

²per·fect \pər-'fekt also 'pər-fikt\ vt (14c) **1** : to bring to final form **2** : to make perfect : IMPROVE, REFINE — **per·fect·er** n

³per·fect \'pər-fikt\ n (1841) : the perfect tense of a language; also : a verb form in the perfect tense

per·fec·ta \pər-'fek-tə\ n [AmerSp quiniela perfecta perfect quiniela] (1967) : a bet in which the bettor picks the first and second place finishers in order — compare QUINIELA, TRIFECTA

perfect binding n (1926) : a book binding in which a layer of adhesive holds the pages and cover together — **per·fect–bound** \'pər-fik(t)-'baünd\ adj

perfect game n (ca. 1949) : a baseball game in which a pitcher allows no hits, no runs, and no opposing batter to reach first base

per·fect·ible \pər-'fek-tə-bəl also 'pər-fik-\ adj (1635) : capable of improvement or perfection — **per·fect·ibil·i·ty** \pər-ˌfek-tə-'bi-lə-tē also ˌpər-fik-\ n

per·fec·tion \pər-'fek-shən\ n [ME perfeccioun, fr. OF perfection, fr. L perfection-, perfectio, fr. perficere] (13c) **1** : the quality or state of being perfect: as **a** : freedom from fault or defect : FLAWLESSNESS **b** : MATURITY **c** : the quality or state of being saintly **2 a** : an exemplification of supreme excellence **b** : an unsurpassable degree of accuracy or excellence **3** : the act or process of perfecting

per·fec·tion·ism \-shə-ˌni-zəm\ n (ca. 1846) **1 a** : the doctrine that the perfection of moral character constitutes a person's highest good **b** : the theological doctrine that a state of freedom from sin is attainable on earth **2** : a disposition to regard anything short of perfection as unacceptable — **per·fec·tion·ist** \-sh(ə-)nist\ n or adj — **per·fec·tion·is·tic** \-ˌfek-shə-'nis-tik\ adj

per·fec·tive \pər-'fek-tiv also 'pər-fik-\ adj (1596) **1** archaic : tending to make perfect **b** : becoming better **2** : expressing action as complete or as implying the notion of completion, conclusion, or result ⟨∼ verb⟩ — **perfective** n — **per·fec·tive·ly** adv — **per·fec·tive·ness** n — **per·fec·tiv·i·ty** \pər-ˌfek-'ti-və-tē also ˌpər-fik-\ n

per·fect·ly \'pər-fik(t)-lē\ adv (14c) **1** : in a perfect manner **2** : to a complete or adequate extent : QUITE ⟨was ∼ happy until now⟩

perfect number n (14c) : an integer (as 6 or 28) the sum of whose integral factors including 1 but excluding itself is equal to itself

perfect participle n (1862) : PAST PARTICIPLE

perfect pitch n (1949) : ABSOLUTE PITCH 2

perfect square n (1856) : an integer (as 9 or 36) whose square root is an integer

per·fer·vid \(ˌ)pər-'fər-vəd, 'pər-\ adj [NL perfervidus, fr. L per- thoroughly + fervidus fervid] (1856) : marked by overwrought or exaggerated emotion : excessively fervent **syn** see IMPASSIONED

per·fid·i·ous \(ˌ)pər-'fi-dē-əs\ adj (1598) : of, relating to, or characterized by perfidy **syn** see FAITHLESS — **per·fid·i·ous·ly** adv — **per·fid·i·ous·ness** n

per·fi·dy \'pər-fə-dē\ *n, pl* **-dies** [L *perfidia*, fr. *perfidus* faithless, fr. *per-* detrimental to + *fides* faith — more at PER-, FAITH] (1592) **1** : the quality or state of being faithless or disloyal : TREACHERY **2** : an act or an instance of disloyalty

per·fo·li·ate \,pər-'fō-lē-ət, 'pər-\ *adj* [NL *perfoliata*, an herb having leaves pierced by the stem, fr. L *per* through + *foliata*, fem. of *foliatus* foliate] (1687) : having the basal part naturally united around the stem ⟨a ~ leaf of a honeysuckle⟩

per·fo·rate \'pər-fə-,rāt\ *vb* **-rat·ed; -rat·ing** [L *perforatus*, pp. of *perforare* to bore through, fr. *per-* through + *forare* to bore — more at BORE] *vt* (1538) **1** : to make a hole through ⟨an ulcer ~s the duodenal wall⟩; *esp* : to make a line of holes in to facilitate separation **2** : to pass through or into by or as if by making a hole ~ *vi* : to penetrate a surface — **per·fo·rate** \'pər-f(ə-)rət, -fə-,rāt\ *adj* — **per·fo·ra·tor** \-fə-,rā-tər\ *n*

per·fo·rat·ed \-fə-,rā-təd\ *adj* (1597) **1** : having a hole or perforations; *esp* : having a specified number of perforations in 20 millimeters ⟨the stamps are ~ 10⟩ **2** : characterized by perforation ⟨a ~ ulcer⟩

per·fo·ra·tion \,pər-fə-'rā-shən\ *n* (15c) **1** : the act or process of perforating **2 a** : a hole or pattern made by or as if by piercing or boring **b** : one of the series of holes between rows of postage stamps in a sheet that serve as an aid in separation

per·force \pər-'fōrs, -'fòrs\ *adv* [ME *par force*, fr. MF, by force] (14c) **1** *obs* : by physical coercion **2** : by force of circumstances

per·form \pə(r)-'fòrm\ *vb* [ME, fr. AF *performer*, alter. of OF *perfournir*, fr. *per-* thoroughly (fr. L) + *fournir* to complete — more at FUR-NISH] *vt* (14c) **1** : to adhere to the terms of : FULFILL ⟨~ a contract⟩ **2** : CARRY OUT, DO **3 a** : to do in a formal manner or according to prescribed ritual **b** : to give a rendition of : PRESENT ~ *vi* **1** : to carry out an action or pattern of behavior : ACT, FUNCTION **2** : to give a performance : PLAY — **per·form·abil·i·ty** \-,fòr-mə-'bi-lə-tē\ *n* — **per·form·able** \-'fòr-mə-bəl\ *adj* — **per·form·er** \-'fòr-mər\ *n*

syn PERFORM, EXECUTE, DISCHARGE, ACCOMPLISH, ACHIEVE, EFFECT, FUL-FILL mean to carry out or into effect. PERFORM implies action that follows established patterns or procedures or fulfills agreed-upon requirements and often connotes special skill ⟨*performed* gymnastics⟩. EXECUTE stresses the carrying out of what exists in plan or in intent ⟨*executed* the hit-and-run⟩. DISCHARGE implies execution and completion of appointed duties or tasks ⟨*discharged* his duties⟩. ACCOMPLISH stresses the successful completion of a process rather than the means of carrying it out ⟨*accomplished* everything they set out to do⟩. ACHIEVE adds to ACCOMPLISH the implication of conquered difficulties ⟨*achieve* greatness⟩. EFFECT adds to ACHIEVE an emphasis on the inherent force in the agent capable of surmounting obstacles ⟨*effected* sweeping reforms⟩. FULFILL implies a complete realization of ends or possibilities ⟨*fulfilled* their ambitions⟩.

per·for·mance \pə(r)-'fòr-mən(t)s\ *n* (15c) **1 a** : the execution of an action **b** : something accomplished : DEED, FEAT **2** : the fulfillment of a claim, promise, or request : IMPLEMENTATION **3 a** : the action of representing a character in a play **b** : a public presentation or exhibition ⟨a benefit ~⟩ **4 a** : the ability to perform : EFFICIENCY **b** : the manner in which a mechanism performs ⟨engine ~⟩ **5** : the manner of reacting to stimuli : BEHAVIOR **6** : the linguistic behavior of an individual : PAROLE; *also* : the ability to speak a certain language — compare COMPETENCE 3

performance art *n* (1971) : a nontraditional art form that consists of or features a performance by the artist — **performance artist** *n*

per·for·ma·tive \-'fòr-mə-tiv\ *adj* (1955) : being or relating to an expression that serves to effect a transaction or that constitutes the performance of the specified act by virtue of its utterance ⟨~ verbs such as *promise* and *congratulate*⟩ — compare CONSTATIVE — **performative** *n*

per·for·ma·to·ry \-mə-,tòr-ē, -,tòr-\ *adj* (1949) : PERFORMATIVE; *also* : of or relating to performance

performing *adj* (1889) : of, relating to, or constituting an art (as drama) that involves public performance ⟨the ~ arts⟩

¹per·fume \'pər-,fyüm, (,)pər-\ *n* [MF *perfum*, prob. fr. OProv. Fr. *perfumar* to perfume, fr. *per-* thoroughly (fr. L) + *fumar* to smoke, fr. L *fumare*, fr. *fumus* smoke — more at FUME] (1533) **1** : the scent of something sweet-smelling **2** : a substance that emits a pleasant odor; *esp* : a fluid preparation of natural essences (as from plants or animals) or synthetics and a fixative used for scenting **syn** see FRAGRANCE

²per·fume \(,)pər-'fyüm, 'pər-,\ *vt* **per·fumed; per·fum·ing** (1538) : to fill or imbue with an odor

per·fum·er \pə(r)-'fyü-mər, 'pər-,\ *n* (ca. 1580) : one that makes or sells perfumes

per·fum·ery \pə(r)-'fyü-mə-rē, -'fyüm-rē\ *n, pl* **-er·ies** (1800) **1 a** : the art or process of making perfume **b** : the products made by a perfumer **2** : an establishment where perfumes are made

per·func·to·ry \pər-'fəŋ(k)-t(ə-)rē\ *adj* [LL *perfunctorius*, fr. L *perfungi* to accomplish, get through with, fr. *per-* through + *fungi* to perform — more at PER-, FUNCTION] (1593) **1** : characterized by routine or superficiality : MECHANICAL ⟨a ~ smile⟩ **2** : lacking in interest or enthusiasm : INDIFFERENT — **per·func·to·ri·ly** \-t(ə-)rə-lē\ *adv* — **per·func·to·ri·ness** \-t(ə-)rē-nəs\ *n*

per·fus·ate \(,)pər-'fyü-,zāt, -zət\ *n* (1915) : a fluid (as a solution pumped through the heart) that is perfused

per·fuse \(,)pər-'fyüz\ *vt* **per·fused; per·fus·ing** [ME, fr. L *perfusus*, pp. of *perfundere* to pour over, fr. *per-* through + *fundere* to pour — more at FOUND] (15c) **1** : SUFFUSE **2 a** : to cause to flow or spread : DIFFUSE **b** : to force a fluid through (an organ or tissue) esp. by way of the blood vessels — **per·fu·sion** \-'fyü-zhən\ *n*

per·fu·sion·ist \(,)pər-'fyü-zhə-nist\ *n* (1964) : a certified medical technician responsible for extracorporeal oxygenation of the blood during open-heart surgery and for the operation and maintenance of equipment (as a heart-lung machine) controlling it

per·go·la \'pər-gə-lə, pər-'gō-\ *n* [It, fr. L *pergula*] (1675) **1** : ARBOR, TRELLIS **2** : a structure usu. consisting of parallel colonnades supporting an open roof of girders and cross rafters

¹per·haps \pər-'haps, 'praps\ *adv* [*per* + *hap*] (1528) : possibly but not certainly : MAYBE

²perhaps *n* (1534) : something open to doubt or conjecture

pe·ri \'pir-ē\ *n* [Per *perī* fairy, genius, fr. MPer *parik*; akin to Av *pairikā* sorceress] (ca. 1780) **1** : a supernatural being in Persian folklore de-

scended from fallen angels and excluded from paradise until penance is accomplished **2** : a beautiful and graceful girl

peri- *prefix* [L, fr. Gk, around, in excess, fr. *peri*; akin to Gk *peran* to pass through — more at FARE] **1** : all around : about ⟨*periscope*⟩ **2** : near ⟨*perihelion*⟩ **3** : enclosing : surrounding ⟨*perineurium*⟩

peri·anth \'per-ē-,an(t)th\ *n* [NL *perianthium*, fr. *peri-* + Gk *anthos* flower — more at ANTHOLOGY] (1828) : the floral structure comprised of the calyx and corolla esp. when the two whorls are fused — see FLOWER illustration

peri·apt \'per-ē-,apt\ *n* [MF or Gk; MF *periapte*, fr. Gk *periapton*, fr. *periaptein* to fasten around (oneself), fr. *peri-* + *haptein* to fasten] (1584) : AMULET

peri·car·di·al \,per-ə-'kär-dē-əl\ *adj* (1654) : of, relating to, or affecting the pericardium; *also* : situated around the heart

peri·car·di·tis \-,kär-də-əm\ *n* [NL] (ca. 1799) : inflammation of the pericardium

peri·car·di·um \-'kär-dē-əm\ *n, pl* **-dia** \-dē-ə\ [ME, fr. ML, fr. Gk *perikardion*, neut. of *perikardios* around the heart, fr. *peri-* + *kardia* heart — more at HEART] (15c) **1** : the conical sac of serous membrane that encloses the heart and the roots of the great blood vessels of vertebrates **2** : a cavity or space that contains the heart of an invertebrate and in arthropods is a part of the hemocoel

peri·carp \'per-ə-,kärp\ *n* [NL *pericarpium*, fr. Gk *perikarpion* pod, fr. *peri-* + *-karpion* -carp] (1759) : the ripened and variously modified walls of a plant ovary — see ENDOCARP illustration

peri·chon·dri·um \,per-ə-'kän-drē-əm\ *n, pl* **-dria** \-drē-ə\ [NL, fr. *peri-* + Gk *chondros* grain, cartilage] (1741) : the membrane of fibrous connective tissue that invests cartilage except at joints — **peri·chon·dral** \-drəl\ *adj*

pe·ric·o·pe \pə-'ri-kə-pē\ *n* [LL, fr. Gk *perikopē* section, fr. *peri-* + *kopē* act of cutting, fr. *koptein* to cut — more at CAPON] (1658) : a selection from a book; *specif* : LECTION 1

peri·cra·ni·um \,per-ə-'krā-nē-əm\ *n, pl* **-nia** \-nē-ə\ [ME *pericraneum*, fr. ML, fr. Gk *perikranion*, neut. of *perikranios* around the skull, fr. *peri-* + *kranion* skull — more at CRANIUM] (15c) : the external periosteum of the skull — **peri·cra·ni·al** \-nē-əl\ *adj*

peri·cy·cle \'per-ə-,si-kəl\ *n* [F *péricycle*, fr. Gk *perikyklos* spherical, fr. *peri-* + *kyklos* circle — more at WHEEL] (ca. 1892) : a thin layer of parenchymatous or sclerenchymatous cells that surrounds the stele in most vascular plants — **peri·cy·clic** \,per-ə-'si-klik, -'si-\ *adj*

peri·derm \'per-ə-,dərm\ *n* [NL *peridermis*, fr. *peri-* + *-dermis*] (1849) : an outer layer of tissue; *esp* : a cortical protective layer of many roots and stems that typically consists of phellem, phellogen, and phelloderm

pe·rid·i·um \pə-'ri-dē-əm\ *n, pl* **pe·rid·ia** \-dē-ə\ [NL, fr. Gk *pēridion*, dim. of *pēra* leather bag] (ca. 1823) : the outer envelope of the sporophore of many fungi

per·i·dot \'per-ə-,dät, -,dō(t)\ *n* [F *péridot*, fr. OF *peritot*] (ca. 1706) : a deep yellowish green transparent olivine used as a gem — **per·i·do·tic** \,per-ə-'dä-tik, -'dō-\ *adj*

pe·ri·do·tite \pə-'ri-də-,tīt\ *n* [F *péridotite*, fr. *péridot*] (1878) : any of a group of granitoid igneous rocks composed of ferromagnesian minerals and esp. olivine — **pe·ri·do·tit·ic** \pə-,ri-də-'ti-tik\ *adj*

peri·gee \'per-ə-(,)jē\ *n* [MF, fr. NL *perigeum*, fr. Gk *perigeion*, fr. neut. of *perigeios* near the earth, fr. *peri-* + *gē* earth] (1594) : the point in the orbit of an object (as a satellite) orbiting the earth that is nearest to the center of the earth; *also* : the point nearest a planet or a satellite (as the moon) reached by an object orbiting it — compare APOGEE — **peri·ge·an** \,per-ə-'jē-ən\ *adj*

pe·rig·y·nous \pə-'ri-jə-nəs\ *adj* [NL *perigynus*, fr. *peri-* + *-gynus* -gynous] (1807) : borne on a ring or cup of the receptacle surrounding a pistil ⟨~ stamens⟩ *also* : having perigynous stamens and petals ⟨~ flowers⟩ — **pe·rig·y·ny** \-nē\ *n*

peri·he·lion \,per-ə-'hēl-yən\ *n, pl* **-he·lia** \-'hēl-yə\ [NL, fr. *peri-* + Gk *hēlios* sun — more at SOLAR] (1666) : the point in the path of a celestial body (as a planet) that is nearest to the sun — compare APH-ELION — **peri·he·lial** \-'hēl-yəl\ *adj*

peri·kar·y·on \-'kar-ē-,än, -ən\ *n, pl* **-kar·ya** \-ē-ə\ [NL, fr. *peri-* + Gk *karyon* nut, kernel — more at CAREEN] (1897) : CELL BODY — **peri·kar·y·al** \-ē-əl\ *adj*

¹per·il \'per-əl\ *n* [ME, fr. OF, fr. L *periculum* — more at FEAR] (13c) **1** : exposure to the risk of being injured, destroyed, or lost : DANGER ⟨fire put the city in ~⟩ **2** : something that imperils : RISK ⟨lessen the ~s of the streets⟩

²peril *vt* **-iled** *also* **-illed; -il·ing** *also* **-il·ling** (1567) : to expose to danger

pe·ril·la \pə-'ri-lə\ *n* [NL] (1900) : any of a genus (*Perilla*) of Asian mints that have a bilabiate fruiting calyx and rugose nutlets

perilla oil *n* (1917) : a light yellow drying oil that is obtained from seeds of perillas

per·il·ous \'per-ə-ləs\ *adj* (14c) : full of or involving peril : HAZARDOUS **syn** see DANGEROUS — **per·il·ous·ly** *adv* — **per·il·ous·ness** *n*

peri·lune \'per-ə-,lün\ *n* [*peri-* + L *luna* moon — more at LUNAR] (1960) : the point in the path of a body orbiting the moon that is nearest to the center of the moon — compare APOLUNE

peri·lymph \-,lim(p)f\ *n* [ISV] (ca. 1839) : the fluid between the membranous and bony labyrinths of the ear

pe·rim·e·ter \pə-'ri-mə-tər\ *n* [ME *perimetre*, fr. L *perimetros*, fr. Gk, fr. *peri-* + *metron* measure — more at MEASURE] (15c) **1 a** : the boundary of a closed plane figure **b** : the length of a perimeter **2** : a line or strip bounding or protecting an area **3** : outer limits — often used in pl.

peri·my·si·um \,per-ə-'mi-zhē-əm, -zē-\ *n, pl* **-sia** \-zhē-ə, -zē-\ [NL, irreg. fr. *peri-* + Gk *mys* mouse, muscle — more at MOUSE] (ca. 1842) : the connective-tissue sheath that surrounds a muscle and forms sheaths for the bundles of muscle fibers

---

\ə\ abut \ᵊ\ kitten, F table \ər\ further \a\ ash \ā\ ace \ä\ mop, mar \aù\ out \ch\ chin \e\ bet \ē\ easy \g\ go \i\ hit \ī\ ice \j\ job \ŋ\ sing \ō\ go \ò\ law \òi\ boy \th\ thin \t͟h\ the \ü\ loot \ù\ foot \y\ yet \zh\ vision \ä, k̲, ⁿ, œ, œ̄, ᵫ, ᵫ̄, ᵉ\ *see* Guide to Pronunciation

peri·na·tal \-'nā-t³l\ *adj* (1952) : occurring in, concerned with, or being in the period around the time of birth ⟨∼ mortality⟩ ⟨∼ care⟩ — **peri·na·tal·ly** \-t³l-(l)ē\ *adv*

peri·ne·um \ˌper-ə-'nē-əm\ *n, pl* **-nea** \-'nē-ə\ [ME, fr. LL *perinaion*, fr. Gk, fr. *peri-* + *inan* to empty out; perh. akin to Skt *iṣṇāti* he sets in motion] (15c) : an area of tissue that marks externally the approximate boundary of the outlet of the pelvis and gives passage to the urinogenital ducts and rectum; *also* : the area between the anus and the posterior part of the external genitalia — **peri·ne·al** \-'nē-əl\ *adj*

peri·neu·ri·um \ˌper-ə-'nur-ē-əm, -'nyūr-\ *n, pl* **-ria** \-ē-ə\ [NL, fr. *peri-* + Gk *neuron* nerve — more at NERVE] (ca. 1842) : the connective tissue sheath that surrounds a bundle of nerve fibers

¹pe·ri·od \'pir-ē-əd\ *n* [ME *pariode*, fr. MF *periode*, fr. ML, L, & Gk; ML *periodus* period of time, punctuation mark, fr. L & Gk; L, rhetorical period, fr. Gk *periodos* circuit, period of time, rhetorical period, fr. *peri-* + *hodos* way] (ca. 1530) **1** : the completion of a cycle, a series of events, or a single action : CONCLUSION **2 a** (1) : an utterance from one full stop to another : SENTENCE (2) : a well-proportioned sentence of several clauses (3) : PERIODIC SENTENCE **b** : a musical structure or melodic section usu. composed of two or more contrasting or complementary phrases and ending with a cadence **3 a** : the full pause with which the utterance of a sentence closes **b** : END, STOP **4** *obs* : GOAL, PURPOSE **5 a** : a point . used to mark the end (as of a declarative sentence or an abbreviation) — often used interjectionally to emphasize that no more need be said ⟨I don't remember — ∼⟩ **b** : a rhythmical unit in Greek verse composed of a series of two or more cola **6 a** : a portion of time determined by some recurring phenomenon **b** (1) : the interval of time required for a cyclic motion or phenomenon to complete a cycle and begin to repeat itself (2) : a number *k* that does not change the value of a periodic function *f* when added to the independent variable; *esp* : the smallest such number **c** : a single cyclic occurrence of menstruation **7 a** : a chronological division : STAGE **b** : a division of geologic time longer than an epoch and included in an era **c** : a stage of culture having a definable place in time and space **8 a** : one of the divisions of the academic day **b** : one of the divisions of the playing time of a game

syn PERIOD, EPOCH, ERA, AGE mean a division of time. PERIOD may designate an extent of time of any length ⟨*periods* of economic prosperity⟩. EPOCH applies to a period begun or set off by some significant or striking quality, change, or series of events ⟨the steam engine marked a new *epoch* in industry⟩. ERA suggests a period of history marked by a new or distinct order of things ⟨the *era* of global communications⟩. AGE is used frequently of a fairly definite period dominated by a prominent figure or feature ⟨the *age* of Samuel Johnson⟩.

²period *adj* (1905) : of, relating to, or representing a particular historical period ⟨∼ furniture⟩ ⟨∼ costumes⟩

pe·ri·od·ic \ˌpir-ē-'ä-dik\ *adj* (1642) **1** : occurring or recurring at regular intervals **2 a** : consisting of or containing a series of repeated stages, processes, or digits : CYCLIC ⟨∼ decimals⟩ ⟨a ∼ vibration⟩ **b** : being a function any value of which recurs at regular intervals **3** : expressed in or characterized by periodic sentences

per·iod·ic acid \ˌpər-(ˌ)ī-'ä-dik-\ *n* [ISV *per-* + *iodic*] (1836) : any of the strongly oxidizing acids (as H_5IO_6 or HIO_4) that are the most highly oxidized acids of iodine

¹pe·ri·od·i·cal \ˌpir-ē-'ä-di-kəl\ *adj* (1601) **1** : PERIODIC 1 **2 a** : published with a fixed interval between the issues or numbers **b** : published in, characteristic of, or connected with a periodical

²periodical *n* (1798) : a periodical publication

periodical cicada *n* (1890) : SEVENTEEN-YEAR LOCUST

pe·ri·od·i·cal·ly \ˌpir-ē-'ä-di-k(ə-)lē\ *adv* (1646) **1** : at regular intervals of time **2** : from time to time : FREQUENTLY

pe·ri·od·ic·i·ty \ˌpir-ē-ə-'di-sə-tē\ *n* (1833) : the quality, state, or fact of being regularly recurrent or having periods

periodic law *n* (1872) : a law in chemistry: the elements when arranged in the order of their atomic numbers show a periodic variation of atomic structure and of most of their properties

periodic sentence *n* (ca. 1928) : a usu. complex sentence that has no subordinate or trailing elements following its principal clause (as in "yesterday while I was walking down the street, I saw him")

periodic table *n* (1895) : an arrangement of chemical elements based on the periodic law

pe·ri·od·i·za·tion \ˌpir-ē-ə-də-'zā-shən\ *n* (1938) : division (as of history) into periods

peri·odon·tal \ˌper-ē-ō-'dän-t³l\ *adj* (1854) **1** : investing or surrounding a tooth **2** : of or affecting periodontal tissues or regions ⟨∼ diseases⟩ — **peri·odon·tal·ly** \-t³l-ē\ *adv*

periodontal membrane *n* (ca. 1903) : the fibrous connective-tissue layer covering the cementum of a tooth and holding it in place in the jawbone

peri·odon·tics \-'dän-tiks\ *n pl but sing or pl in constr* [NL *periodontium* periodontal tissue, fr. *peri-* + Gk *odont-, odous, odōn* tooth — more at TOOTH] (ca. 1944) : a branch of dentistry that deals with diseases of the supporting and investing structures of the teeth including the gums, cementum, periodontal membranes, and alveolar bone — **peri·odon·tist** \-'dän-tist\ *n*

peri·odon·tol·o·gy \-ˌdän-'tä-lə-jē\ *n* (1914) : PERIODONTICS

period piece *n* (1940) : a piece (as of fiction, art, furniture, or music) whose special value lies in its evocation of an historical period

peri·onych·i·um \ˌper-ē-ō-'ni-kē-əm\ *n, pl* **-ia** \-kē-ə\ [NL, fr. *peri-* + Gk *onych-, onyx* nail — more at NAIL] (ca. 1879) : the tissue bordering the root and sides of a fingernail or toenail

peri·os·te·al \ˌper-ē-'äs-tē-əl\ *adj* (1830) **1** : situated around or produced external to bone **2** : of, relating to, or involving the periosteum

peri·os·te·um \-tē-əm\ *n, pl* **-tea** \-tē-ə\ [NL, fr. LL *periosteon*, fr. Gk, neut. of *periosteos* around the bone, fr. *peri-* + *osteon* bone — more at OSSEOUS] (1597) : the membrane of connective tissue that closely invests all bones except at the articular surfaces

peri·os·ti·tis \-ˌäs-'tī-təs\ *n* [NL] (1843) : inflammation of the periosteum

¹peri·pa·tet·ic \ˌper-ə-pə-'te-tik\ *n* (15c) **1** *cap* : a follower of Aristotle or adherent of Aristotelianism **2** : PEDESTRIAN, ITINERANT **3** *pl* : movement or journeys hither and thither

²peripatetic *adj* [MF & L; MF *peripatetique*, fr. L *peripateticus*, fr. Gk *peripatētikos*, fr. *peripatein* to walk up and down, discourse while pacing (as did Aristotle), fr. *peri-* + *patein* to tread; akin to Skt *patha* path — more at FIND] (1566) **1** *cap* : ARISTOTELIAN **2 a** : of, relating to, or given to walking **b** : moving or traveling from place to place : ITINER-

---

PERIODIC TABLE

This is a common long form of the table. Roman numerals and letters heading the vertical columns indicate the groups (there are differences of opinion regarding the letter designations, those given here being probably the most generally used). The horizontal rows represent the periods, with two series removed from the two very long periods and represented below the main table. Atomic numbers are given above the symbols for the elements. Compare ELEMENT table.

IA[1]																	VIIA[3]	Zero[4]
1 H	IIA[2]												IIIA	IVA	VA	VIA	1 H	2 He
3 Li	4 Be												5 B	6 C	7 N	8 O	9 F	10 Ne
11 Na	12 Mg	IIIB	IVB	VB	VIB	VIIB		VIII			IB	IIB	13 Al	14 Si	15 P	16 S	17 Cl	18 Ar
19 K	20 Ca	21 Sc	22 Ti	23 V	24 Cr	25 Mn	26 Fe	27 Co	28 Ni	29 Cu	30 Zn		31 Ga	32 Ge	33 As	34 Se	35 Br	36 Kr
37 Rb	38 Sr	39 Y	40 Zr	41 Nb	42 Mo	43 Tc	44 Ru	45 Rh	46 Pd	47 Ag	48 Cd		49 In	50 Sn	51 Sb	52 Te	53 I	54 Xe
55 Cs	56 Ba	57 *La	72 Hf	73 Ta	74 W	75 Re	76 Os	77 Ir	78 Pt	79 Au	80 Hg		81 Tl	82 Pb	83 Bi	84 Po	85 At	86 Rn
87 Fr	88 Ra	89 #Ac	104 Unq	105 Unp	106 Unh													

*LANTHANIDE SERIES	58 Ce	59 Pr	60 Nd	61 Pm	62 Sm	63 Eu	64 Gd	65 Tb	66 Dy	67 Ho	68 Er	69 Tm	70 Yb	71 Lu
#ACTINIDE SERIES	90 Th	91 Pa	92 U	93 Np	94 Pu	95 Am	96 Cm	97 Bk	98 Cf	99 Es	100 Fm	101 Md	102 No	103 Lr

[1] Group IA (excluding hydrogen) comprises the alkali metals.
[2] Group IIA comprises the alkaline-earth metals.
[3] Group VIIA (excluding hydrogen) comprises the halogens.
[4] Group Zero comprises the noble gases.

ANT — **peri·pa·tet·i·cal·ly** \-ti-k(ə-)lē\ adv — **Peri·pa·tet·i·cism** \-'te-tə-ˌsi-zəm\ n

pe·rip·a·tus \pə-'ri-pə-təs\ n [NL, genus name, fr. Gk peripatos act of walking about, fr. peri- + patein to tread] (ca. 1931) : any of a class or phylum (Onychophora) of primitive tropical wormlike invertebrates that appear intermediate between annelid worms and arthropods

peri·pe·teia \ˌper-ə-pə-'tē-ə, -'tī-\ n [Gk, fr. peripiptein to fall around, change suddenly, fr. peri- + piptein to fall — more at FEATHER] (1591) : a sudden or unexpected reversal of circumstances or situation esp. in a literary work

pe·rip·e·ty \pə-'ri-pə-tē\ n, pl -ties (1753) : PERIPETEIA

¹**pe·riph·er·al** \pə-'ri-f(ə-)rəl\ adj (1808) 1 : of, relating to, involving, or forming a periphery or surface part 2 : of, relating to, or being part of the peripheral nervous system ⟨~ nerves⟩ 3 : of, relating to, or being the outer part of the field of vision ⟨good ~ vision⟩ 4 : AUXILIARY, SUPPLEMENTARY ⟨~ equipment⟩; also : of or relating to computer peripherals — **pe·riph·er·al·ly** adv

²**peripheral** n (1966) : a device connected to a computer to provide communication (as input and output) or auxiliary functions (as additional storage)

peripheral nervous system n (1935) : the part of the nervous system that is outside the central nervous system and comprises the cranial nerves excepting the optic nerve, the spinal nerves, and the autonomic nervous system

pe·riph·ery \pə-'ri-f(ə-)rē\ n, pl -er·ies [MF peripherie, fr. LL peripheria, fr. Gk periphereia, fr. peripherein to carry around, fr. peri- + pherein to carry — more at BEAR] (1571) 1 : the perimeter of a circle or other closed curve; also : the perimeter of a polygon 2 : the external boundary or surface of a body 3 a : the outward bounds of something as distinguished from its internal regions or center : CONFINES b : an area lying beyond the strict limits of a thing

pe·riph·ra·sis \pə-'ri-frə-səs\ n, pl -ra·ses \-ˌsēz\ [L, fr. Gk, fr. periphrazein to express periphrastically, fr. peri- + phrazein to point out] (1533) 1 : use of a longer phrasing in place of a possible shorter form of expression 2 : an instance of periphrasis

peri·phras·tic \ˌper-ə-'fras-tik\ adj (1805) 1 : of, relating to, or characterized by periphrasis 2 : formed by the use of function words or auxiliaries instead of by inflection ⟨more fair is a ~ comparative⟩ — **peri·phras·ti·cal·ly** \-ti-k(ə-)lē\ adv

pe·riph·y·ton \pə-'ri-fə-ˌtän\ n [NL, fr. Gk periphytos (verbal of periphyein to grow around, fr. peri- + phyein to bring forth, grow) + -on (as in plankton) — more at BE] (1945) : organisms (as of algae) that live attached to underwater surfaces — **peri·phyt·ic** \ˌper-ə-'fi-tik\ adj

peri·plast \'per-ə-ˌplast\ n (1853) : PLASMA MEMBRANE; also : a proteinaceous subcellular layer below the plasma membrane esp. of a euglena

pe·rique \pə-'rēk\ n [LaF périque] (1882) : an aromatic fermented Louisiana tobacco used in smoking mixtures

peri·sarc \'per-ə-ˌsärk\ n [ISV peri- + Gk sark-, sarx flesh — more at SARCASM] (ca. 1871) : the outer usu. chitinous integument of a hydroid

peri·scope \-ˌskōp\ n [ISV] (1879) : a tubular optical instrument containing lenses and mirrors by which an observer obtains an otherwise obstructed field of view

peri·scop·ic \ˌper-ə-'skä-pik\ adj (1804) 1 : providing a view all around or on all sides ⟨~ lens⟩ 2 : of or relating to a periscope

per·ish \'per-ish\ vb [ME perisshen, fr. OF periss-, stem of perir, fr. L perire, fr. per- detrimentally + ire to go — more at PER-, ISSUE] vi (14c) 1 : to become destroyed or ruined : DIE ⟨recollection of a past already long since ~ed —Philip Sherrard⟩ ⟨guard against your mistakes or your attempts ~ the thought) to cheat —C. B. Davis⟩ 2 chiefly Brit : DETERIORATE, SPOIL ~ vt 1 chiefly Brit : to cause to die : DESTROY 2 : WEAKEN, BENUMB

per·ish·able \'per-i-shə-bəl\ adj (ca. 1611) : liable to perish : liable to spoil or decay ⟨such ~ products as fruit, vegetables, butter, and eggs⟩ — **per·ish·abil·i·ty** \ˌper-i-shə-'bi-lə-tē\ n — **per·ishable** n

pe·ris·so·dac·tyl \pə-'ri-sə-ˌdak-t²l\ n [NL Perissodactyla, fr. Gk perissos excessive, odd in number + daktylos finger, toe] (1849) : any of an order (Perissodactyla) of nonruminant ungulate mammals (as a horse, a tapir, or a rhinoceros) that usu. have an odd number of toes, molar teeth with transverse ridges on the grinding surface, and the posterior premolars resembling true molars — **perissodactyl** adj

peri·stal·sis \ˌper-ə-'stól-səs, -'stäl-, -'stal-\ n, pl -stal·ses \-ˌsēz\ [NL, fr. Gk peristaltikos peristaltic] (1859) : successive waves of involuntary contraction passing along the walls of a hollow muscular structure (as the esophagus or intestine) and forcing the contents onward

peri·stal·tic \-tik\ adj [Gk peristaltikos, fr. peristellein to wrap around, fr. peri- + stellein to place] (1655) 1 : of, relating to, resulting from, or being peristalsis 2 : having an action suggestive of peristalsis

peristaltic pump n (1962) : a pump in which fluid is forced along by waves of contraction produced mechanically on flexible tubing

peri·stome \'per-ə-ˌstōm\ n [NL peristoma, fr. peri- + Gk stoma mouth — more at STOMACH] (ca. 1796) 1 : the fringe of teeth surrounding the orifice of a moss capsule 2 : the region around the mouth in various invertebrates — **peri·sto·mi·al** \ˌper-ə-'stō-mē-əl\ adj

peri·style \'per-ə-ˌstīl\ n [F péristyle, fr. L peristylum, fr. Gk peristylon, fr. neut. of peristylos surrounded by a colonnade, fr. peri- + stylos pillar — more at STEER] (1612) 1 : a colonnade surrounding a building or court 2 : an open space enclosed by a colonnade

peri·the·ci·um \ˌper-ə-'thē-shē-əm, -sē-\ n, pl -cia \-shē-ə, -sē-\ [NL, fr. peri- + Gk thēkion, dim. of thēkē case — more at TICK] (ca. 1832) : a spherical, cylindrical, or flask-shaped hollow fruiting body in various ascomycetous fungi that contains the asci and usu. opens by a terminal pore — **peri·the·cial** \-'thē-sh(ē-)əl, -sē-əl\ adj

peri·to·ne·um \ˌper-ə-t²n-'ē-əm\ n, pl -ne·ums \-'ē-əmz\ or -nea \-'ē-ə\ [ME, fr. LL, fr. Gk peritonaion, neut. of peritonaios stretched around, fr. peri- + teinein to stretch — more at THIN] (15c) : the smooth transparent serous membrane that lines the cavity of the abdo-

men of a mammal and is folded inward over the abdominal and pelvic viscera — **peri·to·ne·al** \-'ē-əl\ adj — **peri·to·ne·al·ly** \-ə-lē\ adv

peri·to·ni·tis \ˌper-ə-t²n-'ī-təs\ n [NL] (1776) : inflammation of the peritoneum

pe·rit·ri·chous \pə-'ri-tri-kəs\ adj [peri- + Gk trich-, thrix hair] (1877) 1 : having flagella uniformly distributed over the body ⟨~ bacteria⟩ 2 : having a spiral line of modified cilia around the oral disk ⟨~ protozoa⟩ — **pe·rit·ri·chous·ly** adv

peri·wig \'per-i-ˌwig\ n [modif. of MF perruque — more at PERUKE] (1529) : PERUKE — **peri·wigged** \-ˌwigd\ adj

¹**per·i·win·kle** \'per-i-ˌwiŋ-kəl\ n [ME perwinke, fr. OE perwince, fr. (assumed) VL pervinca, short for L vincapervinca] (bef. 12c) 1 : any of several trailing or woody evergreen herbs of the dogbane family: as a : a European creeper (Vinca minor) widely cultivated as a ground cover and for its blue or white flowers — called also myrtle b : a commonly cultivated subshrub (Catharanthus roseus syn. Vinca rosea) of the Old World tropics that is the source of several antineoplastic drugs — called also Madagascar periwinkle 2 : a light purplish blue — called also periwinkle blue

²**periwinkle** n [(assumed) ME, alter. of OE pinewincle, fr. L pina, a kind of mussel (fr. Gk) + OE -wincle (akin to Dan vincle snail shell)] (ca. 1530) : any of various gastropod mollusks: as a : any of a genus (Littorina) of edible littoral marine snails; also : any of various similar or related marine snails b : any of several No. American freshwater snails

²periwinkle a

per·jure \'per-jər\ vt -jured; -jur·ing \'pər-jə-riŋ, 'pòrj-riŋ\ [MF perjurer, fr. L perjurare, fr. per- detrimentally, for the worse + jurare to swear — more at PER-, JURY] (1535) 1 : to make a perjurer of (oneself) 2 obs : to cause to commit perjury

per·jur·er \'pər-jər-ər\ n (15c) : a person guilty of perjury

per·ju·ri·ous \ˌpər-'jùr-ē-əs\ adj (1602) : marked by perjury ⟨~ testimony⟩ — **per·ju·ri·ous·ly** adv

per·ju·ry \'pər-jə-rē, 'pòrj-rē\ n (14c) : the voluntary violation of an oath or vow either by swearing to what is untrue or by omission to do what has been promised under oath : false swearing

¹**perk** \'pərk\ vb [ME] (14c) 1 a : to thrust up the head, stretch out the neck, or carry the body in a bold or insolent manner b : to stick up or out jauntily 2 : to gain in vigor or cheerfulness esp. after a period of weakness or depression — usu. used with up ⟨he's ~ed up noticeably⟩ ~ vt 1 : to make smart or spruce in appearance : FRESHEN, IMPROVE 2 : to thrust up quickly or impudently

²**perk** vi (1656) : PERCOLATE

³**perk** n (1824) : PERQUISITE — usu. used in pl.

perky \'pər-kē\ adj perk·i·er; -est (1855) 1 : briskly self-assured : COCKY 2 : JAUNTY ⟨a ~ . . . waltz —New Yorker⟩ — **perk·i·ly** \-kə-lē\ adv — **perk·i·ness** \-kē-nəs\ n

per·lite \'pər-ˌlīt\ n [F, fr. perle pearl] (1833) : volcanic glass that has a concentric shelly structure, appears as if composed of concretions, is usu. grayish and sometimes spherulitic, and when expanded by heat forms a lightweight aggregate used esp. in concrete and plaster and as a medium for potting plants — **per·lit·ic** \ˌpər-'li-tik\ adj

¹**perm** \'pərm\ n (1927) : PERMANENT

²**perm** vt (1928) : to give (hair) a permanent wave

per·ma·frost \'pər-mə-ˌfròst\ n [permanent + frost] (1943) : a permanently frozen layer at variable depth below the surface in frigid regions of a planet (as earth)

per·ma·nence \'pər-mə-nən(t)s, 'pòrm-nən(t)s\ n (15c) : the quality or state of being permanent : DURABILITY

per·ma·nen·cy \-nən(t)-sē\ n, pl -cies (1555) 1 : PERMANENCE 2 : something permanent

¹**per·ma·nent** \-nənt\ adj [ME, fr. MF, fr. L permanent-, permanens, prp. of permanēre to endure, fr. per- throughout + manēre to remain — more at PER-, MANSION] (15c) : continuing or enduring without fundamental or marked change : STABLE syn see LASTING — **per·manent·ly** adv — **per·ma·nent·ness** n

²**permanent** n (1925) : a long-lasting hair wave or straightening produced by mechanical and chemical means — called also permanent wave

permanent magnet n (1828) : a magnet that retains its magnetism after removal of the magnetizing force

permanent press n (1964) 1 : the process of treating a fabric with a chemical (as a resin) and heat for setting the shape and for aiding wrinkle resistance 2 : material treated by permanent press 3 : the condition of material treated by permanent press — **permanent–press** adj

permanent tissue n (ca. 1928) : plant tissue that has completed its growth and differentiation and is usu. incapable of meristematic activity

permanent tooth n (1836) : any of the second set of teeth of a mammal that follow the milk teeth, typically persist into old age, and in humans are 32 in number

per·man·ga·nate \(ˌ)pər-'maŋ-gə-ˌnāt\ n (1841) 1 : a salt containing the anion MnO_4^-; esp : POTASSIUM PERMANGANATE 2 : the anion MnO_4^- of a permanganate

per·me·abil·i·ty \ˌpər-mē-ə-'bi-lə-tē\ n (1759) 1 : the quality or state of being permeable 2 : the property of a magnetizable substance that determines the degree in which it modifies the magnetic flux in the region occupied by it in a magnetic field

per·me·able \'pər-mē-ə-bəl\ adj (15c) : capable of being permeated : PENETRABLE; esp : having pores or openings that permit liquids or gases to pass through ⟨a ~ membrane⟩ ⟨~ limestone⟩

per·me·ase \'pər-mē-ˌās, -ˌāz\ n [ISV perme- (fr. permeate) + -ase] (1957) : a substance that catalyzes the transport of another substance across a cell membrane

per·me·ate \'pər-mē-ˌāt\ vb -at·ed; -at·ing [L permeatus, pp. of permeare, fr. per- through + meare to go, pass; akin to MW mynet to go,

\ə\ abut \²\ kitten, F table \ər\ further \a\ ash \ā\ ace \ä\ mop, mar \aù\ out \ch\ chin \e\ bet \ē\ easy \g\ go \i\ hit \ī\ ice \j\ job \ŋ\ sing \ō\ go \ò\ law \òi\ boy \th\ thin \th\ the \ü\ loot \ù\ foot \y\ yet \zh\ vision \à, ̲k, ⁿ, œ, œ̄, ᵫ, ūᴱ, ʸ\ see Guide to Pronunciation

Czech *míjet* to pass] *vi* (1656) : to diffuse through or penetrate something ~ *vt* **1** : to spread or diffuse through ⟨a room *permeated* with tobacco smoke⟩ **2** : to pass through the pores or interstices of — **per-me-ative** \-ā-tiv\ *adj*

per-me-ation \ˌpər-mē-'ā-shən\ *n* (ca. 1623) **1** : the quality or state of being permeated **2** : the action or process of permeating

per men-sem \ˌ(ˌ)pər-'men(t)-səm\ *adv* [ML] (1647) : by the month

per-meth-rin \(ˌ)pər-'me-thrən\ *n* [*per-* + *methyl* + *pyreth*rin] (1976) : a synthetic pyrethrin $C_{21}H_{20}Cl_2O_3$ used esp. as an insecticide

Perm-ian \'pər-mē-ən, 'per-\ *adj* [*Perm*, former province in eastern Russia] (1841) : of, relating to, or being the last period of the Paleozoic era or the corresponding system of rocks — see GEOLOGIC TIME table — **Permian** *n*

per mill \(ˌ)pər-'mil\ *adv* [*per* + L *mille* thousand] (1902) : per thousand — **per-mil-lage** \(ˌ)pər-'mi-lij\ *n*

per-mis-si-ble \pər-'mi-sə-bəl\ *adj* [ME, fr. ML *permissibilis*, fr. L *permissus*, pp. of *permittere*] (15c) : that may be permitted : ALLOWABLE — **per-mis-si-bil-i-ty** \-ˌmi-sə-'bi-lə-tē\ *n* — **per-mis-si-ble-ness** \-'mi-sə-bəl-nəs\ *n* — **per-mis-si-bly** \-blē\ *adv*

per-mis-sion \pər-'mi-shən\ *n* [ME, fr. MF, fr. L *permission-, permissio*, fr. *permittere*] (15c) **1** : the act of permitting **2** : formal consent : AUTHORIZATION

per-mis-sive \pər-'mi-siv\ *adj* [ME *permyssyf*, fr. MF *permissif*, fr. L *permissus*] (15c) **1** *archaic* : granted on sufferance : TOLERATED **2 a** : granting or tending to grant permission : TOLERANT **b** : deficient in firmness or control : INDULGENT, LAX **3** : allowing discretion : OPTIONAL ⟨reduced the ~ retirement age from 65 to 62⟩ — **per-mis-sive-ly** *adv* — **per-mis-sive-ness** *n*

¹per-mit \pər-'mit\ *vb* **per-mit-ted; per-mit-ting** [ME *permitten*, fr. L *permittere* to let through, permit, fr. *per-* through + *mittere* to let go, send] *vt* (15c) **1** : to consent to expressly or formally ⟨~ access to records⟩ **2** : to give leave : AUTHORIZE **3** : to make possible ~ *vi* : to give an opportunity : ALLOW ⟨if time ~s⟩ — **per-mit-tee** \pər-ˌmi(t)-'tē, ˌpər-mi(t)-\ *n* — **per-mit-ter** *n*

²per-mit \'pər-ˌmit, pər-'\ *n* (1682) **1** : a written warrant or license granted by one having authority ⟨a gun ~⟩ **2** : PERMISSION

³permit *n* [perh. by folk etymology fr. Sp *palometa*, a kind of pompano, fr. dim. of *paloma* dove, fr. L *palumba, palumbes* — more at PALOMINO] (ca. 1945) : either of two pompanos (*Trachinotus falcatus* and *T. goodei*) that are important game fishes of temperate to tropical waters of the western Atlantic

per-mit-tiv-i-ty \ˌpər-ˌmi-'ti-və-tē, -mə-\ *n* [¹*permit* + -*ivity* (as in *selectivity*)] (1887) : the ability of a dielectric to store electrical potential energy under the influence of an electric field measured by the ratio of the capacitance of a condenser with the material as dielectric to its capacitance with vacuum as dielectric — called also *dielectric constant*

per-mu-ta-tion \ˌpər-myü-'tā-shən\ *n* [ME *permutacioun* exchange, transformation, fr. MF *permutation*, fr. L *permutation-, permutatio*, fr. *permutare*] (14c) **1** : often major or fundamental change (as in character or condition) based primarily on rearrangement of existent elements ⟨land-owners and peasants . . . in the ~s of their tortured interdependence —P. E. Mosley⟩ **2 a** : the act or process of changing the lineal order of an ordered set of objects **b** : an ordered arrangement of a set of objects — **per-mu-ta-tion-al** \-shnəl, -shə-nᵊl\ *adj*

permutation group *n* (1904) : a group whose elements are permutations and in which the product of two permutations is a permutation whose effect is the same as the successive application of the first two

per-mute \pər-'myüt\ *vt* **per-mut-ed; per-mut-ing** [ME, to exchange, fr. MF or L; MF *permuter*, fr. L *permutare*, fr. *per-* + *mutare* to change — more at MUTABLE] (1878) : to change the order or arrangement of; *esp* : to arrange in all possible ways — **per-mut-able** \-'myü-tə-bəl\ *adj*

per-ni-cious \pər-'ni-shəs\ *adj* [ME, fr. MF *pernicieus*, fr. L *perniciosus*, fr. *pernicies* destruction, fr. *per-* + *nec-, nex* violent death — more at NOXIOUS] (15c) **1** : highly injurious or destructive : DEADLY **2** *archaic* : WICKED — **per-ni-cious-ly** *adv* — **per-ni-cious-ness** *n*
syn PERNICIOUS, BANEFUL, NOXIOUS, DELETERIOUS, DETRIMENTAL mean exceedingly harmful. PERNICIOUS implies irreparable harm done through evil or insidious corrupting or undermining ⟨the claim that pornography has a *pernicious* effect on society⟩. BANEFUL implies injury through poisoning or destroying ⟨the *baneful* notion that discipline destroys creativity⟩. NOXIOUS applies to what is both offensive and injurious to the health of a body or mind ⟨*noxious* chemical fumes⟩. DELETERIOUS applies to what has an often unsuspected harmful effect ⟨a diet found to have *deleterious* effects⟩. DETRIMENTAL implies obvious harmfulness to something specified ⟨the *detrimental* effects of excessive drinking⟩.

pernicious anemia *n* (1874) : a severe megaloblastic anemia marked by a progressive decrease in the number of red blood cells and by pallor, weakness, and gastrointestinal and nervous disturbances and associated with malabsorption of vitamin B_{12} due to the absence of intrinsic factor

per-nick-e-ty \pər-'ni-kə-tē\ *adj* [origin unknown] (ca. 1818) : PERSNICKETY

Per-nod \per-'nō, ˌpər-\ *trademark* — used for a French liqueur

pe-ro-ne-al \ˌpər-ō-'nē-əl, pə-'rō-nē-əl\ *adj* [NL *peroneus*, fr. *perone* fibula, fr. Gk *perone*, lit., pin, fr. *peirein* to pierce — more at DIAPIR] (1831) : of, relating to, or located near the fibula

per-oral \(ˌ)pər-'ör-əl, per-, -'ör-, -'är-\ *adj* [ISV] (1908) : occurring through or by way of the mouth — **per-oral-ly** \-ə-lē\ *adv*

per-o-rate \'per-ə-ˌrāt *also* 'per-\ *vi* **-rat-ed; -rat-ing** [L *peroratus*, pp. of *perorare* to declaim at length, wind up an oration, fr. *per-* through + *orare* to speak — more at PER-, ORATION] (1603) **1** : to deliver a long or grandiloquent oration **2** : to make a peroration

per-o-ra-tion \ˌper-ə-'rā-shən *also* ˌpər-\ *n* [ME *peroracyon*, fr. L *peroration-, peroratio*, fr. *perorare*] (15c) **1** : the concluding part of a discourse and esp. an oration **2** : a highly rhetorical speech — **per-o-ra-tion-al** \ˌpər-ə-'rā-shnəl, ˌpər-\, -shə-nᵊl\ *adj*

pe-rov-skite \pə-'räv-ˌskit, -'räf-\ *n* [G *Perowskit*, fr. Count L. A. *Perovskii* †1856 Russ. statesman] (1840) : a yellow, brown, or grayish black mineral sometimes containing rare earth elements

per-ox-i-dase \pə-'räk-sə-ˌdās, -ˌdāz\ *n* (1900) : an enzyme that catalyzes the oxidation of various substances by peroxides

¹per-ox-ide \pə-'räk-ˌsīd\ *n* [ISV] (1804) : an oxide containing a high proportion of oxygen; *esp* : a compound (as hydrogen peroxide) in which oxygen is visualized as joined to oxygen — **per-ox-id-ic** \-ˌräk-'si-dik\ *adj*

²peroxide *vt* **-id-ed; -id-ing** (1906) : to treat with a peroxide; *esp* : to bleach (hair) with hydrogen peroxide

³peroxide *adj* (1920) : having or being bleached hair ⟨a ~ blonde⟩

per-ox-i-some \pə-'räk-sə-ˌsōm\ *n* [*peroxide* + ³-*some*] (1965) : a cytoplasmic cell organelle containing enzymes (as catalase) which act in oxidative reactions and esp. in the production and decomposition of hydrogen peroxide — **per-ox-i-som-al** \-ˌräk-sə-'sō-məl\ *adj*

peroxy- *comb form* [ISV *per-* + *oxy*] : containing the bivalent group O—O ⟨*peroxy*acetyl nitrate⟩

per-oxy-ace-tyl nitrate \pə-ˌräk-sē-ə-'sē-tᵊl-, -'a-sə-tᵊl-, -ˌtēl-\ *n* (1963) : a toxic compound $C_2H_3O_5N$ found esp. in smog

per-pend \(ˌ)pər-'pend\ *vb* [ME, fr. L *perpendere*, fr. *per-* thoroughly + *pendere* to weigh — more at PER-, PENDANT] *vt* (15c) : to reflect on carefully : PONDER ~ *vi* : to be attentive : REFLECT

¹per-pen-dic-u-lar \ˌpər-pən-'di-kyə-lər\ *adj* [ME *perpendiculer*, fr. MF, fr. L *perpendicularis*, fr. *perpendiculum* plumb line, fr. *per-* + *pendēre* to hang — more at PENDANT] (14c) **1 a** : standing at right angles to the plane of the horizon : exactly upright **b** : being at right angles to a given line or plane **2** : extremely steep : PRECIPITOUS **3** *often cap* : of or relating to a medieval English Gothic style of architecture in which vertical lines predominate **4** : relating to, uniting, or consisting of individuals of dissimilar type or on different levels **syn** see VERTICAL — **per-pen-dic-u-lar-i-ty** \-ˌdi-kyə-'lar-ə-tē\ *n* — **per-pen-dic-u-lar-ly** \-'di-kyə-lər-lē\ *adv*

²perpendicular *n* (1571) : a line at right angles to a line or plane (as of the horizon)

per-pe-trate \'pər-pə-ˌtrāt\ *vt* **-trat-ed; -trat-ing** [L *perpetratus*, pp. of *perpetrare*, fr. *per-* through + *patrare* to accomplish, fr. *pater* father — more at FATHER] (1537) : to bring about or carry out (as a crime or deception) : COMMIT — **per-pe-tra-tion** \ˌpər-pə-'trā-shən\ *n* — **per-pe-tra-tor** \'pər-pə-ˌtrā-tər\ *n*

per-pet-u-al \pər-'pe-chə-wəl, -chəl; -'pech-wəl\ *adj* [ME *perpetuel*, fr. MF, fr. L *perpetuus* uninterrupted, fr. *per-* through + *petere* to go to — more at FEATHER] (14c) **1 a** : continuing forever : EVERLASTING **b** (1) : valid for all time (2) : holding (as an office) for life or for an unlimited time **2** : occurring continually : indefinitely long-continued **3** : blooming continuously throughout the season **syn** see CONTINUAL — **per-pet-u-al-ly** *adv*

perpetual calendar *n* (1895) : a table for finding the day of the week for any one of a wide range of dates

perpetual check *n* (ca. 1909) : an endless succession of checks to which an opponent's king may be subjected to force a draw in chess

per-pet-u-ate \pər-'pe-chə-ˌwāt\ *vt* **-at-ed; -at-ing** [L *perpetuatus*, pp. of *perpetuare*, fr. *perpetuus*] (1530) : to make perpetual or cause to last indefinitely ⟨~ the species⟩ — **per-pet-u-a-tion** \-ˌpe-chə-'wā-shən\ *n* — **per-pet-u-a-tor** \-'pe-chə-ˌwā-tər\ *n*

per-pe-tu-i-ty \ˌpər-pə-'tü-ə-tē, -'tyü-\ *n, pl* **-ties** [ME *perpetuite*, fr. MF *perpetuité*, fr. L *perpetuit-, perpetuitas*, fr. *perpetuus*] (15c) **1** : ETERNITY **2** : the quality or state of being perpetual ⟨bequeathed to them in ~⟩ **3 a** : the condition of an estate limited so that it will not take effect or vest within the period fixed by law **b** : an estate so limited **4** : an annuity payable forever

per-phe-na-zine \(ˌ)pər-'fē-nə-ˌzēn, -'fe-\ *n* [blend of *piperazine* and *phen-*] (1957) : a tranquilizing drug $C_{21}H_{26}ClN_3OS$ that is used to control tension, anxiety, and agitation esp. in psychotic conditions

per-plex \pər-'pleks\ *vt* [obs. *perplex*, adj., involved, perplexed, fr. L *perplexus*, fr. *per-* thoroughly + *plexus* involved, fr. pp. of *plectere* to braid, twine — more at PER-, PLY] (1593) **1** : to make unable to grasp something clearly or to think logically and decisively about something ⟨her attitude ~*es* me⟩ ⟨a ~*ing* problem⟩ **2** : to make intricate or involved : COMPLICATE **syn** see PUZZLE

per-plexed \-'plekst\ *adj* (15c) **1** : filled with uncertainty : PUZZLED **2** : full of difficulty — **per-plexed-ly** \-'plek-səd-lē, -'plekst-lē\ *adv*

per-plex-i-ty \pər-'plek-sə-tē\ *n, pl* **-ties** [ME *perplexite*, fr. MF *perplexité*, fr. LL *perplexitat-, perplexitas*, fr. L *perplexus*] (14c) **1** : the state of being perplexed : BEWILDERMENT **2** : something that perplexes **3** : ENTANGLEMENT

per-qui-site \'pər-kwə-zət\ *n* [ME, property acquired by means other than inheritance, fr. ML *perquisitum*, fr. neut. of *perquisitus*, pp. of *perquirere* to purchase, acquire, fr. L, to search for thoroughly, fr. *per-* thoroughly + *quaerere* to seek] (15c) **1** : a privilege, gain, or profit incidental to regular salary or wages; *esp* : one expected or promised **2** : GRATUITY, TIP **3** : something held or claimed as an exclusive right or possession ⟨concepts . . . not the ~s of any particular groups — Gilbert Ryle⟩

per-ron \'pər-ən, pe-rōⁿ\ *n* [F, fr. OF, fr. *perre, pierre* rock, stone, fr. L *petra*, fr. Gk] (1723) : an outdoor stairway leading up to a building entrance; *also* : a platform at its top

per-ry \'per-ē\ *n* [ME *peirrie*, fr. MF *peré*, fr. (assumed) VL *piratum*, fr. L *pirum* pear] (14c) : fermented pear juice often made sparkling

perse \'pərs\ *adj* [ME *pers*, fr. MF, fr. ML *persus*] (15c) : of a dark grayish blue resembling indigo

per se \(ˌ)pər-'sā *also* per-'sā *or* (ˌ)pər-'sē\ *adv* [L] (1572) : by, of, or in itself or oneself or themselves : as such : INTRINSICALLY

per second per second *adv* (1922) : per second every second — used of acceleration

per-se-cute \'pər-si-ˌkyüt\ *vt* **-cut-ed; -cut-ing** [ME, fr. MF *persecuter*, back-formation fr. *persecuteur* persecutor, fr. LL *persecutor*, fr. *persequi* to persecute, fr. L, to pursue, fr. *per-* through + *sequi* to follow — more at SUE] (15c) **1** : to harass in a manner designed to injure, grieve, or afflict; *specif* : to cause to suffer because of belief **2** : to annoy with persistent or urgent approaches (as attacks, pleas, or importunities) : PESTER **syn** see WRONG — **per-se-cu-tee** \ˌpər-si-ˌkyü-'tē\ *n* — **per-se-cu-tive** \'pər-si-ˌkyü-tiv\ *adj* — **per-se-cu-tor** \-ˌkyü-tər\ *n* — **per-se-cu-to-ry** \ˌkyü-ˌtör-ē, -ˌtör-; -ˌkyü-tə-rē\ *adj*

per-se-cu-tion \ˌpər-si-'kyü-shən\ *n* (14c) **1** : the act or practice of persecuting esp. those who differ in origin, religion, or social outlook **2** : the condition of being persecuted, harassed, or annoyed

Per-se-id \'pər-sē-əd\ *n* [L *Perseus*; fr. their appearing to radiate from a point in Perseus] : any of a group of meteors that appear annually about August 11

Per·seph·o·ne \pər-'se-fə-nē\ n [L, fr. Gk *Persephonē*] : a daughter of Zeus and Demeter abducted by Pluto to reign with him over the underworld

Per·seus \'pər-ˌsüs, -sē-əs\ n [L, fr. Gk] **1** : a son of Zeus and Danaë and slayer of Medusa **2** [L (gen. *Persei*), fr. Gk] : a northern constellation between Taurus and Cassiopeia

per·se·ver·ance \ˌpər-sə-'vir-ən(t)s\ n (14c) : the action or condition or an instance of persevering : STEADFASTNESS

per·sev·er·a·tion \pər-ˌse-və-'rā-shən\ n [L *perseveration-, perseveratio,* fr. *perseverare*] (1910) : continuation of something (as repetition of a word) usu. to an exceptional degree or beyond a desired point — **per·sev·er·ate** \-'se-və-ˌrāt\ vi

per·se·vere \ˌpər-sə-'vir\ vi **-vered; -ver·ing** [ME, fr. MF *perseverer,* fr. L *perseverare,* fr. *per-* through + *severus* severe] (14c) : to persist in a state, enterprise, or undertaking in spite of counterinfluences, opposition, or discouragement — **per·se·ver·ing·ly** adv

Per·sian \'pər-zhən, *esp Brit* -shən\ n (14c) **1** : one of the people of Persia: as **a** : one of the ancient Iranians who under Cyrus and his successors founded an empire in southwest Asia **b** : a member of one of the peoples forming the modern Iranian nationality **2 a** : any of several Iranian languages dominant in Persia at different periods **b** : the modern language of Iran and western Afghanistan — see INDO-EUROPEAN LANGUAGES table **3** : a thin soft silk formerly used esp. for linings — **Persian cat** — **Persian** adj

Persian cat n (1824) : any of a breed of stocky round-headed domestic cats that have a long silky coat and thick ruff

Persian lamb n (1889) **1** : a pelt that is obtained from karakul lambs older than those yielding broadtail and that is characterized by very silky tightly curled fur **2** : the young of the karakul sheep that furnishes skins used in furriery

per·si·flage \'pər-si-ˌfläzh, 'per-\ n [F, fr. *persifler* to banter, fr. *per-* thoroughly + *siffler* to whistle, hiss, boo, ultim. fr. L *sibilare*] (1757) : frivolous bantering talk : light raillery

per·sim·mon \pər-'si-mən\ n [Virginia Algonquian *pessemmin*] (1612) **1** : any of a genus (*Diospyros*) of trees of the ebony family with hard fine wood, oblong leaves, and small bell-shaped flowers; *esp* : an American tree (*D. virginiana*) or a Japanese tree (*D. kaki*) **2** : the usu. orange several-seeded globular berry of a persimmon that is edible when fully ripe but usu. extremely astringent when unripe

Persian cat

per·sist \pər-'sist, -'zist\ vi [MF *persister,* fr. L *persistere,* fr. *per-* + *sistere* to take a stand, stand firm; akin to L *stare* to stand — more at STAND] (1538) **1** : to go on resolutely or stubbornly in spite of opposition, importunity, or warning **2** *obs* : to remain unchanged or fixed in a specified character, condition, or position **3** : to be insistent in the repetition or pressing of an utterance (as a question or an opinion) **4** : to continue to exist esp. past a usual, expected, or normal time *syn* see CONTINUE — **per·sist·er** n

per·sis·tence \pər-'sis-tən(t)s, -'zis-\ n (1546) **1** : the action or fact of persisting **2** : the quality or state of being persistent; *esp* : PERSEVERANCE

per·sis·ten·cy \-tən(t)-sē\ n (1597) : PERSISTENCE 2

per·sis·tent \-tənt\ adj [L *persistent-, persistens,* prp. of *persistere*] (1826) **1** : existing for a long or longer than usual time or continuously: as **a** : retained beyond the usual period (a ~ leaf) **b** : continuing without change in function or structure (~ gills) **c** : effective in the open for an appreciable time usu. through slow volatilizing (mustard gas is ~) **d** : degraded only slowly by the environment (~ pesticides) **e** : remaining infective for a relatively long time in a vector after an initial period of incubation (~ viruses) **2** : continuing or inclined to persist in a course **b** : continuing to exist in spite of interference or treatment (a ~ cough) — **per·sis·tent·ly** adv

per·snick·e·ty \pər-'sni-kə-tē\ adj [alter. of *pernickety*] (ca. 1905) **1 a** : fussy about small details : FASTIDIOUS (a ~ teacher) **b** : having the characteristics of a snob **2** : requiring great precision (a ~ job) — **per·snick·e·ti·ness** \-nəs\ n

per·son \'pər-s³n\ n [ME, fr. OF *persone,* fr. L *persona* actor's mask, character in a play, person, prob. fr. Etruscan *phersu* mask, fr. Gk *prosōpa,* pl. of *prosōpon* face, mask — more at PROSOPOPOEIA] (13c) **1** : HUMAN, INDIVIDUAL — sometimes used in combination esp. by those who prefer to avoid *man* in compounds applicable to both sexes (chair*person*) (spokes*person*) **2** : a character or part in or as if in a play : GUISE **3 a** : one of the three modes of being in the Trinitarian Godhead as understood by Christians **b** : the unitary personality of Christ that unites the divine and human natures **4 a** *archaic* : bodily appearance **b** : the body of a human being; *also* : the body and clothing (unlawful search of the ~) **5** : the personality of a human being : SELF **6** : one (as a human being, a partnership, or a corporation) that is recognized by law as the subject of rights and duties **7** : reference of a segment of discourse to the speaker, to one spoken to, or to one spoken of as indicated by means of certain pronouns or in many languages by verb inflection — **per·son·hood** \-ˌhud\ n — **in person** : in one's bodily presence

per·so·na \pər-'sō-nə, -ˌnä\ n, *pl* **per·so·nae** \-(ˌ)nē, -ˌnī\ *or* **personas** [L] (1909) **1** : a character assumed by an author in a written work **2** *a pl* **personas** [NL, fr. L] : an individual's social facade or front that esp. in the analytic psychology of C. G. Jung reflects the role in life the individual is playing — compare ANIMA **b** : the personality that a person (as an actor or politician) projects in public : IMAGE **3** *pl persounae* : a character in a fictional presentation (as a novel or play) — usu. used in pl. (comic *personae*)

per·son·able \'pərs-nə-bəl, 'pər-s³n-ə-bəl\ adj (15c) : pleasant or amiable in person : ATTRACTIVE — **per·son·able·ness** n

per·son·age \'pərs-nij, 'pər-s³n-ij\ n (15c) **1** : a person of rank, note, or distinction; *esp* : one distinguished for presence and personal power **2** : a human individual : PERSON **3** : a dramatic, fictional, or historical character; *also* : IMPERSONATION

per·so·na gra·ta \pər-'sō-nə-'gra-tə, -'grä-\ adj [NL, acceptable person] (1882) : personally acceptable or welcome

---

¹per·son·al \'pərs-nəl, 'pər-s³n-əl\ adj [ME, fr. MF, fr. LL *personalis,* fr. L *persona*] (14c) **1** : of, relating to, or affecting a person : PRIVATE, INDIVIDUAL (~ ambition) (~ financial gain) **2 a** : done in person without the intervention of another; *also* : proceeding from a single person **b** : carried on between individuals directly (a ~ interview) **3** : relating to the person or body **4** : relating to an individual or an individual's character, conduct, motives, or private affairs often in an offensive manner (a ~ insult) **5 a** : being rational and self-conscious (~, responsive government is still possible —John Fischer) **b** : having the qualities of a person rather than a thing or abstraction (a ~ devil) **6** : of, relating to, or constituting personal property (a ~ estate) **7** : denoting grammatical person

²personal n (1861) **1** : a short newspaper paragraph relating to the activities of a person or a group or to personal matters **2** : a short personal communication in a special column of the classified ads section of a newspaper or periodical **3** : PERSONAL FOUL

personal computer n (1977) : MICROCOMPUTER 1

personal effects n pl (1843) : privately owned items (as clothing and jewelry) normally worn or carried on the person

personal equation n (1845) : variation (as in observation) occasioned by the personal peculiarities of an individual; *also* : a correction or allowance made for such variation

personal foul n (ca. 1829) : a foul in a game (as basketball) involving usu. physical contact with or deliberate roughing of an opponent — compare TECHNICAL FOUL

per·son·al·ise *Brit var of* PERSONALIZE

per·son·al·ism \'pərs-nə-ˌli-zəm, 'pər-s³n-ə-\ n (ca. 1846) : a doctrine emphasizing the significance, uniqueness, and inviolability of personality — **per·son·al·ist** \-list\ n *or adj* — **per·son·al·is·tic** \ˌpərs-nə-'lis-tik, ˌpər-s³n-ə-\ adj

per·son·al·i·ty \ˌpər-s³n-'a-lə-tē, ˌpər-'sna-\ n, *pl* **-ties** [ME *personalite,* fr. LL *personalitat-, personalitas,* fr. *personalis*] (15c) **1 a** : the quality or state of being a person **b** : personal existence **2 a** : the condition or fact of relating to a particular person; *specif* : the condition of referring directly to or being aimed disparagingly or hostilely at an individual **b** : an offensively personal remark (angrily resorted to *personalities*) **3** : the complex of characteristics that distinguishes an individual or a nation or group; *esp* : the totality of an individual's behavioral and emotional characteristics **4 a** : distinction or excellence of personal and social traits; *also* : a person having such quality **b** : a person of importance, prominence, renown, or notoriety (a TV ~) *syn* see DISPOSITION

personality inventory n (1932) : any of several tests that attempt to characterize the personality of an individual by objective scoring of replies to a large number of questions concerning his or her own behavior — compare MINNESOTA MULTIPHASIC PERSONALITY INVENTORY

personality test n (1914) : any of several tests that consist of standardized tasks designed to determine various aspects of the personality or the emotional status of the individual examined

per·son·al·ize \'pərs-nə-ˌliz, 'pər-s³n-ə-\ vt **-ized; -iz·ing** (ca. 1741) **1** : PERSONIFY **2** : to make personal or individual; *specif* : to mark as the property of a particular person (*personalized* stationery) — **per·son·al·i·za·tion** \ˌpərs-nə-lə-'zā-shən, ˌpər-s³n-ə-\ n

per·son·al·ly \'pərs-nə-lē, 'pər-s³n-ə-\ adv (14c) **1** : in person (attend to the matter ~) **2** : as a person : in personality (~ attractive but not very trustworthy) **3** : for oneself : as far as oneself is concerned

personal pronoun n (1668) : a pronoun (as *I, you,* or *they*) that expresses a distinction of person

personal property n (1838) : property other than real property consisting of things temporary or movable : CHATTELS

personal tax n (ca. 1935) : DIRECT TAX

per·son·al·ty \'pərs-nəl-tē, 'pər-s³n-əl-\ n, *pl* **-ties** [ME, fr. AF *personalté,* fr. LL *personalitat-, personalitas* personality] (15c) : PERSONAL PROPERTY

per·so·na non gra·ta \pər-'sō-nə-ˌnän-'gra-tə, -'grä-\ adj [NL, unacceptable person] (1904) : personally unacceptable or unwelcome

per·son·ate \'pər-s³n-ˌāt\ vt **-at·ed; -at·ing** (1591) **1 a** : IMPERSONATE, REPRESENT **b** : to assume without authority and with fraudulent intent (some character or capacity) **2** : to invest with personality or personal characteristics (*personating* their gods ridiculous, and themselves past shame —John Milton) — **per·son·a·tion** \ˌpər-s³n-'ā-shən\ n — **per·son·a·tive** \'pər-s³n-ˌā-tiv\ adj — **per·son·a·tor** \-ˌā-tər\ n

per·son-hour \'pər-s³n-ˌau̇(-ə)r\ n (1975) : a unit of one hour's work by one person

per·son·i·fi·ca·tion \pər-ˌsä-nə-fə-'kā-shən\ n (ca. 1755) **1** : attribution of personal qualities; *esp* : representation of a thing or abstraction as a person or by the human form **2** : a divinity or imaginary being representing a thing or abstraction **3** : EMBODIMENT, INCARNATION

per·son·i·fy \pər-'sä-nə-ˌfī\ vt **-fied; -fy·ing** (ca. 1741) **1** : to conceive of or represent as a person or as having human qualities or powers **2** : to be the embodiment or personification of : INCARNATE (a teacher who *personified* patience) — **per·son·i·fi·er** \-ˌfī-(ə)r\ n

per·son·nel \ˌpər-s³n-'el\ n [F, fr. *Personale, Personal,* fr. ML *personale,* fr. LL, neut. of *personalis* personal] (1837) **1 a** : a body of persons usu. employed (as in a factory, office, or organization) **b personnel** pl : PERSONS **2** : a division of an organization concerned with personnel

¹per·spec·tive \pər-'spek-tiv\ n [ME *perspectyf,* fr. ML *perspectivum,* fr. neut. of *perspectivus* of sight, optical, fr. L *perspectus,* pp. of *perspicere* to look through, see clearly, fr. *per-* through + *specere* to look — more at PER-, SPY] (14c) *archaic* : an optical glass (as a telescope)

²perspective n [MF, prob. modif. of OIt *prospettiva,* fr. *prospetto* view, prospect, fr. L *prospectus* — more at PROSPECT] (1563) **1 a** : the technique or process of representing on a plane or curved surface the spatial relation of objects as they might appear to the eye; *specif* : representation in a drawing or painting of parallel lines as converging in order to give the illusion of depth and distance **b** : a picture in per-

---

\ə\ abut \ᵊ\ kitten, F table \ər\ further \a\ ash \ā\ ace \ä\ mop, mar \au̇\ out \ch\ chin \e\ bet \ē\ easy \g\ go \i\ hit \ī\ ice \j\ job \ŋ\ sing \ō\ go \ȯ\ law \ȯi\ boy \th\ thin \th\ the \ü\ loot \u̇\ foot \y\ yet \zh\ vision \ä, k̲, ⁿ, œ, œ̄, ue, ᵫ, ᵊ\ *see* Guide to Pronunciation spective   2   a : the interrelation in which a subject or its parts are mentally viewed ⟨places the issues in proper ∼⟩; *also* : POINT OF VIEW   b : the capacity to view things in their true relations or relative importance ⟨urge you to maintain your ∼ and to view your own task in a larger framework —W. J. Cohen⟩   3   a : a visible scene; *esp* : one giving a distinctive impression of distance : VISTA   b : a mental view or prospect ⟨to gain a broader ∼ on the international scene —*Current Biog.*⟩   4 : the appearance to the eye of objects in respect to their relative distance and positions — **per·spec·tiv·al** \pər-'spek-ti-vəl, ,pər-(,)spek-'ti-vəl\ *adj*

³**perspective** *adj* [ME, optical, fr. ML *perspectivus*] (1570)   **1** *obs* : aiding the vision ⟨his eyes should be like unto the wrong end of a ∼ glass —Alexander Pope⟩   **2** : of, relating to, employing, or seen in perspective ⟨∼ drawing⟩ — **per·spec·tive·ly** *adv*

Per·spex \'pər-,speks\ *trademark* — used for an acrylic plastic consisting essentially of polymethyl methacrylate

per·spi·ca·cious \,pər-spə-'kā-shəs\ *adj* [L *perspicac-, perspicax*, fr. *perspicere*] (1640) : of acute mental vision or discernment : KEEN   syn see SHREWD — **per·spi·ca·cious·ly** *adv* — **per·spi·ca·cious·ness** *n* — **per·spi·cac·i·ty** \-'ka-sə-tē\ *n*

per·spic·u·ous \pər-'spi-kyə-wəs\ *adj* [L *perspicuus* transparent, perspicuous, fr. *perspicere*] (1586) : plain to the understanding esp. because of clarity and precision of presentation ⟨a ∼ argument⟩   syn see CLEAR — **per·spi·cu·ity** \,pər-spə-'kyü-ə-tē\ *n* — **per·spic·u·ous·ly** \pər-'spi-kyə-wəs-lē\ *adv* — **per·spic·u·ous·ness** *n*

per·spi·ra·tion \,pər-spə-'rā-shən\ *n* (1626)   **1** : the action or process of perspiring   **2** : a saline fluid secreted by the sweat glands : SWEAT

per·spi·ra·to·ry \pər-'spi-rə-,tōr-ē, 'pər-sp(ə-)rə-, -,tòr-\ *adj* (1725) : of, relating to, secreting, or inducing perspiration

per·spire \pər-'spīr\ *vi* **per·spired; per·spir·ing** [F *perspirer*, fr. MF, fr. L *per-* through + *spirare* to blow, breathe — more at PER.] (ca. 1682) : to emit matter through the skin; *specif* : to secrete and emit perspiration

per·suad·able \pər-'swā-də-bəl\ *adj* (ca. 1598) : capable of being persuaded

per·suade \pər-'swād\ *vt* **per·suad·ed; per·suad·ing** [L *persuadēre*, fr. *per-* thoroughly + *suadēre* to advise, urge — more at SWEET] (15c)   **1** : to move by argument, entreaty, or expostulation to a belief, position, or course of action   **2** : to plead with : URGE — **per·suad·er** *n*

per·sua·si·ble \-'swā-zə-bəl, -'swā-sə-\ *adj* [MF, fr. L *persuasibilis* persuasive, fr. *persuasus*, pp. of *persuadēre*] (1502) : PERSUADABLE

per·sua·sion \pər-'swā-zhən\ *n* [ME *persuasioun*, fr. MF or L; MF *persuasion*, fr. L *persuasion-, persuasio*, fr. *persuadēre*] (14c)   **1**   a : the act or process or an instance of persuading   b : a persuading argument   c : the ability to persuade : PERSUASIVENESS   2 : the condition of being persuaded   3   a : an opinion held with complete assurance   b : a system of religious beliefs; *also* : a group adhering to a particular system of beliefs   4 : KIND, SORT   syn see OPINION

per·sua·sive \-'swā-siv, -ziv\ *adj* (15c) : tending to persuade — **per·sua·sive·ly** *adv* — **per·sua·sive·ness** *n*

pert \'pərt\ *adj* [ME, open, bold, pert, modif. of OF *apert*, fr. L *apertus* open, fr. pp. of *aperire* to open] (14c)   **1**   a : saucily free and forward : flippantly cocky and assured   b : being trim and chic : JAUNTY ⟨a ∼ little hat⟩   c : piquantly stimulating ⟨is a ∼ notion⟩   2 : LIVELY, VIVACIOUS — **pert·ly** *adv* — **pert·ness** *n*

per·tain \pər-'tān\ *vi* [ME *perteinen*, fr. MF *partenir*, fr. L *pertinēre* to reach to, belong, fr. *per-* through + *tenēre* to hold — more at THIN] (14c)   **1**   a   (1) : to belong as a part, member, accessory, or product   (2) : to belong as an attribute, feature, or function ⟨the destruction and havoc ∼*ing* to war⟩   (3) : to belong as a duty or right ⟨responsibilities that ∼ to fatherhood⟩   b : to be appropriate to something ⟨the criteria . . . will be different from those that ∼ elsewhere —J. B. Conant⟩   2 : to have reference ⟨books ∼*ing* to birds⟩

per·ti·na·cious \,pər-t²n-'ā-shəs\ *adj* [L *pertinac-, pertinax*, fr. *per-* thoroughly + *tenac-, tenax* tenacious, fr. *tenēre*] (1626)   **1**   a : adhering resolutely to an opinion, purpose, or design   b : perversely persistent   2 : stubbornly unyielding or tenacious   syn see OBSTINATE — **per·ti·na·cious·ly** *adv* — **per·ti·na·cious·ness** *n* — **per·ti·nac·i·ty** \-'a-sə-tē\ *n*

per·ti·nence \'pər-t²n-ən(t)s, 'pərt-nən(t)s\ *n* (1659) : the quality or state of being pertinent : RELEVANCE

per·ti·nen·cy \-t²n-ən(t)-sē, -nən(t)-sē\ *n* (1598) : PERTINENCE

per·ti·nent \-t²n-ənt, 'pərt-nənt\ *adj* [ME, fr. MF, fr. L *pertinent-, pertinens*, prp. of *pertinēre*] (14c) : having a clear decisive relevance to the matter in hand   syn see RELEVANT — **per·ti·nent·ly** *adv*

per·turb \pər-'tərb\ *vt* [ME, fr. MF, fr. L *perturbare* to throw into confusion, fr. *per-* + *turbare* to disturb — more at TURBID] (14c)   **1** : to disturb greatly in mind : DISQUIET   2 : to throw into confusion : DISORDER   3 : to cause to experience a perturbation   syn see DISCOMPOSE — **per·turb·able** \-'tər-bə-bəl\ *adj*

per·tur·ba·tion \,pər-tər-'bā-shən, ,pər-,tər-\ *n* (14c)   **1** : the action of perturbing : the state of being perturbed   2 : a disturbance of motion, course, arrangement, or state of equilibrium; *esp* : a disturbance of the regular and usu. elliptical course of motion of a celestial body that is produced by some force additional to that which causes its regular motion — **per·tur·ba·tion·al** \-shnəl, -shə-n²l\ *adj*

per·tus·sis \pər-'tə-səs\ *n* [NL, fr. L *per-* thoroughly + *tussis* cough] (ca. 1799) : WHOOPING COUGH

pe·ruke \pə-'rük\ *n* [MF *perruque*, fr. OIt *parrucca, perrucca* hair, wig] (ca. 1573)   : WIG; *specif* : one of a type popular from the 17th to the early 19th century — **pe·ruked** \-'rükt\ *adj*

pe·ruse \pə-'rüz\ *vt* **pe·rused; pe·rus·ing** [ME, to use up, deal with in sequence, fr. L *per-* thoroughly + ME *usen* to use] (1532)   **1**   a : to examine or consider with attention and in detail : STUDY   b : to look over or through in a casual or cursory manner   2 : READ; *esp* : to read over in an attentive or leisurely manner — **pe·rus·al** \-'rü-zəl\ *n* — **pe·rus·er** *n*

peruke

per·vade \pər-'vād\ *vt* **per·vad·ed; per·vad·ing** [L *pervadere* to go through, pervade, fr. *per-* through + *vadere* to go — more at PER., WADE] (1659) : to become diffused throughout every part of

per·va·sion \pər-'vā-zhən\ *n* (1661) : the action of pervading or condition of being pervaded

per·va·sive \pər-'vā-siv, -ziv\ *adj* (ca. 1750) : that pervades or tends to pervade ⟨a ∼ odor⟩ — **per·va·sive·ly** *adv* — **per·va·sive·ness** *n*

per·verse \(,)pər-'vərs, 'pər-,\ *adj* [ME, fr. L *perversus*, fr. pp. of *pervertere*] (14c)   **1**   a : turned away from what is right or good : CORRUPT   b : IMPROPER, INCORRECT   c : contrary to the evidence or the direction of the judge on a point of law ⟨∼ verdict⟩   2   a : obstinate in opposing what is right, reasonable, or accepted : WRONGHEADED   b : arising from or indicative of stubbornness or obstinacy   3 : marked by peevishness or petulance : CRANKY   syn see CONTRARY — **per·verse·ly** *adv* — **per·verse·ness** *n* — **per·ver·si·ty** \pər-'vər-sə-tē, -ste\ *n*

per·ver·sion \pər-'vər-zhən, -shən\ *n* (14c)   **1** : the action of perverting : the condition of being perverted   2 : a perverted form; *esp* : an aberrant sexual practice esp. when habitual and preferred to normal coitus

per·ver·sive \-'vər-siv, -ziv\ *adj* (1817)   **1** : that perverts or tends to pervert   2 : arising from or indicative of perversion

¹**per·vert** \pər-'vərt\ *vt* [ME, fr. MF *pervertir*, fr. L *pervertere* to overturn, corrupt, pervert, fr. *per-* thoroughly + *vertere* to turn — more at PER., WORTH] (14c)   **1**   a : to cause to turn aside or away from what is good or true or morally right : CORRUPT   b : to cause to turn aside or away from what is generally done or accepted : MISDIRECT   2   a : to divert to a wrong end or purpose : MISUSE   b : to twist the meaning or sense of : MISINTERPRET   syn see DEBASE — **per·vert·er** *n*

²**per·vert** \'pər-,vərt\ *n* (ca. 1661) : one that has been perverted; *specif* : one given to some form of sexual perversion

per·vert·ed \pər-'vər-təd\ *adj* (14c)   **1** : CORRUPT   2 : marked by perversion — **per·vert·ed·ly** *adv* — **per·vert·ed·ness** *n*

per·vi·ous \'pər-vē-əs\ *adj* [L *pervius*, fr. *per-* through + *via* way — more at PER., WAY] (ca. 1614)   **1** : ACCESSIBLE ⟨∼ to reason⟩   2 : PERMEABLE ⟨∼ soil⟩ — **per·vi·ous·ness** *n*

Pe·sach \'pā-,säk\ *n* [Heb *pesaḥ*] (1613) : PASSOVER

pe·se·ta \pə-'sā-tə\ *n* [Sp, fr. dim. of *peso*] (1811) — see MONEY table

pe·se·wa \pə-'sā-wə\ *n* [Twi *pésewa*, lit., penny, penny's worth of gold dust] (1965) — see *cedi* at MONEY table

pes·ky \'pes-kē\ *adj* **pes·ki·er; -est** [prob. irreg. fr. *pest* + *-y*] (1775)   : TROUBLESOME, VEXATIOUS ⟨∼ issues⟩

pe·so \'pā-(,)sō, 'pe-\ *n, pl* **pesos** [Sp, lit., weight, fr. L *pensum* — more at POISE] (1555)   **1** : an old silver coin of Spain and Spanish America equal to eight reals   2 — see MONEY table

pes·sa·ry \'pe-sə-rē\ *n, pl* **-ries** [ME *pessarie*, fr. LL *pessarium*, fr. *pessus, pessum* pessary, fr. Gk *pessos* oval stone for playing checkers, pessary] (14c)   **1** : a vaginal suppository   2 : a device worn in the vagina to support the uterus, remedy a malposition, or prevent conception

pes·si·mism \'pə-sə-,mi-zəm *also* 'pe-zə-\ *n* [F *pessimisme*, fr. L *pessimus* worst — more at PEJORATIVE] (1815)   **1** : an inclination to emphasize adverse aspects, conditions, and possibilities or to expect the worst possible outcome   2   a : the doctrine that reality is essentially evil   b : the doctrine that evil overbalances happiness in life — **pes·si·mist** \-mist\ *n*

pes·si·mis·tic \,pe-sə-'mis-tik *also* ,pe-zə-\ *adj* (1868) : of, relating to, or characterized by pessimism : GLOOMY   syn see CYNICAL — **pes·si·mis·ti·cal·ly** \-ti-k(ə-)lē\ *adv*

pest \'pest\ *n* [MF *peste*, fr. L *pestis*] (1553)   **1** : an epidemic disease associated with high mortality; *specif* : PLAGUE   2 : something resembling a pest in destructiveness; *esp* : a plant or animal detrimental to humans or human concerns (as agriculture or livestock production)   3 : one that pesters or annoys : NUISANCE — **pesty** \'pes-tē\ *adj*

pes·ter \'pes-tər\ *vt* **pes·tered; pes·ter·ing** \-t(ə-)riŋ\ [modif. of MF *empestrer* to hobble, embarrass, fr. (assumed) VL *impastoriare*, fr. L *in-* + ML *pastoria* hobble — more at PASTERN] (1533)   **1** *obs* : OVERCROWD   2 : to harass with petty irritations : ANNOY   syn see WORRY

pest·hole \'pest-,hōl\ *n* (1903) : a place liable to epidemic disease

pest·house \-,haůs\ *n* (1611) : a shelter or hospital for those infected with a pestilential or contagious disease

pes·ti·cide \'pes-tə-,sīd\ *n* (ca. 1925) : an agent used to destroy pests

pes·tif·er·ous \pes-'ti-f(ə-)rəs\ *adj* [ME, fr. L *pestifer* pestilential, noxious, fr. *pestis* + *-fer* -ferous] (15c)   **1** : dangerous to society : PERNICIOUS   2   a : carrying or propagating infection : PESTILENTIAL   b : infected with a pestilential disease   3 : TROUBLESOME, ANNOYING — **pes·tif·er·ous·ly** *adv* — **pes·tif·er·ous·ness** *n*

pes·ti·lence \'pes-tə-lən(t)s\ *n* (14c)   **1** : a contagious or infectious epidemic disease that is virulent and devastating; *esp* : BUBONIC PLAGUE   2 : something that is destructive or pernicious ⟨I'll pour this ∼ into his ear —Shak.⟩

pes·ti·lent \-lənt\ *adj* [ME, fr. L *pestilent-, pestilens* pestilential, fr. *pestis*] (14c)   **1** : destructive of life : DEADLY   2 : injuring or endangering society : PERNICIOUS   3 : causing displeasure or annoyance   4 : INFECTIOUS, CONTAGIOUS ⟨∼ disease⟩ — **pes·ti·lent·ly** *adv*

pes·ti·len·tial \,pes-tə-'len(t)-shəl\ *adj* (14c)   **1**   a : causing or tending to cause pestilence : DEADLY   b : of or relating to pestilence   2 : morally harmful : PERNICIOUS   3 : giving rise to vexation or annoyance : IRRITATING — **pes·ti·len·tial·ly** \-'len(t)-sh(ə-)lē\ *adv*

¹**pes·tle** \'pe-səl, 'pes-t²l\ *n* [ME *pestel*, fr. MF, fr. L *pistillum*, fr. *pinsere* to pound, crush; akin to Gk *ptissein* to crush, Skt *pinaṣṭi* he pounds] (14c)   **1** : a usu. club-shaped implement for pounding or grinding substances in a mortar   2 : any of various devices for pounding, stamping, or pressing

²**pestle** *vb* **pes·tled; pes·tling** \'pe-s(ə-)liŋ, 'pes-t²l-iŋ\ *vt* (15c) *archaic* : to beat, pound, or pulverize with or as if with a pestle ∼ *vi* : to work with a pestle : use a pestle

pes·to \'pes-(,)tō\ *n* [It, fr. *pesto*, adj., pounded, fr. *pestare* to pound, fr. LL *pistare*, freq. of L *pinsere*] (1937) : a sauce made esp. of fresh basil, garlic, oil, pine nuts, and grated cheese

¹**pet** \'pet\ *n* [perh. back-formation fr. ME *pety* small — more at PETTY] (1508)   **1**   a : a pampered and usu. spoiled child   b : a person who is treated with unusual kindness or consideration : DARLING   2   a : a domesticated animal kept for pleasure rather than utility

²**pet** *adj* (1584)   **1** : kept or treated as a pet   2 : expressing fondness or endearment ⟨a ∼ name⟩   3 : FAVORITE ⟨a ∼ project⟩

³**pet** vb **pet·ted; pet·ting** vt (1629) **1 a :** to treat as a pet **b :** to stroke in a gentle or loving manner **2 :** to treat with unusual kindness and consideration : PAMPER ~ vi **:** to engage in amorous embracing, caressing, and kissing : NECK — **pet·ter** n
⁴**pet** n [origin unknown] (1590) **:** a fit of peevishness, sulkiness, or anger
⁵**pet** vi **pet·ted; pet·ting** (1629) **:** to take offense : SULK
peta- comb form [ISV, modif. of Gk penta- penta-] **:** quadrillion 〈peta= electron volts〉
pet·al \'pe-t³l\ n [NL petalum, fr. Gk petalon; akin to Gk petannynai to spread out — more at FATHOM] (ca. 1726) **:** one of the modified often brightly colored leaves of the corolla of a flower — see FLOWER illustration — **pet·aled** or **pet·alled** \-t³ld\ adj — **pet·al·like** \-t³l-‚(l)īk\ adj
pet·al·oid \'pe-t³l-‚óid\ adj (1730) **1 :** resembling a flower petal **2 :** consisting of petaloid elements
pet·al·ous \'pe-t³l-əs\ adj (ca. 1736) **1 :** having petals **2 :** having (such or so many) petals — used in combination 〈polypetalous〉
pe·tard \pə-'tär(d)\ n [MF, fr. peter to break wind, fr. pet expulsion of intestinal gas, fr. L peditum, fr. neut. of peditus, pp. of pedere to break wind; akin to Gk bdein to break wind] (1598) **1 :** a case containing an explosive to break down a door or gate or breach a wall **2 :** a firework that explodes with a loud report
pet·a·sos or **pet·a·sus** \'pe-tə-səs\ n [L & Gk; L petasus, fr. Gk petasos; akin to Gk petannynai to spread out] (1599) **:** a broad-brimmed low= crowned hat worn by ancient Greeks and Romans; esp **:** the winged hat of Hermes
pet·cock \'pet-‚käk\ n [pet- (perh. fr. petty) + cock] (ca. 1864) **:** a small cock, faucet, or valve for releasing a gas (as air) or draining
pe·te·chia \pə-'tē-kē-ə\, n, pl **-chi·ae** \-kē-‚ī\ [NL, fr. It petecchia, ultim. fr. L impetigo] (ca. 1796) **:** a minute reddish or purplish spot containing blood that appears in skin or mucous membrane esp. in some infectious diseases (as typhoid fever) — **pe·te·chi·al** \-kē-əl\ adj
¹**pe·ter** \'pē-tər\ vi [origin unknown] (1846) **1 :** to diminish gradually and come to an end : GIVE OUT — usu. used with out 〈novelists whose creative impetus seems largely to have ~ed out —Times Lit. Supp.〉 **2 :** to become exhausted — usu. used with out
²**peter** n [fr. the name Peter] (ca. 1902) **:** PENIS — often considered vulgar
Pe·ter \'pē-tər\ n [LL Petrus, fr. Gk Petros, fr. petra rock] **1 :** a fisherman of Galilee and one of the twelve apostles **2 :** either of two hortatory letters written to early Christians and included as books of the New Testament — see BIBLE table
Peter Pan \-'pan\ n **1 :** a boy in Sir James Barrie's play Peter Pan who lives without growing older in a never-never land **2 :** an adult who doesn't want to grow up : one who hangs on to adolescent interests and attitudes
Peter Pan collar n (1908) **:** a usu. small flat close-fitting collar with rounded ends that meet at the top in front
Peter Principle n [Laurence J. Peter b1919 Am. (Canad.-born) educator] (1968) **:** an observation: in a hierarchy employees tend to rise to the level of their incompetence
Peter's pence n pl but sing in constr [ME; fr. the tradition that St. Peter founded the papal see] (13c) **1 :** an annual tribute of a penny formerly paid by each householder in England to the papal see **2 :** a voluntary annual contribution made by Roman Catholics to the pope
pet·i·o·lar \‚pe-tē-'ō-lər\ adj (1760) **:** of, relating to, or proceeding from a petiole
pet·i·o·late \'pe-tē-ə-‚lāt, ‚pe-tē-'ō-lət\ adj (ca. 1753) **:** having a stalk or petiole
pet·i·ole \'pe-tē-‚ōl\ n [NL petiolus, fr. L petiolus, peciolus small foot, fruit stalk, prob. alter. of (assumed) L pediciolus, dim. of pediculus, dim. of ped-, pes foot — more at FOOT] (1753) **1 :** a slender stem that supports the blade of a foliage leaf **2 :** PEDUNCLE; specif **:** a slender abdominal segment joining the rest of the abdomen to the thorax in some insects — **pet·i·oled** \-‚ōld\ adj
pet·i·o·lule \'pe-tē-ō-‚lül, ‚pe-tē-'ōl-(‚)yü(ə)l\ n [NL petiolulus, dim. of petiolus] (1832) **:** a stalk of a leaflet of a compound leaf
pet·it \'pe-tē\ adj [ME, small, minor, fr. MF, small] (14c) **:** PETTY 1 — used chiefly in legal compounds
pe·tit bourgeois \pə-'tē-, ‚pe-tē-\ n [F, lit., small bourgeois] (1853) **1 :** a member of the petite bourgeoisie **2 :** PETITE BOURGEOISIE — **petit bourgeois** adj
¹**pe·tite** \pə-'tēt\ adj [F, fem. of petit] (1784) **:** having a small trim figure — usu. used of a woman — **pe·tite·ness** n
²**petite** n (ca. 1929) **:** a clothing size for short women
petite bourgeoisie n [F, lit., small bourgeoisie] (1916) **:** the lower middle class including esp. small shopkeepers and artisans
pe·tit four \‚pe-tē-'fór, pə-‚tē-, -'fór; 'pe-tē-‚, -‚fór; -'fur\ n, pl **petits fours** or **petit fours** \-'fórz, -'fórz, -'fur(z)\ [F, lit., small oven] (1884) **:** a small cake cut from pound or sponge cake and frosted
¹**pe·ti·tion** \pə-'ti-shən\ n [ME, fr. MF, fr. L petition-, petitio, fr. petere to seek, request — more at FEATHER] (14c) **1 :** an earnest request : ENTREATY **2 a :** a formal written request made to an official person or organized body (as a court) **b :** a document embodying such a formal written request **3 :** something asked or requested — **pe·ti·tion·ary** \-'ti-shə-‚ner-ē\ adj
²**petition** vb **pe·ti·tioned; pe·ti·tion·ing** \-'ti-sh(ə-)niŋ\ vt (1607) **:** to make a request to : SOLICIT ~ vi **:** to make a request; esp **:** to make a formal written request — **pe·ti·tion·er** \-sh(ə-)nər\ n
pe·ti·tio prin·ci·pii \pə-‚tē-tē-‚ō-(‚)priŋ-'ki-pē-‚ī, -ē\ n [ML, lit., postulation of the beginning, begging the question] (1531) **:** a logical fallacy in which a premise is assumed to be true without warrant or in which what is to be proved is implicitly taken for granted
pet·it jury \'pe-tē-\ n (15c) **:** a jury of 12 persons impaneled to try and to decide finally upon the facts at issue in causes for trial in a court
petit larceny n (1587) **:** larceny involving property of a value below a legally established minimum
pe·tit-maî·tre \pə-‚tē-'mätr³\ n, pl **petits-maîtres** \same\ [F, lit., small master] (1711) **:** DANDY, FOP
pe·tit mal \'pe-tē-‚mal, -‚mäl\ n [F, lit., small illness] (1874) **:** epilepsy characterized by mild convulsive seizure with transient clouding of consciousness — compare GRAND MAL
pet·it point \'pe-tē-‚póint\ n [F, lit., small point] (1882) **:** TENT STITCH; also **:** embroidery made with this stitch
pet peeve n (ca. 1919) **:** a frequent subject of complaint

petr- or **petri-** or **petro-** comb form [NL, fr. Gk petr-, petro-, fr. petros stone & petra rock] **1 :** stone : rock 〈petrology〉 **2 :** petroleum 〈petrodollar〉
pe·tra·le sole \pə-'trä-lē-\ n [petrale prob. fr. It dial., a flatfish] (1953) **:** a flounder (Eopsetta jordani) chiefly of the Pacific waters of No. America that is an important food fish — called also petrale
Pe·trar·chan sonnet \pi-'trär-kən-, ‚pē-, (‚)pe-\ n [Petrarch (Francesco Petrarca)] (ca. 1909) **:** ITALIAN SONNET
pe·trel \'pe-trəl, 'pē-\ n [alter. of earlier pitteral] (1676) **:** any of numerous seabirds (esp. families Procellariidae and Hydrobatidae); esp **:** one of the smaller long-winged birds that fly far from land — compare STORM PETREL
pe·tri dish \'pē-trē-\ n [Julius R. Petri †1921 Ger. bacteriologist] (1892) **:** a small shallow dish of thin glass or plastic with a loose cover used esp. for cultures in bacteriology
pet·ri·fac·tion \‚pe-trə-'fak-shən\ n (15c) **1 :** the process of petrifying **2 :** something petrified **3 :** the quality or state of being petrified
pet·ri·fi·ca·tion \‚pe-trə-fə-'kā-shən\ n (ca. 1611) **:** PETRIFACTION
pet·ri·fy \'pe-trə-‚fī\ vb **-fied; -fy·ing** [MF petrifier, fr. petr- + -ifier -ify] vt (1594) **1 :** to convert (organic matter) into stone or a substance of stony hardness by the infiltration of water and the deposition of dissolved mineral matter **2 :** to make rigid or inert like stone: **a :** to make lifeless or inactive : DEADEN 〈slogans are apt to ~ a man's thinking —Saturday Rev.〉 **b :** to confound with fear, amazement, or awe 〈a novel about an airline pilot that will ~ you —Martin Levin〉 ~ vi **:** to become stone or of stony hardness or rigidity
Pe·trine \'pē-‚trīn\ adj [LL Petrus Peter] (1846) **1 :** of, relating to, or characteristic of the apostle Peter or the doctrines associated with his name **2 :** of, relating to, or characteristic of Peter the Great or his reign
pet·ro·chem·i·cal \‚pe-trō-'ke-mi-kəl\ n (1942) **:** a chemical isolated or derived from petroleum or natural gas — **pet·ro·chem·is·try** \-'ke-mə-strē\ n
pet·ro·dol·lar \'pe-trō-‚dä-lər\ n (1974) **:** a dollar's worth of foreign exchange obtained by a petroleum-exporting country through sales abroad — usu. used in pl.
pet·ro·gen·e·sis \‚pe-trō-'je-nə-səs\ n [NL] (1901) **:** the origin or formation of rocks — **pet·ro·ge·net·ic** \-jə-'ne-tik\ adj
pet·ro·glyph \'pe-trə-‚glif\ n [F pétroglyphe, fr. pétr- petr- + -glyphe (as in hiéroglyphe hieroglyph)] (1870) **:** a carving or inscription on a rock
pe·trog·ra·phy \pə-'trä-grə-fē, pe-\ n [NL petrographia, fr. petr- + L -graphia -graphy] (1651) **:** the description and systematic classification of rocks — **pe·trog·ra·pher** \-fər\ n — **pet·ro·graph·ic** \‚pe-trə-'gra-fik\ or **pet·ro·graph·i·cal** \-fi-kəl\ adj — **pet·ro·graph·i·cal·ly** \-fi-k(ə-)lē\ adv
pet·rol \'pe-trəl, -‚träl\ n [F essence de pétrole, lit., essence of petroleum] (1895) chiefly Brit **:** GASOLINE
pet·ro·la·tum \‚pe-trə-'lā-təm, -'lä-\ n [NL, fr. ML petroleum] (1887) **:** PETROLEUM JELLY
pe·tro·leum \pə-'trō-lē-əm, -'trōl-yəm\ n [ME, fr. ML, fr. L petr- + oleum oil — more at OIL] (15c) **:** an oily flammable bituminous liquid that may vary from almost colorless to black, occurs in many places in the upper strata of the earth, is a complex mixture of hydrocarbons with small amounts of other substances, and is prepared for use as gasoline, naphtha, or other products by various refining processes
petroleum jelly n (1897) **:** a neutral unctuous odorless tasteless substance obtained from petroleum and used esp. in ointments and dressings
pe·trol·o·gy \pə-'trä-lə-jē, pe-\ n [ISV] (1811) **:** a science that deals with the origin, history, occurrence, structure, chemical composition, and classification of rocks — **pet·ro·log·ic** \‚pe-trə-'lä-jik\ or **pet·ro·log·i·cal** \-ji-kəl\ adj — **pet·ro·log·i·cal·ly** \-ji-k(ə-)lē\ adv — **pe·trol·o·gist** \pə-'trä-lə-jist, pe-\ n
pet·ro·nel \'pe-trə-‚nel\ n [perh. modif. of MF poitrinal, petrinal, fr. poitrinal of the chest, fr. poitrine chest, deriv. of L pector-, pectus — more at PECTORAL] (ca. 1577) **:** a portable firearm resembling a carbine of large caliber
pe·tro·sal \pə-'trō-səl\ adj [NL petrosa petrous portion of the temporal bone, fr. L, fem. of petrosus] (1741) **:** of, relating to, or situated in the region of the petrous portion of the temporal bone or capsule of the inner ear
pe·trous \'pe-trəs, 'pē-\ adj [ME, fr. MF petreux, fr. L petrosus, fr. petra rock, fr. Gk] (14c) **:** of, relating to, or constituting the exceptionally hard and dense portion of the human temporal bone that contains the internal auditory organs
¹**pet·ti·coat** \'pe-tē-‚kōt\ n [ME petycote short tunic, petticoat, fr. pety small + cote coat] (15c) **1 a :** a skirt worn by women, girls, or young children: as **a :** an outer skirt formerly worn by women and small children **b :** a fancy skirt made to show below a draped-up overskirt **c :** an underskirt usu. a little shorter than outer clothing and often made with a ruffled, pleated, or lace edge **d** archaic **:** the skirt of a woman's riding habit **2 a :** a garment characteristic or typical of women **b :** WOMAN **3 :** something (as a valance) resembling a petticoat — **pet·ti·coat·ed** \-‚kō-təd\ adj
²**petticoat** adj (1660) **:** of, relating to, or exercised by women : FEMALE
pet·ti·fog·ger \'pe-tē-‚fó-gər, -‚fä-\ n [prob. fr. petty + obs. E fogger pettifogger] (1576) **1 :** a lawyer whose methods are petty, underhanded, or disreputable : SHYSTER **2 :** one given to quibbling over trifles — **pet·ti·fog** \-‚fäg\ vb — **pet·ti·fog·ging** \-giŋ\ adj or n — **pet·ti·fog·ery** \-g(ə-)rē\ n
petting zoo n (1968) **:** a collection of farm animals or gentle exotic animals for children to pet and feed
pet·tish \'pe-tish\ adj [prob. fr. ⁴pet] (ca. 1591) **:** FRETFUL, PEEVISH — **pet·tish·ly** adv — **pet·tish·ness** n
pet·ti·toes \'pe-tē-‚tōz\ n pl [pl. of obs. pettytoe offal] (1555) **1 :** the feet of a pig used as food **2 :** TOES, FEET
pet·ty \'pe-tē\ adj **pet·ti·er; -est** [ME pety small, minor, alter. of petit]

\ə\ abut \³\ kitten, F table \ər\ further \a\ ash \ā\ ace \ä\ mop, mar
\aú\ out \ch\ chin \e\ bet \ē\ easy \g\ go \i\ hit \ī\ ice \j\ job
\ŋ\ sing \ō\ go \ó\ law \ói\ boy \th\ thin \th\ the \ü\ loot \ú\ foot
\y\ yet \zh\ vision \á, k̲, ⁿ, œ, œ̄, ue, ūe, ˙\ see Guide to Pronunciation

(14c) 1 : having secondary rank or importance : MINOR, SUBORDINATE 2 : having little or no importance or significance 3 : marked by or reflective of narrow interests and sympathies : SMALL-MINDED — **pet‧ti‧ly** \'pe-t°l-ē\ adv — **pet‧ti‧ness** \'pe-tē-nəs\ n
petty cash n (1834) : cash kept on hand for payment of minor items
petty larceny n (1818) : PETIT LARCENY
petty officer n (1760) : a subordinate officer in the navy or coast guard appointed from among the enlisted men — compare NONCOMMISSIONED OFFICER
petty officer first class n (1942) : an enlisted man in the navy or coast guard ranking above a petty officer second class and below a chief petty officer
petty officer second class n (1942) : an enlisted man in the navy or coast guard ranking above a petty officer third class and below a petty officer first class
petty officer third class n (1942) : an enlisted man in the navy or coast guard ranking above a seaman and below a petty officer second class
pet‧u‧lance \'pe-chə-lən(t)s\ n (1610) : the quality or state of being petulant : PEEVISHNESS
pet‧u‧lan‧cy \-lən(t)-sē\ n (1559) archaic : PETULANCE
pet‧u‧lant \-lənt\ adj [L or MF; MF, fr. L petulant-, petulans; akin to L petere to go to, attack, seek — more at FEATHER] (1605) 1 : insolent or rude in speech or behavior 2 : characterized by temporary or capricious ill humor : PEEVISH — **pet‧u‧lant‧ly** adv
pe‧tu‧nia \pi-'tün-yə, -'tyün-\ n [NL, fr. obs. F petun tobacco, fr. Tupi petïma] (1825) : any of a genus (Petunia) of tropical American herbs of the nightshade family with flowers having funnel-shaped corollas
pew \'pyü\ n [ME pewe, fr. MF puie balustrade, fr. L podia, pl. of podium parapet, podium, fr. Gk podion base, dim. of pod-, pous foot — more at FOOT] (14c) 1 : a compartment in the auditorium of a church providing seats for several persons 2 : one of the benches with backs and sometimes doors fixed in rows in a church
pe‧wee \'pē-(,)wē\ n [imit.] (1796) : any of various small olivaceous flycatchers (genus Contopus)
pew‧hold‧er \'pyü-,hōl-dər\ n (1845) : a renter or owner of a pew
pe‧wit var of PEEWIT
pew‧ter \'pyü-tər\ n [ME, fr. MF peutre, fr. (assumed) VL peltrum] (14c) 1 : any of various alloys having tin as chief component; esp : a dull alloy with lead formerly used for domestic utensils 2 : utensils of pewter 3 : a bluish gray — **pewter** adj
pew‧ter‧er \'pyü-tər-ər\ n (14c) : one that makes pewter utensils
pey‧o‧te \pā-'ō-tē\ also **pey‧otl** \-'ō-t°l\ n [MexSp peyote, fr. Nahuatl peyotl] (1849) 1 : a stimulant drug derived from mescal buttons 2 : any of several American cacti (genus Lophophora); esp : MESCAL
pfen‧nig \'fe-nig, -nik, G '(p)fe-nik\ n, pl **pfennig** also **pfen‧nigs** \'fe-nigz, -niks\ or **pfen‧ni‧ge** \'(p)fe-ni-gə, -ni-yə\ [G, fr. OHG pfenning — more at PENNY] (1547) — see deutsche mark at MONEY table
PG \'pē-'jē\ certification mark — used to certify that a motion picture is of such a nature that all ages may be allowed admission but parental guidance is suggested; compare G, NC-17, PG-13, R
PG-13 \-,thər(t)-'tēn\ certification mark — used to certify that a motion picture is of such a nature that persons of all ages may be admitted but parental guidance is suggested esp. for children under 13; compare G, NC-17, PG, R
pH \'pē-'āch\ n [G, fr. Potenz power + H (symbol for hydrogen)] (1909) : a measure of acidity and alkalinity of a solution that is a number on a scale on which a value of 7 represents neutrality and lower numbers indicate increasing acidity and higher numbers increasing alkalinity and on which each unit of change represents a tenfold change in acidity or alkalinity and that is the negative logarithm of the effective hydrogen-ion concentration or hydrogen-ion activity in gram equivalents per liter of the solution; also : the condition represented by a pH number
Phae‧dra \'fē-drə\ n [L, fr. Gk Phaidra] : a daughter of Minos who marries Theseus and falls in love with her stepson Hippolytus
Pha‧ë‧thon \'fā-ə-t°n, -tən, -,thän\ n [L, fr. Gk Phaethōn] : a son of Helios who drives his father's sun-chariot through the sky but loses control and is struck down by a thunderbolt of Zeus
pha‧eton \'fā-ə-t°n\ n [Phaethon] (1742) 1 : any of various light four-wheeled horse-drawn vehicles 2 : TOURING CAR
phage \'fāj\ also 'fäzh\ n [by shortening] (1926) : BACTERIOPHAGE
-phage n comb form [Gk -phagos one that eats, fr. -phagos -phagous] : virus or cell that destroys cells ⟨bacteriophage⟩ ⟨microphage⟩

phaeton 1

-phagia n comb form [NL, fr. Gk] : -PHAGY ⟨dysphagia⟩
phago‧cyte \'fa-gə-,sīt\ n [ISV, fr. Gk phagein + NL -cyta -cyte] (ca. 1884) : a cell (as a white blood cell) that engulfs and consumes foreign material (as microorganisms) and debris — **phago‧cyt‧ic** \,fa-gə-'si-tik\ adj
phago‧cy‧tize \'fa-gə-sə-,tīz, -,sī-\ vt **-tized; -tiz‧ing** (1913) : PHAGOCYTOSE
phago‧cy‧tose \-sə-,tōs, -sī-, -,tōz\ vt **-tosed; -tos‧ing** [back-formation fr. phagocytosis] (1912) : to consume by phagocytosis
phago‧cy‧to‧sis \,fa-gə-sə-'tō-səs, -sī-\ n, pl **-to‧ses** \-,sēz\ [NL] (1889) : the engulfing and usu. the destruction of particulate matter by phagocytes — **phago‧cy‧tot‧ic** \-'tä-tik\ adj
-phagous adj comb form [Gk -phagos, fr. phagein to eat — more at BAKSHEESH] : eating ⟨saprophagous⟩
-phagy n comb form, pl **-phagies** [Gk -phagia, fr. phagein] : eating of a (specified) type or substance ⟨geophagy⟩
pha‧lange \'fā-,lanj, fə-', fā-'\ n [F, fr. Gk phalang-, phalanx] (ca. 1860) : PHALANX 2
pha‧lan‧ge‧al \,fā-lən-'jē-əl, ,fa-; fə-'lan-jē-, fā-\ adj (1831) : of or relating to a phalanx or the phalanges
pha‧lan‧ger \fə-'lan-jər, 'fā-\ n [NL, fr. Gk phalang-, phalanx] (ca. 1774) : any of various small to medium-sized marsupial mammals (family Phalangeridae) of the Australian region that are chiefly arboreal and nocturnal and usu. densely furred

phal‧an‧stery \'fa-lən-,ster-ē\ n, pl **-ster‧ies** [F phalanstère dwelling of a Fourierist community, fr. L phalang-, phalanx + F -stère (as in monastère monastery)] (1846) 1 a : a Fourierist cooperative community b : a self-contained structure housing such a community 2 : something resembling a Fourierist phalanstery
pha‧lanx \'fā-,laŋ(k)s, Brit usu 'fa-\ n, pl **pha‧lanx‧es** or **pha‧lan‧ges** \fə-'lan-(,)jēz, fā-, 'fā-,, Brit usu fa-\ [L phalang-, phalanx, fr. Gk, battle line, digital bone, lit., log — more at BALK] (1553) 1 : a body of heavily armed infantry in ancient Greece formed in close deep ranks and files; broadly : a body of troops in close array 2 pl phalanges : one of the digital bones of the hand or foot of a vertebrate 3 pl usu phalanxes a : a massed arrangement of persons, animals, or things b : an organized body of persons
phal‧a‧rope \'fa-lə-,rōp\ n, pl **-ropes** also **-rope** [F, fr. NL phalaropod-, phalaropus, fr. Gk phalaris coot + pod-, pous foot; akin to Gk phalios having a white spot — more at BALD, FOOT] (ca. 1776) : any of a genus (Phalaropus) of small shorebirds that are related to sandpipers but have lobate toes and are good swimmers
phal‧lic \'fa-lik\ adj (1789) 1 : of or relating to phallicism ⟨a ~ cult⟩ 2 : of, relating to, or resembling a phallus 3 : relating to or being the stage of psychosexual development in psychoanalytic theory during which a child becomes interested in his or her own sexual organs — **phal‧li‧cal‧ly** \-li-k(ə-)lē\ adv
phal‧li‧cism \'fa-lə-,si-zəm\ n (1884) : the worship of the generative principle as symbolized by the phallus
phal‧lo‧cen‧tric \,fa-lə-'sen-trik\ adj (1927) : centered on or emphasizing the masculine point of view
phal‧lus \'fa-ləs\ n, pl **phal‧li** \'fa-,lī\, -,lē\ or **phal‧lus‧es** [L, fr. Gk phallos penis, representation of the penis; prob. akin to L flare to blow — more at BLOW] (ca. 1613) 1 : a symbol or representation of the penis 2 : PENIS
-phane n comb form [Gk phanēs appearing, fr. phainein to show — more at FANCY] : substance having a (specified) form, quality, or appearance ⟨hydrophane⟩
phan‧er‧o‧gam \'fa-nə-rə-,gam, fə-'ner-ə-\ n [F phanérogame, ultim. fr. Gk phaneros visible (fr. phainein) + gamos marriage] (1861) : a seed plant or flowering plant : SPERMATOPHYTE
phan‧er‧o‧phyte \'fa-nə-rə-,fīt, fə-'ner-ə-\ n [Gk phaneros + ISV -phyte] (1913) : a perennial plant that bears its perennating buds well above the surface of the ground
Phan‧er‧o‧zo‧ic \,fa-nə-rə-'zō-ik\ adj [Gk phaneros + E ²-zoic] (1930) : of, relating to, or being an eon of geologic history that comprises the Paleozoic, Mesozoic, and Cenozoic or the corresponding system of rocks — see GEOLOGIC TIME table — **Phanerozoic** n
phan‧tasm \'fan-,ta-zəm\ n [ME fantasme, fr. OF, fr. L phantasma, fr. Gk, fr. phantazein to present to the mind — more at FANCY] (13c) 1 : a product of fantasy: as a : delusive appearance : ILLUSION b : GHOST, SPECTER c : a figment of the imagination 2 : a mental representation of a real object — **phan‧tas‧mal** \fan-'taz-məl\ adj — **phan‧tas‧mic** \-mik\ adj
phan‧tas‧ma \fan-'taz-mə\ n, pl **-ma‧ta** \-mə-tə\ [L] (1598) : PHANTASM 1
phan‧tas‧ma‧go‧ria \(,)fan-,taz-mə-'gȯr-ē-ə, -'gȯr-\ n [F phantasmagorie, fr. phantasme phantasm (fr. OF fantasme) + -agorie (perh. fr. Gk agora assembly) — more at AGORA] (ca. 1802) 1 : an exhibition or display of optical effects and illusions 2 a : a constantly shifting complex succession of things seen or imagined b : a scene that constantly changes 3 : a bizarre or fantastic combination, collection, or assemblage — **phan‧tas‧ma‧gor‧ic** \-'gȯr-ik, -'gȯr-, -'gär-\ or **phan‧tas‧ma‧gor‧i‧cal** \-i-kəl\ adj
phantasy var of FANTASY
¹phan‧tom \'fan-təm\ n [ME fantosme, fantome, fr. MF fantosme, modif. of L phantasma] (14c) 1 a : something (as a specter) apparent to sense but with no substantial existence : APPARITION b : something elusive or visionary : WILL-O'-THE-WISP c : an object of continual dread or abhorrence : BUGBEAR ⟨the ~ of disease and want⟩ 2 : something existing in appearance only 3 : a representation of something abstract, ideal, or incorporeal ⟨she was a ~ of delight —William Wordsworth⟩ — **phan‧tom‧like** \-,līk\ adv or adj
²phantom adj (15c) 1 : of the nature of, suggesting, or being a phantom : ILLUSORY 2 : FICTITIOUS, DUMMY ⟨~ voters⟩
pha‧raoh \'fer-(,)ō, 'far-(,)ō, 'fā-(,)rō\ n, often cap [ME pharao, fr. OE, fr. LL pharaon-, pharao, fr. Gk pharaō, fr. Heb par'ōh, fr. Egypt pr-'',] (bef. 12c) 1 : a ruler of ancient Egypt 2 : TYRANT
pharaoh ant n (ca. 1947) : a little red ant (Monomorium pharaonis) that is a common household pest
phar‧a‧on‧ic \,fer-ā-'ä-nik, ,far-\ adj, often cap [F pharaonique, fr. pharaon pharaoh, fr. LL Pharaon-, Pharao] (ca. 1828) 1 : of, relating to, or characteristic of a pharaoh or the pharaohs 2 : enormous in size or magnitude ⟨~ construction projects⟩
phar‧i‧sa‧ic \,far-ə-'sā-ik\ adj [LL pharisaicus, fr. LGk pharisaikos, fr. Gk pharisaios Pharisee] (1618) 1 : PHARISAICAL 2 cap : of or relating to the Pharisees
phar‧i‧sa‧ical \-'sā-ə-kəl\ adj (1531) 1 : marked by hypocritical censorious self-righteousness — **phar‧i‧sa‧ical‧ly** \-k(ə-)lē\ adv — **phar‧i‧sa‧ical‧ness** \-kəl-nəs\ n
phar‧i‧sa‧ism \'far-ə-(,)sā-,i-zəm\ n [NL pharisaismus, fr. Gk pharisaios] (1610) 1 cap : the doctrines or practices of the Pharisees 2 often cap : pharisaical character, spirit, or attitude : HYPOCRISY
phar‧i‧see \'far-ə-(,)sē\ n [ME pharise, fr. OE farise, fr. LL pharisaeus, fr. Gk pharisaios, fr. Aram pĕrīshayyā, pl. of pĕrīshā, lit., separated] (bef. 12c) 1 cap : a member of a Jewish sect of the intertestamental period noted for strict observance of rites and ceremonies of the written law and for insistence on the validity of their own oral traditions concerning the law 2 : a pharisaical person
¹phar‧ma‧ceu‧ti‧cal \,fär-mə-'sü-ti-kəl\ adj [LL pharmaceuticus, fr. Gk pharmakeutikos, fr. pharmakeuein to administer drugs — more at PHARMACY] (1648) : of, relating to, or engaged in pharmacy or the manufacture and sale of pharmaceuticals ⟨a ~ company⟩ — **phar‧ma‧ceu‧ti‧cal‧ly** \-ti-k(ə-)lē\ adv
²pharmaceutical n (1881) : a medicinal drug
phar‧ma‧cist \'fär-mə-sist\ n (1834) : a person licensed to engage in pharmacy

phar·ma·co- *comb form* [Gk *pharmako-*, fr. *pharmakon*] : medicine : drug ⟨*pharmacology*⟩

phar·ma·co·dy·nam·ics \,fär-mə-kō-dī-'na-miks, -də-\ *n pl but sing in constr* (ca. 1842) : a branch of pharmacology dealing with the reactions between drugs and living systems — **phar·ma·co·dy·nam·ic** \-mik\ *adj* — **phar·ma·co·dy·nam·i·cal·ly** \-mi-k(ə-)lē\ *adv*

phar·ma·cog·no·sy \,fär-mə-'käg-nə-sē\ *n* [ISV, fr. Gk *pharmakon* + *-gnōsia* knowledge, fr. *gnōsis* — more at GNOSIS] (ca. 1885) : descriptive pharmacology dealing with crude drugs and simples — **phar·ma·cog·nos·tic** \-,käg-'näs-tik\ *or* **phar·ma·cog·nos·ti·cal** \-ti-kəl\ *adj*

phar·ma·co·ki·net·ics \-kō-kə-'ne-tiks, -kō-kī-\ *n pl but sing in constr* (1960) **1** : the study of the bodily absorption, distribution, metabolism, and excretion of drugs **2** : the characteristic interactions of a drug and the body in terms of its absorption, distribution, metabolism, and excretion — **phar·ma·co·ki·net·ic** \-tik\ *adj*

phar·ma·col·o·gy \,fär-mə-'kä-lə-jē\ *n* (ca. 1721) **1** : the science of drugs including materia medica, toxicology, and therapeutics **2** : the properties and reactions of drugs esp. with relation to their therapeutic value — **phar·ma·co·log·i·cal** \-kə-'lä-ji-kəl\ *also* **phar·ma·co·log·ic** \-jik\ *adj* — **phar·ma·co·log·i·cal·ly** \-ji-k(ə-)lē\ *adv* — **phar·ma·col·o·gist** \-'kä-lə-jist\ *n*

phar·ma·co·poe·ia *also* **phar·ma·co·pe·ia** \-kə-'pē-ə\ *n* [NL, fr. LGk *pharmakopoiia* preparation of drugs, fr. Gk *pharmako-* + *poiein* to make — more at POET] (1621) **1** : a book describing drugs, chemicals, and medicinal preparations; *esp* : one issued by an officially recognized authority and serving as a standard **2** : a collection or stock of drugs — **phar·ma·co·poe·ial** *also* **phar·ma·co·pe·ial** \-əl\ *adj*

phar·ma·co·ther·a·py \,fär-mə-kō-'ther-ə-pē\ *n* (ca. 1909) : the treatment of disease and esp. mental illness with drugs

phar·ma·cy \'fär-mə-sē\ *n, pl* **-cies** [LL *pharmacia* administration of drugs, fr. Gk *pharmakeia*, fr. *pharmakeuein* to administer drugs, fr. *pharmakon* magic charm, poison, drug] (1651) **1** : the art, practice, or profession of preparing, preserving, compounding, and dispensing medical drugs **2 a** : a place where medicines are compounded or dispensed **b** : DRUGSTORE **3** : PHARMACOPOEIA 2

pha·ryn·geal \,far-ən-'jē-əl, fə-'rin-j(ē-)əl\ *adj* [NL *pharyngeus*, fr. *pharyng-, pharynx*] (1828) : relating to or located or produced in the region of the pharynx

phar·yn·gi·tis \,far-ən-'jī-təs\ *n, pl* **-git·i·des** \-'ji-tə-,dēz\ (ca. 1844) : inflammation of the pharynx

phar·ynx \'far-iŋ(k)s\ *n, pl* **pha·ryn·ges** \fə-'rin-(,)jēz\ *also* **phar·ynx·es** [NL *pharyng-, pharynx*, fr. Gk, throat, pharynx; akin to ON *barki* throat and prob. to L *ferire* to strike — more at BORE] (ca. 1693) **1** : the part of the vertebrate alimentary canal between the cavity of the mouth and the esophagus **2** : a differentiated part of the alimentary canal in some invertebrates that may be thickened and muscular, eversible and toothed, or adapted as a suctorial organ

¹**phase** \'fāz\ *n* [NL *phasis*, fr. Gk, appearance of a star, phase of the moon, fr. *phainein* to show (middle voice, to appear) — more at FANCY] (1812) **1** : a particular appearance or state in a regularly recurring cycle of changes ⟨~s of the moon⟩ **2 a** : a distinguishable part in a course, development, or cycle ⟨the early ~s of her career⟩ **b** : an aspect or part (as of a problem) under consideration **3** : the point or stage in a period of uniform circular motion, harmonic motion, or the periodic changes of any magnitude varying according to a simple harmonic law to which the rotation, oscillation, or variation has advanced considered in its relation to a standard position or assumed instant of starting **4** : a homogeneous, physically distinct, and mechanically separable portion of matter present in a nonhomogeneous physicochemical system **5** : an individual or subgroup distinguishably different in appearance or behavior from the norm of the group to which it belongs; *also* : the distinguishing peculiarity — **pha·sic** \'fā-zik\ *adj* — **in phase** : in a synchronized or correlated manner — **out of phase** : in an unsynchronized manner : not in correlation

²**phase** *vt* **phased; phas·ing** (1904) **1** : to adjust so as to be in a synchronized condition **2** : to conduct or carry out by planned phases **3** : to introduce in stages — often used with *in* ⟨~ in new models⟩

phase–contrast *adj* (1934) : of or employing the phase-contrast microscope

phase–contrast microscope *n* (1947) : a microscope that translates differences in phase of the light transmitted through or reflected by the object into differences of intensity in the image — called also *phase microscope*

phase–down \'fāz-,daùn\ *n* (1964) : a gradual reduction (as in operations)

phase modulation *n* (1930) : modulation of the phase of a radio carrier wave by voice or other signal

phase–out \'fā-,zaùt\ *n* (1958) : a gradual stopping of operations or production : a closing down by phases

phase out *vt* (1940) : to discontinue the practice, production, or use of by phases ⟨*phase out* the old machinery⟩ ~ *vi* : to stop production or operation by phases

-phasia *n comb form* [NL, fr. Gk, speech, fr. *phasis* utterance, fr. *phanai* to speak, say — more at BAN] : speech disorder of a (specified) type ⟨dysphasia⟩

phas·mid \'faz-məd\ *n* [NL *Phasmida*, group name, fr. *Phasma*, type genus, fr. Gk, apparition, fr. *phainein* to show — more at FANCY] (1872) : any of an order (Phasmatodea syn. Phasmida) of large cylindrical or sometimes flattened chiefly tropical insects (as a walking stick) with long strong legs, strictly phytophagous habits, and slight metamorphosis — **phasmid** *adj*

phat·ic \'fa-tik\ *adj* [Gk *phatos*, verbal of *phanai* to speak] (1923) : of, relating to, or being speech used for social or emotive purposes rather than for communicating information — **phat·i·cal·ly** \-ti-k(ə-)lē\ *adv*

pheas·ant \'fe-z²nt\ *n, pl* **pheasant** *or* **pheasants** [ME *fesaunt*, fr. AF, fr. OF *fesan*, fr. L *phasianus*, fr. Gk *phasianos*, fr. *phasianos* of the Phasis River, fr. *Phasis*, river in Colchis] (13c) **1** : any of numerous large often long-tailed and brightly colored Old World gallinaceous birds (*Phasianus* and related genera of the family Phasianidae) including many raised as ornamental or game birds **2** : any of various birds resembling a pheasant

phel·lem \'fe-,lem\ *n* [Gk *phellos* cork + E *-em* (as in *phloem*)] (1887) : a layer of usu. suberized cells produced outwardly by a phellogen

phel·lo·derm \'fe-lə-,dərm\ *n* [Gk *phellos* + ISV *-derm*] (1875) : a layer of parenchyma produced inwardly by a phellogen

phel·lo·gen \'fe-lə-jən\ *n* [Gk *phellos* + ISV *-gen*] (1875) : a secondary meristem that initiates phellem and phelloderm in the periderm of a stem — called also *cork cambium*

phen- *or* **pheno-** *comb form* [obs. *phene* benzene, fr. F *phène*, fr. Gk *phainein* to show; fr. its occurrence in illuminating gas — more at FANCY] **1** : related to or derived from benzene ⟨*phenol*⟩ **2** : containing phenyl ⟨*phenobarbital*⟩

phen·a·caine \'fē-nə-,kān, 'fe-\ *n* [prob. fr. *phenetidine* + *acet-* + *-caine*] (1907) : a crystalline base $C_{18}H_{22}N_2O_2$ or its hydrochloride used as a local anesthetic

phen·ac·e·tin \fi-'na-sə-tən\ *n* [ISV] (1887) : a white crystalline compound $C_{10}H_{13}NO_2$ formerly used to ease pain or fever but withdrawn because of its serious side effects — called also *acetophenetidin*

phen·a·kite \'fe-nə-,kīt, 'fē-\ *or* **phen·a·cite** \-,sit\ *n* [G *Phenakit*, fr. Gk *phenak-, phenax* deceiver; fr. its being easily mistaken for quartz] (ca. 1834) : a glassy mineral that consists of a beryllium silicate and occurs in rhombohedral crystals

phen·an·threne \fə-'nan-,thrēn\ *n* [ISV *phen-* + *anthracene*] (1882) : a crystalline aromatic hydrocarbon $C_{14}H_{10}$ of coal tar isomeric with anthracene

phen·a·zine \'fe-nə-,zēn\ *n* [ISV] (ca. 1900) : a yellowish crystalline base $C_{12}H_8N_2$ used esp. in organic synthesis

phen·cy·cli·dine \(,)fen-'si-klə-,dēn, -'si-, -dən\ *n* [*phen-* + *cycl-* + *-idine*] (1959) : a piperidine derivative $C_{17}H_{25}N$ used esp. as a veterinary anesthetic and sometimes illicitly as a psychedelic drug — called also *angel dust*, PCP

phe·net·ic \fi-'ne-tik\ *adj* [*phenotype* + *-etic* (as in *genetic*)] (1960) : of or relating to taxonomic analysis that emphasizes the overall similarities of characteristics among biological taxa without regard to phylogenetic relationships

phe·net·ics \-tiks\ *n pl but sing in constr* (ca. 1960) : a system of biological classification based on phenetic methods — **phe·net·i·cist** \-'ne-tə-sist\ *n*

phen·met·ra·zine \(,)fen-'me-trə-,zēn\ *n* [*phenyl* + *methyl* + *tetra-* + *azine*] (1956) : a sympathomimetic stimulant $C_{11}H_{15}NO$ used in the form of its hydrochloride as an appetite suppressant

phe·no·bar·bi·tal \,fē-nō-'bär-bə-,töl\ *n* (1918) : a crystalline barbiturate $C_{12}H_{12}N_2O_3$ used as a hypnotic and sedative

phe·no·bar·bi·tone \-bə-,tōn\ *n* (ca. 1932) *chiefly Brit* : PHENOBARBITAL

phe·no·copy \'fē-nə-,kä-pē\ *n* [ISV *phenotype* + *copy*] (1937) : a phenotypic variation that is caused by unusual environmental conditions and resembles the normal expression of a genotype other than its own

phe·no·cryst \-,krist\ *n* [F *phénocryste*, fr. Gk *phainein* to show + *krystallos* crystal — more at FANCY] (ca. 1893) : one of the prominent embedded crystals of a porphyry — **phe·no·crys·tic** \,fē-nə-'kris-tik\ *adj*

phe·nol \'fē-,nōl, -,nól, fi-'\ *n* [ISV *phen-* + *³-ol*] (ca. 1852) **1** : a corrosive poisonous crystalline acidic compound C_6H_5OH present in coal tar and wood tar that in dilute solution is used as a disinfectant **2** : any of various acidic compounds analogous to phenol and regarded as hydroxyl derivatives of aromatic hydrocarbons

phe·no·late \'fē-n²l-,āt\ *n* (1885) : PHENOXIDE

phe·no·lat·ed \'fē-n²l-,ā-təd\ *adj* (1923) : treated, mixed, or impregnated with phenol

¹**phe·no·lic** \fi-'nō-lik, -'nä-\ *adj* (1872) **1 a** : of, relating to, or having the characteristics of a phenol **b** : containing or derived from a phenol **2** : of, relating to, or being a phenolic

²**phenolic** *n* (1924) : a usu. thermosetting resin or plastic made by condensation of a phenol with an aldehyde and used esp. for molding and insulating and in coatings and adhesives — called also *phenolic resin*

phe·nol·o·gy \fi-'nä-lə-jē\ *n* [*phenomena* + *-logy*] (ca. 1884) **1** : a branch of science dealing with the relations between climate and periodic biological phenomena (as bird migration or plant flowering) **2** : periodic biological phenomena (as of a kind of organism) that are correlated with climatic conditions — **phe·no·log·i·cal** \,fē-n²l-'ä-ji-kəl\ *adj* — **phe·no·log·i·cal·ly** \-k(ə-)lē\ *adv*

phe·nol·phtha·lein \,fē-n²l-'tha-lē-ən, -'tha-,lēn, -'thā-\ *n* [ISV] (ca. 1875) : a white or yellowish white crystalline compound $C_{20}H_{14}O_4$ used in analysis as an indicator because its solution is brilliant red in alkalies and is decolorized by acids and in medicine as a laxative

phenol red *n* (1916) : a red crystalline compound $C_{19}H_{14}O_5S$ used esp. as an acid-base indicator

phe·nom \'fē-,näm, fi-'näm\ *n* (ca. 1890) : PHENOMENON; *esp* : a person of phenomenal ability or promise

phe·nom·e·na \fi-'nä-mə-nə, -,nä\ *n, pl* **-nas** (1576) *nonstand* : PHENOMENON

usage Phenomena has been in occasional use as a singular for more than 400 years and its plural *phenomenas* for more than 350. Our evidence shows that it is primarily a speech form used by poets, critics, and professors, among others, but one that sometimes turns up in edited prose ⟨the Borgia were, in modern terms, a media *phenomena* —*Economist*⟩. It is etymologically no more irregular than *stamina*, *agenda*, and *candelabra*, but it has nowhere near the frequency of use that they have, and while they are standard, *phenomena* is still rather borderline.

phe·nom·e·nal \fi-'nä-mə-n²l\ *adj* (1825) : relating to or being a phenomenon: as **a** : known through the senses rather than through thought or intuition **b** : concerned with phenomena rather than with hypotheses **c** : EXTRAORDINARY, REMARKABLE *syn* see MATERIAL — **phe·nom·e·nal·ly** \-n²l-ē\ *adv*

phe·nom·e·nal·ism \-n²l-,i-zəm\ *n* (ca. 1865) **1** : a theory that limits knowledge to phenomena only **2** : a theory that all knowledge is of phenomena and that what is construed to be perception of material objects is simply perception of sense-data — **phe·nom·e·nal·ist** \-ist\

\ə\ abut \²\ kitten, F table \ər\ further \a\ ash \ā\ ace \ä\ mop, mar \aù\ out \ch\ chin \e\ bet \ē\ easy \g\ go \i\ hit \ī\ ice \j\ job \ŋ\ sing \ō\ go \ò\ law \òi\ boy \th\ thin \t̲h̲\ the \ü\ loot \ù\ foot \y\ yet \zh\ vision \à, k̲, ⁿ, œ, œ̄, ue, ū̄, ʸ\ *see* Guide to Pronunciation *n or adj* — **phe·nom·e·nal·is·tic** \-ˌnä-mə-nᵊl-'is-tik\ *adj* — **phe·nom·e·nal·is·ti·cal·ly** \-ti-k(ə-)lē\ *adv*

phe·nom·e·no·log·i·cal \fi-ˌnä-mə-nᵊl-'ä-ji-kəl\ *adj* (ca. 1858) **1 :** of or relating to phenomenology **2 :** PHENOMENAL **3 :** of or relating to phenomenalism — **phe·nom·e·no·log·i·cal·ly** \-k(ə-)lē\ *adv*

phe·nom·e·nol·o·gy \fi-ˌnä-mə-'nä-lə-jē\ *n, pl* **-gies** [G *Phänomenologie,* fr. *Phänomenon* phenomenon + *-logie* -logy] (ca. 1797) **1 :** the study of the development of human consciousness and self-awareness as a preface to philosophy or a part of philosophy **2 a** (1) **:** a philosophical movement that describes the formal structure of the objects of awareness and of awareness itself in abstraction from any claims concerning existence (2) **:** the typological classification of a class of phenomena ⟨the ~ of religion⟩ **b :** an analysis produced by phenomenological investigation — **phe·nom·e·nol·o·gist** \-jist\ *n*

phe·nom·e·non \fi-'nä-mə-ˌnän, -nən\ *n, pl* **-na** \-nə, -ˌnä\ *or* **-nons** [LL *phaenomenon,* fr. Gk *phainomenon,* fr. neut. of *phainomenos,* prp. of *phainesthai* to appear, middle voice of *phainein* to show — more at FANCY] (1605) **1** *pl* **phenomena :** an observable fact or event **2** *pl* **phenomena a :** an object or aspect known through the senses rather than by thought or intuition **b :** a temporal or spatiotemporal object of sensory experience as distinguished from a noumenon **c :** a fact or event of scientific interest susceptible of scientific description and explanation **3 a :** a rare or significant fact or event **b** *pl* **phenomenons :** an exceptional, unusual, or abnormal person, thing, or occurrence
usage see PHENOMENA

phe·no·thi·a·zine \ˌfē-nō-'thī-ə-ˌzēn\ *n* [ISV] (1894) **1 :** a greenish yellow crystalline compound $C_{12}H_9NS$ used as an anthelmintic and insecticide esp. in veterinary practice **2 :** any of various phenothiazine derivatives (as chlorpromazine) that are used as tranquilizing agents esp. in the treatment of schizophrenia

phe·no·type \'fē-nə-ˌtīp\ *n* [G *Phänotypus,* fr. Gk *phainein* to show + *typos* type] (ca. 1911) **:** the visible properties of an organism that are produced by the interaction of the genotype and the environment — **phe·no·typ·ic** \ˌfē-nə-'ti-pik\ *also* **phe·no·typ·i·cal** \-pi-kəl\ *adj* — **phe·no·typ·i·cal·ly** \-pi-k(ə-)lē\ *adv*

phen·ox·ide \fi-'näk-ˌsīd\ *n* (1888) **:** a salt of a phenol esp. in its capacity as a weak acid

phen·tol·amine \fen-'tä-lə-ˌmēn, -mən\ *n* [*phen-* + *tolu*idine + *amine*] (1952) **:** an adrenergic blocking agent $C_{17}H_{19}N_3O$ that is used esp. in the diagnosis and treatment of hypertension due to pheochromocytoma

phe·nyl \'fe-nᵊl, 'fē-\ *n* [ISV] (ca. 1850) **:** a univalent group C_6H_5 that is an aryl group derived from benzene by removal of one hydrogen atom — often used in combination — **phe·nyl·ic** \fi-'ni-lik\ *adj*

phe·nyl·al·a·nine \ˌfe-nᵊl-'a-lə-ˌnēn, ˌfē-\ *n* [ISV] (1883) **:** an essential amino acid $C_9H_{11}NO_2$ that is converted in the normal body to tyrosine

phen·yl·bu·ta·zone \ˌfe-nᵊl-'byü-tə-ˌzōn\ *n* [*phenyl* + *butyric* acid + *pyraz*olone $(C_3H_4N_2O)$] (1952) **:** a drug $C_{19}H_{20}N_2O_2$ that is used for its analgesic and anti-inflammatory properties esp. in the treatment of arthritis, gout, and bursitis

phen·yl·eph·rine \-'e-ˌfrēn, -frən\ *n* [*phenyl* + *epineph*rine] (1947) **:** a sympathomimetic agent $C_9H_{13}NO_2$ that is used in the form of the hydrochloride as a vasoconstrictor, a mydriatic, and by injection to raise the blood pressure

phen·yl·eth·yl·amine \ˌfe-nᵊl-ˌe-thəl-'a-ˌmēn, ˌfē-\ *n* (1939) **:** a neurotransmitter $C_8H_{11}N$ that is an amine resembling amphetamine in structure and pharmacological properties; *also* **:** any of its derivatives

phe·nyl·ke·ton·uria \ˌfe-nᵊl-ˌkē-tᵊn-'úr-ē-ə, ˌfē-, -'yúr-\ *n* [NL, fr. ISV *phenyl* + *ketone* + NL *-uria*] (1935) **:** an inherited human metabolic disease that is characterized by inability to oxidize a metabolic product of phenylalanine and by severe mental deficiency — abbr. *PKU* — **phe·nyl·ke·ton·uric** \-'úr-ik, -'yúr-\ *n or adj*

phen·yl·pro·pa·nol·amine \ˌfe-nᵊl-ˌprō-pə-'nò-lə-ˌmēn, -ˌfē-, -'nò-; -'nò-lə-ˌmēn\ *n* [*phenyl* + *propane* + *-ol* + *amine*] (1947) **:** a sympathomimetic drug $C_9H_{13}NO$ used in the form of its hydrochloride esp. as a nasal and bronchial decongestant and as an appetite suppressant

phen·yl·thio·car·ba·mide \ˌfe-nᵊl-ˌthī-ō-'kär-bə-ˌmīd, ˌfē-\ *n* (1879) **:** a crystalline compound $C_7H_8N_2S$ that is extremely bitter or tasteless depending on the presence or absence of a single dominant gene in the taster — called also *phenylthiourea, PTC*

phen·yl·thio·urea \-ˌthī-ō-yü-'rē-ə\ *n* (1896) **:** PHENYLTHIOCARBAMIDE

phe·nyt·o·in \fə-'ni-tə-wən\ *n* [di*phenyl*hydan*toin*] (1941) **:** a crystalline anticonvulsant compound $C_{15}H_{12}N_2O_2$ used in the form of its sodium salt in the treatment of epilepsy — called also *diphenylhydantoin*

pheo·chro·mo·cy·to·ma \ˌfē-ə-ˌkrō-mə-sə-'tō-mə, -sī-\ *n, pl* **-mas** *or* **-ma·ta** \-mə-tə\ [NL, fr. ISV *pheochromocyte* chromaffin cell + NL *-oma*] (ca. 1929) **:** a tumor that is derived from chromaffin cells and is usu. associated with paroxysmal or sustained hypertension

pher·o·mone \'fer-ə-ˌmōn\ *n* [ISV *phero-,* fr. Gk *pherein* to carry) + *-mone* (as in *hormone*) — more at BEAR] (1959) **:** a chemical substance that is produced by an animal and serves esp. as a stimulus to other individuals of the same species for one or more behavioral responses — **pher·o·mon·al** \ˌfer-ə-'mō-nᵊl\ *adj*

phew *a voiceless bilabial fricative usu. followed by a voiceless* (y)ü *or* ᵫ *sound; often read as* 'f(y)ü\ *interj* (1604) **1 —** used to express relief or fatigue **2 —** used to express disgust at or as if at an unpleasant odor

phi \'fī\ *n* [MGk, fr. Gk *phei*] (ca. 1899) **:** the 21st letter of the Greek alphabet — see ALPHABET table

phi·al \'fī-(ə)l\ *n* [ME, fr. L *phiala,* fr. Gk *phialē*] (14c) **:** VIAL

Phi Be·ta Kap·pa \ˌfī-ˌbā-tə-'ka-pə\ *n* [*Phi Beta Kappa* (Society), fr. *phi* + *beta* + *kappa,* initials of the society's Gk motto *philosophia biou kybernētēs* philosophy the guide of life] (1912) **:** a person winning high scholastic distinction in an American college or university and being elected to membership in a national honor society founded in 1776

phil- *or* **philo-** *comb form* [ME, fr. OF, fr. L, fr. Gk, fr. *philos* dear, friendly] **:** loving **:** having an affinity for ⟨*philo*progenitive⟩

¹-phil *or* **-phile** *n comb form* [F *-phile,* fr. Gk *-philos* -philous] **:** lover **:** one having an affinity for or a strong attraction to ⟨acido*phil*⟩ ⟨Slavo*phile*⟩

²-phil *or* **-phile** *adj comb form* [NL *-philus,* fr. L, fr. Gk *-philos*] **:** loving **:** having a fondness or affinity for ⟨Franco*phile*⟩

Phil·a·del·phia lawyer \ˌfi-lə-'del-fyə-, -ˌfē-ə-\ *n* [*Philadelphia,* Pa.] (1788) **:** a lawyer knowledgeable in even the most minute aspects of the law

Philadelphia pepper pot *n* (1929) **:** PEPPER POT 2b

phil·a·del·phus \ˌfi-lə-'del-fəs\ *n* [NL, fr. Gk *philadelphos* brotherly, fr. *phil-* + *adelphos* brother — more at -ADELPHOUS] (1950) **:** MOCK ORANGE 1

phi·lan·der \fə-'lan-dər\ *vi* **-dered; -der·ing** \-d(ə-)riŋ\ [fr. obs. *philander* lover, philanderer, prob. fr. the name *Philander* (1737) **1 :** to make love to someone with whom marriage is impossible (as because of an existing marriage) or with no intention of proposing marriage **2 :** to have many love affairs — **phi·lan·der·er** \-dər-ər\ *n*

phil·an·throp·ic \ˌfi-lən-'thrä-pik\ *also* **phil·an·throp·i·cal** \-pi-kəl\ *adj* (1789) **1 :** of, relating to, or characterized by philanthropy **:** HUMANITARIAN **2 :** dispensing or receiving aid from funds set aside for humanitarian purposes — **phil·an·throp·i·cal·ly** \-pi-k(ə-)lē\ *adv*

phi·lan·thro·pist \fə-'lan(t)-thrə-pist\ *n* (ca. 1736) **:** one who practices philanthropy

phi·lan·thro·poid \-'pòid\ *n* [blend of *philanthropist* and *anthropoid*] (1945) **:** a person who works for a philanthropic organization

phi·lan·thro·py \-pē\ *n, pl* **-pies** [LL *philanthropia,* fr. Gk *philanthrōpia,* fr. *philanthrōpos* loving people, fr. *phil-* + *anthrōpos* human being] (ca. 1623) **1 :** goodwill to fellowmen; *esp* **:** active effort to promote human welfare **2 a :** a philanthropic act or gift **b :** an organization distributing or supported by philanthropic funds

phi·lat·e·list \fə-'la-tᵊl-ist\ *n* (ca. 1865) **:** a specialist in philately **:** one who collects or studies stamps

phi·lat·e·ly \fə-'la-tᵊl-ē\ *n* [F *philatélie,* fr. *phil-* + Gk *ateleia* tax exemption, fr. *atelēs* free from tax, fr. *a-* + *telos* tax; perh. akin to Gk *tlēnai* to bear; fr. the fact that a stamped letter frees the recipient from paying the mailing charges — more at TOLERATE] (ca. 1865) **:** the collection and study of postage and imprinted stamps **:** stamp collecting — **phil·a·tel·ic** \ˌfi-lə-'te-lik\ *adj* — **phil·a·tel·i·cal·ly** \-li-k(ə-)lē\ *adv*

Phi·le·mon \fə-'lē-mən, fī-\ *n* [Gk *Philēmōn*] **1 :** a friend and probable convert of the apostle Paul **2 :** a letter written by St. Paul to a Christian living in the area of Colossae and included as a book in the New Testament — see BIBLE table **3 :** a poor aged Phrygian in Greek mythology who with his wife Baucis treats a disguised Zeus hospitably and is rewarded by him with a splendid temple

phil·har·mon·ic \ˌfi-lər-'mä-nik, -(ˌ)lär-; ˌfil-(ˌ)här-\ *n* [F *philharmonique,* lit., loving harmony, fr. It *filarmonico,* fr. *fil-* phil- + *armonia* harmony, fr. L *harmonia*] (1843) **:** SYMPHONY ORCHESTRA

phil·hel·lene \(ˌ)fil-'he-ˌlēn\ *or* **phil·hel·len·ic** \ˌfil-hə-'le-nik\ *adj* [Gk *philellēn,* fr. *phil-* + *Hellēn* Hellene] (ca. 1825) **:** admiring Greece or the Greeks — **philhellene** *n* — **phil·hel·le·nism** \(ˌ)fil-'he-lə-ˌni-zəm\ *n* — **phil·hel·le·nist** \-nist\ *n*

-philia *n comb form* [NL, fr. Gk *philia* friendship, fr. *philos* dear] **1 :** friendly feeling toward ⟨Franco*philia*⟩ **2 :** tendency toward ⟨hemo*philia*⟩ **3 :** abnormal appetite or liking for ⟨necro*philia*⟩

-philiac *n comb form* [NL *-philia* + Gk *-akos,* adj. suffix] **1 :** one having a tendency toward ⟨hemo*philiac*⟩ **2 :** one having an abnormal appetite or liking for ⟨copro*philiac*⟩

-philic *adj comb form* [Gk *-philos* -philous] **:** having an affinity for **:** loving ⟨acido*philic*⟩

Phi·lip·pi·ans \fə-'li-pē-ənz\ *n pl but sing in constr* [short for *Epistle to the Philippians*] **:** a hortatory letter written by St. Paul to the Christians of Philippi and included as a book in the New Testament — see BIBLE table

phi·lip·pic \fə-'li-pik\ *n* [MF *philippique,* fr. L & Gk; L *philippica, orationes philippicae,* speeches of Cicero against Mark Antony, trans. of Gk *philippikoi logoi,* speeches of Demosthenes against Philip II of Macedon, lit., speeches relating to Philip] (1592) **:** a discourse or declamation full of bitter condemnation **:** TIRADE

Phil·ip·pine mahogany \'fi-lə-ˌpēn-\ *n* [*Philippine* Islands] (ca. 1924) **:** any of several Philippine dipterocarp timber trees (genera *Shorea, Parashorea,* and *Pentacme*) with wood resembling that of the true mahoganies; *also* **:** its wood

phi·lis·tia \fə-'lis-tē-ə\ *n, pl, often cap* [*Philistia,* ancient country of southwest Palestine] (1857) **:** the class or world of cultural philistines

Phi·lis·tine \'fi-lə-ˌstēn; fə-'lis-tən, -ˌtēn; 'fi-lə-stən\ *n* (14c) **1 :** a native or inhabitant of ancient Philistia **2** *often not cap* **a :** a person who is guided by materialism and is usu. disdainful of intellectual or artistic values **b :** one uninformed in a special area of knowledge — **philistine** *adj, often cap* — **phi·lis·tin·ism** \-lə-ˌstē-ˌni-zəm; -'lis-tə-, -ˌtē-, -lə-stə-\ *n, often cap*

Phil·lips \'fi-ləps\ *adj* [fr. *Phillips,* a trademark, fr. Henry M. *Phillips* 20th cent. Am. engineer] (1935) **:** of, relating to, or being a screw having a head with a cross slot or the corresponding screwdriver

phil·lu·men·ist \fi-'lü-mə-nist\ *n* [*phil-* + L *lumen* light — more at LUMINARY] (1943) **:** one who collects matchbooks or matchbox labels

Phi·loc·te·tes \ˌfi-'läk-tə-ˌtēz, ˌfi-ˌläk-'tē-tēz\ *n* [Gk *Philoktētēs*] **:** a Greek archer who uses the bow of Hercules to slay Paris at Troy

phil·o·den·dron \ˌfi-lə-'den-drən\ *n, pl* **-drons** *or* **-dra** \-drə\ [NL, fr. Gk, neut. of *philodendros* loving trees, fr. *phil-* + *dendron* tree — more at DENDR-] (1877) **:** any of various aroid plants (as of the genus *Philodendron*) that are cultivated for their showy foliage

phi·lol·o·gy \fə-'lä-lə-jē *also* fī-\ *n* [F *philologie,* fr. L *philologia* love of learning and literature, fr. Gk, fr. *philologos* fond of learning and literature, fr. *phil-* + *logos* word, speech — more at LEGEND] (1612) **1 :** the study of literature and of disciplines relevant to literature or to language as used in literature **2 a :** LINGUISTICS; *esp* **:** historical and comparative linguistics **b :** the study of human speech esp. as the vehicle of literature and as a field of study that sheds light on cultural history — **phil·o·log·i·cal** \ˌfi-lə-'lä-ji-kəl\ *adj* — **phil·o·log·i·cal·ly** \-k(ə-)lē\ *adv* — **phi·lol·o·gist** \fə-'lä-lə-jist *also* fī-\ *n*

Phil·o·mel \'fi-lə-ˌmel\ *n* [L *Philomela* Philomela, nightingale] (1579) **:** NIGHTINGALE

Phil·o·me·la \ˌfi-lə-'mē-lə\ *n* [L, fr. Gk *Philomēlē*] **:** an Athenian princess in Greek mythology raped and deprived of her tongue by her brother-in-law Tereus, avenged by the killing of his son, and changed into a nightingale while fleeing from him

phil·o·pro·gen·i·tive \ˌfi-lə-prō-'je-nə-tiv\ *adj* [*phil-* + L *progenitus,* pp. of *progignere* to beget — more at PROGENITOR] (1865) **1 :** tending to produce offspring **:** PROLIFIC **2 :** of, relating to, or characterized by love of offspring — **phil·o·pro·gen·i·tive·ness** *n*

phi·lo·sophe \'fē-lə-'zòf\ *n* [F, lit., philosopher] (1779) : one of the deistic or materialistic writers and thinkers of the 18th century French Enlightenment

phi·los·o·pher \fə-'lä-s(ə-)fər\ *n* [ME, modif. of MF *philosophe*, fr. L *philosophus*, fr. Gk *philosophos*, fr. *phil-* + *sophia* wisdom, fr. *sophos* wise] (14c) **1 a :** a person who seeks wisdom or enlightenment **: SCHOLAR, THINKER b :** a student of philosophy **2 a :** a person whose philosophical perspective makes meeting trouble with equanimity easier **b :** an expounder of a theory in a particular area of experience **c :** one who philosophizes

philosophers' stone *n* (14c) : an imaginary stone, substance, or chemical preparation believed to have the power of transmuting baser metals into gold and sought by alchemists — called also *philosopher's stone*

phil·o·soph·i·cal \,fi-lə-'sä-fi-kəl *also* -'zä-\ *or* **phil·o·soph·ic** \-fik\ (14c) **1 a :** of or relating to philosophers or philosophy **b :** based on philosophy **2 :** characterized by the attitude of a philosopher; *specif* : calm or unflinching in face of trouble, defeat, or loss — **phil·o·soph·i·cal·ly** \-fi-k(ə-)lē\ *adv*

philosophical analysis *n* (1936) : ANALYTIC PHILOSOPHY

phi·los·o·phise *Brit var of* PHILOSOPHIZE

phi·los·o·phize \fə-'lä-sə-,fīz\ *vb* **-phized; -phiz·ing** *vi* (1594) **1 :** to reason in the manner of a philosopher **2 :** to expound a moralizing and often superficial philosophy ~ *vt* : to consider from or bring into conformity with a philosophical point of view — **phi·los·o·phiz·er** *n*

phi·los·o·phy \fə-'lä-s(ə-)fē\ *n, pl* **-phies** [ME *philosophie*, fr. OF, fr. L *philosophia*, fr. Gk, fr. *philosophos* philosopher] (14c) **1 a** (1) : all learning exclusive of technical precepts and practical arts (2) : the sciences and liberal arts exclusive of medicine, law, and theology ⟨a doctor of ~⟩ (3) : the 4-year college course of a major seminary **b** (1) *archaic* : PHYSICAL SCIENCE (2) : ETHICS **c :** a discipline comprising as its core logic, aesthetics, ethics, metaphysics, and epistemology **2 a :** pursuit of wisdom **b :** a search for a general understanding of values and reality by chiefly speculative rather than observational means **c :** an analysis of the grounds of and concepts expressing fundamental beliefs **3 a :** a system of philosophical concepts **b :** a theory underlying or regarding a sphere of activity or thought ⟨the ~ of war⟩ ⟨~ of science⟩ **4 a :** the most general beliefs, concepts, and attitudes of an individual or group **b :** calmness of temper and judgment befitting a philosopher

philosophy of life (1853) **1 :** an overall vision of or attitude toward life and the purpose of life **2** [trans. of G *Lebensphilosophie*] : any of various philosophies that emphasize human life or life in general

-philous *adj comb form* [Gk *-philos*, fr. *philos* dear, friendly] : loving : having an affinity for ⟨hydrophilous⟩

phil·ter *or* **phil·tre** \'fil-tər\ *n* [MF *philtre*, fr. L *philtrum*, fr. Gk *philtron*; akin to Gk *philos* dear] (ca. 1587) **1 :** a potion, drug, or charm held to have the power to arouse sexual passion **2 :** a potion credited with magical power

phi phenomenon \'fī-\ *n* (ca. 1928) : apparent motion resulting from an orderly sequence of stimuli (as lights flashed in rapid succession a short distance apart on a sign) without any actual motion being presented to the eye

phiz \'fiz\ *n* [by shortening & alter. fr. *physiognomy*] (1688) : FACE

phleb- *or* **phlebo-** *comb form* [ME *fleb-*, fr. MF, fr. LL *phlebo-*, fr. Gk *phleb-*, *phlebo-*, fr. *phleb-*, *phleps*; perh. akin to Gk *phlyein*, *phlyzein* to boil over — more at FLUID] : vein ⟨phlebitis⟩

phle·bi·tis \fli-'bī-təs\ *n* [NL] (ca. 1834) : inflammation of a vein

phle·bo·gram \'flē-bə-,gram\ *n* [ISV] (1885) : a figure of a vein or a record of its movements

phle·bog·ra·phy \fli-'bä-grə-fē\ *n* [ISV] (1937) : the process of making phlebograms

phle·bol·o·gy \fli-'bä-lə-jē\ *n* [ISV] (1893) : a branch of medicine concerned with the veins

phle·bo·to·mus fever \fli-'bä-tə-məs-\ *n* [NL *Phlebotomus*, genus of sand flies] (ca. 1923) : SANDFLY FEVER

phle·bot·o·my \fli-'bä-tə-mē\ *n, pl* **-mies** [ME *fleobotomie*, fr. MF *flebotomie*, fr. LL *phlebotomia*, fr. Gk, fr. *phleb-* + *-tomia* -tomy] (14c) : the letting of blood for transfusion, diagnosis, or experiment, and esp. formerly in the treatment of disease — called also *venesection* — **phle·bot·o·mist** \-mist\ *n*

Phleg·e·thon \'fle-gə-,thän\ *n* [L, fr. Gk *Phlegethōn*] : a river of fire in Hades

phlegm \'flem\ *n* [ME *fleume*, fr. MF, fr. LL *phlegmat-*, *phlegma*, fr. Gk, flame, inflammation, phlegm, fr. *phlegein* to burn — more at BLACK] (13c) **1 :** the one of the four humors in early physiology that was considered to be cold and moist and to cause sluggishness **2 :** viscid mucus secreted in abnormal quantity in the respiratory passages **3 a :** dull or apathetic coldness or indifference **b :** intrepid coolness or calm ⟨firmness⟩ — **phlegmy** \'fle-mē\ *adj*

phleg·mat·ic \fleg-'ma-tik\ *adj* (14c) **1 :** resembling, consisting of, or producing the humor phlegm **2 :** having or showing a slow and stolid temperament *syn* see IMPASSIVE — **phleg·mat·i·cal·ly** \-ti-k(ə-)lē\ *adv*

phlo·em \'flō-,em\ *n* [G, fr. Gk *phloios, phloos* bark; perh. akin to Gk *phlein* to teem, abound, *phlyein, phlyzein* to boil over — more at FLUID] (1875) : a complex tissue in the vascular system of higher plants that consists mainly of sieve tubes and elongated parenchyma cells usu. with fibers and that functions in translocation and in support and storage — compare XYLEM

phloem necrosis *n* (1923) : a pathological state in a plant characterized by brown discoloration and disintegration of the phloem; *esp* : a fatal disease of the American elm caused by a mycoplasma-like organism transmitted by a leafhopper (*Scaphoideus luteolus*)

phloem ray *n* (1875) : a vascular ray or part of a vascular ray that is located in phloem — compare XYLEM RAY

phlo·gis·tic \flō-'jis-tik\ *adj* (1733) **1** [NL *phlogiston*] : of or relating to phlogiston **2** [Gk *phlogistos*] : of or relating to inflammations and fevers

phlo·gis·ton \-tən\ *n* [NL, fr. Gk, neut. of *phlogistos* inflammable, fr. *phlogizein* to set on fire, fr. *phlog-*, *phlox* flame, fr. *phlegein*] (1733) : the hypothetical principle of fire regarded formerly as a material substance

phlog·o·pite \'flä-gə-,pīt\ *n* [G *Phlogopit*, fr. Gk *phlogōpos* fiery= looking, fr. *phlog-*, *phlox* + *ōps* face — more at EYE] (1850) : a usu. brown to red form of mica

phlox \'fläks\ *n, pl* **phlox** *or* **phlox·es** [NL, fr. L, a flower, fr. Gk, flame, wallflower] (ca. 1706) : any of a genus (*Phlox* of the family Polemoniaceae, the phlox family) of American annual or perennial herbs that have red, purple, white, or variegated flowers, a salverform corolla with the stamens on its tube, and a 3-valved capsular fruit

phlox

-phobe *n comb form* [Gk *-phobos* fearing] : one fearing or averse to (something specified) ⟨Franco-phobe⟩

pho·bia \'fō-bē-ə\ *n* [-phobia] (1786) : an exaggerated usu. inexplicable and illogical fear of a particular object, class of objects, or situation

-phobia *n comb form* [NL, fr. LL, fr. Gk, fr. *-phobos* fearing, fear, flight, fr. *phebesthai* to flee; akin to Lith *bégti* to flee, OCS *běžati*] **1 :** exaggerated fear of ⟨acrophobia⟩ **2 :** intolerance or aversion for ⟨photophobia⟩

pho·bic \'fō-bik\ *adj* (1897) : of, relating to, affected with, or constituting phobia — **phobic** *n*

-phobic *adj comb form* [F *-phobique*, fr. LL *-phobicus*, fr. Gk *-phobikos*, fr. *-phobia*] **1 a :** having an intolerance or aversion for ⟨photophobic⟩ ⟨Anglophobic⟩ **b :** exhibiting a phobia for ⟨claustrophobic⟩ **2 :** lacking affinity for ⟨hydrophobic⟩

phoe·be \'fē-(,)bē\ *n* [imit.] (1700) : any of a genus (*Sayornis*) of American flycatchers; *esp* : one (*S. phoebe*) of the eastern U.S. that has a slight crest and is plain grayish brown above and yellowish white below

Phoe·be \'fē-bē\ *n* [L, fr. Gk *Phoibē*, fr. *phoibē*, fem. of *phoibos*] : ARTEMIS

Phoe·bus \'fē-bəs\ *n* [L, fr. Gk *Phoibos*, fr. *phoibos* radiant] **1 :** APOLLO **2** *not cap* : SUN

Phoe·ni·cian \fi-'nē-shən, -'ni-\ *n* (14c) **1 :** a native or inhabitant of ancient Phoenicia **2 :** the Semitic language of ancient Phoenicia — **Phoenician** *adj*

phoe·nix \'fē-niks\ *n* [ME *fenix*, fr. OE, fr. L *phoenix*, fr. Gk *phoinix*] (bef. 12c) : a legendary bird which according to one account lived 500 years, burned itself to ashes on a pyre, and rose alive from the ashes to live another period; *also* : a person or thing likened to the phoenix — **phoe·nix·like** \-,līk\ *adj*

phon \'fän\ *n* [ISV, fr. Gk *phōnē* voice, sound] (1932) : the unit of loudness on a scale beginning at zero for the faintest audible sound and corresponding to the decibel scale of sound intensity with the number of phons of a given sound being equal to the decibels of a pure 1000= cycle tone judged by the average listener to be equal in loudness to the given sound

phon- *or* **phono-** *comb form* [L, fr. Gk *phōn-*, *phōno-*, fr. *phōnē* — more at BAN] : sound : voice : speech ⟨phonate⟩ ⟨phonograph⟩

pho·nate \'fō-,nāt\ *vi* (ca. 1890) : to produce vocal sounds and esp. speech — **pho·na·tion** \fō-'nā-shən\ *n*

¹phone \'fōn\ *n* [Gk *phōnē*] (ca. 1866) : a speech sound considered as a physical event without regard to its place in the sound system of a language

²phone *n* [by shortening] (1884) **1 :** TELEPHONE **2 :** EARPHONE

³phone *vb* **phoned; phon·ing** (1889) : TELEPHONE

¹-phone *n comb form* [Gk *-phōnos* sounding, fr. *phōnē*] **1 :** sound ⟨homophone⟩ — often in names of musical instruments and sound-transmitting devices ⟨radiophone⟩ ⟨xylophone⟩ **2 :** speaker of (a specified language) ⟨Francophone⟩

²-phone *adj comb form* [F, fr. Gk *-phōnos*] : of or relating to a population that speaks (a specified language) ⟨Francophone⟩

phone-in \'fōn-,in\ *n* (1968) : a call-in show (as on radio)

pho·ne·mat·ic \,fō-nē-'ma-tik\ *adj* (1936) : PHONEMIC

pho·neme \'fō-,nēm\ *n* [F *phonème*, fr. Gk *phōnēmat-*, *phōnēma* speech sound, utterance, fr. *phōnein* to sound] (ca. 1916) : any of the abstract units of the phonetic system of a language that correspond to a set of similar speech sounds (as the velar \k\ of *cool* and the palatal \k\ of *keel*) which are perceived to be a single distinctive sound in the language

pho·ne·mic \fə-'nē-mik, fō-\ *adj* (ca. 1931) **1 :** of, relating to, or having the characteristics of a phoneme **2 a :** constituting members of different phonemes (as \n\ and \m\ in English) **b :** DISTINCTIVE 2 — **pho·ne·mi·cal·ly** \-mi-k(ə-)lē\ *adv*

pho·ne·mics \-miks\ *n pl but sing in constr* (1936) **1 :** a branch of linguistic analysis that consists of the study of phonemes **2 :** the structure of a language in terms of phonemes — **pho·ne·mi·cist** \-mə-sist\ *n*

pho·net·ic \fə-'ne-tik\ *adj* [NL *phoneticus*, fr. Gk *phōnētikos*, fr. *phōnein* to sound with the voice, fr. *phōnē* voice] (1826) **1 a :** of or relating to spoken language or speech sounds **b :** of or relating to the science of phonetics **2 :** representing the sounds and other phenomena of speech: as **a :** constituting an alteration of ordinary spelling that better represents the spoken language, that employs only characters of the regular alphabet, and that is used in a context of conventional spelling **b :** representing speech sounds by means of symbols that have one value only **c :** employing for speech sounds more than the minimum number of symbols necessary to represent the significant differences in a speaker's speech — **pho·net·i·cal·ly** \-ti-k(ə-)lē\ *adv*

phonetic alphabet *n* (1848) **1 :** a set of symbols (as IPA) used for phonetic transcription **2 :** any of various systems of identifying letters of the alphabet by means of code words in voice communication

pho·ne·ti·cian \,fō-nə-'ti-shən *also* ,fä-\ *n* (1848) : a specialist in phonetics

pho·net·ics \fə-'ne-tiks\ *n pl but sing in constr* (1836) **1 :** the system of speech sounds of a language or group of languages **2 a :** the study and systematic classification of the sounds made in spoken utterance **b :** the practical application of this science to language study

---

\ə\ abut \ᵊ\ kitten, F table \ər\ further \a\ ash \ā\ ace \ä\ mop, mar \aủ\ out \ch\ chin \e\ bet \ē\ easy \g\ go \i\ hit \ī\ ice \j\ job \ŋ\ sing \ō\ go \ò\ law \ói\ boy \th\ thin \t͟h\ the \ü\ loot \ủ\ foot \y\ yet \zh\ vision \à, ḵ, ⁿ, œ, œ̄, ue, ūᴇ, ᵞ\ *see* Guide to Pronunciation

pho·nic \'fä-nik *also* 'fō-\ *adj* (1823) **1** : of, relating to, or producing sound : ACOUSTIC **2 a** : of or relating to the sounds of speech **b** : of or relating to phonics — **pho·ni·cal·ly** \-ni-k(ə-)lē\ *adv*

pho·nics \'fä-niks, *1 is also* 'fō-\ *n pl but sing in constr* (ca. 1684) **1** : the science of sound : ACOUSTICS **2** : a method of teaching beginners to read and pronounce words by learning the phonetic value of letters, letter groups, and esp. syllables

pho·no \'fō-(,)nō\ *n, pl* **phonos** (1909) : PHONOGRAPH

pho·no·car·dio·gram \,fō-nō-'kär-dē-ə-,gram\ *n* [ISV] (1912) : a graphic recording of heart sounds made by means of a microphone, amplifier, and galvanometer

pho·no·car·di·og·ra·phy \-,kär-dē-'ä-grə-fē\ *n* (1916) : the process of producing a phonocardiogram — **pho·no·car·dio·graph** \'kär-dē-ə-,graf\ *n* — **pho·no·car·dio·graph·ic** \-,kär-dē-ə-'gra-fik\ *adj*

pho·no·gram \'fō-nə-,gram\ *n* [ISV] (1860) **1** : a character or symbol used to represent a word, syllable, or phoneme **2** : a succession of orthographic letters that occurs with the same phonetic value in several words (as the *ight* of *bright, fight,* and *flight*) — **pho·no·gram·mic** or **pho·no·gram·ic** \,fō-nə-'gra-mik\ *adj* — **pho·no·gram·mi·cal·ly** or **pho·no·gram·i·cal·ly** \-mi-k(ə-)lē\ *adv*

pho·no·graph \'fō-nə-,graf\ *n* (1877) : an instrument for reproducing sounds by means of the vibration of a stylus or needle following a spiral groove on a revolving disc or cylinder

pho·nog·ra·pher \fə-'nä-grə-fər, fō-\ *n* (1845) : a specialist in phonography

pho·no·graph·ic \,fō-nə-'gra-fik, *1 is also* ,fä-\ *adj* (1828) **1** : of or relating to phonography **2** : of or relating to a phonograph — **pho·no·graph·i·cal·ly** \-fi-k(ə-)lē\ *adv*

pho·nog·ra·phy \fə-'nä-grə-fē, fō-\ *n* (1701) **1** : spelling based on pronunciation **2** : a system of shorthand writing based on sound

pho·no·lite \'fō-n²l-,īt\ *n* [F, fr. G *Phonolith,* fr. *phon-* + *-lith;* fr. its ringing sound when struck] (ca. 1828) : a gray or green volcanic rock consisting essentially of orthoclase and nepheline

pho·nol·o·gy \fə-'nä-lə-jē, fō-\ *n* (1799) **1** : the science of speech sounds including esp. the history and theory of sound changes in a language or in two or more related languages **2** : the phonetics and phonemics of a language at a particular time — **pho·no·log·i·cal** \,fō-n²l-'ä-ji-kəl *also* ,fä-\ *also* **pho·no·log·ic** \-jik\ *adj* — **pho·no·log·i·cal·ly** \-ji-k(ə-)lē\ *adv* — **pho·nol·o·gist** \fō-'nä-lə-jist, fə-\ *n*

pho·non \'fō-,nän\ *n* [*phon-* + ²*-on*] (1932) : a quantum of vibrational energy (as in a crystal)

pho·no·tac·tics \,fō-nə-'tak-tiks\ *n pl but sing in constr* (1956) : the area of phonology concerned with the analysis and description of the permitted sound sequences of a language — **pho·no·tac·tic** \-tik\ *adj*

¹**pho·ny** or **pho·ney** \'fō-nē\ *adj* **pho·ni·er; -est** [perh. alter. of *fawney* gilded brass ring used in the fawney rig, a confidence game, fr. Ir *fáinne* ring, fr. OIr *ánne* — more at ANUS] (1900) : not genuine or real: as **a** (1) : intended to deceive or mislead (2) : intended to defraud : COUNTERFEIT ⟨a ~ $10 bill⟩ ⟨a ~ check⟩ **b** : arousing suspicion : probably dishonest ⟨something ~ about the story⟩ **c** : having no genuine existence : FICTITIOUS ⟨~ publicity stories⟩ **d** : FALSE, SHAM ⟨a ~ name⟩ ⟨~ pearls⟩ **e** : making a false show: as (1) : HYPOCRITICAL (2) : SPECIOUS ⟨has a ~ poetic elegance —*New Republic*⟩ — **pho·ni·ly** \'fō-ni-lē\ *adv* — **pho·ni·ness** \'fō-nē-nəs\ *n*

²**phony** *or* **phoney** \n, pl\ **phonies** (1902) : one that is phony

³**phony** *or* **phoney** *vt* **pho·nied** *or* **pho·neyed; pho·ny·ing** *or* **pho·ney·ing** (ca. 1942) : COUNTERFEIT, FAKE — often used with *up* ⟨a paper *phonied* up on the spur of the moment —William Faulkner⟩

-phony *also* **-phonia** *n comb form* [ME *-phonie,* fr. OF, fr. L *-phonia,* fr. Gk *-phōnia,* fr. *-phōnos* sounding — more at -PHONE] **1** : sound ⟨tele*phony*⟩ **2** *usu* **-phonia** : speech disorder of a (specified) type ⟨dys*phonia*⟩

phooey \'fü-ē\ *interj* (1929) — used to express repudiation or disgust

pho·rate \'fōr-,āt, 'for-\ *n* [*phosphorus* + *thioate* (salt of a thio acid)] (1959) : a very toxic organophosphate systemic insecticide $C_7H_{17}O_2PS_3$ that is used esp. in seed treatments

-phore *n comb form* [NL *-phorus,* fr. Gk *-phoros,* fr. *-phoros* (adj. comb. form) carrying, fr. *pherein* to carry — more at BEAR] : carrier ⟨gameto*phore*⟩

-phoresis *n comb form, pl* **-phoreses** [NL, fr. Gk *phorēsis* act of carrying, fr. *phorein* to carry, wear, freq. of *pherein*] : transmission ⟨electro*phoresis*⟩

phos·gene \'fäz-,jēn\ *n* [Gk *phōs* light + *-genēs* born, produced — more at FANCY, -GEN; fr. its originally having been obtained by the action of sunlight] (1812) : a colorless gas $COCl_2$ of unpleasant odor that is a severe respiratory irritant

phosph- *or* **phospho-** *comb form* [*phosphorus*] **1** : phosphorus ⟨*phos*phide⟩ **2** : phosphate ⟨*phospho*fructokinase⟩

phos·pha·tase \'fäs-fə-,tās, -,tāz\ *n* (1912) : an enzyme that accelerates the hydrolysis and synthesis of organic esters of phosphoric acid and the transfer of phosphate groups to other compounds: **a** : ALKALINE PHOSPHATASE **b** : ACID PHOSPHATASE

phos·phate \'fäs-,fāt\ *n* [F, fr. *acide phosphorique* phosphoric acid] (1795) **1 a** (1) : a salt or ester of a phosphoric acid **b** : the trivalent anion PO_4^{3-} derived from phosphoric acid H_3PO_4 **b** : an organic compound of phosphoric acid in which the acid group is bound to nitrogen or a carboxyl group in a way that permits useful energy to be released (as in metabolism) **2** : an effervescent drink of carbonated water with a small amount of phosphoric acid flavored with fruit syrup **3** : a phosphatic material used for fertilizers

phosphate rock *n* (1870) : a rock that consists largely of calcium phosphate usu. together with other minerals (as calcium carbonate), is used in making fertilizers, and is a source of phosphorus compounds

phos·phat·ic \fäs-'fa-tik, -'fā-\ *adj* (1843) : of, relating to, or containing phosphoric acid or phosphates ⟨~ fertilizers⟩

phos·pha·tide \'fäs-fə-,tīd\ *n* [ISV] (1884) : PHOSPHOLIPID — **phos·pha·tid·ic** \,fäs-fə-'ti-dik\ *adj*

phos·pha·ti·dyl \'fäs-fə-'tī-d²l, fäs-'fa-tə-d²l\ *n* (1941) : any of several univalent groups $(RCOO)_2C_3H_5OPO(OH)$ that are derived from phosphatidic acids

phos·pha·ti·dyl·cho·line \,fäs-fə-,tī-d²l-'kō-,lēn, (,)fäs-,fa-tə-d²l-\ *n* (1954) : LECITHIN

phos·pha·ti·dyl·eth·a·nol·amine \-,e-thə-'nä-lə-,mēn, -'nō-\ *n* (1942) : any of a group of phospholipids that occur esp. in blood plasma and the white matter of the central nervous system — called also *cephalin*

phos·pha·tize \'fäs-fə-,tīz\ *vt* **-tized; -tiz·ing** (1883) **1** : to change to a phosphate or phosphates **2** : to treat with phosphoric acid or a phosphate — **phos·pha·ti·za·tion** \,fäs-fə-tə-'zā-shən, -,fā-\ *n*

phos·pha·tu·ria \,fäs-fə-'tür-ē-ə, -'tyür-\ *n* [NL, fr. ISV *phosphate* + NL *-uria*] (1876) : the excessive discharge of phosphates in the urine

phos·phene \'fäs-,fēn\ *n* [ISV *phos-* + Gk *phainein* to show — more at FANCY] (ca. 1860) : a luminous impression due to excitation of the retina

phos·phide \-,fīd\ *n* [ISV] (1849) : a binary compound of phosphorus with a more electropositive element or group

phos·phine \-,fēn\ *n* [ISV] (1873) **1** : a colorless poisonous flammable gas PH_3 that is a weaker base than ammonia and that is used esp. to fumigate stored grain **2** : any of various derivatives of phosphine analogous to amines but weaker as bases

phos·phite \-,fīt\ *n* (1799) : a salt or ester of phosphorous acid

phos·pho·cre·a·tine \,fäs-(,)fō-'krē-ə-,tēn\ *n* [ISV] (1927) : a compound $C_4H_{10}N_3O_5P$ of creatine and phosphoric acid that is found esp. in vertebrate muscle where it is an energy source for muscle contraction

phos·pho·di·es·ter·ase \-dī-'es-tə-,rās, -,rāz\ *n* (1936) : a phosphatase (as from snake venom) that acts on diesters (as some nucleotides) to hydrolyze only one of the two ester groups

phos·pho·enol·py·ru·vate \,fäs-fō-ə-,nōl-pī-'rü-,vāt, -,nōl-, -,pīr-'yü-\ *n* (1956) : a salt or ester of phosphoenolpyruvic acid

phos·pho·enol·py·ru·vic acid \-pī-'rü-vik-, -,pir-'yü-vik-\ *n* (1959) : the phosphate $H_2C=C(OPO_3H_2)COOH$ of the enol form of pyruvic acid that is formed as an intermediate in carbohydrate metabolism

phos·pho·fruc·to·ki·nase \,fäs-(,)fō-,frək-tō-'kī-,nās, -,frük-, -,frük-, -,nāz\ *n* [*phosph-* + *fructose* + *kinase*] (1947) : an enzyme that functions in carbohydrate metabolism and esp. in glycolysis by catalyzing the transfer of a second phosphate (as from ATP) to fructose

phos·pho·glu·co·mu·tase \-,glü-kō-'myü-,tās, -,tāz\ *n* (1938) : an enzyme that is found in all plant and animal cells and that catalyzes the reversible isomerization of glucose-1-phosphate to glucose-6-phosphate

phos·pho·glyc·er·al·de·hyde \-,gli-sə-'ral-də-,hīd\ *n* (1941) : a phosphate of glyceraldehyde $C_3H_5O_3(H_2PO_3)$ that is formed esp. in anaerobic metabolism of carbohydrates by the splitting of a diphosphate of fructose

phos·pho·glyc·er·ate \,fäs-fō-'gli-sə-,rāt\ *n* (1901) : a salt or ester of phosphoglyceric acid

phos·pho·gly·cer·ic acid \-gli-'ser-ik-\ *n* (1857) : either of two isomeric phosphates $HOOCC_2H_3(OH)OPO_3H_2$ of glyceric acid that are formed as intermediates in photosynthesis and in carbohydrate metabolism

phos·pho·ki·nase \,fäs-fō-'kī-,nās, -,nāz\ *n* (1946) : KINASE

phos·pho·li·pase \-'li-,pās, -,pāz\ *n* (1945) : any of several enzymes that hydrolyze lecithins or phosphatidylethanolamines — called also *lecithinase*

phos·pho·lip·id \-'li-pəd\ *n* (1928) : any of numerous lipids (as lecithins and phosphatidylethanolamines) in which phosphoric acid as well as a fatty acid is esterified to glycerol and which are found in all living cells and in the bilayers of plasma membranes

phos·pho·mono·es·ter·ase \-,mä-nō-'es-tə-,rās, -,rāz\ *n* (1933) : a phosphatase that acts on monoesters

phos·pho·ni·um \fäs-'fō-nē-əm\ *n* [NL] (1871) : a univalent cation PH_4^+ analogous to ammonium and derived from phosphine; *also* : an organic derivative of phosphonium (as $(C_2H_5)_4P^+$)

phos·pho·pro·tein \,fäs-fō-'prō-,tēn, -'prō-tē-ən\ *n* (ca. 1908) : any of various proteins (as casein) that contain combined phosphoric acid

phos·phor \'fäs-fər, -,fór\ *also* **phos·phore** \-,fór, -,fór, -fər\ *n* [L *phosphorus,* fr. Gk *phōsphoros,* lit., light bringer, fr. *phōsphoros* light-bearing, fr. *phōs* light + *pherein* to carry, bring — more at FANCY, BEAR] (1705) : a phosphorescent substance; *specif* : a substance that emits light when excited by radiation

phosphor bronze *n* (1875) : a bronze of great hardness, elasticity, and toughness that contains a small amount of phosphorus

phos·pho·resce \,fäs-fə-'res\ *vi* **-resced; -resc·ing** [prob. backformation fr. *phosphorescent*] (1794) : to exhibit phosphorescence

phos·pho·res·cence \-'re-s²n(t)s\ *n* (1796) **1** : luminescence that is caused by the absorption of radiation at one wavelength followed by delayed reradiation at a different wavelength and that continues for a noticeable time after the incident radiation stops — compare FLUORESCENCE **2** : an enduring luminescence without sensible heat

phos·pho·res·cent \-s²nt\ *adj* (1766) : exhibiting phosphorescence — **phos·pho·res·cent·ly** *adv*

phos·phor·ic \fäs-'fór-ik, -'fär-; 'fäs-f(ə-)rik\ *adj* (1800) : of, relating to, or containing phosphorus esp. with a valence higher than in phosphorous compounds

phosphoric acid *n* (1791) **1** : a syrupy or deliquescent tribasic acid H_3PO_4 used esp. in preparing phosphates (as for fertilizers), in rustproofing metals, and esp. formerly as a flavoring in soft drinks — called also *orthophosphoric acid* **2** : a compound (as pyrophosphoric acid or metaphosphoric acid) consisting of phosphate groups linked directly to each other by oxygen

phos·pho·rite \'fäs-fə-,rīt\ *n* (1796) **1** : a fibrous concretionary apatite **2** : PHOSPHATE ROCK — **phos·pho·rit·ic** \,fäs-fə-'ri-tik\ *adj*

phos·pho·rol·y·sis \,fäs-fə-'rä-lə-səs\ *n* [NL] (1937) : a reversible reaction analogous to hydrolysis in which phosphoric acid functions in a manner similar to that of water with the formation of a phosphate (as glucose-1-phosphate in the breakdown of liver glycogen) — **phos·pho·ro·lyt·ic** \-rō-'li-tik\ *adj*

phos·pho·rous \'fäs-f(ə-)rəs; fäs-'fōr-əs, -'fòr-\ *adj* (1815) : of, relating to, or containing phosphorus esp. with a valence lower than in phosphoric compounds

phosphorous acid *n* (1794) : a deliquescent crystalline acid H_3PO_3 used esp. as a reducing agent and in making phosphites

phos·pho·rus \'fäs-f(ə-)rəs\ *n, often attrib* [NL, fr. Gk *phōsphoros* light-bearing — more at PHOSPHOR] (1645) **1** : a phosphorescent substance or body; *esp* : one that shines or glows in the dark **2** : a nonmetallic element of the nitrogen family that occurs widely esp. as phosphates — see ELEMENT table

phos·pho·ryl \'fäs-fə-,ril\ *n* [ISV] (1871) : a usu. trivalent group PO

phos·phor·y·lase \\fäs-'fòr-ə-ˌlās, -ˌlāz\ *n* (1939) : any of the enzymes that catalyze phosphorolysis with the formation of organic phosphates

phos·phor·y·late \-ˌlāt\ *vt* **-lat·ed; -lat·ing** (1937) : to cause (an organic compound) to take up or combine with phosphoric acid or a phosphorus-containing group — **phos·phor·y·la·tive** \-ˌlā-tiv\ *adj*

phos·phor·y·la·tion \ˌfäs-ˌfòr-ə-'lā-shən\ *n* (1925) : the process of phosphorylating a chemical compound either by reaction with inorganic phosphate or by transfer of phosphate from another organic phosphate; *esp* : the enzymatic conversion of carbohydrates into their phosphoric esters in metabolic processes

phot- *or* **photo-** *comb form* [Gk *phōt-, phōto-,* fr. *phōt-, phōs* — more at FANCY] **1** : light : radiant energy ⟨*photon*⟩ ⟨*photography*⟩ **2** : photograph : photographic ⟨*photoengraving*⟩ **3** : photoelectric ⟨*photocell*⟩

pho·tic \'fō-tik\ *adj* (1843) **1** : of, relating to, or involving light esp. in relation to organisms **2** : penetrated by light esp. of the sun ⟨the ~ zone of the ocean⟩ — **pho·ti·cal·ly** \'fō-ti-k(ə-)lē\ *adv*

¹pho·to \'fō-(ˌ)tō\ *n, pl* **photos** (1860) : PHOTOGRAPH

²photo *vb* (1868) : PHOTOGRAPH

³photo *adj* (1889) : PHOTOGRAPHIC 1

pho·to·au·to·troph \ˌfō-tō-'ò-tə-ˌtròf\ *n* (1949) : a photoautotrophic organism

pho·to·au·to·tro·phic \-ˌó-tə-'trō-fik\ *adj* (1943) : autotrophic and utilizing energy from light ⟨green plants are ~⟩ — **pho·to·au·to·tro·phi·cal·ly** \-fi-k(ə-)lē\ *adv*

pho·to·bi·ol·o·gy \ˌfō-tō-(ˌ)bī-'ä-lə-jē\ *n* [ISV] (1935) : a branch of biology that deals with the effects on living beings of radiant energy (as light) — **pho·to·bi·o·log·i·cal** \-ˌbī-ə-'lä-ji-kəl\ *also* **pho·to·bi·o·log·ic** \-'lä-jik\ *adj* — **pho·to·bi·ol·o·gist** \-(ˌ)bī-'ä-lə-jist\ *n*

pho·to·cath·ode \-'ka-ˌthōd\ *n* [ISV] (1930) : a cathode that emits electrons when exposed to radiant energy and esp. light

pho·to·cell \'fō-tō-ˌsel\ *n* [ISV] (1891) : PHOTOELECTRIC CELL

pho·to·chem·i·cal \ˌfō-tō-'ke-mi-kəl\ *adj* (1859) **1** : of, relating to, or resulting from the chemical action of radiant energy and esp. light ⟨~ smog⟩ **2** : of or relating to photochemistry ⟨~ studies⟩ — **pho·to·chem·i·cal·ly** \-k(ə-)lē\ *adv*

pho·to·chem·is·try \-'ke-mə-strē\ *n* (1867) **1** : a branch of chemistry that deals with the effect of radiant energy in producing chemical changes **2 a** : photochemical properties ⟨the ~ of gases⟩ **b** : photochemical processes ⟨~ of vision⟩ — **pho·to·chem·ist** \-'ke-mist\ *n*

pho·to·chro·mic \ˌfō-tə-'krō-mik\ *adj* [*phot-* + *chrom-* + ¹*-ic*] (1953) **1** : capable of changing color on exposure to radiant energy (as light) ⟨~ glass⟩ **2** : of, relating to, or utilizing the change of color shown by a photochromic substance ⟨a ~ process⟩ — **pho·to·chro·mism** \-ˌmi-zəm\ *n*

pho·to·co·ag·u·la·tion \-kō-ˌa-gyə-'lā-shən\ *n* (1961) : a surgical process of coagulating tissue by means of a precisely oriented high-energy light source (as a laser)

pho·to·com·pose \ˌfō-tō-kəm-'pōz\ *vt* (1929) : to set (as reading matter) by photocomposition — **pho·to·com·pos·er** *n*

pho·to·com·po·si·tion \-ˌkäm-pə-'zi-shən\ *n* (1929) : composition of text directly on film or photosensitive paper for reproduction

pho·to·con·duc·tive \-kən-'dək-tiv\ *adj* (1929) : having, involving, or operating by photoconductivity

pho·to·con·duc·tiv·i·ty \-ˌkän-ˌdək-'ti-və-tē, -kən-\ *n* (1929) : electrical conductivity that is affected by exposure to electromagnetic radiation (as light)

¹pho·to·copy \'fō-tə-ˌkä-pē\ *n* [ISV] (ca. 1909) : a photographic reproduction of graphic matter

²photocopy *vt* (1944) : to make a photocopy of ~ *vi* : to make a photocopy — **pho·to·copi·er** *n*

pho·to·cur·rent \'fō-tō-ˌkər-ənt, -ˌkə-rənt\ *n* (1913) : a stream of electrons produced by photoelectric or photovoltaic effects

pho·to·de·com·po·si·tion \-ˌdē-ˌkäm-pə-'zi-shən\ *n* (1888) : chemical breaking down (as of a pesticide) by means of radiant energy

pho·to·de·grad·able \-di-'grā-də-bəl\ *adj* (1971) : chemically degradable by the action of light ⟨~ plastics⟩

pho·to·de·tec·tor \-di-'tek-tər\ *n* (1947) : any of various devices for detecting and measuring the intensity of radiant energy through photoelectric action

pho·to·di·ode \-'dī-ˌōd\ *n* (1945) : a photoelectric semiconductor device for detecting and often measuring radiant energy (as light)

pho·to·dis·in·te·gra·tion \-di-ˌsin-tə-'grā-shən\ *n* (1935) : disintegration of the nucleus of an atom caused by absorption of radiant energy (as light) — **pho·to·dis·in·te·grate** \-'sin-tə-ˌgrāt\ *vt*

pho·to·dis·so·ci·a·tion \-di-ˌsō-sē-'ā-shən, -shē-\ *n* (1925) : dissociation of the molecules of a substance (as water) caused by absorption of radiant energy — **pho·to·dis·so·ci·ate** \-'sō-sē-ˌāt, -shē-\ *vb*

pho·to·du·pli·ca·tion \-ˌdü-plə-'kā-shən, -dyü-\ *n* (1941) : the process of making photocopies — **pho·to·du·pli·cate** \-'dü-plə-ˌkāt, -'dyü-\ *vb* — **pho·to·du·pli·cate** \-pli-kət\ *n*

pho·to·dy·nam·ic \-(ˌ)dī-'na-mik\ *adj* [ISV] (1909) : of, relating to, or having the property of intensifying or inducing a toxic reaction to light (as in the destruction of cancer cells stained with a light-sensitive dye) in a living system — **pho·to·dy·nam·i·cal·ly** \-mi-k(ə-)lē\ *adv*

pho·to·elec·tric \ˌfō-tō-i-'lek-trik\ *adj* [ISV] (ca. 1879) : involving, relating to, or utilizing any of various electrical effects due to the interaction of radiation (as light) with matter — **pho·to·elec·tri·cal·ly** \-tri-k(ə-)lē\ *adv*

photoelectric cell *n* (1891) : an electronic device whose electrical properties are modified by the action of light

photoelectric effect *n* (1892) : the emission of free electrons from a metal surface when light strikes it

pho·to·elec·tron \ˌfō-tō-i-'lek-ˌträn\ *n* [ISV] (1912) : an electron released in photoemission — **pho·to·elec·tron·ic** \-ˌlek-'trä-nik\ *adj*

pho·to·emis·sion \-i-'mi-shən\ *n* (1916) : the release of electrons from a usu. solid material (as a metal) by means of energy supplied by incidence of radiation and esp. light — **pho·to·emis·sive** \-'mi-siv\ *adj*

pho·to·en·grave \-in-'grāv\ *vt* [back-formation fr. *photoengraving*] (1892) : to make a photoengraving of — **pho·to·en·grav·er** *n*

pho·to·en·grav·ing \-in-'grā-viŋ\ *n* (1872) **1** : a photomechanical process for making linecuts and halftone cuts by photographing an image on a metal plate and then etching **2 a** : a plate made by photoengraving **b** : a print made from such a plate

pho·to—es·say \'fō-tō-ˌe-ˌsā\ *n* (1944) : a group of photographs (as in a book or magazine) arranged to explore a theme or tell a story

pho·to·ex·ci·ta·tion \ˌfō-tō-ˌek-ˌsī-'tā-shən, -ˌek-sə-\ *n* (1918) : the process of exciting the atoms or molecules of a substance by the absorption of radiant energy — **pho·to·ex·cit·ed** \-ik-'sī-təd, -ek-\ *adj*

photo finish *n* (1936) **1** : a race in which contestants are so close that a photograph of them as they cross the finish line has to be examined to determine the winner **2** : a close contest

pho·to·fin·ish·er \ˌfō-tō-'fi-ni-shər\ *n* (ca. 1934) : one who develops and prints photographic film commercially — **pho·to·fin·ish·ing** \-shiŋ\ *n*

pho·to·flash \'fō-tō-ˌflash\ *n* (1930) : FLASH 6f

pho·to·flood \-ˌfləd\ *n* (1933) : an electric lamp that provides intense sustained illumination for taking photographs

pho·to·flu·o·rog·ra·phy \-ˌflü-'rä-grə-fē, -flò-, -flō-\ *n* (1941) : the photography of the image produced on a fluorescent screen by X rays

pho·tog \fə-'täg\ *n* [short for *photographer*] (ca. 1906) : one who takes photographs : PHOTOGRAPHER

pho·to·gen·ic \ˌfō-tə-'je-nik, -'jē-\ *adj* (1839) **1** : produced or precipitated by light ⟨~ dermatitis⟩ **2** : producing or generating light : PHOSPHORESCENT ⟨~ bacteria⟩ **3** : suitable for being photographed ⟨a ~ smile⟩ — **pho·to·ge·ni·cal·ly** \-ni-k(ə-)lē\ *adv*

pho·to·ge·ol·o·gy \ˌfō-tō-jē-'ä-lə-jē\ *n* (1941) : a branch of geology concerned with the identification and study of geological features through the study of aerial or orbital photographs — **pho·to·geo·log·ic** \-jē-ə-'lä-jik\ *also* **pho·to·geo·log·i·cal** \-ji-kəl\ *adj* — **pho·to·ge·ol·o·gist** \-jē-'ä-lə-jist\ *n*

pho·to·gram \'fō-tō-ˌgram\ *n* [ISV] (1859) : a shadowlike photograph made by placing objects between light-sensitive paper and a light source

pho·to·gram·me·try \ˌfō-tə-'gra-mə-trē\ *n* [ISV *photogram* photograph (fr. *phot-* + *-gram*) + *-metry*] (1875) : the science of making reliable measurements by the use of photographs and esp. aerial photographs (as in surveying) — **pho·to·gram·met·ric** \-grə-'me-trik\ *adj* — **pho·to·gram·me·trist** \-'gra-mə-trist\ *n*

¹pho·to·graph \'fō-tə-ˌgraf\ *n* (1839) : a picture or likeness obtained by photography

²photograph *vt* (1839) : to take a photograph of ~ *vi* **1** : to take a photograph **2** : to appear as an image in a photograph ⟨an actress who ~s well⟩

pho·tog·ra·pher \fə-'tä-grə-fər\ *n* (1847) : one who practices photography; *esp* : one who makes a business of taking photographs

pho·to·graph·ic \ˌfō-tə-'gra-fik\ *adj* (1839) **1** : relating to, obtained by, or used in photography **2** : representing nature and human beings with the exactness of a photograph **3** : capable of retaining vivid impressions ⟨a ~ mind⟩ — **pho·to·graph·i·cal·ly** \-fi-k(ə-)lē\ *adv*

pho·tog·ra·phy \fə-'tä-grə-fē\ *n* (1839) : the art or process of producing images on a sensitized surface (as a film) by the action of radiant energy and esp. light

pho·to·gra·vure \ˌfō-tə-grə-'vyùr\ *n* [F, fr. *phot-* + *gravure*] (1879) : a process for printing from an intaglio plate prepared by photographic methods

pho·to·in·duced \ˌfō-tō-in-'düst, -'dyüst\ *adj* (1947) : induced by the action of light — **pho·to·in·duc·tion** \-'dək-shən\ *n* — **pho·to·in·duc·tive** \-'dək-tiv\ *adj*

pho·to·in·ter·pre·ta·tion \-in-ˌtər-prə-'tā-shən, -pə-\ *n* (1923) : the science of identifying and describing objects in photographs — **pho·to·in·ter·pret·er** \-in-'tər-prə-tər\ *n*

pho·to·ion·i·za·tion \-ˌī-ə-nə-'zā-shən\ *n* (1914) : ionization (as in the ionosphere) of a molecule or atom caused by absorption of radiant energy — **pho·to·ion·ize** \-'ī-ə-ˌnīz\ *vt*

pho·to·jour·nal·ism \ˌfō-tō-'jər-nᵊl-ˌi-zəm\ *n* (1938) : journalism in which written copy is subordinate to pictorial usu. photographic presentation of news stories or in which a high proportion of pictorial presentation is used — **pho·to·jour·nal·ist** \-nᵊl-ist\ *n* — **pho·to·jour·nal·is·tic** \-ˌjər-nᵊl-'is-tik\ *adj*

pho·to·ki·ne·sis \-kə-'nē-səs, -ki-\ *n* [NL] (1905) : motion or activity induced by light — **pho·to·ki·net·ic** \-'ne-tik\ *adj*

pho·to·li·thog·ra·phy \-li-'thä-grə-fē\ *n* [ISV] (1856) **1** : lithography in which photographically prepared plates are used **2** : a process involving the photographic transfer of a pattern to a surface for etching (as in producing an integrated circuit) — **pho·to·lith·o·graph** \-'li-thə-ˌgraf\ *n or vt* — **pho·to·lith·o·graph·ic** \-ˌli-thə-'gra-fik\ *adj*

pho·tol·y·sis \fō-'tä-lə-səs\ *n* [NL] (1911) : chemical decomposition by the action of radiant energy — **pho·to·lyt·ic** \ˌfō-tᵊl-'i-tik\ *adj* — **pho·to·lyt·i·cal·ly** \-ti-k(ə-)lē\ *adv*

pho·to·lyze \'fō-tᵊl-ˌīz\ *vt* **-lyzed; -lyz·ing** (1936) : to cause to undergo photolysis — **pho·to·lyz·able** \-ˌī-zə-bəl\ *adj*

pho·to·map \'fō-tō-ˌmap\ *n* (1939) : a photograph which is taken vertically from above (as from an airplane) and upon which a grid and data pertinent to maps have been added — **photomap** *vb*

pho·to·mask \-ˌmask\ *n* (1965) : MASK 2d

pho·to·me·chan·i·cal \ˌfō-tō-mi-'ka-ni-kəl\ *adj* (ca. 1889) : relating to or involving any of various processes for producing printed matter from a photographically prepared surface — **pho·to·me·chan·i·cal·ly** \-ni-k(ə-)lē\ *adv*

pho·tom·e·ter \fō-'tä-mə-tər\ *n* [NL *photometrum,* fr. *phot-* + *-metrum* -meter] (1778) : an instrument for measuring luminous intensity, luminous flux, illumination, or brightness

pho·to·met·ric \ˌfō-tə-'me-trik\ *adj* (ca. 1828) : of or relating to photometry or the photometer — **pho·to·met·ri·cal·ly** \-tri-k(ə-)lē\ *adv*

pho·tom·e·try \fō-'tä-mə-trē\ *n* [NL *photometria,* fr. *phot-* + *-metria* -metry] (1824) : a branch of science that deals with measurement of the intensity of light; *also* : the practice of using a photometer

---

\ə\ abut \ᵊ\ kitten, F table \ər\ further \a\ ash \ā\ ace \ä\ mop, mar \au̇\ out \ch\ chin \e\ bet \ē\ easy \g\ go \i\ hit \ī\ ice \j\ job \ŋ\ sing \ō\ go \ȯ\ law \ȯi\ boy \th\ thin \t̲h̲\ the \ü\ loot \u̇\ foot \y\ yet \zh\ vision \á, k̲, ⁿ, œ, œ̄, ᵫ, ᵫ̄, ᵞ\ *see* Guide to Pronunciation

pho·to·mi·cro·graph \ˌfō-tə-'mī-krə-ˌgraf\ *n* (1858) : a photograph of a microscope image — **pho·to·mi·cro·graph·ic** \-ˌmī-krə-'gra-fik\ *adj* — **pho·to·mi·crog·ra·phy** \-mī-'krä-grə-fē\ *n*

pho·to·mon·tage \-män-'täzh, -mōⁿ(n)-, -'tazh\ *n* [ISV] (1931) : montage using photographic images; *also* : a picture made by photomontage

pho·to·mor·pho·gen·e·sis \ˌfōtə-ˌmȯr-fə-'je-nə-səs\ *n* [NL] (1959) : plant morphogenesis controlled by radiant energy (as light) — **pho·to·mor·pho·gen·ic** \-'je-nik\ *adj*

pho·to·mo·sa·ic \-mō-'zā-ik\ *n* (1942) : a photographic mosaic; *esp* : one composed of aerial or orbital photographs

pho·to·mul·ti·pli·er tube \ˌfō-tō-'məl-tə-ˌplī(-ə)r-\ *n* (1941) : a vacuum tube that detects light esp. from dim sources through the use of photoemission and successive instances of secondary emission to produce enough electrons to generate a useful current — called also *photomultiplier*

pho·to·mu·ral \-'myúr-əl\ *n* (1927) : an enlarged photograph usu. several yards long used on walls esp. as decoration

pho·ton \'fō-ˌtän\ *n* [*phot-* + ²-*on*] (1916) 1 : a unit of intensity of light at the retina equal to the illumination received per square millimeter of a pupillary area from a surface having a brightness of one candle per square meter 2 : a quantum of electromagnetic radiation — **pho·ton·ic** \fō-'tä-nik\ *adj*

pho·to·neg·a·tive \ˌfō-tō-'ne-gə-tiv\ *adj* (1914) : exhibiting negative phototropism or phototaxis

pho·ton·ics \fō-'tä-niks\ *n pl but sing in constr* (1952) : a branch of physics that deals with the properties and applications of photons esp. as a medium for transmitting information

pho·to·nu·cle·ar \ˌfō-tō-'nü-klē-ər, -'nyü-, ÷-kyə-lər\ *adj* (1941) : relating to or caused by the incidence of radiant energy (as gamma rays) on atomic nuclei

pho·to—off·set \-'ȯf-ˌset\ *n* (1926) : offset printing from photolithographic plates

photo opportunity *n* (1972) : a situation or event that lends itself to and is often arranged expressly for the taking of pictures that favorably publicize the individuals photographed

pho·to·ox·i·da·tion \-ˌäk-sə-'dā-shən\ *n* (1888) : oxidation under the influence of radiant energy (as light) — **pho·to·ox·i·da·tive** \-'äk-sə-ˌdā-tiv\ *adj* — **pho·to·ox·i·dize** \-'äk-sə-ˌdīz\ *vb*

pho·to·pe·ri·od \'fō-tə-ˌpir-ē-əd\ *n* (1920) : a recurring cycle of light and dark periods of constant length; *also* : PHOTOPHASE 2 — **pho·to·pe·ri·od·ic** \-ˌpir-ē-'ä-dik\ *adj* — **pho·to·pe·ri·od·i·cal·ly** \-di-k(ə-)lē\ *adv*

pho·to·pe·ri·od·ism \'-ˌpir-ē-ə-ˌdi-zəm\ *n* (ca. 1911) : a plant or animal's response or capacity to respond to photoperiod

pho·to·phase \'fō-tə-ˌfāz\ *n* (1944) 1 : LIGHT REACTION 2 : the light period of a photoperiodic cycle of light and dark

pho·to·pho·bia \ˌfō-tə-'fō-bē-ə\ *n* [NL] (ca. 1799) : intolerance to light; *esp* : painful sensitiveness to strong light

pho·to·pho·bic \-'fō-bik\ *adj* (1858) 1 a : shunning or avoiding light b : growing best under reduced illumination 2 : of or relating to photophobia

pho·to·phore \'fō-tə-ˌfōr, -ˌfȯr\ *n* [ISV] (1898) : a light-emitting organ; *esp* : one of the luminous spots on various marine mostly deep-sea fishes

pho·to·phos·phor·y·la·tion \'fō-tə-ˌfäs-ˌfȯr-ə-'lā-shən\ *n* (1956) : the synthesis of ATP from ADP and phosphate that occurs in a plant using radiant energy absorbed during photosynthesis

phot·op·ic \fōt-'ō-pik, -'ä-pik\ *adj* [NL *photopia*, fr. *phot-* + -*opia*] (1915) : relating to or being vision in bright light with light-adapted eyes that is mediated by the cones of the retina

pho·to·play \'fō-tō-ˌplā\ *n* (1910) : MOTION PICTURE 2

pho·to·po·la·rim·e·ter \ˌfō-tō-ˌpō-lə-'ri-mə-tər\ *n* (ca. 1890) : an instrument used to measure the intensity and polarization of reflected light (as from clouds enveloping a planet)

pho·to·poly·mer \-'päz-lə-mər\ *n* (1932) : a photosensitive plastic used esp. in the manufacture of printing plates

pho·to·pos·i·tive \-'päz-tə-tiv, -'päz-tiv\ *adj* (1914) : exhibiting positive phototropism or phototaxis

pho·to·prod·uct \-'prä-(ˌ)dəkt\ *n* (1926) : a product of a photochemical reaction

pho·to·pro·duc·tion \-prə-'dək-shən\ *n* (1949) : the production of elementary particles (as mesons) as a result of the action of photons on atomic nuclei

pho·to·re·ac·tion \-rē-'ak-shən\ *n* (1909) : a photochemical reaction

pho·to·re·ac·ti·va·tion \-rē-ˌak-tə-'vā-shən\ *n* (1949) : repair of DNA (as of a bacterium) esp. by a light-dependent enzymatic reaction after damage by ultraviolet irradiation — **pho·to·re·ac·ti·vat·ing** \-'ak-tə-ˌvā-tiŋ\ *adj*

photo—realism *n* (1961) : realism in painting characterized by extremely meticulous depiction of detail — **photo—realist** *n or adj*

pho·to·re·cep·tion \-ri-'sep-shən\ *n* (1902) : perception of waves in the range of visible light; *specif* : VISION — **pho·to·re·cep·tive** \-'sep-tiv\ *adj*

pho·to·re·cep·tor \-'sep-tər\ *n* (1906) : a receptor for light stimuli

pho·to·re·con·nais·sance \-ri-'kä-nə-zən(t)s *also* -sən(t)s\ *n* (1940) : reconnaissance in which aerial photographs are taken

pho·to·re·duc·tion \-ri-'dək-shən\ *n* (1888) : chemical reduction under the influence of radiant energy (as light) : photochemical reduction — **pho·to·re·duce** \-ri-'düs, -'dyüs\ *vt*

pho·to·re·pro·duc·tion \-ˌrē-prə-'dək-shən\ *n* (1939) : reproduction by photographic means; *also* : PHOTOCOPY

pho·to·re·sist \'fō-tō-ri-ˌzist, ˌfō-tō-ri-'\ *n* (1953) : a photosensitive resin that loses its resistance to chemical etching when exposed to radiation and is used esp. in the transference of a circuit pattern to a semiconductor chip during the production of an integrated circuit

pho·to·res·pi·ra·tion \ˌfō-tō-ˌres-pə-'rā-shən\ *n* (1945) : oxidation involving production of carbon dioxide during photosynthesis

pho·to·sen·si·tive \-'sen(t)-s(ə-)tiv\ *adj* (1886) : sensitive or sensitized to the action of radiant energy — **pho·to·sen·si·tiv·i·ty** \-ˌsen(t)-sə-'ti-və-tē\ *n*

pho·to·sen·si·ti·za·tion \-ˌsen(t)-s(ə-)tə-'zā-shən\ *n* (ca. 1923) 1 : the process of photosensitizing 2 : the condition of being photosensitized; *esp* : the development of an abnormal capacity to react to sunlight typically by edematous swelling and dermatitis

pho·to·sen·si·tize \-'sen(t)-sə-ˌtīz\ *vt* (ca. 1923) : to make sensitive to the influence of radiant energy and esp. light — **pho·to·sen·si·tiz·er** *n*

pho·to·set \'fō-tō-ˌset\ *vt* -**set; -set·ting** (1957) : PHOTOCOMPOSE — **pho·to·set·ter** *n*

pho·to·sphere \'fō-tə-ˌsfir\ *n* (1664) 1 : a sphere of light or radiance 2 : the luminous surface layer of the sun or a star — **pho·to·spher·ic** \ˌfō-tə-'sfir-ik, -'sfer-\ *adj*

pho·to·stat \'fō-tə-ˌstat\ *vt* (1914) : to copy by a Photostat device

Photostat *trademark* — used for a device for making a photographic copy of graphic matter

pho·to·stat·ic \ˌfō-tə-'sta-tik\ *adj* (1919) : of, made by, or using a Photostat device ⟨a ~ copy⟩ ⟨a ~ process⟩

pho·to·syn·thate \ˌfō-tō-'sin-ˌthāt\ *n* [*photosynthe*sis + -*ate*] (1913) : a product of photosynthesis

pho·to·syn·the·sis \-'sin(t)-thə-səs\ *n* [NL] (1898) : synthesis of chemical compounds with the aid of radiant energy and esp. light; *esp* : formation of carbohydrates from carbon dioxide and a source of hydrogen (as water) in the chlorophyll-containing tissues of plants exposed to light — **pho·to·syn·the·size** \-ˌsīz\ *vi* — **pho·to·syn·thet·ic** \-sin-'the-tik\ *adj* — **pho·to·syn·thet·i·cal·ly** \-ti-k(ə-)lē\ *adv*

pho·to·sys·tem \'fō-tō-ˌsis-təm\ *n* (1964) : either of two photochemical reactions occurring in chloroplasts: a : one that proceeds best in long wavelength light — called also *photosystem I* b : one that proceeds best in short wavelength light — called also *photosystem II*

pho·to·tac·tic \ˌfō-tō-'tak-tik\ *adj* [ISV] (1882) : of, relating to, or exhibiting phototaxis — **pho·to·tac·ti·cal·ly** \-ti-k(ə-)lē\ *adv*

pho·to·tax·is \-'tak-səs\ *n* [NL] (ca. 1890) : a taxis in which light is the directive factor

pho·to·te·leg·ra·phy \-tə-'le-grə-fē\ *n* [ISV] (1886) : FACSIMILE 2

pho·to·tox·ic \-'täk-sik\ *adj* (1942) 1 : rendering the skin susceptible to damage (as sunburn or blisters) upon exposure to light and esp. ultraviolet light 2 : induced by a phototoxic substance — **pho·to·tox·ic·i·ty** \-ˌtäk-'si-sə-tē\ *n*

pho·to·tro·pic \-'trō-pik, -'trä-\ *adj* (ca. 1890) : of, relating to, or capable of phototropism — **pho·to·tro·pi·cal·ly** \-pi-k(ə-)lē\ *adv*

pho·tot·ro·pism \fō-'tä-trə-ˌpi-zəm\ *n* [ISV] (1899) : a tropism in which light is the orienting stimulus

pho·to·tube \'fō-tō-ˌtüb, -ˌtyüb\ *n* (1930) : an electron tube having a photoemissive cathode whose released electrons are drawn to the anode by reason of its positive potential

pho·to·type·set·ting \ˌfō-tō-'tīp-ˌse-tiŋ\ *n* (1931) : PHOTOCOMPOSITION; *esp* : photocomposition done on a keyboard or tape-operated composing machine — **pho·to·type·set·ter** *n*

pho·to·vol·ta·ic \-väl-'tā-ik, -vōl-\ *adj* [ISV] (ca. 1890) : of, relating to, or utilizing the generation of a voltage when radiant energy falls on the boundary between dissimilar substances (as two different semiconductors) — **photovoltaic** *n*

phrag·mo·plast \'frag-mō-ˌplast\ *n* [ISV *phragmo-* (fr. Gk *phragmos* fence, fr. *phrassein* to enclose) + -*plast*] (1912) : the enlarged barrelshaped spindle that is characteristic of the later stages of plant mitosis and within which the cell plate forms

phras·al \'frā-zəl\ *adj* (1871) : of, relating to, or consisting of a phrase ⟨~ prepositions⟩ — **phras·al·ly** \-zə-lē\ *adv*

¹**phrase** \'frāz\ *n* [L *phrasis*, fr. Gk, fr. *phrazein* to point out, explain, tell] (1530) 1 : a characteristic manner or style of expression : DICTION 2 a : a brief expression; *esp* : CATCHWORD b : WORD 3 : a short musical thought typically two to four measures long closing with a cadence 4 : a word or group of words forming a syntactic constituent with a single grammatical function ⟨an adverbial ~⟩ 5 : a series of dance movements comprising a section of a pattern

²**phrase** *vt* **phrased; phras·ing** (1570) 1 a : to express in words or in appropriate or telling terms b : to designate by a descriptive word or phrase 2 : to divide into melodic phrases

phrase book *n* (1594) : a book containing idiomatic expressions of a foreign language and their translation

phrase-mak·er \'frāz-ˌmā-kər\ *n* (1822) 1 : one who coins impressive phrases 2 : one given to making fine-sounding but often hollow and meaningless phrases — **phrase-mak·ing** \-kiŋ\ *n*

phrase-mon·ger \-ˌməŋ-gər, -ˌmäŋ-\ *n* (1815) : PHRASEMAKER 2 — **phrase-mon·ger·ing** \-g(ə-)riŋ\ *n*

phra·se·o·log·i·cal \ˌfrā-zē-ə-'lä-ji-kəl\ *adj* (1664) 1 a : expressed in formal often sententious phrases b : marked by frequently insincere use of such phrases 2 : of or relating to phraseology

phra·se·ol·o·gist \ˌfrā-zē-'ä-lə-jist, frā-'zä-\ *n* (1713) : one who uses sententious or insincere phrases

phra·se·ol·o·gy \-jē\ *n, pl* -**gies** [NL *phraseologia*, irreg. fr. Gk *phrasis* + -*logia* -logy] (1664) 1 : a manner of organizing words and phrases into longer elements : STYLE 2 : choice of words

phras·ing \'frā-ziŋ\ *n* (1611) 1 : style of expression : PHRASEOLOGY 2 : the act, method, or result of grouping notes into musical phrases

phra·try \'frā-trē\ *n, pl* **phratries** [Gk *phratria*, fr. *phratēr* member of the same clan, member of a phratry — more at BROTHER] (1833) 1 : a kinship group forming a subdivision of a Greek phyle 2 : a tribal subdivision; *specif* : an exogamous group typically comprising several totemic clans

phre·at·ic \frē-'a-tik\ *adj* [Gk *phreat-, phrear* well; akin to Arm *atbiwr* spring, OHG *brunno* — more at BURN] (ca. 1890) 1 : of, relating to, or being groundwater 2 : of, relating to, or being an explosion caused by steam derived from groundwater

phre·at·o·phyte \frē-'a-tə-ˌfīt\ *n* [Gk *phreat-, phrear* well + E -*o-* + -*phyte*] (1920) : a deep-rooted plant that obtains its water from the water table or the layer of soil just above it — **phre·at·o·phyt·ic** \-ˌa-tə-'fi-tik\ *adj*

phre·net·ic *var of* FRENETIC

-**phre·nia** *n comb form* [NL, fr. Gk *phren-, phrēn* diaphragm, mind] : disordered condition of mental functions ⟨hebe*phrenia*⟩

phren·ic \'fre-nik\ *adj* [NL *phrenicus*, fr. Gk *phren-, phrēn*] (1704) 1 : of or relating to the diaphragm 2 : of or relating to the mind

phre·nol·o·gy \fri-'nä-lə-jē\ *n* [Gk *phren-, phrēn*] (1805) : the study of the conformation of the skull based on the belief that it is indicative of mental faculties and character — **phre·no·log·i·cal** \ˌfre-nᵊl-'ä-ji-kəl, ˌfrē-\ *adj* — **phre·nol·o·gist** \fri-'nä-lə-jist\ *n*

phren·sy *var of* FRENZY

Phry·gian \'fri-j(ē-)ən\ *n* (15c) **1** : a native or inhabitant of ancient Phrygia **2** : the extinct Indo-European language of the Phrygians — see INDO-EUROPEAN LANGUAGES table — **Phrygian** *adj*

phthal·ic acid \'tha-lik-\ *n* [ISV, short for obs. *naphthalic acid*, fr. *naphthalene*] (1857) : any of three isomeric acids $C_8H_6O_4$ obtained by oxidation of various benzene derivatives

phthalic anhydride *n* (1855) : a crystalline cyclic acid anhydride $C_8H_4O_3$ used esp. in making alkyd resins

phtha·lo·cy·a·nine \,tha-lō-'sī-ə-,nēn, ,thā-\ *n* [ISV *phthalic acid* + *-o-* + *cyanine*] (1933) : a bright greenish blue crystalline compound $C_{32}H_{18}N_8$; *also* : any of several metal derivatives that are brilliant fast blue to green dyes or pigments

phthis·ic \'ti-zik\ *n* [ME *tisike*, fr. MF *tisique*, fr. *tisique* tubercular, fr. L *phthisicus*, fr. Gk *phthisikos*, fr. *phthisis*] (14c) : PHTHISIS — **phthisic** *or* **phthis·i·cal** \-zi-kəl\ *adj*

phthi·sis \'thī-səs, 'ti-, 'fthī- *or with* i *for* ī\ *n, pl* **phthi·ses** \-,sēz\ [L, fr. Gk, fr. *phthinein* to waste away; akin to Skt *kṣinoti* he destroys] (1526) : a progressively wasting or consumptive condition; *esp* : pulmonary tuberculosis

phyco- *comb form* [Gk *phykos* seaweed] : algae ⟨phycology⟩

phy·co·cy·a·nin \,fī-kō-'sī-ə-nən\ *n* [ISV *phyco-* + *cyan-* + ¹-*in*] (1875) : any of various bluish green protein pigments in the cells of blue-green algae

phy·co·er·y·thrin \-'er-i-thrən\ *n* [ISV *phyco-* + *erythr-* + ¹-*in*] (ca. 1868) : any of the red protein pigments in the cells of red algae

phy·col·o·gy \fī-'kä-lə-jē\ *n* (ca. 1847) : ALGOLOGY — **phy·co·log·i·cal** \,fī-kə-'lä-ji-kəl\ *adj* — **phy·col·o·gist** \fī-'kä-lə-jist\ *n*

phy·co·my·cete \,fī-kō-'mī-,sēt, -,mī-'sēt\ *n* [ultim. fr. Gk *phykos* + *mykēt-, mykēs* fungus — more at MYC.] (ca. 1900) : any of a large class (Phycomycetes) of lower fungi that are in many respects similar to algae and are now often assigned to subdivisions (Mastigomycotina and Zygomycotina) — **phy·co·my·ce·tous** \-,mī-'sē-təs\ *adj*

phyl- *or* **phylo-** *comb form* [L, fr. Gk, fr. *phylē, phylon;* akin to Gk *phyein* to bring forth — more at BE] : tribe : race : phylum ⟨phylogeny⟩

phy·lac·tery \fə-'lak-t(ə-)rē\ *n, pl* **-ter·ies** [ME *philaterie*, fr. ML *philaterium*, alter. of LL *phylacterium*, fr. Gk *phylaktērion* amulet, phylactery, fr. *phylassein* to guard, fr. *phylak-, phylax* guard] (14c) **1** : either of two small square leather boxes containing slips inscribed with scriptural passages and traditionally worn on the left arm and on the head by Jewish men during morning weekday prayers **2** : AMULET

phy·le \'fī-(,)lē\ *n, pl* **phy·lae** \-,lē\ [Gk *phylē* tribe, phyle] (1863) : the largest political subdivision among the ancient Athenians

phy·let·ic \fī-'le-tik\ *adj* [ISV *phyl-* + *-etic* (as in *genetic*)] (1881) : of or relating to evolutionary change in a single line of descent without branching — **phy·let·i·cal·ly** \-ti-k(ə-)lē\ *adv*

phyll- *or* **phyllo-** *comb form* [NL, fr. Gk, fr. *phyllon* — more at BLADE] : leaf ⟨phyllome⟩

-phyll *n comb form* [NL *-phyllum*, fr. Gk *phyllon* leaf] : leaf ⟨sporophyll⟩

phylactery 1

phyl·la·ry \'fi-lə-rē\ *n, pl* **-ries** [NL *phyllarium*, fr. Gk *phyllarion*, dim. of *phyllon* leaf] (1857) : one of the involucral bracts subtending the flower head of a composite plant

phyl·lo \'fē-(,)lō, 'fi-\ *n* [NGk, sheet of pastry dough, lit., leaf, fr. Gk *phyllon*] (ca. 1950) : extremely thin pastry dough that is layered to produce a flaky pastry

phyl·lo·clade \'fi-lə-,klād\ *n* [NL *phyllocladium*, fr. *phyll-* + Gk *klados* branch — more at HOLT] (1858) : a flattened stem or branch (as a joint of a cactus) that functions as a leaf

phyl·lode \'fi-,lōd\ *n* [NL *phyllodium*, fr. Gk *phyllōdēs* like a leaf, fr. *phyllon* leaf] (1848) : a flat expanded petiole that replaces the blade of a foliage leaf, fulfills the same functions, and is analogous to a cladophyll

phyl·lo·di·um \fi-'lō-dē-əm\ *n, pl* **-dia** \-dē-ə\ [NL] (ca. 1847) : PHYLLODE

phyl·lome \'fi-,lōm\ *n* [ISV] (1875) : a plant part that is a leaf or is phylogenetically derived from a leaf

phyl·lo·tac·tic \,fi-lə-'tak-tik\ *adj* (1857) : of or relating to phyllotaxis

phyl·lo·tax·is \,fi-lə-'tak-səs\ *also* **phyl·lo·taxy** \'fi-lə-,tak-sē\ *n* [NL *phyllotaxis*, fr. *phyll-* + *-taxis*] (1857) **1** : the arrangement of leaves on a stem and in relation to one another **2** : the study of phyllotaxis and of the laws that govern it

-phyllous *adj comb form* [NL *-phyllus*, fr. Gk *-phyllos*, fr. *phyllon* leaf — more at BLADE] : having (such or so many) leaves, leaflets, or leaflike parts ⟨heterophyllous⟩

phyl·lox·e·ra \,fi-,läk-'sir-ə, fə-'läk-sə-rə\ *n* [NL, fr. *phyll-* + Gk *xēros* dry] (1868) : any of various plant lice (esp. genus *Phylloxera*) that differ from aphids esp. in wing structure and in being continuously oviparous

phy·lo·ge·net·ic \,fī-lō-jə-'ne-tik\ *adj* [ISV, fr. NL *phylogenesis* phylogeny, fr. *phyl-* + *genesis*] (1877) **1** : of or relating to phylogeny **2** : based on natural evolutionary relationships **3** : acquired in the course of phylogenetic development : RACIAL — **phy·lo·ge·net·i·cal·ly** \-ti-k(ə-)lē\ *adv*

phy·log·e·ny \fī-'lä-jə-nē\ *n, pl* **-nies** [ISV] (1872) **1** : the evolutionary history of a kind of organism **2** : the evolution of a genetically related group of organisms as distinguished from the development of the individual organism **3** : the history or course of the development of something (as a word or custom)

phy·lum \'fī-ləm\ *n, pl* **phy·la** \-lə\ [NL, fr. Gk *phylon* tribe, race — more at PHYL.] (1876) **1 a** : a direct line of descent within a group **b** : a group that constitutes or has the unity of a phylum; *esp* : one of the usu. primary divisions of the animal kingdom **2** : a group of languages related more remotely than those of a family or stock

phys ed \'fiz-'ed\ *n* (1955) : PHYSICAL EDUCATION

physi- *or* **physio-** *comb form* [L, fr. Gk, fr. *physis* — more at PHYSICS] **1** : nature ⟨physiography⟩ **2** : physical ⟨physiotherapy⟩

phys·i·at·rist \,fi-zē-'a-trist\ *n* [*physiatrics* physical medicine, fr. Gk *physis* + ISV *-iatrics*] (ca. 1947) : a physician who specializes in physical medicine

¹**phys·ic** \'fi-zik\ *n* [ME *physik* natural science, art of medicine, fr. OF *fisique*, fr. L *physica*, sing., natural science, fr. Gk *physikē*, fr. fem. of *physikos* — more at PHYSICS] (14c) **1 a** : the art or practice of healing disease **b** : the practice or profession of medicine **2** : a medicinal agent or preparation; *esp* : PURGATIVE **3** *archaic* : NATURAL SCIENCE

²**physic** *vt* **phys·icked; phys·ick·ing** (14c) **1** : to treat with or administer medicine to; *esp* : PURGE **2** : HEAL, CURE

¹**phys·i·cal** \'fi-zi-kəl\ *adj* [ME *phisicale* medical, fr. ML *physicalis*, fr. L *physica*] (1597) **1 a** : having material existence : perceptible esp. through the senses and subject to the laws of physical ⟨everything ∼ is measurable by weight, motion, and resistance —Thomas De Quincey⟩ **b** : of or relating to material things **2 a** : of or relating to natural science **b** (1) : of or relating to physics (2) : characterized or produced by the forces and operations of physics **3 a** : of or relating to the body **b** : concerned or preoccupied with the body and its needs : CARNAL **c** : characterized by esp. rugged and forceful physical activity : ROUGH ⟨a ∼ hockey game⟩ ⟨a ∼ player⟩ *syn* see MATERIAL — **phys·i·cal·ly** \-k(ə-)lē\ *adv* — **phys·i·cal·ness** \-kəl-nəs\ *n*

²**physical** *n* (1934) : PHYSICAL EXAMINATION

physical anthropology *n* (1873) : anthropology concerned with the comparative study of human evolution, variation, and classification esp. through measurement and observation — compare CULTURAL ANTHROPOLOGY — **physical anthropologist** *n*

physical education *n* (1830) : instruction in the development and care of the body ranging from simple calisthenic exercises to a course of study providing training in hygiene, gymnastics, and the performance and management of athletic games

physical examination *n* (1884) : an examination of the bodily functions and condition of an individual

physical geography *n* (1808) : geography that deals with the exterior physical features and changes of the earth

phys·i·cal·ism \'fi-zi-kə-,li-zəm\ *n* (ca. 1931) : a thesis that the descriptive terms of scientific language are reducible to terms which refer to spatiotemporal things or events or to their properties — **phys·i·cal·ist** \-list\ *n* — **phys·i·cal·is·tic** \,fi-zi-kə-'lis-tik\ *adj*

phys·i·cal·i·ty \,fi-zə-'ka-lə-tē\ *n, pl* **-ties** (1660) **1** : intensely physical orientation : predominance of the physical usu. at the expense of the mental, spiritual, or social **2** : a physical aspect or quality

physical medicine *n* (1939) : a branch of medicine concerned with the diagnosis and treatment of disease and disability by physical means (as radiation, heat, and electricity) — compare PHYSICAL THERAPY

physical science *n* (1802) : any of the natural sciences (as physics, chemistry, and astronomy) that deal primarily with nonliving materials — **physical scientist** *n*

physical therapy *n* (1922) : the treatment of disease by physical and mechanical means (as massage, regulated exercise, water, light, heat, and electricity) — **physical therapist** *n*

phy·si·cian \fə-'zi-shən\ *n* [ME *fisicien*, fr. OF, fr. *fisique* medicine] (13c) **1** : a person skilled in the art of healing; *specif* : a doctor of medicine **2** : one exerting a remedial or salutary influence

physician's assistant *n* (1970) : a person certified to provide basic medical services usu. under the supervision of a licensed physician — called also *PA, physician assistant*

phys·i·cist \'fi-zə-sist, 'fiz-sist\ *n* (1840) **1** : a specialist in physics **2** *archaic* : a person skilled in natural science

phys·i·co·chem·i·cal \,fi-zi-kō-'ke-mi-kəl\ *adj* (1664) **1** : being physical and chemical **2** : of or relating to chemistry that deals with the physicochemical properties of substances — **phys·i·co·chem·i·cal·ly** \-k(ə-)lē\ *adv*

phys·ics \'fi-ziks\ *n pl but sing or pl in constr* [L *physica*, pl., natural science, fr. Gk *physika*, fr. neut. pl. of *physikos* of nature, fr. *physis* growth, nature, fr. *phyein* to bring forth — more at BE] (1715) **1** : a science that deals with matter and energy and their interactions **2 a** : the physical processes and phenomena of a particular system **b** : the physical properties and composition of something

Phys·io·crat \'fi-zē-ə-,krat\ *n* [F *physiocrate*, fr. *physi-* physi- + *-crate* -crat] (1798) : a member of a school of political economists founded in 18th century France and characterized chiefly by a belief that government policy should not interfere with the operation of natural economic laws and that land is the source of all wealth — **phys·io·crat·ic** \,fi-zē-ə-'kra-tik\ *adj, often cap*

phys·i·og·nom·ic \,fi-zē-ə(g)-'nä-mik\ *also* **phys·i·og·nom·i·cal** \-mi-kəl\ *adj* (1588) : of, relating to, or characteristic of physiognomy or the physiognomy — **phys·i·og·nom·i·cal·ly** \-mi-k(ə-)lē\ *adv*

phys·i·og·no·my \,fi-zē-'ä(g)-nə-mē\ *n, pl* **-mies** [ME *phisonomie*, fr. MF, fr. LL *physiognomonia, physiognomia*, fr. Gk *physiognōmonia*, fr. *physiognōmōn* judging character by the features, fr. *physis* nature, physique, appearance + *gnōmōn* interpreter — more at GNOMON] (14c) **1** : the art of discovering temperament and character from outward appearance **2** : the facial features held to show qualities of mind or character by their configuration or expression **3** : external aspect; *also* : inner character or quality revealed outwardly

phys·i·og·ra·phy \,fi-zē-'ä-grə-fē\ *n* [prob. fr. F *Physiographie*, fr. *physi-* + *-graphie* -graphy] (ca. 1828) : PHYSICAL GEOGRAPHY — **phys·i·og·ra·pher** \-fər\ *n* — **phys·io·graph·ic** \,fi-zē-ō-'gra-fik\ *also* **phys·io·graph·i·cal** \-fi-kəl\ *adj*

phys·i·o·log·i·cal \,fi-zē-ə-'lä-ji-kəl\ *or* **phys·i·o·log·ic** \-jik\ *adj* (1814) **1** : of or relating to physiology **2** : characteristic of or appropriate to an organism's healthy or normal functioning **3** : differing in, involving, or affecting physiological factors ⟨a ∼ strain of bacteria⟩ — **phys·i·o·log·i·cal·ly** \-ji-k(ə-)lē\ *adv*

\ə\ abut \'\ kitten, F table \ər\ further \a\ ash \ā\ ace \ä\ mop, mar \aú\ out \ch\ chin \e\ bet \ē\ easy \g\ go \i\ hit \ī\ ice \j\ job \ŋ\ sing \ō\ go \ó\ law \ói\ boy \th\ thin \t̷h\ the \ü\ loot \ú\ foot \y\ yet \zh\ vision \à, k̲, ⁿ, œ, œ̄, ᵫ, ᵫ̄, ᵞ\ see Guide to Pronunciation

physiological psychology n (1888) : a branch of psychology that deals with the effects of normal and pathological physiological processes on mental life — called also *psychophysiology*

physiological saline n (1896) : a solution of a salt or salts that is essentially isotonic with tissue fluids or blood

phys·i·ol·o·gy \,fi-zē-'ä-lə-jē\ n [L *physiologia* natural science, fr. Gk, fr. *physi-* + *-logia* -logy] (1597) **1** : a branch of biology that deals with the functions and activities of life or of living matter (as organs, tissues, or cells) and of the physical and chemical phenomena involved — compare ANATOMY **2** : the organic processes and phenomena of an organism or any of its parts or of a particular bodily process — **phys·i·ol·o·gist** \-jist\ n

phys·io·pa·thol·o·gy \,fi-zē-ō-pə-'thä-lə-jē, -pä-\ n (ca. 1889) : a branch of biology or medicine that combines physiology and pathology esp. in the study of altered bodily function in disease — **phys·io·path·o·log·ic** \-,pa-thə-'lä-jik\ or **phys·io·path·o·log·i·cal** \-ji-kəl\ adj

phys·io·ther·a·py \,fi-zē-ō-'ther-ə-pē\ n [NL *physiotherapia*, fr. *physi-* + *therapia* therapy] (ca. 1903) : PHYSICAL THERAPY — **phys·io·ther·a·pist** \-'ther-ə-\pist\ n

phy·sique \fə-'zēk\ n [F, fr. *physique* physical, bodily, fr. L *physicus* of nature, fr. Gk *physikos*] (1813) : the form or structure of a person's body : bodily makeup

phy·so·stig·mine \,fi-sə-'stig-,mēn\ n [ISV, fr. NL *Physostigma*, genus of vines that bear the Calabar bean] (1864) : a crystalline tasteless alkaloid $C_{15}H_{21}N_3O_2$ from the Calabar bean that is used in medicine esp. in the form of its salicylate for its anticholinesterase activity

phyt- or **phyto-** comb form [NL, fr. Gk, fr. *phyton*, fr. *phyein* to bring forth — more at BE] : plant ⟨*phytophagous*⟩

phy·tane \'fi-,tān\ n (1907) : an isoprenoid hydrocarbon $C_{20}H_{42}$ that is found esp. associated with fossilized plant remains from the Precambrian and later eras

-phyte n comb form [ISV, fr. Gk *phyton* plant] : plant having a (specified) characteristic or habitat ⟨*xerophyte*⟩

-phytic adj comb form [ISV, fr. Gk *phyton* plant] : like a plant ⟨*holophytic*⟩

phy·to·alex·in \,fi-tō-ə-'lek-sən\ n [ISV *phyt-* + *alexin* substance combating infection, fr. Gk *alexein* to ward off, protect; akin to Skt *rakṣati* he protects] (1949) : a chemical substance produced by a plant to combat infection by a pathogen (as a fungus)

phy·to·chem·i·cal \-'ke-mi-kəl\ adj (ca. 1858) : of, relating to, or being phytochemistry — **phy·to·chem·i·cal·ly** \-mi-k(ə-)lē\ adv

phy·to·chem·is·try \-'ke-mə-strē\ n (1837) : the chemistry of plants, plant processes, and plant products — **phy·to·chem·ist** \-'ke-mist\ n

phy·to·chrome \'fi-tə-,krōm\ n (ca. 1893) : a chromoprotein that is present in traces in many plants and that plays a significant role in initiating floral and developmental processes when activated by red or near-infrared radiation

phy·to·fla·gel·late \,fi-tō-'fla-jə-lət, -,lāt; -flə-'jə-\ n (1935) : any of various organisms (as dinoflagellates) that are considered a subclass (Phytomastigophora syn. Phytomastigina) usu. of algae by botanists and of protozoans by zoologists and that have many characteristics in common with typical algae

phy·to·ge·og·ra·phy \,fi-tō-jē-'ä-grə-fē\ n [ISV] (1847) : the biogeography of plants — **phy·to·ge·og·ra·pher** \-fər\ n — **phy·to·geo·graph·i·cal** \-jē-ə-'gra-fi-kəl\ or **phy·to·geo·graph·ic** \-fik\ adj — **phy·to·geo·graph·i·cal·ly** \-fi-k(ə-)lē\ adv

phy·to·he·mag·glu·ti·nin \-,hē-mə-'glü-t³n-ən\ n (1949) : a proteinaceous hemagglutinin of plant origin used esp. to induce mitosis (as in lymphocytes)

phy·to·hor·mone \-'hòr-,mōn\ n [ISV] (1933) : PLANT HORMONE

phy·ton \'fi-,tän\ n [NL, fr. Gk, plant] (1848) **1** : a structural unit of a plant consisting of a leaf and its associated portion of stem **2** : the smallest part of a stem, root, or leaf that when severed may grow into a new plant — **phy·ton·ic** \fi-'tä-nik\ adj

phy·to·path·o·gen \,fi-tō-'pa-thə-jən\ n (ca. 1930) : an organism parasitic on a plant host — **phy·to·path·o·gen·ic** \-,pa-thə-'je-nik\ adj

phy·to·pa·thol·o·gy \-pə-'thä-lə-jē, -pä-\ n [ISV] (ca. 1859) : plant pathology — **phy·to·path·o·log·i·cal** \-,pa-thə-'lä-ji-kəl\ adj

phy·toph·a·gous \fi-'tä-fə-gəs\ adj (1826) : feeding on plants ⟨a ~ insect⟩

phy·to·plank·ter \,fi-tō-'plan(k)-tər\ n (1944) : a planktonic plant

phy·to·plank·ton \-'plan(k)-tən, -,tän\ n [ISV] (1897) : planktonic plant life — **phy·to·plank·ton·ic** \-,plan(k)-'tä-nik\ adj

phy·to·so·ci·ol·o·gy \,sō-sē-'ä-lə-jē, -shē-\ n (ca. 1928) : a branch of ecology concerned esp. with the structure, composition, and interrelationships of plant communities — **phy·to·so·cio·log·i·cal** \-sē-ə-'lä-ji-kəl\ adj

phy·tos·ter·ol \fi-'täs-tə-,ròl, -,rōl\ n [ISV] (1898) : any of various sterols derived from plants — compare ZOOSTEROL

phy·to·tox·ic \,fi-tə-'täk-sik\ adj (1926) : poisonous to plants — **phy·to·tox·ic·i·ty** \-täk-'si-sə-tē\ n

¹**pi** also **pie** \'pī\ n, pl **pies** [origin unknown] (ca. 1659) **1** : type that is spilled or mixed **2** : a pi character or matrix

²**pi** also **pie** vb **pied; pi·ing** or **pie·ing** vt (1870) : to spill or throw (type or type matter) into disorder ~ vi : to become pied

³**pi** adj (ca. 1940) **1** : not intended to appear in final printing ⟨~ lines⟩ **2** : capable of being inserted only by hand ⟨~ characters⟩

⁴**pi** n, pl **pis** \'piz\ [MGk, fr. Gk *pei*, of Sem origin; akin to Heb *pē* pe] (1823) **1** : the 16th letter of the Greek alphabet — see ALPHABET table **2 a** : the symbol π denoting the ratio of the circumference of a circle to its diameter **b** : the ratio itself : a transcendental number having a value to eight decimal places of 3.14159265

pi·al \'pī-əl, 'pē-\ adj (1889) : of or relating to the pia mater

pia ma·ter \'pī-ə-,mā-tər, 'pē-ə-,mä-\ n [ME, fr. ML, fr. L, tender mother] (14c) : the thin vascular membrane that invests the brain and spinal cord internal to the arachnoid and dura mater

pi·a·nism \'pē-ə-,ni-zəm\ n (1844) **1** : the art or technique of piano playing **2** : the composition or adaptation of music for the piano

¹**pi·a·nis·si·mo** \,pē-ə-'ni-sə-,mō\ adv or adj [It, fr. *piano* softly] (1724) : very softly — used as a direction in music

²**pianissimo** n, pl **-mi** \-(,)mē\ or **-mos** (1883) : a passage played, sung, or spoken very softly

pi·a·nist \pē-'a-nist, 'pē-ə-\ n (ca. 1828) : one who plays the piano; esp : a skilled or professional performer on the piano

pi·a·nis·tic \,pē-ə-'nis-tik\ adj (1881) **1** : of, relating to, or characteristic of the piano **2** : skilled in or well adapted to piano playing — **pi·a·nis·ti·cal·ly** \-ti-k(ə-)lē\ adv

¹**pi·a·no** \pē-'ä-(,)nō\ adv or adj [It, fr. LL *planus* smooth, fr. L, level — more at FLOOR] (1683) : at a soft volume : SOFT — used as a direction in music

²**pi·a·no** \pē-'a-(,)nō also -'ä-\ n, pl **pianos** [It, short for *pianoforte*, fr. *gravicembalo col piano e forte*, lit., harpsichord with soft and loud; fr. the fact that its tones could be varied in loudness] (1803) : a musical instrument having steel wire strings that sound when struck by felt-covered hammers operated from a keyboard

piano accordion n (1860) : an accordion with a keyboard for the right hand resembling and corresponding to the middle register of a piano keyboard

pi·ano·forte \pē-'a-nə-,fōrt, -'ä-, -,fòrt, -,fòr-tē; -,a-nə-'fòr-tē, -,ä-\ n [It] (1767) **1** : FORTEPIANO **2** : PIANO

piano hinge n (1926) : a hinge that has a thin pin joint and extends along the full length of the part to be moved

pi·as·sa·va \,pē-ə-'sä-və\ n [Pg *piassaba*, fr. Tupi *piasawa*] (1835) **1** : any of several stiff coarse fibers obtained from palms and used esp. in cordage or brushes **2** : a palm yielding piassava; esp : either of two Brazilian palms (*Attalia funifera* and *Leopoldinia piassaba*)

pi·as·tre also **pi·as·ter** \pē-'as-tər, -'äs-\ n [F *piastre*, fr. It *piastra* thin metal plate, coin, fr. L *emplastra*, *emplastrum* plaster] (1592) **1** : PIECE OF EIGHT **2** — see *pound* at MONEY table

pi·az·za \pē-'a-zə, -'ä-, l is usu -'at-sə, -'ät-\ n, pl **piazzas** or **pi·az·ze** \-'at-(,)sä, -'ät-\ [It, fr. L *platea* broad street — more at PLACE] (1563) **1** pl **piazze** : an open square esp. in an Italian town **2 a** : an arcaded and roofed gallery **b** dial : VERANDA, PORCH

pi·broch \'pē-,bräk, -,bräk\ n [ScGael *piobaireachd* pipe music] (1719) : a set of martial or mournful variations for the Scottish Highland bagpipe

¹**pic** \'pik\ n, pl **pics** or **pix** \'piks\ [short for *picture*] (1884) **1** : PHOTOGRAPH **2** : MOTION PICTURE

²**pic** \'pik, 'pēk\ n [Sp *pica*, fr. *picar* to prick] (1926) : the picador's lance

¹**pi·ca** \'pī-kə\ n [ML, fr. L, magpie — more at PIE] (1563) : an abnormal desire to eat substances (as chalk or ashes) not normally eaten

²**pica** n [prob. fr. ML, collection of church rules] (1588) **1** : 12-point type **2** : a unit of about ¹⁄₆ inch used in measuring typographic material **3** : a typewriter type providing 10 characters to the linear inch and six lines to the vertical inch

pic·a·dor \'pi-kə-,dòr, ,pi-kə-'\ n, pl **picadors** \-,dòrz, -'dòrz\ or **pic·a·do·res** \,pi-kə-'dòr-ēz, -'dòr-\ [Sp, fr. *picar* to prick, fr. (assumed) VL *piccare* — more at PIKE] (1797) : a horseman in a bullfight who jabs the bull with a lance to weaken its neck and shoulder muscles

pi·ca·ra \'pē-kä-,rä\ n [Sp *pícara*, fem. of *pícaro*] (ca. 1930) : a woman who is a rogue

¹**pi·ca·resque** \,pi-kə-'resk, ,pē-\ adj [Sp *picaresco*, fr. *pícaro*] (1810) : of or relating to rogues or rascals; also : of, relating to, suggesting, or being a type of fiction dealing with the episodic adventures of a usu. roguish protagonist ⟨a ~ novel⟩

²**picaresque** n (1895) : one that is picaresque

pi·ca·ro \'pē-kä-,rō\ n, pl **-ros** [Sp *pícaro*] (1623) : ROGUE, BOHEMIAN

¹**pic·a·roon** or **pick·a·roon** \,pi-kə-'rün\ n [Sp *picarón*, aug. of *pícaro*] (1624) **1** : PIRATE **2** : PICAROO

²**picaroon** vi (1675) : to act as a pirate

¹**pic·a·yune** \,pi-kē-'yün\ n [Prov *picaioun*, a small coin, fr. *picaio* money, fr. *pica* to jingle, of imit. origin] (1804) **1 a** : a Spanish half real piece formerly current in the South **b** : HALF DIME **2** : something trivial

²**picayune** adj (1836) : of little value : PALTRY; also : PETTY, SMALL-MINDED — **pi·ca·yun·ish** \-'yü-nish\ adj

pic·ca·lil·li \,pi-kə-'li-lē\ n [prob. alter. of *pickle*] (1845) : a relish of chopped vegetables and spices

¹**pic·co·lo** \'pi-kə-,lō\ adj [It, small] (ca. 1854) : smaller than ordinary size ⟨a ~ banjo⟩

²**piccolo** n, pl **-los** [It, short for *piccolo flauto* small flute] (1856) : a small shrill flute whose range is an octave higher than that of an ordinary flute — **pic·co·lo·ist** \-,lō-ist\ n

pice \'pīs\ n, pl **pice** [Hindi *paisā*] (1615) : PAISA

pi·ce·ous \'pī-sē-əs\ adj [L *piceus*, fr. *pic-*, *pix* pitch — more at PITCH] (1826) : of, relating to, or resembling pitch; esp : glossy brownish black in color ⟨an insect with a ~ abdomen⟩

¹**pick** \'pik\ vb [ME *piken*, partly fr. (assumed) OE *pician* (akin to MD *picken* to prick); partly fr. MF *piquer* to prick — more at PIKE] vt (14c) **1** : to pierce, penetrate, or break up with a pointed instrument ⟨~ed the hard clay⟩ **2 a** : to remove bit by bit ⟨~ meat from bones⟩ **b** : to remove covering or adhering matter from ⟨~ the bones⟩ **3 a** : to gather by plucking ⟨~ apples⟩ **b** : CHOOSE, SELECT ⟨tried to ~ the shortest route⟩ ⟨she ~ed out the most expensive dress⟩ **c** : to make (one's way) slowly and carefully ⟨~ed his way through the rubble⟩ **4 a** : PILFER, ROB ⟨~ pockets⟩ **b** : to obtain useful information from by questioning — used in such phrases as *pick the brains of* **5** : PROVOKE ⟨~ a quarrel⟩ **6 a** : to dig into : PROBE ⟨~ his teeth⟩ **b** : to pluck (as a guitar) with a pick or with the fingers **c** : to loosen or pull apart with a sharp point ⟨~ wool⟩ **7** : to unlock with a device (as a wire) other than the key ⟨~ a lock⟩ ~ vi **1** : to use or work with a pick **2** : to gather or harvest something by plucking **3** : PILFER — used in the phrase *picking and stealing* **4** : to eat sparingly or mincingly ⟨~ing listlessly at his dinner⟩ — **pick and choose** : to select with care and deliberation — **pick at** : to criticize repeatedly esp. for minor faults : NAG — **pick on 1** : to single out for criticism, teasing, or bullying ⟨*picked on* smaller boys⟩; also : to single out for a particular purpose or for special attention

²**pick** n (15c) **1** : a blow or stroke with a pointed instrument **2 a** : the act or privilege of choosing or selecting : CHOICE ⟨take your ~⟩

piccolo

b : the best or choicest one ⟨the ~ of the herd⟩ **3** : the portion of a crop gathered at one time ⟨the first ~ of peaches⟩ **4** : a screen in basketball
³**pick** n [ME pik] (14c) **1** : a heavy wooden-handled iron or steel tool pointed at one or both ends — compare MATTOCK **2 a** : TOOTHPICK **b** : PICKLOCK **c** : a small thin piece (as of plastic or metal) used to pluck the strings of a stringed instrument **3** : one of the points on the forepart of the blade of a skate used in figure skating **4** : a comb with long widely spaced teeth used to give height to a hair style
⁴**pick** vt [ME pykken to pitch (a tent); akin to ME picchen to pitch] (1523) **1** chiefly dial : to throw or thrust with effort : HURL **2** : to throw (a shuttle) across the loom
⁵**pick** n (1627) **1** dial Eng **a** : the act of pitching or throwing **b** : something thrown **2 a** : a throw of the shuttle **b** : a filling thread
pick·a·back \'pik-ə-,bak, 'pi-kə-\ var of PIGGYBACK
pick–and–roll \'pik-ən(d)-'rōl\ n (ca. 1961) : a basketball play in which a player sets a screen and then cuts toward the basket for a pass
pick–and–shovel adj (1895) : done with or as if with a pick and shovel : LABORIOUS
pick·a·nin·ny or **pic·a·nin·ny** \'pi-kə-,ni-nē, ,pi-kə-'\ n, pl -nies [prob. ultim. fr. Pg pequenino, dim. of pequeno small] (1653) : a black child — often taken to be offensive
pick·ax \'pik-,aks\ n [ME pecaxe, alter. of pikois, fr. OF picois, fr. pic pick, fr. L picus woodpecker — more at PIE] (15c) : ³PICK 1
¹**pick·ed** \'pi-kəd\ adj [ME, fr. ³pick] (14c) chiefly dial : POINTED, PEAKED
²**picked** \'pikt\ adj [¹pick] (ca. 1548) : CHOICE, PRIME
pick·eer \pi-'kir\ vi [prob. modif. of F picorer to maraud, perh. fr. MF pecore sheep, fr. OIt pecora — more at PECORINO] (ca. 1645) archaic : to skirmish in advance of an army; also : SCOUT, RECONNOITER
pick·er \'pi-kər\ n (14c) : one that picks: as **a** : a worker who picks something (as crops) **b** : a tool, implement, or machine used in picking something **c** : a musician who picks a stringed instrument (as a banjo)
pick·er·el \'pi-k(ə-)rəl\ n, pl -el or -els [ME pikerel, dim. of pike] (13c) **1** dial chiefly Brit : a young or small pike **b** : either of two fishes resembling but smaller than the related northern pike: (1) : CHAIN PICKEREL (2) : one (Esox americanus) having green or red fins and a black bar below and slanting away from the eye — compare WALLEYE 3
pick·er·el·weed \-,wēd\ n (1836) : an American shallow-water monocotyledonous plant (Pontederia cordata of the family Pontederiaceae) with large leaves and a spike of blue flowers
¹**pick·et** \'pi-kət\ n [F piquet, fr. MF, fr. piquer to prick — more at PIKE] (ca. 1702) **1** : a pointed or sharpened stake, post, or pale **2 a** : a detached body of soldiers serving to guard an army from surprise **b** : a detachment kept ready in camp for such duty **c** : SENTRY **3** : a person posted by a labor organization at a place of work affected by a strike; also : a person posted for a demonstration or protest
²**picket** vt (1745) **1** : to enclose, fence, or fortify with pickets **2 a** : to guard with a picket **b** : to post as a picket : TETHER **c** : to post pickets at **b** : to walk or stand in front of as a picket ~ vi : to serve as a picket — **pick·et·er** n
pick·et·boat \'pi-kət-,bōt\ n (1866) : a craft used (as by the coast guard) for harbor patrol
picket line n (1856) **1** : a position held by a line of military pickets **2** : a line of pickets picketing a business, organization, or institution
pick·ings \'pi-kiŋz, -kənz\ n pl (1642) : something that is picked or picked up: as **a** : gleanable or eatable fragments : SCRAPS **b** : yield or return for effort expended
¹**pick·le** \'pi-kəl\ n [ME pekille] (15c) **1** : a solution or bath for preserving or cleaning: as **a** : a brine or vinegar solution in which foods are preserved **b** : any of various baths used in industrial cleaning or processing **2** : a difficult situation : PLIGHT ⟨could see no way out of the ~ I was in —R. L. Stevenson⟩ **3** : an article of food that has been preserved in brine or in vinegar; specif : a cucumber that has been so preserved **4** Brit : a mischievous or troublesome person
²**pickle** vt **pick·led; pick·ling** \-k(ə-)liŋ\ (1570) **1** : to treat, preserve, or clean in or with a pickle **2** : to give a light finish to (as furniture) by bleaching or painting and wiping
³**pickle** n [perh. fr. Sc pickle to trifle, pilfer] (1552) **1** Scot : GRAIN, KERNEL **2** Scot : a small quantity
pickled adj (ca. 1552) **1** : preserved in or cured with pickle ⟨~ herring⟩ **2** : DRUNK 1a ⟨gets thoroughly ~ before dinner —New Yorker⟩
pick·lock \'pik-,läk\ n (1553) **1** : BURGLAR **2** : a tool for picking locks
pick–me–up \'pik-mē-,əp\ n (1867) : something that stimulates or restores : TONIC, BRACER
pick·off \'pik-,óf\ n (1939) : a baseball play in which a base runner is picked off
pick off vt (1810) **1** : to shoot or bring down esp. one by one **2** : to put out (a base runner who is off base) with a quick throw (as from the pitcher or catcher) **3** : INTERCEPT ⟨picked off a pass⟩
pick out vt (1540) **1** : DISCERN, MAKE OUT **2** : to play the notes of by ear or one by one ⟨picking out tunes on the piano⟩
pick over vt (1839) : to examine in order to select the best or remove the unwanted
pick·pocket \'pik-,pä-kət\ n (1591) : a thief who picks pockets
pick·proof \-,prüf\ adj (1933) : designed to prevent picking ⟨a ~ lock⟩
pick·thank \-,thaŋk\ n [fr. pick a thank to seek someone's favor] (15c) archaic : SYCOPHANT
¹**pick·up** \'pik-,əp\ n (1848) **1** : one that is picked up: as **a** : a hitchhiker who is given a ride **b** : a temporary chance acquaintance **2** : the act or process of picking up: as **a** : a revival of business activity **b** : ACCELERATION **3** : the conversion of mechanical movements into electrical impulses in the reproduction of sound; also : a device (as on a phonograph) for making such conversion **4 a** (1) : the reception of sound or an image into a radio or television transmitting apparatus for conversion into electrical signals (2) : interference (as with such reception) from an adjacent electrical circuit or system **b** : a device (as a microphone or a television camera) for converting sound or the image of a scene into electrical signals **c** : the place where a broadcast originates **d** : the electrical system for connecting to a broadcasting station a program produced outside the studio **5** : a light truck having

an enclosed cab and an open body with low sides and tailgate — called also pickup truck
²**pickup** adj (1909) : utilizing or comprising local or available personnel esp. without formal organization ⟨a ~ basketball game⟩
pick up vt (14c) **1 a** : to take hold of and lift up **b** : to gather together : COLLECT ⟨picked up all the pieces⟩ **c** : to clean up : TIDY **2** : to take (passengers or freight) into a vehicle **3 a** : to acquire casually or by chance ⟨picked up a valuable antique at an auction⟩ **b** : to acquire by study or experience : LEARN ⟨picking up a great deal of knowledge in the process —Robert Schleicher⟩ **c** : to obtain esp. by payment : BUY ⟨picked up some groceries⟩ **d** : to acquire (a player) esp. from another team through a trade or by financial recompense **e** : to accept for the purpose of paying ⟨offered to pick up the tab⟩ **f** : to come down with : CATCH ⟨picked up a cold⟩ **g** : GAIN ⟨picked up a few yards on the last play⟩ **4 a** : to enter informally into conversation or companionship with (a previously unknown person) ⟨had a brief affair with a girl he picked up in a bar⟩ **b** : to take into custody ⟨the police picked up the fugitive⟩ **5 a** : to catch sight of : PERCEIVE ⟨picked up the harbor lights⟩ **b** : to come to and follow ⟨picked up the outlaw's trail⟩ **c** : to bring within range of sight or hearing ⟨pick up distant radio signals⟩ **d** : UNDERSTAND, CATCH ⟨didn't pick up the hint⟩ **6 a** : REVIVE **b** : INCREASE **7** : to resume after a break : CONTINUE ⟨pick up the discussion tomorrow⟩ **8** : to assume responsibility for guarding (an opponent) in an athletic contest ~ vi **1** : to recover speed, vigor, or activity : IMPROVE ⟨after the strike, business picked up⟩ **2** : to put things in order ⟨was always picking up after her⟩ **3** : to pack up one's belongings ⟨couldn't just pick up and leave⟩ — **pick up on** 1 a : UNDERSTAND, APPRECIATE **b** : to become aware of : NOTICE **2** : to adopt as one's own : TAKE UP
Pick·wick·ian \(,)pik-'wi-kē-ən\ adj [Samuel Pickwick, character in the novel Pickwick Papers (1836–37) by Charles Dickens] (1836) **1** : marked by simplicity and generosity **2** : intended or taken in a sense other than the obvious or literal one
picky \'pi-kē\ adj **pick·i·er; -est** (1917) : FUSSY, CHOOSY ⟨a ~ eater⟩
pi·clo·ram \'pi-klə-,ram, 'pī-\ n [picoline + chlor- + amine] (1965) : a systemic herbicide $C_6H_3Cl_3N_2O_2$ that breaks down only very slowly in the soil
¹**pic·nic** \'pik-(,)nik\ n, often attrib [G or F; G Picknick, fr. F piquenique] (1748) **1** : an excursion or outing with food usu. provided by members of the group and eaten in the open; also : the food provided for a picnic **2** : a pleasant or amusingly carefree experience ⟨I don't expect being married to be a ~ —Josephine Pinckney⟩ **b** : an easy task or feat **3** : a shoulder of pork with much of the butt removed — **pic·nic·ky** \-(,)ni-kē\ adj
²**picnic** vi **pic·nicked; pic·nick·ing** (1842) : to go on a picnic : eat in picnic fashion — **pic·nick·er** n
pico- comb form [ISV, prob. fr. Sp pico small amount, lit., peak, beak] **1** : one trillionth (10^{-12}) part of ⟨picogram⟩ **2** : very small ⟨picornavirus⟩
pi·co·far·ad \,pē-kō-'far-,ad, -əd\ n [ISV] (ca. 1926) : one trillionth of a farad
pi·co·gram \'pē-kō-,gram, -kə-\ n [ISV] (1951) : one trillionth of a gram
pic·o·line \'pi-kə-,lēn, 'pī-\ n [L pic-, pix pitch + ISV ¹-ol + ²-ine — more at PITCH] (1853) : any of the three liquid pyridine bases C_6H_7N used chiefly as solvents and in organic synthesis
pi·co·mole \'pē-kō-,mōl, -kə-\ n (1968) : one trillionth of a mole
pi·cor·na·vi·rus \(,)pē-,kórn-ə-'vī-rəs\ n [pico- + RNA + virus] (1962) : any of a group of small RNA-containing viruses that includes the enteroviruses and rhinoviruses
pi·co·sec·ond \,pē-kō-'se-kənd, -kənt\ n [ISV] (ca. 1962) : one trillionth of a second
¹**pi·cot** \'pē-(,)kō, pē-'\ n [F, lit., small point, fr. MF, fr. pic prick, fr. piquer to prick — more at PIKE] (ca. 1882) : one of a series of small ornamental loops forming an edging on ribbon or lace
²**picot** vt (1926) : to finish with picots
pic·o·tee \,pi-kə-'tē\ n [F picoté pointed, fr. picoter to mark with points, fr. picot] (1727) : a flower (as some carnations or tulips) having one basic color with a margin of another color
picr- or **picro-** comb form [F, fr. Gk pikr-, pikro-, fr. pikros — more at PAINT] : bitter ⟨picric acid⟩
pic·ric acid \'pi-krik-\ n [ISV] (1852) : a toxic explosive yellow crystalline strong acid $C_6H_3N_3O_7$ used esp. in high explosives and as a dye
pic·ro·tox·in \,pi-krō-'täk-sən\ n [ISV] (1815) : a poisonous bitter crystalline stimulant and convulsive drug $C_{30}H_{34}O_{13}$ used intravenously as an antidote for barbiturate poisoning
Pict \'pikt\ n [ME Pihtas, pl., Picts, fr. OE Pihtas, fr. LL Picti] (bef. 12c) : a member of a people of the north of Scotland who are first noted in historical records in the late 3d century and who became amalgamated with the Scots in the mid-8th century — **Pict·ish** \'pik-tish\ adj or n
pic·to·gram \'pik-tə-,gram\ n [ISV picto- (fr. L pictus) + -gram] (1910) : PICTOGRAPH
pic·to·graph \-,graf\ n [L pictus + E -o- + -graph] (1851) **1** : an ancient or prehistoric drawing or painting on a rock wall **2** : one of the symbols belonging to a pictorial graphic system **3** : a diagram representing statistical data by pictorial forms — **pic·to·graph·ic** \,pik-tə-'gra-fik\ adj
pic·tog·ra·phy \pik-'tä-grə-fē\ n (1851) : use of pictographs : PICTURE WRITING 1
¹**pic·to·ri·al** \pik-'tōr-ē-əl, -'tōr-\ adj [LL pictorius, fr. L pictor painter] (1646) **1** : of or relating to a painter, a painting, or the painting or drawing of pictures ⟨~ perspective⟩ **2 a** : of, relating to, or consisting of pictures ⟨~ records⟩ **b** : illustrated by pictures ⟨~ weekly⟩ **c** : consisting of or displaying the characteristics of pictographs **d** : suggesting or conveying visual images ⟨~ poetry⟩ — **pic·to·ri·al·ly** \-ē-ə-lē\ adv — **pic·to·ri·al·ness** n
²**pictorial** n (1844) : a periodical having much pictorial matter

---

\ə\ abut \'ə\ kitten, F table \ər\ further \a\ ash \ā\ ace \ä\ mop, mar \aü\ out \ch\ chin \e\ bet \ē\ easy \g\ go \i\ hit \ī\ ice \j\ job \ŋ\ sing \ō\ go \ó\ law \ói\ boy \th\ thin \th\ the \ü\ loot \ú\ foot \y\ yet \zh\ vision \à, k̟, ⁿ, œ, œ̄, ue, ᵫ, ᵊ\ see Guide to Pronunciation

pic·to·ri·al·ism \-ē-ə-,li-zəm\ *n* (1869) **1** : the use or creation of pictures or visual images **2** : a movement or technique in photography emphasizing artificial often romanticized pictorial qualities — **pic·to·ri·al·ist** \-list\ *adj or n*

pic·to·ri·al·ize \pik-'tōr-ē-ə-,līz, -'tȯr-\ *vt* **-ized; -iz·ing** (1870) : to represent by a picture or illustrate with pictures — **pic·to·ri·al·i·za·tion** \-,tōr-ē-ə-lə-'zā-shən, -,tȯr-\ *n*

¹pic·ture \'pik-chər\ *n* [ME, fr. L *pictura,* fr. *pictus,* pp. of *pingere* to paint — more at PAINT] (15c) **1** : a design or representation made by various means (as painting, drawing, or photography) **2 a** : a description so vivid or graphic as to suggest a mental image or give an accurate idea of something (the book gives a detailed ~ of what is happening) **b** : a mental image **3** : IMAGE, COPY (the ~ of his father) (the very ~ of health) **4 a** : a transitory visible image or reproduction **b** : MOTION PICTURE **c** *pl* : MOVIES **5** : TABLEAU 1, 2 (stage ~s) **6** : SITUATION (took a hard look at his financial ~)

²picture *vt* **pic·tured; pic·tur·ing** \'pik-chə-riŋ, 'pik-shriŋ\ (15c) **1** : to paint or draw a representation, image, or visual conception of : DEPICT; *also* : ILLUSTRATE **2** : to describe graphically in words **3** : to form a mental image of : IMAGINE

picture-book *adj* (1922) : suitable for or suggestive of a picture book: as **a** : PICTURESQUE **b** : PICTURE-PERFECT

picture book *n* (1847) : a book that consists wholly or chiefly of pictures

picture hat *n* (1887) : a woman's dressy hat with a broad brim

picture-perfect *adj* (1981) : completely flawless : PERFECT (made a ~ landing)

pic·ture·phone \'pik-chər-,fōn\ *n* (1956) : VIDEOPHONE

picture-postcard *adj* (1907) : PICTURESQUE, PICTURE-BOOK (a ~ village)

picture puzzle *n* (1898) : JIGSAW PUZZLE

pic·tur·esque \,pik-chə-'resk\ *adj* [F & It; F *pittoresque,* fr. It *pittoresco,* fr. *pittore* painter, fr. L *pictor,* fr. *pingere*] (1703) **1 a** : resembling a picture : suggesting a painted scene **b** : charming or quaint in appearance **2** : evoking mental images : VIVID *syn* see GRAPHIC — **pic·tur·esque·ly** *adv* — **pic·tur·esque·ness** *n*

picture tube *n* (1937) : a cathode-ray tube on which the picture appears in a television receiver

picture window *n* (1938) : an outsize usu. single-paned window designed to frame an exterior view

picture writing *n* (1741) **1** : the recording of events or expression of messages by pictures representing actions or facts **2** : the record or message represented by picture writing

pic·tur·ize \'pik-chə-,rīz\ *vt* **-ized; -iz·ing** (ca. 1846) : to make a picture of : present in pictures; *esp* : to make into a motion picture — **pic·tur·i·za·tion** \,pik-chə-rə-'zā-shən\ *n*

pid·dle \'pi-d²l\ *vi* **pid·dled; pid·dling** \'pid-liŋ, 'pi-d²l-iŋ\ [origin unknown] (1545) **1** : DAWDLE, PUTTER **2** : URINATE

pid·dling \'pid-lən, -liŋ; 'pi-d²l-iŋ\ *adj* (1559) : TRIVIAL, PALTRY

pid·dock \'pi-dək, -dik\ *n* [origin unknown] (1851) : a bivalve mollusk (genus *Pholas* or family Pholadidae) that bores holes in wood, clay, and rocks

pid·gin \'pi-jən\ *n* [*pidgin English*] (1876) : a simplified speech used for communication between people with different languages — **pid·gin·i·za·tion** \,pi-jə-nə-'zā-shən\ *n* — **pid·gin·ize** \'pi-jə-,nīz\ *vt*

pidgin English *n, often cap P* [Chinese Pidgin English *pidgin* business] (1859) : an English-based pidgin; *esp* : one orig. used in parts of the Orient

¹pie \'pī\ *n* [ME, fr. OF, fr. L *pica;* akin to L *picus* woodpecker, OHG *speh*] (13c) : MAGPIE

²pie *n* [ME] (14c) **1** : a meat dish baked with biscuit or pastry crust — compare POTPIE **2** : a dessert consisting of a filling (as of fruit or custard) in a pastry shell or topped with pastry or both **3 a** : AFFAIR, BUSINESS (she wanted her finger . . . in every possible social ~ —Mary Deasy) **b** : what regarded as divisible into shares (giving the less fortunate . . . a larger share of the economic ~ —R. M. Hutchins)

³pie *var of* PI

¹pie·bald \'pī-,bȯld\ *adj* (1594) **1** : of different colors; *esp* : spotted or blotched with black and white **2** : composed of incongruous parts

²piebald *n* (1765) : a piebald animal (as a horse)

¹piece \'pēs\ *n* [ME, fr. OF, fr. (assumed) VL *pettia,* of Gaulish origin; akin to W *peth* thing] (14c) **1** : a part of a whole: as **a** : FRAGMENT (~s of broken glass) **b** : any of the individual members comprising a unit — often used in combination (a five-*piece* band) (a three-*piece* suit) **2** : an object or individual regarded as a unit of a kind or class (a ~ of fruit) **3** : a short distance (down the road a ~) **4** : a standard quantity (as of length, weight, or size) in which something is made or sold **5** : a literary, journalistic, artistic, dramatic, or musical composition **6** : FIREARM **7** : COIN; *also* : TOKEN **8** : a man used in playing a board game; *specif* : a chessman of superior rank **9** : OPINION, VIEW (spoke his ~) **10 a** : an act of copulation — usu. considered vulgar **b** : the female partner in sexual intercourse — usu. considered vulgar *syn* see PART — **of a piece** : ALIKE, CONSISTENT — **piece of one's mind** : a severe scolding : TONGUE-LASHING — **piece of the action** : a share in activity or profit — **to pieces 1** : without reserve or restraint : COMPLETELY **2** : into fragments; *also* : into component parts **3** : out of control (went *to pieces* from shock)

²piece *vt* **pieced; piec·ing** (15c) **1** : to repair, renew, or complete by adding pieces : PATCH **2** : to join onto a whole — often used with *together* (his new book . . . has been *pieced* together from talks —Merle Miller) — **piec·er** *n*

piece by piece *adv* (1560) : by degrees : PIECEMEAL

pièce de ré·sis·tance \pē-,es-də-rə-,zē-'stän(t)s, -rā-, -'stäns\ *n, pl* **pièces de ré·sis·tance** *same*\ [F, lit., piece of resistance] (1839) **1** : the chief dish of a meal **2** : an outstanding item or event : SHOWPIECE

piece-dye \'pēs-,dī\ *vt* (1920) : to dye after weaving or knitting

piece goods *n pl* (1665) : cloth fabrics sold from the bolt at retail in lengths specified by the customer — called also *yard goods*

¹piece·meal \'pēs-,mēl, -'mē(ə)l\ *adv* (14c) **1** : one piece at a time : GRADUALLY **2** : in pieces or fragments : APART

²piecemeal *adj* (1600) : done, made, or accomplished piece by piece or in a fragmentary way (~ reforms in the system)

piece of cake (1936) : something easily done : CINCH, BREEZE

piece of eight (1610) : an old Spanish peso of eight reals

piece of work (1928) : a complicated, difficult, or eccentric person

piece·wise \'pēs-,wīz\ *adv* (1674) : with respect to a number of discrete intervals, sets, or pieces (~ continuous functions)

piece·work \-,wərk\ *n* (1549) : work done by the piece and paid for at a set rate per unit — **piece·work·er** \-,wər-kər\ *n*

pie chart *n* (1922) : a circular chart cut by radii into segments illustrating relative magnitudes or frequencies — called also *circle graph*

pie·crust \'pī-,krəst\ *n* (1582) : the pastry shell of a pie

¹pied \'pīd\ *adj* (14c) : of two or more colors in blotches; *also* : wearing or having a parti-colored coat (a ~ horse)

²pied *past and past part of* PI *or of* PIE

pied-à-terre \pē-,ad-ə-'ter, -,ȧd-ȧ-; ,pyȧ-dä-\ *n, pl* **pieds-à-terre** *same*\ [F, lit., foot to the ground] (1829) : a temporary or second lodging

pied·mont \'pēd-,mänt\ *adj* [*Piedmont,* region of Italy] (1855) : lying or formed at the base of mountains — **piedmont** *n*

pied piper *n, often cap both Ps* [the *Pied Piper,* hero of a German folktale who charmed the rats of Hameln, Germany, into a river] (1925) **1** : one that offers strong but delusive enticement **2** : a leader who makes irresponsible promises **3** : a charismatic person who attracts followers

pie–eyed \'pī-,īd\ *adj* (1904) : INTOXICATED

pie–faced \-,fāst\ *adj* (ca. 1912) : having a round, smooth, or blank face

pieing *pres part of* PI *or of* PIE

pie in the sky (1911) : an unrealistic enterprise or prospect of prosperity — **pie–in–the–sky** *adj*

pie·plant \'pī-,plant\ *n* (ca. 1847) : garden rhubarb

pier \'pir\ *n* [ME *per,* fr. OE, fr. ML *pera*] (12c) **1** : an intermediate support for the adjacent ends of two bridge spans **2** : a structure (as a breakwater) extending into navigable water for use as a landing place or promenade or to protect or form a harbor **3** : a vertical structural support: as **a** : the wall between two openings **b** : PILLAR, PILASTER **c** : a vertical member that supports the end of an arch or lintel **d** : an auxiliary mass of masonry used to stiffen a wall **4** : a structural mount (as for a telescope) usu. of stonework, concrete, or steel

pierce \'pirs\ *vb* **pierced; pierc·ing** [ME *percen,* fr. OF *percer,* fr. (assumed) VL *pertusiare,* fr. L *pertusus,* pp. of *pertundere* to perforate, fr. *per-* through + *tundere* to beat — more at PER-, CONTUSION] *vt* (14c) **1 a** : to run into or through as a pointed weapon does : STAB **b** : to enter or thrust into sharply or painfully **2** : to make a hole through : PERFORATE **3** : to force or make a way into or through **4** : to penetrate with the eye or mind : DISCERN **5** : to penetrate so as to move or touch the emotions of ~ *vi* : to force a way into or through something *syn* see ENTER

pierced *adj* (14c) **1** : having holes; *esp* : decorated with perforations **2** : having the earlobe punctured for an earring (~ ears) **3** : designed for pierced ears (~ earrings)

piercing *adj* (14c) : PENETRATING: as **a** : LOUD, SHRILL (~ cries) **b** : PERCEPTIVE (~ eyes) **c** : penetratingly cold : BITING (a ~ wind) **d** : CUTTING, INCISIVE (~ sarcasm) — **pierc·ing·ly** \'pir-siŋ-lē\ *adv*

pier glass *n* (1703) : a large high mirror; *esp* : one designed to occupy the wall space between windows — called also *pier mirror*

Pi·eri·an \pī-'ir-ē-ən, -'er-\ *adj* (1591) **1** : of or relating to the region of Pieria in ancient Macedonia or to the Muses who were once worshiped there **2** : of or relating to learning or poetry

pie·ro·gi *also* **pi·ro·gi** \pə-'rō-gē, pi-\ *n, pl* **-gi** *also* **-gies** [Pol, pl. of *pieróg* dumpling, pierogi] (1927) : a case of dough filled with a savory filling (as of meat, cheese, or vegetables) and cooked by boiling and then panfrying

Pier·rot \'pē-ə-,rō\ *n* [F, dim. of *Pierre* Peter] (ca. 1770) : a stock comic character of old French pantomime usu. having a whitened face and wearing loose white clothes

pier table *n* (1803) : a table to be placed under a pier glass

pies *pl of* PI *or of* PIE

pie safe *n* (1951) : a cupboard whose doors have decoratively pierced tin panels for ventilation

pie·tà \,pē-(,)ä-'tä, pyä-\ *n, often cap* [It, lit., pity, fr. L *pietat-, pietas*] (1644) : a representation of the Virgin Mary mourning over the dead body of Christ

pi·e·tism \'pī-ə-,ti-zəm\ *n* (1697) **1** *cap* : a 17th century religious movement originating in Germany in reaction to formalism and intellectualism and stressing Bible study and personal religious experience **2 a** : emphasis on devotional experience and practices **b** : affectation of devotion — **pi·e·tist** \'pī-ə-tist\ *adj or n, often cap*

pi·e·tis·tic \,pī-ə-'tis-tik\ *adj* (1830) **1** : of or relating to Pietism **2 a** : of or relating to religious devotion or devout persons **b** : marked by overly sentimental or emotional devotion to religion : RELIGIOSE — **pi·e·tis·ti·cal·ly** \-ti-k(ə-)lē\ *adv*

pi·e·ty \'pī-ə-tē\ *n, pl* **pi·e·ties** [F *pieté* piety, pity, fr. L *pietat-, pietas,* fr. *pius* dutiful, pious] (1565) **1** : the quality or state of being pious: as **a** : fidelity to natural obligations (as to parents) **b** : dutifulness in religion : DEVOUTNESS **2** : an act inspired by piety **3** : a conventional belief or standard : ORTHODOXY *syn* see FIDELITY

piezo- *comb form* [Gk *piezein* to press; perh. akin to Skt *pidayati* squeezes] : pressure (*piezometer*)

pi·e·zo·elec·tric \pē-,ā-(,)zō-ə-'lek-trik, pē-,āt-(,)sō-\ *adj* [ISV] (1883) : of, relating to, marked by, or functioning by means of piezoelectricity — **pi·e·zo·elec·tri·cal·ly** \-tri-k(ə-)lē\ *adv*

pi·e·zo·elec·tric·i·ty \-,lek-'tri-s(ə-)tē\ *n* [ISV] (1883) : electricity or electric polarity due to pressure esp. in a crystalline substance (as quartz)

pi·e·zom·e·ter \,pē-ə-'zä-mə-tər, pē-,āt-'sä-\ *n* (1820) : an instrument for measuring pressure or compressibility; *esp* : one for measuring the change of pressure of a material subjected to hydrostatic pressure — **pi·e·zo·met·ric** \pē-,ā-zə-'me-trik, pē-,āt-sə-\ *adj*

¹pif·fle \'pi-fəl\ *vi* **pif·fled; pif·fling** \-f(ə-)liŋ\ [perh. blend of *piddle* and *trifle*] (ca. 1878) : to talk or act in a trivial, inept, or ineffective way

²piffle *n* (1890) : trivial nonsense (pseudo-scientific ~)

pif·fling \'pi-flən, -f(ə-)liŋ\ *adj* (1894) : of little worth or importance : TRIVIAL

¹pig \'pig\ *n, often attrib* [ME *pigge*] (13c) **1** : a young swine not yet sexually mature; *broadly* : a wild or domestic swine   **2   a** : PORK   **b** : the dressed carcass of a young swine weighing less than 130 pounds (60 kilograms)   **c** : PIGSKIN   **3   a** : one that resembles a pig ⟨an unkempt . . . person is a ∼ —S. S. Hall⟩   **b** : an animal related to or resembling the pig   **4** : a crude casting of metal (as iron)   **5** *slang* : an immoral woman   **6** *slang* : POLICE OFFICER — usu. used disparagingly — **pig·like** \-ˌlik\ *adj*

²pig *vb* **pigged; pig·ging** *vi* (15c)   **1** : FARROW   **2** : to live like a pig ⟨∼ it⟩ ∼ *vt* : FARROW

pig-boat \ˈpig-ˌbōt\ *n* (1921) : SUBMARINE

¹pi·geon \ˈpi-jən\ *n* [ME, fr. MF *pijon*, fr. LL *pipion-, pipio* young bird, fr. L *pipire* to chirp] (14c)   **1** : any of a widely distributed family (Columbidae, order Columbiformes) of birds with a stout body, rather short legs, and smooth and compact plumage; *esp* : a member of any of numerous varieties of the rock dove that exist in domestication and in the feral state in cities and towns throughout most of the world   **2** : a young woman   **3** : an easy mark : DUPE   **4** : CLAY PIGEON

²pigeon *n* [alter. of *pidgin*] (1938) : an object of special concern : BUSINESS

pigeon breast *n* (1842) : a deformity of the chest marked by sharp projection of the sternum

pigeon hawk *n* (ca. 1728)   **1** : a falcon of the No. American population of the merlin   **2** : SHARP-SHINNED HAWK

¹pi·geon·hole \ˈpi-jən-ˌhōl\ *n* (1577)   **1** : a hole or small recess for pigeons to nest in   **2** : a small open compartment (as in a desk or cabinet) for keeping letters or documents   **3** : a neat category which usu. fails to reflect actual complexities

²pigeonhole *vt* (1840)   **1   a** : to place in or as if in the pigeonhole of a desk   **b** : to lay aside : SHELVE ⟨his reports continued to be *pigeonholed* and his advice not taken —Walter Mills⟩   **2** : to assign to a category : CLASSIFY — **pi·geon·hol·er** \-ˌhō-lər\ *n*

pi·geon·ite \ˈpi-jə-ˌnit\ *n* [*Pigeon* Point, northeast Minn. + ¹-*ite*] (1900) : a monoclinic mineral of the pyroxene group

pi·geon-liv·ered \ˈpi-jən-ˌli-vərd\ *adj* (1602) : GENTLE, MILD

pigeon pea *n* (1725) : a leguminous woody herb (*Cajanus cajan*) that has trifoliate leaves, yellow flowers, and somewhat flat pods and is much cultivated esp. in the tropics; *also* : its small highly nutritious seed

pi·geon-toed \ˈpi-jən-ˌtōd\ *adj* (1801) : having the toes turned in

pi·geon·wing \-ˌwiŋ\ *n* (ca. 1808) : a fancy dance step executed by jumping and striking the legs together

pig·fish \ˈpig-ˌfish\ *n* (1860) : a saltwater grunt (*Orthopristis chrysopterus*) that is a food fish found from Long Island southward

pig·gery \ˈpi-gə-rē\ *n, pl* **-ger·ies** (1781)   **1** : a place where swine are kept   **2** : swinish behavior

pig·gin \ˈpi-gən\ *n* [ME *pygyn*] (15c) : a small wooden pail with one stave extended upward as a handle

pig·gish \ˈpi-gish\ *adj* (1792)   **1** : of, relating to, or suggestive of a pig ⟨a ∼ snort⟩   **2** : having qualities (as greediness or stubbornness) associated with a pig — **pig·gish·ly** *adv* — **pig·gish·ness** *n*

pig·gy \ˈpi-gē\ *adj* **pig·gi·er; -est** (ca. 1845) : PIGGISH

¹pig·gy·back \ˈpi-gē-ˌbak\ *adv* [alter. of earlier *a pick pack*, of unknown origin] (1565)   **1** : up on the back and shoulders   **2** : on or as if on the back of another; *esp* : on a railroad flatcar

²piggyback *n* (ca. 1590)   **1** : the act of carrying piggyback   **2** : the movement of loaded truck trailers on railroad flatcars

³piggyback *adj* (1823)   **1** : marked by being up on the shoulders and back ⟨a child needs hugging, tussling, and ∼ rides —Benjamin Spock⟩   **2** : carried or transported piggyback: as   **a** : of or relating to the hauling of truck trailers on railroad flatcars   **b** : of, relating to, or being a radio or television commercial that is presented in addition to other commercials during one commercial break   **c** : being or relating to something carried into space as an extra load by a vehicle (as a spacecraft)

⁴piggyback *vt* (1952)   **1** : to carry up on the shoulders and back   **2** : to haul (as a truck trailer) by railroad car   **3** : to set up or cause to function in conjunction with something larger or more important ∼ *vi* **1** : to haul truck trailers on railroad cars   **2** : to function or be carried on or as if on the back of another

piggy bank *n* (1941) : a coin bank often in the shape of a pig

pig·head·ed \ˈpig-ˌhe-dəd\ *adj* (1620) : willfully or perversely unyielding : OBSTINATE — **pig·head·ed·ly** *adv* — **pig·head·ed·ness** *n*

pig in a poke (1562) : something offered in such a way as to obscure its real nature or worth ⟨unwilling to buy a *pig in a poke*⟩

pig iron *n* (1665) : crude iron that is the direct product of the blast furnace and is refined to produce steel, wrought iron, or ingot iron

pig latin *n, often cap L* (1931) : a jargon that is made by systematic alteration of English (as *ipskay the ointjay* for *skip the joint*)

pig·let \ˈpi-glət\ *n* (1883) : a small usu. young swine

¹pig·ment \ˈpig-mənt\ *n* [L *pigmentum*, fr. *pingere* to paint — more at PAINT] (14c)   **1** : a substance that imparts black or white or a color to other materials; *esp* : a powdered substance that is mixed with a liquid in which it is relatively insoluble and used esp. to impart color to coating materials (as paints) or to inks, plastics, and rubber   **2** : a coloring matter in animals and plants esp. in a cell or tissue; *also* : any of various related colorless substances — **pig·men·tary** \-mən-ˌter-ē\ *adj*

²pigment \-ˌment, -mənt\ *vt* (1900) : to color with or as if with pigment

pig·men·ta·tion \ˌpig-mən-ˈtā-shən, -ˌmen-\ *n* (1866) : coloration with or deposition of pigment; *esp* : an excessive deposition of bodily pigment

pig·my *var of* PYGMY

pi·gno·li \pēn-ˈyō-lē\ *or* **pi·gno·lia** \-lē-ə\ *n* [*pignoli* fr. It, pl. of *pignolo, pinolo,* fr. *pigna, pina* pine cone, fr. L *pinea; pignolia* perh. modif. of *pignoli* — more at PINEAL] (1898) : PINE NUT

pig·nut \ˈpig-ˌnət\ *n* (1666)   **1** : any of several bitter-flavored hickory nuts   **2** : a hickory (as *Carya glabra* and *C. cordiformis*) bearing pignuts

pig out *vi* (1978) *slang* : to eat greedily : GORGE — **pig–out** \ˈpig-ˌaut\ *n*

pig·pen \-ˌpen\ *n* (1803)   **1** : a pen for pigs   **2** : a dirty slovenly place

pig·skin \-ˌskin\ *n* (1855)   **1** : the skin of a swine or leather made of it   **2   a** : a jockey's saddle   **b** : FOOTBALL 2a

pig·stick \-ˌstik\ *vi* (1891) : to hunt the wild boar on horseback with a spear — **pig·stick·er** *n*

pig·sty \ˈpig-ˌsti\ *n* (ca. 1591) : PIGPEN

pig·tail \-ˌtāl\ *n* (1688)   **1** : tobacco in small twisted strands or rolls   **2** : a tight braid of hair

pig·tailed \-ˌtāld\ *adj* (1754) : wearing a pigtail ⟨∼ little girls⟩

pig·weed \-ˌwēd\ *n* (ca. 1801) : any of various strongly growing weedy plants esp. of the goosefoot or amaranth families

piing *pres part of* PI *or of* PIE

pi·ka \ˈpē-kə, ˈpī-\ *n* [perh. fr. Evenki (Tungusic language of Siberia)] (1827) : any of various short-eared small lagomorph mammals (family Ochotonidae) of rocky uplands of Asia and western No. America with relatively short hind legs

pi·ka·ke \ˈpē-kä-ˌkä\ *n* [Hawaiian *pikake*, lit., peacock, fr. E] (1938) : an Asian vine (*Jasminum sambac*) cultivated for its profuse fragrant white flowers

¹pike \ˈpīk\ *n* [ME, fr. OE *pīc* pickax] (13c)   **1** : PIKESTAFF   **2** : a sharp point or spike; *also* : the tip of a spear — **piked** \ˈpīkt\ *adj*

²pike *n* [ME, perh. of Scand origin; akin to Norw dial. *pīk* pointed mountain] (13c) *dial Eng* : a mountain or hill having a peaked summit — used esp. in place names

³pike *n, pl* **pike** *or* **pikes** [ME, fr. ¹*pike*] (14c)   **1   a** : a large elongate long-snouted freshwater bony fish (*Esox lucius*) valued for food and sport and widely distributed in cooler parts of the northern hemisphere — called also *northern, northern pike*   **b** : any of various fishes (family Esocidae) related to the pike: as   (1): MUSKELLUNGE (2): PICKEREL   **2** : any of various fishes resembling the pike in appearance or habits

⁴pike *n* [MF *pique,* fr. *piquer* to prick, fr. (assumed) VL *piccare,* perh. fr. L *piccus* woodpecker — more at PIE] (ca. 1511) : a heavy spear with a very long shaft used by infantry esp. in Europe from the Middle Ages to the 18th century

⁵pike *vt* **piked; pik·ing** (1798) : to pierce, kill, or wound with a pike

⁶pike *vi* **piked; pik·ing** [ME *pyken* (refl.)] (1526)   **1** : to leave abruptly ⟨get lonely and sore, and ∼ out —Sinclair Lewis⟩   **2** : to make one's way ⟨∼ along⟩

⁷pike *n* (1812)   **1** : TURNPIKE   **2** : a railroad or railroad line or system — **down the pike**   **1** : in the course of events ⟨the greatest boxer to come *down the pike* in years⟩   **2** : in the future ⟨today's advances only hint at what's *down the pike*⟩

⁸pike *n* [perh. fr. ³*pike*] (1928) : a body position (as in diving) in which the hips are bent, the knees are straight, the head is pressed forward, and the hands touch the toes or clasp the legs behind or just above the knees

pike·man \ˈpīk-mən\ *n* (1566) : a soldier armed with a pike

pike perch *n* (1842) : a fish (as the walleye) of the perch group that resembles the pike

pik·er \ˈpī-kər\ *n* [*pike* to play cautiously, of unknown origin] (1872)   **1** : one who gambles or speculates with small amounts of money   **2** : one who does things in a small way; *also* : TIGHTWAD, CHEAPSKATE

pike·staff \ˈpīk-ˌstaf\ *n* (14c)   **1** : a spiked staff for use on slippery ground   **2** : the staff of a foot soldier's pike

pi·ki \ˈpē-kē\ *n* [Hopi *píki*] (ca. 1889) : bread made esp. from blue cornmeal and baked in thin sheets by the Indians of the southwestern U.S.

pi·laf *or* **pi·laff** \pi-ˈläf, -ˈlòf; ˈpē-\ *or* **pi·lau** *also* **pi·law** \pi-ˈlò, -ˈlò, ˈpē-ˌ\; *Southern often* ˈpər-(ˌ)lò, -ˌ)lò\ *n* [Turk & Pers; Turk *pilav,* fr. Pers *pilāv*] (1612) : a dish made of seasoned rice and often meat

pi·las·ter \pi-ˈlas-tər, ˈpī-ˌlas-\ *n* [MF *pilastre,* fr. It *pilastro*] (1575) : an upright architectural member that is rectangular in plan and is structurally a pier but architecturally treated as a column and that usu. projects a third of its width or less from the wall

1 pilaster

pil·chard \ˈpil-chərd\ *n* [origin unknown] (ca. 1530)   **1** : a fish (*Sardina pilchardus*) of the herring family resembling the herring and occurring in great schools along the coasts of Europe   **2** : any of several sardines related to the European pilchard

¹pile \ˈpī(ə)l\ *n* [ME, dart, stake, fr. OE *pil,* fr. L *pilum* javelin] (12c)   **1** : a long slender column usu. of timber, steel, or reinforced concrete driven into the ground to carry a vertical load   **2** : a wedge-shaped heraldic charge usu. placed vertically with the broad end up   **3   a** : a target-shooting arrowhead without cutting edges   **b** [L *pilum*] : an ancient Roman foot soldier's heavy javelin

²pile *vt* **piled; pil·ing** (15c) : to drive piles into

³pile *vb* **piled; pil·ing** [ME, fr. ⁴*pile*] *vt* (14c)   **1** : to lay or place in a pile : STACK   **2   a** : to heap in abundance : LOAD ⟨*piled* potatoes on his plate⟩   **b** : to collect little by little into a mass — usu. used with *up* ∼ *vi*   **1** : to form a pile or accumulation — usu. used with *up*   **2** : to move or press forward in or as if in a mass : CROWD ⟨*piled* into a car⟩

⁴pile *n* [ME, fr. MF, fr. L *pila* pillar] (15c)   **1   a** (1) : a quantity of things heaped together   (2) : a heap of wood for burning a corpse or a sacrifice   **b** : any great number or quantity : LOT   **2** : a large building or group of buildings   **3** : a great amount of money : FORTUNE   **4** : REACTOR 3b

⁵pile *n* [ME, fr. L *pilus* hair] (15c)   **1** : a coat or surface of usu. short close fine furry hairs   **2** : a velvety surface produced by an extra set of filling yarns that form raised loops which are cut and sheared — **pile·less** \ˈpī(ə)l-ləs\ *adj*

⁶pile *n* [ME, fr. L *pila* ball] (15c)   **1** : a single hemorrhoid   **2** *pl* : HEMORRHOIDS

\ə\ abut   \ᵊ\ kitten, F table   \ər\ further   \a\ ash   \ā\ ace   \ä\ mop, mar \au\ out   \ch\ chin   \e\ bet   \ē\ easy   \g\ go   \i\ hit   \ī\ ice   \j\ job \ŋ\ sing   \ō\ go   \o\ law   \oi\ boy   \th\ thin   \th\ the   \ü\ loot   \u\ foot \y\ yet   \zh\ vision   \ä, ᵏ, ⁿ, œ, œ̄, ue, ūe, ᵞ\ see Guide to Pronunciation

pi·le·at·ed \'pī-lē-ˌā-təd, 'pi-\ *adj* (ca. 1728) : having a crest covering the pileum

pileated woodpecker *n* (1782) : a large red-crested No. American woodpecker (*Dryocopus pileatus*) that is black with white on the face, neck, and undersides of the wings

piled \'pi(ə)ld\ *adj* (15c) : having a pile ⟨a deep-*piled* rug⟩

pile driver *n* (1772) : a machine for driving down piles with a drop hammer or a steam or air hammer

pi·le·um \'pī-lē-əm\ *n, pl* **pi·lea** \-lē-ə\ [NL, fr. L *pileus, pileum* felt cap; akin to Gk *pilos* felt] (1874) : the top of the head of a bird from the bill to the nape

pile-up \'pī-ˌləp, -ˌəp\ *n* (ca. 1929) **1** : a collision involving usu. several motor vehicles **2** : a jammed tangled mass or pile (as of motor vehicles or people) resulting from collision or accumulation **b** : ACCUMULATION

pi·le·us \'pī-lē-əs\ *n, pl* **pi·lei** \-lē-ˌī\ [NL, fr. L] (1760) **1** : the convex, concave, or flattened spore-bearing structure of some basidiomycetes that is attached superiorly to the stem and typically is expanded with gills or pores on the underside — called also *cap* **2** [L]: a pointed or close-fitting cap worn by ancient Romans

pile-wort \'pī(ə)l-ˌwərt, -ˌwȯrt\ *n* [ME *pyle wort*; fr. its use in treating piles] (15c) : LESSER CELANDINE

pil·fer \'pil-fər\ *vb* **pil·fered; pil·fer·ing** \-f(ə-)riŋ\ [MF *pelfrer,* fr. *pelfre* booty] *vi* (ca. 1548) : STEAL; *esp* : to steal stealthily in small amounts and often again and again ∼ *vt* : STEAL; *esp* : to steal in small quantities *syn* see STEAL — **pil·fer·able** \-f(ə-)rə-bəl\ *adj* — **pil·fer·age** \-f(ə-)rij\ *n* — **pil·fer·er** \-fər-ər\ *n* — **pil·fer·proof** \-ˌprüf\ *adj*

pil·gar·lic \ˌpil-'gär-lik\ *n* [*pilled garlic*] (ca. 1529) **1 a** : a bald head **b** : a bald-headed man **2** : a man looked upon with humorous contempt or mock pity

pil·grim \'pil-grəm\ *n* [ME, fr. OF *peligrin,* fr. LL *pelegrinus,* alter. of L *peregrinus* foreigner, fr. *peregrinus,* adj., foreign, fr. *peregri* abroad, fr. *per* through + *agr-, ager* land — more at FOR, ACRE] (13c) **1** : one who journeys in foreign lands : WAYFARER **2** : one who travels to a shrine or holy place as a devotee **3** *cap* : one of the English colonists settling at Plymouth in 1620

¹pil·grim·age \'pil-grə-mij\ *n* (14c) **1** : a journey of a pilgrim; *esp* : one to a shrine or a sacred place **2** : the course of life on earth

²pilgrimage *vi* **-aged; -ag·ing** (14c) : to go on a pilgrimage

pilgrim bottle *n* (1874) : COSTREL

pil·ing \'pī-liŋ\ *n* (15c) : a structure of piles; *also* : PILES

Pi·li·pi·no \ˌpil-ə-'pē-(ˌ)nō, ˌpē-\ *n* [Tag, lit., Philippine, fr. Sp *Filipino*] (1936) : the Tagalog-based official language of the Republic of the Philippines

¹pill \'pil\ *vb* [ME *pilen, pillen,* partly fr. OE *pilian* to peel, partly fr. MF *piller* to plunder] *vi* (12c) *dial chiefly Eng* : to come off in flakes or scales : PEEL ∼ *vt* **1** *archaic* : to subject to depredation or extortion **2** *dial* : to peel or strip off

²pill *n* [ME *pylle,* fr. MD *pille,* ultim. fr. L *pilula,* fr. dim. of *pila* ball] (14c) **1 a** : medicine in a small rounded mass to be swallowed whole **b** *often cap* : an oral contraceptive — usu. used with *the* **2** : something repugnant or unpleasant that must be accepted or endured **3** : something resembling a pill in size or shape **4** : a disagreeable or tiresome person

³pill *vt* (1736) **1** : to dose with pills **2** : BLACKBALL ∼ *vi* : to become rough with or mat into little balls ⟨brushed woolens often ∼⟩

¹pil·lage \'pil-ij\ *n* [ME, fr. MF, fr. *piller* to plunder, abuse] (14c) **1** : the act of looting or plundering esp. in war **2** : something taken as booty

²pillage *vb* **pil·laged; pil·lag·ing** *vt* (ca. 1592) : to plunder ruthlessly : LOOT ∼ *vi* : to take booty *syn* see RAVAGE — **pil·lag·er** *n*

¹pil·lar \'pi-lər\ *n* [ME *piler,* fr. OF, fr. ML *pilare,* fr. L *pila*] (13c) **1 a** : a firm upright support for a superstructure : POST **b** : a usu. ornamental column or shaft; *esp* : one standing alone for a monument **2** : a chief supporter : PROP **3** : a solid mass of coal, rock, or ore left standing to support a mine roof **4** : a body part that resembles a column — **pil·lar·less** *adj* — **from pillar to post** : from one place or one predicament to another

²pillar *vt* (1607) : to provide or strengthen with or as if with pillars

pil·lar-box \'pil- lər-ˌbäks\ *n* (1858) *Brit* : a pillar-shaped mailbox

pill-box \'pil-ˌbäks\ *n* (1730) **1** : a box for pills; *esp* : a shallow round box of pasteboard **2** : a small low concrete emplacement for machine guns and antitank weapons **3** : a small round hat without a brim; *specif* : a woman's shallow hat with a flat crown and straight sides

pill bug *n* [²*pill;* fr. its rolling into a ball when disturbed] (1843) : WOOD LOUSE

¹pil·lion \'pil-yən\ *n* [ScGael or Ir; ScGael *pillean,* dim. of *peall* covering, couch; Ir *pillín,* dim. of *peall* covering, couch] (1503) **1 a** : a light saddle for women consisting chiefly of a cushion **b** : a pad or cushion put on behind a man's saddle chiefly for a woman to ride on **2** *chiefly Brit* : a motorcycle or bicycle saddle for a passenger

²pillion *adv* (1926) *chiefly Brit* : on or as if on a pillion ⟨ride ∼⟩

¹pil·lo·ry \'pi-lə-rē, 'pil-rē\ *n, pl* **-ries** [ME, fr. OF *pilori*] (13c) **1** : a device formerly used for publicly punishing offenders consisting of a wooden frame with holes in which the head and hands can be locked **2** : a means for exposing one to public scorn or ridicule

²pillory *vt* **-ried; -ry·ing** (ca. 1600) **1** : to set in a pillory as punishment **2** : to expose to public contempt, ridicule, or scorn

¹pil·low \'pi-(ˌ)lō\ *n* [ME *pilwe,* fr. OE *pyle* (akin to OHG *pfuliwi*), fr. L *pulvinus*] (bef. 12c) **1 a** : a support for the head of a reclining person; *esp* : one consisting of a cloth bag filled with feathers, down, sponge rubber, or plastic fiber **b** : something resembling a pillow esp. in form **2** : a cushion or pad tightly stuffed and used as a support for the design and tools in making lace with a bobbin — **pil·lowy** \'pi-lə-wē\ *adj*

²pillow *vt* (1629) **1** : to rest or lay on or as if on a pillow **2** : to serve as a pillow for ∼ *vi* : to lay or rest one's head on or as if on a pillow

pillow block *n* (1844) : a block or standard to support a journal (as of a shaft) : BEARING

pil·low·case \'pi-lə-ˌkās, -lō-\ *n* (1724) : a removable covering for a pillow

pillow lace *n* [fr. its being worked over a pillow on which the pattern is marked] (ca. 1858) : lace made with a bobbin

pillow slip *n* (ca. 1828) : PILLOWCASE

pillow talk *n* (1939) : intimate conversation between lovers in bed

pi·lo·car·pine \ˌpī-lə-'kär-ˌpēn\ *n* [ISV, fr. NL *Pilocarpus jaborandi,* species of tropical shrubs] (1875) : a miotic alkaloid $C_{11}H_{16}N_2O_2$ that is obtained from jaborandi and used esp. in the treatment of glaucoma

pi·lose \'pī-ˌlōs\ *adj* [L *pilosus,* fr. *pilus* hair] (1753) : covered with usu. soft hair — **pi·los·i·ty** \pī-'lä-sə-tē\ *n*

¹pi·lot \'pī-lət\ *n* [MF *pilote,* fr. It *pilota,* alter. of *pedota,* fr. (assumed) MGk *pēdōtēs,* fr. Gk *pēda* steering oars, pl. of *pēdon* oar; prob. akin to Gk *pod-, pous* foot — more at FOOT] (1530) **1 a** : one employed to steer a ship : HELMSMAN **b** : a person who is qualified and usu. licensed to conduct a ship into and out of a port or in specified waters **c** : a person who flies or is qualified to fly an aircraft or spacecraft **2** : GUIDE, LEADER **3** : COWCATCHER **4** : a piece that guides a tool or machine part **5** : a television show produced and filmed or taped as a sample of a proposed series **6** : PILOT LIGHT 2 — **pi·lot·less** \-ləs\ *adj*

²pilot *vt* (1649) **1** : to act as a guide to : lead or conduct over a usu. difficult course **2 a** : to set and conn the course of ⟨∼ a ship⟩ **b** : to act as pilot of ⟨∼ a plane⟩ *syn* see GUIDE

³pilot *adj* (1802) : serving as a guiding or tracing device, an activating or auxiliary unit, or a trial apparatus or operation ⟨a ∼ study⟩

pi·lot·age \'pī-lə-tij\ *n* (ca. 1618) **1** : the action or business of piloting **2** : the compensation paid to a licensed ship's pilot

pilot biscuit *n* (1836) : HARDTACK — called also *pilot bread*

pilot engine *n* (1838) : a locomotive going in advance of a train to make sure that the way is clear

pilot fish *n* (1634) : a pelagic carangid fish (*Naucrates ductor*) that has dark stripes and often swims in company with a shark

pi·lot·house \'pī-lət-ˌhau̇s\ *n* (1846) : a deckhouse for a ship's helmsman containing the steering wheel, compass, and navigating equipment

pilot light *n* (ca. 1890) **1** : an indicator light showing where a switch or circuit breaker is located or whether a motor is in operation or power is on — called also *pilot lamp* **2** : a small permanent flame used to ignite gas at a burner

pilot officer *n* (1919) : a commissioned officer in the British air force who ranks with a second lieutenant in the army

pilot whale *n* (1867) : BLACKFISH 2

pil·sner *or* **pil·sen·er** \'pils-nər, 'pilz-, 'pil-zə-\ *n* [G, lit., of Pilsen (Plzeň), city in the Czech Republic] (1877) **1** : a light beer with a strong flavor of hops **2** : a tall slender footed glass for beer

Pilt·down man \'pilt-ˌdau̇n-\ *n* [*Piltdown,* East Sussex, England] (ca. 1918) : a supposedly very early hominid erroneously reconstructed from a combination of human and animal skeletal remains the latter of which were later found to have been planted by a hoaxer

pil·u·lar \'pil-yə-lər\ *adj* (1802) : of, relating to, or resembling a pill

pil·ule \'pil-(ˌ)yü(ə)l\ *n* [MF, fr. L *pilula* pill — more at PILL] (1543) : a little pill

pi·lus \'pī-ləs\ *n, pl* **pi·li** \-ˌlī\ [L] (ca. 1890) : a hair or a structure (as of a bacterium) resembling a hair

Pi·ma \'pē-mə\ *n, pl* **Pimas** *or* **Pima** (1850) **1** : a member of an American Indian people of southern Arizona and northern Mexico **2** : the Uto-Aztecan language of the Pima people — **Pi·man** \-mən\ *adj*

pi·ma cotton \'pē-mə-, 'pī-\ *n* [*Pima* County, Arizona] (1925) : a cotton that produces fiber of exceptional strength and firmness and that was developed in the southwestern U.S. by selection and breeding of Egyptian cottons

pi·men·to \pə-'men-(ˌ)tō\ *n, pl* **-tos** *or* **-to** [Sp *pimienta* allspice, pepper, fr. LL *pigmenta,* pl. of *pigmentum* plant juice, fr. L, pigment] (1660) **1** : ALLSPICE **2** : PIMIENTO 1

pimento cheese *n* (1916) : a Neufchâtel, process, cream, or occas. cheddar cheese to which ground pimientos have been added

pi·me·son \'pī-ˈme-ˌzän, -ˈmā-, -ˈmē-, -ˌsän\ *n* [²*pi*] (1948) : PION

pi·mien·to \pə-ˈmen-(ˌ)tō, pəm-ˈyen-\ *n, pl* **-tos** [Sp. fr. *pimienta*] (1845) **1** : any of various bluntly conical thick-fleshed sweet peppers of European origin that have a distinctive mild sweet flavor and are used esp. as a garnish, as a stuffing for olives, and as a source of paprika **2** : a plant that bears pimientos

¹pimp \'pimp\ *n* [origin unknown] (1600) : a man who solicits clients for a prostitute

²pimp *vi* (1636) : to work as a pimp

pim·per·nel \'pim-pər-ˌnel, -pər-nəl\ *n* [ME *pimpernele,* fr. MF *pimprenelle,* fr. LL *pimpinella,* a medicinal herb] (14c) : any of a genus (*Anagallis*) of herbs of the primrose family; *esp* : SCARLET PIMPERNEL

pimp·ing \'pim-pən, -piŋ\ *adj* [origin unknown] (1687) **1** : PETTY, INSIGNIFICANT **2** *chiefly dial* : PUNY, SICKLY

pim·ple \'pim-pəl\ *n* [ME *pinple*] (14c) **1** : a small inflamed elevation of the skin : PAPULE; *esp* : PUSTULE **2** : a swelling or protuberance like a pimple — **pim·pled** \-pəld\ *adj* — **pim·ply** \-p(ə-)lē\ *adj*

pimp·mo·bile \'pimp-mō-ˌbēl, -mə-\ *n* (1971) : an ostentatious luxury car of a kind characteristically used by a pimp

¹pin \'pin\ *n* [ME, fr. OE *pinn* (akin to OHG *pfinn* peg), perh. fr. L *pinna* quill, feather — more at PEN] (bef. 12c) **1 a** : a piece of solid material (as wood or metal) used esp. for fastening separate articles together or as a support by which one article may be suspended from another **b** *obs* : the center peg of a target; *also* : the center itself **c** : something that resembles a pin esp. in slender elongated form ⟨an electrical connector ∼⟩ **d** (1) : one of the wooden pieces constituting the target in various games (as bowling) (2) : the peg at which a quoit is pitched (3) : the staff of the flag marking a hole on a golf course **e** : a peg for regulating the tension of the strings of a musical instrument **f** : the part of a key stem that enters a lock **g** (1) : THOLE 1 (2) : a belaying pin **2 a** (1) : a small pointed piece of wire with a head used esp. for fastening cloth (2) : something of small value : TRIFLE **b** : an ornament or emblem fastened to clothing with a pin **c** (1) : BOBBY PIN (2) : HAIRPIN (3) : SAFETY PIN **3** : LEG — usu. used in pl. ⟨wobbly on his ∼s⟩ **4** : a fall in wrestling

²pin *vt* **pinned; pin·ning** (14c) **1 a** : to fasten, join, or secure with a pin **b** : to hold fast or immobile **c** : to present ⟨a young woman⟩ with a fraternity pin as a pledge of affection **2 a** : ATTACH, HANG ⟨*pinned* his hopes on a miracle⟩ **b** : to assign the blame or responsibility for ⟨∼ the robbery on a night watchman⟩ **c** : to define or determine clearly or precisely — usu. used with *down* ⟨it is hard to ∼ down exactly when things changed —Katharine Whittemore⟩ **3 a** : to make (a chess opponent's piece) unable to move without exposing the king to check or a valuable piece to capture **b** *of a wrestler* : to secure a fall over (an opponent)

³pin *adj* (1523)   **1 :** of or relating to a pin   **2** *of leather* **:** having a grain suggesting the heads of pins

pi·ña cloth \'pēn-yə-\ *n* [Sp *piña* pineapple, pinecone, fr. L *pinea* pinecone — more at PINEAL] (ca. 1858) **:** a lustrous transparent cloth of Philippine origin that is woven of silky pineapple fibers

pi·ña co·la·da \'pēn-yə-kō-'lä-də, 'pē-nə-\ *n* [Sp, lit., strained pineapple] (1923) **:** a tall drink made of rum, cream of coconut, and pineapple juice mixed with ice

pin·a·fore \'pin-ə-,fōr, -,fȯr\ *n* [²pin + afore] (1782) **:** a sleeveless usu. low-necked garment fastened in the back and worn as an apron or dress — **pin·a·fored** \-,fōrd, -,fȯrd\ *adj*

pi·ña·ta *or* **pi·na·ta** \pēn-'yä-tə\ *n* [Sp *piñata*, lit., pot, fr. It *pignatta*, prob. fr. *pigna* pinecone — more at PIGNOLI] (1887) **:** a decorated vessel (as a pottery jar) filled with candies, fruits, and gifts and hung from the ceiling to be broken with sticks by blindfolded persons as part of esp. Latin-American festivities (as at Christmas or for a birthday party)

pin·ball machine \'pin-,bȯl-\ *n* (1936) **:** an amusement device in which a ball propelled by a plunger scores points as it rolls down a slanting surface among pins and targets — called also *pinball game*

piñata

pin·bone \'pin-,bōn\ *n* (1640) **:** the hipbone esp. of a quadruped — see COW illustration

pince–nez \'pans-'nā, pan(t)s-\, *n, pl* **pince–nez** \-'nā(z)\ [F, fr. *pincer* to pinch + *nez* nose, fr. L *nasus* — more at NOSE] (1876) **:** eyeglasses clipped to the nose by a spring

pin·cer \'pin(t)-sər, *esp for 1 US often* 'pin-chər\ *n* [ME *pinceour*, fr. (assumed) AF *pinceour*, fr. MF *pincier* to pinch, fr. (assumed) VL *pinctiare*, *punctiare*, fr. L *punctum* puncture — more at POINT] (14c)   **1** *pl but sing or pl in constr* **:** an instrument having two short handles and two grasping jaws working on a pivot and used for gripping things   **b :** a claw (as of a lobster) resembling a pair of pincers **:** CHELA   **2 :** one part of a double envelopment in which two military forces converge on opposite sides of an enemy position — **pin·cer·like** \-,līk\ *adj*

¹pinch \'pinch\ *vb* [ME, fr. (assumed) ONF *pinchier*, fr. (assumed) VL *pinctiare*] *vt* (14c)   **1 a :** to squeeze between the finger and thumb or between the jaws of an instrument   **b :** to prune the tip of (a plant or shoot) usu. to induce branching   **c :** to squeeze or compress painfully   **d :** to cause physical or mental pain to   **e** (1) **:** to cause to appear thin or shrunken   (2) **:** to cause to shrivel or wither   **2 a :** to subject to strict economy or want **:** STRAITEN   **b :** to confine or limit narrowly **:** CONSTRICT   **3 a :** STEAL   **b :** ARREST   **4 :** to sail too close to the wind ~ *vi*   **1 :** COMPRESS, SQUEEZE   **2 :** to be miserly or closefisted   **3 :** to press painfully   **4 :** NARROW, TAPER ⟨the road ~*ed* down to a trail — Cecelia Holland⟩ — **pinch pennies :** to practice strict economy

²pinch *n* (15c)   **1 a :** a critical juncture **:** EMERGENCY   **b** (1) **:** PRESSURE, STRESS   (2) **:** HARDSHIP, PRIVATION   **c :** DEFICIT   **2 a :** an act of pinching **:** SQUEEZE   **b :** as much as may be taken between the finger and thumb ⟨a ~ of snuff⟩   **c :** a very small amount   **3 :** a marked thinning of a vein or bed   **4 a :** THEFT   **b :** a police raid; *also* **:** ARREST *syn* see JUNCTURE

³pinch *n* (1916)   **1 :** SUBSTITUTE ⟨~ runner⟩   **2 :** hit by a pinch hitter ⟨~ homer⟩

pinch bar *n* (1837) **:** a bar similar in form and use to a crowbar and sometimes having an end adapted for pulling spikes or inserting under a heavy wheel that is to be rolled

pinch·beck \'pinch-,bek\ *n* [Christopher *Pinchbeck* †1732 Eng. watchmaker] (1734)   **1 :** an alloy of copper and zinc used esp. to imitate gold in jewelry   **2 :** something counterfeit or spurious — **pinchbeck** *adj*

pinch·er \'pin-chər\ *n* (15c)   **1 :** one that pinches   **2** *pl* **:** PINCERS

pinch–hit \'pinch-'hit, ,pinch-\ *vi* [back-formation fr. *pinch hitter*] (1915)   **1 :** to act or serve in place of another   **2 :** to bat in the place of another esp. when a hit is particularly needed

pinch hit *n* (1927) **:** a hit made by a pinch hitter

pinch hitter *n* (1912) **:** one that pinch-hits

pinch–pen·ny \'pinch-,pe-nē\ *adj* (1582) **:** STINGY, NIGGARDLY

pin curl *n* (1896) **:** a curl made usu. by dampening a strand of hair with water or lotion, coiling it, and securing it by a hairpin or clip

pin·cush·ion \'pin-,kù-shən\ *n* (1632) **:** a small cushion in which pins may be stuck ready for use

¹Pin·dar·ic \pin-'dar-ik\ *adj* (1640)   **1 :** of or relating to the poet Pindar   **2 :** written in the manner or style characteristic of Pindar

²Pindaric *n* (1685)   **1 :** a Pindaric ode   **2** *pl* **:** loose irregular verses similar to those used in Pindaric odes

pin·dling \'pin(d)-lən, -liŋ; 'pin-d²l-ən, -iŋ\ *adj* [perh. alter. of *spindling*] (1861) *dial* **:** PUNY, FRAIL

¹pine \'pin\ *n, often attrib* [ME, fr. OE *pin*, fr. L *pinus*; prob. akin to Gk *pitys* pine] (bef. 12c)   **1 :** any of a genus (*Pinus* of the family Pinaceae, the pine family) of coniferous evergreen trees that have slender elongated needles and include some valuable timber trees and ornamentals   **2 :** the straight-grained white or yellow usu. durable and resinous wood of a pine varying from extreme softness in the white pine to hardness in the longleaf pine   **3 :** any of various Australian coniferous trees (as of the genera *Callitris* or *Araucaria*)   **4 :** PINEAPPLE   **5 :** BENCH 1c — **pin·ey** *also* **piny** \'pi-nē\ *adj*

²pine *vi* **pined**; **pin·ing** [ME, fr. (assumed) OE *pin* punishment, fr. L *poena* — more at PAIN] (14c)   **1 :** to lose vigor, health, or flesh (as through grief) **:** LANGUISH   **2 :** to yearn intensely and persistently esp. for something unattainable ⟨they still *pined* for their lost wealth⟩ *syn* see LONG

pi·ne·al \'pi-nē-əl, pī-'\ *adj* [F *pinéal*, fr. MF, fr. L *pinea* pinecone, fr. fem. of *pineus* of pine, fr. *pinus*] (1681) **:** of, relating to, or being the pineal gland

pi·ne·al·ec·to·my \,pī-nē-ə-'lek-tə-mē, pi-,nē-\ *n* (1915) **:** surgical removal of the pineal gland — **pi·ne·al·ec·to·mize** \-tə-,mīz\ *vt*

pineal gland *n* (1712) **:** a small usu. conical appendage of the brain of all craniate vertebrates that functions primarily as an endocrine organ

and that in a few reptiles has the essential structure of an eye — called also *pineal, pineal body, pineal organ*

pine·ap·ple \'pi-,na-pəl\ *n* (1664)   **1 a :** a tropical monocotyledonous plant (*Ananas comosus* of the family Bromeliaceae, the pineapple family) that has rigid spiny-margined recurved leaves and a short stalk with a dense oblong head of small abortive flowers   **b :** the large edible multiple fruit of the pineapple that consists of the sweet succulent fleshy inflorescence   **2 :** a hand grenade

pineapple guava *n* (ca. 1924) **:** FEIJOA

pine·cone \'pin-,kōn\ *n* (1695) **:** a cone of a pine tree

pine·drops \'pin-,dräps\ *n pl but sing or pl in constr* (1857)   **1 :** a purplish brown leafless saprophytic plant (*Pterospora andromedea*) of the wintergreen family with racemose drooping white flowers   **2 :** BEECHDROPS

pine·land \'pin-,land, -lənd\ *n* (ca. 1658) **:** land naturally dominated by pine forests

pi·nene \'pi-,nēn\ *n* [ISV, fr. L *pinus*] (1885) **:** either of two liquid isomeric unsaturated bicyclic terpene hydrocarbons $C_{10}H_{16}$ of which one is a major constituent of wood turpentine

pine nut *n* (bef. 12c) **:** the edible seed of any of several pines — compare PIÑON

pin·ery \'pi-nə-rē, 'pin-rē\ *n, pl* **-er·ies** (1758)   **1 :** a hothouse or area where pineapples are grown   **2 :** a grove or forest of pine

pine·sap \'pin-,sap\ *n* (1840) **:** any of several yellowish or reddish parasitic or saprophytic herbs (genus *Monotropa*) of the wintergreen family resembling the Indian pipe

pine siskin *n* (1887) **:** a No. American finch (*Carduelis pinus*) with streaked plumage

pine snake *n* (1791)   **1 :** a large constricting snake (*Pituophis melanoleucus*) of the eastern U.S. that is typically white and black and is found esp. in coastal regions from New Jersey southward   **2 :** any of various snakes related to the pine snake

pine tar *n* (1880) **:** tar obtained by destructive distillation of the wood of the pine tree and used esp. in roofing and soaps and in the treatment of skin diseases

pi·ne·tum \pi-'nē-təm\ *n, pl* **pi·ne·ta** \-'nē-tə\ [L, fr. *pinus*] (1842) **:** a plantation of pine trees; *esp* **:** a scientific collection of living coniferous trees

pine·wood \'pin-,wùd\ *n* (1673)   **1 :** a wood of pines — often used in pl. but sing. or pl. in constr.   **2 :** the wood of the pine tree

piney woods *n pl* (1800) **:** woodland of the southern U.S. in which pines are the dominant tree

pin·feath·er \'pin-,fe-thər\ *n* (ca. 1775) **:** a feather not fully developed; *esp* **:** a feather just emerging through the skin

pin·fish \-,fish\ *n* (1878) **:** a small compressed dark green grunt (*Lagodon rhomboides*) that has sharp dorsal spines and is found along the Atlantic coast

pin·fold \-,fōld\ *n* [ME, fr. OE *pundfald*, fr. *pund*- enclosure + *fald* fold] (13c)   **1 :** ²POUND 1a   **2 :** a place of restraint

¹ping \'piŋ\ *n* [imit.] (1835)   **1 :** a sharp sound like that of a striking bullet   **2 :** KNOCK 2b — **ping** *vi*

ping·er \'piŋ-ər\ *n* (1957) **:** a device for producing pulses of sound (as for marking an underwater site or detecting an underwater object)

pin·go \'piŋ-(,)gō\ *n, pl* **pingos** [Inuit *pinguq*] (1938) **:** a low hill or mound forced up by hydrostatic pressure in an area underlain by permafrost

ping–pong \'piŋ-,päŋ, -,pȯŋ\ *vb* (1952) **:** SHIFT, BOUNCE

Ping–Pong \'piŋ-,päŋ, -,pȯŋ\ *trademark* — used for table tennis

pin·head \'pin-,hed\ *n* (1593)   **1 :** the head of a pin   **2 :** something very small or insignificant   **3 :** a very dull or stupid person **:** FOOL

pin·head·ed \-,he-dəd\ *adj* (1901) **:** lacking intelligence or understanding **:** DULL, STUPID — **pin·head·ed·ness** *n*

pin·hole \-,hōl\ *n* (1676) **:** a small hole made by, for, or as if by a pin

¹pin·ion \'pin-yən\ *n* [ME, fr. MF *pignon*, fr. (assumed) VL *pinnion-, pinnio*, fr. L *pinna* feather — more at PEN] (15c)   **1 :** the terminal section of a bird's wing including the carpus, metacarpus, and phalanges; *broadly* **:** WING   **2 :** FEATHER, QUILL; *also* **:** FLIGHT FEATHERS — **pinioned** \-yənd\ *adj*

²pinion *vt* (1558)   **1 a :** to disable or restrain by binding the arms   **b :** to bind fast **:** SHACKLE   **2 :** to restrain (a bird) from flight esp. by cutting off the pinion of one wing

³pinion *n* [F *pignon*, fr. MF *peignon*, fr. *peigne* comb, fr. L *pecten* — more at PECTINATE] (1659)   **1 :** a gear with a small number of teeth designed to mesh with a larger wheel or rack   **2 :** the smaller of a pair or the smallest of a train of gear wheels

¹pink \'piŋk\ *n* [ME, fr. MD *pinke*] (15c) **:** a ship with a narrow overhanging stern — called also *pinkie*

²pink *n* [origin unknown] (1573)   **1 :** any of a genus (*Dianthus* of the family Caryophyllaceae, the pink family) of herbs having a cylindrical many-veined calyx with bracts at its base   **2 a :** the very embodiment **:** PARAGON   **b** (1) **:** one dressed in the height of fashion   (2) **:** ELITE   **c :** highest degree possible **:** HEIGHT ⟨keep their house in the ~ of repair —Rebecca West⟩ — **in the pink :** in the best of health or condition

³pink *n* (1678)   **1 :** any of a group of colors bluish red to red in hue, of medium to high lightness, and of low to moderate saturation   **2 a :** the scarlet color of a fox hunter's coat; *also* **:** a fox hunter's coat of this color   **b :** pink-colored clothing   **c** *pl* **:** light-colored trousers formerly worn by army officers   **3 :** PINKO

⁴pink *adj* (1720)   **1 :** of the color pink   **2 :** holding moderately radical and usu. socialistic political or economic views   **3 :** emotionally moved **:** EXCITED — often used as an intensive ⟨tickled ~⟩ — **pink·ness** *n*

⁵pink *vt* [ME, to thrust] (1503)   **1 a :** to perforate in an ornamental pattern   **b :** to cut a saw-toothed edge on   **2 a :** PIERCE, STAB   **b :** to wound by irony, criticism, or ridicule

pink bollworm *n* (1906) **:** a small dark brown moth (*Pectinophora gossypiella*) whose pinkish larva bores into the flowers and bolls of cotton and is a destructive pest in most cotton-growing regions

---

\ə\ abut \ᵊ\ kitten, F table \ər\ further \a\ ash \ā\ ace \ä\ mop, mar
\aù\ out \ch\ chin \e\ bet \ē\ easy \g\ go \i\ hit \ī\ ice \j\ job
\ŋ\ sing \ō\ go \ò\ law \òi\ boy \th\ thin \th\ the \ü\ loot \ù\ foot
\y\ yet \zh\ vision \à, k̲, ⁿ, œ, œ̄, ᵫ, ᵫ̄, ʸ\ see Guide to Pronunciation

pink–collar *adj* (1977) : of, relating to, or constituting a class of employees in occupations (as nursing and clerical jobs) traditionally held by women

pink elephants *n pl* (1940) : hallucinations arising esp. from heavy drinking or use of narcotics ⟨began to see *pink elephants*⟩

pink-eye \'piŋk-,ī\ *n* (1855) : an acute highly contagious conjunctivitis of humans and various domestic animals

¹pin·kie \'piŋ-kē\ *n* [prob. fr. D *pinkje* small pink, dim. of *pink*, fr. MD *pinke*] (1840) : ¹PINK

²pinkie *or* **pin·ky** \'piŋ-kē\ *n, pl* **pinkies** [prob. fr. D *pinkje*, dim. of *pink* little finger] (ca. 1808) : LITTLE FINGER

pinking shears *n pl* (ca. 1939) : shears with a saw-toothed inner edge on the blades for making a zigzag cut

pink·ish \'piŋ-kish\ *adj* (1784) : somewhat pink; *esp* : tending to be pink in politics — **pink·ish·ness** *n*

pink lady *n* (1936) : a cocktail consisting of gin, brandy, lemon juice, grenadine, and white of egg shaken with ice and strained

pink·ly \'piŋ-klē\ *adv* (1836) : in a pink manner : with a pink hue

pinko \'piŋ-(,)kō\ *n, pl* **pink·os** *also* **pink·oes** (1936) : a person who holds advanced liberal or moderately radical political or economic views

pink·root \'piŋk-,rüt, -,rut\ *n* (1763) : any of several plants (genus *Spigelia*) related to the nux vomica and used as anthelmintics; *esp* : an American woodland herb (*S. marilandica*) sometimes cultivated for its showy red and yellow flowers

pink salmon *n* (1905) : a small spotted Pacific salmon (*Oncorhynchus gorbuscha*) native to the northern Pacific Ocean and adjacent rivers

pink slip *n* (1915) : a notice from an employer that a recipient's employment is being terminated — **pink–slip** *vt*

pin money *n* (1697) **1 a** : money given by a man to his wife for her own use **b** : money set aside for the purchase of incidentals **2** : a trivial amount of money ⟨worked for *pin money*⟩

pin·na \'pi-nə\ *n, pl* **pin·nae** \'pi-,nē, -,nī\ *or* **pinnas** [NL, fr. L, feather, wing — more at PEN] (1785) **1** : a leaflet or primary division of a pinnate leaf or frond **2 a** : a projecting body part (as a feather, wing, or fin) **b** : the largely cartilaginous projecting portion of the external ear — see EAR illustration

pin·nace \'pi-nəs\ *n* [MF *pinace*, prob. fr. OSp *pinaza*, fr. *pino* pine, fr. L *pinus*] (1538) **1** : a light sailing ship; *esp* : one used as a tender **2** : any of various ship's boats

¹pin·na·cle \'pi-ni-kəl\ *n* [ME *pinacle*, fr. MF, fr. LL *pinnaculum* small wing, gable, fr. L *pinna* wing, battlement] (14c) **1** : an upright architectural member generally ending in a small spire and used esp. in Gothic construction to give weight esp. to a buttress **2** : a structure or formation suggesting a pinnacle; *specif* : a lofty peak **3** : the highest point of development or achievement : ACME *syn* see SUMMIT

²pinnacle *vt* **-cled; -cling** \-k(ə-)liŋ\ (14c) **1** : to surmount with a pinnacle **2** : to raise or rear on a pinnacle

pin·nate \'pi-,nāt\ *adj* [NL *pinnatus*, fr. L, feathered, fr. *pinna* feather, wing, fin] (1727) : resembling a feather esp. in having similar parts arranged on opposite sides of an axis like the barbs on the rachis of a feather ⟨~ leaf⟩ — see LEAF illustration — **pin·nate·ly** *adv*

1 pinnacle 1

pin·nat·i·fid \pə-'na-tə-fəd, -,fid\ *adj* [NL *pinnatifidus*, fr. *pinnatus* + L *-fidus* -fid] (ca. 1753) : cleft in a pinnate manner ⟨a ~ leaf⟩

pin·ner \'pi-nər\ *n* (1652) **1** : a woman's cap with long lappets worn in the 17th and 18th centuries **2** : one that pins

pin·ni·ped \'pi-nə-,ped\ *n* [ultim. fr. L *pinna* + *ped-, pes* foot — more at FOOT] (ca. 1842) : any of a suborder (Pinnipedia) of aquatic carnivorous mammals (as a seal or walrus) with all four limbs modified into flippers — **pinniped** *adj*

pin·nule \'pin-(,)yü(ə)l\ *n* [NL *pinnula*, fr. L, dim. of *pinna*] (1748) **1** : any of the secondary branches of a plumose organ esp. of a crinoid **2** : one of the ultimate divisions of a twice pinnate leaf

pin·ny \'pi-nē\ *n, pl* **pinnies** [by shortening & alter.] (1851) *chiefly Brit* : PINAFORE

pin oak *n* (1813) : a pyramidally-crowned oak (*Quercus palustris*) of wet regions of the eastern U.S. that has deeply cleft toothed leaves and rather small nearly hemispherical acorns

pi·noch·le \'pē-,nə-kəl\ *n* [modif. of G dial. *Binokel*, a game resembling bezique, fr. F dial. *binocle*] (1864) : a card game played with a 48-card pack containing two each of A, K, Q, J, 10, 9 in each suit with the object to score points by melding certain combinations of cards or by winning tricks that contain scoring cards; *also* : the meld of queen of spades and jack of diamonds scoring 40 points in this game

pi·no·cy·to·sis \,pī-nə-sə-'tō-səs, ,pi-nə-, -,sī-\ *n, pl* **-to·ses** \-,sēz\ [NL, fr. Gk *pinein* to drink + NL *cyt-* + *-osis* — more at POTABLE] (1895) : the uptake of fluid by a cell by invagination and pinching off of the plasma membrane

pi·no·cy·tot·ic \-'tä-tik\ *or* **pi·no·cyt·ic** \,pi-nə-'si-tik, ,pī-\ *adj* (1959) : of, relating to, or being pinocytosis — **pi·no·cy·tot·i·cal·ly** \-ti-k(ə-)lē\ *adv*

pi·no·le \pi-'nō-lē\ *n* [AmerSp, fr. Nahuatl *pinolli*] (1842) **1** : a finely ground flour made from parched corn **2** : any of various flours resembling pinole and ground from the seeds of other plants

pi·ñon *or* **pin·yon** \'pin-,yōn, -,yän, -yən; pin-'yōn\ *n, pl* **pi·ñons** *or* **pin·yons** *or* **pi·ño·nes** \pin-'yō-nēz\ [AmerSp *piñón*, fr. Sp, pine nut, fr. *piña* pinecone, fr. L *pinea* — more at PINEAL] (1831) : any of various low-growing pines (as *Pinus quadrifolia, P. cembroides, P. edulis,* and *P. monophylla*) of western No. America with edible seeds; *also* : the edible seed of a piñon

pi·not noir \'pē-(,)nō-'nwär, pē-'nō-\ *n, often cap P&N* [F, lit., black Pinot (a grape variety)] (1941) : a dry red wine produced from the same grape as French burgundy

¹pin·point \'pin-,point\ *n* (1849) **1** : something that is extremely small or insignificant **2** : the point of a pin **3** : an extremely small or sharp point

²pinpoint *adj* (1899) **1** : extremely fine or precise **2** : located, fixed, or directed with extreme precision ⟨~ targets⟩ **3** : small as a pinpoint

³pinpoint *vt* (1917) **1** : to locate or aim with great precision or accuracy **2 a** : to fix, determine, or identify with precision **b** : to cause to stand out conspicuously : HIGHLIGHT

¹pin-prick \'pin-,prik\ *n* (1862) **1** : a small puncture made by or as if by a pin **2** : a petty irritation or annoyance

²pinprick *vt* (1899) : to administer pinpricks to ~ *vi* : to administer pinpricks

pins and needles *n pl* (1813) : a pricking tingling sensation in a limb growing numb or recovering from numbness — **on pins and needles** : in a nervous or jumpy state of anticipation

pin·set·ter \'pin-,se-tər\ *n* (1916) : an employee or a mechanical device that spots pins in a bowling alley

pin·spot·ter \-,spä-tər\ *n* (1946) : PINSETTER

pin·stripe \-,strīp\ *n, often attrib* (1897) : a very thin stripe esp. on a fabric; *also* : a suit with such stripes — often used in pl. — **pin·striped** \-,strīpt\ *adj*

pint \'pīnt\ *n* [ME *pinte*, fr. MF, fr. ML *pincta*, prob. fr. (assumed) VL, fem. of *pinctus*, pp. of L *pingere* to paint — more at PAINT] (14c) **1** — see WEIGHT table **2** : a pint pot or vessel

¹pin·ta \'pin-tə, -,tä\ *n* [AmerSp, fr. Sp, spot, mark, fr. (assumed) VL *pincta*] (1825) : a chronic skin disease that is endemic in tropical America, that occurs successively as an initial papule, a generalized eruption, and a patchy loss of pigment, and that is caused by a spirochete (*Treponema careteum*) morphologically indistinguishable from the causative agent of syphilis

²pinta \'pin-tə\ *n* [*pint* + *-a* (as in *cuppa*)] (1959) *Brit* : a pint of milk

pin–ta·ble \'pin-,tā-bəl\ *n* (1936) *Brit* : PINBALL MACHINE

pin·tail \'pin-,tāl\ *n, pl* **pintail** *or* **pintails** (1768) : a bird having elongated central tail feathers; *esp* : a slender duck (*Anas acuta*) of the northern hemisphere with the male having a brown head, a white breast with a white line continuing up the side of the neck, and chiefly gray upperparts

pin·tle \'pin-t³l\ *n* [ME *pintel*, lit., penis, fr. OE; akin to MLG *pint* penis, OE *pinn* pin] (15c) : a usu. upright pivot pin on which another part turns

¹pin·to \'pin-(,)tō\ *n, pl* **pintos** *also* **pintoes** [AmerSp, fr. *pinto* spotted, fr. obs. Sp, fr. (assumed) VL *pinctus*] (1860) : a horse or pony marked with patches of white and another color — compare PIEBALD, SKEWBALD

²pinto *adj* (1865) : PIED, MOTTLED

pinto bean *n* (1916) : a mottled kidney bean that is grown chiefly in the southwestern U.S. for food and for stock feed

pint–size \'pīnt-,sīz\ *or* **pint–sized** \-,sīzd\ *adj* (1936) : SMALL

¹pin-up \'pin-,əp\ *n* (1943) : something fastened to a wall: as **a** : a photograph or poster of a person considered to have glamorous qualities **b** : something (as a lamp) designed for wall attachment

²pinup *adj* (1941) **1** : of or relating to pinups ⟨male ~ calendars⟩ **2** : designed for hanging on a wall ⟨a ~ lamp⟩

pinup girl *n* (1941) : a girl or woman whose glamorous qualities make her a suitable subject for a pinup

pin·wale \'pin-,wāl\ *adj* (1949) *of a fabric* : made with narrow wales

pin·weed \-,wēd\ *n* (1814) : any of a genus (*Lechea*) of herbs of the rockrose family with slender stems, many small leaves, and tiny flowers

¹pin·wheel \-,hwēl, -,wēl\ *n* (1869) **1** : a fireworks device in the form of a revolving wheel of colored fire **2** : a toy consisting of lightweight vanes that revolve at the end of a stick **3** : something (as a galaxy) shaped like a pinwheel

²pinwheel *vi* (ca. 1934) : to move like a pinwheel

pin·worm \-,wərm\ *n* (ca. 1864) **1** : any of numerous small nematode worms (family Oxyuridae) that infest the intestines and esp. the cecum of various vertebrates; *esp* : a worm (*Enterobius vermicularis*) parasitic in humans **2** : any of several rather slender insect larvae that burrow in plant tissue

pinx·ter flower \'piŋ(k)-stər-\ *n* [D *pinkster* Whitsuntide] (1857) : a deciduous pink-flowered azalea (*Rhododendron periclymenoides* syn. *R. nudiflorum*) that is native to rich moist woodlands of eastern No. America

pin·yin \'pin-'yin\ *n, often cap* [Chin (Beijing) *pīnyīn* to spell phonetically, fr. *pīn* to arrange + *yīn* sound, pronunciation] (1963) : a system for romanizing Chinese ideograms in which tones are indicated by diacritics and unaspirated consonants are transcribed as voiced — compare WADE-GILES

pi·on \'pī-,än\ *n* [contr. of *pi-meson*] (1950) : any of four mesons that consist of combinations of two up or down quarks, that may be positive, negative, or neutral, that have a mass about 270 times that of the electron, and that are subject to the strong force — **pi·on·ic** \pī-'ä-nik\ *adj*

¹pi·o·neer \,pī-ə-'nir\ *n* [MF *pionier*, fr. OF *peonier* foot soldier, fr. *peon* foot soldier, fr. ML *pedon-, pedo* — more at PAWN] (1523) **1** : a member of a military unit usu. of construction engineers **2 a** : a person or group that originates or helps open up a new line of thought or activity or a new method or technical development **b** : one of the first to settle in a territory **3** : a plant or animal capable of establishing itself in a bare, barren, or open area and initiating an ecological cycle

²pioneer *vi* (1780) **1** : to act as a pioneer ⟨~ed in the development of airplanes⟩ ~ *vt* **1** : to open or prepare for others to follow; *also* : SETTLE **2** : to originate or take part in the development of

³pioneer *adj* (1840) **1** : ORIGINAL, EARLIEST **2** : relating to or being a pioneer; *esp* : of, relating to, or characteristic of early settlers or their time

pi·ous \'pī-əs\ *adj* [ME, fr. L *pius*] (15c) **1 a** : marked by or showing reverence for deity and devotion to divine worship **b** : marked by conspicuous religiosity ⟨a hypocrite—a thing all ~ words and uncharitable deeds —Charles Reade⟩ **2** : sacred or devotional as distinct from the profane or secular : RELIGIOUS ⟨a ~ opinion⟩ **3** : showing loyal reverence for a person or thing : DUTIFUL **4 a** : marked by sham or hypocrisy **b** : marked by self-conscious virtue : VIRTUOUS **5** : deserving commendation : WORTHY ⟨a ~ effort⟩ — **pi·ous·ly** *adv* — **pi·ous·ness** *n*

¹pip \'pip\ *n* [ME *pippe*, fr. MD (akin to OHG *pfiffiz*), fr. (assumed) VL *pipita*, alter. of L *pituita* phlegm, pip; perh. akin to Gk *pitys* pine — more at PINE] (15c) **1 a** : a disorder of a bird marked by formation of a scale or crust on the tongue **b** : the scale or crust of this disorder **2**

a : any of various human ailments; *esp* : a slight nonspecific disorder **b** *chiefly Brit* : a feeling of irritation or annoyance

²**pip** *vb* **pipped; pip·ping** [imit.] *vi* (1598) **1** : ¹PEEP 1 **2** : to break through the shell of the egg ⟨the chick *pipped*⟩ ∼ *vt* : to break open (the shell of an egg) in hatching

³**pip** *n* [origin unknown] (1604) **1 a** : one of the dots used on dice and dominoes to indicate numerical value **b** : SPOT 2c **2 a** : SPOT, SPECK **b** : ¹SPIKE 6a; *also* : BLIP **3** : an individual rootstock of the lily of the valley **4** : a diamond-shaped insignia of rank worn by a second lieutenant, lieutenant, or captain in the British army

⁴**pip** *n* [short for *pippin*] (1797) **1** : a small fruit seed; *esp* : one of a several-seeded fleshy fruit **2** : one extraordinary of its kind

⁵**pip** *vt* **pipped; pip·ping** [prob. fr. *pip* to blackball, fr. ³*pip* or ⁴*pip*] (1880) *Brit* : to beat by a narrow margin

⁶**pip** *n* [imit.] (1907) *chiefly Brit* : a short high-pitched tone

pip·age *or* **pipe·age** \'pī-pij\ *n* (1612) **1 a** : transportation by means of pipes **b** : the charge for such transportation **2** : material for pipelines : PIPING

pi·pal \'pē-(,)pəl\ *n* [Hindi *pīpal*, fr. Skt *pippala*] (1788) : a large long-lived fig (*Ficus religiosa*) of India

¹**pipe** \'pīp\ *n* [ME, fr. OE *pipa* (akin to OHG *pfīfa* pipe), fr. (assumed) VL *pipa* pipe, fr. L *pipare* to peep, of imit. origin] (bef. 12c) **1 a** : a tubular wind instrument; *specif* : a small fipple flute held in and played by the left hand **b** : one of the tubes of a pipe organ: (1) : FLUE PIPE (2) : REED PIPE **c** : BAGPIPE — usu. used in pl. **d** (1) : VOICE, VOCAL CORD — usu. used in pl. (2) : PIPING 1 **2** : a long tube or hollow body for conducting a liquid, gas, or finely divided solid or for structural purposes **3 a** : a tubular or cylindrical object, part, or passage **b** : a roughly cylindrical and vertical geological formation **c** : the eruptive channel opening into the crater of a volcano **4** : a large cask of varying capacity used esp. for wine and oil **b** : any of various units of liquid capacity based on the size of a pipe; *esp* : a unit equal to 2 hogsheads **5** : a device for smoking usu. consisting of a tube having a bowl at one end and a mouthpiece at the other **6** : SNAP 2c, CINCH — **pipe·ful** \-,fủl\ *n* — **pipe·less** \'pī-pləs\ *adj* — **pipe·like** \'pīp-,līk\ *adj*

²**pipe** *vb* **piped; pip·ing** *vi* (bef. 12c) **1 a** : to play on a pipe **b** : to convey orders by signals on a boatswain's pipe **2 a** : to speak in a high or shrill voice **b** : to emit a shrill sound ∼ *vt* **1 a** : to play (a tune) on a pipe **b** : to utter in the shrill tone of a pipe **2 a** : to lead or cause to go with pipe music **b** (1) : to call or direct by the boatswain's pipe (2) : to receive aboard or attend the departure of by sounding a boatswain's pipe **3** : to trim with piping **4** : to furnish or equip with pipes **5** : to convey by or as if by pipes; *esp* : to transmit by wire or coaxial cable **6** : NOTICE

pipe clay *n* (1777) : highly plastic grayish white clay used esp. in making tobacco pipes and for whitening leather

pipe cleaner *n* (1870) : something used to clean the inside of a pipe; *specif* : a piece of flexible wire in which tufted fabric is twisted and which is used to clean the stem of a tobacco pipe

pipe cutter *n* (ca. 1890) : a tool or machine for cutting pipe; *esp* : a hand tool comprising a grasping device and one or more sharp-edged wheels that cut into the pipe as the tool is rotated

pipe down *vi* [²*pipe*] (1850) : to stop talking or making noise

pipe dream *n* [fr. the fantasies brought about by the smoking of opium] (1896) : an illusory or fantastic plan, hope, or story

pipe·fish \'pīp-,fish\ *n* (1769) : any of various fishes (family Syngnathidae) that are related to the sea horses and have a tube-shaped snout and a long slender body covered with bony plates

pipe fitter *n* (ca. 1883) : a worker who installs and repairs piping

pipe fitting *n* (ca. 1890) **1** : a piece (as a coupling or elbow) used to connect pipes or as accessory to a pipe **2** : the work of a pipe fitter

pipe·line \'pīp-,līn\ *n* (1860) **1** : a line of pipe with pumps, valves, and control devices for conveying liquids, gases, or finely divided solids **2** : a direct channel for information **3** : the processes through which supplies pass from or as if from source to user — **in the pipeline** : undergoing preparation, production, or completion : in the works

pipe of peace (1705) : CALUMET

pipe organ *n* (1885) : ORGAN 1b(1)

pip·er \'pī-pər\ *n* (bef. 12c) : one that plays on a pipe

pi·per·a·zine \pī-'per-ə-,zēn, pī-\ *n* [ISV *piperidine* + *azine*] (1889) : a crystalline heterocyclic base $C_4H_{10}N_2$ used esp. as an anthelmintic

pi·per·i·dine \pī-'per-ə-,dēn, pī-\ *n* [ISV *piperine* + -*idine*] (1854) : a liquid heterocyclic base $C_5H_{11}N$ that has a peppery ammoniacal odor and is obtained usu. by hydrolysis of piperine

pip·er·ine \'pī-pə-,rēn\ *n* [prob. fr. F *pipérine*, fr. L *piper* pepper] (1820) : a white crystalline alkaloid $C_{17}H_{19}NO_3$ that is the chief active constituent of pepper

pip·er·o·nal \pī-'per-ə-,nal\ *n* [ISV *piperine* + -*one* + ³-*al*] (1869) : a crystalline aldehyde $C_8H_6O_3$ with an odor of heliotrope

pip·er·o·nyl bu·tox·ide \pī-'per-ə-,nil-byü-'tāk-,sīd, -n³l-\ *n* [*piperonal* + -*yl* + *butyl* + *oxide*] (1945) : an insecticide $C_{19}H_{30}O_5$; *also* : an oily liquid containing this compound that is used chiefly as a synergist (as for pyrethrum insecticides)

pipe·stone \'pīp-,stōn\ *n* (ca. 1805) : a pink or mottled pink-and-white argillaceous stone used esp. by American Indians to make carved objects (as tobacco pipes)

pipe stop *n* (ca. 1909) : an organ stop composed of flue pipes

pi·pette *also* **pi·pet** \pī-'pet\ *n* [F *pipette*, dim. of *pipe*, cask, fr. (assumed) VL *pipa*, *pippa* pipe] (1839) : a small piece of apparatus which typically consists of a narrow tube into which fluid is drawn by suction (as for dispensing or measurement) and retained by closing the upper end — **pipette** *also* **pipet** *vb*

pipe up *vi* (1889) : SPEAK UP

pipe wrench *n* (ca. 1875) : a wrench for gripping and turning a cylindrical object (as a pipe) usu. by use of two serrated jaws so designed as to grip the pipe when turning in one direction only

¹**pip·ing** \'pī-piŋ\ *n* (13c) **1 a** : a sound, note, or call like that of a pipe **b** : the music of a pipe **2** : a quantity or system of pipes **3** : trimming stitched in seams or along edges (as of clothing, slipcovers, or curtains)

²**piping** *adj* (15c) **1** : SHRILL ⟨a ∼ voice⟩ **2** : TRANQUIL ⟨∼ times of peace —Shak.⟩

piping hot *adj* (14c) : very hot

pip·it \'pip-ət\ *n* [imit.] (1768) : any of various small singing birds (family Motacillidae and esp. genus *Anthus*) resembling the lark

pip·kin \'pip-kən\ *n* [perh. fr. *pipe*] (1565) : a small earthenware or metal pot usu. with a horizontal handle

pip·pin \'pi-pən\ *n* [ME *pepin*, fr. MF] (15c) **1** : any of numerous apples that have usu. yellow or greenish yellow skins strongly flushed with red and are used esp. for cooking **2** : a highly admired or very admirable person or thing

pip–pip \,pi(p)-'pip\ *interj* [prob. fr. *pip-pip*, imitating the sound of a horn] (1907) *Brit* — used to express farewell

pip·sis·se·wa \pip-'si-sə-,wô\ *n* [perh. fr. Eastern Abenaki *kpi-psk^ʷáhsawe*, lit., flower of the woods] (1789) : any of a genus (*Chimaphila* and esp. *C. umbellata*) of evergreen herbs of the wintergreen family with astringent leaves used as a tonic and diuretic

pip–squeak \'pip-,skwēk\ *n* (1910) : one that is small or insignificant

pi·quan·cy \'pē-kən(t)s, -,kwən(t)s\ *n* (1883) : PIQUANCY

pi·quant \'pē-kənt(s)-, 'pi-kwən(t)-\ *n* (1664) : the quality or state of being piquant

pi·quant \'pē-kənt, -,känt; 'pi-kwənt\ *adj* [MF, fr. prp. of *piquer*] (1630) **1** : agreeably stimulating to the palate; *esp* : SPICY **2** : engagingly provocative; *also* : having a lively arch charm *syn* see PUNGENT — **pi·quant·ly** *adv* — **pi·quant·ness** *n*

¹**pique** \'pēk\ *n* (1592) : a transient feeling of wounded vanity : RESENTMENT ⟨a fit of ∼⟩ *syn* see OFFENSE

²**pique** *vt* **piqued; piqu·ing** [F *piquer*, lit., to prick — more at PIKE] (1669) **1** : to arouse anger or resentment in : IRRITATE ⟨what ∼s linguistic conservatives —T. H. Middleton⟩ **2 a** : to excite or arouse by a provocation, challenge, or rebuff ⟨sly remarks to ∼ their curiosity⟩ **b** : PRIDE ⟨he ∼s himself on his skill as a cook⟩ *syn* see PROVOKE

pi·qué *or* **pi·que** \pi-'kā, pē-,\ *n* [F *piqué*, fr. pp. of *piquer* to prick, quilt] (1852) **1** : a durable ribbed clothing fabric of cotton, rayon, or silk **2** : decoration of a tortoiseshell or ivory object with inlaid fragments of gold or silver

pi·quet \pi-'kā, -'ket\ *n* [F] (1646) : a two-handed card game played with 32 cards

pi·ra·cy \'pī-rə-sē\ *n, pl* **-cies** [ML *piratia*, fr. LGk *peirateia*, fr. Gk *peiratēs* pirate] (1537) **1** : an act of robbery on the high seas; *also* : an act resembling such robbery **2** : robbery on the high seas **3** : the unauthorized use of another's production, invention, or conception esp. in infringement of a copyright

pi·ra·gua \pi-'rä-gwə, -'rä-\ *n* [Sp] (1609) **1** : DUGOUT 1 **2** : a 2-masted flat-bottomed boat

pi·ra·nha \pə-'rä-nə, -'rän-yə, -'ran-\ *n* [Pg, fr. Tupi *pira* fish + *áya* tooth] (1869) : any of various usu. small So. American characin fishes (genus *Serrasalmo*) having very sharp teeth and including some that may attack and inflict dangerous wounds upon humans and large animals — called also *caribe*

pi·ra·ru·cu \pi-,rär-ə-'kü\ *n* [Pg, fr. Tupi *pirauruku*, fr. *pira* fish + *uruku* annatto] (1840) : a very large edible bony fish (*Arapaima gigas* of the family Osteoglossidae) of the rivers of northern So. America

¹**pi·rate** \'pī-rət\ *n* [ME, fr. MF or L; MF, fr. L *pirata*, fr. Gk *peiratēs*, fr. *peiran* to attempt — more at FEAR] (14c) : one who commits or practices piracy — **pi·rat·i·cal** \pə-'ra-ti-kəl, pī-\ *adj* — **pi·rat·i·cal·ly** \-k(ə-)lē\ *adv*

²**pirate** *vb* **pi·rat·ed; pi·rat·ing** *vt* (1574) **1** : to commit piracy on **2** : to take or appropriate by piracy; *as* **a** : to reproduce without authorization esp. in infringement of copyright **b** : to lure away from another employer by offers of betterment ∼ *vi* : to commit or practice piracy

pirn \'pərn, 2 *is also* 'pirn\ *n* [ME] (15c) **1** : QUILL 1a(1) **2** *chiefly Scot* : a device resembling a reel

pi·ro·gi *var of* PIEROGI

pi·rogue \'pē-,rōg\ *n* [F, fr. Sp *piragua*, fr. Carib *piraua*] (1666) **1** : DUGOUT 1 **2** : a boat like a canoe

piro·plasm \'pir-ə-,pla-zəm\ *or* **piro·plas·ma** \,pir-ə-'plaz-mə\ *n, pl* **piroplasms** *or* **piro·plas·ma·ta** \,pir-ə-'plaz-mə-tə\ [NL *Piroplasma*, genus of piroplasms] (1901) : BABESIA

pi·rosh·ki *or* **pi·rozh·ki** \pi-'rôsh-kē, ,pir-əsh-'ke\ *n pl* [Russ *pirozhki*, pl. of *pirozhok*, dim. of *pirog* pastry] (1912) : small pastries with meat, cheese, or vegetable filling

pir·ou·ette \,pir-ə-'wet\ *n* [F, lit., teetotum] (1706) : a rapid whirling about of the body; *esp* : a full turn on the toe or ball of one foot in ballet — **pirouette** *vi*

pis *pl of* PI

pis al·ler \,pē-za-'lā\ *n, pl* **pis al·lers** \-'lā(z)\ [F, lit., to go worst] (1676) : a last resource or device : EXPEDIENT

pis·ca·to·ri·al \,pis-kə-'tōr-ē-əl, -'tôr-\ *adj* (1828) : PISCATORY

pis·ca·to·ry \'pis-kə-,tōr-ē, -,tôr-\ *adj* [L *piscatorius*, fr. *piscari* to fish, fr. *piscis*] (1633) : of, relating to, or dependent on fish or fishing

Pi·sce·an \'pī-sē-ən, 'pi-sē-, 'pis-kē-\ *n* (1925) : PISCES 2b

Pi·sces \'pī-(,)sēz *also* 'pi-,sēz *or* 'pis-,kēz\ *n pl but sing in constr* [ME, fr. L (gen. *Piscium*), fr. pl. of *piscis* fish — more at FISH] **1** : a zodiacal constellation directly south of Andromeda **2 a** : the 12th sign of the zodiac in astrology — see ZODIAC table **b** : one born under this sign

pi·sci·cul·ture \'pī-sə-,kəl-chər, 'pis-ə-, 'pis-kə-\ *n* [prob. fr. F, fr. L *piscis* + F *culture* culture] (1859) : fish culture

pi·sci·na \pə-'sē-nə, -'si-\ *n* [ML, fr. L, fishpond, fr. *piscis*] (1793) : a basin with a drain near the altar of a church for disposing of water from liturgical ablutions

\a\ abut \³\ kitten, F table \ər\ further \a\ ash \ā\ ace \ä\ mop, mar
\aủ\ out \ch\ chin \e\ bet \ē\ easy \g\ go \i\ hit \ī\ ice \j\ job
\ŋ\ sing \ō\ go \ȯ\ law \ȯi\ boy \th\ thin \t͟h\ the \ü\ loot \ủ\ foot
\y\ yet \zh\ vision \à, ͟k, ⁿ, œ, œ̄, ɯ̄, ᵫ̄, ʸ\ see Guide to Pronunciation

pis·cine \'pī-,sēn, 'pi-,sīn, 'pis-,kīn\ *adj* [L *piscinus*, fr. *piscis*] (1799) : of, relating to, or characteristic of fish

pis·civ·o·rous \pə-'si-və-rəs, pī-\ *adj* [L *piscis* + E *-vorous*] (1668) : feeding on fishes

pish \'pish\ *interj* (1592) — used to express disdain or contempt

¹pi·si·form \'pī-sə-,fórm\ *adj* [L *pisum* pea + E *-iform* — more at PEA] (1767) : resembling a pea in size or shape

²pisiform *n* (ca. 1771) : a bone on the ulnar side of the carpus in most mammals

pis·mire \'pis-,mīr, 'piz-\ *n* [ME *pissemire*, fr. *pisse* urine + *mire* ant, fr. of Scand origin; akin to ON *maurr* ant; akin to L *formica* ant, Gk *myrmēx*] (14c) : ANT

pis·mo clam \'piz-(,)mō-\ *n, often cap P* [*Pismo* Beach, Calif.] (1913) : a thick-shelled clam (*Tivela stultorum*) of the southwest coast of No. America used extensively for food

pi·so \'pē-(,)sō\ *n* [prob. fr. Tag, fr. Sp *peso*] (ca. 1975) : the peso of the Philippines

pi·so·lite \'pī-sə-,līt\ *n* [NL *pisolithus*, fr. Gk *pisos* pea + *-lithos* -lith] (1708) : a limestone composed of pisiform concretions — **pi·so·lit·ic** \,pī-sə-'li-tik\ *adj*

¹piss \'pis\ *vb* [ME, fr. OF *pissier*, fr. (assumed) VL *pissiare*, of imit. origin] *vi* (14c) : URINATE — sometimes considered vulgar ~ *vt* : to urinate in or on — sometimes considered vulgar

²piss *n* (14c) **1** : URINE — sometimes considered vulgar **2** : an act of urinating — often used with *take*; sometimes considered vulgar

piss·ant \'pis-,ant\ *n, often attrib* [*pissant* ant, fr. ¹*piss* + *ant*] (ca. 1946) : one that is insignificant — used as a generalized term of abuse; sometimes considered vulgar

piss away *vt* (1949) : to fritter away : SQUANDER — sometimes considered vulgar

pissed \'pist\ *adj* (1929) **1** *chiefly Brit* : DRUNK 1a — sometimes considered vulgar **2** : ANGRY, IRRITATED — often used with *off*; sometimes considered vulgar

piss off *vi* (1953) *Brit* : to leave immediately : SCRAM — usu. used as a command; sometimes considered vulgar ~ *vt* : ANGER, IRRITATE — sometimes considered vulgar

pis·soir \pi-'swär\ *n* [F, fr. MF, fr. *pisser* to urinate, fr. OF *pissier*] (1919) : a public urinal usu. located on the street in some European countries

pis·ta·chio \pə-'sta-shē-,ō, -'stä-\ *n, pl* **-chios** [It *pistacchio*, fr. L *pistacium* pistachio nut, fr. Gk *pistakion*, fr. *pistakē* pistachio tree, of Iranian origin; akin to Pers *pistah* pistachio tree] (1598) : a small Asian tree (*Pistacia vera*) of the cashew family whose drupaceous fruit contains a greenish edible seed; *also* : its seed

pis·ta·reen \,pis-tə-'rēn\ *n* [prob. modif. of Sp *peseta* peseta] (1744) : an old Spanish silver piece circulating at a debased rate

piste \'pēst\ *n* [F, fr. MF, fr. OIt *pista*, fr. *pistare* to trample down, pound — more at PISTON] (ca. 1741) : TRAIL; *esp* : a downhill ski trail

pis·til \'pis-t'l\ *n* [NL *pistillum*, fr. L, pestle — more at PESTLE] (1749) : a single carpel or group of fused carpels usu. differentiated into an ovary, style, and stigma — see FLOWER illustration

pis·til·late \'pis-tə-,lāt\ *adj* (ca. 1828) : having pistils; *specif* : having pistils but no stamens

pis·tol \'pis-t'l\ *n* [MF *pistole*, fr. G, fr. MHG *pischulle*, fr. Czech *píšt'ala*, lit., pipe, fife; akin to Czech *pištět* to squeak] (ca. 1570) : a handgun whose chamber is integral with the barrel; *broadly* : HANDGUN — **pistol** *vt*

pis·tole \pis-'tōl\ *n* [MF] (1592) : an old gold 2-escudo piece of Spain; *also* : any of several old gold coins of Europe of approximately the same value

pis·tol·eer \,pis-tə-'lir\ *n* (1832) : one who is armed with a pistol

pistol grip *n* (1874) **1** : a grip of a shotgun or rifle shaped like a pistol stock **2** : a handle shaped like a pistol stock

pistol–whip *vt* (ca. 1942) : to beat with a pistol

pis·ton \'pis-tən\ *n* [F, fr. It *pistone*, fr. *pistare* to pound, fr. OIt, fr. ML, fr. L *pistus*, pp. of *pinsere* to crush — more at PESTLE] (1704) **1** : a sliding piece moved by or moving against fluid pressure which usu. consists of a short cylinder fitting within a cylindrical vessel along which it moves back and forth **2 a** : a sliding valve moving in a cylinder in a brass instrument which when depressed by a finger knob serves to lower the instrument's pitch **b** : a button on an organ console to bring in a previously selected registration

piston pin *n* (1897) : WRIST PIN

piston ring *n* (1867) : a springy split metal ring for sealing the gap between a piston and the cylinder wall

piston rod *n* (1786) : CONNECTING ROD

¹pit \'pit\ *n* [ME, fr. OE *pytt* (akin to OHG *pfuzzi* well), fr. L *puteus* well, pit] (bef. 12c) **1 a** (1) : a hole, shaft, or cavity in the ground (2) : MINE **b** : a scooped-out place used for burning something (as charcoal) **c** : an area often sunken or depressed below the adjacent floor area: as (1) : an enclosure in which animals are made to fight each other (2) : a space at the front of a theater for the orchestra (3) : an area in a securities or commodities exchange in which members trade (as stocks) **2 a** : HELL — used with *the* **b** : a place or situation of futility, misery, or degradation ⟨*c pl* : WORST ⟨it's the ~s⟩ **3 a** : a hollow or indentation esp. in the surface of an organism: as **a** : a natural hollow in the surface of the body **b** : one of the indented scars left in the skin by a pustular disease : POCKMARK **c** : a minute depression in the secondary wall of a plant cell functioning in the intercellular movement of water and dissolved material **4** : any of the areas alongside an auto racecourse used for refueling and repairing the cars during a race — often used in pl. with *the*

²pit *vb* **pit·ted; pit·ting** *vt* (15c) **1 a** : to place, cast, bury, or store in a pit **b** : to make pits in; *esp* : to scar or mark with pits **2 a** : to set (as gamecocks) into or as if into a pit to fight **b** : to set into opposition or rivalry — usu. used with *against* ~ *vi* **1** : to become marked with pits; *esp* : to preserve for a time an indentation made by pressure **2** : to make a pit stop

³pit *n* [D, fr. MD — more at PITH] (1841) : the stone of a drupaceous fruit

⁴pit *vt* **pit·ted; pit·ting** (1913) : to remove the pit from (a fruit)

¹pi·ta \'pē-tə\ *n* [Sp & Pg] (1698) **1** : any of several fiber-yielding plants (as an agave) **2** : the fiber of a pita; *also* : any of several fibers from other sources

²pita *n* [NGk] (1951) : a thin flat bread that can be separated easily into two layers to form a pocket — called also *pita bread*

pit–a–pat \,pit-i-'pat\ *n* [imit.] (1582) : PITTER-PATTER — **pit–a–pat** *adv or adj* — **pit–a–pat** *vi*

pit boss *n* (1949) : a person who supervises the gaming tables in a casino

pit bull *n* (1930) : a dog (as an American Staffordshire terrier) of any of several breeds or a real or apparent hybrid with one or more of these breeds that was developed and is now often trained for fighting and is noted for strength and stamina

pit bull terrier *n* (1945) **1** : PIT BULL **2** : AMERICAN PIT BULL TERRIER

¹pitch \'pich\ *n* [ME *pich*, fr. OE *pic*, fr. L *pic-, pix*; akin to Gk *pissa* pitch, OCS *pĭcĭlŭ*] (bef. 12c) **1** : a black or dark viscous substance obtained as a residue in the distillation of organic materials and esp. tars **2** : any of various bituminous substances **3** : resin obtained from various conifers and often used medicinally **4** : any of various artificial mixtures resembling resinous or bituminous pitches

²pitch *vt* (bef. 12c) : to cover, smear, or treat with or as if with pitch

³pitch *vb* [ME *pichen*] *vt* (13c) **1** : to erect and fix firmly in place ⟨~ a tent⟩ **2** : to throw usu. with a particular objective or toward a particular point ⟨~ hay onto a wagon⟩: as **a** : to throw (a baseball) to a batter **b** : to toss (as coins) so as to fall at or near a mark ⟨~ pennies⟩ **c** : to put aside or discard by or as if by throwing ⟨~ed the trash into the bin⟩ ⟨decided to ~ the whole idea⟩ **3** : to present or advertise for sale esp. in a high-pressure way **4 a** (1) : to cause to be at a particular level or of a particular quality **b** : to set in a particular musical key **b** : to cause to be set at a particular angle : SLOPE **5** : to utter glibly and insincerely ⟨~ a line⟩ **6** : to use as a starting pitcher **b** : to play as pitcher **7** : to hit (a golf ball) in a high arc with backspin so that it rolls very little after striking the green ~ *vi* **1 a** : to fall precipitately or headlong **b** (1) *of a ship* : to have the bow alternately plunge precipitately and rise abruptly (2) *of an aircraft, missile, or spacecraft* : to turn about a lateral axis so that the forward end rises or falls in relation to the after end **c** : BUCK 1 **2** : ENCAMP **3** : to hit upon or happen upon something ⟨~ upon the perfect gift⟩ **4** : to incline downward : SLOPE **5 a** : to throw a ball to a batter **b** : to play ball as a pitcher **c** : to pitch a golf ball **6** : to make a sales pitch *syn* see THROW — **pitch into 1** : ATTACK, ASSAIL **2** : to set to work on energetically

⁴pitch *n* (1542) **1 a** : SLOPE; *also* : degree of slope : RAKE **b** : the distance between any of various things: as (1) : distance between one point on a gear tooth and the corresponding point on the next tooth (2) : distance from any point on the thread of a screw to the corresponding point on an adjacent thread measured parallel to the axis **c** : the theoretical distance a propeller would advance longitudinally in one revolution **d** : the number of teeth or of threads per inch **e** : a unit of width of type based on the number of times a letter can be set in a linear inch **2** : the action or a manner of pitching; *esp* : an up-and-down movement — compare YAW **3** *archaic* : TOP, ZENITH **4** : the relative level, intensity, or extent of some quality or state ⟨tensions rose to a feverish ~⟩ **b** : the property of a sound and esp. a musical tone that is determined by the frequency of the waves producing it : highness or lowness of sound (2) : a standard frequency for tuning instruments **c** (1) : the difference in the relative vibration frequency of the human voice that contributes to the total meaning of speech (2) : a definite relative pitch that is a significant phenomenon in speech **5** : a steep place : DECLIVITY **6** *chiefly Brit* **a** : an outdoor site (as for camping or doing business) **b** : PLAYING FIELD 1 **7** : an all-fours game in which the first card led is a trump **8 a** : an often high-pressure sales presentation **b** : ADVERTISEMENT **9 a** : the delivery of a baseball by a pitcher to a batter **b** : a baseball so thrown : PITCHOUT 2 — **pitched** \'picht\ *adj*

staff notation of pitch 4b(1)

pitch–black \'pich-'blak\ *adj* (1599) : extremely dark or black

pitch·blende \'pich-,blend\ *n* [part trans. of G *Pechblende*, fr. *Pech* pitch + *Blende* blende] (1770) : a brown to black mineral that consists of massive uraninite, has a distinctive luster, contains radium, and is the chief ore-mineral source of uranium

pitch–dark \'pich-'därk\ *adj* (1827) : extremely dark : PITCH-BLACK

pitched battle *n* (1607) : an intensely fought battle in which the opposing forces are locked in close combat

¹pitch·er \'pi-chər\ *n* [ME *picher*, fr. OF *pichier*, fr. ML *bicarius* goblet] (13c) **1** : a container for holding and pouring liquids that usu. has a lip or spout and a handle **2** : a modified leaf of a pitcher plant in which the hollowed petiole and base of the blade form an elongated receptacle — **pitch·er·ful** \-,ful\ *n*

²pitcher *n* (ca. 1722) : one that pitches; *specif* : the player that pitches in a game of baseball

pitcher plant *n* (1819) : a plant (esp. family Sarraceniaceae, the pitcher-plant family) with leaves modified into pitchers in which insects are trapped and digested by means of liquids secreted by the leaves

pitch·fork \'pich-,fórk\ *n* (13c) : a long-handled fork that has two or three long somewhat curved prongs and is used esp. in pitching hay — **pitchfork** *vt*

pitch in *vi* (1843) **1** : to begin to work **2** : to contribute to a common endeavor

pitch·man \'pich-mən\ *n* (ca. 1926) : one who makes a sales pitch: as **a** : one who sells merchandise on the streets or from a concession **b** : one who does radio or TV commercials

pitch·out \'pich-,aút\ *n* (1912) **1** : a pitch in baseball deliberately out of reach of the batter to enable the catcher to put out a base runner esp. with a throw **2** : a lateral pass in football between two backs behind the line of scrimmage — **pitch out** *vi*

pitch pine n (1676) **1** : any of several pines that yield pitch; *esp* : a 3-leaved pine (*Pinus rigida*) of eastern No. America **2** : the wood of a pitch pine

pitch pipe n (1711) : a small reed pipe or flue pipe producing one or more tones to establish the pitch in singing or in tuning an instrument

pitch·pole \'pich-ˌpōl\ vb [*pitchpole* somersault, fr. ³*pitch* + *pole, poll* head] vi (1851) : to turn end over end ⟨the catamaran *pitchpoled*⟩ ~ vt : to cause to turn end over end

pitch·wom·an \-ˌwu̇-mən\ n (1957) : a woman who makes a sales pitch

pitchy \'pi-chē\ adj (15c) **1 a** : full of pitch : TARRY **b** : of, relating to, or having the qualities of pitch **2** : PITCH-BLACK

pit·e·ous \'pi-tē-əs\ adj (14c) : of a kind to move to pity or compassion — **pit·e·ous·ly** adv — **pit·e·ous·ness** n

pit·fall \'pit-ˌfȯl\ n (14c) **1** : TRAP, SNARE; *specif* : a pit flimsily covered or camouflaged and used to capture and hold animals or men **2** : a hidden or not easily recognized danger or difficulty

¹**pith** \'pith\ n [ME, fr. OE *pitha*; akin to MD & MLG *pit* pith, pit] (bef. 12c) **1 a** : a usu. continuous central strand of spongy tissue in the stems of most vascular plants that prob. functions chiefly in storage **b** : any of various loose spongy plant tissues that resemble true pith **c** : the soft or spongy interior of a part of the body **2 a** : the essential part : CORE **b** : substantial quality (as of meaning) **3** : IMPORTANCE

²**pith** vt (1805) **1 a** : to kill (as cattle) by piercing or severing the spinal cord **b** : to destroy the spinal cord or central nervous system of (as a frog) usu. by passing a wire or needle up and down the vertebral canal **2** : to remove the pith from (a plant stem)

pit·head \'pit-ˌhed\ n (1839) *chiefly Brit* : the top of a mining pit or coal shaft; *also* : the immediately adjacent ground and buildings

pith·ec·an·thro·pine \ˌpi-thi-'kan(t)-thrə-ˌpīn\ n (1925) : any of a group of Pleistocene hominids (as Java man, Peking man, and Heidelberg man) that have a smaller cranial capacity than modern humans (*Homo sapiens*) but a greater cranial capacity than the australopithecines, prominent eyebrow ridges, a receding forehead, constriction of the skull behind the eye sockets, and relatively large canine and incisor teeth and that were formerly considered to comprise a genus (*Pithecanthropus*) but are now grouped in a single species (*Homo erectus*) — **pithecanthropine** adj

pith·ec·an·thro·pus \-'kan(t)-thrə-pəs, -ˌkan-'thrō-\ n, pl **-pi** \-ˌpī, -ˌpē\ [NL, fr. Gk *pithēkos* ape + *anthrōpos* human being] (1895) : PITHECANTHROPINE

pith helmet n (1889) : TOPEE

pith ray n (1902) : MEDULLARY RAY

pithy \'pi-thē\ adj **pith·i·er; -est** (1562) **1** : consisting of or abounding in pith **2** : having substance and point : tersely cogent *syn* see CONCISE — **pith·i·ly** \'pi-thə-lē\ adv — **pith·i·ness** \'pi-thē-nəs\ n

piti·able \'pi-tē-ə-bəl\ adj (15c) **1** : deserving or exciting pity : LAMENTABLE **2** : of a kind to evoke mingled pity and contempt esp. because of inadequacy ⟨a ~ excuse⟩ *syn* see CONTEMPTIBLE — **piti·able·ness** n — **piti·ably** \-blē\ adv

piti·er \'pi-tē-ər\ n (1601) : one that pities

piti·ful \'pi-ti-fəl\ adj (14c) **1** *archaic* : full of pity : COMPASSIONATE **2 a** : deserving or arousing pity or commiseration **b** : exciting pitying contempt (as by meanness or inadequacy) — **piti·ful·ly** \-f(ə-)lē\ adv — **piti·ful·ness** \-fəl-nəs\ n

piti·less \'pi-ti-ləs, 'pi-tᵊl-əs\ adj (15c) : devoid of pity : MERCILESS — **piti·less·ly** adv — **piti·less·ness** n

pit·man \'pit-mən\ n (1703) **1** pl **pit·men** \-mən\ : one who works in or near a pit (as in a coal mine) **2** pl **pitmans** : CONNECTING ROD

pi·ton \'pē-ˌtän\ n [F] (1893) : a spike, wedge, or peg that is driven into a rock or ice surface as a support (as for a mountain climber)

pi·tot-stat·ic tube \ˌpē-ˌtō-'sta-tik-\ n, often cap P M (1926) : a device that consists of a pitot tube and a static tube and that measures pressures in such a way that the relative speed of a fluid can be determined

pi·tot tube \'pē-ˌtō-\ n, often cap P [F (*tube de*) *Pitot*, fr. Henri Pitot †1771 Fr. physicist] (ca. 1859) **1** : a device that consists of a tube having a short right-angled bend which is placed vertically in a moving body of fluid with the mouth of the bent part directed upstream and that is used with a manometer to measure the velocity of fluid flow **2** : PITOT-STATIC TUBE

pit saw n (1679) : a handsaw worked by two persons one of whom stands on or above the log being sawed into planks and the other below it usu. in a pit

pit stop n (1932) **1** : a stop at the pits during an automobile race **2 a** : a stop (as during a trip) for fuel, food, or rest or for use of a rest room **b** (1) : a place where a pit stop can be made (2) : an establishment providing food or drink

pit·tance \'pi-tᵊn(t)s\ n [ME *pitance*, fr. OF, piety, pity, fr. ML *pietantia*, fr. *pietant*, *pietans*, prp. of *pietari* to be charitable, fr. L *pietas* piety — more at PITY] (14c) : a small portion, amount, or allowance; *also* : a meager wage or remuneration

pit·ted \'pi-təd\ adj (bef. 12c) : marked with pits

pit·ter-pat·ter \'pi-tər-ˌpa-tər, 'pi-tē-\ n [redupl. of ⁴*patter*] (15c) : a rapid succession of light sounds or beats : PATTER — **pitter-patter** \ˌpi-tər-', ˌpi-tē-'\ adv or adj — **pitter-patter** *same as adj*⟩ vi

pit·ting n (1665) **1** : an arrangement of pits **2** : the action or process of forming pits **3** : the bringing of gamecocks together to fight

pit·tos·po·rum \pə-'täs-pə-rəm\ n [NL, fr. Gk *pitta*, *pissa* pitch + *spora* seed — more at PITCH, SPORE] (1789) : any of various Old World shrubs or trees (genus *Pittosporum* of the family Pittosporaceae) planted esp. as ornamentals in warm regions

¹**pi·tu·i·tary** \pə-'tü-ə-ˌter-ē, -'tyü-\ adj [L *pituita* phlegm; fr. the former belief that the pituitary gland secreted phlegm — more at PIP] (1615) **1** : of or relating to the pituitary gland **2** : caused or characterized by secretory disturbances of the pituitary gland ⟨a ~ dwarf⟩

²**pituitary** n, pl **-tar·ies** (1845) : PITUITARY GLAND

pituitary gland n (1825) : a small oval endocrine organ that is attached to the infundibulum of the brain, consists of an epithelial anterior lobe joined by an intermediate part to a posterior lobe of nervous origin, and produces various internal secretions directly or indirectly impinging on most basic body functions — called also *hypophysis*, *pituitary body*; see BRAIN illustration

pit viper n (ca. 1885) : any of various mostly New World venomous snakes (subfamily Crotalinae of the family Viperidae) with a sensory pit on each side of the head and hollow perforated fangs

¹**pity** \'pi-tē\ n, pl **pit·ies** [ME *pite*, fr. OF *pité*, fr. L *pietat-*, *pietas* piety, pity, fr. *pius* pious] (13c) **1 a** : sympathetic sorrow for one suffering, distressed, or unhappy **b** : capacity to feel pity **2** : something to be regretted ⟨it's a ~ you can't go⟩

syn PITY, COMPASSION, COMMISERATION, CONDOLENCE, SYMPATHY mean the act or capacity for sharing the painful feelings of another. PITY implies tender or sometimes slightly contemptuous sorrow for one in misery or distress ⟨felt *pity* for the captives⟩. COMPASSION implies pity coupled with an urgent desire to aid or to spare ⟨treats the homeless with great *compassion*⟩. COMMISERATION suggests pity expressed outwardly in exclamations, tears, or words of comfort ⟨murmurs of *commiseration* filled the loser's headquarters⟩. CONDOLENCE applies chiefly to formal expression of grief to one who has suffered loss ⟨expressed their *condolences* to the widow⟩. SYMPATHY often suggests a tender concern but can also imply a power to enter into another's emotional experience of any sort ⟨went to my best friend for *sympathy*⟩ ⟨in *sympathy* with her desire to locate her natural parents⟩.

²**pity** vb **pit·ied; pity·ing** vt (15c) : to feel pity for ~ vi : to feel pity

pity·ing adj (1589) : expressing or feeling pity — **pity·ing·ly** \-iŋ-lē\ adv

pit·y·ri·a·sis \ˌpi-ti-'rī-ə-səs\ n [NL, fr. Gk, fr. *pityron* scurf] (ca. 1693) : a condition of humans or domestic animals marked by dry scaling or scurfy patches of skin

più \'pyü, pē-'ü\ adv [It, fr. L *plus*] (1724) : MORE — used to qualify an adverb or adjective used as a direction in music

Pi·ute var of PAIUTE

¹**piv·ot** \'pi-vət\ n [F] (1611) **1** : a shaft or pin on which something turns **2 a** : a person, thing, or factor having a major or central role, function, or effect **b** : a key player or position; *specif* : an offensive position of a basketball player standing usu. with back to the basket to relay passes, shoot, or provide a screen for teammates **3** : the action of pivoting

²**pivot** adj (1796) **1** : turning on or as if on a pivot **2** : PIVOTAL

³**pivot** vi (1841) : to turn on or as if on a pivot ~ vt **1** : to provide with, mount on, or attach by a pivot **2** : to cause to pivot — **pivot·able** \-və-tə-bəl\ adj

piv·ot·al \'pi-və-tᵊl\ adj (1844) **1** : of, relating to, or constituting a pivot **2** : vitally important : CRUCIAL — **piv·ot·al·ly** \-tᵊl-ē\ adv

piv·ot·man \'pi-vət-ˌman\ n (ca. 1814) : one who plays the pivot; *specif* : a center on a basketball team

pivot tooth n (1842) : an artificial crown attached to the root of a tooth by a usu. metallic pin — called also *pivot crown*

pix pl of PIC

pix·el \'pik-səl, -ˌsel\ n [*pix* + *element*] (1969) **1** : any of the small discrete elements that together constitute an image (as on a television screen) **2** : any of the detecting elements of a charge-coupled device used as an optical sensor

¹**pix·ie** or **pixy** \'pik-sē\ n, pl **pix·ies** [origin unknown] (1746) : FAIRY; *specif* : a cheerful mischievous sprite — **pix·ie·ish** \-sē-ish\ adj

²**pixie** or **pixy** adj (1943) : playfully mischievous — **pixi·ness** n

pix·i·lat·ed or **pix·il·lat·ed** \'pik-sə-ˌlā-təd\ adj [irreg. fr. *pixie*] (1848) **1** : somewhat unbalanced mentally; *also* : BEMUSED : WHIMSICAL — **pix·i·la·tion** \ˌpik-sə-'lā-shən\ n

piz·za \'pēt-sə\ n [It, perh. of Gmc origin; akin to OHG *bizzo*, *pizzo* bite, bit, *bizan* to bite — more at BITE] (1935) : an open pie made typically of flattened bread dough spread with a savory mixture usu. including tomatoes and cheese and often other toppings and baked — called also *pizza pie* — **piz·za·like** \-ˌlīk\ adj

piz·zazz or **pi·zazz** \pə-'zaz\ n [origin unknown] (1937) : the quality of being exciting or attractive: use **a** : GLAMOUR **b** : VITALITY — **piz·zazzy** or **pi·zazzy** \-'za-zē\ adj

piz·ze·ria \ˌpēt-sə-'rē-ə\ n [It, fr. *pizza*] (1943) : an establishment where pizzas are made or sold

¹**piz·zi·ca·to** \ˌpit-si-'kä-(ˌ)tō\ n, pl **-ca·ti** \-'kä-(ˌ)tē\ (1845) : a note or passage played by plucking strings

²**pizzicato** adv or adj [It, pp. of *pizzicare* to pluck] (ca. 1854) : by means of plucking instead of bowing — used as a direction in music; compare ARCO

piz·zle \'pi-zəl\ n [prob. fr. Flem *pezel*; akin to LG *pesel* pizzle] (1523) **1** : the penis of an animal **2** : a whip made of a bull's pizzle

pj's \ˌpē-'jāz\ n pl [*pajamas*] (1951) : PAJAMAS

PK \ˌpē-'kā\ n (1943) : PSYCHOKINESIS

pla·ca·ble \'pla-kə-bəl, 'plā-\ adj (1586) : easily placated : TOLERANT, TRACTABLE — **pla·ca·bil·i·ty** \ˌpla-kə-'bi-lə-tē, ˌplā-\ n — **pla·ca·bly** \'pla-kə-blē, 'plā-\ adv

¹**plac·ard** \'pla-kərd, -ˌkärd\ n [ME *placquart* formal document, fr. MF, fr. *plaquier* to plate — more at PLAQUE] (1560) **1** : a notice posted in a public place : POSTER **2** : a small card or metal plaque

²**plac·ard** \-ˌkärd, -kərd\ vt (1813) **1 a** : to cover with or as if with posters **b** : to post in a public place **2** : to announce by or as if by posting

pla·cate \'plā-ˌkāt, 'pla-\ vt **pla·cat·ed; pla·cat·ing** [L *placatus*, pp. of *placare* — more at PLEASE] (1678) : to soothe or mollify esp. by concessions : APPEASE *syn* see PACIFY — **pla·cat·er** n — **pla·cat·ing·ly** \-ˌkā-tiŋ-lē\ adv — **pla·ca·tion** \plā-'kā-shən, pla-\ n — **pla·ca·tive** \'plā-ˌkā-tiv, 'pla-\ adj — **pla·ca·to·ry** \'plā-kə-ˌtōr-ē, 'pla-, -ˌtȯr-\ adj

¹**place** \'plās\ n [ME, fr. OF, open space, fr. L *platea* broad street, fr. Gk *plateia* (*hodos*), fr. fem. of *platys* broad, flat; akin to Skt *pṛthu* broad, L *planta* sole of the foot] (13c) **1 a** : physical environment : SPACE **b** : a way for admission or transit **c** : physical surroundings : ATMOSPHERE **2 a** : an indefinite region or expanse ⟨all over the ~⟩ **b** : a building or locality used for a special purpose ⟨a ~ of learning⟩ ⟨a fine eating ~⟩ **c** *archaic* : the three-dimensional compass of a material object **3 a** : a particular region, center of population, or location ⟨a nice ~ to visit⟩ **b** : a building, part of a building, or area occupied as a home ⟨our summer ~⟩ **4** : a particular part of a surface or body : SPOT **5** : relative position in a scale or series: as **a** : position in a

\ə\ abut \ᵊ\ kitten, F table \ər\ further \a\ ash \ā\ ace \ä\ mop, mar \au̇\ out \ch\ chin \e\ bet \ē\ easy \g\ go \i\ hit \ī\ ice \j\ job \ŋ\ sing \ō\ go \ȯ\ law \ȯi\ boy \th\ thin \t̲h̲\ the \ü\ loot \u̇\ foot \y\ yet \zh\ vision \á, k̲, ⁿ, œ, œ̄, ᵫ, ᵭ, ᵞ\ see Guide to Pronunciation social scale ⟨kept them in their ∼⟩   **b :** a step in a sequence ⟨in the first ∼, it's none of your business⟩   **c :** a position at the conclusion of a competition ⟨finished in last ∼⟩   **6 a :** a proper or designated niche ⟨the ∼ of education in society⟩   **b :** an appropriate moment or point ⟨this is not the ∼ to discuss compensation —Robert Moses⟩   **7 a :** an available seat or accommodation ⟨needs a ∼ to stay⟩   **b :** an empty or vacated position ⟨new ones will take their ∼⟩   **8 :** the position of a figure in relation to others of a row or series; *esp* : the position of a digit within a numeral   **9 a :** remunerative employment : JOB   **b :** prestige accorded to one of high rank : STATUS ⟨an endless quest for preferment and ∼ —*Time*⟩   **10 :** a public square : PLAZA   **11 :** a small street or court   **12 :** second place at the finish (as of a horse race) — **in place 1 :** in an original or proper position   **2 :** in the same spot without forward or backward movement ⟨run *in place*⟩

²**place** *vb* **placed; plac·ing** *vt* (15c)   **1 a :** to put in or as if in a particular place or position : SET   **b :** to present for consideration ⟨a question *placed* before the group⟩   **c :** to put in a particular state ⟨∼ a performer under contract⟩   **d :** to direct to a desired spot : to cause (the voice) to produce free and well resonated singing or speaking tones   **2 a :** to assign to a position in a series or category : RANK   **b :** ESTIMATE ⟨*placed* the value of the estate too high⟩   **c :** to identify by connecting with an associated context ⟨couldn't quite ∼ her face⟩ ⟨police *placed* them at the crime scene⟩   **3 :** to distribute in an orderly manner : ARRANGE   **4 :** to appoint to a position   **5 :** to find a place (as a home or employment) for   **6 a :** to give (an order) to a supplier   **b :** to give an order for ⟨∼ a bet⟩   **c :** to try to establish a connection for ⟨∼ a telephone call⟩ ∼ *vi* : to earn a given spot in a competition; *specif* : to come in second (as in a horse race) — **place·able** \ˈplā-sə-bəl\ *adj*

pla·ce·bo *n, pl* **-bos** (13c)   **1** \plä-ˈchā-(ˌ)bō\ [ME, fr. L, I shall please, fr. *placēre* to please — more at PLEASE]: the Roman Catholic vespers for the dead   **2** \plə-ˈsē-\ [L, I shall please]   **a** (1) : a medication prescribed more for the mental relief of the patient than for its actual effect on a disorder   (2) : an inert or innocuous substance used esp. in controlled experiments testing the efficacy of another substance (as a drug)   **b :** something tending to soothe

placebo effect *n* (1950) : improvement in the condition of a sick person that occurs in response to treatment but cannot be considered due to the specific treatment used

place·hold·er \ˈplās-ˌhōl-dər\ *n* (1958) : a symbol in a mathematical or logical expression that may be replaced by the name of any element of a set

¹**place·kick** \ˈplās-ˌkik\ *n* (1856) : the kicking of a ball (as a football) placed or held in a stationary position on the ground

²**placekick** *vt* (1856)   **1 :** to kick (a ball) from a stationary position   **2 :** to score by means of a placekick — **place·kick·er** *n*

place·less \-ləs\ *adj* (14c) : lacking a fixed location — **place·less·ly** *adv*

place·man \-mən\ *n* (1741) : a political appointee to a public office esp. in 18th century Britain

place mat *n* (1928) : a small often rectangular table mat on which a place setting is laid

place·ment \ˈplās-mənt\ *n* (1844)   **1 :** an act or instance of placing as   **a :** an accurately hit ball (as in tennis) that an opponent cannot return   **b :** the assignment of a person to a suitable place (as a job or a class in school)   **2 :** PLACEKICK

placement test *n* (1928) : a test usu. given to a student entering an educational institution to determine specific knowledge or proficiency in various subjects for the purpose of assignment to appropriate courses or classes

place–name \ˈplās-ˌnām\ *n* (1868) : the name of a geographical locality

pla·cen·ta \plə-ˈsen-tə\ *n, pl* **-centas** *or* **-cen·tae** \-ˈsen-(ˌ)tē\ [NL, fr. L, flat cake, fr. Gk *plakoenta*, acc. of *plakoeis*, fr. *plak-, plax* flat surface — more at FLUKE] (1691)   **1 :** the vascular organ in mammals except monotremes and marsupials that unites the fetus to the maternal uterus and mediates its metabolic exchanges through a more or less intimate association of uterine mucosal with chorionic and usu. allantoic tissues; *also* : an analogous organ in another animal   **2 :** a sporangium-bearing surface; *esp* : the part of the carpel bearing ovules — **pla·cen·tal** \-ˈsen-t³l\ *adj or n*

pla·cen·ta·tion \ˌpla-s³n-ˈtā-shən, plə-ˌsen-\ *n* (1760)   **1 :** the arrangement of placentas and ovules in a plant ovary   **2 a :** the development of the placenta and attachment of the fetus to the uterus during pregnancy   **b :** the morphological type of a placenta

¹**plac·er** \ˈplā-sər\ *n* (1579) : one that places: as   **a :** one that deposits or arranges   **b :** one of the winners in a competition

²**plac·er** \ˈpla-sər\ *n* [Sp, fr. Catal, submarine plain, fr. *plaza* place, fr. L *platea* broad street — more at PLACE] (1848) : an alluvial, marine, or glacial deposit containing particles of valuable mineral and esp. of gold

place setting *n* (1944) : a table service for one person

place value *n* (1911) : the value of the place of a digit in a numeral

plac·id \ˈpla-səd\ *adj* [L *placidus*, fr. *placēre* to please — more at PLEASE] (1626)   **1 :** serenely free of interruption or disturbance ⟨∼ skies⟩ ⟨a ∼ disposition⟩   **2 :** COMPLACENT   *syn* see CALM — **pla·cid·i·ty** \pla-ˈsi-də-tē, plə-\ *n* — **plac·id·ly** \ˈpla-səd-lē\ *adv* — **plac·id·ness** *n*

plack·et \ˈpla-kət\ *n* [origin unknown] (1605)   **1 a :** a slit in a garment (as a skirt) often forming the closure   **b** *archaic* : a pocket esp. in a woman's skirt   **2** *archaic* **a :** PETTICOAT   **b :** WOMAN

plac·oid \ˈpla-ˌkȯid\ *adj* [Gk *plak-, plax* flat surface] (1842) : of, relating to, or being a scale of dermal origin with an enamel-tipped spine characteristic of the elasmobranchs

pla·gal \ˈplā-gəl\ *adj* [ML *plagalis*, ultim. fr. Gk *plagios* oblique, sideways, fr. *plagos* side; akin to L *plaga* net, region, Gk *pelagos* sea] (1597)   **1** *of a church mode* : having the keynote on the 4th scale step — compare AUTHENTIC 4a   **2** *of a cadence* : progressing from the subdominant chord to the tonic — compare AUTHENTIC 4b

plage \ˈpläzh\ *n* [F, beach, luminous surface, fr. It *piaggia* beach, fr. LL *plagia*, fr. Gk *plagios* oblique] (1888)   **1 :** the beach of a seaside resort   **2 :** a bright region on the sun caused by the light emitted by clouds of calcium or hydrogen and often associated with a sunspot

pla·gia·rise *Brit var of* PLAGIARIZE

pla·gia·rism \ˈplā-jə-ˌri-zəm *also* -jē-ə-\ *n* (1621)   **1 :** an act or instance of plagiarizing   **2 :** something plagiarized — **pla·gia·rist** \-rist\ *n* — **pla·gia·ris·tic** \ˌplā-jə-ˈris-tik *also* -jē-ə-\ *adj*

pla·gia·rize \ˈplā-jə-ˌrīz *also* -jē-ə-\ *vb* **-rized; -riz·ing** [*plagiary*] *vt* (1716) : to steal and pass off (the ideas or words of another) as one's own : use (a created production) without crediting the source ∼ *vi* : to commit literary theft : present as new and original an idea or product derived from an existing source — **pla·gia·riz·er** *n*

pla·gia·ry \ˈplā-jē-ˌer-ē, -jə-rē\ *n, pl* **-ries** [L *plagiarius*, lit., plunderer, fr. *plagium* hunting net, fr. *plaga* net] (1601)   **1** *archaic* : one that plagiarizes   **2 :** PLAGIARISM

pla·gio·clase \ˈplā-j(ē-)ə-ˌklās, ˈpla-, -ˌklāz\ *n* [Gk *plagios* oblique + *klasis* breaking, fr. *klan* to break — more at CLAST] (ca. 1868) : a triclinic feldspar; *esp* : one having calcium or sodium in its composition

pla·gio·tro·pic \ˌplā-j(ē-)ə-ˈtrō-pik, ˌpla-, -ˈträ-\ *adj* [Gk *plagios* + ISV *-tropic*] (1882) : having the longer axis inclined away from the vertical

¹**plague** \ˈplāg\ *n* [ME *plage*, fr. MF, fr. LL *plaga*, fr. L, blow; akin to L *plangere* to strike — more at PLAINT] (14c)   **1 a :** a disastrous evil or affliction : CALAMITY   **b :** a destructively numerous influx ⟨a ∼ of locusts⟩   **2 a :** an epidemic disease causing a high rate of mortality : PESTILENCE   **b :** a virulent contagious febrile disease that is caused by a bacterium (*Yersinia pestis*) and that occurs in bubonic, pneumonic, and septicemic forms — called also *black death*   **3 a :** a cause of irritation : NUISANCE   **b :** a sudden unwelcome outbreak ⟨a ∼ of burglaries⟩

²**plague** *vt* **plagued; plagu·ing** (15c)   **1 :** to smite, infest, or afflict with or as if with disease, calamity, or natural evil   **2 a :** to cause worry or distress to : HAMPER, BURDEN   **b :** to disturb or annoy persistently   *syn* see WORRY — **plagu·er** *n*

plagu·ey *or* **plaguy** \ˈplā-gē, ˈple-\ *adj* (1615) : causing irritation or annoyance : TROUBLESOME — **plaguey** *adv* — **plagu·i·ly** \-gə-lē\ *adv*

plaice \ˈplās\ *n, pl* **plaice** [ME *plaice*, fr. MF *plaïs*, fr. LL *platessa*] (13c) : any of various flatfishes; *esp* : a large European flounder (*Pleuronectes platessa*) with red spots

plaid \ˈplad\ *n* [ScGael *plaide*] (1512)   **1 :** a rectangular length of tartan worn over the left shoulder as part of the Scottish national costume   **2 a :** a twilled woolen fabric with a tartan pattern   **b :** a fabric with a pattern of tartan or an imitation of tartan   **3 a :** TARTAN 1   **b :** a pattern of unevenly spaced repeated stripes crossing at right angles — **plaid** *adj* — **plaid·ed** \ˈpla-dəd\ *adj*

¹**plain** \ˈplān\ *vi* [ME, fr. OF *plaindre*, fr. L *plangere* to lament — more at PLAINT] (14c) *archaic* : COMPLAIN

²**plain** *n* [ME, fr. OF, fr. L *planum*, fr. neut. of *planus* flat, plain — more at FLOOR] (14c)   **1 a :** an extensive area of level or rolling treeless country   **b :** a broad unbroken expanse   **2 :** something free from artifice, ornament, or extraneous matter

³**plain** *adj* (14c)   **1** *archaic* : EVEN, LEVEL   **2 :** lacking ornament : UNDECORATED   **3 :** free of extraneous matter : PURE   **4 :** free of impediments to view : UNOBSTRUCTED   **5 a** (1) : evident to the mind or senses : OBVIOUS ⟨it's perfectly ∼ that they will resist⟩   (2) : CLEAR ⟨let me make my meaning ∼⟩   **b :** marked by outspoken candor : free from duplicity or subtlety : BLUNT ⟨∼ talk⟩   **6 a :** belonging to the great mass of humans   **b :** lacking special distinction or affectation : ORDINARY   **7 :** characterized by simplicity : not complicated ⟨∼ home-cooked meals⟩   **8 :** lacking beauty or ugliness   *syn* see COMMON, EVIDENT, FRANK — **plain·ly** *adv* — **plain·ness** \ˈplān-nəs\ *n*

⁴**plain** *adv* (14c) : in a plain manner ⟨saw them clearly and told you ∼ —*Amer. Documentation*⟩

⁵**plain** *adv* [partly fr. ME *plein* entire, complete, fr. MF, full, fr. L *plenus*; partly fr. ⁴*plain* — more at FULL] (1535) : ABSOLUTELY ⟨it ∼ galled me to pay fancy prices —F. R. Buckley⟩

plain-chant \ˈplān-ˌchant\ *n* [F *plain-chant*, lit., plain song] (ca. 1741) : PLAINSONG

plain-clothes \ˈplān-ˈklō(th)z\ *adj* (1866) : dressed in civilian clothes while on duty — used esp. of a police officer

plain-clothes·man \ˈplān-ˈklō(th)z-mən, -ˌman\ *n* (1899) : a plainclothes police officer

plain–Jane \ˈplān-ˈjān\ *adj* [fr. the name *Jane*] (1912) : not fancy or glamorous : ORDINARY

plain–laid \ˈplān-ˈlād\ *adj* (1881) *of a rope* : consisting of three strands laid right-handed

Plain People *n* (1904) : members of any of various Protestant groups (as Mennonites) esp. in the U.S. who wear distinctively plain clothes and adhere to a simple and traditional style of life excluding many conveniences of modern technology

Plains \ˈplānz\ *adj* (1844) : of or relating to No. American Indians of the Great Plains or to their culture

plain sailing *n* (1756) : easy progress over an unobstructed course

plains·man \ˈplānz-mən\ *n* [Great *Plains* + *man*] (1870) : an inhabitant of the plains

plain·song \ˈplān-ˌsȯŋ\ *n* (1513) : a monophonic rhythmically free liturgical chant of any of various Christian rites; *esp* : GREGORIAN CHANT

plain–spo·ken \-ˈspō-kən\ *adj* (1678) : CANDID, FRANK — **plain·spo·ken·ness** \-kən-nəs\ *n*

plaint \ˈplānt\ *n* [ME, fr. MF, fr. L *planctus*, fr. *plangere* to strike, beat one's breast, lament; akin to OHG *fluokhōn* to curse, Gk *plēssein* to strike] (13c)   **1 :** LAMENTATION, WAIL   **2 :** PROTEST, COMPLAINT

plain·text \ˈplān-ˌtekst\ *n* (1918) : the intelligible form of an encrypted text or of its elements — compare CIPHERTEXT

plaint·ful \ˈplānt-fəl\ *adj* (14c) : MOURNFUL

plain·tiff \ˈplān-təf\ *n* [ME *plaintif*, fr. MF, fr. *plaintif*, adj.] (14c) : a person who brings a legal action — compare DEFENDANT

plain·tive \ˈplān-tiv\ *adj* [ME *plaintif* grieving, fr. MF, fr. *plaint*] (1579) : expressive of suffering or woe : MELANCHOLY — **plain·tive·ly** *adv* — **plain·tive·ness** *n*

plain–vanilla *adj* (1975) : lacking special features or qualities : BASIC

plain weave *n* (1888) : a weave in which the threads interlace alternately

plain–woven *adj* (1925) : made in plain weave

plais·ter \ˈplas-tər, ˈpläs-\ *var of* PLASTER

¹**plait** \ˈplāt, ˈplat\ *n* [ME *pleit*, fr. MF, fr. (assumed) VL *plicitum*, fr. neut. of L *plicitus*, pp. of *plicare* to fold — more at PLY] (14c)   **1 :** PLEAT   **2 :** a braid of material (as hair or straw); *specif* : PIGTAIL

²plait *vt* (14c) **1** : PLEAT 1 **2 a** : to interweave the strands or locks of : BRAID **b** : to make by plaiting — **plait·er** *n*

plait·ing *n* (15c) : the interlacing of strands : BRAIDING

¹plan \'plan\ *n* [F, plane, foundation, ground plan; partly fr. L *planum* level ground, fr. neut. of *planus* level; partly fr. F *planter* to plant, fix in place, fr. LL *plantare* — more at FLOOR, PLANT] (1706) **1** : a drawing or diagram drawn on a plane: as **a** : a top or horizontal view of an object **b** : a large-scale map of a small area **2 a** : a method for achieving an end **b** : an often customary method of doing something : PROCEDURE **c** : a detailed formulation of a program of action **d** : GOAL, AIM **3** : an orderly arrangement of parts of an overall design or objective **4** : a detailed program (as for payment or the provision of some service) ⟨pension ∼⟩ — **plan·less** \-ləs\ *adj* — **plan·less·ly** *adv* — **plan·less·ness** *n*

syn PLAN, DESIGN, PLOT, SCHEME, PROJECT mean a method devised for making or doing something or achieving an end. PLAN always implies mental formulation and sometimes graphic representation ⟨*plans* for a house⟩. DESIGN often suggests a particular pattern and some degree of achieved order or harmony ⟨a *design* for a new dress⟩. PLOT implies a laying out in clearly distinguished sections with attention to their relations and proportions ⟨the *plot* of the play⟩. SCHEME stresses calculation of the end in view and may apply to a plan motivated by craftiness and self-interest ⟨a *scheme* to defraud the government⟩. PROJECT often stresses imaginative scope and vision ⟨a *project* to develop the waterfront⟩.

²plan *vb* **planned; plan·ning** *vt* (1728) **1** : to arrange the parts of : DESIGN **2** : to devise or project the realization or achievement of ⟨∼ a program⟩ **3** : to have in mind : INTEND ∼ *vi* : to make plans — **plan·ner** *n*

plan- *or* **plano-** *comb form* [L *planus*] **1** : flat ⟨*plano*sol⟩ **2** : flat and ⟨*plano*-concave⟩

pla·nar \'plā-nər, -,när\ *adj* (1850) **1** : of, relating to, or lying in a plane **2** : two-dimensional in quality — **pla·nar·i·ty** \plā-'nar-ə-tē\ *n*

pla·nar·ia \plə-'nar-ē-ə, -'ner-\ *n* [NL, fr. fem. of LL *planarius* lying on a plane, fr. L *planum* plane] (ca. 1909) : PLANARIAN; *esp* : any of a genus (*Planaria*) of 2-eyed planarian worms

pla·nar·i·an \-ē-ən\ *n* [NL *Planaria*] (ca. 1858) : any of various dark-colored freshwater triclad flatworms (family Planariidae) with two eyespots and a triangular head; *broadly* : TRICLAD

pla·na·tion \plā-'nā-shən\ *n* (1877) : the condition or process of becoming flattened

plan·chet \'plan-chət\ *n* [dim. of *planch* flat plate, fr. MF *planche*] (1611) **1** : a metal disk to be stamped as a coin **2** : a small metal or plastic disk

plan·chette \plan-'shet\ *n* [F, fr. dim. of *planche* plank, fr. L *planca*] (1860) : a small triangular or heart-shaped board supported on casters at two points and a vertical pencil at a third and believed to produce automatic writing when lightly touched by the fingers; *also* : a similar board without a pencil

Planck's constant \'plän(k)s-, 'plaŋ(k)s-\ *n* [Max K.E.L. *Planck*] (1910) : a constant that gives the unvarying ratio of the energy of a quantum of radiation to its frequency and that has an approximate value of 6.626×10^{-34} J·s — symbol *h*

¹plane \'plān\ *vb* **planed; plan·ing** [ME, fr. MF *planer*, fr. LL *planare*, fr. L *planus* level — more at FLOOR] *vt* (14c) **1 a** : to make smooth or even : LEVEL **b** : to make smooth or even by use of a plane **2** : to remove by planing — often used with *away* or *off* ∼ *vi* **1** : to work with a plane **2** : to do the work of a plane — **plan·er** *n*

²plane *n* [ME, fr. MF, fr. L *platanus*, fr. Gk *platanos*; prob. akin to Gk *platys* broad — more at PLACE] (14c) : any of a genus (*Platanus* of the family Platanaceae, the plane-tree family) of trees with large palmately lobed leaves and flowers in globose heads — called also *buttonwood*, *plane tree*, *sycamore*

³plane *n* [ME, fr. MF, fr. LL *plana*, fr. *planare*] (14c) : a tool for smoothing or shaping a wood surface

⁴plane *n* [L *planum*, fr. neut. of *planus* level] (1604) **1 a** : a surface of such nature that a straight line joining two of its points lies wholly in the surface **b** : a flat or level surface **2** : a level of existence, consciousness, or development ⟨on the intellectual ∼⟩ **3 a** : one of the main supporting surfaces of an airplane **b** [by shortening] : AIRPLANE

³plane

⁵plane *adj* [L *planus*] (1704) **1** : having no elevations or depressions : FLAT **2** : of, relating to, or dealing with geometric planes **b** : lying in a plane ⟨a ∼ curve⟩ *syn* see LEVEL

⁶plane *vi* **planed; plan·ing** [ME, fr. MF *planer*, fr. *plain* level, plain] (15c) **1 a** : to fly while keeping the wings motionless **b** : to skim across the surface of the water **2** : to travel by airplane

plane angle *n* (1570) : an angle that for a given dihedral angle is formed by two intersecting lines each of which lies on a face of the dihedral angle and is perpendicular to the edge of the face

plane geometry *n* (1747) : a branch of elementary geometry that deals with plane figures

plane·load \'plān-,lōd\ *n* (1941) : a load that fills an airplane

plane of polarization (1831) : the plane in which the magnetic-vibration component of plane-polarized electromagnetic radiation lies

plane·polarized *adj* (ca. 1853) : vibrating in a single plane ⟨*plane*-polarized light waves⟩

pla·ner tree \'plā-nər-\ *n* [J. J. *Planer* †1789 Ger. botanist] (ca. 1810) : a small-leaved No. American tree (*Planera aquatica*) of the elm family with an oval ribbed fruit

plan·et \'pla-nət\ *n* [ME *planete*, fr. OF, fr. LL *planeta*, modif. of Gk *planēt-, planēs*, lit., wanderer, fr. *planasthai* to wander — more at FLOOR] (13c) **1 a** : any of the seven celestial bodies sun, moon, Venus, Jupiter, Mars, Mercury, and Saturn that in ancient belief have motions of their own among the fixed stars **b** (1) : any of the large bodies that revolve around the sun in the solar system (2) : a similar body associated with another star **c** : EARTH — usu. used with *the* **2** : a celestial body held to influence the fate of human beings **3** : a person or thing of great importance : LUMINARY — **plan·et·like** \-,līk\ *adj*

PLANETS

| NAME | SYMBOL | MEAN DISTANCE FROM THE SUN | | PERIOD OF REVOLUTION | EQUA-TORIAL |
		astronomical units	million miles	IN DAYS OR YEARS	DIAMETER IN MILES
Mercury	☿	0.387	36.0	87.97 d.	3,032
Venus	♀	0.723	67.2	224.70 d.	7,523
Earth	⊕	1.000	92.9	365.26 d.	7,928
Mars	♂	1.524	141.5	686.98 d.	4,218
Jupiter	♃	5.203	483.4	11.86 y.	88,900
Saturn	♄	9.522	884.6	29.46 y.	74,900
Uranus	♅	19.201	1783.8	84.01 y.	31,800
Neptune	♆	30.074	2793.9	164.79 y.	30,800
Pluto	♇	39.725	3690.5	247.69 y.	1,400

plane table *n* (1607) : an instrument consisting essentially of a drawing board on a tripod with a ruler pointed at the object observed and used for plotting the lines of a survey directly from observation

plan·e·tar·i·um \,pla-nə-'ter-ē-əm\ *n*, *pl* **-i·ums** *or* **-ia** \-ē-ə\ (1860) **1** : a model or representation of the solar system **2 a** : an optical device for projecting various celestial images and effects **b** : a building or room housing such a projector

plan·e·tary \'pla-nə-,ter-ē\ *adj* (1607) **1 a** : of, relating to, being, or resembling a planet **b** : ERRATIC, WANDERING **c** : having a motion like that of a planet ⟨∼ electrons⟩ **d** : IMMENSE ⟨the scope of this project has reached ∼ proportions⟩ **2 a** : of, relating to, or belonging to the earth : TERRESTRIAL **b** : GLOBAL, WORLDWIDE **3** : having or consisting of an epicyclic train of gear wheels

planetary nebula *n* (1785) : a usu. compact luminous ring-shaped nebula that is composed of matter which has been ejected from a hot star at its center

planetary science *n* (1969) : PLANETOLOGY — **planetary scientist** *n*

plan·e·tes·i·mal \,pla-nə-'te-sə-məl, -zə-məl\ *n* [planet + -esimal (as in *infinitesimal*)] (1903) : any of numerous small solid celestial bodies that may have existed at an early stage of the development of the solar system

planetesimal hypothesis *n* (1904) : a hypothesis in astronomy: the planets have evolved by aggregation from planetesimals

plan·et·oid \'pla-nə-,tȯid\ *n* (1803) : a small body resembling a planet; *esp* : ASTEROID — **plan·et·oi·dal** \,pla-nə-'tȯi-d⁹l\ *adj*

plan·et·ol·o·gy \,pla-nə-'tä-lə-jē\ *n*, *pl* **-gies** (1907) : a branch of astronomy that deals with the condensed matter of the solar system and esp. with the planets and their moons — **plan·et·o·log·i·cal** \,pla-nə-t⁹l-'ä-ji-kəl\ *adj* — **plan·et·ol·o·gist** \,pla-nə-'tä-lə-jist\ *n*

plan·et·strick·en \'pla-nət-,stri-kən\ *or* **plan·et·struck** \-,strək\ *adj* (1599) **1** *archaic* : affected by the influence of a planet **2** *archaic* : PANIC-STRICKEN

planet wheel *n* (1827) : a gear wheel that revolves around the wheel with which it meshes in an epicyclic train

plan·et·wide \'pla-nət-'wīd\ *adj* (1969) : extending throughout or involving an entire planet

plan·form \'plan-,fȯrm\ *n* (1908) : the contour of an object (as an airplane) or mass as viewed from above

plan·gen·cy \'plan-jən(t)-sē\ *n* (1858) : the quality or state of being plangent

plan·gent \-jənt\ *adj* [L *plangent-, plangens*, prp. of *plangere* to strike, lament — more at PLAINT] (1858) **1** : having a loud reverberating sound **2** : having an expressive and esp. plaintive quality — **plan·gent·ly** *adv*

pla·nim·e·ter \plā-'ni-mə-tər, plə-\ *n* [F *planimètre*, fr. L *planum* plane + F *-mètre* -meter] (ca. 1858) : an instrument for measuring the area of a plane figure by tracing its boundary line

pla·ni·met·ric \,plā-nə-'me-trik\ *adj* (ca. 1828) **1** : of, relating to, or made by means of a planimeter ⟨∼ measurements⟩ **2** : of a map; having no indications of relief — **pla·ni·met·ri·cal·ly** \-tri-k(ə-)lē\ *adv*

plan·ish \'pla-nish\ *vt* [ME *planysshen*, fr. MF *planiss-*, stem of *planir* to make smooth, fr. *plan* level, fr. L *planus* — more at FLOOR] (14c) : to smooth, toughen, and finish (metal) by hammering lightly — **plan·ish·er** *n*

pla·ni·sphere \'pla-nə-,sfir\ *n* [alter. of ME *planisperie*, fr. ML *planisphaerium*, fr. L *planum* plane + *sphaera* sphere] (1571) : a representation of the circles of the sphere on a plane; *esp* : a polar projection of the celestial sphere and the stars on a plane with adjustable circles or other appendages for showing celestial phenomena for any given time — **pla·ni·spher·ic** \,plā-nə-'sfir-ik, -'sfer-\ *adj*

¹plank \'plaŋk\ *n* [ME, fr. ONF *planke*, fr. L *planca*] (13c) **1 a** : a heavy thick board; *esp* : one 2 to 4 inches (5 to 10 centimeters) thick and at least 8 inches (20 centimeters) wide **b** : an object made of a plank or planking **c** : PLANKING **2 a** : an article in the platform of a political party **b** : a principal item of a policy or program

²plank *vt* (15c) **1** : to cover, build, or floor with planks **2** : SET DOWN 1, 2 — usu. used with *down* **3** : to cook and serve on a board ⟨∼ed salmon⟩ ⟨∼ed steak⟩

plank·ing *n* (15c) **1** : the act or process of covering or fitting with planks **2** : a quantity of planks

plank·ter \'plaŋ(k)-tər\ *n* [Gk *planktēr* wanderer, fr. *plazesthai*] (1935) : a planktonic organism

plank·ton \'plaŋ(k)-tən, -,tän\ *n* [G, fr. Gk, neut. of *planktos* drifting, fr. *plazesthai* to wander, drift, middle voice of *plazein* to drive astray; akin to L *plangere* to strike — more at PLAINT] (1891) : the passively floating or weakly swimming usu. minute animal and plant life of a body of water — **plank·ton·ic** \plaŋ(k)-'tä-nik\ *adj*

Planned Parenthood *service mark* — used for research and dissemination of information on contraception

\ə\ abut \ᵊ\ kitten, F table \ər\ further \a\ ash \ā\ ace \ä\ mop, mar
\au̇\ out \ch\ chin \e\ bet \ē\ easy \g\ go \i\ hit \ī\ ice \j\ job
\ŋ\ sing \ō\ go \ȯ\ law \ȯi\ boy \th\ thin \t̶h\ the \ü\ loot \u̇\ foot
\y\ yet \zh\ vision \à, k̲, ⁿ, œ, œ̄, ᵫ, ᵫ̄, ᵞ\ *see* Guide to Pronunciation

plan·ning n (1748) : the act or process of making or carrying out plans; specif : the establishment of goals, policies, and procedures for a social or economic unit ⟨city ∼⟩ ⟨business ∼⟩

plano- — see PLAN-

pla·no·con·cave \ˌplā-nō-(ˌ)kän-ˈkāv, -ˈkän-ˌ\ adj (1693) : flat on one side and concave on the other

pla·no·con·vex \-(ˌ)kän-ˈveks, -ˈkän-ˌ, -kən-ˈ\ adj (1665) : flat on one side and convex on the other

pla·nog·ra·phy \plā-ˈnä-grə-fē, plə-\ n (ca. 1909) : a process (as lithography) for printing from a plane surface — **pla·no·graph·ic** \ˌplā-nə-ˈgra-fik\ adj

pla·no·sol \ˈplā-nə-ˌsäl, -ˌsȯl\ n [plan- + L solum ground, soil] (1938) : any of an intrazonal group of soils that have a strongly leached upper layer over a compacted clay or silt and occur on smooth flat uplands

plan position indicator n (1932) : a radarscope having a sweep synchronized with a usu. rotating antenna so that the radar return can be used to find range and bearing

¹plant \ˈplant\ vb [ME, fr. OE plantian, fr. LL plantare to plant, fix in place, fr. L, to plant, fr. planta plant] vt (bef. 12c) **1 a :** to put or set in the ground for growth ⟨∼ seeds⟩ **b :** to set or sow with seeds or plants **c :** IMPLANT **2 a :** ESTABLISH, INSTITUTE **b :** COLONIZE, SETTLE **c :** to place (animals) in a new locality **d :** to stock with animals **3 a :** to place in or on the ground **b :** to place firmly or forcibly ⟨∼ed a hard blow on his chin⟩ **4 a :** CONCEAL **b :** to covertly place for discovery, publication, or dissemination ∼ vi : to plant something — **plant·able** \ˈplan-tə-bəl\ adj

²plant n [ME plante, fr. OE, fr. L planta] (bef. 12c) **1 a :** a young tree, vine, shrub, or herb planted or suitable for planting **b :** any of a kingdom (Plantae) of living things typically lacking locomotive movement or obvious nervous or sensory organs and possessing cellulose cell walls **2 a :** the land, buildings, machinery, apparatus, and fixtures employed in carrying on a trade or an industrial business **b :** a factory or workshop for the manufacture of a particular product **c :** the total facilities available for production or service **d :** the buildings and other physical equipment of an institution **3 :** an act of planting **4 :** something or someone planted — **plant·like** \-ˌlīk\ adj

Plan·tag·e·net \plan-ˈta-jə-nət, -ˈtaj-nət\ adj [Plantagenet, nickname of the family adopted as surname] (1868) : of or relating to a royal house ruling England from 1154 to 1485 — **Plantagenet** n

¹plan·tain \ˈplan-tᵊn\ n [ME, fr. OF, fr. L plantagin-, plantago, fr. planta sole of the foot; fr. its broad leaves — more at PLACE] (13c) : any of a genus (Plantago of the family Plantaginaceae, the plantain family) of short-stemmed elliptic-leaved herbs with spikes of minute greenish flowers

²plantain n [Sp plántano, plátano plane tree, banana tree, fr. ML plantanus plane tree, alter. of L platanus — more at PLANE] (1555) **1 :** a banana plant (Musa paradisiaca) **2 :** the angular greenish starchy fruit of the plantain that is a staple food in the tropics when cooked

plantain lily n (1882) : any of a genus (Hosta) of perennial plants of the lily family with densely growing basal leaves and racemose white or violet flowers — called also hosta, funkia

plan·tar \ˈplan-tər, -ˌtär\ adj [L plantaris, fr. planta sole — more at PLACE] (ca. 1706) : of or relating to the sole of the foot ⟨∼ wart⟩

plan·ta·tion \plan-ˈtā-shən\ n (1569) **1 :** a usu. large group of plants and esp. trees under cultivation **2 :** a settlement in a new country or region ⟨Plymouth Plantation⟩ **3 a :** a place that is planted or under cultivation **b :** an agricultural estate usu. worked by resident labor

plant·er \ˈplan-tər\ n (14c) **1 :** one that cultivates plants: as **a** (1) : FARMER (2) : one who owns or operates a plantation **b :** a planting machine or implement **2 :** one who settles or founds a place and esp. a new colony **3 :** a container in which ornamental plants are grown

planter's punch n (1924) : a punch made of rum, lime or lemon juice, sugar, water, and sometimes bitters

plant food n (1869) **1 :** FOOD 1b **2 :** FERTILIZER

plant hormone n (1935) : an organic substance other than a nutrient that in minute amounts modifies a plant physiological process; esp : one produced by a plant and active elsewhere than at the site of production

plan·ti·grade \ˈplan-tə-ˌgrād\ adj [F, fr. L planta sole + F -grade] (1831) : walking on the sole with the heel touching the ground ⟨humans are ∼⟩ — **plantigrade** n

plant·ing n (1632) : an area where plants are grown for commercial or decorative purposes; also : the plants cultivated in such an area

plant kingdom n (1884) : a basic group of natural objects that includes all living and extinct plants — compare ANIMAL KINGDOM, MINERAL KINGDOM

plant·let \ˈplant-lət\ n (1816) : a small or young plant

plant louse n (1805) : APHID; also : any of various small insects (as a jumping plant louse) of similar habits

plan·to·cra·cy \plan-ˈtä-krə-sē\ n [planter + -o- + -cracy] (ca. 1846) **1 :** a ruling class made up of planters **2 :** government by planters

plants·man \ˈplants-mən, -ˌman\ n (1881) : a person skilled with plants : an expert gardener or horticulturist

plan·u·la \ˈplan-yə-lə\ n, pl -lae \-ˌlē, -ˌlī\ [NL, fr. L planus level, flat — more at FLOOR] (1870) : the very young usu. flattened oval or oblong free-swimming ciliated larva of a coelenterate

plaque \ˈplak\ n [F, fr. MF, metal sheet, fr. plaquier to plate, fr. MD placken to piece, patch; akin to MD placke piece, MHG placke patch] (1848) **1 a :** an ornamental brooch; esp : the badge of an honorary order **b :** a flat thin piece (as of metal) used for decoration **c :** a commemorative or identifying inscribed tablet **2 a :** a localized abnormal patch on a body part or surface **b :** a film of mucus that harbors bacteria on a tooth **c :** an atherosclerotic lesion **d :** a histopathologic lesion of brain tissue that is characteristic of Alzheimer's disease and consists of a cluster of degenerating nerve endings and dendrites around a core of amyloid **3 :** a clear area in a bacterial culture produced by destruction of cells by a virus

¹plash \ˈplash\ n [prob. imit.] (1513) : SPLASH

²plash vi (1542) : to cause a splashing or spattering effect ∼ vt : to break the surface of (water) : SPLASH

-plasia or **-plasy** n comb form [NL -plasia, fr. Gk plasis molding, fr. plassein] : development : formation ⟨hyperplasia⟩ ⟨homoplasy⟩

plasm \ˈpla-zəm\ n [LL plasma something molded] (1747) : PLASMA

plasm- or **plasmo-** comb form [F, fr. NL plasma] : plasma ⟨plasmodium⟩ ⟨plasmolysis⟩

-plasm n comb form [G -plasma, fr. NL plasma] : formative or formed material (as of a cell or tissue) ⟨endoplasm⟩

plas·ma \ˈplaz-mə\ n [G, fr. LL, something molded, fr. Gk, fr. plassein to mold — more at PLASTER] (1772) **1 :** a green faintly translucent quartz **2** [NL, fr. LL] **a :** the fluid part of blood, lymph, or milk as distinguished from suspended material **b :** the juice that can be expressed from muscle **3 :** PROTOPLASM **4 :** a collection of charged particles (as in the atmospheres of stars or in a metal) containing about equal numbers of positive ions and electrons and exhibiting some properties of a gas but differing from a gas in being a good conductor of electricity and in being affected by a magnetic field — **plas·mat·ic** \plaz-ˈma-tik\ adj

plasma cell n (1888) : a lymphocyte that is a mature antibody-secreting B cell

plas·ma·gel \ˈplaz-mə-ˌjel\ n (1923) : gelated cytoplasm; esp : the outer firm zone of a pseudopodium

plas·ma·gene \-ˌjēn\ n [ISV] (1939) : an extranuclear determiner of hereditary characteristics with a capacity for replication similar to that of a nuclear gene

plasma jet n (1957) : a stream of very hot ionized plasma; also : a device for producing such a stream

plas·ma·lem·ma \ˌplaz-mə-ˈle-mə\ n [NL, fr. plasma + Gk lemma husk — more at LEMMA] (1923) : PLASMA MEMBRANE

plasma membrane n (1900) : a semipermeable limiting layer of cell protoplasm — called also cell membrane; see CELL illustration

plas·ma·phe·re·sis \ˌplaz-mə-fə-ˈrē-səs, -ˈfer-ə-səs\ n [NL, fr. plasm- + Gk aphairesis taking off — more at APHAERESIS] (1914) : a process for obtaining blood plasma without depleting the donor or patient of other blood constituents (as red blood cells) by separating out the plasma from the whole blood and returning the rest to the donor's or patient's circulatory system

plas·ma·sol \ˈplaz-mə-ˌsäl, -ˌsȯl, -ˌsōl\ n (1923) : cytoplasm in the form of a sol esp. in a pseudopodium or amoeboid cell

plasma torch n (1959) : a device that heats a gas by electrical means to form a plasma for high-temperature operations (as melting metal)

plas·mid \ˈplaz-məd\ n [plasma + ²-id] (1952) : an extrachromosomal ring of DNA esp. of bacteria that replicates autonomously

plas·min \-mən\ n (ca. 1866) : a proteolytic enzyme that dissolves the fibrin of blood clots

plas·min·o·gen \plaz-ˈmi-nə-jən\ n (1945) : the precursor of plasmin that is found in blood plasma and serum

plas·mo·des·ma \ˌplaz-mə-ˈdez-mə\ also **plas·mo·desm** \ˈplaz-mə-ˌdezəm\ n, pl **-des·ma·ta** \ˈdez-mə-tə\ or **-des·mas** \ˈdez-məz\ [NL plasmodesma, fr. plasma + Gk desmat-, desma bond, fr. dein to bind — more at DIADEM] (1905) : one of the cytoplasmic strands that pass through openings in some plant cell walls and provide living bridges between cells

plas·mo·di·um \plaz-ˈmō-dē-əm\ n, pl **-dia** \-dē-ə\ [NL, fr. plasm- + -odium thing resembling, fr. Gk -ōdēs like] (1875) **1 a :** a motile multinucleate mass of protoplasm resulting from fusion of uninucleate amoeboid cells; also : an organism (as a stage of a slime mold) that consists of such a structure **b :** SYNCYTIUM 1 **2 :** an individual malaria parasite

plas·mog·a·my \plaz-ˈmä-gə-mē\ n [ISV] (1912) : fusion of the cytoplasm of two or more cells as distinguished from fusion of nuclei

plas·mol·y·sis \plaz-ˈmä-lə-səs\ n [NL] (1883) : shrinking of the cytoplasm away from the wall of a living cell due to outward osmotic flow of water — **plas·mo·lyt·ic** \ˌplaz-mə-ˈli-tik\ adj

plas·mo·lyze \ˈplaz-mə-ˌlīz\ vb **-lyzed; -lyz·ing** vt (1888) : to subject to plasmolysis ∼ vi : to undergo plasmolysis

-plast n comb form [MF -plaste thing molded, fr. LL -plastus, -plastos, fr. plastos molded, fr. plassein] : organized particle or granule : cell ⟨chromoplast⟩

¹plas·ter \ˈplas-tər\ n [ME, fr. OE, fr. L emplastrum, fr. Gk emplastron, fr. emplassein to plaster on, fr. en- + plassein to mold, plaster; perh. akin to L planus level, flat — more at FLOOR] (bef. 12c) **1 :** a medicated or protective dressing that consists of a film (as of cloth or plastic) spread with a usu. medicated substance ⟨adhesive ∼⟩; broadly : something applied to heal and soothe **2 :** a pasty composition (as of lime, water, and sand) that hardens on drying and is used for coating walls, ceilings, and partitions — **plas·tery** \-t(ə-)rē\ adj

²plaster vb **plas·tered; plas·ter·ing** \-t(ə-)riŋ\ vt (14c) **1 :** to overlay or cover with plaster : COAT **2 :** to apply a plaster to **3 a :** to cover over or conceal as if with a coat of plaster **b :** to apply as a coating or incrustation **c :** to smooth down with a sticky or shiny substance ⟨∼ed his hair down⟩ **4 :** to fasten or apply tightly to another surface **5 :** to treat with plaster of paris **6 :** to affix to or place on esp. conspicuously or in quantity **7 :** to inflict heavy damage or loss on esp. by a concentrated or unremitting attack ∼ vi : to apply plaster — **plas·ter·er** \-tər-ər\ n

plas·ter·board \ˈplas-tər-ˌbȯrd, -ˌbȯrd\ n (1897) : a board made of several plies of fiberboard, paper, or felt usu. bonded to a hardened gypsum plaster core and used esp. as wallboard

plaster cast n (1825) **1 :** a sculptor's model in plaster of paris **2 :** a rigid dressing of gauze impregnated with plaster of paris

plas·tered \ˈplas-tərd\ adj (1902) : DRUNK, INTOXICATED

plastering n (15c) **1 :** a coating of or as if of plaster **2 :** a decisive defeat

plaster of par·is \-ˈpar-əs\ often cap 2d P [Paris, France] (15c) : a white powdery slightly hydrated calcium sulfate $CaSO_4·\frac{1}{2}H_2O$ or $2CaSO_4·H_2O$ made by calcining gypsum and used chiefly for casts and molds in the form of a quick-setting paste with water

plaster saint n (1890) : a person without human failings

plas·ter·work \ˈplas-tər-ˌwərk\ n (1600) : plastering often ornate in design used to finish architectural constructions

¹plas·tic \ˈplas-tik\ adj [L plasticus of molding, fr. Gk plastikos, fr. plassein to mold, form] (1632) **1 :** FORMATIVE, CREATIVE ⟨∼ forces in nature⟩ **2 a :** capable of being molded or modeled ⟨∼ clay⟩ **b :** capable of adapting to varying conditions : PLIABLE ⟨ecologically ∼ animals⟩ **3 :** SCULPTURAL **4 :** made or consisting of a plastic **5 :** capable of being deformed continuously and permanently in any direction without rupture **6 :** of, relating to, or involving plastic surgery **7**

: having a quality suggestive of mass-produced plastic goods; *esp* : AR-
TIFICIAL 4 〈~ smiles〉
syn PLASTIC, PLIABLE, PLIANT, DUCTILE, MALLEABLE, ADAPTABLE mean
susceptible of being modified in form or nature. PLASTIC applies to
substances soft enough to be molded yet capable of hardening into the
desired fixed form 〈*plastic* materials allow the sculptor greater free-
dom〉. PLIABLE suggests something easily bent, folded, twisted, or
manipulated 〈*pliable* rubber tubing〉. PLIANT may stress flexibility and
sometimes connote springiness 〈an athletic shoe with a *pliant* sole〉.
DUCTILE applies to what can be drawn out or extended with ease 〈*ductile* metals such as copper〉. MALLEABLE applies to what may be pressed
or beaten into shape 〈the *malleable* properties of gold enhance its
value〉. ADAPTABLE implies the capability of being easily modified to
suit other conditions, needs, or uses 〈computer hardware that is
adaptable〉.
²**plastic** *n* (1905)   **1** : a plastic substance; *specif* : any of numerous
organic synthetic or processed materials that are mostly thermoplastic
or thermosetting polymers of high molecular weight and that can be
made into objects, films, or filaments   **2** : credit cards used for payment — **plas·ticky** \'plas-ti-kē\ *adj*
-plastic *adj comb form* [Gk *-plastikos*, fr. *plassein*]   **1** : developing
: forming 〈thrombo*plastic*〉   **2** : of or relating to 〈something designated by a term ending in *-plasm, -plast, -plasty,* or *-plasy*〉 〈homoplas-
tic〉 〈neo*plastic*〉
plas·ti·cal·ly \'plas-ti-k(ə-)lē\ *adv* (1835)   **1** : in a plastic manner   **2**
: with respect to plastic qualities
plastic art *n* (ca. 1907)   **1** : art (as sculpture or bas-relief) characterized by modeling : three-dimensional art   **2** : visual art (as painting,
sculpture, or film) esp. as distinguished from art that is written (as
poetry or music) — often used in pl.
plastic foam *n* (1943) : EXPANDED PLASTIC
plas·ti·cine *also* **plas·ti·cene** \'plas-tə-,sēn\ *n* [fr. *Plasticine,* a trade-
mark] (1897) : a plastic paste used for models and sculptures
plas·tic·i·ty \pla-'sti-sə-tē\ *n* (ca. 1783)   **1** : the quality or state of
being plastic; *esp* : capacity for being molded or altered   **2** : the ability
to retain a shape attained by pressure deformation   **3** : the capacity of
organisms with the same genotype to vary in developmental pattern, in
phenotype, or in behavior according to varying environmental conditions
plas·ti·cize \'plas-tə-,sīz\ *vt* **-cized; -ciz·ing** (1919)   **1** : to make plastic   **2** : to treat with a plastic 〈a *plasticized* mattress cover〉 — **plas·ti-
ci·za·tion** \,plas-tə-sə-'zā-shən\ *n*
plas·ti·ciz·er \'plas-tə-,sī-zər\ *n* (1925) : one that plasticizes; *specif* : a
chemical added esp. to rubbers and resins to impart flexibility, workability, or stretchability
plastic surgeon *n* (1946) : a specialist in plastic surgery
plastic surgery *n* (1842) : surgery concerned with the repair, restoration, or improvement of lost, injured, defective, or misshapen body
parts
plas·tid \'plas-təd\ *n* [G, fr. Gk *plastos* molded] (1885) : any of various
cytoplasmic organelles (as an amyloplast or chloroplast) of photosynthetic cells that serve in many cases as centers of special metabolic
activities — **plas·tid·i·al** \pla-'sti-dē-əl\ *adj*
plas·ti·sol \'plas-tə-,säl, -,sōl\ *n* [*plastic* + ⁴*sol*] (1946) : a substance
consisting of a mixture of a resin and a plasticizer that can be molded,
cast, or made into a continuous film by application of heat
plas·to·cy·a·nin \,plas-tō-'sī-ə-nən\ *n* [Gk *plastos* + E *cyan-* + ¹*-in*]
(1961) : a copper-containing protein that acts as an intermediary in
photosynthetic electron transport
plas·to·qui·none \,plas-(,)tō-kwi-'nōn, -'kwi-,\ *n* [Gk *plastos* + E *quinone*] (1958) : a plant substance that is related to vitamin K and plays
a role in photosynthetic phosphorylation
plas·tral \'plas-trəl\ *adj* (1889) : of or relating to a plastron
plas·tron \'plas-trən\ *n* [MF, fr. OIt *piastrone,* aug. of *piastra* thin
metal plate — more at PIASTRE] (ca. 1507)   **1 a** : a metal breastplate
formerly worn under the hauberk   **b** : a quilted pad worn in fencing
practice to protect the chest, waist, and the side on which the weapon
is held   **2** : the ventral part of the shell of a tortoise or turtle consisting
typically of nine symmetrically placed bones overlaid by horny plates
3 a : a trimming like a bib for a woman's dress   **b** : DICKEY 1a   **4** : a
thin film of air held by water-repellent hairs of some aquatic insects
-plasty *n comb form* [F *-plastie,* fr. LGk *-plastia* molding, fr. Gk *-plastēs*
molder, fr. *plassein*] : plastic surgery 〈osteo*plasty*〉
-plasy — see -PLASIA
¹**plat** \'plat\ *vt* **plat·ted; plat·ting** [ME, alter. of *plaiten*] (14c) : PLAIT
²**plat** *n* (1535) : PLAIT
³**plat** *n* [prob. alter. of *plot*] (15c)   **1** : a small piece of ground (as a lot
or quadrat) : PLOT   **2** : a plan, map, or chart of a piece of land with
actual or proposed features (as lots); *also* : the land represented
⁴**plat** *vt* **plat·ted; plat·ting** (1751) : to make a plat of
plat·an \'pla-t⁹n\ *n* [ME, fr. L *platanus* — more at PLANE] (14c)
: ²PLANE
plat du jour \,plä-də-'zhùr, ,pla-\, *pl* **plats du jour** *same*\ [F, lit.,
plate of the day] (1906) : a dish that is featured by a restaurant on a
particular day
¹**plate** \'plāt\ *n* [ME, fr. OF, fr. *plate,* fem. of *plat* flat, fr. (assumed) VL
plattus, prob. fr. Gk *platys* broad, flat — more at PLACE] (14c)   **1 a** : a
smooth flat thin piece of material   **b** (1) : forged, rolled, or cast metal
in sheets usu. thicker than ¼ inch (6 millimeters)   (2) : a very thin
layer of metal deposited on a surface of base metal by plating   **c** : one
of the broad metal pieces used in armor; *also* : armor of such plates   **d**
(1) : a lamina or plaque (as of bone or horn) that forms part of an animal body; *esp* : SCUTE   (2) : the thin under portion of the forequarter of
beef; *esp* : the fatty back part — see BEEF illustration   **e** : HOME PLATE
f : any of the large movable segments into which the earth's crust is
divided according to the theory of plate tectonics   **2** [ME; partly fr.
OF *plate* plate, piece of silver; partly fr. OSp *plata* silver, fr. (assumed)
VL *platta* metal plate, fr. fem. of *plattus* flat]   **a** *obs* : a silver coin   **b**
: precious metal; *esp* : silver bullion   **3** [ME, fr. MF *plat* dish, plate, fr.
plat flat]   **a** : domestic hollowware metal or of plated with gold, silver,
or base metals   **b** : a shallow usu. circular vessel from which food is
eaten or served   **c** (1) : a quantity to fill a plate : PLATEFUL   (2) : a
main course served on a plate   (3) : food and service supplied to one
person 〈a dinner at $10 a ~〉   **d** : a prize given to the winner in a

contest   (2) *Brit* : a horse race in which the contestants compete for a
prize of fixed value rather than stakes   **e** : a dish or pouch passed in
taking collections   **f** : a flat glass dish used chiefly for culturing microorganisms   **4 a** : a prepared surface from which printing is done   **b**
: a sheet of material (as glass) coated with a light-sensitive photographic emulsion   **c** (1) : the usu. flat or grid-formed anode of an
electron tube at which electrons collect   (2) : a metallic grid with its
interstices filled with active material that forms one of the structural
units of a battery   **d** : LICENSE PLATE   **5** : a horizontal structural member that provides bearing and anchorage esp. for the trusses of a roof or
the rafters   **6** : the part of a denture that fits to the mouth; *broadly*
: DENTURE   **7** : a full-page illustration often on different paper from the
text pages   **8** : a schedule of matters to deal with 〈have a lot on my ~
now〉 — **plate·ful** \-,fúl\ *n* — **plate·like** \-,līk\ *adj*
²**plate** *vt* **plat·ed; plat·ing** (14c)   **1** : to cover or equip with plate: as   **a**
: to provide with armor plate   **b** : to cover with an adherent layer
mechanically, chemically, or electrically; *also* : to deposit (as a layer)
on a surface   **2** : to make a printing surface from or for   **3** : to fix or
secure with a plate   **4** : to cause (as a runner) to score in baseball
¹**pla·teau** \pla-'tō, 'pla-,\ *n, pl* **plateaus** *or* **pla·teaux** \-'tōz, -,tōz\ [F,
fr. MF, platter, fr. *plat* flat] (1796)   **1 a** : a usu. extensive land area
having a relatively level surface raised sharply above adjacent land on
at least one side : TABLELAND   **b** : a similar undersea feature   **2 a** : a
region of little or no change in a graphic representation   **b** : a relatively stable level, period, or condition   **3** : a level of attainment or
achievement 〈the 500-point ~〉
²**plateau** *vi* (1939) : to reach a level, period, or condition of stability
plate·glass \'plāt-'glas, -,glas\ *adj, often cap* (1968) : of, relating to, or
being the British universities founded in the latter half of the twentieth
century — compare OXBRIDGE, REDBRICK
plate glass *n* (ca. 1741) : rolled, ground, and polished sheet glass
plate·let \'plāt-lət\ *n* (1895) : a minute flattened body (as of ice or a
mineral); *esp* : BLOOD PLATELET
plate·mak·er \'plāt-,mā-kər\ *n* (1904) : a machine for making printing
plates and esp. offset printing plates — **plate·mak·ing** \-kiŋ\ *n*
plat·en \'pla-t⁹n\ *n* [MF *plateine,* fr. *plat*] (1541)   **1** : a flat plate; *esp*
: one that exerts or receives pressure (as in a printing press)   **2** : the
roller of a typewriter or printer
plat·er \'plā-tər\ *n* (1777)   **1** : one that plates   **2 a** : a horse that runs
chiefly in plate races   **b** : a racehorse that competes in the lowest grade
of races
plate rail *n* (1902) : a rail or narrow shelf along the upper part of a
wall for holding plates or ornaments
plat·er·esque \,pla-tə-'resk\ *adj, often cap* [Sp *plateresco,* fr. *platero*
silversmith, fr. *plata* silver] (ca. 1864) : of, relating to, or being a 16th
century Spanish architectural style characterized by elaborate ornamentation suggestive of silver plate
plate tectonics *n pl but sing in constr* (1969) : a theory in geology: the
lithosphere of the earth is divided into a small number of plates which
float on and travel independently over the mantle and much of the
earth's seismic activity occurs at the boundaries of these plates — compare CONTINENTAL DRIFT
plat·form \'plat-,fórm\ *n, often attrib* [MF *plate-forme* diagram, map,
lit., flat form] (1535)   **1** : PLAN, DESIGN   **2** : a declaration of the principles on which a group of persons stands; *esp* : a declaration of principles and policies adopted by a political party or a candidate   **3 a** (1)
: a usu. raised horizontal flat surface; *esp* : a raised flooring (as for
speakers or performers)   (2) : a device or structure incorporating or
providing a platform; *esp* : such a structure on legs used for offshore
drilling (as for oil)   **b** : a place or opportunity for public discussion   **4**
a : a usu. thick layer (as of cork) between the inner sole and outer sole
of a shoe   **b** : a shoe having such a sole   **5** : a vehicle (as a satellite or
aircraft) used for a particular activity or purpose or to carry a usu.
specified kind of equipment
platform balance *n* (1811) : a balance having a platform on which
objects are weighed — called also *platform scale*
platform rocker *n* (1944) : a chair that rocks on a stable platform
platform tennis *n* (1955) : a variation of paddle tennis that is played
on a platform enclosed by a wire fence
pla·ti·na \plə-'tē-nə\ *n* [Sp] (1750) : PLATINUM
plat·ing \'plā-tiŋ\ *n* (1831)   **1** : the act or process of plating   **2 a** : a
coating of metal plates   **b** : a thin coating of metal
plat·i·nize \'pla-t⁹n-,īz\ *vt* **-nized; -niz·ing** (1825) : to cover, treat, or
combine with platinum or a compound of platinum
plat·i·no·cy·a·nide \,pla-t⁹n-ō-'sī-ə-,nīd\ *n* (1845) : a fluorescent complex salt formed by the union of a compound of platinum and cyanide
with another cyanide
plat·i·num \'plat-nəm, 'pla-t⁹n-əm\ *n, often attrib* [NL, fr. Sp *platina,*
fr. dim. of *plata* silver — more at PLATE] (1812)   **1** : a heavy precious
grayish white noncorroding ductile malleable metallic element that
fuses with difficulty and is used esp. in chemical ware and apparatus, as
a catalyst, and in dental and jewelry alloys — see ELEMENT table   **2** : a
moderate gray
platinum blonde *n* (1931)   **1** : a person whose hair is of a pale silvery
blonde color   **2** : the color of the hair of a platinum blonde
plat·i·tude \'pla-tə-,tüd, -,tyüd\ *n* [F, fr. *plat* flat, dull] (1812)   **1** : the
quality or state of being dull or insipid   **2** : a banal, trite, or stale remark
plat·i·tu·di·nal \,pla-tə-'tüd-nəl, -'tyüd-; -'tü-d⁹n-əl, -'tyü-\ *adj* (1870)
: PLATITUDINOUS
plat·i·tu·di·nar·i·an \-,tü-d⁹n-'er-ē-ən, -,tyü-\ *n* (1855) : one given to
the use of platitudes
plat·i·tu·di·nize \-'tü-d⁹n-,īz, -'tyü-\ *vi* **-nized; -niz·ing** [*platitudinous*]
(1885) : to utter platitudes
plat·i·tu·di·nous \-'tüd-nəs, -'tyüd-; -'tü-d⁹n-əs, -'tyü-\ *adj* [*platitude* +
-inous (as in *multitudinous*)] (1862) : having the characteristics of a
platitude : full of platitudes 〈~ remarks〉 — **plat·i·tu·di·nous·ly** *adv*

\ə\ abut \⁹\ kitten, F table \ər\ further \a\ ash \ā\ ace \ä\ mop, mar
\aú\ out \ch\ chin \e\ bet \ē\ easy \g\ go \i\ hit \ī\ ice \j\ job
\ŋ\ sing \ō\ go \ò\ law \òi\ boy \th\ thin \t̲h̲\ the \ü\ loot \ú\ foot
\y\ yet \zh\ vision \à, k̲, ⁿ, œ, œ̄, ue, ūe, ᵞ\ see Guide to Pronunciation

pla·ton·ic \plə-'tä-nik, plā-\ *adj* [L *platonicus,* fr. Gk *platōnikos,* fr. *Platōn* Plato] (1533) **1** *cap* : of, relating to, or characteristic of Plato or Platonism **2 a** : relating to or based on platonic love; *also* : experiencing or professing platonic love **b** : of, relating to, or being a relationship marked by the absence of romance or sex **3** : NOMINAL, THEORETICAL — **pla·ton·i·cal·ly** \-ni-k(ə-)lē\ *adv*

platonic love *n, often cap P* (1631) **1** : love conceived by Plato as ascending from passion for the individual to contemplation of the universal and ideal **2** : a close relationship between two persons in which sexual desire is nonexistent or has been suppressed or sublimated

Pla·to·nism \'plā-t³n-ˌi-zəm\ *n* (ca. 1570) **1 a** : the philosophy of Plato stressing esp. that actual things are copies of transcendent ideas and that these ideas are the objects of true knowledge apprehended by reminiscence **b** : NEOPLATONISM **2** : PLATONIC LOVE — **Pla·to·nist** \-t³n-ist\ *n* — **Pla·to·nis·tic** \ˌplā-t³n-'is-tik\ *adj*

Pla·to·nize \'plā-t³n-ˌīz\ *vb* **-nized; -niz·ing** *vi* (1608) : to adopt, imitate, or conform to Platonic opinions ∼ *vt* : to explain in accordance with or adapt to Platonic doctrines; *esp* : IDEALIZE

¹pla·toon \plə-'tün, pla-\ *n* [F *peloton* small detachment, lit., ball, fr. MF *pelote* little ball — more at PELLET] (1637) **1** : a subdivision of a company-size military unit normally consisting of two or more squads or sections **2** : a group of persons sharing a common characteristic or activity ⟨a ∼ of waiters⟩; *esp* : a group of football players who are trained for either offense or defense and are sent into or withdrawn from the game as a body

²platoon *vt* (1963) : to play (one player) alternately with another player in the same position (as on a baseball team) ∼ *vi* **1** : to alternate with another player at the same position **2** : to use alternate players at the same position

platoon sergeant *n* (1915) : a noncommissioned officer in the army ranking above a staff sergeant and below a first sergeant

Platt·deutsch \'plat-ˌdȯich, 'plät-\ *n* [G, fr. D *Plattduitsch,* lit., Low German, fr. *plat* flat, low + *duitsch* German] (1677) : the Low German speech of northern Germany comprising several dialects

plat·ter \'pla-tər\ *n* [ME *plater,* fr. AF, fr. MF *plat* plate] (13c) **1 a** : a large plate used esp. for serving meat **b** : PLATE 3c(2) **2 a** : a phonograph record — **plat·ter·ful** \-ˌfu̇l\ *n* — **on a platter** : without effort : very easily ⟨can have the presidency *on a platter* —Jonathan Daniels⟩

¹pla·ty \'plā-tē\ *adj* (1533) : resembling a plate; *also* : consisting of plates or flaky layers —used chiefly of soil or mineral formations

²pla·ty \'pla-tē\ *n, pl* **platy** *or* **plat·ys** *or* **plat·ies** [NL *Platypoecilus,* former genus name of the fish] (1931) : either of two live-bearers (*Xiphophorus maculatus* and *X. variatus* of the family Poeciliidae) that are popular aquarium fishes and are noted for variability and brilliant color —called also *platy·fish* \-ˌfish\

platy·hel·minth \ˌpla-ti-'hel-ˌmin(t)th\ *n* [ultim. fr. Gk *platys* broad, flat + *helminth-, helmis* helminth] (ca. 1890) : any of a phylum (Platyhelminthes) of soft-bodied usu. much flattened acoelomate worms (as the planarians, flukes, and tapeworms) — called also *flatworm* — **platy·hel·min·thic** \-hel-'min(t)-thik, -'min-tik\ *adj*

platy·pus \'pla-ti-pəs, -ˌpu̇s\ *n, pl* **platy·pus·es** *also* **platy·pi** \-ˌpī, -ˌpē\ [NL, fr. Gk *platypous* flat-footed, fr. *platys* broad, flat + *pous* foot — more at PLACE, FOOT] (1799) : a small carnivorous aquatic oviparous mammal (*Ornithorhynchus anatinus*) of eastern Australia and Tasmania that has a fleshy bill resembling that of a duck, dense fur, webbed feet, and a broad flattened tail

platypus

platy·rrhine \'pla-ti-ˌrīn\ *adj* (1857) **1** [NL *Platyrrhina,* fr. Gk *platyrrhin-, platyrrhis* broad-nosed, fr. *platys* + *rhin-, rhis* nose] : of, relating to, or being any of a division (Platyrrhina) of monkeys all of which are New World monkeys and are characterized by a broad nasal septum, usu. 36 teeth, and often a prehensile tail **2** [Gk *platyrrhin-, platyrrhis*] : having a short broad nose — **platyrrhine** *n*

plau·dit \'plȯ-dət\ *n* [L *plaudite* applaud, pl. imper. of *plaudere* to applaud] (1624) **1** : an act or round of applause **2** : enthusiastic approval —usu. used in pl. ⟨received the ∼s of the critics⟩

plau·si·bil·i·ty \ˌplȯ-zə-'bi-lə-tē\ *n, pl* **-ties** (1649) **1** : the quality or state of being plausible **2** : something plausible

plau·si·ble \'plȯ-zə-bəl\ *adj* [L *plausibilis* worthy of applause, fr. *plausus,* pp. of *plaudere*] (1565) **1** : superficially fair, reasonable, or valuable but often specious ⟨a ∼ pretext⟩ **2** : superficially pleasing or persuasive ⟨a swindler . . . , then a quack, then a smooth, ∼ gentleman —R. W. Emerson⟩ **3** : appearing worthy of belief ⟨the argument was both powerful and ∼⟩ — **plau·si·ble·ness** *n* — **plau·si·bly** \-blē\ *adv*

plau·sive \'plȯ-ziv, -siv\ *adj* [L *plausus,* pp.] (1600) **1** : manifesting praise or approval **2** *obs* : PLEASING **3** *archaic* : SPECIOUS

¹play \'plā\ *n* [ME, fr. OE *plega;* akin to OE *plegan* to play, MD *pleyen*] (bef. 12c) **1 a** : SWORDPLAY **b** *archaic* : GAME, SPORT **c** : the conduct, course, or action of a game **d** : a particular act or maneuver in a game: as **(1)** : the action during an attempt to advance the ball in football **(2)** : the action in which a player is put out in baseball **e** : the action in which cards are played after bidding in a card game **f** : the moving of a piece in a board game (as chess) **g** : one's turn in a game ⟨it's your ∼⟩ **2 a** *obs* : SEXUAL INTERCOURSE **b** : amorous flirtation : DALLIANCE **3 a** : recreational activity; *esp* : the spontaneous activity of children **b** : absence of serious or harmful intent : JEST ⟨said it in ∼⟩ **c** : the act or an instance of playing on words or speech sounds **d** : GAMING, GAMBLING **4 a (1)** : an act, way, or manner of proceeding : MANEUVER ⟨that was a ∼ to get your fingerprints —Erle Stanley Gardner⟩ **(2)** : DEAL, VENTURE **b (1)** : OPERATION, ACTIVITY ⟨other motives surely come into ∼ —M. R. Cohen⟩ **(2)** : brisk, fitful, or light movement ⟨the gem presented a dazzling ∼ of colors⟩ **(3)** : free or unimpeded motion (as of a part of a machine); *also* : the length or measure of such motion **(4)** : scope or opportunity for action **5** : emphasis or publicity esp. in the news media ⟨wished the country received a better ∼ in the American press —Hugh MacLen-

nan⟩ **6** : a move or series of moves calculated to arouse friendly feelings — usu. used with *make* ⟨made a big ∼ for the girl —Will Herman⟩ **7 a** : the stage representation of an action or story **b** : a dramatic composition : DRAMA   *syn* see FUN — **in play** : in condition or position to be legitimately played — **out of play** : not in play

²play *vi* (bef. 12c) **1 a** : to engage in sport or recreation : FROLIC **b** : to have sexual relations; *esp* : to have promiscuous or illicit sexual relations — usu. used in the phrase *play around* **c (1)** : to move aimlessly about : TRIFLE **(2)** : to toy or fiddle around with something ⟨∼ed with her food⟩ **(3)** : to deal or behave frivolously or mockingly : JEST **(4)** : to deal in a light, speculative, or sportive manner **(5)** : to make use of double meaning or of the similarity of sound of two words for stylistic or humorous effect **2 a** : to take advantage ⟨∼ing on fears⟩ **b (1)** : FLUTTER, FRISK **(2)** : to move or operate in a lively, irregular, or intermittent manner **c** : to move or function freely within prescribed limits **d** : to produce a stream ⟨hoses ∼ing on a fire⟩ **3 a (1)** : to perform music ⟨∼ on a violin⟩ **(2)** : to sound in performance ⟨the organ is ∼ing⟩ **(3)** : to emit sounds ⟨the radio is ∼ing⟩ **(4)** : to reproduce recorded sounds ⟨a record is ∼ing⟩ **b (1)** : to act in a dramatic production **(2)** : SHOW, RUN ⟨what's ∼ing at the theater⟩ **c** : to be suitable for dramatic performance **d** : to act with special consideration so as to gain favor, approval, or sympathy ⟨might ∼ to popular prejudices to serve his political ends —V. L. Parrington⟩ — often used in the phrase *play up to* **4 a** : to engage or take part in a game **b** : to perform in a position in a specified manner ⟨the outfielders were ∼ing deep⟩ **c** : to perform an action during one's turn in a game **d** : GAMBLE **e (1)** : to behave or conduct oneself in a specified way ⟨∼ safe⟩ **(2)** : to feign a specified state or quality ⟨∼ dead⟩ **(3)** : to take part in or assent to some activity : COOPERATE ⟨∼ along with his scheme⟩ **(4)** : to act so as to prove advantageous to another — usu. used in the phrase *play into the hands of* **5** : to gain approval : GO OVER ⟨her idea did not ∼ well⟩ ∼ *vt* **1 a (1)** : to engage in or occupy oneself with ⟨∼ baseball⟩ **(2)** : to engage in (an activity) as a game **(3)** : to deal with, handle, or manage **(4)** : EXPLOIT, MANIPULATE **b** : to pretend to engage in the activities of ⟨∼ war⟩ ⟨children ∼ing house⟩ **c (1)** : to amount to by one's efforts ⟨∼ed an important role in their success⟩ **(2)** : to perform or execute for amusement or to deceive or mock ⟨∼ a trick⟩ **(3)** : WREAK ⟨∼ havoc⟩ **2 a (1)** : to put on a performance of (a play) **(2)** : to act in the character or part of **(3)** : to act or perform in ⟨∼ed leading theaters⟩ **b** : to perform or act the part of ⟨∼ the fool⟩ **3 a (1)** : to contend against in or as if in a game **(2)** : to use as a contestant in a game ⟨the coach did not ∼ him⟩ **(3)** : to perform the duties associated with (a certain position) ⟨∼ed quarterback⟩ **(4)** : to guard or move into position to defend against (an opponent) in a specified manner **b (1)** : to wager in a game : STAKE **(2)** : to make wagers on ⟨∼ the races⟩ **(3)** : to speculate on or in ⟨∼ the stock market⟩ **(4)** : to operate on the basis of ⟨∼ a hunch⟩ **c** : to put into action in a game; *esp* : to remove (a playing card) from one's hand and place usu. faceup on a table in one's turn either as part of a scoring combination or as one's contribution to a trick **d** : to catch or pick up (a batted ball) : FIELD ⟨∼ed the ball barehanded⟩ **e** : to direct the course of (as a ball) : HIT ⟨∼ed a wedge shot to the green⟩; *also* : to cause (a ball or puck) to rebound ⟨∼ed the ball off the backboard⟩ **4 a** : to perform (music) on an instrument ⟨∼ a waltz⟩ **b** : to perform music on ⟨∼ the violin⟩ **c** : to perform music of (a certain composer) **d (1)** : to cause (as a radio or phonograph) to emit sounds **(2)** : to cause the recorded sound or image of (as a record or a magnetic tape) to be reproduced **5 a** : WIELD, PLY **b** : to discharge, fire, or set off with continuous effect ⟨∼ed the hose on the burning building⟩ **c** : to cause to move or operate lightly and irregularly or intermittently **d** : to keep (a hooked fish) in action — **play·abil·i·ty** \ˌplā-ə-'bi-lə-tē\ *n* — **play·able** \'plā-ə-bəl\ *adj* — **play ball** : COOPERATE — **play both ends against the middle** : to set opposing interests against each other to one's own ultimate profit — **play by ear** : to deal with something without previous planning or instructions — **play games** : to try to hide the truth from someone by deceptive means — **play one's cards** : to act with the means available to one — **play possum** : to pretend to be asleep or dead — **play second fiddle** : to take a subordinate position — **play the field** : to date or have romantic connections with more than one person — **play the game** : to act according to a code or set of standards — **play with fire** : to do something risky or dangerous — **play with oneself** : MASTURBATE

pla·ya \'plī-ə\ *n* [Sp, lit., beach, fr. LL *plagia* — more at PLAGE] (1854) : the flat-floored bottom of an undrained desert basin that becomes at times a shallow lake

play·act \'plā-ˌakt\ *vb* [back-formation fr. *playacting*] *vt* (1901) : ACT OUT 1a ∼ *vi* **1 a** : to take part in theatrical performances esp. as a professional **b** : to make believe **2** : to engage in theatrical or insincere behavior — **play·act·ing** *n*

play–action pass *n* (1964) : a pass play in football in which the quarterback fakes a handoff before passing the ball — called also *play-action*

play·back \'plā-ˌbak\ *n* (1929) : an act or instance of reproducing recorded sound or pictures often immediately after recording

play back *vt* (1949) : to perform a playback of (a usu. recently recorded disc or tape)

play·bill \'plā-ˌbil\ *n* (1616) : a bill advertising a play and usu. announcing the cast

Playbill *trademark* — used for a theater program

play·book \-ˌbu̇k\ *n* (1535) **1** : one or more plays in book form **2** : a notebook containing diagrammed football plays

play·boy \-ˌbȯi\ *n* (1907) : a man who lives a life devoted chiefly to the pursuit of pleasure

play–by–play \'plā-bī-ˌplā, ˌplā-bī-\ *adj* (1931) **1** : being or giving a running commentary on a sports event **2** : relating each event as it occurs — **play–by–play** *n*

play down *vt* (1930) : to attach little importance to : MINIMIZE

played out *adj* (ca. 1859) **1** : worn out or used up **2** : tired out : SPENT

play·er \'plā-ər\ *n* (14c) : one that plays: as **a** : a person who plays a game **b** : MUSICIAN **c** : ACTOR **d** : a device that reproduces recorded material (as video images or music) from a usu. specified medium **e**

: one actively involved esp. in a competitive field or process : PARTICIPANT

play·er piano *n* (1907) : a piano containing a mechanism by which it plays automatically

play·fel·low \'plā-,fe-(,)lō\ *n* (1513) : PLAYMATE

play·field \-,fēld\ *n* (1883) : a playground for outdoor athletics

play·ful \'plā-fəl\ *adj* (13c) **1** : full of play : FROLICSOME, SPORTIVE ⟨a ~ kitten⟩ **2** : HUMOROUS, JOCULAR — **play·ful·ly** \-fə-lē\ *adv* — **play·ful·ness** *n*

play·girl \-,gər(-ə)l\ *n* (1938) : a woman who lives a life devoted chiefly to the pursuit of pleasure

play·go·er \-,gō(-ə)r\ *n* (1822) : a person who frequently attends plays

play·ground \-,graünd\ *n* (1794) **1** : a piece of land used for and usu. equipped with facilities for recreation esp. by children **2** : an area known or suited for activity of a specified sort ⟨a vacation ~⟩

play·house \-,haüs\ *n* (bef. 12c) **1** : THEATER **2** : a small house for children to play in

playing card *n* (1543) : one of a set of 24 to 78 thin rectangular pieces of paperboard or plastic marked on one side to show its rank and suit and used in playing any of numerous games

playing field *n* (ca. 1584) **1** : a field for various games; *esp* : the part of a field officially marked off for play **2** : a set of conditions for competition (as in business) — usu. used in such phrases as *a level playing field*

play·land \'plā-,land\ *n* (1918) : PLAYGROUND

play·let \-lət\ *n* (1884) : a short play

play·list \-,list\ *n* (1972) : a list of recordings to be played on the air by a radio station

play·mak·er \-,mā-kər\ *n* (ca. 1942) : a player who leads the offense for a team (as in basketball or hockey) — **play·mak·ing** \-kiŋ\ *n or adj*

play·mate \-,māt\ *n* (1642) : a companion in play

play-off \'plā-,óf\ *n* (1895) **1** : a final contest or series of contests to determine the winner between contestants or teams that have tied **2** : a series of contests played after the end of the regular season to determine a championship

play off *vt* (1807) **1 a** : to set in opposition for one's own gain **b** : to set in contrast **2** : to complete the playing of (an interrupted contest) **3** : to break (a tie) by a play-off

play out *vt* (1596) **1 a** : to perform to the end ⟨*play out* a role⟩ **b** : USE UP, FINISH **2** : UNREEL, UNFOLD ⟨*played out* a length of line —Gordon Webber⟩ ~ *vi* : to become spent or exhausted

play·pen \-,pen\ *n* (1931) : a portable usu. collapsible enclosure in which a baby or young child may play

play·room \-,rüm, -,rüm\ *n* (1819) : RUMPUS ROOM

play·suit \-,süt\ *n* (1908) : a sports and play outfit for women or children that consists usu. of a blouse and shorts

play therapy *n* (1939) : psychotherapy in which a child is encouraged to reveal feelings and conflicts in play rather than by verbalization

play·thing \-,thiŋ\ *n* (1675) : TOY

play·time \-,tīm\ *n* (1661) : a time for play or diversion

play up *n* (1909) : EMPHASIZE; *also* : EXAGGERATE, OVEREMPHASIZE

play·wear \'plā-,war, -,wer\ *n* (1964) : informal clothing worn for leisure activities

play·wright \'plā-,rīt\ *n* [¹*play* + obs. *wright* maker — more at WRIGHT] (1687) : a person who writes plays

play·writ·ing *also* **play·wright·ing** \-,rī-tiŋ\ *n* (1809) : the writing of plays

pla·za \'pla-zə, 'plä-\ *n* [Sp, fr. L *platea* broad street — more at PLACE] (1683) **1 a** : a public square in a city or town **b** : an open area usu. located near urban centers and often featuring walkways, trees and shrubs, places to sit, and sometimes shops **2** : a place on a thoroughfare (as a turnpike) at which all traffic must temporarily stop (as to pay tolls) **3** : an area adjacent to an expressway which has service facilities (as a restaurant, service station, and rest rooms) **5** : SHOPPING CENTER

plea \'plē\ *n* [ME *plaid, plai*, fr. OF *plait, plaid*, fr. ML *placitum*, fr. L, decision, decree, fr. neut. of *placitus*, pp. of *placēre* to please, be decided — more at PLEASE] (13c) **1** : a legal suit or action **2** : an allegation made by a party in support of a cause: as **a** : an allegation of fact — compare DEMURRER **b** (1) : a defendant's answer to a plaintiff's declaration in common-law practice (2) : an accused person's answer to a charge or indictment in criminal practice **c** : a plea of guilty to an indictment **3** : something offered by way of excuse or justification ⟨left early with the ~ of a headache⟩ **4** : an earnest entreaty : APPEAL ⟨their ~ for understanding must be answered⟩ *syn* see APOLOGY

plea bargaining *n* (1964) : the negotiation of an agreement between a prosecutor and a defendant whereby the defendant is permitted to plead guilty to a reduced charge — **plea–bargain** *vi* — **plea bargain** *n*

pleach \'plēch, 'plāch\ *vt* [ME *plechen*, fr. ONF *plechier*, fr. (assumed) VL *plactiare*, alter. of *plectere* to braid — more at PLY] (14c) : INTERLACE, PLAIT

plead \'plēd\ *vb* **plead·ed** \'plē-dəd\ *or* **pled** *also* **plead** \'pled\; **plead·ing** [ME *plaiden* to institute a lawsuit, fr. MF *plaidier*, fr. *plaid* plea] *vi* (13c) **1** : to argue a case or cause in a court of law **2 a** : to make an allegation in an action or other legal proceeding; *esp* : to answer the previous pleading of the other party by denying facts therein stated or by alleging new facts **b** : to conduct pleadings **3** : to make a plea of a specified nature ⟨~ not guilty⟩ **4** : to argue for or against a claim ~ *vt* **1** : to maintain (as a case or cause) in a court of law or other tribunal **2** : to allege in or by way of a legal plea **3** : to offer as a plea usu. in defense, apology, or excuse — **plead·able** \'plē-də-bəl\ *adj* — **plead·er** *n* — **plead·ing·ly** \'plē-diŋ-lē\ *adv*

pleading *n* (14c) **1** : advocacy of a cause in a court of law **2 a** : one of the formal usu. written allegations and counter allegations made alternately by the parties in a legal action or proceeding **b** : the action or process performed by the parties in presenting such formal allegations until a single point at issue is produced **c** : the introduction of one of these allegations and esp. the first one **d** : the body of rules according to which these allegations are framed **3** : the act or an instance of making a plea **4** : a sincere entreaty

pleas·ance \'ple-z°n(t)s\ *n* (14c) **1** : a feeling of pleasure : DELIGHT **2** : a pleasant rest or recreation place usu. attached to a mansion

pleas·ant \'ple-z°nt\ *adj* [ME *plesaunt*, fr. MF *plaisant*, fr. prp. of *plaisir*] (14c) **1** : having qualities that tend to give pleasure : AGREEABLE ⟨a ~ day⟩ **2** : having or characterized by pleasing manners, behavior, or appearance — **pleas·ant·ly** *adv* — **pleas·ant·ness** *n*

pleas·ant·ry \-z°n-trē\ *n, pl* **-ries** (1655) **1** : an agreeable playfulness in conversation : BANTER **2** : a humorous act or remark : JEST **3** : a polite social remark ⟨exchanged *pleasantries*⟩

¹please \'plēz\ *vb* **pleased; pleas·ing** [ME *plesen*, fr. MF *plaisir*, fr. L *placēre*; akin to L *placare* to placate and perh. to Gk *plak-, plax* flat surface — more at FLUKE] *vi* (14c) **1** : to afford or give pleasure or satisfaction **2** : LIKE, WISH ⟨do as you ~⟩ **3** *archaic* : to have the kindness ⟨will you ~ to enter the carriage —Charles Dickens⟩ ~ *vt* **1** : to give pleasure to : GRATIFY **2** : to be the will or pleasure of ⟨may it ~ your Majesty⟩ — **pleas·er** \'plē-zər\ *n*

²please *adv* (1667) **1** — used as a function word to express politeness or emphasis in a request ⟨~ come in⟩ **2** — used as a function word to express polite affirmation ⟨have some tea? *Please*⟩

pleas·ing \'plē-ziŋ\ *adj* (14c) : giving pleasure : AGREEABLE ⟨the sun's ~ warmth⟩ — **pleas·ing·ly** \-lē\ *adv* — **pleas·ing·ness** *n*

plea·sur·able \'plezh-rə-bəl, 'plazh-; 'ple-zhə-, 'plä-\ *adj* (1579) : PLEASANT, GRATIFYING — **plea·sur·abil·i·ty** \,plezh-rə-'bi-lə-tē, ,plazh-; ,ple-zhə-, ,plä-\ *n* — **plea·sur·able·ness** \'plezh-rə-bəl-nəs, 'plazh-; 'ple-zhə-, 'plä-\ *n* — **plea·sur·ably** \-blē\ *adv*

¹plea·sure \'ple-zhər, 'plä-\ *n* [ME *plesure*, alter. of *plesir*, fr. MF *plaisir*, fr. *plaisir* to please] (14c) **1** : DESIRE, INCLINATION ⟨wait upon his ~ — Shak.⟩ **2** : a state of gratification **3** : sensual gratification **b** : frivolous amusement **4** : a source of delight or joy

²pleasure *vb* **plea·sured; plea·sur·ing** \'plezh-riŋ, 'plazh-; 'ple-zhə-, 'plä-\ *vt* (1537) **1** : to give pleasure to : GRATIFY **2** : to give sexual pleasure to ~ *vi* **1** : to take pleasure : DELIGHT **2** : to seek pleasure

pleasure dome *n* (1797) : a place of pleasurable entertainment or recreation : RESORT

plea·sure·less \'ple-zhər-ləs, 'plä-\ *adj* (1814) : giving no pleasure

pleasure principle *n* (1912) : a tendency for individual behavior to be directed toward immediate satisfaction of instinctual drives and immediate relief from pain or discomfort

¹pleat \'plēt\ *vt* [ME *pleten*, fr. *pleit, plete* plait] (14c) **1** : FOLD; *esp* : to arrange in pleats ⟨~ a skirt⟩ **2** : PLAIT **2** — **pleat·er** *n*

²pleat *n* [ME *plete*] (15c) : a fold in cloth made by doubling material over on itself; *also* : something resembling such a fold — **pleat·less** \-ləs\ *adj*

pleb \'pleb\ *n* (1865) : PLEBEIAN

plebe \'plēb\ *n* [obs. *plebe* common people, fr. F *plèbe*, fr. L *plebs*] (1833) : a freshman at a military or naval academy

¹ple·be·ian \pli-'bē-ən\ *n* [L *plebeius* of the common people, fr. *plebs* common people] (1533) **1** : a member of the Roman plebs **2** : one of the common people — **ple·be·ian·ism** \-ə-,ni-zəm\ *n*

²plebeian *adj* (1566) **1** : of or relating to plebeians **2** : crude or coarse in manner or style : COMMON — **ple·be·ian·ly** *adv*

pleb·i·scite \'ple-bə-,sīt, -sət *also* -,sēt\ *n* [L *plebis scitum* law voted by the comitia, lit., decree of the common people] (1860) : a vote by which the people of an entire country or district express an opinion for or against a proposal esp. on a choice of government or ruler — **ple·bi·sci·ta·ry** \ple-'bi-sə-,ter-ē, pli-; ,ple-bə-'sī-tə-rē\ *adj*

plebs \'plebz, 'pleps\ *n, pl* **ple·bes** \'plē-(,)bēz, 'plā-,bäs\ [L] (1647) **1** : the general populace **2** : the common people of ancient Rome

ple·cop·ter·an \pli-'käp-tə-rən\ *n* [NL *Plecoptera*, group name, fr. Gk *plekein* to braid + *pteron* wing — more at PLY, FEATHER] (ca. 1890) : STONE FLY — **plecopteran** *adj*

plec·trum \'plek-trəm\ *n, pl* **plec·tra** \-trə\ *or* **plectrums** [L, fr. Gk *plēktron*, fr. *plēssein* to strike — more at PLAINT] (1626) : ³PICK 2c

¹pledge \'plej\ *n* [ME, security, fr. MF *plege*, fr. LL *plebium*, fr. (assumed) LL *plebere* to pledge, prob. of Gmc origin; akin to OHG *pflegan* to take care of — more at PLIGHT] (14c) **1 a** : a bailment of a chattel as security for a debt or other obligation without involving transfer of title **b** : the chattel so delivered **c** : the contract incidental to such a bailment **2** : the state of being held as a security or guaranty **b** : something given as security for the performance of an act **3** : a token, sign, or earnest of something else **4** : a gage of battle **5** : TOAST **3 6 a** : a binding promise or agreement to do or forbear **b** (1) : a promise to join a fraternity, sorority, or secret society (2) : a person who has so promised

²pledge *vt* **pledged; pledg·ing** (15c) **1** : to make a pledge of; *esp* : PAWN **2** : to drink to the health of **3** : to bind by a pledge **4** : to promise the performance of by a pledge — **pledg·er** \'ple-jər\ *or* **pledg·or** \'ple-jər, ple-'jór\ *n*

pledg·ee \ple-'jē\ *n* (1766) : one to whom a pledge is given

pled·get \'ple-jət\ *n* [origin unknown] (ca. 1540) : a compress or pad used to apply medication to or absorb discharges (as from a wound)

-plegia *n comb form* [NL, fr. Gk -*plēgia*, fr. *plēssein* to strike — more at PLAINT] : paralysis ⟨diplegia⟩

ple·iad \'plē-əd, 'plā-, -,ad, *chiefly Brit* 'plī-\ *n* [F *Pléiade*, group of seven 16th cent. Fr. poets, fr. MF, group of seven tragic poets of ancient Alexandria, fr. Gk *Pleiad-, Pleias*, fr. sing. of *Pleiades*] (ca. 1839) : a group of usu. seven illustrious or brilliant persons or things

Pleiad *n* : any of the Pleiades

Ple·ia·des \'plē-ə-,dēz, 'plā-, *chiefly Brit* 'plī-\ *n pl* [L, fr. Gk] **1** : the seven daughters of Atlas turned into a group of stars in Greek mythology **2** : a conspicuous cluster of stars in the constellation Taurus that includes six stars in the form of a very small dipper

plein air \,plān-'ar, -'er; ple-'nar, -'ner\ *adj* [F, open air] (1894) **1** : of or relating to painting in outdoor daylight **2** : of or relating to a branch of impressionism that attempts to represent outdoor light and air — **plein-air·ism** \plä-'nar-,i-zəm, ple-, -'ner-\ *n* — **plein-air·ist** \-ist\ *n*

pleio- *or* **pleo-** *or* **plio-** *comb form* [Gk *pleion, pleōn* — more at PLUS] : more ⟨*pleio*tropic⟩ ⟨*pleo*morphic⟩ ⟨*Plio*cene⟩

\ə\ abut \ᵊ\ kitten, F table \ər\ further \a\ ash \ā\ ace \ä\ mop, mar \aü\ out \ch\ chin \e\ bet \ē\ easy \g\ go \i\ hit \ī\ ice \j\ job \ŋ\ sing \ō\ go \ò\ law \òi\ boy \th\ thin \th̲\ the \ü\ loot \ù\ foot \y\ yet \zh\ vision \a, k, ⁿ, œ, œ̄, ue, ūe, ᵛ\ *see* Guide to Pronunciation

pleio·tro·pic \ˌplī-ə-'trō-pik, -'trä-\ adj (1938) : producing more than one genic effect; specif : having multiple phenotypic expressions ⟨a ～ gene⟩ — **plei·ot·ro·py** \plī-'ä-trə-pē\ n

Pleis·to·cene \'plīs-tə-ˌsēn\ adj [Gk pleistos most + ISV -cene; akin to Gk pleiōn more] (1839) : of, relating to, or being the earlier epoch of the Quaternary or the corresponding system of rocks — see GEOLOGIC TIME table — **Pleistocene** n

ple·na·ry \'plē-nə-rē, 'ple-\ adj [ME, fr. LL plenarius, fr. L plenus full — more at FULL] (15c) 1 : complete in every respect : ABSOLUTE, UN-QUALIFIED ⟨～ power⟩ 2 : fully attended or constituted by all entitled to be present ⟨a ～ session⟩ **syn** see FULL

plenary indulgence n (1675) : a remission of the entire temporal punishment for sin

ple·nip·o·tent \pli-'ni-pə-tənt\ adj [LL plenipotent-, plenipotens, fr. L plenus + potent-, potens powerful — more at POTENT] (1658) : PLENIPOTENTIARY

¹plen·i·po·ten·tia·ry \ˌple-nə-pə-'ten(t)-sh(ə-)rē, -shē-ˌer-ē\ adj [ML plenipotentiarius, adj. & n., fr. LL plenipotent-, plenipotens] (ca. 1645) 1 : invested with full power 2 : of or relating to a plenipotentiary

²plenipotentiary n, pl -ries (ca. 1656) : a person and esp. a diplomatic agent invested with full power to transact business

plen·ish \'ple-nish\ vt [ME (Sc) plenyssen to fill up, fr. MF pleniss-, stem of plenir, fr. plen full, fr. L plenus] (1513) chiefly Brit : EQUIP

plen·i·tude \'ple-nə-ˌtüd, -ˌtyüd\ n [ME plenitude, fr. MF or L; MF, fr. L plenitudo, fr. plenus] (15c) 1 : the quality or state of being full : COMPLETENESS 2 : a great sufficiency : ABUNDANCE

plen·i·tu·di·nous \ˌple-nə-'tüd-nəs, -'tyüd-; -'tü-dᵊn-əs, -'tyü-\ adj [plenitudin-, plenitudo] (1895) : characterized by plenitude

plen·te·ous \'plen-tē-əs\ adj [ME plentevous, plenteous, fr. MF plentiveus, fr. plentif abundant, fr. plenté plenty] (14c) 1 : FRUITFUL, PRODUCTIVE ⟨a ～ harvest — J. G. Frazer⟩ — usu. used with in or of ⟨the seasons had been ～ in corn —George Eliot⟩ 2 : constituting or existing in plenty ⟨～ grace with thee is found —Charles Wesley⟩ — **plen·te·ous·ly** adv — **plen·te·ous·ness** n

plen·ti·ful \'plen-ti-fəl\ adj (15c) 1 : containing or yielding plenty ⟨a ～ land⟩ 2 : characterized by, constituting, or existing in plenty — **plen·ti·ful·ly** \-f-ə-lē\ adv — **plen·ti·ful·ness** n

syn PLENTIFUL, AMPLE, ABUNDANT, COPIOUS mean more than sufficient without being excessive. PLENTIFUL implies a great or rich supply ⟨peaches are plentiful this summer⟩. AMPLE implies a generous sufficiency to satisfy a particular requirement ⟨ample food to last the winter⟩. ABUNDANT suggests an even greater or richer supply than does PLENTIFUL ⟨streams abundant with fish⟩. COPIOUS stresses largeness of supply rather than fullness or richness ⟨copious examples of bureaucratic waste⟩.

plen·ti·tude \'plen-tə-ˌtüd, -ˌtyüd\ n [by alter. (influenced by plenty)] (1615) : PLENITUDE

¹plen·ty \'plen-tē\ n [ME plente, fr. OF plenté, fr. LL plenitat-, plenitas, fr. L, fullness, fr. plenus full — more at FULL] (13c) 1 a : a full or more than adequate amount or supply ⟨had ～ of time to finish the job⟩ b : a large number or amount ⟨in ～ of trouble⟩ 2 : the quality or state of being copious : PLENTIFULNESS

²plenty adj (14c) 1 : plentiful in amount, number, or supply ⟨if reasons were as ～ as blackberries —Shak.⟩ 2 : AMPLE ⟨～ work to be done —Time⟩

usage Many commentators object to use of sense 2 in writing; it appears to be limited chiefly to spoken English. Sense 1 is literary but is no longer in common use.

³plenty adv (1842) : more than sufficiently : to a considerable degree ⟨the nights were ～ cold —F. B. Gipson⟩

usage Many handbooks advise avoiding the adverb plenty in writing; "use very, quite, or a more precise word," they advise. Actually plenty is often a more precise word than its recommended replacements; very, fully, or quite will not work as well in these typical quotations ⟨it's already plenty hot for us in the kitchen without some dolt opening the oven —C. H. Bridges⟩ ⟨may not be rising quite as rapidly as other health costs, but it is going up plenty fast —Changing Times⟩. It is not used in more formal writing.

ple·num \'ple-nəm, 'plē-\ n, pl -nums or -na \-nə\ [NL, fr. L, neut. of plenus] (1678) 1 a : a space or all space every part of which is full of matter b (1) : a condition in which the pressure of the air in an enclosed space is greater than that of the outside atmosphere (2) : an enclosed space in which such a condition exists 2 : a general assembly of all members esp. of a legislative body 3 : the quality or state of being full

ple·och·ro·ism \plē-'ä-krə-ˌwi-zəm\ n [ISV pleochroic, fr. pleio- + Gk chrōs skin, color] (1857) : the property of a crystal of showing different colors when viewed by light that vibrates parallel to different axes — **pleo·chro·ic** \ˌplē-ə-'krō-ik\ adj

pleo·mor·phic \ˌplē-ə-'mȯr-fik\ adj (1886) : able to assume different forms : POLYMORPHIC ⟨～ bacteria⟩ ⟨a ～ sarcoma⟩ — **pleo·mor·phism** \-ˌfi-zəm\ n

ple·o·nasm \'plē-ə-ˌna-zəm\ n [LL pleonasmus, fr. Gk pleonasmos, fr. pleonazein to be excessive, fr. pleiōn, pleōn more — more at PLUS] (1610) 1 : the use of more words than those necessary to denote mere sense (as in the man he said) : REDUNDANCY 2 : an instance or example of pleonasm — **ple·o·nas·tic** \ˌplē-ə-'nas-tik\ adj — **ple·o·nas·ti·cal·ly** \-ti-k(ə-)lē\ adv

ple·o·pod \'plē-ə-ˌpäd\ n [Gk plein to sail + E -o- + -pod; fr. its use in swimming — more at FLOW] (ca. 1890) : an abdominal limb of a crustacean

ple·ro·cer·coid \ˌplir-ō-'sər-ˌkȯid\ n [Gk plērēs full + kerkos tail — more at FULL] (1906) : the solid elongate infective larva of some tapeworms usu. occurring in the muscles of fishes

ple·si·o·saur \'plē-sē-ə-ˌsȯr, -zē-\ n [ultim. fr. Gk plēsios close (akin to Gk pelas near) + sauros lizard] (1839) : any of a suborder (Plesiosauria) of Mesozoic marine reptiles with dorsoventrally flattened bodies and limbs modified into paddles

pleth·o·ra \'ple-thə-rə\ n [ML, fr. Gk plēthōra, lit., fullness, fr. plēthein to be full — more at FULL] (1541) 1 : a bodily condition characterized by an excess of blood and marked by turgescence and a florid complexion 2 : EXCESS, SUPERFLUITY; also : PROFUSION, ABUNDANCE — **ple·tho·ric** \plə-'thȯr-ik, ple-, -'thär-; 'ple-thə-rik\ adj

---

ple·thys·mo·gram \ple-'thiz-mə-ˌgram, plə-\ n (1894) : a tracing made by a plethysmograph

ple·thys·mo·graph \-ˌgraf\ n [ISV, fr. Gk plēthysmos increase, fr. plēthynein to increase, fr. plēthys mass, quantity, fr. plēthein] (1872) : an instrument for determining and registering variations in the size of an organ or limb resulting from changes in the amount of blood present or passing through it — **ple·thys·mo·graph·ic** \-ˌthiz-mə-'gra-fik\ adj — **ple·thys·mo·graph·i·cal·ly** \-fi-k(ə-)lē\ adv — **pleth·ys·mog·ra·phy** \ˌple-thiz-'mä-grə-fē\ n

pleu·ra \'plu̇r-ə\, n, pl **pleu·rae** \'plu̇r-ˌē, -ˌī\ or **pleuras** [ME, fr. ML, fr. Gk, rib, side] (15c) : the delicate serous membrane that lines each half of the thorax of mammals and is folded back over the surface of the lung of the same side — **pleu·ral** \'plu̇r-əl\ adj

pleu·ri·sy \'plu̇r-ə-sē\ n [ME pluresie, fr. MF pleuresie, fr. LL pleurisis, alter. of L pleuritis, fr. Gk, fr. pleura side] (14c) : inflammation of the pleura usu. with fever, painful and difficult respiration, cough, and exudation of fluid or fibrinous material into the pleural cavity — **pleu·rit·ic** \plu̇-'ri-tik\ adj

pleu·ro·pneu·mo·nia \ˌplu̇r-ō-nu̇-'mō-nyə, -ō-nyü-\ n [NL] (1725) 1 : combined inflammation of the pleura and lungs 2 : an acute febrile and often fatal respiratory disorder of cattle, goats, sheep, and related animals caused by a mycoplasma (Mycoplasma mycoides)

pleuropneumonia-like organism n (1935) : MYCOPLASMA

pleus·ton \'plü-stən, -ˌstän\ n [ISV pleus- (irreg. fr. Gk plein to sail, float) + -on (as in plankton)] (1943) : organisms living in the thin surface layer existing at the air-water interface of a body of fresh water — **pleus·ton·ic** \plü-'stä-nik\ adj

-plex n comb form [partly fr. L -plex (as in duplex); partly fr. complex] 1 : a figure of a given power ⟨googolplex⟩ 2 : a building divided into an often specified number of spaces (as apartments or movie theaters) ⟨fourplex⟩ ⟨multiplex⟩

plex·i·form \'plek-sə-ˌfȯrm\ adj [NL plexus + E -iform] (ca. 1828) : of, relating to, or having the form or characteristics of a plexus

Plex·i·glas \'plek-si-ˌglas\ trademark — used for acrylic plastic sheets and molding powders

plex·us \'plek-səs\ n, pl **plex·us·es** \-sə-səz\ [NL, fr. L plectere to braid — more at PLY] (1682) 1 : a network of anastomosing or interlacing blood vessels or nerves 2 : an interwoven combination of parts or elements in a structure or system

pli·able \'plī-ə-bəl\ adj [ME, fr. MF, fr. plier to bend, fold — more at PLY] (14c) 1 a : supple enough to bend freely or repeatedly without breaking b : yielding readily to others : COMPLAISANT 2 : adjustable to varying conditions **syn** see PLASTIC — **pli·abil·i·ty** \ˌplī-ə-'bi-lə-tē\ n — **pli·able·ness** \'plī-ə-bəl-nəs\ n — **pli·ably** \-blē\ adv

pli·an·cy \'plī-ən(t)-sē\ n (1699) : the quality or state of being pliant

pli·ant \'plī-ənt\ adj (14c) 1 : PLIABLE 1a 2 : easily influenced : YIELDING 3 : suitable for varied uses **syn** see PLASTIC — **pli·ant·ly** adv — **pli·ant·ness** n

pli·ca \'plī-kə\, n, pl **pli·cae** \-ˌkē, -ˌsē\ [ML, fr. L plicare to fold — more at PLY] (ca. 1706) : a fold or folded part; esp : a groove or fold of skin

pli·cate \'plī-ˌkāt\ adj [L plicatus, pp. of plicare] (1760) 1 : folded lengthwise like a fan ⟨a ～ leaf⟩ 2 : having the surface thrown up into or marked with parallel ridges ⟨～ wing cases⟩

pli·ca·tion \plī-'kā-shən\ n (14c) 1 : the act or process of folding : the state of being folded 2 : FOLD

plié \plē-'ā\ n [F, fr. pp. of plier to bend] (1892) : a bending of the knees outward by a ballet dancer with the back held straight

pli·ers \'plī-(ə-)rz\ n pl but sing or pl in constr [²ply] (ca. 1569) : a small pincers for holding small objects or for bending and cutting wire

¹plight \'plīt\ vt [ME, fr. OE plihtan to endanger, fr. pliht danger; akin to OE plēon to expose to danger, OHG pflegan to take care of] (13c) 1 : to put or give in pledge : ENGAGE ⟨～ one's troth⟩ — **plight·er** n

²plight n (13c) : a solemnly given pledge : ENGAGEMENT

³plight n [ME plit condition, fr. AF, fr. (assumed) VL plicitum fold — more at PLAIT] (13c) : an unfortunate, difficult, or precarious situation

plim·soll \'plim(p)-səl, 'plim-ˌsȯl\ n [prob. fr. the supposed resemblance of the upper edge of the shoe's mudguard to the Plimsoll mark on a ship] (1907) Brit : SNEAKER 2

Plimsoll mark n [Samuel Plimsoll †1898 Eng. shipping reformer] (1884) : a load line or a set of load-line markings on an oceangoing cargo ship — called also Plimsoll line

¹plink \'pliŋk\ vb [imit.] vi (1941) 1 : to make a tinkling sound 2 : to shoot at random targets in an informal and noncompetitive manner ～ vt 1 : to cause to make a tinkling sound 2 : to shoot at esp. in a casual manner — **plink·er** n

²plink n (1954) : a tinkling metallic sound

Plimsoll mark: TF tropical freshwater mark; F freshwater mark; T tropical load line; S summer load line; W winter load line; WNA winter load line, North Atlantic

plinth \'plin(t)th\ n [L plinthus, fr. Gk plinthos] (1601) 1 a : the lowest member of a base : SUBBASE b : a block upon which the moldings of an architrave or trim are stopped at the bottom 2 : a usu. square block serving as a base; broadly : any of various bases or lower parts — see BASE illustration 3 : a course of stones forming a continuous foundation or base course

plio- — see PLEIO-

Pli·o·cene \'plī-ə-ˌsēn\ adj (1831) : of, relating to, or being the latest epoch of the Tertiary or the corresponding system of rocks — see GEOLOGIC TIME table — **Pliocene** n

Plio·film \'plī-ə-ˌfilm\ trademark — used for a glossy membrane made of rubber hydrochloride and used esp. for packaging

plique-à-jour \ˌplēk-(ˌ)ä-'zhu̇r\ n [F, lit., braid letting in daylight] (1878) : a style of enameling in which usu. transparent enamels are fused into the openings of a metal filigree to produce an effect suggestive of stained glass

plis·kie or **plis·ky** \'plis-kē\ n, pl pliskies [origin unknown] (1706) chiefly Scot : PRACTICAL JOKE, TRICK

plis·sé or **plis·se** \pli-'sā\ n [F plissé, fr. pp. of plisser to pleat, fr. MF, fr. pli fold, fr. plier to fold — more at PLY] (1873) 1 : a textile finish of permanently puckered designs formed by treating with a sodium hydroxide solution **2** : a fabric with a plissé finish

plod \'pläd\ *vb* **plod·ded; plod·ding** [origin unknown] *vi* (1562) **1** : to work laboriously and monotonously : DRUDGE **2 a** : to walk heavily or slowly : TRUDGE **b** : to proceed slowly or tediously ⟨the movie just ∼s along⟩ ∼ *vt* : to tread slowly or heavily along or over — **plod** *n* — **plod·der** *n* — **plod·ding·ly** \'plä-diŋ-lē\ *adv*

-ploid *adj comb form* [ISV, fr. *diploid* & *haploid*] : having or being a chromosome number that bears (such) a relationship to or is (so many) times the basic chromosome number of a given group ⟨poly*ploid*⟩

ploi·dy \'plöi-dē\ *n* [fr. such words as *diploidy, hexaploidy*] (1939) : degree of repetition of the basic number of chromosomes

PL/1 \,pē-(,)el-'wən\ *n* [programming language (version) *1*] (1965) : a general-purpose language for programming a computer

¹plonk \'pläŋk, 'plöŋk\ *var of* PLUNK

²plonk *n* [short for earlier *plink-plonk*, perh. modif. of F *vin blanc* white wine] (1930) *chiefly Brit* : cheap or inferior wine

plop \'pläp\ *vb* **plopped; plop·ping** [imit.] *vi* (1821) **1** : to fall, drop, or move suddenly with a sound like that of something dropping into water **2** : to allow the body to drop heavily ⟨*plopped* into a chair⟩ ∼ *vt* : to set, drop, or throw heavily — **plop** *n*

plo·sion \'plō-zhən\ *n* (1899) : EXPLOSION 3

plo·sive \'plō-siv\ *n* [short for *explosive*] (1899) : STOP 9 — **plosive** *adj*

¹plot \'plät\ *n* [ME, fr. OE] (bef. 12c) **1 a** : a small area of planted ground ⟨a vegetable ∼⟩ **b** : a small piece of land in a cemetery **c** : a measured piece of land **2** : GROUND PLAN, PLAT **3** : the plan or main story of a literary work **4** : a secret plan for accomplishing a usu. evil or unlawful end : INTRIGUE **5** : a graphic representation (as a chart) — **plot·less** \-ləs\ *adj* — **plot·less·ness** *n*

syn PLOT, INTRIGUE, MACHINATION, CONSPIRACY, CABAL mean a plan secretly devised to accomplish an evil or treacherous end. PLOT implies careful foresight in planning a complex scheme ⟨an assassination *plot*⟩. INTRIGUE suggests secret underhanded maneuvering in an atmosphere of duplicity ⟨backstairs *intrigue*⟩. MACHINATION implies a contriving of annoyances, injuries, or evils by indirect means ⟨the *machinations* of a party boss⟩. CONSPIRACY implies a secret agreement among several people usu. involving treason or great treachery ⟨a *conspiracy* to fix prices⟩. CABAL typically applies to political intrigue involving persons of some eminence ⟨a *cabal* among powerful senators⟩. **syn** see in addition PLAN

²plot *vb* **plot·ted; plot·ting** *vt* (1588) **1 a** : to make a plot, map, or plan of **b** : to mark or note on or as if on a map or chart **2** : to lay out in plots **3** : to locate (a point) by means of coordinates **b** : to locate (a curve) by plotted points **c** : to represent (an equation) by means of a curve so constructed **4** : to plan or contrive esp. secretly **5** : to invent or devise the plot of (a literary work) ∼ *vi* **1** : to form a plot : SCHEME **2** : to be located by means of coordinates ⟨the data ∼ at a single point⟩

Plo·ti·nism \'plō-'tī-,ni-zəm, 'plō-tᵊn-,i-zəm\ *n* (ca. 1890) : the Neoplatonic ideas of the philosopher Plotinus — **Plo·ti·nist** \-'tī-nist, -tᵊn-ist\ *n*

plot·line \'plät-,līn\ *n* (1952) : PLOT 3

plot·tage \'plä-tij\ *n* (1936) : the area included in a plot of land

plot·ter \'plä-tər\ *n* (1588) : one that plots: as **a** : a person who schemes or conspires **b** : a contriver of a literary plot **c** : a device for plotting; *specif* : an instrument that graphs computer output

plot·ty \'plä-tē\ *adj* **plot·ti·er; -est** (1897) : marked by intricacy of plot or intrigue

plough·man's lunch \'plaů-mənz-\ *n* (1970) : a cold lunch served esp. in an English pub typically including bread, cheese, and pickled onions

plo·ver \'plə-vər, 'plō-\ *n, pl* **plover** *or* **plovers** [ME, fr. MF, fr. (assumed) VL *pluviarius*, fr. L *pluvia* rain — more at PLUVIAL] (14c) **1** : any of a family (Charadriidae) of shore-inhabiting birds that differ from the sandpipers in having a short hard-tipped bill and usu. a stouter more compact build **2** : any of various birds (as a turnstone or sandpiper) related to the plovers

¹plow *or* **plough** \'plaů\ *n* [ME, fr. OE *plōh* hide of land; akin to OHG *pfluog* plow] (12c) **1** : an implement used to cut, lift, and turn over soil esp. in preparing a seedbed **2** : any of various devices (as a snowplow) operating like a plow

²plow *or* **plough** *vt* (15c) **1 a** : to turn, break up, or work with a plow **b** : to make (as a furrow) with a plow **2** : to cut into, open, or make furrows or ridges in with or as if with a plow **3** : to cleave the surface of or move through (water) ⟨whales ∼*ing* the ocean⟩ **4** : to clear away snow from with a snowplow ⟨∼ the street⟩ ∼ *vi* **1 a** : to use a plow **b** : to bear or admit of plowing **2 a** : to move in a way resembling that of a plow ⟨the car ∼*ed* into a fence⟩ **b** : to proceed steadily and laboriously ⟨had to ∼ through a stack of letters⟩ — **plow·able** \-ə-bəl\ *adj* — **plow·er** \'plaů-(ə)r\ *n*

plow back *vt* (1930) : to reinvest (profits) in a business — **plow·back** \'plaů-,bak\ *n*

plow·boy \'plaů-,böi\ *n* (1596) **1** : a boy who leads the team drawing a plow **2** : a country youth

plow·man \-mən, -,man\ *n* (13c) **1** : a man who guides a plow **2** : a farm laborer

plow·share \'plaů-,sher, -,shar\ *n* [ME *ploughshare*, fr. *plough* plow + *schare* plowshare — more at SHARE] (14c) : a part of a plow that cuts the furrow

plow under *vt* (1900) : to cause to disappear : BURY, OVERWHELM

ploy \'plöi\ *n* [prob. fr. *employ*] (1722) **1** : ESCAPADE, FROLIC **2 a** : a tactic intended to embarrass or frustrate an opponent **b** : a devised or contrived move : STRATAGEM ⟨a ∼ to get her to open the door —Robert B. Parker⟩

¹pluck \'plək\ *vb* [ME, fr. OE *pluccian;* akin to MHG *pflücken* to pluck] *vt* (bef. 12c) **1** : to pull or pick off or out **2** : to remove something (as hairs) from by or as if by plucking ⟨∼ one's eyebrows⟩ **b** : ROB, FLEECE **3** : to move, remove, or separate forcibly or abruptly ⟨∼*ed* the child from the middle of the street⟩ **4 a** : to pick, pull, or grasp at **b** : to play by sounding the strings with the fingers or a pick ∼ *vi* : to make a sharp pull or twitch — **pluck·er** *n*

²pluck *n* (15c) **1** : an act or instance of plucking or pulling **2** : the heart, liver, lungs, and windpipe of a slaughtered animal esp. as an item of food **3** : courageous readiness to fight or continue against odds : dogged resolution

plucky \'plə-kē\ *adj* **pluck·i·er; -est** (1842) : SPIRITED, BRAVE — **pluck·i·ly** \'plə-kə-lē\ *adv* — **pluck·i·ness** \'plə-kē-nəs\ *n*

¹plug \'pləg\ *n* [D, fr. MD *plugge;* akin to MHG *pfloc* plug] (1627) **1 a** : a piece used to fill a hole : STOPPER **b** : an obtruding or obstructing mass of material resembling a stopper **2** : a flat compressed cake of tobacco **3** : a small core or segment removed from a larger object **4** : something inferior; *esp* : an inferior often aged or unsound horse; *also* : a quiet steady cold-blooded horse usu. of light or moderate weight **5 a** : HYDRANT, FIREPLUG **b** : SPARK PLUG **6** : an artificial angling lure used primarily for casting and made with one or more sets of gang hooks **7** : any of various devices resembling or functioning like a plug: as **a** : a male fitting for making an electrical connection to a live circuit by insertion in a receptacle (as an outlet) **b** : a device for connecting electric wires to a jack **8** : a piece of favorable publicity or a favorable mention usu. incorporated in general matter

²plug *vb* **plugged; plug·ging** *vt* (1630) **1** : to stop, make tight, or secure by inserting a plug **2** : to hit with a bullet : SHOOT **3** : to advertise or publicize insistently ∼ *vi* **1** : to become plugged — usu. used with *up* **2** : to work doggedly and persistently ⟨*plugged* away at her homework⟩ **3** : to fire shots — **plug·ger** *n* — **plug into** : to connect or become connected to by or as if by means of a plug ⟨the city was *plugged into* the new highway system⟩

plugged \'pləgd\ *adj* (1694) **1** *of a coin* : altered by the insertion of a plug of base metal **2** : closed by or as if by a plug : OBSTRUCTED

plug hat *n* (1863) : a man's stiff hat (as a bowler or top hat)

plug–in \'pləg-,in\ *adj* (1922) : designed to be connected to an electric circuit by plugging in ⟨a ∼ toy⟩ — **plug–in** *n*

plug in *vi* (1903) : to establish an electric circuit by inserting a plug ∼ *vt* : to attach or connect to a service outlet

plug·o·la \(,)plə-'gō-lə\ *n* [*plug* + *-ola* (as in *payola*)] (1959) : incidental advertising on radio or television that is not purchased like regular advertising

plug–ug·ly \'pləg-,əg-lē\ *n* (1856) : THUG, TOUGH; *esp* : one hired to intimidate

plum \'pləm\ *n, often attrib* [ME, fr. OE *plūme*, modif. of L *prunum* plum, fr. Gk *proumnon*] (bef. 12c) **1 a** : any of numerous trees and shrubs (genus *Prunus*) with globular to oval smooth-skinned fruits that are drupes with oblong seeds **b** : the edible fruit of a plum **2** : any of various trees with edible fruits resembling plums; *also* : the fruit **3 a** : a raisin when used in desserts **b** : SUGARPLUM **4** : something superior or very desirable; *esp* : something desirable given in return for a favor **5** : a dark reddish purple — **plum·like** \-,līk\ *adj*

plum·age \'plü-mij\ *n* [ME, fr. MF, fr. *plume* feather — more at PLUME] (14c) : the feathers of a bird — **plum·aged** \-mijd\ *adj*

¹plumb \'pləm\ *n* [ME, fr. (assumed) OF *plomb* lead, fr. L *plumbum*] (14c) : a lead weight attached to a line and used to indicate a vertical direction — **out of plumb** *or* **off plumb** : out of vertical or true

²plumb *adv* (15c) **1** : straight down or up : VERTICALLY **2** *chiefly dial* : to a complete degree : ABSOLUTELY ⟨'you're ∼ crazy', she remarked, with easy candor —*Harper's Weekly*⟩ **3** : in a direct manner : EXACTLY; *also* : without interval of time : IMMEDIATELY

³plumb *vt* (15c) **1** : to weight with lead **2 a** : to measure the depth of with a plumb **b** : to examine minutely and critically ⟨∼*ing* the book's complexities⟩ **3** : to adjust or test by a plumb line **4** : to seal with lead **5** [back-formation fr. *plumber*] : to supply with or install as plumbing ∼ *vi* : to work as a plumber

⁴plumb *adj* (15c) **1** : exactly vertical or true **2** : THOROUGH, COMPLETE
syn see VERTICAL

plum·ba·go \,pləm-'bā-(,)gō\ *n, pl* **-gos** [L *plumbagin-, plumbago* galena, fr. *plumbum*] (1747) **1** [NL, fr. L] : any of a genus (*Plumbago* of the family Plumbaginaceae, the plumbago family) of woody chiefly tropical plants with alternate leaves and spikes of showy flowers **2** : GRAPHITE 1

plumb bob *n* (ca. 1840) : the metal bob of a plumb line

plumb·er \'plə-mər\ *n* [ME, fr. MF *plommier, plombier*, fr. L *plumbarius*, fr. *plumbum*] (15c) **1** : a dealer or worker in lead **2** : one who installs, repairs, and maintains piping, fittings, and fixtures involved in the distribution and use of water in a building

plumber's helper *n* (1952) : PLUNGER d — called also *plumber's friend*

plumber's snake *n* (1938) : a long flexible rod or cable usu. of steel that is used to free clogged pipes

plumb·ing \'plə-miŋ\ *n* (1666) **1** : the act of using a plumb **2** : a plumber's occupation or trade **3 a** : the apparatus (as pipes and fixtures) concerned in the distribution and use of water in a building **b** : an internal system that resembles plumbing; *esp* : one consisting of conduits or channels for conveying fluids

plum·bism \'pləm-,bi-zəm\ *n* [L *plumbum* lead] (1876) : lead poisoning esp. when chronic

plumb line *n* (15c) **1** : a line (as of cord) that has at one end a weight (as a plumb bob) and is used esp. to determine verticality **2** : a line directed to the center of gravity of the earth : a vertical line

¹plume \'plüm\ *n* [ME, fr. MF, fr. L *pluma* small soft feather — more at FLEECE] (14c) **1 a** : a feather of a bird: as **a** : a large conspicuous or showy feather **b** : CONTOUR FEATHER **c** : PLUMAGE **d** : a cluster of distinctive feathers **2 a** : material (as a feather, cluster of feathers, or a tuft of hair) worn as an ornament **b** : a token of honor or prowess : PRIZE **3** : something resembling a feather (as in shape, appearance, or lightness): as **a** : a plumose appendage of a plant **b** : an elongated and usu. open and mobile column or band (as of smoke, exhaust gases, or blowing snow) **c** : an animal structure having a main shaft bearing many hairs or filamentous parts; *esp* : a full bushy tail

²plume *vt* **plumed; plum·ing** (15c) **1 a** : to provide or deck with feathers **b** : to array showily **2** : to indulge (oneself) in pride with an obvious or vain display of self-satisfaction **3** *of a bird* **a** : to preen and arrange the feathers of (itself) **b** : to preen and arrange (feathers)

plumed \'plümd\ *adj* (15c) : provided with or adorned with or as if with a plume — often used in combination ⟨a white-*plumed* egret⟩

\ə\ abut \ᵊ\ kitten, F table \ər\ further \a\ ash \ā\ ace \ä\ mop, mar
\aů\ out \ch\ chin \e\ bet \ē\ easy \g\ go \i\ hit \ī\ ice \j\ job
\ŋ\ sing \ō\ go \ö\ law \öi\ boy \th\ thin \t̲h̲\ the \ü\ loot \ů\ foot
\y\ yet \zh\ vision \à, k̲, ⁿ, œ, œ̄, ʊᵉ, ū̄, ᵊ\ *see* Guide to Pronunciation

plume·let \'plüm-lət\ *n* (ca. 1847) : a small tuft or plume

plu·me·ria \plü'mir-ē-ə\ *n* [NL, genus name, fr. Charles *Plumier* †1704 Fr. botanist] (1753) : FRANGIPANI

¹**plum·met** \'plə-mət\ *n* [ME *plomet*, fr. MF *plombet* ball of lead, fr. *plomb* lead, fr. (assumed) OF — more at PLUMB] (14c) : PLUMB; *also* : PLUMB LINE

²**plummet** *vi* (1937) **1 :** to fall perpendicularly ⟨birds ~ed down⟩ **2 :** to drop sharply and abruptly ⟨prices ~ed⟩

plum·my \'plə-mē\ *adj* **plum·mi·er; -est** (1759) **1 a :** full of plums ⟨a rich ~ cake⟩ **b :** CHOICE, DESIRABLE ⟨got a ~ role in the movie⟩ **2 a :** having a plum color **b :** rich and mellow often to the point of affectation ⟨a ~ singing voice⟩

plu·mose \'plü-,mōs\ *adj* (ca. 1727) **1 :** having feathers or plumes : FEATHERED **2 :** FEATHERY

¹**plump** \'pləmp\ *vb* [ME] *vi* (14c) **1 :** to drop, sink, or come in contact suddenly or heavily ⟨~ed down in the chair⟩ **2 :** to favor or decide in favor of someone or something strongly or emphatically — used with *for* ~ *vt* **1 :** to drop, cast, or place suddenly or heavily **2 :** to give support and favorable publicity to

²**plump** *n* (15c) : a sudden plunge, fall, or blow; *also* : the sound made by a plump

³**plump** *adv* (1594) **1 :** with a sudden or heavy drop **2 a :** straight down **b :** straight ahead **3 :** without qualification : DIRECTLY

⁴**plump** *n* [ME *plumpe*] (15c) *chiefly dial* : GROUP, FLOCK ⟨a ~ of ducks rose at the same time —H. D. Thoreau⟩

⁵**plump** *vb* [⁶*plump*] *vt* (1533) : to make plump ~ *vi* : to become plump

⁶**plump** *adj* [ME, dull, blunt, fr. MD *plomp*] (1569) **1 :** having a full rounded usu. pleasing form ⟨a ~ woman⟩ **2 :** AMPLE, ABUNDANT — **plump·ish** \'pləm-pish\ *adj*

plump·en \'pləm-pən\ *vb* (1687) : ⁵PLUMP

¹**plump·er** \'pləm-pər\ *n* [⁵*plump*] (1690) : an object carried in the mouth to fill out the cheeks

²**plumper** *n* [¹*plump*] (ca. 1785) *chiefly Brit* : a vote for only one candidate when two or more are to be elected to the same office

¹**plump·ly** \'pləm-plē\ *adv* (1611) : in a plump way ⟨a ~ pretty girl⟩

²**plumply** *adv* [³*plump*] (1786) : in a wholehearted manner and without hesitation or circumlocution : FORTHRIGHTLY

¹**plump·ness** \'pləmp-nəs\ *n* (1545) : the quality or state of being plump

²**plumpness** *n* (1780) : freedom from hesitation or circumlocution

plum pudding *n* (1711) : a rich boiled or steamed pudding containing fruits and spices

plum tomato *n* (ca. 1900) : a small oblong tomato

plu·mule \'plü-(,)myü(ə)l\ *n* [NL *plumula*, fr. L, dim. of *pluma* small soft feather — more at FLEECE] (ca. 1741) **1 :** the primary bud of a plant embryo usu. situated at the apex of the hypocotyl and consisting of leaves and an epicotyl **2 :** a down feather

plumy \'plü-mē\ *adj* **plum·i·er; -est** (1582) **1 :** DOWNY **2 :** having or resembling plumes

¹**plun·der** \'plən-dər\ *vb* **plun·dered; plun·der·ing** \-d(ə-)riŋ\ [G *plündern*] *vt* (1632) **1 a :** to take the goods of by force (as in war) : ROB **b :** to take by force or wrongfully : STEAL, LOOT **2 :** to make extensive use of as if by plundering : use or use up wrongfully ⟨~ the land⟩ ~ *vi* : to commit robbery or looting — **plun·der·er** \-dər-ər\ *n*

²**plunder** *n* (1643) **1 :** an act of plundering : PILLAGING **2 :** something taken by force, theft, or fraud : LOOT **3** *chiefly dial* : personal or household effects *syn* see SPOIL

plun·der·ous \-d(ə-)rəs\ *adj* (1845) : given to plundering

¹**plunge** \'plənj\ *vb* **plunged; plung·ing** [ME, fr. MF *plonger*, fr. (assumed) VL *plumbicare*, fr. L *plumbum* lead] *vt* (14c) **1 :** to cause to penetrate or enter quickly and forcibly into something **2 :** to cause to enter a state or course of action usu. suddenly, unexpectedly, or violently ~ *vi* **1 :** to thrust or cast oneself into or as if into water **2 a :** to become pitched or thrown headlong or violently forward and downward; *also* : to move oneself in such a manner **b :** to act with reckless haste : enter suddenly or unexpectedly **c :** to bet or gamble heavily and recklessly **3 :** to descend or dip suddenly

²**plunge** *n* (15c) : an act or instance of plunging : DIVE; *also* : SWIM

plung·er \'plən-jər\ *n* (1611) : one that plunges: as **a :** DIVER **b :** a reckless gambler or speculator **c** (1) : a sliding reciprocating piece driven by or against fluid pressure; *esp* : PISTON (2) : a piece with a motion more or less like that of a ram or piston **d :** a rubber suction cup on a handle used to free plumbing traps and waste outlets of obstructions

plunk \'pləŋk\ *vb* [imit.] *vt* (1805) **1 :** to pluck or hit so as to produce a quick, hollow, metallic, or harsh sound **2 :** to set down suddenly : PLUMP ~ *vi* **1 :** to make a plunking sound **2 :** to drop abruptly : DIVE **3 :** to come out in favor of someone or something — used with *for* — **plunk** *n* — **plunk·er** *n*

plunk down *vi* (1891) : to drop abruptly : settle into position ~ *vt* **1 a :** to put down usu. firmly or abruptly ⟨plunked the money *down* on the counter⟩ **b :** to settle (oneself) into position ⟨plunked himself *down* on the bench⟩ **2 :** to pay out

plu·per·fect \,plü-'pər-fikt\ *adj* [ME *pluperfyth*, modif. of LL *plusquamperfectus*, lit., more than perfect] (15c) **1 :** PAST PERFECT **2 :** utterly perfect or complete — **pluperfect** *n*

plu·ral \'plur-əl\ *adj* [ME, fr. MF & L; MF *plurel*, fr. L *pluralis*, fr. *plur-, plus* more — more at PLUS] (14c) **1 :** of, relating to, or constituting a class of grammatical forms usu. used to denote more than one or in some languages more than two ⟨*genetics* is ~ in form but takes a singular verb⟩ **2 :** relating to, consisting of, or containing more than one or more than one kind or class ⟨a ~ society⟩ — **plural** *n* — **plu·ral·ly** \-ə-lē\ *adv*

plu·ral·ism \'plur-ə-,li-zəm\ *n* (1818) **1 :** the holding of two or more offices or positions (as benefices) at the same time **2 :** the quality or state of being plural **3 a :** a theory that there are more than one or more than two kinds of ultimate reality **b :** a theory that reality is composed of a plurality of entities **4 a :** a state of society in which

members of diverse ethnic, racial, religious, or social groups maintain an autonomous participation in and development of their traditional culture or special interest within the confines of a common civilization **b :** a concept, doctrine, or policy advocating this state — **plu·ral·ist** \-list\ *adj or n* — **plu·ral·is·tic** \,plur-ə-'lis-tik\ *adj* — **plu·ral·is·ti·cal·ly** \-ti-k(ə-)lē\ *adv*

plu·ral·i·ty \plu-'ra-lə-tē\ *n, pl* **-ties** (14c) **1 a :** the state of being plural **b :** the state of being numerous **c :** a large number or quantity **2 :** PLURALISM 1; *also* : a benefice held by pluralism **3 a :** a number greater than another **b :** an excess of votes over those cast for an opposing candidate **c :** a number of votes cast for a candidate in a contest of more than two candidates that is greater than the number cast for any other candidate but not more than half the total votes cast

plu·ral·ize \'plur-ə-,līz\ *vt* **-ized; -iz·ing** (1803) : to make plural or express in the plural form — **plu·ral·i·za·tion** \,plur-ə-lə-'zā-shən\ *n*

plu·rip·o·tent \plu-'ri-pə-tənt\ *adj* [L *plur-, plus* more + E *potent*] (1916) : not fixed as to developmental potentialities : having developmental plasticity ⟨~ stem cell⟩

¹**plus** \'pləs\ *adj* [L, adv., more, fr. neut. of *plur-, plus*, adj.; akin to Gk *pleion* more, L *plenus* full — more at FULL] (1579) **1 :** algebraically positive **2 :** having, receiving, or being in addition to what is anticipated **3 a :** falling high in a specified range ⟨a grade of C ~⟩ **b :** greater than that specified **c :** possessing a specified quality to a high degree **4 :** electrically positive **5 :** relating to or being a particular one of the two mating types that are required for successful fertilization in sexual reproduction in some lower plants (as a fungus)

²**plus** *n, pl* **plus·es** \'plə-səz\ *also* **plus·ses** (1654) **1 :** PLUS SIGN **2 :** an added quantity **3 :** a positive factor or quality **4 :** SURPLUS

³**plus** *prep* (1668) **1 :** increased by : with the addition of ⟨four ~ five⟩ ⟨principal ~ interest⟩ ⟨made twelve dollars a week ~ room and board —E. L. Doctorow⟩ **2 :** BESIDES — used chiefly in speech and casual writing ⟨~ all this, as a sedative it has no equal —Groucho Marx⟩

⁴**plus** *conj* (ca. 1950) **1 :** AND ⟨the Smyth Report, ~ an idea and some knowledge of bureaucracy, were all I needed —Pat Frank⟩ ⟨a box-office ~ critical and artistic success —G. J. Nathan⟩ ⟨eats alone, a hot beef sandwich ~ a BLT ~ apple pie —Garrison Keillor⟩ **2 :** in addition to which ⟨it was an achievement. *Plus*, I wrote the story and the musical score —Jackie Gleason⟩ ⟨it's also pretty on my open shelves, ~ it smells good —Nikki Giovanni⟩

usage The preposition *plus* has long been used with a meaning equivalent to *and* (as in "two *plus* two"); it is not, therefore, very surprising that in time people have begun to use it as a conjunction much like *and*. Sense 2 is considered to be an adverb by some commentators. It is used chiefly in speech and in informal writing.

plus fours *n pl* (1920) : loose sports knickers made four inches longer than ordinary knickers

¹**plush** \'pləsh\ *n* [MF *peluche*] (1594) : a fabric with an even pile longer and less dense than velvet pile

²**plush** *adj* (ca. 1645) **1 :** relating to, resembling, or made of plush **2 :** notably luxurious — **plush·ly** *adv* — **plush·ness** *n*

plushy \'plə-shē\ *adj* **plush·i·er; -est** (1611) **1 :** having the texture of or covered with plush **2 :** LUXURIOUS, SHOWY — **plush·i·ness** *n*

plus·sage \'plə-sij\ *n* (1924) : an amount over and above another amount

plus sign *n* (ca. 1907) : a sign + denoting addition or a positive quantity

Plu·to \'plü-(,)tō\ *n* [L *Pluton-, Pluto*, fr. Gk *Ploutōn*] **1 :** the Greek god of the underworld — compare DIS **2** [NL] : the planet with the farthest mean distance from the sun — see PLANET table

plu·toc·ra·cy \plü-'tä-krə-sē\ *n, pl* **-cies** [Gk *ploutokratia*, fr. *ploutos* wealth; akin to Gk *plein* to sail, float — more at FLOW] (1652) **1 :** government by the wealthy **2 :** a controlling class of the wealthy — **plu·to·crat** \'plü-tə-,krat\ *n* — **plu·to·crat·ic** \,plü-tə-'kra-tik\ *adj* — **plu·to·crat·i·cal·ly** \-ti-k(ə-)lē\ *adv*

plu·ton \'plü-,tän\ *n* [prob. back-formation fr. *plutonic*] (1936) : a typically large body of intrusive igneous rock

plu·to·ni·an \plü-'tō-nē-ən\ *adj, often cap* (1667) : of, relating to, or characteristic of Pluto or the lower world : INFERNAL

plu·ton·ic \plü-'tä-nik\ *adj* [L *Pluton-, Pluto*] (1833) **1 :** formed by solidification of magma deep within the earth and crystalline throughout ⟨~ rock⟩ **2** *often cap* : PLUTONIAN

plu·to·ni·um \plü-'tō-nē-əm\ *n* [NL, fr. *Pluton-, Pluto*, the planet Pluto] (1942) : a radioactive metallic element similar chemically to uranium that is formed as the isotope 239 by decay of neptunium and found in minute quantities in pitchblende, that undergoes slow disintegration with the emission of an alpha particle to form uranium 235, and that is fissionable with slow neutrons to yield atomic energy — see ELEMENT table

¹**plu·vi·al** \'plü-vē-əl\ *adj* [L *pluvialis*, fr. *pluvia* rain, fr. fem. of *pluvius* rainy, fr. *pluere* to rain — more at FLOW] (ca. 1656) **1 a :** of or relating to rain **b :** characterized by abundant rain **2** *of a geologic change* : resulting from the action of rain

²**pluvial** *n* (1929) : a prolonged period of wet climate

¹**ply** \'plī\ *vb* **plied; ply·ing** [ME *plien*, short for *applien* to apply] *vt* (14c) **1 a :** to use or wield diligently ⟨busily ~ing his pen⟩ **b :** to practice or perform diligently ⟨~ a trade⟩ **2 :** to keep furnishing or supplying something to ⟨plied us with liquor⟩ **3 a :** to make a practice of rowing or sailing over or on ⟨the boat *plies* the river⟩ **b :** to go or travel regularly over, on, or through ⟨jets ~ing the skies⟩ ~ *vi* **1 :** to apply oneself steadily **2 :** to go or travel regularly ⟨a steamer ~ing between the towns⟩

²**ply** *n, pl* **plies** [³*ply*] (1532) **1 a :** one of several layers (as of cloth) usu. sewn or laminated together **b :** one of the strands in a yarn **c :** one of the veneer sheets forming plywood **d :** a layer of a paper or paperboard **2 :** INCLINATION, BIAS

³**ply** *vt* **plied; ply·ing** [ME *plien* to fold, fr. MF *plier*, fr. L *plicare*; akin to OHG *flehtan* to braid, L *plectere*, Gk *plekein*] (ca. 1909) : to twist together ⟨~ two single yarns⟩

Plym·outh Rock \'pli-məth-\ *n* [*Plymouth Rock*, on which the Pilgrims are supposed to have landed in 1620] (1849) : any of an American breed of medium-sized single-combed dual-purpose domestic fowls

ply·wood \'plī-,wůd\ *n* (1907) : a structural material consisting of sheets of wood glued or cemented together with the grains of adjacent layers arranged at right angles or at a wide angle

-pnea *or* **-pnoea** *n comb form* [NL, fr. Gk *-pnoia*, fr. *pnoia*, fr. *pnein* to breathe] : breath : breathing ⟨hyper*pnea*⟩ ⟨a*pnoea*⟩

pneum- *or* **pneumo-** *comb form* [NL, partly fr. Gk pneum- (fr. *pneuma*); partly fr. Gk *pneumōn* lung]   **1** : air : gas ⟨*pneumo*thorax⟩   **2** : lung ⟨*pneumo*coniosis⟩   **3** : respiration ⟨*pneumo*graph⟩   **4** : pneumonia ⟨*pneumo*coccus⟩

pneu·ma \'nü-mə, 'nyü-\ *n* [Gk] (1884) : SOUL, SPIRIT

pneumat- *or* **pneumato-** *comb form* [Gk, fr. *pneumat-, pneuma*]   **1** : air : vapor : gas ⟨*pneumato*lytic⟩   **2** : respiration ⟨*pneumato*phore⟩

pneu·mat·ic \nù-'ma-tik, nyü-\ *adj* [L *pneumaticus*, fr. Gk *pneumatikos*, fr. *pneumat-, pneuma* air, breath, spirit, fr. *pnein* to breathe — more at SNEEZE] (1659)   **1** : of, relating to, or using gas (as air or wind): **a** : moved or worked by air pressure   **b** (1) : adapted for holding or inflated with compressed air   (2) : having air-filled cavities   **2** : of or relating to the pneuma ⟨SPIRITUAL   **3** : having a well-proportioned feminine figure; *esp* : having a full bust — **pneu·mat·i·cal·ly** \-ti-k(ə-)lē\ *adv* — **pneu·ma·tic·i·ty** \,nü-mə-'ti-sə-tē, ,nyü-\ *n*

pneu·ma·tol·o·gy \,nü-mə-'tä-lə-jē, ,nyü-\ *n* [NL *pneumatologia*, fr. Gk *pneumat-, pneuma* + NL *-logia* -logy] (1678) : the study of spiritual beings or phenomena

pneu·ma·to·lyt·ic \,nü-mə-t²l-'i-tik, ,nyü-; (,)n(y)ü-,ma-\ *adj* [ISV] (1896) : formed or forming by hot vapors or superheated liquids under pressure — used esp. of minerals and ores

pneu·mat·o·phore \nù-'ma-tə-,fór, nyü-, -,fór\ *n* [ISV] (1859)   **1** : a muscular gas-containing sac that serves as a float on a siphonophore colony   **2** : a root often functioning as a respiratory organ in a wetland plant

pneu·mo·coc·cus \,nü-mə-'kä-kəs, ,nyü-\ *n, pl* **-coc·ci** \-'käk-,sī, -,sē; -'kä-,ki, -,kē\ [NL] (1881) : a bacterium (*Streptococcus pneumoniae*) that causes an acute pneumonia involving one or more lobes of the lung — **pneu·mo·coc·cal** \-'kä-kəl\ *adj*

pneu·mo·co·ni·o·sis \,nü-mō-,kō-nē-'ō-səs, ,nyü-\ *n, pl* **-o·ses** \-,sēz\ [NL, fr. *pneum-* + Gk *konis* dust — more at INCINERATE] (1881) : a disease of the lungs caused by the habitual inhalation of irritants (as mineral or metallic particles) — compare BLACK LUNG, SILICOSIS

Pneu·mo·cys·tis ca·ri·nii pneumonia \,nü-mə-'sis-təs-kə-'rī-nē-,ē-, ,nyü-\ *n* [NL *Pneumocystis carinii*, species name] (1964) : a pneumonia that affects individuals whose immunological defenses have been compromised, that is caused by a microorganism (*Pneumocystis carinii*), and that attacks esp. the interstitial tissue of the lungs with marked thickening of the alveolar septa and alveoli

pneu·mo·graph \'nü-mə-,graf, 'nyü-\ *n* [ISV] (1878) : an instrument for recording thoracic movements or volume change during respiration

pneu·mo·nec·to·my \,nü-mə-'nek-tə-mē, ,nyü-\ *n, pl* **-mies** [Gk *pneumōn* + ISV *-ectomy*] (ca. 1895) : excision of an entire lung or of one or more lobes of a lung

pneu·mo·nia \nù-'mō-nyə, nyü-\ *n* [NL, fr. Gk, fr. *pneumōn* lung, alter. of *pleumōn* — more at PULMONARY] (1603) : a disease of the lungs characterized by inflammation and consolidation followed by resolution and caused by infection or irritants

pneu·mon·ic \nù-'mä-nik, nyü-\ *adj* [NL *pneumonicus*, fr. Gk *pneumonikos*, fr. *pneumōn*] (1675)   **1** : of, relating to, or affecting the lungs : PULMONIC, PULMONARY   **2** : of, relating to, or affected with pneumonia

pneu·mo·ni·tis \,nü-mə-'nī-təs, ,nyü-\ *n* [NL, fr. Gk *pneumōn*] (ca. 1834) : inflammation of the lungs

pneu·mo·tho·rax \,nü-mə-'thór-,aks, ,nyü-, -'thór-\ *n* [NL] (1821) : a condition in which air or other gas is present in the pleural cavity and which occurs spontaneously as a result of disease or injury of lung tissue or puncture of the chest wall or is induced as a therapeutic measure to collapse the lung

¹poach \'pōch\ *vt* [ME *pochen*, fr. MF *pocher*, fr. OF *pochier*, lit., to put into a bag, fr. *poche* bag, pocket, of Gmc origin; akin to OE *pocca* bag] (15c) : to cook in simmering liquid

²poach *vb* [MF *pocher*, of Gmc origin; akin to ME *poken* to poke] *vi* (1611)   **1** : to encroach upon esp. for the purpose of taking something   **2** : to trespass for the purpose of stealing game; *also* : to take game or fish illegally ⟨∼ at⟩   **1** : to trespass on ⟨a field ∼ed too frequently by the amateur —*Times Lit. Supp.*⟩   **2 a** : to take (game or fish) by illegal methods   **b** : to appropriate (something) as one's own

¹poach·er \'pō-chər\ *n* [²*poach*] (1614)   **1** : one that trespasses or steals   **2** : one who kills or takes wild animals (as game or fish) illegally

²poacher *n* [¹*poach*] (1861)   **1** : a covered pan containing a plate with depressions or shallow cups in each of which an egg can be cooked over steam rising from boiling water in the bottom of the pan   **2** : a baking dish in which food (as fish) can be poached

po'·boy \'pō-,bói\ *var of* POOR BOY

po·chard \'pō-chərd\ *n* [origin unknown] (1552) : any of numerous rather heavy-bodied diving ducks (esp. genus *Aythya*) with a large head and with feet and legs placed far back under the body

¹pock \'päk\ *n* [ME *pokke*, fr. OE *pocc*; akin to MLG & MD *pocke* pock] (bef. 12c) : a pustule in an eruptive disease (as smallpox); *also* : a spot suggesting such a pustule

²pock *vt* (1841) : to mark with or as if with pocks : PIT

¹pock·et \'pä-kət\ *n* [ME *poket*, fr. ONF *pokete*, dim. of *poke* bag, of Gmc origin; akin to OE *pocca* bag] (15c)   **1 a** : a small bag carried by a person : PURSE   **b** : a small bag that is sewed or inserted in a garment so that it is open at the top or side ⟨coat ∼⟩   **2** : supply of money : MEANS   **3** : RECEPTACLE, CONTAINER: as   **a** : an opening at the corner or side of a billiard table   **b** : a superficial pouch in some animals   **4** : a small often isolated area or group ⟨∼s of unemployment⟩: **a** (1) : a cavity containing a deposit (as of gold, water, or gas)   (2) : a small body of ore   **b** : AIR POCKET   **5** : a place for a batten made by sewing a strip on a sail   **6 a** : the position of a contestant in a race hemmed in by others   **c** : an area formed by blockers from which a football quarterback attempts to pass   **7** : the concave area at the base of the finger sections of a baseball glove or mitt in which the ball is normally caught — **pock·et·ful** \-,fúl\ *n* — **in one's pocket** : in one's control or possession — **in pocket**   **1** : provided with funds   **2** : in the position of having made a profit — **out of pocket**   **1** : low on money or funds   **2** : having suffered a loss

²pocket *vt* (1589)   **1 a** : to put or enclose in or as if in one's pocket ⟨∼ed the change⟩   **b** : to appropriate to one's own use : STEAL   **c** : to refuse assent to (a bill) by a pocket veto   **2** : to put up with : ACCEPT   **3** : to set aside : SUPPRESS ⟨∼ed his pride⟩   **4 a** : to hem in   **b** : to drive (a ball) into a pocket of a pool table   **5** : to cover or supply with pockets — **pock·et·able** \'pä-kə-tə-bəl\ *adj*

³pocket *adj* (1612)   **1 a** : small enough to be carried in the pocket   **b** : SMALL, MINIATURE ⟨a ∼ park⟩   **2 a** : of or relating to money   **b** : carried in or paid from one's own pocket

pocket battleship *n* (1930) : a small German battleship built so as to come within treaty limitations of tonnage and armament

pocket billiards *n pl but usu sing in constr* (1913) : POOL 2b

¹pock·et·book \'pä-kət-,búk\ *n* (1617)   **1** *often* **pocket book** : a small esp. paperback book that can be carried in the pocket   **2** : a flat typically leather folding case for money or personal papers that can be carried in a pocket or handbag   **3 a** : PURSE   **b** : HANDBAG   **4** : financial resources : INCOME

²pocketbook *adj* (1894) : relating to or involving economic interests ⟨∼ issues⟩

pocket borough *n* (1856) : an English constituency controlled before parliamentary reform by a single person or family

pocket edition *n* (1715)   **1** : POCKETBOOK 1   **2** : a miniature form of something

pocket gopher *n* (1873) : GOPHER 2a

pocket–handkerchief *n* (1645) : a handkerchief carried in the pocket

pock·et·knife \'pä-kət-,nif\ *n* (1727) : a knife that has one or more blades that fold into the handle and that can be carried in the pocket

pocket money *n* (1632) : money for small personal expenses

pocket mouse *n* (1884) : any of various nocturnal burrowing rodents (family Heteromyidae) that resemble mice, live in arid parts of western No. America, and have long hind legs and tail and fur-lined cheek pouches

pock·et–size \'pä-kət-,sīz\ *also* **pock·et–sized** \-,sīzd\ *adj* (1907)   **1** : of a size convenient for carrying in the pocket   **2** : SMALL ⟨a ∼ country⟩

pocket veto *n* (1842) : an indirect veto of a legislative bill by an executive through retention of the bill unsigned until after adjournment of the legislature — **pocket veto** *vt*

¹pock·mark \'päk-,märk\ *n* (ca. 1673) : a mark, pit, or depressed scar caused by smallpox or acne; *also* : an imperfection or depression like a pockmark

²pockmark *vt* (1756) : to cover with or as if with pockmarks : PIT

pocket mouse

pocky \'pä-kē\ *adj* (14c) : covered with pocks

po·co \'pō-(,)kō, 'pō-\ *adv* [It, little, fr. L *paucus* — more at FEW] (1724) : to a slight degree : SOMEWHAT — used to qualify a direction in music ⟨∼ allegro⟩

po·co a po·co \'pō-kō-(,)ä-'pō-(,)kō, 'pō-kō-(,)ä-'pō-\ *adv* [It] (ca. 1854) : little by little : GRADUALLY — used as a direction in music

po·co·cu·ran·te \'pō-kō-kyú-'ran-tē, -kú-\ *adj* [It *poco curante* caring little] (1815) : INDIFFERENT, NONCHALANT — **po·co·cu·ran·tism** \-'ran-,ti-zəm\ *n*

po·co·sin \pə-'kō-s³n\ *n* [prob. fr. Virginia or North Carolina Algonquian] (1634) : an upland swamp of the coastal plain of the southeastern U.S.

¹pod \'päd\ *n* [origin unknown] (1573)   **1** : a bit socket in a brace   **2** : a straight groove or channel in the barrel of an auger

²pod *n* [prob. alter. of *cod* bag — more at CODPIECE] (1688)   **1** : a dry dehiscent pericarp or fruit that is composed of one or more carpels; *esp* : LEGUME   **2 a** : an anatomical pouch   **b** : a grasshopper egg case   **3** : a tapered and roughly cylindrical body of ore or mineral   **4** : a usu. protective container or housing: as   **a** : a streamlined compartment (as for fuel) under the wings or fuselage of an aircraft   **b** : a compartment (as for personnel, a power unit, or an instrument) on a ship or craft

³pod *vi* **pod·ded; pod·ding** (1734) : to produce pods

⁴pod *n* [origin unknown] (1832) : a number of animals (as whales) clustered together

-pod *n comb form* [Gk *-podos*, fr. *pod-, pous* foot — more at FOOT] : foot : part resembling a foot ⟨pleo*pod*⟩

po·da·gra \pə-'da-grə\ *n* [ME, fr. L, fr. Gk, lit., foot trap, fr. *pod-, pous* + *agra* hunt, catch; prob. akin to Gk *agein* to drive, lead — more at AGENT] (14c) : a painful condition of the big toe caused by gout

pod corn *n* (1893) : an Indian corn that has each kernel enclosed in a chaffy shell similar to that of other cereals

po·de·sta \,pō-də-'stä\ *n* [It *podestà*, lit., power, fr. L *potestat-, potestas*, irreg. fr. *potis* able — more at POTENT] (1548) : a chief magistrate in a medieval Italian municipality

podgy \'pä-jē\ *adj* **podg·i·er; -est** [*podge* something pudgy] (1846) *chiefly Brit* : PUDGY

po·di·a·try \pə-'dī-ə-trē, pō-\ *n* [Gk *pod-, pous* + E *-iatry*] (1914) : the medical care and treatment of the human foot — called also chiropody — **po·di·at·ric** \,pō-dē-'a-trik\ *adj* — **po·di·a·trist** \pə-'dī-ə-trist, pō-\ *n*

po·di·um \'pō-dē-əm\ *n, pl* **podiums** *or* **po·dia** \-dē-ə\ [L — more at PEW] (1743)   **1** : a low wall serving as a foundation or terrace wall: as   **a** : one around the arena of an ancient amphitheater serving as a base for the tiers of seats   **b** : the masonry under the stylobate of a temple   **2 a** : a dais esp. for an orchestral conductor   **b** : LECTERN

-podium *n comb form, pl* **-podia** [NL, fr. Gk *podion*, dim. of *pod-, pous* foot — more at FOOT] : foot : part resembling a foot ⟨pseudo*podium*⟩

podo·phyl·lin \,pä-də-'fi-lən\ *n* [ISV, fr. NL *Podophyllum*] (1851) : a resin obtained from podophyllum and used in medicine as a caustic

podo·phyl·lum \-'fi-ləm\ *n, pl* **-phyl·li** \-'fi-,lī\ *or* **-phyllums** [NL, fr. *Podophyllum*, genus of herbs including the mayapple] (1842) : the dried rhizome and rootlet of the mayapple that is used as a caustic or as a source of the more effective podophyllin

Po·dunk \'pō-,dəŋk\ *n* [*Podunk*, village in Mass. or locality in Conn.] (1846) : a small, unimportant, and isolated town

---

\ə\ abut   \³\ kitten, F table   \ər\ further   \a\ ash   \ā\ ace   \ä\ mop, mar
\aú\ out   \ch\ chin   \e\ bet   \ē\ easy   \g\ go   \i\ hit   \ī\ ice   \j\ job
\ŋ\ sing   \ō\ go   \ó\ law   \ói\ boy   \th\ thin   \th̲\ the   \ü\ loot   \ú\ foot
\y\ yet   \zh\ vision   \á, k̲, ⁿ, œ, œ̄, ɶ, ɶ̄, ʸ\ *see* Guide to Pronunciation

pod·zol *also* **pod·sol** \'päd-,zòl\ *n* [Russ] (1908) : any of a group of zonal soils that develop in a moist climate esp. under coniferous or mixed forest and have an organic mat and a thin organic-mineral layer above a light gray leached layer resting on a dark illuvial horizon enriched with amorphous clay — **pod·zol·ic** \päd-'zä-lik, -'zò-\ *adj*

pod·zol·i·za·tion *also* **pod·sol·i·za·tion** \,päd-,zò-lə-'zä-shən\ *n* (1912) : a process of soil formation esp. in humid regions involving principally leaching of the upper layers with accumulation of material in lower layers and development of characteristic horizons; *specif* : the development of a podzol — **pod·zol·ize** \'päd-,zò-,līz\ *vb*

po·em \'pō-əm, -im, 'pōm *also* 'pó(-)im, 'pō-,em\ *n* [MF *poeme*, fr. L *poema*, fr. Gk *poiēma*, fr. *poiein*] (15c) **1** : a composition in verse **2** : something suggesting a poem (as in expressiveness, lyricism, or formal grace) ⟨the house we stayed in . . . was itself a ∼ —H. J. Laski⟩

po·e·sy \'pō-ə-zē, -sē\ *n, pl* **po·e·sies** [ME *poesie*, fr. MF, fr. L *poesis*, fr. Gk *poiēsis*, lit., creation, fr. *poiein*] (14c) **1 a** : a poem or body of poems **b** : POETRY **c** : artificial or sentimentalized poetic writing **2** : poetic inspiration

po·et \'pō-ət, -it *also* 'pó(-)it\ *n* [ME, fr. MF *poete*, fr. L *poeta*, fr. Gk *poiētēs* maker, poet, fr. *poiein* to make; akin to Skt *cinoti* he gathers, heaps up] (14c) **1** : one who writes poetry : a maker of verses **2** : one (as a creative artist) of great imaginative and expressive capabilities and special sensitivity to the medium

po·et·as·ter \'pō-ə-,tas-tər\ *n* [NL, fr. L *poeta* + *-aster* -aster] (1599) : an inferior poet

po·et·ess \'pō-ə-təs, 'pō-i- *also* 'pó(-)i-\ *n* (1530) : a girl or woman who is a poet

po·et·ic \pō-'e-tik\ *adj* (1530) **1 a** : of, relating to, or characteristic of poets or poetry **2** : written in verse

po·et·i·cal \-ti-kəl\ *adj* (14c) **1** : POETIC **2** : being beyond or above the truth of history or nature : IDEALIZED ⟨had ∼ ideas about love⟩ — **po·et·i·cal·ly** \-k(ə-)lē\ *adv* — **po·et·i·cal·ness** \-ti-kəl-nəs\ *n*

po·et·i·cism \pō-'e-tə-,si-zəm\ *n* (1847) : an archaic, trite, or strained expression in poetry

po·et·i·cize \-,sīz\ *vt* **-cized; -ciz·ing** (1804) : to give a poetic quality to

poetic justice *n* (ca. 1890) : an outcome in which vice is punished and virtue rewarded usu. in a manner peculiarly or ironically appropriate

poetic license *n* (1819) : LICENSE 4

po·et·ics \pō-'e-tiks\ *n pl but sing or pl in constr* (ca. 1741) **1 a** : a treatise on poetry or aesthetics **b** *also* **po·et·ic** \-'tik\ : poetic theory or practice **2** : poetic feelings or utterances

po·et·ize \'pō-ə-,tīz\ *vb* **-ized; -iz·ing** *vi* (1581) : to compose poetry ∼ *vt* : POETICIZE — **po·et·iz·er** *n*

poet laureate *n, pl* **poets laureate** *or* **poet laureates** (15c) **1** : a poet honored for achievement in his art **2** : a poet appointed for life by an English sovereign as a member of the royal household and formerly expected to compose poems for court and national occasions **3** : one regarded by a country or region as its most eminent or representative poet

po·et·ry \'pō-ə-trē, -i-trē *also* 'pó(-)i-trē\ *n* (14c) **1 a** : metrical writing : VERSE **b** : the productions of a poet : POEMS **2** : writing that formulates a concentrated imaginative awareness of experience in language chosen and arranged to create a specific emotional response through meaning, sound, and rhythm **3 a** : something likened to poetry esp. in beauty of expression **b** : poetic quality or aspect ⟨the ∼ of dance⟩

po–faced \'pō-,fāst\ *adj* [perh. fr. *po* chamber pot, toilet, fr. F *pot* pot] (1934) *Brit* : having an assumed solemn, serious, or earnest expression or manner : piously or hypocritically solemn

pog·o·nip \'päg-ə-,nip\ *n* [Shoshone *payɨnappɨh* cloud] (1865) : a dense winter fog containing frozen particles that is formed in deep mountain valleys of the western U.S.

po·go·noph·o·ran \,pō-gə-'nä-fə-rən\ *n* [NL *Pogonophora*, fr. Gk *pōgōnophora*, neut. pl. of *pōgōnophoros* wearing a beard, fr. *pōgōn* beard + *-phoros* -phore] (1963) : any of a phylum (Pogonophora) of marine wormlike animals of uncertain systematic relationships that live in chitinous tubes, have obscure segmentation, and lack a mouth and digestive tract — **pogonophoran** *adj*

po·go stick \'pō-(,)gō-\ *n* [fr. *Pogo*, a trademark] (1921) : a pole with a strong spring at the bottom and two footrests on which a person stands and moves along with a series of jumps

¹po·grom \'pō-grəm, 'pä-; pō-'gräm, pə-\ *n* [Yiddish, fr. Russ, lit., devastation] (1903) : an organized massacre of helpless people; *specif* : such a massacre of Jews

²pogrom *vt* (1915) : to massacre or destroy in a pogrom

po·grom·ist \'pō-grə-mist, 'pä-; pō-'grä-, pə-\ *n* (1907) : one who organizes or takes part in a pogrom

po·gy \'pō-gē\ *n, pl* **pogies** [by shortening & alter. fr. *poghaden*, perh. fr. Eastern Abenaki] (ca. 1847) : MENHADEN

poi \'pói\ *n, pl* **poi** *or* **pois** [Hawaiian & Samoan] (1823) : a Hawaiian food of taro root cooked, pounded, and kneaded to a paste and often allowed to ferment

-poiesis *n comb form, pl* **-poieses** [NL, fr. Gk *poiēsis* creation — more at POESY] : production : formation ⟨hematopoiesis⟩

-poietic *adj comb form* [Gk *poiētikos* creative, fr. *poiētēs* maker — more at POET] : productive : formative ⟨hematopoietic⟩

poi·gnance \'pói-nyən(t)s *sometimes* 'pói(g)-nən(t)s\ *n* (1769) : POIGNANCY

poi·gnan·cy \'pói-nyən(t)-sē *sometimes* 'pói(g)-nən(t)-sē\ *n, pl* **-cies** (1730) **1** : the quality or state of being poignant **2** : an instance of poignancy

poi·gnant \'pói-nyənt *sometimes* 'pói(g)-nənt\ *adj* [ME *poinaunt*, fr. MF *poignant*, prp. of *poindre* to prick, sting, fr. L *pungere* — more at PUNGENT] (14c) **1** : pungently pervasive ⟨a ∼ perfume⟩ **2 a** (1) : painfully affecting the feelings : PIERCING (2) : deeply affecting : TOUCHING **b** : designed to make an impression : CUTTING ⟨∼ satire⟩ **3 a** : pleasurably stimulating **b** : being to the point : APT **syn** see PUNGENT, MOVING — **poi·gnant·ly** *adv*

poi·ki·lo·therm \'pói-'kē-lə-,thərm, -'ki-\ *n* [Gk *poikilos* variegated + ISV *-therm* — more at PAINT] (1920) : an organism (as a frog) with a variable body temperature that is usu. slightly higher than the temperature of its environment : a cold-blooded organism — **poi·ki·lo·ther·mic** \,pói-kə-lō-'thər-mik\ *adj*

poi·lu \pwäl-'yü, pwä-'lü; 'pwäl-,yü, 'pwä-,lü; pwȧ-lw̄ē\ *n* [F, fr. *poilu* hairy, fr. MF, fr. *poil* hair, fr. L *pilus*] (1914) : a French soldier; *esp* : a front-line soldier in World War I

poin·ci·ana \,pòin(t)-sē-'a-nə, ,p(w)än(t)-\ *n* [NL, fr. De *Poinci*, 17th cent. governor of part of the French West Indies] (1731) : any of several ornamental tropical leguminous trees or shrubs (genera *Caesalpinia* and *Delonix*) formerly placed in their own genus (*Poinciana*) — compare ROYAL POINCIANA

poin·set·tia \pòin-'se-tē-ə, ÷-pòint-, ÷-'se-tə\ *n* [NL, fr. Joel R. *Poinsett* †1851 Am. diplomat] (1836) : any of several spurges (genus *Euphorbia*) with flower clusters subtended by showy involucral bracts; *esp* : a showy Mexican and Central American plant (*E. pulcherrima*) with tapering usu. scarlet bracts that suggest petals and surround small yellow flowers

¹point \'pòint\ *n* [ME, partly fr. OF, puncture, small spot, point in time or space, fr. L *punctum*, fr. neut. of *punctus*, pp. of *pungere* to prick; partly fr. OF *pointe* sharp end, fr. (assumed) VL *puncta*, fr. L, fem. of *punctus*, pp. — more at PUNGENT] (13c) **1 a** (1) : an individual detail : ITEM (2) : a distinguishing detail ⟨tact is one of her strong ∼s⟩ **b** : the most important essential in a discussion or matter ⟨missed the whole ∼ of the joke⟩ **c** : COGENCY **2** *obs* : physical condition **3** : an end or object to be achieved ⟨did not see what ∼ there was in continuing the discussion⟩ **4 a** (1) : a geometric element of which it is postulated that at least two exist and that two suffice to determine a line (2) : a geometric element determined by an ordered set of coordinates **b** (1) : a narrowly localized place having a precisely indicated position ⟨walked to a ∼ 50 yards north of the building⟩ (2) : a particular place : LOCALITY ⟨have come from distant ∼s⟩ **c** (1) : an exact moment ⟨at this ∼ I was interrupted⟩ (2) : a time interval immediately before something indicated : VERGE ⟨at the ∼ of death⟩ **d** (1) : a particular step, stage, or degree in development ⟨had reached the ∼ where nothing seemed to matter anymore⟩ (2) : a definite position in a scale **5 a** : the terminal usu. sharp or narrowly rounded part of something : TIP **b** : a weapon or tool having such a part and used for stabbing or piercing: as (1) : ARROWHEAD (2) : SPEARHEAD **c** (1) : the contact or discharge extremity of an electric device (as a spark plug or distributor) (2) *chiefly Brit* : an electric outlet **6 a** : a projecting usu. tapering piece of land or a sharp prominence **b** (1) : the tip of a projecting body part (2) : TINE 2 (3) *pl* : the extremities or markings of the extremities of an animal esp. when of a color differing from the rest of the body **c** (1) : a railroad switch (2) : the tip of the angle between two rails in a railroad frog **d** : the head of the bow of a stringed instrument **7** : a short musical phrase; *esp* : a phrase in contrapuntal music **8 a** : a very small mark **b** : PUNCTUATION MARK; *esp* : PERIOD (2) : DECIMAL POINT **9** : a lace for tying parts of a garment together used esp. in the 16th and 17th centuries **10** : one of usu. 11 divisions of a heraldic shield that determines the position of a charge **11 a** : one of the 32 equidistant spots of a compass card **b** : the difference of 11¼ degrees between two such successive points **12** : a small detachment ahead of an advance guard or behind a rear guard **13 a** : NEEDLEPOINT 1 **b** : lace made with a bobbin **14** : one of 12 spaces marked off on each side of a backgammon board **15** : a unit of measurement: as **a** (1) : a unit of counting in the scoring of a game or contest (2) : a unit used in evaluating the strength of a bridge hand **b** : a unit of academic credit **c** (1) : a unit used in quoting prices (as of stocks, bonds, and commodities) (2) *pl* : a percentage of the face value of a loan often added as a placement fee or service charge (3) : a percentage of the profits of a business venture (as a motion-picture production) **d** : a unit of about ¹/₇₂ inch used esp. to measure the size of type **16** : the action of pointing: as **a** : the rigidly intent attitude of a hunting dog marking game for a gunner **b** : the action in dancing of extending one leg and arching the foot so that only the tips of the toes touch the floor **17** : a position of a player in various games (as lacrosse); *also* : the player of such a position **18** : a number thrown on the first roll of the dice in craps which the player attempts to repeat before throwing a seven — compare MISSOUT, PASS 13 **19** : credit accruing from creating a good impression ⟨scored ∼s for hard work⟩ — **beside the point** : IRRELEVANT — **in point of** : with regard to : in the matter of ⟨*in point of* law⟩ ⟨*in point of* fact⟩ — **to the point** : RELEVANT, PERTINENT ⟨a suggestion that was *to the point*⟩

²point *vt* (14c) **1 a** : to furnish with a point : SHARPEN ⟨∼ing a pencil with a knife⟩ **b** : to give added force, emphasis, or piquancy to ⟨∼ up a remark⟩ **2** : to scratch out the old mortar from the joints of (as a brick wall) and fill in with new material **3 a** (1) : to mark the pauses or grammatical divisions in : PUNCTUATE (2) : to separate (a decimal fraction) from an integer by a decimal point — usu. used with *off* **b** : to mark (as Hebrew words) with diacritics (as vowel points) **4 a** (1) : to indicate the position or direction of esp. by extending a finger ⟨∼ the way home⟩ (2) : to direct someone's attention to ⟨∼ the way to new knowledge —Elizabeth Hall⟩ — usu. used with *out* or *up* ⟨∼ out a mistake⟩ ⟨∼s up the difference⟩ **b** *of a hunting dog* : to indicate the presence and place of (game) by a point **5 a** : to cause to be turned in a particular direction ⟨∼ a gun⟩ ⟨∼ed the boat upstream⟩ **b** : to extend (a leg) and arch (the foot) in executing a point in dancing ∼ *vi* **1** : to indicate the fact or probability of something specified ⟨everything ∼s to a bright future⟩ **b** : to indicate the position or direction of something esp. by extending a finger ⟨∼ at the map⟩ **c** : to direct attention ⟨can ∼ with pride to their own traditions⟩ **d** : to point game ⟨a dog that ∼s well⟩ **2 a** : to lie extended, aimed, or turned in a particular direction ⟨a directional arrow that ∼ed to the north⟩ **b** : to execute a point in dancing **3** *of a ship* : to sail close to the wind **4** : to train for a particular contest

point–blank \'pòint-'blaŋk\ *adj* (1591) **1 a** : marked by no appreciable drop below initial horizontal line of flight **b** : so close to a target that a missile fired will travel in a straight line to the mark **2** : DIRECT, BLUNT ⟨a ∼ refusal⟩ — **point–blank** *adv*

point count *n* (1950) : a method of evaluating the strength of a hand in bridge by counting points for each high card and usu. for long or short suits; *also* : the value of a hand so evaluated

point d'ap·pui \,pwaⁿ(h)-da-'pwē\ *n, pl* **points d'appui** *same*\ [F, lit., point of support] (1819) : FOUNDATION, BASE

point–de·vice \,pòint-di-'vīs\ *adj* [ME *at point devis* at a fixed point] (1526) *archaic* : marked by punctilious attention to detail : METICULOUS — **point–device** *adv, archaic*

pointe \'pwaⁿ(n)t\ *n* [F *pointe* (*du pied*), lit., tiptoe] (1846) : a ballet position in which the body is balanced on the extreme tip of the toe

¹**point·ed** \'pȯin-təd\ *adj* (14c) **1 a :** having a point **b :** being an arch with a pointed crown; *also* : marked by the use of a pointed arch ⟨∼ architecture⟩ **2 a :** being to the point : PERTINENT **b :** aimed at a particular person or group **3 :** CONSPICUOUS, MARKED ⟨∼ indifference⟩ — **point·ed·ly** *adv* — **point·ed·ness** *n*

²**pointed** *adj* [short for *appointed*] (1523) *obs* : SET, FIXED

poin·telle \,pȯin-'tel\ *n* [perh. fr. ¹*point* + -*elle* (as in *dentelle* lace)] (1953) : an openwork design (as in knitted fabric) typically in the shape of chevrons; *also* : a fabric with this design

point·er \'pȯin-tər\ *n* (1574) **1 a** *pl, cap* : the two stars in the Big Dipper a line through which points to the North Star **b :** one that points out; *esp* : a rod used to direct attention **c :** a computer memory address that contains another address (as of desired data) **2 :** a large strong slender smooth-haired gundog that hunts by scent and indicates the presence of game by pointing **3 :** one that furnishes with points **4 :** a useful suggestion or hint : TIP

point estimate *n* (1966) : the single value assigned to a parameter in point estimation

point estimation *n* (1962) : estimation in which a single value is assigned to a parameter

point guard *n* (1970) : a guard in basketball who is chiefly responsible for running the offense

poin·til·lism \'pwaⁿ(n)-tē-,yi-zəm, 'pȯin-tᵊl-,i-zəm\ *n, often cap* [F *pointillisme*, fr. *pointiller* to stipple, fr. *point* spot — more at POINT] (1901) : the theory or practice in art of applying small strokes or dots of color to a surface so that from a distance they blend together — **poin·til·list** \,pwaⁿ(n)-tē-'yēst, 'pȯin-tᵊl-ist\ *n*

poin·til·lis·tic \,pwaⁿ(n)-tē-'yis-tik, ,pȯin-tᵊl-'is-\ *also* **point·til·list** \,pwaⁿ(n)-tē-'yēst, 'pȯin-tᵊl-ist\ *adj* (1922) **1 :** composed of many discrete details or parts **2 :** of, relating to, or characteristic of pointillism or pointillists

point lace *n* (1672) : NEEDLEPOINT 1

point·less \'pȯint-ləs\ *adj* (1726) **1 :** devoid of meaning : SENSELESS ⟨∼ remark⟩ **2 :** devoid of effectiveness : FLAT ⟨∼ attempts to be funny⟩ — **point·less·ly** *adv* — **point·less·ness** *n*

point man *n* (1903) : a soldier who goes ahead of a patrol; *broadly* : one who is in the forefront (as on a political issue)

point mutation *n* (1925) : mutation due to intramolecular gene reorganization (as by substitution, addition, or deletion of a nucleotide)

point of accumulation (1929) : LIMIT POINT

point of departure (1857) : a starting point esp. in a discussion

point of honor (1612) : a matter seriously affecting one's honor

point of inflection (1743) : INFLECTION POINT

point of no return (1941) **1 :** the point in the flight of an aircraft beyond which the remaining fuel will be insufficient for a return to the starting point with the result that the craft must proceed **2 :** a critical point at which turning back or reversal is not possible

point of view (1720) : a position from which something is considered or evaluated : STANDPOINT

point set topology *n* (1957) : a branch of topology concerned with the properties and theory of topological spaces and metric spaces developed with emphasis on set theory

point source *n* (1903) : a source of radiation (as light) that is concentrated at a point and considered as having no spatial extension

point-to-point *n* (1898) : a cross-country steeplechase

pointy \'pȯin-tē\ *adj* **point·i·er; -est** (1644) **1 :** coming to a rather sharp point **2 :** having parts that stick out sharply here and there

pointy-head \'pȯin-tē-,hed\ *n* (1968) : INTELLECTUAL — usu. used disparagingly — **pointy-head·ed** \-,he-dəd\ *adj*

¹**poise** \'pȯiz\ *n* [ME *poyse* weight, heaviness, fr. MF *pois*, fr. L *pensum*, fr. neut. of *pensus*, pp. of *pendere* to weigh — more at PENDANT] (1555) **1 :** a stably balanced state : EQUILIBRIUM ⟨a ∼ between widely divergent impulses —F. R. Leavis⟩ **2 a :** easy self-possessed assurance of manner : gracious tact in coping or handling; *also* : the pleasantly tranquil interaction between persons of poise ⟨no angry outbursts marred the ∼ of the meeting⟩ **b :** a particular way of carrying oneself : BEARING, CARRIAGE *syn* see TACT

²**poise** *vb* **poised; pois·ing** [ME, to weigh, ponder, fr. MF *pois-*, stem of *peser*, fr. L *pensare* — more at PENSIVE] *vt* (1598) **1 a :** BALANCE; *esp* : to hold or carry in equilibrium ⟨carried a water jar *poised* on her head⟩ **b :** to hold supported or suspended without motion in a steady position ⟨*poised* her fork and gave her guest a knowing look —Louis Bromfield⟩ **2 :** to hold or carry (the head) in a particular way **3 :** to put into readiness : BRACE ∼ *vi* **1 :** to become drawn up into readiness **2 :** HOVER

³**poise** \'pwäz\ *n* [F, fr. Jean Louis Marie *Poiseuille* †1869 Fr. physician and anatomist] (1913) : a centimeter-gram-second unit of viscosity equal to the viscosity of a fluid that would require a shearing force of one dyne to move a square-centimeter area of either of two parallel layers of fluid one centimeter apart with a velocity of one centimeter per second relative to the other layer with the space between the layers being filled with the fluid

poised \'pȯizd\ *adj* (ca. 1643) : having poise: **a :** marked by balance or equilibrium **b :** marked by easy composure of manner or bearing

poi·sha \'pȯi-shə\ *n, pl* **poisha** [Bengali, fr. Hindi *paisā*] (ca. 1976) : the paisa of Bangladesh

¹**poi·son** \'pȯi-zᵊn\ *n* [ME, fr. MF, drink, poisonous drink, poison, fr. L *potion-, potio* drink — more at POTION] (13c) **1 a :** a substance that through its chemical action usu. kills, injures, or impairs an organism **b** (1) : something destructive or harmful (2) : an object of aversion or abhorrence **2 :** a substance that inhibits the activity of another substance or the course of a reaction or process ⟨a catalyst ∼⟩

²**poison** *vt* **poi·soned; poi·son·ing** \'pȯiz-niŋ, 'pȯi-zᵊn-iŋ\ (14c) **1 a :** to injure or kill with poison **b :** to treat, taint, or impregnate with or as if with poison **2 :** to exert a baneful influence on : CORRUPT ⟨∼ed their minds⟩ **3 :** to inhibit the activity, course, or occurrence of — **poi·son·er** \'pȯiz-nər, 'pȯi-zᵊn-ər\ *n*

³**poison** *adj* (1530) **1 :** POISONOUS, VENOMOUS ⟨a ∼ plant⟩ ⟨a ∼ tongue⟩ **2 :** impregnated with poison : POISONED ⟨a ∼ arrow⟩

poison gas *n* (1915) : a poisonous gas or a liquid or a solid giving off poisonous vapors designed (as in chemical warfare) to kill, injure, or disable by inhalation or contact

poison hemlock *n* (ca. 1818) **1 :** a large branching biennial poisonous herb (*Conium maculatum*) of the carrot family with finely divided leaves and white flowers **2 :** WATER HEMLOCK

poison ivy *n* (1784) **1 a :** a climbing plant (*Rhus radicans*) of the cashew family that is esp. common in the eastern and central U.S., that has ternate leaves, greenish flowers, and white berries, and that produces an acutely irritating oil causing a usu. intensely itching skin rash **b :** any of several plants (as poison oak) closely related to poison ivy **2 :** a skin rash caused by poison ivy

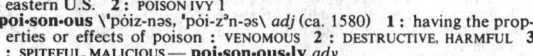

poison oak *n* (1743) **1 :** any of several plants of the same genus (*Rhus*) as poison ivy that produce an oil with similar irritating properties: **a :** a bushy plant (*Rhus diversiloba*) of the Pacific coast **b :** a bushy plant (*Rhus toxicodendron* syn. *R. quercifolia*) of the southeastern U.S. **2 :** POISON IVY 1

poison ivy 1a

poi·son·ous \'pȯiz-nəs, 'pȯi-zⁿ-əs\ *adj* (ca. 1580) **1 :** having the properties or effects of poison : VENOMOUS **2 :** DESTRUCTIVE, HARMFUL **3 :** SPITEFUL, MALICIOUS — **poi·son·ous·ly** *adv*

poison-pen *adj* (1925) : written with malice and spite and usu. anonymously ⟨∼ letter⟩

poison pill *n* (1983) : a financial tactic (as increasing indebtedness) used by a company to deter an unwanted takeover

poison sumac *n* (1817) : a smooth American swamp shrub (*Rhus vernix*) that has pinnate leaves, greenish flowers, and greenish white berries and produces an irritating oil — called also *poison dogwood*

poi·son·wood \'pȯi-zⁿ-,wůd\ *n* (1721) : a poisonous tree (*Metopium toxiferum*) of the cashew family that is native to Florida and the West Indies and has compound leaves, greenish paniculate flowers, and orange-yellow fruits

Pois·son distribution \pwä-'sōⁿ-\ *n* [Siméon D. *Poisson* †1840 Fr. mathematician] (1922) : a probability density function that is often used as a mathematical model of the number of outcomes obtained in a suitable interval of time and space, that has its mean equal to its variance, that is used as an approximation to the binomial distribution, and that has the form

$$f(x) = \frac{e^{-\mu}\mu^x}{x!} \quad \text{where } \mu$$

is the mean and x takes on nonnegative integral values

Poisson's ratio *n* [S. *Poisson*] (1886) : the ratio of transverse to longitudinal strain in a material under tension

¹**poke** \'pōk\ *n* [ME, fr. ONF — more at POCKET] (13c) **1** *chiefly Southern & Midland* : BAG, SACK **2 a :** WALLET **b :** PURSE

²**poke** *vb* **poked; pok·ing** [ME; akin to MD *poken* to poke] *vt* (14c) **1 a** (1) : PROD, JAB ⟨*poked* him in the ribs⟩ (2) : to urge or stir by prodding or jabbing (3) : to cause to prod : THRUST ⟨*poked* a stick at the snake⟩ **b** (1) : PIERCE, STAB (2) : to produce by piercing, stabbing, or jabbing ⟨∼ a hole⟩ **c** (1) : HIT, PUNCH ⟨*poked* him in the nose⟩ (2) : to deliver (a blow) with the fist **2 a :** to cause to project ⟨*poked* her head out of the window⟩ **b :** to make (one's way) by poking ⟨*poked* his way through the ruins⟩ **c :** to interpose or interject in a meddlesome manner ⟨asked him not to ∼ his nose into other people's business⟩ ∼ *vi* **1 a :** to make a prodding, jabbing, or thrusting movement esp. repeatedly **b :** to strike out at something **2 a :** to look about or through something without system : RUMMAGE ⟨*poking* around in the attic⟩ **b :** MEDDLE **3 :** to move or act slowly or aimlessly ⟨just *poked* around and didn't accomplish much⟩ **4 :** to become stuck out or forward : PROTRUDE — **poke fun at :** RIDICULE, MOCK

³**poke** *n* (ca. 1796) **1 a :** a quick thrust : JAB **b :** a blow with the fist : PUNCH **2 :** a projecting brim on the front of a woman's bonnet

⁴**poke** *n* [perh. modif. of Virginia Algonquian *pocone, poughkone* puccoon] (1708) : POKEWEED

poke·ber·ry \'pōk-,ber-ē\ *n* (1774) : the berry of the pokeweed; *also* : POKEWEED

poke bonnet *n* (1820) : a woman's bonnet with a projecting brim at the front

¹**pok·er** \'pō-kər\ *n* (1534) : one that pokes; *esp* : a metal rod for stirring a fire

²**po·ker** \'pō-kər\ *n* [prob. modif. of F *poque*, a card game similar to

poker hands in descending value: *1* five of a kind, *2* royal flush, *3* straight flush, *4* four of a kind, *5* full house, *6* flush, *7* straight, *8* three of a kind, *9* two pairs, *10* one pair

\ə\ abut \ᵊ\ kitten, F table \ər\ further \a\ ash \ā\ ace \ä\ mop, mar \aů\ out \ch\ chin \e\ bet \ē\ easy \g\ go \i\ hit \ī\ ice \j\ job \ŋ\ sing \ō\ go \ȯ\ law \ȯi\ boy \th\ thin \t͟h\ the \ü\ loot \ů\ foot \y\ yet \zh\ vision \ä, k̲, ⁿ, œ, œ̄, ůe, ̄̄ue, ᵊ\ see Guide to Pronunciation poker] (1836) : any of several card games in which a player bets that the value of his or her hand is greater than that of the hands held by others, in which each subsequent player must either equal or raise the bet or drop out, and in which the player holding the highest hand at the end of the betting wins the pot

poker face n [²poker; fr. the poker player's need to conceal emotions during play] (1885) : an inscrutable face that reveals no hint of a person's thoughts or feelings — **po·ker-faced** \'pō-kər-ˌfāst\ adj

poke·weed \'pōk-ˌwēd\ n (1751) : a coarse American perennial herb (Phytolacca americana of the family Phytolaccaceae, the pokeweed family) with racemose white flowers, dark purple juicy berries, a poisonous root, and young shoots sometimes used as potherbs

po·key \'pō-kē\ n, pl **pokeys** [origin unknown] (ca. 1919) slang : JAIL

poky or **pok·ey** \'pō-kē\ adj **pok·i·er; -est** [²poke] (1849) **1** : small and cramped **2** : SHABBY, DULL **3** : annoyingly slow — **pok·i·ly** \-kə-lē\ adv — **pok·i·ness** \-kē-nəs\ n

pol \'päl\ n (ca. 1942) : POLITICIAN

Po·la·bi·an \pō-'lä-bē-ən, -'lä-\ n [Polab, ultim. fr. Polabian po on + Labi, the Elbe River] (1866) **1** or **Po·lab** \pō-'läb\ : a member of a Slavic people formerly dwelling in the basin of the Elbe and on the Baltic coast of Germany **2** : the extinct West Slavic language of the Polabians

Po·lack \'pō-ˌläk, -ˌlak\ n [Pol polak] (1574) **1** obs : a native or inhabitant of Poland **2** : a person of Polish birth or descent — usu. used disparagingly

Po·land Chi·na \'pō-lən(d)-'chī-nə\ n [Poland, Europe + China, Asia] (1879) : any of an American breed of large white-marked black swine

¹po·lar \'pō-lər\ adj [NL polaris, fr. L polus pole] (1551) **1 a** : of or relating to a geographical pole or the region around it **b** : coming from or having the characteristics of such a region **c** (1) : passing over a celestial body's north and south poles ⟨a satellite in a ∼ orbit⟩ (2) : traveling in a polar orbit ⟨a ∼ satellite⟩ **2** : of or relating to one or more poles (as of a magnet) **3** : serving as a guide **4** : diametrically opposite **5** : exhibiting polarity; esp : having a dipole or characterized by molecules having dipoles ⟨a ∼ solvent⟩ **6** : resembling a pole or axis around which all else revolves : PIVOTAL **7** : of, relating to, or expressed in polar coordinates ⟨∼ equations⟩; also : of or relating to a polar coordinate system

²polar n (1848) : a straight line related to a point; specif : the straight line joining the points of contact of the tangents from a point exterior to a conic section

polar bear n (1781) : a large creamy-white bear (Thalarctos maritimus syn. Ursus maritimus) that inhabits arctic regions

polar body n (1888) : a cell that separates from an oocyte during meiosis and that contains a nucleus produced in the first or second meiotic division but very little cytoplasm

polar circle n (1551) : either of the two parallels of latitude each at a distance from a pole of the earth equal to about 23 degrees 27 minutes

polar coordinate n (1816) : either of two numbers that locate a point in a plane by its distance from a fixed point on a line and the angle this line makes with a fixed line

polar front n (1920) : the boundary between the cold air of a polar region and the warmer air of lower latitudes

po·lar·im·e·ter \ˌpō-lə-'ri-mə-tər\ n [ISV, fr. polarization] (ca. 1859) **1** : an instrument for determining the amount of polarization of light or the proportion of polarized light in a partially polarized ray **2** : a polariscope for measuring the amount of rotation of the plane of polarization esp. by liquids — **po·lar·i·met·ric** \pō-ˌlar-ə-'me-trik\ adj — **po·lar·im·e·try** \ˌpō-lə-'ri-mə-trē\ n

Po·lar·is \pə-'lar-əs, -'lär-\ n [NL, fr. polaris polar] : NORTH STAR

po·lar·ise Brit var of POLARIZE

po·lar·i·scope \pō-'lar-ə-ˌskōp\ n [ISV, fr. polarization] (1829) **1** : an instrument for studying the properties of or examining substances in polarized light **2** : POLARIMETER 2 — **po·lar·i·scop·ic** \-ˌlar-ə-'skä-pik\ adj

po·lar·i·ty \pō-'lar-ə-tē, pə-\ n, pl **-ties** (1646) **1** : the quality or condition inherent in a body that exhibits opposite properties or powers in opposite parts or directions or that exhibits contrasted properties or powers in contrasted parts or directions : the condition of having poles **2** : attraction toward a particular object or in a specific direction **3** : the particular state either positive or negative with reference to the two poles or to electrification **4 a** : diametrical opposition **b** : an instance of such opposition

po·lar·i·za·tion \ˌpō-lə-rə-'zā-shən\ n (1812) **1** : the action of polarizing or state of being or becoming polarized: as **a** (1) : the action or process of affecting radiation and esp. light so that the vibrations of the wave assume a definite form (2) : the state of radiation affected by this process **b** : an increase in the resistance of an electrolytic cell often caused by the deposition of gas on one or both electrodes **c** : MAGNETIZATION 2 **2** : division into two opposites **b** : concentration about opposing extremes of groups or interests formerly ranged on a continuum

po·lar·ize \'pō-lə-ˌrīz\ vb **-ized; -iz·ing** [F polariser, fr. NL polaris polar] vt (1811) **1** : to cause (as light waves) to vibrate in a definite pattern **2** : to give physical polarity to **3** : to break up into opposing factions or groupings ⟨a campaign that polarized the electorate⟩ **4** : CONCENTRATE 1 ⟨recreate a cohesive rock community by polarizing . . . an amorphous, fragmented audience —Ellen Willis⟩ ∼ vi : to become polarized — **po·lar·iz·abil·i·ty** \ˌpō-lə-ˌrī-zə-'bi-lə-tē\ n — **po·lar·iz·able** \ˌpō-lə-'rī-zə-bəl\ adj

polar nucleus n (1882) : either of the two nuclei of a seed plant embryo sac that are destined to form endosperm

po·lar·og·ra·phy \ˌpō-lə-'rä-grə-fē\ n [ISV, fr. polarization] (1936) : a method of qualitative or quantitative analysis based on current-voltage curves obtained during electrolysis of a solution with a steadily increasing electromotive force — **po·lar·o·graph·ic** \pō-ˌlar-ə-'gra-fik\ adj — **po·lar·o·graph·i·cal·ly** \-fi-k(ə-)lē\ adv

Po·lar·oid \'pō-lə-ˌröid\ trademark — used esp. for a light-polarizing material used esp. in eyeglasses and lamps to prevent glare or for a camera that develops pictures instantly

po·lar·on \'pō-lə-ˌrän\ n [ISV polar + ²-on] (1946) : a conducting electron in an ionic crystal together with the induced polarization of the surrounding lattice

pol·der \'pōl-dər\ n [D] (1604) : a tract of low land (as in the Netherlands) reclaimed from a body of water (as the sea)

¹pole \'pōl\ n [ME, fr. OE pāl stake, pole, fr. L palus stake; akin to L pangere to fix — more at PACT] (bef. 12c) **1 a** : a long slender usu. cylindrical object (as a length of wood) **b** : a shaft which extends from the front axle of a wagon between wheelhorses and by which the wagon is drawn : TONGUE **c** : a long staff of wood, metal, or fiberglass used in the pole vault **2 a** : a varying unit of length; esp : one measuring 16½ feet (5.03 meters) **b** : a unit of area equal to a square rod (25.293 square meters) **3** : a tree with a breast-high diameter of from 4 to 12 inches (10 to 30 centimeters) **4** : the inside front row position on the starting line for a race

²pole vb **poled; pol·ing** vt (1573) **1** : to act upon with a pole **2** : to impel or push with a pole ∼ vi **1** : to propel a boat with a pole **2** : to use ski poles to gain speed

³pole n [ME, fr. L polus, fr. Gk polos pivot, pole; akin to Gk pelesthai to become, Skt carati he moves, wanders — more at WHEEL] (14c) **1** : either extremity of an axis of a sphere and esp. of the earth's axis **2 a** : either of two related opposites **b** : a point of guidance or attraction **3 a** : either of the two terminals of an electric cell, battery, generator, or motor **b** : one of two or more regions in a magnetized body at which the magnetic flux density is greatest **4** : either of two morphologically or physiologically differentiated areas at opposite ends of an axis in an organism or cell — see BLASTULA illustration **5 a** : the fixed point in a system of polar coordinates that serves as the origin **b** : the point of origin of two tangents to a conic section that determine a polar — **poles apart** : as diametrically opposed as possible

Pole \'pōl\ n [G, of Slavic origin; akin to Pol polak Pole] (1535) **1** : a native or inhabitant of Poland **2** : a person of Polish descent

¹pole·ax \'pō-ˌlaks\ n [ME poleax, pollax, fr. pol, polle poll + ax] (14c) **1** : a battle-ax with a short handle and often a hook or spike opposite the blade; also : one with a long handle used as an ornamental weapon **2** : an ax used in slaughtering cattle

²poleax vt (1882) : to attack, strike, or fell with or as if with a poleax

pole bean n (ca. 1770) : a cultivated bean that is usu. trained to grow upright on supports

pole·cat \'pōl-ˌkat\ n, pl **polecats** or **polecat** [ME polcat, prob. fr. MF poul, pol cock + ME cat; prob. fr. its preying on poultry — more at PULLET] (14c) **1** : any of several carnivorous mammals (as of the genera Mustela or Vormela) of the weasel family; esp : a brown to black European mammal (M. putorius) from which the domesticated ferret is derived **2** : SKUNK

poleis pl of POLIS

pole·less \'pōl-ləs\ adj (1647) : having no pole

po·lem·ic \pə-'le-mik\ n [F polémique, fr. MF, fr. polemique controversial, fr. Gk polemikos warlike, hostile, fr. polemos war; perh. akin to Gk pelemizein to shake, OE eal felo baleful] (1638) **1 a** : an aggressive attack on or refutation of the opinions or principles of another **b** : the art or practice of disputation or controversy — usu. used in pl. but sing. or pl. in constr. **2** : an aggressive controversialist : DISPUTANT — **po·lem·i·cist** \-'le-mə-sist\ n

po·lem·i·cal \-mi-kəl\ also **po·lem·ic** \-mik\ adj (1640) **1** : of, relating to, or being a polemic : CONTROVERSIAL **2** : engaged in or addicted to polemics : DISPUTATIOUS — **po·lem·i·cal·ly** \-mi-k(ə-)lē\ adv

po·lem·i·cize \-'le-mə-ˌsiz\ vi **-cized; -ciz·ing** (1950) : to engage in controversy : deliver a polemic

po·le·mist \pə-'le-mist, 'pä-lə-mist\ n (1825) : one skilled in or given to polemics

pol·e·mize \'pä-lə-ˌmīz\ vi **-mized; -miz·ing** (1828) : POLEMICIZE

po·le·mo·ni·um \ˌpä-lə-'mō-nē-əm\ n [NL, fr. Gk polemōnion, a plant] (1900) : JACOB'S LADDER 1

po·len·ta \pō-'len-tə, pə-, -ˌtä\ n [It, fr. L, crushed and hulled barley; akin to L pollen fine flour] (1764) : mush made of chestnut meal, cornmeal, semolina, or farina

pol·er \'pō-lər\ n (1848) : one that poles a boat

pole·star \'pōl-ˌstär\ n **1** : NORTH STAR **2 a** : a directing principle : GUIDE **b** : a center of attraction

pole vault n (ca. 1890) : a vault with the aid of a pole; specif : a field event consisting of a vault for height over a crossbar — **pole-vault** vi — **pole-vaulter** n

pole·ward \'pōl-wərd\ adv or adj (1875) : toward or in the direction of a pole of the earth ⟨as the sun moves ∼⟩ ⟨∼ variation in temperature⟩

¹po·lice \pə-'lēs\ vt **po·liced; po·lic·ing** [in sense 1, fr. MF policier, police conduct of public affairs; in other senses, fr. ²police] (1589) **1** archaic : GOVERN **2** : to control, regulate, or keep in order by use of police **3** : to make clean and put in order **4 a** : to supervise the operation, execution, or administration of to prevent or detect and prosecute violations of rules and regulations **b** : to exercise such supervision over the policies and activities of **5** : to perform the functions of a police force in or over

²police n, pl **police** often attrib [F, fr. LL politia government, administration, fr. Gk politeia, fr. politēs citizen, fr. polis city, state; akin to Skt pur rampart, Lith pilis castle] (1716) **1 a** : the internal organization or regulation of a political unit through exercise of governmental powers esp. with respect to general comfort, health, morals, safety, or prosperity **b** : control and regulation of affairs affecting the general order and welfare of any unit or area **c** : the system of laws for effecting such control **2 a** : the department of government concerned primarily with maintenance of public order, safety, and health and enforcement of laws and possessing executive, judicial, and legislative powers **b** : the department of government charged with prevention, detection, and prosecution of public nuisances and crimes **3** pl : POLICE FORCE **b** pl : POLICE OFFICERS **4 a** : a private organization resembling a police force ⟨campus ∼⟩ **b** pl : the members of a private police organization **5 a** : the action or process of cleaning and putting in order **b** : military personnel detailed to perform this function

police action n (1933) : a localized military action undertaken without formal declaration of war by regular armed forces against persons (as guerrillas or aggressors) held to be violators of international peace and order

police court n (1823) : a court of record that has jurisdiction over various minor offenses (as breach of the peace) and the power to bind over for trial in a superior court or for a grand jury persons accused of more serious offenses

police dog *n* (1908) **1 :** a dog trained to assist police (as in drug detection) **2 :** GERMAN SHEPHERD

police force *n* (1838) **:** a body of trained officers entrusted by a government with maintenance of public peace and order, enforcement of laws, and prevention and detection of crime

po·lice·man \pə-'lēs-mən\ *n* (1801) **1 :** a member of a police force **2 :** one held to resemble a policeman ⟨making the United States the ∼ for the whole wide world —R. B. Long⟩

police officer *n* (1800) **:** a member of a police force

police power *n* (1827) **:** the inherent power of a government to exercise reasonable control over persons and property within its jurisdiction in the interest of the general security, health, safety, morals, and welfare except where legally prohibited

police procedural *n, pl* **police procedurals** (1967) **:** a mystery story written from the point of view of the police investigating the crime

police reporter *n* (1834) **:** a reporter regularly assigned to cover police news (as crimes and arrests)

police state *n* (1865) **:** a political unit characterized by repressive governmental control of political, economic, and social life usu. by an arbitrary exercise of power by police and esp. secret police in place of regular operation of administrative and judicial organs of the government according to publicly known legal procedures

police station *n* (1846) **:** the headquarters of the police for a locality

po·lice·wom·an \pə-'lēs-,wù-mən\ *n* (1853) **:** a woman who is a member of a police force

¹pol·i·cy \'pä-lə-sē\ *n, pl* **-cies** *often attrib* [ME *policie* government, policy, fr. MF, government, regulation, fr. LL *politia*] (15c) **1 a :** prudence or wisdom in the management of affairs **b :** management or procedure based primarily on material interest **2 a :** a definite course or method of action selected from among alternatives and in light of given conditions to guide and determine present and future decisions **b :** a high-level overall plan embracing the general goals and acceptable procedures esp. of a governmental body

²policy *n, pl* **-cies** [alter. of earlier *police*, fr. MF, certificate, fr. OIt *polizza*, modif. of ML *apodixa* receipt, fr. MGk *apodeixis*, fr. Gk, proof, fr. *apodeiknynai* to demonstrate — more at APODICTIC] (1565) **1 :** a writing whereby a contract of insurance is made **2 a :** a daily lottery in which participants bet that certain numbers will be drawn from a lottery wheel **b :** NUMBER 7a

pol·i·cy·hold·er \'pä-lə-sē-,hōl-dər\ *n* (1851) **:** the owner of an insurance policy

policy science *n* (1950) **:** a social science dealing with the making of high-level policy (as in a government or business)

po·lio \'pō-lē-,ō\ *n* (1931) **:** POLIOMYELITIS

po·lio·my·eli·tis \,pō-lē-(,)ō-,mī-ə-'li-təs\ *n* [NL, fr. Gk *polios* gray + *myelos* marrow — more at FALLOW, MYEL] (1878) **:** an acute infectious virus disease characterized by fever, motor paralysis, and atrophy of skeletal muscles often with permanent disability and deformity and marked by inflammation of nerve cells in the anterior gray matter in each lateral half of the spinal cord — called also *infantile paralysis*

po·lio·vi·rus \'pō-lē-(,)ō-,vī-rəs\ *n* [NL, fr. *polio*myelitis + *virus*] (1953) **:** an enterovirus that occurs in several antigenically distinct forms and is the causative agent of human poliomyelitis

po·lis \'pä-ləs\ *n, pl* **po·leis** \'pä-,lās\ [Gk — more at POLICE] (1894) **:** a Greek city-state; *broadly* **:** a state or society esp. when characterized by a sense of community

-polis *n comb form* [LL, fr. Gk, fr. *polis*] **:** city ⟨megalo*polis*⟩

¹pol·ish \'pä-lish\ *vb* [ME *polisshen*, fr. MF *poliss-*, stem of *polir*, fr. L *polire*] *vt* (14c) **1 :** to make smooth and glossy usu. by friction **:** BURNISH **2 :** to smooth, soften, or refine in manners or condition **3 :** to bring to a highly developed, finished, or refined state **:** PERFECT ∼ *vi* **:** to become smooth or glossy by or as if by friction — **pol·ish·er** *n*

²polish *n* (1704) **1 a :** a smooth glossy surface **:** LUSTER **b :** freedom from rudeness or coarseness **:** CULTURE **c :** a state of high development or refinement **2 :** the action or process of polishing **3 :** a preparation that is used to produce a gloss and often a color for the protection and decoration of a surface ⟨furniture ∼⟩ ⟨nail ∼⟩

¹Pol·ish \'pō-lish\ *adj* [*Pole*] (1674) **:** of, relating to, or characteristic of Poland, the Poles, or Polish

²Polish *n* (1784) **:** the Slavic language of the Poles

polish off *vt* (1829) **:** to finish off or dispose of rapidly or completely

po·lit·bu·ro \'pä-lət-,byùr-(,)ō, 'pō-lət-, pə-'lit-\ *n* [Russ *politbyuro*, fr. *politicheskoe byuro* political bureau] (1925) **:** the principal policy-making and executive committee of a Communist party

po·lite \pə-'līt\ *adj* **po·lit·er; -est** [L *politus*, fr. pp. of *polire*] (1501) **1 a :** of, relating to, or having the characteristics of advanced culture **b :** marked by refined cultural interests and pursuits esp. in arts and belles lettres **2 a :** showing or characterized by correct social usage **b :** marked by an appearance of consideration, tact, deference, or courtesy **c :** marked by a lack of roughness or crudities ⟨∼ literature⟩ **syn** see CIVIL — **po·lite·ly** *adv* — **po·lite·ness** *n*

po·li·tesse \,pä-li-'tes, ,pō-\ *n* [F, fr. MF, cleanness, fr. OIt *pulitezza*, fr. *pulito*, pp. of *pulire* to polish, clean, fr. L *polire*] (1717) **:** formal politeness **:** DECOROUSNESS

pol·i·tic \'pä-lə-,tik\ *adj* [ME *politik*, fr. MF *politique*, fr. L *politicus*, fr. Gk *politikos*, fr. *politēs* citizen — more at POLICE] (15c) **1 :** POLITICAL **2 :** characterized by shrewdness in managing, contriving, or dealing **3 :** sagacious in promoting a policy **4 :** shrewdly tactful **syn** see EXPEDIENT, SUAVE

po·lit·i·cal \pə-'li-ti-kəl\ *adj* [L *politicus*] (1551) **1 a :** of or relating to government, a government, or the conduct of government **b :** of, relating to, or concerned with the making as distinguished from the administration of governmental policy **2 :** of, relating to, involving, or involved in politics and esp. party politics **3 :** organized in governmental terms ⟨∼ units⟩ **4 :** involving or charged or concerned with acts against a government or a political system ⟨∼ prisoners⟩ — **po·lit·i·cal·ly** \-k(ə-)lē\ *adv*

political action committee *n* (1944) **:** a group formed (as by an industry or an issue-oriented organization) to raise and contribute money to the campaigns of candidates likely to advance the group's interests

political correctness *n* (1990) **:** conformity to a belief that language and practices which could offend political sensibilities should be eliminated

political economy *n* (1740) **1 :** ECONOMICS **2 :** the theory or study of the role of public policy in influencing the economic and social welfare of a political unit — **political economist** *n*

po·lit·i·cal·ize \pə-'li-ti-kə-,līz\ *vt* **-ized; -izing** (1869) **:** POLITICIZE — **po·lit·i·cal·i·za·tion** \-,li-ti-kə-lə-'zā-shən\ *n*

politically correct *adj* (1936) **:** conforming to a belief that language and practices which could offend political sensibilities (as in matters of sex or race) should be eliminated

political science *n* (1779) **:** a social science concerned chiefly with the description and analysis of political and esp. governmental institutions and processes — **political scientist** *n*

po·li·ti·cian \,pä-lə-'ti-shən\ *n* (1589) **1 :** a person experienced in the art or science of government; *esp* **:** one actively engaged in conducting the business of a government **2 a :** a person engaged in party politics as a profession **b :** a person primarily interested in political office for selfish or other narrow usu. short-sighted reasons

po·lit·i·cise *Brit var of* POLITICIZE

po·lit·i·cize \pə-'li-tə-,sīz\ *vt* **-cized; -ciz·ing** (1846) **:** to give a political tone or character to ⟨an attempt to ∼ the civil service⟩ — **po·lit·i·ci·za·tion** \-,li-tə-sə-'zā-shən\ *n*

pol·i·tick \'pä-lə-,tik\ *vi* [back-formation fr. *politicking*, n., fr. *politics* + ³-*ing*] (ca. 1934) **:** to engage in often partisan political discussion or activity — **pol·i·tick·er** *n*

po·lit·i·co \pə-'li-ti-,kō\ *n, pl* **-cos** *also* **-coes** [It *politico* or Sp *político*, ultim. fr. L *politicus* political] (1630) **:** POLITICIAN 2

pol·i·tics \'pä-lə-,tiks\ *n pl but sing or pl in constr* [Gk *politika*, fr. neut. pl. of *politikos* political] (ca. 1529) **1 a :** the art or science of government **b :** the art or science concerned with guiding or influencing governmental policy **c :** the art or science concerned with winning and holding control over a government **2 :** political actions, practices, or policies **3 a :** political affairs or business; *esp* **:** competition between competing interest groups or individuals for power and leadership (as in a government) **b :** political life esp. as a principal activity or profession **c :** political activities characterized by artful and often dishonest practices **4 :** the political opinions or sympathies of a person **5 a :** the total complex of relations between people living in society **b :** relations or conduct in a particular area of experience esp. as seen or dealt with from a political point of view ⟨office ∼⟩

pol·i·ty \'pä-lə-tē\ *n, pl* **-ties** [LL *politia* — more at POLICE] (1538) **1 :** political organization **2 :** a specific form of political organization **3 :** a politically organized unit **4 a :** the form or constitution of a politically organized unit **b :** the form of government of a religious denomination

pol·ka \'pōl-kə, 'pō-kə\ *n* [Czech, fr. *Polka* Polish woman, fem. of *Polák* Pole] (1844) **1 :** a vivacious couple dance of Bohemian origin in duple time with a basic pattern of hop-step-close-step **2 :** a lively Bohemian dance tune in ²/₄ time — **polka** *vi*

polka dot \'pō-kə-,dät\ *n* (1884) **:** a dot in a pattern of regularly distributed dots in textile design — **polka–dot** *or* **pol·ka–dot·ted** \-,dä-təd\ *adj*

¹poll \'pōl\ *n* [ME *pol, polle,* fr. MLG] (14c) **1 :** HEAD **2 a :** the top or back of the head **b :** NAPE **3 :** the broad or flat end of a striking tool (as a hammer) **4 a** (1) **:** the casting or recording of the votes of a body of persons (2) **:** a counting of votes cast **b :** the place where votes are cast or recorded — usu. used in pl. ⟨at the ∼s⟩ **c :** the period of time during which votes may be cast at an election **d :** the total number of votes recorded ⟨a heavy ∼⟩ **5 a :** a questioning or canvassing of persons selected at random or by quota to obtain information or opinions to be analyzed **b :** a record of the information so obtained

²poll *vt* (14c) **1 a :** to cut off or cut short the hair or wool of **:** CROP, SHEAR **b :** to cut off or cut short (as wool) **2 a :** to cut off or back the top of (as a tree); *specif* **:** POLLARD **b :** to cut off or cut short the horns of (cattle) **3 a :** to receive and record the votes of **b :** to request each member of to declare a vote individually ⟨∼ the assembly⟩ **4 :** to receive (as votes) in an election **5 :** to question or canvass in a poll **6 :** to test (as several computer terminals sharing a single line) in sequence for messages to be transmitted ∼ *vi* **:** to cast one's vote at a poll — **poll·ee** \pō-'lē\ *n* — **poll·er** \'pō-lər\ *n*

pol·lack *or* **pol·lock** \'pä-lək\ *n, pl* **pollack** *or* **pollock** [ME *poullok,* perh. fr. ScotGael *pollag* or Ir *pollóg*] (15c) **1 :** a commercially important north Atlantic food fish (*Pollachius virens*) related to and resembling the cods but darker **2 :** a commercially important northern Pacific food fish (*Theragra chalcogramma*) of the cod family that closely resembles the pollack — called also *walleye pollack*

¹pol·lard \'pä-lərd\ *n* [²*poll*] (1611) **:** a tree cut back to the trunk to promote the growth of a dense head of foliage

²pollard *vt* (1670) **:** to make a pollard of (a tree)

polled \'pōld\ *adj* (1584) **:** having no horns

pol·len \'pä-lən\ *n* [NL *pollin-, pollen,* fr. L, fine flour] (1760) **1 :** a mass of microspores in a seed plant appearing usu. as a fine dust **2 :** a dusty bloom on the body of an insect

pollen basket *n* (1860) **:** a smooth area on each hind tibia of a bee that is edged by a fringe of stiff hairs and serves to collect and transport pollen — called also *corbicula*

pollen grain *n* (1835) **:** one of the granular microspores that occur in pollen and give rise to the male gametophyte of a seed plant

pol·len·iz·er *also* **pol·lin·iz·er** \'pä-lə-,nī-zər\ *n* [*pollenize* to pollinate] (1897) **:** a plant that is a source of pollen **:** POLLINATOR A

pollen mother cell *n* (1884) **:** a cell that is derived from the hypodermis of the pollen sac and that gives rise by meiosis to four cells each of which develops into a pollen grain

pollen sac *n* (1875) **:** one of the pouches of a seed plant anther in which pollen is formed

---

\ə\ abut \ᵊ\ kitten, F table \ər\ further \a\ ash \ā\ ace \ä\ mop, mar
\aù\ out \ch\ chin \e\ bet \ē\ easy \g\ go \i\ hit \ī\ ice \j\ job
\ŋ\ sing \ō\ go \ò\ law \òi\ boy \th\ thin \t̲h̲\ the \ü\ loot \ù\ foot
\y\ yet \zh\ vision \ä, k̲, ⁿ, œ, œ̄, ᵫ, ᵫ̄, ᵋ\ *see* Guide to Pronunciation

pollen tube *n* (1835) : a tube that is formed by a pollen grain and conveys the sperm nuclei to the embryo sac of an angiosperm or the archegonium of a gymnosperm

pol·lex \'pä-,leks\ *n, pl* **pol·li·ces** \'pä-lə-,sēz\ [NL *pollic-, pollex*, fr. L, thumb, big toe] (ca. 1836) : the first digit of the forelimb : THUMB

pollin- *comb form* [NL *pollin-, pollen*] : pollen ⟨*pollinate*⟩

pol·li·nate \'pä-lə-,nāt\ *vt* **-nat·ed; -nat·ing** (1875) **1 :** to carry out the pollination of **2 :** to mark or smudge with pollen

pol·li·na·tion \,pä-lə-'nā-shən\ *n* (1875) : the transfer of pollen from an anther to the stigma in angiosperms or from the microsporangium to the micropyle in gymnosperms

pol·li·na·tor \'pä-lə-,nā-tər\ *n* (1903) : one that pollinates: as **a :** an agent (as an insect) that pollinates flowers **b :** POLLENIZER 1

pol·lin·i·um \pä-'li-nē-əm\ *n, pl* **-ia** \-nē-ə\ [NL, fr. *pollin-*] (1862) : a coherent mass of pollen grains often with a stalk bearing an adhesive disk that clings to insects

pol·li·no·sis *or* **pol·len·o·sis** \,pä-lə-'nō-səs\ *n* [NL *pollinosis*, fr. *pollin-*] (1925) : an acute recurrent catarrhal disorder caused by allergic sensitivity to specific pollens

poll·ster \'pōl-stər\ *n* (1939) : one that conducts a poll or compiles data obtained by a poll

poll tax *n* (1692) : a tax of a fixed amount per person levied on adults

pol·lut·ant \pə-'lü-t²nt\ *n* (1892) : something that pollutes

pol·lute \pə-'lüt\ *vt* **pol·lut·ed; pol·lut·ing** [ME, fr. L *pollutus*, pp. of *polluere*, fr. *por-* (akin to L *per* through) + *-luere* (akin to L *lutum* mud, Gk *lyma* dirt, defilement) — more at FOR] (14c) **1 a :** to make ceremonially or morally impure : DEFILE **b :** DEBASE 1 ⟨using language to deceive or mislead ~*s* language —Linda C. Lederman⟩ **2 a :** to make physically impure or unclean : BEFOUL, DIRTY **b :** to contaminate (an environment) esp. with man-made waste *syn* see CONTAMINATE — **pol·lut·er** *n* — **pol·lut·ive** \-'lü-tiv\ *adj*

pol·lu·tion \pə-'lü-shən\ *n* (14c) **1 :** the action of polluting esp. by environmental contamination with man-made waste; *also* : the condition of being polluted **2 :** POLLUTANT

Pol·lux \'pä-ləks\ *n* [L, modif. of Gk *Polydeukēs*] **1 :** one of the Dioscuri **2 :** a first-magnitude star in the constellation Gemini

Pol·ly·an·na \,pä-lē-'a-nə\ *n* [*Pollyanna*, heroine of the novel *Pollyanna* (1913) by Eleanor Porter †1920 Am. fiction writer] (1921) : a person characterized by irrepressible optimism and a tendency to find good in everything — **Pollyanna** *adj* — **Pol·ly·an·na·ish** \-'a-nə-ish\ *also* **Pol·ly·an·nish** \-'a-nish\ *adj*

pol·ly·wog *or* **pol·li·wog** \'pä-lē-,wäg, -,wȯg\ *n* [alter. of ME *polwygle*, prob. fr. *pol* poll + *wiglen* to wiggle] (1832) : TADPOLE

po·lo \'pō-(,)lō\ *n* [Balti, ball] (1872) **1 :** a game played by teams of players on horseback using mallets with long flexible handles to drive a wooden ball through goalposts **2 :** WATER POLO — **po·lo·ist** \'pō-(,)lō-ist\ *n*

polo coat *n* (1910) : a tailored overcoat that is made esp. of tan camel's hair and often has stitched edges and a half-belt on the back

po·lo·naise \,pä-lə-'nāz, ,pō-\ *n* [F, fr. fem. of *polonais* Polish, fr. *Pologne* Poland, fr. ML *Polonia* (1773) **1 :** an elaborate overdress with a short=sleeved fitted waist and a draped cutaway overskirt **2 a :** a stately Polish processional dance popular in 19th century Europe **b :** music for this dance in moderate ¾ time

Po·lo·nia \pə-'lō-nē-ə, -nyə\ *n* [NL, Poland, fr. ML] (1944) : people of Polish descent living outside Poland

po·lo·ni·um \pə-'lō-nē-əm\ *n* [NL, fr. ML *Polonia*] (1898) : a radioactive metallic element that is similar chemically to tellurium and bismuth, occurs esp. in pitchblende and radium-lead residues, and emits an alpha particle to form an isotope of lead — see ELEMENT table

Po·lo·ni·us \pə-'lō-nē-əs\ *n* : a garrulous courtier and father of Ophelia and Laertes in Shakespeare's *Hamlet*

polo shirt *n* (1920) : a close-fitting pullover often knit shirt with short or long sleeves and turnover collar or banded neck

polonaise 1

pol·ter·geist \'pōl-tər-,gīst\ *n* [G, fr. *poltern* to knock + *Geist* spirit] (1848) : a noisy usu. mischievous ghost held to be responsible for unexplained noises (as rappings)

¹pol·troon \päl-'trün\ *n* [MF *poultron*, fr. OIt *poltrone*, prob. akin to *poltro* colt, ultim. fr. L *pullus* young of an animal — more at FOAL] (ca. 1529) : a spiritless coward : CRAVEN

²poltroon *adj* (1645) : characterized by complete cowardice

pol·troon·ery \-'trü-nə-rē, -'trün-rē\ *n* (1590) : mean pusillanimity : COWARDICE

poly \'pä-lē\ *n, pl* **pol·ys** \-lēz\ *often attrib* [short for *polymer*] (1942) : a polymerized plastic or something made of this; *esp* : a polyester fiber, fabric, or garment

poly- *comb form* [ME, fr. L, fr. Gk, fr. *polys*; akin to OHG *filu* many, Skt *puru*, L *plenus* full — more at FULL] **1 :** many; several : much : MULTI- ⟨*polychotomous*⟩ ⟨*polygyny*⟩ **2 a :** containing an indefinite number more than one of a (specified) substance ⟨*polysulfide*⟩ **b :** polymeric : polymer of a (specified) monomer ⟨*polyethylene*⟩ ⟨*poly*adenylic acid⟩

poly-A \,pä-lē-'ā\ *n* [*poly-* + adenylic acid] (1957) : RNA or a segment of RNA that is composed of a polynucleotide chain consisting entirely of adenylic acid residues and that codes for polylysine when functioning as messenger RNA in protein synthesis

poly·acryl·amide \,pä-lē-ə-'kri-lə-,mīd\ *n* (1944) : a polyamide of acrylic acid

poly·ac·ry·lo·ni·trile \,pä-lē-a-krə-lō-'nī-trəl, -,trēl\ *n* (1935) : a polymer of acrylonitrile used often as fibers

poly·ad·e·nyl·ic acid \,pä-lē-'ad-kə-,hȯl\ *n* (1956) : POLYA

poly·al·co·hol \,pä-lē-'al-kə-,hȯl\ *n* (1900) : an alcohol (as a diol) that contains more than one hydroxyl group

poly·am·ide \,pä-lē-'a-,mīd, -məd\ *n* [ISV] (1929) : a compound characterized by more than one amide group; *esp* : a polymeric amide (as nylon)

poly·amine \'pä-lē-ə-,mēn, ,pä-lē-'a-,mēn\ *n* (1861) : a compound characterized by more than one amino group

poly·an·dry \'pä-lē-,an-drē\ *n* [Gk *polyandros*, adj., having many husbands, fr. *poly-* + *andr-, anēr* man, husband — more at ANDR-] (1780) : the state or practice of having more than one husband or male mate at one time — compare POLYGAMY, POLYGYNY — **poly·an·drous** \,pä-lē-'an-drəs\ *adj*

poly·an·tha \pä-lē-'an(t)-thə\ *n* [NL, fr. Gk *polyanthos* blooming] (1889) : any of numerous dwarf hybrid roses characterized by many large clusters of small flowers

poly·an·thus \-'an(t)-thəs\ *n, pl* **-an·thus·es** *or* **-an·thi** \-'an-,thī, -,thē\ [NL, fr. Gk *polyanthos* blooming, fr. *poly-* + *anthos* flower — more at ANTHOLOGY] (ca. 1727) **1 :** any of various hybrid primroses **2 :** a narcissus (*Narcissus tazetta*) having small white or yellow flowers arranged in umbels and having a spreading perianth

poly·atom·ic \-ə-'tä-mik\ *adj* [ISV] (1857) : containing more than one and esp. more than two atoms ⟨~ molecules⟩

poly·bro·mi·nat·ed biphenyl \,pä-lē-'brō-mə-,nā-təd-\ *n* (1975) : any of several compounds that are similar to polychlorinated biphenyls in environmental toxicity and in structure but that have various hydrogen atoms replaced by bromine rather than chlorine — called also *PBB*

poly·bu·ta·di·ene \,pä-lē-,byü-tə-'dī-,ēn, -,dī-'\ *n* (1939) : a synthetic rubber that has a high resistance to wear and is used esp. in the manufacture of tires

poly·car·bon·ate \-'kär-bə-,nāt, -nət\ *n* (1930) : any of various tough transparent thermoplastics characterized by high impact strength and high softening temperature

poly·cen·tric \-'sen-trik\ *adj* (1887) : having more than one center (as of development or control): as **a :** having several centromeres ⟨~ chromosomes⟩ ⟨~ cells⟩ **b :** characterized by polycentrism

poly·cen·trism \-'sen-,tri-zəm\ *n* (1956) : the existence of many centers of communist ideological thought; *esp* : the existence of a number of autonomous national communist movements

poly·chaete \'pä-lē-,kēt\ *n* [ultim. fr. Gk *polychaitēs* having much hair, fr. *poly-* + *chaitē* long hair] (1896) : any of a class (Polychaeta) of chiefly marine annelid worms (as clam worms) usu. with paired segmental appendages, separate sexes, and a free-swimming trochophore larva — **polychaete** *adj*

poly·chlo·ri·nat·ed biphenyl \,pä-lē-'klōr-ə-,nā-təd-, -'klȯr-\ *n* (1962) : any of several compounds that are produced by replacing hydrogen atoms in biphenyl with chlorine, have various industrial applications, and are poisonous environmental pollutants which tend to accumulate in animal tissues — called also *PCB*

poly·chot·o·mous \-'kä-tə-məs\ *adj* [*poly-* + *-chotomous* (as in *dichotomous*)] (ca. 1858) : dividing or marked by division into many parts, branches, or classes — **poly·chot·o·my** \-mē\ *n*

poly·chro·mat·ic \-krō-'ma-tik\ *adj* [Gk *polychrōmatos*, fr. *poly-* + *chrōmat-, chrōma* color — more at CHROMATIC] (ca. 1841) **1 :** showing a variety or a change of colors : MULTICOLORED **2 :** being or relating to radiation that is composed of more than one wavelength

poly·chro·mato·phil·ic \-krō-,ma-tə-'fi-lik\ *adj* (1897) : stainable with more than one type of stain and esp. with both acid and basic dyes ⟨~ erythroblasts⟩ — **poly·chro·mato·phil·ia** \-'fi-lē-ə\ *n*

poly·chrome \'pä-lē-,krōm\ *adj* [Gk *polychrōmos*, fr. *poly-* + *chrōma*] (1837) : relating to, made with, or decorated in several colors ⟨~ pottery⟩ — **polychrome** *vt* — **poly·chro·my** \-,krō-mē\ *n*

poly·cis·tron·ic \,pä-lē-sis-'trä-nik\ *adj* (1963) : containing the genetic information of a number of cistrons ⟨~ messenger RNA⟩

poly·clin·ic \-'kli-nik\ *n* [ISV] (ca. 1890) : a clinic or hospital treating diseases of many sorts

poly·clon·al \-'klō-nəl\ *adj* (1914) : produced by or being cells derived from two or more cells of different ancestry or genetic constitution ⟨~ antibodies⟩

poly·con·den·sa·tion \-,kän-,den-'sā-shən, -dən-\ *n* [ISV] (1936) : a chemical condensation leading to the formation of a compound of high molecular weight

poly·con·ic projection \,pä-lē-'kä-nik-\ *n* (ca. 1864) : a map projection consisting of a composite series of concentric cones each of which before being unrolled has been placed over a sphere so as to be tangent to a different parallel of latitude

poly·crys·tal·line \-'kris-tə-lən\ *adj* (1918) **1 :** consisting of crystals variously oriented **2 :** composed of more than one crystal — **poly·crys·tal** \'pä-lē-,kris-t²l\ *n*

poly·cy·clic \,pä-lē-'si-klik, -'sī-\ *adj* [ISV] (1869) : having more than one cyclic component; *esp* : having two or more rings in the molecule

poly·cys·tic \-'sis-tik\ *adj* (1872) : having or involving more than one cyst ⟨~ kidneys⟩ ⟨~ ovaries⟩

poly·cy·the·mia \-(,)sī-'thē-mē-ə\ *n* [NL, fr. *poly-* + *cyt-* + *-hemia*] (ca. 1857) : a condition marked by an abnormal increase in the number of circulating red blood cells; *specif* : POLYCYTHEMIA VERA — **poly·cy·the·mic** \-mik\ *adj*

polycythemia ve·ra \-'vir-ə\ *n* [NL, true polycythemia] (ca. 1925) : polycythemia of unknown cause that is characterized by increase in total blood volume and accompanied by nosebleed, distension of the circulatory vessels, and enlargement of the spleen — called also *erythremia*

poly·cyt·i·dyl·ic acid \,pä-lē-,si-tə-'di-lik-\ *n* (1965) : RNA or a segment of RNA that is composed of a polynucleotide chain consisting entirely of cytosine-containing nucleotides and that codes for a polypeptide chain consisting of proline residues when functioning as messenger RNA in protein synthesis

poly·dac·tyl \-'dak-t²l\ *adj* [Gk *polydaktylos*, fr. *poly-* + *daktylos* digit] (ca. 1890) : having or causing polydactyly

poly·dac·ty·ly \-'dak-t²l-ē\ *n* (1886) : the condition of having more than the normal number of fingers or toes

poly·dip·sia \-'dip-sē-ə\ *n* [NL, fr. *poly-* + Gk *dipsa* thirst] (1660) : excessive or abnormal thirst — **poly·dip·sic** \-sik\ *adj*

poly·dis·perse \-dis-'pərs\ *adj* [*poly-* + L *dispersus* dispersed, fr. pp. of *dispergere* to disperse] (1915) : of, relating to, or characterized by or as particles of varied sizes in the dispersed phase of a disperse system — **poly·dis·per·si·ty** \-'pər-sə-tē\ *n*

poly·elec·tro·lyte \,pä-lē-ə-'lek-trə-,līt\ *n* (ca. 1947) : a substance of high molecular weight (as a protein) that is an electrolyte

poly·em·bry·o·ny \-'em-brē-ə-nē, -(,)em-'brī-\ *n* [ISV *poly-* + *embry-*

on- + ²-y] (1849) **1** : the condition of having several embryos **2** : the production of two or more embryos from one ovule or egg — **poly·em·bry·on·ic** \-,em-brē-'ä-nik\ adj
poly·ene \'pä-lē-,ēn\ n [ISV] (1928) : an organic compound containing many double bonds; esp : one having the double bonds in a long aliphatic hydrocarbon chain — **poly·en·ic** \,pä-lē-'ē-nik\ adj
¹**poly·es·ter** \'pä-lē-,es-tər, ,pä-lē-'\ n [ISV] (1929) : any of a group of polymers that consist basically of repeated units of an ester and are used esp. in making fibers or plastics — **poly·es·ter·i·fi·ca·tion** \-e-,ster-ə-fə-'kā-shən\ n
²**polyester** adj (1975) : characterized by inelegant or unsophisticated middle-class taste ⟨~ suburbs⟩ ⟨~ folks⟩
poly·es·trous \,pä-lē-'es-trəs\ adj (1900) : having more than one period of estrus in a year
poly·eth·yl·ene \-'e-thə-,lēn\ n (ca. 1862) : a polymer of ethylene; esp : any of various partially crystalline lightweight thermoplastics (CH₂CH₂)ₓ that are resistant to chemicals and moisture, have good insulating properties, and are used esp. in packaging and insulation
po·lyg·a·la \pə-'li-gə-lə\ n [NL, genus name, fr. L, milkwort, fr. Gk polygalon, fr. poly- + gala milk — more at GALAXY] (1578) : MILKWORT
poly·gam·ic \,pä-lē-'ga-mik\ adj (1819) : POLYGAMOUS
po·lyg·a·mous \pə-'li-gə-məs\ adj [Gk polygamos, fr. poly- + -gamos -gamous] (1613) **1 a** : relating to or practicing polygamy **b** : having more than one mate at one time ⟨baboons are ~⟩ **2** : bearing both hermaphrodite and unisexual flowers on the same plant
po·lyg·a·my \-mē\ n (ca. 1591) **1** : marriage in which a spouse of either sex may have more than one mate at the same time — compare POLYANDRY, POLYGYNY **2** : the state of being polygamous — **po·lyg·a·mist** \-mist\ n — **po·lyg·a·mize** \-,mīz\ vi
poly·gene \'pä-lē-,jēn\ n [ISV] (1941) : any of a group of nonallelic genes that collectively control the inheritance of a quantitative character or modify the expression of a qualitative character — **poly·gen·ic** \,pä-lē-'jē-nik\ adj
poly·gen·e·sis \,pä-lē-'je-nə-səs\ n [NL] (ca. 1882) : development from more than one source
poly·ge·net·ic \-jə-'ne-tik\ adj (1861) **1** : POLYPHYLETIC **2** : having many distinct sources
¹**poly·glot** \'pä-lē-,glät\ n [²polyglot] (ca. 1645) **1** : one who is polyglot **2** cap : a book containing versions of the same text in several languages; esp : the Scriptures in several languages **3** : a mixture or confusion of languages or nomenclatures
²**polyglot** adj [Gk polyglōttos, fr. poly- + glōtta language — more at GLOSS] (1656) **1 a** : speaking or writing several languages : MULTILINGUAL **b** : composed of numerous linguistic groups ⟨a ~ population⟩ **2** : containing matter in several languages ⟨a ~ sign⟩ **3** : composed of elements from different languages **4** : being widely diverse ⟨as in ethnic or cultural origins⟩ ⟨~ cuisine⟩
poly·glot·ism or **poly·glot·tism** \-,glä-,ti-zəm\ n (1882) : the use of many languages : the ability to speak many languages
poly·gon \'pä-lē-,gän\ n [LL polygonum, fr. Gk polygōnon, fr. neut. of polygōnos polygonal, fr. poly- + gōnia angle — more at -GON] (1571) **1** : a closed plane figure bounded by straight lines **2** : a closed figure on a sphere bounded by arcs of great circles — **po·lyg·o·nal** \pə-'li-gən²l\ adj — **po·lyg·o·nal·ly** \-n²l-ē\ adv
po·lyg·o·num \pə-'li-gə-nəm\ n [NL, fr. Gk polygonon knotgrass, fr. poly- + gony knee — more at KNEE] (ca. 1706) : any of a genus (Polygonum) of herbs of the buckwheat family with a prominent tubular sheath around the base of each petiole, thickened nodes, and flowers that are solitary and axillary or in spiked racemes — called also knotweed
poly·graph \'pä-lē-,graf\ n (1871) : an instrument for recording variations of several different pulsations (as of physiological variables) simultaneously; broadly : LIE DETECTOR — **poly·graph·ic** \,pä-lē-'gra-fik\ adj
po·lyg·ra·pher \'pä-lē-,gra-fər, pə-'li-grə-fər\ n (ca. 1934) : one who operates a polygraph
po·lyg·ra·phist \'pä-lē-,gra-fist, pə-'li-grə-fist\ n (1954) : POLYGRAPHER
po·lyg·y·nous \pə-'li-jə-nəs\ adj (1874) : relating to or practicing polygyny
po·lyg·y·ny \-nē\ n (1780) : the state or practice of having more than one wife or female mate at one time — compare POLYANDRY, POLYGAMY
polyhedral angle n (ca. 1864) : a portion of space partly enclosed by three or more planes whose intersections meet in a vertex
poly·he·dron \,pä-lē-'hē-drən\ n, pl **-drons** or **-dra** \-drə\ [NL] (1570) : a solid formed by plane faces — **poly·he·dral** \-drəl\ adj
poly·he·dro·sis \,pä-lē-hē-'drō-səs\ n, pl **-dro·ses** \-,sēz\ [NL, fr. polyhedron] (1947) : any of several virus diseases of insect larvae characterized by dissolution of tissues and accumulation of polyhedral granules in the resultant fluid
poly·his·tor \,pä-lē-'his-tər\ n [Gk polyistōr very learned, fr. poly- + istōr, histōr learned — more at HISTORY] (1588) : POLYMATH — **poly·his·tor·ic** \-his-'tòr-ik, -'tär-\ adj
poly·hy·droxy \-hī-'dräk-sē\ adj (ca. 1929) : containing more than one hydroxyl group in the molecule
Poly·hym·nia \,pä-lē-'him-nē-ə\ n [L, fr. Gk Polyymnia] : the Greek Muse of sacred song
poly I:C \,pä-lē-'ī-'sē\ or **poly I-poly C** \,pä-lē-'ī-,pä-lē-'sē\ n [poly- + inosinic acid + cytidylic acid] (1969) : a synthetic 2-stranded RNA composed of one strand of polyinosinic acid and one strand of polycytidylic acid that induces interferon formation and has been used experimentally as an anticancer and antiviral agent
poly·ino·sin·ic acid \,pä-lē-,i-nə-'si-nik-, -,ī-nə-\ n [poly- + inosinic acid (C₁₀H₁₃N₄O₈P), fr. Gk in-, is sinew + ISV ²-ose + ¹-in + ¹-ic + acid] (1965) : RNA or a segment of RNA that is composed of a polynucleotide chain consisting entirely of inosinic acid residues
poly·ly·sine \,pä-lē-'lī-,sēn\ n (1947) : a protein whose polypeptide chain consists entirely of lysine residues
poly·math \'pä-lē-,math\ n [Gk polymathēs very learned, fr. poly- + manthanein to learn — more at MATHEMATICAL] (1621) : a person of encyclopedic learning — **polymath** or **poly·math·ic** \,pä-lē-'ma-thik\ adj — **poly·ma·thy** \'pä-lē-,ma-thē, pä-lə-,ma-thē\ n
poly·mer \'pä-lə-mər\ n [ISV, back-formation fr. polymeric, fr. Gk polymerēs having many parts, fr. poly- + meros part — more at MERIT] (1866) : a chemical compound or mixture of compounds formed by

polymerization and consisting essentially of repeating structural units — **poly·mer·ic** \,pä-lə-'mer-ik\ adj — **poly·mer·ism** \pə-'li-mə-,ri-zəm, 'pä-lə-mə-\ n
poly·mer·ase \'pä-lə-mə-,rās, -,rāz\ n (1958) : any of several enzymes that catalyze the formation of DNA or RNA from precursor substances in the presence of preexisting DNA or RNA acting as a template
polymerase chain reaction n (1987) : an in vitro technique for rapidly synthesizing large quantities of a given DNA segment that involves separating the DNA into its two complementary strands, using DNA polymerase to synthesize two-stranded DNA from each single strand, and repeating the process
po·ly·mer·i·sa·tion, po·ly·mer·ise chiefly Brit var of POLYMERIZATION, POLYMERIZE
po·ly·mer·i·za·tion \pə-,li-mə-rə-'zā-shən, ,pä-lə-mə-rə-\ n [ISV] (1872) **1** : a chemical reaction in which two or more molecules combine to form larger molecules that contain repeating structural units — compare ASSOCIATION 5 **2** : reduplication of parts in an organism
po·ly·mer·ize \pə-'li-mə-,rīz, 'pä-lə-mə-\ vb **-ized; -iz·ing** vt (1865) : to subject to polymerization ~ vi : to undergo polymerization
poly·meth·yl methacrylate \,pä-lē-,me-thəl-\ n (1936) : a thermoplastic resin of polymerized methyl methacrylate which is characterized by its optical clarity (as in a contact lens)
poly·morph \'pä-lē-,mòrf\ n [ISV] (ca. 1828) **1** : a polymorphic organism; also : one of the several forms of such an organism **2** : any of the crystalline forms of a polymorphic substance
poly·mor·phism \,pä-lē-'mòr-,fi-zəm\ n (1839) : the quality or state of being able to assume different forms: as **a** : existence of a species in several forms independent of the variations of sex **b** : the property of crystallizing in two or more forms with distinct structure — **poly·mor·phic** \-fik\ adj — **poly·mor·phi·cal·ly** \-fi-k(ə-)lē\ adv
poly·mor·pho·nu·cle·ar \,-mòr-fə-'nü-klē-ər, -'nyü-\ adj (1897) of a leukocyte : having the nucleus complexly lobed — **polymorphonuclear** n
poly·mor·phous \-'mòr-fəs\ adj [Gk polymorphous, fr. poly- + -morphos -morphous] (1785) : having, assuming, or occurring in various forms, characters, or styles : POLYMORPHIC ⟨a ~ rash⟩ ⟨~ sexuality⟩ — **poly·mor·phous·ly** adv
polymorphous perverse adj (1909) : relating to or exhibiting infantile sexual tendencies in which the genitals are not yet identified as the sole or principal sexual organs nor coitus as the goal of erotic activity
poly·myx·in \,pä-lē-'mik-sən\ n [ISV, fr. NL polymyxa, fr. poly- + Gk myxa mucus — more at MUCUS] (1947) : any of several toxic antibiotics obtained from a soil bacterium (Bacillus polymyxa) and active against gram-negative bacteria
Poly·ne·sian \,pä-lə-'nē-zhən, -shən\ n (1807) **1** : a member of any of the indigenous peoples of Polynesia **2** : a group of Austronesian languages spoken in Polynesia — **Polynesian** adj
poly·neu·ri·tis \,pä-lē-nù-'rī-təs, -nyù-\ n [NL] (1886) : neuritis of several peripheral nerves at the same time
Poly·ni·ces \,pä-lə-'nī-sēz\ n [L, fr. Gk Polyneikēs] : a son of Oedipus for whom the Seven against Thebes mount their expedition
¹**poly·no·mi·al** \,pä-lə-'nō-mē-əl\ n [poly- + -nomial (as in binomial)] (1674) : a mathematical expression of one or more algebraic terms each of which consists of a constant multiplied by one or more variables raised to a nonnegative integral power (as a + bx + cx²)
²**polynomial** adj (ca. 1704) : relating to, composed of, or expressed as one or more polynomials ⟨~ functions⟩ ⟨~ equations⟩
poly·nu·cle·ar \,pä-lē-'nü-klē-ər, -'nyü-, ÷-kyə-lər\ adj [ISV] (1908) : chemically polycyclic esp. with respect to the benzene ring — used chiefly of aromatic hydrocarbons that are important as pollutants and possibly as carcinogens
poly·nu·cle·o·tide \-'nü-klē-ə-,tīd, -'nyü-\ n [ISV] (1911) : a polymeric chain of nucleotides
po·lyn·ya \,pä-lən-'yä\ n, pl **polynyas** also **po·lyn·yi** \-'yē\ [Russ polyn'ya] (1853) : an area of open water in sea ice
poly·ole·fin \,pä-lē-'ō-lə-fən\ n (1930) : a polymer of an alkene (as polyethylene)
poly·oma virus \,pä-lē-'ō-mə-\ n [NL polyoma, fr. poly- + -oma] (1958) : a papovavirus of rodents that is associated with various kinds of tumors — called also polyoma
poly·on·y·mous \,pä-lē-'ä-nə-məs\ adj [Gk polyōnymos, fr. poly- + onoma, onyma name — more at NAME] (1678) : having or known by various names
pol·yp \'pä-ləp\ n [MF polype octopus, nasal tumor, fr. L polypus, fr. Gk polypous, fr. poly- + pous foot — more at FOOT] (1742) **1** : a coelenterate that has typically a hollow cylindrical body closed and attached at one end and opening at the other by a central mouth surrounded by tentacles armed with nematocysts **2** : a projecting mass of swollen and hypertrophied or tumorous membrane — **pol·yp·oid** \-lə-,pòid\ adj
poly·pep·tide \,pä-lē-'pep-,tīd\ n [ISV] (1903) : a molecular chain of amino acids — **poly·pep·tid·ic** \-(,)pep-'ti-dik\ adj
poly·pet·al·ous \-'pe-t²l-əs\ adj [NL polypetalus, fr. poly- + petalum petal] (ca. 1704) : having or consisting of separate petals
poly·pha·gia \-'fā-j(ē-)ə\ n [Gk polyphagia, fr. polyphagos] (ca. 1693) : excessive appetite or eating
po·lyph·a·gous \pə-'li-fə-gəs\ adj [Gk polyphagos eating too much, fr. poly- + -phagos -phagous] (1815) : feeding on or utilizing many kinds of food — **po·lyph·a·gy** \-jē\ n
poly·phase \'pä-lē-,fāz\ adj [ISV] (1891) : having or producing two or more phases ⟨a ~ machine⟩ ⟨a ~ current⟩
poly·pha·sic \,pä-lē-'fā-zik\ adj (1922) : consisting of two or more phases
Poly·phe·mus \,pä-lə-'fē-məs\ n [L, fr. Gk Polyphēmos] : a Cyclops whom Odysseus blinds in order to escape from his cave

\ə\ abut \²\ kitten, F table \ər\ further \a\ ash \ā\ ace \ä\ mop, mar \aú\ out \ch\ chin \e\ bet \ē\ easy \g\ go \i\ hit \ī\ ice \j\ job \ŋ\ sing \ō\ go \ò\ law \òi\ boy \th\ thin \t̲h̲\ the \ü\ loot \ú\ foot \y\ yet \zh\ vision \à, k̲, ⁿ, œ, œ̄, ɯ, ūē, ᵜ\ see Guide to Pronunciation

poly·phe·nol \,pä-lē-'fē-,nōl, -fi-'\ n [ISV] (1894) : a polyhydroxy phenol — **poly·phe·no·lic** \-fi-'nō-lik, -'nä-\ adj

poly·phil·o·pro·gen·i·tive \-,fi-lə-prō-'je-nə-tiv\ adj (1919) : extremely prolific : PHILOPROGENITIVE

poly·phone \'pä-lē-,fōn\ n (1872) : a symbol or sequence of symbols having more than one phonemic value (as a in English)

poly·phon·ic \,pä-lē-'fä-nik\ or **po·lyph·o·nous** \pə-'li-fə-nəs\ adj (1782) 1 : of, relating to, or marked by polyphony 2 : being a polyphone — **poly·phon·i·cal·ly** \,pä-lē-'fä-ni-k(ə-)lē\ or **po·lyph·o·nous·ly** adv

polyphonic prose n (1916) : a freely rhythmical prose employing characteristic devices of verse (as alliteration and assonance)

po·lyph·o·ny \pə-'li-fə-nē\ n [Gk polyphōnia variety of tones, fr. polyphōnos having many tones or voices, fr. poly- + phōnē voice — more at BAN] (ca. 1864) : a style of musical composition in which two or more independent melodies are juxtaposed in harmony

poly·phy·let·ic \,pä-lē-()fi-'le-tik\ adj [ISV, fr. Gk polyphylos of many tribes, fr. poly- + phylē tribe — more at PHYL-] (1875) : of, relating to, or derived from different ancestral stocks; specif : relating to or being a taxonomic group that includes members (as genera or species) from different ancestral lineages — **poly·phy·let·i·cal·ly** \-ti-k(ə-)lē\ adv

pol·yp·ide \'pä-lə-,pīd\ n [polyp + Gk -idēs, patronymic suffix] (1850) : one of the individual zooids of a bryozoan colony

poly·ploid \'pä-lē-,plȯid\ adj [ISV] (1920) : having or being a chromosome number that is a multiple greater than two of the monoploid number — **polyploid** n — **poly·ploi·dy** \-,plȯi-dē\ n

po·lyp·nea \,pä-'lip-nē-ə, pə-\ n [NL] (ca. 1890) : rapid or panting respiration

poly·po·dy \'pä-lə-,pō-dē\ n, pl **-dies** [ME polypodie, fr. L polypodium, fr. Gk polypodion, fr. poly- + pod-, pous foot — more at FOOT] (14c) : any of a genus (Polypodium) of chiefly epiphytic ferns with creeping rhizomes; esp : either of two ferns (P. vulgare of Eurasia and P. virginianum of No. America) with relatively narrow entire segments

polypody

poly·pro·pyl·ene \,pä-lē-'prō-pə-,lēn\ n (1935) : any of various thermoplastic plastics or fibers that are polymers of propylene

po·lyp·tych \'pä-ləp-,tik, pə-'lip-tik\ n [Gk polyptychos having many folds, fr. poly- + ptychē fold, fr. ptyssein to fold] (1859) : an arrangement of four or more panels (as of a painting) usu. hinged and folding together

poly·rhythm \'pä-lē-,ri-thəm\ n (1929) : the simultaneous combination of contrasting rhythms in music — **poly·rhyth·mic** \,pä-lē-'rith-mik\ adj — **poly·rhyth·mi·cal·ly** \-mi-k(ə-)lē\ adv

poly·ri·bo·nu·cle·o·tide \,pä-lē-,rī-bō-'nü-klē-ə-,tīd, -'nyü-\ n (1956) : a polynucleotide in which the mononucleotides are ribonucleotides

poly·ri·bo·some \-'rī-bə-,sōm\ n (1962) : a cluster of ribosomes linked together by a molecule of messenger RNA and forming the site of protein synthesis — **poly·ri·bo·som·al** \-,rī-bə-'sō-məl\ adj

poly·sac·cha·ride \-'sa-kə-,rīd\ n [ISV] (1892) : a carbohydrate that can be decomposed by hydrolysis into two or more molecules of monosaccharides; esp : any of the more complex carbohydrates (as cellulose, starch, or glycogen)

po·ly·se·mous \,pä-lē-'sē-məs, pə-'li-sə-məs\ adj [LL polysemus, fr. Gk polysēmos, fr. poly- + sēma sign] (1884) : having multiple meanings — **po·ly·se·my** \-,mē\ n

poly·some \'pä-lē-,sōm\ n (1962) : POLYRIBOSOME

poly·sor·bate \,pä-lē-'sȯr-,bāt\ n (1950) : any of several emulsifiers used in the preparation of some pharmaceuticals or foods

po·lys·ti·chous \pə-'lis-ti-kəs\ adj [Gk polystichos, fr. poly- + stichos row — more at DISTICH] (ca. 1890) : arranged in several rows

poly·sty·rene \,pä-lē-'stī-,rēn\ n (1927) : a polymer of styrene; esp : a rigid transparent thermoplastic that has good physical and electrical insulating properties and is used esp. in molded products, foams, and sheet materials

poly·sul·fide \-'səl-,fīd\ n [ISV] (1849) : a sulfide containing two or more atoms of sulfur in the molecule

poly·syl·lab·ic \-sə-'la-bik\ adj [ML polysyllabus, fr. Gk polysyllabos, fr. poly- + syllabē syllable] (1782) 1 : having more than one and usu. more than three syllables 2 : characterized by words of many syllables — **poly·syl·lab·i·cal·ly** \-bi-k(ə-)lē\ adv

poly·syl·la·ble \'pä-lē-,si-lə-bəl, ,pä-lē-'\ n [modif. of ML polysyllaba, fr. fem. of polysyllabus] (1570) : a polysyllabic word

poly·syn·ap·tic \-sə-'nap-tik\ adj (1964) : involving two or more synapses in the central nervous system (∼ reflexes) — **poly·syn·ap·ti·cal·ly** \-ti-k(ə-)lē\ adv

poly·syn·de·ton \-'sin-də-,tän\ n [NL, fr. LGk, neut. of polysyndetos using many conjunctions, fr. Gk poly- + syndetos bound together, conjunctive — more at ASYNDETON] (ca. 1577) : repetition of conjunctions in close succession (as in we have ships and men and money and stores)

¹**poly·tech·nic** \-'tek-nik\ adj [F polytechnique, fr. Gk polytechnos skilled in many arts, fr. poly- + technē art — more at TECHNICAL] (1805) : relating to or devoted to instruction in many technical arts or applied sciences

²**polytechnic** n (1836) : a polytechnic school

poly·tene \'pä-lē-,tēn\ adj [ISV] (1935) : relating to, being, or having chromosomes each of which consists of many strands with the corresponding chromomeres in contact — **poly·te·ny** \-,tē-nē\ n

poly·the·ism \'pä-lē-(,)thē-,i-zəm\ n [F polytheisme, fr. LGk polytheos polytheistic, fr. Gk, of many gods, fr. poly- + theos god] (1613) : belief in or worship of more than one god — **poly·the·ist** \-,thē-ist\ adj or n — **poly·the·is·tic** \,pä-lē-thē-'is-tik\ also **poly·the·is·ti·cal** \-'is-ti-kəl\ adj

poly·thene \'pä-lə-,thēn\ n [by contr.] (1939) chiefly Brit : POLYETHYLENE

poly·to·nal·i·ty \,pä-lē-tō-'na-lə-tē\ n (1923) : the simultaneous use of two or more musical keys — **poly·ton·al** \-'tō-n²l\ adj — **poly·ton·al·ly** \-²l-ē\ adv

poly·typ·ic \,pä-lē-'ti-pik\ adj (1888) : represented by several or many types or subdivisions (a ∼ species of organism)

poly·un·sat·u·rat·ed \,pä-lē-,ən-'sa-chə-,rā-təd\ adj (1932) of an oil or fatty acid : having many double or triple bonds in a molecule — compare MONOUNSATURATED

poly·ure·thane \,pä-lē-'yùr-ə-,thān\ n [ISV] (1944) : any of various polymers that contain NHCOO linkages and are used esp. in flexible and rigid foams, elastomers, and resins (as for coatings)

poly·uria \-'yùr-ē-ə\ n [NL] (ca. 1842) : excessive secretion of urine

poly·va·lent \-'vā-lənt also pə-'li-və-lənt\ adj [ISV] (1881) 1 : having a chemical valence greater usu. than two 2 : effective against, sensitive toward, or counteracting more than one exciting agent (as a toxin or antigen) — **poly·va·lence** \-lən(t)s\ n

poly·vi·nyl \,pä-lē-'vī-n²l\ adj [ISV] (1927) : of, relating to, or being a polymerized vinyl compound, resin, or plastic — often used in combination

polyvinyl chloride n (1933) : a polymer of vinyl chloride used esp. for electrical insulation, films, and pipes — abbr. PVC

poly·wa·ter \'pä-lē-,wȯ-tər, -,wä-\ n [polymeric water] (1969) : water condensed into a glass capillary tube and formerly held to be a stable form with special properties

Pom \'päm\ n (1912) Austral & NewZeal : POMMY — usu. used disparagingly

pom·ace \'pə-məs, 'pä-\ n [ME pomys, prob. fr. ML pomacium cider, fr. LL pomum apple, fr. L, fruit] (15c) 1 : the dry or pulpy residue of material (as fruit, seeds, or fish) from which a liquid (as juice or oil) has been pressed or extracted 2 : something crushed to a pulpy mass

po·ma·ceous \pō-'mā-shəs\ adj [NL pomaceus, fr. LL pomum] (1708) 1 : of or relating to apples 2 [pome] : resembling a pome

po·made \pō-'mād, -'mäd\ n [MF pommade ointment formerly made from apples, fr. It pomata, fr. pomo apple, fr. LL pomum] (1562) : a perfumed ointment; esp : a fragrant hair dressing — **pomade** vt

po·man·der \'pō-,man-dər, pō-'\ n [ME, modif. of MF pome d'ambre, lit., apple or ball of amber] (15c) 1 : a mixture of aromatic substances enclosed in a perforated bag or box and used to scent clothes and linens or formerly carried as a guard against infection; also : a clove-studded orange or apple used for the same purposes 2 : a box or hollow fruit-shaped ball for holding pomander

po·ma·tum \pō-'mā-təm, -'mä-\ n [NL, fr. LL pomum apple] (1562) : POMADE

pome \'pōm\ n [ME, fr. MF pome, pomme apple, pome, ball, ultim. fr. LL pomum] (15c) : a fleshy fruit (as an apple or pear) consisting of an outer thickened fleshy layer and a central core with usu. five seeds enclosed in a capsule

pome·gran·ate \'pä-mə-,gra-nət; 'päm-,gra-nət, 'pəm-\ n [ME poumgrenet, fr. MF pomme grenate, lit., seedy apple] (14c) 1 : a thick-skinned several-celled reddish berry that is about the size of an orange and has many seeds with pulpy crimson arils of tart flavor 2 : a widely cultivated tropical Old World tree (Punica granatum of the family Punicaceae) bearing pomegranates

pom·e·lo \'pä-mə-,lō\ n, pl **-los** [alter. of earlier pompelmous, fr. D pompelmoes] (1858) 1 : GRAPEFRUIT 2 : SHADDOCK

Pom·er·a·nian \,pä-mə-'rā-nē-ən, -nyən\ n (1760) 1 : any of a breed of very small compact long-haired dogs 2 : a native or inhabitant of Pomerania — **Pomeranian** adj

pom·mée \pä-'mā, ,pə-\ adj [F, fr. MF pomme apple, ball] (1725) of a heraldic cross : having the end of each arm terminating in a ball or disk — see CROSS illustration

¹**pom·mel** \'pə-məl, 'pä-\ n [ME pomel, fr. MF, fr. (assumed) VL pomellum ball, knob, fr. dim. of LL pomum apple] (14c) 1 : the knob on the hilt of a sword or saber 2 : the protuberance at the front and top of a saddle 3 : either of a pair of removable rounded or U-shaped handles used on the top of a pommel horse

²**pom·mel** \'pə-məl\ vt **-meled** or **-melled; -mel·ing** or **-mel·ling** \'pə-mə-liŋ, 'pəm-liŋ\ [¹pommel] (1530) : PUMMEL

pommel horse n (1908) 1 : a gymnastics apparatus for swinging and balancing feats that consists of a padded rectangular or cylindrical form with two pommels on the top and that is supported in a horizontal position above the floor 2 : an event in which the pommel horse is used

pommel horse 1

Pom·my or **Pom·mie** \'pä-mē\ n, pl **Pommies** [by shortening & alter. fr. pomegranate, alter. of Jimmy Grant, rhyming slang for immigrant] (1912) Austral & NewZeal : BRITON; esp : an English immigrant — usu. used disparagingly

Po·mo \'pō-(,)mō\ n, pl **Pomo** or **Pomos** (1852) : a member of an American Indian people of northern California

po·mol·o·gy \pō-'mä-lə-jē\ n [NL pomologia, fr. L pomum fruit + -logia -logy] (1818) : the science and practice of fruit growing — **po·mo·log·i·cal** \,pō-mə-'lä-ji-kəl\ adj — **po·mol·o·gist** \pō-'mä-lə-jist\ n

pomp \'pämp\ n [ME, fr. MF pompe, fr. L pompa procession, pomp, fr. Gk pompē act of sending, escort, procession, pomp, fr. pempein to send] (14c) 1 : a show of magnificence : SPLENDOR (every day begins … in a ∼ of flaming colours —F. D. Ommanney) 2 : a ceremonial or festival display (as a train of followers or a pageant) 3 : ostentatious display : VAINGLORY b : an ostentatious gesture or act

pom·pa·dour \'päm-pə-,dȯr, -,dȯ\ n [Marquise de Pompadour] (1756) 1 a : a man's style of hairdressing in which the hair is combed into a high mound in front b : a woman's style of hairdressing in which the hair is brushed into a loose full roll around the face 2 : hair dressed in a pompadour — **pom·pa·doured** \-,dȯrd, -,dȯrd\ adj

pom·pa·no \'päm-pə-,nō, 'pəm-\ n, pl **-no** or **-nos** [AmerSp pámpano, fr. Sp, a percoid fish (Sparus auratus), lit., vine leaf, fr. L pampinus] (1778) 1 : a carangid food fish (Trachinotus carolinus) of the southern Atlantic and Gulf coasts of No. America; broadly : any of several related fishes 2 : a small bluish or greenish butterfly (Peprilus simillimus) of the Pacific coast

¹**pom–pom** \'päm-,päm\ n [alter. of pompon] (1897) 1 : an ornamental ball or tuft used esp. on clothing, caps, or costumes 2 : a handheld usu. brightly colored fluffy ball flourished by cheerleaders

²pom–pom n [imit.; fr. the sound of its discharge] (1899) : a multibarreled automatic antiaircraft gun of 20 to 40 millimeters mounted esp. on ships

pom·pon \'päm-,pän\ n [F, fr. MF pompe tuft of ribbons] (1753) **1** : ¹POM-POM 1 **2** : a chrysanthemum or dahlia with small rounded flower heads

pom·pos·i·ty \päm-'pä-sə-tē\ n, pl **-ties** (1620) **1** : pompous demeanor, speech, or behavior **2** : a pompous gesture, habit, or act

pomp·ous \'päm-pəs\ adj (15c) **1** : excessively elevated or ornate ⟨∼ rhetoric⟩ **2** : having or exhibiting self-importance : ARROGANT ⟨a ∼ politician⟩ **3** : relating to or suggestive of pomp : MAGNIFICENT — **pomp·ous·ly** adv — **pomp·ous·ness** n

ponce \'pän(t)s\ n [origin unknown] (1872) Brit : PIMP; also : a male homosexual — usu. used disparagingly

pon·cho \'pän-(,)chō\ n, pl **ponchos** [AmerSp, fr. Araucanian] (1717) **1** : a blanket with a slit in the middle so that it can be slipped over the head and worn as a sleeveless garment **2** : a waterproof garment resembling a poncho and having an integral hood

¹pond \'pänd\ n [ME ponde artificially confined body of water, prob. alter. of pounde enclosure — more at POUND] (14c) : a body of water usu. smaller than a lake

²pond vt (1694) : to block (as a stream) to create a pond ∼ vi : to collect in or form a pond

pon·der \'pän-dər\ vb **pon·dered; pon·der·ing** \-d(ə-)riŋ\ [ME, fr. MF ponderer, fr. L ponderare to weigh, ponder, fr. ponder-, pondus weight — more at PENDANT] vt (14c) **1** : to weigh in the mind : APPRAISE ⟨∼ed their chances of success⟩ **2** : to think about : reflect on ⟨∼ed the events of the day⟩ ∼ vi : to think or consider esp. quietly, soberly, and deeply — **pon·der·er** \-dər-ər\ n

syn PONDER, MEDITATE, MUSE, RUMINATE mean to consider or examine attentively or deliberately. PONDER implies a careful weighing of a problem or, often, prolonged inconclusive thinking about a matter ⟨pondered the course of action⟩. MEDITATE implies a definite focusing of one's thoughts on something so as to understand it deeply ⟨meditated on the meaning of life⟩. MUSE suggests a more or less focused daydreaming as in remembrance ⟨mused upon childhood joys⟩. RUMINATE implies going over the same matter in one's thoughts again and again but suggests little of either purposive thinking or rapt absorption ⟨ruminated on past disappointments⟩.

pon·der·a·ble \'pän-d(ə-)rə-bəl\ adj [LL ponderabilis, fr. ponderare] (1813) : important enough to be worth considering : APPRECIABLE — **syn** SEE PERCEPTIBLE

pon·der·o·sa pine \,pän-də-'rō-sə-, -zə-\ n [NL ponderosa, specific epithet of Pinus ponderosa, fr. L, fem. of ponderosus ponderous] (1878) : a tall pine (Pinus ponderosa) of western No. America with long needles usu. in groups of 2 or 3; also : its strong reddish straight-grained wood — called also **ponderosa**

pon·der·ous \'pän-d(ə-)rəs\ adj [ME, fr. MF pondereux, fr. L ponderosus, fr. ponder-, pondus weight] (15c) **1** : of very great weight **2** : unwieldy or clumsy because of weight and size **3** : oppressively or unpleasantly dull : LIFELESS ⟨∼ prose⟩ **syn** see HEAVY — **pon·der·ous·ly** adv — **pon·der·ous·ness** n

pond lily n (1748) : WATER LILY

pond scum n (ca. 1890) **1** : SPIROGYRA; also : any of various related algae **2** : a mass of tangled algal filaments in stagnant waters

pond skater n (1895) : WATER STRIDER

pond·weed \'pänd-,wēd\ n (1578) : any of a genus (Potamogeton of the family Potamogetonaceae, the pondweed family) of aquatic plants with jointed usu. rooting stems, 2-ranked floating or submerged leaves, and spikes of greenish flowers

pone \'pōn\ n [modif. of Virginia Algonquian appone] (1634) Southern & Midland : CORN PONE

pon·gee \,pän-'jē, 'pän-,\ n, often attrib [Chin (Beijing) běnjī, fr. běn own + jī loom] (1711) : a thin soft fabric of Chinese origin woven from raw silk; also : an imitation of this fabric in cotton or a synthetic fiber (as of polyester or rayon)

pon·gid \'pän-jəd, 'päŋ-gəd\ n [ultim. fr. Kongo mpongi ape] (1950) : any of a family (Pongidae) of apes that includes the chimpanzee, gorilla, and orangutan — **pongid** adj

¹pon·iard \'pän-yərd\ n [MF poignard, fr. poing fist, fr. L pugnus fist — more at PUNGENT] (1588) : a dagger with a usu. slender blade of triangular or square cross section

²poniard vt (1601) : to pierce or kill with a poniard

pons \'pänz\ n, pl **pon·tes** \'pän-,tēz\ [NL, short for pons Varolii] (1831) : a broad mass of chiefly transverse nerve fibers conspicuous on the ventral surface of the brain of man and lower mammals at the anterior end of the medulla oblongata — see BRAIN illustration

pons asi·no·rum \'pänz-,a-sə-'nōr-əm, -'nȯr-\ n [NL, lit., asses' bridge, name applied to the proposition that the base angles of an isosceles triangle are equal] (1751) : a critical test of ability or understanding; also : STUMBLING BLOCK

pons Va·ro·lii \-və-'rō-lē-,ī, -lē-,ē\ n [NL, lit., bridge of Varoli, fr. Costanzo Varoli †1575 Ital. surgeon and anatomist] (ca. 1693) : PONS

pon·ti·fex \'pän-tə-,feks\ n, pl **pon·tif·i·ces** \pän-'ti-fə-,sēz\ [L pontific-, pontifex, fr. pont-, pons bridge + facere to make — more at FIND, DO] (ca. 1580) : a member of the council of priests in ancient Rome

pon·tiff \'pän-təf\ n [F pontif, fr. L pontific-, pontifex] (1626) **1** : PONTIFEX **2** : BISHOP; specif : POPE

¹pon·tif·i·cal \pän-'ti-fi-kəl\ n (14c) **1** : episcopal attire; specif : the insignia of the episcopal order worn by a prelate when celebrating a pontifical mass — usu. used in pl. **2** : a book containing the forms for sacraments and rites performed by a bishop

²pontifical adj [ME, fr. L pontificalis, fr. pontific-, pontifex] (15c) **1 a** : of or relating to a pontiff or pontifex **b** : celebrated by a prelate of episcopal rank with distinctive ceremonies ⟨∼ mass⟩ **2** : POMPOUS **3** : pretentiously dogmatic — **pon·tif·i·cal·ly** \-k(ə-)lē\ adv

¹pon·tif·i·cate \pän-'ti-fi-kət, -,kāt\ n [ME, fr. L pontificatus, fr. pontific-, pontifex] (15c) : the state, office, or term of office of a pontiff

²pon·tif·i·cate \pän-'ti-fə-,kāt\ vi **-cat·ed; -cat·ing** [ML pontificatus, pp. of pontificare, fr. L pontific-, pontifex] (1818) **1 a** : to officiate as a pontiff **b** : to celebrate pontifical mass **2** : to speak or express opinions in a pompous or dogmatic way — **pon·tif·i·ca·tion** \(,)pän-,ti-fə-'kā-shən\ n — **pon·tif·i·ca·tor** \-,kā-tər\ n

pon·til \'pän-t³l\ n [F, perh. fr. It puntello, dim. of punto point, fr. L punctus — more at POINT] (1832) : PUNTY — called also **pontil rod**

pon·tine \'pän-,tīn\ adj [NL pont-, pons pons] (1889) : of or relating to the pons

Pont l'É·vêque \,pōⁿ-lā-'vek\ n [Pont l'Évêque, town in France] (ca. 1889) : a soft surface-ripened cheese firmer, yellower, and having less surface mold than Camembert

¹pon·toon \pän-'tün\ n [F ponton, fr. L ponton-, ponto] (1690) **1** : a flat-bottomed boat (as a lighter); esp : a flat-bottomed boat or portable float used in building a floating temporary bridge **2** : a float esp. of a seaplane

²pontoon n [perh. alter. of vingt-et-un] (ca. 1917) Brit : BLACKJACK 5

po·ny \'pō-nē\ n, pl **ponies** [prob. fr. obs. F poulenet, dim. of F poulain colt, fr. ML pullanus, fr. L pullus young of an animal, foal — more at FOAL] (1659) **1 a** : a small horse; esp : one of any of several breeds of very small stocky animals noted for their gentleness and endurance **b** : a bronco, mustang, or similar horse of the western U.S. **c** : RACEHORSE — usu. used in pl. **2** : something smaller than standard: as **a** : a small beer glass **b** : a small liqueur glass typically holding one ounce **3** : a literal translation of a foreign language text; esp : one used surreptitiously by students in preparing or reciting lessons

pony express n, often cap P&E (1860) : a rapid postal and express system that operated across the western U.S. in 1860–1861 by relays of horses and riders

po·ny·tail \'pō-nē-,tāl\ n (1951) : a hairstyle in which the hair is pulled together and banded at the back of the head so as to resemble a pony's tail — **po·ny·tailed** \-,tāld\ adj

po·ny up \'pō-nē-\ vb **po·nied up; po·ny·ing up** [origin unknown] vt (1824) : to pay (money) esp. in settlement of an account ⟨ponied up $12.50 for the fine —Newsweek⟩ ∼ vi : PAY

Pon·zi scheme \'pän-zē-\ n [Charles A. Ponzi †1949 Am. (Ital.-born) swindler] (1973) : an investment swindle in which some early investors are paid off with money put up by later ones in order to encourage more and bigger risks

-poo \,pü, 'pü\ suffix [origin unknown] — used as a disparaging diminutive ⟨cutesy-poo⟩

¹pooch \'püch\ vb [alter. of ¹pouch] (ca. 1923) chiefly dial : BULGE

²pooch n [origin unknown] (1924) : DOG

pood \'püd, 'püt\ n [Russ pud, fr. ORuss, fr. ON pund pound — more at POUND] (1554) : a Russian unit of weight equal to about 36.11 pounds (16.38 kilograms)

poo·dle \'pü-d³l\ n [G Pudel, short for Pudelhund, fr. pudeln to splash + Hund dog] (1820) **1** : a dog of any of three breeds of active intelligent heavy-coated solid-colored dogs — compare TOY POODLE **2** : a fabric with a nubby or coarsely looped surface that resembles a poodle's coat — called also **poodle cloth**

¹poof \'püf, 'pu̇f\ interj (1824) — used to express disdain or dismissal or to suggest instantaneous occurrence

²poof also **poove** \'püv, 'pu̇v\ n, pl **poofs** also **pooves** [perh. alter. of ²puff] (ca. 1860) Brit : a male homosexual — usu. used disparagingly

poof·ter \'püf-tər, 'pu̇f-\ also **poof·tah** \-tə\ n [by alter.] (1903) Brit : POOF — usu. used disparagingly

pooh \'pü, 'pu̇\ interj (1602) — used to express contempt or disapproval

pooh–bah \'pü-,bä, -,bȯ\ n, often cap P&B [Pooh-Bah, character in Gilbert and Sullivan's opera The Mikado (1885) bearing the title Lord-High-Everything-Else] (1888) **1** : a person holding many public or private offices **2** : a person in high position or of great influence

pooh–pooh \'pü-(,)pü, pü-'\ also **pooh** \'pü\ vb [pooh] vi (1827) : to express contempt or impatience ∼ vt : to express contempt for or make light of : DISMISS

¹pool \'pü(ə)l\ n [ME, fr. OE pōl; akin to OHG pfuol pool] (bef. 12c) **1 a** (1) : a small and rather deep body of usu. fresh water (2) : a quiet place in a stream (3) : a body of water forming above a dam **b** : something resembling a pool ⟨a ∼ of light⟩ **2** : a small body of standing liquid **3** : a continuous area of porous sedimentary rock that yields petroleum or gas **4** : SWIMMING POOL

²pool vi (1626) **1** : to form a pool **2** of blood : to accumulate or become static (as in the veins of a bodily part)

³pool n [F poule, lit., hen, fr. OF, fem. of poul cock — more at PULLET] (ca. 1712) **1 a** : an aggregate stake to which each player of a game has contributed **b** : all the money bet by a number of persons on a particular event **2 a** : a game played on an English billiard table in which each of the players stakes a sum and the winner takes all **b** : any of various games of billiards played on an oblong table having 6 pockets with usu. 15 object balls **3** : an aggregation of the interests or property of different persons made to further a joint undertaking by subjecting them to the same control and a common liability **4** : a readily available supply: as **a** : the whole quantity of a particular material present in the body and available for function or the satisfying of metabolic demands **b** : a body product (as blood) collected from many donors and stored for later use **c** : a group of people available for some purpose ⟨a shrinking ∼ of applicants⟩ ⟨typing ∼⟩ **5** : GENE POOL

⁴pool vt (1879) : to combine (as resources) in a common fund or effort

pool·room \'pü(ə)l-,rüm, -,rum\ n (1861) **1** : a room in which bookmaking is carried on **2** : a room for the playing of pool

pool·side \-,sīd\ n (1921) : the area surrounding a swimming pool

¹poop \'püp\ n [ME, fr. MF poupe, fr. L puppis] (15c) **1** obs : STERN **2** : an enclosed superstructure at the stern of a ship above the main deck

²poop vt (1748) **1** : to break over the stern of **2** : to ship (a sea or wave) over the stern

³poop vb [origin unknown] vt (ca. 1932) slang : to put out of breath; also : to tire out ∼ vi, slang : to become exhausted ⟨∼ out⟩

⁴poop n [perh. alter. of ³poop] (ca. 1941) slang : INFORMATION, SCOOP

\ə\ abut \³\ kitten, F table \ər\ further \a\ ash \ā\ ace \ä\ mop, mar \au̇\ out \ch\ chin \e\ bet \ē\ easy \g\ go \i\ hit \ī\ ice \j\ job \ŋ\ sing \ō\ go \ȯ\ law \ȯi\ boy \th\ thin \t̲h̲\ the \ü\ loot \u̇\ foot \y\ yet \zh\ vision \â, k̲, ⁿ, œ, œ̄, ɷ, ūe, ᵫ\ see Guide to Pronunciation

⁵poop n [poop, v., to defecate, break wind, fr. ME poupen to make a gulping sound; of imit. origin] (1965) : EXCREMENT
poop deck n (1840) : a partial deck above a ship's main afterdeck
poop·er–scoop·er \'pü-pər-,skü-pər\ n [⁵poop] (1976) : a device used for picking up the droppings of a pet (as a dog) for disposal
poor \'pür, 'pôr\ adj [ME poure, fr. OF povre, fr. L pauper; akin to L paucus little and to L parere to give birth to, produce — more at FEW, PARE] (13c) **1 a** : lacking material possessions **b** : of, relating to, or characterized by poverty **2 a** : less than adequate : MEAGER **b** : small in worth **3** : exciting pity ⟨you ~ thing⟩ **4 a** : inferior in quality or value **b** : HUMBLE, UNPRETENTIOUS **c** : MEAN, PETTY **5** : LEAN, EMACIATED **6** : BARREN, UNPRODUCTIVE — used of land **7** : INDIFFERENT, UNFAVORABLE **8** : lacking a normal or adequate supply of something specified — often used in combination ⟨oil-poor countries⟩ — **poor·ish** \-ish\ adj — **poor·ness** n
poor box n (1621) : a box (as in a church) for alms for the poor
poor boy \'pô(r)-,bói\ n (ca. 1941) : SUBMARINE 2
Poor Clare \-'klar, -'kler\ n (1608) : a member of an austere order of nuns founded by St. Clare under the direction of St. Francis in Assisi, Italy, in 1212
poor farm \'pür-,färm, 'pôr-\ n (1852) : a farm maintained at public expense for the support and employment of needy persons
poor·house \-,haús\ n (1792) : a place maintained at public expense to house needy or dependent persons
poor law n (1752) : a law providing for or regulating the public relief or support of the poor
¹poor·ly \'pür-lē, 'pôr-\ adv (13c) : in a poor condition or manner; esp : in an inferior or imperfect way : BADLY ⟨sang ~⟩
²poor·ly adj (1750) : somewhat ill : INDISPOSED
poor–mouth \'pür-,maúth, 'pôr-, -,maúth\ vi (1964) : to plead poverty as a defense or excuse ~ vt : to speak disparagingly of
poor mouth \-,maúth\ n (1822) : an exaggerated claim of poverty
poor–spir·it·ed \-'spir-ə-təd\ adj (1670) : lacking zest, confidence, or courage — **poor·spir·it·ed·ly** adv — **poor·spir·it·ed·ness** n
poor white n (1819) : a member of an inferior or underprivileged white social group — often taken to be offensive
¹pop \'päp\ vb **popped; pop·ping** [ME poppen, of imit. origin] vt (15c) **1** : to strike or knock sharply : HIT **2** : to push, put, or thrust suddenly and often deftly **3** : to cause to explode or burst open **4** : to fire at : SHOOT **5** : to take (pills) esp. frequently or habitually **6** : to open with a pop ⟨~ a cold beer⟩ ~ vi **1 a** : to go, come, or appear suddenly — often used with up **b** : to escape or break away from something (as a point of attachment) usu. suddenly or unexpectedly **2** : to make or burst with a sharp sound : EXPLODE **3** : to protrude from the sockets **4** : to shoot with a firearm **5** : to hit a pop fly — often used with up or out — **pop the question** : to propose marriage
²pop n (1591) **1** : a sharp explosive sound **2** : a shot from a gun **3** : SODA POP **4** : POP FLY — **a pop** : for each one : APIECE ⟨tickets at $10 a pop⟩
³pop adv (1621) : like or with a pop : SUDDENLY
⁴pop n [short for poppa] (1838) : FATHER
⁵pop adj [by shortening] (1880) **1** : POPULAR ⟨~ music⟩ **a** : of or relating to popular music ⟨~ singer⟩ **b** : of or relating to the popular culture disseminated through the mass media ⟨~ psychology⟩ ⟨~ grammarians⟩ ⟨~ society⟩ **2 a** : of or relating to pop art ⟨~ painter⟩ **b** : having, using, or imitating themes or techniques characteristic of pop art ⟨~ movie⟩
⁶pop n (1954) **1** : pop music **2** : POP ART **3** : pop culture
pop art n (1957) : art in which commonplace objects (as road signs, hamburgers, comic strips, or soup cans) are used as subject matter and are often physically incorporated in the work — **pop artist** n
pop·corn \'päp-,kórn\ n (1823) : an Indian corn (Zea mays praecox) whose kernels on exposure to heat burst open to form a white starchy mass; also : the kernels esp. after popping
pope \'pōp\ n [ME, fr. OE pāpa, fr. LL papa, fr. Gk pappas, papas, title of bishops, lit., papa] (bef. 12c) **1** often cap : a prelate who as bishop of Rome is the head of the Roman Catholic Church **2** : one that resembles a pope (as in authority) **3 a** : the Eastern Orthodox or Coptic patriarch of Alexandria **b** : a priest of an Eastern church
pop·ery \'pō-p(ə-)rē\ n (ca. 1534) : ROMAN CATHOLICISM — usu. used disparagingly
pop eye \'päp-,ī\ n [back-formation fr. pop-eyed] (1828) : an eye staring and bulging (as from excitement) — **pop–eyed** \-,īd\ adj
pop fly n (1887) : a high fly ball in baseball
pop·gun \'päp-,gən\ n (1622) : a toy gun that usu. shoots a cork and produces a popping sound
pop·in·jay \'pä-pən-,jā\ n [ME papejay parrot, fr. MF papegai, papejai, fr. Ar babghā'] (14c) : a strutting supercilious person
pop·ish \'pō-pish\ adj [pope] (1528) : ROMAN CATHOLIC — often used disparagingly
pop·lar \'pä-plər\ n [ME poplere, fr. MF pouplier, fr. pouple poplar, fr. L populus] (14c) **1 a** : any of a genus (Populus) of slender catkin-bearing quick-growing trees (as an aspen or cottonwood) of the willow family **b** : the wood of a poplar **2** : TULIP TREE 1
pop·lin \'pä-plən\ n [F papeline] (1710) : a strong fabric in plain weave with crosswise ribs
pop·li·te·al \,pä-plə-'tē-əl and also pä-'pli-tē-əl\ adj [NL popliteus, fr. L poplit-, poples ham of the knee] (1786) : of or relating to the back part of the leg behind the knee joint
pop off vi (1764) **1 a** : to die unexpectedly **b** : to leave suddenly **2** : to talk thoughtlessly and often loudly or angrily
pop·over \'päp-,ō-vər\ n (1876) : a hollow quick bread shaped like a muffin and made from a thin batter of eggs, milk, and flour
pop·pa \'pä-pə\ var of PAPA
pop·per \'pä-pər\ n (1750) **1** : one that pops; esp : a utensil for popping corn **2** slang : a vial of amyl nitrite or butyl nitrite esp. when used illicitly as an aphrodisiac
pop·pet \'pä-pət\ n [ME popet — more at PUPPET] (15c) **1 a** Midland : DOLL **b** obs : MARIONETTE **2** chiefly Brit : DEAR **3 a** : an upright support or guide of a machine that is fastened at the bottom only **b** : a valve that rises perpendicularly to or from its seat
pop·pied \'pä-pēd\ adj (1818) **1** archaic : growing or overgrown with poppies **2** : DROWSY

¹pop·ple \'pä-pəl\ n [ME popul, fr. OE, fr. L populus] (14c) chiefly dial : POPLAR 1
²popple n [popple, vb., fr. ME poplen to bubble, ripple, prob. of imit. origin] (1875) : a choppy sea
pop·py \'pä-pē\ n, pl **poppies** [ME popi, fr. OE popæg, popig, modif. of L papaver] (bef. 12c) **1 a** : any of a genus (Papaver of the family Papaveraceae, the poppy family) of chiefly annual or perennial herbs with milky juice, showy regular flowers, and capsular fruits including the opium poppy and several forms cultivated as ornamentals **b** : an extract or decoction of poppy used medicinally **2** : a strong reddish orange
pop·py·cock \'pä-pē-,käk\ n [D dial. pappekak, lit., soft dung, fr. D pap pap + kak dung] (1865) : empty talk or writing : NONSENSE
pop·py·head \-,hed\ n (1839) : a raised ornament often in the form of a finial generally used on the tops of the upright ends of seats in Gothic churches
poppy seed n (14c) : the seed of a poppy used chiefly as a topping or flavoring for baked goods
pop quiz n (ca. 1960) : an unscheduled or unannounced quiz
Pop·si·cle \'päp-,si-kəl, -sə-\ trademark — used for flavored and colored water frozen on a stick
pop–top \'päp-,täp\ n (1965) : a closure that can be pulled by hand to open a can
pop·u·lace \'päp-yə-ləs\ n [MF, fr. It popolaccio rabble, aug. of popolo the people, fr. L populus] (1572) **1** : the common people : MASSES **2** : POPULATION
pop·u·lar \'pä-pyə-lər\ adj [L popularis, fr. populus the people, a people] (1548) **1** : of or relating to the general public **2** : suitable to the majority: as **a** : adapted to or indicative of the understanding and taste of the majority ⟨a ~ history of the war⟩ **b** : suited to the means of the majority : INEXPENSIVE ⟨sold at ~ prices⟩ **3** : frequently encountered or widely accepted **4** : commonly liked or approved ⟨a very ~ girl⟩ syn see COMMON — **pop·u·lar·ly** adv
popular front n, often cap P&F (1936) : a coalition esp. of leftist political parties against a common opponent; specif : one sponsored and dominated by Communists as a device for gaining power
pop·u·lar·ise Brit var of POPULARIZE
pop·u·lar·i·ty \,pä-pyə-'lar-ə-tē\ n (1601) : the quality or state of being popular
pop·u·lar·ize \'pä-pyə-lə-,rīz\ vb **-ized; -iz·ing** vi (1593) : to cater to popular taste ~ vt : to make popular: as **a** : to cause to be liked or esteemed **b** : to present in generally understandable or interesting form — **pop·u·lar·i·za·tion** \,pä-pyə-lə-rə-'zä-shən\ n — **pop·u·lar·iz·er** \'pä-pyə-lə-,rī-zər\ n
popular sovereignty n (1848) **1** : a doctrine in political theory that government is created by and subject to the will of the people **2** : a pre-Civil War doctrine asserting the right of the people living in a newly organized territory to decide by vote of their territorial legislature whether or not slavery would be permitted there
pop·u·late \'pä-pyə-,lāt\ vt **-lat·ed; -lat·ing** [ML populatus, pp. of populare to people, fr. L populus people] (1578) **1** : to have a place in : OCCUPY, INHABIT **2 a** : to furnish or provide with inhabitants : PEOPLE **b** : to provide with members
pop·u·la·tion \,pä-pyə-'lä-shən\ n [LL population-, populatio, fr. L populus] (1612) **1 a** : the whole number of people or inhabitants in a country or region **b** : the total of individuals occupying an area or making up a whole **c** : the total of particles at a particular energy level — used esp. of atoms in a laser **2** : the act or process of populating **3 a** : a body of persons or individuals having a quality or characteristic in common **b** (1) : the organisms inhabiting a particular locality (2) : a group of interbreeding organisms that represents the level of organization at which speciation begins **4** : a group of individual persons, objects, or items from which samples are taken for statistical measurement — **pop·u·la·tion·al** \-shnəl, -shə-n³l\ adj
population explosion n (1953) : a pyramiding of numbers of a biological population; esp : the recent great increase in human numbers resulting from increased survival and exponential population growth
¹pop·u·list \'pä-pyə-list\ n [L populus the people] (1892) **1** : a member of a political party claiming to represent the common people; esp, often cap : a member of a U.S. political party formed in 1891 primarily to represent agrarian interests and to advocate the free coinage of silver and government control of monopolies **2** : a believer in the rights, wisdom, or virtues of the common people — **pop·u·lism** \-,li-zəm\ n — **pop·u·lis·tic** \,pä-pyə-'lis-tik\ adj
²populist adj (1893) **1** often cap : of, relating to, or characterized by populism **2** : POPULAR 1, 2
pop·u·lous \'pä-pyə-ləs\ adj [ME, fr. L populosus, fr. populus people] (15c) **1 a** : densely populated **b** : having a large population **2 a** : NUMEROUS **b** : filled to capacity — **pop·u·lous·ly** adv — **pop·u·lous·ness** n
pop–up \'päp-,əp\ n (1906) : POP FLY
por·bea·gle \'pór-,bē-gəl\ n [Corn porgh-bugel] (1758) : a small viviparous shark (Lamna nasus) chiefly of the No. Atlantic Ocean with a pointed nose and crescent-shaped tail
por·ce·lain \'pór-s(ə-)lən, 'pór-\ n [MF porcelaine cowrie shell, porcelain, fr. It porcellana, fr. porcello vulva, lit., little pig, fr. L porcellus, dim. of porcus pig, vulva; fr. the shape of the shell — more at FARROW] (ca. 1530) : a hard, fine-grained, sonorous, nonporous, and usu. translucent and white ceramic ware that consists essentially of kaolin, quartz, and feldspar and is fired at high temperatures — **por·ce·lain·like** \-,līk\ adj — **por·ce·la·ne·ous** or **por·cel·la·ne·ous** \,pór-sə-'lä-nē-əs, ,pór-\ adj
porcelain enamel n (1883) : a fired-on opaque glassy coating on metal (as steel)
por·ce·lain·ize \'pór-s(ə-)lə-,nīz, 'pór-\ vt **-ized; -iz·ing** (1951) : to fire a glassy coating on (as steel)
porch \'pórch, 'pôrch\ n [ME porche, fr. OF, fr. L porticus portico, fr. porta gate; akin to L portus port — more at FORD] (14c) **1** : a covered area adjoining an entrance to a building and usu. having a separate roof **2** obs : PORTICO
por·cine \'pór-,sīn\ adj [L porcinus, fr. porcus pig — more at FARROW] (ca. 1656) : of, relating to, or suggesting swine

por·ci·no \pȯr-'chē-(,)nō\ n, pl **-ni** \-(,)nē\ [It, short for *fungo porcino*, lit., porcine mushroom] (1976) : a wild edible boletus mushroom (esp. *Boletus edulis*)

por·cu·pine \'pȯr-kyə-,pīn\ n, pl **porcupines** also **porcupine** [ME *porkepin*, fr. MF *porc espin*, fr. OIt *porcospino*, fr. L *porcus* pig + *spina* spine, prickle] (15c) : any of various relatively large rodents having stiff sharp erectile bristles mingled with the hair and constituting an Old World terrestrial family (Hystricidae) and a New World arboreal family (Erethizontidae)

porcupine fish n (1681) : any of several bony fishes (family Diodontidae) having sharp spines covering the body; esp : a spotted chiefly tropical fish (*Diodon hystrix*) that is olive to brown above with white below

¹pore \'pȯr, 'pȯr\ vi **pored; por·ing** [ME *pouren*] (13c) 1 : to gaze intently 2 : to read studiously or attentively — usu. used with *over* 3 : to reflect or meditate steadily

²pore n [ME, fr. MF, fr. L *porus*, fr. Gk *poros* passage, pore — more at FARE] (14c) 1 : a minute opening esp. in an animal or plant; esp : one by which matter passes through a membrane 2 : a small interstice (as in soil) admitting absorption or passage of liquid — **pored** \'pȯrd, 'pȯrd\ adj

pore fungus n (1922) : a fungus (family Boletaceae or Polyporaceae) having the spore-bearing surface within tubes or pores

por·gy \'pȯr-gē\ n, pl **porgies** also **porgy** [alter. of *pargo*, fr. Sp & Pg, fr. L *phager*, fr. Gk *phagros*] (1671) 1 : a blue-spotted crimson food fish (*Pagrus pagrus* of the family Sparidae) of the eastern and western Atlantic; also : any of various fishes of the same family 2 [alter. of *pogy*] : any of various bony fishes (as a menhaden) of families other than that of the porgy

pork \'pȯrk, 'pȯrk\ n [ME, fr. OF *porc* pig, fr. L *porcus* — more at FARROW] (14c) 1 : the fresh or salted flesh of swine when dressed for food 2 : government money, jobs, or favors used by politicians as patronage

pork barrel n (1909) : government projects or appropriations yielding rich patronage benefits; also : PORK 2

pork belly n (ca. 1950) : an uncured side of pork

pork·er \'pȯr-kər, 'pȯr-\ n (1657) : HOG; esp : a young pig fattened for table use as fresh pork

pork·pie hat \'pȯrk-,pī-, 'pȯrk-\ n [fr. its shape] (1860) : a hat with a low telescoped crown, flat top, and brim turned up all around or up in back and down in front

¹porky \'pȯr-kē, 'pȯr-\ adj **pork·i·er; -est** (1852) : resembling a pig : FAT

²por·ky \'pȯr-kē\ n, pl **porkies** (1900) : PORCUPINE

porn \'pȯrn\ also **por·no** \'pȯr-(,)nō\ n, often attrib (1962) : PORNOGRAPHY

por·nog·ra·pher \pȯr-'nä-grə-fər\ n (1850) : one who produces pornography

por·nog·ra·phy \-fē\ n [Gk *pornographos*, adj., writing about prostitutes, fr. *pornē* prostitute + *graphein* to write; akin to Gk *pernanai* to sell, *poros* journey — more at FARE, CARVE] (ca. 1864) 1 : the depiction of erotic behavior (as in pictures or writing) intended to cause sexual excitement 2 : material (as books or a photograph) that depicts erotic behavior and is intended to cause sexual excitement 3 : the depiction of acts in a sensational manner so as to arouse a quick intense emotional reaction (the ~ of violence) — **por·no·graph·ic** \,pȯr-nə-'gra-fik\ adj — **por·no·graph·i·cal·ly** \-fi-k(ə-)lē\ adv

porny \'pȯr-nē\ adj **porn·i·er; -est** (1961) : of, relating to, involved in, or being pornography

po·ros·i·ty \pə-'rä-sə-tē, pȯ-\ n, pl **-ties** (14c) 1 a : the quality or state of being porous b : the ratio of the volume of interstices of a material to the volume of its mass 2 : PORE

po·rous \'pȯr-əs, 'pȯr-\ adj (14c) 1 a : possessing or full of pores b : containing vessels (hardwood is ~) 2 a : permeable to fluids b : permeable to outside influences (his imagination is astonishingly ~ —Elizabeth Hardwick) 3 : capable of being penetrated (~ national boundaries) (a ~ defense) — **po·rous·ly** adv — **po·rous·ness** n

por·phyr·ia \pȯr-'fir-ē-ə\ n [NL, fr. ISV *porphyrin*] (1923) : any of several usu. hereditary abnormalities of porphyrin metabolism characterized by excretion of excess porphyrins in the urine

por·phy·rin \'pȯr-fə-rən\ n [ISV, fr. Gk *porphyra* purple] (1910) : any of various compounds with a structure that consists essentially of four pyrrole rings joined by four =CH— groups; esp : one (as chlorophyll or hemoglobin) containing a central metal atom and usu. exhibiting biological activity

por·phy·rit·ic \,pȯr-fə-'ri-tik\ adj [ML *porphyriticus*, fr. Gk *porphyritikos*, fr. *porphyritēs* (*lithos*) porphyry] (15c) 1 : of or relating to porphyry 2 : having distinct crystals (as of feldspar) in a relatively fine-grained base

por·phy·rop·sin \,pȯr-fə-'räp-sən\ n [Gk *porphyra* purple + E *-opsin* (as in *rhodopsin*)] (1930) : a purple pigment in the retinal rods of freshwater fishes that resembles rhodopsin

por·phy·ry \'pȯr-f(ə-)rē\ n, pl **-ries** [ME *porphiri*, fr. ML *porphyrium*, alter. of L *porphyrites*, fr. Gk *porphyrītēs* (*lithos*), lit., stone like Tyrian purple, fr. *porphyra* purple] (15c) 1 : a rock consisting of feldspar crystals embedded in a compact dark red or purple groundmass 2 : an igneous rock of porphyritic texture

por·poise \'pȯr-pəs\ n [ME *porpoys*, fr. MF *porpois*, fr. ML *porcopiscis*, fr. L *porcus* pig + *piscis* fish — more at FARROW, FISH] (14c) 1 : any of a family (Phocoenidae) of small gregarious toothed whales; esp : a blunt-snouted usu. largely black whale (*Phocoena phocoena*) of the No. Atlantic and Pacific 5 to 8 feet (1.5 to 2.4 meters) long 2 : DOLPHIN 1a

por·rect \pə-'rekt, pä-\ adj [L *porrectus*, pp. of *porrigere* to stretch out, fr. *por-* forward + *regere* to direct — more at PORTEND, RIGHT] (15c) : extended forward (~ antennae)

por·ridge \'pȯr-ij, 'pär-\ n [alter. of *pottage*] (ca. 1643) : a soft food made by boiling meal of grains or legumes in milk or water until thick — **por·ridgy** \-i-jē\ adj

por·rin·ger \-ən-jər\ n [alter. of ME *poteger*, *potinger*, fr. AF *potager*, fr. MF *potager* of pottage, fr. *potage* pottage] (1522) : a low usu. metal bowl with a handle and usu. flat and pierced handle

¹port \'pȯrt, 'pȯrt\ n [ME, fr. OE & OF, fr. L *portus* — more at FORD] (bef. 12c) 1 : a place where ships may ride secure from storms : HAVEN 2 a : a harbor town or city where ships may take on or discharge cargo b : AIRPORT 3 : PORT OF ENTRY

²port n [ME *porte*, fr. MF, gate, door, fr. L *porta* passage, gate; akin to L *portus* port] (bef. 12c) 1 *chiefly Scot* : GATE 2 a : an opening (as in a valve seat or valve face) for intake or exhaust of a fluid b : the area of opening in a cylinder face of a passageway for the working fluid in an engine; also : such a passageway 3 a : an opening in a vessel's side (as for admitting light or loading cargo) b *archaic* : the cover for a porthole 4 : a hole in an armored vehicle or fortification through which guns may be fired 5 : a hardware interface by which a computer communicates with another device or system

³port n [ME, fr. MF, fr. *porter* to carry, fr. L *portare*] (14c) 1 : the manner of bearing oneself 2 *archaic* : STATE 3 3 : the position in which a military weapon is carried at the command *port arms*

⁴port vt [³*port*] (1580) : to turn or put (a helm) to the left — used chiefly as a command

⁵port n [prob. fr. ¹*port* or ²*port*] (ca. 1625) : the left side of a ship or aircraft looking forward — called also *larboard*; compare STARBOARD — **port** adj

⁶port n [*Oporto*, Portugal] (1691) : a sweet fortified wine of rich taste and aroma made in Portugal; also : a similar wine made elsewhere

¹por·ta·ble \'pȯr-tə-bəl, 'pȯr-\ adj [ME, fr. MF, fr. LL *portabilis*, fr. L *portare* to carry — more at FARE] (14c) 1 a : capable of being carried or moved about (a ~ TV) (a ~ sawmill) b : usable on many computers without modification (~ software) 2 *archaic* : BEARABLE — **por·ta·bil·i·ty** \,pȯr-tə-'bi-lə-tē, ,pȯr-\ n — **por·ta·bly** \'pȯr-tə-blē, 'pȯr-\ adv

²portable n (1883) : something that is portable

¹por·tage \'pȯr-tij, 'pȯr-, 3 is also pȯr-'täzh\ n [ME, fr. MF, fr. *porter* to carry] (15c) 1 : the labor of carrying or transporting 2 *archaic* : the cost of carrying : PORTERAGE 3 a : the carrying of boats or goods overland from one body of water to another or around an obstacle (as a rapids) b : the route followed in making such a transfer

²por·tage \'pȯr-tij, 'pȯr-; pȯr-'täzh\ vb **por·taged; por·tag·ing** vt (1864) : to carry over a portage ~ vi : to move gear over a portage

¹por·tal \'pȯr-t²l, 'pȯr-\ n [ME, fr. MF, fr. ML *portale* city gate, porch, fr. neut. of *portalis* of a gate, fr. L *porta* gate — more at PORT] (14c) 1 : DOOR, ENTRANCE; esp : a grand or imposing one 2 : the whole architectural composition surrounding and including the doorways and porches of a church 3 : the approach or entrance to a bridge or tunnel 4 : a communicating part or area of an organism; *specif* : the point at which something (as a pathogen) enters the body

²portal adj [NL *porta* transverse fissure of the liver, fr. L, gate] (1845) 1 : of or relating to the transverse fissure on the underside of the liver where most of the vessels enter 2 : of, relating to, or being a portal vein

portal system n [*portal vein*] (1851) : a system of veins that begins and ends in capillaries

portal-to-portal adj (1943) : of or relating to the time spent by a worker in traveling between the entrance to an employer's property and the worker's actual job site (as in a mine) (~ pay)

portal vein n [²*portal*] (1845) : a vein that collects blood from one part of the body and distributes it in another through capillaries; esp : a vein carrying blood from the digestive organs and spleen to the liver

por·ta·men·to \,pȯr-tə-'men-(,)tō, ,pȯr-\ n, pl **-men·ti** \-(,)tē\ [It, lit., act of carrying, fr. *portare* to carry, fr. L] (1771) : a continuous gliding movement from one tone to another (as by the voice)

por·ta·pak or **por·ta·pack** \'pȯr-tə-,pak, 'pȯr-\ n [*portable* + ¹*pack*] (1970) : a small portable combined videotape recorder and camera

port arms n [fr. the command *port arms!*] (ca. 1890) : a position in the manual of arms in which the rifle is held diagonally in front of the body with the muzzle pointing upward to the left; also : a command to assume this position

por·ta·tive \'pȯr-tə-tiv, 'pȯr-\ adj [ME *portatif*, fr. MF, fr. L *portatus*, pp. of *portare*] (14c) : PORTABLE

port·cul·lis \pȯrt-'kə-ləs, pȯrt-\ n [ME *port colice*, fr. MF *porte coleice*, lit., sliding door] (14c) : a grating of iron hung over the gateway of a fortified place and lowered between grooves to prevent passage

port de bras \,pȯr-də-'brä\ n [F, lit., carriage of the arm] (1912) : the technique and practice of arm movement in ballet

Port du Sa·lut \,pȯr-də-sə-'lü, -sȧ-; -səl-'yü, -sȧl-\ n [F *port-du-salut*, *port-salut*, fr. *Port du Salut*, Trappist abbey in northwest France] (1881) : a semisoft pressed ripened cheese of usu. mild flavor originated by Trappist monks in France

Porte \'pȯrt, 'pȯrt\ n [F, short for *Sublime Porte*, lit., sublime gate; fr. the gate of the sultan's palace where justice was administered] (15c) : the government of the Ottoman empire

portcullis

porte co·chere \,pȯrt-kō-'sher, ,pȯrt-\ n [F *porte cochère*, lit., coach door] (1698) 1 : a passageway through a building or screen wall designed to let vehicles pass from the street to an interior courtyard 2 : a roofed structure extending from the entrance of a building over an adjacent driveway and sheltering those getting in or out of vehicles

por·tend \pȯr-'tend, pȯr-\ vt [ME, fr. L *portendere*, fr. *por-* forward (akin to *per* through) + *tendere* to stretch — more at FOR, THIN] (15c) 1 : to give an omen or anticipatory sign of : BODE 2 : INDICATE, SIGNIFY

por·tent \'pȯr-,tent, 'pȯr-\ n [L *portentum*, fr. neut. of *portentus*, pp. of *portendere*] (ca. 1587) 1 : something that foreshadows a coming event : OMEN 2 : prophetic indication or significance : MARVEL, PRODIGY

por·ten·tous \pȯr-'ten-təs, pȯr-\ adj (15c) 1 : of, relating to, or constituting a portent 2 : eliciting amazement or wonder : PRODIGIOUS 3 a : being a grave or serious matter (~ decisions) b : self-consciously

\ə\ abut \ᵊ\ kitten, F table \ər\ further \a\ ash \ā\ ace \ä\ mop, mar \aú\ out \ch\ chin \e\ bet \ē\ easy \g\ go \i\ hit \ī\ ice \j\ job \ŋ\ sing \ō\ go \ȯ\ law \ȯi\ boy \th\ thin \th\ the \ü\ loot \ú\ foot \y\ yet \zh\ vision \ȧ, k̟, ⁿ, œ, œ̄, ɶ, ū̄, ᵂ\ see Guide to Pronunciation solemn or important : POMPOUS   **c** : ponderously excessive ⟨that discipline's overwrought, ~ phrases —R. M. Coles⟩   *syn* see OMINOUS — **por·ten·tous·ly** *adv* — **por·ten·tous·ness** *n*

¹**por·ter** \'pōr-tər, 'pȯr-\ *n* [ME, fr. OF *portier*, fr. LL *portarius*, fr. L *porta* gate — more at PORT] (13c) *chiefly Brit* : a person stationed at a door or gate to admit or assist those entering

²**porter** *n* [ME *portour*, fr. MF *porteour*, fr. LL *portator*, fr. L *portare* to carry — more at FARE] (14c)   **1** : a person who carries burdens; *esp* : one employed to carry baggage for patrons at a hotel or transportation terminal   **2** : a parlor-car or sleeping-car attendant who waits on passengers and makes up berths   **3** [short for *porter's beer*]: a heavy dark brown beer brewed from browned or charred malt   **4** : a person who does routine cleaning (as in a hospital or office)

³**porter** *vt* (1609) : to transport or carry as or as if by a porter   ~ *vi* : to act as a porter

por·ter·age \-tə-rij\ *n* (15c) : a porter's work; *also* : the charge for it

por·ter·house \'pōr-tər-,haus, 'pȯr-\ *n* (ca. 1758)   **1** *archaic* : a house where malt liquor (as porter) is sold   **2** : a large steak cut from the thick end of the short loin to contain a T-shaped bone and a large piece of tenderloin — see BEEF illustration

port·fo·lio \pōrt-'fō-lē-,ō, pȯrt-\ *n, pl* **-lios** [It *portafoglio*, fr. *portare* to carry (fr. L) + *foglio* leaf, sheet, fr. L *folium* — more at BLADE] (1722)   **1** : a hinged cover or flexible case for carrying loose papers, pictures, or pamphlets   **2** [fr. the use of such a case to carry documents of state] : the office and functions of a minister of state or member of a cabinet   **3** : the securities held by an investor : the commercial paper held by a financial house (as a bank)   **4** : a set of pictures (as drawings or photographs) either bound in book form or loose in a folder

port·hole \'pōrt-,hōl, 'pȯrt-\ *n* [²port] (ca. 1591)   **1** : an opening (as a window) with a cover or closure esp. in the side of a ship or aircraft   **2** : a port through which to shoot \ ²PORT 2

Por·tia \'pōr-shə, 'pȯr-\ *n* : the heroine in Shakespeare's *The Merchant of Venice*

por·ti·co \'pōr-ti-,kō, 'pȯr-\ *n, pl* **-coes** *or* **-cos** [It, fr. L *porticus* — more at PORCH] (1605)   : a colonnade or covered ambulatory esp. in classical architecture and often at the entrance of a building

por·tiere \pōr-'tyer, pȯr-, -'tir; 'pōr-tē-ər, 'pȯr-\ *n* [F *portière*, fr. OF, fem. of *portier* porter, doorkeeper] (1843) : a curtain hanging across a doorway

¹**por·tion** \'pōr-shən, 'pȯr-\ *n* [ME, fr. OF, fr. L *portion-, portio*; akin to L *part-, pars* part] (14c)   **1** : an individual's part or share of something: as   **a** : a share received by gift or inheritance   **b** : DOWRY   **c** : enough food esp. of one kind to serve one person at one meal   **2** : an individual's lot, fate, or fortune : one's share of good and evil   **3** : an often limited part set off or abstracted from a whole ⟨give but that ~ which yourself proposed —Shak.⟩   *syn* see PART, FATE

²**portion** *vt* **por·tioned; por·tion·ing** \-sh(ə-)niŋ\ (14c)   **1** : to divide into portions : DISTRIBUTE   **2** : to allot a dowry to : DOWER

por·tion·less \-shən-ləs\ *adj* (1782) : having no portion; *esp* : having no dowry or inheritance

port·land cement \'pōrt-lən(d)-, 'pȯrt-\ *n* [Isle of *Portland*, England; fr. its resemblance to a limestone found there] (1824) : a hydraulic cement made by finely pulverizing the clinker produced by calcining to incipient fusion a mixture of clay and limestone or similar materials

port·ly \'pōrt-lē, 'pȯrt-\ *adj* **port·li·er; -est** [³port] (15c)   **1** : DIGNIFIED, STATELY   **2** : heavy or rotund of body : STOUT — **port·li·ness** *n*

¹**port·man·teau** \pōrt-'man-(,)tō, pȯrt-\ *n, pl* **-teaus** *or* **-teaux** \-(,)tōz\ [MF *portemanteau*, fr. *porter* to carry + *manteau* mantle, fr. L *mantellum* — more at PORT] (1579)   **1** : a large suitcase   **2** : a word or morpheme whose form and meaning are derived from a blending of two or more distinct forms (as *smog* from *smoke* and *fog*)

²**portmanteau** *adj* (1909)   **1** : combining more than one use or quality   **2** : being a portmanteau ⟨a ~ word⟩

port of call (1884)   **1** : an intermediate port where ships customarily stop for supplies, repairs, or transshipment of cargo   **2** : a stop included on an itinerary

port of entry (1840)   **1** : a place where foreign goods may be cleared through a customhouse   **2** : a place where an alien may be permitted to enter a country

por·trait \'pōr-trət, 'pȯr-, -,trāt\ *n* [MF, fr. pp. of *portraire*] (1570)   **1** : PICTURE; *esp* : a pictorial representation (as a painting) of a person usu. showing the face   **2** : a sculptured figure : BUST, STATUE   **3** : a graphic portrayal in words

por·trait·ist \-trə-tist, -,trā-\ *n* (1866) : a maker of portraits

por·trai·ture \'pōr-trə-,chùr, 'pȯr-, -chər, -,tyùr, -,tùr\ *n* (14c)   **1** : the making of portraits : PORTRAYAL   **2** : PORTRAIT

por·tray \pōr-'trā, pȯr-, por-\ *vt* [ME *portraien*, fr. MF *portraire*, fr. L *protrahere* to draw forth, reveal, expose — more at PROTRACT] (14c)   **1** : to make a picture of : DEPICT   **2** **a** : to describe in words   **b** : to play the role of : ENACT — **por·tray·er** *n*

por·tray·al \-'trā(-ə)l\ *n* (ca. 1847)   **1** : the act or process or an instance of portraying : REPRESENTATION   **2** : PORTRAIT, TRAIT

por·tress \'pōr-trəs, 'pȯr-\ *n* (15c) : a female porter: as   **a** : a doorkeeper in a convent or apartment house   **b** : CHARWOMAN

Port Roy·al·ist \pōrt-'rȯi-ə-list, pȯrt-\ *n* [F *port-royaliste*, fr. *Port-Royal*, a convent near Versailles, France] (ca. 1741) : a member or adherent of a 17th century French Jansenist lay community noted for its logicians and educators

Port Sa·lut \,pȯr-sə-'lü, -sa-; -səl-'yü, -sal-\ *n* (1902) : PORT DU SALUT

Por·tu·guese \'pōr-chə-,gēz, 'pȯr-, -,gēs; ,pōr-chə-', pȯr-\ *n, pl* **Portuguese** [Pg *português*, adj. & n., fr. *Portugal*] (1534)   **1 a** : a native or inhabitant of Portugal   **b** : one who is of Portuguese descent   **2** : the Romance language of Portugal and Brazil — **Portuguese** *adj*

Portuguese man–of–war *n, pl* **Portuguese man–of–wars** *also* **Portuguese men–of–war** (1707) : any of a genus (*Physalia*) of large tropical and subtropical pelagic siphonophores having a crested bladderlike float which bears the colony

Portuguese man-of-war

comprised of three types of zooids on the lower surface with one of the three having nematocyst-equipped tentacles

por·tu·la·ca \,pōr-chə-'la-kə, ,pȯr-\ *n* [NL, fr. L, purslane, fr. *portula*, dim. of *porta* gate; fr. the lid of its capsule — more at PORT] (1548) : any of a genus (*Portulaca*) of mainly tropical succulent herbs of the purslane family; *esp* : a widely cultivated plant (*P. grandiflora*) with showy flowers and small conical leaves

port–wine stain \'pōrt-'wīn-, 'pȯrt-\ *n* (ca. 1909) : a reddish purple superficial hemangioma of the skin commonly occurring as a birthmark

po·sa·da \pə-'sä-də\ *n* [Sp, fr. *posar* to lodge, fr. LL *pausare*] (1763) : an inn in Spanish-speaking countries

¹**pose** \'pōz\ *vb* **posed; pos·ing** [ME, fr. MF *poser*, (assumed) VL *pausare*, fr. LL, to stop, rest, pause, fr. L *pausa* pause] *vt* (14c)   **1 a** : to present for attention or consideration ⟨let me ~ a question⟩   **b** : to put or set forth : OFFER ⟨this attitude ~s a threat to our hopes for peace⟩   **2 a** : to put or set in place   **b** : to place (as a model) in a studied attitude   ~ *vi*   **1** : to assume a posture or attitude usu. for artistic purposes   **2** : to affect an attitude or character usu. to deceive or impress

²**pose** *n* (1818)   **1** : a sustained posture; *esp* : one assumed for artistic effect   **2** : an attitude, role, or characteristic assumed for effect

syn POSE, AIR, AIRS, AFFECTATION, MANNERISM mean an adopted way of speaking or behaving. POSE implies an attitude deliberately assumed in order to impress others ⟨her shyness was just a *pose*⟩. AIR may suggest natural acquirement through environment or way of life ⟨a traveler's sophisticated *air*⟩. AIRS always implies artificiality and pretentiousness ⟨snobbish *airs*⟩. AFFECTATION applies to a trick of speech or behavior that strikes the observer as insincere ⟨the posh accent is an *affectation*⟩. MANNERISM applies to an acquired eccentricity that has become a habit ⟨gesturing with a cigarette was her most noticeable *mannerism*⟩.

³**pose** *vt* **posed; pos·ing** [short for earlier *appose*, fr. ME *apposen*, alter. of *opposen* to oppose] (1592) : PUZZLE, BAFFLE

Po·sei·don \pə-'sī-d[']n\ *n* [L, fr. Gk *Poseidōn*] : the Greek god of the sea — compare NEPTUNE

¹**pos·er** \'pō-zər\ *n* [³pose] (1793) : a puzzling or baffling question

²**poser** *n* [¹pose] (1888) : a person who poses

po·seur \pō-'zər\ *n* [F, lit., poser, fr. *poser*] (1872) : a person who pretends to be what he or she is not : an affected or insincere person

posh \'päsh\ *adj* [origin unknown] (1918) : ELEGANT, FASHIONABLE — **posh·ly** *adv* — **posh·ness** *n*

pos·it \'pä-zət\ *vt* **pos·it·ed** \'pä-zə-təd, 'päz-təd\; **pos·it·ing** \'pä-zə-tiŋ, 'päz-tiŋ\ [L *positus*, pp. of *ponere*] (1647)   **1** : to dispose or set firmly : FIX   **2** : to assume or affirm the existence of : POSTULATE   **3** : to propose as an explanation : SUGGEST

¹**po·si·tion** \pə-'zi-shən\ *n* [ME *posycion*, fr. MF *position*, fr. L *position-, positio*, fr. *ponere* to lay down, put, place, fr. (assumed) OL *posinere*, fr. *po-* away (akin to OCS *po-*, perfective prefix, Gk *apo* away) + L *sinere* to leave — more at OF] (14c)   **1** : an act of placing or arranging: as   **a** : the laying down of a proposition or thesis   **b** : an arranging in order   **2** : a point of view adopted and held to ⟨made my ~ on the issue clear⟩   **3 a** : the point or area occupied by a physical object ⟨took her ~ at the head of the line⟩   **b** : a certain arrangement of bodily parts ⟨rose to a standing ~⟩   **4 a** : a market commitment in securities or commodities; *also* : the inventory of a market trader   **5 a** : relative place, situation, or standing ⟨is now in a ~ to make decisions on his own⟩   **b** : social or official rank or status   **c** : an employment for which one has been hired : JOB ⟨a ~ with a brokerage firm⟩   **d** : a situation that confers advantage or preference

²**position** *vt* **po·si·tioned; po·si·tion·ing** \pə-'zi-sh(ə-)niŋ\ (1817) : to put in proper position; *also* : LOCATE

po·si·tion·al \pə-'zi-sh(ə-)nəl\ *adj* (1571)   **1** : of, relating to, or fixed by position ⟨~ astronomy⟩   **2** : involving little movement ⟨~ warfare⟩   **3** : dependent on position or environment or context ⟨the front-articulated \k\ in \kē\ *key* and the back-articulated \k\ in \kül\ *cool* are ~ variants⟩ — **po·si·tion·al·ly** *adv*

positional notation *n* (1941) : a system of expressing numbers in which the digits are arranged in succession, the position of each digit has a place value, and the number is equal to the sum of the products of each digit by its place value

position effect *n* (1930) : genetic effect that is due to interaction of adjacent genes and that is modified when the spatial relationships of the genes change (as by chromosomal inversion)

position paper *n* (1949) : a detailed report that recommends a course of action on a particular issue

¹**pos·i·tive** \'pä-zə-tiv, 'päz-tiv\ *adj* [ME, fr. MF *positif*, fr. L *positivus*, fr. *positus*, pp. of *ponere*] (14c)   **1 a** : formally laid down or imposed : PRESCRIBED ⟨~ laws⟩   **b** : expressed clearly or peremptorily ⟨her answer was a ~ no⟩   **c** : fully assured : CONFIDENT   **2 a** : of, relating to, or constituting the degree of comparison that is expressed in English by the unmodified and uninflected form of an adjective or adverb and denotes no increase or diminution   **b** (1) : independent of changing circumstances : UNCONDITIONED   (2) : relating to or constituting a motion or device that is definite, unyielding, constant, or certain in its action ⟨a ~ system of levers⟩   **c** (1) : INCONTESTABLE ⟨~ proof⟩   (2) : UNQUALIFIED ⟨a ~ disgrace⟩   **3 a** : not fictitious : REAL ⟨a ~ influence for good in the community⟩   **b** : active and effective in social or economic function rather than merely maintaining peace and order ⟨a ~ government⟩   **4 a** : having or expressing actual existence or quality as distinguished from deprivation or deficiency ⟨~ change in temperature⟩: as   (1) : capable of being constructively applied   (2) : not speculative : EMPIRICAL   **b** : having rendition of light and shade similar in tone to the tones of the original subject ⟨a ~ photographic image⟩   **c** : that is or is generated in a direction arbitrarily or customarily taken as that of increase or progression ⟨~ rotation of the earth⟩ ⟨we are making some ~ progress⟩   **d** : directed or moving toward a source of stimulation ⟨a ~ taxis⟩   **e** : real and numerically greater than zero ⟨+2 is a ~ integer⟩   **5 a** (1) : being, relating to, or charged with electricity of which the proton is the elementary unit and which predominates in a glass body after being rubbed with silk   (2) : having more protons than electrons ⟨a ~ ion⟩   **b** (1) : having higher electric potential and constituting the part from which the current flows to the external circuit ⟨the ~ terminal of a discharging storage battery⟩   (2) : being an electron-collecting electrode of an electron tube   **6 a** [...]

: marked by or indicating acceptance, approval, or affirmation **b**
: affirming the presence of that sought or suspected to be present ⟨a ∼
test for blood⟩ **7** *of a lens* : converging light rays and forming a real
inverted image *syn* see SURE — **pos·i·tive·ly** \-lē\ *for emphasis often*
,pä-zə-'tiv-\ *adv* — **pos·i·tive·ness** \'pä-zə-tiv-nəs, ,päz-tiv-\ *n*
²**positive** *n* (1530) : something positive: as **a** (1) : the positive degree
of comparison in a language (2) : a positive form of an adjective or
adverb **b** : something of which an affirmation can be made : REALITY
c : a positive photograph or a print from a negative
positive definite *adj* (1907) **1** : having a positive value for all values
of the constituent variables ⟨*positive definite* quadratic forms⟩ **2** *of a
matrix* : having the characteristic roots real and positive
positive law *n* (14c) : law established or recognized by governmental
authority — compare NATURAL LAW
pos·i·tiv·ism \'pä-zə-ti,vi-zəm, 'päz-ti-\ *n* [F *positivisme*, fr. *positif* positive + *-isme* -ism] (1847) **1 a** : a theory that theology and metaphysics are earlier imperfect modes of knowledge and that positive knowledge is based on natural phenomena and their properties and relations
as verified by the empirical sciences **b** : LOGICAL POSITIVISM **2** : the
quality or state of being positive — **pos·i·tiv·ist** \-vist\ *adj or n* —
pos·i·tiv·is·tic \,pä-zə-ti-'vis-tik, ,päz-ti-\ *adj* — **pos·i·tiv·is·ti·cal·ly**
\-ti-k(ə-)lē\ *adv*
pos·i·tiv·i·ty \,pä-zə-'ti-və-tē\ *n, pl* **-ties** (1659) **1** : the quality or
state of being positive **2** : something that is positive
pos·i·tron \'pä-zə-,trän\ *n* [*positive* + *-tron* (as in *electron*)] (1933) : a
positively charged particle having the same mass and magnitude of
charge as the electron and constituting the antiparticle of the electron
positron–emission tomography *n* (1979) : tomography in which a
cross-sectional image of regional metabolism is obtained by a usu.
color-coded cathode-ray tube representation of the distribution of
gamma radiation given off in the collision of electrons in cells with
positrons emitted by radionuclides incorporated into metabolic substances
pos·i·tro·ni·um \,pä-zə-'trō-nē-əm\ *n* (1945) : a short-lived system that
consists of a positron and an electron bound together and is suggestive
of a hydrogen atom
pos·se \'pä-sē\ *n* [ML *posse comitatus*, lit., power or authority of the
county] (1645) **1** : a large group often with a common interest **2** : a
body of persons summoned by a sheriff to assist in preserving the public peace usu. in an emergency **3** : a group of people temporarily organized to make a search (as for a lost child)
pos·sess \pə-'zes *also* -'ses\ *vt* [ME, fr. MF *possesser* to have possession
of, take possession of, fr. L *possessus*, pp. of *possidēre*, fr. *potis* able,
having the power + *sedēre* to sit — more at POTENT, SIT] (14c) **1 a**
: to have and hold as property : OWN **b** : to have as an attribute,
knowledge, or skill **2 a** : to take into one's possession **b** : to enter
into and control firmly : DOMINATE ⟨was ∼ed by demons⟩ **c** : to
bring or cause to fall under the influence, possession, or control of
some emotional or intellectual state ⟨melancholy ∼es her⟩ **3** *obs*
: to instate as owner **b** : to make the owner or holder — used in passive construction to indicate simple possession ⟨∼ed of riches⟩ ⟨∼ed of
knowledge and experience⟩ — **pos·ses·sor** *n*
pos·sessed *adj* (1534) **1 a** (1) : influenced or controlled by something (as an evil spirit or a passion) (2) : MAD, CRAZED **b** : urgently
desirous to do or have something **2** *obs* : held as a possession **3**
: SELF-POSSESSED, CALM — **pos·sessed·ly** \-'ze-səd-lē, -'zest-lē *also* -'se-
səd- *or* -'sest-\ *adv* — **pos·sessed·ness** \-'ze-səd-nəs, -'zest-nəs *also*
-'se-səd- *or* -'sest-\ *n*
pos·ses·sion \-'ze-shən *also* -'se-\ *n* (14c) **1 a** : the act of having or
taking into control **b** : control or occupancy of property without
regard to ownership **c** : OWNERSHIP **d** : control of the ball or puck **2**
: something owned, occupied, or controlled : PROPERTY **3 a** : domination by something (as an evil spirit, a passion, or an idea) **b** : a
psychological state in which an individual's normal personality is replaced by another **c** : the fact or condition of being self-controlled —
pos·ses·sion·al \-'zesh-nəl, -'ze-shə-n³l *also* -'sesh-nəl *or* -'se-shə-n³l\
adj — **pos·ses·sion·less** \-'ze-shən-ləs, -'se-\ *adj*
¹**pos·ses·sive** \pə-'ze-siv *also* -'se-\ *adj* (15c) **1** : of, relating to, or
constituting a word, a word group, or a grammatical case that denotes
ownership or a relation analogous to ownership **2** : manifesting possession or the desire to own or dominate — **pos·ses·sive·ly** *adv* —
pos·ses·sive·ness *n*
²**possessive** *n* (15c) **1** : a possessive word or word group **2 a** : the
possessive case **b** : a word in the possessive case
possessive adjective *n* (1870) : a pronominal adjective expressing
possession
possessive pronoun *n* (15c) : a pronoun that derives from a personal
pronoun and denotes possession and analogous relationships
pos·ses·so·ry \pə-'ze-sə-rē, -'zes-rē *also* -'se-sə-rē *or* -'ses-rē\ *adj* (15c)
1 : of, arising from, or having the nature of possession ⟨∼ rights⟩ **2**
: having possession **3** : characteristic of a possessor : POSSESSIVE
pos·set \'pä-sət\ *n* [ME *poshet, possot*] (15c) : a hot drink of sweetened
and spiced milk curdled with ale or wine
pos·si·bil·i·ty \,pä-sə-'bi-lə-tē\ *n, pl* **-ties** (14c) **1** : the condition or
fact of being possible **2** *archaic* : one's utmost power, capacity, or
ability **3** : something that is possible **4** : potential or prospective
value — usu. used in pl. ⟨the house had great possibilities⟩
pos·si·ble \'pä-sə-bəl\ *adj* [ME, fr. MF, fr. L *possibilis*, fr. *posse* to be
able, fr. *potis, pote* able + *esse* to be — more at POTENT, IS] (14c) **1 a**
: being within the limits of ability, capacity, or realization **b** : being
what may be done or may occur according to nature, custom, or manners **2 a** : being something that may or may not occur **b** : being
something that may or may not be true or actual ⟨∼ explanation⟩ **3**
: having an indicated potential ⟨a ∼ housing site⟩
syn POSSIBLE, PRACTICABLE, FEASIBLE mean capable of being realized.
POSSIBLE implies that a thing may certainly exist or occur given the
proper conditions ⟨a *possible* route up the west face of the mountain⟩.
PRACTICABLE implies that something may be effected by available
means or under current conditions ⟨a *practicable* route up the west
face of the mountain⟩. FEASIBLE applies to what is likely to work or be
useful in attaining the end desired ⟨commercially *feasible* for mass
production⟩.
pos·si·bly \-blē\ *adv* (14c) **1** : in a possible manner : by any possibility **2** : by merest chance : PERHAPS

pos·sum \'pä-səm\ *n* (1613) : OPOSSUM
¹**post** \'pōst\ *n* [ME, fr. OE, fr. L *postis*; prob. akin to L *por-* forward
and to L *stare* to stand — more at PORTEND, STAND] (bef. 12c) **1** : a
piece (as of timber or metal) fixed firmly in an upright position esp. as a
stay or support : PILLAR, COLUMN **2** : a pole or stake set up to mark or
indicate something; *esp* : a pole that marks the starting or finishing
point of a horse race **3** : a metallic fitting attached to an electrical
device (as a storage battery) for convenience in making connections **4**
: GOALPOST **5** : the metal stem of a pierced earring
²**post** *vt* (1633) **1 a** : to publish, announce, or advertise by or as if by
use of a placard **b** : to denounce by public notice **c** : to enter on a
public listing **d** : to forbid (property) to trespassers under penalty of
legal prosecution by notices placed along the boundaries **e** : SCORE
⟨∼ed a 70 in the final round⟩ **2** : to affix to a usual place (as a wall)
for public notices : PLACARD
³**post** *n* [MF *poste* relay station, courier, fr. OIt *posta* relay station, fr.
fem. of *posto*, pp. of *porre* to place, fr. L *ponere* — more at POSITION]
(1507) **1** *obs* : COURIER **2** *archaic* : one of a series of stations for
keeping horses for relays **b** : the distance between any two such consecutive stations : STAGE **3** *chiefly Brit* **a** : a nation's organization for
handling mail; *also* : the mail handled **b** : a single dispatch of mail **c**
: POST OFFICE **d** : POSTBOX
⁴**post** *vi* (1533) **1** : to travel with post-horses **2** : to ride or travel with
haste : HURRY **3** : to rise from the saddle and return to it in rhythm
with a horse's trot ∼ *vt* **1** *archaic* : to dispatch in haste **2** : MAIL ⟨∼
a letter⟩ **3 a** : to transfer or carry from a book of original entry to a
ledger **b** : to make transfer entries in **4** : to make familiar with a
subject : INFORM ⟨kept her ∼ed on the latest gossip⟩
⁵**post** *adv* (1549) : with post-horses : EXPRESS
⁶**post** *n* [MF *poste*, fr. OIt *posto*, fr. pp. of *porre* to place] (1598) **1 a**
: the place at which a sentry is stationed; *esp* : a sentry's beat or station **b** : a station or task to which one is assigned **c** : the place at
which a body of troops is stationed : CAMP **d** : a local subdivision of a
veterans' organization **e** : one of two bugle calls sounded (as in the
British army) at tattoo **2 a** : an office or position to which a person
is appointed **b** : a player position in basketball that is the focal point
of the offense; *specif* : PIVOT 2b **3 a** : TRADING POST, SETTLEMENT **b**
: a trading station on the floor of a stock exchange
⁷**post** *vt* (1683) **1 a** : to station in a given place ⟨guards were ∼ed at
the doors⟩ **b** : to carry ceremoniously to a position ⟨∼ing the colors⟩
2 *chiefly Brit* : to assign to a unit, position, or location (as in the military or civil service) **3** : to put up (as bond)
post- *prefix* [ME, fr. L, fr. *post*; akin to Lith *pas* at, Gk *apo* away from
— more at OF] **1 a** : after : subsequent : later ⟨*postdate*⟩ **b** : behind
: posterior : following after ⟨*post*lude⟩ ⟨*post*consonantal⟩ **2 a** : subsequent to : later than ⟨*post*operative⟩ **b** : posterior to ⟨*post*orbital⟩

post-abor·tion	post–Ein·stein·ian	post·mat·ing
post·ac·ci·dent	post·elec·tion	post·me·di·e·val
post·ad·o·les·cent	post·em·bry·o·nal	post·mid·night
post·am·pu·ta·tion	post·em·bry·on·ic	post·neo·na·tal
post·apoc·a·lyp·tic	post·emer·gen·cy	post·or·gas·mic
post·ar·rest	post·en·ceph·a·lit·ic	post·pol·li·na·tion
post·atom·ic	post·ep·i·lep·tic	post·pres·i·den·tial
post·bac·ca·lau·re·ate	post·ex·er·cise	post·pri·ma·ry
post·base	post·ex·pe·ri·ence	post·pris·on
post·bib·li·cal	post·ex·per·i·men·tal	post·psy·cho·an·a·lyt·ic
post·bour·geois	post·ex·po·sure	post·pu·ber·ty
post·burn	post·fault	post·pu·bes·cent
post·cap·i·tal·ist	post·fire	post·race
post–Chris·tian	post·flight	post·re·ces·sion
post·co·i·tal	post·frac·ture	post–Ref·or·ma·tion
post·col·lege	post·freeze	post·res·ur·rec·tion
post·col·le·giate	post–Freud·ian	post·re·tire·ment
post·co·lo·nial	post·game	post·rev·o·lu·tion·ary
post·con·cep·tion	post·gla·cial	post·ri·ot
post·con·cert	post·grad·u·a·tion	post·ro·man·tic
post·con·quest	post·har·vest	post·sea·son
post·con·so·nan·tal	post·hem·or·rhag·ic	post·sec·ond·ary
post·con·ven·tion	post·hol·i·day	post·show
post·cop·u·la·to·ry	post·ho·lo·caust	post·stim·u·la·tion
post·cor·o·nary	post·hos·pi·tal	post·stim·u·la·to·ry
post·coup	post·im·pact	post·stim·u·lus
post·crash	post·im·pe·ri·al	post·strike
post·cri·sis	post·in·au·gu·ral	post·sur·gi·cal
post–Dar·win·i·an	post·in·de·pen·dence	post·tax
post·dead·line	post·in·dus·tri·al	post·teen
post·de·bate	post·in·fec·tion	post·trau·mat·ic
post·deb·u·tante	post·in·jec·tion	post·treat·ment
post·de·liv·ery	post·in·oc·u·la·tion	post·trial
post·de·po·si·tion·al	post·ir·ra·di·a·tion	post·vac·ci·nal
post·de·pres·sion	post·is·che·mic	post·vac·ci·na·tion
post·de·val·u·a·tion	post·iso·la·tion	post·va·got·o·my
post·dive	post·land·ing	post·va·sec·to·my
post·di·ves·ti·ture	post·launch	post–Vic·to·ri·an
post·di·vorce	post·lib·er·a·tion	post·war
post·drug	post·mar·i·tal	post·wean·ing
post·ed·it·ing	post·mas·tec·to·my	post·work·shop

post·age \'pōs-tij\ *n* (1654) **1** : the fee for postal service **2** : adhesive
stamps or printed indicia representing postal fees
postage–due stamp *n* (1893) : a special adhesive stamp that is applied
by a post office to mail bearing insufficient postage
postage meter *n* (1927) : a machine that prints postal indicia on pieces
of mail, records the amount of postage, and subtracts it from a total
paid amount for which the machine has been set

\ə\ abut \ᵊ\ kitten, F table \ər\ further \a\ ash \ā\ ace \ä\ mop, mar
\au̇\ out \ch\ chin \e\ bet \ē\ easy \g\ go \i\ hit \ī\ ice \j\ job
\ŋ\ sing \ō\ go \ȯ\ law \ȯi\ boy \th\ thin \t͟h\ the \ü\ loot \u̇\ foot
\y\ yet \zh\ vision \a̤, k̲, ⁿ, œ, œ̄, ᵫ, ᵫ̄, ᵞ\ see Guide to Pronunciation

postage–stamp *adj* (1938) : suggesting a postage stamp in size : very small ⟨~ yards⟩

postage stamp *n* (1840) : a government adhesive stamp or imprinted stamp for use on mail as evidence of prepayment of postage

post·al \'pōs-t³l\ *adj* (1843) **1** : of or relating to the mails or the post office **2** : conducted by mail ⟨~ chess⟩

postal card *n* (1872) **1** : a card officially stamped and issued by the government for use in the mail : POSTCARD

postal order *n* (1883) *Brit* : MONEY ORDER

postal service *n* (ca. 1920) : POST OFFICE 1

postal union *n* (1875) : an association of governments setting up uniform regulations and practices for international mail

post·ax·i·al \,pōst-'ak-sē-əl\ *adj* (1872) : of or relating to the ulnar side of the vertebrate forelimb or the fibular side of the hind limb; *also* : of or relating to the side of an animal or side of one of its limbs that is posterior to the axis of its body or limb

post-bag \'pōs(t)-,bag\ *n* (1813) **1** *Brit* : MAILBAG **2** *Brit* : a single batch of mail : LETTERS

post·bel·lum \,pōs(t)-'be-ləm\ *adj* [L *post bellum* after the war] (1874) : of, relating to, or characteristic of the period following a war and esp. following the American Civil War

post-box \'pōs(t)-,bäks\ *n* (1754) : MAILBOX; *esp* : a public mailbox

post-boy \-,bȯi\ *n* (1707) : POSTILION

post-card \'pōs(t)-,kärd\ *n* (1870) **1** : POSTAL CARD 1 **2** : a card on which a message may be written for mailing without an envelope and to which the sender must affix a stamp — **post-card-like** \-,līk\ *adj*

post·ca·va \,pōs(t)-'kā-və\ *n* [NL] (1882) : the inferior vena cava of vertebrates higher than fishes — **post·ca·val** \-vəl\ *adj*

post chaise *n* (1712) : a carriage usu. having a closed body on four wheels and seating two to four persons

post·clas·si·cal \,pōs(t)-'kla-si-kəl\ *or* **post·clas·sic** \-sik\ *adj* (1867) : of or relating to a period (as in art, literature, or civilization) following a classical one

post·code \'pōs(t)-,kōd\ *n* (1967) : a code (as of numbers and letters) used similarly to the zip code esp. in the United Kingdom and Australia

post–com·mu·nion \,pōs(t)-kə-'myü-nyən\ *n, often cap P&C* [ML *postcommunion-, postcommunio,* fr. L *post-* + LL *communio* communion] (15c) : a liturgically variable prayer following the communion at Mass

post·cra·ni·al \-'krā-nē-əl\ *adj* (1913) : of or relating to the part of the body caudal to the head ⟨~ skeleton⟩ ⟨~ fossil remains⟩ — **post·cra·ni·al·ly** *adv*

post·date \pōs(t)-'dāt, 'pōs(t)-,\ *vt* (1624) **1 a** : to date with a date later than that of execution ⟨~ a check⟩ **b** : to assign (an event) to a date subsequent to that of actual occurrence **2** : to follow in time

post·di·lu·vi·an \,pōs(t)-də-'lü-vē-ən, -dī-\ *adj* [*post-* + L *diluvium* flood — more at DELUGE] (1680) : of or relating to the period after the flood described in the Bible — **postdiluvian** *n*

¹post·doc \'pōs(t)-,däk\ *n* (1968) : one engaged in postdoctoral study or research

²postdoc *adj* (1970) : POSTDOCTORAL

post–doc·tor·al \,pōs(t)-'däk-t(ə-)rəl, 'pōs(t)-,\ *also* **post–doc·tor·ate** \-t(ə-)rət\ *adj* (1936) : being beyond the doctoral level: **a** : of or relating to advanced academic or professional work beyond a doctor's degree ⟨a ~ fellowship⟩ **b** : engaged in such work ⟨~ scholars⟩

post·emer·gence \,pōst-i-'mər-jən(t)s\ *adj* (1940) : used or occurring in the stage between the emergence of a seedling and the maturity of a crop plant ⟨~ herbicides⟩ ⟨~ development⟩

¹post·er \'pōs-tər\ *n* [⁴*post*] (1605) *archaic* : a swift traveler

²poster *n* [²*post*] (1838) : a bill or placard for posting often in a public place; *esp* : one that is decorative or pictorial

poster color *n* (1925) : an opaque watercolor paint with a gum or glue-size binder sold usu. in jars — called also *poster paint*

poste res·tante \,pōst-'res-'tänt\ *n* [F, lit., waiting mail] (1768) *chiefly Brit* : GENERAL DELIVERY

¹pos·te·ri·or \pō-'stir-ē-ər, pä-\ *adj* [L, compar. of *posterus* coming after, fr. *post* after — more at POST] (1534) **1** : later in time : SUBSEQUENT **2** : situated behind: as **a** : CAUDAL **b** *of the human body or its parts* : DORSAL **3** *of a plant part* : ADAXIAL, SUPERIOR — **pos·te·ri·or·ly** *adv*

²pos·te·ri·or \pä-'stir-ē-ər, pō-\ *n* (ca. 1616) : the hinder parts of the body; *specif* : BUTTOCKS

pos·te·ri·or·i·ty \(,)pō-,stir-ē-'or-ə-tē, (,)pä-, -'är-\ *n* (14c) : the quality or state of being later or subsequent

pos·ter·i·ty \pä-'ster-ə-tē\ *n* [ME *posterite,* fr. MF *posterité,* fr. L *posteritat-, posteritas,* fr. *posterus* coming after] (14c) **1** : the offspring of one progenitor to the furthest generation **2** : all future generations

pos·tern \'pōs-tərn, 'päs-\ *n* [ME *posterne,* fr. OF, alter. of *posterle,* fr. LL *posterula,* dim. of *postera* back door, fr. L, fem. of *posterus*] (14c) **1** : a back door or gate **2** : a private or side entrance or way — **postern** *adj*

pos·tero·lat·er·al \,päs-tə-rō-'la-t(ə-)rəl\ *adj* [*posterior* + *-o-* + *lateral*] (1852) : posterior and lateral in position or direction

post exchange *n* (1892) : a store at a military installation that sells merchandise and services to military personnel and authorized civilians

post·ex·il·ic \,pōst-(,)eg-'zi-lik\ *adj* (1871) : of or relating to the period of Jewish history between the end of the exile in Babylon in 538 B.C. and A.D. 1

post·face \'pōst-,fās, -,fäs; pōs-fás\ *n* [F, fr. *post-* + *-face* (as in *préface* preface)] (1782) : a brief article or note (as of explanation) placed at the end of a publication

post·fem·i·nist \,pōst-'fe-mə-nist\ *adj* (1983) : of, relating to, occurring in, or being the period following widespread advocacy and acceptance of feminism

post·fix \'pōs(t)-,fiks\ *adj* [*post-* + *-fix* (as in *prefix*)] (1973) : characterized by placement of an operator after its operand or after its two operands if it is a binary operator — compare INFIX, PREFIX

post–free \'pōs(t)-'frē\ *adj* (1723) *chiefly Brit* : POSTPAID

post·gan·gli·on·ic \,pōs(t)-,gan-glē-'ä-nik\ *adj* (1897) : distal to a ganglion; *specif* : of, relating to, or being an axon arising from a cell body within an autonomic ganglion — compare PREGANGLIONIC

¹post·grad·u·ate \-'gra-jə-wət, -,wāt, -'graj-wət\ *adj* (1858) : GRADUATE 2

²postgraduate *n* (ca. 1890) : a student continuing formal education after graduation from high school or college

¹post·haste \'pōst-'hāst\ *n* [³*post*] (1545) *archaic* : great haste

²posthaste *adv* (1593) : with all possible speed

³posthaste *adj* (1604) *obs* : SPEEDY, IMMEDIATE ⟨requires your . . . ~ appearance —Shak.⟩

post hoc \'pōst-'häk\ *adj* [NL *post hoc, ergo propter hoc* after this, therefore because of this] (1704) **1** : relating to or being the fallacy of arguing from temporal sequence to a causal relation **2** : formulated after the fact ⟨a *post hoc* rationalization⟩

post-hole \'pōst-,hōl\ *n* (1703) : a hole dug for a post (as to support a fence or wall)

post horn *n* (1675) : a simple straight or coiled brass or copper wind instrument with cupped mouthpiece used esp. by guards of mail coaches of the 18th and 19th centuries

post horn

post–horse \'pōst-,hȯrs\ *n* [³*post*] (1527) : a horse for use esp. by couriers or mail carriers

post·hu·mous \'päs-chə-məs *also* -tə-, -tyə-, -thə-; päst-'hyü-məs, 'pōst-, -'yü-\ *adj* [L *posthumus,* alter. of *postumus* late-born, posthumous, fr. superl. of *posterus* coming after — more at POSTERIOR] (1619) **1** : born after the death of the father **2** : published after the death of the author **3** : following or occurring after death ⟨~ fame⟩ — **post·hu·mous·ly** *adv* — **post·hu·mous·ness** *n*

post·hyp·not·ic \,pōst-hip-'nä-tik, -ip-\ *adj* [ISV] (1890) : of, relating to, or characteristic of the period following a hypnotic trance

pos·tiche \pä-'tēsh\ *n* [F, fr. Sp. *postizo*] (1886) : WIG; *esp* : TOUPEE 2

pos·til·ion *or* **pos·til·lion** \pō-'stil-yən, pə-\ *n* [MF *postillon* mail carrier using post-horses, fr. It *postiglione,* fr. *posta* post — more at POST] (ca. 1611) : one who rides as a guide on the near horse of one of the pairs attached to a coach or post chaise esp. without a coachman

Post·im·pres·sion·ism \,pōst-im-'pre-shə-,ni-zəm\ *n* [F *postimpressionisme,* fr. *post-* + *impressionisme* impressionism] (1910) : a theory or practice of art originating in France in the last quarter of the 19th century that in revolt against impressionism stresses variously volume, picture structure, or expressionism — **Post·im·pres·sion·ist** \-'pre-sh(ə-)nist\ *adj or n* — **Post·im·pres·sion·is·tic** \-,pre-shə-'nis-tik\ *adj*

¹post·ing \'pōs-tiŋ\ *n* [⁴*post*] (1682) **1** : the act of transferring an entry or item from a book of original entry to the proper account in a ledger **2** : the record in a ledger account resulting from the transfer of an entry or item from a book of original entry

²posting *n* [⁷*post*] (1880) : appointment to a post or a command

Post–Kant·ian \,pōs(t)-'kan-tē-ən, -'kän-\ *adj* (1843) : of or relating to the idealist philosophers (as Fichte, Schelling, and Hegel) following Kant and developing some of his ideas

post·lap·sar·i·an \-,lap-'ser-ē-ən\ *adj* [*post-* + L *lapsus* slip, fall — more at LAPSE] (1733) : of, relating to, or characteristic of the time or state after the fall of mankind

post·lit·er·ate \-'li-tə-rət *also* -'li-trət\ *adj* (1965) : relating to or occurring after the introduction of the electronic media

post·lude \'pōst-,lüd\ *n* [*post-* + *-lude* (as in *prelude*)] (1851) **1** : a closing piece of music; *esp* : an organ voluntary at the end of a church service **2** : a closing phase (as of an epoch or a literary work)

post·man \'pōs(t)-mən, -,man\ *n* (1529) : MAILMAN

¹post·mark \-,märk\ *n* (1678) : an official postal marking on a piece of mail; *specif* : a mark showing the post office and date of mailing

²postmark *vt* (1716) : to put a postmark on

post·mas·ter \-,mas-tər\ *n* (1513) **1** : one who has charge of a post office **2** : one who has charge of a station for the accommodation of travelers or who supplies post-horses — **post·mas·ter·ship** \-,ship\ *n*

postmaster general *n, pl* **postmasters general** (1626) : an official in charge of a national post office department or agency

post·men·o·paus·al \,pōs(t)-,me-nə-'pȯ-zəl\ *adj* (1928) **1** : having undergone menopause **2** : occurring after menopause

post me·ri·di·em \-mə-'ri-dē-əm, -,em\ *adj* [L] (1647) : being after noon — abbr. *p.m.*

post·mil·le·nar·i·an·ism \-,mi-lə-'ner-ē-ə-,ni-zəm\ *n* (ca. 1890) : POST-MILLENNIALISM — **postmillenarian** *adj or n*

post·mil·len·ni·al \-mə-'le-nē-əl\ *adj* (1851) **1** : coming after or relating to the period after the millennium **2** : holding or relating to post-millennialism

post·mil·len·ni·al·ism \-ə-,li-zəm\ *n* (1879) : the theological doctrine that the second coming of Christ will occur after the millennium — **post·mil·len·ni·al·ist** \-ə-list\ *n*

post·mis·tress \'pōs(t)-,mis-trəs\ *n* (1697) : a woman who is a postmaster

post·mod·ern \,pōs(t)-'mä-dərn, -̣'mä-d(ə-)rən\ *adj* (1949) : of, relating to, or being any of several movements (as in art, architecture, or literature) that are reactions against the philosophy and practices of modern movements and are typically marked by revival of traditional elements and techniques — **post·mod·ern·ism** \-dər-,ni-zəm\ *n* — **post·mod·ern·ist** \-nist\ *adj or n*

¹post·mor·tem \,pōs(t)-'mȯr-təm\ *adj* [L *post mortem* after death] (ca. 1836) **1** : done, occurring, or collected after death ⟨~ tissue specimens⟩ **2** : following the event

²postmortem *n* (1850) **1** : an analysis or discussion of an event after it is over **2** : AUTOPSY 1

postmortem examination *n* (1837) : AUTOPSY 1

post·na·sal drip \'pōst-,nā-zəl-\ *n* (1949) : flow of mucous secretion from the posterior part of the nasal cavity onto the wall of the pharynx occurring usu. as a chronic accompaniment of an allergic state

post·na·tal \-'nā-t³l\ *adj* [ISV] (ca. 1859) : occurring or being after birth; *specif* : of or relating to an infant immediately after birth ⟨~ care⟩ — **post·na·tal·ly** *adv*

post·nup·tial \-'nəp-shəl, -chəl, ÷-chə-wəl\ *adj* (1807) : made or occurring after marriage or mating

post oak *n* [²*post*] (1775) : an oak (*Quercus stellata*) of the eastern and central U.S. having hard durable wood

¹post–obit \pōst-'ō-bət, *esp Brit* -'ä-bit\ *n* (1751) : POST-OBIT BOND

²post–obit *adj* [L *post obitum* after death] (ca. 1834) : occurring or taking effect after death

post–obit bond *n* (1788) : a bond made by a reversioner to secure a loan and payable out of his reversion

post office *n* (1652) **1 :** a government department or agency handling the transmission of mail **2 :** a local branch of a national post office handling the mail for a particular place or area **3 :** a game in which a player acting as postmaster or postmistress may exact a kiss from one of the opposite sex as payment for the pretended delivery of a letter

post·op·er·a·tive \ˌpōst-ˈä-p(ə-)rə-tiv, -pə-ˌrā-\ *adj* [ISV] (ca. 1890) **1 :** following a surgical operation ⟨∼ care⟩ **2 :** having undergone a surgical operation ⟨a ∼ patient⟩ — **post·op·er·a·tive·ly** *adv*

post·or·bit·al \-ˈör-bə-tᵊl\ *adj* (ca. 1836) : situated behind the eye socket

post·paid \ˈpōs(t)-ˈpād\ *adj* (1653) : having the postage paid by the sender and not chargeable to the receiver

post·par·tum \ˈpōs(t)-ˈpär-təm\ *adj* [NL *post partum* after birth] (1846) **1 :** following parturition ⟨∼ period⟩ **2 :** being in the postpartum period ⟨∼ mothers⟩ — **postpartum** *adv*

post·pone \(ˌ)pōs(t)-ˈpōn\ *vt* **post·poned; post·pon·ing** [L *postponere* to place after, postpone, fr. *post-* + *ponere* to place — more at POSITION] (ca. 1520) **1 :** to put off to a later time : DEFER **2 a :** to place later (as in a sentence) than the normal position in English ⟨∼ an adjective⟩ **b :** to place later in order of precedence, preference, or importance *syn* see DEFER — **post·pon·able** \-ˈpō-nə-bəl\ *adj* — **post·pone·ment** \-ˈpōn-mənt\ *n* — **post·pon·er** *n*

post·po·si·tion \ˌpōs(t)-pə-ˈzi-shən, ˈpōs(t)-pə-ˌ\ *n* [F, fr. *postposer* to place after, fr. L *postponere* (perf. indic. *postposui*)] (ca. 1638) : the placing of a grammatical element after a word to which it is primarily related in a sentence; *also* : such a word or particle esp. when functioning as a preposition — **post·po·si·tion·al** \ˌpōs(t)-pə-ˈzish-nəl, -ˈzi-shə-nᵊl\ *adj* — **post·po·si·tion·al·ly** *adv*

post·pos·i·tive \-ˈpä-zə-tiv, -ˈpäz-tiv\ *adj* (1786) : placed after or at the end of another word — **post·pos·i·tive·ly** *adv*

post·pran·di·al \ˈpōs(t)-ˈpran-dē-əl\ *adj* (1820) : occurring after a meal

post·pro·duc·tion \ˌpōs(t)-prə-ˈdək-shən, ˈpōs(t)-prə-ˌ, -prō-\ *n* (1953) : the period following filming or taping in which a motion picture or television show is readied for public presentation

post road *n* (1657) : a route over which mail is carried

post·script \ˈpōs(t)-ˌskript\ *n* [NL *postscriptum*, fr. L, neut. of *postscriptus*, pp. of *postscribere* to write after, fr. *post-* + *scribere* to write — more at SCRIBE] (1551) : a note or series of notes appended to a completed letter, article, or book

post·syn·ap·tic \ˌpōs(t)-sə-ˈnap-tik\ *adj* (1909) **1 :** occurring after synapsis ⟨a ∼ chromosome⟩ **2 :** relating to, occurring in, or being part of a nerve cell by which a wave of excitation is conveyed away from a synapse — **post·syn·ap·ti·cal·ly** \-ti-k(ə-)lē\ *adv*

post·ten·sion \-ˈten(t)-shən\ *vt* (1950) : to apply tension to (reinforcing steel) after concrete has set

post·test \ˈpōs(t)-ˌtest\ *n* (ca. 1951) : a test given to students after completion of an instructional program or segment and often used in conjunction with a pretest to measure their achievement and the effectiveness of the program

post time *n* [¹*post*] (1941) : the designated time for the start of a horse race

post·tran·scrip·tion·al \ˌpōs(t)-tran(t)-ˈskrip-shnəl, -shə-nᵊl\ *adj* (1969) : occurring, acting, or existing after genetic transcription

post·trans·fu·sion \-tran(t)s-ˈfyü-zhən\ *adj* (1944) **1 :** caused by transfused blood **2 :** occurring after blood transfusion ⟨∼ shock⟩

post·trans·la·tion·al \-tran(t)s-ˈlā-shnəl, -shə-nᵊl\ *adj* (1975) : occurring or existing after genetic translation

post–traumatic stress disorder *n* (1980) : a psychological reaction occurring after a highly stressing event that is usu. characterized by depression, anxiety, flashbacks, recurrent nightmares, and avoidance of reminders of the event — called also *post-traumatic stress syndrome*

pos·tu·lan·cy \ˈpäs-chə-lən(t)-sē\ *n, pl* **-cies** (ca. 1883) **1 :** the quality or state of being a postulant **2 :** the period during which a person remains a postulant

pos·tu·lant \ˈpäs-chə-lənt\ *n* [F, petitioner, candidate, postulant, fr. MF, fr. prp. of *postuler* to demand, solicit, fr. L *postulare*] (1759) **1 :** a person admitted to a religious order as a probationary candidate for membership **2 :** a person on probation before being admitted as a candidate for holy orders in the Episcopal Church

¹pos·tu·late \ˈpäs-chə-ˌlāt\ *vt* **-lat·ed; -lat·ing** [L *postulatus*, pp. of *postulare*; akin to L *poscere* to ask, OHG *forscōn* to search, Skt *prcchati* he asks — more at PRAY] (1593) **1 :** DEMAND, CLAIM **2 a :** to assume or claim as true, existent, or necessary : depend upon or start from the postulate of **b :** to assume as a postulate or axiom (as in logic or mathematics) — **pos·tu·la·tion** \ˌpäs-chə-ˈlā-shən\ *n* — **pos·tu·la·tion·al** \-shnəl, -shə-nᵊl\ *adj*

²pos·tu·late \ˈpäs-chə-lət, -ˌlāt\ *n* [ML *postulatum*, fr. neut. of *postulatus*, pp. of *postulare* to assume, fr. L, to demand] (1646) **1 :** a hypothesis advanced as an essential presupposition, condition, or premise of a train of reasoning : AXIOM 3

pos·tu·la·tor \-ˌlā-tər\ *n* (1863) : an official who presents a plea for beatification or canonization in the Roman Catholic Church — compare DEVIL'S ADVOCATE

pos·tur·al \ˈpäs-chə-rəl\ *adj* (1857) : of, relating to, or involving posture

¹pos·ture \ˈpäs-chər\ *n* [F, fr. It *postura*, fr. L *positura*, fr. *positus*, pp. of *ponere* to place — more at POSITION] (ca. 1586) **1 a :** the position or bearing of the body whether characteristic or assumed for a special purpose ⟨erect ∼⟩ **b :** the pose of a model or artistic figure **2 :** state or condition at a given time esp. with respect to capability in particular circumstances ⟨maintain a competitive ∼ in the market⟩ ⟨put the country in a ∼ of defense⟩ **3 :** a conscious mental or outward behavioral attitude ⟨takes a neutral ∼ toward the discussions⟩

²posture *vb* **pos·tured; pos·tur·ing** *vt* (ca. 1645) : to cause to assume a given posture : POSE ∼ *vi* **1 :** to assume a posture; *esp* : to strike a pose for effect **2 :** to assume an artificial or pretended attitude : ATTITUDINIZE — **pos·tur·er** \-chər-ər\ *n*

post·vo·cal·ic \ˌpōs(t)-vō-ˈka-lik, -və-\ *adj* [ISV] (1892) : immediately following a vowel

po·sy \ˈpō-zē\ *n, pl* **posies** [alter. of *poesy*] (1533) **1 :** a brief sentiment, motto, or legend **2 a :** BOUQUET, NOSEGAY **b :** FLOWER

¹pot \ˈpät\ *n* [ME, fr. OE *pott*; akin to MLG *pot* pot] (bef. 12c) **1 a**

: a usu. rounded metal or earthen container used chiefly for domestic purposes (as in cooking or for holding liquids or growing plants); *also* : any of various technical or industrial vessels or enclosures resembling or likened to a household pot ⟨the ∼ of a still⟩ **b :** POTFUL ⟨a ∼ of coffee⟩ **2 :** an enclosed framework of wire, wood, or wicker for catching fish or lobsters **3 a :** a large amount (as of money) **b** (1) : the total of the bets at stake at one time (2) : one round in a poker game **c :** the common fund of a group **4 :** POTSHOT **5 :** POTBELLY **6 :** RUIN ⟨gone to ∼⟩ **7** *Brit* : a shot in snooker in which a ball is pocketed

²pot *vb* **pot·ted; pot·ting** *vt* (1616) **1 a :** to place in a pot **b :** to pack or preserve (as cooked and chopped meat) in a sealed pot, jar, or can often with aspic **2 :** to shoot with a potshot **3 :** to make or shape (earthenware) as a potter **4 :** to embed (as electronic components) in a container with an insulating or protective material (as plastic) ∼ *vi* : to take a potshot

³pot *n* [perh. modif. of MexSp *potiguaya*] (1938) : MARIJUANA

¹po·ta·ble \ˈpō-tə-bəl\ *adj* [ME, fr. LL *potabilis*, fr. L *potare* to drink; akin to L *bibere* to drink, Gk *pinein*] (15c) : suitable for drinking — **po·ta·bil·i·ty** \ˌpō-tə-ˈbi-lə-tē\ *n* — **po·ta·ble·ness** \ˈpō-tə-bəl-nəs\ *n*

²potable *n* (1623) : a liquid that is suitable for drinking; *esp* : an alcoholic beverage

po·tage \pō-ˈtäzh\ *n* [MF, fr. OF, pottage] (1567) : a thick soup

pot ale *n* (1812) : the residue of fermented wort left in a still after the distillation of whiskey or alcohol and used for feeding swine

pot·ash \ˈpät-ˌash\ *n* [sing. of *pot ashes*] (ca. 1648) **1 :** potassium carbonate esp. from wood ashes **2 :** potassium or a potassium compound esp. as used in agriculture or industry

po·tas·sic \pə-ˈta-sik\ *adj* (1858) : of, relating to, or containing potassium

po·tas·si·um \pə-ˈta-sē-əm\ *n, often attrib* [NL, fr. *potassa* potash, fr. E *potash*] (ca. 1807) : a silver-white soft light low-melting univalent metallic element of the alkali metal group that occurs abundantly in nature esp. combined in minerals — see ELEMENT table

potassium–argon *adj* (1953) : being or relating to a method of dating paleontological or geological materials based on the radioactive decay of potassium to argon that has taken place in a specimen

potassium bromide *n* (1873) : a crystalline salt KBr with a saline taste that is used as a sedative and in photography

potassium carbonate *n* (1885) : a white salt K_2CO_3 that forms a strongly alkaline solution and is used in making glass and soap

potassium chlorate *n* (1885) : a crystalline salt $KClO_3$ that is used as an oxidizing agent in matches, fireworks, and explosives

potassium chloride *n* (1885) : a crystalline salt KCl occurring as a mineral and in natural waters and used esp. as a fertilizer

potassium cyanide *n* (1885) : a very poisonous crystalline salt KCN used esp. in gold and silver extraction from ore

potassium dichromate *n* (1885) : a soluble salt $K_2Cr_2O_7$ forming large orange-red crystals used esp. in dyeing, in photography, and as an oxidizing agent

potassium hydroxide *n* (1885) : a white deliquescent solid KOH that dissolves in water with much heat to form a strongly alkaline and caustic liquid and is used chiefly in making soap and as a reagent

potassium nitrate *n* (1885) : a crystalline salt KNO_3 that occurs as a product of nitrification in arable soils, is a strong oxidizer, and is used esp. in making gunpowder, as a fertilizer, and in medicine

potassium permanganate *n* (1869) : a dark purple salt $KMnO_4$ used as an oxidizer and disinfectant

potassium sorbate *n* (1960) : a potassium salt $C_6H_7KO_2$ of sorbic acid used esp. as a food preservative

potassium sulfate *n* (1885) : a white crystalline compound K_2SO_4 used esp. as a fertilizer

po·ta·tion \pō-ˈtā-shən\ *n* [ME *potacioun*, fr. MF *potation*, fr. L *potation-*, *potatio* act of drinking, fr. *potare* to drink — more at POTABLE] (15c) **1 :** a usu. alcoholic drink or brew **2 :** the act or an instance of drinking or inhaling; *also* : the portion taken in one such act

po·ta·to \pə-ˈtā-(ˌ)tō, -tə, *dial* pə-ˈdā-, bə-\ *n, pl* **-toes** *often attrib* [Sp *batata*, fr. Taino] (1565) **1 :** SWEET POTATO **2 a :** an erect So. American herb (*Solanum tuberosum*) of the nightshade family widely cultivated as a vegetable crop **b :** the edible starchy tuber of a potato — called also *Irish potato, white potato*

potato beetle *n* (1821) : COLORADO POTATO BEETLE

potato blight *n* (1879) : any of several destructive fungus diseases of the potato

potato bug *n* (1799) : COLORADO POTATO BEETLE

potato chip *n* (1878) : a thin slice of white potato that has been fried until crisp and then usu. salted

potato leafhopper *n* (1921) : a small green white-spotted leafhopper (*Empoasca fabae*) of the eastern and southern U.S. that is a serious pest on many cultivated plants and esp. on the potato

potato 2a

potato pancake *n* (1935) : a fried flat cake of grated potato mixed with raw egg and usu. grated onion and spices

potato tu·ber·worm \-ˈtü-bər-ˌwərm, -ˈtyü-\ *n* (1920) : a grayish brown moth (*Phthorimaea operculella* of the family Gelechiidae) whose larva mines the leaves and bores in the stems esp. of potato and tobacco plants and commonly overwinters in potato tubers

pot–au–feu \ˌpät-ō-ˈfə(r), pō-tō-ˈfœ̄\ *n, pl* **pot–au–feu** [F, lit., pot on the fire] (1791) : a French boiled dinner of meat and vegetables

pot·bel·lied \ˈpät-ˌbe-lēd\ *adj* (1657) : having a potbelly

potbellied stove *n* (1933) : a stove with a rounded or bulging body — called also *potbelly stove*

pot·bel·ly \ˈpät-ˌbe-lē\ *n* (ca. 1714) **1 :** an enlarged, swollen, or protruding abdomen **2 :** POTBELLIED STOVE

pot·boil \ˈpät-ˌbȯil\ *vi* (1867) : to produce potboilers

\ə\ **abut** \ᵊ\ **kitten, F table** \ər\ **further** \a\ **ash** \ā\ **ace** \ä\ **mop, mar**

\aù\ **out** \ch\ **chin** \e\ **bet** \ē\ **easy** \g\ **go** \i\ **hit** \ī\ **ice** \j\ **job**

\ŋ\ **sing** \ō\ **go** \ȯ\ **law** \ȯi\ **boy** \th\ **thin** \t̲h̲\ **the** \ü\ **loot** \ù\ **foot**

\y\ **yet** \zh\ **vision** \ä, k̲, ⁿ, œ, œ̄, ue̲, uē̲, ᵝ\ *see* Guide to Pronunciation

pot·boil·er \-ˌbȯi-lər\ n (1864) : a usu. inferior work (as of art or literature) produced chiefly for profit

pot–bound \'pät-ˌbau̇nd\ adj (1850) of a potted plant : having roots so densely matted as to allow little or no space for further growth

pot·boy \-ˌbȯi\ n (1795) : a boy who serves drinks in a tavern

pot cheese n (1812) : COTTAGE CHEESE

po·teen also **po·theen** \pə-'tēn, -'chēn, -'tyēn, -'thēn\ n [Ir poitín, lit., small pot, dim. of pota pot] (1812) : whiskey illicitly distilled in Ireland

Po·tem·kin village \pə-'tem(p)-kən-\ n [Grigori Potëmkin, who supposedly built impressive fake villages along a route Catherine the Great was to travel] (1937) : an impressive facade or show designed to hide an undesirable fact or condition

po·tence \'pō-t²n(t)s\ n (15c) : POTENCY

po·ten·cy \'pō-t²n(t)-sē\ n, pl **-cies** (15c) 1 a : FORCE, POWER b : the quality or state of being potent c : the ability or capacity to achieve or bring about a particular result 2 : POTENTIALITY 1

¹po·tent \'pō-t²nt\ adj [ME, fr. L potent-, potens (prp. of posse to be able), fr. L potis, pote able; akin to Goth brūthfaths bridegroom, Gk posis husband, Skt pati master] (15c) 1 : having or wielding force, authority, or influence : POWERFUL 2 : achieving or bringing about a particular result : EFFECTIVE 3 a : chemically or medicinally effective ⟨a ~ vaccine⟩ b : rich in a characteristic constituent 4 : able to copulate — usu. used of the male — **po·tent·ly** adv

²potent adj [obs. E potent crutch] (1610) of a heraldic cross : having flat bars across the ends of the arms — see CROSS illustration

po·ten·tate \'pō-t²n-ˌtāt\ n (15c) : RULER, SOVEREIGN: broadly : one who wields great power or sway

¹po·ten·tial \pə-'ten(t)-shəl\ adj [ME potencial, fr. LL potentialis, fr. potentia potentiality, fr. L, power, fr. potent-, potens] (14c) 1 : existing in possibility : capable of development into actuality ⟨~ benefits⟩ 2 : expressing possibility; specif : of, relating to, or constituting a verb phrase expressing possibility, liberty, or power by the use of an auxiliary with the infinitive of the verb (as in "it may rain") syn see LATENT — **po·ten·tial·ly** \-'ten(t)-sh(ə-)lē\ adv

²potential n (1817) 1 : something that can develop or become actual ⟨a ~ for violence⟩ b : PROMISE 2 2 a : any of various functions from which the intensity or the velocity at any point in a field may be readily calculated b : the work required to move a unit positive charge from a reference point (as at infinity) to a point in question c : POTENTIAL DIFFERENCE

potential difference n (1896) : the difference in potential between two points that represents the work involved or the energy released in the transfer of a unit quantity of electricity from one point to another

potential energy n (1853) : the energy that a piece of matter has because of its position or because of the arrangement of parts

po·ten·ti·al·i·ty \pə-ˌten(t)-shē-'a-lə-tē\ n, pl **-ties** (1625) 1 : the ability to develop or come into existence 2 : POTENTIAL 1

po·ten·ti·ate \pə-'ten(t)-shē-ˌāt\ vt **-at·ed; -at·ing** (1817) : to make effective or active or more effective or more active; also : to augment the activity of (as a drug) synergistically — **po·ten·ti·a·tion** \-ˌten(t)-shē-'ā-shən\ n — **po·ten·ti·a·tor** \-'ten(t)-shē-ˌā-tər\ n

po·ten·til·la \ˌpō-t²n-'ti-lə\ n [NL, fr. ML, garden heliotrope, fr. L potent-, potens] (1548) : CINQUEFOIL 1

po·ten·ti·om·e·ter \pə-ˌten(t)-shē-'ä-mə-tər\ n [ISV potential + -o- + -meter] (1881) 1 : an instrument for measuring electromotive forces 2 : VOLTAGE DIVIDER — **po·ten·ti·o·met·ric** \-sh(ē-)ə-'me-trik\ adj

pot·ful \'pät-ˌfu̇l\ n (14c) 1 : as much or as many as a pot will hold 2 : a large amount ⟨makes a ~ of money —John Corry⟩

pot hat n (1798) : a hat with a stiff crown; esp : DERBY

pot·head \'pät-ˌhed\ n (1959) : a person who smokes marijuana

¹poth·er \'pä-thər\ n [origin unknown] (1591) 1 : confused or fidgety flurry or activity : COMMOTION b : agitated talk or controversy usu. over a trivial matter 2 : a choking cloud of dust or smoke 3 : mental turmoil

²pother vb **poth·ered; poth·er·ing** \'pä-thə-riŋ, 'päth-riŋ\ vt (1692) : to put into a pother ~ vi : to be in a pother

pot·herb \'pät-ˌərb, -ˌhərb\ n (1538) : a usu. leafy herb that is cooked for use as greens; also : one (as mint) used to season food

pot holder n (1944) : a small cloth pad used for handling hot cooking utensils or containers

pot·hole \'pät-ˌhōl\ n (1826) 1 a : a circular hole formed in the rocky bed of a river by the grinding action of stones or gravel whirled round by the water b : a sizable rounded often water-filled depression in land 2 : a pot-shaped hole in a road surface — **pot·holed** \-ˌhōld\ adj

pot·hook \-ˌhu̇k\ n (15c) 1 : an S-shaped hook for hanging pots and kettles over an open fire 2 : a written character resembling a pothook

pot·house \-ˌhau̇s\ n (1724) : TAVERN 1

pot·hunt·er \-ˌhən-tər\ n (1781) 1 : one who hunts game for food 2 : an amateur archaeologist — **pot·hunt·ing** \-tiŋ\ n

po·tion \'pō-shən\ n [ME pocioun, fr. MF potion, fr. L potion-, potio drink, potion, fr. potare to drink — more at POTABLE] (14c) : a mixture of liquids (as liquor or medicine)

¹pot·latch \'pät-ˌlach\ n [Chinook Jargon patlač, fr. Nootka paλpač] (ca. 1861) 1 : a ceremonial feast of the American Indians of the northwest coast marked by the host's lavish distribution of gifts or sometimes destruction of property to demonstrate wealth and generosity with the expectation of eventual reciprocation 2 Northwest : a social event or celebration

²potlatch vt (1898) 1 : to give (as a gift) esp. with the expectation of a gift in return 2 : to hold or give a potlatch for (as a tribe or group) ~ vi : to hold or give a potlatch

pot lik·ker \-'li-kər\ Southern & Midland var of POT LIQUOR

pot·line \'pät-ˌlin\ n (1944) : a row of electrolytic cells used in the production of aluminum

pot liquor n (1744) : the liquid left in a pot after cooking something

pot·luck \'pät-'lək, 1b also -ˌlək\ n (1592) 1 a : the regular meal available to a guest for whom no special preparations have been made b : a communal meal to which people bring food to share — usu. used attributively ⟨a ~ supper⟩ 2 : whatever is offered or available in given circumstances or at a given time

pot marigold n (1814) : a calendula (Calendula officinalis) grown esp. for ornament

po·tom·e·ter \pō-'tä-mə-tər\ n [Gk poton drink (akin to Gk pinein to drink) + E -meter — more at POTABLE] (1884) : an apparatus for mea-

suring the rate of transpiration in a plant by determining the amount of water absorbed

pot·pie \'pät-'pī, -ˌpī\ n (ca. 1792) : pastry-covered meat and vegetables cooked in a deep dish

pot·pour·ri \ˌpō-pu̇-'rē\ n [F pot pourri, lit., rotten pot] (1749) 1 : a mixture of flowers, herbs, and spices that is usu. kept in a jar and used for scent 2 : a miscellaneous collection : MEDLEY ⟨a ~ of the best songs and sketches —Current Biog.⟩

pot roast n (1881) : a piece of beef cooked by braising usu. on top of the stove

pot·sherd \'pät-ˌshərd\ n [ME pot-sherd, fr. pot + sherd shard] (14c) : a pottery fragment

¹pot·shot \-ˌshät\ n [fr. the notion that such a shot is unsportsmanlike and worthy only of one whose object is to fill the cooking pot] (1858) 1 : a shot taken from ambush or at a random or easy target 2 : a critical remark made in a random or sporadic manner

²potshot vb **potshot; pot·shot·ting** vi (1918) : to take a potshot ~ vt : to attack or shoot with a potshot

pot still n (1799) : a still used esp. in the distillation of Irish grain whiskey and Scotch malt whiskey in which the heat of the fire is applied directly to the pot containing the mash

pot·stone \'pät-ˌstōn\ n (1771) : a more or less impure steatite used esp. in prehistoric times to make cooking vessels

pot·tage \'pä-tij\ n [ME potage, fr. OF, fr. pot pot, of Gmc origin; akin to OE pott pot] (13c) : a thick soup of vegetables and often meat

pot·ted \'pä-təd\ adj (1646) 1 chiefly Brit : preserved in a pot, jar, or can 2 : planted or grown in a pot 3 chiefly Brit : briefly and superficially summarized ⟨a dull, pedestrian ~ history —Times Lit. Supp.⟩ 4 slang : DRUNK 1a

¹pot·ter \'pä-tər\ n (bef. 12c) : one that makes pottery

²potter vi [prob. freq. of E dial. pote to poke] (1829) : PUTTER — **pot·ter·er** \'pä-tər-ər\ n — **pot·ter·ing·ly** \'pä-tə-riŋ-lē\ adv

potter's clay n (15c) : a plastic clay suitable for making pottery — called also potter's earth

potter's field n [fr. the mention in Mt 27:7 of the purchase of a potter's field for use as a graveyard] (1777) : a public burial place for paupers, unknown persons, and criminals

potter's wheel n (ca. 1741) : a usu. horizontal disk revolving on a vertical spindle and carrying the clay being shaped by a potter

pot·tery \'pä-tə-rē\ n, pl **-ter·ies** (15c) 1 : a place where clayware is made and fired 2 a : the art or craft of the potter b : the manufacture of clayware 3 : CLAYWARE: esp : earthenware as distinguished on the one hand from porcelain and stoneware and on the other from brick and tile

pot·tle \'pä-t²l\ n [ME potel, fr. MF, fr. pot] (14c) : a container holding a half gallon (1.9 liters)

pot·to \'pä-(ˌ)tō\ n, pl **pottos** [perh. fr. Wolof pata, a tailless monkey] (1705) : any of several African primates (genera Arctocebus and Perodicticus); esp : a West African primate (P. potto) that has a vestigial index finger and tail

potter's wheel

Pott's disease \'päts-\ n [Percivall Pott †1788 Eng. surgeon] (1835) : tuberculosis of the spine with destruction of bone resulting in curvature of the spine

¹pot·ty \'pä-tē\ adj **pot·ti·er; -est** [prob. fr. ¹pot] (ca. 1860) 1 Brit : TRIVIAL, INSIGNIFICANT 2 chiefly Brit : slightly crazy : SNOBBISH

²potty n, pl **potties** (ca. 1942) : a small child's pot for urination or defecation

pot·ty–chair \-ˌcher, -ˌchar\ n (1943) : a child's chair having an open seat under which a receptacle in placed for toilet training

pot·zer \'pät-sər\ var of PATZER

¹pouch \'pau̇ch\ n [ME pouche, fr. MF, of Gmc origin; akin to OE pocca bag] (14c) 1 : a small drawstring bag carried on the person 2 a : a bag of small or moderate size for storing or transporting goods; specif : a lockable bag for first-class mail or diplomatic dispatches b chiefly Scot : POCKET c : PACKET 3 : an anatomical structure resembling a pouch — **pouched** \'pau̇cht\ adj

²pouch vt (ca. 1566) 1 : to put or form into or as if into a pouch 2 : to transmit by pouch ~ vi 1 : to bulge or stick out or down in a manner suggesting a pouch ⟨~ing cheeks⟩ 2 : to transmit mail or dispatches by pouch

pouchy \'pau̇-chē\ adj **pouch·i·er; -est** (1828) : having, tending to have, or resembling a pouch ⟨~ insomniac eyes —Graham Greene⟩

pouf also **pouffe** \'pu̇f\ n [F pouf, something inflated, of imit. origin] (1817) 1 : PUFF 3b(3) 2 : a bouffant or fluffy part of a garment or accessory 3 : OTTOMAN — **poufed** or **pouffed** \'pu̇ft\ adj

Pouil·ly–Fuis·sé \ˌpü-yē-fwē-'sā\ n [Solutré-Pouilly and Fuissé, villages in France] (1927) : a dry white burgundy from an area west of Mâcon, France

Pouil·ly–Fu·mé \ˌpü-yē-fü-'mā, -fǖ-\ n [F, fr. Pouilly-sur-Loire, village in France + fumé, pp. of fumer to smoke, fr. L fumare, fr. fumus smoke — more at FUME] (1935) : a dry white wine from the Loire valley of France

pou·larde also **pou·lard** \pu̇-'lärd\ n [F poularde] (1732) : a pullet sterilized to produce fattening

poult \'pōlt\ n [ME polet, pulte young fowl — more at PULLET] (15c) : a young fowl; esp : a young turkey

poul·ter·er \'pōl-tər-ər\ n [alter. of ME pulter, fr. MF pouletier] (1638) : one that deals in poultry

poul·ter's measure \'pōl-tərz-\ n [obs. poulter poulterer, fr. ME pulter; fr. the former practice of occas. giving one or two extra when counting eggs by dozens] (1576) : a meter in which lines of 12 and 14 syllables alternate

¹poul·tice \'pōl-təs\ n [ME pultes, fr. ML, lit., pap, fr. L, pl. of pult-, puls porridge] (15c) : a soft usu. heated and sometimes medicated mass spread on cloth and applied to sores or other lesions

²poultice vt **-ticed; -tic·ing** (1730) : to apply a poultice to

poul·try \'pōl-trē\ *n* [ME *pultrie,* fr. MF *pouleterie,* fr. OF, fr. *pouletier* poulterer, fr. *poulet* — more at PULLET] (14c) : domesticated birds kept for eggs or meat

poul·try·man \-mən\ *n* (ca. 1574)   1 : one who raises domestic fowls esp. on a commercial scale for the production of eggs and meat   2 : one who deals in poultry or poultry products

¹**pounce** \'paủn(t)s\ *n* [ME, talon] (15c) : the claw of a bird of prey

²**pounce** *vi* **pounced; pounc·ing** (1744)   1 a : to swoop upon and seize something with or as if with talons   b : to seize upon and make capital of something (as another's blunder or an opportunity)   2 : to make a sudden assault or approach

³**pounce** *n* (1841) : the act of pouncing

⁴**pounce** *vt* **pounced; pounc·ing** [MF *poncer,* fr. *ponce*] (1535) : to dust, rub, finish, or stencil with pounce

⁵**pounce** *n* [F *ponce* pumice, fr. MF, fr. LL *pomic-, pomex,* alter. of L *pumic-, pumex* — more at FOAM] (1706)   1 : a fine powder formerly used to prevent ink from spreading   2 : a fine powder for making stenciled patterns

poun·cet-box \'paủn(t)-sət-\ *n* [prob. fr. (assumed) MF *poncette* small pounce bag] (1596) *archaic* : a box for carrying pomander

¹**pound** \'paủnd\ *n, pl* **pounds** *also* **pound** [ME, fr. OE *pund,* fr. L *pondo* pound, fr. abl. of *pondus* weight — more at PENDANT] (bef. 12c)   1 : any of various units of mass and weight; *specif* : a unit now in general use among English-speaking peoples equal to 16 avoirdupois ounces or 7000 grains or 0.45359237 kilogram — see WEIGHT table   2 a : the basic monetary unit of the United Kingdom — called also *pound sterling*   b : any of numerous basic monetary units of other countries — see MONEY table   c : ²LIRA

²**pound** *n* [ME, enclosure, fr. OE *pund-*] (14c)   1 a : an enclosure for animals; *esp* : a public enclosure for stray or unlicensed animals ⟨a dog ~⟩   b : a depot for holding impounded personal property until redeemed by the owner ⟨a car ~⟩   2 : a place or condition of confinement   3 : an enclosure within which fish are kept or caught; *esp* : the inner compartment of a fish trap or pound net

³**pound** *n* (1562) : an act or sound of pounding

⁴**pound** *vb* [alter. of ME *pounen,* fr. OE *pūnian*] *vt* (1594)   1 : to reduce to powder or pulp by beating   2 a : to strike heavily or repeatedly   b : to produce with or as if with repeated vigorous strokes — usu. used with *out* ⟨~ out a story on the typewriter⟩   c : to inculcate by insistent repetition : DRIVE ⟨day after day the facts were ~ed home to them — Ivy B. Priest⟩   3 : to move along heavily or persistently ⟨~ed the pavements looking for work⟩   ~ *vi*   1 : to strike heavy repeated blows   2 : PULSATE, THROB ⟨my heart was ~ing⟩   3 a : to move with or make a heavy repetitive sound   b : to work hard and continuously — usu. used with *away*

¹**pound·age** \'paủn-dij\ *n* (ca. 1500)   1 : a charge per pound of weight   2 : weight in pounds

²**poundage** *n* (1554) : IMPOUNDMENT 1

pound·al \'paủn-d°l\ *n* [¹*pound* + *-al* (as in *quintal*)] (1879) : a unit of force equal to the force that would give a free mass of one pound an acceleration of one foot per second per second

pound cake *n* [fr. the original recipe prescribing a pound of each of the principal ingredients] (1747) : a rich butter cake made with a large proportion of eggs and shortening

¹**pound·er** \'paủn-dər\ *n* (bef. 12c)   1 : one that pounds   2 : a tool used for pounding

²**pounder** *n* (1684)   1 : a gun throwing a projectile of a specified weight — usu. used in combination ⟨the ship was armed with six-*pounders*⟩   2 : one having a usu. specified weight or value in pounds — usu. used in combination ⟨caught a ten-*pounder*⟩

pound-fool·ish \'paủn(d)-'fü-lish\ *adj* [fr. the phrase *penny-wise and pound-foolish*] (1607) : imprudent in dealing with large sums or large matters

pound mile *n* (1939) : the transport of one pound of mail or express for one mile

pound net *n* (1865) : a fish trap consisting of a netting arranged into a directing wing and an enclosure with a narrow entrance

pound sign *n* (1980)   1 : the symbol £   2 : the symbol #

¹**pour** \'pōr, 'por\ *vb* [ME] *vt* (14c)   1 a : to cause to flow in a stream   b : to dispense from a container ⟨~ed drinks for everyone⟩   2 : to supply or produce freely or copiously   3 : to give full expression to : VENT ⟨~ed out his feelings⟩   ~ *vi*   1 : to move with a continuous flow   2 : to rain hard   3 : to move or come continuously : STREAM ⟨complaints ~ed in⟩ — **pour·able** \'pōr-ə-bəl, 'por-\ *adj* — **pour·er** \-ər\ *n* — **pour·ing·ly** \-iŋ-lē\ *adv*

²**pour** *n* (1790)   1 : the action of pouring : STREAM   2 a : an instance of pouring or an amount poured   b : a heavy fall of rain : DOWNPOUR

pour·boire \púr-'bwär\ *n* [F, fr. *pour boire* for drinking] (1817) : TIP, GRATUITY

pour·par·ler \¸púr-pär-'lā\ *n* [F, fr. MF, fr. *pourparler* to discuss, fr. OF, fr. *pour* for, before + *parler* to speak — more at PURCHASE, PARLEY] (1795) : a discussion preliminary to negotiations

pour·point \'púr-¸pöint, -¸pwant\ *n* [ME *purpuint,* fr. MF *pourpoint,* fr. OF *porpoint,* fr. *porpoint,* adj., quilted, alter. of (assumed) VL *perpunctus,* pp. of *perpungere* to perforate, fr. L *per* through + *pungere* to prick, pierce — more at PUNGENT] (14c) : a padded and quilted doublet

pour point \'pōr-¸pöint, 'por-\ *n* (1922) : the lowest temperature at which a substance flows under specified conditions

pousse-ca·fé \¸püs-(¸)ka-'fā\ *n* [F, lit., coffee chaser] (1880) : an after-dinner drink consisting of several liqueurs of different colors and specific gravities poured so as to remain in separate layers

pous·sette \pü-'set\ *vi* **pous·sett·ed; pous·sett·ing** [F, game in which contestants cross pins with each attempting to get his pin on top, fr. *pousser* to push] (1812) : to swing in a semicircle with hands joined with one's partner in a country-dance

¹**pout** \'paủt\ *vb* [ME] *vi* (14c)   1 a : to show displeasure by thrusting out the lips or wearing a sullen expression   b : SULK   2 : PROTRUDE   ~ *vt* : to cause to protrude ⟨~ed her lips⟩

²**pout** *n* (1591)   1 : a protrusion of the lips expressive of displeasure   2 *pl* : a fit of pique

³**pout** *n, pl* **pout** *or* **pouts** [prob. fr. (assumed) ME *poute,* a fish with a large head, fr. OE *-pūte;* akin to ME *pouten* to pout] (1591) : any of several large-headed fishes (as a bullhead or eelpout)

pout·er \'paủ-tər\ *n* (1725)   1 : a domestic pigeon of a breed characterized by erect carriage and a dilatable crop   2 : one that pouts

pouty \'paủ-tē\ *adj* (1863)   1 : SULKY 1   2 : expressive of displeasure

pov·er·ty \'pä-vər-tē\ *n, often attrib* [ME *poverte,* fr. OF *poverté,* fr. L *paupertat-, paupertas,* fr. *pauper* poor — more at POOR] (12c)   1 a : the state of one who lacks a usual or socially acceptable amount of money or material possessions   b : renunciation as a member of a religious order of the right as an individual to own property   2 : SCARCITY, DEARTH   3 a : debility due to malnutrition   b : lack of fertility ⟨~ of the soil⟩

syn POVERTY, INDIGENCE, PENURY, WANT, DESTITUTION mean the state of one with insufficient resources. POVERTY may cover a range from extreme want of necessities to an absence of material comforts ⟨the extreme *poverty* of the slum dwellers⟩. INDIGENCE implies seriously straitened circumstances ⟨the *indigence* of her years as a graduate student⟩. PENURY suggests a cramping or oppressive lack of money ⟨a catastrophic illness that condemned them to years of *penury*⟩. WANT and DESTITUTION imply extreme poverty that threatens life itself through starvation or exposure ⟨lived in a perpetual state of *want*⟩ ⟨the widespread *destitution* in countries beset by famine⟩.

poverty line *n* (1901) : a level of personal or family income below which one is classified as poor according to governmental standards — called also *poverty level*

pov·er·ty-strick·en \-¸stri-kən\ *adj* (1803) : very poor : DESTITUTE

¹**pow** \'pō, 'paủ\ *n* [alter. of *poll*] (1724) : HEAD, POLL

²**pow** \'paủ\ *n* [imit.] (1881) : a sound of a blow or explosion

POW \¸pē-(¸)ō-'də-bəl-(¸)yü, -¸b-(¸)yü; -'däb-(¸)yü\ *n* (ca. 1919) : PRISONER OF WAR

¹**pow·der** \'paủ-dər\ *vb* **pow·dered; pow·der·ing** \'paủ-d(ə-)riŋ\ *vt* (13c)   1 : to sprinkle or cover with or as if with powder   2 : to reduce or convert to powder   3 : to hit (as a ball) very hard   ~ *vi*   1 : to become powder   2 : to apply cosmetic powder — **pow·der·er** \-dər-ər\ *n*

²**powder** *n, often attrib* [ME *poudre,* fr. OF, fr. L *pulver-, pulvis* dust; prob. akin to Skt *palāva* chaff] (14c)   1 : matter in a finely divided state : particulate matter   2 a : a preparation in the form of fine particles esp. for medicinal or cosmetic use   b : fine dry light snow   3 : any of various solid explosives used chiefly in gunnery and blasting — **pow·der·less** \-ləs\ *adj* — **pow·der·like** \-¸līk\ *adj*

powder blue *n* (1896) : a pale blue

powder horn *n* (1533) : a flask for carrying gunpowder; *esp* : one made of the horn of an ox or cow

powder keg *n* (1855)   1 : a small usu. metal cask for holding gunpowder or blasting powder   2 : something liable to explode

powder metallurgy *n* (1933) : a branch of science or an art concerned with the production of powdered metals or of metallic objects by compressing a powdered metal or alloy with or without other materials and heating without thoroughly melting to solidify and strengthen

powder monkey *n* (1682) : one who carries or has charge of explosives (as in blasting operations)

powder-puff *adj* (1939) : of, relating to, or being a competitive activity or event for women ⟨a ~ football game⟩

powder puff *n* (ca. 1704) : a small fluffy device (as a pad) for applying cosmetic powder

powder room *n* (ca. 1937)   1 : a rest room for women   2 : a lavatory in the main living area of a house

pow·dery \'paủ-də-rē\ *adj* (15c)   1 a : resembling or consisting of powder ⟨~ snow⟩   b : easily reduced to powder : CRUMBLING   2 : covered with or as if with powder

powdery mildew *n* (1889)   1 : an ascomycetous fungus (family Erysiphaceae) producing abundant powdery conidia on the host   2 : a plant disease caused by a powdery mildew

¹**pow·er** \'paủ-(ə)r\ *n, often attrib* [ME, fr. OF *poeir, poeir* to be able, fr. (assumed) VL *potēre,* alter. of L *posse* — more at POTENT] (13c)   1 a (1) : ability to act or produce an effect (2) : ability to get extra base hits (3) : capacity for being acted upon or undergoing an effect   b : legal or official authority, capacity, or right   2 a : possession of control, authority, or influence over others   b : one having such power; *specif* : a sovereign state   c : a controlling group : ESTABLISHMENT — often used in the phrase *the powers that be*   d *archaic* : a force of armed men   e *chiefly dial* : a large number or quantity   3 a : physical might   b : mental or moral efficacy   c : political control or influence   4 *pl* : an order of angels — see CELESTIAL HIERARCHY   5 a : the number of times as indicated by an exponent that a number occurs as a factor in a product; *also* : the product itself   b : CARDINAL NUMBER 2   6 a : a source or means of supplying energy; *esp* : ELECTRICITY   b : MOTIVE POWER   c : the time rate at which work is done or energy emitted or transferred   7 : MAGNIFICATION 2b   8 : SCOPE, COMPREHENSIVENESS   9 : the probability of rejecting the null hypothesis in a statistical test when a particular alternative hypothesis happens to be true

syn POWER, AUTHORITY, JURISDICTION, CONTROL, COMMAND, SWAY, DOMINION mean the right to govern or rule or determine. POWER implies possession of ability to wield force, permissive authority, or substantial influence ⟨the *power* to mold public opinion⟩. AUTHORITY implies the granting of power for a specific purpose within specified limits ⟨gave her attorney the *authority* to manage her estate⟩. JURISDICTION applies to official power exercised within prescribed limits ⟨the bureau having *jurisdiction* over alcohol and firearms⟩. CONTROL stresses the power to direct and restrain ⟨you are responsible for the students under your *control*⟩. COMMAND implies the power to make arbitrary decisions and compel obedience ⟨the army officer in *command*⟩. SWAY suggests the extent or scope of exercised power or influence ⟨an empire that extended its *sway* over the known world⟩. DOMINION stresses sovereign power or supreme authority ⟨given *dominion* over all the animals⟩.

syn POWER, FORCE, ENERGY, STRENGTH, MIGHT mean the ability to exert

\ə\ abut \ᵊ\ kitten, F table \ər\ further \a\ ash \ā\ ace \ä\ mop, mar \aủ\ out \ch\ chin \e\ bet \ē\ easy \g\ go \i\ hit \ī\ ice \j\ job \ŋ\ sing \ō\ go \ò\ law \òi\ boy \th\ thin \th\ the \ü\ loot \ù\ foot \y\ yet \zh\ vision \ȧ, k̫, ⁿ, œ, œ̄, ue, ue̅, ᵊ\ *see* Guide to Pronunciation effort. POWER may imply latent or exerted physical, mental, or spiritual ability to act or be acted upon ⟨the awesome *power* of flowing water⟩. FORCE implies the actual effective exercise of power ⟨used enough *force* to push the door open⟩. ENERGY applies to power expended or capable of being transformed into work ⟨a worker with boundless *energy*⟩. STRENGTH applies to the quality or property of a person or thing that makes possible the exertion of force or the withstanding of strain, pressure, or attack ⟨use weight training to build your *strength*⟩. MIGHT implies great or overwhelming power or strength ⟨the belief that *might* makes right⟩.

²**power** *vt* (1540) **1** : to supply with power and esp. motive power **2** : to give impetus to ~ *vi* **1** : to move about by means of motive power **2** : to move with great speed or force

³**power** *adj* (1949) **1** : relating to or utilizing power ⟨plays a ~ game⟩; *also* : POWERFUL 1 ⟨a ~ critic⟩ **2** : of, relating to, or being a meal at which influential people discuss business or politics

power base *n* (1959) : a base of political support

pow·er·boat \'paù(-ə)r-ˌbōt\ *n* (1908) : MOTORBOAT

power broker *n* (1961) : a person (as in politics) able to exert strong influence through control of votes or individuals

pow·er-dive \-ˌdiv\ *vi* (1937) : to make a power dive ~ *vt* : to cause to power-dive

power dive *n* (1930) : a dive of an airplane accelerated by the power of the engine

pow·er·ful \'paù(-ə)r-fəl\ *adj* (15c) **1** : having great power, prestige, or influence **2** : leading to many or important deductions ⟨a ~ set of postulates⟩ — **pow·er·ful·ly** \-f(ə-)lē\ *adv*

power function *n* (1957) **1** : a function of a parameter under statistical test whose value for a particular value of the parameter is the probability of rejecting the null hypothesis if that value of the parameter happens to be true **2** : a function (as $f(x) = ax^k$) that equals the product of a constant and a power of the independent variable

pow·er·house \'paù(-ə)r-ˌhaùs\ *n* (ca. 1890) **1 a** : POWER PLANT 1 **b** : a source of influence or inspiration **2** : one having great power: as **a** : one having great drive, energy, or ability **b** : an athletic team characterized by strong aggressive play

pow·er·less \-ləs\ *adj* (15c) **1** : devoid of strength or resources **2** : lacking the authority or capacity to act — **pow·er·less·ly** *adv* — **pow·er·less·ness** *n*

power mower *n* (1940) : a motor-driven lawn mower

power of attorney (1747) : a legal instrument authorizing one to act as the attorney or agent of the grantor

power pack *n* (1936) : a unit for converting a power supply (as from a battery or household electrical circuit) to a voltage suitable for an electronic device

power plant *n* (1890) **1** : an electric utility generating station **2** : an engine and related parts supplying the motive power of a self-propelled object (as a rocket or automobile)

power play *n* (1947) **1** : a military, diplomatic, political, or administrative maneuver in which power is brought to bear **2 a** : a concentrated attack in football in which the ballcarrier is preceded by a mass of blockers **b** : a situation in ice hockey in which one team temporarily has more players on the ice than the other team because of a penalty

power politics *n pl but sing or pl in constr* (1926) : politics based primarily on the use of power (as military and economic strength) as a coercive force rather than on ethical precepts

power series *n* (1893) : an infinite series whose terms are successive integral powers of a variable multiplied by constants

power shovel *n* (1909) : a power-operated excavating machine consisting of a boom or crane that supports a lever arm with a large bucket at the end of it

power station *n* (1901) : POWER PLANT 1

power steering *n* (1932) : automotive steering with engine power used to amplify the torque applied at the steering wheel by the driver

power structure *n* (1950) **1** : a group of persons having control of an organization : ESTABLISHMENT **2** : the hierarchical interrelationships existing within a controlling group

power sweep *n* (1964) : SWEEP 7b

power take-off *n* (1929) : a supplementary mechanism (as on a tractor) enabling the engine power to be used to operate nonautomotive apparatus (as a pump or saw)

power train *n* (1943) : the intervening mechanism by which power is transmitted from an engine to a propeller or axle that it drives

power up *vt* (1970) : to cause to operate ⟨*power up* the computer⟩ — **pow·er-up** \'paù(-ə)r-ˌəp\ *n*

¹**pow·wow** \'paù-ˌwaù\ *n* [Narraganset *powwaw* or Massachuset *pauwau*] (1625) **1** : an American Indian medicine man **2 a** : an American Indian ceremony (as for victory in war) **b** : an American Indian social gathering or fair usu. including competitive dancing **3 a** : a social get-together **b** : a meeting for discussion

²**powwow** *vi* (1642) : to hold a powwow

¹**pox** \'päks\ *n, pl* **pox** *or* **pox·es** (1550) **1 a** : a virus disease (as chicken pox) characterized by pustules or eruptions **b** *archaic* : SMALLPOX **c** : SYPHILIS **2** : a disastrous evil ⟨a ~ on him⟩

²**pox** *vt* (1601) *archaic* : to infect with a pox and esp. with syphilis

pox·vi·rus \'päks-ˌvī-rəs\ *n* (1941) : any of a group of relatively large round, brick-shaped, or ovoid DNA-containing animal viruses (as the causative agent of smallpox) that have a fluffy appearance caused by a covering of tubules and threads

poz·zo·la·na \ˌpät-sə-'lä-nə\ *or* **poz·zo·lan** \'pät-sə-lən\ *n* [It *pozzolana*] (1706) : finely divided siliceous or siliceous and aluminous material that reacts chemically with slaked lime at ordinary temperature and in the presence of moisture to form a strong slow-hardening cement — **poz·zo·la·nic** \ˌpät-sə-'la-nik, -'lä-\ *adj*

PPO \ˌpē-(ˌ)pē-'ō\ *n, pl* **PPOs** [preferred provider organization] (1983) : an organization providing health care that gives economic incentives to the individual purchaser of a health-care contract to patronize certain physicians, laboratories, and hospitals that agree to supervision and reduced fees — compare HMO

prac·ti·ca·ble \'prak-ti-kə-bəl\ *adj* (1670) **1** : capable of being put into practice or of being done or accomplished : FEASIBLE **2** : capable of being used : USABLE *syn* see POSSIBLE — **prac·ti·ca·bil·i·ty** \ˌprak-

---

ti-kə-'bi-lə-tē\ *n* — **prac·ti·ca·ble·ness** \'prak-ti-kə-bəl-nəs\ *n* — **prac·ti·ca·bly** \-blē\ *adv*

¹**prac·ti·cal** \'prak-ti-kəl\ *adj* [ME, fr. LL *practicus*, fr. Gk *praktikos*, fr. *prassein* to pass over, fare, do; akin to Gk *peran* to pass through — more at FARE] (15c) **1 a** : of, relating to, or manifested in practice or action : not theoretical or ideal ⟨a ~ question⟩ ⟨for all ~ purposes⟩ **b** : being such in practice or effect : VIRTUAL ⟨a ~ failure⟩ **2** : actively engaged in some course of action or occupation ⟨a ~ farmer⟩ **3** : capable of being put to use or account : USEFUL ⟨he had a ~ knowledge of French⟩ **4 a** : disposed to action as opposed to speculation or abstraction **b** (1) : qualified by practice or practical training ⟨a good ~ mechanic⟩ (2) : designed to supplement theoretical training by experience **5** : concerned with voluntary action and ethical decisions ⟨~ reason⟩ — **prac·ti·cal·i·ty** \ˌprak-ti-'ka-lə-tē\ *n* — **prac·ti·cal·ness** \'prak-ti-kəl-nəs\ *n*

²**practical** *n* (1925) : an examination requiring demonstration of some practical skill ⟨a zoology ~⟩

practical art *n* (ca. 1925) : an art (as woodworking) that serves ordinary or material needs — usu. used in pl.

practical joke *n* (ca. 1847) : a prank intended to trick or embarrass someone or cause physical discomfort — **practical joker** *n*

prac·ti·cal·ly \'prak-ti-k(ə-)lē\ *adv* (1623) **1** : in a practical manner ⟨look ~ at the problem⟩ **2** : ALMOST, NEARLY ⟨~ everyone went to the party⟩

practical nurse *n* (1921) : a nurse who cares for the sick professionally without having the training or experience required of a registered nurse; *esp* : LICENSED PRACTICAL NURSE

practical theology *n* (ca. 1909) : the study of the institutional activities of religion (as preaching, church administration, pastoral care, and liturgics)

¹**prac·tice** *or* **prac·tise** \'prak-təs\ *vb* **prac·ticed** *or* **prac·tised; prac·tic·ing** *or* **prac·tis·ing** [ME *practisen*, fr. MF *practiser*, fr. *practique*, *pratique* practice, n., fr. LL *practice*, fr. Gk *praktikē*, fr. fem. of *praktikos*] *vt* (14c) **1 a** : CARRY OUT, APPLY ⟨~ what you preach⟩ **b** : to do or perform often, customarily, or habitually ⟨~ politeness⟩ **c** : to be professionally engaged in ⟨~ medicine⟩ **2 a** : to perform or work at repeatedly so as to become proficient ⟨~ the act⟩ **b** : to train by repeated exercises ⟨~ pupils in penmanship⟩ **3** *obs* : PLOT ~ *vi* **1** : to do repeated exercises for proficiency **2** : to pursue a profession actively **3** *archaic* : INTRIGUE **4** : to do something customarily **5** : to take advantage of someone ⟨he *practised* on their credulity with huge success —*Times Lit. Supp.*⟩ — **prac·tic·er** *n*

²**practice** *also* **practise** *n* (15c) **1 a** : actual performance or application ⟨ready to carry out in ~ what they advocated in principle⟩ **b** : a repeated or customary action ⟨had this irritating ~⟩ **c** : the usual way of doing something ⟨local ~s⟩ **d** : the form, manner, and order of conducting legal suits and prosecutions **2 a** : systematic exercise for proficiency ⟨~ makes perfect⟩ **b** : the condition of being proficient through systematic exercise ⟨get in ~⟩ **3 a** : the continuous exercise of a profession **b** : a professional business; *esp* : one constituting an incorporeal property *syn* see HABIT

prac·ticed *or* **prac·tised** \'prak-təst\ *adj* (1568) **1** : EXPERIENCED, SKILLED **2** : learned by practice

prac·tice–teach \'prak-təs-ˈtēch\ *vi* **-taught** \-'tòt\; **-teach·ing** [back-formation fr. *practice teaching*] (1952) : to engage in practice teaching — **practice teacher** *n*

practice teaching *n* (ca. 1913) : teaching by a student under the supervision of an experienced teacher

prac·tic·ing *or* **prac·tis·ing** *adj* (ca. 1625) : actively engaged in a specified career or way of life ⟨a ~ physician⟩

prac·ti·cum \'prak-ti-kəm\ *n* [G *Praktikum*, fr. LL *practicus* practical] (ca. 1909) : a course of study designed esp. for the preparation of teachers and clinicians that involves the supervised practical application of previously studied theory

prac·ti·tion·er \prak-'ti-sh(ə-)nər\ *n* [alter. of earlier *practician*, fr. ME (Sc) *pratician*, fr. MF *practicien*, fr. *pratique*] (1535) **1** : one who practices; *esp* : one who practices a profession **2** *Christian Science* : an authorized healer

prae·ci·pe \'pre-sə-ˌpē, 'prē-\ *n* [ME *presepe*, fr. ML *praecipe*, fr. L imper. of *praecipere* to instruct — more at PRECEPT] (15c) **1** : any of various legal writs commanding a person to do something or to appear and show cause why he or she should not **2** : a written order requesting a clerk or prothonotary of a court to issue a writ and specifying the contents of the writ

prae·di·al *var of* PREDIAL

prae·mu·ni·re \ˌprē-myü-'nīr-ē\ *n* [ME *praemunire facias*, fr. ML, that you cause to warn; fr. prominent words in the writ] (1529) : an offense against the English Crown punishable chiefly by forfeiture and orig. committed by asserting papal legal supremacy in England

prae·no·men \prē-'nō-mən\ *n, pl* **-nomens** *or* **-no·mi·na** \-'nä-mə-nə, -'nō-\ [L, fr. *prae-* pre- + *nomen* name — more at NAME] (1706) : the first of the usual three names of an ancient Roman male

prae·sid·i·um *var of* PRESIDIUM

prae·tor \'prē-tər\ *n* [ME *pretor*, fr. L *praetor*] (15c) : an ancient Roman magistrate ranking below a consul and having chiefly judicial functions — **prae·to·ri·al** \prē-'tōr-ē-əl, -'tòr-\ *adj* — **prae·tor·ship** \'prē-tər-ˌship\ *n*

prae·to·ri·an \prē-'tōr-ē-ən, -'tòr-\ *adj* (15c) **1** *often cap* : of, forming, or resembling the Roman imperial bodyguard **2** : of or relating to a praetor — **praetorian** *n, often cap*

prag·mat·ic \prag-'ma-tik\ *also* **prag·mat·i·cal** \-ti-kəl\ *adj* [L *pragmaticus* skilled in law or business, fr. Gk *pragmatikos*, fr. *pragmat-, pragma* deed, fr. *prassein* to do — more at PRACTICAL] (1616) **1** *archaic* **a** (1) : BUSY (2) : OFFICIOUS **b** : OPINIONATED **2** : relating to matters of fact or practical affairs often to the exclusion of intellectual or artistic matters : practical as opposed to idealistic ⟨~ men of power have had no time or inclination to deal with ... social morality —K. B. Clark⟩ **3** : relating to or being in accordance with philosophical pragmatism — **pragmatic** *n* — **prag·mat·i·cal·ly** \-ti-k(ə-)lē\ *adv*

prag·ma·ti·cism \prag-'ma-tə-ˌsi-zəm\ *n* (1905) : the philosophic doctrine of C. S. Peirce — **prag·ma·ti·cist** \-sist\ *n*

prag·mat·ics \prag-'ma-tiks\ *n pl but sing or pl in constr* (1937) **1** : a branch of semiotic that deals with the relation between signs or linguistic expressions and their users **2** : linguistics concerned with the relationship of sentences to the environment in which they occur

pragmatic sanction *n* (1643) : a solemn decree of a sovereign on a matter of primary importance and with the force of fundamental law

prag·ma·tism \'prag-mə-ˌti-zəm\ *n* (ca. 1864) **1** : a practical approach to problems and affairs ⟨tried to strike a balance between principles and ∼⟩ **2** : an American movement in philosophy founded by C. S. Peirce and William James and marked by the doctrines that the meaning of conceptions is to be sought in their practical bearings, that the function of thought is to guide action, and that truth is preeminently to be tested by the practical consequences of belief — **prag·ma·tist** \-mə-tist\ *adj or n* — **prag·ma·tis·tic** \ˌprag-mə-'tis-tik\ *adj*

prai·rie \'prer-ē\ *n, often attrib* [F, fr. (assumed) VL *prataria*, fr. L *pratum* meadow] (ca. 1682) **1** : land in or predominantly in grass **2** : a tract of grassland: as **a** : a large area of level or rolling land in the Mississippi valley that in its natural uncultivated state usu. has deep fertile soil, a cover of tall coarse grasses, and few trees **b** : one of the dry treeless plateaus east of the Rocky Mountains that merge on their east side with the prairies proper and are characterized by shorter grasses and drier less fertile soil

prairie chicken *n* (1691) : a grouse (*Tympanuchus cupido*) chiefly of the prairies of the central U.S.; *also* : a closely related smaller grouse (*T. pallidicinctus*)

prairie dog *n* (1774) : any of a genus (*Cynomys*) of gregarious burrowing rodents of the squirrel family chiefly of central and western U.S. plains; *esp* : a black-tailed rodent (*C. ludovicianus*) that usu. lives in extensive colonial burrows

prairie schooner *n* (1841) : a covered wagon used by pioneers in cross-country travel — called also *prairie wagon*

prairie soil *n* (1817) : any of a zonal group of soils developed in a temperate relatively humid climate under tall grass

prairie wolf *n* (1804) : COYOTE

prairie dog

¹**praise** \'prāz\ *vb* **praised; prais·ing** [ME, fr. OF *preisier* to prize, praise, fr. LL *pretiare* to prize, fr. L *pretium* price — more at PRICE] *vt* (13c) **1** : to express a favorable judgment of : COMMEND **2** : to glorify (a god or saint) esp. by the attribution of perfections ∼ *vi* : to express praise — **prais·er** *n*

²**praise** *n* (14c) **1** **a** : an expression of approval : COMMENDATION **b** : WORSHIP **2 a** : VALUE, MERIT **b** *archaic* : one that is praised

praise·wor·thy \'prāz-ˌwər-thē\ *adj* (15c) : LAUDABLE — **praise·wor·thi·ly** \-thə-lē\ *adv* — **praise·wor·thi·ness** \-thē-nəs\ *n*

Pra·krit \'prä-ˌkrit, -ˌkrət\ *n* [Skt *prākṛta* natural, vulgar] (1766) : any or all of the ancient Indo-Aryan languages or dialects other than Sanskrit — see INDO-EUROPEAN LANGUAGES table

pra·line \'prä-ˌlēn, 'prā-, 'prò-\ *n* [F, fr. Count Plessis-*Praslin* †1675 Fr. soldier] (1723) : a confection of nuts and sugar: **a** : almonds cooked in boiling sugar until brown and crisp **b** : a patty of creamy brown sugar and pecan meats

prall·tril·ler \'präl-ˌtri-lər\ *n* [G, fr. *prallen* to rebound + *Triller* trill] (ca. 1841) : a musical ornament made by a quick alternation of a principal tone with the tone above

¹**pram** \'präm, 'pram\ *n* [MD *praem* & MLG *prām*] (1548) : a small lightweight nearly flat-bottomed boat with a broad transom and usu. squared-off bow

²**pram** \'pram\ *n* [by shortening & alter. fr. *perambulator*] (1884) *chiefly Brit* : BABY CARRIAGE

¹**prance** \'pran(t)s\ *vb* **pranced; pranc·ing** [ME *prauncen*] *vi* (14c) **1** : to spring from the hind legs or move by so doing **2** : to ride on a prancing horse **3** : to walk or move in a spirited manner : STRUT; *also* : to dance about ∼ *vt* : to cause (a horse) to prance — **pranc·er** \'pran(t)-sər\ *n*

²**prance** *n* (1751) : an act or instance of prancing; *specif* : a prancing movement

pran·di·al \'pran-dē-əl\ *adj* [L *prandium* late breakfast, luncheon] (1820) : of or relating to a meal

prang \'praŋ\ *vt* [origin unknown] (1941) *chiefly Brit* : to have an accident with : cause to crash — **prang** *n, chiefly Brit*

¹**prank** \'praŋk\ *n* [obs. *prank* to play tricks] (ca. 1529) : TRICK: **a** *obs* : a malicious act **b** : a mildly mischievous act **c** : a ludicrous act

²**prank** *vb* [prob. fr. D *pronken* to strut; akin to MHG *gebrunkel* glitter of metal] *vi* (15c) : to show oneself off ∼ *vt* : to dress or adorn gaily or showily

prank·ish \'praŋ-kish\ *adj* (1827) **1** : full of pranks ⟨a ∼ child⟩ **2** : having the nature of a prank ⟨∼ acts⟩ — **prank·ish·ly** *adv* — **prank·ish·ness** *n*

prank·ster \'praŋ(k)-stər\ *n* (1927) : a person who plays pranks

prase \'prāz, 'präs\ *n* [F, fr. L *prasius*, fr. Gk *prasios*, adj., of the color of a leek, fr. *prason* leek; akin to L *porrum* leek] (1788) : a chalcedony that is translucent and yellowish green

pra·seo·dym·i·um \ˌprā-zē-ō-'di-mē-əm, ˌprä-sē-\ *n* [NL, alter. of *praseodidymium*, irreg. fr. Gk *prasios*, adj. + NL *didymium* didymium] (1885) : a yellowish white trivalent metallic element of the rare-earth group used chiefly in the form of its salts in coloring glass greenish yellow — see ELEMENT table

prate \'prāt\ *vi* **prat·ed; prat·ing** [ME, fr. MD; akin to MLG *pratten* to pout] (15c) : to talk long and idly : CHATTER — **prate** *n* — **prat·er** *n* — **prat·ing·ly** \'prā-tiŋ-lē\ *adv*

prat·fall \'prat-ˌfòl\ *n* [*prat* buttocks + *fall*] (1938) **1** : a fall on the buttocks **2** : a humiliating mishap or blunder

pra·tin·cole \'pra-t²n-ˌkōl, 'prä-, -tiŋ-\ *n* [ultim. fr. L *pratum* meadow + *incola* inhabitant, fr. *in-* + *colere* to cultivate — more at WHEEL] (1773) : any of several Old World shore-inhabiting birds (genera *Glareolus* and *Stiltia* of the family Glareolidae) with a short bill and a forked tail

pra·tique \pra-'tēk\ *n* [F, lit., practice — more at PRACTICE] (1609) : clearance given an incoming ship by the health authority of a port

¹**prat·tle** \'pra-t²l\ *vb* **prat·tled; prat·tling** \'prat-liŋ, 'prä-t²l-iŋ\ [LG *pratelen*; akin to MD *praten* to prate] *vi* (1532) **1** : PRATE **2** : to utter or make meaningless sounds suggestive of the chatter of children : BAB-

BLE ∼ *vt* : to say in an unaffected or childish manner — **prat·tler** \'prat-lər, 'prä-t²l-ər\ *n* — **prat·tling·ly** \-liŋ-lē, -t²l-iŋ-\ *adv*

²**prattle** *n* (1555) **1** : trifling or empty talk **2** : a sound that is meaningless, repetitive, and suggestive of the chatter of children

prau \'praù, 'prä-ˌü\ *n* [Malay *pěrahu*] (1582) : any of various Indonesian boats usu. without a deck that are propelled esp. by sails or paddles

¹**prawn** \'pròn, 'prän\ *n* [ME *prane*] (15c) : any of numerous widely distributed edible decapod crustaceans (as of the genera *Pandalus* and *Peneus*) that resemble shrimps and have large compressed abdomens; *also* : SHRIMP

²**prawn** *vi* (1886) : to fish for or with prawns — **prawn·er** *n*

prax·e·ol·o·gy \ˌprak-sē-'ä-lə-jē\ *n* [alter. of earlier *praxiology*, fr. *praxis* + *-o-* + *-logy*] (1904) : the study of human action and conduct — **prax·e·o·log·i·cal** \-sē-ə-'lä-ji-kəl\ *adj*

prax·is \'prak-səs\ *n, pl* **prax·es** \-ˌsēz\ [ML, fr. Gk, doing, action, fr. *prassein* to do, practice — more at PRACTICAL] (1581) : ACTION, PRACTICE: as **a** : exercise or practice of an art, science, or skill **b** : customary practice or conduct

pray \'prā\ *vb* [ME, fr. OF *preier*, fr. L *precari*, fr. *prec-, prex* request, prayer; akin to OHG *frāgēn* to ask, Skt *pṛcchati* he asks] *vt* (13c) **1** : ENTREAT, IMPLORE — often used as a function word in introducing a question, request, or plea ⟨∼ be careful⟩ **2** : to get or bring by praying ∼ *vi* **1** : to make a request in a humble manner **2** : to address God or a god with adoration, confession, supplication, or thanksgiving

¹**prayer** \'prar, 'prer\ *n, often attrib* [ME, fr. MF *preiere*, fr. ML *precaria*, fr. L, fem. of *precarius* obtained by entreaty, fr. *prec-, prex*] (14c) **1 a** (1) : an address (as a petition) to God or a god in word or thought ⟨said a ∼ for the success of the voyage⟩ (2) : a set order of words used in praying **b** : an earnest request or wish **2** : the act or practice of praying to God or a god ⟨kneeling in ∼⟩ **3** : a religious service consisting chiefly of prayers — often used in pl. **4** : something prayed for **5** : a slight chance ⟨haven't got a ∼⟩

²**pray·er** \'prā-ər, 'pret-(-ə)r\ *n* [ME *prayere*, fr. *prayen* to pray + ²*-er*] (14c) : one that prays : SUPPLIANT

prayer beads \'prar-, 'prer-\ *n pl* (1630) : a string of beads by which prayers are counted; *specif* : ROSARY

prayer book *n* (ca. 1597) : a book containing prayers and often other forms and directions for worship

prayer·ful \'prar-fəl, 'prer-\ *adj* (1626) **1** : DEVOUT **2** : EARNEST, SINCERE — **prayer·ful·ly** \-fə-lē\ *adv* — **prayer·ful·ness** *n*

prayer meeting *n* (1780) : a usu. informal gathering for worship and prayer; *esp* : a Protestant worship service usu. held on a week night — called also *prayer service*

prayer rug *n* (ca. 1890) : a small Oriental rug used by Muslims to kneel on when praying

prayer shawl *n* (1905) : TALLITH

prayer wheel *n* (1814) : a cylinder of wood or metal that revolves on an axis and contains written prayers and that is used in praying by Tibetan Buddhists

praying mantis *n* (ca. 1890) : MANTIS; *esp* : a European mantis (*Mantis religiosa*) that has been introduced into the U.S. — called also *praying mantid*

pre- *prefix* [ME, fr. OF & L; OF, fr. L *prae-*, fr. *prae* in front of, before — more at FOR] **1 a** (1) : earlier than : prior to : before ⟨Precambrian⟩ ⟨prehistoric⟩ (2) : preparatory or prerequisite to ⟨premedical⟩ **b** : in advance : beforehand ⟨precancel⟩ ⟨prepay⟩ **2** : in front of : anterior to ⟨preaxial⟩ ⟨premolar⟩

pre·ad·mis·sion	pre·crease	pre·fro·zen
pre·adult	pre·cri·sis	pre·game
pre·ag·ri·cul·tur·al	pre·cut	pre·gen·i·tal
pre·an·es·thet·ic	pre·dawn	pre·har·vest
pre·an·nounce	pre·de·fine	pre·head·ache
pre·ap·prove	pre·de·liv·ery	pre·hir·ing
pre·ar·range	pre·de·par·ture	pre·hol·i·day
pre·ar·range·ment	pre·des·ig·nate	pre·hu·man
pre·as·sem·bled	pre·de·val·u·a·tion	pre·in·au·gu·ral
pre·as·sign	pre·de·vel·op·ment	pre·in·cor·po·ra·tion
pre·bake	pre·din·ner	pre·in·duc·tion
pre·bat·tle	pre·dis·charge	pre·in·dus·tri·al
pre·bib·li·cal	pre·dis·cov·ery	pre·in·ter·view
pre·book	pre·dive	pre·in·va·sion
pre·break·fast	pre·drill	pre·kin·der·gar·ten
pre·cap·i·tal·ist	pre·dy·nas·tic	pre·launch
pre·chill	pre·elec·tion	pre·life
pre·Christ·mas	pre·elec·tric	pre·lit·er·ary
pre·clear	pre·em·bar·go	pre·log·i·cal
pre·clear·ance	pre·em·ploy·ment	pre·lunch
pre·code	pre·en·roll·ment	pre·lun·cheon
pre·co·i·tal	pre·erect	pre·made
pre·col·lege	pre·es·tab·lish	pre·man·u·fac·ture
pre·col·le·giate	pre·eth·i·cal	pre·mar·i·tal
pre·co·lo·nial	pre·ex·per·i·ment	pre·mar·i·tal·ly
pre·com·bus·tion	pre·fade	pre·mar·ket
pre·com·mit·ment	pre·fas·cist	pre·mar·ket·ing
pre·com·pute	pre·feu·dal	pre·mar·riage
pre·com·put·er	pre·fight	pre·meal
pre·con·cert	pre·file	pre·mea·sure
pre·con·quest	pre·filled	pre·me·di·e·val
pre·con·so·nan·tal	pre·fi·nance	pre·meet
pre·con·struct·ed	pre·fire	pre·mei·ot·ic
pre·con·ven·tion	pre·flame	pre·men·o·paus·al
pre·con·vic·tion	pre·flight	pre·merg·er
pre·cool	pre·for·mat	pre·mi·gra·tion
pre·cop·u·la·to·ry	pre·for·mu·late	pre·mod·ern
pre·crash	pre·fresh·man	pre·mod·i·fi·ca·tion

\ə\ abut \²\ kitten, F table \ər\ further \a\ ash \ā\ ace \ä\ mop, mar \aù\ out \ch\ chin \e\ bet \ē\ easy \g\ go \i\ hit \ī\ ice \j\ job \ŋ\ sing \ō\ go \ò\ law \òi\ boy \th\ thin \th\ the \ü\ loot \ù\ foot \y\ yet \zh\ vision \à, ḵ, ⁿ, œ, œ̄, ue, ūe, ᵞ\ see Guide to Pronunciation

pre·mod·i·fy
pre·moist·en
pre·mold
pre·molt
pre·mor·al
pre·my·cot·ic
pre·noon
pre·no·ti·fi·ca·tion
pre·no·ti·fy
pre·num·ber
pre·open·ing
pre·op·er·a·tion·al
pre·or·der
pre·paste
pre·per·for·mance
pre·pill
pre·plan
pre·por·tion
pre·pre·pared
pre·pres·i·den·tial
pre·price
pre·pro·duc·tion
pre·pro·gram
pre·psy·che·del·ic
pre·pub·li·ca·tion
pre·punch
pre·pu·pal
pre·pur·chase
pre·qual·i·fi·ca·tion
pre·qual·i·fy
pre·race

pre·re·ces·sion
pre·re·cord·ed
pre·re·hears·al
pre·re·lease
pre·re·quire
pre·re·tire·ment
pre·re·turn
pre·re·view
pre·re·vi·sion·ist
pre·rev·o·lu·tion
pre·rev·o·lu·tion·ary
pre·rinse
pre·ri·ot
pre·rock
pre·ro·man·tic
pre·sale
pre·sched·ule
pre·screen
pre·sea·son
pre·sen·tence
pre·sen·tenc·ing
pre·ser·vice
pre·set
pre·set·tle·ment
pre·show
pre·slaugh·ter
pre·sleep
pre·slice
pre·song
pre·spec·i·fy
pre·split
pre·stamp

pre·ster·il·ize
pre·stor·age
pre·strike
pre·struc·ture
pre·sum·mit
pre·sur·gery
pre·sweet·en
pre·symp·tom·at·ic
pre·tape
pre·tax
pre·tech·no·log·i·cal
pre·tele·vi·sion
pre·ter·mi·na·tion
pre·the·a·ter
pre·tour·na·ment
pre·train
pre·trav·el
pre·treat
pre·treat·ment
pre·trial
pre·trimmed
pre·type
pre·uni·fi·ca·tion
pre·uni·ver·si·ty
pre·vi·a·ble
pre·war
pre·warn
pre·wash
pre·wean·ing
pre·work
pre·wrap

preach \'prēch\ vb [ME prechen, fr. OF prechier, fr. LL praedicare, fr. L, to proclaim publicly, fr. prae- pre- + dicare to proclaim — more at DICTION] vi (13c) 1 : to deliver a sermon 2 : to urge acceptance or abandonment of an idea or course of action; specif : to exhort in an officious or tiresome manner ~ vt 1 : to set forth in a sermon ⟨~ the gospel⟩ 2 : to advocate earnestly ⟨~ed revolution⟩ 3 : to deliver (as a sermon) publicly 4 : to bring, put, or affect by preaching ⟨~ed the . . . church out of debt —Amer. Guide Series: Va.⟩ — **preach·er** n — **preach·ing·ly** \'prē-chiŋ-lē\ adv

preach·i·fy \'prē-cha-ˌfī\ vi -**ified**; -**ify·ing** (1775) : to preach ineptly or tediously

preach·ment \'prēch-mənt\ n (14c) 1 : the act or practice of preaching 2 : SERMON, EXHORTATION; specif : a tedious or unwelcome one

preachy \'prē-chē\ adj **preach·i·er**; -est (1819) : marked by obvious moral exhortation : DIDACTIC — **preach·i·ly** \-cha-lē\ adv — **preach·i·ness** \-chē-nas\ n

pre·ad·ap·ta·tion \ˌprē-ˌa-ˌdap-'tā-shən\ n (1886) 1 : the possession by an organism or taxonomic group of characters that are not adapted to the ancestral environment but favor survival in some other environment 2 : a preadaptive character

pre·adapt·ed \ˌprē-ə-'dap-təd\ adj (1915) : characterized by preadaptation

pre·adap·tive \-'dap-tiv\ adj (1915) : of, relating to, or characterized by preadaptation

pre·ad·o·les·cence \ˌprē-ˌa-d²l-'e-s²n(t)s\ n (1930) : the period of human development just preceding adolescence; specif : the period between the approximate ages of 9 and 12 — **pre·ad·o·les·cent** \-s²nt\ adj or n

pre·am·ble \'prē-ˌam-bəl, prē-'\ n [ME, fr. MF preambule, fr. ML preambulum, fr. LL, neut. of praeambulus walking in front of, fr. L prae- + ambulare to walk] (14c) 1 : an introductory statement; esp : the introductory part of a constitution or statute that usu. states the reasons for and intent of the law 2 : an introductory fact or circumstance; esp : one indicating what is to follow

pre·amp \'prē-ˌamp\ n (1949) : PREAMPLIFIER

pre·am·pli·fi·er \(ˌ)prē-'am-plə-ˌfī-(ə)r\ n (1935) : an amplifier designed to amplify extremely weak electrical signals before they are fed to additional amplifier circuits

pre·atom·ic \ˌprē-ə-'tä-mik\ adj (1914) : of or relating to a time before the use of the atomic bomb and atomic energy

pre·ax·i·al \(ˌ)prē-'ak-sē-əl\ adj (1872) : situated in front of an axis of the body

preb·end \'pre-bənd\ n [ME prebende, fr. MF, fr. ML praebenda, fr. LL, subsistence allowance granted by the state, fr. L, fem. of praebendus, gerundive of praebēre to offer, fr. prae- + habēre to hold — more at GIVE] (15c) 1 : a stipend furnished by a cathedral or collegiate church to a clergyman (as a canon) in its chapter 2 : PREBENDARY — **pre·ben·dal** \pri-'ben-d²l, 'pre-bən-\ adj

preb·en·dary \'pre-bən-ˌder-ē\ n, pl -**dar·ies** (15c) 1 : a clergyman receiving a prebend for officiating and serving in the church 2 : an honorary canon in a cathedral chapter

pre·bi·o·log·i·cal \ˌprē-ˌbī-ə-'lä-ji-kəl\ also **pre·bi·o·log·ic** \-jik\ adj (1953) : of, relating to, or being chemical or environmental precursors of the origin of life ⟨~ molecules⟩

pre·bi·ot·ic \ˌprē-bī-'ä-tik\ adj (1958) : PREBIOLOGICAL

pre·cal·cu·lus \(ˌ)prē-'kal-kyə-ləs\ adj (1964) : relating to or being mathematical prerequisites for the study of calculus — **precalculus** n

Pre·cam·bri·an \(ˌ)prē-'kam-brē-ən, -'kam-\ adj (1864) : of, relating to, or being the earliest era of geological history or the corresponding system of rocks characterized esp. by the appearance of single-celled organisms and is equivalent to the Archean and Proterozoic eons — see GEOLOGIC TIME table — **Precambrian** n

¹**pre·can·cel** \(ˌ)prē-'kan(t)-səl\ vt (1921) : to cancel (a postage stamp) in advance of use — **pre·can·cel·la·tion** \ˌprē-ˌkan(t)-sə-'lā-shən\ n

²**precancel** n (1929) : a precanceled postage stamp

pre·can·cer·ous \(ˌ)prē-'kan(t)s-rəs, -'kan(t)-sə-\ adj [ISV] (1882) : tending to become cancerous ⟨a ~ lesion⟩

pre·car·i·ous \pri-'kar-ē-əs, -'ker-\ adj [L precarius obtained by entreaty, uncertain — more at PRAYER] (1646) 1 : depending on the will or pleasure of another 2 : dependent on uncertain premises : DUBIOUS ⟨~ generalizations⟩ 3 a : dependent on chance circumstances, unknown conditions, or uncertain developments b : characterized by a lack of security or stability that threatens with danger syn see DANGEROUS — **pre·car·i·ous·ly** adv — **pre·car·i·ous·ness** n

pre·cast \ˌprē-'kast, 'prē-ˌ\ adj (1914) : being concrete that is cast in the form of a structural element (as a panel or beam) before being placed in final position

prec·a·to·ry \'pre-kə-ˌtōr-ē, -ˌtȯr-\ adj [LL precatorius, fr. L precari to pray — more at PRAY] (1636) : expressing a wish

pre·cau·tion \pri-'kȯ-shən\ n [F précaution, fr. LL praecaution-, praecautio, fr. L praecavēre to guard against, fr. prae- + cavēre to be on one's guard — more at HEAR] (1603) 1 : care taken in advance : FORESIGHT ⟨warned of the need for ~⟩ 2 : a measure taken beforehand to prevent harm or secure good : SAFEGUARD — **pre·cau·tion·ary** \-shə-ˌner-ē\ adj

pre·cede \pri-'sēd\ vb **pre·ced·ed**; **pre·ced·ing** [ME, fr. MF preceder, fr. L praecedere, fr. prae- pre- + cedere to go] vt (15c) 1 : to surpass in rank, dignity, or importance 2 : to be, go, or come ahead or in front of 3 : to be earlier than 4 : to cause to be preceded : PREFACE ~ vi : to go or come before

pre·ce·dence \'pre-sə-dən(t)s, pri-'sē-d²n(t)s\ n (1588) 1 a obs : ANTECEDENT b : the fact of preceding in time 2 a : the right to superior honor on a ceremonial or formal occasion b : the order of ceremonial or formal preference c : priority of importance ⟨your safety takes ~⟩

pre·ce·den·cy \-d²n(t)-sē, -d²n(t)-sē\ n (1612) : PRECEDENCE

¹**prec·e·dent** \pri-'sē-d²nt, 'pre-sə-dənt\ adj [ME, fr. MF, fr. L praecedent-, praecedens, prp. of praecedere] (15c) : prior in time, order, arrangement, or significance

²**prec·e·dent** \'pre-sə-dənt\ n (15c) 1 : an earlier occurrence of something similar 2 a : something done or said that may serve as an example or rule to authorize or justify a subsequent act of the same or an analogous kind ⟨a verdict that had no ~⟩ b : the convention established by such a precedent or by long practice 3 : a person or thing that serves as a model

pre·ced·ing \pri-'sē-diŋ\ adj (15c) : that immediately precedes in time or place ⟨the ~ day⟩ ⟨~ paragraphs⟩

syn PRECEDING, ANTECEDENT, FOREGOING, PREVIOUS, PRIOR, FORMER, ANTERIOR mean being before. PRECEDING usu. implies being immediately before in time or in place ⟨the preceding sentence⟩. ANTECEDENT applies to order in time and may suggest a causal relation ⟨conditions antecedent to the revolution⟩. FOREGOING applies chiefly to statements ⟨the foregoing remarks⟩. PREVIOUS and PRIOR imply existing or occurring earlier, but PRIOR often adds an implication of greater importance ⟨a child from a previous marriage⟩ ⟨a prior obligation⟩. FORMER implies always a definite comparison or contrast with something that is latter ⟨the former name of the company⟩. ANTERIOR applies to position before or ahead of usu. in space, sometimes in time or order ⟨the anterior lobe of the brain⟩.

pre·cen·sor \(ˌ)prē-'sen(t)-sər\ vt (1942) : to censor (a publication or film) before its release to the public

pre·cen·tor \pri-'sen-tər\ n [LL praecentor, fr. L praecinere to sing before, fr. prae- + canere to sing — more at CHANT] (1613) : a leader of the singing of a choir or congregation — **pre·cen·to·ri·al** \ˌprē-ˌsen-'tȯr-ē-əl, -'tȯr-\ adj — **pre·cen·tor·ship** \pri-'sen-tər-ˌship\ n

pre·cept \'prē-ˌsept\ n [ME, fr. L praeceptum, fr. neut. of praeceptus, pp. of praecipere to take beforehand, instruct, fr. prae- + capere to take — more at HEAVE] (14c) 1 : a command or principle intended esp. as a general rule of action 2 : an order issued by legally constituted authority to a subordinate official syn see LAW

pre·cep·tive \pri-'sep-tiv\ adj (15c) : giving precepts : DIDACTIC

pre·cep·tor \pri-'sep-tər, 'prē-ˌ\ n (15c) 1 a : TEACHER, TUTOR b : the headmaster or principal of a school 2 : the head of a preceptory of Knights Templars — **pre·cep·tor·ship** \-ˌship\ n

¹**pre·cep·to·ri·al** \ˌprē-ˌsep-'tōr-ē-əl, ˌprē-, -'tȯr-\ adj (ca. 1741) : of, relating to, or making use of preceptors

²**preceptorial** n (ca. 1952) : a college course that emphasizes independent reading, discussion in small groups, and individual conferences with the teacher

pre·cep·to·ry \pri-'sep-t(ə-)rē, 'prē-ˌ\ n, pl -**ries** (1540) 1 : a subordinate house or community of the Knights Templars; broadly : COMMANDERY 1 2 : COMMANDERY 2

pre·cess \prē-'ses, 'prē-ˌ\ vb [back-formation fr. precession] vi (1892) : to progress with a movement of precession ~ vt : to cause to process

pre·ces·sion \prē-'se-shən\ n [NL praecession-, praecessio, fr. ML, act of preceding, fr. L praecedere to precede] (1879) : a comparatively slow gyration of the rotation axis of a spinning body about another line intersecting it so as to describe a cone — **pre·ces·sion·al** \-'sesh-nəl, -'se-shə-n²l\ adj

precession of the equinoxes (1621) : a slow westward motion of the equinoxes along the ecliptic caused by the gravitational action of sun and moon upon the protuberant matter about the earth's equator

pre–Chel·le·an \(ˌ)prē-'she-lē-ən\ adj (1916) : of or relating to a Lower Paleolithic culture preceding the Abbevillian and characterized by crudely flaked stone hand axes

pre–Chris·tian \-'kris-chən, -'krish-\ adj (1828) : of, relating to, or being a time before the beginning of the Christian era

pré·cieux \prā-syœ\ or **pré·cieuse** \-syœz\ adj [F précieux, masc., & précieuse, fem., lit., precious, fr. MF precios] (1727) : PRECIOUS 3

pre·cinct \'prē-ˌsiŋ(k)t\ n [ME, fr. ML praecinctum, fr. L, neut. of praecinctus, pp. of praecingere to gird about, fr. prae- pre- + cingere to gird — more at CINCTURE] (15c) 1 : a part of a territory with definite bounds or functions often established for administrative purposes : DISTRICT: as a : a subdivision of a county, town, city, or ward for election purposes b : a division of a city for police control 2 a : an enclosure bounded by the walls of a building — often used in pl. b : a sphere of thought, action, or influence — often used in pl. 3 a pl : the region immediately surrounding a place : ENVIRONS b : PLACE, LOCALE 4 : BOUNDARY — often used in pl. ⟨a ruined tower within the ~s of the squire's grounds —T. L. Peacock⟩

pre·ci·os·i·ty \ˌpre-shē-'ä-sə-tē, -sē-\ n, pl -**ties** (1866) 1 : fastidious refinement 2 : an instance of preciosity

¹**pre·cious** \'pre-shəs\ adj [ME, fr. MF precios, fr. L pretiosus, fr. pretium price — more at PRICE] (13c) 1 : of great value or high price 2 : highly esteemed or cherished 3 : excessively refined : AFFECTED 4 : GREAT, THOROUGHGOING ⟨~ scoundrel⟩ — **pre·cious·ness** n

²precious *adv* (1595) : VERY, EXTREMELY ⟨has ~ little to say⟩
pre·cious·ly *adv* (14c) **1** : in a precious manner **2** : PRECIOUS
pre·ci·pe *var of* PRAECIPE
prec·i·pice \'pre-s(ə-)pəs\ *n* [MF, fr. L *praecipitium*, fr. *praecipit-*, *praeceps* headlong, fr. *prae-* + *caput* head — more at HEAD] (1613) **1** : a very steep or overhanging place **2** : a hazardous situation; *broadly* : BRINK
pre·cip·i·ta·ble \pri-'si-pə-tə-bəl\ *adj* (1670) : capable of being precipitated
pre·cip·i·tance \pri-'si-pə-tən(t)s\ *n* (1667) : PRECIPITANCY
pre·cip·i·tan·cy \-tən(t)-sē\ *n* (1646) : undue hastiness or suddenness
¹pre·cip·i·tant \-tənt\ *adj* (1671) : PRECIPITATE — **pre·cip·i·tant·ly** *adv* — **pre·cip·i·tant·ness** *n*
²precipitant *n* (ca. 1685) : a precipitating agent; *esp* : one that causes the formation of a precipitate
¹pre·cip·i·tate \pri-'si-pə-ˌtāt\ *vb* **-tat·ed; -tat·ing** [L *praecipitatus*, pp. of *praecipitare*, fr. *praecipit-*, *praeceps*] (1528) **1 a** : to throw violently : HURL ⟨the quandaries into which the release of nuclear energy has *precipitated* mankind —A. B. Arons⟩ **b** : to throw down **2** : to bring about esp. abruptly ⟨~ a scandal that would end with his expulsion —John Cheever⟩ **3 a** : to cause to separate from solution or suspension **b** : to cause (vapor) to condense and fall or deposit ~ *vi* **1 a** : to fall headlong **b** : to fall or come suddenly into some condition **2** : to move or act precipitately **3 a** : to separate from solution or suspension **b** : to condense from a vapor and fall as rain or snow — **pre·cip·i·ta·tive** \-ˌtā-tiv\ *adj* — **pre·cip·i·ta·tor** \-ˌtā-tər\ *n*
²pre·cip·i·tate \pri-'si-pə-tət, -ˌtāt\ *n* [NL *praecipitatum*, fr. L, neut. of *praecipitatus*] (1594) **1** : a substance separated from a solution or suspension by chemical or physical change usu. as an insoluble amorphous or crystalline solid **2** : a product, result, or outcome of some process or action
³pre·cip·i·tate \pri-'si-pə-tət\ *adj* (1615) **1 a** : falling, flowing, or rushing with steep descent **b** : PRECIPITOUS, STEEP **2** : exhibiting violent or unwise speed — **pre·cip·i·tate·ly** *adv* — **pre·cip·i·tate·ness** *n*
syn PRECIPITATE, HEADLONG, ABRUPT, IMPETUOUS, SUDDEN mean showing undue haste or unexpectedness. PRECIPITATE stresses lack of due deliberation and implies prematureness of action ⟨the army's *precipitate* withdrawal⟩. HEADLONG stresses rashness and lack of forethought ⟨a *headlong* flight from arrest⟩. ABRUPT stresses curtness and a lack of warning or ceremony ⟨an *abrupt* refusal⟩. IMPETUOUS stresses extreme impatience or impulsiveness ⟨an *impetuous* lover proposing marriage⟩. SUDDEN stresses unexpectedness and sharpness or violence of action ⟨flew into a *sudden* rage⟩.
pre·cip·i·ta·tion \pri-ˌsi-pə-'tā-shən\ *n* (1502) **1** : the quality or state of being precipitate : HASTINESS **2** : an act, process, or instance of precipitating; *esp* : the process of forming a precipitate **3** : something precipitated: as **a** : a deposit on the earth of hail, mist, rain, sleet, or snow; *also* : the quantity of water deposited **b** : PRECIPITATE 1
pre·cip·i·tin \pri-'si-pə-tən\ *n* [ISV, fr. *precipitate*] (1900) : an antibody that forms a precipitate when it unites with its antigen
pre·cip·i·tin·o·gen \pri-ˌsi-pə-'ti-nə-jən\ *n* (1904) : an antigen that stimulates the production of a specific precipitin
pre·cip·i·tous \pri-'si-pə-təs\ *adj* [F *précipiteux*, fr. MF, fr. L *precipitium* precipice] (1613) **1** : PRECIPITATE 3 **2 a** : very steep, perpendicular, or overhanging in rise or fall ⟨a ~ slope⟩ **b** : having precipitous sides ⟨a ~ gorge⟩ **c** : having a very steep ascent ⟨a ~ street⟩ **syn** see STEEP — **pre·cip·i·tous·ly** *adv* — **pre·cip·i·tous·ness** *n*
pré·cis \prā-'sē, 'prā-(ˌ)sē\ *n, pl* **pré·cis** \-'sēz, -(ˌ)sēz\ [F, fr. *précis* precise] (1760) : a concise summary of essential points, statements, or facts
pre·cise \pri-'sis\ *adj* [ME, fr. MF *precis*, fr. L *praecisus*, pp. of *praecidere* to cut off, fr. *prae-* + *caedere* to cut] (15c) **1** : exactly or sharply defined or stated **2** : minutely exact **3** : strictly conforming to a pattern, standard, or convention **4** : distinguished from every other ⟨at just that ~ moment⟩ **syn** see CORRECT — **pre·cise·ness** *n*
pre·cise·ly *adv* (14c) : EXACTLY ⟨~ two o'clock⟩ — sometimes used as an intensive ⟨was popular ~ because he was so kind⟩
pre·ci·sian \pri-'si-zhən\ *n* (1571) **1** : a person who stresses or practices scrupulous adherence to a strict standard esp. of religious observance or morality **2** : PURITAN
¹pre·ci·sion \pri-'si-zhən\ *n* (1740) **1** : the quality or state of being precise : EXACTNESS **2 a** : the degree of refinement with which an operation is performed or a measurement stated — compare ACCURACY 2b **b** : the accuracy (as in binary or decimal places) with which a number can be represented usu. expressed in terms of the number of computer words available for representation ⟨double ~ arithmetic permits the representation of an expression by two computer words⟩ **3** : RELEVANCE 2 — **pre·ci·sion·ist** \-'si-zhə-nist, -'sizh-nist\ *n*
²precision *adj* (1875) **1** : adapted for extremely accurate measurement or operation **2** : held to low tolerance in manufacture **3** : marked by precision of execution
pre·clin·i·cal \(ˌ)prē-'kli-ni-kəl\ *adj* (1926) **1** : of, relating to, or concerned with the period preceding clinical manifestations **2** : of, relating to, or being the period in medical or dental education preceding the clinical study of medicine or dentistry
pre·clude \pri-'klüd\ *vt* **pre·clud·ed; pre·clud·ing** [L *praecludere*, fr. *prae-* + *claudere* to close — more at CLOSE] (1629) **1** *archaic* : CLOSE **2** : to make impossible by necessary consequence : rule out in advance — **pre·clu·sion** \-'klü-zhən\ *n* — **pre·clu·sive** \-'klü-siv, -ziv\ *adj* — **pre·clu·sive·ly** *adv*
pre·co·cial \pri-'kō-shəl\ *adj* [NL *praecoces* precocial birds, fr. L, pl. of *praecoc-, praecox*] (ca. 1872) : capable of a high degree of independent activity from birth ⟨ducklings are ~⟩ — compare ALTRICIAL
pre·co·cious \pri-'kō-shəs\ *adj* [L *praecoc-, praecox* early ripening, precocious, fr. *prae-* + *coquere* to cook — more at COOK] (1650) **1** : exceptionally early in development or occurrence **2** : exhibiting mature qualities at an unusually early age — **pre·co·cious·ly** *adv* — **pre·co·cious·ness** *n* — **pre·coc·i·ty** \pri-'kä-sə-tē\ *n*
pre·cog·ni·tion \(ˌ)prē-ˌkäg-'ni-shən\ *n* [LL *praecognition-, praecognitio*, fr. L *praecognoscere* to know beforehand, fr. *prae-* + *cognoscere* to know — more at COGNITION] (ca. 1611) : clairvoyance relating to an event or state not yet experienced — **pre·cog·ni·tive** \(ˌ)prē-'käg-nə-tiv\ *adj*

pre–Co·lum·bi·an \ˌprē-kə-'ləm-bē-ən\ *adj* (1888) : preceding or belonging to the time before the arrival of Columbus in America
pre·con·ceive \ˌprē-kən-'sēv\ *vt* (1558) : to form (as an opinion) prior to actual knowledge or experience ⟨*preconceived* notions⟩
pre·con·cep·tion \-kən-'sep-shən\ *n* (1625) **1** : a preconceived idea **2** : PREJUDICE
pre·con·cert \ˌprē-kən-'sərt\ *vt* (1748) : to settle by prior agreement
¹pre·con·di·tion \ˌprē-kən-'di-shən\ *n* (1825) : PREREQUISITE
²precondition *vt* (1922) : to put in a proper or desired condition or frame of mind esp. in preparation
¹pre·con·scious \(ˌ)prē-'kän(t)-shəs\ *adj* (1860) : not present in consciousness but capable of being recalled without encountering any inner resistance or repression — **pre·con·scious·ly** *adv*
²preconscious *n* (ca. 1922) : the preconscious part of the psyche esp. in psychoanalysis
pre·con·tact \ˌprē-'kän-ˌtakt\ *adj* (ca. 1909) : of or relating to the period before contact of an indigenous people with an outside culture
pre·cook \(ˌ)prē-'kúk\ *vt* (1926) : to cook partially or entirely before final cooking or reheating
pre·crit·i·cal \-'kri-ti-kəl\ *adj* (1881) : prior to the development of critical capacity
pre·cur·sor \pri-'kər-sər, 'prē-,\ *n* [ME *precursoure*, fr. L *praecursor*, fr. *praecurrere* to run before, fr. *prae-* pre- + *currere* to run — more at CURRENT] (15c) **1 a** : one that precedes and indicates the approach of another **b** : PREDECESSOR **2** : a substance, cell, or cellular component from which another substance, cell, or cellular component is formed **syn** see FORERUNNER — **pre·cur·so·ry** \-'kərs-rē, -'kər-sə-\ *adj*
pre·da·ceous *or* **pre·da·cious** \pri-'dā-shəs\ *adj* [L *praedari* to prey upon (fr. *praeda* prey) + E -*aceous* or -*acious* (as in *rapacious*) — more at PREY] (1713) **1** : living by preying on other animals : PREDATORY **2** *usu* **predacious** : tending to devour or despoil : RAPACIOUS — **pre·da·ceous·ness** *n* — **pre·dac·i·ty** \-'da-sə-tē\ *n*
pre·date \(ˌ)prē-'dāt\ *vt* (ca. 1864) : ANTEDATE
pre·da·tion \pri-'dā-shən\ *n* [ME *predacion*, fr. L *praedation-, praedatio*, fr. *praedari*] (15c) **1** : the act of preying or plundering : DEPREDATION **2** : a mode of life in which food is primarily obtained by the killing and consuming of animals
predation pressure *n* (1942) : the effects of predation on a natural community esp. with respect to the survival of species preyed upon
pred·a·tor \'pre-də-tər, -ˌtȯr\ *n* (1912) **1** : one that preys, destroys, or devours **2** : an animal that lives by predation
pred·a·to·ry \'pre-də-ˌtȯr-ē, -ˌtȯr-\ *adj* (1589) **1 a** : of, relating to, or practicing plunder, pillage, or rapine **b** : inclined or intended to injure or exploit others for personal gain or profit ⟨~ pricing practices⟩ **2** : living by predation : PREDACEOUS; *also* : adapted to predation
pre·de·cease \ˌprē-di-'sēs\ *vb* **-ceased; -ceas·ing** *vt* (1593) : to die before (another person) ~ *vi* : to die first — **predecease** *n*
pre·de·ces·sor \'pre-də-ˌse-sər, 'prē-; ˌpre-də-', ˌprē-\ *n* [ME *predecessour*, fr. MF *predecesseur*, fr. LL *praedecessor*, fr. L *prae-* pre- + *decessor* retiring governor, fr. *decedere* to depart, retire from office — more at DECEASE] (14c) **1** : one that precedes; *esp* : a person who has previously occupied a position or office to which another has succeeded **2** *archaic* : ANCESTOR
pre·des·ti·nar·i·an \(ˌ)prē-ˌdes-tə-'ner-ē-ən, ˌprē-des-\ *n* [predestination + -*arian*] (1667) : one who believes in predestination — **predestinarian** *adj* — **pre·des·ti·nar·i·an·ism** \-ē-ə-ˌni-zəm\ *n*
¹pre·des·ti·nate \prē-'des-tə-nət, -ˌnāt\ *adj* [ME, fr. L *praedestinatus*, pp. of *praedestinare*] (14c) : destined, fated, or determined beforehand
²pre·des·ti·nate \-ˌnāt\ *vt* **-nat·ed; -nat·ing** [ME, fr. L *praedestinatus*, pp.] (15c) **1** : to foreordain to an earthly or eternal lot or destiny by divine decree **2** *archaic* : PREDETERMINE
pre·des·ti·na·tion \(ˌ)prē-ˌdes-tə-'nā-shən, ˌprē-des-\ *n* (14c) **1** : the act of predestinating : the state of being predestinated **2** : the doctrine that God in consequence of his foreknowledge of all events infallibly guides those who are destined for salvation
pre·des·ti·na·tor \prē-'des-tə-ˌnā-tər\ *n* (1579) **1** *archaic* : PREDESTINARIAN **2** : one who predestines
pre·des·tine \(ˌ)prē-'des-tən\ *vt* [ME, fr. MF or L; MF *predestiner*, fr. L *praedestinare*, fr. *prae-* + *destinare* to determine — more at DESTINE] (14c) : to destine, decree, determine, appoint, or settle beforehand; *esp* : PREDESTINATE 1
pre·de·ter·mi·na·tion \ˌprē-di-ˌtər-mə-'nā-shən\ *n* (1647) **1** : the act of predetermining : the state of being predetermined: as **a** : the ordaining of events beforehand **b** : a fixing or settling in advance **2** : a purpose formed beforehand
pre·de·ter·mine \ˌprē-di-'tər-mən\ *vt* [LL *praedeterminare*, fr. L *prae-* + *determinare* to determine] (1625) **1 a** : FOREORDAIN, PREDESTINE **b** : to determine beforehand **2** : to impose a direction or tendency on beforehand
pre·de·ter·min·er \-di-'tər-mə-nər\ *n* (1959) : a limiting noun modifier (as *both* or *all*) characterized by occurrence before the determiner in a noun phrase
pre·di·a·be·tes \ˌprē-ˌdi-ə-'bē-tēz, -təs\ *n* (1935) : an inapparent abnormal state that precedes the development of clinically evident diabetes — **pre·di·a·bet·ic** \-'be-tik\ *adj or n*
pre·di·al \'prē-dē-əl\ *adj* [ME *prediall*, fr. ML *praedialis*, fr. L *praedium* landed property, fr. *praed-, praes* bondsman, fr. *prae-* + *vad-, vas* surety — more at WED] (15c) : of or relating to land or its products
¹pred·i·ca·ble \'pre-di-kə-bəl\ *n* [ML *praedicabile*, fr. neut. of *praedicabilis*] (1551) : something that may be predicated; *esp* : one of the five most general kinds of attribution in traditional logic that include genus, species, difference, property, and accident
²predicable *adj* [ML *praedicabilis*, fr. LL *praedicare* to predicate] (ca. 1598) : capable of being asserted
pre·dic·a·ment \pri-'di-kə-mənt, *1 is usu* ˌpre-di-kə-\ *n* [ME, fr. LL *praedicamentum*, fr. *praedicare*] (14c) **1** : the character, status, or

\ə\ abut \ᵊ\ kitten, F table \ər\ further \a\ ash \ā\ ace \ä\ mop, mar \aú\ out \ch\ chin \e\ bet \ē\ easy \g\ go \i\ hit \ī\ ice \j\ job \ŋ\ sing \ō\ go \ò\ law \òi\ boy \th\ thin \t͟h\ the \ü\ loot \ú\ foot \y\ yet \zh\ vision \á, k̲, ⁿ, œ, œ̄, ᵫ, ᵫ̄, ᵌ\ *see* Guide to Pronunciation classification assigned by a predication; *specif* : CATEGORY 1   2 : CONDITION, STATE; *esp* : a difficult, perplexing, or trying situation

¹pred·i·cate \'pre-di-kət\ *n* [ME, fr. LL *praedicatum*, fr. neut. of *praedicatus*] (15c) **1 a** : something that is affirmed or denied of the subject in a proposition in logic   **b** : a term designating a property or relation   **2** : the part of a sentence or clause that expresses what is said of the subject and that usu. consists of a verb with or without objects, complements, or adverbial modifiers — **pred·i·ca·tive** \-kə-tiv, -ˌkā-\ *adj* — **pred·i·ca·tive·ly** *adv*

²pred·i·cate \'pre-də-ˌkāt\ *vt* **-cat·ed; -cat·ing** [LL *praedicatus*, pp. of *praedicare* to assert, predicate logically, preach, fr. L, to proclaim publicly, assert — more at PREACH] (1552) **1 a** : AFFIRM, DECLARE   **b** *archaic* : PREACH   **2 a** : to assert to be a quality, attribute, or property — used with following of ⟨~s intelligence of humans⟩   **b** : to make (a term) the predicate in a proposition   **3** : FOUND, BASE — usu. used with *on* ⟨the theory is *predicated* on recent findings⟩   **4** : IMPLY

³pred·i·cate \'pre-di-kət\ *adj* (1887) : completing the meaning of a copula ⟨~ adjective⟩ ⟨~ noun⟩

predicate calculus *n* (1950) : the branch of symbolic logic that uses symbols for quantifiers and for arguments and predicates of propositions as well as for unanalyzed propositions and logical connectives — called also *functional calculus;* compare PROPOSITIONAL CALCULUS

predicate nominative *n* (1887) : a noun or pronoun in the nominative or common case completing the meaning of a copula

pred·i·ca·tion \ˌpre-də-'kā-shən\ *n* [ME *predicacion*, fr. MF *predication*, fr. L *praedication-*, *praedicatio*, fr. *praedicare*] (14c) **1** *archaic* : an act of proclaiming or preaching   **b** : SERMON   **2** : an act or instance of predicating: as   **a** : the expression of action, state, or quality by a grammatical predicate   **b** : the logical affirmation of something about another; *esp* : assignment of something to a class

pred·i·ca·to·ry \'pre-di-kə-ˌtȯr-ē, -ˌtȯr-\ *adj* [LL *praedicatorius*, fr. *praedicare* to preach] (1611) : of or relating to preaching

pre·dict \pri-'dikt\ *vb* [L *praedictus*, pp. of *praedicere*, fr. *prae-* pre- + *dicere* to say — more at DICTION] *vt* (ca. 1632) : to declare or indicate in advance; *esp* : foretell on the basis of observation, experience, or scientific reason ~ *vi* : to make a prediction   *syn* see FORETELL — **pre·dict·abil·i·ty** \-ˌdik-tə-'bi-lə-tē\ *n* — **pre·dict·able** \-'dik-tə-bəl\ *adj* — **pre·dic·tive** \-'dik-tiv\ *adj* — **pre·dic·tive·ly** \-lē\ *adv* — **pre·dic·tor** \-'dik-tər\ *n*

pre·dict·ably \-'dik-tə-blē\ *adv* (1914) **1** : in a manner that can be predicted ⟨works quickly and ~⟩   **2** : as one could predict : as one would expect ⟨~, the politicians howled⟩

pre·dic·tion \pri-'dik-shən\ *n* (1561) **1** : an act of predicting   **2** : something that is predicted : FORECAST

pre·di·gest \ˌprē-dī-'jest, -də-\ *vt* (1663) **1** : to subject to predigestion   **2** : to simplify for easy use ⟨~ed classics for children⟩

pre·di·ges·tion \-'jes-chən, -'jesh-\ *n* (ca. 1612) : artificial or natural partial digestion of food ⟨enzymatic ~⟩ ⟨microbial ~⟩

pre·di·lec·tion \ˌpre-dᵊl-'ek-shən, ˌprē-\ *n* [F *prédilection*, fr. ML *praediligere* to love more, prefer, fr. L *prae-* + *diligere* to love — more at DILIGENT] (1742) : an established preference for something

syn PREDILECTION, PREPOSSESSION, PREJUDICE, BIAS mean an attitude of mind that predisposes one to favor something. PREDILECTION implies a strong liking deriving from one's temperament or experience ⟨a *predilection* for horror movies⟩. PREPOSSESSION suggests a fixed conception likely to preclude objective judgment of anything counter to it ⟨a *prepossession* against technology⟩. PREJUDICE usu. implies an unfavorable prepossession and connotes a feeling rooted in suspicion, fear, or intolerance ⟨a mindless *prejudice* against the unfamiliar⟩. BIAS implies an unreasoned and unfair distortion of judgment in favor of or against a person or thing ⟨the common *bias* against overweight people⟩.

pre·dis·pose \ˌprē-di-'spōz\ *vt* (1646) **1** : to dispose in advance ⟨a good teacher ~s children to learn⟩   **2** : to make susceptible ⟨malnutrition ~s one to disease⟩ ~ *vi* : to bring about susceptibility   *syn* see INCLINE — **pre·dis·po·si·tion** \ˌprē-ˌdis-pə-'zi-shən\ *n*

pred·nis·o·lone \pred-'ni-sə-ˌlōn\ *n* [blend of *prednisone* and *-ol*] (1955) : a glucocorticoid $C_{21}H_{28}O_5$ that is a dehydrogenated analogue of hydrocortisone and is used esp. as an anti-inflammatory drug

pred·ni·sone \'pred-nə-ˌsōn *also* -ˌzōn\ *n* [prob. fr. *pregnane* ($C_{21}H_{36}$) + *diene* (compound containing two double bonds) + *cortisone*] (1955) : a glucocorticoid $C_{21}H_{26}O_5$ that is a dehydrogenated analogue of cortisone and is used as an anti-inflammatory agent esp. in the treatment of arthritis, as an antineoplastic agent, and as an immunosuppressant

pre·doc·tor·al \ˌprē-'däk-t(ə-)rəl\ *adj* (1937) : of, relating to, or engaged in academic study leading to the doctoral degree

pre·dom·i·nance \pri-'dä-mə-nən(t)s, -'däm-nən(t)s\ *n* (1602) : the quality or state of being predominant

pre·dom·i·nan·cy \-nən(t)-sē\ *n* (1598) : PREDOMINANCE

pre·dom·i·nant \-nənt\ *adj* [MF, fr. ML *praedominant-*, *praedominans*, prp. of *praedominari* to predominate, fr. L *prae-* + *dominari* to rule, govern — more at DOMINATE] (1576) **1** : having superior strength, influence, or authority : PREVAILING   **2** : being most frequent or common   *syn* see DOMINANT

pre·dom·i·nant·ly \-nənt-lē\ *adv* (1681) : for the most part : MAINLY

¹pre·dom·i·nate \-nət\ *adj* [alter. of *predominant*] (1591) : PREDOMINANT — **pre·dom·i·nate·ly** *adv*

²pre·dom·i·nate \pri-'dä-mə-ˌnāt\ *vb* [ML *praedominatus*, pp. of *praedominari*] *vi* (1594) **1** : to hold advantage in numbers or quantity   **2** : to exert controlling power or influence : PREVAIL ~ *vt* : to exert control over : DOMINATE — **pre·dom·i·na·tion** \-ˌdä-mə-'nā-shən\ *n*

pree \'prē\ *vt* **preed; pree·ing** [alter. of *preve* to prove, test, fr. ME *preven*, fr. OF *preuv-*, stem of *prover* to prove] (1680) *Scot* : to taste tentatively : SAMPLE

pre·eclamp·sia \ˌprē-i-'klam(p)-sē-ə\ *n* [NL] (1923) : a toxic condition developing in late pregnancy that is characterized by a sudden rise in blood pressure, excessive weight gain, generalized edema, albuminuria, severe headache, and visual disturbances — **pre·eclamp·tic** \-'klam(p)-tik\ *adj*

pre·emer·gence \ˌprē-ə-'mər-jən(t)s\ *adj* (1935) : used or occurring before emergence of seedlings above the ground ⟨~ herbicides⟩

pre·emer·gent \-jənt\ *adj* (1959) : PREEMERGENCE

pree·mie \'prē-mē\ *n* [*premature* + *-ie*] (1927) : a premature baby

pre·em·i·nence \prē-'e-mə-nən(t)s\ *n* (13c) : the quality or state of being preeminent : SUPERIORITY

pre·em·i·nent \-nənt\ *adj* [ME, fr. LL *praeeminent-*, *praeeminens*, fr. L, prp. of *praeeminēre* to be outstanding, fr. *prae-* + *eminēre* to stand out — more at EMINENT] (15c) : having paramount rank, dignity, or importance : OUTSTANDING — **pre·em·i·nent·ly** *adv*

pre·empt \prē-'em(p)t\ *vb* [back-formation fr. *preemption*] *vt* (1850) **1** : to acquire (as land) by preemption   **2** : to seize upon to the exclusion of others : take for oneself ⟨the movement was then ~ed by a lunatic fringe⟩   **3** : to replace with something considered to be of greater value or priority : take precedence over ⟨the program did not appear, having been ~ed by a baseball game —Robert MacNeil⟩   **4** : to gain a commanding or preeminent place in   **5** : to prevent from happening or taking place : FORESTALL, PRECLUDE ~ *vi* : to make a preemptive bid in bridge — **pre·emp·tor** \-'em(p)-tər\ *n*

pre·emp·tion \-'em(p)-shən\ *n* [ML *praeemption-*, *praeemptio* previous purchase, fr. *praeemere* to buy before, fr. L *prae-* + *emere* to buy — more at REDEEM] (1602) **1 a** : the right of purchasing before others; *esp* : one given by the government to the actual settler upon a tract of public land   **b** : the purchase of something under this right   **2** : a prior seizure or appropriation : a taking possession before others

pre·emp·tive \-'em(p)-tiv\ *adj* (1855) **1 a** : of or relating to preemption   **b** : having power to preempt   **2** *of a bid in bridge* : higher than necessary and intended to shut out bids by the opponents   **3** : giving a stockholder first option to purchase new stock in an amount proportionate to his existing holdings   **4** : marked by the seizing of the initiative : initiated by oneself ⟨a ~ attack⟩ — **pre·emp·tive·ly** *adv*

¹preen \'prēn\ *n* [ME *prene*, fr. OE *prēon*; akin to MHG *pfrieme* awl] (bef. 12c) **1** *dial chiefly Brit* : PIN   **2** *dial chiefly Brit* : BROOCH

²preen \(1572) *chiefly Scot* : PIN

³preen *vb* [ME *preinen*] *vt* (14c) **1** : to dress or smooth (oneself) up : PRIMP   **2** *of a bird* : to trim or dress with a bill   **3** : to pride or congratulate (oneself) for achievement ~ *vi* **1** : to make oneself sleek : GLOAT, SWELL — **preen·er** *n*

pre·en·gi·neered \ˌprē-ˌen-jə-'nird\ *adj* (1951) : constructed of or employing prefabricated modules ⟨a ~ building⟩

pre·ex·il·ic \ˌprē-eg-'zi-lik\ *adj* (1880) : previous to the exile of the Jews to Babylon in about 600 B.C.

pre·ex·ist \ˌprē-ig-'zist\ *vt* (1599) : to exist earlier or before ~ *vt* : ANTEDATE

pre·ex·is·tence \-ig-'zis-tən(t)s\ *n* (ca. 1652) : existence in a former state or previous to something else; *specif* : existence of the soul before its union with the body — **pre·ex·is·tent** \-tənt\ *adj*

pre·fab \(ˌ)prē-'fab, 'prē-ˌ\ *n* (1937) : a prefabricated structure — **prefab** *adj*

pre·fab·ri·cate \(ˌ)prē-'fa-bri-ˌkāt\ *vt* (1932) **1** : to fabricate the parts of a factory so that construction consists mainly of assembling and uniting standardized parts   **2** : to produce artificially — **pre·fab·ri·ca·tion** \ˌprē-ˌfa-bri-'kā-shən\ *n*

¹pref·ace \'pre-fəs\ *n* [ME, fr. MF, fr. ML *prephatia*, alter. of L *praefation-*, *praefatio* foreword, fr. *praefari* to say beforehand, fr. *prae-* pre- + *fari* to say — more at BAN] (14c) **1** *often cap* : a variable doxology beginning with the Sursum Corda and ending with the Sanctus in traditional eucharistic liturgies   **2** : the introductory remarks of a speaker or author   **3** : APPROACH, PRELIMINARY

²preface *vb* **pref·aced; pref·ac·ing** *vi* (1619) : to make introductory remarks ~ *vt* **1** : to say or write as preface ⟨a note *prefaced* to the manuscript⟩   **2** : PRECEDE, HERALD   **3** : to introduce by or begin with a preface   **4** : to stand in front of ⟨a porch ~s the entrance⟩   **5** : to be a preliminary to — **pref·ac·er** *n*

pref·a·to·ry \'pre-fə-ˌtȯr-ē, -ˌtȯr-\ *adj* [L *praefari*] (1675) **1** : of, relating to, or constituting a preface   **2** : located in front

pre·fect \'prē-ˌfekt\ *n* [ME, fr. MF, fr. L *praefectus*, fr. pp. of *praeficere* to place at the head of, fr. *prae-* + *facere* to make — more at DO] (14c) **1** : any of various high officials or magistrates of differing functions and ranks in ancient Rome   **2** : a chief officer or chief magistrate   **3** : a student monitor in a private school

prefect apostolic *n* (ca. 1888) : a Roman Catholic clergyman and usu. a priest with quasi-episcopal jurisdiction over a district of a missionary territory

pre·fec·ture \'prē-ˌfek-chər\ *n* (15c) **1** : the office or term of office of a prefect   **2** : the official residence of a prefect   **3** : the district governed by a prefect — **pre·fec·tur·al** \'prē-ˌfek-chə-rəl, pri-'\ *adj*

prefecture apostolic *n* (1911) : the district under a prefect apostolic

pre·fer \pri-'fər\ *vt* **pre·ferred; pre·fer·ring** [ME *preferren*, fr. MF *preferer*, fr. L *praeferre* to put before, prefer, fr. *prae-* + *ferre* to carry — more at BEAR] (14c) **1** : to promote or advance to a rank or position   **2** : to like better or best ⟨~s sports to reading⟩ ⟨~s to watch TV⟩   **3** : to give (a creditor) priority   **4** *archaic* : to put or set forward or before someone : RECOMMEND   **5** : to bring or lay against someone ⟨won't ~ charges⟩   **6** : to bring forward or lay before one for consideration — **pre·fer·rer** *n*

pref·er·a·ble \'pre-f(ə-)rə-bəl, 'pre-fər-bəl *also* pri-'fər-ə-bəl\ *adj* (1666) : having greater value or desirability : being preferred — **pref·er·a·bil·i·ty** \ˌpre-f(ə-)rə-'bi-lə-tē\ *n* — **pref·er·a·bly** \-blē\ *adv*

pref·er·ence \'pre-fərn(t)s, 'pre-f(ə-)rən(t)s\ *n* [ME *preferraunce*, fr. MF *preferance*, fr. ML *praeferentia*, fr. L *praeferent-*, *praeferens*, prp. of *praeferre*] (15c) **1 a** : the act of preferring : the state of being preferred   **b** : the power or opportunity of choosing   **2** : one that is preferred   **3** : the act, fact, or principle of giving advantages to some over others   **4** : priority in the right to demand and receive satisfaction of an obligation   **5** : ORIENTATION 2 ⟨sexual ~⟩   *syn* see CHOICE

pref·er·en·tial \ˌpre-fə-'ren(t)-shəl\ *adj* (1849) **1** : showing preference   **2** : employing or creating a preference in trade relations   **3** : designed to permit expression of preference among candidates ⟨a ~ primary⟩   **4** : giving preference esp. in hiring to union members ⟨a ~ shop⟩ — **pref·er·en·tial·ly** \-'ren(t)-sh(ə-)lē\ *adv*

pre·fer·ment \pri-'fər-mənt\ *n* (15c) **1 a** : advancement or promotion in dignity, office, or station   **b** : a position or office of honor or profit   **2** : priority or seniority in right esp. to receive payment or to purchase property on equal terms with others   **3** : the act of bringing forward (as charges)

preferred stock *n* (ca. 1859) : stock guaranteed priority by a corporation's charter over common stock in the payment of dividends and usu. in the distribution of assets

pre·fig·u·ra·tion \(ˌ)prē-ˌfi-gyə-'rā-shən, -gə-\ n (14c) **1** : the act of prefiguring : the state of being prefigured **2** : something that prefigures

pre·fig·u·ra·tive \ˌprē-'fi-gyə-rə-tiv, -gə-\ adj (1504) : of, relating to, or showing by prefiguration — **pre·fig·u·ra·tive·ly** adv — **pre·fig·u·ra·tive·ness** n

pre·fig·ure \prē-'fi-gyər, esp Brit -'fi-gər\ vt [ME, fr. LL praefigurare, fr. L prae- pre- + figurare to shape, picture, fr. figura figure] (15c) **1** : to show, suggest, or announce by an antecedent type, image, or likeness **2** : to picture or imagine beforehand : FORESEE — **pre·fig·ure·ment** \-mənt\ n

¹pre·fix vt [ME, fr. MF prefixer, fr. pre- + fixer to fix, fr. fix fixed, fr. L fixus — more at FIX] (15c) **1** \(ˌ)prē-'fiks\ : to fix or appoint beforehand **2** \'prē-ˌ\ [partly fr. ²prefix] : to place in front; esp : to add as a prefix (~ a syllable to a word)

²pre·fix \'prē-ˌfiks\ n [NL praefixum, fr. L, neut. of praefixus, pp. of praefigere to fasten before, fr. prae- + figere to fasten — more at FIX] (1646) **1** : an affix attached to the beginning of a word, base, or phrase and serving to produce a derivative word or an inflectional form — compare SUFFIX **2** : a title used before a person's name — **pre·fix·al** \'prē-ˌfik-səl, prē-'\ adj

³pre·fix \same as ²\ adj (1971) : characterized by placement of an operator before its operand or before its two operands if it is a binary operator — compare INFIX, POSTFIX

pre·fo·cus \(ˌ)prē-'fō-kəs\ vt (1948) : to focus beforehand (as automotive headlights before installation)

pre·form \'prē-ˌfórm, (ˌ)prē-'\ vt [L praeformare, fr. prae- + formare to form, fr. forma form] (1601) **1** : to form or shape beforehand **2** : to bring to approximate preliminary shape and size — **pre·form** \'prē-ˌfórm\ n

pre·for·ma·tion \ˌprē-fór-'mā-shən\ n (1732) **1** : previous formation **2** : the now discredited theory that every germ cell contains the organism of its kind fully formed and that development involves merely an increase in size — compare EPIGENESIS 1, HOMUNCULUS 2 — **pre·for·ma·tion·ist** \-sh(ə-)nist\ n or adj

¹pre·fron·tal \(ˌ)prē-'frən-tᵊl\ adj (1854) : anterior to or involving the anterior part of a frontal structure (a ~ bone)

²prefrontal n (1854) : a prefrontal part (as a bone)

pre·gan·gli·on·ic \ˌprē-ˌgaŋ-glē-'ä-nik\ adj (1895) : proximal to a ganglion; specif : of, relating to, or being a usu. medullated axon arising from a cell body in the central nervous system and terminating in an autonomic ganglion — compare POSTGANGLIONIC

preg·na·ble \'preg-nə-bəl\ adj [alter. of ME prenable, fr. MF — more at IMPREGNABLE] (14c) : vulnerable to capture (a ~ fort) — **preg·na·bil·i·ty** \ˌpreg-nə-'bi-lə-tē\ n

preg·nan·cy \'preg-nən(t)-sē\ n, pl -cies (15c) **1** : the quality of being pregnant (as in meaning) **2** : the condition of being pregnant : GESTATION **3** : an instance of being pregnant

¹preg·nant \'preg-nənt\ adj [ME preignant, fr. MF, fr. prp. of preindre to press, fr. L premere — more at PRESS] (14c) archaic : COGENT

²pregnant adj [ME, fr. L praegnant-, praegnans, alter. of praegnas, fr. prae- pre- + -gnas (akin to gignere to give birth to) — more at KIN] (15c) **1** : abounding in fancy, wit, or resourcefulness : INVENTIVE (all this has been said ... by great and ~ artists —Times Lit. Supp.) **2** : rich in significance or implication : MEANINGFUL, PROFOUND (the ~ phrases of the Bible —Edmund Wilson) (a ~ pause) **3** : containing unborn young within the body : GRAVID **4** : having possibilities of development or consequence : involving important issues : MOMENTOUS (draw inspiration from the heroic achievements of that ~ age —Kemp Malone) **5** obs : INCLINED, DISPOSED (your own most ~ and vouchsafed ear —Shak.) **6** : FULL, TEEMING — **preg·nant·ly** adv

preg·nen·o·lone \preg-'ne-nᵊl-ˌōn\ n [ISV pregnene (C₂₁H₃₄) + ¹-ol + -one] (1936) : an unsaturated hydroxy steroid ketone $C_{21}H_{32}O_2$ that is formed by the oxidation of steroids (as cholesterol) and yields progesterone on dehydrogenation

pre·heat \(ˌ)prē-'hēt\ vt (1898) : to heat beforehand; esp : to heat (an oven) to a designated temperature before using for cooking — **pre·heat·er** n

pre·hen·sile \prē-'hen(t)-səl, -'hen-ˌsīl\ adj [F préhensile, fr. L prehensus, pp. of prehendere to seize — more at GET] (ca. 1785) **1** : adapted for seizing or grasping esp. by wrapping around (~ tail) **2** : gifted with mental grasp or moral or aesthetic perception — **pre·hen·sil·i·ty** \(ˌ)prē-ˌhen-'si-lə-tē\ n

pre·hen·sion \prē-'hen(t)-shən\ n (ca. 1828) **1** : the act of taking hold, seizing, or grasping **2 a** : mental understanding : COMPREHENSION **b** : apprehension by the senses

pre·His·pan·ic \ˌprē-(h)is-'pa-nik\ adj (1919) : of, relating to, or being the time prior to Spanish conquests in the western hemisphere

pre·his·to·ri·an \ˌprē-(h)is-'tór-ē-ən, -'tór-\ n (1893) : an archaeologist who specializes in prehistory

pre·his·tor·ic \ˌprē-(h)is-'tór-ik, -'tär-\ also **pre·his·tor·i·cal** \-i-kəl\ adj (1851) **1** : of, relating to, or existing in times antedating written history **2** : of or relating to a language in a period of its development from which contemporary records of its sounds and forms have not been preserved — **pre·his·tor·i·cal·ly** \-i-k(ə-)lē\ adv

pre·his·to·ry \ˌprē-'his-t(ə-)rē\ n (1871) **1** : the study of prehistoric humankind **2** : a history of the antecedents of an event, situation, or thing **3** : the prehistoric period of human evolution

pre·hom·i·nid \-'hä-mə-nəd\ n [ultim. fr. L pre- + homin-, homo human being — more at HOMAGE] (1939) : any of various extinct primates resembling or ancestral to humans — **prehominid** adj

pre·ig·ni·tion \ˌprē-ig-'ni-shən\ n (1898) : ignition in an internal combustion engine while the inlet valve is open or before compression is completed

pre·im·plan·ta·tion \ˌprē-ˌim-ˌplan-'tā-shən\ adj (1945) : of, involving, or being an embryo before uterine implantation

pre·judge \(ˌ)prē-'jəj\ vt [MF prejuger, fr. L praejudicare, fr. prae- + judicare to judge — more at JUDGE] (1579) : to judge before hearing or before full and sufficient examination — **pre·judg·er** n — **pre·judg·ment** \-'jəj-mənt\ n

¹prej·u·dice \'pre-jə-dəs\ n [ME, fr. OF, fr. L praejudicium previous judgment, damage, fr. prae- + judicium judgment — more at JUDICIAL] (13c) **1** : injury or damage resulting from some judgment or action of another in disregard of one's rights; esp : detriment to one's legal rights or claims **2 a** (1) : preconceived judgment or opinion (2) : an adverse opinion or leaning formed without just grounds or before sufficient knowledge **b** : an instance of such judgment or opinion **c** : an irrational attitude of hostility directed against an individual, a group, a race, or their supposed characteristics syn see PREDILECTION

²prejudice vt -diced; -dic·ing (15c) **1** : to injure or damage by some judgment or action (as in a case of law) **2** : to cause to have prejudice

prej·u·diced \-dəst\ adj (1579) : resulting from or having a prejudice or bias for or esp. against

prej·u·di·cial \ˌpre-jə-'di-shəl\ adj (15c) **1** : tending to injure or impair : DETRIMENTAL **2** : leading to premature judgment or unwarranted opinion — **prej·u·di·cial·ly** \-'di-sh(ə-)lē\ adv — **prej·u·di·cial·ness** \-shəl-nəs\ n

prel·a·cy \'pre-lə-sē\ n, pl -cies (14c) **1** : the office or dignity of a prelate **2** : episcopal church government

pre·lap·sar·i·an \ˌprē-ˌlap-'ser-ē-ən\ adj [pre- + L lapsus slip, fall — more at LAPSE] (1879) : characteristic of or belonging to the time or state before the fall of mankind

prel·ate \'pre-lət also 'prē-ˌlāt\ n [ME prelat, fr. OF, fr. ML praelatus, lit., one receiving preferment, fr. L (pp. of praeferre to prefer), fr. prae- + latus, pp. of ferre to carry — more at TOLERATE, BEAR] (13c) : an ecclesiastic (as a bishop or abbot) of superior rank

prel·a·ture \'pre-lə-ˌchúr, -chər, -ˌtyúr, -ˌtúr\ n (1607) **1** : PRELACY 1 **2** : a body of prelates

pre·lect \pri-'lekt\ vi [L praelectus, pp. of praelegere to read, fr. prae- + legere to read — more at LEGEND] (1785) : to discourse publicly : LECTURE — **pre·lec·tion** \-'lek-shən\ n

pre·li·ba·tion \ˌprē-li-'bā-shən\ n [L praelibation-, praelibatio, fr. prae- libare to taste beforehand, fr. prae- + libare to pour as an offering, taste — more at LIBATION] (1526) : FORETASTE

pre·lim \'prē-ˌlim, pri-'\ n or adj (1891) : PRELIMINARY

¹pre·lim·i·nary \pri-'li-mə-ˌner-ē\ n, pl -nar·ies [F préliminaires, pl., fr. ML praeliminaris, adj., preliminary, fr. L prae- pre- + limin-, limen threshold] (1656) : something that precedes or is introductory or preparatory: as **a** : a preliminary scholastic examination **b** pl, Brit : FRONT MATTER **c** : a preliminary heat or trial (as of a race) **d** : a minor match preceding the main event (as of a boxing card)

²preliminary adj (ca. 1667) : coming before and usu. forming a necessary prelude to something else — **pre·lim·i·nar·i·ly** \-ˌli-mə-'ner-ə-lē\ adv

pre·lit·er·ate \ˌprē-'li-t(ə-)rət\ adj (1925) **1 a** : not yet employing writing as a cultural medium **b** : lacking the use of writing **2** : antedating the use of writing — **preliterate** n

¹pre·lude \'prel-ˌyüd, 'prāl-; 'prē-ˌlüd, 'prā-; sense 1 also 'prē-ˌlüd\ n [MF, fr. ML praeludium, fr. L praeludere to play beforehand, fr. prae- + ludere to play — more at LUDICROUS] (1561) **1** : an introductory performance, action, or event preceding and preparing for the principal or a more important matter **2 a** : a musical section or movement introducing the theme or chief subject (as of a fugue or suite) or serving as an introduction to an opera or oratorio **b** : an opening voluntary **c** : a separate concert piece usu. for piano or orchestra and based entirely on a short motif

²prelude vb **pre·lud·ed; pre·lud·ing** vt (1655) **1** : to serve as a prelude to **2** : to play as a prelude ~ vi : to serve or serve as a prelude; esp : to play a musical introduction — **pre·lud·er** n

pre·lu·sion \pri-'lü-zhən\ n [L praelusion-, praelusio, fr. praeludere] (1597) : PRELUDE, INTRODUCTION

pre·lu·sive \-'lü-siv, -ziv\ adj (1605) : constituting or having the form of a prelude : INTRODUCTORY — **pre·lu·sive·ly** adv

pre·ma·lig·nant \ˌprē-mə-'lig-nənt\ adj (ca. 1897) : PRECANCEROUS

pre·man \(ˌ)prē-'man, 'prē-ˌman\ n (1921) : any of several extinct primates ancestral to humans and esp. recent humans

pre·ma·ture \ˌprē-mə-'túr, -'tyúr, -'chúr also ˌpre-\ adj [L praematurus too early, fr. prae- + maturus ripe, mature] (ca. 1529) : happening, arriving, existing, or performed before the proper, usual, or intended time; esp : born after a gestation period of less than 37 weeks (~ babies) — **premature** n — **pre·ma·ture·ly** adv — **pre·ma·ture·ness** n — **pre·ma·tu·ri·ty** \-'tyúr-ə-tē, -'túr-, -'chúr-\ n

pre·max·il·la \ˌprē-mak-'si-lə\ n [NL] (1866) : either of a pair of bones of the upper jaw of vertebrates between and in front of the maxillae — **pre·max·il·lary** \(ˌ)prē-'mak-sə-ˌler-ē, chiefly Brit ˌprē-mak-'si-lə-rē\ adj or n

¹pre·med \(ˌ)prē-'med, 'prē-ˌmed\ n (ca. 1928) : a premedical student or course of study

²premed adj (1950) : PREMEDICAL

pre·med·i·cal \(ˌ)prē-'me-di-kəl\ adj (1904) : preceding and preparing for the professional study of medicine

pre·med·i·tate \(ˌ)prē-'me-də-ˌtāt\ vb [L praemeditatus, pp. of praemeditari, fr. prae- + meditari to meditate] vt (ca. 1548) : to think about and revolve in the mind beforehand ~ vi : to think, consider, or deliberate beforehand — **pre·med·i·ta·tor** \-ˌtā-tər\ n

pre·med·i·tat·ed \(ˌ)prē-'me-də-ˌtā-təd\ adj (1590) : characterized by fully conscious willful intent and a measure of forethought and planning (~ murder) — **pre·med·i·tat·ed·ly** adv

pre·med·i·ta·tion \(ˌ)prē-ˌme-də-'tā-shən\ n (15c) : an act or instance of premeditating; specif : consideration or planning of an act beforehand that shows intent to commit that act

pre·med·i·ta·tive \(ˌ)prē-'me-də-ˌtā-tiv\ adj (1858) : given to or characterized by premeditation

pre·men·stru·al \(ˌ)prē-'men(t)-strə-wəl, -strəl\ adj (1885) : of, relating to, occurring in, or being the period just preceding menstruation (~ tension) (~ women) — **pre·men·stru·al·ly** adv

premenstrual syndrome n (1982) : a varying group of symptoms manifested by some women prior to menstruation that may include emotional instability, irritability, insomnia, fatigue, anxiety, depression, headache, edema, and abdominal pain — abbr. PMS

pre·mie var of PREEMIE

\ə\ abut \ᵊ\ kitten, F table \ər\ further \a\ ash \ā\ ace \ä\ mop, mar \aú\ out \ch\ chin \e\ bet \ē\ easy \g\ go \i\ hit \ī\ ice \j\ job \ŋ\ sing \ō\ go \ó\ law \ói\ boy \th\ thin \t̶h̶\ the \ü\ loot \ú\ foot \y\ yet \zh\ vision \à, k̲, ⁿ, œ, œ̄, ᵫ, ᵫ̄, ᵊ\ see Guide to Pronunciation

¹**pre·mier** \pri-'mir, -'myir, -'mē-ər; 'prē-„ 'pre-,\ *adj* [ME *primier,* fr. MF *premier* first, chief, fr. L *primarius* of the first rank — more at PRIMARY] (15c) **1 :** first in position, rank, or importance **2 :** first in time **:** EARLIEST

²**premier** *n* [F, fr. *premier,* adj.] (1711) **:** PRIME MINISTER — **pre·mier·ship** \-,ship\ *n*

pre·mier dan·seur \prə-myä-däⁿ-sœr\ *n* [F] (1828) **:** the principal male dancer in a ballet company

¹**pre·miere** \pri-'myer, -'mir, -'mē-ər; ,pri-mē-'er\ *adj* [alter. of ¹*premier*] (1768) **:** PREMIER

²**premiere** *also* **pre·mière** *same as* ¹PREMIERE\ *n* [F *première,* fr. fem. of *premier* first] (1889) **1 :** a first performance or exhibition ⟨the ~ of a play⟩ **2 :** the chief actress of a theatrical cast

³**premiere** *also* **pre·mière** *or* **pre·mier** *same as* ¹PREMIERE\ *vb* **pre·miered** *also* **pre·mièred; pre·mier·ing** *also* **pre·mièr·ing** *vt* (1933) **:** to give a first public performance of ~ *vi* **1 :** to have a first public performance **2 :** to appear for the first time as a star performer

pre·mière dan·seuse \prə-myer-däⁿ-sœz\ *n* [F] (1828) **:** PRIMA BALLERINA

pre·mil·le·nar·i·an·ism \,prē-,mi-lə-'ner-ē-ə-,ni-zəm\ *n* (1844) **:** PREMILLENNIALISM — **pre·mil·le·nar·i·an** \-ē-ən\ *adj or n*

pre·mil·len·ni·al \,prē-mə-'le-nē-əl\ *adj* (1846) **1 :** coming before a millennium **2 :** holding or relating to premillennialism — **pre·mil·len·ni·al·ly** \-nē-ə-lē\ *adv*

pre·mil·len·ni·al·ism \-nē-ə-,li-zəm\ *n* (ca. 1883) **:** the view that Christ's return will usher in a future millennium of Messianic rule mentioned in Revelation — **pre·mil·len·ni·al·ist** \-nē-ə-list\ *n*

¹**prem·ise** *also* **prem·iss** \'pre-məs\ *n* [in sense 1, fr. ME *premisse,* fr. MF, fr. ML *praemissa,* fr. L, fem. of *praemissus,* pp. of *praemittere* to place ahead, fr. *prae-* pre- + *mittere* to send; in other senses, fr. ME *premisses,* fr. ML *praemissa,* fr. L, neut. pl. of *praemissus*] (14c) **1 a :** a proposition antecedently supposed or proved as a basis of argument or inference; *specif* **:** either of the first two propositions of a syllogism from which the conclusion is drawn **b :** something assumed or taken for granted **:** PRESUPPOSITION **2** *pl* **:** matters previously stated; *specif* **:** the preliminary and explanatory part of a deed or of a bill in equity **3** *pl* [fr. its being identified in the premises of the deed] **a :** a tract of land with the buildings thereon **b :** a building or part of a building usu. with its appurtenances (as grounds)

²**prem·ise** \'pre-məs *also* pri-'miz\ *vt* **prem·ised; prem·is·ing** (1526) **1 a :** to set forth beforehand as an introduction or a postulate **b :** to offer as a premise in an argument **2 :** POSTULATE **3 :** to base on certain assumptions

¹**pre·mi·um** \'prē-mē-əm\ *n* [L *praemium* booty, profit, reward, fr. *prae-* + *emere* to take, buy — more at REDEEM] (1601) **1 a :** a reward or recompense for a particular act **b :** a sum over and above a regular price paid chiefly as an inducement or incentive **c :** a sum in advance of or in addition to the nominal value of something ⟨bonds callable at a ~ of six percent⟩ **d :** something given free or at a reduced price with the purchase of a product or service **2 :** the consideration paid for a contract of insurance **3 :** a high value or a value in excess of that normally or usu. expected ⟨put a ~ on accuracy⟩

²**premium** *adj* (1844) **:** of exceptional quality or amount; *also* **:** higher‐priced

¹**pre·mix** \,(,)prē-'miks, 'prē-,\ *vt* (1927) **:** to mix before use

²**pre·mix** \'prē-,miks\ *n* (1937) **:** a mixture of ingredients designed to be mixed with other ingredients before use

pre·mo·lar \,(,)prē-'mō-lər\ *adj* (ca. 1859) **:** situated in front of or preceding the molar teeth; *esp* **:** being or relating to those teeth of a mammal in front of the true molars and behind the canines when the latter are present — **premolar** *n*

pre·mon·ish \-'mä-nish\ *vt* (1526) *archaic* **:** FOREWARN ~ *vi, archaic* **:** to give warning in advance

pre·mo·ni·tion \,prē-mə-'ni-shən, ,pre-\ *n* [ME, fr. MF, fr. LL *praemonition-, praemonitio,* fr. L *praemonēre* to warn in advance, fr. *prae-* + *monēre* to warn — more at MIND] (15c) **1 :** previous notice or warning **:** FOREWARNING **2 :** anticipation of an event without conscious reason **:** PRESENTIMENT

pre·mon·i·to·ry \pri-'mä-nə-,tōr-ē, -,tòr-\ *adj* (1647) **:** giving warning ⟨a ~ symptom⟩ — **pre·mon·i·to·ri·ly** \-,mä-nə-'tòr-ə-lē, -'tōr-\ *adv*

Pre·mon·stra·ten·sian \,prē-,män(t)-strə-'ten(t)-shən\ *n* [ML *praemonstratensis,* fr. *praemonstratensis* of Prémontré, fr. *Praemonstratus* Prémontré] (1695) **:** a member of an order of canons regular founded by St. Norbert at Prémontré near Laon, France, in 1120

pre·mune \(,)prē-'myün\ *adj* [back-formation fr. *premunition*] (1948) **:** exhibiting premunition

pre·mu·ni·tion \,prē-myù-'ni-shən\ *n* [L *praemunition-, praemunitio* advance fortification, fr. *praemunire* to fortify in advance, fr. *prae-* + *munire* to fortify — more at MUNITION] (1607) **1** *archaic* **:** an advance provision of protection **2 a :** resistance to a disease due to the existence of its causative agent in a state of physiological equilibrium in the host **b :** immunity to a particular infection due to previous presence of the causative agent

pre·name \'prē-,nām\ *n* (1894) **:** FORENAME

pre·na·tal \,(,)prē-'nā-t²l\ *adj* (1826) **1 :** occurring, existing, or performed before birth ⟨~ care⟩ ⟨the ~ period⟩ **2 :** providing or receiving prenatal medical care ⟨a ~ clinic⟩ ⟨~ patients⟩ — **pre·na·tal·ly** \-t²l-ē\ *adv*

¹**pre·nom·i·nate** \(,)prē-'nä-mə-nət\ *adj* [LL *praenominatus,* pp. of *praenominare* to name before, fr. L *prae-* + *nominare* to name — more at NOMINATE] (1513) *obs* **:** previously mentioned

²**pre·nom·i·nate** \-,nāt\ *vt* (1547) *obs* **:** to mention previously — **pre·nom·i·na·tion** \(,)prē-,nä-mə-'nā-shən\ *n, obs*

pre·no·tion \(,)prē-'nō-shən, 'prē-,\ *n* [L *praenotion-, praenotio* preconception, fr. *prae-* + *notio* idea, conception — more at NOTION] (1588) **1 :** PRESENTIMENT, PREMONITION **2 :** PRECONCEPTION

¹**pren·tice** \'pren-təs\ *n* [ME *prentis,* short for *apprentis*] (14c) **:** APPRENTICE 1, LEARNER — **prentice** *adj*

²**prentice** *vt* **pren·ticed; pren·tic·ing** (1598) **:** APPRENTICE

pre·nup·tial \,(,)prē-'nəp-shəl, -chəl, ÷-chə-wəl\ *adj* (1869) **:** made or occurring before marriage ⟨a ~ agreement⟩

pre·oc·cu·pan·cy \(,)prē-'ä-kyə-pən(t)-sē\ *n* (ca. 1755) **1 :** an act or the right of taking possession before another **2 :** the condition of being completely busied or preoccupied

pre·oc·cu·pa·tion \(,)prē-,ä-kyə-'pā-shən\ *n* (1603) **1 :** an act of preoccupying **:** the state of being preoccupied **2 a :** extreme or excessive concern with something **b :** something that preoccupies one

pre·oc·cu·pied \(,)prē-'ä-kyə-,pīd\ *adj* (1842) **1 :** previously applied to another group and unavailable for use in a new sense — used of a biological generic or specific name **2 a :** lost in thought; *also* **:** absorbed in some preoccupation **b :** already occupied

pre·oc·cu·py \-,pī\ *vt* [L *praeoccupare,* lit., to seize in advance, fr. *prae-* + *occupare* to seize, occupy] (1567) **1 :** to engage or engross the interest or attention of beforehand or preferentially **2 :** to take possession of or fill beforehand or before another

pre·op·er·a·tive \(,)prē-'ä-p(ə-)rə-tiv, -,rā-\ *adj* (1904) **:** occurring before a surgical operation — **pre·op·er·a·tive·ly** *adv*

pre·or·dain \,prē-òr-'dān\ *vt* (1533) **:** to decree or ordain in advance **:** FOREORDAIN — **pre·or·dain·ment** \-mənt\ *n* — **pre·or·di·na·tion** \(,)prē-,ór-d²n-'ā-shən\ *n*

pre·ovu·la·to·ry \(,)prē-'äv-yə-lə-,tōr-ē, -,tòr-, -'ōv-\ *adj* (1935) **:** occurring or existing in or typical of the period immediately preceding ovulation ⟨~ oocytes⟩ ⟨a ~ surge of luteinizing hormone⟩

pre-owned \(,)prē-'ōnd, 'prē-,\ *adj* (1964) **:** SECONDHAND

¹**prep** \'prep\ *n* (1862) **1 :** PREPARATION **2 :** PREPARATORY SCHOOL **3 :** a preliminary trial for a racehorse

²**prep** *vb* **prepped; prep·ping** *vi* (1915) **1 :** to attend preparatory school **2** [short for *prepare*] **:** to get ready ~ *vt* **1 :** to prepare for operation or examination

pre·pack·age \(,)prē-'pa-kij\ *vt* (1945) **:** to package (as food or a manufactured article) before offering for sale to the consumer

prep·a·ra·tion \,pre-pə-'rā-shən\ *n* [ME *preparacion,* fr. MF *preparation,* fr. L *praeparation-, praeparatio,* fr. *praeparare* to prepare] (14c) **1 :** the action or process of making something ready for use or service or of getting ready for some occasion, test, or duty **2 :** a state of being prepared **:** READINESS **3 :** a preparatory act or measure **4 :** something that is prepared; *specif* **:** a medicinal substance made ready for use ⟨a ~ for colds⟩

¹**pre·par·a·tive** \pri-'par-ə-tiv\ *n* (14c) **:** something that prepares the way for or serves as a preliminary to something else **:** PREPARATION

²**preparative** *adj* (ca. 1530) **:** PREPARATORY — **pre·par·a·tive·ly** *adv*

pre·pa·ra·tor \pri-'par-ə-tər\ *n* (1762) **:** one that prepares; *specif* **:** a person who prepares scientific specimens or museum displays

pre·pa·ra·to·ry \pri-'par-ə-,tōr-ē, -,tòr- *also* 'pre-p(ə-)rə-\ *adj* (15c) **:** preparing or serving to prepare for something **:** INTRODUCTORY — **pre·pa·ra·to·ri·ly** \pri-,par-ə-'tōr-ə-lē, -'tòr- *also* ,pre-p(ə-)rə-\ *adv*

preparatory school *n* (1822) **1 :** a usu. private school preparing students primarily for college **2** *Brit* **:** a private elementary school preparing students primarily for British public schools

preparatory to *prep* (1649) **:** in preparation for

pre·pare \pri-'par, -'per\ *vb* **pre·pared; pre·par·ing** [ME, fr. MF *preparer,* fr. L *praeparare,* fr. *prae-* pre- + *parare* to procure, prepare — more at PARE] *vt* (15c) **1 a :** to make ready beforehand for some purpose, use, or activity ⟨~ food for dinner⟩ **b :** to put in a proper state of mind ⟨is prepared to listen⟩ **2 :** to work out the details of **:** plan in advance ⟨*preparing* strategy for the coming campaign⟩ **3 a :** to put together **:** COMPOUND ⟨~ a prescription⟩ **b :** to put into written form ⟨~ a report⟩ ~ *vi* **:** to get ready ⟨*preparing* for a career⟩ — **pre·par·er** *n*

prepared *adj* (1663) **:** subjected to a special process or treatment — **pre·pared·ly** \-'pard-lē, -'perd-; -'par-əd-, -'per-\ *adv* — **pre·pared·ness** \pri-'par-əd-nəs, -'per- *also* -'pard-nəs *or* -'perd-nəs\ *n* (1590) **:** the quality or state of being prepared; *esp* **:** a state of adequate preparation in case of war

pre·pay \(,)prē-'pā\ *vt* **-paid** \-'pād\; **-pay·ing** (1839) **:** to pay or pay the charge on in advance — **pre·pay·ment** \-'pā-mənt\ *n*

pre·pense \pri-'pen(t)s\ *adj* [by shortening & alter. fr. earlier *purpensed,* fr. ME, pp. of *purpensen* to deliberate, premeditate, fr. MF *purpenser,* fr. OF, fr. *pur-* for + *penser* to think — more at PURCHASE, PENSIVE] (1702) **:** planned beforehand **:** PREMEDITATED — usu. used postpositively ⟨malice ~⟩ — **pre·pense·ly** *adv*

pre·plant \,prē-'plant, 'prē-,\ *also* **pre·plant·ing** \-'plan-tiŋ\ *adj* (1961) **:** occurring or used before planting a crop ⟨~ soil fertilization⟩

pre·pon·der·ance \pri-'pän-d(ə-)rən(t)s\ *n* (1681) **1 :** a superiority in weight, power, importance, or strength **2 a :** a superiority or excess in number or quantity **b :** MAJORITY

pre·pon·der·an·cy \-d(ə-)rən(t)-sē\ *n* (1646) **:** PREPONDERANCE

pre·pon·der·ant \pri-'pän-d(ə-)rənt\ *adj* (15c) **1 :** having superior weight, force, or influence **2 :** having greater prevalence **syn** see DOMINANT — **pre·pon·der·ant·ly** *adv*

¹**pre·pon·der·ate** \pri-'pän-də-,rāt\ *vb* **-at·ed; -at·ing** [L *praeponderatus,* pp. of *praeponderare,* fr. *prae-* + *ponder-, pondus* weight — more at PENDANT] *vi* (1623) **1 :** to exceed in weight **2 :** to exceed in influence, power, or importance **3 :** to exceed in numbers ~ *vt* **1** *archaic* **:** OUTWEIGH **2** *archaic* **:** to weigh down — **pre·pon·der·a·tion** \-,pän-də-'rā-shən, ,prē-\ *n*

²**pre·pon·der·ate** \-'pän-də-rət\ *adj* (1802) **:** PREPONDERANT — **pre·pon·der·ate·ly** *adv*

prep·o·si·tion \,pre-pə-'zi-shən\ *n* [ME *preposicioun,* fr. L *praeposition-, praepositio,* fr. *praeponere* to put in front, fr. *prae-* pre- + *ponere* to put — more at POSITION] (14c) **:** a function word that typically combines with a noun phrase to form a phrase which usu. expresses a modification or predication — **prep·o·si·tion·al** \-'zish-nəl, -'zi-shə-n²l\ *adj* — **prep·o·si·tion·al·ly** *adv*

pre·pos·i·tive \(,)prē-'pä-zə-tiv, -'päz-tiv\ *adj* [LL *praepositivus,* fr. L *praepositus,* pp. of *praeponere*] (1583) **:** put before **:** PREFIXED — **pre·pos·i·tive·ly** *adv*

pre·pos·sess \,prē-pə-'zes *also* -'ses\ *vt* (1614) **1** *obs* **:** to take previous possession of **2 :** to cause to be preoccupied **3 :** to influence beforehand esp. favorably

pre·pos·sess·ing *adj* (1642) **1** *archaic* **:** creating prejudice **2 :** tending to create a favorable impression **:** ATTRACTIVE

pre·pos·ses·sion \,prē-pə-'ze-shən *also* -'se-\ *n* (1648) **1** *archaic* **:** prior possession **2 :** an attitude, belief, or impression formed beforehand **:** PREJUDICE **3 :** an exclusive concern with one idea or object **:** PREOCCUPATION **syn** see BIGOTRY

pre·pos·ter·ous \pri-'päs-t(ə-)rəs\ *adj* [L *praeposterus,* lit., in the wrong order, fr. *prae-* + *posterus* hinder, following — more at POSTERIOR]

(1542) : contrary to nature, reason, or common sense : ABSURD — **pre·pos·ter·ous·ly** *adv* — **pre·pos·ter·ous·ness** *n*

pre·po·ten·cy \(ˌ)prē-'pō-t°n(t)-sē\ *n* (1646) **1** : the quality or state of being prepotent : PREDOMINANCE **2** : unusual ability of an individual or strain to transmit its characters to offspring because of homozygosity for numerous dominant genes

pre·po·tent \-t°nt\ *adj* [ME, fr. L *praepotent-, praepotens*, fr. *prae-* + *potens* powerful — more at POTENT] (15c) **1 a** : having exceptional power, authority, or influence **b** : exceeding others in power **2** : exhibiting genetic prepotency — **pre·po·tent·ly** *adv*

¹prep·py *or* **prep·pie** \'pre-pē\ *n, pl* **prep·pies** [¹*prep*] (1967) **1** : a student at or a graduate of a preparatory school **2** : a person deemed to dress or behave like a preppy

²preppy *or* **preppie** *adj* (1967) **1** : relating to, characteristic of, or being a preppy **2** : relating to or being a style of dress characterized esp. by classic clothing and neat appearance — **prep·pi·ly** \'pre-pə-lē\ *adv* — **prep·pi·ness** \'pre-pē-nəs\ *n*

pre·pran·di·al \(ˌ)prē-'pran-dē-əl\ *adj* (1822) : of, relating to, or suitable for the time just before dinner ⟨a ~ drink⟩

pre·preg \ˌprē-'preg, 'prē-,\ *n* [*pre-* + im(*pregn*ated)] (1954) : a reinforcing or molding material (as paper or glass cloth) already impregnated with a synthetic resin

¹pre·print \'prē-ˌprint, ˌprē-'print\ *n* (1889) **1** : an issue of a technical paper often in preliminary form before its publication in a journal **2** : something (as an advertisement) printed before the rest of the publication in which it is to appear

²pre·print \(ˌ)prē-'print\ *vt* (1926) : to print in advance for later use

pre·pro·cess \(ˌ)prē-'prä-ˌses, -'prō-, -səs\ *vt* (1942) : to do preliminary processing of (as data) — **pre·pro·ces·sor** \-ˌse-sər, -sə-sər, -ˌsôr\ *n*

pre·pro·fes·sion·al \ˌprē-prə-'fesh-nəl, -'fe-shə-n°l\ *adj* (1926) : of or relating to the period preceding specific study for or practice of a profession

prep school *n* (1895) : PREPARATORY SCHOOL

pre·pu·ber·al \(ˌ)prē-'pyü-b(ə-)rəl\ *adj* (ca. 1935) : PREPUBERTAL

pre·pu·ber·tal \-bər-t°l\ *adj* (1859) : of or relating to prepuberty

pre·pu·ber·ty \-bər-tē\ *n* (1922) : the period immediately preceding puberty

pre·pu·bes·cence \ˌprē-pyü-'be-s°n(t)s\ *n* (1916) : PREPUBERTY

pre·pu·bes·cent \-s°nt\ *adj* (1904) : PREPUBERTAL — **prepubescent** *n*

pre·puce \'prē-ˌpyüs\ *n* [ME, fr. MF, fr. L *praeputium*] (15c) : FORESKIN; *also* : a similar fold investing the clitoris — **pre·pu·tial** \prē-'pyü-shəl\ *adj*

pre·quel \'prē-kwəl\ *n* [*pre-* + -*quel* (as in *sequel*)] (1972) : a literary or dramatic work whose story precedes that of an earlier work

Pre–Rapha·el·ite \(ˌ)prē-'ra-fē-ə-ˌlīt, -'rä-, -'rä-\ *n* (1850) **1 a** : a member of a brotherhood of artists formed in England in 1848 to restore the artistic principles and practices regarded as characteristic of Italian art before Raphael **b** : an artist or writer influenced by this brotherhood **2** : a modern artist dedicated to restoring early Renaissance ideals or methods — **Pre–Raphaelite** *adj* — **Pre–Ra·pha·el·it·ism** \-ˌli-ˌti-zəm\ *n*

pre·reg·is·tra·tion \ˌprē-ˌre-jə-'strā-shən\ *n* (1967) : a special registration (as for returning students) prior to an official registration period — **pre·reg·is·ter** \(ˌ)prē-'re-jə-stər\ *vi*

pre·req·ui·site \(ˌ)prē-'re-kwə-zət\ *n* (1633) : something that is necessary to an end or to the carrying out of a function — **prerequisite** *adj*

pre·rog·a·tive \pri-'rä-gə-tiv\ *n* [ME, fr. MF & L; MF, fr. L *praerogativa*, Roman century voting first in the comitia, privilege, fr. fem. of *praerogativus* voting first, fr. *praerogatus*, pp. of *praerogare* to ask for an opinion before another, fr. *prae-* + *rogare* to ask — more at RIGHT] (15c) **1 a** : an exclusive or special right, power, or privilege as (1) : one belonging to an office or an official body (2) : one belonging to a person, group, or class of individuals (3) : one possessed by a nation as an attribute of sovereignty **b** : the discretionary power inhering in the British Crown **2** : a distinctive excellence — **pre·rog·a·tived** \-tivd\ *adj*

¹pres·age \'pre-sij, *also* pri-'sāj\ *n* [ME, fr. L *praesagium*, fr. *praesagire* having a foreboding, fr. *prae-* + *sagus* prophetic — more at SEEK] (14c) **1** : something that foreshadows or portends a future event : OMEN **2** : an intuition or feeling of what is going to happen in the future **3** *archaic* : PROGNOSTICATION **4** : warning or indication of the future — **pre·sage·ful** \pri-'sāj-fəl\ *adj*

²pres·age \'pre-sij, pri-'sāj\ *vb* **pre·saged; pre·sag·ing** *vt* (1562) **1** : to give an omen or warning of : FORESHADOW **2** : FORETELL, PREDICT ~ *vi* : to make or utter a prediction — **pre·sag·er** *n, obs*

pre·sanc·ti·fied \(ˌ)prē-'saŋ(k)-ti-ˌfīd\ *adj* (1758) : consecrated at a previous service — used of eucharistic elements

pres·by·ope \'prez-bē-ˌōp, 'pres-bē-, -pē-\ *n* [prob. fr. F, fr. Gk *presbys* old man + *ōps* eye — more at EYE] (ca. 1857) : one affected with presbyopia

pres·by·o·pia \ˌprez-bē-'ō-pē-ə, ˌpres-\ *n* [NL] (1793) : a visual condition which becomes apparent esp. in middle age and in which loss of elasticity of the lens of the eye causes defective accommodation and inability to focus sharply for near vision — **pres·by·o·pic** \-'ō-pik, -'ä-\ *adj or n*

pres·by·ter \'prez-bə-tər, 'pres-\ *n* [LL, elder, priest, fr. Gk *presbyteros*, compar. of *presbys* old man, elder; akin to Gk *pro* before and Gk *bainein* to go — more at FOR, COME] (1597) **1** : a member of the governing body of an early Christian church **2** : a member of the order of priests in churches having episcopal hierarchies that include bishops, priests, and deacons **3** : ELDER 4b — **pres·byt·er·ate** \prez-'bi-tə-rət, pres-, -ˌrāt\ *n*

¹pres·by·te·ri·al \ˌprez-bə-'tir-ē-əl, ˌpres-\ *adj* (ca. 1600) : of or relating to presbyters or a presbytery — **pres·by·te·ri·al·ly** \-ē-ə-lē\ *adv*

²presbyterial *n, often cap* (1928) : an organization of Presbyterian women associated with a presbytery

¹Pres·by·te·ri·an \-ē-ən\ *n* (1640) : a member of a Presbyterian church

²Presbyterian *adj* (1641) **1** *often not cap* : characterized by a graded system of representative ecclesiastical bodies (as presbyteries) exercising legislative and judicial powers **2** : of, relating to, or constituting a Protestant Christian church that is presbyterian in government and traditionally Calvinistic in doctrine — **Pres·by·te·ri·an·ism** \-ē-ə-ˌni-zəm\ *n*

pres·by·tery \'prez-bə-ˌter-ē, 'pres-, -bə-trē\ *n, pl* **-ter·ies** [ME & LL;

ME *presbytory* part of church reserved for clergy, fr. LL *presbyterium* group of presbyters, part of church reserved for clergy, fr. Gk *presbyterion* group of presbyters, fr. *presbyteros* elder, priest] (15c) **1** : the part of a church reserved for the officiating clergy **2** : a ruling body in presbyterian churches consisting of the ministers and representative elders from congregations within a district **3** : the jurisdiction of a presbytery **4** : the house of a Roman Catholic parish priest

¹pre·school \'prē-ˌskül, (ˌ)prē-\ *adj* (1914) : of, relating to, or constituting the period in a child's life from infancy to the age of five or six that ordinarily precedes attendance at elementary school

²pre·school \'prē-ˌskül\ *n* (ca. 1925) : NURSERY SCHOOL, KINDERGARTEN

pre·school·er \-ˌskü-lər\ *n* (1946) **1** : a child not yet old enough for school **2** : a child attending a preschool

pre·science \'pre-sh(ē-)ən(t)s, 'prē-, -s(ē-)ən(t)s\ *n* [ME, fr. LL *praescientia*, fr. L *praescient-, praesciens*, prp. of *praescire* to know beforehand, fr. *prae-* + *scire* to know — more at SCIENCE] (14c) : foreknowledge of events: **a** : divine omniscience **b** : human anticipation of the course of events : FORESIGHT — **pre·scient** \-sh(ē-)ənt, -s(ē-)ənt\ *adj* — **pre·scient·ly** *adv*

pre·sci·en·tif·ic \ˌprē-ˌsī-ən-'ti-fik\ *adj* (1858) : of, relating to, or having the characteristics of a period before the rise of modern science or a state prior to the application of the scientific method

pre·scind \pri-'sind\ *vb* [L *praescindere* to cut off in front, fr. *prae-* + *scindere* to cut — more at SHED] *vi* (1650) : to withdraw one's attention ~ *vt* : to detach for purposes of thought

pre·score \(ˌ)prē-'skōr, -'skȯr\ *vt* (1937) : to record (as sound) in advance for use when the corresponding scenes are photographed in making movies

pre·scribe \pri-'skrīb\ *vb* **pre·scribed; pre·scrib·ing** [ME, fr. L *praescribere* to write at the beginning, dictate, order, fr. *prae-* + *scribere* to write — more at SCRIBE] *vi* (15c) **1** : to lay down a rule : DICTATE **2** [ME, fr. ML *praescribere*, fr. L, to write at the beginning] : to claim a title to something by right of prescription **3** : to write or give medical prescriptions **4** : to become by prescription invalid or unenforceable ~ *vt* **1 a** : to lay down as a guide, direction, or rule of action : ORDAIN **b** : to specify with authority **2** : to designate or order the use of as a remedy — **pre·scrib·er** *n*

pre·script \'prē-ˌskript, pri-'\ *adj* [ME, fr. L *praescriptus*, pp.] (ca. 1540) : prescribed as a rule — **pre·script** \'prē-ˌskript\ *n*

pre·scrip·tion \pri-'skrip-shən\ *n* [partly fr. ME *prescripcion* [partly fr. ME *prescripcion* establishment of a claim, fr. MF *prescription*, fr. LL *praescription-, praescriptio*, fr. L, act of writing at the beginning, order, limitation of subject matter, fr. *praescribere*; partly fr. L *praescription-, praescriptio* order] (14c) **1 a** : the establishment of a claim of title to something under common law usu. by use and enjoyment for a period fixed by statute **b** : the right or title acquired under common law by such possession **2** : the process of making claim to something by long use and enjoyment **3** : the action of laying down authoritative rules or directions **4 a** : a written direction for a therapeutic or corrective agent; *specif* : one for the preparation and use of a medicine **b** : a prescribed medicine **c** : something like a doctor's prescription ⟨~s for economic recovery⟩ **5 a** : ancient or long continued custom **b** : a claim founded upon ancient custom or long continued use **6** : something prescribed as a rule

prescription drug *n* (1951) : a drug that can be obtained only by means of a physician's prescription

pre·scrip·tive \pri-'skrip-tiv\ *adj* (1748) **1** : serving to prescribe ⟨~ rules of usage⟩ **2** : acquired by, founded on, or determined by prescription or by long-standing custom — **pre·scrip·tive·ly** *adv*

pre·se·lect \ˌprē-sə-'lekt\ *vt* (ca. 1859) : to choose in advance usu. on the basis of a particular criterion — **pre·se·lec·tion** \-'lek-shən\ *n*

pre·sell \(ˌ)prē-'sel\ *vt* **-sold** \-'sōld\; **-sell·ing** (1947) **1** : to precondition (as a customer) for subsequent purchase or create advance demand for (as a product) esp. through marketing strategies **2** : to sell in advance ⟨raised money to publish the book by *preselling* film rights⟩

pres·ence \'pre-z°n(t)s\ *n* (14c) **1** : the fact or condition of being present **2** : the part of space within one's immediate vicinity **b** : the neighborhood of one of superior esp. royal rank **3** *archaic* : COMPANY **2a** : one that is present: as **a** : the actual person or thing that is present **b** : something present of a visible or concrete nature **5 a** : the bearing, carriage, or air of a person; *esp* : stately or distinguished bearing **b** : a quality of poise and effectiveness that enables a performer to achieve a close relationship with his audience **6** : something (as a spirit) felt or believed to be present

presence of mind (1665) : self-control so maintained in an emergency or in an embarrassing situation that one can say or do the right thing

¹pres·ent \'pre-z°nt\ *n* [ME, fr. OF, fr. *presenter*] (13c) : something presented : GIFT

²pre·sent \pri-'zent\ *vb* [ME, fr. OF *presenter*, fr. L *praesentare*, fr. *praesent-, praesens*, adj.] *vt* (14c) **1 a** (1) : to bring or introduce into the presence of someone esp. of superior rank or status (2) : to introduce socially **b** : to bring (as a play) before the public **2** : to make a gift to **3** : to give or bestow formally **4 a** : to lay (as a charge) before a court as an object of inquiry **b** : to bring a formal public charge, indictment, or presentment against **5** : to nominate to a benefice **6 a** : to offer to view : SHOW **b** : to bring to one's attention ⟨this ~s a problem⟩ **7** : to act the part of : PERFORM **8** : to aim, point, or direct (as a weapon) so as to face something or in a particular direction ~ *vi* **1** : to present a weapon **2** : to become manifest **3** : to come forward as a patient **4** : to make a presentation *syn* see GIVE — **pre·sent·er** *n*

³pres·ent \'pre-z°nt\ *adj* [ME, fr. OF, fr. L *praesent-, praesens*, fr. prp. of *praeesse* to be before one, fr. *prae-* + *esse* to be — more at IS] (14c) **1** : now existing or in progress **2** : being in view or at hand **b** : existing in something mentioned or under consideration **3** : constituting the one actually involved, at hand, or being considered **4** : of, relating to, or constituting a verb tense that is expressive of pres-

\ə\ abut \ᵊ\ kitten, F table \ər\ further \a\ ash \ā\ ace \ä\ mop, mar \au̇\ out \ch\ chin \e\ bet \ē\ easy \g\ go \i\ hit \ī\ ice \j\ job \ŋ\ sing \ō\ go \ȯ\ law \ȯi\ boy \th\ thin \th̲\ the \ü\ loot \u̇\ foot \y\ yet \zh\ vision \ä, k̲, ⁿ, œ, œ̄, ᵫ, ᵫ̄, ᵍ\ *see* Guide to Pronunciation ent time or the time of speaking **5** *obs* : ATTENTIVE **6** *archaic* : IN-STANT, IMMEDIATE — **pres·ent·ness** *n*

⁴pres·ent \'pre-z²nt\ *n* (14c) **1 a** *obs* : present occasion or affair **b** *pl* : the present words or statements; *specif* : the legal instrument or other writing in which these words are used **2 a** : the present tense of a language **b** : a verb form in the present tense **3** : the present time — **at present** : at or during this time : NOW

pre·sent·able \pri-'zen-tə-bəl\ *adj* (ca. 1626) **1** : capable of being presented **2** : being in condition to be seen or inspected esp. by the critical — **pre·sent·abil·i·ty** \-,zen-tə-'bi-lə-tē\ *n* — **pre·sent·able·ness** \-'zen-tə-bəl-nəs\ *n* — **pre·sent·ably** \-blē\ *adv*

pre·sent arms \pri-'zent-\ *n* [fr. the command *present arms!*] (ca. 1884) **1** : a position in the manual of arms in which the rifle is held vertically in front of the body **2** : a command to assume the position of present arms or to give a hand salute

pre·sen·ta·tion \,prē-,zen-'tā-shən, ,pre-z²n-, ,prē-z²n-\ *n* (15c) **1 a** : the act of presenting **b** : the act, power, or privilege esp. of a patron of applying to the bishop or ordinary for instituting someone into a benefice **2** : something presented: as **a** : a symbol or image that represents something **b** : something offered or given : GIFT **c** : something set forth for the attention of the mind **d** : a descriptive or persuasive account (as by a salesman of a product) **3** : the position in which the fetus lies in the uterus in labor with respect to the mouth of the uterus **4** : an immediate object of perception, cognition, or memory **5** *often cap* : a church feast on November 21 celebrating the presentation of the Virgin Mary in the temple **6** : the method by which radio, navigation, or radar information is given to the operator (as the pilot of an airplane) — **pre·sen·ta·tion·al** \-shnəl, -shə-n²l\ *adj*

pre·sen·ta·tive \pri-'zen-tə-tiv, 'pre-z²n-,tā-\ *adj* (ca. 1842) : known, knowing, or capable of being known directly rather than through cogitation

pre·sent–day \'pre-z²nt-'dā\ *adj* (1887) : now existing or occurring

pre·sen·tee \,pre-z²n-'tē, pri-,zen-\ *n* (15c) : one who is presented or to whom something is presented

pre·sen·tient \pri-'sen(t)-sh(ē-)ənt, 'pre-; pri-'zen(t)-\ *adj* [L *praesentient-, praesentiens*, prp. of *praesentire*] (1814) : having a presentiment

pre·sen·ti·ment \pri-'zen-tə-mənt\ *n* [F *pressentiment*, fr. MF, fr. *pressentir* to have a presentiment, fr. L *praesentire* to feel beforehand, fr. *prae- + sentire* to feel — more at SENSE] (1714) : a feeling that something will or is about to happen : PREMONITION — **pre·sen·ti·men·tal** \-,zen-tə-'men-t²l\ *adj*

pres·ent·ism \'pre-z²n-,ti-zəm\ *n* [³*present*] (1923) : an outlook dominated by present-day attitudes and experiences — **pres·ent·ist** \-z²n-tist\ *adj*

pres·ent·ly \'pre-z²nt-lē\ *adv* (14c) **1 a** *archaic* : at once **b** : before long : without undue delay **2** : at the present time : NOW

usage Both senses 1b and 2 are flourishing in current English, but many commentators have objected to sense 2. Since this sense has been in continuous use since the 15th century, it is not clear why it is objectionable. Perhaps a note in the *Oxford English Dictionary* (1909) that the sense has been obsolete since the 17th century in literary English is to blame, but the note goes on to observe that the sense is in regular use in most English dialects. The last citation in that dictionary is from a 1901 Leeds newspaper, written in Standard English. Sense 2 is most common in contexts relating to business and politics ⟨the fastest-rising welfare cost is Medicaid, *presently* paid by the states and cities —William Safire⟩

pre·sent·ment \pri-'zent-mənt\ *n* (14c) **1** : the act of presenting to an authority a formal statement of a matter to be dealt with; *specif* : the notice taken or statement made by a grand jury of an offense from their own knowledge without a bill of indictment laid before them **2** : the act of offering at the proper time and place a document (as a bill of exchange) that calls for acceptance or payment by another **3 a** : the act of presenting to view or consciousness **b** : something set forth, presented, or exhibited **c** : the aspect in which something is presented

present participle *n* (1864) : a participle that typically expresses present action in relation to the time expressed by the finite verb in its clause and that in English is formed with the suffix *-ing* and is used in the formation of the progressive tenses

present perfect *adj* (1887) : of, relating to, or constituting a verb tense that is formed in English with *have* and that expresses action or state completed at the time of speaking — **present perfect** *n*

present tense *n* (14c) : the tense of a verb that expresses action or state in the present time and is used of what occurs or is true at the time of speaking and of what is habitual or characteristic or is always or necessarily true, that is sometimes used to refer to action in the past, and that is sometimes used for future events

present value *n* (1831) : the sum of money which if invested now at a given rate of compound interest will accumulate exactly to a specified amount at a specified future date

pres·er·va·tion·ist \,pre-zər-'vā-sh(ə-)nist\ *n* (1927) : one who advocates preservation (as of a biological species or a historical landmark)

¹pre·ser·va·tive \pri-'zər-və-tiv\ *adj* (14c) : having the power of preserving

²preservative *n* (15c) : something that preserves or has the power of preserving; *specif* : an additive used to protect against decay, discoloration, or spoilage

¹pre·serve \pri-'zərv\ *vb* **pre·served; pre·serv·ing** [ME, fr. MF *preserver*, fr. ML *praeservare*, fr. LL, to observe beforehand, fr. L *prae- + servare* to keep, guard, observe — more at CONSERVE] *vt* (14c) **1** : to keep safe from injury, harm, or destruction : PROTECT **2** : to keep alive, intact, or free from decay : MAINTAIN **3 a** : to keep or save from decomposition **b** : to can, pickle, or similarly prepare for future use **4** : to keep up and reserve for personal or special use ~ *vi* **1** : to make preserves **2** : to raise and protect game for purposes of sport **3** : to be able to be preserved (as by canning) — **pre·serv·abil·i·ty** \-,zər-və-'bi-lə-tē\ *n* — **pre·serv·able** \-'zər-və-bəl\ *adj* — **pres·er·va·tion** \,pre-zər-'vā-shən\ *n* — **pre·serv·er** \-'zər-vər\ *n*

²preserve *n* (1600) **1** : fruit canned or made into jams or jellies or cooked whole or in large pieces in a syrup so as to keep its shape — often used in pl. **2** : an area restricted for the protection and preservation of natural resources (as animals or trees); *esp* : one used primarily for regulated hunting or fishing **3** : something regarded as reserved for certain persons

pre·shrink \(,)prē-'shriŋk, *esp Southern* -'sriŋk\ *vt* **-shrank** \-'shraŋk, -'sraŋk\; **-shrunk** \-'shrəŋk, -'sraŋk\ (1926) : to shrink (as a fabric) before making into a garment so that it will not shrink much when washed

pre·side \pri-'zīd\ *vi* **pre·sid·ed; pre·sid·ing** [L *praesidēre* to guard, preside over, fr. *prae- + sedēre* to sit — more at SIT] (1608) **1** : to exercise guidance, direction, or control **2 a** : to occupy the place of authority : act as president, chairman, or moderator **b** : to occupy a position similar to that of a president or chairman **3** : to occupy a position of featured instrumental performer — usu. used with *at* ⟨*presided* at the organ⟩ — **pre·sid·er** *n*

pres·i·den·cy \'pre-zə-dən(t)-sē, 'prez-dən(t)- *also* 'pre-zə-,den(t)-sē\ *n, pl* **-cies** (1591) **1 a** : the office of president **b** (1) : the office of president of the U.S. (2) : the American governmental institution comprising the office of president and various associated administrative and policy-making agencies **2** : the term during which a president holds office **3** : the action or function of one that presides : SUPERINTENDENCE **4** : a Mormon executive council of the church or a stake consisting of a president and two counselors

pres·i·dent \'pre-zə-dənt, 'prez-dənt, 'pre-zə-,dent *in rapid speech* 'pre-z²nt\ *n* [ME, fr. MF, fr. L *praesident-, praesidens*, fr. prp. of *praesidēre*] (14c) **1** : an official chosen to preside over a meeting or assembly **2** : an appointed governor of a subordinate political unit **3** : the chief officer of an organization (as a corporation or institution) usu. entrusted with the direction and administration of its policies **4** : the presiding officer of a governmental body **5 a** : an elected official serving as both chief of state and chief political executive in a republic having a presidential government **b** : an elected official having the position of chief of state but usu. only minimal political powers in a republic having a parliamentary government — **pres·i·den·tial** \,pre-zə-'den(t)-shəl, ,prez-'den(t)-\ *adj* — **pres·i·den·tial·ly** \-sh(ə-)lē\ *adv* — **pres·i·dent·ship** \'pre-zə-dənt-,ship, 'prez-dənt-, 'pre-zə-,dent-\ *n*

presidential government *n* (1902) : a system of government in which the president is constitutionally independent of the legislature

Presidents' Day *n* (1952) : WASHINGTON'S BIRTHDAY 2

pre·sid·i·al \pri-'si-dē-əl, prī-, -'zi-\ *adj* [LL *praesidialis*, fr. L *praesidium* garrison, fr. *praes* guard, governor, fr. *praesidēre*] (1611) **1** [F *présidial*, fr. MF, alter. of *presidal*, fr. LL *praesidalis* of a provincial governor, fr. L *praesid-, praeses*] : PROVINCIAL **2** : of, having, or constituting a garrison **3** : of or relating to a president : PRESIDENTIAL

pre·sid·i·ary \-dē-,er-ē\ *adj* (1599) : PRESIDIAL 2

pre·si·dio \pri-'sē-dē-,ō, -'si-, -'zē-, -'zi-\ *n, pl* **-di·os** [Sp, fr. L *praesidium*] (1763) : a garrisoned place; *esp* : a military post or fortified settlement in areas currently or orig. under Spanish control

pre·sid·i·um \pri-'si-dē-əm, prī-, -'zi-\ *n, pl* **-ia** \-dē-ə\ *or* **-iums** [Russ *prezidium*, fr. L *praesidium* garrison] (1920) **1** : a permanent executive committee selected esp. in Communist countries to act for a larger body **2** : a nongovernmental executive committee

pre·sig·ni·fy \(,)prē-'sig-nə-,fī\ *vt* [L *praesignificare*, fr. *prae- + significare* to signify] (1586) : to intimate or signify beforehand : PRESAGE

¹pre·soak \(,)prē-'sōk\ *vt* (1919) : to soak beforehand

²pre·soak \'prē-,sōk\ *n* (1919) **1** : an instance of presoaking **2** : a preparation used in presoaking clothes

pre–So·crat·ic \,prē-sə-'kra-tik, -sō-\ *adj* (1871) : of or relating to Greek philosophers before Socrates — **pre–Socratic** *n*

pre·sort \(,)prē-'sȯrt\ *vt* (1951) : to sort (outgoing mail) by zip code usu. before delivery to a post office

¹press \'pres\ *n* [ME *presse*, fr. OF, fr. *presser* to press] (13c) **1 a** : a crowd or crowded condition : THRONG **b** : a thronging or crowding forward or together **2 a** : an apparatus or machine by which a substance is cut or shaped, an impression of a body is taken, a material is compressed, pressure is applied to a body, liquid is expressed, or a cutting tool is fed into the work by pressure **b** : a building containing presses or a business using presses **3** : CLOSET, CUPBOARD **4 a** : an action of pressing or pushing : PRESSURE **b** : an aggressive pressuring defense employed in basketball often over the entire court area **5** : the properly smoothed and creased condition of a freshly pressed garment ⟨out of ~⟩ **6 a** : PRINTING PRESS **b** : the act or the process of printing **c** : a printing or publishing establishment **7 a** : the gathering and publishing or broadcasting of news : JOURNALISM **b** : newspapers, periodicals, and often radio and television news broadcasting **c** : news reporters, publishers, and broadcasters **d** : comment or notice in newspapers and periodicals ⟨is getting a good ~⟩ **8** : any of various pressure devices (as one for keeping sporting gear from warping when not in use) **9** : a lift in weight lifting in which the weight is raised to shoulder height and then smoothly extended overhead without assist from the legs — compare CLEAN AND JERK, SNATCH

²press *vb* [ME, fr. MF *presser*, fr. L *pressare*, freq. of *premere* to press; prob. akin to Russ *naperet* to press] *vt* (14c) **1** : to act upon through steady pushing or thrusting force exerted in contact : SQUEEZE **2 a** : ASSAIL, HARASS **b** : AFFLICT, OPPRESS **3 a** : to squeeze out the juice or contents of **b** : to squeeze with apparatus or instruments to a desired density, smoothness, or shape **4 a** : to exert influence on : CONSTRAIN **b** : to try hard to persuade : BESEECH, ENTREAT **5** : to move by means of pressure **6 a** : to lay stress or emphasis on **b** : to insist on or request urgently **7** : to follow through (a course of action) **8** : to clasp in affection or courtesy **9** : to make (a phonograph record) from a matrix ~ *vi* **1** : to crowd closely : MASS **2** : to force or push one's way **3** : to seek urgently : CONTEND **4** : to require haste or speed in action **5** : to exert pressure **6** : to take or hold a press **7** : to employ a press in basketball — **press·er** *n* — **press the flesh** : to greet and shake hands with people esp. while campaigning for political office

³press *vb* [alter. of, obs. *prest* to enlist by giving pay in advance] *vt* (1578) **1** : to force into service esp. in an army or navy : IMPRESS **2 a** : to take by authority esp. for public use : COMMANDEER **b** : to take and force into any usu. emergency service ~ *vi* : to impress men as soldiers or sailors

⁴press *n* (1599) **1** : impressment into service esp. in a navy **2** *obs* : a warrant for impressing recruits

press agent *n* [¹*press*] (1883) : an agent employed to establish and maintain good public relations through publicity — **press–agent** *vb* — **press–agent·ry** \-'ā-jən-trē\ *n*

press·board \'pres-,bōrd, -,bȯrd\ *n* (1849) **1 :** IRONING BOARD; *esp* : a small one for sleeves **2 :** a strong highly glazed composition board resembling vulcanized fiber

press box *n* (1889) : a space reserved for reporters (as at a stadium)

press cloth *n* (1899) : a cloth used between an iron and a garment

press conference *n* (1937) : an interview or announcement given by a public figure to the press by appointment

press–gang \'pres-,gaŋ\ *n* [⁴*press*] (1693) : a detachment of men under command of an officer empowered to force men into military or naval service — **press–gang** *vt*

press·ing *adj* (1616) **1 :** urgently important : CRITICAL **2 :** EARNEST, WARM — **press·ing·ly** \'pre-siŋ-lē\ *adv*

press kit *n* (1968) : a collection of promotional materials for distribution to the press

press·man \'pres-mən, -,man\ *n* (1598) **1 :** an operator of a press; *esp* : the operator of a printing press **2** *Brit* : NEWSPAPERMAN

press·mark \-,märk\ *n* [¹*press* (closet)] (1802) *chiefly Brit* : a mark or number assigned to a book to indicate its location in a library

press of sail (1794) : the fullest amount of sail that a ship can crowd on — called also *press of canvas*

pres·sor \'pre-,sȯr, -sər\ *adj* [LL, one that presses, fr. L *premere* to press — more at PRESS] (ca. 1890) : raising or tending to raise blood pressure; *also* : involving vasoconstriction

press·room \'pres-,rüm, -,rùm\ *n* (1683) **1 :** a room in a printing plant containing the printing presses **2 :** a room (as at the White House) for the use of members of the press

press·run \-,rən\ *n* (1945) : a continuous operation of a printing press producing a specified number of copies; *also* : the number of copies printed

press secretary *n* (1951) : a person officially in charge of press relations for a usu. prominent public figure ⟨the President's *press secretary*⟩

press–up \'pres-,əp\ *n* (1936) *Brit* : PUSH-UP

¹pres·sure \'pre-shər\ *n* [ME, fr. LL *pressura*, fr. L, action of pressing, pressure, fr. *pressus*, pp. of *premere*] (14c) **1 a :** the burden of physical or mental distress **b :** the constraint of circumstance : the weight of social or economic imposition **2 :** the application of force to something by something else in direct contact with it : COMPRESSION **3** *archaic* : IMPRESSION, STAMP **4 a :** the action of a force against an opposing force **b :** the force or thrust exerted over a surface divided by its area **c :** ELECTROMOTIVE FORCE **5 :** the stress or urgency of matters demanding attention : EXIGENCY ⟨people who work well under ∼⟩ **6 :** the force of selection that results from one or more agents and tends to reduce a population of organisms ⟨population ∼⟩ ⟨predation ∼⟩ **7 :** atmospheric pressure **8 :** a sensation aroused by moderate compression of a body part or surface — **pres·sure·less** *adj*

²pressure *vt* **pres·sured; pres·sur·ing** \'pre-sh(ə-)riŋ\ (1938) **1 :** to apply pressure to **2 :** PRESSURIZE **3 :** to cook in a pressure cooker

pressure cabin *n* (1935) : a pressurized cabin

pressure cooker *n* (1915) **1 :** an airtight utensil for quick cooking or preserving of foods by means of superheated steam under pressure **2 :** a situation or environment that is fraught with emotional or social pressures — **pressure–cook** *vb*

pressure gauge *n* (1862) : a gauge for indicating fluid pressure

pressure group *n* (1928) : an interest group organized to influence public and esp. government policy but not to elect candidates to office

pressure point *n* (1909) : a point where a blood vessel runs near a bone and can be compressed (as to check bleeding) by the application of pressure against the bone

pressure suit *n* (1936) : an inflatable suit for high-altitude or space flight to protect the body from low pressure

pressure wave *n* (1942) : a wave (as a sound wave) in which the propagated disturbance is a variation of pressure in a material medium — called also *P-wave*

pres·sur·ise *Brit var of* PRESSURIZE

pres·sur·ize \'pre-shə-,rīz\ *vt* **-ized; -iz·ing** (1938) **1 :** to confine the contents of under a pressure greater than that of the outside atmosphere; *esp* : to maintain near-normal atmospheric pressure in during high-altitude or spaceflight (as by means of a supercharger) **2 :** to apply pressure to **3 :** to design to withstand pressure — **pres·sur·i·za·tion** \,pre-sh(ə-)rə-'zā-shən\ *n* — **pres·sur·iz·er** *n*

press·work \'pres-,wərk\ *n* (1771) : the operation, management, or product of a printing press; *esp* : the branch of printing concerned with the actual transfer of ink from form or plates to paper

prest \'prest\ *adj* [ME, fr. OF, fr. L *praestus* — more at PRESTO] (14c) *obs* : READY

pres·ti·dig·i·ta·tion \,pres-tə-,di-jə-'tā-shən\ *n* [F, fr. *prestidigitateur* prestidigitator, fr. *preste* nimble, quick (fr. It *presto*) + L *digitus* finger — more at DIGIT] (1859) : SLEIGHT OF HAND, LEGERDEMAIN — **pres·ti·dig·i·ta·tor** \-'di-jə-,tā-tər\ *n*

pres·tige \pre-'stēzh, -'stēj\ *n, often attrib* [F, fr. MF, conjuror's trick, illusion, fr. L *praestigiae*, pl., conjuror's tricks, fr. *praestringere* to graze, blunt, constrict, fr. *prae-* + *stringere* to bind tight — more at STRAIN] (1829) **1 :** standing or estimation in the eyes of people : weight or credit in general opinion **2 :** commanding position in people's minds *syn* see INFLUENCE — **pres·tige·ful** \-fəl\ *adj*

pres·ti·gious \pre-'sti-jəs, -'stē- *also* prə-\ *adj* [L *praestigiosus*, fr. *praestigiae*] (1546) **1** *archaic* : of, relating to, or marked by illusion, conjuring, or trickery **2 :** having prestige : HONORED — **pres·ti·gious·ly** *adv* — **pres·ti·gious·ness** *n*

pres·tis·si·mo \pre-'sti-sə-,mō\ *adv or adj* [It, fr. *presto* + *-issimo*, suffix denoting a high degree] (ca. 1724) : faster than presto — used as a direction in music

¹pres·to \'pres-(,)tō\ *adv or adj* [It, quick, quickly, fr. L *praestus* ready, fr. *praesto*, adv., on hand; akin to L *prae* before — more at FOR] (ca. 1599) **1 :** suddenly as if by magic : IMMEDIATELY **2 :** at a rapid tempo — used as a direction in music

²presto *n, pl* **prestos** (1869) : a presto musical passage or movement

¹pre·stress \(,)prē-'stres\ *vt* (1934) : to introduce internal stresses into (as a structural beam) to counteract the stresses that will result from applied load (as in incorporating cables under tension in concrete)

²pre·stress \'prē-,stres, ,prē-'\ *n* (1934) **1 :** the stresses introduced in prestressing **2 :** the process of prestressing **3 :** the condition of being prestressed

pre·sum·able \pri-'zü-mə-bəl\ *adj* (1692) : capable of being presumed : acceptable as an assumption

pre·sum·ably \-blē\ *adv* (1846) : by reasonable assumption

pre·sume \pri-'züm\ *vb* **pre·sumed; pre·sum·ing** [ME, fr. LL & MF; LL *praesumere* to dare, fr. L, to anticipate, assume, fr. *prae-* + *sumere* to take; MF *presumer* to assume, fr. L *praesumere* — more at CONSUME] *vt* (14c) **1 :** to undertake without leave or clear justification : DARE **2 :** to expect or assume esp. with confidence **3 :** to suppose to be true without proof ⟨*presumed* innocent until proved guilty⟩ **4 :** to take for granted : IMPLY ∼ *vi* **1 :** to act or proceed presumptuously or on a presumption **2 :** to go beyond what is right or proper — **pre·sumed·ly** \-'zü-məd-lē, -'zümd-lē\ *adv* — **pre·sum·er** *n*

presuming *adj* (15c) : PRESUMPTUOUS — **pre·sum·ing·ly** \-'zü-miŋ-lē\ *adv*

pre·sump·tion \pri-'zəm(p)-shən\ *n* [ME *presumpcioun*, fr. OF *presumption*, fr. LL & L; LL *praesumption-*, *praesumptio* presumptuous attitude, fr. L, assumption, fr. *praesumere*] (13c) **1 :** presumptuous attitude or conduct : AUDACITY **2 a :** an attitude or belief dictated by probability : ASSUMPTION **b :** the ground, reason, or evidence lending probability to a belief **3 :** a legal inference as to the existence or truth of a fact not certainly known that is drawn from the known or proved existence of some other fact

pre·sump·tive \-'zəm(p)-tiv\ *adj* (15c) **1 :** based on probability or presumption **2 :** giving grounds for reasonable opinion or belief **3 :** being an embryonic precursor with the potential for forming a particular structure or tissue in the normal course of development ⟨∼ retina⟩ — **pre·sump·tive·ly** *adv*

pre·sump·tu·ous \pri-'zəm(p)-chə-wəs, -chəs, -shəs\ *adj* [ME, fr. MF *presumptueux*, fr. LL *praesumptuosus*, irreg. fr. *praesumptio*] (14c) : overstepping due bounds (as of propriety or courtesy) : taking liberties — **pre·sump·tu·ous·ly** *adv* — **pre·sump·tu·ous·ness** *n*

pre·sup·pose \,prē-sə-'pōz\ *vt* [ME, fr. MF *presupposer*, fr. ML *praesupponere* (perf. indic. *praesupposui*), fr. L *prae-* + ML *supponere* to suppose — more at SUPPOSE] (15c) **1 :** to suppose beforehand **2 :** to require as an antecedent in logic or fact — **pre·sup·po·si·tion** \(,)prē-,sə-pə-'zi-shən\ *n* — **pre·sup·po·si·tion·al** \-'zish-nəl, -'zi-shə-nᵊl\ *adj*

pre·syn·ap·tic \,prē-sə-'nap-tik\ *adj* (1909) : situated or occurring just before a nerve synapse — **pre·syn·ap·ti·cal·ly** \-ti-k(ə-)lē\ *adv*

pret–a–por·ter *or* **prêt–à–por·ter** \,pret-ä-pȯr-'tā\ *n* [F, ready to wear] (1959) : ready-to-wear clothes

¹pre·teen \'prē-'tēn, -,tēn\ *n* (1952) : a boy or girl not yet 13 years old

²preteen *adj* (1954) **1 :** relating to or produced for children esp. in the 9 to 12 year-old age group ⟨∼ fashions⟩ **2 :** being younger than 13

pre·teen–ag·er \(,)prē-'tē-nā-jər\ *n* (1965) : PRETEEN

¹pre·tend \pri-'tend\ *vb* [ME, fr. L *praetendere* to allege as an excuse, lit., to stretch out, fr. *prae-* pre- + *tendere* to stretch — more at THIN] *vt* (15c) **1 :** to give a false appearance of being, possessing, or performing ⟨does not ∼ to be a psychiatrist⟩ **2 a :** to make believe : FEIGN ⟨∼ed deafness⟩ **b :** to claim, represent, or assert falsely ⟨∼ing an emotion he could not really feel⟩ **3** *archaic* : VENTURE, UNDERTAKE ∼ *vi* **1 :** to feign an action, part, or role in play **2 :** to put in a claim *syn* see ASSUME

²pretend *adj* (1911) : IMAGINARY, MAKE-BELIEVE

pre·tend·ed *adj* (1607) : professed or avowed but not genuine ⟨∼ affection⟩ — **pre·tend·ed·ly** *adv*

pre·tend·er \pri-'ten-dər\ *n* (1609) : one that pretends: as **a :** one who lays claim to something; *specif* : a claimant to a throne who is held to have no just title **b :** one who makes a false or hypocritical show

pre·tense *or* **pre·tence** \'prē-,ten(t)s, pri-'\ *n* [ME, fr. MF *pretensse*, fr. (assumed) ML *praetensa*, fr. LL, fem. of *praetensus*, pp. of L *praetendere*] (15c) **1 :** a claim made or implied; *esp* : one not supported by fact **2 a :** mere ostentation : PRETENTIOUSNESS ⟨confuse dignity with pomposity and ∼ —Bennett Cerf⟩ **b :** a pretentious act or assertion **3 :** an inadequate or insincere attempt to attain a certain condition or quality **4 :** professed rather than real intention or purpose : PRETEXT ⟨was there under false ∼s⟩ **5 :** MAKE-BELIEVE, FICTION **6 :** false show : SIMULATION ⟨saw through his ∼ of indifference⟩

¹pre·ten·sion \pri-'ten(t)-shən\ *n* (15c) **1 :** an allegation of doubtful value : PRETEXT **2 :** a claim or an effort to establish a claim **3 :** a claim or right to attention or honor because of merit **4 :** an aspiration or intention that may or may not reach fulfillment ⟨has serious literary ∼s⟩ **5 :** VANITY, PRETENTIOUSNESS *syn* see AMBITION — **pre·ten·sion·less** \-ləs\ *adj*

²pre·ten·sion \,prē-'ten(t)-shən\ *vt* [*pre-* + ²*tension*] (1937) : PRESTRESS

pre·ten·tious \pri-'ten(t)-shəs\ *adj* [F *prétentieux*, fr. *prétention* pretension, fr. ML *praetention-*, *praetentio*, fr. L *praetendere*] (1837) **1 :** characterized by pretension: as **a :** making usu. unjustified or excessive claims (as of value or standing) ⟨the ∼ fraud who assumes a love of culture that is alien to him —Richard Watts⟩ **b :** expressive of affected, unwarranted, or exaggerated importance, worth, or stature ⟨∼ language⟩ ⟨∼ houses⟩ **2 :** making demands on one's skill, ability, or means : AMBITIOUS ⟨the ∼ daring of the Green Mountain Boys in crossing the lake —*Amer. Guide Series: Vt.*⟩ *syn* see SHOWY — **pre·ten·tious·ly** *adv* — **pre·ten·tious·ness** *n*

¹pret·er·it *or* **pret·er·ite** \'pre-tə-rət\ *adj* [ME *preterit*, fr. MF, fr. L *praeteritus*, fr. pp. of *praeterire* to go by, pass, fr. *praeter* beyond, past, by (fr. compar. of *prae* before) + *ire* to go — more at FOR, ISSUE] (14c) *archaic* : BYGONE, FORMER

²preterit *or* **preterite** *n* (14c) : PAST TENSE

pre·term \(,)prē-'tərm, 'prē-,\ *adj* (1928) : of, relating to, being, or brought forth by premature birth ⟨∼ infant⟩ ⟨∼ labor⟩

pre·ter·mi·nal \(,)prē-'tərm-nəl, -'tər-mə-\ *adj* (1947) : occurring before death ⟨∼ cancer⟩

pre·ter·mis·sion \,prē-tər-'mi-shən\ *n* [L *praetermission-*, *praetermissio*, fr. *praetermittere*] (1583) : the act or an instance of pretermitting : OMISSION

\ə\ abut \ᵊ\ kitten, F table \ər\ further \a\ ash \ā\ ace \ä\ mop, mar \aù\ out \ch\ chin \e\ bet \ē\ easy \g\ go \i\ hit \ī\ ice \j\ job \ŋ\ sing \ō\ go \ȯ\ law \ȯi\ boy \th\ thin \th\ the \ü\ loot \ù\ foot \y\ yet \zh\ vision \ä, k̲, ⁿ, œ, œ̄, ue, ūe, ᵊ\ *see* Guide to Pronunciation

pre·ter·mit \-'mit\ vt **-mit·ted; -mit·ting** [L praetermittere, fr. praeter by, past + mittere to let go, send] (1538)   **1** : to let pass without mention or notice : OMIT   **2** : to leave undone : NEGLECT   **3** : SUSPEND, BREAK OFF

pre·ter·nat·u·ral \ˌprē-tər-'na-chə-rəl, -'nach-rəl\ adj [ML praeternaturalis, fr. L praeter naturam beyond nature] (1580)   **1** : existing outside of nature   **2** : exceeding what is natural or regular : EXTRAORDINARY ⟨wits trained to ~ acuteness by the debates —G. L. Dickinson⟩   **3** : inexplicable by ordinary means; esp : PSYCHIC ⟨~ phenomena⟩ — **pre·ter·nat·u·ral·ly** \-'na-chə-rə-lē, 'nach-rə-, 'na-chər-\ adv — **pre·ter·nat·u·ral·ness** \-'na-chə-rəl-nəs, -'nach-rəl-\ n

pre·test \'prē-ˌtest\ n (1926) : a preliminary test: as   **a** : a test of the effectiveness or safety of a product prior to its sale   **b** : a test to evaluate the preparedness of students for further studies — **pre·test** \(ˌ)prē-'test\ vt

pre·text \'prē-ˌtekst\ n [L praetextus, fr. praetexere to assign as a pretext, screen, extend in front, fr. prae- + texere to weave — more at TECHNICAL] (1513) : a purpose or motive alleged or an appearance assumed in order to cloak the real intention or state of affairs   syn see APOLOGY

pre·tor, pre·to·ri·an var of PRAETOR, PRAETORIAN

pret·ti·fy \'pri-ti-ˌfī, 'pur-, 'pru-\ vt **-fied; -fy·ing** (1850) : to make pretty — **pret·ti·fi·ca·tion** \ˌpri-ti-fə-'kā-shən, ˌpur-, ˌpru-\ n — **pret·ti·fi·er** \'pri-ti-ˌfi(-ə)r, 'pur-, 'pru-\ n

pret·ti·ness \'pri-tē-nəs, 'pur-, 'pru-\ n (1649)   **1** : the quality or state of being pretty   **2** : something pretty

¹pret·ty \'pri-tē, 'pur- also 'pru-\ adj **pret·ti·er; -est** [ME praty, prety, fr. OE prættig tricky, fr. prætt trick; akin to ON prettr trick] (15c)   **1 a** : ARTFUL, CLEVER   **b** : PAT, APT   **2 a** : pleasing by delicacy or grace   **b** : having conventionally accepted elements of beauty   **c** : appearing or sounding pleasant or nice but lacking strength, force, manliness, purpose, or intensity ⟨~ words that make no sense —Elizabeth B. Browning⟩   **3 a** : MISERABLE, TERRIBLE ⟨a ~ mess you've gotten us into⟩   **b** chiefly Scot : STOUT   **4** : moderately large : CONSIDERABLE ⟨a very ~ profit⟩ ⟨cost a ~ penny⟩   syn see BEAUTIFUL — **pret·ti·ly** \-t²l-ē\ adv — **pret·ty·ish** \-tē-ish\ adj

²pret·ty \'pur-tē, 'pri-tē also 'pru-tē; before "near(ly)" often 'pərt or 'prit or 'prút\ adv (1565)   **1** : in some degree : MODERATELY ⟨~ cold weather⟩   **2** : in a pretty manner : PRETTILY ⟨pop vocalists who can sing ~ —Gerald Levitch⟩

   usage Some handbooks complain that pretty is overworked and recommend the selection of a more specific word or restrict pretty to informal or colloquial contexts. Pretty is used to tone down a statement and is in wide use across the whole spectrum of English. It is common in informal speech and writing but is neither rare nor wrong in serious discourse ⟨he may, if he feels well off or clever, qualify himself as a doctor —G. B. Shaw⟩ ⟨a return to those traditions of American foreign policy which worked pretty well for over a century —H. S. Commager⟩ ⟨the arguments for buying expensive books have to be pretty cogent —Times Lit. Supp.⟩

³pret·ty \'pri-tē, 'pur-tē also 'pru-tē\ n, pl **pretties** (1736)   **1** pl : dainty clothes; esp : LINGERIE   **2** : a pretty person or thing

⁴pret·ty \same as ³\ vt **pret·tied; pret·ty·ing** (1909) : to make pretty — usu. used with up ⟨curtains to ~ up the room⟩

pret·zel \'pret-səl\ n [G Brezel, ultim. fr. L brachiatus having branches like arms, fr. brachium arm — more at BRACE] (ca. 1838) : a brittle or chewy glazed usu. salted slender bread often shaped like a loose knot

pre·vail \pri-'vā(ə)l\ vi [ME, fr. L praevalēre, fr. prae- pre- + valēre to be strong — more at WIELD] (15c)   **1** : to gain ascendancy through strength or superiority : TRIUMPH   **2** : to be or become effective or effectual   **3** : to use persuasion successfully ⟨~ed on him to sing⟩   **4** : to be frequent : PREDOMINATE ⟨the west winds that ~ in the mountains⟩   **5** : to be or continue in use or fashion : PERSIST ⟨a custom that still ~s⟩

prev·a·lence \'pre-və-lən(t)s, 'prev-lən(t)s\ n (1713)   **1** : the quality or state of being prevalent   **2** : the degree to which something is prevalent; esp : the percentage of a population that is affected with a particular disease at a given time

prev·a·lent \-lənt\ adj [L praevalent-, praevalens very powerful, fr. prp. of praevalēre] (1576)   **1** archaic : POWERFUL   **2** : being in ascendancy : DOMINANT   **3** : generally or widely accepted, practiced, or favored : WIDESPREAD — **prevalent** n — **prev·a·lent·ly** adv

pre·var·i·cate \pri-'var-ə-ˌkāt\ vi **-cat·ed; -cat·ing** [L praevaricatus, pp. of praevaricari to act in collusion, lit., to straddle, fr. prae- + varicare to straddle, fr. varus bowlegged] (ca. 1631) : to deviate from the truth : EQUIVOCATE   syn see LIE — **pre·var·i·ca·tion** \-ˌvar-ə-'kā-shən\ n — **pre·var·i·ca·tor** \-'var-ə-ˌkā-tər\ n

pre·ve·nient \pri-'vēn-yənt\ adj [L praevenient-, praeveniens, prp. of praevenire] (ca. 1656) : ANTECEDENT, ANTICIPATORY — **pre·ve·nient·ly** adv

pre·vent \pri-'vent\ vb [ME, to anticipate, fr. L praeventus, pp. of praevenire to come before, anticipate, forestall, fr. prae- + venire to come — more at COME] vt (15c)   **1** archaic   **a** : to be in readiness for ⟨as an occasion⟩   **b** : to meet or satisfy in advance   **c** : to act ahead of   **d** : to go or arrive before   **2** : to deprive of power or hope of acting or succeeding   **3** : to keep from happening or existing ⟨steps to ~ war⟩   **4** : to hold or keep back : HINDER, STOP — often used with from ~ vi : to interpose an obstacle — **pre·vent·abil·i·ty** \-ˌven-tə-'bi-lə-tē\ n — **pre·vent·able** also **pre·vent·ible** \-'ven-tə-bəl\ adj — **pre·vent·er** n

   syn PREVENT, ANTICIPATE, FORESTALL mean to deal with beforehand. PREVENT implies taking advance measures against something possible or probable ⟨measures taken to prevent leaks⟩. ANTICIPATE may imply merely getting ahead of another by being a precursor or forerunner or it may imply checking another's intention by acting first ⟨anticipated the question by making a statement⟩. FORESTALL implies a getting ahead so as to stop or interrupt something in its course ⟨hoped to forestall the sale⟩.

pre·ven·ta·tive \-'ven-tə-tiv\ adj or n (ca. 1666) : PREVENTIVE

pre·ven·tion \pri-'ven(t)-shən\ n (1582) : the act of preventing or hindering

¹pre·ven·tive \-'ven-tiv\ n (ca. 1639) : something that prevents; esp : something used to prevent disease

²preventive adj (1639)   **1** : devoted to or concerned with prevention

: PRECAUTIONARY ⟨~ steps against soil erosion⟩   **2** : undertaken to forestall anticipated hostile action ⟨a ~ coup⟩ — **pre·ven·tive·ly** adv — **pre·ven·tive·ness** n

pre·ver·bal \(ˌ)prē-'vər-bəl\ adj (1921)   **1** : occurring before the verb   **2** : having not yet acquired the faculty of speech ⟨a ~ child⟩

¹pre·view \'prē-ˌvyü\ vt (1607)   **1** : to see beforehand; specif : to view or to show in advance of public presentation   **2** : to give a preliminary survey of — **pre·view·er** \-ˌvyü-ər\ n

²preview n (1922)   **1** : an advance showing or performance ⟨as of a motion picture or play⟩   **2** also **pre·vue** \-ˌvyü\ : a showing of snatches from a motion picture advertised for appearance in the near future — called also trailer   **3** : an advance statement, sample, or survey

pre·vi·ous \'prē-vē-əs\ adj [L praevius leading the way, fr. prae- pre- + via way — more at WAY] (1625)   **1** : going before in time or order : PRIOR   **2** : acting too soon : PREMATURE   syn see PRECEDING — **pre·vi·ous·ly** adv — **pre·vi·ous·ness** n

previous question n (ca. 1715) : a parliamentary motion to put the pending question to an immediate vote without further debate or amendment that if defeated has the effect of permitting resumption of debate

previous to prep (1702) : PRIOR TO, BEFORE

¹pre·vi·sion \prē-'vi-zhən\ n [ME previsioun, fr. OF prevision, fr. LL praevision-, praevisio, fr. L praevidēre to foresee, fr. prae- + vidēre to see — more at WIT] (15c)   **1** : FORESIGHT, PRESCIENCE   **2** : FORECAST, PROGNOSTICATION — **pre·vi·sion·al** \-'vizh-nəl, -'vi-zhə-n²l\ adj — **pre·vi·sion·ary** \-'vi-zhə-ˌner-ē\ adj

²prevision vt **pre·vi·sioned; pre·vi·sion·ing** \-'vi-zhə-niŋ, -'vizh-niŋ\ (1891) : FORESEE

pre·vo·cal·ic \ˌprē-vō-'ka-lik, -və-\ adj [ISV] (1899) : immediately preceding a vowel

pre·vo·ca·tion·al \ˌprē-vō-'kā-shnəl, -shə-n²l\ adj (1914) : given or required before admission to a vocational school

pre·writ·ing \'prē-ˌri-tiŋ\ n (1968) : the formulation and organization of ideas preparatory to writing

prexy \'prek-sē\ also **prex** \'preks\ n, pl **prex·ies** also **prex·es** [prexy fr. prex, by shortening & alter. fr. president] (1871) slang : PRESIDENT — used chiefly of a college president

¹prey \'prā\ n, pl **prey** also **preys** [ME preie, fr. OF, fr. L praeda; akin to L prehendere to grasp, seize — more at GET] (13c)   **1** archaic : SPOIL, BOOTY   **2 a** : an animal taken by a predator as food   **b** : one that is helpless or unable to resist attack : VICTIM ⟨was ~ to his own appetites⟩   **3** : the act or habit of preying

²prey vi **preyed; prey·ing** [ME, fr. OF preier, fr. L praedari, fr. praeda] (14c)   **1** : to make raids for the sake of booty   **2 a** : to seize and devour prey   **b** : to commit violence or robbery or fraud   **3** : to have an injurious, destructive, or wasting effect — **prey·er** n

prez \'prez\ n, pl **prez·es** \'pre-zəz\ [by shortening & alter.] (1892) slang : PRESIDENT

Pri·am \'prī-əm, -ˌam\ n [L Priamus, fr. Gk Priamos] : the father of Hector and Paris and king of Troy during the Trojan War

pri·a·pic \prī-'ā-pik, -'a-\ adj [L priapus lecher, fr. Priapus] (1786)   **1** : PHALLIC   **2** : relating to or preoccupied with virility

Pri·a·pus \prī-'ā-pəs\ n [L, fr. Gk Priapos] : a Greek and Roman god of gardens and male generative power

¹price \'pris\ n [ME pris, fr. OF, fr. L pretium price, money; prob. akin to Skt prati- against, in return — more at PROS-] (13c)   **1** archaic : VALUE, WORTH   **2 a** : the quantity of one thing that is exchanged or demanded in barter or sale for another   **b** : the amount of money given or set as consideration for the sale of a specified thing   **3** : the terms for the sake of which something is done or undertaken: as   **a** : an amount sufficient to bribe one ⟨believed every man had his ~⟩   **b** : a reward for the apprehension or death of a person ⟨an outlaw with a ~ on his head⟩   **4** : the cost at which something is obtained ⟨the ~ of freedom is restraint —J. Irwin Miller⟩

²price vt **priced; pric·ing** (15c)   **1** : to set a price on   **2** : to find out the price of   **3** : to drive by raising prices excessively ⟨priced themselves out of the market⟩ — **pric·er** n

price-cut·ter \'pris-ˌkə-tər\ n (1901) : one that reduces prices esp. to a level designed to cripple competition — **price-cut·ting** \-tiŋ\ n

priced \'prist\ adj (1722) : having a specified price — used in combination ⟨low-priced merchandise⟩

price-earnings ratio n (1961) : a measure of the value of a common stock determined as the ratio of its market price to its earnings per share and usu. expressed as a simple numeral

price-fix·ing \'pris-ˌfik-siŋ\ n (1920) : the setting of prices artificially ⟨as by producers or government⟩ contrary to free market operations

price index n (1886) : an index number expressing the level of a group of commodity prices relative to the level of the prices of the same commodities during an arbitrarily chosen base period and used to indicate changes in the level of prices from one period to another

price·less \'pris-ləs\ adj (1593)   **1 a** : having a value beyond any price : INVALUABLE   **b** : costly because of rarity or quality : PRECIOUS   **2** : having worth in terms of other than market value   **3** : delightfully amusing, odd, or absurd — **price·less·ly** adv

price support n (1945) : artificial maintenance of prices ⟨as of a raw material⟩ at some predetermined level usu. through government action

price tag n (1881)   **1** : a tag on merchandise showing the price at which it is offered for sale   **2** : PRICE, COST

price war n (1925) : commercial competition characterized by the repeated cutting of prices below those of competitors

pric·ey also **pricy** \'pri-sē\ adj **pric·i·er; -est** (1932) : EXPENSIVE

¹prick \'prik\ n [ME prikke, fr. OE prica; akin to MD pric prick] (bef. 12c)   **1** : a mark or shallow hole made by a pointed instrument   **2 a** : a pointed instrument or weapon   **b** : a sharp projecting organ or part   **3** : an instance of pricking or the sensation of being pricked: as   **a** : a nagging or sharp feeling of remorse, regret, or sorrow   **b** : a slight sharply localized discomfort ⟨the ~ of a needle⟩   **4** : PENIS — usu. considered vulgar   **5** : a spiteful or contemptible man often having some authority — usu. considered vulgar

²prick vt (bef. 12c)   **1** : to pierce slightly with a sharp point   **2** : to affect with anguish, grief, or remorse ⟨doubt began to ~ him —Philip Hale⟩   **3** : to ride, guide, or urge on with or as if with spurs : GOAD   **4** : to mark, distinguish, or note by means of a small mark   **5** : to trace or outline with punctures   **6** : to remove ⟨a young seedling⟩ from the seedbed to another suitable for further growth — usu. used with *out* **7** : to cause to be or stand erect ⟨a dog ~*ing* its ears⟩ ~ *vi* **1 a** : to prick something or cause a pricking sensation **b** : to feel discomfort as if from being pricked **2 a** : to urge a horse with the spur **b** : to ride fast **3** : THRUST **4** : to become directed upward : POINT — **prick up one's ears** : to listen intently

prick·er \'pri-kər\ *n* (14c) **1** : one that pricks: as **a** : a rider of horses **b** : a military light horseman **2 a** : THORN, PRICKLE **b** : BRIER

prick·et \'pri-kət\ *n* [ME *priket*, fr. *prikke*] (15c) **1 a** : a spike on which a candle is stuck **b** : a candlestick with such a point **2 a** : a buck in the second year of life

¹**prick·le** \'pri-kəl\ *n* [ME *prikle*, fr. OE *pricle*; akin to OE *prica* prick] (15c) **1** : a fine sharp process or projection; *esp* : a sharp pointed emergence arising from the epidermis or bark of a plant **2** : a prickling or tingling sensation

²**prickle** *vb* **prick·led; prick·ling** \-k(ə-)liŋ\ *vt* (1513) **1** : to prick slightly **2** : to produce prickles in ~ *vi* : to cause or feel a prickling, tingling, or stinging sensation

prick·ly \'pri-k(ə-)lē\ *adj* **prick·li·er; -est** (1578) **1** : full of or covered with prickles **2** : distinguished from related kinds by the presence of prickles **3** : marked by prickling : STINGING ⟨a ~ sensation⟩ **3 a** : TROUBLESOME, VEXATIOUS ⟨~ issues⟩ **b** : easily irritated ⟨had a ~ disposition⟩ — **prick·li·ness** *n*

prickly ash *n* (1709) : a prickly aromatic shrub or small tree (*Zanthoxylum americanum*) of the rue family with yellowish flowers

prickly heat *n* (1736) : a noncontagious cutaneous eruption of red pimples with intense itching and tingling caused by inflammation around the sweat ducts

prickly pear *n* (1612) **1** : OPUNTIA; *esp* : any of those with flat spiny joints — called also *prickly pear cactus;* compare CHOLLA **2** : the pulpy pear-shaped edible fruit of various prickly pears (as *Opuntia ficus-indica*)

prickly poppy *n* (1724) : any of a genus (*Argemone*) of plants of the poppy family with white or yellow flowers and prickly leaves and fruits

¹**pride** \'prīd\ *n* [ME, fr. OE *prȳde*, fr. *prūd* proud — more at PROUD] (bef. 12c) **1** : the quality or state of being proud: as **a** : inordinate self-esteem : CONCEIT **b** : a reasonable or justifiable self-respect **c** : delight or elation arising from some act, possession, or relationship ⟨parental ~⟩ **2** : proud or disdainful behavior or treatment : DISDAIN **3 a** : ostentatious display **b** : highest pitch : PRIME **4** : a source of pride : the best in a group or class **5** : a company of lions **6** : a showy or impressive group ⟨a ~ of dancers⟩

²**pride** *vt* **prid·ed; prid·ing** (13c) : to indulge (as oneself) in pride

pride·ful \'prīd-fəl\ *adj* (15c) : full of pride: as **a** : DISDAINFUL, HAUGHTY **b** : EXULTANT, ELATED — **pride·ful·ly** \-fə-lē\ *adv* — **pride·ful·ness** *n*

pride of place (1605) : the highest or first position

prie–dieu \(,)prē-'dyə(r), prē-dyœ̄\ *n, pl* **prie–dieux** \-'dyə(r)(z), -dyœ̄(z)\ [F, lit., pray God] (1760) **1** : a kneeling bench designed for use by a person at prayer and fitted with a raised shelf on which the elbows or a book may be rested **2** : a low armless upholstered chair with a high straight back

pri·er \'prī(-ə)r\ *n* (1552) : one that pries; *esp* : an inquisitive person

priest \'prēst\ *n* [ME *preist*, fr. OE *prēost*, ultim. fr. LL *presbyter* — more at PRESBYTER] (bef. 12c) : one authorized to perform the sacred rites of a religion esp. as a mediatory agent between humans and God; *specif* : an Anglican, Eastern Orthodox, or Roman Catholic clergyman ranking below a bishop and above a deacon

prie-dieu 1

priest·ess \'prēs-təs\ *n* (1693) **1** : a woman authorized to perform the sacred rites of a religion **2** : a woman regarded as a leader (as of a movement)

priest·hood \'prēst-,hùd, 'prē-,stùd\ *n* (bef. 12c) **1** : the office, dignity, or character of a priest **2** : the whole body of priests

priest·ly \'prēst-lē\ *adj* (bef. 12c) **1** : of or relating to a priest or the priesthood : SACERDOTAL **2** : characteristic of or befitting a priest — **priest·li·ness** *n*

priest–rid·den \'prēst-,ri-d²n\ *adj* (1653) : controlled or oppressed by a priest

¹**prig** \'prig\ *n* [*prig* to steal] (1610) : THIEF

²**prig** *n* [prob. fr. ¹*prig*] (1676) **1** *archaic* : FOP **2** *archaic* : FELLOW, PERSON **3** : one who offends or irritates by observance of proprieties (as of speech or manners) in a pointed manner or to an obnoxious degree — **prig·gery** \-gə-rē\ *n* — **prig·gish** \'pri-gish\ *adj* — **prig·gish·ly** *adv* — **prig·gish·ness** *n*

prig·gism \'pri-,gi-zəm\ *n* (ca. 1805) : stilted adherence to convention

¹**prill** \'pril\ *vt* [origin unknown] (1944) : to convert (as a molten solid) into spherical pellets usu. by forming into a spray and allowing the drops to solidify

²**prill** *n* (1952) : a pellet made by prilling

¹**prim** \'prim\ *vt* **primmed; prim·ming** [origin unknown] (1706) **1** : to give a prim or demure expression to ⟨*primming* her thin lips after every mouthful —John Buchan⟩ **2** : to dress primly

²**prim** *adj* **prim·mer; prim·mest** (1709) **1 a** : stiffly formal and proper : DECOROUS **b** : PRUDISH **2** : NEAT, TRIM ⟨~ hedges⟩ — **prim·ly** *adv* — **prim·ness** *n*

pri·ma ballerina \'prē-mə-\ *n* [It, leading ballerina] (1870) : the principal female dancer in a ballet company

pri·ma·cy \'prī-mə-sē\ *n* (14c) **1** : the state of being first (as in importance, order, or rank) : PREEMINENCE ⟨the ~ of intellectual and esthetic over materialistic values —T. R. McConnell⟩ **2** : the office, rank, or preeminence of an ecclesiastical primate

pri·ma don·na \,pri-mə-'dä-nə, ,prē-\ *n, pl* **prima donnas** [It, lit., first lady] (1782) **1** : a principal female singer in an opera or concert organization **2** : an extremely sensitive, vain, or undisciplined person

¹**pri·ma fa·cie** \,prī-mə-'fā-shə, -shē, -sē also -shē-,ē, -sē-,ē\ *adv* [ME, fr. L] (15c) : at first view : on the first appearance

²**prima facie** *adj* (1800) **1** : true, valid, or sufficient at first impression : APPARENT ⟨the theory . . . gives a *prima facie* solution —R. J. Butler⟩

2 : SELF-EVIDENT **3** : legally sufficient to establish a fact or a case unless disproved ⟨*prima facie* evidence⟩

pri·mal \'prī-məl\ *adj* [ML *primalis*, fr. L *primus* first — more at PRIME] (1602) **1** : ORIGINAL, PRIMITIVE ⟨village life continued in its ~ innocence —Van Wyck Brooks⟩ **2** : first in importance : FUNDAMENTAL ⟨our ~ concern⟩

pri·mal·i·ty \prī-'ma-lə-tē\ *n* (1919) : the property of being a prime number

primal scream therapy *n* (1971) : psychotherapy in which the patient recalls and reenacts a particularly disturbing past experience usu. occurring early in life and expresses normally repressed anger or frustration esp. through spontaneous and unrestrained screams, hysteria, or violence — called also *primal therapy*

pri·mar·i·ly \prī-'mer-ə-lē also prə-, chiefly Brit 'prī-mər-ə-lē\ *adv* (1601) **1** : for the most part : CHIEFLY ⟨has now become ~ a residential town —S. P. B. Mais⟩ **2** : in the first place : ORIGINALLY

¹**pri·ma·ry** \'prī-,mer-ē, 'prī-mə-rē\ *adj* [ME, fr. LL *primarius* basic, primary, fr. L, principal, fr. *primus*] (15c) **1 a** : first in order of time or development : PRIMITIVE ⟨the ~ stage of civilization⟩ **b** : of or relating to formations of the Paleozoic and earlier periods **2 a** : of first rank, importance, or value : PRINCIPAL ⟨the ~ purpose⟩ **b** : BASIC, FUNDAMENTAL ⟨security is a ~ need⟩ **c** : of, relating to, or constituting the principal quills of a bird's wing **d** : of or relating to agriculture, forestry, and the extractive industries or their products **e** : expressive of present or future time ⟨~ tense⟩ **f** : of, relating to, or constituting the strongest of the three or four degrees of stress recognized by most linguists ⟨the first syllable of *basketball* carries ~ stress⟩ **3 a** : DIRECT, FIRSTHAND ⟨~ sources of information⟩ **b** : not derivable from other colors, odors, or tastes **c** : preparatory to something else in a continuing process ⟨~ instruction⟩ **d** : of or relating to a primary school ⟨~ education⟩ **e** : belonging to the first group or order in successive divisions, combinations, or ramifications ⟨~ nerves⟩ **f** : of, relating to, or constituting the inducing current or its circuit in an induction coil or transformer **g** : directly derived from ores ⟨~ metals⟩ **h** : of, relating to, or being the amino acid sequence in proteins ⟨~ protein structure⟩ **4** : resulting from the substitution of one of two or more atoms or groups in a molecule; *esp* : being or characterized by a carbon atom having a bond to only one other carbon atom **5** : of, relating to, involving, or derived from primary meristem ⟨~ tissue⟩ ⟨~ growth⟩ **6** : of, relating to, or involved in the production of organic substances by green plants ⟨~ productivity⟩

²**primary** *n, pl* **-ries** (ca. 1772) **1** : something that stands first in rank, importance, or value : FUNDAMENTAL — usu. used in pl. **2** : the celestial body around which one or more other celestial bodies revolve; *esp* : the more massive one. brighter component of a binary star system **3** : one of the usu. 9 or 10 strong quills on the distal joint of a bird's wing — see WING illustration **4 a** : PRIMARY COLOR **b** : a primary color sensation **5 a** : CAUCUS **b** : an election in which qualified voters nominate or express a preference for a particular candidate or group of candidates for political office, choose party officials, or select delegates for a party convention **6** : the coil that is connected to the source of electricity in an induction coil or transformer — called also *primary coil*

primary atypical pneumonia *n* (ca. 1944) : any of a group of pneumonias (as Q fever and psittacosis) caused esp. by viruses, mycoplasmas, rickettsias, and chlamydias

primary cell *n* (1902) : a cell that converts chemical energy into electrical energy by irreversible chemical reactions

primary color *n* (1612) : any of a set of colors from which all other colors may be derived

primary meristem *n* (1875) : meristem (as procambium) derived from the apical meristem

primary root *n* (ca. 1890) : the root of a plant that develops first and originates from the radicle

primary school *n* (1802) **1** : a school usu. including the first three grades of elementary school but sometimes also including kindergarten **2** : ELEMENTARY SCHOOL

primary syphilis *n* (ca. 1890) : the first stage of syphilis that is marked by the development of a chancre and the spread of the causative spirochete in the tissues of the body

primary tooth *n* (ca. 1898) : MILK TOOTH

primary wall *n* (ca. 1933) : the first-formed wall of a plant cell that is produced around the protoplast and usu. has plasmodesmata

pri·mate \'prī-,māt *or esp for 1* -mət\ *n* [ME *primat*, fr. OF, fr. ML *primat-, primas* archbishop, fr. L, leader, fr. *primus*] (13c) **1** *often cap* : a bishop who has precedence in a province, group of provinces, or a nation **2** *archaic* : one first in authority or rank : LEADER **3** [NL *Primates*, fr. L, pl. of *primat-, primas*] : any of an order (Primates) of mammals comprising humans, apes, monkeys, and related forms (as lemurs and tarsiers) — **pri·mate·ship** \-,ship\ *n* — **pri·ma·tial** \prī-'mā-shəl\ *adj*

pri·ma·tol·o·gy \,prī-mə-'tä-lə-jē\ *n* (1926) : the study of primates esp. other than recent humans (*Homo sapiens*) — **pri·ma·to·log·i·cal** \-mə-t²l-'ä-ji-kəl\ *adj* — **pri·ma·tol·o·gist** \-mə-'tä-lə-jist\ *n*

¹**prime** \'prīm\ *n* [ME, fr. OE *prim*, fr. L *prima hora* first hour] (bef. 12c) **1** *often cap* : the second of the canonical hours **b** : the first hour of the day usu. considered either as 6 a.m. or the hour of sunrise **2 a** : the earliest stage **b** : SPRING **c** : YOUTH **3** : the most active, thriving, or successful stage or period ⟨in the ~ of his life⟩ **4** : the chief or best individual or part : PICK ⟨~ of the flock, and choicest of the stall —Alexander Pope⟩ **5** : PRIME NUMBER **6 a** : the first note or tone of a musical scale : TONIC **b** : the interval between two notes on the same staff degree **7** : the symbol ′ **8** : PRIME RATE

²**prime** *adj* [ME, fr. MF, fem. of *prin* first, fr. L *primus*; akin to L *prior*] (14c) **1** : first in time : ORIGINAL **2 a** : of, relating to, or being a prime number **b** : RELATIVELY PRIME **b** : having no polynomial factors other than itself and no monomial factors other than 1 ⟨a

\ə\ abut \ᵊ\ kitten, F table \ər\ further \a\ ash \ā\ ace \ä\ mop, mar \aù\ out \ch\ chin \e\ bet \ē\ easy \g\ go \i\ hit \ī\ ice \j\ job \ŋ\ sing \ō\ go \ò\ law \òi\ boy \th\ thin \t͟h\ the \ü\ loot \ù\ foot \y\ yet \zh\ vision \á, k̲, ⁿ, œ, œ̄, ᵫ, ūᵫ, ʸ\ see Guide to Pronunciation

~ polynomial⟩ **c** : expressed as a product of prime factors (as prime numbers and prime polynomials) ⟨a ~ factorization⟩ **3 a** : first in rank, authority, or significance : PRINCIPAL **b** : having the highest quality or value ⟨~ farmland⟩ **c** : of the highest grade regularly marketed — used of meat and esp. beef **4** : not deriving from something else : PRIMARY — **prime·ly** *adv* — **prime·ness** *n*

³**prime** *vb* **primed; prim·ing** [prob. fr. ¹*prime*] *vt* (1513) **1** : FILL, LOAD **2 a** : to prepare for firing by supplying with priming **b** : to insert a primer into (a cartridge case) **3** : to apply the first color, coating, or preparation to ⟨~ a wall⟩ **4** : to put into working order by filling or charging with something ⟨~ a pump with water⟩ **5** : to instruct beforehand : COACH ⟨*primed* the witness⟩ **6** : STIMULATE ~ *vi* : to become prime — **prime the pump** : to take steps to encourage the growth or functioning of something

prime cost *n* (1718) : the combined total of raw material and direct labor costs incurred in production; *broadly* : cost less vendor's or agent's commission for charges

prime meridian *n* (ca. 1859) : the meridian of 0 degrees longitude which runs through the original site of the Royal Observatory at Greenwich, England, and from which other longitudes are reckoned

prime minister *n* (1655) **1** : the chief minister of a ruler or state **2** : the official head of a cabinet or ministry; *esp* : the chief executive of a parliamentary government — **prime ministerial** *adj* — **prime ministership** *n* — **prime ministry** *n*

prime mover *n* [trans. of ML *primus motor*] (1809) **1 a** : an initial source of motive power (as a windmill, waterwheel, turbine, or internal combustion engine) designed to receive and modify force and motion as supplied by some natural source and apply them to drive machinery **b** : a powerful tractor or truck usu. with all-wheel drive **2** : the self-moved being that is the source of all motion **3** : the original or most effective force in an undertaking or work ⟨education is . . . a *prime mover* of cultural and societal change —R. C. Buck⟩

prime number *n* (1570) : any integer other than 0 or ± 1 that is not divisible without remainder by any other integers except ± 1 and ± the integer itself

¹**prim·er** \'pri-mər, *chiefly Brit* 'pri-mər\ *n* [ME, fr. ML *primarium*, fr. LL, neut. of *primarius* primary] (14c) **1** : a small book for teaching children to read **2** : a small introductory book on a subject

²**prim·er** \'pri-mər\ *n* (1819) **1** : a device for priming; *esp* : a cap, tube, or wafer containing percussion powder or compound used to ignite an explosive charge **2** : material used in priming a surface — called also *prime coat* **3** : a molecule (as a short strand of RNA or DNA) whose presence is required for formation of another molecule (as a longer chain of DNA)

prime rate *n* (1958) : an interest rate formally announced by a bank to be the lowest available at a particular time to its most credit-worthy customers — called also *prime interest rate*

pri·me·ro \pri-'mer-(,)ō, -'mir-\ *n* [modif. of Sp *primera*, fr. fem. of *primer* first, fr. L *primarius*] (1533) : a card game popular in the 16th and 17th centuries

prime time *n* (1958) **1** : the time period when the television or radio audience is the largest; *also* : prime-time television **2** : the choicest or busiest time — **prime-time** *adj*

pri·me·val \pri-'mē-vəl\ *adj* [L *primaevus*, fr. *primus* first + *aevum* age — more at AYE] (1662) **1** : of or relating to the earliest ages (as of the world or human history) : ANCIENT, PRIMITIVE ⟨100 acres of ~ forest which has never felt an ax —Mary R. Zimmer⟩ **2** : PRIMORDIAL 1b — **pri·me·val·ly** \-və-lē\ *adv*

priming *n* (15c) **1** : the act of one that primes **2** : the explosive used in priming a charge **3** : ²PRIMER 2

pri·mip·a·ra \pri-'mi-pə-rə\ *n, pl* **-ras** *or* **-rae** \-,rē, -,rī\ [L, fr. *primus* first + *-para* -para] (ca. 1842) **1** : an individual bearing a first offspring **2** : an individual that has borne only one offspring — **pri·mip·a·rous** \pri-'mi-pə-rəs\ *adj*

¹**prim·i·tive** \'pri-mə-tiv\ *adj* [ME *primitif*, fr. L *primitivus* first formed, fr. *primitiae* first fruits, fr. *primus* first — more at PRIME] (14c) **1 a** : not derived : ORIGINAL, PRIMARY **b** : assumed as a basis; *esp* : AXIOMATIC ⟨~ concepts⟩ **2 a** : of or relating to the earliest age or period : PRIMEVAL ⟨the ~ church⟩ **b** : closely approximating an early ancestral type : little evolved ⟨~ mammals⟩ **c** : belonging to or characteristic of an early stage of development : CRUDE, RUDIMENTARY ⟨~ technology⟩ **d** : of, relating to, or constituting the assumed parent speech of related languages ⟨~ Germanic⟩ **3 a** : ELEMENTAL, NATURAL ⟨our ~ feelings of vengeance —John Mackwood⟩ **b** : of, relating to, or produced by a people or culture that is nonindustrial and often nonliterate and tribal ⟨~ art⟩ **c** : NAIVE **d** (1) : SELF-TAUGHT, UNTUTORED ⟨~ craftsmen⟩ (2) : produced by a self-taught artist ⟨a ~ painting⟩ — **prim·i·tive·ly** *adv* — **prim·i·tive·ness** *n* — **prim·i·tiv·i·ty** \,pri-mə-'ti-və-tē\ *n*

²**primitive** *n* (15c) **1 a** : something primitive; *specif* : a primitive idea, term, or proposition **b** : a root word **2 a** (1) : an artist of an early period of a culture or artistic movement (2) : a later imitator or follower of such an artist **b** (1) : a self-taught artist (2) : an artist whose work is marked by directness and naïveté **c** : a work of art produced by a primitive artist **d** : a typically rough or simple usu. handmade and antique home accessory or furnishing **3 a** : a member of a primitive people **b** : an unsophisticated person

prim·i·tiv·ism \'pri-mə-ti-,vi-zəm\ *n* (1861) **1** : belief in the superiority of a simple way of life close to nature **b** : belief in the superiority of nonindustrial society to that of the present **2** : the style of art of primitive peoples or primitive artists — **prim·i·tiv·ist** \-vist\ *n or adj* — **prim·i·tiv·is·tic** \,pri-mə-ti-'vis-tik\ *adj*

¹**pri·mo** \'prē-(,)mō\ *n, pl* **primos** [It, fr. *primo* first, fr. L *primus*] (1792) : the first or leading part (as in a duet or trio)

²**pri·mo** \'prē-(,)mō, 'prē-\ *adv* [L, fr. *primus*] (ca. 1901) : in the first place

³**pri·mo** \'prē-(,)mō\ *adj* [prob. fr. It, chief, first] (1972) *slang* : of the finest quality : EXCELLENT

pri·mo·gen·i·tor \,pri-mō-'je-nə-tər\ *n* [LL, fr. L *primus* + *genitor* begetter, fr. *gignere* to beget — more at KIN] (1654) : ANCESTOR, FOREFATHER

pri·mo·gen·i·ture \-,chür, -chər, -,tyür, -,tür\ *n* [LL *primogenitura*, fr. L *primus* + *genitura* birth, fr. *genitus*, pp. of *gignere*] (1602) **1** : the

state of being the firstborn of the children of the same parents **2** : an exclusive right of inheritance belonging to the eldest son

pri·mor·di·al \pri-'mȯr-dē-əl\ *adj* [ME, fr. LL *primordialis*, fr. L *primordium* origin, fr. *primus* first + *ordiri* to begin — more at PRIME, ORDER] (14c) **1 a** : first created or developed : PRIMEVAL 1 **b** : existing in or persisting from the beginning (as of a solar system or universe) ⟨a ~ gas cloud⟩ **c** : earliest formed in the growth of an individual or organ : PRIMITIVE **2** : FUNDAMENTAL, PRIMARY ⟨~ human joys —Sir Winston Churchill⟩ — **pri·mor·di·al·ly** \-dē-ə-lē\ *adv*

pri·mor·di·um \-dē-əm\ *n, pl* **-dia** \-dē-ə\ [NL, fr. L] (1671) : the rudiment or commencement of a part or organ

primp \'primp\ *vb* [perh. alter. of ¹*prim*] *vt* (1801) : to dress, adorn, or arrange in a careful or finicky manner ~ *vi* : to dress or groom oneself carefully ⟨~s for hours before a date⟩

prim·rose \'prim-,rōz\ *n* [ME *primerose*, fr. MF, fr. *prime* (fem. of *prin* prime) + *rose* rose — more at PRIME, ROSE] (14c) **1** : any of a genus (*Primula* of the family Primulaceae, the primrose family) of perennial herbs with large tufted basal leaves and showy variously colored flowers — compare EVENING PRIMROSE

primrose path *n* (1602) **1** : a path of ease or pleasure and esp. sensual pleasure ⟨himself the *primrose path* of dalliance treads —Shak.⟩ **2** : a path of least resistance

primrose yellow *n* (1882) **1** : a light to moderate greenish yellow **2** : a light to moderate yellow

prim·u·la \'prim-yə-lə\ *n* [ML, fr. *primula veris*, lit., first fruit of spring] (1753) : PRIMROSE

pri·mum mo·bi·le \'pri-məm-'mō-bə-lē, 'prē-\ *n, pl* **primum mobiles** [ME, fr. ML, lit., first moving thing] (15c) : the outermost concentric sphere conceived in medieval astronomy as carrying the spheres of the fixed stars and the planets in its daily revolution

pri·mus \'pri-məs\ *n, often cap* [ML, one who is first, magnate, fr. L, first — more at PRIME] (1724) : the presiding bishop of the Scottish Episcopal Church

pri·mus in·ter pa·res \'pri-məs-,in-tər-'par-ēz, 'prē-məs-\ *n* [L] (1813) : first among equals

prince \'prin(t)s\ *n* [ME, fr. OF, fr. L *princip-, princeps* leader, initiator, fr. *primus* first + *capere* to take — more at HEAVE] (13c) **1 a** : MONARCH, KING **b** : the ruler of a principality or state **2** : a male member of a royal family; *esp* : a son of the sovereign **3** : a nobleman of varying rank and status **4** : one likened to a prince; *esp* : a man of high rank or of high standing in his class or profession — **prince·ship** \'prin(t)s-,ship\ *n*

Prince Al·bert \-'al-bərt\ *n* [*Prince Albert* Edward (later Edward VII king of England)] (1884) : a double-breasted frock coat with the upper part fitted to the body

Prince Charming *n* [*Prince Charming*, hero of the fairy tale *Cinderella* by Charles Perrault] (1862) : a suitor who fulfills the dreams of his beloved; *also* : a man of often specious charm toward women

prince consort *n, pl* **princes consort** (1861) : the husband of a reigning queen

prince·dom \'prin(t)s-dəm, -təm\ *n* (1560) **1** : the jurisdiction, sovereignty, rank, or estate of a prince **2** : PRINCIPALITY **3** — usu. used in pl.

prince·let \'prin(t)s-lət\ *n* (1682) : PRINCELING

prince·li·ness \-lē-nəs\ *n* (1571) **1** : princely conduct or character **2** : LUXURY, MAGNIFICENCE

prince·ling \'prin(t)s-liŋ\ *n* (1794) : a petty or insignificant prince

prince·ly \'prin(t)s-lē\ *adj* **prince·li·er; -est** (15c) **1** : of or relating to a prince : ROYAL **2** : befitting a prince : NOBLE, MAGNIFICENT ⟨~ manners⟩ ⟨a ~ sum⟩ — **princely** *adv*

Prince of Wales \-'wā(ə)lz\ *n* (15c) : the male heir apparent to the British throne — used as a title only after it has been specif. conferred by the sovereign

prince's-feath·er \'prin(t)-səz-,fe-thər\ *n* (1629) : a showy widely cultivated annual plant (*Amaranthus hybridus erythrostachys*) of the amaranth family having dense usu. red spikes of flowers

¹**prin·cess** \'prin(t)-səs, 'prin-,ses, (*usual Brit*) prin-'ses\ *n* (14c) **1** *archaic* : a woman having sovereign power **2** : a female member of a royal family; *esp* : a daughter or granddaughter of a sovereign **3** : the consort of a prince **4** : one likened to a princess; *esp* : a woman of high rank or of high standing in her class or profession ⟨a pop music ~⟩

²**princess** *same as* ¹\ *or* **prin·cesse** \prin-'ses\ *adj* [F *princesse* princess, fr. *prince*] (1867) : close-fitting and usu. with gores from neck to flaring hemline ⟨a ~ gown⟩

Princess Royal *n, pl* **Princesses Royal** (ca. 1649) : the eldest daughter of a British sovereign — a title granted for life and used only after it has been specif. conferred by the sovereign

¹**prin·ci·pal** \'prin(t)-s(ə-)pəl, -sə-bəl\ *adj* [ME, fr. OF, fr. L *principalis*, fr. *princip-, princeps*] (14c) **1** : most important, consequential, or influential : CHIEF **2** : of, relating to, or constituting principal or a principal *usage* see PRINCIPLE — **prin·ci·pal·ly** \-sə-p(ə-)lē, -sə-bə-lē, -splē\ *adv*

²**principal** *n* (14c) **1** : a person who has controlling authority or is in a leading position: as **a** : a chief or head man or woman **b** : the chief executive officer of an educational institution **c** : one who employs another to act as agent subject to the employer's general control and instruction; *specif* : the person from whom an agent's authority derives **d** : the chief or an actual participant in a crime **e** : the person primarily or ultimately liable on a legal obligation **f** : a leading performer : STAR **2** : a matter or thing of primary importance: as **a** (1) : a capital sum placed at interest, due as a debt, or used as a fund **(2)** : the corpus of an estate, portion, devise, or bequest **b** : the construction that gives shape and strength to a roof and is usu. one of several trusses; *broadly* : the most important member of a piece of framing *usage* see PRINCIPLE — **prin·ci·pal·ship** \'prin(t)-s(ə-)pəl-,ship, -sə-bəl-\ *n*

principal diagonal *n* (1965) : the diagonal in a square matrix that runs from upper left to lower right

prin·ci·pal·i·ty \,prin(t)-sə-'pa-lə-tē\ *n, pl* **-ties** (14c) **1 a** : the state,

Prince Albert

office, or authority of a prince **b** : the position or responsibilities of a principal (as of a school) **2** : the territory or jurisdiction of a prince : the country that gives title to a prince **3** *pl* : an order of angels — see CELESTIAL HIERARCHY

principal parts *n pl* (1870) : a series of verb forms from which all the other forms of a verb can be derived including in English the infinitive, the past tense, and the present and past participles

prin·cip·i·um \prin-ˈsi-pē-əm, prin-ˈki-\ *n, pl* **-ia** \-pē-ə\ [L, beginning, basis] (1600) : a fundamental principle

prin·ci·ple \ˈprin(t)-s(ə-)pəl, -sə-bəl\ *n* [ME, modif. of MF *principe*, fr. L *principium* beginning, fr. *princip-, princeps* initiator — more at PRINCE] (14c) **1 a** : a comprehensive and fundamental law, doctrine, or assumption **b** (1) : a rule or code of conduct (2) : habitual devotion to right principles ⟨a man of ∼⟩ **c** : the laws or facts of nature underlying the working of an artificial device **2** : a primary source : ORIGIN **3 a** : an underlying faculty or endowment ⟨such ∼s of human nature as greed and curiosity⟩ **b** : an ingredient (as a chemical) that exhibits or imparts a characteristic quality **4** *cap, Christian Science* : a divine principle : GOD — **in principle** : with respect to fundamentals ⟨prepared to accept the proposition *in principle*⟩
usage Although nearly every handbook and many dictionaries warn against confusing *principle* and *principal*, many people still do. *Principle* is only a noun; *principal* is both adjective and noun. If you are unsure which noun you want, read the definitions in this dictionary.

prin·ci·pled \-s(ə-)pəld, -sə-bəld\ *adj* (1642) : exhibiting, based on, or characterized by principles — often used in combination

prin·cox \ˈprin-ˌkäks, ˈprin-\ *n* [origin unknown] (1540) *archaic* : a pert youth : COXCOMB

prink \ˈprink\ *vb* [prob. alter. of ²*prank*] (1576) : PRIMP — **prink·er** *n*

¹**print** \ˈprint\ *n* [ME *preinte*, fr. MF, fr. *preint*, pp. of *preindre* to press, fr. L *premere* — more at PRESS] (14c) **1 a** : a mark made by pressure : IMPRESSION **b** : something impressed with a print or formed in a mold **2 a** : printed state or form **b** : the printing industry **3 a** : PRINTED MATTER **b** *pl* : printed publications **4** : printed letters : TYPE **5 a** (1) : a copy made by printing (2) : a reproduction of an original work of art (as a painting) made by a photomechanical process (3) : an original work of art (as a woodcut, etching, or lithograph) intended for graphic reproduction and produced by or under the supervision of the artist who designed it **b** : cloth with a pattern or figured design applied by printing; *also* : an article of such cloth **c** : a photographic or motion-picture copy; *esp* : one made from a negative — **in print** : procurable from the publisher — **out of print** : not procurable from the publisher

²**print** *vt* (14c) **1 a** : to impress something in or on **b** : to stamp (as a mark) in or on something **2 a** : to make a copy of by impressing paper against an inked printing surface **b** (1) : to impress (as wallpaper) with a design or pattern (2) : to impress (a pattern or design) on something **c** : to publish in print **d** : PRINT OUT; *also* : to display on a surface (as a computer screen) for viewing **3** : to write in letters shaped like those of ordinary roman text type **4** : to make (a positive picture) on a sensitized photographic surface from a negative or a positive ∼ *vi* **1 a** : to work as a printer **b** : to produce printed matter **2** : to produce something in printed form **3** : to write or hand-letter in imitation of unjoined printed characters

³**print** *adj* (1953) : of, relating to, or writing for printed publications ⟨∼ journalists⟩

print·able \ˈprin-tə-bəl\ *adj* (1837) **1** : capable of being printed or of being printed from **2** : considered fit to publish — **print·abil·i·ty** \ˌprin-tə-ˈbi-lə-tē\ *n*

printed circuit *n* (1946) : a circuit for electronic apparatus made by depositing conductive material in continuous paths from terminal to terminal on an insulating surface

printed matter *n* (1876) : matter printed by and of various mechanical processes that is eligible for mailing at a special rate

print·er \ˈprin-tər\ *n* (1504) : one that prints: as **a** : a person engaged in printing **b** : a device used for printing; *esp* : a machine for printing from photographic negatives **c** : a device (as a dot matrix printer) that produces printout

printer's devil *n* (1763) : an apprentice in a printing office

print·ery \ˈprin-tə-rē\ *n, pl* **-er·ies** (1638) : PRINTING OFFICE

print·head \ˈprint-ˌhed\ *n* (1968) : a usu. movable part of a computer printer that contains the printing elements

print·ing *n* (14c) **1** : the act or product of one that prints **2** : reproduction in printed form **3** : the art, practice, or business of a printer **4** : IMPRESSION 4c **5** *pl* : paper to be printed on

printing office *n* (1733) : an establishment where printing is done

printing press *n* (1588) : a machine that produces printed copies

print·less \ˈprint-ləs\ *adj* (1610) : making, bearing, or taking no imprint

print·mak·ing \-ˌmā-kin\ *n* (1928) : the design and production of prints by an artist — **print·mak·er** \-kər\ *n*

print·out \ˈprint-ˌaût\ *n* (1953) : a printed record produced automatically (as by a computer)

print out *vt* (1953) : to make a printout of

pri·on \ˈprē-ˌän\ *n* [*protinaceous* + *infectious* + ²*on*] (1982) : a protein particle that lacks nucleic acid and is sometimes held to be the cause of various infectious diseases of the nervous system (as scrapie and Creutzfeldt-Jakob disease)

¹**pri·or** \ˈprī(-ə)r\ *n* [ME, fr. OE & OF; both fr. ML, fr. LL, administrator, fr. L, former, superior] (bef. 12c) **1** : the superior ranking next to the abbot of a monastery **2** : the superior of a house or group of houses of any of various religious communities — **pri·or·ate** \ˈprī-ə-rət\ *n* — **pri·or·ship** \ˈprī(-ə)r-ˌship\ *n*

²**prior** *adj* [L, former, superior, compar. of OL *pri* before; akin to L *priscus* ancient, *prae* before — more at FOR] (1714) **1** : earlier in time or order : PREVIOUS ⟨by ∼ agreement⟩ **2** : taking precedence (as in importance) *syn* see PRECEDING — **pri·or·ly** *adv*

pri·or·ess \ˈprī-ə-rəs\ *n* (14c) : a nun corresponding in rank to a prior

pri·or·i·tize \prī-ˈȯr-ə-ˌtīz, -ˈär-; ˈprī-ə-rə-\ *vt* **-tized; -tiz·ing** (1964) : to list or rate (as projects or goals) in order of priority *usage* see -IZE — **pri·or·i·ti·za·tion** \prī-ˌȯr-ə-tə-ˈzā-shən, -är-; ˌprī-ə-rə-\ *n*

pri·or·i·ty \prī-ˈȯr-ə-tē, -ˈär-\ *n, pl* **-ties** (14c) **1 a** (1) : the quality or state of being prior (2) : precedence in date or position of publication — used of taxa **b** (1) : superiority in rank, position, or privilege

(2) : legal precedence in exercise of rights over the same subject matter **2** : a preferential rating; *esp* : one that allocates rights to goods and services usu. in limited supply ⟨that project has top ∼⟩ **3** : something given or meriting attention before competing alternatives

prior restraint *n* (1951) : governmental prohibition imposed on expression before the expression actually takes place

prior to *prep* (1714) : in advance of : BEFORE
usage Sometimes termed pompous or affected, *prior to* is a synonym of *before* that most often appears in rather formal contexts, such as the annual reports of corporations. It may occas. emphasize the notion of anticipation ⟨if page makeup decisions are verified and approved *prior to* typesetting, proofreading of pages afterward becomes unnecessary —*Publishers Weekly*⟩. It is also used sometimes in less formal contexts ⟨they have taught her how to walk ⟨which I thought she did rather well *prior to* the expenditure of the 200 bucks⟩ —Groucho Marx (letter)⟩.

pri·o·ry \ˈprī-(ə-)rē\ *n, pl* **-ries** [ME *priorie*, fr. AF, fr. ML *prioria*, fr. *prior*] (13c) : a religious house under a prior or prioress

prise \ˈprīz\ *chiefly Brit var of* ⁵PRIZE

prism \ˈpri-zəm\ *n* [LL *prismat-, prisma*, fr. Gk, lit., anything sawn, fr. *priein* to saw] (1570) **1** : a polyhedron with two polygonal faces lying in parallel planes and with the other faces parallelograms **2 a** : a transparent body that is bounded in part by two nonparallel plane faces and is used to refract or disperse a beam of light **b** : a prism-shaped decorative glass luster **3** : a crystal form whose faces are parallel to one axis; *esp* : one whose faces are parallel to the vertical axis **4** : a medium that distorts, slants, or colors whatever is viewed through it

pris·mat·ic \priz-ˈma-tik\ *adj* (1709) **1** : relating to, resembling, or constituting a prism **2 a** : formed by a prism **b** : resembling the colors formed by refraction of light through a prism ⟨∼ effects⟩ **3** : highly colored : BRILLIANT ⟨∼ lyrics⟩ **4** : having such symmetry that a general form with faces cutting all axes at unspecified intercepts is a prism ⟨∼ crystals⟩ — **pris·mat·i·cal·ly** \-ti-k(ə-)lē\ *adv*

pris·ma·toid \ˈpriz-mə-ˌtȯid\ *n* [LL *prismat-, prisma* prism] (ca. 1890) : a polyhedron that has all of its vertices in two parallel planes

pris·moid \ˈpriz-ˌmȯid\ *n* (ca. 1704) : a prismatoid whose parallel bases have the same number of sides — **pris·moi·dal** \priz-ˈmȯi-d²l\ *adj*

¹**pris·on** \ˈpri-z²n\ *n* [ME, fr. OF, fr. L *prehension-, prehensio* act of seizing, fr. *prehendere* to seize — more at GET] (12c) **1** : a state of confinement or captivity **2** : a place of confinement esp. for lawbreakers; *specif* : an institution (as one under state jurisdiction) for confinement of persons convicted of serious crimes — compare JAIL

²**prison** *vt* (14c) : IMPRISON, CONFINE

prison camp *n* (ca. 1908) **1** : a camp for the confinement of reasonably trustworthy prisoners usu. employed on government projects **2** : a camp for prisoners of war or political prisoners

pris·on·er \ˈpriz-nər, ˈpri-z²n-ər\ *n* (14c) **1** : a person deprived of liberty and kept under involuntary restraint, confinement, or custody; *esp* : one on trial or in prison **2** : someone restrained as if in prison ⟨a ∼ of her own conscience⟩

prisoner of war (1678) : a person captured in war; *esp* : a member of the armed forces of a nation who is taken by the enemy during combat

prisoner's base *n* (ca. 1773) : a game in which players on each of two teams seek to tag and imprison players of the other team who have ventured out of their home territory

pris·sy \ˈpri-sē\ *adj* **pris·si·er; -est** [prob. blend of *prim* and *sissy*] (1895) : being prim and precise : FINICKY — **pris·si·ly** \ˈpri-sə-lē\ *adv* — **pris·si·ness** \ˈpri-sē-nəs\ *n*

pris·tane \ˈpris-ˌtān\ *n* [L *pristis* shark, sawfish; fr. its presence in the liver oils of sharks] (1923) : an isoprenoid hydrocarbon $C_{19}H_{40}$ that usu. accompanies phytane

pris·tine \ˈpris-ˌtēn, pri-ˈstēn, *esp Brit* ˈpris-ˌtīn\ *adj* [L *pristinus*; akin to L *prior*] (1534) **1** : belonging to the earliest period or state : ORIGINAL ⟨the hypothetical ∼ lunar atmosphere⟩ **2 a** : not spoiled, corrupted, or polluted (as by civilization) : PURE ⟨a ∼ forest⟩ **b** : fresh and clean as or as if new ⟨∼ hard-backs in uniform editions to fill our built-in bookcases —Michiko Kakutani⟩ — **pris·tine·ly** *adv*

prith·ee \ˈpri-thē, -thē\ *interj* [alter. of (*I*) *pray thee*] (ca. 1591) *archaic* — used to express a wish or request

pri·va·cy \ˈprī-və-sē, *esp Brit* ˈpri-\ *n, pl* **-cies** (15c) **1 a** : the quality or state of being apart from company or observation : SECLUSION **b** : freedom from unauthorized intrusion ⟨one's right to ∼⟩ **2** *archaic* : a place of seclusion **3 a** : SECRECY **b** : a private matter : SECRET

pri·vat·do·cent *or* **pri·vat·do·zent** \pri-ˈvät-(ˌ)dō(t)-ˌsent\ *n* [G *Privatdozent*, fr. *privat* private + *Dozent* teacher, fr. L *docent-, docens*, prp. of *docēre* to teach — more at DOCILE] (1854) : an unsalaried university lecturer or teacher in German-speaking countries remunerated directly by students' fees

¹**pri·vate** \ˈprī-vət\ *adj* [ME *privat*, fr. L *privatus*, fr. pp. of *privare* to deprive, release, fr. *privus* private, individual; prob. akin to L *pro* for, in front of — more at FOR] (14c) **1 a** : intended for or restricted to the use of a particular person, group, or class ⟨a ∼ park⟩ **b** : belonging to or concerning an individual person, company, or interest ⟨a ∼ house⟩ **c** (1) : restricted to the individual or arising independently of others ⟨∼ opinion⟩ (2) : carried on by the individual independently of the usual institutions ⟨∼ study⟩; *also* : being educated by independent study or a tutor or in a private school ⟨∼ students⟩ **d** : not general in effect ⟨a ∼ statute⟩ **e** : of, relating to, or receiving hospital service in which the patient has more privileges than a semiprivate or ward patient **2 a** (1) : not holding public office or employment ⟨a ∼ citizen⟩ (2) : not related to one's official position : PERSONAL ⟨∼ correspondence⟩ **b** : being a private ⟨a ∼ soldier⟩ **3 a** : withdrawn from company or observation : SEQUESTERED ⟨a ∼ retreat⟩ **b** : not known or intended to be known publicly : SECRET **c** : preferring to keep personal affairs to oneself : valuing privacy highly **d** : unsuitable for

---

public use or display   **4** : not having shares that can be freely traded on the open market ⟨a ∼ company⟩ — **pri·vate·ly** *adv* — **pri·vate-ness** *n*

²private *n* (15c)   **1** *archaic* : one not in public office   **2** *obs* : PRIVACY   **3** *pl* : PRIVATE PARTS   **4 a** : a person of low rank in various organizations (as a police or fire department)   **b** : an enlisted man of the lowest rank in the marine corps or of one of the two lowest ranks in the army — **in private** : not openly or in public

private detective *n* (1868) : PRIVATE INVESTIGATOR

private enterprise *n* (1844) : FREE ENTERPRISE

pri·va·teer \ˌprī-və-ˈtir\ *n* (1664) : an armed private ship licensed to attack enemy shipping; *also* : a sailor on such a ship — **privateer** *vi*

private eye *n* (1938) : PRIVATE INVESTIGATOR

private first class *n* (1918) : an enlisted man ranking in the army above a private and below a corporal and in the marine corps above a private and below a lance corporal

private investigator *n* (1940) : a person not a member of a police force who is licensed to do detective work (as investigation of suspected wrongdoing or searching for missing persons)

private law *n* (1773) : a branch of law concerned with private persons, property, and relationships — compare PUBLIC LAW

private parts *n pl* (1785) : the external genital and excretory organs

private school *n* (1857) : a school that is established, conducted, and primarily supported by a nongovernmental agency

private treaty *n* (1858) : a sale of property on terms determined by conference of the seller and buyer — compare AUCTION

pri·va·tion \prī-ˈvā-shən\ *n* [ME *privacion*, fr. MF *privation*, fr. L *privation-, privatio*, fr. *privare* to deprive] (14c)   **1** : an act or instance of depriving : DEPRIVATION   **2** : the state of being deprived; *esp* : lack of what is needed for existence

pri·vat·ise *Brit var of* PRIVATIZE

pri·vat·ism \ˈprī-və-ˌti-zəm\ *n* [*private*] (1950) : the attitude of being uncommitted to or avoiding involvement in anything beyond one's immediate interests

¹priv·a·tive \ˈpri-və-tiv\ *adj* (14c) : constituting or predicating privation or absence of a quality (as the prefixes *a-, un-, non-*) — **priv·a·tive·ly** *adv*

²priv·a·tive *n* (1588) : a privative term, expression, or proposition; *also* : a privative prefix or suffix

pri·vat·ize \ˈprī-və-ˌtīz\ *vt* (1948) : to make private; *esp* : to change (as a business or industry) from public to private control or ownership — **pri·vat·iza·tion** \ˌprī-və-tə-ˈzā-shən\ *n*

priv·et \ˈpri-vət\ *n* [origin unknown] (1542) : a European deciduous shrub (*Ligustrum vulgare*) of the olive family with semievergreen leaves and small white flowers that is widely used for hedges; *broadly* : any of various congeneric shrubs

¹priv·i·lege \ˈpriv-lij, ˈpri-və-\ *n* [ME, fr. OF, fr. L *privilegium* law for or against a private person, fr. *privus* private + *leg-, lex* law] (12c) : a right or immunity granted as a peculiar benefit, advantage, or favor : PREROGATIVE; *esp* : such a right or immunity attached specif. to a position or an office

²privilege *vt* **-leged; -leg·ing** (14c) : to grant a privilege to

priv·i·leged \-lijd\ *adj* (14c)   **1** : having or enjoying one or more privileges ⟨∼ classes⟩   **2** : not subject to the usual rules or penalties because of some special circumstance; *esp* : not subject to disclosure in a court of law ⟨a ∼ communication⟩

priv·i·ty \ˈpri-və-tē\ *n, pl* **-ties** [ME *privite* privacy, secret, fr. OF *privité*, fr. ML *privitat-, privatas*, fr. L *privus* private — more at PRIVATE] (1523)   **1 a** : a relationship between persons who successively have a legal interest in the same right or property   **b** : an interest in a transaction, contract, or legal action to which one is not a party arising out of a relationship to one of the parties   **2** : private or joint knowledge of a private matter; *esp* : cognizance implying concurrence

¹privy \ˈpri-vē\ *adj* [ME *prive*, fr. OF *privé*, fr. L *privatus* private] (14c)   **1 a** : PRIVATE, WITHDRAWN   **b** : SECRET   **2** : belonging or relating to a person in one's individual rather than official capacity   **3** : admitted as one sharing in a secret ⟨∼ to the conspiracy⟩ — **priv·i·ly** \-və-lē\ *adv*

²privy *n, pl* **priv·ies** (14c)   **1 a** : a small building having a bench with holes through which the user may defecate or urinate   **b** : TOILET 3b   **2** : a person having a legal interest of privity

privy council *n* (14c)   **1** *archaic* : a secret or private council   **2** *cap P&C* : a body of officials and dignitaries chosen by the British monarch as an advisory council to the Crown usu. functioning through its committees   **3** : a usu. appointive advisory council to an executive — **privy councillor** *n*

privy purse *n* (1765) : an allowance for the private expenses of the British sovereign

prix fixe \ˈprē-ˈfēks, -ˈfiks\ *n* [F, fixed price] (1883) : a complete meal offered at a fixed price; *also* : the price charged

¹prize \ˈprīz\ *n* [ME *pris* prize, price — more at PRICE] (14c)   **1** : something offered or striven for in competition or in contests of chance; *also* : PREMIUM 1d   **2** : something exceptionally desirable   **3** *archaic* : a contest for a reward : COMPETITION

²prize *adj* (1803)   **1 a** : awarded or worthy of a prize   **b** : awarded as a prize   **c** : entered for the sake of a prize ⟨a ∼ drawing⟩   **2** : outstanding of a kind ⟨raised ∼ hogs⟩

³prize *vt* **prized; priz·ing** [ME *prisen*, fr. MF *prisier*, fr. LL *pretiare*, fr. L *pretium* price, value — more at PRICE] (14c)   **1** : to estimate the value of : RATE   **2** : to value highly : ESTEEM   *syn* see APPRECIATE

⁴prize *n* [ME *prise*, fr. MF, act of taking, fr. *prendre* to take, fr. L *prehendere* — more at GET] (14c)   **1** : something taken by force, stratagem, or threat; *esp* : property lawfully captured at sea in time of war   **2** : an act of capturing or taking; *esp* : the wartime capture of a ship and its cargo at sea   *syn* see SPOIL

⁵prize *vt* **prized; priz·ing** [*prize* lever] (1686) : to press, force, or move with a lever : PRY

prize-fight \ˈprīz-ˌfīt\ *n* (1824) : a professional boxing match — **prize-fight·er** \-ˌfī-tər\ *n*

prize-fight·ing \-ˌfī-tiŋ\ *n* (1706) : professional boxing

prize money *n* (1748)   **1** : a part of the proceeds of a captured ship formerly divided among the officers and men making the capture   **2** : money offered in prizes

priz·er \ˈprī-zər\ *n* (1599) *archaic* : one that contends for a prize

prize-win·ner \ˈprīz-ˌwi-nər\ *n* (1893) : a winner of a prize

prize-win·ning \-ˌwi-niŋ\ *adj* (1919) : having won or of a quality to win a prize ⟨a ∼ design⟩

¹pro \ˈprō\ *n, pl* **pros** [ME, fr. L, prep., for — more at FOR] (15c)   **1** : an argument or evidence in affirmation ⟨an appraisal of the ∼s and cons⟩   **2** : the affirmative side or one holding it

²pro *adv* [*pro-*] (15c) : on the affirmative side : in affirmation ⟨much has been written ∼ and con⟩

³pro *prep* [L] (1837) : in favor of : FOR

⁴pro *n or adj* (1866) : PROFESSIONAL

¹pro- *prefix* [ME, fr. OF, fr. L, fr. Gk, before, forward, forth, for, fr. *pro* — more at FOR]   **1 a** : earlier than : prior to : before ⟨prothalamion⟩   **b** : rudimentary : PROT- ⟨pronucleus⟩   **c** : precursory ⟨proinsulin⟩   **2 a** : located in front of or at the front of : anterior to ⟨procephalic⟩ ⟨proventriculus⟩   **b** : front : anterior ⟨prothorax⟩   **3** : projecting ⟨prognathous⟩

²pro- *prefix* [L *pro* in front of, before, for, forward — more at FOR]   **1** : taking the place of : substituting for ⟨procathedral⟩ ⟨procaine⟩   **2** : favoring : supporting : championing ⟨pro-American⟩

proa \ˈprō-ə\ *var of* PRAU

pro·abor·tion \ˌprō-ə-ˈbȯr-shən\ *adj* (1972) : favoring the legalization of abortion — **pro·abor·tion·ist** \-sh(ə-)nist\ *n*

pro·ac·tive \(ˌ)prō-ˈak-tiv\ *adj* (1933)   **1** [¹*pro-*] : relating to, caused by, or being interference between previous learning and the recall or performance of later learning ⟨∼ inhibition of memory⟩   **2** [²*pro-* + *reactive*] : acting in anticipation of future problems, needs, or changes

prob·a·bi·lism \ˈprä-bə-bə-ˌli-zəm\ *n* [F *probabilisme*, fr. L *probabilis* probable] (ca. 1843)   **1** : a theory that in disputed moral questions any solidly probable course may be followed even though an opposed course is or appears more probable   **2** : a theory that certainty is impossible esp. in the sciences and that probability suffices to govern belief and action — **prob·a·bi·list** \-list\ *adj or n*

prob·a·bi·lis·tic \ˌprä-bə-bə-ˈlis-tik\ *adj* (1864)   **1** : of or relating to probabilism   **2** : of, relating to, or based on probability — **prob·a·bi·lis·ti·cal·ly** *adv*

prob·a·bil·i·ty \ˌprä-bə-ˈbi-lə-tē\ *n, pl* **-ties** (15c)   **1** : the quality or state of being probable   **2** : something (as an event or circumstance) that is probable   **3 a** (1) : the ratio of the number of outcomes in an exhaustive set of equally likely outcomes that produce a given event to the total number of possible outcomes   (2) : the chance that a given event will occur   **b** : a branch of mathematics concerned with the study of probabilities   **4** : a logical relation between statements such that evidence confirming one confirms the other to some degree

probability density *n* (1939) : PROBABILITY DENSITY FUNCTION; *also* : a particular value of a probability density function

probability density function *n* (1957)   **1** : PROBABILITY FUNCTION   **2** : a function of a continuous random variable whose integral over an interval gives the probability that its value will fall within the interval

probability distribution *n* (1937) : PROBABILITY FUNCTION; *also* : PROBABILITY DENSITY FUNCTION 2

probability function *n* (1906) : a function of a discrete random variable that gives the probability that a specified value will occur

¹prob·a·ble \ˈprä-bə-bəl, ˈprä(b)-bəl\ *adj* [ME, provable, fr. MF, fr. L *probabilis* commendable, probable, fr. *probare* to test, approve, prove — more at PROVE] (1606)   **1** : supported by evidence strong enough to establish presumption but not proof ⟨a ∼ hypothesis⟩   **2** : establishing a probability ⟨∼ evidence⟩   **3** : likely to be or become true or real ⟨∼ events⟩

²probable *n* (1647) : one that is probable

probable cause *n* (ca. 1676) : a reasonable ground for supposing that a charge is well-founded

prob·a·bly \ˈprä-bə-blē, ˈprä(b)-blē\ *adv* (1613) : insofar as seems reasonably true, factual, or to be expected : without much doubt ⟨is ∼ happy⟩ ⟨it will ∼ rain⟩

pro·band \ˈprō-ˌband, prō-ˈ\ *n* [L *probandus*, gerundive of *probare*] (ca. 1929) : SUBJECT 3c(2)

pro·bang \ˈprō-ˌbaŋ\ *n* [origin unknown] (1657) : a slender flexible rod with a sponge on one end used esp. for removing obstructions from the esophagus

¹pro·bate \ˈprō-ˌbāt, *Brit also* -bit\ *n* [ME *probat*, fr. L *probatum*, neut. of *probatus*, pp. of *probare*] (15c)   **1 a** : the action or process of proving before a competent judicial authority that a document offered for official recognition and registration as the last will and testament of a deceased person is genuine   **b** : the judicial determination of the validity of a will   **2** : the officially authenticated copy of a probated will

²pro·bate \-ˌbāt\ *vt* **pro·bat·ed; pro·bat·ing** (1570)   **1** : to establish (a will) by probate as genuine and valid   **2** : to put (a convicted offender) on probation

probate court *n* (ca. 1847) : a court that has jurisdiction chiefly over the probate of wills and administration of deceased persons' estates

pro·ba·tion \prō-ˈbā-shən\ *n* [ME *probacioun*, fr. MF *probation*, fr. L *probation-, probatio*, fr. *probare*] (15c)   **1** : critical examination and evaluation or subjection to such examination and evaluation   **2 a** : subjection of an individual to a period of testing and trial to ascertain fitness (as for a job or school)   **b** : the action of suspending the sentence of a convicted offender and giving the offender freedom during good behavior under the supervision of a probation officer   **c** : the state or a period of being subject to probation — **pro·ba·tion·al** \-shnəl, -shə-nᵊl\ *adj* — **pro·ba·tion·al·ly** *adv* — **pro·ba·tion·ary** \-shə-ˌner-ē\ *adj*

pro·ba·tion·er \-sh(ə-)nər\ *n* (1603)   **1** : a person (as a newly admitted student nurse) whose fitness is being tested during a trial period   **2** : a convicted offender on probation

probation officer *n* (1880) : an officer appointed to investigate, report on, and supervise the conduct of convicted offenders on probation

pro·ba·tive \ˈprō-bə-tiv\ *adj* (15c)   **1** : serving to test or try : EXPLORATORY   **2** : serving to prove : SUBSTANTIATING

pro·ba·to·ry \ˈprō-bə-ˌtōr-ē, -ˌtȯr-\ *adj* (1625) : PROBATIVE

¹probe \ˈprōb\ *n* [ML *proba* examination, fr. L *probare*] (1580)   **1 a** : a slender medical instrument used esp. for exploration (as of a wound or bodily cavity)   **2 a** : any of various testing devices or substances: as   (1) : a pointed metal tip for making electrical contact with a circuit element being checked   (2) : a usu. small object that is inserted into something so as to test conditions at a given point   (3) : a device used to penetrate or send back information esp. from outer space or a celestial body (4) : a device (as an ultrasound generator) or a substance (as DNA in genetic research) used to obtain specific information for diagnostic or experimental purposes **b** : a pipe on the receiving airplane thrust into the drogue of the delivering airplane in air refueling **3 a** : the action of probing **b** : a penetrating or critical investigation **c** : a tentative exploratory advance or survey

²**probe** *vb* **probed; prob·ing** *vt* (1649) **1** : to search into and explore with great thoroughness : subject to a penetrating investigation **2** : to examine with a probe ⟨unmanned vehicles *probed* space⟩ ~ *vi* : to make a searching exploratory investigation **syn** see ENTER — **prob·er** *n*

pro·ben·e·cid \prō-'be-nə-səd\ *n* [irreg. fr. *propyl* + *benzoic ac*id] (1950) : a drug $C_{13}H_{19}NO_4S$ that acts on renal tubular function and is used to increase the concentration of some drugs (as penicillin) in the blood by inhibiting their excretion and to increase the excretion of urates in gout

prob·it \'präb-ət\ *n* [*probability unit*] (1934) : a unit of measurement of statistical probability based on deviations from the mean of a normal distribution

pro·bi·ty \'prō-bə-tē\ *n* [ME *probite*, fr. MF *probité*, fr. L *probitat-, probitas*, fr. *probus* honest — more at PROVE] (15c) : adherence to the highest principles and ideals : UPRIGHTNESS **syn** see HONESTY

¹**prob·lem** \'präb-ləm, -b'm, -,blem\ *n* [ME *probleme*, fr. MF, fr. L *problema*, fr. Gk *problēma*, lit., obstacle, fr. *proballein* to throw forward, fr. *pro-* forward + *ballein* to throw — more at PRO-, DEVIL] (14c) **1 a** : a question raised for inquiry, consideration, or solution **b** : a proposition in mathematics or physics stating something to be done **2 a** : an intricate unsettled question **b** : a source of perplexity, distress, or vexation **c** : difficulty in understanding or accepting ⟨I have a ~ with your saying that⟩ **syn** see MYSTERY

²**problem** *adj* (1894) **1** : dealing with a problem of conduct or social relationship ⟨a ~ play⟩ **2** : difficult to deal with ⟨a ~ child⟩

¹**prob·lem·at·ic** \,präb-lə-'ma-tik\ *or* **prob·lem·at·i·cal** \-ti-kəl\ *adj* (1609) **1 a** : posing a problem : difficult to solve or decide **b** : not definite or settled : UNCERTAIN ⟨their future remains ~⟩ **c** : open to question or debate : QUESTIONABLE **2** : expressing or supporting a possibility **syn** see DOUBTFUL — **prob·lem·at·i·cal·ly** \-ti-k(ə-)lē\ *adv*

²**problematic** *n* (1957) : something that is problematic : a problematic aspect or concern

pro bono \,prō-'bō-(,)nō\ *adj* [L *pro bono publico* for the public good] (1970) : being, involving, or doing legal work donated esp. for the public good ⟨*pro bono* work⟩

pro·bos·ci·de·an \,prə-,bä-sə-'dē-ən\ *or* **pro·bos·cid·i·an** \,prə-,bä-'si-dē-ən, (,)prō-\ *n* [ultim. fr. *proboscid-, proboscis*] (ca. 1859) : any of an order (Proboscidea) of large mammals comprising the elephants and extinct related forms — **proboscidean** *adj*

pro·bos·cis \prə-'bä-səs, -'bäs-kəs\ *n, pl* **-bos·cis·es** *also* **-bos·ci·des** \-'bä-sə-,dēz\ [L, fr. Gk *proboskis*, fr. *pro-* + *boskein* to feed] (1576) **1 a** : the trunk of an elephant; *also* : any long flexible snout **b** : the human nose esp. when prominent **2** : any of various elongated or extensible tubular processes (as the sucking organ of a butterfly) on the oral region of an invertebrate

pro·caine \'prō-,kān\ *n* [ISV ²*pro-* + -*caine*] (1918) : a basic ester $C_{13}H_{20}N_2O_2$ of para-aminobenzoic acid; *also* : its crystalline hydrochloride used as a local anesthetic

pro·cam·bi·um \(,)prō-'kam-bē-əm\ *n* [NL] (1875) : the part of the primary meristem of a plant that forms cambium and primary vascular tissues — **pro·cam·bi·al** \-bē-əl\ *adj*

pro·car·ba·zine \prō-'kär-bə-,zēn, -zən\ *n* [*propyl* + *carbamic* acid + *azine*] (1965) : an antineoplastic drug $C_{12}H_{19}N_3O$ that is a monoamine oxidase inhibitor used in the form of its hydrochloride esp. in the palliative treatment of Hodgkin's disease

pro·cary·ote *var of* PROKARYOTE

pro·ca·the·dral \,prō-kə-'thē-drəl\ *n* (1868) : a parish church used as a cathedral

¹**pro·ce·dur·al** \prə-'sē-jə-rəl, -'sēj-rəl\ *adj* (1889) : of or relating to procedure; *esp* : of or relating to the procedure used by courts or other bodies administering substantive law — **pro·ce·dur·al·ly** *adv*

²**procedural** *n* (1974) : a realistic crime novel with a specific focus ⟨a courtroom ~⟩; *esp* : POLICE PROCEDURAL

procedural due process *n* (1938) : DUE PROCESS 1

pro·ce·dure \prə-'sē-jər\ *n* [F *procédure*, fr. MF, fr. *proceder*] (ca. 1611) **1 a** : a particular way of accomplishing something or of acting **b** : a step in a procedure **2 a** : a series of steps followed in a regular definite order ⟨legal ~⟩ ⟨a surgical ~⟩ **b** : a series of instructions for a computer that has a name by which it can be called into action **3 a** : a traditional or established way of doing things **b** : PROTOCOL 3a

pro·ceed \prō-'sēd, prə-\ *vi* [ME *proceden*, fr. MF *proceder*, fr. L *procedere*, fr. *pro-* forward + *cedere* to go — more at PRO-] (14c) **1** : to come forth from a source : ISSUE **2 a** : to continue after a pause or interruption **b** : to go on in an orderly regulated way **3 a** : to begin and carry on an action, process, or movement **b** : to be in the process of being accomplished **4** : to move along a course : ADVANCE **syn** see SPRING

pro·ceed·ing *n* (15c) **1** : legal action ⟨a divorce ~⟩ **2** : PROCEDURE 3 *pl* : EVENTS, HAPPENINGS **4** : TRANSACTION **5** *pl* : an official record of things said or done

pro·ceeds \'prō-,sēdz\ *n pl* (1665) **1** : the total amount brought in ⟨the ~ of a sale⟩ **2** : the net amount received (as for a check or from an insurance settlement) after deduction of any discount or charges

pro·ce·phal·ic \,prō-sə-'fa-lik\ *adj* (1874) : relating to, forming, or situated on or near the front of the head

pro·cer·coid \(,)prō-'sər-,kȯid\ *n* [*pro-* + Gk *kerkos* tail] (1926) : the solid first parasitic larva of some tapeworms that develops usu. in the body cavity of a copepod

¹**pro·cess** \'prä-,ses, 'prō-, -səs\ *n, pl* **pro·cess·es** \-,se-səz, -sə-, -,sēz\ [ME *proces*, fr. MF, fr. L *processus*, fr. *procedere*] (14c) **1 a** : PROGRESS, ADVANCE ⟨in the ~ of time⟩ **b** : something going on : PROCEEDING **2 a** (1) : a natural phenomenon marked by gradual changes that lead toward a particular result ⟨the ~ of growth⟩ (2) : a natural continuing activity or function ⟨such life ~*es* as breathing⟩ **b** : a series of actions or operations conducing to an end; *esp* : a continuous operation or treatment esp. in manufacture **3 a** : the whole course of

proceedings in a legal action **b** : the summons, mandate, or writ used by a court to compel the appearance of the defendant in a legal action or compliance with its orders **4** : a prominent or projecting part of an organism or organic structure ⟨a bone ~⟩ **5** : ⁵CONK

²**process** *vt* (1532) **1 a** : to proceed against by law : PROSECUTE **b** (1) : to take out a summons against (2) : to serve a summons on **2 a** : to subject to a special process or treatment (as in the course of manufacture) **b** (1) : to subject to or handle through an established usu. routine set of procedures (~ insurance claims) (2) : to subject to examination or analysis ⟨computers ~ data⟩ **c** : to work (hair) into a conk

³**process** *adj* (1888) **1** : treated or made by a special process esp. when involving synthesis or artificial modification **2** : made by or used in a mechanical or photomechanical duplicating process **3** : of or involving illusory effects usu. introduced during processing of the film

⁴**pro·cess** \prə-'ses\ *vi* [back-formation fr. ¹*procession*] (1814) *chiefly Brit* : to move in a procession

process cheese *n* (1926) : a cheese made by blending several lots of cheese — called also *processed cheese*

pro·cess·ible *or* **pro·cess·able** \'prä-,se-sə-bəl, 'prō-\ *adj* (1954) : suitable for processing : capable of being processed — **pro·cess·ibil·i·ty** *or* **pro·cess·abil·i·ty** \,prä-,se-sə-'bi-lə-tē, ,prō-\ *n*

¹**pro·ces·sion** \prə-'se-shən\ *n* [ME *processioun*, fr. OF *procession*, fr. LL & L; LL *procession-, processio* religious procession, fr. L, act of proceeding, fr. *procedere*] (12c) **1 a** : a group of individuals moving along in an orderly often ceremonial way **b** : SUCCESSION, SEQUENCE **2 a** : continuous forward movement : PROGRESSION **b** : EMANATION ⟨the Holy Spirit's ~ from the Father⟩

²**procession** *vi* (1691) *archaic* : to go in procession

¹**pro·ces·sion·al** \prə-'sesh-nəl, -'se-shə-n'l\ *n* (15c) **1** : a book containing material for a procession **2** : a musical composition (as a hymn) designed for a procession **3** : a ceremonial procession

²**processional** *adj* (ca. 1611) : of, relating to, or moving in a procession — **pro·ces·sion·al·ly** *adv*

pro·ces·sor \'prä-,se-sər, 'prō-\ *n* (1909) **1** : one that processes ⟨scrap ~⟩ ⟨agricultural ~⟩ **2 a** (1) : COMPUTER (2) : the part of a computer system that operates on data — called also *central processing unit* **b** : a computer program (as a compiler) that puts another program into a form acceptable to the computer **3** : FOOD PROCESSOR

pro·cès-ver·bal \,prō-,sā-vər-'bäl, -(,)ver-\ *n, pl* **pro·cès-ver·baux** \-'bō\ [F, lit., verbal trial] (1635) : an official written record

pro-choice \(,)prō-'chȯis\ *adj* (1975) : favoring the legalization of abortion — **pro-choic·er** \-'chȯi-sər\ *n*

pro·claim \prō-'klām, prə-\ *vt* [ME *proclamen*, fr. MF or L; MF *proclamer*, fr. L *proclamare*, fr. *pro-* before + *clamare* to cry out — more at PRO-, CLAIM] (14c) **1 a** : to declare publicly, typically insistently, proudly, or defiantly and in either speech or writing : ANNOUNCE **b** : to give outward indication of : SHOW **2** : to declare or declare to be solemnly, officially, or formally ⟨~ an amnesty⟩ ⟨~ the country a republic⟩ **3** : to praise or glorify openly or publicly : EXTOL **syn** see DECLARE — **pro·claim·er** *n*

proc·la·ma·tion \,prä-klə-'mā-shən\ *n* [ME *proclamacion*, fr. MF *proclamation*, fr. L *proclamation-, proclamatio*, fr. *proclamare*] (14c) **1** : the action of proclaiming : the state of being proclaimed **2** : something proclaimed; *specif* : an official formal public announcement

pro·clit·ic \(,)prō-'kli-tik\ *n* [NL *procliticus*, fr. Gk *pro-* + LL -*cliticus* (as in *encliticus* enclitic)] (ca. 1864) : a clitic that is associated with a following word — **proclitic** *adj*

pro·cliv·i·ty \prō-'kli-və-tē\ *n, pl* **-ties** [L *proclivitas*, fr. *proclivis* sloping, prone, fr. *pro-* forward + *clivus* slope — more at PRO-, DECLIVITY] (ca. 1591) : an inclination or predisposition toward something; *esp* : a strong inherent inclination toward something objectionable **syn** see LEANING

Procne \'präk-nē\ *n* [L, fr. Gk *Proknē*] : the wife of Tereus who is changed into a swallow while fleeing from him

pro·con·sul \(,)prō-'kän(t)-səl\ *n* [ME, fr. L, fr. *pro consule* for a consul] (14c) **1** : a governor or military commander of an ancient Roman province **2** : an administrator in a modern colony, dependency, or occupied area usu. with wide powers — **pro·con·su·lar** \-s(ə-)lər\ *adj* — **pro·con·su·late** \-s(ə-)lət\ *n* — **pro·con·sul·ship** \-səl-,ship\ *n*

pro·cras·ti·nate \prə-'kras-tə-,nāt, prō-\ *vb* **-nat·ed; -nat·ing** [L *procrastinatus*, pp. of *procrastinare*, fr. *pro-* forward + *crastinus* of tomorrow, fr. *cras* tomorrow] *vt* (1588) : to put off intentionally and habitually ~ *vi* : to put off intentionally the doing of something that should be done **syn** see DELAY — **pro·cras·ti·na·tion** \-,kras-tə-'nā-shən\ *n* — **pro·cras·ti·na·tor** \-'kras-tə-,nā-tər\ *n*

pro·cre·ant \'prō-krē-ənt\ *adj* (1588) **1** : producing offspring **2** *archaic* : of or relating to procreation

pro·cre·ate \-,āt\ *vb* **-at·ed; -at·ing** [L *procreatus*, pp. of *procreare*, fr. *pro-* forth + *creare* to create — more at PRO-, CREATE] *vt* (1536) : to beget or bring forth (offspring) : PROPAGATE ~ *vi* : to beget or bring forth offspring : REPRODUCE — **pro·cre·ation** \,prō-krē-'ā-shən\ *n* — **pro·cre·ative** \'prō-krē-,ā-tiv\ *adj* — **pro·cre·ator** \-,ā-tər\ *n*

pro·crus·te·an \prə-'krəs-tē-ən, prō-\ *adj, often cap* (ca. 1846) **1** : of, relating to, or typical of Procrustes **2** : marked by arbitrary often ruthless disregard of individual differences or special circumstances

procrustean bed *n, often cap P* (1844) : a scheme or pattern into which someone or something is arbitrarily forced

Pro·crus·tes \prə-'krəs-(,)tēz, prō-\ *n* [L, fr. Gk *Prokroustēs*] : a villainous son of Poseidon in Greek mythology who forces travelers to fit into his bed by stretching their bodies or cutting off their legs

pro·cryp·tic \(,)prō-'krip-tik\ *adj* [*pro-* (as in *protect*) + *cryptic*] (1891) : of, relating to, or being a concealing pattern or shade of coloring esp. in insects

proc·to·dae·um \,präk-tə-'dē-əm\ *n, pl* **-daea** \-'dē-ə\ *or* **-dae·ums** [NL, fr. Gk *prōktos* anus + *hodos* way] (1878) : the posterior ectoder-

\ə\ abut \ᵊ\ kitten, F table \ər\ further \a\ ash \ā\ ace \ä\ mop, mar \aú\ out \ch\ chin \e\ bet \ē\ easy \g\ go \i\ hit \ī\ ice \j\ job \ŋ\ sing \ō\ go \ȯ\ law \ȯi\ boy \th\ thin \t͟h\ the \ü\ loot \ú\ foot \y\ yet \zh\ vision \ā, k̲, ⁿ, œ, œ̄, ᵫ, ᵫ̄, ᵜ\ see Guide to Pronunciation mal part of the alimentary canal formed in the embryo by invagination of the outer body wall

proc·tol·o·gy \präk-ˈtä-lə-jē\ n [Gk prōktos + E -logy] (1899) : a branch of medicine dealing with the structure and diseases of the anus, rectum, and sigmoid colon — **proc·to·log·ic** \ˌpräk-tə-ˈlä-jik\ or **proc·to·log·i·cal** \-ji-kəl\ adj — **proc·tol·o·gist** \präk-ˈtä-lə-jist\ n

proc·tor \ˈpräk-tər\ n [ME procutour procurator, proctor, alter. of procuratour] (14c) : SUPERVISOR, MONITOR: specif : one appointed to supervise students (as at an examination) — **proctor** vb — **proc·to·ri·al** \präk-ˈtȯr-ē-əl, -ˈtȯr-\ adj — **proc·tor·ship** \ˈpräk-tər-ˌship\ n

pro·cum·bent \prō-ˈkəm-bənt\ adj [L procumbent-, procumbens, prp. of procumbere to fall or lean forward, fr. pro- forward + -cumbere to lie down] (1668) 1 : being or having stems that trail along the ground without rooting 2 : lying face down

proc·u·ra·tion \ˌprä-kyə-ˈrā-shən\ n [ME procuratioun, fr. MF procuration, fr. L procuration-, procuratio, fr. procurare] (15c) 1 a : the act of appointing another as one's agent or attorney b : the authority vested in one so appointed 2 : the action of obtaining something (as supplies) : PROCUREMENT

proc·u·ra·tor \ˈprä-kyə-ˌrā-tər\ n (14c) 1 : one that manages another's affairs : AGENT 2 : an officer of the Roman empire entrusted with management of the financial affairs of a province and often having administrative powers as agent of the emperor — **proc·u·ra·to·ri·al** \ˌprä-kyə-rə-ˈtȯr-ē-əl, -ˈtȯr-\ adj

pro·cure \prə-ˈkyu̇r, prō-\ vb **pro·cured; pro·cur·ing** [ME, fr. LL procurare, fr. L, to take care of, fr. pro- for + cura care] vt (14c) 1 a : to get possession of : obtain by particular care and effort b : to get and make available for promiscuous sexual intercourse 2 : BRING ABOUT, ACHIEVE ∼ vi : to procure women — **pro·cur·able** \-ˈkyu̇r-ə-bəl\ adj — **pro·cure·ment** \-ˈkyu̇r-mənt\ n

pro·cur·er \-ˈkyu̇r-ər\ n (1538) : one that procures; esp : PANDER

Pro·cy·on \ˈprō-sē-ˌän, ˈprä-, -ən\ n [L, fr. Gk Prokyōn, lit., fore-dog; fr. its rising before Sirius] : the brightest star in the constellation Canis Minor

¹prod \ˈpräd\ vb **prod·ded; prod·ding** [origin unknown] vt (1535) 1 a : to thrust a pointed instrument into : PRICK b : to incite to action : STIR 2 : to poke or stir as if with a prod ∼ vi : to urge someone on — **prod·der** n

²prod n (ca. 1787) 1 : a pointed instrument used to prod 2 : an incitement to act

¹prod·i·gal \ˈprä-di-gəl\ adj [L prodigus, fr. prodigere to drive away, squander, fr. pro-, prod- forth + agere to drive — more at PRO-, AGENT] (ca. 1520) 1 : recklessly extravagant 2 : characterized by wasteful expenditure : LAVISH 3 : yielding abundantly : LUXURIANT — often used with of ⟨nature has been so ∼ of her bounty —H. T. Buckle⟩ syn see PROFUSE — **prod·i·gal·i·ty** \ˌprä-də-ˈga-lə-tē\ n — **prod·i·gal·ly** \ˈprä-di-g(ə-)lē\ adv

²prodigal n (1596) : one who spends or gives lavishly and foolishly

pro·di·gious \prə-ˈdi-jəs\ adj (15c) 1 a obs : being an omen : PORTENTOUS b archaic : resembling or befitting a prodigy : STRANGE, UNUSUAL 2 : exciting amazement or wonder 3 : extraordinary in bulk, quantity, or degree : ENORMOUS syn see MONSTROUS — **pro·di·gious·ly** adv — **pro·di·gious·ness** n

prod·i·gy \ˈprä-də-jē\ n, pl **-gies** [ME, fr. L prodigium monster, fr. pro-, prod- + -igium (akin to aio I say) — more at ADAGE] (15c) 1 a : a portentous event : OMEN b : something extraordinary or inexplicable 2 a : an extraordinary, marvelous, or unusual accomplishment, deed, or event b : a highly talented child or youth

pro·dro·mal \(ˌ)prō-ˈdrō-məl\ adj (1716) : PRECURSORY; esp : marked by prodromes

pro·drome \ˈprō-ˌdrōm\ n [F, lit., precursor, fr. Gk prodromos, fr. pro- before + dromos act of running, racecourse — more at PRO-, DROMEDARY] (ca. 1834) : a premonitory symptom of disease

¹pro·duce \prə-ˈdüs, prō-, -ˈdyüs\ vb **pro·duced; pro·duc·ing** [ME (Sc), fr. L producere, fr. pro- forward + ducere to lead — more at TOW] vt (15c) 1 : to offer to view or notice 2 : to give birth or rise to : YIELD 3 : to extend in length, area, or volume ⟨∼ a side of a triangle⟩ 4 : to present to the public on the stage or screen or over radio or television 5 a : to cause to have existence or to happen : BRING ABOUT b : to give being, form, or shape to : MAKE; esp : MANUFACTURE 6 : to compose, create, or bring out by intellectual or physical effort 7 : to cause to accrue ∼ vi : to bear, make, or yield something — **pro·duc·ible** \-ˈdü-sə-bəl, -ˈdyü-\ adj

²pro·duce \ˈprä-(ˌ)düs, ˈprō- also -(ˌ)dyüs\ n (1695) 1 a : something produced b : the amount produced : YIELD 2 : agricultural products and esp. fresh fruits and vegetables as distinguished from grain and other staple crops 3 : the progeny usu. of a female animal

pro·duc·er \prə-ˈdü-sər, prō-, -ˈdyü-\ n (1513) 1 : one that produces; esp : one that grows agricultural products or manufactures crude materials into articles of use 2 : a furnace or apparatus that produces combustible gas to be used for fuel by circulating air or a mixture of air and steam through a layer of incandescent fuel 3 : a person who supervises or finances the production of a stage or screen production or radio or television program 4 : any of various organisms (as a green plant) which produce their own organic compounds from simple precursors (as carbon dioxide and inorganic nitrogen) and many of which are food sources for other organisms — compare CONSUMER

producer gas n (1895) : a fuel gas made in a producer and consisting chiefly of carbon monoxide, hydrogen, and nitrogen

producer goods n pl (1948) : goods (as tools and raw materials) used to produce other goods and satisfy human wants only indirectly

prod·uct \ˈprä-(ˌ)dəkt\ n [in sense 1, fr. ME, fr. ML productum, fr. L, something produced, fr. neut. of productus, pp. of producere; in other senses, fr. L productum] (15c) 1 : the number or expression resulting from the multiplication together of two or more numbers or expressions 2 a : something produced b : something resulting from or necessarily following from a set of conditions ⟨a ∼ of his environment⟩ 3 : the amount, quantity, or total produced 4 : CONJUNCTION 5

pro·duc·tion \prə-ˈdək-shən, prō-\ n (15c) 1 : something produced : PRODUCT b (1) : a literary or artistic work (2) : a work presented on the stage or screen or over the air c : something exaggerated out of proportion to its importance 2 a : the act or process of producing b : the creation of utility; esp : the making of goods avail-

able for use 3 : total output esp. of a commodity or an industry — **pro·duc·tion·al** \-shnəl, -shə-nᵊl\ adj

production control n (1929) : systematic planning, coordinating, and directing of all manufacturing activities and influences to insure having goods made on time, of adequate quality, and at reasonable cost

production line n (1935) : LINE 6j

pro·duc·tive \prə-ˈdək-tiv, prō-\ adj (1612) 1 : having the quality or power of producing esp. in abundance ⟨∼ fishing waters⟩ 2 : effective in bringing about ⟨investigating committees have been ∼ of much good —R. K. Carr⟩ 3 a : yielding results, benefits, or profits b : yielding or devoted to the satisfaction of wants or the creation of utilities 4 : continuing to be used in the formation of new words or constructions ⟨un- is a ∼ prefix⟩ 5 : raising mucus or sputum (as from the bronchi) ⟨a ∼ cough⟩ — **pro·duc·tive·ly** adv — **pro·duc·tive·ness** n

pro·duc·tiv·i·ty \ˌprō-dək-ˈti-və-tē, ˌprä-, prə-, prō-\ n (ca. 1810) 1 : the quality or state of being productive 2 : rate of production esp. of food by the utilization of solar energy by producer organisms

pro·em \ˈprō-ˌem, -əm\ n [ME proheme, fr. MF, fr. L prooemium, fr. Gk prooimion, fr. pro- + oimē song; prob. akin to Hitt išamai- song, Skt syati he binds — more at SINEW] (14c) 1 : preliminary comment : PREFACE 2 : PRELUDE — **pro·emi·al** \prō-ˈē-mē-əl, -ˈe-\ adj

pro·en·zyme \(ˌ)prō-ˈen-ˌzīm\ n [ISV] (ca. 1900) : ZYMOGEN

pro·es·trus \(ˌ)prō-ˈes-trəs\ n [NL] (1923) : a period immediately preceding estrus characterized by preparatory physiological changes

prof \ˈpräf\ n (1838) : PROFESSOR

pro·fam·i·ly \ˌprō-ˈfam-lē, -ˈfa-mə-\ adj (1926) 1 : favoring or encouraging traditional family structures and values 2 : opposing abortion and often birth control

prof·a·na·tion \ˌprä-fə-ˈnā-shən, ˌprō-\ n (1552) : the act or an instance of profaning

pro·fa·na·to·ry \prō-ˈfa-nə-ˌtōr-ē, prə-, -ˈfā-, -ˌtȯr-\ adj (1853) : tending to profane : DESECRATING

¹pro·fane \prō-ˈfān, prə-\ vt **pro·faned; pro·fan·ing** [ME prophanen, fr. L profanare, fr. profanus] (14c) 1 : to treat (something sacred) with abuse, irreverence, or contempt : DESECRATE 2 : to debase by a wrong, unworthy, or vulgar use — **pro·fan·er** n

²profane adj [ME prophane, fr. MF, fr. L profanus, fr. pro- before + fanum temple — more at PRO-, FEAST] (15c) 1 : not concerned with religion or religious purposes : SECULAR 2 : not holy because unconsecrated, impure, or defiled : UNSANCTIFIED 3 : serving to debase or defile what is holy : IRREVERENT 4 a : not being among the initiated b : not possessing esoteric or expert knowledge — **pro·fane·ly** adv — **pro·fane·ness** \-ˈfān-nəs\ n

pro·fan·i·ty \prō-ˈfa-nə-tē, prə-\ n, pl **-ties** (1607) 1 a : the quality or state of being profane b : the use of profane language 2 a : profane language b : an utterance of profane language

pro·fess \prə-ˈfes, prō-\ vb [in sense 1, fr. ME, fr. profes, adj., having professed one's vows, fr. MF, fr. LL professus, fr. L, pp. of profitēri to profess, confess, fr. pro- before + fatēri to acknowledge; in other senses, fr. L professus, pp. — more at CONFESS] vt (14c) 1 : to receive formally into a religious community following a novitiate by acceptance of the required vows 2 a : to declare or admit openly or freely : AFFIRM b : to declare in words or appearances only : PRETEND, CLAIM 3 : to confess one's faith in or allegiance to 4 a : to practice or claim to be versed in (a calling or profession) b : to teach as a professor ∼ vi 1 : to make a profession or avowal 2 obs : to profess friendship

pro·fessed \-ˈfest\ adj (ca. 1569) 1 : openly and freely declared or acknowledged : AFFIRMED 2 : professing to be qualified; also : EXPERT 3 : pretended, alleged — **pro·fessed·ly** \prə-ˈfe-səd-lē, -ˈfest-lē\ adv (1570) 1 : by profession or declaration : AVOWEDLY 2 : with pretense : ALLEGEDLY

pro·fes·sion \prə-ˈfe-shən\ n [ME professioun, fr. OF profession, fr. LL & L, fr. L profession-, professio, fr. L, public declaration, fr. profitēri] (13c) 1 : the act of taking the vows of a religious community 2 : an act of openly declaring or publicly claiming a belief, faith, or opinion : PROTESTATION 3 : an avowed religious faith 4 a : a calling requiring specialized knowledge and often long and intensive academic preparation b : a principal calling, vocation, or employment c : the whole body of persons engaged in a calling

¹pro·fes·sion·al \prə-ˈfesh-nəl, -ˈfe-shə-nᵊl\ adj (ca. 1748) 1 a : of, relating to, or characteristic of a profession b : engaged in one of the learned professions c (1) : characterized by or conforming to the technical or ethical standards of a profession (2) : exhibiting a courteous, conscientious, and generally businesslike manner in the workplace 2 a : participating for gain or livelihood in an activity or field of endeavor often engaged in by amateurs ⟨a ∼ golfer⟩ b : having a particular profession as a permanent career ⟨a ∼ soldier⟩ c : engaged in by persons receiving financial return ⟨∼ football⟩ 3 : following a line of conduct as though it were a profession ⟨a ∼ patriot⟩ — **pro·fes·sion·al·ly** adv

²professional n (1811) : one that is professional; esp : one that engages in a pursuit or activity professionally

professional corporation n (1970) : a corporation organized by one or more licensed individuals (as a doctor or lawyer) esp. for the purpose of providing professional services and obtaining tax advantages

pro·fes·sion·al·ism \-ˈfesh-nə-ˌli-zəm, -ˈfe-shə-nᵊl-ˌi-\ n (1856) 1 : the conduct, aims, or qualities that characterize or mark a profession or a professional person 2 : the following of a profession (as athletics) for gain or livelihood

pro·fes·sion·al·ize \-ˌlīz, -ˌīz\ vt **-ized; -iz·ing** (1856) : to give a professional character to — **pro·fes·sion·al·i·za·tion** \-ˌfesh-nə-lə-ˈzā-shən, -ˌfe-shə-nᵊl-ə-\ n

pro·fes·sor \prə-ˈfe-sər\ n (14c) 1 : one that professes, avows, or declares 2 a : a faculty member of the highest academic rank at an institution of higher education b : a teacher at a university, college, or sometimes secondary school c : one that teaches or professes special knowledge of an art, sport, or occupation requiring skill — **pro·fes·so·ri·al** \ˌprō-fə-ˈsōr-ē-əl, ˌprä-, -ˈsȯr-\ adj — **pro·fes·so·ri·al·ly** \-ē-ə-lē\ adv — **pro·fes·sor·ship** \prə-ˈfe-sər-ˌship\ n

pro·fes·sor·ate \prə-ˈfe-sə-rət\ n (1860) : the office, term of office, or position of a professor

pro·fes·so·ri·at \prə-fə-ˈsȯr-ē-ət, ˌprä-, -ˈsȯr-, -ē-ˌat\ or **pro·fes·so·ri·ate** \-ət, -ˌāt\ n [modif. of F professorat, fr. professeur professor, fr. L professor, fr. profitēri] (1858) 1 : the body of college and university teachers at an institution or in society 2 : the office, duties, or position of a professor

¹prof·fer \'prä-fər\ *vt* **prof·fered; prof·fer·ing** \-f(ə-)riŋ\ [ME *profren*, fr. AF *profrer*, fr. OF *poroffrir*, fr. *por-* forth (fr. L *pro-*) + *offrir* to offer — more at PRO-] (14c) : to present for acceptance : TENDER, OFFER

²proffer *n* (14c) : OFFER, SUGGESTION

pro·fi·cien·cy \prə-'fi-shən(t)-sē\ *n* (1544) 1 : advancement in knowledge or skill : PROGRESS 2 : the quality or state of being proficient

pro·fi·cient \-shənt\ *adj* [L *proficient-, proficiens*, prp. of *proficere* to go forward, accomplish, fr. *pro-* forward + *facere* to make — more at PRO-, DO] (ca. 1590) : well advanced in an art, occupation, or branch of knowledge — **proficient** *n* — **pro·fi·cient·ly** *adv*
   syn PROFICIENT, ADEPT, SKILLED, SKILLFUL, EXPERT mean having great knowledge and experience in a trade or profession. PROFICIENT implies a thorough competence derived from training and practice ⟨*proficient* in translating foreign languages⟩. ADEPT implies special aptitude as well as proficiency ⟨*adept* at doing long division⟩. SKILLED stresses mastery of technique ⟨a *skilled* surgeon⟩. SKILLFUL implies individual dexterity in execution or performance ⟨*skillful* drivers⟩. EXPERT implies extraordinary proficiency and often connotes knowledge as well as technical skill ⟨*expert* in the evaluation of wines⟩.

¹pro·file \'prō-,fīl\ *n* [It *profilo*, fr. *profilare* to draw in outline, fr. *pro-* forward (fr. L) + *filare* to spin, fr. LL — more at FILE] (ca. 1656) 1 : a representation of something in outline; *esp* : a human head or face represented or seen in a side view 2 : an outline seen or represented in sharp relief : CONTOUR 3 : a side or sectional elevation: as a : a drawing showing a vertical section of the ground b : a vertical section of a soil from the ground surface to the underlying unweathered material 4 : a set of data often in graphic form portraying the significant features of something ⟨a corporation's earnings ~⟩; *esp* : a graph representing the extent to which an individual exhibits traits or abilities as determined by tests or ratings 5 : a concise biographical sketch 6 : degree or level of public exposure ⟨trying to keep a low ~⟩ ⟨a job with a high ~⟩   *syn* see OUTLINE

²profile *vt* **pro·filed; pro·fil·ing** (1715) 1 : to represent in profile or by a profile : produce (as by drawing, writing, or graphing) a profile of 2 : to shape the outline of by passing a cutter around — **pro·fil·er** *n*

¹prof·it \'prä-fət\ *n, often attrib* [ME, fr. MF, fr. L *profectus* advance, profit, fr. *proficere*] (14c) 1 : a valuable return : GAIN 2 : the excess of returns over expenditure in a transaction or series of transactions; *esp* : the excess of the selling price of goods over their cost 3 : net income usu. for a given period of time 4 : the ratio of profit for a given year to the amount of capital invested or to the value of sales 5 : the compensation accruing to entrepreneurs for the assumption of risk in business enterprise as distinguished from wages or rent — **prof·it·less** \-ləs\ *adj* — **prof·it·wise** \-,wīz\ *adv*

²profit *vi* (14c) 1 : to be of service or advantage : AVAIL 2 : to derive benefit : GAIN 3 : to make a profit ~ *vt* : to be of service to : BENEFIT

prof·it·able \'prä-fə-tə-bəl, 'präf-tə-bəl\ *adj* (14c) : affording profits : yielding advantageous returns or results — **prof·it·abil·i·ty** \,prä-fə-tə-'bi-lə-tē\ *n* — **prof·it·able·ness** \'prä-fə-tə-bəl-nəs\ *n* — **prof·it·ably** \-blē\ *adv*

profit and loss *n* (1588) : a summary account used at the end of an accounting period to collect the balances of the nominal accounts so that the net profit or loss may be shown

prof·i·teer \,prä-fə-'tir\ *n* (1912) : one who makes what is considered an unreasonable profit esp. on the sale of essential goods during times of emergency — **profiteer** *vi*

pro·fit·er·ole \prə-'fi-tə-,rōl\ *n* [F, perh. fr. *profit* profit] (1884) : a miniature cream puff with a sweet or savory filling

profit sharing *n* (1881) : a system or process under which employees receive a part of the profits of an industrial or commercial enterprise

profit system *n* (1945) : FREE ENTERPRISE

prof·li·ga·cy \'prä-fli-gə-sē\ *n* (1738) : the quality or state of being profligate

¹prof·li·gate \'prä-fli-gət, -,gāt\ *adj* [L *profligatus*, fr. pp. of *profligare* to strike down, fr. *pro-* forward, down + *-fligare* (akin to *fligere* to strike); akin to Gk *phlibein* to squeeze] (1647) 1 : completely given up to dissipation and licentiousness 2 : wildly extravagant : PRODIGAL — **prof·li·gate·ly** *adv*

²profligate *n* (1709) : a person given to wildly extravagant and usu. grossly self-indulgent expenditure

pro·flu·ent \'prä-,flü-ənt, 'prō-; prō-'flü-\ *adj* [ME, fr. L *profluent-, profluens*, prp. of *profluere* to flow forth, fr. *pro-* forth + *fluere* to flow — more at PRO-, FLUID] (15c) : flowing copiously or smoothly

pro for·ma \(,)prō-'fȯr-mə\ *adj* [L, for form] (ca. 1580) 1 : made or carried out in a perfunctory manner or as a formality 2 : provided in advance to prescribe form or describe items ⟨*pro forma* invoice⟩

¹pro·found \prə-'faůnd, prō-\ *adj* [ME, fr. MF *profond* deep, fr. L *profundus*, fr. *pro-* before + *fundus* bottom — more at PRO-, BOTTOM] (14c) 1 a : having intellectual depth and insight b : difficult to fathom or understand 2 a : extending far below the surface b : coming from, reaching to, or situated at a depth : DEEP-SEATED ⟨a ~ sigh⟩ 3 a : characterized by intensity of feeling or quality b : all encompassing : COMPLETE ⟨~ sleep⟩ — **pro·found·ly** \-'faůn(d)-lē\ *adv* — **pro·found·ness** \-'faůn(d)-nəs\ *n*

²profound *n* (1621) *archaic* : something that is very deep; *specif* : the depths of the sea

pro·fun·di·ty \prə-'fən-də-tē\ *n, pl* **-ties** [ME *profundite*, fr. MF *profundité*, fr. L *profunditat-, profunditas* depth, fr. *profundus*] (15c) 1 a : intellectual depth b : something profound or abstruse 2 : the quality or state of being profound or deep

pro·fuse \prə-'fyüs, prō-\ *adj* [ME, fr. L *profusus*, pp. of *profundere* to pour forth, fr. *pro-* forth + *fundere* to pour — more at FOUND] (15c) 1 : pouring forth liberally : EXTRAVAGANT ⟨~ in their thanks⟩ 2 : exhibiting great abundance : BOUNTIFUL ⟨a ~ harvest⟩ — **pro·fuse·ly** *adv* — **pro·fuse·ness** *n*
   syn PROFUSE, LAVISH, PRODIGAL, LUXURIANT, LUSH, EXUBERANT mean giving or given out in great abundance. PROFUSE implies pouring forth without restraint ⟨uttered *profuse* apologies⟩. LAVISH suggests an unstinted or unmeasured profusion ⟨a *lavish* wedding reception⟩. PRODIGAL implies reckless or wasteful lavishness threatening to lead to early exhaustion of resources ⟨*prodigal* spending⟩. LUXURIANT suggests a rich and splendid abundance ⟨*luxuriant* side-whiskers⟩. LUSH suggests

rich, soft luxuriance ⟨a *lush* green lawn⟩. EXUBERANT implies marked vitality or vigor in what produces abundantly ⟨an *exuberant* imagination⟩.

pro·fu·sion \-'fyü-zhən\ *n* (1545) 1 : lavish expenditure : EXTRAVAGANCE 2 : the quality or state of being profuse 3 : great quantity : lavish display or supply ⟨snow falling in ~⟩

¹prog \'präg\ *vi* **progged; prog·ging** [origin unknown] (1624) *chiefly dial* : to search about; *esp* : FORAGE

²prog *n* (1655) *chiefly dial* : FOOD, VICTUALS

pro·gen·i·tor \prō-'je-nə-tər, prə-\ *n* [ME, fr. MF *progeniteur*, fr. L *progenitor*, fr. *progignere* to beget, fr. *pro-* forth + *gignere* to beget — more at KIN] (14c) 1 a : an ancestor in the direct line : FOREFATHER b : a biologically ancestral form 2 : PRECURSOR, ORIGINATOR ⟨~s of socialist ideas —*Times Lit. Supp.*⟩

prog·e·ny \'prä-jⁿ-ē\ *n, pl* **-nies** [ME *progenie*, fr. MF, fr. L *progenies*, fr. *progignere*] (14c) 1 a : DESCENDANTS, CHILDREN b : offspring of animals or plants 2 : OUTCOME, PRODUCT 3 : a body of followers, disciples, or successors

pro·ges·ta·tion·al \,prō-,jes-'tā-shnəl, -shə-nⁿl\ *adj* (1923) : preceding pregnancy or gestation; *esp* : of, relating to, inducing, or constituting the modifications of the female mammalian system associated esp. with ovulation and corpus luteum formation ⟨~ hormones⟩

pro·ges·ter·one \prō-'jes-tə-,rōn\ *n* [*progestin* + *-sterone*] (1935) : a female steroid sex hormone $C_{21}H_{30}O_2$ that is secreted by the corpus luteum to prepare the endometrium for implantation and later by the placenta during pregnancy to prevent rejection of the developing embryo or fetus

pro·ges·tin \-'jes-tən\ *n* [*pro-* + *gestation* + ¹-*in*] (1930) : a progestational hormone; *esp* : PROGESTERONE

pro·ges·to·gen \-'jes-tə-jən\ *n* [*progestational* + *-ogen* (as in *estrogen*)] (1942) : any of several progestational steroids (as progesterone) — **pro·ges·to·gen·ic** \-,jes-tə-'je-nik\ *adj*

pro·glot·tid \(,)prō-'glä-təd\ *n* [NL *proglottis*] (1878) : a segment of a tapeworm containing both male and female reproductive organs

pro·glot·tis \(,)prō-'glä-təs\ *n, pl* **-glot·ti·des** \-'glä-tə-,dēz\ [NL *proglottid-, proglottis*, fr. Gk *proglōttis* tip of the tongue, fr. *pro-* + *glōtta* tongue — more at GLOSS] (1855) : PROGLOTTID

prog·na·thism \'präg-nə-,thi-zəm, präg-'nā-\ *n* (ca. 1864) : prognathous condition

prog·na·thous \-thəs\ *adj* (1836) : having the jaws projecting beyond the upper part of the face

prog·no·sis \präg-'nō-səs\ *n, pl* **-no·ses** \-,sēz\ [LL, fr. Gk *prognōsis*, lit., foreknowledge, fr. *progignōskein* to know before, fr. *pro-* + *gignōskein* to know — more at KNOW] (1655) 1 : the prospect of recovery as anticipated from the usual course of disease or peculiarities of the case 2 : FORECAST, PROGNOSTICATION

¹prog·nos·tic \präg-'näs-tik\ *n* [ME *pronostique*, fr. MF, fr. L *prognosticum*, fr. Gk *prognōstikon*, fr. neut. of *prognōstikos* foretelling, fr. *progignōskein*] (14c) 1 : something that foretells : PORTENT 2 : PROGNOSTICATION, PROPHECY

²prognostic *adj* (1603) : of, relating to, or serving as ground for prognostication or a prognosis ⟨~ weather charts⟩ ⟨favorable ~ signs⟩

prog·nos·ti·cate \präg-'näs-tə-,kāt\ *vt* **-cat·ed; -cat·ing** (15c) 1 : to foretell from signs or symptoms : PREDICT 2 : PRESAGE   *syn* see FORETELL — **prog·nos·ti·ca·tive** \-,kā-tiv\ *adj* — **prog·nos·ti·ca·tor** \-,kā-tər\ *n*

prog·nos·ti·ca·tion \(,)präg-,näs-tə-'kā-shən\ *n* (15c) 1 : an indication in advance : FORETOKEN 2 a : an act, the fact, or the power of prognosticating : FORECAST b : FOREBODING

pro·grade \'prō-,grād\ *adj* [L *pro-* forward + E *-grade* (as in *retrograde*)] (1967) : having or being a direction of rotation or revolution that is counterclockwise as viewed from the north pole of the sky or a planet

¹pro·gram \'prō-,gram, -grəm\ *n* [F *programme* agenda, public notice, fr. Gk *programma*, fr. *prographein* to write before, fr. *pro-* before + *graphein* to write — more at CARVE] (1633) 1 [LL *programma*, fr. Gk] : a public notice 2 a : a brief usu. printed outline of the order to be followed, of the features to be presented, and the persons participating (as in a public exercise or performance) b : the performance of a program; *esp* : a performance broadcast on radio or television 3 : a plan or system under which action may be taken toward a goal 4 : CURRICULUM 5 : PROSPECTUS, SYLLABUS 6 a : a plan for the programming of a mechanism (as a computer) b : a sequence of coded instructions that can be inserted into a mechanism (as a computer); *also* : such a sequence that is part of an organism's genotype or behavioral repertoire

²program *also* **programme** *vt* **-grammed** *or* **-gramed; -gram·ming** *or* **-gram·ing** (1896) 1 a : to arrange or furnish a program of or for : BILL b : to enter in a program 2 : to work out a sequence of operations to be performed by (a mechanism) : provide with a program 3 a : to insert a program for (a particular action) into or as if into a mechanism b : to control by or as if by a program c (1) : to code in an organism's program (2) : to provide with a biological program ⟨cells *programmed* to synthesize hemoglobin⟩ 4 : to predetermine the thinking, behavior, or operations of as if by computer programming ⟨children are *programmed* into violence —Lisa A. Richette⟩ — **pro·gram·ma·bil·i·ty** \(,)prō-,gra-mə-'bi-lə-tē\ *n* — **pro·gram·ma·ble** \'prō-,gra-mə-bəl\ *adj or n*

program director *n* (1953) : one in charge of planning and scheduling program material for a radio or television station or network

pro·gram·mat·ic \,prō-grə-'ma-tik\ *adj* (1896) 1 : relating to program music 2 : of, relating to, resembling, or having a program — **pro·gram·mat·i·cal·ly** \-ti-k(ə-)lē\ *adv*

programme *chiefly Brit var of* PROGRAM

programmed instruction *n* (1962) : instruction through information given in small steps with each requiring a correct response by the learner before going on to the next step

---

\ə\ abut \ᵊ\ kitten, F table \ər\ further \a\ ash \ā\ ace \ä\ mop, mar
\aů\ out \ch\ chin \e\ bet \ē\ easy \g\ go \i\ hit \ī\ ice \j\ job
\ŋ\ sing \ō\ go \ȯ\ law \ȯi\ boy \th\ thin \t͟h\ the \ü\ loot \ů\ foot
\y\ yet \zh\ vision \à, k̲, ⁿ, œ, œ̄, ue, ūe, ʸ\ *see* Guide to Pronunciation

pro·gram·mer also **pro·gram·er** \'prō-,gra-mər, -grə-\ n (ca. 1890) : one that programs: as **a** : a person who prepares and tests programs for devices (as computers) **b** : one that programs a mechanism **c** : one that prepares instructional or educational programs

pro·gram·ming also **pro·gram·ing** \-miŋ\ n (1940) **1** : the planning, scheduling, or performing of a program **2 a** : the process of instructing or learning by means of an instructional program **b** : the process of preparing an instructional program

program music n (1879) : music intended to suggest a sequence of images or incidents

program trading n (1985) : computerized trading of large blocks of stocks in one market against stock index futures in another

¹**prog·ress** \'prä-grəs, -,gres, US also & Brit usu 'prō-,gres\ n [ME, fr. L progressus advance, fr. progredi to go forth, fr. pro- forward + gradi to go — more at PRO-, GRADE] (15c) **1 a** (1) : a royal journey marked by pomp and pageant (2) : a state procession **b** : a tour or circuit made by an official (as a judge) **c** : an expedition, journey, or march through a region **2** : a forward or onward movement (as to an objective or to a goal) : ADVANCE **3** : gradual betterment; esp : the progressive development of mankind — **in progress** : going on : OCCURRING

²**pro·gress** \prə-'gres\ vi (1539) **1** : to move forward : PROCEED **2** : to develop to a higher, better, or more advanced stage

pro·gres·sion \prə-'gre-shən\ n (15c) **1** : a sequence of numbers in which each term is related to its predecessor by a uniform law **2 a** : the action or process of progressing : ADVANCE **b** : a continuous and connected series : SEQUENCE **3 a** : succession of musical tones or chords **b** : the movement of musical parts in harmony **c** : SEQUENCE 2c — **pro·gres·sion·al** \-'gresh-nəl, -'gre-shə-nᵊl\ adj

¹**pro·gres·sive** \prə-'gre-siv\ adj (ca. 1612) **1** : of, relating to, or characterized by progress **b** : making use of or interested in new ideas, findings, or opportunities **c** : of, relating to, or constituting an educational theory marked by emphasis on the individual child, informality of classroom procedure, and encouragement of self-expression **2** : of, relating to, or characterized by progression **3** : moving forward or onward : ADVANCING **4 a** : increasing in extent or severity ⟨a ~ disease⟩ **b** : increasing in rate as the base increases ⟨a ~ tax⟩ **5** often cap : of or relating to political Progressives **6** : of, relating to, or constituting a verb form that expresses action or state in progress at the time of speaking or a time spoken of — **pro·gres·sive·ly** adv — **pro·gres·sive·ness** n

²**progressive** n (1846) **1 a** : one that is progressive **b** : one believing in moderate political change and esp. social improvement by governmental action **2** cap : a member of any of various U.S. political parties: as **a** : a member of a predominantly agrarian minor party that around 1912 split off from the Republicans; specif : BULL MOOSE **b** : a follower of Robert M. La Follette in the presidential campaign of 1924 **c** : a follower of Henry A. Wallace in the presidential campaign of 1948

Progressive Conservative adj (1944) : of or relating to a major political party in Canada traditionally advocating economic nationalism and close ties with the United Kingdom and the Commonwealth — **Progressive Conservative** n

pro·gres·siv·ism \prə-'gre-si-,vi-zəm\ n (1892) **1** : the principles, beliefs, or practices of progressives **2** cap : the political and economic doctrines advocated by the Progressives **3** : the theories of progressive education — **pro·gres·siv·ist** \-vist\ n or adj — **pro·gres·siv·is·tic** \-,gre-si-'vis-tik\ adj

pro·gres·siv·i·ty \,prō-(,)gre-'si-və-tē\ n (1883) : the quality or state of being a progressive tax

pro·hib·it \prō-'hi-bət, prə-\ vt [ME, fr. L prohibitus, pp. of prohibēre to keep off, fr. pro- forward + habēre to hold — more at PRO-, GIVE] (15c) **1** : to forbid by authority : ENJOIN **2 a** : to prevent from doing something **b** : PRECLUDE syn see FORBID

pro·hi·bi·tion \,prō-ə-'bi-shən also ,prō-hə-\ n (14c) **1** : the act of prohibiting by authority **2** : an order to restrain or stop **3** often cap : the forbidding by law of the manufacture, transportation, and sale of alcoholic liquors except for medicinal and sacramental purposes

pro·hi·bi·tion·ist \-sh(ə-)nist\ n (ca. 1846) : one who favors prohibition; esp. cap : a member of a minor U.S. political party advocating prohibition

pro·hib·i·tive \prō-'hi-bə-tiv, prə-\ adj (15c) **1** : tending to prohibit or restrain **2** : tending to preclude use or purchase ⟨~ costs⟩ **3** : almost certain to perform as predicted ⟨a ~ favorite⟩ — **pro·hib·i·tive·ly** adv — **pro·hib·i·tive·ness** n

pro·hib·i·to·ry \-'hi-bə-,tōr-ē, -,tôr-\ adj (ca. 1591) : PROHIBITIVE

pro·insulin \(,)prō-'in(t)-s(ə-)lən\ n (1916) : a single-chain pancreatic polypeptide precursor of insulin that gives rise to the double chain of insulin by loss of the middle part of the molecule

¹**proj·ect** \'prä-,jekt, -jikt also 'prō-\ n [ME proiecte, fr. ML projectum, fr. L, neut. of projectus, pp. of proicere to throw forward, fr. pro- + jacere to throw — more at JET] (15c) **1 a** : a specific plan or design : SCHEME **2** obs : IDEA **3** : a planned undertaking: as **a** : a definitely formulated piece of research **b** : a large usu. government-supported undertaking **c** : a task or problem engaged in usu. by a group of students to supplement and apply classroom studies **4** : a usu. public housing development consisting of houses or apartments built and arranged according to a single plan syn see PLAN

²**pro·ject** \prə-'jekt\ vb [partly modif. of MF projeter, fr. OF porjeter to throw forward, fr. por- (fr. L porro forward; akin to Gk pro forward) + jeter to throw; partly fr. L projectus, pp. — more at FOR, JET] vt (15c) **1 a** : to devise in the mind : DESIGN **b** : to plan, figure, or estimate for the future ⟨~ expenditures for the coming year⟩ **2** : to throw or cast forward : THRUST **3** : to put or set forth : present for consideration **4** : to cause to protrude **5** : to cause (light or shadow) to fall into space or (an image) to fall on a surface ⟨~ a beam of light⟩ **6** : to reproduce (as a point, line, or area) on a surface by motion in a prescribed direction **7** : to display outwardly esp. to an audience ⟨~ an image⟩ ⟨an actress who could ~ amorality —Current Biog.⟩ **8** : to attribute (one's own ideas, feelings, or characteristics) to other people or to objects ⟨a nation is an entity on which one can ~ many of the worst of one's instincts —Times Lit. Supp.⟩ ~ vi **1** : to jut out : PROTRUDE **2 a** : to come across vividly : give an impression **b** : to make oneself heard clearly — **pro·ject·able** \-'jek-tə-bəl\ adj

¹**pro·jec·tile** \prə-'jek-tᵊl, -,til, chiefly Brit 'prä-,jik-,til\ n (1665) **1** : a

body projected by external force and continuing in motion by its own inertia; esp : a missile for a weapon (as a firearm) **2** : a self-propelling weapon (as a rocket)

²**projectile** adj (1715) **1** : projecting or impelling forward ⟨a ~ force⟩ **2** : capable of being thrust forward

pro·jec·tion \prə-'jek-shən\ n (1557) **1 a** : a systematic presentation of intersecting coordinate lines on a flat surface upon which features from the curved surface of the earth or the celestial sphere may be mapped **b** : the process or technique of reproducing a spatial object upon a plane or curved surface or a line by projecting its points; also : a graph or figure so formed **2** : a transforming change **3** : the act of throwing or thrusting forward **4** : the forming of a plan : SCHEMING **5 a** (1) : a jutting out (2) : a part that juts out **b** : a view of a building or architectural element **6 a** : the act of perceiving a mental object as spatially and sensibly objective; also : something so perceived **b** : the attribution of one's own ideas, feelings, or attitudes to other people or to objects; esp : the externalization of blame, guilt, or responsibility as a defense against anxiety **7** : the display of motion pictures by projecting an image from them upon a screen **8 a** : the act of projecting esp. to an audience **b** : control of the volume, clarity, and distinctness of a voice to gain greater audibility **9** : an estimate of future possibilities based on a current trend — **pro·jec·tion·al** \-shnəl, -shə-nᵊl\ adj

syn PROJECTION, PROTRUSION, PROTUBERANCE, BULGE mean an extension beyond the normal line or surface. PROJECTION implies a jutting out esp. at a sharp angle ⟨those projections along the wall are safety hazards⟩. PROTRUSION suggests a thrusting out so that the extension seems a deformity ⟨the bizarre protrusions of a coral reef⟩. PROTUBERANCE implies a growing or swelling out in rounded form ⟨a skin disease marked by warty protuberances⟩. BULGE suggests an expansion caused by internal pressure ⟨bulges in the floor⟩.

projection booth n (ca. 1928) : a booth in a theater or hall for housing and operating a projector and esp. a motion-picture projector

pro·jec·tion·ist \prə-'jek-sh(ə-)nist\ n (1922) : one that makes projections: as **a** : CARTOGRAPHER **b** : a person who operates a motion-picture projector or television equipment

pro·jec·tive \prə-'jek-tiv\ adj (1682) **1** : relating to, produced by, or involving geometric projection **2** : of or relating to something that indicates the psychodynamic constitution of an individual ⟨~ tests⟩ — **pro·jec·tive·ly** adv

projective geometry n (1885) : a branch of geometry that deals with the properties of configurations that are unaltered by projection

pro·jec·tor \prə-'jek-tər\ n (1596) **1** : one that plans a project; specif : PROMOTER **2** : one that projects: as **a** : a device for projecting a beam of light **b** : an optical instrument for projecting an image upon a surface **c** : a machine for projecting motion pictures on a screen **3** : an imagined line from an object to a surface along which projection takes place

pro·jet \prō-'zhā, 'prō-,\ n, pl **projets** \-'zhā(z), -,zhā(z)\ [F, fr. MF pourget, fr. pourjeter, projeter] (1808) **1** : PLAN; esp : a draft of a proposed measure or treaty **2** : a projected or proposed design

pro·kary·ote \(,)prō-'kar-ē-,ōt\ n [NL Prokaryotes, proposed subdivision of protists, fr. ¹pro- + kary- + -otes, pl. n. suffix, fr. Gk -ōtos — more at -OTIC] (1963) : a cellular organism (as a bacterium or a blue-green alga) that does not have a distinct nucleus — compare EUKARYOTE — **pro·kary·ot·ic** \-,kar-ē-'ä-tik\ adj

pro·lac·tin \prō-'lak-tən\ n [²pro- + lact- + ¹-in] (1932) : a protein hormone of the anterior lobe of the pituitary that induces lactation

pro·la·min or **pro·la·mine** \'prō-lə-mən, -,mēn\ n [ISV proline + ammonia + ¹-in, ²-ine] (1908) : any of various simple proteins (as zein) that are found esp. in seeds and are insoluble in absolute alcohol or water

pro·lan \'prō-,lan\ n [G, fr. L proles progeny — more at PROLETARIAN] (1931) : either of two gonadotrophic hormones: **a** : FOLLICLE-STIMULATING HORMONE **b** : LUTEINIZING HORMONE

¹**pro·lapse** \'prō-,laps, 'prō-,\ n [NL prolapsus, fr. LL, fall, fr. L prolabi to fall or slide forward, fr. pro- forward + labi to slide — more at PRO-, SLEEP] (ca. 1834) : the falling down or slipping of a body part from its usual position or relations

²**pro·lapse** \prō-'laps\ vi **pro·lapsed; pro·laps·ing** (1876) : to undergo prolapse

pro·late \'prō-,lāt\ adj [L prolatus (pp. of proferre to bring forward, extend) fr. pro- forward + latus, pp. of ferre to carry — more at BEAR, TOLERATE] (1694) : EXTENDED; esp : elongated in the direction of a line joining the poles ⟨a ~ spheroid⟩

prole \'prōl\ n or adj (1887) : PROLETARIAN

pro·leg \'prō-,leg, -,läg\ n (1816) : a fleshy leg that occurs on an abdominal segment of some insect larvae but not in the adult

pro·le·gom·e·non \,prō-li-'gä-mə-,nän, -nən\ n, pl **-e·na** \-nə\ [Gk, neut. pres. pass. part. of prolegein to say beforehand, fr. pro- before + legein to say — more at LEGEND] (ca. 1652) : prefatory remarks; specif : a formal essay or critical discussion serving to introduce and interpret an extended work — **pro·le·gom·e·nous** \-nəs\ adj

pro·lep·sis \prō-'lep-səs\ n, pl **-lep·ses** \-,sēz\ [Gk prolēpsis, fr. prolambanein to take beforehand, fr. pro- before + lambanein to take — more at LATCH] (1578) : ANTICIPATION: as **a** : the representation or assumption of a future act or development as if presently existing or accomplished **b** : the application of an adjective to a noun in anticipation of the result of the action of the verb (as in "while yon slow oxen turn the furrowed plain") — **pro·lep·tic** \-'lep-tik\ adj — **pro·lep·ti·cal·ly** \-ti-k(ə-)lē\ adv

pro·le·tar·i·an \,prō-lə-'ter-ē-ən\ n [L proletarius, fr. proles progeny, fr. pro- forth + -oles (akin to alere to nourish) — more at OLD] (1658) : a member of the proletariat — **proletarian** adj

pro·le·tar·i·an·ise Brit var of PROLETARIANIZE

pro·le·tar·i·an·ize \-'ter-ē-ə-,nīz\ vt **-ized; -iz·ing** (1887) : to reduce to a proletarian status or level — **pro·le·tar·i·an·i·za·tion** \-,ter-ē-ə-nə-'zā-shən\ n

pro·le·tar·i·at \,prō-lə-'ter-ē-ət, -'tar-, -ē-,at\ n [F prolétariat, fr. L proletarius] (1853) **1** : the lowest social or economic class of a community **2** : the laboring class; esp : the class of industrial workers who lack their own means of production and hence sell their labor to live

pro–life \\(,)prō-'līf\\ *adj* (1961) : ANTIABORTION — **pro–lif·er** \\-'lī-fər\\ *n*

pro·lif·er·ate \\prə-'li-fə-,rāt\\ *vb* **-at·ed; -at·ing** [back-formation fr. *proliferation*, fr. F *prolifération*, fr. *proliférer* to proliferate, fr. *prolifère* reproducing freely, fr. L *proles* + *-fer* -ferous] *vi* (1873) **1** : to grow by rapid production of new parts, cells, buds, or offspring **2** : to increase in number as if by proliferating : MULTIPLY ~ *vt* : to cause to grow by proliferating — **pro·lif·er·a·tion** \\-,li-fə-'rā-shən\\ *n* — **pro·lif·er·a·tive** \\-'li-fə-,rā-tiv, -f(ə-)rə-tiv\\ *adj*

pro·lif·ic \\prə-'li-fik\\ *adj* [F *prolifique*, fr. L *proles*] (1650) **1** : producing young or fruit esp. freely : FRUITFUL **2** *archaic* : causing abundant growth, generation, or reproduction **3** : marked by abundant inventiveness or productivity ⟨a ~ composer⟩ *syn* see FERTILE — **pro·lif·i·ca·cy** \\-'li-fi-kə-sē\\ *n* — **pro·lif·i·cal·ly** \\-fi-k(ə-)lē\\ *adv* — **pro·lif·ic·ness** \\-fik-nəs\\ *n*

pro·li·fic·i·ty \\,prō-lə-'fi-sə-tē\\ *n* (1725) : prolific power or character

pro·line \\'prō-,lēn\\ *n* [G *Prolin*] (1904) : an amino acid C₅H₉NO₂ that can be synthesized by animals from glutamate

pro·lix \\prō-'liks, 'prō-(,)\\ *adj* [ME, fr. MF & L; MF *prolixe*, fr. L *prolixus* extended, fr. *pro-* forward + *liquēre* to be fluid — more at LIQUID] (15c) **1** : unduly prolonged or drawn out : too long **2** : marked by or using an excess of words *syn* see WORDY — **pro·lix·i·ty** \\prō-'lik-sə-tē\\ *n* — **pro·lix·ly** *adv*

pro·loc·u·tor \\prō-'lä-kyə-tər\\ *n* [ME, fr. L, fr. *pro-* for + *locutor* speaker, fr. *loqui* to speak] (15c) **1** : one who speaks for another : SPOKESMAN **2** : presiding officer : CHAIRMAN

pro·log·ize \\'prō-,lô-,gīz, -,lä-; -lə-,jīz\\ *or* **pro·logu·ize** \\-,lô-,gīz, -,lä-\\ *vi* **-log·ized** *or* **-logu·ized; -log·iz·ing** *or* **-logu·iz·ing** (1608) : to write or speak a prologue

pro·logue *also* **pro·log** \\'prō-,lòg, -,läg\\ *n* [ME *prolog*, fr. MF *prologue*, fr. L *prologus* preface to a play, fr. Gk *prologos* part of a Greek play preceding the entry of the chorus, fr. *pro-* before + *legein* to speak — more at PRO-, LEGEND] (14c) **1** : the preface or introduction to a literary work **2 a** : a speech often in verse addressed to the audience by an actor at the beginning of a play **b** : the actor speaking such a prologue **3** : an introductory or preceding event or development

pro·long \\prə-'lòn\\ *vt* [ME, fr. MF *prolonguer*, fr. LL *prolongare*, fr. L *pro-* forward + *longus* long] (15c) **1** : to lengthen in time : CONTINUE **2** : to lengthen in extent, scope, or range *syn* see EXTEND — **pro·long·er** \\-'lòn-ər\\ *n*

pro·lon·ga·tion \\(,)prō-,lòn-'gā-shən, prə-\\ *n* (15c) **1** : an extension or lengthening in time or duration **2** : an expansion or continuation in extent, scope, or range

pro·lu·sion \\prō-'lü-zhən\\ *n* [L *prolusion-, prolusio*, fr. *proludere* to play beforehand, fr. *pro-* before + *ludere* to play — more at LUDICROUS] (1601) **1** : a preliminary trial or exercise : PRELUDE **2** : an introductory and often tentative discourse — **pro·lu·so·ry** \\-'lü-sə-rē, -zə-; -'lüz-rē, -'lüz-\\ *adj*

prom \\'präm\\ *n* [short for *promenade*] (1894) **1** : a formal dance given by a high school or college class **2** *Brit* : PROMENADE 2

¹prom·e·nade \\,prä-mə-'nād, -'näd\\ *vb* **-nad·ed; -nad·ing** [²*promenade*] *vi* (1588) **1** : to take or go on a promenade **2** : to perform a promenade in a dance ~ *vt* : to walk about in or on — **prom·e·nad·er** *n*

²promenade *n* [F, fr. *promener* to take for a walk, fr. L *prominare* to drive forward, fr. *pro-* forward + *minare* to drive — more at AMENABLE] (1648) **1** : a place for strolling **2** : a leisurely walk or ride esp. in a public place for pleasure or display **3 a** : a ceremonious opening of a formal ball consisting of a grand march of all the guests **b** : a figure in a square dance in which couples move counterclockwise in a circle

promenade deck *n* (1829) : an upper deck or an area on a deck of a passenger ship where passengers stroll

Pro·me·the·an \\prə-'mē-thē-ən\\ *adj* (1588) : of, relating to, or resembling Prometheus, his experiences, or his art; *esp* : daringly original or creative

Pro·me·theus \\-thē-əs, -,thyüs\\ *n* [L, fr. Gk *Promētheus*] : a Titan who is chained and tortured by Zeus for stealing fire from heaven and giving it to mankind

pro·me·thi·um \\-thē-əm\\ *n* [NL, fr. L *Prometheus*] (1948) : a radioactive metallic element of the rare-earth group obtained as a fission product of uranium or from neutron-irradiated neodymium — see ELEMENT table

prom·i·nence \\'prä-mə-nən(t)s, 'präm-nən(t)s\\ *n* (1598) **1** : something prominent : PROJECTION ⟨a rocky ~⟩ **2** : the quality, state, or fact of being prominent or conspicuous **3** : a mass of gas resembling a cloud that arises from the chromosphere of the sun

prom·i·nent \\-nənt\\ *adj* [L *prominent-, prominens*, fr. prp. of *prominēre* to jut forward, fr. L *pro-* forward + -*minēre* (akin to *mont-, mons* mountain) — more at MOUNT] (15c) **1** : standing out or projecting beyond a surface or line : PROTUBERANT **2 a** : readily noticeable : CONSPICUOUS **b** : widely and popularly known : LEADING *syn* see NOTICEABLE — **prom·i·nent·ly** *adv*

pro·mis·cu·i·ty \\,prä-mə-'skyü-ə-tē, ,prō-\\ *n, pl* **-ties** (ca. 1849) **1** : a miscellaneous mixture or mingling of persons or things **2** : promiscuous sexual behavior

pro·mis·cu·ous \\prə-'mis-kyə-wəs\\ *adj* [L *promiscuus*, fr. *pro-* forth + *miscēre* to mix — more at PRO-, MIX] (1603) **1** : composed of all sorts of persons or things **2** : not restricted to one class, sort, or person : INDISCRIMINATE ⟨education . . . cheapened through the ~ distribution of diplomas —Norman Cousins⟩ **3** : not restricted to one sexual partner **4** : CASUAL, IRREGULAR ⟨~ eating habits⟩ — **pro·mis·cu·ous·ly** *adv* — **pro·mis·cu·ous·ness** *n*

¹prom·ise \\'prä-məs\\ *n* [ME *promis*, fr. L *promissum*, fr. neut. of *promissus*, pp. of *promittere* to send forth, promise, fr. *pro-* forth + *mittere* to send] (15c) **1 a** : a declaration that one will do or refrain from doing something specified **b** : a legally binding declaration that gives the person to whom it is made a right to expect or to claim the performance or forbearance of a specified act **2** : reason to expect something ⟨little ~ of relief⟩; *esp* : ground for expectation of success, improvement, or excellence ⟨shows considerable ~⟩ **3** : something that is promised

²promise *vb* **prom·ised; prom·is·ing** *vt* (15c) **1** : to pledge to do, bring about, or provide ⟨~ aid⟩ **2** *archaic* : WARRANT, ASSURE **3** *chiefly dial* : BETROTH **4** : to suggest beforehand : give promise of

⟨dark clouds ~ rain⟩ ~ *vi* **1** : to make a promise **2** : to give ground for expectation : be imminent — **prom·is·ee** \\,prä-mə-'sē\\ *n* — **prom·i·sor** \\'prä-mə-sər\\ *n*

promised land *n* (1667) : something good and esp. a place or condition believed to promise final satisfaction or realization of hopes

prom·is·ing \\'prä-mə-siŋ\\ *adj* (1601) : full of promise : likely to succeed or to yield good results — **prom·is·ing·ly** \\-siŋ-lē\\ *adv*

prom·is·so·ry \\'prä-mə-,sōr-ē, -,sòr-\\ *adj* [ME *promissorye*, fr. ML *promissorius*, fr. L *promittere*] (15c) : containing or conveying a promise or assurance

promissory note *n* (1710) : a written promise to pay at a fixed or determinable future time a sum of money to a specified individual or to bearer

pro·mo \\'prō-(,)mō\\ *n, pl* **promos** *often attrib* [short for *promotional*] (1946) : a promotional announcement, blurb, or appearance

prom·on·to·ry \\'prä-mən-,tōr-ē, -,tòr-\\ *n, pl* **-ries** [L *promunturium, promontorium;* prob. akin to *prominēre* to jut forth — more at PROMINENT] (1548) **1 a** : a high point of land or rock projecting into a body of water **b** : a prominent mass of land overlooking or projecting into a lowland **2** : a bodily prominence

pro·mote \\prə-'mōt\\ *vt* **pro·mot·ed; pro·mot·ing** [ME, fr. L *promotus*, pp. of *promovēre*, lit., to move forward, fr. *pro-* forward + *movēre* to move] (14c) **1 a** : to advance in station, rank, or honor : RAISE **b** : to change (a pawn) into a piece in chess by moving to the eighth rank **c** : to advance (a student) from one grade to the next higher grade **2 a** : to contribute to the growth or prosperity of : FURTHER ⟨~ international understanding⟩ **b** : to help bring (as an enterprise) into being : LAUNCH **c** : to present (merchandise) for buyer acceptance through advertising, publicity, or discounting **3** *slang* : to get possession of by doubtful means or by ingenuity *syn* see ADVANCE — **pro·mot·abil·i·ty** \\-,mō-tə-'bi-lə-tē\\ *n* — **pro·mot·able** \\-'mō-tə-bəl\\ *adj*

pro·mot·er \\-'mō-tər\\ *n* (14c) **1** : one that promotes; *esp* : one who assumes the financial responsibilities of a sporting event (as a boxing match) including contracting with the principals, renting the site, and collecting gate receipts **2** *obs* : PROSECUTOR **3** : a substance that in very small amounts is able to increase the activity of a catalyst **4** : a binding site in a DNA chain at which RNA polymerase binds to initiate transcription of messenger RNA by one or more nearby structural genes

pro·mo·tion \\prə-'mō-shən\\ *n* (15c) **1** : the act or fact of being raised in position or rank : PREFERMENT **2** : the act of furthering the growth or development of something; *esp* : the furtherance of the acceptance and sale of merchandise through advertising, publicity, or discounting — **pro·mo·tion·al** \\-shnəl, -shə-nᵊl\\ *adj*

pro·mo·tive \\-'mō-tiv\\ *adj* (1644) : tending or serving to promote — **pro·mo·tive·ness** *n*

¹prompt \\'präm(p)t\\ *vt* [ME, fr. ML *promptare*, fr. L *promptus* prompt] (14c) **1** : to move to action : INCITE **2** : to assist (one acting or reciting) by suggesting or saying the next words of something forgotten or imperfectly learned : CUE **3** : to serve as the inciting cause of — **prompt·er** *n*

²prompt *adj* (1784) : of or relating to prompting actors

³prompt *adj* [ME, fr. MF or L; MF, fr. L *promptus* ready, prompt, fr. pp. of *promere* to bring forth, fr. *pro-* forth + *emere* to take — more at REDEEM] (15c) **1** : being ready and quick to act as occasion demands **2** : performed readily or immediately ⟨~ assistance⟩ *syn* see QUICK — **prompt·ly** \\'präm(p)t-lē, 'präm-plē\\ *adv* — **prompt·ness** \\'präm(p)t-nəs, 'prämp-nəs\\ *n*

⁴prompt *n, pl* **prompts** \\'präm(p)ts, 'prämps\\ (1597) **1** [¹*prompt*] : something that prompts : REMINDER **2** [³*prompt*] : a limit of time given for payment of an account for goods purchased; *also* : the contract by which this time is fixed

prompt·book \\'präm(p)t-,bük, 'prämp-,bük\\ *n* (1809) : a copy of a play with directions for performance used by a theater prompter

promp·ti·tude \\'präm(p)-tə-,tüd, -,tyüd\\ *n* [ME, fr. MF or LL; MF, fr. LL *promptitudo*, fr. L *promptus*] (15c) : the quality or habit of being prompt : PROMPTNESS

prompt side *n* (1824) **1** : the side of the stage adjacent to the prompter's corner **2** : the side of the stage to the right of an actor facing the audience

pro·mul·gate \\'prä-məl-,gāt; prō-'məl-, prə-', 'prō-(,)\\ *vt* **-gat·ed; -gat·ing** [L *promulgatus*, pp. of *promulgare*, fr. *pro-* forward + -*mulgare* (prob. akin to *mulgēre* to milk, extract) — more at EMULSION] (1530) **1** : to make known by open declaration : PROCLAIM **2 a** : to make known or public the terms of (a proposed law) **b** : to put (a law) into action or force *syn* see DECLARE — **pro·mul·ga·tion** \\,prä-məl-'gā-shən; ,prō-(,)məl-, (,)prō-\\ *n* — **pro·mul·ga·tor** \\'prä-məl-,gā-tər; prō-'məl-, prə-', 'prō-(,)\\ *n*

pro·na·tion \\prō-'nā-shən\\ *n* [*pronate*, fr. LL *pronatus*, pp. of *pronare* to bend forward, fr. L *pronus*] (1666) **1** : rotation of the hand and forearm so that the palm faces backwards or downwards **2** : rotation of the medial bones in the midtarsal region of the foot inward and downward so that in walking the foot tends to come down on its inner margin — **pro·nate** \\'prō-,nāt\\ *vb*

pro·na·tor \\'prō-,nā-tər\\ *n* (ca. 1741) : a muscle that produces pronation

prone \\'prōn\\ *adj* [ME, fr. L *pronus* bent forward, tending; akin to L *pro* forward — more at FOR] (14c) **1** : having a tendency or inclination : being likely ⟨~ to forget names⟩ ⟨*accident-prone*⟩ **2 a** : having the front or ventral surface downward **b** : lying flat or prostrate — **prone** *adv* — **prone·ly** *adv* — **prone·ness** \\'prōn-nəs\\ *n*

syn PRONE, SUPINE, PROSTRATE, RECUMBENT mean lying down. PRONE implies a position with the front of the body turned toward the supporting surface ⟨push-ups require a *prone* position⟩. SUPINE implies lying on one's back and suggests inertness or abjectness ⟨lying *supine* on the couch⟩. PROSTRATE implies lying full-length as in submission, defeat, or physical collapse ⟨a runner fell *prostrate* at the finish line⟩.

\\ə\\ abut \\ᵊ\\ kitten, F table \\ər\\ further \\a\\ ash \\ā\\ ace \\ä\\ mop, mar
\\aù\\ out \\ch\\ chin \\e\\ bet \\ē\\ easy \\g\\ go \\i\\ hit \\ī\\ ice \\j\\ job
\\ŋ\\ sing \\ō\\ go \\ò\\ law \\òi\\ boy \\th\\ thin \\t͟h\\ the \\ü\\ loot \\ù\\ foot
\\y\\ yet \\zh\\ vision \\ä, k̯, ⁿ, œ, œ̄, ᵫ, īē, ᶴ\\ *see* Guide to Pronunciation

RECUMBENT implies the posture of one sleeping or resting ⟨a patient comfortably *recumbent* in a hospital bed⟩. *syn* see in addition LIABLE

pro·neph·ros \(,)prō-'ne-frəs, -,fräs\ *n* [NL, fr. Gk *pro-* + *nephros* kidney — more at NEPHRITIS] (1881) : either member of the first and most anterior pair of the three successive paired vertebrate renal organs that functions in the adults of amphioxus and some lampreys, functions temporarily in larval fishes and amphibians, and is present but nonfunctional in embryos of reptiles, birds, and mammals — compare MESONEPHROS, METANEPHROS — **pro·neph·ric** \-frik\ *adj*

¹prong \'prȯŋ, 'präŋ\ *n* [ME *pronge*] (15c) **1** : FORK **2** : a tine of a fork **3** : a slender pointed or projecting part: as **a** : a fang of a tooth **b** : a point of an antler **4** : something resembling a prong

²prong *vt* (1848) : to stab, pierce, or break up with a pronged device

pronged \'prȯŋd, 'präŋd\ *adj* (1767) **1** : having a usu. specified number of prongs — usu. used in combination ⟨a three-*pronged* fork⟩ **2** : having a usu. specified number of parts or approaches ⟨a two-*pronged* strategy⟩

prong·horn \'prȯŋ-,hȯrn, 'präŋ-\ *n, pl* **pronghorn** *or* **pronghorns** (1823) : a ruminant mammal (*Antilocapra americana*) of treeless parts of western No. America that resembles an antelope — called also *pronghorn antelope*

pronghorn

pro·nom·i·nal \prō-'nä-mə-n³l, -'näm-nəl\ *adj* [LL *pronominalis*, fr. L *pronomin-, pronomen*] (1680) **1** : of, relating to, or constituting a pronoun **2** : resembling a pronoun in identifying or specifying without describing ⟨the ~ adjective *this* in *this* dog⟩ — **pro·nom·i·nal·ly** *adv*

pro·noun \'prō-,naun\ *n* [ME *pronom*, fr. L *pronomin-, pronomen*, fr. *pro-* for + *nomin-, nomen* name — more at PRO-, NAME] (1530) : any of a small set of words in a language that are used as substitutes for nouns or noun phrases and whose referents are named or understood in the context

pro·nounce \prə-'naun(t)s\ *vb* **pro·nounced; pro·nounc·ing** [ME, fr. MF *prononcier*, fr. L *pronuntiare*, fr. *pro-* forth + *nuntiare* to report, fr. *nuntius* messenger — more at PRO-] *vt* (14c) **1** : to declare officially or ceremoniously ⟨the minister *pronounced* them husband and wife⟩ **2** : to declare authoritatively or as an opinion ⟨doctors *pronounced* him fit to resume duties⟩ **3 a** : to employ the organs of speech to produce ⟨~ these words⟩; *esp* : to say correctly ⟨I can't ~ his name⟩ **b** : to represent in printed characters the spoken counterpart of (an orthographic representation) ⟨both dictionaries ~ *clique* the same⟩ **4** : RECITE ⟨speak the speech, I pray you, as I *pronounced* it to you —Shak.⟩ ~ *vi* **1** : to pass judgment **2** : to produce the components of spoken language — **pro·nounce·abil·i·ty** \-,naun(t)-sə-'bi-lə-tē\ *n* — **pro·nounce·able** \-'naun(t)-sə-bəl\ *adj* — **pro·nounc·er** *n*

pro·nounced \-'naun(t)st\ *adj* (ca. 1741) : strongly marked : DECIDED — **pro·nounc·ed·ly** \-'naun(t)-səd-lē, -'naun(t)st-lē\ *adv*

pro·nounce·ment \prə-'naun(t)s-mənt\ *n* (1593) **1** : a usu. formal declaration of opinion **2** : an authoritative announcement

pronouncing *adj* (1764) : relating to or indicating pronunciation ⟨a ~ dictionary⟩

pron·to \'prän-,tō\ *adv* [Sp, fr. L *promptus* prompt] (ca. 1740) : without delay

¹pro·nu·clear \(,)prō-'nü-klē-ər, -'nyü-, -÷-kyə-lər\ *adj* [*pronucleus*] (ca. 1890) : of, relating to, or resembling a pronucleus

²pronuclear *adj* [²*pro-* + *nuclear*] (1971) : advocating the use of nuclear-powered generating stations

pro·nu·cle·us \(,)prō-'nü-klē-əs, -'nyü-\ *n* [NL] (1880) : the haploid nucleus of a male or female gamete (as an egg or sperm) up to the time of fusion with that of another gamete in fertilization

pro·nun·ci·a·men·to \prō-,nən(t)-sē-ə-'men-(,)tō\ *n, pl* **-tos** *or* **-toes** [modif. of Sp *pronunciamiento*, fr. *pronunciar* to pronounce, fr. L *pronuntiare*] (1835) : PROCLAMATION, PRONOUNCEMENT

pro·nun·ci·a·tion \prə-,nən(t)-sē-'ā-shən *also* ÷-,naun(t)-\ *n* [ME *pronunciacion*, fr. MF *prononciation*, fr. L *pronuntiation-, pronuntiatio*, fr. *pronuntiare*] (15c) : the act or manner of pronouncing something — **pro·nun·ci·a·tion·al** \-shnəl, -shə-n³l\ *adj*

¹proof \'prüf\ *n* [ME, alter. of *preove*, fr. OF *preuve*, fr. LL *proba*, fr. L *probare* to prove — more at PROVE] (13c) **1 a** : the cogency of evidence that compels acceptance by the mind of a truth or a fact **b** : the process or an instance of establishing the validity of a statement esp. by derivation from other statements in accordance with principles of reasoning **2** *obs* : EXPERIENCE **3** : something that induces certainty or establishes validity **4** *archaic* : the quality or state of having been tested or tried; *esp* : unyielding hardness **5** : evidence operating to determine the finding or judgment of a tribunal **6 a** *pl* **proofs** *or* **proof** : a copy (as of typeset text) made for examination or correction **b** : a test impression of an engraving, etching, or lithograph **c** : a coin that is struck from a highly-polished die on a polished planchet, is not intended for circulation, and sometimes differs in metallic content from coins of identical design struck for circulation **d** : a test photographic print made from a negative **7** : a test applied to articles or substances to determine whether they are of standard or satisfactory quality **8 a** : the minimum alcoholic strength of proof spirit **b** : strength with reference to the standard for proof spirit; *specif* : alcoholic strength indicated by a number that is twice the percent by volume of alcohol present ⟨whiskey of 90 ~ is 45% alcohol⟩

²proof *adj* (1592) **1** : able to resist or repel ⟨boots that were . . . ~ against cold and wet —Robertson Davies⟩ — often used in combination ⟨wind*proof*⟩ **2** : used in proving or testing or as a standard of comparison **3** : of standard strength or quality or alcoholic content

³proof *vt* (1745) **1 a** : to make or take a proof or test of **b** : PROOFREAD **2** : to give a resistant quality to **3** : to activate (yeast) by mixing with water and sometimes sugar or milk — **proof·er** *n*

proof·read \'prüf-,rēd\ *vt* **-read** \-,red\; **-read·ing** [back-formation fr. *proofreader*] (1920) : to read and mark corrections in (as a proof)

proof·read·er \-,rē-dər\ *n* (1832) : a person who proofreads

proof·room \'prüf-,rüm, -,rum\ *n* (1903) : a room for proofreading

proof spirit *n* (1790) : an alcoholic liquor or mixture of ethanol and water that contains 50% ethanol by volume at 60°F (16°C)

PROOFREADERS' MARKS

Mark	Meaning
℧ or ɤ or ℸ	delete; take *it* out
⊃	close up; print as o̶ne word
ℬ̶	delete and clo̶s̶e up
∧ or ⟩ or ⅄	caret; insert here ⟨something⟩
#	insert a space
eq#	space evenly∧ where∧indicated
stet	let marked t̶e̶x̶t̶ stand as set
tr	transpo̶s̶e̶; change⌢order⌢the⌢
/	used to separate two or more marks and often as a concluding stroke at the end of an insertion
[⌐	set farther to the left
⌐ set⌐	farther to the right
⌢	set a͡e or f͡l as ligatures æ or fl
=	straighten alignment
‖ ‖	straighten or align
✗	imperfect or broken character
⧠	indent or insert em quad space
¶	begin a new paragraph
ⓢⓟ	spell out ⟨set 5 lbs⟩ as five pounds⟩
cap	set in capitals ⟨CAPITALS⟩
sm cap or s.c.	set in small capitals ⟨SMALL CAPITALS⟩
lc	set in L̸owercase ⟨lowercase⟩
ital	set in italic ⟨*italic*⟩
rom	set in roman ⟨roman⟩
bf	set in boldface ⟨**boldface**⟩
= or -/ or ≃ or /H/	hyphen
$\frac{1}{N}$ or en or /N/	en dash ⟨1965–72⟩
$\frac{1}{M}$ or em or /M/	em — or long — dash
∨	superscript or superior ⟨³as in πr^2⟩
∧	subscript or inferior ⟨₂as in H_2O⟩
◇ or ⤬	centered ⟨⦁for a centered dot in $p \cdot q$⟩
⸝	comma
⸍	apostrophe
⊙	period
; or ;/	semicolon
: or ⊙	colon
⸌⸍ or ⸜⸝	quotation marks
(/)	parentheses
[/]	brackets
ok/?	query to author: has this been set as intended?
⊥ or ⊥¹	push down a ₤work-up
ꝰ¹	turn over an inve̲rted letter
wf¹	wrong font; a character of the wrong size or esp. style

¹ The last three symbols are unlikely to be needed in marking proofs of photocomposed matter.

¹prop \'präp\ *n* [ME *proppe*, fr. MD, stopper; akin to MLG *proppe* stopper] (15c) : something that props or sustains : SUPPORT

²prop *vt* **propped; prop·ping** (1538) **1 a :** to support by placing something under or against — often used with *up* **b :** to support by placing against something **2 :** SUSTAIN, STRENGTHEN

³prop *n* (1841) : PROPERTY 3

⁴prop *n* (1914) : PROPELLER

prop- *comb form* [ISV, fr. *propionic (acid)*] : related to propionic acid ⟨*propane*⟩ ⟨*propyl*⟩

pro·pae·deu·tic \,prō-pi-'dü-tik, -'dyü-\ *n* [Gk *propaideuein* to teach beforehand, fr. *pro-* before + *paideuein* to teach, fr. *paid-, pais* child — more at PRO-, FEW] (1798) : preparatory study or instruction — **pro·paedeutic** *adj*

pro·pa·gan·da \,prä-pə-'gan-də, ,prō-\ *n* [NL, fr. *Congregatio de propaganda fide* Congregation for propagating the faith, organization established by Pope Gregory XV †1623] (1718) **1** *cap* : a congregation of the Roman curia having jurisdiction over missionary territories and related institutions **2 :** the spreading of ideas, information, or rumor for the purpose of helping or injuring an institution, a cause, or a person **3 :** ideas, facts, or allegations spread deliberately to further one's cause or to damage an opposing cause; *also* : a public action having such an effect — **pro·pa·gan·dist** \-dist\ *n or adj* — **pro·pa·gan·dis·tic** \-,gan-'dis-tik\ *adj* — **pro·pa·gan·dis·ti·cal·ly** \-ti-k(ə-)lē\ *adv*

pro·pa·gan·dize \-'gan-,dīz\ *vb* **-dized; -diz·ing** *vt* (1844) **1 :** to subject to propaganda; *also* : to carry on propaganda for ~ *vi* : to carry on propaganda — **pro·pa·gan·diz·er** \-,dī-zər\ *n*

prop·a·gate \'prä-pə-,gāt\ *vb* **-gat·ed; -gat·ing** [L *propagatus*, pp. of *propagare* to set slips, propagate, fr. *propages* slip, offspring, fr. *pro-* before + *pangere* to fasten — more at PRO-, PACT] *vt* (ca. 1570) **1 :** to cause to continue or increase by sexual or asexual reproduction **2 :** to pass along to offspring **3 a :** to cause to spread out and affect a greater number or greater area : EXTEND **b :** to foster growing knowledge of, familiarity with, or acceptance of (as an idea or belief) : PUBLICIZE **c :** to transmit (as sound or light) through a medium ~ *vi* **1** : to multiply sexually or asexually **2 :** INCREASE, EXTEND **3 :** to travel through space or a material — used of wave energy (as light, sound, or radio waves) — **prop·a·ga·ble** \'prä-pə-gə-bəl\ *adj* — **prop·a·ga·tive** \-,gā-tiv\ *adj* — **prop·a·ga·tor** \-,gā-tər\ *n*

prop·a·ga·tion \,prä-pə-'gā-shən\ *n* (15c) : the act or action of propagating: as **a :** increase (as of a kind of organism) in numbers **b :** the spreading of something (as a belief) abroad or into new regions **c** : enlargement or extension (as of a crack) in a solid body

prop·a·gule \'prä-pə-,gyü(ə)l\ *n* [NL *propagulum*, fr. L *propages* slip] (1858) : a structure (as a cutting, a seed, or a spore) that propagates a plant

pro·pane \'prō-,pān\ *n* [ISV *prop-* + *-ane*] (1866) : a heavy flammable gaseous alkane C₃H₈ found in crude petroleum and natural gas and used esp. as fuel and in chemical synthesis

pro·pel \prə-'pel\ *vt* **pro·pelled; pro·pel·ling** [ME *propellen*, fr. L *propellere*, fr. *pro-* before + *pellere* to drive — more at FELT] (15c) : to drive forward or onward by or as if by means of a force that imparts motion

¹pro·pel·lant *also* **pro·pel·lent** \-'pe-lənt\ *adj* (1644) : capable of propelling

²propellant *also* **propellent** *n* (1814) : something that propels: as **a :** an explosive for propelling projectiles **b :** fuel plus oxidizer used by a rocket engine **c :** a gas kept under pressure in a bottle or can for expelling the contents when the pressure is released

pro·pel·ler *also* **pro·pel·lor** \prə-'pe-lər\ *n* (1780) : one that propels; *esp* : a device that consists of a central hub with radiating blades placed and twisted so that each forms part of a helical surface and that is used to propel a vehicle (as a ship or airplane)

pro·pend \prō-'pend\ *vi* [L *propendēre*, fr. *pro-* before + *pendēre* to hang — more at PENDANT] (1545) *obs* : INCLINE

pro·pense \prō-'pen(t)s\ *adj* [L *propensus*, pp. of *propendēre*] (1528) *archaic* : leaning or inclining toward : DISPOSED

pro·pen·si·ty \prə-'pen(t)-sə-tē\ *n, pl* **-ties** (1570) : an often intense natural inclination or preference *syn* see LEANING

¹prop·er \'prä-pər\ *adj* [ME *propre* proper, own, fr. MF, fr. L *proprius* own] (14c) **1 a :** referring to one individual only **b :** belonging to one : OWN **c :** appointed for the liturgy of a particular day **d :** represented heraldically in natural color **2 :** belonging characteristically to a species or individual : PECULIAR **3** *chiefly dial* : GOOD-LOOKING, HANDSOME **4 :** very good : EXCELLENT **5** *chiefly Brit* : UTTER, ABSOLUTE **6 :** strictly limited to a specified thing, place, or idea ⟨the city ~⟩ **7 a :** strictly accurate : CORRECT **b** *archaic* : VIRTUOUS, RESPECTABLE **c :** strictly decorous : GENTEEL **8 :** marked by suitability, rightness, or appropriateness : FIT **9 :** being a mathematical subset (as a subgroup) that does not contain all the elements of the inclusive set from which it is derived *syn* see FIT — **prop·er·ly** *adv* — **prop·er·ness** *n*

²proper *n* (15c) **1 :** the parts of the Mass that vary according to the liturgical calendar **2 :** the part of a missal or breviary containing the proper of the Mass and the offices proper to the holy days of the liturgical year

³proper *adv* (15c) *chiefly dial* : in a thorough manner : COMPLETELY

proper adjective *n* (1905) : an adjective that is formed from a proper noun and that is usu. capitalized in English

pro·per·din \prō-'pər-d³n\ *n* [prob. fr. ¹*pro-* + L *perdere* to destroy + E ¹*-in* — more at PERDITION] (1954) : a serum protein that participates in destruction of bacteria, neutralization of viruses, and lysis of red blood cells

proper fraction *n* (1674) : a fraction in which the numerator is less or of lower degree than the denominator

proper noun *n* (ca. 1890) : a noun that designates a particular being or thing, does not take a limiting modifier, and is usu. capitalized in English — called *also* proper name

prop·er·tied \'prä-pər-tēd\ *adj* (ca. 1772) : possessing property

prop·er·ty \'prä-pər-tē\ *n, pl* **-ties** [ME *proprete*, fr. MF *propreté*, fr. L *proprietat-, proprietas*, fr. *proprius* own] (14c) **1 a :** a quality or trait belonging and esp. peculiar to an individual or thing **b :** an effect that an object has on another object or on the senses **c :** VIRTUE **3 d :** an attribute common to all members of a class **2 a :** something owned or possessed; *specif* : a piece of real estate **b :** the exclusive right to possess, enjoy, and dispose of a thing : OWNERSHIP **c :** something to

which a person or business has a legal title **d :** one (as a performer) under contract whose work is esp. valuable **3 :** an article or object used in a play or motion picture except painted scenery and costumes *syn* see QUALITY — **prop·er·ty·less** \-ləs\ *adj* — **prop·er·ty·less·ness** \-nəs\ *n*

property damage insurance *n* (ca. 1946) : insurance protecting against all or part of an individual's legal liability for damage done (as by his or her automobile) to the property of another

property right *n* (1903) : a legal right or interest in or against specific property

property tax *n* (1808) : a tax levied on real or personal property

pro·phage \'prō-,fāj, -,fäzh\ *n* (1951) : an intracellular form of a bacteriophage in which it is harmless to the host, is usu. integrated into the hereditary material of the host, and reproduces when the host does

pro·phase \-,fāz\ *n* [ISV] (1884) **1 :** the initial stage of mitosis and of the mitotic division of meiosis characterized by the condensation of chromosomes consisting of two chromatids, disappearance of the nucleolus and nuclear membrane, and formation of mitotic spindle **2 :** the initial stage of the first division of meiosis in which the chromosomes become visible, homologous pairs of chromosomes undergo synapsis and crossing over, chiasmata appear, chromosomes condense with homologues visible as tetrads, and the nuclear membrane and nucleolus disappear — compare DIAKINESIS, DIPLOTENE, LEPTOTENE, PACHYTENE, ZYGOTENE — **pro·pha·sic** \(,)prō-'fā-zik\ *adj*

proph·e·cy *also* **proph·e·sy** \'prä-fə-sē\ *n, pl* **-cies** *also* **-sies** [ME *prophecie*, fr. OF, fr. LL *prophetia*, fr. Gk *prophēteia*, fr. *prophētēs* prophet] (13c) **1 :** an inspired utterance of a prophet **2 :** the function or vocation of a prophet; *specif* : the inspired declaration of divine will and purpose **3 :** a prediction of something to come

proph·e·sy \'prä-fə-,sī\ *vb* **-sied; -sy·ing** [ME *prophesien*, fr. MF *prophesier*, fr. OF, fr. *prophecie*] *vt* (14c) **1 :** to utter by or as if by divine inspiration **2 :** to predict with assurance or on the basis of mystic knowledge **3 :** PREFIGURE ~ *vi* **1 :** to speak as if divinely inspired **2 :** to give instruction in religious matters : PREACH **3 :** to make a prediction *syn* see FORETELL — **proph·e·si·er** \-,sī(-ə)r\ *n*

proph·et \'prä-fət\ *n* [ME *prophete*, fr. OF, fr. L *propheta*, fr. Gk *prophētēs*, fr. *pro* for + *phanai* to speak — more at FOR, BAN] (12c) **1 :** one who utters divinely inspired revelations; *specif, often cap* : the writer of one of the prophetic books of the Old Testament **2 :** one gifted with more than ordinary spiritual and moral insight; *esp* : an inspired poet **3 :** one who foretells future events : PREDICTOR **4 :** an effective or leading spokesman for a cause, doctrine, or group **5** *Christian Science* : a spiritual seer **b :** disappearance of material sense before the conscious facts of spiritual Truth — **proph·et·hood** \-,hůd\ *n*

proph·et·ess \'prä-fə-təs\ *n* (14c) : a woman who is a prophet

pro·phet·ic \prə-'fe-tik\ *also* **pro·phet·i·cal** \-'fe-ti-kəl\ *adj* (15c) **1** : of, relating to, or characteristic of a prophet or prophecy **2 :** foretelling events : PREDICTIVE — **pro·phet·i·cal·ly** \-ti-k(ə-)lē\ *adv*

Proph·ets \'prä-fəts\ *n pl* : the second part of the Jewish scriptures — see BIBLE table

¹pro·phy·lac·tic \,prō-fə-'lak-tik *also* ,prä-\ *adj* [Gk *prophylaktikos*, fr. *prophylassein* to be on guard, fr. *pro-* before + *phylassein* to guard, fr. *phylak-, phylax* guard] (1574) **1 :** guarding from or preventing disease **2 :** tending to prevent or ward off : PREVENTIVE — **pro·phy·lac·ti·cal·ly** \-ti-k(ə-)lē\ *adv*

²prophylactic *n* (1642) : something prophylactic; *esp* : a device and esp. a condom for preventing venereal infection or conception

pro·phy·lax·is \-'lak-səs\ *n, pl* **-lax·es** \-'lak-,sēz\ [NL, fr. Gk *prophylaktikos*] (ca. 1842) : measures designed to preserve health (as of an individual or of society) and prevent the spread of disease

¹pro·pine \prə-'pēn, -'pin\ *vt* **pro·pined; pro·pin·ing** [ME, fr. MF *propiner*, fr. L *propinare* to present, drink to someone's health, fr. Gk *propinein* lit., to drink first, fr. *pro-* + *pinein* to drink — more at POTABLE] (15c) *chiefly Scot* : to present or give esp. as a token of friendship

²propine *n* (15c) *Scot* : a gift in return for a favor

pro·pin·qui·ty \prə-'piŋ-kwə-tē\ *n* [ME *propinquite*, fr. L *propinquitat-, propinquitas* kinship, proximity, fr. *propinquus* near, akin to *prope* near — more at APPROACH] (14c) **1 :** nearness of blood : KINSHIP **2 :** nearness in place or time : PROXIMITY

pro·pi·o·nate \'prō-pē-ə-,nāt\ *n* [ISV] (1862) : a salt or ester of propionic acid

pro·pi·on·ic acid \,prō-pē-'ä-nik-\ *n* [ISV ¹*pro-* + Gk *piōn* fat; akin to Skt *pivan* swelling, fat] (1850) : a liquid sharp-odored fatty acid C₃H₆O₂ found in milk and distillates of wood, coal, and petroleum

pro·pi·ti·ate \prō-'pi-shē-,āt\ *vt* **-at·ed; -at·ing** [L *propitiatus*, pp. of *propitiare*, fr. *propitius* propitious] (1583) : to gain or regain the favor or goodwill of : APPEASE, CONCILIATE *syn* see PACIFY — **pro·pi·ti·a·tor** \-,ā-tər\ *n*

pro·pi·ti·a·tion \prō-,pi-shē-'ā-shən\ *n* (14c) **1 :** the act of propitiating **2 :** something that propitiates; *specif* : an atoning sacrifice

pro·pi·ti·a·to·ry \prō-'pi-shē(-ə)-,tōr-ē, -,tòr-\ *adj* (1551) **1 :** intended to propitiate : EXPIATORY **2 :** of or relating to propitiation

pro·pi·tious \prə-'pi-shəs\ *adj* [ME *propicious*, fr. L *propitius*, prob. fr. *pro-* for + *petere* to seek — more at PRO-, FEATHER] (15c) **1 :** favorably disposed : BENEVOLENT **2 :** being of good omen : AUSPICIOUS ⟨~ sign⟩ **3 :** tending to favor : ADVANTAGEOUS *syn* see FAVORABLE — **pro·pi·tious·ly** *adv* — **pro·pi·tious·ness** *n*

pro·plas·tid \(,)prō-'plas-təd\ *n* [ISV] (1922) : a minute cytoplasmic body from which a plastid is formed

prop·man \'präp-,man\ *n* (ca. 1937) : a man in charge of stage properties

prop·o·lis \'prä-pə-ləs\ *n* [ME *propoleos*, fr. ML, alter. of L *propolis*, fr. Gk, fr. *pro-* for + *polis* city — more at PRO-, POLICE] (15c) : a brownish resinous material of waxy consistency collected by bees from the buds of trees and used as a cement

---

\ə\ abut \ᵊ\ kitten, F table \ər\ further \a\ ash \ā\ ace \ä\ mop, mar \aů\ out \ch\ chin \e\ bet \ē\ easy \g\ go \i\ hit \ī\ ice \j\ job \ŋ\ sing \ō\ go \ò\ law \òi\ boy \th\ thin \t͟h\ the \ü\ loot \ů\ foot \y\ yet \zh\ vision \ä, k̲, ⁿ, œ, œ̄, ᵫ, ū̆, ᵞ\ *see* Guide to Pronunciation

pro·pone \prə-'pōn\ *vt* **pro·poned; pro·pon·ing** [ME (Sc), fr. L *proponere* — more at PROPOUND] (14c) **1** *Scot* : PROPOSE, PROPOUND **2** *Scot* : to put forward (a defense)

pro·po·nent \prə-'pō-nənt, 'prō-\ *n* [L *proponent-, proponens*, prp. of *proponere*] (1588) : one who argues in favor of something : ADVOCATE

¹pro·por·tion \prə-'pōr-shən, -'por-\ *n* [ME *proporcion*, fr. MF *proportion*, fr. L *proportion-, proportio*, fr. *pro* for + *portion-, portio* portion — more at FOR] (14c) **1** : harmonious relation of parts to each other or to the whole : BALANCE, SYMMETRY **2 a** : proper or equal share ⟨each did her ~ of the work⟩ **b** : QUOTA, PERCENTAGE **3** : the relation of one part to another or to the whole with respect to magnitude, quantity, or degree : RATIO **4** : SIZE, DIMENSION **5** : a statement of equality between two ratios in which the first of the four terms divided by the second equals the third divided by the fourth (as in 4/2 = 10/5) — compare EXTREME 1b, MEAN 1c — **in proportion** : PROPORTIONAL 1

²proportion *vt* **pro·por·tioned; pro·por·tion·ing** \-sh(ə-)niŋ\ (14c) **1** : to adjust (a part or thing) in size relative to other parts or things **2** : to make the parts of harmonious or symmetrical **3** : APPORTION, ALLOT

pro·por·tion·able \-sh(ə-)nə-bəl\ *adj* (14c) : PROPORTIONAL, PROPORTIONATE — **pro·por·tion·ably** \-blē\ *adv, archaic*

¹pro·por·tion·al \prə-'pōr-shnəl, -'por-, -shə-nᵊl\ *n* (14c) : a number or quantity in a proportion

²proportional *adj* (15c) **1 a** : corresponding in size, degree, or intensity **b** : having the same or a constant ratio ⟨corresponding sides of similar triangles are ~⟩ **2** : regulated or determined in size or degree with reference to proportions ⟨a ~ system of immigration quotas⟩ — **pro·por·tion·al·i·ty** \-,pōr-shə-'na-lə-tē, -,por-\ *n* — **pro·por·tion·al·ly** \-'pōr-shnə-lē, -'por-, -shə-nᵊl-ē\ *adv*

proportional parts *n pl* (ca. 1890) : fractional parts of the difference between successive entries in a table for use in linear interpolation

proportional representation *n* (1870) : an electoral system designed to represent in a legislative body each political group or party in proportion to its actual voting strength in the electorate

proportional tax *n* (ca. 1943) : a tax in which the tax rate remains constant regardless of the amount of the tax base

¹pro·por·tion·ate \prə-'pōr-sh(ə-)nət, -'por-\ *adj* (14c) : PROPORTIONAL 1 — **pro·por·tion·ate·ly** *adv*

²pro·por·tion·ate \-shə-,nāt\ *vt* **-at·ed; -at·ing** (1570) : to make proportionate : PROPORTION

pro·pos·al \prə-'pō-zəl\ *n* (1653) **1** : an act of putting forward or stating something for consideration **2 a** : something proposed : SUGGESTION **b** : OFFER; *specif* : an offer of marriage

pro·pose \prə-'pōz\ *vb* **pro·posed; pro·pos·ing** [ME, fr. MF *proposer*, fr. L *proponere* (perf. indic. *proposui*) — more at PROPOUND] *vi* (14c) **1** : to form or put forward a plan or intention ⟨man ~s, but God disposes⟩ **2** *obs* : to engage in talk or discussion **3** : to make an offer of marriage ~ *vt* **1 a** : to set before the mind (as for discussion, imitation, or action) ⟨~ a plan for settling the dispute⟩ **b** : to set before someone and esp. oneself as an aim or intent ⟨*proposed* to spend the summer in Italy⟩ **2 a** : to set forth for acceptance or rejection ⟨~ terms for peace⟩ **b** : to recommend to fill a place or vacancy : NOMINATE ⟨~ them for membership⟩ **c** : to offer as a toast ⟨~ the happiness of the couple⟩ — **pro·pos·er** *n*

¹prop·o·si·tion \,prä-pə-'zi-shən\ *n* (14c) **1 a** (1) : something offered for consideration or acceptance : PROPOSAL (2) : a request for sexual intercourse **b** : the point to be discussed or maintained in argument usu. stated in sentence form near the outset **c** : a theorem or problem to be demonstrated or performed **2 a** : an expression in language or signs of something that can be believed, doubted, or denied or is either true or false **b** : the objective meaning of a proposition **3** : something of an indicated kind ⟨getting there is a tough ~⟩ ⟨the farm was never a paying ~⟩ — **prop·o·si·tion·al** \-'zish-nəl, -'zish-shə-nᵊl\ *adj*

²proposition *vt* **-si·tioned; -si·tion·ing** \-'zi-sh(ə-)niŋ\ (1924) : to make a proposal to (someone); *esp* : to suggest sexual intercourse to

propositional calculus *n* (1903) : the branch of symbolic logic that uses symbols for unanalyzed propositions and logical connectives only — called also *sentential calculus*; compare PREDICATE CALCULUS

propositional function *n* (1903) **1** : SENTENTIAL FUNCTION **2** : something that is designated or expressed by a sentential function

pro·pos·i·tus \prō-'pä-zə-təs\ *n, pl* **-i·ti** \-,tī\ [NL, fr. L, pp. of *proponere*] (1899) : the person immediately concerned : SUBJECT

pro·pound \prə-'paůnd\ *vt* [alter. of earlier *propone*, fr. ME (Sc) *proponen*, fr. L *proponere* to display, propound, fr. *pro-* before + *ponere* to put, place — more at PRO-, POSITION] (1537) : to offer for discussion or consideration — **pro·pound·er** *n*

pro·poxy·phene \prō-'päk-sə-,fēn\ *n* [*prop-* + *oxy* + *-phene* (alter. of *phenyl*)] (1955) : an analgesic $C_{22}H_{29}NO_2$ structurally related to methadone but less addicting that is administered in the form of its hydrochloride

pro·prae·tor *or* **pro·pre·tor** \(,)prō-'prē-tər\ *n* [L *propraetor*, fr. *pro-* (as in *proconsul*) + *praetor*] (ca. 1580) : a praetor of ancient Rome sent out to govern a province

pro·pran·o·lol \prō-'pra-nə-,lȯl, -,lōl\ *n* [*propyl* + *propanol* + *-ol*] (1964) : a beta-adrenergic blocking agent $C_{16}H_{21}NO_2$ used in the form of its hydrochloride in the treatment of abnormal heart rhythms and angina pectoris

¹pro·pri·e·tary \prə-'prī-ə-,ter-ē\ *n, pl* **-tar·ies** (15c) **1** : one that possesses, owns, or holds exclusive right to something; *specif* : PROPRIETOR 1 **2** : something that is used, produced, or marketed under exclusive legal right of the inventor or maker; *specif* : a drug (as a patent medicine) that is protected by secrecy, patent, or copyright against free competition as to name, product, composition, or process of manufacture **3** : a business secretly owned by and run as a cover for an intelligence organization

²proprietary *adj* [LL *proprietarius*, fr. L *proprietas* property — more at PROPERTY] (1589) **1** : of, relating to, or characteristic of a proprietor ⟨~ rights⟩ **2** : used, made, or marketed by one having the exclusive legal right ⟨a ~ process⟩ **3** : privately owned and managed and run as a profit-making organization ⟨a ~ clinic⟩

pro·pri·e·tor \prə-'prī-ə-tər\ *n* [alter. of ¹*proprietary*] (1637) **1** : one granted ownership of a colony (as one of the original American colonies) and full prerogatives of establishing a government and distributing land **2 a** : one who has the legal right or exclusive title to something : OWNER **b** : one having an interest (as control or present use) less than absolute and exclusive right — **pro·pri·e·tor·ship** \-,ship\ *n*

pro·pri·e·to·ri·al \prə-,prī-ə-'tōr-ē-əl, prō-, -'tȯr-\ *adj* (1851) : PROPRIETARY 1

pro·pri·e·tress \-'prī-ə-trəs\ *n* (1692) : a woman who is a proprietor

pro·pri·e·ty \prə-'prī-ə-tē\ *n, pl* **-ties** [ME *propriete*, fr. MF *proprieté, propreté* property, quality of a person or thing — more at PROPERTY] (14c) **1** *obs* : true nature **2** *obs* : a special characteristic : PECULIARITY **3** : the quality or state of being proper : APPROPRIATENESS **4 a** : conformity to what is socially acceptable in conduct or speech **b** : fear of offending against conventional rules of behavior esp. between the sexes **c** *pl* : the customs and manners of polite society

pro·pri·o·cep·tion \,prō-prē-ō-'sep-shən\ *n* [*proprioceptive* + *-ion*] (1906) : the reception of stimuli produced within the organism

pro·pri·o·cep·tive \-'sep-tiv\ *adj* [L *proprius* own + E *-ceptive* (as in *receptive*)] (1906) : of, relating to, or being stimuli arising within the organism

pro·pri·o·cep·tor \-tər\ *n* [NL, fr. L *proprius* + NL *-ceptor* (as in *receptor*)] (1906) : a sensory receptor (as a muscle spindle) excited by proprioceptive stimuli

prop root *n* (1905) : a root that serves as a prop or support to the plant

prop·to·sis \präp-'tō-səs, prō-'tō-\ *n* [NL, fr. LL, falling forward, fr. Gk *proptōsis*, fr. *propiptein* to fall forward, fr. *pro-* forward + *piptein* to fall — more at PRO-, FEATHER] (1676) : forward projection or displacement esp. of the eyeball

pro·pul·sion \prə-'pəl-shən\ *n* [L *propellere* to propel] (1626) **1** : the action or process of propelling **2** : something that propels

pro·pul·sive \-'pəl-siv\ *adj* [L *propulsus*] (1758) : tending or having power to propel

pro·pyl \'prō-pəl\ *n, often attrib* [ISV *prop-* + *-yl*] (1850) : either of two isomeric alkyl groups C_3H_7 derived from propane — often used in combination

pro·py·lae·um \,prä-pə-'lē-əm, -pi-\ *n, pl* **-laea** \-'lē-ə\ [L, fr. Gk *propylaion*, fr. *pro-* before + *pylē* gate — more at PRO-] (ca. 1706) : a vestibule or entrance of architectural importance before a building or enclosure — often used in pl.

pro·pyl·ene \'prō-pə-,lēn\ *n* (1850) : a flammable gaseous hydrocarbon C_3H_6 obtained by cracking petroleum hydrocarbons and used chiefly in organic synthesis

propylene glycol *n* (1885) : a sweet hygroscopic viscous liquid $C_3H_8O_2$ made esp. from propylene and used esp. as an antifreeze and solvent and in brake fluids

pro ra·ta \(,)prō-'rä-tə, -'rä-, -'ra-\ *adv* [L] (1575) : proportionately according to an exactly calculable factor (as share or liability) — **pro rata** *adj*

pro·rate \(,)prō-'rāt, 'prō-\ *vb* **pro·rat·ed; pro·rat·ing** [*pro rata*] *vt* (1860) : to divide, distribute, or assess proportionately ~ *vi* : to make a pro rata distribution — **pro·ra·tion** \prō-'rā-shən\ *n*

pro·ro·gate \'prō-rə-,gāt\ *vt* **-gat·ed; -gat·ing** (1534) : PROROGUE — **pro·ro·ga·tion** \,prō-rə-'gā-shən\ *n*

pro·rogue \prə-'rōg\ *vb* **pro·rogued; pro·rogu·ing** [ME *prorogen*, fr. MF *proroger*, fr. L *prorogare*, fr. *pro-* before + *rogare* to ask — more at PRO-, RIGHT] *vt* (15c) **1** : DEFER, POSTPONE **2** : to terminate a session of (as a British parliament) by royal prerogative ~ *vi* : to suspend or end a legislative session

pros *pl of* PRO

pros- *prefix* [LL, fr. Gk, fr. *proti, pros* face to face with, toward, in addition to, near; akin to Skt *prati-* near, toward, against, in return, Gk *pro* before — more at FOR] : in front ⟨*prosencephalon*⟩

pro·sa·ic \prō-'zā-ik\ *adj* [LL *prosaicus*, fr. L *prosa* prose] (ca. 1656) **1 a** : characteristic of prose as distinguished from poetry : FACTUAL **b** : DULL, UNIMAGINATIVE **2** : EVERYDAY, ORDINARY — **pro·sa·i·cal·ly** \-'zā-ə-k(ə-)lē\ *adv*

pro·sa·ism \'prō-(,)zā-ji-zəm\ *n* (1787) **1** : a prosaic manner, style, or quality **2** : a prosaic expression

pro·sa·ist \[L *prosa* prose] (1803) **1** \'prō-(,)zā-ist, -zā-,ist\ : a prose writer **2** \prō-'zā-ist\ : a prosaic person

pro·sa·teur \,prō-zä-'tər\ *n* [F, fr. It *prosatore*, fr. ML *prosator*, fr. L *prosa*] (1880) : a writer of prose

pro·sau·ro·pod \prō-'sȯr-ə-,päd\ *n* [NL *Prosauropoda*, fr. ¹*pro-* + *Sauropoda* — more at SAUROPOD] (1941) : any of a group (Prosauropoda) of chiefly herbivorous Triassic dinosaurs that are prob. ancestral to sauropods

pro·sce·ni·um \prō-'sē-nē-əm\ *n* [L, fr. Gk *proskēnion* front of the building forming the background for a dramatic performance, stage, fr. *pro-* + *skēnē* building forming the background for a dramatic performance — more at SCENE] (1606) **1 a** : the stage of an ancient Greek or Roman theater **b** : the part of a modern stage in front of the curtain **c** : the wall that separates the stage from the auditorium and provides the arch that frames it **2** : FOREGROUND

pro·sciut·to \prō-'shü-(,)tō\ *n, pl* **-ti** \-(,)tē\ *or* **-tos** [It, alter. of *presciutto*, fr. *pre-* (fr. L *prae-* pre-) + *asciutto* dried out, fr. L *exsuctus*, fr. pp. of *exsugere* to suck out, fr. *ex-* + *sugere* to suck — more at SUCK] (ca. 1929) : dry-cured spiced Italian ham usu. sliced thin

pro·scribe \prō-'skrīb\ *vt* **pro·scribed; pro·scrib·ing** [L *proscribere* to publish, proscribe, fr. *pro-* before + *scribere* to write — more at SCRIBE] (1560) **1** : to condemn or forbid as harmful or unlawful : PROHIBIT **2** : to publish the name of as condemned to death with the property of the condemned forfeited to the state — **pro·scrib·er** *n*

pro·scrip·tion \prō-'skrip-shən\ *n* [ME *proscripcion*, fr. L *proscription-, proscriptio*, fr. *proscribere*] (14c) **1** : the act of proscribing : the state of being proscribed **2** : an imposed restraint or restriction : PROHIBITION — **pro·scrip·tive** \-'skrip-tiv\ *adj* — **pro·scrip·tive·ly** *adv*

¹prose \'prōz\ *n* [ME, fr. MF, fr. L *prosa*, fr. fem. of *prorsus, prosus*, straightforward, being in prose, contr. of *proversus*, pp. of *provertere* to turn forward, fr. *pro-* forward + *vertere* to turn — more at PRO-, WORTH] (14c) **1 a** : the ordinary language people use in speaking or writing **b** : a literary medium distinguished from poetry esp. by its greater irregularity and variety of rhythm and its closer correspondence to the patterns of everyday speech **2** : a prosaic style, quality, or condition

²prose *adj* (14c) **1** : of, relating to, or written in prose **2** : PROSAIC

³prose *vi* **prosed; pros·ing** (1642) **1** : to write prose **2** : to write or speak in a prosaic manner

pro·sec·tor \prō-'sek-tər\ n [prob. fr. F prosecteur, fr. LL prosector anatomist, fr. L prosecare to cut away, fr. pro- forth + secare to cut — more at PRO-, SAW] (ca. 1857) : a person who makes dissections for anatomic demonstrations

pros·e·cute \'prä-si-ˌkyüt\ vb -cut·ed; -cut·ing [ME, fr. L prosecutus, pp. of prosequi to pursue — more at PURSUE] vt (15c) **1** : to follow to the end : pursue until finished ⟨was ... ordered to ~ the war with ... vigor —Marjory S. Douglas⟩ **2** : to engage in : PERFORM **3 a** : to bring legal action against for redress or punishment of a crime or violation of law ⟨prosecuted them for fraud⟩ **b** : to institute legal proceedings with reference to ⟨~ a claim⟩ ~ vi : to institute and carry on a legal suit or prosecution — **pros·e·cut·able** \ˌprä-sə-'kyü-tə-bəl\ adj

prosecuting attorney n (1833) : an attorney who conducts proceedings in a court on behalf of the government : DISTRICT ATTORNEY

pros·e·cu·tion \ˌprä-si-'kyü-shən\ n (1567) **1** : the act or process of prosecuting; specif : the institution and continuance of a criminal suit involving the process of pursuing formal charges against an offender to final judgment **2** : the party by whom criminal proceedings are instituted or conducted **3** obs : PURSUIT

pros·e·cu·tor \'prä-si-ˌkyü-tər\ n (ca. 1670) **1** : a person who institutes an official prosecution before a court **2** : PROSECUTING ATTORNEY

pros·e·cu·to·ri·al \ˌprä-si-kyü-'tōr-ē-əl, -'tor-\ adj (1968) : of, relating to, or being a prosecutor or prosecution

¹**pros·e·lyte** \'prä-sə-ˌlīt\ n [ME proselite, fr. LL proselytus proselyte, alien resident, fr. Gk prosēlytos, fr. pros near + -ēlytos (akin to ēlythe he went) — more at PROS-, ELASTIC] (14c) : a new convert; specif : a convert to Judaism

²**proselyte** vb -lyt·ed; -lyt·ing (1624) : PROSELYTIZE

pros·e·ly·tise Brit var of PROSELYTIZE

pros·e·ly·tism \'prä-sə-ˌli-ˌti-zəm, 'prä-s(ə-)lə-\ n (ca. 1660) **1** : the act of becoming or condition of being a proselyte : CONVERSION **2** : the act or process of proselytizing

pros·e·ly·tize \'prä-s(ə-)lə-ˌtīz\ vb -tized; -tiz·ing vi (1679) **1** : to induce someone to convert to one's faith **2** : to recruit someone to join one's party, institution, or cause ~ vt : to recruit or convert esp. to a new faith, institution, or cause — **pros·e·ly·ti·za·tion** \ˌprä-s(ə-)lə-tə-'zā-shən, ˌprä-sə-ˌlī-tə-\ n — **pros·e·ly·tiz·er** \'prä-s(ə-)lə-ˌtī-zər\ n

pro·sem·i·nar \(ˌ)prō-'se-mə-ˌnär\ n (ca. 1922) : a directed course of study like a graduate seminar but often open to advanced undergraduates

pros·en·ceph·a·lon \ˌpräs-ˌen-'se-fə-ˌlän, -lən\ n [NL] (1846) : FOREBRAIN — **pros·en·ce·phal·ic** \-sə-'fa-lik\ adj

prose poem n (1842) : a composition in prose that has some of the qualities of a poem — **prose poet** n

pros·er \'prō-zər\ n (1627) **1** : a writer of prose **2** : one who talks or writes tediously

Pro·ser·pi·na \prə-'sər-pə-nə\ or **Pros·er·pine** \'prä-sər-ˌpīn\ n [L] : PERSEPHONE

pro·sim·i·an \prō-'si-mē-ən\ n [NL Prosimii, fr. ¹pro- + L simia ape — more at SIMIAN] (ca. 1890) : any of a suborder (Prosimii) of lower primates (as lemurs) — **prosimian** adj

pro·sit \'prō-zət, -sət\ or **prost** \'prōst\ interj [G, fr. L prosit may it be beneficial, fr. prodesse to be useful — more at PROUD] (1846) : — used to wish good health esp. before drinking

pro·so \'prō-(ˌ)sō\ n [Russ] (1917) : MILLET 1a

pros·o·branch \'prä-sə-ˌbraŋk\ n, pl -branchs [NL Prosobranchia, fr. proso- in front (fr. Gk prosō forward) + branchia gills fr. Gk)] (1851) : any of a subclass (Prosobranchia) of gastropod mollusks that have the loop of visceral nerves twisted into a figure eight, the sexes usu. separate, and usu. an operculum — **prosobranch** adj

pro·sod·ic \prə-'sä-dik also -'zä-\ or **pro·sod·i·cal** \-di-kəl\ adj (1774) : of or relating to prosody — **pro·sod·i·cal·ly** \-di-k(ə-)lē\ adv

pros·o·dy \'prä-sə-dē, -zə-\ n, pl -dies [ME, fr. L prosodia accent of a syllable, fr. Gk prosōidia song sung to instrumental music, accent, fr. pros in addition to + ōidē song — more at PROS-, ODE] (15c) **1** : the study of versification; esp : the systematic study of metrical structure **2** : a particular system, theory, or style of versification **3** : the rhythmic and intonational aspect of language — **pros·o·dist** \-dist\ n

pro·so·ma \(ˌ)prō-'sō-mə\ n [NL, fr. Gk pro- + sōma body] (1872) : the anterior region of the body of an invertebrate when not readily analyzable into its primitive segmentation; esp : CEPHALOTHORAX

pros·o·pog·ra·phy \ˌprä-sə-'pä-grə-fē\ n [NL prosopographia, fr. Gk prosōpon person + -graphia -graphy] (1929) : a study that identifies and relates a group of persons or characters within a particular historical or literary context — **pros·o·po·graph·i·cal** \-pə-'gra-fi-kəl\ adj

pro·so·po·poe·ia \ˌprä-sə-ˌpō-'pē-ə, ˌprä-sə-pə-\ n [L, fr. Gk prosōpopoiia, fr. prosōpon mask, person (fr. pros- + ōps face) + poiein to make — more at EYE, POET] (ca. 1555) **1** : a figure of speech in which an imaginary or absent person is represented as speaking or acting **2** : PERSONIFICATION

¹**pros·pect** \'prä-ˌspekt\ n [ME, fr. L prospectus view, prospect, fr. prospicere to look forward, exercise foresight, fr. pro- forward + specere to look — more at PRO-, SPY] (15c) **1** : EXPOSURE **2 a** (1) : an extensive view (2) : a mental consideration : SURVEY **b** : a place that commands an extensive view : LOOKOUT **c** : something extended to the view : SCENE **d** archaic : a sketch or picture of a scene **3** obs : ASPECT **4 a** : the act of looking forward : ANTICIPATION **b** : a mental picture of something to come : VISION **c** : something that is awaited or expected : POSSIBILITY **d** pl (1) : financial expectations (2) : CHANCES **5** : a place showing signs of containing a mineral deposit **6 a** : a potential buyer or customer **b** : a likely candidate — **in prospect** : possible or likely for the future

syn PROSPECT, OUTLOOK, ANTICIPATION, FORETASTE mean an advance realization of something to come. PROSPECT implies expectation of a particular event, condition, or development of definite interest or concern ⟨the prospect of a quiet weekend⟩. OUTLOOK suggests a forecasting of the future ⟨a favorable outlook for the economy⟩. ANTICIPATION implies a prospect or outlook that involves advance suffering or enjoyment of what is foreseen ⟨the anticipation of her arrival⟩. FORETASTE implies an actual though brief or partial experience of something forthcoming ⟨the frost was a foretaste of winter⟩.

²**pros·pect** \'prä-ˌspekt, chiefly Brit prə-'\ vi (1841) : to explore an area esp. for mineral deposits ~ vt : to inspect (a region) for mineral deposits; broadly : EXPLORE — **pros·pec·tor** \-ˌspek-tər, -'spek-\ n

pro·spec·tive \prə-'spek-tiv also 'prä-ˌ, prō-\ adj (ca. 1699) **1** : relating to or effective in the future **2 a** : likely to come about : EXPECTED ⟨the ~ benefits of this law⟩ **b** : likely to be or become ⟨a ~ mother⟩ — **pro·spec·tive·ly** adv

pro·spec·tus \prə-'spek-təs, prä-\ n, pl -tus·es [L, prospect] (1765) **1** : a preliminary printed statement that describes an enterprise (as a business or publication) and that is distributed to prospective buyers, investors, or participants **2** : something (as a statement or situation) that forecasts the course or nature of something

pros·per \'prä-spər\ vb pros·pered; pros·per·ing \-p(ə-)riŋ\ [ME, fr. MF prosperer, fr. L prosperare to cause to succeed, fr. prosperus favorable] vi (14c) **1** : to succeed in an enterprise or activity; esp : to achieve economic success **2** : to become strong and flourishing ~ vt : to cause to succeed or thrive

pros·per·i·ty \prä-'sper-ə-tē\ n (13c) : the condition of being successful or thriving; esp : economic well-being

Pros·pe·ro \'präs-pə-ˌrō\ n : the rightful duke of Milan in Shakespeare's The Tempest

pros·per·ous \'präs-p(ə-)rəs\ adj [ME, fr. MF prospereus, fr. L prosperus] (15c) **1** : AUSPICIOUS, FAVORABLE **2 a** : marked by success or economic well-being **b** : enjoying vigorous and healthy growth : FLOURISHING — **pros·per·ous·ly** adv — **pros·per·ous·ness** n

pross \'präs\ or **pros·sie** \'prä-sē\ or **pros·tie** \'präs-tē\ n (ca. 1902) slang : PROSTITUTE 1a

pros·ta·cy·clin \ˌpräs-tə-'sī-klən\ n [prosta- (as in prostaglandin) + cycl- + ¹-in] (1976) : a prostaglandin that is a metabolite of arachidonic acid, inhibits platelet aggregation, and dilates blood vessels

pros·ta·glan·din \ˌpräs-tə-'glan-dən\ n [prostate gland + ¹-in; fr. its occurrence in the seminal fluid of animals] (1936) : any of various oxygenated unsaturated cyclic fatty acids of animals that perform a variety of hormonelike actions (as in controlling blood pressure or smooth muscle contraction)

pros·tate \'präs-ˌtāt\ n [NL prostata prostate gland, fr. Gk prostatēs, fr. proïstanai to put in front, fr. pro- before + histanai to cause to stand — more at PRO-, STAND] (1646) : PROSTATE GLAND — **pros·tat·ic** \prä-'sta-tik\ adj

pros·ta·tec·to·my \ˌpräs-tə-'tek-tə-mē\ n, pl -mies (ca. 1890) : surgical removal or resection of the prostate gland

prostate gland n (1828) : a firm partly muscular partly glandular body that is situated about the base of the mammalian male urethra and secretes an alkaline viscid fluid which is a major constituent of the ejaculatory fluid

pros·ta·tism \'präs-tə-ˌti-zəm\ n (ca. 1900) : disease of the prostate; esp : a disorder resulting from obstruction of the bladder neck by an enlarged prostate

pros·ta·ti·tis \ˌpräs-tə-'tī-təs\ n [NL] (ca. 1844) : inflammation of the prostate gland

pros·the·sis \präs-'thē-səs, 'präs-thə-\ n, pl -the·ses \-ˌsēz\ [NL, fr. Gk, addition, fr. prostithenai to add to, fr. pros- in addition to + tithenai to put — more at PROS-, DO] (ca. 1900) : an artificial device to replace a missing part of the body

pros·thet·ic \präs-'the-tik\ adj (ca. 1890) **1** : of or relating to a prosthesis or prosthetics **2** : of, relating to, or constituting a nonprotein group of a conjugated protein — **pros·thet·i·cal·ly** \-ti-k(ə-)lē\ adv

pros·thet·ics \-tiks\ n pl but sing or pl in constr (ca. 1894) : the surgical or dental specialty concerned with the design, construction, and fitting of prostheses

pros·thet·ist \'präs-thə-tist\ n (1902) : a specialist in prosthetics

pros·tho·don·tics \ˌpräs-thə-'dän-tiks\ n pl but sing or pl in constr [NL prosthodontia, fr. prosthesis + -odontia] (1947) : prosthetic dentistry

pros·tho·don·tist \-'dän-tist\ n (1917) : a specialist in prosthodontics

¹**pros·ti·tute** \'präs-tə-ˌtüt, -ˌtyüt\ vt -tut·ed; -tut·ing [L prostitutus, pp. of prostituere, fr. pro- before + statuere to station — more at PRO-, STATUTE] (1530) **1** : to offer indiscriminately for sexual intercourse esp. for money **2** : to devote to corrupt or unworthy purposes : DEBASE ⟨~ one's talents⟩ — **pros·ti·tu·tor** \-ˌtü-tər, -ˌtyü-\ n

²**prostitute** adj (1563) : devoted to corrupt purposes : PROSTITUTED

³**prostitute** n (1613) **1 a** : a woman who engages in promiscuous sexual intercourse esp. for money : WHORE **b** : a male who engages in sexual and esp. homosexual practices for money **2** : a person (as a writer or painter) who deliberately debases his or her talents (as for money)

pros·ti·tu·tion \ˌpräs-tə-'tü-shən, -'tyü-\ n (1553) **1** : the act or practice of indulging in promiscuous sexual relations esp. for money **2** : the state of being prostituted : DEBASEMENT

pro·sto·mi·um \prō-'stō-mē-əm\ n -mia \-mē-ə\ [NL, fr. Gk pro- + stoma mouth — more at STOMACH] (1870) : the portion of the head of various worms that is situated in front of the mouth — **pro·sto·mi·al** \-mē-əl\ adj

¹**pros·trate** \'prä-ˌstrāt\ adj [ME prostrat, fr. L prostratus, pp. of prosternere, fr. pro- before + sternere to spread out, throw down — more at STREW] (14c) **1** : stretched out with face on the ground in adoration or submission; also : lying flat **2** : completely overcome and lacking vitality, will, or power to rise ⟨was ~ from the heat⟩ **3** : trailing on the ground : PROCUMBENT ⟨~ shrub⟩ **syn** see PRONE

²**pros·trate** \'prä-ˌstrāt, esp Brit prä-'\ vt pros·trat·ed; pros·trat·ing (15c) **1** : to throw or put into a prostrate position **2** : to put (oneself) in a humble and submissive posture or state ⟨the whole town had to ~ itself in official apology —Claudia Cassidy⟩ **3** : to reduce to submission, helplessness, or exhaustion ⟨was prostrated with grief⟩

pros·tra·tion \prä-'strā-shən\ n (14c) **1 a** : the act of assuming a prostrate position **b** : the state of being in a prostrate position : ABASEMENT **2 a** : complete physical or mental exhaustion : COL-

\ə\ abut \ᵊ\ kitten, F table \ər\ further \a\ ash \ā\ ace \ä\ mop, mar \au̇\ out \ch\ chin \e\ bet \ē\ easy \g\ go \i\ hit \ī\ ice \j\ job \ŋ\ sing \ō\ go \ȯ\ law \ȯi\ boy \th\ thin \t͟h\ the \ü\ loot \u̇\ foot \y\ yet \zh\ vision \à, k̟, ⁿ, œ, œ̄, ᵫ, ᵫ̄, �\ see Guide to Pronunciation

LAPSE **b** : the process of being made powerless or the condition of powerlessness ⟨the country suffered economic ∼ after the war⟩

prosy \'prō-zē\ *adj* **pros·i·er; -est** [¹*prose*] (1814) : lacking in qualities that seize the attention or strike the imagination : COMMONPLACE: *esp* : tediously dull in speech or manner — **pros·i·ly** \-zə-lē\ *adv* — **pros·i·ness** \-zē-nəs\ *n*

prot- *or* **proto-** *comb form* [ME *protho-*, fr. MF, fr. LL *proto-*, fr. Gk *prōt-*, *prōto-*, fr. *prōtos*; akin to Gk *pro* before — more at FOR] **1 a** : first in time ⟨*proto*history⟩ **b** : beginning : giving rise to ⟨*proto*planet⟩ **2** : parent substance of a (specified) substance ⟨*prot*actinium⟩ **3** : first formed : primary ⟨*proto*xylem⟩ **4** *cap* : relating to or constituting the recorded or assumed language that is ancestral to a language or to a group of related languages or dialects ⟨*Proto*-Indo-European⟩

prot·ac·tin·i·um \,prō-,tak-'ti-nē-əm\ *n* [NL] (1918) : a shiny radioactive metallic element of relatively short life — see ELEMENT table

pro·tag·o·nist \prō-'ta-gə-nist\ *n* [Gk *prōtagōnistēs*, fr. *prōt-* prot- + *agōnistēs* competitor at games, actor, fr. *agōnizesthai* to compete, fr. *agōn* contest, competition at games — more at AGONY] (1671) **1 a** : the principal character in a literary work (as a drama or story) **b** : a leading actor, character, or participant in a literary work or real event **2** : a leader, proponent, or supporter of a cause : CHAMPION **3** : a muscle that by its contraction actually causes a particular movement

prot·amine \'prō-tə-,mēn\ *n* [ISV *prot-* + *amine*] (1874) : any of various strongly basic proteins of relatively low molecular weight that are rich in arginine and are found associated esp. with DNA in place of histone in the sperm cells of various animals (as fish)

prot·a·sis \'prä-tə-səs\ *n*, *pl* **-a·ses** \-,sēz\ [LL, fr. Gk, premise of a syllogism, conditional clause, fr. *proteinein* to stretch out before, put forward, fr. *pro-* + *teinein* to stretch — more at THIN] (ca. 1568) **1** : the introductory part of a play or narrative poem **2** : the subordinate clause of a conditional sentence — compare APODOSIS — **pro·tat·ic** \prä-'ta-tik, prō-\ *adj*

prote- *or* **proteo-** *comb form* [ISV, fr. F *protéine*] : protein ⟨*proteo*lysis⟩ ⟨*prote*ose⟩

pro·tea \'prō-tē-ə\ *n* [NL, fr. L *Proteus* Proteus] (1825) : any of a genus (*Protea* of the family Proteaceae, the protea family) of evergreen shrubs often grown for their showy bracts and dense flower heads

pro·te·an \'prō-tē-ən, prō-'tē-\ *adj* (1598) **1** : of or resembling Proteus in having a varied nature or ability to assume different forms **2** : displaying great diversity or variety : VERSATILE

pro·te·ase \'prō-tē-,ās, -,āz\ *n* [ISV] (1903) : any of numerous enzymes that hydrolyze proteins and are classified according to the most prominent functional group (as serine or cysteine) at the active site — called also *proteinase*

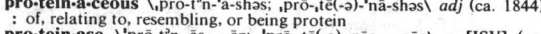

protea

pro·tect \prə-'tekt\ *vt* [ME, fr. L *protectus*, pp. of *protegere*, fr. *pro-* in front + *tegere* to cover — more at PRO-, THATCH] (15c) **1** : to cover or shield from exposure, injury, or destruction : GUARD **2** : to maintain the status or integrity of esp. through financial or legal guarantees: as **a** : to save from contingent financial loss **b** : to foster or shield from infringement or restriction ⟨salesmen with ∼ed territories⟩; *specif* : to restrict competition for (as domestic industries) by means of tariffs or trade controls *syn* see DEFEND — **pro·tec·tive** \-'tek-tiv\ *adj* — **pro·tec·tive·ly** *adv* — **pro·tec·tive·ness** *n*

pro·tec·tant \prə-'tek-tənt\ *n* (1935) : a protecting agent

pro·tec·tion \prə-'tek-shən\ *n* (14c) **1** : the act of protecting : the state of being protected **2 a** : one that protects **b** : supervision or support of one that is smaller and weaker **3** : the freeing of the producers of a country from foreign competition in their home market by restrictions (as high duties) on foreign competitive goods **4 a** : immunity from prosecution purchased by criminals through bribery **b** : money extorted by racketeers posing as a protective association **5** : COVERAGE 1a

pro·tec·tion·ist \-sh(ə-)nist\ *n* (1844) : an advocate of government economic protection for domestic producers through restrictions on foreign competitors — **pro·tec·tion·ism** \-shə-,ni-zəm\ *n* — **protectionist** *adj*

protective tariff *n* (1838) : a tariff intended primarily to protect domestic producers rather than to yield revenue

pro·tec·tor \prə-'tek-tər\ *n* (14c) **1 a** : one that protects : GUARDIAN **b** : a device used to prevent injury : GUARD **2 a** : one having the care of a kingdom during the king's minority : REGENT **b** : the executive head of the Commonwealth of England, Scotland, and Ireland from 1653 to 1659 — called also *Lord Protector of the Commonwealth* — **pro·tec·tor·ship** \-,ship\ *n*

pro·tec·tor·al \-'tek-t(ə-)rəl\ *adj* (1657) : of or relating to a protector or protectorate

pro·tec·tor·ate \-'tek-t(ə-)rət\ *n* (1692) **1 a** : government by a protector **b** *cap* : the government of England (1653–59) under the Cromwells **c** : the rank, office, or period of rule of a protector **2 a** : the relationship of superior authority assumed by one power or state over a dependent one **b** : the dependent political unit in such a relationship

pro·tec·to·ry \-'tek-t(ə-)rē\ *n*, *pl* **-ries** (1885) : an institution for the protection and care usu. of homeless or delinquent children

pro·tec·tress \-'tek-trəs\ *n* (1570) : a woman who is a protector

pro·té·gé \'prō-tə-,zhā, ,prō-tə-'\ *n* [F, fr. pp. of *protéger* to protect, fr. L *protegere*] (1787) : one who is protected or trained or whose career is furthered by a person of experience, prominence, or influence

pro·té·gée \'prō-tə-,zhā, ,prō-tə-'\ *n* [F, fem. of *protégé*] (1778) : a female protégé

pro·tein \'prō-,tēn *also* 'prō-tē-ən\ *n*, *often attrib* [F *protéine*, fr. LGk *prōteios* primary, fr. Gk *prōtos* first — more at PROT-] (ca. 1844) **1** : any of numerous naturally occurring extremely complex substances that consist of amino-acid residues joined by peptide bonds, contain the elements carbon, hydrogen, nitrogen, oxygen, usu. sulfur, and occas. other elements (as phosphorus or iron), and include many essential biological compounds (as enzymes, hormones, or immunoglobulins) **2** : the total nitrogenous material in plant or animal substances

pro·tein·a·ceous \,prō-,tē³n-'ā-shəs; ,prō-,tē(-ə)-'nā-shəs\ *adj* (ca. 1844) : of, relating to, resembling, or being protein

pro·tein·ase \'prō-t³n-,ās, -,āz; 'prō-,tē(ə)-,nās, -,nāz\ *n* [ISV] (ca. 1929) : PROTEASE

pro·tein·uria \,prō-,tē³n-'úr-ē-ə, -'yúr-; ,prō-,tē(-ə)-'núr-ē-ə, -'nyúr-\ *n* [NL, fr. ISV *protein* + NL *-uria*] (1911) : the presence of excess protein in the urine

pro tem \(,)prō-'tem\ *adv* (1828) : PRO TEMPORE

pro tem·po·re \prō-'tem-pə-rē\ *adv* [ME, fr. L] (15c) : for the time being

pro·tend \prō-'tend\ *vb* [ME, fr. L *protendere*, fr. *pro-* + *tendere* to stretch — more at THIN] *vt* (15c) 1 *archaic* : to stretch forth **2** *archaic* : EXTEND ∼ *vi*, *archaic* : STICK OUT, PROTRUDE

pro·ten·sive \-'ten(t)-siv\ *adj* [L *protensus*, pp. of *protendere*] (1671) **1** *archaic* : having continuance in time **2** *archaic* : having lengthwise extent or extensiveness — **pro·ten·sive·ly** *adv*

pro·teo·gly·can \,prō-tē-ə-'gli-,kan\ *n* [ISV] (1968) : any of a class of glycoproteins of high molecular weight that are found esp. in the extracellular matrix of connective tissue

pro·te·ol·y·sis \,prō-tē-'ä-lə-səs\ *n* [NL] (1880) : the hydrolysis of proteins or peptides with formation of simpler and soluble products

pro·teo·lyt·ic \,prō-tē-ə-'li-tik\ *adj* (1877) : of, relating to, or producing proteolysis — **pro·teo·lyt·i·cal·ly** \-ti-k(ə-)lē\ *adv*

pro·te·ose \'prō-tē-,ōs, -,ōz\ *n* [ISV] (ca. 1890) : any of various water-soluble protein derivatives formed by partial hydrolysis of proteins

Pro·te·ro·zo·ic \,prä-tə-rə-'zō-ik, ,prō-\ *adj* [Gk *proteros* former, earlier (fr. *pro* before) + ISV *-zoic* — more at FOR] (1899) : of, relating to, or being the eon of geologic time or the corresponding system of rocks that includes the interval between the Archean and Phanerozoic eons, perhaps exceeds in length all of subsequent geological time, and is marked by rocks that contain fossils indicating the first appearance of eukaryotic organisms (as algae) — see GEOLOGIC TIME table — **Proterozoic** *n*

¹pro·test \'prō-,test\ *n* [ME, fr. MF, fr. *protester*] (15c) **1 a** : a solemn declaration of opinion and usu. of dissent: as **a** : a sworn declaration that payment of a note or bill has been refused and that all responsible signers or debtors are liable for resulting loss or damage **b** : a declaration made esp. before or while paying that a tax is illegal and that payment is not voluntary **2** : the act of objecting or a gesture of disapproval ⟨resigned in ∼⟩; *esp* : a usu. organized public demonstration of disapproval **3** : a complaint, objection, or display of unwillingness usu. to an idea or a course of action ⟨went under ∼⟩ **4** : an objection made to an official or a governing body of a sport

²pro·test \prə-'test, 'prō-,, prō-'\ *vb* [ME, fr. MF *protester*, fr. L *protestari*, fr. *pro-* forth + *testari* to call to witness — more at PRO-, TESTAMENT] *vt* (15c) **1** : to make solemn declaration or affirmation of ⟨∼ my innocence⟩ **2** : to execute or have executed a formal protest against (as a bill or note) **3** : to make a statement or gesture in objection to ⟨∼ed the abuses of human rights⟩ ∼ *vi* **1** : to make a protestation **2** : to make or enter a protest *syn* see ASSERT — **pro·test·er** *or* **pro·tes·tor** \-'tes-tər, -,tes-\ *n*

¹prot·es·tant \'prä-tə-stənt, 2 *is also* prə-'tes-\ *n* [MF, fr. L *protestant-*, *protestans*, prp. of *protestari*] (1539) **1** *cap* **a** : any of a group of German princes and cities presenting a defense of freedom of conscience against an edict of the Diet of Spires in 1529 intended to suppress the Lutheran movement **b** : a member of any of several church denominations denying the universal authority of the Pope and affirming the Reformation principles of justification by faith alone, the priesthood of all believers, and the primacy of the Bible as the only source of revealed truth; *broadly* : a Christian not of a Catholic or Eastern church **2** : one who makes or enters a protest — **Prot·es·tant·ism** \'prä-təs-tən-,ti-zəm\ *n*

²protestant *adj* (1539) **1** *cap* : of or relating to Protestants, their churches, or their religion **2** : making or sounding a protest ⟨the two ∼ ladies up and marched out —*Time*⟩

Protestant ethic *n* (1926) : an ethic that stresses the virtue of hard work, thrift, and self-discipline

pro·tes·ta·tion \,prä-təs-'tā-shən, ,prō-, -,tes-\ *n* (14c) : the act of protesting : a solemn declaration or avowal

pro·te·us \'prō-tē-əs\ *n*, *pl* **-tei** \-tē-,ī\ [NL, fr. L, Proteus] (1896) : any of a genus (*Proteus*) of aerobic usu. motile enterobacteria that include saprophytes in decaying organic matter and forms associated with urinary tract infections

Pro·teus \'prō-,tyüs, -tē-əs, -,tüs\ *n* [L, fr. Gk *Prōteus*] : a Greek sea god capable of assuming different forms

pro·tha·la·mi·on \,prō-thə-'lā-mē-ən, -,än\ *or* **pro·tha·la·mi·um** \-mē-əm\ *n*, *pl* **-mia** \-mē-ə\ [NL, fr. Gk *pro-* + *thalamion* (as in *epithalamion*)] (1597) : a song in celebration of a marriage

pro·thal·li·um \prō-'tha-lē-əm\ *n*, *pl* **-thal·lia** \-lē-ə\ [NL, fr. *pro-* + *thallus*] (1858) **1** : the gametophyte of a pteridophyte (as a fern) that is typically a small flat green thallus attached to the soil by rhizoids **2** : a greatly reduced structure of a seed plant corresponding to the pteridophyte prothallium

pro·thal·lus \-'tha-ləs\ *n* [NL] (1854) : PROTHALLIUM

proth·e·sis \'prä-thə-səs\ *n*, *pl* **-e·ses** \-,sēz\ [LL, alter. of *prosthesis*, fr. Gk, lit., addition — more at PROSTHESIS] (ca. 1550) : the addition of a sound to the beginning of a word (as in Old French *estat*—whence English *estate*—from Latin *status*) — **pro·thet·ic** \prä-'the-tik\ *adj*

pro·tho·no·ta·ry \prō-'thä-nə-,ter-ē, ,prō-thə-'nō-tə-rē\ *or* **pro·to·no·ta·ry** \prō-'tä-nə-,ter-ē, ,prō-tə-'nō-tə-rē\ *n*, *pl* **-ries** [ME *prothonotarie*, fr. LL *protonotarius*, fr. *prot-* + L *notarius* stenographer — more at NOTARY PUBLIC] (15c) : a chief clerk of any of various courts of law — **pro·tho·no·tar·i·al** \prō-,thä-nə-'ter-ē-əl, ,prō-thə-nō-'ter-ē-əl\ *adj*

pro·tho·rac·ic \,prō-thə-'ra-sik\ *adj* (1826) : of or relating to the prothorax

prothoracic gland *n* (1887) : one of a pair of thoracic endocrine organs in some insects that control molting

pro·tho·rax \(,)prō-'thōr-,aks, -'thōr-\ *n* [NL *prothorac-*, *prothorax*, fr. ¹*pro-* + *thorax*] (1826) : the anterior segment of the thorax of an insect — see INSECT illustration

pro·throm·bin \(,)prō-'thräm-bən\ *n* [ISV] (1898) : a plasma protein produced in the liver in the presence of vitamin K and converted into thrombin in the clotting of blood

pro·tist \'prō-(,)tist\ *n* [NL *Protista*, fr. Gk, neut. pl. of *prōtistos* very first, primal, fr. superl. of *prōtos* first —more at PROT-] (1889) : any of a taxonomic group and esp. a kingdom (Protista) of unicellular, colonial, or multicellular organisms usu. including the protozoans and most algae and in various classifications prokaryotes, some or all fungi, and the sponges — **pro·tis·tan** \prō-'tis-tən\ *adj or n*

pro·ti·um \'prō-tē-əm, 'prō-shē-\ *n* [NL, fr. Gk *prōtos* first] (1933) : the ordinary light hydrogen isotope of atomic mass 1

proto- — see PROT-

pro·to·col \'prō-tə-ˌkȯl, -ˌkōl, -ˌkäl, -kəl\ *n* [MF *prothocole*, fr. ML *protocollum*, fr. LGk *prōtokollon* first sheet of a papyrus roll bearing data of manufacture, fr. Gk *prōt-* prot- + *kollan* to glue together, fr. *kolla* glue; perh. akin to MD *helen* to glue] (1541) **1** : an original draft, minute, or record of a document or transaction **2 a** : a preliminary memorandum often formulated and signed by diplomatic negotiators as a basis for a final convention or treaty **b** : the records or minutes of a diplomatic conference or congress that show officially the agreements arrived at by the negotiators **3 a** : a code prescribing strict adherence to correct etiquette and precedence (as in diplomatic exchange and in the military services) **b** : a set of conventions governing the treatment and esp. the formatting of data in an electronic communications system **4** : a detailed plan of a scientific or medical experiment, treatment, or procedure

pro·to·derm \'prō-tə-ˌdərm\ *n* [ISV] (ca. 1932) : the outer primary meristem of a plant or plant part

pro·to·gal·axy \ˌprō-tō-'ga-lək-sē\ *n* (1950) : a cloud of gas believed to be the precursor to a galaxy

pro·to·his·to·ry \-'his-t(ə-)rē\ *n* [ISV] (1903) : the study of human beings in the times that immediately antedate recorded history — **pro·to·his·to·ri·an** \-(h)is-'tōr-ē-ən, -'tȯr-\ *n* — **pro·to·his·tor·ic** \-'tȯr-ik, -'tär-\ *adj*

pro·to·hu·man \-'hyü-mən, -'yü-\ *adj* (ca. 1909) : of, relating to, or resembling an early hominid (as an australopithecine) — **protohuman** *n*

pro·to·lan·guage \'prō-tō-ˌlaŋ-gwij\ *n* (1948) : an assumed or recorded ancestral language

pro·to·mar·tyr \'prō-tō-ˌmär-tər\ *n* [ME *prothomartir*, fr. MF, fr. LL *protomartyr*, fr. LGk *prōtomartyr-, prōtomartys*, fr. Gk *prōt-* + *martyr-, martys* martyr] (15c) : the first martyr in a cause or region

pro·ton \'prō-ˌtän\ *n* [Gk *prōton*, neut. of *prōtos* first — more at PROT-] (1920) : an elementary particle that is identical with the nucleus of the hydrogen atom, that along with neutrons is a constituent of all other atomic nuclei, that carries a positive charge numerically equal to the charge of an electron, and that has a mass of 1.673×10^{-24} gram — **pro·ton·ic** \prō-'tä-nik\ *adj*

pro·ton·ate \'prō-tə-ˌnāt\ *vb* **-at·ed; -at·ing** *vt* (1945) : to add a proton to ∼ *vi* : to acquire an additional proton — **pro·ton·ation** \ˌprō-tə-'nā-shən\ *n*

pro·to·ne·ma \ˌprō-tə-'nē-mə\ *n, pl* **-ne·ma·ta** \-'nē-mə-tə, -'ne-\ [NL *protonemat-, protonema*, fr. *prot-* + Gk *nēma* thread — more at NEMAT-] (1857) : the primary usu. filamentous thalloid stage of the gametophyte in mosses and in some liverworts comparable to the prothallium in ferns — **pro·to·ne·mal** \-'nē-məl\ *adj* — **pro·to·ne·ma·tal** \-'nē-mə-t³l, -'ne-\ *adj*

protonotary apostolic or **prothonotary apostolic** *n, pl* **protonotaries apostolic** or **prothonotaries apostolic** (1682) : a priest of the chief college of the papal curia who keeps records of consistories and canonizations and signs papal bulls; *also* : an honorary member of this college

proton synchrotron *n* (1947) : a synchrotron in which protons are accelerated by means of frequency modulation of the radio-frequency accelerating voltage so that they have energies of billions of electron volts

pro·to·path·ic \ˌprō-tə-'pa-thik\ *adj* [ISV, fr. MGk *prōtopathēs* affected first, fr. Gk *prōt-* prot- + *pathos* experience, suffering — more at PATHOS] (1905) : of, relating to, or being cutaneous sensory reception responsive only to rather gross stimuli

pro·to·phlo·em \-'flō-ˌem\ *n* (1884) : the first-formed phloem that develops from procambium, consists of narrow thin-walled cells capable of a limited amount of stretching, and is usu. associated with a region of rapid growth

pro·to·plan·et \'prō-tō-ˌpla-nət\ *n* (1949) : a hypothetical whirling gaseous mass within a giant cloud of gas and dust that rotates around a sun and is believed to give rise to a planet — **pro·to·plan·e·tary** \ˌprō-tō-'pla-nə-ˌter-ē\ *adj*

pro·to·plasm \'prō-tə-ˌpla-zəm\ *n* [G *Protoplasma*, fr. *prot-* + NL *plasma*] (1848) **1** : the organized colloidal complex of organic and inorganic substances (as proteins and water) that constitutes the living nucleus, cytoplasm, plastids, and mitochondria of the cell **2** : CYTOPLASM — **pro·to·plas·mic** \ˌprō-tə-'plaz-mik\ *adj*

pro·to·plast \'prō-tə-ˌplast\ *n* [MF *protoplaste*, fr. LL *protoplastus* first human, fr. Gk *prōtoplastos* first formed, fr. *prōt-* prot- + *plastos* formed, fr. *plassein* to mold — more at PLASTER] (1532) **1** : one that is formed first : PROTOTYPE **2** : a plant cell that has had its cell wall removed; *also* : the nucleus, cytoplasm, and plasma membrane of a cell as distinguished from inert walls and inclusions

pro·to·por·phy·rin \ˌprō-tō-'pȯr-f(ə-)rən\ *n* [ISV] (1925) : a purple porphyrin acid $C_{34}H_{34}N_4O_4$ obtained from hemin or heme by removal of bound iron

pro·to·star \'prō-tō-ˌstär\ *n* (1947) : a cloud of gas and dust in space believed to develop into a star

pro·to·stele \'prō-tə-ˌstēl, ˌprō-tə-'stē-lē\ *n* (1901) : a stele forming a solid rod with the phloem surrounding the xylem — **pro·to·ste·lic** \ˌprō-tə-'stē-lik\ *adj*

pro·to·stome \'prō-tə-ˌstōm\ *n* [NL *Protostomia*, fr. *prot-* + Gk *stoma* mouth — more at STOMACH] (ca. 1961) : any of a major group (Protostomia) of bilateral metazoan animals (as mollusks, annelids, and arthropods) characterized in typical forms by determinate and spiral cleavage, formation of a mouth and anus directly from the blastopore, and formation of the coelom by splitting of the embryonic mesoderm — compare DEUTEROSTOME

pro·to·troph \'prō-tə-ˌtröf, -ˌträf\ *n* [back-formation fr. *prototrophic*] (1946) : a prototrophic individual

pro·to·tro·phic \ˌprō-tə-'trō-fik\ *adj* [ISV] (1900) : having the nutritional requirements of the normal or wild type — **pro·to·tro·phy** \prō-'tä-trə-fē\ *n*

pro·to·typ·al \ˌprō-tə-'tī-pəl\ *adj* (ca. 1693) : PROTOTYPICAL

pro·to·type \'prō-tə-ˌtīp\ *n* [F, fr. Gk *prōtotypon*, fr. neut. of *prōtotypos* archetypal, fr. *prōt-* + *typos* type] (1552) **1** : an original model on which something is patterned : ARCHETYPE **2** : an individual that exhibits the essential features of a later type **3** : a standard or typical example **4** : a first full-scale and usu. functional form of a new type or design of a construction (as an airplane)

pro·to·typ·i·cal \ˌprō-tə-'ti-pi-kəl\ *also* **pro·to·typ·ic** \-pik\ *adj* (1650) : of, relating to, or being a prototype — **pro·to·typ·i·cal·ly** \-pi-k(ə-)lē\ *adv*

pro·to·xy·lem \ˌprō-tə-'zī-ləm, -ˌlem\ *n* (1887) : the first-formed xylem developing from procambium and consisting of narrow cells with annular, spiral, or scalariform wall thickenings

pro·to·zo·al \ˌprō-tə-'zō-əl\ *adj* (1890) : of or relating to protozoans

pro·to·zo·an \-'zō-ən\ *n* [NL *Protozoa*, fr. *prot-* + *-zoa*] (ca. 1864) : any of a phylum or subkingdom (Protozoa) of chiefly motile and heterotrophic unicellular protists (as amoebas, trypanosomes, sporozoans, and paramecia) that are represented in almost every kind of habitat and include some pathogenic parasites of humans and domestic animals — **protozoan** *adj*

pro·to·zo·ol·o·gy \-zō-'ä-lə-jē, -zə-'wä-\ *n* [NL *Protozoa* + ISV *-logy*] (1904) : a branch of zoology dealing with protozoans — **pro·to·zo·ol·o·gist** \-zō-'ä-lə-jist, -zə-'wä-\ *n*

pro·to·zo·on \-'zō-ˌän\ *n, pl* **-zoa** \-'zō-ə\ [NL, fr. sing. of *Protozoa*] (ca. 1853) : PROTOZOAN

pro·tract \prō-'trakt, prə-\ *vt* [L *protractus*, pp. of *protrahere*, lit., to draw forward, fr. *pro-* forward + *trahere* to draw — more at PRO-] (1540) **1** *archaic* : DELAY, DEFER **2** : to prolong in time or space : CONTINUE **3** : to extend forward or outward — compare RETRACT 1 **syn** see EXTEND — **pro·trac·tive** \-'trak-tiv\ *adj*

protracted meeting *n* (1832) : a protracted revival meeting

pro·trac·tile \-'trak-t³l, -ˌtīl\ *adj* [L *protractus*] (1828) : capable of being thrust out ⟨∼ jaws⟩

pro·trac·tion \-'trak-shən\ *n* [LL *protraction-, protractio* act of drawing out, fr. *protrahere*] (1535) **1** : the act of protracting : the state of being protracted **2** : the drawing to scale of an area of land

pro·trac·tor \-'trak-tər\ *n* (ca. 1611) **1 a** : one that protracts **b** : a muscle that extends a part **2** : an instrument for laying down and measuring angles in drawing and plotting

pro·trep·tic \-'trep-tik\ *n* [LL *protrepticus* hortatory, encouraging, fr. Gk *protreptikos*, fr. *protrepein* to turn forward, urge on, fr. *pro-* + *trepein* to turn] (ca. 1656) : an utterance (as a speech) designed to instruct and persuade — **protreptic** *adj*

pro·trude \prō-'trüd\ *vb* **pro·trud·ed; pro·trud·ing** [L *protrudere*, fr. *pro-* + *trudere* to thrust — more at THREAT] *vt* (1620) **1** *archaic* : to thrust forward **2** : to cause to project ∼ *vi* : to jut out from the surrounding surface or context ⟨a handkerchief *protruding* from his breast pocket⟩ — **pro·tru·si·ble** \-'trü-sə-bəl, -zə-\ *adj*

pro·tru·sion \prō-'trü-zhən\ *n* [L *protrudere*] (1646) **1** : the act of protruding : the state of being protruded **2** : something (as a part or excrescence) that protrudes **syn** see PROJECTION

pro·tru·sive \-'trü-siv, -ziv\ *adj* (1646) **1** *archaic* : thrusting forward **2** : PROMINENT, PROTUBERANT ⟨a ∼ jaw⟩ **3** : OBTRUSIVE, PUSHING ⟨a coarse ∼ manner⟩ — **pro·tru·sive·ly** *adv* — **pro·tru·sive·ness** *n*

pro·tu·ber·ance \prō-'tü-b(ə-)rən(t)s, -'tyü-\ *n* (1646) **1** : something that is protuberant **2** : the quality or state of being protuberant **syn** see PROJECTION

pro·tu·ber·ant \-b(ə-)rənt\ *adj* [LL *protuberant-, protuberans*, prp. of *protuberare* to bulge out, fr. L *pro-* forward + *tuber* excrescence, swelling; perh. akin to L *tumēre* to swell — more at THUMB] (1646) **1** : thrusting out from a surrounding or adjacent surface often as a rounded mass : PROMINENT **2** : forcing itself into consciousness : OBTRUSIVE — **pro·tu·ber·ant·ly** *adv*

proud \'praud\ *adj* [ME, fr. OE *prūd*, prob. fr. OF *prod, prud, prou* capable, good, valiant, fr. LL *prode* advantage, advantageous, back-formation fr. L *prodesse* to be advantageous, fr. *pro-, prod-* for, in favor + *esse* to be — more at PRO-, IS] (bef. 12c) **1** : feeling or showing pride: as **a** : having or displaying excessive self-esteem **b** : much pleased : EXULTANT **c** : having proper self-respect **2 a** : marked by stateliness : MAGNIFICENT **b** : giving reason for pride : GLORIOUS ⟨the ∼*est* moment in her life⟩ **3** : VIGOROUS, SPIRITED ⟨a ∼ steed⟩ **4** *chiefly Brit* : raised above a surrounding area ⟨a ∼ design on a stamp⟩ — **proud·ly** *adv*

syn PROUD, ARROGANT, HAUGHTY, LORDLY, INSOLENT, OVERBEARING, SUPERCILIOUS, DISDAINFUL mean showing scorn for inferiors. PROUD may suggest an assumed superiority or loftiness ⟨too *proud* to take charity⟩. ARROGANT implies a claiming for oneself of more consideration or importance than is warranted ⟨a conceited and *arrogant* executive⟩. HAUGHTY suggests a consciousness of superior birth or position ⟨a *haughty* aristocrat⟩. LORDLY implies pomposity or an arrogant display of power ⟨a *lordly* condescension⟩. INSOLENT implies contemptuous haughtiness ⟨ignored by an *insolent* waiter⟩. OVERBEARING suggests a tyrannical manner or an intolerable insolence ⟨an *overbearing* supervisor⟩. SUPERCILIOUS implies a cool, patronizing haughtiness ⟨an aloof and *supercilious* manner⟩. DISDAINFUL suggests a more active and openly scornful superciliousness ⟨*disdainful* of their social inferiors⟩.

proud flesh *n* (14c) : an excessive growth of granulation tissue (as in an ulcer)

proud·ful \'praud-fəl\ *adj* (14c) *chiefly dial* : marked by or full of pride

proud-heart·ed \-'här-təd\ *adj* (14c) : proud in spirit : HAUGHTY

proust·ite \'prü-ˌstīt\ *n* [F, fr. Joseph L. *Proust* †1826 Fr. chemist] (1835) : a mineral that consists of a red silver arsenic sulfide and occurs in crystals or massively

---

\ə\ abut \ᵊ\ kitten, F table \ər\ further \a\ ash \ā\ ace \ä\ mop, mar \aú\ out \ch\ chin \e\ bet \ē\ easy \g\ go \i\ hit \ī\ ice \j\ job \ŋ\ sing \ō\ go \ó\ law \ói\ boy \th\ thin \t͟h\ the \ü\ loot \ú\ foot \y\ yet \zh\ vision \á, k̠, ⁿ, œ, œ̄, ɶ, ɶ̄, ʸ\ *see* Guide to Pronunciation

pro·vas·cu·lar \(,)prō-'vas-kyə-lər\ adj (ca. 1948) : of, relating to, or being procambium

prove \'prüv\ vb **proved; proved** or **prov·en** \'prü-vən, Brit also 'prō-\; **prov·ing** \'prü-viŋ\ [ME, fr. OF prover, fr. L probare to test, approve, prove, fr. probus good, honest, fr. pro- for, in favor + -bus (akin to OE bēon to be) — more at PRO-, BE] vt (13c) **1** archaic : to learn or find out by experience **2 a** : to test the truth, validity, or genuineness of ⟨the exception ~s the rule⟩ ⟨~ a will at probate⟩ **b** : to test the worth or quality of; specif : to compare against a standard — sometimes used with up or out **c** : to check the correctness of (as an arithmetic result) **3 a** : to establish the existence, truth, or validity of (as by evidence or logic) ⟨~ a theorem⟩ ⟨the charges were never proved in court⟩ **b** : to demonstrate as having a particular quality or worth ⟨the vaccine has been proven effective after years of tests⟩ ⟨proved herself a great actress⟩ **4** : to show (oneself) to be worthy or capable ⟨eager to ~ myself in the new job⟩ **~** vi : to turn out esp. after trial or test ⟨the new drug proved effective⟩ — **prov·able** \'prü-və-bəl\ adj — **prov·able·ness** n — **prov·ably** \-blē\ adv — **prov·er** \'prü-vər\ n

usage The past participle proven, orig. the past participle of preve, a Middle English variant of prove that survived in Scotland, has gradually worked its way into standard English over the past three and a half centuries. It seems to have first become established in legal use and to have come only slowly into literary use. Tennyson was one of its earliest frequent users, prob. for metrical reasons. It was disapproved by 19th century grammarians, one of whom included it in a list of "words that are not words." Surveys made some 30 or 40 years ago indicated that proved was about four times as frequent as proven. But our evidence for the last 10 or 15 years shows this no longer to be the case. As a past participle proven is now about as frequent as proved in all contexts. As an attributive adjective ⟨proved or proven gas reserves⟩ proven is much more common than proved.

prov·e·nance \'präv-nən(t)s, 'prä-və-,nän(t)s\ n [F, fr. provenir to come forth, originate, fr. L provenire, fr. pro- forth + venire to come — more at PRO-, COME] (1785) **1** : ORIGIN, SOURCE **2** : the history of ownership of a valued object or work of art or literature

¹Pro·ven·çal \,prō-,vän-'säl, ,prä-vən-, sense 1 also prə-'ven(t)-səl\ adj [MF, fr. Provence Provence] (1589) **1** : of, relating to, or characteristic of Provence or the people of Provence **2** or **Pro·ven·çale** : cooked with garlic, onion, mushrooms, tomato, olive oil, and herbs ⟨scallops ~⟩

²Pro·ven·çal \,prō-,vän-'säl, ,prä-vən-\ n (1600) **1** : a native or inhabitant of Provence **2** : a Romance language spoken in southern France; esp : the dialect of this language spoken in Provence

prov·en·der \'prä-vən-dər\ n [ME, fr. MF provende, provendre, fr. ML provenda, alter. of praebenda prebend] (14c) **1** : dry food for domestic animals — more at FEED **2** : FOOD, VICTUALS

pro·ve·nience \prə-'vē-nyən(t)s, -nē-ən(t)s\ n [alter. of provenance] (1882) : ORIGIN, SOURCE

prov·en·ly \'prü-vən-lē, Brit also 'prō-\ adv (1887) : demonstrably as stated : without doubt or uncertainty

pro·ven·tric·u·lus \,prō-ven-'tri-kyə-ləs\ n, pl **-li** \-,lī, -,lē\ [NL] (ca. 1836) **1** : the glandular or true stomach of a bird that is situated between the crop and gizzard **2** : a muscular dilatation of the foregut in most mandibulate insects that is armed internally with chitinous teeth or plates for triturating food **3** : the thin-walled sac in front of the gizzard of an earthworm

prove out vi (1941) : to turn out to be satisfactory or as expected

¹prov·erb \'prä-,vərb\ n [ME proverbe, fr. MF, fr. L proverbium, fr. pro- + verbum word — more at WORD] (14c) **1** : a brief popular epigram or maxim : ADAGE **2** : BYWORD **4**

²proverb vt (14c) **1** : to speak of proverbially **2** obs : to provide with a proverb

pro-verb \'prō-,vərb, -'vərb\ n (1907) : a form of the verb do used to avoid repetition of a verb (as do in "act as I do")

pro·ver·bi·al \prə-'vər-bē-əl\ adj (1548) **1** : of, relating to, or resembling a proverb **2** : that has become a proverb or byword : commonly spoken of ⟨the ~ smoking gun⟩ — **pro·ver·bi·al·ly** \-ə-lē\ adv

Prov·erbs \'prä-,vərbz\ n pl but sing in constr : a collection of moral sayings and counsels forming a book of canonical Jewish and Christian Scripture — see BIBLE table

pro·vide \prə-'vīd\ vb **pro·vid·ed; pro·vid·ing** [ME, fr. L providere, lit., to see ahead, fr. pro- forward + videre to see — more at PRO-, WIT] vi (15c) **1** : to take precautionary measures ⟨~ for the common defense —U.S. Constitution⟩ **2** : to make a proviso or stipulation ⟨the constitution . . . ~s for an elected two-chamber legislature —Current Biog.⟩ **3** : to make preparation to meet a need ⟨~ for entertainment⟩; esp : to supply something for sustenance or support ⟨~s for the poor⟩ **~** vt **1** archaic : to prepare or get ready in advance **2 a** : to supply or make available (something wanted or needed) ⟨provided new uniforms for the band⟩; also : AFFORD ⟨curtains ~ privacy⟩ **b** : to make something available to ⟨~ the children with free balloons⟩ **3** : to have as a condition : STIPULATE ⟨the contract ~s that certain deadlines will be met⟩

provided conj [ME, pp. of providen to provide] (15c) : on condition that : with the understanding : IF **usage** see PROVIDING

prov·i·dence \'prä-və-dən(t)s, -,den(t)s\ n [ME, fr. MF, fr. L providentia, fr. provident-, providens] (14c) **1 a** often cap : divine guidance or care **b** cap : God conceived as the power sustaining and guiding human destiny **2** : the quality or state of being provident

prov·i·dent \-dənt, -,dent\ adj [ME, fr. L provident-, providens, fr. prp. of providere] (15c) **1** : making provision for the future : PRUDENT **2** : FRUGAL, SAVING — **prov·i·dent·ly** adv

prov·i·den·tial \,prä-və-'den(t)-shəl\ adj (1648) **1** : of, relating to, or determined by Providence **2** archaic : marked by foresight : PRUDENT **3** : occurring by or as if by an intervention of Providence ⟨a ~ escape⟩ **syn** see LUCKY — **prov·i·den·tial·ly** \-'den(t)-sh(ə-)lē\ adv

pro·vid·er \prə-'vī-dər\ n (1523) : one that provides; esp : BREADWINNER

providing conj [ME, prp. of providen] (15c) : on condition that : in case **usage** Although occas. still disapproved, providing is as well established as a conjunction as provided is. Provided is more common.

prov·ince \'prä-vən(t)s\ n [ME, fr. MF, fr. L provincia] (14c) **1 a** : a country or region brought under the control of the ancient Roman government **b** : an administrative district or division of a country **c** pl : all of a country except the metropolises **2 a** : a division of a country forming the jurisdiction of an archbishop or metropolitan **b** : a territorial unit of a religious order **3 a** : a biogeographic division of less rank than a region **b** : an area that exhibits essential continuity of geological history; also : one characterized by particular structural or petrological features **4 a** : proper or appropriate function or scope : SPHERE **b** : a department of knowledge or activity **syn** see FUNCTION

¹pro·vin·cial \prə-'vin(t)-shəl\ n [in sense 1, fr. ME, fr. MF or ML; MF, fr. ML provincialis, fr. provincia ecclesiastical province; in other senses, fr. L provincialis, fr. provincia province] (14c) **1** : the superior of a province of a Roman Catholic religious order **2** : one living in or coming from a province **3 a** : a person of local or restricted interests or outlook **b** : a person lacking urban polish or refinement

²provincial adj (14c) **1** : of, relating to, or coming from a province **2 a** : limited in outlook : NARROW **b** : lacking the polish of urban society : UNSOPHISTICATED **3** : of or relating to a decorative style (as in furniture) marked by simplicity, informality, and relative plainness; esp : FRENCH PROVINCIAL — **pro·vin·cial·ly** \-'vin(t)-sh(ə-)lē\ adv

pro·vin·cial·ism \-shə-,li-zəm\ n (1770) **1** : a dialectal or local word, phrase, or idiom **2** : the quality or state of being provincial

pro·vin·cial·ist \-'vin(t)-sh(ə-)list\ n (1656) : a native or inhabitant of a province

pro·vin·ci·al·i·ty \prə-,vin(t)-shē-'a-lə-tē\ n, pl **-ties** (1782) **1** : PROVINCIALISM **2** : an act or instance of provincialism

pro·vin·cial·ize \-'vin(t)-shə-,līz\ vt **-ized; -iz·ing** (1829) : to make provincial — **pro·vin·cial·i·za·tion** \-,vin(t)-sh(ə-)lə-'zā-shən\ n

proving ground n (ca. 1890) **1** : a place for scientific experimentation or testing (as of vehicles or weapons) **2** : a place where something is developed or tried out

pro·vi·rus \(,)prō-'vī-rəs\ n [NL] (1949) : a form of a virus that is integrated into the genetic material of a host cell and by replicating with it can be transmitted from one cell generation to the next without causing lysis — **pro·vi·ral** \-rəl\ adj

¹pro·vi·sion \prə-'vi-zhən\ n [ME, fr. MF, fr. LL & L; LL provision-, provisio act of providing, fr. L, foresight, fr. providere to see ahead — more at PROVIDE] (14c) **1 a** : the act or process of providing **b** : the fact or state of being prepared beforehand **c** : a measure taken beforehand to deal with a need or contingency : PREPARATION ⟨made ~ for replacements⟩ **2** : a stock of needed materials or supplies; esp : a stock of food — usu. used in pl. **3** : PROVISO, STIPULATION

²provision vt **pro·vi·sioned; pro·vi·sion·ing** \-'vi-zhə-niŋ, -'vizh-niŋ\ (1809) : to supply with provisions

¹pro·vi·sion·al \prə-'vizh-nəl, -'vi-zhə-nᵊl\ adj (1601) : serving for the time being : TEMPORARY — **pro·vi·sion·al·ly** adv

²provisional n (1886) : a postage stamp for use until a regular issue appears — compare DEFINITIVE

pro·vi·sion·ary \prə-'vi-zhə-,ner-ē\ adj (1617) : PROVISIONAL

pro·vi·sion·er \-'vi-zhə-nər, -'vizh-nər\ n (1866) : a furnisher of provisions

pro·vi·so \prə-'vī-(,)zō\ n, pl **-sos** or **-soes** [ME, fr. ML proviso quod provided that] (15c) **1** : an article or clause (as in a contract) that introduces a condition **2** : a conditional stipulation

pro·vi·so·ry \-'vī-zə-rē, -'viz-rē\ adj (ca. 1611) **1** : containing or subject to a proviso : CONDITIONAL **2** : PROVISIONAL

pro·vi·ta·min \(,)prō-'vī-tə-mən\ n (1927) : a precursor of a vitamin convertible into the vitamin in an organism

Pro·vo \'prō-(,)vō\ n, pl **Provos** [Provisional I.R.A., name of the faction + ¹-o] (1971) : a member of the extremist faction of the Irish Republican Army

pro·vo·ca·teur \prō-,vä-kə-'tər\ n (1919) : AGENT PROVOCATEUR

pro·vo·ca·tion \,prä-və-'kā-shən\ n [ME provocacioun, fr. MF provocation, fr. L provocation-, provocatio, fr. provocare] (14c) **1** : the act of provoking : INCITEMENT **2** : something that provokes, arouses, or stimulates

pro·voc·a·tive \prə-'vä-kə-tiv\ adj (15c) : serving or tending to provoke, excite, or stimulate — **provocative** n — **pro·voc·a·tive·ly** adv — **pro·voc·a·tive·ness** n

pro·voke \prə-'vōk\ vt **pro·voked; pro·vok·ing** [ME, fr. MF provoquer, fr. L provocare, fr. pro- forth + vocare to call, fr. voc-, vox voice — more at PRO-, VOICE] (14c) **1** archaic : to arouse to a feeling or action **b** : to incite to anger **2 a** : to call forth (as a feeling or action) : EVOKE ⟨~ laughter⟩ **b** : to stir up purposely ⟨~ a fight⟩ **c** : to provide the needed stimulus for ⟨will ~ a lot of discussion⟩ — **pro·vok·er** n

syn PROVOKE, EXCITE, STIMULATE, PIQUE, QUICKEN mean to arouse as if by pricking. PROVOKE directs attention to the response called forth ⟨my stories usually provoke laughter⟩. EXCITE implies a stirring up or moving profoundly ⟨news that excited anger and frustration⟩. STIMULATE suggests a rousing out of lethargy, quiescence, or indifference ⟨stimulating conversation⟩. PIQUE suggests stimulating by mild irritation or challenge ⟨that remark piqued my interest⟩. QUICKEN implies beneficially stimulating and making active or lively ⟨the high salary quickened her desire to have the job⟩. **syn** see in addition IRRITATE

pro·vok·ing \-'vō-kiŋ\ adj (1642) : causing mild anger : ANNOYING — **pro·vok·ing·ly** \-kiŋ-lē\ adv

pro·vo·lo·ne \,prō-və-'lō-nē\ n [It, aug. of provola, a kind of cheese] (1912) : a usu. firm pliant often smoked cheese of Italian origin

pro·vost \'prō-,vōst, 'prä-vəst, 'prō-vəst, esp attrib ,prō-(,)vō\ n [ME, fr. OE profost & OF provost, fr. ML propositus, alter. of praepositus, fr. L, one in charge, director, fr. pp. of praeponere to place at the head — more at PREPOSITION] (bef. 12c) **1** : the chief dignitary of a collegiate or cathedral chapter **2** : the chief magistrate of a Scottish burgh **3** : the keeper of a prison **4** : a high-ranking university administrative officer

provost court n (1864) : a military court usu. for the trial of minor offenses within an occupied hostile territory

provost guard n (1862) : a police detail of soldiers under the authority of the provost marshal

provost marshal n (1535) : an officer who supervises the military police of a command

¹prow \'prau\ adj [ME, fr. MF prou — more at PROUD] (14c) archaic : VALIANT, GALLANT

²prow \'praů, *archaic* 'prō\ *n* [MF *proue*, prob. fr. OIt dial. *prua*, fr. L *prora*, fr. Gk *prōira*] (1555) **1 :** the bow of a ship **: STEM 2 :** a pointed projecting front part

prow·ess \'praů-əs *also* 'prō-\ *n* [ME *prouesse*, fr. OF *proesse*, fr. *prou*] (13c) **1 :** distinguished bravery; *esp* : military valor and skill **2 :** extraordinary ability ⟨his ∼ on the football field⟩

¹prowl \'praů(ə)l\ *vb* [ME *prollen*] *vi* (14c) : to move about or wander stealthily in or as if in search of prey ∼ *vt* : to roam over in a predatory manner — **prowl·er** \'praů-lər\ *n*

²prowl *n* (1803) : an act or instance of prowling — **on the prowl** : in the act of prowling; *also* : in search of something ⟨his fourth wife had just left him, and he was *on the prowl* again —Mary McCarthy⟩

prowl car *n* (1937) : SQUAD CAR

prox·e·mics \präk-'sē-miks\ *n pl but sing or pl in constr* [*proximity* + *-emics* (as in *phonemics*)] (1963) : the study of the nature, degree, and effect of the spatial separation individuals naturally maintain (as in various social and interpersonal situations) and of how this separation relates to environmental and cultural factors — **prox·e·mic** \-mik\ *adj*

prox·i·mal \'präk-sə-məl\ *adj* [L *proximus*] (1727) **1 :** situated close to **: PROXIMATE 2 :** next to or nearest the point of attachment or origin, a central point, or the point of view; *esp* : located toward the center of the body — compare DISTAL **3 :** of, relating to, or being the mesial and distal surfaces of a tooth — **prox·i·mal·ly** \-mə-lē\ *adv*

proximal convoluted tubule *n* (ca. 1899) : the convoluted portion of the vertebrate nephron that lies between Bowman's capsule and the loop of Henle and functions esp. in the resorption of sugar, sodium and chloride ions, and water from the glomerular filtrate — called also *proximal tubule*

prox·i·mate \'präk-sə-mət\ *adj* [L *proximatus*, pp. of *proximare* to approach, fr. *proximus* nearest, next, superl. of *prope* near — more at APPROACH] (1661) **1 :** immediately preceding or following (as in a chain of events, causes, or effects) ⟨∼, rather than ultimate, goals — Reinhold Niebuhr⟩ **2 a :** very near **: CLOSE b :** soon forthcoming **: IMMINENT — prox·i·mate·ly** *adv* — **prox·i·mate·ness** *n*

prox·im·i·ty \präk-'si-mə-tē\ *n* [MF *proximité*, fr. L *proximitat-*, *proximitas*, fr. *proximus*] (15c) : the quality or state of being proximate **: CLOSENESS**

proximity fuze *n* (1945) : a fuze for a projectile that uses the principle of radar to detect the presence of a target within the projectile's effective range

prox·i·mo \'präk-sə-,mō\ *adj* [L *proximo mense* in the next month] (1855) : of or occurring in the next month after the present

proxy \'präk-sē\ *n, pl* **prox·ies** [ME *procucie*, contr. of *procuracie*, fr. AF, fr. ML *procuratia*, alter. of L *procuratio* procuration] (15c) **1 :** the agency, function, or office of a deputy who acts as a substitute for another **2 a :** authority or power to act for another **b :** a document giving such authority; *specif* : a power of attorney authorizing a specified person to vote corporate stock **3 :** a person authorized to act for another **: PROCURATOR — proxy** *adj*

proxy marriage *n* (1900) : a marriage celebrated in the absence of one of the contracting parties who is represented at the ceremony by a proxy

prude \'prüd\ *n* [F, good woman, prudish woman, short for *prude-femme* good woman, fr. OF *prode femme*] (1704) : a person who is excessively or priggishly attentive to propriety or decorum; *esp* : a woman who shows or affects extreme modesty

pru·dence \'prü-d°n(t)s\ *n* [ME, fr. MF, fr. L *prudentia*, alter. of *providentia* — more at PROVIDENCE] (14c) **1 :** the ability to govern and discipline oneself by the use of reason **2 :** sagacity or shrewdness in the management of affairs **3 :** skill and good judgment in the use of resources **4 :** caution or circumspection as to danger or risk

pru·dent \-d°nt\ *adj* [ME, fr. MF, fr. L *prudent-*, *prudens*, contr. of *provident-*, *providens* — more at PROVIDENT] (14c) : characterized by, arising from, or showing prudence: as **a :** marked by wisdom or judiciousness **b :** shrewd in the management of practical affairs **c :** marked by circumspection **: DISCREET d :** PROVIDENT, FRUGAL **syn** see WISE — **pru·dent·ly** *adv*

pru·den·tial \prü-'den(t)-shəl\ *adj* (15c) **1 :** of, relating to, or proceeding from prudence **2 :** exercising prudence esp. in business matters — **pru·den·tial·ly** \-'den(t)-sh(ə-)lē\ *adv*

prud·ery \'prü-d(ə-)rē\ *n, pl* **-er·ies** (1709) **1 :** the characteristic quality or state of a prude **2 :** a prudish act or remark

prud·ish \'prü-dish\ *adj* (1717) : marked by prudery **: PRIGGISH — prud·ish·ly** *adv* — **prud·ish·ness** *n*

pru·i·nose \'prü-ə-,nōs\ *adj* [L *pruinosus* covered with hoarfrost, fr. *pruina* hoarfrost — more at FREEZE] (ca. 1826) : covered with whitish dust or bloom ⟨∼ stems⟩

¹prune \'prün\ *n* [ME, fr. MF, plum, fr. L *prunum* — more at PLUM] (14c) : a plum dried or capable of drying without fermentation

²prune *vb* **pruned; prun·ing** [ME *prouynen*, fr. MF *proignier*, prob. alter. of *provigner* to layer, fr. *provain* layer, fr. L *propagin-*, *propago*, fr. *pro-* forward + *pangere* to fix — more at PRO-, PACT] *vt* (15c) **1 a :** to reduce esp. by eliminating superfluous matter ⟨*pruned* the text⟩ ⟨∼ the budget⟩ **b :** to remove as superfluous ⟨∼ away all ornamentation⟩ **2 :** to cut off or cut back parts of for better shape or more fruitful growth ∼ *vi* : to cut away what is unwanted or superfluous — **prun·er** *n*

pru·nel·la \prü-'ne-lə\ *also* **pru·nelle** \-'nel\ *n* [F *prunelle*, lit., sloe, fr. dim. of *prune* plum] (1670) **1 :** a twilled woolen dress fabric **2 :** a heavy woolen fabric used for the uppers of shoes

pruning hook *n* (1611) : a pole bearing a curved blade for pruning plants

pru·nus \'prü-nəs\ *n* [NL, fr. L, plum tree, fr. Gk *proumnē*] (1901) : any of a genus (*Prunus*) of drupaceous trees or shrubs of the rose family that have showy clusters of usu. white or pink flowers first appearing in the spring often before the leaves including many grown for ornament or for their fruit (as the plum, cherry, or apricot)

pru·ri·ence \'průr-ē-ən(t)s\ *n* (1781) : the quality or state of being prurient

pru·ri·en·cy \-ən(t)-sē\ *n* (1795) : PRURIENCE

pru·ri·ent \-ənt\ *adj* [L *prurient-*, *pruriens*, prp. of *prurire* to itch, crave; akin to L *pruna* glowing coal, Skt *plosati* he singes, and prob. to L *pruina* hoarfrost — more at FREEZE] (1592) : marked by or arousing an immoderate or unwholesome interest or desire; *esp* : marked by, arousing, or appealing to unusual sexual desire — **pru·ri·ent·ly** *adv*

pru·ri·go \prü-'rī-(,)gō, -'rē-\ *n* [NL, fr. L, itch, fr. *prurire*] (ca. 1646) : a chronic inflammatory skin disease marked by itching papules

pru·rit·ic \-'ri-tik\ *adj* (1899) : of, relating to, or marked by itching

pru·ri·tus \-'rī-təs, -'rē-\ *n* [L, fr. *prurire*] (1653) : ITCH 1a

Prus·sian blue \'prə-shən-\ *n* [*Prussia*, Germany] (1724) **1 :** any of numerous blue iron pigments formerly regarded as ferric ferrocyanide **2 :** a dark blue crystalline hydrated ferric ferrocyanide $Fe_4[Fe(CN)_6]_3 \cdot xH_2O$ used as a test for ferric iron **3 :** a greenish blue

prus·sian·ise *Brit var of* PRUSSIANIZE

Prus·sian·ism \'prə-shə-,ni-zəm\ *n* (1856) : the practices or policies (as the advocacy of militarism) held to be typically Prussian

prus·sian·ize \-,nīz\ *vt* **-ized; -iz·ing** *often cap* (1861) : to make Prussian in character or principle (as in authoritarian control or rigid discipline) — **prus·sian·i·za·tion** \,prə-shə-nə-'zā-shən\ *n*

pru·tah *or* **pru·ta** \prü-'tä\ *n, pl* **pru·toth** \-'tōt, -'tōth, -'tōs\ *or* **pru·tot** \-'tōt, -'tōs\ [NHeb *pĕrūṭāh*, fr. LHeb, a small coin] (1949) **1 :** a former monetary unit of Israel equivalent to $\frac{1}{1000}$ pound **2 :** a coin representing one prutah

¹pry \'prī\ *vi* **pried; pry·ing** [ME *prien*] (14c) : to look closely or inquisitively; *also* : to make a nosy or presumptuous inquiry

²pry *vt* **pried; pry·ing** [prob. back-formation fr. ⁵*prize*] (ca. 1806) **1 :** to raise, move, or pull apart with a lever **: PRIZE 2 :** to extract, detach, or open with difficulty ⟨*pried* the secret out of my sister⟩

³pry *n* (1823) **1 :** a tool for prying **2 :** LEVERAGE

pry·er *var of* PRIER

prying *adj* (1552) : impertinently or officiously inquisitive or interrogatory **syn** see CURIOUS — **pry·ing·ly** \-iŋ-lē\ *adv*

Prze·wal·ski's horse \psha-'väl-skēz-, shə-, ,pər-zhə-'väl-\ *n* [Nikolaĭ M. *Przhevalskiĭ* †1888 Russ. soldier & explorer] (1881) : a small stocky bay- or dun-colored wild horse (*Equus caballus przewalskii* syn. *E. przewalskii*) of central Asia having a large head and short erect mane — called also *Prze·wal·ski horse* \-skē-\

psalm \'säm, 'sälm, 'sȯm, 'sȯlm, *NewEng also* 'sȧm\ *n, often cap* [ME, fr. OE *psealm*, fr. LL *psalmus*, fr. Gk *psalmos*, lit., twanging of a harp, fr. *psallein* to pluck, play a stringed instrument] (bef. 12c) : a sacred song or poem used in worship; *esp* : one of the biblical hymns collected in the Book of Psalms

psalm·book \-,bůk\ *n* (12c) *archaic* : PSALTER

psalm·ist \'sä-mist, 'säl-, 'sȯ-, 'sȯl-, *NewEng also* 'sȧ-mist\ *n* (15c) : a writer or composer of esp. biblical psalms

psalm·o·dy \'sä-mə-dē, 'säl-, 'sȯ-, 'sȯl, *NewEng also* 'sȧ-mə-dē\ *n* [ME *psalmodie*, fr. LL *psalmodia*, fr. LGk *psalmōidia*, lit., singing to the harp, fr. Gk *psalmos* + *aidein* to sing — more at ODE] (14c) **1 :** the act, practice, or art of singing psalms in worship **2 :** a collection of psalms

Psalms \'sämz, 'sälmz, 'sȯmz, 'sȯlmz, *NewEng also* 'sȧmz\ *n pl but sing in constr* : a collection of sacred poems forming a book of canonical Jewish and Christian Scripture — see BIBLE table

Psal·ter \'säl-tər, 'sȯl-\ *n* [ME, fr. OE *psalter* & OF *psaltier*, fr. LL *psalterium*, fr. LGk *psaltērion*, fr. Gk, psaltery] (bef. 12c) : the Book of Psalms; *also* : a collection of Psalms for liturgical or devotional use

psal·te·ri·um \säl-'tir-ē-əm, sȯl-\ *n, pl* **-ria** \-ē-ə\ [NL, fr. LL, psalter; fr. the resemblance of the folds to the pages of a book] (ca. 1846) **: OMASUM**

psal·tery *also* **psal·try** \'säl-t(ə-)rē, 'sȯl-\ *n, pl* **-ter·ies** *also* **-tries** [ME *psalterie*, fr. MF, fr. L *psalterium*, fr. Gk *psaltērion*, fr. *psallein* to play on a stringed instrument] (14c) : an ancient musical instrument resembling the zither

p's and q's \,pēz-°n-'kyüz\ *n pl* [fr. the phrase *mind one's p's and q's*, alluding to the difficulty a child learning to write has in distinguishing between *p* and *q*] (1779) **1 :** something (as one's manners) that one should be mindful of ⟨better watch his *p's and q's* when I get a six-gun of my own —Jean Stafford⟩ **2 :** best behavior ⟨being on her *p's and q's* for two solid days was too much —Guy McCrone⟩

pse·phol·o·gy \sē-'fä-lə-jē, si-\ *n* [Gk *psēphos* pebble, ballot, vote; fr. the use of pebbles by the ancient Greeks in voting] (1952) : the scientific study of elections — **pse·pho·log·i·cal** \,sē-fə-'lä-ji-kəl\ *adj* — **pse·phol·o·gist** \sē-'fä-lə-jist\ *n*

pseud \'süd\ *n* [short for *pseudo-intellectual*] (1964) *Brit* : a person who pretends to be an intellectual

pseud- *or* **pseudo-** *comb form* [ME, fr. LL, fr. Gk, fr. *pseudēs*, fr. *pseudesthai* to lie; akin to Arm *sut* lie and prob. to Gk *psychein* to breathe — more at PSYCH-] **1 :** false : spurious ⟨*pseudo*classic⟩ ⟨*pseudo*podium⟩

pseud·ep·i·graph \sü-'de-pə-,graf\ *n* (1884) : PSEUDEPIGRAPHON 2

pseud·ep·i·gra·phon \,sü-di-'p-grə-,fän\ *n, pl* **-pha** \-fə\ [NL, sing. of *pseudepigrapha*, fr. Gk, neut. pl. of *pseudepigraphos* falsely inscribed, fr. *pseud-* + *epigraphein* to inscribe — more at EPIGRAM] (1692) **1 *pl* : APOCRYPHA 2 :** any of various pseudonymous or anonymous Jewish religious writings of the period 200 B.C. to 200 A.D.; *esp* : one of such writings (as the Psalms of Solomon) not included in any canon of biblical Scripture — usu. used in pl.

pseud·epig·ra·phy \-fē\ *n* [Gk *pseudepigraphos*] (ca. 1842) : the ascription of false names of authors to works

pseu·do \'sü-(,)dō\ *adj* [ME, fr. *pseudo-*] (15c) : being apparently rather than actually as stated **: SHAM, SPURIOUS** ⟨distinction between true and ∼ humanism —K. F. Reinhardt⟩

pseu·do·al·lele \,sü-dō-ə-'lē(ə)l\ *n* (1948) : any of two or more closely linked genes that act usu. as if a single member of an allelic pair but occas. undergo crossing-over and recombination

pseu·do·cho·lin·es·ter·ase \'sü-dō-,kō-lə-'nes-tə-,rās, -,rāz\ *n* (1943) **: CHOLINESTERASE 2**

pseu·do·clas·sic \,sü-dō-'kla-sik\ *adj* (1899) : pretending to be or erroneously regarded as classic — **pseudoclassic** *n*

pseu·do·clas·si·cism \'kla-sə-,si-zəm\ *n* (1871) : imitative representation of classicism in literature and art

\ə\ abut \²\ kitten, F table \ər\ further \a\ ash \ā\ ace \ä\ mop, mar \aů\ out \ch\ chin \e\ bet \ē\ easy \g\ go \i\ hit \ī\ ice \j\ job \ŋ\ sing \ō\ go \ȯ\ law \ȯi\ boy \th\ thin \t̲h̲\ the \ü\ loot \ů\ foot \y\ yet \zh\ vision \ȧ, k̲, ⁿ, œ, œ̄, ɾ, ụ̄, ʸ\ see Guide to Pronunciation

pseu·do·coel \'sü-də-ˌsēl\ n (1887) : a body cavity that is not a product of gastrulation and is not lined with a well-defined mesodermal membrane

pseu·do·coe·lom·ate \ˌsü-dō-'sē-lə-ˌmāt\ n (1940) : an invertebrate (as a nematode or rotifer) having a body cavity that is a pseudocoel — **pseudocoelomate** adj

pseu·do·cy·e·sis \-sī-'ē-səs\ n [NL, fr. pseud- + cyesis pregnancy, fr. Gk kyēsis, fr. kyein to be pregnant — more at CYME] (ca. 1817) : a psychosomatic state that occurs without conception and is marked by some of the physical symptoms and changes in hormonal balance of pregnancy

pseu·do·mo·nad \ˌsü-də-'mō-ˌnad, -nəd\ n [NL Pseudomonad-, Pseudomonas] (1921) : any of a genus (Pseudomonas) of gram-negative rod-shaped motile bacteria including some that produce a greenish fluorescent water-soluble pigment and some that are saprophytes or plant or animal pathogens

pseu·do·mo·nas \-nəs\ n, pl **-mo·na·des** \-'mō-nə-ˌdēz, -'mä-\ [NL, fr. pseud- + monad-, monas monad] (1903) : PSEUDOMONAD

pseu·do·morph \'sü-də-ˌmȯrf\ n [prob. fr. F pseudomorphe, fr. pseud- + -morphe -morph] (1849) 1 : a mineral having the characteristic outward form of another species 2 : a deceptive or irregular form — **pseu·do·mor·phic** \ˌsü-də-'mȯr-fik\ adj — **pseu·do·mor·phism** \-ˌfi-zəm\ n — **pseu·do·mor·phous** \-fəs\ adj

pseu·do·nym \'sü-dⁿ-ˌim\ n [F pseudonyme, fr. Gk pseudōnymos bearing a false name, fr. pseud- + onyma name — more at NAME] (1833) : a fictitious name; esp : PEN NAME

pseu·do·nym·i·ty \ˌsü-dⁿ-'i-mə-tē\ n (1877) : the use of a pseudonym; also : the fact or state of being signed with a pseudonym

pseu·don·y·mous \sü-'dä-nə-məs\ adj [Gk pseudōnymos] (ca. 1706) : bearing or using a fictitious name ⟨a ∼ report⟩; also : being a pseudonym — **pseu·don·y·mous·ly** adv — **pseu·don·y·mous·ness** n

pseu·do·pa·ren·chy·ma \ˌsü-dō-pə-'reŋ-kə-mə\ n [NL] (1875) : compactly interwoven short-celled filaments in a thallophyte that resemble parenchyma of higher plants — **pseu·do·par·en·chy·ma·tous** \-ˌpar-ən-'ki-mə-təs, -'ki-\ adj

pseu·do·pod \'sü-də-ˌpäd\ n [NL pseudopodium] (1874) : PSEUDOPODIUM — **pseu·dop·o·dal** \sü-'dä-pə-dˀl\ or **pseu·do·po·di·al** \ˌsü-də-'pō-dē-əl\ adj

pseu·do·po·di·um \ˌsü-də-'pō-dē-əm\ n, pl **-po·dia** \-dē-ə\ [NL] (1854) 1 : a temporary protrusion or retractile process of the cytoplasm of a cell that functions (as in an amoeba) esp. in a locomotor or food gathering capacity — see AMOEBA illustration 2 : a slender leafless branch of the gametophyte in various mosses that often bears gemmae

pseu·do·preg·nan·cy \ˌsü-dō-'preg-nən(t)-sē\ n (1860) 1 : PSEUDOCYESIS 2 : an anestrous state resembling pregnancy that occurs in various mammals usu. after an infertile copulation — **pseu·do·preg·nant** \-nənt\ adj

pseu·do·ran·dom \-'ran-dəm\ adj (1949) : being or involving entities (as numbers) that are selected by a definite computational process but that satisfy one or more standard tests for statistical randomness

pseu·do·sci·ence \-'sī-ən(t)s\ n (1844) : a system of theories, assumptions, and methods erroneously regarded as scientific — **pseu·do·sci·en·tif·ic** \-ˌsī-ən-'ti-fik\ adj — **pseu·do·sci·en·tist** \-'sī-ən-tist\ n

pseu·do·scor·pi·on \-'skȯr-pē-ən\ n [NL Pseudoscorpiones, fr. pseud- + L scorpion-, scorpio scorpion] (1835) : any of a widely distributed order (Pseudoscorpionida syn. Pseudoscorpiones) of tiny arachnids that have no caudal stinger and feed on tiny invertebrates (as insects and mites)

pseu·do·so·phis·ti·ca·tion \'sü-dō-sə-ˌfis-tə-'kā-shən\ n (1965) : false or feigned sophistication — **pseu·do·so·phis·ti·cat·ed** \-sə-'fis-ti-ˌkā-təd\ adj

pseu·do·tu·ber·cu·lo·sis \-ˌtü-bər-kyə-'lō-səs, -tyü-\ n [NL] (1900) : any of several diseases that are characterized by the formation of granulomas resembling tubercular nodules but are not caused by the tubercle bacillus

pshaw \'shȯ\ interj (1673) — used to express irritation, disapproval, contempt, or disbelief

¹psi \'sī, 'psī\ n [ME, fr. ML, fr. LGk, fr. Gk psei] (15c) : the 23d letter of the Greek alphabet — see ALPHABET table

²psi \'sī\ n [prob. by shortening & alter. fr. psychic] (ca. 1946) : parapsychological psychic phenomena or powers

psi·lo·cy·bin \ˌsī-lə-'sī-bən\ n [NL Psilocybe, fungus genus + ¹-in] (1958) : a hallucinogenic indole $C_{12}H_{17}N_2O_4P$ obtained from a fungus (Psilocybe mexicana)

psi·lo·phyte \'sī-lə-ˌfīt\ n [NL Psilophyton, genus of plants, fr. Gk psilos bare, mere (prob. akin to Gk psēn to rub) + phyton plant — more at PHYT-] (ca. 1911) : any of an order (Psilophytales) of extinct simple dichotomously branched plants from the Paleozoic of Europe and eastern Canada that include the oldest known land plants with vascular structure — **psi·lo·phyt·ic** \ˌsī-lə-'fi-tik\ adj

psi particle \'sī-, 'psī-\ n (1974) : J/PSI PARTICLE

psit·ta·cine \'si-tə-ˌsīn\ adj [L psittacinus, fr. psittacus parrot, fr. Gk psittakos] (1874) : of or relating to the parrots — **psittacine** n

psit·ta·co·sis \ˌsi-tə-'kō-səs\ n [NL, fr. L psittacus] (1897) : an infectious disease of birds caused by a bacterium (Chlamydia psittaci), marked by diarrhea and wasting, and transmissible to humans in whom it usu. occurs as an atypical pneumonia accompanied by high fever — **psit·ta·cot·ic** \-'kä-tik, -'kō-\ adj

pso·cid \'sō-səd\ n [ultim. fr. NL Psocus, genus of lice] (1891) : any of an order (Psocoptera syn. Corrodentia) of minute usu. winged primitive insects (as a book louse)

pso·ri·a·sis \sə-'rī-ə-səs\ n [NL, fr. Gk psōriasis, fr. psōrian to have the itch, fr. psōra itch; akin to Gk psēn to rub] (ca. 1684) : a chronic skin disease characterized by circumscribed red patches covered with white scales — **pso·ri·at·ic** \ˌsȯr-ē-'a-tik, ˌsȯr-\ adj or n

psych also **psyche** \'sīk\ vt **psyched; psych·ing** [by shortening] (1917) 1 : PSYCHOANALYZE 2 a : to anticipate correctly the intentions or actions of : OUTGUESS b : to analyze or figure out (as a problem or course of action) ⟨I ∼ed it all out by myself and decided —David Hulburd⟩ 3 a : to make psychologically uneasy : INTIMIDATE, SCARE ⟨pressure doesn't ∼ me —Jerry Quarry⟩ — often used with out

b : to make (as oneself) psychologically ready esp. for performance — often used with up ⟨∼ed herself up for the race⟩

psych- or **psycho-** comb form [Gk, fr. psychē breath, principle of life, life, soul, fr. psychein to breathe; akin to Skt babhasti he blows] 1 : mind : mental processes and activities ⟨psychodynamic⟩ ⟨psychology⟩ 2 : psychological methods ⟨psychoanalysis⟩ ⟨psychotherapy⟩ 3 : brain ⟨psychosurgery⟩ 4 : mental and ⟨psychosomatic⟩

psych·as·the·nia \ˌsī-kəs-'thē-nē-ə\ n [NL] (1900) : a neurotic state characterized esp. by phobias, obsessions, or compulsions that one knows are irrational — **psych·as·then·ic** \-'the-nik\ adj or n

Psy·che \'sī-kē\ n [L, fr. Gk psychē soul] 1 : a princess loved by Cupid 2 not cap [Gk psychē] a : SOUL, SELF b : MIND

psy·che·de·lia \ˌsī-kə-'dēl-yə\ n [NL, fr. E psychedelic] (1967) : the world of people, phenomena, or items associated with psychedelic drugs

¹psy·che·del·ic \ˌsī-kə-'de-lik\ n [irreg. fr. psych- + Gk dēloun to show, fr. dēlos evident; akin to Skt didēti it shines, L dies day — more at DEITY] (1956) : a psychedelic drug (as LSD)

²psychedelic adj (1957) 1 a : of, relating to, or being drugs (as LSD) capable of producing abnormal psychic effects (as hallucinations) and sometimes psychic states resembling mental illness b : produced by or associated with the use of psychedelic drugs ⟨a ∼ experience⟩ 2 : imitating, suggestive of, or reproducing effects (as distorted or bizarre images or sounds) resembling those produced by psychedelic drugs ⟨∼ color schemes⟩ — **psy·che·del·i·cal·ly** \-'de-li-k(ə-)lē\ adv

psy·chi·a·try \sə-'kī-ə-trē, sī-\ n [prob. fr. F psychiatrie, fr. psychiatre psychiatrist, fr. psych- psych- + Gk iatros physician — more at -IATRY] (ca. 1846) : a branch of medicine that deals with mental, emotional, or behavioral disorders — **psy·chi·at·ric** \ˌsī-kē-'a-trik\ adj — **psy·chi·at·ri·cal·ly** \-tri-k(ə-)lē\ adv — **psy·chi·a·trist** \sə-'kī-ə-trist, sī-\ n

¹psy·chic \'sī-kik\ also **psy·chi·cal** \-ki-kəl\ adj [Gk psychikos of the soul, fr. psychē soul] (1642) 1 : of or relating to the psyche : PSYCHOGENIC 2 : lying outside the sphere of physical science or knowledge : immaterial, moral, or spiritual in origin or force 3 : sensitive to nonphysical or supernatural forces and influences : marked by extraordinary or mysterious sensitivity, perception, or understanding — **psy·chi·cal·ly** \-ki-k(ə-)lē\ adv

²psychic n (1871) 1 a : a person apparently sensitive to nonphysical forces b : MEDIUM 2d 2 : psychic phenomena

psy·cho \'sī-(ˌ)kō\ n, pl **psychos** [short for psychopath] (1942) : a deranged or psychopathic person — not used technically — **psycho** adj

psy·cho·acous·tics \ˌsī-kō-ə-'kü-stiks\ n pl but sing in constr (1948) : a branch of science dealing with hearing, the sensations produced by sounds, and the problems of communication — **psy·cho·acous·tic** \-stik\ adj

psy·cho·ac·tive \ˌsī-kō-'ak-tiv\ adj (1961) : affecting the mind or behavior ⟨∼ drugs⟩

psy·cho·anal·y·sis \ˌsī-kō-ə-'na-lə-səs\ n [NL] (1906) : a method of analyzing psychic phenomena and treating emotional disorders that involves treatment sessions during which the patient is encouraged to talk freely about personal experiences and esp. about early childhood and dreams — **psy·cho·an·a·lyst** \-'a-nˀl-ist\ n

psy·cho·an·a·lyt·ic \-ˌa-nˀl-'i-tik\ also **psy·cho·an·a·lyt·i·cal** \-ti-kəl\ adj (1906) : of, relating to, or employing psychoanalysis or its principles and techniques — **psy·cho·an·a·lyt·i·cal·ly** \-ti-k(ə-)lē\ adv

psy·cho·an·a·lyze \-'a-nˀl-ˌīz\ vt (1911) : to treat by means of psychoanalysis

psy·cho·bab·ble \ˌsī-kō-ˌba-bəl\ n (1975) : a predominantly metaphorical language for expressing one's feelings; also : psychological jargon — **psy·cho·bab·bler** \-ˌba-blər\ n

psy·cho·bi·og·ra·phy \ˌsī-kō-bī-'ä-grə-fē, -bī-ä-\ n (1931) : a biography written from a psychodynamic or psychoanalytic point of view; also : the application of such a point of view when writing a biography — **psy·cho·bi·og·ra·pher** \-fər\ n — **psy·cho·bio·graph·i·cal** \-ˌbī-ə-gra-fi-kəl\ adj

psy·cho·bi·ol·o·gy \-bī-'ä-lə-jē\ n [ISV] (1902) : the study of mental functioning and behavior in relation to other biological processes — **psy·cho·bi·o·log·i·cal** \-ˌbī-ə-'lä-ji-kəl\ also **psy·cho·bi·o·log·ic** \-jik\ adj — **psy·cho·bi·ol·o·gist** \-bī-'ä-lə-jist\ n

psy·cho·chem·i·cal \-'ke-mi-kəl\ n (1956) : a psychoactive chemical — **psychochemical** adj

psy·cho·dra·ma \-'drä-mə, -'dra-\ n (1937) 1 : an extemporized dramatization designed to afford catharsis and social relearning for one or more of the participants from whose life history the plot is abstracted 2 : a dramatic narrative or event characterized by psychological overtones — **psy·cho·dra·mat·ic** \-drə-'ma-tik\ adj

psy·cho·dy·nam·ics \-dī-'na-miks, -də-\ n pl but sing or pl in constr (1874) 1 : the psychology of mental or emotional forces or processes developing esp. in early childhood and their effects on behavior and mental states 2 : explanation or interpretation (as of behavior or mental states) in terms of mental or emotional forces or processes 3 : motivational forces acting esp. at the unconscious level — **psy·cho·dy·nam·ic** \-mik\ adj — **psy·cho·dy·nam·i·cal·ly** \-mi-k(ə-)lē\ adv

psy·cho·gen·e·sis \-'je-nə-səs\ n [NL] (1838) 1 : the origin and development of mental functions, traits, or states 2 : development from mental as distinguished from physical origins — **psy·cho·ge·net·ic** \-jə-'ne-tik\ adj

psy·cho·gen·ic \-'je-nik\ adj (1902) : originating in the mind or in mental or emotional conflict — **psy·cho·gen·i·cal·ly** \-ni-k(ə-)lē\ adv

psy·cho·graph \'sī-kə-ˌgraf\ n (1916) : PSYCHOBIOGRAPHY

psy·cho·his·to·ry \ˌsī-kō-ˌhis-t(ə-)rē\ n (1934) : historical analysis or interpretation employing psychological and psychoanalytic methods; also : a work of history employing such methods — **psy·cho·his·to·ri·an** \ˌsī-kō-(h)is-'tōr-ē-ən, -'tȯr-, -'tär-\ n — **psy·cho·his·to·ri·cal** \-'tȯr-i-kəl, -'tär-\ adj

psy·cho·ki·ne·sis \ˌsī-kō-kə-'nē-səs, -kī-\ n [NL] (1914) : movement of physical objects by the mind without use of physical means — compare PRECOGNITION, TELEKINESIS — **psy·cho·ki·net·ic** \-'ne-tik\ adj

psy·cho·lin·guis·tics \ˌsī-kō-liŋ-'gwis-tiks\ n pl but sing in constr (1936) : the study of the mental faculties involved in the perception, production, and acquisition of language — **psy·cho·lin·guist** \-'liŋ-gwist\ n — **psy·cho·lin·guis·tic** \-tik\ adj

psy·cho·log·i·cal \ˌsī-kə-'lä-ji-kəl\ also **psy·cho·log·ic** \-jik\ adj (ca. 1688) 1 a : of or relating to psychology b : MENTAL 2 : directed

toward the will or toward the mind specif. in its conative function ⟨∼ warfare⟩ — **psy·cho·log·i·cal·ly** \-ji-k(ə-)lē\ adv
psychological moment n (1871) : the occasion when the mental atmosphere is most certain to be favorable to the full effect of an action or event
psy·chol·o·gise Brit var of PSYCHOLOGIZE
psy·chol·o·gism \sī-ˈkä-lə-ˌji-zəm\ n (1858) : a theory that applies psychological conceptions to the interpretation of historical events or logical thought
psy·chol·o·gize \-ˌjiz\ vb -gized; -giz·ing vi (1810) : to speculate in psychological terms or on psychological motivations ∼ vt : to explain or interpret in psychological terms
psy·chol·o·gy \-jē\ n, pl -gies [NL psychologia, fr. psych- + -logia -logy] (1653) 1 : the science of mind and behavior 2 a : the mental or behavioral characteristics of an individual or group b : the study of mind and behavior in relation to a particular field of knowledge or activity 3 : a treatise on psychology — **psy·chol·o·gist** \-jist\ n
psy·cho·met·ric \ˌsī-kə-ˈme-trik\ adj (1854) : of or relating to psychometrics or psychometry — **psy·cho·met·ri·cal·ly** \-tri-k(ə-)lē\ adv
psy·cho·me·tri·cian \-mə-ˈtri-shən\ n (ca. 1939) 1 : a person (as a clinical psychologist) who is skilled in the administration and interpretation of objective psychological tests 2 : a psychologist who devises, constructs, and standardizes psychometric tests
psy·cho·met·rics \-ˈme-triks\ n pl but sing in constr (ca. 1924) : the psychological theory or technique of mental measurement
psy·chom·e·try \sī-ˈkä-mə-trē\ n (ca. 1842) 1 : divination of facts concerning an object or its owner through contact with or proximity to the object 2 : PSYCHOMETRICS
psy·cho·mo·tor \ˌsī-kə-ˈmō-tər\ adj [ISV] (1878) : of or relating to motor action directly proceeding from mental activity
psy·cho·neu·ro·sis \ˌsī-kō-n(y)u̇-ˈrō-səs, -nyu̇-\ n [NL] (1883) : NEUROSIS; esp : a neurosis based on emotional conflict in which an impulse that has been blocked seeks expression in a disguised response or symptom — **psy·cho·neu·rot·ic** \-ˈrä-tik\ adj or n
psy·cho·path \ˈsī-kə-ˌpath\ n [ISV] (1885) : a mentally ill or unstable person; esp : a person having a psychopathic personality
¹psy·cho·path·ic \ˌsī-kə-ˈpa-thik\ adj (1847) : of, relating to, or characterized by psychopathy — **psy·cho·path·i·cal·ly** \-thi-k(ə-)lē\ adv
²psychopathic n (ca. 1890) : PSYCHOPATH
psychopathic personality n (ca. 1923) 1 : an emotionally and behaviorally disordered state characterized by clear perception of reality except for the individual's social and moral obligations and often by the pursuit of immediate personal gratification in criminal acts, drug addiction, or sexual perversion 2 : an individual having a psychopathic personality
psy·cho·pa·thol·o·gy \ˌsī-kō-pə-ˈthä-lə-jē, -pa-\ n [ISV] (1847) : the study of psychological and behavioral dysfunction occurring in mental disorder or in social disorganization; also : such dysfunction — **psy·cho·path·o·log·ic** \-ˌpa-thə-ˈlä-jik\ or **psy·cho·path·o·log·i·cal** \-ji-kəl\ adj — **psy·cho·path·o·log·i·cal·ly** \-ji-k(ə-)lē\ adv — **psy·cho·pa·thol·o·gist** \-pə-ˈthä-lə-jist, -pa-\ n
psy·chop·a·thy \sī-ˈkä-pə-thē\ n [ISV] (1847) : mental disorder; esp : extreme mental disorder marked usu. by egocentric and antisocial activity
psy·cho·phar·ma·col·o·gy \ˌsī-kō-ˌfär-mə-ˈkä-lə-jē\ n (1920) : the study of the effect of drugs on the mind and behavior — **psy·cho·phar·ma·co·log·i·cal** \-mə-kə-ˈlä-ji-kəl\ or **psy·cho·phar·ma·co·log·ic** \-jik\ adj — **psy·cho·phar·ma·col·o·gist** \-ˈkä-lə-jist\ n
psy·cho·phys·i·cal \ˌsī-kō-ˈfi-zi-kəl\ adj (1847) : of or relating to psychophysics; also : sharing mental and physical qualities — **psy·cho·phys·i·cal·ly** \-k(ə-)lē\ adv
psychophysical parallelism n (1894) : PARALLELISM 4
psy·cho·phys·ics \ˌsī-kō-ˈfi-ziks\ n pl but sing in constr [ISV] (1878) : a branch of psychology concerned with the effect of physical processes (as intensity of stimulation) on the mental processes of an organism — **psy·cho·phys·i·cist** \-ˈfi-zə-sist, -ˈfiz-sist\ n
psy·cho·phys·i·o·log·i·cal \ˌsī-kō-ˌfi-zē-ə-ˈlä-ji-kəl\ also **psy·cho·phys·i·o·log·ic** \-jik\ adj (1839) 1 : of or relating to physiological psychology 2 : combining or involving mental and bodily processes — **psy·cho·phys·i·o·log·i·cal·ly** \-ji-k(ə-)lē\ adv
psy·cho·phys·i·ol·o·gy \-ˌfi-zē-ˈä-lə-jē\ n [ISV] (1839) : PHYSIOLOGICAL PSYCHOLOGY — **psy·cho·phys·i·ol·o·gist** \-jist\ n
psy·cho·sex·u·al \-ˈsek-shə-wəl, -shwəl, -shəl\ adj (1897) 1 : of or relating to the mental, emotional, and behavioral aspects of sexual development 2 : of or relating to mental or emotional attitudes concerning sexual activity 3 : of or relating to the physiological psychology of sex — **psy·cho·sex·u·al·ly** adv
psy·cho·sex·u·al·i·ty \-ˌsek-shə-ˈwa-lə-tē\ n (1910) : the psychic factors of sex
psy·cho·sis \sī-ˈkō-səs\ n, pl -cho·ses \-ˌsēz\ [NL] (1847) : fundamental mental derangement (as schizophrenia) characterized by defective or lost contact with reality
psy·cho·so·cial \ˌsī-kō-ˈsō-shəl\ adj (1899) 1 : involving both psychological and social aspects ⟨∼ adjustment in marriage⟩ 2 : relating social conditions to mental health ⟨∼ medicine⟩ — **psy·cho·so·cial·ly** \-ˈsō-sh(ə-)lē\ adv
psy·cho·so·mat·ic \-sə-ˈma-tik\ adj [ISV] (1863) 1 : of, relating to, concerned with, or involving both mind and body ⟨the ∼ nature of man —Herbert Ratner⟩ 2 : of, relating to, involving, or concerned with bodily symptoms caused by mental or emotional disturbance ⟨∼ illness⟩ ⟨∼ medicine⟩ — **psy·cho·so·mat·i·cal·ly** \-ti-k(ə-)lē\ adv
psy·cho·so·mat·ics \-sə-ˈma-tiks\ n pl but sing in constr (1938) : a branch of medical science dealing with interrelationships between the mind or emotions and the body and esp. with the relation of psychic conflict to somatic symptomatology
psy·cho·sur·gery \-ˈsər-jə-rē, -ˈsərj-rē\ n (1936) : cerebral surgery employed in treating psychic symptoms — **psy·cho·sur·geon** \-ˈsər-jən\ n — **psy·cho·sur·gi·cal** \-ˈsər-ji-kəl\ adj
psy·cho·syn·the·sis \-ˈsin(t)-thə-səs\ n (1919) : a form of psychotherapy combining psychoanalytic techniques with meditation and exercise
psy·cho·ther·a·peu·tic \-ˌther-ə-ˈpyü-tik\ adj [ISV] (ca. 1888) : of, relating to, or used in psychotherapy — **psy·cho·ther·a·peu·ti·cal·ly** \-ti-k(ə-)lē\ adv

psy·cho·ther·a·py \-ˈther-ə-pē\ n [ISV] (ca. 1890) : treatment of mental or emotional disorder or of related bodily ills by psychological means — **psy·cho·ther·a·pist** \-pist\ n
psy·chot·ic \sī-ˈkä-tik\ adj (ca. 1890) : of, relating to, marked by, or affected with psychosis ⟨a ∼ patient⟩ ⟨∼ behavior⟩ — **psychotic** n — **psy·chot·i·cal·ly** \-ti-k(ə-)lē\ adv
psy·choto·mi·met·ic \sī-ˌkä-tō-mə-ˈme-tik, -mī-\ adj [psychotic + -o- + mimetic] (1957) : of, relating to, involving, or inducing psychotic alteration of behavior and personality ⟨∼ drugs⟩ — **psychotomimetic** n — **psy·choto·mi·met·i·cal·ly** \-ti-k(ə-)lē\ adv
psy·cho·tro·pic \ˌsī-kə-ˈtrō-pik\ adj (1948) : acting on the mind ⟨∼ drugs⟩ — **psychotropic** n
psych–out \ˈsik-ˌau̇t\ n (1971) : an act or an instance of psyching someone out
psychro- comb form [Gk, fr. psychros, fr. psychein to cool] : cold ⟨psychrometer⟩
psy·chrom·e·ter \sī-ˈkrä-mə-tər\ n [ISV] (1838) : a hygrometer consisting essentially of two similar thermometers with the bulb of one being kept wet so that the cooling that results from evaporation makes it register a lower temperature than the dry one and with the difference between the readings constituting a measure of the dryness of the atmosphere — **psy·chro·met·ric** \ˌsī-krə-ˈme-trik\ adj — **psy·chrom·e·try** \sī-ˈkrä-mə-trē\ n
psy·chro·phil·ic \ˌsī-krō-ˈfi-lik\ adj (ca. 1903) : thriving at a relatively low temperature ⟨∼ bacteria⟩
psyl·la \ˈsi-lə\ n [NL, genus name, fr. Gk, flea; akin to L pulex flea, Skt plusi] (1852) : any of various plant lice (family Psyllidae) including economically important plant pests — compare PEAR PSYLLA
psyl·lid \si-ləd\ n [ultim. fr. NL Psylla] (1899) : PSYLLA — **psyllid** adj
psyl·li·um seed \ˈsi-lē-əm-\ n [NL psyllium, fr. Gk psyllion fleawort, fr. psylla] (1897) : the seed of a fleawort (esp. Plantago psyllium) that has the property of swelling and becoming gelatinous when moist and is used as a mild laxative — called also psyllium
psy·war \ˈsī-ˌwȯr\ n [by shortening] (1951) : psychological warfare
ptar·mi·gan \ˈtär-mi-gən\ n, pl -gan or -gans [modif. of ScGael tarmachan] (1599) : any of various grouses (genus Lagopus) of northern regions with completely feathered feet
PT boat \ˌpē-ˈtē-, ˈpē-\ n [patrol torpedo] (1941) : a small fast patrol craft usu. armed with torpedoes, machine guns, and depth charges — called also PT
PTC \ˌpē-(ˌ)tē-ˈsē\ n (1932) : PHENYLTHIOCARBAMIDE
pter·an·o·don \tə-ˈra-nə-ˌdän, -ˈrä-\ n [NL, fr. Gk pteron wing + anodōn toothless fr. an- + odōn, odous tooth — more at FEATHER, TOOTH] (1877) : any of a genus (Pteranodon) of Cretaceous pterosaurs having a backwardly directed bony crest on the skull and a wingspan of about 25 feet (7.7 meters)

ptarmigan: A summer plumage; B winter plumage

pterid- or **pterido-** comb form [Gk pterid-, pteris; akin to Gk pteron wing, feather] : fern ⟨pteridology⟩
pter·i·dine \ˈter-ə-ˌdēn\ n [ISV pterin + -idine] (ca. 1943) : a yellow crystalline bicyclic base C₆H₄N₄ that is a structural constituent esp. of various animal pigments
pter·i·dol·o·gy \ˌter-ə-ˈdä-lə-jē\ n (1855) : the study of ferns — **pter·i·do·log·i·cal** \ˌter-ə-də-ˈlä-ji-kəl\ adj — **pter·i·dol·o·gist** \-ˈdä-lə-jist\ n
pte·ri·do·phyte \tə-ˈri-də-ˌfīt, ˈter-ə-dō-\ n [NL Pteridophyta, fr. Gk pterid-, pteris fern + phyton plant — more at PHYT-] (1880) : any of a division (Pteridophyta) of vascular plants (as a fern) that have roots, stems, and leaves but lack flowers or seeds
pte·ri·do·sperm \tə-ˈri-də-ˌspərm, ˈter-ə-dō-\ n [ISV] (1904) : SEED FERN
pter·in \ˈter-ən\ n [ISV pter- (fr. Gk pteron wing) + ¹-in; fr. its being a factor in the pigments of butterfly wings] (1934) : any of various compounds that contain the bicyclic ring system characteristic of pteridine
ptero·dac·tyl \ˌter-ə-ˈdak-t⁵l\ n [NL Pterodactylus, genus of reptiles, fr. Gk pteron wing + daktylos finger — more at FEATHER] (1830) : any of various pterosaurs (suborder Pterodactyloidea) of the Late Jurassic and Cretaceous having a rudimentary tail and a beak with reduced dentition; broadly : PTEROSAUR
ptero·pod \ˈter-ə-ˌpäd\ n [NL Pteropoda, group name, fr. Gk pteron wing + NL -poda] (1835) : any of the opisthobranch mollusks comprising two orders (Thecosomata and Gymnosomata) and having the anterior lobes of the foot expanded into broad thin winglike swimming organs
ptero·saur \ˈter-ə-ˌsȯr\ n [NL Pterosauria, fr. Gk pteron wing + sauros lizard] (1862) : any of an order (Pterosauria) of extinct flying reptiles existing from the Late Triassic throughout the Jurassic and most of the Cretaceous and having a featherless wing membrane extending from the side of the body along the arm to the end of the greatly elongated fourth digit
pter·o·yl·glu·tam·ic acid \ˌter-ə-ˌwil-glü-ˈta-mik-\ n [ISV pteroyl (the radical (C₁₃H₁₁N₅O₃)CO) + glutamic acid] (1943) : FOLIC ACID
¹pter·y·goid \ˈter-ə-ˌgȯid\ adj [NL pterygoides, fr. Gk pterygoeidēs, lit., shaped like a wing, fr. pteryg-, pteryx wing; akin to Gk pteron wing — more at FEATHER] (1722) : of, relating to, or lying in the region of the inferior part of the sphenoid bone of the vertebrate skull
²pterygoid n (1831) : a pterygoid part (as a bone, muscle, or nerve)
pterygoid process n (1741) : a process extending downward from each side of the sphenoid bone in humans and other mammals

---

\ə\ abut \ᵊ\ kitten, F table \ər\ further \a\ ash \ā\ ace \ä\ mop, mar \au̇\ out \ch\ chin \e\ bet \ē\ easy \g\ go \i\ hit \ī\ ice \j\ job \ŋ\ sing \ō\ go \ȯ\ law \ȯi\ boy \th\ thin \th\ the \ü\ loot \u̇\ foot \y\ yet \zh\ vision \à, k̲, ⁿ, œ, œ̄, ᴜᴇ, ᵫ, ʸ\ see Guide to Pronunciation

pter·y·la \'ter-ə-lə\ *n, pl* **-lae** \-,lē, -,lī\ [NL, fr. Gk *pteron* + *hylē* wood, forest] (1867) : one of the definite areas of the skin of a bird on which feathers grow

Ptol·e·ma·ic \,tä-lə-'mā-ik\ *adj* [Gk *Ptolemaikos*, fr. *Ptolemaios* Ptolemy] (1674) **1** : of or relating to Ptolemy the geographer and astronomer who flourished at Alexandria about A.D. 130 **2** : of or relating to the Greco-Egyptian Ptolemies ruling Egypt from 323 to 30 B.C.

Ptolemaic system *n* (ca. 1771) : the system of planetary motions according to which the earth is at the center with the sun, moon, and planets revolving around it

pto·maine \'tō-,mān, tō-'\ *n* [It *ptomaina*, fr. Gk *ptōma* fall, fallen body, corpse, fr. *piptein* to fall — more at FEATHER] (1880) : any of various organic bases which are formed by the action of putrefactive bacteria on nitrogenous matter and some of which are poisonous

ptomaine poisoning *n* (1893) : food poisoning caused by bacteria or bacterial products

pto·sis \'tō-səs\ *n, pl* **pto·ses** \-,sēz\ [NL, fr. Gk *ptōsis* act of falling, fr. *piptein*] (1743) : a sagging or prolapse of an organ or part; *esp* : a drooping of the upper eyelid

pty·a·lin \'tī-ə-lən\ *n* [Gk *ptyalon* saliva, fr. *ptyein* to spit — more at SPEW] (1845) : an amylase found in the saliva of many animals that converts starch into sugar

pty·a·lism \-,li-zəm\ *n* [NL *ptyalismus*, fr. Gk *ptyalismos*, fr. *ptyalizein* to salivate, fr. *ptyalon*] (1676) : an excessive flow of saliva

p-type \'pē-,tip\ *adj* [*positive type*] (1946) : relating to or being a semiconductor in which charge is carried by holes — compare N-TYPE

pub \'pəb\ *n* (ca. 1859) **1** *chiefly Brit* : PUBLIC HOUSE 2 **2** : an establishment where alcoholic beverages are sold and consumed

pub crawler *n* (1910) : one who goes from bar to bar — **pub–crawl** *vi* — **pub crawl** *n*

pu·ber·tal \'pyü-bər-t²l\ *or* **pu·ber·al** \'pyü-bə-rəl\ *adj* [*pubertal* fr. *puberty; puberal* fr. ML *puberalis*, fr. L *puber*] (ca. 1837) : of or relating to puberty

pu·ber·ty \'pyü-bər-tē\ *n* [ME *puberte*, fr. L *pubertas*, fr. *puber* pubescent] (14c) **1** : the condition of being or the period of becoming first capable of reproducing sexually marked by maturing of the genital organs, development of secondary sex characteristics, and in the human and in higher primates by the first occurrence of menstruation in the female **2** : the age at which puberty occurs often construed legally as 14 in boys and 12 in girls

pu·ber·u·lent \pyü-'ber-ə-lənt, -yə-lənt\ *adj* [L *puber* pubescent + E *-ulent* (as in *pulverulent*)] (ca. 1859) : covered with fine pubescence

pu·bes \'pyü-(,)bēz\ *n, pl* **pubes** [NL, fr. L, manhood, body hair, pubic region; akin to L *puber* pubescent] (ca. 1570) **1** : the hair that appears on the lower part of the hypogastric region at puberty **2** : the pubic region

pu·bes·cence \pyü-'be-s²n(t)s\ *n* (15c) **1** : the quality or state of being pubescent **2** : a pubescent covering or surface

pu·bes·cent \-s²nt\ *adj* [L *pubescent-, pubescens*, prp. of *pubescere* to reach puberty, become covered as with hair, fr. *pubes*] (1646) **1 a** : arriving at or having reached puberty **b** : of or relating to puberty **2** : covered with fine soft short hairs — compare VILLOUS

pu·bic \'pyü-bik\ *adj* (1831) : of, relating to, or situated in or near the region of the pubes or the pubis

pu·bis \'pyü-bəs\ *n, pl* **pubes** \-(,)bēz\ [NL *os pubis*, lit., bone of the pubic region] (1597) : the ventral and anterior of the three principal bones composing either half of the pelvis — called also *pubic bone*

¹**pub·lic** \'pə-blik\ *adj* [ME *publique*, fr. MF, fr. L *publicus*; akin to L *populus* the people] (14c) **1 a** : exposed to general view : OPEN **b** : WELL-KNOWN, PROMINENT **c** : PERCEPTIBLE, MATERIAL **2 a** : of, relating to, or affecting all the people or the whole area of a nation or state ⟨~ law⟩ **b** : of or relating to a government **c** : of, relating to, or being in the service of the community or nation **3 a** : of or relating to people in general : UNIVERSAL **b** : GENERAL, POPULAR **4** : of or relating to business or community interests as opposed to private affairs : SOCIAL **5** : devoted to the general or national welfare : HUMANITARIAN **6 a** : accessible to or shared by all members of the community **b** : capitalized in shares that can be freely traded on the open market — often used with *go* — **pub·lic·ness** *n*

²**public** *n* (15c) **1** : a place accessible or visible to the public — usu. used in the phrase *in public* **2** : the people as a whole : POPULACE **3** : a group of people having common interests or characteristics; *specif* : the group at which a particular activity or enterprise aims

public–address system *n* (1923) : an apparatus including a microphone and loudspeakers used for broadcasting to a large audience in an auditorium or outdoors

pub·li·can \'pə-bli-kən\ *n* [ME, fr. OF, fr. L *publicanus* tax farmer, fr. *publicum* public revenue, fr. neut. of *publicus*] (13c) **1 a** : a Jewish tax collector for the ancient Romans **b** : a collector of taxes or tribute **2** *chiefly Brit* : the licensee of a public house

public assistance *n* (1884) : government aid to needy, blind, aged, or disabled persons and to dependent children

pub·li·ca·tion \,pə-blə-'kā-shən\ *n* [ME *publicacioun*, fr. MF *publication*, fr. L *publication-, publicatio*, fr. *publicare*, fr. *publicus* public] (14c) **1** : the act or process of publishing **2** : a published work

public defender *n* (1918) : a lawyer usu. holding public office whose duty is to defend accused persons unable to pay for legal assistance

public domain *n* (1832) **1** : land owned directly by the government **2** : the realm embracing property rights that belong to the community at large, are unprotected by copyright or patent, and are subject to appropriation by anyone

public health *n* (1617) : the art and science dealing with the protection and improvement of community health by organized community effort and including preventive medicine and sanitary and social science

public house *n* (1658) **1** : INN, HOSTELRY **2** *chiefly Brit* : a licensed saloon or bar

pub·li·cise *Brit var of* PUBLICIZE

pub·li·cist \'pə-blə-sist\ *n* (1792) **1 a** : an expert in international law **b** : an expert or commentator on public affairs **2** : one that publicizes; *specif* : PRESS AGENT

pub·lic·i·ty \(,)pə-'bli-sə-tē, -'blis-tē\ *n* (1791) **1** : the quality or state of being public **2 a** : an act or device designed to attract public interest; *specif* : information with news value issued as a means of gaining

public attention or support **b** : the dissemination of information or promotional material **c** : paid advertising **d** : public attention or acclaim

pub·li·cize \'pə-blə-,sīz\ *vt* **-cized; -ciz·ing** (1925) : to bring to the attention of the public : ADVERTISE

public land *n* (1789) : land owned by a government; *specif* : that part of the U.S. public domain subject to sale or disposal under the homestead laws

public law *n* (1773) **1** : a legislative enactment affecting the public at large **2** : a branch of law concerned with regulating the relations of individuals with the government and the organization and conduct of the government itself — compare PRIVATE LAW

pub·lic·ly \'pə-bli-klē\ *also* **pub·li·cal·ly** \-li-k(ə-)lē\ *adv* (1567) **1** : in a manner observable by or in a place accessible to the public : OPENLY **2 a** : by the people generally **b** : by a government

public officer *n* (1925) : a person who has been legally elected or appointed to office and who exercises governmental functions

public relations *n pl but usu sing in constr, often attrib* (1807) : the business of inducing the public to have understanding for and goodwill toward a person, firm, or institution; *also* : the degree of understanding and goodwill achieved

public sale *n* (1678) : AUCTION 1

public school *n* (1580) **1** : an endowed secondary boarding school in Great Britain offering a classical curriculum and preparation for the universities or public service **2** : a free tax-supported school contolled by a local governmental authority

public servant *n* (1676) : a government official or employee

public service *n* (ca. 1576) **1** : the business of supplying a commodity (as electricity or gas) or service (as transportation) to any or all members of a community **2** : a service rendered in the public interest **3** : governmental employment; *esp* : CIVIL SERVICE

public–service corporation *n* (1904) : a quasi-public corporation

public speaking *n* (1762) **1** : the act or process of making speeches in public **2** : the art of effective oral communication with an audience

public–spirited *adj* (1677) : motivated by devotion to the general welfare — **pub·lic–spir·it·ed·ness** *n*

public television *n* (1965) : television supported by public funds and private contributions rather than by commercials

public utility *n* (1903) : a business organization (as an electric company) performing a public service and subject to special governmental regulation

public works *n pl* (1676) : works (as schools, highways, docks) constructed for public use or enjoyment esp. when financed and owned by the government

pub·lish \'pə-blish\ *vb* [ME, modif. of MF *publier*, fr. L *publicare*, fr. *publicus* public] *vt* (14c) **1 a** : to make generally known **b** : to make public announcement of **2 a** : to disseminate to the public **b** : to produce or release for distribution; *specif* : PRINT 2c **c** : to issue the work of (an author) ~ *vi* **1** : to put out an edition **2** : to have one's work accepted for publication — **pub·lish·able** \-bli-shə-bəl\ *adj*

pub·lish·er \'pə-bli-shər\ *n* (15c) : one that publishes something; *esp* : a person or corporation whose business is publishing

pub·lish·ing \-shiŋ\ *n* (1580) : the business or profession of the commercial production and issuance of literature, information, musical scores or sometimes recordings, or art ⟨newspaper ~⟩ ⟨software ~⟩

puc·coon \(,)pə-'kün\ *n* [Virginia Algonquian *poughkone*] (1612) **1** : any of several American plants (as bloodroot) yielding a red or yellow pigment **2** : a pigment from a puccoon

puce \'pyüs\ *n* [F, lit., flea, fr. L *pulic-, pulex* — more at PSYLLA] (1882) : a dark red

¹**puck** \'pək\ *n* [ME *puke*, fr. OE *pūca*; akin to ON *pūki* devil] (bef. 12c) **1** *archaic* : an evil spirit : DEMON **2** : a mischievous sprite : HOBGOBLIN; *specif, cap* : ROBIN GOODFELLOW

²**puck** *n* [E dial. *puck* to poke, hit, prob. fr. Ir *poc* butt, stroke in hurling, lit., buck (male deer)] (1891) : a vulcanized rubber disk used in ice hockey

pucka *var of* PUKKA

¹**puck·er** \'pə-kər\ *vb* **puck·ered; puck·er·ing** \-k(ə-)riŋ\ [prob. irreg. fr. ¹*poke*] *vi* (1598) : to become wrinkled or constricted ~ *vt* : to contract into folds or wrinkles

²**pucker** *n* (ca. 1750) : a fold or wrinkle in a normally even surface

puck·ery \'pə-k(ə-)rē\ *adj* (1748) : that puckers or causes puckering

puck·ish \'pə-kish\ *adj* [¹*puck*] (1874) : IMPISH, WHIMSICAL — **puck·ish·ly** *adv* — **puck·ish·ness** *n*

pud \'püd\ *n* (1706) *Brit* : PUDDING

pud·ding \'pu̇-diŋ\ *n* [ME] (13c) **1** : BLOOD SAUSAGE **2 a** (1) : a boiled or baked soft food usu. with a cereal base ⟨corn ~⟩ (2) : a dessert of a soft, spongy, or thick creamy consistency ⟨chocolate ~⟩ (3) *Brit* : DESSERT 1 **b** : a dish often containing suet or having a suet crust and orig. boiled in a bag ⟨steak and kidney ~⟩

pudding stone *n* (1753) : CONGLOMERATE

¹**pud·dle** \'pə-d²l\ *n* [ME *podel*; akin to LG *pudel* puddle, OE *pudd* ditch] (14c) **1** : a very small pool of usu. dirty or muddy water **2 a** : an earthy mixture (as of clay, sand, and gravel) worked while wet into a compact mass that becomes impervious to water when dry **b** : a thin mixture of soil and water for puddling plants

²**puddle** *vb* **pud·dled; pud·dling** \'pəd-liŋ, 'pə-d²l-iŋ\ *vi* (15c) : to dabble or wade around in a puddle ~ *vt* **1** : to make muddy or turbid : MUDDLE **2 a** : to work (a wet mixture of earth or concrete) into a dense impervious mass **b** : to subject (iron) to the process of puddling **3 a** : to strew with puddles **b** : to compact (soil) esp. by working when too wet **c** : to dip the roots of (a plant) in a thin mud before transplanting — **pud·dler** \'pəd-lər, 'pə-d²l-ər\ *n*

puddle duck *n* (1877) : DABBLER b

puddle jumper *n* (1942) *slang* : LIGHTPLANE

pud·dling \'pəd-liŋ, 'pə-d²l-iŋ\ *n* (1839) : the process of converting pig iron into wrought iron or rarely steel by subjecting it to heat and frequent stirring in a furnace in the presence of oxidizing substances

pu·den·cy \'pyü-d²n(t)-sē\ *n* [L *pudentia*, fr. *pudent-, pudens*, prp. of *pudēre* to be ashamed, be ashamed] (1611) : MODESTY

pu·den·dum \pyü-'den-dəm\ *n, pl* **-da** \-də\ [NL, sing. of L *pudenda*, fr. neut. pl. of *pudendus*, gerundive of *pudēre* to be ashamed] (1634) : the external genital organs of a human being and esp. of a woman — usu. used in pl. — **pu·den·dal** \-d²l\ *adj*

pudgy \'pə-jē\ *adj* **pudg·i·er; -est** [origin unknown] (1836) : being short and plump : CHUBBY — **pudg·i·ness** *n*
pu·di·bund \'pyü-də-ˌbənd\ *adj* [L *pudibundus*, fr. *pudēre* to be ashamed + *-bundus* (as in *moribundus* moribund)] (ca. 1656) : PRUDISH
pueb·lo \'pwe-(ˌ)blō; pü-'e-, pyü-\ *n, pl* **-los** [Sp, village, lit., people, fr. L *populus*] (1808) **1 a** : the communal dwelling of an Indian village of Arizona, New Mexico, and adjacent areas consisting of contiguous flat-roofed stone or adobe houses in groups sometimes several stories high **b** : an Indian village of the southwestern U.S. **2** *cap* : a member of a group of Indian peoples of the southwestern U.S.
pu·er·ile \'pyü-(ə)r-əl, -,il\ *adj* [F or L; F *puéril*, fr. L *puerilis*, fr. *puer* boy, child; akin to Skt *putra* son, child and perh. to Gk *pais* boy, child — more at FEW] (1661) **1** : JUVENILE **2** : CHILDISH. SILLY ⟨∼ remarks⟩ — **pu·er·ile·ly** \-ə(l)-lē, -ˌīl-lē\ *adv* — **pu·er·il·i·ty** \ˌpyü-(ə)r-'i-lə-tē\ *n*
pu·er·il·ism \'pyü-(ə)r-ə-ˌli-zəm, 'pyü(-ə)r-ˌi-\ *n* (1924) : childish behavior esp. as a symptom of mental disorder
pu·er·per·al \pyü-'ər-p(ə-)rəl\ *adj* [L *puerpera* woman in childbirth, fr. *puer* child + *parere* to give birth to — more at PARE] (1768) : of, relating to, or occurring during childbirth or the period immediately following ⟨∼ infection⟩ ⟨∼ depression⟩
puerperal fever *n* (1768) : an abnormal condition that results from infection of the placental site following delivery or abortion and is characterized in mild form by fever but in serious cases the infection may spread through the uterine wall or pass into the bloodstream — called also *childbed fever, puerperal sepsis*
pu·er·pe·ri·um \ˌpyü-ər-'pir-ē-əm\ *n, pl* **-ria** \-ē-ə\ [L, fr. *puerpera*] (ca. 1890) : the period between childbirth and the return of the uterus to its normal size
1puff \'pəf\ *vb* [ME, fr. OE *pyffan*, of imit. origin] *vi* (bef. 12c) **1 a** (1) : to blow in short gusts (2) : to exhale forcibly **b** : to breathe hard : PANT **c** : to emit small whiffs or clouds (as of smoke) often as an accompaniment to vigorous action ⟨∼ at a pipe⟩ **2** : to speak or act in a scornful, conceited, or exaggerated manner **3 a** : to become distended : SWELL — usu. used with *up* **b** : to open or appear in or as if in a puff **4** : to form a chromosomal puff ∼ *vt* **1 a** : to emit, propel, blow, or expel by or as if by puffs : WAFT **b** : to draw on (as a cigar, cigarette, or pipe) with intermittent exhalations of smoke **2 a** : to distend with or as if with air or gas : INFLATE **b** : to make proud or conceited : ELATE **c** (1) : to praise extravagantly and usu. with exaggeration (2) : ADVERTISE
2puff *n* (13c) **1 a** : an act or instance of puffing : WHIFF **b** : a slight explosive sound accompanying a puff **c** : a perceptible cloud or aura emitted in a puff **d** : DRAW 1a **2 a** : a light round hollow pastry **3 a** : a slight swelling : PROTUBERANCE **b** : a fluffy mass: as (1) : POUF 2 (2) : a small fluffy pad for applying cosmetic powder (3) : a soft loose roll of hair (4) : a quilted bed covering **4** : a commendatory or promotional notice or review **5** : an enlarged region of a chromosome that is associated with intensely active genes involved in RNA synthesis — **puff·i·ness** \'pə-fē-nəs\ *n* — **puffy** \'pə-fē\ *adj*
puff adder *n* (1789) **1** : a thick-bodied extremely venomous African viper (*Bitis arietans*) **2** : HOGNOSE SNAKE
puff·ball \'pəf-,bȯl\ *n* (1649) : any of various globose and often edible fungi (esp. family Lycoperdaceae) that discharge ripe spores in a smokelike cloud when pressed or struck
puff·er \'pə-fər\ *n* (1629) **1** : one that puffs **2 a** : any of a family (Tetraodontidae) of chiefly tropical marine bony fishes which can distend themselves to a globular form and most of which are highly poisonous — called also *blowfish, globefish* **b** : any of various fish of the same order (Tetraodontiformes syn. Plectognathi) as the puffers
puff·ery \'pə-f(ə-)rē\ *n* (1782) : exaggerated commendation esp. for promotional purposes : HYPE

puffer 2a

puf·fin \'pə-fən\ *n* [ME *pophyn*] (14c) : any of several seabirds (genera *Fratercula* and *Lunda*) having a short neck and a deep grooved partly colored laterally compressed bill
puff pastry *n* (1611) : a pastry dough containing many alternating layers of butter and dough or the light flaky pastry made from it — called also *puff paste*
1pug \'pəg\ *n* [obs. *pug* hobgoblin, monkey] (1789) **1** : a small sturdy compact dog of a breed of Asian origin with a close coat, tightly curled tail, and broad wrinkled face **2 a** : PUG NOSE **b** : a close knot or coil of hair : BUN
2pug *vt* **pugged; pug·ging** [origin unknown] (1843) : to work and mix (as clay) when wet esp. to make more homogeneous and easier to handle (as in throwing or molding wares)
3pug *n* [by shortening & alter. fr. *puglist*] (1858) : 1BOXER 1
4pug *n* [Hindi *pag* foot] (1865) : FOOTPRINT; *esp* : a print of a wild mammal
pug·ga·ree *or* **pug·a·ree** *or* **pug·gree** \'pə-g(ə-)rē\ *n* [Hindi *pagri* turban] (1665) : a light scarf wrapped around a sun helmet or used as a hatband
pu·gi·lism \'pyü-jə-ˌli-zəm\ *n* [L *pugil* boxer; akin to L *pugnus* fist — more at PUNGENT] (1791) : 2BOXING — **pu·gi·lis·tic** \ˌpyü-jə-'lis-tik\ *adj*
pu·gi·list \'pyü-jə-list\ *n* (1790) : FIGHTER; *esp* : a professional boxer
pug·mark \'pəg-ˌmärk\ *n* (1922) : 4PUG
pug mill *n* [2pug] (1824) : a machine in which materials (as clay and water) are mixed, blended, or kneaded into a desired consistency
pug·na·cious \ˌpəg-'nä-shəs\ *adj* [L *pugnac-, pugnax*, fr. *pugnare* to fight — more at PUNGENT] (1642) : having a quarrelsome or combative nature : TRUCULENT *syn* see BELLIGERENT — **pug·na·cious·ly** *adv* — **pug·na·cious·ness** *n* — **pug·nac·i·ty** \-'na-sə-tē\ *n*
pug nose *n* [1pug] (1778) : a nose having a slightly concave bridge and flattened nostrils — **pug-nosed** \'pəg-ˌnōzd\ *adj*
puis·ne \'pyü-nē\ *adj* [MF *puisné* younger — more at PUNY] (1688) *chiefly Brit* : inferior in rank ⟨∼ judge⟩ — **puisne** *n*

puis·sance \'pwi-s³n(t)s, 'pyü-ə-sən(t)s, pyü-'i-s³n(t)s\ *n* [ME, fr. MF, fr. OF, fr. *puissant* powerful, fr. *poeir* to be able, be powerful — more at POWER] (15c) : STRENGTH, POWER
puis·sant \-s³nt, -sənt\ *adj* (15c) : having puissance : POWERFUL
puke \'pyük\ *vb* **puked; puk·ing** [origin unknown] (1600) : VOMIT — **puke** *n*
puk·ka \'pə-kə\ *adj* [Hindi *pakkā* cooked, ripe, solid, fr. Skt *pakva; akin to Gk *pessein* to cook — more at COOK] (1698) : GENUINE. AUTHENTIC: *also* : FIRST-CLASS
pul \'pül\ *n, pl* **puls** \'pülz\ *or* **pul** [Per *pūl*] (1927) — see *afghani* at MONEY table
pu·la \'pü-lə, 'pyü-\ *n, pl* **pula** [Tswana, lit., rain (used as a greeting)] (1976) — see MONEY table
Pu·las·ki \pə-'las-kē, pyü-\ *n* [Edward C. *Pulaski*, 20th cent. Am. forest ranger] (1924) : a single-bit ax with an adze-shaped hoe extending from the back
pul·chri·tude \'pəl-krə-ˌtüd, -,tyüd\ *n* [ME, fr. L *pulchritudin-, pulchritudo*, fr. *pulchr-, pulcher* beautiful] (15c) : physical comeliness — **pul·chri·tu·di·nous** \ˌpəl-krə-'tüd-nəs, -'tyüd-; -'tü-d³n-əs, -'tyü-\ *adj*
pule \'pyü(ə)l\ *vi* **puled; pul·ing** [prob. imit.] (1534) : WHINE. WHIMPER
pu·li \'pü-lē, 'pyü-\ *n, pl* **pu·lik** \-lik\ *or* **pulis** \-lēz\ [Hung] (1936) : any of a breed of medium-sized Hungarian sheepdogs with a thick woolly coat hanging in long thin cords
Pu·lit·zer prize \'pu̇-lət-sər-, 'pyü-\ *n* (1918) : any of various annual prizes (as for outstanding literary or journalistic achievement) established by the will of Joseph Pulitzer — called also *Pulitzer*
1pull \'pu̇l *also* 'pəl\ *vb* [ME, fr. OE *pullian*; akin to MLG *pulen* to shell, cull] *vt* (bef. 12c) **1 a** : to exert force upon so as to cause or tend to cause motion toward the force **b** : to stretch (cooking candy) repeatedly ⟨∼ taffy⟩ **c** : to strain abnormally ⟨∼ a tendon⟩ **d** : to hold back (a racehorse) from winning **e** : to work (an oar) by drawing back strongly **2 a** : to draw out from the skin ⟨∼ feathers from a rooster's tail⟩ **b** : to pluck from a plant or by the roots ⟨∼ flowers⟩ ⟨∼ turnips⟩ **c** : EXTRACT ⟨∼ a tooth⟩ **3** : to hit (a ball) toward the left from a right-handed swing or toward the right from a left-handed swing — compare PUSH **4** : to draw apart : REND. TEAR **5** : to print (as a proof) by impression **6** : to remove from a place or situation ⟨∼ the engine⟩ ⟨∼ed the pitcher in the third inning⟩ ⟨∼ed the show⟩ **7** : to bring (a weapon) into the open ⟨∼ed a knife⟩ **8 a** : COMMIT. PERPETRATE ⟨∼ a robbery⟩ ⟨∼ a prank⟩ **b** : to carry out as an assignment or duty **9** : PUT ON. ASSUME ⟨∼ a grin⟩ **10 a** : to draw the support or attention of : ATTRACT ⟨∼ votes⟩ — often used with *in* **b** : OBTAIN. SECURE ⟨∼ed a B in the course⟩ **11** : to demand or obtain an advantage over someone by the assertion of ⟨∼ rank⟩ ∼ *vi* **1 a** : to use force in drawing, dragging, or tugging **b** : to move esp. through the exercise of mechanical energy ⟨the car ∼ed clear of the rut⟩ **c** (1) : to take a drink (2) : to draw hard in smoking ⟨∼ed at a pipe⟩ **d** : to strain against the bit **2** : to draw a gun **3** : to admit of being pulled **4** : to feel or express strong sympathy : ROOT ⟨∼ing for my team to win⟩ **5** *of an offensive lineman in football* : to move back from the line of scrimmage and toward one flank to provide blocking for a ballcarrier — **pull·er** *n* — **pull a fast one** : to perpetrate a trick or fraud — **pull punches** *also* **pull a punch** : to refrain from using all the force at one's disposal — **pull oneself together** : to regain one's composure — **pull one's leg** : to deceive someone playfully : HOAX — **pull one's weight** : to do one's full share of the work — **pull out all the stops** : to use all one's resources without restraint — **pull stakes** *or* **pull up stakes** : to move out : LEAVE — **pull strings** *also* **pull wires** : to exert hidden influence or control — **pull the plug** 1 : to disconnect a medical life-support system **2** : to withdraw essential esp. financial support — **pull the rug from under** : to weaken or unsettle esp. by removing support or assistance from — **pull the string** : to throw a change-up — **pull the wool over one's eyes** : to blind to the true situation : HOODWINK — **pull together** : to work in harmony : COOPERATE
2pull *n, often attrib* (14c) **1 a** : the act or an instance of pulling **b** (1) : a draft of liquid (2) : an inhalation of smoke **c** : the effort expended in moving ⟨∼ uphill⟩ **2** : force required to overcome resistance to pulling ⟨trigger ∼⟩ **2 a** : ADVANTAGE **b** : special influence **3** : PROOF 6a **4** : a device for pulling something or for operating by pulling ⟨drawer ∼⟩ **5** : a force that attracts, compels, or influences : ATTRACTION **6** : an injury resulting from abnormal straining or stretching ⟨a muscle ∼⟩ ⟨a groin ∼⟩
pull away *vi* (ca. 1934) **1** : to draw oneself back or away : WITHDRAW **2** : to move off or ahead
pull-back \'pu̇l-ˌbak\ *n* (1668) : a pulling back; *esp* : an orderly withdrawal of troops from a position or area
pull down *vt* (15c) **1 a** : DEMOLISH. DESTROY **b** : to hunt down : OVERCOME **2 a** : to bring to a lower level : REDUCE **b** : to depress in health, strength, or spirits **3** : to draw as wages or salary
pul·let \'pu̇-lət\ *n* [ME *polet* young fowl, fr. MF *poulet*, fr. OF, dim. of *poul* cock, fr. LL *pullus*, fr. L, young of an animal, chicken, sprout — more at FOAL] (14c) : a young hen; *specif* : a hen of the domestic chicken less than a year old
pul·ley \'pu̇-lē\ *n, pl* **pulleys** [ME *pouley*, fr. MF *poulie*, prob. ultim. fr. Gk *polos* axis, pole — more at POLE] (14c) **1** : a sheave or small wheel with a grooved rim and with or without the block in which it runs used singly with a rope or chain to change the direction and point of application of a pulling force and in various combinations to increase the applied force esp. for lifting weights **2** : a pulley or pulleys with ropes to form a tackle that constitutes one of the simple machines **3** : a wheel used to transmit power by means of a band, belt, cord, rope, or chain passing over its rim
pull in *vi* (1605) **1** : CHECK. RESTRAIN **2** : ARREST ∼ *vi* : to arrive at a destination or come to a stop

\ə\ abut \³\ kitten, F table \ər\ further \a\ ash \ā\ ace \ä\ mop, mar \au̇\ out \ch\ chin \e\ bet \ē\ easy \g\ go \i\ hit \ī\ ice \j\ job \ŋ\ sing \ō\ go \ȯ\ law \ȯi\ boy \th\ thin \t͟h\ the \ü\ loot \u̇\ foot \y\ yet \zh\ vision \ā, k̲, ⁿ, œ, œ̄, ue, ᵫ, ᵊ\ see Guide to Pronunciation

Pull·man \'pul-mən\ *n* [George M. *Pullman*] (1867)   **1** : a railroad passenger car with specially comfortable furnishings for day or esp. for night travel   **2** : a large suitcase

pull off *vt* (1883) : to carry out despite difficulties : accomplish successfully against odds

pul·lo·rum disease \pə-'lör-əm-, -'lòr-\ *n* [NL *pullorum* (specific epithet of *Salmonella pullorum*), fr. L, of chickens (gen. pl. of *pullus*)] (1929) : a destructive typically diarrheal salmonellosis esp. of young domestic chickens that is caused by a bacterium (*Salmonella pullorum*)

pull·out \'pul-,aut\ *n* (1825)   **1** : the act or an instance of pulling out: as   **a** : the action in which an airplane goes from a dive to horizontal flight   **b** : PULLBACK   **2** : something that can be pulled out

pull out *vi* (1855)   **1** : LEAVE, DEPART   **2** : WITHDRAW

¹**pull·over** \'pul-,ō-vər\ *n* (1899) : a pullover garment (as a sweater)

²**pullover** *adj* (1907) : put on by being pulled over the head

pull over *vi* (1930) : to steer one's vehicle to the side of the road ~ *vt* : to cause to pull over ⟨*pulled* him *over* for speeding⟩

pull round *vi* (1891) *chiefly Brit* : to regain one's health ~ *vt, chiefly Brit* : to restore to good health

pull tab *n* (1963) : a metal tab (as on a can) pulled to open the container

pull through *vi* (1852) : to survive a dangerous or difficult situation ~ *vt* : to help survive a dangerous or difficult situation

pul·lu·late \'pəl-yə-,lāt\ *vi* **-lat·ed; -lat·ing** [L *pullulatus*, pp. of *pullulare*, fr. *pullulus*, dim. of *pullus* chicken, sprout — more at FOAL] (1619)   **1 a** : GERMINATE, SPROUT   **b** : to breed or produce freely   **2** : SWARM, TEEM — **pul·lu·la·tion** \,pəl-yə-'lā-shən\ *n*

pull-up \'pul-,əp\ *n* (1938) : CHIN-UP

pull up *vt* (1623)   **1** : to bring to a stop : HALT   **2** : CHECK, REBUKE ~ *vi*   **1 a** : to check oneself   **b** : to come to an often abrupt halt : STOP   **2** : to draw even with others in a race

pul·mo·nary \'pul-mə-,ner-ē, 'pəl-\ *adj* [L *pulmonarius*, fr. *pulmon-, pulmo* lung; akin to Gk *pleumōn* lung, Skt *kloman* right lung] (1704)   **1** : relating to, functioning like, or associated with the lungs   **2** : PULMONATE   **3** : carried on by the lungs

pulmonary artery *n* (1704) : an artery that conveys venous blood from the heart to the lungs — see HEART illustration

pulmonary circulation *n* (ca. 1890) : the passage of blood from the right side of the heart through arteries to the lungs where it picks up oxygen and is returned to the left side of the heart by veins

pulmonary vein *n* (1704) : a valveless vein that returns oxygenated blood from the lungs to the heart

¹**pul·mo·nate** \'pul-mə-,nāt, 'pəl-\ *adj* [L *pulmon-, pulmo* lung] (ca. 1859)   **1** : having lungs or organs resembling lungs   **2** : of or relating to a subclass (Pulmonata) of gastropod mollusks having a respiratory sac and comprising most land snails and slugs and many freshwater snails

²**pulmonate** *n* (1883) : a pulmonate gastropod

pul·mon·ic \pul-'mä-nik, ,pəl-\ *adj* [L *Pulmotor, pulmo*] (1661) : PULMONARY

pul·mo·tor \'pul-,mō-tər, 'pəl-\ *n* [fr. *Pulmotor*, a trademark] (1911) : a respiratory apparatus for pumping oxygen or air into and out of the lungs (as of an asphyxiated person)

¹**pulp** \'pəlp\ *n* [ME *pulpe*, fr. MF *poulpe*, fr. L *pulpa* flesh, pulp] (14c)   **1 a** (1) : the soft, succulent part of a fruit usu. composed of mesocarp   (2) : stem pith when soft and spongy   **b** : a soft mass of vegetable matter (as of apples) from which most of the water has been extracted by pressure   **c** : the soft sensitive tissue that fills the central cavity of a tooth — see TOOTH illustration   **d** : a material prepared by chemical or mechanical means from various materials (as wood or rags) for use in making paper and cellulose products   **2** : pulverized ore mixed with water   **3 a** : pulpy condition or character   **b** : something in such a condition or having such a character   **4** : a magazine or book printed on cheap paper (as newsprint) and often dealing with sensational material — **pulp·i·ness** \'pəl-pē-nəs\ *n* — **pulpy** \'pəl-pē\ *adj*

²**pulp** *vt* (1683)   **1** : to reduce to pulp : cause to appear pulpy   **2** : to deprive of the pulp   **3** : to produce or reproduce (written matter) in pulp form ~ *vi* : to become pulp or pulpy — **pulp·er** *n*

pulp·al \'pəl-pəl\ *adj* (1903) : of or relating to pulp esp. of a tooth ⟨a ~ abscess⟩ — **pulp·al·ly** \'pəl-pə-lē\ *adv*

pul·pit \'pul-,pit *also* 'pəl-, -,pət\ *n* [ME, fr. L *pulpitum*, fr. L, staging, platform] (14c)   **1** : an elevated platform or high reading desk used in preaching or conducting a worship service   **2 a** : the preaching profession   **b** : a preaching position

pulp·wood \'pəlp-,wud\ *n* (1885) : a wood (as of aspen, hemlock, pine, or spruce) used in making pulp for paper

pul·que \'pül-,kā; 'pül-kē, 'pül-\ *n* [MexSp] (1693) : a Mexican alcoholic beverage made from the fermented sap of various agaves (as *Agave atrovirens*)

pul·sant \'pəl-sənt\ *adj* (1709) : pulsating with activity

pul·sar \'pəl-,sär\ *n* [*pulse* + *-ar* (as in *quasar*)] (1968) : a celestial source of pulsating electromagnetic radiation (as radio waves) characterized by a short relatively constant interval (as .033 second) between pulses that is held to be a rotating neutron star

pul·sate \'pəl-,sāt *also* ,pəl-'\ *vi* **pul·sat·ed; pul·sat·ing** [L *pulsatus*, pp. of *pulsare*, freq. of *pellere*] (1794)   **1** : to exhibit a pulse or pulsation : BEAT   **2** : to throb or move rhythmically : VIBRATE

pul·sa·tile \'pəl-sə-t°l, -,til\ *adj* (1541) : of or marked by pulsation

pul·sa·tion \,pəl-'sā-shən\ *n* (1541)   **1** : rhythmical throbbing or vibrating (as of an artery); *also* : a single beat or throb   **2** : a periodically recurring alternate increase and decrease of a quantity (as pressure, volume, or voltage)

pul·sa·tor \'pəl-,sā-tər, ,pəl-'\ *n* (1890) : something that beats or throbs in working

¹**pulse** \'pəls\ *n* [ME *puls*, fr. OF *pouls* porridge, fr. L *pult-, puls*, prob. fr. Gk *poltos*] (13c) : the edible seeds of various leguminous crops (as peas, beans, or lentils); *also* : a plant yielding pulse

²**pulse** *n* [ME *puls*, fr. MF *pouls*, fr. L *pulsus*, lit., beating, fr. *pellere* to drive, push, beat — more at FELT] (14c)   **1 a** : a regular throbbing caused in the arteries by the contractions of the heart   **b** : the palpable beat resulting from such pulse as detected in a superficial artery; *also* : the number of individual beats in a specified time period (as one minute) ⟨a resting ~ of 70⟩   **2 a** : underlying sentiment or opinion or an

indication of it   **b** : VITALITY   **3 a** : rhythmical beating, vibrating, or sounding   **b** : BEAT, THROB   **4 a** : a transient variation of a quantity (as electrical current or voltage) whose value is normally constant   **b** (1) : an electromagnetic wave or modulation thereof of brief duration   (2) : a brief disturbance of pressure in a medium; *esp* : a sound wave or short train of sound waves   **5** : a dose of a substance esp. when applied over a short period of time ⟨*pulse*-labeled DNA⟩

³**pulse** *vb* **pulsed; puls·ing** *vi* (15c) : to exhibit a pulse or pulsation : THROB ~ *vt*   **1** : to drive by or as if by a pulsation   **2** : to cause to pulsate   **3 a** : to produce or modulate (as electromagnetic waves) in the form of pulses ⟨*pulsed* waves⟩   **b** : to cause (an apparatus) to produce pulses — **puls·er** *n*

pulse–jet engine \'pəls-'jet-\ *n* (1949) : a jet engine designed to produce a pulsating thrust by the intermittent flow of hot gases

pul·ver·a·ble \'pəl-və-rə-bəl, 'pəlv-rə-\ *adj* (ca. 1617) : capable of being pulverized

pul·ver·ise *Brit var of* PULVERIZE

pul·ver·ize \'pəl-və-,rīz\ *vb* **-ized; -iz·ing** [ME, fr. MF *pulveriser*, fr. LL *pulverizare*, fr. L *pulver-, pulvis* dust, powder — more at POWDER] *vt* (15c)   **1** : to reduce (as by crushing, beating, or grinding) to very small particles : ATOMIZE   **2** : ANNIHILATE, DEMOLISH ~ *vi* : to become pulverized — **pul·ver·iz·able** \,pəl-və-'rī-zə-bəl\ *adj* — **pul·ver·i·za·tion** \,pəl-və-rə-'zā-shən, ,pəlv-rə-\ *n* — **pul·ver·iz·er** \'pəl-və-,rī-zər\ *n*

pul·ver·u·lent \,pəl-'ver-yə-lənt, -'ver-ə-\ *adj* [L *pulverulentus* dusty, fr. *pulver-, pulvis*] (ca. 1656)   **1** : consisting of or reducible to fine powder   **2** : being or looking dusty : CRUMBLY

pul·vil·lus \,pəl-'vi-ləs\ *n, pl* **-vil·li** \-'vi-,lī, -,(,)lē\ [NL, fr. L, dim. of *pulvinus*] (ca. 1826) : one of the lobed hairy adhesive organs that terminate the feet of dipteran flies

pul·vi·nus \,pəl-'vī-nəs, -'vē-\ *n, pl* **-vi·ni** \-'vī-,nī, -'vē-(,)nē\ [NL, fr. L, cushion] (1857) : a mass of large thin-walled cells surrounding a vascular strand at the base of a petiole or petiolule and functioning in turgor movements of leaves or leaflets

pu·ma \'pü-mə, 'pyü-\ *n, pl* **pumas** *also* **puma** [Sp, fr. Quechua] (1777) : COUGAR; *also* : the fur or pelt of a cougar

pum·ice \'pə-məs\ *n* [ME *pomis*, fr. MF, fr. L *pumic-, pumex* — more at FOAM] (15c) : a volcanic glass full of cavities and very light in weight used esp. in powder form for smoothing and polishing — **pu·mi·ceous** \pyü-'mi-shəs, ,pə-\ *adj*

pum·ic·ite \'pə-mə-,sīt\ *n* (1916) : PUMICE

pum·mel \'pə-məl\ *vb* **-meled** *also* **-melled; -mel·ing** *also* **-mel·ling** \'pə-mə-liŋ, 'pəm-liŋ\ [alter. of *pommel*] (1548) : POUND, BEAT

pum·me·lo *var of* POMELO

¹**pump** \'pəmp\ *n* [ME *pumpe, pompe*, fr. MLG *pumpe* or MD *pompe*, perh. fr. Sp *bomba*, of imit. origin] (15c)   **1** : a device that raises, transfers, or compresses fluids or that attenuates gases esp. by suction or pressure or both   **2** : HEART   **3** : an act or the process of pumping   **4** : an energy source (as light) for pumping atoms or molecules   **5** : a mechanism (as the sodium pump) for pumping atoms, ions, or molecules

²**pump** *vi* (1508)   **1** : to work a pump : raise or move a fluid with a pump   **2** : to exert oneself to pump or as if to pump something   **3** : to move in a manner that resembles the action of a pump handle ~ *vt*   **1 a** : to raise (as water) with a pump   **b** : to draw fluid from with a pump   **2** : to pour forth, deliver, or draw with or as if with a pump ⟨~ed money into the economy⟩ ⟨~ new life into the classroom⟩   **3 a** : to question persistently   **b** : to elicit by persistent questioning   **4 a** : to operate by manipulating a lever   **b** : to manipulate as if operating a pump handle ⟨~ed my hand warmly⟩   **c** : to cause to move with an action resembling that of a pump handle ⟨a runner ~ing her arms⟩   **5** : to transport (as ions) against a concentration gradient by the expenditure of energy   **6 a** : to excite (as atoms or molecules) esp. so as to cause emission of coherent monochromatic electromagnetic radiation (as in a laser)   **b** : to energize (as a laser) by pumping — **pump iron** : to lift weights

³**pump** *n* [origin unknown] (1555) : a shoe that grips the foot chiefly at the toe and heel; *esp* : a close-fitting woman's dress shoe with a moderate to high heel

pumped storage *n* (1927) : a hydroelectric system in which electricity is generated during periods of high demand by the use of water that has been pumped into a reservoir at a higher altitude during periods of low demand

pump·er \'pəm-pər\ *n* (1660) : one that pumps; *esp* : a fire truck equipped with a pump

pum·per·nick·el \'pəm-pər-,ni-kəl\ *n* [G, fr. *pumpern* to break wind + *Nickel* goblin; fr. its reputed indigestibility] (1756) : a dark coarse sourdough bread made of unbolted rye flour

pump·kin \'pəm(p)-kən, ÷'pəŋ-kən\ *n, often attrib* [alter. of earlier *pumpion*, modif. of F *popon, pompon* melon, pumpkin, fr. L *pepon-, pepo*, fr. Gk *pepōn, pepōn* ripened; akin to Gk *pessein* to cook, ripen — more at COOK] (1654)   **1 a** : the usu. round orange fruit of a vine (*Cucurbita pepo*) of the gourd family widely cultivated as food   **b** : WINTER CROOKNECK   **c** *Brit* : any of various large-fruited winter squashes (*C. maxima*)   **2** : a usu. hairy prickly vine that produces pumpkins

pump·kin·seed \-,sēd\ *n* (1814) : a brilliantly colored No. American freshwater sunfish (*Lepomis gibbosus*) with a reddish spot on the operculum

pump priming *n* (1936) : government investment expenditures designed to induce a self-sustaining expansion of economic activity

pump up *vt* (1791)   **1 a** : to fill with enthusiasm or excitement   **b** : to fill with or as if with air : INFLATE   **2** : INCREASE 1

¹**pun** \'pən\ *n* [perh. fr. It *puntiglio* fine point, quibble — more at PUNCTILIO] (1662) : the usu. humorous use of a word in such a way as to suggest two or more of its meanings or the meaning of another word similar in sound

²**pun** *vi* **punned; pun·ning** (1670) : to make puns

pu·na \'pü-nə\ *n* [AmerSp, fr. Quechua] (1613) : a treeless windswept tableland or basin in the higher Andes

¹**punch** \'pənch\ *vb* [ME, fr. MF *poinçonner* to prick, stamp, fr. *poinçon* puncheon] *vt* (14c)   **1 a** : PROD, POKE   **b** : DRIVE, HERD ⟨~ing cattle⟩   **2 a** : to strike with a forward thrust esp. of the fist   **b** : to drive or push forcibly by or as if by a punch   **c** : to hit (a ball) with less than a full swing   **3** : to emboss, cut, perforate, or make with or as if with a

punch **4 a** : to push down so as to produce a desired result ⟨~ buttons on a jukebox⟩ **b** : to hit or press down the operating mechanism of ⟨~ a time clock⟩ ⟨~ a typewriter⟩ **c** : to produce by or as if by punching keys ⟨~ out a tune on the piano⟩ **d** : to enter (as data) by punching keys **5** : to give emphasis to ~ *vi* : to perform the action of punching something — **punch·er** *n*

²**punch** *n* (14c) **1** : the action of punching **2** : a quick blow with or as if with the fist **3** : effective energy or forcefulness ⟨a story that packs a ~⟩ ⟨political ~⟩ — **punch·less** \'pənch-ləs\ *adj* — **to the punch** : to the first blow or to decisive action — usu. used with *beat*

³**punch** *n* [prob. short for *puncheon*] (14c) **1 a** : a tool usu. in the form of a short rod of steel that is variously shaped at one end for different operations (as forming, perforating, embossing, or cutting) **b** : a short tapering steel rod for driving the heads of nails below a surface **c** : a steel die faced with a letter in relief that is forced into a softer metal to form an intaglio matrix from which foundry type is cast **d** : a device or machine for cutting holes or notches (as in paper or cardboard) **2** : a hole or notch from a perforating operation

⁴**punch** *n* [perh. fr. Hindi *pāc* five, fr. Skt *pañca*; akin to Gk *pente* five; fr. its orig. having five ingredients — more at FIVE] (1632) : a hot or cold drink that is usu. a combination of hard liquor, wine, or beer and nonalcoholic beverages; *also* : a drink that is a mixture of nonalcoholic beverages

Punch–and–Judy show \,pənch-ən-'jü-dē-\ *n* (1876) : a traditional puppet show in which the little hook-nosed humpback Punch fights comically with his wife Judy

punch·ball \'pənch-,bȯl\ *n* (1932) : baseball adapted for small areas in which a rubber ball is hit with a fist instead of a bat

punch·board \-,bōrd, -,bȯrd\ *n* (1912) : a small board that has many holes each filled with a rolled-up printed slip to be punched out on payment of a nominal sum in an effort to obtain a slip that entitles the player to a designated prize

punch bowl *n* (1692) : a large bowl from which a beverage (as punch) is served

punch–drunk \'pənch-,drəŋk\ *adj* [²*punch*] (1918) **1** : suffering cerebral injury from many minute brain hemorrhages as a result of repeated head blows received in boxing **2** : behaving as if punch-drunk : DAZED, CONFUSED

punched card \'pəncht-\ *n* (1919) : a card in which holes are punched in designated positions to represent data — called also *Hollerith card*, *punch card*

¹**pun·cheon** \'pən-chən\ *n* [ME *ponson*, fr. MF *poinçon* pointed tool, king post, fr. (assumed) VL *punction-*, *punctio* pointed tool, fr. L, action of pricking, fr. *pungere* to prick — more at PUNGENT] (14c) **1 a** : a pointed tool for piercing or for working on stone **2 a** : a short upright framing timber **b** : a split log or heavy slab with the face smoothed

²**puncheon** *n* [ME *poncion*, fr. MF *ponchon*, *poinçon*, of unknown origin] (15c) : a large cask of varying capacity

punch in *vi* (1926) : to record the time of one's arrival or beginning work by punching a time clock

pun·chi·nel·lo \,pən-chə-'ne-(,)lō\ *n* [modif. of It dial. *polecenella*] (1666) **1** *cap* : a fat short humpbacked clown or buffoon in Italian puppet shows **2** *pl* **-los** : a squat grotesque person

punching bag *n* (1886) : a stuffed or inflated bag that is usu. suspended for free movement and that is punched for exercise or for training in boxing

punch line *n* (1921) : the sentence, statement, or phrase (as in a joke) that makes the point

punch–out \'pənch-,aut\ *n* (1928) : FISTFIGHT

punch out *vi* (1973) **1** : to record the time of one's stopping work or departure by punching a time clock **2** : to bail out of an aircraft using an ejection seat ~ *vt* **1** : to beat up **2** : STRIKE OUT

punch press *n* (1911) : a press equipped with cutting, shaping, or combination dies for working on material (as metal)

punch–up \'pənch-,əp\ *n* (1958) *chiefly Brit* : FISTFIGHT

punch up *vt* (ca. 1959) : to give energy or forcefulness to ⟨jokes added to *punch up* a speech⟩

punchy \'pən-chē\ *adj* **punch·i·er; -est** (1917) **1** : having punch : FORCEFUL, SPIRITED **2** : PUNCH-DRUNK

punc·tate \'pəŋk-,tāt\ *adj* [NL *punctatus*, fr. L *punctum* point — more at POINT] (ca. 1760) **1** : marked with minute spots or depressions ⟨a ~ leaf⟩ **2** : characterized by dots or points ⟨~ skin lesions⟩ — **punc·ta·tion** \,pəŋk-'tā-shən\ *n*

punc·til·io \,pəŋk-'ti-lē-,ō\ *n*, *pl* **-i·os** [It & Sp; It *puntiglio* point of honor, scruple, fr. Sp *puntillo*, fr. dim. of *punto* point, fr. L *punctum*] (1596) **1** : a minute detail of conduct in a ceremony or in observance of a code **2** : careful observance of forms (as in social conduct)

punc·til·i·ous \-lē-əs\ *adj* (1634) : marked by or concerned about precise accordance with the details of codes or conventions *syn* see CAREFUL — **punc·til·i·ous·ly** *adv* — **punc·til·i·ous·ness** *n*

punc·tu·al \'pəŋk-chə-wəl, -chəl\ *adj* [ME, having a sharp point, fr. ML *punctualis* of a point, fr. L *punctus* pricking, point, fr. *pungere* to prick — more at PUNGENT] (1675) : being on time ⟨*punctual* payment⟩ — **punc·tu·al·i·ty** \,pəŋk-chə-'wa-lə-tē\ *n* — **punc·tu·al·ly** \'pəŋk-chə-wə-lē, -chə-lē\ *adv*

punc·tu·ate \'pəŋk-chə-,wāt\ *vb* **-at·ed; -at·ing** [ML *punctuatus*, pp. of *punctuare* to point, provide with punctuation marks, fr. L *punctus* point] *vt* (ca. 1818) **1** : to mark or divide (written matter) with punctuation marks **2** : to break into or interrupt at intervals ⟨the steady click of her needles *punctuated* the silence —Edith Wharton⟩ **3** : ACCENTUATE, EMPHASIZE ~ *vi* : to use punctuation marks — **punc·tu·a·tor** \-,wā-tər\ *n*

punctuated equilibrium *n* (1978) : evolution that is characterized by long periods of stability in the characteristics of an organism and short periods of rapid change during which new forms appear esp. from small subpopulations of the ancestral form in restricted parts of its geographic range; *also* : a theory or model of evolution emphasizing this — compare GRADUALISM 2

punc·tu·a·tion \,pəŋk-chə-'wā-shən\ *n* (ca. 1539) **1** : the act of punctuating : the state of being punctuated **2** : the act or practice of inserting standardized marks or signs in written matter to clarify the meaning and separate structural units; *also* : a system of punctuation **3** : something that contrasts or accentuates

PUNCTUATION MARKS

.	period (*or* full stop)
,	comma
;	semicolon
:	colon
'	apostrophe
' '	quotation marks, single (*or chiefly Brit* inverted commas)
" "	quotation marks, double (*or chiefly Brit* inverted commas)
« »	guillemets
?	question mark (*or* interrogation point)
¿ ?	question marks, Spanish
!	exclamation point
¡ !	exclamation points, Spanish
‽	interrobang
/	slash (*or diagonal or slant or solidus or* virgule)
. . . *or*	ellipsis (*or* suspension points)
-	hyphen
⸗	double hyphen
–	dash (*or* en dash)
—	dash (*or* em dash)
~	swung dash
( )	parentheses (*or* brackets)
[ ]	brackets, square (*or* braces)
⟨ ⟩	brackets, angle
{ }	braces (*or* curly brackets)

punctuation mark *n* (1860) : any of various standardized marks or signs used in punctuation

¹**punc·ture** \'pəŋk-chər\ *n* [ME, fr. L *punctura*, fr. *punctus*, pp. of *pungere*] (14c) **1** : an act of puncturing **2** : a hole, wound, or perforation made by puncturing **3** : a minute depression

²**puncture** *vb* **punc·tured; punc·tur·ing** \'pəŋk-chə-riŋ, 'pəŋk-shriŋ\ *vt* (1699) **1** : to pierce with or as if with a pointed instrument or object **2** : to make useless or ineffective as if by a puncture : DEFLATE ~ *vi* : to become punctured

puncture vine *n* (1911) : an Old World annual prostrate herb (*Tribulus terrestris*) of the caltrop family that has hard spiny pods and is a troublesome weed esp. in the western U.S. — called also *caltrop*, *puncture-weed*

pun·dit \'pən-dət\ *n* [Hindi *paṇḍit*, fr. Skt *paṇḍita*, learned] (1672) **1** : PANDIT **2** : a learned man : TEACHER **3** : one who gives opinions in an authoritative manner : CRITIC — **pun·dit·ry** \-də-trē\ *n*

pung \'pəŋ\ *n* [short for earlier *tow-pong*, of Algonquian origin; akin to Micmac *tobâgun* drag made with skin] (1825) *NewEng* : a sleigh with a box-shaped body

pun·gen·cy \'pən-jən(t)-sē\ *n* (1649) : the quality or state of being pungent

pun·gent \-jənt\ *adj* [L *pungent-*, *pungens*, prp. of *pungere* to prick, sting; akin to L *pugnus* fist, *pugnare* to fight, Gk *pygmē* fist] (1597) **1** : sharply painful **2** : having a stiff and sharp point ⟨~ leaves⟩ **3 a** : marked by a sharp incisive quality : CAUSTIC ⟨a ~ critic⟩ ⟨~ language⟩ **b** : being sharp and to the point **4** : causing a sharp or irritating sensation; *esp* : ACRID — **pun·gent·ly** *adv*

syn PUNGENT, PIQUANT, POIGNANT, RACY mean sharp and stimulating to the mind or the senses. PUNGENT implies a sharp, stinging, or biting quality esp. of odors ⟨a cheese with a *pungent* odor⟩. PIQUANT suggests a power to whet the appetite or interest through tartness or mild pungency ⟨a *piquant* sauce⟩. POIGNANT suggests something is sharply or piercingly effective in stirring one's consciousness or emotions ⟨felt a *poignant* sense of loss⟩. RACY implies having a strongly characteristic natural quality fresh and unimpaired ⟨spontaneous, *racy* prose⟩.

pun·gle \'pən-gəl\ *vb* **pun·gled; pun·gling** \'pən-g(ə-)liŋ\ [Sp *póngale* put it down] *vt* (1851) : to make a payment or contribution of (money) — usu. used with *up* ~ *vi* : to make a payment — usu. used with *up*

¹**Pu·nic** \'pyü-nik\ *adj* [L *punicus*, fr. *Poenus* inhabitant of Carthage; akin to Gk *Phoinix* Phoenician] (1533) **1** : of or relating to Carthage or the Carthaginians **2** : FAITHLESS, TREACHEROUS

²**Punic** *n* (1673) : the Phoenician dialect of ancient Carthage

pun·ish \'pə-nish\ *vb* [ME *punisshen*, fr. MF *puniss-*, stem of *punir*, fr. L *punire*, fr. *poena* penalty — more at PAIN] *vt* (14c) **1 a** : to impose a penalty on for a fault, offense, or violation **b** : to inflict a penalty for the commission of (an offense) in retribution or retaliation **2 a** : to deal with roughly or harshly **b** : to inflict injury on : HURT ~ *vi* : to inflict punishment — **pun·ish·abil·i·ty** \,pə-nish-ə-'bi-lə-tē\ *n* — **pun·ish·able** \'pə-nish-ə-bəl\ *adj* — **pun·ish·er** *n*

syn PUNISH, CHASTISE, CASTIGATE, CHASTEN, DISCIPLINE, CORRECT mean to inflict a penalty on in requital for wrongdoing. PUNISH implies subjecting to a penalty for wrongdoing ⟨*punished* for stealing⟩. CHASTISE may apply to either the infliction of corporal punishment or to verbal censure or denunciation ⟨*chastised* his son for neglecting his studies⟩. CASTIGATE usu. implies a severe, typically public censure ⟨an editorial *castigating* the entire city council⟩. CHASTEN suggests any affliction or trial that leaves one humbled or subdued ⟨*chastened* by a landslide election defeat⟩. DISCIPLINE implies a punishing or chastening in order to bring under control ⟨parents must *discipline* their children⟩. CORRECT implies punishing aimed at reforming an offender ⟨the function of prison is to *correct* the wrongdoer⟩.

pun·ish·ment \'pə-nish-mənt\ *n* (15c) **1** : the act of punishing **2 a**

\ə\ **abut** \ᵊ\ **kitten**, F **table** \ər\ **further** \a\ **ash** \ā\ **ace** \ä\ **mop, mar** \au\ **out** \ch\ **chin** \e\ **bet** \ē\ **easy** \g\ **go** \i\ **hit** \ī\ **ice** \j\ **job** \ŋ\ **sing** \ō\ **go** \ȯ\ **law** \ȯi\ **boy** \th\ **thin** \t̲h̲\ **the** \ü\ **loot** \u̇\ **foot** \y\ **yet** \zh\ **vision** \a̱, k̲, ⁿ, œ, œ̄, ᵫ, ᵫ̄, ᵞ\ *see* Guide to Pronunciation

: suffering, pain, or loss that serves as retribution **b** : a penalty inflicted on an offender through judicial procedure **3** : severe, rough, or disastrous treatment

pu·ni·tion \pyü-'ni-shən\ *n* [ME *punicion*, fr. MF *punition*, fr. L *punition-*, *punitio*, fr. *punire*] (15c) : PUNISHMENT

pu·ni·tive \'pyü-nə-tiv\ *adj* [F *punitif*, fr. ML *punitivus*, fr. L *punitus*, pp. of *punire*] (1624) : inflicting, involving, or aiming at punishment — **pu·ni·tive·ly** *adv* — **pu·ni·tive·ness** *n*

punitive damages *n pl* (ca. 1890) : damages awarded in excess of normal compensation to the plaintiff to punish a defendant for a serious wrong

Pun·ja·bi \pən-'jä-bē, -'ja-\ *n* [Hindi *panjābī*, fr. *pañjābī* of Punjab, fr. Per *panjābī*, fr. *Panjāb* Punjab] (1846) **1** : PANJABI 1 **2** : a native or inhabitant of the Punjab region of the northwestern Indian subcontinent — **Punjabi** *adj*

¹punk \'pəŋk\ *n* [origin unknown] (1596) **1** *archaic* : PROSTITUTE **2** [prob. partly fr. ³*punk*] : NONSENSE, FOOLISHNESS **3 a** : a young inexperienced person : BEGINNER, NOVICE; *esp* : a young man **b** : a usu. petty gangster, hoodlum, or ruffian **c** : a youth used as a homosexual partner **4 a** : PUNK ROCK **b** : a punk rock musician **c** : one who affects punk styles

²punk *adj* (1896) **1** : very poor : INFERIOR ⟨played a ~ game⟩ **2** : being in poor health ⟨said that she was feeling ~⟩ **3 a** : of or relating to punk rock **b** : relating to or being a style (as of dress or hair) inspired by punk rock — **punk·ish** \'pəŋ-kish\ *adj*

³punk *n* [perh. alter. of *spunk*] (1687) **1** : wood so decayed as to be dry, crumbly, and useful for tinder **2** : a dry spongy substance prepared from fungi (genus *Fomes*) and used to ignite fuses esp. of fireworks

pun·kah \'pəŋ-kə\ *n* [Hindi *pākhā*] (1787) : a fan used esp. in India that consists of a canvas-covered frame suspended from the ceiling and that is operated by a cord

punk·er \'pəŋ-kər\ *n* (1977) : ¹PUNK 4b, c

pun·kie *also* **pun·ky** \'pəŋ-kē\ *n, pl* **punkies** [New York D *punki*, modif. of Delaware (Munsee) *pónkwəs*] (1769) : BITING MIDGE

pun·kin \'pəŋ-kən\ *var of* PUMPKIN

punk rock *n* (1971) : rock music marked by extreme and often deliberately offensive expressions of alienation and social discontent — **punk rocker** *n*

¹punky *adj* [¹*punk*] (1872) : resembling punk in being soft or rotted — **punk·i·ness** *n*

²punky *adj* [¹*punk*] (1972) : resembling or typical of a punk

pun·net \'pə-nət\ *n* [origin unknown] (ca. 1822) *Brit* : a small basket for fruits or vegetables

Pun·nett square \'pə-nət-\ *n* [Reginald C. Punnett †1967 Eng. geneticist] (1942) : an *n* × *n* square used in genetics to calculate the frequencies of the different genotypes and phenotypes among the offspring of a cross

pun·ny \'pə-nē\ *adj* **pun·ni·er; -est** (1947) : constituting or involving a pun

pun·ster \'pən(t)-stər\ *n* (1700) : one who is given to punning

¹punt \'pənt\ *n* [(assumed) ME, fr. OE, fr. L *ponton-*, *ponto*] (bef. 12c) : a long narrow flat-bottomed boat with square ends usu. propelled with a pole

²punt *vt* (1816) : to propel (as a punt) with a pole

³punt *vi* [F *ponter*, fr. *ponte* point in some games, play against the banker, fr. Sp *punto* point, fr. L *punctum* — more at POINT] (1712) **1** : to play at a gambling game against the banker **2** *Brit* : GAMBLE

⁴punt *vb* [origin unknown] *vt* (1845) : to kick (a football or soccer ball) with the top of the foot before the ball which is dropped from the hands hits the ground ~ *vi* : to punt a ball

⁵punt *n* (1845) : the act or an instance of punting a ball

⁶punt \'pùnt\ *n* [Ir, pound, fr. E *pound*] (1975) : the monetary pound of Ireland

punt·er \'pən-tər\ *n* (ca. 1706) : one that punts: as **a** *chiefly Brit* : a person who gambles; *esp* : one who bets against a bookmaker : one who uses a punt in boating **c** : one who punts a ball

punt formation *n* (1949) : an offensive football formation in which a back making a punt stands approximately 10 yards behind the line and the other backs are in blocking position close to the line

pun·ty \'pən-tē\ *n, pl* **punties** [F *pontil*] (1662) : a metal rod used for fashioning hot glass

pu·ny \'pyü-nē\ *adj* **pu·ni·er; -est** [MF *puisné* younger, lit., born afterward, fr. *puis* afterward + *né* born] (1593) : slight or inferior in power, size, or importance : WEAK — **pu·ni·ly** \'pyü-n²l-ē\ *adv* — **pu·ni·ness** \'pyü-nē-nəs\ *n*

¹pup \'pəp\ *n* [short for *puppy*] (1773) : a young dog; *also* : one of the young of various animals (as a seal or rat)

²pup *vi* **pupped; pup·ping** (1773) : to give birth to pups

pu·pa \'pyü-pə\ *n, pl* **pu·pae** \-(,)pē *also* -,pī\ *or* **pupas** [NL, fr. L *pupa* doll] (1815) : an intermediate usu. quiescent stage of a metamorphic insect (as a bee, moth, or beetle) that occurs between the larva and the imago, is usu. enclosed in a cocoon or protective covering, and undergoes internal changes by which larval structures are replaced by those typical of the imago — **pu·pal** \'pyü-pəl\ *adj*

pu·par·i·um \pyü-'par-ē-əm, -pär-\ *n, pl* **pu·par·ia** \-ē-ə\ [NL, fr. *pupa*] (1815) : a rigid outer shell formed from the larval skin that covers some pupae (as of a dipteran fly)

pu·pate \'pyü-,pāt\ *vi* **pu·pat·ed; pu·pat·ing** (ca. 1879) : to become a pupa : pass through a pupal stage — **pu·pa·tion** \pyü-'pā-shən\ *n*

pup·fish \'pəp-,fish\ *n* (1949) : any of several killifishes (genus *Cyprinodon* or the family Cyprinodontidae) esp. of warm streams and springs of the western U.S.

¹pu·pil \'pyü-pəl\ *n* [ME *pupille* minor ward, fr. MF, fr. L *pupillus* male ward (fr. dim. of *pupus* boy) & *pupilla* female ward, fr. dim. of *pupa* girl, doll] (1536) **1** : a child or young person in school or in the charge of a tutor or instructor : STUDENT **2** : one who has been taught or influenced by a famous or distinguished person

²pupil *n* [MF *pupille*, fr. L *pupilla*, fr. dim. of *pupa* doll; fr. the tiny image of oneself seen reflected in another's eye] (1567) : the contractile aperture in the iris of the eye — **pu·pil·lary** \'pyü-pə-,ler-ē\ *adj*

pu·pil·age *or* **pu·pil·lage** \'pyü-pə-lij\ *n* (ca. 1599) : the state or period of being a pupil

pup·pet \'pə-pət\ *n, often attrib* [ME *popet*, fr. MF *poupette*, dim. of

(assumed) *poupe* doll, fr. L *pupa*] (1538) **1 a** : a small-scale figure (as of a person or animal) usu. with a cloth body and hollow head that fits over and is moved by the hand **b** : MARIONETTE **2** : DOLL 1 **3** : one whose acts are controlled by an outside force or influence — **pup·pet·like** \-,līk\ *adj*

pup·pe·teer \,pə-pə-'tir\ *n* (ca. 1923) : one who manipulates puppets

pup·pet·ry \'pə-pə-trē\ *n, pl* **-ries** (1528) **1** : the production or creation of puppets or puppet shows **2** : the art of manipulating puppets

pup·py \'pə-pē\ *n, pl* **puppies** [ME *popi*, fr. MF *poupée* doll, toy, fr. (assumed) *poupe* doll] (1591) : a young domestic dog; *specif* : one less than a year old — **pup·py·hood** \-,hùd\ *n* — **pup·py·ish** \-ish\ *adj* — **pup·py·like** \-,līk\ *adj*

puppy dog *n* (1595) : a domestic dog; *esp* : one having the lovable attributes of a puppy

puppy love *n* (1834) : transitory affection felt by a boy or girl for one of the opposite sex

pup tent *n* (1863) : a low small tent for two persons usu. consisting of two halves fastened together

Pu·ra·na \pù-'rä-nə\ *n, often cap* [Skt *purāna*, fr. *purāna* ancient, fr. *purā* formerly; akin to Skt *pura* before, Gk *para* beside, *pro* before — more at FOR] (1696) : one of a class of Hindu sacred writings chiefly from A.D. 300 to A.D. 750 comprising popular myths and legends and other traditional lore — **Pu·ra·nic** \-nik\ *adj*

pur·blind \'pər-,blīnd\ *adj* [ME *pur blind*, fr. *pur* purely, wholly, fr. *pur* pure] (14c) **1 a** *obs* : wholly blind **b** : partly blind **2** : lacking in vision, insight, or understanding : OBTUSE — **pur·blind·ly** \-,blīn(d)-lē\ *adv* — **pur·blind·ness** \-,blīn(d)-nəs\ *n*

¹pur·chase \'pər-chəs\ *vb* **pur·chased; pur·chas·ing** [ME *purchacen*, fr. OF *purchacier* to seek to obtain, fr. *por-*, *pur-* for, forward (modif. of L *pro-*) + *chacier* to pursue, chase — more at PRO-] *vt* (14c) **1 a** *archaic* : GAIN, ACQUIRE **b** : to acquire (real estate) by means other than descent or inheritance **c** : to obtain by paying money or its equivalent : BUY **d** : to obtain by labor, danger, or sacrifice **2** : to apply a device for obtaining a mechanical advantage to (as something to be moved); *also* : to move by a purchase **3** : to constitute the means for buying ⟨our dollars ~ less each year⟩ ~ *vi* : to purchase something — **pur·chas·able** \-chə-sə-bəl\ *adj* — **pur·chas·er** *n*

²purchase *n* (14c) **1** : an act or instance of purchasing **2** : something obtained esp. for a price in money or its equivalent **3 a** (1) : a mechanical hold or advantage applied to the raising or moving of heavy bodies (2) : an apparatus or device by which advantage is gained **b** (1) : an advantage (as a firm hold or position) used in applying one's power ⟨clutching the steering wheel for more ~ —Barry Crump⟩ (2) : a means of exerting power

pur·dah \'pər-də\ *n* [Hindi *parda*, lit., screen, veil] (1865) **1** : seclusion of women from public observation among Muslims and some Hindus esp. in India **2** : a state of seclusion or concealment

pure \'pyùr\ *adj* **pur·er; pur·est** [ME *pur*, fr. OF, fr. L *purus*; akin to OHG *fowen* to sift, Skt *punāti* he cleanses, MIr *úr* fresh, new] (14c) **1 a** (1) : unmixed with any other matter ⟨~ gold⟩ (2) : free from dust, dirt, or taint ⟨~ food⟩ (3) : SPOTLESS, STAINLESS **b** : free from harshness or roughness and being in tune — used of a musical tone **c** *of a vowel* : characterized by no appreciable alteration of articulation during utterance **2 a** : being thus and no other : SHEER, UNMITIGATED ⟨~ folly⟩ **b** (1) : ABSTRACT, THEORETICAL (2) : A PRIORI ⟨~ mechanics⟩ **c** : not directed toward exposition of reality or solution of practical problems ⟨~ literature⟩ **d** : being nonobjective and to be appraised on formal and technical qualities only ⟨~ form⟩ **3 a** (1) : free from what vitiates, weakens, or pollutes (2) : containing nothing that does not properly belong **b** : free from moral fault or guilt **c** : marked by chastity : CONTINENT **d** (1) : of pure blood and unmixed ancestry (2) : homozygous and breeding true for one or more characters **e** : ritually clean *syn* see CHASTE — **pure·ness** *n*

pure–blood·ed \'pyùr-,blə-dəd\ *or* **pure–blood** \-,bləd\ *adj* (1821) : FULL-BLOODED 1 — **pure-blood** \-,bləd\ *n*

pure·bred \-'bred, -,bred\ *adj* (1868) : bred from members of a recognized breed, strain, or kind without admixture of other blood over many generations — **pure·bred** \-,bred\ *n*

pure democracy *n* (ca. 1910) : democracy in which the power is exercised directly by the people rather than through representatives

¹pu·ree *or* **pu·rée** \pyù-'rā, -'rē\ *n* [F *purée*, fr. MF, fr. fem. of *puré*, pp. of *purer* to purify, strain, fr. L *purare* to purify, fr. *purus*] (1707) **1** : a paste or thick liquid suspension usu. made from cooked food ground finely **2** : a thick soup made of pureed vegetables

²puree *vt* **pu·reed; pu·ree·ing** (1928) : to make a puree of

pure imaginary *n* (1947) : a complex number that is the product of a real number other than zero and the imaginary unit — **pure imaginary** *adj*

pure·ly \'pyùr-lē\ *adv* (14c) **1** : WHOLLY, COMPLETELY ⟨a selection based ~ on merit⟩ **2** : without admixture of anything injurious or foreign **3** : SIMPLY, MERELY ⟨read ~ for relaxation⟩ **4** : in a chaste or innocent manner

pur·fle \'pər-fəl\ *vt* **pur·fled; pur·fling** [ME *purfilen*, fr. MF *porfiler*, fr. (assumed) VL *profilare*, fr. L *pro-* forward + LL *filare* to spin — more at PRO-, FILE] (14c) : to ornament the border or edges of — **purfle** *n*

pur·ga·tion \,pər-'gā-shən\ *n* (14c) : the act or result of purging

¹pur·ga·tive \'pər-gə-tiv\ *adj* [ME *purgatif*, fr. MF, fr. LL *purgativus*, fr. L *purgatus*, pp.] (15c) : purging or tending to purge

²purgative *n* (1626) : a purging medicine : CATHARTIC

pur·ga·to·ri·al \,pər-gə-'tōr-ē-əl, -'tor-\ *adj* (15c) **1** : of, relating to, or suggestive of purgatory **2** : cleansing of sin : EXPIATORY

pur·ga·to·ry \'pər-gə-,tōr-ē, -,tor-\ *n, pl* **-ries** [ME or AF or ML; AF *purgatorie*, fr. ML *purgatorium*, fr. LL, neut. of *purgatorius* purging, fr. L *purgare*] (13c) **1** : an intermediate state after death for expiatory purification; *specif* : a place or state of punishment wherein according to Roman Catholic doctrine the souls of those who die in God's grace may make satisfaction for past sins and so become fit for heaven **2** : a place or state of temporary suffering or misery

¹purge \'pərj\ *vb* **purged; purg·ing** [ME, fr. MF *purgier*, fr. L *purigare, purgare* to purify, purge, fr. *purus* pure + *-igare* (akin to *agere* to drive, do) — more at ACT] *vt* (14c) **1 a** : to clear of guilt **b** : to free from moral or ceremonial defilement **2 a** : to cause evacuation from (as the bowels) **b** (1) : to make free of something unwanted ⟨~ a manhole of gas⟩ ⟨~ yourself of fear⟩ (2) : to free (as a boiler) of sediment or relieve (as a steam pipe) of trapped air by bleeding **c** (1) : to rid (as a nation or party) by a purge (2) : to get rid of ⟨the leaders had been *purged*⟩ ⟨~ money-losing operations⟩ ~ *vi* **1** : to become purged **2** : to have or produce frequent evacuations **3** : to cause purgation — **purg·er** *n*

²**purge** *n* (1563) **1** : something that purges; *esp* : PURGATIVE **2 a** : an act or instance of purging **b** : the removal of elements or members regarded as undesirable and esp. as treacherous or disloyal

pu·ri \'puṙ-ē\ *n*, *pl* **puri** *or* **puris** [Hindi *pūri*, fr. Skt *pūra*] (ca. 1885) : a puffy fried wheat cake of India

pu·ri·fi·ca·tion \ˌpyu̇r-ə-fə-'kā-shən\ *n* (14c) : the act or an instance of purifying or of being purified

pu·ri·fi·ca·tor \'pyu̇r-ə-fə-ˌkā-tər\ *n* (1853) **1** : a linen cloth used to wipe the chalice after celebration of the Eucharist **2** : one that purifies

pu·ri·fi·ca·to·ry \pyu̇r-'i-fi-kə-ˌtȯr-ē, 'pyu̇r-(ə-)fə-kə-, -ˌtȯr-\ *adj* (1610) : serving, tending, or intended to purify

pu·ri·fy \'pyu̇r-ə-ˌfī\ *vb* **-fied; -fy·ing** [ME *purifien*, fr. MF *purifier*, fr. L *purificare*, fr. L *purus* + *-ificare* -ify] *vt* (14c) : to make pure: as **a** : to clear from material defilement or imperfection **b** : to free from guilt or moral or ceremonial blemish **c** : to free from undesirable elements ~ *vi* : to grow or become pure or clean — **pu·ri·fi·er** \-ˌfī(-ə)r\ *n*

Pu·rim \'pu̇r-im, 'pyu̇r-, -ˌēm; pu̇-'rim, pyu̇-, -'rēm\ *n* [Heb *pūrīm*, lit., lots; fr. the casting of lots by Haman (Esth 9:24–26)] (1535) : a Jewish holiday celebrated on the 14th of Adar in commemoration of the deliverance of the Jews from the massacre plotted by Haman

pu·rine \'pyu̇r-ˌēn\ *n* [G *Purin*, fr. L *purus* pure + NL *uricus* uric (fr. E *uric*) + G *-in* ²-ine] (1898) **1** : a crystalline base $C_5H_4N_4$ that is the parent of compounds of the uric-acid group **2** : a derivative of purine; *esp* : a base (as adenine or guanine) that is a constituent of DNA or RNA

pur·ism \'pyu̇r-ˌi-zəm\ *n* (1803) **1** : an example of rigid adherence to or insistence on purity or nicety esp. in use of words; *esp* : a word, phrase, or sense used chiefly by purists **2** : the quality or practice of adherence to purity esp. in language

pur·ist \'pyu̇r-ist\ *n* (ca. 1706) : one who adheres strictly and often excessively to a tradition; *esp* : one preoccupied with the purity of a language and its protection from the use of foreign or altered forms — **pu·ris·tic** \pyu̇-'ris-tik\ *adj* — **pu·ris·ti·cal·ly** \-ti-k(ə-)lē\ *adv*

¹**pu·ri·tan** \'pyu̇r-ə-t³n\ *n* [prob. fr. LL *puritas* purity] (1572) **1** *cap* : a member of a 16th and 17th century Protestant group in England and New England opposing as unscriptural the ceremonial worship and the prelacy of the Church of England **2** : one who practices or preaches a more rigorous or professedly purer moral code than that which prevails

²**puritan** *adj*, *often cap* (1589) : of or relating to puritans, the Puritans, or puritanism

pu·ri·tan·i·cal \ˌpyu̇r-ə-'ta-ni-kəl\ *adj* (1607) **1** : PURITAN **2** : of, relating to, or characterized by a rigid morality — **pu·ri·tan·i·cal·ly** \-k(ə-)lē\ *adv*

pu·ri·tan·ism \'pyu̇r-ə-t³n-ˌi-zəm\ *n* (1573) **1** *cap* : the beliefs and practices characteristic of the Puritans **2** : strictness and austerity esp. in matters of religion or conduct

pu·ri·ty \'pyu̇r-ə-tē\ *n* [ME *purete*, fr. OF *pureté*, fr. LL *puritat-, puritas*, fr. L *purus* pure] (13c) **1** : the quality or state of being pure **2** : SATURATION 4a

Pur·kin·je cell \(ˌ)pər-'kin-jē-\ *n* [Jan *Purkinje*] (ca. 1890) : any of numerous nerve cells that occupy the middle layer of the cerebellar cortex and are characterized by a large globose body with massive dendrites directed outward and a single slender axon directed inward

Purkinje fiber *n* (ca. 1890) : any of the modified cardiac muscle fibers that have few nuclei, granulated central cytoplasm, and sparse peripheral striations and make up a network of conducting tissue in the myocardium

¹**purl** \'pər(-ə)l\ *n* [ME] (14c) **1** : gold or silver thread or wire for embroidering or edging **2** : the intertwisting of thread that knots a stitch usu. along an edge **3** : PURL STITCH

²**purl** *vt* (1526) **1 a** : to embroider with gold or silver thread **b** : to edge or border with gold or silver embroidery **2** : to knit in purl stitch ~ *vi* : to do knitting in purl stitch

³**purl** *n* [perh. of Scand origin; akin to Norw *purla* to ripple] (ca. 1522) **1** : a purling or swirling stream or rill **2** : a gentle murmur or movement (as of purling water)

⁴**purl** *vi* (1591) **1** : EDDY, SWIRL **2** : to make a soft murmuring sound like that of a purling stream

pur·lieu \'pərl-(ˌ)yü, 'pər-(ˌ)lü\ *n* [ME *purlewe* land severed from an English royal forest by perambulation, fr. AF *puralé* perambulation, fr. OF *puraler* to go through, fr. *pur-* for, through + *aler* to go — more at PURCHASE] (15c) **1 a** : an outlying or adjacent district **b** *pl* : ENVIRONS, NEIGHBORHOOD **2 a** : a frequently visited place : HAUNT **b** *pl* : CONFINES, BOUNDS

pur·lin \'pər-lən\ *n* [origin unknown] (15c) : a horizontal member in a roof

pur·loin \(ˌ)pər-'lȯin, 'pər-ˌ\ *vt* [ME, to put away, misappropriate, fr. AF *purloigner*, fr. OF *porloigner* to put off, delay, fr. *por-* forward + *loing* at a distance, fr. L *longe*, fr. *longus* long — more at PURCHASE, LONG] (15c) : to appropriate wrongfully and often by a breach of trust *syn* see STEAL — **pur·loin·er** *n*

purl stitch *n* [¹*purl*] (1885) : a knitting stitch usu. made with the yarn at the front of the work by inserting the right needle into the front of a loop on the left needle from the right, catching the yarn with the right needle, and bringing it through to form a new loop — compare KNIT STITCH

pu·ro·my·cin \ˌpyu̇r-ə-'mī-s³n\ *n* [*purine* + *-o-* + *-mycin*] (1953) : an antibiotic $C_{22}H_{29}N_7O_5$ that is obtained from an actinomycete (*Streptomyces alboniger*) and is used esp. as a potent inhibitor of protein synthesis

¹**pur·ple** \'pər-pəl\ *adj* **pur·pler** \-p(ə-)lər\; **pur·plest** \-p(ə-)ləst\ [ME *purpel*, alter. of *purper*, fr. OE *purpuran* of purple, gen. of *purpure* purple color, fr. L *purpura*, fr. Gk *porphyra*] (bef. 12c) **1** : REGAL, IMPERIAL **2** : of the color purple **3 a** : highly rhetorical : ORNATE **b** : marked by profanity

²**purple** *n* (15c) **1 a** (1) : cloth dyed purple (2) : a garment of such color; *esp* : a purple robe worn as an emblem of rank or authority **b**

(1) : TYRIAN PURPLE (2) : any of various colors that fall about midway between red and blue in hue **c** (1) : a mollusk (as of the genus *Purpura*) yielding a purple dye and esp. the Tyrian purple of ancient times (2) : a pigment or dye that colors purple **2 a** : imperial or regal rank or power **b** : high rank or station

³**purple** *vb* **pur·pled; pur·pling** \-p(ə-)liŋ\ *vt* (15c) : to make purple ~ *vi* : to become purple

pur·ple·heart \'pər-pəl-ˌhärt\ *n* (1796) : a strong durable purplish wood that is obtained from various leguminous trees (genus *Peltogyne*); *also* : a tree producing such wood

Purple Heart *n* (1932) : a U.S. military decoration awarded to any member of the armed forces wounded or killed in action

purple loosestrife *n* (1548) : an Old World marsh herb (*Lythrum salicaria*) of the loosestrife family that is naturalized in the eastern U.S. and has long spikes of purple flowers

purple martin *n* (1743) : a large swallow (*Progne subis*) of No. America the males of which have bluish black plumage

purple passage *n* [trans. of L *pannus purpureus* purple patch; fr. the traditional splendor of purple cloth as contrasted with plainer materials] (1895) **1** : a passage conspicuous for brilliance or effectiveness in a work that is dull, commonplace, or uninspired **2** *chiefly Brit* : a piece of obtrusively ornate writing — called also *purple patch*

purple scale *n* (ca. 1909) : a brownish or purplish armored scale (*Lepidosaphes beckii*) that is destructive to citrus fruit

pur·plish \'pər-p(ə-)lish\ *adj* (1562) : somewhat purple

pur·ply \'pər-p(ə-)lē\ *adj* (1725) : PURPLISH

¹**pur·port** \'pər-ˌpȯrt, -ˌpȯrt\ *n* [ME, fr. AF, content, tenor, fr. *purporter* to contain, fr. OF *porporter* to convey, fr. *por-* forward + *porter* to carry — more at PURCHASE, PORT] (15c) : meaning conveyed, professed, or implied : IMPORT; *also* : SUBSTANCE, GIST

²**pur·port** \(ˌ)pər-'pȯrt, -'pȯrt\ *vt* (1528) **1** : to have the often specious appearance of being, intending, or claiming (something implied or inferred) ⟨a book that ~s to be an objective analysis⟩; *also* : CLAIM ⟨foreign novels which he ~s to have translated —Mary McCarthy⟩ **2** : INTEND, PURPOSE

pur·port·ed \-'pȯr-təd, -'pȯr-\ *adj* (1894) : REPUTED, ALLEGED ⟨took gullible tourists to ~ ancient sites⟩

pur·port·ed·ly \-lē\ *adv* (1942) : as it is purported : OSTENSIBLY, ALLEGEDLY

¹**pur·pose** \'pər-pəs\ *n* [ME *purpos*, fr. OF, fr. *purposer* to purpose, fr. L *proponere* (perf. indic. *proposui*) to propose — more at PROPOUND] (14c) **1 a** : something set up as an object or end to be attained : INTENTION **b** : RESOLUTION, DETERMINATION **2** : a subject under discussion or an action in course of execution *syn* see INTENTION — **on purpose** : by intent : INTENTIONALLY

²**purpose** *vt* **pur·posed; pur·pos·ing** (14c) : to propose as an aim to oneself

pur·pose–built \ˌpər-pəs-'bilt\ *adj* (1954) *chiefly Brit* : built for a particular purpose

pur·pose·ful \'pər-pəs-fəl\ *adj* (1853) **1** : having a purpose: as **a** : MEANINGFUL ⟨~ activities⟩ **b** : INTENTIONAL ⟨~ ambiguity⟩ **2** : full of determination ⟨a ~ man⟩ — **pur·pose·ful·ly** \-fə-lē\ *adv* — **pur·pose·ful·ness** *n*

pur·pose·less \-ləs\ *adj* (ca. 1552) : having no purpose : AIMLESS, MEANINGLESS — **pur·pose·less·ly** *adv* — **pur·pose·less·ness** *n*

pur·pose·ly \-lē\ *adv* (15c) : with a deliberate or express purpose

pur·po·sive \'pər-pə-siv, (ˌ)pər-'pō-\ *adj* (1855) **1** : serving or effecting a useful function though not as a result of planning or design **2** : having or tending to fulfill a conscious purpose or design : PURPOSEFUL — **pur·po·sive·ly** *adv* — **pur·po·sive·ness** *n*

pur·pu·ra \'pər-pyə-rə, -pə-rə\ *n* [NL, fr. L, purple color] (1753) : any of several hemorrhagic states characterized by patches of purplish discoloration resulting from extravasation of blood into the skin and mucous membranes — **pur·pu·ric** \ˌpər-'pyu̇r-ik\ *adj*

pur·pure \'pər-pyər\ *n* [ME, fr. OE, purple] (1535) : the heraldic color purple

¹**purr** \'pər\ *n* [imit.] (1601) : a low vibratory murmur typical of an apparently contented or pleased cat

²**purr** *vi* (1620) **1** : to make a purr or a sound like a purr ⟨cars ~ing along the highway⟩ **2 a** : to speak in a manner that resembles a purr **b** : to speak in a malicious catty manner — **purr·ing·ly** \-iŋ-lē\ *adv*

¹**purse** \'pərs\ *n* [ME *purs*, fr. OE, modif. of ML *bursa*, fr. LL, ox hide, fr. Gk *byrsa*] (bef. 12c) **1 a** : a small bag for money (2) : a receptacle (as a pocketbook) for carrying money and often other small objects **b** : a receptacle (as a pouch) shaped like a purse **2 a** : RESOURCES, FUNDS **b** : a sum of money offered as a prize or present; *also* : the total amount of money offered in prizes for a given event — **purse·like** \-ˌlīk\ *adj*

²**purse** *vt* **pursed; purs·ing** (14c) **1** : to put into a purse **2** : PUCKER, KNIT

purse–proud \'pərs-ˌprȧud\ *adj* (1681) : proud because of one's wealth esp. in the absence of other distinctions

purs·er \'pər-sər\ *n* [ME, fr. *purs* purse] (15c) **1** : an official on a ship responsible for papers and accounts and on a passenger ship also for the comfort and welfare of passengers **2** : a steward on an airliner

purse seine *n* (1870) : a large seine designed to be set by two boats around a school of fish and so arranged that after the ends have been brought together the bottom can be closed — **purse seiner** *n* — **purse seining** *n*

purse strings *n pl* (15c) : financial resources; *also* : control over these resources

purse seine

purs·lane \'pər-slən, -ˌslän\ *n* [ME, fr. MF *porcelaine*, fr. LL *porcillagin-, porcillago*, alter. of L *porcillaca*, alter. of *portulaca*] (14c) : any of a

\ə\ abut \³\ kitten, F table \ər\ further \a\ ash \ā\ ace \ä\ mop, mar \au̇\ out \ch\ chin \e\ bet \ē\ easy \g\ go \i\ hit \ī\ ice \j\ job \ŋ\ sing \ō\ go \ȯ\ law \ȯi\ boy \th\ thin \t͟h\ the \ü\ loot \u̇\ foot \y\ yet \zh\ vision \ä, k̲, ⁿ, œ, œ̄, ᵫ, ᵜ\ see Guide to Pronunciation family (Portulacaceae, the purslane family) of cosmopolitan usu. succulent herbs; *esp* : a fleshy-leaved trailing plant (*Portulaca oleracea*) with tiny yellow flowers that is a common troublesome weed but is sometimes eaten as a potherb or in salads

pur·su·ance \'pər-'sü-ən(t)s\ *n* (1605) : the act of pursuing; *esp* : a carrying out or into effect : PROSECUTION ⟨in ~ of his duties⟩

pur·su·ant to \-ənt-\ *prep* (1648) : in carrying out : in conformity with : ACCORDING TO

pur·sue \pər-'sü, -'syü\ *vb* **pur·sued; pur·su·ing** [ME, fr. AF *pursuer*, fr. OF *poursuir*, fr. L *prosequi*, fr. *pro-* forward + *sequi* to follow — more at PRO-, SUE] *vt* (14c) **1** : to follow in order to overtake, capture, kill, or defeat **2** : to find or employ measures to obtain or accomplish : SEEK ⟨~ a goal⟩ **3** : to proceed along ⟨~s a northern course⟩ **4 a** : to engage in ⟨~ a hobby⟩ **b** : to follow up or proceed with ⟨~ an argument⟩ **5** : to continue to afflict : HAUNT ⟨was *pursued* by horrible memories⟩ **6** : ²CHASE 1c ⟨*pursued* by dozens of fans⟩ ~ *vi* : to go in pursuit **syn** see CHASE — **pur·su·er** *n*

pur·suit \pər-'süt, -'syüt\ *n* [ME, fr. MF *poursuite*, fr. *poursuir*] (14c) **1** : the act of pursuing **2** : an activity that one engages in as a vocation, profession, or avocation : OCCUPATION **syn** see WORK

pursuit plane *n* (ca. 1918) : a fighter plane esp. of the period before World War II

pur·sui·vant \'pər-si-vənt, -swi-\ *n* [ME *pursevant* attendant of a herald, fr. MF *poursuivant*, lit., follower, fr. prp. of *poursuir, poursuivre* to pursue] (14c) **1** : an officer of arms ranking below a herald but having similar duties **2** : FOLLOWER, ATTENDANT

¹**pur·sy** \'pə-sē, 'pər-sē\ *adj* **pur·si·er; -est** [ME, fr. AF *pursif*, alter. of MF *polsif*, fr. *poulser, polser* to beat, push, pant — more at PUSH] (15c) **1** : short-winded esp. because of corpulence **2** : FAT — **pur·si·ness** *n*

²**pur·sy** \'pər-sē\ *adj* **purs·i·er; -est** [¹*purse*] (1552) **1** : having a puckered appearance **2** : PURSE-PROUD

pur·te·nance \'pərt-nən(t)s, 'pər-tⁿn-ən(t)s\ *n* [ME, lit., appendage, modif. of MF *partenance*, fr. *partenir* to pertain — more at PERTAIN] (15c) : ENTRAILS, PLUCK

pu·ru·lence \'pyür-ə-lən(t)s, 'pyür-yə-\ *n* (1597) : the quality or state of being purulent; *also* : PUS

pu·ru·lent \-lənt\ *adj* [L *purulentus*, fr. *pur-, pus* pus] (1597) **1** : containing, consisting of, or being pus ⟨a ~ discharge⟩ **2** : accompanied by suppuration

pur·vey \(,)pər-'vā, 'pər-,\ *vt* **pur·veyed; pur·vey·ing** [ME *purveien*, fr. MF *porveeir*, fr. L *providēre* to provide] (14c) **1** : to supply (as provisions) usu. as a matter of business **2** : PEDDLE 2

pur·vey·ance \-ən(t)s\ *n* (14c) : the act or process of purveying or procuring

pur·vey·or \-ər\ *n* (14c) **1** : one that purveys **2** : VICTUALLER, CATERER

pur·view \'pər-,vyü\ *n* [ME *purveu*, fr. AF *purveu est* it is provided (opening phrase of a statute)] (15c) **1 a** : the body or enacting part of a statute **b** : the limit, purpose, or scope of a statute **2** : the range or limit of authority, competence, responsibility, concern, or intention **3** : range of vision, understanding, or cognizance

pus \'pəs\ *n* [L *pur-, pus* — more at FOUL] (1541) : thick opaque usu. yellowish white fluid matter formed by suppuration and composed of exudate containing white blood cells, tissue debris, and microorganisms

Pu·sey·ism \'pyü-zē-,i-zəm, -sē-\ *n* [Edward Bouverie *Pusey*] (1838) : TRACTARIANISM — **Pu·sey·ite** \-,īt\ *n*

¹**push** \'push\ *vb* [ME *pushen*, fr. MF *poulser* to beat, push, fr. OF, fr. L *pulsare*, freq. of *pellere* to drive, strike — more at FELT] *vt* (13c) **1 a** : to press against with force in order to drive or impel **b** : to move or endeavor to move away or ahead by steady pressure without striking **2 a** : to thrust forward, downward, or outward **b** : to cause to increase ⟨~ prices to record levels⟩ **c** : to hit (a ball) toward the right from a right-handed swing or toward the left from a left-handed swing — compare PULL 3 **a** : to press or urge forward to completion **b** : to urge or press the advancement, adoption, or practice of ⟨~ed a bill in the legislature⟩; *esp* : to make aggressive efforts to sell ⟨we're ~ing ham this week⟩ **c** : to engage in the illicit sale of (narcotics) **4** : to bear hard upon so as to involve in difficulty ⟨poverty ~ed them to the breaking point⟩ **5** : to approach in age or number ⟨grandmother must be ~ing 75⟩ ~ *vi* **1** : to press against something with steady force in or as if in order to impel **2** : to press forward energetically against opposition **3** : to exert oneself continuously, vigorously, or obtrusively to gain an end ⟨~ing for higher wages⟩ — **push one's luck** : to take an increasing risk

²**push** *n* (1563) **1** : a vigorous effort to attain an end : DRIVE **a** : a military assault or offensive **b** : an advance that overcomes obstacles **c** : a campaign to promote a product **2** : a time for action : EMERGENCY **3 a** : an act of pushing : SHOVE **b** (1) : a physical force steadily applied in a direction away from the body exerting it (2) : a nonphysical pressure : INFLUENCE, URGE **c** : vigorous enterprise or energy **4 a** : an exertion of influence to promote another's interests **b** : stimulation to activity : IMPETUS — **push comes to shove** : a decisive moment comes ⟨backed down when *push came to shove*⟩

push around *vt* (1923) : to impose on contemptuously

push·ball \'push-,bȯl\ *n* (1896) : a game in which each of two sides endeavors to push an inflated orig. leather-covered ball six feet (1.8 meters) in diameter across its opponents' goal; *also* : the ball used

push–bike \-,bīk\ *n* (1913) *Brit* : BICYCLE — called also *push bicycle*

push broom *n* (1926) : a long-handled wide brush that is designed to be pushed and is used for sweeping

push–button *adj* (1916) **1** : operated or done by means of push buttons ⟨a ~ phone⟩ **2** : using or dependent on complex and more or less self-operating mechanisms that are put in operation by a simple act comparable to pushing a button ⟨~ warfare⟩

push button *n* (1878) : a small button or knob that when pushed operates something esp. by closing an electric circuit

push·cart \'push-,kärt\ *n* (1893) : a cart or barrow pushed by hand

push·chair \-,cher, -,char\ *n* (1921) *chiefly Brit* : STROLLER

push·down \-,daün\ *n* (1961) : a store of data (as in a computer) from which the most recently stored item must be the first retrieved — called also *pushdown list, pushdown stack*

push·er \'pu̇-shər\ *n* (1591) : one that pushes; *esp* : one that pushes illegal drugs

push·ful \-fəl\ *adj* (1896) *chiefly Brit* : PUSHING — **push·ful·ness** *n*, *chiefly Brit*

push·ing *adj* (1692) **1** : marked by ambition, energy, enterprise, and initiative **2** : marked by tactless forwardness or officious intrusiveness

push off *vi* (1925) : SET OUT ⟨we *pushed off* for home⟩

push on *vi* (1718) : to continue on one's way : PROCEED

push·over \'push-,ō-vər\ *n* (1906) **1** : something accomplished without difficulty : SNAP **2** : an opponent who is easy to defeat or a victim who is capable of no effective resistance **3** : someone unable to resist an attraction or appeal : SUCKER

push·pin \-,pin\ *n* (1907) : a pin that has a roughly cylindrical head and that is easily inserted and withdrawn (as from a bulletin board)

push–pull \-'pu̇l\ *adj* (1922) : relating to or being an arrangement of two electronic circuit elements (as transistors) such that an alternating input causes them to send current through a load alternately ⟨a ~ circuit⟩ — **push–pull** *n*

Push·tu \'pəsh-(,)tü\ *var of* PASHTO

Push·tun *var of* PASHTUN

push–up \'push-,əp\ *n* (1942) : a conditioning exercise performed in a prone position by raising and lowering the body with the straightening and bending of the arms while keeping the back straight and supporting the body on the hands and toes

pushy \'pu̇-shē\ *adj* **push·i·er; -est** (1936) : aggressive often to an objectionable degree : FORWARD — **push·i·ly** \'pu̇-shə-lē\ *adv* — **push·i·ness** \'pu̇-shē-nəs\ *n*

pu·sil·la·nim·i·ty \,pyü-sə-lə-'ni-mə-tē *also* ,pyü-zə-\ *n* (14c) : the quality or state of being pusillanimous : COWARDLINESS

pu·sil·lan·i·mous \,pyü-sə-'la-nə-məs\ *adj* [LL *pusillanimis*, fr. L *pusillus* very small (dim. of *pusus* boy) + *animus* spirit; perh. akin to L *puer* child — more at PUERILE, ANIMATE] (1586) : lacking courage and resolution : marked by contemptible timidity **syn** see COWARDLY — **pu·sil·lan·i·mous·ly** *adv*

¹**puss** \'pu̇s\ *n* [origin unknown] (ca. 1530) **1** : CAT **2** : GIRL

²**puss** *n* [Ir *pus* mouth] (ca. 1890) *slang* : FACE

puss·ley \'pu̇s-lē\ *n* [by alter.] (1833) : PURSLANE

¹**pussy** \'pu̇-sē\ *n, pl* **puss·ies** [¹*puss*] (1726) **1** : CAT **2** : a catkin of the pussy willow

²**pus·sy** \'pu̇-sē\ *n, pl* **pussies** [perh. of LG or Scand origin; akin to ON *püss* pocket, pouch, LG *püse* vulva, OE *pusa* bag] (ca. 1879) **1** : VULVA — usu. considered vulgar **2 a** : SEXUAL INTERCOURSE — usu. considered vulgar **b** : the female partner in sexual intercourse — usu. considered vulgar

³**pus·sy** \'pə-sē\ *adj* **pus·si·er; -est** (ca. 1890) : full of or resembling pus

⁴**pus·sy** \'pə-sē\ *var of* ¹PURSY

pussy·cat \'pu̇-sē-,kat\ *n* (1805) **1** : CAT **2** : one that is weak, compliant, or amiable : SOFTY

pussy·foot \'pu̇-sē-,fu̇t\ *vi* (1903) **1** : to tread or move warily or stealthily **2** : to refrain from committing oneself — **pussy·foot·er** *n*

pussy·toes \'pu̇-sē-,tōz\ *or* **puss·y's–toes** \-,sēz-\ *n pl but sing or pl in constr* (1892) : any of a genus (*Antennaria*) of woolly or hoary chiefly temperate composite herbs that have small usu. whitish discoid flower heads and a pappus formed of club-shaped bristles

pussy willow *n* (1869) : a willow (as the American *Salix discolor*) having large cylindrical silky aments

¹**pus·tu·lant** \'pəs-chə-lənt; 'pəs-tyə-, -tə-\ *n* (1871) : an agent (as a chemical) that induces pustule formation

²**pustulant** *adj* (ca. 1890) : producing pustules

pus·tu·lar \-lər\ *adj* (1739) **1** : of, relating to, or resembling pustules **2** : covered with pustular prominences : PUSTULATED

pus·tu·lat·ed \-,lā-təd\ *adj* (1732) : covered with pustules

pus·tu·la·tion \,pəs-chə-'lā-shən, ,pəs-tyə-, -tə-\ *n* (ca. 1860) **1** : the act of producing pustules : the state of having pustules **2** : PUSTULE

pus·tule \'pəs-(,)chü(ə)l, -(,)tyü(ə)l, -(,)tü(ə)l\ *n* [ME, fr. L *pustula*; akin to Lith *pusti* to blow, Gk *physa* breath] (14c) **1** : a small circumscribed elevation of the skin containing pus and having an inflamed base **2** : a small often distinctively colored elevation or spot resembling a blister or pimple

¹**put** \'pu̇t\ *vb* **put; put·ting** [ME *putten;* akin to OE *putung* instigation, MD *poten* to plant] *vt* (12c) **1 a** : to place in a specified position or relationship : LAY ⟨~ the book on the table⟩ **b** : to move in a specified direction : SET ⟨~ to send (as a weapon or missile) into or through something : THRUST (2) : to throw with an overhand pushing motion ⟨~ the shot⟩ **d** : to bring into a specified state or condition ⟨a reapportionment . . . that was ~ into effect at the September primaries — *Current Biog.*⟩ **2 a** : to cause to endure or suffer something : SUBJECT ⟨~ traitors to death⟩ **b** : IMPOSE, INFLICT ⟨~ a special tax on luxuries⟩ **3 a** : to set before one for judgment or decision ⟨~ the question⟩ **b** : to call for a formal vote on ⟨~ the motion⟩ **4 a** (1) : to convey into another form ⟨want to ~ my feelings into words⟩ (2) : to translate into another language or style ⟨~ the poem into English⟩ (3) : ADAPT ⟨lyrics ~ to music⟩ **b** : EXPRESS, STATE ⟨*putting* it mildly⟩ **5 a** : to devote (oneself) to an activity or end ⟨~ himself to winning back their confidence⟩ **b** : APPLY ⟨~ her mind to the problem⟩ **c** : ASSIGN ⟨~ them to work⟩ **d** : to cause to perform an action : URGE ⟨~ the horse over the fence⟩ **e** : IMPEL, INCITE ⟨~ him into a frenzy⟩ **6 a** : REPOSE, REST ⟨~s his faith in reason⟩ **b** : INVEST ⟨~ her money in the company⟩ **7 a** : to give as an estimate ⟨~ the time as about eleven⟩ **b** : ATTACH, ATTRIBUTE ⟨~s a high value on their friendship⟩ **c** : IMPUTE ⟨~ the blame on the partners⟩ **8** : BET, WAGER ⟨~ $2 on the favorite⟩ ~ *vi* **1** : to start in motion : GO; *esp* : to leave in a hurry **2** *of a ship* : to take a specified course ⟨~ down the river⟩ — **put forth 1 a** : ASSERT, PROPOSE **b** : to make public : ISSUE **2** : to bring into action : EXERT **3** : to produce or send out by growth ⟨*put forth* leaves⟩ **4** : to start out — **put forward** : PROPOSE ⟨*put forward* a theory⟩ — **put in mind** : REMIND — **put one's finger on** : IDENTIFY ⟨*put his finger* on the cause of the trouble⟩ — **put one's foot down** : to take a firm stand — **put one's foot in one's mouth** : to make a tactless or embarrassing blunder — **put paid to** *Brit* : to finish off : WIPE OUT — **put the arm on or put the bite on** : to ask for money — **put the finger on** : to inform on ⟨*put the finger on* . . . heroin pushers —Barrie Zwicker⟩ — **put the make on** : to make sexual advances toward — **put to bed** : to make the final preparations for printing (as a newspaper) — **put together 1** : to create as a unified whole : CONSTRUCT **2**

: ADD, COMBINE — **put to it** : to give difficulty to : press hard ⟨had been *put to it* to keep up⟩

²put *n* (14c) **1** : a throw made with an overhand pushing motion; *specif* : the act or an instance of putting the shot **2** : an option to sell a specified amount of a security (as a stock) or commodity (as wheat) at a fixed price at or within a specified time — compare CALL 3d

³put *adj* (1848) : being in place : FIXED, SET ⟨stay ~ until I call⟩

put about *vi* (1748) *of a ship* : to change direction : go on another tack ~ *vt* : to cause to change course or direction

put across *vt* (1919) **1** : PUT OVER 3 **2** : to convey effectively or forcefully

put—and—take \ˌpu̇t-ᵊn-ˈtāk\ *n* (1922) : any of various games of chance played with a teetotum or with dice in which players contribute to a pool and take from it according to the instructions on the top or dice

pu·ta·tive \ˈpyü-tə-tiv\ *adj* [ME, fr. LL *putativus*, fr. L *putatus*, pp. of *putare* to think] (15c) **1** : commonly accepted or supposed **2** : assumed to exist or to have existed — **pu·ta·tive·ly** *adv*

put away *vt* (14c) **1 a** : DISCARD, RENOUNCE ⟨to *put* grief *away* is disloyal to the memory of the departed —H. A. Overstreet⟩ **b** : DIVORCE **2** : to eat or drink up : CONSUME **3 a** : to confine esp. in a mental institution **b** : BURY **c** : KILL

put by *vt* (15c) **1** *archaic* : REJECT **2** : to lay aside : SAVE

put—down \ˈpu̇t-ˌdau̇n\ *n* (1962) : an act or instance of putting down; *esp* : a humiliating remark : SQUELCH

put down *vt* (14c) **1** : to bring to an end : STOP ⟨*put down* a riot⟩ **2 a** : DEPOSE, DEGRADE **b** : DISPARAGE, BELITTLE ⟨mentioned his poetry only to *put it down*⟩ **c** : DISAPPROVE, CRITICIZE ⟨was *put down* for the way she dressed⟩ **d** : HUMILIATE, SQUELCH ⟨*put* him *down* with a sharp retort⟩ **3** : to make ineffective : CHECK ⟨*put down* the gossip⟩ **4** : to do away with (as an injured, sick, or aged animal) : DESTROY **5 a** : to put in writing ⟨*put* it *down* truthfully⟩ **b** : to enter in a list ⟨*put* me *down* for a donation⟩ **6 a** : to place in a category ⟨I *put* him *down* as a hypochondriac —O. S. J. Gogarty⟩ **b** : ATTRIBUTE ⟨*put* it *down* to inexperience⟩ **7** : to pack or preserve for future use **8** : CONSUME ⟨*putting down* helping after helping —Carson McCullers⟩ — **put down roots** : to establish a permanent residence

put in *vt* (15c) **1** : to make a formal offer or declaration of ⟨*put in* a plea of guilty⟩ **2** : to come in with : INTERPOSE ⟨*put in* a word for his brother⟩ **3** : to spend (time) esp. at some occupation or job ⟨*put in* six hours at the office⟩ **4** : PLANT ⟨*put in* a crop⟩ ~ *vi* **1** : to call at or enter a place; *esp* : to enter a harbor or port **2** : to make an application, request, or offer — often used with *for* ⟨had to retire and *put in* for a pension —Seymour Nagan⟩

put·log \ˈpu̇t-ˌlȯg, ˈpət-, -ˌläg\ *n* [prob. alter. of earlier *putlock*, perh. fr. ³*put* + ²*lock*] (1645) : one of the short timbers that support the flooring of a scaffold

put off *vt* (14c) **1 a** : DISCONCERT **b** : REPEL **2 a** : to hold back to a later time **b** : to induce to wait ⟨*put* the bill collector *off*⟩ **3** : to rid oneself of : TAKE OFF **4** : to sell or pass fraudulently

¹put—on \ˈpu̇t-ˌȯn, -ˌän\ *adj* (1621) : PRETENDED, ASSUMED

²put—on \ˈpu̇t-ˌȯn, -ˌän\ *n* (ca. 1927) **1** : an instance of putting someone on ⟨conversational ~s are related to old-fashioned joshing —Jacob Brackman⟩ **2** : PARODY, SPOOF ⟨a kind of ~ of every pretentious film ever made —C. A. Ridley⟩

put on *vt* (15c) **1 a** : to dress oneself in : DON **b** : to make part of one's appearance or behavior **c** : FEIGN ⟨*put* a saintly manner *on*⟩ **2** : to cause to act or operate : APPLY ⟨*put on* more speed⟩ **3 a** : ADD ⟨*put on* weight⟩ **b** : EXAGGERATE, OVERSTATE ⟨he's *putting* it *on* when he makes such claims⟩ **4** : PERFORM, PRODUCE ⟨*put on* a play⟩ **5 a** : to mislead deliberately esp. for amusement ⟨the interviewer . . . must be put down — or possibly, *put on* —Melvin Maddocks⟩ **b** : KID ⟨you're *putting* me *on*⟩

put·out \ˈpu̇t-ˌau̇t\ *n* (1885) : the retiring of a base runner or batter by a defensive player in baseball

put out *vt* (14c) **1** : EXTINGUISH ⟨*put* the fire *out*⟩ **2** : EXERT, USE ⟨*put out* considerable effort⟩ **3** : PUBLISH, ISSUE **4** : to produce for sale **5 a** : DISCONCERT, EMBARRASS **b** : ANNOY, IRRITATE ⟨don't *put* yourself *out* for us⟩ **6** : to cause to be out (as in baseball or cricket) ~ *vi* **1** : to set out from shore **2** : to make an effort **3** : to engage in sexual intercourse

put over *vt* (1528) **1** : POSTPONE, DELAY **2** : PUT ACROSS 2 **3** : to achieve or carry through by deceit or trickery ⟨*put one over* on me⟩

pu·tre·fac·tion \ˌpyü-trə-ˈfak-shən\ *n* [ME *putrefaccion*, fr. LL *putrefaction-, putrefactio*, fr. L *putrefacere*] (14c) **1** : the decomposition of organic matter; *esp* : the typically anaerobic splitting of proteins by bacteria and fungi with the formation of foul-smelling incompletely oxidized products **2** : the state of being putrefied : CORRUPTION — **pu·tre·fac·tive** \-ˈfak-tiv\ *adj*

pu·tre·fy \ˈpyü-trə-ˌfī\ *vb* **-fied; -fy·ing** [ME *putrefien*, fr. MF & L; MF *putrefier*, fr. L *putrefacere*, fr. *putrēre* to be rotten + *facere* to make — more at DO] (14c) *vt* : to make putrid ~ *vi* : to undergo putrefaction **syn** see DECAY

pu·tres·cence \pyü-ˈtres-ᵊn(t)s\ *n* (1646) : the state of being putrescent

pu·tres·cent \-ˈs°nt\ *adj* [L *putrescent-, putrescens*, prp. of *putrescere* to grow rotten, incho. of *putrēre*] (1732) **1** : undergoing putrefaction : becoming putrid **2** : of or relating to putrefaction

pu·tres·ci·ble \-ˈtre-sə-bəl\ *adj* (1797) : liable to become putrid

pu·tres·cine \-ˈtre-ˌsēn\ *n* [ISV, fr. L *putrescere*] (1887) : a crystalline slightly poisonous ptomaine $C_4H_{12}N_2$ that occurs in small amounts in virtually all living things

pu·trid \ˈpyü-trəd\ *adj* [L *putridus*, fr. *putrēre* to be rotten, fr. *puter, putris* rotten; akin to L *putēre* to stink — more at FOUL] (1598) **1 a** : being in a state of putrefaction : ROTTEN **b** : of, relating to, or characteristic of putrefaction : FOUL ⟨a ~ odor⟩ **2 a** : morally corrupt **b** : totally objectionable **syn** see MALODOROUS — **pu·trid·i·ty** \pyü-ˈtri-də-tē\ *n* — **pu·trid·ly** \ˈpyü-trəd-lē\ *adv*

putsch \ˈpu̇ch\ *n* [G] (1920) : a secretly plotted and suddenly executed attempt to overthrow a government

putsch·ist \ˈpu̇-chist\ *n* (1898) : one who takes part in a putsch

putt \ˈpət\ *n* [Sc, lit., shove, gentle push, fr. *putt, put* to put] (1743) : a golf stroke made on a putting green to cause the ball to roll into or near the hole — **putt** *vb*

put·tee \ˌpə-ˈtē, pu̇-; ˈpə-tē\ *n* [Hindi *paṭṭī* strip of cloth, fr. Skt *paṭṭikā*] (1886) **1** : a cloth strip wrapped around the leg from ankle to knee **2 a** : a usu. leather legging secured by a strap or catch or by laces

puttees

¹put·ter \ˈpu̇t-ər\ *n* (14c) : one that puts ⟨a ~ of questions⟩

²putt·er \ˈpə-tər\ *n* (1743) **1** : a golf club used in putting **2** : one that putts

³put·ter \ˈpə-tər\ *vi* [alter. of *potter*] (ca. 1877) **1** : to move or act aimlessly or idly **2** : to work at random : TINKER — **put·ter·er** \-tər-ər\ *n*

put through *vt* (1852) **1** : to carry to a successful conclusion ⟨*put through* a number of reforms⟩ **2 a** : to make a telephone connection for **b** : to obtain a connection for (a telephone call)

putt·ing green \ˈpə-tiŋ-\ *n* (1841) : a smooth grassy area at the end of a golf fairway containing the hole; *also* : a similar area usu. with many holes that is used for practice

put·to \ˈpü-(ˌ)tō\ *n, pl* **put·ti** \-(ˌ)tē\ [It, lit., boy, fr. (assumed) VL *puttus*, alter. of L *putus*; akin to L *puer* boy — more at PUERILE] (1644) : a figure of an infant boy esp. in European art of the Renaissance — usu. used in pl.

¹put·ty \ˈpə-tē\ *n, pl* **putties** [F *potée* potter's glaze, lit., potful, fr. OF, fr. *pot* pot — more at POTTAGE] (ca. 1706) **1 a** : a doughlike material typically made of whiting and linseed oil that is used esp. to fasten glass in window frames and to fill crevices in woodwork **b** : any of various substances resembling putty in appearance, consistency, or use **2** : a light brownish gray to light grayish brown color **3** : one who is easily manipulated ⟨is ~ in her hands⟩ — **put·ty·less** *adj* — **put·ty·like** *adj*

²putty *vt* **put·tied; put·ty·ing** (1734) : to use putty on or apply putty to

putty knife *n* (1858) : an implement with a broad flat metal blade used esp. for applying putty and for scraping

put·ty·root \ˈpə-tē-ˌrüt, -ˌru̇t\ *n* (1817) : a No. American orchid (*Aplectrum hyemale*) having a slender naked rootstock and producing a solitary leaf and a scape bearing a raceme of brownish flowers

put—up \ˈpu̇t-ˌəp\ *adj* (1810) : arranged secretly beforehand

put up *vt* (14c) **1 a** : to place in a container or receptacle ⟨*put* his lunch *up* in a bag⟩ **b** : to put away (a sword) in a scabbard : SHEATHE **c** : to prepare so as to preserve for later use : CAN **d** : to put in storage **2** : to start (game) from cover **3** : to nominate for election **4** : to offer up (as a prayer) **5** : SET 16 **6** : to offer for public sale ⟨*put* their possessions *up* for auction⟩ **7** : to give food and shelter to : ACCOMMODATE **8** : to arrange (as a plot or scheme) with others ⟨*put up* a job to steal the jewels⟩ **9** : BUILD, ERECT **10 a** : to make a display of ⟨*put up* a bluff⟩ **b** : to engage in ⟨*put up* a struggle against odds⟩ **11 a** : CONTRIBUTE, PAY **b** : to offer as a prize or stake **12** *chiefly Brit* : to increase the amount of : RAISE ~ *vi* : LODGE — **put up to** : INCITE, INSTIGATE ⟨they *put* him *up to* playing the prank⟩ — **put up with** : to endure or tolerate without complaint or attempt at reprisal

put—up·on \ˈpu̇t-ə-ˌpȯn, -ˌpän\ *adj* (1920) : imposed upon : taken advantage of

¹puz·zle \ˈpə-zəl\ *vb* **puz·zled; puz·zling** \ˈpə-zə-liŋ, ˈpəz-liŋ\ [origin unknown] *vt* (1602) **1** : to offer or represent to (as a person) a problem difficult to solve or a situation difficult to resolve : challenge mentally; *also* : to exert (as oneself) over such a problem or situation ⟨they *puzzled* their wits to find a solution⟩ **2** *archaic* : COMPLICATE, ENTANGLE **3** : to solve with difficulty or ingenuity ⟨~ out an answer to a riddle⟩ ~ *vi* **1** : to be uncertain as to action or choice **2** : to attempt a solution of a puzzle by guesswork or experiment — **puz·zler** \ˈpə-zə-lər, ˈpəz-lər\ *n*

syn PUZZLE, PERPLEX, BEWILDER, DISTRACT, NONPLUS, CONFOUND, DUMBFOUND mean to baffle and disturb mentally. PUZZLE implies existence of a problem difficult to solve ⟨the persistent fever *puzzled* the doctor⟩. PERPLEX adds a suggestion of worry and uncertainty esp. about making a necessary decision ⟨a behavior that *perplexed* her friends⟩. BEWILDER stresses a confusion of mind that hampers clear and decisive thinking ⟨a *bewildering* number of possibilities⟩. DISTRACT implies agitation or uncertainty induced by conflicting preoccupations or interests ⟨*distracted* by personal problems⟩. NONPLUS implies a bafflement that makes orderly planning or deciding impossible ⟨the remark left us utterly *nonplussed*⟩. CONFOUND implies temporary mental paralysis caused by astonishment or profound abasement ⟨the tragic news *confounded* us all⟩. DUMBFOUND suggests intense but momentary confounding; often the idea of astonishment is so stressed that it becomes a near synonym of astound ⟨was at first too *dumbfounded* to reply⟩.

²puzzle *n* (ca. 1612) **1** : the state of being puzzled : PERPLEXITY **2 a** : something that puzzles **b** : a question, problem, or contrivance designed for testing ingenuity **syn** see MYSTERY

puz·zle·head·ed \ˈpə-zəl-ˌhe-dəd\ *adj* (ca. 1784) : having or based on confused attitudes or ideas — **puz·zle·head·ed·ness** *n*

puz·zle·ment \ˈpə-zəl-mənt\ *n* (1822) **1** : the state of being puzzled : PERPLEXITY **2** : PUZZLE

puzzling *adj* (1666) : difficult to understand or solve — **puz·zling·ly** *adv*

P—wave \ˈpē-ˌwāv\ *n* [by shortening] (1936) : PRESSURE WAVE

py- *or* **pyo-** *comb form* [Gk, fr. *pyon* pus — more at FOUL] : pus ⟨*pyemia*⟩ ⟨*pyorrhea*⟩

pya \ˈpyä, pē-ˈä\ *n* [Burmese] (1952) — see *kyat* at MONEY table

pyc·nid·i·um \pik-ˈni-dē-əm\ *n, pl* **-ia** \-dē-ə\ [NL, fr. Gk *pyknos* dense] (1857) : a flask-shaped fruiting body bearing conidiophores and conidia on the interior and occurring in various imperfect fungi and ascomycetes — **pyc·nid·i·al** \-dē-əl\ *adj*

\ə\ abut \ᵊ\ kitten, F table \ər\ further \a\ ash \ā\ ace \ä\ mop, mar \au̇\ out \ch\ chin \e\ bet \ē\ easy \g\ go \i\ hit \ī\ ice \j\ job \ŋ\ sing \ō\ go \ȯ\ law \ȯi\ boy \th\ thin \t̷h\ the \ü\ loot \u̇\ foot \y\ yet \zh\ vision \ȧ, k̲, ⁿ, œ, œ̄, ᵫ, ᵬ, ʸ\ *see* Guide to Pronunciation

pyc·no·go·nid \pik-'nä-gə-nəd, ,pik-nə-'gä-nəd\ n [ultim. fr. Gk *pyknos* + *gony* knee — more at KNEE] (1881) : SEA SPIDER

pyc·nom·e·ter \pik-'nä-mə-tər\ n [Gk *pyknos* + ISV -*meter*] (1858) : a standard vessel often provided with a thermometer for measuring and comparing the densities of liquids or solids

pye–dog \'pī-,dög\ n [perh. fr. Hindi *pāhī* outsider] (1864) : a half-wild dog common about Asian villages

pyel- or **pyelo-** comb form [NL, pelvis, fr. Gk *pyelos* basin; akin to Gk *plynein* to wash, *plein* to sail — more at FLOW] : renal pelvis ⟨*pyel*itis⟩

py·eli·tis \,pī-ə-'lī-təs\ n [NL] (ca. 1842) : inflammation of the lining of the renal pelvis

py·elo·ne·phri·tis \,pī-(ə-)lō-ni-'frī-təs\ n [NL] (1866) : inflammation of both the lining of the pelvis and the parenchyma of the kidney — **py·elo·ne·phrit·ic** \-'frī-tik\ adj

py·emia \pī-'ē-mē-ə\ n [NL] (ca. 1857) : septicemia caused by pus-forming bacteria and accompanied by multiple abscesses

py·gid·i·um \pī-'ji-dē-əm\ n, pl -**ia** \-dē-ə\ [NL, fr. Gk *pygidion*, dim. of *pygē* rump] (ca. 1849) : a caudal structure or the terminal body region of various invertebrates — **py·gid·i·al** \-dē-əl\ adj

pyg·mae·an or **pyg·me·an** \pig-'mē-ən, 'pig-mē-\ adj [L *pygmaeus*] (1667) : PYGMY

Pyg·ma·lion \pig-'māl-yən, -'mä-lē-ən\ n [L, fr. Gk *Pygmaliōn*] : a king of Cyprus who makes a female figure of ivory that is brought to life for him by Aphrodite

pyg·moid \'pig-,móid\ adj (ca. 1930) : resembling or having the characteristics of the Pygmies

pyg·my \'pig-mē\ n, pl **pygmies** [ME *pigmei*, fr. L *pygmaeus* of a pygmy, dwarfish, fr. Gk *pygmaios*, fr. *pygmē* fist, measure of length — more at PUNGENT] (14c) **1** often cap : any of a race of dwarfs described by ancient Greek authors **2** cap : any of a small people of equatorial Africa ranging under five feet (1.5 meters) in height **3 a** : a short insignificant person : DWARF **b** : something very small of its kind — **pygmy** adj

pygmy chimpanzee n (1962) : an anthropoid ape (*Pan paniscus*) of Zaire that has a lighter build than the related common chimpanzee (*P. troglodytes*) — called also *pygmy chimp*

py·ja·mas \pə-'jä-məz\ n, pl *chiefly Brit var of* PAJAMAS

pyk·nic \'pik-nik\ adj [ISV, fr. Gk *pyknos* dense, stocky] (1925) : characterized by shortness of stature, broadness of girth, and powerful muscularity : ENDOMORPHIC — **pyknic** n

py·lon \'pī-,län, -lən\ n [Gk *pylōn*, fr. *pylē* gate] (1850) **1 a** : a usu. massive gateway **b** : an ancient Egyptian gateway building in a truncated pyramidal form **c** : a monumental mass flanking an entranceway or an approach to a bridge **2 a** *chiefly Brit* : a tower for supporting either end of usu. a number of wires over a long span **b** : any of various towerlike structures **3 a** : a post or tower marking a prescribed course of flight for an airplane **b** : TRAFFIC CONE **4** : a rigid structure on the outside of an aircraft for supporting something (as an engine or missile) — see AIRPLANE illustration

py·lo·ric \pī-'lór-ik, pə-, -'lór-\ adj (1807) : of or relating to the pylorus; *also* : of, relating to, or situated in or near the posterior part of the stomach

py·lo·rus \-əs\ n, pl **py·lo·ri** \-'lór-ī, -(,)ē\ [LL, fr. Gk *pylōros*, lit., gatekeeper, fr. *pylē*] (1615) : the opening from the vertebrate stomach into the intestine

pyo·der·ma \,pī-ə-'dər-mə\ n [NL] (1930) : a bacterial skin inflammation marked by pus-filled lesions

pyo·gen·ic \-'je-nik\ adj [ISV] (ca. 1847) : producing pus ⟨~ bacteria⟩; *also* : marked by pus production ⟨~ meningitis⟩

py·or·rhea \,pī-ə-'rē-ə\ n [NL] (1878) : purulent inflammation of the sockets of the teeth leading usu. to loosening of the teeth

pyr- or **pyro-** comb form [ME, fr. MF, fr. LL, fr. Gk, fr. *pyr* — more at FIRE] **1** : fire : heat ⟨*pyro*meter⟩ ⟨*pyr*heliometer⟩ **2 a** : produced by or as if by the action of heat ⟨*pyro*electricity⟩ **b** : derived from a corresponding ortho acid by loss of one molecule of water from two molecules of acid ⟨*pyro*phosphoric acid⟩ **3** : fever ⟨*pyro*genic⟩

pyr·acan·tha \,pī-rə-'kan(t)-thə\ n [NL, fr. Gk *pyrakantha*, a tree, fr. *pyr-* + *akantha* thorn] (1705) : any of a small genus (*Pyracantha*) of Eurasian thorny evergreen or semievergreen shrubs of the rose family with alternate leaves, corymbs of white flowers, and small red or orange pomes

py·ral·id \pī-'ra-ləd\ n [ultim. fr. L *pyralis*, fly fabled as living in fire, fr. Gk, fr. *pyr* fire] (ca. 1890) : any of a very large heterogeneous family (Pyralidae) of mostly small slender long-legged moths — **pyralid** adj

¹**pyr·a·mid** \'pir-ə-,mid\ n [L *pyramid-*, *pyramis*, fr. Gk] (1549) **1 a** : an ancient massive structure found esp. in Egypt having typically a square ground plan, outside walls in the form of four triangles that meet in a point at the top, and inner sepulchral chambers **b** : a structure or object of similar form **2** : a polyhedron having for its base a polygon and for faces triangles with a common vertex — see VOLUME table **3 a** : a crystalline form each face of which intersects the vertical axis and either two lateral axes or in the tetragonal system one lateral axis **4** : an anatomical structure resembling a pyramid: as **a** : any of the conical masses that project from the renal medulla into the kidney pelvis **b** : either of two large bundles of motor fibers from the cerebral cortex that reach the medulla oblongata and are continuous with the pyramidal tracts of the spinal cord **5** : an immaterial structure built on a broad supporting base and narrowing gradually to an apex ⟨the socioeconomic ~⟩ — **py·ra·mi·dal** \pə-'ra-mə-d²l, ,pir-ə-'mi-\ adj — **py·ra·mi·dal·ly** adv — **pyr·a·mid·i·cal** \,pir-ə-'mi-di-kəl\ adj

pyramid 2

²**pyramid** vi (ca. 1900) **1** : to speculate (as on a security or commodity exchange) by using paper profits as margin for additional transactions **2** : to increase rapidly and progressively step by step on a broad base ~ vt **1** : to arrange or build up as if on the base of a pyramid **2** : to use (as profits) in speculative pyramiding **3** : to increase the impact of (as a tax assessed at the production level) on the ultimate consumer by treating as a cost subject to markup

pyramidal tract n (ca. 1890) : any of four columns of motor fibers that run in pairs on each side of the spinal cord and are continuations of the pyramids of the medulla oblongata

Pyr·a·mus \'pir-ə-məs\ n [L, fr. Gk *Pyramos*] : a legendary youth of Babylon who dies for love of Thisbe

py·ran \'pir-,an\ n [ISV] (1904) : either of two cyclic compounds C_5H_6O that contain five carbon atoms and one oxygen atom in the ring

py·ra·nose \'pī-rə-,nōs, -,nōz\ n [ISV] (1927) : a monosaccharide in the form of a cyclic hemiacetal containing a pyran ring

py·ran·o·side \pī-'ra-nə-,sīd\ n (1932) : a glycoside containing the pyran ring

pyr·ar·gy·rite \pī-'rär-jə-,rīt\ n [G *Pyrargyrit*, fr. Gk *pyr-* + *argyros* silver — more at ARGENT] (1849) : a mineral consisting of silver antimony sulfide that occurs in rhombohedral crystals or in massive form and has a dark red or black color with a metallic luster

pyre \'pīr\ n [L *pyra*, fr. Gk, fr. *pyr* fire — more at FIRE] (1658) : a combustible heap for burning a dead body as a funeral rite; *broadly* : a pile of material to be burned ⟨a ~ of dead leaves⟩

py·re·noid \pī-'rē-,nóid, 'pī-rə-\ n [ISV, fr. NL *pyrena* stone of a fruit, fr. Gk *pyrēn*; akin to Gk *pyros* wheat grain, wheat — more at FURZE] (ca. 1875) : one of the protein bodies in the chromatophores of various lower organisms (as some algae) that act as centers for starch deposition

py·re·thrin \pī-'rē-thrən, -'re-\ n [ISV, fr. L *pyrethrum*] (1924) : either of two oily liquid esters $C_{21}H_{28}O_3$ and $C_{22}H_{28}O_5$ having insecticidal properties and occurring esp. in the flowers of pyrethrum

py·re·throid \-'rē-,thróid, -'re-\ n [*pyrethr*in + -*oid*] (1949) : any of various synthetic compounds that are related to the pyrethrins and resemble them in insecticidal properties — **pyrethroid** adj

py·re·thrum \pī-'rē-thrəm, -'re-\ n [L, pellitory, fr. Gk *pyrethron*, fr. *pyr* fire] (ca. 1543) **1** : any of several chrysanthemums with finely divided often aromatic leaves including ornamentals as well as important sources of insecticides **2** : an insecticide made from the dried heads of any of several Old World chrysanthemums

py·ret·ic \pī-'re-tik\ adj [NL *pyreticus*, fr. Gk *pyretikos*, fr. *pyretos* fever, fr. *pyr*] (ca. 1858) : of or relating to fever : FEBRILE

Py·rex \'pir-,eks\ trademark — used for borosilicate glass and glassware resistant to heat, chemicals, and electricity

py·rex·ia \pī-'rek-sē-ə\ n [NL, fr. Gk *pyressein* to be feverish, fr. *pyretos*] (1769) : abnormal elevation of body temperature : FEVER — **py·rex·i·al** \-sē-əl\ adj — **py·rex·ic** \-sik\ adj

pyr·he·li·om·e·ter \,pīr-,hē-lē-'ä-mə-tər, ,pir-\ n [ISV] (1863) : an instrument for measuring the sun's radiant energy as received at the earth — **pyr·he·lio·met·ric** \-lē-ə-'me-trik\ adj

py·ric \'pī-rik, 'pir-ik\ adj [F *pyrique*, fr. Gk *pyr*] (1946) : resulting from, induced by, or associated with burning

pyr·i·dine \'pir-ə-,dēn\ n [*pyr-* + -*ide* + ²-*ine*] (1851) : a toxic water-soluble flammable liquid base C_5H_5N of pungent odor that is the parent of many naturally occurring organic compounds and is used as a solvent and as a denaturant for alcohol and in the manufacture of pharmaceuticals and waterproofing agents

pyr·i·dox·al \,pir-ə-'däk-,sal\ n [ISV, fr. *pyridoxine*] (1944) : a crystalline aldehyde $C_8H_9NO_3$ of the vitamin B_6 group that occurs as a phosphate and is active as a coenzyme

pyr·i·dox·amine \,pir-ə-'däk-sə-,mēn\ n [ISV *pyridoxine* + *amine*] (1944) : a crystalline amine $C_8H_{12}N_2O_2$ of the vitamin B_6 group that occurs as a phosphate and is active as a coenzyme

pyr·i·dox·ine \,pir-ə-'däk-,sēn, -sən\ n [*pyridine* + *ox-* + ²-*ine*] (1939) : a crystalline phenolic alcohol $C_8H_{11}NO_3$ of the vitamin B_6 group found esp. in cereals and convertible in the organism into pyridoxal and pyridoxamine

pyr·i·form \'pir-ə-,fórm\ adj [NL *pyriformis*, fr. ML *pyrum* pear (alter. of L *pirum*) + L -*iformis* -iform] (1741) : having the form of a pear

py·ri·meth·amine \,pir-ə-'me-thə-,mēn\ n [*pyrimidine* + *ethyl* + *amine*] (1952) : a folic acid antagonist $C_{12}H_{13}ClN_4$ used in the treatment of malaria and of toxoplasmosis

py·rim·i·dine \pī-'ri-mə-,dēn, pə-\ n [ISV, alter. of *pyridine*] (1885) **1** : a feeble organic base $C_4H_4N_2$ of penetrating odor **2** : a derivative of pyrimidine; *esp* : a base (as cytosine, thymine, or uracil) that is a constituent of DNA or RNA

py·rite \'pī-,rīt\ n [L *pyrites*] (1588) : a common mineral that consists of iron disulfide, has a pale brass-yellow color and metallic luster, and is burned in making sulfur dioxide and sulfuric acid

py·rites \pə-'rī-tēz, pī-; 'pī-,rīts\ n, pl **pyrites** [L, flint, fr. Gk *pyritēs* or in fire, fr. *pyr* fire] (1543) : any of various metallic-looking sulfides of which pyrite is the commonest — **py·rit·ic** \-'ri-tik\ adj

py·ro·cat·e·chol \,pī-rō-'ka-tə-,kól, -,kōl\ n [ISV] (1890) : a crystalline phenol $C_6H_6O_2$ obtained by pyrolysis of various natural substances (as resins and lignins) but usu. made synthetically and used esp. as a photographic developer and in organic synthesis

py·ro·clas·tic \-'klas-tik\ adj [ISV] : formed by or involving fragmentation as a result of volcanic or igneous action

py·ro·elec·tric·i·ty \,pī-rō-ə-,lek-'tri-sə-tē, -ē-,lek-\ n [ISV] (ca. 1834) : a state of electrical polarization produced (as in a crystal) by a change of temperature — **py·ro·elec·tric** \-'lek-trik\ adj

py·ro·gal·lol \,pī-rō-'ga-,lól, -,lōl; -'gó-\ n [ISV *pyro-* + *gallic* (acid) + ¹-*ol*] (1876) : a poisonous bitter crystalline phenol $C_6H_6O_3$ with weak acid properties that is obtained usu. by pyrolysis of gallic acid and used esp. as a mild reducing agent (as in photographic developing)

py·ro·gen \'pī-rə-jən\ n [ISV] (ca. 1890) : a fever-producing substance

py·ro·gen·ic \,pī-rō-'je-nik\ adj [ISV] (1853) **1** : producing or produced by heat or fever **2** : of or relating to igneous origin — **py·ro·ge·nic·i·ty** \,pī-rō-jə-'ni-sə-tē\ n

py·ro·la \pī-'rō-lə\ n [NL, prob. fr. L *pirum* pear] (1578) : WINTERGREEN I

py·ro·lig·ne·ous acid \,pī-rō-'lig-nē-əs-\ n [F *pyroligneux*, fr. *pyr-* + *ligneux* woody, fr. L *lignosus*, fr. *lignum* wood — more at LIGNEOUS] (ca. 1790) : an acid reddish brown aqueous liquid containing chiefly acetic acid, methanol, wood oils, and tars that is obtained by destructive distillation of wood

py·ro·lu·site \,pī-rō-'lü-,sīt\ n [G *Pyrolusit*, fr. Gk *pyr-* + *lousis* washing, fr. *louein* to wash — more at LYE] (1828) : a mineral consisting of manganese dioxide that is of an iron-black or dark steel-gray color and metallic luster, is usu. soft, and is the most important ore of manganese

py·rol·y·sate \pī-'rä-lə-,zāt, -,sāt\ or **py·rol·y·zate** \-,zāt\ n (1944) : a product of pyrolysis

py·rol·y·sis \pī-'rä-lə-səs\ *n* [NL] (ca. 1890) : chemical change brought about by the action of heat — **py·ro·lyt·ic** \ˌpī-rə-'li-tik\ *adj* — **py·ro·lyt·i·cal·ly** \-ti-k(ə-)lē\ *adv*

py·ro·lyze *also* **py·ro·lize** \'pī-rə-ˌlīz\ *vt* **-lyzed** *also* **-lized; -lyz·ing** *also* **-liz·ing** (1932) : to subject to pyrolysis — **py·ro·lyz·able** \ˌpī-rə-'lī-zə-bəl\ *adj* — **py·ro·lyz·er** *n*

py·ro·man·cy \-ˌman(t)-sē\ *n* [ME *pyromancie*, fr. MF, fr. LL *pyromantia*, fr. Gk *pyromanteia*, fr. *pyr* fire + *manteia* divination — more at -MANCY] (14c) : divination by means of fire or flames

py·ro·ma·nia \ˌpī-rō-'mā-nē-ə, -nyə\ *n* [NL] (ca. 1842) : an irresistible impulse to start fires — **py·ro·ma·ni·ac** \-nē-ˌak\ *n* — **py·ro·ma·ni·a·cal** \-mə-'nī-ə-kəl\ *adj*

py·ro·met·al·lur·gy \-'me-t³l-ˌər-jē, *esp Brit* -mə-'ta-lər-\ *n* [ISV] (1908) : chemical metallurgy depending on heat action (as roasting and smelting) — **py·ro·met·al·lur·gi·cal** \-ˌme-t³l-'ər-ji-kəl\ *adj*

py·rom·e·ter \pī-'rä-mə-tər\ *n* [ISV] (1796) : an instrument for measuring temperatures esp. when beyond the range of mercurial thermometers — **py·ro·met·ric** \ˌpī-rə-'me-trik\ *adj* — **py·ro·met·ri·cal·ly** \-tri-k(ə-)lē\ *adv* — **py·rom·e·try** \pī-'rä-mə-trē\ *n*

py·ro·mor·phite \ˌpī-rə-'mȯr-ˌfīt\ *n* [G *Pyromorphit*, fr. Gk *pyr-* + *morphē* form] (ca. 1814) : a mineral consisting essentially of a lead chloride and phosphate

py·ro·nine \'pī-rə-ˌnēn\ *n* [ISV, irreg. fr. *pyr-* + ²-*ine*] (1895) : any of several basic xanthene dyes used chiefly as biological stains

py·ro·nin·o·phil·ic \ˌpī-rə-ˌnē-nə-'fi-lik\ *adj* (1946) : staining selectively with pyronines ⟨~ cells⟩

py·rope \'pīr-ˌōp\ *n* [ME *pirope*, a red gem, fr. MF, fr. L *pyropus*, a red bronze, fr. Gk *pyrōpos*, lit., fiery-eyed, fr. *pyr-* + *ōp-, ōps* eye — more at EYE] (1804) : a magnesium-aluminum garnet that is deep red in color and is frequently used as a gem

py·ro·phor·ic \ˌpī-rə-'fȯr-ik, -'fär-\ *adj* [NL *pyrophorus*, fr. Gk *pyrophoros* fire-bearing, fr. *pyr-* + *-phoros* carrying — more at -PHORE] (1836) **1** : igniting spontaneously **2** : emitting sparks when scratched or struck esp. with steel

py·ro·phos·phate \-'fäs-ˌfāt\ *n* (1836) : a salt or ester of pyrophosphoric acid

py·ro·phos·pho·ric acid \-ˌfäs-'fȯr-ik-, -'fär-; -'fäs-f(ə-)rik-\ *n* [ISV] (1832) : a crystalline acid $H_4P_2O_7$ formed when orthophosphoric acid is heated or prepared in the form of salts by heating acid salts of orthophosphoric acid

py·ro·phyl·lite \ˌpī-rō-'fi-ˌlīt, pī-'rä-fə-ˌlīt\ *n* [G *Pyrophyllit*, fr. Gk *pyr-* + *phyllon* leaf — more at BLADE] (1830) : a white or greenish mineral that is a hydrous aluminum silicate, resembles talc, occurs in a foliated form or in compact masses, and is used esp. in ceramic wares

py·ro·sis \pī-'rō-səs\ *n* [NL, fr. Gk *pyrōsis* burning, fr. *pyroun* to burn, fr. *pyr* fire — more at FIRE] (1789) : HEARTBURN

¹**py·ro·tech·nic** \ˌpī-rə-'tek-nik\ *also* **py·ro·tech·ni·cal** \-ni-kəl\ *adj* [F *pyrotechnique*, fr. Gk *pyr* fire + *technē* art — more at TECHNICAL] (1825) : of or relating to pyrotechnics — **py·ro·tech·ni·cal·ly** \-ni-k(ə-)lē\ *adv*

²**pyrotechnic** *n* (1840) **1 a** : FIREWORK **b** : any of various similar devices (as for igniting a rocket or producing an explosion) **2 a** : a combustible substance used in a firework

py·ro·tech·nics \ˌpī-rə-'tek-niks\ *n pl* (1729) **1** *sing or pl in constr* : the art of making or the manufacture and use of fireworks **2 a** : a display of fireworks **b** : a spectacular display (as of extreme virtuosity) ⟨verbal ~⟩ ⟨keyboard ~⟩ — **py·ro·tech·nist** \-'tek-nist\ *n*

py·rox·ene \pī-'räk-ˌsēn, pə-\ *n* [F *pyroxène*, fr. Gk *pyr-* + *xenos* stranger] (1800) : any of a group of igneous-rock-forming silicate minerals that contain calcium, sodium, magnesium, iron, or aluminum, usu. occur in short prismatic crystals or massive form, are often laminated, and vary in color from white to dark green or black — **py·rox·e·nic** \ˌpī-ˌräk-'sē-nik, pə-, 'se-\ *adj* — **py·rox·e·noid** \pī-'räk-sə-ˌnȯid, pə-\ *adj or n*

py·rox·e·nite \pī-'räk-sə-ˌnīt, pə-\ *n* (ca. 1862) : an igneous rock that is free from olivine and is composed essentially of pyroxene — **py·rox·e·nit·ic** \-ˌräk-sə-'ni-tik\ *adj*

py·rox·y·lin \pī-'räk-sə-lən, pə-\ *n* [ISV *pyr-* + Gk *xylon* wood] (ca. 1847) **1** : a flammable mixture of nitrocelluloses used esp. in making plastics and water-repellent coatings (as lacquers) **2** : a pyroxylin product

Pyr·rha \'pir-ə\ *n* [L, fr. Gk] : the wife of Deucalion

pyr·rhic \'pir-ik\ *n* [L *pyrrhichius*, fr. Gk (*pous*) *pyrrhichios*, fr. *pyrrhichē*, a kind of dance] (1626) : a metrical foot consisting of two short or unaccented syllables

Pyr·rhic \'pir-ik\ *adj* [*Pyrrhus*, king of Epirus who sustained heavy losses in defeating the Romans] (1885) : achieved at excessive cost ⟨a ~ victory⟩; *also* : costly to the point of negating or outweighing expected benefits ⟨a great but ~ act of ingenuity⟩

Pyr·rho·nism \'pir-ə-ˌni-zəm\ *n* [F *pyrrhonisme*, fr. *Pyrrhon* Pyrrho, 4th cent. B.C. Gk. philosopher, fr. Gk *Pyrrhōn*] (ca. 1670) **1** : the doctrines of a school of ancient extreme skeptics who suspended judgment on every proposition — compare ACADEMICISM **2** : total or radical skepticism — **Pyr·rho·nist** \-nist\ *n*

pyr·rho·tite \'pir-ə-ˌtīt\ *n* [modif. of G *Pyrrhotin*, fr. Gk *pyrrhotēs* redness, fr. *pyrrhos* red, fr. *pyr* fire — more at FIRE] (1868) : a bronze-colored mineral of metallic luster that consists of ferrous sulfide and is attracted by a magnet

Pyr·rhus \'pir-əs\ *n* [L, fr. Gk *Pyrrhos*] : a son of Achilles and slayer of Priam at the taking of Troy

pyr·role \'pir-ˌōl\ *n* [Gk *pyrrhos*] (1835) : a toxic liquid heterocyclic compound C_4H_5N that has a ring consisting of four carbon atoms and one nitrogen atom, polymerizes readily in air, and is the parent compound of many biologically important substances (as bile pigments, porphyrins, and chlorophyll); *broadly* : a derivative of pyrrole — **pyr·rol·ic** \pi-'rō-lik\ *adj*

py·ru·vate \pī-'rü-ˌvāt\ *n* (1855) : a salt or ester of pyruvic acid

py·ru·vic acid \pī-'rü-vik-\ *n* [ISV *pyr-* + L *uva* grapes; fr. its importance in fermentation — more at UVULA] (1838) : a 3-carbon keto acid $C_3H_4O_3$ that in carbohydrate metabolism is an important intermediate product formed as pyruvate by glycolysis

¹**Py·thag·o·re·an** \pə-ˌtha-gə-'rē-ən, (ˌ)pī-\ *n* (1550) : any of a group professing to be followers of the Greek philosopher Pythagoras

²**Pythagorean** *adj* (ca. 1580) : of, relating to, or associated with the Greek philosopher Pythagoras, his philosophy, or the Pythagoreans

Py·thag·o·re·an·ism \-'rē-ə-ˌni-zəm\ *n* (ca. 1727) : the doctrines and theories of Pythagoras and the Pythagoreans who developed some basic principles of mathematics and astronomy, originated the doctrine of the harmony of the spheres, and believed in metempsychosis, the eternal recurrence of things, and the mystical significance of numbers

Pythagorean theorem *n* (ca. 1909) : a theorem in geometry: the square of the length of the hypotenuse of a right triangle equals the sum of the squares of the lengths of the other two sides

Pyth·i·ad \'pi-thē-ˌad, -əd\ *n* [Gk *Pythia*, the Pythian games, fr. neut. pl. of *pythios*] (1842) : the 4-year period between celebrations of the Pythian games in ancient Greece

¹**Pyth·i·an** \'pi-thē-ən\ *adj* [L *pythius* of Delphi, fr. Gk *pythios*, fr. *Pythō* Pytho, name for Delphi, Greece] (1603) **1** : of or relating to games celebrated at Delphi every four years **2** : of or relating to Delphi or its oracle of Apollo

²**Pythian** *n* (1903) : KNIGHT OF PYTHIAS

Pyth·i·as \'pi-thē-əs\ *n* [Gk] : a friend of Damon condemned to death by Dionysius of Syracuse

py·thon \'pī-ˌthän, -thən\ *n* [L, monstrous serpent killed by Apollo, fr. Gk *Pythōn*, fr. *Pythō Delphi*] (1836): any of various large constricting snakes (as a boa); *esp* : any of the large oviparous snakes (subfamily Pythoninae of the family Boidae) of Africa, Asia, Australia, and adjacent islands that include some of the largest existing snakes

py·tho·ness \'pī-thə-nəs, 'pi-\ *n* [ME *Phitonesse*, fr. MF *pithonisse*, fr. LL *pythonissa*, fr. Gk *Pythōn*, spirit of divination, perh. fr. *Pythō*, seat of the Delphic oracle] (14c) **1** : a woman who practices divination **2** : a prophetic priestess of Apollo — **py·thon·ic** \pi-'thä-nik\ *adj*

python

py·uria \pī-'yur-ē-ə\ *n* [NL] (ca. 1811) : pus in the urine; *also* : a condition characterized by pus in the urine

pyx \'piks\ *n* [ME, fr. ML *pyxis*, fr. L, box, fr. Gk, fr. *pyxos* box (shrub)] (15c) **1** : a container for the reserved host; *esp* : a small round metal receptacle used to carry the Eucharist to the sick **2** : a box used in a mint for deposit of sample coins reserved for testing weight and fineness

pyx·ie \'pik-sē\ *n* [by shortening & alter. fr. NL *Pyxidanthera*] (1882) : a creeping evergreen dicotyledonous shrub (*Pyxidanthera barbulata* of the family Diapensiaceae) of the sandy pine barrens of the Atlantic coast of the U.S. that has white or pink pentamerous flowers

pyx·is \'pik-səs\ *n, pl* **pyx·i·des** \-sə-ˌdēz\ [NL, fr. L, box] (1845) : a capsular fruit that dehisces so that the upper part falls off like a cap

\ə\ **abut** \ᵊ\ **kitten**, F **table** \ər\ **further** \a\ **ash** \ā\ **ace** \ä\ **mop, mar** \au̇\ **out** \ch\ **chin** \e\ **bet** \ē\ **easy** \g\ **go** \i\ **hit** \ī\ **ice** \j\ **job** \ŋ\ **sing** \ō\ **go** \ȯ\ **law** \ȯi\ **boy** \th\ **thin** \t͟h\ **the** \ü\ **loot** \u̇\ **foot** \y\ **yet** \zh\ **vision** \à, ḵ, ⁿ, œ, œ̄, ᵫ, ᵫ̄, ʸ\ *see* Guide to Pronunciation

q \'kyü\ *n, pl* **q's** *or* **qs** \'kyüz\ *often cap, often attrib* (bef. 12c) **1 a** : the 17th letter of the English alphabet   **b** : a graphic representation of this letter   **c** : a speech counterpart of orthographic *q* **2** : a graphic device for reproducing the letter *q* **3** : one designated *q* esp. as the 17th in order or class **4** : something shaped like the letter Q

Q–boat \'kyü-ˌbōt\ *n* (1918) : Q-SHIP

Q fever \'kyü-\ *n* [*query*] (1937) : a disease that is characterized by high fever, chills, and muscular pains, is caused by a rickettsial bacterium (*Coxiella burnetii*), and is transmitted by raw milk, by droplet infection, or by ticks

qin·tar \kyin-'tär, kin-\ *n, pl* **qin·dar·ka** \-'där-kə\ *also* **qintars** *or* **qindars** \-'därz\ [Alb] (ca. 1929) — see *lek* at MONEY table

qi·vi·ut \'kē-vē-ət, -vē-ˌüt\ *n* [Inuit] (1958) : the wool of the undercoat of the musk ox

qoph \'kōf\ *n* [Heb *qōph*] (ca. 1823) : the 19th letter of the Hebrew alphabet — see ALPHABET table

Q–ship \'kyü-ˌship\ *n* (1919) : an armed ship disguised as a merchant or fishing ship to decoy enemy submarines into gun range

q.t. \ˌkyü-'tē\ *n, often cap Q&T* [abbr.] (ca. 1887) : QUIET — usu. used in the phrase *on the q.t.*

qua \'kwä *also* 'kwā\ *prep* [L, which way, as, fr. abl. sing. fem. of *qui* who — more at WHO] (1647) : in the capacity or character of : AS ⟨confusion of the role of scientist ∼ scientist with that of scientist as citizen —Philip Handler⟩

quaa·lude \'kwä-ˌlüd\ *n* [fr. *Quaalude,* a trademark] (1966) : a tablet or capsule of methaqualone

¹quack \'kwak\ *vi* [alter. of *queck* to quack, fr. ME *queken,* fr. *queke,* interj., of imit. origin] (14c) : to make the characteristic cry of a duck

²quack *n* (1839) : a noise made by quacking

³quack *vi* [⁴*quack*] (1628) : to act like a quack

⁴quack *n* [short for *quacksalver*] (1638) **1** : CHARLATAN 2 **2** : a pretender to medical skill — **quack·ish** \'kwa-kish\ *adj*

⁵quack *adj* (1653) : of, relating to, or characteristic of a quack; *esp* : pretending to cure diseases

quack·ery \'kwa-k(ə-)rē\ *n* (ca. 1711) : the practices or pretensions of a quack

quack grass \'kwak-\ *n* [alter. of *quick* (grass), alter. of *quitch* (grass)] (ca. 1818) : a European grass (*Agropyron repens*) that is naturalized throughout No. America as a weed and spreads by creeping rhizomes — called also *couch grass, quitch, twitch, witchgrass*

quack·sal·ver \'kwak-ˌsal-vər\ *n* [obs. D (now *kwakzalver*)] (1579) : CHARLATAN, QUACK

¹quad \'kwäd\ *n* (1820) : QUADRANGLE

²quad *n* [short for *quadrat*] (ca. 1879) : a type-metal space that is 1 en or more in width

³quad *vt* **quad·ded; quad·ding** (1888) : to fill out (as a typeset line) with blank space

⁴quad *n* (1896) : QUADRUPLET

⁵quad *adj* (1970) : QUADRAPHONIC

⁶quad *n* (1971) : quadraphonic sound

⁷quad *n* [short for *quadrillion*] (1974) : a unit of energy equal to one quadrillion British thermal units

quad·ran·gle \'kwä-ˌdraŋ-gəl\ *n* [ME, fr. MF, fr. LL *quadriangulum,* fr. L, neut. of *quadriangulus* quadrangular, fr. *quadri-* + *angulus* angle] (15c) **1** : QUADRILATERAL **2 a** : a 4-sided enclosure esp. when surrounded by buildings **b** : the buildings enclosing a quadrangle **3** : a tract of country represented by one of a series of map sheets (as published by the U.S. Geological Survey) — **qua·dran·gu·lar** \kwä-'draŋ-gyə-lər\ *adj*

quad·rant \'kwä-drənt\ *n* [ME, fr. L *quadrant-, quadrans* fourth part; akin to L *quattuor* four — more at FOUR] (15c) **1 a** : an instrument for measuring altitudes consisting commonly of a graduated arc of 90 degrees with an index or vernier and usu. having a plumb line or spirit level for fixing the vertical or horizontal direction **b** : a device or mechanical part shaped like or suggestive of the quadrant of a circle **2 a** : an arc of 90 degrees that is one quarter of a circle **b** : the area bounded by a quadrant and two radii **3 a** : any of the four parts into which a plane is divided by rectangular coordinate axes lying in that plane **b** : any of the four quarters into which something is divided by two real or imaginary lines that intersect each other at right angles — **qua·dran·tal** \kwä-'dran-tᵊl\ *adj*

quadrant 2

Qua·dran·tid \kwä-'dran-təd\ *n* [NL *Quadrant-, Quadrans (Muralis)* mural quadrant, a group of stars in the constellation Draco from which the shower appears to radiate] : any of a group of meteors that appear annually about January 3

quad·ra·phon·ic *also* **quad·ri·phon·ic** \ˌkwä-drə-'fä-nik\ *adj* [irreg. fr. *quadri-* + *-phonic* (as in *stereophonic*)] (ca. 1970) : of, relating to, or using four channels for the transmission, recording, or reproduction of sound — **quad·ra·phon·ics** *or* **quad·ri·phon·ics** \-niks\ *n pl but sing in constr*

quad·rat \'kwä-drət, -ˌdrat\ *n* [alter. of ²*quadrate*] (1683) **1** : ²QUAD 2 : a usu. rectangular plot used for ecological or population studies

¹quad·rate \'kwä-ˌdrāt, -drət\ *adj* [ME, fr. L *quadratus,* pp. of *quadrare* to make square, fit, fr. *quadrum* square; akin to L *quattuor* four] (14c) **1** : being square or approximately square **2** *of a heraldic cross* : expanded into a square at the junction of the arms — see CROSS illustration **3** : of, relating to, or constituting a bony or cartilaginous element of each side of the skull to which the lower jaw is articulated in most vertebrates below mammals

²quadrate *n* (15c) **1** : an approximately square or cubical area, space, or body **2** : a quadrate bone

qua·drat·ic \kwä-'dra-tik\ *adj* (1668) : involving terms of the second degree at most ⟨∼ function⟩ ⟨∼ equations⟩ — **quadratic** *n* — **qua·drat·i·cal·ly** \-ti-k(ə-)lē\ *adv*

quadratic form (1859) : a homogeneous polynomial (as $x^2 + 5xy + y^2$) of the second degree

quad·ra·ture \'kwä-drə-ˌchùr, -chər, -ˌtyùr, -ˌtùr\ *n* (1591) **1** : a configuration in which two celestial bodies (as the moon and the sun) have an angular separation of 90 degrees as seen from the earth **2** : the process of finding a square equal in area to a given area

quad·ren·ni·al \kwä-'dre-nē-əl\ *adj* (ca. 1656) **1** : consisting of or lasting for four years **2** : occurring or being done every four years — **quadrennial** *n* — **qua·dren·ni·al·ly** \-nē-ə-lē\ *adv*

quad·ren·ni·um \-nē-əm\ *n, pl* **-ni·ums** *or* **-nia** \-nē-ə\ [L *quadriennium,* fr. *quadri-* + *annus* year — more at ANNUAL] (1754) : a period of four years

quadri- *or* **quadr-** *or* **quadru-** *comb form* [ME, fr. L *quattuor* four] **1 a** : four ⟨*quadri*lateral⟩ ⟨*quadru*manous⟩ **b** : square ⟨*quadric*⟩ **2** : fourth ⟨*quadri*centennial⟩

quad·ric \'kwä-drik\ *adj* [ISV] (1858) : QUADRATIC ⟨∼ surface⟩ — used where there are more than two variables — **quadric** *n*

quad·ri·cen·ten·ni·al \ˌkwä-drə-sen-'te-nē-əl\ *n* (1882) : a 400th anniversary or its celebration

quad·ri·ceps \'kwä-drə-ˌseps\ *n* [NL *quadricipit-, quadriceps,* fr. *quadri-* + *-cipit-, -ceps* (as in *bicipit-, biceps* biceps)] (1840) : the greater extensor muscle of the front of the thigh that is divided into four parts

qua·dri·ga \kwä-'drē-gə\ *n, pl* **-gae** \-ˌgī\ [L, sing. of *quadrigae* team of four, contr. of *quadrijugae,* fem. pl. of *quadrijugus* yoked four abreast, fr. *quadri-* + *jungere* to yoke, join — more at YOKE] (ca. 1741) : a chariot drawn by four horses abreast

¹quad·ri·lat·er·al \ˌkwä-drə-'la-t(ə-)rəl\ *n* [L *quadrilaterus* four-sided, fr. *quadri-* + *later-, latus* side] (1650) : a polygon of four sides

²quadrilateral *adj* (1656) : having four sides

¹qua·drille \kwä-'dril, kwə-, kə-\ *n* [F, group of knights engaged in a carousel, fr. Sp *cuadrilla* troop, fr. dim. of *cuadra* square, fr. L *quadra, quadrum*] (1726) : a four-handed variant of ombre popular esp. in the 18th century **2** : a square dance for four couples made up of five or six figures chiefly in ⁶⁄₈ and ²⁄₄ time; *also* : music for this dance

²quadrille *adj* [F *quadrillé*] (ca. 1885) : marked with squares or rectangles

qua·dril·lion \kwä-'dril-yən\ *n* [F, fr. MF, fr. *quadri-* + *-illion* (as in *million*)] (1674) — see NUMBER table — **quadrillion** *adj* — **qua·dril·lionth** \-yən(t)th\ *adj or n*

quad·ri·par·tite \ˌkwä-drə-'pär-ˌtīt\ *adj* [ME, fr. L *quadripartitus,* fr. *quadri-* + *partitus,* pp. of *partire* to divide, fr. *part-, pars* part] (15c) **1** : consisting of or divided into four parts **2** : shared or participated in by four parties or persons ⟨a ∼ agreement⟩

quad·ri·ple·gic \ˌkwä-drə-'plē-jik\ *n* [*quadriplegia,* fr. NL] (1921) : one affected with paralysis of both arms and both legs — **quad·ri·ple·gia** \-j(ē-)ə\ *n*

¹quad·ri·va·lent \ˌkwä-drə-'vā-lənt, *in sense 2* kwä-'dri-və-lənt\ *adj* [ISV] (1865) **1** : TETRAVALENT **2** : composed of four homologous chromosomes synapsed in meiotic prophase

²quadrivalent *n* (1923) : a quadrivalent chromosomal group

qua·driv·i·al \kwä-'dri-vē-əl\ *adj* (15c) **1** : of or relating to the quadrivium **2** : having four ways or roads meeting in a point

qua·driv·i·um \-vē-əm\ *n* [LL, fr. L, crossroads, fr. *quadri-* + *via* way — more at WAY] (1804) : a group of studies consisting of arithmetic, music, geometry, and astronomy and forming the upper division of the seven liberal arts in medieval universities — compare TRIVIUM

qua·droon \kwä-'drün\ *n* [modif. of Sp *cuarterón,* fr. *cuarto* fourth, fr. L *quartus* — more at QUART] (1707) : a person of one-quarter black ancestry

qua·dru·ma·nous \kwä-'drü-mə-nəs\ *adj* [ultim. fr. L *quadri-* + *manus* hand — more at MANUAL] (1819) : of, relating to, or being the primates excluding humans as they are distinguished by hand-shaped feet

qua·drum·vir \kwä-'drəm-vər\ *n* [back-formation fr. *quadrumvirate*] (1790) : a member of a quadrumvirate

qua·drum·vi·rate \-və-rət\ *n* [*quadri-* + *-umvirate* (as in *triumvirate*)] (1752) : a group or association of four

quad·ru·ped \'kwä-drə-ˌped\ *n* [L *quadruped-, quadrupes,* fr. *quadruped-, quadrupes,* adj., having four feet, fr. *quadri-* + *ped-, pes* foot — more at FOOT] (1646) : an animal having four feet — **quadruped** *adj* — **qua·dru·pe·dal** \kwä-'drü-pə-dᵊl, ˌkwä-drə-'pe-\ *adj*

¹qua·dru·ple \kwä-'drü-pəl, -'drə-; 'kwä-drə-\ *vb* **qua·dru·pled; qua·dru·pling** \-p(ə-)liŋ\ *vt* (14c) : to make four times as great or as many ∼ *vi* : to become four times as great or as numerous

²quadruple *n* (15c) : a sum four times as great as another

³quadruple *adj* [MF or L; MF, fr. L *quadruplus,* fr. *quadri-* + *-plus* multiplied by — more at -FOLD] (1557) **1** : having four units or members **2** : marked by four beats per measure ⟨∼ meter⟩ — **qua·dru·ply** \-'drü-plē, -'drə-, -drə-\ *adv* — **qua·dru·plic·i·ty** \ˌkwä-drü-'pli-sə-tē\ *n*

qua·dru·plet \kwä-'drü-plət, -'drə-; 'kwä-drə-plət\ *n* (1787) **1** : one of four offspring born at one birth **2** : a combination of four of a kind **3** : a group of four musical notes to be performed in the time ordinarily given to three of the same kind

¹qua·dru·pli·cate \kwä-'drü-pli-kət\ *adj* [L *quadruplicatus,* pp. of *quadruplicare* to quadruple, fr. *quadruplic-, quadruplex* fourfold, fr. *quadri-* + *-plic-, -plex* fold — more at -FOLD] (1657) **1** : consisting of or existing in four corresponding or identical parts or examples ⟨∼ invoices⟩ **2** : being the fourth of four things exactly alike

²qua·dru·pli·cate \-plə-ˌkāt\ *vt* **-cat·ed; -cat·ing** (ca. 1661) **1** : to make quadruple or fourfold **2** : to prepare in quadruplicate — **qua·dru·pli·ca·tion** \-ˌdrü-pli-'kā-shən\ *n*

³qua·dru·pli·cate \kwä-'drü-pli-kət\ *n* (1790) **1** : four copies all alike — used with *in* ⟨typed in ∼⟩ **2** : one of four things exactly alike; *specif* : one of four identical copies

quad·ru·pole \'kwä-drə-ˌpōl\ *n* [ISV *quadri-* + *pole*] (1922) : a system composed of two dipoles of equal but oppositely directed moment

quae·re \'kwir-ē, 'kwer-\ *n* [L, imper. of *quaerere* to seek, question] (1589) *archaic* : QUERY

quaes·tor \'kwe-stər, 'kwē-\ *n* [ME *questor,* fr. L *quaestor,* fr. *quaerere*] (14c) : one of numerous ancient Roman officials concerned chiefly with financial administration

quaff \'kwäf, 'kwaf\ *vb* [origin unknown] *vi* (1523) : to drink deeply ∼ *vt* : to drink (a beverage) deeply — **quaff** *n* — **quaff·er** *n*

quag \'kwag, 'kwäg\ *n* [origin unknown] (1589) : MARSH, BOG

quag·ga \'kwa-gə, 'kwä-\ *n* [obs. Afrik (now *kwagga*), fr. Khoikhoi *quácha*] (1785) : an extinct mammal (*Equus quagga*) of southern Africa related to the zebras

quag·gy \'kwa-gē, 'kwä-\ *adj* (1610) **1** : MARSHY **2** : FLABBY

quag·mire \'kwag-ˌmīr, 'kwäg-\ *n* (ca. 1580) **1** : soft miry land that shakes or yields under the foot **2** : a difficult, precarious, or entrapping position : PREDICAMENT

qua·hog *also* **qua·haug** \'kō-ˌhòg, 'kwò-, 'kwō-, -ˌhäg\ *n* [Narraganset *poquaûhock*] (1753) : a thick-shelled edible clam (*Mercenaria mercenaria*) of the U.S.

quai \'kā\ *n* [F, fr. MF *cai* — more at QUAY] (1862) : QUAY

quaich *or* **quaigh** \'kwäk\ *n* [ScGael *cuach*] (1546) *chiefly Scot* : a small shallow drinking vessel with ears for use as handles

¹quail \'kwā(ə)l\ *n, pl* **quail** *or* **quails** [ME *quaille*, fr. MF, fr. ML *quaccula*, of imit. origin] (14c) : any of numerous small gallinaceous birds: as **a** : an Old World migratory game bird (*Coturnix coturnix*) **b** : BOBWHITE

²quail *vb* [ME, fr. MD *quelen*] *vi* (15c) **1 a** *chiefly dial* : WITHER, DECLINE **b** : to give way : FALTER ⟨his courage never ~*ed*⟩ **2** : to recoil in dread or terror : COWER ⟨the strongest ~ before financial ruin —Samuel Butler †1902⟩ ~ *vt, archaic* : to make fearful *syn* see RECOIL

quail

quaint \'kwānt\ *adj* [ME *cointe*, fr. OF, fr. L *cognitus*, pp. of *cognoscere* to know — more at COGNITION] (13c) **1** *obs* : EXPERT, SKILLED **2 a** : marked by skillful design ⟨~ with many a device in India ink —Herman Melville⟩ **b** : marked by beauty or elegance **3 a** : unusual or different in character or appearance : ODD ⟨figures of fun, ~ people —Herman Wouk⟩ **b** : pleasingly or strikingly old-fashioned or unfamiliar *syn* see STRANGE — **quaint·ly** *adv* — **quaint·ness** *n*

¹quake \'kwāk\ *vi* **quaked; quak·ing** [ME, fr. OE *cwacian*] (bef. 12c) **1** : to shake or vibrate usu. from shock or instability **2** : to tremble or shudder usu. from cold or fear

²quake *n* (14c) : an instance of shaking or trembling (as of the earth or moon); *esp* : EARTHQUAKE

quak·er \'kwā-kər\ *n* (1597) **1** : one that quakes **2** *cap* : FRIEND 5 — **Quak·er·ish** \'kwā-k(ə-)rish\ *adj* — **Quak·er·ism** \-kə-ˌri-zəm\ *n* — **Quak·er·ly** \-kər-lē\ *adj*

Quaker gun *n* [fr. opposition to war as a basic Quaker tenet] (1809) : a dummy piece of artillery usu. made of wood

quak·er·la·dies \ˌkwā-kər-'lā-dēz\ *n pl* (1871) : BLUETS

quaking aspen *n* (1843) : an aspen (*Populus tremuloides*) chiefly of the U.S. and Canada that has small nearly circular leaves with flattened petioles and finely serrate margins

qua·le \'kwä-lē, -ˌlā\ *n, pl* **qua·lia** \'kwä-lē-ə\ [L, neut. of *qualis* of what kind] (1675) **1** : a property (as redness) considered apart from things having the property : UNIVERSAL **2** : a property as it is experienced as distinct from any source it might have in a physical object

qual·i·fi·able \ˌkwä-lə-'fī-bəl\ *adj* (1611) : capable of qualifying or being qualified

qual·i·fi·ca·tion \ˌkwä-lə-fə-'kā-shən\ *n* (ca. 1544) **1** : a restriction in meaning or application : a limiting modification ⟨this statement requires without ~⟩ **2 a** *obs* : NATURE **b** *archaic* : CHARACTERISTIC **3 a** : a quality or skill that fits a person (as for an office) ⟨the applicant with the best ~s⟩ **b** : a condition or standard that must be complied with (as for the attainment of a privilege) ⟨a ~ for membership⟩

qual·i·fied \'kwä-lə-ˌfīd\ *adj* (1558) **1 a** : fitted (as by training or experience) for a given purpose : COMPETENT **b** : having complied with the specific requirements or precedent conditions (as for an office or employment) : ELIGIBLE **2** : limited or modified in some way ⟨~ approval⟩ — **qual·i·fied·ly** \-ˌfī(-ə)d-lē\ *adv*

qual·i·fi·er \-ˌfī(-ə)r\ *n* (1561) : one that qualifies: as **a** : one that satisfies requirements or meets a specified standard **b** : a word (as an adjective) or word group that limits or modifies the meaning of another word (as a noun) or word group

qual·i·fy \'kwä-lə-ˌfī\ *vb* **-fied; -fy·ing** [MF *qualifier*, fr. ML *qualificare*, fr. L *qualis*] *vt* (1533) **1 a** : to reduce from a general to a particular or restricted form : MODIFY **b** : to make less harsh or strict : MODERATE **c** : to alter the strength or flavor of **d** : to limit or modify the meaning of (as a noun) **2** : to characterize by naming an attribute : DESCRIBE ⟨cannot ~ it as . . . either glad or sorry —T. S. Eliot⟩ **3 a** : to fit by training, skill, or ability for a special purpose **b** (1) : to declare competent or adequate : CERTIFY (2) : to invest with legal capacity : LICENSE ~ *vi* **1** : to be or become fit (as for an office) : meet the required standard **2** : to acquire legal or competent power or capacity ⟨has just *qualified* as a lawyer⟩ **3 a** : to exhibit a required degree of ability in a preliminary contest ⟨*qualified* for the finals⟩ **b** : to shoot well enough to earn a marksmanship badge

qual·i·ta·tive \'kwä-lə-ˌtā-tiv\ *adj* (1607) : of, relating to, or involving quality or kind — **qual·i·ta·tive·ly** *adv*

qualitative analysis *n* (1842) : chemical analysis designed to identify the components of a substance or mixture

¹qual·i·ty \'kwä-lə-tē\ *n, pl* **-ties** [ME *qualite*, fr. OF *qualité*, fr. L *qualitat-, qualitas*, fr. *qualis* of what kind; akin to L *qui* who — more at WHO] (14c) **1 a** : peculiar and essential character : NATURE ⟨her ethereal ~ —Gay Talese⟩ **b** : an inherent feature : PROPERTY ⟨had a ~ of stridence, dissonance —Roald Dahl⟩ **c** : CAPACITY, ROLE ⟨in the ~ of reader and companion —Joseph Conrad⟩ **2 a** : degree of excellence : GRADE ⟨the ~ of competing air service —*Current Biog.*⟩ **b** : superiority in kind ⟨merchandise of ~⟩ **3 a** : social status : RANK **b** : ARISTOCRACY **4 a** : a distinguishing attribute : CHARACTERISTIC ⟨possesses many fine *qualities*⟩ **b** *archaic* : an acquired skill : ACCOMPLISHMENT **5** : the character in a logical proposition of being affirmative or negative **6** : vividness of hue **7 a** : TIMBRE **b** : the identifying character of a vowel sound determined chiefly by the resonance of the vocal chambers in uttering it **8** : the attribute of an elementary sensation that makes it fundamentally unlike any other sensation

syn QUALITY, PROPERTY, CHARACTER, ATTRIBUTE mean an intelligible feature by which a thing may be identified. QUALITY is a general term

applicable to any trait or characteristic whether individual or generic ⟨material with a silky *quality*⟩. PROPERTY implies a characteristic that belongs to a thing's essential nature and may be used to describe a type or species ⟨the *property* of not conducting heat⟩. CHARACTER applies to a peculiar and distinctive quality of a thing or a class ⟨remarks of an unseemly *character*⟩. ATTRIBUTE implies a quality ascribed to a thing or a being ⟨the traditional *attributes* of a military hero⟩.

²quality *adj* (1701) : being of high quality

quality assurance *n* (1982) : a program for the systematic monitoring and evaluation of the various aspects of a project, service, or facility to ensure that standards of quality are being met

quality circle *n* (1980) : a group of employees who volunteer to meet regularly to discuss and propose solutions to problems (as of quality or productivity) in the workplace

quality control *n* (1935) : an aggregate of activities (as design analysis and inspection for defects) designed to ensure adequate quality esp. in manufactured products — **quality controller** *n*

quality point *n* (1948) : GRADE POINT

quality point average *n* (ca. 1972) : GRADE POINT AVERAGE

qualm \'kwäm *also* 'kwòm *or* 'kwälm\ *n* [origin unknown] (ca. 1530) **1** : a sudden attack of illness, faintness, or nausea **2** : a sudden access of usu. disturbing emotion (as doubt or fear) **3** : a feeling of uneasiness about a point esp. of conscience or propriety — **qualmy** *adj*

syn QUALM, SCRUPLE, COMPUNCTION, DEMUR mean a misgiving about what one is doing or going to do. QUALM implies an uneasy fear that one is not following one's conscience or better judgment ⟨no *qualms* about plagiarizing⟩. SCRUPLE implies doubt of the rightness of an act on grounds of principle ⟨no *scruples* against buying stolen goods⟩. COMPUNCTION implies a spontaneous feeling of responsibility or compassion for a potential victim ⟨had *compunctions* about lying⟩. DEMUR implies hesitation caused by objection to an outside suggestion or influence ⟨accepted her decision without *demur*⟩.

qualm·ish \'kwä-mish *also* 'kwò- *or* 'kwäl-\ *adj* (1548) **1 a** : feeling qualms : NAUSEATED **b** : overly scrupulous : SQUEAMISH **2** : of, relating to, or producing qualms — **qualm·ish·ly** *adv* — **qualm·ish·ness** *n*

qua·mash \'kwä-mish\ *var of* CAMAS

quan·da·ry \'kwän-d(ə-)rē\ *n, pl* **-ries** [origin unknown] (1579) : a state of perplexity or doubt

quan·tal \'kwän-t⁰l\ *adj* (1933) **1** [L *quanti* how many, pl. of *quantus*] : of, relating to, or having only two experimental alternatives (as dead or alive, all or none) **2** [*quantum*] : of or relating to a quantum

quan·ti·fi·ca·tion \ˌkwän-tə-fə-'kā-shən\ *n* (ca. 1840) : the operation of quantifying — **quan·ti·fi·ca·tion·al** \-shnəl, -shə-n⁰l\ *adj* — **quan·ti·fi·ca·tion·al·ly** *adv*

quan·ti·fi·er \'kwän-tə-ˌfi(-ə)r\ *n* (1876) : one that quantifies: as **a** : a prefixed operator that binds the variables in a logical formula by specifying their quantity **b** : a limiting noun modifier (as *five* in "the five young men") expressive of quantity and characterized by occurrence before the descriptive adjectives in a noun phrase

quan·ti·fy \-ˌfī\ *vt* **-fied; -fy·ing** [ML *quantificare*, fr. L *quantus* how much] (ca. 1840) **1 a** : to limit by a quantifier (2) : to bind by prefixing a quantifier **b** : to make explicit the logical quantity of **2** : to determine, express, or measure the quantity of — **quan·ti·fi·able** \ˌkwän-tə-'fī-ə-bəl\ *adj*

quan·ti·tate \'kwän-tə-ˌtāt\ *vt* **-tat·ed; -tat·ing** [back-formation fr. *quantitative*] (1927) **1** : to measure or estimate the quantity of; *esp* : to measure or determine precisely **2** : to express in quantitative terms — **quan·ti·ta·tion** \ˌkwän-tə-'tā-shən\ *n*

quan·ti·ta·tive \'kwän-tə-ˌtā-tiv\ *adj* [ML *quantitativus*, fr. L *quantitat-, quantitas* quantity] (1581) **1** : of, relating to, or expressible in terms of quantity **2** : of, relating to, or involving the measurement of quantity or amount **3** : based on quantity; *specif, of classical verse* : based on temporal quantity or duration of sounds — **quan·ti·ta·tive·ly** *adv* — **quan·ti·ta·tive·ness** *n*

quantitative analysis *n* (ca. 1847) : chemical analysis designed to determine the amounts or proportions of the components of a substance

quantitative inheritance *n* (ca. 1929) : genic inheritance of a character (as human skin color) controlled by polygenes

quan·ti·ty \'kwän-tə-tē\ *n, pl* **-ties** [ME *quantite*, fr. MF *quantité*, fr. L *quantitat-, quantitas*, fr. *quantus* how much, how large; akin to L *quam* how, as, *quando* when, *qui* who — more at WHO] (14c) **1 a** : an indefinite amount or number **b** : a determinate or estimated amount **c** : total amount or number **d** : a considerable amount or number — often used in pl. ⟨generous *quantities* of luck —H. E. Putsch⟩ **2 a** : the aspect in which a thing is measurable in terms of greater, less, or equal of or increasing or decreasing magnitude **b** : the subject of a mathematical operation **c** : an individual considered with respect to a given situation ⟨an unknown ~ . . . as attorney general —Tom Wicker⟩ **3 a** : duration and intensity of speech sounds as distinct from their individual quality or phonemic character; *specif* : the relative length or brevity of a prosodic syllable in some languages (as Greek and Latin) **b** : the relative duration or time length of a speech sound or sound sequence **4** : the character of a logical proposition as being universal, particular, or singular

quantity theory *n* (1888) : a theory in economics: changes in the price level tend to vary directly with the amount of money in circulation and the rate of its circulation

quan·tize \'kwän-ˌtiz\ *vt* **quan·tized; quan·tiz·ing** [*quantum*] (1922) **1** : to subdivide (as energy) into small but measurable increments **2** : to calculate or express in terms of quantum mechanics — **quan·ti·za·tion** \ˌkwän-tə-'zā-shən\ *n* — **quan·tiz·er** \'kwän-ˌti-zər\ *n*

¹quan·tum \'kwän-təm\ *n, pl* **quan·ta** \'kwän-tə\ [L, neut. of *quantus* how much] (1567) **1 a** : QUANTITY, AMOUNT **b** : PORTION, PART **c** : gross quantity : BULK **2 a** : any of the very small increments or parcels into which many forms of energy are subdivided **b** : any of the

\a\ abut \⁰\ kitten, F table \ər\ further \a\ ash \ā\ ace \ä\ mop, mar \aù\ out \ch\ chin \e\ bet \ē\ easy \g\ go \i\ hit \ī\ ice \j\ job \ŋ\ sing \ō\ go \ò\ law \òi\ boy \th\ thin \t͟h\ the \ü\ loot \ù\ foot \y\ yet \zh\ vision \à, ᵏ, ⁿ, œ, œ̄, ᵫ, ᵫ̄, ʸ\ *see* Guide to Pronunciation small subdivisions of a quantized physical magnitude (as magnetic moment)

²quantum *adj* (1942) : LARGE, SIGNIFICANT ⟨a ~ improvement⟩

quantum chromodynamics *n pl but sing in constr* (1975) : a theory of fundamental particles based on the assumption that quarks are distinguished by differences in color and are held together (as in hadrons) by an exchange of gluons

quantum electrodynamics *n pl but usu sing in constr* (1927) : quantum mechanics applied to electrical interactions (as between nuclear particles)

quantum field theory *n* (1948) : a theory in physics: the interaction of two separate physical systems (as particles) is attributed to a field that extends from one to the other and is manifested in a particle exchange between the two systems

quantum jump *n* (1926) **1** : an abrupt transition (as of an electron, an atom, or a molecule) from one discrete energy state to another **2** : QUANTUM LEAP

quantum leap *n* (1956) : an abrupt change, sudden increase, or dramatic advance

quantum mechanics *n pl but sing or pl in constr* (1922) : a theory of matter that is based on the concept of the possession of wave properties by elementary particles, that affords a mathematical interpretation of the structure and interactions of matter on the basis of these properties, and that incorporates within it quantum theory and the uncertainty principle — called also *wave mechanics* — **quantum mechanical** *adj* — **quantum mechanically** *adv*

quantum number *n* (1902) : any of a set of integers or half odd integers that indicate the magnitude of various discrete quantities (as electric charge) of a particle or system and that serve to define its state

quantum theory *n* (1912) : a theory in physics based on the concept of the subdivision of radiant energy into finite quanta and applied to numerous processes involving transference or transformation of energy in an atomic or molecular scale

¹quar·an·tine \'kwȯr-ən-ˌtēn, 'kwär-\ *n* [partly modif. of F *quarantaine*, fr. OF, fr. *quarante* forty, fr. L *quadraginta*, fr. *quadra*- (akin to *quattuor* four) + *-ginta* (akin to *viginti* twenty); partly modif. of It *quarantena* quarantine of a ship, fr. *quaranta* forty, fr. L *quadraginta* — more at FOUR, VIGESIMAL] (1609) **1** : a period of 40 days **2 a** : a term during which a ship arriving in port and suspected of carrying contagious disease is held in isolation from the shore **b** : a regulation placing a ship in quarantine **c** : a place where a ship is detained during quarantine **3 a** : a restraint upon the activities or communication of persons or the transport of goods designed to prevent the spread of disease or pests **b** : a place in which those under quarantine are kept **4** : a state of enforced isolation

²quarantine *vb* **-tined; -tin·ing** *vt* (1804) **1** : to detain in or exclude by quarantine **2** : to isolate from normal relations or communication ⟨~ an aggressor⟩ **~** *vi* : to establish or declare a quarantine

quare \'kwar, 'kwer, 'kwär\ *dial var of* ¹QUEER

quark \'kwȯrk, 'kwärk\ *n* [coined by Murray Gell-Mann] (1964) : any of several elementary particles that are postulated to come in pairs (as in the up and down varieties) of similar mass with one member having a charge of +²/₃ and the other a charge of −¹/₃ and are held to make up hadrons

¹quar·rel \'kwȯr-(-ə)l, 'kwär-(-ə)l\ *n* [ME, fr. OF, square-headed arrow, building stone, fr. (assumed) VL *quadrellum*, dim. of L *quadrum* square — more at QUADRATE] (13c) : a square-headed bolt or arrow esp. for a crossbow

²quarrel *n* [ME *querele*, fr. MF, complaint, fr. L *querela*, fr. *queri* to complain] (14c) **1** : a ground of dispute or complaint ⟨have no ~ with a different approach⟩ **2** : a usu. verbal conflict between antagonists : ALTERCATION

³quarrel *vi* **-reled** *or* **-relled; -rel·ing** *or* **-rel·ling** (14c) **1** : to find fault ⟨many people ~ with the idea —*Johns Hopkins Mag.*⟩ **2** : to contend or dispute actively ⟨~*ed* frequently with his superiors —*London Calling*⟩ — **quar·rel·er** *or* **quar·rel·ler** *n*

quar·rel·some \'kwȯr-(-ə)l-səm, 'kwär-(-ə)l-\ *adj* (1596) : apt or disposed to quarrel in an often petty manner : CONTENTIOUS *syn* see BELLIGERENT — **quar·rel·some·ly** *adv* — **quar·rel·some·ness** *n*

quar·ri·er \'kwȯr-ē-ər, 'kwär-\ *n* (14c) : a worker in a stone quarry

¹quar·ry \'kwȯr-ē, 'kwär-\ *n, pl* **quarries** [ME *querre* entrails of game given to the hounds, fr. MF *cuiree*, fr. *cuir* skin, hide (on which the entrails were placed), fr. L *corium* — more at CUIRASS] (14c) **1** *obs* : a heap of the game killed in a hunt **2** : GAME; *specif* : game hunted with hawks **3** : one that is sought or pursued : PREY

²quarry *n, pl* **quarries** [ME *quarey*, alter. of *quarrere*, fr. MF *quarriere*, fr. (assumed) OF *quarre* squared stone, fr. L *quadrum* square] (14c) **1** : an open excavation usu. for obtaining building stone, slate, or limestone **2** : a rich source

³quarry *vb* **quar·ried; quar·ry·ing** *vt* (1774) **1** : to dig or take from or as if from a quarry ⟨~ marble⟩ **2** : to make a quarry in ⟨~ a hill⟩ **~** *vi* : to delve in or as if in a quarry

⁴quarry *n, pl* **quarries** [alter. of ¹*quarrel*] (1555) : a diamond-shaped pane of glass, stone, or tile

quarrying *n* (ca. 1828) : the business, occupation, or act of extracting useful material (as building stone) from quarries

quar·ry·man \'kwȯr-ē-mən, 'kwär-\ *n* (15c) : QUARRIER

quart \'kwȯrt\ *n* [ME, fr. MF *quarte*, fr. OF, fr. fem. of *quart*, adj., fourth, fr. L *quartus*; akin to L *quattuor* four — more at FOUR] (14c) **1** — see WEIGHT table **2** : a vessel or measure having a capacity of one quart

¹quar·tan \'kwȯr-t°n\ *adj* [ME *quarteyne*, fr. MF (*fievre*) *quartaine* quartan fever, fr. L (*febris*) *quartana*, fr. *quartana* of the fourth, fr. *quartus*] (14c) : occurring every fourth day reckoning inclusively; *specif* : recurring at approximately 72-hour intervals

²quartan *n* (14c) : an intermittent fever that recurs at approximately 72-hour intervals; *esp* : a quartan malaria

¹quar·ter \'kwȯr-tər *also* 'kȯ(r)-\ *n* [ME, fr. OF *quartier*, fr. L *quartarius*, fr. *quartus* fourth] (14c) **1** : one of four equal parts into which something is divisible : a fourth part ⟨in the top ~ of his class⟩ **2** : any of various units of capacity or weight equal to or derived from one fourth of some larger unit **3** : any of various units of length or area equal to one fourth of some larger unit **4** : the fourth part of a measure of time: as **a** : one of a set of four 3-month divisions of a year

⟨business was up during the third ~⟩ **b** : a school term of about 12 weeks **c** : QUARTER HOUR ⟨a ~ after three⟩ **5 a** : a coin worth a quarter of a dollar **b** : the sum of 25 cents **6 a** : one limb of a quadruped with the adjacent parts; *esp* : one fourth part of the carcass of a slaughtered animal including a leg **b** *pl, Brit* : HINDQUARTER **2 7 a** : the region or direction lying under any of the four divisions of the horizon **b** : one of the four parts into which the horizon is divided or the cardinal point corresponding to it **c** : a compass point or direction other than the cardinal points **d** (1) : an unspecified person or group ⟨financial help from many ~s —*Current Biog.*⟩ (2) : a point, direction, or place not definitely identified ⟨the view to the rear ~ —*Consumer Reports*⟩ **8 a** : a division or district of a town or city ⟨he describes the immigrant ~ —Alfred Kazin⟩ **b** : the inhabitants of such a quarter **9 a** : an assigned station or post **b** *pl* : an assembly of a ship's company for ceremony, drill, or emergency **c** *pl* : living accommodations : LODGINGS ⟨show you to your ~s⟩ **10** : merciful consideration of an opponent; *specif* : the clemency of not killing a defeated enemy **11** : a fourth part of the moon's period **12** : the side of a horse's hoof between the toe and the heel — see HOOF illustration **13 a** : any of the four parts into which a heraldic field is divided **b** : a bearing or charge occupying the first fourth part of a heraldic field **14** : the state of two machine parts that are exactly at right angles to one another or are spaced about a circle so as to subtend a right angle at the center of the circle **15 a** : the stern area of a ship's side **b** : the part of the yardarm outside the slings **16** : one side of the upper of a shoe or boot from heel to vamp **17** : one of the four equal periods into which the playing time of some games is divided

²quarter *vt* (14c) **1 a** : to cut or divide into four equal or nearly equal parts ⟨~ an apple⟩ ⟨condemned to be hanged, drawn, and ~*ed*⟩ **b** *archaic* : DIVIDE **2** : to provide with lodging or shelter **3** : to crisscross (an area) in many directions **4 a** : to arrange or bear (as different coats of arms) quarterly on one escutcheon **b** : to add (a coat of arms) to others on one escutcheon **c** : to divide (a shield) into distinct sections (as by stripes) **5** : to adjust or locate (as cranks) at right angles in a machine **~** *vi* **1** : LODGE, DWELL **2** : to crisscross a district **3** : to change from one quarter to another ⟨the moon ~s⟩ **4** : to strike on a ship's quarter ⟨the wind was ~*ing*⟩

³quarter *adj* (14c) : consisting of or equal to a quarter

quar·ter·age \'kwȯ(r)-tə-rij\ *n* (14c) : a quarterly payment, tax, wage, or allowance

¹quar·ter·back \'kwȯ(r)-tər-ˌbak\ *n* (1879) **1** : an offensive back in football who usu. lines up behind the center, calls the signals, and directs the offensive play of the team **2** : one who gives direction and leadership

²quarterback *vt* (1944) **1** : to direct the offensive play of (as a football team) **2** : to give executive direction to : BOSS ⟨~*ed* the original buying syndicate —*Time*⟩ **~** *vi* : to play quarterback

quarterback sneak *n* (ca. 1923) : a usu. quick run with the ball by a quarterback into the middle of the offensive line

quar·ter·bound \'kwȯ(r)-tər-ˈbau̇nd\ *adj* (ca. 1888) *of a book* : bound in material of two qualities with the material of better quality on the spine only — **quarter binding** *n*

quarter day *n* (15c) *chiefly Brit* : the day which begins a quarter of the year and on which a quarterly payment often falls due

quar·ter·deck \'kwȯ(r)-tər-ˌdek\ *n* (1627) **1** : the stern area of a ship's upper deck **2** : a part of a deck on a naval vessel set aside by the captain for ceremonial and official use

¹quar·ter·fi·nal \ˌkwȯ(r)-tər-ˈfī-n°l\ *n* (1927) **1** *pl* : a quarterfinal round **2** : a quarterfinal match — **quar·ter·fi·nal·ist** \-n°l-ist\ *n*

²quarterfinal *adj* (ca. 1934) **1** : immediately preceding the semifinal in an elimination tournament **2** : of or participating in a quarterfinal

quarter horse *n* [fr. its high speed for distances up to a quarter of a mile] (1834) : any of a breed of compact muscular saddle horses characterized by great endurance and by high speed for short distances

quarter hour *n* (1883) **1** : any of the quarter points of an hour **2** : fifteen minutes **3** : a unit of academic credit representing an hour of class (as lecture class) or three hours of laboratory work each week for an academic quarter

¹quar·ter·ing \'kwȯ(r)-tə-riŋ\ *n* (15c) **1 a** : the division of an escutcheon containing different coats of arms into four or more compartments **b** : a quarter of an escutcheon or the coat of arms on it **2** : a line of usu. noble or distinguished ancestry

quarter horse

²quartering *adj* (ca. 1692) **1** : coming from a point well abaft the beam of a ship but not directly astern ⟨~ waves⟩ **2** : lying at right angles

¹quar·ter·ly \'kwȯ(r)-tər-lē\ *adv* (14c) **1** : in heraldic quarters or quarterings **2** : at 3-month intervals

²quarterly *adj* (15c) **1** : computed for or payable at 3-month intervals ⟨~ premium⟩ **2** : recurring, issued, or spaced at 3-month intervals **3** : divided into heraldic quarters or compartments

³quarterly *n, pl* **-lies** (1830) : a periodical published four times a year

Quarterly Meeting *n* (1675) : an organizational unit of the Society of Friends usu. composed of several Monthly Meetings

quar·ter·mas·ter \'kwȯ(r)-tər-ˌmas-tər\ *n* (15c) **1** : a petty officer who attends to a ship's helm, binnacle, and signals **2** : an army officer who provides clothing and subsistence for a body of troops

quar·tern \'kwȯ(r)-tərn\ *n* [ME *quarteron*, fr. OF, quarter of a pound, quarter of a hundred, fr. *quartier* quarter] (14c) : a fourth part (as of a unit of measurement)

quarter note *n* (1763) : a musical note with the time value of ¹/₄ of a whole note — see NOTE illustration

quarter rest *n* (ca. 1890) : a musical rest corresponding in time value to a quarter note — see REST illustration

quar·ter·sawn \'kwȯ(r)-tər-ˈsȯn\ *also* **quar·ter·sawed** \-ˈsȯd\ *adj* (ca. 1890) : sawed from quartered logs so that the annual rings are nearly at right angles to the wide face — used of boards and planks

quarter section *n* (1804) : a tract of land that is half a mile square and contains 160 acres in the U.S. government system of land surveying

quarter sessions *n pl* (1577) : a former English local court with limited original and appellate criminal and sometimes civil jurisdiction and often administrative functions held quarterly usu. by two justices of the peace in a county or by a recorder in a borough

quar·ter·staff \'kwȯ(r)-tər-,staf\ *n, pl* **-staves** \-,stavz, -,stävz\ (1550) : a long stout staff formerly used as a weapon and wielded with one hand in the middle and the other between the middle and the end

quarter tone *n* (ca. 1776) **1** : a musical interval of one half a semitone **2** : a tone at an interval of one quarter

quar·tet *also* **quar·tette** \kwȯr-'tet\ *n* [It *quartetto*, fr. *quarto* fourth, fr. L *quartus* — more at QUART] (1773) **1** : a musical composition for four instruments or voices **2** : a group or set of four; *esp* : the performers of a quartet

quar·tic \'kwȯr-tik\ *adj* [L *quartus* fourth] (ca. 1890) : of the fourth degree ⟨~ equation⟩ — **quartic** *n*

quar·tile \'kwȯr-,tīl, -t'l\ *n* [ISV, fr. L *quartus*] (1879) : any of the three values that divide the items of a frequency distribution into four classes with each containing one fourth of the total population; *also* : any one of the four classes

quar·to \'kwȯr-(,)tō\ *n, pl* **quartos** [L, abl. of *quartus* fourth] (1589) **1** : the size of a piece of paper cut four from a sheet; *also* : paper or a page of this size **2** : a book printed on quarto pages

quartz \'kwȯrts\ *n* [G *Quarz*] (ca. 1631) **1** : a mineral consisting of silicon dioxide occurring in colorless and transparent or colored hexagonal crystals or in crystalline masses **2** : a quartz crystal that when placed in an electric field oscillates at a constant frequency and is used to control devices which require precise regulation ⟨a ~ watch⟩ — **quartz·ose** \'kwȯrt-,sōs\ *adj*

quartz glass *n* (1903) : vitreous silica prepared from pure quartz and noted for its transparency to ultraviolet radiation

quartz heater *n* (1980) : a portable electric radiant heater that has heating elements sealed in quartz-glass tubes producing infrared radiation in front of a reflective backing

quartz–iodine lamp *n* (ca. 1964) : an incandescent lamp that has a quartz bulb and a tungsten filament with the bulb containing iodine which reacts with the vaporized tungsten to prevent excessive blackening of the bulb

quartz·ite \'kwȯrt-,sīt\ *n* [ISV] (ca. 1847) : a compact granular rock composed of quartz and derived from sandstone by metamorphism — **quartz·it·ic** \kwȯrt-'si-tik\ *adj*

qua·sar \'kwā-,zär *also* -,sär\ *n* [*quasi-stellar*] (1964) : any of a class of celestial objects that resemble stars but whose large redshift and apparent brightness imply extreme distance and huge energy output

¹quash \'kwäsh, 'kwȯsh\ *vt* [ME *quashen* to smash, fr. MF *quasser*, *casser*, fr. L *quassare* to shake violently, shatter, freq. of *quatere* to shake] (13c) : to suppress or extinguish summarily and completely ⟨~ a rebellion⟩

²quash *vt* [ME *quassen*, fr. MF *casser*, *quasser* to annul, fr. LL *cassare*, fr. L *cassus* void] (14c) : to nullify esp. by judicial action ⟨~ an indictment⟩

qua·si \'kwā-,zī, -,sī; 'kwä-zē, -sē\ *adj* [*quasi-*] (1642) **1** : having some resemblance usu. by possession of certain attributes ⟨a ~ corporation⟩ **2** : having a legal status only by operation or construction of law and without reference to intent ⟨a ~ contract⟩

quasi- *comb form* [L *quasi* as if, as it were, approximately, fr. *quam* as + *si* if — more at QUANTITY, SO] **1** : in some sense or degree ⟨*quasi*periodic⟩ **2** : resembling in some degree ⟨*quasi*particle⟩

qua·si–ju·di·cial \,kwä-,zī-jü-'di-shəl, -,sī-, ,kwä-zē-, -sē-\ *adj* (1836) **1** : having a partly judicial character by possession of the right to hold hearings on and conduct investigations into disputed claims and alleged infractions of rules and regulations and to make decisions in the general manner of courts ⟨~ bodies⟩ **2** : essentially judicial in character but not within the judicial power or function esp. as constitutionally defined ⟨~ review⟩ — **qua·si–ju·di·cial·ly** \-'di-sh(ə-)lē\ *adv*

qua·si–leg·is·la·tive \-'le-jəs-,lā-tiv\ *adj* (ca. 1934) **1** : having a partly legislative character by possession of the right to make rules and regulations having the force of law ⟨a ~ agency⟩ **2** : essentially legislative in character but not within the legislative power or function esp. as constitutionally defined ⟨~ powers⟩

Qua·si·mo·do \,kwä-si-'mō-(,)dō, ,kwä-zi-\ *n* [ML *quasi modo geniti infantes* as newborn babes (words of the introit for Low Sunday)] (ca. 1847) : LOW SUNDAY

qua·si·par·ti·cle \,kwä-,zī-'pär-ti-kəl, -,sī-, ,kwä-zē-, -sē-\ *n* (1957) : a composite entity (as a vibration in a solid) that is analogous in its behavior to a single particle

qua·si·pe·ri·od·ic \-,pir-ē-'ä-dik\ *adj* (ca. 1890) : almost but not quite periodic; *esp* : periodic on a small scale but unpredictable at some larger scale — **qua·si·pe·ri·od·ic·i·ty** \-,pir-ē-ə-'di-sə-tē\ *n*

qua·si–pub·lic \-'pə-blik\ *adj* (1888) : essentially public (as in services rendered) although under private ownership or control

qua·si–stel·lar object \-'ste-lər-\ *n* (1964) : QUASAR

quas·sia \'kwä-shə\ *n* [NL, genus name of a So. American tree, fr. *Quassi* 18th cent. Surinam slave who discovered the medicinal value of quassia] (1770) : a drug from the heartwood of various tropical trees of the ailanthus family used esp. as a bitter tonic and remedy for roundworms in children and as an insecticide

qua·ter·cen·te·na·ry \,kwä-tər-(,)sen-'te-nə-rē, -'sen-t²n-,er-ē, -sen-'tē-nə-rē\ *n* [L *quater* four times + E *centenary* — more at QUATERNION] (1883) : a year marking a 400th anniversary

¹qua·ter·na·ry \'kwä-tə(r),ner-ē, kwə-'tər-nə-rē\ *adj* [L *quaternarius*, fr. *quaterni* four each] (1605) **1 a** : of, relating to, or consisting of four units or members **b** : of, relating to, or being a number system with a base of four **2** *cap* : of, relating to, or being the geological period from the end of the Tertiary to the present time or the corresponding system of rocks — see GEOLOGIC TIME table **3** : consisting of, containing, or being an atom bonded to four other atoms

²quaternary *n, pl* **-ries** (1880) **1** *cap* : the Quaternary period or system of rocks **2** : a member of a group fourth in order or rank

quaternary ammonium compound *n* (ca. 1934) : any of numerous strong bases and their salts derived from ammonium by replacement of the hydrogen atoms with organic radicals and important esp. as surface-active agents, disinfectants, and drugs

qua·ter·ni·on \kwə-'tər-nē-ən, kwä-\ *n* [ME *quaternyoun*, fr. LL *quaternion-*, *quaternio*, fr. L *quaterni* four each, fr. *quater* four times; akin to L *quattuor* four — more at FOUR] (14c) **1** : a set of four parts, things, or persons **2 a** : a generalized complex number that is composed of a real number and a vector and that depends on one real and three imaginary units **b** *pl* : the calculus of quaternions

qua·ter·ni·ty \kwə-'tər-nə-tē, kwä-\ *n, pl* **-ties** [LL *quaternitas*, fr. L *quaterni* four each] (1529) : a union of a group or set of four

qua·train \'kwä-,trān, kwä-'\ *n* [MF, fr. *quatre* four, fr. L *quattuor*] (1582) : a unit or group of four lines of verse

qua·tre·foil \'ka-tər-,fȯil, 'ka-trə-\ *n* [ME *quaterfoil* set of four leaves, fr. MF *quatre* + ME *-foil* (as in *trefoil*)] (15c) **1** : a conventionalized representation of a flower with four petals or of a leaf with four leaflets **2** : a 4-lobed foliation in architecture

quat·tro·cen·to \,kwä-trō-'chen-(,)tō\ *n, often cap* [It, lit., four hundred, fr. *quattro* four (fr. L *quattuor*) + *cento* hundred — more at CINQUECENTO] (ca. 1854) : the 15th century esp. with reference to Italian literature and art

quat·tu·or·de·cil·lion \,kwä-tə-,wȯr-di-'sil-yən\ *n, often attrib* [L *quattuordecim* fourteen (fr. *quattuor* four + *decem* ten) + E *-illion* (as in *million*) — more at TEN] (ca. 1903) — see NUMBER table

¹qua·ver \'kwä-vər\ *vb* **qua·vered; qua·ver·ing** \'kwä-və-riŋ, 'kwäv-riŋ\ [ME, freq. of *quaven* to tremble] *vi* (15c) **1** : TREMBLE **2** : TRILL **3** : to utter sound in tremulous tones ~ *vt* : to utter quaveringly — **qua·ver·ing·ly** *adv* — **qua·very** \'kwä-və-rē, 'kwäv-rē\ *adj*

²quaver *n* (1570) **1** : EIGHTH NOTE **2** : TRILL 1 **3** : a tremulous sound

quay \'kē, 'kā, 'kwā\ *n* [alter. of earlier *key*, fr. ME, fr. MF dial. *cai*, prob. of Celt origin; akin to Bret *kae* hedge, enclosure; akin to OE *hecg* hedge] (1696) : a structure built parallel to the bank of a waterway for use as a landing place

quay·age \-ij\ *n* (ca. 1756) **1** : a charge for use of a quay **2** : room on or for quays **3** : a system of quays

quay·side \-,sīd\ *n* (1903) : land bordering a quay

quean \'kwēn, 'kwän\ *n* [ME *quene*, fr. OE *cwene*; akin to OE *cwēn* woman, queen] (bef. 12c) **1** : a disreputable woman; *specif* : PROSTITUTE **2** *chiefly Scot* : WOMAN; *esp* : one that is young or unmarried

quea·sy *also* **quea·zy** \'kwē-zē\ *adj* **quea·si·er; -est** [ME *coysy*, *qwesye*] (15c) **1 a** : causing nausea ⟨~ motion⟩ **b** : suffering from nausea : NAUSEATED **2** : full of doubt : HAZARDOUS **3 a** : causing uneasiness **b** (1) : DELICATE, SQUEAMISH (2) : ill at ease — **quea·si·ly** \-zə-lē\ *adv* — **quea·si·ness** \-zē-nəs\ *n*

Que·bec \kwi-'bek *also* ki-\ *n* (1952) — a communications code word for the letter *q*

Que·be·cois *or* **Qué·bé·cois** *or* **Qué·be·cois** \,kā-bə-'kwä, -,be-\ *n, pl* **Quebecois** *or* **Québécois** *or* **Québecois** \-'kwä(z)\ [F *québécois*, *québecois*, fr. *Québec* Quebec] (1873) : a native or inhabitant of Quebec; *specif* : a French-speaking native or inhabitant of Quebec — **Quebecois** *or* **Québécois** *or* **Québecois** *adj*

que·bra·cho \kā-'brä-(,)chō, ki-\ *n* [AmerSp, alter. of *quiebracha*, fr. Sp *quiebra* it breaks + *hacha* ax] (ca. 1881) **1** : any of several trees of southern So. America with hard wood: as **a** : a tree (*Aspidosperma quebracho*) of the dogbane family which occurs in Argentina and Chile and whose dried bark is used as a respiratory sedative in dyspnea and in asthma **b** : a chiefly Argentine tree (*Schinopsis lorentzii*) of the cashew family with dense wood rich in tannins **2 a** : the wood of a quebracho **b** : a tannin-rich extract of the Argentine quebracho used in tanning leather

Que·chua \'ke-chə-wə, 'kech-wə\ *n, pl* **Quechua** *or* **Quechuas** [Sp, prob. fr. Southern Peruvian Quechua *qheswa* (*simi*), lit., valley speech] (1840) **1** : a family of languages spoken by Indian peoples of Peru, Bolivia, Ecuador, Chile, and Argentina **2 a** : a member of an Indian people of central Peru **b** : a group of peoples forming the dominant element of the Inca Empire — **Que·chu·an** \-wən\ *adj or n*

¹queen \'kwēn\ *n* [ME *quene*, fr. OE *cwēn* woman, queen; akin to Goth *qens* wife, Gk *gynē* woman, Skt *jani*] (bef. 12c) **1 a** : the wife or widow of a king **b** : the wife or widow of a tribal chief **2 a** : a female monarch **b** : a female chieftain **3 a** : a woman eminent in rank, power, or attractions ⟨a movie ~⟩ **b** : a goddess or a thing personified as female and having supremacy in a specified realm **c** : an attractive girl or woman; *esp* : a beauty contest winner **4** : the most privileged piece of each color in a set of chessmen having the power to move in any direction across any number of unoccupied squares **5** : a playing card marked with a stylized figure of a queen **6** : the fertile fully developed female of social bees, ants, and termites whose function is to lay eggs **7** : a mature female cat kept esp. for breeding **8** : a male homosexual; *esp* : an effeminate one — often used disparagingly

²queen *vi* (1611) **1** : to act like a queen; *esp* : to put on airs — usu. used with *it* ⟨~*s it* over her friends⟩ **2** : to become a queen in chess ~ *vt* : to promote (a pawn) to a queen in chess

Queen Anne \-'an\ *adj* [*Queen Anne* of England] (1863) **1** : of, relating to, or having the characteristics of a style of furniture originating in England under Dutch influence esp. during the first half of the 18th century that is marked by extensive use of upholstery, marquetry, and oriental fabrics **2** : of, relating to, or having the characteristics of a style of English building of the early 18th century characterized by modified classic ornament and the use of red brickwork in which even relief ornament is carved

Queen Anne's lace *n* (1895) : a widely naturalized Eurasian biennial herb (*Daucus carota*) which has a whitish acrid taproot and from which the cultivated carrot originated — called also *wild carrot*

queen consort *n, pl* **queens consort** (1765) : the wife of a reigning king

queen·ly \'kwēn-lē\ *adj* **queen·li·er; -est** (15c) **1** : of, relating to, or befitting a queen **2** : having royal rank **3** : MONARCHICAL — **queen·li·ness** *n* — **queenly** *adv*

queen mother *n* (1577) : a queen dowager who is mother of the reigning sovereign

---

\ə\ abut \ᵊ\ kitten, F table \ər\ further \a\ ash \ā\ ace \ä\ mop, mar \au̇\ out \ch\ chin \e\ bet \ē\ easy \g\ go \i\ hit \ī\ ice \j\ job \ŋ\ sing \ō\ go \ȯ\ law \ȯi\ boy \th\ thin \t̲h̲\ the \ü\ loot \u̇\ foot \y\ yet \zh\ vision \a̧, k̲, ⁿ, œ, œ̄, ᵫ, ᵫ̄, ᵜ\ see Guide to Pronunciation

queen post *n* (1823) : one of two vertical tie posts in a truss (as of a roof)

queen regnant *n, pl* **queens regnant** (ca. 1639) : a queen reigning in her own right

Queen's Bench *n* (ca. 1809) : a division of the English superior courts system that hears civil and criminal court cases — used during the reign of a queen

de gf queen posts

Queen's Counsel *n* (ca. 1860) : a barrister selected to serve as counsel to the British crown — used during the reign of a queen

queen·ship \'kwēn-,ship\ *n* (1536) **1** : the rank, dignity, or state of being a queen **2** : a regal quality like that of a queen

queen·side \-,sīd\ *n* (1897) : the side of a chessboard containing the file on which the queen sits at the beginning of the game

queen–size *adj* (1959) **1** : having dimensions of approximately 60 inches by 80 inches (about 1.5 by 2.0 meters) — used of a bed; compare FULL-SIZE, KING-SIZE, TWIN-SIZE **2** : of a size that fits a queen-size bed ⟨a ~ sheet⟩

queen substance *n* (1954) : a pheromone secreted by queen bees that is consumed by worker bees and inhibits ovary development

1queer \'kwir\ *adj* [origin unknown] (1508) **1 a** : WORTHLESS, COUNTERFEIT ⟨~ money⟩ **b** : QUESTIONABLE, SUSPICIOUS **2 a** : differing in some odd way from what is usual or normal **b** (1) : ECCENTRIC, UNCONVENTIONAL (2) : mildly insane : TOUCHED **c** : absorbed or interested to an extreme or unreasonable degree : OBSESSED **d** : HOMOSEXUAL — usu. used disparagingly **3** : not quite well *syn* see STRANGE — **queer·ish** \-ish\ *adj* — **queer·ly** *adv* — **queer·ness** *n*

2queer *vt* (ca. 1812) **1** : to spoil the effect or success of ⟨~ one's plans⟩ **2** : to put or get into an embarrassing or disadvantageous situation

3queer *n* (ca. 1812) : one that is queer; *esp* : HOMOSEXUAL — usu. used disparagingly

1quell \'kwel\ *vt* [ME, to kill, quell, fr. OE *cwellan* to kill; akin to OHG *quellen* to torture, kill, *quāla* torment, Lith *gelti* to hurt] (13c) **1** : to thoroughly overwhelm and reduce to submission or passivity ⟨~ a riot⟩ **2** : QUIET, PACIFY ⟨~ fears⟩ — **quell·er** *n*

2quell *n* [ME, fr. *quellen* to kill] (15c) **1** *obs* : SLAUGHTER **2** *archaic* : the power of quelling

quench \'kwench\ *vb* [ME, fr. OE *-cwencan*; akin to OE *-cwincan* to vanish, OFris *quinka*] (12c) **1 a** : PUT OUT, EXTINGUISH ⟨~ put out the light or fire of ⟨~ glowing coals with water⟩ **c** : to cool (as heated metal) suddenly by immersion (as in oil or water) **d** : to cause to lose heat or warmth ⟨you have ~ed the warmth of France toward you —Alfred Tennyson⟩ **2 a** : to bring (something immaterial) to an end typically by satisfying, damping, cooling, or decreasing ⟨a rational understanding of the laws of nature can ~ impossible desires —Lucius Garvin⟩ ⟨the praise that ~es all desire to read the book —T. S. Eliot⟩ **b** : to terminate by or as if by destroying : ELIMINATE ⟨the Commonwealth party ~ed a whole generation of play-acting —Margery Bailey⟩ ⟨~ a rebellion⟩ **c** : to relieve or satisfy with liquid ⟨~ed his thirst at a wayside spring⟩ ~ *vi* **1** : to become extinguished : COOL **2** : to become calm : SUBSIDE — **quench·able** \'kwen-chə-bəl\ *adj* — **quench·er** *n* — **quench·less** \'kwench-ləs\ *adj*

que·nelle \kə-'nel\ *n* [F, fr. G *Knödel* dumpling, fr. MHG; akin to OHG *knoto* knot — more at KNOT] (1845) : a poached oval dumpling of pureed forcemeat (as of pike) often served in a cream sauce

quer·ce·tin \'kwər-sə-tən\ *n* [ISV, fr. L *quercetum* oak forest, fr. *quercus* oak — more at FIR] (1857) : a yellow crystalline pigment $C_{15}H_{10}O_7$ occurring usu. in the form of glycosides in various plants

quer·cit·ron \'kwər-,si-trən, ,kwər-'\ *n* [blend of NL *Quercus* and ISV *citron*] (1794) **1** : a large timber oak (*Quercus velutina*) of the eastern and central U.S. **2** : the bark of the quercitron that is rich in tannin and a dye containing quercetin; *also* : the dye

que·rist \'kwir-əst, 'kwer-\ *n* [L *quaerere* to ask] (1633) : one who inquires

quern \'kwərn\ *n* [ME, fr. OE *cweorn*; akin to OHG *quirn* hand mill, OCS *žrůny*] (bef. 12c) : a primitive hand mill for grinding grain

quer·u·lous \'kwer-yə-ləs, -ə-ləs *also* 'kwir-\ *adj* [ME *querelose*, fr. L *querulus*, fr. *queri* to complain] (15c) **1** : habitually complaining **2** : FRETFUL, WHINING ⟨a ~ voice⟩ — **quer·u·lous·ly** *adv* — **quer·u·lous·ness** *n*

1que·ry \'kwir-ē, 'kwer-\ *n, pl* **queries** [alter. of earlier *quere*, fr. L *quaere*, imper. of *quaerere* to ask] (ca. 1635) **1** : QUESTION, INQUIRY **2** : a question in the mind : DOUBT **3** : QUESTION MARK

2query *vt* **que·ried; que·ry·ing** (1654) **1** : to ask questions of esp. with a desire for authoritative information **2** : to ask questions about esp. in order to resolve a doubt **3** : to put as a question **4** : to mark with a query *syn* see ASK — **que·ri·er** *n*

que·sa·dil·la \,kā-sə-'dē-ə *also* -'thē- *or* -'thēl-yə\ *n* [MexSp, fr. Sp cheese pastry, dim. of *quesada*, fr. *queso* cheese, fr. L *caseus*] (1944) : a wheat tortilla filled with a savory mixture, folded, fried in deep fat, and topped with cheese

1quest \'kwest\ *n* [ME, search, pursuit, investigation, inquest, fr. MF *queste* search, pursuit, fr. (assumed) VL *quaesta*, fr. L, fem. of *quaestus*, pp. of *quaerere*] (14c) **1 a** : a jury of inquest **b** : INVESTIGATION **2** : an act or instance of seeking **a** : PURSUIT, SEARCH **b** : a chivalrous enterprise in medieval romance usu. involving an adventurous journey **3** *obs* : a person or group of persons who search or make inquiry

2quest *vi* (14c) **1** *of a dog* **a** : to search a trail **b** : BAY **2** : to go on a quest ~ *vt* **1** : to search for **2** : to ask for — **quest·er** *n*

1ques·tion \'kwes-chən, 'kwesh-\ *n* [ME, fr. MF, fr. L *quaestion-, quaestio*, fr. *quaerere* to seek, ask] (14c) **1 a** (1) : an interrogative expression often used to test knowledge (2) : an interrogative sentence or clause **b** : a subject or aspect in dispute or open for discussion : ISSUE: *broadly* : PROBLEM, MATTER **c** (1) : a subject or point of debate or a proposition to be voted on in a meeting (2) : the bringing of such to a vote **d** : the specific point at issue **2 a** : an act or instance of asking : INQUIRY **b** : INTERROGATION; *also* : a judicial or official investigation **c** : torture as part of an examination **d** (1) : OBJECTION, DISPUTE ⟨true beyond ~⟩ (2) : room for doubt or objection ⟨little ~ of his skill⟩ (3) : CHANCE, POSSIBILITY ⟨no ~ of escape⟩

2question *vt* (15c) **1** : to ask a question of or about **2** : to interrogate

intensively : CROSS-EXAMINE **3 a** : DOUBT, DISPUTE **b** : to subject to analysis : EXAMINE ~ *vi* : to ask questions : INQUIRE *syn* see ASK — **ques·tion·er** *n*

ques·tion·able \'kwes-chə-nə-bəl, 'kwesh-, *in rapid speech* 'kwesh-nə-\ *adj* (1590) **1** *obs* : inviting inquiry **2** *obs* : liable to judicial inquiry or action **3** : affording reason for being doubted, questioned, or challenged : not certain or exact : PROBLEMATIC ⟨milk of ~ purity⟩ ⟨a ~ decision⟩ **4** : attended by well-grounded suspicions of being immoral, crude, false, or unsound : DUBIOUS ⟨~ motives⟩ *syn* see DOUBTFUL — **ques·tion·able·ness** *n* — **ques·tion·ably** \-blē\ *adv*

ques·tion·ary \'kwes-chə-,ner-ē, 'kwesh-\ *n, pl* **-ar·ies** (1887) : QUESTIONNAIRE

ques·tion·less \'kwes-chən-ləs, 'kwesh-\ *adj* (1532) **1** : INDUBITABLE, UNQUESTIONABLE **2** : UNQUESTIONING

question mark *n* (1869) **1** : something unknown, unknowable, or uncertain **2** : a mark ? used in writing and printing at the conclusion of a sentence to indicate a direct question

ques·tion·naire \,kwes-chə-'nar, -'ner, ,kwesh-\ *n* [F, fr. *questionner* to question, fr. MF, *question*, n.] (1899) **1** : a set of questions for obtaining statistically useful or personal information from individuals **2** : a written or printed questionnaire often with spaces for answers **3** : a survey made by the use of a questionnaire

question time *n* (1885) : a period in a session of a British parliamentary body during which members may put questions to ministers on matters concerning their departments

ques·tor \'kwes-tər\ *var of* QUAESTOR

quet·zal \ket-'säl, -'sal\ *n, pl* **quetzals** *or* **quet·za·les** \-'sä-(,)lās, -'sa-\ [AmerSp, fr. Nahuatl *quetzalli* tail coverts of the quetzal] (1827) **1** : a Central American trogon (*Pharomachrus mocinno*) that has brilliant green plumage above, a red breast, and in the male long upper tail coverts **2** *pl* **quetzales** — see MONEY table

Quet·zal·co·a·tl \,kwet-səl-kə-'wä-t²l, ,ket-, -səl-'kwä-; ket-,säl-, -,sal-\ *n* [Nahuatl *Quetzalcōātl*] : a chief Toltec and Aztec god identified with the wind and air and represented by a feathered serpent

1queue \'kyü\ *n* [F, lit., tail, fr. L *cauda, coda*] (1748) **1** : a braid of hair usu. worn hanging at the back of the head **2** : a waiting line esp. of persons or vehicles **3 a** : a sequence of messages or jobs held in auxiliary storage awaiting transmission or processing **b** : a data structure that consists of a list of records such that records are added at one end and removed from the other

2queue *vb* **queued; queu·ing** *or* **queue·ing** *vt* (1777) : to arrange or form in a queue ~ *vi* : to line up or wait in a queue — often used with *up* — **queu·er** *n*

1quib·ble \'kwi-bəl\ *vb* **quib·bled; quib·bling** \-b(ə-)liŋ\ *vi* (1656) **1** : to evade the point of an argument by caviling about words **2 a** : CAVIL, CARP **b** : BICKER ~ *vt* : to subject to quibbles — **quib·bler** \-b(ə-)lər\ *n*

2quibble *n* [prob. dim. of obs. *quib* quibble] (1670) **1** : an evasion of or shift from the point **2** : a minor objection or criticism

quiche \'kēsh\ *n* [F, fr. F dial. (Lorraine)] (1941) : an unsweetened custard pie usu. having a savory filling (as spinach, mushrooms, or ham)

quiche lor·raine \-lə-'rän, -lò-\ *n, often cap L* [F, quiche of Lorraine] (1941) : a quiche containing cheese and bacon bits

1quick \'kwik\ *adj* [ME *quik*, fr. OE *cwic*; akin to ON *kvikr* living, L *vivus* living, *vivere* to live, Gk *bios, zōē* life] (bef. 12c) **1** : not dead : LIVING, ALIVE **2** : acting or capable of acting with speed: as **a** (1) : fast in understanding, thinking, or learning : mentally agile ⟨a ~ wit⟩ ⟨~ thinking⟩ (2) : reacting to stimuli with speed and keen sensitivity (3) : aroused immediately and intensely ⟨~ tempers⟩ **b** (1) : fast in development or occurrence ⟨a ~ succession of events⟩ (2) : done or taking place with rapidity ⟨gave them a ~ look⟩ **c** : marked by speed, readiness, or promptness of physical movement ⟨walked with ~ steps⟩ **d** : inclined to hastiness (as in action or response) ⟨~ to criticize⟩ **e** : capable of being easily and speedily prepared ⟨a ~ and tasty dinner⟩ **3** *archaic* **a** : not stagnant : RUNNING, FLOWING **b** : MOVING, SHIFTING ⟨~ mud⟩ **4** *archaic* : FIERY, GLOWING **5** *obs* **a** : PUNGENT **b** : CAUSTIC **6** *archaic* : PREGNANT **7** : having a sharp angle ⟨a ~ turn in the road⟩ — **quick·ly** *adv* — **quick·ness** *n*

syn QUICK, PROMPT, READY, APT mean able to respond without delay or hesitation or indicative of such ability. QUICK stresses instancy of response and is likely to connote native rather than acquired power ⟨quick reflexes⟩ ⟨a keen quick mind⟩. PROMPT is more likely to connote training and discipline that fits one for instant response ⟨prompt emergency medical care⟩. READY suggests facility or fluency in response ⟨backed by a pair of ready assistants⟩. APT stresses the possession of qualities (as intelligence, a particular talent, or a strong bent) that makes quick effective response possible ⟨an apt student⟩ ⟨her answer was apt and to the point⟩. *syn* see in addition FAST

2quick *n* (bef. 12c) **1 quick** *pl* : living beings **2** [prob. of Scand origin; akin to ON *kvika* sensitive flesh, fr. *kvikr* living] **a** : a painfully sensitive spot or area of flesh (as that underlying a fingernail or toenail) **b** : the inmost sensibilities ⟨hurt to the ~ by the remark⟩ **c** : the very center of something : HEART **3** *archaic* : LIFE 11

3quick *adv* (14c) : in a quick manner

quick assets *n pl* (1891) : cash, accounts receivable, and other current assets excluding inventories

quick bread *n* (1918) : bread made with a leavening agent (as baking powder or baking soda) that permits immediate baking of the dough or batter mixture

quick·en \'kwi-kən\ *vb* **quick·ened; quick·en·ing** \'kwi-kə-niŋ, 'kwik-niŋ\ *vt* (14c) **1 a** : to make alive : REVIVE **b** : to cause to be enlivened : STIMULATE **2** *archaic* : KINDLE **b** : to cause to burn more intensely **3** : to make more rapid : HASTEN, ACCELERATE ⟨~ed her steps⟩ **4 a** : to make (a curve) sharper **b** : to make (a slope) steeper ~ *vi* **1** : to quicken something **2** : to come to life; *esp* : to enter into a phase of active growth and development ⟨seeds ~ing in the

quetzal 1

soil⟩ **3** : to reach the stage of gestation at which fetal motion is felt **4** : to shine more brightly ⟨watched the dawn ~*ing* in the east⟩ **5** : to become more rapid ⟨her pulse ~*ed* at the sight⟩ — **quick·en·er** \'kwi-kə-nər, 'kwik-nər\ *n*

syn QUICKEN, ANIMATE, ENLIVEN, VIVIFY mean to make alive or lively. QUICKEN stresses a sudden renewal of life or activity esp. in something inert ⟨the arrival of spring *quickens* the earth⟩. ANIMATE emphasizes the imparting of motion or vitality to what is or might be mechanical or artificial ⟨happiness *animated* his conversation⟩. ENLIVEN suggests a stimulus that arouses from dullness or boredom ⟨*enlivened* her lectures with humorous anecdotes⟩. VIVIFY implies a freshening or energizing through renewal of vitality ⟨new blood needed to *vivify* the dying club⟩. *syn* see in addition PROVOKE

quick fix *n* (1970) : an expedient usu. temporary or inadequate solution to a problem

quick-freeze \'kwik-'frēz\ *vt* **-froze** \-'frōz\; **-fro·zen** \-'frō-z²n\; **-freez·ing** (1930) : to freeze (food) for preservation so rapidly that ice crystals formed are too small to rupture the cells and the natural juices and flavor are preserved

quick·ie \'kwi-kē\ *n, often attrib* (ca. 1926) : something done or made in a hurry: as **a** : a quickly and usu. cheaply produced work (as a motion picture or book) **b** : a hastily performed act of sexual intercourse

quick kick *n* (ca. 1940) : a punt in football on first, second, or third down made from a running or passing formation and designed to take the opposing team by surprise

quick·lime \'kwik-,līm\ *n* (14c) : ¹LIME 2a

quick·sand \'kwik-,sand\ *n* (14c) **1** : sand readily yielding to pressure; *esp* : a deep mass of loose sand mixed with water into which heavy objects readily sink **2** : something that entraps or frustrates

quick·set \-,set\ *n* (15c) *chiefly Brit* : plant cuttings set in the ground to grow esp. in a hedgerow; *also* : a hedge or thicket esp. of hawthorn grown from quickset

¹**quick·sil·ver** \-,sil-vər\ *n* (bef. 12c) : MERCURY 2a

²**quicksilver** *adj* (1655) : resembling or suggestive of quicksilver; *esp* : MERCURIAL 3

quick·step \-,step\ *n* (ca. 1811) : a spirited march tune usu. accompanying a march in quick time

quick–tem·pered \-'tem-pərd\ *adj* (1830) : easily angered : IRASCIBLE

quick time *n* (ca. 1802) : a rate of marching in which 120 steps each 30 inches in length are taken in one minute

quick–wit·ted \'kwik-'wi-təd\ *adj* (1530) : quick in perception and understanding : mentally alert *syn* see INTELLIGENT — **quick–wit·ted·ly** *adv* — **quick–wit·ted·ness** *n*

¹**quid** \'kwid\ *n, pl* **quid** *also* **quids** [origin unknown] (1688) *Brit* : a pound sterling

²**quid** *n* [E dial., cud, fr. ME *quide*, fr. OE *cwidu, cwudu* — more at CUD] (ca. 1727) : a cut or wad of something chewable

quid·di·ty \'kwi-də-tē\ *n, pl* **-ties** [ME *quidite*, fr. ML *quidditat-, quidditas* essence, fr. L *quid* what, neut. of *quis* who — more at WHO] (14c) **1** : whatever makes something the type that it is : ESSENCE **2** **a** : a trifling point : QUIBBLE **b** : CROTCHET, ECCENTRICITY

quid·nunc \'kwid-,nəŋk\ *n* [L *quid nunc* what now?] (1709) : a person who seeks to know all the latest news or gossip : BUSYBODY

quid pro quo \,kwid-,prō-'kwō\ *n* [NL, something for something] (1591) : something given or received for something else; *also* : a deal arranging a quid pro quo

qui·es·cence \kwī-'e-s²n(t)s, kwē-\ *n* (ca. 1631) : the quality or state of being quiescent

qui·es·cent \-s²nt\ *adj* [L *quiescent-, quiescens,* prp. of *quiescere* to become quiet, rest, fr. *quies*] (1605) **1** : marked by inactivity or repose : tranquilly at rest **2** : causing no trouble or symptoms ⟨~ gallstones⟩ *syn* see LATENT — **qui·es·cent·ly** *adv*

¹**qui·et** \'kwī-ət\ *n* [ME, fr. L *quiet-, quies* rest, quiet — more at WHILE] (14c) : the quality or state of being quiet : TRANQUILLITY — **on the quiet** : in a secretive manner : in secret

²**quiet** *adj* [ME, fr. MF, fr. L *quietus,* fr. pp. of *quiescere*] (14c) **1** **a** : marked by little or no motion or activity : CALM ⟨a ~ sea⟩ **b** : GENTLE, EASYGOING ⟨a ~ temperament⟩ **c** : not interfered with ⟨~ reading⟩ **d** : enjoyed in peace and relaxation ⟨a ~ cup of tea⟩ **2** **a** : free from noise or uproar : STILL **b** : UNOBTRUSIVE, CONSERVATIVE ⟨~ clothes⟩ **3** : SECLUDED ⟨a ~ nook⟩ — **qui·et·ly** *adv* — **qui·et·ness** *n*

³**quiet** *adv* (1573) : in a quiet manner ⟨a *quiet*-running engine⟩

⁴**quiet** *vb* [ME, fr. LL *quietare* to set free, to calm, fr. L *quietus*] *vt* (14c) **1** : to cause to be quiet : CALM **2** : to make secure by freeing from dispute or question ⟨~ title to a property⟩ ~ *vi* : to become quiet — usu. used with *down* — **qui·et·er** *n*

qui·et·en \'kwī-ə-t²n\ *vb* **qui·et·ened; qui·et·en·ing** \'kwī-ət-niŋ, 'kwī-ə-t²n-iŋ\ (ca. 1828) *chiefly Brit* : QUIET

qui·et·ism \'kwī-ə-,ti-zəm\ *n* (1687) **1** **a** : a system of religious mysticism teaching that perfection and spiritual peace are attained by annihilation of the will and passive absorption in contemplation of God and divine things **b** : a passive withdrawn attitude or policy toward the world or worldly affairs **2** : a state of calmness or passivity — **qui·et·ist** \-tist\ *adj or n* — **qui·et·ist·ic** \,kwī-ə-'tis-tik\ *adj*

qui·etude \'kwī-ə-,tüd, -,tyüd\ *n* [MF, fr. LL *quietudo,* fr. L *quietus*] (1597) : a quiet state : REPOSE

qui·etus \kwī-'ē-təs, -'ā-\ *n* [ME *quietus est,* fr. ML, he is quit, formula of discharge from obligation] (1540) **1** : final settlement (as of a debt) **2** : removal from activity; *esp* : DEATH **3** : something that quiets or represses

quiff \'kwif\ *n* [origin unknown] (ca. 1890) *Brit* : a prominent forelock

¹**quill** \'kwil\ *n* [ME *quil* hollow reed, bobbin; akin to MHG *kil* large feather] (15c) **1** **a** (1) : a bobbin, spool, or spindle on which filling yarn is wound (2) : a hollow shaft often surrounding another shaft and used in various mechanical devices **b** : a roll of dried bark ⟨cinnamon ~*s*⟩ **2** **a** (1) : the hollow horny shaft of a feather — see FEATHER illustration (2) : FEATHER; *esp* : one of the large stiff feathers of the wing or tail **b** : one of the hollow sharp spines of a porcupine or hedgehog **c** : ³PEN **3** : something made from or resembling the quill of a feather; *esp* : a pen for writing **4** : a float for a fishing line

²**quill** *vt* (1783) **1** : to pierce with quills **2** **a** : to wind (thread or yarn) on a quill **b** : to make a series of small rounded ridges in (cloth)

quill·back \'kwil-,bak\ *n, pl* **quillback** *or* **quillbacks** (1882) : any of

several suckers; *esp* : a small fish (*Carpiodes cyprinus*) of central and eastern No. America that has the first ray of the dorsal fin much elongated

quill·work \-,wərk\ *n* (1843) : ornamental work in porcupine or bird quills

¹**quilt** \'kwilt\ *n* [ME *quilte* mattress, quilt, fr. OF *cuilte,* fr. L *culcita* mattress] (14c) **1** : a bed coverlet of two layers of cloth filled with padding (as down or batting) held in place by ties or stitched designs **2** : something that is quilted or resembles a quilt

²**quilt** *vt* (1555) **1** **a** : to fill, pad, or line like a quilt **b** (1) : to stitch, sew, or cover with lines or patterns like those used in quilts (2) : to stitch (designs) through layers of cloth **c** : to fasten between two pieces of material **2** : to stitch or sew in layers with padding in between ~ *vi* **1** : to make quilts **2** : to do quilted work — **quilt·er** *n*

quilt·ing *n* (1609) **1** : material that is quilted or used for making quilts **2** : the process of quilting

quin·a·crine \'kwi-nə-,krēn\ *n* [*quin*ine + *acr*idine] (ca. 1934) : an antimalarial drug derived from acridine and used esp. in the form of its dihydrochloride $C_{23}H_{30}ClN_3O·2HCl·2H_2O$

quince \'kwin(t)s\ *n* [ME *quynce* quinces, pl. of *coyn, quyn* quince, fr. MF *coin,* fr. L *cotoneum,* alter. *cydonium,* fr. Gk *kydōnion*] (14c) **1** : the fruit of a central Asian tree (*Cydonia oblonga*) of the rose family that resembles a hard-fleshed yellow apple and is used esp. in preserves **2** : a tree that bears quinces

quin·cen·te·na·ry \,kwin-sen-'te-nə-rē, -'sen-²n-,er-ē, *esp Brit* -sen-'tē-nə-rē\ *n* [L *quinque* five + E *centenary*] (1879) : a 500th anniversary or its celebration — **quincentenary** *adj*

quin·cen·ni·al \-sen-'te-nē-əl\ *n* [L *quinque* five + E *centennial*] (1884) : QUINCENTENARY — **quincentennial** *adj*

quin·cunx \'kwin-,kəŋ(k)s\ *n* [L *quincunc-, quincunx,* lit., five twelfths, fr. *quinque* five + *uncia* twelfth part — more at FIVE, OUNCE] (1658) : an arrangement of five things in a square or rectangle with one at each corner and one in the middle — **quin·cun·cial** \kwin-'kən(t)-shəl\ *or* **quin·cunx·ial** \-'kəŋk-sē-əl\ *adj*

quince 1

quin·de·cil·lion \,kwin-di-'sil-yən\ *n, often attrib* [L *quindec*im fifteen (fr. *quinque* five + *decem* ten) + E *-illion* (as in *million*) — more at TEN] (1903) — see NUMBER table

quin·i·dine \'kwi-nə-,dēn\ *n* [ISV, fr. *quinine*] (1836) : an alkaloid $C_{20}H_{24}N_2O_2$ that is stereoisomeric with quinine and is used in treating cardiac rhythm irregularities

qui·nie·la \kwin-'ye-lə\ *or* **qui·nel·la** \kwi-'ne-lə\ *n* [AmerSp *quiniela,* a game of chance resembling a lottery] (1905) : a bet in which the bettor picks the first and second place finishers but need not designate their order of finish in order to win — compare PERFECTA

qui·nine \'kwī-,nīn *also* 'kwi- *or* kwi-'nīn *or* ki-'nēn *or* kwi-'nēn\ *n* [Sp *quina* cinchona, fr. Quechua *kina* bark] (1826) **1** : a bitter crystalline alkaloid $C_{20}H_{24}N_2O_2$ from cinchona bark used in medicine **2** : a salt of quinine used esp. as an antipyretic, antimalarial, and bitter tonic

quinine water *n* (1953) : TONIC WATER

qui·noa \'kēn-,wä\ *n* [Sp, fr. Quechua *kinua*] (1625) : a pigweed (*Chenopodium quinoa*) of the high Andes whose seeds are ground and widely used as food in Peru

quin·o·line \'kwi-n²l-,ēn\ *n* [ISV *quin*ine + ³*-ol* + ²*-ine*] (1845) **1** : a pungent oily nitrogenous base C_9H_7N obtained usu. by distillation of coal tar or by synthesis from aniline that is the parent compound of many alkaloids, drugs, and dyes **2** : a derivative of quinoline

qui·none \kwi-'nōn, 'kwi-,\ *n* [ISV *quin*ine + *-one*] (1853) **1** : either of two isomeric cyclic crystalline compounds $C_6H_4O_2$ that are di-keto derivatives of dihydro-benzene **2** : any of various usu. yellow, orange, or red quinonoid compounds including several that are biologically important as coenzymes, hydrogen acceptors, or vitamins

qui·no·noid \kwi-'nō-,nóid, 'kwi-nə-\ *or* **quin·oid** \'kwi-,nóid\ *adj* (1878) : resembling quinone esp. in having a benzene nucleus containing two double bonds within the nucleus

quin·quen·ni·al \kwin-'kwe-nē-əl, kwaŋ-\ *adj* (15c) **1** : consisting of or lasting for five years **2** : occurring or being done every five years — **quinquennial·ly** *adv* — **quin·quen·ni·al·ly** \-nē-ə-lē\ *adv*

quin·quen·ni·um \-nē-əm\ *n, pl* **-ni·ums** *or* **-nia** \-nē-ə\ [L, fr. *quinque* five + *annus* year — more at FIVE, ANNUAL] (1621) : a period of five years

quin·sy \'kwin-zē\ *n* [ME *quinesie,* fr. MF *quinancie,* fr. LL *cynanche,* fr. Gk *kynanchē,* fr. *kyn-, kyōn* dog + *anchein* to strangle — more at HOUND, ANGER] (14c) : an abscess in the tissue around a tonsil usu. resulting from bacterial infection and often accompanied by pain and fever

quint \'kwint\ *n* (1935) : QUINTUPLET

quin·ta \'kin-tə, 'kēn-\ *n* [Sp & Pg, *quinta,* farm rented at one fifth of its income, fr. L, fem. of *quintus* fifth] (1754) : a country villa or estate esp. in Portugal or Latin America

quin·tain \'kwin-t²n\ *n* [ME *quintaine,* fr. MF, perh. fr. L *quintana* street in a Roman camp separating the fifth maniple from the sixth where a market was held, fr. fem. of *quintanus* fifth in rank, fr. *quintus* fifth] (15c) : an object to be tilted at; *esp* : a post with a revolving crosspiece that has a target at one end and a sandbag at the other end

quin·tal \'kwin-t²l, 'kan-\ *n* [ME, fr. MF, fr. ML *quintale,* fr. Ar *qintār,* fr. LGk *kentēnarion,* fr. LL *centenarium,* fr. L, neut. of *centenarius* consisting of a hundred — more at CENTENARY] (15c) **1** : HUNDREDWEIGHT **2** : a unit of weight equal to 100 kilograms (about 220 pounds)

quin·tes·sence \kwin-'te-s²n(t)s\ *n* [ME, fr. MF *quinte essence,* fr. ML *quinta essentia,* lit., fifth essence] (15c) **1** : the fifth and highest ele-

\ə\ abut \²\ kitten, F table \ər\ further \a\ ash \ā\ ace \ä\ mop, mar \aú\ out \ch\ chin \e\ bet \ē\ easy \g\ go \i\ hit \ī\ ice \j\ job \ŋ\ sing \ō\ go \ó\ law \ói\ boy \th\ thin \t̲h\ the \ü\ loot \ú\ foot \y\ yet \zh\ vision \à, k̲, ⁿ, œ, œ̄, ᴜᴇ, ᵫ, ᵞ\ *see* Guide to Pronunciation ment in ancient and medieval philosophy that permeates all nature and is the substance composing the celestial bodies **2** : the essence of a thing in its purest and most concentrated form **3** : the most typical example or representative — **quin·tes·sen·tial** \,kwin-tə-'sen(t)-shəl\ *adj* — **quin·tes·sen·tial·ly** *adv*

quin·tet *also* **quin·tette** \kwin-'tet\ *n* [quintet fr. It *quintetto*, fr. *quinto* fifth, fr. L *quintus; quintette* fr. F, fr. It *quintetto*] (1811) **1** : a musical composition or movement for five instruments or voices **2** : a group or set of five: as **a** : the performers of a quintet **b** : a basketball team

¹quin·tic \'kwin-tik\ *adj* [L *quintus* fifth] (1853) : of the fifth degree

²quintic *n* (1856) : a polynomial or a polynomial equation of the fifth degree

quin·tile \'kwin-,tīl\ *n* [L *quintus* + E ²-*ile*] (ca. 1928) : any of the four values that divide the items of a frequency distribution into five classes with each containing one fifth of the total population; *also* : any one of the five classes

quin·til·lion \kwin-'til-yən\ *n* [L *quintus* + E -*illion* (as in *million*)] (1674) — see NUMBER table — **quintillion** *adj* — **quin·til·lionth** \-yən(t)th\ *adj or n*

¹quin·tu·ple \kwin-'tü-pəl, -'tyü-, -'tə-; 'kwin-tə-\ *adj* [MF, fr. ML *quintuplus*, fr. L *quintus* fifth + *-plus* -fold; akin to L *quinque* five — more at FIVE, -FOLD] (1570) **1** : being five times as great or as many **2** : having five units or members **3** : marked by five beats per measure \~ meter\ — **quintuple** *n*

²quintuple *vb* **quin·tu·pled; quin·tu·pling** \-p(ə-)liŋ\ *vt* (1639) : to make five times as great or as many \~ vi : to become five times as much or as numerous

quin·tu·plet \kwin-'tə-plət, -'tü-, -'tyü-; 'kwin-tə-\ *n* (1873) **1** : a combination of five of a kind **2** : one of five offspring born at one birth

¹quin·tu·pli·cate \kwin-'tü-pli-kət, -'tyü-\ *adj* [ML *quintuplicatus*, pp. of *quintuplicare* to quintuple, fr. *quintuplus* quintuple] (1656) **1** : consisting of or existing in five corresponding or identical parts or examples \~ invoices\ **2** : being the fifth of five things exactly alike \file the ~ copy\

²quintuplicate *n* (1851) **1** : one of five things exactly alike; *specif* : one of five identical copies **2** : five copies all alike — used with *in* \typed in ~\

³quin·tu·pli·cate \-plə-,kāt\ *vt* -**cat·ed; -cat·ing** (ca. 1890) **1** : to make quintuple or fivefold **2** : to prepare in quintuplicate

¹quip \'kwip\ *n* [earlier *quippy*, perh. fr. L *quippe* indeed, to be sure (often ironic), fr. *quid* what — more at QUIDDITY] (1532) **1 a** : a clever usu. taunting remark : GIBE **b** : a witty or funny observation or response usu. made on the spur of the moment : QUIBBLE, EQUIVOCATION **2** : something strange, droll, curious, or eccentric : ODDITY

²quip *vb* **quipped; quip·ping** *vi* (1579) : to make quips : GIBE \~ *vt* : to jest or gibe at — **quip·per** \'kwi-pər\ *n*

quip·ster \'kwip-stər\ *n* (1876) : one who is given to quipping

qui·pu \'kē-(,)pü\ *n* [Sp *quipo*, fr. Quechua *khipu*] (1704) : a device made of a main cord with smaller varicolored cords attached and knotted and used by the ancient Peruvians (as for calculating)

¹quire \'kwir\ *n* [ME *quair* four sheets of paper folded once, collection of sheets, fr. MF *quaer*, fr. (assumed) VL *quaternum* set of four, fr. L *quaterni* four each, set of four — more at QUATERNION] (15c) : a collection of 24 or sometimes 25 sheets of paper of the same size and quality : one twentieth of a ream

²quire *var of* CHOIR

Qui·ri·nus \kwə-'ri-nəs, -'rē-\ *n* [L] : an early state god of the Romans later identified with Romulus

¹quirk \'kwərk\ *n* [origin unknown] (1565) **1 a** : an abrupt twist or curve **b** : a peculiar trait : IDIOSYNCRASY **c** : ACCIDENT, VAGARY \a ~ of fate\ **2** : a groove separating a bead or other molding from adjoining members — **quirk·i·ly** \'kwər-kə-lē\ *adv* — **quirk·i·ness** \-kē-nəs\ *n* — **quirk·ish** \'kwər-kish\ *adj* — **quirky** \-kē\ *adj*

²quirk *vb* (1596) : CURVE, TWIST \~ed his eyebrows\

¹quirt \'kwərt\ *n* [MexSp *cuarta*] (1845) : a riding whip with a short handle and a rawhide lash

²quirt *vt* (1887) : to strike or drive with a quirt

quis·ling \'kwiz-liŋ\ *n, often attrib* [Vidkun *Quisling* †1945 Norw. politician who collaborated with the Nazis] (1940) : TRAITOR 2, COLLABORATOR — **quis·ling·ism** \-liŋ,-i-zəm\ *n*

¹quit \'kwit\ *adj* [ME *quite, quit*, fr. OF *quite*] (13c) : released from obligation, charge, or penalty; *esp* : FREE

²quit *vb* **quit** *also* **quit·ted; quit·ting** [ME *quiten, quitten*, fr. MF *quiter, quitter*, fr. OF, fr. *quite* free of, released, lit., at rest, fr. L *quietus* quiet, at rest] *vt* (13c) **1** : to make full payment of : PAY UP \~ a debt\ **2** : to set free : RELIEVE, RELEASE \~ oneself of fear\ **3** : CONDUCT, ACQUIT \the youths ~ themselves like men\ **4** : to depart from or out of **b** : to leave the company of **c** : GIVE UP 1, 2 \~ a job\ \~ smoking\ \~ *vi* **1** : to cease normal, expected, or necessary action **2** : to give up employment **3** : to admit defeat : GIVE UP *syn* see STOP

³quit *n* (ca. 1923) : the act or an instance of quitting a job

quitch \'kwich\ *n* [(assumed) ME *quicche*, fr. OE *cwice*; akin to OHG *quecca* couch grass] (bef. 12c) : QUACK GRASS

quit·claim \'kwit-,klām\ *vt* (14c) : to release or relinquish a legal claim to; *esp* : to release a claim to or convey by a quitclaim deed — **quit·claim** *n*

quitclaim deed *n* (1756) : a legal instrument used to release one person's right, title, or interest to another without providing a guarantee or warranty of title

quite \'kwit\ *adv* [ME, fr. *quite*, adj., quit] (14c) **1** : WHOLLY, COMPLETELY \not ~ finished\ **2** : to an extreme : POSITIVELY \~ sure\ — often used as an intensifier with *a* \~ a swell guy\ \~ a beauty\ **3** : to a considerable extent : RATHER \~ near\ *usage* see PLENTY — **quite a bit** : a considerable amount — **quite a few** : MANY

quit·rent \'kwit-,rent\ *n* (15c) : a fixed rent payable to a feudal superior in commutation of services; *specif* : a fixed rent due from a socage tenant

quits \'kwits\ *adj* [ME, quit, prob. fr. ML *quittus*, alter. of L *quietus* at rest] (15c) : being on even terms by repayment or requital

quit·tance \'kwi-t³n(t)s\ *n* (14c) **1 a** : discharge from a debt or an obligation **b** : a document evidencing quittance **2** : RECOMPENSE, REQUITAL

quit·ter \'kwi-tər\ *n* (1611) : one that quits; *esp* : one that gives up too easily : DEFEATIST

quit·tor \'kwi-tər\ *n* [ME *quiture* pus, prob. fr. OF, act of boiling, fr. L *coctura*, fr. *coctus*, pp. of *coquere* to cook — more at COOK] (1703) : a purulent inflammation of the feet esp. of horses and donkeys

¹quiv·er \'kwi-vər\ *n* [ME, fr. MF *quivre*, of Gmc origin; akin to OE *cocer* quiver, OHG *kohhari*] (14c) **1** : a case for carrying or holding arrows **2** : the arrows in a quiver

²quiver *vi* **quiv·ered; quiv·er·ing** \'kwi-və-riŋ, 'kwiv-riŋ\ [ME, prob. fr. *quiver* agile, quick; akin to OE *cwiferlice* zealously] (15c) : to shake or move with a slight trembling motion — **quiv·er·ing·ly** *adv*

³quiver *n* (1786) : the act or action of quivering : TREMOR

qui vive \kē-'vēv\ *n* [F *qui-vive*, fr. *qui vive?* long live who?, challenge of a French sentry] (1726) : ALERT, LOOKOUT — used in the phrase *on the qui vive*

qui·xote \'kwik-sət, kē-'hō-tē, -'ō-\ *n, often cap* [Don *Quixote*, hero of the novel *Don Quixote de la Mancha* (1605, 1615) by Cervantes] (1648) : a quixotic person — **quix·o·tism** \'kwik-sə-,ti-zəm\ *n* — **quix·o·try** \-sə-trē\ *n*

quix·ot·ic \kwik-'sä-tik\ *adj* [Don *Quixote*] (1815) **1** : foolishly impractical esp. in the pursuit of ideals; *esp* : marked by rash lofty romantic ideas or extravagantly chivalrous action **2** : CAPRICIOUS, UNPREDICTABLE *syn* see IMAGINARY — **quix·ot·i·cal** \-ti-kəl\ *adj* — **quix·ot·i·cal·ly** \-ti-k(ə-)lē\ *adv*

¹quiz \'kwiz\ *n, pl* **quiz·zes** [origin unknown] (1749) **1** : an eccentric person : PRACTICAL JOKE **3** : the act or action of quizzing; *specif* : a short oral or written test

²quiz *vt* **quizzed; quiz·zing** (1794) **1** : to make fun of : MOCK **2** : to look at inquisitively **3** : to question closely — **quiz·zer** *n*

quiz·mas·ter \'kwiz-,mas-tər\ *n* (1943) : one who puts the questions to contestants in a quiz show

quiz show *n* (1944) : an entertainment program (as on radio or television) in which contestants answer questions — called also *quiz program*

quiz·zi·cal \'kwi-zi-kəl\ *adj* (1800) **1** : comically quaint **2** : mildly teasing or mocking \a ~ remark\ **3** : expressive of puzzlement, curiosity, or disbelief \raised a ~ eyebrow\ — **quiz·zi·cal·i·ty** \,kwi-zə-'ka-lə-tē\ *n* — **quiz·zi·cal·ly** \'kwi-zi-k(ə-)lē\ *adv*

quod \'kwäd\ *n* [origin unknown] (ca. 1700) *slang Brit* : PRISON

quod·li·bet \'kwäd-lə-,bet\ *n* [ME, fr. ML *quodlibetum*, fr. L *quodlibet*, neut. of *quilibet* any whatever, fr. *qui* who, what + *libet* it pleases, fr. *libēre* to please — more at WHO, LOVE] (14c) **1** : a philosophical or theological point proposed for disputation; *also* : a disputation on such a point **2** : a whimsical combination of familiar melodies or texts

¹quoin \'kòin, 'kwòin\ *n* [alter. of ¹*coin*] (1532) **1 a** : a solid exterior angle (as of a building) **b** : one of the members (as a block) forming a quoin and usu. differentiated from the adjoining walls by material, texture, color, size, or projection **2** : the keystone or a voussoir of an arch **3** : a wooden or expandable metal block used by printers to lock up a form within a chase

²quoin *vt* (1683) **1** : to equip (a type form) with quoins **2** : to provide with quoins \~ed walls\

quoin 1b

¹quoit \'kòit, 'kwòit, 'kwät\ *n* [ME *coite*] (15c) **1** : a flattened ring of iron or circle of rope used in a throwing game **2** *pl but sing in constr* : a game in which the quoits are thrown at an upright pin in an attempt to ring the pin or come as near to it as possible

²quoit *vt* (1597) : to throw like a quoit

quon·dam \'kwän-dəm, -,dam\ *adj* [L, at one time, formerly, fr. *quom, cum* when; akin to L *qui* who — more at WHO] (1539) : FORMER, SOMETIME \a ~ friend\

Quon·set \'kwän(t)-sət, 'kwän-zət\ *trademark* — used for a prefabricated shelter set on a foundation of bolted steel trusses and built of a semicircular arching roof of corrugated metal insulated with wood fiber

quo·rum \'kwòr-əm, 'kwòr-\ *n* [ME, quorum of justices of the peace, fr. L, of whom, gen. pl. of *qui* who; fr. the wording of the commission formerly issued to justices of the peace] (1602) **1** : a select group **2** : the number (as a majority) of officers or members of a body that when duly assembled is legally competent to transact business **3** : a Mormon body comprising those in the same grade of priesthood

quo·ta \'kwō-tə\ *n* [ML, fr. L *quota pars* how great a part] (1618) **1** : a proportional part or share; *esp* : the share or proportion assigned to each in a division or to each member of a body **2** : the number or amount constituting a proportional share

quot·able \'kwō-tə-bəl *also* 'kò-\ *adj* (1811) : fit for or worth quoting — **quot·abil·i·ty** \,kwō-tə-'bi-lə-tē *also* ,kò-\ *n*

quo·ta·tion \kwō-'tā-shən *also* kò-\ *n* (1646) **1 a** : the act or process of quoting **b** (1) : the naming or publishing of current bids and offers or prices of securities or commodities (2) : the bids, offers, or prices so named or published; *esp* : the highest bid and lowest offer for a particular security in a given market at a given time **2** : something that is quoted; *esp* : a passage referred to, repeated, or adduced

quotation mark *n* (ca. 1859) : one of a pair of punctuation marks " " or ' ' used chiefly to indicate the beginning and the end of a quotation in which the exact phraseology of another or of a text is directly cited

¹quote \'kwōt *also* 'kòt\ *vb* **quot·ed; quot·ing** [ML *quotare* to mark the number of, number references, fr. L *quotus* of what number or quantity, fr. *quot* how many, (as) many as; akin to L *qui* who — more at WHO] *vt* (1582) **1** : to speak or write (a passage) from another usu. with credit acknowledgment **b** : to repeat a passage from esp. in substantiation or illustration **2** : to cite in illustration \~ cases\ **3 a** : to state (the current price or bid-offer spread) for a commodity, stock, or bond **b** : to give exact information on **4** : to set off by quotation marks \~ *vi* : to inform a hearer or reader that matter following is quoted — **quot·er** *n*

²quote *n* (1888) **1** : QUOTATION **2** : QUOTATION MARK — often used orally to indicate the beginning of a direct quotation

quoth \'kwōth *also* 'kòth\ *vb past* [ME, past of *quethen* to say, fr. OE *cwethan*; akin to OHG *quedan* to say] (bef. 12c) *archaic* : SAID — used chiefly in the first and third persons with a postpositive subject

quo·tha \'kwō-thə\ *interj* [alter. of *quoth he*] (1519) *archaic* — used esp. to express surprise or contempt

quo·tid·i·an \kwō-'ti-dē-ən\ *adj* [ME *cotidian*, fr. MF, fr. L *quotidianus, cotidianus*, fr. *quotidie* every day, fr. *quot* (as) many as + *dies* day — more at DEITY] (14c) **1** : occurring every day ⟨~ fever⟩ **2 a** : belonging to each day : EVERYDAY ⟨~ routine⟩ **b** : COMMONPLACE, ORDINARY ⟨~ drabness⟩ — **quotidian** *n*

quo·tient \'kwō-shənt\ *n* [ME *quocient*, modif. of L *quotiens* how many times, fr. *quot* how many] (15c) **1** : the number resulting from the division of one number by another **2** : the numerical ratio usu. multiplied by 100 between a test score and a measurement on which that score might be expected largely to depend **3** : QUOTA, SHARE

quotient group *n* (1893) : a group whose elements are the cosets of a normal subgroup of a given group — called also *factor group*

quotient ring *n* (ca. 1958) : a ring whose elements are the cosets of an ideal in a given ring

quo war·ran·to \‚kwō-wə-'rän-(‚)tō, -'ran-; -'wȯr-ən-‚tō, -'wär-\ *n* [ME *quo waranto*, fr. ML *quo warranto* by what warrant; fr. the wording of the writ] (15c) **1 a** : an English writ formerly requiring a person to show by what authority he exercises a public office, franchise, or liberty **b** : a legal proceeding for a like purpose begun by an information **2** : the legal action begun by a quo warranto

Qur·an *also* **Qur·an** \kə-'ran, -'rän; kü-'ran, -'rän\ *var of* KORAN

QWER·TY \'kwər-tē, 'kwer-\ *n, often not cap* [fr. the first six letters in the second row of the keyboard] (1929) : a standard typewriter keyboard — called also *QWERTY keyboard*

r \'är\ *n, pl* **r's** *or* **rs** \'ärz\ *often cap, often attrib* (bef. 12c) **1 a** : the 18th letter of the English alphabet **b** : a graphic representation of this letter **c** : a speech counterpart of orthographic *r* **2** : a graphic device for reproducing the letter *r* **3** : one designated *r* esp. as the 18th in order or class **4** : something shaped like the letter R **R** *certification mark* — used to certify that a motion picture is of such a nature that admission is restricted to persons over a specified age (as 17) unless accompanied by a parent or guardian; compare G, NC-17, PG, PG-13

Ra \'rä\ *n* [Egypt *r*'] : the Egyptian sun-god and chief deity

ra·ba·to \rə-'bä-(‚)tō\ *n, pl* **-tos** [modif. of MF *rabat*, lit., act of turning down, fr. *rabattre*] (1591) : a wide lace-edged collar of the early 17th century often stiffened to stand high at the back

¹rab·bet \'ra-bət\ *n* [ME *rabet*, fr. MF *rabat* act of beating down, fr. OF *rabattre* to beat down, reduce — more at REBATE] (14c) : a channel, groove, or recess cut out of the edge or face of a surface; *esp* : one intended to receive another member (as a panel)

²rabbet *vt* (15c) **1** : to unite the edges of in a rabbet joint **2** : to cut a rabbet in ⟨~ *vi* : to become joined by a rabbet

rabbet joint *n* (ca. 1828) : a joint formed by fitting together rabbeted boards or timbers

rab·bi \'ra-‚bī\ *n* [ME, fr. OE, fr. LL, fr. Gk *rhabbi*, fr. Heb *rabbi* my master, fr. *rabh* master + -*ī* my] (bef. 12c) **1** : MASTER, TEACHER — used by Jews as a term of address **2** : a Jew qualified to expound and apply the halakah and other Jewish law **3** : a Jew trained and ordained for professional religious leadership; *specif* : the official leader of a Jewish congregation

rab·bin \'ra-bən\ *n* [F] (1579) : RABBI

rab·bin·ate \'ra-bə-nət, -‚nät\ *n* (1702) **1** : the office or tenure of a rabbi **2** : the whole body of rabbis

rab·bin·ic \rə-'bi-nik, ra-\ *or* **rab·bin·i·cal** \-ni-kəl\ *adj* (1612) **1** : of or relating to rabbis or their writings **2** : of or preparing for the rabbinate **3** : comprising or belonging to any of several sets of Hebrew characters simpler than the square Hebrew letters — **rab·bin·i·cal·ly** \-ni-k(ə-)lē\ *adv*

Rabbinic Hebrew *n* (ca. 1909) : the Hebrew used esp. by medieval rabbis

rab·bin·ism \'ra-bə-‚ni-zəm\ *n* (1652) : rabbinic teachings and traditions

¹rab·bit \'ra-bət\ *n, pl* **rabbit** *or* **rabbits** *often attrib* [ME *rabet*, prob. fr. MF dial. (Walloon) *robett*, fr. MD *robe*] (14c) **1** : any of a family (Leporidae) of long-eared short-tailed lagomorph mammals with long hind legs: **a** : any of various lagomorphs that are born naked, blind, and helpless, that are sometimes gregarious, and that include esp. the cottontails of the New World and a small Old World mammal (*Oryctolagus cuniculus*) that is the source of various domestic breeds **b** : HARE **2** : the pelt of a rabbit **3** : WELSH RABBIT **4 a** : a figure of a rabbit sped mechanically along the edge of a dog track as an object of pursuit **b** : a runner in a long-distance race who sets a fast pace for the field in the first part of the race — **rab·bity** \-bə-tē\ *adj*

²rabbit *vi* (1852) : to hunt rabbits — **rab·bit·er** *n*

rab·bit·brush \'ra-bət-‚brəsh\ *n* (ca. 1890) : any of several low branching composite shrubs (genus *Chrysothamnus* and esp. *C. nauseosus*) of the alkali plains of western No. America that are characterized by linear entire leaves and clusters of golden yellow or white flowers

rabbit ears *n pl* (1952) : an indoor dipole television antenna consisting of two usu. extensible rods connected to a base to form a V shape

rabbit fever *n* (1925) : TULAREMIA

rabbit punch *n* (1915) : a short chopping blow delivered to the back of the neck or the base of the skull — **rabbit–punch** *vt*

rab·bit·ry \'ra-bə-trē\ *n, pl* **-ries** (1838) : a place where domestic rabbits are kept; *also* : a rabbit-raising enterprise

¹rab·ble \'ra-bəl\ *n* [ME *rabel* pack of animals] (14c) **1** : a disorganized or confused collection of things **2 a** : a disorganized or disorderly crowd of people : MOB **b** : the lowest class of people

²rabble *vt* **rab·bled; rab·bling** \-b(ə-)liŋ\ (1644) : to insult or assault by or as a mob

rab·ble·ment \'ra-bəl-mənt\ *n* (1548) **1** : RABBLE **2** : DISTURBANCE

rab·ble–rous·er \'ra-bəl-‚raú-zər\ *n* (1843) : one that stirs up (as to hatred or violence) the masses of the people : DEMAGOGUE — **rab·ble–rous·ing** \-ziŋ\ *n or adj*

Ra·be·lai·sian \‚ra-bə-'lā-zhən, -zē-ən\ *adj* (1817) **1** : of, relating to, or characteristic of Rabelais or his works **2** : marked by gross robust humor, extravagance of caricature, or bold naturalism

Ra·bi \'rə-bē\ *n* [Ar *rabī*] (ca. 1769) : either of two months of the Islamic year: **a** : the 3d month **b** : the 4th month — see MONTH table

ra·bic \'rä-bik\ *adj* (1885) : of or relating to rabies

ra·bid \'ra-bəd *also* 'rā-\ *adj* [L *rabidus* mad, fr. *rabere*] (1611) **1 a** : extremely violent : FURIOUS **b** : going to extreme lengths in expressing or pursuing a feeling, interest, or opinion **2** : affected with rabies — **ra·bid·i·ty** \rə-'bi-də-tē, ra-, rä-\ *n* — **ra·bid·ly** \'ra-bəd-lē *also* 'rä-\ *adv* — **ra·bid·ness** *n*

ra·bies \'rā-bēz\ *n, pl* **rabies** [NL, fr. L, madness, fr. *rabere* to rave — more at RAGE] (ca. 1598) : an acute virus disease of the nervous system of warm-blooded animals usu. transmitted through the bite of a rabid animal and typically characterized by increased salivation, abnormal behavior, and eventual paralysis and death

rac·coon \ra-'kün *also* rə-\ *n, pl* **raccoon** *or* **raccoons** [Virginia Algonquian *raugroughcun, arocoun*] (1608) **1 a** : a small nocturnal carnivore (*Procyon lotor*) of No. America that is chiefly gray, has a black mask and bushy ringed tail, lives chiefly in trees, and has a varied diet including small animals, fruits, and nuts **b** : the pelt of this animal **2** : any of several animals resembling or related to the raccoon

raccoon dog *n* (1868) : a small omnivorous canid (*Nyctereutes procyonoides*) of eastern Asia having a long yellowish brown coat and facial markings resembling that of a raccoon — called also *tanuki*

¹race \'rās\ *n* [ME *ras*, fr. ON *rás*; akin to OE *rǣs* rush] (14c) **1** *chiefly Scot* : the act of running **2 a** : a strong or rapid current of water flowing through a narrow channel **b** : a watercourse used industrially **c** : the current flowing in such a course **3 a** : a set course or duration of time **b** : the course of life **4 a** : a contest of speed **b** *pl* : a meeting in which several races (as for horses) are run **c** : a contest or rivalry involving progress toward a goal ⟨pennant ~⟩ **5** : a track or channel in which something rolls or slides; *specif* : a groove (as for the balls) in a bearing — see ROLLER BEARING illustration

²race *vb* **raced; rac·ing** *vi* (15c) **1** : to compete in a race **2** : to go or move at top speed or out of control **3** : to revolve too fast under a diminished load ⟨~ *vt* **1** : to engage in a race with **2** : to enter in a race **b** : to drive or ride at high speed **c** : to transport or propel at maximum speed **3** : to speed (as an engine) without a working load or with the transmission disengaged

³race *n* [MF, generation, fr. OIt *razza*] (1580) **1** : a breeding stock of animals **2 a** : a family, tribe, people, or nation belonging to the same stock **b** : a class or kind of people united by community of interests, habits, or characteristics ⟨the English ~⟩ **3 a** : an actually or potentially interbreeding group within a species; *also* : a taxonomic category (as a subspecies) representing such a group **b** : BREED **c** : a division of mankind possessing traits that are transmissible by descent and sufficient to characterize it as a distinct human type **4** *obs* : inherited temperament or disposition **5** : distinctive flavor, taste, or strength

race·course \'rās-‚kōrs, -‚kȯrs\ *n* (1764) **1** : a course for racing **2** : RACEWAY 1

race·horse \-‚hȯrs\ *n* (ca. 1626) : a horse bred or kept for racing

ra·ce·mate \rā-'sē-‚māt, rə-; 'ra-sə-\ *n* (1907) : a racemic compound or mixture

ra·ceme \rā-'sēm, rə-\ *n* [L *racemus* bunch of grapes; prob. akin to Gk *rhag-, rhax* grape] (1785) : a simple inflorescence (as in the lily-of-the-valley) in which the flowers are borne on short stalks of about equal length at equal distances along an elongated axis and open in succession toward the apex — see INFLORESCENCE illustration

ra·ce·mic \-'sē-mik\ *adj* (1892) : of, relating to, or constituting a compound or mixture that is composed of equal amounts of dextrorotatory and levorotatory forms of the same compound and is not optically active

ra·ce·mi·za·tion \rā-‚sē-mə-'zā-shən, rə-; ‚ra-sə-mə-\ *n* (1895) : the action or process of changing from an optically active compound into a

---

\ə\ abut \ᵊ\ kitten, F table \ər\ further \a\ ash \ā\ ace \ä\ mop, mar
\aú\ out \ch\ chin \e\ bet \ē\ easy \g\ go \i\ hit \ī\ ice \j\ job
\ŋ\ sing \ō\ go \ȯ\ law \ȯi\ boy \th\ thin \t̲h̲\ the \ü\ loot \ú\ foot
\y\ yet \zh\ vision \á, k̲, ⁿ, œ, œ̄, ue, ūe, ᵞ\ *see* Guide to Pronunciation

racemic compound or mixture — **ra·ce·mize** \'rā-'sē-,mīz, rə-; 'ra-sə-\ *vb*

ra·ce·mose \'ra-sə-,mōs; rā-'sē-, rə-\ *adj* [L *racemosus* full of clusters, fr. *racemus*] (1698) : having or growing in the form of a raceme

rac·er \'rā-sər\ *n* (1649) **1** : one that races or is used for racing **2** : any of various active American colubrid snakes (genus *Coluber* and *Mastigophis*); *esp* : BLACK RACER

race riot *n* (1890) : a riot caused by racial dissensions or hatreds

race runner *n* (1915) : a No. American lizard (*Cnemidophorus sex-lineatus*) that moves swiftly

race·track \'rās-,trak\ *n* (1859) : a usu. oval course for racing

race·track·er \-,tra-kər\ *n* (1953) : one who frequents a racetrack

race·walk·ing \-,wò-kiŋ\ *n* (1962) : the competitive sport of racing at a fast walk while maintaining continuous foot contact with the ground and keeping the supporting leg straight — **race·walk·er** \-kər\ *n*

race·way \-,wā\ *n* (1828) **1** : a canal for a current of water **2** : a channel for loosely holding electrical wires in buildings **3** : ¹RACE 5 **4** : a course for racing; *esp* : a track for harness racing

rach·et \'ra-chət\ *var of* RATCHET

ra·chis \'rā-kəs, 'ra-\ *n, pl* **ra·chis·es** *also* **ra·chi·des** \'ra-kə-,dēz, 'rā-\ [NL *rachid-, rachis*, fr. Gk *rhachis*; akin to Gk *rhachos* thorn, Lith *ražas* dry twig, tine] (1842) **1** : SPINAL COLUMN **2** : an axial structure: as **a** (1) : the elongated axis of an inflorescence (2) : an extension of the petiole of a compound leaf that bears the leaflets **b** : the distal part of the shaft of a feather that bears the web

ra·chit·ic \rə-'ki-tik\ *adj* [NL *rachitis* rickets, fr. Gk *rachitis* spinal disease, fr. *rhachis*] (1797) : RICKETY

ra·cial \'rā-shəl\ *adj* (1862) **1** : of, relating to, or based on a race **2** : existing or occurring between races — **ra·cial·ly** \-shə-lē\ *adv*

ra·cial·ism \'rā-shə-,li-zəm\ *n* (1907) : RACISM — **ra·cial·ist** \-list\ *n or adj* — **ra·cial·is·tic** \,rā-shə-'lis-tik\ *adj*

rac·ing \'rā-siŋ\ *n* (1680) : the sport or profession of engaging in or holding races

racing form *n* (1946) : an information sheet giving details of past performance (as for racehorses) for use by bettors

rac·ism \'rā-,si-zəm *also* -,shi-\ *n* (1936) **1** : a belief that race is the primary determinant of human traits and capacities and that racial differences produce an inherent superiority of a particular race **2** : racial prejudice or discrimination — **rac·ist** \-sist *also* -shist\ *n or adj*

¹rack \'rak\ *n* [ME *rak*, prob. of Scand origin; akin to Sw dial. *rak* wreck; akin to OE *wrecan* to drive — more at WREAK] (14c) : a wind-driven mass of high often broken clouds

²rack *vi* (1590) : to fly or scud in high wind

³rack *n* [ME, prob. fr. MD *rec* framework; akin to OE *reccan* to stretch, Gk *oregein* — more at RIGHT] (14c) **1** : a framework for holding fodder for livestock **2** : an instrument of torture on which a body is stretched **3 a** (1) : a cause of anguish or pain (2) : acute suffering **b** : the action of straining or wrenching **4** : a framework, stand, or grating on or in which articles are placed **5** : a frame placed in a stream to stop fish and floating or suspended matter **6 a** : a bar with teeth on one face for gearing with a pinion or worm gear to transform rotary motion to linear motion or vice versa (as in an automobile steering mechanism or microscope drawtube) **b** : a notched bar used as a ratchet to engage with a pawl, click, or detent **7** : a pair of antlers **8** : a triangular frame used to set up the balls in a pool game; *also* : the balls as set up — **rack·ful** \-,fùl\ *n* — **on the rack** : under great mental or emotional stress

⁴rack *vt* (15c) **1** : to torture on the rack **2** : to cause to suffer torture, pain, or anguish **3 a** : to stretch or strain violently (~ed his brains) **b** : to raise (rents) oppressively **c** : to harass or oppress with high rents or extortions **4** : to work or treat (material) on a rack **5** : to work by a rack and pinion or worm so as to extend or contract (~ a camera) **6** : to seize (as parallel ropes of a tackle) together **7** : to place (as pool balls) in a rack ~ *vi* : to become forced out of shape or out of plumb *syn* see AFFLICT — **rack·er** *n* — **rack·ing·ly** \'ra-kiŋ-lē\ *adv*

⁵rack *vt* [ME *rakken*, fr. OProv *arraca*, fr. *raca* stems and husks of pressed grapes] (15c) : to draw off (as wine) from the lees

⁶rack *vi* [prob. alter. of ¹*rock*] (1530) *of a horse* : to go at a rack

⁷rack *n* (1580) : either of two gaits of a horse: **a** : PACE 4b **b** : a fast showy 4-beat gait

⁸rack *n* [perh. fr. ³*rack*] (1570) **1** : the neck and spine of a forequarter of veal, pork, or esp. mutton **2** : the rib section of a foresaddle of lamb used for chops or as a roast — see LAMB illustration

⁹rack *n* [alter. of *wrack*] (1599) : DESTRUCTION (~ and ruin)

¹rack·et *also* **rac·quet** \'ra-kət\ *n* [MF *raquette*, ultim. fr. Ar *rāhah* palm of the hand] (ca. 1520) **1** : a lightweight implement that consists of a netting (as of nylon) stretched in a usu. oval open frame with a handle attached and that is used for striking the ball or shuttlecock in various games (as tennis, racquets, or badminton) **2** *usu* **racquets** *pl but sing in constr* : a game for two or four players with ball and racket on a 4-walled court

²racket *n* [origin unknown] (1565) **1** : confused clattering noise : CLAMOR **2 a** : social whirl or excitement **b** : the strain of exciting or trying experiences **3 a** : a fraudulent scheme, enterprise, or activity **b** : a usu. illegitimate enterprise made workable by bribery or intimidation **c** : an easy and lucrative means of livelihood **d** *slang* : OCCUPATION, BUSINESS

³racket *vi* (1609) **1** : to engage in active social life **2** : to move with or make a racket

¹rack·e·teer \,ra-kə-'tir\ *n* (1928) : one who obtains money by an illegal enterprise usu. involving intimidation

²racketeer *vi* (1928) : to carry on a racket ~ *vt* : to practice extortion on

racket 1: *A* tennis, *B* racquetball, *C* badminton

rack·ety \'ra-kə-tē\ *adj* (1773) **1** : NOISY **2** : FLASHY, ROWDY **3** : RICKETY

rack·le \'ra-kəl\ *adj* [ME *rakel*] (14c) *chiefly Scot* : IMPETUOUS

rack railway *n* (1884) : a railway having between its rails a rack that meshes with a gear wheel or pinion of the locomotive for traction on steep grades

rack–rent *vt* (1748) : to subject to rack rent

rack rent *n* [⁴*rack*] (1607) **1** : an excessive or unreasonably high rent **2** *Brit* : the highest rent that can be earned on a property

rack–rent·er \'rak-,ren-tər\ *n* (1680) : one that pays or exacts rack rent

rack up *vt* (1949) : ACCUMULATE, GAIN (*racked up* their tenth victory)

ra·clette \ra-'klet, rä-\ *n* [F, lit., scraper, fr. *racler* to scrape, fr. MF, fr. OProv *rasclar*, fr. (assumed) VL *rasiculare*, fr. L *rasus*, pp. of *radere* to scrape — more at RODENT] (ca. 1949) : a Swiss dish consisting of cheese melted over a fire and then scraped onto bread or boiled potatoes; *also* : the cheese used in this dish

ra·con \'rā-,kän\ *n* [*radar beacon*] (1945) : RADAR BEACON

ra·con·teur \,ra-,kän-'tər, -kən-\ *n* [F, fr. MF, fr. *raconter* to tell, fr. OF, fr. *re-* + *aconter, acompter* to tell, count — more at ACCOUNT] (1828) : a person who excels in telling anecdotes

ra·coon *var of* RACCOON

rac·quet·ball \'ra-kət-,bòl\ *n* (1968) : a game similar to handball that is played on a 4-walled court with a short-handled racket and a larger ball

¹racy \'rā-sē\ *adj* **rac·i·er; -est** [³*race*] (ca. 1650) **1 a** : full of zest or vigor **b** : having a strongly marked quality : PIQUANT (a ~ flavor) **c** : RISQUÉ, SUGGESTIVE **2 a** : having the distinctive quality of something in its original or most characteristic form *syn* see PUNGENT — **rac·i·ly** \'rā-sə-lē\ *adv* — **rac·i·ness** \-sē-nəs\ *n*

²racy *adj* **rac·i·er; -est** [¹*race*] (1841) : having a body fitted for racing : long-bodied and lean

¹rad \'rad\ *n* [*radiation absorbed dose*] (1918) : a unit of absorbed dose of ionizing radiation equal to an energy of 100 ergs per gram of irradiated material

²rad *adj* (1982) *slang* : COOL 7, RADICAL

ra·dar \'rā-,där\ *n, often attrib* [*radio detecting and ranging*] (1941) : a device or system consisting usu. of a synchronized radio transmitter and receiver that emits radio waves and processes their reflections for display and is used esp. for detecting and locating objects (as aircraft) or surface features (as of a planet)

radar astronomy *n* (1959) : astronomy in which celestial bodies in the solar system are studied by analyzing the return of radio waves directed at them

radar beacon *n* (1945) : a radar transmitter that upon receiving a radar signal emits a signal which reinforces the normal reflected signal or which introduces a code into the reflected signal esp. for identification purposes

ra·dar·scope \'rā-,där-,skōp\ *n* [*radar* + *oscilloscope*] (1945) : the oscilloscope or screen serving as the visual indicator in a radar receiver

¹rad·dle \'ra-d²l\ *n* [ME *radel*, fr. dim. of *rad-, red* red] (14c) : RED OCHER

²raddle *vt* **rad·dled; rad·dling** \'rad-liŋ, 'ra-d²l-iŋ\ (1631) : to mark or paint with raddle

³raddle *vt* **rad·dled; rad·dling** \'rad-liŋ, 'ra-d²l-iŋ\ [E dial. *raddle* supple stick interwoven with others as in making a fence] (1671) : to twist together : INTERWEAVE

rad·dled \'ra-d²ld\ *adj* [origin unknown] (1694) **1** : being in a state of confusion : lacking composure **2** : BROKEN-DOWN, WORN

radi- *or* **radio-** *comb form* [F, fr. L *radius* ray] **1** : radiant energy : radiation (*radio*active) (*radio*opaque) **2** : radioactive (*radio*element) **3** : radium : X rays (*radio*therapy) **4** : radioactive isotopes esp. as produced artificially (*radio*carbon) **5** : radio (*radio*telegraphy)

¹ra·di·al \'rā-dē-əl\ *adj* [ML *radialis*, fr. L *radius* ray] (1570) **1** : arranged or having parts arranged like rays **2 a** : relating to, placed like, or moving along a radius **b** : characterized by divergence from a center **3** : of, relating to, or adjacent to a bodily radius **4** : developing uniformly around a central axis — **ra·di·al·ly** \-ə-lē\ *adv*

²radial *n* (1872) **1 a** : a radial part **b** : RAY 2 **2** : a body part (as an artery) lying near or following the course of the radius **3** : a pneumatic tire in which the ply cords that extend to the beads are laid at approximately 90 degrees to the centerline of the tread — called also *radial-ply tire, radial tire*

radial cleavage *n* (1973) : holoblastic cleavage that is typical of deuterostomes and that is characterized by arrangement of the blastomeres of each upper tier directly over those of the next lower tier resulting in radial symmetry around the pole to pole axis of the embryo — compare SPIRAL CLEAVAGE

radial engine *n* (1909) : a usu. internal combustion engine with cylinders arranged radially like the spokes of a wheel

radial ker·a·tot·o·my \-,ker-ə-'tä-tə-mē\ *n* (1980) : multiple incision of the cornea in a radial pattern that is performed to correct myopia

radial symmetry *n* (ca. 1890) : the condition of having similar parts regularly arranged around a central axis — **radially symmetrical** *adj*

ra·di·an \'rā-dē-ən\ *n* (1879) : a unit of plane angular measurement that is equal to the angle at the center of a circle subtended by an arc equal in length to the radius

ra·di·ance \'rā-dē-ən(t)s\ *n* (1601) **1** : the quality or state of being radiant **2** : a deep pink **3** : the flux density of radiant energy per unit solid angle and per unit projected area of radiating surface

ra·di·an·cy \-ən(t)-sē\ *n* (1646) : RADIANCE

¹ra·di·ant \'rā-dē-ənt\ *adj* (15c) **1 a** : radiating rays or reflecting beams of light **b** : vividly bright and shining : GLOWING (a ~) **2** : marked by or expressive of love, confidence, or happiness (a ~ smile) **3 a** : emitted or transmitted by radiation **b** : emitting or relating to radiant heat *syn* see BRIGHT — **ra·di·ant·ly** *adv*

²radiant *n* (ca. 1741) : something that radiates: as **a** : a point in the heavens at which the visible parallel paths of meteors appear to meet when traced backward **b** : the part of a gas or electric heater that becomes incandescent

radiant energy *n* (ca. 1890) : energy traveling as electromagnetic waves

radiant flux *n* (1917) : the rate of emission or transmission of radiant energy

radiant heat n (1794) : heat transmitted by radiation as contrasted with that transmitted by conduction or convection

¹**ra·di·ate** \'rā-dē-ˌāt\ vb **-at·ed; -at·ing** [L radiatus, pp. of radiare, fr. radius ray] vi (ca. 1619) **1** : to proceed in a direct line from or toward a center **2** : to send out rays : shine brightly **3 a** : to issue in or as if in rays **b** : to evolve by adaptive radiation ~ vt **1** : to send out in or as if in rays **2** : IRRADIATE, ILLUMINATE **3** : to spread abroad or around as if from a center

²**ra·di·ate** \'rā-dē-ət, -ˌāt\ adj (1668) : having rays or radial parts: as **a** : having ray flowers **b** : characterized by radial symmetry : radially symmetrical — **ra·di·ate·ly** adv

ra·di·a·tion \ˌrā-dē-'ā-shən\ n (15c) **1 a** : the action or process of radiating **b** : the process of emitting radiant energy in the form of waves or particles **c** (1) : the combined processes of emission, transmission, and absorption of radiant energy (2) : the transfer of heat by radiation — compare CONDUCTION, CONVECTION **2 a** : something that is radiated **b** : energy radiated in the form of waves or particles **3** : radial arrangement **4** : ADAPTIVE RADIATION **5** : RADIATOR — **ra·di·a·tion·al** \-shnəl, -shə-nᵊl\ adj — **ra·di·a·tion·less** \-shən-ləs\ adj — **ra·di·a·tive** \'rā-dē-ˌā-tiv\ adj

radiation sickness n (1924) : sickness that results from exposure to radiation and is commonly marked by fatigue, nausea, vomiting, loss of teeth and hair, and in more severe cases by damage to blood-forming tissue with decrease in red and white blood cells and with bleeding

ra·di·a·tor \'rā-dē-ˌā-tər, dial 'ra-\ n (1836) : one that radiates: as **a** : any of various devices (as a nest of pipes or tubes) for transferring heat from a fluid within to an area or object outside **b** : a transmitting antenna

¹**rad·i·cal** \'ra-di-kəl\ adj [ME, fr. LL radicalis, fr. L radic-, radix root — more at ROOT] (14c) **1** : of, relating to, or proceeding from a root: as **a** (1) : of or growing from the root of a plant ⟨~ tubers⟩ (2) : growing from the base of a stem, from a rootlike stem, or from a stem that does not rise above the ground ⟨~ leaves⟩ **b** : of, relating to, or constituting a linguistic root **c** : of or relating to a mathematical root **d** : designed to remove the root of a disease or all diseased tissue ⟨~ surgery⟩ **2** : of or relating to the origin : FUNDAMENTAL **3 a** : marked by a considerable departure from the usual or traditional : EXTREME **b** : tending or disposed to make extreme changes in existing views, habits, conditions, or institutions **c** : of, relating to, or constituting a political group associated with views, practices, and policies of extreme change **d** : advocating extreme measures to retain or restore a political state of affairs ⟨the ~ right⟩ **4** slang : EXCELLENT, COOL — **rad·i·cal·ness** n

²**radical** n (1641) **1 a** : a root part **b** : a basic principle : FOUNDATION **2 a** : ROOT 6 **b** : a sound or letter belonging to a radical **3** : one who is radical **4** : FREE RADICAL; also : a group of atoms bonded together that is considered an entity in various kinds of reactions **5 a** : a mathematical expression indicating a root by means of a radical sign **b** : RADICAL SIGN

radical chic n (1970) : a fashionable practice among socially prominent people of associating with radicals or members of minority groups

rad·i·cal·ise Brit var of RADICALIZE

rad·i·cal·ism \'ra-di-kə-ˌli-zəm\ n (1820) **1** : the quality or state of being radical **2** : the doctrines or principles of radicals

rad·i·cal·ize \-kə-ˌlīz\ vt **-ized; -iz·ing** (1830) : to make radical esp. in politics — **rad·i·cal·i·za·tion** \ˌra-di-kə-lə-'zā-shən\ n

rad·i·cal·ly \'ra-di-k(ə-)lē\ adv (15c) **1** : in origin or essence **2** : in a radical or extreme manner

radical sign n (1668) : the sign √ or ⱽ placed before an expression to denote that the square root is to be extracted or that the root marked by an index (as in ᵛ or ᵛ for the cube root) is to be extracted

rad·i·cand \ˌra-də-'kand\ n [L radicandum, neut. of radicandus, gerundive of radicarī (ca. 1890) : the quantity under a radical sign

ra·dic·chio \ra-'di-kē-ō\ n [It, chicory, fr. (assumed) VL radiculus, alter. of L radicula] (1968) : a chicory of a red variety with variegated leaves that is used as a salad green

radices pl of RADIX

rad·i·cle \'ra-di-kəl\ n [L radicula, dim. of radic-, radix] (1671) **1** : the lower part of the axis of a plant embryo or seedling: **a** : the embryonic root of a seedling **b** : HYPOCOTYL **c** : the hypocotyl and the root together **2** : RADICAL

ra·dic·u·lar \ra-'di-kyə-lər, ra-\ adj (1830) **1** : of or relating to a plant radicle **2** : of, relating to, or involving a nerve root ⟨~ pain⟩

radii pl of RADIUS

¹**ra·dio** \'rā-dē-ˌō\ adj [²radio or radio-] (1887) **1** : of, relating to, or operated by radiant energy **2** : of or relating to electric currents or phenomena (as electromagnetic radiation) of frequencies between about 15,000 and 10¹¹ hertz **3** : of, relating to, or used in radio or a radio set **b** : specializing in radio or associated with the radio industry **c** (1) : transmitted by radio (2) : making or participating in radio broadcasts **d** : controlled or directed by radio

²**radio** n, pl **ra·di·os** [short for radiotelegraphy] (1903) **1 a** : the wireless transmission and reception of electric impulses or signals by means of electromagnetic waves **b** : the use of these waves for the wireless transmission of electric impulses into which sound is converted **2 a** : a radio message **3** : a radio receiving set **4 a** : a radio transmitting station **b** : a radio broadcasting organization **c** : the radio broadcasting industry **d** : communication by radio

³**radio** vt (1913) **1** : to send or communicate by radio **2** : to send a radio message to ~ vi : to send or communicate something by radio

radio- — see RADI-

ra·dio·ac·tive \ˌrā-dē-ō-'ak-tiv\ adj [ISV] (1898) : of, caused by, or exhibiting radioactivity — **ra·dio·ac·tive·ly** adv

ra·dio·ac·tiv·i·ty \-ak-'ti-və-tē\ n [ISV] (1899) : the property possessed by some elements (as uranium) or isotopes (as carbon 14) of spontaneously emitting energetic particles (as electrons or alpha particles) by the disintegration of their atomic nuclei; also : the rays emitted

ra·dio·al·ler·go·sor·bent \ˌrā-dē-ō-ə-ˌlər-gō-'sȯr-bənt\ adj [radi- + allergen + -o- + sorbent] (1967) : relating to or being a blood analysis that tests for allergen-specific antibodies and is used to detect allergic reactions

radio astronomy n (1948) : astronomy dealing with radio waves received from outside the earth's atmosphere — **radio astronomer** n — **radio astronomical** adj

ra·dio·au·to·graph \ˌrā-dē-ō-'ȯ-tə-ˌgraf\ n (1941) : AUTORADIOGRAPH — **ra·dio·au·to·graph·ic** \-ˌȯ-tə-'gra-fik\ adj — **ra·dio·au·tog·ra·phy** \-ȯ-'tä-grə-fē\ n

radio beacon n (1919) : a radio transmitting station that transmits special radio signals for use (as on a landing field) in determining the direction or position of those receiving them

ra·dio·bi·ol·o·gy \ˌrā-dē-ō-bī-'ä-lə-jē\ n (1919) : a branch of biology dealing with the effects of radiation or radioactive materials on biological systems — **ra·dio·bi·o·log·i·cal** \-ˌbī-ə-'lä-ji-kəl\ also **ra·dio·bi·o·log·ic** \-jik\ adj — **ra·dio·bi·o·log·i·cal·ly** \-ji-k(ə-)lē\ adv — **ra·dio·bi·ol·o·gist** \-bī-'ä-lə-jist\ n

radio car n (1925) : an automobile equipped with radio communication

ra·dio·car·bon \ˌrā-dē-ō-'kär-bən\ n, often attrib [ISV] (1939) : radioactive carbon; esp : CARBON 14

radiocarbon dating n (1951) : CARBON DATING — **radiocarbon-date** \-'dāt\ vt

ra·dio·chem·is·try \ˌrā-dē-ō-'ke-mə-strē\ n (1904) : a branch of chemistry dealing with radioactive substances and phenomena including tracer studies — **ra·dio·chem·i·cal** \-'ke-mi-kəl\ adj — **ra·dio·chem·i·cal·ly** \-k(ə-)lē\ adv — **ra·dio·chem·ist** \-'ke-mist\ n

ra·dio·chro·ma·to·gram \-krō-'ma-tə-ˌgram, -kra-\ n (1951) : a chromatogram revealing one or more radioactive substances

radio compass n (1918) : a direction finder used in navigation

ra·dio·ecol·o·gy \ˌrā-dē-ō-i-'kä-lə-jē\ n (1956) : the study of the effects of radiation and radioactive substances on ecological communities

ra·dio·el·e·ment \-'e-lə-mənt\ n [ISV] (1903) : a radioactive element

radio frequency n (1915) : any of the electromagnetic wave frequencies that lie in the range extending from below 3 kilohertz to about 300 gigahertz and that include the frequencies used for radio and television transmission

RADIO FREQUENCIES

CLASS	ABBREVIATION	RANGE
extremely low frequency	ELF	below 3 kilohertz
very low frequency	VLF	3 to 30 kilohertz
low frequency	LF	30 to 300 kilohertz
medium frequency	MF	300 to 3000 kilohertz
high frequency	HF	3 to 30 megahertz
very high frequency	VHF	30 to 300 megahertz
ultrahigh frequency	UHF	300 to 3000 megahertz
superhigh frequency	SHF	3 to 30 gigahertz
extremely high frequency	EHF	30 to 300 gigahertz

radio galaxy n (1960) : a galaxy that is a powerful source of radio waves

ra·dio·gen·ic \ˌrā-dē-ō-'je-nik\ adj (1935) : produced by or determined from radioactivity ⟨~ isotopes⟩ ⟨~ tumors⟩

ra·dio·gram \'rā-dē-ō-ˌgram\ n (1896) **1** : RADIOGRAPH **2** : a message transmitted by radiotelegraphy **3** [short for radiogramophone] Brit : a combined radio receiver and record player

¹**ra·dio·graph** \-ˌgraf\ n (1896) : a picture produced on a sensitive surface by a form of radiation other than visible light; specif : an X-ray or gamma ray photograph — **ra·dio·graph·ic** \ˌrā-dē-ō-'gra-fik\ adj — **ra·dio·graph·i·cal·ly** \-fi-k(ə-)lē\ adv

²**radiograph** vt (1896) : to make a radiograph of

ra·di·og·ra·phy \ˌrā-dē-'ä-grə-fē\ n [ISV] (1896) : the art, act, or process of making radiographs

ra·dio·im·mu·no·as·say \ˌrā-dē-ō-i-myə-nō-'a-ˌsā, -i-ˌmyü-, -a-'sā\ n (1961) : immunoassay of a substance that has been radioactively labeled — **ra·dio·im·mu·no·as·say·able** \-ə-bəl\ adj

ra·dio·iso·tope \ˌrā-dē-ō-'ī-sə-ˌtōp\ n [ISV] (1946) : a radioactive isotope — **ra·dio·iso·to·pic** \-ˌī-sə-'tä-pik, -'tō-\ adj — **ra·dio·iso·to·pi·cal·ly** \-pi-k(ə-)lē\ adv

ra·dio·la·bel \-'lā-bəl\ vt (1953) : to label with a radioactive atom or substance

ra·dio·lar·i·an \ˌrā-dē-ō-'lar-ē-ən, -'ler-\ n [ultim. fr. LL radiolus small sunbeam, fr. dim. of L radius ray — more at RAY] (1877) : any of three classes (Acantharia, Polycystina, and Phaeodaria) of usu. spherical marine protozoans having radiating threadlike pseudopodia and often a siliceous skeleton of spicules — **radiolarian** adj

ra·dio·log·i·cal \ˌrā-dē-ə-'lä-ji-kəl\ or **ra·dio·log·ic** \-jik\ adj (1909) **1** : of or relating to radiology **2** : of or relating to nuclear radiation — **ra·dio·log·i·cal·ly** \-k(ə-)lē\ adv

ra·di·ol·o·gist \ˌrā-dē-'ä-lə-jist\ n (1906) : a physician specializing in the use of radiant energy for diagnostic and therapeutic purposes

ra·di·ol·o·gy \-jē\ n (1900) **1** : a branch of medicine concerned with the use of radiant energy (as X rays and radium) in the diagnosis and treatment of disease **2** : the science of radioactive substances and high-energy radiations

ra·dio·lu·cent \ˌrā-dē-ō-'lü-sᵊnt\ adj (1917) : partly or wholly permeable to radiation ⟨~ tissues⟩ — **ra·dio·lu·cen·cy** \-sᵊn(t)-sē\ n

ra·di·ol·y·sis \ˌrā-dē-'ä-lə-səs\ n [NL] (1948) : chemical decomposition by the action of radiation — **ra·dio·lyt·ic** \-dē-ə-'li-tik\ adj

ra·dio·man \'rā-dē-ō-ˌman\ n (1921) : a radio operator or technician

ra·di·om·e·ter \ˌrā-dē-'ä-mə-tər\ n (1875) : an instrument for measuring the intensity of radiant energy by the torsional twist of suspended vanes that are blackened on

radiometer

\ə\ abut \ᵊ\ kitten, F table \ər\ further \a\ ash \ā\ ace \ä\ mop, mar \aú\ out \ch\ chin \e\ bet \ē\ easy \g\ go \i\ hit \ī\ ice \j\ job \ŋ\ sing \ō\ go \ȯ\ law \ȯi\ boy \th\ thin \th\ the \ü\ loot \ú\ foot \y\ yet \zh\ vision \á, k, ⁿ, œ, œ̄, ᵫ, ᵫ̄, ᵛ\ see Guide to Pronunciation one side and exposed to a source of radiant energy; *also* : an instrument for measuring electromagnetic or acoustic radiation — **ra·di·om·e·try** \-mə-trē\ *n*

ra·dio·met·ric \ˌrä-dē-ō-'me-trik\ *adj* [ISV] (1877) **1** : relating to, using, or measured by a radiometer **2** : of or relating to the measurement of geologic time by means of the rate of disintegration of radioactive elements — **ra·dio·met·ri·cal·ly** \-tri-k(ə-)lē\ *adv*

ra·dio·mi·met·ic \-mə-'me-tik, -mī-\ *adj* [ISV] (1947) : producing effects similar to those of radiation

ra·dio·nu·clide \ˌrä-dē-ō-'nü-ˌklīd, -'nyü-\ *n* (1947) : a radioactive nuclide

ra·di·opaque \ˌrä-dē-ō-'pāk\ *adj* (ca. 1923) : being opaque to various forms of radiation (as X rays)

ra·dio·phar·ma·ceu·ti·cal \ˌrä-dē-ō-ˌfär-mə-'sü-ti-kəl\ *n* (1952) : a radioactive drug used for diagnostic or therapeutic purposes — **radiopharmaceutical** *adj*

ra·dio·phone \'rä-dē-ə-ˌfōn\ *n* (1919) : RADIOTELEPHONE

ra·dio·pho·to \ˌrä-dē-ō-'fō-(ˌ)tō\ *n* (1929) : a picture transmitted by radio

ra·dio·pro·tec·tive \-prə-'tek-tiv\ *adj* (1956) : serving to protect or aiding in protecting against the injurious effect of radiations ⟨∼ drugs⟩ — **ra·dio·pro·tec·tion** \-'tek-shən\ *n*

radio range *n* (1929) : a radio facility for aircraft navigation

ra·dio·sen·si·tive \ˌrä-dē-ō-'sen(t)-sə-tiv, -'sen)t-stiv\ *adj* (1920) : sensitive to the effects of radiant energy ⟨∼ cancer cells⟩ — **ra·dio·sen·si·tiv·i·ty** \-ˌsen(t)-sə-'ti-və-tē\ *n*

ra·dio·sonde \'rä-dē-ō-ˌsänd\ *n* [ISV] (1937) : a miniature radio transmitter that is carried aloft (as by an unmanned balloon) with instruments for broadcasting the humidity, temperature, and pressure

radio spectrum *n* (1929) : the region of the electromagnetic spectrum usu. including frequencies below 300,000 megahertz in which radio or radar transmission and detection techniques may be used

radio star *n* (1948) : a cosmic radio source; *esp* : a point source of radio emissions

ra·dio·stron·ti·um \ˌrä-dē-ō-'strän(t)-sh(ē-)əm, -'strän-tē-əm\ *n* [NL] (1941) : radioactive strontium; *esp* : STRONTIUM 90

ra·dio·tele·graph \-'te-lə-ˌgraf\ *n* [ISV] (1903) : WIRELESS TELEGRAPHY — **ra·dio·te·leg·ra·phy** \-tə-'le-grə-fē\ *n*

ra·dio·te·lem·e·try \-tə-'le-mə-trē\ *n* (1951) **1** : TELEMETRY **2** : BIOTELEMETRY — **ra·dio·tele·met·ric** \-ˌte-lə-'me-trik\ *adj*

ra·dio·tele·phone \-'te-lə-ˌfōn\ *n* [ISV] (1904) : an apparatus for carrying on wireless telephony by radio waves — **ra·dio·te·le·pho·ny** \-tə-'le-fə-nē, -'te-lə-ˌfō-nē\ *n*

radio telescope *n* (1929) : a radio receiver-antenna combination used for observation in radio astronomy

ra·dio·ther·a·py \ˌrä-dē-ō-'ther-ə-pē\ *n* [ISV] (1903) : the treatment of disease with radiation (as X rays) — **ra·dio·ther·a·pist** \-pist\ *n*

ra·dio·tho·ri·um \-'thȯr-ē-əm, -'thȯr-\ *n* [NL] (1905) : a radioactive isotope of thorium with the mass number 228

ra·dio·trac·er \'rä-dē-ō-ˌträ-sər\ *n* (1946) : a radioactive tracer

ra·dio·ul·na \ˌrä-dē-ō-'əl-nə\ *n* [NL] (1960) : a single bone in the forelimb of an amphibian (as a frog) that represents fusion of the separate radius and ulna of higher vertebrate forms

radio wave *n* (1916) : an electromagnetic wave with radio frequency

rad·ish \'ra-dish\ *also* 're-\ *n* [ME, alter. of OE *rædic*, fr. L *radic-, radix* root, radish — more at ROOT] (15c) : the pungent fleshy root of a widely cultivated Eurasian plant (*Raphanus sativus*) of the mustard family usu. eaten raw; *also* : a plant that produces radishes

ra·di·um \'rä-dē-əm\ *n, often attrib* [NL, fr. L *radius* ray] (1899) : an intensely radioactive brilliant white metallic element that resembles barium chemically, occurs in combination in minute quantities in minerals (as pitchblende or carnotite), emits alpha particles and gamma rays to form radon, and is used chiefly in luminous materials and in the treatment of cancer — see ELEMENT table

radium therapy *n* (1904) : RADIOTHERAPY

ra·di·us \'rä-dē-əs\ *n, pl* **ra·dii** \-dē-ˌī\ *also* **ra·di·us·es** [L, ray, radius] (ca. 1611) **1** : a line segment extending from the center of a circle or sphere to the circumference or bounding surface **2 a** : the bone on the thumb side of the human forearm; *also* : a corresponding part of vertebrates above fishes **b** : the third and usu. largest vein of an insect's wing **3 a** : the length of a radius ⟨a truck with a short turning ∼⟩ **b** : the circular area defined by a stated radius **c** : a bounded or circumscribed area **4** : a radial part **5** : the distance from a center line or point to an axis of rotation

radius of curvature (ca. 1753) : the reciprocal of the curvature of a curve

radius vector *n* (ca. 1753) **1 a** : the line segment or its length from a fixed point to a variable point **b** : the linear polar coordinate of a variable point **2** : a straight line joining the center of an attracting body (as the sun) with that of a body (as a planet) in orbit around it

ra·dix \'rä-diks\ *n, pl* **ra·di·ces** \'rä-də-ˌsēz, 'ra-\ *or* **ra·dix·es** \'rä-dik-səz\ [L, root — more at ROOT] (1798) **1** : the base of a number system or of logarithms **2** : the primary source

ra·dome \'rä-ˌdōm\ *n* [*radar dome*] (ca. 1944) : a plastic housing sheltering the antenna assembly of a radar set esp. on an airplane

ra·don \'rä-ˌdän\ *n* [ISV, fr. *radium*] (1918) : a heavy radioactive gaseous element formed by the decay of radium — see ELEMENT table

rad·u·la \'ra-jə-lə\ *n, pl* **-lae** \-ˌlē, -ˌlī\ *also* **-las** [NL, fr. L, scraper, fr. *radere* to scrape — more at RODENT] (ca. 1859) : a horny band or ribbon in mollusks other than bivalves that bears minute teeth on its dorsal surface and tears up food and draws it into the mouth — **rad·u·lar** \-lər\ *adj*

rad·waste \'rad-ˌwäst\ *n, often attrib* [by shortening] (1973) : radioactive waste

raff \'raf\ *n* [ME *raf* rubbish] (14c) : RIFFRAFF

raf·fia \'ra-fē-ə\ *n* [Malagasy *rafia*] (1882) : the fiber of the raffia palm used esp. for tying plants and making baskets and hats

raffia palm *n* (1897) : a pinnate-leaved palm (*Raphia farinifera* syn. *R. ruffia*) of Madagascar that is valued for the fiber from its leafstalks

raf·fi·nose \'ra-fə-ˌnōs, -ˌnōz\ *n* [F, fr. *raffiner* to refine, fr. re- + *affiner* to make fine, fr. a- ad- (fr. L *ad*-) + *fin* fine] (1876) : a crystalline slightly sweet sugar $C_{18}H_{32}O_{16}$ obtained commercially from cottonseed meal and present in many plant products

raff·ish \'ra-fish\ *adj* (1801) **1** : marked by or suggestive of flashy vulgarity or crudeness **2** : marked by a careless unconventionality : RAKISH — **raff·ish·ly** *adv* — **raff·ish·ness** *n*

¹raf·fle \'ra-fəl\ *vb* **raf·fled; raf·fling** \'ra-f(ə-)liŋ\ *vi* (ca. 1680) : to engage in a raffle ∼ *vt* : to dispose of by means of a raffle ⟨∼ off a turkey⟩

²raffle *n* [ME *rafle*, a dice game, fr. MF, dice game in which all the stakes can be won in a throw, lit., rake for a fire, fr. MHG *raffel* rake for a fire, fr. *raffen* to snatch, gather] (1766) : a lottery in which the prize is won by one of numerous persons buying chances

³raffle *n* [prob. fr. F *rafle* act of snatching, sweeping, fr. MF, rake for a fire] (1881) : RUBBISH; *esp* : a jumble or tangle of nautical equipment

raf·fle·sia \rə-'flē-zh(ē-)ə, ra-\ *n* [NL, fr. Sir Stamford *Raffles* †1826 Eng. colonial administrator] (1830) : any of a genus (*Rafflesia* of the family Rafflesiaceae) of Malaysian dicotyledonous plants that are parasitic in other plants and have fleshy usu. foul-smelling apetalous flowers emerging from the host, imbricated scales in place of leaves, and no stems

¹raft \'raft\ *n* [ME *raft* rafter, raft, fr. ON *raptr* rafter] (15c) **1 a** : a collection of logs or timber fastened together for conveyance by water **b** : a flat structure for support or transportation on water **2** : a floating cohesive mass **3** : an aggregation of animals (as waterfowl) resting on the water

²raft *vt* (1706) **1** : to transport in the form of or by means of a raft; *also* : to convey (as pebbles) in floating ice or masses of organic material **2** : to make into a raft ∼ *vi* : to travel by raft

³raft *n* [alter. of *raff* jumble] (1830) : a large collection or number

¹raft·er \'raf-tər\ *n* [ME, fr. OE *ræfter*; akin to ON *raptr* rafter] (bef. 12c) : any of the parallel beams that support a roof — see RIDGEPOLE illustration — **raf·tered** \-tərd\ *adj*

²raft·er \'raf-tər\ *n* [²*raft*] (1809) **1** : one who maneuvers logs into position and binds them into rafts **2** : one who travels by raft

rafts·man \'raf(t)s-mən\ *n* (1775) : a man engaged in rafting

¹rag \'rag\ *n* [ME *ragge*, fr. (assumed) OE *ragg*, fr. ON *rǫgg* tuft, shagginess] (14c) **1 a** : a waste piece of cloth **b** *pl* : clothes usu. in poor or ragged condition **c** : CLOTHING ⟨the ∼ trade⟩ **2** : something resembling a rag **3** : NEWSPAPER

²rag *n* [ME *ragge*] (14c) **1** : any of various hard rocks **2** : a large roofing slate that is rough on one side

³rag *vt* **ragged; rag·ging** [origin unknown] (1739) **1** : to rail at : SCOLD **2** : TORMENT, TEASE

⁴rag *n* (1864) *chiefly Brit* : an outburst of boisterous fun; *also* : PRANK

⁵rag *n* [short for *ragtime*] (1897) : a composition in ragtime

ra·ga \'rä-gə\ *n* [Skt *rāga*, lit., color, tone; akin to Skt *rajyati* it reddens, Gk *rhezein* to dye] (1788) **1** : one of the ancient traditional melodic patterns or modes in Indian music **2** : an improvisation based on a traditional raga — compare TALA

rag·a·muf·fin \'ra-gə-ˌmə-fən\ *n* [ME *Ragamuffyn*, name for a ragged, oafish person] (1581) : a ragged often disreputable person; *esp* : a poorly clothed often dirty child

rag·bag \'rag-ˌbag\ *n* (1820) **1** : a bag for scraps **2** : a miscellaneous collection

rag doll *n* (1853) : a stuffed usu. painted cloth doll

¹rage \'rāj\ *n* [ME, fr. OF, fr. LL *rabia*, fr. L *rabies* rage, madness, fr. *rabere* to be mad; akin to Skt *rabhas* violence] (14c) **1 a** : violent and uncontrolled anger **b** : a fit of violent wrath **c** *archaic* : INSANITY **2** : violent action (as of wind or sea) **3** : an intense feeling : PASSION **4** : a fad pursued with intense enthusiasm ⟨was all the ∼⟩ **syn** see ANGER, FASHION

²rage *vi* **raged; rag·ing** (14c) **1** : to be in a rage **2** : to be in tumult **3** : to prevail uncontrollably

rag·ged \'ra-gəd\ *adj* (14c) **1** : roughly unkempt **2** : having an irregular edge or outline **3 a** : torn or worn to tatters **b** : worn-out from stress and strain ⟨ran herself ∼⟩ **4** : wearing tattered clothes **5 a** : STRAGGLY **b** : executed in an irregular or uneven manner **c** *of a sound* : HARSH, DISSONANT — **rag·ged·ly** *adv* — **rag·ged·ness** *n*

ragged robin *n* (1741) : a perennial herb (*Lychnis flos-cuculi*) cultivated for its pink flowers with narrow-lobed petals

rag·gedy \'ra-gə-dē\ *adj* (1890) : RAGGED

rag·gle-tag·gle \'ra-gəl-ˌta-gəl\ *adj* [irreg. fr. *ragtag*] (1904) : MOTLEY

ra·gi \'ra-gē, 'rä-\ *n* [perh. fr. Deccan Hindi *rāgī*] (1792) : an Old World cereal grass (*Eleusine coracana*) yielding a staple food crop esp. in India and Africa; *also* : the seeds of ragi used for food

raging *adj* (15c) **1** : causing great pain or distress **2** : VIOLENT, WILD **3** : EXTRAORDINARY, TREMENDOUS ⟨a ∼ success⟩

rag·lan \'ra-glən\ *n* [F.J.H. Somerset, Baron *Raglan* †1855 Brit. field marshal] (ca. 1859) : a loose overcoat with raglan sleeves

raglan sleeve *n* (ca. 1924) : a sleeve that extends to the neckline with slanted seams from the underarm to the neck

rag·man \'rag-ˌman\ *n* (1586) : a man who collects or deals in rags

Rag·na·rok \'rag-nə-ˌräk, -rək\ *n* [ON *Ragnarǫk*, lit., fate of the gods, fr. *ragna*, gen. pl. of *regin* gods + *rǫk* fate, course (later rendered as *Ragnarøkkr*, lit., twilight of the gods)] : the final destruction of the world in the conflict between the Aesir and the powers of Hel led by Loki — called also *Twilight of the Gods*

ra·gout \ra-'gü\ *n* [F *ragoût*, fr. *ragoûter* to revive the taste, fr. MF *ragouster*, fr. re- + a- ad- (fr. L *ad*-) + *goust* taste, fr. L *gustus*; akin to L *gustare* to taste — more at CHOOSE] (ca. 1657) **1** : well-seasoned meat and vegetables cooked in a thick sauce **2** : MIXTURE, MÉLANGE

rag·pick·er \'rag-ˌpi-kər\ *n* (1860) : one who collects rags and refuse for a livelihood

rag·tag \'rag-ˌtag\ *adj* [*ragtag and bobtail*] (1882) **1** : RAGGED, UNKEMPT **2** : MOTLEY **2** ⟨a ∼ bunch of misfits⟩

ragtag and bobtail *n* [¹*rag* + ¹*tag*] (1820) : RABBLE

rag·time \'rag-ˌtīm\ *n* [prob. fr. *ragged* + *time*] (1897) **1** : rhythm characterized by strong syncopation in the melody with a regularly accented accompaniment **2** : music having ragtime rhythm

rag·top \-ˌtäp\ *n* (1953) : a convertible automobile

rag·weed \-ˌwēd\ *n* (1790) : any of various chiefly No. American weedy composite herbs (genus *Ambrosia*) that produce highly allergenic pollen

rag·wort \-ˌwərt, -ˌwȯrt\ *n* (14c) : any of several senecios; *esp* : TANSY RAGWORT

rah \'rä, 'rȯ\ *interj* (1870) : HURRAH — used esp. to cheer on a team

rah–rah \'rä-(,)rä, 'rö-(,)rö\ *adj* [redupl. of *rah*] (1911) : marked by the enthusiastic expression of college spirit

¹raid \'rād\ *n* [ME (Sc) *rade*, fr. OE *rād* ride, raid — more at ROAD] (15c) **1 a :** a hostile or predatory incursion **b :** a surprise attack by a small force **2 a :** a brief foray outside one's usual sphere **b :** a sudden invasion by officers of the law **c :** a daring operation against a competitor **d :** the recruiting of personnel (as faculty, executives, or athletes) from competing organizations **3 :** the act of mulcting public money **4 :** an attempt by professional operators to depress stock prices by concerted selling

²raid *vi* (1865) : to conduct or take part in a raid ~ *vt* : to make a raid on

raid·er \'rā-dər\ *n* (1863) : one that raids: as **a :** a fast lightly armed ship operating against merchant shipping **b :** a soldier specially trained for close-range fighting **c :** one that attempts a raid. hostile takeover of a business corporation ⟨corporate ~s⟩

¹rail \'rā(ə)l\ *n* [ME *raile*, fr. MF *reille* ruler, bar, fr. L *regula* ruler, fr. *regere* to keep straight, direct, rule — more at RIGHT] (14c) **1 a :** a bar extending from one post or support to another and serving as a guard or barrier **b :** a structural member or support **2 a :** RAILING 1 **b :** a light structure serving as a guard at the outer edge of a ship's deck **c :** a fence bounding a racetrack **3 :** a bar of rolled steel forming a track for wheeled vehicles **b :** TRACK **c :** RAILROAD

²rail *vt* (14c) : to provide with a railing : FENCE

³rail *n, pl* **rail** *or* **rails** [ME *raile*, fr. MF *raale*] (15c) : any of numerous wading birds (family Rallidae, the rail family) that are of small or medium size and have short rounded wings, a short tail, and usu. very long toes which enable them to run on the soft mud of marshes

⁴rail *vi* [ME, fr. MF *railler* to mock, fr. OProv *ralhar* to babble, joke, fr. (assumed) VL *ragulare* to bray, fr. LL *ragere* to neigh] (15c) : to revile or scold in harsh, insolent, or abusive language **syn** see SCOLD — **rail·er** *n*

rail·bird \'rā(ə)l-,bərd\ *n* (1892) : a racing enthusiast who sits on or near the track rail to watch a race or workout

rail·bus \-,bəs\ *n* (1933) : a passenger car with an automotive engine for operation on rails

rail·car \-,kär\ *n* (1834) **1 :** a railroad car **2 :** a self-propelled railroad car

rail·head \'rā(ə)l-,hed\ *n* (1896) : a point on a railroad at which traffic may originate or terminate

rail·ing \'rā-liŋ\ *n* (15c) **1 :** a barrier consisting of a rail and supports **2 :** RAILS; *also* : material for making rails

rail·lery \'rā-lə-rē\ *n, pl* **-ler·ies** [F *raillerie*, fr. MF, fr. *railler* to mock] (1653) **1 :** good-natured ridicule : BANTER **2 :** JEST

¹rail·road \'rā(ə)l-,rōd, 're(ə)l-; 're-,rōd\ *n* (1825) : a permanent road having a line of rails fixed to ties and laid on a roadbed and providing a track for cars or equipment drawn by locomotives or propelled by self-contained motors; *also* : such a road and its assets constituting a single property

²railroad *vt* (1877) **1 a :** to convict with undue haste and by means of false charges or insufficient evidence **b :** to push through hastily or without due consideration **2 :** to transport by railroad ~ *vi* : to work for a railroad company — **rail·road·er** *n*

railroad flat *n* (1947) : an apartment having a series of narrow rooms arranged in line

rail·road·ing *n* (1870) : construction or operation of a railroad

railroad worm *n* (1909) **1** [prob. fr. its dissemination by railroad] : APPLE MAGGOT **2** [fr. the rows of luminescent spots along its sides making it resemble a lighted train]: the larva or wingless female of any of several So. American beetles (genus *Phrixothrix* of the family Cantharidae)

rail–split·ter \'rā(ə)l-,spli-tər\ *n* (1860) : one that makes logs into fence rails

rail·way \-,wā\ *n* (1812) : RAILROAD; *esp* : a railroad operating with light equipment or within a small area

rai·ment \'rā-mənt\ *n* [ME *rayment*, short for *arrayment*, fr. *arrayen* to array] (15c) : CLOTHING, GARMENTS

¹rain \'rān\ *n, often attrib* [ME *reyn*, fr. OE *regn, rēn*; akin to OHG *regan* rain] (bef. 12c) **1 a :** water falling in drops condensed from vapor in the atmosphere **b :** the descent of this water **c :** water that has fallen as rain : RAINWATER **2 a :** a fall of rain : RAINSTORM **b** *pl* : the rainy season **3 :** rainy weather **4 :** a heavy fall of particles or bodies

²rain *vi* (bef. 12c) **1 :** to send down rain **2 :** to fall as water in drops from the clouds **3 :** to fall like rain ~ *vt* **1 :** to pour down **2 :** to bestow abundantly — **rain cats and dogs** : to rain heavily

rain·bird \'rān-,bərd\ *n* (1555) : any of numerous birds (esp. of the family Cuculidae) whose cries are popularly believed to augur rain

rain·bow \-,bō\ *n* (bef. 12c) **1 :** an arc or circle that exhibits in concentric bands the colors of the spectrum and that is formed opposite the sun by the refraction and reflection of the sun's rays in raindrops, spray, or mist **2 :** a multicolored array : a wide assortment or range **3** [fr. the impossibility of reaching the rainbow, at whose foot a pot of gold is said to be buried]: an illusory goal or hope **4 :** RAINBOW TROUT — **rain·bow·like** *adj*

rainbow fish *n* (1888) : any of numerous brilliantly colored fishes (as a wrasse, parrot fish, or guppy)

rainbow runner *n* (1940) : a large brilliantly marked blue and yellow carangid food and sport fish (*Elagatis bipinnulata*) common in warm seas

rainbow trout *n* (1882) : a large stout-bodied salmonid fish (*Oncorhynchus mykiss* syn. *Salmo gairdneri*) of western No. America that is related to the Pacific salmon and is typically greenish above and white on the belly with a pink, red, or lavender stripe along each side of the body and with profuse black dots — compare STEELHEAD

rain check *n* (1884) **1 :** a ticket stub good for a later performance when the scheduled one is rained out **2 :** an assurance of a deferred extension of an offer; *esp* : an assurance that a customer can take advantage of a

rainbow trout

sale later if the item or service offered is not available (as by being sold out)

rain·coat \'rān-,kōt\ *n* (1830) : a waterproof or water-resistant coat

rain·drop \-,dräp\ *n* (bef. 12c) : a drop of rain

rain·fall \-,föl\ *n* (1854) **1 :** the amount of precipitation usu. measured by the depth in inches **2 :** RAIN 2a

rain forest *n* (1903) **1 :** a tropical woodland with an annual rainfall of at least 100 inches (254 centimeters) and marked by lofty broad-leaved evergreen trees forming a continuous canopy — called also *tropical rain forest* **2 :** TEMPERATE RAIN FOREST

rain gauge *n* (1769) : an instrument for measuring the quantity of precipitation

rain·mak·er \'rān-,mā-kər\ *n* (1775) **1 :** a person who produces or attempts to produce rain by artificial means **2 :** a person (as a partner in a law firm) who brings in new business; *also* : a person whose influence can initiate progress or ensure success — **rain·mak·ing** \-,mā-'kiŋ\ *n*

rain out *vt* (1928) : to interrupt or prevent by rain

rain·proof \'rān-,prüf\ *adj* (1831) : impervious to rain

rain·spout \-,spaut\ *n* (1922) : GUTTER 1a; *also* : DOWNSPOUT

rain·squall \-,skwöl\ *n* (1849) : a squall accompanied by rain

rain·storm \-,störm\ *n* (1816) : a storm of or with rain

rain tree *n* (ca. 1900) : MONKEYPOD

rain·wash \'rān-,wösh, -,wäsh\ *n* (1876) : the washing away of material by rain; *also* : the material so washed away

rain·wa·ter \-,wö-tər, -,wä-\ *n* (bef. 12c) : water fallen as rain that has not collected soluble matter from the soil and is therefore soft

rain·wear \-,war, -,wer\ *n* (1939) : waterproof or water-resistant clothing

rainy \'rā-nē\ *adj* **rain·i·er; -est** (bef. 12c) : marked by, abounding with, or bringing rain

rainy day *n* (ca. 1580) : a period of want or need

¹raise \'rāz\ *vb* **raised; rais·ing** [ME, fr. ON *reisa* — more at REAR] *vt* (13c) **1 :** to cause or help to rise to a standing position **2 a** : AWAKEN, AROUSE **b :** to stir up : INCITE ⟨~ a rebellion⟩ **c :** to flush (game) from cover **d :** to recall from or as if from death **e :** to establish radio communication with **3 a :** to set upright by lifting or building **b :** to lift higher **c :** to place higher in rank or dignity : ELEVATE **d :** HEIGHTEN, INVIGORATE ⟨~ the spirits⟩ **e :** to end or suspend the operation or validity of ⟨~ a siege⟩ **4 :** to get together for a purpose : COLLECT ⟨~ funds⟩ **5 a :** to breed and bring (an animal) to maturity **b :** GROW, CULTIVATE ⟨~ cotton⟩ **c :** to bring up (a child) : REAR **6 a :** to give rise to : PROVOKE ⟨~ a commotion⟩ **b :** to give voice to ⟨~ a cheer⟩ **7 :** to bring up for consideration or debate ⟨~ an issue⟩ **8 a :** to increase the strength, intensity, or pitch of **b :** to increase the degree of **c :** to cause to rise in level or amount ⟨~ the rent⟩ **d (1) :** to increase the amount of (a poker bet) **(2) :** to bet more than (a previous bettor) **e (1) :** to make a higher bridge bid in (a partner's suit) **(2) :** to increase the bid of (one's partner) **9 :** to make light and porous ⟨~ dough⟩ **10 :** to cause to ascend **11 :** to multiply (a quantity) by itself a specified number of times **12 :** to bring in sight on the horizon by approaching ⟨~ land⟩ **13 a :** to bring up the nap of (cloth) **b :** to cause (as a blister) to form on the skin **14 :** to increase the nominal value of fraudulently ⟨~ a check⟩ **15 :** to articulate (a sound) with the tongue in a higher position ~ *vi* **1** *dial* : RAISE **2 :** to increase a bet or bid **syn** see LIFT — **rais·er** *n* — **raise Cain** *or* **raise hell 1 :** to act wildly : create a disturbance **2 :** to scold or upbraid someone esp. loudly — **raise eyebrows** : to cause surprise or astonishment

²raise *n* (1538) **1 :** an act of raising or lifting **2 :** a rising stretch of road : an upward grade : RISE **3 :** an increase in amount: as **a :** an increase of a bet or bid **b :** an increase in wages or salary **4 :** a vertical or inclined opening or passageway connecting one mine working area with another at a higher level

raised *adj* (1599) **1 a :** done in relief **b :** having a nap **2 :** leavened with yeast rather than with baking powder or baking soda

rai·sin \'rā-z⁰n\ *n* [ME, fr. MF, grape, fr. L *racemus* cluster of grapes or berries — more at RACEME] (14c) : a grape of any of several varieties that has been dried in the sun or by artificial heat

rai·son d'être *also* **rai·son d'etre** \,rā-,zōⁿ-'detr⁰\ *n* [F] (1864) : reason or justification for existence

raj \'räj\ *n* [Hindi *rāj*, fr. Skt *rājya*; akin to Skt *rājan* king] (1800) : RULE; *esp, often cap* : the former British rule of the Indian subcontinent

ra·ja *or* **ra·jah** \'rä-jə, -(,)jä, -zhə, -(,)zhä\ *n* [Hindi *rājā*, fr. Skt *rājan* king — more at ROYAL] (1555) **1 :** an Indian or Malay prince or chief **2 :** the bearer of a title of nobility among the Hindus

Ra·jab \rə-'jab\ *n* [Ar] (ca. 1771) : the 7th month of the Islamic year — see MONTH table

Ra·jas·tha·ni \,rä-jə-'stä-nē, ,rä-zhə-\ *n* [Hindi *Rājasthānī*, fr. *Rājasthān* Rajasthan] (1901) : the Indo-Aryan dialects of Rajasthan

Raj·put *or* **Raj·poot** \'räj-,püt, 'räzh-\ *n* [Hindi *rājpūt*, fr. Skt *rājaputra* king's son, fr. *rājan* king + *putra* son — more at FEW] (1598) : a member of a dominant military caste of northern India

¹rake \'rāk\ *n* [ME, fr. OE *racu*; akin to OHG *rehho* rake] (bef. 12c) **1 a :** an implement equipped with projecting prongs to gather material (as leaves) or for loosening or smoothing the surface of the ground **b** : a machine for gathering hay **2 :** an implement like a rake

²rake *vt* **raked; rak·ing** (14c) **1 :** to gather, loosen, or smooth with or as if with a rake **2 :** to gain rapidly or in abundance ⟨~ in a fortune⟩ **3 a :** to touch in passing over lightly **b :** SCRATCH **4 :** to censure severely **5 :** to search through : RANSACK **6 :** to sweep the length of esp. with gunfire : ENFILADE **7 :** to glance over rapidly — **rak·er** *n*

³rake *n* [origin unknown] (1626) **1 :** inclination from the perpendicular; *esp* : the overhang of a ship's bow or stern **2 :** inclination from the horizontal : SLOPE **3 :** the angle between the top cutting surface of a tool and a plane perpendicular to the surface of the work **4 :** the

\ə\ abut \⁰\ kitten, F table \ər\ further \a\ ash \ā\ ace \ä\ mop, mar
\aů\ out \ch\ chin \e\ bet \ē\ easy \g\ go \i\ hit \ī\ ice \j\ job
\ŋ\ sing \ō\ go \ö\ law \öi\ boy \th\ thin \th\ the \ü\ loot \ů\ foot
\y\ yet \zh\ vision \á, k̟, ⁿ, œ, œ̄, ᵫ, ᵫ̄, ʸ\ see Guide to Pronunciation

angle between a wing-tip edge that is sensibly straight in planform and the plane of symmetry of an airplane
⁴**rake** *vi* **raked; rak·ing** (1691) : to incline from the perpendicular
⁵**rake** *n* [short for *rakehell*] (1653) : a dissolute person : LIBERTINE
rake-hell \'rāk-,hel\ *n* (1554) : LIBERTINE 2 — **rakehell** *or* **rake·hel·ly** \-,he-lē\ *adj*
rake-off \'rāk-,óf\ *n* [*rake off*, fr. the use of a rake by a croupier to collect the operator's profits in a gambling casino] (1888) : a percent-age or cut taken (as by an operator)
rake up *vt* (1581) : to make known or public : UNCOVER ⟨*rake up a* scandal⟩
ra·ki \rə-'kē; 'ra·kē, 'rä-\ *n* [Turk, fr. Ar *'araqī*, lit., of liquor, fr. *'araq* liquor, arrack] (1675) : a Turkish liqueur flavored with aniseed
¹**rak·ish** \'rā-kish\ *adj* [⁵*rake*] (1706) : of, relating to, or characteristic of a rake : DISSOLUTE
²**rakish** *adj* [prob. fr. ⁴*rake*; fr. the raking masts of pirate ships] (1824) **1** : having a trim or streamlined appearance suggestive of speed ⟨a ~ ship⟩ **2** : dashingly or carelessly unconventional : JAUNTY ⟨~ clothes⟩
rak·ish·ly *adv* (1838) : in a rakish manner
rak·ish·ness *n* (ca. 1828) : the quality or state of being rakish
rale \'ral, 'räl\ *n* [F *râle*, fr. *râler* to make a rattling sound in the throat] (1828) : an abnormal sound heard accompanying the normal respira-tory sounds on auscultation of the chest
ral·len·tan·do \,rä-lən-'tän-(,)dō\ *adv or adj* [It, lit., slowing down, verbal of *rallentare* to slow down again, fr. *re-* + *allentare* to slow down, fr. LL, fr. L *al-* ad- + *lentus* slow, pliant — more at LITHE] (ca. 1811) : RITARDANDO
¹**ral·ly** \'ra-lē\ *vb* **ral·lied; ral·ly·ing** [F *rallier*, fr. OF *ralier*, fr. *re-* + *alier* to unite — more at ALLY] *vt* (1603) **1 a** : to muster for a com-mon purpose **b** : to recall to order **2 a** : to arouse for action **b** : to rouse from depression or weakness ~ *vi* **1** : to come together again to renew an effort **2** : to join in a common cause **3** : RECOVER, RE-BOUND **4** : to engage in a rally
²**rally** *n, pl* **rallies** (1651) **1 a** : a mustering of scattered forces to renew an effort **b** : a summoning up of strength or courage after weakness or dejection **c** : a recovery of price after a decline **d** : a renewed offensive **2** : a mass meeting intended to arouse group enthu-siasm **3** : a series of shots interchanged between players (as in tennis) before a point is won **4** *also* **ral·lye** [F *rallye*, fr. E ¹*rally*] : an auto-mobile competition using public roads and ordinary traffic rules with the object of maintaining a specified average speed between check-points over a route unknown to the participants until the start of the event
³**rally** *vt* **ral·lied; ral·ly·ing** [F *railler* to mock, rally — more at RAIL] (1668) : to attack with raillery : BANTER
ral·ly·ing \'ra-lē-iŋ\ *n* (1957) : the sport of driving in automobile rallies
¹**ram** \'ram\ *n* [ME, fr. OE *ramm;* akin to OHG *ram*] (bef. 12c) **1 a** : a male sheep **b** *cap* : ARIES **2 a** : BATTERING RAM **b** : a warship with a heavy beak at the prow for piercing an enemy ship **3** : any of various guided pieces for exerting pressure or for driving or forcing something by impact: **a** : the plunger of a hydrostatic press or force pump **b** : the weight that strikes the blow in a pile driver
²**ram** *vb* **rammed; ram·ming** [ME *rammen*, prob. fr. *ram*, n.] *vi* (14c) **1** : to strike with violence : CRASH **2** : to move with extreme rapidity ~ *vt* **1** : to force in by or as if by driving **2 a** : to make compact (as by pounding) **b** : CRAM, CROWD **3** : to force passage or acceptance of ⟨~ home an idea⟩ **4** : to strike against violently — **ram·mer** *n*
RAM \'ram\ *n* (1957) : RANDOM-ACCESS MEMORY
Ra·ma \'rä-mə\ *n* [Skt *Rāma*] : a deity or deified hero of later Hindu-ism worshiped as an avatar of Vishnu
Ram·a·dan \'rä-mə-,dän, ,rä-mə-'\ *n* [Ar *Ramadān*] (ca. 1595) : the 9th month of the Islamic year observed as sacred with fasting practiced daily from dawn to sunset — see MONTH table
ra·mate \'rā-,māt\ *adj* [L *ramus* branch — more at RAMIFY] (1897) : RAMOSE
¹**ram·ble** \'ram-bəl\ *vb* **ram·bled; ram·bling** \-b(ə-)liŋ\ [perh. fr. ME *romblen*, freq. of *romen* to roam] *vi* (1620) **1 a** : to move aimlessly from place to place **b** : to explore idly **2** : to talk or write in a desul-tory or long-winded wandering fashion **3** : to grow or extend irregu-larly ~ *vt* : to wander over : ROAM *syn* see WANDER — **ram·bling-ly** \-b(ə-)liŋ-lē\ *adv*
²**ramble** *n* (1654) : a leisurely excursion for pleasure; *esp* : an aimless walk
ram·bler \'ram-blər\ *n* (1624) **1** : one that rambles **2** : any of vari-ous climbing roses with long flexible canes and rather small often dou-ble flowers in large clusters **3** : RANCH HOUSE
ram·bouil·let \,ram-bə-'lā, -bü-'yā\ *n, often cap* [*Rambouillet*, France] (1906) : any of a breed of large sturdy sheep de-veloped in France
ram·bunc·tious \ram-'bəŋk-shəs\ *adj* [prob. alter. of *rumbustious*] (1830) : marked by uncontrollable exuberance : UNRULY — **ram·bunc·tious·ly** *adv* — **ram·bunc·tious·ness** *n*
ram·bu·tan \ram-'bü-t*ə*n\ *n* [Malay] (1707) : a bright red spiny Malayan fruit closely related to the litchi; *also* : a tree (*Nephelium lappaceum*) of the soapberry family that bears this fruit
ram·e·kin *also* **ram·e·quin** \'ram-kən, 'ra-mi-\ *n* [F *ramequin*, fr. LG *ramken*, dim. of *ram* cream] (ca. 1706) **1** : a preparation of cheese esp. with bread crumbs or eggs baked in a mold or shell **2** : an individual baking dish
ra·met \'rā-,met\ *n* [L *ramus* branch] (1929) : an independent member of a clone
ra·mie \'rā-mē, 'ra-\ *n* [Malay *rami*] (1832) **1** : an Asian perennial plant (*Boehmeria nivea*) of the nettle family **2 a** : the strong lustrous bast fiber of ramie capable of being spun or woven **b** : fabric made of ramie often resembling linen or silk
ram·i·fi·ca·tion \,ra-mə-fə-'kā-shən\ *n* (1665) **1 a** : BRANCH, OFF-SHOOT **b** : a branched structure **2 a** : the act or process of branching

rambouillet

b : arrangement of branches (as on a plant) **3** : CONSEQUENCE, OUT-GROWTH ⟨the ~s of a problem⟩
ram·i·fy \'ra-mə-,fī\ *vb* **-fied; -fy·ing** [ME *ramifien*, fr. MF *ramifier*, fr. ML *ramificare*, fr. L *ramus* branch; akin to L *radix* root — more at ROOT] *vi* (15c) **1** : to split up into branches or constituent parts **2** : to send forth branches or extensions ~ *vt* **1** : to cause to branch **2** : to separate into divisions
Ra·mism \'rä-,mi-zəm\ *n* [Petrus *Ramus* †1572 Fr. philosopher] (1710) : the doctrines of Ramus based on opposition to Aristotelianism and advocacy of a new logic blended with rhetoric — **Ra·mist** \-mist\ *n or adj*
ram·jet \'ram-,jet\ *n* (1942) : a jet engine that consists essentially of a hollow tube without mechanical components and depends on the air-craft's speed of flight for the air compression necessary to produce the thrust obtained from the expansion of gases caused by the combustion of fuel
ra·mose \'rā-,mōs, rä-'\ *adj* [L *ramosus*, fr. *ramus* branch] (1689) : consist-ing of or having branches ⟨a ~ sponge⟩
¹**ramp** \'ramp\ *vb* [ME, fr. MF *ramper* to crawl, rear, of Gmc origin; akin to OHG *rimpfan* to wrinkle — more at RUMPLE] *vi* (14c) **1 a** : to stand or advance menacingly with forelegs or with arms raised **b** : to move or act furiously **2** : to creep up — used esp. of plants ~ *vt* [⁴*ramp* (electrical waveform)] : to increase or decrease esp. at a con-stant rate — usu. used with *up* or *down* ⟨~ up production⟩
²**ramp** *n* (1671) : the act or an instance of ramping
³**ramp** *n* [back-formation fr. *ramps*, alter. of *rams*, fr. ME, fr. OE *hramsa;* akin to OHG *ramusia* ramp, Gk *krommyon* onion] (1598) : any of various alliums used for food
⁴**ramp** *n* [F *rampe*, fr. *ramper*, fr. MF] (1778) **1** : a short bend, slope, or curve usu. in the vertical plane where a handrail or coping changes its direction **2 a** : a sloping way: as **a** : a sloping floor, walk, or road-way leading from one level to another **b** : a stairway for entering or leaving an airplane **c** : a slope for launching boats : APRON 2h
¹**ram·page** \'ram-,pāj, (,)ram-'\ *vi* **ram·paged; ram·pag·ing** [Sc] (1808) : to rush wildly about
²**ram·page** \'ram-,pāj\ *n* (1861) : a course of violent, riotous, or reck-less action or behavior — **ram·pa·geous** \ram-'pā-jəs\ *adj* — **ram·pa·geous·ly** *adv* — **ram·pa·geous·ness** *n*
ram·pan·cy \'ram-pən(t)-sē\ *n* (1664) : the quality or state of being rampant
ram·pant \'ram-pənt *also* -,pant\ *adj* [ME, fr. MF, prp. of *ramper*] (14c) **1 a** : rearing upon the hind legs with forelegs extended **b** : standing on one hind foot with one foreleg raised above the other and the head in profile — used of a heraldic animal **2 a** : marked by a menacing wildness, extravagance, or absence of restraint **b** : WIDE-SPREAD **3** : having one impost or abutment higher than the other ⟨a ~ arch⟩ — **ram·pant·ly** *adv*
ram·part \'ram-,pärt, -pərt\ *n* [MF, fr. *ramparer* to fortify, fr. *re-* + *emparer* to defend, fr. OProv *antparar*, fr. (assumed) VL *anteparare*, fr. L *ante* before + *parare* to prepare — more at ANTE-, PARE] (1536) **1** : a protective barrier : BULWARK **2** : a broad embankment raised as a fortification and usu. surmounted by a parapet **3** : a wall-like ridge (as of rock fragments, earth, or debris)
ram·pike \-,pīk\ *n* [origin unknown] (1853) : an erect broken or dead tree
¹**ram·rod** \'ram-,räd\ *n* (1757) **1** : a rod for ramming home the charge in a muzzle-loading firearm **2** : a cleaning rod for small arms **3** : BOSS, OVERSEER
²**ramrod** *adj* (1905) : marked by rigidity, severity, or stiffness
³**ramrod** *vt* (ca. 1940) : to direct, supervise, and control
ram·shack·le \'ram-,sha-kəl\ *adj* [alter. of earlier *ransackled*, fr. pp. of obs. *ransackle*, freq. of *ransack*] (1830) **1** : appearing ready to collapse : RICKETY **2** : carelessly or loosely constructed
rams·horn \'ramz-,hórn\ *n* (1901) : any of various snails (as genera *Planorbis, Helisoma,* and *Planorbarius*) often used as aquarium scaven-gers
ra·mus \'rā-məs\ *n, pl* **ra·mi** \-,mī\ [NL, fr. L, branch — more at RAM-IFY] (1803) **1** : a projecting part, elongated process, or branch: as **a** : the posterior more or less vertical part on each side of the lower jaw that articulates with the skull **b** : a branch of a nerve
ran *past of* RUN
¹**ranch** \'ranch\ *n* [MexSp *rancho* small ranch, fr. Sp, camp, hut & Sp dial., small farm, fr. OSp *rancharse* to take up quarters, fr. MF *se ranger* to take up a position, fr. *ranger* to set in a row — more at RANGE] (1831) **1** : a large farm for raising horses, beef cattle, or sheep **2** : a farm or area devoted to a particular specialty : RANCH HOUSE
²**ranch** *vi* (1866) : to live or work on a ranch ~ *vt* **1** : to work as a rancher on **2** : to raise on a ranch
ranch dressing *n* (1984) : a creamy salad dressing usu. containing milk or buttermilk and mayonnaise
ranch·er \'ran-chər\ *n* (1836) : one who owns or works on a ranch
ran·che·ro \ran-'cher-(,)ō, rän-\ *n, pl* **-ros** [MexSp, fr. *rancho*] (1826) : RANCHER; *also* : RANCH 1
ranch house *n* (1862) **1** : the main dwelling house on a ranch **2** : a one-story house typically with a low-pitched roof and an open plan
ranch·man \'ranch-mən\ *n* (1856) : RANCHER
ran·cho \'ran-(,)chō, 'rän-\ *n, pl* **ranchos** [MexSp, small ranch] (1808) : RANCH 1
ran·cid \'ran(t)-səd\ *adj* [L *rancidus*, fr. *rancēre* to be rancid] (1646) **1** : having a rank smell or taste **2** : OFFENSIVE — **ran·cid·i·ty** \ran-'si-də-tē\ *n* — **ran·cid·ness** \'ran(t)-səd-nəs\ *n*
ran·cor \'ran-kər, -,kôr\ *n* [ME *rancour*, fr. MF *ranceur*, fr. LL *rancor* rancidity, rancor, fr. L *rancēre*] (14c) : bitter deep-seated ill will *syn* see ENMITY
ran·cor·ous \'raŋ-k(ə-)rəs\ *adj* (1590) : marked by rancor — **ran·cor·ous·ly** *adv*
ran·cour *Brit var of* RANCOR
rand \'rand, 'ränd, 'ränt\ *n, pl* **rand** [the *Rand*, So. Africa] (ca. 1932) **1** — see MONEY table **2** : a former monetary unit of Botswana, Leso-tho, and Swaziland
R and D *n* (1966) : research and development
¹**ran·dom** \'ran-dəm\ *n* [ME, impetuosity, fr. MF *random*, fr. OF, fr. *randir* to run, of Gmc origin; akin to OHG *rinnan* to run — more at

RUN] (1561) : a haphazard course — **at random** : without definite aim, direction, rule, or method

²**random** *adj* (1565) **1 a** : lacking a definite plan, purpose, or pattern **b** : made, done, or chosen at random ⟨read ~ passages from the book⟩ **2 a** : relating to, having, or being elements or events with definite probability of occurrence ⟨~ processes⟩ **b** : being or relating to a set or to an element of a set each of whose elements has equal probability of occurrence ⟨a ~ sample⟩; *also* : characterized by procedures designed to obtain such sets or elements ⟨~ sampling⟩ — **ran·dom·ly** *adv* — **ran·dom·ness** *n*

syn RANDOM, HAPHAZARD, CASUAL mean determined by accident rather than design. RANDOM stresses lack of definite aim, fixed goal, or regular procedure ⟨a *random* selection of books⟩. HAPHAZARD applies to what is done without regard for regularity or fitness or ultimate consequence ⟨a *haphazard* collection of rocks⟩. CASUAL suggests working or acting without deliberation, intention, or purpose ⟨a *casual* collector⟩.

³**random** *adv* (1618) : in a random manner

random–access *adj* (1953) : permitting access to stored data in any order the user desires

random–access memory *n* (1955) : a computer memory that provides the main internal storage available to the user for programs and data — called also *RAM*; compare READ-ONLY MEMORY

ran·dom·ize \'ran-də-ˌmīz\ *vt* **-ized; -iz·ing** (1926) : to select, assign, or arrange in a random way — **ran·dom·i·za·tion** \ˌran-də-mə-'zā-shən\ *n* — **ran·dom·iz·er** *n*

randomized block *n* (ca. 1942) : an experimental design (as in horticulture) in which different treatments are distributed in random order in a block or plot — called also *randomized block design*

random variable *n* (1949) : a variable that is itself a function of the result of a statistical experiment in which each outcome has a definite probability of occurrence — called also *variate*

random walk *n* (1941) : a process (as Brownian motion or genetic drift) consisting of a sequence of steps (as movements or changes in gene frequency) each of whose characteristics (as magnitude and direction) is determined by chance

¹**randy** \'ran-dē\ *adj* [prob. fr. obs. *rand* to rant] (1698) **1** *chiefly Scot* : having a coarse manner **2** : LUSTFUL, LECHEROUS

²**randy** *n*, *pl* **rand·ies** (1762) *chiefly Scot* : a scolding or dissolute woman

rang *past of* RING

¹**range** \'rānj\ *n*, *often attrib* [ME, row of persons, fr. MF *renge*, fr. OF *rengier* to range] (14c) **1 a** (1) : a series of things in a line : ROW (2) : a series of mountains (3) : one of the north-south rows of townships in a U.S. public-land survey that are numbered east and west from the principal meridian of the survey **b** : an aggregate of individuals in one order **c** : a direction line **2** : a cooking stove that has an oven and a flat top with burners or heating elements **3 a** : a place that may be ranged over **b** : an open region over which animals (as livestock) may roam and feed **c** : the region throughout which a kind of organism or ecological community naturally lives or occurs **4** : the act of ranging about **5 a** (1) : the horizontal distance to which a projectile can be propelled (2) : the horizontal distance between a weapon and target **b** : the maximum distance a vehicle or craft can travel without refueling **c** (1) : a place where shooting is practiced (2) : DRIVING RANGE **6 a** : the space or extent included, covered, or used : SCOPE **b** : the extent of pitch covered by a melody or lying within the capacity of a voice or instrument **7 a** : a sequence, series, or scale between limits ⟨a wide ~ of patterns⟩ **b** : the limits of a series : the distance or extent between possible extremes **c** : the difference between the least and greatest values of an attribute or of the variable of a frequency distribution **8 a** : the set of values a function may take on **b** : the class of admissible values of a variable **9** : LINE 11

syn RANGE, GAMUT, COMPASS, SWEEP, SCOPE, ORBIT mean the extent that lies within the powers of something (as to cover or control). RANGE is a general term indicating the extent of one's perception or the extent of powers, capacities, or possibilities ⟨the entire *range* of human experience⟩. GAMUT suggests a graduated series running from one possible extreme to another ⟨a performance that ran the *gamut* of emotions⟩. COMPASS implies a sometimes limited extent of perception, knowledge, or activity ⟨your concerns lie beyond the narrow *compass* of this study⟩. SWEEP suggests extent, often circular or arc-shaped, of motion or activity ⟨the book covers the entire *sweep* of criminal activity⟩. SCOPE is applicable to an area of activity, predetermined and limited, but somewhat flexible (as time went on, the *scope* of the investigation widened⟩. ORBIT suggests an often circumscribed range of activity or influence within which forces work toward accommodation ⟨within that restricted *orbit* they tried to effect social change⟩.

²**range** *vb* **ranged; rang·ing** [ME, fr. MF *ranger*, fr. OF *renc*, *reng* line, place, row — more at RANK] *vt* (14c) **1 a** : to set in a row or in the proper order **b** : to place among others in a position or situation **c** : to assign to a category : CLASSIFY **2 a** : to rove over or through **b** : to sail or pass along **3** : to arrange (an anchor cable) on deck **4** : to graze (livestock) on a range **5** : to determine or give the elevation necessary for (a gun) to propel a projectile to a given distance ~ *vi* **1 a** : to roam at large or freely **b** : to move over an area so as to explore it **2** : to take a position **3 a** : to correspond in direction or line : ALIGN **b** : to extend in a particular direction **4** : to have range **5** : to change or differ within limits **6** *of an organism* : to live or occur in or be native to a region **7** : to obtain the range of an object by instrument (as radar or laser)

range finder *n* (1872) **1** : an instrument used in gunnery to determine the distance of a target **2** : a surveying instrument (as a transit) for determining quickly the distances, bearings, and elevations of distant objects **3** : a usu. built-in adjustable optical device for focusing a camera that automatically indicates the correct focus (as when two parts of a split image are brought together)

range·land \'rānj-ˌland\ *n* (1935) : land used or suitable for range

rang·er \'rān-jər\ *n* (14c) **1 a** : the keeper of a British royal park or forest **b** : FOREST RANGER **2** : one that ranges **3 a** : one of a body of organized armed men who range over a region esp. to enforce the law **b** : a soldier specially trained in close-range fighting and in raiding tactics

rangy \'rān-jē\ *adj* **rang·i·er; -est** (1868) **1** : able to range for considerable distances **2 a** : long-limbed and long-bodied ⟨~ cattle⟩ **b**

: being tall and slender **3** : having room for ranging **4** : having great scope — **rang·i·ness** *n*

ra·ni *or* **ra·nee** \rä-'nē, 'rä-ˌnē\ *n* [Hindi *rānī*, fr. Skt *rājñī*, fem. of *rājan* king — more at ROYAL] (1673) : a Hindu queen : a rajah's wife

ra·nid \'ra-nəd, 'rā-\ *n* [ultim. fr. L *rana* frog] (ca. 1934) : any of a large family (Ranidae) of frogs distinguished by slightly dilated transverse sacral processes

¹**rank** \'raŋk\ *adj* [ME, fr. OE *ranc* overbearing, strong; akin to ON *rakkr* erect and perh. to OE *riht* right — more at RIGHT] (13c) **1** : luxuriantly or excessively vigorous in growth **2** : offensively gross or coarse : FOUL **3** *obs* : grown too large **4 a** : shockingly conspicuous ⟨must lecture him on his ~ disloyalty —David Walden⟩ **b** : OUTRIGHT — used as an intensive ⟨~ beginners⟩ **5** *archaic* : LUSTFUL, RUTTISH **6** : offensive in odor or flavor; *esp* : RANCID **7** : PUTRID, FESTERING **8** : high in amount or degree : FRAUGHT *syn* see MALODOROUS, FLAGRANT — **rank·ly** *adv* — **rank·ness** *n*

²**rank** *n* [ME, fr. MF *renc*, *reng*, of Gmc origin; akin to OHG *hring* ring — more at RING] (14c) **1 a** : ROW, SERIES **b** : a row of people **c** (1) : a line of soldiers ranged side by side in close order (2) *pl* : ARMED FORCES (3) *pl* : the body of enlisted personnel **d** : any of the rows of squares that extend across a chessboard perpendicular to the files **e** *Brit* : STAND 6 **2 a** : relative standing or position **b** : a degree or position of dignity, eminence, or excellence : DISTINCTION ⟨soon took ~ as a leading attorney —J. D. Hicks⟩ **c** : high social position ⟨the privileges of ~⟩ **d** : a grade of official standing in a hierarchy **3** : an orderly arrangement : FORMATION **4** : an aggregate of individuals classed together — usu. used in pl. **5** : the order according to some statistical characteristic (as the score on a test) **6** : any of a series of classes of coal based on increasing alteration of the parent vegetable matter, increasing carbon content, and increasing fuel value **7** : the number of linearly independent rows or columns in a matrix

³**rank** *vt* (1573) **1** : to arrange in lines or in a regular formation **2** : to determine the relative position of : RATE **3** : to take precedence of ~ *vi* **1** : to form or move in ranks **2** : to take or have a position in relation to others

rank and file *n* (1598) **1** : the enlisted personnel of an armed force **2** : the individuals who constitute the body of an organization, society, or nation as distinguished from the leaders — **rank–and–file** \ˌraŋk-ⁿn-'fīl\ *adj* — **rank and fil·er** \-'fī-lər\ *n*

rank correlation *n* (1907) : a measure of correlation depending on rank

rank·er \'raŋ-kər\ *n* (1878) : one who serves or has served in the ranks; *esp* : a commissioned officer promoted from the ranks

Ran·kine \'raŋ-kən\ *adj* [William J. M. *Rankine* †1872 Scot. engineer & physicist] (ca. 1926) : being, according to, or relating to an absolute temperature scale on which the unit of measurement equals a Fahrenheit degree and on which the freezing point of water is 491.67° and the boiling point 671.67°

rank·ing *adj* (1862) : having a high position: as **a** : FOREMOST ⟨~ poet⟩ **b** : being next to the chairman in seniority ⟨~ committee member⟩

ran·kle \'raŋ-kəl\ *vb* **ran·kled; ran·kling** \-k(ə-)liŋ\ [ME *ranclen* to fester, fr. MF *rancler*, fr. OF *draoncler*, *raoncler*, fr. *draoncle*, *raoncle* festering sore, fr. ML *dracunculus*, fr. L, dim. of *draco* serpent — more at DRAGON] *vi* (1606) **1** : to cause anger, irritation, or deep bitterness **2** : to feel anger and irritation ~ *vt* : to cause irritation or bitterness in

ran·sack \'ran-ˌsak, (ˌ)ran-'\ *vt* [ME *ransaken*, fr. ON *rannsaka*, fr. *rann* house + *-saka* (akin to OE *sēcan* to seek) — more at SEEK] (13c) **1 a** : to search thoroughly **b** : to examine closely and carefully **2** : to search through to commit robbery : PLUNDER — **ran·sack·er** *n*

¹**ran·som** \'ran(t)-səm\ *n* [ME *ransoun*, fr. OF *rançon*, fr. L *redemption-*, *redemptio* — more at REDEMPTION] (13c) **1** : a consideration paid or demanded for the release of someone or something from captivity **2** : the act of ransoming

²**ransom** *vt* (14c) **1** : to deliver esp. from sin or its penalty **2** : to free from captivity or punishment by paying a price *syn* see RESCUE — **ran·som·er** *n*

¹**rant** \'rant\ *vb* [obs. D *ranten*, *randen*] *vi* (1602) **1** : to talk in a noisy, excited, or declamatory manner **2** : to scold vehemently ~ *vt* : to utter in a bombastic declamatory fashion — **rant·er** *n* — **rant·ing·ly** \'ran-tiŋ-lē\ *adv*

²**rant** *n* (1649) **1 a** : a bombastic extravagant speech **b** : bombastic extravagant language **2** *dial Brit* : a rousing good time

ran·u·la \'ran-yə-lə\ *n* [NL, dim. fr. L swelling on the tongue of cattle, fr. dim. of *rana* frog] (15c) : a cyst formed under the tongue by obstruction of a gland duct

ra·nun·cu·lus \rə-'nəŋ-kyə-ləs\ *n*, *pl* **-lus·es** *or* **-li** \-ˌlī, -ˌlē\ [NL, fr. L, fr. dim. of *rana* frog] (1543) : BUTTERCUP

¹**rap** \'rap\ *n* [ME *rappe*] (14c) **1** : a sharp blow or knock **2 a** : a sharp rebuke or criticism **b** : a negative and often undeserved reputation or charge — usu. used with *bum* or *bad* ⟨given a bum ~ by the press⟩ **3 a** : the responsibility for or adverse consequences of an action ⟨refused to take the ~⟩ **b** : a criminal charge **c** : a prison sentence

²**rap** *vb* **rapped; rap·ping** *vt* (14c) **1** : to strike with a sharp blow **2** : to utter suddenly and forcibly **3** : to cause to be or come by raps ⟨~ the meeting to order⟩ **4** : to criticize sharply ~ *vi* **1** : to strike a quick sharp blow **2** : to make a short sharp sound

³**rap** *vt* **rapped** *also* **rapt** \'rapt\; **rap·ping** [back-formation fr. *rapt*] (1528) **1** : to snatch away or upward **2** : ENRAPTURE

⁴**rap** *n* [perh. fr. ¹*rap*] (1834) : a minimum amount or degree (as of care or consideration) : the least bit ⟨doesn't care a ~⟩

⁵**rap** *vi* **rapped; rap·ping** [perh. fr. ¹*rap*] (1929) **1** : to talk freely and frankly **2** : to perform rap music

---

\ə\ abut \ᵊ\ kitten, F table \ər\ further \a\ ash \ā\ ace \ä\ mop, mar \aú\ out \ch\ chin \e\ bet \ē\ easy \g\ go \i\ hit \ī\ ice \j\ job \ŋ\ sing \ō\ go \ò\ law \òi\ boy \th\ thin \t̲h̲\ the \ü\ loot \ù\ foot \y\ yet \zh\ vision \á, k̲, ⁿ, œ, œ̄, ᵫ, ᵫ̄, ᵊ\ *see* Guide to Pronunciation

⁶rap n (1967) **1 :** TALK, CONVERSATION; also : a line of talk : PATTER **2 a :** a rhythmic chanting often in unison of usu. rhymed couplets to a musical accompaniment **b :** a piece so performed

ra·pa·cious \rə-'pā-shəs\ adj [L rapac-, rapax, fr. rapere to seize — more at RAPID] (1651) **1 :** excessively grasping or covetous **2 :** living on prey **3 :** RAVENOUS **syn** see VORACIOUS — **ra·pa·cious·ly** adv — **ra·pa·cious·ness** n

ra·pac·i·ty \rə-'pa-sə-tē\ n (1543) **:** the quality of being rapacious

¹rape \'rāp\ n [ME, fr. L rapa, rapum turnip, rape; akin to OHG rāba turnip, rape, Lith rópė] (14c) **:** a European herb (Brassica napus) of the mustard family grown as a forage crop for sheep and hogs and for its seeds which yield rapeseed oil and are a bird food — called also CANOLA

²rape vt raped; rap·ing [ME, fr. L rapere] (14c) **1 a** archaic **:** to seize and take away by force **b :** DESPOIL **2 :** to commit rape on — **rap·er** n — **rap·ist** \'rā-pist\ n

³rape n (14c) **1 :** an act or instance of robbing or despoiling or carrying away a person by force **2 a :** sexual intercourse with a woman by a man without her consent and chiefly by force or deception — compare STATUTORY RAPE **b :** unlawful sexual intercourse by force or threat other than by a man with a woman **3 :** an outrageous violation

⁴rape n [F râpe grape stalk] (1657) **:** grape pomace

rape·seed \'rāp-ˌsēd\ n (1577) **:** the seed of the rape plant

rapeseed oil n (1816) **:** a nondrying or semidrying oil obtained from rapeseed and turnip seed and used chiefly as a lubricant, illuminant, and food — called also rape oil; compare CANOLA OIL

Ra·pha·el \'ra-fē-əl, 'rä-, -ˌel\ n [LL, fr. Gk Rhaphaēl, fr. Heb Rĕphā'ēl] **:** one of the four archangels named in Hebrew tradition

ra·phe \'rā-(ˌ)fē\ n [NL, fr. Gk raphē seam, fr. rhaptein to sew] (ca. 1753) **1 :** the seamlike union of the two lateral halves of a part or organ (as the tongue) having externally a ridge or furrow **2 a :** the part of the stalk of an anatropous ovary that is united in growth to the outside covering and forms a ridge along the body of the ovule **b :** the median line or slit of a diatom's valve

ra·phia \'rā-fē-ə, 'ra-\ n [NL, genus of palms, fr. Malagasy rafia raffia] (ca. 1866) **:** RAFFIA

raph·ide \'ra-ˌfīd\ n, pl **raph·ides** \'ra-ˌfīdz, 'ra-fə-ˌdēz\ [F & NL; F raphide, fr. NL raphides, pl., fr. Gk rhaphides, pl. of rhaphid-, rhaphis needle, fr. rhaptein] (ca. 1842) **:** any of the needle-shaped crystals usu. of calcium oxalate that develop as metabolic by-products in plant cells

¹rap·id \'ra-pəd\ adj [L rapidus seizing, sweeping, rapid, fr. rapere to seize, sweep away; akin to Lith aprėpti to embrace] (1634) **:** marked by a fast rate of motion, activity, succession, or occurrence **syn** see FAST — **rap·id·ly** adv — **rap·id·ness** n

²rapid n (1765) **:** a part of a river where the current is fast and the surface is usu. broken by obstructions — usu. used in pl. but sing. or pl. in constr.

rapid eye movement n (1916) **:** a rapid conjugate movement of the eyes associated esp. with REM sleep

rapid eye movement sleep n (1965) **:** REM SLEEP

rap·id-fire \ˌra-pəd-'fīr\ adj (1890) **1 :** firing or adapted for firing shots in rapid succession **2 :** marked by rapidity, liveliness, or sharpness

ra·pid·i·ty \rə-'pi-də-tē, ra-\ n (1654) **:** the quality or state of being rapid

rapid transit n (1873) **:** fast passenger transportation (as by subway) in urban areas

ra·pi·er \'rā-pē-ər\ n [MF (espee) rapiere] (1553) **:** a straight 2-edged sword with a narrow pointed blade

rap·ine \'ra-pən, -ˌpīn\ n [ME rapyne, fr. L rapina, fr. rapere to seize, rob] (15c) **:** PILLAGE, PLUNDER

ra·pi·ni also **rap·pi·ni** \ra-'pē-nē\ n [It rapini, pl. of rapino, dim. of rapo turnip, fr. L rapum — more at RAPE] (1942) **:** BROCCOLI RABE

rap·pa·ree \ˌra-pə-'rē\ n [Ir rapaire, ropaire, lit., thruster, stabber, fr. rop thrust, stab] (1690) **1 :** an Irish irregular soldier or bandit **2 :** VAGABOND, PLUNDERER

rap·pee \ra-'pā\ n [F (tabac) râpé, lit., grated tobacco] (ca. 1740) **:** a pungent snuff made from dark tobacco leaves

rap·pel \ra-'pel, ra-\ vi **-pelled** also **-peled**; **-pel·ling** also **-pel·ing** [F, lit., recall, fr. OF rapel, fr. rapeler to recall, fr. re- + apeler to appeal, call — more at APPEAL] (1944) **:** to descend (as from a cliff) by sliding down a rope passed under one thigh, across the body, and over the opposite shoulder or through a special friction device — **rappel** n

rap·pen \'räp-ən\ n, pl **rappen** [G, fr. G dial., lit., raven] (1838) **:** the centime of Switzerland

rap·per \'ra-pər\ n (1640) **:** one that raps or is used for rapping: as **a :** a door knocker **b :** a performer of rap music

rap·port \ra-'pōr, rə-, -'pȯr\ n [F, fr. rapporter to bring back, refer, fr. OF raporter to bring back, fr. re- + aporter to bring, fr. L apportare, fr. ad- ad- + portare to carry — more at FARE] (ca. 1661) **:** RELATION; esp **:** relation marked by harmony, conformity, accord, or affinity

rap·por·teur \ˌra-ˌpȯr-'tər, -ˌpȯr-\ n [MF, fr. rapporter to bring back, report] (ca. 1500) **:** a person who gives reports (as at a meeting of a learned society)

rap·proche·ment \ˌra-ˌprōsh-'mäⁿ, -ˌprȯsh-; ra-'prōsh-\ n [F, fr. rapprocher to bring together, fr. MF, fr. re- + approcher to approach, fr. OF aprochier] (1809) **:** establishment of or state of having cordial relations

rap·scal·lion \rap-'skal-yən\ n [alter. of earlier rascallion, irreg. fr. rascal] (1699) **:** RASCAL, NE'ER-DO-WELL

rap sheet n (1960) **:** a police arrest record esp. for an individual

rapt \'rapt\ adj [ME, fr. L raptus, pp. of rapere to seize — more at RAPID] (14c) **1 :** lifted up and carried away **2 :** transported with emotion : ENRAPTURED **3 :** wholly absorbed : ENGROSSED — **rapt·ly** \'rap(t)-lē\ adv — **rapt·ness** \'rap(t)-nəs\ n

rap·tor \'rap-tər, -ˌtȯr\ n [NL Raptores, former order name, fr. L, pl. of raptor plunderer, fr. rapere] (1873) **:** BIRD OF PREY

rap·to·ri·al \rap-'tȯr-ē-əl, -'tȯr-\ adj (1823) **1 :** PREDACEOUS 1 **2 :** adapted to seize prey **3 :** of, relating to, or being a bird of prey

¹rap·ture \'rap-chər\ n [L raptus] (1629) **1 a :** a state or experience of being carried away by overwhelming emotion **b :** a mystical experience in which the spirit is exalted to a knowledge of divine things **2 :** an expression or manifestation of ecstasy or passion **syn** see ECSTASY — **rap·tur·ous** \'rap-chə-rəs, 'rap-shrəs\ adj — **rap·tur·ous·ly** adv — **rap·tur·ous·ness** n

²rapture vt **rap·tured; rap·tur·ing** (1637) **:** ENRAPTURE

rapture of the deep (1953) **:** NITROGEN NARCOSIS

ra·ra avis \ˌrar-ə-'ā-vəs, ˌrer-; ˌrär-ə-'ä-wəs\ n, pl **ra·ra avis·es** \-'ā-və-səz\ or **ra·rae aves** \ˌrär-ˌī-'ā-ˌwās\ [L, rare bird] (1607) **:** RARITY 2

¹rare \'rar, 'rer\ adj **rar·er; rar·est** [ME, fr. L rarus] (14c) **1 :** marked by wide separation of component particles : THIN ⟨∼ air⟩ **2 a :** marked by unusual quality, merit, or appeal : DISTINCTIVE **b :** superlative or extreme of its kind **3 :** seldom occurring or found : UNCOMMON **syn** see CHOICE, INFREQUENT — **rare·ness** n

²rare adj **rar·er; rar·est** [alter. of earlier rere, fr. ME, fr. OE hrēre boiled lightly; akin to OE hrēran to stir, OHG hruoren] (1784) **:** cooked so that the inside is still red ⟨∼ roast beef⟩

rare bird n (1890) **:** RARITY 2, RARA AVIS

rare·bit \'rar-bət, 'rer-\ n [(Welsh) rarebit] (ca. 1785) **:** WELSH RABBIT

rare earth n (1875) **1 :** any of a group of similar oxides of metals or a mixture of such oxides occurring together in widely distributed but relatively scarce minerals **2 :** RARE EARTH ELEMENT

rare earth element n (1942) **:** any of a series of metallic elements of which the oxides are classed as rare earths and which include the elements of the lanthanide series and sometimes yttrium and scandium — called also rare earth metal

rar·ee-show \'rar-ē-ˌshō, 'rer-\ n [alter. of rare show] (1684) **:** a small display or scene viewed in a box : PEEP SHOW; broadly **:** an unusual or amazing show or spectacle

rar·e·fac·tion \ˌrar-ə-'fak-shən, ˌrer-\ n [F or ML; F raréfaction, fr. ML rarefactio-, rarefactio, fr. L rarefacere to rarefy] (1603) **1 :** the action or process of rarefying **2 :** the quality or state of being rarefied **3 :** a state or region of minimum pressure in a medium traversed by compressional waves (as sound waves) — **rar·e·fac·tion·al** \-shnəl, -shə-nᵊl\ adj

rar·e·fied also **rar·i·fied** \'rar-ə-ˌfīd, 'rer-\ adj (1941) **1 :** of, relating to, or interesting to a select group : ESOTERIC **2 :** very high

rar·e·fy also **rar·i·fy** \-ə-ˌfī\ vb **-fied; -fy·ing** [ME rarefien, rarifien, fr. MF rarefier, modif. of L rarefacere, fr. rarus rare + facere to make — more at DO] vt (14c) **1 :** to make rare, thin, porous, or less dense **:** to expand without the addition of matter **2 :** to make more spiritual, refined, or abstruse ∼ vi **:** to become less dense

rare·ly \'rar-lē, 'rer-\ adv (1552) **1 :** not often : SELDOM **2 :** with rare skill : EXCELLENTLY **3 :** in an extreme or exceptional manner

rare-ripe \'rar-ˌrīp, 'rer-\ n [E dial. rare early + E ripe] (1722) **1 :** an early ripening fruit or vegetable **2** dial **:** GREEN ONION

rar·ing \'rar-ən, 'rer-, -iŋ\ adj [fr. prp. of E dial. rare to rear, alter. of E rear] (1909) **:** full of enthusiasm or eagerness ⟨ready and ∼ to go⟩

rar·i·ty \'rar-ə-tē, 'rer-\ n, pl **-ties** (1542) **1 :** the quality, state, or fact of being rare **2 :** one that is rare

ras·bo·ra \raz-'bȯr-ə, -'bȯr-\ n [NL] (1931) **:** any of a genus (Rasbora) of tiny brilliantly colored cyprinid freshwater fishes often kept in tropical aquariums

ras·cal \'ras-kəl\ n [ME rascaile rabble, one of the rabble] (15c) **1 :** a mean, unprincipled, or dishonest person **2 :** a mischievous person or animal — **rascal** adj

ras·cal·i·ty \ra-'ska-lə-tē\ n, pl **-ties** (ca. 1577) **1 :** RABBLE **2 a :** the character or actions of a rascal : KNAVERY **b :** a rascally act

ras·cal·ly \'ras-kə-lē\ adj (1594) **:** of or characteristic of a rascal — **rascally** adv

rase \'rāz\ vt **rased; ras·ing** [ME, fr. MF raser, fr. (assumed) VL rasare, freq. of L radere to scrape, shave — more at RODENT] (14c) **1** archaic **:** ERASE **2** archaic **:** RAZE 2

¹rash \'rash\ adv [ME (northern dial.) rasch quickly; akin to OHG rasc fast] (15c) archaic **:** in a rash manner

²rash adj (1509) **1 :** marked by or proceeding from undue haste or lack of deliberation or caution **2** obs **:** quickly effective **syn** see ADVENTUROUS — **rash·ly** adv — **rash·ness** n

³rash n [obs. F rache scurf, fr. (assumed) VL rasica, fr. rasicare to scratch, fr. L rasus, pp. of radere] (1709) **1 :** an eruption on the body **2 :** a large number of instances in a short period ⟨a ∼ of complaints⟩

rash·er \'ra-shər\ n [perh. fr. obs. rash to cut, fr. ME rashen] (1592) **:** a thin slice of bacon or ham broiled or fried; also **:** a portion consisting of several such slices

¹rasp \'rasp\ vb [ME, fr. (assumed) MF rasper, of Gmc origin; akin to OHG raspōn to scrape together] vt (14c) **1 :** to rub with something rough; specif **:** to abrade with a rasp **2 :** to grate upon : IRRITATE **3 :** to utter in a raspy tone ∼ vi **1 :** SCRAPE **2 :** to produce a grating sound — **rasp·er** n — **rasp·ing·ly** \'ras-piŋ-lē\ adv

²rasp n (ca. 1512) **1 :** a coarse file with cutting points instead of lines **2 :** something used for rasping **3 a :** an act of rasping **b :** a rasping sound, sensation, or effect

rasp·ber·ry \'raz-ˌber-ē, -b(ə-)rē\ n [E dial. rasp raspberry + E berry] (ca. 1616) **1 a :** any of various usu. black or red edible berries that are aggregate fruits consisting of numerous small drupes on a fleshy receptacle and that are usu. rounder and smaller than the closely related blackberries **b :** a plant (genus Rubus) of the rose family that bears raspberries **2** [short for raspberry tart, rhyming slang for fart] **:** a sound of contempt made by protruding the tongue between the lips and expelling air forcibly to produce a vibration; broadly **:** an expression of disapproval or contempt

raspy \'ras-pē\ adj (1838) **1 :** HARSH, GRATING **2 :** IRRITABLE

Ras·ta \'ras-tə, 'räs-\ n (1955) **:** RASTAFARIAN — **Rasta** adj

Ras·ta·far·i·an \ˌras-tə-'far-ē-ən, ˌräs-tə-'fär-\ n [Ras Tafari, precoronation name of Haile Selassie] (1955) **:** an adherent of Rastafarianism — **Rastafarian** adj

Ras·ta·far·i·an·ism \-ē-ə-ˌni-zəm\ n (1968) **:** a religious cult among black Jamaicans that teaches the eventual redemption of blacks and their return to Africa, employs the ritualistic use of marijuana, forbids the cutting of hair, and venerates Haile Selassie as a god

ras·ter \'ras-tər\ n [G, fr. L raster, rastrum rake, fr. radere to scrape] (1934) **:** a scan pattern (as of the electron beam in a cathode-ray tube) in which an area is scanned from side to side in lines from top to bottom; also **:** a pattern of closely spaced rows of dots that form the image on a cathode-ray tube (as of a television or computer display)

ra·sure \'rā-shər, -zhər\ *n* [MF, fr. L *rasura*, fr. *rasus*, pp. of *radere*] (1508) : ERASURE, OBLITERATION

¹rat \'rat\ *n* [ME, fr. OE *ræt*; akin to OHG *ratta* rat and perh. to L *rodere* to gnaw — more at RODENT] (bef. 12c) **1 a** : any of numerous rodents (*Rattus* and related genera) differing from the related mice by considerably larger size and by structural details (as of the teeth) **b** : any of various similar rodents **2** : a contemptible person: as **a** : one who betrays or deserts friends or associates **b** : SCAB 3b **c** : IN-FORMER 2 **3** : a pad over which a woman's hair is arranged **4** : a person who spends much time esp. idly in a specified place ⟨a mall ∼⟩ — **rat·like** \-ˌlīk\ *adj*

²rat *vb* **rat·ted; rat·ting** *vi* (1812) **1** : to betray, desert, or inform on one's associates — usu. used with *on* **2** : to catch or hunt rats **3** : to work as a scab ∼ *vt* : to give (hair) the effect of greater quantity by use of a rat

rat·able *or* **rate·able** \'rā-tə-bəl\ *adj* (1503) : capable of being rated, estimated, or apportioned — **rat·ably** \-blē\ *adv*

rat·a·fia \ˌra-tə-ˈfē-ə\ *n* [F] (1699) **1** : a liqueur made from an infusion of macerated fruit or fruit juice in a liquor (as brandy) and often flavored with almonds **2** : a sweet biscuit made of almond paste

rat-a-plan \ˌra-tə-ˌplan\ *n* [F, of imit. origin] (ca. 1848) : the iterative sound of beating ⟨a rolling ∼ of drums⟩ —*Time*)

rat–a–tat \'ra-tə-ˌtat\ *or* **rat–a–tat–tat** \ˌra-tə-ˌta(t)-'tat\ *n* [imit.] (1681) : a rapid succession of knocking, tapping, or cracking sounds

ra·ta·tou·ille \ˌra-ˌta-'twē, ˌrä-ˌtä-, -'tü-ē\ *n* [F, fr. blend of *ratouiller* to disturb, shake and *tatouiller* to stir] (ca. 1877) : a seasoned stew made of eggplant, tomatoes, green peppers, squash, and sometimes meat

rat·bag \'rat-ˌbag\ *n* (1890) *chiefly Austral* : a stupid, eccentric, or disagreeable person

rat–bite fever *n* (1910) : either of two febrile bacterial diseases of humans usu. transmitted by the bite of a rat

rat cheese *n* (1939) : CHEDDAR

¹ratch·et \'ra-chət\ *n* [alter. of earlier *rochet*, fr. F, alter. of MF *rocquet* ratchet, bobbin, of Gmc origin; akin to OHG *rocko* distaff — more at ROCK] (1654) **1** : a mechanism that consists of a bar or wheel having inclined teeth into which a pawl drops so that motion can be imparted to the wheel or bar, governed, or prevented and that is used in a hand tool (as a wrench or screwdriver) to allow effective motion in one direction only **2** : a pawl or detent for holding or propelling a ratchet wheel

²ratchet *vt* (1973) : to cause to move by steps or degrees — usu. used with *up* or *down* ⟨tried to ∼ down the debt⟩ ∼ *vi* : to proceed by steps or degrees

ratchet wheel *n* (1777) : a toothed wheel held in position or turned by an engaging pawl

ratchet wheel: *1* wheel, *2* reciprocating lever, *3* pawl for communicating motion, *4* pawl for preventing backward motion

¹rate \'rāt\ *vb* **rat·ed; rat·ing** [ME] *vt* (14c) **1** : to rebuke angrily or violently **2** *obs* : to drive away by scolding ∼ *vi* : to voice angry reprimands

²rate *n* [ME, fr. MF, fr. ML *rata*, fr. L (*pro*) *rata* (*parte*) according to a fixed proportion] (15c) **1 a** : reckoned value : VALUATION **b** *obs* : ESTIMATION **2** *obs* : a fixed quantity **3 a** : a fixed ratio between two things **b** : a charge, payment, or price fixed according to a ratio, scale, or standard: as (1) : a charge per unit of a public-service commodity (2) : a charge per unit of freight or passenger service (3) : a unit charge or ratio used by a government for assessing property taxes (4) *Brit* : a local tax **4 a** : a quantity, amount, or degree of something measured per unit of something else **b** : an amount of payment or charge based on another amount; *specif* : the amount of premium per unit of insurance **5** : relative condition or quality : CLASS — **at any rate** : in any case : ANYWAY

³rate *vb* **rat·ed; rat·ing** *vt* (15c) **1** *obs* : ALLOT **2 a** : to set an estimate on : VALUE, ESTEEM ⟨black is *rated* very high this season⟩ **b** : to determine or assign the relative rank or class of : GRADE ⟨∼ a seaman⟩ **c** : to estimate the normal capacity or power of **3** : CONSIDER, REGARD ⟨was *rated* an excellent pianist⟩ **4** : to fix the amount of premium to be charged per unit of insurance on **5** : to have a right to : DESERVE ⟨she *rated* special privileges⟩ ∼ *vi* : to enjoy a status of special privilege ⟨rarely ∼s with the boss⟩ *syn* see ESTIMATE

ra·tel \'rä-t²l, 'rā-\ *n* [Afrik, lit., rattle, fr. D, fr. MD — more at RATTLE] (1777) : an African or Asian nocturnal carnivorous mammal (*Mellivora capensis*) of the weasel family that resembles a badger

rate·me·ter \'rāt-ˌmē-tər\ *n* (1949) : an instrument that indicates the counting rate of an electronic counter

rate of change (ca. 1939) : a value that results from dividing the change in a function of a variable by the change in the variable ⟨velocity is the *rate of change* in distance with respect to time⟩

rate of exchange (ca. 1741) : the amount of one currency that will buy a given amount of another

rate of interest (1785) : the percentage usu. on an annual basis that is paid for the use of money borrowed from another

rate·pay·er \'rāt-ˌpā-ər\ *n* (1845) **1** *Brit* : TAXPAYER **2** : one who pays for the consumption of electricity according to established rates

rat·er \'rā-tər\ *n* (1611) **1** : one that rates; *specif* : a person who estimates or determines a rating **2** : one having a specified rating or class — usu. used in combination ⟨first-*rater*⟩

rat fink *n* (1964) : FINK, INFORMER

rat·fish \'rat-ˌfish\ *n* (1882) : CHIMAERA; *esp* : a silvery iridescent white-spotted chimaera (*Hydrolagus colliei*) of cold deep waters of the Pacific coast of No. America

rathe \'rāth, 'rath\ *adj* [ME, quick, fr. OE *hræth*, alter. of *hræd*; akin to OHG *hrad* quick] (14c) *archaic* : EARLY ⟨bring the ∼ primrose that forsaken dies —John Milton⟩

rath·er \'ra-thər, 'rä-, 'rə- *also* 're-; *interjectionally* 'ra-'thər, 'rä-\ *adv* [ME, fr. OE *hrathor*, compar. of *hrathe* quickly; akin to OHG *rado* quickly, OE *hræd* quick] (bef. 12c) **1** : with better reason or more propriety : more properly ⟨this you should pity ∼ than despise — Shak.⟩ **2** : more readily or willingly : PREFERABLY ⟨I'd ∼ not go⟩ ⟨would ∼ read than watch television⟩ — often used interjectionally to express affirmation **3** : more correctly speaking ⟨my father, or ∼ my stepfather⟩ **4** : to the contrary : INSTEAD ⟨was no better but ∼ grew

worse —Mk 5:26 (RSV)⟩ **5** : in some degree : SOMEWHAT ⟨it's ∼ warm⟩ — often used as a mild intensive ⟨spent ∼ a lot of money⟩ — **the rather** *archaic* : the more quickly or readily

rather than *conj* (14c) : and not ⟨obscures *rather than* resolves the problem⟩ ⟨why do one thing *rather than* another?⟩

raths·kel·ler \'rät-ˌske-lər, 'rat-, 'rath-\ *n* [obs. G (now *Ratskeller*), city-hall basement restaurant, fr. *Rat* council + *Keller* cellar] (1900) : a usu. basement tavern or restaurant

rat·i·cide \'ra-tə-ˌsīd\ *n* (1908) : a substance for killing rats

rat·i·fy \'ra-tə-ˌfī\ *vt* **-fied; -fy·ing** [ME *ratifien*, fr. MF *ratifier*, fr. ML *ratificare*, fr. L *ratus* determined, fr. pp. of *reri* to calculate — more at REASON] (14c) : to approve and sanction formally : CONFIRM ⟨∼ a treaty⟩ — **rat·i·fi·ca·tion** \ˌra-tə-fə-ˈkā-shən\ *n* — **rat·i·fi·er** \'ra-tə-ˌfī(-ə)r\ *n*

ra·ti·né \ˌra-tə-'nā\ *or* **ra·tine** \ˌra-tə-'nā, ra-'tēn\ *n* [F *ratiné*] (ca. 1914) **1** : a nubby ply yarn of various fibers made by twisting under tension a thick and a thin yarn **2** : a rough bulky fabric usu. woven loosely in plain weave from ratiné yarns

rat·ing \'rā-tiŋ\ *n* (1702) **1** : a classification according to grade; *specif* : a military or naval specialist classification **2** *chiefly Brit* : a naval enlisted man **3 a** : relative estimate or evaluation : STANDING ⟨the school has a good academic ∼⟩ **b** : an estimate of an individual's or business's credit and responsibility **c** : an estimate of the percentage of the public listening to or viewing a particular radio or television program **4** : a stated operating limit of a machine expressible in power units (as kilowatts of a direct-current generator) or in characteristics (as voltage)

ra·tio \'rā-(ˌ)shō, -shē-ˌō\ *n, pl* **ra·tios** [L, computation, reason — more at REASON] (1660) **1 a** : the indicated quotient of two mathematical expressions **b** : the relationship in quantity, amount, or size between two or more things : PROPORTION **2** : the expression of the relative values of gold and silver as determined by a country's currency laws

ra·ti·o·ci·nate \ˌra-tē-'ō-sə-ˌnāt, ˌra-shē-, -'ä-\ *vi* **-nat·ed; -nat·ing** [L *ratiocinatus*, pp. of *ratiocinari* to reckon, fr. *ratio* + *-cinari* (as in *vaticinari* to prophesy) — more at VATICINATE] (1643) : REASON — **ra·ti·o·ci·na·tor** \-ˌā-tər\ *n*

ra·ti·o·ci·na·tion \-ˌō-s²n-'ā-shən, -ˌä-\ *n* (ca. 1530) **1** : the process of exact thinking : REASONING **2** : a reasoned train of thought — **ra·ti·o·ci·na·tive** \-'ō-s²n-ˌā-tiv, -'ä-\ *adj*

¹ra·tion \'ra-shən, 'rā-\ *n* [F, fr. L *ration-, ratio* computation, reason] (ca. 1711) **1 a** : a food allowance for one day **b** *pl* : FOOD, PROVISIONS **2** : a share esp. as determined by supply

²ration *vt* **ra·tioned; ra·tion·ing** \'ra-sh(ə-)niŋ, 'rā-\ (1859) **1** : to supply with or put on rations **2 a** : to distribute as rations — often used with *out* **b** : to distribute equitably **c** : to use sparingly

¹ra·tio·nal \'rash-nəl, 'ra-shə-n²l\ *adj* [ME *racional*, fr. L *rationalis*, fr. *ration-, ratio*] (14c) **1 a** : having reason or understanding **b** : relating to, based on, or agreeable to reason : REASONABLE ⟨a ∼ explanation⟩ ⟨∼ behavior⟩ **2** : involving only multiplication, division, addition, and subtraction and only a finite number of times **3** : relating to, consisting of, or being one or more rational numbers ⟨a ∼ root of an equation⟩ — **ra·tio·nal·ly** *adv* — **ra·tio·nal·ness** *n*

²rational *n* (1606) : something rational; *specif* : RATIONAL NUMBER

ra·tio·nale \ˌra-shə-'nal\ *n* [L, neut. of *rationalis*] (1657) **1** : an explanation of controlling principles of opinion, belief, practice, or phenomena **2** : an underlying reason : BASIS

rational function *n* (1885) : a function that is the quotient of two polynomials; *also* : POLYNOMIAL

ra·tio·nal·ise *Brit var of* RATIONALIZE

ra·tio·nal·ism \'rash-nə-ˌli-zəm, 'ra-shə-n²l-ˌi-\ *n* (1827) **1** : reliance on reason as the basis for establishment of religious truth **2 a** : a theory that reason is in itself a source of knowledge superior to and independent of sense perceptions **b** : a view that reason and experience rather than the nonrational are the fundamental criteria in the solution of problems **3** : FUNCTIONALISM — **ra·tio·nal·ist** \-nə-list, -n²l-ist\ *n* — **rationalist** *or* **ra·tio·nal·is·tic** \ˌrash-nə-'lis-tik, ˌra-shə-n²l-'is-\ *adj* — **ra·tio·nal·is·ti·cal·ly** \-ti-k(ə-)lē\ *adv*

ra·tio·nal·i·ty \ˌra-shə-'na-lə-tē\ *n, pl* **-ties** (1628) **1** : the quality or state of being rational **2** : the quality or state of being agreeable to reason : REASONABLENESS **3** : a rational opinion, belief, or practice — usu. used in pl.

ra·tio·nal·ize \'rash-nə-ˌlīz, 'ra-shə-n²l-ˌīz\ *vb* **-ized; -iz·ing** *vt* (1803) **1** : to free (a mathematical expression) from irrational parts ⟨∼ a denominator⟩ **2** : to bring into accord with reason or cause something to seem reasonable: as **a** : to substitute a natural for a supernatural explanation of ⟨∼ a myth⟩ **b** : to attribute (one's actions) to rational and creditable motives without analysis of true and esp. unconscious motives ⟨*rationalized* his dislike of his brother⟩ **3** : to apply the principles of scientific management to (as an industry or its operations) for a desired result (as increased efficiency) ∼ *vi* : to provide plausible but untrue reasons for conduct — **ra·tio·nal·iz·able** \ˌrash-nə-'lī-zə-bəl, ˌra-shə-n²l-'ī-\ *adj* — **ra·tio·nal·i·za·tion** \ˌrash-nə-lə-'zā-shən, ˌra-shə-n²l-ə-\ *n* — **ra·tio·nal·iz·er** \'rash-nə-ˌlī-zər, 'ra-shə-n²l-ˌī-\ *n*

rational number *n* (1904) : an integer or the quotient of an integer divided by a nonzero integer

rat·ite \'ra-ˌtīt\ *n* [ultim. fr. L *ratitus* marked with the figure of a raft, fr. *ratis* raft] (ca. 1890) : a bird with a flat breastbone; *esp* : any of various mostly flightless birds (as an ostrich, rhea, emu, moa, or kiwi) with small or rudimentary wings and no keel on the sternum that are prob. of polyphyletic origin and are assigned to a number of different orders — **ratite** *adj*

rat·line \'rat-lən\ *n* [ME *radelyng*] (15c) : any of the small transverse ropes attached to the shrouds of a ship so as to form the steps of a rope ladder

¹ra·toon \ra-'tün\ *n* [Sp *retoño*, fr. *retoñar* to sprout, fr. *re-* (fr. L) + *otoñar* to grow in autumn, fr. *otoño* autumn, fr. L *autumnus*] (1631) **1**

\ə\ abut \'ə\ kitten, F table \ər\ further \a\ ash \ā\ ace \ä\ mop, mar \aù\ out \ch\ chin \e\ bet \ē\ easy \g\ go \i\ hit \ī\ ice \j\ job \ŋ\ sing \ō\ go \ò\ law \òi\ boy \th\ thin \t̲h̲\ the \ü\ loot \ù\ foot \y\ yet \zh\ vision \á, k̲, ⁿ, œ, œ̄, ūe, ū̄e, ʸ\ see Guide to Pronunciation

: a shoot of a perennial plant (as sugarcane)　**2** : a crop (as of bananas) produced on ratoons

²**ra·toon** *vi* (1756) : to sprout or spring up from the root ～ *vt* : to grow or produce (a crop) from or on ratoons

rat race *n* (1939) : strenuous, wearisome, and usu. competitive activity or rush

rats \'rats\ *interj* (1890) — used to express disappointment, frustration, or disgust

rat snake *n* (1860) : any of numerous large harmless rat-eating colubrid snakes (esp. genus *Elaphe*) — called also *chicken snake*

rat·tail \'rat-ˌtāl\ *n* (1705)　**1** : a horse's tail with little or no hair　**2** : GRENADIER 2

rattail cactus *n* (1900) : a commonly cultivated tropical American cactus (*Aporocactus flagelliformis*) with showy crimson flowers

rat–tail file *n* (1744) : a round slender tapered file

rat·tan \ra-'tan, rə-\ *n* [Malay *rotan*] (1660)　**1** : a rattan cane or switch　**2 a** : a climbing palm (esp. of the genera *Calamus* and *Daemonorops*) with very long tough stems　**b** : a part of the stem of a rattan used esp. for walking sticks and wickerwork

rat·teen \ra-'tēn\ *n* [F *ratine*] (1685) *archaic* : a coarse woolen fabric

rat·ter \'ra-tər\ *n* (1857) : one that catches rats; *specif* : a rat-catching dog or cat

¹**rat·tle** \'ra-t⁽ə⁾l\ *vb* **rat·tled; rat·tling** \'rat-liŋ, 'ra-t⁽ə⁾l-iŋ\ [ME *ratelen*; akin to MD *ratel* rattle] *vi* (14c)　**1** : to make a rapid succession of short sharp noises ⟨the windows *rattled* in the wind⟩　**2** : to chatter incessantly and aimlessly　**3** : to move with a clatter or rattle; *also* : to be or move about in a place or station too large or grand ⟨*rattled* around the big old house⟩ ～ *vt*　**1** : to say, perform, or affect in a brisk lively fashion ⟨*rattled* off four magnificent backhands —Kim Chapin⟩　**2** : to cause to make a rattling sound　**3** : ROUSE; *specif* : to beat (a cover) for game　**4** : to upset to the point of loss of poise and composure　*syn* see EMBARRASS

²**rattle** *n* (1519)　**1 a** : a device that produces a rattle; *specif* : a case containing pellets used as a baby's toy　**b** : the sound-producing organ on a rattlesnake's tail　**2 a** : a rapid succession of sharp clattering sounds　**b** : NOISE, RACKET　**3** : a throat noise caused by air passing through mucus and heard esp. at the approach of death

³**rattle** *vt* **rat·tled; rat·tling** \'rat-liŋ, 'ra-t⁽ə⁾l-iŋ\ [irreg. fr. *ratline*] (1729) : to furnish with ratlines

rat·tle·brain \'ra-t⁽ə⁾l-ˌbrān\ *n* (1709) : a flighty or thoughtless person — **rat·tle·brained** \-ˌbrānd\ *adj*

rat·tler \'rat-lər, 'ra-t⁽ə⁾l-ər\ *n* (15c)　**1** : one that rattles　**2** : RATTLESNAKE

rat·tle·snake \'ra-t⁽ə⁾l-ˌsnāk\ *n* (1630) : any of the American pit vipers comprising two genera (*Crotalus* and *Sistrurus*) and having horny interlocking joints at the end of the tail that make a sharp rattling sound when shaken

rattlesnake plantain *n* (1778) : an orchid (genus *Goodyera*) with checked or mottled leaves

rattlesnake root *n* (1682) : any of various plants formerly believed to be distasteful to rattlesnakes or effective against their venom: as　**a** : any of a genus (*Prenanthes* and esp. *P. altissima*) of composite plants that have lobed or pinnatifid leaves and small heads of drooping ligulate flowers　**b** : SENECA SNAKEROOT

rattlesnake weed *n* (1760) : a hawkweed (*Hieracium venosum*) with purple-veined leaves

rat·tle·trap \'ra-t⁽ə⁾l-ˌtrap\ *n* (1822) : something rattly or rickety; *esp* : an old car — **rattletrap** *adj*

¹**rat·tling** \'rat-liŋ\ *adj* (1560)　**1** : LIVELY, BRISK ⟨moved at a ～ pace⟩　**2** : extraordinarily good : SPLENDID — **rat·tling·ly** \-liŋ-lē\ *adv*

²**rattling** *adv* (1829) : to an extreme degree : VERY ⟨a ～ good argument —E. A. Betts⟩

rat·tly \'rat-lē, 'ra-t⁽ə⁾l-ē\ *adj* (1881) : likely to rattle : making a rattle

rat·ton \'ra-t⁰n, 'rä-\ *n* [ME *raton*, dim. of *rat*, prob. of Gmc origin; akin to OE *ræt* rat] (14c) *chiefly dial* : RAT

rat·trap \'ra(t)-ˌtrap\ *n* (15c)　**1** : a trap for rats　**2** : a dirty dilapidated structure　**3** : a hopeless situation

rat trap cheese *n* (1927) : CHEDDAR

rat·ty \'ra-tē\ *adj* **rat·ti·er; -est** (1865)　**1 a** : infested with rats　**b** : of, relating to, or suggestive of a rat　**2** : SHABBY, UNKEMPT ⟨a ～ brown overcoat —John Lardner⟩　**3 a** : DESPICABLE, TREACHEROUS　**b** : IRRITABLE ⟨feeling ～ as hell —Richard Bissell⟩

rau·cous \'ro-kəs\ *adj* [L *raucus* hoarse; akin to L *ravis* hoarseness] (1769)　**1** : disagreeably harsh or strident : HOARSE ⟨～ voices⟩　**2** : boisterously disorderly ⟨a . . . ～ frontier town —Truman Capote⟩　*syn* see LOUD — **rau·cous·ly** *adv* — **rau·cous·ness** *n*

raunch \'ronch, 'ränch\ *n* [back-formation fr. *raunchy*] (1964) : VULGARITY, LEWDNESS

raun·chy \'ron-chē, 'rän-\ *adj* **raun·chi·er; -est** [origin unknown] (1939)　**1** : SLOVENLY, DIRTY ⟨a ～ panhandler⟩; *also* : very smelly ⟨～ sneakers⟩　**2** : OBSCENE, SMUTTY ⟨～ jokes⟩ — **raun·chi·ly** \'ron-chə-lē, 'rän-\ *adv* — **raun·chi·ness** \-chē-nəs\ *n*

rau·wol·fia \raù-'wùl-fē-ə, rȯ-\ *n* [NL, fr. Leonhard *Rauwolf* †1596 Ger. botanist] (1752)　**1** : any of a large pantropical genus (*Rauwolfia* syn. *Rauwolfia*) of somewhat poisonous trees and shrubs of the dogbane family that yield emetic and purgative substances　**2** : a medicinal extract from the root of an Asian rauwolfia (*Rauwolfia serpentina*) used in the treatment of hypertension and mental disorders

¹**rav·age** \'ra-vij\ *n* [F, fr. MF, fr. *ravir* to ravish — more at RAVISH] (ca. 1611)　**1** : an act or practice of ravaging　**2** : damage resulting from ravaging : violently destructive effect ⟨the ～s of time⟩

²**ravage** *vb* **rav·aged; rav·ag·ing** *vt* (ca. 1611) : to wreak havoc on : affect destructively ～ *vi* : to commit destructive actions — **rav·age·ment** \-vij-mənt\ *n* — **rav·ag·er** *n*

syn RAVAGE, DEVASTATE, WASTE, SACK, PILLAGE, DESPOIL mean to lay waste by plundering or destroying. RAVAGE implies violent often cumulative depredation and destruction ⟨a hurricane *ravaged* the coast⟩. DEVASTATE implies the complete ruin and desolation of a wide area ⟨an earthquake *devastated* the city⟩. WASTE may imply producing the same

result by a slow process rather than sudden and violent action ⟨years of drought had *wasted* the area⟩. SACK implies carrying off all valuable possessions from a place ⟨barbarians *sacked* ancient Rome⟩. PILLAGE implies ruthless plundering at will but without the completeness suggested by SACK ⟨settlements *pillaged* by Vikings⟩. DESPOIL applies to looting or robbing of a place or person without suggesting accompanying destruction ⟨the Nazis *despoiled* the art museums⟩.

¹**rave** \'rāv\ *vb* **raved; rav·ing** [ME] *vi* (14c)　**1 a** : to talk irrationally in or as if in delirium　**b** : to speak out wildly　**c** : to talk with extreme enthusiasm ⟨*raved* about its beauty⟩　**2** : to move or advance violently : STORM ⟨the iced gusts still ～ and beat —John Keats⟩ ～ *vt* : to utter in madness or frenzy — **rav·er** *n*

²**rave** *n* (1598)　**1** : an act or instance of raving　**2** : an extravagantly favorable criticism ⟨the play received the critics' ～s⟩

¹**rav·el** \'ra-vəl\ *vb* **-eled** *or* **-elled; -el·ing** *or* **-el·ling** \'rav-liŋ, 'ra-və-\ [D *rafelen*, fr. *rafel* loose thread] *vt* (1582)　**1 a** : to separate or undo the texture of : UNRAVEL　**b** : to undo the intricacies of : DISENTANGLE　**2** : ENTANGLE, CONFUSE ～ *vi*　**1** *obs* : to become entangled or confused　**2** : to become unwoven, untwisted, or unwound : FRAY　**3** : BREAK UP, CRUMBLE — **rav·el·er** \'rav-lər, 'ra-və-\ *n* — **rav·el·ment** \'ra-vəl-mənt\ *n*

²**ravel** *n* (1634) : an act or result of raveling: as　**a** : something tangled　**b** : something raveled out; *specif* : a loose thread

rav·el·ing *or* **rav·el·ling** *n* (1658) : RAVEL b

¹**ra·ven** \'rā-vən\ *n* [ME, fr. OE *hræfn*; akin to OHG *hraban* raven, L *corvus*, Gk *korax*] (bef. 12c) : a large glossy black corvine bird (*Corvus corax*) of Europe, Asia, northern Africa, and America

²**raven** *adj* (1634) : shiny and black like a raven's feathers ⟨～ hair⟩

³**rav·en** \'ra-vən\ *vb* **rav·ened; rav·en·ing** \'ra-və-niŋ, 'rav-niŋ\ [MF *raviner* to rush, take by force, fr. *ravine* rapine] *vt* (1530)　**1** : to devour greedily　**2** : DESPOIL ⟨men . . . ～ the earth, destroying its resources —*New Yorker*⟩ ～ *vi*　**1** : to feed greedily　**2** : to prowl for food : PREY　**3** : PLUNDER — **rav·en·er** \'ra-və-nər, 'rav-nər\ *n*

raven

rav·en·ous \'ra-və-nəs, 'rav-nəs\ *adj* (15c)　**1** : RAPACIOUS ⟨～ wolves⟩　**2** : very eager or greedy for food, satisfaction, or gratification ⟨～ appetite⟩　*syn* see VORACIOUS — **rav·en·ous·ly** *adv* — **rav·en·ous·ness** *n*

rav·in \'ra-vən\ *n* [ME, fr. MF *ravine*] (14c)　**1** : PLUNDER, PILLAGE　**2 a** : an act or habit of preying　**b** : something seized as prey

ra·vine \rə-'vēn\ *n* [F, fr. MF, rapine, rush, fr. L *rapina* rapine] (1760) : a small narrow steep-sided valley that is larger than a gully and smaller than a canyon and that is usu. worn by running water

rav·ined \'ra-vənd\ *adj* (1606) *obs* : RAPACIOUS, RAVENOUS

¹**rav·ing** \'rā-viŋ\ *adj* (14c) : irrational, incoherent, wild, or extravagant utterance or declamation — usu. used in pl.

²**raving** *adj* (15c)　**1** : talking wildly or irrationally ⟨a ～ lunatic⟩　**2** : RAVISHING ⟨a ～ beauty⟩

rav·i·o·li \ˌra-vē-'ō-lē, ˌrä-\ *n, pl* **ravioli** *also* **rav·i·o·lis** \-lēz\ [It, fr. It dial., pl. of *raviolo*, lit., little turnip, dim. of *rava* turnip, fr. L *rapa* — more at RAPE] (ca. 1611) : pasta in the form of little cases of dough containing a savory filling (as of meat or cheese)

rav·ish \'ra-vish\ *vt* [ME *ravisshen*, fr. MF *raviss-*, stem of *ravir*, fr. (assumed) VL *rapire*, alter. of L *rapere* to seize, rob — more at RAPID] (14c)　**1 a** : to seize and take away by violence　**b** : to overcome with emotion (as joy or delight) ⟨～ed by the scenic beauty⟩　**c** : RAPE 2　**2** : PLUNDER, ROB — **rav·ish·er** *n* — **rav·ish·ment** \-mənt\ *n*

rav·ish·ing \'ra-vi-shiŋ\ *adj* (14c) : unusually attractive, pleasing, or striking — **rav·ish·ing·ly** \-shiŋ-lē\ *adv*

¹**raw** \'rȯ\ *adj* **raw·er** \'rȯ(-ə)r\; **raw·est** \'rȯ-əst\ [ME, fr. OE *hrēaw*; akin to OHG *hrō* raw, L *crudus* raw, *cruor* blood, Gk *kreas* flesh] (bef. 12c)　**1** : not cooked　**2 a** (1) : being in or nearly in the natural state : not processed or purified ⟨～ fibers⟩ ⟨～ sewage⟩　(2) : not diluted or blended ⟨～ spirits⟩　**b** : unprepared or imperfectly prepared for use　**c** : not being in polished, finished, or processed form ⟨～ data⟩ ⟨a ～ draft of a thesis⟩　**3 a** (1) : having the surface abraded or chafed　(2) : very irritated ⟨a ～ sore throat⟩　**b** : lacking covering : NAKED　**c** : not protected : susceptible to hurt ⟨～ emotions⟩　**4 a** : lacking experience or understanding : GREEN ⟨a ～ recruit⟩　**b** (1) : marked by absence of refinements　(2) : VULGAR, COARSE　**c** : not tempered : UNBRIDLED ⟨～ power⟩　**5** : disagreeably damp or cold　*syn* see RUDE — **raw·ly** *adv* — **raw·ness** *n*

²**raw** *n* (1823) : a raw place or state — **in the raw**　**1** : in a natural, unrefined, or crude state　**2** : NAKED ⟨slept *in the raw*⟩

raw bar *n* (1943) : a counter (as in a restaurant) that serves raw shellfish

raw·boned \'rȯ-ˌbōnd\ *adj* (1591) : relatively thin with prominent bone structure; *also* : heavy-framed and rugged but not attractively built　*syn* see LEAN

raw deal *n* (ca. 1912) : an instance of unfair treatment

¹**raw·hide** \'rȯ-ˌhīd\ *n* (1829)　**1** : a whip of untanned hide　**2** : untanned cattle skin

²**rawhide** *vt* **raw·hid·ed; raw·hid·ing** (1858)　**1** : to whip or drive with or as if with a rawhide　**2** : CHASTISE 2

ra·win·sonde \'rā-wən-ˌsänd\ *n* [*radar* + *wind* + radio*sonde*] (1946) : a radiosonde tracked by a radio direction-finding device to determine the velocity of winds aloft

raw material *n* (1796) : crude or processed material that can be converted by manufacture, processing, or combination into a new and useful product ⟨wheat . . . is *raw material* for the flour mill —C. A. Koepke⟩; *broadly* : something with a potential for improvement, development, or elaboration ⟨perplexities are often the *raw material* of discoveries —Agnes M. Clerke⟩

raw score *n* (1920) : an individual's actual achievement score (as on a test) before being adjusted for relative position in the test group

rax \'raks\ *vb* [ME (northern dial.) *raxen*, fr. OE *raxan*; akin to OE *reccan* to stretch — more at RACK] (bef. 12c) *chiefly Scot* : STRETCH

¹ray \'rā\ *n* [ME *raye*, fr. MF *raie*, fr. L *raia*] (14c) : any of an order (Rajiformes) of cartilaginous fishes (as stingrays and skates) having the body flattened dorsoventrally, the eyes on the upper surface, and enlarged pectoral fins fused with the head

²ray *n* [ME, fr. MF *rai*, fr. L *radius* rod, ray] (14c) **1 a** : any of the lines of light that appear to radiate from a bright object **b** : a beam of radiant energy (as light) of small cross section **c** (1) : a stream of material particles traveling in the same line (as in radioactive phenomena) (2) : a single particle of such a stream **2 a** : light cast by rays : RADIANCE **b** : a moral or intellectual light **3** : a thin line suggesting a ray: as **a** : any of a group of lines diverging from a common center **b** : HALF LINE **4 a** : one of the bony rods that extend and support the membrane in the fin of a fish **b** : one of the radiating divisions of the body of a radiate animal (as a starfish) **5 a** : a branch or flower stalk of an umbel **b** (1) : MEDULLARY RAY (2) : VASCULAR RAY **c** : RAY FLOWER 1 **6** : PARTICLE, TRACE ⟨~ of hope⟩ — **rayed** \'rād\ *adj*

³ray *vi* (1598) **1 a** : to shine in or as if in rays **b** : to issue as rays **2** : to extend like the radii of a circle : RADIATE ~ *vt* **1** : to emit in rays **2** : to furnish or mark with rays

ray flower *n* (1842) **1** : one of the marginal flowers of the head in a composite plant (as the aster) that also has disk flowers **2** : the entire head in a plant (as chicory) that lacks disk flowers

Ray·leigh scattering \'rā-lē-\ *n* [John W. S. *Rayleigh*] (1937) : scattering of light by particles small enough to render the effect selective so that different colors are deflected through different angles

ray·less \'rā-ləs\ *adj* (1747) : having, admitting, or emitting no rays; *esp* : DARK — **ray·less·ness** *n*

rayless goldenrod *n* (1923) : a shrubby to herbaceous composite plant (*Haplopappus heterophyllus* syn. *Isocoma wrightii*) esp. of open saline ground from Texas to Arizona and northern Mexico that lacks ray flowers and causes trembles in cattle

ray·on \'rā-ˌän\ *n* [irreg. fr. ²*ray*] (1924) **1** : any of a group of smooth textile fibers made from regenerated cellulose by extrusion through minute holes **2** : a rayon yarn, thread, or fabric

raze \'rāz\ *vt* **razed; raz·ing** [alter. of *rase*] (1536) **1 a** *archaic* : ERASE **b** : to scrape, cut, or shave off **2** : to destroy to the ground : DEMOLISH — **raz·er** *n*

ra·zee \rä-'zē\ *n* [F (*vaisseau*) *rasé*, lit., cut-off ship] (1794) : a wooden warship with the upper deck cut away

ra·zor \'rā-zər\ *n* [ME *rasour*, fr. OF *raseor*, fr. *raser* to raze, shave — more at RASE] (14c) : a keen-edged cutting instrument for shaving or cutting hair

ra·zor·back \'rā-zər-ˌbak\ *n* (1849) : a thin-bodied long-legged feral hog chiefly of the southeastern U.S.

ra·zor–backed \-ˌbakt\ *or* **ra·zor·back** \-ˌbak\ *adj* (1829) : having a sharp narrow back ⟨a ~ horse⟩

ra·zor·bill \-ˌbil\ *n* (1674) : a No. Atlantic auk (*Alca torda*) with the plumage black above and white below and a compressed sharp-edged bill — called also *razor-billed auk*

razor clam *n* (1882) : any of a family (Solenidae) of marine bivalve mollusks having a long narrow thin shell

¹razz \'raz\ *n* [short for *razzberry* sound of contempt, alter. of *raspberry*] (ca. 1919) : RASPBERRY 2

²razz *vt* (1921) : HECKLE, DERIDE ⟨the fans ~ed the visiting players⟩

razz·a·ma·tazz \ˌra-zə-mə-'taz\ *chiefly Brit var of* RAZZMATAZZ

raz·zle–daz·zle \ˌra-zəl-'da-zəl\ *n* [redupl. of *dazzle*] (1889) **1** : a state of confusion or hilarity **2** : a complex maneuver (as in sports) designed to confuse an opponent **3** : a confusing or colorful often gaudy action or display — **razzle–dazzle** *adj*

razz·ma·tazz \ˌraz-mə-'taz\ *n* [prob. alter. of razzle-dazzle] (1942) **1** : RAZZLE-DAZZLE 3 **2** : DOUBLE-TALK 2 **3** : VIM, ZING

RBI \ˌär-(ˌ)bē-'ī, 'ri-bē\ *n, pl* **RBIs** *or* **RBI** [*run batted in*] (1948) : a run in baseball that is driven in by a batter; *also* : official credit to a batter for driving in a run ⟨led the league in ~s⟩

r color *n* (1937) : an acoustic effect of a simultaneously articulated \r\ imparted to a vowel by retroflexion or constriction of the tongue — **r–col·ored** \'är-ˌkə-lərd\ *adj*

-rd *symbol* — used after the figure 3 to indicate the ordinal number *third* ⟨3*rd*⟩ ⟨83*rd*⟩

¹re \'rā\ *n* [ML, fr. the syllable sung to this note in a medieval hymn to St. John the Baptist] (14c) : the 2d tone of the diatonic scale in solmization

²re \'rā, 'rē\ *prep* [L, abl. of *res* thing — more at REAL] (1707) : with regard to : IN RE

re- *prefix* [ME, fr. OF, fr. L *re-*, *red-* back, again, against] **1** : again : anew ⟨retell⟩ **2** : back : backward ⟨recall⟩

re·ac·cel·er·ate	re·an·i·ma·tion	re·as·sem·bly
re·ac·cept	re·an·nex	re·as·sert
re·ac·ces·sion	re·an·nex·a·tion	re·as·ser·tion
re·ac·cli·ma·tize	re·ap·pear	re·as·sess
re·ac·cred·it	re·ap·pear·ance	re·as·sess·ment
re·ac·cred·i·ta·tion	re·ap·pli·ca·tion	re·as·sign
re·ac·quaint	re·ap·ply	re·as·sign·ment
re·ac·quire	re·ap·point	re·as·sume
re·ac·qui·si·tion	re·ap·point·ment	re·at·tach
re·ac·ti·vate	re·ap·prais·al	re·at·tach·ment
re·ac·ti·va·tion	re·ap·praise	re·at·tain
re·ad·dress	re·ap·pro·pri·ate	re·at·tempt
re·ad·just	re·ap·prove	re·at·tri·bute
re·ad·just·ment	re·ar·gue	re·at·tri·bu·tion
re·ad·mis·sion	re·ar·gu·ment	re·au·tho·ri·za·tion
re·ad·mit	re·arous·al	re·au·tho·rize
re·adopt	re·arouse	re·awak·en
re·af·firm	re·ar·range	re·bait
re·af·fir·ma·tion	re·ar·range·ment	re·bal·ance
re·af·fix	re·ar·rest	re·bap·tism
re·al·lo·cate	re·ar·tic·u·late	re·bap·tize
re·al·lo·ca·tion	re·as·cend	re·be·gin
re·anal·y·sis	re·as·cent	re·bid
re·an·a·lyze	re·as·sem·blage	re·bind
re·an·i·mate	re·as·sem·ble	re·blend

re·bloom	re·dis·til·la·tion	re·ig·nite
re·board	re·di·vide	re·ig·ni·tion
re·boil	re·di·vi·sion	re·im·age
re·book	re·don	re·im·merse
re·boot	re·draft	re·im·plant
re·bore	re·draw	re·im·plan·ta·tion
re·bot·tle	re·dream	re·im·port
re·breed	re·drill	re·im·por·ta·tion
re·buri·al	re·dub	re·im·pose
re·bury	re·el·i·gi·bil·i·ty	re·im·po·si·tion
re·buy	re·el·i·gi·ble	re·in·cor·po·rate
re·cal·cu·late	re·emerge	re·in·cor·po·ra·tion
re·cal·cu·la·tion	re·emer·gence	re·in·dict
re·cal·i·brate	re·emis·sion	re·in·dict·ment
re·cal·i·bra·tion	re·emit	re·in·fes·ta·tion
re·cen·tral·i·za·tion	re·em·pha·sis	re·in·flate
re·cen·tri·fuge	re·em·pha·size	re·in·fla·tion
re·cer·ti·fi·ca·tion	re·em·ploy	re·in·hab·it
re·cer·ti·fy	re·em·ploy·ment	re·ini·ti·ate
re·chal·lenge	re·en·coun·ter	re·in·ject
re·chan·nel	re·en·dow	re·in·jec·tion
re·char·ter	re·en·er·gize	re·in·jure
re·check	re·en·gage	re·in·ju·ry
re·cho·reo·graph	re·en·gage·ment	re·ink
re·chris·ten	re·en·gi·neer	re·in·ner·vate
re–Chris·tian·ize	re·en·grave	re·in·ner·va·tion
re·chro·mato·graph	re·en·list	re·in·oc·u·late
re·chro·ma·tog·ra·phy	re·en·list·ment	re·in·oc·u·la·tion
re·cir·cu·late	re·en·roll	re·in·sert
re·cir·cu·la·tion	re·en·throne	re·in·ser·tion
re·clad	re·equip	re·in·spect
re·clas·si·fi·ca·tion	re·equip·ment	re·in·spec·tion
re·clas·si·fy	re·erect	re·in·spire
re·clothe	re·es·ca·late	re·in·stal
re·cock	re·es·ca·la·tion	re·in·stal·la·tion
re·cod·i·fi·ca·tion	re·es·tab·lish	re·in·sti·tute
re·cod·i·fy	re·es·tab·lish·ment	re·in·sti·tu·tion·al·i·za·tion
re·col·o·ni·za·tion	re·es·ti·mate	re·in·ter
re·col·o·nize	re·eval·u·ate	re·in·ter·view
re·col·or	re·eval·u·a·tion	re·in·tro·duce
re·com·bine	re·ex·am·i·na·tion	re·in·tro·duc·tion
re·com·mence	re·ex·am·ine	re·in·vade
re·com·mence·ment	re·ex·pe·ri·ence	re·in·va·sion
re·com·mis·sion	re·ex·plore	re·in·ves·ti·gate
re·com·pi·la·tion	re·ex·port	re·in·ves·ti·ga·tion
re·com·pile	re·ex·por·ta·tion	re·in·vig·o·rate
re·com·pu·ta·tion	re·ex·pose	re·in·vig·o·ra·tion
re·com·pute	re·ex·po·sure	re·in·vig·o·ra·tor
re·con·ceive	re·ex·press	re·jack·et
re·con·cen·trate	re·face	re·judge
re·con·cen·tra·tion	re·feed	re·jug·gle
re·con·cep·tion	re·feel	re·key
re·con·cep·tu·al·i·za·tion	re·fence	re·key·board
re·con·cep·tu·al·ize	re·fight	re·kin·dle
re·con·dense	re·fig·ure	re·knit
re·con·fig·u·ra·tion	re·file	re·la·bel
re·con·fig·ure	re·find	re·lac·quer
re·con·nect	re·fire	re·land·scape
re·con·nec·tion	re·fix	re·launch
re·con·quer	re·float	re·learn
re·con·quest	re·fold	re·lend
re·con·se·crate	re·forge	re·li·cense
re·con·se·cra·tion	re·for·mat	re·li·cen·sure
re·con·sol·i·date	re·for·mu·late	re·light
re·con·tact	re·for·mu·la·tion	re·link
re·con·tam·i·nate	re·for·ti·fi·ca·tion	re·liq·ue·fy
re·con·tam·i·na·tion	re·for·ti·fy	re·load
re·con·tex·tu·al·ize	re·found	re·lock
re·con·tour	re·foun·da·tion	re·look
re·con·vene	re·frame	re·lu·bri·cate
re·con·ver·sion	re·freeze	re·lu·bri·ca·tion
re·con·vert	re·fry	re·mar·ket
re·con·vict	re·fur·nish	re·mar·riage
re·con·vic·tion	re·gain	re·mar·ry
re·con·vince	re·gath·er	re·mate
re·copy	re·gear	re·ma·te·ri·al·ize
re·cork	re·gild	re·mea·sure
re·cross	re·give	re·mea·sure·ment
re·cul·ti·vate	re·glaze	re·meet
re·date	re·grade	re·melt
re·ded·i·cate	re·graft	re·merge
re·ded·i·ca·tion	re·grant	re·mi·gra·tion
re·de·fect	re·green	re·mil·i·ta·ri·za·tion
re·de·liv·er	re·grind	re·mil·i·ta·rize
re·de·liv·ery	re·groom	re·mix
re·de·pos·it	re·groove	re·mo·bi·li·za·tion
re·de·ter·mi·na·tion	re·growth	re·mo·bi·lize
re·de·ter·mine	re·han·dle	re·moist·en
re·di·ges·tion	re·hang	re·mold
re·dis·cov·er	re·heat	re·mon·e·ti·za·tion
re·dis·cov·ery	re·hinge	re·mon·e·tize
re·dis·cuss	re·hire	re·mo·ti·vate
re·dis·play	re·hos·pi·tal·i·za·tion	re·mo·ti·va·tion
re·dis·pose	re·hos·pi·tal·ize	re·my·thol·o·gize
re·dis·po·si·tion	re·hu·man·ize	re·nail
re·dis·solve	re·hyp·no·tize	re·name
re·dis·till	re·iden·ti·fy	re·na·tion·al·i·za·tion

\ə\ abut \ʰ\ kitten, F table \ər\ further \a\ ash \ā\ ace \ä\ mop, mar \au̇\ out \ch\ chin \e\ bet \ē\ easy \g\ go \i\ hit \ī\ ice \j\ job \ŋ\ sing \ō\ go \ȯ\ law \ȯi\ boy \th\ thin \t͟h\ the \ü\ loot \u̇\ foot \y\ yet \zh\ vision \à, k̲, ⁿ, œ, œ̄, ᵫ, ᵫ̄, ᵉ\ *see* Guide to Pronunciation

re·na·tion·al·ize
re·nest
re·num·ber
re·ob·serve
re·oc·cu·pa·tion
re·oc·cu·py
re·oc·cur
re·oc·cur·rence
re·oil
re·op·er·ate
re·op·er·a·tion
re·or·ches·trate
re·or·ches·tra·tion
re·ori·ent
re·ori·en·tate
re·ori·en·ta·tion
re·out·fit
re·ox·i·da·tion
re·ox·i·dize
re·pack
re·paint
re·park
re·patch
re·pat·tern
re·pave
re·peg
re·peo·ple
re·pho·to·graph
re·phrase
re·plan
re·plas·ter
re·plate
re·pledge
re·plot
re·plumb
re·pol·ish
re·poll
re·pop·u·lar·ize
re·pop·u·late
re·pop·u·la·tion
re·pot
re·pres·sur·ize
re·price
re·pri·vat·i·za·tion
re·pri·vat·ize
re·pro·vi·sion
re·pump
re·punc·tu·a·tion
re·pur·chase
re·pu·ri·fy
re·rack
re·raise
re·read
re·read·ing
re·re·cord
re·reg·is·ter
re·reg·is·tra·tion
re·reg·u·late
re·reg·u·la·tion

re·re·lease
re·re·mind
re·re·peat
re·re·view
re·rig
re·roof
re·route
re·sail
re·sam·ple
re·saw
re·school
re·score
re·screen
re·sculpt
re·seal
re·seal·able
re·sea·son
re·seat
re·se·cure
re·see
re·seg·re·gate
re·seg·re·ga·tion
re·sell
re·sell·er
re·sen·si·tize
re·sen·tence
re·ser·vice
re·set·tle
re·set·tle·ment
re·sew
re·shin·gle
re·shoe
re·shoot
re·show
re·sight
re·sil·ver
re·site
re·size
re·slate
re·soak
re·so·cial·i·za·tion
re·so·cial·ize
re·sod
re·sol·der
re·sole
re·so·lid·i·fi·ca·tion
re·so·lid·i·fy
re·sow
re·spir·i·tu·al·ize
re·spot
re·spray
re·sprout
re·sta·bi·lize
re·stack
re·stage
re·stamp
re·stim·u·late
re·stim·u·la·tion
re·stock

re·stoke
re·strength·en
re·stress
re·study
re·stuff
re·style
re·sub·mis·sion
re·sub·mit
re·sum·mon
re·sup·ply
re·sur·vey
re·syn·the·sis
re·syn·the·size
re·sys·tem·a·tize
re·tack·le
re·tag
re·tar·get
re·taste
re·teach
re·team
re·test
re·tex·ture
re·thread
re·tie
re·tight·en
re·tile
re·time
re·trace
re·trans·fer
re·trans·form
re·trans·for·ma·tion
re·trans·mis·sion
re·trans·mit
re·try
re·tune
re·type
re·uni·fy
re·uni·fi·ca·tion
re·up·hol·ster
re·uti·li·za·tion
re·uti·lize
re·vac·ci·nate
re·vac·ci·na·tion
re·val·i·date
re·val·i·da·tion
re·val·o·ri·za·tion
re·val·o·rize
re·vict·ual
re·vi·su·al·i·za·tion
re·vote
re·warm
re·wash
re·weigh
re·wet
re·wire
re·wrap
re·zone

're \(ə)r\ *vb* (1591) : ARE ⟨you're right⟩

re·ab·sorb \ˌrē-əb-ˈsȯrb, -ˈzȯrb\ *vt* (ca. 1774) : to take up (something previously secreted or emitted) ⟨sugars ~ed in the kidney⟩; *also* : RE-SORB 2

¹reach \ˈrēch\ *vb* [ME *rechen*, fr. OE *rǣcan*; akin to OHG *reichen* to reach, Lith *raižytis* to stretch oneself] *vt* (bef. 12c) 1 a : to stretch out : EXTEND b : THRUST 2 a : to touch or grasp by extending a part of the body (as a hand) or an object ⟨couldn't ~ the apple⟩ b : to pick up and draw toward one : TAKE c (1) : to extend to ⟨the shadow ~ed the wall⟩ (2) : to get up to or as far as : come to ⟨your letter ~ed me yesterday⟩ ⟨his voice ~ed the last rows⟩ ⟨they hoped to ~ an agreement⟩ d (1) : ENCOMPASS (2) : to make an impression on (3) : to communicate with 3 : to hand over : PASS ~ *vi* 1 a : to make a stretch with or as if with one's hand b : to strain after something 2 a : PROJECT, EXTEND ⟨his land ~es to the river⟩ b : to arrive at or come to something ⟨as far as the eye could ~⟩ 3 : to sail on a reach — **reach·able** \ˈrē-chə-bəl\ *adj* — **reach·er** *n*

²reach *n* (1536) 1 : a continuous stretch or expanse: as a : a straight portion of a stream or river 2 a (1) : the action or an act of reaching (2) : an individual part of a progression or journey b (1) : a reachable distance ⟨within ~⟩ (2) : ability to reach ⟨had a long ~⟩ c : an extent or range esp. of knowledge or comprehension 3 : a bearing shaft or coupling pole; *esp* : the rod joining the hind axle to the forward bolster of a wagon 4 : the tack sailed by a ship with the wind coming just forward of the beam or with the wind directly abeam or abaft the beam 5 : ECHELON, LEVEL — usu. used in pl. ⟨the higher ~es of academic life⟩

reach—me—down \ˈrēch-mē-ˌdau̇n\ *adj or n* (1862) *chiefly Brit* : HAND-ME-DOWN

re·act \rē-ˈakt\ *vb* [NL *reactus*, pp. of *reagere*, fr. L *re-* + *agere* to act — more at AGENT] *vi* (1644) 1 : to exert a reciprocal or counteracting force or influence — often used with *on* or *upon* 2 : to respond to a stimulus 3 : to act in opposition to a force or influence — usu. used with *against* 4 : to move or tend in a reverse direction 5 : to undergo chemical reaction ~ *vt* : to cause to react

re·ac·tance \rē-ˈak-tən(t)s\ *n* (1893) : the part of the impedance of an alternating-current circuit that is due to capacitance or inductance or both and that is expressed in ohms

re·ac·tant \-tənt\ *n* (ca. 1920) : a substance that enters into and is altered in the course of a chemical reaction

re·ac·tion \rē-ˈak-shən\ *n* (ca. 1611) 1 a : the act or process or an instance of reacting b : resistance or opposition to a force, influence, or movement; *esp* : tendency toward a former and usu. outmoded political or social order or policy 2 : a response to some treatment, situ-

ation, or stimulus ⟨her stunned ~ to the news⟩; *also* : such a response expressed verbally ⟨critical ~ to the play⟩ 3 : bodily response to or activity aroused by a stimulus: a : an action induced by vital resistance to another action; *esp* : the response of tissues to a foreign substance (as an antigen or infective agent) b : depression or exhaustion due to excessive exertion or stimulation c : heightened activity and overaction succeeding depression or shock d : a mental or emotional disorder forming an individual's response to his or her life situation 4 : the force that a body subjected to the action of a force from another body exerts in the opposite direction 5 a (1) : chemical transformation or change : the interaction of chemical entities (2) : the state resulting from such a reaction b : a process involving change in atomic nuclei

re·ac·tion·ary \rē-ˈak-shə-ˌner-ē\ *adj* (1840) : relating to, marked by, or favoring reaction; *esp* : ultraconservative in politics — **reactionary** *n* — **re·ac·tion·ary·ism** \-ˌi-zəm\ *n*

re·ac·tive \rē-ˈak-tiv\ *adj* (1794) 1 : of, relating to, or marked by reaction or reactance 2 a : readily responsive to a stimulus b : occurring as a result of stress or emotional upset ⟨~ depression⟩ — **re·ac·tive·ly** *adv* — **re·ac·tive·ness** *n* — **re·ac·tiv·i·ty** \(ˌ)rē-ˌak-ˈti-və-tē\ *n*

re·ac·tor \rē-ˈak-tər\ *n* (ca. 1904) 1 : one that reacts 2 : a device (as a coil, winding, or conductor of small resistance) used to introduce reactance into an alternating-current circuit 3 a : a vat for an industrial chemical reaction b : a device for the controlled release of nuclear energy (as for producing heat)

¹read \ˈrēd\ *vb* read \ˈred\; read·ing \ˈrē-diŋ\ [ME *reden* to advise, interpret, read, fr. OE *rǣdan* to advise, Skt *rādhnoti* he achieves, prepares] *vt* (bef. 12c) 1 a (1) : to receive or take in the sense of (as letters or symbols) esp. by sight or touch (2) : to study the movements of (as lips) with mental formulation of the communication expressed (3) : to utter aloud the printed or written words of ⟨~ them a story⟩ b : to learn from what one has seen or found in writing or printing c : to deliver aloud by or as if by reading; *specif* : to utter interpretively d (1) : to become acquainted with or look over the contents of (as a book) (2) : to make a study of ⟨~ law⟩ (3) : to read the works of e : to check (as copy or proof) for errors f (1) : to receive and understand (a voice message) by radio (2) : UNDERSTAND, COMPREHEND 2 a : to interpret the meaning or significance of ⟨~ palms⟩ b : FORETELL, PREDICT ⟨able to ~ his fortune⟩ 3 : to recognize or interpret as if by reading: as a : to learn the nature of by observing outward expression or signs ⟨~s him like a book⟩ b : to note the action or characteristics of in order to anticipate what will happen ⟨a good canoeist ~s the rapids⟩ ⟨a golfer ~ing a green⟩; *also* : to predict the movement of (a putt) by reading a green c : to anticipate by observation of an opponent's position or movement ⟨~ a blitz⟩ 4 a : to attribute a meaning to (as something read) : INTERPRET ⟨how do you ~ this passage⟩ b : to attribute (a meaning) to something read or considered ⟨~ a nonexistent meaning into her words⟩ 5 : to use as a substitute for or in preference to another word or phrase in a particular passage, text, or version ⟨~ *hurry* for *harry*⟩ — often used to introduce a clarifying substitute for a euphemistic or misleading word or phrase ⟨a friendly, ~ nosy, coworker⟩ 6 : INDICATE ⟨the thermometer ~s zero⟩ 7 : to interpret (a musical work) in performance 8 a : to acquire (information) from storage; *esp* : to sense the meaning of (data) in recorded and coded form — used of a computer or data processor b : to read the coded information on (as a floppy disk) ~ *vi* 1 a : to perform the act of reading words : read something b (1) : to learn something by reading (2) : to pursue a course of study 2 a : to yield a particular meaning or impression when read b : to be readable or read in a particular manner or to a particular degree ⟨this book ~s smoothly⟩ 3 : to consist of specific words, phrases, or other similar elements ⟨a passage that ~s differently in older versions⟩ — **read between the lines** : to understand more than is directly stated — **read the riot act** 1 : to order a mob to disperse 2 a : to order or warn to cease something b : to protest vehemently c : to reprimand severely

²read \ˈred\ *adj* (1586) : instructed by or informed through reading

³read \ˈrēd\ *n* (1825) 1 *chiefly Brit* : a period of reading ⟨it was a night . . . for a ~ and a long sleep —William Sansom⟩ 2 : something (as a book) that is read ⟨a novel that's a good ~⟩ 3 : the action or an instance of reading

read·able \ˈrē-də-bəl\ *adj* (15c) : able to be read easily: as a : LEGIBLE b : interesting to read — **read·abil·i·ty** \ˌrē-də-ˈbi-lə-tē\ *n* — **read·able·ness** \ˈrē-də-bəl-nəs\ *n* — **read·ably** \-blē\ *adv*

read·er \ˈrē-dər\ *n* (bef. 12c) 1 a : one that reads : one appointed to read to others: as (1) : LECTOR (2) : one chosen to read aloud selected material in a Christian Science church or society c (1) : PROOFREADER (2) : one who evaluates manuscripts (3) : one who reads periodical literature to discover items of special interest or value d : an employee who reads and records the indications of meters e : a teacher's assistant who reads and marks student papers 2 *Brit* : one who reads lectures or expounds subjects to students 3 a : a device for projecting a readable image of a transparency b : a unit that scans material recorded (as on punched cards) for storage or computation 4 a : a book for instruction and practice esp. in reading b : ANTHOLOGY

read·er·ly \-lē\ *adj* (1959) : of, relating to, or typical of a reader

read·er·ship \-ˌship\ *n* (1719) 1 a : the quality or state of being a reader b : the office or position of a reader 2 : the mass or a particular group of readers ⟨a magazine's ~⟩

read·i·ly \ˈre-də-lē\ *adv* (14c) : in a ready manner: as a : without hesitating : WILLINGLY ⟨~ accepted advice⟩ b : without much difficulty : EASILY ⟨for reasons that anyone could ~ understand⟩

read·ing \ˈrē-diŋ\ *n* (bef. 12c) 1 : the act of reading 2 a : material read or for reading b : extent of material read 3 a : a particular version b : data indicated by an instrument 4 a : a particular interpretation of something (as a law) b : a particular performance of something (as a musical work) 5 : an indication of a certain state of affairs ⟨a study to get some ~ of shoppers' preferences⟩

reading desk *n* (1703) : LECTERN

reading frame *n* (1965) : any of the three possible ways of reading a sequence of nucleotides as a series of triplets

read—only memory *n* (1961) : a usu. small computer memory that contains special-purpose information (as a program) which cannot be altered — called also *ROM*; compare RANDOM-ACCESS MEMORY

read·out \'rēd-ˌaut\ *n* (1652) **1 :** the process of reading **2 a :** the process of removing information from an automatic device (as an electronic computer) and displaying it in an understandable form **b :** the information removed from such a device and displayed or recorded (as by magnetic tape or printing device) **c :** an electronic device that presents information in visual form **3 :** the radio transmission of data or pictures from a space vehicle

read out *vt* (1600) **1 a :** to read aloud **b :** to produce a readout of **2 :** to expel from an organization or group

¹ready \'re-dē\ *adj* **read·i·er; -est** [ME *redy;* akin to OE *gerǣde* ready, Goth ga*raiths* arranged] (13c) **1 a :** prepared mentally or physically for some experience or action **b :** prepared for immediate use ⟨dinner is ∼⟩ **2 a :** willingly disposed : INCLINED ⟨∼ to agree to his proposal⟩ **b :** likely to do something indicated ⟨a house that looks ∼ to collapse⟩ **3 :** displayed readily and spontaneously ⟨a ∼ wit⟩ **4 :** immediately available ⟨had little ∼ cash⟩ *syn* see QUICK — **read·i·ness** *n* — **at the ready :** ready for immediate use ⟨kept their guns *at the ready*⟩

²ready *vt* **read·ied; ready·ing** (14c) **:** to make ready

ready box *n* (1942) **:** a box placed near a gun (as on a ship) to hold ammunition kept ready for immediate use

¹ready–made \ˌred-ē-'mād\ *adj* (15c) **1 :** made beforehand esp. for general sale ⟨∼ suits⟩ **2 :** lacking originality or individuality **3 :** readily available ⟨her illness provided a ∼ excuse⟩

²ready–made *n* (1882) **1 :** something (as a garment) that is ready‑made **2** *usu* **ready·made** [F *ready-made*, fr. E] **:** a commonplace artifact (as a comb or a pair of ice tongs) selected and displayed as a work of art

ready room *n* (1941) **:** a room in which pilots or astronauts are briefed and await orders

ready–to–wear *adj* (1895) **1** *of clothing* **:** READY-MADE **2 :** dealing in ready-made clothins ⟨∼ stores⟩ — **ready–to–wear** *n*

ready–wit·ted \ˌre-dē-'wi-təd\ *adj* (1581) **:** QUICK-WITTED

re·af·for·es·ta·tion \ˌrē-ə-ˌfōr-ə-'stā-shən, -ˌfär-\ *n* (1884) *chiefly Brit* **:** REFORESTATION — **re·af·for·est** \-'fōr-əst, -'fär-\ *vt, chiefly Brit*

re·agent \rē-'ā-jənt\ *n* [NL *reagent-, reagens,* prp. of *reagere* to react — more at REACT] (1797) **:** a substance used (as in detecting or measuring a component, in preparing a product, or in developing photographs) because of its chemical or biological activity

re·ag·gre·gate \(ˌ)rē-'a-gri-ˌgāt\ *vt* (1849) **:** to cause to re-form into an aggregate or a whole — **re·ag·gre·gate** \-gət\ *n* — **re·ag·gre·ga·tion** \-ˌa-gri-'gā-shən\ *n*

re·agin \rē-'ā-jən, -gən\ *n* [ISV, fr. *reagent*] (ca. 1911) **1 :** a substance in the blood of persons with syphilis responsible for positive serological reactions for syphilis **2 :** an antibody in the blood of individuals with some forms of allergy possessing the power of passively sensitizing the skin of normal individuals — **re·agin·ic** \ˌrē-ə-'ji-nik, -'gi-\ *adj*

¹re·al \'rē(-ə)l, 'ri(-ə)l\ *adj* [ME, real, relating to things (in law), fr. MF, fr. ML & LL; ML *realis* relating to things (in law), fr. LL, real, fr. L *res* thing, fact; akin to Skt *rayi* property] (14c) **1 :** of or relating to fixed, permanent, or immovable things (as lands or tenements) **2 a :** not artificial, fraudulent, illusory, or apparent : GENUINE ⟨∼ gold⟩; *also* **:** being precisely what the name implies ⟨a ∼ professional⟩ **b** (1) **:** occurring in fact ⟨a story of ∼ life⟩ (2) **:** of or relating to practical or everyday concerns or activities ⟨left school to live in the ∼ world⟩ (3) **:** existing as a physical entity and having properties that deviate from an ideal, law, or standard ⟨a ∼ gas⟩ — compare IDEAL 3b **c :** having objective independent existence ⟨unable to believe that what he saw was ∼⟩ **d :** FUNDAMENTAL, ESSENTIAL **e** (1) **:** belonging to or having elements or components that belong to the set of real numbers ⟨the ∼ roots of an equation⟩ ⟨a ∼ matrix⟩ (2) **:** concerned with or containing real numbers ⟨∼ analysis⟩ (3) **:** REAL-VALUED ⟨∼ variable⟩ **f :** measured by purchasing power ⟨∼ income⟩ ⟨∼ dollars⟩ **g :** COMPLETE, UTTER ⟨a ∼ fiasco⟩ **3** *of a particle* **:** capable of being detected — compare VIRTUAL **1** — **re·al·ness** *n* — **for real 1 :** in earnest : SERIOUSLY ⟨fighting *for real*⟩ **2 :** GENUINE ⟨couldn't believe the threats were *for real*⟩

²real *n* (ca. 1626) **:** a real thing; *esp* **:** a mathematically real quantity

³real *adv* (1718) **:** VERY ⟨he was ∼ cool —H. M. McLuhan⟩

usage Most handbooks consider the adverb *real* to be informal and more suitable to speech than writing. Our evidence shows these observations to be true in the main, but *real* is becoming increasingly common in writing of an informal, conversational style. It is used as an intensifier only and is not interchangeable with *really* except in that use.

⁴re·al \rā-'äl\ *n, pl* **reals** *or* **re·ales** \-'ä-(ˌ)lās\ [Sp, fr. real royal, fr. L *regalis* — more at ROYAL] (1555) **:** a former monetary unit and coin of Spain and its possessions

⁵re·al \rā-'äl\ *n, pl* **reals** *or* **reis** \'rāsh, 'rās, 'rāzh, 'rāz\ [Pg, fr. real royal, fr. L *regalis*] (1951) **1 :** a former monetary unit and coin of Portugal **2** — see MONEY table

real estate *n* (1666) **:** property in buildings and land

real focus *n* (1909) **:** a point at which rays (as of light) converge or from which they diverge

re·al·gar \rē-'al-ˌgär, -gər\ *n* [ME, fr. ML, fr. Catal. Ar *rahj al-ghār* powder of the mine] (15c) **:** an orange-red mineral consisting of arsenic sulfide and having a resinous luster

re·a·lia \rē-'ā-lē-ə, -'ā-\ *n pl* [LL, neut. pl. of *realis* real] (1937) **:** objects or activities used to relate classroom teaching to the real life esp. of peoples studied

re·align \ˌrē-ə-'līn\ *vt* (1899) **:** to align again; *esp* **:** to reorganize or make new groupings of — **re·align·ment** \-mənt\ *n*

real image *n* (1899) **:** an optical image formed of real foci

re·al·ism \'rē-ə-ˌli-zəm, 'ri-ə-\ *n* (1817) **1 :** concern for fact or reality and rejection of the impractical and visionary **2 a :** a doctrine that universals exist outside the mind; *specif* **:** the conception that an abstract term names an independent and unitary reality **b :** the conception that objects of sense perception or cognition exist independently of the mind — compare NOMINALISM **3 :** fidelity in art and literature to nature or to real life and to accurate representation without idealization — **re·al·ist** \-list\ *adj or n* — **re·al·is·tic** \ˌrē-ə-'lis-tik, ˌri-ə-\ *adj* — **re·al·is·ti·cal·ly** \-ti-k(ə-)lē\ *adv*

re·al·i·ty \rē-'a-lə-tē\ *n, pl* **-ties** (1550) **1 :** the quality or state of being real **2 a** (1) **:** a real event, entity, or state of affairs ⟨his dream became a ∼⟩ (2) **:** the totality of real things and events ⟨trying to escape from ∼⟩ **b :** something that is neither derivative nor dependent but exists necessarily — **in reality :** in actual fact

reality check *n* (1986) **:** something that clarifies or serves as a reminder of reality often by correcting a misconception

re·al·i·za·tion \ˌrē-ə-lə-'zā-shən, ˌri-ə-\ *n* (ca. 1611) **1 :** the action of realizing; the state of being realized **2 :** something realized

re·al·ize \'rē-ə-ˌlīz, 'ri-ə-\ *vt* **-ized; -iz·ing** [F *réaliser,* fr. MF *realiser,* fr. real real] (ca. 1611) **1 a :** to bring into concrete existence : ACCOMPLISH ⟨finally *realized* her goal⟩ **b :** to cause to seem real : make appear real ⟨a book in which the characters are carefully *realized*⟩ **2 a :** to convert into actual money ⟨*realized* assets⟩ **b :** to bring or get by sale, investment, or effort : GAIN **3 :** to conceive vividly as real : be fully aware of ⟨did not ∼ the risk she was taking⟩ *syn* see THINK — **re·al·iz·able** \ˌrē-ə-'lī-zə-bəl, ˌri-ə\ *adj* — **re·al·iz·er** *n*

real–life *adj* (1938) **:** existing or occurring in reality : drawn from or drawing on actual events or situations ⟨∼ problems⟩ ⟨∼ drama⟩

re·al·ly \'rē-(ə-)lē, 'ri-\ *adv* (15c) **1 a :** in reality : ACTUALLY ⟨things as they ∼ are⟩ ⟨there was nothing peculiar about her doing this, ∼ —Peter Taylor⟩ **b :** TRULY, UNQUESTIONABLY — used as an intensifier ⟨a ∼ beautiful day⟩ **2** — used to emphasize an assertion ⟨you ∼ should read Yeats⟩ ⟨∼, you're being ridiculous⟩

realm \'relm\ *n* [ME *realme,* fr. OF *reialme,* alter. of *reialme,* fr. L *regimen* rule — more at REGIMEN] (13c) **1 :** KINGDOM 2 **2 :** SPHERE, DOMAIN ⟨within the ∼ of possibility⟩ **3 :** a primary marine or terrestrial biogeographic division of the earth's surface

real number *n* (1909) **:** one of the numbers that have no imaginary parts and comprise the rationals and the irrationals

real part *n* (1949) **:** the term in a complex number (as 2 in 2 + 3*i*) that does not contain the imaginary unit as a factor

re·al·po·li·tik \rā-'äl-ˌpō-li-ˌtēk\ *n, often cap* [G, fr. *real* actual + *Politik* politics] (1914) **:** politics based on practical and material factors rather than on theoretical or ethical objectives

real presence *n, often cap R&P* (1559) **:** the doctrine that Christ is actually present in the Eucharist

real time *n* (1953) **:** the actual time during which something takes place ⟨the computer may partly analyze the data in *real time* as it comes in⟩ —R. H. March⟩ — **real–time** *adj*

Re·al·tor \'rē(-ə)l-tər, -ˌtör, ÷'rē-lə-tər *also* rē-'al-tər\ *collective mark* — used for a real estate agent who is a member of the National Association of Realtors

re·al·ty \'rē(-ə)l-tē\ *n* [*real* + *-ty* (as in *property*)] (1670) **:** REAL ESTATE

real–valued *adj* (1965) **:** taking on only real numbers for values

real–world *adj* (1963) **:** REAL-LIFE

¹ream \'rēm\ *n* [ME *reme,* fr. MF *raime,* fr. Ar *rizmah,* lit., bundle] (14c) **1 :** a quantity of paper being 20 quires or variously 480, 500, or 516 sheets **2 :** a great amount — usu. used in pl.

²ream *vt* [perh. fr. (assumed) ME *remen* to open up, fr. OE *rēman;* akin to OE *rȳman* to open up, *rūm* space — more at ROOM] (1815) **1 a :** to widen the opening of (a hole) : COUNTERSINK **b** (1) **:** to enlarge or dress out (a hole) with a reamer (2) **:** to enlarge the bore of (as a gun) in this way **c :** to remove by reaming **2 a :** to press out with a reamer **b :** to press out the juice of (as an orange) with a reamer **3** : CHEAT, VICTIMIZE **4 :** REPRIMAND

ream·er \'rē-mər\ *n* (1825) **:** one that reams: as **a :** a rotating finishing tool with cutting edges used to enlarge or shape a hole **b :** a fruit juice extractor with a ridged and pointed center rising from a shallow dish

reamer a

reamer b

reap \'rēp\ *vb* [ME *repen,* fr. OE *reopan*] *vt* (bef. 12c) **1 a** (1) **:** to cut with a sickle, scythe, or reaping machine (2) **:** to clear of a crop by reaping **b :** to gather by reaping **:** HARVEST **2 :** OBTAIN, WIN ∼ *vi* **:** to reap something

reap·er \'rē-pər\ *n* (bef. 12c) **:** one that reaps; *esp* **:** any of various machines for reaping grain

reap–hook \'rēp-ˌhúk\ *n* (1591) **:** a hand implement with a hook-shaped blade used in reaping

re·ap·por·tion \ˌrē-ə-'pōr-shən, -'pör-\ *vt* (ca. 1828) **:** to apportion (as a house of representatives) anew ∼ *vi* **:** to make a new apportionment — **re·ap·por·tion·ment** \-shən-mənt\ *n*

¹rear \'rir\ *vt4 & vi2 are also* 'rar *or* 'rer\ *vb* [ME *reren,* fr. OE *rǣran;* akin to ON *reisa* to raise, OE *rīsan* to rise] *vt* (bef. 12c) **1 :** to erect by building : CONSTRUCT **2 :** to raise upright **3 a** (1) **:** to breed and raise (an animal) for use or market (2) **:** BRING UP 1 **b :** to cause (as plants) to grow **4 :** to cause (a horse) to rise up on the hind legs ∼ *vi* **1 :** to rise high **2** *of a horse* **:** to rise up on the hind legs *syn* see LIFT — **rear·er** *n*

²rear \'rir\ *n* [ME *rere,* short for *rerewarde* rearward] (14c) **1 :** the back part of something: as **a :** the unit (as of an army) or area farthest from the enemy **b :** the part of something located opposite its front ⟨the ∼ of a house⟩ **c :** BUTTOCKS **2 :** the space or position at the back ⟨moved to the ∼⟩

³rear \'rir\ *adj* [ME *rere-,* fr. MF *rere* backward, behind, fr. L *retro-* — more at RETRO] (14c) **:** being at the back

⁴rear \'rir\ *adv* (1855) **:** toward or from the rear — usu. used in combination ⟨a *rear*-driven car⟩

rear admiral *n* (1589) **:** a commissioned officer in the navy who ranks above a commodore and in the coast guard who ranks above a captain and whose insignia is two stars

rear echelon *n* (ca. 1934) **:** an element of a military headquarters or unit located at a considerable distance from the front and concerned esp. with administrative and supply duties

rear–end \'rir-'end, -ˌend\ *vt* (1957) **:** to crash into the back of (as an automobile)

rear end *n* (ca. 1930) **:** BUTTOCKS

rear·guard \'rir-ˌgärd\ *adj* (1898) **:** of or relating to resistance esp. to sweeping social forces ⟨fought a ∼ action against automation⟩

\ə\ abut \ᵊ\ kitten, F table \ər\ further \a\ ash \ā\ ace \ä\ mop, mar
\aú\ out \ch\ chin \e\ bet \ē\ easy \g\ go \i\ hit \ī\ ice \j\ job
\ŋ\ sing \ō\ go \ò\ law \òi\ boy \th\ thin \ṯẖ\ the \ü\ loot \ú\ foot
\y\ yet \zh\ vision \ä, k̟, ⁿ, œ, œ̄, ɷ, ᵫ, ᵜ\ see Guide to Pronunciation

rear guard \-'gärd, -ˌgärd\ n [MF reregarde, fr. OF, fr. rere + garde guard] (1659) : a military detachment detailed to bring up and protect the rear of a main body or force

re·arm \(ˌ)rē-'ärm\ vt (1871) : to arm (as a nation or a military force) again with new or better weapons ~ vi : to become armed again — **re·ar·ma·ment** \-'är-mə-mənt\ n

rear·most \'rir-ˌmōst\ adj (1718) : farthest in the rear : LAST

rear·view mirror \'rir-ˌvyü-\ n (1926) : a mirror (as in an automobile) that gives a view of the area behind a vehicle

¹rear·ward \'rir-wȯrd\ n [ME rerewarde, fr. AF; akin to OF reregarde rear guard] (14c) : REAR; esp : the rear division (as of an army)

²rear·ward \-wȯrd\ adj [²rear + -ward] (1598) 1 : located at, near, or toward the rear   2 : directed toward the rear

³rear·ward \-wȯrd\ also **rear·wards** \-wȯrdz\ adv (1625) : at, near, or toward the rear : BACKWARD

¹rea·son \'rē-zⁿn\ n [ME resoun, fr. OF raison, fr. L ration-, ratio reason, computation, fr. reri to calculate, think; prob. akin to Goth rathjo account, explanation] (13c) 1 a : a statement offered in explanation or justification (gave ~s that were quite satisfactory)   b : a rational ground or motive (a good ~ to act soon)   c : a sufficient ground of explanation or of logical defense; esp : something (as a principle or law) that supports a conclusion or explains a fact (the ~s behind her client's action)   d : the thing that makes some fact intelligible : CAUSE (the ~ for earthquakes) (the real ~ why he wanted me to stay — Graham Greene)   2 a (1) : the power of comprehending, inferring, or thinking esp. in orderly rational ways : INTELLIGENCE   (2) : proper exercise of the mind   (3) : SANITY   b : the sum of the intellectual powers   3 archaic : treatment that affords satisfaction — **in reason** : RIGHTLY, JUSTIFIABLY — **within reason** : within reasonable limits — **with reason** : with good cause

²reason vb **rea·soned; rea·son·ing** \'rēz-niŋ, 'rē-zⁿn-iŋ\ vi (15c) 1 a obs : to take part in conversation, discussion, or argument   b : to talk with another so as to influence his actions or opinions (can't ~ with her)   2 : to use the faculty of reason so as to arrive at conclusions ~ vt 1 archaic : to justify or support with reasons   2 : to persuade or influence by the use of reason   3 : to discover, formulate, or conclude by the use of reason (a carefully ~ed analysis) syn see THINK — **rea·son·er** \'rēz-nər, 'rē-zⁿn-ər\ n

rea·son·able \'rēz-nə-bəl, 'rē-zⁿn-ə-bəl\ adj (14c) 1 a : being in accordance with reason (a ~ theory)   b : not extreme or excessive (~ requests)   c : MODERATE, FAIR (a ~ chance) (a ~ price)   d : INEXPENSIVE   2 a : having the faculty of reason   b : possessing sound judgment — **rea·son·abil·i·ty** \ˌrēz-nə-'bi-lə-tē, ˌrē-zⁿn-ə-\ n — **rea·son·able·ness** \'rēz-nə-bəl-nəs, 'rē-zⁿn-ə-\ n — **rea·son·ably** \-blē\ adv

reasoning n (14c) 1 : the use of reason; esp : the drawing of inferences or conclusions through the use of reason   2 : an instance of the use of reason : ARGUMENT

rea·son·less \'rē-zⁿn-ləs\ adj (14c) 1 : not having the faculty of reason (a ~ brute)   2 : not reasoned : SENSELESS (~ hostility)   3 : not based on or supported by reasons (a ~ accusation) — **rea·son·less·ly** adv

re·as·sur·ance \ˌrē-ə-'shu̇r-ən(t)s\ n (ca. 1811) 1 : the action of reassuring : the state of being reassured   2 : REINSURANCE

re·as·sure \ˌrē-ə-'shu̇r\ vt (1598) 1 : to assure anew (reassured him that the work was on schedule)   2 : to restore to confidence (felt reassured by their earnest promise to do better)   3 : REINSURE — **re·as·sur·ing·ly** \-'shu̇r-iŋ-lē\ adv

re·ata \rē-'ä-tə, -'ä-\ n [AmerSp — more at LARIAT] (1846) : LARIAT

Ré·au·mur \ˌrā-ō-'myu̇r, 'rā-ō-\ adj [René Antoine Ferchault de Réaumur] (1814) : relating to or conforming to a thermometric scale on which the boiling point of water is at 80° above the zero of the scale and the freezing point is at zero

¹reave \'rēv\ vb **reaved** or **reft** \'reft\; **reav·ing** [ME reven, fr. OE rēafian; akin to OHG roubôn to rob, L rumpere to break] vi (bef. 12c) : PLUNDER, ROB ~ vt 1 archaic a (1) : ROB, DESPOIL   (2) : to deprive one of   b : SEIZE   2 archaic : to carry or tear away — **reav·er** n

²reave vt **reaved** or **reft** \'reft\; **reav·ing** [ME reven, prob. modif. of ON rifa to rive] (13c) archaic : BURST

reb \'reb\ n [short for rebel] (1862) : JOHNNY REB

Reb \'reb\ n [Yiddish, fr. Heb rabbī my master, rabbi] (1882) : RABBI, MISTER — used as a title

re·bar \'rē-ˌbär\ n [reinforcing bar] (1953) : a steel rod with ridges for use in reinforced concrete

re·bar·ba·tive \ri-'bär-bə-tiv\ adj [F rébarbatif, fr. MF, fr. rebarber to be repellent, fr. re- + barbe beard, fr. L barba — more at BEARD] (1892) : REPELLENT, IRRITATING — **re·bar·ba·tive·ly** adv

¹re·bate \'rē-ˌbāt, ri-'\ vb **re·bat·ed; re·bat·ing** [ME, fr. MF rabattre to beat down again, fr. OF, fr. re- + abattre to beat down, fr. a- (fr. L ad-) + battre to beat, fr. L battuere] vt (14c) 1 : to reduce the force or activity of : DIMINISH   2 : to reduce the sharpness of : BLUNT   3 a : to make a rebate of   b : to give a rebate to ~ vi : to give rebates — **re·bat·er** n

²re·bate \'rē-ˌbāt\ n (1656) : a return of a part of a payment

³re·bate \'ra-bət, 'rē-ˌbāt\ chiefly Brit var of RABBET

re·ba·to \ri-'bä-(ˌ)tō\ var of RABATO

reb·be \'re-bə\ n [Yiddish rebe, fr. Heb rabbi rabbi] (1881) : a Jewish spiritual leader or teacher : RABBI

re·bec or **re·beck** \'rē-ˌbek, 're-(ˌ)bek\ n [ME rebecke, fr. MF rebec, alter. of OF rebebe, fr. OProv rebeb, fr. Ar rabāb] (15c) : an ancient bowed instr. 3-stringed musical instrument with a pear-shaped body and slender neck

Re·bek·ah \ri-'be-kə\ n [Heb Ribhqāh] : the wife of Isaac

¹reb·el \'re-bəl\ adj [ME, fr. OF rebelle, fr. L rebellis, fr. re- + bellum war, fr. OL duellum] (14c) 1 a : opposing or taking arms against a government or ruler   b : of or relating to rebels (the ~ camp)   2 : DISOBEDIENT, REBELLIOUS

²reb·el n (14c) : one who rebels or participates in a rebellion

³re·bel \ri-'bel\ vi **re·belled; re·bel·ling** (14c) 1 a : to oppose or disobey one in authority or control   b : to renounce and resist by force the authority of one's government   2 a : to act in

rebec

or show opposition or disobedience (rebelled against the conventions of polite society)   b : to feel or exhibit anger or revulsion (rebelled at the injustice of life)

re·bel·lion \ri-'bel-yən\ n (14c) 1 : opposition to one in authority or dominance   2 a : open, armed, and usu. unsuccessful defiance of or resistance to an established government   b : an instance of such defiance or resistance

syn REBELLION, REVOLUTION, UPRISING, REVOLT, INSURRECTION, MUTINY mean an outbreak against authority. REBELLION implies an open formidable resistance that is often unsuccessful (open rebellion against the officers). REVOLUTION applies to a successful rebellion resulting in a major change (as in government) (a political revolution that toppled the monarchy). UPRISING implies a brief, limited and often immediately ineffective rebellion (quickly put down the uprising). REVOLT and INSURRECTION imply an armed uprising that quickly fails or succeeds (a revolt by the Young Turks that surprised party leaders) (an insurrection of oppressed laborers). MUTINY applies to group insubordination or insurrection esp. against naval authority (a mutiny led by the ship's cook).

re·bel·lious \-yəs\ adj (15c) 1 a : given to or engaged in rebellion (~ troops)   b : of, relating to, or characteristic of a rebel or rebellion (a ~ speech)   2 : resisting treatment or management : REFRACTORY — **re·bel·lious·ly** adv — **re·bel·lious·ness** n

rebel yell n (1863) : a prolonged high-pitched yell often uttered by Confederate soldiers in the U.S. Civil War

re·birth \(ˌ)rē-'bərth, 'rē-\ n (1837) 1 a : a new or second birth : METEMPSYCHOSIS   b : spiritual regeneration   2 : RENAISSANCE, REVIVAL (a ~ of nationalism)

Re·blo·chon \rə-blō-'shōⁿ\ n [F reblochon, fr. F dial. (Savoy)] (1908) : a semisoft creamy mild-flavored French cheese

reb·o·ant \'re-bə-wənt\ adj [L reboant-, reboans, prp. of reboare to resound, fr. re- + boare to cry aloud, roar, fr. Gk boan, of imit. origin] (1830) : marked by reverberation

re·born \(ˌ)rē-'bȯrn\ adj (1598) : born again : REGENERATED, REVIVED

¹re·bound \'rē-ˌbau̇nd, ri-'\ vb [ME, fr. MF rebondir, fr. OF, fr. re- + bondir to bound — more at BOUND] vi (14c) 1 a : to spring back on or as if on collision or impact with another body   b : to recover from setback or frustration   2 : REECHO   3 : to gain possession of a rebound in basketball ~ vt : to cause to rebound — **re·bound·er** \'rē-ˌbau̇n-dər, ri-'\ n

²re·bound \'rē-ˌbau̇nd, ri-'\ n (1530) 1 a : the action of rebounding : RECOIL   b : an upward leap or movement : RECOVERY (a sharp ~ in prices)   2 a : a basketball or hockey puck that rebounds   b : the act or an instance of gaining possession of a basketball rebound (leads the league in ~s)   3 : a reaction to setback, frustration, or crisis (on the ~ from an unhappy love affair)

re·bo·zo \ri-'bō-(ˌ)zō, -(ˌ)sō\ n, pl **-zos** [Sp, shawl, fr. rebozar to muffle, alter. of embozar to muffle, prob. fr. (assumed) VL imbucciare, fr. L in- + bucca cheek] (1807) : a long scarf worn chiefly by Mexican women

re·branch \(ˌ)rē-'branch\ vi (1888) : to form secondary branches

re·broad·cast \(ˌ)rē-'brȯd-ˌkast\ vt **-cast; -cast·ing** (1923) 1 : to broadcast again (a radio or television program being simultaneously received from another source)   2 : to repeat (a broadcast) at a later time — **rebroadcast** n

re·buff \ri-'bəf\ vt [MF rebuffer, fr. OIt ribuffare to reprimand, fr. ribuffo reprimand] (ca. 1586) : to reject or criticize sharply : SNUB — **rebuff** n

re·build \(ˌ)rē-'bild\ vb **-built** \-'bilt\; **-build·ing** vt (1537) 1 a : to make extensive repairs to : RECONSTRUCT (~ a war-torn city)   b : to restore to a previous state (~ inventories)   2 : to make extensive changes in : REMODEL (~ society) ~ vi : to build again (planned to ~ after the fire) syn see MEND

¹re·buke \ri-'byük\ vt **re·buked; re·buk·ing** [ME, fr. ONF rebuker] (14c) 1 a : to criticize sharply : REPRIMAND   b : to serve as a rebuke to   2 : to turn back or keep down : CHECK   syn see REPROVE — **re·buk·er** n

²rebuke n (15c) : an expression of strong disapproval : REPRIMAND

re·bus \'rē-bəs\ n [L, by things, abl. pl. of res thing — more at REAL] (1605) : a representation of words or syllables by pictures of objects or by symbols whose names resemble the intended words or syllables in sound; also : a riddle made up of such pictures or symbols

re·but \ri-'bət\ vb **re·but·ted; re·but·ting** [ME, fr. MF reboter, fr. re- + boter to butt — more at BUTT] vt (14c) 1 : to drive or beat back : REPEL   2 a : to contradict or oppose by formal legal argument, plea, or countervailing proof   b : to expose the falsity of : REFUTE ~ vi : to make or furnish an answer or counter proof — **re·but·ta·ble** \-'bə-tə-bəl\ adj

re·but·tal \ri-'bə-tⁿl\ n (1830) : the act of rebutting esp. in a legal suit; also : argument or proof that rebuts

¹re·but·ter \-'bə-tər\ n [AF rebuter, fr. OF reboter to rebut] (1540) : the answer of a defendant in matter of fact to a plaintiff's surrejoinder

²rebutter n (1794) : one that rebuts

re·cal·ci·trance \ri-'kal-sə-trən(t)s\ n (1856) : the state of being recalcitrant

re·cal·ci·tran·cy \-trən(t)-sē\ n (1869) : RECALCITRANCE

re·cal·ci·trant \-trənt\ adj [LL recalcitrant-, recalcitrans, prp. of recalcitrare to be stubbornly disobedient, fr. L, to kick back, fr. re- + calcitrare to kick, fr. calc-, calx heel] (1843) 1 : obstinately defiant of authority or restraint   2 a : difficult to manage or operate   b : not responsive to treatment   c : RESISTANT (this subject is ~ both to observation and to experiment —G. G. Simpson) syn see UNRULY — **recalcitrant** n

¹re·call \ri-'kȯl\ vt (1582) 1 a : to call back (was ~ed to active duty)   b : to bring back to mind (~ those early years)   c : to remind one of : RESEMBLE (a playwright who ~s the Elizabethan dramatists)   2 : CANCEL, REVOKE   3 : RESTORE, REVIVE   syn see REMEMBER — **re·call·abil·i·ty** \-ˌkȯ-lə-'bi-lə-tē\ n — **re·call·able** \-'kȯ-lə-bəl\ adj — **re·call·er** n

²re·call \ri-'kȯl, 'rē-\ n (1611) 1 : a call to return (a ~ of workers after a layoff)   2 : the right or procedure by which an official may be removed by vote of the people   3 : remembrance of what has been learned or experienced   4 : the act of revoking   5 : a public call by a manufacturer for the return of a product that may be defective or contaminated

re·ca·mier \ˌrā-käm-ˈyā\ *n* [fr. its appearance in a portrait of Mme. Récamier by Jacques-Louis David] (1924) : a sometimes backless couch with a high curved headrest and low footrest

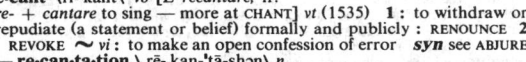

recamier

re·can·a·li·za·tion \(ˌ)rē-ˌka-nᵊl-ə-ˈzā-shən\ *n* (1953) : the process of restoring flow to or reuniting an interrupted channel of a bodily tube (as a blood vessel or vas deferens) — **re·can·a·lize** \-kə-ˈna-ˌlīz, -ˈka-nᵊl-ˌīz\ *vt*

re·cant \ri-ˈkant\ *vb* [L *recantare*, fr. *re-* + *cantare* to sing — more at CHANT] *vt* (1535) **1** : to withdraw or repudiate (a statement or belief) formally and publicly : RENOUNCE **2** : REVOKE ~ *vi* : to make an open confession of error *syn* see ABJURE — **re·can·ta·tion** \ˌrē-ˌkan-ˈtā-shən\ *n*

¹re·cap \ˈrē-ˌkap\ *n* [by shortening] (ca. 1926) : RECAPITULATION

²re·cap \ˈrē-ˌkap, ri-ˈ\ *vb* **re·capped; re·cap·ping** (1945) : RECAPITULATE

³re·cap \ˈrē-ˌkap\ *n* [⁴*recap*] (1940) : RETREAD 1

⁴re·cap \(ˌ)rē-ˈkap\ *vt* **re·capped; re·cap·ping** [*re-* + ¹*cap*] (1941) : RETREAD — **re·cap·pa·ble** \-ˈka-pə-bəl\ *adj*

re·cap·i·tal·i·za·tion \(ˌ)rē-ˌka-pə-tᵊl-ə-ˈzā-shən, -ˌkap-tᵊl-\ *n* (1920) : a revision of the capital structure of a corporation

re·cap·i·tal·ize \(ˌ)rē-ˈka-pə-tᵊl-ˌīz, (ˌ)rē-ˈkap-tᵊl-\ *vt* (1904) : to change the capital structure of

re·ca·pit·u·late \ˌrē-kə-ˈpi-chə-ˌlāt\ *vb* **-lat·ed; -lat·ing** [LL *recapitulatus*, pp. of *recapitulare* to restate by heads, sum up, fr. L *re-* + *capitulum* division of a book — more at CHAPTER] *vt* (1570) : to repeat the principal points or stages of : SUMMARIZE ~ *vi* : SUM UP

re·ca·pit·u·la·tion \-ˌpi-chə-ˈlā-shən\ *n* (14c) **1** : a concise summary **2** : the hypothetical occurrence in an individual organism's development of successive stages resembling the series of ancestral types from which it has descended so that the ontogeny of the individual is a recapitulation of the phylogeny of its group **3** : the third section of a sonata form

¹re·cap·ture \(ˌ)rē-ˈkap-chər\ *n* (1752) **1 a** : the act of retaking **b** : an instance of being retaken **2** : the retaking of a prize or goods under international law **3** : a government seizure under law of earnings or profits beyond a fixed amount

²recapture *vt* (1799) **1 a** : to capture again **b** : to experience again ⟨by no effort of the imagination could she ~ the ecstasy —Ellen Glasgow⟩ **2** : to take (as a portion of earnings or profits above a fixed amount) by law or through negotiations under law

re·cast \(ˌ)rē-ˈkast\ *vt* **-cast; -cast·ing** (1603) : to cast again ⟨~ a gun⟩ ⟨~ a play⟩; *also* : REMODEL, REFASHION ⟨~s his political image to fit the times⟩ — **re·cast** \ˈrē-ˌkast, (ˌ)rē-ˈ\ *n*

rec·ce \ˈre-kē\ *n, often attrib* [by shortening & alter.] (1941) : RECONNAISSANCE

¹re·cede \ri-ˈsēd\ *vi* **re·ced·ed; re·ced·ing** [ME, fr. L *recedere* to go back, fr. *re-* + *cedere* to go] (15c) **1 a** : to move back or away : WITHDRAW **b** : to slant backward **2** : to grow less or smaller : DIMINISH, DECREASE

syn RECEDE, RETREAT, RETRACT, BACK mean to move backward. RECEDE implies a gradual withdrawing from a forward or high fixed point in time or space ⟨the flood waters gradually *receded*⟩. RETREAT implies withdrawal from a point or position reached ⟨*retreating* soldiers⟩. RETRACT implies drawing back from an extended position ⟨a cat *retracting* its claws⟩. BACK is used with *up, down, out,* or *off* to refer to any retrograde motion ⟨*backed* off on the throttle⟩.

²re·cede \(ˌ)rē-ˈsēd\ *vt* [*re-* + *cede*] (1771) : to cede back to a former possessor

¹re·ceipt \ri-ˈsēt\ *n* [ME *receite*, fr. ONF, fr. ML *recepta*, prob. fr. L, neut. pl. of *receptus*, pp. of *recipere* to receive] (14c) **1** : RECIPE **2 a** *obs* : RECEPTACLE **b** *archaic* : a revenue office **3** : the act or process of receiving **4** : something received — usu. used in pl. **5** : a writing acknowledging the receiving of goods or money

²receipt *vt* (1787) **1** : to give a receipt for or acknowledge the receipt of **2** : to mark as paid

re·ceiv·able \ri-ˈsē-və-bəl\ *adj* (14c) **1** : capable of being received **2** : subject to call for payment ⟨notes ~⟩

re·ceiv·ables \-bəlz\ *n pl* (1863) : amounts of money receivable

re·ceive \ri-ˈsēv\ *vb* **re·ceived; re·ceiv·ing** [ME, fr. ONF *receivre*, fr. L *recipere*, fr. *re-* + *capere* to take — more at HEAVE] *vt* (14c) **1** : to come into possession of : ACQUIRE ⟨~ a gift⟩ **2 a** : to act as a receptacle or container for ⟨the cistern ~s water from the roof⟩ **b** : to assimilate through the mind or senses ⟨~ new ideas⟩ **3 a** : to permit to enter : ADMIT **b** : WELCOME, GREET **c** : to react to in a specified manner **4** : to accept as authoritative, true, or accurate : BELIEVE **5 a** : to support the weight or pressure of : BEAR **b** : to take (a mark or impression) from the weight of something ⟨some clay ~s clear impressions⟩ **c** : ACQUIRE, EXPERIENCE ⟨*received* his early schooling at home⟩ **d** : to suffer the hurt or injury of ⟨*received* a broken nose⟩ ~ *vi* **1** : to be a recipient **2** : to be at home to visitors ⟨~s on Tuesdays⟩ **3** : to convert incoming radio waves into perceptible signals **4** : to prepare to take possession of the ball from a kick in football

received *adj* (15c) : generally accepted : COMMON ⟨a healthy skepticism about ~ explanations —B. K. Lewalski⟩

Received Pronunciation *n* (1869) : the pronunciation of Received Standard

Received Standard *n* (1913) : a traditionally prestigious form of English spoken at the English public schools, at the universities of Oxford and Cambridge, and by many educated British people elsewhere

re·ceiv·er \ri-ˈsē-vər\ *n* (14c) : one that receives: as **a** : TREASURER **b** (1) : a person appointed to hold in trust and administer property under litigation (2) : a person appointed to settle the affairs of a business involving a public interest or to manage a corporation during reorganization **c** : one that receives stolen goods : FENCE **d** : a device for converting signals (as electromagnetic waves) into audio or visual form: as (1) : a device in a telephone for converting electric impulses or varying current into sound (2) : a radio receiver with a tuner and am-

plifier on one chassis **e** (1) : CATCHER (2) : a member of the offensive team in football eligible to catch a forward pass

receiver general *n, pl* **receivers general** (15c) : a public officer in charge of the treasury (as of Massachusetts)

re·ceiv·er·ship \ri-ˈsē-vər-ˌship\ *n* (15c) **1** : the office or function of a receiver **2** : the state of being in the hands of a receiver

receiving blanket *n* (1926) : a small lightweight blanket used to wrap an infant (as after bathing)

receiving end *n* (1937) : the position of being a recipient or esp. a victim — usu. used in the phrase *on the receiving end*

receiving line *n* (1933) : a group of people who stand in a line and individually welcome guests (as at a wedding reception)

re·cen·cy \ˈrē-sᵊn(t)-sē\ *n* (1612) : the quality or state of being recent

re·cen·sion \ri-ˈsen(t)-shən\ *n* [L *recension-, recensio* enumeration, fr. *recensēre* to review, fr. *re-* + *censēre* to assess, tax — more at CENSOR] (ca. 1828) **1** : a critical revision of a text **2** : a text established by critical revision

re·cent \ˈrē-sᵊnt\ *adj* [ME, fr. MF or L; MF, fr. L *recent-, recens;* perh. akin to Gk *kainos* new] (15c) **1 a** : having lately come into existence : NEW, FRESH **b** : of or relating to a time not long past **2** *cap* : HOLOCENE — **re·cent·ness** *n*

re·cent·ly *adv* (1533) : during a recent period of time : LATELY

re·cep·ta·cle \ri-ˈsep-ti-kəl\ *n* [ME, fr. L *receptaculum*, fr. *receptare* to receive, freq. of *recipere* to receive] (15c) **1** : one that receives and contains something : CONTAINER **2** [NL *receptaculum*, fr. L] **a** : the end of the flower stalk upon which the floral organs are borne **b** : a modified branch bearing sporangia in a cryptogamous plant **3** : a mounted female electrical fitting that contains the live parts of the circuit

re·cep·tion \ri-ˈsep-shən\ *n* [ME *recepcion*, fr. MF or L; MF *reception*, fr. L *reception-, receptio, recipere*] (15c) **1** : the act or action or an instance of receiving: as **a** : RECEIPT ⟨the ~ and distribution of funds⟩ **b** : ADMISSION ⟨~ into the church⟩ **c** : RESPONSE, REACTION ⟨the play met with a mixed ~⟩ **d** : the receiving of a radio or television broadcast **e** : the catching of a forward pass by a receiver **2** : a social gathering often for the purpose of extending a formal welcome

re·cep·tion·ist \-sh(ə-)nist\ *n* (1901) : a person employed to greet telephone callers, visitors, patients, or clients

re·cep·tive \ri-ˈsep-tiv\ *adj* (15c) **1** : able or inclined to receive; *esp* : open and responsive to ideas, impressions, or suggestions **2 a** *of a sensory end organ* : fit to receive and transmit stimuli **b** : SENSORY — **re·cep·tive·ly** *adv* — **re·cep·tive·ness** *n* — **re·cep·tiv·i·ty** \ˌrē-ˌsep-ˈti-və-tē, ri-\ *n*

re·cep·tor \ri-ˈsep-tər\ *n* (1898) : RECEIVER: as **a** : a cell or group of cells that receives stimuli : SENSE ORGAN **b** : a chemical group or molecule (as a protein) on the cell surface or in the cell interior that has an affinity for a specific chemical group, molecule, or virus

¹re·cess \ˈrē-ˌses, ri-ˈ\ *n* [L *recessus*, fr. *recedere* to recede] (1531) **1** : the action of receding : RECESSION **2** : a hidden, secret, or secluded place or part **3 a** : INDENTATION, CLEFT ⟨a deep ~ in the hill⟩ **b** : ALCOVE ⟨a ~ lined with books⟩ **4** : a suspension of business or procedure often for rest or relaxation ⟨children playing at ~⟩

²recess *vt* (1809) **1** : to put into a recess ⟨~ed lighting⟩ **2** : to make a recess in **3** : to interrupt for a recess ~ *vi* : to take a recess

¹re·ces·sion \ri-ˈse-shən\ *n* (ca. 1652) **1** : the act or action of receding : WITHDRAWAL **2** : a departing procession (as of clergy and choir at the end of a church service) **3** : a period of reduced economic activity — **re·ces·sion·ary** \-shə-ˌner-ē\ *adj*

²re·ces·sion \(ˌ)rē-ˈse-shən\ *n* [*re-* + *cession*] (1828) : the act of ceding back to a former possessor

¹re·ces·sion·al \ri-ˈsesh-nəl, -ˈse-shə-nᵊl\ *adj* (1867) : of or relating to withdrawal

²recessional *n* (1867) **1** : a hymn or musical piece at the conclusion of a service or program **2** : ¹RECESSION 2

¹re·ces·sive \ri-ˈse-siv\ *adj* (ca. 1673) **1 a** : tending to recede **b** : WITHDRAWN **2 2 a** : producing little or no phenotypic effect when occurring in heterozygous condition with a contrasting allele ⟨~ genes⟩ **b** : expressed only when the determining gene is in the homozygous condition ⟨~ traits⟩ — **re·ces·sive·ly** *adv* — **re·ces·sive·ness** *n*

²recessive *n* (1900) **1** : an organism possessing one or more recessive characters **2** : a recessive character or gene

re·charge \(ˌ)rē-ˈchärj\ *vt* (1598) **1** : to make a new attack **2** : to regain energy or spirit ~ *vt* (1) : to charge again; *esp* : to restore anew the active materials in (a storage battery) **2** : to inspire or invigorate afresh : RENEW — **re·charge** \(ˌ)rē-ˈchärj, ˈrē-ˌ\ *n* — **re·charge·able** \(ˌ)rē-ˈchär-jə-bəl\ *adj* — **re·charg·er** \-jər\ *n*

ré·chauf·fé \ˌrā-shō-ˈfā, -ˈshō-ˌ\ *n* [F, fr. pp. of *réchauffer* warmed-over, fr. pp. of *réchauffer* to warm over, fr. *ré- re-* + *chauffer* to warm, fr. MF *chaufer* — more at CHAFE] (1805) **1** : REHASH **2** : a warmed-over dish of food

re·cheat \ri-ˈchēt\ *n* [ME *rechate*, fr. *rechaten* to blow the recheat, fr. MF *rachater* to assemble, rally, fr. *re-* + *achater* to acquire, fr. (assumed) VL *accaptare* — more at CATE] (15c) : a hunting call sounded on a horn to assemble the hounds

re·cher·ché \rə-ˌsher-ˈshā, -ˈsher-ˌ\ *adj* [F, fr. pp. of *rechercher* to seek out, fr. MF *rechercher* — more at RESEARCH] (1722) **1 a** : EXQUISITE, CHOICE **b** : EXOTIC, RARE : excessively refined : AFFECTED : PRETENTIOUS, OVERBLOWN

re·cid·i·vism \ri-ˈsi-də-ˌvi-zəm\ *n* (1886) : a tendency to relapse into a previous condition or mode of behavior; *esp* : relapse into criminal behavior

re·cid·i·vist \-vist\ *n* [F *récidiviste*, fr. *récidiver* to relapse, fr. ML *recidivare*, fr. L *recidivus* recurring, fr. *recidere* to fall back, fr. *re-* + *cadere* to fall — more at CHANCE] (1880) : one who relapses; *specif* : an habitual criminal — **recidivist** *adj* — **re·cid·i·vis·tic** \-ˌsi-də-ˈvis-tik\ *adj*

rec·i·pe \ˈre-sə-(ˌ)pē\ *n* [L, take, imper. of *recipere* to take, receive — more at RECEIVE] (1584) **1** : PRESCRIPTION 4a **2** : a set of instructions

---

\ə\ abut \ᵊ\ kitten, F table \ər\ further \a\ ash \ā\ ace \ä\ mop, mar \au̇\ out \ch\ chin \e\ bet \ē\ easy \g\ go \i\ hit \ī\ ice \j\ job \ŋ\ sing \ō\ go \o̊\ law \o̊i\ boy \th\ thin \th̲\ the \ü\ loot \u̇\ foot \y\ yet \zh\ vision \à, k̲, ⁿ, œ, œ̄, ᵫ, ūᵉ, ʸ\ see Guide to Pronunciation for making something from various ingredients **3** : a formula or procedure for doing or attaining something ⟨a ~ for success⟩

re·cip·i·ent \ri-'si-pē-ənt\ n [L recipient-, recipiens, prp. of recipere] (1558) : one that receives : RECEIVER — **recipient** adj

¹re·cip·ro·cal \ri-'si-prə-kəl\ adj [L reciprocus returning the same way, alternating] (1570) **1 a** : inversely related : OPPOSITE **b** : of, constituting, or resulting from paired crosses in which the kind that supplies the male parent of the first cross supplies the female parent of the second cross and vice versa **2** : shared, felt, or shown by both sides **3** : serving to reciprocate : consisting of or functioning as a return in kind ⟨the ~ devastation of nuclear war⟩ **4 a** : mutually corresponding ⟨agreed to extend ~ privileges to each other's citizens⟩ **b** : marked by or based on reciprocity ⟨~ trade agreements⟩ — **re·cip·ro·cal·ly** \-k(ə-)lē\ adv

²reciprocal n (1570) **1** : something in a reciprocal relationship to another **2** : either of a pair of numbers (as ⅔ and ³/₂ or 9 and ⅑) whose product is one; broadly : MULTIPLICATIVE INVERSE

reciprocal pronoun n (1844) : a pronoun (as each other) used when its referents are predicated to bear the same relationship to one another

re·cip·ro·cate \ri-'si-prə-ˌkāt\ vb -cat·ed; -cat·ing vt (1607) **1** : to give and take mutually **2** : to return in kind or degree ⟨~ a compliment gracefully⟩ ~ vi **1** : to make a return for something ⟨we hope to ~ for your kindness⟩ **2** : to move forward and backward alternately ⟨a reciprocating valve⟩ — **re·cip·ro·ca·tor** \-ˌkā-tər\ n
syn RECIPROCATE, RETALIATE, REQUITE, RETURN mean to give back usu. in kind or in quantity. RECIPROCATE implies a mutual or equivalent exchange or a paying back of what one has received ⟨reciprocated their hospitality by inviting them for a visit⟩. RETALIATE usu. implies a paying back of injury in exact kind, often vengefully ⟨the enemy retaliated by executing their prisoners⟩. REQUITE implies a paying back according to one's preference and often not equivalently ⟨requited her love with cold indifference⟩. RETURN implies a paying or giving back ⟨returned their call⟩ ⟨return good for evil⟩.

reciprocating engine n (1822) : an engine in which the to-and-fro motion of one or more pistons is transformed into the rotary motion of a crankshaft

re·cip·ro·ca·tion \ri-ˌsi-prə-'kā-shən\ n (1561) **1 a** : a mutual exchange **b** : a return in kind or of like value **2** : an alternating motion — **re·cip·ro·ca·tive** \-'si-prə-ˌkā-tiv, -kə-\ adj

rec·i·proc·i·ty \ˌre-sə-'prä-s(ə-)tē\ n, pl -ties (1766) **1** : the quality or state of being reciprocal : mutual dependence, action, or influence **2** : a mutual exchange of privileges; specif : a recognition by one of two countries or institutions of the validity of licenses or privileges granted by the other

re·ci·sion \ri-'si-zhən\ n [MF, alter. of rescision, fr. LL rescission-, rescissio rescission] (1611) : an act of rescinding : CANCELLATION

re·cit·al \ri-'sī-t³l\ n (1536) **1 a** : a detailed account : ENUMERATION ⟨a ~ of names and dates⟩ **b** : the act or process or an instance of reciting **c** : DISCOURSE, NARRATION ⟨a colorful ~ of a night on the town⟩ **2 a** : a concert given by an individual musician or dancer or by a dance troupe **b** : a public exhibition of skill given by music or dance pupils — **re·cit·al·ist** \-t³l-ist\ n

rec·i·ta·tion \ˌre-sə-'tā-shən\ n (15c) **1** : the act of enumerating ⟨a ~ of relevant details⟩ **2** : the act or an instance of reading or repeating aloud esp. publicly **3 a** : a student's oral reply to questions **b** : a class period esp. in association with and for review of a lecture

rec·i·ta·tive \ˌre-sə-tə-'tēv, ˌres-tə-\ n [It recitativo, fr. recitare to recite, fr. L] (1656) **1** : a rhythmically free vocal style that imitates the natural inflections of speech and that is used for dialogue and narrative in operas and oratorios; also : a passage to be delivered in this style **2** : RECITATION **2** — **recitative** adj

rec·i·ta·ti·vo \-'tē-(ˌ)vō\ n, pl -vi \-(ˌ)vē\ or -vos [It] (1645) : RECITATIVE 1

re·cite \ri-'sīt\ vb re·cit·ed; re·cit·ing [ME, to state formally, fr. MF or L; MF reciter to recite, fr. L recitare, fr. re- + citare to summon — more at CITE] vt (15c) **1** : to repeat from memory or read aloud publicly **2 a** : to relate in full ⟨~s dull anecdotes⟩ **b** : to give a recital of : DETAIL ⟨recited a catalog of offenses⟩ **3** : to repeat or answer questions about (a lesson) ~ vi **1** : to repeat or read aloud something memorized or prepared **2** : to reply to a teacher's question on a lesson — **re·cit·er** n

reck \'rek\ vb [ME, to take heed, fr. OE reccan; akin to OHG ruohhen to take heed] vi (bef. 12c) **1** : WORRY, CARE **2** archaic : to be of account or interest : MATTER ~ vt **1** archaic : to care for : REGARD **2** archaic : to matter to : CONCERN

reck·less \'re-kləs\ adj (bef. 12c) **1** : marked by lack of proper caution : careless of consequences **2** : IRRESPONSIBLE ⟨~ charges⟩ syn see ADVENTUROUS — **reck·less·ly** adv — **reck·less·ness** n

reck·on \'re-kən\ vb reck·oned; reck·on·ing \'rek-niŋ, 'rek-niŋ\ [ME rekenen, fr. OE -recenian (as in gerecenian to narrate); akin to OE reccan] vt (13c) **1 a** : COUNT ⟨~ the days till Christmas⟩ **b** : ESTIMATE, COMPUTE ⟨~ the height of a building⟩ **c** : to determine by reference to a fixed basis ⟨the existence of the U.S. is ~ed from the Declaration of Independence⟩ **2** : to regard or think of as : CONSIDER **3** chiefly dial : THINK, SUPPOSE ⟨I — I've outlived my time —Ellen Glasgow⟩ ~ vi **1** : to settle accounts **2** : to make a calculation **3 a** : JUDGE **b** chiefly dial : SUPPOSE, THINK **4** : to accept something as certain : place reliance ⟨I — on your promise to help⟩ — **reckon with** : to take into consideration — **reckon without** : to fail to consider : IGNORE

reckoning n (14c) **1** : the act or an instance of reckoning: as **a** : ACCOUNT, BILL **b** : COMPUTATION **c** : calculation of a ship's position **2** : a settling of accounts ⟨day of ~⟩ **3** : a summing up

re·claim \ri-'klām\ vt [ME reclamen, fr. MF reclamer to call back, fr. L reclamare to cry out against, fr. re- + clamare to cry out — more at CLAIM] (14c) **1 a** : to recall from wrong or improper conduct : REFORM **b** : TAME, SUBDUE **2 a** : to rescue from an undesirable state **b** : to make available for human use by changing natural conditions ⟨~ swampland⟩ **3** : to obtain from a waste product or by-product : RECOVER **4 a** : to demand or obtain the return of **b** : to regain possession of syn see RESCUE — **re·claim·able** \-'klā-mə-bəl\ adj

rec·la·ma·tion \ˌre-klə-'mā-shən\ n [F réclamation, fr. L reclamation-, reclamatio, fr. reclamare] (1633) : the act or process of reclaiming: as **a** : REFORMATION, REHABILITATION **b** : restoration to use : RECOVERY

ré·clame \rā-'kläm\ n [F, advertising, fr. réclamer to appeal, fr. MF reclamer] (1883) **1** : a gift for dramatization or publicity : SHOWMANSHIP **2** : public acclaim : VOGUE

re·cline \ri-'klīn\ vb re·clined; re·clin·ing [ME, fr. MF or L; MF recliner, fr. L reclinare, fr. re- + clinare to bend — more at LEAN] vt (15c) : to cause or permit to incline backwards ~ vi **1** : to lean or incline backwards **2** : REPOSE, LIE

re·clin·er \-'klī-nər\ n (1928) : a chair with an adjustable back and footrest

re·clos·able \(ˌ)rē-'klō-zə-bəl\ adj (1965) : capable of being tightly closed again after opening ⟨~ packages of bacon⟩

¹re·cluse \'re-ˌklüs, ri-'klüs, 're-ˌklüz\ adj [ME, fr. OF reclus, lit., shut up, fr. LL reclusus, pp. of recludere to shut up, fr. L re- + claudere to close — more at CLOSE] (13c) : marked by withdrawal from society : SOLITARY — **re·clu·sive** \ri-'klü-siv, -ziv\ adj — **re·clu·sive·ly** adv — **re·clu·sive·ness** n

²recluse n (13c) : a person who leads a secluded or solitary life

re·clu·sion \ri-'klü-zhən\ n (15c) : the state of being recluse

rec·og·nise chiefly Brit var of RECOGNIZE

rec·og·ni·tion \ˌre-kig-'ni-shən, -kəg-\ n [ME recognicion, fr. L recognition-, recognitio, fr. recognoscere] (15c) **1** : the action of recognizing : the state of being recognized: as **a** : ACKNOWLEDGMENT; esp : formal acknowledgment of the political existence of a government or nation **b** : knowledge or feeling that someone or something present has been encountered before **2** : special notice or attention **3** : the sensing and encoding of printed or written data by a machine ⟨optical character ~⟩ ⟨magnetic ink character ~⟩

re·cog·ni·zance \ri-'käg-nə-zən(t)s, -'kä-nə-\ n [ME, alter. of reconissaunce, fr. MF reconoissance recognition, fr. reconoistre to recognize] (14c) **1 a** : an obligation of record entered into before a court or magistrate requiring the performance of an act (as appearance in court) usu. under penalty of a money forfeiture ⟨released on his own ~⟩ **b** : the sum liable to forfeiture upon such an obligation **2** archaic : TOKEN, PLEDGE

rec·og·nize \'re-kig-ˌnīz, -kəg-\ vt -nized; -niz·ing [modif. of MF reconoiss-, stem of reconoistre, fr. L recognoscere, fr. re- + cognoscere to know — more at COGNITION] (ca. 1532) **1** : to acknowledge formally: as **a** : to admit as being lord or sovereign **b** : to admit as being of a particular status **c** : to admit as being one entitled to be heard : give the floor to **d** : to acknowledge the de facto existence or the independence of **2** : to acknowledge or take notice of in some definite way: as **a** : to acknowledge with a show of appreciation ⟨~ an act of bravery with the award of a medal⟩ **b** : to acknowledge acquaintance with ⟨~ a neighbor with a nod⟩ **3 a** : to perceive to be something or someone previously known ⟨recognized the word⟩ **b** : to perceive clearly : REALIZE — **rec·og·niz·abil·i·ty** \ˌre-kig-ˌnī-zə-'bi-lə-tē, -kəg-\ n — **rec·og·niz·able** \'re-kəg-ˌnī-zə-bəl, -kig-\ adj — **rec·og·niz·ably** \-blē\ adv — **rec·og·niz·er** n

¹re·coil \ri-'kȯi(ə)l\ vi [ME reculen, fr. MF reculer, fr. re- + cul backside — more at CULET] (14c) **1 a** : to fall back under pressure **b** : to shrink back physically or emotionally **2** : to spring back to or as if to a starting point : REBOUND **3** obs : DEGENERATE
syn RECOIL, SHRINK, FLINCH, WINCE, BLENCH, QUAIL mean to draw back in fear or distaste. RECOIL implies a start or movement away through shock, fear, or disgust ⟨recoiled at the suggestion of stealing⟩. SHRINK suggests an instinctive recoil through sensitiveness, scrupulousness, or cowardice ⟨shrank from the unpleasant truth⟩. FLINCH implies a failure to endure pain or face something dangerous or frightening with resolution ⟨faced her accusers without flinching⟩. WINCE suggests a slight involuntary physical reaction (as a start or recoiling) ⟨winced in pain⟩. BLENCH implies fainthearted flinching ⟨stood their ground without blenching⟩. QUAIL suggests shrinking and cowering in fear ⟨quailed before the apparition⟩.

²re·coil \'rē-ˌkȯil, ri-'kȯi(ə)l\ n (14c) **1** : the act or action of recoiling; esp : the kickback of a gun upon firing **2** : REACTION ⟨the ~ from the rigors of Calvinism —Edmund Wilson⟩

re·coil·less \-ˌkȯil-ləs, -'kȯi(ə)l-\ adj (1943) : venting expanding propellant gas before recoil is produced ⟨~ rifle⟩ ⟨~ airgun⟩

recoil–operated adj (1942) of a firearm : utilizing the movement of parts in recoil to operate the action

re·coin \(ˌ)rē-'kȯin\ vt (1685) : to coin again or anew; esp : REMINT — **re·coin·age** \-'kȯi-nij\ n

rec·ol·lect \ˌre-kə-'lekt\ vb [ML recollectus, pp. of recolligere, fr. L, to gather again] (1559) **1** : to bring back to the level of conscious awareness : REMEMBER ⟨trying to ~ the name⟩ **2** : to remind (oneself) of something temporarily forgotten ~ vi : to call something to mind syn see REMEMBER

re·col·lect \ˌrē-kə-'lekt\ vt [partly fr. L recollectus, pp. of recolligere, fr. re- + colligere to collect; partly fr. re- + collect] (1604) : to collect again; esp : RALLY, RECOVER

re·col·lect·ed \ˌrē-kə-'lek-təd\ adj (1627) : COMPOSED, CALM

rec·ol·lec·tion \ˌre-kə-'lek-shən\ n (1624) **1 a** : tranquillity of mind **b** : religious contemplation **2 a** : the action or power of recalling to mind **b** : something recalled to the mind syn see MEMORY

re·com·bi·nant \(ˌ)rē-'käm-bə-nənt\ adj (1942) **1** : relating to or exhibiting genetic recombination ⟨~ progeny⟩ **2** : relating to or containing recombinant DNA; also : produced by recombinant DNA technology — **recombinant** n

recombinant DNA n (1975) : genetically engineered DNA prepared in vitro by cutting up DNA molecules and splicing together specific DNA fragments usu. from more than one species of organism

re·com·bi·na·tion \ˌrē-ˌkäm-bə-'nā-shən\ n (1903) : the formation by the processes of crossing-over and independent assortment of new combinations of genes in progeny that did not occur in the parents — **re·com·bi·na·tion·al** \-shnəl, -shə-n³l\ adj

rec·om·mend \ˌre-kə-'mend\ vt [ME, to praise, fr. ML recommendare, fr. L re- + commendare to commend] (14c) **1 a** : to present as worthy of acceptance or trial ⟨~ed the medicine⟩ **b** : to endorse as fit, worthy, or competent ⟨~s her for the position⟩ **2** : ENTRUST, COMMIT ⟨~ed his soul to God⟩ **3** : to make acceptable ⟨has other points to ~ it⟩ **4** : ADVISE ⟨~ that the matter be dropped⟩ — **rec·om·mend·able** \-'men-də-bəl\ adj — **rec·om·men·da·to·ry** \-də-ˌtȯr-ē, -ˌtȯr-\ adj

rec·om·men·da·tion \ˌre-kə-mən-'dā-shən, -ˌmen-\ *n* (15c) **1 a** : the act of recommending **b** : something (as a procedure) recommended **2** : something that recommends or expresses commendation

re·com·mit \ˌrē-kə-'mit\ *vt* (1621) **1** : to refer (as a bill) back to a committee **2** : to entrust or consign again — **re·com·mit·ment** \-mənt\ *n* — **re·com·mit·tal** \-'mi-t²l\ *n*

¹**rec·om·pense** \'re-kəm-ˌpen(t)s\ *vt* **-pensed; -pens·ing** [ME, fr. MF *recompenser*, fr. LL *recompensare*, fr. L *re-* + *compensare* to compensate] (15c) **1 a** : to give something to by way of compensation (as for a service rendered or damage incurred) **b** : to pay for **2** : to return in kind : REQUITE *syn* see PAY

²**recompense** *n* (15c) : an equivalent or a return for something done, suffered, or given : COMPENSATION ⟨offered in ~ for injuries⟩

re·com·pose \ˌrē-kəm-'pōz\ *vt* (1611) **1** : to compose again : REAR-RANGE **2** : to restore to composure — **re·com·po·si·tion** \(ˌ)rē-ˌkäm-pə-'zi-shən\ *n*

re·con \ri-'kän, 'rē-ˌkän\ *n* (1918) : RECONNAISSANCE

rec·on·cile \'re-kən-ˌsīl\ *vb* **-ciled; -cil·ing** [ME, fr. MF or L; MF *reconciler*, fr. L *reconciliare*, fr. *re-* + *conciliare* to conciliate] *vt* (14c) **1 a** : to restore to friendship or harmony ⟨*reconciled* the factions⟩ **b** : SETTLE, RESOLVE ⟨~ differences⟩ **2** : to make consistent or congruous ⟨~ an ideal with reality⟩ **3** : to cause to submit to or accept something unpleasant ⟨was *reconciled* to hardship⟩ **4 a** : to check (a financial account) against another for accuracy **b** : to account for ~ *vi* : to become reconciled *syn* see ADAPT — **rec·on·cil·abil·i·ty** \ˌre-kən-ˌsī-lə-'bi-lə-tē\ *n* — **rec·on·cil·able** \ˌre-kən-'sī-lə-bəl, 're-kən-\ *adj* — **rec·on·cile·ment** \'re-kən-ˌsīl-mənt\ *n* — **rec·on·cil·er** *n*

rec·on·cil·i·a·tion \ˌre-kən-ˌsi-lē-'ā-shən\ *n* [ME, fr. L *reconciliation-, reconciliatio*, fr. *reconciliare*] (14c) **1** : the action of reconciling : the state of being reconciled **2** : the Roman Catholic sacrament of penance — **rec·on·cil·ia·to·ry** \-'sil-yə-ˌtōr-ē, -'si-lē-ə-, -ˌtōr-\ *adj*

re·con·dite \'re-kən-ˌdīt, ri-'kän-\ *adj* [L *reconditus*, pp. of *recondere* to conceal, fr. *re-* + *condere* to store up, fr. *com-* + *-dere* to put — more at COM-, DO] (1649) **1** : hidden from sight : CONCEALED **2** : difficult or impossible for one of ordinary understanding or knowledge to comprehend : DEEP ⟨a ~ subject⟩ **3** : of, relating to, or dealing with something little known or obscure ⟨~ fact about the origin of the holiday — Floyd Dell⟩ — **re·con·dite·ly** *adv* — **re·con·dite·ness** *n*

re·con·di·tion \ˌrē-kən-'di-shən\ *vt* (1920) **1** : to restore to good condition (as by replacing parts) **2** : to condition (as a person or a person's attitudes) anew; *also* : to reinstate (a response) in an organism

re·con·firm \ˌrē-kən-'fərm\ *vt* (1611) : to confirm again; *also* : to establish more strongly — **re·con·fir·ma·tion** \(ˌ)rē-ˌkän-fər-'mā-shən\ *n*

re·con·nais·sance \ri-'kä-nə-zən(t)s, -sən(t)s\ *n* [F, lit., recognition, fr. MF *reconoissance* — more at RECOGNIZANCE] (1810) : a preliminary survey to gain information; *esp* : an exploratory military survey of enemy territory

re·con·noi·ter *or* **re·con·noi·tre** \ˌrē-kə-'nȯi-tər, ˌre-kə-\ *vb* **-noi·tered** *or* **-noi·tred; -noi·ter·ing** *or* **-noi·tring** \-'nȯi-tə-riŋ, -'nȯi-triŋ\ [obs. F *reconnoître*, lit., to recognize, fr. MF *reconoistre* — more at RECOGNIZE] *vt* (1707) : to make a reconnaissance of ~ *vi* : to engage in reconnaissance

re·con·sid·er \ˌrē-kən-'si-dər\ *vt* (1571) : to consider again esp. with a view to changing or reversing ~ *vi* : to consider something again — **re·con·sid·er·a·tion** \-ˌsi-də-'rā-shən\ *n*

re·con·sti·tute \(ˌ)rē-'kän(t)-stə-ˌtüt, -ˌtyüt\ *vt* (1812) : to constitute again or anew; *esp* : to restore to a former condition by adding water — **re·con·sti·tu·tion** \(ˌ)rē-ˌkän(t)-stə-'tü-shən, -'tyü-\ *n*

re·con·struct \ˌrē-kən-'strəkt\ *vt* (1768) : to construct again: as **a** : to establish or assemble again **b** : to build up again mentally : RE-CREATE ⟨~ing a lost civilization⟩ — **re·con·struct·ible** \-'strək-tə-bəl\ *adj* — **re·con·struc·tive** \-tiv\ *adj* — **re·con·struc·tor** \-tər\ *n*

re·con·struc·tion \ˌrē-kən-'strək-shən\ *n* (1791) **1** : the action of reconstructing : the state of being reconstructed **b** *often cap* : the reorganization and reestablishment of the seceded states in the Union after the American Civil War **2** : something reconstructed

re·con·struc·tion·ism \-shə-ˌni-zəm\ *n*, *often cap* (1942) **1** : a movement in 20th century American Judaism that advocates a creative adjustment to contemporary conditions through the cultivation of traditions and folkways shared by all Jews **2** : advocacy of post-Civil War reconstruction — **re·con·struc·tion·ist** \-sh(ə-)nist\ *adj or n*, *often cap*

reconstructive surgery *n* (1943) : surgery to restore function or normal appearance by remaking defective organs or parts

re·con·vey \ˌrē-kən-'vā\ *vt* (1506) : to convey back to a previous position or owner — **re·con·vey·ance** \-'vā-ən(t)s\ *n*

¹**re·cord** \ri-'kȯrd\ *vb* [ME, lit., to recall, fr. OF *recorder*, fr. L *recordari*, fr. *re-* + *cord-, cor* heart — more at HEART] *vt* (14c) **1 a** (1) : to set down in writing : furnish written evidence of (2) : to deposit an authentic official copy of ⟨~ a deed⟩ **b** : to state for or as if for the record ⟨voted in favor but ~ed certain reservations⟩ **c** (1) : to register permanently by mechanical means ⟨earthquake shocks ~ed by a seismograph⟩ (2) : INDICATE, READ ⟨the thermometer ~ed 90°⟩ **2** : to give evidence of **3** : to cause (as sound, visual images, or data) to be registered on something (as a disc or magnetic tape) in reproducible form ~ *vi* : to record something — **re·cord·able** \-'kȯr-də-bəl\ *adj*

²**re·cord** \'re-kərd *also* -ˌkȯrd\ *n* (14c) **1** : the state or fact of being recorded **2** : something that records: as **a** : something that recalls or relates past events **b** : an official document that records the acts of a public body or officer **c** : an authentic official copy of a document deposited with a legally designated officer **d** : the official copy of the papers used in a law case **3 a** (1) : a body of known or recorded facts about something or someone esp. with reference to a particular sphere of activity that often forms a discernible pattern ⟨a good academic ~⟩ ⟨a liberal voting ~⟩ (2) : a collection of related items of information (as in a database) treated as a unit **b** (1) : an attested top performance (2) : an unsurpassed statistic **4** : something on which sound or visual images have been recorded; *specif* : a disc with a spiral groove carrying recorded sound for phonograph reproduction — **for the record** : for public knowledge : on the record — **off the record** : not for publication ⟨spoke *off the record*⟩ ⟨remarks that were *off the record*⟩ — **of record** : being documented or attested ⟨a partner *of record* in several firms⟩ — **on record 1** : in the position of having

publicly declared oneself ⟨went *on record* as opposed to higher taxes⟩ **2** : being known, published, or documented ⟨the judge's opinion is *on record*⟩ — **on the record** : for publication

³**record** *same as* ²\ *adj* (1893) : of, relating to, or being one that is extraordinary among or surpasses others of its kind

re·cor·da·tion \ˌre-kȯr-'dā-shən, ˌrē-, ri-\ *n* (ca. 1812) : the action or process of recording

record changer *n* (1931) : a phonograph with a device that automatically positions and plays successively each of a stack of records; *also* : the automatic device on a record changer

re·cord·er \ri-'kȯr-dər\ *n* (15c) **1 a** : the chief judicial magistrate of some British cities and boroughs **b** : a municipal judge with criminal jurisdiction of first instance and sometimes limited civil jurisdiction **2** : one that records **3** : any of a group of wind instruments ranging from soprano to bass that are characterized by a conical tube, a whistle mouthpiece, and eight finger holes

recorder 3

re·cord·ing \ri-'kȯr-diŋ\ *n* (1932) : RECORD 4

re·cord·ist \ri-'kȯr-dist\ *n* (ca. 1930) : one who records sound (as on magnetic tape)

¹**re·count** \ri-'kaunt\ *vt* [ME, fr. MF *reconter*, fr. *re-* + *conter* to count, relate — more at COUNT] (15c) : to relate in detail : NARRATE — **re·count·er** *n*

²**re·count** \(ˌ)rē-'kaunt\ *vt* [*re-* + *count*] (1764) : to count again

³**re·count** \'rē-ˌkaunt, (ˌ)rē-'\ *n* (1884) : a second or fresh count

re·coup \ri-'küp\ *vb* [F *recouper* to cut back, fr. OF, fr. *re-* + *couper* to cut — more at COPE] *vt* (1628) **1 a** : to get an equivalent for (as losses) : make up for **b** : REIMBURSE, COMPENSATE ⟨~ a person for losses⟩ **2** : REGAIN ⟨an attempt to ~ his fortune⟩ ~ *vi* : to make good or make up for something lost; *also* : RECUPERATE — **re·coup·able** \-'kü-pə-bəl\ *adj* — **re·coup·ment** \-'küp-mənt\ *n*

re·course \'rē-ˌkōrs, -ˌkȯrs, ri-'\ *n* [ME *recours*, fr. MF, fr. LL *recursus*, fr. L, act of running back, fr. *recurrere* to run back — more at RECUR] (14c) **1 a** : a turning to someone or something for help or protection **b** : a source of help or strength : RESORT **2** : the right to demand payment from the maker or endorser of a negotiable instrument (as a check)

re·cov·er \ri-'kə-vər\ *vb* **re·cov·ered; re·cov·er·ing** \-'kə-və-riŋ, -'kəv-riŋ\ [ME, fr. MF *recoverer*, fr. L *recuperare*, fr. *re-* + (assumed) L *cape-rare*, fr. L *capere* to take — more at HEAVE] *vt* (14c) **1** : to get back : REGAIN **2 a** : to bring back to normal position or condition ⟨stumbled, then ~ed himself⟩ **b** *archaic* : RESCUE **3 a** : to make up for ⟨~ increased costs through higher prices⟩ **b** : to gain by legal process **4** *archaic* : REACH **5** : to find or identify again ⟨~ a comet⟩ **6 a** : to obtain from an ore, a waste product, or a by-product **b** : to save from loss and restore to usefulness : RECLAIM ~ *vi* **1** : to regain a normal position or condition (as of health) ⟨~ing from a cold⟩ **2** : to obtain a final legal judgment in one's favor — **re·cov·er·abil·i·ty** \-ˌkə-və-rə-'bi-lə-tē, -ˌkəv-rə-\ *n* — **re·cov·er·able** \-'kə-və-rə-bəl, -'kəv-rə-\ *adj* — **re·cov·er·er** \-'kə-vər-ər\ *n*

re·cov·er \(ˌ)rē-'kə-vər\ *vt* (15c) : to cover again or anew

re·cov·ery \ri-'kə-və-rē, -'kəv-rē\ *n*, *pl* **-er·ies** (15c) : the act, process, or an instance of recovering; *esp* : an economic upturn (as after a depression)

recovery room *n* (1916) : a hospital room equipped for meeting postoperative emergencies

¹**rec·re·ant** \'re-krē-ənt\ *adj* [ME, fr. MF, fr. prp. of *recroire* to renounce one's cause in a trial by battle, fr. *re-* + *croire* to believe, fr. L *credere* — more at CREED] (14c) **1** : crying for mercy : COWARDLY **2** : unfaithful to duty or allegiance

²**recreant** *n* (15c) **1** : COWARD **2** : APOSTATE, DESERTER

rec·re·ate \'re-krē-ˌāt\ *vb* **-at·ed; -at·ing** [L *recreatus*, pp. of *recreare*] *vt* (1530) : to give new life or freshness to : REFRESH ~ *vi* : to take recreation — **rec·re·a·tive** \-ˌā-tiv\ *adj*

re·cre·ate \ˌrē-krē-'āt\ *vt* (1587) : to create again; *esp* : to form anew in the imagination — **re·cre·at·able** \-'ā-tə-bəl\ *adj* — **re·cre·a·tion** \-'ā-shən\ *n* — **re·cre·a·tive** \-'ā-tiv\ *adj* — **re·cre·a·tor** \-'ā-tər\ *n*

rec·re·a·tion \ˌre-krē-'ā-shən\ *n* [ME *recreacion*, fr. MF *recreation*, fr. L *recreation-, recreatio* restoration to health, fr. *recreare* to create anew, restore, refresh, fr. *re-* + *creare* to create] (15c) : refreshment of strength and spirits after work; *also* : a means of refreshment or diversion : HOBBY — **rec·re·a·tion·al** \-shnəl, -shə-n²l\ *adj*

recreational vehicle *n* (1966) : a vehicle designed for recreational use (as in camping); *esp* : MOTOR HOME

rec·re·a·tion·ist \-sh(ə-)nist\ *n* (1904) : a person who seeks recreation esp. in the outdoors

recreation room *n* (1854) **1** : a room (as a rumpus room) used for recreation and relaxation — called also *rec room* **2** : a public room (as in a hospital) for recreation and social activities

re·crim·i·na·tion \ri-ˌkri-mə-'nā-shən\ *n* [ML *recrimination-, recriminatio*, fr. *recriminare* to make a retaliatory charge, fr. L *re-* + *criminari* to accuse — more at CRIMINATE] (ca. 1611) : a retaliatory accusation; *also* : the making of such accusations ⟨endless ~⟩ — **re·crim·i·nate** \-'kri-mə-ˌnāt\ *vi* — **re·crim·i·na·tive** \-ˌnā-tiv\ *adj* — **re·crim·i·na·to·ry** \-'kri-mə-nə-ˌtōr-ē, -'krim-nə-, -ˌtōr-\ *adj*

re·cru·desce \ˌrē-krü-'des\ *vi* **-desced; -desc·ing** [L *recrudescere* to become raw again, fr. *re-* + *crudescere* to become raw, fr. *crudus* raw — more at RAW] (1884) : to break out or become active again

re·cru·des·cence \-'de-s²n(t)s\ *n* (ca. 1721) : a new outbreak after a period of abatement or inactivity : RENEWAL

\ə\ abut \²\ kitten, F table \ər\ further \a\ ash \ā\ ace \ä\ mop, mar \au\ out \ch\ chin \e\ bet \ē\ easy \g\ go \i\ hit \ī\ ice \j\ job \ŋ\ sing \ō\ go \o\ law \oi\ boy \th\ thin \th\ the \ü\ loot \u\ foot \y\ yet \zh\ vision \à, k, ⁿ, œ, œ̄, ue, ūe, ᵘ\ see Guide to Pronunciation

re·cru·des·cent \-s°nt\ *adj* (ca. 1727) : breaking out again : RENEWING

¹re·cruit \ri-'krüt\ *vt* (1643) **1 a** (1) : to fill up the number of (as an army) with new members : REINFORCE (2) : to enlist as a member of an armed service **b** : to increase or maintain the number of ⟨America ~*ed* her population from Europe⟩ **c** : to secure the services of : ENGAGE, HIRE **d** : to seek to enroll ⟨~ students⟩ **2** : REPLENISH **3** : to restore or increase the health, vigor, or intensity of ~ *vi* : to enlist new members — **re·cruit·er** *n*

²recruit *n* [F *recrute*, *recrue* fresh growth, new levy of soldiers, fr. MF, fr. *recroistre* to grow up again, fr. L *recrescere*, fr. *re-* + *crescere* to grow — more at CRESCENT] (ca. 1645) **1 a** : a fresh or additional supply **2** : a newcomer to a field or activity; *specif* : a newly enlisted or drafted member of the armed forces **3** : a former enlisted man of the lowest rank in the army

re·cruit·ment \ri-'krüt-mənt\ *n* (ca. 1828) **1** : the action or process of recruiting **2** : the process of adding new individuals to a population or subpopulation (as of breeding individuals) by growth, reproduction, immigration, and stocking; *also* : a measure (as in numbers or biomass) of recruitment

re·crys·tal·lize \(ˌ)rē-'kris-tə-ˌlīz\ *vb* (1797) : to crystallize again or repeatedly — **re·crys·tal·li·za·tion** \(ˌ)rē-ˌkris-tə-lə-'zā-shən\ *n*

rec·tal \'rek-t°l\ *adj* (ca. 1859) : relating to, affecting, or being near the rectum — **rec·tal·ly** *adv*

rect·an·gle \'rek-ˌtaŋ-gəl\ *n* [ML *rectangulus* having a right angle, fr. L *rectus* right + *angulus* angle — more at RIGHT, ANGLE] (1571) : a parallelogram all of whose angles are right angles; *esp* : one with adjacent sides of unequal length

rect·an·gu·lar \rek-'taŋ-gyə-lər\ *adj* (1624) **1** : shaped like a rectangle ⟨a ~ area⟩ **2 a** : crossing, lying, or meeting at a right angle ⟨~ axes⟩ **b** : having edges, surfaces, or faces that meet at right angles : having faces or surfaces shaped like rectangles ⟨~ parallelepipeds⟩ ⟨a ~ solid⟩ — **rect·an·gu·lar·i·ty** \(ˌ)rek-ˌtaŋ-gyə-'lar-ə-tē\ *n* — **rect·an·gu·lar·ly** \rek-'taŋ-gyə-lər-lē\ *adv*

rectangular coordinate *n* (ca. 1864) : a Cartesian coordinate of a Cartesian coordinate system whose straight-line axes or coordinate planes are perpendicular

rec·ti·fi·able \'rek-tə-ˌfī-ə-bəl\ *adj* [*rectify* (to determine the length of an arc)] (1816) : having finite length ⟨a ~ curve⟩ — **rec·ti·fi·abil·i·ty** \ˌrek-tə-ˌfī-ə-'bi-lə-tē\ *n*

rec·ti·fi·er \'rek-tə-ˌfī(-ə)r\ *n* (1611) : one that rectifies; *specif* : a device for converting alternating current into direct current

rec·ti·fy \'rek-tə-ˌfī\ *vt* **-fied; -fy·ing** [ME *rectifien*, fr. MF *rectifier*, fr. ML *rectificare*, fr. L *rectus* right — more at RIGHT] (14c) **1** : to set right : REMEDY **2** : to purify (as alcohol) esp. by repeated or fractional distillation **3** : to correct by removing errors : ADJUST ⟨~ the calendar⟩ **4** : to make (an alternating current) unidirectional **syn** see CORRECT — **rec·ti·fi·ca·tion** \ˌrek-tə-fə-'kā-shən\ *n*

rec·ti·lin·e·ar \ˌrek-tə-'li-nē-ər\ *adj* [LL *rectilineus*, fr. L *rectus* + *linea* line] (1659) **1** : moving in or forming a straight line ⟨~ motion⟩ **2** : characterized by straight lines **3** : PERPENDICULAR **3** — **rec·ti·lin·e·ar·ly** *adv*

rec·ti·tude \'rek-tə-ˌtüd, -ˌtyüd\ *n* [ME, fr. MF, fr. LL *rectitudo*, fr. L *rectus* straight, right] (15c) **1** : the quality or state of being straight **2** : moral integrity : RIGHTEOUSNESS **3** : the quality or state of being correct in judgment or procedure

rec·ti·tu·di·nous \ˌrek-tə-'tüd-nəs, -'tyüd-; -'tü-dᵊn-əs, -'tyü-\ *adj* [LL *rectitudin-, rectitudo* rectitude] (1897) **1** : characterized by rectitude **2** : piously self-righteous

rec·to \'rek-(ˌ)tō\ *n, pl* **rectos** [NL *recto* (*folio*) on the right-hand leaf] (1824) **1** : the side of a leaf (as of a manuscript) that is to be read first **2** : a right-hand page — compare VERSO

rec·tor \'rek-tər\ *n* [ME, fr. L, fr. *regere* to direct — more at RIGHT] (14c) **1** : one that directs : LEADER **2 a** : a clergyman (as of the Protestant Episcopal Church) in charge of a parish **b** : an incumbent of a Church of England benefice in full possession of its rights **c** : a Roman Catholic priest directing a church with no pastor or one whose pastor has other duties **3** : the head of a university or school — **rec·tor·ate** \-t(ə-)rət\ *n* — **rec·to·ri·al** \rek-'tōr-ē-əl, -'tȯr-\ *adj* — **rec·tor·ship** \'rek-tər-ˌship\ *n*

rec·to·ry \'rek-t(ə-)rē\ *n, pl* **-ries** (1594) **1** : a benefice held by a rector **2** : a residence of a rector or a parish priest

rec·trix \'rek-triks\ *n, pl* **rec·tri·ces** \'rek-trə-ˌsēz, rek-'trī-(ˌ)sēz\ [NL, fr. L, fem. of *rector* one that directs] (1768) : any of the quill feathers of a bird's tail that are important in controlling flight direction — see BIRD illustration

rec·tum \'rek-təm\ *n, pl* **rectums** *or* **rec·ta** \-tə\ [ME, fr. ML, fr. *rectum intestinum*, lit., straight intestine] (15c) : the terminal part of the intestine from the sigmoid flexure to the anus

rec·tus \'rek-təs\ *n, pl* **rec·ti** \-ˌtī, -ˌtē\ [NL, fr. *rectus musculus* straight muscle] (ca. 1704) : any of several straight muscles (as of the abdomen)

re·cum·ben·cy \ri-'kəm-bən(t)-sē\ *n, pl* **-cies** (1646) : the state of leaning, resting, or reclining : REPOSE; *also* : a recumbent position

re·cum·bent \-bənt\ *adj* [L *recumbent-, recumbens,* prp. of *recumbere* to lie down, fr. *re-* + *-cumbere* to lie down; akin to L *cubare* to lie] (1705) **1 a** : suggestive of repose : LEANING, RESTING **b** : lying down **2** : representing a person lying down ⟨a ~ statue⟩ **syn** see PRONE

re·cu·per·ate \ri-'kü-pə-ˌrāt, -'kyü-\ *vb* **-at·ed; -at·ing** [L *recuperatus,* pp. of *recuperare* — more at RECOVER] *vt* (1542) : to get back : REGAIN ~ *vi* : to regain a former state or condition; *esp* : to recover health or strength — **re·cu·per·a·tion** \-ˌkü-pə-'rā-shən, -ˌkyü-\ *n*

re·cu·per·a·tive \-'kü-pə-ˌrā-tiv, -'kyü-, -p(ə-)rə-tiv\ *adj* (ca. 1828) **1** : of or relating to recuperation ⟨~ powers⟩ **2** : aiding in recuperation : RESTORATIVE

re·cur \ri-'kər\ *vi* **re·curred; re·cur·ring** [ME *recurren* to return, fr. L *recurrere*, lit., to run back, fr. *re-* + *currere* to run — more at CAR] (1529) **1** : to have recourse : RESORT **2** : to go back in thought or discourse **3 a** : to come up again for consideration **b** : to come again to mind **4** : to occur again after an interval : occur time after time — **re·cur·rence** \-'kər-ən(t)s, -'kə-rən(t)s\ *n*

re·cur·rent \-'kər-ənt, -'kə-rənt\ *adj* [L *recurrent-, recurrens,* prp. of *recurrere*] (1611) **1** : running or turning back in a direction opposite to a former course — used of various nerves and branches of vessels in

the arms and legs **2** : returning or happening time after time ⟨~ complaints⟩ — **re·cur·rent·ly** *adv*

recurring decimal *n* (1801) : REPEATING DECIMAL

re·cur·sion \ri-'kər-zhən\ *n* [LL *recursion-, recursio,* fr. *recurrere*] (1616) **1** : RETURN **2** : the determination of a succession of elements (as numbers or functions) by operation on one or more preceding elements according to a rule or formula involving a finite number of steps **3** : a computer programming technique involving the use of a procedure, subroutine, function, or algorithm that calls itself in a step having a termination condition so that successive repetitions are processed up to the critical step until the condition is met at which time the rest of each repetition is processed from the last one called to the first — compare ITERATION

re·cur·sive \ri-'kər-siv\ *adj* (1934) **1** : of, relating to, or involving recursion ⟨a ~ function in a computer program⟩ **2** : of, relating to, or constituting a procedure that can repeat itself indefinitely ⟨a ~ rule in a grammar⟩ — **re·cur·sive·ly** *adv* — **re·cur·sive·ness** *n*

re·curved \(ˌ)rē-'kərvd\ *adj* (1597) : curved backward or inward

re·cu·san·cy \'re-kyə-zən(t)-sē, ri-'kyü-\ *n* (ca. 1600) : the act or state of being a recusant

re·cu·sant \-zənt\ *n* [L *recusant-, recusans,* prp. of *recusare* to refuse, fr. *re-* + *causari* to give a reason, fr. *causa* cause, reason] (ca. 1553) **1** : an English Roman Catholic of the time from about 1570 to 1791 who refused to attend services of the Church of England and thereby committed a statutory offense **2** : one who refuses to accept or obey established authority — **recusant** *adj*

re·cuse \ri-'kyüz\ *vt* **re·cused; re·cus·ing** [ME, to refuse, fr. MF *recuser,* fr. L *recusare*] (1949) : to disqualify (oneself) as judge in a particular case; *broadly* : to remove (oneself) from participation to avoid a conflict of interest — **re·cus·al** \-'kyü-zəl\ *n*

re·cut \(ˌ)rē-'kət, 're-\ *vt* (1664) **1** : to cut again **2** : to edit (as a film) anew

¹re·cy·cle \(ˌ)rē-'sī-kəl\ *vt* (1926) **1** : to pass again through a series of changes or treatments: as **a** : to process (as liquid body waste, glass, or cans) in order to regain material for human use **b** : RECOVER 6 **2** : to adapt to a new use : ALTER **3** : to bring back : REUSE ⟨~s a number of good anecdotes —Larry McMurtry⟩ **4** : to make ready for reuse ⟨a plan to ~ vacant tenements⟩ ~ *vi* **1** : to return to an earlier point in a countdown **2** : to return to an original condition so that operation can begin again — used of an electronic device — **re·cy·cla·ble** \-k(ə-)lə-bəl\ *adj or n* — **re·cy·cler** \-k(ə-)lər\ *n*

²recycle *n* (1926) : the process of recycling

¹red \'red\ *adj* **red·der; red·dest** [ME, fr. OE *rēad;* akin to OHG *rōt* red, L *ruber & rufus,* Gk *erythros*] (bef. 12c) **1 a** : of the color red **b** : having red as a distinguishing color **2 a** (1) : flushed esp. with anger or embarrassment (2) : RUDDY, FLORID (3) : being or having skin of a coppery hue **b** : BLOODSHOT ⟨eyes ~ from crying⟩ **c** : in the color range between a moderate orange and russet or bay **d** : tinged with red : REDDISH **3** : heated to redness : GLOWING **4 a** : inciting or endorsing radical social or political change esp. by force **b** *often cap* : COMMUNIST *often cap* : of or relating to a communist country and esp. to the U.S.S.R.

²red *n* (bef. 12c) **1** : a color whose hue resembles that of blood or of the ruby or is that of the long-wave extreme of the visible spectrum **2** : red clothing ⟨the lady in ~⟩ **3** : one that is of a red or reddish color: as **a** : RED WINE **b** : an animal with a red or reddish coat **4 a** : a pigment or dye that colors red **b** : a shade or tint of red **5 a** : one who advocates the violent overthrow of an existing social or political order **b** *cap* : COMMUNIST **6** [fr. the bookkeeping practice of entering debit items in red ink] : the condition of showing a loss — usu. used with *the* ⟨in the ~⟩; compare BLACK

re·dact \ri-'dakt\ *vt* [ME, fr. L *redactus,* pp. of *redigere*] (15c) **1** : to put in writing : FRAME **2** : to select or adapt for publication : EDIT

re·dac·tion \-'dak-shən\ *n* [F *rédaction,* fr. LL *redaction-, redactio* act of reducing, compressing, fr. L *redigere* to bring back, reduce, fr. *red-, re-* + *agere* to lead — more at AGENT] (1785) **1** : an act or instance of redacting something **2** : a work that has been redacted : EDITION, VERSION — **re·dac·tion·al** \-shnəl, -shə-n°l\ *adj*

re·dac·tor \-'dak-tər\ *n* (1816) : one who redacts a work; *esp* : EDITOR

red admiral *n* (1840) : a nymphalid butterfly (*Vanessa atalanta*) that is common in both Europe and America, has broad orange-red bands on the forewings, and feeds chiefly on nettles in the larval stage

red alert *n* (ca. 1951) : the final stage of alert in which enemy attack appears imminent; *broadly* : a state of alert brought on by impending danger

red alga *n* (1852) : any of a division (Rhodophyta) of chiefly marine algae that have predominantly red pigmentation

red admiral

red ant *n* (1667) : any of various reddish ants (as the pharaoh ant)

red·ar·gue \ri-'där-(ˌ)gyü\ *vt* **-gued; -gu·ing** [ME, fr. L *redarguere,* fr. *red-* + *arguere* to demonstrate, prove — more at ARGUE] (1627) *archaic* : CONFUTE, DISPROVE

red–bait \'red-ˌbāt\ *vb, often cap R, vt* (1940) : to subject (as a person or group) to red-baiting ~ *vi* : to engage in red-baiting — **red–bait·er** *n, often cap R*

red–bait·ing *n, often cap R* (1928) : the act of attacking or persecuting as a Communist or as communistic

red bay *n* (ca. 1730) : a small tree (*Persea borbonia*) of the southern U.S. that has dark red heartwood

red·bel·ly dace \'red-'be-lē-\ *n* (1884) : either of two small brightly marked No. American cyprinid fishes (*Phoxinus eos* and *P. erythrogaster*) — called also *red-bel·lied dace* \-lēd-\

red·bird \'red-ˌbərd\ *n* (1669) : any of several birds (as a cardinal, several tanagers, or the bullfinch) with predominantly red plumage

red blood cell *n* (1910) : any of the hemoglobin-containing cells that carry oxygen to the tissues and are responsible for the red color of vertebrate blood — called also *erythrocyte, red blood corpuscle, red cell, red corpuscle*

red–blood·ed \'red-'blə-dəd\ *adj* (1881) : VIGOROUS, LUSTY

red·bone \'red-ˌbōn\ *n* (1916) : any of a breed of moderate-sized speedy dark red or red and tan coonhounds of American origin

red·breast \'red-ˌbrest\ *n* (15c) **1** : a bird (as a robin) with a reddish breast **2** : a reddish-bellied sunfish (*Lepomis auritus*) of the eastern U.S. — called also *red-breasted bream*

red·brick \-ˌbrik\ *adj* (1943) **1** : built of red brick **2** *often cap* [fr. the common use of red brick in constructing the buildings of recently founded universities] : of, relating to, or being the British Universities founded in the 19th or early 20th century — compare OXBRIDGE, PLATE-GLASS

red·bud \-ˌbəd\ *n* (1705) : any of several leguminous trees (genus *Cercis*) with usu. pale rosy pink flowers

red bug *n* (1804) *Southern & Midland* : CHIGGER 2

red·cap \'red-ˌkap\ *n* (1918) : a baggage porter (as at a railroad station) — compare SKYCAP

red–carpet *adj* [fr. the traditional laying down of a red carpet for important guests to walk on] (1952) : marked by ceremonial courtesy ⟨~ treatment⟩

red carpet *n* (1951) : a greeting or reception marked by ceremonial courtesy — usu. used in the phrase *roll out the red carpet*

red cedar *n* (1682) **1** : a common juniper (*Juniperus virginiana*) chiefly of the eastern U.S. that has dark green closely imbricated scale-like leaves; *also* : a related tree (*J. silicicola*) of the southeastern U.S. **2** : an arborvitae (*Thuja plicata*) of the Pacific Northwest **3** : the red or reddish brown wood of a red cedar

red cent *n* (ca. 1839) : PENNY — used for emphasis in negative constructions

red clover *n* (bef. 12c) : a Eurasian clover (*Trifolium pratense*) that has globose heads of reddish purple flowers and is widely cultivated as a hay, forage, and cover crop

red·coat \'red-ˌkōt\ *n* (1520) : a British soldier esp. in America during the Revolutionary War

red coral *n* (ca. 1864) : a gorgonian (*Corallium nobile*) of the Mediterranean and adjacent parts of the Atlantic having a hard stony skeleton of a delicate red or pink color used for ornaments and jewelry

Red Cross *n* (1863) : a red Greek cross on a white background used as the emblem of the International Red Cross

red currant *n* (1622) : either of two currants (*Ribes sativum* and *R. rubrum*) often cultivated for their fruit; *also* : the fruit

¹**redd** \'red\ *vb* **redd·ed** *or* **redd; redd·ing** [ME (Sc), to clear, perh. alter. of *ridden* — more at RID] *vt* (ca. 1520) *chiefly dial* : to set in order — usu. used with *up* or *out* ~ *vi, chiefly dial* : to make things tidy — usu. used with *up*

²**redd** *n* [origin unknown] (1808) : the spawning ground or nest of various fishes

red deer *n* (15c) : ELK 1b — used for one of the Old World elk

red·den \'re-dᵊn\ *vb* **red·dened; red·den·ing** \'red-niŋ, 'red-ᵊn-iŋ\ *vt* (ca. 1611) : to make red or reddish ~ *vi* : to become red; *esp* : BLUSH

red·dish \'re-dish\ *adj* (14c) : tinged with red — **red·dish·ness** *n*

red dog *n* (1953) : BLITZ 2b — **red dog** *vb*

red drum *n* (1709) : CHANNEL BASS

¹**rede** \'rēd\ *vt* [ME — more at READ] (bef. 12c) **1** *dial* : to give counsel to : ADVISE **2** *dial* : INTERPRET, EXPLAIN

²**rede** *n* (bef. 12c) **1** *chiefly dial* : COUNSEL, ADVICE **2** *archaic* : ACCOUNT, STORY

red·ear \'red-ˌir\ *n* (ca. 1948) : a common sunfish (*Lepomis microlophus*) of the southern and eastern U.S. resembling the bluegill but having the back part of the operculum bright orange-red — called also *redear sunfish, shellcracker*

re·dec·o·rate \(ˌ)rē-'de-kə-ˌrāt\ *vt* (ca. 1611) : to freshen or change in appearance : REFURBISH ~ *vi* : to freshen or change a decorative scheme — **re·dec·o·ra·tion** \(ˌ)rē-ˌde-kə-'rā-shən\ *n* — **re·dec·o·ra·tor** \(ˌ)rē-'de-kə-ˌrā-tər\ *n*

re·deem \ri-'dēm\ *vt* [ME *redemen*, modif. of MF *redimer*, fr. L *redimere*, fr. *re-*, *red-* re- + *emere* to take, buy; akin to Lith *imti* to take] (15c) **1 a** : to buy back : REPURCHASE **b** : to get or win back **2** : to free from what distresses or harms : as **a** : to free from captivity by payment of ransom **b** : to extricate from or help to overcome something detrimental **c** : to release from blame or debt : CLEAR **d** : to free from the consequences of sin **3** : to change for the better : REFORM **4** : REPAIR, RESTORE **5 a** : to free from a lien by payment of an amount secured thereby **b** (1) : to remove the obligation of by payment ⟨the U.S. Treasury ~s savings bonds on demand⟩ (2) : to exchange for something of value ⟨~ trading stamps⟩ **c** : to make good : FULFILL **6 a** : to atone for : EXPIATE **b** (1) : to offset the bad effect of (2) : to make worthwhile : RETRIEVE **syn** see RESCUE — **re·deem·able** \-'dē-mə-bəl\ *adj*

re·deem·er \-'dē-mər\ *n* (15c) : a person who redeems; *esp, cap* : JESUS

re·deem·ing \-'dē-miŋ\ *adj* (1631) : serving to offset or compensate for a defect ⟨her performance is the film's ~ feature⟩

re·de·fine \ˌrē-di-'fīn\ *vt* (1872) **1** : to define (as a concept) again : REFORMULATE ⟨had to ~ their terms⟩ **2 a** : to reexamine or reevaluate esp. with a view to change **b** : TRANSFORM 1c — **re·def·i·ni·tion** \ˌrē-ˌde-fə-'ni-shən\ *n*

re·demp·tion \ri-'dem(p)-shən\ *n* [ME *redempcioun*, fr. MF *redemption*, fr. L *redemption-, redemptio*, fr. *redimere* to redeem] (14c) : the act, process, or an instance of redeeming

re·demp·tion·er \-sh(ə-)nər\ *n* (1771) : an immigrant to America in the 18th and 19th centuries who obtained passage by becoming an indentured servant

re·demp·tive \-'dem(p)-tiv\ *adj* (15c) : of, relating to, or bringing about redemption

Re·demp·tor·ist \ri-'dem(p)-t(ə-)rist\ *n* [F *rédemptoriste*, fr. LL *redemptor* redeemer, fr. L, contractor, fr. *redimere*] (ca. 1842) : a member of the Congregation of the Most Holy Redeemer founded by St. Alphonsus Liguori in Scala, Italy, in 1732 and devoted to preaching

re·demp·to·ry \ri-'dem(p)-t(ə-)rē\ *adj* (1602) : serving to redeem

re·de·ploy \ˌrē-di-'plȯi\ *vt* (1945) : to transfer from one area or activity to another ~ *vi* : to relocate men or equipment — **re·de·ploy·ment** \-mənt\ *n*

re·de·scribe \ˌrē-di-'skrīb\ *vt* (1871) : to describe anew or again; *esp* : to give a new and more complete description to (a biological taxon)

re·de·scrip·tion \-'skrip-shən\ *n* (1884) : a new and more complete description esp. of a biological taxon

re·de·sign \ˌrē-di-'zīn\ *vt* (1891) : to revise in appearance, function, or content — **redesign** *n*

re·de·vel·op \ˌrē-di-'ve-ləp\ *vt* (1882) : to develop again; *esp* : REDESIGN, REBUILD — **re·de·vel·op·er** *n*

re·de·vel·op·ment \-mənt\ *n* (1873) : the act or process of redeveloping; *esp* : renovation of a blighted area

red–eye \'red-ˌī\ *n* (1819) **1** : cheap whiskey **2** : a late night or overnight flight

red–eye gravy \'red-ˌī-\ *n* (1947) : gravy made from the juices of ham and often flavored with coffee

red fescue *n* (1900) : a perennial pasture and turf grass (*Festuca rubra*) of Eurasia and No. America with creeping rootstocks, erect culms, and reddish spikelets

red·fish \'red-ˌfish\ *n* (15c) : any of various reddish fishes: as **a** (1) : a marine scorpaenid food fish (*Sebastes marinus*) of the northern coasts of Europe and No. America that is usu. bright rose-red when mature — called also *rosefish* (2) : a fish (*Sebastes mentella*) related to the redfish **b** : CHANNEL BASS

red flag *n* (1777) **1** : a warning signal **2** : something that attracts usu. irritated attention

red flannel hash *n* (ca. 1907) : hash made esp. from beef, potatoes, and beets

red fox *n* (1778) : a usu. orange-red to reddish brown Holarctic fox (*Vulpes vulpes*) that has a white-tipped tail

red giant *n* (1916) : a star that has low surface temperature and a diameter that is large relative to the sun

red–green blindness *n* (1888) : dichromatism in which the spectrum is seen in tones of yellow and blue — called also *red-green color blindness*

Red Guard *n* (1966) : a member of a paramilitary youth organization in China in the 1960s

red gum *n* (1788) **1 a** : any of several Australian eucalyptus trees (esp. *Eucalyptus camaldulensis, E. amygdalina,* and *E. calophylla*) **b** : eucalyptus gum **2** : SWEET GUM

red–hand·ed \'red-'han-dəd\ *adv or adj* (1819) : in the act of committing a crime or misdeed ⟨caught ~⟩

red·head \'red-ˌhed\ *n* (1664) **1** : a person having red hair **2** : a No. American duck (*Aythya americana*) resembling the related canvasback but having a shorter bill with a black tip and in the male a brighter reddish head

red·head·ed \-ˌhe-dəd\ *adj* (1565) : having red hair or a red head

red heat *n* (1686) : the state of being red-hot; *also* : the temperature at which a substance is red-hot

red herring *n* (15c) **1** : a herring cured by salting and slow smoking to a dark brown color **2** [fr. the practice of drawing a red herring across a trail to confuse hunting dogs] : something that distracts attention from the real issue

red·horse \'red-ˌhȯrs\ *n* (1796) : any of numerous large suckers (genus *Moxostoma*) of No. American rivers and lakes with the males having red fins esp. in the breeding season

red–hot \'red-'hät\ *adj* (14c) : extremely hot: as **a** : glowing with heat **b** : exhibiting or marked by intense emotion, enthusiasm, or violence ⟨a ~ campaign⟩ **c** : FRESH, NEW ⟨~ news⟩ **d** : extremely popular

red hot *n* (1835) **1** : one who shows intense emotion or partisanship **2** : HOT DOG 1 **3** : a small red candy strongly flavored with cinnamon

re·dia \'rē-dē-ə\ *n, pl* **re·di·ae** \-dē-ˌē\ *also* **re·di·as** [NL, fr. Francesco *Redi* †1698² Ital. naturalist] (1877) : a larva produced within the sporocyst of many trematodes that produces another generation of rediae or develops into a cercaria — **re·di·al** \-dē-əl\ *adj*

re·di·al \'rē-ˌdī(-ə)l, rē-'\ *n* (1980) : a function on a telephone that automatically repeats the dialing of the last number called; *also* : a button that invokes this function — **re·dial** *vb*

Red Indian *n* (1831) *chiefly Brit* : AMERICAN INDIAN

red·in·gote \'re-din-ˌgōt\ *n* [F, modif. of E *riding coat*] (1793) : a fitted outer garment: as **a** : a double-breasted coat with wide flat cuffs and collar worn by men in the 18th century **b** : a woman's lightweight coat open at the front **c** : a dress with a front gore of contrasting material

red ink *n* [fr. the use of red ink in financial statements to indicate a loss] (1926) **1** : a business loss : DEFICIT **2** : the condition of showing a business loss

red·in·te·grate \ri-'din-tə-ˌgrāt, rē-\ *vt* [ME, fr. L *redintegratus*, pp. of *redintegrare*, fr. *re-*, *red-* re- + *integrare* to make complete — more at INTEGRATE] (15c) *archaic* : to restore to a former and esp. sound state

red·in·te·gra·tion \ri-ˌdin-tə-'grā-shən, rē-\ *n* (15c) **1** *archaic* : restoration to a former state **2 a** : revival of the whole of a previous mental state when a phase of it recurs **b** : arousal of any response by a part of the complex of stimuli that originally aroused that response — **red·in·te·gra·tive** \-'din-tə-ˌgrā-tiv\ *adj*

re·di·rect \ˌrē-də-'rekt, ˌrē-(ˌ)dī-\ *vt* (1844) : to change the course or direction of — **re·di·rec·tion** \-'rek-shən\ *n*

¹**re·dis·count** \(ˌ)rē-'dis-ˌkaunt, ˌrē-dis-'\ *vt* (1866) : to discount again (as commercial paper) — **re·dis·count·able** \-ˌkaun-tə-bəl, -'kaun-\ *adj*

²**re·dis·count** \(ˌ)rē-'dis-ˌkaunt\ *n* (1892) **1** : the act or process of rediscounting **2** : negotiable paper that is rediscounted

re·dis·trib·ute \ˌrē-də-'stri-byət\ *vt* (1611) **1** : to alter the distribution of : REALLOCATE **2** : to spread to other areas — **re·dis·tri·bu·tion** \(ˌ)rē-ˌdis-trə-'byü-shən\ *n* — **re·dis·tri·bu·tion·al** \-shnəl, -shə-nᵊl\ *adj* — **re·dis·trib·u·tive** \ˌrē-də-'stri-byə-tiv\ *adj*

redingote a

\ə\ abut \ᵊ\ kitten, F table \ər\ further \a\ ash \ā\ ace \ä\ mop, mar \au̇\ out \ch\ chin \e\ bet \ē\ easy \g\ go \i\ hit \ī\ ice \j\ job \ŋ\ sing \ō\ go \ȯ\ law \ȯi\ boy \th\ thin \tẖ\ the \ü\ loot \u̇\ foot \y\ yet \zh\ vision \ä, k̲, ⁿ, œ, œ̄, ue, ue̅, ᵊ\ *see* Guide to Pronunciation

re·dis·tri·bu·tion·ist \(ˌ)rē-ˌdis-trə-'byü-sh(ə-)nist\ *n* (1979) : one that believes in or advocates a welfare state

re·dis·trict \(ˌ)rē-'dis-(ˌ)trikt\ *vt* (1850) : to divide anew into districts; *specif* : to revise the legislative districts of ~ *vi* : to revise legislative districts

red·i·vi·vus \ˌred-ə-'vī-vəs, -'vē-\ *adj* [LL, fr. L, reused] (1675) : brought back to life : REBORN — used postpositively

red lead *n* (15c) : an orange-red to brick-red lead oxide Pb₃O₄ used in storage-battery plates, in glass and ceramics, and as a paint pigment

red leaf *n* (1909) : any of several plant diseases characterized by reddening of the foliage

red·leg \'red-ˌleg, -ˌlāg\ *n* (1900) : ARTILLERYMAN

red–legged grasshopper *n* (1867) : a widely distributed and sometimes highly destructive small No. American grasshopper (*Melanoplus femur-rubrum*) with red hind legs — called also *red-legged locust*

red–let·ter \'red-ˌle-tər\ *adj* [fr. the practice of marking holy days in red letters in church calendars] (1704) : of special significance

red light *n* (1849) : a warning signal; *esp* : a red traffic signal

red–light district *n* (1900) : a district in which houses of prostitution are numerous

¹red·line \'red-'līn\ *n* (1952) : a recommended safety limit : the fastest, farthest, or highest point or degree considered safe; *also* : the red line which marks this point on a gauge

²red·line \'red-ˌlīn, -'līn\ *vi* (1968) : to withhold home-loan funds or insurance from neighborhoods considered poor economic risks ~ *vt* : to discriminate against in housing or insurance

red·ly \'red-lē\ *adv* (1611) : in a red manner : with red color

red man *n* (1725)   **1** : AMERICAN INDIAN   **2** *cap R&M* [Improved Order of *Red Men*] : a member of a major benevolent and fraternal order

red maple *n* (1770) : a common tree (*Acer rubrum*) of the eastern and central U.S. that grows chiefly on moist soils, has reddish twigs and flowers, and yields a lighter and softer wood than the sugar maple

red marrow *n* (1900) : reddish bone marrow that is the seat of blood-cell production

red mass *n, often cap R&M* (1889) : a votive mass of the Holy Spirit celebrated in red vestments esp. at the opening of courts and congresses

red mite *n* (1894) : any of several mites having a red color: as   **a** : EUROPEAN RED MITE   **b** : CITRUS RED MITE

red mulberry *n* (1717) : a No. American forest tree (*Morus rubra*) with toothed leaves and soft durable wood; *also* : its edible usu. purple fruit

red mullet *n* (1762) : GOATFISH

red·neck \'red-ˌnek\ *n* (1830)   **1** : a white member of the Southern rural laboring class — sometimes used disparagingly   **2** : a person whose behavior and opinions are similar to those attributed to rednecks — often used disparagingly — **redneck** *also* **red-necked** \-ˌnekt\ *adj*

red·ness \-nəs\ *n* (bef. 12c) : the quality or state of being red or red-hot

re·do \(ˌ)rē-'dü\ *vt* **-did** \-'did\; **-done** \-'dən\; **-do·ing** \-'dü-iŋ\; **-does** \-'dəz\ (1597)   **1** : to do over or again   **2** : REDECORATE — **re·do** \'rē-ˌdü, ˌrē-'dü\ *n*

red oak *n* (1634)   **1** : any of numerous American oaks (as *Quercus rubra* and *Quercus falcata*) that have four stamens in each floret, acorns with the inner surface of the shell lined with woolly hairs, the acorn cap covered with thin scales, and leaf veins that usu. run beyond the margin of the leaf to form bristles   **2** : the wood of red oak

red ocher *n* (1572) : a red earthy hematite used as a pigment

red·o·lence \'re-dᵊl-ən(t)s\ *n* (15c)   **1** : an often pungent or agreeable odor   **2** : the quality or state of being redolent   *syn* see FRAGRANCE

red·o·lent \-ənt\ *adj* [ME, fr. MF, fr. L redolent-, redolens, prp. of redolēre to emit a scent, fr. re-, red- + olēre to smell — more at ODOR] (15c)   **1** : exuding fragrance : AROMATIC   **2** **a** : full of a specified fragrance : SCENTED ⟨air ~ of seaweed⟩   **b** : EVOCATIVE, SUGGESTIVE ⟨a city ~ of antiquity⟩   *syn* see ODOROUS — **red·o·lent·ly** *adv*

red osier *n* (1807) : a common shrubby No. American dogwood (*Cornus sericea* syn. *C. stolonifera*) with reddish purple twigs, white flowers, and globose blue or whitish fruit

re·dou·ble \(ˌ)rē-'də-bəl\ *vt* (15c)   **1** : to make twice as great in size or amount; *broadly* : INTENSIFY, STRENGTHEN   **2** **a** *obs* : to echo back   **b** *archaic* : REPEAT ~ *vi*   **1** : to become redoubled   **2** *archaic* : RESOUND   **3** : to double an opponent's double in bridge — **redouble** *n*

re·doubt \ri-'daut\ *n* [F redoute, fr. It ridotto, fr. ML reductus secret place, fr. L, withdrawn, fr. pp. of reducere to lead back — more at REDUCE] (ca. 1608)   **1** **a** : a small usu. temporary enclosed defensive work   **b** : a defended position : protective barrier   **2** : a secure retreat : STRONGHOLD

re·doubt·able \ri-'dau-tə-bəl\ *adj* [ME redoutable, fr. MF, fr. redouter to dread, fr. re- + douter to doubt] (15c)   **1** : causing fear or alarm : FORMIDABLE   **2** : ILLUSTRIOUS, EMINENT; *broadly* : worthy of respect — **re·doubt·ably** \-blē\ *adv*

re·dound \ri-'daund\ *vi* [ME, fr. MF redonder, fr. L redundare, fr. re-, red- re- + unda wave — more at WATER] (14c)   **1** *archaic* : to become swollen : OVERFLOW   **2** : to have an effect for good or ill ⟨new power alignments which may or may not ~ to the faculty's benefit —G. W. Bonham⟩   **3** : to become transferred or added : ACCRUE   **4** : REBOUND, REFLECT

red·out \'red-ˌaut\ *n* (1942) : a condition in which centripetal acceleration (as that created when an aircraft abruptly enters a dive) drives blood to the head and causes reddening of the visual field and headache

re·dox \'rē-ˌdäks\ *adj* [reduction + oxidation] (1928) : of or relating to oxidation-reduction

red panda *n* (1955) : PANDA 1

red–pen·cil \'red-ˌpen(t)-səl\ *vt* (1946)   **1** : CENSOR   **2** : CORRECT, REVISE

red pepper *n* (ca. 1591) : CAYENNE PEPPER

red pine *n* (1809)   **1** : a No. American pine (*Pinus resinosa*) that has reddish bark and two long needles in each cluster   **2** : the relatively hard wood of the red pine that consists chiefly of sapwood

red·poll \'red-ˌpōl\ *n* (1738) : either of two small finches (genus *Carduelis* syn. *Acanthis*) having brownish streaked plumage and a red or rosy crown; *esp* : one (*C. flammea*) found in northern regions of both of the New and Old World

red poll *n, often cap R&P* [alter. of *red polled*] (1891) : any of a breed of large hornless red beef cattle of English origin

¹re·dress \ri-'dres\ *vt* [ME, fr. MF redresser, fr. OF redrecier, fr. re- + drecier to make straight — more at DRESS] (14c)   **1** **a** (1) : to set right : REMEDY   (2) : to make up for : COMPENSATE   **b** : to remove the cause of (a grievance or complaint)   **c** : to exact reparation for : AVENGE   **2** *archaic*   **a** : to requite (a person) for a wrong or loss   **b** : HEAL   *syn* see CORRECT — **re·dress·er** *n*

²re·dress \ri-'dres, 'rē-ˌ\ *n* (14c)   **1** **a** : relief from distress   **b** : means or possibility of seeking a remedy ⟨without ~⟩   **2** : compensation for wrong or loss : REPARATION   **3** **a** : an act or instance of redressing   **b** : RETRIBUTION, CORRECTION

red ribbon *n* (1927) : a red ribbon usu. with appropriate words or markings awarded the second-place winner in a competition

red·root \'red-ˌrüt, -ˌrut\ *n* (1709)   **1** : a perennial herb (*Lachnanthes caroliniana* syn. *L. tinctoria*) of the bloodwort family of the eastern U.S. whose red root is the source of a dye   **2** : NEW JERSEY TEA   **3** : BLOODROOT   **4** : a pigweed (*Amaranthus retroflexus*) that bears greenish flowers in dense spikes with bracts almost twice as long as the sepals

red rust *n* (1846)   **1** : the uredinial stage of a rust   **2** : the diseased condition produced by red rust

red salmon *n* (1881) : SOCKEYE

red–shaft·ed flicker \'red-'shaf-təd-\ *n* (1846) : a flicker of western No. America with light red on the underside of the tail and wings, a gray nape with no red, and in the male red on each cheek

red·shank \'red-ˌshaŋk\ *n* (1525) : a common Old World sandpiper (*Tringa totanus*) with pale red legs and feet

red·shift \'red-'shift\ *n* (1923) : a displacement of the spectrum of a celestial body toward longer wavelengths that is a consequence of the Doppler effect or the gravitational field of the source — **red·shift·ed** *adj*

red·shirt \'red-ˌshort\ *n* [fr. the red jersey commonly worn by such a player in practice scrimmages against the regulars] (1955) : a college athlete who is kept out of varsity competition for a year in order to extend eligibility — **redshirt** *vb*

red–shoul·dered hawk \-ˌshōl-dərd-\ *n* (1812) : a common No. American hawk (*Buteo lineatus*) that has a banded tail and a light spot on the underside of the wings toward the tips

red sin·dhi \'sin-dē\ *n* [¹red + sindhi one belonging to Sind, Pakistan] (1946) : any of a breed of humped rather small red dairy cattle developed in southwestern Asia and extensively used for crossbreeding with European stock in tropical areas

red siskin *n* (1948) : a finch (*Carduelis cucullata*) of northern So. America that is scarlet with black head, wings, and tail

red·skin \'red-ˌskin\ *n* (1699) : AMERICAN INDIAN — usu. taken to be offensive

red snapper *n* (1755) : any of various reddish fishes (as of the genera *Lutjanus* and *Sebastes*) including several food fishes

red snow *n* (1678) : snow colored by various airborne dusts or by a growth of algae (as of the genus *Chlamydomonas*) that contain red pigment and live in the upper layer of snow; *also* : an alga causing red snow

red soil *n* (1889) : any of a group of zonal soils that develop in a warm temperate moist climate under deciduous or mixed forests and that have thin organic and organic-mineral layers overlying a yellowish brown leached layer resting on an illuvial red horizon — called also *red podzolic soil*

red spider *n* (1646) : SPIDER MITE

red spruce *n* (1777) : a spruce (*Picea rubens*) of eastern No. America that has pubescent twigs and yellowish green needles and is an important source of lumber and pulpwood

red squill *n* (1738)   **1** : a red-bulbed form of squill (*Urginea maritima*)   **2** : a rat poison derived from the bulb of red squill

red squirrel *n* (1682) : a common and widely distributed No. American squirrel (*Tamiasciurus hudsonicus*) that has reddish upper parts and is smaller than the gray squirrel

red star *n* (1903) : a star having a very low surface temperature and a red color

red·start \'red-ˌstärt\ *n* [red + obs. *start* handle, tail] (ca. 1570)   **1** : a small Old World songbird (*Phoenicurus phoenicurus*) of the family Turdidae) with the male having a white brow, black throat, and chestnut breast and tail   **2** : an American warbler (*Setophaga ruticilla* of the family Parulidae) with a black and orange male

red–tailed hawk \'red-ˌtāld-\ *n* (1805) : a widely distributed chiefly rodent-eating New World hawk (*Buteo jamaicensis*) that is usu. mottled dusky above and white streaked dusky and tinged with buff below and has a rather short typically reddish tail — called also *red-tail*

red-tailed hawk

red tape *n* [fr. the red tape formerly used to bind legal documents in England] (1736) : official routine or procedure marked by excessive complexity which results in delay or inaction

red tide *n* (1904) : seawater discolored by the presence of large numbers of dinoflagellates (esp. of the genera *Gonyaulax* and *Gymnodinium*) which produce a toxin poisonous esp. to many forms of marine vertebrate life and to humans who consume contaminated shellfish — compare SAXITOXIN

red·top \'red-ˌtäp\ *n* (1790) : any of various grasses (genus *Agrostis*) with usu. reddish panicles; *esp* : an important forage and lawn grass (*A. alba* syn. *A. gigantea*) of eastern No. America

re·duce \ri-'düs, -'dyüs\ *vb* **re·duced; re·duc·ing** [ME, to lead back, fr. L reducere, fr. re- + ducere to lead — more at TOW] (14c)   **1** : to draw together or cause to converge : CONSOLIDATE ⟨~ all the questions to one⟩   **b** (1) : to diminish in size, amount, extent, or number ⟨~ taxes⟩ ⟨~ the likelihood of war⟩   (2) : to decrease the volume and concentrate the flavor of by boiling ⟨add the wine and ~ the sauce for two minutes⟩   **c** : to narrow down : RESTRICT ⟨the Indians were reduced to small reservations⟩   **d** : to make shorter : ABRIDGE   **2** *archaic* : to restore to righteousness : SAVE   **3** : to bring to a specified state or condition ⟨the impact of the movie reduced them to tears⟩   **4** **a** : to force to capitulate **b** : FORCE, COMPEL **5 a** : to bring to a systematic form or character ⟨∼ natural events to laws⟩ **b** : to put down in written or printed form ⟨∼ an agreement to writing⟩ **6** : to correct (as a fracture) by bringing displaced or broken parts back into their normal positions **7 a** : to lower in grade or rank : DEMOTE **b** : to lower in condition or status : DOWNGRADE **8 a** : to diminish in strength or density **b** : to diminish in value **9 a** (1) : to change the denominations or form of without changing the value (2) : to construct a geometrical figure similar to but smaller than (a given figure) **b** : to transpose from one form into another : CONVERT **c** : to change (an expression) to an equivalent but more fundamental expression ⟨∼ a fraction⟩ **10** : to break down (as by crushing or grinding) : PULVERIZE **11 a** : to remove to the metallic state by removal of nonmetallic elements ⟨∼ an ore by heat⟩ **b** : DEOXIDIZE **c** : to combine with or subject to the action of hydrogen **d** (1) : to change (an element or ion) from a higher to a lower oxidation state (2) : to add one or more electrons (to an atom or ion or molecule) **12** : to change (a stressed vowel) to an unstressed vowel ∼ *vi* **1 a** (1) : to become diminished or lessened; *esp* : to lose weight by dieting (2) : to become reduced ⟨ferrous iron ∼s to ferric iron⟩ **b** : to become concentrated or consolidated **c** : to undergo meiosis **2** : to become converted or equated *syn* see DECREASE, CONQUER — **re·duc·er** *n* — **re·duc·ibil·i·ty** \-,dü-sə-'bil-ə-tē, -,dyü-\ *n* — **re·duc·ible** \-'dü-sə-bəl, -'dyü-\ *adj* — **re·duc·ibly** \-blē\ *adv*

reducing agent *n* (1885) : a substance that reduces a chemical compound usu. by donating electrons

re·duc·tant \ri-'dək-tənt\ *n* (1925) : REDUCING AGENT

re·duc·tase \-,tās, -,tāz\ *n* (1902) : an enzyme that catalyzes reduction

re·duc·tio ad ab·sur·dum \ri-'dək-tē-,ō-,ad-əb-'sər-dəm, -'dək-sē-ō-, -shē-, -'zər-\ *n* [LL, lit., reduction to the absurd] (1741) **1** : disproof of a proposition by showing an absurdity to which it leads when carried to its logical conclusion **2** : the carrying of something to an absurd extreme

re·duc·tion \ri-'dək-shən\ *n* [ME *reduccion* restoration, fr. MF *reduction*, fr. LL & L; LL *reduction-, reductio* reduction (in a syllogism), fr. L, restoration, fr. *reducere*] (1546) **1** : the act or process of reducing : the state of being reduced **2 a** : something made by reducing **b** : the amount by which something is reduced **3** [Sp *reducción*, fr. L *reductio-, reductio*] : a So. American Indian settlement directed by Jesuit missionaries **4** : MEIOSIS 2; *specif* : production of the gametic chromosome number in the first meiotic division — **re·duc·tion·al** \-shnəl, -shə-nᵊl\ *adj*

reduction division *n* (1891) : the usu. first division of meiosis in which chromosome reduction occurs; *also* : MEIOSIS 2

reduction gear *n* (1896) : a combination of gears used to reduce the input speed (as of a marine turbine) to a lower output speed (as of a ship's propeller)

re·duc·tion·ism \ri-'dək-shə-,ni-zəm\ *n* (1943) **1** : the attempt to explain all biological processes by the same explanations (as by physical laws) that chemists and physicists use to interpret inanimate matter; *also* : the theory that complete reductionism is possible **2** : a procedure or theory that reduces complex data or phenomena to simple terms; *esp* : OVERSIMPLIFICATION — **re·duc·tion·ist** \-sh(ə-)nist\ *n or adj* — **re·duc·tion·is·tic** \-,dək-shə-'nis-tik\ *adj*

re·duc·tive \ri-'dək-tiv\ *adj* (1633) **1** : of, relating to, causing, or involving reduction **2** : of or relating to reductionism : REDUCTIONISTIC — **re·duc·tive·ly** *adv* — **re·duc·tive·ness** *n*

re·dun·dan·cy \ri-'dən-dən(t)-sē\ *n, pl* **-cies** (ca. 1602) **1 a** : the quality or state of being redundant : SUPERFLUITY **b** : the use of redundant components; *also* : such components **c** *chiefly Brit* : dismissal from a job esp. by layoff **2** : PROFUSION, ABUNDANCE **3 a** : superfluous repetition : PROLIXITY **b** : an act or instance of needless repetition **4** : the part of a message that can be eliminated without loss of essential information

re·dun·dant \-dənt\ *adj* [L *redundant-, redundans,* prp. of *redundare* to overflow — more at REDOUND] (1594) **1** : exceeding what is necessary or normal : SUPERFLUOUS **b** : characterized by or containing an excess; *specif* : using more words than necessary **c** : characterized by similarity or repetition ⟨a group of particularly ∼ brick buildings⟩ **d** *chiefly Brit* : no longer needed for a job and hence laid off **2** : PROFUSE, LAVISH **3** : serving as a duplicate for preventing failure of an entire system (as a spacecraft) upon failure of a single component — **re·dun·dant·ly** *adv*

re·du·pli·cate \ri-'dü-pli-,kāt, 'rē-, -'dyü-\ *vt* [LL *reduplicatus,* pp. of *reduplicare,* fr. L *re-* + *duplicare* to double — more at DUPLICATE] (ca. 1570) **1** : to make or perform again : COPY, REPEAT **2** : to form (a word) by reduplication — **re·du·pli·cate** \-kət\ *adj*

re·du·pli·ca·tion \ri-,dü-pli-'kā-shən, ,rē-, -'dyü-\ *n* (1555) **1** : an act or instance of doubling or reiterating **2 a** : an often grammatically functional repetition of a radical element or a part of it occurring usu. at the beginning of a word and often accompanied by change of the radical vowel **b** (1) : a word or form produced by reduplication (2) : the repeated element in such a word or form **3** : ANADIPLOSIS — **re·du·pli·ca·tive** \ri-'dü-pli-,kā-tiv, 'rē-, -'dyü-\ *adj* — **re·du·pli·ca·tive·ly** *adv*

re·du·vi·id \ri-'dü-vē-əd, -'dyü-\ *n* [ultim. fr. L *reduvia* hangnail] (1888) : ASSASSIN BUG — **reduviid** *adj*

re·dux \(,)rē-'dəks, 'rē-,\ *adj* [L, returning, fr. *reducere* to lead back] (1873) : brought back — used postpositively

red·ware \'red-,war, -,wer\ *n* (ca. 1797) : earthenware pottery made of clay containing considerable iron oxide

red water *n* (1594) : any of several cattle diseases characterized by hematuria

red wheat *n* (1523) : a wheat that has red grains

red wine *n* (ca. 1754) : a wine with a predominantly red color derived during fermentation from the natural pigment in the skins of dark≈colored grapes

red·wing \'red-,wiŋ\ *n* (1657) **1** : a European thrush (*Turdus iliacus* syn. *T. musicus*) having the underwing coverts red **2** : RED-WINGED BLACKBIRD

red–winged blackbird \'red-,wiŋd-\ *n* (1797) : a No. American blackbird (*Agelaius phoeniceus*) of which the adult male is black with a patch of bright scarlet at the bend of the wings bordered behind with yellow or buff — called also *redwing blackbird*

red wolf *n* (1840) : a wolf (*Canis rufus* syn. *C. niger*) orig. of the southeastern U.S.

red·wood \'red-,wud\ *n* (1634) **1** : any of various woods yielding a red dye **2** : a tree that yields a red dyewood or produces red or reddish wood **3 a** : a commercially important coniferous timber tree (*Sequoia sempervirens*) of the bald cypress family that grows chiefly in coastal California and sometimes reaches a height of 360 feet (110 meters) — called also *coast redwood* **b** : its brownish red durable wood

red worm *n* (1935) : BLOODWORM

re·echo \(,)rē-'e-(,)kō\ *vi* (1590) : to repeat or return an echo : echo again or repeatedly : REVERBERATE ∼ *vt* : to echo back : REPEAT

¹**reed** \'rēd\ *n* [ME *rede,* fr. OE *hrēod;* akin to OHG *hriot* reed] (bef. 12c) **1 a** : any of various tall grasses with slender often prominently jointed stems that grow esp. in wet areas **b** : a stem of a reed **c** : a person or thing too weak to rely on : one easily swayed or overcome **2** : a growth or mass of reeds; *specif* : reeds for thatching **3** : ARROW **4** : a wind instrument made from the hollow joint of a plant **5** : an ancient Hebrew unit of length equal to 6 cubits **6 a** : a thin elastic tongue (as of cane, wood, metal, or plastic) fastened at one end over an air opening in a wind instrument (as a clarinet, organ pipe, or accordion) and set in vibration by an air current **b** : a woodwind instrument that produces sound by the vibrating of a reed against the mouthpiece ⟨the ∼s of an orchestra⟩ **7** : a device on a loom resembling a comb and used to space warp yarns evenly **8** : REEDING 1a — **reed·like** \-,līk\ *adj*

²**reed** *vt* (1951) : MILL 2

reed·buck \'rēd-,bək\ *n, pl* **reedbuck** *also* **reedbucks** (1834) : any of a genus (*Redunca*) of fawn-colored African antelopes in which the females are hornless

reed·ed \'rē-dəd\ *adj* (1829) : decorated with reeds or reeding ⟨a bed with ∼ posts⟩

re·ed·i·fy \(,)rē-'e-də-,fī\ *vt* **-fied; -fy·ing** [ME *reedifien,* fr. MF *reedifier,* fr. LL *reaedificare,* fr. L *re-* + *aedificare* to build — more at EDIFY] (15c) *Brit* : REBUILD

reed·ing \'rē-diŋ\ *n* (1815) **1 a** : a small convex molding — see MOLDING illustration **b** : decoration by series of readings **2** : MILLING

re·edit \(,)rē-'e-dət\ *vt* (1797) : to edit again : make a new edition of — **re·edi·tion** \,rē-ə-'di-shən\ *n*

reed·man \'rēd-,man\ *n* (1938) : one who plays a reed instrument

reed organ *n* (1851) : a keyboard wind instrument in which the wind acts on a set of free reeds

reed pipe *n* (ca. 1741) : a pipe-organ pipe producing its tone by vibration of a beating reed in a current of air

re·ed·u·cate \(,)rē-'e-jə-,kāt\ *vt* (1808) : to train again; *esp* : to rehabilitate through education — **re·ed·u·ca·tion** \(,)rē-,e-jə-'kā-shən\ *n* — **re·ed·u·ca·tive** \(,)rē-'e-jə-,kā-tiv\ *adj*

reedy \'rē-dē\ *adj* **reed·i·er; -est** (14c) **1** : abounding in or covered with reeds **2** : made of or resembling reeds; *esp* : SLENDER, FRAIL **3** : having the tone quality of a reed instrument — **reed·i·ness** \-nəs\ *n*

¹**reef** \'rēf\ *n* [ME *riff,* fr. ON *rif;* akin to OE *ribb* rib] (14c) **1** : a part of a sail taken in or let out in regulating size **2** : reduction in sail area by reefing

²**reef** *vt* (1667) **1** : to reduce the area of (a sail) by rolling or folding a portion **2** : to lower or bring inboard (a spar) wholly or partially ∼ *vi* : to reduce a sail by taking in a reef — **reef·able** \'rē-fə-bəl\ *adj*

³**reef** *n* [D *rif,* prob. of Scand origin; akin to ON *rif* reef of a sail] (1584) **1 a** : a chain of rocks or coral or a ridge of sand at or near the surface of water **b** : a hazardous obstruction **2** : LODE, VEIN — **reefy** \'rē-fē\ *adj*

¹**reef·er** \'rē-fər\ *n* (1818) **1** : one that reefs **2** : a close-fitting usu. double-breasted jacket or coat of thick cloth

²**reef·er** \-fər\ *n* [by shortening & alter.] (1914) **1** : REFRIGERATOR **2** : a refrigerator car, truck, trailer, or ship

³**reef·er** *n* [prob. modif. of MexSp *grifa*] (1931) : a marijuana cigarette; *also* : MARIJUANA 2

reef knot *n* (1841) : a square knot used in reefing a sail

¹**reek** \'rēk\ *n* [ME *rek,* fr. OE *rēc;* akin to OHG *rouh* smoke] (bef. 12c) **1** *chiefly dial* : SMOKE **2** : VAPOR, FOG **3** : a strong or disagreeable fume or odor

²**reek** *vi* (bef. 12c) **1** : to emit smoke or vapor **2 a** : to give off or become permeated with a strong or offensive odor **b** : to give a strong impression of some constituent quality or feature ⟨a neighborhood that ∼s of poverty⟩ **3** : EMANATE ∼ *vt* **1** : to subject to the action of smoke or vapor **2** : EXUDE, GIVE OFF ⟨a politician who ∼s charm⟩ — **reek·er** *n* — **reeky** \'rē-kē\ *adj*

¹**reel** \'rē(ə)l\ *n* [ME, fr. OE *hrēol;* akin to ON *hrœll* weaver's reed, Gk *krekein* to weave] (bef. 12c) **1** : a revolvable device on which something flexible is wound: as **a** : a small windlass at the butt of a fishing rod for the line **b** *chiefly Brit* : a spool or bobbin for sewing thread **c** : a flanged spool for photographic film; *esp* : one for motion pictures **2** : a quantity of something wound on a reel

²**reel** *vt* (14c) **1** : to wind on or as if on a reel **2** : to draw by reeling a line ⟨∼ a fish in⟩ ∼ *vi* : to turn a reel — **reel·able** \'rē-lə-bəl\ *adj*

³**reel** *vb* [ME *relen,* prob. fr. *reel,* n.] *vi* (14c) **1 a** : to turn or move round and round **b** : to be in a whirl **2** : to behave in a violent disorderly manner **3** : to waver or fall back (as from a blow) **4** : to walk or move unsteadily ∼ *vt* : to cause to reel

⁴**reel** *n* (1572) : a reeling motion

⁵**reel** *n* [prob. fr. ⁴*reel*] (ca. 1585) **1** : a lively Scottish-Highland dance; *also* : the music for this dance **2** : VIRGINIA REEL

re·elect \,rē-ə-'lekt\ *vt* (1601) : to elect for another term in office — **re·elec·tion** \-'lek-shən\ *n*

reel·er \'rē-lər\ *n* (ca. 1598) **1** : one that reels **2** : a motion picture having a specified number of reels ⟨a two-*reeler*⟩

reel off *vt* (1837) **1** : to tell or recite readily and usu. at length ⟨*reel off* a few jokes to break the ice⟩ **2** : to chalk up usu. as a series

\ə\ abut \ᵊ\ kitten, F table \ər\ further \a\ ash \ā\ ace \ä\ mop, mar \au̇\ out \ch\ chin \e\ bet \ē\ easy \g\ go \i\ hit \ī\ ice \j\ job \ŋ\ sing \ō\ go \ȯ\ law \ȯi\ boy \th\ thin \t͟h\ the \ü\ loot \u̇\ foot \y\ yet \zh\ vision \à, k̲, ⁿ, œ, œ̄, ᵫ, ᵫ̄, Ꙩ\ *see* Guide to Pronunciation

reel–to–reel *adj* (1961) : of, relating to, or utilizing magnetic tape that requires threading on a take-up reel ⟨a ~ tape recorder⟩

re·em·broi·der \‚rē-əm-'brói-dər\ *vt* (1927) : to outline a design (as on lace) with embroidery stitching

re·en·act \‚rē-ə-'nakt\ *vt* (ca. 1676) **1** : to enact (as a law) again **2** : to act or perform again **3** : to repeat the actions of (an earlier event or incident) — **re·en·act·ment** \-'nak(t)-mənt\ *n*

re·en·force \‚rē-ən-'fórs, -'fórs\ *var of* REINFORCE

re·en·ter \(‚)rē-'en-tər\ *vt* (15c) **1** : to enter (something) again **2** : to return to and enter ~ *vi* : to enter again

re·en·trance \(‚)rē-'en-trən(t)s\ *n* (1594) : REENTRY

¹re·en·trant \-'trant\ *adj* (1781) : directed inward

²reentrant *n* (1899) **1** : one that reenters : one that is reentrant **3** : an indentation in a landform

re·en·try \(‚)rē-'en-trē\ *n* (15c) **1** : a retaking possession; *esp* : entry by a lessor on leased premises on the tenant's failure to perform the conditions of the lease **2** : a second or new entry **3** : a playing card that will enable a player to regain the lead **4** : the action of reentering the earth's atmosphere after travel in space

reest \'rēst\ *vi* [prob. short for Sc *arrest* to arrest, fr. ME (Sc) *arreisten*, fr. MF *arester* — more at ARREST] (1786) *chiefly Scot* : BALK

¹reeve \'rēv\ *n* [ME *reve*, fr. OE *gerēfa*, fr. *ge-* (associative prefix) + *-rēfa* (akin to OE *-rōf* number, OHG *ruova*) — more at CO-] (bef. 12c) **1** : a local administrative agent of an Anglo-Saxon king **2** : a medieval English manor officer responsible chiefly for overseeing the discharge of feudal obligations **3 a** : the council president in some Canadian municipalities **b** : a local official charged with enforcement of specific regulations ⟨deer ~⟩

²reeve \'rēv\ *vb* **rove** \'rōv\ *or* **reeved; reev·ing** [origin unknown] *vt* (1627) **1** : to pass (as a rope) through a hole or opening **2** : to fasten by passing through a hole or around something **3** : to pass a rope through ~ *vi, of a rope* : to pass through a block or similar device

³reeve *n* [origin unknown] (1634) : the female of the ruff (sandpiper)

ref \'ref\ *n* (1899) : a referee in a game or sport

re·fash·ion \(‚)rē-'fa-shən\ *vt* (1803) : REMAKE, ALTER

re·fect \ri-'fekt\ *vt* [L *refectus*, pp. of *reficere*] (14c) *archaic* : to refresh with food or drink

re·fec·tion \ri-'fek-shən\ *n* [ME *refeccioun*, fr. MF *refection*, fr. L *refection-, refectio*, fr. *reficere* to restore, fr. *re-* + *facere* to make — more at DO] (14c) **1** : refreshment of mind, spirit, or body; *esp* : NOURISHMENT **2 a** : the taking of refreshment **b** : food and drink together : REPAST

re·fec·to·ry \ri-'fek-t(ə-)rē\ *n, pl* **-ries** [LL *refectorium*, fr. L *reficere*] (15c) : a dining hall (as in a monastery or college)

refectory table *n* (1923) : a long table with heavy legs

re·fel \ri-'fel\ *vt* **re·felled; re·fel·ling** [L *refellere* to prove false, refute, fr. *re-* + *fallere* to deceive] (1530) *obs* : REJECT, REPULSE

re·fer \ri-'fər\ *vb* **re·ferred; re·fer·ring** [ME *referren*, fr. L *referre* to bring back, report, refer, fr. *re-* + *ferre* to carry — more at BEAR] *vt* (14c) **1 a (1)** : to think of, regard, or classify within a general category or group **(2)** : to explain in terms of a general cause **b** : to allot to a particular place, stage, or period **c** : to regard as coming from or located in a specific area **2 a** : to send or direct for treatment, aid, information, or decision ⟨~ a patient to a specialist⟩ ⟨~ a bill back to a committee⟩ **b** : to direct for testimony or guaranty as to character or ability ~ *vi* **1 a** : to have relation or connection : RELATE **b** : to direct attention usu. by clear and specific mention ⟨no one *referred* to yesterday's quarrel⟩ **2** : to have recourse : glance briefly ⟨*referred* frequently to his notes while speaking⟩ — **re·fer·able** \'re-f(ə-)rə-bəl, ri-'fər-ə-\ *adj* — **re·fer·rer** \ri-'fər-ər\ *n*

¹ref·er·ee \‚re-fə-'rē\ *n* (1621) **1** : one to whom a thing is referred: as **a** : a person to whom a legal matter if referred for investigation and report or for settlement **b** : a person who reviews a paper and esp. a technical paper and recommends that it should or should not be published **c** *chiefly Brit* : REFERENCE 4a **2** : a sports official usu. having final authority in administering a game

²referee *vb* **-eed; -ee·ing** *vt* (1889) **1** : to conduct (as a match or game) as referee **2** : to arbitrate (as a legal matter) as a judge or third party **b** : to review (as a technical paper) before publication ~ *vi* : to act as a referee

¹ref·er·ence \'re-fərn(t)s, 're-f(ə-)rən(t)s\ *n* (1589) **1** : the act of referring or consulting **2** : a bearing on a matter : RELATION ⟨in ~ to your recent letter⟩ **3** : something that refers: as **a** : ALLUSION, MENTION **b** : something (as a sign or indication) that refers a reader or consulter to another source of information (as a book or passage) **c** : consultation of sources of information **4** : one referred to or consulted: as **a** : a person to whom inquiries as to character or ability can be made **b** : a statement of the qualifications of a person seeking employment or appointment given by someone familiar with the person **c (1)** : a source of information (as a book or passage) to which a reader or consulter is referred **(2)** : a work (as a dictionary or encyclopedia) containing useful facts or information **d** : DENOTATION, MEANING

²reference *adj* (1856) : used or usable for reference; *esp* : constituting a standard for measuring or constructing

³reference *vt* **-enced; -enc·ing** (1891) **1 a** : to supply with references **b** : to cite in or as a reference **2** : to put in a form (as a table) adapted to easy reference

reference mark *n* (1856) : a conventional mark (as *, †, or ‡) placed in written or printed text to direct the reader's attention esp. to a footnote

ref·er·en·dum \‚re-fə-'ren-dəm\ *n, pl* **-da** \-də\ *or* **-dums** [NL, fr. L, neut. of *referendus*, gerundive of *referre* to refer] (1847) **1 a** : the principle or practice of submitting to popular vote a measure passed on or proposed by a legislative body or by popular initiative **b** : a vote on a measure so submitted **2** : a diplomatic agent's note asking for government instructions

ref·er·ent \'re-f(ə)rənt\ *n* [L *referent-, referens*, prp. of *referre*] (1844) : one that refers or is referred to; *esp* : the thing that a symbol (as a word or sign) stands for — **referent** *adj*

ref·er·en·tial \‚re-fə-'ren(t)-shəl\ *adj* (1660) : of, containing, or constituting a reference — **ref·er·en·tial·i·ty** \-‚ren(t)-shē-'a-lə-tē\ *n* — **ref·er·en·tial·ly** \-'ren(t)-sh(ə-)lē\ *adv*

re·fer·ral \ri-'fər-əl\ *n* (1927) **1** : the act, action, or an instance of referring ⟨gave the patient a ~ to a specialist⟩ **2** : one that is referred

¹re·fill \(‚)rē-'fil\ *vt* (1681) : to fill again : REPLENISH ~ *vi* : to become filled again — **re·fill·able** \-'fi-lə-bəl\ *adj*

²re·fill \'rē-‚fil\ *n* (1886) **1** : a product or a container and a product used to refill the exhausted supply of a device **2** : something provided again; *esp* : a second or later filling of a medical prescription

re·fi·nance \‚rē-fə-'nan(t)s, (‚)rē-'fī-, ‚rē-(‚)fī-\ *vt* (1908) : to renew or reorganize the financing of ~ *vi* : to finance something anew

re·fine \ri-'fīn\ *vb* **re·fined; re·fin·ing** *vt* (1582) **1** : to free (as metal, sugar, or oil) from impurities or unwanted material **2** : to free from moral imperfection : ELEVATE **3** : to improve or perfect by pruning or polishing ⟨~ a poetic style⟩ **4** : to reduce in vigor or intensity **5** : to free from what is coarse, vulgar, or uncouth ~ *vi* **1** : to become pure or perfected **2** : to make improvement by introducing subtleties or distinctions — **re·fin·er** *n*

re·fined \ri-'fīnd\ *adj* (1588) **1** : FASTIDIOUS, CULTIVATED **2** : free from impurities **3** : PRECISE, EXACT ⟨a ~ test for radioactivity⟩

re·fine·ment \ri-'fīn-mənt\ *n* (ca. 1611) **1** : the action or process of refining **2** : the quality or state of being refined : CULTIVATION **3 a** : a refined feature or method **b** : a highly refined distinction : SUBTLETY **c** : a contrivance or device intended to improve or perfect

re·fin·ery \ri-'fī-nə-rē, -'fin-rē\ *n, pl* **-er·ies** (ca. 1741) : a building and equipment for refining or processing (as oil or sugar)

re·fin·ish \(‚)rē-'fi-nish\ *vt* (1931) : to give (as furniture) a new surface ~ *vi* : to refinish furniture — **re·fin·ish·er** *n*

¹re·fit \(‚)rē-'fit\ *vt* (1666) : to fit out or supply again ~ *vi* : to obtain repairs or fresh supplies or equipment

²re·fit \'rē-‚fit, (‚)rē-\ *n* (1799) : the action of refitting; *esp* : a refitting and renovating of a ship

re·fla·tion \(‚)rē-'flā-shən\ *n* [*re-* + *-flation* (as in *deflation*)] (1932) : restoration of deflated prices to a desirable level — **re·flate** \(‚)rē-'flāt\ *vb* — **re·fla·tion·ary** \-shə-‚ner-ē\ *adj*

re·flect \ri-'flekt\ *vb* [ME, fr. L *reflectere* to bend back, fr. *re-* + *flectere* to bend] *vt* (15c) **1** *archaic* : to turn into or away from a course : DEFLECT **2** : to prevent passage of and cause to change direction ⟨a mirror ~s light⟩ **3** : to bend or fold back **4** : to give back or exhibit as an image, likeness, or outline : MIRROR ⟨the clouds were ~*ed* in the water⟩ **5** : to bring or cast as a result ⟨his attitude ~s little credit on his judgment⟩ **6** : to make manifest or apparent : SHOW ⟨the pulse ~s the condition of the heart⟩ **7** : REALIZE, CONSIDER ~ *vi* **1** : to throw back light or sound **2 a** : to think quietly and calmly **b** : to express a thought or opinion resulting from reflection **3 a** : to tend to bring reproach or discredit ⟨an investigation that ~s on all the members of the department⟩ **b** : to bring about a specified appearance or characterization ⟨an act which ~s well on him⟩ **c** : to have a bearing or influence *syn* see THINK

re·flec·tance \ri-'flek-tən(t)s\ *n* (1926) : the fraction of the total radiant flux incident upon a surface that is reflected and that varies according to the wavelength distribution of the incident radiation — called also *re·flec·tiv·i·ty* \‚rē-‚flek-'ti-və-tē, ri-\

reflecting telescope *n* (ca. 1704) : REFLECTOR 2

re·flec·tion \ri-'flek-shən\ *n* [ME, alter. of *reflexion*, fr. LL *reflexion-, reflexio* act of bending back, fr. L *reflectere*] (14c) **1** : an instance of reflecting; *esp* : the return of light or sound waves from a surface **2** : the production of an image by or as if by a mirror **3 a** : the action of bending or folding back **b** : a reflected part : FOLD **4** : something produced by reflecting: as **a** : an image given back by a reflecting surface **b** : an effect produced by an influence ⟨the high crime rate is a ~ of our violent society⟩ **5** : an often obscure or indirect criticism : REPROACH ⟨no ~ on his character⟩ **6** : a thought, idea, or opinion formed or a remark made as a result of meditation **7** : consideration of some subject matter, idea, or purpose **8** *obs* : turning back : RETURN **9** *a* : a transformation of a figure in which each point is replaced by a point symmetric with respect to a line or plane **b** : a transformation that involves reflection in more than one axis of a rectangular coordinate system — **re·flec·tion·al** \-shnəl, -shə-nᵊl\ *adj*

re·flec·tive \ri-'flek-tiv\ *adj* (1627) **1** : capable of reflecting light, images, or sound waves **2** : marked by reflection : THOUGHTFUL, DELIBERATIVE **3** : of, relating to, or caused by reflection ⟨~ glare⟩ **4** : REFLEXIVE 3 — **re·flec·tive·ly** *adv* — **re·flec·tive·ness** *n*

re·flec·tom·e·ter \‚rē-‚flek-'tä-mə-tər, ri-\ *n* (1891) : a device for measuring the reflectance of radiant energy (as light) — **re·flec·tom·e·try** \-mə-trē\ *n*

re·flec·tor \ri-'flek-tər\ *n* (1665) **1** : one that reflects; *esp* : a polished surface for reflecting light or other radiation **2** : a telescope in which the principal focusing element is a mirror

re·flec·tor·ize \-'tə-‚rīz\ *vt* **-ized; -iz·ing** (1940) **1** : to make reflecting **2** : to provide with reflectors

¹re·flex \'rē-‚fleks\ *n* [L *reflexus*, pp. of *reflectere* to reflect] (1508) **1 a** : reflected heat, light, or color **b** : a mirrored image **c** : a copy exact in essential or peculiar features **2 a** : an automatic and often inborn response to a stimulus that involves a nerve impulse passing inward from a receptor to a nerve center and thence outward to an effector (as a muscle or gland) without reaching the level of consciousness — compare HABIT **b** : the process that culminates in a reflex and comprises reception, transmission, and reaction — called also *reflex action* **c** *pl* : the power of acting or responding with adequate speed **d** : a way of thinking or behaving **3** : a linguistic element (as a word or sound) or system (as writing) that is derived from a prior and esp. an older element or system ⟨*boat* is the ~ of Old English *bāt*⟩

²reflex *adj* [L *reflexus*] (1649) **1** : directed back on the mind or its operations : INTROSPECTIVE **2** : bent, turned, or directed back : REFLECTED ⟨a stem with ~ leaves⟩ **3** : produced or carried out in reaction, resistance, or return **4** *of an angle* : being between 180° and 360° **5** : of, relating to, or produced by a reflex without intervention of consciousness — **re·flex·ly** *adv*

reflex arc *n* (1882) : the complete nervous path involved in a reflex

re·flexed \'rē-‚flekst, ri-\ *adj* [L *reflexus* + E ¹*-ed*] (1733) : bent or curved backward or downward ⟨~ petals⟩ ⟨~ leaves⟩

re·flex·ion *chiefly Brit var of* REFLECTION

¹re·flex·ive \ri-'flek-siv\ *adj* [ML *reflexivus*, fr. L *reflexus*] (1640) **1 a** : directed or turned back on itself **b** : marked by or capable of reflection : REFLECTIVE **2** : of, relating to, characterized by, or being a relation that exists between an entity and itself ⟨the relation "is equal to" ~ but the relation "is the father of" is not⟩ **3** : of, relating to, or constituting an action (as in "he perjured himself") directed back on the agent or the grammatical subject **4** : characterized by habitual and unthinking behavior — **re·flex·ive·ly** *adv* — **re·flex·ive·ness** *n* — **re·flex·iv·i·ty** \ˌrē-ˌflek-'si-və-tē, ri-\ *n*

²**reflexive** *n* (1866) : REFLEXIVE PRONOUN

reflexive pronoun *n* (1867) : a pronoun referring to the subject of the sentence, clause, or verbal phrase in which it stands; *specif* : a personal pronoun compounded with -*self*

re·flex·ol·o·gy \ˌrē-ˌflek-'sä-lə-jē\ *n* [ISV] (1923) **1** : the study and interpretation of behavior in terms of simple and complex reflexes **2** : massage of the hands or feet based on the belief that pressure applied to specific points on these extremities benefits other parts of the body

re·flow \(ˌ)rē-'flō\ *vi* (14c) **1** : to flow back **2** : to flow in again — **re·flow** \'rē-ˌflō\ *n*

ref·lu·ence \'re-ˌflü-ən(t)s, re-'flü-\ *n* (15c) *archaic* : REFLUX 1

re·flu·ent \-ənt\ *adj* [ME, fr. L *refluent-, refluens*, prp. of *refluere* to flow back, fr. *re-* + *fluere* to flow — more at FLUID] (15c) : flowing back

¹**re·flux** \'rē-ˌfləks\ *n* [ME, fr. ML *refluxus*, fr. L *re-* + *fluxus* flow — more at FLUX] (15c) **1** : a flowing back : EBB **2** : a process of refluxing or condition of being refluxed

²**re·flux** \-'fləks, 'rē-\ *vt* (1926) : to cause to flow back or return; *esp* : to heat so that the vapors formed condense and return to be heated again

re·fo·cus \(ˌ)rē-'fō-kəs\ *vt* (ca. 1865) **1** : to focus again **2** : to change the emphasis or direction of ⟨had ~ed his life⟩ ~ *vi* **1** : to focus something again **2** : to change emphasis or direction

re·for·es·ta·tion \(ˌ)rē-ˌför-ə-'stā-shən, -ˌfär-\ *n* (1887) : the action of renewing forest cover by planting seeds or young trees — **re·for·est** \(ˌ)rē-'för-əst, -'fär-\ *vt*

¹**re·form** \ri-'förm\ *vb* [ME, fr. MF *reformer*, fr. L *reformare*, fr. *re-* + *formare* to form, fr. *forma* form] *vt* (14c) **1 a** : to put or change into an improved form or condition **b** : to amend or improve by change of form or removal of faults or abuses **2** : to put an end to (an evil) by enforcing or introducing a better method or course of action **3** : to induce or cause to abandon evil ways ⟨~ a drunkard⟩ **4 a** : to subject (hydrocarbons) to cracking **b** : to produce (as gasoline or gas) by cracking ~ *vi* : to become improved for the better *syn* see CORRECT — **re·form·abil·i·ty** \ˌför-mə-'bi-lə-tē\ *n* — **re·form·able** \-'för-mə-bəl\ *adj*

²**reform** *n* (1663) **1** : amendment of what is defective, vicious, corrupt, or depraved **2** : a removal or correction of an abuse, a wrong, or errors **3** *cap* : REFORM JUDAISM

³**reform** *adj* (1819) : relating to or favoring reform

re—form \ˌrē-'förm\ *vt* (14c) : to form again ~ *vi* : to take form again ⟨the ice ~ed on the lake⟩

re·for·mate \ri-'för-ˌmāt, -mət\ *n* (1949) : a product of hydrocarbon reforming

ref·or·ma·tion \ˌre-fər-'mā-shən\ *n* (15c) **1** : the act of reforming : the state of being reformed **2** *cap* : a 16th century religious movement marked ultimately by rejection or modification of some Roman Catholic doctrine and practice and establishment of the Protestant churches — **ref·or·ma·tion·al** \-shnəl, -shə-n²l\ *adj*

re·for·ma·tive \ri-'för-mə-tiv\ *adj* (1593) : intended or tending to reform

¹**re·for·ma·to·ry** \ri-'för-mə-ˌtōr-ē, -ˌtor-\ *adj* (1589) : REFORMATIVE

²**reformatory** *n, pl* -**ries** (1834) : a penal institution to which esp. young or first offenders are committed for training and reformation

re·formed *adj* (1563) **1** : changed for the better **2** *cap* : PROTESTANT; *specif* : of or relating to the chiefly Calvinist Protestant churches formed in various continental European countries

reformed spelling *n* (ca. 1934) : any of several methods of spelling English words that use letters with more phonetic consistency than conventional spelling and that usu. discard some silent letters (as in *pedagog* for *pedagogue*)

re·form·er \ri-'för-mər\ *n* (1548) **1** : one that works for or urges reform **2** *cap* : a leader of the Protestant Reformation **3** : an apparatus for cracking oils or gases to form specialized products

re·form·ism \ri-'för-ˌmi-zəm\ *n* (1904) : a doctrine, policy, or movement of reform — **re·form·ist** \-mist\ *n or adj*

Reform Judaism *n* (ca. 1905) : Judaism marked by a liberal approach in nonobservance of much legal tradition regarded as irrelevant to the present and in shortening and simplification of traditional ritual — compare CONSERVATIVE JUDAISM, ORTHODOX JUDAISM

reform school *n* (ca. 1859) : a reformatory for boys or girls

re·fract \ri-'frakt\ *vt* [L *refractus*, pp. of *refringere* to break open, break up, fr. *re-* + *frangere* to break — more at BREAK] (1612) **1 a** : to subject (as a ray of light) to refraction **b** : to alter or distort as if by refraction ⟨to ~ that familiar world through the mind and heart of a romantic ... woman —Anton Myrer⟩ **2** : to determine the refracting power of

re·frac·tile \-'frak-t²l, -ˌtīl\ *adj* (ca. 1849) : capable of refracting : REFRACTIVE

refracting telescope *n* (1764) : REFRACTOR

re·frac·tion \ri-'frak-shən\ *n* (1603) **1** : deflection from a straight path undergone by a light ray or energy wave in passing obliquely from one medium (as air) into another (as glass) in which its velocity is different **2** : the change in the apparent position of a celestial body due to bending of the light rays emanating from it as they pass through the atmosphere; *also* : the correction to be applied to the apparent position of a body because of this bending **3** : the action of distorting an image by viewing through a medium; *also* : an instance of this

refraction 1: *a* light ray, *b* reflected ray, *c* refracted ray

re·frac·tive \ri-'frak-tiv\ *adj* (1673) **1** : having power to refract **2** : relating or due to refraction — **re·frac·tive·ly** *adv* — **re·frac·tive·ness** *n* — **re·frac·tiv·i·ty** \ˌrē-ˌfrak-'ti-və-tē, ri-\ *n*

refractive index *n* (1839) : INDEX OF REFRACTION

re·frac·tom·e·ter \ˌrē-ˌfrak-'tä-mə-tər, ri-\ *n* [ISV] (ca. 1859) : an instrument for measuring indices of refraction — **re·frac·to·met·ric** \ri-ˌfrak-tə-'me-trik\ *adj* — **re·frac·tom·e·try** \ˌrē-ˌfrak-'tä-mə-trē, ri-\ *n*

re·frac·tor \ri-'frak-tər\ *n* (1769) : a telescope whose principal focusing element is a lens

¹**re·frac·to·ry** \ri-'frak-t(ə-)rē\ *adj* [alter. of *refractary*, fr. L *refractarius*, irreg. fr. *refragari* to oppose, fr. *re-* + *-fragari* (as in *suffragari* to support with one's vote)] (1606) **1** : resisting control or authority : STUBBORN, UNMANAGEABLE **2 a** : resistant to treatment or cure ⟨a ~ lesion⟩ **b** : unresponsive to stimulus **c** : IMMUNE, INSUSCEPTIBLE ⟨after recovery they were ~ to infection⟩ **3** : difficult to fuse, corrode, or draw out; *esp* : capable of enduring high temperature *syn* see UNRULY — **re·frac·to·ri·ly** \-t(ə-)rə-lē; ˌrē-ˌfrak-'tōr-ə-lē, ri-, -'tor-\ *adv* — **re·frac·to·ri·ness** \ri-'frak-t(ə-)rē-nəs\ *n*

²**refractory** *n, pl* -**ries** (1627) : a refractory person or thing; *esp* : a heat-resisting ceramic material

refractory period *n* (ca. 1880) : the brief period immediately following the response esp. of a muscle or nerve before it recovers the capacity to make a second response — called also *refractory phase*

¹**re·frain** \ri-'frān\ *vb* [ME *refreynen*, fr. MF *refreiner, refrener*, fr. L *refrenare*, fr. *re-* + *frenum* bridle — more at FRENUM] *vt* (14c) *archaic* : CURB, RESTRAIN ~ *vi* : to keep oneself from doing, feeling, or indulging in something and esp. from following a passing impulse — **re·frain·ment** \-mənt\ *n*

²**refrain** *n* [ME *refreyn*, fr. MF *refrain*, fr. *refraindre, refreindre* to resound, fr. L *refringere* to break up] (14c) : a regularly recurring phrase or verse esp. at the end of each stanza or division of a poem or song : CHORUS; *also* : the musical setting of a refrain

re·fran·gi·ble \ri-'fran-jə-bəl\ *adj* [irreg. fr. L *refringere* to break up] (1673) : capable of being refracted — **re·fran·gi·bil·i·ty** \-ˌfran-jə-'bi-lə-tē\ *n* — **re·fran·gi·ble·ness** \-'fran-jə-bəl-nəs\ *n*

re·fresh \ri-'fresh\ *vb* [ME *refresshen*, fr. MF *refreschir*, fr. OF, fr. *re-* + *freis* fresh — more at FRESH] *vt* (14c) **1** : to restore strength and animation to : REVIVE **2** : to freshen up : RENOVATE **3 a** : to restore or maintain by renewing supply : REPLENISH **b** : AROUSE, STIMULATE ⟨let me ~ your memory⟩ **4** : to run water over or restore water to ~ *vi* **1** : to become refreshed **2** : to take refreshment **3** : to lay in fresh provisions *syn* see RENEW

re·fresh·en \ri-'fre-shən, ˌrē-\ *vt* [*re-* + *freshen*] (1782) : REFRESH

re·fresh·er \ri-'fre-shər\ *n* (15c) **1** : something (as a drink) that refreshes **2** : REMINDER **3** : review or instruction designed esp. to keep one abreast of professional developments ⟨~ course⟩

re·fresh·ing \-shiŋ\ *adj* (ca. 1580) : serving to refresh; *esp* : agreeably stimulating because of freshness or newness — **re·fresh·ing·ly** \-shiŋ-lē\ *adv*

re·fresh·ment \ri-'fresh-mənt\ *n* (14c) **1** : the act of refreshing : the state of being refreshed **2 a** : something (as food or drink) that refreshes **b** *pl* (1) : a light meal (2) : assorted light foods

re·fried beans \'rē-ˌfrīd-\ *n pl* (1957) : beans cooked with seasonings, fried, then mashed and fried again

¹**re·frig·er·ant** \ri-'fri-jə-rənt, -'frij-rənt\ *adj* (1599) : allaying heat or fever

²**refrigerant** *n* (1676) : a refrigerant agent or agency: as **a** : a medication for reducing body heat **b** : a substance used in refrigeration

re·frig·er·ate \ri-'fri-jə-ˌrāt\ *vt* -**at·ed; -at·ing** [L *refrigeratus*, pp. of *refrigerare*, fr. *re-* + *frigerare* to cool, fr. *frigor-, frigus* cold — more at FRIGID] (1534) : to make or keep cold or cool; *specif* : to freeze or chill (as food) for preservation — **re·frig·er·a·tion** \-ˌfri-jə-'rā-shən\ *n*

re·frig·er·a·tor \ri-'fri-jə-ˌrā-tər\ *n* (1803) : something that refrigerates; *esp* : a room or appliance for keeping food or other items cool

reft *past of* REAVE

re·fu·el \(ˌ)rē-'fyü(-ə)l\ *vt* (1811) : to provide with additional fuel ~ *vi* : to take on additional fuel

¹**ref·uge** \'re-(ˌ)fyüj *also* -(ˌ)fyüzh\ *n* [ME, fr. MF, fr. L *refugium*, fr. *refugere* to escape, fr. *re-* + *fugere* to flee — more at FUGITIVE] (14c) **1** : shelter or protection from danger or distress **2** : a place that provides shelter or protection **3** : something to which one has recourse in difficulty

²**refuge** *vb* **ref·uged; ref·ug·ing** *vt* (1594) : to give refuge to ~ *vi* : to seek or take refuge

ref·u·gee \ˌre-fyu̇-'jē, 're-fyu̇-\\ *n* [F *réfugié*, pp. of (*se*) *réfugier* to take refuge, fr. L *refugium*] (1685) : one that flees; *esp* : a person who flees to a foreign country or power to escape danger or persecution — **ref·u·gee·ism** \-ˌi-zəm\ *n*

re·fu·gi·um \ri-'fyü-jē-əm\ *n, pl* -**gia** \-jē-ə\ [NL, fr. L, refuge] (1943) : an area of relatively unaltered climate that is inhabited by plants and animals during a period of continental climatic change (as a glaciation) and remains as a center of relict forms from which a new dispersion and speciation may take place after climatic readjustment

re·ful·gence \ri-'fu̇l-jən(t)s, -'fəl-\ *n* [L *refulgentia*, fr. *refulgent-, refulgens*, prp. of *refulgere* to shine brightly, fr. *re-* + *fulgēre* to shine — more at FULGENT] (1634) : a radiant or resplendent quality or state : BRILLIANCE — **re·ful·gent** \-jənt\ *adj*

¹**re·fund** \ri-'fənd, 'rē-\ *vb* [ME, fr. MF & L; MF *refonder*, fr. L *refundere*, lit., to pour back, fr. *re-* + *fundere* to pour — more at FOUND] (15c) **1** : to give or put back **2** : to return (money) in restitution, repayment, or balancing of accounts — **re·fund·abil·i·ty** \-ˌfən-də-'bi-lə-tē\ *n* — **re·fund·able** \-'fən-də-bəl\ *adj*

²**re·fund** \'rē-ˌfənd\ *n* (1866) **1** : the act of refunding **2** : a sum refunded

³**re·fund** \(ˌ)rē-'fənd\ *vt* [*re-* + ²*fund*] (ca. 1860) : to fund again

re·fur·bish \ri-'fər-bish\ *vt* (1611) : to brighten or freshen up : RENOVATE — **re·fur·bish·er** *n* — **re·fur·bish·ment** \-bish-mənt\ *n*

re·fus·al \ri-'fyü-zəl\ *n* (15c) **1** : the act of refusing or denying **2** : the opportunity or right of refusing or taking before others

¹**re·fuse** \ri-'fyüz\ *vb* **re·fused; re·fus·ing** [ME, fr. MF *refuser*, fr.

\ə\ abut \²\ kitten, F table \ər\ further \a\ ash \ā\ ace \ä\ mop, mar \au̇\ out \ch\ chin \e\ bet \ē\ easy \g\ go \i\ hit \ī\ ice \j\ job \ŋ\ sing \ō\ go \ȯ\ law \ȯi\ boy \th\ thin \t͟h\ the \ü\ loot \u̇\ foot \y\ yet \zh\ vision \ä, k̲, ⁿ, œ, œ̅, ᵫ, ᵫ̅, ᵜ\ *see* Guide to Pronunciation (assumed) VL *refusare*, perh. blend of L *refutare* to refute and *recusare* to demur — more at RECUSE] *vt* (14c) **1 :** to express oneself as unwilling to accept ⟨~ a gift⟩ ⟨~ a promotion⟩ **2 a :** to show or express unwillingness to do or comply with ⟨*refused* to answer the question⟩ **b :** DENY ⟨they were *refused* admittance to the game⟩ **3** *obs* : GIVE UP, RENOUNCE **4** *of a horse* : to decline to jump or leap over ~ *vi* : to withhold acceptance, compliance, or permission **syn** see DECLINE — **re·fus·er** *n*

²**ref·use** \'re-ˌfyüs, -ˌfyüz\ *n* [ME, fr. MF *refus* rejection, fr. OF, fr. *refuser*] (14c) **1 :** the worthless or useless part of something : LEAVINGS **2 :** TRASH, GARBAGE

³**ref·use** \'re-ˌfyüs, -ˌfyüz\ *adj* (15c) : thrown aside or left as worthless

re·fuse·nik *also* **re·fus·nik** \ri-'fyüz-(ˌ)nik\ *n* [part trans. of Russ *otkaznik*, fr. *otkaz* refusal] (1974) : a Soviet citizen and esp. a Jew refused permission to emigrate

ref·u·ta·tion \ˌre-fyü-'tā-shən\ *n* (ca. 1548) : the act or process of refuting

re·fute \ri-'fyüt\ *vt* **re·fut·ed; re·fut·ing** [L *refutare* to check, suppress, refute] (1597) **1 :** to prove wrong by argument or evidence : show to be false or erroneous **2 :** to deny the truth or accuracy of ⟨*refuted* the allegations⟩ — **re·fut·able** \-'fyü-tə-bəl\ *adj* — **re·fut·ably** \-blē\ *adv* — **re·fut·er** *n*

reg \'reg\ *n* [by shortening] (ca. 1925) : REGULATION ⟨federal ~s⟩

re·gal \'rē-gəl\ *adj* [ME, fr. MF or L; MF, fr. L *regalis* — more at ROYAL] (14c) **1 :** of, relating to, or suitable for a king **2 :** of notable excellence or magnificence : SPLENDID — **re·gal·i·ty** \ri-'ga-lə-tē\ *n* — **re·gal·ly** \'rē-gə-lē\ *adv*

¹**re·gale** \ri-'gā(ə)l\ *vb* **re·galed; re·gal·ing** [F *régaler*, fr. MF, fr. *re·gale*, n.] *vt* (ca. 1656) **1 :** to entertain sumptuously : feast with delicacies **2 :** to give pleasure or amusement to ⟨*regaled* us with tall tales⟩ ~ *vi* : to feast oneself : FEED

²**regale** *n* [F *régal*, fr. MF *regale*, fr. *re-* + *galer* to have a good time — more at GALLANT] (1670) **1 :** a sumptuous feast **2 :** a choice piece esp. of food

re·ga·lia \ri-'gāl-yə\ *n pl* [ML, fr. L, neut. pl. of *regalis*] (ca. 1540) **1 :** royal rights or prerogatives **2 a :** the emblems, symbols, or paraphernalia indicative of royalty **b :** decorations or insignia indicative of an office or membership **3 :** special dress; *esp* : FINERY

¹**re·gard** \ri-'gärd\ *n* [ME, fr. MF, fr. OF, fr. *regarder*] (14c) **1** *archaic* : APPEARANCE **2 a :** ATTENTION, CONSIDERATION ⟨due ~ should be given to all facets of the question⟩ **b :** a protective interest : CARE ⟨ought to have more ~ for his health⟩ **3 :** LOOK, GAZE **4 a :** the worth or estimation in which something or someone is held ⟨a man of small ~⟩ **b** (1) : a feeling of respect and affection : ESTEEM ⟨his hard work won him the ~ of his colleagues⟩ (2) *pl* : friendly greetings implying such feeling ⟨give him my ~s⟩ **5 :** a basis of action or opinion : MOTIVE **6 :** an aspect to be taken into consideration : RESPECT ⟨is a small school, and is fortunate in this ~⟩ **7** *obs* : INTENTION — **in regard to** : with respect to : CONCERNING — **with regard to** : in regard to

²**regard** *vb* [ME, fr. MF *regarder* to look back at, regard, fr. OF, fr. *re-* + *garder* to guard, look at — more at GUARD] *vt* (14c) **1 :** to consider and appraise usu. from a particular point of view ⟨is highly ~ed as a mechanic⟩ **2 :** to pay attention to : take into consideration or account **3 a :** to show respect or consideration for **b :** to hold in high esteem **4 :** to look at **5** *archaic* : to relate to ~ *vi* **1 :** to look attentively : GAZE **2 :** to pay attention : HEED — **as regards** : with respect to : CONCERNING

syn REGARD, RESPECT, ESTEEM, ADMIRE mean to recognize the worth of a person or thing. REGARD is a general term that is usu. qualified ⟨he is highly *regarded* in the profession⟩. RESPECT implies a considered evaluation or estimation ⟨after many years they came to *respect* her views⟩. ESTEEM implies greater warmth of feeling accompanying a high valuation ⟨no citizen of the town was more highly *esteemed*⟩. ADMIRE suggests usu. enthusiastic appreciation and often deep affection ⟨a friend that I truly *admire*⟩.

re·gar·dant \ri-'gär-dᵊnt\ *adj* [ME *regardand*, fr. MF *regardant*, prp. of *regarder*] (15c) : looking backward over the shoulder — used of a heraldic animal

re·gard·ful \ri-'gärd-fəl\ *adj* (ca. 1586) **1 :** HEEDFUL, OBSERVANT **2 :** full or expressive of regard or respect : RESPECTFUL — **re·gard·ful·ly** \-fə-lē\ *adv* — **re·gard·ful·ness** *n*

re·gard·ing *prep* (1866) : with respect to : CONCERNING

¹**re·gard·less** \ri-'gärd-ləs\ *adj* (1591) : HEEDLESS, CARELESS — **re·gard·less·ly** *adv* — **re·gard·less·ness** *n*

²**regardless** *adv* (1872) : despite everything ⟨went ahead with their plans ~⟩ *usage* see IRREGARDLESS

regardless of *prep* (1784) : without taking into account ⟨accepts all *regardless of* age⟩; *also* : in spite of ⟨*regardless of* our mistakes⟩

re·gat·ta \ri-'gä-tə, -'ga-\ *n* [It *regata*] (1652) : a rowing, speedboat, or sailing race or a series of such races

re·gen·cy \'rē-jən(t)-sē\ *n, pl* **-cies** (15c) **1 :** the office, jurisdiction, or government of a regent or body of regents **2 :** a body of regents **3 :** the period of rule of a regent or body of regents

Regency *adj* (1880) : of, relating to, or characteristic of the styles of George IV's regency as Prince of Wales during the period 1811–20

re·gen·er·a·cy \ri-'je-nə-rə-sē, -'jen-rə-\ *n* (1626) : the state of being regenerated

¹**re·gen·er·ate** \-rət\ *adj* [ME *regenerat*, fr. L *regeneratus*, pp. of *regenerare* to regenerate, fr. *re-* + *generare* to beget — more at GENERATE] (15c) **1 :** formed or created again **2 :** spiritually reborn or converted **3 :** restored to a better, higher, or more worthy state — **re·gen·er·ate·ly** *adv* — **re·gen·er·ate·ness** *n*

²**re·gen·er·ate** \ri-'je-nə-ˌrāt\ *vb* (1541) **1 :** to become formed again **2 :** to become regenerate : REFORM **3 :** to undergo regeneration ~ *vt* **1 a :** to subject to spiritual regeneration **b :** to change radically and for the better **2 a :** to generate or produce anew; *esp* : to replace (a body part) by a new growth of tissue **b :** to produce again chemically sometimes in a physically changed form **3 :** to restore to original strength or properties — **re·gen·er·a·ble** \-'je-nə-rə-bəl, -'jen-rə-\ *adj*

³**re·gen·er·ate** *same as* ¹\ *n* (ca. 1569) : one that is regenerated: as **a** : an individual who is spiritually reborn **b** (1) : an organism that has undergone regeneration (2) : a regenerated body part

regenerated cellulose *n* (1904) : cellulose obtained in a changed form by chemical treatment (as of a cellulose solution or derivative)

re·gen·er·a·tion \ri-ˌje-nə-'rā-shən, ˌrē-\ *n* (14c) **1 :** an act or the process of regenerating : the state of being regenerated **2 :** spiritual renewal or revival **3 :** renewal or restoration of a body or bodily part after injury or as a normal process **4 :** utilization by special devices of heat or other products that would ordinarily be lost

re·gen·er·a·tive \ri-'je-nə-ˌrā-tiv, -'je-nə-rə-, -'jen-rə-\ *adj* (14c) **1 :** of, relating to, or marked by regeneration **2 :** tending to regenerate

re·gen·er·a·tor \ri-'je-nə-ˌrā-tər\ *n* (ca. 1550) **1 :** one that regenerates **2 :** a device used esp. with hot-air engines or gas furnaces in which incoming air or gas is heated by contact with masses (as of brick) previously heated by outgoing hot air or gas

re·gent \'rē-jənt\ *n* [ME, fr. MF or ML; MF, fr. ML *regent-, regens*, fr. L, prp. of *regere* to rule — more at RIGHT] (15c) **1 :** one who governs a kingdom in the minority, absence, or disability of the sovereign **2 :** one who rules or reigns : GOVERNOR **3 :** a member of a governing board (as of a state university) — **regent** *adj* — **re·gent·al** \-jən-tᵊl\ *adj*

reg·gae \'re-(ˌ)gā, 'rā-\ *n* [origin unknown] (1968) : popular music of Jamaican origin that combines native styles with elements of rock and soul music and is performed at moderate tempos with the accent on the offbeat

reg·i·cide \'re-jə-ˌsīd\ *n* [L *reg-, rex* king + E *-cide* — more at ROYAL] (ca. 1548) **1 :** one who kills a king **2 :** the killing of a king — **reg·i·ci·dal** \ˌre-jə-'sī-dᵊl\ *adj*

re·gime *also* **ré·gime** \rā-'zhēm, ri- *also* ri-'jēm\ *n* [F *régime*, fr. L *regimin-, regimen*] (1776) **1 a :** REGIMEN 1 **b :** a regular pattern of occurrence or action (as of seasonal rainfall) **c :** the characteristic behavior or orderly procedure of a natural phenomenon or process **2 a :** mode of rule or management **b :** a form of government ⟨a socialist ~⟩ **c :** a government in power ⟨predicted that the new ~ would fall⟩ **d :** a period of rule

reg·i·men \'re-jə-mən *also* 're-jə-ˌmen\ *n* [ME, fr. L *regimin-, regimen* rule, fr. *regere* to rule] (14c) **1 a :** a systematic plan (as of diet, therapy, or medication) esp. when designed to improve and maintain the health of a patient **b :** a regular course of action and esp. of strenuous training ⟨the daily ~ of a top ballet dancer⟩ **2 :** GOVERNMENT, RULE **3 :** REGIME 1c

¹**reg·i·ment** \'re-jə-mənt, 'rej-mənt\ *n* [ME, fr. MF, fr. LL *regimentum*, fr. L *regere*] (14c) **1** *archaic* : governmental rule **2 :** a military unit consisting usu. of a number of battalions

²**reg·i·ment** \'re-jə-ˌment\ *vt* (1617) **1 :** to form into or assign to a regiment **2 a :** to organize rigidly esp. for the sake of regulation or control ⟨~ an entire country⟩ **b :** to subject to order or uniformity — **reg·i·men·ta·tion** \ˌre-jə-mən-'tā-shən, -ˌmen-\ *n*

reg·i·men·tal \ˌre-jə-'men-tᵊl\ *adj* (1659) **1 :** of or relating to a regiment **2 :** AUTHORITATIVE, DICTATORIAL

reg·i·men·tals \-tᵊlz\ *n pl* (1742) **1 :** a regimental uniform **2 :** military dress

re·gion \'rē-jən\ *n* [ME, fr. MF, fr. L *region-, regio*, fr. *regere* to rule] (14c) **1 :** an administrative area, division, or district; *esp* : the basic administrative unit for local government in Scotland **2 a :** an indefinite area of the world or universe ⟨few unknown ~s left on earth⟩ **b :** a broad geographical area distinguished by similar features ⟨the Appalachian ~⟩ **c** (1) : a major world area that supports a characteristic fauna (2) : an area characterized by the prevalence of one or more vegetational climax types **3 a :** any of the major subdivisions into which the body or one of its parts is divisible **b :** an indefinite area surrounding a specified body part ⟨a pain in the ~ of the heart⟩ **4 :** a sphere of activity or interest : FIELD **5 :** any of the zones into which the atmosphere is divided according to height or the sea according to depth **6 :** an open connected set together with none, some, or all of the points on its boundary ⟨a simple closed curve divides a plane into two ~s⟩

¹**re·gion·al** \'rēj-nəl, 'rē-jə-nᵊl\ *adj* (15c) **1 :** affecting a particular region : LOCALIZED **2 :** of, relating to, characteristic of, or serving a region ⟨a ~ high school⟩ **3 :** marked by regionalism ⟨~ art⟩

²**regional** *n* (1936) : something (as a branch of an organization or an edition of a magazine) that serves a region

re·gion·al·ism \'rēj-nə-ˌli-zəm, 'rē-jə-nᵊl-ˌi-\ *n* (1881) **1 a :** consciousness of and loyalty to a distinct region with a homogeneous population **b :** development of a political or social system based on one or more such areas **2 :** emphasis on regional locale and characteristics in art or literature **3 :** a characteristic feature (as of speech) of a geographic area — **re·gion·al·ist** \-list, -ist\ *n or adj* — **re·gion·al·is·tic** \ˌrēj-nə-'lis-tik, ˌrē-jə-nᵊl-'is-\ *adj*

re·gion·al·ize \'rēj-nə-ˌlīz, 'rē-jə-nᵊl-ˌīz\ *vt* **-ized; -iz·ing** (1921) : to divide into regions or administrative districts : arrange regionally — **re·gion·al·i·za·tion** \ˌrēj-nə-lə-'zā-shən, ˌrē-jə-nᵊl-ə-\ *n*

re·gion·al·ly \'rēj-nə-lē, 'rē-jə-nᵊl-ē\ *adv* (1879) : on a regional basis

re·gis·seur *or* **ré·gis·seur** \ˌrā-zhi-'sər\ *n* [F *régisseur*, fr. *régir* to direct, fr. L *regere* to rule] (1828) : a director responsible for staging a theatrical work (as a ballet)

¹**reg·is·ter** \'re-jə-stər\ *n* [ME *registre*, fr. MF, fr. ML *registrum*, alter. of LL *regesta*, pl., register, fr. L, neut. pl. of *regestus*, pp. of *regerere* to bring back, pile up, collect, fr. *re-* + *gerere* to bear] (14c) **1 :** a written record containing regular entries of items or details **2 a :** a book or system of public records **b :** a roster of qualified or available individuals ⟨a civil service ~⟩ **3 :** an entry in a register **4 a :** a set of organ pipes of like quality : STOP **b** (1) : the range of a human voice or a musical instrument (2) : a portion of such a range similarly produced or of the same quality **c :** any of the varieties of a language that a speaker uses in a particular social context ~ **5 a :** a device regulating admission of air to fuel **b :** a grille often with shutters for admitting heated air or for ventilation **6 :** REGISTRATION, REGISTRY **7 a :** an automatic device registering a number or a quantity **b :** a number or quantity so registered **8 :** a condition of correct alignment or proper relative position **9 :** a device (as in a computer) for storing small amounts of data; *esp* : one in which data can be both stored and operated on

²**register** *vb* **reg·is·tered; reg·is·ter·ing** \-st(ə-)riŋ\ *vt* (14c) **1 a :** to make or secure official entry of in a register **b :** to enroll formally esp. as a voter or student **c :** to record automatically : INDICATE **d :** to

make a record of : NOTE **e** : PERCEIVE; *also* : COMPREHEND **2** : to make or adjust so as to correspond exactly **3** : to secure special protection for (a piece of mail) by prepayment of a fee **4** : to convey an impression of : EXPRESS **5** : ACHIEVE ⟨~*ed* an impressive victory⟩ ~ *vi* **1 a** : to enroll one's name in a register ⟨~*ed* at the hotel⟩ **b** : to enroll one's name officially as a prerequisite for voting **c** : to enroll formally as a student **2 a** : to correspond exactly **b** : to be in correct alignment or register **3** : to make or convey an impression

³**register** *n* [prob. alter. of ME *registrer*] (ca. 1532) : REGISTRAR

registered *adj* (1861) **1 a** : having the owner's name entered in a register ⟨~ security⟩ **b** : recorded as the owner of a security **2** : recorded on the basis of pedigree or breed characteristics in the studbook of a breed association **3** : qualified formally or officially

registered mail *n* (1886) : mail recorded in the post office of mailing and at each successive point of transmission and guaranteed special care in delivery

registered nurse *n* (1896) : a graduate trained nurse who has been licensed by a state authority after qualifying for registration

register ton *n* (ca. 1909) : TON 1a

reg·is·tra·ble \'re-jə-strə-bəl\ *also* **reg·is·ter·able** \-st(ə-)rə-bəl\ *adj* (1765) : capable of being registered

reg·is·trant \'re-jə-strənt\ *n* (ca. 1890) : one that registers or is registered

reg·is·trar \'re-jə-ˌsträr\ *n* [alter. of ME *registrer*, fr. MF *registreur*, fr. *registrer* to register, fr. ML *registrare*, fr. *registrum*] (1675) : an official recorder or keeper of records: as **a** : an officer of an educational institution responsible for registering students, keeping academic records, and corresponding with applicants and evaluating their credentials **b** : an admitting officer at a hospital **c** *chiefly Brit* : RESIDENT 3

reg·is·tra·tion \ˌre-jə-'strā-shən\ *n* (ca. 1566) **1** : the act of registering **2** : an entry in a register **3** : the number of individuals registered : ENROLLMENT **4 a** : the art or act of selecting and adjusting pipe organ stops **b** : the combination of stops selected for performing a particular organ work **5** : a document certifying an act of registering

reg·is·try \'re-jə-strē\ *n, pl* **-tries** (1589) **1** : REGISTRATION, ENROLLMENT **2** : the nationality of a ship according to its entry in a register : FLAG **3** : a place of registration **4** : an official record book **b** : an entry in a registry

re·gius professor \ˌrē-j(ē-)əs-\ *n* [NL, royal professor] (1621) : a holder of a professorship founded by royal subsidy at a British university

reg·let \'re-glət\ *n* [F *réglet*, fr. MF *reglet* straightedge, fr. *regle* rule, fr. L *regula* — more at RULE] (1664) **1** : a flat narrow architectural molding **2** : a strip of wood used like a lead between lines of type

reg·nal \'reg-n²l\ *adj* [ML *regnalis*, fr. L *regnum* reign — more at REIGN] (1612) : of or relating to a king or his reign; *specif* : calculated from a monarch's accession to the throne ⟨in his eighth ~ year⟩

reg·nant \'reg-nənt\ *adj* [L *regnant-, regnans*, prp. of *regnare* to reign, fr. *regnum*] (1600) **1** : exercising rule : REIGNING **2 a** : having the chief power : DOMINANT **b** : of common or widespread occurrence

reg·num \'reg-nəm\ *n, pl* **reg·na** \-nə\ [L] (ca. 1890) : KINGDOM

reg·o·lith \'re-gə-ˌlith\ *n* [Gk *rhēgos* blanket + E *-lith*; akin to Gk *rhezein* to dye — more at RAGA] (1897) : unconsolidated residual or transported material that overlies the solid rock on the earth, moon, or a planet

reg·o·sol \'re-gə-ˌsäl, -ˌsȯl\ *n* [*rego-* (as in *regolith*) + L *solum* soil — more at SOLE] (1949) : any of a group of azonal soils consisting chiefly of imperfectly consolidated material and having no clear-cut and specific morphology

re·greet \ˌ(ˌ)rē-'grēt\ *vt* (1593) *archaic* : to greet in return

regreets *n pl* (1596) *obs* : GREETINGS

¹**re·gress** \'rē-ˌgres\ *n* [ME, fr. L *regressus*, fr. *regredi* to go back, fr. *re-* + *gradi* to go — more at GRADE] (14c) **1 a** : an act or the privilege of going or coming back **b** : REENTRY 1 **2** : movement backward to a previous and esp. worse or more primitive state or condition **3** : the act of reasoning backward

²**re·gress** \ri-'gres\ *vi* (1552) **1 a** : to make or undergo regress : RETROGRADE **b** : to be subject to or exhibit regression **2** : to tend to approach or revert to a mean ~ *vt* : to induce a state of psychological regression in — **re·gres·sor** \-'gre-sər\ *n*

re·gres·sion \ri-'gre-shən\ *n* (1597) **1** : the act or an instance of regressing **2** : a trend or shift toward a lower or less perfect state: as **a** : progressive decline of a manifestation of disease **b** (1) : gradual loss of differentiation and function by a body part esp. as a physiological change accompanying aging (2) : gradual loss of memories and acquired skills **c** : reversion to an earlier mental or behavioral level **d** : a functional relationship between two or more correlated variables that is often empirically determined from data and is used esp. to predict values of one variable when given values of the others ⟨the ~ of *y* on *x* is linear⟩; *specif* : a function that yields the mean value of a random variable under the condition that one or more independent variables have specified values **3** : retrograde motion

re·gres·sive \ri-'gre-siv\ *adj* (1634) **1** : tending to regress or produce regression **2** : being, characterized by, or developing in the course of an evolutionary process involving increasing simplification of bodily structure **3** : decreasing in rate as the base increases ⟨a ~ tax⟩ — **re·gres·sive·ly** *adv* — **re·gres·sive·ness** *n* — **re·gres·siv·i·ty** \ˌrē-ˌgre-'si-və-tē\ *n*

¹**re·gret** \ri-'gret\ *vb* **re·gret·ted; re·gret·ting** [ME *regretten*, fr. MF *regreter*, fr. OF, fr. *re-* + *-greter* (perh. of Gmc origin; akin to ON *grāta* to weep) — more at GREET] *vt* (14c) **1 a** : to mourn the loss or death of **b** : to miss very much **2 a** : to be very sorry for ⟨~*s* his mistakes⟩ ~ *vi* : to experience regret — **re·gret·ter** *n*

²**regret** *n* (1590) **1** : sorrow aroused by circumstances beyond one's control or power to repair **2 a** : an expression of distressing emotion (as sorrow or disappointment) **b** *pl* : a note politely declining an invitation *syn* see SORROW — **re·gret·ful** \-'gret-fəl\ *adj* — **re·gret·ful·ness** *n*

re·gret·ful·ly \ri-'gret-fə-lē\ *adv* (1682) **1** : with regret **2** : it is to be regretted

re·gret·ta·ble \ri-'gre-tə-bəl\ *adj* (1603) : deserving regret

re·gret·ta·bly \-blē\ *adv* (1866) **1** : to a regrettable extent ⟨a ~ steep decline in wages⟩ **2** : it is to be regretted ⟨~, they could not attend⟩

re·group \ˌ(ˌ)rē-'grüp\ *vt* (1885) **1** : to form into a new grouping ⟨in order to subtract 129 from 531 ~ 531 into 5 hundreds, 2 tens, and 11 ones⟩ ⟨~ military forces⟩ ~ *vi* **1** : to reorganize (as after a setback) for renewed activity **2** : to alter the tactical formation of a military force

re·grow \ˌ(ˌ)rē-'grō\ *vb* **-grew** \-'grü\; **-grown** \-'grōn\; **-grow·ing** *vt* (1872) : to grow (as a missing part) anew ~ *vi* : to continue growth after interruption or injury

¹**reg·u·lar** \'re-gyə-lər, 're-g(ə-)lər\ *adj* [ME *reguler*, fr. MF, fr. LL *regularis* regular, fr. L, of a bar, fr. *regula* rule — more at RULE] (14c) **1** : belonging to a religious order **2 a** : formed, built, arranged, or ordered according to some established rule, law, principle, or type **b** (1) : both equilateral and equiangular ⟨a ~ polygon⟩ (2) : having faces that are congruent regular polygons and all the polyhedral angles congruent ⟨a ~ polyhedron⟩ *of a flower* : having the arrangement of floral parts exhibiting radial symmetry with members of the same whorl similar in form **3 a** : ORDERLY, METHODICAL ⟨~ habits⟩ **b** : recurring, attending, or functioning at fixed or uniform intervals ⟨a ~ income⟩ ⟨a ~ churchgoer⟩ **4 a** : constituted, conducted, or done in conformity with established or prescribed usages, rules, or discipline **b** : NORMAL, STANDARD: as (1) : ABSOLUTE, COMPLETE ⟨a ~ fool⟩ ⟨the office seemed like a ~ madhouse⟩ (2) : thinking or behaving in an acceptable, normal, or agreeable manner ⟨was a ~ guy⟩ **c** (1) : conforming to the normal or usual manner of inflection (2) : WEAK 7 **d** *of a postage stamp* : issued in large numbers over a long period for general use in prepayment of postage **5** : of, relating to, or constituting the permanent standing military force of a state ⟨~ army⟩ ⟨~ soldiers⟩

syn REGULAR, NORMAL, TYPICAL, NATURAL mean being of the sort or kind that is expected as usual, ordinary, or average. REGULAR stresses conformity to a rule, standard, or pattern ⟨the club's *regular* monthly meeting⟩. NORMAL implies lack of deviation from what has been discovered or established as the most usual or expected ⟨*normal* behavior for a two-year-old⟩. TYPICAL implies showing all important traits of a type, class, or group and may suggest lack of strong individuality ⟨a *typical* small town⟩. NATURAL applies to what conforms to a thing's essential nature, function, or mode of being ⟨the *natural* love of a mother for her child⟩.

²**regular** *n* (15c) **1** : one who is regular: as **a** : one of the regular clergy **b** : a soldier in a regular army **c** : one who can be trusted or depended on ⟨a party ~⟩ **d** : a player on an athletic team who usu. starts every game **e** : one who is usu. present or participating; *esp* : a long-standing regular customer **2** : something of average or medium size; *esp* : a clothing size designed to fit a person of average height

reg·u·lar·i·ty \ˌre-gyə-'lar-ə-tē\ *n, pl* **-ties** (1603) **1** : the quality or state of being regular **2** : something that is regular

reg·u·lar·ize \'re-gyə-lə-ˌrīz\ *vt* **-ized; -iz·ing** (1833) : to make regular by conformance to law, rules, or custom — **reg·u·lar·i·za·tion** \ˌre-gyə-lə-rə-'zā-shən\ *n*

reg·u·lar·ly \'re-gyə-lər-lē, 're-gyə(r)-lē\ *adv* (14c) **1** : in a regular manner **2** : on a regular basis : at regular intervals

regular solid *n* (1841) : any of the five possible regular polyhedrons that include the regular forms of the tetrahedron, hexahedron, octahedron, dodecahedron, and icosahedron

reg·u·late \'re-gyə-ˌlāt\ *vt* **-lat·ed; -lat·ing** [ME, fr. LL *regulatus*, pp. of *regulare*, fr. L *regula* rule] (15c) **1 a** : to govern or direct according to rule **b** (1) : to bring under the control of law or constituted authority (2) : to make regulations for or concerning ⟨~ the industries of a country⟩ **2** : to bring order, method, or uniformity to ⟨~ one's habits⟩ **3** : to fix or adjust the time, amount, degree, or rate of ⟨~ the pressure of a tire⟩ — **reg·u·la·tive** \-ˌlā-tiv\ *adj* — **reg·u·la·to·ry** \-lə-ˌtȯr-ē, -ˌtȯr-\ *adj*

¹**reg·u·la·tion** \ˌre-gyə-'lā-shən, ˌre-gə-\ *n* (1665) **1** : the act of regulating : the state of being regulated **2 a** : an authoritative rule dealing with details or procedure ⟨safety ~*s*⟩ **b** : a rule or order issued by an executive authority or regulatory agency of a government and having the force of law **3 a** : the process of redistributing material (as in an embryo) to restore a damaged or lost part independent of new tissue growth **b** : the mechanism by which an early embryo maintains normal development see LAW

²**regulation** *adj* (ca. 1839) : conforming to regulations : OFFICIAL

reg·u·la·tor \'re-gyə-ˌlā-tər\ *n* (1655) **1** : one that regulates **2** : REGULATORY GENE

regulatory gene *or* **regulator gene** *n* (1961) : a gene that regulates the expression of one or more structural genes by controlling the production of a protein (as a genetic repressor) which regulates their rate of transcription

reg·u·lus \'re-gyə-ləs\ *n* [NL, fr. L, petty king, fr. *reg-, rex* king — more at ROYAL] **1** *cap* : a first-magnitude star in the constellation Leo **2** [ML, metallic antimony, fr. L] : the more or less impure mass of metal formed beneath the slag in smelting and reducing ores

re·gur·gi·tate \ˌ(ˌ)rē-'gər-jə-ˌtāt\ *vb* **-tat·ed; -tat·ing** [ML *regurgitatus*, pp. of *regurgitare*, fr. L *re-* + LL *gurgitare* to engulf, fr. L *gurgit-, gurges* whirlpool — more at VORACIOUS] *vi* (1653) : to become thrown or poured back ~ *vt* : to throw or pour back or out from or as if from a cavity ⟨~ food⟩ ⟨memorized facts to ~ on the exam⟩

re·gur·gi·ta·tion \ˌ(ˌ)rē-ˌgər-jə-'tā-shən\ *n* (1601) : an act of regurgitating: as **a** : the casting up of incompletely digested food (as by some birds in feeding their young) **b** : the backward flow of blood through a defective heart valve

re·hab \'rē-ˌhab\ *n, often attrib* [short for *rehabilitation* or *rehabilitate*] (1941) **1** : the action or process of rehabilitating : REHABILITATION 2 **2** : a rehabilitated building or dwelling — **rehab** *vt* — **re·hab·ber** \-ˌha-bər\ *n*

re·ha·bil·i·tant \ˌrē-ə-'bi-lə-tənt, ˌrē-hə-\ *n* (1961) : a disabled person undergoing rehabilitation

re·ha·bil·i·tate \ˌrē-ə-'bi-lə-ˌtāt, ˌrē-hə-\ *vt* **-tat·ed; -tat·ing** [ML *rehabilitatus*, pp. of *rehabilitare*, fr. L *re-* + LL *habilitare* to habilitate] (ca. 1581) **1 a** : to restore to a former capacity : REINSTATE **b** : to

\ə\ abut \ᵊ\ kitten, F table \ər\ further \a\ ash \ā\ ace \ä\ mop, mar
\au̇\ out \ch\ chin \e\ bet \ē\ easy \g\ go \i\ hit \ī\ ice \j\ job
\ŋ\ sing \ō\ go \ȯ\ law \ȯi\ boy \th\ thin \t̲h̲\ the \ü\ loot \u̇\ foot
\y\ yet \zh\ vision \á, k̲, ⁿ, œ, œ̄, ᵫ, ᵈ, ʸ\ see Guide to Pronunciation

restore to good repute : reestablish the good name of **2 a :** to restore to a former state (as of efficiency, good management, or solvency) ⟨~ slum areas⟩ **b :** to restore or bring to a condition of health or useful and constructive activity — **re·ha·bil·i·ta·tion** \-ˌbi-lə-ˈtā-shən\ n — **re·ha·bil·i·ta·tive** \-ˈbi-lə-ˌtā-tiv\ adj — **re·ha·bil·i·ta·tor** \-ˌtā-tər\ n

¹re·hash \(ˌ)rē-ˈhash\ vt (ca. 1822) **1 :** to talk over or discuss again **2 :** to present or use again in another form without substantial change or improvement

²re·hash \ˈrē-ˌhash\ n (1849) **1 :** something that is rehashed **2 :** the action or process of rehashing

re·hear \(ˌ)rē-ˈhir\ vt **-heard** \-ˈhərd\; **-hear·ing** \-ˈhir-iŋ\ (1756) : to hear again or anew esp. judicially

rehearing n (1686) : a second or new hearing by the same tribunal

re·hears·al \ri-ˈhər-səl\ n (14c) **1 :** something recounted or told again : RECITAL **2 a :** a private performance or practice session preparatory to a public appearance **b :** a practice exercise : TRIAL

re·hearse \ri-ˈhərs\ vb **re·hearsed; re·hears·ing** [ME rehersen, fr. MF rehercier, lit., to harrow again, fr. re- + hercier to harrow, fr. herce harrow — more at HEARSE] vt (14c) **1 a :** to say again : REPEAT **b :** to recite aloud in a formal manner **2 :** to present an account of : RELATE ⟨~ a familiar story⟩ **3 :** to recount in order : ENUMERATE ⟨rehearsed their demands⟩ **4 a :** to give a rehearsal of **b :** to train or make proficient by rehearsal **5 :** to perform or practice as if in a rehearsal ~ vi : to engage in a rehearsal — **re·hears·er** n

re·house \(ˌ)rē-ˈhau̇z\ vt (1820) : to house again or anew esp : to establish in a new or different housing unit of a better quality

re·hy·drate \(ˌ)rē-ˈhī-ˌdrāt\ vt (1943) : to restore fluid to (something dehydrated) — **re·hy·drat·able** \-ˌdrā-tə-bəl\ adj — **re·hy·dra·tion** \ˌrē-ˌhī-ˈdrā-shən\ n

reichs·mark \ˈrīks-ˌmärk\ n, pl **reichsmarks** also **reichsmark** [G, fr. Reich empire, kingdom + Mark mark] (1924) : the German mark from 1925 to 1948

re·ifi·ca·tion \ˌrā-ə-fə-ˈkā-shən, ˌrē-\ n (1846) : the process or result of reifying

re·ify \ˈrā-ə-ˌfī, ˈrē-\ vt **re·ified; re·ify·ing** [L res thing — more at REAL] (1854) : to regard (something abstract) as a material or concrete thing

¹reign \ˈrān\ n [ME regne, fr. OF, fr. L regnum, fr. reg-, rex king — more at ROYAL] (13c) **1 a :** royal authority : SOVEREIGNTY ⟨under the ~ of the Stuart kings⟩ **b :** the dominion, sway, or influence of one resembling a monarch ⟨the ~ of the Puritan ministers⟩ **2 :** the time during which one (as a sovereign) reigns

²reign vi (14c) **1 a :** to possess or exercise sovereign power : RULE **b :** to hold office as chief of state although possessing little governing power ⟨in England the sovereign ~s but does not rule⟩ **2 :** to exercise authority in the manner of a monarch **3 :** to be predominant or prevalent ⟨chaos ~ed in the classroom⟩

reign of terror [Reign of Terror, a period of the French Revolution that was conspicuous for mass executions of political suspects] (1801) : a state or a period of time marked by violence often committed by those in power that produces widespread terror

re·imag·ine \ˌrē-i-ˈma-jən\ vt (ca. 1934) : to imagine again or anew; esp : to form a new conception of : RE-CREATE

re·im·burse \ˌrē-əm-ˈbərs\ vt **-bursed; -burs·ing** [re- + obs. E imburse to put in the pocket, pay, fr. ML imbursare, fr. L in- in- + ML bursa purse — more at PURSE] (1611) **1 :** to pay back to someone : REPAY ⟨~ travel expenses⟩ **2 :** to make restoration or payment of an equivalent to ⟨~ him for his traveling expenses⟩ syn see PAY — **re·im·burs·able** \-ˈbər-sə-bəl\ adj — **re·im·burse·ment** \-ˈbərs-mənt\ n

re·im·pres·sion \ˌrē-əm-ˈpre-shən\ n (1684) : REPRINT a

¹rein \ˈrān\ n [ME reine, fr. MF rene, fr. (assumed) VL retina, fr. L retinēre to restrain — more at RETAIN] (14c) **1 :** a strap fastened to a bit by which a rider or driver controls an animal — usu. used in pl. **2 a :** a restraining influence : CHECK ⟨kept a tight ~ on the proceedings⟩ **b :** controlling or guiding power — usu. used in pl. ⟨the ~s of government⟩ **3 :** opportunity for unhampered activity or use ⟨gave full ~ to her imagination⟩

²rein vt (15c) **1 :** to control or direct with or as if with reins **2 :** to check or stop by or as if by a pull at the reins ⟨~ed in her horse⟩ ⟨couldn't ~ his impatience⟩ ~ vi **1** archaic : to submit to the use of reins **2 :** to stop or slow up one's horse or oneself by or as if by pulling the reins

re·in·car·nate \ˌrē-ən-ˈkär-ˌnāt, (ˌ)rē-ˈin-\ vt (1858) : to incarnate again

re·in·car·na·tion \ˌrē-(ˌ)in-(ˌ)kär-ˈnā-shən\ n (1858) **1 a :** the action of reincarnating **b :** rebirth in new bodies or forms of life; esp : a rebirth of a soul in a new human body **2 :** a fresh embodiment

rein·deer \ˈrān-ˌdir\ n [ME reindere, fr. ON hreinn reindeer + ME deer animal, deer] (14c) : CARIBOU — used esp. for the Old World caribou

reindeer moss n (ca. 1753) : a gray, erect, tufted, and much-branched lichen (Cladonia rangiferina) that forms extensive patches in arctic and north-temperate regions, constitutes a large part of the food of caribou, and is sometimes eaten by humans — called also reindeer lichen

re·in·dus·tri·al·i·za·tion \ˌrē-in-ˌdəs-trē-ə-lə-ˈzā-shən\ n (1979) : a policy of stimulating economic growth esp. through government aid to revitalize and modernize aging industries and encourage growth of new ones — **re·in·dus·tri·al·ize** \-ˈdəs-trē-ə-ˌlīz\ vb

re·in·fec·tion \ˌrē-ən-ˈfek-shən\ n (1882) : infection following recovery from or superimposed on infection of the same type

re·in·force \ˌrē-ən-ˈfōrs, -ˈfȯrs\ vb [re- + inforce, alter. of enforce] vt (1600) **1 :** to strengthen or increase by fresh additions ⟨~ our troops⟩ ⟨were reinforcing their pitching staff⟩ **2 :** to strengthen by additional assistance, material, or support : make stronger or more pronounced ⟨~ levees⟩ ⟨~ the elbows of a jacket⟩ ⟨~ ideas⟩ **3 :** to stimulate (as an experimental animal or a student) with a reinforcer; also : to encourage (a response) with a reinforcer ~ vi : to seek or get reinforcements — **re·in·force·able** \-ˈfōr-sə-bəl, -ˈfȯr-\ adj

reinforced concrete n (1902) : concrete in which metal (as steel) is embedded so that the two materials act together in resisting forces

re·in·force·ment \ˌrē-ən-ˈfōrs-mənt, -ˈfȯrs-\ n (1617) **1 :** the action of reinforcing : the state of being reinforced **2 :** something that reinforces

re·in·forc·er \-ˈfōr-sər, -ˈfȯr-\ n (1955) : a stimulus (as a reward or the

removal of an electric shock) that increases the probability of a desired response in operant conditioning by being applied or effected following the desired response

reins \ˈrānz\ n pl [ME, fr. MF & L; MF, fr. L renes] (14c) **1 a :** KIDNEYS **b :** the region of the kidneys : LOINS **2 :** the seat of the feelings or passions

reins·man \ˈrānz-mən\ n (1855) : a skilled driver or rider of horses

re·in·state \ˌrē-ən-ˈstāt\ vt **-stat·ed; -stat·ing** (1628) **1 :** to place again (as in possession or in a former position) **2 :** to restore to a previous effective state — **re·in·state·ment** \-ˈstāt-mənt\ n

re·in·sur·ance \ˌrē-ən-ˈshu̇r-ən(t)s also \(ˌ)rē-in-\ n (1755) : insurance by another insurer of all or a part of a risk previously assumed by an insurance company

re·in·sure \ˌrē-ən-ˈshu̇r\ vt (1755) **1 :** to insure again by transferring to another insurance company all or a part of a liability assumed **2 :** to insure again by assuming all or a part of the liability of an insurance company already covering a risk ~ vi : to provide increased insurance — **re·in·sur·er** n

re·in·te·grate \(ˌ)rē-ˈin-tə-ˌgrāt\ vt [ML reintegratus, pp. of reintegrare to renew, reinstate, fr. L re- + integrare to integrate] (1626) : to integrate again into an entity : restore to unity — **re·in·te·gra·tion** \(ˌ)rē-ˌin-tə-ˈgrā-shən\ n — **re·in·te·gra·tive** \(ˌ)rē-ˈin-tə-ˌgrā-tiv\ adj

re·in·ter·pret \ˌrē-ən-ˈtər-prət, -pət\ vt (1611) : to interpret again; specif : to give a new or different interpretation to — **re·in·ter·pre·ta·tion** \-ˌtər-prə-ˈtā-shən, -pə-\ n

re·in·vent \ˌrē-ən-ˈvent\ vt (1686) **1 :** to make as if for the first time something already invented ⟨~ the wheel⟩ **2 :** to remake or redo completely **3 :** to bring into use again — **re·in·ven·tion** \-ˈven(t)-shən\ n

re·in·vest \ˌrē-ən-ˈvest\ vt (1611) **1 :** to invest again or anew **2 a :** to invest (as income from investments) in additional securities **b :** to invest (as earnings) in a business rather than distribute as dividends or profits

re·in·vest·ment \-ˈves(t)-mənt\ n (1611) **1 :** the action of reinvesting : the state of being reinvested **2 :** a second or repeated investment

reis pl of REAL

re·is·sue \(ˌ)rē-ˈi-(ˌ)shü, chiefly Brit -ˈis-(ˌ)yü\ vi (ca. 1618) : to come forth again ~ vt : to issue again; esp : to cause to become available again — **reissue** n

re·it·er·ate \rē-ˈi-tə-ˌrāt\ vt **-at·ed; -at·ing** [ME, fr. L reiteratus, pp. of reiterare to repeat, fr. re- + iterare to iterate] (15c) : to state or do over again or repeatedly sometimes with wearying effect — **re·it·er·a·tion** \(ˌ)rē-ˌi-tə-ˈrā-shən\ n — **re·it·er·a·tive** \rē-ˈi-tə-ˌrā-tiv, -t(ə-)rə-tiv\ adj — **re·it·er·a·tive·ly** adv

Rei·ter's syndrome \ˈrī-tərz-\ n [Hans Reiter †1969 Ger. physician] (ca. 1947) : a disease that is usu. initiated by infection in genetically predisposed individuals and is characterized usu. by recurrence of arthritis, conjunctivitis, and urethritis — called also Reiter's disease

reive \ˈrēv\ vb **reived; reiv·ing** [ME (Sc) reifen, fr. OE rēafian to rob — more at REAVE] (bef. 12c) Scot : RAID — **reiv·er** n, Scot

¹re·ject \ri-ˈjekt\ vt [ME, fr. L rejectus, pp. of reicere, fr. re- + jacere to throw — more at JET] (15c) **1 a :** to refuse to accept, consider, submit to, take for some purpose, or use ⟨~ed the suggestion⟩ ⟨~ a manuscript⟩ **b :** to refuse to hear, receive, or admit : REBUFF, REPEL ⟨parents who ~ their children⟩ **c :** to refuse as lover or spouse **2** obs : to cast off **3 :** THROW BACK, REPULSE **4 :** to spew out **5 :** to subject to immunological rejection syn see DECLINE — **re·ject·er** or **re·jec·tor** \-ˈjek-tər\ n — **re·ject·ing·ly** \-tiŋ-lē\ adv — **re·jec·tive** \-ˈjek-tiv\ adj

²re·ject \ˈrē-ˌjekt\ n (ca. 1555) : a rejected person or thing; esp : one rejected as not wanted, unsatisfactory, or not fulfilling standard requirements

re·ject·ee \ri-ˌjek-ˈtē, ˌrē-\ n (1941) : one that is rejected; esp : a person rejected as unfit for military service

re·jec·tion \ri-ˈjek-shən\ n (ca. 1552) **1 a :** the action of rejecting : the state of being rejected **b :** the immunological process of sloughing off foreign tissue or an organ (as a transplant) by the recipient organism **2 :** something rejected

rejection slip n (1906) : a printed slip enclosed with a rejected manuscript returned by an editor to an author

re·jig·ger \(ˌ)rē-ˈji-gər\ vt [re- + ³jigger] (1942) : ALTER, REARRANGE

re·joice \ri-ˈjȯis\ vb **re·joiced; re·joic·ing** [ME, fr. MF rejoiss-, stem of rejoir, fr. re- + joir to rejoice, fr. L gaudēre — more at JOY] vt (14c) : to give joy to : GLADDEN ~ vi : to feel joy or great delight — **re·joic·er** n — **re·joic·ing·ly** \-ˈjȯi-siŋ-lē\ adv — **rejoice in** : HAVE, POSSESS

rejoicing n (14c) **1 :** the action of one that rejoices **2 :** an instance, occasion, or expression of joy : FESTIVITY

re·join \ri-ˈjȯin, vt 1 is (ˌ)rē-\ vb [ME, fr. MF rejoin-, stem of rejoindre, fr. re- + OF joindre to join — more at JOIN] vt (15c) : to answer the replication of the plaintiff ~ vt **1 :** to join again **2 :** to say often sharply or critically in response esp. as a reply to a reply syn see ANSWER

re·join·der \ri-ˈjȯin-dər\ n [ME rejoiner, fr. MF rejoindre to rejoin] (15c) **1 :** the defendant's answer to the plaintiff's replication **2 :** REPLY; specif : an answer to a reply

re·ju·ve·nate \ri-ˈjü-və-ˌnāt\ vb **-nat·ed; -nat·ing** [re- + L juvenis young — more at YOUNG] vt (1807) **1 a :** to make young or youthful again : give new vigor to **b :** to restore to an original or new state ⟨~ old cars⟩ **2 a :** to stimulate (a stream) to renewed erosive activity esp. by uplift **b :** to develop youthful features of topography in ~ vi : to cause or undergo rejuvenation syn see RENEW — **re·ju·ve·na·tion** \ri-ˌjü-və-ˈnā-shən, ˌrē-\ n — **re·ju·ve·na·tor** \ri-ˈjü-və-ˌnā-tər\ n

re·ju·ve·nes·cence \ri-ˌjü-və-ˈne-sən(t)s, ˌrē-\ n [ML rejuvenescere to become young again, fr. L re- + juvenescere to become young, fr. juvenis] (ca. 1631) : a renewal of youthfulness or vigor : REJUVENATION — **re·ju·ve·nes·cent** \-s³nt\ adj

¹re·lapse \ri-ˈlaps, ˈrē-\ n [ME, fr. ML relapsus, fr. L relabi to slide back, fr. re- + labi to slide — more at SLEEP] (15c) **1 :** the act or an instance of backsliding, worsening, or subsiding **2 :** a recurrence of symptoms of a disease after a period of improvement

²re·lapse \ri-ˈlaps\ vi **re·lapsed; re·laps·ing** (1568) **1 :** to slip or fall back into a former worse state **2 :** SINK, SUBSIDE ⟨~ into deep thought⟩ — **re·laps·er** n

relapsing fever *n* (1849) : a variable acute epidemic disease that is marked by recurring high fever usu. lasting 3 to 7 days and is caused by a spirochete (genus *Borrelia*) transmitted by the bites of lice and ticks

re·late \ri-'lāt\ *vb* **re·lat·ed; re·lat·ing** [L *relatus* (pp. of *referre* to carry back), fr. *re-* + *latus,* pp. of *ferre* to carry — more at TOLERATE, BEAR] *vt* (1530) **1 :** to give an account of : TELL **2 :** to show or establish logical or causal connection between ⟨seeks to ∼ crime to poverty⟩ ∼ *vi* **1 :** to apply or take effect retroactively **2 :** to have relationship or connection ⟨the readings ∼ to his lectures⟩ **3 :** to have or establish a relationship : INTERACT ⟨the way a child ∼s to a teacher⟩ **4 :** to respond esp. favorably ⟨can't ∼ to that kind of music⟩ — **re·lat·able** \-'lā-tə-bəl\ *adj* — **re·lat·er** *or* **re·la·tor** \-'lā-tər\ *n*

related *adj* (ca. 1663) **1 :** connected by reason of an established or discoverable relation **2 :** connected by common ancestry or sometimes by marriage **3 :** having close harmonic connection — used of tones, chords, or tonalities — **re·lat·ed·ly** *adv* — **re·lat·ed·ness** *n*

re·la·tion \ri-'lā-shən\ *n* [ME *relacioun,* fr. MF *relation,* fr. L *relation-, relatio,* fr. *referre* (pp. *relatus*) to carry back] (14c) **1 :** the act of telling or recounting : ACCOUNT **2 :** an aspect or quality (as resemblance) that connects two or more things or parts as being or belonging or working together or as being of the same kind ⟨the ∼ of time and space⟩; *specif* : a property (as one expressed by *is equal to, is less than,* or *is the brother of*) that holds between an ordered pair of objects **3 :** the referring by a legal fiction of an act to a prior date as the time of its taking effect **4 a** (1) : a person connected by consanguinity or affinity : RELATIVE (2) : a person legally entitled to a share of the property of an intestate **b :** relationship by consanguinity or affinity : KINSHIP **5 :** REFERENCE, RESPECT ⟨in ∼ to⟩ **6 :** the attitude or stance which two or more persons or groups assume toward one another ⟨race ∼s⟩ **7 a :** the state of being mutually or reciprocally interested (as in social or commercial matters) **b** *pl* (1) : DEALINGS, AFFAIRS ⟨foreign ∼s⟩ (2) : INTERCOURSE (3) : SEXUAL INTERCOURSE

re·la·tion·al \-shnəl, -shə-nᵊl\ *adj* (1662) **1 :** of or relating to kinship **2 :** characterized or constituted by relations **3 :** having the function chiefly of indicating a relation of syntax ⟨*has* is notional in *he has luck,* ∼ in *he has gone*⟩ **4 :** relating to, using, or being a method of organizing data in a database so that it is perceived by the user as a set of tables — **re·la·tion·al·ly** *adv*

relational grammar *n* (1982) : a grammar based on a theory in which grammatical relations (as subject or object) are primitives in terms of which syntactic operations are defined

re·la·tion·ship \-shən-,ship\ *n* (ca. 1744) **1 :** the state of being related or interrelated ⟨studied the ∼ between the variables⟩ **2 :** the relation connecting or binding participants in a relationship: as **a :** KINSHIP **b :** a specific instance or type of kinship **3 a :** a state of affairs existing between those having relations or dealings ⟨had a good ∼ with his family⟩ **b :** a romantic or passionate attachment

¹rel·a·tive \'re-lə-tiv\ *n* (14c) **1 :** a word referring grammatically to an antecedent **2 :** a thing having a relation to or connection with or necessary dependence on another thing **3 a :** a person connected with another by blood or affinity **b :** an animal or plant related to another by common descent **4 :** a relative term

²relative *adj* (15c) **1 :** introducing a subordinate clause qualifying an expressed or implied antecedent ⟨∼ pronoun⟩; *also* : introduced by such a connective ⟨∼ clause⟩ **2 :** RELEVANT, PERTINENT ⟨matters ∼ to world peace⟩ **3 :** not absolute or independent : COMPARATIVE ⟨the ∼ isolation of life in the country⟩ **4 :** having the same key signature — used of major and minor keys and scales **5 :** expressed as the ratio of the specified quantity (as an error in measuring) to the total magnitude (as the value of a measured quantity) or to the mean of all the quantities involved

relative humidity *n* (1820) : the ratio of the amount of water vapor actually present in the air to the greatest amount possible at the same temperature

rel·a·tive·ly *adv* (1561) : to a relative degree or extent : SOMEWHAT

relatively prime *adj* (ca. 1890) *of integers* : having no common factors except +1 and −1 ⟨12 and 25 are *relatively prime*⟩

relative to *prep* (1660) : with regard to : in connection with

relative wind *n* (ca. 1918) : the motion of the air relative to a body in it

rel·a·tiv·ism \'re-lə-ti-,vi-zəm\ *n* (1865) **1 a :** a theory that knowledge is relative to the limited nature of the mind and the conditions of knowing **b :** a view that ethical truths depend on the individuals and groups holding them **2 :** RELATIVITY — **rel·a·tiv·ist** \-vist\ *n*

rel·a·tiv·is·tic \,re-lə-ti-'vis-tik\ *adj* (1886) **1 :** of, relating to, or characterized by relativity or relativism **2 :** moving at a velocity such that there is a significant change in properties (as mass) in accordance with the theory of relativity ⟨a ∼ electron⟩ — **rel·a·tiv·is·ti·cal·ly** \-'vis-ti-k(ə-)lē\ *adv*

rel·a·tiv·i·ty \,re-lə-'ti-və-tē\ *n, pl* **-ties** (ca. 1834) **1 a :** the quality or state of being relative **b :** something that is relative **2 :** the state of being dependent for existence on or determined in nature, value, or quality by relation to something else **3 a :** a theory which is based on the two postulates (1) that the speed of light in a vacuum is constant and independent of the source or observer and (2) that the mathematical forms of the laws of physics are invariant in all inertial systems and which leads to the assertion of the equivalence of mass and energy and of change in mass, dimension, and time with increased velocity — called also *special relativity, special theory of relativity* **b :** an extension of the theory to include gravitation and related acceleration phenomena — called also *general relativity, general theory of relativity* **4 :** RELATIVISM 1b

rel·a·tiv·ize \'re-lə-tə-,vīz\ *vt* **-ized; -iz·ing** (1935) : to treat or describe as relative

re·lax \ri-'laks\ *vb* [ME, fr. L *relaxare,* fr. *re-* + *laxare* to loosen, fr. *laxus* loose — more at SLACK] *vt* (15c) **1 :** to make less tense or rigid : SLACKEN ⟨∼ed his grip⟩ **2 :** to make less severe or stringent : MODIFY ⟨∼ immigration laws⟩ **3 :** to make soft or enervated **4 :** to relieve from nervous tension ∼ *vi* **1 :** to become lax, weak, or loose : REST **2 :** to become less intense or severe ⟨hoped the committee would ∼ in its opposition⟩ **3** *of a muscle or muscle fiber* : to become inactive and lengthen **4 :** to cast off social restraint, nervous tension, or anxiety ⟨couldn't ∼ in crowds⟩ **5 :** to seek rest or recreation ⟨∼ at the seashore⟩ **6 :** to relieve constipation **7 :** to attain equilibrium following

the abrupt removal of some influence (as light, high temperature, or stress) — **re·lax·er** *n*

¹re·lax·ant \ri-'lak-sənt\ *adj* (1771) : of, relating to, or producing relaxation ⟨an anesthetic and ∼ agent⟩

²relaxant *n* (ca. 1847) : a substance (as a drug) that relaxes; *specif* : one that relieves muscular tension

re·lax·a·tion \,rē-,lak-'sā-shən, ri-,lak-, *esp Brit* ,re-lək-\ *n* (1548) **1 :** the act of relaxing or state of being relaxed **2 :** easy or recreative state, activity, or pastime : DIVERSION **3 :** the lengthening that characterizes inactive muscle fibers or muscles

re·laxed \ri-'lakst\ *adj* (1623) **1 :** freed from or lacking in precision or stringency **2 :** set or being at rest or at ease **3 :** easy of manner : INFORMAL — **re·laxed·ly** \-'lak-səd-lē, -'lakst-lē\ *adv* — **re·laxed·ness** \-'lak-səd-nəs, -'laks(t)-nəs\ *n*

re·lax·in \ri-'lak-sən\ *n* (1930) : a sex hormone of the corpus luteum that facilitates birth by causing relaxation of the pelvic ligaments

¹re·lay \'rē-,lā\ *n* (1659) **1 a :** a supply (as of horses) arranged beforehand for successive relief **b :** a number of persons who relieve others in some work ⟨worked in ∼s around the clock⟩ **2 a :** a race between teams in which each team member successively covers a specified portion of the course **b :** one of the divisions of a relay **3 :** an electromagnetic device for remote or automatic control that is actuated by variation in conditions of an electric circuit and that operates in turn other devices (as switches) in the same or a different circuit **4 :** SERVOMOTOR **5 :** the act of passing along (as a message or ball) by stages; *also* : one of such stages

²re·lay \'rē-,lā, ri-'lā\ *vt* **re·layed; re·lay·ing** [ME, to hunt with relays, fr. MF *relaier,* fr. OF, fr. *re-* + *laier* to leave — more at DELAY] (1788) **1 a :** to place or dispose in relays **b :** to provide with relays **2 :** to pass along by relays ⟨news was ∼ed to distant points⟩ **3 :** to control or operate by a relay

³re·lay \(,)rē-'lā\ *vt* **-laid** \-'lād\; **-lay·ing** [*re-* + ¹*lay*] (1757) : to lay again ⟨∼ track⟩

¹re·lease \ri-'lēs\ *vt* **re·leased; re·leas·ing** [ME *relesen,* fr. MF *relessier,* fr. L *relaxare* to relax] (14c) **1 :** to set free from restraint, confinement, or servitude ⟨∼ hostages⟩ ⟨∼ pent-up emotions⟩ ⟨∼ the brakes⟩; *also* : to let go : DISMISS ⟨released from her job⟩ **2 :** to relieve from something that confines, burdens, or oppresses ⟨was released from her promise⟩ **3 :** to give up in favor of another : RELINQUISH ⟨∼ a claim to property⟩ **4 :** to give permission for publication, performance, exhibition, or sale of; *also* : to make available to the public ⟨the commission *released* its findings⟩ ⟨∼ a new movie⟩ *syn* see FREE — **re·leas·able** \-'lē-sə-bəl\ *adj*

²release *n* (14c) **1 :** relief or deliverance from sorrow, suffering, or trouble **2 a :** discharge from obligation or responsibility **b** (1) : relinquishment of a right or claim (2) : an act by which a legal right is discharged; *specif* : a conveyance of a right in lands or tenements to another having an estate in possession **3 a :** the act or an instance of liberating or freeing (as from restraint) **b :** the act or manner of concluding a musical tone or phrase **c :** the act or manner of ending a sound : the movement of one or more vocal organs in quitting the position for a speech sound **4 :** an instrument effecting a legal release **5 :** the state of being freed **6 :** a device adapted to hold or release a mechanism as required **7 a :** the act of permitting performance or publication; *also* : PERFORMANCE, PUBLICATION ⟨became a best-seller on its ∼⟩ **b :** the matter released; *esp* : a statement prepared for the press

re·lease \(,)rē-'lēs\ *vt* (1828) : to lease again

released time *n* (1941) : time off from regularly scheduled activities (as school) given to take part in some other specified activity

release print *n* (1937) : a motion-picture film released for public showing

re·leas·er \ri-'lē-sər\ *n* (15c) : one that releases; *specif* : a stimulus that serves as the initiator of complex reflex behavior

rel·e·gate \'re-lə-,gāt\ *vt* **-gat·ed; -gat·ing** [L *relegatus,* pp. of *relegare,* fr. *re-* + *legare* to send with a commission — more at LEGATE] (1599) **1 :** to send into exile : BANISH **2 :** ASSIGN: as **a :** to assign to a place of insignificance or oblivion : put out of sight or mind **b :** to assign to an appropriate place or situation on the basis of classification or appraisal **c :** to submit to someone or something for appropriate action : DELEGATE *syn* see COMMIT — **rel·e·ga·tion** \,re-lə-'gā-shən\ *n*

re·lent \ri-'lent\ *vb* [ME, to melt, soften, fr. AF *relenter,* fr. *re-* + L *lentare* to bend, fr. *lentus* soft, pliant, slow — more at LITHE] *vi* (1526) **1 a :** to become less severe, harsh, or strict usu. from reasons of humanity **b :** to cease resistance : GIVE IN : LET UP, SLACKEN ∼ *vt, obs* : SOFTEN, MOLLIFY *syn* see YIELD

re·lent·less \-ləs\ *adj* (1592) : showing or promising no abatement of severity, intensity, strength, or pace : UNRELENTING ⟨∼ pressure⟩ ⟨a ∼ campaign⟩ — **re·lent·less·ly** *adv* — **re·lent·less·ness** *n*

rel·e·vance \'re-lə-vən(t)s\ *n* (1733) **1 a :** relation to the matter at hand **b :** practical and esp. social applicability : PERTINENCE ⟨giving ∼ to college courses⟩ **2 :** the ability (as of an information retrieval system) to retrieve material that satisfies the needs of the user

rel·e·van·cy \-vən(t)-sē\ *n, pl* **-cies** (1561) : RELEVANCE; *also* : something relevant

rel·e·vant \'re-lə-vənt\ *adj* [ML *relevant-, relevans,* fr. L, prp. of *relevare* to raise up — more at RELIEVE] (1560) **1 a :** having significant and demonstrable bearing on the matter at hand **b :** affording evidence tending to prove or disprove the matter at issue or under discussion ⟨∼ testimony⟩ **c :** having social relevance **2 :** PROPORTIONAL, RELATIVE — **rel·e·vant·ly** *adv*

syn RELEVANT, GERMANE, MATERIAL, PERTINENT, APPOSITE, APPLICABLE, APROPOS mean relating to or bearing upon the matter in hand. RELEVANT implies a traceable, significant, logical connection ⟨found material *relevant* to her case⟩. GERMANE may additionally imply a fitness for or appropriateness to the situation or occasion ⟨a point not *germane* to the discussion⟩. MATERIAL implies so close a relationship that it cannot be dispensed with without serious alteration of the case ⟨facts

---

\ə\ abut \ᵊ\ kitten, F table \ər\ further \a\ ash \ā\ ace \ä\ mop, mar \aú\ out \ch\ chin \e\ bet \ē\ easy \g\ go \i\ hit \ī\ ice \j\ job \ŋ\ sing \ō\ go \ò\ law \òi\ boy \th\ thin \t͟h\ the \ü\ loot \ú\ foot \y\ yet \zh\ vision \à, k̲, ⁿ, œ, œ̄, ᵫ, ᵫ̄, ᵊ\ *see* Guide to Pronunciation material to the investigation⟩. PERTINENT stresses a clear and decisive relevance ⟨a *pertinent* observation⟩. APPOSITE suggests a felicitous relevance ⟨add an *apposite* quotation to the definition⟩. APPLICABLE suggests the fitness of bringing a general rule or principle to bear upon a particular case ⟨the rule is not *applicable* in this case⟩. APROPOS suggests being both relevant and opportune ⟨the quip was *apropos*⟩.

re·li·abil·i·ty \ri-ˌlī-ə-ˈbi-lə-tē\ *n* (1816) **1** : the quality or state of being reliable **2** : the extent to which an experiment, test, or measuring procedure yields the same results on repeated trials

¹re·li·able \ri-ˈlī-ə-bəl\ *adj* (1569) **1** : suitable or fit to be relied on : DEPENDABLE **2** : giving the same result on successive trials — **re·li·able·ness** *n* — **re·li·ably** \-blē\ *adv*

²reliable *n* (1890) : one that is reliable

re·li·ance \ri-ˈlī-ən(t)s\ *n* (1607) **1** : the act of relying : the state of being reliant **2** : something or someone relied on

re·li·ant \-ənt\ *adj* (1859) : having reliance on something or someone : DEPENDENT — **re·li·ant·ly** *adv*

rel·ic \ˈre-lik\ *n* [ME *relik*, fr. OF *relique*, fr. ML *reliquia*, fr. LL *reliquiae*, pl., remains of a martyr, fr. L, remains, fr. *relinquere* to leave behind — more at RELINQUISH] (13c) **1 a** : an object esteemed and venerated because of association with a saint or martyr **b** : SOUVENIR, MEMENTO **2** *pl* : REMAINS, CORPSE **3** : a survivor or remnant left after decay, disintegration, or disappearance **4** : a trace of some past or outmoded practice, custom, or belief

¹rel·ict \ˈre-likt\ *n* [in sense 1, fr. ME *relicte*, fr. LL *relicta*, fem. of *relictus*, pp. of *relinquere*; in senses 2 & 3, fr. *relict* residual, adj., fr. L *relictus*] (15c) **1** : WIDOW **2** : a persistent remnant of an otherwise extinct flora or fauna or kind of organism **3 a** : a relief feature or rock remaining after other parts have disappeared **b** : something left unchanged

²relict *adj* (15c) : of, relating to, or being a relict ⟨~ populations⟩

re·lic·tion \ri-ˈlik-shən\ *n* [L *reliction-*, *relictio* act of leaving behind, fr. *relinquere*] (ca. 1676) **1** : the gradual recession of water leaving land permanently uncovered **2** : land uncovered by reliction

¹re·lief \ri-ˈlēf\ *n* [ME, fr. MF, fr. OF, fr. *relever* to relieve] (14c) **1** : a payment made by a feudal tenant to a lord on succeeding to an inherited estate **2 a** : removal or lightening of something oppressive, painful, or distressing **b** : WELFARE 2a **c** : military assistance to an endangered post or force **d** : means of breaking or avoiding monotony or boredom : DIVERSION **3** : release from a post or from the performance of duty **4** : one that takes the place of another on duty **5** : legal remedy or redress **6** [F] **a** : a mode of sculpture in which forms and figures are distinguished from a surrounding plane surface **b** : sculpture or a sculptural form executed in this mode **c** : projecting detail, ornament, or figures **7** : sharpness of outline due to contrast ⟨a roof in bold ~ against the sky⟩ **8** : the elevations or inequalities of a land surface **9** : the pitching done by a relief pitcher ⟨two innings of hitless ~⟩

relief 6b

²relief *adj* (1838) **1** : providing relief **2** : characterized by surface inequalities **3** : of or used in letterpress

relief map *n* (1876) : a map representing topographic relief

relief pitcher *n* (ca. 1949) : a baseball pitcher who takes over for another during a game

relief printing *n* (1875) : LETTERPRESS 1

re·lieve \ri-ˈlēv\ *vb* **re·lieved**; **re·liev·ing** [ME *releven*, fr. MF *relever* to raise, relieve, fr. L *relevare*, fr. *re-* + *levare* to raise — more at LEVER] *vt* (14c) **1 a** : to free from a burden : give aid or help to **b** : to set free from an obligation, condition, or restriction **c** : to ease of a burden, wrong, or oppression by judicial or legislative interposition **2 a** : to bring about the removal or alleviation of : MITIGATE **b** : ROB, DEPRIVE **3 a** : to release from a post, station, or duty **b** : to take the place of **4** : to remove or lessen the monotony of **5 a** : to set off by contrast **b** : to raise in relief **6** : to discharge the bladder or bowels of (oneself) ~ *vi* **1** : to bring or give relief **2** : to stand out in relief **3** : to serve as a relief pitcher — **re·liev·able** \-ˈlē-və-bəl\ *adj*

syn RELIEVE, ALLEVIATE, LIGHTEN, ASSUAGE, MITIGATE, ALLAY mean to make something less grievous. RELIEVE implies a lifting of enough of a burden to make it tolerable ⟨took an aspirin to *relieve* the pain⟩. ALLEVIATE implies temporary or partial lessening of pain or distress ⟨the lotion *alleviated* the itching⟩. LIGHTEN implies reducing a burdensome or depressing weight ⟨good news would *lighten* our worries⟩. ASSUAGE implies softening or sweetening what is harsh or disagreeable ⟨ocean breezes *assuaged* the intense heat⟩. MITIGATE suggests a moderating or countering of the effect of something violent or painful ⟨the need to *mitigate* barbaric laws⟩. ALLAY implies an effective calming or soothing of fears or alarms ⟨*allayed* their fears⟩.

re·lieved \ri-ˈlēvd\ *adj* (1869) : experiencing or showing relief esp. from anxiety or pent-up emotions — **re·liev·ed·ly** \-ˈlē-vəd-lē\ *adv*

re·liev·er \ri-ˈlē-vər\ *n* (15c) : one that relieves; *esp* : RELIEF PITCHER

re·lie·vo \ri-ˈlē-(ˌ)vō, rēl-ˈyā-(ˌ)vō\ *n*, *pl* **-vos** [It *rilievo*, fr. *rilevare* to raise, fr. L *relevare*] (1625) : RELIEF 6

re·li·gio- \ri-ˈli-jē-ō\ *comb form* : religion and ⟨religio-political⟩

re·li·gion \ri-ˈli-jən\ *n* [ME *religioun*, fr. L *religion-*, *religio* supernatural constraint, sanction, religious practice, perh. fr. *religare* to restrain, tie back — more at RELY] (13c) **1 a** : the state of a religious ⟨a nun in her 20th year of ~⟩ **b** (1) : the service and worship of God or the supernatural (2) : commitment or devotion to religious faith or observance **2** : a personal set or institutionalized system of religious attitudes, beliefs, and practices **3** *archaic* : scrupulous conformity : CONSCIENTIOUSNESS **4** : a cause, principle, or system of beliefs held to with ardor and faith — **re·li·gion·less** *adj*

re·li·gion·ist \-ˈli-jə-nist, -ˈlij-nist\ *n* (1653) : a person adhering to a religion; *esp* : a religious zealot

re·li·gi·ose \ri-ˈli-jē-ˌōs\ *adj* [*religion* + ¹*-ose*] (1853) : RELIGIOUS; *esp* : excessively, obtrusively, or sentimentally religious — **re·li·gi·os·i·ty** \-ˌli-jē-ˈä-sə-tē\ *n*

¹re·li·gious \ri-ˈli-jəs\ *adj* [ME, fr. OF *religieus*, fr. L *religiosus*, fr. *religio*] (13c) **1** : relating to or manifesting faithful devotion to an

acknowledged ultimate reality or deity ⟨a ~ person⟩ ⟨~ attitudes⟩ **2** : of, relating to, or devoted to religious beliefs or observances **3 a** : scrupulously and conscientiously faithful **b** : FERVENT, ZEALOUS — **re·li·gious·ly** *adv* — **re·li·gious·ness** *n*

²religious *n*, *pl* **religious** [ME, fr. OF *religieus*, fr. *religieus*, adj.] (13c) : a member of a religious order under monastic vows

re·line \(ˌ)rē-ˈlīn\ *vt* (1851) : to put new lines on or a new lining in

re·lin·quish \ri-ˈliŋ-kwish, -ˈlin-\ *vt* [ME *relinquisshen*, fr. MF *relinquiss-*, stem of *relinquir*, fr. L *relinquere* to leave behind, fr. *re-* + *linquere* to leave — more at LOAN] (15c) **1** : to withdraw or retreat from : leave behind **2** : GIVE UP ⟨~ a title⟩ **3 a** : to stop holding physically : RELEASE ⟨slowly ~ed his grip on the bar⟩ **b** : to give over possession or control of : YIELD ⟨few leaders willingly ~ power⟩ — **re·lin·quish·ment** \-mənt\ *n*

syn RELINQUISH, YIELD, RESIGN, SURRENDER, ABANDON, WAIVE mean to give up completely. RELINQUISH usu. does not imply strong feeling but may suggest some regret, reluctance, or weakness ⟨*relinquished* her crown⟩. YIELD implies concession or compliance or submission to force ⟨the troops *yielded* ground grudgingly⟩. RESIGN emphasizes voluntary relinquishment or sacrifice without struggle ⟨*resigned* her position⟩. SURRENDER implies a giving up after a struggle to retain or resist ⟨*surrendered* their claims⟩. ABANDON stresses finality and completeness in giving up ⟨*abandoned* all hope⟩. WAIVE implies conceding or forgoing with little or no compulsion ⟨*waived* the right to a trial by jury⟩.

reli·quary \ˈre-lə-ˌkwer-ē\ *n*, *pl* **-quar·ies** [F *reliquaire*, fr. ML *reliquiarium*, fr. *reliquia* relic — more at RELIC] (ca. 1656) : a container or shrine in which sacred relics are kept

re·lique \ri-ˈlēk, ˈre-lik\ *archaic var of* RELIC

re·liq·ui·ae \ri-ˈli-kwē-ˌī, -kwē-ˌē\ *n pl* [L — more at RELIC] (1654) : remains of the dead : RELICS

¹rel·ish \ˈre-lish\ *n* [alter. of ME *reles* taste, fr. OF, something left behind, release, fr. *relessier* to release] (1530) **1** : characteristic flavor; *esp* : pleasing or zestful flavor **2** : a quantity just sufficient to flavor or characterize : TRACE **3 a** : enjoyment of or delight in something that satisfies one's tastes, inclinations, or desires ⟨eat with great ~⟩ **b** : a strong liking : INCLINATION ⟨has little ~ for sports⟩ **4 a** : something adding a zestful flavor; *esp* : a condiment (as of pickles or green tomatoes) eaten with other food to add flavor **b** : APPETIZER, HORS D'OEUVRE

²relish *vt* (1586) **1** : to add relish to **2** : to be pleased or gratified by : ENJOY **3** : to eat or drink with pleasure **4** : to appreciate with taste and discernment ~ *vi* **1** : to have a characteristic or pleasing taste — **rel·ish·able** \ˈre-li-shə-bəl\ *adj*

re·live \(ˌ)rē-ˈliv\ *vi* (1548) : to live again ~ *vt* : to live over again; *esp* : to experience again in the imagination

re·lo·cate \(ˌ)rē-ˈlō-ˌkāt, ˌrē-lō-ˈ\ *vt* (1834) : to locate again : establish or lay out in a new place ~ *vi* : to move to a new location — **re·lo·cat·able** \-ˈlō-ˌkā-tə-bəl, -ˌlō-ˈkā-\ *adj* — **re·lo·ca·tion** \ˌrē-lō-ˈkā-shən\ *n*

re·lo·cat·ee \ˌrē-lə-ˌkā-ˈtē, ˌrē-ˌlō-kə-ˈtē\ *n* (1954) : one who moves to a new location : one that is relocated

re·lu·cent \ri-ˈlü-sᵊnt\ *adj* [L *relucent-*, *relucens*, pp. of *relucēre* to shine back, fr. *re-* + *lucēre* to shine — more at LIGHT] (15c) : reflecting light : SHINING

re·luct \ri-ˈləkt\ *vi* [L *reluctari*] (1547) : to show reluctance

re·luc·tance \ri-ˈlək-tən(t)s\ *n* (1710) **1** : the quality or state of being reluctant **2** : the opposition offered in a magnetic circuit to magnetic flux; *specif* : the ratio of the magnetic potential difference to the corresponding flux

re·luc·tan·cy \-tən(t)-sē\ *n* (1634) : RELUCTANCE

re·luc·tant \ri-ˈlək-tənt\ *adj* [L *reluctant-*, *reluctans*, prp. of *reluctari* to struggle against, fr. *re-* + *luctari* to struggle] (1667) : feeling or showing aversion, hesitation, or unwillingness ⟨~ to get involved⟩; *also* : having or assuming a specified role unwillingly ⟨a ~ hero⟩ **syn** see DISINCLINED — **re·luc·tant·ly** *adv*

re·luc·tate \ri-ˈlək-ˌtāt\ *vi* **-tat·ed**; **-tat·ing** (1643) : RELUCT — **re·luc·ta·tion** \ri-ˌlək-ˈtā-shən, ˌrē-\ *n*

re·lume \(ˌ)rē-ˈlüm\ *vt* **re·lumed**; **re·lum·ing** [irreg. tr. LL *reluminare*, fr. L *re-* + *luminare* to light up — more at ILLUMINATE] (1604) *archaic* : to light or light up again : REKINDLE

re·ly \ri-ˈlī\ *vi* **re·lied**; **re·ly·ing** [ME *relien* to rally, fr. MF *relier* to connect, rally, fr. L *religare* to tie back — more at LIGATURE] (1574) **1** : to be dependent ⟨the system on which we ~ for water⟩ **2** : to have confidence based on experience ⟨someone you can ~ on⟩ — **re·li·er** \-ˈlī(-ə)r\ *n*

rem \ˈrem\ *n* [roentgen equivalent man] (1947) : the dosage of an ionizing radiation that will cause the same biological effect as one roentgen of X-ray or gamma-ray exposure

REM \ˈrem\ *n* (1957) : RAPID EYE MOVEMENT

¹re·main \ri-ˈmān\ *vi* [ME, fr. MF *remaindre*, fr. L *remanēre*, fr. *re-* + *manēre* to remain — more at MANSION] (14c) **1 a** : to be a part not destroyed, taken, or used up ⟨only a few ruins ~⟩ **b** : to be something yet to be shown, done, or treated ⟨it ~s to be seen⟩ **2** : to stay in the same place or with the same person or group; *esp* : to stay behind **3** : to continue unchanged ⟨the fact ~s that we can't go⟩

²remain *n* (15c) **1** *obs* : STAY **2** : a remaining part or trace — usu. used in pl. **3** *pl* : a dead body

¹re·main·der \ri-ˈmān-dər\ *n* [ME, fr. AF, fr. MF *remaindre*] (14c) **1** : an interest or estate in property that follows and is dependent on the termination of a prior intervening possessory estate created at the same time by the same instrument **2 a** : a remaining group, part, or trace **b** (1) : the number left after a subtraction (2) : the final undivided part after division that is less or of lower degree than the divisor **3** : a book sold at a reduced price by the publisher after sales have slowed

²remainder *adj* (1567) : LEFTOVER, REMAINING

³remainder *vt* **-dered**; **-der·ing** \-d(ə-)riŋ\ (1904) : to dispose of as remainders

remainder theorem *n* (1886) : a theorem in algebra: if $f(x)$ is a polynomial in x then the remainder on dividing $f(x)$ by $x - a$ is $f(a)$

¹re·make \(ˌ)rē-ˈmāk\ *vt* **-made** \-ˈmād\; **-mak·ing** (ca. 1635) : to make anew or in a different form — **re·mak·er** \-ˈmā-kər\ *n*

²re·make \ˈrē-ˌmāk\ *n* (1936) : one that is remade; *esp* : a new version of a motion picture

re·man \(,)rē-'man\ *vt* (1666) **1** : to man again or anew **2** : to imbue with courage again

re·mand \ri-'mand\ *vt* [ME *remaunden*, fr. MF *remander*, fr. LL *remandare* to send back word, fr. L *re-* + *mandare* to order — more at MANDATE] (15c) : to order back: as **a** : to send back (a case) to another court or agency for further action **b** : to return to custody pending trial or for further detention — **remand** *n*

rem·a·nence \'re-mə-nən(t)s, ri-'mā-\ *n* (ca. 1880) : the magnetic induction remaining in a magnetized substance no longer under external magnetic influence

rem·a·nent \-nənt\ *adj* [ME, fr. L *remanent-, remanens*, prp. of *remanēre* to remain] (15c) **1** : RESIDUAL, REMAINING **2** : of, relating to, or characterized by remanence

re·man·u·fac·ture \(,)rē-,ma-nyə-'fak-chər, -,ma-nə-\ *vt* (1851) : to manufacture into a new product — **remanufacture** *n* — **re·man·u·fac·tur·er** \-chər-ər\ *n*

re·map \(,)rē-'map\ *vt* (1931) : to map again; *also* : to lay out in a new pattern

¹**re·mark** \ri-'märk\ *n* [F *remarque*, fr. MF, fr. *remarquer* to remark, fr. *re-* re- + *marquer* to mark — more at MARQUE] (1660) **1** : the act of remarking : NOTICE **2** : an expression of opinion or judgment **3** : mention of that which deserves attention or notice

²**remark** *vt* (1675) **1** : to take notice of : OBSERVE **2** : to express as an observation or comment : SAY ~ *vi* : to notice something and comment thereon — used with *on* or *upon*

re·mark·able \ri-'mär-kə-bəl\ *adj* (ca. 1604) : worthy of being or likely to be noticed esp. as being uncommon or extraordinary *syn* see NOTICEABLE — **re·mark·able·ness** *n*

re·mark·ably \-blē\ *adv* (1638) **1** : in a remarkable manner ⟨~ talented⟩ **2** : as is remarkable ⟨~, no one was hurt⟩

re·marque \ri-'märk\ *n* [F *remarque* remark, note, fr. MF, fr. *remarquer*] (1882) **1** : a drawn, etched, or incised scribble or sketch done on the margin of a plate or stone and removed before the regular printing **2** : a proof taken before remarques have been removed

re·mas·ter \(,)rē-'mas-tər\ *vt* (1964) : to create a new master of esp. by altering or enhancing the sound quality of an older recording

re·match \(,)rē-'mach, 'rē-,\ *n* (1941) : a second match between the same contestants or teams

re·me·di·a·ble \ri-'mē-dē-ə-bəl\ *adj* (15c) : capable of being remedied — **re·me·di·abil·i·ty** \ri-,mē-dē-ə-'bi-lə-tē\ *n*

re·me·di·al \ri-'mē-dē-əl\ *adj* (1651) **1** : intended as a remedy **2** : concerned with the correction of faulty study habits and the raising of a pupil's general competence ⟨~ reading courses⟩; *also* : receiving or requiring remedial instruction ⟨~ students⟩ — **re·me·di·al·ly** \-ə-lē\ *adv*

re·me·di·ate \ri-'mē-dē-ət\ *adj* (1605) *archaic* : REMEDIAL

re·me·di·a·tion \ri-,mē-dē-'ā-shən\ *n* (1818) : the act or process of remedying ⟨~ of reading problems⟩ — **re·me·di·ate** \-'mē-dē-,āt\ *vt*

¹**rem·e·dy** \'re-mə-dē\ *n, pl* **rem·e·dies** [ME *remedie*, fr. AF, fr. L *remedium*, fr. *re-* + *mederi* to heal — more at MEDICAL] (13c) **1** : a medicine, application, or treatment that relieves or cures a disease **2** : something that corrects or counteracts **3** : the legal means to recover a right or to prevent or obtain redress for a wrong — **rem·e·di·less** *adj*

²**remedy** *vt* **-died; -dy·ing** (15c) : to provide or serve as a remedy for : RELIEVE ⟨~ a social evil⟩ *syn* see CORRECT

re·mem·ber \ri-'mem-bər\ *vb* **-bered; -ber·ing** \-b(ə-)riŋ\ [ME *remembren*, fr. MF *remembrer*, fr. LL *rememorari*, fr. L *re-* + LL *memorari* to be mindful of, fr. *memor* mindful — more at MEMORY] *vt* (14c) **1** : to bring to mind or think of again ⟨~s the old days⟩ **2** *archaic* **a** : BETHINK 1b **b** : REMIND **3** **a** : to keep in mind for attention or consideration ⟨~s friends at Christmas⟩ **b** : REWARD ⟨was ~ed in the will⟩ **4** : to retain in the memory ⟨~ the facts until the test is over⟩ **5** : to convey greetings from ⟨~ me to her⟩ **6** : RECORD, COMMEMORATE ~ *vi* **1** : to exercise or have the power of memory **2** : to have a recollection or remembrance — **re·mem·ber·abil·i·ty** \-,mem-b(ə-)rə-'bi-lə-tē\ *n* — **re·mem·ber·able** \-'mem-b(ə-)rə-bəl\ *adj* — **re·mem·ber·er** \-bər-ər\ *n*

syn REMEMBER, RECOLLECT, RECALL, REMIND, REMINISCE mean to bring an image or idea from the past into the mind. REMEMBER implies a keeping in memory that may be effortless or unwilled ⟨*remembers* that day as though it were yesterday⟩. RECOLLECT implies a bringing back to mind what is lost or scattered ⟨as near as I can *recollect*⟩. RECALL suggests an effort to bring back to mind and often to re-create in speech ⟨can't *recall* the words of the song⟩. REMIND suggests a jogging of one's memory by an association or similarity ⟨that *reminds* me of a story⟩. REMINISCE implies a casual often nostalgic recalling of experiences long past and gone ⟨old college friends like to *reminisce*⟩.

re·mem·brance \ri-'mem-brən(t)s *also* -bə-rən(t)s\ *n* (14c) **1** : the state of bearing in mind **2** **a** : the ability to remember : MEMORY **b** : the period over which one's memory extends **3** : act of recalling to mind **4** : a memory of a person, thing, or event **5** **a** : something that serves to keep in or bring to mind : REMINDER **b** : COMMEMORATION, MEMORIAL **c** : a greeting or gift recalling or expressing friendship or affection *syn* see MEMORY

Remembrance Day *n* (1918) : November 11 set aside in commemoration of the end of hostilities in 1918 and 1945 and observed as a legal holiday in Canada; *also* : REMEMBRANCE SUNDAY

re·mem·branc·er \ri-'mem-brən(t)-sər\ *n* (15c) **1** : any of several English officials **2** : one that reminds

Remembrance Sunday *n* (1942) : a Sunday that is usu. closest to November 11 and that in Great Britain is set aside in commemoration of the end of hostilities in 1918 and 1945

re·mex \'rē-,meks\ *n, pl* **rem·i·ges** \'re-mə-,jēz\ [NL *remig-, remex*, fr. L, oarsman, fr. *remus* oar + *agere* to drive — more at ROW, AGENT] (1767) : a primary or secondary quill feather of the wing of a bird

re·mind \ri-'mīnd\ *vt* (1660) : to put in mind of something : cause to remember *syn* see REMEMBER — **re·mind·er** *n*

re·mind·ful \-'mīn(d)-fəl\ *adj* (1810) **1** : MINDFUL **2** : tending to remind : SUGGESTIVE, EVOCATIVE

rem·i·nisce \,re-mə-'nis\ *vi* **-nisced; -nisc·ing** [back-formation fr. *reminiscence*] (1829) : to indulge in reminiscence *syn* see REMEMBER — **rem·i·nis·cer** \-'ni-sər\ *n*

rem·i·nis·cence \-'ni-s°n(t)s\ *n* (1589) **1** : apprehension of a Platonic idea as if it had been known in a previous existence **2** **a** : recall to

mind of a long-forgotten experience or fact **b** : the process or practice of thinking or telling about past experiences **3** **a** : a remembered experience **b** : an account of a memorable experience — often used in pl. **4** : something so like another as to be regarded as an unconscious repetition, imitation, or survival *syn* see MEMORY

rem·i·nis·cent \-s°nt\ *adj* [L *reminiscent-, reminiscens*, prp. of *reminisci* to remember, fr. *re-* + *-minisci* (akin to L *ment-, mens* mind) — more at MIND] (1765) **1** : of the character of or relating to reminiscence **2** : marked by or given to reminiscence **3** : tending to remind : SUGGESTIVE — **rem·i·nis·cent·ly** *adv*

rem·i·nis·cen·tial \,re-mə-(,)ni-'sen(t)-shəl\ *adj* (1646) : REMINISCENT

re·mint \(,)rē-'mint\ *vt* (1823) : to melt down (old or worn coin) and make into new coin

re·mise \ri-'mīz\ *vt* **re·mised; re·mis·ing** [ME, fr. MF *remis*, pp. of *remettre* to put back, fr. L *remittere* to send back] (15c) : to give, grant, or release a claim to : DEED

re·miss \ri-'mis\ *adj* [ME, fr. L *remissus*, fr. pp. of *remittere* to send back, relax] (15c) **1** : negligent in the performance of work or duty : CARELESS **2** : showing neglect or inattention : LAX *syn* see NEGLIGENT — **re·miss·ly** *adv* — **re·miss·ness** *n*

re·mis·si·ble \ri-'mi-sə-bəl\ *adj* (1577) : capable of being forgiven ⟨~ sins⟩ — **re·mis·si·bly** \-blē\ *adv*

re·mis·sion \ri-'mi-shən\ *n* (13c) **1** : the act or process of remitting **2** : a state or period during which something is remitted

¹**re·mit** \ri-'mit\ *vb* **re·mit·ted; re·mit·ting** [ME *remitten*, fr. L *remittere* to send back, fr. *re-* + *mittere* to send] *vt* (14c) **1** **a** : to lay aside (a mood or disposition) partly or wholly **b** : to desist from (an activity) **c** : to let (as attention or diligence) slacken : RELAX **2** **a** : to release from the guilt or penalty of ⟨~ sins⟩ **b** : to refrain from exacting ⟨~ a tax⟩ **c** : to cancel or refrain from inflicting ⟨~ the penalty⟩ **d** : to give relief from (suffering) **3** : to submit or refer for consideration, judgment, decision, or action; *specif* : REMAND **4** : to restore or consign to a former status or condition **5** : POSTPONE, DEFER **6** : to send (money) to a person or place esp. in payment of a demand, account, or draft ~ *vi* **1** **a** : to abate in force or intensity : MODERATE **b** *of a disease or abnormality* : to abate symptoms for a period **2** : to send money (as in payment) — **re·mit·ment** \-'mit-mənt\ *n* — **re·mit·ta·ble** \-'mi-tə-bəl\ *adj* — **re·mit·ter** *n*

²**re·mit** \ri-'mit, 'rē-,\ *n* (15c) **1** : an act of remitting **2** : something remitted to another person or authority

re·mit·tal \ri-'mi-t°l\ *n* (1596) : REMISSION

re·mit·tance \ri-'mi-t°n(t)s\ *n* (1705) **1** **a** : a sum of money remitted **b** : an instrument by which money is remitted **2** : transmittal of money (as to a distant place)

remittance man *n* (1886) : one living abroad on remittances from home

re·mit·tent \ri-'mi-t°nt\ *adj* [L *remittent-, remittens*, prp. of *remittere*] (1693) *of a disease* : marked by alternating periods of abatement and increase of symptoms

¹**rem·nant** \'rem-nənt\ *n* [ME, contr. of *remenant*, fr. MF, fr. prp. of *remenoir* to remain, fr. L *remanēre* — more at REMAIN] (14c) **1** **a** : a usu. small part, member, or trace remaining **b** : a small surviving group — often used in pl. **2** : an unsold or unused end of piece goods

²**remnant** *adj* (1550) : still remaining

re·mod·el \(,)rē-'mä-d°l\ *vt* (1789) : to alter the structure of : REMAKE

re·mon·strance \ri-'män(t)-strən(t)s\ *n* (1585) **1** : an earnest presentation of reasons for opposition or grievance; *esp* : a document formally stating such points **2** : an act or instance of remonstrating

re·mon·strant \-strənt\ *adj* (1641) : vigorously objecting or opposing — **remonstrant** *n* — **re·mon·strant·ly** *adv*

re·mon·strate \'re-mən-,strāt, ri-'män-\ *vb* **-strat·ed; -strat·ing** [ML *remonstratus*, pp. of *remonstrare* to demonstrate, fr. L *re-* + *monstrare* to show — more at MUSTER] *vi* (1695) : to present and urge reasons in opposition : EXPOSTULATE — usu. used with *with* ~ *vt* : to say or plead in protest, reproof, or opposition — **re·mon·stra·tion** \,re-mən-strā-shən, ri-'män-\ *n* — **re·mon·stra·tive** \ri-'män(t)-strə-tiv\ *adj* — **re·mon·stra·tive·ly** *adv* — **re·mon·stra·tor** \'re-mən-,strā-tər, ri-'män-\ *n*

rem·o·ra \'re-mə-rə *also* ri-'mor-ə *or* -'mor-\ *n* [LL, fr. L, delay, fr. *remorari* to delay, fr. *re-* + *morari* to delay — more at MORATORIUM] (1567) **1** : any of a family (Echeneididae) of marine bony fishes that have the anterior dorsal fin modified into a suctorial disk on the head by means of which they cling esp. to other fishes **2** : HINDRANCE, DRAG

re·morse \ri-'mors\ *n* [ME, fr. MF *remors*, fr. ML *remorsus*, fr. LL, act of biting again, fr. L *remordēre* to bite again, fr. *re-* + *mordēre* to bite — more at MORDANT] (14c) **1** : a gnawing distress arising from a sense of guilt for past wrongs : SELF-REPROACH **2** *obs* : COMPASSION *syn* see PENITENCE

remoras on tiger shark

re·morse·ful \-'mors-fəl\ *adj* (1592) : motivated or marked by remorse — **re·morse·ful·ly** \-fə-lē\ *adv* — **re·morse·ful·ness** *n*

re·morse·less \-ləs\ *adj* (1593) **1** : having no remorse : MERCILESS **2** : RELENTLESS — **re·morse·less·ly** *adv* — **re·morse·less·ness** *n*

¹**re·mote** \ri-'mōt\ *adj* **re·mot·er; -est** [ME, fr. L *remotus*, fr. pp. of *removēre* to remove] (15c) **1** : separated by an interval or space greater than usual (an involucre ~ from the flower) **2** : far removed in space, time, or relation : DIVERGENT ⟨the ~ past⟩ ⟨comments ~ from the truth⟩ **3** : OUT-OF-THE-WAY, SECLUDED ⟨a ~ cabin in the hills⟩ **4** : acting, acted on, or controlled indirectly or from a distance ⟨~

\ə\ abut \ᵊ\ kitten, F table \ər\ further \a\ ash \ā\ ace \ä\ mop, mar \aù\ out \ch\ chin \e\ bet \ē\ easy \g\ go \i\ hit \ī\ ice \j\ job \ŋ\ sing \ō\ go \ò\ law \òi\ boy \th\ thin \ṯh\ the \ü\ loot \ù\ foot \y\ yet \zh\ vision \à, ḵ, ⁿ, œ, œ̄, ᵫ, ᵫ̄, ᵊ\ *see* Guide to Pronunciation computer operation); *also* : relating to the acquisition of information about a distant object (as by radar or photography) without coming into physical contact with it 〈~ sensing〉 **5** : not arising from a primary or proximate action **6** : small in degree : SLIGHT 〈a ~ possibility〉 **7** : distant in manner : ALOOF — **re·mote·ly** *adv* — **re·mote·ness** *n*

²remote *n* (1937) **1** : a radio or television program or a portion of a program originating outside the studio **2** : REMOTE CONTROL 2

remote control *n* (1904) **1** : control (as by radio signal) of operation from a point at some distance removed **2** : a device or mechanism for controlling something from a distance

re·mo·tion \ri-'mō-shən\ *n* (15c) **1** : the quality or state of being remote **2** : the act of removing : REMOVAL **3** *obs* : DEPARTURE

¹re·mount \(,)rē-'maůnt\ *vb* [ME, partly fr. *re-* + *mounten* to mount, partly fr. MF *remonter*, fr. *re-* + *monter* to mount] *vt* (15c) **1** : to mount (something) again 〈~ a picture〉 **2** : to furnish remounts to ~ *vi* **1** : to mount again **2** : REVERT

²re·mount \'rē-,maůnt, (,)rē-'\ *n* (1781) : a fresh horse to replace one no longer available

re·mov·al \ri-'mü-vəl\ *n* (1597) : the act or process of removing : the fact of being removed

¹re·move \ri-'müv\ *vb* **re·moved; re·mov·ing** [ME, fr. OF *removoir*, fr. L *removēre*, fr. *re-* + *movēre* to move] *vt* (14c) **1 a** : to change the location, position, station, or residence of 〈~ soldiers to the front〉 **b** : to transfer (a legal proceeding) from one court to another **2** : to move by lifting, pushing aside, or taking away or off 〈~ your hat〉 **3** : to dismiss from office **4** : to get rid of : ELIMINATE 〈~ a tumor surgically〉 ~ *vi* **1** : to change location, station, or residence 〈*removing* from the city to the suburbs〉 **2** : to go away **3** : to be capable of being removed — **re·mov·abil·i·ty** \-,mü-və-'bi-lə-tē\ *n* — **re·mov·able** *also* **re·move·able** \ri-'mü-və-bəl\ *adj* — **re·mov·able·ness** \-'mü-və-bəl-nəs\ *n* — **re·mov·ably** \-blē\ *adv* — **re·mov·er** *n*

²remove *n* (1553) **1** : REMOVAL; *specif* : MOVE 2c **2 a** : a distance or interval separating one person or thing from another **b** : a degree or stage of separation

removed *adj* (ca. 1548) **1 a** : distant in degree of relationship **b** : of a younger or older generation 〈a second cousin's child is a second cousin once ~〉 **2** : separate or remote in space, time, or character

REM sleep *n* (1965) : a state of sleep that recurs cyclically several times during a normal period of sleep and that is characterized by increased neuronal activity of the forebrain and midbrain, by depressed muscle tone, and esp. in humans by dreaming, rapid eye movements, and vascular congestion of the sex organs — called also *paradoxical sleep, rapid eye movement sleep*

re·mu·da \ri-'mü-də, -'myü-\ *n* [AmerSp, relay of horses, fr. Sp, exchange, fr. *remudar* to exchange, fr. *re-* + *mudar* to change, fr. L *mutare* — more at MUTABLE] (ca. 1892) : the herd of horses from which those to be used for the day are chosen

re·mu·ner·ate \ri-'myü-nə-,rāt\ *vt* **-at·ed; -at·ing** [L *remuneratus,* pp. of *remunerare* to recompense, fr. *re-* + *munerare* to give, fr. *muner-, munus* gift — more at MEAN] (1523) **1** : to pay an equivalent for 〈their services were generously *remunerated*〉 **2** : to pay an equivalent to for a service, loss, or expense : RECOMPENSE   *syn* see PAY — **re·mu·ner·a·tor** \-,rā-tər\ *n* — **re·mu·ner·a·to·ry** \-rə-,tōr-ē, -,tȯr-\ *adj*

re·mu·ner·a·tion \ri-,myü-nə-'rā-shən\ *n* (15c) **1** : something that remunerates : RECOMPENSE, PAY **2** : an act or fact of remunerating

re·mu·ner·a·tive \ri-'myü-nə-rə-tiv, -,rā-\ *adj* (ca. 1677) **1** : serving to remunerate **2** : providing remuneration : PROFITABLE — **re·mu·ner·a·tive·ly** *adv* — **re·mu·ner·a·tive·ness** *n*

Re·mus \'rē-məs\ *n* [L] : a son of Mars slain by his twin brother Romulus

re·nais·sance \,re-nə-'sän(t)s, -'zän(t)s, -'säⁿs, -'zäⁿs, 're-nə-,, *chiefly Brit* ri-'nā-sⁿt)s\ *n, often attrib* [F, fr. MF, rebirth, fr. *renaistre* to be born again, fr. L *renasci*, fr. *re-* + *nasci* to be born — more at NATION] (1845) **1** *cap* **a** : the transitional movement in Europe between medieval and modern times beginning in the 14th century in Italy, lasting into the 17th century, and marked by a humanistic revival of classical influence expressed in a flowering of the arts and literature and by the beginnings of modern science **b** : the period of the Renaissance **c** : the neoclassic style of architecture prevailing during the Renaissance **2** *often cap* : a movement or period of vigorous artistic and intellectual activity **3** : REBIRTH, REVIVAL

Renaissance man *n* (1906) : a person who has wide interests and is expert in several areas

re·nal \'rē-nⁿl\ *adj* [F or LL; F *rénal,* fr. LL *renalis,* fr. L *renes* kidneys] (ca. 1656) : relating to, involving, or located in the region of the kidneys : NEPHRITIC

renal clearance *n* (1948) : CLEARANCE 3

re·na·scence \ri-'na-sⁿt)s, -'nä-\ *n, often cap* (1727) : RENAISSANCE

re·na·scent \-sⁿt\ *adj* [L *renascent-, renascens,* prp. of *renasci*] (ca. 1727) : rising again into being or vigor

re·na·ture \(,)rē-'nā-chər\ *vt* **re·na·tured; re·na·tur·ing** \-'nā-chə-riŋ, -'nāch-riŋ\ [*re-* + *denature*] (1926) : to restore (as a denatured protein) to an original or normal condition — **re·na·tur·a·tion** \(,)rē-,nā-chə-'rā-shən\ *n*

ren·con·tre \rän-kōⁿtrᵊ, ren-'kän-tər\ *or* **ren·coun·ter** \ren-'kaůn-tər\ *n* [*rencounter* fr. MF *rencontre, rencontrer; rencontre* fr. F] (1523) **1** : a hostile meeting or a contest between forces or individuals : COMBAT **2** : a casual meeting

ren·coun·ter \ren-'kaůn-tər\ *vt* [MF *rencontrer* to meet by chance or in hostility, fr. *re-* + *encontrer* to encounter] (1549) *archaic* : to meet casually

rend \'rend\ *vb* **rent** \'rent\ *also* **rend·ed** \'ren-dəd\; **rend·ing** [ME, fr. OE *rendan;* akin to OFris *renda* to tear and perh. to Skt *randhra* hole] *vt* (bef. 12c) **1** : to remove from place by violence : WREST **2** : to split or tear apart or in pieces by violence **3** : to tear (the hair or clothing) as a sign of anger, grief, or despair **4 a** : to lacerate mentally or emotionally **b** : to pierce with sound **c** : to divide (as a nation) into contesting factions ~ *vi* **1** : to perform an act of tearing or splitting **2** : to become torn or split   *syn* see TEAR

¹ren·der \'ren-dər\ *vb* **ren·dered; ren·der·ing** \-d(ə-)riŋ\ [ME *rendren,* fr. MF *rendre* to give back, yield, fr. (assumed) VL *rendere,* alter. of L *reddere,* partly fr. *re-* + *dare* to give & partly fr. *re-* + *-dere* to put — more at DATE, DO] *vt* (14c) **1 a** : to melt down 〈~ suet〉; *also* : to

extract by melting 〈~ lard〉 **b** : to treat so as to convert into industrial fats and oils or fertilizer **2 a** : to transmit to another : DELIVER **b** : GIVE UP, YIELD **c** : to furnish for consideration, approval, or information: as (1) : to hand down (a legal judgment) (2) : to agree on and report (a verdict) **3 a** : to give in return or retribution **b** (1) : GIVE BACK, RESTORE (2) : REFLECT, ECHO **c** : to give in acknowledgment of dependence or obligation : PAY **d** : to do (a service) for another **4 a** (1) : to cause to be or become : MAKE 〈enough rainfall . . . to ~ irrigation unnecessary —P. E. James〉 〈~ed him helpless〉 (2) : IMPART **b** (1) : to reproduce or represent by artistic or verbal means : DEPICT (2) : to give a performance of (3) : to produce a copy or version of (the documents are ~ed in the original French) (4) : to execute the motions of 〈~ a salute〉 **c** : TRANSLATE **5** : to direct the execution of : ADMINISTER 〈~ justice〉 **6** : to apply a coat of plaster or cement directly to ~ *vi* : to give recompense — **ren·der·able** \-d(ə-)rə-bəl\ *adj* — **ren·der·er** \-dər-ər\ *n*

²render *n* (1647) : a return esp. in goods or services due from a feudal tenant to his lord

¹ren·dez·vous \'rän-di-,vü, -dā-\ *n, pl* **ren·dez·vous** \-,vüz\ [MF, fr. *rendez vous* present yourselves] (1591) **1 a** : a place appointed for assembling or meeting **b** : a place of popular resort : HAUNT **2 a** : meeting at an appointed place and time **3** : the process of bringing two spacecraft together

²rendezvous *vb* **-voused** \-,vüd\; **-vous·ing** \-,vü-iŋ\; **-vouses** \-,vüz\ *vi* (ca. 1645) : to come together at a rendezvous ~ *vt* **1** : to bring together at a rendezvous **2** : to meet at a rendezvous

ren·di·tion \ren-'di-shən\ *n* [obs. F, fr. MF, alter. of *reddition,* fr. LL *reddition-, redditio,* fr. L *reddere* to return] (1601) : the act or result of rendering: as **a** : SURRENDER **b** : TRANSLATION **c** : PERFORMANCE, INTERPRETATION

ren·dzi·na \ren-'jē-nə\ *n* [Pol *rędzina* rich limy soil] (1922) : any of a group of dark grayish brown intrazonal soils developed in grassy regions of high to moderate humidity from soft calcareous marl or chalk

¹ren·e·gade \'re-ni-,gäd\ *n* [Sp *renegado,* fr. ML *renegatus,* fr. pp. of *renegare* to deny, fr. L *re-* + *negare* to deny — more at NEGATE] (1583) **1** : a deserter from one faith, cause, or allegiance to another **2** : an individual who rejects lawful or conventional behavior

²renegade *vi* **-gad·ed; -gad·ing** (ca. 1611) : to become a renegade

³renegade *adj* (1705) **1** : having deserted a faith, cause, or religion for a hostile one **2** : having rejected tradition : UNCONVENTIONAL

re·nege \ri-'nig, -'neg, -'nēg, -'näg\ *vb* **re·neged; re·neg·ing** [ML *renegare*] *vt* (1548) : DENY, RENOUNCE ~ *vi* **1** *obs* : to make a denial **2** : REVOKE **3** : to go back on a promise or commitment — **re·neg·er** *n*

re·ne·go·tia·ble \,rē-ni-'gō-sh(ē-ə)-bəl\ *adj* (1943) : subject to renegotiation 〈~ mortgages〉 〈~ rates〉

re·ne·go·ti·ate \,rē-ni-'gō-shē-,āt\ *vt* (ca. 1934) : to negotiate again (as to adjust interest rates or repayments or to get new money) 〈~ a loan〉 〈~ a contract〉 — **re·ne·go·ti·a·tion** \,rē-ni-,gō-shē-'ā-shən, -sē-'ā-\ *n*

re·new \ri-'nü, -'nyü\ *vt* (14c) **1** : to make like new : restore to freshness, vigor, or perfection 〈as we ~ our strength in sleep〉 **2** : to make new spiritually : REGENERATE **3 a** : to restore to existence : REVIVE **b** : to make extensive changes in : REBUILD **4** : to do again : REPEAT **5** : to begin again : RESUME **6** : REPLACE, REPLENISH 〈~ water in a tank〉 **7 a** : to grant or obtain an extension of or on 〈~ a license〉 **b** : to grant or obtain an extension on the loan of 〈~ a library book〉 ~ *vi* **1** : to become new or as new **2** : to begin again : RESUME **3** : to make a renewal (as of a lease) — **re·new·er** *n*

syn RENEW, RESTORE, REFRESH, RENOVATE, REJUVENATE mean to make like new. RENEW implies a restoration of what had become faded or disintegrated so that it seems like new 〈efforts to *renew* the splendor of the old castle〉. RESTORE implies a return to an original state after depletion or loss 〈*restored* a fine piece of furniture〉. REFRESH implies the supplying of something necessary to restore lost strength, animation, or power 〈a *refreshing* drink〉. RENOVATE suggests a renewing by cleansing, repairing, or rebuilding 〈the apartment has been entirely *renovated*〉. REJUVENATE suggests the restoration of youthful vigor, powers, or appearance 〈the change in jobs *rejuvenated* her spirits〉.

re·new·able \-'nü-ə-bəl, -'nyü-\ *adj* (1727) **1** : capable of being renewed 〈~ contracts〉 **2** : capable of being replaced by natural ecological cycles or sound management practices 〈~ resources〉 — **re·new·abil·i·ty** \-,nü-ə-'bi-lə-tē, -,nyü-\ *n* — **re·new·ably** \-'nü-ə-blē, -'nyü-\ *adv*

re·new·al \ri-'nü-əl, -'nyü-\ *n* (ca. 1686) **1** : the act or process of renewing : REPETITION **2** : the quality or state of being renewed **3** : something (as a subscription to a magazine) renewed **4** : something used for renewing; *specif* : an expenditure that betters existing fixed assets **5** : the rebuilding of a large area (as of a city) by a public authority

reni- *or* **reno-** *comb form* [L *renes* kidneys] : kidney 〈*reni*form〉

re·ni·form \'rē-nə-,fȯrm, 're-\ *adj* [NL *reniformis,* fr. *reni-* + *-formis* -form] (ca. 1753) : suggesting a kidney in outline

re·nin \'rē-nən, 're-\ *n* [ISV, fr. L *renes*] (1906) : a proteolytic enzyme of the kidney that plays a major role in the release of angiotensin

re·ni·ten·cy \'re-nə-tən(t)-sē, ri-'nī-tⁿt)\ *n* (1613) : RESISTANCE, OPPOSITION

re·ni·tent \'re-nə-tənt, ri-'nī-tⁿnt\ *adj* [F or L; F *rénitent, renitens,* prp. of *reniti* to resist, fr. *re-* + *niti* to strive — more at NISUS] (1701) **1** : resisting physical pressure **2** : resisting constraint or compulsion : RECALCITRANT

ren·min·bi \'ren-'min-'bē\ *n, pl* **ren·min·bi** [Chin (Beijing) *rénmínbì,* fr. *rénmín* people + *bì* currency] (1957) : the currency of the People's Republic of China consisting of yuan

ren·net \'re-nət\ *n* [ME, fr. (assumed) ME *rennen* to cause to coagulate, fr. OE *gerennan,* fr. *ge-* together + (assumed) OE *rennan* to cause to run; akin to OHG *rennen* to cause to run, OE *rinnan* to run — more at CO-, RUN] (15c) **1 a** : the contents of the stomach of an unweaned animal and esp. a calf **b** : the lining membrane of a stomach or one of its compartments (as the fourth of a ruminant) used for curdling milk; *also* : a preparation of the stomach of animals used for this purpose **2 a** : RENNIN **b** : a substitute for rennin

ren·nin \'re-nən\ *n* [*rennet* + ¹-*in*] (1897) : an enzyme that coagulates milk and is used in making cheese and junkets; *esp* : one from the mucous membrane of the stomach of a calf

re·no·gram \'rē-nə-ˌgram\ *n* (1952) : a photographic depiction of the course of renal excretion of a radioactively labeled substance — **re·no·graph·ic** \ˌrē-nə-'gra-fik\ *adj* — **re·nog·ra·phy** \rē-'nä-grə-fē\ *n*

re·nom·i·nate \(ˌ)rē-'nä-mə-ˌnāt\ *vt* (1864) : to nominate again esp. for a succeeding term — **re·nom·i·na·tion** \(ˌ)rē-ˌnä-mə-'nä-shən\ *n*

re·nounce \ri-'naůn(t)s\ *vb* **re·nounced; re·nounc·ing** [ME, fr. MF *renoncer*, fr. L *renuntiare*, fr. *re-* + *nuntiare* to report, fr. *nuntius* messenger] *vt* (14c) **1** : to give up, refuse, or resign usu. by formal declaration ⟨~ his errors⟩ **2** : to refuse to follow, obey, or recognize any further : REPUDIATE ⟨~ the authority of the church⟩ ~ *vi* **1** : to make a renunciation **2** : to fail to follow suit in a card game *syn* see ABDICATE, ABJURE — **re·nounce·ment** \-'naůn(t)s-mənt\ *n* — **re·nounc·er** *n*

re·no·vas·cu·lar \ˌrē-nō-'vas-kyə-lər\ *adj* (1961) : of, relating to, or involving the blood vessels of the kidneys ⟨~ hypertension⟩

ren·o·vate \'re-nə-ˌvāt\ *vt* **-vat·ed; -vat·ing** [L *renovatus*, pp. of *renovare*, fr. *re-* + *novare* to make new, fr. *novus* new — more at NEW] (ca. 1522) **1** : to restore to a former better state (as by cleaning, repairing, or rebuilding) **2** : to restore to life, vigor, or activity : REVIVE ⟨the church was *renovated* by a new ecumenical spirit⟩ *syn* see RENEW — **ren·o·va·tion** \ˌre-nə-'vā-shən\ *n* — **ren·o·va·tive** \'re-nə-ˌvā-tiv\ *adj* — **ren·o·va·tor** \-ˌvā-tər\ *n*

¹re·nown \ri-'naůn\ *n* [ME, fr. MF *renon*, fr. OF, fr. *renomer* to celebrate, fr. *re-* + *nomer* to name, fr. L *nominare*, fr. *nomin-, nomen* name — more at NAME] (14c) **1** : a state of being widely acclaimed and highly honored : FAME **2** *obs* : REPORT, RUMOR

²renown *vt* (15c) : to give renown to

re·nowned *adj* (14c) : having renown : CELEBRATED *syn* see FAMOUS

¹rent \'rent\ *n* [ME *rente*, fr. OF, income from a property, fr. (assumed) VL *rendita*, fr. fem. of *renditus*, pp. of *rendere* to yield — more at RENDER] (12c) **1** : property (as a house) rented or for rent **2 a** : a usu. fixed periodical return made by a tenant or occupant of property to the owner for the possession and use thereof; *esp* : an agreed sum paid at fixed intervals by a tenant to the landlord **b** : the amount paid by a hirer of personal property to the owner for the use thereof **3 a** : the portion of the income of an economy (as of a nation) attributable to land as a factor of production in addition to capital and labor **b** : ECONOMIC RENT — **for rent** : available for use or service in return for payment

²rent *vt* (15c) **1** : to grant the possession and enjoyment of in exchange for rent **2** : to take and hold under an agreement to pay rent ~ *vi* **1** : to be for rent **2 a** : to obtain the possession and use of a place or article in exchange for rent **b** : to allow the possession and use of property in exchange for rent *syn* see HIRE — **rent·abil·i·ty** \ˌren-tə-'bi-lə-tē\ *n* — **rent·able** \'ren-tə-bəl\ *adj*

³rent *past and past part of* REND

⁴rent *n* [E dial. *rent* to rend, fr. ME, alter. of *renden* — more at REND] (1535) **1** : an opening made by or as if by rending : a split in a party or organized group : SCHISM **3** : an act or instance of rending

rent–a–car \'rent-ə-ˌkär\ *n* (1935) : a rented car

¹rent·al \'ren-t°l\ *n* (14c) **1** : an amount paid or collected as rent **2** : something that is rented **3** : an act of renting **4** : a business that rents something

²rental *adj* (15c) **1 a** : of or relating to rent **b** : available for rent **2** : dealing in rental property ⟨a ~ agency⟩

rental library *n* (1928) : a commercially operated library (as in a store) that lends books at a fixed charge per book per day — called also *lending library*

rent control *n* (1931) : government regulation of the amount charged as rent for housing and often also of eviction — **rent–controlled** *adj*

rente \'räⁿ(n)t\ *n* [F] (1873) : a government security (as in France) paying interest; *also* : the interest paid

rent·er \'ren-tər\ *n* (1655) : one that rents; *specif* : the lessee or tenant of property

ren·tier \räⁿ-tyā\ *n* [F, fr. OF, fr. *rente*] (ca. 1847) : a person who lives on income from property or securities

rent strike *n* (1964) : a refusal by a group of tenants to pay rent (as in protest against high rates)

re·nun·ci·a·tion \ri-ˌnən(t)-sē-'ā-shən\ *n* [ME, fr. L *renuntiation-, renuntiatio*, fr. *renuntiare* to renounce] (14c) : the act or practice of renouncing : REPUDIATION; *specif* : ascetic self-denial — **re·nun·ci·a·tive** \ri-'nən(t)-sē-ˌā-tiv\ *adj* — **re·nun·ci·a·to·ry** \-sē-ə-ˌtōr-ē, -ˌtȯr-\ *adj*

re·of·fer \(ˌ)rē-'ȯ-fər, -'ä-\ *vt* (1920) : to offer (a security issue) for public sale

re·open \(ˌ)rē-'ō-pən, -'ō-p°m\ *vt* (1733) **1** : to open again **2 a** : to take up again : RESUME ⟨~ discussion⟩ **b** : to resume discussion or consideration of ⟨~ a contract⟩ **3** : to begin again ~ *vi* : to open again ⟨school ~s in September⟩

¹re·or·der \(ˌ)rē-'ȯr-dər\ *vt* (1656) **1** : to arrange in a different way **2** : to give a reorder for ~ *vi* : to place a reorder

²reorder *n* (1901) : an order like a previous order placed with the same supplier

re·or·ga·ni·za·tion \(ˌ)rē-ˌȯr-gə-nə-'zā-shən, -ˌȯrg-nə-\ *n* (1813) : the act or process of reorganizing : the state of being reorganized; *esp* : the financial reconstruction of a business concern — **re·or·ga·ni·za·tion·al** \-shnəl, -shə-n°l\ *adj*

re·or·ga·nize \(ˌ)rē-'ȯr-gə-ˌnīz\ *vt* (ca. 1686) : to organize again or anew ~ *vi* : to undergo reorganization — **re·or·ga·niz·er** *n*

reo·vi·rus \ˌrē-ō-'vī-rəs\ *n* [*r*espiratory *e*nteric *o*rphan (i.e., unidentified) *virus*] (1959) : any of a group of double-stranded RNA viruses lacking a lipoprotein envelope that includes many pathogens of plants or animals

¹rep \'rep\ *n* (ca. 1705) *slang* : REPUTATION; *esp* : status in a group (as a gang)

²rep *n* (1848) : REPRESENTATIVE ⟨sales ~s⟩

³rep *or* **repp** \'rep\ *n* [F *reps*, modif. of E *ribs*, pl. of *rib*] (1860) : a plain-weave fabric with prominent rounded crosswise ribs

⁴rep *n* (1925) : REPERTORY 2b, 3

⁵rep *n* [*r*oentgen *e*quivalent *p*hysical] (1947) : the dosage of an ionizing radiation that will develop the same amount of energy upon absorption in human tissue as one roentgen of X-ray or gamma-ray exposure

⁶rep *n* [short for *repetition*] (1978) : a repetition of a specified movement or exercise (as in weight lifting)

re·pack·age \(ˌ)rē-'pa-kij\ *vt* (1946) : to package again or anew; *specif* : to put into a more efficient or attractive form — **re·pack·ag·er** *n*

¹re·pair \ri-'par, -'per\ *vi* [ME, fr. MF *repairier* to go back to one's country, fr. LL *repatriare*, fr. L *re-* + *patria* native country — more at EXPATRIATE] (14c) **1 a** : to betake oneself : GO ⟨~ed to the judge's chambers⟩ **b** : to come together : RALLY **2** *obs* : RETURN

²repair *n* (14c) **1** : the act of repairing : RESORT **2** : a popular gathering place

³repair *vb* [ME, fr. MF *reparer*, fr. L *reparare*, fr. *re-* + *parare* to prepare — more at PARE] *vt* (14c) **1 a** : to restore by replacing a part or putting together what is torn or broken : FIX ⟨~ a shoe⟩ **b** : to restore to a sound or healthy state : RENEW ⟨~ his strength⟩ **2** : to make good : compensate for : REMEDY ⟨~ a gap in my reading⟩ ~ *vi* : to make repairs *syn* see MEND — **re·pair·abil·i·ty** \-ˌpar-ə-'bi-lə-tē, -ˌper-\ *n* — **re·pair·able** \-'par-ə-bəl, -'per-\ *adj* — **re·pair·er** \-'par-ər, -'per-\ *n*

⁴repair *n* (15c) **1 a** : an instance or result of repairing **b** : the act or process of repairing **c** : the replacement of destroyed cells or tissues by new formations **2 a** : relative condition with respect to soundness or need of repairing **b** : the state of being in good or sound condition

re·pair·man \ri-'par-ˌman, -'per-, -mən\ *n* (1871) : one who repairs; *specif* : one whose occupation is to make repairs in a mechanism

re·pand \ri-'pand\ *adj* [L *repandus* spread out, fr. *repandere* to open wide, fr. *re-* + *pandere* to spread — more at FATHOM] (ca. 1760) : having a slightly undulating margin ⟨a ~ leaf⟩ ⟨a ~ colony of bacteria⟩

rep·a·ra·ble \'re-p(ə-)rə-bəl\ *adj* (1570) : capable of being repaired

rep·a·ra·tion \ˌre-pə-'rā-shən\ *n* [ME, fr. MF, fr. LL *reparation-, reparatio*, fr. L *reparare*] (14c) **1 a** : a repairing or keeping in repair **b** *pl* : REPAIRS **2 a** : the act of making amends, offering expiation, or giving satisfaction for a wrong or injury **b** : something done or given as amends or satisfaction **3** : the payment of damages : INDEMNIFICATION; *specif* : compensation in money or materials payable by a defeated nation for damages to or expenditures sustained by another nation as a result of hostilities with the defeated nation — usu. used in pl.

re·par·a·tive \ri-'par-ə-tiv\ *adj* (1656) **1** : of, relating to, or effecting repair **2** : serving to make amends

rep·ar·tee \ˌre-pər-'tē, -ˌpär-, -'tā\ *n* [F *repartie*, fr. *repartir* to retort, fr. MF, fr. *re-* + *partir* to divide — more at PART] (ca. 1645) **1 a** : a quick and witty reply **b** : a succession or interchange of clever retorts : amusing and usu. light sparring with words **2** : adroitness and cleverness in reply : skill in repartee *syn* see WIT

¹re·par·ti·tion \ˌre-ˌpär-'ti-shən, ˌrē-\ *n* [prob. fr. Sp *repartición*, fr. *repartir* to distribute, fr. *re-* + *partir* to divide, fr. L *partire* — more at PART] (1555) : DISTRIBUTION

²re·par·ti·tion \ˌrē-ˌpär-'ti-shən\ *n* [*re-* + *partition*] (1835) : a second or additional dividing or distribution

re·pass \(ˌ)rē-'pas\ *vb* [ME, fr. MF *repasser*, fr. OF, fr. *re-* + *passer* to pass] *vi* (15c) : to pass again esp. in the opposite direction : RETURN ~ *vt* **1** : to pass through, over, or by again ⟨~ the house⟩ **2** : to cause to pass again **3** : to adopt again ⟨~ed the resolution⟩ — **re·pas·sage** \-'pa-sij\ *n*

¹re·past \ri-'past, 're-ˌ\ *n* [ME, fr. MF, fr. OF, fr. *repaistre* to feed, fr. *re-* + *paistre* to feed, fr. L *pascere* — more at FOOD] (14c) **1** : something taken as food : MEAL **2** : the act or time of taking food

²re·past \ri-'past\ *vt* (15c) *obs* : FEED ~ *vi* : to take food : FEAST

re·pa·tri·ate \(ˌ)rē-'pā-trē-ˌāt, -'pa-\ *vt* **-at·ed; -at·ing** [LL *repatriatus*, pp. of *repatriare* to go back to one's country — more at REPAIR] (1611) : to restore or return to the country of origin, allegiance, or citizenship ⟨~ prisoners of war⟩ — **re·pa·tri·ate** \-trē-ət, -trē-ˌāt\ *n* — **re·pa·tri·a·tion** \(ˌ)rē-ˌpā-trē-'ā-shən, -ˌpa-\ *n*

re·pay \(ˌ)rē-'pā\ *vb* **-paid** \-'pād\; **-pay·ing** *vt* (15c) **1 a** : to pay back ⟨~ a loan⟩ **b** : to give or inflict in return or requital ⟨~ evil for evil⟩ **2** : to make a return payment to : COMPENSATE, REQUITE **3** : to make requital for : RECOMPENSE ⟨the success that ~s hard work⟩ ~ *vi* : to make return payment or requital *syn* see PAY — **re·pay·able** \-'pā-ə-bəl\ *adj* — **re·pay·ment** \-'pā-mənt\ *n*

re·peal \ri-'pē(ə)l\ *vt* [ME *repelen*, fr. MF *repeler*, fr. OF, fr. *re-* + *apeler* to appeal, fr. L *appellare*] (14c) **1** : to rescind or annul by authoritative act; *esp* : to revoke or abrogate by legislative enactment : ABANDON, RENOUNCE **3** *obs* : to summon to return : RECALL — **repeal** *n* — **re·peal·able** \-'pē-lə-bəl\ *adj*

re·peal·er \ri-'pē-lər\ *n* (1765) : one that repeals; *specif* : a legislative act that abrogates an earlier act

¹re·peat \ri-'pēt\ *vb* [ME *repeten*, fr. MF *repeter*, fr. L *repetere* to return to, repeat, fr. *re-* + *petere* to go to, seek — more at FEATHER] *vt* (14c) **1 a** : to say or state again **b** : to say over from memory : RECITE **c** : to say after another **2 a** : to make, do, or perform again ⟨~ an experiment⟩ **b** : to make appear again ⟨the curtains ~ the wallpaper pattern⟩ ⟨will ~ the program tomorrow⟩ **c** : to go through or experience again ⟨had to ~ third grade⟩ **3** : to express or present (oneself) again in the same words, terms, or form ~ *vi* : to say, do, or accomplish something again; *esp* : to win (as a sports championship) another time in succession — **re·peat·abil·i·ty** \-ˌpē-tə-'bi-lə-tē\ *n* — **re·peat·able** \-'pē-tə-bəl\ *adj*

²re·peat \ri-'pēt, 're-ˌ\ *n* (15c) **1** : something repeated : REPETITION **b** : a musical passage to be repeated in performance; *also* : a sign placed before and after such a passage **c** : a usu. transcribed repetition of a radio or television program **d** : a genetic duplication in which the duplicated parts are adjacent to each other along the chromosome **2** : the act of repeating

re·peat·ed \ri-'pē-təd\ *adj* (1611) **1** : renewed or recurring again and again ⟨~ changes of plan⟩ **2** : said, done, or presented again

re·peat·ed·ly *adv* (ca. 1718) : AGAIN AND AGAIN

re·peat·er \ri-'pē-tər\ *n* (1598) : one that repeats: as **a**

repeat 1b

\ə\ abut \ᵊ\ kitten, F table \ər\ further \a\ ash \ā\ ace \ä\ mop, mar \aů\ out \ch\ chin \e\ bet \ē\ easy \g\ go \i\ hit \ī\ ice \j\ job \ŋ\ sing \ō\ go \ȯ\ law \ȯi\ boy \th\ thin \t̲h̲\ the \ü\ loot \ů\ foot \y\ yet \zh\ vision \ä, k̲, ⁿ, œ, œ̄, ue, ūe, ᵊ\ *see* Guide to Pronunciation

: one who relates or recites   **b** : a watch or clock with a striking mechanism that upon pressure of a spring will indicate the time in hours or quarters and sometimes minutes   **c** : a firearm having a magazine that holds a number of cartridges loaded one at a time into the chamber by the action of the piece   **d** : an habitual violator of the laws   **e** : one who votes illegally by casting more than one ballot in an election   **f** : a student enrolled in a class or course for a second or subsequent time   **g** : a device for receiving electronic communication signals and delivering corresponding amplified ones

re·peat·ing *adj* (1824) *of a firearm* : designed to load cartridges from a magazine

repeating decimal *n* (1773) : a decimal in which after a certain point a particular digit or sequence of digits repeats itself indefinitely — compare TERMINATING DECIMAL

re·pe·chage \,re-pə-'shäzh, 're-pə-,\ *n* [F *repêchage* second chance, reexamination for a candidate who has failed, fr. *repêcher* to fish out, rescue, fr. *re-* + *pêcher* to fish, fr. L *piscari* — more at PISCATORY] (1928) : a trial heat (as in rowing) in which first-round losers are given another chance to qualify for the semifinals

re·pel \ri-'pel\ *vb* **re·pelled; re·pel·ling** [ME *repellen*, fr. L *repellere*, fr. *re-* + *pellere* to drive — more at FELT] *vt* (15c) **1 a** : to drive back : REPULSE   **b** : to fight against : RESIST   **2** : TURN AWAY, REJECT ⟨*repelled* the insinuation⟩   **3 a** : to drive away : DISCOURAGE ⟨foul words and frowns must not ~ a lover —Shak.⟩   **b** : to be incapable of adhering to, mixing with, taking up, or holding   **c** : to force away or apart or tend to do so by mutual action at a distance   **4** : to cause aversion in : DISGUST   ~ *vi* : to cause aversion — **re·pel·ler** *n*

re·pel·len·cy \ri-'pe-lən(t)-sē\ *n* (1747) : the quality or capacity of repelling

1re·pel·lent *also* **re·pel·lant** \ri-'pe-lənt\ *adj* [L *repellent-, repellens*, prp. of *repellere*] (1643) **1** : serving or tending to drive away or ward off — often used in combination ⟨a mosquito-*repellent* spray⟩   **2** : arousing aversion or disgust : REPULSIVE — **re·pel·lent·ly** *adv*

2repellent *also* **repellant** *n* (1661) : something that repels; *esp* : a substance that repels insects

1re·pent \ri-'pent\ *vb* [ME, fr. OF *repentir*, fr. *re-* + *pentir* to be sorry, fr. L *paenitēre* — more at PENITENT] *vi* (14c) **1** : to turn from sin and dedicate oneself to the amendment of one's life   **2 a** : to feel regret or contrition   **b** : to change one's mind   ~ *vt* **1** : to cause to feel regret or contrition   **2** : to feel sorrow, regret, or contrition for — **re·pent·er** *n*

2re·pent \'rē-pənt\ *adj* [L *repent-, repens*, prp. of *repere* to creep — more at REPTILE] (1669) : CREEPING, PROSTRATE ⟨~ stems⟩

re·pen·tance \ri-'pen-t³n(t)s\ *n* (14c) : the action or process of repenting esp. for misdeeds or moral shortcomings   *syn* see PENITENCE

re·pen·tant \-t³nt\ *adj* (13c) **1** : experiencing repentance : PENITENT   **2** : expressive of repentance — **re·pen·tant·ly** *adv*

re·per·cus·sion \,rē-pər-'kə-shən, ,re-\ *n* [L *repercussion-, repercussio*, fr. *repercutere* to drive back, fr. *re-* + *percutere* to beat — more at PERCUSSION] (1536) **1** : REFLECTION, REVERBERATION   **2 a** : an action or effect given or exerted in return : a reciprocal action or effect   **b** : a widespread, indirect, or unforeseen effect of an act, action, or event — usu. used in pl. — **re·per·cus·sive** \-'kə-siv\ *adj*

rep·er·toire \'re-pə(r)-,twär\ *n* [F *répertoire*, fr. LL *repertorium*] (1847) **1 a** : a list or supply of dramas, operas, pieces, or parts that a company or person is prepared to perform   **b** : a supply of skills, devices, or expedients ⟨part of the ~ of a quarterback⟩; *broadly* : AMOUNT, SUPPLY ⟨an endless ~ of summer clothes⟩   **c** : a list or supply of capabilities ⟨the instruction ~ of a computer⟩   **2 a** : the complete list or supply of dramas, operas, or musical works available for performance ⟨our modern orchestral ~⟩   **b** : the complete list or supply of skills, devices, or ingredients used in a particular field, occupation, or practice ⟨the ~ of literary criticism⟩

rep·er·to·ry \'re-pə(r)-,tōr-ē, -,tor-\ *n, pl* **-ries** [LL *repertorium* list, fr. L *reperire* to find, fr. *re-* + *parere* to produce — more at PARE] (1593) **1** : a place where something may be found : REPOSITORY   **2 a** : REPERTOIRE   **b** : a company that presents several different plays, operas, or pieces usu. alternately in the course of a season at one theater   **c** : a theater housing such a company   **3** : the production and presentation of plays by a repertory company ⟨acting in ~⟩

rep·e·tend \'re-pə-,tend\ *n* [L *repetendus* to be repeated, gerundive of *repetere* to repeat] (1728) : a repeated sound, word, or phrase; *specif* : REFRAIN

rep·e·ti·tion \,re-pə-'ti-shən\ *n* [ME *repeticioun*, fr. L *repetition-, repetitio*, fr. *repetere* to repeat] (15c) **1** : the act or an instance of repeating or being repeated   **2** : MENTION, RECITAL — **rep·e·ti·tion·al** \-'tish-nəl, -'ti-shə-n³l\ *adj*

rep·e·ti·tious \-'ti-shəs\ *adj* (1675) : characterized or marked by repetition; *esp* : tediously repeating — **rep·e·ti·tious·ly** *adv* — **rep·e·ti·tious·ness** *n*

re·pet·i·tive \ri-'pe-tə-tiv\ *adj* (1839) **1** : containing repetition   **2** : REPETITIOUS — **re·pet·i·tive·ly** *adv* — **re·pet·i·tive·ness** *n*

re·pine \ri-'pīn\ *vi* (ca. 1530) **1** : to feel or express dejection or discontent   **2** : to long for something — **re·pin·er** *n*

re·place \ri-'plās\ *vt* (1595) **1** : to restore to a former place or position ⟨~ cards in a file⟩   **2** : to take the place of esp. as a substitute or successor   **3** : to put something new in the place of ⟨~ a worn carpet⟩ — **re·place·able** \-'plā-sə-bəl\ *adj* — **re·plac·er** *n*

syn REPLACE, DISPLACE, SUPPLANT, SUPERSEDE mean to put out of a usual or proper place or into the place of another. REPLACE implies a filling of a place once occupied by something lost, destroyed, or no longer usable or adequate ⟨*replaced* the broken window⟩. DISPLACE implies an ousting or dislodging ⟨war had *displaced* thousands⟩. SUPPLANT implies either a dispossessing or usurping of another's place, possessions, or privileges or an uprooting of something and its replacement with something else ⟨was abruptly *supplanted* in her affections by another⟩. SUPERSEDE implies replacing a person or thing that has become superannuated, obsolete, or otherwise inferior ⟨the new edition *supersedes* all previous ones⟩.

re·place·ment \ri-'plās-mənt\ *n* (ca. 1790) **1** : the action or process of replacing : the state of being replaced   **2** : one that replaces another esp. in a job or function

replacement set *n* (1959) : a set of elements any one of which may be used to replace a given variable or placeholder in a mathematical sentence or expression (as an equation)

re·plant \(,)rē-'plant\ *vt* (1575) **1** : to plant again or anew   **2** : to provide with new plants   **3** : to subject to replantation

re·plan·ta·tion \,rē-(,)plan-'tā-shən\ *n* (1870) : reattachment or reinsertion of a bodily part (as a limb or tooth) after separation from the body

1re·play \(,)rē-'plā\ *vt* (1884) : to play again or over

2re·play \'rē-,plā\ *n* (1895) **1 a** : an act or instance of replaying   **b** : the playing of a tape (as a videotape)   **2** : REPETITION, REENACTMENT ⟨don't want a ~ of our old mistakes⟩

re·plead·er \(,)rē-'plē-dər\ *n* [*replead* to plead again + *-er* (as in *misnomer*)] (1607) **1** : a second legal pleading   **2** : the right of pleading again granted usu. when the issue raised is immaterial or insufficient

re·plen·ish \ri-'ple-nish\ *vb* [ME *replenisshen*, fr. MF *repleniss-*, stem of *replenir* to fill, fr. OF, fr. *re-* + *plein* full, fr. L *plenus* — more at FULL] *vt* (14c) **1 a** : to fill with persons or animals : STOCK   **b** *archaic* : to supply fully : PERFECT   **c** : to fill with inspiration or power : NOURISH   **2 a** : to fill or build up again ⟨~ed his glass⟩   **b** : to make good : REPLACE   ~ *vi* : to become full : fill up again — **re·plen·ish·able** \-ni-shə-bəl\ *adj* — **re·plen·ish·er** *n* — **re·plen·ish·ment** \-nish-mənt\ *n*

re·plete \ri-'plēt\ *adj* [ME, fr. MF & L; MF *replet*, fr. L *repletus*, pp. of *replēre* to fill up, fr. *re-* + *plēre* to fill — more at FULL] (14c) **1** : fully or abundantly provided or filled ⟨a book ~ with ... delicious details —William Safire⟩   **2 a** : abundantly fed   **b** : FAT, STOUT   **3** : COMPLETE   *syn* see FULL — **re·plete·ness** *n*

re·ple·tion \ri-'plē-shən\ *n* (14c) **1** : the act of eating to excess : the state of being fed to excess : SURFEIT   **2** : the condition of being filled up or overcrowded   **3** : fulfillment of a need or desire : SATISFACTION

1re·plev·in \ri-'ple-vən\ *n* [ME, fr. AF *replevine*, fr. *replevir* to give security, fr. OF, fr. *re-* + *plevir* to pledge, fr. (assumed) LL *plebere* — more at PLEDGE] (15c) **1** : the recovery by a person of goods or chattels claimed to be wrongfully taken or detained upon the person's giving security to try the matter in court and return the goods if defeated in the action   **2** : the writ or the common-law action whereby goods and chattels are replevied

2replevin *vt* (1678) : REPLEVY

1re·plevy \ri-'ple-vē\ *n, pl* **re·plev·ies** [ME, fr. AF *replevir*, v.] (15c) : REPLEVIN

2replevy *vt* **re·plev·ied; re·plevy·ing** (1596) : to take or get back by a writ for replevin — **re·plevi·able** \-vē-ə-bəl\ *adj*

rep·li·ca \'re-pli-kə\ *n* [It, repetition, fr. *replicare* to repeat, fr. LL, fr. L, to fold back — more at REPLY] (1824) **1** : an exact reproduction (as of a painting) executed by the original artist ⟨a ~ of this was painted ... this year —Constance Strachey⟩   **2** : a copy exact in all details ⟨DNA makes a ~ of itself⟩ ⟨sailed a ~ of the Viking ship⟩; *broadly* : COPY ⟨this faithful, pathetic ~ of a Midwestern suburb —G. F. Kennan⟩   *syn* see REPRODUCTION

rep·li·ca·ble \'re-plə-kə-bəl\ *adj* (1950) : capable of replication ⟨~ experimental results⟩ — **rep·li·ca·bil·i·ty** \,re-plə-kə-'bi-lə-tē\ *n*

rep·li·case \'re-pli-,kās, -,kāz\ *n* [*replication* + *-ase*] (1963) : a polymerase that promotes synthesis of a particular RNA in the presence of a template of RNA

1rep·li·cate \'re-plə-,kāt\ *vb* **-cat·ed; -cat·ing** [LL *replicatus*, pp. of *replicare*] *vt* (15c) : DUPLICATE, REPEAT ⟨~ a statistical experiment⟩   ~ *vi* : to undergo replication : produce a replica of itself ⟨virus particles *replicating* in cells⟩

2rep·li·cate \-kət\ *adj* (1922) : MANIFOLD, REPEATED

3rep·li·cate \-kət\ *n* (1929) : one of several identical experiments, procedures, or samples

rep·li·ca·tion \,re-plə-'kā-shən\ *n* (14c) **1 a** : ANSWER, REPLY   **b** (1) : an answer to a reply : REJOINDER   (2) : a plaintiff's reply to a defendant's plea, answer, or counterclaim   **2** : ECHO, REVERBERATION   **3 a** : COPY, REPRODUCTION   **b** : the action or process of reproducing   **4** : performance of an experiment or procedure more than once; *esp* : systematic or random repetition of agricultural test rows or plats to reduce error

rep·li·ca·tive \'re-pli-,kā-tiv\ *adj* (ca. 1890) : of, relating to, involved in, or characterized by replication ⟨the ~ form of tobacco mosaic virus⟩

rep·li·con \'re-pli-,kän\ *n* [*replicate* + *2-on*] (1963) : a linear or circular section of DNA or RNA which replicates sequentially as a unit

1re·ply \ri-'plī\ *vb* **re·plied; re·ply·ing** [ME *replien*, fr. MF *replier* to fold again, fr. L *replicare* to fold back, fr. *re-* + *plicare* to fold — more at PLY] *vi* (14c) **1 a** : to respond in words or writing   **b** : ECHO, RESOUND   **c** : to make a legal replication   **2** : to do something in response; *specif* : to return gunfire or an attack   ~ *vt* : to give as an answer   *syn* see ANSWER — **re·pli·er** \-'plī-(ə)r\ *n*

2reply *n, pl* **replies** (1560) **1** : something said, written, or done in answer or response   **2** : REPLICATION 1b(2)

re·po \'rē-,pō\ *n, pl* **repos** [by shortening & alter.] (1963) : REPURCHASE AGREEMENT

re·po·lar·i·za·tion \,rē-,pō-lə-rə-'zā-shən\ *n* (1922) : polarization of a muscle fiber, cell, or membrane following depolarization — **re·po·lar·ize** \(,)rē-'pō-lə-,rīz\ *vb*

1re·port \ri-'pōrt, -'port\ *n* [ME, fr. MF, fr. OF, fr. *reporter* to report, fr. L *reportare*, fr. *re-* + *portare* to carry — more at FARE] (14c) **1 a** : common talk or an account spread by common talk : RUMOR   **b** : quality of reputation ⟨a witness of good ~⟩   **2 a** : a usu. detailed account or statement ⟨a news ~⟩   **b** : an account or statement of a judicial opinion or decision   **c** : a usu. formal record of the proceedings of a meeting or session   **3** : an explosive noise — **on report** : subject to disciplinary action

2report *vt* (14c) **1 a** : to give an account of : RELATE   **b** : to describe as being in a specified state ⟨~ed him much improved⟩   **2 a** : to serve as carrier of (a message)   **b** : to relate the words or sense of (something said)   **c** : to make a written record or summary of   **d** (1) : to watch for and write about the newsworthy aspects or developments of : COVER   (2) : to prepare or present an account of for broadcast   **3 a** (1) : to give a formal or official account or statement of ⟨the treasurer ~ed a balance of ten dollars⟩   (2) : to return or present (a matter referred for consideration) with conclusions or recommendations   **b** : to announce or relate as the result of investigation ⟨~ed no sign of dis-

ease⟩ **c** : to announce the presence, arrival, or sighting of **d** : to make known to the proper authorities ⟨~ a fire⟩ **e** : to make a charge of misconduct against ~ *vi* **1 a** : to give an account : TELL **b** : to present oneself **c** : to account for oneself ⟨~ed sick on Friday⟩ **2** : to make, issue, or submit a report **3** : to act in the capacity of a reporter
re·port·able \ri-'pōr-tə-bəl, -'pȯr-\ *adj* (1858) **1** : worth reporting ⟨~ news⟩ **2** : required by law to be reported ⟨~ income⟩ ⟨~ diseases⟩
re·port·age \ri-'pȯr-tij, -'pȯr-, *esp for 2* ˌre-pȯr-'täzh, ˌre-ˌpȯr-'\ *n* [F, fr. *reporter* to report] (ca. 1864) **1 a** : the act or process of reporting news **b** : something (as news) that is reported **2** : writing intended to give an account of observed or documented events
report card *n* (1920) **1** : a report on a student that is periodically submitted by a school to the student's parents or guardian **2** : an evaluation of performance
re·port·ed·ly \ri-'pōr-təd-lē, -'pȯr-\ *adv* (1901) : according to report
re·port·er \ri-'pȯr-tər, -'pȯr-\ *n* (14c) : one that reports: as **a** : one who makes authorized statements of law decisions or legislative proceedings **b** : one who makes a shorthand record of a speech or proceeding **c** (1) : one employed by a newspaper, magazine, or television company to gather and report news (2) : one who broadcasts news — **re·por·to·ri·al** \ˌre-pə(r)-'tōr-ē-əl, ˌrē-, -'tȯr-\ *adj* — **re·por·to·ri·al·ly** \-ē-ə-lē\ *adv*
report out *vt* (1907) : to return after consideration and often with revisions to a legislative body for action ⟨after much debate the committee *reported* the bill *out*⟩
report stage *n* (ca. 1906) : the stage in the British legislative process preceding the third reading and concerned esp. with amendments and details
re·pos·al \ri-'pō-zəl\ *n* (1605) *obs* : the act of reposing
¹**re·pose** \ri-'pōz\ *vb* **re·posed; re·pos·ing** [ME, fr. MF *reposer*, fr. OF, fr. LL *repausare*, fr. L *re-* + LL *pausare* to stop, fr. L *pausa* pause] *vi* (15c) : to lay at rest ~ *vi* **1** : to lie at rest **b** : to lie dead ⟨*reposing* in state⟩ **c** : to remain still or concealed **2** : to take a rest **3** *archaic* : RELY **4** : to rest for support : LIE
²**repose** *n* (1509) **1 a** : a state of resting after exertion or strain; *esp* : rest in sleep **b** : eternal or heavenly rest ⟨pray for the ~ of a soul⟩ **2 a** : a place of rest : PEACE, TRANQUILLITY ⟨the ~ of the bayous⟩ **c** : a harmony in the arrangement of parts and colors that is restful to the eye **3** : lack of activity : QUIESCENCE **b** : cessation or absence of activity, movement, or animation ⟨the face in ~ is grave and thoughtful⟩ **4** : composure of manner : POISE
³**re·pose** *vt* **re·posed; re·pos·ing** [ME, to replace, fr. L *reponere* (perf. indic. *reposui*)] (15c) **1** *archaic* : to put away or set down : DEPOSIT **2 a** : to place (as confidence or trust) in someone or something **b** : to place for control, management, or use
re·pose·ful \ri-'pōz-fəl\ *adj* (1852) : of a kind to induce ease and relaxation — **re·pose·ful·ly** \-fə-lē\ *adv* — **re·pose·ful·ness** *n*
re·pos·it *vt* **re·pos·it·ed** \-'pä-zə-təd, -'päz-təd\; **re·pos·it·ing** \-'pä-zə-tiŋ, -'päz-tiŋ\ [L *repositus*, pp. of *reponere* to replace, fr. *re-* + *ponere* to place — more at POSITION] (ca. 1641) **1** \ri-'pä-zət\ : DEPOSIT, STORE **2** \(ˌ)rē-\ : to put back in place : REPLACE
¹**re·po·si·tion** \ˌrē-pə-'zi-shən, ˌre-\ *n* (1588) : the act of repositing : the state of being reposited
²**re·po·si·tion** \ˌrē-pə-'zi-shən\ *vt* (ca. 1859) **1** : to change the position of **2** : to revise the marketing strategy of (a product or a company) so as to increase sales
¹**re·pos·i·to·ry** \ri-'pä-zə-ˌtōr-ē, -ˌtȯr-\ *n, pl* **-ries** (15c) **1** : a place, room, or container where something is deposited or stored : DEPOSITORY **2** : a side altar in a Roman Catholic church where the consecrated Host is reserved from Maundy Thursday until Good Friday **3** : one that contains or stores something nonmaterial ⟨considered the book a ~ of knowledge⟩ **4** : a place or region richly supplied with a natural resource **5** : a person to whom something is confided or entrusted
²**repository** *adj* (1950) *of a drug* : designed to act over a prolonged period ⟨~ penicillin⟩
re·pos·sess \ˌrē-pə-'zes *also* -'ses\ *vt* (15c) **1 a** : to regain possession of **b** : to resume possession of in default of the payment of installments due **2** : to restore to possession — **re·pos·ses·sion** \-'ze-shən *also* -'se-\ *n* — **re·pos·ses·sor** \-'ze-sər *also* -'se-\ *n*
¹**re·pous·sé** \rə-ˌpü-'sā, -'pü-ˌ\ *adj* [F, lit., pushed back] (1858) **1** : shaped or ornamented with patterns in relief made by hammering or pressing on the reverse side — used esp. of metal **2** : formed in relief
²**repoussé** *n* (1858) **1** : repoussé work **2** : repoussé decoration
re·pow·er \(ˌ)rē-'paú(-ə)r\ *vt* (1954) : to provide again or anew with power; *esp* : to provide (as a boat) with a new engine
repp *var of* REP
rep·re·hend \ˌre-pri-'hend\ *vt* [ME, fr. L *reprehendere*, lit., to hold back, fr. *re-* + *prehendere* to grasp — more at GET] (14c) : to voice disapproval of : CENSURE *syn* see CRITICIZE
rep·re·hen·si·ble \ˌre-pri-'hen(t)-sə-bəl\ *adj* (14c) : worthy of or deserving reprehension : CULPABLE ⟨~ conduct⟩ — **rep·re·hen·si·bil·i·ty** \-ˌhen(t)-sə-'bi-lə-tē\ *n* — **rep·re·hen·si·ble·ness** \-'hen(t)-sə-bəl-nəs\ *n* — **rep·re·hen·si·bly** \-blē\ *adv*
rep·re·hen·sion \-'hen(t)-shən\ *n* [ME *reprehensioun*, fr. MF or L; MF *reprehension*, fr. L *reprehension-, reprehensio*, fr. *reprehendere*] (14c) : the act of reprehending : CENSURE
rep·re·hen·sive \-'hen(t)-siv\ *adj* (1589) : serving to reprehend : conveying reprehension or reproof
rep·re·sent \ˌre-pri-'zent\ *vb* [ME, fr. MF *representer*, fr. L *repraesentare*, fr. *re-* + *praesentare* to present] *vt* (14c) **1** : to bring clearly before the mind : PRESENT ⟨a book which ~s the character of early America⟩ **2** : to serve as a sign or symbol of ⟨the flag ~s our country⟩ **3** : to portray or exhibit in art : DEPICT **4** : to serve as the counterpart or image of : TYPIFY ⟨a movie hero who ~s the ideals of the culture⟩ **5 a** : to produce on the stage **b** : to act the part or role of **6 a** (1) : to take the place of in some respect (2) : to act in the place of or for usu. by legal right **b** : to serve esp. in a legislative body by delegated authority usu. resulting from election **7** : to describe as having a specified character or quality ⟨~s himself as a friend⟩ **8 a** : to give one's impression and judgment of : state in a manner intended to affect action or judgment **b** : to point out in protest or remonstrance **9** : to serve as a specimen, example, or instance of **10 a** : to form an image or representation of in the mind **b** (1) : to apprehend (an ob-

ject) by means of an idea (2) : to recall in memory **11** : to correspond to in essence : CONSTITUTE ~ *vi* : to make representations against something : PROTEST — **rep·re·sent·able** \-'zen-tə-bəl\ *adj* — **rep·re·sent·er** *n*
re–pre·sent \ˌrē-pri-'zent\ *vt* (1564) : to present again or anew — **re–pre·sen·ta·tion** \ˌrē-ˌprē-ˌzen-'tā-shən, -ˌpre-zⁿn-, -ˌprē-zⁿn-\ *n*
rep·re·sen·ta·tion \ˌre-pri-ˌzen-'tā-shən, -zən-\ *n* (15c) **1** : one that represents: as **a** : an artistic likeness or image **b** (1) : a statement or account made to influence opinion or action (2) : an incidental or collateral statement of fact on the faith of which a contract is entered into **c** : a dramatic production or performance **d** (1) : a usu. formal statement made against something or to effect a change (2) : a usu. formal protest **2** : the act or action of representing : the state of being represented: as **a** : REPRESENTATIONALISM 2 **b** (1) : the action or fact of one person standing for another so as to have the rights and obligations of the person represented (2) : the substitution of an individual or class in place of a person (as a child for a deceased parent) **c** : the action of representing or the fact of being represented esp. in a legislative body **3** : the body of persons representing a constituency — **rep·re·sen·ta·tion·al** \-shnəl, -shə-nⁿl\ *adj* — **rep·re·sen·ta·tion·al·ly** *adv*
rep·re·sen·ta·tion·al·ism \-shnə-ˌli-zəm, -shə-nⁿl-ˌi-\ *n* (1899) **1** : the doctrine that the immediate object of knowledge is an idea in the mind distinct from the external object which is the occasion of perception **2** : the theory or practice of realistic representation in art — **rep·re·sen·ta·tion·al·ist** \-list, -ist\ *n*
¹**rep·re·sen·ta·tive** \ˌre-pri-'zen-tə-tiv\ *adj* (1532) **1** : serving to represent **2 a** : standing or acting for another esp. through delegated authority **b** : of, based on, or constituting a government in which the many are represented by persons chosen from among them usu. by election **3** : serving as a typical or characteristic example ⟨a ~ moviegoer⟩ **4** : of or relating to representation or representationalism — **rep·re·sen·ta·tive·ly** *adv* — **rep·re·sen·ta·tive·ness** *n* — **rep·re·sen·ta·tiv·i·ty** \-ˌzen-tə-'ti-və-tē\ *n*
²**representative** *n* (1647) **1** : a typical example of a group, class, or quality : SPECIMEN **2** : one that represents another or others: as **a** (1) : one that represents a constituency as a member of a legislative body (2) : a member of the house of representatives of the U.S. Congress or a state legislature **b** : one that represents another as agent, deputy, substitute, or delegate usu. being invested with the authority of the principal **c** : one that represents a business organization **d** : one that represents another as successor or heir
re·press \ri-'pres\ *vb* [ME, fr. L *repressus*, pp. of *reprimere* to check, fr. *re-* + *premere* to press — more at PRESS] *vt* (14c) **1 a** : to check by or as if by pressure : CURB ⟨injustice was ~ed⟩ **b** : to put down by force : SUBDUE ⟨~ a disturbance⟩ **2 a** : to hold in by self-control ⟨~ed a laugh⟩ **b** : to prevent the natural or normal expression, activity, or development of ⟨~ed her anger⟩ **3** : to exclude from consciousness **4** : to inactivate (a gene or formation of a gene product) by allosteric combination at a DNA binding site ~ *vi* : to take repressive action — **re·press·ibil·i·ty** \-ˌpre-sə-'bi-lə-tē\ *n* — **re·press·ible** \-'pre-sə-bəl\ *adj* — **re·pres·sive** \-'pre-siv\ *adj* — **re·pres·sive·ly** *adv* — **re·pres·sive·ness** *n*
re–press \(ˌ)rē-'pres\ *vt* (14c) : to press again ⟨~ a record⟩
re·pressed \ri-'prest\ *adj* (1665) **1** : subjected to or marked by repression **2** : characterized by restraint
re·pres·sion \ri-'pre-shən\ *n* (1533) **1 a** : the action or process of repressing : the state of being repressed ⟨~ of unpopular opinions⟩ **b** : an instance of repressing ⟨racial ~s⟩ **2 a** : a process by which unacceptable desires or impulses are excluded from consciousness and left to operate in the unconscious **b** : an item so excluded — **re·pres·sion·ist** \-sh(ə-)nist\ *adj*
re·pres·sor \ri-'pre-sər\ *n* [NL] (1611) : one that represses; *esp* : a protein that is determined by a regulatory gene, binds to a genetic operator, and inhibits the initiation of transcription of messenger RNA
re·priev·al \ri-'prē-vəl\ *n* (ca. 1586) *archaic* : REPRIEVE
¹**re·prieve** \ri-'prēv\ *vt* **re·prieved; re·priev·ing** [alter. of earlier *repry*, perh. fr. MF *repris*, pp. of *reprendre* to take back] (1596) **1** : to delay the punishment of (as a condemned prisoner) **2** : to give relief or deliverance to for a time
²**reprieve** *n* (1592) **1** : the act of reprieving : the state of being reprieved **2** : a formal temporary suspension of the execution of a sentence esp. of death **b** (1) : an order or warrant for a reprieve **3** : a temporary respite (as from pain or trouble)
¹**rep·ri·mand** \'re-prə-ˌmand\ *n* [F *réprimande*, fr. L *reprimenda*, fem. of *reprimendus*, gerundive of *reprimere* to check — more at REPRESS] (1636) : a severe or formal reproof
²**reprimand** *vt* (1681) : to reprove sharply or censure formally usu. from a position of authority *syn* see REPROVE
¹**re·print** \ri-'print\ *vt* (1551) : to print again : make a reprint of
²**re·print** \'rē-ˌprint, (ˌ)rē-'\ *n* (1611) : a reproduction of printed matter: as **a** : a subsequent printing of a book already published that preserves the identical text of the previous printing **b** : OFFPRINT **c** : matter (as an article) that has appeared in print before
re·print·er \(ˌ)rē-'prin-tər\ *n* (1689) : one that publishes a reprint
re·pri·sal \ri-'prī-zəl\ *n* [ME *reprisail*, fr. MF *reprisaille*, fr. OIt *ripresaglia*, fr. *ripreso*, pp. of *riprendere* to take back, fr. *ri-* re- (fr. L *re-*) + *prendere* to take, fr. L *prehendere* — more at GET] (15c) **1 a** : the act or practice in international law of resorting to force short of war in retaliation for damage or loss suffered **b** : an instance of such action **2** *obs* : PRIZE **3** : the regaining of something (as by recapture) **4** : something (as a sum of money) given or paid in restitution — usu. used in pl. **5** : a retaliatory act
¹**re·prise** \ri-'prēz, *1 is also* -'prīz\ *n* [ME, fr. MF, lit., action of taking back, fr. OF, fr. *reprendre* to take back, fr. *re-* + *prendre* to take, fr. L *prehendere*] (15c) **1** : a deduction or charge made yearly out of a manor or estate — usu. used in pl. **2** : a recurrence, renewal, or re-

---

\ə\ abut \ᵊ\ kitten, F table \ər\ further \a\ ash \ā\ ace \ä\ mop, mar
\aú\ out \ch\ chin \e\ bet \ē\ easy \g\ go \i\ hit \ī\ ice \j\ job
\ŋ\ sing \ō\ go \ȯ\ law \ȯi\ boy \th\ thin \t̲h̲\ the \ü\ loot \ú\ foot
\y\ yet \zh\ vision \à, k̲, ⁿ, œ, œ̄, ᴜᴇ, ᵫ, ᵌ\ *see* Guide to Pronunciation

sumption of an action **3 a :** a musical repetition: (1) : the repetition of the exposition preceding the development (2) : RECAPITULATION **b :** a repeated performance : REPETITION

²**re·prise** \ri-'prīz, *3 is* -'prēz\ *vt* **re·prised; re·pris·ing** [MF *reprise* action of taking back] (15c) **1** *archaic* : TAKE BACK; *esp* : to recover by force **2** *archaic* : COMPENSATE **3 a :** to repeat the performance of **b :** RECAPITULATE

re·pris·ti·nate \(ˌ)rē-'pris-tə-ˌnāt\ *vt* **-nat·ed; -nat·ing** [*re-* + *pristine* + ⁴*-ate*] (1659) : to restore to an original state or condition — **re·pris·ti·na·tion** \(ˌ)rē-ˌpris-tə-'nā-shən\ *n*

re·pro \'rē-(ˌ)prō\ *n, pl* **repros** [short for *reproduction*] (1946) **1 :** a clear sharp proof made esp. from a letterpress printing surface to serve as photographic copy for a printing plate **2 :** REPRODUCTION 2

¹**re·proach** \ri-'prōch\ *n* [ME *reproche*, fr. MF, fr. OF, fr. *reprochier* to reproach, fr. (assumed) VL *repropiare*, fr. L *re-* + *prope* near — more at APPROACH] (14c) **1 :** an expression of rebuke or disapproval **2 :** the act or action of reproaching or disapproving (was beyond ∼) **3 a :** a cause or occasion of blame, discredit, or disgrace **b :** DISCREDIT, DISGRACE **4** *obs* : one subjected to censure or scorn — **re·proach·ful** \-fəl\ *adj* — **re·proach·ful·ly** \-fə-lē\ *adv* — **re·proach·ful·ness** *n*

²**reproach** *vt* (14c) **1 :** to express disappointment in or displeasure with (a person) for conduct that is blameworthy or in need of amendment **2 :** to make (something) a matter of reproach **3 :** to bring into discredit **syn** see REPROVE — **re·proach·able** \-'prō-chə-bəl\ *adj* — **re·proach·er** *n* — **re·proach·ing·ly** \-'prō-chiŋ-lē\ *adv*

rep·ro·bance \'re-prə-bən(t)s\ *n* (1604) *archaic* : REPROBATION

¹**rep·ro·bate** \'re-prə-ˌbāt\ *vt* **-bat·ed; -bat·ing** [ME, fr. LL *reprobatus*, pp. of *reprobare* — more at REPROVE] (15c) **1 :** to condemn strongly as unworthy, unacceptable, or evil (*reprobating* the laxity of the age) **2 :** to foreordain to damnation **3 :** to refuse to accept : REJECT **syn** see CRITICIZE — **rep·ro·ba·tive** \'re-prə-ˌbā-tiv\ *adj* — **rep·ro·ba·to·ry** \-bə-ˌtōr-ē, -ˌtȯr-\ *adj*

²**reprobate** *adj* (15c) **1** *archaic* : rejected as worthless or not standing a test : CONDEMNED **2 a :** foreordained to damnation **b :** morally corrupt : DEPRAVED **3 :** expressing or involving reprobation **4 :** of, relating to, or characteristic of a reprobate

³**reprobate** *n* (1545) : a reprobate person

rep·ro·ba·tion \ˌre-prə-'bā-shən\ *n* (14c) : the act of reprobating or the state of being reprobated

re·pro·cess \(ˌ)rē-'prä-ˌses, -'prō-, -səs\ *vt* (1921) : to subject to a special process or treatment in preparation for reuse; *esp* : to extract uranium and plutonium from (the spent fuel rods of a nuclear reactor) for use again as fuel

re·pro·duce \ˌrē-prə-'düs, -'dyüs\ *vt* (1611) : to produce again: as **a :** to produce (new individuals of the same kind) by a sexual or asexual process **b :** to cause to exist again or anew (∼ water from steam) **c :** to imitate closely (sound-effects can ∼ the sound of thunder) **d :** to present again **e :** to make a representation (as an image or copy) of (∼ a face on canvas) **f :** to revive mentally : RECALL **g :** to translate (a recording) into sound ∼ *vi* **1 :** to undergo reproduction **2 :** to produce offspring — **re·pro·duc·er** *n* — **re·pro·duc·ibil·i·ty** \-ˌdü-sə-'bi-lə-tē, -ˌdyü-\ *n* — **re·pro·duc·ible** \-'dü-sə-bəl, -'dyü-\ *adj or n* — **re·pro·duc·ibly** \-blē\ *adv*

re·pro·duc·tion \ˌrē-prə-'dək-shən\ *n* (1659) **1 :** the act or process of reproducing; *specif* : the process by which plants and animals give rise to offspring and which fundamentally consists of the segregation of a portion of the parental body by a sexual or an asexual process and its subsequent growth and differentiation into a new individual **2 :** something reproduced : COPY **3 :** young seedling trees in a forest

syn REPRODUCTION, DUPLICATE, COPY, FACSIMILE, REPLICA mean a thing made to closely resemble another. REPRODUCTION implies an exact or close imitation of an existing thing (*reproductions* from the museum's furniture collection). DUPLICATE implies a double or counterpart exactly corresponding to another thing (a *duplicate* of a house key). COPY applies esp. to one of a number of things reproduced mechanically (printed a thousand *copies* of the lithograph). FACSIMILE suggests a close reproduction often of graphic matter that may differ in scale (a *facsimile* of a rare book). REPLICA implies the exact reproduction of a particular item in all details (a *replica* of the Mayflower) but not always in the same scale (miniature *replicas* of classic cars).

reproduction proof *n* (1945) : REPRO 1

¹**re·pro·duc·tive** \ˌrē-prə-'dək-tiv\ *adj* (1753) : of, relating to, or capable of reproduction — **re·pro·duc·tive·ly** *adv*

²**reproductive** *n* (1934) : an actual or potential parent; *specif* : a sexually functional social insect

re·pro·gram \(ˌ)rē-'prō-ˌgram, -grəm\ *vt* (1959) : to program anew; *esp* : to write new programs for (as a computer) ∼ *vi* : to rewrite or revise a program esp. of a computer — **re·pro·gram·ma·ble** \-'prō-ˌgra-mə-bəl, -ˌprō-'gra-\ *adj*

re·prog·ra·phy \ri-'prä-grə-fē\ *n* [*reproduction* + *-graphy*] (1956) : facsimile reproduction (as by photocopying) of graphic matter — **re·prog·ra·pher** \-grə-fər\ *n* — **re·pro·graph·ic** \ˌrē-prə-'gra-fik, ˌre-\ *adj* — **re·pro·graph·ics** \-fiks\ *n pl*

re·proof \ri-'prüf\ *n* [ME *reprof*, fr. MF *reprove*, fr. OF, fr. *reprover*] (14c) : criticism for a fault : REBUKE

re·prove \ri-'prüv\ *vb* **re·proved; re·prov·ing** [ME, fr. MF *reprover*, fr. LL *reprobare* to disapprove, condemn, fr. L *re-* + *probare* to test, approve — more at PROVE] *vt* (14c) **1 :** to scold or correct usu. gently or with kindly intent **2 :** to express disapproval of : CENSURE (it is not for me to ∼ popular taste —D. W. Brogan) **3** *obs* : DISPROVE, REFUTE **4** *obs* : CONVINCE, CONVICT ∼ *vi* : to express rebuke or reproof — **re·prov·er** *n* — **re·prov·ing·ly** \-'prü-viŋ-lē\ *adv*

syn REPROVE, REBUKE, REPRIMAND, ADMONISH, REPROACH, CHIDE mean to criticize adversely. REPROVE implies an often kindly intent to correct a fault (gently *reproved* my table manners). REBUKE suggests a sharp or stern reproof (the papal letter *rebuked* dissenting clerics). REPRIMAND implies a severe, formal, often public or official rebuke (*reprimanded* by the ethics committee). ADMONISH suggests earnest or friendly warning and counsel (*admonished* by my parents to control expenses). REPROACH and CHIDE suggest displeasure or disappointment expressed in mild reproof or scolding (*reproached* him for tardiness) (*chided* by their mother for untidiness).

¹**rep·tile** \'rep-ˌtil, -t⁵l\ *n* [ME *reptil*, fr. MF or LL; MF *reptile* (fem.), fr. LL *reptile* (neut.), fr. neut. of *reptilis* creeping, fr. L *reptus*, pp. of *repere* to crawl; akin to Lith *replioti* to crawl] (14c) **1 :** an animal that crawls or moves on its belly (as a snake) or on small short legs (as a lizard) **2 :** any of a class (Reptilia) of air-breathing vertebrates that include the alligators and crocodiles, lizards, snakes, turtles, and extinct related forms (as dinosaurs and pterosaurs) and are characterized by a completely ossified skeleton with a single occipital condyle, a distinct quadrate bone usu. immovably articulated with the skull, ribs attached to the sternum, and a body usu. covered with scales or bony plates **3 :** a groveling or despised person

²**reptile** *adj* (1607) : characteristic of a reptile : REPTILIAN

¹**rep·til·ian** \rep-'ti-lē-ən, -'til-yən\ *adj* (ca. 1846) **1 :** resembling or having the characteristics of the reptiles **2 :** of or relating to the reptiles **3 :** cold-bloodedly treacherous (a ∼ villain —Theodore Dreiser)

²**reptilian** *n* (ca. 1847) : REPTILE 2

re·pub·lic \ri-'pə-blik\ *n* [F *république*, fr. MF *republique*, fr. L *respublica*, fr. *res* thing, wealth + *publica*, fem. of *publicus* public — more at REAL, PUBLIC] (1604) **1 a** (1) : a government having a chief of state who is not a monarch and who in modern times is usu. a president (2) : a political unit (as a nation) having such a form of government **b** (1) : a government in which supreme power resides in a body of citizens entitled to vote and is exercised by elected officers and representatives responsible to them and governing according to law (2) : a political unit (as a nation) having such a form of government **c :** a usu. specified republican government of a political unit (the French Fourth *Republic*) **2 :** a body of persons freely engaged in a specified activity (the ∼ of letters) **3 :** a constituent political and territorial unit of the former nations of Czechoslovakia, the U.S.S.R., or Yugoslavia

¹**re·pub·li·can** \ri-'pə-bli-kən\ *n* (1697) **1 :** one that favors or supports a republican form of government **2** *cap* **a :** a member of a political party advocating republicanism **b :** a member of the Democratic-Republican party or of the Republican party of the U.S.

²**republican** *adj* (1712) **1 a :** of, relating to, or having the characteristics of a republic **b :** favoring, supporting, or advocating a republic **c :** belonging or appropriate to one living in or supporting a republic (∼ simplicity) **2** *cap* **a :** DEMOCRATIC-REPUBLICAN **b :** of, relating to, or constituting the one of the two major political parties evolving in the U.S. in the mid-19th century that is usu. primarily associated with business, financial, and some agricultural interests and is held to favor a restricted governmental role in economic life

re·pub·li·can·ism \ri-'pə-bli-kə-ˌni-zəm\ *n* (1689) **1 :** adherence to or sympathy for a republican form of government **2 :** the principles or theory of republican government **3** *cap* **a :** the principles, policy, or practices of the Republican party of the U.S. **b :** the Republican party or its members

re·pub·li·can·ize \-kə-ˌnīz\ *vt* **-ized; -iz·ing** (1797) : to make republican in character, form, or principle

re·pub·li·ca·tion \(ˌ)rē-ˌpə-blə-'kā-shən\ *n* (1730) **1 :** the act or action of republishing : the state of being republished **2 :** something that has been republished

re·pub·lish \(ˌ)rē-'pə-blish\ *vt* (1592) **1 :** to publish again or anew **2 :** to execute (a will) anew — **re·pub·lish·er** *n*

re·pu·di·ate \ri-'pyü-dē-ˌāt\ *vt* **-at·ed; -at·ing** [L *repudiatus*, pp. of *repudiare*, fr. *repudium* rejection of a prospective spouse, divorce, prob. fr. *re-* + *pudēre* to shame] (1545) **1 :** to divorce or separate formally from (a woman) **2 :** to refuse to have anything to do with : DISOWN **3 a :** to refuse to accept; *esp* : to reject as unauthorized or as having no binding force **b :** to reject as untrue or unjust (∼ a charge) **4 :** to refuse to acknowledge or pay **syn** see DECLINE — **re·pu·di·a·tor** \-ˌā-tər\ *n*

re·pu·di·a·tion \ri-ˌpyü-dē-'ā-shən\ *n* (1545) : the act of repudiating : the state of being repudiated; *esp* : the refusal of public authorities to acknowledge or pay a debt — **re·pu·di·a·tion·ist** \-sh(ə-)nist\ *n*

re·pugn \ri-'pyün\ *vb* [ME, fr. MF & L; MF *repugner*, fr. L *repugnare*] *vi* (14c) *archaic* : to offer opposition, objection, or resistance ∼ *vt* : to contend against : OPPOSE

re·pug·nance \ri-'pəg-nən(t)s\ *n* (15c) **1 a :** the quality or fact of being contradictory or inconsistent **b :** an instance of such contradiction or inconsistency **2 :** strong dislike, distaste, or antagonism

re·pug·nan·cy \-nən(t)-sē\ *n, pl* **-cies** (15c) : REPUGNANCE

re·pug·nant \-nənt\ *adj* [ME, opposed, contradictory, incompatible, fr. MF, fr. L *repugnant-, repugnans*, prp. of *repugnare* to fight against, fr. *re-* + *pugnare* to fight — more at PUNGENT] (15c) **1 :** INCOMPATIBLE, INCONSISTENT **2** *archaic* : HOSTILE **3 :** exciting distaste or aversion — **re·pug·nant·ly** *adv*

¹**re·pulse** \ri-'pəls\ *vt* **re·pulsed; re·puls·ing** [L *repulsus*, pp. of *repellere* to repel] (15c) **1 :** to drive or beat back : REPEL **2 :** to repel by discourtesy, coldness, or denial **3 :** to cause repulsion in

²**repulse** *n* (1533) **1 :** REBUFF, REJECTION **2 :** the action of repelling an attacker : the fact of being repelled

re·pul·sion \ri-'pəl-shən\ *n* (15c) **1 :** the action of repulsing : the state of being repulsed **2 :** the action of repelling : the force with which bodies, particles, or like forces repel one another **3 :** a feeling of aversion : REPUGNANCE

re·pul·sive \-siv\ *adj* (1598) **1 :** tending to repel or reject : COLD, FORBIDDING **2 :** serving or able to repulse **3 :** arousing aversion or disgust — **re·pul·sive·ly** *adv* — **re·pul·sive·ness** *n*

re·pur·chase agreement \(ˌ)rē-'pər-chəs-\ *n* (1952) : a contract giving the seller of securities (as treasury bills) the right to repurchase after a stated period and the buyer the right to retain interest earnings

rep·u·ta·ble \'re-pyə-tə-bəl\ *adj* (1674) **1 :** enjoying good repute : held in esteem **2 :** employed widely or sanctioned by good writers — **rep·u·ta·bil·i·ty** \ˌre-pyə-tə-'bi-lə-tē\ *n* — **rep·u·ta·bly** \'re-pyə-tə-blē\ *adv*

rep·u·ta·tion \ˌre-pyə-'tā-shən\ *n* [ME *reputacioun*, fr. L *reputation-, reputatio* consideration, fr. *reputare*] (14c) **1 a :** overall quality or character as seen or judged by people in general **b :** recognition by other people of some characteristic or ability (has the ∼ of being clever) **2 :** a place in public esteem or regard : good name — **rep·u·ta·tion·al** \-shnəl, -shə-n⁵l\ *adj*

¹**re·pute** \ri-'pyüt\ *vt* **re·put·ed; re·put·ing** [ME, fr. MF *reputer*, fr. L *reputare* to reckon up, think over, fr. *re-* + *putare* to reckon] (15c) : BELIEVE, CONSIDER

²**re·pute** n (1551) **1 :** the character or status commonly ascribed to one **:** REPUTATION **2 :** the state of being favorably known, spoken of, or esteemed

reputed adj (1549) **1 :** having a good repute **:** REPUTABLE **2 :** being such according to reputation or popular belief

re·put·ed·ly adv (1687) **:** according to reputation or general belief

¹**re·quest** \ri-ˈkwest\ n [ME requeste, fr. MF, fr. (assumed) VL requa-esta, fr. fem. of requaestus, pp. of requaerere to require] (14c) **1 :** the act or an instance of asking for something **2 :** something asked for **3 :** the condition or fact of being requested ⟨available on ~⟩ **4 :** the state of being sought after **:** DEMAND

²**request** vt (1533) **1 :** to make a request to or of ⟨~ed her to write a paper⟩ **2 :** to ask as a favor or privilege ⟨~s to be excused⟩ **3** obs **:** to ask (a person) to come or go to a thing or place **4 :** to ask for ⟨~ed a brief delay⟩　syn see ASK — **re·quest·er** or **re·quest·or** \-ˈkwes-tər\ n

re·qui·em \ˈre-kwē-əm also ˈrā- or ˈrē-\ n [ME, fr. L (first word of the introit of the requiem mass), acc. of requies rest, fr. re- + quies quiet, rest — more at WHILE] (14c) **1 :** a mass for the dead **2 a :** a solemn chant (as a dirge) for the repose of the dead **b :** something that resembles such a solemn chant **3 a :** a musical setting of the mass for the dead **b :** a musical composition in honor of the dead

requiem shark n [obs. F requiem shark, alter. of F requin] (1900) **:** any of a family (Carcharhinidae) of sharks (as the tiger shark) that includes some dangerous to humans

re·qui·es·cat \ˌre-kwē-ˈes-ˌkät, -ˌkat; ˌrā-kwē-ˈes-ˌkät\ n [L, may he (or she) rest, fr. requiescere to rest, fr. re- + quiescere to be quiet, fr. quies] (1824) **:** a prayer for the repose of a dead person

re·quire \ri-ˈkwīr\ vb **re·quired; re·quir·ing** [ME requeren, fr. MF requerre, fr. (assumed) VL requaerere to seek for, need, require, alter. of L requirere, fr. re- + quaerere to seek, ask] vt (14c) **1 a :** to claim or ask for by right and authority **b** archaic **:** REQUEST **2 a :** to call for as suitable or appropriate ⟨the occasion ~s formal dress⟩ **b :** to demand as necessary or essential **:** have a compelling need for ⟨all living beings ~ food⟩ **3 :** to impose a compulsion or command on **:** COMPEL **4** chiefly Brit **:** to feel or be obliged — used with a following infinitive ⟨one does not ~ to be a specialist —Elizabeth Bowen⟩ ~ vi, archaic **:** ASK　syn see DEMAND

re·quire·ment \-ˈkwīr-mənt\ n (1662) **:** something required: **a :** something wanted or needed **:** NECESSITY ⟨production was not sufficient to satisfy military ~s⟩ **b :** something essential to the existence or occurrence of something else **:** CONDITION ⟨failed to meet the school's ~s for graduation⟩

req·ui·site \ˈre-kwə-zət\ adj [ME, fr. L requisitus, pp. of requirere] (15c) **:** ESSENTIAL, NECESSARY — **requisite** n — **req·ui·site·ness** n

req·ui·si·tion \ˌre-kwə-ˈzi-shən\ n [ME requisicion, fr. MF or ML; MF requisition, fr. ML requisition-, requisitio, fr. L, act of searching, fr. requirere] (15c) **1 a :** the act of formally requiring or calling upon someone to perform an action **b :** a formal demand made by one nation upon another for the surrender or extradition of a fugitive from justice **2 a :** the act of requiring something to be furnished **b :** a demand or application made usu. with authority: as **(1) :** a demand made by military authorities upon civilians for supplies or other needs **(2) :** a written request for something authorized but not made available automatically **3 :** the state of being in demand or use — **requisition** vt

re·quit·al \ri-ˈkwī-tᵊl\ n (1582) **1 :** something given in return, compensation, or retaliation **2 :** the act or action of requiting **:** the state of being requited

re·quite \ri-ˈkwīt\ vt **re·quit·ed; re·quit·ing** [re- + obs. quite to quit, pay, fr. ME quiten — more at QUIT] (1529) **1 a :** to make return for **:** REPAY **b :** to make retaliation for **:** AVENGE **2 :** to make suitable return to for a benefit or service or for an injury　syn see RECIPROCATE — **re·quit·er** n

re·ra·di·ate \(ˌ)rē-ˈrā-dē-ˌāt\ vt (1913) **:** to radiate again or anew; esp **:** to emit (energy) in the form of radiation after absorbing incident radiation — **re·ra·di·a·tion** \(ˌ)rē-ˌrā-dē-ˈā-shən\ n

rere·dos \ˈrer-ə-ˌdäs also ˈrir-ə-ˌdäs or ˈrir-ˌdäs\ n [ME, fr. AF areredos, fr. MF arrere behind + dos back, fr. L dorsum — more at ARREAR] (14c) **:** a usu. ornamental wood or stone screen or partition wall behind an altar

rereward n [ME rewarde, fr. AF, fr. OF rere behind + ONF warde guard; akin to OF garde guard — more at REAR GUARD] (14c) obs **:** REAR GUARD

¹**re·run** \(ˌ)rē-ˈrən\ vt **-ran** \-ˈran\; **-run; -run·ning** (1804) **:** to run again or anew

²**re·run** \ˈrē-ˌrən, (ˌ)rē-ˈ\ n (ca. 1934) **:** the act or action or an instance of rerunning **:** REPETITION; esp **:** a movie or television show that is rerun

res \ˈräs, ˈrēz\ n, pl **res** [L — more at REAL] (1851) **:** a particular thing **:** MATTER — used esp. in legal phrases

res ad·ju·di·ca·ta \ˈrēz-ə-ˌjü-di-ˈkä-tə\ n [LL] (1902) **:** RES JUDICATA

re·sal·able \(ˌ)rē-ˈsā-lə-bəl\ adj (1866) **:** fit for resale

re·sale \ˈrē-ˌsāl, (ˌ)rē-ˈsā(ə)l\ n (1625) **1 :** the act of selling again usu. to a new party **2 a :** a secondhand sale **b :** an additional sale to the same buyer

re·scale \(ˌ)rē-ˈskā(ə)l\ vt (1944) **:** to plan, establish, or formulate on a new and usu. smaller scale

re·sched·ule \(ˌ)rē-ˈske-(ˌ)jü(ə)l, -jəl, Canad also -ˈshe-, Brit usu -ˈshe-(ˌ)dyü(ə)l\ vt (1965) **:** to schedule or plan again according to a different timetable; esp **:** to defer required payment of (a debt or loan)

re·scind \ri-ˈsind\ vt [L rescindere to annul, fr. re- + scindere to cut — more at SHED] (1643) **1 :** to take away **:** REMOVE **2 a :** TAKE BACK, CANCEL ⟨refused to ~ the order⟩ **b :** to abrogate (a contract) and restore the parties to the positions they would have occupied had there been no contract **3 :** to make void (as an act) by action of the enacting authority or a superior authority **:** REPEAL — **re·scind·er** n — **re·scind·ment** \-ˈsin(d)-mənt\ n

reredos

re·scis·sion \ri-ˈsi-zhən\ n [LL rescission-, rescissio, fr. L rescindere] (1611) **:** an act of rescinding

re·scis·so·ry \-ˈsi-zə-rē, -ˈsi-sə-\ adj (1605) **:** relating to or tending to or having the effect of rescission

re·script \ˈrē-ˌskript\ n [ME rescripte, fr. L rescriptum, fr. neut. of rescriptus, pp. of rescribere to write in reply, fr. re- + scribere to write — more at SCRIBE] (15c) **1 :** a written answer of a Roman emperor or of a pope to a legal inquiry or petition **2 :** an official or authoritative order, decree, edict, or announcement **3 :** an act or instance of rewriting

res·cue \ˈres-(ˌ)kyü\ vt **res·cued; res·cu·ing** [ME, fr. MF rescourre, fr. OF, fr. re- + escourre to shake out, fr. L excutere, fr. ex- + quatere to shake] (14c) **:** to free from confinement, danger, or evil **:** SAVE, DELIVER: as **a :** to take (as a prisoner) forcibly from custody **b :** to recover (as a prize) by force **c :** to deliver (as a place under siege) by armed force — **res·cu·able** \-ə-bəl\ adj — **rescue** n — **res·cu·er** n
syn RESCUE, DELIVER, REDEEM, RANSOM, RECLAIM, SAVE mean to set free from confinement or danger. RESCUE implies freeing from imminent danger by prompt or vigorous action ⟨rescued the crew of a sinking ship⟩. DELIVER implies release usu. of a person from confinement, temptation, slavery, or suffering ⟨delivered his people from bondage⟩. REDEEM implies releasing from bondage or penalties by giving what is demanded or necessary ⟨job training designed to redeem school dropouts from chronic unemployment⟩. RANSOM specif. applies to buying out of captivity ⟨tried to ransom the kidnap victim⟩. RECLAIM suggests a bringing back to a former state or condition of someone or something abandoned or debased ⟨reclaimed long-abandoned farms⟩. SAVE may replace any of the foregoing terms; it may further imply a preserving or maintaining for usefulness or continued existence ⟨an operation that saved my life⟩.

rescue mission n (1902) **:** a city religious mission seeking to convert and rehabilitate the down-and-out

¹**re·search** \ri-ˈsərch, ˈrē-ˌ\ n [MF recerche, fr. recerchier to investigate thoroughly, fr. OF, fr. re- + cerchier to search — more at SEARCH] (1577) **1 :** careful or diligent search **2 :** studious inquiry or examination; esp **:** investigation or experimentation aimed at the discovery and interpretation of facts, revision of accepted theories or laws in the light of new facts, or practical application of such new or revised theories or laws **3 :** the collecting of information about a particular subject

²**research** vt (1593) **1 :** to search or investigate exhaustively ⟨~ a problem⟩ **2 :** to do research for ⟨~ a book⟩ ~ vi **:** to engage in research — **re·search·able** \ri-ˈsər-chə-bəl, ˈrē-ˌ\ adj — **re·search·er** n

re·search·ist \ri-ˈsər-chist, ˈrē-ˌ\ n (1921) **:** one engaged in research

re·seau \rā-ˈzō, ri-\ n, pl **re·seaux** \-ˈzōz\ [F réseau, fr. OF resel, dim. of rais net, fr. L retis, rete] (1578) **1 :** a net ground or foundation in lace **2 :** a grid photographed by a separate exposure onto a plate containing star images to facilitate astronomical measurements

re·sect \ri-ˈsekt\ vt [L resectus, pp. of resecare to cut off, fr. re- + secare to cut — more at SAW] (1846) **:** to perform resection on — **re·sect·abil·i·ty** \ˌsek-tə-ˈbi-lə-tē\ n — **re·sect·able** \-ˈsek-tə-bəl\ adj

re·sec·tion \ri-ˈsek-shən\ n (1775) **:** the surgical removal of part of an organ or structure

re·se·da \ˈrā-zə-ˌdä\ n [F réséda, fr. réséda, a mignonette] (1873) **:** a grayish green color

re·seed \(ˌ)rē-ˈsēd\ vt (1888) **1 :** to sow seed on again or anew **2 :** to maintain (itself) by self-sown seed ~ vi **:** to maintain itself by self= sown seed

re·sem·blance \ri-ˈzem-blən(t)s\ n (14c) **1 a :** the quality or state of resembling; esp **:** correspondence in appearance or superficial qualities **b :** a point of likeness **:** SIMILARITY **2 :** REPRESENTATION, IMAGE **3** archaic **:** characteristic appearance **4** obs **:** PROBABILITY　syn see LIKENESS

re·sem·blant \-blənt\ adj (14c) **:** marked by or showing resemblance

re·sem·ble \ri-ˈzem-bəl\ vt **re·sem·bled; re·sem·bling** \-b(ə-)liŋ\ [ME, fr. MF resembler, ressembler, fr. OF, fr. re- + sembler to be like, seem, fr. L similare to copy, fr. similis like — more at SAME] (14c) **1 :** to be like or similar to **2** archaic **:** to represent as like

re·send \(ˈ)rē-ˈsend\ vt **-sent** \-ˈsent\; **-send·ing** (1554) **:** to send again or back

re·sent \ri-ˈzent\ vt [F ressentir to be emotionally sensible of, fr. OF, fr. re- + sentir to feel, fr. L sentire — more at SENSE] (1628) **:** to feel or express annoyance or ill will at

re·sent·ful \-fəl\ adj (1656) **1 :** full of resentment **:** inclined to resent **2 :** caused or marked by resentment — **re·sent·ful·ly** \-fə-lē\ adv — **re·sent·ful·ness** n

re·sent·ment \ri-ˈzent-mənt\ n (1619) **:** a feeling of indignant displeasure or persistent ill will at something regarded as a wrong, insult, or injury　syn see OFFENSE

re·ser·pine \ri-ˈsər-ˌpēn, -pən\ n [G Reserpin, prob. irreg. fr. NL Rauwolfia serpentina, a species of rauwolfia] (1952) **:** an alkaloid $C_{33}H_{40}N_2O_9$ extracted esp. from the root of rauwolfias and used in the treatment of hypertension, mental disorders, and tension states

res·er·va·tion \ˌre-zər-ˈvā-shən\ n (15c) **1 :** an act of reserving something: as **a (1) :** the act or fact of a grantor's reserving some newly created thing out of the thing granted **(2) :** the right or interest so reserved **b :** the setting of limiting conditions or withholding from complete exposition ⟨answered without ~⟩ **c :** an arrangement to have something (as a hotel room) held for one's use; also **:** a promise, guarantee, or record of such engagement **2 a :** a limiting condition ⟨agreed, but with ~s⟩ **b :** DOUBT, MISGIVING ⟨had serious ~s about marriage⟩ **3 :** something reserved: as **a :** a tract of public land set aside (as for use by American Indians) **b :** an area in which hunting is not permitted; esp **:** one set aside as a secure breeding place — **res·er·va·tion·ist** \-sh(ə-)nist\ n

¹**re·serve** \ri-ˈzərv\ vt **re·served; re·serv·ing** [ME, fr. MF reserver, fr. L reservare, lit., to keep back, fr. re- + servare to keep — more at CONSERVE] (14c) **1 a :** to hold in reserve **:** keep back ⟨~ grain for seed⟩

\ə\ abut \ᵊ\ kitten, F table \ər\ further \a\ ash \ā\ ace \ä\ mop, mar \aù\ out \ch\ chin \e\ bet \ē\ easy \g\ go \i\ hit \ī\ ice \j\ job \ŋ\ sing \ō\ go \ȯ\ law \ȯi\ boy \th\ thin \t̲h̲\ the \ü\ loot \ù\ foot \y\ yet \zh\ vision \à, k̟, ⁿ, œ, œ̄, ue, ūe, ᵜ\ see Guide to Pronunciation

b : to set aside (part of the consecrated elements) at the Eucharist for future use   **c** : to retain or hold over to a future time or place : DEFER ⟨~ one's judgment on a plan⟩   **d** : to make legal reservation of **2** : to set or have set aside or apart ⟨~ a hotel room⟩   *syn* see KEEP — re-serv·a·ble \-'zər-və-bəl\ *adj*

²**reserve** *n, often attrib* (1648)   **1** : something reserved or set aside for a particular purpose, use, or reason: as **a** (1) : a military force withheld from action for later decisive use — usu. used in pl.   (2) : forces not in the field but available   (3) : the military forces of a country not part of the regular services; *also* : RESERVIST   **b** : a tract (as of public land) set apart : RESERVATION   **2** : something stored or kept available for future use or need : STOCK   **3** : an act of reserving : QUALIFICATION   **4** **a** : restraint, closeness, or caution in one's words and actions   **b** : forbearance from making a full explanation, complete disclosure, or free expression of one's mind   **5** *archaic* : SECRET   **6** **a** : money or its equivalent kept in hand or set apart usu. to meet liabilities   **b** : the liquid resources of a nation for meeting international payments   **7** : SUBSTITUTE   **8** : RESERVE PRICE   **9** : a wine made from select grapes, bottled on the maker's premises, and aged specially and often longer — **in reserve** : held back for future or special use

reserve bank *n* (1905) : a central bank holding reserves of other banks

reserve clause *n* (1944) : a clause formerly placed in a professional athlete's contract that reserved for the club the exclusive right automatically to renew the contract and that bound the athlete to the club until retirement or until the athlete was traded or released

re·served \ri-'zərvd\ *adj* (1601)   **1** : restrained in words and actions   **2** : kept set apart or aside for future or special use   *syn* see SILENT — **re·serv·ed·ly** \-'zər-vəd-lē\ *adv* — **re·serv·ed·ness** \-'zər-vəd-nəs\ *n*

reserved power *n* (1838) : a political power reserved by a constitution to the exclusive jurisdiction of a specified political authority

reserve price *n* (1919) : a price announced at an auction as the lowest that will be considered

re·serv·ist \ri-'zər-vist\ *n* (1876) : a member of a military reserve

res·er·voir \'re-zə-₋vwär, -zər-, -₋vwȯr *also* -₋vȯi\ *n* [F *réservoir*, fr. MF, fr. *reserver*] (1690)   **1** : a place where something is kept in store: as **a** : an artificial lake where water is collected and kept in quantity for use   **b** : a part of an apparatus in which a liquid is held   **c** : SUPPLY, STORE ⟨a large ~ of educated people⟩   **2** : an extra supply : RESERVE   **3** : an organism in which a parasite that is pathogenic for some other species lives and multiplies without damaging its host; *also* : a noneconomic organism within which a pathogen of economic or medical importance flourishes

re·set \(₋)rē-'set\ *vt* **-set; -set·ting** (1655)   **1** : to set again or anew ⟨~ type⟩ ⟨~ a diamond⟩ ⟨~ a circuit breaker⟩   **2** : to change the reading of often to zero ⟨~ an odometer⟩ — **re·set** \'rē-₋set\ *n* — **re·set·ta·ble** \-'se-tə-bəl\ *adj*

res ges·tae \'räs-'ges-₋tī, 'rēz-'jes-(₋)tē\ *n pl* [L] (1616) : things done; *esp* : the facts that form the environment of a litigated issue and are admissible in evidence

resh \'räsh\ *n* [Heb *rēsh*] (ca. 1823) : the 20th letter of the Hebrew alphabet — see ALPHABET table

re·shape \(₋)rē-'shāp\ *vt* (1827) : to give a new form or orientation to : REORGANIZE — **re·shap·er** *n*

re·shuf·fle \(₋)rē-'shə-fəl\ *vt* (1830)   **1** : to shuffle (as cards) again   **2** : to reorganize usu. by the redistribution of existing elements ⟨the cabinet was *reshuffled* by the prime minister⟩ — **reshuffle** *n*

re·sid \ri-'zid\ *n* (1967) : RESIDUAL OIL

re·side \ri-'zīd\ *vi* **re·sid·ed; re·sid·ing** [ME, fr. MF or L; MF *resider*, fr. L *residēre* to sit back, remain, abide, fr. *re-* + *sedēre* to sit — more at SIT] (15c)   **1** **a** : to be in residence as the incumbent of a benefice or office   **b** : to dwell permanently or continuously : occupy a place as one's legal domicile   **2** **a** : to be present as an element or quality   **b** : to be vested as a right — **re·sid·er** *n*

res·i·dence \'re-zə-dən(t)s, 'rez-dən(t)s, 're-zə-₋den(t)s\ *n* (14c)   **1** **a** : the act or fact of dwelling in a place for some time   **b** : the act or fact of living or regularly staying at or in some place for the discharge of a duty or the enjoyment of a benefit   **2** **a** (1) : the place where one actually lives as distinguished from one's domicile or a place of temporary sojourn   (2) : DOMICILE 2a   **b** : the place where a corporation is actually or officially established   **c** : the status of a legal resident   **3** **a** : a building used as a home : DWELLING   **b** : housing or a unit of housing provided for students   **4** **a** : the period or duration of abode in a place   **b** : a period of active and esp. full-time study, research, or teaching at a college or university — **in residence** : engaged to live and work at a particular place often for a specified time ⟨poet *in residence* at a university⟩

residence time *n* (1954) : the duration of persistence of a mass or substance in a medium or place

res·i·den·cy \'re-zə-dən(t)-sē, 'rez-dən(t)-, 're-zə-₋den(t)-\ *n, pl* **-cies** (1579)   **1** : a usu. official place of residence   **2** : a territory in a protected state in which the powers of the protecting state are executed by a resident agent   **3** : a period of advanced training in a medical specialty after graduation from medical school and licensing to practice medicine

¹**res·i·dent** \'re-zə-dənt, 'rez-dənt, 're-zə-₋dent\ *adj* [ME, fr. L *resident-, residens*, prp. of *residēre*] (14c)   **1** **a** : living in a place for some length of time : RESIDING   **b** : serving in a regular or full-time capacity ⟨the ~ engineer for a highway department⟩; *also* : being in residence   **2** : PRESENT, INHERENT   **3** : not migratory

²**resident** *n* (15c)   **1** : one who resides in a place   **2** : a diplomatic agent residing at a foreign court or seat of government; *esp* : one exercising authority in a protected state as representative of the protecting power   **3** : a physician serving a residency

resident commissioner *n* (1902)   **1** : a nonvoting representative of a dependency in the U.S. House of Representatives   **2** : a resident administrator in a British colony or possession

res·i·den·tial \₋re-zə-'den(t)-shəl, ₋rez-'den(t)-\ *adj* (1654)   **1** **a** : used as a residence or by residents   **b** : providing living accommodations for students ⟨a ~ college⟩   **2** : restricted to or occupied by residences ⟨a ~ neighborhood⟩   **3** : of or relating to residence or residences — **res·i·den·tial·ly** \-'den(t)-shə-)lē\ *adv*

¹**res·id·u·al** \ri-'zi-jə-wəl, -jəl; -'zij-wəl\ *n* [L *residuum* residue] (1557)   **1** : REMAINDER, RESIDUUM: as   **a** : the difference between results obtained by observation and by computation from a formula or between

the mean of several observations and any one of them   **b** : a residual product or substance   **c** : an internal aftereffect of experience or activity that influences later behavior; *esp* : a disability remaining from a disease or operation   **2** : a payment (as to an actor or writer) for each rerun after an initial showing (as of a TV show)

²**residual** *adj* (1570)   **1** : of, relating to, or constituting a residue   **2** : leaving a residue that remains effective for some time — **re·sid·u·al·ly** *adv*

residual oil *n* (ca. 1948) : fuel oil that remains after the removal of valuable distillates (as gasoline) from petroleum and that is used esp. by industry — called also **resid**

residual power *n* (1919) : power held to remain at the disposal of a governmental authority after an enumeration or delegation of specified powers to other authorities

re·sid·u·ary \ri-'zi-jə-₋wer-ē\ *adj* (1726) : of, relating to, or constituting a residue ⟨~ estate⟩

res·i·due \'re-zə-₋dü, -₋dyü\ *n* [ME, fr. MF *residu*, fr. L *residuum*, fr. neut. of *residuus* left over, fr. *residēre* to remain] (14c) : something that remains after a part is taken, separated, or designated : REMNANT, REMAINDER: as   **a** : the part of a testator's estate remaining after the satisfaction of all debts, charges, allowances, and previous devises and bequests   **b** : the remainder after subtracting a multiple of a modulus from an integer or a power of the integer that can appear as the second of the two terms in an appropriate congruence ⟨2 and 7 are ~s of 12 modulo 5⟩   **c** : a constituent structural unit (as a group or monomer) of a usu. complex molecule ⟨amino acid ~s from hydrolysis of protein⟩

residue class *n* (1948) : the set of elements (as integers) that leave the same remainder when divided by a given modulus

re·sid·u·um \ri-'zi-jə-wəm\ *n, pl* **re·sid·ua** \-wə\ [L] (1672) : something residual: as   **a** : RESIDUE a   **b** : a residual product (as from the distillation of petroleum)

re·sign \ri-'zīn\ *vb* [ME, fr. MF *resigner*, fr. L *resignare*, lit., to unseal, cancel, fr. *re-* + *signare* to sign, seal — more at SIGN] *vt* (14c)   **1** : RELEGATE, CONSIGN; *esp* : to give (oneself) over without resistance ⟨~ed herself to her fate⟩   **2** : to give up deliberately; *esp* : to renounce (as a right or position) by a formal act   ~ *vi*   **1** : to give up one's office or position : QUIT   **2** : to accept something as inevitable : SUBMIT   *syn* see RELINQUISH, ABDICATE — **re·sign·ed·ly** \-'zī-nəd-lē\ *adv* — **re·signed·ness** \-'zī-nəd-nəs\ *n* — **re·sign·er** \-'zī-nər\ *n*

re·sign \(₋)rē-'sīn\ *vt* (1805) : to sign again   ~ *vi* : to sign up again

res·ig·na·tion \₋re-zig-'nā-shən\ *n* (14c)   **1** **a** : an act or instance of resigning something : SURRENDER   **b** : a formal notification of resigning   **2** : the quality or state of being resigned : SUBMISSIVENESS

re·sile \ri-'zī(ə)l\ *vi* **re·siled; re·sil·ing** [LL & L; LL *resilire* to withdraw, fr. L, to recoil] (1529) : RECOIL, RETRACT; *esp* : to return to a prior position

re·sil·ience \ri-'zil-yən(t)s\ *n* (1824)   **1** : the capability of a strained body to recover its size and shape after deformation caused esp. by compressive stress   **2** : an ability to recover from or adjust easily to misfortune or change

re·sil·ien·cy \-yən-sē\ *n* (ca. 1836) : RESILIENCE

re·sil·ient \-yənt\ *adj* [L *resilient-, resiliens*, prp. of *resilire* to jump back, recoil, fr. *re-* + *salire* to leap — more at SALLY] (1674) : characterized or marked by resilience: as   **a** : capable of withstanding shock without permanent deformation or rupture   **b** : tending to recover from or adjust easily to misfortune or change   *syn* see ELASTIC — **re·sil·ient·ly** *adv*

¹**res·in** \'re-z²n\ *n* [ME, fr. MF *resine*, fr. L *resina*; akin to Gk *rhētinē* pine resin] (14c)   **1** **a** : any of various solid or semisolid amorphous fusible flammable natural organic substances that are usu. transparent or translucent and yellowish to brown, are formed esp. in plant secretions, are soluble in organic solvents (as ether) but not in water, are electrical nonconductors, and are used chiefly in varnishes, printing inks, plastics, and sizes and in medicine   **b** : ROSIN   **2** **a** : any of a large class of synthetic products that have some of the physical properties of natural resins but are different chemically and are used chiefly in plastics   **b** : any various products made from a natural resin or a natural polymer — **res·in·ous** \'re-z²n-əs, 'rez-nəs\ *adj*

²**resin** *vt* **res·ined; res·in·ing** \'re-z²n-iŋ, 'rez-niŋ\ (1865) : to treat with resin

res·in·ate \'re-z²n-₋āt\ *vt* **-at·ed; -at·ing** (ca. 1890) : to impregnate or flavor with resin

resin canal *n* (1884) : a tubular intercellular space in gymnosperms and some angiosperms that is lined with epithelial cells which secrete resin — called also **resin duct**

res·in·oid \'re-z²n-₋ȯid\ *n* (1880) : GUM RESIN

¹**re·sist** \ri-'zist\ *vb* [ME, fr. MF or L; MF *resister*, fr. L *resistere*, fr. *re-* + *sistere* to take a stand; akin to L *stare* to stand — more at STAND] *vi* (14c) : to exert force in opposition   ~ *vt*   **1** : to exert oneself so as to counteract or defeat   **2** : to withstand the force or effect of   *syn* see OPPOSE

²**resist** *n* (1836) : something (as a coating) that protects against a chemical, electrical, or physical action

re·sis·tance \ri-'zis-tən(t)s\ *n* (14c)   **1** **a** : an act or instance of resisting : OPPOSITION   **b** : a means of resisting   **2** : the ability to resist; *esp* : the inherent capacity of a living being to resist untoward circumstances (as disease, malnutrition, or toxic agents)   **3** : an opposing or retarding force   **4** **a** : the opposition offered by a body or substance to the passage through it of a steady electric current   **b** : a source of resistance   **5** *often cap* : an underground organization of a conquered or nearly conquered country engaging in sabotage and secret operations against occupation forces and collaborators

¹**re·sis·tant** \-tənt\ *adj* (15c) : giving or capable of resistance — often used in combination ⟨wrinkle-*resistant* clothes⟩

²**resistant** *n* (1600) : one that resists : RESISTER

re·sist·er \ri-'zis-tər\ *n* (14c) : one that resists; *esp* : one who actively opposes the policies of a government

re·sist·ibil·i·ty \ri-₋zis-tə-'bi-lə-tē\ *n* (1617)   **1** : the quality or state of being resistible   **2** : ability to resist

re·sist·ible \ri-'zis-tə-bəl\ *adj* (1608) : capable of being resisted

re·sis·tive \ri-'zis-tiv\ *adj* (1603) : marked by resistance — often used in combination ⟨fire-*resistive* material⟩ — **re·sis·tive·ly** *adv* — **re·sis·tive·ness** *n*

re·sis·tiv·i·ty \ri-₋zis-'ti-və-tē, ₋rē-\ *n, pl* **-ties** (1885)   **1** : the longitudinal electrical resistance of a uniform rod of unit length and unit cross-sectional area : the reciprocal of conductivity **2** : capacity for resisting : RESISTANCE

re·sist·less \ri-'zist-ləs\ *adj* (1586) **1** : IRRESISTIBLE **2** : offering no resistance — **re·sist·less·ly** *adv* — **re·sist·less·ness** *n*

re·sis·tor \ri-'zis-tər\ *n* (1905) : a device that has electrical resistance and that is used in an electric circuit for protection, operation, or current control

re·sit·ting \(,)rē-'si-tiŋ\ *n* (1661) : a sitting (as of a legislature) for a second time : another sitting

res ju·di·ca·ta \'rēz-,jü-di-'kä-tə\ *n* [L, judged matter] (1693) : a matter finally decided on its merits by a court having competent jurisdiction and not subject to litigation again between the same parties

re·sol·u·ble \ri-'zäl-yə-bəl\ *adj* [LL *resolubilis*, fr. L *resolvere* to resolve, unloose] (1602) : capable of being resolved

¹res·o·lute \'re-zə-,lüt, -lət\ *adj* [L *resolutus*, pp. of *resolvere*] (1533) **1** : marked by firm determination : RESOLVED **2** : BOLD, STEADY *syn* see FAITHFUL — **res·o·lute·ly** \-,lüt-lē, -lət-; ,re-zə-'lüt-\ *adv* — **res·o·lute·ness** \-,lüt-nəs, -lət-, -'lüt-\ *n*

²resolute *n* (1602) : a resolute person

res·o·lu·tion \,re-zə-'lü-shən\ *n* [ME, fr. MF or L; MF *resolution*, fr. L *resolution-, resolutio*, fr. *resolvere*] (14c) **1** : the act or process of reducing to simpler form: as **a** : the act of analyzing a complex notion into simpler ones **b** : the act of answering : SOLVING **c** : the act of determining **d** : the passing of a voice part from a dissonant to a consonant tone or the progression of a chord from dissonance to consonance **e** : the separating of a chemical compound or mixture into its constituents **f** (1) : the division of a prosodic element into its component parts (2) : the substitution in Greek or Latin prosody of two short syllables for a long syllable **g** : the analysis of a vector into two or more vectors of which it is the sum **h** : the process or capability of making distinguishable the individual parts of an object, closely adjacent optical images, or sources of light **2** : the subsidence of a pathological state (as inflammation) **3 a** : something that is resolved ⟨made a ~ to mend my ways⟩ **b** : firmness of resolve **4** : a formal expression of opinion, will, or intent voted by an official body or assembled group **5** : the point in a literary work at which the chief dramatic complication is worked out *syn* see COURAGE

¹re·solve \ri-'zälv, -'zölv *also* -'zäv *or* -'zöv\ *vb* **re·solved; re·solv·ing** [ME, fr. L *resolvere* to unloose, dissolve, fr. *re-* + *solvere* to loosen, release — more at SOLVE] *vt* (14c) **1** *obs* : DISSOLVE, MELT **2 a** : BREAK UP, SEPARATE ⟨the prism *resolved* the light into a play of color⟩; *also* : to change by disintegration **b** : to reduce by analysis ⟨~ the problem into simple elements⟩ **c** : to distinguish between or make independently visible adjacent parts of **d** : to separate (a racemic compound or mixture) into the two components **3** : to cause resolution of (a pathological state) **4 a** : to deal with successfully : clear up ⟨~ doubts⟩ ⟨~ a dispute⟩ **b** : to find an answer to **c** : to make clear or understandable **d** : to find a mathematical solution of **e** : to split up (as a vector) into two or more components esp. in assigned directions **5** : to reach a firm decision about ⟨~ to get more sleep⟩ ⟨~ disputed points in a text⟩ **6 a** : to declare or decide by a formal resolution and vote **b** : to change by resolution or formal vote ⟨the house *resolved* itself into a committee⟩ **7** : to make (as voice parts) progress from dissonance to consonance **8** : to work out the resolution of (as a play) ~ *vi* **1** : to become separated into component parts; *also* : to become reduced by dissolving or analysis **2** : to form a resolution : DETERMINE **3** : CONSULT, DELIBERATE **4** : to progress from dissonance to consonance *syn* see DECIDE — **re·solv·able** \-'zäl-və-bəl, -'zöl- *also* -'zäv-ə- *or* -'zöv-ə-\ *adj* — **re·solv·er** *n*

²resolve *n* (1591) **1** : fixity of purpose : RESOLUTENESS **2** : something that is resolved **3** : a legal or official determination; *esp* : a formal resolution

re·sol·vent \ri-'zäl-vənt, -'zöl-\ *n* (1851) : a means of solving something (as an equation) — **resolvent** *adj*

resolving power *n* (1879) **1** : the ability of an optical system to form distinguishable images of objects separated by small angular distances **2** : the ability of a photographic film or plate to reproduce the fine detail of an optical image

res·o·nance \'re-z²n-ən(t)s, 'rez-nən(t)s\ *n* (15c) **1 a** : the quality or state of being resonant **b** (1) : a vibration of large amplitude in a mechanical or electrical system caused by a relatively small periodic stimulus of the same or nearly the same period as the natural vibration period of the system (2) : the state of adjustment that produces resonance in a mechanical or electrical system **2 a** : the intensification and enriching of a musical tone by supplementary vibration **b** : a quality imparted to voiced sounds by vibration in anatomical resonating chambers or cavities (as the mouth or the nasal cavity) **c** : a quality of richness or variety **d** : a quality of evoking response ⟨how much ~ the scandal seems to be having —*U.S. News & World Report*⟩ **3** : the sound elicited on percussion of the chest **4** : the conceptual alternation of a chemical species (as a molecule or ion) between two or more equivalent allowed structural representations differing only in the placement of electrons that aids in understanding the actual state of the species as an amalgamation of its possible structures and the usu. higher-than-expected stability of the species **5 a** : the enhancement of an atomic, nuclear, or particle reaction or a scattering event by excitation of internal motion in the system **b** : MAGNETIC RESONANCE **6** : an extremely short-lived elementary particle **7** : a synchronous gravitational relationship of two celestial bodies (as moons) that orbit a third (as a planet) which can be expressed as a simple ratio of their orbital periods

res·o·nant \'re-z²n-ənt, 'rez-nənt\ *adj* (1592) **1** : continuing to sound : ECHOING **2 a** : capable of inducing resonance **b** : relating to or exhibiting resonance **3 a** : intensified and enriched by or as if by resonance **b** : marked by grandiloquence — **resonant** *n* — **res·o·nant·ly** *adv*

res·o·nate \'re-z²n-,āt\ *vb* **-nat·ed; -nat·ing** [L *resonatus*, pp. of *resonare* to resound — more at RESOUND] *vi* (1873) **1** : to produce or exhibit resonance **2** : to respond as if by resonance ⟨~ to the music⟩; *also* : to have a repetitive pattern that resembles resonance **3** : to relate harmoniously ~ *vt* : to subject to resonating

res·o·na·tor \-,ā-tər\ *n* (ca. 1869) : something that resounds or resonates: as **a** : a hollow metallic container for producing microwaves or

a piezoelectric crystal put into oscillation by the oscillations of an outside source **b** : a device for increasing the resonance of a musical instrument

re·sorb \(,)rē-'sörb, -'zörb\ *vb* [L *resorbēre*, fr. *re-* + *sorbēre* to suck up — more at ABSORB] *vt* (1640) **1** : to swallow or suck in again **2** : to break down and assimilate (something previously differentiated) ~ *vi* : to undergo resorption

res·or·cin \rə-'zör-s²n\ *n* [ISV *res-* (fr. L *resina* resin) + *orcin*, a phenol (C₇H₈O₂)] (ca. 1868) : RESORCINOL

res·or·cin·ol \-,öl, -,ōl\ *n* (1881) : a crystalline phenol C₆H₆O₂ obtained from various resins or artificially and used esp. in making dyes, pharmaceuticals, and resins

re·sorp·tion \(,)rē-'sörp-shən, -'zörp-\ *n* [L *resorbēre*] (ca. 1820) : the action or process of resorbing something — **re·sorp·tive** \-tiv\ *adj*

¹re·sort \ri-'zört\ *n* [ME, fr. MF, resource, recourse, fr. *resortir* to rebound, resort, fr. OF, fr. *re-* + *sortir* to escape, sally] (14c) **1 a** : one that affords aid or refuge : RESOURCE ⟨went to them as a last ~⟩ **b** : RECOURSE **2 a** : frequent, habitual, or general visiting ⟨a place of popular ~⟩ **b** : persons who frequent a place : THRONG **c** (1) : a frequently visited place : HAUNT (2) : a place providing recreation and entertainment esp. to vacationers *syn* see RESOURCE

²resort *vi* (15c) **1** : to go esp. frequently or habitually : REPAIR **2** : to have recourse ⟨~ to force⟩

re·sort \(,)rē-'sört\ *vt* (1889) : to sort again

re·sort·er \ri-'zör-tər\ *n* (1917) : a frequenter of resorts

re·sound \ri-'zaund *also* -'saund\ *vb* [ME *resounen*, fr. MF *resoner*, fr. L *resonare*, fr. *re-* + *sonare* to sound — more at SOUND] *vi* (14c) **1** : to become filled with sound : REVERBERATE **2 a** : to sound loudly **b** : to produce a sonorous or echoing sound **3** : to become renowned ~ *vt* **1** : to extol loudly or widely : CELEBRATE **2** : ECHO, REVERBERATE **3** : to sound or utter in full resonant tones

re·sound·ing *adj* (15c) **1** : producing or characterized by resonant sound : RESONATING **2 a** : impressively sonorous **b** : EMPHATIC, UNEQUIVOCAL ⟨a ~ success⟩ — **re·sound·ing·ly** \-'zaun-diŋ-lē *also* -'saun-\ *adv*

re·source \'rē-,sörs, -,sörs, -,zörs, -,zörs, ri-'\ *n* [F *ressource*, fr. OF *ressourse* relief, resource, fr. *resourdre* to relieve, lit., to rise again, fr. L *resurgere* — more at RESURRECTION] (1611) **1 a** : a source of supply or support : an available means — usu. used in pl. **b** : a natural source of wealth or revenue — often used in pl. **c** : computable wealth — usu. used in pl. **d** : a source of information or expertise **2** : something to which one has recourse in difficulty : EXPEDIENT **3** : a possibility of relief or recovery **4** : a means of spending one's leisure time **5** : an ability to meet and handle a situation : RESOURCEFULNESS

syn RESOURCE, RESORT, EXPEDIENT, SHIFT, MAKESHIFT, STOPGAP mean something one turns to in the absence of the usual means or source of supply. RESOURCE and RESORT apply to anything one falls back upon ⟨exhausted all of their *resources*⟩ ⟨a last *resort*⟩. EXPEDIENT may apply to any device or contrivance used when the usual one is not at hand or not possible ⟨a flimsy *expedient*⟩. SHIFT implies a tentative or temporary imperfect expedient ⟨desperate *shifts* to stave off foreclosure⟩. MAKESHIFT implies an inferior expedient adopted because of urgent need or countenanced through indifference ⟨old equipment employed as a *makeshift*⟩. STOPGAP applies to something used temporarily as an emergency measure ⟨a new law intended only as a *stopgap*⟩.

re·source·ful \ri-'sörs-fəl, -'sörs-, -'zörs-, -'zörs-\ *adj* (1851) : able to meet situations : capable of devising ways and means — **re·source·ful·ly** \-fə-lē\ *adv* — **re·source·ful·ness** *n*

¹re·spect \ri-'spekt\ *n* [ME, fr. L *respectus*, lit., act of looking back, fr. *respicere* to look back, regard, fr. *re-* + *specere* to look — more at SPY] (14c) **1** : a relation or reference to a particular thing or situation ⟨remarks having ~ to an earlier plan⟩ **2** : an act of giving particular attention : CONSIDERATION **3 a** : high or special regard : ESTEEM **b** : the quality or state of being esteemed **c** *pl* : expressions of respect or deference ⟨paid our ~s⟩ **4** : PARTICULAR, DETAIL ⟨a good plan in some ~s⟩ — **in respect of** *chiefly Brit* : with respect to : CONCERNING — **in respect to** : with respect to : CONCERNING — **with respect to** : with reference to : in relation to

²respect *vt* (1560) **1 a** : to consider worthy of high regard : ESTEEM **b** : to refrain from interfering with **2** : to have reference to : CONCERN *syn* see REGARD — **re·spect·er** *n*

¹re·spect·able \ri-'spek-tə-bəl\ *adj* (1599) **1** : worthy of respect : ESTIMABLE **2** : decent or correct in character or behavior : PROPER **3 a** : fair in size or quantity ⟨~ amount⟩ **b** : moderately good : TOLERABLE **4** : fit to be seen : PRESENTABLE ⟨~ clothes⟩ — **re·spect·abil·i·ty** \-,spek-tə-'bi-lə-tē\ *n* — **re·spect·able·ness** \-'spek-tə-bəl-nəs\ *n* — **re·spect·ably** \-blē\ *adv*

²respectable *n* (1814) : a respectable person

re·spect·ful \ri-'spekt-fəl\ *adj* (1687) : marked by or showing respect or deference — **re·spect·ful·ly** \-fə-lē\ *adv* — **re·spect·ful·ness** *n*

re·spect·ing *prep* (1611) **1** : in view of : CONSIDERING **2** : with respect to : CONCERNING

re·spec·tive \ri-'spek-tiv\ *adj* (1592) **1** *obs* : PARTIAL, DISCRIMINATIVE **2** : PARTICULAR, SEPARATE ⟨their ~ homes⟩ — **re·spec·tive·ness** *n*

re·spec·tive·ly *adv* (1605) **1** : in particular : SEPARATELY ⟨could not recognize the solutions as salty or sour, ~⟩ **2** : in the order given ⟨Mary and Anne were ~ 12 and 16 years old⟩

re·spell \(,)rē-'spel\ *vt* (1806) : to spell again or in another way; *esp* : to spell out according to a phonetic system — **re·spell·ing** \-'spe-liŋ\ *n*

re·spi·ra·ble \'res-p(ə-)rə-bəl, ri-'spī-rə-\ *adj* (1779) : fit for breathing; *also* : capable of being taken in by breathing ⟨~ particles of ash⟩

res·pi·ra·tion \,res-pə-'rā-shən\ *n* [ME *respiracioun*, fr. L *respiration-, respiratio*, fr. *respirare*] (15c) **1 a** : the placing of air or dissolved gases in intimate contact with the circulating medium of a multicellular organism (as by breathing) **b** : a single complete act of breathing **2** : the physical and chemical processes by which an organism supplies its cells and tissues with the oxygen needed for metabolism and relieves

\ə\ abut \ᵊ\ kitten, F table \ər\ further \a\ ash \ā\ ace \ä\ mop, mar \aú\ out \ch\ chin \e\ bet \ē\ easy \g\ go \i\ hit \ī\ ice \j\ job \ŋ\ sing \ō\ go \ó\ law \ói\ boy \th\ thin \t̲h̲\ the \ü\ loot \ú\ foot \y\ yet \zh\ vision \ä, k̲, ⁿ, œ, œ̄, ᵫ, ᵬ̄, �\ see Guide to Pronunciation them of the carbon dioxide formed in energy-producing reactions **3** : any of various energy-yielding oxidative reactions in living matter — **re·spi·ra·to·ry** \'res-p(ə-)rə-ˌtōr-ē, ri-'spī-rə-, -ˌtȯr-\ *adj*

res·pi·ra·tor \'res-pə-ˌrā-tər\ *n* (1836) **1** : a device worn over the mouth or nose for protecting the respiratory tract **2** : a device for maintaining artificial respiration

respiratory pigment *n* (1896) : any of various permanently or intermittently colored conjugated proteins and esp. hemoglobin that function in the transfer of oxygen in cellular respiration

respiratory quotient *n* (ca. 1890) : a ratio indicating the relation of the volume of carbon dioxide given off in respiration to that of the oxygen consumed

respiratory system *n* (1940) : a system of organs subserving the function of respiration and in air-breathing vertebrates consisting typically of the lungs and their nervous and circulatory supply and the channels by which these are continuous with the outer air

re·spire \ri-'spīr\ *vb* **re·spired; re·spir·ing** [ME, fr. L *respirare*, fr. re- + *spirare* to blow, breathe] *vi* (15c) **1** : BREATHE; *specif* : to inhale and exhale air successively **2** *of a cell or tissue* : to take up oxygen and produce carbon dioxide through oxidation ~ *vt* : BREATHE

res·pi·rom·e·ter \ˌres-pə-'rä-mə-tər\ *n* (ca. 1883) : an instrument for studying the character and extent of respiration — **res·pi·ro·met·ric** \-rō-'me-trik\ *adj* — **res·pi·rom·e·try** \-'rä-mə-trē\ *n*

¹re·spite \'res-pət *also* ri-'spit, *Brit usu* 'res-ˌpīt\ *n* [ME *respit*, fr. OF, fr. ML *respectus*, fr. L, act of looking back — more at RESPECT] (13c) **1** : a period of temporary delay; *esp* : REPRIEVE 1b **2** : an interval of rest or relief

²respite *vt* **re·spit·ed; re·spit·ing** (14c) **1** : to grant a respite to **2** : PUT OFF, DELAY

re·splen·dence \ri-'splen-dən(t)s\ *n* (15c) : the quality or state of being resplendent : SPLENDOR

re·splen·den·cy \-dən(t)-sē\ *n* (1611) : RESPLENDENCE

re·splen·dent \-dənt\ *adj* [L *resplendent-, resplendens*, prp. of *resplendēre* to shine back, fr. re- + *splendēre* to shine — more at SPLENDID] (15c) : shining brilliantly : characterized by a glowing splendor ⟨meadows ~ with wildflowers —*Outdoor World*⟩ **syn** see SPLENDID — **re·splen·dent·ly** *adv*

¹re·spond \ri-'spänd\ *n* (15c) : an engaged pillar supporting an arch or closing a colonnade or arcade

²respond *vb* [MF *respondre*, fr. L *respondēre* to promise in return, answer, fr. re- + *spondēre* to promise — more at SPOUSE] *vi* (1719) **1** : to say something in return : make an answer ⟨~ to criticism⟩ **2** **a** : to react in response ⟨~ed to a call for help⟩ **b** : to show favorable reaction ⟨~ to surgery⟩ **3** : to be answerable ⟨~ in damages⟩ ~ *vt* : REPLY **syn** see ANSWER — **re·spond·er** \-'spän-dər\ *n*

¹re·spon·dent \ri-'spän-dənt\ *n* [L *respondent-, respondens*, prp. of *respondēre*] (1528) **1** : one who responds: as **a** : one who maintains a thesis in reply **b** (1) : one who answers in various legal proceedings (as in equity cases) (2) : the prevailing party in the lower court **c** : a person who responds to a poll **2** : a reflex that occurs in response to a specific external stimulus — compare OPERANT

²respondent *adj* (1726) **1** : making response : RESPONSIVE; *esp* : being a respondent at law **2** : relating to or being behavior or responses to a stimulus that are followed by a reward ⟨~ conditioning⟩ — compare OPERANT 3

re·sponse \ri-'spän(t)s\ *n* [ME & L; ME *respounse*, fr. MF *respons*, fr. L *responsum* reply, fr. neut. of *responsus*, pp. of *respondēre*] (14c) **1** : an act of responding **2** : something constituting a reply or a reaction: as **a** : a verse, phrase, or word sung or said by the people or choir after or in reply to the officiant in a liturgical service **b** : the activity or inhibition of previous activity of an organism or any of its parts resulting from stimulation **c** : the output of a transducer or detecting device resulting from a given input

re·spon·si·bil·i·ty \ri-ˌspän(t)-sə-'bi-lə-tē\ *n, pl* **-ties** (1787) **1** : the quality or state of being responsible: as **a** : moral, legal, or mental accountability **b** : RELIABILITY, TRUSTWORTHINESS **2** : something for which one is responsible : BURDEN

re·spon·si·ble \ri-'spän(t)-sə-bəl\ *adj* (1643) **1** **a** : liable to be called on to answer **b** : liable to be called to account as the primary cause, motive, or agent ⟨a committee ~ for the job⟩ (2) : being the cause or explanation ⟨mechanical defects were ~ for the accident⟩ **c** : liable to legal review or in case of fault to penalties **2** **a** : able to answer for one's conduct and obligations : TRUSTWORTHY **b** : able to choose for oneself between right and wrong **3** : marked by or involving responsibility or accountability ⟨~ financial policies⟩ ⟨a ~ job⟩ **4** : politically answerable; *esp* : required to submit to the electorate if defeated by the legislature — used esp. of the British cabinet — **re·spon·si·ble·ness** *n* — **re·spon·si·bly** \-blē\ *adv*

syn RESPONSIBLE, ANSWERABLE, ACCOUNTABLE, AMENABLE, LIABLE mean subject to being held to account. RESPONSIBLE implies holding a specific office, duty, or trust ⟨the bureau *responsible* for revenue collection⟩. ANSWERABLE suggests a relation between one having a moral or legal obligation and a court or other authority charged with oversight of its observance ⟨an intelligence agency *answerable* to Congress⟩. ACCOUNTABLE suggests imminence of retribution for unfulfilled trust or violated obligation ⟨elected officials are *accountable* to the voters⟩. AMENABLE and LIABLE stress the fact of subjection to review, censure, or control by a designated authority under certain conditions ⟨laws are *amenable* to judicial review⟩ ⟨not *liable* for the debts of the former spouse⟩.

re·spon·sions \ri-'spän(t)-shənz\ *n pl* [ME *responcioun* response, sum to be paid, fr. MF or ML; MF *responsion*, fr. ML *responsion-, responsio*, fr. L, answer, fr. *respondēre*] (1813) : an examination required for matriculation as an undergraduate at Oxford

re·spon·sive \ri-'spän(t)-siv\ *adj* (15c) **1** : giving response : constituting a response : ANSWERING ⟨a ~ glance⟩ ⟨~ aggression⟩ **2** : quick to respond or react appropriately or sympathetically : SENSITIVE **3** : using responses ⟨~ worship⟩ — **re·spon·sive·ly** *adv* — **re·spon·sive·ness** *n*

re·spon·so·ry \ri-'spän(t)s-(ə-)rē\ *n, pl* **-ries** [ME, fr. ML *responsorius*, fr. L *respondēre*] (15c) : a set of versicles and responses sung or said after or during a lection

re·spon·sum \ri-'spän(t)-səm\ *n, pl* **-sa** \-sə\ [NL, fr. L, reply, response] (1896) : a written decision from a rabbinic authority in response to a submitted question or problem

res pu·bli·ca \'räs-'pü-bli-ˌkä\ *n* [L — more at REPUBLIC] (ca. 1898) **1** : COMMONWEALTH, STATE, REPUBLIC **2** : COMMONWEAL

res·sen·ti·ment \rə-ˌsäⁿ-tē-'mäⁿ\ *n* [F, resentment, fr. *ressentir* to resent — more at RESENT] (1941) : deep-seated resentment, frustration, and hostility accompanied by a sense of being powerless to express these feelings directly

¹rest \'rest\ *n* [ME, fr. OE; akin to OHG *rasta* rest and perh. to OHG *ruowa* calm] (bef. 12c) **1** : REPOSE, SLEEP; *specif* : a bodily state characterized by minimal functional and metabolic activities **2** **a** : freedom from activity or labor **b** : a state of motionlessness or inactivity **c** : the repose of death **3** : a place for resting or lodging **4** : peace of mind or spirit **5** **a** (1) : a rhythmic silence in music (2) : a character representing such a silence **b** : a brief pause in reading **6** : something used for support — **at rest 1** : resting or reposing esp. in sleep or death **2** : QUIESCENT, MOTIONLESS **3** : free of anxieties

rest 5a(2): *1* whole, *2* half, *3* quarter, *4* eighth, *5* sixteenth

²rest *vi* (bef. 12c) **1** **a** : to get rest by lying down; *esp* : SLEEP **b** : to lie dead **2** : to cease from action or motion : refrain from labor or exertion **3** : to be free from anxiety or disturbance **4** : to sit or lie fixed or supported ⟨a column ~s on its pedestal⟩ **5** **a** : to remain confident : TRUST ⟨cannot ~ on that assumption⟩ **b** : to be based or founded ⟨the verdict ~ed on several sound precedents⟩ **6** : to remain for action or accomplishment ⟨the answer ~s with you⟩ **7** *of farmland* : to remain idle or uncropped **8** : to bring to an end voluntarily the introduction of evidence in a law case ~ *vt* **1** : to give rest to **2** : to set at rest **3** : to place on or against a support **4** : to cause to be firmly fixed ⟨~ed all hope in his child⟩ **5** : to stop voluntarily from presenting evidence pertinent to (a case at law) — **rest·er** *n*

³rest *n* [ME *reste*, lit., stoppage, short for *areste*, fr. MF, fr. OF, fr. *arester* to arrest] (14c) : a projection or attachment on the side of the breastplate of medieval armor for supporting the butt of a lance

⁴rest *n* [ME, fr. MF *reste*, fr. *rester* to remain, fr. L *restare*, fr. re- + *stare* to stand — more at STAND] (15c) : something that remains over : REMAINDER ⟨ate the ~ of the candy⟩ — **for the rest** : with regard to remaining issues or needs

re·start \(ˌ)rē-'stärt\ *vt* (1845) **1** : to start anew (as an activity) after interruption ~ *vi* : to resume operation — **re·start** \'rē-ˌstärt, (ˌ)re-'\ *n* — **re·start·able** \-'stär-tə-bəl\ *adj*

re·state \(ˌ)rē-'stāt\ *vt* (ca. 1713) : to state again or in another way

re·state·ment \-mənt\ *n* (1803) **1** : something that is restated **2** : the act of restating

res·tau·rant \'res-t(ə-)rənt, -tə-ˌränt, -ˌtränt, -tərnt\ *n* [F, fr. prp. of *restaurer* to restore, fr. L *restaurare*] (1827) : a business establishment where meals or refreshments may be procured

res·tau·ra·teur \ˌres-tə-rə-'tər\ *also* **res·tau·ran·teur** \-ˌrän-\ *n* [F *restaurateur*, fr. LL *restaurator* restorer, fr. L *restaurare*] (1796) : the operator or proprietor of a restaurant

rest·ful \'rest-fəl\ *adj* (14c) **1** : marked by, affording, or suggesting rest and repose ⟨a ~ color scheme⟩ **2** : being at rest : QUIET **syn** see COMFORTABLE — **rest·ful·ly** \-fə-lē\ *adv* — **rest·ful·ness** *n*

rest home *n* (1926) : an establishment that provides housing and general care for the aged or the convalescent

rest house *n* (1807) : a building used for shelter by travelers

rest·ing *adj* (14c) **1** : being or characterized by dormancy : QUIESCENT ⟨a ~ spore⟩ ⟨bulbs in the ~ state⟩ **2** : not undergoing or marked by division : VEGETATIVE ⟨a ~ nucleus⟩

res·ti·tute \'res-tə-ˌtüt, -ˌtyüt\ *vb* **-tut·ed; -tut·ing** [L *restitutus*, pp. of *restituere*] *vt* (ca. 1500) **1** : to restore to a former state or position **2** : GIVE BACK; REFUND ~ *vi* : to undergo restitution

res·ti·tu·tion \ˌres-tə-'tü-shən, -'tyü-\ *n* [ME, fr. MF, fr. L *restitution-, restitutio*, fr. *restituere* to restore, fr. re- + *statuere* to set up — more at STATUTE] (14c) **1** : an act of restoring or a condition of being restored: as **a** : a restoration of something to its rightful owner **b** : a making good of or giving an equivalent for some injury **2** : a legal action serving to cause restoration of a previous state

res·tive \'res-tiv\ *adj* [ME *restyf*, fr. MF *restif*, fr. *rester* to stop behind, remain] (15c) **1** : stubbornly resisting control : BALKY **2** : marked by impatience : FIDGETY **syn** see CONTRARY — **res·tive·ly** *adv* — **res·tive·ness** *n*

rest·less \'rest-ləs\ *adj* (bef. 12c) **1** : lacking or denying rest : UNEASY ⟨a ~ night⟩ **2** : continuously moving : UNQUIET ⟨the ~ sea⟩ **3** : characterized by or manifesting unrest esp. of mind ⟨~ pacing⟩; *also* : CHANGEFUL, DISCONTENTED — **rest·less·ly** *adv* — **rest·less·ness** *n*

rest mass *n* (1914) : the mass of a body exclusive of additional mass the body acquires by its motion according to the theory of relativity

re·stor·able \ri-'stōr-ə-bəl, -'stȯr-\ *adj* (1611) : fit for restoring or reclaiming

re·stor·al \-əl\ *n* (1611) : RESTORATION

res·to·ra·tion \ˌres-tə-'rä-shən\ *n* (14c) **1** : an act of restoring or the condition of being restored: as **a** : a bringing back to a former position or condition : REINSTATEMENT ⟨the ~ of peace⟩ **b** : RESTITUTION **c** : a restoring to an unimpaired or improved condition ⟨the ~ of a painting⟩ **d** : the replacing of missing teeth or crowns **2** : something that is restored; *esp* : a representation or reconstruction of the original form (as of a fossil or a building) **3** *cap* **a** : the reestablishment of the monarchy in England in 1660 under Charles II **b** : the period in English history usu. held to coincide with the reign of Charles II but sometimes extended through the reign of James II

¹re·stor·ative \ri-'stȯr-ə-tiv, -'stōr-\ *adj* (14c) : of or relating to restoration; *esp* : having power to restore

²restorative *n* (15c) : something that serves to restore to consciousness, vigor, or health

re·store \ri-'stōr, -'stȯr\ *vt* **re·stored; re·stor·ing** [ME, fr. OF *restorer*, fr. L *restaurare* to renew, rebuild, alter. of *instaurare* to renew] (14c) **1** : GIVE BACK, RETURN **2** : to put or bring back into existence or use **3** : to bring back to or put back into a former or original state : RENEW **4** : to put again in possession of something *syn* see RENEW — **re‑stor·er** *n*

re·strain \ri-'strān\ *vt* [ME *restraynen*, fr. MF *restraindre*, fr. L *restringere* to restrain, restrict, fr. *re-* + *stringere* to bind tight — more at STRAIN] (14c) **1 a** : to prevent from doing, exhibiting, or expressing something ⟨∼ed the child from jumping⟩ **b** : to limit, restrict, or keep under control ⟨try to ∼ your anger⟩ **2** : to moderate or limit the force, effect, development, or full exercise of ⟨∼ trade⟩ **3** : to deprive of liberty; *esp* : to place under arrest or restraint — **re·strain·able** \-'strā-nə-bəl\ *adj* — **re·strain·er** *n*
syn RESTRAIN, CHECK, CURB, BRIDLE mean to hold back from or control in doing something. RESTRAIN suggests holding back by force or persuasion from acting or from going to extremes ⟨*restrained* themselves from laughing⟩. CHECK implies restraining or impeding a progress, activity, or impetus ⟨trying to *check* government spending⟩. CURB suggests an abrupt or drastic checking ⟨learn to *curb* your appetite⟩. BRIDLE implies keeping under control by subduing or holding in ⟨*bridle* an impulse to throw the book down⟩.
re·strained \ri-'strānd\ *adj* (14c) : marked by restraint : being without excess or extravagance — **re·strain·ed·ly** \-'strā-nəd-lē\ *adv*
restraining order *n* (ca. 1876) **1** : a preliminary legal order sometimes issued to keep a situation unchanged pending decision upon an application for an injunction **2** : a legal order issued against an individual to restrict or prohibit access or proximity to another specified individual
re·straint \ri-'strānt\ *n* [ME, fr. MF *restrainte*, fr. *restraindre*] (15c) **1 a** : an act of restraining : the state of being restrained **b** (1) : a means of restraining : a restraining force or influence (2) : a device that restricts movement ⟨a ∼ for children riding in cars⟩ **2** : a control over the expression of one's emotions or thoughts
re·strict \ri-'strikt\ *vt* [L *restrictus*, pp. of *restringere*] (1535) **1** : to confine within bounds : RESTRAIN **2** : to place under restrictions as to use or distribution *syn* see LIMIT
re·strict·ed *adj* (ca. 1828) **1** : subject or subjected to restriction: as **a** : not general : LIMITED ⟨the decision had a ∼ effect⟩ **b** : available to the use of particular groups or specif. excluding others ⟨a ∼ country club⟩ **c** : not intended for general circulation or release ⟨a ∼ document⟩ — **re·strict·ed·ly** *adv*
re·stric·tion \ri-'strik-shən\ *n* [ME *restriccioun*, fr. LL *restriction-*, *restrictio*, fr. L *restringere*] (15c) **1** : something that restricts: as **a** : a regulation that restricts or restrains ⟨∼s for hunters⟩ **b** : a limitation on the use or enjoyment of property or a facility **2** : an act of restricting : the condition of being restricted
restriction enzyme *n* (1965) : any of various enzymes that break DNA into fragments at specific sites in the interior of the molecule — called also *restriction endonuclease*
re·stric·tion·ism \-shə-,ni-zəm\ *n* (1937) : a policy or philosophy favoring restriction (as of trade or immigration) — **re·stric·tion·ist** \-sh(ə-)nist\ *adj or n*
re·stric·tive \ri-'strik-tiv\ *adj* (1579) **1 a** : of or relating to restriction **b** : serving or tending to restrict ⟨∼ regulations⟩ **2** : limiting the reference of a modified word or phrase **3** : prohibiting further negotiation — **restrictive** *n* — **re·stric·tive·ly** *adv* — **re·stric·tiveness** *n*
restrictive clause *n* (ca. 1895) : a descriptive clause that is essential to the definiteness of the word it modifies ⟨as *that you ordered* in "the book that you ordered is out of print"⟩
re·strike \(,)rē-'strik, 'rē-,\ *n* (1899) : a coin or medal struck from an original die at some time after the original issue
rest room *n* (1899) : a room or suite of rooms providing toilets and lavatories
re·struc·ture \(,)rē-'strək-chər\ *vt* (1942) : to change the makeup, organization, or pattern of ∼ *vi* : to restructure something
¹re·sult \ri-'zəlt\ *vi* [ME, fr. ML *resultare*, fr. L, to rebound, fr. *re-* + *saltare* to leap — more at SALTATION] (15c) **1 a** : to proceed or arise as a consequence, effect, or conclusion ⟨death ∼ed from the disease⟩ **b** : to have an issue or result ⟨the disease ∼ed in death⟩ **2** : REVERT 2
²result *n* (1647) **1** : something that results as a consequence, issue, or conclusion; *also* : beneficial or tangible effect : FRUIT **2** : something obtained by calculation or investigation — **re·sult·ful** \-fəl\ *adj* — **re·sult·less** \-ləs\ *adj*
¹re·sul·tant \ri-'zəl-t³nt\ *adj* (1639) : derived from or resulting from something else — **re·sul·tant·ly** *adv*
²resultant *n* (1815) : something that results : OUTCOME; *specif* : the single vector that is the sum of a given set of vectors
re·sume \ri-'züm\ *vb* **re·sumed; re·sum·ing** [ME, fr. MF or L; MF *resumer*, fr. L *resumere*, fr. *re-* + *sumere* to take up, take — more at CONSUME] *vt* (15c) **1** : to assume or take again : REOCCUPY ⟨*resumed* his seat by the fire —Thomas Hardy⟩ **2** : to return to or begin again after interruption ⟨*resumed* her work⟩ **3** : to take back to oneself **4** : to pick up again **5** : REITERATE, SUMMARIZE ∼ *vi* : to begin again something interrupted
ré·su·mé *or* **re·su·me** *or* **re·su·mé** \'re-zə-,mā, ,re-zə-' *also* 'rā- *or* ,rā-\ *n* [F *résumé*, fr. pp. of *résumer* to resume, summarize, fr. MF *resumer*] (1804) **1** : SUMMARY **2** : CURRICULUM VITAE
re·sump·tion \ri-'zəm(p)-shən\ *n* [ME, fr. MF or LL; MF *resomption*, fr. LL *resumption-*, *resumptio*, fr. L *resumere*] (15c) **1** : an act or instance of resuming : RECOMMENCEMENT **2** : a return to payment in specie
re·su·pi·nate \ri-'sü-pə-,nāt\ *adj* [L *resupinatus*, pp. of *resupinare* to bend back to a supine position, fr. *re-* + *supinus* supine] (ca. 1776) **1** : inverted in position ⟨∼ orchid flowers⟩ **2** : having or being a fruiting body lying flat on the substrate with the hymenium at the periphery or over the whole surface ⟨∼ fungi⟩ ⟨∼ sporophores⟩
re·sur·face \(,)rē-'sər-fəs\ *vt* (1894) : to provide with a new or fresh surface ∼ *vi* : to come again to the surface (as of the water); *broadly* : to appear or show up again — **re·sur·fac·er** \-fə-sər\ *n*
re·surge \ri-'sərj\ *vi* **re·surged; re·surg·ing** [L *resurgere*] (1575) : to undergo a resurgence
re·sur·gence \ri-'sər-jən(t)s\ *n* (ca. 1834) : a rising again into life, activity, or prominence : RENASCENCE

re·sur·gent \-jənt\ *adj* [L *resurgent-*, *resurgens*, prp. of *resurgere*] (1808) : undergoing or tending to produce resurgence
res·ur·rect \,re-zə-'rekt\ *vt* [back-formation fr. *resurrection*] (1772) **1** : to raise from the dead **2** : to bring to view, attention, or use again
res·ur·rec·tion \,re-zə-'rek-shən\ *n* [ME, fr. LL *resurrection-*, *resurrectio* act of rising from the dead, fr. *resurgere* to rise from the dead, fr. L, to rise again, fr. *re-* + *surgere* to rise — more at SURGE] (14c) **1 a** *cap* : the rising of Christ from the dead **b** *often cap* : the rising again to life of all the human dead before the final judgment **c** : the state of one risen from the dead **2** : RESURGENCE, REVIVAL **3** *Christian Science* : a spiritualization of thought : material belief that yields to spiritual understanding — **res·ur·rec·tion·al** \-shnəl, -shə-n³l\ *adj*
res·ur·rec·tion·ist \-sh(ə-)nist\ *n* (1776) **1** : BODY SNATCHER **2** : one who resurrects
re·sus·ci·tate \ri-'sə-sə-,tāt\ *vb* **-tat·ed; -tat·ing** [L *resuscitatus*, pp. of *resuscitare* to reawaken, fr. *re-* + *suscitare* to rouse, fr. *sub-*, *sus-* up + *citare* to put in motion, stir — more at SUB-, CITE] *vt* (1532) : to revive from apparent death or from unconsciousness; *also* : REVITALIZE ∼ *vi* : COME TO, REVIVE — **re·sus·ci·ta·tion** \ri-,sə-sə-'tā-shən, ,rē-\ *n* — **re·sus·ci·ta·tive** \ri-'sə-sə-,tā-tiv\ *adj*
re·sus·ci·ta·tor \ri-'sə-sə-,tā-tər\ *n* (ca. 1843) : one that resuscitates; *specif* : an apparatus used to restore respiration (as to a partially asphyxiated person)
ret \'ret\ *vb* **ret·ted; ret·ting** [ME, fr. MD] *vt* (14c) : to soak (as flax) to loosen the fiber from the woody tissue ∼ *vi* : to become retted
re·ta·ble \'rē-,tā-bəl, ri-'\ *n* [F, fr. MF, modif. of OProv *retaule*, alter. of *reretaule*, ultim. fr. L *retro-* + *tabula* board, tablet] (ca. 1823) : a raised shelf above an altar for the altar cross, the altar lights, and flowers
¹re·tail \'rē-,tāl, *esp for 2 also* ri-'tā(ə)l\ *vb* [ME, fr. MF *retaillier* to cut back, divide into pieces, fr. OF, fr. *re-* + *taillier* to cut — more at TAILOR] *vt* (15c) **1** : to sell in small quantities directly to the ultimate consumer **2** : TELL, RETELL ∼ *vi* : to sell at retail — **re·tail·er** *n*
²re·tail \'rē-,tāl\ *n* (15c) : the sale of commodities or goods in small quantities to ultimate consumers; *also* : the industry of such selling — **at retail 1** : at a retailer's price **2** : ⁴RETAIL
³re·tail \'rē-,tāl\ *adj* (1601) : of, relating to, or engaged in the sale of commodities at retail ⟨∼ trade⟩
⁴re·tail \'rē-,tāl\ *adv* (1784) : in small quantities : from a retailer
re·tail·ing \'rē-,tā-liŋ\ *n* (14c) : the activities involved in the selling of goods to ultimate consumers for personal or household consumption
re·tain \ri-'tān\ *vt* [ME *reteinen*, *retainen*, fr. MF *retenir*, fr. L *retinēre* to hold back, keep, restrain, fr. *re-* + *tenēre* to hold — more at THIN] (15c) **1 a** : to keep in possession or use **b** : to keep in one's pay or service; *specif* : to employ by paying a retainer **c** : to keep in mind or memory : REMEMBER **2** : to hold secure or intact *syn* see KEEP
retained object *n* (ca. 1904) : an object of a verb in the predicate of a passive construction (as *me* in "a book was given me" and *book* in "I was given a book")
¹re·tain·er \ri-'tā-nər\ *n* (1540) **1 a** : a person attached or owing service to a household; *esp* : SERVANT **b** : EMPLOYEE **2** : one that retains **3** : any of various devices used for holding something
²retainer *n* [ME *reteiner* act of withholding, fr. *reteinen* + AF *-er* (as in *weyver* waiver)] (1775) **1** : the act of a client by which the services of a lawyer, counselor, or adviser are engaged **2** : a fee paid to a lawyer or professional adviser for advice or services or for a claim on services when needed
¹re·take \(,)rē-'tāk\ *vt* **-took** \-'túk\; **-tak·en** \-'tā-kən\; **-tak·ing** (15c) **1** : to take or receive again **2** : RECAPTURE **3** : to photograph again
²re·take \'rē-,tāk\ *n* (1916) : a subsequent filming, photographing, or recording undertaken to improve upon the first; *also* : an instance of this
re·tal·i·ate \ri-'ta-lē-,āt\ *vb* **-at·ed; -at·ing** [LL *retaliatus*, pp. of *retaliare*, fr. L *re-* + *talio* legal retaliation] *vt* (1611) : to repay (as an injury) in kind ∼ *vi* : to return like for like; *esp* : to get revenge *syn* see RECIPROCATE — **re·tal·i·a·tion** \ri-,ta-lē-'ā-shən, ,rē-\ *n* — **re·tal·ia·tive** \ri-'ta-lē-,ā-tiv\ *adj* — **re·tal·i·a·to·ry** \-'tal-yə-,tōr-ē, -'ta-lē-ə-, -,tòr-\ *adj*
¹re·tard \ri-'tärd\ *vb* [ME, fr. MF or L; MF *retarder*, fr. L *retardare*, fr. *re-* + *tardus* slow] *vt* (15c) : to slow up esp. by preventing or hindering advance or accomplishment : IMPEDE **2** : to delay academic progress by failure to promote ∼ *vi* : to undergo retardation *syn* see DELAY — **re·tard·er** *n*
²re·tard \'rē-,tärd\ *n* (1788) **1** \ri-'tärd\ : a holding back or slowing down : RETARDATION **2** \'rē-,tärd\ : a retarded person; *also* : a person held to resemble a retarded person in behavior — often taken to be offensive
re·tar·dant \ri-'tär-d³nt\ *adj* (1642) : serving or tending to retard ⟨a growth-*retardant* substance⟩ — **retardant** *n*
re·tar·date \-'tär-,dāt, -dət\ *n* (1915) : a mentally retarded person
re·tar·da·tion \,rē-,tär-'dā-shən, ri-\ *n* (15c) **1** : an act or instance of retarding **2** : the extent to which something is retarded **3** : a musical suspension; *specif* : one that resolves upward **4 a** : an abnormal slowness of thought or action; *also* : less than normal intellectual competence usu. characterized by an IQ of less than 70 **b** : slowness in development or progress
re·tard·ed \ri-'tär-dəd\ *adj* (1895) : slow or limited in intellectual or emotional development or academic progress
retch \'rech, *esp Brit* 'rēch\ *vb* [(assumed) ME *rechen* to spit, retch, fr. OE *hrǣcan* to spit, hawk; akin to OE *hrǣkja* to spit] *vt* (ca. 1798) : VOMIT 1 ∼ *vi* : to make an effort to vomit; *also* : VOMIT — **retch** *n*
re·te \'rē-tē, 'rā-\ *n*, *pl* **re·tia** \'rē-tē-ə, 'rā-\ [NL, fr. L, net] (1541) : a network esp. of blood vessels or nerves : PLEXUS **2** : an anatomical part resembling or including a network
re·tell \(,)rē-'tel\ *vt* **-told** \-'tōld\; **-tell·ing** (1593) **1** : to tell again or in another form **2** : to count again
re·tell·ing *n* (1883) : a new version of a story ⟨a ∼ of a Greek legend⟩
re·ten·tion \ri-'ten(t)-shən\ *n* [ME *retencioun*, fr. L *retention-*, *retentio*,

\ə\ abut \³\ kitten, F table \ər\ further \a\ ash \ā\ ace \ä\ mop, mar
\aú\ out \ch\ chin \e\ bet \ē\ easy \g\ go \i\ hit \ī\ ice \j\ job
\ŋ\ sing \ō\ go \ò\ law \òi\ boy \th\ thin \th\ the \ü\ loot \ú\ foot
\y\ yet \zh\ vision \ä, k̲, ⁿ, œ, œ̄, ᴜᴇ, ᵫ, ᵛ\ *see* Guide to Pronunciation

fr. *retinēre* to retain — more at RETAIN] (14c) **1 a** : the act of retaining : the state of being retained **b** : abnormal retaining of a fluid or secretion in a body cavity **2 a** : power of retaining : RETENTIVENESS **b** : an ability to retain things in mind; *specif* : a preservation of the aftereffects of experience and learning that makes recall or recognition possible **3** : something retained

re·ten·tive \-'ten-tiv\ *adj* [ME *retentif*, fr. MF & ML; MF, fr. ML *retentivus*, fr. L *retentus*, pp. of *retinēre*] (14c) : having the power, property, or capacity of retaining (soils ~ of moisture); *esp* : retaining knowledge easily — **re·ten·tive·ly** *adv* — **re·ten·tive·ness** *n*

re·ten·tiv·i·ty \ˌrē-ˌten-'ti-və-tē, ri-\ *n* (1881) : the power of retaining; *specif* : the capacity for retaining magnetism after the action of the magnetizing force has ceased

re·think \(ˌ)rē-'thiŋk\ *vb* **-thought** \-'thȯt\; **-think·ing** *vt* (1700) : to think about again : RECONSIDER ~ *vi* : to engage in reconsideration — **re·think** \'rē-ˌthiŋk, -'thiŋk\ *n* — **re·think·er** *n*

ret·i·cence \'re-tə-sən(t)s\ *n* (1603) **1** : the quality or state of being reticent : RESERVE, RESTRAINT **2** : an instance of being reticent **3** : RELUCTANCE 1

ret·i·cen·cy \-sən(t)-sē\ *n, pl* **-cies** (1617) : RETICENCE

ret·i·cent \-sənt\ *adj* [L *reticent-, reticens*, prp. of *reticēre* to keep silent, fr. *re-* + *tacēre* to be silent — more at TACIT] (ca. 1834) **1** : inclined to be silent or uncommunicative in speech : RESERVED **2** : restrained in expression, presentation, or appearance (the room has an aspect of ~ dignity —A. N. Whitehead) **3** : RELUCTANT *syn* see SILENT — **ret·i·cent·ly** *adv*

ret·i·cle \'re-ti-kəl\ *n* [L *reticulum* network] (ca. 1731) : a scale on transparent material (as in an optical instrument) used esp. for measuring or aiming

re·tic·u·lar \ri-'ti-kyə-lər\ *adj* (1597) **1 a** : RETICULATE **b** : of, relating to, or forming a reticulum **2** : INTRICATE

reticular formation *n* (1887) : a mass of nerve cells and fibers situated primarily in the brain stem and functioning upon stimulation esp. in arousal of the organism

¹re·tic·u·late \-lət, -ˌlāt\ *adj* [L *reticulatus*, fr. *reticulum*] (1658) **1** : resembling a net; *esp* : having veins, fibers, or lines crossing (a ~ leaf) **2** : being or involving evolutionary change dependent on genetic recombination involving diverse interbreeding populations — **re·tic·u·late·ly** *adv*

²re·tic·u·late \-ˌlāt\ *vb* **-lat·ed; -lat·ing** [back-formation fr. *reticulated*, adj., reticulate] *vt* (1787) : to divide, mark, or construct so as to form a network ~ *vi* : to become reticulated

re·tic·u·la·tion \ri-ˌti-kyə-'lā-shən\ *n* (1671) : a reticulated formation : NETWORK; *also* : something reticulated

ret·i·cule \'re-ti-ˌkyü(ə)l\ *n* [F *réticule*, fr. L *reticulum* network, network bag, fr. dim. of *rete* net] (ca. 1738) **1** : RETICLE **2** : a woman's drawstring bag used esp. as a carryall

re·tic·u·lo·cyte \ri-'ti-kyə-lō-ˌsīt\ *n* [NL *reticulum* + ISV *-cyte*] (1922) : an immature red blood cell that appears esp. during regeneration of lost blood and has a fine basophilic reticulum formed of ribosomal remains

re·tic·u·lo·en·do·the·li·al \ri-ˌti-kyə-lō-ˌen-də-'thē-lē-əl\ *adj* [NL *reticulum* + *endothelium*] (ca. 1923) : of, relating to, or being the reticuloendothelial system

reticuloendothelial system *n* (ca. 1923) : a diffuse system of cells arising from mesenchyme and comprising all the phagocytic cells of the body except the circulating white blood cells

re·tic·u·lum \ri-'ti-kyə-ləm\ *n* [NL, fr. L, network] (ca. 1658) **1** : the second compartment of the stomach of a ruminant in which folds of the mucous membrane form hexagonal cells — compare ABOMASUM, OMASUM, RUMEN **2** : a reticular structure : NETWORK; *esp* : interstitial tissue composed of reticulum cells

reticulum cell *n* (1912) : one of the branched anastomosing reticuloendothelial cells that form an intricate interstitial network ramifying through other tissues and organs

retin- *or* **retino-** *comb form* [*retina*] **1** : retina (*retinitis*) (*retinoscopy*) **2** : retinal (*retinene*)

ret·i·na \'re-t²n-ə, 're-t-nə\ *n, pl* **retinas** *or* **ret·i·nae** \-t²n-ˌē, -ˌī\ [ME *rethina*, fr. ML *retina*, prob. fr. L *rete* net] (14c) : the sensory membrane that lines the eye, is composed of several layers including one containing the rods and cones, and functions as the immediate instrument of vision by receiving the image formed by the lens and converting it into chemical and nervous signals which reach the brain by way of the optic nerve — see EYE illustration

ret·i·nac·u·lum \ˌre-t²n-'a-kyə-ləm\ *n, pl* **-la** \-lə\ [NL, fr. L, halter, cable, fr. *retinēre* to hold back — more at RETAIN] (ca. 1825) : a small structure on the forewings of many lepidopterous insects (as a noctuid moth) that catches and holds the frenulum

¹ret·i·nal \'re-t²n-əl, 're-t-nəl\ *adj* (1838) : of, relating to, involving, or being a retina

²ret·i·nal \'re-t²n-ˌal, -ˌôl\ *n* [*retin-* + ³-*al*] (1944) : a yellowish to orange aldehyde $C_{20}H_{28}O$ derived from vitamin A that in combination with proteins forms the visual pigments of the retinal rods and cones

ret·i·nene \'re-t²n-ˌēn\ *n* (1934) : RETINAL

ret·i·ni·tis \ˌre-t²n-'ī-təs\ *n* [NL] (1861) : inflammation of the retina

retinitis pig·men·to·sa \-ˌpig-mən-'tō-sə, -(ˌ)men-, -zə\ *n* [NL, pigmented retinitis] (1861) : any of several hereditary progressive degenerative diseases of the eye marked by night blindness in the early stages, atrophy and pigment changes in the retina, constriction of the visual field, and eventual blindness

ret·i·no·blas·to·ma \ˌre-t²n-ō-ˌblas-'tō-mə\ *n* [*retin-* + *blast-* + -*oma*] (1924) : a malignant tumor of the retina that develops during childhood, is derived from retinal germ cells, and is associated with a chromosomal abnormality

ret·i·no·ic acid \ˌre-t²n-'ō-ik-\ *n* (1965) : an acid $C_{20}H_{28}O_2$ derived from vitamin A and used esp. in the treatment of acne

ret·i·noid \'re-t²n-ˌȯid\ *n* (1976) : any of various synthetic or naturally occurring analogues of vitamin A

ret·i·nol \'re-t²n-ˌȯl, -ˌôl\ *n* [*retin-* + ¹-*ol*; fr. its being the source of retinal] (1960) : the chief and typical vitamin A

ret·i·nop·a·thy \ˌre-t²n-'ä-pə-thē\ *n* (1932) : any of various noninflammatory disorders of the retina including some that cause blindness

ret·i·nos·co·py \ˌre-t²n-'äs-kə-pē\ *n* (1884) : observation of the retina of the eye esp. to determine the state of refraction

---

ret·i·no·tec·tal \ˌre-t²n-ō-'tek-təl\ *adj* [*retin-* + *tectum* + ¹-*al*] (1951) : of, relating to, or being the nerve fibers connecting the retina and the tectum of the midbrain (~ pathways)

ret·i·nue \'re-t²n-ˌü, -ˌyü\ *n* [ME *retenue*, fr. MF, fr. fem. of *retenu*, pp. of *retenir* to retain] (14c) : a group of retainers or attendants

re·tin·u·la \re-'tin-yə-lə\ *n, pl* **-lae** \-ˌlē, -ˌlī\ *also* **-las** [NL, dim. of ML *retina*] (1878) : the neural receptor of a single facet of an arthropod compound eye — **re·tin·u·lar** \-lər\ *adj*

re·tir·ant \ri-'tī-rənt\ *n* (1948) : RETIREE

re·tire \ri-'tīr\ *vb* **re·tired; re·tir·ing** [MF *retirer*, fr. *re-* + *tirer* to draw] *vi* (1533) **1** : to withdraw from action or danger : RETREAT **2** : to withdraw esp. for privacy **3** : to move back : RECEDE **4** : to withdraw from one's position or occupation : conclude one's working or professional career **5** : to go to bed ~ *vt* **1** : WITHDRAW: as **a** : to march (a military force) away from the enemy **b** : to withdraw from circulation or from the market : RECALL **c** : to withdraw from usual use or service **2** : to cause to retire from one's position or occupation **3 a** : to put out (a batter or batsman) in baseball or cricket **b** : to cause (a side) to end a turn at bat in baseball **4** : to win permanent possession of (as a trophy)

re·tired \ri-'tīrd\ *adj* (1590) **1** : SECLUDED (~ village) **2** : withdrawn from one's position or occupation : having concluded one's working or professional career **3** : received by or due to one in retirement — **re·tired·ly** \-'tī-rəd-lē, -'tīrd-\ *adv* — **re·tired·ness** \-'tīrd-nəs\ *n*

re·tir·ee \ri-ˌtī-'rē\ *n* (1945) : a person who has retired from a working or professional career

¹re·tire·ment \ri-'tīr-mənt\ *n* (1596) **1 a** : an act of retiring : the state of being retired **b** : withdrawal from one's position or occupation or from active working life **c** : the age at which one normally retires (reaches ~ in May) **2** : a place of seclusion or privacy

²retirement *adj* (1919) : of, relating to, or designed for retired persons

re·tir·ing \ri-'tīr-iŋ\ *adj* (1766) : RESERVED, SHY — **re·tir·ing·ly** \-iŋ-lē\ *adv* — **re·tir·ing·ness** *n*

re·tool \(ˌ)rē-'tül\ *vt* (1927) **1** : to reequip with tools **2** : REORGANIZE

¹re·tort \ri-'tȯrt\ *vb* [L *retortus*, pp. of *retorquēre*, lit., to twist back, hurl back, fr. *re-* + *torquēre* to twist — more at TORTURE] *vt* (1557) **1** : to pay or hurl back : RETURN (~ an insult) **2 a** : to make a reply to **b** : to say in reply **3** : to answer (as an argument) by a counter argument ~ *vi* **1** : to answer back usu. sharply **2** : to return an argument or charge **3** : RETALIATE *syn* see ANSWER

²retort *n* (1600) **1** : a quick, witty, or cutting reply; *esp* : one that turns back or counters the first speaker's words

³re·tort \ri-'tȯrt, 'rē-ˌ\ *n* [MF *retorte*, fr. ML *retorta*, fr. L, fem. of *retortus*; fr. its shape] (1605) : a vessel or chamber in which substances are distilled or decomposed by heat

⁴re·tort \ri-'tȯrt, 'rē-\ *vt* (1850) : to treat (as oil shale) by heating in a retort

retort pouch \ri-'tȯrt-, 'rē-\ *n* (1977) : a flexible package in which prepared food is hermetically sealed for long-term unrefrigerated storage

¹re·touch \(ˌ)rē-'təch\ *vb* [F *retoucher*, fr. MF, fr. *re-* + *toucher* to touch] *vt* (1685) **1** : to rework in order to improve : TOUCH UP **2** : to alter (as a photographic negative) to produce a more desirable appearance **3** : to color (new growth of hair) to match previously dyed, tinted, or bleached hair ~ *vi* : to make or give retouches — **re·touch·er** *n*

²re·touch \'rē-ˌtəch, (ˌ)rē-'\ *n* (1703) : the act, process, or an instance of retouching; *esp* : the retouching of a new growth of hair

retort

re·tract \ri-'trakt\ *vb* [ME, fr. L *retractus*, pp. of *retrahere* — more at RETREAT] *vt* (15c) **1** : to draw back or in (cats ~ their claws) **2 a** : TAKE BACK, WITHDRAW (~ a confession) **b** : DISAVOW ~ *vi* **1** : to draw or pull back **2** : to recant or disavow something *syn* see ABJURE, RECEDE — **re·tract·able** \-'trak-tə-bəl\ *adj*

re·trac·tile \ri-'trak-t²l, -ˌtīl\ *adj* (1777) : capable of being drawn back or in (~ claws) — **re·trac·til·i·ty** \ˌrē-ˌtrak-'ti-lə-tē, ri-\ *n*

re·trac·tion \ri-'trak-shən\ *n* (14c) **1** : an act of recanting; *specif* : a statement made by one retracting **2** : an act of retracting : the state of being retracted **3** : the ability to retract

re·trac·tor \ri-'trak-tər\ *n* (1837) : one that retracts: as **a** : a surgical instrument for holding open the edges of a wound **b** : a muscle that draws in an organ or part

re·train \(ˌ)rē-'trān\ *vt* (1918) : to train again or anew ~ *vi* : to become trained again — **re·train·able** \-'trā-nə-bəl\ *adj*

re·tral \'rē-trəl, 're-\ *adj* [L *retro* back — more at RETRO-] (1875) **1** : situated at or toward the back : POSTERIOR **2** : BACKWARD, RETROGRADE — **re·tral·ly** \-trə-lē\ *adv*

re·trans·late \ˌrē-tran(t)s-'lāt, -tranz-\ *vt* (1860) : to translate (a translation) into another language; *also* : to give a new form to ~ *vi* : to retranslate something — **re·trans·la·tion** \-'lā-shən\ *n*

¹re·tread \(ˌ)rē-'tred\ *vt* **re·tread·ed; re·tread·ing** (1907) **1** : to bond or vulcanize a new tread to the prepared surface of (a worn tire) **2** : to make over as if new (~ an old plot)

²re·tread \'rē-ˌtred\ *n* (1914) **1** : a retreaded tire **2** : something made or done again esp. in slightly revised form : REMAKE **3 a** : one (as a retired person) who is retrained for work **b** : one (as an athlete) who has previously held the same or a similar position

re—tread \(ˌ)rē-'tred\ *vt* **-trod** \-'träd\; **-trod·den** \-'trä-d²n\ *or* **-trod; -tread·ing** (1598) : to tread again

¹re·treat \ri-'trēt\ *n* [ME *retret*, fr. MF *retrait*, fr. pp. of *retraire* to withdraw, fr. L *retrahere*, fr. *re-* + *trahere* to draw] (14c) **1 a** (1) : an act or process of withdrawing esp. from what is difficult, dangerous, or disagreeable (2) : the process of receding from a position or state attained (the ~ of a glacier) (the slow ~ of an epidemic) **b** (1) : the usu. forced withdrawal of troops from an enemy or from an advanced position (2) : a signal for retreating **c** (1) : a signal given by bugle at the beginning of a military flag-lowering ceremony (2) : a military flag-lowering ceremony **2** : a place of privacy or safety : REFUGE **3** : a period of group withdrawal for prayer, meditation, study, and instruction under a director

²retreat *vi* (15c) **1 :** to make a retreat : WITHDRAW **2 :** to slope backward ~ *vt* : to draw or lead back : REMOVE; *specif* : to move (a piece) back in chess **syn** see RECEDE — **re•treat•er** *n*

re•treat•ant \-'trē-t²nt\ *n* (1880) : a person on a religious retreat

re•trench \ri-'trench\ *vb* [obs. F *retrencher* (now *rancher*), fr. MF *retrenchier*, fr. re- + *trenchier* to cut] *vt* (1625) **1 a :** CUT DOWN, REDUCE **b :** to cut out : EXCISE **2 :** to pare away : REMOVE ~ *vi* : to make retrenchments; *specif* : ECONOMIZE **syn** see SHORTEN

re•trench•ment \-mənt\ *n* (ca. 1600) : REDUCTION, CURTAILMENT; *specif* : a cutting of expenses

re•tri•al \(¸)rē-'trī(-ə)l\ *n* (1875) : a second trial, experiment, or test; *specif* : a second judicial trial

ret•ri•bu•tion \¸re-trə-'byü-shən\ *n* [ME *retribucioun*, fr. MF *retribution*, fr. LL *retribution-, retributio*, fr. L *retribuere* to pay back, fr. re- + *tribuere* to pay — more at TRIBUTE] (14c) **1 :** RECOMPENSE, REWARD **2 :** the dispensing or receiving of reward or punishment esp. in the hereafter **3 :** something given or exacted in recompense; *esp* : PUNISHMENT

re•trib•u•tive \ri-'tri-byə-tiv\ *adj* (1678) : of, relating to, or marked by retribution — **re•trib•u•tive•ly** *adv*

re•trib•u•to•ry \-byə-¸tȯr-ē, -¸tȯr-\ *adj* (ca. 1615) : RETRIBUTIVE

re•triev•al \ri-'trē-vəl\ *n* (ca. 1643) **1 :** an act or process of retrieving **2 :** possibility of being retrieved or of recovering ⟨beyond ~⟩

¹re•trieve \ri-'trēv\ *vb* **re•trieved; re•triev•ing** [ME *retreven*, modif. of MF *retrouver* to find again, fr. re- + *trouver* to find, fr. (assumed) VL *tropare* to find, compose — more at TROUBADOUR] *vt* (15c) **1 :** to discover and bring in (killed or wounded game) **2 :** to call to mind again **3 :** to get back again : REGAIN **4 a :** RESCUE, SALVAGE **b :** to return (as a ball or shuttlecock that is difficult to reach) successfully **5 :** RESTORE, REVIVE ⟨his writing ~s the past⟩ **6 :** to remedy the evil consequences of : CORRECT **7 :** to get and bring back; *esp* : to recover (as information) from storage ~ *vi* : to bring in game ⟨a dog that ~s well⟩; *also* : to bring back an object thrown by a person — **re•triev•abil•i•ty** \-¸trē-və-'bi-lə-tē\ *n* — **re•triev•able** \-'trē-və-bəl\ *adj*

²retrieve *n* (1575) **1 :** RETRIEVAL **2 :** the successful return of a ball that is difficult to reach or control (as in tennis)

re•triev•er \ri-'trē-vər\ *n* (15c) : one that retrieves; *esp* : a dog of any of several breeds (as a golden retriever) having a heavy water-resistant coat and used esp. for retrieving game

ret•ro \'re-(¸)trō\ *adj* [F *rétro*, short for *rétrospectif* retrospective] (1974) : relating to, reviving, or being the styles or esp. the fashions of the past : fashionably nostalgic or old-fashioned ⟨a ~ look⟩

retro- *prefix* [ME, fr. L, fr. *retro*, fr. re- + *-tro* (as in *intro* within) — more at INTRO-] **1 :** backward : back ⟨*retro*-rocket⟩ **2 :** situated behind ⟨*retro*peritoneal⟩

ret•ro•ac•tion \¸re-trō-'ak-shən\ *n* (ca. 1738) **1** [*retroactive*] : retroactive operation (as of a law or tax) **2** [*retro*- + *action*] : a reciprocal action : REACTION

ret•ro•ac•tive \-'ak-tiv\ *adj* [F *rétroactif*, fr. L *retroactus*, pp. of *retroagere* to drive back, reverse, fr. *retro*- + *agere* to drive — more at AGENT] (1611) : extending in scope or effect to a prior time or to conditions that existed or originated in the past; *esp* : made effective on a date prior to enactment, promulgation, or imposition ⟨~ tax⟩ — **ret•ro•ac•tive•ly** *adv*

ret•ro•cede \¸re-trō-'sēd\ *vb* **-ced•ed; -ced•ing** [L *retrocedere*, fr. *retro*- + *cedere* to go, cede] *vi* (1654) : to go back : RECEDE ~ *vt* [F *rétrocéder*, fr. ML *retrocedere*, fr. L *retro*- + *cedere* to cede] : to cede back (as a territory) — **ret•ro•ces•sion** \-'se-shən\ *n*

ret•ro•dict \¸re-trə-'dikt\ *vt* [*retro*- + *predict*] (1949) : to utilize present information or ideas to infer or explain (a past event or state of affairs) ⟨~ past eclipses⟩ — **ret•ro•dic•tion** \-'dik-shən\ *n* — **ret•ro•dic•tive** \-'dik-tiv\ *adj*

ret•ro•en•gine \'re-trō-¸en-jən\ *n* (1965) : RETRO-ROCKET

ret•ro•fire \-¸fīr\ *vt* (1961) : to cause (a retro-rocket) to become ignited ~ *vi*, of a retro-rocket : to become ignited — **retrofire** *n*

ret•ro•fit \¸re-trō-'fit\ *vt* (1953) **1 :** to furnish (as a computer, airplane, or building) with new or modified parts or equipment not available or considered necessary at the time of manufacture **2 :** to install (new or modified parts or equipment) in something previously manufactured or constructed — **retrofit** *n*

ret•ro•flex \'re-trə-¸fleks\ *adj* [NL *retroflexus*, fr. L *retro*- + *flexus*, pp. of *flectere* to bend] (1776) **1 :** turned or bent abruptly backward **2 :** articulated with the tongue tip turned up or curled back just under the hard palate ⟨~ vowel⟩

ret•ro•flex•ion or **ret•ro•flec•tion** \¸re-trə-'flek-shən\ *n* (1845) **1 :** the state of being bent back; *esp* : the bending back of an organ (as a uterus) upon itself **2 :** the act or process of bending back **3 :** retroflex articulation

ret•ro•gra•da•tion \¸re-trō-grā-'dā-shən, -grə-\ *n* (ca. 1545) : the action or process of retrograding

¹ret•ro•grade \'re-trə-¸grād\ *adj* [ME, fr. L *retrogradus*, fr. *retrogradi*] (14c) **1 a** (1) of a celestial body : having a direction contrary to that of the general motion of similar bodies (2) : having or being a direction of rotation or revolution that is clockwise as viewed from the north pole of the sky or a planet **b :** moving, occurring, or performed in a backward direction or opposite to the usual direction ⟨a ~ step⟩ ⟨~ peristalsis⟩ **c :** contrary to the normal order : INVERSE **2 :** tending toward or resulting in a worse or previous state **3** *archaic* : CONTRADICTORY, OPPOSED **4 :** characterized by retrogression **5 :** affecting a period prior to a precipitating cause ⟨~ amnesia⟩ **6 :** RETRO — **ret•ro•grade•ly** *adv*

²retrograde *adv* (ca. 1619) : BACKWARD, REVERSELY

³retrograde *vb* [L *retrogradi*, fr. *retro*- + *gradi* to go — more at GRADE] *vt* (1582) *archaic* : to turn back : REVERSE ~ *vi* **1 a :** to go back : RETREAT **b :** to go back over or recapitulate something **2 :** to decline to a worse condition

ret•ro•gress \¸re-trə-'gres\ *vi* [L *retrogressus*, pp. of *retrogradi*] (1819) : to move backward : REVERT

ret•ro•gres•sion \-'gre-shən\ *n* (1646) **1 :** REGRESSION **3 2 :** return to a former and less complex level of development or organization

ret•ro•gres•sive \-'gre-siv\ *adj* (1802) : characterized by retrogression: as **a :** going or directed backward **b :** declining from a better to a worse state **c :** passing from a higher to a lower level of organization ⟨~ evolution⟩ — **ret•ro•gres•sive•ly** *adv*

ret•ro•pack \'re-trō-¸pak\ *n* (1962) : a system of auxiliary rockets on a spacecraft that produces thrust in the direction opposite to the motion of the spacecraft and that is used to reduce speed

ret•ro•per•i•to•ne•al \¸re-trō-¸per-ə-t²n-'ē-əl\ *adj* (1874) : situated behind the peritoneum — **ret•ro•per•i•to•ne•al•ly** \-ə-lē\ *adv*

ret•ro•re•flec•tion \¸re-trō-ri-'flek-shən\ *n* (ca. 1965) : the action or use of a retroreflector — **ret•ro•re•flec•tive** \-'flek-tiv\ *adj*

ret•ro•re•flec•tor \-'flek-tər\ *n* (1946) : a device that reflects radiation (as light) so that the paths of the rays are parallel to those of the incident rays

ret•ro•rock•et \'re-trō-¸rä-kət\ *n* (1957) : an auxiliary rocket engine (as on a spacecraft) used in decelerating

re•trorse \'rē-¸trȯrs\ *adj* [L *retrorsus*, contr. of *retroversus*] (ca. 1825) : bent backward or downward

¹ret•ro•spect \'re-trə-¸spekt\ *n* [prob. fr. *retro*- + *prospect*] (1602) **1** *archaic* : reference to or regard of a precedent or authority **2 :** a review of or meditation on past events — **in retrospect :** in considering the past or a past event

²retrospect *adj* (1709) : RETROSPECTIVE

³retrospect *vi* (1659) **1 :** to engage in retrospection **2 :** to refer back : REFLECT ~ *vt* : to go back over in thought

ret•ro•spec•tion \¸re-trə-'spek-shən\ *n* (1674) : the act or process or an instance of surveying the past

¹ret•ro•spec•tive \-'spek-tiv\ *adj* (1664) **1 a** (1) : of, relating to, or given to retrospection (2) : based on memory ⟨a ~ report⟩ **b :** being a retrospective ⟨a ~ exhibition⟩ **2 :** affecting things past : RETROACTIVE — **ret•ro•spec•tive•ly** *adv*

²retrospective *n* (1932) : a generally comprehensive exhibition or performance of the work of an artist over a span of years

re•trous•sé \rə-¸trü-'sā, rə-'trü-¸, ¸re-trü-'\ *adj* [F, fr. pp. of *retrousser* to tuck up, fr. MF, fr. re- + *trousser* to truss, tuck up — more at TRUSS] (1802) : turned up ⟨~ nose⟩

ret•ro•ver•sion \¸re-trō-'vər-zhən *also* -shən\ *n* [L *retroversus* turned backward, fr. *retro*- + *versus*, pp. of *vertere* to turn — more at WORTH] (1776) **1 :** the bending backward of the uterus and cervix **2 :** the act or process of turning back or regressing

ret•ro•vi•rus \'re-trō-¸vī-rəs\ *n* (1975) : any of a group of RNA-containing viruses (as HIV) that produce reverse transcriptase by means of which DNA is produced using their RNA as a template and incorporated into the genome of infected cells and that include numerous tumorigenic viruses — **ret•ro•vi•ral** \-rəl\ *adj*

ret•si•na \ret-'sē-nə\ *n* [NGk, perh. fr. It *resina* resin, fr. L — more at RESIN] (1940) : a resin-flavored Greek wine

¹re•turn \ri-'tərn\ *vb* [ME *retournen*, fr. MF *retourner*, fr. re- + *tourner* to turn — more at TURN] *vi* (14c) **1 a :** to go back or come back again ⟨~ home⟩ **b :** to go back in thought or practice : REVERT ⟨soon ~ed to her old habit⟩ **2 :** to pass back to an earlier possessor **3 :** REPLY, RETORT ~ *vt* **1 :** to give (as an official account) to a superior **b** *Brit* : to elect (a candidate) as attested by official report or returns **c :** to bring back (as a writ or verdict) to an office or tribunal **2 a :** to bring, send, or put back to a former or proper place ⟨~ the gun to its holster⟩ **b :** to restore to a former or to a normal state **3 a :** to send back : VISIT — usu. used with *on* or *upon* **b** *obs* : RETORT **4 :** to bring in (as profit) : YIELD **5 a :** to give or perform in return : REPAY ⟨~ a compliment⟩ **b :** to give back to the owner **c :** REFLECT ⟨~ an echo⟩ **6 :** to cause (as a wall) to continue in a different direction (as at a right angle) **7 :** to lead (a specified suit or specified card of a suit) in response to a partner's earlier lead **8 a :** to hit back (a ball or shuttlecock) **b :** to run with (a football) after a change of possession (as by a punt or a fumble) **syn** see RECIPROCATE — **re•turn•er** *n*

²return *n* (14c) **1 a :** the act of coming back to or from a place or condition **b :** a regular or frequent returning : RECURRENCE **2 a** (1) : the delivery of a legal order (as a writ) to the proper officer or court (2) : an endorsed certificate stating an official's action in the execution of such an order (3) : the sending back of a commission with the certificate of the commissioners **b :** an account or formal report **c** (1) : a report of the results of balloting — usu. used in pl. ⟨election ~s⟩ (2) : an official declaration of the election of a candidate (3) *chiefly Brit* : ELECTION **d** (1) : a formal statement on a required legal form showing taxable income, allowable deductions and exemptions, and the computation of the tax due (2) : a list of taxable property **3 a** : the continuation usu. at a right angle of the face or of a member of a building or of a molding or group of moldings **b :** a turn, bend, or winding back (as in a rod, stream, or trench) **c :** a means for conveying something (as water) back to its starting point **4 a :** a quantity of goods, consignment, or cargo coming back in exchange for goods sent out as a mercantile venture **b :** the value of or profit from such venture **c** (1) : the profit from labor, investment, or business : YIELD (2) *pl* : RESULTS **d** : the rate of profit in a process of production per unit of cost **5 a** : the act of returning something to a former place, condition, or ownership : RESTITUTION **b** : something returned; *esp*, *pl* : unsold publications returned to the publisher for cash or credit **6 a** : something given in repayment or reciprocation **b** : ANSWER, RETORT **7 :** an answering play: as **a :** a lead in a suit previously led by one's partner in a card game **b :** the action or an instance of returning a ball (as in football or tennis) — **in return :** in compensation or repayment

³return *adj* (1676) **1 a :** having or formed by a change of direction ⟨a ~ facade⟩ **b :** doubled on itself ⟨a ~ flue⟩ **2 :** played, delivered, or given in return : taking place for the second time ⟨a ~ meeting for the two champions⟩ **3 :** used or taken on returning ⟨the ~ road⟩ **4 :** returning or permitting return ⟨a ~ valve⟩ **5 :** of, relating to, or causing a return to a place or condition

¹re•turn•able \ri-'tər-nə-bəl\ *adj* (15c) **1 :** legally required to be returned, delivered, or argued at a specified time or place ⟨a writ ~ on the date indicated⟩ **2 a :** capable of returning or of being returned (as for reuse) **b :** permitted to be returned

---

\ə\ abut \²\ kitten, F table \ər\ further \a\ ash \ā\ ace \ä\ mop, mar \aú\ out \ch\ chin \e\ bet \ē\ easy \g\ go \i\ hit \ī\ ice \j\ job \ŋ\ sing \ō\ go \ò\ law \òi\ boy \th\ thin \th\ the \ü\ loot \ù\ foot \y\ yet \zh\ vision \à, ᴋ, ⁿ, œ, œ̄, ᴜᴇ, ūᴇ, ᵛ\ see Guide to Pronunciation

²**returnable** n (1963) : something designed to be returned (as for recycling); esp : a returnable beverage container

re·turn·ee \ri-,tər-'nē\ n (1944) : one who returns; esp : one returning to the U.S. after military service overseas

re·tuse \ri-'tüs, -'tyüs\ adj [L retusus blunted, fr. pp. of retundere to pound back, blunt, fr. re- + tundere to beat, pound — more at CONTUSION] (ca. 1753) : having the apex rounded or obtuse with a slight notch

¹**Reu·ben** \'rü-bən\ n [Heb Rĕ'ūbhēn] : a son of Jacob and the traditional eponymous ancestor of one of the tribes of Israel

²**Reuben** n [prob. fr. Reuben Kulakofsky †1960 Am. grocer] (1956) : a grilled sandwich of corned beef, Swiss cheese, and sauerkraut usu. on rye bread

³**Reuben** n [Reuben L. Goldberg †1970 Am. cartoonist] (1958) : a statuette awarded annually by a professional organization for notable achievement in cartoon artistry

re·union \(,)rē-'yün\ n (1610) 1 : an act of reuniting : the state of being reunited 2 : a reuniting of persons after separation

re·union·ist \-yə-nist\ n (1866) : an advocate of reunion (as of sects or parties) — **re·union·is·tic** \(,)rē-,yün-yə-'nis-tik\ adj

re·unite \,rē-yü-'nīt\ vb [ML reunitus, pp. of reunire, fr. L re- + LL unire to unite — more at UNITE] vt (15c) : to bring together again ~ vi : to come together again : REJOIN

re-up \(,)rē-'əp\ vi [re- + sign up] (ca. 1906) : to enlist again

re·us·able \(,)rē-'yü-zə-bəl\ adj (1943) : capable of being used again or repeatedly — **re·us·abil·i·ty** \(,)rē-,yü-zə-'bi-lə-tē\ n

¹**re·use** \(,)rē-'yüz\ vt (1843) : to use again esp. after reclaiming or reprocessing (the need to ~ scarce resources)

²**reuse** \-'yüs\ n (1866) : further or repeated use

¹**rev** \'rev\ n [short for revolution] (ca. 1890) : a revolution of a motor

²**rev** vb **revved**; **rev·ving** vt (1920) 1 a : to step up the number of revolutions per minute of — often used with up (~ up the engine) b : INCREASE — used with up (~ up production) 2 : to drive or operate esp. at high speed — often used with up 3 : to make more active or effective — used with up 4 : to stir up : EXCITE — usu. used with up ~ vi 1 : to operate at an increased speed of revolution — usu. used with up 2 : to increase in amount or activity — used with up

re·val·u·ate \(,)rē-'val-yə-,wāt\ vt [back-formation fr. revaluation] (1921) : REVALUE; specif : to increase the value of (as currency) — **re·val·u·a·tion** \(,)rē-,val-yə-'wā-shən\ n

re·val·ue \(,)rē-'val-(,)yü\ vt (1592) 1 : to value (as currency) anew 2 : to make a new valuation of : REAPPRAISE

re·vamp \(,)rē-'vamp\ vt (1850) 1 : REMAKE, REVISE 2 : RENOVATE, RECONSTRUCT — **re·vamp** \'rē-, ri-'\ n

re·vanche \rə-'vänsh\ n [F, fr. MF, alter. of revenche — more at REVENGE] (1882) : REVENGE; esp : a usu. political policy designed to recover lost territory or status — **re·vanch·ism** \-'vän-,shi-zəm\ n

¹**re·vanch·ist** \-'vän-shist\ n (1926) : one who advocates a policy of revanche

²**revanchist** adj (1948) : of or relating to a policy of revanche

re·vas·cu·lar·i·za·tion \,rē-,vas-kyə-lə-rə-'zā-shən\ n (1951) : a surgical procedure for the provision of a new, additional, or augmented blood supply to a body part or organ

¹**re·veal** \ri-'vē(ə)l\ vt [ME revelen, fr. MF reveler, fr. L revelare to uncover, reveal, fr. re- + velare to cover, veil, fr. velum veil] (14c) 1 : to make known through divine inspiration 2 : to make (something secret or hidden) publicly or generally known (~ a secret) 3 : to open up to view : DISPLAY (the uncurtained window ~ed a cluttered room) — **re·veal·able** \-'vē-lə-bəl\ adj — **re·veal·er** n
syn REVEAL, DISCLOSE, DIVULGE, TELL, BETRAY mean to make known what has been or should be concealed. REVEAL may apply to supernatural or inspired revelation of truths beyond the range of ordinary human vision or reason (divine will as revealed in sacred writings). DISCLOSE may imply a discovering but more often an imparting of information previously kept secret (candidates must disclose their financial assets). DIVULGE implies a disclosure involving some impropriety or breach of confidence (refused to divulge an anonymous source). TELL implies an imparting of necessary or useful information (told them what he had overheard). BETRAY implies a divulging that represents a breach of faith or an involuntary or unconscious disclosure (a blush that betrayed her).

²**reveal** n [alter. of earlier revale, fr. ME revalen to lower, fr. MF revaler, fr. re- + val valley — more at VALE] (1688) : the side of an opening (as for a window) between a frame and the outer surface of a wall; also : JAMB

re·veal·ing adj (ca. 1925) : allowing a look at or an understanding of something inner or hidden : INSIGHTFUL — **re·veal·ing·ly** adv

re·veal·ment \ri-'vē(ə)l-mənt\ n (1584) : an act of revealing

re·veg·e·tate \(,)rē-'ve-jə-,tāt\ vt (1804) : to provide (barren or denuded land) with a new vegetative cover — **re·veg·e·ta·tion** \(,)rē-,ve-jə-'tā-shən\ n

rev·eil·le \'re-və-lē, Brit ri-'va-li or -'ve-\ n [modif. of F réveillez, imper. pl. of réveiller to awaken, fr. MF reveiller, fr. re- + eveiller to awaken, fr. (assumed) VL exvigilare, fr. L ex- + vigilare to keep watch, stay awake — more at VIGILANT] (1644) 1 : a signal to get up mornings 2 : a bugle call at about sunrise signaling the first military formation of the day; also : the formation so signaled

¹**rev·el** \'re-vəl\ vi -eled or -elled; -el·ing or -el·ling \'re-və-liŋ, 'rev-liŋ\ [ME, fr. MF reveler, lit., to rebel, fr. L rebellare] (14c) 1 : to take part in a revel : CAROUSE 2 : to take intense pleasure or satisfaction

²**revel** n (14c) : a usu. wild party or celebration

rev·e·la·tion \,re-və-'lā-shən\ n [ME, fr. MF, fr. LL revelation-, revelatio, fr. L revelare to reveal] (14c) 1 a : an act of revealing or communicating divine truth b : something that is revealed by God to humans 2 a : an act of revealing to view or making known b : something that is revealed; esp : an enlightening or astonishing disclosure (shocking ~s) c : a pleasant often enlightening surprise (her talent was a ~) 3 cap : an apocalyptic writing addressed to early Christians of Asia Minor and included as a book in the New Testament — called also Apocalypse; see BIBLE table

Rev·e·la·tions \-shənz\ n pl but sing in constr : REVELATION 3

rev·e·la·tor \'re-və-,lā-tər\ n (1801) : one that reveals; esp : one that reveals the will of God

re·ve·la·to·ry \'re-və-lə-,tōr-ē, -,tōr-, ri-'ve-lə-\ adj (1882) : of or relating to revelation : serving to reveal something

rev·el·er or **rev·el·ler** \'re-və-lər, 'rev-lər\ n (14c) : one who engages in revelry

rev·el·ry \'re-vəl-rē\ n (15c) : noisy partying or merrymaking

rev·e·nant \'re-və-,nän, -nənt\ n [F, fr. prp. of revenir to return] (1827) : one that returns after death or a long absence — **revenant** adj

¹**re·venge** \ri-'venj\ vt **re·venged**; **re·veng·ing** [ME, fr. MF revengier, fr. OF, fr. re- + vengier to avenge — more at VENGEANCE] (14c) 1 : to avenge (as oneself) 2 : to inflict injury in return for (~ an insult) — **re·veng·er** n

²**revenge** n [MF revenge, revenche, fr. revengier, revenchier to revenge] (ca. 1547) 1 : a desire for revenge 2 : an act or instance of retaliating in order to get even 3 : an opportunity for getting satisfaction

re·venge·ful \ri-'venj-fəl\ adj (ca. 1586) : full of or prone to revenge : determined to get even — **re·venge·ful·ly** \-fə-lē\ adv — **re·venge·ful·ness** n

rev·e·nue \'re-və-,nü, -,nyü\ n, often attrib [ME, fr. MF, fr. revenir to return, fr. L revenire, fr. re- + venire to come — more at COME] (15c) 1 : the total income produced by a given source (a property expected to yield a large annual ~) 2 : the gross income returned by an investment 3 : the yield of sources of income (as taxes) that a political unit (as a nation or state) collects and receives into the treasury for public use 4 : a government department concerned with the collection of the national revenue

revenue bond n (1856) : a bond issued by a public agency authorized to build, acquire, or improve a revenue-producing property (as a toll road) and payable out of revenue derived from such property

rev·e·nu·er \'re-və-,nü-ər, -,nyü-\ n (1880) : a revenue officer or boat

revenue stamp n (1862) : a stamp (as on a cigar box) for use as evidence of payment of a tax

revenue tariff n (1820) : a tariff intended wholly or primarily to produce public revenue — compare PROTECTIVE TARIFF

re·verb \ri-'vərb, 'rē-,\ n [short for reverberation] (1953) : an electronically produced echo effect in recorded music; also : a device for producing reverb

re·ver·ber·ant \ri-'vər-b(ə-)rənt\ adj (ca. 1798) 1 : tending to reverberate 2 : marked by reverberation : RESONANT — **re·ver·ber·ant·ly** adv

¹**re·ver·ber·ate** \-bə-,rāt\ vb -at·ed; -at·ing [L reverberatus, pp. of reverberare, fr. re- + verberare to lash, fr. verber rod — more at VERVAIN] vt (15c) 1 : REFLECT 2 : REPEL 3 : ECHO ~ vi 1 a : to become driven back b : to become reflected 2 : to continue in or as if in a series of echoes : RESOUND

²**re·ver·ber·ate** \-b(ə-)rət\ adj (1603) : REVERBERANT

re·ver·ber·a·tion \ri-,vər-bə-'rā-shən\ n (14c) 1 : an act of reverberating : the state of being reverberated 2 a : something that is reverberated b : an effect or impact that resembles an echo

re·ver·ber·a·tive \ri-'vər-bə-,rā-tiv, -b(ə-)rə-\ adj (1716) 1 : constituting reverberation 2 : tending to reverberate

re·ver·ber·a·to·ry \ri-'vər-b(ə-)rə-,tōr-ē, -bə-,tōr-, -,tòr-\ adj (1605) : acting by reverberation

reverberatory furnace n (1672) : a furnace in which heat is radiated from the roof onto the material treated

¹**re·vere** \ri-'vir\ vt **re·vered**; **re·ver·ing** [L revereri, fr. re- + vereri to fear, respect — more at WARY] (ca. 1661) : to show devoted deferential honor to : regard as worthy of great honor (~ the aged) (~ tradition)
syn REVERE, REVERENCE, VENERATE, WORSHIP, ADORE mean to honor and admire profoundly and respectfully. REVERE stresses deference and tenderness of feeling (a professor revered by generations of students). REVERENCE presupposes an intrinsic merit and inviolability in the one honored and a corresponding depth of feeling in the one honoring (reverenced the academy's code of honor). VENERATE implies a holding as holy or sacrosanct because of character, association, or age (heroes still venerated). WORSHIP implies homage usu. expressed in words or ceremony (worships their memory). ADORE implies love and stresses the notion of an individual and personal attachment (a doctor adored by her patients).

²**revere** n [by alter.] (ca. 1934) : REVERS

¹**rev·er·ence** \'rev-rən(t)s, 're-və-; 're-vərn(t)s\ n (14c) 1 : honor or respect felt or shown : DEFERENCE; esp : profound adoring awed respect 2 : a gesture of respect (as a bow) 3 : the state of being revered 4 : one held in reverence — used as a title for a clergyman syn see HONOR

²**reverence** vt -enced; -enc·ing (14c) : to regard or treat with reverence syn see REVERE — **rev·er·enc·er** n

¹**rev·er·end** \'rev-rənd, 're-və-; 're-vərnd\ adj [ME, fr. MF, fr. L reverendus, gerundive of revereri] (15c) 1 : worthy of reverence : REVERED 2 a : of or relating to the clergy b : being a member of the clergy — used as a title (the Reverend Mr. Doe) (the Reverend John Doe) (the Reverend Mrs. Jane Doe)

²**reverend** n (1608) : a member of the clergy — sometimes used in pl. as a title

rev·er·ent \'rev-rənt, 're-və-; 're-vərnt\ adj [ME, fr. L reverent-, reverens, prp. of revereri] (14c) : expressing or characterized by reverence : WORSHIPFUL — **rev·er·ent·ly** adv

rev·er·en·tial \,re-və-'ren(t)-shəl\ adj (ca. 1555) 1 : expressing or having a quality of reverence (~ awe) 2 : inspiring reverence — **rev·er·en·tial·ly** \-'ren(t)-sh(ə-)lē\ adv

rev·er·ie also **re·very** \'re-və-rē, 're-vrē\ n, pl rev·er·ies [F rêverie, fr. MF, delirium, fr. resver, rever to wander, be delirious] (1657) 1 : DAYDREAM 2 : the condition of being lost in thought

re·vers \ri-'vir, -'ver\ n, pl re·vers \-'virz, -'verz\ [F, lit., reverse, fr. MF, fr. revers, adj.] (1869) : a lapel esp. on a woman's garment

re·ver·sal \ri-'vər-səl\ n (15c) 1 : an act or the process of reversing 2 : a conversion of a photographic positive into a negative or vice versa 3 : a change of fortune usu. for the worse

¹**re·verse** \ri-'vərs\ adj [ME revers, fr. MF, fr. L reversus, pp. of revertere to turn back — more at REVERT] (14c) 1 a : opposite or contrary to a previous or normal condition (~ order) b : having the back presented to the observer or opponent 2 : coming from the rear of a military force 3 : acting, operating, or arranged in a manner contrary to the usual 4 : effecting reverse movement (~ gear) 5 : so made

that the part which normally prints in color appears white against a colored background — **re·verse·ly** adv

²reverse vb **re·versed; re·vers·ing** vt (14c) **1 a :** to turn completely about in position or direction **b :** to turn upside down **:** INVERT **2 :** ANNUL: as **a :** to overthrow, set aside, or make void (a legal decision) by a contrary decision **b :** to cause to take an opposite point of view **c :** to change to the contrary ⟨~ a policy⟩ **3 :** to cause to go in the opposite direction; esp **:** to cause (as an engine) to perform its action in the opposite direction ~ vi **1 :** to turn or move in the opposite direction **2 :** to put a mechanism (as an engine) in reverse — **re·vers·er** n — **reverse field :** to make a sudden reversal in direction or opinion **syn** REVERSE, TRANSPOSE, INVERT mean to change to the opposite position. REVERSE is the most general term and may imply change in order, side, direction, meaning ⟨reversed his position on the trade agreement⟩. TRANSPOSE implies a change in order or relative position of units often through exchange of position ⟨transposed the letters to form an anagram⟩. INVERT applies chiefly to turning upside down or inside out ⟨a stamp with an inverted picture of an airplane⟩.

³reverse n (14c) **1 :** something directly contrary to something else **:** OPPOSITE **2 :** an act or instance of reversing; esp **:** DEFEAT, SETBACK **3 :** the back part of something **4 a** (1) **:** a gear that reverses something; also **:** the whole mechanism brought into play when such a gear is used (2) **:** movement in reverse **b :** an offensive play in football in which a back moving in one direction gives the ball to a player moving in the opposite direction — **in reverse :** in an opposite manner or direction

reverse discrimination n (1969) **:** discrimination against whites or males (as in employment or education)

reverse osmosis n (1955) **:** the movement of fresh water through a semipermeable membrane when pressure is applied to a solution (as seawater) on one side of it

reverse tran·scrip·tase \-ˌtran-ˈskrip-(ˌ)tās, -(ˌ)tāz\ n (1971) **:** a polymerase that catalyzes the formation of DNA using RNA as a template and that is found esp. in retroviruses

reverse transcription n (1971) **:** the process of synthesizing double-stranded DNA using RNA as a template and reverse transcriptase as a catalyst

¹re·vers·ible \ri-ˈvər-sə-bəl\ adj (1648) **:** capable of being reversed or of reversing: as **a :** capable of going through a series of actions (as changes) either backward or forward ⟨a ~ chemical reaction⟩ **b :** having two finished usable sides ⟨~ fabric⟩ **c :** wearable with either side out ⟨a ~ coat⟩ — **re·vers·ibil·i·ty** \-ˌvər-sə-ˈbi-lə-tē\ n — **re·vers·ibly** \-ˈvər-sə-blē\ adv

²reversible n (1863) **:** a reversible cloth or article of clothing

re·ver·sion \ri-ˈvər-zhən, -shən\ n [ME, fr. MF, fr. L reversion-, reversio act of returning, fr. revertere] (15c) **1 a :** the part of a simple estate remaining in the control of its owner after the owner has granted therefrom a lesser particular estate **b :** a future interest in property left in the control of a grantor or the grantor's successor **2 :** the right of succession or future possession or enjoyment **3 a :** an act or the process of returning (as to a former condition) **b :** a return toward an ancestral type or condition **:** reappearance of an ancestral character **4 :** an act or instance of turning the opposite way **:** the state of being so turned **5 :** a product of reversion; specif **:** an organism with an atavistic character **:** THROWBACK

re·ver·sion·al \-ˈvərzh-nəl, -ˈvərsh-; -ˈvər-zhə-nᵊl, -shə-\ adj (1675) **:** REVERSIONARY

re·ver·sion·ary \-ˈvər-zhə-ˌner-ē, -shə-\ adj (1720) **:** of, relating to, constituting, or involving esp. a legal reversion

re·ver·sion·er \-ˈvərzh-nər, -ˈvərsh-; -ˈvər-zhə-nər, -shə-\ n (1614) **:** one that has or is entitled to a reversion; broadly **:** one having a vested right to a future estate

re·vert \ri-ˈvərt\ vi [ME, fr. MF revertir, fr. L revertere, v.t., to turn back & reverti, v.i., to return, come back, fr. re- + vertere, verti to turn — more at WORTH] (15c) **1 :** to come or go back (as to a former condition, period, or subject) **2 :** to return to the proprietor or his heirs at the end of a reversion **3 :** to return to an ancestral type — **re·vert·er** n — **re·vert·ible** \-ˈvər-tə-bəl\ adj

re·ver·tant \ri-ˈvər-tᵊnt\ n (1955) **:** a mutant gene, individual, or strain that regains a former capability (as the production of a particular protein) by undergoing further mutation ⟨yeast ~s⟩ — **revertant** adj

re·vest \(ˌ)rē-ˈvest\ vt (1561) **:** REINSTATE, REINVEST

re·vet \ri-ˈvet\ vt **re·vet·ted; re·vet·ting** [F revêtir, lit., to clothe again, dress up, fr. L revestire, fr. re- + vestire to clothe — more at VEST] (1812) **:** to face (as an embankment) with a revetment

re·vet·ment \-ˈvet-mənt\ n (1779) **1 :** a facing (as of stone or concrete) to sustain an embankment **2 :** EMBANKMENT; esp **:** a barricade to provide shelter (as against bomb fragments or strafing)

¹re·view \ri-ˈvyü\ n [ME, fr. MF reveue, fr. revoir to look over, fr. re- + voir to see — more at VIEW] (15c) **1 a :** a formal military inspection **b :** a military ceremony honoring a person or an event **2 :** REVISION 1a **3 :** a general survey (as of the events of a period) **4 :** an act or the process of reviewing **5 :** judicial reexamination (as of the proceedings of a lower tribunal by a higher) **6 a :** a critical evaluation (as of a book or play) **b :** a magazine devoted chiefly to reviews and essays **7 a :** a retrospective view or survey (as of one's life) **b** (1) **:** renewed study of material previously studied (2) **:** an exercise facilitating such study **8 :** REVUE

²re·view \ri-ˈvyü, 1 is also ˈrē-\ vb [in senses 1 & 2, fr. re- + view; in other senses, fr. ¹review] vt (1576) **1 :** to view or see again **2 :** to examine or study again; esp **:** to reexamine judicially **3 :** to look back on **:** take a retrospective view of **4 a :** to go over or examine critically or deliberately ⟨~ed the results of the study⟩ **b :** to give a critical evaluation of ⟨~ a novel⟩ **5 :** to hold a review of ⟨~ troops⟩ ~ vi **1 :** to study material again **:** make a review ⟨~ for a test⟩ **2 :** to write reviews — **re·view·able** \ri-ˈvyü-ə-bəl\ adj

re·view·er \ri-ˈvyü-ər\ n (1651) **:** one that reviews; esp **:** a writer of critical reviews

re·vile \ri-ˈvī(ə)l\ vb **re·viled; re·vil·ing** [ME, fr. MF reviler to despise, fr. re- + vil vile] vt (14c) **:** to subject to verbal abuse **:** VITUPERATE ~ vi **:** to use abusive language **:** RAIL **syn** see SCOLD — **re·vile·ment** \-ˈvī(ə)l-mənt\ n — **re·vil·er** n

re·vis·al \ri-ˈvī-zəl\ n (1612) **:** an act of revising **:** REVISION

¹re·vise \ˈrē-ˌvīz, ri-ˈ\ n (1591) **1 :** an act of revising **:** REVISION **2 :** a printing proof that incorporates changes marked in a previous proof

²re·vise \ri-ˈvīz\ vb **re·vised; re·vis·ing** [MF reviser, fr. L revisere to look at again, freq. of revidēre to see again, fr. re- + vidēre to see — more at WIT] vt (1596) **1 a :** to look over again in order to correct or improve ⟨~ a manuscript⟩ **b** Brit **:** to study again **:** REVIEW **2 a :** to make a new, amended, improved, or up-to-date version of ⟨~ a dictionary⟩ **b :** to provide with a new taxonomic arrangement ⟨revising the alpine ferns⟩ ~ vi, Brit **:** REVIEW 1 **syn** see CORRECT — **re·vis·able** \-ˈvī-zə-bəl\ adj — **re·vis·er** or **re·vi·sor** \-ˈvī-zər\ n

Revised Standard Version n (1946) **:** a revision of the American Standard Version of the Bible published in 1946 and 1952

Revised Version n (1880) **:** a British revision of the Authorized Version of the Bible published in 1881 and 1885

re·vi·sion \ri-ˈvi-zhən\ n (1611) **1 a :** an act of revising **b :** a result of revising **:** ALTERATION **2 :** a revised version — **re·vi·sion·ary** \-zhə-ˌner-ē\ adj

re·vi·sion·ism \ri-ˈvi-zhə-ˌni-zəm\ n (1903) **1 :** a movement in revolutionary Marxian socialism favoring an evolutionary rather than a revolutionary spirit **2 :** advocacy of revision (as of a doctrine or policy or in historical analysis) — **re·vi·sion·ist** \-nist\ n or adj

¹re·vis·it \(ˌ)rē-ˈvi-zət\ vt (15c) **:** to visit again **:** return to ⟨~ the old neighborhood⟩; also **:** to consider or take up again ⟨reluctant to ~ past disputes⟩

²revisit n (1623) **:** a second or subsequent visit

re·vi·so·ry \ri-ˈvī-zə-rē, -ˈvīz-rē\ adj (ca. 1841) **:** having the power or purpose to revise ⟨a ~ committee⟩ ⟨a ~ function⟩

re·vi·tal·ise Brit var of REVITALIZE

re·vi·tal·ize \(ˌ)rē-ˈvī-tᵊl-ˌīz\ vt **-ized; -iz·ing** (1869) **:** to give new life or vigor to — **re·vi·tal·i·za·tion** \(ˌ)rē-ˌvī-tᵊl-ə-ˈzā-shən\ n

re·viv·al \ri-ˈvī-vəl\ n (1651) **1 :** an act or instance of reviving **:** the state of being revived: as **a :** renewed attention to or interest in something **b :** a new presentation or publication of something old **c** (1) **:** a period of renewed religious interest (2) **:** an often highly emotional evangelistic meeting or series of meetings **2 :** restoration of force, validity, or effect (as to a contract)

re·viv·al·ism \-ˈvī-və-ˌli-zəm\ n (1815) **1 :** the spirit or methods characteristic of religious revivals **2 :** a tendency or desire to revive or restore

re·viv·al·ist \-ˈvī-və-list, -ˈvīv-list\ n (1820) **1 :** one who conducts religious revivals; specif **:** a clergyman who travels about to conduct revivals **2 :** one who revives or restores something disused — **reviv·alist** adj — **re·viv·al·is·tic** \-ˌvī-və-ˈlis-tik\ adj

re·vive \ri-ˈvīv\ vb **re·vived; re·viv·ing** [ME, fr. MF revivre, fr. L revivere to live again, fr. re- + vivere to live — more at QUICK] vi (15c) **:** to return to consciousness or life **:** become active or flourishing again ~ vt **1 :** to restore to consciousness or life **2 :** to restore from a depressed, inactive, or unused state **:** bring back **3 :** to renew in the mind or memory — **re·viv·able** \-ˈvī-və-bəl\ adj — **re·viv·er** n

re·viv·i·fy \rē-ˈvi-və-ˌfī\ vt [F révivifier, fr. LL revivificare, fr. L re- + LL vivificare to vivify] (1675) **:** to give new life to **:** REVIVE — **re·viv·i·fi·ca·tion** \-ˌvi-və-fə-ˈkā-shən\ n

re·vi·vis·cence \ˌrē-ˌvi-və-ˈvi-sᵊn(t)s, ri-\ n [L reviviscere to come to life again, fr. re- + viviscere to come to life, fr. vivus alive, living — more at QUICK] (1626) **:** an act of reviving **:** the state of being revived — **re·vivis·cent** \-sᵊnt\ adj

rev·o·ca·ble \ˈre-və-kə-bəl also ri-ˈvō-\ also **re·vok·able** \ri-ˈvō-kə-bəl\ adj [ME, fr. MF, fr. L revocabilis, fr. revocare] (15c) **:** capable of being revoked

rev·o·ca·tion \ˌre-və-ˈkā-shən; ri-ˌvō-, ˌrē-\ n [ME, fr. MF, fr. L revocation-, revocatio, fr. revocare] (15c) **:** an act or instance of revoking

¹re·voke \ri-ˈvōk\ vb **re·voked; re·vok·ing** [ME, fr. MF revoquer, fr. L revocare, fr. re- + vocare to call, fr. voc-, vox voice — more at VOICE] vt (14c) **1 :** to annul by recalling or taking back **:** RESCIND ⟨~ a will⟩ **2 :** to bring or call back ~ vi **:** to fail to follow suit when able in a card game in violation of the rules — **re·vok·er** n

²revoke n (1709) **:** an act or instance of revoking in a card game

¹re·volt \ri-ˈvōlt also -ˈvòlt\ vb [MF revolter, fr. OIt rivoltare to overthrow, fr. (assumed) VL revolvitare, freq. of L revolvere to revolve, roll back] vi (1539) **1 :** to renounce allegiance or subjection (as to a government) **:** REBEL **2 a :** to experience disgust or shock **b :** to turn away with disgust ~ vt **:** to cause to turn away or shrink with disgust or abhorrence — **re·volt·er** n

²revolt n (1560) **1 :** a renouncing of allegiance (as to a government or party); esp **:** a determined armed uprising **2 :** a movement or expression of vigorous dissent **syn** see REBELLION

re·volt·ing adj (1806) **:** extremely offensive — **re·volt·ing·ly** adv

re·vo·lute \ˈre-və-ˌlüt\ adj [L revolutus, pp. of revolvere] (ca. 1753) **:** rolled backward or downward ⟨a leaf with ~ margins⟩

rev·o·lu·tion \ˌre-və-ˈlü-shən\ n [ME revolucioun, fr. MF revolution, fr. LL revolution-, revolutio, fr. L revolvere to revolve] (14c) **1 a** (1) **:** the action by a celestial body of going round in an orbit or elliptical course; also **:** apparent movement of such a body round the earth (2) **:** the time taken by a celestial body to make a complete round in its orbit (3) **:** the rotation of a celestial body on its axis **b :** completion of a course (as of years); also **:** the period made by the regular succession of a measure of time or by a succession of similar events **c** (1) **:** a progressive motion of a body round an axis so that any line of the body parallel to the axis returns to its initial position while remaining parallel to the axis in transit and usu. at a constant distance from it (2) **:** motion of any figure about a center or axis ⟨~ of a right triangle about one of its legs generates a cone⟩ (3) **:** ROTATION 1b **2 a :** a sudden, radical, or complete change **b :** a fundamental change in political organization; esp **:** the overthrow or renunciation of one government or ruler and the substitution of another by the governed **c :** activity or movement designed to effect fundamental changes in the socioeconomic situation **d :** a fundamental change in the way of

\ə\ abut \ᵊ\ kitten, F table \ər\ further \a\ ash \ā\ ace \ä\ mop, mar \au̇\ out \ch\ chin \e\ bet \ē\ easy \g\ go \i\ hit \ī\ ice \j\ job \ŋ\ sing \ō\ go \ȯ\ law \ȯi\ boy \th\ thin \t͟h\ the \ü\ loot \u̇\ foot \y\ yet \zh\ vision \à, ḵ, ⁿ, œ, œ̄, ue, ūe, ᵊ\ see Guide to Pronunciation thinking about or visualizing something : a change of paradigm ⟨the Copernican ∼⟩ **e** : a changeover in use or preference esp. in technology ⟨the computer ∼⟩ ⟨the foreign car ∼⟩ *syn* see REBELLION

¹**rev·o·lu·tion·ary** \-shə-,ner-ē\ *adj* (1774) **1 a** : of, relating to, or constituting a revolution ⟨∼ war⟩ **b** : tending to or promoting revolution ⟨a ∼ party⟩ **c** : constituting or bringing about a major or fundamental change ⟨∼ styling⟩ ⟨a ∼ new product⟩ **2** *cap* : of or relating to the American Revolution or to the period in which it occurred — **rev·o·lu·tion·ar·i·ly** \-,lü-shə-'ner-ə-lē\ *adv* — **rev·o·lu·tion·ar·i·ness** \-'lü-shə-,ner-ē-nəs\ *n*

²**revolutionary** *n, pl* **-ar·ies** (1850) **1** : one engaged in a revolution **2** : an advocate or adherent of revolutionary doctrines

rev·o·lu·tion·ise *Brit var of* REVOLUTIONIZE

rev·o·lu·tion·ist \,re-və-'lü-sh(ə-)nist\ *n* (1710) : REVOLUTIONARY — **revolutionist** *adj*

rev·o·lu·tion·ize \-shə-,nīz\ *vb* **-ized; -iz·ing** *vt* (1797) **1** : to overthrow the established government of **2** : to imbue with revolutionary doctrines **3** : to change fundamentally or completely ∼ *vi* : to engage in revolution — **rev·o·lu·tion·iz·er** *n*

re·volve \ri-'välv, -'võlv *also* -'väv *or* -'võv\ *vb* **re·volved; re·volv·ing** [ME, fr. L *revolvere* to roll back, cause to return, fr. *re-* + *volvere* to roll — more at VOLUBLE] *vt* (15c) **1** : to turn over at length in the mind : PONDER ⟨∼ a scheme⟩ **2 a** *obs* : to cause to go round in an orbit : ROTATE 1 ∼ *vi* **1** : RECUR 2 **a** : to ponder something **b** : to remain under consideration ⟨ideas *revolved* in his mind⟩ **3 a** : to move in a curved path round a center or axis **b** : to turn or roll round on an axis **4** : to come to a main or central point : CENTER ⟨the dispute *revolved* around wages⟩ — **re·volv·able** \-'väl-və-bəl, -'võl- *also* -'vä-və- *or* -'võ-və-\ *adj*

re·volv·er \ri-'väl-vər, -'võl- *also* -'vä-vər *or* -'võ-vər\ *n* (ca. 1835) **1** : one that revolves **2** : a handgun with a cylinder of several chambers brought successively into line with the barrel and discharged with the same hammer

revolving *adj* (1599) **1** : tending to revolve or recur; *esp* : recurrently available **2** : turning around on or as if on an axis ⟨a ∼ platform⟩

revolving charge account *n* (1967) : a charge account under which payment is made in monthly installments and includes a carrying charge

revolving credit *n* (1919) : a credit which may be used repeatedly up to the limit specified after partial or total repayments have been made

revolving-door *adj* (1973) : characterized by a frequently repeated cycle of leaving and returning ⟨∼ governments⟩

revolving fund *n* (1920) : a fund set up for specified purposes with the proviso that repayments to the fund may be used again for these purposes

re·vue \ri-'vyü\ *n* [F, fr. MF *reveue* review — more at REVIEW] (1872) : a theatrical production consisting typically of brief loosely connected often satirical skits, songs, and dances

re·vulsed \ri-'vəlst\ *adj* [L *revulsus,* pp. of *revellere* + E *-ed*] (ca. 1934) : affected with or having undergone revulsion

re·vul·sion \ri-'vəl-shən\ *n* [L *revulsion-, revulsio* act of tearing away, fr. *revellere* to pluck away, fr. *re-* + *vellere* to pluck — more at VULNERABLE] (1609) **1** : a strong pulling or drawing away : WITHDRAWAL **2 a** : a sudden or strong reaction or change **b** : a sense of utter distaste or repugnance — **re·vul·sive** \-'vəl-siv\ *adj*

revved *past and past part of* REV

revving *pres part of* REV

re·wake \(,)rē-'wāk\ *vb* **-waked** *or* **-woke** \-'wōk\; **-waked** *or* **-wo·ken** \-'wō-kən\ *or* **-woke; -wak·ing** *vt* (1593) : to waken again or anew ∼ *vi* : to become awake again

re·wak·en \(,)rē-'wā-kən\ *vb* (1638) : REWAKE

¹**re·ward** \ri-'wȯrd\ *vt* [ME, fr. ONF *rewarder* to regard, reward, fr. *re-* + *warder* to watch, guard, of Gmc origin; akin to OHG *wartēn* to watch — more at WARD] (14c) **1** : to give a reward to or for **2** : RECOMPENSE — **re·ward·able** \-'wȯr-də-bəl\ *adj* — **re·ward·er** *n*

²**reward** *n* (14c) **1** : something that is given in return for good or evil done or received and esp. that is offered or given for some service or attainment **2** : a stimulus administered to an organism following a correct or desired response that increases the probability of occurrence of the response

re·ward·ing *adj* (1697) **1** : yielding or likely to yield a reward : VALUABLE, SATISFYING ⟨∼ experience⟩ **2** : serving as a reward ⟨a ∼ smile of thanks⟩ — **re·ward·ing·ly** *adv*

¹**re·wind** \(,)rē-'wīnd\ *vt* **-wound** \-'waùnd\; **-wind·ing** (1717) : to wind again; *esp* : to reverse the winding of (as film)

²**re·wind** \'rē-,wind, (,)rē-'\ *n* (1926) **1** : something that rewinds or is rewound **2** : an act of rewinding

re·word \(,)rē-'wərd\ *vt* (1602) **1** : to repeat in the same words **2** : to alter the wording of; *also* : to restate in other words

re·work \(,)rē-'wərk\ *vt* (1842) : to work again or anew: as **a** : REVISE **b** : to reprocess (as used material) for further use

¹**re·write** \(,)rē-'rīt\ *vb* **-wrote** \-'rōt\; **-writ·ten** \-'ri-t³n\; **-writ·ing** \-'rī-tiŋ\ *vt* (1567) **1** : to write in reply **2** : to make a revision of (as a story) : cause to be revised: as **a** : to put (contributed material) into form for publication **b** : to alter (previously published material) for use in another publication ∼ *vi* : to revise something previously written — **re·writ·er** *n*

²**re·write** \'rē-,rīt\ *n* (1914) **1** : a piece of writing (as a news story) constructed by rewriting **2** : an act or instance of rewriting

re·write man \'rē-,rīt-,man\ *n* (1901) : a newspaperman who specializes in rewriting

re·write rule \'rē-,rīt-\ *n* (1961) : a rule in a grammar which specifies the constituents of a single symbol

rex \'reks\ *n, pl* **rex·es** *or* **rex** [modif. of F *castorrex, castorex,* a variety of rabbit, perh. fr. L *castor* beaver + *rex* king — more at CASTOR, ROYAL] (1920) : an animal (as a domestic rabbit) showing a genetic recessive variation in which the guard hairs are very short or entirely

rex

lacking; *esp* : any of the slender domestic cats having a short curly undercoat and no guard hairs and belonging to either of two breeds

Reye's syndrome \'rīz-, 'rāz-\ *n* [R.D.K. *Reye* †1977 Austral. pathologist] (1965) : an often fatal encephalopathy esp. of childhood characterized by fever, vomiting, fatty infiltration of the liver, and swelling of the kidneys and brain — called also *Reye syndrome*

rey·nard \'rā-nərd, 're-, -,när(d)\ *n, often cap* [ME *Renard,* name of the fox who is hero of the Fr. beast epic *Roman de Renart,* fr. MF *Renart, Renard*] (14c) : FOX

Rey·nolds number \'re-n³ldz-\ *n* [Osborne *Reynolds* †1912 Eng. physicist] (1910) : a number characteristic of the flow of a fluid in a pipe or past an obstruction

R factor \'är-\ *n* [resistance] (1962) : a group of genes present in some bacteria that provide a basis for resistance to antibiotics and can be transferred from cell to cell by conjugation

Rh \,är-'āch\ *adj* (1940) : of, relating to, or being an Rh factor ⟨∼ antigens⟩ ⟨∼ sensitization in pregnancy⟩

rhabdo- *comb form* [LGk, fr. Gk *rhabdos* rod — more at VERVAIN] : rodlike structure ⟨*rhabdo*virus⟩

rhab·do·coele \'rab-də-,sēl\ *n* [NL *Rhabdocoela,* fr. *rhabdo-* + NL *-coela -coele*] (ca. 1909) : a turbellarian worm (order Rhabdocoela) with an unbranched intestine

rhab·dom \'rab-,däm, -dəm\ *or* **rhab·dome** \-,dōm\ *n* [NL, fr. LGk *rhabdōma* bundle of rods, fr. Gk *rhabdos* rod] (1878) : one of the minute rodlike structures in the retinulae in the compound eyes of arthropods

rhab·do·man·cy \'rab-də-,man(t)-sē\ *n* [LGk *rhabdomanteia,* fr. Gk *rhabdos* rod + *-manteia* -mancy] (1646) : divination by rods or wands — **rhab·do·man·cer** \-,man(t)-sər\ *n*

rhab·do·mere \-,mir\ *n* (ca. 1884) : a division of a rhabdom

rhab·do·myo·sar·co·ma \'rab-(,)dō-,mī-ə-sär-'kō-mə\ *n, pl* **-mas** *or* **-ma·ta** \-mə-tə\ [NL, fr. *rhabdo-* + *myo-* + *sarcoma*] (1898) : a malignant tumor composed of striated muscle fibers

rhab·do·vi·rus \-,vī-rəs\ *n* [NL] (1966) : any of a group of RNA-containing rod- or bullet-shaped viruses found in plants and animals and including the causative agents of rabies and vesicular stomatitis

rhad·a·man·thine \,ra-də-'man(t)-thən, -'man(t)-,thīn\ *adj, often cap* [*Rhadamanthus*] (1840) : rigorously strict or just

Rhad·a·man·thus \,ra-də-'man(t)-thəs\ *n* : a judge of the underworld in Greek mythology

Rhae·to-Ro·mance \,rē-tō-rō-'man(t)s, -tō-rə-; -'rō-,man(t)s\ *adj* **Rhae·to-Ro·man·ic** \-rō-'ma-nik\ *n* [L *Rhaetus* of Rhaetia, ancient Roman province] (1867) : a group of Romance languages spoken in eastern Switzerland and northeastern Italy

rham·nose \'ram-,nōs, -,nōz\ *n* [ISV, fr. NL *Rhamnus,* genus of the buckthorn; fr. its being produced from a plant of this genus] (1888) : a crystalline sugar $C_6H_{12}O_5$ that occurs usu. in the form of a glycoside in many plants and is obtained in the common dextrorotatory L form

rhap·sode \'rap-,sōd\ *n* [F, fr. Gk *rhapsōidos*] (1834) : RHAPSODIST

rhap·sod·ic \rap-'sä-dik\ *also* **rhap·sod·i·cal** \-di-kəl\ *adj* (1782) **1** : extravagantly emotional : RAPTUROUS **2** : resembling or characteristic of a rhapsody — **rhap·sod·i·cal·ly** \-di-k(ə-)lē\ *adv*

rhap·so·dist \'rap-sə-dist\ *n* (ca. 1656) **1** : a professional reciter of epic poems **2** : one who writes or speaks rhapsodically

rhap·so·dize \-sə-,dīz\ *vi* **-dized; -diz·ing** (1806) : to speak or write in a rhapsodic manner ⟨∼ about a new book⟩

rhap·so·dy \'rap-sə-dē\ *n, pl* **-dies** [L *rhapsodia,* fr. Gk *rhapsōidia* recitation of selections from epic poetry, rhapsody, fr. *rhapsōidos* rhapsodist, fr. *rhaptein* to sew, stitch together + *aidein* to sing — more at ODE] (1542) **1** : a portion of an epic poem adapted for recitation **2** *archaic* : a miscellaneous collection **3 a** (1) : a highly emotional utterance (2) : a highly emotional literary work (3) : effusively rapturous or extravagant discourse **b** : RAPTURE, ECSTASY **4** : a musical composition of irregular form having an improvisatory character

rhat·a·ny \'ra-t³n-ē\ *n* [Sp *ratania* & Pg *ratânhia*] (1808) **1** : the dried root of either of two So. American shrubs (*Krameria triandra* and *K. argentea* of the family Krameriaceae) used as an astringent **2** : a plant yielding rhatany

rhea \'rē-ə\ *n* [NL, genus of birds, prob. fr. L *Rhea,* mother of Zeus, fr. Gk] (1797) : either of two So. American ratite birds (*Rhea americana* and *Pterocnemia pennata* of the family Rheidae) that resemble but are smaller than the African ostrich and that have three toes, a fully feathered head and neck, an undeveloped tail, and pale gray to brownish feathers that droop over the rump and back

rhe·bok \'rē-,bäk\ *n* [Afrik *reebok,* fr. D, male roe deer, fr. *ree* roe + *boc* buck] (1834) : a brownish gray antelope (*Pelea capreolus*) of southern Africa

rhe·ni·um \'rē-nē-əm\ *n* [NL, fr. L *Rhenus* Rhine River] (1925) : a rare heavy metallic element that resembles manganese, is obtained either as a powder or as a silver-white hard metal, and is used in catalysts and thermocouples — see ELEMENT table

rheo- *comb form* [Gk *rhein* to flow — more at STREAM] : flow : current ⟨*rheo*stat⟩

rhe·ol·o·gy \rē-'ä-lə-jē\ *n* [ISV] (1929) : a science dealing with the deformation and flow of matter; *also* : the ability to flow or be deformed — **rhe·o·log·i·cal** \,rē-ə-'lä-ji-kəl\ *adj* — **rhe·o·log·i·cal·ly** \-k(ə-)lē\ *adv* — **rhe·ol·o·gist** \rē-'ä-lə-jist\ *n*

rhe·om·e·ter \rē-'ä-mə-tər\ *n* [ISV] (ca. 1859) : an instrument for measuring flow (as of viscous substances)

rheo·stat \'rē-ə-,stat\ *n* (1843) : a resistor for regulating a current by means of variable resistances — **rheo·stat·ic** \,rē-ə-'sta-tik\ *adj*

rhe·sus monkey \'rē-səs-\ *n* [NL *Rhesus,* genus of monkeys, fr. L, a mythical king of Thrace, fr. Gk *Rhēsos*] (1841) : a pale brown Asian macaque (*Macaca mulatta*) often used in medical research

rhe·tor \'rē-,tȯr, -tər\ *n* [ME *rethor,* fr. L *rhetor,* fr. Gk *rhētōr*] (14c) : RHETORICIAN 1

rhet·o·ric \'re-tə-rik\ *n* [ME *rethorik,* fr. MF *rethorique,* fr. L *rhetorica,* fr. Gk *rhētorikē,* lit., art of oratory, fr. fem. of *rhētorikos* of an orator, fr. *rhētōr* orator, rhetorician, fr. *eirein* to say, speak — more at WORD] (14c) **1 a** : the art of speaking or writing effectively: as **a** : the study of principles and rules of composition formulated by critics of ancient times **b** : the study of writing or speaking as a means of communication or persuasion **2 a** : skill in the effective use of speech **b** : a type

or mode of language or speech; *also* : insincere or grandiloquent language **3** : verbal communication : DISCOURSE
rhe·tor·i·cal \ri-'tor-i-kəl, -'tär-\ *also* **rhe·tor·ic** \ri-'tor-ik, -'tär-\ *adj* (15c) **1 a** : of, relating to, or concerned with rhetoric **b** : employed for rhetorical effect; *esp* : asked merely for effect with no answer expected ⟨a ~ question⟩ **2 a** : given to rhetoric : GRANDILOQUENT **b** : VERBAL — **rhe·tor·i·cal·ly** \-i-k(ə-)lē\ *adv*
rhet·o·ri·cian \,ret-ə-'ri-shən\ *n* (15c) **1 a** : a master or teacher of rhetoric **b** : ORATOR **2** : an eloquent or grandiloquent writer or speaker
rheum \'rüm\ *n* [ME *reume*, fr. MF, fr. L *rheuma*, fr. Gk, lit., flow, flux, fr. *rhein* to flow — more at STREAM] (14c) **1** : a watery discharge from the mucous membranes esp. of the eyes or nose **2** *archaic* : TEARS — **rheumy** \'rü-mē\ *adj*
¹**rheu·mat·ic** \rü-'ma-tik\ *adj* [ME *rewmatik* subject to rheum, fr. L *rheumaticus*, fr. Gk *rheumatikos*, fr. *rheumat-, rheuma*] (1711) : of, relating to, characteristic of, or affected with rheumatism — **rheu·mat·i·cal·ly** \-ti-k(ə-)lē\ *adv*
²**rheumatic** *n* (1884) : one affected with rheumatism
rheumatic fever *n* (1782) : an acute disease that occurs chiefly in children and young adults and is characterized by fever, by inflammation and pain in and around the joints, and by inflammatory involvement of the pericardium and heart valves
rheu·ma·tism \'rü-mə-,ti-zəm, 'rü-\ *n* [L *rheumatismus* flux, rheum, fr. Gk *rheumatismos*, fr. *rheumatizesthai* to suffer from a flux, fr. *rheumat-, rheuma* flux] (1677) **1** : any of various conditions characterized by inflammation or pain in muscles, joints, or fibrous tissue ⟨muscular ~⟩ **2** : RHEUMATOID ARTHRITIS
rheu·ma·tiz \-,tiz\ *n* (1760) *chiefly dial* : RHEUMATISM
rheu·ma·toid \-,tȯid\ *adj* [ISV, fr. *rheumatism*] (1871) : characteristic of or affected with rheumatoid arthritis
rheumatoid arthritis *n* (1859) : a usu. chronic disease of unknown cause that is characterized esp. by pain, stiffness, inflammation, swelling, and sometimes destruction of joints
rheumatoid factor *n* (1960) : an autoantibody of high molecular weight that is usu. present in rheumatoid arthritis
rheu·ma·tol·o·gy \,rü-mə-'tä-lə-jē, ,rü-\ *n* (ca. 1941) : a medical science dealing with rheumatic diseases — **rheu·ma·tol·o·gist** \-jist\ *n*
Rh factor \,är-'ach-\ *n* [*rhesus* monkey (in which it was first detected)] (1942) : any of one or more genetically determined antigens present in the red blood cells of most persons and of higher animals and capable of inducing intense immunogenic reactions
rhin- *or* **rhino-** *comb form* [NL, fr. Gk, fr. *rhin-, rhis*] : nose ⟨*rhino*plasty⟩
rhi·nal \'rī-nᵊl\ *adj* (ca. 1859) : of or relating to the nose : NASAL
rhin·en·ceph·a·lon \,rī-(,)nen-'se-fə-,län, -lən\ *n* [NL] (1846) : the chiefly olfactory part of the forebrain — **rhin·en·ce·phal·ic** \,rī-,nen-sə-'fa-lik\ *adj*
rhine·stone \'rīn-,stōn\ *n* [*Rhine* River] (ca. 1888) : a colorless imitation stone of high luster made of glass, paste, or gem quartz — **rhine-stoned** \-,stȯnd\ *adj*
Rhine wine \'rīn-\ *n* (1843) **1** : a usu. white wine produced in the Rhine valley **2** : a wine similar to Rhine wine produced elsewhere
rhi·ni·tis \rī-'nī-təs\ *n* [NL] (ca. 1884) : inflammation of the mucous membrane of the nose
¹**rhi·no** \'rī-(,)nō\ *n* [origin unknown] (1670) : MONEY, CASH
²**rhino** *n, pl* **rhino** *or* **rhinos** (1884) : RHINOCEROS
rhi·noc·er·os \rī-'näs-rəs, rə-, -'nä-sə-\ *n, pl* **-noc·er·os·es** *or* **-noc·er·os** *or* **-noc·eri** \-'näs-sə-,rī\ [ME *rinoceros*, fr. L *rhinocerot-, rhinoceros*, fr. Gk *rhinokerōt-, rhinokerōs*, fr. *rhin-* + *keras* horn — more at HORN] (14c) : any of a family (Rhinocerotidae) of large heavyset herbivorous perissodactyl mammals of Africa and Asia that have one or two upright keratinous horns on the snout and thick gray to brown skin with little hair
rhinoceros beetle *n* (1681) : any of various large chiefly tropical scarab beetles (subfamily Dynastinae) having projecting horns on thorax and head

rhinoceros beetle

rhi·no·plas·ty \'rī-nō-,plas-tē\ *n, pl* **-ties** (1842) : plastic surgery on the nose usu. for cosmetic purposes
rhi·nos·co·py \rī-'näs-kə-pē\ *n* [ISV] (1861) : examination of the nasal passages
rhi·no·vi·rus \,rī-nō-'vī-rəs\ *n* [NL] (1961) : any of a group of picornaviruses that are related to the enteroviruses and are associated with disorders of the upper respiratory tract (as the common cold)
rhiz- *or* **rhizo-** *comb form* [NL, fr. Gk, fr. *rhiza* — more at ROOT] : root ⟨*rhizo*plane⟩
-rhiza *or* **-rrhiza** *n comb form, pl* **-zae** *or* **-zas** [NL, fr. Gk *rhiza*] : root : part resembling a root or roots ⟨*coleorhiza*⟩ ⟨*mycorrhiza*⟩
rhi·zo·bi·um \rī-'zō-bē-əm\ *n, pl* **-bia** \-bē-ə\ [NL, fr. *rhiz-* + Gk *bios* life — more at QUICK] (1921) : any of a genus (*Rhizobium*) of small heterotrophic soil bacteria capable of forming symbiotic nodules on the roots of leguminous plants and of there becoming bacteroids that fix atmospheric nitrogen — **rhi·zo·bi·al** \-bē-əl\ *adj*
rhi·zoc·to·nia \,rī-,zäk-'tō-nē-ə\ *n* [NL, fr. *rhiz-* + Gk *-ktonos* killing, fr. *kteinein* to kill; akin to Skt *kṣaṇoti* he wounds] (1897) : any of a form genus (*Rhizoctonia*) of imperfect fungi that includes major plant pathogens
rhi·zoid \'rī-,zȯid\ *n* (1875) : a rootlike structure — **rhi·zoi·dal** \rī-'zȯi-dᵊl\ *adj*
rhi·zo·ma·tous \rī-'zō-mə-təs\ *adj* [ISV, fr. NL *rhizomat-, rhizoma*] (1847) : having, resembling, or being a rhizome ⟨~ plants⟩
rhi·zome \'rī-,zōm\ *n* [NL *rhizomat-, rhizoma*, fr. Gk *rhizōmat-, rhizōma* mass of roots, fr. *rhizoun* to cause to take root, fr. *rhiza* root — more at ROOT] (1845) : a somewhat elongate usu. horizontal subterranean plant stem that is often thickened by deposits of reserve food material, produces shoots above and roots below, and is distinguished from a true root in possessing buds, nodes, and usu. scalelike leaves — **rhi·zo·mic** \rī-'zō-mik, -'zä-\ *adj*

rhi·zo·plane \'rī-zə-,plān\ *n* (1949) : the external surface of roots together with closely adhering soil particles and debris
rhi·zo·pod \'rī-zə-,päd\ *n* [NL *Rhizopoda*, fr. *rhiz-* + *-poda* -pod] (1851) : any of a superclass (Rhizopoda) of usu. creeping protozoans (as an amoeba or a foraminifer) having lobate or rootlike pseudopodia
rhi·zo·pus \'rī-zə-pəs, -,püs\ *n* [NL, fr. *rhiz-* + Gk *pous* foot — more at FOOT] (1887) : any of a genus (*Rhizopus*) of mold fungi including some economically valuable forms and some plant or animal pathogens (as a bread mold)
rhi·zo·sphere \-,sfir\ *n* [ISV] (1929) : soil that surrounds and is influenced by the roots of a plant
rhi·zot·o·my \rī-'zä-tə-mē\ *n, pl* **-mies** [ISV] (1911) : the operation of cutting the anterior or posterior spinal nerve roots
Rh–neg·a·tive \,är-,äch-'ne-gə-tiv\ *adj* (1945) : lacking Rh factor in the blood
rho \'rō\ *n* [Gk *rhō*, of Sem origin; akin to Heb *rēsh* resh] (15c) : the 17th letter of the Greek alphabet — see ALPHABET table
rhod- *or* **rhodo-** *comb form* [NL, fr. L, fr. Gk, fr. *rhodon* rose — more at ROSE] : rose : red ⟨*rhodolite*⟩
rho·da·mine \'rō-də-,mēn\ *n, often cap* [ISV] (1888) : any of a group of yellowish red to blue fluorescent dyes; *esp* : a brilliant bluish red dye made by fusing an amino derivative of phenol with phthalic anhydride and used esp. in coloring paper and as a biological stain
Rhode Island Red *n* [*Rhode Island*, U.S. state] (1896) : any of an American breed of general-purpose domestic fowls having a long heavy body, smooth yellow or reddish legs, and rich brownish red plumage
Rhode Island White *n* (ca. 1923) : any of an American breed of domestic fowls resembling Rhode Island Reds but having pure white plumage
Rhodes grass \'rōdz-\ *n* [Cecil J. *Rhodes*] (1915) : an African perennial grass (*Chloris gayana*) widely cultivated as a forage grass esp. in dry regions
Rho·de·sian man \rō-'dē-zh(ē-)ən-\ *n* [Northern *Rhodesia*, Africa] (1921) : an extinct African hominid (*Homo sapiens rhodesiensis*) having long bones of modern type, a skull with prominent brow ridges and large face but human palate and dentition, and a simple but relatively large brain
Rhodesian Ridge·back \-'rij-,bak\ *n* (1925) : any of an African breed of powerful long-bodied hunting dogs having a dense harsh short tan coat with a characteristic crest of reversed hair along the spine
Rhodes scholar \'rōd(z)-\ *n* (1902) : a holder of one of numerous scholarships founded under the will of Cecil J. Rhodes that can be used at Oxford University for two or three years and are open to candidates from the Commonwealth and the U.S.
rho·di·um \'rō-dē-əm\ *n* [NL, fr. Gk *rhodon* rose] (1804) : a white hard ductile metallic element that is resistant to acids, occurs in platinum ores, and is used in alloys with platinum — see ELEMENT table
rho·do·chro·site \,rō-də-'krō-,sīt\ *n* [G *Rhodocrosit*, fr. Gk *rhodochrōs* rose-colored, fr. *rhod-* + *chrōs* color — more at CHROMATIC] (1836) : a rose red mineral consisting essentially of manganese carbonate
rho·do·den·dron \,rō-də-'den-drən\ *n* [NL, fr. L, oleander, fr. Gk, fr. *rhod-* + *dendron* tree — more at DENDR-] (1664) : any of a genus (*Rhododendron*) of the heath family of widely cultivated shrubs and trees with alternate leaves and showy flowers; *esp* : one with leathery evergreen leaves as distinguished from a deciduous azalea
rho·do·lite \'rō-dᵊl-,īt\ *n* (1882) : a pink or purple garnet used as a gem
rho·do·mon·tade *var of* RODOMONTADE
rho·do·nite \'rō-dᵊn-,īt\ *n* [G *Rhodonit*, fr. Gk *rhodon* rose] (1823) : a pale red triclinic mineral that consists essentially of manganese silicate and is used as an ornamental stone
rho·dop·sin \rō-'däp-sən\ *n* [ISV *rhod-* + Gk *opsis* sight, vision + ISV *-in* — more at OPTIC] (1886) : a red photosensitive pigment in the retinal rods of marine fishes and most higher vertebrates that is important in vision in dim light — called also *visual purple*
rho·do·ra \rō-'dōr-ə, -'dȯr-\ *n* [NL, alter. of L *rodarum*, a plant] (ca. 1731) : an azalea (*Rhododendron canadense*) of northeastern No. America that has spring-flowering pink blossoms
rhomb \'räm(b)\ *n, pl* **rhombs** \'rämz\ [MF *rhombe*, fr. L *rhombus*] (ca. 1578) **1** : RHOMBUS **2** : RHOMBOHEDRON
rhomb- *or* **rhombo-** *comb form* [NL, fr. Gk *rhombos*] : rhombus ⟨*rhomb*encephalon⟩
rhomb·en·ceph·a·lon \,räm-(,)ben-'se-fə-,län, -lən\ *n* [NL] (1897) : HINDBRAIN 1
rhom·bic \'räm-bik\ *adj* (1701) **1** : having the form of a rhombus **2** : ORTHORHOMBIC
rhom·bo·he·dron \,räm-bō-'hē-drən\ *n, pl* **-drons** *or* **-dra** \-drə\ [NL] (1836) : a parallelepiped whose faces are rhombuses — **rhom·bo·he·dral** \-drəl\ *adj*
¹**rhom·boid** \'räm-,bȯid\ *n* [MF *rhomboïde*, fr. L *rhomboides*, fr. Gk *rhomboeidēs* resembling a rhombus, fr. *rhombos*] (1570) : a parallelogram with no right angles and with adjacent sides of unequal length
²**rhom·boid** \'räm-,bȯid\ *or* **rhom·boi·dal** \räm-'bȯi-dᵊl\ *adj* (1693) : shaped somewhat like a rhombus or rhomboid
rhom·boi·de·us \räm-'bȯi-dē-əs\ *n, pl* **-dei** \-dē-,ī\ [NL, fr. L *rhomboides* rhomboid] (ca. 1836) : either of two muscles that lie beneath the trapezius muscle and connect the spinous processes of various vertebrae with the medial border of the scapula
rhom·bus \'räm-bəs\ *n, pl* **rhom·bus·es** *or* **rhom·bi** \-,bī, -,bē\ [L, fr. Gk *rhombos* piece of wood whirled on a string, lozenge, fr. *rhembein* to whirl] (ca. 1567) : a parallelogram with four equal sides and sometimes one with no right angles
rhon·chus \'räŋ-kəs\ *n, pl* **rhon·chi** \'räŋ-,kī\ [LGk, fr. *rhenchein* to snore, wheeze; prob. akin to OIr *sreinnid* he snores] (1829) : a whistling or snoring sound heard on auscultation of the chest when the air channels are partly obstructed
Rh–pos·i·tive \,är-,äch-'pä-zə-tiv, -'päz-tiv\ *adj* (1942) : containing Rh factor in the red blood cells

\ə\ abut \ᵊ\ kitten, F table \ər\ further \a\ ash \ā\ ace \ä\ mop, mar \aù\ out \ch\ chin \e\ bet \ē\ easy \g\ go \i\ hit \ī\ ice \j\ job \ŋ\ sing \ō\ go \ȯ\ law \ȯi\ boy \th\ thin \t̲h̲\ the \ü\ loot \ù\ foot \y\ yet \zh\ vision \à, k̲, ⁿ, œ, œ̄, ue, ūe, ᵞ\ see Guide to Pronunciation

rhu·barb \'rü-ˌbärb\ *n* [ME *rubarbe*, fr. MF *reubarbe*, fr. ML *reubarbarum*, alter. of *rha barbarum*, lit., barbarian rhubarb] (15c) **1 :** any of a genus (*Rheum*) of Asian plants of the buckwheat family having large leaves with thick succulent petioles often used as food **2 :** the dried rhizome and roots of any of several rhubarbs grown in China and Tibet and used as a purgative and stomachic **3 :** a heated dispute or controversy

rhumb \'rəm(b)\ *n, pl* **rhumbs** \'rəmz\ [Sp *rumbo* rhumb, rhumb line] (1578) **1 :** a line or course on a single bearing **2 :** any of the points of the mariner's compass

rhumba *var of* RUMBA

rhumb line *n* [Sp *rumbo*] (ca. 1795) **:** a line on the surface of the earth that follows a single compass bearing and makes equal oblique angles with all meridians — called also loxodrome

rhus \'rüs\ *n, pl* **rhus·es** *or* **rhus** [NL, fr. L, sumac, fr. Gk *rhous*] (ca. 1611) **:** any of a genus (*Rhus*) of shrubs and trees (as sumac or poison ivy) of the cashew family that are native to temperate and warm regions, have compound trifoliolate or pinnate leaves, and sometimes produce substances causing dermatitis

¹rhyme \'rīm\ *n* [ME *rime*, fr. OF] (13c) **1 a** (1) **:** rhyming verse (2) **:** POETRY **b :** a composition in verse that rhymes **2 a :** correspondence in terminal sounds of units of composition or utterance (as two or more words or lines of verse) **b :** one of two or more words thus corresponding in sound **c :** correspondence of other than terminal word sounds: as (1) **:** ALLITERATION (2) **:** INTERNAL RHYME **3 :** RHYTHM, MEASURE — **rhyme·less** *adj*

²rhyme *vb* **rhymed; rhym·ing** *vt* (14c) **1 :** to relate or praise in rhyming verse **2 a :** to put into rhyme **b :** to compose (verse) in rhyme **c :** to cause to rhyme: use as rhyme ~ *vi* **1 :** to make rhymes; *also* **:** to compose rhyming verse **2** *of a word or verse* **:** to end in syllables that are rhymes **3 :** to be in accord: HARMONIZE — **rhym·er** *n*

rhyme or reason *n* (15c) **:** good sense or reason

rhyme royal \-'rȯi(-ə)l\ *n* (ca. 1841) **:** a stanza of seven lines in iambic pentameter with a rhyme scheme of *ababbcc*

rhyme scheme *n* (1917) **:** the arrangement of rhymes in a stanza or a poem

rhyme·ster \'rīm(p)-stər\ *n* (1589) **:** an inferior poet

rhyming slang *n* (1859) **:** slang in which the word intended is replaced by a word or phrase that rhymes with it (as *loaf of bread* for *head*) or the first part of the phrase (as *loaf* for *head*)

rhyn·cho·ce·pha·lian \ˌriŋ-kō-sə-'fāl-yən\ *n* [ultim. fr. Gk *rhynchos* beak, snout + *kephalē* head — more at CEPHALIC] (1886) **:** any of an order (Rhynchocephalia) of reptiles resembling lizards that includes the tuatara as the only living member — **rhynchocephalian** *adj*

rhy·o·lite \'rī-ə-ˌlīt\ *n* [G *Rhyolith*, fr. Gk *rhyax* stream, stream of lava (fr. *rhein*) + G *-lith* -lite] (1868) **:** a very acid volcanic rock that is the lava form of granite — **rhy·o·lit·ic** \ˌrī-ə-'li-tik\ *adj*

rhythm \'ri-thəm\ *n* [MF & L; MF *rhythme*, fr. L *rhythmus*, fr. Gk *rhythmos*, prob. fr. *rhein* to flow — more at STREAM] (1560) **1 a :** an ordered recurrent alternation of strong and weak elements in the flow of sound and silence in speech **b :** a particular example or form of rhythm ⟨iambic ~⟩ **2 a :** the aspect of music comprising all the elements (as accent, meter, and tempo) that relate to forward movement **b :** a characteristic rhythmic pattern ⟨rumba ~⟩; *also* **:** ¹METER **2 c :** the group of instruments in a band supplying the rhythm — called also *rhythm section* **3 a :** movement or fluctuation marked by the regular recurrence or natural flow of related elements **b :** the repetition in a literary work of phrase, incident, character type, or symbol **4 :** a regularly recurrent quantitative change in a variable biological process ⟨a circadian ~⟩ — compare BIORHYTHM **5 :** the effect created by the elements in a play, movie, or novel that relate to the temporal development of the action **6 :** RHYTHM METHOD

rhythm and blues *n* (1949) **:** popular music typically including elements of blues and black folk music and marked by a strong beat and simple chord structure

rhythm band *n* (ca. 1943) **:** a band usu. composed of schoolchildren who play simple percussion instruments (as rhythm sticks, sleigh bells, or tambourines) to learn fundamentals of coordination and music

rhyth·mic \'rith-mik\ *or* **rhyth·mi·cal** \-mi-kəl\ *adj* (1589) **1 :** marked by or moving in pronounced rhythm **2 :** of, relating to, or involving rhythm — **rhyth·mi·cal·ly** \-mi-k(ə-)lē\ *adv*

rhyth·mic·i·ty \rith-'mi-sə-tē\ *n* (1901) **:** the state of being rhythmic or of responding rhythmically

rhyth·mics \'rith-miks\ *n pl but sing or pl in constr* (ca. 1859) **:** the science or theory of rhythms

rhyth·mist \'ri-thə-mist, 'rith-mist\ *n* (1864) **:** one who studies or has a feeling for rhythm

rhyth·mize \-ˌmīz\ *vt* **-mized; -miz·ing** (1885) **:** to order or compose rhythmically — **rhyth·mi·za·tion** \ˌri-thə-mə-'zā-shən, ˌrith-mə-\ *n*

rhythm method *n* (1940) **:** a method of birth control involving continence during the period in which ovulation is most likely to occur

rhythm stick *n* (1952) **:** one of a pair of plain or notched wood sticks that are struck or rubbed together to produce various percussive sounds and are used esp. by young children in rhythm bands

rhyt·i·dome \'ri-tə-ˌdōm, 'rī-\ *n* [Gk *rhytidōma* wrinkle, fr. *rhytidoun* to wrinkle, fr. *rhytid-, rhytis* wrinkle] (1881) **:** the bark external to the last formed periderm

rhy·ton \'ri-ˌtän\ *n* [Gk, neut. of *rhytos* flowing, fr. *rhein* to flow — more at STREAM] (1850) **:** any of various ornate drinking vessels of ancient times typically shaped in part like an animal or animal's head

¹ri·al \rē-'ȯl, -'äl\ *n* [Per., fr. Ar *riyāl* riyal] (1932) — see MONEY table

²rial *var of* RIYAL

ri·al·to \rē-'al-(ˌ)tō\ *n, pl* **-tos** [*Rialto*, island and district in Venice] (1549) **1 :** EXCHANGE, MARKETPLACE **2 :** a theater district

ri·ant \'rī-ənt, 'rē-; rē-'än\ *adj* [MF, prp. of *rire* to laugh, fr. L *ridēre*] (1567) **:** GAY, MIRTHFUL — **ri·ant·ly** \'rī-ənt-lē, 'rē-\ *adv*

ri·a·ta \rē-'a-tə, -'ä-\ *n* [modif. of AmerSp *reata*] (1846) **:** LARIAT

¹rib \'rib\ *n* [ME, fr. OE *ribb*; akin to OHG *rippi* rib, OCS *rebro*, and prob. to Gk *erephein* to roof over] (bef. 12c) **1 a :** any of the paired curved bony or partly cartilaginous rods that stiffen the walls of the body of most vertebrates and protect the viscera **b :** a cut of meat including a rib — see BEEF illustration **c** [fr. the account of Eve's creation from Adam's rib in Gen 2:21–22] **:** WIFE **2 :** something resembling a rib in shape or function: as **a** (1) **:** a traverse member of the frame of a ship that runs from keel to deck (2) **:** a light fore-and-aft member in an airplane's wing **b :** one of the stiff strips supporting an umbrella's fabric **c :** one of the arches in Romanesque and Gothic vaulting meeting and crossing one another and dividing the whole vaulted space into triangles **3 :** an elongated ridge: as **a** (1) **:** a vein of an insect's wing (2) **:** one of the primary veins of a leaf **b :** one of the ridges in a knitted or woven fabric

²rib *vt* **ribbed; rib·bing** (ca. 1547) **1 :** to furnish or enclose with ribs **2 :** to form vertical ridges in in knitting — **rib·ber** *n*

³rib *n* [⁴rib] (1929) **1 :** JOKE **2 :** PARODY

⁴rib *vt* **ribbed; rib·bing** [prob. fr. ¹*rib*; fr. the tickling of the ribs to cause laughter] (1930) **:** to poke fun at: KID — **rib·ber** *n*

¹rib·ald \'ri-bəld *also* 'ri-ˌbȯld, 'rī-ˌbȯld\ *n* [ME, fr. MF *ribaut, ribauld* wanton, rascal, fr. *riber* to be wanton, of Gmc origin; akin to OHG *riban* to be wanton, lit., to rub] (13c) **:** a ribald person

²ribald *adj* (1508) **1 :** CRUDE, OFFENSIVE ⟨~ language⟩ **2 :** characterized by or using coarse indecent humor *syn* see COARSE

rib·ald·ry \'ri-bəl-drē *also* 'rī-\ *n, pl* **-ries** (14c) **1 :** a ribald quality or element **2 a :** ribald language or humor **b :** an instance of ribald language or humor

rib·and \'ri-bənd\ *n* [ME, alter. of *riban*] (15c) **:** a ribbon used esp. as a decoration

ri·ba·vi·rin \ˌrī-bə-'vī-rən\ *n* [perh. fr. *ribonucleic acid* + *virus* + ¹-*in*] (1976) **:** a synthetic broad-spectrum antiviral nucleoside $C_8H_{12}N_4O_5$

rib·band \'ri(b)-ˌband, 'ri-bən(d)\ *n* [¹*rib* + ¹*band*] (1711) **:** a long narrow strip or bar used in shipbuilding; *esp* **:** one bent and bolted longitudinally to the frames to hold them in position during construction

rib·bing \'ri-biŋ\ *n* (1564) **:** an arrangement of ribs

¹rib·bon \'ri-bən\ *n* [ME *riban*, fr. MF *riban, ruban*] (14c) **1 a :** a flat or tubular narrow closely woven fabric (as of silk or rayon) used for trimmings or knitting **b :** a narrow fabric used for tying packages **c :** a piece of usu. multicolored ribbon worn as a military decoration or in place of a medal **d :** a strip of colored satin given for winning a place in a competition **2 :** a strip of inked fabric (as in a typewriter) **3** *pl* **:** reins for controlling an animal **4 :** TATTER, SHRED — usu. used in pl. **5 :** RIBBAND — **rib·bon·like** \-ˌlīk\ *adj*

²ribbon *vt* (1716) **1 a :** to adorn with ribbons **b :** to divide into ribbons **c :** to cover with or as if with ribbons **2 :** to rip to shreds

ribbon development *n* (1927) **:** a system of buildings built side by side along a road

rib·bon·fish \'ri-bən-ˌfish\ *n* (ca. 1798) **:** any of a family (Trachipteridae) of elongate greatly compressed marine bony fishes (as a dealfish)

ribbon worm *n* (1855) **:** NEMERTEAN

rib·by \'ri-bē\ *adj* (1849) **:** showing or marked by ribs

rib cage *n* (1909) **:** the bony enclosing wall of the chest consisting chiefly of the ribs and the structures connecting them

ri·bes \'rī-(ˌ)bēz\ *n, pl* **ribes** [NL, fr. ML, currant, fr. Ar *ribās* rhubarb] (1543) **:** any of a genus (*Ribes*) of shrubs (as a currant or a gooseberry) of the saxifrage family that have small racemose variously colored flowers and pulpy two-seeded to many-seeded berries

rib eye *n* (1926) **:** the large piece of meat that lies along the outer side of the rib (as of a steer)

rib·grass \'rib-ˌgras\ *n* (ca. 1500) **:** ¹PLANTAIN; *esp* **:** an Old World plantain (*Plantago lanceolata*) with long narrow ribbed leaves

rib·let \'ri-blət\ *n* (1943) **:** one of the rib ends in the strip of breast of lamb or veal — see LAMB illustration

ribo- *comb form* [*ribose*] **1 :** ribose ⟨*riboflavin*⟩ **2 :** ribonucleic acid ⟨*ribosome*⟩

ri·bo·fla·vin \ˌrī-bə-'flā-vən, 'rī-bə-ˌ\ *n* [ISV *ribo-* + L *flavus* yellow — more at BLUE] (1935) **:** a yellow crystalline compound $C_{17}H_{20}N_4O_6$ that is a growth-promoting member of the vitamin B complex and occurs both free (as in milk) and combined (as in liver) — called also *vitamin B₂, vitamin G*

ri·bo·nu·cle·ase \ˌrī-bō-'nü-klē-ˌās, -'nyü-, -ˌāz\ *n* (1942) **:** an enzyme that catalyzes the hydrolysis of RNA

ri·bo·nu·cle·ic acid \ˌrī-bō-nü-'klē-ik-, -nyü-, -klā-\ *n* (1931) **:** RNA

ri·bo·nu·cleo·pro·tein \-ˌnü-klē-ō-'prō-ˌtēn, -'prō-tē-ən\ *n* (1940) **:** a nucleoprotein that contains RNA

ri·bo·nu·cle·o·side \-'nü-klē-ə-ˌsīd, -'nyü-\ *n* (1931) **:** a nucleoside that contains ribose

ri·bo·nu·cle·o·tide \-ˌtīd\ *n* (1929) **:** a nucleotide that contains ribose and occurs esp. as a constituent of RNA

ri·bose \'rī-ˌbōs, -ˌbōz\ *n* [ISV, fr. *ribonic acid* (an acid $C_5H_{10}O_6$ obtained by oxidation of ribose)] (1892) **:** a pentose $C_5H_{10}O_5$ found esp. in the dextrorotatory form and obtained esp. from RNA

ribosomal RNA *n* (1961) **:** RNA that is a fundamental structural element of ribosomes

ri·bo·some \'rī-bə-ˌsōm\ *n* (1958) **:** any of the RNA-rich cytoplasmic granules that are sites of protein synthesis — see CELL illustration — **ri·bo·som·al** \ˌrī-bə-'sō-məl\ *adj*

rib roast *n* (ca. 1890) **:** a cut of meat containing the large piece that lies along the outer side of the rib — see BEEF illustration

rib·wort \'rib-ˌwərt, -ˌwȯrt\ *n* (14c) **:** RIBGRASS

rice \'rīs\ *n* [ME *rys*, fr. OF *ris*, fr. OIt *riso*, fr. Gk *oryza, oryzon*, of Iranian origin; akin to Pashto *wriže* rice; akin to Skt *vrihi* rice] (13c) **:** the starchy seeds of an annual cereal grass (*Oryza sativa*) that are cooked and used for food; *also* **:** this cereal grass that occurs in southeastern Asia and is widely cultivated in warm climates for its seeds and by-products

rice·bird \'rīs-ˌbərd\ *n* (1731) **:** any of several small birds common in rice fields; *esp* **:** BOBOLINK

rice paper *n* [fr. its resemblance to paper made from rice straw] (1822) **:** a thin papery material made from the pith of a small Asian tree or shrub (*Tetrapanax papyriferum*) of the ginseng family

rice polishings *n pl* (ca. 1934) **:** the inner bran layer of rice rubbed off in milling

ric·er \'rī-sər\ *n* (1896) **:** a kitchen utensil in which soft foods are pressed through a perforated container to produce strings

ri·cer·car \ˌrē-(ˌ)chər-'kär\ *or* **ri·cer·ca·re** \-'kä-(ˌ)rā\ *n, pl* **ricercars** *or* **ri·cer·ca·ri** \-'kä-(ˌ)rē\ [It, fr. *ricercare* to seek again, seek out, fr. *ri-* re- (fr. L *re-*) + *cercare* to seek, fr. LL *circare* to go about — more at SEARCH] (1789) **:** any of various usu. keyboard musical forms esp. of the 16th and 17th centuries in either quasi-improvisatory toccata style or strict polyphonic fugal style

rich \'rich\ *adj* [ME *riche,* fr. OE *rice;* akin to OHG *rihhi* rich, OE *rice* kingdom, OHG *rihhi,* n.; all fr. prehistoric Gmc words borrowed fr. Celt words akin to OIr *rí* (gen. *ríg*) king — more at ROYAL] (bef. 12c) **1 :** having abundant possessions and esp. material wealth **2 a :** having high value or quality **b :** well supplied ⟨a city ~ in traditions⟩ **3 :** magnificently impressive : SUMPTUOUS **4 a :** vivid and deep in color ⟨a ~ red⟩ **b :** full and mellow in tone and quality ⟨a ~ voice⟩ **c :** having a strong fragrance ⟨~ perfumes⟩ **5 :** highly productive or remunerative ⟨a ~ mine⟩ **6 a :** having abundant plant nutrients ⟨~ soil⟩ **b :** highly seasoned, fatty, oily, or sweet ⟨~ foods⟩ **c :** high in the combustible component ⟨a ~ fuel mixture⟩ **d :** high in some component ⟨cholesterol-*rich* foods⟩ **7 a :** ENTERTAINING; *also* : LAUGHABLE **b :** MEANINGFUL, SIGNIFICANT ⟨~ allusions⟩ **c :** LUSH ⟨~ meadows⟩ **8 :** pure or nearly pure ⟨~ lime⟩ — **rich·ness** *n*
syn RICH, WEALTHY, AFFLUENT, OPULENT mean having goods, property, and money in abundance. RICH implies having more than enough to gratify normal needs or desires ⟨became *rich* through shrewd investing⟩. WEALTHY stresses the possession of property and intrinsically valuable things ⟨*wealthy* landowners⟩. AFFLUENT suggests prosperity and an increasing wealth ⟨an *affluent* society⟩. OPULENT suggests lavish expenditure and display of great wealth, more often applying to things than people ⟨an *opulent* mansion⟩.

Rich·ard Roe \,rich-ǝrd-'rō\ *n* (1768) : a party to legal proceedings whose true name is unknown — compare JOHN DOE
rich·en \'ri-chǝn\ *vt* **rich·ened; rich·en·ing** \'ri-chǝ-niŋ, 'rich-niŋ\ (1878) : to make rich or richer
rich·es \'ri-chǝz\ *n pl* [ME, sing. or pl., fr. *richesse,* lit., richness, fr. OF, fr. *riche* rich, of Gmc origin; akin to OE *rice* rich] (13c) : things that make one rich : WEALTH
rich·ly \'rich-lē\ *adv* [ME *richely,* fr. OE *riclice,* fr. *rice* rich] (bef. 12c) **1 :** in a rich manner **2 :** in full measure : AMPLY ⟨praise ~ deserved⟩
Rich·ter scale \'rik-tǝr-\ *n* [Charles F. *Richter*] (1938) : an open-ended logarithmic scale for expressing the magnitude of a seismic disturbance (as an earthquake) in terms of the energy dissipated in it with 1.5 indicating the smallest earthquake that can be felt, 4.5 an earthquake causing slight damage, and 8.5 a very devastating earthquake
ri·cin \'rī-sᵊn, 'ri-\ *n* [L *ricinus* castor-oil plant] (1896) : a poisonous protein in the castor bean
ri·cin·ole·ic acid \,rī-sᵊn-ō-'lē-ik-, ,ri-, -'lā-\ *n* [L *ricinus* + E *oleic acid*] (1848) : an oily unsaturated hydroxy fatty acid $C_{18}H_{34}O_3$ that occurs in castor oil as a glyceride and yields esters important as plasticizers
¹rick \'rik\ *n* [ME *reek,* fr. OE *hrēac;* akin to ON *hraukr* rick] (bef. 12c) **1 :** a stack (as of hay) in the open air **2 :** a pile of material (as cordwood) split from short logs
²rick *vt* (1623) : to pile (as hay) in ricks
³rick *vt* [perh. fr. ME *wrikken* to move unsteadily] (1798) *chiefly Brit* : WRENCH, SPRAIN
rick·ets \'ri-kǝts\ *n pl but sing in constr* [origin unknown] (1634) : a deficiency disease that affects the young during the period of skeletal growth, is characterized esp. by soft and deformed bones, and is caused by failure to assimilate and use calcium and phosphorus normally due to inadequate sunlight or vitamin D
rick·ett·sia \ri-'ket-sē-ǝ\ *n, pl* **-si·as** *or* **-si·ae** \-sē-,ē, -,ī\ *also* **-sia** [NL, genus name, fr. Howard T. *Ricketts* †1910 Am. pathologist] (1919) : any of a family (Rickettsiaceae) of rod-shaped, coccoid, or diplococcus-shaped, often pleomorphic bacteria that cause various diseases (as typhus) — **rick·ett·si·al** \-sē-ǝl\ *adj*
rick·ety \'ri-kǝ-tē\ *adj* (1683) **1 :** affected with rickets **2 a :** lacking stability or firmness : SHAKY ⟨a ~ coalition⟩ **b :** in unsound physical condition ⟨~ veterans⟩ ⟨~ stairs⟩
rick·ey \'ri-kē\ *n, pl* **rickeys** [prob. fr. the name *Rickey*] (1895) : a drink containing liquor, lime juice, sugar, and soda water; *also* : a similar drink without liquor
rick·rack *or* **ric·rac** \'rik-,rak\ *n* [redupl. of ⁴*rack*] (1884) : a flat braid woven to form zigzags and used esp. as trimming on clothing
rick·sha *or* **rick·shaw** \'rik-,shò\ *n* [alter. of *jinrikisha*] (1887) : a small covered 2-wheeled vehicle usu. for one passenger that is pulled by one man and that was used orig. in Japan
¹ric·o·chet \'ri-kǝ-,shā, *Brit also* -,shet\ *n* [F] (1769) : a glancing rebound (as of a projectile off a flat surface); *also* : an object that ricochets
²ricochet *vi* **-cheted** \-,shād\ *or* **-chet·ted** \-,she-tǝd\; **-chet·ing** \-,shā-iŋ\ *or* **-chet·ting** \-,she-tiŋ\ (1828) : to skip with or as if with glancing rebounds
ri·cot·ta \ri-'kä-tǝ, -'kò-\ *n* [It, fem. of pp. of *ricuocere* to cook again, fr. L *recoquere,* fr. *re-* + *coquere* to cook — more at COOK] (1877) : a white unripened whey cheese of Italy that resembles cottage cheese; *also* : a similar cheese made in the U.S. from whole or skim milk
ric·tal \'rik-tᵊl\ *adj* (1825) : of or relating to the rictus
ric·tus \'rik-tǝs\ *n* [NL, fr. L, open mouth, fr. *ringi* to open the mouth; akin to OCS *rǫgǔ* mockery] (1827) **1 :** the gape of a bird's mouth **2 a :** the mouth orifice **b :** a gaping grin or grimace
rid \'rid\ *vt* **rid** *also* **rid·ded; rid·ding** [ME *ridden* to clear, fr. ON *rythja;* akin to OHG *riutan* to clear land] (13c) **1** *archaic* : SAVE, RESCUE **2 :** to make free : RELIEVE, DISENCUMBER ⟨~ the language of impropriety⟩ ⟨be ~ of worries⟩ ⟨get ~ of that junk⟩
rid·dance \'ri-dᵊn(t)s\ *n* (1533) **1 :** an act of ridding **2 :** DELIVERANCE, RELIEF — often used in the phrase *good riddance*
rid·den \'ri-dᵊn\ *adj* (1653) **1 :** harassed, oppressed, or obsessed by — usu. used in combination ⟨guilt-*ridden*⟩ ⟨debt-*ridden*⟩ **2 :** excessively full of or supplied with — usu. used in combination ⟨slum-*ridden*⟩
¹rid·dle \'ri-dᵊl\ *n* [ME *redels, ridel,* fr. OE *rǣdelse* opinion, conjecture, riddle; akin to OE *rǣdan* to interpret — more at READ] (bef. 12c) **1 :** a mystifying, misleading, or puzzling question posed as a problem to be solved or guessed : CONUNDRUM, ENIGMA **2 :** something or someone difficult to understand *syn* see MYSTERY
²riddle *vb* **rid·dled; rid·dling** \'rid-liŋ, 'rid-ᵊl-iŋ\ *vi* (1571) : to speak in or propound riddles ~ *vt* **1 :** to find the solution of : EXPLAIN **2 :** to set a riddle for : PUZZLE — **rid·dler** \'rid-lǝr, 'ri-dᵊl-ǝr\ *n*
³riddle *n* [ME *riddil,* fr. OE *hriddel;* akin to L *cribrum* sieve, *cernere* to sift — more at CERTAIN] (bef. 12c) : a coarse sieve
⁴riddle *vt* **rid·dled; rid·dling** \'rid-liŋ, 'ri-dᵊl-iŋ\ (13c) **1 :** to separate

(as grain from chaff) with a riddle : SCREEN **2 :** to pierce with many holes ⟨*riddled* the car with bullets⟩ **3 :** to spread through : PERMEATE ⟨a book *riddled* with errors⟩
rid·dling \'rid-liŋ, 'ri-dᵊl-iŋ\ *adj* (1591) : containing or presenting riddles
¹ride \'rīd\ *vb* **rode** \'rōd\ *or chiefly dial* **rid** \'rid\; **rid·den** \'ri-dᵊn\ *or chiefly dial* **rid** *or* **rode; rid·ing** \'rī-diŋ\ [ME, fr. OE *rīdan;* akin to OHG *rītan* to ride, MIr *réidid* he rides] *vi* (bef. 12c) **1 a :** to sit and travel on the back of an animal that one directs **b :** to travel in or on a conveyance **2 :** to travel as if on a conveyance : be borne ⟨rode on a wave of popularity⟩ **3 a :** to lie moored or anchored ⟨a ship ~s at anchor⟩ **b :** SAIL **c :** to move like a floating object ⟨the moon rode in the sky⟩ **4 :** to become supported on a point or surface **5 a :** to travel over a surface ⟨the car ~s well⟩ **b :** to move on the body ⟨shorts that ~ up⟩ **6 :** to continue without interference ⟨let it ~⟩ **7 a :** to be contingent : DEPEND ⟨plans on which the future ~s⟩ **b :** to become bet ⟨a lot of money *riding* on the favorite⟩ ~ *vt* **1 a :** to travel on ⟨~ a bike⟩ ⟨~ the bus⟩ **b :** to move with like a rider ⟨~ the waves⟩ **2 a :** to traverse by conveyance ⟨rode 500 miles⟩ **b :** to ride a horse in ⟨~ a race⟩ **3 :** SURVIVE, OUTLAST — usu. used with *out* ⟨rode out the gale⟩ **4 :** to traverse on horseback to inspect or maintain ⟨~ fence⟩ **5 :** to mount in copulation **6 a :** OBSESS, OPPRESS ⟨ridden by anxiety⟩ **b :** to harass persistently : NAG **c :** TEASE, RIB **7 :** CARRY, CONVEY **8 :** to project over : OVERLAP **9 :** to give with (a punch) to soften the impact **10 :** to keep in partial engagement by resting a foot continuously on the pedal ⟨~ the brakes⟩ — **rid·able** *or* **ride·able** \'rī-dǝ-bǝl\ *adj* — **ride circuit :** to hold court in the various towns of a judicial circuit — **ride for a fall :** to court disaster — **ride herd on :** to keep a check on — **ride high :** to experience success — **ride shotgun :** to ride in the front passenger seat of a motor vehicle
²ride *n* (1759) **1 :** an act of riding; *esp* : a trip on horseback or by vehicle **2 :** a way (as a road or path) suitable for riding **3 :** any of various mechanical devices (as at an amusement park) for riding on **4 a :** a trip on which gangsters take a victim to murder him **b :** something likened to such a trip ⟨take the taxpayers for a ~⟩ **5 :** a means of transportation **6 :** the qualities of travel comfort in a vehicle
rid·er \'rī-dǝr\ *n* (14c) **1 :** one that rides **2 a :** an addition to a document often attached on a separate piece of paper **b :** a clause appended to a legislative bill to secure a usu. distinct object **3 :** something used to overlie another or to move along on another piece — **rid·er·less** \-lǝs\ *adj*
rid·er·ship \'rī-dǝr-,ship\ *n* (1968) : the number of persons who ride a system of public transportation
¹ridge \'rij\ *n* [ME *rigge,* fr. OE *hrycg;* akin to OHG *hrukki* ridge, back] (bef. 12c) **1 :** an elevated body part (as along the backbone) **2 :** a range of hills or mountains **3 :** an elongate elevation on an ocean bottom **4 :** an elongate crest or a linear series of crests **5 :** a raised strip (as of plowed ground) **5 :** the line of intersection at the top between the opposite slopes or sides of a roof — **ridged** \'rijd\ *adj*
²ridge *vb* **ridged; ridg·ing** *vt* (1523) : to form into a ridge ~ *vi* : to extend in ridges
ridge·line \'rij-,līn\ *n* (1833) : a line marking or following a ridge top
ridge·ling *or* **ridg·ling** \'rij-liŋ\ *n* [perh. fr. ¹*ridge;* fr. the supposition that the undescended testis remains near the animal's back] (1555) **1 :** a partially castrated male animal **2 :** a male animal having one or both testes retained in the inguinal canal
ridge·pole \'rij-,pōl\ *n* (1788) **1 :** the horizontal pole at the top of a tent **2 :** the highest horizontal timber in a roof against which the upper ends of the rafters are fixed
ridgy \'ri-jē\ *adj* (1697) : having or rising in ridges

1 ridgepole, 2 rafters

¹rid·i·cule \'ri-dǝ-,kyü(ǝ)l\ *n* [F or L; F, fr. L *ridiculum* jest] (1690) : the act of exposing to laughter : DERISION, MOCKERY
²ridicule *vt* **-culed; -cul·ing** (ca. 1700) : to make fun of — **rid·i·cul·er** *n*
syn RIDICULE, DERIDE, MOCK, TAUNT mean to make an object of laughter of. RIDICULE implies a deliberate often malicious belittling ⟨consistently *ridiculed* everything she said⟩. DERIDE suggests contemptuous and often bitter ridicule ⟨*derided* their efforts to start their own business⟩. MOCK implies scorn often ironically expressed as by mimicry or sham deference ⟨youngsters began to *mock* the helpless wino⟩. TAUNT suggests jeeringly provoking insult or challenge ⟨hometown fans *taunted* the visiting team⟩.
ri·dic·u·lous \rǝ-'di-kyǝ-lǝs\ *adj* [L *ridiculosus* (fr. *ridiculum* jest, fr. neut. of *ridiculus*) or *ridiculus,* lit., laughable, fr. *ridēre* to laugh] (1550) : arousing or deserving ridicule : ABSURD, PREPOSTEROUS *syn* see LAUGHABLE — **ri·dic·u·lous·ly** *adv* — **ri·dic·u·lous·ness** *n*
¹rid·ing \'rī-diŋ\ *n* (14c) : the action or state of one that rides
²rid·ing *adj* (15c) **1 :** used for or when riding ⟨a ~ horse⟩ ⟨~ boots⟩ **2 :** operated by a rider ⟨a ~ mower⟩
³rid·ing \'rī-diŋ\ *n* [ME *-redying* or *trithing,* alter. of (assumed) OE *thriding,* fr. ON *thrithjungr* third part, fr. *thrithi* third; akin to OE *thridda* third — more at THIRD] (15c) **1 :** one of the three administrative jurisdictions into which Yorkshire, England, was formerly divided **2 :** an administrative jurisdiction or electoral district in a British dominion (as Canada)
rid·ley \'rid-lē\ *n* [origin unknown] (1926) : either of two sea turtles: **a :** one (*Lepidochelys kempii*) of the Gulf of Mexico and the Atlantic coast of the U.S. — called also *Kemp's ridley* **b :** one (*L. olivacea*) of the Pacific, Atlantic, and Indian oceans
ri·dot·to \ri-'dä-(,)tō\ *n, pl* **-tos** [It, retreat, place of entertainment, redoubt — more at REDOUBT] (1722) : a public entertainment consisting of music and dancing often in masquerade popular in 18th century England

\ǝ\ abut \ᵊ\ kitten, F table \ǝr\ further \a\ ash \ā\ ace \ä\ mop, mar
\au̇\ out \ch\ chin \e\ bet \ē\ easy \g\ go \i\ hit \ī\ ice \j\ job
\ŋ\ sing \ō\ go \ȯ\ law \ȯi\ boy \th\ thin \t̶h̶\ the \ü\ loot \u̇\ foot
\y\ yet \zh\ vision \á, k̲, ⁿ, œ, œ̄, ǔ, ū̄, ʸ\ see Guide to Pronunciation

ri·el \rē-'el\ *n* [origin unknown] (1956) — see MONEY table

Rie·mann·ian geometry \rē-'mä-nē-ən-\ *n* [G. F. B. *Riemann*] (1904) : a non-Euclidean geometry in which straight lines are geodesics and in which the parallel postulate is replaced by the postulate that every pair of straight lines intersects

Rie·mann integral \'rē-,män-, -mən-\ *n* (1914) : a definite integral defined as the limit of sums found by partitioning the interval comprising the domain of definition into subintervals, by finding the sum of products each of which consists of the width of a subinterval multiplied by the value of the function at some point in it, and by letting the maximum width of the subintervals approach zero

Ries·ling \'rēz-liŋ, 'rēs-\ *n* [G] (1833) : a white wine that ranges from dry to very sweet and is made from a single variety of grape orig. grown in Germany; *also* : the grape

ri·fam·pin \rī-'fam-pən\ *or* **ri·fam·pi·cin** \rī-'fam-pə-sən\ *n* [ISV, alter. of rifamycin, antibiotic derived from *Streptomyces mediterranei*] (1966) : a semisynthetic antibiotic $C_{43}H_{58}N_4O_{12}$ that acts against some viruses and bacteria esp. by inhibiting RNA synthesis

rife \'rīf\ *adj* [ME *ryfe*, fr. OE *rȳfe*; akin to ON *rifr* abundant] (12c) **1** : prevalent esp. to an increasing degree ⟨fear was ~ in the people⟩ **2** : ABUNDANT, COMMON **3** : copiously supplied : ABOUNDING — usu. used with *with* ⟨~ with rumors⟩ — **rife** *adv* — **rife·ly** *adv*

¹**riff** \'rif\ *n* [prob. by shortening & alter. fr. *refrain*] (1935) **1** : an ostinato phrase (as in jazz) typically supporting a solo improvisation; *also* : a piece based on such a phrase **2** : a short succint usu. witty comment; *also* : BIT, ROUTINE

²**riff** *vi* (1950) : to perform a riff

³**riff** *vb* [short for *riffle*] (1952) : RIFFLE, SKIM ⟨~ pages⟩

Riff \'rif\ *n, pl* **Riffs** *or* **Riffi** \'ri-fē\ *or* **Riff** (1903) : a Berber of the Rif Mountains in northern Morocco

Riff·ian \'ri-fē-ən\ *n* (1867) : RIFF

¹**rif·fle** \'ri-fəl\ *vb* **rif·fled; rif·fling** \'ri-f(ə-)liŋ\ [²*riffle*] *vi* (1752) **1** : to form, flow over, or move in riffles **2** : to flip cursorily : THUMB ⟨~ through the catalog⟩ ~ *vt* **1** : to ruffle slightly : RIPPLE **2 a** : to leaf through hastily; *specif* : to leaf (as a stack of paper) by sliding a thumb along the edge of the leaves **b** : to shuffle (playing cards) by separating the deck into two parts and riffling with the thumbs so the cards intermix **3** : to manipulate (small objects) idly between the fingers

²**riffle** *n* [perh. alter. of *ruffle*] (1785) **1 a** : a shallow extending across a streambed and causing broken water **b** : a stretch of water flowing over a riffle **2** : a small wave or succession of small waves : RIPPLE **3 a** : any of various contrivances (as blocks or rails) laid on the bottom of a sluice or launder to make a series of grooves or interstices to catch and retain a mineral (as gold) **b** : a groove or interstice so formed **4** : a cleat or bar fastened to an inclined surface in a gold-washing apparatus to catch and hold mineral grains **5** [¹*riffle*] **a** : the act or process of shuffling (as cards) **b** : the sound made while doing this

rif·fler \'ri-flər\ *n* [F *rifloir*, fr. *rifler* to file, rifle] (ca. 1797) : a small filing or scraping tool

riff·raff \'rif-,raf\ *n* [ME *ryffe raffe*, fr. *rif and raf* every single one, fr. MF *rif et raf* completely, fr. *rifler* to scratch, plunder + *raffe* act of sweeping] (15c) **1 a** : disreputable persons **b** : RABBLE **c** : one of the riffraff **2** : REFUSE, RUBBISH — **riffraff** *adj*

¹**ri·fle** \'ri-fəl\ *vb* **ri·fled; ri·fling** \-f(ə-)liŋ\ [ME, fr. MF *rifler* to scratch, file, plunder, of Gmc origin; akin to OHG *riffilōn* to saw, obs. D *riffelen* to scrape] *vt* (14c) **1** : to ransack esp. with the intent to steal **2** : to steal and carry away ~ *vi* : to engage in ransacking and stealing — **ri·fler** \-f(ə-)lər\ *n*

²**rifle** *vt* **ri·fled; ri·fling** \-f(ə-)liŋ\ [perh. fr. F *rifler* to scratch, file] (1635) : to cut spiral grooves into the bore of ⟨*rifled* arms⟩ ⟨*rifled* pipe⟩

³**rifle** *n* (1770) **1 a** : a shoulder weapon with a rifled bore **b** : a rifled artillery piece **2** *pl* : soldiers armed with rifles

⁴**rifle** *vt* **ri·fled; ri·fling** \-f(ə-)liŋ\ [³*rifle*] (1937) : to propel (as a ball) with great force or speed

ri·fle-bird \'ri-fəl-,bərd\ *n* (1831) : any of several birds of paradise (genus *Ptiloris*)

ri·fle·man \-mən\ *n* (1775) **1** : a soldier armed with a rifle **2** : one skilled in shooting with a rifle

ri·fle·ry \'rī-fəl-rē\ *n* (1935) : the practice of shooting at targets with a rifle

ri·fling \'rī-f(ə-)liŋ\ *n* (1797) **1** : the act or process of making spiral grooves **2** : a system of spiral grooves in the surface of the bore of a gun causing a projectile when fired to rotate about its longer axis

¹**rift** \'rift\ *n* [ME, of Scand origin; akin to Dan & Norw *rift* fissure, ON *rifa* to rive — more at RIVE] (14c) **1 a** : FISSURE, CREVASSE **b** : FAULT **5 2** : a clear space or interval **3** : BREACH, ESTRANGEMENT

²**rift** *vi* (14c) : to burst open ~ *vt* **1** : CLEAVE, DIVIDE ⟨hills were ~ed by the earthquake⟩ **2** : PENETRATE

rift valley *n* (1894) : an elongated valley formed by the depression of a block of the earth's crust between two faults or groups of faults of approximately parallel strike

¹**rig** \'rig\ *vt* **rigged; rig·ging** [ME *riggen*] (15c) **1** : to fit out (as a ship) with rigging **2** : CLOTHE, DRESS — usu. used with *out* **3** : to furnish with special gear : EQUIP **4 a** : to put in condition or position for use : ADJUST, ARRANGE ⟨a car *rigged* for manual control⟩ **b** : CONSTRUCT ⟨~ up a temporary shelter⟩

²**rig** *n* (1822) **1** : the distinctive shape, number, and arrangement of sails and masts of a ship **2** : EQUIPAGE; *esp* : a carriage with its horse **3** : CLOTHING, DRESS **4** : tackle, equipment, or machinery fitted for a specified purpose ⟨an oil-drilling ~⟩ **5** : a tractor-trailer combination

³**rig** *vt* **rigged; rig·ging** [*rig*, n., a swindle] (1851) **1** : to manipulate or control usu. by deceptive or dishonest means ⟨~ an election⟩ **2** : to fix in advance for a desired result ⟨~ a quiz program⟩

rig·a·doon \,ri-gə-'dün\ *or* **ri·gau·don** \rē-gō-dōⁿ\ *n* [F *rigaudon*] (1691) : a lively dance of the 17th and 18th centuries; *also* : the music for a rigadoon

rig·a·ma·role *var of* RIGMAROLE

rig·a·to·ni \,ri-gə-'tō-nē\ *n* [It, pl., fr. *rigato* furrowed, fluted, fr. pp. of *rigare* to furrow, flute, fr. *riga* line, of Gmc origin; akin to OHG *riga* line — more at ROW] (ca. 1923) : pasta made in short wide fluted tubes

Ri·gel \'rī-jəl, -gəl; 'ri-jəl\ *n* [Ar *Rijl*, lit., foot] : a first-magnitude star in the left foot of the constellation Orion

rig·ger \'ri-gər\ *n* (1611) **1** : one that rigs **2** : a long slender pointed sable paintbrush

rig·ging \'ri-giŋ, -gən\ *n* (1594) **1 a** : lines and chains used aboard a ship esp. in working sail and supporting masts and spars **b** : a similar network (as in theater scenery) used for support and manipulation **2** : CLOTHING

¹**right** \'rīt\ *adj* [ME, fr. OE *riht*; akin to OHG *reht* right, L *rectus* straight, right, *regere* to lead straight, direct, rule, *rogare* to ask, Gk *oregein* to stretch out] (bef. 12c) **1** : RIGHTEOUS, UPRIGHT **2** : being in accordance with what is just, good, or proper ⟨~ conduct⟩ **3 a** : agreeable to a standard **b** : conforming to facts or truth : CORRECT ⟨the ~ answer⟩ **4** : SUITABLE, APPROPRIATE ⟨the ~ man for the job⟩ **5** : STRAIGHT ⟨a ~ line⟩ **6** : GENUINE, REAL **7 a** : of, relating to, situated on, or being the side of the body which is away from the heart and on which the hand is stronger in most people **b** : located nearer to the right hand than to the left **c** : located to the right of an observer facing the object specified or directed as the right arm would point when raised out to the side **d** (1) : located on the right of an observer facing in the same direction as the object specified ⟨stage ~⟩ (2) : located on the right when facing downstream ⟨the ~ bank of a river⟩ **8** : having the axis perpendicular to the base ⟨~ cone⟩ **9** : of, relating to, or constituting the principal or more prominent side of an object ⟨made sure the socks were ~ side out⟩ **10** : acting or judging in accordance with truth or fact ⟨time proved her ~⟩ **11 a** : being in good physical or mental health or order ⟨not in his ~ mind⟩ **b** : being in a correct or proper state ⟨put things ~⟩ **12** : most favorable or desired : PREFERABLE; *also* : socially acceptable ⟨knew all the ~ people⟩ **13** *often cap* : of, adhering to, or constituted by the Right esp. in politics *syn* see CORRECT — **right·ness** *n*

²**right** *n* [ME, fr. OE *riht*, fr. *riht*, adj.] (bef. 12c) **1** : qualities (as adherence to duty or obedience to lawful authority) that together constitute the ideal of moral propriety or merit moral approval **2** : something to which one has a just claim: as **a** : the power or privilege to which one is justly entitled **b** (1) : the interest that one has in a piece of property — often used in pl. ⟨mineral ~s⟩ (2) *pl* : the property interest possessed under law or custom and agreement in an intangible thing esp. of a literary and artistic nature ⟨film ~s of the novel⟩ **3** : something that one may properly claim as due **4** : the cause of truth or justice **5 a** : RIGHT HAND 1a; *also* : a blow struck with this hand ⟨gave him a hard ~ on the jaw⟩ **b** : the location or direction of the right side ⟨woods on his ~⟩ **c** : the part on the right side **d** : RIGHT FIELD **6 a** : the true account or correct interpretation **b** : the quality or state of being factually correct **7** *often cap* : the part of a legislative chamber located to the right of the presiding officer **b** : the members of a continental European legislative body occupying the right as a result of holding more conservative political views than other members **8 a** *often cap* : individuals sometimes professing opposition to change in the established order and favoring traditional attitudes and practices and sometimes advocating the forced establishment of an authoritarian order (as in government) **b** *often cap* : a conservative position **9 a** : a privilege given stockholders to subscribe pro rata to a new issue of securities generally below market price **b** : the negotiable certificate evidencing such privilege — usu. used in pl. — **right·most** \-,mōst\ *adj* — **by rights** : with reason or justice : PROPERLY — **in one's own right** : by virtue of one's own qualifications or properties — **of right 1** : as an absolute right **2** : legally or morally exactable — **to rights** : into proper order

³**right** *adv* (bef. 12c) **1** : according to right ⟨live ~⟩ **2** : in the exact location, position, or moment : PRECISELY ⟨~ at his fingertips⟩ ⟨quit ~ then and there⟩ **3** : in a suitable, proper, or desired manner ⟨knew he wasn't doing it ~⟩ **4** : in a direct line, course, or manner : DIRECTLY, STRAIGHT ⟨go ~ home⟩ ⟨came ~ out and said it⟩ **5** : according to fact or truth : TRULY ⟨guessed ~⟩ **6 a** : all the way ⟨windows ~ to the floor⟩ **b** : in a complete manner ⟨felt ~ at home⟩ **7** : without delay : IMMEDIATELY ⟨~ after lunch⟩ **8** : to a great degree : VERY ⟨a ~ pleasant day⟩ **9** : on or to the right ⟨looked left and ~⟩

⁴**right** *vt* (bef. 12c) **1 a** : to do justice to : redress the injuries of ⟨so just is God to ~ the innocent —Shak.⟩ **b** : JUSTIFY, VINDICATE ⟨felt the need to ~ himself in court⟩ **2** : AVENGE ⟨vows to ~ the injustice done to his family⟩ **3 a** : to adjust or restore to the proper state or condition ⟨~ the economy⟩ **b** : to bring or restore to an upright position ⟨~ a capsized boat⟩ ~ *vi* : to become upright — **right·er** *n*

right and left *adv* (1829) : on both or all sides : in every direction : EVERYWHERE

right angle *n* (15c) : the angle bounded by two lines perpendicular to each other : an angle of 90° or $1/2 \pi$ radians — **right-an·gled** \'rīt-'aŋ-gəld\ *or* **right-an·gle** \-gəl\ *adj*

right ascension *n* (15c) : the arc of the celestial equator between the vernal equinox and the point where the hour circle through the given body intersects the equator reckoned eastward commonly in terms of the corresponding interval of sidereal time in hours, minutes, and seconds

right away *adv* (1818) : without delay or hesitation : IMMEDIATELY

right circular cone *n* (ca. 1889) : CONE 1a

right circular cylinder *n* (1877) : a cylinder with the bases circular and with the axis joining the two centers of the bases perpendicular to the planes of the two bases

righ·teous \'rī-chəs\ *adj* [alter. of earlier *rightuous*, alter. of ME *rightwise, rightwos*, fr. OE *rihtwis*, fr. *riht*, n., right + *wis* wise] (1535) **1** : acting in accord with divine or moral law : free from guilt or sin **2 a** : morally right or justifiable ⟨a ~ decision⟩ **b** : arising from an outraged sense of justice or morality ⟨~ indignation⟩ **3** *slang* : GENUINE, GOOD *syn* see MORAL — **righ·teous·ly** *adv* — **righ·teous·ness** *n*

right field *n* (1857) **1** : the part of the baseball outfield to the right of the outfielder looking out from home plate **2** : the position of the player defending right field — **right fielder** *n*

right·ful \'rīt-fəl\ *adj* (14c) **1** : JUST, EQUITABLE **2 a** : having a just or legally established claim : LEGITIMATE ⟨the ~ owner⟩ **b** : held by

right circular cylinder: *1* axis

right or just claim : LEGAL 〈~ authority〉 **3** : PROPER, FITTING 〈assured of his ~ place in history —Brian Duff〉 — **right·ful·ly** \-fə-lē\ *adv* — **right·ful·ness** *n*

right–hand \'rīt-,hand\ *adj* (1592) **1** : situated on the right **2** : RIGHT-HANDED **3** : chiefly relied on 〈~ man〉

right hand *n* (bef. 12c) **1 a** : the hand on a person's right side **b** : an indispensable person **2 a** : the right side **b** : a place of honor

right–hand·ed \-'han-dəd\ *adj* (14c) **1** : using the right hand habitually or more easily than the left; *also* : swinging from right to left 〈a ~ batter〉 **2** : relating to, designed for, or done with the right hand **3 a** : having the same direction or course as the movement of the hands of a watch viewed from in front : CLOCKWISE **b** : having a spiral structure or form that ascends or advances to the right 〈a ~ screw〉 〈a ~ double helix of DNA〉 **4** *of a door* : opening to the right away from one — **right–handed** *adv* — **right–hand·ed·ly** *adv* — **right–hand·ed·ness** *n*

right–hand·er \-'han-dər\ *n* (1857) **1** : a blow struck with the right hand **2** : a right-handed person; *esp* : a right-handed pitcher

right·ism \'rīt-,i-zəm\ *n, often cap* (1939) **1** : the principles and views of the Right **2** : advocacy of or adherence to the doctrines of the Right — **right·ist** \'rī-tist\ *n or adj, often cap*

right·ly \'rīt-lē\ *adv* (bef. 12c) **1** : in accordance with right conduct : FAIRLY, JUSTLY **2** : in the right or proper manner : PROPERLY, FITTINGLY **3** : according to truth or fact : CORRECTLY, EXACTLY

right–mind·ed \-'mīn-dəd\ *adj* (ca. 1586) : having a right or honest mind 〈a ~ citizen〉 — **right–mind·ed·ness** *n*

right now *adv* (14c) **1** : RIGHT AWAY **2** : at present

righ·to \,rīt-'ō, 'rī-(,)tō\ *interj* (1896) — used to express cheerful concurrence, assent, or understanding

right off *adv* (1790) : RIGHT AWAY : at once — **right off the bat** : RIGHT OFF

right–of–way \,rīt-ə(v)-'wā\ *n, pl* **rights–of–way** *also* **right–of–ways** (1768) **1** : a legal right of passage over another person's ground **2 a** : the area over which a right-of-way exists **b** : the strip of land over which is built a public road **c** : the land occupied by a railroad esp. for its main line **d** : the land used by a public utility (as for a transmission line) **3 a** : a precedence in passing accorded to one vehicle over another by custom, decision, or statute **b** : the right of traffic to take precedence **c** : the right to take precedence over others 〈gave the bill the ~ in the Senate〉

right on *adj* (1925) **1** : exactly correct — often used interjectionally to express agreement **2** *usu* **right–on** : attuned to the spirit of the times

Right Reverend (15c) — used as a title for high ecclesiastical officials

right shoulder arms *n* (1902) : a position in the manual of arms in which the butt of the rifle is held in the right hand with the barrel resting on the right shoulder; *also* : a command to assume this position

right–to–life \'rīt-tə-'līf\ *adj* (1973) : opposed to abortion — **right–to–lif·er** \-'lī-fər\ *n*

right–to–work *adj* (1949) : opposing or banning the closed shop and the union shop

right triangle *n* (1924) : a triangle having a right angle — see TRIANGLE illustration

right·ward \'rīt-wərd\ *adj* (1825) : being toward or on the right

right whale *n* (1725) : any of a family (Balaenidae) of baleen whales having very long baleen, a large head on a stocky body, a smooth throat, and short broad rounded flippers

right whale

right wing *n* (1905) **1** : the rightist division of a group or party **2** : RIGHT 8 — **right–wing** \'rīt-'wiŋ, -,wiŋ\ *adj* — **right–wing·er** \'rīt-'wiŋ-ər, ,rīt-\ *n*

righ·ty \'rī-tē\ *n, pl* **right·ies** (1949) : RIGHT-HANDER 2

rig·id \'ri-jəd\ *adj* [ME *rigide*, fr. MF or L, fr. L *rigidus*, fr. *rigēre* to be stiff] (15c) **1 a** : deficient in or devoid of flexibility 〈~ price controls〉 〈a ~ bar of metal〉 **b** : appearing stiff and unyielding 〈his face ~ with pain〉 **2 a** : inflexibly set in opinion **b** : strictly observed 〈adheres to a ~ schedule〉 **3** : firmly inflexible rather than lax or indulgent 〈a ~ disciplinarian〉 **4** : precise and accurate in procedure 〈~ control of the manufacturing process〉 **5** *of an airship* : having the outer shape maintained by a fixed framework — **rig·id·ly** *adv* — **rig·id·ness** *n*

syn RIGID, RIGOROUS, STRICT, STRINGENT mean extremely severe or stern. RIGID implies uncompromising inflexibility 〈*rigid* rules of conduct〉. RIGOROUS implies the imposition of hardship and difficulty 〈the *rigorous* training of recruits〉. STRICT emphasizes undeviating conformity to rules, standards, or requirements 〈*strict* enforcement of the law〉. STRINGENT suggests severe, tight restriction or limitation 〈*stringent* standards of admission〉. **syn** see in addition STIFF

ri·gid·i·fy \rə-'ji-də-,fī\ *vb* **-fied; -fy·ing** *vt* (1842) : to make rigid ~ *vi* : to become rigid — **ri·gid·i·fi·ca·tion** \-,ji-də-fə-'kā-shən\ *n*

ri·gid·i·ty \rə-'ji-də-tē\ *n, pl* **-ties** (1624) **1** : the quality or state of being rigid **2** : one that is rigid (as in form or conduct)

rig·ma·role \'ri-gə-mə-,rōl, 'rig-mə-\ *n* [alter. of obs. *ragman roll* long list, catalog] (ca. 1736) **1** : confused or meaningless talk **2** : a complex and ritualistic procedure

rig·or \'ri-gər\ *n* [ME *rigour*, fr. MF *rigueur*, fr. L *rigor*, lit., stiffness, fr. *rigēre* to be stiff] (14c) **1 a** (1) : harsh inflexibility in opinion, temper, or judgment : SEVERITY (2) : the quality of being unyielding or inflexible : STRICTNESS (3) : severity of life : AUSTERITY **b** : an act or instance of strictness, severity, or cruelty **2** : a tremor caused by a chill **3** : a condition that makes life difficult, challenging, or uncomfortable; *esp* : extremity of cold **4** : strict precision : EXACTNESS 〈logical ~〉 **5 a** *obs* : RIGIDITY, STIFFNESS **b** : rigidness or torpor of organs or tissue that prevents response to stimuli

rig·or·ism \'ri-gə-,ri-zəm\ *n* (1704) : rigidity in principle or practice — **rig·or·ist** \-rist\ *n or adj* — **rig·or·is·tic** \,ri-gə-'ris-tik\ *adj*

rig·or mor·tis \,ri-gər-'mȯr-təs *also chiefly Brit* ,rī-,gȯr-\ *n* [NL, stiffness of death] (ca. 1847) : temporary rigidity of muscles occurring after death

rig·or·ous \'ri-g(ə-)rəs\ *adj* (15c) **1** : manifesting, exercising, or favoring rigor : very strict **2 a** : marked by extremes of temperature or climate **b** : HARSH, SEVERE **3** : scrupulously accurate : PRECISE **syn** see RIGID — **rig·or·ous·ly** *adv* — **rig·or·ous·ness** *n*

rig·our *chiefly Brit var of* RIGOR

rijst·ta·fel \'ris-,tä-fəl\ *n* [D, fr. *rijst* rice + *tafel* table] (1889) : an Indonesian meal consisting of rice and a variety of accompanying dishes (as meat, seafood, and vegetables)

Riks·mål *or* **Riks·maal** \'riks-,mȯl, 'rēks-\ *n* [Norw., fr. *rik* kingdom + *mål* speech] (1913) : BOKMÅL

rile \'rī(ə)l\ *vt* **riled; ril·ing** [var. of *roil*] (1825) **1** : to make agitated and angry : UPSET **2** : ROIL 1 **syn** see IRRITATE

ril·ey \'rī-lē\ *adj* (1805) **1** : TURBID **2** : ANGRY

[1]rill \'ril\ *n* [D *ril* or LG *rille*; akin to OE *rith* rivulet] (1538) : a very small brook

[2]rill *vi* (1610) : to flow like a rill

[3]rill \'ril\ *or* **rille** \'ril, 'ri-lə\ *n* [G *Rille*, lit., channel made by a small stream, fr. LG, rill] (1868) : any of several long narrow valleys on the moon's surface

rill·et \'ri-lət\ *n* (1538) : a little rill

ril·lettes \ri-'lets, -'yet\ *n pl* [F, pl., dim. of *rille*, sing., piece of pork, fr. MF, dial. var. of *reille* board, lath, fr. L *regula* straightedge — more at RULE] (1889) : cooked shredded meat (as pork or duck) or fish preserved in fat

[1]rim \'rim\ *n* [ME, fr. OE *rima*; akin to ON *rimi* strip of land] (13c) **1 a** : BRINK **b** : the outer often curved or circular edge or border of something **2 a** : the outer part of a wheel joined to the hub usu. by spokes **b** : a removable outer metal band on an automobile wheel to which the tire is attached **3** : FRAME 4c(1) — **rim·less** \-ləs\ *adj*

[2]rim *vb* **rimmed; rim·ming** *vt* (1794) **1** : to serve as a rim for : BORDER 〈cliffs *rimming* the camp〉 **2** : to run around the rim of 〈putts that ~ the cup〉 ~ *vi* : to form or show a rim

[1]rime \'rim\ *n* [ME *rim*, fr. OE *hrim*; akin to ON *hrim* frost] (bef. 12c) **1** : FROST 1b **2** : an accumulation of granular ice tufts on the windward sides of exposed objects that is formed from supercooled fog or cloud and built out directly against the wind **3** : CRUST, INCRUSTATION 〈a ~ of snow〉

[2]rime *vt* **rimed; rim·ing** (ca. 1755) : to cover with or as if with rime

[3]rime, rime·ster *var of* RHYME, RHYMESTER

rim–fire \'rim-,fīr\ *adj* (1868) *of a cartridge* : having the priming distributed in the rim of the shell — **rimfire** *n*

rim·land \'rim-,land\ *n* (1944) : a region on the periphery of the heartland

rimmed \'rimd\ *adj* (1729) : having a rim — usu. used in combination 〈dark-*rimmed* glasses〉 〈red-*rimmed* eyes〉

rim·rock \'rim-,räk\ *n* (1860) **1** : a top stratum or overlying strata of resistant rock of a plateau that outcrops to form a vertical face **2** : the edge or face of a rimrock outcrop

rimy \'rī-mē\ *adj* **rim·i·er; -est** [OE *hrīmig*, fr. *hrīm*] (bef. 12c) : covered with rime : FROSTY

rind \'rīnd, *dial* 'rīn\ *n* [ME, fr. OE; akin to OHG *rinda* bark, and prob. to OE *rendan* to rend] (bef. 12c) **1** : the bark of a tree **2** : a usu. hard or tough outer layer : PEEL, CRUST 〈grated lemon ~〉 — **rind·ed** \'rīn-dəd\ *adj*

rin·der·pest \'rin-dər-,pest\ *n* [G, fr. *Rinder*, pl., cattle + *Pest* pestilence] (1865) : an acute infectious febrile disease of ruminant mammals (as cattle) that is caused by a virus and is marked by diarrhea and inflammation of mucous membranes

[1]ring \'riŋ\ *n* [ME, fr. OE *hring*; akin to OHG *hring* ring, OCS *krọgŭ* circle] (bef. 12c) **1** : a circular band for holding, connecting, hanging, pulling, packing, or sealing 〈a key ~〉 〈a towel ~〉 **2** : a circlet usu. of precious metal worn on the finger **3 a** : a circular line, figure, or object (smoke ~) **b** : an encircling arrangement 〈a ~ of suburbs〉 **c** : a circular or spiral course — often used in pl. in the phrase *run rings around* **4 a** (1) : an often circular space esp. for exhibitions or competitions; *esp* : such a space at a circus (2) : a structure containing such a ring **b** : a square enclosure in which boxers or wrestlers contest **5** : a band believed to be composed of rocky fragments revolving around a planet (as Saturn) **6** : ANNUAL RING **7 a** : an exclusive combination of persons for a selfish and often corrupt purpose (as to control a market) 〈a wheat ~〉 **b** : GANG **8** : the field of a political contest : RACE **9** : food in the shape of a circle **10** : an arrangment of atoms represented in formulas or models in a cyclic manner — called *also* cycle **11** : a set of mathematical elements that is closed under two binary operations of which the first forms a commutative group with the set and the second is associative over the set and is distributive with respect to the first operation **12** *pl* **a** : a pair of usu. rubber-covered metal rings suspended from a ceiling or crossbar to a height of approximately eight feet above the floor and used for hanging, swinging, and balancing feats in gymnastics **b** : an event in gymnastics competition in which the rings are used **13** : [2]BOXING 〈ended his ~ career〉 — **ring–like** \'riŋ-līk\ *adj*

[2]ring *vb* **ringed; ring·ing** *vt* (14c) **1** : to provide with a ring **2** : to place or form a ring around : ENCIRCLE 〈police ~ed the building〉 **3** : GIRDLE 2 **4** : to throw a ringer over (the peg) in a game (as horseshoes or quoits) ~ *vi* **1 a** : to move in a ring **b** : to rise in the air spirally **2** : to form or take the shape of a ring

\ə\ abut \ᵊ\ kitten, F table \ər\ further \a\ ash \ā\ ace \ä\ mop, mar \au̇\ out \ch\ chin \e\ bet \ē\ easy \g\ go \i\ hit \ī\ ice \j\ job \ŋ\ sing \ō\ go \ȯ\ law \ȯi\ boy \th\ thin \t̷h\ the \ü\ loot \u̇\ foot \y\ yet \zh\ vision \á, k̲, ⁿ, œ, œ̄, ue, ūe, ᶜ\ *see* Guide to Pronunciation

³**ring** *vb* **rang** \'raŋ\; **rung** \'rəŋ\; **ring·ing** \'riŋ-iŋ\ [ME, fr. OE *hringan*; akin to ON *hringja* to ring] *vi* (bef. 12c) **1 :** to sound resonantly or sonorously ⟨the doorbell *rang*⟩ ⟨cheers *rang* out⟩ **2 a :** to be filled with a reverberating sound : RESOUND ⟨the halls *rang* with laughter⟩ **b :** to have the sensation of being filled with a humming sound ⟨his ears *rang*⟩ **3 :** to cause something to ring ⟨~ for the butler⟩ **4 a :** to be filled with talk or report ⟨the whole land *rang* with her fame⟩ **b :** to have great renown **c :** to sound repetitiously ⟨their praise *rang* in his ears⟩ **5 :** to have a sound or character expressive of some quality ⟨a story that ~s true⟩ **6** *chiefly Brit* **:** to make a telephone call — usu. used with *up* ~ *vt* **1 :** to cause to sound esp. by striking **2 :** to make (a sound) by or as if by ringing a bell **3 :** to announce by or as if by ringing **4 :** to repeat often, loudly, or earnestly **5 a :** to summon esp. by bell **b** *chiefly Brit* **:** TELEPHONE — usu. used with *up* — **ring a bell :** to arouse a response ⟨that name *rings a bell*⟩ — **ring down the curtain :** to conclude a performance or an action — **ring off the hook :** to ring frequently or constantly with incoming calls ⟨the telephone was *ringing off the hook*⟩ — **ring the changes** *or* **ring changes :** to run through the range of possible variations — **ring up the curtain :** to begin a performance or an action

⁴**ring** *n* (1549) **1 :** a set of bells **2 :** a clear resonant sound made by or resembling that made by vibrating metal **3 :** resonant tone : SONORITY **4 :** a loud sound continued, repeated, or reverberated **5 :** a sound or character expressive of some particular quality ⟨the story had a familiar ~⟩ **6 a :** the act or an instance of ringing **b :** a telephone call ⟨give me a ~ in the morning⟩

ring–a–le·vio \,riŋ-ə-'lē-vē-,ō\ *or* **ring–a–lie·vo** \-'lē-(,)vō\ *n* [alter. of earlier *ring relievo*, fr. ¹*ring* + *relieve*] (ca. 1901) **:** a game in which players on one team are given time to hide and are then sought out by members of the other team who try to capture them, keep them in a place of confinement, and keep them from being released by their teammates

ring–around–a–rosy \,riŋ-ə-,raûn-də-'rō-zē\ *or* **ring–around–the–rosy** \-,raûn(d)-thə-\ *n* (ca. 1886) **:** a children's singing game in which players dance around in a circle and at a given signal squat — called also *ring-a-rosy* \,riŋ-ə-'rō-zē\

ring–bark \'riŋ-,bärk\ *vt* (1892) **:** GIRDLE 2

ring binder *n* (1929) **:** a loose-leaf binder in which split metal rings attached to a metal back hold the perforated sheets of paper

ring·bolt \'riŋ-,bōlt\ *n* (1599) **:** an eyebolt with a ring through its eye

ring·bone \-,bōn\ *n* (1523) **:** a bony outgrowth on the pastern bones of the horse usu. producing lameness

ring dance *n* (1600) **:** ROUND DANCE 1

ring·dove \'riŋ-,dəv\ *n* (1538) **1 :** a chiefly European pigeon (*Columba palumbus*) with a whitish patch on each side of the neck and wings edged with white **2 :** a small dove (*Streptopelia risoria*) of southeastern Europe and Asia — called also *ringed turtle dove*

ringed \'riŋd\ *adj* (14c) **1 :** encircled or marked with or as if with rings **2 :** composed or formed of rings

¹**ring·er** \'riŋ-ər\ *n* (15c) **1 :** one that sounds esp. by ringing **2 a** (1) **:** one that enters a competition under false representations (2) **:** IMPOSTER, FAKE **b :** one that strongly resembles another — often used with *dead* ⟨he's a dead ~ for the senator⟩

²**ringer** *n* (1863) **:** one that encircles or puts a ring around (as a quoit or horseshoe that lodges so as to surround the peg)

Ring·er's solution \'riŋ-ərz-\ *n* [Sidney *Ringer* †1910 Eng. physician] (1893) **:** a balanced aqueous solution that contains chloride, sodium, potassium, calcium, bicarbonate, and phosphate ions and that is used in physiological experiments to provide a medium essentially isotonic to many animal tissues — called also *Ringer solution*

ring finger *n* (bef. 12c) **:** the third finger esp. of the left hand counting the forefinger as the first

ring·git \'riŋ-git\ *n*, *pl* **ringgit** *or* **ringgits** [Malay, lit., toothed, serrated] (1967) — see MONEY table

ring·ing \'riŋ-iŋ\ *adj* (14c) **1 :** clear and full in tone : RESOUNDING ⟨a ~ baritone⟩ **2 :** vigorously unequivocal : DECISIVE ⟨a ~ condemnation of immorality⟩ — **ring·ing·ly** \-iŋ-lē\ *adv*

ring·lead·er \'riŋ-,lē-dər\ *n* (1503) **:** a leader of a ring of individuals engaged esp. in improper or unlawful activities

ring·let \'riŋ-lət\ *n* (1555) **1 :** a small ring or circle **2 :** CURL; *esp* **:** a long curl of hair

ring·mas·ter \'riŋ-,mas-tər\ *n* (1873) **:** one in charge of performances in a ring (as of a circus); *broadly* **:** a supervisor or moderator esp. of a performance or presentation

ring·neck \-,nek\ *n* (1791) **:** a ring-necked animal

ring–necked \'riŋ-,nekt\ *or* **ring–neck** \'riŋ-,nek\ *adj* (1817) **:** having a ring of color about the neck

ring–necked duck *n* (1831) **:** an American scaup duck (*Aythya collaris*) that has a white ring around the bill and in the male a faint narrow chestnut ring encircling the neck

ring–necked pheasant *n* (1834) **:** a Eurasian pheasant (*Phasianus colchicus*) that has been widely introduced as a game bird in No. America and that has a white neck ring and an iridescent green and purplish head with red wattles around the eyes

ring off *vi* (1882) *chiefly Brit* **:** HANG UP 1

ring–po·rous \'riŋ-,pōr-əs, -,pȯr-\ *adj* (1902) **:** having vessels more numerous and usu. larger in cross section in the springwood with a resulting more or less distinct line between the springwood and the last season's wood — compare DIFFUSE-POROUS

ring road *n* (1928) *chiefly Brit* **:** a highway skirting an urban area

¹**ring·side** \'riŋ-,sīd\ *n* (1866) **1 :** the area just outside a ring esp. in which a contest occurs **2 :** a place from which one may have a close view

²**ringside** *adj* (1896) **:** being at the ringside ⟨a ~ seat⟩

ring-necked pheasant

ring spot *n* (1923) **1 :** a lesion of plant tissue consisting of yellowish, purplish, or necrotic, often concentric rings **2 :** a viral disease of plants that is characterized by ring spots

ring stand *n* (ca. 1865) **:** a metal stand consisting of a long upright rod attached to a heavy rectangular base that is used with rings and clamps for supporting laboratory apparatus

ring·straked \'riŋ-,strākt\ *adj* (1611) *archaic* **:** marked with circular stripes

ring·tail \-,tāl\ *n* (1844) **1 :** RACCOON **2 :** a carnivore (*Bassariscus astutus*) of the western U.S. and Mexico that is related to and resembles the raccoon — called also *cacomistle, civet cat, ringtail cat, ringtailed cat* **3 :** CAPUCHIN 3

ring–tailed \-,tā(ə)ld\ *adj* (1729) **1 :** having a tail marked with rings of differing colors **2 :** having a tail carried in a form approximating a circle ⟨a ~ Afghan hound⟩

ring–taw \-,tȯ\ *n* (1828) **:** a game of marbles in which marbles are placed in a circle on the ground and shot at from the edge of the circle with the object being to knock them out of the circle

ring–toss \-,tȯs, -,täs\ *n* (1871) **:** a game in which the object is to toss a ring so that it will fall over an upright stick

ring up *vt* (1937) **1 :** to total and record esp. by means of a cash register **2 :** ACHIEVE ⟨*rang up* many social triumphs⟩

ring·worm \'riŋ-,wərm\ *n* (15c) **:** any of several contagious fungal diseases of the skin, hair, or nails of humans and domestic animals that are characterized by ring-shaped discolored skin patches covered with vesicles and scales

rink \'riŋk\ *n* [ME (Sc) *rinc* area in which a contest takes place, fr. MF *renc* place, row — more at RANK] (1787) **1 a :** a smooth extent of ice marked off for curling or ice hockey **b :** a surface of ice for ice-skating; *also* **:** a building containing such a rink **c :** an enclosure for roller-skating **2 :** an alley for lawn bowling **3 :** a team in bowls or curling

rinky–dink \'riŋ-kē-,diŋk\ *adj* [origin unknown] (1913) **1 :** SMALL-TIME **2 :** OLD-FASHIONED

¹**rinse** \'rin(t)s, *esp dial* 'rench\ *vt* **rinsed; rins·ing** [ME *rincen*, fr. MF *rincer*, fr. (assumed) VL *recentiare*, fr. L *recent-, recens* fresh, recent] (14c) **1 :** to cleanse by flushing with liquid (as water) — often used with *out* ⟨~ out the mouth⟩ **2 a :** to cleanse (as of soap used in washing) by clear water **b :** to treat (hair) with a rinse **3 :** to remove (dirt or impurities) by washing lightly or in water only — **rins·er** *n*

²**rinse** *n* (1837) **1 :** the act or process of rinsing **2 a :** liquid used for rinsing **b :** a solution that temporarily tints hair

rins·ing \'riŋ\ *n* (1818) **1 :** DREGS, RESIDUE — usu. used in pl. **2 :** water that has been used for rinsing — usu. used in pl.

rio·ja \rē-'ō-(,)hä\ *n, often cap* (1907) **:** a wine from the Rioja region of Spain; *esp* **:** a dry red wine from this region

¹**ri·ot** \'rī-ət\ *n* [ME, fr. OF, dispute, fr. *rioter* to quarrel] (13c) **1** *archaic* **a :** profligate behavior : DEBAUCHERY **b :** unrestrained revelry **c :** noise, uproar, or disturbance made by revelers **2 a :** public violence, tumult, or disorder **b :** a violent public disorder; *specif* **:** a tumultuous disturbance of the public peace by three or more persons assembled together and acting with a common intent **3 :** a random or disorderly profusion ⟨the woods were a ~ of color⟩ **4 :** one that is wildly amusing ⟨the new comedy is a ~⟩

²**riot** *vi* (14c) **1 :** to indulge in revelry or wantonness **2 :** to create or engage in a riot — **ri·ot·er** *n*

riot act *n* [the *Riot Act*, English law of 1715 providing for the dispersal of riots upon command of legal authority] (1819) **:** a vigorous reprimand or warning — used in the phrase *read the riot act*

riot gun *n* (1916) **:** a small arm used to disperse rioters rather than to inflict serious injury or death; *esp* **:** a short-barreled shotgun

ri·ot·ous \'rī-ə-təs\ *adj* (15c) **1 a :** of the nature of a riot : TURBULENT **b :** participating in riot **2 :** ABUNDANT, EXUBERANT ⟨the garden was ~ with flowers⟩ — **ri·ot·ous·ly** *adv* — **ri·ot·ous·ness** *n*

¹**rip** \'rip\ *vb* **ripped; rip·ping** [prob. fr. Flem *rippen* to strip off roughly] *vt* (15c) **1 a :** to tear or split apart or open **b :** to saw or split (wood) with the grain **2 :** to slash or slit with or as if with a sharp blade **3 :** to hit sharply ⟨*ripped* a double to left field⟩ **4 :** to utter violently : spit out ⟨*ripped* out an oath⟩ **5 :** CRITICIZE, PUT DOWN ~ *vi* **1 :** to become ripped : REND **2 :** to rush headlong ⟨*ripped* past second base⟩ **syn** see TEAR — **rip into :** to tear into : ATTACK

²**rip** *n* (1711) **1 :** a rent made by ripping : TEAR **2 :** CUT 5b

³**rip** *n* [perh. fr. ²*rip*] (1775) **1 :** a body of water made rough by the meeting of opposing tides, currents, or winds **2 :** a current of water roughened by passing over an irregular bottom **3 :** RIP CURRENT

⁴**rip** *n* [perh. by shortening & alter. fr. *reprobate*] (1797) **:** a dissolute person : LIBERTINE

ri·par·i·an \rə-'per-ē-ən, rī-\ *adj* [L *riparius* — more at RIVER] (ca. 1841) **:** relating to or living or located on the bank of a natural watercourse (as a river) or sometimes of a lake or a tidewater

riparian right *n* (ca. 1860) **:** a right (as access to or use of the shore, bed, and water) of one owning riparian land

rip cord *n* (1907) **1 :** a cord by which the gasbag of a balloon may be ripped open for a limited distance to release the gas quickly and so cause immediate descent **2 :** a cord or wire pulled in making a descent to release the pilot parachute which lifts the main parachute out of its container

rip current *n* (1936) **:** a strong usu. narrow surface current flowing outward from a shore that results from the return flow of waves and wind-driven water

ripe \'rīp\ *adj* **rip·er; rip·est** [ME, fr. OE *ripe*; akin to OE *ripan, reopan* to reap] (bef. 12c) **1 :** fully grown and developed : MATURE **2 :** having mature knowledge, understanding, or judgment **3 :** of advanced years : LATE ⟨lived to a ~ old age⟩ **4 a :** SUITABLE, APPROPRIATE ⟨the time seemed ~ for the experiment⟩ **b :** fully prepared : READY ⟨the colonies were ~ for revolution⟩ **5 a :** brought by aging to full flavor or the best state : MELLOW ⟨~ cheese⟩ **b :** SMELLY, STINKING **6 :** ruddy, plump, or full like ripened fruit **7 :** INDECENT ⟨~ language⟩ — **ripe·ly** *adv* — **ripe·ness** *n*

rip·en \'rī-pən, 'rī-p'm\ *vb* **rip·ened; rip·en·ing** \'rī-pə-niŋ, 'rīp-niŋ\ *vi* (1561) **:** to grow or become ripe ~ *vt* **1 :** to make ripe **2 a :** to bring to completeness or perfection **b :** to age or cure (cheese) to develop characteristic flavor, odor, body, texture, and color **c :** to improve flavor and tenderness of (beef or game) by aging under refrigeration — **rip·en·er** \'rī-pə-nər, 'rīp-nər\ *n*

ri·pie·no \ri-'pyā-(,)nō, -'pye-\ *n, pl* **-ni** \-(,)nē\ *or* **-nos** [It, lit., filled up] (ca. 1930) : TUTTI

rip-off \'rip-,óf\ *n* (1969) **1** : an act or instance of stealing : THEFT; *also* : a financial exploitation **2** : a usu. cheap exploitive imitation

rip off *vt* (1967) **1 a** : ROB; *also* : CHEAT, DEFRAUD **b** : STEAL **2** : to copy or imitate blatantly or unscrupulously **3** : to perform, achieve, or score quickly or easily ⟨*ripped off* 10 straight points⟩

ri·poste \ri-'pōst\ *n* [F, modif. of It *risposta*, lit., answer, fr. *ripondere* to respond, fr. L *respondēre*] (1707) **1** : a fencer's quick return thrust following a parry **2** : a retaliatory verbal sally : RETORT **3** : a retaliatory maneuver or measure — **riposte** *vb*

ripped \'ript\ *adj* (1970) *slang* : being under the influence of alcohol or drugs : HIGH, STONED

rip·per \'ri-pər\ *n* (1611) **1** : one that rips; *esp* : a machine used to break up solid material (as rock or ore) **2** : an excellent example or instance of its kind

rip·ping \'ri-piŋ\ *adj* [prob. fr. prp. of ¹*rip*] (1846) *chiefly Brit* : EXCELLENT, DELIGHTFUL ⟨wrote me some ~ letters⟩ ⟨had a ~ time⟩

¹**rip·ple** \'ri-pəl\ *vb* **rip·pled; rip·pling** \-p(ə-)liŋ\ [perh. freq. of ¹*rip*] *vi* (ca. 1671) **1 a** : to become lightly ruffled or covered with small waves **b** : to flow in small waves **c** : to fall in soft undulating folds ⟨the scarf *rippled* to the floor⟩ **2** : to flow with a light rise and fall of sound or inflection ⟨laughter *rippled* over the audience⟩ **3** : to move with an undulating motion or so as to cause ripples ⟨the canoe *rippled* through the water⟩ **4** : to have or produce a ripple effect : SPREAD ⟨the news *rippled* outwards⟩ ~ *vt* **1** : to stir up small waves on **2** : to impart a wavy motion or appearance to ⟨*rippling* his arm muscles⟩ **3** : to utter or play with a slight rise and fall of sound — **rip·pler** \-p(ə-)lər\ *n*

²**ripple** *n* (1755) **1 a** : a shallow stretch of rough water in a stream **b** (1) : the ruffling of the surface of water (2) : a small wave **2 a** : RIPPLE MARK **b** : a sound like that of rippling water ⟨a ~ of laughter⟩ **c** : a usu. slight noticeable effect or reaction — **rip·ply** \'ri-p(ə-)lē\ *adj*

ripple effect *n* (1966) : a spreading, pervasive, and usu. unintentional effect or influence ⟨the automotive industry has a *ripple effect* on many other industries⟩ — compare DOMINO EFFECT

ripple mark *n* (1833) **1** : one of a series of small ridges produced esp. on sand by the action of wind, a current of water, or waves **2** : a striation across the grain of wood esp. on the tangential surface — **rip·ple-marked** \'ri-pəl-,märkt\ *adj*

¹**rip·rap** \'rip-,rap\ *n* [obs. *riprap* sound of rapping] (1833) **1** : a foundation or sustaining wall of stones or chunks of concrete thrown together without order (as in deep water); *also* : a layer of this or similar material on an embankment slope to prevent erosion **2** : material used for riprap

²**riprap** *vt* (1848) **1** : to form a riprap in or upon **2** : to strengthen or support with a riprap

rip-roar·ing \'rip-'rōr-iŋ, -'rór-\ *adj* (1834) : noisily excited or exciting

rip·saw \'rip-,só\ *n* (1846) : a coarse-toothed saw used to cut wood in the direction of the grain — compare CROSSCUT SAW

rip-snort·er \'rip-'snór-tər\ *n* (1840) : something extraordinary : HUMDINGER ⟨the finale was a ~⟩ — **rip-snort·ing** \-tiŋ\ *adj*

rip·stop \'rip-,stäp\ *adj* (1949) : of, relating to, or being a fabric woven with a double thread at regular intervals so that small tears do not spread ⟨~ nylon⟩ — **ripstop** *n*

rip·tide \'rip-,tīd\ *n* (1862) : RIP CURRENT

Rip·u·ar·i·an \,rip-yə-'wer-ē-ən\ *adj* [ML *Ripuarius*] (1781) : of, relating to, or constituting a group of Franks settling in the 4th century on the Rhine near Cologne

Rip van Win·kle \,rip-(,)van-'wiŋ-kəl, -vən-\ *n* : a ne'er-do-well in a story in Washington Irving's *Sketch Book* who sleeps for 20 years

¹**rise** \'rīz\ *vi* **rose** \'rōz\; **ris·en** \'ri-z°n\; **ris·ing** \'rī-ziŋ\ [ME, fr. OE *risan*; akin to OHG *rīsan* to rise] (bef. 12c) **1 a** : to assume an upright position esp. from lying, kneeling, or sitting **b** : to get up from sleep or from one's bed **2** : to return from death **3** : to take up arms ⟨~ in rebellion⟩ **4** : to respond warmly : APPLAUD — usu. used with *to* ⟨the audience *rose* to his verve and wit⟩ **5** *chiefly Brit* : to end a session : ADJOURN **6** : to appear above the horizon ⟨the sun ~s at six⟩ **7 a** : to move upward : ASCEND **b** : to increase in height, size, or volume ⟨the river *rose* after the heavy rains⟩ **8** : to extend above other objects ⟨mountain peaks *rose* to the west⟩ **9 a** : to become heartened or elated ⟨his spirits *rose*⟩ **b** : to increase in fervor or intensity ⟨my anger *rose* as I thought about the insult⟩ **10 a** : to attain a higher level or rank ⟨officers who *rose* from the ranks⟩ **b** : to increase in quantity or number **11 a** : to take place : HAPPEN **b** : to come into being : ORIGINATE **12** : to follow as a consequence : RESULT **13** : to exert oneself to meet a challenge ⟨~ to the occasion⟩ *syn* see SPRING

²**rise** \'rīz\ *also* 'rīs\ *n* (15c) **1 a** : a spot higher than surrounding ground : HILLTOP **b** : an upward slope ⟨a ~ in the road⟩ **2 a** : an act of rising or a state of being risen: as **a** : a movement upward : ASCENT **b** : emergence (as of the sun) above the horizon **c** : the upward movement of a fish to seize food or bait **3** : BEGINNING, ORIGIN ⟨the river had its ~ in the mountain⟩ **4** : the distance or elevation of one point above another **5 a** : an increase esp. in amount, number, or volume **b** *chiefly Brit* : RAISE 3b **c** : an increase in price, value, rate, or sum ⟨a ~ in the cost of living⟩ **6** : an angry reaction ⟨got a ~ out of him⟩ **7** : the distance from the crotch to the waistline on pants

ris·er \'rī-zər\ *n* (15c) **1** : one that rises (as from sleep) **2** : the upright member between two stair treads **3** : a stage platform on which performers are placed for greater visibility **4** : a vertical pipe (as for water or gas) or a vertical portion of an electric wiring system **5** : one of the straps that connects a parachutist's harness with the shroud lines

ris·i·bil·i·ty \,ri-zə-'bi-lə-tē\ *n, pl* **-ties** (1620) **1** : LAUGHTER **2** : the ability or inclination to laugh — often used in pl. ⟨our risibilities support us as we skim over the surface of a deep issue —J. A. Pike⟩

ris·i·ble \'ri-zə-bəl\ *adj* [LL *risibilis*, fr. L *risus*, pp. of *ridēre* to laugh] (1557) **1 a** : capable of laughing **b** : disposed to laugh **2** : arousing or provoking laughter; *esp* : LAUGHABLE **3** : associated with, relating to, or used in laughter ⟨~ muscles⟩

ris·i·bles \-bəlz\ *n pl* (1785) : sense of the ridiculous : sense of humor

¹**ris·ing** \'rī-ziŋ\ *n* (14c) : INSURRECTION, UPRISING

²**rising** *adv* (ca. 1772) : approaching a stated age : NEARLY ⟨a red cow ~ four years old —*Lancaster (Pa.) Jour.*⟩

rising diphthong *n* (1888) : a diphthong in which the second element is more sonorous than the first (as \wi\ in \'kwit\ *quit*)

rising rhythm *n* (1881) : rhythm with stress occurring regularly on the last syllable of each foot — compare FALLING RHYTHM

¹**risk** \'risk\ *n* [F *risque*, fr. It *risco*] (ca. 1661) **1** : possibility of loss or injury : PERIL **2** : someone or something that creates or suggests a hazard **3 a** : the chance of loss or the perils to the subject matter of an insurance contract; *also* : the degree of probability of such loss **b** : a person or thing that is a specified hazard to an insurer ⟨a poor ~ for insurance⟩ **c** : an insurance hazard from a specified cause or source ⟨war ~⟩ — **risk·less** \'ris-kləs\ *adj* — **at risk** : exposed to a usu. specified danger or loss ⟨patients *at risk* of infection⟩

²**risk** *vt* (ca. 1687) **1** : to expose to hazard or danger ⟨~ed her life⟩ **2** : to incur the risk or danger of ⟨~ed breaking his neck⟩ — **risk·er** *n*

risk capital *n* (1944) : VENTURE CAPITAL

risky \'ris-kē\ *adj* **risk·i·er; -est** (1827) : attended with risk or danger : HAZARDOUS *syn* see DANGEROUS — **risk·i·ness** *n*

ri·sor·gi·men·to \(,)rē-,zòr-ji-'men-(,)tō, -,sòr-\ *n, pl* **-tos** [It, lit., rising again, fr. *risorgere* to rise again, fr. L *resurgere* — more at RESURRECTION] (1902) : a time of renewal or renaissance : REVIVAL; *specif* : the 19th century movement for Italian political unity

ri·sot·to \ri-'sò-(,)tō, -'zò-\ *n, pl* **-tos** [It, fr. *riso* rice — more at RICE] (1855) : rice cooked in meat stock and seasoned (as with Parmesan cheese or saffron)

ris·qué \ri-'skā\ *adj* [F, fr. pp. of *risquer* to risk, fr. *risque*] (1867) : verging on impropriety or indecency : OFF-COLOR

Rit·a·lin \'ri-tə-lən\ *trademark* — used for methylphenidate

ri·tard \ri-'tärd\ *n* (ca. 1890) : RITARDANDO

¹**ri·tar·dan·do** \ri-,tär-'dän-(,)dō, rē-\ *adv or adj* [It, fr. L *retardandum*, gerund of *retardare* to retard] (ca. 1811) : with a gradual slackening in tempo — used as a direction in music

²**ritardando** *n, pl* **-dos** (1889) : a ritardando passage

rite \'rīt\ *n* [ME, fr. L *ritus*; akin to Gk *arithmos* number — more at ARITHMETIC] (14c) **1 a** : a prescribed form or manner governing the words or actions for a ceremony **b** : the liturgy of a church or group of churches **2** : a ceremonial act or action ⟨initiation ~s⟩ **3** : a division of the Christian church using a distinctive liturgy

rite de pas·sage \,rēt-də-pa-'säzh, -pä-\ *n, pl* **rites de passage** \,rēt(s)-də-\ [F] (1911) : RITE OF PASSAGE

rite of passage (1909) : a ritual associated with a crisis or a change of status (as marriage, illness, or death) for an individual

ri·tor·nel·lo \,ri-tar-'ne-(,)lō, ,ri-,tór-\ *n, pl* **-nel·li** \-'ne-(,)lē\ *or* **-nellos** [It, dim. of *ritorno* return, fr. *ritornare* to return, fr. *ri-* re- + *tornare* to turn, fr. L, to turn on a lathe — more at TURN] (1675) **1 a** : a short recurrent instrumental passage in a vocal composition **b** : an instrumental interlude in early opera **2** : a tutti passage in a concerto or rondo refrain

¹**rit·u·al** \'ri-chə-wəl, -chəl; 'rich-wəl\ *adj* [L *ritualis*, fr. *ritus* rite] (1570) **1** : of or relating to rites or a ritual : CEREMONIAL ⟨a ~ dance⟩ **2** : according to religious law or social custom ⟨~ purity⟩ — **rit·u·al·ly** *adv*

²**ritual** *n* (1649) **1** : the established form for a ceremony; *specif* : the order of words prescribed for a religious ceremony **2 a** : ritual observance; *specif* : a system of rites **b** : a ceremonial act or action **c** : the customarily repeated often formal act or series of acts

rit·u·al·ism \'ri-chə-wə-,li-zəm, -chə-,li-; 'rich-wə-\ *n* (1843) **1** : the use of ritual **2** : excessive devotion to ritual — **rit·u·al·ist** \-list\ *n* — **rit·u·al·is·tic** \,ri-chə-wə-'lis-tik, -chə-'lis-; ,rich-wə-\ *adj* — **rit·u·al·is·ti·cal·ly** \-ti-k(ə-)lē\ *adv*

rit·u·al·ize \-,līz\ *vb* **-ized; -iz·ing** *vt* (1842) : to practice ritualism ~ *vt* **1** : to make a ritual of **2** : to impose a ritual on — **rit·u·al·i·za·tion** \,ri-chə-wə-lə-'zā-shən, -chə-lə-; ,rich-wə-\ *n*

ritzy \'rit-sē\ *adj* **ritz·i·er; -est** [*Ritz* hotels, noted for their opulence] (1920) **1** : SNOBBISH **2** : ostentatiously smart ; FASHIONABLE, POSH — **ritz·i·ness** *n*

¹**ri·val** \'rī-vəl\ *n* [MF or L; MF, fr. L *rivalis* one using the same stream as another, rival in love, fr. *rivalis* of a stream, fr. *rivus* stream — more at RUN] (1577) **1 a** : one of two or more striving to reach or obtain something that only one can possess **b** : one striving for competitive advantage **2** *obs* : COMPANION, ASSOCIATE **3** : one that equals another in desired qualities : PEER

²**rival** *adj* (1590) : having the same pretensions or claims : COMPETING

³**rival** *vb* **ri·valed** *or* **ri·valled; ri·val·ing** *or* **ri·val·ling** \'riv-(ə-)liŋ\ *vi* (1605) : to act as a rival : COMPETE ~ *vt* **1** : to be in competition with **2** : to strive to equal or excel : EMULATE **3** : to possess qualities or aptitudes that approach or equal (those of another)

ri·val·rous \'rī-vəl-rəs\ *adj* (1812) : given to rivalry : COMPETITIVE

ri·val·ry \'rī-vəl-rē\ *n, pl* **-ries** (1598) : the act of rivaling : the state of being a rival : COMPETITION

rive \'rīv\ *vb* **rived** \'rīvd\; **riv·en** \'ri-vən\ *also* **rived; riv·ing** \'rī-viŋ\ [ME, fr. ON *rīfa*; akin to Gk *ereipein* to tear down] *vt* (14c) **1 a** : to wrench open or tear apart or to pieces : REND **b** : to split with force or violence ⟨lightning *rived* the tree⟩ **2 a** : to divide into pieces : SHATTER **b** : FRACTURE ~ *vi* : to become split : CRACK *syn* see TEAR

riv·er \'ri-vər\ *n, often attrib* [ME *rivere*, fr. OF, fr. (assumed) VL *riparia*, fr. L, fem. of *riparius* riparian, fr. *ripa* bank, shore; perh. akin to Gk *ereipein* to tear down] (14c) **1 a** : a natural stream of water of usu. considerable volume **b** : WATERCOURSE **2** : something resembling a river ⟨a ~ of lava⟩ **b** *pl* : large or overwhelming quantities ⟨drank ~s of coffee⟩ — **up the river** : to or in prison ⟨takes the rap and goes *up the river* —Nigel Balchin⟩

river·bank \'ri-vər-,baŋk\ *n* (1565) : the bank of a river

riv·er·bed \-,bed\ *n* (1833) : the channel occupied by a river

river blindness *n* (1953) : ONCHOCERCIASIS

riv·er·boat \-,bōt\ *n* (1565) : a boat for use on a river

\ə\ abut \°\ kitten, F table \ər\ further \a\ ash \ā\ ace \ä\ mop, mar
\aú\ out \ch\ chin \e\ bet \ē\ easy \g\ go \i\ hit \ī\ ice \j\ job
\ŋ\ sing \ō\ go \ó\ law \ói\ boy \th\ thin \th\ the \ü\ loot \ú\ foot
\y\ yet \zh\ vision \ä, k, °, œ, œ̄, ue, üe, ™\ *see* Guide to Pronunciation

river duck *n* (1837) : DABBLER b

riv·er·front \-ˌfrənt\ *n* (1855) : the land or area along a river

river horse *n* (1601) : HIPPOPOTAMUS

riv·er·ine \'ri-və-ˌrīn, -ˌrēn\ *adj* (1860) **1** : relating to, formed by, or resembling a river **2** : living or situated on the banks of a river

riv·er·side \'ri-vər-ˌsīd\ *n* (14c) : the side or bank of a river

riv·er·ward \-wərd\ *or* **riv·er·wards** \-wərdz\ *adv or adj* (1833) : toward a river

¹riv·et \'ri-vət\ *n* [ME *ryvette*, fr. MF *rivet*, fr. *river* to attach] (15c) : a headed pin or bolt of metal used for uniting two or more pieces by passing the shank through a hole in each piece and then beating or pressing down the plain end so as to make a second head

²rivet *vt* (15c) **1** : to fasten with or as if with rivets **2** : to upset the end or point of (as a metallic pin, rod, or bolt) by beating or pressing so as to form a head **3** : to fasten firmly ⟨they ... these feelings ... tightly together —Michael Novak⟩ **4** : to attract and hold (as the attention) completely — **riv·et·er** *n*

riv·et·ing \'ri-və-tiŋ\ *adj* (1677) : having the power to fix the attention : ENGROSSING, FASCINATING — **riv·et·ing·ly** \-lē\ *adv*

ri·vi·era \ˌri-vē-'er-ə, ri-'vyer-\ *n, often cap* [fr. the *Riviera*, region in southeastern France and northwestern Italy] (1766) : a coastal region frequented as a resort area and usu. marked by a mild climate

ri·vi·ère \ri-vē-'er, 'ri-ˌvyer\ *n* [F, lit., river, fr. OF *rivere*] (1879) : a necklace of precious stones (as diamonds)

riv·u·let \'ri-vyə-lət, -və-\ *n* [It *rivoletto*, dim. of *rivolo*, fr. L *rivulus*, dim. of *rivus* stream — more at RUN] (1587) : a small stream

¹ri·yal \rē-'yäl, -'yal\ *n* [Ar *riyāl*, fr. Sp *real* real] (1928) — see MONEY table

²riyal *var of* RIAL

RN \ˌär-'en\ *n* (1903) : REGISTERED NURSE

RNA \ˌär-(ˌ)en-'ā\ *n* [ribonucleic acid] (1948) : any of various nucleic acids that contain ribose and uracil as structural components and are associated with the control of cellular chemical activities — compare MESSENGER RNA, RIBOSOMAL RNA, TRANSFER RNA

RNA polymerase *n* (ca. 1962) : any of a group of enzymes that promote the synthesis of RNA using DNA or RNA as a template

RN·ase \ˌär-'en-ˌās, -ˌāz\ *or* **RNA·ase** \ˌär-(ˌ)en-'ā-ˌās, -'ā-ˌāz\ *n* [RNA + -*ase*] (1957) : RIBONUCLEASE

¹roach \'rōch\ *n, pl* **roach** *also* **roach·es** [ME *roche*, fr. MF] (13c) **1** : a silver-green European freshwater cyprinid fish (*Rutilus rutilus*); *also* : any of various related fishes (as some shiners) **2** : any of several American freshwater sunfishes (family Centrarchidae)

²roach *n* [origin unknown] (1794) **1** : a curved cut in the edge of a sail to prevent chafing or to secure a better fit **2** : a roll of hair brushed straight back from the forehead or side of the head

³roach *vt* (1818) **1** : to cut (as a horse's mane) so that the remainder stands upright **2** : to cause to arch; *specif* : to brush (the hair) in a roach — often used with *up*

⁴roach *n* [by shortening] (ca. 1848) **1** : COCKROACH **2** : the butt of a marijuana cigarette

roach back *n* (1874) : an arched back (as of a dog)

roach clip *n* (1968) : a metal clip that resembles tweezers and is used by marijuana smokers to hold a roach — called also *roach holder*

road \'rōd\ *n* [ME *rode*, fr. OE *rād* ride, journey; akin to OE *rīdan* to ride] (14c) **1** : ROADSTEAD — often used in pl. **2 a** : an open way for vehicles, persons, and animals; *esp* : one lying outside of an urban district : HIGHWAY **b** : ROADBED 2b **3** : ROUTE, PATH **4** : RAILWAY **5** : a series of scheduled visits or appearances (as games or performances) in several locations or the travel necessary to make these visits ⟨the team is on the ∼⟩ ⟨on tour with the musical's ∼ company⟩ — **road·less** \'rōd-ləs\ *adj* — **down the road** : in or into the future

road·abil·i·ty \ˌrō-də-'bi-lə-tē\ *n* (ca. 1914) : the qualities (as steadiness and balance) desirable in an automobile on the road

road agent *n* (1863) : a highwayman who formerly operated esp. on stage routes in unsettled districts

road·bed \'rōd-ˌbed\ *n* (ca. 1840) **1 a** : the bed on which the ties, rails, and ballast of a railroad rest **b** : the ballast or the upper surface of the ballast on which the ties rest **2 a** : the earth foundation of a road prepared for surfacing **b** : the part of the surface of a road traveled by vehicles

road·block \-ˌbläk\ *n* (1940) **1 a** : a barricade often with traps or mines for holding up an enemy at a point on a road covered by fire **b** : a road barricade set up esp. by law enforcement officers **2** : an obstruction in a road **3** : something (as a fact, condition, or countermeasure) that blocks progress or prevents accomplishment of an objective — **roadblock** *vt*

road hog *n* (1891) : a driver of an automotive vehicle who obstructs others esp. by occupying part of another's traffic lane

road·hold·ing \'rōd-ˌhōl-diŋ\ *n* (1932) *chiefly Brit* : the qualities of an automobile that tend to make it respond precisely to the driver's steering

road·house \'rōd-ˌhau̇s\ *n* (1857) : an inn or tavern usu. outside city limits providing liquor and usu. meals, dancing, and often gambling

road·ie \'rō-dē\ *n* [*road* + -*ie*] (1969) : one who works (as by moving heavy equipment) for traveling entertainers

road·kill \'rōd-ˌkil\ *n* (1979) : an animal that has been killed on a road by a motor vehicle — **road–killed** \-ˌkild\ *adj*

road map *n* (1883) **1** : a map showing roads esp. for automobile travel **2 a** : a detailed plan to guide progress toward a goal **b** : a detailed explanation

road metal *n* (1818) : broken stone or cinders used in making and repairing roads or ballasting railroads

road racing *n* (1828) : racing over public roads; *esp* : automobile racing over roads or over a closed course designed to simulate public roads — **road race** *n*

road roller *n* (ca. 1876) : one that rolls roadways; *specif* : a machine with heavy wide smooth rollers for compacting roadbeds

road·run·ner \'rōd-ˌrə-nər\ *n*

(1856) : a largely terrestrial bird (*Geococcyx californianus*) of the cuckoo family that has a long tail and a crest, is a speedy runner, and ranges from the southwestern U.S. to Mexico; *also* : a closely related bird (*G. velox*) of Mexico and Central America

roadrunner

road show *n* (1908) **1** : a theatrical performance given by a troupe on tour **2** : a special engagement of a new motion picture usu. at increased prices **3** : a promotional presentation or meeting conducted in a series of locations

road·side \'rōd-ˌsīd\ *n* (1744) : the strip of land along a road : the side of a road — **roadside** *adj*

road·stead \'rōd-ˌsted\ *n* (1556) : a place less enclosed than a harbor where ships may ride at anchor

road·ster \'rōd-stər\ *n* (1818) **1 a** : a horse for riding or driving on roads **b** : a utility saddle horse of the hackney type **2 a** : a light carriage : BUGGY **b** : an automobile with an open body that seats two and has a folding fabric top and a luggage compartment in the rear

road test *n* (1906) **1** : a test of a vehicle under practical operating conditions on the road **2** : a test on the road of a person's driving ability as a requirement for a driver's license — **road test** *vt*

road·way \'rōd-ˌwā\ *n* (1600) **1 a** : the strip of land over which a road passes **b** : ROAD; *specif* : ROADBED 2b **2** : the part of a bridge used by vehicles

road·work \-ˌwərk\ *n* (1869) **1** : work done in constructing or repairing roads **2** : conditioning for an athletic contest (as a boxing match) consisting mainly of long runs

road·wor·thy \-ˌwər-t̲h̲ē\ *adj* (1819) : fit for use on the road — **road·wor·thi·ness** *n*

roam \'rōm\ *vb* [ME *romen*] *vi* (14c) **1** : to go from place to place without purpose or direction : WANDER **2** : to travel purposefully unhindered through a wide area ⟨cattle ∼ing in search of water⟩ ∼ *vt* : to range or wander over *syn* see WANDER — **roam** *n* — **roam·er** *n*

¹roan \'rōn\ *also* \'rō-ən\ *adj* [MF, fr. OSp *roano*] (1530) : having the base color (as red, black, or brown) muted and lightened by admixture of white hairs ⟨a ∼ horse⟩ ⟨a ∼ calf⟩

²roan *n* (1580) **1** : an animal (as a horse) with a roan coat — usu. used of a red roan when unqualified **2** : the color of a roan horse — used esp. when the base color is red

³roan *n* [origin unknown] (1818) : sheepskin tanned with sumac and colored and finished to imitate morocco

¹roar \'rōr, 'ror\ *vb* [ME *roren*, fr. OE *rārian*; akin to OHG *rērēn* to bleat] *vi* (bef. 12c) **1** : to utter or emit a full loud prolonged sound **b** : to sing or shout with full force **2 a** : to make or emit a loud confused sound (as background reverberation or rumbling) **b** : to laugh loudly **3 a** : to be boisterous or disorderly **b** : to proceed or rush with great noise or commotion **4** : to make a loud noise during inhalation (as that of a horse affected with roaring) ∼ *vt* **1** : to utter or proclaim with a roar **2** : to cause to roar

²roar *n* (14c) **1** : the deep cry of a wild animal **2** : a loud deep cry (as of pain or anger) **3** : a loud continuous confused sound ⟨the ∼ of the crowd⟩ **4** : a boisterous outcry

roar·er \'rōr-ər, 'ror-\ *n* (14c) **1** : one that roars **2** : a horse subject to roaring

¹roar·ing \'rōr-iŋ, 'ror-\ *adj* (14c) **1** : making or characterized by a sound resembling a roar : LOUD ⟨∼ applause⟩ **2** : marked by prosperity esp. of a temporary nature : BOOMING **3** : INTENSE, UTTER ⟨in the ∼ heat⟩ ⟨a ∼ success⟩ — **roar·ing·ly** *adv*

²roaring *adv* (1697) : EXTREMELY ⟨was ∼ hungry —Herman Wouk⟩

³roaring *n* (1823) : noisy inhalation in a horse caused by nerve paralysis and muscular atrophy and constituting an unsoundness

roaring boy *n* (ca. 1590) : a noisy street bully esp. of Elizabethan and Jacobean England who intimidated passersby

¹roast \'rōst\ *vb* [ME *rosten*, fr. OF *rostir*, of Gmc origin; akin to OHG *rōsten* to roast] *vt* (13c) **1 a** : to cook by exposing to dry heat (as in an oven or before a fire) or by surrounding with hot embers, sand, or stones ⟨∼ a potato in ashes⟩ **b** : to dry and parch by exposure to heat ⟨∼ coffee⟩ **2** : to heat (inorganic material) with access of air and without fusing to effect change (as expulsion of volatile matter, oxidation, or removal of sulfur from sulfide ores) **3** : to heat to excess ⟨∼ed by the summer sun⟩ **4** : to subject to severe criticism or ridicule ⟨films have been ∼ed by most critics —H. J. Seldes⟩ **5** : to honor (a person) at a roast ∼ *vi* **1** : to cook food by heat **2** : to undergo being roasted

²roast *n* (14c) **1** : a piece of meat suitable for roasting **2** : a gathering at which food is roasted before an open fire or in hot ashes or sand **3** : an act or process of roasting; *specif* : severe banter or criticism **4** : a banquet honoring a person (as a celebrity) who is subjected to humorous tongue-in-cheek ridicule by friends

³roast *adj* (14c) : that has been roasted ⟨∼ beef⟩

roast·er \'rōs-tər\ *n* (15c) **1** : one that roasts **2** : a device for roasting **3** : something adapted to roasting: as **a** : a suckling pig **b** : a bird fit for roasting; *esp* : a young chicken of more than four pounds (1.8 kilograms) dressed weight

roast·ing ear \'rōs-tiŋ-ˌir, sense 2 usu \'rōs-s²n-ˌir *or* \'rōs-ˌnir\ *n* (1650) **1** : an ear of young corn roasted or suitable for roasting usu. in the husk **2** *chiefly Southern & Midland* : an ear of corn suitable for boiling or steaming

rob \'räb\ *vb* **robbed; rob·bing** [ME *robben*, fr. OF *rober*, of Gmc origin; akin to OHG *roubōn* to rob — more at REAVE] *vt* (13c) **1 a** (1) : to take something away from by force : steal from (2) : to take personal property from by violence or threat **b** (1) : to remove valuables without right from (a place) (2) : to take the contents of (a receptacle) **c** : to take away as loot : STEAL ⟨∼ jewelry⟩ **2 a** : to deprive of something due, expected, or desired **b** : to withhold unjustly or injuriously ∼ *vi* : to commit robbery — **rob·ber** *n*

usage Sense *vt* 1c, in which the direct object is the thing stolen, is sometimes considered to be wrong, or perhaps archaic. The sense has been in use since the 13th century and is found in earlier literature ⟨contrive to *rob* the honey and subvert the hive —John Dryden⟩. It is still in use though not as common as other senses ⟨then *robbed* $100 after the clerk fled —*Springfield (Mass.) Morning Union*⟩.

ro·ba·lo \'rō-bä-(ˌ)lō\ *n, pl* **-los** *or* **-lo** [Sp] (ca. 1890) : SNOOK 1

ro·band \'rō-ˌband, -bənd\ *n* [prob. fr. MD *rabant*] (1762) : a piece of spun yarn or marline used to fasten the head of a sail to a spar

robber baron *n* (1878) : an American capitalist of the latter part of the 19th century who became wealthy through exploitation (as of natural resources, governmental influence, or low wage scales)

robber fly *n* (1871) : any of a family (Asilidae) of predaceous flies including some closely resembling bumblebees

rob·bery \'rä-b(ə-)rē\ *n, pl* **-ber·ies** (13c) : the act or practice of robbing; *specif* : larceny from the person or presence of another by violence or threat

¹**robe** \'rōb\ *n* [ME, fr. OF, robe, booty, of Gmc origin; akin to OHG *roubōn* to rob] (13c) **1 a** : a long flowing outer garment; *esp* : one used for ceremonial occasions or as a symbol of office or profession **b** : a loose garment (as a bathrobe) for informal wear esp. at home **2** : COVERING, MANTLE ⟨peaks on the axis of the range in their ∼s of snow and light —John Muir †1914⟩ **3** : a covering of pelts or fabric for the lower body used while driving or at outdoor events

²**robe** *vb* **robed; rob·ing** *vt* (14c) : to clothe or cover with or as if with a robe ∼ *vi* **1** : to put on a robe **2** : DRESS

robe de cham·bre \‚rōb-də-'shäⁿbr²‚, -'shäm-brə\ *n, pl* **robes de chambre** \‚rōb(z)-\ [F] (1731) : DRESSING GOWN

rob·in \'rä-bən\ *n* [short for *robin redbreast*] (1549) **1 a** : a small chiefly European thrush (*Erithacus rubecula*) resembling a warbler and having a brownish olive back and orangish face and breast **b** : any of various Old World songbirds that are related to or resemble the European robin **2** : a large No. American thrush (*Turdus migratorius*) with olivaceous to slate gray upperparts, blackish head and tail, black and whitish streaked throat, and dull reddish breast and underparts

Rob·in Good·fel·low \'rä-bən-'gùd-‚fe-(‚)lō\ *n* : a mischievous sprite in English folklore

Robin Hood \-‚hùd\ *n* [*Robin Hood,* legendary Eng. outlaw who gave to the poor what he stole from the rich] (1597) : a person or group likened to a heroic outlaw; *esp* : one that robs the rich and gives to the poor

robin red·breast \-'red-‚brest\ *n* [ME, fr. *Robin,* nickname for *Robert*] (15c) : ROBIN

Rob·in·son Cru·soe \'rä-bə(n)-sən-'krü-(‚)sō\ *n* : a shipwrecked sailor in Defoe's *Robinson Crusoe* who lives for many years on a desert island

Rob·in·son projection \'rä-bən-sən-\ *n* [Arthur H. *Robinson b*1915 Am. geographer] (1978) : a compromise map projection showing the poles as lines rather than points and more accurately portraying high latitutude lands and water to land ratio

ro·ble \'rō-(‚)blä\ *n* [AmerSp, fr. Sp. oak, fr. L *robur*] (1864) : any of several oaks of California and Mexico

ro·bot \'rō-‚bät, -bət\ *n* [Czech, fr. *robota* compulsory labor; akin to OHG *arabeit* trouble, L *orbus* orphaned — more at ORPHAN] (1923) **1 a** : a machine that looks like a human being and performs various complex acts (as walking or talking) of a human being; *also* : a similar but fictional machine whose lack of capacity for human emotions is often emphasized **b** : an efficient insensitive person who functions automatically **2** : a device that automatically performs complicated often repetitive tasks **3** : a mechanism guided by automatic controls — **ro·bot·ism** \'rō-‚bä-‚ti-zəm, -bə-\ *n*

ro·bot·ic \rō-'bä-tik, rə-\ *adj* (1941) **1** : of or relating to mechanical robots **2** : having the characteristics of a robot ⟨performs with ∼ consistency⟩ — **ro·bot·i·cal·ly** \-ti-k(ə-)lē\ *adv*

ro·bot·ics \rō-'bä-tiks\ *n pl but sing in constr* (1941) : technology dealing with the design, construction, and operation of robots in automation

ro·bot·i·za·tion \‚rō-‚bä-tə-'zā-shən, -bə-\ *n* (ca. 1927) **1** : AUTOMATION **2** : the process of turning a human being into a robot

ro·bot·ize \'rō-‚bä-‚tīz, -bə-\ *vt* **-ized; -iz·ing** (1927) **1** : to make automatic : equip with robots **2** : to turn (a human being) into a robot

Rob Roy \'räb-'ròi\ *n* [*Rob Roy,* nickname of Robert McGregor †1734 Scot. freebooter] (1919) : a manhattan made with Scotch whisky

ro·bust \rō-'bəst, 'rō-(‚)bəst\ *adj* [L *robustus* oaken, strong, fr. *robor-, robur* oak, strength] (1549) **1 a** : having or exhibiting strength or vigorous health **b** : having or showing vigor, strength, or firmness ⟨a ∼ debate⟩ ⟨a ∼ faith⟩ **c** : strongly formed or constructed : STURDY ⟨a ∼ plastic⟩ **2** : ROUGH, RUDE ⟨stories . . . laden with ∼, down-home imagery —*Playboy*⟩ **3** : requiring strength or vigor ⟨∼ work⟩ **4** : FULL-BODIED ⟨∼ coffee⟩; *also* : HEARTY ⟨a ∼ dinner⟩ **5** : relating to, resembling, or being any of the primitive, relatively large, heavyset hominids (genus *Australopithecus* and esp. *A. robustus* and *A. boisei*) characterized esp. by heavy molars and small incisors adapted to a vegetarian diet — compare GRACILE 3 *see* HEALTHY — **ro·bust·ly** *adv* — **ro·bust·ness** \-'bəs(t)-nəs, -(‚)bəs(t)-\ *n*

ro·bus·ta \rō-'bəs-tə\ *n, often attrib* [NL *robusta,* specific epithet of *Coffea robusta,* syn. of *Coffea canephora*] (1909) **1** : a coffee (*Coffea canephora*) that is indigenous to central Africa but has been introduced elsewhere (as in Java) **2 a** : the seed of robusta coffee **b** : coffee brewed from the seed of robusta coffee

ro·bus·tious \rō-'bəs-chəs\ *adj* (ca. 1548) **1** : ROBUST **2** : vigorous in a rough or unrefined way : BOISTEROUS — **ro·bus·tious·ly** *adv* — **ro·bus·tious·ness** *n*

roc \'räk\ *n* [Ar *rukhkh*] : a legendary bird of great size and strength believed to inhabit the Indian Ocean area

ro·caille \rō-'kī, rä-\ *n* [F, lit., stone debris, fr. MF *roquailles,* pl., rocky terrain, fr. *roc* rock, alter. of *roche,* fr. (assumed) VL *rocca*] (1856) **1** : a style of ornament developed in the 18th century and characterized by sinuous foliate forms **2** : ROCOCO

Roche limit \'rōsh-, 'rōsh-\ *n* [E. A. *Roche* †1883 Fr. mathematician] (1889) : the distance between a planet's center and its satellite within which the satellite cannot approach without becoming disrupted

Ro·chelle salt \rō-'shel-\ *n* [La *Rochelle,* France] (1753) : a crystalline salt KNaC₄H₄O₆·4H₂O that is a mild purgative

roche mou·ton·née \'rōsh-‚mü-t^an-'ā, 'rōsh-\ *n, pl* **roches mou·ton·nées** *same or* -'āz\ [F, lit., fleecy rock] (1843) : an elongate rounded ice-sculptured hillock of bedrock

roch·et \'rä-chət\ *n* [ME, fr. MF, fr. OF, fr. (assumed) OF *roc* coat, of Gmc origin; akin to OHG *roc* coat] (13c) : a white linen vestment resembling a surplice with close-fitting sleeves worn esp. by bishops and privileged prelates

¹**rock** \'räk\ *vb* [ME *rokken,* fr. OE *roccian;* akin to OHG *rucken* to cause to move] *vt* (12c) **1 a** : to move back and forth in or as if in a

cradle **b** : to wash (placer gravel) in a cradle **2 a** : to cause to sway back and forth ⟨a boat ∼ed by the waves⟩ **b** (1) : to cause to shake violently (2) : to daze with or as if with a vigorous blow ⟨a hard right ∼ed the contender⟩ (3) : to astonish or disturb greatly ⟨the scandal ∼ed the community⟩ ∼ *vi* **1** : to become moved backward and forward under often violent impact; *also* : to move gently back and forth **2** : to move forward at a steady pace; *also* : to move forward at a high speed ⟨the train ∼ed through the countryside⟩ **3** : to sing, dance to, or play rock music *syn see* SHAKE — **rock the boat** : to do something that disturbs the equilibrium of a situation

²**rock** *n, often attrib* (1823) **1** : a rocking movement **2** : popular music usu. played on electronically amplified instruments and characterized by a persistent heavily accented beat, much repetition of simple phrases, and often country, folk, and blues elements

³**rock** *n* [ME *roc,* fr. MD *rocke;* akin to OHG *rocko* distaff] (14c) **1** : DISTAFF **2** : the wool or flax on a distaff

⁴**rock** *n* [ME *rokke,* fr. ONF *roque,* fr. (assumed) VL *rocca*] (14c) **1 a** : large mass of stone forming a cliff, promontory, or peak **2** : a concreted mass of stony material; *also* : broken pieces of such masses **3** : consolidated or unconsolidated solid mineral matter; *also* : a particular mass of it **4 a** : something like a rock in firmness: (1) : FOUNDATION, SUPPORT (2) : REFUGE ⟨a ∼ of independent thought . . . in an ocean of parochialism —Thomas Molnar⟩ **b** : something that threatens or causes disaster — often used in pl. **5 a** : a flavored stick candy with color running through **b** : ROCK CANDY 1 **6** *slang* **a** : GEM **b** : DIAMOND **7 a** : a small crystallized mass of crack cocaine **b** : CRACK 9 — **rock** *adj* — **rock·like** \'räk-‚līk\ *adj* — **between a rock and a hard place** *also* **between the rock and the hard place** : in a difficult or uncomfortable position with no attractive way out — **on the rocks 1** : in or into a state of destruction or wreckage ⟨their marriage went *on the rocks*⟩ **2** : over ice cubes ⟨bourbon *on the rocks*⟩

rock·a·bil·ly \'rä-kə-‚bi-lē\ *n* [²*rock* + *-a-* (as in *rock-a-bye,* phrase used to put a child to sleep) + hill*billy*] (1956) : pop music marked by features of rock and country music

rock and roll *n* (1954) : ²ROCK 2

rock and roller *n* (1956) : ROCKER 3

rock·a·way \'rä-kə-‚wä\ *n* [perh. fr. *Rockaway,* New Jersey] (1846) : a light low four-wheel carriage with a fixed top and open sides

rock bass *n* (1811) : a brown spotted sunfish (*Ambloplites rupestris*) found esp. in the upper Mississippi valley and Great Lakes region

rock–bottom *adj* (1884) : being the very lowest ⟨∼ off-season rates⟩; *also* : FUNDAMENTAL ⟨the ∼ question⟩

rock bottom *n* (1890) : the lowest or most fundamental part or level

rock·bound \'räk-‚baùnd\ *adj* (1840) : fringed, surrounded, or covered with rocks : ROCKY

rock brake *n* (ca. 1850) : any of several ferns that grow chiefly on or among rocks

rock candy *n* (1723) **1** : boiled sugar crystallized in large masses on string **2** : ⁴ROCK 5a

rock climbing *n* (1892) : mountain climbing on rocky cliffs — **rock climb** *vi* — **rock climber** *n*

Rock Cornish *n* (1956) : a crossbred domestic fowl produced by interbreeding Cornish and white Plymouth Rock fowls and used esp. for small roasters

rock crystal *n* (1666) : CRYSTAL 1

rock dove *n* (1655) : a bluish gray dove (*Columba livia*) of Europe and Asia that is the ancestor of many domesticated pigeons and of the feral pigeons found in cities and towns throughout most of the world — called also *rock pigeon*

rock·er \'rä-kər\ *n* (1760) **1 a** : either of two curving pieces of wood or metal on which an object (as a cradle) rocks **b** : any of various objects (as a rocking chair or an infant's toy having a seat placed between side pieces) that rock on rockers **c** : any of various objects in the form of a rocker or with parts resembling a rocker (as a skate with a curved blade) **d** (1) : any of the curved stripes at the lower part of a chevron worn by a noncommissioned officer above the rank of sergeant (2) : the curved stripe at the upper part of a chevron worn by a chief petty officer **2** : any of various devices that work with a rocking motion **3** : a rock performer, song, or enthusiast — **off one's rocker** : in a state of extreme confusion or insanity ⟨went *off her rocker,* and had to be put away —Mervyn Wall⟩

rocker arm *n* (1860) : a center-pivoted lever to push an automotive engine valve down

rock·ery \'rä-k(ə-)rē\ *n, pl* **-er·ies** [⁴*rock* + *-ery*] (1845) *chiefly Brit* : ROCK GARDEN

¹**rock·et** \'rä-kət, rä-'ket\ *n* [MF *roquette,* fr. OIt *rochetta,* dim. of *ruca arugula,* fr. L *eruca*] (1530) : any of several plants of the mustard family: as **a** : ARUGULA **b** : DAME'S ROCKET

²**rock·et** \'rä-kət\ *n, often attrib* [It *rocchetta,* lit., small distaff, fr. dim. of *rocca* distaff, of Gmc origin; akin to OHG *rocko* distaff] (1611) **1 a** : a firework consisting of a case partly filled with a combustible composition fastened to a guiding stick and propelled through the air by the rearward discharge of the gases liberated by combustion **b** : a similar device used as an incendiary weapon or as a propelling unit (as for a lifesaving line) **2** : a jet engine that operates on the same principle as the firework rocket, consists essentially of a combustion chamber and an exhaust nozzle, carries either liquid or solid propellants which provide the fuel and oxygen needed for combustion and thus make the engine independent of the oxygen of the air, and is used esp. for the propulsion of a missile (as a bomb or shell) or a vehicle (as an airplane) **3** : rocket-propelled bomb, missile, or projectile

³**rock·et** \'rä-kət\ *vt* (1837) : to convey or propel by means of or as if by a rocket ∼ *vi* **1** : to rise up swiftly, spectacularly, and with force **2** : to travel rapidly in or as if in a rocket

rock·e·teer \‚rä-kə-'tir\ *n* (1832) **1** : one who fires, pilots, or rides in a rocket **2** : a scientist who specializes in rocketry

rocket plane *n* (1928) : an airplane propelled by rockets

\ə\ abut \ᵊ\ kitten, F table \ər\ further \a\ ash \ā\ ace \ä\ mop, mar \aù\ out \ch\ chin \e\ bet \ē\ easy \g\ go \i\ hit \ī\ ice \j\ job \ŋ\ sing \ō\ go \ò\ law \òi\ boy \th\ thin \ṯẖ\ the \ü\ loot \ù\ foot \y\ yet \zh\ vision \ä, k̲, ⁿ, œ, œ̄, ue, ᵫ, ᵍ\ *see* Guide to Pronunciation

rock·et·ry \'rä-kə-trē\ n (1930) : the study of, experimentation with, or use of rockets
rocket ship n (1927) : a rocket-propelled spaceship
rocket sled n (1954) : a rocket-propelled vehicle that runs usu. on a single rail and that is used esp. in aeronautical experimentation
rock·fall \'räk-,fȯl\ n (1924) : a mass of falling or fallen rocks
rock-fish \-,fish\ n (1598) : any of various important market fishes that live among rocks or on rocky bottoms: as **a** : any of numerous scorpaenid fishes (esp. genus *Sebastes*) **b** : STRIPED BASS **c** : any of several groupers
rock garden n (1836) : a garden laid out among rocks or decorated with rocks and adapted for the growth of particular kinds of plants (as alpines)
rock hind n (ca. 1867) : a red-spotted tan to olive brown grouper (*Epinephelus adscensionis*) of the Atlantic esp. from Massachusetts to southeastern Brazil
rock·hop·per \'räk-,hä-pər\ n (1875) : a small penguin (*Eudyptes crestatus*) with a short thick bill and a yellow crest
rock hound n (1915) **1** : a specialist in geology **2** : an amateur rock and mineral collector — **rock·hound·ing** \'räk-,haún-diŋ\ n
rock·i·ness \'rä-kē-nəs\ n (1611) : the quality or state of being rocky
rocking chair n (1766) : a chair mounted on rockers
rocking horse n (1724) : a toy horse mounted on rockers — called also *hobbyhorse*
rock·ling \'rä-kliŋ\ n (1602) : any of several small rather elongate marine bony fishes (esp. genera *Enchelyopus* and *Gaidropsarus*) of the cod family
rock lobster n (1884) **1** : SPINY LOBSTER **2** : the flesh of a spiny lobster esp. when canned or frozen for use as food
rock maple n (1775) : SUGAR MAPLE 1
rock 'n' roll, rock 'n' roller var of ROCK AND ROLL, ROCK AND ROLLER
rock oil n (1668) : PETROLEUM
rock pigeon n (1611) : ROCK DOVE
rock rabbit n (1840) **1** : HYRAX **2** : PIKA
rock–ribbed \'räk-'ribd\ adj (1776) **1** : [1]ROCKY 1 **2** : firm and inflexible in doctrine or integrity ⟨a ~ conservative community —John Hale⟩
rock·rose \'räk-,rōz\ n (1731) : any of various shrubs or woody herbs (family Cistaceae, the rockrose family) with simple entire leaves and a capsular fruit
rock salt n (1707) : common salt occurring in solid form as a mineral; *also* : salt artificially prepared in large crystals or masses
rock·shaft \'räk-,shaft\ n (ca. 1864) : a shaft that oscillates on its journals instead of revolving
rock tripe n (1854) : any of various dark leathery umbilicate foliose lichens (as of the genus *Umbilicaria*) that are widely distributed on rocks in boreal and alpine areas and are sometimes used as food
rock wallaby n (1841) : any of various medium-sized kangaroos (genus *Petrogale*)
rock·weed \'räk-,wēd\ n (1626) : any of various coarse brown algae (family Fucaceae, esp. genera *Fucus* and *Ascophyllum*) growing in marine environments attached to rocks
rock wool n (ca. 1909) : mineral wool made by blowing a jet of steam through molten rock (as limestone or siliceous rock) or through slag and used chiefly for heat and sound insulation
[1]**rock·y** \'rä-kē\ adj **rock·i·er; -est** [ME *rokky*, fr. *rokke* rock] (15c) **1** : abounding in or consisting of rocks **2** : difficult to impress or affect : INSENSITIVE **3** : firmly held : STEADFAST
[2]**rocky** adj **rock·i·er; -est** [[1]*rock*] (1737) **1** : UNSTABLE, WOBBLY **2** : physically upset or mentally confused (as from drinking excessively) **3** : marked by obstacles : DIFFICULT ⟨a financially ~ year —Michael Murray⟩
Rocky Mountain sheep n [*Rocky Mountains*, No. America] (1817) : BIGHORN
Rocky Mountain spotted fever n (1905) : an acute disease that is characterized by chills, fever, prostration, pains in muscles and joints, and a red to purple eruption and that is caused by a rickettsia (*Rickettsia rickettii*) usu. transmitted by an ixodid tick and esp. either the American dog tick or a wood tick (*Dermacentor andersoni*)
[1]**ro·co·co** \rə-'kō-(,)kō, rō-kə-'kō\ n (1840) : rococo work or style
[2]**rococo** adj [F, irreg. fr. *rocaille* rocaille] (1841) **1** : of or relating to an artistic style esp. of the 18th century characterized by fanciful curved asymmetrical forms and elaborate ornamentation **b** : of or relating to an 18th century musical style marked by light gay ornamentation and departure from thorough-bass and polyphony **2** : excessively ornate or intricate
rod \'räd\ n [ME, fr. OE *rodd*; akin to ON *rudda* club] (bef. 12c) **1 a** (1) : a straight slender stick growing on or cut from a tree or bush (2) : OSIER (3) : a stick or bundle of twigs used to punish; *also* : PUNISHMENT (4) : a shepherd's cudgel (5) : a pole with a line and usu. a reel attached for fishing **b** (1) : a slender bar (as of wood or metal) (2) : a bar or staff for measuring (3) : SCEPTER; *also* : a wand or staff carried as a badge of office (as of marshal) **2 a** : a unit of length — see WEIGHT table **b** : a square rod **3** : any of the long rod-shaped photosensitive receptors in the retina responsive to faint light — compare CONE 3a **4** : a rod-shaped bacterium **5** *slang* : HANDGUN — **rod·less** \-ləs\ adj — **rod·like** \-,līk\ adj
rode past and chiefly dial past part of RIDE
ro·dent \'rō-d²nt\ n [ultim. fr. L *rodent-, rodens*, prp. of *rodere* to gnaw; akin to L *radere* to scrape, scratch, Skt *radati* he gnaws] (1859) **1** : any of an order (Rodentia) of relatively small gnawing mammals (as a mouse, a squirrel, or a beaver) that have in both jaws a single pair of incisors with a chisel-shaped edge **2** : a small mammal (as a rabbit or a shrew) other than a true rodent — **rodent** adj
ro·den·ti·cide \rō-'den-tə-,sīd\ n (ca. 1935) : an agent that kills, repels, or controls rodents
rodent ulcer n [L *rodent-, rodens* gnawing] (1853) : a chronic persisting ulcer of the exposed skin and esp. of the face that is destructive locally, spreads slowly, and is usu. a carcinoma derived from basal cells — called also *rodent cancer*
[1]**ro·deo** \'rō-dē-,ō, rə-'dā-(,)ō\ n, pl **ro·de·os** [Sp, fr. *rodear* to surround, fr. *rueda* wheel, fr. L *rota* — more at ROLL] (1834) **1** : ROUNDUP **2 a** : a public performance featuring bronco riding, calf roping, steer wrestling, and Brahma bull riding **b** : a contest resembling a rodeo

[2]**rodeo** vi (1951) : to participate in a rodeo
rod·man \'räd-mən, -,man\ n (1853) : a surveyor's assistant who holds the leveling rod
ro·do·mon·tade \,rä-də-mən-'tād, ,rō-, -'täd\ n [MF, fr. It *Rodomonte*, character in *Orlando Innamorato* by Matteo M. Boiardo] (1612) **1** : a bragging speech **2** : vain boasting or bluster : RANT — **rodomontade** adj
[1]**roe** \'rō\ n, pl **roe** or **roes** [ME *ro*, fr. OE *rā*; akin to OHG *rēh* roe] (bef. 12c) : DOE
[2]**roe** n [ME *roof, roughe, row*; akin to ON *hrogn* roe and prob. to Lith *kurkulai* frog's eggs] (15c) **1** : the eggs of a fish esp. when still enclosed in the ovarian membrane **2** : the eggs or ovaries of an invertebrate (as the coral of a lobster)
roe·buck \'rō-,bək\ n, pl **roebuck** or **roebucks** (14c) : ROE DEER; *esp* : the male roe deer
roe deer n (1575) : either of two small European or Asian deer (*Capreolus capreolus* and *C. pygarus*) that have erect cylindrical antlers forked at the summit, are reddish brown in summer and grayish in winter, have a white rump patch, and are noted for their nimbleness and grace
[1]**roent·gen** \'rent-gən, 'rənt-, -jən, -shən\ adj [ISV, fr. Wilhelm *Röntgen*] (1896) : of or relating to X rays ⟨~ examinations⟩
[2]**roentgen** n (1922) : the international unit of x-radiation or gamma radiation equal to the amount of radiation that produces in one cubic centimeter of dry air at 0°C and standard atmospheric pressure ionization of either sign equal to one electrostatic unit of charge
roent·gen·o·gram \-gə-nə-,gram, -jə-, -shə-\ n [ISV] (ca. 1904) : a photograph made with X rays
roent·gen·og·ra·phy \,rent-gə-'nä-grə-fē, ,rənt-, -jə-, -shə-\ n [ISV] (1905) : photography by means of X rays — **roent·gen·o·graph·ic** \-nə-'gra-fik\ adj — **roent·gen·o·graph·i·cal·ly** \-fi-k(ə-)lē\ adv
roent·gen·ol·o·gy \-'nä-lə-jē\ n [ISV] (1905) : a branch of radiology that deals with the use of X rays for diagnosis or treatment of disease — **roent·gen·o·log·ic** \-nə-'lä-jik\ or **roent·gen·o·log·i·cal** \-ji-kəl\ adj — **roent·gen·o·log·i·cal·ly** \-ji-k(ə-)lē\ adv — **roent·gen·ol·o·gist** \-'nä-lə-jist\ n
roentgen ray n, often cap 1st R (ca. 1890) : X RAY
ro·ga·tion \rō-'gā-shən\ n [ME *rogacion*, fr. LL *rogation-, rogatio*, fr. L, questioning, fr. *rogare* to ask — more at RIGHT] (14c) **1** : LITANY, SUPPLICATION **2** : the religious observance of the Rogation Days — often used in pl.
Rogation Day n (15c) : any of the days of prayer esp. for the harvest observed on the three days before Ascension Day and by Roman Catholics also on April 25
rog·er \'rä-jər\ interj [fr. *Roger*, former communications code word for the letter *r*] (ca. 1941) — used esp. in radio and signaling to indicate that a message has been received and understood
[1]**rogue** \'rōg\ n [origin unknown] (1561) **1** : VAGRANT, TRAMP **2** : a dishonest or worthless person : SCOUNDREL **3** : a mischievous person : SCAMP **4** : a horse inclined to shirk or misbehave **5** : an individual exhibiting a chance and usu. inferior biological variation — **rogu·ish** \'rō-gish\ adj — **rogu·ish·ly** adv — **rogu·ish·ness** n
[2]**rogue** vi **rogued; rogu·ing** or **rogue·ing** (1766) : to weed out inferior, diseased, or nontypical individuals from a crop plant or a field
[3]**rogue** adj (1872) **1** of an animal : being vicious and destructive **2** : resembling or suggesting a rogue elephant esp. in being isolated and dangerous or uncontrollable ⟨capsized by a ~ wave⟩
rogue elephant n (1859) : a vicious elephant that separates from the herd and roams alone
rogu·ery \'rō-g(ə-)rē\ n, pl **-er·ies** (1592) **1** : an act or behavior characteristic of a rogue **2** : mischievous play
rogues' gallery n (1859) : a collection of pictures of persons arrested as criminals; *also* : a collection or list likened to a rogues' gallery ⟨a *rogues' gallery* of infectious diseases⟩
roil \'rȯi)l, vt 2 is also 'rī(ə)l\ vb [origin unknown] vt (1590) **1 a** : to make turbid by stirring up the sediment or dregs of **b** : to stir up : DISTURB, DISORDER **2** : RILE 1 ~ vi : to move turbulently : be in a state of turbulence or agitation
roily \'rȯi-lē\ adj (1823) **1** : full of sediment or dregs : MUDDY : TURBULENT ⟨~ waters⟩
[1]**rois·ter** \'rȯi-stər\ n [MF *rustre* lout, alter. of *ruste*, fr. *ruste*, adj., rude, rough, fr. L *rusticus* rural — more at RUSTIC] (1551) archaic : one that roisters : ROISTERER
[2]**roister** vi **rois·tered; rois·ter·ing** \-st(ə-)riŋ\ (1582) : to engage in noisy revelry : CAROUSE — **rois·ter·er** \-stər-ər\ n — **rois·ter·ous** \-st(ə-)rəs\ adj — **rois·ter·ous·ly** adv
Ro·land \'rō-lənd\ n [F] : a stalwart defender of the Christians against the Saracens in the Charlemagne legends who is killed at Roncesvalles
role also **rôle** \'rōl\ n [F *rôle*, lit., roll, fr. OF *rolle*] (1606) **1 a** (1) : a character assigned or assumed (2) : a socially expected behavior pattern usu. determined by an individual's status in a particular society **b** : a part played by an actor or singer **2** : a function or part performed esp. in a particular operation or process ⟨played a major ~ in the negotiations⟩ **3** : an identifier attached to an index term to show functional relationships between terms
role model n (1957) : a person whose behavior in a particular role is imitated by others
role–play \'rōl-,plā, -'plā\ vt (1949) : ACT OUT ⟨students were asked to ~ the thoughts and feelings of each character —R. G. Lambert⟩ ~ vi : to play a role
rolf \'rȯlf also 'rōf\ vt, often cap (1970) : to practice Rolfing on — **rolf·er** \'rȯl-fər also 'rō-\ n, often cap
Rolf·ing \'rȯl-fiŋ also 'rōl-\ service mark — used for a system of muscle massage intended to serve as both physical and emotional therapy
[1]**roll** \'rōl\ n [ME *rolle*, fr. OF, fr. L *rotulus*, dim. of *rota* wheel; akin to OHG *rad* wheel, W *rhod*, Skt *ratha* wagon] (13c) **1 a** (1) : a written document that may be rolled up : SCROLL; *specif* : a document containing an official or formal record ⟨the ~s of parliament⟩ (2) : a manuscript book **b** : a list of names or related items : CATALOG **c** : an official list: as (1) : MUSTER ROLL (2) : a list of members of a school or class or of members of a legislative body **2** : something that is rolled up into a cylinder or ball or rounded as if rolled: as **a** : a quantity (as of fabric or paper) rolled up to form a single package **b** : a hairdo in which some or all of the hair is rolled or curled up or under ⟨a

pageboy ~⟩ **c :** any of various food preparations rolled up for cooking or serving; *esp* : a small piece of baked yeast dough **d :** a cylindrical twist of tobacco **e :** a flexible case (as of leather) in which articles may be rolled and fastened by straps or clasps **f** (1) : paper money folded or rolled into a wad (2) *slang* : BANKROLL **3 :** something that performs a rolling action or movement : ROLLER: as **a : a** wheel for making decorative lines on book covers; *also* : a design impressed by such a tool **b :** a typewriter platen
²**roll** *vb* [ME, fr. MF *roller*, fr. (assumed) VL *rotulare*, fr. L *rotulus*] *vt* (14c) **1 a :** to impel forward by causing to turn over and over on a surface **b :** to cause to revolve by turning over and over on or as if on an axis **c :** to cause to move in a circular manner **d :** to form into a mass by turning over and over **e :** to impel forward with an easy continuous motion **2 a :** to put a wrapping around : ENFOLD, ENVELOP **b :** to wrap wholly or partly around : shape into a ball or roll; *also* : to produce by such shaping ⟨~ed his own cigarettes⟩ **3 a :** to press, spread, or level with a roller : make smooth, even, or compact ⟨hulled and ~ed oats⟩ **b :** to spread out : EXTEND ⟨~ out the red carpet⟩ **4 a :** to move on rollers or wheels **b :** to cause to begin operating or moving ⟨~ the cameras⟩ **5 a :** to sound with a full reverberating tone ⟨~ed out the words⟩ **b :** to make a continuous beating sound upon : sound a roll upon ⟨~ed their drums⟩ **c :** to utter with a trill ⟨~ed his *r*'s⟩ **d :** to play (a chord) in arpeggio style **6 :** to rob (a drunk, sleeping, or unconscious person) usu. by going through the pockets ~ *vi* **1 a :** to move along a surface by rotation without sliding **b** (1) : to turn over and over ⟨the children ~ed in the grass⟩ (2) : to luxuriate in an abundant supply : WALLOW ⟨fairly ~ing in money⟩ **2 a :** to move onward or around as if by completing a revolution : ELAPSE, PASS ⟨the months ~ on⟩ **b :** to shift the gaze continually ⟨eyes ~ing in terror⟩ **c :** to revolve on an axis **3 :** to move about : ROAM, WANDER **4 a :** to go forward in an easy, gentle, or undulating manner ⟨the waves ~ed in⟩ **b :** to flow in a continuous stream : POUR ⟨money was ~ing in⟩ **c :** to flow as part of a stream of words **d :** to have an undulating contour ⟨~ing prairie⟩ **e :** to lie extended : STRETCH **5 a :** to travel in a vehicle **b :** to become carried on a stream **c :** to move on wheels **6 a :** to make a deep reverberating sound ⟨the thunder ~s⟩ **b :** TRILL **7 a :** to swing from side to side ⟨the ship heaved and ~ed⟩ **b :** to walk with a swinging gait : SWAY **c :** to move so as to lessen the impact of a blow — used with *with* ⟨~ed with the punch⟩ **8 a :** to take the form of a cylinder or ball **b :** to respond to rolling in a specified way **9 a :** to get under way : begin to move or operate **b :** to move forward : develop and maintain impetus; *esp* : to proceed or progress with notable ease or success ⟨the team was ~ing⟩ **10 a :** BOWL **b :** to execute a somersault **11** *of a football quarterback* : to run toward one flank usu. parallel to the line of scrimmage esp. before throwing a pass — often used with *out* — **roll the bones :** to shoot craps
³**roll** *n* (1688) **1 a :** a sound produced by rapid strokes on a drum **b** : a sonorous and often rhythmical flow of speech **c :** a heavy reverberatory sound ⟨the ~ of cannon⟩ **d :** a chord in arpeggio style **e :** a trill of some birds (as a canary) **2 :** a rolling movement or an action or process involving such movement ⟨a ~ of the dice⟩ ⟨an airplane's takeoff ~⟩: as **a :** a swaying movement of the body **b :** a side-to-side movement (as of a ship or train) **c** (1) : a flight maneuver in which a complete revolution about the longitudinal axis of an airplane is made with the horizontal direction of flight being approximately maintained (2) : the motion of an aircraft or spacecraft about its longitudinal axis **d :** SOMERSAULT **e :** the movement of a curling stone after impact with another stone — **on a roll :** in the midst of a series of successes : on a hot streak — sometimes used with a modifier ⟨has been *on a* brilliant *roll*⟩
roll·back \'rōl-ˌbak\ *n* (1942) : the act or an instance of rolling back ⟨a government-ordered ~ of gasoline prices⟩
roll back *vt* (1942) **1 :** to reduce (as a commodity price) to or toward a previous level on a national scale **2 :** to cause to retreat or withdraw : push back **3 :** RESCIND ⟨attempted to *roll back* antipollution standards⟩
roll bar *n* (ca. 1952) : an overhead metal bar on an automobile that is designed to protect the occupant in case of a rollover
roll cage *n* (1966) : a protective framework of metal bars encasing the driver of a vehicle (as a racing car)
roll call *n* (1775) **1 :** the act or an instance of calling off a list of names (as for checking attendance); *also* : a time for a roll call **2** : ⁶LIST 1
¹**roll·er** \'rō-lər\ *n* (13c) **1 a :** a revolving cylinder over or on which something is moved or which is used to press, shape, spread, or smooth something **b :** a cylinder or rod on which something (as a shade) is rolled up **2 a :** a long heavy ocean wave **b :** a tumbler pigeon **3** : one that rolls or performs a rolling operation **4 :** a slowly rolling ground ball
²**roll·er** \'rō-lər\ *n* [G, fr. *rollen* to roll, reverberate, fr. MF *roller* — more at ROLL] (1678) **1 :** any of numerous mostly brightly colored nonpasserine Old World birds (family Coraciidae) that perform rolling aerial dives during courtship displays **2 :** a canary having a song in which the notes are soft and run together
roller bearing *n* (1857) : a bearing in which the journal rotates in peripheral contact with a number of rollers usu. contained in a cage
roll·er–coast·er \'rō-lər-ˌkō-stər, 'rō-lə-ˌkō-\ *adj* (1940) : marked by numerous ups and downs ⟨an entertainer's ~ career⟩
roll·er coast·er \'rō-lər-ˌkō-stər, 'rō-lē-ˌkō-\ *n* (1888) **1 :** an elevated railway (as in an amusement park) constructed with sharp curves and steep inclines on which cars roll **2 :** something resembling a roller coaster; *esp* : behavior, events, or experiences characterized by sudden and extreme changes ⟨an emotional *roller coaster*⟩
Roller Derby *service mark* — used for an entertainment involving two roller-skating teams on an oval track in which each team attempts to maneuver a skater into position to score points by circling the track and lapping opponents within a given time period

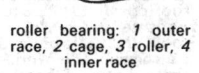

roller bearing: *1* outer race, *2* cage, *3* roller, *4* inner race

roller rink *n* (1885) : RINK 1c
roller skate *n* (1863) : a shoe with a set of wheels attached for skating over a flat surface; *also* : a metal frame with wheels attached that can be fitted to the sole of a shoe — **roller–skate** *vi* — **roller skater** *n*
roller towel *n* (1845) : an endless towel hung from a roller
Rolle's theorem \'rōlz-, 'rōlz-\ *n* [Michel *Rolle* †1719 Fr. mathematician] (ca. 1891) : a theorem in mathematics: if a curve is continuous, crosses the x-axis at two points, and has a tangent at every point between the two intercepts, its tangent is parallel to the x-axis at some point between the intercepts
roll film *n* (1895) : a strip of film for still camera use wound on a spool
rol·lick \'rä-lik\ *vi* [origin unknown] (1826) : to move or behave in a carefree joyous manner : FROLIC — **rollick** *n*
rol·lick·ing \'rä-li-kiŋ\ *adj* (1811) : boisterously carefree, joyful, or high-spirited ⟨a ~ adventure film⟩
rolling hitch *n* (ca. 1769) : a hitch for fastening a line to a spar or to the standing part of another line that will not slip when the pull is parallel to the spar or line — see KNOT illustration
rolling mill *n* (1787) : an establishment where metal is rolled into plates and bars
rolling pin *n* (ca. 1589) : a long cylinder for rolling out dough
rolling stock *n* (1853) : the wheeled vehicles owned and used by a railroad or motor carrier
roll–neck \'rōl-ˌnek\ *n, often attrib* (1943) *Brit* : TURTLENECK — **roll-necked** \-ˌnekt\ *adj*
roll–off \'rō-ˌlȯf\ *n* (1947) : a play-off match in bowling
roll·out \'rō-ˌlaȯt\ *n* (1952) **1 :** the public introduction of a new aircraft; *broadly* : the widespread public introduction of a new product **2** : a football play in which the quarterback rolls to the left or right
roll out *vi* (1884) : to get out of bed ~ *vt* : to introduce (as a new product) esp. for widespread sale to the public
roll·over \'rō-ˌlō-vər\ *n* (1945) **1 :** the act or process of rolling over **2** : a motor vehicle accident in which the vehicle overturns
roll over *vt* (1949) **1 a :** to defer payment of (an obligation) **b :** to renegotiate the terms of (a financial agreement) **2 :** to place (invested funds) in a new investment of the same kind : REINVEST ⟨*roll over* IRA funds⟩
roll–over arm *n* (ca. 1925) : a fully upholstered chair or sofa arm curving outward from the seat
roll–top desk \'rōl-ˌtäp-\ *n* (1887) : a writing desk with a sliding cover often of parallel slats fastened to a flexible backing

rolltop desk

roll up *vt* (1859) : to increase or acquire by successive accumulations : ACCUMULATE ⟨*rolled up* a large majority⟩ ~ *vi* **1 :** to become larger by successive accumulations **2 :** to arrive in a vehicle
¹**ro·ly–po·ly** \ˌrō-lē-'pō-lē\ *adj* [redupl. of *roly*, fr. ²*roll*] (1820) : being short and pudgy : ROTUND
²**roly–poly** *n, pl* **-lies** (1836) **1 :** a roly≠ poly person or thing **2** *Brit* : a sweet dough spread with a filling, rolled, and baked or steamed — called also *roly-poly pudding*
Rom \'rōm\ *n, pl* **Rom** *also* **Roma** \'rō-mə\ [Romany, married man, husband, male Gypsy, fr. Skt *domba, doma* low caste male musician] (1841) : GYPSY 1
ROM \'räm\ *n* (1966) : READ-ONLY MEMORY
Ro·ma·ic \rō-'mā-ik\ *n* [NGk *Rhōmaiikos*, fr. Gk *Rhōmaïkos* Roman, fr. *Rhōmē* Rome] (1810) : the modern Greek vernacular — **Romaic** *adj*
ro·maine \rō-'mān, 'rō-ˌ\ *n* [F, fr. fem. of *romain* Roman, fr. L *Romanus*] (1907) : a lettuce that belongs to a cultivar of garden lettuce (*Lactuca sativa*) and has long crisp leaves and columnar heads — called also *cos lettuce*
ro·man \rō-'mäⁿ\ *n* [F, fr. OF *romans* romance] (1765) : a metrical romance
¹**Ro·man** \'rō-mən\ *n* [partly fr. ME, fr. OE, fr. L *Romanus*, adj. & n., fr. *Roma* Rome; partly fr. ME *Romain*, fr. OF, fr. L *Romanus*] [bef. 12c] **1 :** a native or resident of Rome **2 :** ROMAN CATHOLIC — often taken to be offensive **3** *not cap* : roman letters or type
²**Roman** *adj* (14c) **1 :** of or relating to Rome or the people of Rome; *specif* : characteristic of the ancient Romans ⟨~ fortitude⟩ **2 a** : LATIN 1a **b :** of or relating to the Latin alphabet **3** *not cap* : of or relating to a type style with upright characters — compare ITALIC **4** : of or relating to the see of Rome or the Roman Catholic Church **5** : having a semicircular intrados ⟨~ arch⟩ **6 :** having a prominent slightly aquiline bridge ⟨~ nose⟩
ro·man à clef \rō-ˌmä(ⁿ)n-(ˌ)ä-'klā\ *n, pl* **romans à clef** \-ˌmäⁿ-(ˌ)zä-\ [F, lit., novel with a key] (1893) : a novel in which real persons or actual events figure under disguise
Roman candle *n* (1834) : a cylindrical firework that discharges at intervals balls or stars of fire
¹**Roman Catholic** *n* (1605) : a member of the Roman Catholic Church
²**Roman Catholic** *adj* (1614) : of, relating to, or being a Christian church having a hierarchy of priests and bishops under the pope, a liturgy centered in the Mass, veneration of the Virgin Mary and saints, clerical celibacy, and a body of dogma including transubstantiation and papal infallibility
Roman Catholicism *n* (ca. 1823) : the faith, doctrine, or polity of the Roman Catholic Church
¹**ro·mance** \rō-'man(t)s, rə-; 'rō-ˌ\ *n* [ME *romauns*, fr. OF *romans* French, something written in French, fr. L *romanice* in the Roman manner, fr. *romanicus* Roman, fr. *Romanus*] (14c) **1 a** (1) : a medieval tale based on legend, chivalric love and adventure, or the supernatural (2) : a prose narrative treating imaginary characters involved in

\ə\ abut \ˀ\ kitten, F table \ər\ further \a\ ash \ā\ ace \ä\ mop, mar \aȯ\ out \ch\ chin \e\ bet \ē\ easy \g\ go \i\ hit \ī\ ice \j\ job \ŋ\ sing \ō\ go \ȯ\ law \ȯi\ boy \th\ thin \t͟h\ the \ü\ loot \u̇\ foot \y\ yet \zh\ vision \ä, k̲, ⁿ, œ, œ̄, ᵫ, ᵫ̄, ᵊ\ see Guide to Pronunciation events remote in time or place and usu. heroic, adventurous, or mysterious (3) : a love story **b** : a class of such literature **2** : something (as an extravagant story or account) that lacks basis in fact **3** : an emotional attraction or aura belonging to an esp. heroic era, adventure, or activity **4** : LOVE AFFAIR **5** *cap* : the Romance languages

²romance *vb* **ro·manced; ro·manc·ing** *vi* (1671) **1** : to exaggerate or invent detail or incident **2** : to entertain romantic thoughts or ideas ~ *vt* **1** : to try to influence or curry favor with esp. by lavishing personal attention, gifts, or flattery **2** : to carry on a love affair with

³romance *n* (ca. 1854) : a short instrumental piece in ballad style

Ro·mance \rō-'man(t)s, rə-; 'rō-,\ *adj* (1690) : of, relating to, or being any of several languages developed from Latin (as Italian, French, and Spanish)

ro·manc·er \rō-'man(t)-sər, rə-; 'rō-,\ *n* (1654) **1** : a writer of romance **2** : one that romances

Roman collar *n* (ca. 1890) : CLERICAL COLLAR

Ro·man·esque \,rō-mə-'nesk\ *adj* (1819) : of or relating to a style of architecture developed in Italy and western Europe between the Roman and the Gothic styles and characterized in its development after 1000 by the use of the round arch and vault, substitution of piers for columns, decorative use of arcades, and profuse ornament — **Romanesque** *n*

ro·man–fleuve \rō-,män-'flœv, -'flə(r)v\ *n, pl* **ro·mans–fleuves** \-,män-'flœv, 'flə(r)v(z)\ [F, lit., river novel] (1935) : a novel in the form of a long usu. easygoing chronicle of a social group (as a family or a community)

Roman holiday *n* (1886) **1** : a time of debauchery or of sadistic enjoyment **2** : a destructive or tumultuous disturbance : RIOT

Ro·ma·nian \rü-'mā-nē-ən, rō-, -nyən\ *n* (1868) **1** : a native or inhabitant of Romania **2** : the Romance language of the Romanians

Ro·man·ic \rō-'ma-nik\ *adj* (1708) : ROMANCE — **Romanic** *n*

ro·man·ise *Brit var of* ROMANIZE

Ro·man·ism \'rō-mə-,ni-zəm\ *n* (1674) : ROMAN CATHOLICISM — often taken to be offensive

Ro·man·ist \-nist\ *n* (1523) **1** : ROMAN CATHOLIC — often taken to be offensive **2** : a specialist in the language, culture, or law of ancient Rome — **Romanist** *or* **Ro·man·is·tic** \,rō-mə-'nis-tik\ *adj*

ro·man·ize \'rō-mə-,nīz\ *vt* **-ized; -iz·ing** (1607) **1** *often cap* : to make Roman in character **2** : to write or print (as a language) in the Latin alphabet (~ Chinese) **3** *cap* **a** : to convert to Roman Catholicism **b** : to give a Roman Catholic character to — **ro·man·i·za·tion** \,rō-mə-nə-'zā-shən\ *n, often cap*

roman law *n, often cap R* (1660) : the legal system of the ancient Romans that includes written and unwritten law, is based on the traditional law and the legislation of the city of Rome, and in form comprises legislation of the assemblies, resolves of the senate, enactments of the emperors, edicts of the praetors, writings of the jurisconsults, and the codes of the later emperors

Roman numeral *n* (1735) : a numeral in a system of notation that is based on the ancient Roman system — see NUMBER table

Ro·ma·no \rə-'mä-(,)nō, rō-\ *n* [It, Roman, fr. L *Romanus*] (1908) : a hard sharp cheese of Italian origin that is often served grated

Ro·mans \'rō-mənz\ *n pl but sing in constr* : a letter on doctrine written by St. Paul to the Christians of Rome and included as a book in the New Testament — see BIBLE table

Ro·mansh *or* **Ro·mansch** \rō-'mänch, -'manch\ *n* [Romansh *romonsch*] (1663) : the Rhaeto-Romance dialects spoken in the Grisons, Switzerland

¹ro·man·tic \rō-'man-tik, rə-\ *adj* [F *romantique*, fr. obs. *romant* romance, fr. OF *romans*] (1650) **1** : consisting of or resembling a romance **2** : having no basis in fact : IMAGINARY **3** : impractical in conception or plan : VISIONARY **4** : marked by the imaginative or emotional appeal of what is heroic, adventurous, remote, mysterious, or idealized **b** *often cap* : of, relating to, or having the characteristics of romanticism **c** : of or relating to music of the 19th century characterized by an emphasis on subjective emotional qualities and freedom of form; *also* : of or relating to a composer of this music **5** **a** : having an inclination for romance : responsive to the appeal of what is idealized, heroic, or adventurous **b** : marked by expressions of love or affection **c** : conducive to or suitable for lovemaking **6** : of, relating to, or constituting the part of the hero esp. in a light comedy — **ro·man·ti·cal·ly** \-ti-k(ə-)lē\ *adv*

²romantic *n* (1679) **1** : a romantic person, trait, or component **2** *cap* : a romantic writer, artist, or composer

ro·man·ti·cise *Brit var of* ROMANTICIZE

ro·man·ti·cism \rō-'man-tə-,si-zəm, rə-\ *n* (1823) **1** *often cap* **a** (1) : a literary, artistic, and philosophical movement originating in the 18th century, characterized chiefly by a reaction against neoclassicism and an emphasis on the imagination and emotions, and marked esp. in English literature by sensibility and the use of autobiographical material, an exaltation of the primitive and the common man, an appreciation of external nature, an interest in the remote, a predilection for melancholy, and the use in poetry of older verse forms (2) : an aspect of romanticism **b** : adherence to a romantic attitude or style **2** : the quality or state of being romantic — **ro·man·ti·cist** \-sist\ *n, often cap*

ro·man·ti·cize \-'man-tə-,sīz\ *vb* **-cized; -ciz·ing** *vt* (1818) : to make romantic : treat as idealized or heroic ~ *vi* **1** : to hold romantic ideas **2** : to present details, incidents, or people in a romantic way — **ro·man·ti·ci·za·tion** \-,man-tə-sə-'zā-shən\ *n*

Ro·ma·ny \'rä-mə-nē, 'rō-\ *n, pl* **Romanies** [Romany *romani*, fem. of *romano*, adj., Gypsy, fr. *rom* Gypsy man — more at ROM] (ca. 1812) **1** : GYPSY 1 **2** : the Indo-Aryan language of the Gypsies — **Romany** *adj*

ro·maunt \rō-'mȯnt, -'mänt\ *n* [ME, fr. MF *romant*] (1530) *archaic* : ROMANCE 1a(1)

rom·el·dale \'rä-məl-,dāl\ *n, often cap* [blend of *Romney* (Marsh), *Rambouillet*, and *Corriedale*] (ca. 1948) : any of an American breed of utility sheep yielding a heavy fleece of fine wool and producing a quickly maturing high-grade market lamb

¹Ro·meo \'rō-mē-,ō, *in Shak also* 'rōm-(,)yō\ *n, pl* **Ro·me·os** **1** : the hero of Shakespeare's *Romeo and Juliet* who dies for love of Juliet **2** : a male lover

²Romeo (1952) — a communications code word for the letter *r*

Rom·ish \'rō-mish\ *adj* (1531) : ROMAN CATHOLIC — usu. used disparagingly — **Rom·ish·ly** *adv* — **Rom·ish·ness** *n*

Rom·ney Marsh \'räm-nē-, 'rəm-\ *n* [*Romney Marsh*, pasture tract in England] (1832) : any of a British breed of hardy long-wooled mutton-type sheep esp. adapted to damp or marshy regions — called also *Romney*

¹romp \'rämp, 'rȯmp\ *n* [partly alter. of ²ramp; partly alter. of *ramp* bold woman] (1706) **1** : one that romps; *esp* : a romping girl or woman **2** **a** : high-spirited, carefree, and boisterous play **b** : something suggestive of such play: as (1) : a light fast-paced narrative, dramatic, or musical work usu. in a comic mood (2) : an episode of lovemaking **3** : an easy winning pace; *also* : RUNAWAY

²romp *vi* [alter. of ¹ramp] (1709) **1** : to run or play in a lively, carefree, or boisterous manner **2** : to move or proceed in a brisk, easy, or playful manner **3** : to win a contest easily

romp·er \'räm-pər, 'rȯm-\ *n* (1842) **1** : one that romps **2** : a one-piece garment esp. for children with the lower part shaped like bloomers — usu. used in pl.

Rom·u·lus \'räm-yə-ləs\ *n* [L] : a son of Mars and legendary founder of Rome

ron·deau \'rän-(,)dō, rän-'dō\ *n, pl* **ron·deaux** \-(,)dōz, -'dōz\ [MF *rondel, rondeau*] (1525) **1** **a** : a fixed form of verse based on two rhyme sounds and consisting usu. of 13 lines in three stanzas with the opening words of the first line of the first stanza used as an independent refrain after the second and third stanzas **b** : a poem in this form **2** : a monophonic trouvère song with a 2-part refrain

ron·del \'rän-d'l, rän-'del\ *or* **ron·delle** \rän-'del\ *n* [ME, fr. OF, lit., small circle — more at ROUNDEL] (14c) **1** *usu rondelle* : a circular object; *esp* : a circular jewel or jeweled ring **2** **a** *usu rondel* : a fixed form of verse based on two rhyme sounds and consisting usu. of 14 lines in three stanzas in which the first two lines of the first stanza are repeated as the refrain of the second and third stanzas **b** : a poem in this form **c** : RONDEAU 1

ron·de·let \,rän-də-'let, -'lā\ *n* (15c) : a modified rondeau consisting usu. of seven lines in which the first line of four syllables is repeated as the third line and as the final line or refrain and the remaining lines are made up of eight syllables each

ron·do \'rän-(,)dō, rän-'dō\ *n, pl* **rondos** [It *rondò*, fr. MF *rondeau*] (1797) **1** : an instrumental composition typically with a refrain recurring four times in the tonic and with three couplets in contrasting keys **2** : the musical form of a rondo used esp. for a movement in a concerto or sonata

ron·dure \'rän-jər, -(,)dyu̇r, -(,)du̇r\ *n* [F *rondeur* roundness, fr. MF, fr. *rond* round, fr. OF *roont* — more at ROUND] (ca. 1600) **1** : ROUND 1a **2** : gracefully rounded curvature

ron·yon \'rən-yən, 'rän-\ *n* [perh. modif. of MF *rogne* scab] (1598) *obs* : a mangy or scabby creature

rood \'rüd\ *n* [ME, fr. OE *rōd* rod, rood; akin to OHG *ruota* rod and perh. to ORuss *ratište* lance] (bef. 12c) **1** : a cross or crucifix symbolizing the cross on which Jesus Christ died; *specif* : a large crucifix on a beam or screen at the entrance of the chancel of a medieval church **2** **a** : any of various units of land area; *esp* : a British unit equal to ¼ acre **b** : any of various units of length; *esp* : a British unit equal to seven or eight yards or sometimes a rod

¹roof \'rüf, 'ru̇f\ *n, pl* **roofs** \'rüfs, 'ru̇fs *also* 'rüvz, 'ru̇vz\ [ME, fr. OE *hrōf*; akin to ON *hrōf* roof of a boathouse and perh. to OCS *stropŭ* roof] (bef. 12c) **1** **a** (1) : the cover of a building (2) : material used for a roof : ROOFING **b** : the roof of a dwelling conventionally designating the home itself (didn't have a ~ over my head) (they share the same ~) **2** **a** : the highest point : SUMMIT **b** : an upper limit : CEILING **3** **a** : the vaulted upper boundary of the mouth **b** : a covering structure of any of various parts of the body (~ of the skull) **4** : something suggesting a roof: as **a** : a canopy of leaves and branches **b** : the top over the passenger section of a vehicle — **roofed** \'rüft, 'ru̇ft\ *adj* — **roof·less** \'rü-fləs, 'ru̇-\ *adj* — **roof·like** \-,līk\ *adj*

roof 1a(1): *1* gambrel, *2* mansard, *3* hip, *4* lean-to

²roof *vt* (15c) **1** **a** : to cover with or as if with a roof **b** : to provide with a particular kind of roof or roofing — often used in combination (slate-*roofed* houses) **2** : to constitute a roof — **roof·er** *n*

roof garden *n* (1893) : a restaurant or nightclub at the top of a building often in connection with or decorated to suggest an outdoor garden

roof·ing *n* (15c) : material for a roof

roof·line \'rüf-,līn, 'ru̇f-\ *n* (1857) : the profile of a roof (as of a house)

¹roof·top \-,täp\ *n* (1611) : ROOF; *esp* : the outer surface of a usu. flat roof (sunning themselves on the ~)

²rooftop *adj* (1935) : situated or taking place on a rooftop

roof-tree \'rüf-,trē, 'ru̇f-\ *n* (14c) : RIDGEPOLE

¹rook \'ru̇k\ *n* [ME, fr. OE *hrōc*; akin to OHG *hruoch* rook] (bef. 12c) : a common Old World gregarious bird (*Corvus frugilegus*) about the size and color of the related American crow but having a bare patch of skin at the base of the bill

²rook *vt* (ca. 1590) : to defraud by cheating or swindling

³**rook** n [ME rok, fr. MF roc, fr. Ar rukhkh, fr. Per rukh] (14c) : either of two pieces of the same color in a set of chessmen having the power to move along the ranks or files across any number of unoccupied squares — called also *castle*

rook·ery \'rú-kə-rē\ n, pl **-er·ies** (1725) **1 a** : the nests or breeding place of a colony of rooks; *also* : a colony of rooks **b** : a breeding ground or haunt esp. of gregarious birds or mammals; *also* : a colony of such birds or mammals **2** : a crowded dilapidated tenement or group of dwellings **3** : a place teeming with like individuals

rook·ie \'rú-kē\ n [perh. alter. of recruit] (1892) **1** : RECRUIT; *also* : NOVICE **2** : a first-year participant in a major professional sport

rooky \'rú-kē\ adj (1605) : full of or containing rooks

¹**room** \'rüm, 'rúm\ n [ME, fr. OE rūm; akin to OHG rūm room, L rur-, rus open land] (bef. 12c) **1** : an extent of space occupied by or sufficient or available for something ⟨in the country where there is ~ to run and play⟩ **2** a obs : an appropriate or designated position, post, or station **b** : PLACE, STEAD ⟨in whose ~ I am now assuming the pen —Sir Walter Scott⟩ **3 a** : a partitioned part of the inside of a building; *esp* : such a part used as a lodging **b** : the people in a room **4 a** : suitable or fit occasion or opportunity : CHANCE ⟨left no ~ for doubt⟩ — **roomed** \'rümd, 'rúmd\ adj

²**room** vi (1817) : to occupy a room esp. as a lodger ~ vt : to accommodate with lodgings

room and board n (1955) : lodging and food usu. furnished for a set price or as part of wages

room·er \'rü-mər, 'rú-\ n (ca. 1871) : one who occupies a rented room in another's house

room·ette \rü-'met, rú-\ n (1937) : a small private single room on a railroad sleeping car

room·ful \'rüm-,fúl, 'rúm-\ n (1710) : as much or as many as a room will hold; *also* : the persons or objects in a room

rooming house n (1893) : a house where lodgings are provided for rent

rooming-in \'rü-miŋ-'in, 'rú-\ n (1943) : an arrangement in a hospital whereby a newborn infant is kept in a crib at the mother's bedside instead of in a nursery

room·mate \'rüm-,māt, 'rúm-\ n (1789) : one of two or more persons sharing the same room or living quarters — called also *room·ie* \'rü-mē, 'rú-\

room service n (1930) : service provided to hotel guests in their rooms; *also* : the hotel department responsible for such service ⟨ordered a meal from *room service*⟩

roomy \'rü-mē, 'rú-\ adj **room·i·er; -est** (1627) **1** : having ample room : SPACIOUS **2** of a female mammal : having a large or well-proportioned body suited for breeding — **room·i·ness** n

roor·back \'rúr-,bak\ n [fr. an attack on James K. Polk in 1844 purporting to quote from an invented book by a Baron von *Roorback*] (1855) : a defamatory falsehood published for political effect

roose \'rüz\ vt [ME rusen, fr. ON hrōsa] (14c) *chiefly dial* : PRAISE

¹**roost** \'rüst\ n [ME, fr. OE hrōst; akin to OS hrōst attic] (bef. 12c) **1 a** : a support on which birds rest **b** : a place where winged animals and esp. birds customarily roost **2** : a group of birds (as fowl) roosting together

²**roost** vi (1530) **1** : to settle down for rest or sleep : PERCH **2** : to settle oneself as if on a roost ~ vt : to supply a roost for or put to roost

roost·er \'rüs-tər also 'rús-\ n (1772) **1 a** : an adult male domestic fowl : COCK **b** : an adult male of various birds other than the domestic fowl **2** : a cocky or vain man

rooster tail n (1946) : a high arching spray of water thrown up behind a fast-moving motorboat

¹**root** \'rüt, 'rút\ n, often attrib [ME, fr. OE rōt, fr. ON; akin to OE wyrt root, L radix, Gk rhiza] (12c) **1 a** : the usu. underground part of a seed plant body that originates usu. from the hypocotyl, functions as an organ of absorption, aeration, and food storage or as a means of anchorage and support, and differs from a stem esp. in lacking nodes, buds, and leaves **b** : any subterranean plant part (as a true root or a bulb, tuber, rootstock, or other modified stem) esp. when fleshy and edible **2 a** : the part of a tooth within the socket; *also* : any of the processes into which this part is often divided — see TOOTH illustration **b** : the enlarged basal part of a hair within the skin **c** : the proximal end of a nerve **d** : the part of an organ or physical structure by which it is attached to the body ⟨the ~ of the tongue⟩ **3 a** : something that is an origin or source (as of a condition or quality) ⟨the love of money is the ~ of all evil —1 Tim 6:10 (AV)⟩ **b** : one or more progenitors of a group of descendants — usu. used in pl. **c** : an underlying support : BASIS **d** : the essential core : HEART — often used in the phrase at root **e** : close relationship with an environment : TIE — usu. used in pl. **4 a** : a quantity taken an indicated number of times as an equal factor ⟨2 is a fourth ~ of 16⟩ **b** : a number that reduces an equation to an identity when it is substituted for one variable **5 a** : the lower part : BASE **b** : the part by which an object is attached to something else **6** : the simple element inferred as the basis from which a word is derived by phonetic change or by extension (as composition or the addition of an affix or inflectional ending) **7** : the tone from whose overtones a chord is composed : the lowest tone of a chord in normal position *syn* see ORIGIN — **root·ed** \'rü-təd, 'rú-\ adj — **root·less** \'rü-ləs, 'rút-\ adj — **root·less·ness** n — **root·like** \-,līk\ adj

²**root** vt (14c) **1 a** : to furnish with or enable to develop roots **b** : to fix or implant by or as if by roots **2** : to remove altogether by or as if by pulling out by the roots — usu. used with out ⟨~ out dissenters⟩ ~ vi **1** : to grow roots or take root **2** : to have an origin or base

³**root** vb [alter. of wroot, fr. ME wroten, fr. OE wrōtan; akin to OHG ruozzan to root] vi (1532) **1** : to turn up or dig in the earth with the snout : GRUB **2** : to poke or dig about ~ vt : to turn over, dig up, or discover and bring to light — usu. used with out ⟨~ out the cause of the problem⟩

⁴**root** \'rüt also 'rút\ vi [perh. alter. of ²rout] (1889) **1** : to noisily applaud or encourage a contestant or team : CHEER **2** : to wish the success of or lend support to someone or something — **root·er** n

root·age \'rü-tij, 'rú-\ n (ca. 1895) **1** : a developed system of roots **2** : ROOT 3a

root beer n (1843) : a sweetened carbonated beverage flavored with extracts of roots (as sarsaparilla) and herbs

root canal n (1893) : the part of the pulp cavity lying in the root of a tooth; *also* : a dental operation to save a tooth by removing the contents of its root canal and filling the cavity with a protective substance

root cap n (1875) : a protective cap of parenchyma cells that covers the terminal meristem in most root tips

root cellar n (1822) : a pit used for the storage esp. of root crops

root crop n (1834) : a crop (as turnips) grown for its enlarged roots

root·ed·ness \'rü-təd-nəs, 'rú-\ n (1642) : the quality or state of having roots

root hair n (1857) : a filamentous extension of an epidermal cell near the tip of a rootlet that functions in absorption of water and minerals

root·hold \'rüt-,hōld, 'rút-\ n (1864) **1** : the anchorage of a plant to soil through the growing and spreading of roots **2** : a place where plants may obtain a roothold

root knot n (1889) : a plant disease caused by nematodes that produce characteristic enlargements on the roots and stunt the growth of the plant

root-knot nematode n (1922) : any of several small plant-parasitic nematodes (genus *Meloidogyne*) that cause root knot

root·let \'rüt-lət, 'rút-\ n (ca. 1793) : a small root

root-mean-square n (1895) : the square root of the arithmetic mean of the squares of a set of numbers

root pressure n (1875) : the chiefly osmotic pressure by which water rises into the stems of plants from the roots

root rot n (1883) : any of various plant diseases characterized by decay of the roots and caused esp. by fungi

root·stock \'rüt-,stäk, 'rút-\ n (1832) **1** : a rhizomatous underground part of a plant **2** : a stock for grafting consisting of a root or a piece of root; *broadly* : STOCK 3b

rooty \'rü-tē, 'rú-\ adj (15c) : full or consisting of roots ⟨~ soil⟩

¹**rope** \'rōp\ n [ME, fr. OE rāp; akin to OHG reif hoop] (bef. 12c) **1 a** : a large stout cord of strands of fibers or wire twisted or braided together **b** : a long slender strip of material used as rope ⟨rawhide ~⟩ **c** : a hangman's noose **d** : LARIAT **2** : a row or string consisting of things united by or as if by braiding, twining, or threading ⟨~ of pearls⟩ **3** pl : special or basic techniques or procedures ⟨show him the ~s⟩ **4** : LINE DRIVE — **rope·like** \-,līk\ adj — **on the ropes** : in a defensive and often helpless position

²**rope** vb **roped; rop·ing** vt (14c) **1 a** : to bind, fasten, or tie with a rope or cord **b** : to partition, separate, or divide by a rope ⟨~ off the street⟩ **c** : LASSO **2** : to draw as if with a rope : LURE ~ vi : to take the form of or twist in the manner of rope — **rop·er** n

rope-danc·er \'rōp-,dan(t)-sər\ n (1648) : one that dances, walks, or performs acrobatic feats on a rope high in the air — **rope-danc·ing** \-siŋ\ n

rop·ery \'rō-p(ə-)rē\ n [prob. fr. the thought that the perpetrator deserved the gallows] (1592) *archaic* : roguish tricks or banter

rope tow n (1948) : SKI TOW 1

rope·walk \'rōp-,wók\ n (1672) : a long covered walk, building, or room where ropes are manufactured

rope·walk·er \-,wó-kər\ n (1615) : an acrobat who walks on a rope high in the air

rope·way \-,wā\ n (1889) **1** : an endless aerial cable moved by a stationary engine and used to transport freight (as logs and ore) **2** : a fixed cable or a pair of fixed cables between supporting towers serving as a track for suspended passenger or freight carriers

ropy also **rop·ey** \'rō-pē\ adj **rop·i·er; -est** (15c) **1 a** : capable of being drawn into a thread : VISCOUS; *also* : tending to adhere in stringy masses **b** : having a gelatinous or slimy quality from bacterial or fungal contamination ⟨~ milk⟩ ⟨~ flour⟩ **2 a** : resembling rope **b** : MUSCULAR, SINEWY **3** usu **ropey**, slang : extremely unsatisfactory : LOUSY — **rop·i·ness** n

roque \'rōk\ n [alter. of croquet] (1899) : croquet played on a hard-surfaced court with a raised border

Roque·fort \'rōk-fərt\ trademark — used for a pungent French blue cheese made from sheep's milk

ro·que·laure \,rō-kə-'lór, ,rä-, -'lór\ n [F, fr. the Duc de *Roquelaure* †1738 Fr. marshal] (1716) : a knee-length cloak worn esp. in the 18th and 19th centuries

ror·qual \'rór-kwəl, -,kwól\ n [F, fr. Norw rørhval, fr. ON reytharhvalr, fr. reythr rorqual + hvalr whale] (1827) : any of a family (Balaenopteridae) of large baleen whales (as a blue whale or humpback whale) having the skin of the throat marked with deep longitudinal furrows

Ror·schach \'rór-,shäk\ adj (1927) : of, relating to, used in connection with, or resulting from the Rorschach test

Rorschach test n [Hermann *Rorschach* †1922 Swiss psychiatrist] (1927) : a personality and intelligence test in which a subject interprets inkblot designs in terms of what they reveal intellectual and emotional factors — called also *Rorschach, Rorschach inkblot test*

ro·sa·ceous \rō-'zā-shəs\ adj [ultim. fr. L rosa] (1731) **1** : of or relating to the rose family **2** : of, relating to, or resembling a rose esp. in having a 5-petaled regular corolla

ro·sar·i·an \rō-'zar-ē-ən, -'zer-\ n (1864) : a cultivator of roses

ro·sa·ry \'rō-zə-rē, 'rōz-rē\ n, pl **-ries** [ML rosarium, fr. L rose garden, fr. neut. of rosarius of roses, fr. rosa rose] (1547) **1** often cap : a Roman Catholic devotion consisting of meditation on usu. five sacred mysteries during recitation of five decades of Hail Marys of which each begins with an Our Father and ends with a Gloria Patri **2** : a string of beads used in counting prayers esp. of the Roman Catholic rosary

rosary pea n (ca. 1866) **1** : a tropical leguminous twining herb (*Abrus precatorius*) that bears jequirity beans and has a root used as a substitute for licorice — called also *Indian licorice, jequirity bean* **2** : JEQUIRITY BEAN 1

ros·coe \'räs-(,)kō\ n [prob. fr. the name Roscoe] (ca. 1914) *slang* : HANDGUN

¹**rose** past of RISE

²**rose** \'rōz\ n [ME, fr. OE, fr. L rosa; akin to Gk rhodon rose, Per gul]

\ə\ abut \ᵊ\ kitten, F table \ər\ further \a\ ash \ā\ ace \ä\ mop, mar \aú\ out \ch\ chin \e\ bet \ē\ easy \g\ go \i\ hit \ī\ ice \j\ job \ŋ\ sing \ō\ go \ó\ law \ói\ boy \th\ thin \th\ the \ü\ loot \ú\ foot \y\ yet \zh\ vision \ä, ḵ, ⁿ, œ, œ̄, ᵫ, ᵫ̄, ᵞ\ see Guide to Pronunciation (bef. 12c) **1 a** : any of a genus (*Rosa* of the family Rosaceae, the rose family) of usu. prickly shrubs with pinnate leaves and showy flowers having five petals in the wild state but being often double or partly double under cultivation **b** : the flower of a rose **2** : something resembling a rose in form: as **a** (1) : COMPASS CARD (2) : a circular card with radiating lines used in other instruments **b** : a rosette esp. on a shoe **c** : ROSE CUT **3** *pl* : a comfortable situation or an easily accomplished task ⟨it was not all sunshine and ∼s —Anthony Lewis⟩ **4** : a moderate purplish red **5** : a plane curve which consists of three or more loops meeting at the origin and whose equation in polar coordinates is of the form ρ = *a* sin *n*θ or ρ = *a* cos *n*θ where *n* is an integer greater than zero — **rose-like** \-ˌlīk\ *adj* — **under the rose** : SUB ROSA

³**rose** *adj* (14c) **1 a** : containing or used for roses **b** : of or relating to a rose **c** : flavored, scented, or colored with or like roses **2** : of the color rose

ro·sé \rō-ˈzā\ *n* [F] (1897) : a light pink table wine made from red grapes by removing the skins after fermentation has begun

rose·ate \ˈrō-zē-ət, -zē-ˌāt\ *adj* [L *roseus* rosy, fr. *rosa*] (1589) **1** : resembling a rose esp. in color **2** : overly optimistic : viewed favorably — **ro·se·ate·ly** *adv*

roseate spoonbill *n* (ca. 1785) : a spoonbill (*Ajaia ajaja*) that is found from the southern U.S. to Patagonia and has chiefly pink plumage

rose-bay \ˈrōz-ˌbā\ *n* (1760) **1** : RHODODENDRON; *esp* : GREAT LAUREL **2** : FIREWEED b

rosebay rhododendron *n* (ca. 1949) : GREAT LAUREL

rose—breast·ed grosbeak \ˈrōz-ˌbres-təd-\ *n* (1810) : a grosbeak (*Pheucticus ludovicianus*) chiefly of eastern No. America that in the male is chiefly black and white with a rose-red breast and in the female is grayish brown with a streaked breast

rose-bud \ˈrōz-ˌbəd\ *n* (15c) : the bud of a rose

rose-bush \-ˌbúsh\ *n* (1587) : a shrub that produces roses

rose chafer *n* (1704) : a common No. American beetle (*Macrodactylus subspinosus*) that feeds on plant roots as a larva and on leaves and flowers (as of rose or grapevines) as an adult — called also *rose bug*

rose—col·ored \ˈrōz-kə-lərd\ *adj* (1526) **1** : having a rose color **2** : seeing or seen in a promising light : OPTIMISTIC

rose—colored glasses *n pl* (1950) : favorably disposed opinions : optimistic eyes ⟨views the world through *rose-colored glasses*⟩

rose cut *n* (ca. 1842) : a form in which gems (as diamonds) are cut that usu. has a flat circular base and facets in two ranges rising to a point — **rose—cut** *adj*

rose fever *n* (1851) : hay fever occurring in the spring or early summer — called also *rose cold*

rose-fish \ˈrōz-ˌfish\ *n* (1731) : REDFISH

rose geranium *n* (1832) : any of several pelargoniums grown for their fragrant 3- to 5-lobed leaves and small pink flowers

rose hip *n* (1857) : the ripened accessory fruit of a rose that consists of a fleshy receptacle enclosing numerous achenes

ro·se·ma·ling \ˈrō-zə-ˌmä-liŋ, -sə-\ *n* [Norw, fr. *rose* rose + *maling* painting] (1942) : painted or sometimes carved decoration (as on furniture, walls, or wooden dinnerware) in Scandinavian peasant style that consists esp. of floral designs and inscriptions

rose mallow *n* (1857) : any of several hibiscuses with large rose-colored flowers; *esp* : a showy plant (*Hibiscus moscheutos*) of the salt marshes of the eastern U.S.

rose-mary \ˈrōz-ˌmer-ē\ *n, pl* **-mar·ies** [ME *rosmarine*, fr. L *rosmarinus*, fr. *ros-* ros dew + *marinus* of the sea; akin to Skt *rasa* sap, juice — more at MARINE] (14c) : a fragrant shrubby mint (*Rosmarinus officinalis*) of southern Europe and Asia Minor; *also* : its leaves used as a seasoning

rose of Jer·i·cho \-ˈjer-i-ˌkō\ *n* [ME, fr. *Jericho*, ancient city in Palestine] (15c) : an Asian plant (*Anastatica hierochuntica*) of the mustard family that rolls up when dry and expands when moistened

rose of Shar·on \-ˈshar-ən, -ˈsher-\ [Plain of *Sharon*, Palestine] (ca. 1847) : a commonly cultivated Asian shrub or small tree (*Hibiscus syriacus*) having showy bell-shaped rose, purple, or white flowers

rose oil *n* (1552) : a fragrant essential oil obtained from roses and used chiefly in perfumery and in flavoring

ro·se·o·la \ˌrō-zē-ˈō-lə, rō-ˈzē-ə-lə\ *n* [NL, fr. L *roseus* rosy, fr. *rosa* rose] (ca. 1818) : a rose-colored eruption in spots or a disease marked by such an eruption; *esp* : ROSEOLA INFANTUM — **ro·se·o·lar** \-lər\ *adj*

roseola in·fan·tum \-in-ˈfan-təm\ *n* [NL, infant roseola] (ca. 1935) : a mild disease of infants and children characterized by fever lasting usu. three days followed by an eruption of rose-colored spots

rose pink *n* (ca. 1859) : a moderate pink

rose slug *n* (1877) : the slimy green larva of either of two sawflies (*Claudius isomerus* and *Endelomyia aethiops*) that feed on the parenchyma of and skeletonize the leaves of roses

ro·set \ˈrō-zət\ *n* [alter. of ME *rosin*] (14c) *chiefly Scot* : RESIN

Ro·set·ta stone \rō-ˈzet-ə-\ *n* [*Rosetta*, Egypt] (ca. 1859) **1** : a black basalt stone found in 1799 that bears an inscription in hieroglyphics, demotic characters, and Greek and is celebrated for having given the first clue to the decipherment of Egyptian hieroglyphics **2** : one that gives a clue to understanding

ro·sette \rō-ˈzet\ *n* [F, lit., small rose, fr. OF, fr. *rose*, fr. L *rosa*] (1790) **1** : an ornament usu. made of material gathered or pleated so as to resemble a rose and worn as a badge of office, as evidence of having won a decoration (as the Medal of Honor), or as trimming **2** : a disk of foliage or a floral design usu. in relief used as a decorative motif **3** : a structure or color marking on an animal suggestive of a rosette; *esp* : one of the groups of spots on a leopard **4** : a cluster of leaves in crowded circles or spirals arising basally from a crown (as in the dandelion) or apically from an axis with greatly shortened internodes (as in many tropical palms) **5** : a food decoration or garnish in the shape of a rose ⟨icing ∼s⟩ ⟨carrot ∼s⟩

rose-wa·ter \ˈrōz-ˌwò-tər, -ˌwä-\ *adj* (1840) **1** : affectedly nice or delicate **2** : having the odor of rose water

rose water *n* (14c) : a watery solution of the odoriferous constituents of the rose used as a perfume or a flavoring

rose window *n* (1773) : a circular window filled with tracery

rose-wood \ˈrōz-ˌwüd\ *n* (1660) : any of various tropical trees (esp. genus *Dalbergia*) yielding valuable cabinet woods of a dark red or purplish color streaked and variegated with black; *also* : the wood

Rosh Ha·sha·nah \ˌräsh-(h)ə-ˈshä-nə, ˌrōsh-, -ˈshō-\ *n* [LHeb *rōsh hashshānāh*, lit., beginning of the year] (1846) : the Jewish New Year observed on the first and by Orthodox and Conservative Jews also on the second of Tishri

Ro·si·cru·cian \ˌrō-zə-ˈkrü-shən, ˌrä-\ *n* [Christian *Rosenkreutz* (NL *Rosae Crucis*) reputed 15th cent. founder of the movement] (1624) **1** : an adherent of a 17th and 18th century movement devoted to esoteric wisdom with emphasis on psychic and spiritual enlightenment **2** : a member of one of several organizations held to be descended from the Rosicrucians — **Rosicrucian** *adj* — **Ro·si·cru·cian·ism** \-shə-ˌni-zəm\ *n*

rose window

ros·i·ly \ˈrō-zə-lē\ *adv* (1809) **1** : in an optimistic manner **2** : with a rosy color or tinge

¹**ros·in** \ˈrä-z²n, ˈrò-, *dial* ˈró-zəm\ *n* [ME, modif. of MF *resine* resin] (13c) : a translucent amber-colored to almost black brittle friable resin that is obtained by chemical means from the oleoresin or deadwood of pine trees or from tall oil and used esp. in making varnish, paper size, soap, and soldering flux and in rosining violin bows

²**rosin** *vt* **ros·ined; ros·in·ing** \ˈräz-niŋ, ˈröz-; ˈrä-z²n-iŋ, ˈró-\ (15c) : to rub or treat (as the bow of a violin) with rosin

ros·in·weed \ˈrä-z²n-ˌwēd, ˈró-\ *n* (1831) : any of several American plants (as the compass plant) having resinous foliage or a resinous odor

ros·tel·lum \rä-ˈste-ləm\ *n* [NL, fr. L, dim. of *rostrum* beak] (ca. 1826) : a small process resembling a beak : a diminutive rostrum: as **a** : an extension of the stigma of an orchid flower **b** : an anterior prolongation of the head of a tapeworm bearing hooks — **ros·tel·lar** \rä-ˈste-lər\ *adj*

ros·ter \ˈräs-tər *also* ˈròs- *or* ˈrós-\ *n* [D *rooster*, lit., gridiron; fr. the parallel lines] (1727) **1 a** : a roll or list of personnel **b** : such a list giving the order in which a duty is to be performed ⟨duty ∼⟩ **c** : the persons listed on a roster **2** : an itemized list

ros·tral \ˈräs-trəl *also* ˈròs-\ *adj* [NL *rostralis*, fr. L *rostrum*] (1709) **1** : of or relating to a rostrum **2** : situated toward the oral or nasal region: as **a** *of a part of the spinal cord* : SUPERIOR 6a **b** *of a part of the brain* : ANTERIOR, VENTRAL — **ros·tral·ly** \-trə-lē\ *adv*

ros·trate \ˈräs-ˌtrāt, -trət *also* ˈròs-\ *adj* (ca. 1819) : having a rostrum

ros·trum \ˈräs-trəm *also* ˈròs-\ *n, pl* **ros·tra** \-trə\ *or* **rostrums** [L, beak, ship's beak, fr. *rodere* to gnaw — more at RODENT] (1542) **1** [L *Rostra*, pl., a platform for speakers in the Roman Forum decorated with the beaks of captured ships, fr. pl. of *rostrum*] **a** : an ancient Roman platform for public orators **b** : a stage for public speaking **c** : a raised platform on a stage **2** : the curved end of a ship's prow; *esp* : the beak of a war galley **3** : a bodily part or process suggesting a bird's bill: as **a** : the beak, snout, or proboscis of any of various insects or arachnids **b** : the often spinelike anterior median prolongation of the carapace of a crustacean (as a crayfish or lobster)

rosy \ˈrō-zē\ *adj* **ros·i·er; -est** (14c) **1 a** : of the color rose **b** : having a pinkish usu. healthy-looking complexion : BLOOMING **c** : marked by blushes **2** : characterized by or tending to promote optimism — **ros·i·ness** *n*

¹**rot** \ˈrät\ *vb* **rot·ted; rot·ting** [ME *roten*, fr. OE *rotian*; akin to OHG *rōzzēn* to rot] *vi* (bef. 12c) **1 a** : to undergo decomposition from the action of bacteria or fungi **b** : to become unsound or weak (as from use or chemical action) **2 a** : to go to ruin : DETERIORATE **b** : to become morally corrupt : DEGENERATE ∼ *vt* : to cause to decompose or deteriorate with or as if with rot **syn** see DECAY

²**rot** *n* (14c) **1 a** : the process of rotting : the state of being rotten : DECAY **b** : something rotten or rotting **2 a** *archaic* : a wasting putrescent disease **b** : any of several parasitic diseases esp. of sheep marked by necrosis and wasting **c** : plant disease marked by breakdown of tissues and caused esp. by fungi or bacteria **3** : NONSENSE — often used interjectionally

ro·ta \ˈrō-tə\ *n* [L, wheel — more at ROLL] (1673) **1** *chiefly Brit* **a** : a fixed order of rotation (as of persons or duties) **b** : a roll or list of persons : ROSTER **2** *cap* [ML, fr. L] : a tribunal of the papal curia exercising jurisdiction esp. in matrimonial cases appealed from diocesan courts

ro·ta·me·ter \ˈrō-tə-ˌmē-tər, rō-ˈta-mə-tər\ *n* [L *rota* + E *-meter*] (1907) : a gauge that consists of a graduated glass tube containing a free float for measuring the flow of a fluid

Ro·tar·i·an \rō-ˈter-ē-ən\ *n* [*Rotary (club)*] (1911) : a member of a major national and international service club

¹**ro·ta·ry** \ˈrō-tə-rē\ *adj* [ML *rotarius*, fr. L *rota* wheel] (ca. 1731) **1 a** : turning on an axis like a wheel **b** : taking place about an axis ⟨∼ motion⟩ **2** : having an important part that turns on an axis ⟨∼ cutter⟩ **3** : characterized by rotation **4** : of, relating to, or being a press in which paper is printed by rotation in contact with a curved printing surface attached to a cylinder

²**rotary** *n, pl* **-ries** (ca. 1888) **1** : a rotary machine **2** : a road junction formed around a central circle about which traffic moves in one direction only — called also *circle, traffic circle*

rotary cultivator *n* (1926) : ROTOTILLER

rotary engine *n* (1837) **1** : any of various engines (as a turbine) in which power is applied to vanes or similar parts constrained to move in a circular path **2** : a radial engine in which the cylinders revolve about a stationary crankshaft

rotary—wing aircraft *n* (1935) : ROTORCRAFT; *specif* : HELICOPTER — usu. used in pl.

¹**ro·tate** \ˈrō-ˌtāt\ *adj* [L *rota*] (1785) : having the parts flat and spreading or radiating like the spokes of a wheel ⟨∼ blue flowers⟩

²**ro·tate** \ˈrō-ˌtāt, *esp Brit* rō-ˈ\ *vb* **ro·tat·ed; ro·tat·ing** [L *rotatus*, pp. of *rotare*, fr. *rota* wheel — more at ROLL] *vi* (1808) **1** : to turn about an axis or a center : REVOLVE; *esp* : to move in such a way that all particles follow circles with a common angular velocity about a common axis **2 a** : to perform an act, function, or operation in turn **b** : to pass or alternate in a series ∼ *vt* **1 a** : to cause to turn or move about an

axis or a center **b** : to cause (a plane region or line) to sweep out a volume or surface by moving around an axis so that each of its points remains at a constant distance from the axis ⟨generate a torus by *rotating* a circle about an external line⟩ **2** : to cause to grow in rotation ⟨~ crops⟩ **3** : to cause to pass or act in a series : ALTERNATE **4** : to exchange (individuals or units) with others — **ro·tat·able** \'rō-,tā-tə-bəl *also* rō-'\ *adj*

ro·ta·tion \rō-'tā-shən\ *n* (1555) **1 a** (1) : the action or process of rotating on or as if on an axis or center (2) : the act or an instance of rotating something **b** : one complete turn : the angular displacement required to return a rotating body or figure to its original orientation **2 a** : return or succession in a series ⟨~ of the seasons⟩ **b** : the growing of different crops in succession in one field usu. in a regular sequence **3** : the turning of a body part about its long axis as if on a pivot **4** : a game of pool in which all 15 object balls are shot in numerical order **5** : the series of pitchers on a baseball team who regularly start successive games in turn — **ro·ta·tion·al** \-shnəl, -shə-nᵊl\ *adj*

ro·ta·tive \'rō-,tā-tiv *also* rō-'\ *adj* (1778) **1** : turning like a wheel : ROTARY **2** : relating to, occurring in, or characterized by rotation — **ro·ta·tive·ly** *adv*

ro·ta·tor \'rō-,tā-tər *also* rō-'\ *n* (1676) : one that rotates or causes rotation; *esp*, *pl* **-tors** *or* **-tor·es** \,rō-tə-'tōr-,ēz, -'tór-\ : a muscle that partially rotates a part on its axis

rotator cuff *n* (1961) : a supporting and strengthening structure of the shoulder joint that is made up of the capsule of the shoulder joint blended with tendons and muscles as they pass to the capsule or across it to insert on the head of the humerus

ro·ta·to·ry \'rō-tə-,tōr-ē, -,tór-, *Brit* -t(ə-)ri *also* rō-'tā-tə-ri\ *adj* (1755) **1** : of, relating to, or producing rotation **2** : occurring in rotation

ro·ta·vi·rus \'rō-tə-,vī-rəs\ *n* [NL, fr. L *rota* wheel + NL *virus*] (1974) : a reovirus that has a double-layered capsid and that causes diarrhea esp. in infants

¹rote \'rōt\ *n* [ME, fr. MF, of Gmc origin; akin to OHG *hruozza* crowd] (14c) : ³CROWD 1

²rote *n* [ME] (14c) **1** : the use of memory usu. with little intelligence ⟨learn by ~⟩ **2** : routine or repetition carried out mechanically or unthinkingly ⟨a joyless sense of order, ~, and commercial hustle —L. L. King⟩

³rote *adj* (1641) **1** : learned or memorized by rote **2** : MECHANICAL 3a

⁴rote *n* [perh. of Scand origin; akin to ON *rauta* to roar — more at ROUT] (1610) : the noise of surf on the shore

ro·te·none \'rōt-ᵊn-,ōn\ *n* [ISV, fr. Jp *roten* derris plant] (1924) : a crystalline insecticide $C_{23}H_{22}O_6$ that is obtained from the roots of several tropical plants (as a derris) and is of low toxicity for warm-blooded animals and is used esp. in home gardens

rot·gut \'rät-,gət\ *n* (1633) : cheap or inferior liquor

ro·ti \'rō-tē\ *n* [Hindi *roti* bread; akin to Skt *rotika*, kind of bread] (1920) : a round soft flat unleavened bread; *also* : such a bread wrapped around a filling and eaten as a sandwich

ro·ti·fer \'rō-tə-fər\ *n* [ultim. fr. L *rota* + *-fer*] (1793) : any of a class (Rotifera of the phylum Aschelminthes) of minute usu. microscopic but many-celled chiefly freshwater aquatic invertebrates having the anterior end modified into a retractile disk bearing circles of strong cilia that often give the appearance of rapidly revolving wheels

ro·tis·ser·ie \rō-'tis-rē, -'ti-sə-\ *n* [F *rôtisserie*, fr. MF *rostisserie*, fr. *rostir* to roast — more at ROAST] (ca. 1920) **1** : a restaurant specializing in broiled and barbecued meats **2** : an appliance fitted with a spit on which food is rotated before or over a source of heat

ro·to \'rō-(,)tō\ *n*, *pl* **rotos** (1926) : ROTOGRAVURE

ro·to·gra·vure \,rō-tə-grə-'vyúr\ *n* [G *Rotogravur*, blend of L *rota* wheel and G *Photogravur* photogravure] (1913) **1** : PHOTOGRAVURE 2 : a section of a newspaper devoted to rotogravure pictures

ro·tor \'rō-tər\ *n* [contr. of *rotator*] (1903) **1** : a part that revolves in a stationary part; *esp* : the rotating member of an electrical machine **2** : a complete system of horizontal rotating blades that supplies lift for a rotorcraft

ro·tor·craft \-,kraft\ *n*, *pl* **rotorcraft** (1940) : an aircraft (as a helicopter) whose lift is derived principally from rotating airfoils

ro·to·till \'rō-tō-,til\ *vt* [back-formation fr. *rototiller*] (1939) : to till or plow (soil) with a rototiller

ro·to·till·er \-,ti-lər\ *n* [fr. *Rototiller*, a trademark] (1923) : a landscaping implement with engine-powered rotating blades used to lift and turn over soil

¹rot·ten \'rä-t³n\ *adj* [ME *roten*, fr. ON *rotinn*; akin to OE *rotian* to rot] (13c) **1** : having rotted : PUTRID **2** : morally corrupt **3** : extremely unpleasant or inferior ⟨a ~ day⟩ ⟨a ~ job⟩ **4** : very uncomfortable ⟨feeling ~⟩ **5** : of very poor quality : LOUSY, ABOMINABLE ⟨a ~ show⟩ ⟨what ~ luck⟩ — **rot·ten·ly** *adv* — **rot·ten·ness** \-t³n-(n)əs\ *n*

²rotten *adv* (1880) : to an extreme degree (spoiled ~)

rotten borough *n* (1812) : an election district that has many fewer inhabitants than other election districts with the same voting power

rot·ten·stone \'rä-t³n-,stōn\ *n* (1677) : a decomposed siliceous limestone used for polishing

rot·ter \'rä-tər\ *n* (1894) : a thoroughly objectionable person

rott·wei·ler \'rät-,wī-lər\ *n*, *often cap* [G, fr. *Rottweil*, city in Germany] (1907) : any of a breed of tall powerful black-and-tan short-haired dogs of German origin that are commonly used as guard dogs

ro·tund \rō-'tənd, 'rō-,\ *adj* [L *rotundus*, prob. alter. of (assumed) OL *retundus*; akin to L *rota* wheel — more at ROLL] (1705) **1** : marked by roundness : ROUNDED **2** : marked by fullness of sound or cadence : OROTUND, SONOROUS ⟨a master of ~ phrase⟩ **3** : notably plump : CHUBBY — **ro·tun·di·ty** \rō-'tən-də-tē\ *n* — **ro·tund·ly** \-'tənd-lē, 'rō-,\ *adv* — **ro·tund·ness** \rō-'tən(d)-nəs, 'rō-,\ *n*

rottweiler

ro·tun·da \rō-'tən-də\ *n* [It *rotonda*, fr. L *rotunda*, fem. of *rotundus*] (ca. 1700) **1** : a round building; *esp* : one covered by a dome **2 a** : a large round room **b** : a large central area (as in a hotel)

ro·tu·ri·er \rō-'tür-ē-,ā, -'tyúr-\ *n* [MF] (1586) : a person not of noble birth

rou·ble *var of* RUBLE

roué \rù-'ā\ *n* [F, lit., broken on the wheel, fr. pp. of *rouer* to break on the wheel, fr. ML *rotare*, fr. L, to rotate; fr. the feeling that such a person deserves this punishment] (1800) : a man devoted to a life of sensual pleasure : RAKE

¹rouge \'rüzh, *esp Southern* 'rüj\ *n* [F, fr. MF, fr. *rouge* red, fr. L *rubeus* reddish — more at RUBY] (1753) **1** : any of various cosmetics for coloring the cheeks or lips red **2** : a red powder consisting essentially of ferric oxide used in polishing glass, metal, or gems and as a pigment

²rouge *vb* **rouged; roug·ing** *vt* (1777) **1** : to apply rouge to **2** : to cause to redden ~ *vi* : to use rouge

¹rough \'rəf\ *adj* **rough·er; rough·est** [ME, fr. OE *rūh*; akin to OHG *rūh* rough, Lith *raukas* wrinkle] (bef. 12c) **1 a** : marked by inequalities, ridges, or projections on the surface : COARSE **b** : covered with or made up of coarse and often shaggy hair ⟨*rough*-coated collie⟩ — compare SMOOTH, WIREHAIRED **c** (1) : having a broken, uneven, or bumpy surface ⟨~ terrain⟩ (2) : difficult to travel through or penetrate : WILD ⟨into the ~ woods —P. B. Shelley⟩ **2 a** : TURBULENT, TEMPESTUOUS ⟨~ seas⟩ **b** (1) : characterized by harshness, violence, or force (2) : presenting a challenge : DIFFICULT ⟨~ to deal with —R. M. McAlmon⟩ **3** : coarse or rugged in character or appearance: as **a** : harsh to the ear **b** : crude in style or expression ⟨~ INDELICATE **d** : marked by a lack of refinement or grace : UNCOUTH **4 a** : CRUDE, UNFINISHED ⟨~ carpentry⟩ **b** : executed or ventured hastily, tentatively, or imperfectly ⟨a ~ draft⟩ ⟨~ estimate⟩; *also* : APPROXIMATE ⟨this gives a ~ idea⟩ — **rough·ish** \'rə-fish\ *adj* — **rough·ness** \'rəf-nəs\ *n*

syn ROUGH, HARSH, UNEVEN, RUGGED, SCABROUS mean not smooth or even. ROUGH implies points, bristles, ridges, or projections on the surface ⟨a *rough* wooden board⟩. HARSH implies a surface or texture distinctly unpleasant to the touch ⟨a *harsh* fabric that chafes the skin⟩. UNEVEN implies a lack of uniformity in height, breadth, or quality ⟨an old house with *uneven* floors⟩. RUGGED implies irregularity or roughness of land surface and connotes difficulty of travel ⟨a *rugged* landscape⟩. SCABROUS implies scaliness or prickliness of surface ⟨a *scabrous* leaf⟩. **syn** see in addition RUDE

²rough *adv* (14c) : ROUGHLY 1

³rough *n* (15c) **1** : uneven ground covered with high grass, brush, and stones; *specif* : such ground bordering a golf fairway **2** : the rugged or disagreeable side or aspect ⟨hiking-camping admirers of nature in the ~ —Eleanor Stirling⟩ **3 a** : something in a crude, unfinished, or preliminary state **b** : broad outline : general terms ⟨the question . . . has been discussed in ~ —*Manchester Guardian Weekly*⟩ **c** : a hasty preliminary drawing or layout **4** : ROWDY

⁴rough *vt* (1763) **1** : ROUGHEN **2 a** : to subject to abuse : MANHANDLE, BEAT — usu. used with *up* **b** : to subject to unnecessary and intentional violence in a sport **3** : to calk or otherwise roughen (a horse's shoes) to prevent slipping **4 a** : to shape, make, or dress in a rough or preliminary way **b** : to indicate the chief lines of ⟨~ out the structure of a building⟩ — **rough·er** *n* — **rough it** : to live under harsh or primitive conditions

rough·age \'rə-fij\ *n* (ca. 1900) : FIBER 1d; *also* : food containing much indigestible material acting as fiber

rough–and–ready \,rə-fən-'re-dē\ *adj* (1810) : crude in nature, method, or manner but effective in action or use

¹rough–and–tum·ble \-'təm-bəl\ *n* (1792) : rough disorderly unrestrained fighting or struggling; *also* : INFIGHTING

²rough–and–tumble *adj* (1832) **1** : marked by rough-and-tumble ⟨grew up in a ~ atmosphere —E. J. Kahn⟩; *also* : ROUGH-AND-READY **2** : put together haphazardly : MAKESHIFT ⟨a ~ fence⟩

rough bluegrass *n* (ca. 1925) : a forage grass (*Poa trivialis*) of Eurasia and northern Africa that is naturalized in No. America

rough breathing *n* (1899) **1** : a mark ' used in Greek over some initial vowels to show that they are aspirated or over ρ to show that it is voiceless **2** : the sound indicated by a mark ' over a Greek vowel or ρ

¹rough·cast \'rəf-,kast, *for* 2 *also* -'kast\ *vt* **-cast; -cast·ing** (1565) **1** : to plaster (as a wall) with roughcast **2** : to shape or form roughly

²rough·cast \-,kast\ *n* (1579) **1** : a rough model **2** : a plaster of lime mixed with shells or pebbles used for covering buildings **3** : a rough surface finish (as of a plaster wall)

rough cut *n* (1937) : a print of an incompletely edited motion picture

¹rough–dry \'rəf-'drī\ *vt* (1837) : to dry (laundry) without smoothing or ironing

²rough–dry *adj* (1856) : being dry after laundering but not ironed or smoothed over ⟨~ clothes⟩

rough·en \'rə-fən\ *vb* **rough·ened; rough·en·ing** \'rə-fə-niŋ, 'rəf-niŋ\ *vt* (1582) : to make rough or rougher ⟨her hands were ~ed by work —Ellen Glasgow⟩ ~ *vi* : to become rough

rough fish *n* (1843) : a fish that is neither a sport fish nor an important food for sport fishes

rough–hew \'rəf-'hyü\ *vt* **-hewed; -hewn** \-'hyün\; **-hew·ing** (1530) **1** : to hew (as timber) coarsely without smoothing or finishing **2** : to form crudely

rough–hewn \-'hyün\ *adj* (1530) **1** : being in a rough, unsmoothed, or unfinished state : crudely formed ⟨~ beams⟩ **2** : lacking refinement ⟨he was rather attractive, in a ~ kind of way —Jan Speas⟩

¹rough·house \'rəf-,haús\ *n* (1887) : violence or rough boisterous play

²rough·house \-,haús, -,haúz\ *vb* **rough·housed; rough·hous·ing** *vt* (1902) : to treat in a boisterously rough manner ~ *vi* : to engage in roughhouse

rough·leg \'rəf-,leg, -,läg\ *n* (1895) : ROUGH-LEGGED HAWK

\ə\ abut \³\ kitten, F table \ər\ further \a\ ash \ā\ ace \ä\ mop, mar \aú\ out \ch\ chin \e\ bet \ē\ easy \g\ go \i\ hit \ī\ ice \j\ job \ŋ\ sing \ō\ go \ó\ law \ói\ boy \th\ thin \t̲h̲\ the \ü\ loot \ú\ foot \y\ yet \zh\ vision \à, k̲, ⁿ, œ, œ̄, ue̲, ūe̲, ᵞ\ see Guide to Pronunciation

rough–legged hawk n (1811) : a large circumpolar arctic hawk (*Buteo lagopus*) that winters southward and typically has a white tail with a wide black band or bands at the tip

rough lemon n (1900) 1 : a hybrid lemon that forms a large spreading thorny tree, bears rough-skinned nearly globular acid fruit, and is important chiefly as a rootstock for other citrus trees 2 : the fruit of a rough lemon

rough·ly \'rə-flē\ adv (14c) 1 : in a rough manner: as a : with harshness or violence ⟨treated the prisoner ~⟩ b : in crude fashion : IMPERFECTLY ⟨~ dressed lumber⟩ 2 : without completeness or exactness : APPROXIMATELY ⟨~ 20 percent⟩

¹**rough·neck** \'rəf-,nek\ n (1836) 1 a : a rough or uncouth person b : ROWDY, TOUGH 2 : a worker of an oil-well-drilling crew other than the driller

²**roughneck** adj (1916) : having the characteristics of or suitable for a roughneck

rough·ri·der \'rəf-'rī-dər\ n (1733) 1 : one who is accustomed to riding unbroken or little-trained horses 2 usu **Rough Rider** : a member of the 1st U.S. Volunteer Cavalry regiment in the Spanish–American War commanded by Theodore Roosevelt

¹**rough·shod** \-,shäd\ adj (ca. 1688) 1 : shod with calked shoes 2 : marked by tyrannical force ⟨~ rule⟩

²**roughshod** adv (1813) : in a roughshod manner ⟨rode ~ over the opposition⟩

rough trade n (ca. 1935) : male homosexuals who are or affect to be rugged and potentially violent; also : such a homosexual

rouille \'rü-ē, rüy\ n [F, lit., rust; fr. its color] (1951) : a peppery garlic sauce

rou·lade \rü-'läd\ n [F, lit., act of rolling] (ca. 1706) 1 : a florid vocal embellishment sung to one syllable 2 : a slice of usu. stuffed meat that is rolled, browned, and steamed or braised

rou·leau \rü-'lō\ n, pl **rou·leaux** \-'lōz\ [F] (1693) 1 : a little roll; esp : a roll of coins put up in paper

¹**rou·lette** \rü-'let\ n [F, lit., small wheel, fr. OF roelete, dim. of roele small wheel, fr. LL rotella, dim. of L rota wheel — more at ROLL] (1745) 1 : a gambling game in which players bet on which compartment of a revolving wheel a small ball will come to rest in 2 a : any of various toothed wheels or disks (as for producing rows of dots on engraved plates or for making short consecutive incisions in paper to facilitate subsequent division) b : tiny slits between rows of stamps in a sheet that are made by a roulette and serve as an aid in separation — compare PERFORATION

²**roulette** vt **rou·lett·ed; rou·lett·ing** (1867) : to make roulettes in

Rou·ma·nian \rü-'mā-nē-ən, -nyən\ var of RUMANIAN

¹**round** \'raünd\ adj [ME, fr. OF roont, fr. L rotundus — more at ROTUND] (14c) 1 a (1) : having every part of the surface or circumference equidistant from the center (2) : CYLINDRICAL ⟨a ~ peg⟩ b : approximately round ⟨a ~ face⟩ 2 : well filled out : PLUMP, SHAPELY 3 a : COMPLETE, FULL ⟨a ~ dozen⟩ ⟨a ~ ton⟩ b : approximately correct; esp : exact only to a specific decimal or place (use the ~ number 1400 for the exact figure 1411) c : substantial in amount : AMPLE ⟨a good ~ price —T. B. Costain⟩ 4 : direct in utterance : OUTSPOKEN ⟨a ~ oath⟩ 5 : moving in or forming a circle 6 a : brought to completion or perfection : FINISHED b : presented with lifelike fullness or vividness 7 : delivered with a swing of the arm ⟨a ~ blow⟩ 8 a : having full or unimpeded resonance or tone : SONOROUS b : pronounced with rounded lips : LABIALIZED 9 : of or relating to handwriting predominantly curved rather than angular — **round·ness** \'raün(d)-nəs\ n

²**round** adv (14c) : AROUND 1, 2b, 3, 4, 5

³**round** n (14c) 1 a : something (as a circle, globe, or ring) that is round b (1) : a knot of people (2) : a circle of things 2 : ROUND DANCE 1 3 : a musical canon sung in unison in which each part is continuously repeated 4 a : a rung of a ladder or a chair b : a rounded molding 5 a : a circling or circuitous path or course b : motion in a circle or a curving path 6 a : a route or circuit habitually covered (as by a security guard or police officer) b : a series of similar or customary calls or stops ⟨making the ~s of his friends —Current Biog.⟩; esp : a series of regularly scheduled professional calls on hospital patients made by a doctor or nurse — usu. used in pl. 7 : a drink of liquor apiece served at one time to each person in a group ⟨I'll buy the next ~⟩ 8 : a sequence of recurring routine or repetitive actions or events ⟨went about my ~ of chores⟩ ⟨the newest ~ of talks⟩ 9 : a period of time that recurs in a fixed pattern ⟨the daily ~⟩ 10 a : one shot fired by a weapon or by each man in a military unit b : a unit of ammunition consisting of the parts necessary to fire one shot 11 a : a unit of action in a contest or game which comprises a stated period, covers a prescribed distance, includes a specified number of plays, or gives each player one turn b : a division of a tournament in which each contestant plays an opponent 12 : a prolonged burst (as of applause) 13 a : a cut of meat (as beef) esp. between the rump and the lower leg — see BEEF illustration b : a slice of food ⟨a ~ of bread⟩ 14 : a rounded or curved part — **in the round** 1 : in full sculptured form unattached to a background 2 : with an inclusive or comprehensive view or representation 3 : with a center stage surrounded by an audience ⟨theater *in the round*⟩

⁴**round** vt (14c) 1 a : to make round b (1) : to make (the lips) round and protruded (as in the pronunciation of \ü\) (2) : to pronounce with lip rounding : LABIALIZE 2 a : GO AROUND b : to pass part of the way around 3 : ENCIRCLE, ENCOMPASS 4 : to bring to completion or perfection — often used with *off* or *out* 5 : to express as a round number — often used with *off* ⟨11.3572 ~ed off to two decimal places becomes 11.36⟩ ~ vi 1 a : to become round, plump, or shapely b : to reach fullness or completion 2 : to follow a winding course : BEND — **round on** 1 : to turn against : ASSAIL

⁵**round** prep (1602) 1 : AROUND 2 : all during : THROUGHOUT ⟨~ the year⟩

⁶**round** vt [alter. of ME rounen, fr. OE rūnian; akin to OE rūn mystery — more at RUNE] (ca. 1529) 1 archaic : WHISPER 2 archaic : to speak to in a whisper

¹**round·about** \'raün-də-,baút\ adj (1608) : CIRCUITOUS, INDIRECT ⟨had to take a ~ course⟩ — **round·about·ness** n

²**roundabout** n (1755) 1 : a circuitous route : DETOUR 2 Brit : MERRY-GO-ROUND 3 : a short close-fitting jacket worn by men and boys esp. in the 19th century 4 Brit : ROTARY 2

round angle n (ca. 1934) : an angle of 360° or 2 π radians

round clam n (ca. 1843) : QUAHOG

round dance n (1683) 1 : a folk dance in which participants form a ring and move in a prescribed direction 2 : a ballroom dance in which couples progress around the room 3 : a series of movements performed by a bee to indicate that a source of food is nearby

round·ed \'raün-dəd\ adj (1712) 1 : made round : flowing rather than jagged or angular 2 : fully developed — **round·ed·ness** n

roun·del \'raün-d°l\ n [ME, fr. OF rondel, fr. roont round — more at ROUND] (14c) 1 : a round figure or object (as a circular panel, window, or niche) 2 a : RONDEL 2a b : an English modified rondeau

roun·de·lay \'raün-də-,lā\ n [ME, modif. of MF rondelet, dim. of rondel] (15c) 1 : a simple song with a refrain 2 : a poem with a refrain recurring frequently or at fixed intervals as in a rondel

round·er \'raün-dər\ n (1828) 1 pl but sing in constr : a game of English origin that is played with ball and bat and that somewhat resembles baseball 2 : a dissolute person : WASTREL 3 : one that rounds by hand or by machine 4 : a boxing match lasting a specified number of rounds — usu. used in combination ⟨a 10-*rounder*⟩

Round·head \'raünd-,hed\ n [fr. the Puritans' cropping their hair short in contrast to the Cavaliers] (1642) 1 : a member of the parliamentary party in England at the time of Charles I and Oliver Cromwell 2 : PURITAN 1

round·head·ed \-'he-dəd\ adj (1729) : having a round head; specif : BRACHYCEPHALIC — **round·head·ed·ness** n

round·house \'raünd-,haús\ n (1589) 1 archaic : LOCKUP 2 : a circular building for housing and repairing locomotives 3 : a blow delivered with a wide swing

round·ish \'raún-dish\ adj (1545) : somewhat round

round lot n (ca. 1902) : the standard unit of trading in a security market usu. amounting to 100 shares of stock

round·ly \'raünd-lē\ adv (15c) 1 a : in a complete or thorough manner : THOROUGHLY ⟨~ disliked⟩ ⟨~ satisfying⟩ b : by nearly everyone : WIDELY ⟨~ praised⟩ 2 : in a plainspoken manner : BLUNTLY ⟨told them ~ they would get no help⟩ 3 : with vigor or asperity ⟨~ attacked the plan⟩

round–rob·in \'raünd-,rä-bən\ n [fr. the name Robin] (1730) 1 a : a written petition, memorial, or protest to which the signatures are affixed in a circle so as not to indicate who signed first b : a statement signed by several persons c : something (as a letter) sent in turn to the members of a group each of whom signs and forwards it sometimes after adding comment 2 : ROUND TABLE 2 3 : a tournament in which every contestant meets every other contestant in turn 4 : SERIES, ROUND

round–shoul·dered \'raün(d)-,shōl-dərd\ adj (1586) : having the shoulders stooping or rounded

rounds·man \'raün(d)z-mən\ n (1795) 1 : one that makes rounds 2 : a supervisory police officer of the grade of sergeant or just below

round steak n (1876) : a steak cut from the round of beef — see BEEF illustration

round ta·ble \'raün(d)-,tā-bəl\ n (14c) 1 a cap R&T : the large circular table of King Arthur and his knights b : the knights of King Arthur 2 usu **round·ta·ble** : a conference for discussion or deliberation by several participants; also : the participants in such a conference

round–the–clock adj (1937) : AROUND-THE-CLOCK

round–trip \'raünd-,trip\ n, often attrib (1860) : a trip to a place and back usu. over the same route

round–up \'raün-,dəp\ n (1873) 1 a (1) : the act or process of collecting animals (as cattle) by riding around them and driving them in (2) : the cowboys and ranch personnel engaged in a cattle roundup b : a gathering in of scattered persons or things ⟨a ~ of all suspects⟩ 2 : a summary of information ⟨a ~ of the news⟩

round up vt (1844) 1 : to collect (as cattle) by means of a roundup 2 : to gather in or bring together from various quarters

round window n (ca. 1903) : FENESTRA 1b

round·wood \'raünd-,wúd\ n (1910) : timber used (as for poles) without being squared by sawing or hewing

round·worm \'raünd-,wərm\ n (1565) : NEMATODE; also : a related round-bodied unsegmented worm (as a spiny-headed worm) as distinguished from a flatworm

roup \'rüp, 'raúp\ n [origin unknown] (ca. 1808) : TRICHOMONIASIS c

¹**rouse** \'raúz\ vb **roused; rous·ing** [ME, to shake the feathers] vt (1531) 1 archaic : to cause to break from cover 2 a : to stir up : EXCITE ⟨was roused to fury⟩ b : to arouse from or as if from sleep or repose : AWAKEN ~ vi 1 : to become aroused : AWAKEN 2 : to become stirred — **rouse·ment** \'raúz-mənt\ n — **rous·er** n

²**rouse** n (ca. 1802) : an act or instance of rousing; esp : an excited stir

³**rouse** n [alter. (fr. misdivision of to drink carouse) of carouse] (1602) 1 obs : DRINK, TOAST 2 archaic : CAROUSAL

rouse·about \'raúz-ə-,baút\ n (1861) Austral : an unskilled worker

rous·ing \'raú-ziŋ\ adj (1641) 1 : giving rise to excitement : STIRRING b : BRISK, LIVELY 2 : EXCEPTIONAL, SUPERLATIVE — **rous·ing·ly** adv

Rous sarcoma \'raús-\ n [F. Peyton Rous †1970 Am. physician] (ca. 1925) : a readily transplantable malignant fibrosarcoma of chickens that is caused by a specific carcinogenic virus

Rous·seau·ism \rü-'sō-,i-zəm\ n (1865) 1 : the philosophical, educational, and political doctrines of Jean Jacques Rousseau 2 : the return to or glorification of a simpler and more primitive way of life — **Rous·seau·ist** \-ist\ n — **Rous·seau·is·tic** \,rü-,sō-'is-tik, rü-\ adj

roust \'raúst\ vt [alter. of ¹rouse] (1658) : to drive (as from bed) roughly or unceremoniously

roust·about \'raús-tə-,baút\ n (1868) 1 a : DECKHAND b : LONGSHOREMAN 2 : an unskilled or semiskilled laborer esp. in an oil field or refinery 3 : a circus worker who erects and dismantles tents, cares for the grounds, and handles animals and equipment

roust·er \'raús-tər\ n (1883) 1 : DECKHAND 2 : LONGSHOREMAN

¹**rout** \'raút\ n [ME route, fr. MF, troop, defeat, fr. (assumed) VL rupta, fr. L, fem. of ruptus, pp. of rumpere to break — more at REAVE] (13c) 1 : a crowd of people : THRONG; specif : RABBLE 2b 2 a : DISTURBANCE b archaic : FUSS 3 : a fashionable gathering

²**rout** \'rōt, 'rüt\ *vi* [ME *rowten,* fr. ON *rauta;* akin to OE *rēotan* to weep, L *rudere* to roar] (14c) *dial chiefly Brit* : to low loudly : BELLOW — used of cattle

³**rout** \'raut\ *vb* [alter. of ³*root*] *vi* (ca. 1564) **1** : to poke around with the snout : ROOT ⟨pigs ~*ing* in the earth⟩ **2** : to search haphazardly ~ *vt* **1 a** *archaic* : to dig up with the snout **b** : to gouge out or make a furrow in (as wood or metal) **2 a** : to force out as if by digging — usu. used with *out* **b** : to cause to emerge esp. from bed **3** : to come up with : UNCOVER

⁴**rout** \'raut\ *n* [MF *route* troop, defeat] (1598) **1** : a state of wild confusion or disorderly retreat **2 a** : a disastrous defeat : DEBACLE **b** : a precipitate flight

⁵**rout** \'raut\ *vt* (1600) **1 a** : to disorganize completely : DEMORALIZE **b** : to put to precipitate flight **c** : to defeat decisively or disastrously ⟨the discomfiture of seeing their party ~*ed* at the polls —A. N. Holcombe⟩ **2** : to drive out : DISPEL

¹**route** \'rüt, 'raut\ *n* [ME, fr. OF, fr. (assumed) VL *rupta* (*via*), lit., broken way, fr. L *rupta,* fem. of *ruptus,* pp.] (13c) **1 a** : a traveled way : HIGHWAY ⟨the main ~ north⟩ **b** : a means of access : CHANNEL ⟨the ~ to social mobility —T. F. O'Dea⟩ **2** : a line of travel : COURSE **3 a** : an established or selected course of travel or action **b** : an assigned territory to be systematically covered ⟨a newspaper ~⟩

²**route** *vt* **rout·ed; rout·ing** (1832) **1** : to send by a selected route : DIRECT ⟨was *routed* along the scenic shore road⟩ **2** : to divert in a specified direction

route·man \'rüt-mən, 'raut-,man\ *n* (1918) : one who is responsible for making sales or deliveries on an assigned route

¹**rout·er** \'rau-tər\ *n* (1846) : one that routs: as **a** : a routing plane **b** : a machine with a revolving vertical spindle and cutter for milling out the surface of wood or metal

²**rout·er** \'rü-tər, 'raù-\ *n* (1903) : one that routes

³**rout·er** \'rü-tər, 'raù-\ *n* [*route* (race of a mile or more)] (ca. 1951) : a horse trained for distance races

route step *n* (1867) : a style of marching in which troops maintain prescribed intervals but are not required to keep in step or to maintain silence — called also *route march*

route·way \'rüt-,wā, 'raut-\ *n* (1946) *chiefly Brit* : ROUTE 3a

routh \'rauth, 'rüth\ *n* [origin unknown] (ca. 1689) *chiefly Scot* : PLENTY

¹**rou·tine** \rü-'tēn\ *n* [F, fr. MF, fr. *route* traveled way] (1676) **1 a** : a regular course of procedure ⟨if resort to legal action becomes a campus ~ —J. A. Perkins⟩ **b** : habitual or mechanical performance of an established procedure ⟨the ~ of factory work⟩ **2** : a reiterated speech or formula ⟨the old "After you" ~ —Ray Russell⟩ **3** : a worked-out part (as of an entertainment or sports contest) that may be often repeated ⟨a dance ~⟩ ⟨a gymnastic ~⟩; *esp* : a theatrical number **4** : a sequence of computer instructions for performing a particular task

²**rou·tine** \rü-'tēn, 'rü-\ *adj* (1817) **1** : of a commonplace or repetitious character : ORDINARY **2** : of, relating to, or being in accordance with established procedure ⟨~ business⟩ — **rou·tine·ly** *adv*

rou·tin·ize \rü-'tē-,nīz, 'rü-t^ən-,īz\ *vt* **-ized; -iz·ing** (1921) : to discipline in or reduce to a routine — **rou·tin·i·za·tion** \(,)rü-,tē-nə-'zā-shən, ,rü-t^ən-ə-\ *n*

roux \'rü\ *n, pl* **roux** \'rüz\ [F, fr. *beurre roux* brown butter] (1813) : a cooked mixture of flour and fat used as a thickening agent in a soup or a sauce

¹**rove** \'rōv\ *vb* **roved; rov·ing** [ME *roven* to shoot at random, wander] *vi* (1536) : to move aimlessly : ROAM ~ *vt* : to wander through or over   *syn* see WANDER

²**rove** *n* (1606) : an act or instance of wandering

³**rove** *past and past part of* REEVE

⁴**rove** *vt* **roved; rov·ing** [origin unknown] (1789) : to join (textile fibers) with a slight twist and draw out into roving

⁵**rove** *n* (1789) : ROVING

rove beetle *n* [perh. fr. ¹*rove*] (ca. 1771) : any of a family (Staphylinidae) of often predatory active beetles having a long body and very short wing covers beneath which the wings are folded transversely — called also *staphylinid*

¹**rov·er** \'rō-vər\ *n* [ME, fr. MD, fr. *roven* to rob; akin to OE *rēafian* to reave — more at REAVE] (14c) : PIRATE

²**rov·er** \'rō-vər\ *n* [ME, fr. *roven*] (15c) **1** : a random or long-distance mark in archery — usu. used in pl. **2** : WANDERER, ROAMER **3** : a player who is not assigned to a specific position on a team and who plays wherever needed **4** : a vehicle for exploring the surface of an extraterrestrial body (as the moon or Mars)

¹**rov·ing** \'rō-viŋ\ *adj* [¹*rove*] (1596) **1 a** : capable of being shifted from place to place : MOBILE **b** : not restricted as to location or area of concern **2** : inclined to ramble or stray ⟨a ~ fancy⟩

²**roving** *n* [⁴*rove*] (1802) : a slightly twisted roll or strand of usu. textile fibers

¹**row** \'rō\ *vb* [ME, fr. OE *rōwan;* akin to MHG *rüejen* to row, L *remus* oar] *vi* (bef. 12c) **1** : to propel a boat by means of oars **2** : to move by or as if by the propulsion of oars ~ *vt* **1 a** : to propel with or as if with oars **b** : to be equipped with (a specified number of oars) **c** (1) : to participate in (a rowing match) (2) : to compete against in rowing (3) : to pull (an oar) in a crew **2** : to transport in an oar-propelled boat — **row·er** \'rō(-ə)r\ *n*

²**row** *n* (1832) : an act or instance of rowing

³**row** *n* [ME *rawe;* akin to OE *rǣw* row, OHG *riga* line, and perh. to Skt *rikhati* he scratches] (13c) **1** : a number of objects arranged in a usu. straight line ⟨a ~ of bottles⟩; *also* : the line along which such objects are arranged ⟨planted the corn in parallel ~s⟩ **2 a** : WAY, STREET **b** : a street or area dominated by a specific kind of enterprise or occupancy ⟨doctors' ~⟩ **3** : TWELVE-TONE ROW **4 a** : a continuous strip usu. running horizontally or parallel to a base line **b** : a horizontal arrangement of items — **in a row** : one after another : SUCCESSIVELY

⁴**row** *vt* (1657) : to form into rows

⁵**row** \'raù\ *n* [origin unknown] (1746) : a noisy disturbance or quarrel

⁶**row** \'raù\ *vi* (1797) : to engage in a row : have a quarrel

row·an \'raù-ən, 'rō-ən\ *n* [of Scand origin; akin to ON *reynir* rowan; akin to OE *rēad* red — more at RED] (1804) **1 a** : a Eurasian mountain ash (*Sorbus aucuparia*) with flat corymbs of white flowers followed by small red pomes **b** : an American mountain ash (*Sorbus americana*) with flat corymbs of white flowers followed by small orange red pomes **2** : the fruit of a rowan

row·an·ber·ry \-,ber-ē\ *n* (1814) : ROWAN 2

rowan 1b: leaves and fruit

row·boat \'rō-,bōt\ *n* (1538) : a small boat designed to be rowed

¹**row·dy** \'raù-dē\ *adj* **row·di·er; -est** [perh. irreg. fr. ⁵*row*] (1819) : coarse or boisterous in behavior : ROUGH; *also* : characterized by such behavior ⟨~ local bars⟩ — **row·di·ly** \'raù-d^əl-ē\ *adv* — **row·di·ness** \'raù-dē-nəs\ *n* — **rowdy·ish** \-ish\ *adj*

²**rowdy** *n, pl* **rowdies** (1819) : a rowdy person : TOUGH

row·dy·ism \'raù-dē-,i-zəm\ *n* (1842) : rowdy character or behavior

¹**row·el** \'raù(-ə)l\ *n* [ME *rowelle,* fr. MF *rouelle* small wheel, fr. OF *roele* — more at ROULETTE] (15c) : a revolving disk with sharp marginal points at the end of a spur

²**rowel** *vt* **-eled** *or* **-elled; -el·ing** *or* **-el·ling** (1599) **1** : to goad with or as if with a rowel **2** : VEX, TROUBLE

row·en \'raù-ən\ *n* [ME *rowein,* fr. (assumed) ONF *rewain;* akin to OF *regain* aftermath, fr. *re-* + *gain* aftermath, of Gmc origin; akin to OHG *weida* pasture, *weidanōn* to hunt for food — more at GAIN] (15c) : AFTERMATH 1

row house *n* (1936) : one of a series of houses connected by common sidewalls and forming a continuous group

row·ing \'rō-iŋ\ *n* (bef. 12c) **1** : the propelling of a boat by means of oars : the action of one that rows **2** : the sport of racing in shells

rowing boat *n* (1820) *chiefly Brit* : ROWBOAT

rowing machine *n* (1848) : an exercise machine that simulates the action of rowing

row·lock \'rä-lək, 'rə-; 'rō-,läk\ *n* [prob. by alter.] (ca. 1750) *chiefly Brit* : OARLOCK

¹**roy·al** \'ròi(-ə)l\ *adj* [ME *roial,* fr. MF, fr. L *regalis,* fr. *reg-, rex* king; akin to OIr *rī* (gen. *rig*) king, Skt *rājan* to rule — more at RIGHT] (14c) **1 a** : of kingly ancestry ⟨the ~ family⟩ **b** : of, relating to, or subject to the crown ⟨the ~ estates⟩ **c** : being in the crown's service ⟨Royal Air Force⟩ **2 a** : suitable for royalty : MAGNIFICENT **b** : requiring no exertion : EASY ⟨there is no ~ road to logic —Justus Buchler⟩ **3 a** : of superior size, magnitude, or quality ⟨a patronage of ~ dimensions —J. H. Plumb⟩ — often used as an intensive ⟨a ~ pain⟩ **b** : established or chartered by the crown **4** : of, relating to, or being a part (as a mast, sail, or yard) next above the topgallant — **roy·al·ly** \'ròi-ə-lē\ *adv*

²**royal** *n* (14c) **1** : a person of royal blood **2** : a small sail on the royal mast immediately above the topgallant sail **3** : a stag of 8 years or more having antlers with at least 12 points

royal blue *n* (1789) : a vivid purplish blue

royal flush *n* (ca. 1868) : a straight flush having an ace as the highest card — see POKER illustration

roy·al·ism \'ròi-ə-,li-zəm\ *n* (1793) : MONARCHISM

roy·al·ist \-list\ *n* (1643) **1** *often cap* : an adherent of a king or of monarchical government: as **a** : CAVALIER 3 **b** : TORY 4 **2** : a reactionary business tycoon — **royalist** *adj*

royal jelly *n* (1817) : a highly nutritious secretion of the pharyngeal glands of the honeybee that is fed to the very young larvae in a colony and to all queen larvae

royal palm *n* (1861) : any of a genus (*Roystonea*) of palms chiefly of the Caribbean region; *esp* : a tall graceful pinnate-leaved palm (*R. regia*) native to Cuba that is widely planted for ornament

royal poinciana *n* (ca. 1900) : a showy tropical tree (*Delonix regia* syn. *Poinciana regia*) widely planted for its immense racemes of scarlet and orange flowers — called also *flamboyant, peacock flower*

royal purple *n* (1661) : a dark reddish purple

roy·al·ty \'ròi(-ə)l-tē\ *n, pl* **-ties** [ME *roialte,* fr. MF *roialte,* fr. OF, fr. *roial*] (14c) **1 a** : royal status or power : SOVEREIGNTY **b** : a right or perquisite of a sovereign (as a percentage paid to the crown of gold or silver taken from mines) **2** : regal character or bearing : NOBILITY **3 a** : persons of royal lineage **b** : a person of royal rank ⟨how to address *royalties* —George Santayana⟩ **c** : a privileged class **4** : a right of jurisdiction granted to an individual or corporation by a sovereign **5 a** : a share of the product or profit reserved by the grantor esp. of an oil or mining lease **b** : a payment made to an author or composer for each copy of a work sold or to an inventor for each article sold under a patent

royster *var of* ROISTER

roz·zer \'rä-zər\ *n* [origin unknown] (1893) *slang Brit* : POLICE OFFICER

RPG \,är-(,)pē-'jē\ *n* [*report program generator*] (1966) : a computer language that generates programs from the user's specifications esp. to produce business reports

RPV \,är-(,)pē-'vē\ *n* [*remotely piloted vehicle*] (1970) : an unmanned aircraft flown by remote control and used esp. for reconnaissance

-rrhagia *n comb form* [NL, fr. Gk, fr. *rhēgnynai* to break, burst; prob. akin to Lith *rėžti* to cut] : abnormal or excessive discharge or flow ⟨metro*rrhagia*⟩

-rrhea *n comb form* [ME *-ria,* fr. LL *-rrhoea,* fr. Gk *-rrhoia,* fr. *rhoia,* fr. *rhein* to flow — more at STREAM] : flow : discharge ⟨logo*rrhea*⟩ ⟨leu-ko*rrhea*⟩

-rrhiza — see -RHIZA

-rrhoea *chiefly Brit var of* -RRHEA

rRNA \,är-(,)är-(,)en-'ā\ *n* (ca. 1965) : RIBOSOMAL RNA

ru·a·na \rü-'ä-nə\ *n* [AmerSp, fr. Sp, woolen fabric] (1903) : a woolen covering resembling a poncho

¹**rub** \'rəb\ *vb* **rubbed; rub·bing** [ME *rubben;* akin to Icel *rubba* to

---

\ə\ abut \^ə\ kitten, F table \ər\ further \a\ ash \ā\ ace \ä\ mop, mar
\aù\ out \ch\ chin \e\ bet \ē\ easy \g\ go \i\ hit \ī\ ice \j\ job
\ŋ\ sing \ō\ go \ò\ law \òi\ boy \th\ thin \t̲h̲\ the \ü\ loot \ù\ foot
\y\ yet \zh\ vision \á, k̲, ⁿ, œ, œ̄, ue, ūe, ^y\ see Guide to Pronunciation

scrape] *vi* (14c)   **1   a :** to move along the surface of a body with pressure : GRATE   **b**   (1) : to fret or chafe with or as if with friction   (2) : to cause discontent, irritation, or anger   **2 :** to continue in a situation usu. with slight difficulty ⟨in spite of financial difficulties, he is *rubbing* along⟩   **3 :** to admit of being rubbed (as for erasure or obliteration) ∼ *vt*   **1   a :** to subject to or as if to the action of something moving esp. back and forth with pressure and friction   **b**   (1) : to cause (a body) to move with pressure and friction along a surface   (2) : to treat in any of various ways by rubbing   **c :** to bring into reciprocal back-and-forth or rotary contact   **2 :** ANNOY, IRRITATE — **rub elbows** *or* **rub shoulders :** to associate closely : MINGLE — **rub one's nose in :** to bring forcefully or repeatedly to one's attention — **rub the wrong way :** to arouse the antagonism or displeasure of : IRRITATE
²**rub** *n* (1586)   **1   a :** an unevenness of surface (as of the ground in lawn bowling)   **b :** OBSTRUCTION, DIFFICULTY ⟨the ∼ is that so few of the scholars have any sense of this truth themselves —Benjamin Farrington⟩   **c :** something grating to the feelings (as a gibe or harsh criticism)   **d :** something that mars serenity   **2 :** the application of friction with pressure ⟨an alcohol ∼⟩
Ru·bai·yat stanza \'rü-bē-ät-, -,bī-, -,at-\ *n* [*The Rubáiyát of Omar Khayyám*, quatrains translated by Edward FitzGerald (1859)] (1940) : an iambic pentameter quatrain with a rhyme scheme *aaba*
ru·basse \rü-'bas, 'rü-,\ *n* [F *rubace*, irreg. fr. *rubis* ruby — more at RUBY] (ca. 1890) : a quartz stained a ruby red
ru·ba·to \rü-'bä-(,)tō\ *n, pl* **-tos** [It, lit., robbed] (ca. 1883) : a fluctuation of tempo within a musical phrase often against a rhythmically steady accompaniment
¹**rub·ber** \'rə-bər\ *n* (1536)   **1 :** one that rubs **a :** an instrument or object (as a rubber eraser) used in rubbing, polishing, scraping, or cleaning   **c :** something that prevents rubbing or chafing   **2** [fr. its use in erasers]   **a :** an elastic substance that is obtained by coagulating the milky juice of any of various tropical plants (as of the genera *Hevea* and *Ficus*), is essentially a polymer of isoprene, and is prepared as sheets and then dried — called also *caoutchouc, india rubber*   **b :** any of various synthetic rubberlike substances   **c :** natural or synthetic rubber modified by chemical treatment to increase its useful properties (as toughness and resistance to wear) and used esp. in tires, electrical insulation, and waterproof materials   **3 :** something made of or resembling rubber: as   **a :** a rubber overshoe   **b**   (1) : a rubber tire   (2) : the set of tires on a vehicle   **c :** a rectangular slab of white rubber in the middle of a baseball infield on which a pitcher stands while pitching   **d :** CONDOM — **rubber** *adj*
²**rubber** *n* [origin unknown] (1599)   **1 :** a contest consisting of an odd number of games won by the side that takes a majority (as two out of three)   **2 :** an odd game played to determine the winner of a tie
rubber band *n* (1886) : a continuous band of rubber used in various ways (as for holding together a sheaf of papers)
rubber bridge *n* (1936) : a form of contract bridge in which settlement is made at the end of each rubber
rubber cement *n* (1886) : an adhesive consisting typically of a dispersion of vulcanized rubber in an organic solvent
rubber check *n* [fr. its coming back like a bouncing rubber ball] (1926) : a check returned by a bank because of insufficient funds in the payer's account
rub·ber·ized \'rə-bə-,rīzd\ *adj* (1908) : coated or saturated with rubber or a rubber solution
rub·ber·like \'rə-bər-,līk\ *adj* (1922) : resembling rubber esp. in physical properties (as elasticity and toughness)
¹**rub·ber·neck** \-,nek\ *n* (ca. 1896)   **1 :** an overly inquisitive person   **2 :** TOURIST; *esp* : one on a guided tour
²**rubberneck** *vi* (1896)   **1 :** to look about, stare, or listen with exaggerated curiosity   **2 :** to go on a tour : SIGHTSEE — **rub·ber·neck·er** \-,ne-kər\ *n*
rubber plant *n* (1888) : a plant that yields rubber; *esp* : a tall tropical Asian tree (*Ficus elastica*) of the mulberry family that is frequently dwarfed as an ornamental
rubber–stamp *vt* (1918)   **1 :** to approve, endorse, or dispose of as a matter of routine or at the command of another   **2 :** to mark with a rubber stamp
rubber stamp *n* (1881)   **1 :** a stamp of rubber for making imprints   **2   a :** a person who echoes or imitates others   **b :** a body or person that approves or endorses a program or policy with little or no dissent or discussion   **3 :** a stereotyped copy or expression ⟨the usual *rubber stamps* of criticism —H. L. Mencken⟩   **b :** a routine endorsement or approval — **rubber–stamp** *adj*
rubber tree *n* (1847) : a tree that yields rubber; *esp* : a So. American tree (*Hevea brasiliensis*) of the spurge family that is cultivated in plantations and is a chief source of rubber
rub·bery \'rə-b(ə-)rē\ *adj* (1907) : resembling rubber (as in elasticity, consistency, or texture) ⟨∼ legs⟩
rub·bing \'rə-biŋ\ *n* (1845) : an image of a raised, incised, or textured surface obtained by placing paper over it and rubbing the paper with a colored substance
rubbing alcohol *n* (ca. 1931) : a cooling and soothing liquid for external application that contains approximately 70 percent denatured ethyl alcohol or isopropanol
rub·bish \'rə-bish, *dial* -bij\ *n* [ME *robys*] (15c)   **1 :** useless waste or rejected matter : TRASH   **2 :** something that is worthless or nonsensical ⟨few real masterpieces are forgotten and not much ∼ survives —William Bridges-Adams⟩ — **rub·bishy** \-bə-shē\ *adj*
¹**rub·ble** \'rə-bəl\ *n* [ME *robyl*] (14c)   **1   a :** broken fragments (as of rock) resulting from the decay or destruction of a building ⟨fortifications knocked into ∼ —C. S. Forester⟩   **b :** a miscellaneous confused mass or group of usu. broken or worthless things ⟨lay in a pile of ∼, only this time there was more of it, additional gear having hit the deck —K. M. Dodson⟩   **2 :** waterworn or rough broken stones or bricks used in coarse masonry or in filling courses of walls   **3 :** rough stone as it comes from the quarry

rubber tree

²**rubble** *vt* **rub·bled; rub·bling** \-b(ə-)liŋ\ (1926) : to reduce to rubble
rub-down \'rəb-,daùn\ *n* (1896) : a brisk rubbing of the body
rube \'rüb\ *n* [*Rube*, nickname for *Reuben*] (1896) : an awkward unsophisticated person : RUSTIC
¹**ru·be·fa·cient** \,rü-bə-'fā-shənt\ *adj* [L *rubefacient-, rubefaciens*, prp. of *rubefacere* to make red, fr. *rubeus* reddish + *facere* to make — more at RUBY, DO] (1804) : causing redness (as of the skin)
²**rubefacient** *n* (1805) : a substance for external application that produces redness of the skin
Rube Gold·berg \'rüb-'gōl(d)-,bərg\   *also* **Rube Gold·berg·i·an** \-,bər-gē-ən, -,bərg-yən\ *adj* [*Reuben* (*Rube*) L. *Goldberg* †1970 Am. cartoonist] (1931) : accomplishing by complex means what seemingly could be done simply ⟨a kind of *Rube Goldberg* contraption . . . with five hundred moving parts —L. T. Grant⟩; *also* : characterized by such complex means
ru·bel·la \rü-'be-lə\ *n* [NL, fr. L, fem. of *rubellus* reddish, fr. *ruber* red — more at RED] (1883) : GERMAN MEASLES
ru·bel·lite \rü-'be-,līt, 'rü-bə-,līt\ *n* [L *rubellus*] (ca. 1796) : a red tourmaline used as a gem
Ru·ben·esque \,rü-bə-'nesk\ *adj* (1925) : of, relating to, or suggestive of the painter Rubens or his works; *esp* : plump or rounded usu. in a pleasing or attractive way ⟨a ∼ figure⟩
ru·be·o·la \,rü-bē-'ō-lə, rü-'bē-ə-lə\ *n* [NL, fr. neut. pl. of (assumed) NL *rubeolus* reddish, fr. L *rubeus*] (1803) : MEASLES
Ru·bi·con \'rü-bi-,kän\ *n* [L *Rubicon-, Rubico*, river of northern Italy forming part of the boundary between Cisalpine Gaul and Italy whose crossing by Julius Caesar in 49 B.C. was regarded by the Senate as an act of war] (1626)   **1 :** a bounding or limiting line; *esp* : one that when crossed commits a person irrevocably
ru·bi·cund \'rü-bi-(,)kənd\ *adj* [ME *rubicunde*, fr. L *rubicundus*, fr. *rubēre* to be red; akin to L *rubeus*] (15c) : RUDDY — **ru·bi·cun·di·ty** \,rü-bi-'kən-də-tē\ *n*
ru·bid·i·um \rü-'bi-dē-əm\ *n* [NL, fr. L *rubidus* red, fr. *rubēre*] (1861) : a soft silvery metallic element of the alkali metal group that reacts violently with water and bursts into flame spontaneously in air — see ELEMENT table
rub in *vt* (1851) : to harp on (as something unpleasant) : EMPHASIZE
ru·bi·ous \'rü-bē-əs\ *adj* (1601) : RED, RUBY
ru·ble \'rü-bəl\ *n* [Russ *rubl'*] (1554) — see MONEY table
rub off *vi* (1950) : to become transferred ⟨bad habits *rubbed off* on them⟩ ⟨carbon *rubs off* on your hands⟩ — **rub–off** \'rəb-,óf\ *n*
rub out *vt* (14c)   **1 :** to obliterate or extinguish by or as if by rubbing   **2 :** to destroy completely; *specif* : KILL, MURDER ⟨somebody *rubbed* him out . . . with a twenty-two —Raymond Chandler⟩ — **rub-out** \'rəb-,aùt\ *n*
ru·bric \'rü-brik, -,brik\ *n* [ME *rubrike* red ocher, heading in red letters of part of a book, fr. MF *rubrique*, fr. L *rubrica*, fr. *rubr-, ruber* red] (14c)   **1   a :** an authoritative rule; *esp* : a rule for conduct of a liturgical service   **b**   (1) : NAME, TITLE; *specif* : the title of a statute   (2) : something under which a thing is classed : CATEGORY ⟨the sensations falling under the general ∼, "pressure" —F. A. Geldard⟩   **c :** an explanatory or introductory commentary : GLOSS; *specif* : an editorial interpolation   **2 :** a heading of a part of a book or manuscript done or underlined in a color (as red) different from the rest   **3 :** an established rule, tradition, or custom — **rubric** *or* **ru·bri·cal** \-bri-kəl\ *adj* — **ru·bri·cal·ly** \-bri-k(ə-)lē\ *adv*
ru·bri·cate \'rü-bri-,kāt\ *vt* **-cat·ed; -cat·ing** (1570)   **1 :** to write or print as a rubric   **2 :** to provide with a rubric — **ru·bri·ca·tion** \,rü-bri-'kā-shən\ *n* — **ru·bri·ca·tor** \'rü-bri-,kā-tər\ *n*
rub up *vt* (1572)   **1 :** to revive or refresh knowledge of : RECALL   **2 :** to improve the keenness of (a mental faculty)
ru·bus \'rü-bəs\ *n, pl* **rubus** [NL, fr. L, blackberry] (ca. 1921) : any of a genus (*Rubus*) of plants (as a blackberry or a raspberry) of the rose family having 3- to 7-foliolate or simple lobed leaves, white or pink flowers, and a mass of carpels ripening into an aggregate fruit composed of many drupelets
¹**ru·by** \'rü-bē\ *n, pl* **rubies** [ME, fr. MF *rubis, rubi*, alter. of *robin*, fr. ML *rubinus*, fr. L *rubeus* reddish; akin to L *ruber* red — more at RED] (14c)   **1   a :** a precious stone that is a red corundum   **b :** something (as a watch bearing) made of ruby   **2   a :** the dark red color of the ruby   **b :** something resembling a ruby in color
²**ruby** *adj* (1508) : of the color ruby
ruby glass *n* (1797) : glass of a deep red color containing selenium, an oxide of copper, or a chloride of gold
ruby spinel *n* (1839) : a usu. red spinel used as a gem
ru·by·throat \'rü-bē-,thrōt\ *n* (ca. 1783) : RUBY-THROATED HUMMINGBIRD
ru·by–throat·ed hummingbird \'rü-bē-,thrō-təd-\ *n* (ca. 1782) : a hummingbird (*Archilochus colubris*) of eastern No. America having a bright green back, whitish underparts, and in the adult male a red throat with metallic reflections
ruche \'rüsh\ *or* **ruch·ing** \'rü-shiŋ\ *n* [F *ruche* lit., beehive, fr. ML *rusca* bark] (1827) : a pleated, fluted, or gathered strip of fabric used for trimming — **ruched** \'rüsht\ *adj*
¹**ruck** \'rək\ *n* [ME, of Scand origin; akin to ON *hraukr* rick — more at RICK] (15c)   **1   a :** the usual run of persons or things : GENERALITY ⟨trying to rise above the ∼ —Richard Holt⟩   **b :** an indistinguishable gathering : JUMBLE   **2 :** the persons or things following the vanguard ⟨finished the race in the ∼⟩
²**ruck** *vb* [*ruck*, n., wrinkle] (1812) : PUCKER, WRINKLE
ruck·sack \'rək-,sak, 'rük-\ *n* [G, fr. G dial., fr. *Rucken* back + *Sack* sack] (1866) : KNAPSACK
ruck·us \'rə-kəs *also* 'rü- *or* 'rù-\ *n* [prob. blend of *ruction* and *rumpus*] (ca. 1890) : ROW, DISTURBANCE ⟨raise a ∼⟩
ruc·tion \'rək-shən\ *n* [perh. by shortening & alter. fr. *insurrection*] (ca. 1825)   **1 :** a noisy fight   **2 :** DISTURBANCE, UPROAR
rud·beck·ia \,rəd-'be-kē-ə, rüd-\ *n* [NL, fr. Olof *Rudbeck* †1702 Swed. scientist] (ca. 1759) : any of a genus (*Rudbeckia*) of No. American perennial composite herbs having showy flower heads with mostly yellow ray flowers and a conical chaffy receptacle
rudd \'rəd, 'rùd\ *n* [prob. fr. *rud* redness, red ocher, fr. ME *rude*, fr. OE *rudu* — more at RUDDY] (1526) : a freshwater European cyprinid fish (*Scardinius erythrophthalmus*) resembling the roach
rud·der \'rə-dər\ *n* [ME *rother*, fr. OE *rōther* paddle; akin to OE *rōwan*

to row] (14c) **1** : a flat piece or structure of wood or metal attached upright to the stern of a boat or ship so that it can be turned causing the vessel's head to turn in the same direction **2** : a movable auxiliary airfoil on an airplane usu. attached at the rear end that serves to control direction of flight in the horizontal plane — see AIRPLANE illustration **3** : a guiding force or strategy — **rud·der·less** \-ləs\ *adj*

rud·der·post \-ˌpōst\ *n* (1691) **1** : the shaft of a rudder **2** : an additional sternpost in a ship with a single screw propeller to which the rudder is attached

¹**rud·dle** \ˈrə-dᵊl\ *n* [dim. of *rud* red ocher] (1538) : RED OCHER
²**ruddle** *vt* **rud·dled; rud·dling** \ˈrəd-liŋ, ˈrə-dᵊl-iŋ\ (1718) : to color with or as if with red ocher : REDDEN
rud·dock \ˈrə-dək, ˈrù-\ *n* [ME *ruddok*, fr. OE *rudduc*; akin to OE *rudu*] (bef. 12c) *archaic* : ROBIN 1a
rud·dy \ˈrə-dē\ *adj* **rud·di·er; -est** [ME *rudi*, fr. OE *rudig*, fr. *rudu* redness; akin to OE *rēad* red — more at RED] (bef. 12c) **1** : having a healthy reddish color **2** : RED, REDDISH **3** *Brit* — used as an intensive ⟨bellowed like a ~ bull when he wanted food —Doreen Tovey⟩ — **rud·di·ly** \ˈrə-dᵊl-ē\ *adv* — **rud·di·ness** \ˈrə-dē-nəs\ *n*
ruddy duck *n* (1814) : an American duck (*Oxyura jamaicensis*) which has a wedge-shaped tail of stiff sharp feathers, a broad bill, and white cheeks and the adult male of which has rich brownish red on the upper side and a blue bill during breeding season
rude \ˈrüd\ *adj* **rud·er; rud·est** [ME, fr. MF, fr. L *rudis*; prob. akin to L *rudus* rubble] (14c) **1 a** : being in a rough or unfinished state : CRUDE ⟨~ line illustrations⟩ **b** : NATURAL, RAW ⟨~ cotton⟩ **c** : PRIMITIVE, UNDEVELOPED ⟨peasants use ~ wooden plows —Jack Raymond⟩ **d** : SIMPLE, ELEMENTAL ⟨landscape done in ~ whites, blacks, deep browns —Richard Harris⟩ **2** : lacking refinement or delicacy: **a** : IGNORANT, UNLEARNED **b** : INELEGANT, UNCOUTH **c** : offensive in manner or action : DISCOURTEOUS **d** : UNCIVILIZED, SAVAGE **e** : COARSE, VULGAR **3** : marked by or suggestive of lack of training or skill : INEXPERIENCED ⟨~ workmanship⟩ **4** : ROBUST, STURDY ⟨in ~ health⟩ **5** : occurring abruptly and disconcertingly ⟨a ~ awakening⟩ — **rude·ly** *adv*

syn RUDE, ROUGH, CRUDE, RAW mean lacking in social refinement. RUDE implies ignorance of or indifference to good form; it may suggest intentional discourtesy ⟨*rude* behavior⟩. ROUGH is likely to stress lack of polish and gentleness ⟨*rough* manners⟩. CRUDE may apply to thought or behavior limited to the gross, the obvious, or the primitive and ignorant of civilized amenities ⟨a *crude* joke⟩. RAW suggests being untested, inexperienced, or unfinished ⟨turning *raw* youths into polished performers⟩.

rude·ness *n* (14c) **1** : the quality or state of being rude **2** : a rude action
¹**ru·der·al** \ˈrü-də-rəl\ *adj* [NL *ruderalis*, fr. L *ruder-, rudus* rubble] (ca. 1858) : growing where the natural vegetational cover has been disturbed by humans ⟨~ weeds of old fields and roadsides⟩
²**ruderal** *n* (ca. 1928) : a weedy and commonly introduced plant growing where the vegetational cover has been interrupted
ru·di·ment \ˈrü-də-mənt\ *n* [L *rudimentum* beginning, fr. *rudis* raw, rude] (1548) **1** : a basic principle or element or a fundamental skill — usu. used in pl. ⟨teaching themselves the ~s of rational government — G. B. Galanti⟩ **2 a** : something unformed or undeveloped : BEGINNING — usu. used in pl. ⟨the ~s of a plan⟩ **b** (1) : a body part so deficient in size or structure as to be entirely unable to perform its normal function (2) : an organ just beginning to develop : ANLAGE — **ru·di·men·tal** \ˌrü-də-ˈmen-tᵊl\ *adj*
ru·di·men·ta·ry \ˌrü-də-ˈmen-tə-rē, -ˈmen-trē\ *adj* (1839) **1** : consisting in first principles : FUNDAMENTAL ⟨had only a ~ formal education —D. J. Boorstin⟩ **2** : of a primitive kind ⟨the equipment of these past empire-builders was ~ —A. J. Toynbee⟩ **3** : very imperfectly developed or represented esp. by a vestige ⟨the ~ tail of a hyrax⟩ — **ru·di·men·tar·i·ly** \-ˌmen-ˈter-ə-lē, -ˈmen-trə-lē\ *adv* — **ru·di·men·ta·ri·ness** \-ˈmen-tə-rē-nəs, -ˈmen-trē-\ *n*
¹**rue** \ˈrü\ *n* [ME *rewe*, fr. OE *hrēow*; akin to OHG *hriuwa* sorrow] (bef. 12c) : REGRET, SORROW
²**rue** *vb* **rued; ru·ing** *vt* (12c) : to feel penitence, remorse, or regret for ~ *vi* : to feel sorrow, remorse, or regret
³**rue** *n* [ME, fr. MF, fr. L *ruta*, fr. Gk *rhytē*] (13c) : a European strong-scented perennial woody herb (*Ruta graveolens* of the family Rutaceae, the rue family) that has bitter leaves used medicinally
rue anemone *n* (ca. 1818) : a delicate vernal No. American herb (*Anemonella thalictroides*) of the buttercup family with white flowers resembling those of the wood anemone
rue·ful \ˈrü-fəl\ *adj* (13c) **1** : exciting pity or sympathy : PITIABLE ⟨~ squalid poverty . . . by every wayside —John Morley⟩ **2** : MOURNFUL, REGRETFUL ⟨troubled her with a ~ disquiet —W. M. Thackeray⟩ — **rue·ful·ly** \-fə-lē\ *adv* — **rue·ful·ness** *n*
ru·fes·cent \rü-ˈfe-sᵊnt\ *adj* [L *rufescent-, rufescens*, prp. of *rufescere* to become reddish, fr. *rufus* red — more at RED] (1817) : REDDISH
¹**ruff** *also* **ruffe** \ˈrəf\ *n* [ME *ruf*] (15c) : a small freshwater European perch (*Acerina cernua*)
²**ruff** *n* [prob. back-formation fr. *ruffle*] (1555) **1** : a large round collar of pleated muslin or linen worn by men and women of the late 16th and early 17th centuries **2** : a fringe or frill of long hairs or feathers growing around or on the neck **3** : a common Eurasian sandpiper (*Philomachus pugnax*) whose male during the breeding season has a large ruff of erectile feathers on the neck — **ruffed** \ˈrəft\ *adj*
³**ruff** *vb* [MF *roffler*] *vi* (1598) : to take a trick with a trump ~ *vt* : to play a trump on (a card previously led or played)
⁴**ruff** *n* (ca. 1828) : the act of trumping
ruffed grouse *n* (ca. 1782) : a No. American grouse (*Bonasa umbellus*) of heavy forests that has a ruff of erectile black feathers in the male that is lighter and less conspicuous in the female

ruff 1

ruf·fi·an \ˈrə-fē-ən\ *n* [MF *rufian*] (1531) : a brutal person : BULLY — **ruffian** *adj* — **ruf·fi·an·ism** \-ə-ˌni-zəm\ *n* — **ruf·fi·an·ly** *adj*

¹**ruf·fle** \ˈrə-fəl\ *vb* **ruf·fled; ruf·fling** \-f(ə-)liŋ\ [ME *ruffelen*; akin to LG *ruffelen* to crumple] *vt* (14c) **1 a** : ROUGHEN, ABRADE **b** : TROUBLE, VEX ⟨is not *ruffled* by such barbs —Bruce Anderson⟩ **2 a** : to erect (as feathers) in or like a ruff **3 a** : to flip through (as pages) **b** : SHUFFLE **4** : to make into a ruffle ~ *vi* : to become ruffled ⟨their dispositions ~ perceptibly —*Life*⟩
²**ruffle** *n* (1534) **1 a** : COMMOTION, BRAWL **2** : a state or cause of irritation **3 a** : a strip of fabric gathered or pleated on one edge **b** : ²RUFF 2 **4** : an unevenness or disturbance of surface : RIPPLE — **ruf·fly** \-f(ə-)lē\ *adj*
³**ruffle** *n* [*ruff* a drumbeat] (ca. 1802) : a low vibrating drumbeat less loud than a roll
ru·fi·yaa \ˈrü-fē-ˌyä\ *n, pl* **rufiyaa** [prob. fr. Divehi (Indo-Aryan language of the Maldive Islands), fr. Hindi *rupiyā, rūpaiyā* rupee] (1982) — see MONEY table
RU 486 \ˈär-ˌyü-ˌfōr-ˌā-tē-ˈsiks, -ˌfȯr-\ *n* [Roussel-UCLAF, the drug's Fr. manufacturer + *486*, laboratory serial number] (1983) : a drug $C_{29}H_{35}NO_2$ taken orally to induce abortion esp. early in pregnancy by blocking the body's use of progesterone
ru·fous \ˈrü-fəs\ *adj* [L *rufus* red — more at RED] (1782) : REDDISH
rug \ˈrəg\ *n* [(assumed) ME, rag, tuft, of Scand origin; akin to ON *rogg* tuft] (1591) **1** : LAP ROBE **2** : a piece of thick heavy fabric that usu. has a nap or pile and is used as a floor covering **3** : a floor mat of an animal pelt ⟨a bearskin ~⟩ **4** *slang* : TOUPEE 2 **5** *Brit* : a blanket for an animal (as a horse or dog)
ru·ga \ˈrü-gə\ *n, pl* **ru·gae** \-ˌgī, -ˌgē, -ˌjē\ [NL, fr. L, wrinkle — more at CORRUGATE] (1775) : an anatomical fold or wrinkle esp. of the viscera — usu. used in pl.
rug·by \ˈrəg-bē\ *n, often cap* [Rugby School, Rugby, England] (1864) : a football game in which play is continuous without time-outs or substitutions, interference and forward passing are not permitted, and kicking, dribbling, lateral passing, and tackling are featured
rug·ged \ˈrə-gəd\ *adj* [ME, fr. (assumed) ME *rug*] (14c) **1** *obs* : SHAGGY, HAIRY **2** : having a rough uneven surface : JAGGED ⟨~ mountains⟩ **3** : TURBULENT, STORMY ⟨~ weather⟩ **4 a** : seamed with wrinkles and furrows : WEATHERED — used of a human face **b** : showing facial signs of strength ⟨~ good looks⟩ **5 a** : AUSTERE, STERN **b** : COARSE, RUDE **c** : rough and strong in character **6 a** : presenting a severe test of ability, stamina, or resolution **b** : strongly built or constituted ⟨ROBUST ⟨those that survive are stalwart, ~ men —L. D. Stamp⟩ *syn* see ROUGH — **rug·ged·ly** *adv* — **rug·ged·ness** *n*
rug·ged·ize \ˈrə-gə-ˌdīz\ *vt* **-ized; -iz·ing** (1950) : to strengthen (as a machine) for better resistance to wear, stress, and abuse ⟨a *ruggedized* camera⟩ — **rug·ged·i·za·tion** \ˌrə-gə-də-ˈzā-shən\ *n*
rug·ger \ˈrə-gər\ *n* [by alter.] *Brit* : RUGBY; *also* : a rugby player
ru·go·la \ˈrü-gə-lə\ *n* [prob. fr. It dial.; akin to It dial. *ruga* arugula, It *ruca* — more at ROCKET] (1973) : ARUGULA
ru·go·sa rose \rü-ˈgō-sə-, -zə-\ *n* [NL *rugosa*, specific epithet of *Rosa rugosa* rugose rose] (1892) : any of various garden roses descended from a rose (*Rosa rugosa*) introduced from China and Japan — called *also rugosa*
ru·gose \ˈrü-ˌgōs\ *adj* [L *rugosus*, fr. *ruga*] (1676) **1** : full of wrinkles ⟨~ cheeks⟩ **2** : having the veinlets sunken and the spaces between elevated ⟨~ leaves of the sage⟩ — **ru·gos·i·ty** \rü-ˈgä-sə-tē\ *n*
ru·gu·lose \ˈrü-gyə-ˌlōs\ *adj* [NL *rugula*, dim. of L *ruga*] (ca. 1819) : having small rugae : finely wrinkled
¹**ru·in** \ˈrü-ən, -ˌin; ˈrün\ *n* [ME *ruine*, fr. MF, fr. L *ruina*, fr. *ruere* to rush headlong, fall, collapse] (12c) **1 a** *archaic* : a falling down : COLLAPSE ⟨from age to age . . . the crash of ~ fitfully resounds —William Wordsworth⟩ **b** : physical, moral, economic, or social collapse **2 a** : the state of being ruined — archaic except in pl. ⟨the city lay in ~s⟩ **b** : the remains of something destroyed — usu. used in pl. ⟨the ~s of an ancient temple⟩ ⟨the ~s of his life⟩ **3** : a cause of destruction **4 a** : the action of destroying, laying waste, or wrecking **b** : DAMAGE, INJURY **5** : a ruined building, person, or object — **ru·in·ate** \-ˌnāt, -nət\ *adj* — **ruinate** \-ˌnāt\ *vt*
²**ruin** *vt* (1585) **1** : to reduce to ruins : DEVASTATE **2 a** : to damage irreparably **b** : BANKRUPT, IMPOVERISH ⟨~ed by stock speculation⟩ **3** : to subject to frustration, failure, or disaster ⟨will ~ your chances of promotion⟩ ~ *vi* : to become ruined — **ru·in·er** *n*
ru·in·a·tion \ˌrü-ə-ˈnā-shən\ *n* (1664) : RUIN, DESTRUCTION
ru·in·ous \ˈrü-ə-nəs\ *adj* (14c) **1** : DILAPIDATED, RUINED **2** : causing or tending to cause ruin — **ru·in·ous·ly** *adv* — **ru·in·ous·ness** *n*
¹**rule** \ˈrül\ *n* [ME *reule*, fr. OF, fr. L *regula* straightedge, rule, fr. *regere* to direct — more at RIGHT] (13c) **1 a** : a prescribed guide for conduct or action **b** : the laws or regulations prescribed by the founder of a religious order for observance by its members **c** : an accepted procedure, custom, or habit **d** (1) : a usu. written order or direction made by a court regulating court practice or the action of parties (2) : a legal precept or doctrine **e** : a regulation or bylaw governing procedure or controlling conduct **2 a** (1) : a usu. valid generalization (2) : a generally prevailing quality, state, or mode ⟨fair weather was the ~ yesterday —*N.Y. Times*⟩ **b** : a standard of judgment : CRITERION **c** : a regulating principle **d** : a determinate method for performing a mathematical operation and obtaining a certain result **3 a** : the exercise of authority or control : DOMINION **b** : a period during which a specified ruler or government exercises control **4 a** : a strip of material marked off in units used esp. for measuring : RULER 3, TAPE MEASURE **b** : a metal strip with a type-high face that prints a linear design; *also* : a linear design produced by or as if by such a strip *syn* see LAW — **as a rule** : for the most part : GENERALLY
²**rule** *vb* **ruled; rul·ing** (13c) **1 a** : to exert control, direction, or influence on ⟨the passions that ~ our minds⟩ **b** : to exercise control over esp. by curbing or restraining ⟨~ a fractious horse⟩ ⟨*ruled* his appetites firmly⟩ **2 a** : to exercise authority or power over often harshly or arbitrarily ⟨the speaker *ruled* the legislature with an iron hand⟩ **b** : to be preeminent in : DOMINATE **3** : to determine and de-

\ə\ abut \ᵊ\ kitten, F table \ər\ further \a\ ash \ā\ ace \ä\ mop, mar \aù\ out \ch\ chin \e\ bet \ē\ easy \g\ go \i\ hit \ī\ ice \j\ job \ŋ\ sing \ō\ go \ȯ\ law \ȯi\ boy \th\ thin \t̲h̲\ the \ü\ loot \ù\ foot \y\ yet \zh\ vision \ä, k̲, ⁿ, œ, œ̄, ᵫ, ᵫ̄, ʸ\ see Guide to Pronunciation

clare authoritatively; *esp* : to command or determine judicially **4 a** (1) : to mark with lines drawn along or as if along the straight edge of a ruler (2) : to mark (a line) on a paper with a ruler **b** : to arrange in a line **~** *vi* **1 a** : to exercise supreme authority **b** : to be first in importance or prominence : PREDOMINATE ⟨the physical did not ~ in her nature —Sherwood Anderson⟩ **2** : to exist in a specified state or condition **3** : to lay down a legal rule *syn* see DECIDE
ruled surface *n* (1862) : a surface generated by a moving straight line with the result that through every point on the surface a line can be drawn lying wholly in the surface
rule·less \'rül-ləs\ *adj* (15c) : not restrained or regulated by law
rule of the road (1871) : a customary practice (as driving always on a particular side of the road or yielding the right of way) developed in the interest of safety and often subsequently reinforced by law; *esp* : any of the rules making up a code governing ships in matters relating to mutual safety
rule of thumb (1692) **1** : a method of procedure based on experience and common sense **2** : a general principle regarded as roughly correct but not intended to be scientifically accurate
rule out *vt* (1869) **1** : EXCLUDE, ELIMINATE **2** : to make impossible : PREVENT ⟨heavy rain *ruled out* the picnic⟩
rul·er \'rü-lər\ *n* (14c) **1** : one that rules; *specif* : SOVEREIGN **2** : a worker or a machine that rules paper **3** : a smooth-edged strip (as of wood or metal) that is usu. marked off in units (as inches) and is used as a straightedge or for measuring — **rul·er·ship** \-,ship\ *n*
¹**rul·ing** \'rü-liŋ\ *n* (15c) : an official or authoritative decision, decree, statement, or interpretation (as by a judge on a point of law)
²**ruling** *adj* (1593) **1 a** : exerting power or authority ⟨the ~ party⟩ **b** : CHIEF, PREDOMINATING ⟨a ~ passion⟩ **2** : generally prevailing
ruly \'rü-lē\ *adj* [back-formation fr. *unruly*] (15c) : OBEDIENT, ORDERLY ⟨a ~ crowd⟩
¹**rum** \'rəm\ *n* [prob. short for obs. *rumbullion* rum] (1654) **1** : an alcoholic beverage distilled from a fermented cane product (as molasses) **2** : alcoholic liquor ⟨the demon ~⟩
²**rum** *adj* **rum·mer; rum·mest** [origin unknown] (1752) **1** *chiefly Brit* : QUEER, ODD ⟨writing is a ~ trade . . . and what is all right one day is all wrong the next —Angela Thirkell⟩ **2** *chiefly Brit* : DIFFICULT, DANGEROUS
ru·ma·ki \rə-'mä-kē\ *n* [perh. modif. of Jp *harumaki*, trans. of Chin (Beijing) *chūnjuǎn* spring roll] (1961) : a cooked appetizer made of pieces of usu. marinated chicken liver wrapped together with sliced water chestnuts in bacon slices
Ru·ma·nian \rü-'mā-nē-ən, -nyən\ *n* (1878) : ROMANIAN — **Rumanian** *adj*
rum·ba \'rəm-bə, 'rùm-, 'rüm-\ *n* [AmerSp] (1922) : a ballroom dance of Cuban origin in ³/₄ or ⁴/₄ time with a basic pattern of step-close-step and marked by a delayed transfer of weight and pronounced hip movements; *also* : the music for this dance
¹**rum·ble** \'rəm-bəl\ *vb* **rum·bled; rum·bling** \-b(ə-)liŋ\ [ME; akin to MHG *rummeln* to rumble] *vi* (14c) **1** : to make a low heavy rolling sound ⟨thunder *rumbling* in the distance⟩ **2** : to travel with a low reverberating sound ⟨wagons *rumbled* into town⟩ **3** : to speak in a low rolling tone **4** : to engage in a rumble **~** *vt* **1** : to utter or emit in a low rolling voice **2** *Brit* : to reveal or discover the true character of — **rum·bler** \-b(ə-)lər\ *n*
²**rumble** *n* (14c) **1 a** : a low heavy continuous reverberating often muffled sound (as of thunder) **b** : low frequency noise in phonographic playback caused by the transmission of mechanical vibrations by the turntable to the pickup **2** : a seat for servants behind the body of a carriage **3 a** : widespread expression of dissatisfaction or unrest **b** : a street fight esp. among gangs
rumble seat *n* (1912) : a folding seat in the back of an automobile (as a coupe or roadster) not covered by the top
rum·bling \'rəm-bliŋ\ *n* (14c) **1** : RUMBLE **2** : general but unofficial talk or opinion often of dissatisfaction — usu. used in pl. ⟨~s of political trouble —Anthony Burgess⟩
rum·bly \'rəm-b(ə-)lē\ *adj* (1874) : tending to rumble or rattle
rum·bus·tious \,rəm-'bəs-chəs\ *adj* [alter. of *robustious*] (1778) *chiefly Brit* : RAMBUNCTIOUS — **rum·bus·tious·ly** *adv*, *chiefly Brit* — **rum·bus·tious·ness** *n*, *chiefly Brit*
ru·men \'rü-mən\ *n, pl* **ru·mi·na** \-mə-nə\ *or* **rumens** [NL *rumin-, rumen*, fr. L] (ca. 1728) : the large first compartment of the stomach of a ruminant in which cellulose is broken down by the action of symbiotic microorganisms — compare ABOMASUM, OMASUM, RETICULUM — **ru·mi·nal** \-mə-n³l\ *adj*
¹**ru·mi·nant** \'rü-mə-nənt\ *n* (1661) : a ruminant mammal
²**ruminant** *adj* (1691) **1 a** (1) : chewing the cud (2) : characterized by chewing again what has been swallowed **b** : of or relating to a suborder (Ruminantia) of even-toed hoofed mammals (as sheep, giraffes, deer, and camels) that chew the cud and have a complex usu. 4-chambered stomach **2** : given to or engaged in contemplation : MEDITATIVE ⟨stood there with her hands clasped in this attitude of ~ relish —Thomas Wolfe⟩ — **ru·mi·nant·ly** *adv*
ru·mi·nate \'rü-mə-,nāt\ *vb* **-nat·ed; -nat·ing** [L *ruminatus*, pp. of *ruminari* to chew the cud, muse upon, fr. *rumin-, rumen* rumen; perh. akin to Skt *romantha* act of chewing the cud] *vt* (1533) **1** : to go over in the mind repeatedly and often casually or slowly **2** : to chew repeatedly for an extended period **~** *vi* **1** : to chew again what has been chewed slightly and swallowed : chew the cud **2** : to engage in contemplation : REFLECT *syn* see PONDER — **ru·mi·na·tion** \,rü-mə-'nā-shən\ *n* — **ru·mi·na·tive** \'rü-mə-,nā-tiv\ *adj* — **ru·mi·na·tive·ly** *adv* — **ru·mi·na·tor** \-,nā-tər\ *n*
¹**rum·mage** \'rə-mij\ *vb* **rum·maged; rum·mag·ing** [²*rummage*] (ca. 1595) **1** : to make a thorough search or investigation **2** : to engage in an undirected or haphazard search **~** *vt* **1** : to make a thorough search through : RANSACK ⟨*rummaged* the attic⟩ **2** : to examine minutely and completely **3** : to discover by searching — **rum·mag·er** *n*
²**rummage** *n* [obs. E *rummage* act of packing cargo, modif. of MF *arrimage*] (1598) **1 a** : a confused miscellaneous collection **b** : items for sale at a rummage sale **2** : a thorough search esp. among a confusion of objects
rummage sale *n* (ca. 1858) : a usu. informal sale of miscellaneous goods; *esp* : a sale of donated articles conducted by a nonprofit organization (as a church or charity) to help support its programs

rum·mer \'rə-mər\ *n* [G or D; G *Römer*, fr. D *roemer*] (1654) : a large-bowled footed drinking glass often elaborately etched or engraved
¹**rum·my** \'rə-mē\ *adj* **rum·mi·er; -est** [²*rum*] (1828) : QUEER, ODD ⟨were still feeling a little ~ from our trip up the escalator —*New Yorker*⟩
²**rummy** *n, pl* **rummies** [¹*rum*] (1851) : DRUNKARD
³**rummy** *n* [perh. fr. ¹*rummy*] (1915) : any of several card games for two or more players in which each player tries to assemble groups of three or more cards of the same rank or suit and to be the first to meld them all
ru·mor \'rü-mər\ *n* [ME *rumour*, fr. MF, fr. L *rumor* clamor, gossip; akin to OE *rēon* to lament, Skt *rauti* he roars] (14c) **1** : talk or opinion widely disseminated with no discernible source **2** : a statement or report current without known authority for its truth **3** *archaic* : talk or report of a notable person or event **4** : a soft low indistinct sound : MURMUR
²**rumor** *vt* or **ru·mored;** **ru·mor·ing** (1594) : to tell or spread by rumor
ru·mor·mon·ger \-,məŋ-gər, -,mäŋ-\ *n* (1884) : a person who spreads rumors — **ru·mor·mon·ger·ing** \-gər-iŋ\ *n*
ru·mour \'rü-mər\ *chiefly Brit var of* RUMOR
rump \'rəmp\ *n* [ME, of Scand origin; akin to Icel *rumpr* rump; akin to MHG *rumph* torso] (15c) **1 a** : the upper rounded part of the hindquarters of a quadruped mammal **b** : BUTTOCKS **c** : the sacral or dorsal part of the posterior end of a bird **2** : a cut of meat (as beef) between the loin and round — see BEEF illustration **3** : a small or inferior remnant or offshoot; *esp* : a group (as a parliament) carrying on in the name of the original body after the departure or expulsion of a large number of its members
¹**rum·ple** \'rəm-pəl\ *n* (ca. 1520) : FOLD, WRINKLE
²**rumple** *vb* **rum·pled; rum·pling** \-p(ə-)liŋ\ [D *rompelen*; akin to OHG *rimpfan* to wrinkle] *vt* (1603) **1** : WRINKLE, CRUMPLE **2** : to make unkempt : TOUSLE **~** *vi* : to become rumpled
rum·ply \'rəm-p(ə-)lē\ *adj* **rum·pli·er; -est** (1833) : having rumples
rum·pus \'rəm-pəs\ *n* [origin unknown] (1764) : a usu. noisy commotion
rumpus room *n* (1939) : a room usu. in the basement of a home that is used for games, parties, and recreation
rum·run·ner \'rəm-,rə-nər\ *n* (1920) : a person or ship engaged in bringing prohibited liquor ashore or across a border — **rum-run·ning** \-,rə-niŋ\ *adj or n*
¹**run** \'rən\ *vb* **ran** \'ran\ *also chiefly dial* **run; run; run·ning** [ME *ronnen*, alter. of *rinnen*, v.i. (fr. OE *iernan*, *rinnan* & ON *rinna*) & of *rennen*, v.t., fr. ON *renna*; akin to OHG *rinnan*, v.i., to run, Skt *riṇāti* he causes to flow, and prob. to L *rivus* stream] *vi* (bef. 12c) **1 a** : to go faster than a walk; *specif* : to go steadily by springing steps so that both feet leave the ground for an instant in each step **b** *of a horse* : to move at a fast gallop **c** : FLEE, RETREAT, ESCAPE ⟨dropped the gun and *ran*⟩ **d** : to utilize a running play on offense — used of a football team **2 a** : to go without restraint : move freely about at will ⟨let chickens ~ loose⟩ **b** : to keep company : CONSORT ⟨a ram *running* with ewes⟩ ⟨*ran* with a wild crowd when he was young⟩ **c** : to sail before the wind in distinction from reaching or sailing close-hauled **d** : ROAM, ROVE ⟨*running* about with no overcoat⟩ **3 a** : to go rapidly or hurriedly : HASTEN ⟨~ and fetch the doctor⟩ **b** : to go in urgency or distress : RESORT ⟨~s to mother at every little difficulty⟩ **c** : to make a quick, easy, or casual trip or visit ⟨*ran* over to borrow some sugar⟩ **4 a** : to contend in a race **b** : to enter into an election contest **5 a** : to move on or as if on wheels : GLIDE ⟨file drawers *running* on ball bearings⟩ **b** : to roll forward rapidly or freely **c** : to pass or slide freely ⟨a rope ~s through the pulley⟩ **d** : to ravel lengthwise ⟨stockings guaranteed not to ~⟩ **6** : to sing or play a musical passage quickly ⟨~ up the scale⟩ **7 a** : to go back and forth : PLY ⟨the train ~s between New York and Washington⟩ **b** *of fish* : to migrate or move in considerable numbers; *esp* : to move up or down a river to spawn **8 a** : TURN, ROTATE ⟨a swiftly *running* grindstone⟩ **b** : FUNCTION, OPERATE ⟨the engine ~s on gasoline⟩ **9 a** (1) : to continue in force, operation, or production ⟨the contract has two more years to ~⟩ ⟨the play *ran* for six months⟩ (2) : to have a specified duration, extent, or length ⟨the manuscript ~s nearly 500 pages⟩ **b** : to accompany as a valid obligation or right ⟨a right-of-way that ~s with the land⟩ **c** : to continue to accrue or become payable ⟨interest on the loan ~s from July 1st⟩ **10** : to pass from one state to another ⟨~ into debt⟩ **11 a** : to flow rapidly or under pressure **b** : MELT, FUSE **c** : SPREAD, DISSOLVE ⟨colors guaranteed not to ~⟩ **d** : to discharge pus or serum ⟨a *running* sore⟩ **12 a** : to develop rapidly in some specific direction; *esp* : to throw out an elongated shoot of growth **b** : to tend to produce or develop a specified quality or feature ⟨they ~ to big noses in that family⟩ **13 a** : to lie in or take a certain direction ⟨the boundary line ~s east⟩ **b** : to lie or extend in relation to something **c** : to go back : REACH **d** (1) : to be in a certain form or expression ⟨the letter ~s as follows⟩ (2) : to be in a certain order of succession **14 a** : to occur persistently ⟨musical talent ~s in the family⟩ **b** (1) : to remain of a specified size, amount, character, or quality ⟨profits were *running* high⟩ (2) : to have or maintain a relative position or condition (as in a race) ⟨*ran* third⟩ ⟨*running* late⟩ **c** : to exist or occur in a continuous range of variation ⟨shades ~ from white to dark gray⟩ **15 a** : to spread or pass quickly from point to point ⟨chills *ran* up her spine⟩ **b** : to be current : CIRCULATE ⟨speculation *ran* rife⟩ **~** *vt* **1 a** : to cause (an animal) to go rapidly : ride or drive fast **b** : to bring to a specified condition by or as if by running ⟨*ran* himself to death⟩ **c** : to go in pursuit of : HUNT, CHASE ⟨dogs that ~ deer⟩ **d** : to follow the trail of backward : TRACE ⟨*ran* the rumor to its source⟩ **e** : to enter, register, or enroll as a contestant in a race **f** : to put forward as a candidate for office **2 a** : to drive (livestock) esp. to a grazing place **b** : to provide pasturage for (livestock) **c** : to keep or maintain (livestock) on or as if on pasturage **3 a** : to pass over or traverse with speed **b** : to accomplish or perform by or as if by running ⟨*ran* a great race⟩ ⟨*running* errands for a bank⟩ **c** : to slip or go through or past ⟨~ a blockade⟩ ⟨~ a red light⟩ **4 a** : to cause to penetrate or enter : THRUST ⟨*ran* a splinter into her toe⟩ **b** : STITCH **c** : to cause to pass : LEAD ⟨~ a wire in from the antenna⟩ **d** : to cause to collide ⟨*ran* his head into a post⟩ **e** : SMUGGLE ⟨~ guns⟩ **5** : to cause to pass lightly or quickly over, along, or into something ⟨*ran* her eye down the list⟩ **6 a** : to cause or allow (as a vehicle or a vessel) to go in a specified manner or direction

⟨*ran* the car off the road⟩ **b :** OPERATE ⟨~ a lathe⟩ **c :** to direct the business or activities of : MANAGE, CONDUCT ⟨~ a factory⟩ **7 a :** to be full of or drenched with ⟨streets *ran* blood⟩ **b :** CONTAIN, ASSAY **8 a** : to cause to move or flow in a specified way or into a specified position ⟨~ cards into a file⟩ **b :** to cause to produce a flow (as of water) ⟨~ the faucet⟩; *also :* to prepare by running a faucet ⟨~ a hot bath⟩ **9 a** : to melt and cast in a mold ⟨~ bullets⟩ **b :** TREAT, PROCESS, REFINE ⟨~ oil in a still⟩ ⟨~ a problem through a computer⟩ **10 :** to make oneself liable to : INCUR ⟨*ran* the risk of discovery⟩ **11 :** to mark out : DRAW ⟨~ a contour line on a map⟩ **12 a :** to permit (as charges) to accumulate before settling ⟨~ an account at the grocery⟩ — often used with *up* ⟨*ran* up a large phone bill⟩ **b :** COST 1 ⟨rooms that ~ $50 a night⟩ **13 a :** to produce by or as if by printing — usu. used with *off* ⟨*ran* off 10,000 copies of the first edition⟩ **b :** to carry in a printed medium : PRINT ⟨every newspaper *ran* the story⟩ **14 a :** to make (a series of counts) without a miss ⟨~ 19 in an inning in billiards⟩ **b :** to lead winning cards of (a suit) successively **c :** to alter by addition ⟨*ran* his record to six wins and four losses⟩ **15 :** to make (a golf ball) roll forward after alighting — **run across :** to meet with or discover by chance — **run a fever** *or* **run a temperature :** to have a fever — **run after 1 :** PURSUE, CHASE; *esp :* to seek the company of **2 :** to take up with : FOLLOW ⟨*run after* new theories⟩ — **run against 1 :** to meet suddenly or unexpectedly **2 :** to work or take effect unfavorably : DISFAVOR, OPPOSE — **run foul of 1 :** to collide with ⟨*ran foul of* a hidden reef⟩ **2 :** to come into conflict with ⟨*run foul of* the law⟩ — **run into 1 a :** to change or transform into : BECOME **b :** to merge with **c :** to mount up to ⟨their yearly income often *runs into* six figures⟩ **2 a :** to collide with **b :** to meet by chance ⟨*ran into* an old classmate the other day⟩ — **run low on :** to approach running out of ⟨*running low on* options⟩ — **run rings around :** to show marked superiority over : defeat decisively or overwhelmingly — **run riot 1** : to act wildly or without restraint **2 :** to occur in profusion ⟨daffodils *running riot*⟩ — **run short :** to become insufficient — **run short of** : to use up : run low on — **run to :** to mount up to ⟨the book *runs to* 500 pages⟩ — **run upon :** to run across : meet with

usage The past tense *run* still survives in speech in southern England and in the speech esp. of older people in some parts of the U.S. It was formerly used in literature, and was a standard variant in our dictionaries from 1828 until 1934. Grammarians have generally opposed it, and many people consider it nonstandard. Just about everybody uses *ran* in writing now.

²run *n* (14c) **1 a :** an act or the action of running : continued rapid movement **b :** a quickened gallop **c :** a migration of fish (as up or down a river) esp. to spawn; *also :* such fish in the process of migration **d :** a running race ⟨a mile ~⟩ **e :** a score made in baseball by a runner reaching home plate safely **f :** strength or ability to run **g :** a gain of a usu. specified distance made on a running play in football ⟨scored on a 25-yard ~⟩; *also :* a running play **h :** a sustained usu. aggressive effort (as to win or obtain something) ⟨making a ~ at the championship⟩ **2 a** *chiefly Midland :* CREEK **b :** something that flows in the course of an operation or during a particular time ⟨the first ~ of sap in sugar maples⟩ **3 a :** the stern of the underwater body of a ship from where it begins to curve or slope upward and inward **b :** the direction in which a vein of ore lies **c :** a direction of secondary or minor cleavage : GRAIN ⟨the ~ of a mass of granite⟩ **d :** a horizontal distance (as that covered by a flight of stairs) **e :** general tendency or direction **4** : a continuous period or series esp. of things of identical or similar sort ⟨a ~ of bad luck⟩: as **a :** a rapid passage up or down a scale in vocal or instrumental music **b :** a number of rapid small dance steps executed in even tempo **c :** the act of making successively a number of successful shots or strokes; *also :* the score thus made ⟨a ~ of 20 in billiards⟩ **d :** an unbroken course of performances or showings **e :** a set of consecutive measurements, readings, or observations **f :** persistent and heavy demands from depositors, creditors, or customers ⟨a ~ on a bank⟩ **g :** SEQUENCE 2b **5 :** the quantity of work turned out in a continuous operation ⟨a press ~ of 10,000 copies⟩ **6 :** the usual or normal kind, character, type, or group ⟨the average ~ of students⟩ **7 a :** the distance covered in a period of continuous traveling or sailing **b :** a course or trip esp. if mapped out and traveled with regularity **c** : a news reporter's regular territory : BEAT **d :** freedom of movement in or access to a place or area ⟨has the ~ of the house⟩ **8 a :** the period during which a machine or plant is in continuous operation **b** : the use of machinery for a single set of processing procedures ⟨a computer ~⟩ **9 a :** a way, track, or path frequented by animals **b :** an enclosure for domestic animals where they may feed or exercise ⟨*Austral* (1) : a large area of land used for grazing ⟨a sheep ~⟩ (2) : RANCH, STATION ⟨*run*-holder⟩ **d :** an inclined passageway **10 a** : an inclined course (as for skiing or bobsledding) **b :** a support (as a track, pipe, or trough) on which something runs **11 a :** a ravel in a knitted fabric (as in hosiery) caused by the breaking of stitches **b :** a paint defect caused by excessive flow **12** *pl but sing or pl in constr* : DIARRHEA — used with *the* — **on the run 1 :** in haste : without pausing ⟨ate lunch *on the run*⟩ **2 :** in retreat : in flight (as from the law) ⟨an escaped convict *on the run*⟩

³run *adj* (1774) **1 a :** being in a melted state ⟨~ butter⟩ **b :** made from molten material : cast in a mold ⟨~ metal⟩ **2** *of fish :* having made a migration or spawning run ⟨a fresh ~ salmon⟩ **3 :** exhausted or winded from running

run·about \ˈrən-ə-ˌbau̇t\ *n* (1549) **1 :** one who wanders about : STRAY **2 :** a light usu. open wagon, car, or motorboat

run·a·gate \ˈrə-nə-ˌgāt\ *n* [alter. of *renegate*, fr. ML *renegatus* — more at RENEGADE] (1547) **1 :** VAGABOND **2 :** FUGITIVE, RUNAWAY

run along *vi* (1902) : to go away : be on one's way : DEPART

run-around \ˈrə-nə-ˌrau̇nd\ *n* (1915) **1 :** deceptive or delaying action esp. in response to a request ⟨tired of getting the ~⟩ **2 :** matter typeset in shortened measure to run around something (as a cut)

¹run·a·way \ˈrə-nə-ˌwā\ *n* (1547) **1 :** one that runs away from danger, duty, or restraint : FUGITIVE **2 :** the act of running away out of control; *also :* something (as a horse) that is running out of control **3 :** a one-sided or overwhelming victory

²runaway *adj* (1548) **1 a :** running away : FUGITIVE **b :** leaving to gain special advantages (as lower wages) or avoid disadvantages (as governmental or union restrictions) ⟨~ shipping firms⟩ ⟨a ~ shop⟩ **2** : accomplished by elopement or during flight **3 :** won by or having a

long lead ⟨a ~ success⟩; *also :* extremely successful ⟨a ~ best-seller⟩ **4** : subject to uncontrolled changes ⟨~ inflation⟩ **5 :** being or operating out of control ⟨a ~ oil well⟩ ⟨a ~ nuclear reactor⟩

run away *vi* (13c) **1 a :** to leave quickly in order to avoid or escape something **b :** to leave home; *esp :* ELOPE **2 :** to run out of control : STAMPEDE, BOLT **3 :** to gain a substantial lead : win by a large margin — **run away with 1 :** to take away in haste or secretly; *esp :* STEAL **2 :** to outshine the others in (a theatrical performance) **3 :** to carry or drive beyond prudent or reasonable limits ⟨your imagination *ran away with* you⟩

run-back \ˈrən-ˌbak\ *n* (1929) : a run made in football after catching an opponent's kick or intercepting a pass

run-ci-ble spoon \ˈrən(t)-sə-bəl-\ *n* [coined with an obscure meaning by Edward Lear] (1871) : a sharp-edged fork with three broad curved prongs

run-ci-nate \ˈrən(t)-sə-ˌnāt\ *adj* [L *runcinatus*, pp. of *runcinare* to plane off, fr. *runcina* plane] (1776) : pinnately cut with the lobes pointing downward ⟨~ leaves of the dandelion⟩ — see LEAF illustration

run-dle \ˈrən-dᵊl\ *n* [ME *roundel* circle — more at ROUNDEL] (1565) **1** : a step of a ladder : RUNG **2 :** the drum of a windlass or capstan

rund·let *or* **run-let** \ˈrən(d)-lət\ *n* [ME *roundelet*, fr. MF *rondelet* — more at ROUNDELAY] (14c) : a small barrel : KEG

run-down \ˈrən-ˌdau̇n\ *n* (1908) **1 :** a play in baseball in which a base runner who is caught off base is chased by two or more opposing players who throw the ball from one to another in an attempt to tag the runner out **2 :** a item-by-item report or review : SUMMARY

run–down \ˈrən-ˈdau̇n\ *adj* (1866) **1 :** WORN-OUT, EXHAUSTED **2** : completely unwound **3 :** being in poor repair : DILAPIDATED

run down *vt* (ca. 1578) **1 a :** to collide with and knock down **b :** to run against and cause to sink **2 a :** to chase to exhaustion or until captured **b :** to trace the source of **c :** to tag out (a base runner) between bases on a rundown **3 :** DISPARAGE ~ *vi* **1 :** to cease to operate because of the exhaustion of motive power ⟨the clock *ran down*⟩ **2 :** to decline in physical condition or vigor

rune \ˈrün\ *n* [ON & OE *rūn* mystery, runic character, writing; akin to OHG *rūna* secret discussion, OIr *rún* mystery] (1690) **1 :** any of the characters of any of several alphabets used by the Germanic peoples from about the 3d to the 13th centuries **2 :** MYSTERY, MAGIC **3** [Finn *runo*, of Gmc origin; akin to ON *rūn*] **a :** a Finnish or Old Norse poem **b :** POEM, SONG — **ru·nic** \ˈrü-nik\ *adj*

rune 1: Anglo-Saxon runic alphabet

¹rung *past part of* RING

²rung \ˈrəŋ\ *n* [ME, fr. OE *hrung* crossbar; akin to Goth *hrunga* staff and perh. to OE *hring* ring — more at RING] (14c) **1 a :** a rounded part placed as a crosspiece between the legs of a chair **b :** one of the crosspieces of a ladder **2** *Scot :* a heavy staff or cudgel **3 :** a spoke of a wheel **4 :** a level in a hierarchy ⟨rise a few ~s on the social scale — H. W. Van Loon⟩

run–in \ˈrən-ˌin\ *n* (1857) **1** *Brit :* the final part of a race or racetrack **2 :** ALTERCATION, QUARREL **3 :** something inserted as a substantial addition in copy or typeset matter

run in *vt* (1817) **1 a :** to insert as additional matter **b :** to make (typeset matter) continuous without a paragraph or other break **2 :** to arrest for a usu. minor offense **3** *chiefly Brit :* to operate (a new machine) carefully until there is sufficient running ~ *vi* **:** to pay a casual visit

run-less \ˈrən-ləs\ *adj* (1921) : scoring or allowing no runs

run-let \ˈrən-lət\ *n* (ca. 1755) : RIVULET, STREAMLET

run-nel \ˈrə-nᵊl\ *n* [alter. of ME *rinel*, fr. OE *rynel*; akin to OE *rinnan* to run — more at RUN] (bef. 12c) : RIVULET, STREAMLET

run-ner \ˈrə-nər\ *n* (14c) **1 :** one that runs : RACER **b :** BASE RUNNER **c :** BALLCARRIER **2 :** MESSENGER **b :** one that smuggles or distributes illicit or contraband goods (as drugs, liquor, or guns) **3** : any of several large active carangid fishes **4 a :** either of the longitudinal pieces on which a sled or sleigh slides **b :** the part of a skate that slides on the ice : BLADE **c :** the support of a drawer or a sliding door **5 a :** a growth produced by a plant in running; *esp :* STOLON 1a **b :** a plant that forms or spreads by means of runners **c :** a twining vine (as a scarlet runner) **6 a :** a long narrow carpet for a hall or staircase **b :** a narrow decorative cloth cover for a table or dresser top

runner bean *n* (1882) *chiefly Brit :* SCARLET RUNNER

run-ner-up \ˈrə-nə-ˌrəp, ˌrə-nə-ˈ\ *n, pl* **run-ners–up** \-nər-ˌzəp, -ˈzəp\ *also* **runner–ups** (1842) : the competitor that does not win first place in a contest; *esp :* one that finishes in second place

¹run-ning \ˈrə-niŋ\ *n* (bef. 12c) **1 a :** the action of running **b :** RACE **2 :** physical condition for running **3 :** MANAGEMENT, CARE — **in the running 1 :** competing in a contest **2 :** having a chance to win a contest — **out of the running 1 :** not competing in a contest **2** : having no chance of winning a contest

²running *adj* (14c) **1 :** CURSIVE, FLOWING **2 :** FLUID, RUNNY **3 a :** INCESSANT, CONTINUOUS ⟨a ~ battle⟩ **b :** made during the course of a process or activity ⟨a ~ commentary on the game⟩ **4 :** measured in a straight line ⟨cost of lumber per ~ foot⟩ **5 a :** initiated or performed while running or with a running start ⟨~ catch⟩ **b :** of, relating to, or being a football play in which the ball is advanced by running rather than by passing ⟨their ~ game was off⟩ **c :** designed for use by runners ⟨a ~ track⟩ ⟨~ shoes⟩ **6 :** fitted or trained for running rather than walking, trotting, or jumping ⟨a ~ horse⟩

³running *adv* (1719) : in succession : CONSECUTIVELY ⟨three days ~⟩

running back *n* (1924) : a football back (as a halfback or fullback) who carries the ball on running plays

---

\ə\ abut \ᵊ\ kitten, F table \ər\ further \a\ ash \ā\ ace \ä\ mop, mar \au̇\ out \ch\ chin \e\ bet \ē\ easy \g\ go \i\ hit \ī\ ice \j\ job \ŋ\ sing \ō\ go \ȯ\ law \ȯi\ boy \th\ thin \t̲h̲\ the \ü\ loot \u̇\ foot \y\ yet \zh\ vision \ä, k̲, ⁿ, œ, œ̄, ue, u̅e, ᵁ\ *see* Guide to Pronunciation

running board *n* (1817) : a footboard esp. at the side of an automobile

running dog *n* (1927) : one who
does someone else's bidding
: LACKEY

running gear *n* (1662) **1** : the
working and carrying parts of a
machine (as a locomotive) **2** : the
parts of an automobile chassis not
used in developing, transmitting, and
controlling power

running board

running hand *n* (1648) : handwriting in which the letters are usu. slanted and the words formed without
lifting the pen

running head *n* (1839) : a headline repeated on consecutive pages (as
of a book) — called also *running headline*

running knot *n* (1648) : a knot that slips along the rope or line round
which it is tied; *esp* : an overhand slipknot

running light *n* (1881) : any of the lights carried by a vehicle (as a
ship) under way at night that indicate size, position, and course

running mate *n* (1868) **1** : a horse entered in a race to set the pace for
a horse of the same owner or stable **2** : a candidate running for a
subordinate place on a ticket; *esp* : the candidate for vice-president **3**
: COMPANION

running start *n* (1926) : FLYING START 1

running stitch *n* (1848) : a small even stitch run in and out in cloth

running title *n* (1668) : the title or short title of a volume printed at
the top of left-hand text pages or sometimes of all text pages

running water *n* (1912) : water distributed through pipes and fixtures
⟨a cabin with hot and cold *running water*⟩

run·ny \'rə-nē\ *adj* (1817) : having a tendency to run: as **a** : extremely or excessively soft and liquid ⟨a ~ dough⟩ **b** : secreting a thin
flow of mucus ⟨a ~ nose⟩

run-off \'rən-ˌóf\ *n* (1873) **1** : a final race, contest, or election to decide an earlier one that has not resulted in a decision in favor of any
one competitor **2** : the portion of precipitation on land that ultimately reaches streams often with dissolved or suspended material

run off *vt* (1683) **1 a** : to recite, compose, or produce rapidly **b** : to
cause to be run or played to a finish **c** : to decide (as a race) by a run-off **d** : CARRY OUT **2** : to drain off : DRAW OFF **3 a** : to drive off (as
trespassers) **b** : to steal (as cattle) by driving away ~ *vi* : RUN AWAY
1 — **run off with** : to carry off : STEAL

run-of-paper \ˌrən-əv-'pā-pər\ *adj* (ca. 1923) : to be placed anywhere
in a newspaper at the option of the editor ⟨~ advertisement⟩

run-of-the-mill \ˌrən-ə(v)-thə-'mil\ *adj* (1930) : not outstanding in
quality or rarity : AVERAGE, ORDINARY

run-of-the-mine \-'mīn\ *or* **run-of-mine** \-əv-'mīn\ *adj* (1903) **1**
: not graded ⟨~ coal⟩ **2** : RUN-OF-THE-MILL

¹run-on \'rən-ˌón, -ˌän\ *adj* (1877) : continuing without rhetorical
pause from one line of verse into another

²run-on \-ˌón, -ˌän\ *n* (ca. 1909) : something (as a dictionary entry)
that is run on

run on *vi* (15c) **1** : to talk or narrate at length **2** : to keep going
: CONTINUE ~ *vt* **1** : to continue (matter in type) without a break or
a new paragraph : RUN IN **2** : to place or add (as an entry in a dictionary) at the end of a paragraphed item

run-on sentence *n* (1914) : a sentence containing a comma splice

run out *vi* (14c) **1 a** : to come to an end : EXPIRE ⟨time *ran out*⟩ **b**
: to become exhausted or used up ⟨the gasoline *ran out*⟩ **2** : to jut out
~ *vt* **1** : to finish out (as a course, series, or contest) : COMPLETE **2 a**
: to fill out (a typeset line) with quads, leaders, or ornaments **b** : to
set (as the first line of a paragraph) with a hanging indention **3** : to
exhaust (oneself) in running **4** : to cause to leave by force or coercion
: EXPEL — **run out of** : to use up the available supply of — **run out
on** : DESERT

run-over \'rən-ˌō-vər\ *n* (1927) : matter for publication that exceeds
the space allotted

run-over \'rən-ˌō-vər\ *adj* (ca. 1934) : extending beyond the allotted
space

run over *vi* (15c) **1** : to exceed a limit **2** : OVERFLOW ~ *vt* **1** : to go
over, examine, repeat, or rehearse quickly **2** : to collide with, knock
down, and often drive over ⟨*ran over* a dog⟩

runt \'rənt\ *n* [origin unknown] (1501) **1** *chiefly Scot* : a hardened
stalk or stem of a plant **2** : an animal unusually small of its kind; *esp*
: the smallest of a litter of pigs **3** : a person of small stature — **runt-i-
ness** \'rən-tē-nəs\ *n* — **runt-ish** \-tish\ *adj* — **runty** \-tē\ *adj*

run-through \'rən-ˌthrü\ *n* (1923) : a usu. cursory reading, summary,
or rehearsal

run through *vt* (15c) **1** : PIERCE **2** : to spend or consume wastefully
and rapidly **3** : to read or rehearse without pausing **4 a** : CARRY
OUT, DO **b** : to subject to a process

run-up \'rən-ˌəp\ *n* (1834) **1** : the act of running up something **2** : a
usu. sudden increase in volume or price **3** *chiefly Brit* : a period immediately preceding an action or event

run up *vi* (1664) **1** : to grow rapidly : shoot up ~ *vt* **1** : to increase by
bidding : bid up **2** : to stitch together quickly **3** : to erect hastily **4**
: to achieve by accumulating ⟨*ran up* a big lead⟩

run-way \'rən-ˌwā\ *n* (1833) **1 a** : a beaten path made by animals **b**
: a passageway for animals **2** : a paved strip of ground on a landing
field for the landing and takeoff of airplanes **3 a** : a narrow platform
from a stage into an auditorium **b** : a platform along which models
walk in a fashion show **4** : RUN 10b **5** : the area or path along which
a jumper, pole vaulter, or javelin thrower runs

ru·pee \rü-'pē, 'rü-ˌpē\ *n* [Hindi *rūpaiyā*, fr. Skt *rūpya* coined silver]
(1610) — see MONEY table

ru·pi·ah \rü-'pē-ə\ *n, pl* **rupiah** *or* **rupiahs** [Malay, fr. Hindi *rūpaiyā*
rupee] (1947) — see MONEY table

¹rup·ture \'rəp(t)-shər\ *n* [ME *ruptur*, fr. MF or L; MF *rupture*, fr. L
ruptura fracture, fr. *ruptus*, pp. of *rumpere* to break — more at REAVE]
(15c) **1** : breach of peace or concord; *specif* : open hostility or war
between nations **2 a** : the tearing apart of a tissue ⟨~ of the heart
muscle⟩ ⟨~ of an intervertebral disk⟩ **b** : HERNIA **3** : a breaking apart
or the state of being broken apart

²rupture *vb* **rup·tured; rup·tur·ing** \-sh(ə-)riŋ\ *vt* (1739) **1 a** : to
part by violence : BREAK, BURST **b** : to create or induce a breach of **2**
: to produce a rupture in ~ *vi* : to have or undergo a rupture

ru·ral \'rúr-əl\ *adj* [ME, fr. MF, fr. L *ruralis*, fr. *rur-, rus* open land —
more at ROOM] (15c) : of or relating to the country, country people or
life, or agriculture — **ru·ral·i·ty** \rú-'ra-lə-tē\ *n* — **ru·ral·ly** \'rúr-ə-
lē\ *adv*

rural dean *n* (ca. 1628) : DEAN 1b

rural free delivery *n* (1892) : free delivery of mail to a rural area —
called also *rural delivery*

ru·ral·ist \'rúr-ə-list\ *n* (1739) : one who lives in a rural area

rural route *n* (1898) : a mail-delivery route in a rural free delivery area

rur·ban \'rər-bən, 'rúr-\ *adj* [blend of *rural* and *urban*] (1918) : of,
relating to, or constituting an area which is chiefly residential but
where some farming is carried on

Ru·ri·tan \'rúr-ə-tən\ *n* [*Ruritan National*, a service club] (1968) : a
member of a major national service club

Ru·ri·ta·ni·an \ˌrúr-ə-,tā-nē-ən, ˌrúr-ə-'\ *adj* [*Ruritania*, fictional kingdom in the novel *Prisoner of Zenda* (1894) by Anthony Hope] (1896)
: of, relating to, or having the characteristics of an imaginary place of
high romance

ruse \'rüs, 'rüz\ *n* [F, fr. MF, fr. *ruser* to dodge, deceive] (1625) : a wily
subterfuge   *syn* see TRICK

¹rush \'rəsh\ *n* [ME, fr. OE *rysc;* akin to MHG *rusch* rush, Lith *regzti* to
knit] (bef. 12c) : any of various monocotyledonous often tufted marsh
plants (as of the genera *Juncus* and *Scirpus* of the family Juncaceae, the
rush family) with cylindrical often hollow stems which are used in
bottoming chairs and plaiting mats — **rushy** \'rə-shē\ *adj*

²rush *vb* [ME *russhen*, fr. MF *ruser* to put to flight, repel, deceive, fr. L
recusare to refuse — more at RECUSANT] *vi* (14c) **1** : to move forward,
progress, or act with haste or eagerness or without preparation **2** : to
advance a football by running plays ⟨~*ed* for a total of 150 yards⟩ ~
vt **1** : to push or impel on or forward with speed, impetuosity, or
violence **2** : to perform in a short time or at high speed **3** : to urge to
an unnatural or extreme speed ⟨don't ~ me⟩ **4** : to run toward or
against in attack : CHARGE **5 a** : to carry (a ball) forward in a running play **b** : to move in quickly on (a kicker or passer) to hinder,
prevent, or block a kick or pass — used esp. of defensive linemen **6 a**
: to lavish attention on : COURT **b** : to try to secure a pledge of membership (as in a fraternity) from

³rush *n* (14c) **1 a** : a violent forward motion **b** : ATTACK, ONSET
: a surging of emotion **2 a** : a burst of activity, productivity, or
speed **b** : a sudden insistent demand **3** : a thronging of people usu.
to a new place in search of wealth ⟨gold ~⟩ **4 a** : the act of carrying
a football during a game : running play **b** : the action or an instance
of rushing a passer or kicker in football ⟨pass ~⟩ **5 a** : a round of
attention usu. involving extensive social activity **b** : a drive by a fraternity or sorority to recruit new members **6** : a print of a motion-
picture scene processed directly after the shooting for review by the
director or producer — usu. used in pl. **7 a** : the immediate pleasurable feeling produced by a drug (as heroin or amphetamine) — called
also *flash* **b** : a sudden feeling of intense pleasure or euphoria : THRILL

⁴rush *adj* (1887) : requiring or marked by special speed or urgency ⟨~
orders⟩ ⟨the ~ season⟩ ⟨a ~ job⟩

rush candle *n* (1591) : RUSHLIGHT

rush·ee \ˌrə-'shē\ *n* (ca. 1916) : a college or university student who is
being rushed by a fraternity or sorority

rush·er \'rə-shər\ *n* (1654) : one that rushes; *esp* : BALLCARRIER

rush hour *n* (1898) : a period of the day when the demands esp. of
traffic or business are at a peak

rush·ing *n* (1883) : the act of advancing a football by running plays
: the use of running plays; *also* : yardage gained by running plays

rush·light \'rəsh-ˌlit\ *n* (1710) : a candle that consists of the pith of a
rush dipped in grease

rusk \'rəsk\ *n* [modif. of Sp & Pg *rosca* coil, twisted roll] (1595) **1**
: hard crisp bread orig. used as ship's stores **2** : a sweet or plain
bread baked, sliced, and baked again until dry and crisp

Russ \'rəs, 'rüs, 'rús\ *n, pl* **Russ** *or* **Russ·es** [ultim. fr. ORuss *Rus'* the
East Slavic-speaking lands] (1537) : RUSSIAN — **Russ** *adj*

¹rus·set \'rə-sət\ *n* [ME, fr. OF *rousset*, fr. *rousset*, adj., russet, fr. *rous*
russet, fr. L *russus* red; akin to L *ruber* red — more at RED] (13c) **1**
: coarse homespun usu. reddish brown cloth **2** : a strong brown **3**
: any of various winter apples having russet rough skins **4** : IDAHO

²russet *adj* (15c) : of the color russet

rus·set·ing *also* **rus·set·ting** \'rə-sə-tiŋ\ *n* (1912) : a brownish roughened area on the skin of fruit (as apples) caused by injury

Rus·sia leather \'rə-shə-\ *n* [*Russia*, Europe] (1658) : leather made by
tanning various skins with willow, birch, or oak and then rubbing the
flesh side with a phenolic oil distilled from a European birch — called
also *Russia calf*

Rus·sian \'rə-shən\ *n* (1538) **1 a** : a native or inhabitant of Russia
b : a member of the dominant Slavic-speaking ethnic group of Russia
c : a person of Russian descent **2** : a Slavic language of the Russian
people spoken as a second language by many non-Russian ethnic
groups of the Soviet Union and its successor states — **Russian** *adj* —
Rus·sian·ness \-nəs\ *n*

Russian blue *n, often cap B* (1889) : any of a breed of slender long-
bodied large-eared domestic cats with short silky bluish gray fur

Russian dressing *n* (1922) : a dressing (as of mayonnaise or oil and
vinegar) with added chili sauce, chopped pickles, or pimientos

Rus·sian·ize \'rə-shə-ˌnīz\ *vt* **-ized; -iz·ing** (1831) : to make Russian
— **Rus·sian·i·za·tion** \ˌrə-shə-nə-'zā-shən\ *n*

Russian olive *n* (1913) : a chiefly silvery Eurasian large shrub or small
tree (*Elaeagnus angustifolia* of the family Elaeagnaceae) cultivated esp.
as a shelterbelt plant

Russian roulette *n* (1937) **1** : an act of bravado consisting of spinning the cylinder of a revolver loaded with one cartridge, pointing the
muzzle at one's own head, and pulling the trigger **2** : something resembling Russian roulette in its potential for disaster ⟨taking cocaine is
playing *Russian roulette* —Jonathan Nicholas⟩

Russian thistle *n* (1894) : a prickly European saltwort (*Salsola kali*)
that is a serious pest in No. America — called also *Russian tumbleweed*

Russian wolfhound *n* (1872) : BORZOI

Rus·si·fy \\'rə-sə-ˌfī\\ *vt* **-fied; -fy·ing** (1865) : RUSSIANIZE — **Rus·si·fi·ca·tion** \\ˌrə-sə-fə-'kā-shən\\ *n*
Russ·ki *or* **Russ·ky** *or* **Russ·kie** \\'rəs-kē, 'rùs-\\ *n, pl* **Russkies** *or* **Russkis** [Russ *russkiĭ*, adj. & n., Russian, fr. ORuss, fr. *Rus'*] (1858) : RUSSIAN 1
Rus·so- \\'rə-(ˌ)sō, ˌrə-, -(ˌ)shō\\ *comb form* [*Russia & Russian*] : Russian and ⟨the *Russo*-Japanese war⟩
¹**rust** \\'rəst\\ *n* [ME, fr. OE *rūst*; akin to OE *rēad* red — more at RED] (bef. 12c) **1 a** : the reddish brittle coating formed on iron esp. when chemically attacked by moist air and composed essentially of hydrated ferric oxide **b** : a comparable coating produced on a metal other than iron by corrosion **c** : something resembling rust : ACCRETION **2** : corrosive or injurious influence or effect **3** : any of numerous destructive diseases of plants produced by fungi (order Uredinales) and characterized by usu. reddish brown pustular lesions; *also* : a fungus causing this **4** : a strong reddish brown
²**rust** *vi* (13c) **1** : to form rust : become oxidized ⟨iron ∼*s*⟩ **2** : to degenerate esp. from inaction, lack of use, or passage of time ⟨most men would . . . have allowed their faculties to ∼ —T. B. Macaulay⟩ **3** : to become reddish brown as if with rust ⟨the leaves slowly ∼*ed*⟩ **4** : to be affected with a rust fungus ∼ *vt* **1** : to cause (a metal) to form rust ⟨keep up your bright swords, for the dew will ∼ them —Shak.⟩ **2** : to impair or corrode by or as if by time, inactivity, or deleterious use **3** : to cause to become reddish brown : turn the color of rust
rust belt *n, often cap R&B* (1983) : the northeastern and midwestern states of the U.S. in which heavy industry has declined
rust bucket *n* (1945) : an old and dilapidated ship
¹**rus·tic** \\'rəs-tik\\ *also* **rus·ti·cal** \\-ti-kəl\\ *adj* [ME *rustik*, fr. MF *rustique*, fr. L *rusticus*, fr. *rus* open land — more at ROOM] (15c) **1** : of, relating to, or suitable for the country : RURAL **2 a** : made of the rough limbs of trees ⟨∼ furniture⟩ **b** : finished by rusticating ⟨a ∼ joint in masonry⟩ **3 a** : characteristic of or resembling country people **b** : lacking in social graces or polish **4** : appropriate to the country (as in plainness or sturdiness) ⟨heavy ∼ boots⟩ — **rus·ti·cal·ly** \\-ti-k(ə-)lē\\ *adv* — **rus·tic·i·ty** \\ˌrəs-'ti-sə-tē\\ *n*
²**rustic** *n* (ca. 1550) **1** : an inhabitant of a rural area **2 a** : an awkward coarse person **b** : an unsophisticated rural person
rus·ti·cate \\'rəs-tə-ˌkāt\\ *vb* **-cat·ed; -cat·ing** *vi* (1660) : to go into or reside in the country : follow a rustic life ∼ *vt* **1** *chiefly Brit* : to suspend from school or college **2** : to build or face with usu. rough-surfaced masonry blocks having beveled or rebated edges producing pronounced joints ⟨a *rusticated* facade⟩ **3 a** : to compel to reside in the country **b** : to cause to become rustic : implant rustic mannerisms in — **rus·ti·ca·tion** \\ˌrəs-ti-'kā-shən\\ *n* — **rus·ti·ca·tor** \\'rəs-ti-ˌkā-tər\\ *n*
¹**rus·tle** \\'rə-səl\\ *vb* **rus·tled; rus·tling** \\'rə-s(ə-)liŋ\\ [ME *rustelen*] *vi* (14c) **1** : to make or cause a rustle **2 a** : to act or move with energy or speed **b** : to forage food **3** : to steal cattle ∼ *vt* **1** : to cause to rustle **2 a** : to obtain by one's own exertions — often used with *up* ⟨able to ∼ up $5,000 bail —Jack McCallum⟩ **b** : FORAGE **3** : to steal (as livestock) esp. from a farm or ranch — **rus·tler** \\-s(ə-)lər\\ *n*
²**rustle** *n* (1759) : a quick succession or confusion of small sounds
rust mite *n* (1884) : any of various small gall mites that burrow in the surface of leaves or fruits usu. producing brown or reddish patches
rust·proof \\'rəst-ˌprüf\\ *adj* (1691) : incapable of rusting
¹**rusty** \\'rəs-tē\\ *adj* **rust·i·er; -est** (bef. 12c) **1** : affected by or as if by rust; *esp* : stiff with or as if with rust **2** : inept and slow through lack of practice or old age **3 a** : of the color rust **b** : dulled in color or appearance by age and use ⟨a ∼ old suit of clothes⟩ **4** : OUTMODED **5** : HOARSE, GRATING — **rust·i·ly** \\-tə-lē\\ *adv* — **rust·i·ness** \\-tē-nəs\\ *n*
²**rus·ty** \\'rəs-tē\\ *adj* **rus·ti·er; -est** [alter. of *restive*] (1625) *chiefly dial* : ILL-NATURED, SURLY
¹**rut** \\'rət\\ *n* [ME *rutte*, fr. MF *rut* roar, fr. LL *rugitus*, fr. L *rugire* to roar; akin to MIr *rucht* roar, OCS *rūžati* to neigh] (15c) **1** : an annually recurrent state of sexual excitement in the male deer; *broadly* : sexual excitement in a mammal (as estrus in the female) esp. when periodic **2** : the period during which rut normally occurs — often used with *the*
²**rut** *vi* **rut·ted; rut·ting** (1625) : to be in or enter into a state of rut
³**rut** *n* [perh. modif. of MF *route* way, route] (1580) **1 a** : a track worn by a wheel or by habitual passage **b** : a groove in which something runs **c** : CHANNEL, FURROW **2** : a usual or fixed practice; *esp* : a monotonous routine ⟨fall easily into a conversational ∼⟩
⁴**rut** *vt* **rut·ted; rut·ting** (1607) : to make a rut in : FURROW
ru·ta·ba·ga \\ˌrü-tə-'bā-gə, ˌrü-, -'be-; 'rü-tə-ˌ, 'rü-\\ *n* [Sw dial. *rotabagge*, fr. *rot* root + *bagge* bag] (1799) : a turnip (*Brassica napus napobrassica*) that usu. produces a large yellowish root
ruth \\'rüth\\ *n* [ME *ruthe*, fr. *ruen* to rue] (13c) **1** : compassion for the misery of another **2** : sorrow for one's own faults : REMORSE
Ruth \\'rüth\\ *n* [Heb *Rūth*] **1** : a Moabite woman who accompanied Naomi to Bethlehem and became the ancestress of David **2** : a short narrative book of canonical Jewish and Christian Scriptures — see BIBLE table
ru·the·ni·um \\rü-'thē-nē-əm\\ *n* [NL, fr. ML *Ruthenia* Ruthenia] (1848) : a hard brittle grayish polyvalent rare metallic element occurring in platinum ores and used in hardening platinum alloys — see ELEMENT table
ruth·er·ford·ium \\ˌrə-thə(r)-'fór-dē-əm\\ *n* [NL, fr. Ernest *Rutherford*] (1969) : UNNILQUADIUM
ruth·ful \\'rüth-fəl\\ *adj* (13c) **1** : full of ruth : TENDER **2** : full of sorrow : WOEFUL **3** : causing sorrow — **ruth·ful·ly** \\-fə-lē\\ *adv* — **ruth·ful·ness** *n*
ruth·less \\'rüth-ləs *also* 'rüth-\\ *adj* (14c) : having no ruth : MERCILESS, CRUEL — **ruth·less·ly** *adv* — **ruth·less·ness** *n*
ru·ti·lant \\'rü-tᵊl-ənt\\ *adj* [ME *rutilaunt*, fr. L *rutilant-, rutilans*, pp. of *rutilare* to glow reddish, fr. *rutilus* ruddy; prob. akin to L *ruber* red — more at RED] (15c) : having a reddish glow
ru·tile \\'rü-ˌtēl\\ *n* [G *Rutil*, fr. L *rutilus*] (1803) : a mineral that consists of titanium dioxide usu. with a little iron, is typically of a reddish brown color but sometimes deep red or black, and has a brilliant metallic or adamantine luster
rut·tish \\'rə-tish\\ *adj* (1601) : inclined to rut : LUSTFUL — **rut·tish·ly** *adv* — **rut·tish·ness** *n*
rut·ty \\'rə-tē\\ *adj* **rut·ti·er; -est** (1596) : full of ruts
RV \\ˌär-'vē\\ *n* (1967) : RECREATIONAL VEHICLE
R–value \\'är-ˌval-(ˌ)yü\\ *n* [prob. fr. thermal *resistance*] (1948) : a measure of resistance to the flow of heat through a given thickness of a material (as insulation) with higher numbers indicating better insulating properties — compare U-VALUE
Rx \\ˌär-'eks\\ *n* [alter. of ℞, symbol used at the beginning of a prescription, abbr. for L *recipe*, lit., take — more at RECIPE] (1926) : a medical prescription
-ry *n suffix* [ME *-rie*, fr. OF, short for *-erie -ery*] : -ERY ⟨wizard*ry*⟩ ⟨citizen*ry*⟩ ⟨ancient*ry*⟩
rya \\'rē-ə\\ *n* [*Rya*, village in southwest Sweden] (1945) : a Scandinavian handwoven rug with a deep resilient comparatively flat pile; *also* : the weave typical of this rug
¹**rye** \\'rī\\ *n* [ME, fr. OE *ryge*; akin to OHG *rocko* rye, Lith *rugys*] (bef. 12c) **1** : a hardy annual grass (*Secale cereale*) that is widely grown for grain and as a cover crop **2** : the seeds of rye **3** : RYE BREAD **4** : RYE WHISKEY
²**rye** *n* [Romany *rai* gentleman, master, fr. Skt *rājan* king — more at ROYAL] (1851) : a male Gypsy
rye bread *n* (1579) : bread made wholly or in part of rye flour; *esp* : a light bread often with caraway seeds
rye·grass \\'rī-ˌgras\\ *n* (1747) : any of several grasses (genus *Lolium*); *esp* : either of two grasses (*L. perenne* and *L. multiflorum*) that are used esp. for pasture, a cover crop, or lawn grass
rye whiskey *n* (1785) : a whiskey distilled from rye or from rye and malt

---

s \\'es\\ *n, pl* **s's** *or* **ss** \\'e-səz\\ *often cap, often attrib* (bef. 12c) **1 a** : the 19th letter of the English alphabet **b** : a graphic representation of this letter **c** : a speech counterpart of orthographic *s* **2** : a graphic device for reproducing the letter *s* **3** : one designated *s* esp. as the 19th in an order or class **4** [abbr. for *satisfactory*] **a** : a grade rating a student's work as satisfactory **b** : one graded or rated with an S **5** : something shaped like the letter S
¹**-s** \\s *after a voiceless consonant,* z *after a voiced consonant or a vowel*\\ *n pl suffix* [ME *-es, -s,* fr. OE *-as,* nom. & acc. pl. ending of some masc. nouns; akin to OS *-os*] — used to form the plural of most nouns that do not end in *s, z, sh, ch,* or postconsonantal *y* ⟨head*s*⟩ ⟨book*s*⟩ ⟨boy*s*⟩ ⟨belief*s*⟩, to form the plural of proper nouns that end in postconsonantal *y* ⟨Mary*s*⟩, and with or without a preceding apostrophe to form the plural of abbreviations, numbers, letters, and symbols used as nouns ⟨MC*s*⟩ ⟨PhD'*s*⟩ ⟨4*s*⟩ ⟨the 1940'*s*⟩ ⟨$*s*⟩ ⟨B's⟩ ; compare ¹-ES
²**-s** *adv suffix* [ME *-es, -s,* pl. ending of nouns, fr. *-es,* gen. sing. ending of nouns (functioning adverbially), fr. OE *-es*] — used to form adverbs denoting usual or repeated action or state ⟨always at home Sunday*s*⟩ ⟨morning*s* he stops by the newsstand⟩
³**-s** *vb suffix* [ME (Northern & North Midland dial.) *-es,* fr. OE (Northumbrian dial.) *-es, -as,* prob. fr. OE *-es, -as,* 2d sing. pres. indic. ending — more at -EST] — used to form the third person singular present of most verbs that do not end in *s, z, sh, ch,* or postconsonantal *y* ⟨falls⟩ ⟨takes⟩ ⟨plays⟩; compare ²-ES
¹**'s** \\s *same as* -'s\\ *vb* [contr. of *is, has, does*] (1584) **1 a** : IS ⟨she's here⟩ **b** : WAS ⟨when's the last time you ate?⟩ **2** : HAS ⟨he's seen them⟩ **3** : DOES ⟨what's he want?⟩
²**'s** \\s\\ *pron* [by contr.] (1588) : US — used with *let* ⟨let's⟩
-'s \\s *after voiceless consonants other than* s, sh, ch; z *after vowels and voiced consonants other than* z, zh, j; əz *after* s, sh, ch, z, zh, j\\ *n suffix or pron suffix* [ME *-es, -s,* gen. sing. ending, fr. OE *-es;* akin to OHG *-es,* gen. sing. ending, Gk *-oio, -ou,* Skt *-asya*] — used to form the possessive of singular nouns ⟨boy's⟩, of plural nouns not ending in *s* ⟨children's⟩,

---

\\ə\\ abut \\ᵊ\\ kitten, F table \\ər\\ further \\a\\ ash \\ā\\ ace \\ä\\ mop, mar
\\aù\\ out \\ch\\ chin \\e\\ bet \\ē\\ easy \\g\\ go \\i\\ hit \\ī\\ ice \\j\\ job
\\ŋ\\ sing \\ō\\ go \\ȯ\\ law \\ȯi\\ boy \\th\\ thin \\t̲h̲\\ the \\ü\\ loot \\ù\\ foot
\\y\\ yet \\zh\\ vision \\ȧ, k̟, ⁿ, œ, œ̄, ue, ūe, ᵞ\\ see Guide to Pronunciation

of some pronouns ⟨anyone's⟩, and of word groups functioning as nouns ⟨the man in the corner's hat⟩ or pronouns ⟨someone else's⟩

Saa·nen \'sä-nən, 'zä-\ *n* [*Saanen*, locality in southwest Switzerland] (1906) : any of a Swiss breed of usu. white and hornless short-haired dairy goats

sab·a·dil·la \,sa-bə-'di-lə, -'dē-yə\ *n* [Sp *cebadilla*] (1812) : a Mexican plant (*Schoenocaulon officinalis*) of the lily family; *also* : its seeds that are used as a source of veratrine and in insecticides

sa·ba·yon \sá-bá-yōⁿ\ *n* [F, modif. of It *zabaione*] (1906) : ZABAGLIONE

sab·bat \'sa-bət\ *n, often cap* [F, lit., sabbath, fr. L *sabbatum*] (1652) : a midnight assembly of diabolists (as witches and sorcerers) held esp. in medieval and Renaissance times to renew allegiance to the devil through mystic rites and orgies

¹Sab·ba·tar·i·an \,sa-bə-'ter-ē-ən\ *n* [L *sabbatarius*, fr. *sabbatum* sabbath](1613) **1** : one who observes the Sabbath on Saturday in conformity with the letter of the fourth commandment **2** : an adherent of Sabbatarianism

²Sabbatarian *adj* (ca. 1631) **1** : of or relating to the Sabbath **2** : of or relating to the Sabbatarians or Sabbatarianism

Sab·ba·tar·i·an·ism \,sa-bə-'ter-ē-ə-,ni-zəm\ *n* (ca. 1674) : strict and often rigorous observance of the Sabbath

Sab·bath \'sa-bəth\ *n* [ME *sabat*, fr. OF & OE, fr. L *sabbatum*, fr. Gk *sabbaton*, fr. Heb *shabbāth*, lit., rest] (bef. 12c) **1 a** : the seventh day of the week observed from Friday evening to Saturday evening as a day of rest and worship by Jews and some Christians **b** : Sunday observed among Christians as a day of rest and worship **2** : a time of rest

¹sab·bat·i·cal \sə-'ba-ti-kəl\ *or* **sab·bat·ic** \-tik\ *adj* [LL *sabbaticus*, fr. Gk *sabbatikos*, fr. *sabbaton*] (1645) **1** : of or relating to the sabbath ⟨∼ laws⟩ **2** : of or relating to a sabbatical year

²sabbatical *n* (1903) **1** : SABBATICAL YEAR **2** : LEAVE 1b **3** : a break or change from a normal routine (as of employment)

sabbatical year *n* (1599) **1** *often cap S* : a year of rest for the land observed every seventh year in ancient Judea **2** : a leave often with pay granted usu. every seventh year (as to a college professor) for rest, travel, or research — called also *sabbatical leave*

Sa·bel·li·an \sə-'be-lē-ən\ *n* [L *Sabellus* Sabine] (1601) **1** : a member of one of a group of early Italian peoples including Sabines and Samnites **2** : one or all of several little known languages or dialects of ancient Italy presumably closely related to Oscan and Umbrian — **Sabellian** *adj*

¹sa·ber *or* **sa·bre** \'sä-bər\ *n* [F *sabre*, modif. of G dial. *Sabel*, fr. MHG, prob. of Slav origin; akin to Russ *sablya* saber] (1680) **1** : a cavalry sword with a curved blade, thick back, and guard **2 a** : a light fencing or dueling sword having an arched guard that covers the back of the hand and a tapering flexible blade with a full cutting edge along one side and a partial cutting edge on the back at the tip — compare ÉPÉE, FOIL **b** : the sport of fencing with the saber

saber 1

²saber *or* **sabre** *vt* **sa·bered** *or* **sa·bred; sa·ber·ing** *or* **sa·bring** \-b(ə-)riŋ\ (1790) : to strike, cut, or kill with a saber

sa·ber·met·rics \,sä-bər-'me-triks\ *n pl but sing in constr* [*saber-* (fr. Society for American Baseball Research) + *-metrics* (as in *econometrics*)] (1982) : the statistical analysis of baseball data — **sa·ber·me·tri·cian** \,sä-bər-mə-'tri-shən\ *n*

saber rattling *n* (1922) : ostentatious display of military power

saber saw *n* (1953) : a light portable electric saw with a pointed reciprocating blade

sa·ber–toothed \'sä-bər-,tütht\ *adj* (1849) : having long sharp canine teeth

saber–toothed tiger *n* (1849) : any of numerous extinct cats (as genus *Smilodon*) widely distributed from the Oligocene through the Pleistocene and characterized by long curving upper canines — called also *saber-toothed cat*

sa·bin \'sä-bən\ *n* [Wallace C. W. Sabine †1919 Am. physicist] (1934) : a unit of acoustic absorption equivalent to the absorption by one square foot of a perfect absorber

Sa·bine \'sä-,bīn, *esp Brit* 'sa-\ *n* [ME *Sabin*, fr. L *Sabinus*] (14c) **1** : a member of an ancient people of the Apennines northeast of Latium **2** : the Italic language of the Sabine people — **Sabine** *adj*

¹sa·ble \'sä-bəl\ *n, pl* **sables** [ME, sable or its fur, the heraldic color black, black, fr. MF, sable or its fur, the heraldic color black, fr. MLG *sabel* sable or its fur, fr. MHG *zobel*, of Slav origin; akin to Russ *sobol'* sable or its fur] (14c) **1 a** : the heraldic color black **b** : black clothing worn in mourning — usu. used in pl. **2 a** *or pl* **sable** (1) : a carnivorous mammal (*Martes zibellina*) of the weasel family that occurs chiefly in northern Asia (2) : any of various animals related to the sable **b** : the fur or pelt of a sable **3 a** : the usu. dark brown color of the fur of the sable **b** : a grayish yellowish brown

²sable *adj* (15c) **1** : of the color black **2** : DARK, GLOOMY

sa·ble·fish \-,fish\ *n* (1917) : a large spiny-finned gray to blackish bony fish (*Anoplopoma fimbria* of the family Anoplomatidae) of the Pacific coast that is an important food fish and has a liver rich in vitamins

sa·bot \sa-'bō, 'sa-(,)bō, *for 1b also* 'sa-bət\ *n* [F] (1607) **1 a** : a wooden shoe worn in various European countries **b** (1) : a strap across the instep in a shoe esp. of the sandal type (2) : a shoe having a sabot strap **2** : a thrust-transmitting carrier that positions a missile in a gun barrel or launching tube and that prevents the escape of gas ahead of the missile **3** : SHOE 5

¹sab·o·tage \'sa-bə-,täzh\ *n* [F, fr. *saboter* to clatter with sabots, botch, sabotage, fr. *sabot*] (1910) **1** : destruction of an employer's property (as tools or materials) or the hindering of manufacturing by discontented workers **2** : destructive or obstructive action carried on by a civilian or enemy agent to hinder a nation's war effort **3 a** : an act or process tending to hamper or hurt **b** : deliberate subversion

²sabotage *vb* **-taged; -tag·ing** (1913) : to practice sabotage on

sab·o·teur \,sa-bə-'tər, -'tür, -'tyůr\ *n* [F, fr. *saboter*] (1921) : one that practices sabotage

sa·bra \'sä-brə\ *n, often cap* [NHeb *ṣabhār*, lit., prickly pear] (1945) : a native-born Israeli

sac \'sak\ *n* [F, lit., bag, fr. L *saccus* — more at SACK] (1741) : a pouch within an animal or plant often containing a fluid ⟨a synovial ∼⟩ — **sac-like** \-,līk\ *adj*

Sac \'sak, 'sôk\ *var of* SAUK

sa·ca·huis·te \,sa-kə-'wis-tə, ,sä-, -tē\ *or* **sa·ca·huis·ta** \-tə\ *n* [MexSp *zacahuiscle*, fr. (assumed) Nahuatl *zacahuitztli*, fr. Nahuatl *zacatl* grass, hay + *huitztli* thorn] (1896) : a bear grass (*Nolina texana*) that may cause poisoning in livestock

sac·a·ton \'sa-kə-,tōn\ *n* [AmerSp *zacatón*, fr. *zacate* coarse grass, fr. Nahuatl *zacatl*] (1846) : a coarse perennial grass (*Sporobolus wrightii*) of the southwestern U.S. that is used for hay in alkaline regions

sac·cade \sa-'käd\ *n* [F, twitch, jerk, fr. MF, fr. *saquer* to pull, draw] (1938) : a small rapid jerky movement of the eye esp. as it jumps from fixation on one point to another (as in reading) — **sac·cad·ic** \-'kä-dik\ *adj*

sac·cate \'sa-,kāt\ *adj* [NL *saccatus*, fr. L *saccus*] (1830) : having the form of a sac or pouch ⟨∼ pollen grains⟩

sacchar- *or* **sacchari-** *or* **saccharo-** *comb form* [L *saccharum*, fr. Gk *sakcharon*, fr. Prakrit *sakkharā*, fr. Skt *śarkarā* gravel, sugar] : sugar ⟨*saccharify*⟩ ⟨*saccharometer*⟩

sac·cha·rase \'sa-kə-,rās, -,rāz\ *n* [ISV] (1920) : INVERTASE

sac·cha·ride \'sa-kə-,rīd\ *n* (1895) : a simple sugar, combination of sugars, or polymerized sugar : CARBOHYDRATE

sac·char·i·fi·ca·tion \sə-,kar-ə-fə-'kā-shən\ *n* (1839) : the process of breaking a complex carbohydrate (as starch or cellulose) into simple sugars — **sac·char·i·fy** \sə-'kar-ə-,fī, sa-\ *vt*

sac·cha·rim·e·ter \,sa-kə-'ri-mə-tər\ *n* [ISV] (1874) : a device for measuring the amount of sugar in a solution; *specif* : a polarimeter so used

sac·cha·rin \'sa-k(ə-)rən\ *n* [ISV] (1885) : a crystalline compound $C_7H_5NO_3S$ that is unrelated to the carbohydrates, is several hundred times sweeter than cane sugar, and is used as a calorie-free sweetener

sac·cha·rine \'sa-k(ə-)rən, -kə-,rēn, -kə-,rīn\ *adj* [L *saccharum*] (ca. 1674) **1 a** : of, relating to, or resembling that of sugar ⟨∼ taste⟩ **b** : yielding or containing sugar ⟨∼ vegetables⟩ **2** : overly or sickishly sweet ⟨∼ flavor⟩ **3** : ingratiatingly or affectedly agreeable or friendly **4** : overly sentimental : MAWKISH — **sac·cha·rin·i·ty** \,sa-kə-'ri-nə-tē\ *n*

sac·cha·roi·dal \,sa-kə-'rói-d°l\ *adj* (1838) : having or being a fine granular texture like that of loaf sugar ⟨∼ marble⟩

sac·cha·rom·e·ter \-'rä-mə-tər\ *n* (1784) : SACCHARIMETER; *esp* : a hydrometer with a special scale

sac·cha·ro·my·ces \-rō-'mī-(,)sēz\ *n* [NL, fr. *sacchar-* + *-myces* fungus, fr. Gk *mykēs* — more at MYC-] (1873) : any of a genus (*Saccharomyces* of the family Saccharomycetaceae) of usu. unicellular yeasts (as a brewer's yeast) that are distinguished by their sparse or absent mycelium and by their facility in reproducing asexually by budding

sac·cu·lar \'sa-kyə-lər\ *adj* (ca. 1859) : resembling a sac ⟨a ∼ aneurysm⟩

sac·cu·lat·ed \-,lä-təd\ *also* **sac·cu·late** \-,lāt, -lət\ *adj* (ca. 1836) : having or formed of a series of saccular expansions — **sac·cu·la·tion** \,sa-kyə-'lā-shən\ *n*

sac·cule \'sa-(,)kyü(ə)l\ *n* [NL *sacculus*, fr. L, dim. of *saccus* bag — more at SACK] (ca. 1839) : a little sac; *specif* : the smaller chamber of the membranous labyrinth of the ear

sac·cu·lus \'sa-kyə-ləs\ *n, pl* **-li** \-,lī, -,lē\ [NL] (1748) : SACCULE

sac·er·do·tal \,sa-sər-'dō-t°l, ,sa-kər-\ *adj* [ME, fr. MF, fr. L *sacerdotalis*, fr. *sacerdot-, sacerdos* priest, fr. *sacer* sacred + *-dot-, -dos* (akin to *facere* to make) — more at SACRED, DO] (15c) **1** : of or relating to priests or a priesthood : PRIESTLY **2** : of, relating to, or suggesting sacerdotalism — **sac·er·do·tal·ly** \-t°l-ē\ *adv*

sac·er·do·tal·ism \-t°l-,i-zəm\ *n* (1856) : religious belief emphasizing the powers of priests as essential mediators between God and mankind — **sac·er·do·tal·ist** \-t°l-ist\ *n*

sac fungus *n* (ca. 1929) : ASCOMYCETE

sa·chem \'sä-chəm, 'sa-\ *n* [Narraganset *sâchim*] (1622) **1** : a No. American Indian chief; *esp* : the chief of a confederation of the Algonquian tribes of the No. Atlantic coast **2** : a Tammany leader — **sa·chem·ic** \-'che-mik, sa-\ *adj*

Sa·cher torte \'sä-kər-, 'zä-\ *n* [G *Sachertorte*, fr. *Sacher* (name of a family of 19th and 20th cent. Austrian restaurant proprietors) + G *Torte* torte] (1906) : a rich chocolate torte with an apricot jam filling

sa·chet \sa-'shā\ *n* [MF, fr. OF, dim. of *sac* bag — more at SAC] (15c) **1** : a small bag or packet **2** : a small bag containing a perfumed powder or potpourri used to scent clothes and linens — **sa·cheted** \-'shād\ *adj*

¹sack \'sak\ *n* [ME *sak* bag, sackcloth, fr. OE *sacc*, fr. L *saccus* bag & LL *saccus* sackcloth, both fr. Gk *sakkos* bag, sackcloth, of Sem origin; akin to Heb *śaq* bag, sackcloth] (bef. 12c) **1** : a usu. rectangular-shaped bag (as of paper, burlap, or canvas) **2** : the amount contained in a sack; *esp* : a fixed amount of a commodity used as a unit of measure **3 a** : a woman's loose-fitting dress **b** : a short usu. loose-fitting coat for women and children — compare SACQUE **4** : DISMISSAL **5 a** : HAMMOCK, BUNK **b** : BED **6** : a base in baseball **7** : an instance of sacking the quarterback in football — **sack·ful** \-,fůl\ *n*

²sack *vt* (14c) **1** : to put in or as if in a sack **2** : to dismiss esp. summarily **3** : to tackle (the quarterback) behind the line of scrimmage in football — **sack·er** *n*

³sack *n* [modif. of MF *sec* dry, fr. L *siccus*; prob. akin to OHG *sihan* to filter, Skt *siñcati* he pours] (ca. 1532) : any of several white wines imported to England from Spain and the Canary Islands during the 16th and 17th centuries

⁴sack *vt* [⁵*sack*] (ca. 1547) **1** : to plunder (as a town) esp. after capture **2** : to strip of valuables : LOOT *syn* see RAVAGE — **sack·er** *n*

⁵sack *n* [MF *sac*, fr. OIt *sacco*, lit., bag, fr. L *saccus*] (1549) : the plundering of a captured town

sack·but \'sak-(,)bət\ *n* [MF *saqueboute*, lit., hooked lance, fr. OF, fr. *saquer* to pull + *boter* to push — more at BUTT] (1533) : the medieval and Renaissance trombone

sack·cloth \'sa(k)-,klóth\ *n* [¹*sack*] (13c) **1** : a coarse cloth of goat or camel's hair or of flax, hemp, or cotton **2** : a garment of sackcloth worn as a sign of mourning or penitence

sack coat *n* (1847) : a man's jacket with a straight back

sack·ing \'sa-kiŋ\ n (1707) : material for sacks; *esp* : a coarse fabric (as burlap)

sack out vi [¹*sack*] (1946) : to go to bed : go to sleep

sack race n (1859) : a jumping race in which each contestant's legs are enclosed in a sack

sacque \'sak\ n [alter. of ¹*sack*] (1846) **1** : SACK 3a, b **2** : an infant's usu. short jacket that fastens at the neck

¹sa·cral \'sa-krəl, 'sā-\ adj (1767) : of, relating to, or lying near the sacrum

²sa·cral \'sā-krəl, 'sa-\ adj [L *sacr-, sacer* — more at SACRED] (1882) : HOLY, SACRED

sac·ra·ment \'sa-krə-mənt\ n [ME *sacrement, sacrament,* fr. OF & LL; OF, fr. LL *sacramentum,* fr. L, oath of allegiance, obligation, fr. *sacrare* to consecrate] (13c) **1 a** : a Christian rite (as baptism or the Eucharist) that is believed to have been ordained by Christ and that is held to be a means of divine grace or to be a sign or symbol of a spiritual reality **b** : a religious rite or observance comparable to a Christian sacrament **2** *cap* **a** : COMMUNION 2a **b** : BLESSED SACRAMENT **3** : something likened to a religious sacrament ⟨saw voting as a ∼ of democracy⟩

¹sac·ra·men·tal \,sa-krə-'men-t²l\ adj (15c) **1** : of, relating to, or having the character of a sacrament **2** : suggesting a sacrament (as in sacredness) — **sac·ra·men·tal·ly** \-t²l-ē\ adv

²sacramental n (15c) : an action or object (as the rosary) of ecclesiastical origin that serves to express or increase devotion

sac·ra·men·tal·ism \-t²l-,i-zəm\ n (1861) : belief in or use of sacramental rites, acts, or objects; *specif* : belief that the sacraments are inherently efficacious and necessary for salvation

sac·ra·men·tal·ist \-t²l-ist\ n (1840) **1** : SACRAMENTARIAN **2** : an adherent of sacramentalism

Sac·ra·men·tar·i·an \,sa-krə-,men-'ter-ē-ən, -mən-\ n (1535) **1** : one who interprets sacraments as merely visible symbols **2** : SACRAMENTALIST — **Sacramentarian** adj — **Sac·ra·men·tar·i·an·ism** \-ē-ə-,ni-zəm\ n

sa·crar·i·um \sə-'krer-ē-əm, sa-, sā-\ n, pl **-ia** \-ē-ə\ [ML, fr. L, shrine, fr. *sacr-, sacer* sacred] (1727) **1 a** : SANCTUARY 1b **b** : SACRISTY **c** : PISCINA **2** : an ancient Roman shrine or sanctuary in a temple or a home holding sacred objects

sa·cred \'sā-krəd\ adj [ME, fr. pp. of *sacren* to consecrate, fr. OF *sacrer,* fr. L *sacrare,* fr. *sacr-, sacer* sacred; akin to L *sancire* to make sacred, Hitt *šaklāi-* rite] (14c) **1 a** : dedicated or set apart for the service or worship of a deity ⟨a tree ∼ to the gods⟩ **b** : devoted exclusively to one service or use (as of a person or purpose) ⟨a fund ∼ to charity⟩ **2 a** : worthy of religious veneration : HOLY **b** : entitled to reverence and respect **3** : of or relating to religion : not secular or profane ⟨∼ music⟩ **4** *archaic* : ACCURSED **5 a** : UNASSAILABLE, INVIOLABLE **b** : highly valued and important ⟨a ∼ responsibility⟩ — **sa·cred·ly** adv — **sa·cred·ness** n

sacred baboon n [fr. its veneration by the ancient Egyptians] (ca. 1890) : HAMADRYAS BABOON

sacred cow n [fr. the veneration of the cow by Hindus] (1910) : one that is often unreasonably immune from criticism or opposition

sacred mushroom n (1930) **1** : any of various New World hallucinogenic fungi (genus *Psilocybe*) used esp. in some Indian ceremonies **2** : MESCAL BUTTON

¹sac·ri·fice \'sa-krə-,fīs, *also* -fəs *or* -,fiz\ n [ME, fr. OF, fr. L *sacrificium,* fr. *sacr-, sacer* + *facere* to make — more at DO] (13c) **1** : an act of offering to a deity something precious; *esp* : the killing of a victim on an altar **2** : something offered in sacrifice **3 a** : destruction or surrender of something for the sake of something else **b** : something given up or lost ⟨the ∼s made by parents⟩ **4** : LOSS ⟨goods sold at a ∼⟩ **5** : SACRIFICE HIT

²sacrifice vb **-ficed; -fic·ing** vt (14c) **1** : to offer as a sacrifice **2** : to suffer loss of, give up, renounce, injure, or destroy esp. for an ideal, belief, or end **3** : to sell at a loss ∼ vi **1** : to make or perform the rites of a sacrifice **2** : to make a sacrifice hit in baseball — **sac·ri·fic·er** n

sacrifice fly n (1944) : an outfield fly in baseball caught by a fielder after which a runner scores

sacrifice hit n (1880) : a bunt in baseball that allows a runner to advance one base while the batter is put out

sac·ri·fi·cial \,sa-krə-'fi-shəl\ adj (1607) **1** : of, relating to, of the nature of, or involving sacrifice **2** : of or relating to a metal that serves as the anode and is electrolytically consumed instead of another metal that is present — **sac·ri·fi·cial·ly** \-shə-lē\ adv

sac·ri·lege \'sa-krə-lij\ n [ME, fr. MF, fr. L *sacrilegium,* fr. *sacrilegus* one who steals sacred things, fr. *sacr-, sacer* + *legere* to gather, steal — more at LEGEND] (14c) **1** : a technical and not necessarily intrinsically outrageous violation (as improper reception of a sacrament) of what is sacred because consecrated to God **2** : gross irreverence toward a hallowed person, place, or thing — **sac·ri·le·gious** \÷,sa-krə-'li-jəs *also* -'lē-\ adj — **sac·ri·le·gious·ly** adv — **sac·ri·le·gious·ness** n

sac·ris·tan \'sa-krə-stən\ n [ME, fr. ML *sacristanus,* fr. L *sacr-, sacer*] (14c) : a person in charge of the sacristy and ceremonial equipment; *also* : SEXTON

sac·ris·ty \'sa-krə-stē\ n, pl **-ties** [ME *sacristie,* fr. ML *sacristia,* fr. *sacrista* sacristan, fr. L *sacr-, sacer*] (15c) : a room in a church where sacred vessels and vestments are kept and where the clergy vests

¹sa·cro·il·i·ac \,sa-krō-'i-lē-,ak, ,sā-\ adj [prob. fr. F *sacro-iliaque,* fr. NL *sacrum* + F *iliaque* iliac] (1831) : of, relating to, or being the region of juncture of the sacrum and ilium

²sacroiliac n (1936) : the sacroiliac region; *also* : its firm fibrous cartilage

sac·ro·sanct \'sa-krō-,saŋ(k)t\ adj [L *sacrosanctus,* prob. fr. *sacro sanctus* hallowed by a sacred rite] (1601) **1** : most sacred or holy : INVIOLABLE **2** : treated as if holy : immune from criticism or violation ⟨politically ∼ programs⟩ — **sac·ro·sanc·ti·ty** \,sa-krō-'saŋ(k)-tə-tē\ n

sa·crum \'sā-krəm, 'sa-\ n, pl **sa·cra** \'sa-krə, 'sā-\ [NL, fr. LL *os sacrum* last bone of the spine, lit., holy bone, trans. of Gk *hieron osteon*] (1753) : the part of the vertebral column that is directly connected with or forms a part of the pelvis and in humans consists of five fused vertebrae

sad \'sad\ adj **sad·der; sad·dest** [ME, fr. OE *sæd* sated; akin to OHG *sat* sated, L *satis* enough] (13c) **1 a** : affected with or expressive of

grief or unhappiness : DOWNCAST **b** (1) : causing or associated with grief or unhappiness : DEPRESSING ⟨∼ news⟩ (2) : REGRETTABLE, DEPLORABLE ⟨a ∼ relaxation of morals —C. W. Cunnington⟩ **c** : of little worth **2** : of a dull somber color — **sad·ly** adv — **sad·ness** n

sad·den \'sa-d²n\ vb **sad·dened; sad·den·ing** \'sad-niŋ, 'sa-d²n-iŋ\ vt (1628) : to make sad ∼ vi : to become sad

¹sad·dle \'sa-d²l\ n, *often attrib* [ME *sadel,* fr. OE *sadol;* akin to OHG *satul* saddle] (bef. 12c) **1 a** (1) : a girthed usu. padded and leather-covered seat for the rider of an animal (as a horse) (2) : a part of a driving harness comparable to a saddle that is used to keep the breeching in place **b** : a seat to be straddled by the rider of a vehicle (as a bicycle) **2 a** : a device mounted as a support and often shaped to fit the object held **3 a** : a ridge connecting two higher elevations **b** : a pass in a mountain range **4 a** : both sides of the

saddle 1a(1): *1* western, *2* English

unsplit back of a carcass including both loins **b** : a colored marking on the back of an animal ⟨the ∼ : the rear part of a male fowl's back extending to the tail — see DUCK illustration **5** : the central part of the backbone of the binding of a book **6** : a piece of leather across the instep of a shoe — **sad·dle·less** \-d²l-(l)əs\ adj — **in the saddle** : in control

²saddle vb **sad·dled; sad·dling** \'sad-liŋ, 'sa-d²l-iŋ\ vt (bef. 12c) **1** : to put a saddle on **2 a** : to place under a burden or encumbrance **b** : to place (an onerous responsibility) on a person or group ∼ vi : to mount a saddled horse

sad·dle·bag \'sa-d²l-,bag\ n (1773) : one of a pair of covered pouches laid across the back of a horse behind the saddle or hanging over the rear wheel of a bicycle or motorcycle

saddle blanket n (1737) : a folded blanket or pad under a saddle to prevent galling the horse

sad·dle·bow \'sa-d²l-,bō\ n (bef. 12c) : the arch in or the pieces forming the front of a saddle

sad·dle·bred \-,bred\ n (1948) : AMERICAN SADDLEBRED

sad·dle·cloth \-,klòth\ n (15c) : a cloth placed under or over a saddle

sad·dled prominent \'sa-d²ld-\ n [fr. the hump or prominence on the back of the larva] (1910) : a moth (*Heterocampa guttivitta*) whose larva is a serious defoliator of hardwood trees in the eastern and midwestern U.S.

saddle horn n (1856) : a hornlike prolongation of the pommel of a stock saddle

saddle horse n (1662) : a horse suited for or trained for riding

saddle leather n (1832) : leather made of cowhide that is vegetable tanned and used esp. for saddlery; *also* : smooth polished leather simulating this

sad·dler \'sad-lər\ n (14c) : one that makes, repairs, or sells saddles and other furnishings for horses

sad·dlery \'sad-lə-rē, 'sa-d²l-rē\ n, pl **-dler·ies** (15c) : the trade, articles of trade, or shop of a saddler

saddle seat n (1895) : a slightly concave chair seat (as of a Windsor chair) with sometimes a thickened ridge at the center front

saddle shoe n (1939) : an oxford-style shoe having a saddle of contrasting color or leather — called also *saddle oxford*

saddle soap n (1889) : a mild soap used for cleansing and conditioning leather

saddle sore n (1946) **1** : a gall or open sore developing on the back of a horse at points of pressure from an ill-fitting or ill-adjusted saddle **2** : an irritation or sore on parts of the rider chafed by the saddle

sad·dle·tree \'sa-d²l-,trē\ n (15c) : the frame of a saddle

Sad·du·ce·an \,sa-jə-'sē-ən, ,sa-dyə-\ adj (1593) : of or relating to the Sadducees

Sad·du·cee \'sa-jə-,sē, 'sa-dyə-\ n [ME *saducee,* fr. OE *sadduce,* fr. LL *sadducaeus,* fr. Gk *saddoukaios,* fr. LHeb *şāddūqî*] (bef. 12c) : a member of a Jewish party of the intertestamental period consisting of a traditional ruling class of priests and rejecting doctrines not in the Law (as resurrection, retribution in a future life, and the existence of angels) — **Sad·du·cee·ism** \-,i-zəm\ n

sa·dhe \'(t)sä-də, -dē\ n [Heb *şādhē*] (ca. 1899) : the 18th letter of the Hebrew alphabet — see ALPHABET table

sa·dhu *also* **sad·dhu** \'sä-(,)dü\ n [Skt *sādhu*] (1845) : a usu. Hindu mendicant ascetic

sad·iron \'sad-,ī(-ə)rn\ n [*sad* (compact, heavy) + *iron*] (1761) : a flatiron pointed at both ends and having a removable handle

sa·dism \'sā-,di-zəm, 'sa-\ n [ISV, fr. Marquis de *Sade*] (1888) **1** : a sexual perversion in which gratification is obtained by the infliction of physical or mental pain on others (as on a love object) — compare MASOCHISM **2 a** : delight in cruelty **b** : excessive cruelty — **sa·dist** \'sā-dist, 'sa-\ n — **sa·dis·tic** \sə-'dis-tik *also* sā- *or* sa-\ adj — **sa·dis·ti·cal·ly** \-ti-k(ə-)lē\ adv

sa·do·mas·och·ism \,sā-(,)dō-'ma-sə-,ki-zəm, ,sa-, -'ma-zə-\ n [ISV *sadism* + *-o-* + *masochism*] (1922) : the derivation of pleasure from the infliction of physical or mental pain either on others or on oneself — **sa·do·mas·och·ist** \-kist\ n *or adj* — **sa·do·mas·och·is·tic** \-,ma-sə-'kis-tik, -,ma-zə-\ adj

sad sack n (1943) : an inept person; *esp* : an inept soldier — **sad–sack** adj

Sa·far \sə-'fär\ n [Ar *şafar*] (ca. 1771) : the 2d month of the Islamic year — see MONTH table

sa·fa·ri \sə-'fär-ē, -'far-\ n [Ar *safarīy* of a trip] (1896) **1** : the caravan and equipment of a hunting expedition esp. in eastern Africa; *also*

\ə\ abut \²\ kitten, F table \ər\ further \a\ ash \ā\ ace \ä\ mop, mar \au̇\ out \ch\ chin \e\ bet \ē\ easy \g\ go \i\ hit \ī\ ice \j\ job \ŋ\ sing \ō\ go \ȯ\ law \ȯi\ boy \th\ thin \t͟h\ the \ü\ loot \u̇\ foot \y\ yet \zh\ vision \á, k̲, ⁿ, œ, œ̄, ue, ū̄, ʸ\ see Guide to Pronunciation

: such a hunting expedition **2** : JOURNEY, EXPEDITION 〈an arctic ~〉 —
safari *vi*
safari jacket *n* (1951) : a usu. belted shirt jacket with pleated expansible pockets
safari suit *n* (1967) : a safari jacket with matching pants
¹safe \'sāf\ *adj* **saf·er; saf·est** [ME *sauf*, fr. OF, fr. L *salvus* safe, healthy; akin to L *solidus* solid, Gk *holos* whole, safe, Skt *sarva* entire] (14c) **1** : free from harm or risk : UNHURT **2 a** : secure from threat of danger, harm, or loss **b** : successful at getting to a base in baseball without being put out **3** : affording safety or security from danger, risk, or difficulty **4** *obs, of mental or moral faculties* : HEALTHY, SOUND **5 a** : not threatening danger : HARMLESS **b** : unlikely to produce controversy or contradiction **6 a** : not likely to take risks : CAUTIOUS **b** : TRUSTWORTHY, RELIABLE — **safe** *or* **safe·ly** *adv* — **safe·ness** *n*
²safe *n* (15c) **1** : a place or receptacle to keep articles (as valuables) safe **2** : CONDOM
safe–con·duct \'sāf-'kän-(,)dəkt\ *n* [ME *sauf conduit*, fr. OF, safe conduct] (14c) **1** : protection given a person passing through a military zone or occupied area **2** : a document authorizing safe-conduct
safe-crack·er \'sāf-,kra-kər\ *n* (ca. 1825) : one that breaks open safes to steal — **safe-crack·ing** \-,kiŋ\ *n*
safe–deposit box *n* (1882) : a box (as in the vault of a bank) for safe storage of valuables — called also *safety-deposit box*
¹safe·guard \'sāf-,gärd\ *n* [ME *saufgarde*, fr. MF *saufegarde*, fr. OF, fr. *sauve* safe + *garde* guard] (14c) **1 a** : PASS, SAFE-CONDUCT **b** : CONVOY, ESCORT **2 a** : a precautionary measure, stipulation, or device **b** : a technical contrivance to prevent accident
²safeguard *vt* (15c) **1** : to provide a safeguard for **2** : to make safe : PROTECT *syn* see DEFEND
safe house *n* (1946) : a place where one may engage in secret activities or take refuge
safe-keep·ing \'sāf-'kē-piŋ\ *n* (15c) **1** : the act or process of preserving in safety **2** : the state of being preserved in safety
safe·light \'sāf-,līt\ *n* (1903) : a darkroom lamp with a filter to screen out rays that are harmful to sensitive film or paper
safe sex *n* (1985) : sexual activity and esp. sexual intercourse in which various measures (as the use of latex condoms or the practice of monogamy) are taken to avoid disease (as AIDS) transmitted by sexual contact
¹safe·ty \'sāf-tē\ *n, pl* **safeties** [ME *saufte*, fr. MF *sauveté*, fr. OF, fr. *sauve*, fem. of *sauf* safe] (14c) **1** : the condition of being safe from undergoing or causing hurt, injury, or loss **2** : a device (as on a weapon or a machine) designed to prevent inadvertent or hazardous operation **3 a** (1) : a situation in football in which a member of the offensive team is tackled behind its own goal line that counts two points for the defensive team — compare TOUCHBACK (2) : a member of a defensive backfield in football who occupies the deepest position in order to receive a kick, defend against a forward pass, or stop a ballcarrier **b** : a billiard shot made with no attempt to score or so as to leave the balls in an unfavorable position for the opponent **c** : BASE HIT
²safety *vt* **safe·tied; safe·ty·ing** (1940) : to protect against failure, breakage, or accident 〈~ a rifle〉
safety belt *n* (ca. 1858) : a belt fastening a person to an object (as a car seat) to prevent falling or injury
safety glass *n* (1919) : transparent material that is made by laminating a sheet of transparent plastic between sheets of clear glass and is used esp. for windows (as of automobiles) likely to be subjected to shock or impact
safety lamp *n* (1816) : a miner's lamp constructed to avoid explosion in an atmosphere containing flammable gas usu. by enclosing the flame in fine wire gauze
safe·ty·man \'sāf-tē-,man\ *n* (1927) : SAFETY 3a(2)
safety match *n* (1863) : a match capable of being struck and ignited only on a specially prepared friction surface
safety net *n* (1950) : something that provides security against misfortune or difficulty
safety pin *n* (1857) : a pin in the form of a clasp with a guard covering its point when fastened
safety razor *n* (ca. 1875) : a razor provided with a guard for the blade to prevent deep cuts in the skin
safety valve *n* (1813) **1** : an automatic escape or relief valve (as for a steam boiler) **2** : an outlet for pent-up energy or emotion **3** : something that relieves the pressure of overcrowding
saf·flow·er \'sa-,flaú(-ə)r\ *n* [MF *saffleur*, fr. OIt *saffiore*, fr. Ar *aṣfar*, a yellow plant] (1642) : a widely cultivated Old World composite herb (*Carthamus tinctorius*) with large orange or red flower heads and seeds rich in oil; *also* : a red dyestuff prepared from the flower heads
safflower oil *n* (ca. 1857) : an edible drying oil obtained from the seeds of the safflower
saf·fron \'sa-frən\ *n* [ME, fr. OF *safran*, fr. ML *safranum*, fr. Ar *za'-farān*] (13c) **1 a** : the deep orange aromatic pungent dried stigmas of a purple-flowered crocus (*Crocus sativus*) used to color and flavor foods and formerly as a dyestuff and in medicine **b** : the crocus supplying saffron **2** : a moderate orange to orange yellow
saf·ra·nine \'sa-frə-,nēn, -nən\ *or* **saf·ra·nin** \-nən\ *n* [ISV, fr. F or G *safran* saffron] (1868) **1** : any of various usu. red synthetic dyes that are amino derivatives of bases **2** : any of various mixtures of safranine salts used in dyeing and as biological stains
saf·role \'saf-,rōl\ *n* [ISV, fr. sass*afras* + -*ole*] (1869) : a poisonous oily cyclic ether $C_{10}H_{10}O_2$ that is the principal component of sassafras oil and is used chiefly in perfumery
¹sag \'sag\ *vb* **sagged; sag·ging** [ME *saggen*, prob. of Scand origin; akin to Sw *sacka* to sag] *vi* (14c) **1** : to droop, sink, or settle from or as if from pressure or loss of tautness **2 a** : to lose firmness, resiliency, or vigor 〈spirits *sagging* from overwork〉 **b** : to decline esp. from a thriving state **3** : DRIFT **4** : to fail to stimulate or retain interest 〈~〉 *vt* : to cause to sag : leave slack in
²sag *n* (1580) **1** : a tendency to drift (as of a ship to leeward) **2 a** : a sagging part 〈the ~ in a rope〉 **b** : a drop or depression below the surrounding area **c** : an instance or amount of sagging **3** : a temporary decline (as in the price of a commodity)
sa·ga \'sä-gə *also* 'sa-\ *n* [ON — more at SAW] (1709) **1** : a prose narrative recorded in Iceland in the 12th and 13th centuries of historic or legendary figures and events of the heroic age of Norway and Iceland

2 : a modern heroic narrative resembling the Icelandic saga **3** : a long detailed account 〈a ~ of the Old South〉
sa·ga·cious \sə-'gā-shəs, si-\ *adj* [L *sagac-, sagax*, fr. *sagire* to perceive keenly; akin to L *sagus* prophetic — more at SEEK] (1607) **1** *obs* : keen in sense perception **2 a** : of keen and farsighted penetration and judgment : DISCERNING 〈~ judge of character〉 **b** : caused by or indicating acute discernment 〈~ purchase of stock〉 *syn* see SHREWD — **sa·ga·cious·ly** *adv* — **sa·ga·cious·ness** *n*
sa·gac·i·ty \sə-'ga-sə-tē, si-\ *n* (15c) : the quality of being sagacious
sag·a·more \'sa-gə-,mōr, -,mȯr\ *n* [Eastern Abenaki *sàkama*] (1613) **1** : a subordinate chief of the Algonquian Indians of the No. Atlantic coast **2** : SACHEM 1
saga novel *n* (ca. 1938) : ROMAN-FLEUVE
¹sage \'sāj\ *adj* **sag·er; sag·est** [ME, fr. OF, fr. (assumed) VL *sapius*, fr. L *sapere* to taste, have good taste, be wise; akin to Oscan *sipus* knowing, OS an*sebbian* to perceive] (14c) **1 a** : wise through reflection and experience **b** *archaic* : GRAVE, SOLEMN **2** : proceeding from or characterized by wisdom, prudence, and good judgment 〈~ advice〉 *syn* see WISE — **sage·ly** *adv* — **sage·ness** *n*
²sage *n* (14c) **1** : one (as a profound philosopher) distinguished for wisdom **2** : a mature or venerable man of sound judgment
³sage *n* [ME, fr. MF *sauge*, fr. L *salvia*, fr. *salvus* healthy; fr. its use as a medicinal herb — more at SAFE] (14c) **1** : a mint (*Salvia officinalis*) with grayish green aromatic leaves used esp. in flavoring meats; *broadly* : SALVIA **2** : SAGEBRUSH
sage·brush \'sāj-,brəsh\ *n* (1850) : any of several No. American hoary composite subshrubs (genus *Artemisia*); *esp* : one (*A. tridentata*) having a bitter juice and an odor resembling sage and often covering vast tracts of alkaline plains in the western U.S.
sage cheese *n* (1699) : a cheese similar to mild cheddar flecked with green and flavored with sage
sage grouse *n* (1876) : a large grouse (*Centrocercus urophasianus*) of the dry sagebrush plains of western No. America that has mottled gray and buff plumage with a contrasting black belly
sag·ger *or* **sag·gar** \'sa-gər\ *n* [prob. alter. of *safeguard*] (1752) : a box made of fireclay in which delicate ceramic pieces are fired
sag·it·tal \'sa-jə-t²l\ *adj* [ME *sagittale*, fr. ML *sagittalis*, fr. L *sagitta* arrow] (14c) **1** : of or relating to the suture between the parietal bones of the skull **2** : of, relating to, situated in, or being the median plane of the body or any plane parallel thereto — **sag·it·tal·ly** \-t²l-ē, -ta-lē\ *adv*
Sag·it·tar·i·an \,sa-jə-'ter-ē-ən\ *n* (1911) : SAGITTARIUS 2b
Sag·it·tar·i·us \-ē-əs\ *n* [L (gen. *Sagittarii*), lit., archer, fr. *sagitta* arrow] **1** : a southern zodiacal constellation pictured as a centaur shooting an arrow and containing the point in the sky where the center of the Milky Way galaxy is located **2 a** : the 9th sign of the zodiac in astrology — see ZODIAC table **b** : one born under the sign of Sagittarius
sag·it·tate \'sa-jə-,tāt\ *adj* [L *sagitta*] (1760) : shaped like an arrowhead; *specif* : elongated, triangular, and having the two basal lobes prolonged downward 〈~ leaf〉 — see LEAF illustration
sa·go \'sā-(,)gō\ *n, pl* **sagos** [Malay *sagu* sago palm] (ca. 1580) : a dry granulated or powdered starch prepared from the pith of a sago palm and used in foods and as textile stiffening
sago palm *n* (1769) : a plant that yields sago; *esp* : any of various lofty pinnate-leaved Indian and Malaysian palms (genus *Metroxylon*)
sa·gua·ro \sə-'wär-ə, -'gwär-, -ō\ *n, pl* **-ros** [MexSp] (1856) : an arborescent cactus (*Carnegiea gigantea*) of desert regions of the southwestern U.S. and Mexico that has a tall columnar simple or sparsely branched trunk of up to 60 feet (18 meters) and bears white flowers and edible fruit
Sa·hap·ti·an \sə-'hap-tē-ən\ *var of* SHAHAPTIAN
sa·hib \'sä-,hib, -,(h)ēb, -,hä-\ *n* [Hindi *sāheb*, fr. Ar *ṣāhib*] (1673) : SIR, MASTER — used esp. among the native inhabitants of colonial India when addressing or speaking of a European of some social or official status
¹said past and past part of SAY
²said \'sed\ *adj* [pp. of *say*] (14c) : AFOREMENTIONED
¹sail \'sā(ə)l\, *as last element in compounds often* s*əl\ *n* [ME, fr. OE *segl*; akin to OHG *segal* sail] (bef. 12c) **1 a** (1) : an extent of fabric (as canvas) by means of which wind is used to propel a ship through water (2) : the sails of a ship **b** *pl usu* **sail** : a ship equipped with sails **2** : an extent of fabric used in propelling a wind-driven vehicle (as an iceboat) **3** : something that resembles a sail; *esp* : a streamlined conning tower on a submarine **4** : a passage by a sailing craft : CRUISE — **sailed** \'sā(ə)ld\ *adj* — **under sail** : in motion with sails set

sail 1a (of a schooner): *1* flying jib, *2* jib, *3* forestaysail, *4* foresail, *5* fore gaff-topsail, *6* main-topmast staysail, *7* mainsail, *8* main gaff= topsail

²sail *vi* (bef. 12c) **1 a** : to travel on water in a ship **b** : YACHT **2 a** : to travel on water by the action of wind upon sails or by other means **b** : to move or proceed easily, gracefully, nonchalantly, or without resistance 〈~ed through all sorts of contradictions —Vicki Hearne〉 〈the bill ~ed through the legislature〉 **3** : to begin a water voyage 〈~ with the tide〉 ~ *vt* **1 a** : to travel on (water) by means of motive power (as sail) **b** : to glide through **2** : to direct or manage the motion of (as a ship) — **sail·able** \'sā-lə-bəl\ *adj* — **sail into** : to attack vigorously or sharply 〈*sailed into* me for being late〉
sail·board \'sā(ə)l-,bȯrd, -,bȯrd\ *n* (1962) : a modified surfboard having a mast mounted on a universal joint and sailed by one person standing up — **sail-board·ing** *n*
sail·boat \'sā(ə)l-,bōt\ *n* (1798) : a boat usu. propelled by sail — **sail·boat·er** \-,bō-tər\ *n* — **sail·boat·ing** *n*
sail·cloth \-,klȯth\ *n* (13c) : a heavy canvas used for sails, tents, or upholstery; *also* : a lightweight canvas used for clothing
sail·er \'sā-lər\ *n* (15c) : a ship or boat esp. having specified sailing qualities
sail·fish \'sā(ə)l-,fish\ *n* (1879) : any of a genus (*Istiophorus* and esp. *I. platypterus*) of billfishes having a very large dorsal fin

sail·ing \'sā-liŋ\ n (bef. 12c) **1 a :** the technical skill of managing a ship : NAVIGATION **b :** the method of determining the course to be followed to reach a given point **2 a :** the sport of handling or riding in a sailboat **b :** a departure from a port
sail·or \'sā-lər\ n [alter. of *sailer*] (ca. 1642) **1 a :** one that sails; *esp* : MARINER **b** (1) : a member of a ship's crew (2) : SEAMAN 2b **2 :** a traveler by water **3 :** a stiff straw hat with a low flat crown and straight circular brim
sailor collar n (1895) : a broad collar having a square flap across the back and tapering to a V in the front
sail·or's–choice \,sā-lərz-'chȯis\ n (1850) : any of several small grunts of the Western Atlantic: as **a :** PINFISH **b :** PIGFISH
sail·plane \'sā(ə)l-,plān\ n (1922) : a glider of such design that it is able to rise in an upward air current — **sailplane** vi — **sail·plan·er** n
sai·min \'sī-'min\ n [prob. fr. Chin (Guangdong) *sai mihn* fine noodles] (1949) : a Hawaiian noodle soup
sain \'sān\ vt [ME, fr. OE *segnian*, fr. LL *signare*, fr. L, to mark — more at SIGN] (bef. 12c) **1** *dial Brit* : to make the sign of the cross on (oneself) **2** *dial Brit* : BLESS
sain·foin \'sān-,fȯin, 'san-\ n [F, fr. MF, fr. *sain* healthy (fr. L *sanus*) + *foin* hay, fr. L *fenum*] (1626) : a pink-flowered Eurasian perennial leguminous herb (*Onobrychis viciaefolia* syn. *O. viciifolia*) grown for forage
¹saint \'sānt, *before a name* (,)sānt *or* sənt\ n [ME, fr. OF, fr. LL *sanctus*, fr. L, sacred, fr. pp. of *sancire* to make sacred — more at SACRED] (13c) **1 :** one officially recognized esp. through canonization as preeminent for holiness **2 a :** one of the spirits of the departed in heaven **b :** ANGEL 1a **3 a :** one of God's chosen and holy. Christian people **b** *cap* : a member of any of various Christian bodies; *specif* : LATTER-DAY SAINT **4 :** one eminent for piety or virtue **5 :** an illustrious predecessor — **saint·dom** \'sānt-dəm\ n — **saint·like** \'sānt-,līk\ adj
²saint \'sānt\ vt (13c) : to recognize or designate as a saint; *specif* : CANONIZE
Saint Ag·nes' Eve \-'ag-nə-səz-, -'ag-nəs-\ n [*St. Agnes*] (1820) : the night of January 20 when a woman is traditionally held to have a revelation of her future husband
Saint An·drew's cross \-'an-,drüz-\ n [*St. Andrew* †ab A.D. 60, apostle who, according to tradition, was crucified on a cross of this type] (1615) : a figure of a cross that has the form of two intersecting oblique bars — see CROSS illustration
Saint An·tho·ny's cross \-'an(t)-thə-nēz-, *chiefly Brit* -'an-tə-\ n [*St. Anthony*] (1885) : TAU CROSS
Saint Anthony's fire n (14c) : any of several inflammations or gangrenous conditions (as erysipelas or ergotism) of the skin
saint au·gus·tine grass \-'ȯ-gə-,stēn-\ n, *often cap S&A* [prob. fr. *St. Augustine*, Fla.] (1900) : a perennial much-branched creeping grass (*Stenotaphrum secundatum*) of the southern U.S. that is valuable as a sand binder and as sod grass
Saint Ber·nard \-bər-'närd\ n [the hospice of Grand *St. Bernard*, where such dogs were first bred] (1839) : any of a Swiss alpine breed of tall powerful working dogs used esp. formerly in aiding lost travelers
saint·ed \'sān-təd\ adj (1598) **1 :** befitting or relating to a saint **2** : SAINTLY, PIOUS **3 :** entered into heaven : DEAD **4 :** much admired : IDOLIZED
Saint El·mo's fire \'sānt-'el-(,)mōz-\ n [*St. Elmo* (*Erasmus*) †303 Ital. bishop & patron saint of sailors] (1814) : a flaming phenomenon sometimes seen in stormy weather at prominent points on an airplane or ship and on land that is of the nature of a brush discharge of electricity — called also *Saint Elmo's light*
Saint Emi·lion \,saⁿ-tā-mēl-'yōⁿ\ n [*Saint-Émilion*, village in SW France] (1833) : a red Bordeaux wine
saint·hood \'sānt-,hu̇d\ n (1550) **1 :** the quality or state of being a saint **2 :** saints as a group
Saint John's bread \-'jänz-,bred\ n (1591) : CAROB 2
Saint–John's–wort \-,wȯrt, -,wȯrt\ n [*St. John* the Baptist] (15c) : any of a genus (*Hypericum* of the family Guttiferae, the Saint-John's-wort family) of herbs and shrubs with showy pentamerous yellow flowers
Saint Lou·is encephalitis \-'lü-əs-\ n [*St. Louis*, Mo.] (1934) : a No. American viral encephalitis that is transmitted by several culex mosquitoes
saint·ly \'sānt-lē\ adj **saint·li·er; -est** (1534) : relating to, resembling, or befitting a saint : HOLY — **saint·li·ness** n
Saint Mar·tin's summer \-'mär-tⁿz-\ n [*Saint Martin's* Day, November 11] (1591) : Indian summer when occurring in November
Saint Pat·rick's Day \-'pa-triks-\ n (1844) : March 17 observed by the Roman Catholic Church in honor of St. Patrick and celebrated in Ireland in commemoration of his death
saint's day n (15c) : a day in a church calendar on which a saint is commemorated
saint·ship \'sānt-,ship\ n (1631) : SAINTHOOD 1
Saint Val·en·tine's Day \-'va-lən-,tīnz-\ n [*St. Valentine* †ab270 Ital. priest] (14c) : February 14 observed in honor of St. Valentine and as a time for sending valentines
Saint Vi·tus' dance \-'vī-təs-, -'vī-tə-səz-\ n [*St. Vitus*, 3d cent. Christian child martyr] (1621) : CHOREA — called also *Saint Vitus's dance* *same*\
saith \'seth, 'sā-ith\ *archaic pres 3d sing of* SAY
saithe \'sāth, 'sāth\ n, pl **saithe** [of Scand origin; akin to ON *seithr* coalfish] (1632) : POLLACK
Sai·va \'sī-və, 'shī-\ n [Skt *Śaiva*, fr. *Śiva* Siva] (1810) : a member of a major Hindu sect devoted to the cult of Siva — **Sai·vism** \-,vi-zəm\ n
¹sake \'sāk\ n [ME, dispute, guilt, purpose, fr. OE *sacu* guilt, action at law; akin to OHG *sahha* action at law, cause, OE *sēcan* to seek — more at SEEK] (13c) **1 :** END, PURPOSE ⟨for the ~ of argument⟩ **2 a :** the good, advantage, or enhancement of some entity (as an ideal) ⟨free to pursue learning as its own ~ —M. S. Eisenhower⟩ **b :** personal or social welfare, safety, or benefit
²sa·ke *or* **sa·ki** \'sä-kē\ n [Jp *sake*] (1687) : a Japanese alcoholic beverage of fermented rice usu. served hot
sa·ker \'sā-kər\ n [ME *sagre*, fr. MF *sacre*, fr. Ar *ṣaqr*] (15c) : an Old World falcon (*Falco cherrug*) used in falconry
Sak·ti \'säk-tē, 'shäk-\, **Sak·tism** *var of* SHAKTI, SHAKTISM
sal \'sal\ n [ME, fr. L — more at SALT] (14c) : SALT

¹sa·laam \sə-'läm\ n [Ar *salām*, lit., peace] (1613) **1 :** a salutation or ceremonial greeting in the East **2 :** an obeisance performed by bowing very low and placing the right palm on the forehead
²salaam vt (1693) : to greet or pay homage to with a salaam ~ vi : to perform a salaam
sal·able *or* **sale·able** \'sā-lə-bəl\ adj (1530) : capable of being or fit to be sold : MARKETABLE — **sal·abil·i·ty** \,sā-lə-'bi-lə-tē\ n
sa·la·cious \sə-'lā-shəs\ adj [L *salac-, salax*, fr. *salire* to move spasmodically, leap — more at SALLY] (ca. 1645) **1 :** arousing or appealing to sexual desire or imagination : LASCIVIOUS **2 :** LECHEROUS, LUSTFUL — **sa·la·cious·ly** adv — **sa·la·cious·ness** n
sal·ad \'sa-ləd\ n [ME *salade*, fr. MF, fr. OProv *salada*, fr. *salar* to salt, fr. *sal* salt, fr. L] (14c) **1 a :** green vegetables (as lettuce, endive, or romaine) and often tomatoes, cucumbers, or radishes served with dressing **b :** a dish of meat, fish, shellfish, eggs, fruits, or vegetables singly or in combination usu. served cold with a dressing **2 :** a green vegetable or herb grown for salad; *esp* : LETTUCE **3 :** a usu. incongruous mixture : HODGEPODGE
salad bar n (1973) : a self-service counter (as in a restaurant) featuring an array of salad makings and dressings
salad days n pl (1606) : time of youthful inexperience or indiscretion ⟨my *salad days* when I was green in judgment —Shak.⟩; *also* : an early flourishing period : HEYDAY
salad dressing n (ca. 1839) : a dressing either uncooked (as French dressing) or cooked (as a boiled dressing) that is used for salad
salad oil n (1537) : an edible vegetable oil suitable for use in salad dressings
sa·lal \sə-'lal, sa-\ n [Chinook Jargon, fr. Lower Chinook *sálal*] (1825) : a small shrub (*Gaultheria shallon*) of the heath family found on the Pacific coast of No. America and bearing edible grape-sized dark purple berries
sal·a·man·der \'sa-lə-,man-dər *also* ,sa-lə-'\ n [ME *salamandre*, fr. MF, fr. L *salamandra*, fr. Gk] (14c) **1 :** a mythical animal having the power to endure fire without harm **2 :** an elemental being in the theory of Paracelsus inhabiting fire **3 :** any of numerous amphibians (order Caudata) superficially resembling lizards but scaleless and covered with a soft moist skin and breathing by gills in the larval stage **4** : an article used in connection with fire: as **a :** a cooking utensil for browning a food (as pastry or pudding) **b :** a portable stove **c :** a cooking device with an overhead heat source like a broiler — **sal·a·man·drine** \,sa-lə-'man-drən\ adj
sa·la·mi \sə-'lä-mē\ n [It, pl. of *salame* salami, fr. *salare* to salt, fr. *sale* salt, fr. L *sal* — more at SALT] (1852) : a highly seasoned sausage of pork and beef either dried or fresh
sal ammoniac n [ME *sal armoniak*, fr. L *sal ammoniacus*, lit., salt of Ammon] (14c) : AMMONIUM CHLORIDE
sa·lar·i·at \sə-'lar-ē-ət, -'ler-\ n [F, fr. *salaire* salary (fr. L *salarium*) + *-ariat* on the pattern of *prolétariat* proletariat] (1917) : the class or body of salaried persons usu. as distinguished from wage earners
sal·a·ry \'sal-rē, 'sa-lə-\ n, pl **-ries** [ME *salarie*, fr. L *salarium* pension, salary, fr. neut. of *salarius* of salt, fr. *sal* salt — more at SALT] (13c) : fixed compensation paid regularly for services — **sal·a·ried** \-rēd\ adj
sal·a·ry·man \-,man\ n [Jp *sarari-man*, fr. E *salary* + *man*] (1962) : a Japanese white-collar businessman
sal·chow \'sal-,kaú, -,kȯv, -(,)kō\ n [Ulrich *Salchow* †1949 Swed. figure skater] (1940) : a figure-skating jump with a takeoff from the back inside edge of one skate followed by a full turn in the air and a landing on the back outside edge of the opposite skate
sale \'sā(ə)l\ n [ME, fr. OE *sala*, fr. ON — more at SELL] (bef. 12c) **1** : the act of selling; *specif* : the transfer of ownership of and title to property from one person to another for a price **2 a :** opportunity of selling or being sold : DEMAND **b :** distribution by selling **3 :** public disposal to the highest bidder : AUCTION **4 :** a selling of goods at bargain prices **5** *pl* **a :** operations and activities involved in promoting and selling goods or services ⟨vice-president in charge of ~s⟩ **b** : gross receipts — **for sale :** available for purchase — **on sale 1** : for sale **2 :** available for purchase at a reduced price
sa·lep \'sa-ləp, -,lep\ n [F or Sp, both fr. Ar dial. *sahlab*, perh. alter. of Ar (*khuṣy ath-*)*tha'lab*, lit., testicles of the fox] (1736) : the starchy or mucilaginous dried tubers of various Old World orchids (esp. genus *Orchis*) used for food or in medicine
sal·e·ra·tus \,sa-lə-'rā-təs\ n [NL *sal aeratus* aerated salt] (1837) : a leavening agent consisting of potassium or sodium bicarbonate
sale·room \'sā(ə)l-,rüm, -,rúm\ *chiefly Brit var of* SALESROOM
sales \'sā(ə)lz\ adj (1913) : of, relating to, or used in selling
sales·clerk \'sā(ə)lz-,klərk\ n (1926) : a salesperson in a store
sales·girl \-,gər(-ə)l\ n (1887) : SALESWOMAN
Sa·le·sian \sə-'lē-zhən, sā-\ n (1884) : a member of the Society of St. Francis de Sales founded by St. John Bosco in Turin, Italy in the 19th century and devoted chiefly to education
sales·la·dy \'sā(ə)lz-,lā-dē\ n (1856) : SALESWOMAN
sales·man \'sā(ə)lz-mən\ n (1523) : one who sells in a given territory, in a store, or by telephone
sales·man·ship \-,ship\ n (1880) **1 :** the skill or art of selling **2** : ability or effectiveness in selling or in presenting persuasively ⟨political ~⟩
sales·peo·ple \-,pē-pəl\ n pl (1876) : persons employed to sell goods or services
sales·per·son \-,pər-sⁿn\ n (1901) : a salesman or saleswoman
sales·room \'sā(ə)lz-,rüm, -,rúm\ n (1840) : a place where goods are displayed for sale; *esp* : an auction room
sales slip n (1926) : a receipt for a purchase
sales tax n (1921) : a tax levied on the sale of goods and services that is usu. calculated as a percentage of the purchase price and collected by the seller

\ə\ abut \ᵊ\ kitten, F table \ər\ further \a\ ash \ā\ ace \ä\ mop, mar \aú\ out \ch\ chin \e\ bet \ē\ easy \g\ go \i\ hit \ī\ ice \j\ job \ŋ\ sing \ō\ go \ȯ\ law \ȯi\ boy \th\ thin \t̲h̲\ the \ü\ loot \ú\ foot \y\ yet \zh\ vision \á, k̲, ⁿ, œ, œ̄, ᵫ, ūᵊ, ᵞ\ *see* Guide to Pronunciation

sales·wom·an \'sā(ə)lz-ˌwu̇-mən\ n (1704) : a woman who sells in a given territory, in a store, or by telephone

sal·ic \'sa-lik\ adj [by alter.] (1902) : SIALIC

Sa·lic \'sā-lik, 'sa-\ adj [MF or ML; MF salique, fr. ML Salicus, fr. LL Salii Salic Franks] (ca. 1548) : of, relating to, or being a Frankish people that settled on the IJssel river early in the 4th century

sal·i·cin \'sa-lə-sən\ n [F salicine, fr. L salic-, salix willow — more at SALLOW] (1830) : a bitter white crystalline glucoside $C_{13}H_{18}O_7$ found in the bark and leaves of several willows and poplars and used in medicine like salicylic acid

Salic law n (1599) **1** : a rule held to derive from the legal code of the Salic Franks excluding females from the line of succession to a throne **2** : the legal code of the Salic Franks

sa·lic·y·late \sə-'li-sə-ˌlāt\ n (1842) : a salt or ester of salicylic acid

sal·i·cyl·ic acid \ˌsa-lə-'si-lik-\ n [ISV, fr. salicyl (the group HOC₆-H₄CO)] (1840) : a crystalline phenolic acid $C_7H_6O_3$ used esp. in the form of salts and other derivatives as an analgesic and antipyretic

sa·lience \'sā-lyən(t)s, -lē-ən(t)s\ n (1836) **1** : the quality or state of being salient **2** : a striking point or feature : HIGHLIGHT

sa·lien·cy \-lyən(t)-sē, -lē-ən(t)-\ n, pl -cies (1664) : SALIENCE

¹sa·lient \'sā-lyənt, -lē-ənt\ adj [L salient-, saliens, prp. of salire to leap — more at SALLY] (1646) **1** : moving by leaps or springs : JUMPING **2** : jetting upward ⟨a ~ fountain⟩ **3 a** : projecting beyond a line, surface, or level **b** : standing out conspicuously : PROMINENT; esp : of notable significance ⟨similar to . . . Prohibition, but there are a couple of ~ differences —Tony Gibbs⟩ **syn** see NOTICEABLE — **sa·lient·ly** adv

²salient n (1828) : something (as a promontory) that projects outward or upward from its surroundings; esp : an outwardly projecting part of a fortification, trench system, or line of defense

¹sa·line \'sā-ˌlēn, -ˌlīn\ adj [ME, fr. L salinus, fr. sal salt — more at SALT] (15c) **1** : consisting of or containing salt ⟨a ~ solution⟩ **2** : of, relating to, or resembling salt : SALTY ⟨a ~ taste⟩ **3** : consisting of or relating to the salts of the alkali metals or of magnesium ⟨a ~ cathartic⟩ — **sa·lin·i·ty** \sā-'li-nə-tē, sə-\ n

²saline n (1662) **1 a** : a metallic salt; esp : a salt of potassium, sodium, or magnesium with a cathartic action **2** : a saline solution; esp : one isotonic with body fluids

sa·li·nize \'sa-lə-ˌnīz also 'sā-\ vt **-nized; -niz·ing** (1926) : to treat or impregnate with salt — **sa·li·ni·za·tion** \ˌsa-lə-nə-'zā-shən also ˌsā-\ n

sa·li·nom·e·ter \ˌsa-lə-'nä-mə-tər, ˌsā-\ n [ISV saline + -o- + -meter] (1844) : an instrument (as a hydrometer) for measuring the amount of salt in a solution

Sa·lique \'sā-lik, 'sa-; sə-'lēk, sä-\ var of SALIC

Salis·bury steak \'so̐lz-ˌber-ē-, 'salz-, -b(ə-)rē-\ n [J. H. Salisbury, 19th cent. Eng. physician] (1897) : ground beef mixed with egg, milk, bread crumbs, and seasonings and formed into a large patty and cooked

Sa·lish \'sā-lish\ n (1831) **1** : a group of American Indian peoples of British Columbia and the northwestern U.S. **2** : the family of languages spoken by the Salish peoples — **Sa·lish·an** \-li-shən\ adj or n

sa·li·va \sə-'lī-və\ n [L] (15c) : a slightly alkaline secretion of water, mucin, protein, salts, and often a starch-splitting enzyme (as ptyalin) that is secreted into the mouth by salivary glands, lubricates ingested food, and often begins the breakdown of starches

sal·i·vary \'sa-lə-ˌver-ē\ adj (1709) : of or relating to saliva or the glands that secrete it; esp : producing or carrying saliva

sal·i·vate \'sa-lə-ˌvāt\ vi **-vat·ed; -vat·ing** (ca. 1706) **1** : to have a flow of saliva esp. in excess **2** : DROOL 2 — **sal·i·va·tion** \ˌsa-lə-'vā-shən\ n — **sal·i·va·tor** \'sa-lə-ˌvā-tər\ n

Salk vaccine \'so̐k-, 'so̐lk-\ n [Jonas Salk] (1954) : a vaccine consisting of poliomyelitis virus inactivated with formaldehyde

sal·let \'sa-lət\ n [ME, fr. MF sallade] (15c) : a light 15th century helmet with or without a visor and with a projection over the neck

¹sal·low \'sa-(ˌ)lō\ n [ME, fr. OE sealh; akin to OHG salha sallow, L salix willow] (bef. 12c) : any of several Old World broad-leaved willows (as Salix caprea) including important sources of charcoal and tanbark

²sallow adj [ME salowe, fr. OE salu; akin to OHG salo murky, Russ solovyĭ yellowish gray] (bef. 12c) : of a grayish greenish yellow color — **sal·low·ish** \'sa-lə-wish\ adj — **sal·low·ness** \'sa-lō-nəs, -lə-\ n

¹sal·ly \'sa-lē\ n, pl **sallies** [MF saillie, fr. OF, fr. saillir to rush forward, fr. L salire to leap; akin to Gk hallesthai to leap] (1560) **1** : an action of rushing or bursting forth; esp : a sortie of troops from a defensive position to attack the enemy **2 a** : a brief outbreak : OUTBURST **b** : a witty or imaginative saying : QUIP **3** : a venture or excursion usu. off the beaten track : JAUNT

²sally vi **sal·lied; sal·ly·ing** (1560) **1** : to leap out or burst forth suddenly **2** : SET OUT, DEPART — often used with forth

Sal·ly Lunn \ˌsa-lē-'lən\ n [Sally Lunn, 18th cent. Eng. baker] (1780) : a slightly sweetened yeast-leavened bread

sally port n (1649) : a gate or passage in a fortified place for use by troops making a sortie

sal·ma·gun·di \ˌsal-mə-'gən-dē\ n [F salmigondis] (ca. 1674) **1 a** : a salad plate of chopped meats, anchovies, eggs, and vegetables arranged in rows for contrast and dressed with a salad dressing **2** : a heterogeneous mixture : POTPOURRI

sal·mi \'sal-mē\ n [F salmis, short for salmigondis] (1759) : a ragout of partly roasted game stewed in a rich sauce

salm·on \'sa-mən\ n, pl **salmon** also **salmons** [ME samon, fr. MF, fr. L salmon-, salmo] (13c) **1 a** : a large anadromous salmonid fish (Salmo salar) of the No. Atlantic noted as a game and food fish — called also Atlantic salmon **b** : any of various anadromous salmonid fishes other than the salmon; esp : PACIFIC SALMON **c** : a fish (as a barramunda) resembling a salmon **2** : the variable color of salmon's flesh averaging a strong yellowish pink

salm·on·ber·ry \-ˌber-ē\ n (1844) : a showy red-flowered raspberry (Rubus spectabilis) of the Pacific coast; also : its edible salmon-colored fruit

sal·mo·nel·la \ˌsal-mə-'ne-lə\ n, pl **-nel·lae** \-'ne-(ˌ)lē, -ˌlī\ or **-nellas** or **-nella** [NL, fr. Daniel E. Salmon †1914 Am. veterinarian] (1913) : any of a genus (Salmonella) of usu. motile enterobacteria that are pathogenic for humans and other warm-blooded animals and cause food poisoning, gastrointestinal inflammation, typhoid fever, or septicemia

sal·mo·nel·lo·sis \ˌsal-mə-(ˌ)ne-'lō-səs\ n, pl **-lo·ses** \-ˌsēz\ [NL] (ca. 1913) : infection with or disease caused by salmonellae

sal·mo·nid \'sa-mə-nid, 'sal-\ n [NL Salmonidae, fr. Salmon-, Salmo, genus name, fr. L salmo salmon] (1868) : any of a family (Salmonidae) of elongate bony fishes (as a salmon or trout) that have the last three vertebrae upturned — **salmonid** adj

salm·on·oid \'sa-mə-ˌno̐id\ n (ca. 1842) : SALMONID; also : a related fish — **salmonoid** adj

salmon pink n (1882) : a strong yellowish pink

Sa·lo·me \sə-'lō-mē, 'sa-lə-\ n [LL, fr. Gk Salōmē] : a niece of Herod Antipas given the head of John the Baptist as a reward for her dancing

sa·lom·e·ter \sā-'lä-mə-tər, sə-\ n [L sal salt + E -o- + -meter] (1860) : a hydrometer for indicating the percentage of salt in a solution

sa·lon \sə-'län, 'sa-ˌlän, sa-'lōⁿ\ n [F] (1699) **1** : an elegant apartment or living room (as in a fashionable home) **2** : a fashionable assemblage of notables (as literary figures, artists, or statesmen) held by custom at the home of a prominent person **3 a** : a hall for exhibition of art **b** cap : an annual exhibition of works of art **4** : a stylish business establishment or shop ⟨a beauty ~⟩

sa·loon \sə-'lün\ n [F salon, fr. It salone, aug. of sala hall, of Gmc origin; akin to OHG sal hall; akin to Lith sala village] (1728) **1** a chiefly Brit : SALON 1 **b** chiefly Brit : an often elaborately decorated public hall **c** (1) : a usu. large public cabin on a ship (as for dining) (2) : the living area on a yacht **d** chiefly Brit : SALON 4 **e** : BARROOM 2 : SALON 2 **3** Brit **a** : PARLOR CAR **b** : SEDAN 2a — called also saloon car

salp \'salp\ also **sal·pa** \'sal-pə\ n [NL, fr. L, a kind of deep-sea fish, fr. Gk salpē] (1835) : any of various transparent barrel-shaped or fusiform free-swimming tunicates (class Thaliacea) abundant in warm seas

sal·pi·glos·sis \ˌsal-pə-'glä-səs\ n [NL, irreg. fr. Gk salpinx trumpet + glōssa tongue — more at GLOSS] (1827) : any of a small genus (Salpiglossis) of Chilean herbs of the nightshade family with large funnel-shaped varicolored flowers often strikingly marked

sal·pin·gi·tis \ˌsal-pən-'jī-təs\ n [NL, fr. salping-, salpinx fallopian or eustachian tube, fr. Gk, trumpet] (1860) : inflammation of a fallopian or eustachian tube

sal·sa \'sȯl-sə, 'säl-\ n [Sp, lit., sauce, fr. L, fem. of salsus salted — more at SAUCE] (ca. 1962) **1** : a spicy sauce of tomatoes, onions, and hot peppers **2** : popular music of Latin American origin that has absorbed characteristics of rhythm and blues, jazz, and rock

sal·si·fy \'sal-sə-fē, -ˌfī\ n [F salsifis, fr. It salsefica, sassefrica] (ca. 1706) : a European biennial composite herb (Tragopogon porrifolius) with a long fusiform edible root — called also oyster plant, vegetable oyster

sal soda n (15c) : WASHING SODA

¹salt \'so̐lt\ n [ME, fr. OE sealt; akin to OHG salz salt, Lith saldus sweet, L sal salt, Gk hals salt, sea] (bef. 12c) **1 a** : a crystalline compound NaCl that consists of sodium chloride, is abundant in nature, and is used esp. to season or preserve food or in industry — called also common salt **b** : a substance (as washing soda) resembling common salt **c** pl (1) : a mineral or saline mixture (as Epsom salts) used as an aperient or cathartic (2) : SMELLING SALTS **d** : any of numerous compounds that result from replacement of part or all of the acid hydrogen of an acid by a metal or a group acting like a metal : an ionic crystalline compound **2** : a container for salt at table — often used in the phrases above the salt and below the salt alluding to the former custom of seating persons of higher rank above and those of lower rank below a saltcellar placed in the middle of a long table **3 a** : an ingredient that gives savor, piquancy, or zest : FLAVOR ⟨a people . . . full of life, vigor, and the ~ of personality —Clifton Fadiman⟩ **b** : sharpness of wit : PUNGENCY **c** : COMMON SENSE **d** : RESERVE, SKEPTICISM — usu. used in the phrases with a grain of salt and with a pinch of salt **e** : a dependable steadfast person or group of people — usu. used in the phrase salt of the earth **4** : SAILOR ⟨a tale worthy of an old ~⟩ **5** : KEEP 3 — usu. used in the phrase worth one's salt — **salt·like** \-ˌlīk\ adj

²salt vt (bef. 12c) **1 a** : to treat, provide, or season with common salt **b** : to preserve (food) with salt or in brine **c** : to supply (as an animal) with salt **2** : to give flavor or piquancy to (as a story) **3** : to enrich (as a mine) artificially by secretly placing valuable mineral in some of the working places **4** : to sprinkle with or as if with a salt — **salt·er** \'so̐l-tər\ n

³salt adj (bef. 12c) **1 a** : SALINE, SALTY **b** : being or inducing the one of the four basic taste sensations that is suggestive of seawater — compare BITTER, SOUR, SWEET **2** : cured or seasoned with salt : SALTED **3** : overflowed with salt water ⟨a ~ pond⟩ **4** : SHARP, PUNGENT — **salt·ness** n

⁴salt adj [by shortening & alter. fr. assaut, fr. ME a sawt, fr. MF a saut, lit., on the jump] (1598) obs : LUSTFUL, LASCIVIOUS

salt-and-pepper adj (1915) : having black-and-white or dark and light color intermingled in small flecks ⟨a ~ suit⟩

sal·ta·rel·lo \ˌsal-tə-'re-(ˌ)lō, ˌsäl-\ n, pl **-los** [It, fr. saltare to jump, fr. L] (ca. 1724) : an Italian dance with a lively hop step beginning each measure

sal·ta·tion \sal-'tā-shən, so̐l-\ n [L saltation-, saltatio, fr. saltare to leap, dance, freq. of salire to leap — more at SALLY] (1646) **1 a** : the action or process of leaping or jumping **b** : DANCE **2 a** : the origin of a new species or a higher taxon in essentially a single evolutionary step that in some esp. former theories is held to be due to a major mutation or to unknown causes — compare DARWINISM, NEO-DARWINISM, PUNCTUATED EQUILIBRIUM **b** : MUTATION — used esp. of bacteria and fungi

sal·ta·to·ri·al \ˌsal-tə-'tȯr-ē-əl, ˌso̐l-, -'tȯr-\ adj (1789) : relating to, marked by, or adapted for leaping ⟨~ legs of a grasshopper⟩

sal·ta·to·ry \'sal-tə-ˌtȯr-ē, 'so̐l-, -ˌtȯr-\ adj (1656) **1** archaic : of or relating to dancing **2** : proceeding by leaps rather than by gradual transitions : DISCONTINUOUS

salt away vt (ca. 1890) : to lay away (as money) safely : SAVE

salt·box \'so̐lt-ˌbäks\ n (1876) : a frame

saltbox

dwelling with two stories in front and one behind and a roof with a long rear slope

salt·bush \-,bůsh\ *n* (1863) : any of various shrubby plants of the goosefoot family that thrive in dry alkaline soil; *esp* : any of numerous oraches that are important browse plants in dry regions

salt·cel·lar \'sôlt-,se-lər\ *n* [ME *salt saler*, fr. *salt* + *saler* saltcellar, fr. MF, fr. L *salarius* of salt — more at SALARY] (14c) : a small container for holding salt at the table

salt dome *n* (1908) : a domical anticline in sedimentary rock that has a mass of rock salt as its core

salt flat *n* (1816) : a salt-encrusted flat area resulting from evaporation of a former body of water

salt gland *n* (1950) : a gland (as of a marine bird) capable of excreting a concentrated salt solution

salt grass *n* (1704) : a grass (esp. *Distichlis spicata*) native to an alkaline habitat (as a salt marsh)

sal·tim·boc·ca \,sôl-təm-'bô-kə\ *n* [It, fr. *saltare* to jump + *in* in + *bocca* mouth] (1937) : scallops of veal prepared with sage, slices of ham, and sometimes cheese and served with a wine sauce

sal·tine \sôl-'tēn\ *n* (1907) : a thin crisp cracker usu. sprinkled with salt

salt·ing \'sôl-tiŋ\ *n* (1712) *chiefly Brit* : land flooded regularly by tides — usu. used in pl.

sal·tire \'sôl-,tīr, 'sal-\ *n* [ME *sautire*, fr. MF *saultoir* X-shaped animal barricade that can be jumped over by people, saltire, fr. *saulter* to jump, fr. L *saltare* — more at SALTATION] (14c) : a heraldic charge consisting of a cross formed by a bend and a bend sinister crossing in the center

salt lake *n* (1763) : a landlocked body of water that has become salty through evaporation

salt·less \'sôlt-ləs\ *adj* (14c) 1 : having no salt 2 : INSIPID

salt lick *n* (1751) : LICK 3

salt marsh *n* (bef. 12c) : flat land subject to overflow by salt water

salt out *vt* (1939) : to precipitate, coagulate, or separate (as a dissolved substance or lyophilic sol) esp. from a solution by the addition of salt ~ *vi* : to become salted out

salt pan *n* (15c) : an undrained natural depression in which water gathers and leaves a deposit of salt on evaporation

salt·pe·ter \'sôlt-'pē-tər\ *n* [ME *salt petre*, alter. of *salpetre*, fr. MF, fr. ML *sal petrae*, lit., salt of the rock] (14c) 1 : POTASSIUM NITRATE 2 : SODIUM NITRATE

salt pork *n* (1723) : fat pork cured in salt or brine

salt·shak·er \'sôlt-,shā-kər\ *n* (1895) : a container with a perforated top for sprinkling salt

salt·wa·ter \'sôlt-,wô-tər, -,wä-\ *adj* (bef. 12c) : relating to, living in, located near, or consisting of salt water

salt·works \'sôlt-,wərks\ *n pl but sing or pl in constr* (1565) : a plant where salt is prepared commercially

salt·wort \-,wərt, -,wôrt\ *n* (1568) 1 : any of a genus (*Salsola*) of plants (as the Russian thistle) of the goosefoot family of which some have been used in making soda ash 2 : a low-growing strong-smelling coastal shrub (*Batis maritima* of the family Bataceae) of warm parts of the New World

salty \'sôl-tē\ *adj* **salt·i·er; -est** (15c) 1 : of, seasoned with, or containing salt 2 : smacking of the sea or nautical life 3 a : PIQUANT b : EARTHY, CRUDE ⟨~ language⟩ — **salt·i·ly** \-tə-lē\ *adv* — **salt·i·ness** \-tē-nəs\ *n*

sa·lu·bri·ous \sə-'lü-brē-əs\ *adj* [L *salubris*; akin to *salvus* safe, healthy — more at SAFE] (1547) : favorable to or promoting health or well-being *syn* see HEALTHFUL — **sa·lu·bri·ous·ly** *adv* — **sa·lu·bri·ous·ness** *n* — **sa·lu·bri·ty** \-'brə-tē\ *n*

sa·lu·ki \sə-'lü-kē\ *n* [Ar *salūqiy* of Saluq, fr. *Salūq* Saluq, ancient city in Arabia] (1809) : any of an ancient northern African and Asian breed of tall swift slender hunting dogs having long narrow heads, long silky ears, and a smooth silky coat

sal·u·tary \'sal-yə-,ter-ē\ *adj* [MF *salutaire*, fr. L *salutaris*, fr. *salut-, salus* health] (15c) 1 : producing a beneficial effect : REMEDIAL ⟨~ influences⟩ 2 : promoting health : CURATIVE *syn* see HEALTHFUL — **sal·u·tar·i·ly** \,sal-yə-'ter-ə-lē\ *adv* — **sal·u·tar·i·ness** \'sal-yə-,ter-ē-nəs\ *n*

sal·u·ta·tion \,sal-yə-'tā-shən\ *n* (14c) 1 a : an expression of greeting, goodwill, or courtesy by word, gesture, or ceremony b *pl* : REGARDS 2 : the word or phrase of greeting (as *Gentlemen* or *Dear Sir* or *Madam*) that conventionally comes immediately before the body of a letter — **sal·u·ta·tion·al** \-shnəl, -shə-n'l\ *adj*

sa·lu·ta·to·ri·an \sə-,lü-tə-'tôr-ē-ən, -'tôr-\ *n* (ca. 1847) : the student usu. having the second highest rank in a graduating class who delivers the salutatory address at the commencement exercises

1sa·lu·ta·to·ry \sə-'lü-tə-,tôr-ē, -,tôr-\ *adj* (1702) : of or relating to a salutation : expressing or containing a welcome or greeting

2salutatory *n, pl* **-ries** (1779) : an address or statement of welcome or greeting

1sa·lute \sə-'lüt\ *vb* **sa·lut·ed; sa·lut·ing** [ME, fr. L *salutare*, fr. *salut-, salus* health, safety, greeting, fr. *salvus* safe, healthy — more at SAFE] *vt* (14c) 1 a : to address with expressions of kind wishes, courtesy, or honor b : to give a sign of respect, courtesy, or goodwill to : GREET 2 : to become apparent to (one of the senses) 3 a : to honor (as a person, nation, or event) by a conventional military or naval ceremony b : to show respect and recognition to (a military superior) by assuming a prescribed position c : to express commendation of : PRAISE ~ *vi* : to make a salute — **sa·lut·er** *n*

2salute *n* (14c) 1 : GREETING, SALUTATION 2 a : a sign, token, or ceremony expressing goodwill, compliment, or respect ⟨the festival was a ~ to the arts⟩ b : the position (as of the hand) or the entire attitude of a person saluting a superior 3 : FIRECRACKER

sal·u·tif·er·ous \,sal-yə-'ti-f(ə-)rəs\ *adj* [L *salutifer*, fr. *salut-, salus* + -*i-* + -*fer* -ferous] (ca. 1540) : SALUTARY

salv·able \'sal-və-bəl\ *adj* [LL *salvare* to save — more at SAVE] (1667) : capable of being saved or salvaged

1sal·vage \'sal-vij\ *n* [F, fr. MF, fr. *salver* to save — more at SAVE] (1645) 1 a : compensation paid for saving a ship or its cargo from the perils of the sea or for the lives and property rescued in a wreck b : the act of saving or rescuing a ship or its cargo c : the act of saving or rescuing property in danger (as from fire) 2 a : property saved

from destruction in a calamity (as a wreck or fire) b : something extracted (as from rubbish) as valuable or useful

2salvage *vt* **sal·vaged; sal·vag·ing** (1889) : to rescue or save esp. from wreckage or ruin — **sal·vage·abil·i·ty** \,sal-vi-jə-'bi-lə-tē\ *n* — **sal·vage·able** \'sal-vi-jə-bəl\ *adj* — **sal·vag·er** *n*

sal·var·san \'sal-vər-,san\ *n* [fr. *Salvarsan*, a trademark] (1909) : ARSPHENAMINE

sal·va·tion \sal-'vā-shən\ *n* [ME, fr. OF, fr. LL *salvation-, salvatio*, fr. *salvare* to save — more at SAVE] (13c) 1 a : deliverance from the power and effects of sin b : the agent or means that effects salvation c *Christian Science* : the realization of the supremacy of infinite Mind over all bringing with it the destruction of the illusion of sin, sickness, and death 2 : liberation from ignorance or illusion 3 a : preservation from destruction or failure b : deliverance from danger or difficulty — **sal·va·tion·al** \-shnəl, -shə-n'l\ *adj*

Salvation Army *n* (1878) : an international religious and charitable group organized on military lines and founded in 1865 by William Booth for evangelizing and social betterment (as of the poor)

sal·va·tion·ism \sal-'vā-shə-,ni-zəm\ *n* (1883) : religious teaching emphasizing the saving of the soul

Sal·va·tion·ist \-sh(ə-)nist\ *n* (1882) 1 : a soldier or officer of the Salvation Army 2 *often not cap* : EVANGELIST — **salvationist** *adj, often cap*

1salve \'sav, 'säv, 'sav, 'salv, 'sälv\ *n* [ME, fr. OE *sealf*; akin to OHG *salba* salve, Gk *olpē* oil flask] (bef. 12c) 1 : an unctuous adhesive substance for application to wounds or sores 2 : a remedial or soothing influence or agency ⟨a ~ to their hurt feelings⟩

2salve *vt* **salved; salv·ing** (bef. 12c) 1 : to remedy (as disease) with or as if with a salve 2 : QUIET, ASSUAGE ⟨give him a raise in salary to ~ his feelings —Upton Sinclair⟩

3salve \'salv\ *vt* **salved; salv·ing** [back-formation fr. *salvage*] (ca. 1706) : SALVAGE — **salv·or** \'sal-vər, -,vôr\ *n*

sal·ver \'sal-vər\ *n* [modif. of F *salve*, fr. Sp *salva* sampling of food to detect poison, tray, fr. *salvar* to save, sample food to detect poison, fr. LL *salvare* to save — more at SAVE] (ca. 1661) : a tray esp. for serving food or beverages

sal·ver·form \'sal-vər-,fôrm\ *adj* (1821) : tubular with a spreading limb — used of a gamopetalous corolla

sal·via \'sal-vē-ə\ *n* [NL, fr. L, sage — more at SAGE] (1601) : any of a large and widely distributed genus (*Salvia*) of herbs and shrubs of the mint family having a 2-lipped open calyx and two anthers; *esp* : one (*S. splendens*) with scarlet flowers

sal·vif·ic \sal-'vi-fik\ *adj* [LL *salvificus*, fr. L *salvus* safe + -*ficus* -fic] (1591) : having the intent or power to save or redeem ⟨the ~ life and death of Christ —E. A. Walsh⟩

1sal·vo \'sal-(,)vō\ *n, pl* **salvos** *or* **salvoes** [It *salva*, fr. F *salve*, fr. L, hail!, fr. *salvus* healthy — more at SAVE] (1591) 1 a : a simultaneous discharge of two or more guns in military action or as a salute b : the release all at one time of a rack of bombs or rockets (as from an airplane) c : a series of shots by an artillery battery with each gun firing one round in turn after a prescribed interval d : the bombs or projectiles released in a salvo 2 : something suggestive of a salvo: a : a sudden burst ⟨a ~ of cheers⟩ b : a spirited attack ⟨the first ~ of a political campaign⟩

2salvo *vt* (1839) : to release a salvo of ~ *vi* : to fire a salvo

3salvo *n, pl* **salvos** [ML *salvo jure* with the right reserved] (1621) 1 : a mental reservation : PROVISO 2 : a means of safeguarding one's name or honor or allaying one's conscience : SALVE

sal vo·la·ti·le \,sal-və-'la-t'l-ē\ *n* [NL, lit., volatile salt] (1654) : SMELLING SALTS

SAM \'sam, ,es-(,)ā-'em\ *n* (1950) : a surface-to-air missile

sa·ma·ra \'sa-mə-rə; sə-'mar-ə, -'mär-\ *n* [NL, fr. L, seed of the elm] (1577) : a dry indehiscent usu. one-seeded winged fruit (as of an ash or elm tree) — called also **key**

Sa·mar·i·tan \sə-'mar-ə-t'n, -'mer-\ *n* [ME, fr. OE, fr. LL *samaritanus*, n. & adj., fr. Gk *Samaritēs* inhabitant of Samaria, fr. *Samaria*] (bef. 12c) 1 : a native or inhabitant of Samaria 2 [fr. the parable of the good Samaritan in Lk 10:30–37] : one ready and generous in helping those in distress — **samaritan** *adj, often cap*

sa·mar·i·um \sə-'mer-ē-əm, -'mar-\ *n* [NL, fr. F *samarskite*] (1879) : a pale gray lustrous metallic element used esp. in alloys that form permanent magnets — see ELEMENT table

sa·mar·skite \sə-'mär-,skīt, 'sa-mər-\ *n* [G *Samarskit*, fr. V. E. *Samarskiĭ*-Bykhovets †1870 Russ. mining engineer] (1849) : a black or brownish black orthorhombic mineral that is a complex oxide of rare earths, uranium, iron, lead, thorium, niobium, tantalum, and tin

sam·ba \'sam-bə, 'säm-\ *n* [Pg] (1885) : a Brazilian dance of African origin with a basic pattern of step-close-step-close and characterized by a dip and spring upward at each beat of the music; *also* : the music for this dance — **samba** *vi*

sam·bar *or* **sam·bur** \'säm-bər, 'sam-\ *n* [Hindi *sābar*, fr. Skt *śambara*] (1698) : a large Asian deer (*Cervus unicolor*) with the male having strong 3-pointed antlers and long coarse hair on the throat

sam·bo \'sam-(,)bō, 'säm-\ *n* [Russ, fr. *samozashchita bez oruzhiya* self-defense without weapons] (1972) : an international style of wrestling employing judo techniques

Sam Browne \'sam-'braůn\ *n* [Sir *Samuel James Browne* †1901 Brit. army officer] (1915) : a leather belt for a dress uniform supported by a light strap passing over the right shoulder

1same \'sām\ *adj* [ME, fr. ON *samr*; akin to OHG *sama* same, L *simulis* like, *simul* together, at the same time, *similis* like, *sem-* one, Gk *homos* same, *hama* together, *hen-, heis* one] (13c) 1 a : resembling in every relevant respect b : conforming in every respect — used with *as* 2 a : being one without addition, change, or discontinuance : IDENTICAL b : being the one under discussion or already referred to 3 : corresponding so closely as to be indistinguishable 4 : equal in size, shape,

\ə\ abut \'\ kitten, F table \ər\ further \a\ ash \ā\ ace \ä\ mop, mar \aů\ out \ch\ chin \e\ bet \ē\ easy \g\ go \i\ hit \ī\ ice \j\ job \ŋ\ sing \ō\ go \ò\ law \ói\ boy \th\ thin \th\ the \ü\ loot \ů\ foot \y\ yet \zh\ vision \à, k, n, œ, œ, ue, ūe, '\ see Guide to Pronunciation value, or importance — usu. used with *the* or a demonstrative (as *that, those*) in all senses

syn SAME, SELFSAME, VERY, IDENTICAL, EQUIVALENT, EQUAL mean not different or not differing from one another. SAME may imply and SELFSAME always implies that the things under consideration are one thing and not two or more things ⟨took the *same* route⟩ ⟨derived from the *selfsame* source⟩. VERY, like SELFSAME, may imply identity, or, like SAME, may imply likeness in kind ⟨the *very* point I was trying to make⟩. IDENTICAL may imply selfsameness or suggest absolute agreement in all details ⟨their test answers were *identical*⟩. EQUIVALENT implies amounting to the same thing in worth or significance ⟨two houses *equivalent* in market value⟩. EQUAL implies being identical in value, magnitude, or some specified quality ⟨*equal* shares in the business⟩.

²**same** *pron* (14c) **1** : something identical with or similar to another **2** : something or someone previously mentioned or described — often used with *the* or a demonstrative (as *that, those*) in both senses — **all the same** *or* **just the same** : despite everything : NEVERTHELESS

³**same** *adv* (1766) **1** : in the same manner — used with *the* or a demonstrative (as *that, those*)

sa·mekh \'sä-ˌmek\ *n* [Heb *sāmekh*] (1823) : the 15th letter of the Hebrew alphabet — see ALPHABET table

same·ness \'säm-nəs\ *n* (1581) **1** : the quality or state of being the same : IDENTITY, SIMILARITY **2** : MONOTONY, UNIFORMITY

sam·i·sen \'sa-mə-ˌsen\ *n* [Jp] (1864) : a 3-stringed Japanese musical instrument resembling a banjo

sa·mite \'sa-ˌmīt, 'sā-\ *n* [ME *samit*, fr. MF, fr. ML *examitum, samitum*, fr. MGk *hexamiton*, fr. Gk, neut. of *hexamitos* of six threads, fr. *hexa-* + *mitos* thread of the warp] (13c) : a rich medieval silk fabric interwoven with gold or silver

sa·miz·dat \'sä-mēz-ˌdät\ *n* [Russ, fr. *sam-* self + *izdatel*'stvo publishing house] (1967) : a system in the U.S.S.R. and countries within its orbit by which government-suppressed literature was clandestinely printed and distributed; *also* : such literature

sam·let \'sam-lət\ *n* [irreg. fr. *salmon* + *-let*] (1655) : PARR

Sam·mar·i·nese \ˌ(ˌ)sa(m)-ˌmar-ə-'nēz, -'nēs\ *n, pl* **-ne·si** \-'nä-zē\ [It *sammarinese*, fr. *San Marino*] (1938) : a native or inhabitant of San Marino

Sam·nite \'sam-ˌnīt\ *n* [*Samnium*, Italy] (14c) : a member of an ancient people of central Italy

Sa·mo·an \sə-'mō-ən\ *n* (1846) **1** : the Polynesian language of the Samoans **2** : a native or inhabitant of Samoa — **Samoan** *adj*

Samoa time *n* (1983) : the time of the 11th time zone west of Greenwich that includes American Samoa

sam·o·var \'sa-mə-ˌvär\ *n* [Russ, fr. *samo-* self + *varit*' to boil] (1830) **1** : an urn with a spigot at its base used esp. in Russia to boil water for tea **2** : an urn similar to a Russian samovar with a device for heating the contents

samovar 1

Sam·o·yed *also* **Sam·o·yede** \'sa-mə-ˌyed, -ˌmȯi-\ *n* [Russ *samoed*] (1589) **1** : a member of any of a group of peoples inhabiting the far north of European Russia and parts of northwestern Siberia **2** : the family of Uralic languages spoken by the Samoyed people **3** : any of a Siberian breed of medium-sized white or cream-colored sled dogs — **Samoyed** *adj* — **Sam·o·yed·ic** \ˌsa-mə-'ye-dik, -ˌmȯi-\ *adj*

samp \'samp\ *n* [modif. of Narraganset *nasáump* corn mush] (1643) : coarse hominy or a boiled cereal made from it

sam·pan \'sam-ˌpan\ *n* [Chin (Guangdong) *sàam-báan*, fr. *sàam* three + *báan* board, plank] (1620) : a flat-bottomed Chinese skiff usu. propelled by two short oars

sam·phire \'sam-ˌfīr\ *n* [alter. of earlier *sampiere*, fr. MF (*herbe de*) *Saint Pierre*, lit., St. Peter's herb] (1545) **1** : a fleshy European seacoast plant (*Crithmum maritimum*) of the carrot family that is sometimes pickled **2** : a common glasswort (*Salicornia europaea*) that is sometimes pickled

¹**sam·ple** \'sam-pəl\ *n* [ME, fr. MF *essample*, fr. L *exemplum* — more at EXAMPLE] (15c) **1** : a representative part or a single item from a larger whole or group esp. when presented for inspection or shown as evidence of quality : SPECIMEN **2** : a finite part of a statistical population whose properties are studied to gain information about the whole **syn** see INSTANCE

²**sample** *vt* **sam·pled; sam·pling** \-p(ə-)liŋ\ (1767) : to take a sample of or from; *esp* : to judge the quality of by a sample : TEST ⟨*sampled* his output for defects⟩ ⟨~ a wine⟩

³**sample** *adj* (1820) : serving as an illustration or example ⟨~ questions⟩

¹**sam·pler** \'sam-plər\ *n* (1523) : a decorative piece of needlework typically having letters or verses embroidered on it in various stitches as an example of skill

²**sam·pler** \-p(ə-)lər\ *n* (1778) **1** : one that collects, prepares, or examines samples **2** : something containing representative specimens or selections ⟨a ~ of nineteen poets —K. E. Judd⟩; *also* : ASSORTMENT

sample space *n* (1951) : a set in which all of the possible outcomes of a statistical experiment are represented

sam·pling \'sam-pliŋ, *for 1 & 3* -p(ə-)liŋ\ *n* (1778) **1** : the act, process, or technique of selecting a suitable sample; *specif* : the act, process, or technique of selecting a representative part of a population for the purpose of determining parameters or characteristics of the whole population **2** : a small part selected as a sample for inspection or analysis ⟨ask a ~ of people which candidate they favor⟩ **3** : the introduction or promotion of a product by distributing trial packages of it

sam·sa·ra \səm-'sär-ə\ *n* [Skt *saṃsāra*, lit., passing through] (1886) : the indefinitely repeated cycles of birth, misery, and death caused by karma

Sam·son \'sam(p)-sən\ *n* [LL, fr. Gk *Sampsōn*, fr. Heb *Shimshōn*] : a Hebrew hero who wreaked havoc among the Philistines by means of his great strength

Sam·so·ni·an \sam(p)-'sō-nē-ən\ *adj* [*Samson*] (ca. 1623) : of heroic strength or proportions : MIGHTY

Sam·u·el \'sam-yə-wəl, -yəl\ *n* [LL, fr. Gk *Samouel*, fr. Heb *Shĕmū'ēl*]

1 : the early Hebrew judge who successively anointed Saul and David king **2** : either of two narrative and historical books of canonical Jewish and Christian Scriptures — see BIBLE table

sam·u·rai \'sa-mə-ˌrī, 'sam-yə-\ *n, pl* **samurai** [Jp] (1727) **1** : a military retainer of a Japanese daimyo practicing the code of conduct of Bushido **2** : the warrior aristocracy of Japan

San \'sän\ *n* (1876) **1** *pl in constr* : BUSHMEN **2** : BUSHMAN 2

san·a·tive \'sa-nə-tiv\ *adj* [ME *sanatif*, fr. MF, fr. LL *sanativus*, fr. L *sanatus*, pp. of *sanare* to cure, fr. *sanus* healthy] (15c) : having the power to cure or heal : CURATIVE, RESTORATIVE

san·a·to·ri·um \ˌsa-nə-'tōr-ē-əm, -'tȯr-\ *n, pl* **-riums** *or* **-ria** \-ē-ə\ [NL, fr. LL, neut. of *sanatorius* curative, fr. *sanare*] (1839) **1** : an establishment that provides therapy combined with a regimen (as of diet and exercise) for treatment or rehabilitation **2 a** : an institution for rest and recuperation (as of convalescents) **b** : an establishment for the treatment of the chronically ill

san·be·ni·to \ˌsan-bə-'nē-(ˌ)tō, ˌsam-\ *n, pl* **-tos** [Sp *sambenito*, fr. *San Benito* St. Benedict of Nursia] (ca. 1560) **1** : a sackcloth coat worn by penitents on being reconciled to the church **2** : a Spanish Inquisition garment resembling a scapular and being either yellow with red crosses for the penitent or black with painted devils and flames for the impenitent condemned to an auto-da-fé

San·cerre \sä-ser\ *n* [*Sancerre*, village in France] (ca. 1946) : a dry white wine from the Loire valley of France

San·cho Pan·za \ˌsan-chō-'pan-zə, ˌsän-chō-'pän-\ *n* [Sp] : the squire of Don Quixote in Cervantes' *Don Quixote*

sanc·ti·fi·ca·tion \ˌsaŋ(k)-tə-fə-'kā-shən\ *n* (14c) **1** : an act of sanctifying **2 a** : the state of being sanctified **b** : the state of growing in divine grace as a result of Christian commitment after baptism or conversion

sanc·ti·fi·er \'saŋ(k)-tə-ˌfī(-ə)r\ *n* (1548) : one that sanctifies; *specif, cap* : HOLY SPIRIT

sanc·ti·fy \-ˌfī\ *vt* **-fied; -fy·ing** [ME *sanctifien*, fr. MF *sanctifier*, fr. LL *sanctificare*, fr. L *sanctus* sacred — more at SAINT] (14c) **1** : to set apart to a sacred purpose or to religious use : CONSECRATE **2** : to free from sin : PURIFY **3 a** : to impart or impute sacredness, inviolability, or respect to **b** : to give moral or social sanction to **4** : to make productive of holiness or piety ⟨observe the day of the sabbath, to ~ it — Deut 5:12 (DV)⟩

sanc·ti·mo·nious \ˌsaŋ(k)-tə-'mō-nē-əs, -nyəs\ *adj* (1603) **1** : affecting piousness : hypocritically devout; *also* : indicative of affected piousness ⟨the king's ~ rebuke —G. B. Shaw⟩ **2** *obs* : possessing sanctity : HOLY — **sanc·ti·mo·nious·ly** *adv* — **sanc·ti·mo·nious·ness** *n*

sanc·ti·mo·ny \'saŋ(k)-tə-ˌmō-nē\ *n, pl* **-nies** [MF *sanctimonie*, fr. L *sanctimonia*, fr. *sanctus*] (ca. 1541) **1** *obs* : HOLINESS **2** : affected or hypocritical holiness

¹**sanc·tion** \'saŋ(k)-shən\ *n* [MF or L; MF, fr. L *sanction-*, *sanctio*, fr. *sancire* to make holy — more at SACRED] (15c) **1** : a formal decree; *esp* : an ecclesiastical decree **2 a** *obs* : a solemn agreement : OATH **b** : something that makes an oath binding **3** : the detriment, loss of reward, or coercive intervention annexed to a violation of a law as a means of enforcing the law **4 a** : a consideration, principle, or influence (as of conscience) that impels to moral action or determines moral judgment **b** : a mechanism of social control for enforcing a society's standards **c** : explicit or official approval, permission, or ratification : APPROBATION **5** : an economic or military coercive measure adopted usu. by several nations in concert for forcing a nation violating international law to desist or yield to adjudication

²**sanction** *vt* **sanc·tioned; sanc·tion·ing** \-sh(ə-)niŋ\ (1778) **1** : to make valid or binding usu. by a formal procedure (as ratification) **2** : to give effective or authoritative approval or consent to **syn** see APPROVE — **sanc·tion·able** \-sh(ə-)nə-bəl\ *adj*

sanc·ti·ty \'saŋ(k)-tə-tē\ *n, pl* **-ties** [ME *saunctite*, fr. MF *saincteté*, fr. L *sanctitat-, sanctitas*, fr. *sanctus* sacred] (14c) **1** : holiness of life and character : GODLINESS **2 a** : the quality or state of being holy or sacred : INVIOLABILITY **b** *pl* : sacred objects, obligations, or rights

sanc·tu·ary \'saŋ(k)-chə-ˌwer-ē\ *n, pl* **-ar·ies** [ME *sanctuarie*, fr. MF *saintuarie*, fr. LL *sanctuarium*, fr. L *sanctus*] (14c) **1** : a consecrated place: as **a** : the ancient Hebrew temple at Jerusalem or its holy of holies **b** (1) : the most sacred part of a religious building (as the part of a Christian church in which the altar is placed) (2) : the room in which general worship services are held (3) : a place (as a church or a temple) for worship **2 a** (1) : a place of refuge and protection (2) : a refuge for wildlife where predators are controlled and hunting is illegal **b** : the immunity from law attached to a sanctuary

sanc·tum \'saŋ(k)-təm\ *n, pl* **sanctums** *also* **sanc·ta** \-tə\ [LL, fr. L, neut. of *sanctus* sacred] (1577) **1** : a sacred place **2** : a place where one is free from intrusion (an editor's ~) ⟨the inner ~s of research⟩

sanc·tum sanc·to·rum \ˌsaŋ(k)-təm-ˌsaŋ(k)-'tōr-əm, -'tȯr-\ *n* [LL] (1558) **1** *pl* **HOLIES OF HOLIES** **2** : SANCTUM 2

Sanc·tus \'saŋ(k)-təs; 'säŋ(k)-təs, -ˌtüs\ *n* [ME, fr. LL *Sanctus, sanctus, sanctus* Holy, holy, holy, opening of a hymn sung by the angels in Isa 6:3] (15c) : an ancient Christian hymn of adoration sung or said immediately before the prayer of consecration in traditional liturgies

Sanctus bell *n* (15c) : a bell rung by the server at several points (as at the Sanctus) during the mass

¹**sand** \'sand\ *n* [ME, fr. OE; akin to OHG *sant* sand, L *sabulum*, Gk *psammos*] (bef. 12c) **1 a** : a loose granular material that results from the disintegration of rocks, consists of particles smaller than gravel but coarser than silt, and is used in mortar, glass, abrasives, and foundry molds **b** : soil containing 85 percent or more of sand and a maximum of 10 percent of clay; *broadly* : sandy soil **2 a** : a tract of sand : BEACH **b** : a sandbank or sandbar **3** : the sand in an hourglass; *also* : the moments of a lifetime — usu. used in pl. ⟨the ~s of this government run out very rapidly —H. J. Laski⟩ **4** : an oil-producing formation of sandstone or unconsolidated sand **5** : firm resolution **6** : a yellowish gray color

²**sand** *vt* (14c) **1** : to sprinkle or dust with or as if with sand **2** : to cover or fill with sand **3** : to smooth or dress by grinding or rubbing with an abrasive (as sandpaper)

san·dal \'san-d°l\ *n* [ME *sandalie*, fr. L *sandalium*, fr. Gk *sandalion*, dim. of *sandalon* sandal] (14c) **1** : a shoe consisting of a sole strapped to the foot **2** : a low-cut shoe that fastens by an ankle strap **3** : a strap to hold on a slipper or low shoe **4** : a rubber overshoe cut very low — **san-daled** \'san-d³ld\ adj

san-dal-wood \-ˌwůd\ n [sandal sandalwood (fr. ME, fr. MF, fr. ML sandalum, fr. LGk santalon, ultim. fr. Skt candana, of Dravidian origin; akin to Tamil cāntu sandalwood tree) + ²wood] (ca. 1511) **1** : the compact close-grained fragrant yellowish heartwood of a parasitic tree (Santalum album of the family Santalaceae, the sandalwood family) of southern Asia much used in ornamental carving and cabinetwork; also : the tree that yields this wood **2** : any of various trees other than the sandalwood some of which yield dyewoods; also : the fragrant wood of such a tree

sandalwood oil n (1851) : an essential oil obtained from sandalwood: as **a** : a pale yellow somewhat viscous aromatic liquid obtained from a sandalwood (Santalum album) and used chiefly in perfumes and soaps **b** : an oil obtained from a sandalwood (Eucarya spicata) of Australia

san-da-rac \'san-də-ˌrak\ n [L sandaraca red coloring, fr. Gk sandarakē realgar, red pigment from realgar] (1543) : a brittle faintly aromatic translucent resin obtained from a northern African tree (Tetraclinis articulata) of the cypress family and used chiefly in making varnish and as incense; also : a similar resin obtained from any of several Australian trees (genus Callitris) of the same family

¹sand-bag \'san(d)-ˌbag\ n (1590) : a bag filled with sand and used in fortifications, as ballast, or as a weapon

²sandbag vt (1860) **1** : to bank, stop up, or weight with sandbags **2 a** : to hit or stun with or as if with a sandbag **b** : to treat unfairly or harshly **c** : to coerce by crude means ⟨are raiding the Treasury and sandbagging the government —C. W. Ferguson⟩ **d** : to conceal or misrepresent one's true position, potential, or intent esp. in order to take advantage of — **sand-bag-ger** n

sand-bank \'san(d)-ˌbaŋk\ n (15c) : a large deposit of sand forming a mound, hillside, bar, or shoal

sand-bar \-ˌbär\ n (1766) : a ridge of sand built up by currents esp. in a river or in coastal waters

¹sand-blast \-ˌblast\ n (1871) : a stream of sand projected by compressed air (as for engraving, cutting, or cleaning glass or stone)

²sandblast vt (1888) : to affect or treat with or as if with a sandblast — **sand-blast-er** n

sand-blind \'san(d)-ˌblīnd\ adj [ME, prob. fr. (assumed) ME samblind, fr. OE sam- half (akin to OHG sāmi- half) + blind — more at SEMI-] (15c) : having poor eyesight : PURBLIND

sand bluestem n (ca. 1946) : a tall rhizomatous grass (Andropogon hallii) of the western U.S. used for forage and as a soil binder

sand-box \'san(d)-ˌbäks\ n (1688) : a box or receptacle containing loose sand: as **a** : a shaker for sprinkling sand on wet ink **b** : a box that contains sand for children to play in

sand-bur \'san(d)-ˌbər\ n (1830) : any of a genus (Cenchrus) of grasses producing spikelets enclosed in ovoid spiny involucres that form burs; also : one of these burs

sand-cast \-ˌkast\ vt -cast; -cast-ing (1928) : to make (a casting) by pouring metal in a sand mold

sand casting n (1926) : a casting made in a mold of sand

sand crack n (1754) : a fissure in the wall of a horse's hoof often causing lameness

sand dab n (1946) : any of several Pacific flounders (genus Citharichthys of the family Bothidae); esp : a common food fish (C. sordidus)

sand dollar n (1884) : any of numerous flat circular sea urchins (order Clypeasteroida) that live chiefly in shallow water on sandy bottoms

sand-er \'san-dər\ n (1627) : one that sands: as **a** : a device for spreading sand on newly surfaced or icy roads; also : the device together with the truck that bears it **b** : a machine or device that smooths, polishes, or scours by means of abrasive material usu. in the form of a disk or belt — called also sanding machine

sand-er-ling \'san-dər-liŋ\ n [sand + -erling, perh. fr. OE yrthling, kind of bird found in fields, lit., plowman, fr. yrth, earth plowing, fr. erian to plow — more at ARABLE] (1602) : a small widely distributed sandpiper (Calidris alba) with pale gray and white plumage in winter

sand flea n (1796) **1** : a flea (as a chigoe) found in sandy places **2** : BEACH FLEA

sand fly n (1736) : any of various small biting dipteran flies (families Psychodidae, Simuliidae, and Ceratopogonidae)

sand-fly fever \'san(d)-ˌflī-\ n (1910) : a virus disease of brief duration that is characterized by fever, headache, pain in the eyes, malaise, and leukopenia and is transmitted by the bite of a sand fly (Phlebotomus papatasii) — called also phlebotomus fever

sand-glass \'san(d)-ˌglas\ n (1556) : an instrument (as an hourglass) for measuring time by the running of sand

sand-grouse \-ˌgraůs\ n (1783) : any of numerous birds (family Pteroclidae) of arid parts of southern Europe, Asia, and Africa that are closely related to the pigeons but have precocial downy young

san-dhi \'san-dē, 'sän-, 'sən-\ n [Skt saṃdhi, lit., placing together] (1806) : modification of the sound of a morpheme (as a word or affix) conditioned by syntactic context in which it is uttered (as pronunciation of -ed as \d\ in glazed and as \t\ in paced or occurrence of a in a cow and of an in an old cow)

sand-hill crane \'sand-ˌhil-\ n (1805) : a crane (Grus canadensis) of No. America and Siberia that has a red crown and is chiefly bluish gray tinged with a sandy yellow

sand-hog \'sand-ˌhòg, -ˌhäg\ n (1903) : a laborer who works in a caisson in driving underwater tunnels

San-di-nis-ta \ˌsan-də-'nēs-tə, ˌsän-\ n [AmerSp, fr. Augusto César Sandino †1933 Nicaraguan rebel leader] (1974) : a member of a military and political coalition taking power in Nicaragua in 1979

S and L n (1951) : SAVINGS AND LOAN ASSOCIATION

sand lance n (1776) : any of several small elongate marine bony fishes (genus Ammodytes of the family Ammodytidae) that associate in large schools and remain buried in sandy beaches at ebb tide — called also sand eel, sand launce

sand lily n (ca. 1900) : a western No. American spring herb (Leucocrinum montanum) of the lily family with narrow linear leaves and fragrant salverform flowers

sand-lot \'san(d)-ˌlät\ n (1878) : a vacant lot esp. when used (as by children) for usu. unorganized sports — **sandlot** adj — **sand-lot-ter** \-ˌlä-tər\ n

sand-man \'san(d)-ˌman\ n : a genie in folklore who makes children sleepy by sprinkling sand in their eyes

sand myrtle n (1814) : a variable low-branching evergreen upland shrub (Leiophyllum buxifolium) of the heath family found in the southeastern U.S.

sand-paint-ing \'san(d)-ˌpān-tiŋ\ n (1900) : a Navajo and Pueblo Indian ceremonial design made of various materials (as colored sands) on a flat surface of sand or buckskin

¹sand-pa-per \-ˌpā-pər\ n (1825) : paper covered on one side with abrasive material (as sand) glued fast and used for smoothing and polishing — **sand-pa-pery** \-p(ə-)rē\ adj

²sandpaper vt (1846) : to rub with or as if with sandpaper

sand-pile \'san(d)-ˌpīl\ n (1901) : a pile of sand; esp : sand for children to play in

sand-pip-er \-ˌpī-pər\ n (1674) : any of numerous small shorebirds (family Scolopacidae) distinguished from the related plovers chiefly by the longer and soft-tipped bill

sand-pit \-ˌpit\ n (1898) Brit : SAND-BOX b

sand-shoe \-ˌshü\ n (1855) chiefly Austral & NewZeal : TENNIS SHOE

sand-soap \'san(d)-ˌsōp\ n (1854) : a gritty soap for all-purpose cleaning

sand-spur \-ˌspər\ n (ca. 1898) : SAND-BUR

sand-stone \-ˌstōn\ n (1668) : a sedimentary rock consisting of usu. quartz sand united by some cement (as silica or calcium carbonate)

sandpiper

sand-storm \-ˌstörm\ n (1774) : a windstorm (as in a desert) driving clouds of sand before it

sand table n (1812) **1** : a table holding sand for children to mold **2** : a table bearing a relief model of a terrain built to scale for study or demonstration esp. of military tactics

sand trap n (1922) : an artificial hazard on a golf course consisting of a depression containing sand

sand verbena n (1898) : any of several western No. American herbs (genus Abronia) of the four-o'clock family with flowers like the verbena; esp : either of two plants (A. latifolia and A. umbellata) of the Pacific coast

¹sand-wich \'san(d)-ˌwich, 'sam-\ n [John Montagu, 4th Earl of Sandwich †1792 Eng. diplomat] (1762) **1 a** : two or more slices of bread or a split roll having a filling in between **b** : one slice of bread covered with food **2** : something resembling a sandwich; esp : composite structural material consisting of layers often of high-strength facings bonded to a low strength central core

²sandwich vt (1861) **1** : to make into or as if into a sandwich; esp : to insert or enclose between usu. two things of another quality or character **2** : to make a place for — often used with in or between

sandwich board n (1897) : two usu. hinged boards designed for hanging from the shoulders with one board before and one behind and used esp. for advertising or picketing

sandwich coin n (1965) : a clad coin

sandwich man n (1864) : one who wears a sandwich board

sand-worm \'san(d)-ˌwərm\ n (1776) : any of various sand-dwelling polychaete worms: as **a** : any of several large burrowing worms (esp. genus Nereis) often used as bait **b** : LUGWORM

sand-wort \'san(d)-ˌwort, -ˌwòrt\ n (1597) : any of a genus (Arenaria) of low tufted herbs of the pink family growing usu. in dry sandy regions

sandy \'san-dē\ adj sand-i-er; -est (bef. 12c) **1 a** : consisting of or containing sand : full of sand **b** : sprinkled with sand **2** : of the color sand — **sand-i-ness** n

sane \'sān\ adj san-er; san-est [L sanus healthy, sane] (1628) **1** : proceeding from a sound mind : RATIONAL **2** : mentally sound; esp : able to anticipate and appraise the effect of one's actions **3** : healthy in body syn see WISE — **sane-ly** adv — **sane-ness** \'sān-nəs\ n

San-for-ized \'san-fə-ˌrīzd\ trademark — used for fabrics that are shrunk by a mechanical process before being manufactured into articles (as clothing)

sang past of SING

san-ga-ree \ˌsaŋ-gə-'rē\ n [Sp sangría, lit., act of bleeding, fr. sangre blood, fr. L sanguin-, sanguis] (1736) **1** : a sweetened iced drink of wine or sometimes of ale, beer, or liquor garnished with nutmeg **2** : SANGRIA

sang-froid \ˈsäⁿ-ˈf(r)wä\ n [F sang-froid, lit., cold blood] (1750) : self-possession or imperturbability esp. under strain syn see EQUANIMITY

San-greal \'san-grā(ə)l, 'saŋ-\ n [ME Sangrayll, fr. MF Saint Graal Holy Grail] : GRAIL

san-gria \saŋ-'grē-ə, san-\ n [Sp] (1736) : a usu. iced punch made of red wine, fruit juice, and soda water

san-gui-nar-ia \ˌsaŋ-gwə-'ner-ē-ə, -'när-\ n [NL, fr. L, an herb that stanches blood, fr. fem. of sanguinarius sanguinary] (1808) **1** : BLOODROOT **2** : the rhizome and roots of a bloodroot used as an expectorant and emetic

san-gui-nary \'saŋ-gwə-ˌner-ē\ adj [L sanguinarius, fr. sanguin-, sanguis blood] (1623) **1** : BLOODTHIRSTY, MURDEROUS ⟨~ hatred⟩ **2** : attended by bloodshed : BLOODY ⟨this bitter and ~ war —T. H. D. Mahoney⟩ **3** : consisting of blood ⟨a ~ stream⟩ syn see BLOODY — **san-gui-nar-i-ly** \ˌsaŋ-gwə-'ner-ə-lē\ adv

¹san-guine \'saŋ-gwən\ adj [ME sanguin, fr. MF, fr. L sanguineus, fr. sanguin-, sanguis] (14c) **1** : BLOODRED **2 a** : consisting of or relating to blood **b** : BLOODTHIRSTY, SANGUINARY **c** *of the complexion* : RUDDY **3** : having blood as the predominating bodily humor; *also* : having the bodily conformation and temperament held characteristic of such predominance and marked by sturdiness, high color, and cheerfulness **4** : CONFIDENT, OPTIMISTIC — **san·guine·ly** *adv* — **san·guine·ness** \-gwən-nəs\ *n* — **san·guin·i·ty** \saŋ-ˈgwi-nə-tē, san-\ *n*

²sanguine *n* (1500) : a moderate to strong red

san·guin·e·ous \saŋ-ˈgwi-nē-əs, saŋ-\ *adj* [L *sanguineus*] (ca. 1520) **1** : BLOODRED **2** : of, relating to, or involving bloodshed : BLOODTHIRSTY **3** : of, relating to, or containing blood

San·he·drin \san-ˈhe-drən, sän-; san-ˈhē-, ˈsa-nə-\ *n* [LHeb *sanhedhrīn* (*gēdhōlāh*) (great) Sanhedrin, fr. Gk *synedrion* council, fr. *synedros* sitting in council, fr. *syn-* + *hedra* seat — more at SIT] (1588) : the supreme council and tribunal of the Jews during postexilic times headed by a High Priest and having religious, civil, and criminal jurisdiction

san·i·cle \ˈsa-ni-kəl\ *n* [ME, fr. MF, fr. ML *sanicula*] (14c) : any of several plants sometimes held to have healing powers; *esp* : a plant (genus *Sanicula*) of the carrot family with a root used in folk medicine as an anodyne or astringent

san·i·tar·i·an \ˌsa-nə-ˈter-ē-ən\ *n* (1859) : a specialist in sanitary science and public health (milk ~)

san·i·tar·i·um \ˌsa-nə-ˈter-ē-əm\ *n, pl* **-i·ums** *or* **-ia** \-ē-ə\ [NL, fr. L *sanitat-, sanitas* health] (1851) : SANATORIUM

san·i·tary \ˈsa-nə-ˌter-ē\ *adj* [F *sanitaire*, fr. L *sanitas*] (1842) **1** : of or relating to health (~ measures) **2** : of, relating to, or used in the disposal esp. of domestic waterborne waste (~ sewage) **3** : characterized by or readily kept in cleanliness (~ packages) — **san·i·tar·i·ly** \ˌsa-nə-ˈter-ə-lē\ *adv*

sanitary landfill *n* (1968) : LANDFILL

sanitary napkin *n* (1917) : a disposable absorbent pad used postpartum or during menstruation to absorb the uterine flow

sanitary ware *n* (1872) : ceramic plumbing fixtures (as sinks, lavatories, or toilet bowls)

san·i·tate \ˈsa-nə-ˌtāt\ *vt* **-tat·ed; -tat·ing** [back-formation fr. *sanitation*] (1882) : to make sanitary esp. by providing with sanitary appliances or facilities

san·i·ta·tion \ˌsa-nə-ˈtā-shən\ *n* (1848) **1** : the act or process of making sanitary **2** : the promotion of hygiene and prevention of disease by maintenance of sanitary conditions

san·i·tize \ˈsa-nə-ˌtīz\ *vt* **-tized; -tiz·ing** [L *sanitas*] (1836) **1** : to make sanitary (as by cleaning or sterilizing) **2** : to make more acceptable by removing unpleasant or undesired features (~ a document) — **san·i·ti·za·tion** \ˌsa-nə-tə-ˈzā-shən\ *n*

san·i·to·ri·um \ˌsa-nə-ˈtōr-ē-əm, -ˈtȯr-\ *n, pl* **-ri·ums** *or* **-ria** \-ē-ə\ [by alter. (influenced by *sanitarium*)] (1917) : SANATORIUM

san·i·ty \ˈsa-nə-tē\ *n* [ME *sanite*, fr. L *sanitat-, sanitas* health, sanity, fr. *sanus* healthy, sane] (15c) : the quality or state of being sane; *esp* : soundness or health of mind

San Ja·cin·to Day \ˌsan-jə-ˈsin-tə-, -hə-ˌsin-\ *n* (1907) : April 21 observed as a legal holiday in Texas in commemoration of the battle of San Jacinto in 1836 by which independence from Mexico was won

San Jo·se scale \ˌsan-(h)ō-\ *n* [*San Jose*, Calif.] (1887) : a scale insect (*Quadraspidiotus perniciosus*) prob. of Asian origin that is naturalized in the U.S. and is destructive to fruit trees

sank *past of* SINK

San·khya \ˈsän-kyə\ *n* [Skt *sāṁkhya*, lit., based on calculation] (1788) : an orthodox Hindu philosophy teaching salvation through knowledge of the dualism of matter and souls

sann hemp \ˈsən-, ˈsän-\ *n* [Hindi *san*] (1939) : SUNN

san·nup \ˈsa-nəp\ *n* [Eastern Abenaki *sénape* man, male human] (1628) : a married male American Indian

sann·ya·si \(ˌ)sən-ˈyä-sē\ *or* **sann·ya·sin** \-ˈyä-sᵊn\ *n* [Hindi *sannyāsī*, fr. Skt *sannyāsin*] (1613) : a Hindu mendicant ascetic

¹sans \ˈsanz\ *prep* [ME *saun, sans*, fr. MF *san, sans*, modif. of L *sine* without — more at SUNDER] (14c) : WITHOUT (my love to thee is sound, ~ crack or flaw —Shak.)

²sans \ˈsanz\ *n, pl* **sans** (ca. 1909) : SANS SERIF

sans-cu·lotte \ˌsanz-kü-ˈlät, -kyü-\ *n* [F *sans-culotte*, lit., without breeches] (1790) **1** : an extreme radical republican in France at the time of the Revolution **2** : a radical or violent extremist in politics — **sans·cu·lott·ic** \-ˈlä-tik\ *adj* — **sans·cu·lott·ish** \-ˈti-zəm\ *n*

san·sei \ˈsän-ˈsā, ˈsän-\ *n, pl* **sansei** *often cap* [Jp *san* third + *sei* generation] (1940) : a son or daughter of nisei parents who is born and educated in America and esp. in the U.S.

san·se·vie·ria \ˌsan(t)-sə-ˈvir-ē-ə\ *n* [NL, fr. Raimondo di Sangro, prince of *San Severo* †1774 Ital. scholar] (1804) : any of a genus (*Sansevieria*) of tropical herbs of the agave family with showy mottled sword-shaped leaves usu. yielding a strong fiber

San·skrit \ˈsan-ˌskrit, ˈsan(t)-skrət\ *n* [Skt *saṁskṛta*, lit., perfected, fr. *sam* together + *karoti* he makes] (1696) **1** : an ancient Indo-Aryan language that is the classical language of India and of Hinduism **2** : classical Sanskrit together with the older Vedic and various later modifications of classical Sanskrit — see INDO-EUROPEAN LANGUAGES table — **Sanskrit** *adj* — **San·skrit·ic** \san-ˈskri-tik\ *adj* — **San·skrit·ist** \ˈsanˌskri-tist\ *n*

sans ser·if *or* **san·ser·if** \san-ˈser-əf, ˈsanz-\ *n* [prob. fr. *sans* + modif. of D *schreef* stroke — more at SERIF] (1830) : a letter or typeface with no serifs

San·ta Ana \ˌsan-tə-ˈa-nə\ *n* [*Santa Ana* Mountains in southern Calif.] (1880) : a strong hot dry foehn wind from the north, northeast, or east in southern California

San·ta Claus \ˈsan-tə-ˌklȯz *also* ˈsan-tē-\ *n* [modif. of D *Sinterklaas*, alter. of *Sint Nikolaas* Saint Nicholas] : a plump white-bearded and red-suited old man in modern folklore who delivers presents to good children at Christmastime — called also *Santa*

San·ta Ger·tru·dis \ˌsan-tə-(ˌ)gər-ˈtrü-dəs\ *n* [*Santa Gertrudis*, section

sansevieria

of the King Ranch, Kingsville, Texas] (1942) : any of a breed of red beef cattle developed from a Brahman-shorthorn cross and valued for their hardiness in hot climates

San·te·ria *also* **San·te·ría** \ˌsan-tə-ˈrē-ə, ˌsän-\ *n* [AmerSp *santería*, fr. *santero* practitioner of Santeria, fr. *santo* Yoruba deity, lit., saint's image, saint, fr. Sp] (1950) : a religion practiced orig. in Cuba in which Yoruba deities are identified with Roman Catholic saints

san·tir \sän-ˈtir\ *or* **san·tour** \-ˈtu̇r\ *n* [Ar *sanṭīr, sanṭūr*, fr. Gk *psaltērion* psaltery] (1853) : a Persian dulcimer

san·to \ˈsän-(ˌ)tō\ *n, pl* **santos** [Sp, lit., saint, fr. LL *sanctus* — more at SAINT] (1834) : a painted or carved wooden image of a saint common esp. in Mexico and the southwestern U.S.

san·to·li·na \ˌsan-tᵊl-ˈē-nə\ *n* [NL, alter. of L *santonica*, an herb, fem. of *santonicus* of the Santoni, fr. *Santoni*, a people of Aquitania] (1578) : any of a genus (*Santolina*) of Mediterranean composite subshrubs that have dissected leaves and clustered flower heads lacking ray flowers

san·to·nin \ˈsan-tᵊn-ən, san-ˈtä-nən\ *n* [ISV, fr. NL *santonica*, fr. L] (1838) : a poisonous slightly bitter crystalline compound $C_{15}H_{18}O_3$ found esp. in the unopened flower heads of several artemisias (esp. *Artemisia maritima*) and used as an anthelmintic

¹sap \ˈsap\ *n* [ME, fr. OE *sæp*; akin to OHG *saf* sap] (bef. 12c) **1 a** : the fluid part of a plant; *specif* : a watery solution that circulates through a plant's vascular system **b** (1) : a body fluid (as blood) essential to life, health, or vigor (2) : bodily health and vigor **2 a** : a foolish gullible person **3** : BLACKJACK, BLUDGEON — **sap·less** \ˈsa-pləs\ *adj* — **sap·less·ness** \-nəs\ *n*

²sap *vt* **sapped; sap·ping** (1725) **1** : to drain or deprive of sap **2** : to knock out with a sap

³sap *vb* **sapped; sap·ping** [MF *sapper*, fr. OIt *zappare*, fr. *zappa* hoe] *vi* (1598) : to proceed by digging a sap ~ *vt* **1** : to subvert by digging or eroding the substratum or foundation : UNDERMINE **2 a** : to gradually diminish the supply or intensity of (*sapped* her strength) **b** : to weaken or exhaust the energy or vitality of **3** : to operate against or pierce by a sap *syn* see WEAKEN

⁴sap *n* [MF *sape*, fr. *saper*] (1642) : the extension of a trench to a point beneath an enemy's fortifications

sap green *n* (1578) : a strong yellow green

sap·head \ˈsap-ˌhed\ *n* (1798) : a weak-minded stupid person : SAP — **sap·head·ed** \-ˈhe-dəd\ *adj*

sa·phe·nous \sə-ˈfē-nəs, ˈsa-fə-nəs\ *adj* [saphena saphenous vein, fr. ME, fr. ML, fr. Ar *sāfin*] (1840) : of, relating to, associated with, or being either of the two chief superficial veins of the leg (~ nerve)

sap·id \ˈsa-pəd\ *adj* [L *sapidus* tasty, fr. *sapere* to taste — more at SAGE] (1623) **1** : having flavor : FLAVORFUL **2** *archaic* : agreeable to the mind — **sa·pid·i·ty** \sa-ˈpi-də-tē\ *n, archaic*

sa·pi·ence \ˈsā-pē-ən(t)s, ˈsa-\ *n* [ME, fr. MF, fr. L *sapientia*, fr. *sapient-, sapiens*, prp.] (14c) : WISDOM, SAGACITY

sa·pi·ens \ˈsa-pē-ənz, ˈsā-, -ˌenz\ *adj* [NL (specific epithet of *Homo sapiens*), fr. L, prp. of *sapere*] (1939) : of, relating to, or being recent humans (*Homo sapiens*) as distinguished from various fossil hominids

sa·pi·ent \ˈsā-pē-ənt, ˈsa-\ *adj* [ME, fr. MF, fr. L *sapient-, sapiens*, prp. of *sapere* to taste, be wise — more at SAGE] (15c) : possessing or expressing great sagacity *syn* see WISE — **sa·pi·ent·ly** *adv*

sap·ling \ˈsa-pliŋ, -plən\ *n* (14c) **1** : a young tree; *specif* : one not over four inches in diameter at breast height **2** : YOUTH 2a

sap·o·dil·la \ˌsa-pə-ˈdi-lə, -ˈdē-yə\ *n* [Sp *zapotillo*, dim. of *zapote* sapodilla, fr. Nahuatl *tzapotl*] (1697) : a tropical evergreen tree (*Manilkara zapota* syn. *Achras zapota* of the family Sapotaceae, the sapodilla family) with hard reddish wood, a latex that yields chicle, and a rough-skinned brownish edible fruit; *also* : its fruit

sa·po·ge·nin \ˌsa-pə-ˈje-nən, sə-ˈpä-jə-nən\ *n* [ISV *saponin* + *-genin* (compound formed from another compound)] (ca. 1862) : a nonsugar portion of a saponin that is typically obtained by hydrolysis, has either a complex terpenoid or a steroidal structure, and in the latter case forms a practicable starting point in the synthesis of steroid hormones

sap·o·na·ceous \ˌsa-pə-ˈnā-shəs\ *adj* [NL *saponaceus*, fr. L *sapon-, sapo* soap, of Gmc origin; akin to OE *sāpe* soap] (1710) : resembling or having the qualities of soap — **sap·o·na·ceous·ness** *n*

sa·pon·i·fy \sə-ˈpä-nə-ˌfī\ *vb* **-fied; -fy·ing** [F *saponifier*, fr. L *sapon-, sapo*] *vt* (1821) : to convert (as fat) into soap; *specif* : to hydrolyze (a fat) with alkali to form a soap and glycerol ~ *vi* : to undergo saponifying — **sa·pon·i·fi·able** \-ˌfī-ə-bəl\ *adj* — **sa·pon·i·fi·ca·tion** \-ˌpä-nə-fə-ˈkā-shən\ *n* — **sa·pon·i·fi·er** \-ˈpä-nə-ˌfī(-ə)r\ *n*

sa·po·nin \ˈsa-pə-nən, sə-ˈpō-\ *n* [F *saponine*, fr. L *sapon-, sapo*] (1831) : any of various mostly toxic glucosides that occur in plants (as soapwort or soapbark) and are characterized by the property of producing a soapy lather; *esp* : a hygroscopic amorphous saponin mixture used esp. as a foaming and emulsifying agent and detergent

sap·o·nite \ˈsa-pə-ˌnīt\ *n* [Sw *saponit*, fr. L *sapon-, sapo* soap] (ca. 1849) : a hydrous magnesium aluminum silicate occurring in soft soapy amorphous masses and filling veins and cavities (as in serpentine)

sap·per \ˈsa-pər\ *n* (1626) **1** : a military specialist in field fortification work (as sapping) **2** : a military demolitions specialist

¹sap·phic \ˈsa-fik\ *adj* (1501) **1** *cap* : of or relating to the Greek lyric poet Sappho **2** : of, relating to, or consisting of a 4-line strophe made up of chiefly trochaic and dactylic feet **3** : LESBIAN 2

²sapphic *n* (1586) **1** : a verse having the metrical pattern of one of the first three lines of a sapphic strophe **2** : a sapphic strophe

sap·phire \ˈsa-ˌfī(ə)r\ *n* [ME *safir*, fr. OF, fr. L *sapphirus*, fr. Gk *sappheiros*, perh. of Sem origin; akin to Heb *sappīr* sapphire] (13c) **1 a** : a gem variety of corundum in transparent or translucent crystals of a color other than red; *esp* : one of a transparent rich blue **b** : a gem of such corundum **2** : a deep purplish blue color — **sapphire** *adj*

sap·phi·rine \ˈsa-fə-ˌrīn, ˈsa-ˌfir-ˌēn, sa-ˈfī-rən\ *adj* (15c) **1** : made of sapphire **2** : resembling sapphire esp. in color

sap·phism \ˈsa-ˌfi-zəm\ *n* [*Sappho* + *-ism*; fr. the belief that Sappho was homosexual] (ca. 1890) : LESBIANISM

sap·pi·ness \ˈsa-pē-nəs\ *n* (1552) **1** : the state of being full of or smelling of sap **2** : the quality or state of being sappy : FOOLISHNESS

sap·py \ˈsa-pē\ *adj* **sap·pi·er; -est** (12c) **1** : abounding with sap **2** : resembling or consisting largely of sapwood **3 a** : overly sweet or sentimental **b** : lacking in good sense : SILLY

sapr- *or* **sapro-** *comb form* [NL, fr. Gk *sapros* rotten] **1** : dead or decaying organic matter ⟨*saprophyte*⟩ **2** : decay : putrefaction ⟨*saprogenic*⟩

sap·ro·gen·ic \,sa-prə-'je-nik\ *adj* (1876) : of, causing, or resulting from putrefaction — **sap·ro·ge·nic·i·ty** \-jə-'ni-sə-tē\ *n*

sap·ro·lite \'sa-prə-,līt\ *n* (1894) : disintegrated rock that lies in its original place

sa·proph·a·gous \sa-'präf-ə-gəs\ *adj* [NL *saprophagus*, fr. *sapr-* + *-phagus* -phagous] (1819) : feeding on decaying matter

sap·ro·phyte \'sa-prə-,fīt\ *n* [ISV] (1875) : a saprophytic organism; *esp* : a plant living on dead or decaying organic matter

sap·ro·phyt·ic \,sa-prə-'fi-tik\ *adj* (1882) : obtaining food by absorbing dissolved organic material; *esp* : obtaining nourishment osmotically from the products of organic breakdown and decay — **sap·ro·phyt·i·cal·ly** \-ti-k(ə-)lē\ *adv*

sap·ro·zo·ic \,sa-prə-'zō-ik\ *adj* (ca. 1920) : SAPROPHYTIC — used of animals (as protozoans)

sap·sa·go \sap-'sä-(,)gō, 'sap-sə-,gō\ *n* [modif. of G *Schabziger*] (ca. 1846) : a very hard green skim-milk cheese flavored with the powdered leaves of an aromatic legume (*Trigonella coerulea*)

sap·suck·er \'sap-,sə-kər\ *n* (1805) : any of a genus (*Sphyrapicus*) of small No. American woodpeckers that drill holes in trees in order to obtain sap and insects for food

sap·wood \-,wüd\ *n* (1791) : the younger softer living or physiologically active outer portion of wood that lies between the cambium and the heartwood and is more permeable, less durable, and usu. lighter in color than the heartwood

sar·a·band *or* **sar·a·bande** \'sar-ə-,band\ *n* [F *sarabande*, fr. Sp *zarabanda*] (1616) **1** : a stately court dance of the 17th and 18th centuries resembling the minuet **2** : the music for the saraband in slow triple time with accent on the second beat

Sar·a·cen \'sar-ə-sən\ *n* [ME, fr. OE, fr. LL *Saracenus*, fr. LGk *Sarakēnos*] (bef. 12c) : a member of a nomadic people of the deserts between Syria and Arabia; *broadly* : ARAB — **Saracen** *adj* — **Sar·a·cen·ic** \,sar-ə-'se-nik\ *adj*

Sa·rah \'ser-ə, 'sar-ə, 'sä-rə\ *n* [Heb *Śārāh*] **1** : the wife of Abraham and mother of Isaac **2** : a kinswoman of Tobias married to him

sa·ran \sə-'ran\ *n* [fr. *Saran*, a trademark] (1940) : a tough flexible thermoplastic resin

sarape \sə-'rä-pē\ *var of* SERAPE

Sar·a·to·ga trunk \,sar-ə-'tō-gə-\ *n* [*Saratoga* Springs, N.Y.] (1858) : a large traveling trunk usu. with a rounded top

sarc- *or* **sarco-** *comb form* [Gk *sark-, sarko-*, fr. *sark-, sarx*] **1** : flesh ⟨*sarcoid*⟩ **2** : striated muscle ⟨*sarcolemma*⟩

sar·casm \'sär-,ka-zəm\ *n* [F or LL; F *sarcasme*, fr. LL *sarcasmos*, fr. Gk *sarkasmos*, fr. *sarkazein* to tear flesh, bite the lips in rage, sneer, fr. *sark-, sarx* flesh; prob. akin to Av *thwarəs-* to cut] (1550) **1** : a sharp and often satirical or ironic utterance designed to cut or give pain ⟨tired of continual ∼s⟩ **2 a** : a mode of satirical wit depending for its effect on bitter, caustic, and often ironic language that is usu. directed against an individual **b** : the use or language of sarcasm ⟨this is no time to indulge in ∼⟩ *syn* see WIT

sar·cas·tic \sär-'kas-tik\ *adj* (1695) **1** : having the character of sarcasm ⟨∼ criticism⟩ **2** : given to the use of sarcasm : CAUSTIC ⟨a ∼ critic⟩ — **sar·cas·ti·cal·ly** \-ti-k(ə-)lē\ *adv*

syn SARCASTIC, SATIRIC, IRONIC, SARDONIC mean marked by bitterness and a power or will to cut or sting. SARCASTIC implies an intentional inflicting of pain by deriding, taunting, or ridiculing ⟨a critic famous mainly for his *sarcastic* remarks⟩. SATIRIC implies that the intent of the ridiculing is censure and reprobation ⟨a *satiric* look at contemporary sexual mores⟩. IRONIC implies an attempt to be amusing or provocative by saying usu. the opposite of what is meant ⟨made the *ironic* observation that the government could always be trusted⟩. SARDONIC implies scorn, mockery, or derision that is manifested by either verbal or facial expression ⟨surveyed the scene with a *sardonic* smile⟩.

¹sarce·net \'sär-snət\ *n* [ME, fr. AF *sarzinett*] (15c) : a soft thin silk in plain or twill weaves; *also* : a garment made of this

²sarcenet *adj* (1521) **1** *archaic* : made of sarcenet **2** *archaic* : soft like sarcenet

sar·coid \'sär-,kȯid\ *n* (1899) **1** : any of various diseases characterized esp. by the formation of nodules in the skin **2** : a nodule characteristic of sarcoid or of sarcoidosis

sar·coid·o·sis \,sär-,kȯi-'dō-səs\ *n, pl* **-o·ses** \-,sēz\ [NL] (1936) : a chronic disease of unknown cause that is characterized by the formation of nodules esp. in the lymph nodes, lungs, bones, and skin

sar·co·lem·ma \,sär-kə-'le-mə\ *n* [NL, fr. *sarc-* + Gk *lemma* husk — more at LEMMA] (1840) : the thin transparent homogeneous sheath enclosing a striated muscle fiber — **sar·co·lem·mal** \-məl\ *adj*

sar·co·ma \sär-'kō-mə\ *n, pl* **-mas** *also* **-ma·ta** \-mə-tə\ [NL, fr. Gk *sarkōmat-, sarkōma* fleshy growth, fr. *sarkoun* to grow flesh, fr. *sark-, sarx*] (1804) : a malignant neoplasm arising in tissue of mesodermal origin (as connective tissue, bone, cartilage, or striated muscle) — **sar·co·ma·tous** \sär-'kō-mə-təs\ *adj*

sar·co·ma·to·sis \(,)sär-,kō-mə-'tō-səs\ *n, pl* **-to·ses** \-,sēz\ [NL] (ca. 1890) : a disease characterized by the presence and spread of sarcomas

sar·co·mere \'sär-kə-,mir\ *n* (1891) : any of the repeating structural units of striated muscle fibrils

sar·coph·a·gus \sär-'kä-fə-gəs\ *n, pl* **-gi** \-,gī, -,jī, -,gē\ *also* **-gus·es** [L *sarcophagus* (*lapis*) limestone used for coffins, fr. Gk (*lithos*) *sarkophagos*, lit., flesh-eating stone, fr. *sark-* sarc- + *phagein* to eat — more at BAKSHEESH] (1619) : a stone coffin; *broadly* : COFFIN

sar·co·plasm \'sär-kə-,pla-zəm\ *n* [NL *sarcoplasma*] (1899) : the cytoplasm of a striated muscle fiber — **sar·co·plas·mic** \-'plaz-mik\ *adj*

sarcoplasmic reticulum *n* (1953) : the specialized endoplasmic reticulum of cardiac muscle and skeletal striated muscle that functions esp. as a storage and release area for calcium

sar·cop·tic mange \(,)sär-'käp-tik-\ *n* [NL *Sarcoptes*, genus name, fr. *sarc-* + Gk *koptein* to cut — more at CAPON] (1886) : mange caused by mites (genus *Sarcoptes*) burrowing in the skin esp. of the head and face

sar·co·some \'sär-kə-,sōm\ *n* [NL *sarcosoma*, fr. *sarc-* + *-soma* -some] (1899) : a mitochondrion of a striated muscle fiber — **sar·co·som·al** \,sär-kə-'sō-məl\ *adj*

sard \'särd\ *n* [F *sarde*, fr. L *sarda*] (14c) : a reddish brown variety of chalcedony sometimes classified as a variety of carnelian

sardar *var of* SIRDAR

sar·dine \sär-'dēn\ *n, pl* **sardines** *also* **sardine** [ME *sardeine*, fr. MF *sardine*, fr. L *sardina*] (14c) **1** : any of several small or immature clupeid fishes; *esp* : the young of the European pilchard (*Sardina pilchardus*) when of a size suitable for preserving for food **2** : any of various small fishes (as an anchovy) resembling the true sardines or similarly preserved for food

Sar·din·ian \sär-'di-nē-ən, -'din-yən\ *n* (1598) **1** : a native or inhabitant of Sardinia **2** : the Romance language of central and southern Sardinia — **Sardinian** *adj*

sar·don·ic \sär-'dä-nik\ *adj* [F *sardonique*, fr. Gk *sardonios*] (1638) : disdainful or skeptically humorous : derisively mocking ⟨a ∼ comment⟩ ⟨his ∼ expression⟩ *syn* see SARCASTIC — **sar·don·i·cal·ly** \-ni-k(ə-)lē\ *adv*

sar·don·i·cism \sär-'dä-nə-,si-zəm\ *n* (1926) : sardonic quality or humor

sar·don·yx \sär-'dä-niks *also* 'sär-d°n-iks\ *n* [ME *sardonix*, fr. L *sardonyx*, fr. Gk] (14c) : an onyx having parallel layers of sard

sar·gas·so \sär-'ga-(,)sō\ *n, pl* **-sos** [Pg *sargaço*] (1598) **1** : GULFWEED, SARGASSUM **2** : a mass of floating vegetation and esp. sargassums

sar·gas·sum \sär-'ga-səm\ *n* [NL, genus name, fr. ISV *sargasso*] (ca. 1890) : any of a genus (*Sargassum*) of brown algae that have a branching thallus with lateral outgrowths differentiated as leafy segments, air bladders, or spore-bearing structures ; GULFWEED

sarge \'särj\ *n* [by shortening & alter.] (1867) : SERGEANT

sa·ri *also* **sa·ree** \'sär-ē\ *n* [Hindi *sāṛī*, fr. Skt *śāṭī* strip of cloth] (1785) : a garment of southern Asian women that consists of several yards of lightweight cloth draped so that one end forms a skirt and the other a head or shoulder covering

sa·rin \'sär-ən, zä-'rēn\ *n* [G] (1951) : an extremely toxic chemical warfare agent $C_4H_{10}FO_2P$ that is a powerful cholinesterase inhibitor

sark \'särk\ *n* [ME (Sc) *serk*, fr. OE *serc*; akin to ON *serkr* shirt] (bef. 12c) *dial chiefly Brit* : SHIRT

sa·rod *also* **sa·rode** \sə-'rōd\ *n* [Hindi *sarod*, fr. Per] (1865) : a lute of northern India — **sa·rod·ist** \-'rō-dist\ *n*

sa·rong \sə-'rȯŋ, -'räŋ\ *n* [Malay] (1830) : a loose garment made of a long strip of cloth wrapped around the body that is worn as a skirt or dress by men and women chiefly of the Malay Archipelago and the Pacific islands

Sar·pe·don \sär-'pē-d°n\ *n* [L, fr. Gk *Sarpēdōn*] : a son of Zeus and Europa and king of Lycia killed in the Trojan War

sar·ra·ce·nia \,sar-ə-'sē-nē-ə, -'se-\ *n* [NL, fr. Michel *Sarrazin* †1734 Fr. physician & naturalist] (1884) : any of a genus (*Sarracenia* of the family Sarraceniaceae) that includes the insectivorous bog pitcher plants of eastern No. America

sari

sar·sa·pa·ril·la \,sas-pə-'ri-lə, ,särs-, -'re-; ,sa-sə-, ,sär-sə-\ *n* [Sp *zarzaparrilla*, fr. *zarza* bush + *parrilla*, dim. of *parra* vine] (1577) **1 a** : any of various tropical American greenbriers **b** : the dried roots of a sarsaparilla used esp. as a flavoring **2** : any of various plants (as wild sarsaparilla) that resemble or are used as a substitute for sarsaparilla **3** : a sweetened carbonated beverage flavored with sassafras and oil distilled from a European birch

sarsenet *var of* SARCENET

sar·to·ri·al \sär-'tȯr-ē-əl, sə(r)-, -'tȯr-\ *adj* [ML *sartor*] (1823) : of or relating to a tailor or tailored clothes; *broadly* : of or relating to clothes — **sar·to·ri·al·ly** \-ē-ə-lē\ *adv*

sar·to·ri·us \sär-'tȯr-ē-əs, -'tȯr-\ *n, pl* **-rii** \-ē-,ī, -ē-,ē\ [NL, fr. ML *sartor* tailor, fr. L *sarcire* to mend] (1704) : a muscle that crosses the front of the thigh obliquely, assists in rotating the leg to the cross-legged position in which the knees are spread wide apart, and in humans is the longest muscle

Sar·um \'sar-əm, 'ser-\ *adj* [*Sarum*, old borough near Salisbury, England] (1570) : of or relating to the Roman rite as modified in Salisbury and used in England, Wales, and Ireland before the Reformation

¹sash \'sash\ *n* [Ar *shāsh* muslin] (1681) : a band worn about the waist or over one shoulder and used as a dress accessory or the emblem of an honorary or military order — **sashed** \'sasht\ *adj*

²sash *n, pl* **sash** *also* **sash·es** [prob. modif. of F *châssis* chassis (taken as pl.)] (1681) : the framework in which panes of glass are set in a window or door; *also* : such a framework together with its panes forming a usu. movable part of a window

¹sa·shay \sa-'shā *also* si-\ *vi* [alter. of *chassé*] (1836) **1** : to make a chassé **2 a** : WALK, GLIDE, GO **b** : to strut or move about in an ostentatious or conspicuous manner **c** : to proceed or move in a diagonal or sideways manner

²sashay *n* [by alter.] (1900) **1** : TRIP, EXCURSION **2** : a square-dance figure in which partners sidestep in a circle around each other with the man moving behind the woman **3** : CHASSÉ

sa·shi·mi \'sä-shə-mē\ *n* [Jp] (1880) : a Japanese dish consisting of thinly sliced raw fish served with a sauce for dipping

sas·ka·toon \,sas-kə-'tün\ *n* [modif. of Cree *misa·skwato·min* serviceberry fruit] (1810) : SERVICEBERRY

Sas·quatch \'sas-,kwach, -,kwäch\ *n* [Halkomelem (Salishan language of southwestern British Columbia) *sésc̣əc*] (1929) : a hairy creature like a human being reported to exist in the northwestern U.S. and western Canada and said to be a primate between 6 and 15 feet (1.8 and 4.6 meters) tall — called also *bigfoot*

¹sass \'sas\ *n* [alter. of ¹*sauce*] (1835) : impudent speech

²sass *vt* (1856) : to talk impudently or disrespectfully to

sas·sa·fras \'sa-sə-,fras\ *n* [Sp *sasafrás*] (1577) **1** : an eastern No. American tree (*Sassafras albidum*) of the laurel family having both

\ə\ abut \ʼ\ kitten, F table \ər\ further \a\ ash \ā\ ace \ä\ mop, mar
\aú\ out \ch\ chin \e\ bet \ē\ easy \g\ go \i\ hit \ī\ ice \j\ job
\ŋ\ sing \ō\ go \ȯ\ law \ȯi\ boy \th\ thin \t͟h\ the \ü\ loot \ú\ foot
\y\ yet \zh\ vision \á, ḵ, ⁿ, œ, œ̄, ᵫ, ᵫ̄, ᵊ\ see Guide to Pronunciation

ovate and lobed aromatic leaves **2** : the carcinogenic dried root bark of the sassafras used formerly as a diaphoretic or flavoring agent

¹Sas·sa·ni·an *or* **Sa·sa·ni·an** \sə-'sä-nē-ən, sa-'sä-\ *adj* (1788) : of, relating to, or having the characteristics of the Sassanid dynasty of ancient Persia or its art or architecture

²Sassanian *or* **Sasanian** *n* (1855) : SASSANID

Sas·sa·nid *or* **Sa·sa·nid** \sə-'sä-nəd, -'sa-; 'sa-s²n-əd\ *n* [NL *Sassanidae*, Sassanids, fr. *Sassan*, founder of the dynasty] (1776) : a member of a dynasty of Persian kings of the 3d to 7th centuries — **Sassanid** *or* **Sasanid** *adj*

sassy \'sa-sē\ *adj* **sass·i·er; -est** [alter. of *saucy*] (1833) **1** : IMPUDENT, SAUCY **2** : VIGOROUS, LIVELY **3** : distinctively smart and stylish ⟨a ~ black-and-white bow tie⟩ —Jean Stafford⟩

sat *past and past part of* SIT

Sa·tan \'sā-t²n\ *n* [ME, fr. OE, fr. LL, fr. Gk, fr. Heb *śāṭān* adversary] (bef. 12c) : the adversary of God and lord of evil in Judaism and Christianity

sa·tang \sə-'täŋ\ *n, pl* **satang** *or* **satangs** [Thai *sataṅ*] (ca. 1915) — see *baht* at MONEY table

sa·tan·ic \sə-'ta-nik, sā-\ *adj* (1667) **1** : of, relating to, or characteristic of Satan or satanism ⟨~ pride⟩ ⟨~ rites⟩ **2** : characterized by extreme cruelty or viciousness — **sa·tan·i·cal·ly** \-ni-k(ə-)lē\ *adv*

sa·tan·ism \'sā-t²n-,i-zəm\ *n, often cap* (1565) **1** : innate wickedness : DIABOLISM **2** : obsession with or affinity for evil; *specif* : the worship of Satan marked by the travesty of Christian rites — **sa·tan·ist** \-ist\ *n, often cap*

satch·el \'sa-chəl\ *n* [ME *sachel*, fr. MF, fr. LL *saccellum*, dim. of L *sacculus*, dim. of *saccus* bag — more at SACK] (14c) : a small bag often with a shoulder strap — **satch·el·ful** \-,fùl\ *n*

¹sate \'sat\ *archaic past of* SIT

²sate \'sāt\ *vt* **sat·ed; sat·ing** [prob. by shortening & alter. fr. *satiate*] (1602) **1** : to cloy with overabundance : GLUT **2** : to appease (as a thirst) by indulging to the full *syn* see SATIATE

sa·teen \sa-'tēn, sə-\ *n* [alter. of *satin*] (ca. 1878) : a smooth durable lustrous fabric usu. made of cotton in satin weave

sat·el·lite \'sa-t²l-,it\ *n* [MF, fr. L *satellit-, satelles* attendant] (ca. 1548) **1** : a hired agent or obsequious follower : MINION, SYCOPHANT **2 a** : a celestial body orbiting another of larger size **b** : a manufactured object or vehicle intended to orbit the earth, the moon, or another celestial body **3** : someone or something attendant, subordinate, or dependent; *esp* : a country politically and economically dominated or controlled by another more powerful country **4** : a usu. independent urban community situated near but not immediately adjacent to a large city — **satellite** *adj*

satellite DNA *n* (1969) : a fraction of a eukaryotic organism's DNA that differs in density from most of its DNA as determined by centrifugation, that apparently consists of short repetitive nucleotide sequences, that does not undergo transcription, and that in some organisms (as the mouse) is found esp. in centromeric regions

sa·tem \'sä-təm\ *adj* [Av *satəm* hundred; fr. the fact that its initial sound (derived fr. an alveolar fricative) is the representative of an IE palatal stop — more at HUNDRED] (1901) : of, relating to, or constituting an Indo-European language group in which the palatal stops became in prehistoric times palatal or alveolar fricatives — compare CENTUM

sa·ti \(,)sə-'tē, 'sə-,tē\ *var of* SUTTEE

sa·tia·ble \'sā-shə-bəl\ *adj* (1570) : capable of being appeased or satisfied

¹sa·tiate \'sā-sh(ē-)ət\ *adj* (15c) : filled to satiety

²sa·ti·ate \'sā-shē-,āt\ *vt* **-at·ed; -at·ing** [L *satiatus*, pp. of *satiare*, fr. *satis* enough — more at SAD] (15c) : to satisfy (as a need or desire) fully or to excess — **sa·ti·a·tion** \,sä-shē-'ā-shən, ,sä-sē-\ *n*

syn SATIATE, SATE, SURFEIT, CLOY, PALL, GLUT, GORGE mean to fill to repletion. SATIATE and SATE may sometimes imply only complete satisfaction but more often suggest repletion that has destroyed interest or desire ⟨years of globe-trotting had *satiated* their interest in travel⟩ ⟨readers were *sated* with sensationalistic stories⟩. SURFEIT implies a nauseating repletion ⟨*surfeited* themselves with junk food⟩. CLOY stresses the disgust or boredom resulting from such surfeiting ⟨sentimental pictures that *cloy* after a while⟩. PALL emphasizes the loss of ability to stimulate interest or appetite ⟨a life of leisure eventually begins to *pall*⟩. GLUT implies excess in feeding or supplying ⟨a market *glutted* with diet books⟩. GORGE suggests glutting to the point of bursting or choking ⟨*gorged* themselves with chocolate⟩.

sa·ti·ety \sə-'tī-ə-tē *also* 'sā-sh(ē-)ə-\ *n* [MF *satiete*, fr. L *satietat-, satietas*, fr. *satis*] (1533) **1** : the quality or state of being fed or gratified to or beyond capacity : SURFEIT, FULLNESS **2** : the revulsion or disgust caused by overindulgence or excess

¹sat·in \'sa-t²n\ *n* [ME, fr. MF, prob. fr. Ar *zaytūnī*, lit., of Zaytūn, seaport in China during the Middle Ages] (14c) : a fabric (as of silk) in satin weave with lustrous face and dull back

²satin *adj* (1521) **1** : made of or covered with satin **2** : suggestive of satin esp. in smooth lustrous appearance or silkiness to touch

sat·in·et \,sa-t²n-'et\ *n* (1703) **1** : a thin silk satin or imitation satin **2** : a variation of satin weave used in making satinet

satin stitch *n* (1684) : an embroidery stitch nearly alike on both sides and worked so closely as to resemble satin

satin weave *n* (ca. 1883) : a weave in which warp threads interlace with filling threads to produce a smooth-faced fabric

sat·in·wood \'sa-t²n-,wùd\ *n* (1792) **1 a** : an East Indian tree (*Chloroxylon swietenia*) of the rue family that yields a lustrous yellowish brown wood **b** : a tree (as *Zanthoxylum flavum* of the rue family) with wood resembling true satinwood **2** : the wood of a satinwood

satin stitch

sat·iny \'sat-nē, 'sa-t²n-ē\ *adj* (1786) : having or resembling the soft usu. lustrous smoothness of satin

sat·ire \'sa-,tīr\ *n* [MF or L; MF, fr. L *satura, satira*, perh. fr. (*lanx*) *satura* dish of mixed ingredients, fr. fem. of *satur* well-fed; akin to L *satis* enough — more at SAD] (1501) **1** : a literary work holding up human vices and follies to ridicule or scorn **2** : trenchant wit, irony, or sarcasm used to expose and discredit vice or folly *syn* see WIT

sa·tir·ic \sə-'tir-ik\ *or* **sa·tir·i·cal** \-i-kəl\ *adj* (1509) **1** : of, relating to, or constituting satire ⟨~ writers⟩ **2** : manifesting or given to satire *syn* see SARCASTIC — **sa·tir·i·cal·ly** \-i-k(ə-)lē\ *adv*

sat·i·rise *Brit var of* SATIRIZE

sat·i·rist \'sa-tə-rist\ *n* (1589) : one that satirizes; *esp* : a writer of satire

sat·i·rize \-,rīz\ *vb* **-rized; -riz·ing** *vi* (1601) : to utter or write satire ~ *vt* : to censure or ridicule by means of satire — **sat·i·riz·a·ble** \,sa-tə-'rī-zə-bəl\ *adj*

sat·is·fac·tion \,sa-təs-'fak-shən\ *n* [ME, fr. MF, fr. LL *satisfaction-, satisfactio*, fr. L, reparation, amends, fr. *satisfacere* to satisfy] (14c) **1 a** : the payment through penance of the temporal punishment incurred by a sin **b** : reparation for sin that meets the demands of divine justice **2 a** : fulfillment of a need or want **b** : the quality or state of being satisfied : CONTENTMENT **c** : a source or means of enjoyment : GRATIFICATION **3 a** : compensation for a loss or injury : ATONEMENT, RESTITUTION **b** : the discharge of a legal obligation or claim **c** : VINDICATION **4** : convinced assurance or certainty ⟨proved to the ~ of the court⟩

sat·is·fac·to·ry \,sa-təs-'fak-t(ə-)rē\ *adj* (15c) : giving satisfaction : ADEQUATE — **sat·is·fac·to·ri·ly** \-t(ə-)rə-lē\ *adv* — **sat·is·fac·to·ri·ness** *n*

sat·is·fi·able \,sa-təs-'fī-ə-bəl\ *adj* (1609) : capable of being satisfied

sat·is·fy \'sa-təs-,fī\ *vb* **-fied; -fy·ing** [ME *satisfien*, fr. MF *satisfier*, modif. of L *satisfacere*, fr. *satis* enough + *facere* to do, make — more at SAD, DO] (15c) *vt* **1 a** : to carry out the terms of (as a contract) : DISCHARGE **b** : to meet a financial obligation to **2** : to make reparation to (an injured party) : INDEMNIFY **3 a** : to make happy : PLEASE **b** : to gratify to the full : APPEASE **4 a** : CONVINCE **b** : to put an end to (doubt or uncertainty) : DISPEL **5 a** : to conform to (as specifications) : be adequate to (an end in view) **b** : to make true by fulfilling a condition ⟨values that ~ an equation⟩ ⟨~ a hypothesis⟩ ~ *vi* : to be adequate : SUFFICE; *also* : PLEASE *syn* see PAY — **sat·is·fy·ing·ly** \-iŋ-lē\ *adv*

sa·to·ri \sə-'tōr-ē, sä-, -'tòr-\ *n* [Jp] (1727) : a state of intuitive illumination sought in Zen Buddhism

sa·trap \'sā-,trap *also* 'sa-,trap *or* 'sa-trəp\ *n* [ME, fr. L *satrapes*, fr. Gk *satrapēs*, fr. OPer *khshathrapāvan*, lit., protector of the dominion] (14c) **1** : the governor of a province in ancient Persia **2 a** : RULER **b** : a subordinate official : HENCHMAN

sa·tra·py \'sā-trə-pē, 'sa-, -,tra-pē\ *n, pl* **-pies** (1603) : the territory or jurisdiction of a satrap

sat·su·ma \sat-'sü-mə, 'sat-sə-\ *n* [*Satsuma*, former province in Kyushu, Japan] (1882) **1** : any of several cultivated mandarin trees that bear medium-sized largely seedless fruits with thin smooth skin **2** : the fruit of a satsuma

sat·u·ra·ble \'sach-rə-bəl, 'sa-chə-\ *adj* (1570) : capable of being saturated

sat·u·rant \-rənt\ *n* (ca. 1775) : something that saturates

¹sat·u·rate \'sa-chə-,rāt\ *vt* **-rat·ed; -rat·ing** [L *saturatus*, pp. of *saturare*, fr. *satur* well-fed — more at SATIRE] (1538) **1** : to satisfy fully : SATIATE **2** : to treat, furnish, or charge with something to the point where no more can be absorbed, dissolved, or retained ⟨water *saturated* with salt⟩ **3 a** : to fill completely with something that permeates or pervades ⟨book is *saturated* with Hollywood, old and new —Newgate Callendar⟩ **b** : to load to capacity **4** : to cause to combine till there is no further tendency to combine *syn* see SOAK — **sat·u·ra·tor** \-,rā-tər\ *n*

²sat·u·rate \'sach-rət, 'sa-chə-\ *adj* (1782) : SATURATED

sat·u·rat·ed \'sa-chə-,rā-təd\ *adj* (1728) **1** : full of moisture : made thoroughly wet **2 a** : being a solution that is unable to absorb or dissolve any more of a solute at a given temperature and pressure **b** : being an organic compound having no double or triple bonds between carbon atoms **3** *of a color* : having high saturation : PURE

sat·u·ra·tion \,sa-chə-'rā-shən\ *n* (ca. 1554) **1 a** : the act of saturating : the state of being saturated **b** : SATIETY, SURFEIT **2** : conversion of an unsaturated to a saturated chemical compound (as by hydrogenation) **3 a** : a state of maximum impregnation: as **a** : complete infiltration : PERMEATION **b** : the presence in air of the most water possible under existent pressure and temperature **c** : magnetization to the point beyond which a further increase in the intensity of the magnetizing force will produce no further magnetization **4 a** : chromatic purity : freedom from dilution with white **b** (1) : degree of difference from the gray having the same lightness — used of an object color (2) : degree of difference from the achromatic light-source color of the same brightness — used of a light-source color; compare HUE 2c **5** : the supplying of a market with as much of a product as it will absorb **6** : an overwhelming concentration of military forces or firepower

Sat·ur·day \'sa-tər-dē, -,dā\ *n* [ME *saterday*, fr. OE *sæterndæg* akin to OFris *saterdei*, fr. L *Saturnus* Saturn + OE *dæg* day] (bef. 12c) : the seventh day of the week — **Sat·ur·days** \-dēz, -(,)dāz\ *adv*

Saturday night special *n* (1968) : a cheap easily concealed handgun

Sat·urn \'sa-tərn\ *n* [L *Saturnus*] **1** : a Roman god of agriculture and father by Ops of Jupiter **2** : the planet 6th in order from the sun — see PLANET table

sat·ur·na·lia \,sa-tər-'nāl-yə, -'nā-lē-ə\ *n pl but sing or pl in constr* [L, fr. neut. pl. of *saturnalis* of Saturn, fr. *Saturnus*] (1591) **1** *cap* : the festival of Saturn in ancient Rome beginning on Dec. 17 **2** *sing, pl* **saturnalias** *also* **saturnalia** **a** : an unrestrained often licentious celebration : ORGY **b** : EXCESS, EXTRAVAGANCE — **sat·ur·na·lian** \-'nāl-yən, -'nā-lē-ən\ *adj* — **sat·ur·na·lian·ly** *adv*

Sa·tur·ni·an \sa-'tər-nē-ən, sə-\ *adj* (1557) **1** : of, relating to, or influenced by the planet Saturn **2** *archaic* : of or relating to the god Saturn or the golden age of his reign

sa·tur·ni·id \-nē-əd\ *n* [NL *Saturniidae*, fr. *Saturnia*, genus of moths, fr. L, daughter of the god Saturn] (ca. 1909) : any of a family (Saturniidae) of usu. large stout strong-winged moths (as a luna moth or a cecropia moth) with hairy bodies — **saturniid** *adj*

sat·ur·nine \'sa-tər-,nīn\ *adj* (15c) **1** : born under or influenced astrologically by the planet Saturn **2 a** : cold and steady in mood : slow to act or change **b** : of a gloomy or surly disposition **c** : having a sardonic aspect ⟨a ~ smile⟩ *syn* see SULLEN

sat·urn·ism \'sa-tər-,ni-zəm\ *n* [*saturn* lead] (1855) : LEAD POISONING

sa·tya·gra·ha \\(,)sə-'tyä-grə-hə, 'sə-tyə-\ *n* [New Skt *satyāgraha*, fr. Skt *satya* truth + *āgraha* persistence] (1920) : pressure for social and political reform through friendly passive resistance practiced by M. K. Gandhi and his followers in India

sa·tyr \'sā-tər, *chiefly Brit* 'sa-\ *n* [ME, fr. L *satyrus*, fr. Gk *satyros*] **1** *often cap* : a sylvan deity in Greek mythology having certain characteristics of a horse or goat and fond of Dionysian revelry **2 a** : a lecherous man **b** : one having satyriasis **3** : any of various usu. brown and gray satyrid butterflies — **sa·tyr·ic** \sā-'tir-ik, sə-, sa-\ *adj*

sa·ty·ri·a·sis \,sā-tə-'rī-ə-səs, ,sa-\ *n* [LL, fr. Gk, fr. *satyros*] (15c) : excessive or abnormal sexual craving in the male

sa·ty·rid \sə-'tī-rəd\ *n* [NL *Satyridae*, ultim. fr. Gk *satyros*] (1901) : any of a family (Satyridae) of usu. brownish butterflies that feed on grasses as larvae and have one or more forewing veins swollen basally — **satyrid** *adj*

satyr play *n* (1929) : a comic play of ancient Greece burlesquing a mythological subject and having a chorus representing satyrs

¹sauce \'sôs, *usu* 'sas *for* 4\ *n* [ME, fr. MF, fr. L *salsa*, fem. of *salsus* salted, fr. pp. of *sallere* to salt, fr. *sal* salt — more at SALT] (14c) **1 a** : a condiment or relish for food; *esp* : a fluid dressing or topping **2** : something that adds zest or piquancy **3** : stewed fruit eaten with other food or as a dessert **4** : pert or impudent language or actions **5** *slang* : LIQUOR — used with *the*

²sauce \'sôs, *usu* 'sas *for* 3\ *vt* **sauced; sauc·ing** (15c) **1 a** : to dress with relish or seasoning **b** : to cover or serve with a sauce **2 a** *archaic* : to modify the harsh or unpleasant characteristics of **b** : to give zest or piquancy to **3** : to be rude or impudent to

sauce·boat \'sôs-,bōt\ *n* (1747) : a low boat-shaped pitcher for serving sauces and gravies

sauce·box \'sôs-,bäks, 'sas-\ *n* (1588) : a saucy impudent person

sauce·pan \'sôs-,pan, *esp Brit* -pən\ *n* (1686) : a small deep cooking pan with a handle

sau·cer \'sô-sər\ *n* [ME, plate containing sauce, fr. MF *saussier*, fr. *sausse, sauce*] (1607) **1** : a small shallow dish in which a cup is set at table **2** : something resembling a saucer esp. in shape; *esp* : FLYING SAUCER — **sau·cer·like** \-,līk\ *adj*

saucy \'sô-sē, 'sa-\ *adj* **sauc·i·er; -est** (1508) **1** : served with or having the consistency of sauce **2 a** : impertinently bold and impudent **b** : amusingly forward and flippant : IRREPRESSIBLE **3** : SMART, TRIM ⟨a ~ little hat⟩ — **sauc·i·ly** \-sə-lē\ *adv* — **sauc·i·ness** \-sē-nəs\ *n*

sau·er·bra·ten \'saŭ-(ə)r-,brä-t²n\ *n* [G, fr. *sauer* sour + *Braten* roast meat] (1889) : oven-roasted or pot-roasted beef marinated before cooking in vinegar with peppercorns, garlic, onions, and bay leaves

sau·er·kraut \'saŭ(-ə)r-,kraŭt\ *n* [G, fr. *sauer* soŭr + *Kraut* greens] (1617) : cabbage cut fine and fermented in a brine made of its own juice with salt

sau·ger \'sô-gər\ *n* [origin unknown] (1882) : a pike perch (*Stizostedion canadense*) similar to but smaller than the walleye

saugh *or* **sauch** \'säk, 'sòk\ *n* [ME (Sc) *sauch*, fr. OE *salh*, alter. of *sealh* — more at SALLOW] (bef. 12c) *chiefly Scot* : SALLOW

Sauk \'sòk\ *n, pl* **Sauk** *or* **Sauks** (1762) : a member of an American Indian people formerly living in what is now Wisconsin

Saul \'sòl\ *n* [LL *Saulus*, fr. Gk *Saulos*, fr. Heb *Shā'ūl*] **1** : the first king of Israel **2** : the apostle Paul — called also *Saul of Tarsus*

sau·na \'sô-nə, 'saŭ-nə\ *n* [Finn] (1891) **1** : a Finnish steam bath in which the steam is provided by water thrown on hot stones; *also* : a bathhouse or room used for such a bath **2** : a dry heat bath; *also* : a room or cabinet used for such a bath

saun·ter \'sòn-tər, 'sän-\ *vi* [prob. fr. ME *santren* to muse] (ca. 1667) : to walk about in an idle or leisurely manner : STROLL — **saunter** *n* — **saun·ter·er** \-tər-ər\ *n*

sau·rel \sô-'rel\ *n* [F, fr. L *saurus* horse mackerel, fr. Gk *sauros* horse mackerel, lizard] (1882) : JACK MACKEREL

sau·ri·an \'sòr-ē-ən\ *n* [NL *Sauria*, fr. NL *saurus* lizard, fr. Gk *sauros*] (ca. 1829) : any of a suborder (Sauria) of reptiles including the lizards and in older classifications the crocodiles and various extinct forms (as the dinosaurs and ichthyosaurs) that resemble lizards — **saurian** *adj*

saur·is·chi·an \(,)sò-'ris-kē-ən\ *n* [NL *Saurischia*, fr. Gk *sauros* lizard + NL *ischium* ischium] (ca. 1891) : any of an order (Saurischia) of herbivorous or carnivorous dinosaurs (as a brontosaurus) that have a triradiate pelvis with the pubis typically pointed forward — compare ORNITHISCHIAN — **saurischian** *adj*

sau·ro·pod \'sòr-ə-,päd\ *n* [NL *Sauropoda*, fr. Gk *sauros* lizard + NL -*poda*] (ca. 1891) : any of a suborder (Sauropoda) of quadrupedal saurischian dinosaurs comprising herbivorous forms with a long neck and tail, small head, and more or less plantigrade 5-toed limbs — **sauro·pod** *adj*

sau·ry \'sòr-ē\ *n, pl* **sauries** [NL *saurus* lizard] (ca. 1771) **1** : a slender long-beaked fish (*Scombresox saurus*) related to the needlefishes and found in temperate parts of the Atlantic **2** : a widely distributed fish (*Cololabis saira*) of the Pacific similar to the related Atlantic saury

sau·sage \'sò-sij\ *n* [ME *sausige*, fr. ONF *saussiche*, fr. LL *salsicia*, fr. L *salsus* salted — more at SAUCE] (15c) : a highly seasoned minced meat (as pork) usu. stuffed in casings of prepared animal intestine; *also* : a link or patty of sausage

¹sau·té *also* **sau·te** \sô-'tā, sō-\ *n* [F, fr. pp. of *sauter* to jump, fr. L *saltare* — more at SALTATION] (1813) : a sautéed dish — **sauté** *adj*

²sauté *also* **saute** *vt* **sau·téed** *or* **sau·téd; sau·té·ing** (1859) : to fry in a small amount of fat

sau·ternes \sō-'tərn, sò-, -'tern\ *n, often cap* [F, fr. *Sauternes*, commune in France] (1711) **1** : a full-bodied sweet white wine from the Bordeaux region of France **2** *usu* **sauterne** : a semidry to semisweet American white wine that is a blend of several grapes

sau·vi·gnon blanc \,sō-vēn-'yōⁿ-'bläⁿ\ *n* [F, white sauvignon (variety of grape)] (1941) : a dry white wine made from a grape orig. grown in Bordeaux and the Loire valley

¹sav·age \'sa-vij\ *adj* [ME *sauvage*, fr. MF, fr. ML *salvaticus*, alter. of L *silvaticus* of the woods, wild, fr. *silva* wood, forest] (13c) **1 a** : not domesticated or under human control : UNTAMED ⟨~ beasts⟩ **b** : lacking the restraints normal to civilized human beings : FIERCE, FEROCIOUS **2** : WILD, UNCULTIVATED ⟨seldom have I seen such ~ scenery —Douglas Carruthers⟩ **3 a** : BOORISH, RUDE ⟨the ~ bad manners of most motorists —M. P. O'Connor⟩ **b** : MALICIOUS **4** : lacking complex or advanced culture : UNCIVILIZED *syn* see FIERCE — **sav·age·ly** *adv* — **sav·age·ness** *n*

²savage *n* (15c) **1** : a person belonging to a primitive society **2** : a brutal person **3** : a rude or unmannerly person

³savage *vt* **sav·aged; sav·ag·ing** (1880) : to attack or treat brutally

sav·age·ry \'sa-vij-rē, -vi-jə-\ *n, pl* **-ries** (1595) **1 a** : the quality of being savage **b** : an act of cruelty or violence **2** : an uncivilized state

sav·ag·ism \'sa-vi-,ji-zəm\ *n* (1796) : SAVAGERY

sa·van·na *also* **sa·van·nah** \sə-'va-nə\ *n* [Sp *zavana*, fr. Taino *zabana*] (1555) **1** : a treeless plain esp. in Florida **2** : a tropical or subtropical grassland containing scattered trees and drought-resistant undergrowth

sa·vant \sa-'vänt, sə-, -'väⁿ; sə-'vant, 'sa-vənt\ *n* [F, fr. MF, fr. prp. of *savoir* to know, fr. L *sapere* to be wise — more at SAGE] (1719) **1** : a person of learning; *esp* : one with detailed knowledge in some specialized field (as of science or literature) **2** : IDIOT SAVANT 1

sav·a·rin \'sa-və-rən\ *n* [F, fr. Anthelme Brillat-*Savarin* †1826 Fr. politician, writer, and gourmet] (1877) : a rich yeast cake baked in a ring mold and soaked in a rum or kirsch syrup

sa·vate \sə-'vät, sa-, -'vat\ *n* [F, lit., old shoe] (1862) : a form of boxing in which blows are delivered with either the hands or the feet

¹save \'sāv\ *vb* **saved; sav·ing** [ME, fr. OF *salver*, fr. LL *salvare*, fr. L *salvus* safe — more at SAFE] *vt* (13c) **1 a** : to deliver from sin **b** : to rescue or deliver from danger or harm **c** : to preserve or guard from injury, destruction, or loss **2 a** : to put aside as a store or reserve : ACCUMULATE ⟨to spend less by ⟨~ 25%⟩⟩ **3 a** : to make unnecessary : AVOID ⟨it ~s an hour's driving⟩ **b** (1) : to keep from being lost to an opponent (2) : to prevent an opponent from scoring or winning **4** : MAINTAIN, PRESERVE ⟨~ appearances⟩ ~ *vi* **1** : to rescue or deliver someone **2 a** : to put aside money **b** : to avoid unnecessary waste or expense : ECONOMIZE **c** : to spend less money ⟨buy now and ~⟩ **3** : to make a save *syn* see RESCUE — **sav·able** *or* **save·able** \'sā-və-bəl\ *adj* — **sav·er** *n*

²save *n* (1890) **1** : a play that prevents an opponent from scoring or winning **2** : the action of a relief pitcher in baseball in successfully protecting a team's lead

³save *prep* [ME *sauf*, fr. MF, fr. *sauf*, adj., safe — more at SAFE] (14c) : other than : BUT, EXCEPT ⟨no hope ~ one⟩

⁴save *conj* (14c) **1** : except for the fact that : ONLY — used with *that* ⟨of his earlier years little is known, ~ that he studied violin —J. N. Burk⟩ **2** : BUT, EXCEPT — used before a word often taken to be the subject of a clause ⟨no one knows about it ~ she⟩

save-all \'sā-,vòl\ *n* (ca. 1645) : something that prevents waste, loss, or damage (as a receptacle for catching waste products for further utilization)

sav·e·loy \'sa-və-,lòi\ *n* [modif. of F *cervelas*, fr. MF, fr. OIt *cervellata*, lit., pig's brains, fr. *cervello* brain, fr. L *cerebellum* — more at CEREBELLUM] (1837) *Brit* : a ready-cooked highly seasoned dry sausage

sav·in \'sa-vən\ *n* [ME, fr. MF *savine*, fr. L (*herba*) *sabina*, lit., Sabine plant] (14c) **1** : a Eurasian juniper (*Juniperus sabina*) with dark foliage and small yellowish green berries **2** : RED CEDAR 1

¹sav·ing \'sā-viŋ\ *n* [ME, fr. gerund of *saven* to save] (14c) **1** : preservation from danger or destruction : DELIVERANCE **2** : the act or an instance of economizing **3 a** *pl* : money put by **b** : the excess of income over consumption expenditures — often used in pl. **c** : a usu. specified lower cost — often used in pl. ⟨a ~s of 50%⟩

²saving *prep* [ME, fr. prp. of *saven*] (14c) **1** : EXCEPT, SAVE **2** : without disrespect to

³saving *conj* (15c) : EXCEPT, SAVE

saving grace *n* (1597) : a redeeming quality or factor

savings account *n* (1911) : an account (as in a bank) on which interest is usu. paid and from which withdrawals can be made usu. only by presentation of a passbook or by written authorization on a prescribed form

savings and loan association *n* (ca. 1924) : a cooperative association organized to hold savings of members in the form of dividend-bearing shares and to invest chiefly in home mortgage loans

savings bank *n* (1817) : a bank organized to hold funds of individual depositors in interest-bearing accounts and to make long-term investments (as in home mortgage loans)

savings bond *n* (1948) : a nontransferable registered U.S. bond issued in denominations of $50 to $10,000

sav·ior *or* **sav·iour** \'sāv-yər *also* -,yòr\ *n* [ME *saveour*, fr. MF, fr. LL *salvator*, fr. *salvare* to save] (14c) **1** : one that saves from danger or destruction **2** : one who brings salvation; *specif, cap* : JESUS 1

sa·voir faire \,sav-,wär-'far, -'fer\ *n* [F *savoir-faire*, lit., knowing how to do] (1815) : capacity for appropriate action; *esp* : a polished sureness in social behavior *syn* see TACT

¹sa·vor *also* **sa·vour** \'sā-vər\ *n* [ME, fr. OF, fr. L *sapor*, fr. *sapere* to taste — more at SAGE] (13c) **1** : the taste or smell of something **2** : a particular flavor or smell **3** : a distinctive quality — **sa·vor·less** \-ləs\ *adj* — **sa·vor·ous** \'sā-vər-əs, 'sāv-rəs\ *adj*

²savor *also* **savour** *vb* **sa·vored; sa·vor·ing** \'sā-vər-iŋ, 'sāv-riŋ\ *vi* (14c) : to have a specified smell or quality : SMACK ~ *vt* **1** : to give flavor to : SEASON **2 a** : to have experience of : TASTE **b** : to taste or smell with pleasure : RELISH **c** : to delight in : ENJOY — **sa·vor·er** \'sā-vər-ər\ *n*

¹sa·vory *also* **sa·voury** \'sā-və-rē, 'sāv-rē\ *adj* (13c) : having savor: as **a** : piquantly pleasant to the mind ⟨a ~ collection of essays⟩ **b** : morally exemplary : EDIFYING ⟨his reputation was anything but ~⟩ **c** : pleasing to the sense of taste esp. by reason of effective seasoning *syn* see PALATABLE — **sa·vor·i·ly** \-rə-lē\ *adv* — **sa·vor·i·ness** \-rē-nəs\ *n*

²savory *also* **savoury** *n, pl* **sa·vor·ies** (1661) *Brit* : a dish of stimulating flavor served usu. at the end of dinner but sometimes as an appetizer

³sa·vo·ry \'sā-və-rē, 'sāv-rē\ *n, pl* **-ries** [ME *saverey*] (14c) : either of two aromatic mints: **a** : SUMMER SAVORY **b** : WINTER SAVORY

Sa·voy·ard \sə-'vòi-,ärd, -'vòi-'ärd, ,sav-,wä-'yär(d)\ *n* [*Savoy* The-

---

\ə\ abut \'ə\ kitten, F table \ər\ further \a\ ash \ā\ ace \ä\ mop, mar \aŭ\ out \ch\ chin \e\ bet \ē\ easy \g\ go \i\ hit \ī\ ice \j\ job \ŋ\ sing \ō\ go \ò\ law \òi\ boy \th\ thin \t̲h̲\ the \ü\ loot \ŭ\ foot \y\ yet \zh\ vision \á, k̲, ⁿ, œ, œ̄, ue, ūe, 'ᵉ\ see Guide to Pronunciation ater, London, built for the presentation of Gilbert and Sullivan operas] (1890) : a devotee, performer, or producer of the comic operas of W. S. Gilbert and A. S. Sullivan

sa·voy cabbage \sə-'vȯi-, 'sa-ˌvȯi-\ *n, often cap S* [trans. of F *chou de Savoie* cabbage of Savoy (1707) : a cabbage with compact heads of wrinkled and curled leaves

¹sav·vy \'sa-vē\ *vb* **sav·vied; sav·vy·ing** [alter. of *sabi* know (in English-based creoles and pidgins), fr. Pg *sabe* he knows, fr. *saber* to know, fr. L *sapere* to be wise — more at SAGE] (1785) : UNDERSTAND

²savvy *n* (ca. 1785) : practical know-how ⟨political ∼⟩ — **savvy** *adj*

¹saw *past of* SEE

²saw \'sȯ\ *n* [ME *sawe*, fr. OE *sagu*; akin to OHG *sega* saw, L *secare* to cut] (bef. 12c) : a hand or power tool or a machine used to cut hard material (as wood, metal, or bone) and equipped usu. with a toothed blade or disk — **saw·like** \-ˌlīk\ *adj*

³saw *vb* **sawed** \'sȯd\; **sawed** *or* **sawn** \'sȯn\; **saw·ing** \'sȯ-(ə)iŋ\ *vt* (13c) **1 :** to cut with a saw **2 :** to produce or form by cutting with a saw **3 :** to slash as though with a saw ∼ *vi* **1 a :** to use a saw **b :** to cut with or as if with a saw **2 :** to undergo cutting with a saw **3 :** to make motions as though using a saw ⟨∼ed at the reins⟩ — **saw·er** \'sȯ(-ə)r\ *n*

⁴saw *n* [ME *sawe*, fr. OE *sagu* discourse; akin to OHG & ON *saga* tale, OE *secgan* to say — more at SAY] (bef. 12c) : MAXIM, PROVERB

saw·bones \'sȯ-ˌbōnz\ *n, pl* **sawbones** *or* **saw·bones·es** (1837) *slang* **:** PHYSICIAN, SURGEON

saw·buck \'sȯ-ˌbək\ *n* (1850) **1** *slang* **:** a 10-dollar bill **2 :** SAWHORSE; *esp* **:** one with X-shaped ends

saw·dust \'sȯ-(ˌ)dəst\ *n* (1530) : fine particles (as of wood) made by a saw in cutting

sawed–off \'sȯ-ˌdȯf\ *adj* (1869) **1 :** having an end sawed off ⟨a ∼ shotgun⟩ **2 :** of less than average height

saw·fish \'sȯ-ˌfish\ *n* (1664) : any of a family (Pristidae) of large elongate rays that resemble sharks but have a long flattened snout with a row of serrate structures along each edge and that live in tropical and subtropical shallow seas and in or near the mouths of rivers

saw·fly \-ˌflī\ *n* (1773) : any of numerous hymenopterous insects (superfamily Tenthredinoidea) with the female usu. having a sawlike ovipositor and with the larva resembling a plant-feeding caterpillar

saw grass *n* (1822) : any of various sedges (as of the genus *Cladium*) having the edges of the leaves set with minute sharp teeth

saw·horse \'sȯ-ˌhȯrs\ *n* (1778) : a frame on which wood is laid for sawing by hand; *esp* **:** HORSE 2b

saw·log \-ˌlȯg, -ˌläg\ *n* (1756) : a log of suitable size for sawing into lumber

saw·mill \-ˌmil\ *n* (1553) : a mill or machine for sawing logs

saw·ney \'sȯ-nē\ *n* [perh. fr. *sawney* Scotsman, fr. Sc. alter. of *Sandy*, short for *Alexander*] (ca. 1700) *chiefly Brit* **:** FOOL, SIMPLETON — **sawney** *adj*

saw palmetto *n* (1797) : any of several shrubby palms chiefly of the southern U.S. and West Indies that have spiny-toothed petioles; *esp* **:** a common palm (*Serenoa repens*) of the southeastern U.S. with a usu. creeping stem

saw set *n* (1846) : an instrument used to set the teeth of saws

saw·tim·ber \'sȯ-ˌtim-bər\ *n* (1901) : timber suitable for sawing into lumber

saw·tooth \-ˌtüth\ *adj* (ca. 1859) : having serrations : arranged or having parts arranged like the teeth of a saw ⟨a ∼ roof⟩

saw–toothed \-'tütht\ *adj* (ca. 1857) **1 :** having teeth like those of a saw ⟨a ∼ shark⟩ **2 :** SAWTOOTH

saw–whet owl \'sȯ-ˌhwet-, -ˌwet-\ *n* [fr. the supposed resemblance of its cry to the sound made in filing a saw] (1834) : a very small harsh-voiced No. American owl (*Aegolius acadicus*) that is largely dark brown above and chestnut streaked with white beneath — called also *saw-whet*

saw·yer \'sȯ-yər, 'sȯi-ər\ *n* (13c) **1 :** one that saws **2 :** any of several large longicorn beetles whose larvae bore large holes in timber or dead wood **3 :** a tree fast in the bed of a stream with its branches projecting to the surface

sax \'saks\ *n* (ca. 1923) : SAXOPHONE

sax·horn \'saks-ˌhȯrn\ *n* [Antoine Sax †1894 Belgian instrument maker + E *horn*] (1844) : any of a group of valved brass instruments ranging from soprano to bass and characterized by a conical tube, oval shape, and cup-shaped mouthpiece

sax·ic·o·lous \sak-'si-kə-ləs\ *adj* [L *saxum* rock (akin to L *secare* to cut) + E *-colous* — more at SAW] (1856) : inhabiting or growing among rocks ⟨∼ lichens⟩

sax·i·frage \'sak-sə-frij, -ˌfräj\ *n* [ME, fr. MF, fr. LL *saxifraga*, fr. L, fem. of *saxifragus* breaking rocks, fr. *saxum* rock + *frangere* to break — more at BREAK] (14c) : any of a genus (*Saxifraga* of the family Saxifragaceae, the saxifrage family) of chiefly perennial herbs with showy pentamerous flowers and often with basal tufted leaves

sax·i·tox·in \ˌsak-sə-'täk-sən\ *n* [*saxi-* (fr. NL *Saxidomus giganteus*, species of butter clam from which it is isolated) + *toxin*] (1962) : a potent nonprotein neurotoxin $C_{10}H_{17}N_7O_4 \cdot 2HCl$ that originates in dinoflagellates (genus *Gonyaulax*) found in red tides and that sometimes occurs in and renders toxic normally edible mollusks which feed on them

Sax·on \'sak-sən\ *n* [ME, fr. LL *Saxones* Saxons, of Gmc origin; akin to OE *Seaxan* Saxons] (13c) **1 a** (1) : a member of a Germanic people that entered and conquered England with the Angles and Jutes in the 5th century A.D. and merged with them to form the Anglo-Saxon people (2) : an Englishman or lowlander as distinguished from a Welshman, Irishman, or Highlander **b :** a native or inhabitant of Saxony **2 a :** the Germanic language or dialect of any of the Saxon peoples **b :** the Germanic element in the English language esp. as distinguished from the French and Latin — **Saxon** *adj*

sax·o·ny \'sak-s(ə-)nē\ *n, pl* **-nies** *often cap* [*Saxony*, Germany] (1842) **1 a :** a fine soft woolen fabric **b :** a fine closely twisted knitting yarn **2 :** a Wilton jacquard carpet

sax·o·phone \'sak-sə-ˌfōn\ *n* [F, fr. Antoine Sax

saxophone

†1894 Belgian instrument maker + F *-phone*] (1851) : one of a group of single-reed woodwind instruments ranging from soprano to bass and characterized by a conical metal tube and finger keys — **sax·o·phon·ic** \ˌsak-sə-'fō-nik, -'fä-\ *adj* — **sax·o·phon·ist** \'sak-sə-ˌfō-nist, *esp Brit* sak-'sä-fə-\ *n*

sax·tu·ba \'saks-ˌtü-bə, -ˌtyü-\ *n* [Antoine Sax + E *tuba*] (1856) : a bass saxhorn

¹say \'sā, *Southern also* 'se\ *vb* **said** \'sed, *esp when subject follows* səd\; **say·ing** \'sā-iŋ\; **says** \'sez, *sometimes* 'sāz, *esp when subject follows* səz\ [ME, fr. OE *secgan*; akin to OHG *sagēn* to say, Lith *sakyti*, Gk *ennepein* to speak, tell] *vt* (bef. 12c) **1 a :** to express in words : STATE **b :** to state as opinion or belief : DECLARE **2 a :** UTTER, PRONOUNCE **b :** RECITE, REPEAT ⟨∼ your prayers⟩ **3 a :** INDICATE, SHOW ⟨the clock ∼s five minutes after twelve⟩ **b :** to give expression to : COMMUNICATE ⟨a glance that *said* all that was necessary⟩ ∼ *vi* : to express oneself : SPEAK — **say·er** \'sā-ər, 'se-ər\ *n* — **say uncle** : to admit defeat — **that is to say** : in other words : in effect

²say *n, pl* **says** \'sāz, *Southern also* 'sez\ (1571) **1** *archaic* : something that is said : STATEMENT **2 :** an expression of opinion ⟨had my ∼⟩ **3 :** a right or power to influence action or decision; *esp* **:** the authority to make final decisions

³say *adv* [fr. imper. of ¹*say*] (1596) **1 :** ABOUT, APPROXIMATELY ⟨the property is worth, ∼, four million dollars⟩ **2 :** for example : AS ⟨if we compress any gas, ∼ oxygen⟩

say·able \'sā-ə-bəl, 'se-\ *adj* (1856) **1 :** capable of being said **2 :** capable of being spoken effectively or easily ⟨readings in ∼ Chinese — *Linguistic Reporter*⟩

say·est \'sā-əst\ *archaic 2d person sing of* SAY

say·ing \'sā-iŋ, 'se-\ *n* (14c) : something said; *esp* **:** ADAGE

say–so \'sā-(ˌ)sō, 'se-\ *n* (1637) **1 a :** one's unsupported assertion or assurance **b :** an authoritative pronouncement ⟨left the hospital on the ∼ of his doctor⟩ **2 :** a right of final decision ⟨has the ultimate ∼ on what will be taught⟩

say·yid \'sī-yəd, 'sā-; 'sid, 'säd\ *n* [Ar] (1788) **1 :** an Islamic chief or leader **2 :** LORD, SIR — used as a courtesy title for a Muslim of rank or lineage

Saz·e·rac \'sa-zə-ˌrak\ *trademark* — used for a cocktail with a whiskey base

¹scab \'skab\ *n* [ME, of Scand origin; akin to OSw *skabbr* scab; akin to OE *sceabb* scab, L *scabere* to scratch — more at SHAVE] (13c) **1 :** scabies of domestic animals **2 :** a crust of hardened blood and serum over a wound **3 a :** a contemptible person **b** (1) : a worker who refuses to join a labor union (2) : a union member who refuses to strike or returns to work before a strike has ended (3) : a worker who accepts employment or replaces a union worker during a strike (4) : one who works for less than union wages or on nonunion terms **4 :** any of various bacterial or fungus diseases of plants characterized by crustaceous spots; *also* **:** one of the spots

²scab *vi* **scabbed; scab·bing** (1683) **1 :** to become covered with a scab **2 :** to act as a scab

scab·bard \'ska-bərd\ *n* [ME *scaubert*, fr. AF *escaubers*] (13c) : a sheath for a sword, dagger, or bayonet — **scabbard** *vt*

scab·by \'ska-bē\ *adj* **scab·bi·er; -est** (15c) **1 a :** covered with or full of scabs ⟨∼ skin⟩ **b :** diseased with scab ⟨a ∼ animal⟩ ⟨∼ potatoes⟩ **2 :** MEAN, CONTEMPTIBLE ⟨a ∼ trick⟩

sca·bies \'skā-bēz\ *n, pl* **scabies** [L, fr. *scabere* to scratch] (1814) : contagious itch or mange esp. with exudative crusts that is caused by parasitic mites (esp. *Sarcoptes scabiei*) — **sca·bi·et·ic** \ˌskā-bē-'e-tik\ *adj*

¹sca·bi·ous \'skā-bē-əs, 'ska-\ *n* [ME *scabiose*, fr. ML *scabiosa*, fr. L, fem. of *scabiosus*, adj.] (14c) : any of a genus (*Scabiosa*) of Old World herbs of the teasel family with terminal flower heads subtended by a leafy involucre

²scabious *adj* [L *scabiosus*, fr. *scabies*] (1603) **1 :** SCABBY **2 :** of, relating to, or resembling scabies ⟨∼ eruptions⟩

scab·land \'skab-ˌland\ *n* (1904) : a region characterized by elevated tracts of rocky land with little or no soil cover and traversed or isolated by postglacial dry stream channels — usu. used in pl.

sca·brous \'ska-brəs *also* 'skā-\ *adj* [L *scabr-, scaber* rough, scurfy; akin to L *scabere* to scratch — more at SCAB] (1646) **1 :** DIFFICULT, KNOTTY ⟨a ∼ problem⟩ **2 :** rough to the touch: as **a :** having small raised dots, scales, or points ⟨a ∼ leaf⟩ **b :** covered with raised, roughened, or unwholesome patches ⟨∼ paint⟩ ⟨yellowed ∼ skin⟩ **3 :** dealing with suggestive, indecent, or scandalous themes : SALACIOUS; *also* **:** SQUALID *syn* see ROUGH — **sca·brous·ly** *adv* — **sca·brous·ness** *n*

¹scad \'skad\ *n, pl* **scad** *also* **scads** [origin unknown] (1602) : any of several carangid fishes (esp. of the genus *Decapterus*)

²scad *n* [prob. alter. of E dial. *scald* a multitude] (1869) : a large number or quantity — usu. used in pl. ⟨∼s of money⟩

scaf·fold \'ska-fəld *also* -ˌfōld\ *n* [ME, fr. ONF *escafaut*, modif. of (assumed) VL *catafalicum*, fr. Gk *kata-* cata- + L *fala* siege tower] (14c) **1 a :** a temporary or movable platform for workers (as bricklayers, painters, or miners) to stand or sit on when working at a height above the floor or ground **b :** a platform on which a criminal is executed (as by hanging or beheading) **c :** a platform at a height above ground or floor level **2 :** a supporting framework

scaf·fold·ing \-fəl-diŋ, -ˌfōl-\ *n* (14c) : a system of scaffolds; *also* **:** material for scaffolds

scag \'skag\ *n* [origin unknown] (1967) *slang* **:** HEROIN

sca·glio·la \skal-'yō-lə, -'yȯ-lə\ *n, often attrib* [It, lit., little chip] (1747) : an imitation marble used for floors, columns, and ornamental interior work

scal·able \'skā-lə-bəl\ *adj* (ca. 1580) : capable of being scaled

sca·lade \skə-'lād, -'läd\ *or* **sca·la·do** \-'lä-(ˌ)dō, -'lä-\ *n, pl* **-lades** *or* **-la·dos** [obs. It *scalada*, fr. *scalare* to scale, fr. *scala* ladder, staircase, fr. LL — more at SCALE] (1591) *archaic* : ESCALADE

¹sca·lar \'skā-lər, -ˌlär\ *adj* [L *scalaris*, fr. *scalae* stairs, ladder — more at SCALE] (ca. 1656) **1 :** having an uninterrupted series of steps : GRADUATED ⟨∼ chain of authority⟩ ⟨∼ cells⟩ **2 a :** capable of being represented by a point on a scale ⟨∼ quantity⟩ **b :** of or relating to a scalar or scalar product ⟨∼ multiplication⟩

²scalar *n* (1846) **1 :** a real number rather than a vector **2 :** a quantity (as mass or time) that has a magnitude describable by a real number and no direction

sca·la·re \skə-'lär-ē, -'ler-, -'lär-\ *n* [NL, specific epithet, fr. L, neut. of *scalaris*; fr. the barred pattern on its body] (1928) : a black and silver laterally compressed So. American cichlid fish (*Pterophyllum scalare*) popular in aquariums

sca·lar·i·form \skə-'lar-ə-,fórm\ *adj* [NL *scalariformis*, fr. L *scalaris* + *-iformis* -iform] (1836) : resembling a ladder esp. in having transverse bars or markings like the rungs of a ladder ⟨∼ cells in plants⟩ — **sca·lar·i·form·ly** *adv*

scalar product *n* (1878) : a real number that is the product of the lengths of two vectors and the cosine of the angle between them — called also *dot product, inner product*

scal·a·wag \'ska-li-,wag\ *n* [origin unknown] (ca. 1848) **1** : SCAMP, REPROBATE **2** : a white Southerner acting in support of the reconstruction governments after the American Civil War often for private gain

¹scald \'skóld\ *vb* [ME, fr. ONF *escalder*, fr. LL *excaldare* to wash in warm water, fr. L *ex-* + *calida, calda* warm water, fr. fem. of *calidus* warm, fr. *calēre* to be warm — more at LEE] *vt* (13c) **1** : to burn with or as if with hot liquid or steam **2 a** : to subject to the action of boiling water or steam **b** : to bring to a temperature just below the boiling point ⟨∼ milk⟩ **3** : SCORCH ∼ *vi* **1** : to scald something **2** : to become scalded

²scald *n* (1601) **1** : an injury to the body caused by scalding **2** : an act or process of scalding **3** : any of various conditions or diseases of plants or fruits marked esp. by a usu. brownish discoloration of tissue

³scald *adj* [*scall* + ¹-*ed*] (1561) **1** *archaic* : SCABBY, SCURFY **2** *archaic* : SHABBY, CONTEMPTIBLE

⁴scald \'skóld, 'skäld\ *var of* SKALD

⁵scald \'skóld\ *adj* [alter. of *scalded*] (1791) : subjected to scalding ⟨coffee . . . with ∼ cream —Charles Kingsley⟩

scald·ing \'skól-diŋ\ *adj* (13c) **1** : hot enough to scald ⟨∼ water⟩ **2 a** : having or producing the feeling of being burned ⟨∼ sun⟩ ⟨∼ sand⟩ **b** : SCATHING ⟨∼ criticism⟩

¹scale \'skā(ə)l\ *n* [ME, bowl, scale of a balance, fr. ON *skál*; akin to ON *skel* shell — more at SHELL] (14c) **1 a** : either pan or tray of a balance **b** : a beam that is supported freely in the center and has two pans of equal weight suspended from its ends — usu. used in pl. **2** : an instrument or machine for weighing

²scale *vb* **scaled; scal·ing** *vt* (1603) : to weigh in scales ∼ *vi* : to have a specified weight on scales

³scale *n* [ME, fr. MF *escale*, of Gmc origin; akin to OE *scealu* shell, husk — more at SHELL] (14c) **1 a** : a small, flattened, rigid, and definitely circumscribed plate forming part of the external body covering esp. of a fish **b** : a small thin plate suggesting a fish scale ⟨∼s of mica⟩ ⟨the ∼s on a moth's wing⟩ **c** : the scaly covering of a scaled animal **2 a** : a small thin dry lamina shed (as in many skin diseases) from the skin **3** : a thin coating, layer, or incrustation: **a** : usu. black scaly coating of oxide forming on the surface of a metal (as iron) when it is heated for processing **b** : a hard incrustation usu. rich in sulfate of calcium that is deposited on the inside of a vessel (as a boiler) in which water is heated **4 a** : a modified leaf protecting a seed plant bud before expansion **b** : a thin, membranous, chaffy, or woody bract **5 a** : any of the small overlapping usu. metal pieces forming the outer surface of scale armor **b** : SCALE ARMOR **6 a** : SCALE INSECT **b** : infestation with or disease caused by scale insects — **scaled** \'skā(ə)ld\ *adj* — **scale·less** \'skā(ə)l-ləs\ *adj*

⁴scale *vb* **scaled; scal·ing** *vt* (15c) **1** : to remove the scale or scales from (as by scraping) **2** : to take off in thin layers or scales **3** : to form scale on ⟨hard water ∼s a boiler⟩ **4** : to throw (as a thin flat stone) so that the edge cuts the air or so that it skips on water : SKIM ∼ *vi* **1** : to separate and come off in scales : FLAKE **2** : to shed scales ⟨scaling skin⟩ **3** : to become encrusted with scale

⁵scale *vb* **scaled; scal·ing** [ME, fr. ⁶*scale*] *vt* (14c) **1 a** : to attack with or take by means of scaling ladders ⟨∼ a castle wall⟩ **b** : to climb up or reach by means of a ladder ⟨∼ to reach the highest point of : SURMOUNT **2 a** : to arrange in a graduated series ⟨∼ a test⟩ **b** (1) : to measure by or as if by a scale (2) : to measure or estimate the sound content of (as logs) **c** : to pattern, make, regulate, set, or estimate according to some rate or standard : ADJUST ⟨a production schedule *scaled* to actual need⟩ — often used with *down* or *up* ⟨∼ down imports⟩ ∼ *vi* **1** : to climb by or as if by a ladder **2** : to rise in a graduated series **3** : MEASURE

⁶scale *n* [ME, fr. LL *scala* ladder, staircase, fr. L *scalae*, pl., stairs, rungs, ladder, fr. L *scandere* to climb — more at SCAN] (15c) **1 a** *obs* : LADDER **b** *archaic* : a means of ascent **2** : a graduated series of musical tones ascending or descending in order of pitch according to a specified scheme of their intervals **3** : something graduated esp. when used as a measure or rule: as **a** : a series of marks or points at known intervals used to measure distances (as the height of the mercury in a thermometer) **b** : an indication of the relationship between the distances on a map and the corresponding actual distances ⟨a ∼ of taxation⟩ **4 a** : a graduated series or scheme of rank or order ⟨a ∼ of taxation⟩ **b** : MINIMUM WAGE 2 **5 a** : a proportion between two sets of dimensions (as between those of a drawing and its original) **b** : a distinctive relative size, extent, or degree ⟨projects done on a large ∼⟩ **6** : a graded series of tests or of performances used in rating individual intelligence or achievement — **scale** *adj* — **to scale** : according to the proportions of an established scale of measurement ⟨floor plans drawn to scale⟩

⁷scale *n* [⁵*scale*] (ca. 1587) **1** *obs* : ESCALADE **2** : an estimate of the amount of sound lumber in logs or standing timber

scale armor *n* (1842) : armor of small metallic scales on leather or cloth

scale–down \'skā(ə)l-,daún\ *n* (1931) : a reduction according to a fixed ratio ⟨a ∼ of debts⟩

scale insect *n* (1840) : any of numerous small but very prolific homopterous insects (superfamily Coccoidea) that have winged males, wingless scale-covered females attached to the host plant, and young that suck the juices of plants and some of which are economic pests — compare LAC

scale-like \'skā(ə)l-,līk\ *adj* (1883) : resembling a scale ⟨∼ design⟩; *specif* : reduced to a minute appressed element resembling a scale

sca·lene \'skā-,lēn, skā-\ *adj* [LL *scalenus*, fr. Gk *skalēnos*, lit., uneven; perh. akin to Gk *skolios* crooked, *skelos* leg — more at ISOSCELES]

(1734) *of a triangle* : having the three sides of unequal length — see TRIANGLE illustration

scal·er \'skā-lər\ *n* (1568) **1** : one that scales **2** : a dental instrument for removing tartar from teeth **3** : an electronic device that operates a recorder or produces an output pulse after a specified number of input impulses

scale-up \'skā-,ləp\ *n* (1945) : an increase according to a fixed ratio

scall \'skól\ *n* [ME, fr. ON *skalli* bald head; akin to Sw *skulle* skull] (14c) : a scurf or scabby disorder (as of the scalp)

scal·lion \'skal-yən\ *n* [ME *scaloun*, fr. AF *scalun*, fr. (assumed) VL *escalonia*, fr. L *ascalonia (caepa)* onion of Ascalon, fr. fem. of *ascalonius* of Ascalon, fr. *Ascalon, Ascalo* Ascalon, seaport in southern Palestine] (14c) **1** : SHALLOT **2** : LEEK **3** : an onion forming a thick basal portion without a bulb; *also* : GREEN ONION

¹scal·lop \'skä-ləp, 'ska-, 'skó-\ *n* [ME *scalop*, fr. MF *escalope* shell, of Gmc origin; akin to MD *schelpe* shell] (15c) **1 a** : any of numerous marine bivalve lamellibranch mollusks (family Pectinidae) that have a radially ribbed shell with the edge undulated and that swim by opening and closing the valves **b** : the adductor muscle of a scallop as an article of food **2 a** : a valve or shell of a scallop **b** : a baking dish shaped like a valve of a scallop **3** : one of a continuous series of circle segments or angular projections forming a border **4** : PATTYPAN **5** [F *escalope*, prob. fr. MF, shell]: a thin slice of boneless meat (as veal)

²scallop *vt* (1737) **1** [fr. the use of a scallop shell as a baking dish]: to bake in a sauce usu. covered with seasoned bread or cracker crumbs ⟨∼ed potatoes⟩ **2 a** : to shape, cut, or finish in scallops **b** : to form scallops in ∼ *vi* : to gather or dredge scallops

scal·lop·er \-lə-pər\ *n* (ca. 1881) **1** : a person who dredges for or gathers scallops **2** : a boat equipped and used to dredge for scallops

scal·lo·pi·ni *or* **sca·lop·pi·ne** \,skä-lə-'pē-nē, ,ska-\ *n* [It *scaloppine*, ultim. fr. F *escalope* thin slice of meat, prob. fr. MF, shell] (1946) : thin slices of meat (as veal) sautéed or coated with flour and fried

scal·ly·wag *var of* SCALAWAG

sca·lo·gram \'skā-lə-,gram\ *n* [⁶*scale* + *-o-* + *-gram*] (1944) : an arrangement of items (as problems on a test or features of speech) in ascending order so that the presence or accomplishment of an item at one level implies the presence of or the capability to accomplish items at all lower levels

¹scalp \'skalp\ *n* [ME, of Scand origin; akin to ON *skálpr* sheath; akin to MD *schelpe* shell] (14c) **1 a** : the part of the integument of the human head usu. covered with hair in both sexes **b** : the part of an animal (as a wolf or fox) corresponding to the human scalp **2 a** : a part of the human scalp with attached hair cut or torn from an enemy as a token of victory or accomplishment (as by Indian warriors of No. America) **b** : a trophy of victory or accomplishment **3** *chiefly Scot* : a projecting mass of bare ground or rock

²scalp *vt* (1676) **1 a** : to deprive of the scalp **b** : to remove an upper part from **2** : to remove a desired constituent from and discard the rest **3** : to buy and sell so as to make small quick profits ⟨∼ stocks⟩ ⟨∼ grain⟩; *esp* : to resell at greatly increased prices ⟨∼ theater tickets⟩ ∼ *vi* **1** : to take scalps **2** : to profit by slight market fluctuations — **scalp·er** *n*

scal·pel \'skal-pəl *also* skal-'pel\ *n* [L *scalpellus, scalpellum*, dim. of *scalper, scalprum* chisel, knife, fr. *scalpere* to scratch, carve] (1742) : a small straight thin-bladed knife used esp. in surgery

scalp lock *n* (1826) : a long tuft of hair on the crown of the otherwise shaved head esp. of a warrior of some American Indian tribes

scaly \'skā-lē\ *adj* **scal·i·er; -est** (14c) **1 a** : covered with, composed of, or rich in scale or scales **b** : FLAKY **2** : of or relating to scaly animals **3** : DESPICABLE, POOR **4** : infested with scale insects ⟨∼ fruit⟩ — **scal·i·ness** *n*

scaly anteater *n* (1840) : PANGOLIN

scam \'skam\ *n* [origin unknown] (1963) : a fraudulent or deceptive act or operation ⟨an insurance ∼⟩

scam·mo·ny \'ska-mə-nē\ *n, pl* **-nies** [ME *scamonie*, fr. OE *scammoniam*, fr. L *scammonia*, fr. Gk *skammōnia*] (bef. 12c) **1** : a twining convolvulus (*Convolvulus scammonia*) of Asia Minor with a large thick root **2 a** : the dried root of scammony **b** : a cathartic resin obtained from scammony

¹scamp \'skamp\ *n* [obs. *scamp* to roam about idly] (1808) **1** : RASCAL, ROGUE **2** : an impish or playful young person — **scamp·ish** \'skam-pish\ *adj*

²scamp *vt* [origin unknown] (1837) : to perform or deal with in a hasty, neglectful, or imperfect manner

¹scam·per \'skam-pər\ *vi* **scam·pered; scam·per·ing** \-p(ə-)riŋ\ [prob. fr. obs. D *schampen* to flee, fr. MF *escamper*, fr. It *scampare*, fr. (assumed) VL *excampare* to decamp, fr. L *ex-* + *campus* field] (1691) : to run nimbly and usu. playfully about

²scamper *n* (1697) : a playful or hurried run or movement

scam·pi \'skam-pē, 'skäm-\ *n, pl* **scampi** [It, pl. of *scampo*, a European lobster] (1925) : SHRIMP; *esp* : large shrimp prepared with a garlic flavored sauce

¹scan \'skan\ *vb* **scanned; scan·ning** [ME *scannen*, fr. LL *scandere*, fr. L, to climb; akin to MIr *sceinnid* he springs, Skt *skandati* he leaps] *vt* (14c) **1** : to read or mark so as to show metrical structure **2** : to examine by point-by-point observation or checking: **a** : to investigate thoroughly by checking point by point and often repeatedly ⟨a fire lookout *scanning* the hills with binoculars⟩ **b** : to glance from point to point of often hastily, casually, or in search of a particular item ⟨∼ the want ads looking for a job⟩ **3 a** : to examine esp. systematically with a sensing device (as a photometer or a beam of radiation) usu. to obtain information **b** : to pass an electron beam over and convert (an image) into variations of electrical properties (as voltage) that convey information electronically **c** : to pass over in the formation of an image ⟨the electron beam ∼s the picture tube⟩ ∼ *vi* **1** : to scan verse **2** : to conform to a metrical pattern *syn* see SCRUTINIZE — **scan·na·ble** \'ska-nə-bəl\ *adj*

\ə\ abut \ʹ\ kitten, F table \ər\ further \a\ ash \ā\ ace \ä\ mop, mar \aú\ out \ch\ chin \e\ bet \ē\ easy \g\ go \i\ hit \ī\ ice \j\ job \ŋ\ sing \ō\ go \ó\ law \ói\ boy \th\ thin \t̲h\ the \ü\ loot \ú\ foot \y\ yet \zh\ vision \á, k̲, ⁿ, œ, œ̄, ue, ūe, ʸ\ *see* Guide to Pronunciation

²**scan** n (1706) **1** : the act or process of scanning **2** : a radar or television trace **3** **a** : a depiction (as a photograph) of the distribution of a radioactive material in something (as a bodily organ) **b** : an image of a bodily part produced (as by computer) by combining radiographic data obtained from several angles or sections

¹**scan-dal** \'skan-d³l\ n [ME, fr. LL *scandalum* stumbling block, offense, fr. Gk *skandalon* trap, stumbling block, offense; akin to L *scandere* to climb] (13c) **1** **a** : discredit brought upon religion by unseemly conduct in a religious person **b** : conduct that causes or encourages a lapse of faith or of religious obedience in another **2** : loss of or damage to reputation caused by actual or apparent violation of morality or propriety : DISGRACE **3** **a** : a circumstance or action that offends propriety or established moral conceptions or disgraces those associated with it **b** : a person whose conduct offends propriety or morality **4** : malicious or defamatory gossip **5** : indignation, chagrin, or bewilderment brought about by a flagrant violation of morality, propriety, or religious opinion *syn* see OFFENSE

²**scandal** vt (1592) 1 obs : DISGRACE **2** chiefly dial : DEFAME, SLANDER

scan-dal-ise chiefly Brit var of SCANDALIZE

scan-dal-ize \'skan-də-₁līz\ vt -ized; -iz-ing (1566) **1** : to speak falsely or maliciously of **2** archaic : to bring into reproach **3** : to offend the moral sense of : SHOCK

scan-dal-mon-ger \'skan-d³l-₁məŋ-gər, -₁mäŋ-\ n (1721) : a person who circulates scandal — **scan-dal-mon-ger-ing** \-g(ə-)riŋ\ n

scan-dal-ous \'skan-d³l-əs\ adj (1603) **1** : LIBELOUS, DEFAMATORY **2** : offensive to propriety or morality : SHOCKING — **scan-dal-ous-ly** adv — **scan-dal-ous-ness** n

scandal sheet n (1904) : a newspaper or periodical dealing to a large extent in scandal and gossip

scan-dent \'skan-dənt\ adj [L scandent-, scandens, prp. of scandere to climb — more at SCAN] (ca. 1682) : characterized by a climbing mode of growth ⟨~ stems⟩ ⟨~ vines⟩

Scan-di-an \'skan-dē-ən\ adj [L Scandia] (1668) **1** : SCANDINAVIAN **2** : of or relating to the languages of Scandinavia — **Scandian** n

Scan-di-na-vian \₁skan-də-¹nā-vē-ən, -vyən\ n (1766) **1** : the North Germanic languages **2** **a** : a native or inhabitant of Scandinavia **b** : a person of Scandinavian descent — **Scandinavian** adj

scan-di-um \'skan-dē-əm\ n [NL, fr. L Scandia, ancient name of southern Scandinavian peninsula] (1879) : a white metallic element found in association with rare earth elements — see ELEMENT table

scan-ner \'ska-nər\ n (1557) : one that scans: as **a** : a device for sensing recorded data **b** : a device (as a CAT scanner) used for scanning something (as the human body)

scanning electron microscope n (1953) : an electron microscope in which a beam of focused electrons moves across the object with the secondary electrons produced by the object and the electrons scattered by the object being collected to form a three-dimensional image on a cathode-ray tube — called also *scanning microscope* — **scanning electron microscopy** n

scanning tunneling microscope n (1983) : a microscope that makes use of the phenomenon of electron tunneling to map the positions of individual atoms in a surface or to move atoms around on a surface — **scanning tunneling microscopy** n

scan-sion \'skan(t)-shən\ n [LL scansion-, scansio, fr. L, act of climbing, fr. scandere] (1671) : the analysis of verse to show its meter

¹**scant** \'skant\ adj [ME, fr. ON skamt, neut. of skammr short] (14c) **1** dial **a** : excessively frugal **b** : not prodigal : CHARY **2** **a** : barely or scarcely sufficient; esp : not quite coming up to a stated measure **b** : lacking in amplitude or quantity **3** : having a small or insufficient supply ⟨he's fat, and ~ of breath —Shak.⟩ *syn* see MEAGER — **scant-ly** adv — **scant-ness** n

²**scant** adv (15c) dial : SCARCELY, HARDLY

³**scant** vt (ca. 1580) **1** : to provide an incomplete supply of **2** : to make small, narrow, or meager **3** : to give scant attention to : SLIGHT **4** : to provide with a meager or inadequate portion or supply : STINT

scant-ies \'skan-tēz\ n pl [blend of ¹scant and panties] (1929) : abbreviated panties for women

scant-ling \'skant-liŋ, -lən\ n [alter. of ME scantilon, lit., mason's or carpenter's gauge, fr. ONF escantillon] (1555) **1** **a** : the dimensions of timber and stone used in building **b** : the dimensions of a frame or strake used in shipbuilding **2** : a small quantity, amount, or proportion : MODICUM **3** : a small piece of lumber (as an upright piece in house framing)

scanty \'skan-tē\ adj scant-i-er; -est [E dial. scant scanty supply, fr. ME, fr. ON skamt, fr. neut. of skammr short] (1660) : limited or less than sufficient in degree, quantity, or extent *syn* see MEAGER — **scant-i-ly** \'skan-t³l-ē\ adv — **scant-i-ness** \'skan-tē-nəs\ n

¹**scape** \'skāp\ vb scaped; scap-ing [ME, short for escapen] (13c) : ESCAPE

²**scape** n [L scapus shaft, stalk — more at SHAFT] (1601) **1** : a peduncle arising at or beneath the surface of the ground in an acaulescent plant (as the tulip); broadly : a flower stalk **2** : the shaft of an animal part (as an antenna or feather)

³**scape** n [landscape] (1773) : a view or picture of a scene — usu. used in combination ⟨cityscape⟩

¹**scape-goat** \'skāp-₁gōt\ n [¹scape; intended as trans. of Heb 'azāzēl (prob. name of a demon), as if 'ēz 'ōzēl goat that departs—Lev 16:8 (AV)] (1530) **1** : a goat upon whose head are symbolically placed the sins of the people after which he is sent into the wilderness in the biblical ceremony for Yom Kippur **2** **a** : one that bears the blame for others **b** : one that is the object of irrational hostility

²**scapegoat** vt (1943) : to make a scapegoat of — **scape-goat-ism** \-₁gō-₁ti-zəm\ n

scape-grace \'skāp-₁grās\ n [¹scape] (1809) : an incorrigible rascal

scaph-oid \'ska-₁fȯid\ n [NL scaphoides, fr. Gk skaphoeidēs, fr. skaphos boat] (1846) : the bone of the thumb side of the carpus that is the largest in the proximal row; also : the navicular bone of the tarsus — **scaphoid** adj

scap-o-lite \'ska-pə-₁līt\ n [F, fr. L scapus shaft + F -o- + -lite; fr. the prismatic shape of its crystals] (1802) : any of a group of minerals that are essentially complex silicates of aluminum, calcium, and sodium and that include some used as semiprecious stones

sca-pose \'skā-₁pōs\ adj (ca. 1903) : bearing, resembling, or consisting of a scape ⟨the terminal ~ flowers of a pyrola⟩

scap-u-la \'ska-pyə-lə\ n, pl **-lae** \-₁lē, -₁lī\ or **-las** [NL, fr. L, shoulder blade, shoulder] (1578) : either of a pair of large triangular bones lying one in each dorsal lateral part of the thorax, being the principal bone of the corresponding half of the shoulder girdle, and articulating with the corresponding clavicle or coracoid — called also *shoulder blade*

¹**scap-u-lar** \-lər\ n [ME scapulare, fr. LL, fr. L scapula shoulder] (15c) **1** **a** : a long wide band of cloth with an opening for the head worn front and back over the shoulders as part of a monastic habit **b** : a pair of small cloth squares joined by shoulder tapes and worn under the clothing on the breast and back as a sacramental and often also as a badge of a third order or confraternity **2** **a** : SCAPULA **b** : one of the feathers covering the base of a bird's wing — see BIRD illustration

²**scapular** adj [NL scapularis, fr. scapula] (1713) : of or relating to the shoulder, the scapula, or scapulars

scapular medal n (1912) : a medal worn in place of a sacramental scapular

¹**scar** \'skär\ n [ME skere, fr. ON sker skerry; prob. akin to ON skera to cut — more at SHEAR] (14c) **1** : an isolated or protruding rock **2** : a steep rocky eminence : a bare place on the side of a mountain

²**scar** n [ME escare, scar, fr. MF escare scab, fr. LL eschara, fr. Gk, hearth, brazier, scab] (14c) **1** **a** : a mark left (as in the skin) by the healing of injured tissue **2** **a** : a mark left on a stem or branch by a fallen leaf or harvested fruit **b** : CICATRIX **2** **3** : a mark or indentation resulting from damage or wear **4** : a lasting moral or emotional injury ⟨one of his men had been killed . . . in a manner that left a ~ upon his mind —H. G. Wells⟩ — **scar-less** \-ləs\ adj

³**scar** vb scarred; scar-ring vt (1555) **1** : to mark with a scar **2** : to do lasting injury to ~ vi **1** : to form a scar **2** : to become scarred

scar-ab \'skar-əb\ n [MF scarabee, fr. L scarabaeus] (1579) **1** : any of a family (Scarabaeidae) of stout-bodied beetles (as a dung beetle) with lamellate or flabellate antennae **2** : a stone or faience beetle used in ancient Egypt as a talisman, ornament, and a symbol of resurrection

scar-a-bae-us \₁skar-ə-¹bē-əs\ n [L] (1664) : SCARAB 2

scar-a-mouch or **scar-a-mouche** \'skar-ə-₁müsh, -₁müch, -₁maüch\ n [F Scaramouche, fr. It Scaramuccia, fr. scaramuccia skirmish] (1662) **1** cap : a stock character in the Italian commedia dell'arte that burlesques the Spanish don and is characterized by boastfulness and cowardliness **2** **a** : a cowardly buffoon **b** : RASCAL, SCAMP

¹**scarce** \'skers, 'skars\ adj scarc-er; scarc-est [ME scars, fr. ONF escars, fr. (assumed) VL excarpsus, lit., plucked out, pp. of L excarpere to pluck out — more at EXCERPT] (14c) **1** : deficient in quantity or number compared with the demand : not plentiful or abundant **2** : intentionally absent ⟨made himself ~ at inspection time⟩ *syn* see INFREQUENT — **scarce-ness** n

²**scarce** adv (15c) : SCARCELY, HARDLY

scarce-ly adv (14c) **1** **a** : by a narrow margin : only just ⟨had ~ rung the bell when the door flew open —Agnes S. Turnbull⟩ **b** : almost not ⟨could ~ see for the fog⟩ **2** **a** : certainly not ⟨could ~ interfere⟩ **b** : probably not ⟨there could ~ have been found a leader better equipped —V. L. Parrington⟩

scar-ci-ty \'sker-sə-tē, 'skar-, -stē\ n, pl **-ties** (14c) : the quality or state of being scarce; esp : want of provisions for the support of life

¹**scare** \'sker, 'skar\ vb scared; scar-ing [ME skerren, fr. ON skirra, fr. skjarr shy, timid] vt (13c) : to frighten esp. suddenly : ALARM ~ vi : to become scared — **scar-er** n

²**scare** n (ca. 1548) **1** : a sudden fright **2** : a widespread state of alarm : PANIC — **scare** adj

scare-crow \'sker-₁krō, 'skar-\ n (1573) **1** **a** : an object usu. suggesting a human figure that is set up to frighten birds away from crops **b** : something frightening but harmless **2** : a skinny or ragged person

scared adj (1590) : thrown into or being in a state of fear, fright, or panic ⟨~ of snakes⟩ ⟨~ to go out⟩

scaredy–cat \'sker-dē-₁kat, 'skar-\ n [scared (pp. of scare) + ¹-y + cat] (1948) : an unduly fearful person

scare-head \'sker-₁hed, 'skar-\ n (1887) : a big, sensational, or alarming newspaper headline

scare-mon-ger \-₁məŋ-gər, -₁mäŋ-\ n (1888) : one inclined to raise or excite alarms esp. needlessly

scare up vt (1841) : to find or get together with considerable labor or difficulty : scrape up ⟨managed to scare up the money⟩

¹**scarf** \'skärf\ n, pl **scarfs** [ME skarf, prob. of Scand origin; akin to ON skarfr scarf] (15c) **1** : either of the chamfered or cutaway ends that fit together to form a scarf joint **2** : a joint made by chamfering, halving, or notching two pieces to correspond and lapping and bolting them — called also *scarf joint*

²**scarf** also **scarph** \'skärf\ vt (1627) **1** : to unite by a scarf joint **2** : to form a scarf on

³**scarf** n, pl **scarves** \'skärvz\ or **scarfs** [ONF escarpe sash, sling] (1555) **1** **a** : a military or official sash usu. indicative of rank **b** archaic : TIPPET **3** **2** : a broad band of cloth worn about the shoulders, around the neck, or over the head **3** : RUNNER 6b

⁴**scarf** vt (1598) **1** : to wrap, cover, or adorn with or as if with a scarf **2** : to wrap or throw on (a scarf or mantle) loosely

⁵**scarf** vt [by alter.] (ca. 1960) : ³SCOFF 1 ⟨~ed down my sandwich⟩

scarf-pin \'skärf-₁pin\ n (1859) : TIEPIN

scarf-skin \'skärf-₁skin\ n [³scarf] (1615) : EPIDERMIS; esp : that forming the cuticle of a nail

scar-i-fi-ca-tion \₁skar-ə-fə-¹kā-shən, ₁sker-\ n (14c) **1** : the act or process of scarifying **2** : a mark or marks made by scarifying

¹**scar-i-fy** \'skar-ə-₁fī, 'sker-\ vt -fied; -fy-ing [ME scarifien, fr. MF scarifier, fr. LL scarificare, alter. of L scarifare, fr. Gk skariphasthai to scratch an outline, sketch — more at SCRIBE] (14c) **1** : to make scratches or small cuts in (as the skin) ⟨~ an area for vaccination⟩ **2** : to lacerate the feelings of **3** : to break up and loosen the surface of (as a field or road) **4** : to cut or soften the wall of (a hard seed) to hasten germination — **scar-i-fi-er** \-₁fī-(ə)r\ n

²**scarify** vt -fied; -fy-ing (1794) : SCARE, FRIGHTEN — **scar-i-fy-ing-ly** \-₁fī-iŋ-lē\ adv

scar·i·ous \'sker-ē-əs, 'skar-\ *adj* [NL *scariosus*] (ca. 1806) : dry and membranous in texture ⟨a ~ bract⟩

scar·la·ti·na \‚skär-lə-'tē-nə\ *n* [NL, fr. ML *scarlata* scarlet] (1803) : SCARLET FEVER — **scar·la·ti·nal** \-'tē-n⁹l\ *adj*

¹**scar·let** \'skär-lət\ *n* [ME *scarlat, scarlet,* fr. OF or ML; OF *escarlate,* fr. ML *scarlata,* fr. Per *saqalāt,* a kind of rich cloth] (13c) **1** : scarlet cloth or clothes **2** : any of various bright reds

²**scarlet** *adj* (14c) **1** : of the color scarlet **2 a** : grossly and glaringly offensive ⟨sinning in flagrant and ~ fashion —G. W. Johnson⟩ **b** [fr. the use of the word in Isa 1:18 & Rev 17:1–6 (AV)] : of, characterized by, or associated with sexual immorality ⟨a ~ woman⟩

scarlet fever *n* (1676) : an acute contagious febrile disease caused by hemolytic streptococci (esp. various strains of *Streptococcus pyogenes*) and characterized by inflammation of the nose, throat, and mouth, generalized toxemia, and a red rash

scarlet letter *n* [fr. such a letter in the novel *The Scarlet Letter* (1850) by Nathaniel Hawthorne] (1850) : a scarlet A worn as a punitive mark of adultery

scarlet pimpernel *n* (1855) **1** : a common pimpernel (*Anagallis arvensis*) having scarlet, white, or purplish flowers that close in cloudy weather **2** [*Scarlet Pimpernel,* assumed name of the hero of *The Scarlet Pimpernel* (1905), novel by Baroness Orczy] : a person who rescues others from mortal danger by smuggling them across a border

scarlet runner *n* (1806) : a tropical American high-climbing bean (*Phaseolus coccineus*) that has large bright red flowers and red-and-black seeds and is grown widely as an ornamental and as a food bean — called also *scarlet runner bean*

scarlet sage *n* (ca. 1890) : a garden salvia (*Salvia splendens*) of Brazil with long racemes of intense typically scarlet flowers

scarlet tanager *n* (1810) : a common American tanager (*Piranga olivacea*) with the male having scarlet plumage and black wings during the breeding season and the female having chiefly olive plumage

scarp \'skärp\ *n* [It *scarpa*] (1589) **1** : the inner side of a ditch below the parapet of a fortification **2** **a** : a line of cliffs produced by faulting or erosion — see FAULT illustration **b** : a low steep slope along a beach caused by wave erosion — **scarped** *adj*

scar·per \'skär-pər\ *vi* [prob. ultim. fr. It *scappare,* fr. (assumed) VL *excappare* — more at ESCAPE] (ca. 1846) *Brit* : FLEE, RUN AWAY; *broadly* : LEAVE, DEPART

scar·ry \'skär-ē\ *adj* [²*scar*] (1653) : bearing marks of wounds : SCARRED

¹**scart** \'skärt\ *vb* [ME, alter. of *scratten* to scratch] (14c) *chiefly Scot* : SCRATCH, SCRAPE

²**scart** *n* (ca. 1585) *chiefly Scot* : SCRATCH, MARK; *esp* : one made in writing

scar tissue *n* (1875) : the connective tissue forming a scar and composed chiefly of fibroblasts in recent scars and largely of dense collagenous fibers in old scars

scary \'sker-ē, 'skar-\ *adj* **scar·i·er; -est** (1582) **1** : causing fright : ALARMING ⟨a ~ story⟩ **2** : easily scared : TIMID **3** : feeling alarm or fright : FRIGHTENED — **scar·i·ly** \'sker-ə-lē, 'skar-\ *adv*

¹**scat** \'skat\ *vi* **scat·ted; scat·ting** [*scat,* interj. used to drive away a cat] (1838) **1** : to go away quickly **2** : to move fast : SCOOT

²**scat** *n* [perh. fr. Gk *skat-, skōr* excrement — more at SCATOLOGY] (1927) : an animal fecal dropping

³**scat** *n* [origin unknown] (1929) : jazz singing with nonsense syllables

⁴**scat** *vi* **scat·ted; scat·ting** (1935) : to improvise nonsense syllables usu. to an instrumental accompaniment : sing scat

scat·back \'skat-‚bak\ *n* [¹*scat* + *back*] (1945) : an offensive back in football who is an esp. fast and elusive ballcarrier

¹**scathe** \'skāth, 'skäth\ *n* [ME *skathe,* fr. ON *skathi;* akin to OE *sceatha* injury, Gk *askēthēs* unharmed] (13c) : HARM, INJURY — **scatheless** \-ləs\ *adj*

²**scathe** \'skāth\ *vt* **scathed; scath·ing** (13c) **1** : to do harm to; *specif* : SCORCH, SEAR **2** : to assail with withering denunciation

scath·ing \'skā-thiŋ\ *adj* (1794) : bitterly severe ⟨a ~ condemnation⟩ *syn* see CAUSTIC — **scath·ing·ly** \-thiŋ-lē\ *adv*

sca·tol·o·gy \ska-'tä-lə-jē, skə-\ *n* [Gk *skat-, skōr* excrement; akin to OE *scearn* dung, L *muscerdae* mouse droppings] (1876) **1** : interest in or treatment of obscene matters esp. in literature **2** : the biologically oriented study of excrement (as for taxonomic purposes or for the determination of diet) — **scat·o·log·i·cal** \‚ska-t⁹l-'ä-ji-kəl\ *adj*

scatt \'skat\ *n* [ME *scat,* fr. ON *skattr;* akin to OE *sceat* property, money, a small coin, OCS *skotǔ* domestic animal] (13c) *archaic* : TAX, TRIBUTE

¹**scat·ter** \'ska-tər\ *vb* [ME *scateren*] *vt* (14c) **1** **a** : to cause to separate widely **b** : to cause to vanish **2** *archaic* : to fling away heedlessly : SQUANDER **3** : to distribute irregularly **4** : to sow by casting in all directions : STREW **5** **a** : to reflect irregularly and diffusely **b** : to cause (a beam of radiation) to diffuse or disperse **6** : to divide into ineffectual small portions ~ *vi* **1** : to separate and go in various directions : DISPERSE **2** : to occur or fall irregularly or at random — **scat·ter·er** \-tər-ər\ *n*

syn SCATTER, DISPERSE, DISSIPATE, DISPEL mean to cause to separate or break up. SCATTER implies a force that drives parts or units irregularly in many directions ⟨the bowling ball *scattered* the pins⟩. DISPERSE implies a wider separation and a complete breaking up of a mass or group ⟨police *dispersed* the crowd⟩. DISSIPATE stresses complete disintegration or dissolution and final disappearance ⟨the fog was *dissipated* by the morning sun⟩. DISPEL stresses a driving away or getting rid of as if by scattering ⟨an authoritative statement that *dispelled* all doubt⟩.

²**scatter** *n* (1642) **1** : the act of scattering **2** : a small quantity or number irregularly distributed or strewn about : SCATTERING **3** : the state or extent of being scattered; *esp* : DISPERSION

scat·ter·ation \‚ska-tə-'rā-shən\ *n* (1776) **1** : the act or process of scattering : the state of being scattered **2** : the movement of people and industry away from the city; *also* : the resulting regional urbanization **3** : a policy of distributing funds and energies in too many ineffectively small units

scat·ter·brain \'ska-tər-‚brān\ *n* (1790) : a giddy heedless person

scat·ter·brained \-‚brānd\ *adj* (1747) : having the characteristics of a scatterbrain

scatter diagram *n* (1925) : a two-dimensional graph in rectangular coordinates consisting of points whose coordinates represent values of two variables under study

scat·ter·good \'ska-tər-‚gu̇d\ *n* (1577) : a wasteful person : SPENDTHRIFT

scat·ter·gram \-‚gram\ *n* (1938) : SCATTER DIAGRAM

scat·ter·gun \-‚gən\ *n or adj* (1836) : SHOTGUN

¹**scat·ter·ing** *n* (14c) **1** : an act or process in which something scatters or is scattered **2** : something scattered: as **a** : a small number or quantity interspersed here and there ⟨a ~ of visitors⟩ **b** : the random change in direction of the particles constituting a beam or wave front due to collision with particles of the medium traversed

²**scattering** *adj* (15c) **1** : going in various directions **2** : found or placed far apart and in no order **3** : divided among many or several ⟨~ votes⟩ — **scat·ter·ing·ly** \'ska-tə-riŋ-lē\ *adv*

scatter rug *n* (1926) : a rug of such a size that several can be used in a room

scat·ter·shot \'ska-tər-‚shät\ *adj* (1951) : broadly and often randomly inclusive : SHOTGUN

scat·ty \'ska-tē\ *adj* **scat·ti·er; -est** [prob. fr. *scatterbrain* + ¹*-y*] (1911) *chiefly Brit* : CRAZY

scaup \'skȯp\ *n, pl* **scaup** *or* **scaups** [short for *scaup duck; scaup* prob. alter. of *scalp* bed of shellfish] (1797) : either of two diving ducks (*Aythya affinis* or *A. marila*) with the male having a glossy purplish or greenish head and a black breast and tail

scav·enge \'ska-vənj, -vinj\ *vb* **scav·enged; scav·eng·ing** [back-formation fr. *scavenger*] *vt* (ca. 1644) **1** **a** (1) : to remove (as dirt or refuse) from an area (2) : to clean away dirt or refuse from : CLEANSE ⟨~ a street⟩ **b** : to feed on (carrion or refuse) **2** **a** : to remove (burned gases) from the cylinder of an internal combustion engine after a working stroke **b** : to remove (as an undesirable constituent) from a substance or region by chemical or physical means **c** : to clean and purify (molten metal) by taking up foreign elements in chemical union **3** : to salvage from discarded or refuse material; *also* : to salvage usable material from ~ *vi* : to work or act as a scavenger

scav·en·ger \'ska-vən-jər\ *n* [alter. of earlier *scavager,* fr. ME *skawager* customs collector, fr. *skawage* customs, fr. ONF *escauwage* inspection, fr. *escauwer* to inspect, of Gmc origin; akin to OE *scēawian* to look at — more at SHOW] (1530) **1** *chiefly Brit* : a person employed to remove dirt and refuse from streets **2** : one that scavenges: as **a** : a garbage collector **b** : a junk collector **c** : a chemically active substance acting to make innocuous or remove an undesirable substance **3** : an organism that feeds habitually on refuse or carrion

scavenger hunt *n* (1936) : a game in which players try to acquire without buying specified items within a time limit

sce·na \'shā-(‚)nä\ *n* [It, lit., scene, fr. L] (1819) : an elaborate solo vocal composition that consists of a recitative usu. followed by one or more aria sections

sce·nar·io \sə-'nar-ē-‚ō, -'ner-\ *n, pl* **-i·os** [It, fr. L *scaenarium* place for erecting stages, fr. *scaena* stage] (1878) **1** **a** : an outline or synopsis of a play; *esp* : a plot outline used by actors of the commedia dell'arte **b** : the libretto of an opera **2** **a** : SCREENPLAY **b** : SHOOTING SCRIPT **3** : a sequence of events esp. when imagined; *esp* : an account or synopsis of a possible course of action or events ⟨his ~ for a settlement envisages . . . reunification —Selig Harrison⟩

sce·nar·ist \-'nar-ist, -'ner-\ *n* (1920) : a writer of scenarios

scend \'send\ *n* [perh. short for *ascend*] (ca. 1883) **1** : the lift of a wave : SEND **2** : the upward movement of a pitching ship

scene \'sēn\ *n* [MF, stage, fr. L *scena, scaena* stage, scene, prob. fr. Etruscan, fr. Gk *skēnē* shelter, tent, building forming the background for a dramatic performance, stage; perh. akin to Gk *skia* shadow — more at SHINE] (1540) **1** : one of the subdivisions of a play: as **a** : a division of an act presenting continuous action in one place **b** : a single situation or unit of dialogue in a play ⟨the love ~⟩ **c** : a motion-picture or television episode or sequence **2** **a** : a stage setting **b** : a real or imaginary prospect suggesting a stage setting ⟨a sylvan ~⟩ **3** : the place of an occurrence or action : LOCALE ⟨~ of the crime⟩ **4** : an exhibition of anger or indecorous behavior ⟨make a ~⟩ **5** **a** : sphere of activity ⟨the drug ~⟩ **b** : SITUATION ⟨a bad ~⟩ — **behind the scenes 1** : out of public view; *also* : in secret **2** : in a position to see the hidden workings ⟨taken *behind the scenes* and told just how in fact the actual government . . . has operated —William Clark⟩

scen·ery \'sē-nə-rē, 'sēn-rē\ *n, pl* **-er·ies** (1770) **1** : the painted scenes or hangings and accessories used on a theater stage **2** : a picturesque view or landscape

scene·shift·er \'sēn-‚shif-tər\ *n* (1752) : a worker who moves the scenes in a theater

scene–steal·er \-‚stē-lər\ *n* (1949) : an actor who attracts attention when another is intended to be the center of attention

sce·nic \'sē-nik, 'se-\ *also* **sce·ni·cal** \-ni-kəl\ *adj* (1623) **1** : of or relating to the stage, a stage setting, or stage representation **2** : of or relating to natural scenery ⟨a ~ view⟩ **3** : representing graphically an action, event, or episode ⟨a ~ bas-relief⟩ — **sce·ni·cal·ly** \-ni-k(ə-)lē\ *adv*

scenic railway *n* (1894) *chiefly Brit* : a miniature railway (as in an amusement park) with artificial scenery along the way

sce·nog·ra·phy \sē-'nä-grə-fē\ *n* [Gk *skēnographia* painting of scenery, fr. *skēnē* + *-graphia* -graphy] (1645) : the art of perspective representation esp. as applied to the painting of stage scenery (as by the ancient Greeks) — **sce·nog·ra·pher** \-grə-fər\ *n* — **sce·no·graph·ic** \‚sē-nə-'gra-fik\ *adj*

¹**scent** \'sent\ *n* [ME *sent,* fr. *senten*] (14c) **1** : effluvia from a substance that affect the sense of smell: as **a** : an odor left by an animal on a surface passed over **b** : a characteristic or particular odor; *esp* : one that is agreeable **2** : power of smelling : sense of smell ⟨a keen ~⟩ **b** : power of detection : NOSE ⟨a ~ for heresy⟩ **3** : a course of pursuit or discovery ⟨throw one off the ~⟩ **4** : INKLING, INTIMATION

\ə\ **abut** \⁹\ **kitten,** F **table** \ər\ **further** \a\ **ash** \ā\ **ace** \ä\ **mop, mar** \au̇\ **out** \ch\ **chin** \e\ **bet** \ē\ **easy** \g\ **go** \i\ **hit** \ī\ **ice** \j\ **job** \ŋ\ **sing** \ō\ **go** \ȯ\ **law** \ȯi\ **boy** \th\ **thin** \t̲h̲\ **the** \ü\ **loot** \u̇\ **foot** \y\ **yet** \zh\ **vision** \ä, k̲, ⁿ, œ, œ̄, ue, ūe, ⁱ\ *see* Guide to Pronunciation

⟨a ~ of trouble⟩ **5** : PERFUME 2 **6** : bits of paper dropped in the game of hare and hounds **7** : a mixture prepared for use as a lure in hunting or fishing *syn* see FRAGRANCE, SMELL — **scent·less** \'sent-ləs\ *adj*

²scent *vb* [ME *senten*, fr. MF *sentir* to feel, smell, fr. L *sentire* to perceive, feel — more at SENSE] *vt* (15c) **1 a** : to perceive by the olfactory organs : SMELL **b** : to get or have an inkling of ⟨~ trouble⟩ **2** : to imbue or fill with odor ⟨~ed the air with perfume⟩ ~ *vi* **1** : to yield an odor of some specified kind ⟨this ~s of sulfur⟩; *also* : to bear indication or suggestions **2** : to use the nose in seeking or tracking prey

scent·ed *adj* (1666) : having scent: as **a** : having the sense of smell **b** : having a perfumed smell **c** : having or exhaling an odor

¹scep·ter \'sep-tər\ *n* [ME *sceptre*, fr. MF *ceptre*, fr. L *sceptrum*, fr. Gk *skēptron* staff, scepter, fr. *skēptesthai* to prop oneself — more at SHAFT] (14c) **1** : a staff or baton borne by a sovereign as an emblem of authority **2** : royal or imperial authority : SOVEREIGNTY

²scepter *vt* **scep·tered; scep·ter·ing** \-t(ə-)riŋ\ (1526) : to invest with the scepter in token of royal authority

scep·tered \'sep-tərd\ *adj* (1513) **1** : invested with a scepter or sovereign authority **2** : of or relating to a sovereign or to royalty

scep·tic, scep·ti·cal, scep·ti·cism *var of* SKEPTIC, SKEPTICAL, SKEPTICISM

sceptre *Brit var of* SCEPTER

scha·den·freu·de \'shä-d°n-ˌfrȯi-də\ *n, often cap* [G, fr. *Schaden* damage + *Freude* joy] (1895) : enjoyment obtained from the troubles of others

¹sched·ule \'ske-(ˌ)jü(ə)l, -jəl, *Canad also* 'she-, *Brit usu* 'she-(ˌ)dyü(ə)l\ *n* [alter. of ME *cedule*, fr. MF, slip of paper, note, fr. LL *schedula* slip of paper, dim. of (assumed) L *scheda* strip of papyrus, prob. back-formation fr. L *schedium* impromptu speech, fr. Gk *schedion*, fr. neut. of *schedios* casual; akin to Gk *schedon* near at hand, *echein* to seize, have] (1560) **1 a** *obs* : a written document **b** : a statement of supplementary details appended to a legal or legislative document **2** : a written or printed list, catalog, or inventory; *also* : TIMETABLE 1 **3** : PROGRAM; *esp* : a procedural plan that indicates the time and sequence of each operation ⟨finished on ~⟩ **4** : a body of items to be dealt with : AGENDA **5** : a governmental list of drugs all subject to the same legal restrictions and controls

²schedule *vt* **sched·uled; sched·ul·ing** (1862) **1 a** : to place in a schedule **b** : to make a schedule of **2** : to appoint, assign, or designate for a fixed time — **sched·ul·er** *n*

schee·lite \'shā-ˌlīt\ *n* [G *Scheelit*, fr. Karl W. *Scheele* †1786 Swed. chemist] (ca. 1837) : a mineral consisting of the tungstate of calcium that is a source of tungsten and its compounds

Sche·her·a·zade \shə-ˌher-ə-'zäd; -'zä-də, -dē\ *n* [G *Scheherazade*, fr. Per *Shirazād*] : the fictional wife of an oriental king and the narrator of the tales in the *Arabian Nights' Entertainments*

sche·ma \'skē-mə\ *n, pl* **sche·ma·ta** \-mə-tə\ *also* **schemas** [Gk *schēmat-, schēma*] (ca. 1890) **1** : a diagrammatic presentation; *broadly* : a structured framework or plan : OUTLINE **2** : a mental codification of experience that includes a particular organized way of perceiving cognitively and responding to a complex situation or set of stimuli

¹sche·mat·ic \ski-'ma-tik\ *adj* [NL *schematicus*, fr. Gk *schēmat-, schēma*] (1701) : of or relating to a scheme or schema — **sche·mat·i·cal·ly** \-ti-k(ə-)lē\ *adv*

²schematic *n* (1929) : a schematic drawing or diagram

sche·ma·tism \'skē-mə-ˌti-zəm\ *n* (1660) : the disposition of constituents in a pattern or according to a scheme : DESIGN; *also* : a particular systematic disposition of parts

sche·ma·tize \'skē-mə-ˌtīz\ *vt* **-tized; -tiz·ing** [Gk *schēmatizein*, fr. *schēmat-, schēma*] (1828) **1** : to form or to form into a scheme or systematic arrangement **2** : to express or depict schematically — **sche·ma·ti·za·tion** \ˌskē-mə-tə-'zā-shən\ *n*

¹scheme \'skēm\ *n* [L *schemat-, schema* arrangement, figure, fr. Gk *schēmat-, schēma*, fr. *echein* to have, hold, be in (such) a condition; akin to OE *sige* victory, Skt *sahate* he prevails] (1610) **1 a** *archaic* (1) : a mathematical or astronomical diagram (2) : a representation of the astrological aspects of the planets at a particular time **b** : a graphic sketch or outline **2** : a concise statement or table : EPITOME **3** : a plan or program of action; *esp* : a crafty or secret one **4** : a systematic or organized framework : DESIGN *syn* see PLAN

²scheme *vb* **schemed; schem·ing** *vt* (1767) : to form a scheme for ~ *vi* : to form plans; *also* : PLOT, INTRIGUE — **schem·er** *n*

schem·ing *adj* (ca. 1828) : given to forming schemes; *esp* : shrewdly devious and intriguing

¹scher·zan·do \skert-'sän-(ˌ)dō\ *adv or adj* [It, fr. verbal of *scherzare* to joke, of Gmc origin; akin to MHG *scherzen* to leap for joy, joke; perh. akin to Gk *skairein* to gambol] (ca. 1811) : in sportive manner : PLAYFULLY — used as a direction in music indicating style and tempo ⟨allegretto ~⟩

²scherzando *n, pl* **-dos** (ca. 1876) : a passage or movement in scherzando style

scher·zo \'skert-(ˌ)sō\ *n, pl* **scherzos** *or* **scher·zi** \-(ˌ)sē\ [It, lit., joke, fr. *scherzare*] (1852) : a sprightly humorous instrumental musical composition or movement commonly in quick triple time

Schick test \'shik-\ *n* [Béla *Schick*] (1916) : a serological test for susceptibility to diphtheria by cutaneous injection of a diluted diphtheria toxin that causes an area of reddening and induration in susceptible individuals

Schiff's reagent \'shifs-\ *n* [Hugo *Schiff* †1915 Ger. chemist] (1897) : a solution of fuchsine decolorized by treatment with sulfur dioxide that gives a useful test for aldehydes because they restore the dye's color — called also *Schiff reagent* \'shif-\; compare FEULGEN REACTION

schil·ler \'shi-lər\ *n* [G] (1885) : a bronzy iridescent luster (as of a mineral)

schil·ling \'shi-liŋ\ *n* [G, fr. OHG *skilling*, a gold coin — more at SHILLING] (1753) — see MONEY table

schip·per·ke \'ski-pər-kē, 'shi-, -kə; -pərk\ *n* [Flem, dim. of *schipper* skipper; fr. its use as a watchdog on boats — more at SKIPPER] (1887) : any of a Belgian breed of small stocky black dogs with foxy head and heavy coat

schism \'si-zəm, 'ski- *also* 'shi-; *among clergy usu* 'si-\ *n* [ME *scisme*, fr. MF *cisme*, fr. LL *schismat-, schisma*, fr. Gk, cleft, division, fr. *schizein* to split — more at SHED] (14c) **1** : DIVISION, SEPARATION; *also* : DIS-

CORD, DISHARMONY **2 a** : formal division in or separation from a church or religious body **b** : the offense of promoting schism

¹schis·mat·ic \siz-'ma-tik, ski-\ *n* (14c) : one who creates or takes part in schism

²schismatic *also* **schis·mat·i·cal** \-ti-kəl\ *adj* (15c) : of, relating to, or guilty of schism — **schis·mat·i·cal·ly** \-ti-k(ə-)lē\ *adv*

schis·ma·tize \'siz-mə-ˌtīz, 'skiz-\ *vb* **-tized; -tiz·ing** *vi* (1601) : to take part in schism; *esp* : to make a breach of union (as in the church) ~ *vt* : to induce into schism

schist \'shist\ *n* [F *schiste*, fr. L *schistos* (*lapis*), lit., fissile stone, fr. Gk *schistos* that may be split, fr. *schizein*] (ca. 1782) : a metamorphic crystalline rock that has a closely foliated structure and can be split along approximately parallel planes

schis·tose \'shis-ˌtōs\ *adj* (1794) : of or relating to schist : having the character or structure of a schist — **schis·tos·i·ty** \shis-'tä-sə-tē\ *n*

schis·to·some \'shis-tə-ˌsōm\ *n* [NL *Schistosoma*, fr. Gk *schistos* + *sōma* body] (1905) : any of a genus (*Schistosoma*) of elongated trematode worms with the sexes separate that parasitize the blood vessels of birds and mammals and cause a destructive human schistosomiasis; *broadly* : a worm of the family (Schistosomatidae) that includes this genus — **schis·to·som·al** \ˌshis-tə-'sō-məl\ *adj* — **schistosome** *adj*

schis·to·so·mi·a·sis \ˌshis-tə-sō-'mī-ə-səs\ *n, pl* **-a·ses** \-ˌsēz\ [NL, fr. *Schistosoma*] (1906) : infestation with or disease caused by schistosomes; *specif* : a severe endemic disease of humans in much of Asia, Africa, and So. America marked esp. by blood loss and tissue damage

schiz- or schizo- *comb form* [NL, fr. Gk *schizo-*, fr. *schizein* to split — more at SHED] **1** : cleft ⟨*schizocarp*⟩ **2** : characterized by or involving cleavage ⟨*schizogony*⟩ **3** : schizophrenia ⟨*schizoid*⟩

schizo \'skit-(ˌ)sō\ *n, pl* **schiz·os** (1945) : a schizophrenic individual

schizo·carp \'ski-zə-ˌkärp, 'skit-sə-\ *n* [ISV] (1870) : a dry compound fruit that splits at maturity into several indehiscent one-seeded carpels

schi·zog·o·ny \ski-'zä-gə-nē, skit-'sä-\ *n* [NL *schizogonia*, fr. *schiz-* + L *-gonia* -gony] (1887) : asexual reproduction by multiple segmentation characteristic of sporozoans (as the malaria parasite) — **schizo·gon·ic** \ˌski-zə-'gä-nik, ˌskit-sə-\ *or* **schi·zog·o·nous** \ski-'zä-gə-nəs, skit-'sä-gə-\ *adj*

schiz·oid \'skit-ˌsȯid\ *adj* [ISV] (1924) : characterized by, resulting from, tending toward, or suggestive of schizophrenia — **schizoid** *n*

schiz·ont \'skit-ˌzänt, 'skit-ˌsänt\ *n* [ISV] (1900) : a multinucleate sporozoan that reproduces by schizogony

schizo·phrene \'skit-sə-ˌfrēn\ *n* [ISV, prob. back-formation fr. NL *schizophrenia*] (1925) : one affected with schizophrenia : SCHIZOPHRENIC

schizo·phre·nia \ˌskit-sə-'frē-nē-ə\ *n* [NL] (1912) **1** : a psychotic disorder characterized by loss of contact with the environment, by noticeable deterioration in the level of functioning in everyday life, and by disintegration of personality expressed as disorder of feeling, thought (as in hallucinations and delusions), and conduct — called also *dementia praecox* **2** : contradictory or antagonistic qualities or attitudes ⟨both parties . . . have exhibited ~ over the desired outcome —Elizabeth Drew⟩ — **schizo·phren·ic** \-'fre-nik\ *adj or n* — **schizo·phren·i·cal·ly** \-ni-k(ə-)lē\ *adv*

schizy *or* **schiz·zy** \'skit-sē\ *adj* [by shortening & alter.] (1927) : SCHIZOID

schle·miel \shlə-'mē(ə)l\ *n* [Yiddish *shlemil*] (1892) : an unlucky bungler : CHUMP

schlepp *or* **schlep** \'shlep\ *vb* [Yiddish *shlepn*, fr. MHG *sleppen*, fr. MLG *slēpen*] *vt* (1922) : DRAG, HAUL ~ *vi* : to proceed or move slowly, tediously, or awkwardly

schlie·ren \'shlir-ən\ *n pl* [G] (1898) **1** : small masses or streaks in an igneous rock that differ in composition from the main body **2** : regions of varying refraction in a transparent medium often caused by pressure or temperature differences and detectable esp. by photographing the passage of a beam of light — **schlie·ric** \'shlir-ik\ *adj*

schlock \'shläk\ *also* **schlocky** \'shlä-kē\ *adj* [perh. fr. Yiddish *shlak* evil, nuisance, lit., blow, fr. MHG *slag, slac*, fr. OHG *slag*, fr. *slahan* to strike — more at SLAY] (1915) : of low quality or value — **schlock** *n*

schm- or shm- \shm\ *prefix* [Yiddish *shm-*] — used to form a rhyming term of derision by replacing the initial consonant or consonant cluster of a word or by preceding the initial vowel ⟨fancy, schmancy, I prefer plain⟩ ⟨Godfather-shmodfather—enough already —Judith Crist⟩

schmaltz *also* **schmalz** \'shmȯlts, 'shmälts\ *n* [Yiddish *shmalts*, lit., rendered fat, fr. MHG *smalz*; akin to OHG *smelzan* to melt — more at SMELT] (1935) **1** : sentimental or florid music or art **2** : SENTIMENTALITY — **schmaltzy** \'shmȯlt-sē, 'shmält-\ *adj*

schmear *or* **schmeer** \'shmir\ *n* [Yiddish *shmir* smear; akin to OHG *smero* grease — more at SMEAR] (1965) : an aggregate of related things ⟨the whole ~⟩

Schmidt camera \'shmit-\ *n* [B. *Schmidt* †1935 Ger. optical scientist] (1936) : a photographic telescope with specialized optics that correct for spherical aberration and coma — called also *Schmidt telescope*

schmo *or* **schmoe** \'shmō\ *n, pl* **schmoes** [origin unknown] (1947) *slang* : JERK 4

schmooze *or* **shmooze** \'shmüz\ *vi* [Yiddish *shmuesn*, fr. *schmues*, talk, fr. Heb *shēmu'ōth* news, rumor] (1897) : to converse informally : CHAT

schmuck \'shmək\ *n* [Yiddish *shmok*, lit., penis] (1892) *slang* : JERK 4

schnapps \'shnaps\ *n, pl* **schnapps** [G *Schnaps*, lit., dram of liquor, fr. LG *snaps* dram, mouthful, fr. *snappen* to snap] (1818) : any of various liquors of high alcoholic content; *esp* : strong Holland gin

schnau·zer \'shnaut-sər, 'shnaü-zər\ *n* [G, fr. *Schnauze* snout — more at SNOUT] (1923) : a dog of any of three breeds that originated in Germany and are characterized by a wiry coat, long head, small ears, heavy eyebrows, and long hair on the muzzle: **a** : STANDARD SCHNAUZER **b** : GIANT SCHNAUZER **c** : MINIATURE SCHNAUZER

schnit·zel \'shnit-səl\ *n* [G, lit., shaving, chip, dim. of *Schnitz* slice, fr. MHG *snitz*; akin to OHG *snidan* to cut, OE *snithan*, and perh. to Czech *snět* bough] (1854) : a seasoned and garnished veal cutlet

schnook \'shnük\ *n* [origin unknown] (1940) *slang* : a stupid or unimportant person : DOLT

schnor·kel \'shnȯr-kəl\ *var of* SNORKEL

schnor·rer \'shnȯr-, 'shnȯr-\ *n* [Yiddish *shnorer*] (1892) : BEGGAR; *esp* : one who wheedles others into supplying his wants

schnoz·zle \'shnä-zəl\ *n* [prob. modif. of Yiddish *shnoitsl*, dim. of *shnoits* snout; akin to G *Schnauze* snout, muzzle — more at SNOUT] (1937) *slang* : NOSE

scho·la can·to·rum \ˌskō-lə-kan-'tōr-əm, -'tòr-\ *n, pl* **scho·lae can·torum** \-ˌlē-, -ˌlā-, -ˌlī-\ [ML, school of singers] (1782) **1** : a singing school esp. for church choristers; *specif* : the choir or choir school of a monastery or of a cathedral **2** : an enclosure designed for a choir and located in the center of the nave in early church buildings

schol·ar \'skä-lər\ *n* [ME *scoler*, fr. OE *scolere* & OF *escoler*, fr. ML *scholaris*, fr. LL, of a school, fr. L *schola* school] (bef. 12c) **1** : one who attends a school or studies under a teacher : PUPIL **2 a** : one who has done advanced study in a special field **b** : a learned person **3** : a holder of a scholarship

schol·ar·ly \-lē\ *adj* (1638) : of, characteristic of, or suitable to learned persons : LEARNED, ACADEMIC

schol·ar·ship \-ˌship\ *n* (ca. 1536) **1** : a grant-in-aid to a student (as by a college or foundation) **2** : the character, qualities, activity, or attainments of a scholar : LEARNING **3** : a fund of knowledge and learning ⟨drawing on the ∼ of the ancients⟩ *syn* see KNOWLEDGE

Scholarship level *n* (1947) : S LEVEL

¹**scho·las·tic** \skə-'las-tik\ *adj* [ML & L; ML *scholasticus* of the schoolmen, fr. L, of a school, fr. Gk *scholastikos*, fr. *scholazein* to keep a school, fr. *scholē* school] (1596) **1 a** *often cap* : of or relating to Scholasticism ⟨∼ theology⟩ ⟨∼ philosophy⟩ **b** : suggestive or characteristic of a scholastic esp. in subtlety or aridity : PEDANTIC ⟨dull ∼ reports⟩ **2** : of or relating to schools or scholars; *esp* : of or relating to high school or secondary school — **scho·las·ti·cal·ly** \-ti-k(ə-)lē\ *adv*

²**scholastic** *n* (1644) **1 a** *cap* : a Scholastic philosopher **b** : PEDANT, FORMALIST **2** [NL *scholasticus*, fr. L *scholasticus*, adj.] : a student in a scholasticate **3** : one who adopts academic or traditional methods in art

scho·las·ti·cate \skə-'las-tə-ˌkāt, -ti-kət\ *n* [NL *scholasticatus*, fr. *scholasticus* student in a scholasticate] (1875) : a college-level school of general study for those preparing for membership in a Roman Catholic religious order

scho·las·ti·cism \skə-'las-tə-ˌsi-zəm\ *n* (ca. 1782) **1** *cap* **a** : a philosophical movement dominant in western Christian civilization from the 9th until the 17th century and combining religious dogma with the mystical and intuitional tradition of patristic philosophy esp. of St. Augustine and later with Aristotelianism **b** : NEO-SCHOLASTICISM **2 a** : close adherence to the traditional teachings or methods of a school or sect **b** : pedantic adherence to scholarly methods

scho·li·ast \'skō-lē-ˌast, -lē-əst\ *n* [MGk *scholiastēs*, fr. *scholiazein* to write scholia on, fr. Gk *scholion*] (1583) : a maker of scholia : COMMENTATOR, ANNOTATOR — **scho·li·as·tic** \ˌskō-lē-'as-tik\ *adj*

scho·li·um \'skō-lē-əm\ *n, pl* **-lia** \-lē-ə\ *or* **-li·ums** [NL, fr. Gk *scholion* comment, scholium, fr. dim. of *scholē* lecture] (1535) **1** : a marginal annotation or comment (as on the text of a classic by an early grammarian) **2** : a remark or observation subjoined but not essential to a demonstration or a train of reasoning

¹**school** \'skül\ *n* [ME *scole*, fr. OE *scōl*, fr. L *schola*, fr. Gk *scholē* leisure, discussion, lecture, school; perh. akin to Gk *echein* to hold — more at SCHEME] (bef. 12c) **1** : an organization that provides instruction: as **a** : an institution for the teaching of children **b** : COLLEGE, UNIVERSITY **c** (1) : a group of scholars and teachers pursuing knowledge together that with similar groups constituted a medieval university (2) : one of the four faculties of a medieval university (3) : an institution for specialized higher education often associated with a university ⟨the ∼ of engineering⟩ **d** : an establishment offering specialized instruction ⟨a secretarial ∼⟩ ⟨driving ∼s⟩ **2 a** (1) : the process of teaching or learning esp. at a school (2) : attendance at a school (3) : a session of a school **b** : a school building **c** : the students attending a school; *also* : its teachers and students **3** : a source of knowledge ⟨experience was his ∼⟩ **4 a** : persons who hold a common doctrine or follow the same teacher (as in philosophy, theology, or medicine) ⟨the Aristotelian ∼⟩ **b** : a group of artists under a common influence **c** : persons of similar opinions or behavior ⟨other ∼s of thought⟩ **5** : the regulations governing military drill of individuals or units; *also* : the exercises carried out ⟨the ∼ of the soldier⟩

²**school** *vt* (15c) **1 a** : to teach or drill in a specific knowledge or skill ⟨well ∼ed in languages⟩ **b** : to discipline or habituate to something ⟨∼ oneself in patience⟩ **2** : to educate in an institution of learning *syn* see TEACH

³**school** *n* [ME *scole*, fr. MD *schole*; akin to OE *scolu* multitude and prob. to OE *scylian* to separate — more at SKILL] (15c) : a large number of fish or aquatic animals of one kind swimming together

⁴**school** *vi* (1597) : to swim or feed in a school ⟨bluefish are ∼ing⟩

school–age *adj* (1741) : old enough to go to school ⟨∼ children⟩

school·bag \'skül-ˌbag\ *n* (1895) : a bag for carrying schoolbooks and school supplies

school board *n* (1836) : a board in charge of local public schools

school·book \-ˌbùk\ *n* (1745) : a school textbook

¹**school·boy** \-ˌbói\ *n* (1588) : a boy attending school

²**schoolboy** *adj* (1687) **1** : of, relating to, or characteristic of a schoolboy ⟨∼ pranks⟩ **2** : of, relating to, or being a sport for high school or prep school boys; *also* : being one who participates in such sports ⟨a former ∼ and collegiate goalie —D. J. Barr⟩

school·boy·ish \-ˌbói-ish\ *adj* (1831) : SCHOOLBOY 1

school bus *n* (1908) : a vehicle used for transporting children to or from school or on activities connected with school

school·child \'skül-ˌchīld\ *n* (1840) : a child attending school

school committee *n* (1787) : SCHOOL BOARD

school district *n* (1809) : a unit for administration of a public-school system often comprising several towns within a state

school·fel·low \'skül-ˌfe-(ˌ)lō\ *n* (15c) : SCHOOLMATE

school·girl \-ˌgər(-ə)l\ *n* (1777) : a girl attending school

school·house \-ˌhaùs\ *n* (14c) : a building used as a school and esp. as an elementary school

school·ing *n* (15c) **1 a** : instruction in school : EDUCATION **b** : training, guidance, or discipline derived from experience **2** *archaic* : REPROOF **3** : the cost of instruction and maintenance at school **4** : the training of a horse to service; *esp* : the teaching and exercising of horse and rider in the formal techniques of equitation

school·kid \'skül-ˌkid\ *n* (1938) : a child or teenager attending school

school–leav·er \'skül-ˌlē-vər\ *n* (1925) *Brit* : one who has left school usu. after completing a course of study

school·man \'skül-mən, -ˌman\ *n* (ca. 1540) **1 a** : one skilled in academic disputation **b** *cap* : SCHOLASTIC 1a **2** : EDUCATOR 1, 2b

school·marm \-ˌmä(r)m\ *or* **school·ma'am** \-ˌmäm, -ˌmam\ *n* [*school* + *marm*, alter. of *ma'am*] (1831) **1** : a woman schoolteacher esp. in a rural or small-town school **2** : a person who exhibits characteristics attributed to schoolteachers (as strict adherence to arbitrary rules) — **school·marm·ish** \-ˌmä(r)-mish\ *adj*

school·mas·ter \-ˌmas-tər\ *n* (13c) **1** : a man who teaches school **2** : one that disciplines or directs **3** : a reddish brown edible snapper (*Lutjanus apodus*) of the tropical Atlantic and the Gulf of Mexico — **school·mas·ter·ish** \-ˌmas-tə-rish\ *adj* — **school·mas·ter·ly** *adj*

school·mate \-ˌmāt\ *n* (1563) : a companion at school

school·mis·tress \-ˌmis-trəs\ *n* (15c) : a woman who teaches school

school·room \-ˌrüm, -ˌrùm\ *n* (1773) : CLASSROOM

school·teach·er \-ˌtē-chər\ *n* (ca. 1847) : one who teaches school

school·time \-ˌtīm\ *n* (1740) **1** : the time for beginning a session of school or during which school is held **2** : the period of life spent in school or in study

school·work \-ˌwərk\ *n* (1857) : lessons done in class or assigned to be done at home

schoo·ner \'skü-nər\ *n* [origin unknown] (1716) **1** : a typically 2-masted fore-and-aft rigged vessel with a foremast and a mainmast stepped nearly amidships **2** : a larger-than-usual drinking glass (as for beer) **3** : PRAIRIE SCHOONER

schooner rig *n* (1866) : FORE-AND-AFT RIG — **schoo·ner–rigged** \'skü-nə(r)-ˌrigd\ *adj*

schooner 1

schorl \'shór(-ə)l\ *n* [G *Schörl*] (1779) : TOURMALINE; *esp* : tourmaline of the black variety

schot·tische \'shä-tish, shä-'tēsh\ *n* [G, fr. *schottisch* Scottish, fr. *Schotte* Scotsman; akin to OE *Scottas* Scots] (1849) **1** : a round dance resembling a slow polka **2** : music for the schottische

schrod *var of* SCROD

Schrö·ding·er equation \'shrā-diŋ-ər, 'shrōē-, 'shrə(r)-\ *n* [Erwin *Schrödinger*] (1936) : an equation that describes the wave nature of elementary particles and is fundamental to the description of the properties of all matter

schtick *var of* SHTICK

schuss \'shùs, 'shüs\ *vi* [*schuss*, n., fr. G *Schuss*, lit., shot, fr. OHG *scuz* — more at SHOT] (1940) : to ski directly down a slope at high speed — **schuss** *n*

schuss·boom·er \-ˌbü-mər\ *n* (1953) : a skier who schusses

schwa \'shwä\ *n* [G, fr. Heb *schĕwā*] (1895) **1** : an unstressed mid-central vowel (as the usual sound of the first and last vowels of the English word *America*) **2** : the symbol ə used for the schwa sound and less widely for a similarly articulated stressed vowel (as in *cut*)

Schwann cell \'shwän-\ *n* [Theodor *Schwann* †1882 Ger. naturalist] (ca. 1909) : the myelin-secreting cell surrounding a myelinated nerve fiber between two nodes of Ranvier

schwar·me·rei \ˌshver-mə-'rī\ *n* [G *Schwärmerei*, fr. *schwärmen* to be enthusiastic, lit., to swarm] (1845) : excessive or unwholesome sentiment

sci·at·ic \sī-'a-tik\ *adj* [MF *sciatique*, fr. LL *sciaticus*, alter. of L *ischiadicus* of sciatica, fr. Gk *ischiadikos*, fr. *ischiad-, ischias* sciatica, fr. *ischion* ischium] (1586) **1** : of, relating to, or situated near the hip **2** : of, relating to, or caused by sciatica ⟨∼ pains⟩

sci·at·i·ca \sī-'a-ti-kə\ *n* [ME, fr. ML, fr. LL, fem. of *sciaticus*] (14c) : pain along the course of a sciatic nerve esp. in the back of the thigh; *broadly* : pain in the lower back, buttocks, hips, or adjacent parts

sciatic nerve *n* (1741) : either of the pair of largest nerves in the body that arise one on each side from the nerve plexus supplying the posterior limb and pelvic region and that pass out of the pelvis and down the back of the thigh

sci·ence \'sī-ən(t)s\ *n* [ME, fr. MF, fr. L *scientia*, fr. *scient-, sciens* having knowledge, fr. prp. of *scire* to know; prob. akin to Skt *chyati* he cuts off, L *scindere* to split — more at SHED] (14c) **1** : the state of knowing : knowledge as distinguished from ignorance or misunderstanding **2 a** : a department of systematized knowledge as an object of study ⟨the ∼ of theology⟩ **b** : something (as a sport or technique) that may be studied or learned like systematized knowledge ⟨have it down to a ∼⟩ **3 a** : knowledge or a system of knowledge covering general truths or the operation of general laws esp. as obtained and tested through scientific method **b** : such knowledge or such a system of knowledge concerned with the physical world and its phenomena : NATURAL SCIENCE **4** : a system or method reconciling practical ends with scientific laws ⟨culinary ∼⟩ **5** *cap* : CHRISTIAN SCIENCE

science fiction *n* (1851) : fiction dealing principally with the impact of actual or imagined science on society or individuals or having a scientific factor as an essential orienting component

sci·en·tial \sī-'en(t)-shəl\ *adj* (15c) **1** : relating to or producing knowledge or science **2** : having efficient knowledge : CAPABLE

sci·en·tif·ic \ˌsī-ən-'ti-fik\ *adj* [ML *scientificus* producing knowledge, fr. L *scient-, sciens* + *-i-* + *-ficus* -fic] (1589) : of, relating to, or exhibiting the methods or principles of science — **sci·en·tif·i·cal·ly** \-fi-k(ə-)lē\ *adv*

scientific method *n* (1854) : principles and procedures for the systematic pursuit of knowledge involving the recognition and formulation of a problem, the collection of data through observation and experiment, and the formulation and testing of hypotheses

\ə\ abut \ᵊ\ kitten, F table \ər\ further \a\ ash \ā\ ace \ä\ mop, mar \aù\ out \ch\ chin \e\ bet \ē\ easy \g\ go \i\ hit \ī\ ice \j\ job \ŋ\ sing \ō\ go \ò\ law \òi\ boy \th\ thin \th\ the \ü\ loot \ù\ foot \y\ yet \zh\ vision \à, k̄, ⁿ, œ, œ̄, ᵫ, ᵫ̄, ᵊ\ *see* Guide to Pronunciation

scientific notation n (ca. 1934) : a widely used floating-point system in which numbers are expressed as products consisting of a number between 1 and 10 multiplied by an appropriate power of 10

sci·en·tism \'sī-ən-,ti-zəm\ n (1877) **1** : methods and attitudes typical of or attributed to the natural scientist **2** : an exaggerated trust in the efficacy of the methods of natural science applied to all areas of investigation (as in philosophy, the social sciences, and the humanities)

sci·en·tist \'sī-ən-tist\ n [L scientia] (1834) **1** : a person learned in science and esp. natural science : a scientific investigator **2** cap : CHRISTIAN SCIENTIST

sci·en·tize \'sī-ən-,tīz\ vt **-tized; -tiz·ing** (1917) : to treat with a scientific approach 〈the attempt to ∼ reality, to name it and classify it — John Fowles〉

sci–fi \'sī-'fī\ adj [science fiction] (1955) : of, relating to, or being science fiction 〈a ∼ film〉 — **sci–fi** n

sci·li·cet \'ske-li-,ket; 'sī-lə-,set, 'si-\ adv [ME, fr. L, surely, to wit, fr. scire to know + licet it is permitted, fr. licēre to be permitted — more at LICENSE] (14c) : TO WIT, NAMELY

scil·la \'si-lə, 'ski-\ n [NL, fr. L, squill — more at SQUILL] (1824) : any of a genus (Scilla) of Old World bulbous herbs of the lily family with narrow basal leaves and pink, blue, or white racemose flowers

scim·i·tar \'si-mə-tər, -,tär\ n [It scimitarra] (ca. 1548) : a saber having a curved blade with the edge on the convex side and used chiefly by Arabs and Turks

scimitar

scin·tig·ra·phy \sin-'ti-grə-fē\ n [scintillation + -graphy; fr. the scintillation counter used to record radiation on the picture] (1958) : a diagnostic technique in which a two-dimensional picture of a bodily radiation source is obtained by the use of radioisotopes — **scin·ti·graph·ic** \,sin-tə-'gra-fik\ adj

scin·til·la \sin-'ti-lə\ n [L] (1692) : SPARK, TRACE

scin·til·lant \'sin-t°l-ənt\ adj (1737) : that scintillates : SPARKLING — **scin·til·lant·ly** adv

scin·til·late \'sin-t°l-,āt\ vb **-lat·ed; -lat·ing** [L scintillatus, pp. of scintillare to sparkle, fr. scintilla spark] vi (ca. 1623) **1** : to emit sparks : SPARK **2** : to emit quick flashes as if throwing off sparks : SPARKLE ∼ vt : to throw off as a spark or as sparkling flashes 〈∼ witticisms〉 — **scin·til·la·tor** \-,ā-tər\ n

scin·til·lat·ing (1883) : brilliantly lively, stimulating, or witty 〈∼ conversation〉

scin·til·la·tion \,sin-t°l-'ā-shən\ n (ca. 1623) **1** : an act or instance of scintillating; esp : rapid changes in the brightness of a celestial body **2 a** : a spark or flash emitted in scintillating **b** : a flash of light produced in a phosphor by an ionizing event **3** : a brilliant outburst (as of wit) **4** : a flash of the eye

scintillation counter n (1948) : a device for detecting and registering individual scintillations (as in radioactive emission)

scin·til·lom·e·ter \,sin-t°l-'ä-mə-tər\ n [L scintilla + ISV -o- + -meter] (1877) : SCINTILLATION COUNTER

sci·o·lism \'sī-ə-,li-zəm\ n [LL sciolus smatterer, fr. dim. of L scius knowing, fr. scire to know — more at SCIENCE] (1816) : a superficial show of learning — **sci·o·list** \-list\ n — **sci·o·lis·tic** \,sī-ə-'lis-tik\ adj

sci·on \'sī-ən\ n [ME, fr. MF cion, fr. Gmc origin; akin to OHG chīnan to sprout, split open, OE cīnan to gape] (13c) **1** : a detached living portion of a plant joined to a stock in grafting and usu. supplying solely aerial parts to a graft **2** : DESCENDANT, CHILD

sci·re fa·cias \,sī-rē-'fā-sh(ē-)əs\ n [ME, fr. ML, you should cause to know] (15c) **1** : a judicial writ founded on some matter of record and requiring the party proceeded against to show cause why the record should not be enforced, annulled, or vacated **2** : a legal proceeding instituted by a scire facias

sci·roc·co \shi-'rä-(,)kō, sə-\ n var of SIROCCO

scir·rhous \'sir-əs, 'skir-\ adj [NL scirrhosus, fr. scirrhus scirrhous tumor, fr. Gk skiros, skirrhos overgrown land, hardened tumor] (1563) : of, relating to, or being a hard slow-growing malignant tumor having a preponderance of fibrous tissue

scis·sile \'si-səl, -,sīl\ adj [F, fr. L scissilis, fr. scissus, pp. of scindere to split — more at SHED] (1621) : capable of being cut smoothly or split easily 〈a ∼ peptide bond〉

scis·sion \'si-zhən\ n [ME scissione, fr. MF scission, fr. LL scission-, scissio, fr. L scindere] (15c) **1** : a division or split in a group or union : SCHISM **2** : an action or process of cutting, dividing, or splitting : the state of being cut, divided, or split

¹scis·sor \'si-zər\ n [ME sisoure, fr. MF cisoire, fr. LL cisorium cutting instrument, irreg. fr. L caedere to cut] (15c) : SCISSORS

²scissor vt **scis·sored; scis·sor·ing** \'si-zə-riŋ, 'siz-riŋ\ (1612) : to cut, cut up, or cut off with scissors or shears

scis·sors \'si-zərz\ n pl but sing or pl in constr (14c) **1** : a cutting instrument having two blades whose cutting edges slide past each other **2 a** : a gymnastic feat in which the leg movements suggest the opening and closing of scissors **b** : SCISSORS HOLD

scissors–and–paste adj (1902) : being a compilation rather than an effort of original and independent investigation

scissors hold n (1909) : a wrestling hold in which the legs are locked around the head or body of an opponent

scissors kick n (ca. 1930) : a swimming kick used esp. in sidestrokes in which the legs move like scissors

scis·sor–tailed flycatcher \'si-zər-,tāld-\ n (ca. 1909) : a flycatcher (Muscivora forficata) of the southern U.S., Mexico, and Central America that has a deeply forked tail — called also scissortail

sclaff \'sklaf\ vi [Sc, sclaff, n., lit., blow with the palm; prob. of imit. origin] (1893) : to scrape the ground instead of hitting the ball cleanly on a golf stroke — **sclaff** n — **sclaff·er** n

scler– or **sclero–** comb form [NL, fr. Gk sklēr-, sklēro-, fr. sklēros — more at SKELETON] **1** : hard 〈sclerite〉 〈scleroderma〉 **2** : hardness 〈sclerometer〉

sclera \'skler-ə\ n [NL, fr. Gk sklēros] (1888) : the dense fibrous opaque white outer coat enclosing the eyeball except the part covered by the cornea — see EYE illustration — **scler·al** \-əl\ adj

scler·e·id \'skler-ē-əd\ n [ISV, irreg. fr. Gk sklēros] (ca. 1900) : a variably shaped sclerenchymatous cell of a higher plant that is often nearly isodiametric

scler·en·chy·ma \sklə-'reŋ-kə-mə\ n [NL] (1875) : a protective or supporting tissue in higher plants composed of cells with walls thickened and often lignified — **scler·en·chy·ma·tous** \,skler-ən-'ki-mə-təs, -'kī-\ adj

scler·ite \'skler-,īt\ n [ISV] (1861) : a hard chitinous or calcareous plate, piece, or spicule (as of the arthropod integument)

sclero·der·ma \,skler-ə-'dər-mə\ n [NL] (ca. 1860) : a usu. slowly progressive disease marked by the deposition of fibrous connective tissue in the skin and often in internal organs

scle·rom·e·ter \sklə-'rä-mə-tər\ n [ISV] (ca. 1879) : an instrument for determining the relative hardnesses of materials

sclero·pro·tein \,skler-ō-'prō-,tēn, -'prō-tē-ən\ n [ISV] (1907) : any of various fibrous proteins esp. from connective and skeletal tissues

scle·ros·ing \sklə-'rō-siŋ, -ziŋ\ adj [NL sclerosis + E ¹-ing] (1885) : causing or characterized by sclerosis 〈∼ agents〉

scle·ro·sis \sklə-'rō-səs\ n [ME sclirosis tumor, fr. ML, fr. Gk sklērōsis hardening, fr. sklēroun to harden, fr. sklēros] (1846) : pathological hardening of tissue esp. from overgrowth of fibrous tissue or increase in interstitial tissue; also : a disease characterized by sclerosis

¹scle·rot·ic \sklə-'rä-tik\ adj (1543) **1** : being or relating to the sclera **2** : of, relating to, or affected with sclerosis **3** : grown rigid or unresponsive esp. with age 〈∼ institutions〉

²sclerotic n [ML sclerotica, fr. (assumed) Gk sklērōtos, verbal of Gk sklēroun to harden] (1690) : SCLERA

sclerotic coat n (1741) : SCLERA

scler·o·tin \'skler-ə-tən, sklə-'rō-t²n\ n [prob. scler- + -tin (as in chitin)] (1940) : an insoluble tanned protein permeating and stiffening the chitin of the cuticle of arthropods

scle·ro·tium \sklə-'rō-sh(ē-)əm\ n, pl **-tia** \-sh(ē-)ə\ [NL, fr. (assumed) Gk sklērōtos] (1871) : a compact mass of hardened mycelium stored with reserve food material that in some higher fungi becomes detached and remains dormant until a favorable opportunity for growth occurs — **scle·ro·tial** \-'rō-shəl\ adj

scler·o·tized \'skler-ə-,tīzd\ adj [¹sclerotic + -ize + ¹-ed] (ca. 1890) : hardened esp. by the formation of sclerotin 〈∼ insect cuticle〉 — **scler·o·ti·za·tion** \,skler-e-tə-'zā-shən\ n

¹scoff \'skäf, 'skof\ n [ME scof, prob. of Scand origin; akin to obs. Dan skof jest; akin to OFris skof mockery] (14c) **1** : an expression of scorn, derision, or contempt : GIBE **2** : an object of scorn, mockery, or derision

²scoff vi (14c) : to show contempt by derisive acts or language ∼ vt : to treat or address with derision : MOCK — **scoff·er** n

syn SCOFF, JEER, GIBE, FLEER, SNEER, FLOUT mean to show one's contempt in derision or mockery. SCOFF stresses insolence, disrespect, or incredulity as motivating the derision 〈scoffed at their concerns〉. JEER suggests a coarser more undiscriminating derision 〈the crowd jeered at the prisoners〉. GIBE implies taunting either good-naturedly or in sarcastic derision 〈hooted and gibed at the umpire〉. FLEER suggests grinning or grimacing derisively 〈the saucy jackanapes fleered at my credulity〉. SNEER stresses insulting by contemptuous facial expression, phrasing, or tone of voice 〈sneered at anything romantic〉. FLOUT stresses contempt shown by refusal to heed 〈flouted the conventions of polite society〉.

³scoff vb [alter. of dial. scaff to eat greedily] vt (1846) **1** : to eat greedily **2** : SEIZE — often used with up ∼ vi : to eat something greedily

scoff·law \-,lo\ n (1924) : a contemptuous law violator

¹scold \'skōld\ n [ME scald, scold, perh. of Scand origin; akin to ON skáld poet, skald, Icel skálda to make scurrilous verse] (12c) **1 a** : one who scolds habitually or persistently **b** : a woman who disturbs the public peace by noisy and quarrelsome or abusive behavior **2** : SCOLDING

²scold vi (14c) **1** obs : to quarrel noisily **2** : to find fault noisily or angrily ∼ vt : to censure severely or angrily : REBUKE — **scold·er** n

syn SCOLD, UPBRAID, BERATE, RAIL, REVILE, VITUPERATE mean to reproach angrily and abusively. SCOLD implies rebuking in irritation or ill temper justly or unjustly 〈angrily scolding the children〉. UPBRAID implies censuring on definite and usu. justifiable grounds 〈upbraided her assistants for poor research〉. BERATE suggests prolonged and often abusive scolding 〈berated continually by an overbearing boss〉. RAIL (at or against) stresses an unrestrained berating 〈railed loudly at their insolence〉. REVILE implies a scurrilous, abusive attack prompted by anger or hatred 〈an alleged killer reviled in the press〉. VITUPERATE suggests a violent reviling 〈was vituperated for betraying his friends〉.

scold·ing n (1547) **1** : the action of one who scolds **2** : a harsh reproof

sco·le·cite \'skä-lə-,sīt, 'skō-\ n [G Skolezit, fr. Gk skōlēk-, skōlēx worm; fr. the motion of some forms when heated] (ca. 1823) : a zeolite mineral that is a hydrous calcium aluminum silicate and occurs in radiating groups of crystals, in fibrous masses, and in nodules

sco·lex \'skō-,leks\ n, pl **sco·li·ces** \-lə-,sēz\ also **sco·le·ces** \'skō-lə-,sēz, 'skä-\ [NL scolic-, scolex, fr. Gk skōlēk-, scolex; akin to Gk skolios crooked, skelos leg — more at ISOSCELES] (1855) : the head of a tapeworm either in the larva or adult stage

sco·li·o·sis \,skō-lē-'ō-səs\ n, pl **-oses** \-,sēz\ [NL, fr. Gk skoliōsis crookedness of a bodily part, fr. skolios] (ca. 1706) : a lateral curvature of the spine — **sco·li·ot·ic** \-'ä-tik\ adj

scol·lop \'skä-ləp, 'skó-\ var of SCALLOP

scol·o·pen·dra \,skä-lə-'pen-drə\ n [NL, genus of centipedes, fr. L, a kind of millipede, fr. Gk skolopendra] (1608) : CENTIPEDE

scom·broid \'skäm-,bróid\ n [ultim. fr. Gk skombros mackerel] (ca. 1842) : any of a suborder (Scombroidei) of marine bony fishes (as mackerels, tunas, albacores, bonitos, and swordfishes) of great economic importance as food fishes — **scombroid** adj

¹sconce \'skän(t)s\ n [ME, fr. MF esconse screened lantern, fr. OF, fr. fem. of escons, pp. of escondre to hide, fr. L abscondere — more at ABSCOND] (15c) **1** : a bracket candlestick or group of candlesticks; also : an electric light fixture patterned on a candle sconce **2** : HEAD, SKULL

²sconce n [D schans, fr. G Schanze] (1571) : a detached defensive work

scone \'skōn, 'skän\ *n* [perh. fr. D *schoonbrood* fine white bread, fr. *schoon* pure, clean + *brood* bread] (1513) : a rich quick bread cut into usu. triangular shapes and cooked on a griddle or baked on a sheet

¹scoop \'sküp\ *n* [ME *scope,* fr. MD *schope;* akin to OHG *skepfen* to shape — more at SHAPE] (14c) **1 a :** a large ladle **b :** a deep shovel or similar implement for digging, dipping, or shoveling **c :** a usu. hemispherical utensil for dipping food **d :** a small spoon-shaped utensil or instrument for cutting or gouging **2 :** the action of scooping **3 a :** a hollow place : CAVITY **b :** a part forming or surrounding an opening for channeling a fluid (as air) into a desired path **4 a :** information esp. of immediate interest **b :** BEAT 5b **5 :** a rounded and usu. low-cut neckline on a woman's garment — called also *scoop neck* — **scoop·ful** \-,fül\ *n*

²scoop *vt* (14c) **1 a :** to take out or up with or as if with a scoop : DIP **b :** to pick up quickly or surreptitiously with or as if with a sweep of the hand — often used with *up* **2 :** to empty by ladling out the contents **3 :** to make hollow : DIG OUT **4 :** BEAT 5a(2) — **scoop·er** *n*

scoot \'sküt\ *vi* [perh. of Scand origin; akin to ON *skjōta* to shoot — more at SHOOT] (1758) **1 :** to move swiftly **2 :** to slide esp. while seated ⟨~ over and let me sit down⟩ — **scoot** *n*

scoot·er \'skü-tər\ *n* (1916) **1 :** a child's foot-operated vehicle consisting of a narrow footboard between two wheels tandem with an upright steering handle attached to the front wheel **2 :** MOTOR SCOOTER

scop \'shōp, 'skōp, 'skäp\ *n* [OE; akin to OHG *schof* poet] (bef. 12c) : an Old English bard or poet

¹scope \'skōp\ *n* [It *scopo* purpose, goal, fr. Gk *skopos;* akin to Gk *skeptesthai* to watch, look at — more at SPY] (ca. 1555) **1 :** INTENTION, OBJECT **2 :** space or opportunity for unhampered motion, activity, or thought **3 :** extent of treatment, activity, or influence **4 :** range of operation: as **a :** the range of a logical operator : a string in predicate calculus that is governed by a quantifier **b :** a grammatical constituent that determines the interpretation of a predicate or quantifier *syn* see RANGE

²scope *n* [-*scope*] (1872) **1 :** an instrument (as a telescope or radarscope) for viewing **2 :** HOROSCOPE

³scope *vt* **scoped; scop·ing** [perh. fr. ²*scope*] (1974) : to look at esp. for the purpose of evaluation — often used with *out* ⟨*scoped* her out from across the room —Tim Allis⟩

-scope *n comb form* [NL *-scopium,* fr. Gk *skopion;* akin to Gk *skeptesthai*] : means (as an instrument) for viewing or observing ⟨endo*scope*⟩ ⟨spectro*scope*⟩

sco·pol·amine \skō-'pä-lə-,mēn, -mən\ *n* [G *Scopolamin,* fr. NL *Scopolia,* genus of plants + G *Amin* amine] (1892) : a poisonous alkaloid $C_{17}H_{21}NO_4$ found in various plants (as jimsonweed) of the nightshade family and used esp. as a truth serum or usu. with morphine as a sedative in surgery and obstetrics — called also *hyoscine*

-scopy *n comb form* [Gk *-skopia,* fr. *skeptesthai*] : viewing : observation ⟨spectro*scopy*⟩

scor·bu·tic \skór-'byü-tik\ *adj* [NL *scorbuticus,* fr. *scorbutus* scurvy, prob. of Gmc origin; akin to OE *scurf* scurf] (1655) : of, relating to, producing, or affected with scurvy

¹scorch \'skórch\ *vb* [ME; akin to ME *scorcnen,* prob. of Scand origin; akin to ON *skorpna* to shrivel up — more at SHRIMP] *vt* (14c) **1 :** to burn a surface of so as to change its color and texture **2 :** to dry or shrivel with or as if with intense heat : PARCH **b :** to afflict painfully with censure or sarcasm **3 :** DEVASTATE; *esp* : to destroy (as property of possible use to an advancing enemy) before abandoning — used in the phrase *scorched earth* ~ *vi* **1 :** to become scorched **2 :** to travel at great and usu. excessive speed **3 :** to cause intense heat or mental anguish ⟨~*ing* sun⟩ ⟨~*ing* fury⟩ — **scorch·ing·ly** \'skór-chiŋ-lē\ *adv*

²scorch *n* (15c) **1 :** a result of scorching **2 :** a browning of plant tissues usu. from disease or heat

³scorch *vt* [ME, perh. blend of *scoren* to score and *scocchen* to scotch] (14c) *dial Brit* : CUT, SLASH

scorched *adj* (1590) : parched or discolored by scorching

scorch·er \'skór-chər\ *n* (1842) : one that scorches; *esp* : a very hot day

¹score \'skōr, 'skór\ *n, pl* **scores** [ME *scor,* fr. ON *skor* notch, tally, twenty; akin to OE *scieran* to cut — more at SHEAR] (14c) **1** *or pl* **score 1 :** TWENTY **b :** a group of 20 things — often used in combination with a cardinal number ⟨four*score*⟩ **c :** an indefinitely large number **2 a :** a line (as a scratch or incision) made with or as if with a sharp instrument **b** (1) **:** a mark used as a starting point or goal (2) **:** a mark used for keeping account **3 a :** an account or reckoning orig. kept by making marks on a tally **b :** amount due : INDEBTEDNESS **4 :** GRUDGE ⟨a ~ to settle⟩ **5 a :** REASON, GROUND **b :** SUBJECT, TOPIC **6 a :** the copy of a musical composition in written or printed notation **b :** a musical composition; *specif* : the music for a movie or theatrical production **c :** a complete description of a dance composition in choreographic notation **7 a :** a number that expresses accomplishment (as in a game or test) or excellence (as in quality) either absolutely in points gained or by comparison to a standard **b :** an act (as a goal, run, or touchdown) in any of various games or contests that gains points **8 :** success in obtaining something (as money or drugs) esp. through illegal or irregular means **9 :** the stark inescapable facts of a situation ⟨knows the ~⟩

²score *vb* **scored; scor·ing** *vt* (14c) **1 a :** to keep a record or account of by or as if by notches on a tally : RECORD **b :** to enter in a record **c :** to mark with significant lines or notches (as in keeping account) **2 :** to mark with lines, grooves, scratches, or notches **3 :** BERATE, SCOLD; *also* : DENOUNCE **4 a** (1) **:** to make (a score) in a game or contest ⟨*scored* a touchdown⟩ ⟨*scored* three points⟩ (2) **:** to enable (a base runner) to make a score (3) **:** to have as a value in a game or contest **b** (1) **:** ACHIEVE, WIN ⟨*scored* a dazzling success⟩ (2) **:** ACQUIRE ⟨help a traveler ~ local drugs —Poitor Koper⟩ **5 :** to determine the merit of : GRADE **6 a :** to write or arrange (music) for a specific performance medium **b :** to make an orchestration of **c :** to compose a score for (a movie) ~ *vi* **1 :** to keep score in a game or contest **2 :** to make a score in a game or contest **3 a :** to gain or have the advantage **b :** to be successful: as (1) **:** to succeed in having sexual intercourse (2) **:** to manage to obtain illicit drugs **c :** ³RATE — **scor·er** *n* — **score points :** to gain favor, status, or advantage

score·board \'skōr-,bórd, 'skór-,bórd\ *n* (1826) : a large board for displaying the score of a game or match

score·card \-,kärd\ *n* (ca. 1877) : a card for recording the score of a game

score·keep·er \-,kē-pər\ *n* (1880) : one that keeps score; *specif* : an official who records the score during a game or contest

score·less \-ləs\ *adj* (1885) : having no score

sco·ria \'skōr-ē-ə, 'skór-\ *n, pl* **-ri·ae** \-ē-,ē, -ē-,ī\ [ME, fr. L, fr. Gk *skōria,* fr. *skōr* excrement — more at SCATOLOGY] (14c) **1 :** the refuse from melting of metals or reduction of ores : SLAG **2 :** rough vesicular cindery lava — **sco·ri·a·ceous** \,skōr-ē-'ā-shəs, ,skór-\ *adj*

¹scorn \'skórn\ *n* [ME, fr. OF *escarn,* of Gmc origin; akin to OHG *scern* jest] (13c) **1 :** open dislike and disrespect or derision often mixed with indignation **2 :** an expression of contempt or derision **3 :** an object of extreme disdain, contempt, or derision : something contemptible

²scorn *vt* (13c) : to treat with scorn : reject or dismiss as contemptible or unworthy ⟨~*ed* the traditions of their ancestors⟩ ⟨~*ed* to reply to the charge⟩ ~ *vi* : to show disdain or derision : SCOFF *syn* see DESPISE — **scorn·er** *n*

scorn·ful \'skórn-fəl\ *adj* (14c) : full of scorn : CONTEMPTUOUS — **scorn·ful·ly** \-fə-lē\ *adv* — **scorn·ful·ness** *n*

scor·pae·nid \skór-'pē-nəd\ *n* [ultim. fr. Gk *skorpaina,* a kind of fish] (1885) : any of a family (Scorpaenidae) of marine spiny-finned fishes that includes the scorpion fishes — **scorpaenid** *adj*

Scor·pio \'skór-pē-,ō\ *n* [L (gen. *Scorpionis*), fr. Gk *Skorpios,* lit., scorpion] **1 :** SCORPIUS **2 a :** the 8th sign of the zodiac in astrology — see ZODIAC table **b :** one born under this sign

scor·pi·on \'skór-pē-ən\ *n* [ME, fr. OF, fr. L *scorpion-, scorpio,* fr. Gk *skorpios*] (12c) **1 a :** any of an order (Scorpionida) of nocturnal arachnids that have an elongated body and a narrow segmented tail bearing a venomous stinger at the tip **b** *cap* : SCORPIO **2 :** a scourge prob. studded with metal **3 :** something that incites to action like the sting of an insect

scorpion 1a

scorpion fish *n* (1661) : any of various scorpaenid fishes; *esp* : one (as genus *Scorpaena*) with a venomous spine on the dorsal fin

scorpion fly *n* (1668) : any of a family (Panorpidae) of insects that have cylindrical bodies, a long beak with biting mouthparts, and the male genitalia enlarged into a swollen bulb; *broadly* : an insect of the order (Mecoptera) that includes this family

Scor·pi·us \'skór-pē-əs\ *n* [L (gen. *Scorpii*), fr. Gk *Skorpios,* lit., scorpion] : a southern zodiacal constellation partly in the Milky Way and between Libra and Sagittarius

scot \'skät\ *n* [ME, fr. ON *skot* shot, contribution — more at SHOT] (14c) : money assessed or paid

Scot \'skät\ *n* [ME *Scottes* Scots, fr. OE *Scottas* fr. LL *Scotus*] (bef. 12c) **1 :** a member of a Celtic people of northern Ireland settling in Scotland about A.D. 500 **2 a :** a native or inhabitant of Scotland **b :** a person of Scottish descent

scot and lot *n* (15c) **1 :** a parish assessment formerly laid on subjects in Great Britain according to their ability to pay **2 :** obligations of all kinds taken as a whole

¹scotch \'skäch\ *vt* [ME *scocchen* to gash] (15c) **1** *archaic* : CUT, GASH, SCORE; *also* : WOUND ⟨we have ~*ed* the snake, not killed it —Shak.⟩ **2** : to put an end to ⟨~*ed* rumors of a military takeover⟩

²scotch *n* (15c) : a superficial cut : SCORE

³scotch *n* [origin unknown] (1639) : a chock to prevent rolling or slipping

⁴scotch *vt* (1642) **1 :** to block with a chock **2 :** HINDER, THWART

¹Scotch \'skäch\ *adj* [contr. of *Scottish*] (1591) **1 :** SCOTTISH **2 :** inclined to frugality

²Scotch *n* (ca. 1700) **1 :** SCOTS **2** *pl in constr* : the people of Scotland **3** *often not cap* : whiskey distilled in Scotland esp. from malted barley — called also *Scotch whisky*

³Scotch *trademark* — used for any of numerous adhesive tapes

Scotch broom *n* (ca. 1818) : a deciduous broom (*Cytisus scoparius*) of western Europe that is widely cultivated for its bright yellow or partly red flowers and that has become a pest in some areas (as California)

Scotch broth *n* (1834) : a soup made from beef or mutton and vegetables and thickened with barley

Scotch egg *n* (1809) : a hard-boiled egg wrapped in sausage meat, covered with bread crumbs, and fried

Scotch–Irish *adj* (1744) : of, relating to, or descended from Scottish settlers in northern Ireland

Scotch·man \'skäch-mən\ *n* (15c) : SCOTSMAN

Scotch pine *n* (1731) : a pine (*Pinus sylvestris*) of northern Europe and Asia with spreading or pendulous branches, short rigid twisted needles, and hard yellow wood that provides valuable timber

Scotch terrier *n* (1810) : SCOTTISH TERRIER

Scotch verdict *n* (1912) **1 :** a verdict of not proven that is allowed by Scottish criminal law in some cases instead of a verdict of not guilty **2** : an indecisive decision or pronouncement

Scotch·wom·an \'skäch-,wü-mən\ *n* (1818) : SCOTSWOMAN

Scotch woodcock *n* (1879) : buttered toast spread with anchovy paste and scrambled egg

sco·ter \'skō-tər\ *n, pl* **scoters** *or* **scoter** [origin unknown] (ca. 1674) : any of a genus (*Melanitta*) of sea ducks esp. of northern coasts of Europe and No. America that have males with chiefly black plumage

scot–free \'skät-'frē\ *adj* [*scot*] (1528) : completely free from obligation, harm, or penalty

sco·tia \'skō-sh(ē-)ə, -tē-ə\ *n* [L, fr. Gk *skotia,* fr. fem. of *skotios* dark, shadowy, fr. *skotos* darkness — more at SHADE] (1563) : a concave

\a\ abut \ᵊ\ kitten, F table \ər\ further \a\ ash \ā\ ace \ä\ mop, mar \aú\ out \ch\ chin \e\ bet \ē\ easy \g\ go \i\ hit \ī\ ice \j\ job \ŋ\ sing \ō\ go \ò\ law \òi\ boy \th\ thin \t͟h\ the \ü\ loot \ú\ foot \y\ yet \zh\ vision \à, k̲, ⁿ, œ, œ̄, ᵫ, ᵫ̄, ʸ\ *see* Guide to Pronunciation molding used esp. in classical architecture in the bases of columns — see BASE illustration

Scot·ic \'skä-tik\ *adj* (1796) : of or relating to the ancient Scots

Sco·tism \'skō-,ti-zəm\ *n* (ca. 1871) : the doctrines of Duns Scotus — **Sco·tist** \'skō-tist\ *n*

Scot·land Yard \,skät-lən(d)-'yärd\ *n* [*Scotland Yard*, street in London, formerly the headquarters of the metropolitan police] (1864) : the detective department of the London metropolitan police

sco·to·ma \skə-'tō-mə\ *n, pl* **-mas** *or* **-ma·ta** \-mə-tə\ [NL, fr. ML, dimness of vision, fr. Gk *skotōmat-, skotōma*, fr. *skotoun* to darken, fr. *skotos*] (1875) : a blind or dark spot in the visual field

sco·to·pic \skə-'tō-pik, -'tä-\ *adj* [NL *scotopia* scotopic vision, fr. Gk *skotos* darkness + NL *-opia*] (1915) : relating to or being vision in dim light with dark-adapted eyes which involves only the retinal rods as light receptors

¹**Scots** \'skäts\ *adj* [ME *Scottis*, alter. of *Scottish*] (14c) : SCOTTISH — used esp. of the people and language and in legal context

²**Scots** *n* (1542) : the English language of Scotland

Scots·man \'skäts-mən\ *n* (14c) : a native or inhabitant of Scotland

Scots pine *n* (1797) *chiefly Brit* : SCOTCH PINE

Scots·wom·an \'skäts-,wú-mən\ *n* (1820) : a woman who is a native or inhabitant of Scotland

Scot·ti·cism \'skä-tə-,si-zəm\ *n* [LL *scotticus* of the ancient Scots, fr. *Scotus* Scot] (1706) : a word, phrase, or expression characteristic of Scottish English

Scot·tie \'skä-tē\ *n* (ca. 1896) **1** : SCOTSMAN **2** : SCOTTISH TERRIER

¹**Scot·tish** \'skä-tish\ *adj* [ME, fr. *Scottes* Scotsmen] (13c) : of, relating to, or characteristic of Scotland, Scots, or the Scots — **Scot·tish·ness** \-nəs\ *n*

²**Scottish** *n* (1759) : SCOTS

Scottish deerhound *n* (1891) : any of an old breed of dogs of Scottish origin that have the general form of a greyhound but are larger and taller with a rough coat

Scottish Gaelic *n* (1956) : the Gaelic language of Scotland

Scottish rite *n* (1903) **1** : a ceremonial observed by one of the Masonic systems **2** : a system or organization that observes the Scottish rite and confers the 4th through the 33d degrees

Scottish terrier *n* (1837) : any of an old Scottish breed of terrier that has short legs, a large head with small erect ears and a powerful muzzle, a broad deep chest, and a very hard coat of wiry hair

Scottish terrier

scoun·drel \'skaún-drəl\ *n* [origin unknown] (1589) : a disreputable person : RASCAL — **scoundrel** *adj* — **scoun·drel·ly** \-drə-lē\ *adj*

¹**scour** \'skaú(-ə)r\ *vb* [ME, prob. fr. MD *schuren*, fr. OF *escurer*, fr. LL *excurare* to clean off, fr. L, to take good care of, fr. *ex-* + *curare* to care for, fr. *cura* care] *vt* (13c) **1 a** : to rub hard esp. with a rough material for cleansing **b** : to remove by rubbing hard and washing **2** *archaic* : to clear (a region) of enemies or outlaws **3** : to clean by purging : PURGE **4** : to remove dirt and debris from (as a pipe or ditch) **5** : to free from foreign matter or impurities by or as if by washing ⟨∼ wool⟩ **6** : to clear, dig, or remove by or as if by a powerful current of water ∼ *vi* **1** : to perform a process of scouring **2** : to suffer from diarrhea or dysentery **3** : to become clean and bright by rubbing — **scour·er** *n*

²**scour** *n* (1681) **1** : a place scoured by running water **2** : scouring action (as of a glacier) **3** : DIARRHEA, DYSENTERY — usu. used in pl. but sing. or pl. in constr. **4** : SCOURING 1; *also* : damage done by scouring action

³**scour** *vb* [ME *scuren*, prob. of Scand origin; akin to Sw *skura* to rush] *vi* (14c) : to move about quickly esp. in search ∼ *vt* : to go through or range over in or as if in a search

¹**scourge** \'skərj *also* 'skȯrj, 'skȯrj, 'skúrj\ *n* [ME, fr. AF *escorge*, fr. (assumed) OF *escorgier* to whip, fr. OF *es-* ex- + L *corrigia* whip] (13c) **1** : WHIP; *esp* : one used to inflict pain or punishment **2** : an instrument of punishment or criticism **3** : a cause of widespread or great affliction

²**scourge** *vt* **scourged; scourg·ing** (13c) **1** : FLOG, WHIP **2 a** : to punish severely **b** : AFFLICT **c** : to drive as if by blows of a whip **d** : CHASTISE — **scourg·er** *n*

scour·ing \'skaúr-iŋ\ *n* (1588) **1** : material removed by scouring or cleaning **2** : the lowest rank of society — usu. used in pl.

scouring rush *n* (ca. 1818) : EQUISETUM; *esp* : one (*Equisetum hyemale*) with strongly siliceous stems formerly used for scouring

scouse \'skaús\ *n* (1840) **1** : LOBSCOUSE **2** *cap* **a** : SCOUSER **b** : a dialect of English spoken in Liverpool

Scous·er \'skaú-sər\ *n* (1959) : a native or inhabitant of Liverpool, England

¹**scout** \'skaút\ *vb* [ME, fr. MF *escouter* to listen, fr. L *auscultare* — more at AUSCULTATION] *vi* (14c) **1** : to explore an area to obtain information (as about an enemy) **2 a** : to make a search **b** : to work as a talent scout ∼ *vt* **1** : to observe in order to obtain information or evaluate **2** : to explore in order to obtain information **3** : to find by making a search — often used with *up*

²**scout** *n* (1534) **1 a** : one sent to obtain information; *esp* : a soldier, ship, or plane sent out in war to reconnoiter **b** : WATCHMAN, LOOKOUT **c** : TALENT SCOUT **2 a** : the act of scouting **b** : a scouting expedition : RECONNAISSANCE **3** *often cap* : a member of any of various scouting movements: as **a** : BOY SCOUT **b** : GIRL SCOUT **4** : INDIVIDUAL, PERSON — used chiefly in the phrase *good scout*

³**scout** *vb* [prob. of Scand origin; akin to ON *skúti* taunt; akin to OE *scēotan* to shoot — more at SHOOT] *vt* (1605) **1** : MOCK **2** : to reject scornfully ∼ *vi* : SCOFF

scout car *n* (1933) **1** : a military reconnaissance vehicle **2** : SQUAD CAR

scout·craft \'skaút-,kraft\ *n* (1908) : the craft, skill, or practice of a scout

scout·er \'skaú-tər\ *n* (1642) **1** : one that scouts **2** *often cap* : an adult leader in the Boy Scouts of America

scouth \'skúth, 'skaúth\ *n* [origin unknown] (1591) *Scot* : PLENTY

scout·ing \'skaú-tiŋ\ *n* (1644) **1** : the action of one that scouts **2** *often cap* : the activities of various national and worldwide organizations for youth directed to developing character, citizenship, and individual skills

scout·mas·ter \'skaút-,mas-tər\ *n* (1579) : the leader of a band of scouts; *specif* : the adult leader of a troop of Boy Scouts

scow \'skaú\ *n* [D *schouw*; akin to OHG *scalta* punt pole] (1669) : a large flat-bottomed boat with broad square ends used chiefly for transporting bulk material (as ore, sand, or refuse)

¹**scowl** \'skaú(ə)l\ *vb* [ME *skoulen*, prob. of Scand origin; akin to Dan *skule* to scowl] *vi* (14c) **1** : to contract the brow in an expression of displeasure **2** : to exhibit a threatening aspect ∼ *vt* : to express with a scowl — **scowl·er** *n* — **scowl·ing·ly** \'skaú-liŋ-lē\ *adv*

²**scowl** *n* (1500) : a facial expression of displeasure : FROWN

¹**scrab·ble** \'skra-bəl\ *vb* **scrab·bled; scrab·bling** \-b(ə-)liŋ\ [D *schrabbelen* to scratch] *vi* (1537) **1** : SCRAWL, SCRIBBLE **2** : to scratch, claw, or grope about clumsily or frantically **3 a** : SCRAMBLE, CLAMBER **b** : to struggle by or as if by scraping or scratching ⟨∼ for survival⟩ ∼ *vt* **1** : SCRAMBLE **2** : SCRIBBLE — **scrab·bler** \-b(ə-)lər\ *n*

²**scrabble** *n* (1842) **1** : SCRIBBLE **2** : a repeated scratching or clawing **3** : SCRAMBLE

scrab·bly \'skra-b(ə-)lē\ *adj* (1945) **1** : SCRATCHY, RASPY **2** : SPARSE, SCRUBBY

¹**scrag** \'skrag\ *n* [perh. alter. of ²*crag*] (1542) **1** : a rawboned or scrawny person or animal **2** : the lean end of a neck of mutton or veal; *broadly* : NECK — called also *scrag end*

²**scrag** *vt* **scragged; scrag·ging** (1756) **1 a** : to execute by hanging or garroting **b** : to wring the neck of **2 a** : CHOKE **b** : MANHANDLE 1 **c** : KILL, MURDER

scrag·gly \'skra-g(ə-)lē\ *adj* (1869) : irregular in form or growth ⟨∼ hills⟩ ⟨a ∼ beard⟩; *also* : UNKEMPT

scrag·gy \'skra-gē\ *adj* **scrag·gi·er; -est** [ME *scraggi*; akin to E dial. *scrag* tree stump, uneven ground, ME *scrogge* bush] (13c) **1** : ROUGH, JAGGED; *also* : SCRAGGLY

²**scraggy** *adj* **scrag·gi·er; -est** [¹*scrag*] (1611) : being lean and long : SCRAWNY

¹**scram** \'skram\ *vi* **scrammed; scram·ming** [short for *scramble*] (ca. 1928) : to go away at once ⟨∼, you're not wanted⟩

²**scram** *n* (1953) : a rapid emergency shutdown of a nuclear reactor

¹**scram·ble** \'skram-bəl\ *vb* **scram·bled; scram·bling** \-b(ə-)liŋ\ [perh. alter. of ¹*scrabble*] *vi* (ca. 1586) **1 a** : to move or climb hastily on all fours **b** : to move with urgency or panic **2 a** : to struggle eagerly or unceremoniously for possession of something ⟨∼ for front seats⟩ **b** : to get or gather something with difficulty or in irregular ways ⟨∼ for a living⟩ **3** : to spread or grow irregularly : SPRAWL, STRAGGLE **4** : to take off quickly in response to an alert **5** *of a football quarterback* : to run with the ball after the pass protection breaks down ∼ *vt* **1** : to collect by scrambling **2 a** : to toss or mix together : JUMBLE **b** : to prepare (eggs) by stirring during frying **3** : to cause or order (a fighter-interceptor group) to scramble **4** : to disarrange the elements of a transmission (as a telephone or television signal) in order to make unintelligible to interception — **scram·bler** \-b(ə-)lər\ *n*

²**scramble** *n* (1674) **1** : the act or an instance of scrambling **2** : a disordered mass : JUMBLE ⟨a ... ∼ of patterns and textures —*Vogue*⟩ **3** : a rapid emergency takeoff of fighter-interceptor planes

scran·nel \'skra-nᵊl\ *adj* [origin unknown] (1637) : HARSH, UNMELODIOUS

¹**scrap** \'skrap\ *n, often attrib* [ME, fr. ON *skrap* scraps; akin to ON *skrapa* to scrape] (14c) **1** *pl* : fragments of discarded or leftover food **2 a** : a small detached piece ⟨a ∼ of paper⟩ **b** : a fragment of something written, printed, or spoken ⟨∼s of conversation⟩ **c** : the least bit ⟨not a ∼ of evidence⟩ **3** *pl* : CRACKLINGS **4** *a* : fragments of stock removed in manufacturing **b** : manufactured articles or parts rejected or discarded and useful only as material for reprocessing; *esp* : waste and discarded metal

²**scrap** *vt* **scrapped; scrap·ping** (ca. 1891) **1** : to convert into scrap **2** : to abandon or get rid of as no longer of enough worth or effectiveness to retain ⟨∼ outworn methods⟩ *syn* see DISCARD

³**scrap** *n* [origin unknown] (ca. 1889) : FIGHT

⁴**scrap** *vi* **scrapped; scrap·ping** (ca. 1895) : QUARREL, FIGHT

scrap·book \'skrap-,búk\ *n* (1825) : a blank book in which miscellaneous items (as newspaper clippings or pictures) are collected and preserved

¹**scrape** \'skrāp\ *vb* **scraped; scrap·ing** [ME, fr. ON *skrapa*; akin to OE *scrapian* to scrape, L *scrobis* ditch, Russ *skresti* to scrape] *vt* (14c) **1 a** : to remove from a surface by usu. repeated strokes of an edged instrument **b** : to make (a surface) smooth or clean with strokes of an edged instrument or an abrasive **2 a** : to grate harshly over or against **b** : to damage or injure the surface of by contact with a rough surface **c** : to draw roughly or noisily over a surface **3** : to collect by or as if by scraping — often used with *up* or *together* ⟨∼ up the price of a ticket⟩ ∼ *vi* **1** : to move in sliding contact with a rough surface **2** : to accumulate money by small economies **3** : to draw back the foot along the ground in making a bow **4** : to make one's way with difficulty or succeed by a narrow margin ⟨just *scraped* by at school⟩ — **scrap·er** *n* — **scrape a leg** : to make a low bow

²**scrape** *n* (15c) **1 a** : the act or process of scraping **b** : a sound made by scraping **c** : damage or injury caused by scraping : ABRASION ⟨bumps and ∼s⟩ **2 a** : a bow made with a drawing back of the foot along the ground **b** : a distressing encounter ⟨a ∼ with death⟩ **b** : QUARREL, FIGHT

scrap heap *n* (ca. 1902) **1** : a pile of discarded metal **2** : the place where useless things are discarded

scra·pie \'skrā-pē\ *n* [¹*scrape*] (1910) : a usu. fatal disease of the nervous system esp. of sheep that is characterized by twitching, intense itching, excessive thirst, emaciation, weakness, and finally paralysis

scrap·page \'skra-pij\ *n* (ca. 1909) **1** : the scrapping of discarded objects (as automobiles) **2** : the rate at which objects are scrapped

scrap·per \'skra-pər\ *n* (1874) : FIGHTER, QUARRELER

scrap·pi·ly \'skra-pə-lē\ *adv* (1886) : in a scrappy manner

scrap·pi·ness \'skra-pē-nəs\ *n* (1867) : the quality or state of being scrappy

scrap·ple \'skra-pəl\ *n* [dim. of ¹*scrap*] (1855) : a seasoned mixture of ground meat (as pork) and cornmeal set in a mold and served sliced and fried

¹scrap·py \'skra-pē\ *adj* **scrap·pi·er; -est** [¹*scrap*] (1837) : consisting of scraps ⟨~ meals⟩

²scrappy *adj* **scrap·pi·er; -est** [³*scrap*] (ca. 1896) **1** : QUARRELSOME **2** : having an aggressive and determined spirit : FEISTY

¹scratch \'skrach\ *vb* [ME *scracchen*, prob. blend of *scratten* to scratch and *cracchen* to scratch] *vt* (15c) **1** : to scrape or dig with the claws or nails **2** : to rub and tear or mark the surface of with something sharp or jagged **3** : to scrape or rub lightly (as to relieve itching) **4** : to scrape together : collect with difficulty or by effort **5** : to write or draw on a surface **6 a** : to cancel or erase by or as if by drawing a line through **b** : to withdraw (an entry) from competition **7** : SCRIBBLE, SCRAWL **8** : to scrape along a rough surface ⟨~ a match⟩ ~ *vi* **1** : to use the claws or nails in digging, tearing, or wounding **2** : to scrape or rub oneself lightly (as to relieve itching) **3** : to gather money or get a living by hard work and esp. through irregular means and sacrifice **4** : to make a thin grating sound **5** : to withdraw from a contest or engagement **6** : to make a scratch in billiards or pool — **scratch·er** *n* — **scratch one's back** : to accommodate with a favor esp. in expectation of like return — **scratch the surface** : to make a superficial effort or modest start

²scratch *n* (ca. 1586) **1** : a mark or injury produced by scratching; *also* : a slight wound **2** : SCRAWL, SCRIBBLE **3** : the sound made by scratching **4 a** : the starting line in a race **b** : a point at the beginning of a project at which nothing has been done ahead of time ⟨build a school system from ~⟩ **5 a** : a test of courage **b** : satisfactory condition, level, or performance ⟨not up to ~⟩ **6** : a contestant whose name is withdrawn **7** : poultry feed (as mixed grains) scattered on the litter or ground esp. to induce birds to exercise — called also *scratch feed* **8 a** : a shot in billiards or pool that ends a player's turn; *specif* : a shot in pool in which the cue ball falls into the pocket **b** : a shot that scores by chance : FLUKE **9** *slang* : MONEY, FUNDS

³scratch *adj* (1897) **1** : made as or used for a tentative effort **2** : made or done by chance and not as intended ⟨a ~ shot⟩ **3** : arranged or put together with little selection : HAPHAZARD ⟨a ~ team⟩ **4** : having no handicap or allowance ⟨a ~ golfer⟩ **5** : made from scratch : made with basic ingredients ⟨a ~ cake⟩

scratch·board \'skrach-ˌbōrd, -ˌbȯrd\ *n* (ca. 1908) : a black-surfaced cardboard having an undercoat of white clay on which an effect resembling engraving is achieved by scratching away portions of the surface to produce white lines

scratch hit *n* (1903) : a batted ball not solidly hit yet credited to the batter as a base hit

scratch pad *n* (1895) : a pad of scratch paper

scratch paper *n* (1899) : paper that may be used for casual writing

scratch sheet *n* (1939) : a racing publication listing competitors scratched from races and giving odds

scratch test *n* (1937) : a test for allergic susceptibility made by rubbing an extract of an allergy-producing substance into small breaks or scratches in the skin

scratchy \'skra-chē\ *adj* **scratch·i·er; -est** (1827) **1** : marked or made with scratches ⟨~ drawing⟩ ⟨~ handwriting⟩ **2** : likely to scratch : PRICKLY ⟨~ undergrowth⟩ **3** : making a scratching noise **4** : uneven in quality : RAGGED **5** : causing tingling or itching : IRRITATING ⟨~ wool⟩ — **scratch·i·ly** \-chə-lē\ *adv* — **scratch·i·ness** \-chē-nəs\ *n*

scrawl \'skrȯl\ *vb* [origin unknown] *vt* (1612) : to write or draw awkwardly, hastily, or carelessly ~ *vi* : to write awkwardly or carelessly — **scrawl** *n* — **scrawl·er** *n* — **scrawly** \'skrȯ-lē\ *adj*

scraw·ny \'skrȯ-nē\ *adj* **scraw·ni·er; -est** [origin unknown] (1833) : exceptionally thin and slight or meager in body ⟨~ scrub cattle⟩ *syn* see LEAN — **scraw·ni·ness** *n*

screak \'skrēk\ *vi* [of Scand origin; akin to ON *skrækja* to screech] (ca. 1500) : to make a harsh shrill noise : SCREECH — **screak** *n* — **screaky** \'skrē-kē\ *adj*

¹scream \'skrēm\ *vb* [ME *scremen*; akin to MD *schreem* scream] *vi* (12c) **1 a** (1) : to voice a sudden sharp loud cry (2) : to produce harsh high tones **b** : to make a noise resembling a scream ⟨a ~ing siren⟩ **c** : to move with great rapidity **2 a** : to speak or write with intense or hysterical emotion **b** : to protest or complain vehemently **c** : to laugh hysterically **3** : to produce a vivid startling effect ~ *vt* : to utter with or as if with a scream

²scream *n* (1605) **1** : a loud sharp penetrating cry or noise **2** : one that is very funny

scream·er \'skrē-mər\ *n* (1712) **1** : one that screams **2** : any of a small family (Anhimidae) of So. American wetland birds having a large body, long legs, and spurred wings **3** : a sensationally startling headline

scream·ing *adj* (1848) **1** : so striking or conspicuous as to attract notice as if by screaming ⟨~ headlines⟩ ⟨a ~ need for reform⟩ ⟨dressed in ~ red⟩ **2** : so funny as to provoke screams of laughter ⟨a ~ farce⟩ — **scream·ing·ly** *adv*

screaming mee·mies \-ˈmē-mēz\ *n pl but sing in constr* [origin unknown] (1942) : nervous hysteria : JITTERS

scree \'skrē\ *n* [of Scand origin; akin to ON *skritha* landslide, fr. *skrītha* to creep; akin to OHG *scritan* to go, Lith *skriesti* to turn] (ca. 1781) : an accumulation of loose stones or rocky debris lying on a slope or at the base of a hill or cliff : TALUS

¹screech \'skrēch\ *n* (1560) **1** : a high shrill piercing cry usu. expressing pain or terror **2** : a sound resembling a screech

²screech *vb* [alter. of earlier *scritch*, fr. ME *scrichen*; akin to ON *skrækja* to screech] *vi* (1577) **1** : to utter a high shrill piercing cry : make an outcry usu. in terror or pain **2** : to make a shrill high-pitched sound resembling a screech; *also* : to move with such a sound ⟨the car ~ed to a stop⟩ ~ *vt* : to utter with or as if with a screech — **screech·er** *n*

screech owl *n* (1593) **1** : BARN OWL **2** : any of numerous New World owls (genus *Otus*); *esp* : a small No. American owl (*O. asio*) with a pair of tufts of lengthened feathers on the head resembling ears

screechy \'skrē-chē\ *adj* (ca. 1830) : producing a screech

screed \'skrēd\ *n* [ME *screde* fragment, alter. of OE *scrēade* — more at

SHRED] (ca. 1789) **1 a** : a lengthy discourse **b** : an informal piece of writing **2** : a strip (as of plaster of the thickness planned for the coat) laid on as a guide **3** : a leveling device drawn over freshly poured concrete

¹screen \'skrēn\ *n* [ME *screne*, fr. MF *escren*, fr. MD *scherm*; akin to OHG *skirm* shield; prob. akin to Skt *carman* skin, *krnāti* he injures — more at SHEAR] (14c) **1** : a protective or ornamental device (as a movable partition) shielding an area from heat or drafts or from view **2** : something that shelters, protects, or hides: as **a** : a growth or stand of trees, shrubs, or plants **b** : a protective formation of troops, ships, or planes **c** : something that covers or disguises the true nature (as of an activity or feeling) ⟨greets strangers with a ~ of excessive friendliness —Tony Schwartz⟩ **d** (1) : a maneuver in various sports (as basketball or ice hockey) whereby an opponent is legally impeded or his view of the play is momentarily blocked (2) : SCREEN PASS **3 a** : a perforated plate or cylinder or a meshed wire or cloth fabric usu. mounted and used to separate coarser from finer parts **b** : a system for examining and separating into different groups **c** : a piece of apparatus designed to prevent agencies in one part from affecting other parts ⟨an optical ~⟩ ⟨an electric ~⟩ ⟨a magnetic ~⟩ **d** : a frame holding a usu. metallic netting used esp. in a window or door to exclude pests (as insects) **4 a** : a flat surface on which a picture or series of pictures is projected or reflected **b** : the surface on which the image appears in an electronic display (as in a television set, radar receiver, or computer terminal) **5** : a glass plate ruled with crossing opaque lines through which an image is photographed in making a halftone **6** : the motion-picture medium or industry

²screen *vt* (15c) **1** : to guard from injury or danger **2 a** : to give shelter or protection to with or as if with a screen **b** : to separate with or as if with a screen; *also* : to shield (an opponent) from a play or from view of a play **3 a** : to pass (as coal, gravel, or ashes) through a screen to separate the fine part from the coarse; *also* : to remove by a screen **b** (1) : to examine usu. methodically in order to make a separation into different groups (2) : to select or eliminate by a screening process **4** : to provide with a screen to keep out pests (as insects) **5 a** (1) : to present (as a motion picture) for viewing on a screen (2) : to view the presentation of (as a motion picture) **b** : to present in a motion picture ~ *vi* **1** : to appear on a motion-picture screen **2** : to provide a screen in a game or sport *syn* see HIDE — **screen·able** \'skrē-nə-bəl\ *adj* — **screen·er** *n*

screen·ing \'skrē-niŋ\ *n* (1725) **1** : the act or process of one that screens **2** *pl but sing or pl in constr* : material (as waste or fine coal) separated out by means of a screen **3** : metal or plastic mesh (as for window screens) **4** : a showing of a motion picture

screen·land \'skrēn-ˌland\ *n* (1925) : FILMDOM

screen memory *n* (1923) : a recollection of early childhood that may be falsely recalled or magnified in importance and that masks another memory of deep emotional significance

screen pass *n* (ca. 1949) : a forward pass in football to a receiver at or behind the line of scrimmage who is protected by a screen of blockers

screen·play \'skrēn-ˌplā\ *n* (1916) : the script and often shooting directions of a story prepared for motion-picture production

screen test *n* (1927) : a short film sequence for assessing the ability or suitability of a person for a motion-picture role — **screen–test** *vt*

screen·writ·er \'skrēn-ˌrī-tər\ *n* (1921) : a writer of screenplays

¹screw \'skrü\ *n* [ME, fr. MF *escroe* female screw, nut, fr. ML *scrofa*, fr. L, sow] (15c) **1 a** : a simple machine of the inclined plane type consisting of a spirally grooved solid cylinder and a correspondingly grooved hollow cylinder into which it fits **b** : a nail-shaped or rod-shaped piece with a spiral groove and a slotted or recessed head designed to be inserted into material by rotating (as with a screwdriver) and used for fastening pieces of solid material together **2 a** : a screw-like form : SPIRAL **b** : a turn of a screw; *also* : a twist like the turn of a screw **c** : a screwlike device (as a corkscrew) **3** : a worn-out horse **4** *chiefly Brit* : a small packet (as of tobacco) **5** : a prison guard **6** : one who bargains shrewdly; *also* : SKINFLINT **7** : a propeller esp. of a ship **8 a** : THUMBSCREW **2 b** : pressure or punitive measures intended to coerce — used chiefly in the phrase *put the screws on* or *put the screws to* **9 a** : an act of sexual intercourse — usu. considered vulgar **b** : a partner in sexual intercourse — usu. considered vulgar — **screw·like** \-ˌlīk\ *adj* — **have a screw loose** : to be mentally unbalanced

²screw *vt* (1605) **1 a** (1) : to attach, fasten, or close by means of a screw (2) : to unite or separate by means of a screw or a twisting motion ⟨~ the two pieces together⟩ (3) : to press tightly in a device (as a vise) operated by a screw (4) : to operate, tighten, or adjust by means of a screw (5) : to torture by means of a thumbscrew **b** : to cause to rotate spirally about an axis **2 a** (1) : to twist into strained configurations : CONTORT ⟨~ed up his face⟩ (2) : SQUINT (3) : CRUMPLE **b** : to furnish with a spiral groove or ridge : THREAD **3** : to increase the intensity, quantity, or capability of ⟨trying to ~ up courage to confess —Will Scott⟩ **4 a** (1) : to mistreat or exploit through extortion, trickery, or unfair actions; *esp* : to deprive of or cheat out of something due or expected ⟨~ed out of a job⟩ (2) : to treat so as to bring about injury or loss (as to a person's reputation) ⟨use the available Federal machinery to ~ our political enemies —J. W. Dean III⟩ — often used as a generalized curse ⟨~ you!⟩ **b** : to extract by pressure or threat **5** : to copulate with — usu. considered vulgar ~ *vi* **1** : to rotate like or as a screw **2** : to turn or move with a twisting or writhing motion **3** : COPULATE — usu. considered vulgar — **screw·er** *n*

screw around *vi* (1939) **1** : to waste time with unproductive activity : DALLY **2** : to have sexual relations with someone outside of a marriage or steady relationship : be sexually promiscuous

¹screw·ball \'skrü-ˌbȯl\ *n* (1928) **1** : a baseball pitch that spins and breaks in the opposite direction to a curve **2** : a whimsical, eccentric, or crazy person : ZANY

\ə\ abut \ᵊ\ kitten, F table \ər\ further \a\ ash \ā\ ace \ä\ mop, mar \aú\ out \ch\ chin \e\ bet \ē\ easy \g\ go \i\ hit \ī\ ice \j\ job \ŋ\ sing \ō\ go \ȯ\ law \ȯi\ boy \th\ thin \t̷h\ the \ü\ loot \ü\ foot \y\ yet \zh\ vision \à, k̵, ⁿ, œ, œ̄, ᵫ, ᵫ̄, ᵞ\ see Guide to Pronunciation

²**screwball** adj (ca. 1936) : crazily eccentric or whimsical : ZANY

screw·bean \'skrü-,bēn\ n (1866) 1 : a leguminous shrub or small tree (*Prosopis pubescens*) of the southwestern U.S. and northern Mexico — called also *screwbean mesquite* 2 : a spirally twisted sweet pod that is the fruit of the screwbean

screw·driv·er \'skrü-,drī-vər\ n (1779) 1 : a tool for turning screws 2 : vodka and orange juice served with ice

screw eye n (1873) : a wood screw with a head in the form of a loop

screw jack n (1719) : a screw-operated jack for lifting, exerting pressure, or adjusting position (as of a machine part)

screw pine n (1836) : any of a genus (*Pandanus* of the family Pandanaceae, the screw-pine family) of tropical monocotyledonous Old World plants with slender palmlike stems, often huge prop roots, and terminal crowns of swordlike leaves

screw propeller n (1839) : PROPELLER

screw thread n (ca. 1812) 1 : the projecting helical rib of a screw 2 : one complete turn of a screw thread

screw·up \'skrü-,əp\ n (ca. 1960) 1 : one who screws up 2 : BOTCH, BLUNDER

screw up vt (1680) 1 : to tighten, fasten, or lock by or as if by a screw 2 a : BUNGLE, BOTCH b : to cause to act or function in a crazy or confused way : CONFOUND, DISTURB ~ vi : to botch an activity or undertaking

screw·worm \'skrü-,wərm\ n (1879) : a blowfly (*Cochliomyia hominivorax*) of the warmer parts of America whose larva develops in sores or wounds or in the nostrils of mammals including humans with serious or sometimes fatal results; *esp* : its larva 2 : any of several flies other than the screwworm and esp. their larvae which parasitize the flesh of mammals

screwy \'skrü-ē\ adj **screw·i·er; -est** (1887) 1 : crazily absurd, eccentric, or unusual 2 : CRAZY, INSANE — **screw·i·ness** n

scrib·al \'skrī-bəl\ adj (1857) : of, relating to, or due to a scribe

scrib·ble \'skri-bəl\ vb **scrib·bled; scrib·bling** \-b(ə-)liŋ\ [ME *scriblen*, fr. ML *scribillare*, fr. L *scribere* to write] vt (15c) 1 : to write hastily or carelessly without regard to legibility or form 2 : to cover with careless or worthless writings or drawings ~ vi : to write or draw hastily and carelessly — **scribble** n

scrib·bler \'skri-b(ə-)lər\ n (ca. 1553) 1 : one that scribbles 2 : a minor or insignificant author

¹**scribe** \'skrīb\ n [ME, fr. L *scriba* official writer, fr. *scribere* to write; akin to Gk *skariphasthai* to scratch an outline] (14c) 1 : one of a learned class in ancient Israel through New Testament times studying the Scriptures and serving as copyists, editors, teachers, and jurists 2 a : an official or public secretary or clerk b : a copier of manuscripts 3 : WRITER; *specif* : JOURNALIST

²**scribe** vi **scribed; scrib·ing** (1782) : to work as a scribe : WRITE

³**scribe** vt **scribed; scrib·ing** [prob. short for *describe*] (1678) 1 : to mark a line on by cutting or scratching with a pointed instrument 2 : to make by cutting or scratching

⁴**scribe** n (1812) : SCRIBER

scrib·er \'skrī-bər\ n (ca. 1836) : a sharp-pointed tool for making marks and esp. for marking off material (as wood or metal) to be cut

scrieve \'skrēv\ vi [of Scand origin; akin to ON *skrefa* to stride] (1785) *Scot* : to move along swiftly and smoothly

scrim \'skrim\ n [origin unknown] (1792) 1 : a durable plain-woven usu. cotton fabric for use in clothing, curtains, building, and industry 2 : a theater drop that appears opaque when a scene in front is lighted and transparent or translucent when a scene in back is lighted 3 : something likened to a theater scrim

¹**scrim·mage** \'skri-mij\ n [ME *scrymmage*, alter. of *skyrmissh* skirmish] (15c) 1 a : a minor battle : SKIRMISH b : a confused fight : SCUFFLE 2 a : the interplay between two football teams that begins with the snap of the ball and continues until the ball is dead b : practice play (as in football or basketball) between two squads

²**scrimmage** vb **scrim·maged; scrim·mag·ing** vi (ca. 1825) : to take part in a scrimmage ~ vt : to play a scrimmage against — **scrimmag·er** n

scrimmage line n (ca. 1909) : LINE OF SCRIMMAGE

scrimp \'skrimp\ vb [perh. of Scand origin; akin to Sw *skrympa* to shrink, MLG *schrempen* to contract — more at SHRIMP] vt (ca. 1774) 1 : to be stingy in providing for 2 : to make too small, short, or scanty ~ vi : to be frugal or stingy — **scrimpy** \'skrim-pē\ adj

scrim·shan·der \'skrim-,shan-dər\ n [origin unknown] (1851) : a person who creates scrimshaw

¹**scrim·shaw** \'skrim-,shȯ\ vb [origin unknown] vt (ca. 1826) : to carve or engrave into scrimshaw ~ vi : to produce scrimshaw

²**scrimshaw** n (ca. 1864) 1 : any of various carved or engraved articles made orig. by American whalers usu. from baleen or whale ivory 2 : scrimshawed work 3 : the art, practice, or technique of producing scrimshaw

¹**scrip** \'skrip\ n [ME *scrippe*, fr. ML *scrippum* pilgrim's knapsack] (13c) *archaic* : a small bag or wallet

²**scrip** n [alter. of *script*] (1590) 1 : a short writing (as a certificate, schedule, or list) 2 : a small piece 3 a : any of various documents used as evidence that the holder or bearer is entitled to receive something (as a fractional share of stock or an allotment of land) b : paper currency or a token issued for temporary use in an emergency

¹**script** \'skript\ n [ME, fr. L *scriptum*, fr. neut. of *scriptus*, pp. of *scribere* to write — more at SCRIBE] (14c) 1 a : something written : TEXT b : an original or principal instrument or document c (1) : MANUSCRIPT 1 (2) : the written text of a stage play, screenplay, or broadcast; *specif* : the one used in production or performance 2 a : a style of printed letters that resembles handwriting b : written characters : HANDWRITING c : ALPHABET 3 : a plan of action

²**script** vt (1935) 1 : to prepare a script for or from 2 : to provide carefully considered details for (as a plan of action)

script·er \'skrip-tər\ n (1939) : SCRIPTWRITER

scrip·to·ri·um \skrip-'tōr-ē-əm, -'tȯr-\ n, pl **-ria** \-ē-ə\ [ML, fr. L *scribere*] (1774) : a copying room for the scribes in a medieval monastery

scrip·tur·al \'skrip(t)-sh(ə-)rəl\ adj (1641) : of, relating to, contained in, or according to a sacred writing; *esp* : BIBLICAL — **scrip·tur·al·ly** adv

scrip·ture \'skrip(t)-shər\ n [ME, fr. LL *scriptura*, fr. L, act or product of writing, fr. *scriptus*] (14c) 1 a (1) *cap* : the books of the Bible —

often used in pl. (2) *often cap* : a passage from the Bible b : a body of writings considered sacred or authoritative 2 : something written ⟨the primitive man's awe for any ~ —George Santayana⟩

script·writ·er \'skript-,rī-tər\ n (1935) : a person who writes scripts

scriv·en·er \'skriv-nər, 'skri-və-\ n [ME *scriveiner*, alter. of *scrivein*, fr. MF *escrivein*, fr. (assumed) VL *scriban-, scriba*, alter. of L *scriba* scribe] (14c) 1 : a professional or public copyist or writer : SCRIBE 2 : NOTARY PUBLIC

scrod \'skräd\ n [origin unknown] (1841) : a young fish (as a cod or haddock); *esp* : one split and boned for cooking

scrof·u·la \'skro-fyə-lə, 'skrä-\ n [NL, back-formation fr. LL *scrofulae*, pl., swellings of the lymph nodes of the neck, fr. pl. of *scrofula*, dim. of L *scrofa* breeding sow] (1791) : tuberculosis of lymph nodes esp. in the neck

scrof·u·lous \-ləs\ adj (1612) 1 : of, relating to, or affected with scrofula 2 a : having a diseased run-down appearance b : morally contaminated

¹**scroll** \'skrōl\ n [ME *scrowle*, blend of *rolle* roll and *scrowe* scrap, scroll (fr. MF *escroue*, of Gmc origin; akin to OE *scrēade* shred)] (15c) 1 a : a roll (as of papyrus, leather, or parchment) for writing a document b *archaic* : a written message c : ROSTER, LIST d : a riband with rolled ends often inscribed with a motto 2 a : something resembling a scroll in shape; *esp* : a spiral or convoluted form in ornamental design derived from the curves of a loosely or partly rolled parchment scroll b : the curved head of a bowed stringed musical instrument — see VIOLIN illustration

²**scroll** vi (1973) : to move text or graphics up or down or across a display screen as if by unrolling a scroll ~ vt : to cause (text or graphics on a display screen) to move in scrolling

scroll saw n (1851) 1 : FRETSAW 2 : JIGSAW 1

scroll·work \'skrōl-,wərk\ n (1739) : ornamentation characterized by scrolls; *esp* : fancy designs in wood often made with a scroll saw

scrooge \'skrüj\ n, *often cap* [Ebenezer *Scrooge*, character in the story *A Christmas Carol* (1843) by Charles Dickens] (1899) : a miserly person

scro·tum \'skrō-təm\ n, pl **scro·ta** \-tə\ or **scrotums** [L; akin to L *scrautum* quiver] (1597) : the external pouch that in most mammals contains the testes — **scro·tal** \'skrō-t²l\ adj

scrouge \'skrauj, 'skrüj\ vb **scrouged; scroug·ing** [alter. of E dial. *scruze* to squeeze] (1755) *chiefly dial* : CROWD, PRESS

scrounge \'skraunj\ vb **scrounged; scroung·ing** [alter. of E dial. *scrunge* to wander about idly] vt (ca. 1909) 1 : STEAL, SWIPE 2 a : to get as needed by or as if by foraging, scavenging, or borrowing 3 : FINAGLE, WHEEDLE — often used with *up* ~ vi : to search about and turn up something needed from whatever source is available; *also* : to actively seek money, work, or sustenance from any available source — **scroung·er** n

scroungy \'skraun-jē\ adj **scroung·i·er; -est** (ca. 1960) : being shabby, dirty, or unkempt

¹**scrub** \'skrəb\ n, *often attrib* [ME, alter. of *schrobbe* shrub — more at SHRUB] (14c) 1 a : a stunted tree or shrub b : vegetation consisting chiefly of scrubs c : a tract covered with scrub 2 : a domestic animal of mixed or unknown parentage and usu. inferior conformation : MONGREL 3 : a person of insignificant size or standing 4 : a player not belonging to the first string

²**scrub** vb **scrubbed; scrub·bing** [of LG or Scand origin; akin to MLG & MD *schrubben* to scrub, Sw *skrubba*] vt (ca. 1595) 1 a (1) : to clean with hard rubbing : SCOUR (2) : to remove by scrubbing b : to subject to friction : RUB 2 : WASH 6c(2) 3 : CANCEL, ELIMINATE ~ vi 1 : to use hard rubbing in cleaning 2 : to prepare for surgery by scrubbing oneself — **scrub·ba·ble** \'skrə-bə-bəl\ adj

³**scrub** n (1621) 1 : an act or instance of scrubbing; *esp* : CANCELLATION 2 : one that scrubs

¹**scrubbed** \'skrə-bəd\ adj [¹*scrub*] (1596) *archaic* : SCRUBBY 1

²**scrubbed** \'skrəbd\ adj [fr. pp. of ²*scrub*] (1948) : giving the impression of being clean or wholesome as if from scrubbing ⟨days when studios manufactured ~ public images for their stars —Sally Helgesen⟩

scrub·ber \'skrə-bər\ n (1839) : one that scrubs; *esp* : an apparatus for removing impurities esp. from gases

scrub brush n (1897) : a brush with hard bristles for heavy cleaning — called also *scrubbing brush*

scrub·by \'skrə-bē\ adj **scrub·bi·er; -est** [¹*scrub*] (1591) 1 : inferior in size or quality : STUNTED ⟨~ cattle⟩ 2 : covered with or consisting of scrub 3 : SHABBY, PALTRY

scrub·land \'skrəb-,land\ n (1779) : land covered with scrub

scrub nurse n (1905) : a nurse who assists the surgeon in an operating room

scrub oak n (1766) : any of various chiefly American oaks (as *Quercus ilicifolia* of the northeastern U.S.) of small size and usu. shrubby habit

scrub pine n (1791) : a pine of dwarf, straggly, or scrubby growth usu. by reason of environmental conditions; *specif* : a pine tree unsuitable for lumber by reason of inferior or defective growth

scrub typhus n (1929) : TSUTSUGAMUSHI DISEASE

scrub·wom·an \'skrəb-,wu̇-mən\ n (1873) : CHARWOMAN

scruff \'skrəf\ n [alter. of earlier *scuff*, of unknown origin] (1790) : the back of the neck : NAPE

scruffy \'skrə-fē\ adj **scruff·i·er; -est** [E dial. *scruff* something worthless] (1871) : UNKEMPT, SLOVENLY, SHAGGY — **scruff·i·ly** \-fə-lē\ adv — **scruff·i·ness** \-fē-nəs\ n

scrum \'skrəm\ n [short for *scrummage*, alter. of *scrimmage*] (1857) or **scrum·mage** \'skrə-mij\ : a rugby play in which the forwards of each side come together in a tight formation and struggle to gain possession of the ball when it is tossed in among them 2 *Brit* : MADHOUSE 2 — **scrummage** vi

scrump·tious \'skrəm(p)-shəs\ adj [perh. alter. of *sumptuous*] (1830) : DELIGHTFUL, EXCELLENT; *esp* : DELICIOUS — **scrump·tious·ly** adv

¹**scrunch** \'skrənch, 'skrünch\ vb [alter. of ¹*crunch*] vt (ca. 1790) 1 : CRUNCH, CRUSH 2 a : to draw or squeeze together tightly b : CRUMPLE — often used with *up* c : to cause (as one's features) to draw together — usu. used with *up* ~ vi 1 : to move with or make a crunching sound 2 : CROUCH, HUNCH; *also* : SQUEEZE

²**scrunch** n (1857) : a crunching sound

¹**scru·ple** \'skrü-pəl\ n [ME *scriple*, fr. L *scrupulus* a unit of weight, dim. of *scrupus* sharp stone] (14c) 1 — see WEIGHT table 2 : a minute part or quantity : IOTA

²scruple *n* [ME *scrupul*, fr. MF *scrupule*, fr. L *scrupulus*, dim. of *scrupus* source of uneasiness, lit., sharp stone] (15c) **1** : an ethical consideration or principle that inhibits action **2** : the quality or state of being scrupulous **3** : mental reservation *syn* see QUALM

³scruple *vi* **scru·pled; scru·pling** \-p(ə-)liŋ\ (1627) **1** : to have scruples **2** : to show reluctance on grounds of conscience : HESITATE

scru·pu·los·i·ty \ˌskrü-pyə-ˈlä-sə-tē\ *n* (1526) **1** : the quality or state of being scrupulous **2** : ²SCRUPLE 1

scru·pu·lous \ˈskrü-pyə-ləs\ *adj* [ME, fr. L *scrupulosus*, fr. *scrupulus*] (15c) **1** : having moral integrity : acting in strict regard for what is considered right or proper **2** : punctiliously exact : PAINSTAKING ⟨working with ~ care⟩ *syn* see UPRIGHT, CAREFUL — **scru·pu·lous·ly** *adv* — **scru·pu·lous·ness** *n*

scru·ta·ble \ˈskrü-tə-bəl\ *adj* [LL *scrutabilis* searchable, fr. L *scrutari*] (ca. 1600) : capable of being deciphered : COMPREHENSIBLE

scru·ti·neer \ˌskrü-t²n-ˈir\ *n* (1557) **1** : one that examines **2** *Brit* : one who takes or counts votes

scru·ti·nise *Brit var of* SCRUTINIZE

scru·ti·nize \ˈskrü-t²n-ˌīz\ *vb* **-nized; -niz·ing** *vt* (1671) : to examine closely and minutely ~ *vi* : to make a scrutiny — **scru·ti·niz·er** *n*
syn SCRUTINIZE, SCAN, INSPECT, EXAMINE mean to look at or over. SCRUTINIZE stresses close attention to minute detail ⟨*scrutinized* the hospital bill⟩. SCAN implies a surveying from point to point often suggesting a cursory overall observation ⟨*scanned* the wine list⟩. INSPECT implies scrutinizing for errors or defects ⟨*inspected* my credentials⟩. EXAMINE suggests a scrutiny in order to determine the nature, condition, or quality of a thing ⟨*examined* the specimens⟩.

scru·ti·ny \ˈskrü-t²n-ē, ˈskrüt-nē\ *n, pl* **-nies** [L *scrutinium*, fr. *scrutari* to search, examine, prob. fr. *scruta* trash] (1604) **1** : a searching study, inquiry, or inspection : EXAMINATION **2** : a searching look **3** : close watch : SURVEILLANCE

scu·ba \ˈskü-bə\ *n, often attrib* [*s*elf-*c*ontained *u*nderwater *b*reathing *a*pparatus] (1952) : an apparatus utilizing a portable supply of compressed gas (as air) supplied at a regulated pressure and used for breathing while swimming underwater

scuba diver *n* (1958) : one who swims underwater with the aid of scuba gear — **scuba dive** *vi*

¹scud \ˈskəd\ *vi* **scud·ded; scud·ding** [prob. of Scand origin; akin to Norw *skudda* to push] (1532) **1** : to move or run swiftly esp. as if driven forward **2** : to run before a gale

²scud *n* (1609) **1** : the action of scudding : RUSH **2 a** : loose vapory clouds driven swiftly by the wind **b** (1) : a slight sudden shower (2) : mist, rain, snow, or spray driven by the wind **3** : a gust of wind

scu·do \ˈskü-(ˌ)dō\ *n, pl* **scu·di** \-(ˌ)dē\ [It, lit., shield, fr. L *scutum* — more at ESQUIRE] (1644) **1** : a gold or silver coin formerly used in Italy **2** : a unit of value equivalent to a scudo

¹scuff \ˈskəf\ *vb* [prob. of Scand origin; akin to Sw *skuffa* to push] *vi* (1768) **1 a** : to walk without lifting the feet : SHUFFLE **b** : to poke or shuffle a foot in exploration or embarrassment **2** : to become scratched, chipped, or roughened by wear ~ *vt* **1** : ³CUFF **2 a** : to scrape (the feet) along a surface while walking or back and forth while standing **b** : to poke at with the toe **3** : to scratch, gouge, or wear away the surface of

²scuff *n* (1899) **1 a** : a noise of or as if of scuffing **b** : the act or an instance of scuffing **c** : a mark or injury caused by scuffing **2** : a flat-soled slipper without quarter or heel strap — compare MULE

scuf·fle \ˈskə-fəl\ *vi* **scuf·fled; scuf·fling** \-f(ə-)liŋ\ [prob. of Scand origin; akin to Sw *skuffa* to push] (1590) **1 a** : to struggle at close quarters with disorder and confusion **b** : to struggle (as by working odd jobs) to get by **2 a** : to move with a quick shuffling gait : SCURRY **b** : SHUFFLE — **scuffle** *n*

scuffle hoe *n* (1856) : a garden hoe that has both edges sharpened and can be pushed forward or drawn back

¹scull \ˈskəl\ *n* [ME *sculle*] (14c) **1 a** : an oar used at the stern of a boat to propel it forward with a thwartwise motion **b** : either of a pair of oars usu. less than 10 feet (3 meters) in length and operated by one person **2** : a racing shell propelled by one or two persons using sculls

²scull *vt* (1624) : to propel (a boat) by sculls or by a large oar worked thwartwise ~ *vi* : to scull a boat — **scull·er** *n*

scul·lery \ˈskə-lə-rē, ˈskəl-rē\ *n, pl* **-ler·ies** [ME, department of household in charge of dishes, fr. MF *escuelerie*, fr. *escuelle* bowl, fr. L *scutella* drinking bowl — more at SCUTTLE] (15c) : a room for cleaning and storing dishes and cooking utensils and for doing messy kitchen work

scul·lion \ˈskəl-yən\ *n* [ME *sculion*, fr. MF *escouillon* dishcloth, alter. of *escouvillon*, fr. *escouve* broom, fr. L *scopae*, lit., twigs bound together] (15c) : a kitchen helper

scul·pin \ˈskəl-pən\ *n, pl* **sculpins** *also* **sculpin** [origin unknown] (1672) **1** : any of a family (Cottidae) of spiny large-headed broad-mouthed often scaleless bony fishes **2** : a scorpion fish (*Scorpaena guttata*) of the southern California coast caught for food and sport

sculpin 1

sculpt \ˈskəlpt\ *vb* [F *sculpter*, alter. of obs. *sculper*, fr. L *sculpere*] (1864) : CARVE, SCULPTURE

sculp·tor \ˈskəlp-tər\ *n* [L, fr. *sculpere*] (1634) : an artist who makes sculptures

sculp·tress \-trəs\ *n* (1662) : a woman artist who makes sculptures

sculp·tur·al \ˈskəlp-chə-rəl, ˈskəlp-shrəl\ *adj* (1819) **1** : of or relating to sculpture **2** : resembling sculpture : SCULPTURESQUE — **sculp·tur·al·ly** *adv*

¹sculp·ture \ˈskəlp-chər\ *n* [ME, fr. L *sculptura*, fr. *sculptus*, pp. of *sculpere* to carve, alter. of *scalpere* to scratch, carve] (14c) **1 a** : the action or art of processing (as by carving, modeling, or welding) plastic or hard materials into works of art **b** (1) : work produced by sculpture (2) : a three-dimensional work of art (as a statue) **2** : impressed or raised markings or a pattern of such esp. on a plant or animal part

²sculpture *vb* **sculp·tured; sculp·tur·ing** \ˈskəlp-chə-riŋ, ˈskəlp-shriŋ\ *vt* (1645) **1 a** : to form an image or representation of from solid material (as wood or stone) **b** : to form into a three-dimensional work of art **2** : to change (the form of the earth's surface) by natural

processes (as erosion and deposition) **3** : to shape by or as if by carving or molding ~ *vi* : to work as a sculptor

sculp·tur·esque \ˌskəlp-chə-ˈresk\ *adj* (1835) : done in the manner of or resembling sculpture — **sculp·tur·esque·ly** *adv*

¹scum \ˈskəm\ *n* [ME, fr. MD *schum*; akin to OHG *scūm* foam] (14c) **1 a** : extraneous matter or impurities risen to or formed on the surface of a liquid often as a foul filmy covering **b** : the scoria of metals in a molten state : DROSS **c** : a slimy film on a solid or gelatinous object **2 a** : REFUSE **b** : a low, vile, or worthless person or group of people — **scum·my** \ˈskə-mē\ *adj*

²scum *vi* **scummed; scum·ming** (1661) : to become covered with or as if with scum

scum·bag \ˈskəm-ˌbag *also* -ˌbāg\ *n* (1967) *slang* : a dirty or despicable person

¹scum·ble \ˈskəm-bəl\ *vt* **scum·bled; scum·bling** \-b(ə-)liŋ\ [perh. freq. of ²*scum*] (1798) **1 a** : to make (as color or a painting) less brilliant by covering with a thin coat of opaque or semiopaque color **b** : to apply (a color) in this manner **2 a** : to soften the lines or colors of (a drawing) by rubbing lightly

²scumble *n* (1834) **1** : the act or effect of scumbling **2** : a material used for scumbling

scun·gil·li \skün-ˈjē-lē, -ˈgē-, -ˈji-\ *n* [It dial. (Neapolitan) *scuncigli*, pl. of *scunciglio* conch] (1945) : conch used as food

¹scun·ner \ˈskə-nər\ *vi* [ME (Sc) *skunniren*] (14c) *chiefly Scot* : to be in a state of disgusted irritation

²scunner *n* (ca. 1520) : an unreasonable or extreme dislike or prejudice

scup \ˈskəp\ *n, pl* **scup** *also* **scups** [short for *scuppaug*, modif. of Narraganset *mishcùppaûog*] (ca. 1848) : a porgy (*Stenotomus chrysops*) occurring along the Atlantic coast of the U.S. chiefly from No. Carolina to Maine and used as a panfish

¹scup·per \ˈskə-pər\ *n* [ME *skopper*] (15c) **1** : an opening cut through the bulwarks of a ship so that water falling on deck may flow overboard **2** : an opening in the wall of a building through which water can drain from a floor or flat roof

²scupper *vt* [origin unknown] (1899) *Brit* : to defeat or put an end to : DO IN 1a

scup·per·nong \-,nȯŋ, -,näŋ\ *n* [*Scuppernong*, river and lake in No. Carolina] (1811) **1** : MUSCADINE; *esp* : a cultivated muscadine with yellowish green plum-flavored fruits **2** : a sweet aromatic amber-colored wine made from scuppernongs

scurf \ˈskərf\ *n* [ME, fr. OE, of Scand origin; akin to Icel *skurfa* scurf; akin to OHG *scorf* scurf, OE *sceorfan* to scarify] (bef. 12c) **1** : thin dry scales detached from the epidermis esp. in an abnormal skin condition; *specif* : DANDRUFF **2 a** : something like flakes or scales adhering to a surface **b** : the foul remains of something adherent **3 a** : a scaly deposit or covering on some plant parts; *also* : a localized or general darkening and roughening of a plant surface usu. more pronounced than russeting **b** : a plant disease characterized by scurf — **scurfy** \ˈskər-fē\ *adj*

scur·rile *or* **scur·ril** \ˈskər-əl, ˈskə-rəl\ *adj* [MF *scurrile*, fr. L *scurrilis*, fr. *scurra* buffoon] (1567) : SCURRILOUS

scur·ril·i·ty \skə-ˈri-lə-tē\ *n, pl* **-ties** (1508) **1** : the quality or state of being scurrilous **2 a** : scurrilous or abusive language **b** : an offensively rude or abusive remark

scur·ri·lous \ˈskər-ə-ləs, ˈskə-rə-\ *adj* (1576) **1 a** : using or given to coarse language **b** : being vulgar and evil ⟨~ imposters who used a religious exterior to rob poor people —Edwin Benson⟩ **2** : containing obscenities, abuse, or slander ⟨a . . . campaign filled with ~ charges and countercharges —A. D. Graeff⟩ — **scur·ri·lous·ly** *adv* — **scur·ri·lous·ness** *n*

scur·ry \ˈskər-ē, ˈskə-rē\ *vi* **scur·ried; scur·ry·ing** [short for *hurry-scurry*, redupl. of *hurry*] (1810) **1** : to move in or as if in a brisk pace : SCAMPER **2** : to move around in an agitated, confused, or fluttering manner — **scurry** *n*

¹scur·vy \ˈskər-vē\ *n* [²*scurvy*] (ca. 1565) : a disease marked by spongy gums, loosening of the teeth, and a bleeding into the skin and mucous membranes and caused by a lack of vitamin C

²scurvy *adj* [*scurf*] (1579) : disgustingly mean or contemptible : DESPICABLE ⟨a ~ trick⟩ *syn* see CONTEMPTIBLE — **scur·vi·ly** \-və-lē\ *adv* — **scur·vi·ness** \-vē-nəs\ *n*

scurvy grass *n* (1597) : a cruciferous herb (as *Cochlearia officinalis*) formerly believed useful in preventing or treating scurvy

scut \ˈskət\ *n* [origin unknown] (ca. 1530) : a short erect tail (as of a hare)

scu·tage \ˈskü-tij, ˈskyü-\ *n* [ME, fr. ML *scutagium*, fr. L *scutum* shield — more at ESQUIRE] (15c) : a tax levied on a vassal or a knight in lieu of military service

¹scutch \ˈskəch\ *vt* [obs. F *escoucher*, fr. (assumed) VL *excuticare* to beat out, fr. L *excutere*, fr. *ex-* + *quatere* to shake, strike] (1733) : to separate the woody fiber from (flax or hemp) by beating

²scutch *n* (ca. 1791) **1** : SCUTCHER **2** : a bricklayer's hammer for cutting, trimming, and dressing bricks

scutch·eon \ˈskə-chən\ *n* [ME *scochon*, fr. MF *escuchon*] (14c) : ESCUTCHEON

scutch·er \ˈskə-chər\ *n* (1776) : an implement or machine for scutching flax or cotton

scute \ˈsküt, ˈskyüt\ *n* [NL *scutum*, fr. L, shield — more at ESQUIRE] (1898) : an external bony or horny plate or large scale

scu·tel·late \ˈskü-tə-ˌlāt, skyü-; ˈsk(y)ü-t²l-ˌāt\ *or* **scu·tel·lat·ed** \ˈsk(y)ü-t²l-ˌā-təd\ *adj* (1785) : having or covered with scutella

scu·tel·lum \skü-ˈte-ləm, skyü-\ *n, pl* **-la** \-lə\ [NL, dim. of L *scutum* shield] (ca. 1760) **1** : a hard plate or scale (as on the thorax of an insect or the tarsus of a bird) **2** : the shield-shaped cotyledon of a monocotyledon — **scu·tel·lar** \-lər\ *adj*

scut·ter \ˈskə-tər\ *vi* [alter. of ²*scuttle*] (1781) : SCURRY, SCAMPER

¹scut·tle \ˈskə-t²l\ *n* [ME *scutel*, fr. L *scutella* drinking bowl, tray, dim. of *scutra* platter] (15c) : a shallow open basket for carrying some-

\ə\ abut \ᵊ\ kitten, F table \ər\ further \a\ ash \ā\ ace \ä\ mop, mar \aú\ out \ch\ chin \e\ bet \ē\ easy \g\ go \i\ hit \ī\ ice \j\ job \ŋ\ sing \ō\ go \ȯ\ law \ȯi\ boy \th\ thin \th\ the \ü\ loot \ù\ foot \y\ yet \zh\ vision \ä, k̟, ⁿ, œ, œ̄, ᵾ, ᵫ, � y\ see Guide to Pronunciation thing (as grain or garden produce) **2** : a metal pail that usu. has a bail and a sloped lip and is used esp. for carrying coal

²scuttle n [ME skottell] (15c) **1** : a small opening in a wall or roof furnished with a lid: as **a** : a small opening or hatchway in the deck of a ship large enough to admit a person and with a lid for covering it **b** : a small hole in the side or bottom of a ship fitted with a covering or glazed **2** : a covering that closes a scuttle

³scuttle vt **scut·tled; scut·tling** \'skət-liŋ, 'skə-t²l-iŋ\ (1642) **1** : to cut a hole through the bottom, deck, or side of (a ship); specif : to sink or attempt to sink by making holes through the bottom **2** : DESTROY, WRECK; also : SCRAP 2

⁴scuttle n [perh. blend of scud and shuttle] (1623) **1** : a quick shuffling pace **2** : a short swift run

⁵scuttle vi **scut·tled; scut·tling** \'skət-liŋ, 'skə-t²l-iŋ\ (1657) : SCURRY

scut·tle·butt \'skə-t²l-,bət\ n [²scuttle + ³butt] (1805) **1 a** : a cask on shipboard to contain fresh water for a day's use **b** : a drinking fountain on a ship or at a naval or marine installation **2** : RUMOR, GOSSIP

scu·tum \'skü-təm, 'skyü-\ n, pl **scu·ta** \-tə\ [NL, fr. L, shield — more at ESQUIRE] (1771) : a bony, horny, or chitinous plate : SCUTE

scut work \'skət-\ n [prob. fr. medical argot scut junior intern] (ca. 1962) : routine and often menial labor

scuz·zy \'skə-zē\ adj **scuz·zi·er; -est** [origin unknown] (1969) slang : dirty, shabby, or foul in condition or character

Scyl·la \'si-lə\ n [L, fr. Gk Skyllē] : a nymph changed into a monster in Greek mythology who terrorizes mariners in the Strait of Messina — **between Scylla and Charybdis** : between two equally hazardous alternatives

scy·phis·to·ma \sī-'fis-tə-mə\ n, pl **-mae** \-(,)mē\ also **-mas** [NL, fr. L scyphus cup + Gk stoma mouth — more at STOMACH] (1878) : a sexually produced scyphozoan larva that ultimately repeatedly constricts transversely to form free-swimming medusae

scy·pho·zo·an \,si-fə-'zō-ən\ n [NL Scyphozoa, fr. L scyphus + NL -zoa] (ca. 1909) : any of a class (Scyphozoa) of coelenterates that comprise jellyfishes lacking a true polyp and usu. a velum — **scyphozoan** adj

¹scythe \'sīth, 'sī\ n [ME sithe, fr. OE sīthe; akin to OE sagu saw — more at SAW] (bef. 12c) : an implement used for mowing (as grass) and composed of a long curving blade fastened at an angle to a long handle

²scythe vb **scythed; scyth·ing** vi (ca. 1580) : to use a scythe ~ vt : to cut with or as if with a scythe

Scyth·i·an \'si-thē-ən, -thē-\ n [L Scytha, fr. Gk Skythēs] (15c) **1** : a member of an ancient nomadic people inhabiting Scythia **2** : the Iranian language of the Scythians — **Scythian** adj

sea \'sē\ n [ME see, fr. OE sǣ; akin to OHG sē sea, Goth saiws] (bef. 12c) **1 a** : a great body of salty water that covers much of the earth; broadly : the waters of the earth as distinguished from the land and air **b** : a body of salt water of second rank more or less landlocked ⟨the Mediterranean ~⟩ **c** : OCEAN **d** : an inland body of water — used esp. for names of such bodies ⟨the Caspian Sea⟩ ⟨the Sea of Galilee⟩ **2 a** : surface motion on a large body of water or its direction; also : a large swell or wave — often used in pl. ⟨heavy ~s⟩ **b** : the disturbance of the ocean or other body of water due to the wind **3** : something likened to the sea esp. in vastness ⟨the crowd was a ~ of faces⟩ **4** : the seafaring life **5** : ³MARE — **sea** adj — **at sea 1** : on the sea; specif : on a sea voyage **2** : LOST, BEWILDERED — **to sea** : to or on the open waters of the sea

sea anchor n (1769) : a drag typically of canvas thrown overboard to retard the drifting of a ship or seaplane and to keep its head to the wind

sea anemone n (1742) : any of numerous usu. solitary anthozoan polyps (order Actiniaria) whose form, bright and varied colors, and cluster of tentacles superficially resemble a flower

sea·bag \'sē-,bag\ n (1919) : a cylindrical canvas bag used esp. by a sailor for clothes and other gear

sea bass n (1765) **1** : any of numerous marine bony fishes (family Serranidae) that are usu. smaller and more active than the groupers; esp : a food and sport fish (Centropristis striata) of the Atlantic coast of the U.S. **2** : any of numerous croakers or drums including noted sport and food fishes

sea·bed \-,bed\ n (1838) : the floor of a sea or ocean

Sea·bee \'sē-(,)bē\ n [alter. of cee + bee; fr. the initials of construction battalion] (1942) : a member of one of the U.S. Navy construction battalions for building naval shore facilities in combat zones

sea·bird \'sē-,bərd\ n (1589) : a bird (as a gull or albatross) frequenting the open ocean

sea biscuit n (ca. 1690) : HARDTACK 1

sea·board \'sē-,bōrd, -,bȯrd\ n (1788) : SEACOAST; also : the country bordering a seacoast — **seaboard** adj

sea·boot \-,büt\ n (1851) : a very high waterproof boot used esp. by sailors and fishermen

sea·borg·i·um \sē-'bȯr-gē-əm\ n [NL, fr. Glenn T. Seaborg] (1994) : UNNILHEXIUM

sea·borne \-,bōrn, -,bȯrn\ adj (1823) **1** : borne over or on the sea ⟨a ~ invasion⟩ **2** : carried on by oversea shipping ⟨~ trade⟩

sea bream n (ca. 1530) : any of numerous marine bony fishes (as of the family Sparidae)

sea breeze n (1697) : a cooling breeze blowing generally in the daytime inland from the sea

sea captain n (1612) : the master esp. of a merchant vessel

sea change n (1610) **1** archaic : a change brought about by the sea **2** : a marked change : TRANSFORMATION

sea chest n (1669) : a sailor's storage chest for personal property

sea·coast \'sē-,kōst\ n (14c) : the shore or border of the land adjacent to the sea

sea cow n (1613) : SIRENIAN

sea·craft \'sē-,kraft\ n (1727) **1** : skill in navigation **2** : seagoing ships

sea crayfish n (1601) : SPINY LOBSTER

sea cucumber n (1601) : any of a class (Holothurioidea) of echinoderms having a tough muscular elongate body with tentacles surrounding the mouth — called also holothurian

sea devil n (1634) : DEVILFISH 1

sea dog n (1823) : a veteran sailor

sea duck n (1753) : a diving duck (as a scoter, merganser, or eider) that frequents the sea

sea duty n (1946) : duty in the U.S. Navy performed with a deployable unit (as a ship or aircraft squadron)

sea eagle n (1668) : any of various fish-eating eagles (esp. genus Haliaeetus)

Sea Explorer n (1948) : an Explorer in a scouting program that teaches seamanship

sea fan n (1633) : a gorgonian with a fan-shaped skeleton; esp : one (Gorgonia flabellum) of Florida and the West Indies

sea·far·er \'sē-,far-ər, -,fer-\ n [sea + ¹fare + ²-er] (1513) : MARINER

sea·far·ing \-,far-iŋ, -,fer-\ n (1592) : the use of the sea for travel or transportation — **seafaring** adj

sea fire n (1814) : marine bioluminescence

sea·floor \'sē-,flȯr, -,flȯr\ n (1855) : SEABED

sea·food \-,füd\ n (1836) : edible marine fish and shellfish

sea·fowl \-,faül\ n (14c) : SEABIRD

sea·front \-,frənt\ n (1879) : the waterfront of a seaside place

sea·girt \'sē-,gərt\ adj (1616) : surrounded by the sea

sea·go·ing \-,gō-iŋ, -,gȯ(-)iŋ\ adj (1828) : OCEANGOING

sea grape n (1806) : a tree (Coccoloba uvifera) of the buckwheat family that inhabits sandy shores from Florida to So. America, has rounded leaves, and bears clusters of purple to whitish edible berries

sea grass n (1578) : any of various grasslike plants that inhabit coastal areas; esp : EELGRASS 1

sea green n (1598) **1** : a moderate green or bluish green **2** : a moderate yellow green

sea·gull \'sē-,gəl\ n (1542) : a gull frequenting the sea; broadly : GULL

sea hare n (1593) : any of various large opisthobranch mollusks (esp. genus Aplysia) that have an arched back and two anterior tentacles and have the shell much reduced or missing

sea holly n (1548) : a European coastal herb (Eryngium maritimum) of the carrot family with spiny leaves and pale blue flowers

sea horse n (ca. 1500) **1** : WALRUS 2 **a** : a mythical creature half horse and half fish **3** : any of a genus (Hippocampus of the family Syngnathidae) of small bony fishes that have the head angled downward toward the body which is carried vertically and are equipped with a prehensile tail

sea island cotton n, often cap S&I [Sea Islands, chain of islands off the southeastern U.S. coast] (1805) : a cotton (Gossypium barbadense) with esp. long silky fiber — called also sea island

sea kale n (1699) : a succulent Eurasian perennial herb (Crambe maritima) of the mustard family used as a potherb

sea king n (1819) : a Norse pirate chief

sea horse 3

¹seal \'sē(ə)l\ n, pl **seals** also **seal** [ME sele, fr. OE seolh; akin to OHG selah seal] (bef. 12c) **1** : any of numerous carnivorous marine mammals (families Phocidae and Otariidae) that live chiefly in cold regions and have limbs modified into webbed flippers adapted primarily to swimming; esp : a fur seal or hair seal as opposed to a sea lion **2 a** : the pelt of a fur seal **b** : leather made from the skin of a seal **3** : a dark brown

²seal vi (1828) : to hunt seals

³seal n [ME seel, fr. OF, fr. L sigillum seal, fr. dim. of signum sign, seal — more at SIGN] (13c) **1 a** : something that confirms, ratifies, or makes secure : GUARANTEE, ASSURANCE **b** (1) : a device with a cut or raised emblem, symbol, or word used esp. to certify a signature or authenticate a document (2) : a medallion or ring face bearing such a device incised so that it can be impressed on wax or moist clay; also : a piece of wax or a wafer bearing such an impression **c** : an impression, device, or mark given the effect of a common-law seal by statute law or by American local custom recognized by judicial decision **d** : a usu. ornamental adhesive stamp that may be used to close a letter or package; esp : one given in a fund-raising campaign **2 a** : something that secures (as a wax seal on a document) **b** : a closure that must be broken to be opened and thus reveals tampering **c** (1) : a tight and perfect closure (as against the passage of gas or water) (2) : a device to prevent the passage or return of gas or air into a pipe or container **3** : a seal that is symbol or mark of office — **under seal** : with an authenticating seal affixed

⁴seal vt (14c) **1 a** : to confirm or make secure by or as if by a seal **b** : to solemnize for eternity (as a marriage) by a Mormon rite **2 a** : to set or affix an authenticating seal to; also : AUTHENTICATE, RATIFY **b** : to mark with a stamp or seal usu. as an evidence of standard exactness, legal size, weight, or capacity, or merchantable quality **3 a** : to fasten with or as if with a seal to prevent tampering **b** : to close or make secure against access, leakage, or passage by a fastening or coating **c** : to fix in position or close breaks in with a filling (as of plaster) **4** : to determine irrevocably or indisputably ⟨that answer ~ed our fate⟩

sea lamprey n (1879) : a large anadromous lamprey (Petromyzon marinus) that has a mottled upper surface, is an ectoparasite of fish, and is sometimes used as food

sea·lane \'sē-,lān\ n (1927) : an established sea route

seal·ant \'sē-lənt\ n (1944) : a sealing agent (radiator ~)

sea lavender n (1597) : any of a genus (Limonium) of chiefly perennial herbs of the plumbago family with small flowers and basal leaves

sea lawyer n (1848) : an argumentative captious sailor

sealed–beam \'sē(ə)l(d)-'bēm\ adj (1939) : being an electric lamp with a prefocused reflector and lens sealed in the lamp vacuum

sea legs n pl (1712) : bodily adjustment to the motion of a ship indicated esp. by ability to walk steadily and by freedom from seasickness

¹seal·er \'sē-lər\ n (15c) **1** : an official who attests or certifies conformity to a standard of correctness **2** : a coat (as of size) applied to prevent subsequent coats of paint or varnish from sinking in

²sealer n (1842) : a person or a ship engaged in hunting seals

sea lettuce n (1668) : any of a genus (Ulva) of seaweeds with green fronds sometimes eaten as salad

sea level n (1806) : the level of the surface of the sea esp. at its mean position midway between mean high and low water

sea lily n (1876) : CRINOID; esp : a stalked crinoid

sealing wax n (14c) : a resinous composition that is plastic when warm and is used for sealing (as letters, dry cells, or cans)

sea lion n (1697) : any of several Pacific eared seals (as genera *Eumetopius* and *Zalophus*) that are usu. larger than the related fur seals and lack a thick underfur

seal off vt (1931) : to close tightly

seal point n [¹*seal* (the color)] (1939) : a coat color of cats characterized by a cream or fawn body with dark brown points; *also* : a Siamese cat with such coloring

seal ring n (1608) : a finger ring engraved with a seal : SIGNET RING

seal·skin \'sē(ə)l-,skin\ n (14c) 1 : the fur or pelt of a fur seal 2 : a garment (as a jacket, coat, or cape) of sealskin — **sealskin** adj

Sea·ly·ham terrier \'sē-lē-,ham-, *esp Brit* -lē-əm-\ n [*Sealyham*, Pembrokeshire, Wales] (1907) : any of a breed of short-legged long-headed strong-jawed heavy-boned chiefly white terriers developed in Wales

¹seam \'sēm\ n [ME *seem*, fr. OE *sēam*; akin to OE *sīwian* to sew — more at SEW] (bef. 12c) 1 a : the joining of two pieces (as of cloth or leather) by sewing usu. near the edge b : the stitching used in such a joining 2 : the space between adjacent planks or strakes of a ship 3 a : a line, groove, or ridge formed by the abutment of edges b : a thin layer or stratum (as of rock) between distinctive layers; *also* : a bed of valuable mineral and esp. coal irrespective of thickness c : a line left by a cut or wound; *also* : WRINKLE 4 : a weak or vulnerable area or gap (found a ~ in the zone defense) — **seam·like** \-,līk\ adj — **at the seams** : ENTIRELY, COMPLETELY (falling apart *at the seams*)

²seam vt (1582) 1 a : to join by sewing b : to join as if by sewing (as by welding, riveting, or heat-sealing) 2 : to mark with lines suggesting seams ~ vi : to become fissured or ridgy — **seam·er** n

sea·maid \'sē-,mād\ *or* **sea–maid·en** \-,mā-dᵊn\ n (1590) : MERMAID; *also* : a goddess or nymph of the sea

sea·man \'sē-mən\ n (bef. 12c) 1 : SAILOR, MARINER 2 a : any of the three ranks below petty officer in the navy or coast guard b : an enlisted man in the navy or coast guard ranking above a seaman apprentice and below a petty officer

seaman apprentice n (1947) : an enlisted man in the navy or coast guard ranking above a seaman recruit and below a seaman

sea·man·like \'sē-mən-,līk\ adj (1796) : characteristic of or befitting a competent seaman

sea·man·ly \-lē\ adj (1798) : SEAMANLIKE

seaman recruit n (1947) : an enlisted man of the lowest rank in the navy or coast guard

sea·man·ship \'sē-mən-,ship\ n (1766) : the art or skill of handling, working, and navigating a ship

sea·mark \-,märk\ n (15c) 1 : a line on a coast marking the tidal limit 2 : an elevated object serving as a beacon to mariners

sea mew n (15c) : SEAGULL; *esp* : a common gull (*Larus canus*) chiefly of Europe and northwestern No. America

sea mile n (1796) : NAUTICAL MILE

seam·less \'sēm-ləs\ adj (15c) 1 : having no seams 2 : having no awkward transitions or indications of disparity : perfectly smooth (a ~ fusion of beauty and intelligence —Jack Kroll *et al.*) — **seam·less·ly** \-lē\ adv — **seam·less·ness** \-nəs\ n

sea·mount \'sē-,maunt\ n (1941) : a submarine mountain rising above the deep-sea floor

sea mouse n (ca. 1520) : any of various large broad marine polychaete worms (esp. genus *Aphrodite*) having hairlike setae

seam·ster \'sēm(p)-stər *also* 'sem(p)-\ n [ME *semester, semster*, fr. OE *sēamestre* seamstress, tailor, fr. *sēam* seam] (bef. 12c) : a person employed at sewing; *esp* : TAILOR

seam·stress \-strəs\ n (1644) : a woman whose occupation is sewing

seamy \'sē-mē\ adj **seam·i·er; -est** (1604) 1 *archaic* : having the rough side of the seam showing 2 a : UNPLEASANT b : DEGRADED, SORDID — **seam·i·ness** n

sé·ance \'sā-,än(t)s, -,äⁿs, sā-'\ n [F, fr. *seoir* to sit, fr. L *sedēre* — more at SIT] (1803) 1 : SESSION, SITTING 2 : a spiritualist meeting to receive spirit communications

sea nettle n (1601) : a stinging jellyfish; *esp* : one (*Chrysaora quinquecirrha*) occurring esp. in Atlantic estuaries from Cape Cod to the West Indies

sea oats n *pl but sing or pl in constr* (1894) : a tall grass (*Uniola panicolata*) that has panicles resembling those of the oat, grows chiefly on the coast of the southern U.S., and is useful as a sand binder

sea onion n (14c) : SQUILL 1a

sea otter n (1664) : a rare marine otter (*Enhydra lutris*) of the northern Pacific coasts that may attain a length of six feet (two meters), is chiefly brown but with lighter coloration on the back of the head and neck, and feeds largely on shellfish

sea pen n (1763) : any of numerous anthozoans (order Pennatulacea) growing in colonies with a feathery form

sea-piece \'sē-,pēs\ n (1656) : SEASCAPE 2

sea pink (1731) 1 : THRIFT 4 2 : any of a genus (*Sabatia*) of smooth slender No. American herbs of the gentian family typically having pink or white cymose flowers

sea-plane \-,plān\ n (1913) : an airplane designed to take off from and land on the water

sea·port \'sē-,pōrt, -,pȯrt\ n (1596) : a port, harbor, or town accessible to seagoing ships

sea power n (1849) 1 : a nation having formidable naval strength 2 : naval strength

sea puss \-,pùs\ n [alter. of dial. *seapoose* tidal stream, fr. Unquachog (Algonquian language of Long Island) *seépus* river] (ca. 1891) : a swirling or along shore undertow

sea-quake \'sē-,kwāk\ n [*sea* + earth*quake*] (1680) : a submarine earthquake

¹sear *var of* SERE

²sear \'sir\ vb [ME *seren*, fr. OE *sēarian* to become sere, fr. *sēar* sere] vi (bef. 12c) : to cause withering or drying ~ vt 1 : to make withered and dry : PARCH 2 : to burn, scorch, or injure with or as if with sudden application of intense heat — **sear·ing·ly** \-iŋ-lē\ adv

³sear n (1874) : a mark or scar left by searing

⁴sear n [prob. fr. MF *serre* grasp, fr. *serrer* to press, grasp, fr. LL *serare* to bolt, latch, fr. L *sera* bar for fastening a door] (1596) : the catch that holds the hammer of a gun's lock at cock or half cock

¹search \'sərch\ vb [ME *cerchen*, fr. MF *cerchier* to go about, survey, search, fr. LL *circare* to go about, fr. L *circum* round about — more at CIRCUM-] vt (14c) 1 : to look into or over carefully or thoroughly in an effort to find or discover something: as a : to examine in seeking something (~ed the north field) b : to look through or explore by inspecting possible places of concealment or investigating suspicious circumstances c : to read thoroughly : CHECK; *esp* : to examine a public record or register for information about (~ land titles) d : to examine for articles concealed on the person e : to look at as if to discover or penetrate intention or nature 2 : to uncover, find, or come to know by inquiry or scrutiny — usu. used with *out* ~ vi 1 : to look or inquire carefully (~ed for the papers) 2 : to make painstaking investigation or examination — **search·able** \'sər-chə-bəl\ adj — **search·er** n — **search·ing·ly** \-chiŋ-lē\ adv

²search n (15c) 1 a : an act of searching (a ~ for food) (go in ~ of help) b : an act of boarding and inspecting a ship on the high seas in exercise of right of search 2 *obs* : a party that searches 3 : power or range of penetrating; *also* : a penetrating effect

search·less \'sərch-ləs\ adj (1605) : INSCRUTABLE, IMPENETRABLE

search·light \-,līt\ n (1883) : an apparatus for projecting a powerful beam of light; *also* : a beam of light projected by it

search warrant n (1818) : a warrant authorizing a search (as of a house) for stolen goods or unlawful possessions

sea robin n (1814) : any of a family (Triglidae) of marine bony fishes typically having a spiny armored head and the bottom three rays of the pectoral fin on each side free of membrane and modified for use as feelers or in crawling — called also *gurnard*

sea room n (ca. 1554) : room for maneuver at sea

sea rover n (ca. 1580) : one that roves the sea; *specif* : PIRATE

sea–run \'sē-'rən\ adj (1885) : ANADROMOUS (a ~ salmon)

sea·scape \'sē-,skāp\ n (1799) 1 : a view of the sea 2 : a picture representing a scene at sea

sea scorpion n (1896) 1 : SCULPIN 1 2 : EURYPTERID

Sea Scout n (1911) : SEA EXPLORER

sea serpent n (1774) : a large marine animal resembling a serpent often reported to have been seen but never proved to exist

sea·shell \'sē-,shel\ n (bef. 12c) : the shell of a marine animal and esp. a mollusk

sea·shore \-,shȯr, -,shȯr\ n (1526) 1 a : land adjacent to the sea : SEACOAST b : NATIONAL SEASHORE 2 : all the ground between the ordinary high-water and low-water marks : FORESHORE

sea·sick \-,sik\ adj (ca. 1566) : affected with or suggestive of seasickness

sea·sick·ness \-nəs\ n (1625) : motion sickness experienced on the water

sea·side \'sē-,sīd\ n (13c) : the district or land bordering the sea : country adjacent to the sea : SEASHORE — **seaside** adj

sea slug n (1779) 1 : HOLOTHURIAN 2 : a naked marine gastropod; *specif* : NUDIBRANCH

sea snake n (1755) 1 : SEA SERPENT 2 : any of numerous venomous aquatic chiefly viviparous elapid snakes of warm seas

¹sea·son \'sē-zᵊn\ n [ME, fr. MF *saison*, fr. OF, fr. L *sation-, satio* action of sowing, fr. *serere* to sow — more at SOW] (14c) 1 a : a time characterized by a particular circumstance or feature (in a ~ of religious awakening —F. A. Christie) b : a suitable or natural time or occasion (when my ~ comes to sit on David's throne —John Milton) c : an indefinite period of time : WHILE (sent home again to her father for a ~ —Francis Hackett) 2 a : a period of the year characterized by or associated with a particular activity or phenomenon (hay fever ~): as (1) : a period associated with some phase or activity of agriculture (as growth or harvesting) (2) : a period in which an animal engages in some activity (as migrating or mating); *also* : ESTRUS, HEAT (3) : the period normally characterized by a particular kind of weather (a long rainy ~) (4) : a period marked by special activity esp. in some field (the theatrical ~) (tourist ~) (5) : a period in which a place is most frequented b : one of the four quarters into which the year is commonly divided c : the time of a major holiday 3 : YEAR (a boy of seven ~s) 4 [ME *sesoun*, fr. *sesounen* to season] : SEASONING 5 : the schedule of official games played or to be played by a sports team during a playing season (try to get through the ~ undefeated) 6 : OFF-SEASON (closed for the ~) — **in season** 1 : at the right time 2 : at the stage of greatest fitness (as for eating) (peaches are *in season*) 3 : legally available to be hunted or caught — **out of season** : not in season

²season vb **sea·soned; sea·son·ing** \'sēz-niŋ, 'sē-zᵊn-iŋ\ [ME *sesounen*, fr. MF *assaisoner* to ripen, season, fr. OF, fr. *a-* (fr. L *ad-*) + *saison* season] vt (14c) 1 a : to give (food) more flavor or zest by adding seasoning or savory ingredients b : to give a distinctive quality to as if by seasoning; *esp* : to make more agreeable (advice ~ed with wit) c *archaic* : to qualify by admixture : TEMPER 2 a : to treat (as wood or a skillet) so as to prepare for use b : to make fit by experience (a ~ed veteran) ~ vi : to become seasoned

sea·son·able \'sēz-nə-bəl, 'sē-zᵊn-ə-bəl\ adj (14c) 1 : suitable to the season or circumstances : TIMELY (a ~ frost) 2 : occurring in good or proper time : OPPORTUNE (a ~ time for discussion) — **sea·son·able·ness** n — **sea·son·ably** \-blē\ adv

sea·son·al \'sēz-nəl, 'sē-zᵊn-əl\ adj (1838) 1 : of, relating to, or varying in occurrence according to the season (~ storms) (~ fruits) 2 : affected or caused by seasonal need or availability (~ unemployment) (~ industries) — **sea·son·al·i·ty** \,sē-zᵊn-'a-lə-tē\ n — **sea·son·al·ly** \'sēz-nə-lē, 'sē-zᵊn-ə-lē\ adv

seasonal affective disorder n (1985) : depression that tends to recur as the days grow shorter during the fall and winter

sea·son·er \'sēz-nər, 'sē-zᵊn-ər\ n (1598) : one that seasons: as a : a user of seasonings (a heavy ~) b : SEASONING

sea·son·ing \'sēz-niŋ, 'sē-zᵊn-iŋ\ n (1580) : something that serves to season; *esp* : an ingredient (as a condiment, spice, or herb) added to food primarily for the savor that it imparts

---

\a\ abut \ᵊ\ kitten, F table \ər\ further \a\ ash \ā\ ace \ä\ mop, mar \aù\ out \ch\ chin \e\ bet \ē\ easy \g\ go \i\ hit \ī\ ice \j\ job \ŋ\ sing \ō\ go \ȯ\ law \ȯi\ boy \th\ thin \t͟h\ the \ü\ loot \ù\ foot \y\ yet \zh\ vision \ä, k̟, ⁿ, œ, œ̄, ue, ūe, ᵞ\ *see* Guide to Pronunciation

sea·son·less \'sē-z²n-ləs\ *adj* (1816)   **1** : exhibiting no seasonal changes   **2** : not restricted to a particular season; *esp* : suitable for wearing in any season ⟨~ fabrics⟩

season ticket *n* (1820) : a ticket (as to all of a club's home games or for specified daily transportation) valid during a specified time

sea spider *n* (1666) : any of various small long-legged marine arthropods (class Pycnogonida) that superficially resemble spiders

sea squirt *n* (1850) : ASCIDIAN

sea star *n* (1569) : STARFISH

sea stores *n pl* (1659) : supplies (as of foodstuffs) laid in before starting on a sea voyage

sea·strand \'sē-ˌstrand\ *n* (bef. 12c) : SEASHORE

¹seat \'sēt\ *n* [ME *sete*, fr. ON *sæti*; akin to OE *gesete* seat, *sittan* to sit] (13c)   **1 a** : a special chair of one in eminence; *also* : the status represented by it   **b** : a chair, stool, or bench intended to be sat in or on   **c** : the particular part of something on which one rests in sitting ⟨the ~ of a chair⟩ ⟨trouser ~⟩   **d** : BUTTOCKS   **2 a** : a seating accommodation ⟨a ~ for the game⟩ ⟨a 200-*seat* restaurant⟩   **b** : a right of sitting ⟨lost his ~ in Congress⟩   **c** : membership on an exchange   **3 a** : a place where something specified is prevalent : CENTER ⟨a ~ of learning⟩   **b** : a place from which authority is exercised ⟨the county ~⟩   **c** : a bodily part in which some function or condition is centered ⟨the brain as the ~ of the mind⟩   **4** : posture in or way of sitting on horseback   **5 a** : a part at or forming the base of something   **b** : a part (as a socket) or surface on or in which another part or surface rests — **by the seat of one's pants** : using experience and intuition rather than mechanical aids or formal theory

²seat *vt* (1593)   **1 a** : to install in a seat of dignity or office   **b** (1) : to cause to sit or assist in finding a seat   (2) : to provide seats for ⟨a theater ~*ing* 1000 persons⟩   **c** : to put in a sitting position   **2** : to repair the seat of or provide a new seat for   **3** : to fit to or with a seat ⟨~ a valve⟩ — *vi*   **1** *archaic* : to take one's seat or place   **2** : to fit correctly on a seat

seat belt *n* (1932) : an arrangement of straps designed to hold a person steady in a seat (as in an airplane or automobile)

seat·er \'sē-tər\ *n* (1693)   **1** : one that seats   **2** : one that has a specified number of seats — used in combination ⟨a two-*seater* jet⟩

seat·ing \'sē-tiŋ\ *n* (ca. 1859)   **1** : the act of providing with seats   **2 a** : material for covering or upholstering seats   **b** : a seat on or in which something rests ⟨a valve ~⟩

seat·mate \'sēt-ˌmāt\ *n* (1859) : one with whom one shares a seat (as in a vehicle with double or paired seats)

seat–of–the–pants *adj* (1942) : employing or based on personal experience, judgment, and effort rather than technological aids or formal theory ⟨~ navigation⟩ ⟨a ~ decision⟩

sea·train \'sē-ˌtrān\ *n* (1932) : a seagoing ship equipped for carrying a train of railroad cars

sea trout *n* (1745)   **1** : any of various trouts or chars that as adults inhabit the sea but ascend rivers to spawn   **2** : any of various marine fishes resembling trouts: as **a** : WEAKFISH 1   **b** : SPOTTED SEA TROUT

sea turtle *n* (1612) : any of two families (Cheloniidae and Dermochelyidae) of widely distributed marine turtles with the feet modified into paddles that include the green turtle, leatherback, hawksbill, loggerhead, and ridley

sea urchin *n* (1591) : any of numerous echinoderms (class Echinoidea) that are usu. enclosed in thin brittle globular tests covered with movable spines

sea·wall \'sē-ˌwȯl\ *n* (15c) : a wall or embankment to protect the shore from erosion or to act as a breakwater

¹sea·ward \'sē-wərd\ *n* (14c) : the direction or side away from land and toward the open sea

²seaward *also* **sea·wards** \-wərdz\ *adv* (1517) : toward the sea

³seaward *adj* (ca. 1621)   **1** : directed or situated toward the sea   **2** : coming from the sea ⟨a ~ wind⟩

sea wasp *n* (1910) : any of various scyphozoan jellyfishes (order or suborder Cubomedusae) that sting virulently and sometimes fatally

sea·wa·ter \'sē-ˌwȯ-tər, -ˌwä-\ *n* (bef. 12c) : water in or from the sea

sea·way \-ˌwā\ *n* (bef. 12c)   **1** : the sea as a route for travel; *also* : an ocean traffic lane   **2** : a moderate or rough sea   **3** : a deep inland waterway that admits oceangoing shipping

sea·weed \-ˌwēd\ *n* (1577)   **1** : a mass or growth of marine plants   **2** : a plant growing in the sea; *esp* : a marine alga (as a kelp)

sea whip *n* (1775) : any of various gorgonian corals with elongated flexible unbranched or little-branched skeletons

sea·wor·thy \'sē-ˌwər-thē\ *adj* (1807) : fit or safe for a sea voyage ⟨a ~ ship⟩ — **sea·wor·thi·ness** \-thē-nəs\ *n*

sea wrack *n* (1551) : SEAWEED; *esp* : seaweed cast ashore in masses

se·ba·ceous \si-'bā-shəs\ *adj* [L *sebaceus* made of tallow, fr. *sebum* tallow] (1728)   **1** : secreting sebum ⟨~ glands⟩   **2** : of, relating to, or being fatty material : FATTY ⟨a ~ exudate⟩

se·ba·cic acid \si-ˌbā-sik-, ˌsē-, -ˈbā-\ *n* [ISV, fr. L *sebaceus*] (1790) : a crystalline dicarboxylic acid $C_{10}H_{18}O_4$ used esp. in the manufacture of synthetic resins

seb·or·rhea \ˌseb-ə-'rē-ə\ *n* [NL, fr. L *sebum* + NL *-rrhea*] (ca. 1860) : abnormally increased secretion and discharge of sebum — **seb·or·rhe·ic** \-'rē-ik\ *adj*

se·bum \'sē-bəm\ *n* [NL, tallow, grease] (ca. 1860) : fatty lubricant matter secreted by sebaceous glands of the skin

sec \'sek\ *adj* [F, lit., dry — more at SACK] (1863) *of champagne* : moderately dry

se·cant \'sē-ˌkant, -kənt\ *n* [NL *secant-, secans*, fr. L, prp. of *secare* to cut — more at SAW] (1593)   **1** : a straight line cutting a curve at two or more points — see CIRCLE illustration   **2** : a straight line drawn from the center of a circle through one end of a circular arc to a tangent drawn from the other end of the arc   **3 a** : a trigonometric function that for an acute angle is the ratio of the hypotenuse of a right triangle of which the angle is considered part and the leg adjacent to the angle   **b** : a trigonometric function sec θ that is the reciprocal of the cosine for all real numbers θ for which the cosine is not zero and that is exactly equal to the secant of an angle of measure θ in radians

sec·a·teur \ˌse-kə-'tər, 'se-kə-ˌ\ *n* [F *sécateur*, fr. L *secare* to cut] (1881) *chiefly Brit* : pruning shears — usu. used in pl.

¹sec·co \'se-(ˌ)kō\ *n* [It, fr. L *siccus* — more at SACK] (1852) : the art of painting on dry plaster

²secco *adj or adv* [It, lit., dry] (ca. 1854)   **1** : short and very staccato — used as a direction in music   **2** *of a recitative* : accompanied only by the instruments playing the continuo

se·cede \si-'sēd\ *vi* **se·ced·ed; se·ced·ing** [L *secedere*, fr. *sed-, se-* apart (fr. *sed, se* without) + *cedere* to go — more at SUICIDE] (ca. 1755) : to withdraw from an organization (as a religious communion or political party or federation) — **se·ced·er** *n*

se·cern \si-'sərn\ *vt* [L *secernere* to separate — more at SECRET] (ca. 1656) : to discriminate in thought : DISTINGUISH

se·ces·sion \si-'se-shən\ *n* [L *secession-, secessio*, fr. *secedere*] (1604)   **1** : withdrawal into privacy or solitude : RETIREMENT   **2** : formal withdrawal from an organization

se·ces·sion·ist \-'se-sh(ə-)nist\ *n* (ca. 1860) : one who joins in a secession or maintains that secession is a right — **se·ces·sion·ism** \-shə-ˌni-zəm\ *n* — **secessionist** *adj*

se·clude \si-'klüd\ *vt* **se·clud·ed; se·clud·ing** [ME, to keep away, fr. L *secludere* to separate, seclude, fr. *se-* apart + *claudere* to close — more at SECEDE, CLOSE] (ca. 1533)   **1** *obs* : to exclude from a privilege, rank, or dignity : DEBAR   **2** : to remove or separate from intercourse or outside influence : ISOLATE   **3** : SHUT OFF, SCREEN

secluded *adj* (1604)   **1** : screened or hidden from view : SEQUESTERED ⟨a ~ valley⟩   **2** : living in seclusion : SOLITARY ⟨~ monks⟩ — **se·clud·ed·ly** *adv* — **se·clud·ed·ness** *n*

se·clu·sion \si-'klü-zhən\ *n* [ML *seclusion-, seclusio*, fr. L *secludere*] (ca. 1616)   **1** : the act of secluding : the condition of being secluded   **2** : a secluded or isolated place   *syn* see SOLITUDE — **se·clu·sive** \-'klü-siv, -ziv\ *adj* — **se·clu·sive·ly** *adv* — **se·clu·sive·ness** *n*

seco·bar·bi·tal \ˌse-kō-'bär-bə-ˌtȯl\ *n* [fr. *Seconal*, a trademark + *barbital*] (1951) : a barbiturate $C_{12}H_{18}N_2O_3$ that is used chiefly in the form of its bitter hygroscopic sodium salt as a hypnotic and sedative

Sec·o·nal \'se-kə-ˌnȯl, -ˌnal, -n²l\ *trademark* — used for a preparation of secobarbital

¹sec·ond \'se-kənd *also* -kənt, *esp before a consonant* -kən, -k²ŋ\ *adj* [ME, fr. OF, fr. L *secundus* second, following, favorable, fr. *sequi* to follow — more at SUE] (13c)   **1 a** : next to the first in place or time ⟨was ~ in line⟩   **b** (1) : next to the first in value, excellence, or degree ⟨his ~ choice of schools⟩   (2) : INFERIOR, SUBORDINATE ⟨was ~ to none⟩   **c** : ranking next below the top of a grade or degree in authority or precedence ⟨~ mate⟩   **d** : ALTERNATE, OTHER ⟨elects a mayor every ~ year⟩   **e** : resembling or suggesting a prototype : ANOTHER ⟨a ~ Thoreau⟩   **f** : ingrained by discipline, training, or effort : ACQUIRED ⟨~ nature⟩   **g** : being the forward gear or speed next higher than first in a motor vehicle   **2** : relating to or having a part typically subordinate to and lower in pitch than the first part in concerted or ensemble music — **second** *or* **sec·ond·ly** *adv*

²second *n* (14c)   **1 a** — see NUMBER table   **b** : one that is next after the first in rank, position, authority, or precedence ⟨the ~ in line⟩   **2** : one that assists or supports another; *esp* : the assistant of a duelist or boxer   **3 a** : the musical interval embracing two diatonic degrees   **b** : a tone at this interval; *specif* : SUPERTONIC   **c** : the harmonic combination of two tones a second apart   **4** *pl* : merchandise that is usu. slightly flawed and does not meet the manufacturer's standard for firsts or irregulars   **b** : an article of such merchandise   **5** : the act or declaration by which a parliamentary motion is seconded   **6** : a place next below the first in a competition, examination, or contest   **7** : SECOND BASE   **8** : the second forward gear or speed of a motor vehicle   **9** *pl* : a second helping of food

³second *n* [ME *secunde*, fr. ML *secunda*, fr. L, fem. of *secundus* second; fr. its being the second sexagesimal division of a unit, as minute is the first] (14c)   **1 a** : the 60th part of a minute of angular measure   **b** : the 60th part of a minute of time : 1/86,400 part of the mean solar day; *specif* : the base unit of time in the International System of Units that is equal to the duration of 9,192,631,770 periods of the radiation corresponding to the transition between the two hyperfine levels of the ground state of the cesium-133 atom   **2** : an instant of time : MOMENT

⁴second *vt* [L *secundare*, fr. *secundus* second, favorable] (ca. 1586)   **1 a** : to give support or encouragement to : ASSIST   **b** : to support (a fighting person or group) in combat : bring up reinforcements for   **2 a** : to support or assist in contention or debate   **b** : to endorse (a motion or a nomination) so that debate or voting may begin   **3** \si-'känd\ *chiefly Brit* : to release (as a military officer) from a regularly assigned position for temporary duty with another unit or organization — **sec·ond·er** *n*

¹sec·ond·ary \'se-kən-ˌder-ē\ *adj* (14c)   **1 a** : of second rank, importance, or value   **b** : of, relating to, or constituting the second strongest of the three or four degrees of stress recognized by most linguists ⟨the fourth syllable of *basketball team* carries ~ stress⟩   **c** *of a tense* : expressive of past time   **2 a** : immediately derived from something original, primary, or basic   **b** : of, relating to, or being the induced current or its circuit in an induction coil or transformer ⟨~ voltage⟩   **c** : characterized by or resulting from the substitution of two atoms or groups in a molecule ⟨a ~ salt⟩; *esp* : being, characterized by, or attached to a carbon atom having bonds to two other carbon atoms   **d** (1) : not first in order of occurrence or development   (2) : produced by activity of formative tissue and esp. cambium other than that at a growing point ⟨~ growth⟩ ⟨~ phloem⟩   **3 a** : of, relating to, or being the second order or stage in a series   **b** : of, relating to, or being the second segment of the wing of a bird or the quills of this segment   **c** : of or relating to a secondary school ⟨~ education⟩ — **sec·ond·ar·i·ly** \ˌse-kən-'der-ə-lē\ *adv* — **sec·ond·ar·i·ness** \'se-kən-ˌder-ē-nəs\ *n*

²secondary *n, pl* **-ar·ies** (15c)   **1** : one occupying a subordinate or auxiliary position rather than that of a principal   **2** : a defensive football backfield   **3** : the coil through which the secondary current passes in an induction coil or transformer — called also *secondary coil*   **4** : any of the quill feathers of the forearm of a bird — see WING illustration

secondary cell *n* (ca. 1909) : STORAGE BATTERY

secondary color *n* (1831) : a color formed by mixing primary colors in equal or equivalent quantities

secondary emission *n* (1931) : the emission of electrons from a surface that is bombarded by particles (as electrons or ions) from a primary source

secondary radiation *n* (1900) : radiation emitted by molecules or atoms after bombardment by a primary radiation

secondary road *n* (1903) **1 :** a road not of primary importance **2 :** a feeder road

secondary root *n* (1861) **:** one of the branches of a primary root

secondary school *n* (1835) **:** a school intermediate between elementary school and college and usu. offering general, technical, vocational, or college-preparatory courses

secondary sex characteristic *n* (1927) **:** a physical characteristic (as the breasts of a female mammal or the breeding plumage of a male bird) that appears in members of one sex at puberty or in seasonal breeders at the breeding season and is not directly concerned with reproduction — called also *secondary sexual characteristic*

secondary syphilis *n* (1885) **:** the second stage of syphilis that appears from 2 to 6 months after primary infection, that is marked by lesions esp. in the skin but also in organs and tissues, and that lasts from 3 to 12 weeks

second banana *n* (1953) **:** a comedian who plays a supporting role to a top banana; *broadly* **:** a person in a subservient position

second base *n* (1845) **1 :** the base that must be touched second by a base runner in baseball **2 :** the player position for defending the area on the first-base side of second base — **second baseman** *n*

sec·ond–best \ˌse-kən(d)-ˈbest, -kᵊn-\ *adj* (14c) **:** next to the best

¹second best *n* (1708) **:** one that is below or after the best

²second best *adv* (1777) **:** in second place

second blessing *n* (1891) **:** sanctification as a second gift of the Holy Spirit that follows an initial experience of conversion

second childhood *n* (1641) **:** DOTAGE

second–class *adj* (ca. 1838) **1 :** of or relating to a second class **2 :** MEDIOCRE; *also* **:** socially, politically, or economically deprived

second class *n* (1810) **1 :** the second and esp. next to highest group in a classification **2 :** CABIN CLASS **3 :** a class of U.S. or Canadian mail comprising periodicals sent to regular subscribers

Second Coming *n* (1644) **:** the coming of Christ as judge on the last day

second–degree burn *n* (1937) **:** a burn marked by pain, blistering, and superficial destruction of dermis with edema and hyperemia of the tissues beneath the burn

Second Empire *adj* (1873) **:** of, relating to, or characteristic of a style (as of furniture) developed in France under Napoleon III and marked by heavy ornate modification of Empire styles

second estate *n, often cap S&E* (ca. 1935) **:** the second of the traditional political classes; *specif* **:** NOBILITY

second fiddle *n* (1809) **:** one that plays a supporting or subservient role

second growth *n* (1829) **:** forest trees that come up naturally after removal of the first growth by cutting or by fire

sec·ond–guess \ˌse-kᵊn-ˈges, -kən(d)-\ *vt* (1941) **1 :** to criticize or question actions or decisions of (someone) often after the results of those actions or decisions are known ⟨meet almost every morning and, over coffee, ~ the local coach —Bruce Newman⟩; *also* **:** to engage in such criticism of (an action or decision) ⟨~ the general's strategy⟩ **2 :** to seek to anticipate or predict ⟨lived royally by his ability to ~ the stock market —*Time*⟩ — **sec·ond–guess·er** *n*

¹sec·ond–hand \ˈse-kən(d)-ˈhand\ *adj* (1654) **1 a :** received from or through an intermediary **:** BORROWED **b :** DERIVATIVE ⟨~ ideas⟩ **2 a :** acquired after being used by another **:** not new ⟨~ books⟩ **b :** dealing in secondhand merchandise ⟨a ~ bookstore⟩

²secondhand *adv* (1849) **:** at second hand **:** INDIRECTLY

¹second hand \ˌse-kən(d)-ˈhand\ *n* (1588) **:** an intermediate person or means **:** INTERMEDIARY — usu. used in the phrase *at second hand*

²second hand \ˈsek-ən(d)-ˌ\ *n* (1759) **:** the hand marking seconds on a timepiece

secondhand smoke *n* (1976) **:** tobacco smoke that is exhaled by smokers and inhaled by persons nearby

second lieutenant *n* (1702) **:** a commissioned officer of the lowest rank in the army, air force, or marine corps

second mortgage *n* (1912) **:** a mortgage the lien of which is subordinate to that of a first mortgage

se·con·do \si-ˈkōn-(ˌ)dō, -ˈkän-\ *n, pl* **-di** \-(ˌ)dē\ [It, fr. *secondo*, adj., second, fr. L *secundus*] (1792) **:** the second part in a concerted piece; *esp* **:** the lower part (as in a piano duet)

second person *n* (1672) **1 a :** a set of linguistic forms (as verb forms, pronouns, and inflectional affixes) referring to the person or thing addressed in the utterance in which they occur **b :** a linguistic form belonging to such a set **2 :** reference of a linguistic form to the person or thing addressed in the utterance in which it occurs

sec·ond–rate \ˌse-kən(d)-ˈrāt\ *adj* (1669) **:** of second or inferior quality or value **:** MEDIOCRE — **sec·ond–rate·ness** *n* — **sec·ond–rat·er** \-ˈrā-tər\ *n*

Second Reader *n* (1895) **:** a member of a Christian Science church or society chosen for a term of office to assist the First Reader in conducting services by reading aloud selections from the Bible

second reading *n* (1647) **1 :** the stage in the British legislative process following the first reading and usu. providing for debate on the principal features of a bill before its submission to a committee for consideration of details **2 :** the stage in the U.S. legislative process that occurs when a bill has been reported back from committee and that provides an opportunity for full debate and amendment before a vote is taken on the question of a third reading

second sight *n* (1616) **:** the capacity to see remote or future objects or events **:** CLAIRVOYANCE, PRECOGNITION

second–story man *n* (1886) **:** a burglar who enters a house by an upstairs window

sec·ond–string \ˌse-kən(d)-ˈstriŋ, ˌse-kᵊn-\ *adj* [fr. the reserve bowstring carried by an archer in case the first breaks] (1922) **:** being a substitute as distinguished from a regular (as on a ball team)

second thought *n* (1633) **:** reconsideration or a revised opinion of a previous often hurried decision ⟨began to have *second thoughts*⟩

second wind *n* (1824) **:** renewed energy or endurance

second world *n, often cap S&W* [after *third world*] (1973) **:** the Communist nations as a political and economic bloc

se·cre·cy \ˈsē-krə-sē\ *n, pl* **-cies** [alter. of earlier *secretie*, fr. ME *secretee*, fr. *secre* secret, fr. MF *secré*, fr. L *secretus*] (1575) **1 :** the condition of being hidden or concealed **2 :** the habit or practice of keeping secrets or maintaining privacy or concealment

¹se·cret \ˈsē-krət\ *adj* [ME, fr. MF, fr. L *secretus*, fr. pp. of *secernere* to separate, distinguish, fr. *se-* apart + *cernere* to sift — more at SECEDE, CERTAIN] (14c) **1 a :** kept from knowledge or view **:** HIDDEN **b :** marked by the habit of discretion **:** CLOSEMOUTHED **c :** working with hidden aims or methods **:** UNDERCOVER ⟨a ~ agent⟩ **d :** not acknowledged **:** UNAVOWED ⟨a ~ bride⟩ **e :** conducted in secret ⟨a ~ trial⟩ **2 :** remote from human frequentation or notice **:** SECLUDED **3 :** revealed only to the initiated **:** ESOTERIC **4 :** constructed so as to elude observation or detection ⟨a ~ panel⟩ **5 :** containing information whose unauthorized disclosure could endanger national security — compare CONFIDENTIAL, TOP SECRET — **se·cret·ly** *adv*

syn SECRET, COVERT, STEALTHY, FURTIVE, CLANDESTINE, SURREPTITIOUS, UNDERHANDED mean done without attracting observation. SECRET implies concealment on any grounds for any motive ⟨met at a *secret* location⟩. COVERT stresses the fact of not being open or declared ⟨*covert* intelligence operations⟩. STEALTHY suggests taking pains to avoid being seen or heard esp. in some misdoing ⟨the *stealthy* step of a burglar⟩. FURTIVE implies a sly or cautious stealthiness ⟨lovers exchanging *furtive* glances⟩. CLANDESTINE implies secrecy usu. for an evil, illicit, or unauthorized purpose and often emphasizes the fear of being discovered ⟨a *clandestine* meeting of conspirators⟩. SURREPTITIOUS applies to action or behavior done secretly often with skillful avoidance of detection and in violation of custom, law, or authority ⟨the *surreptitious* stockpiling of weapons⟩. UNDERHANDED stresses fraud or deception ⟨an *underhanded* trick⟩.

²secret *n* (14c) **1 a :** something kept hidden or unexplained **:** MYSTERY **b :** something kept from the knowledge of others or shared only confidentially with a few **c :** a method, formula, or process used in an art or a manufacturing operation and divulged only to those of one's own company or craft **d** *pl* **:** the practices or knowledge making up the shared discipline or culture of an esoteric society **2 :** a prayer traditionally said inaudibly by the celebrant just before the preface of the mass **3 :** something that serves as a specific or key to a desired end ⟨the ~ of longevity⟩ — **in secret :** in a private place or manner

se·cre·ta·gogue \si-ˈkrē-tə-ˌgäg\ *n* [*secretion* + *-agogue*] (1919) **:** a substance stimulating secretion (as by the stomach or pancreas)

sec·re·tar·i·at \ˌse-krə-ˈter-ē-ət, -ē-ˌat\ *n* [F *secrétariat*, fr. ML *secretariatus*, fr. *secretarius*] (1811) **1 :** the office of secretary **2 :** a secretarial corps; *specif* **:** the clerical staff of an organization **3 :** the administrative department of a governmental organization

sec·re·tary \ˈse-krə-ˌter-ē, *in rapid speech also* ˈsek-ˌter-, *esp Brit* ˈse-k(r)ə-ˌtrē\ *n, pl* **-tar·ies** [ME *secretarie*, fr. ML *secretarius*, confidential employee, secretary, fr. L *secretum* secret, fr. neut. of *secretus*] (15c) **1 :** one employed to handle correspondence and manage routine and detail work for a superior **2 a :** an officer of a business concern who may keep records of directors' and stockholders' meetings and of stock ownership and transfer and help supervise the company's legal interests **b :** an officer of an organization or society responsible for its records and correspondence **3 :** an officer of state who superintends a government administrative department **4 a :** WRITING DESK, ESCRITOIRE **b :** a writing desk with a top section for books — **sec·re·tar·i·al** \ˌse-krə-ˈter-ē-əl\ *adj* — **sec·re·tary·ship** \ˈse-krə-ˌter-ē-ˌship\ *n*

secretary 4b

secretary bird *n* [prob. fr. the resemblance of its crest to a bunch of quill pens stuck behind the ear] (1824) **:** a large long-legged African bird of prey (*Sagittarius serpentarius* of the family Sagittariidae) that feeds largely on reptiles

secretary–general *n, pl* **secretaries–general** (1701) **:** a principal administrative officer

secret ballot *n* (1917) **:** AUSTRALIAN BALLOT

¹se·crete \si-ˈkrēt\ *vt* **se·cret·ed; se·cret·ing** [back-formation fr. *secretion*] (1707) **:** to form and give off (a secretion)

²se·crete \si-ˈkrēt, ˈsē-ˌkrət\ *vt* **se·cret·ed; se·cret·ing** [alter. of obs. *secret*, fr. ¹*secret*] (1741) **1 :** to deposit or conceal in a hiding place **2 :** to appropriate secretly **:** ABSTRACT *syn* see HIDE

se·cre·tin \si-ˈkrē-tᵊn\ *n* [*secretion* + ¹*-in*] (1902) **:** an intestinal proteinaceous hormone capable of stimulating secretion by the pancreas and liver

se·cre·tion \si-ˈkrē-shən\ *n* [F *sécrétion*, fr. L *secretion-, secretio* separation, fr. *secernere* to separate — more at SECRET] (1646) **1 a :** the process of segregating, elaborating, and releasing some material either functionally specialized (as saliva) or isolated for excretion (as urine) **b :** a product of secretion formed by an animal or plant; *esp* **:** one performing a specific useful function in the organism **2** [²*secrete*] **:** the act of hiding something **:** CONCEALMENT — **se·cre·tion·ary** \-shə-ˌner-ē\ *adj*

se·cre·tive \ˈsē-krə-tiv, si-ˈkrē-\ *adj* [back-formation fr. *secretiveness*, part trans. of F *secrétivité*] (1853) **:** disposed to secrecy **:** not open or outgoing in speech, activity, or purposes *syn* see SILENT — **se·cre·tive·ly** *adv* — **se·cre·tive·ness** *n*

se·cre·tor \si-ˈkrē-tər\ *n* (1941) **:** an individual of blood group A, B, or AB who secretes the antigens characteristic of these blood groups in bodily fluids (as saliva)

se·cre·to·ry \ˈsē-krə-ˌtōr-ē, *esp Brit* si-ˈkrē-t(ə-)rē\ *adj* (1692) **:** of, relating to, or promoting secretion; *also* **:** produced by secretion

secret partner *n* (ca. 1909) **:** a partner whose membership in a partnership is kept secret from the public

secret police *n* (1823) **:** a police organization operating for the most part in secrecy and esp. for the political purposes of its government often with terroristic methods

secret service *n* (1737) **1 :** a governmental service of a secret nature

\ə\ abut \ᵊ\ kitten, F table \ər\ further \a\ ash \ā\ ace \ä\ mop, mar \aù\ out \ch\ chin \e\ bet \ē\ easy \g\ go \i\ hit \ī\ ice \j\ job \ŋ\ sing \ō\ go \ò\ law \òi\ boy \th\ thin \th̲\ the \ü\ loot \ù\ foot \y\ yet \zh\ vision \ä, k̲, ⁿ, œ, œ̄, ᵫ, ᵫ̄, ᵕ\ *see* Guide to Pronunciation

2 *cap both Ss* : a division of the U.S. Treasury Department charged chiefly with the suppression of counterfeiting and the protection of the president

secret society *n* (1829) : any of various oath-bound societies often devoted to brotherhood, moral discipline, and mutual assistance

sect \'sekt\ *n* [ME *secte*, fr. MF & LL & L; MF, group, sect, fr. LL *secta* organized ecclesiastical body, fr. L, course of action, way of life, prob. fr. *sectari* to pursue, freq. of *sequi* to follow — more at SUE] (14c) **1 a** : a dissenting or schismatic religious body; *esp* : one regarded as extreme or heretical **b** : a religious denomination **2** *archaic* : SEX 1 ⟨so is all her ~ —Shak.⟩ **3 a** : a group adhering to a distinctive doctrine or to a leader **b** : PARTY **c** : FACTION

¹sec·tar·i·an \sek-'ter-ē-ən\ *adj* (1649) **1** : of, relating to, or characteristic of a sect or sectarian **2** : limited in character or scope : PAROCHIAL — **sec·tar·i·an·ism** \-ē-ə-ˌni-zəm\ *n*

²sectarian *n* (1819) **1** : an adherent of a sect **2** : a narrow or bigoted person

sec·tar·i·an·ize \sek-'ter-ē-ə-ˌnīz\ *vb* -**ized**; -**iz·ing** *vi* (1842) : to act as sectarians ~ *vt* : to make sectarian

sec·ta·ry \'sek-tə-rē\ *n, pl* -**ries** (1556) : a member of a sect

sec·tile \'sek-t³l, -ˌtīl\ *adj* [L *sectilis*, fr. *sectus*, pp. of *secare*] (1805) : capable of being severed by a knife with a smooth cut — **sec·til·i·ty** \sek-'ti-lə-tē\ *n*

¹sec·tion \'sek-shən\ *n* [L *section-, sectio*, fr. *secare* to cut — more at SAW] (1559) **1 a** : the action or an instance of cutting or separating by cutting **b** : a part set off by or as if by cutting **2** : a distinct part or portion of something written (as a chapter, law, or newspaper) **3 a** : the profile of something as it would appear if cut through by an intersecting plane **b** : the plane figure resulting from the cutting of a solid by a plane **4** : a natural subdivision of a taxonomic group **5** : a character § used as a mark for the beginning of a section and as a reference mark **6** : a piece of land one square mile in area forming one of the 36 subdivisions of a township **7** : a distinct part of a territorial or political area, community, or group of people **8 a** : a part that may be, is, or is viewed as separated ⟨chop the stalks into ~s⟩ ⟨the northern ~ of the route⟩ **b** : one segment of a fruit : CARPEL **9** : a basic military unit usu. having a special function **10** : a very thin slice (as of tissue) suitable for microscopic examination **11 a** : one of the classes formed by dividing the students taking a course **b** : one of the discussion groups into which a conference or organization is divided **12 a** : a part of a permanent railroad way under the care of a particular crew **b** : one of two or more vehicles or trains which run on the same schedule **13** : one of several component parts that may be assembled or reassembled ⟨a bookcase in ~s⟩ **14** : a division of an orchestra composed of one class of instruments **15** : SIGNATURE 3b *syn* see PART

²section *vb* **sec·tioned**; **sec·tion·ing** \-sh(ə-)niŋ\ *vt* (1819) **1** : to cut or separate into sections **2** : to represent in sections ~ *vi* : to become cut or separated into parts

¹sec·tion·al \'sek-shnəl, -shə-n³l\ *adj* (1806) **1** : of or relating to a section **b** : local or regional rather than general in character ⟨~ interests⟩ **2** : consisting of or divided into sections ⟨~ furniture⟩ — **sec·tion·al·ly** *adv*

²sectional *n* (1901) : a piece of furniture made up of modular units capable of use separately or in various combinations

sec·tion·al·ism \'sek-shnə-ˌli-zəm, -shə-n³l-ˌi-\ *n* (1855) : an exaggerated devotion to the interests of a region

Section Eight *n* [*Section VIII*, Army Regulation 615-360, in effect from December 1922 to July 1944] (1943) : a discharge from the U.S. Army for military inaptitude or undesirable habits or traits of character; *also* : a soldier receiving such a discharge

section gang *n* (1890) : a crew of track workers employed to maintain a railroad section

section hand *n* (1873) : a laborer belonging to a section gang

¹sec·tor \'sek-tər, -ˌtòr\ *n* [LL, fr. L, cutter, fr. *secare* to cut — more at SAW] (1570) **1 a** : a geometric figure bounded by two radii and the included arc of a circle **b** (1) : a subdivision of a defensive military position (2) : a portion of a military front or area of operation **c** : an area or portion resembling a sector ⟨bilingual ~ of town —David Kleinberg⟩ **d** : a sociological, economic, or political subdivision of society ⟨greater cooperation between the public and private ~s —Peter Chapman⟩ **2** : a mathematical instrument consisting of two rulers connected at one end by a joint and marked with several scales **3** : a subdivision of a track on a computer disk

²sector \-tər\ *vt* **sec·tored**; **sec·tor·ing** \-t(ə-)riŋ\ (1884) : to divide into or furnish with sectors

sec·to·ri·al \sek-'tòr-ē-əl, -'tòr-\ *adj* (1803) **1** : of, relating to, or having the shape of a sector of a circle **2** *of a chimera* : having a sector of variant growth interposed in an otherwise normal body of tissue

¹sec·u·lar \'se-kyə-lər\ *adj* [ME, fr. OF *seculer*, fr. LL *saecularis*, fr. *saeculum* the present world, fr. L, generation, age, century, world; akin to W *hoedl* lifetime] (14c) **1 a** : of or relating to the worldly or temporal ⟨~ concerns⟩ **b** : not overtly or specif. religious ⟨~ music⟩ **c** : not ecclesiastical or clerical ⟨~ courts⟩ ⟨~ landowners⟩ **2 a** : not bound by monastic vows or rules; *specif* : of, relating to, or forming clergy not belonging to a religious order or congregation ⟨a ~ priest⟩ **3 a** : occurring once in an age or a century **b** : existing or continuing through ages or centuries **c** : of or relating to a long term of indefinite duration — **sec·u·lar·i·ty** \ˌse-kyə-'lar-ə-tē\ *n* — **sec·u·lar·ly** \'se-kyə-lər-lē\ *adv*

²secular *n, pl* **seculars** *or* **secular** (14c) **1** : a secular ecclesiastic (as a diocesan priest) **2** : LAYMAN

secular humanism *n* (1933) : HUMANISM 3; *esp* : humanistic philosophy viewed as a nontheistic religion antagonistic to traditional religion — **secular humanist** *n or adj*

sec·u·lar·ise *Brit var of* SECULARIZE

sec·u·lar·ism \'se-kyə-lə-ˌri-zəm\ *n* (1851) : indifference to or rejection or exclusion of religion and religious considerations — **sec·u·lar·ist** \-rist\ *n* — **secularist** *or* **sec·u·lar·is·tic** \ˌse-kyə-lə-'ris-tik\ *adj*

sec·u·lar·ize \'se-kyə-lə-ˌrīz\ *vt* -**ized**; -**iz·ing** (1611) **1** : to make secular **2** : to transfer from ecclesiastical to civil or lay use, possession, or control **3** : to convert to or imbue with secularism — **sec·u·lar·i·za·tion** \ˌse-kyə-lə-rə-'zā-shən\ *n* — **sec·u·lar·iz·er** *n*

se·cund \si-'kənd, 'sē-ˌ\ *adj* [L *secundus* following — more at SECOND] (ca. 1777) : having some part or element arranged on one side only

¹se·cure \si-'kyùr\ *adj* **se·cur·er; -est** [L *securus* safe, secure, fr. *se* without + *cura* care — more at SUICIDE] (ca. 1533) **1 a** *archaic* : unwisely free from fear or distrust : OVERCONFIDENT **b** : easy in mind : CONFIDENT **c** : assured in opinion or expectation : having no doubt **2 a** : free from danger **b** : free from risk of loss **c** : affording safety ⟨a ~ hideaway⟩ **d** : TRUSTWORTHY, DEPENDABLE ⟨~ foundation⟩ **3** : ASSURED 1 ⟨~ victory⟩ — **se·cure·ly** *adv* — **se·cure·ness** *n*

²secure *vb* **se·cured; se·cur·ing** *vt* (1593) **1 a** : to relieve from exposure to danger : act to make safe against adverse contingencies ⟨~ a supply line from enemy raids⟩ **b** : to put beyond hazard of losing or of not receiving : GUARANTEE ⟨~ the blessings of liberty —U.S. Constitution⟩ **c** : to give pledge of payment to (a creditor) or of (an obligation) ⟨~ a note by a pledge of collateral⟩ **2 a** : to take (a person) into custody : hold fast : PINION **b** : to make fast : SEAL ⟨~ a door⟩ **3 a** : to get secure usu. lasting possession or control of ⟨~ a job⟩ **b** : BRING ABOUT, EFFECT **4** : to release (naval personnel) from work or duty ~ *vi* **1** *of naval personnel* : to stop work : go off duty **2** *of a ship* : to tie up : BERTH *syn* see ENSURE — **se·cur·er** *n*

se·cure·ment \si-'kyùr-mənt\ *n* (1622) **1** *obs* : PROTECTION **2** : the act or process of securing

se·cu·ri·tize \si-'kyùr-ə-ˌtīz\ *vt* -**tized**; -**tiz·ing** (1981) : to consolidate (as mortgage loans) and sell to other investors for resale to the public in the form of securities — **se·cu·ri·ti·za·tion** \-ˌkyùr-ə-tə-'zā-shən\ *n*

se·cu·ri·ty \si-'kyùr-ə-tē\ *n, pl* -**ties** (15c) **1** : the quality or state of being secure: as **a** : freedom from danger : SAFETY **b** : freedom from fear or anxiety **c** : freedom from the prospect of being laid off ⟨job ~⟩ **2 a** : something given, deposited, or pledged to make certain the fulfillment of an obligation **b** : SURETY **3** : an evidence of debt or of ownership (as a stock certificate or bond) **4 a** : something that secures : PROTECTION **b** (1) : measures taken to guard against espionage or sabotage, crime, attack, or escape (2) : an organization or department whose task is security

security blanket *n* (1968) **1** : a blanket carried by a child as a protection against anxiety **2** : a usu. familiar object whose presence dispels anxiety

Security Council *n* (1944) : a permanent council of the United Nations with primary responsibility for maintaining peace and security

security interest *n* (1951) : the rights that a creditor has in the personal property of a debtor that secures an obligation : LIEN

security police *n* (1920) **1** : police engaged in counterespionage **2** : AIR POLICE

se·dan \si-'dan\ *n* [origin unknown] (1635) **1** : a portable often covered chair that is designed to carry one person and that is borne on poles by two men **2 a** : a 2- or 4-door automobile seating 4 or more persons and usu. having a permanent top — compare COUPE **b** : a motorboat having one passenger compartment

sedan 1

¹se·date \si-'dāt\ *adj* [L *sedatus*, fr. pp. of *sedare* to calm; akin to *sedēre* to sit — more at SIT] (1663) : keeping a quiet steady attitude or pace : UNRUFFLED *syn* see SERIOUS — **se·date·ly** *adv* — **se·date·ness** *n*

²sedate *vt* **se·dat·ed; se·dat·ing** [back-formation fr. *sedative*] (1945) : to dose with sedatives

se·da·tion \si-'dā-shən\ *n* (1543) **1** : the inducing of a relaxed easy state esp. by the use of sedatives **2** : a state resulting from an as if from sedation

¹sed·a·tive \'se-də-tiv\ *adj* [ME, alleviating pain, fr. MF *sedatif*, fr. ML *sedativus*, fr. L *sedatus*] (1795) : tending to calm, moderate, or tranquilize nervousness or excitement

²sedative *n* (1797) : a sedative agent or drug

sed·en·tary \'se-d³n-ˌter-ē\ *adj* [MF *sedentaire*, fr. L *sedentarius*, fr. *sedent-, sedens*, prp. of *sedēre* to sit — more at SIT] (1598) **1** : not migratory : SETTLED ⟨~ birds⟩ **2** : doing or requiring much sitting ⟨~ permanently attached ⟨~ barnacles⟩

se·der \'sā-dər\ *n, often cap* [Heb *sēdher* order] (1865) : a Jewish home or community service including a ceremonial dinner held on the first or first and second evenings of the Passover in commemoration of the exodus from Egypt

se·de·runt \sə-'dir-ənt, -'der-\ *n* [L, there (they) sat (fr. *sedēre* to sit), word used to introduce list of those attending a session — more at SIT] (1825) : a prolonged sitting (as for discussion)

sedge \'sej\ *n* [ME *segge*, fr. OE *secg*; akin to MHG *segge* sedge, OE *sagu* saw — more at SAW] (bef. 12c) : any of a family (Cyperaceae, the sedge family) of usu. tufted marsh plants differing from the related grasses in having achenes and solid stems; *esp* : any of a cosmopolitan genus (*Carex*) — **sedgy** \'se-jē\ *adj*

se·di·lia \sə-'dēl-yə, -'dil-, *esp Brit* -'dīl-\ *n pl* [L, pl. of *sedile* seat, fr. *sedēre*] (1793) : seats on the south side of the chancel for the celebrant, deacon, and subdeacon

¹sed·i·ment \'se-də-mənt\ *n* [MF, fr. L *sedimentum* settling, fr. *sedēre* to sit, sink down] (1547) **1** : the matter that settles to the bottom of a liquid **2** : material deposited by water, wind, or glaciers

²sed·i·ment \-ˌment\ *vt* (1859) **1** : to deposit as sediment ~ *vi* **1** : to settle to the bottom in a liquid **2** : to deposit sediment

sed·i·ment·able \ˌse-də-'men-tə-bəl\ *adj* (1943) : capable of being sedimented by centrifugation ⟨~ ribosomal particles⟩

sed·i·men·ta·ry \ˌse-də-'men-tə-rē, -'men-trē\ *adj* (1830) **1** : of, relating to, or containing sediment ⟨~ deposits⟩ **2** : formed by or from deposits of sediment ⟨~ rock⟩

sed·i·men·ta·tion \ˌse-də-mən-'tā-shən, -ˌmen-\ *n* (1874) : the action or process of forming or depositing sediment : SETTLING

sed·i·men·tol·o·gy \ˌse-də-mən-'tä-lə-jē, -ˌmen-\ *n* (1932) : a branch of science that deals with sedimentary rocks and their inclusions — **sed·i·men·to·log·ic** \-ˌmen-t³l-'ä-jik\ *or* **sed·i·men·to·log·i·cal** \-ji-kəl\ *adj* — **sed·i·men·to·log·i·cal·ly** \-ji-k(ə-)lē\ *adv* — **sed·i·men·tol·o·gist** \-mən-'tä-lə-jist, -ˌmen-\ *n*

se·di·tion \si-'di-shən\ *n* [ME, fr. MF, fr. L *sedition-, seditio*, lit., separation, fr. *se-* apart + *ition-, itio* act of going, fr. *ire* to go — more at

SECEDE, ISSUE] (14c) : incitement of resistance to or insurrection against lawful authority

se·di·tious \si-'di-shəs\ *adj* (15c) **1** : disposed to arouse or take part in or guilty of sedition **2** : of, relating to, or tending toward sedition — **se·di·tious·ly** *adv* — **se·di·tious·ness** *n*

se·duce \si-'düs, -'dyüs\ *vt* **se·duced; se·duc·ing** [ME, fr. LL *seducere*, fr. L, to lead away, fr. *se-* apart + *ducere* to lead — more at TOW] (15c) **1** : to persuade to disobedience or disloyalty **2** : to lead astray usu. by persuasion or false promises **3** : to carry out the physical seduction of : entice to sexual intercourse **4** : ATTRACT *syn* see LURE — **se·duc·er** *n*

se·duce·ment \-mənt\ *n* (1586) **1** : SEDUCTION **2** : something that serves to seduce

se·duc·tion \si-'dək-shən\ *n* [MF, fr. LL *seduction-, seductio*, fr. L, act of leading aside, fr. *seducere*] (1526) **1** : the act of seducing to wrong; *esp* : the often unlawful enticement of a female to sexual intercourse **2** : something that seduces : TEMPTATION **3** : something that attracts or charms

se·duc·tive \-'dək-tiv\ *adj* (1771) : tending to seduce : having alluring or tempting qualities 〈a ~, sometimes disingenuous man —Thatcher Freund〉 〈a ~ spring morning〉 — **se·duc·tive·ly** *adv* — **se·duc·tive·ness** *n*

se·duc·tress \-'dək-trəs\ *n* [obs. *seductor* male seducer, fr. LL, fr. *seducere* to seduce] (1803) : a woman who seduces

se·du·li·ty \si-'dü-lə-tē, -'dyü-\ *n* (1542) : sedulous activity : DILIGENCE

sed·u·lous \'se-jə-ləs\ *adj* [L *sedulus*, fr. *sedulo* sincerely, diligently, fr. *se* without + *dolus* guile — more at SUICIDE] (1540) **1** : involving or accomplished with careful perseverance 〈a ~ craftsmanship〉 **2** : diligent in application or pursuit 〈a ~ student〉 *syn* see BUSY — **sed·u·lous·ly** *adv* — **sed·u·lous·ness** *n*

se·dum \'sē-dəm\ *n* [NL, fr. L, houseleek] (1760) : any of a genus (*Sedum*) of fleshy widely distributed herbs of the orpine family — compare STONECROP

¹see \'sē\ *vb* **saw** \'só\; **seen** \'sēn\; **see·ing** \'sē-iŋ\ [ME *seen*, fr. OE *sēon*; akin to OHG *sehan* to see and perh. to L *sequi* to follow — more at SUE] *vt* (bef. 12c) **1 a** : to perceive by the eye : to perceive or detect as if by sight **2 a** : to have experience of : UNDERGO 〈~ army service〉 **b** : to come to know : DISCOVER **c** : to be the setting or time of 〈the last fifty years have *seen* a sweeping revolution in science —Barry Commoner〉 **3 a** : to form a mental picture of : VISUALIZE 〈can still ~ her as she was years ago〉 **b** : to perceive the meaning or importance of : UNDERSTAND **c** : to be aware of : RECOGNIZE 〈~'s only our faults〉 **d** : to imagine as a possibility : SUPPOSE 〈couldn't ~ him as a crook〉 **4 a** : EXAMINE, WATCH 〈want to ~ how she handles the problem〉 **b** (1) : READ (2) : to read of **c** : to attend as a spectator 〈~ a play〉 **5 a** : to take care of : provide for 〈had enough money to ~ us through〉 **b** : to make sure 〈~ that order is kept〉 **6 a** : to regard as : JUDGE **b** : to prefer to have 〈I'll ~ him hanged first〉 〈I'll ~ you dead before I accept your terms〉 **c** : to find acceptable or attractive 〈can't understand what he ~s in her〉 **7 a** : to call on : VISIT **b** (1) : to keep company with esp. in courtship or dating 〈had been ~ing each other for a year〉 (2) : to grant an interview to : RECEIVE 〈the president will ~ you now〉 **8** : ACCOMPANY, ESCORT 〈~ the guests to the door〉 **9** : to meet (a bet) in poker or to equal the bet of (a player) : CALL ~ *vi* **1 a** : to give or pay attention **b** : to look about **2 a** : to have the power of sight **b** : to apprehend objects by sight : to perceive objects as if by sight **3** : to grasp something mentally **4** : to make investigation or inquiry — **see·able** \-ə-bəl\ *adj* — **see after** : to attend to : care for — **see eye to eye** : to have a common viewpoint : AGREE — **see things** : HALLUCINATE — **see through** : to grasp the true nature of 〈*saw through* the scheme〉 — **see to** : to attend to : care for

²see *n* [ME *se*, fr. OF, fr. L *sedes* seat; akin to L *sedēre* to sit — more at SIT] (14c) **1** *archaic* : CATHEDRA **b** : a cathedral town **c** : a seat of a bishop's office, power, or authority **2** : the authority or jurisdiction of a bishop

¹seed \'sēd\ *n, pl* **seed** *or* **seeds** [ME, fr. OE *sǣd*; akin to OHG *sāt* seed, OE *sāwan* to sow — more at SOW] (bef. 12c) **1 a** (1) : the grains or ripened ovules of plants used for sowing (2) : the fertilized ripened ovule of a flowering plant containing an embryo and capable normally of germination to produce a new plant; *broadly* : a propagative plant structure (as a spore or small dry fruit) **b** : a propagative animal structure: (1) : MILT, SEMEN (2) : a small egg (as of an insect) (3) : a developmental form of a lower animal suitable for transplanting; *specif* : SPAT **c** : the condition or stage of bearing seed 〈in ~〉 **2** : PROGENY **3** : a source of development or growth : GERM 〈sowed the ~s of discord〉 **4** : something (as a tiny particle or a bubble in glass) that resembles a seed in shape or size **5** : a competitor who has been seeded in a tournament — **seed** *adj* — **seed·ed** \'sē-dəd\ *adj* — **seed·less** \'sēd-ləs\ *adj* — **seed·like** \-,līk\ *adj* — **go to seed** *or* **run to seed** **1** : to develop seed **2** : DECAY

²seed *vi* (14c) **1** : to bear or shed seed **2** : to sow seed : PLANT ~ *vt* **1 a** : to plant seeds in : SOW 〈~ land to grass〉 **b** : to furnish with something that causes or stimulates growth or development **c** : INOCULATE **d** : to supply with nuclei (as of crystallization or condensation); *esp* : to treat (a cloud) with solid particles to convert water droplets into ice crystals in an attempt to produce precipitation **e** : to cover or permeate by or as if by scattering something 〈~ed [the] sea-lanes with thousands of magnetic mines —Otto Friedrich〉 **2** : PLANT 1a **3** : to extract the seeds from (as raisins) **4 a** : to schedule (tournament players or teams) so that superior ones will not meet in early rounds **b** : to rank (a contestant) relative to others in a tournament on the basis of previous record 〈the top-*seeded* tennis star〉

seed·bed \'sēd-,bed\ *n* (1660) **1** : soil or a bed of soil prepared for planting seed **2** : a place or source of growth or development

seed·cake \-,kāk\ *n* (1573) **1** : a cake or cookie containing aromatic seeds (as sesame or caraway) **2** : OIL CAKE

seed coat *n* (1796) : an outer protective covering of a seed

seed·eat·er \'sēd-,ē-tər\ *n* (ca. 1879) : a bird (as a finch) whose diet consists basically of seeds

seed·er \'sē-dər\ *n* (1868) **1** : an implement for planting or sowing seeds **2** : a device for seeding fruit **3** : one that seeds clouds

seed fern *n* (1927) : any of an order (Pteridospermales) of extinct cycadophytes with foliage like that of ferns and with naked seeds

seed leaf *n* (ca. 1693) : COTYLEDON 2

seed·ling \'sēd-liŋ\ *n* (1660) **1** : a young plant grown from seed **2 a** : a young tree before it becomes a sapling **b** : a nursery plant not yet transplanted — **seedling** *adj*

seed money *n* (1943) : money used for setting up a new enterprise

seed oyster *n* (1885) : a young oyster esp. of a size for transplantation

seed pearl *n* (1553) **1** : a very small and often irregular pearl **2** : minute pearls imbedded in some binding material

seed plant *n* (1707) : a plant that bears seeds; *specif* : SPERMATOPHYTE

seed·pod \'sēd-,päd\ *n* (1718) : ²POD 1

seeds·man \'sēdz-mən\ *n* (1601) **1** : one who sows seeds **2** : a dealer in seeds

seed stock *n* (1926) : a supply (as of seed) for planting; *broadly* : a source of new individuals 〈a *seed stock* of trout in the streams〉

seed tick *n* (1705) : the 6-legged larva of a tick

seed·time \'sēd-,tīm\ *n* (bef. 12c) **1** : the season of sowing **2** : a period of original development

seedy \'sē-dē\ *adj* **seed·i·er; -est** (1574) **1** : containing or full of seeds 〈a ~ fruit〉 **2** : inferior in condition or quality: as **a** : SHABBY, RUN-DOWN 〈~ clothes〉 **b** : somewhat disreputable : SQUALID 〈a ~ district〉 〈~ entertainment〉 **c** : slightly unwell : DEBILITATED 〈felt ~ and went home early〉 — **seed·i·ly** \'sē-d'l-ē\ *adv* — **seed·i·ness** \'sē-dē-nəs\ *n*

¹see·ing \'sē-iŋ\ *conj* (1503) : INASMUCH AS — often used with *as* or *that*

²seeing *n* (1903) : the quality of the images of celestial bodies observed telescopically

Seeing Eye *trademark* — used for a guide dog trained to lead the blind

seek \'sēk\ *vb* **sought** \'sót\; **seek·ing** [ME *seken*, fr. OE *sēcan*; akin to OHG *suohhen* to seek, L *sagus* prophetic, Gk *hēgeisthai* to lead] *vt* (bef. 12c) **1** : to resort to : go to **2 a** : to go in search of : look for **b** : to try to discover **3** : to ask for : REQUEST 〈~s advice〉 **4** : to try to acquire or gain : aim at 〈~ fame〉 **5** : to make an attempt : TRY — used with *to* and an infinitive 〈governments . . . ~ to keep the bulk of their people contented —D. M. Potter〉 ~ *vi* **1** : to make a search or inquiry **2 a** : to be sought **b** : to be lacking 〈in critical judgment . . . they were sadly to ~ —*Times Lit. Supp.*〉 — **seek·er** *n*

seel \'sēl\ *vt* [ME *selen*, alter. of *silen*, fr. MF *siller*, fr. ML *ciliare*, fr. L *cilium* eyelid] (15c) **1** : to close the eyes of (as a hawk) by drawing threads through the eyelids **2** *archaic* : to close up (one's eyes)

see·ly \'sē-lē\ *adj* [ME *sely* — more at SILLY] (14c) *archaic* : pitiable esp. because of weak physical or mental condition : FRAIL

seem \'sēm\ *vi* [ME *semen*, of Scand origin; akin to ON *sœma* to honor, *sœmr* fitting, *samr* same — more at SAME] (13c) **1** : to appear to the observation or understanding **2** : to give the impression of being

¹seem·ing *n* (15c) : external appearance as distinguished from true character : LOOK

²seeming *adj* (ca. 1557) : having an often deceptive or delusive appearance on superficial examination 〈their wealth gave them a ~ security〉 *syn* see APPARENT — **seem·ing·ly** \'sē-miŋ-lē\ *adv*

seem·ly \'sēm-lē\ *adj* **seem·li·er; -est** [ME *semely*, fr. ON *sœmiligr*, fr. *sœmr* fitting] (13c) **1 a** : GOOD-LOOKING, HANDSOME **b** : agreeably fashioned : ATTRACTIVE **2** : conventionally proper : DECOROUS **3** : suited to the occasion, purpose, or person : FIT — **seem·li·ness** *n* — **seemly** *adv*

seen *past part of* SEE

¹seep \'sēp\ *vi* [alter. of earlier *sipe*, fr. ME *sipen*, fr. OE *sipian*; akin to MLG *sipen* to seep] (1790) **1** : to flow or pass slowly through fine pores or small openings : OOZE 〈water ~ed in through a crack〉 **2 a** : to enter or penetrate slowly 〈fear of nuclear war had ~ed into the national consciousness —Tip O'Neill〉 **b** : to become diffused or spread 〈a sadness ~ed through his being —Agnes S. Turnbull〉

²seep *n* (ca. 1825) **1 a** : a spot where a fluid (as water, oil, or gas) contained in the ground oozes slowly to the surface and often forms a pool **b** : a small spring **2** : SEEPAGE — **seepy** \'sē-pē\ *adj*

seep·age \'sē-pij\ *n* (ca. 1825) **1** : the process of seeping : OOZING **2** : a quantity of fluid that has seeped (as through porous material)

¹seer \'sir, 'sē-ər\ *n* (14c) **1** : one that sees **2 a** : one that predicts events or developments **b** : a person credited with extraordinary moral and spiritual insight **3** : one that practices divination esp. by concentrating on a glass or crystal globe

²seer *n, pl* **seers** *or* **seer** [Hindi *ser*] (1618) : an Indian unit of weight equal to 2.057 pounds (0.9330 kilograms)

seer·ess \'sir-əs, 'sē-ər-əs\ *n* (1845) : a woman who predicts events or developments : PROPHETESS

seer·suck·er \'sir-,sə-kər\ *n* [Hindi *śīrsaker*, fr. Per *shīr-o-shakar*, lit., milk and sugar] (1722) : a light fabric of linen, cotton, or rayon usu. striped and slightly puckered

¹see·saw \'sē-,só\ *n* [prob. fr. redupl. of ³*saw*] (1704) **1** : an alternating up-and-down or backward-and-forward motion or movement; *also* : a contest or struggle in which now one side now the other has the lead **2 a** : a pastime in which two children or groups of children ride on opposite ends of a plank balanced in the middle so that one end goes up as the other goes down **b** : the plank or apparatus so used — **seesaw** *adj*

²seesaw *vi* (1712) **1 a** : to move backward and forward or up and down **b** : to play at seesaw **2** : ALTERNATE ~ *vt* : to cause to move in seesaw fashion

¹seethe \'sēth\ *vb* **seethed; seeth·ing** [ME *sethen*, fr. OE *sēothan*; akin to OHG *siodan* to seethe] *vt* (bef. 12c) **1** *archaic* : BOIL, STEW **2** : to soak or saturate in a liquid ~ *vi* **1** *archaic* : BOIL **2 a** : to be in a state of rapid agitated movement **b** : to churn or foam as if boiling **3** : to suffer violent internal excitement

²seethe *n* (1816) : a state of seething : EBULLITION

seething *adj* (14c) **1** : intensely hot : BOILING 〈a ~ inferno〉 **2** : constantly moving or active : AGITATED

\ə\ abut \ᵊ\ kitten, F table \ər\ further \a\ ash \ā\ ace \ä\ mop, mar
\aú\ out \ch\ chin \e\ bet \ē\ easy \g\ go \i\ hit \ī\ ice \j\ job
\ŋ\ sing \ō\ go \ó\ law \ói\ boy \th\ thin \t͟h\ the \ü\ loot \ú\ foot
\y\ yet \zh\ vision \á, k̲, ⁿ, œ, œ̄, ǔe, ūe, ʸ\ *see* Guide to Pronunciation

see–through \'sē-ˌthrü\ adj (1945) : TRANSPARENT 1
¹seg·ment \'seg-mənt\ n [L segmentum, fr. secare to cut — more at SAW] (1570) **1 a :** a separate piece of something : BIT, FRAGMENT ⟨chop the stalks into short ∼s⟩ **b :** one of the constituent parts into which a body, entity, or quantity is divided or marked off by or as if by natural boundaries ⟨all ∼s of the population agree⟩ **2 :** a portion cut off from a geometric figure by one or more points, lines, or planes: as **a :** the part of a circular area bounded by a chord and an arc of that circle or so much of the area as is cut off by the chord **b :** the part of a sphere cut off by a plane or included between two parallel planes **c :** the finite part of a line between two points in the line **syn** see PART — **seg·men·tary** \-mən-ˌter-ē\ adj
²seg·ment \-ˌment\ vt (1859) : to separate into segments : give off as segments
seg·men·tal \seg-'men-t³l\ adj (1816) **1 :** of, relating to, or having the form of a segment and esp. the sector of a circle ⟨∼ fanlight⟩ **2 :** of, relating to, or composed of somites or metameres : METAMERIC **3 a :** divided into segments ⟨∼ knowledge⟩ **b :** PARTIAL, INCOMPLETE **c :** resulting from segmentation — **seg·men·tal·ly** \-t³l-ē\ adv
seg·men·ta·tion \ˌseg-mən-'tā-shən, -ˌmen-\ n (1851) : the process of dividing into segments; esp : the formation of many cells from a single cell (as in a developing egg)
segmentation cavity n (1888) : BLASTOCOEL
seg·ment·ed \'seg-ˌmen-təd, seg-\ adj (1854) : divided into or composed of segments or sections ⟨∼ worms⟩
se·gno \'sān-(ˌ)yō\ n, pl **segnos** [It, sign, fr. L signum — more at SIGN] (1908) : a notational sign; specif : the sign that marks the beginning or end of a musical repeat
se·go lily \'sē-(ˌ)gō-\ n [sego the bulb of the sego lily, fr. Southern Paiute siyo?o] (1913) : a mariposa lily (Calochortus nuttallii) of western No. America having mostly white or in some areas mostly yellow flowers mottled with a darker color
seg·re·gant \'se-gri-gənt\ n (1926) : a genetic segregate
¹seg·re·gate \'se-gri-ˌgāt\ vb **-gat·ed; -gat·ing** [L segregatus, pp. of segregare, fr. se- apart + greg-, grex herd — more at SECEDE] vt (1542) **1 :** to separate or set apart from others or from the general mass : ISOLATE **2 :** to cause or force the separation of (as from the rest of society) ∼ vi **1 :** SEPARATE, WITHDRAW **2 :** to practice or enforce a policy of segregation **3 :** to undergo genetic segregation — **seg·re·ga·tive** \-ˌgā-tiv\ adj
²seg·re·gate \'se-gri-gət, -ˌgāt\ n (1871) : one that is in some respect segregated; esp : one that differs genetically from the parental line because of genetic segregation
segregated adj (1652) **1 a :** set apart or separated from others of the same kind or group ⟨a ∼ account in a bank⟩ **b :** divided in facilities or administered separately for members of different groups or races ⟨∼ education⟩ **c :** restricted to members of one group or one race by a policy of segregation ⟨∼ schools⟩ **2 :** practicing or maintaining segregation esp. of races ⟨∼ states⟩
seg·re·ga·tion \ˌse-gri-'gā-shən\ n (1555) **1 :** the act or process of segregating : the state of being segregated **2 a :** the separation or isolation of a race, class, or ethnic group by enforced or voluntary residence in a restricted area, by barriers to social intercourse, by separate educational facilities, or by other discriminatory means **b :** the separation for special treatment or observation of individuals or items from a larger group ⟨∼ of gifted children into accelerated classes⟩ **3 :** the separation of allelic genes that occurs typically during meiosis
seg·re·ga·tion·ist \-sh(ə-)nist\ n (1913) : a person who believes in or practices segregation esp. of races — **segregationist** adj
¹se·gue \'se-(ˌ)gwā, 'sā-\ vb imper [It, there follows, fr. seguire to follow, fr. L sequi — more at SUE] (ca. 1740) **1 :** proceed to what follows without pause — used as a direction in music **2 :** perform the music that follows like that which has preceded — used as a direction in music
²segue vi **se·gued; se·gue·ing** (ca. 1913) **1 :** to proceed without pause from one musical number or theme to another **2 :** to make a transition without interruption from one activity, topic, scene, or part to another
³segue n (ca. 1937) : the act or an instance of segueing
se·gui·dil·la \ˌse-gə-'dē-yə, -'dēl-yə\ n [Sp, dim. of seguida, a dance, lit., sequence, fr. seguido, pp. of seguir to follow, fr. L sequi] (1763) **1 a :** a Spanish dance with many regional variations **b :** the music for such a dance **2 :** a Spanish stanza of four or seven short partly assonant verses
sei·cen·to \sā-'chen-(ˌ)tō\ n [It, lit., six-hundred, fr. sei six (fr. L sex) + cento hundred — more at SIX, CINQUECENTO] (ca. 1902) : the 17th century; specif : the 17th century period in Italian literature and art
seiche \'sāsh, 'sēch\ n [F] (ca. 1839) : an oscillation of the surface of a landlocked body of water (as a lake) that varies in period from a few minutes to several hours
sei·del \'sī-d³l, 'zī-\ n [G, fr. MHG sīdel, fr. L situla bucket] (1908) : a large glass for beer
Seid·litz powders \'sed-ləts-\ n pl [Sedlitz, (Sedlčany), village in Bohemia; fr. the similarity of their effect to that of the water of the village] (1815) : effervescing salts consisting of one powder of sodium bicarbonate and Rochelle salt and another of tartaric acid that are mixed in water and drunk as a mild cathartic
sei·gneur \sēn-'yər\ n, often cap [MF, fr. ML senior, fr. L adj., elder — more at SENIOR] (1592) **1 :** a man of rank or authority; esp : the feudal lord of a manor **2 :** a member of the landed gentry of Canada
sei·gneur·ial \-'yúr-ē-əl, -'yər-\ adj (1656) : of, relating to, or befitting a seigneur
sei·gneury \'sān-yə-rē\ n, pl **-gneur·ies** (1683) **1 a :** the territory under the government of a feudal lord **b :** a landed estate held in Canada by feudal tenure until 1854 **2 :** the manor house of a Canadian seigneur
sei·gnior \sān-'yòr, 'sān-ˌ\ n [ME seigniour, fr. MF seigneur] (15c) : SEIGNEUR 1
sei·gnior·age or **sei·gnor·age** \'sān-yə-rij\ n [ME seigneurage, fr. MF,

right of the lord (esp. to coin money), fr. seigneur] (15c) : a government revenue from the manufacture of coins calculated as the difference between the face value and the metal value of the coins
sei·gniory or **sei·gnory** \'sān-yə-rē\ n, pl **-gnior·ies** or **-gnor·ies** (14c) **1 :** LORDSHIP, DOMINION; specif : the power or authority of a feudal lord **2 :** the territory over which a lord holds jurisdiction
sei·gno·ri·al \sān-'yòr-ē-əl, -'yòr-\ adj (1818) : of, relating to, or befitting a seignior : MANORIAL
¹seine \'sān\ n [ME, fr. OE segne, fr. L sagena, fr. Gk sagēnē] (bef. 12c) : a large net with sinkers on one edge and floats on the other that hangs vertically in the water and is used to enclose fish when its ends are pulled together or are drawn ashore
²seine vb **seined; sein·ing** vi (1836) : to fish with or catch fish with a seine ∼ vt : to fish for or in with a seine
sein·er \'sā-nər\ n (1602) **1 :** one who fishes with a seine **2 :** a boat used for seining
sei·sin or **sei·zin** \'sē-z³n\ n [ME seisine, fr. OF saisine, fr. saisir to seize — more at SEIZE] (14c) **1 :** the possession of land or chattels **2 :** the possession of a freehold estate in land by one having title thereto
seis·mic \'sīz-mik, 'sīs-\ adj [Gk seismos shock, earthquake, fr. seiein to shake; prob. akin to Av thwaēshō fear] (1858) **1 :** of, subject to, or caused by an earthquake; also : of or relating to an earth vibration caused by something else (as an explosion or the impact of a meteorite) **2 :** of or relating to a vibration on a celestial body (as the moon) comparable to a seismic event on earth **3 :** having a strong or widespread impact : EARTHSHAKING ⟨∼ social changes⟩ — **seis·mi·cal·ly** \-mi-k(ə-)lē\ adv
seis·mic·i·ty \sīz-'mi-sə-tē, sīs-\ n (1902) : the relative frequency and distribution of earthquakes
seismo- comb form [Gk, fr. seismos] : earthquake : vibration ⟨seismometer⟩
seis·mo·gram \'sīz-mə-ˌgram, 'sīs-\ n [ISV] (ca. 1891) : the record of an earth tremor by a seismograph
seis·mo·graph \-ˌgraf\ n [ISV] (1858) : an apparatus to measure and record vibrations within the earth and of the ground — **seis·mog·ra·pher** \sīz-'mä-grə-fər, sīs-\ n — **seis·mo·graph·ic** \ˌsīz-mə-'gra-fik, ˌsīs-\ adj — **seis·mog·ra·phy** \sīz-'mä-grə-fē, sīs-\ n
seis·mol·o·gy \sīz-'mä-lə-jē, sīs-\ n [ISV] (1858) : a science that deals with earthquakes and with artificially produced vibrations of the earth — **seis·mo·log·i·cal** \ˌsīz-mə-'lä-ji-kəl, ˌsīs-\ adj — **seis·mol·o·gist** \sīz-'mä-lə-jist, sīs-\ n
seis·mom·e·ter \sīz-'mä-mə-tər, sīs-\ n (1841) : a seismograph measuring the actual movements of the ground (as on the earth or the moon) — **seis·mo·met·ric** \ˌsīz-mə-'me-trik, ˌsīs-\ adj
seis·mom·e·try \sīz-'mä-mə-trē, sīs-\ n [ISV] (1858) : the scientific study of earthquakes
sei whale \'sā-, 'sī-\ n [part trans. of Norw seihval, fr. sei coalfish + hval whale] (1912) : a common and widely distributed dark gray rorqual (Balaenoptera borealis) that has a ridge on the top of the head and grows to a length of nearly 60 feet (18 meters) — called also sei
seize \'sēz\ vb **seized; seiz·ing** [ME saisen, fr. OF saisir to put in possession of, fr. ML sacire, of Gmc origin; perh. akin to OHG sezzen to set — more at SET] vt (14c) **1 a** usu **seise** \'sēz\ : to vest ownership of a freehold estate in **b** usu **seise** : to put in possession of something ⟨the biographer will be seized of all pertinent papers⟩ **2 a :** to take possession of : CONFISCATE **b :** to take possession of by legal process **3 a :** to possess or take by force : CAPTURE **b :** to take prisoner : ARREST **4 a :** to take hold of : CLUTCH **b :** to possess oneself of : GRASP **c :** to understand fully and distinctly : APPREHEND **5 a :** to attack or overwhelm physically : AFFLICT ⟨suddenly seized with an acute illness —H. G. Armstrong⟩ **b :** to possess (as one's mind) completely or overwhelmingly ⟨seized the popular imagination —Basil Davenport⟩ **6 :** to bind or fasten together with a lashing of small stuff (as yarn, marline, or fine wire) ∼ vi **1 :** to take or lay hold suddenly or forcibly **2 a :** to cohere to a relatively moving part through excessive pressure, temperature, or friction — used esp. of machine parts (as bearings, brakes, or pistons) **b :** to fail to operate due to the seizing of a part — used of an engine **syn** see TAKE — **seiz·er** n
seizing n (14c) **1 a :** the cord or lashing used in binding or fastening **b :** the fastening so made — see KNOT illustration **2 :** the operation of fastening together or lashing with tarred small stuff
sei·zure \'sē-zhər\ n (15c) **1 a :** the act, action, or process of seizing : the state of being seized **b :** the taking possession of person or property by legal process **2 :** a sudden attack (as of disease) ⟨an epileptic ∼⟩
se·jant \'sē-jənt\ adj [modif. of MF seant, prp. of seoir to sit, fr. L sedēre — more at SIT] (ca. 1500) : SITTING — used of a heraldic animal
sel \'sel\ chiefly Scot var of SELF
se·la·chi·an \sə-'lā-kē-ən\ n [ultim. fr. Gk selachos cartilaginous phosphorescent fish; akin to Gk selas brightness] (1835) : any of a variously defined group (Selachii) of cartilaginous fishes that includes all the elasmobranchs or all elasmobranchs except the chimaeras, the existing sharks and rays or in its most restricted use the existing sharks as distinguished from the rays — **selachian** adj
se·lag·i·nel·la \sə-ˌla-jə-'ne-lə\ n [NL, fr. L selagin-, selago, a plant resembling the savin] (1835) : any of a genus (Selaginella) of mossy lower tracheophytes that are related to or grouped with the club mosses and have branching stems and scalelike leaves and produce one-celled sporangia containing both megaspores and microspores
se·lah \'sē-lə, -ˌlä\ interj [Heb selāh] (1530) — a term of uncertain meaning found in the Hebrew text of the Psalms and Habakkuk carried over untranslated into some English versions
sel·couth \'sel-ˌküth\ adj [ME, fr. OE selcūth, seldan seldom + cūth known — more at UNCOUTH] (bef. 12c) archaic : UNUSUAL, STRANGE
¹sel·dom \'sel-dəm\ adv [ME, fr. OE seldan; akin to OHG seltan seldom] (bef. 12c) : in few instances : RARELY, INFREQUENTLY
²seldom adj (13c) : RARE, INFREQUENT
¹se·lect \sə-'lekt\ adj [L selectus, pp. of seligere to select, fr. se- apart (fr. sed, se without) + legere to gather, select — more at SUICIDE, LEGEND] (1565) **1 :** chosen from a number or group by fitness or preference **2 a :** of special value or excellence : SUPERIOR, CHOICE **b :** exclusively or fastidiously chosen often with regard to social, economic, or cultural characteristics **3 :** judicious or restrictive in choice : DISCRIMINATING

⟨pleased with the ~ appreciation of his books —Osbert Sitwell⟩ — **se·lect·able** \sə-'lek-tə-bəl\ *adj* — **se·lect·ness** \sə-'lek(t)-nəs\ *n* — **se·lec·tor** \sə-'lek-tər\ *n*
²**select** *vt* (1567) : to choose (as by fitness or excellence) from a number or group : pick out ~ *vi* : to make a choice
³**select** *n* (1610) : one that is select — often used in pl.
se·lect·ed *adj* (1590) : SELECT; *specif* : of a higher grade or quality than the ordinary
se·lect·ee \sə-,lek-'tē\ *n* (1940) **1** : one inducted into military service under selective service **2** : one who is chosen from a group by fitness or preference
se·lec·tion \sə-'lek-shən\ *n* (ca. 1623) **1 a** : the act or process of selecting : the state of being selected **2** : one that is selected : CHOICE; *also* : a collection of selected things **3** : a natural or artificial process that results or tends to result in the survival and propagation of some individuals or organisms but not of others with the result that the inherited traits of the survivors are perpetuated — compare DARWINISM, NATURAL SELECTION *syn* see CHOICE
se·lec·tion·ist \-sh(ə-)nist\ *n* (1892) : one who considers natural selection a fundamental factor in evolution — **selectionist** *adj*
se·lec·tive \sə-'lek-tiv\ *adj* (1625) **1** : of, relating to, or characterized by selection : selecting or tending to select **2** : highly specific in activity or effect ⟨~ pesticides⟩ ⟨~ absorption⟩ — **se·lec·tive·ly** *adv* — **se·lec·tive·ness** *n* — **se·lec·tiv·i·ty** \sə-,lek-'ti-və-tē, ,sē-\ *n*
selective service *n* (1917) : a system under which men are called up for military service : DRAFT
se·lect·man \si-'lek(t)-,man, -,lek(t)-'man, -'lek(t)-mən; 'sē-,lek(t)-,man\ *n* (1635) : one of a board of officials elected in towns of all New England states except Rhode Island to serve as the chief administrative authority of the town
¹**selen-** *or* **seleno-** *comb form* [L *selen-*, fr. Gk *selēn-*, fr. *selēnē*— more at SELENIUM] : moon ⟨*selenium*⟩ ⟨*selenology*⟩
²**selen-** *or* **seleni-** *comb form* [Sw, fr. NL *selenium*] : selenium ⟨*seleniferous*⟩
sel·e·nate \'se-lə-,nāt\ *n* [Sw *selenat*, fr. *selen* of or containing selenium, fr. NL *selenium*] (1818) : a salt containing the anion SeO_4^{2-}
Se·le·ne \sə-'lē-nē\ *n* : the Greek goddess of the moon
sel·e·nide \'se-lə-,nīd\ *n* (1849) : a binary compound of selenium with a more electropositive element or group
sel·e·nif·er·ous \,se-lə-'ni-f(ə-)rəs\ *adj* (1823) : containing or yielding selenium ⟨~ vegetation⟩ ⟨~ soils⟩
sel·e·nite \'se-lə-,nīt\ *n* [ME *selinete*, fr. L *selenites*, fr. Gk *selēnitēs* (*lithos*), lit., stone of the moon, fr. *selēnē*; fr. the belief that it waxed and waned with the moon] (15c) : a variety of gypsum occurring in transparent crystals or crystalline masses
se·le·ni·um \sə-'lē-nē-əm\ *n* [NL, fr. Gk *selēnē* moon, fr. *selas* brightness] (1818) : a nonmetallic element that resembles sulfur and tellurium chemically, is obtained chiefly as a by-product in copper refining, and is a photoconductive semiconductor in its crystalline form — see ELEMENT table
selenium cell *n* (1880) : an insulated strip of selenium mounted with electrodes and used as a photoconductive element
se·le·no·cen·tric \sə-,lē-nə-'sen-trik\ *adj* [ISV] (ca. 1852) : of or relating to the center of the moon; *also* : referred to or involving the moon as a center
sel·e·nol·o·gy \,se-lə-'nä-lə-jē\ *n* (1821) : a branch of astronomy that deals with the moon — **se·le·no·log·i·cal** \,se-lə-nō-'lä-ji-kəl, sə-,lē-nᵊl-'ä-\ *adj* — **sel·e·nol·o·gist** \,se-lə-'nä-lə-jist\ *n*
Se·leu·cid \sə-'lü-səd, ssl-'yü-\ *n* [NL *seleucides*, fr. *Seleucus I*] (1851) : a member of a Greek dynasty ruling Syria and at various times other Asian territories from 312 B.C. to 64 B.C. — **Seleucid** *adj*
¹**self** \'self, *Southern also* 'sef\ *pron* [ME *intensive pron.*), fr. OE; akin to OHG *selb*, intensive pron., and prob. to L *suus* one's own — more at SUICIDE] (bef. 12c) : MYSELF, HIMSELF, HERSELF ⟨check payable to ~⟩
²**self** *adj* (bef. 12c) **1** *obs* : IDENTICAL, SAME **2** *obs* : belonging to oneself : OWN **3 a** : having a single character or quality throughout; *specif* : having one color only ⟨a ~ flower⟩ **b** : of the same kind (as in color, material, or pattern) as something with which it is used ⟨a ~ trimming⟩
³**self** *n*, *pl* **selves** \'selvz, *Southern also* 'sevz\ (13c) **1 a** : the entire person of an individual **b** : the realization or embodiment of an abstraction **2 a** (1) : an individual's typical character or behavior ⟨her true ~ was revealed⟩ (2) : an individual's temporary behavior or character ⟨his better ~⟩ **b** : a person in prime condition ⟨feel like my old ~ today⟩ **3** : the union of elements (as body, emotions, thoughts, and sensations) that constitute the individuality and identity of a person **4** : personal interest or advantage **5** : material that is part of an individual organism ⟨ability of the immune system to distinguish ~ from nonself⟩
⁴**self** *vt* (1914) **1** : INBREED **2** : to pollinate with pollen from the same flower or plant ~ *vi* : to undergo self-pollination
self- *comb form* [ME, fr. OE, fr. *self*] **1 a** : oneself or itself ⟨*self*-supporting⟩ **b** : of oneself or itself ⟨*self*-abasement⟩ **c** : by oneself or itself ⟨*self*-propelled⟩ **2 a** : to, with, for, or toward oneself or itself ⟨*self*-consistent⟩ ⟨*self*-addressed⟩ ⟨*self*-love⟩ **b** : of or in oneself or itself inherently ⟨*self*-evident⟩ **c** : from or by means of oneself or itself ⟨*self*-fertile⟩

self–abase·ment	self–ad·ver·tis·er	self–cas·ti·ga·tion
self–ab·ne·gat·ing	self–af·fir·ma·tion	self–cen·sor·ship
self–ab·ne·ga·tion	self–ag·gran·dize·ment	self–char·ac·ter·i·za·tion
self–ac·cel·er·at·ing	self–ag·gran·diz·ing	self–clas·si·fi·ca·tion
self–ac·cep·tance	self–alien·ation	self–clean·ing
self–ac·cu·sa·tion	self–anoint·ed	self–com·mand
self–ac·cu·sa·to·ry	self–ap·prais·al	self–com·mun·ing
self–ac·cus·ing	self–ap·pro·ba·tion	self–com·mu·nion
self–ac·knowl·edged	self–as·sess·ment	self–com·pla·cen·cy
self–ad·just·ing	self–as·sign·ment	self–com·pla·cent
self–ad·min·is·ter	self–au·then·ti·cat·ing	self–con·dem·na·tion
self–ad·min·is·tra·tion	self–avowed	self–con·demned
self–ad·mit·ted	self–bet·ter·ment	self–con·firm·ing
self–ad·mit·ted·ly	self–can·cel	self–con·se·cra·tion
self–ad·u·la·to·ry	self–care	self–con·sti·tut·ed
self–ad·vance·ment	self–car·i·ca·ture	self–con·sum·ing
self–ad·ver·tise·ment	self–cas·ti·gate	self–con·tempt

self–cre·at·ed	self–ex·plain·ing	self–per·pet·u·at·ing
self–cre·a·tion	self–ex·tinc·tion	self–per·pet·u·a·tion
self–crit·i·cal	self–fi·nance	self–pla·gia·rism
self–crit·i·cism	self–formed	self–pleas·ing
self–cri·tique	self–gen·er·ate	self–po·lic·ing
self–cul·ti·va·tion	self–giv·ing	self–praise
self–cul·ture	self–guid·ed	self–pre·oc·cu·pa·tion
self–damn·ing	self–hate	self–pre·oc·cu·pied
self–de·base·ment	self–ha·tred	self–pre·serv·ing
self–de·ceit	self–heal·ing	self–pro·claimed
self–de·ceive	self–help	self–pro·duced
self–de·cep·tion	self–hum·bling	self–pro·fessed
self–de·feat·ing	self–hu·mil·i·a·tion	self–pro·mot·er
self–de·lud·ed	self–hyp·no·sis	self–pro·mot·ing
self–de·lud·ing	self–idol·a·try	self–pro·mo·tion
self–de·lu·sion	self–im·posed	self–pro·tec·tion
self–den·i·grat·ing	self–im·prove·ment	self–pro·tec·tive
self–den·i·gra·tion	self–im·prov·er	self–pro·tec·tive·ness
self–de·pen·dence	self–in·duced	self–pun·ish·ing
self–de·pen·dent	self–in·fat·u·at·ed	self–pun·ish·ment
self–de·pre·cat·ing	self–in·fla·tion	self–raised
self–de·pre·cat·ing·ly	self–in·flict·ed	self–re·crim·i·na·tion
self–de·pre·ca·tion	self–ini·ti·at·ed	self–ref·er·en·tial
self–de·pre·ca·to·ry	self–in·struct·ed	self–re·fer·ring
self–de·pre·ci·a·tion	self–in·struc·tion	self–re·flex·ive
self–de·scribed	self–in·struc·tion·al	self–ref·or·ma·tion
self–de·scrip·tion	self–in·ter·view	self–reg·u·la·tion
self–de·scrip·tive	self–in·vent·ed	self–reg·u·la·tive
self–de·vel·op·ment	self–in·ven·tion	self–reg·u·la·to·ry
self–de·vour·ing	self–iso·la·tion	self–re·in·forc·ing
self–dif·fer·en·ti·a·tion	self–la·beled	self–re·new·al
self–di·rect·ed	self–lac·er·at·ing	self–re·new·ing
self–di·rect·ing	self–lac·er·a·tion	self–re·nounc·ing
self–di·rec·tion	self–loath·ing	self–re·nun·ci·a·tion
self–di·rec·tive	self–lock·ing	self–re·proach
self–dis·gust	self–lu·bri·cat·ing	self–re·proach·ful
self–dis·play	self–lu·mi·nous	self–re·proof
self–dis·sat·is·fac·tion	self–main·te·nance	self–re·prov·ing
self–doubt	self–man·age·ment	self–re·straint
self–ed·u·cat·ed	self–mas·tery	self–rid·i·cule
self–ed·u·cat·ing	self–med·i·ca·tion	self–sat·i·riz·ing
self–ed·u·ca·tion	self–mock·ery	self–se·lect·ed
self–ef·face·ment	self–mock·ing	self–se·lec·tion
self–ef·fac·ing	self–mor·ti·fi·ca·tion	self–set
self–eman·ci·pa·tion	self–mo·ti·vat·ed	self–sur·ren·der
self–emas·cu·la·tion	self–mu·ti·lat·ing	self–sus·tained
self–en·closed	self–mu·ti·la·tion	self–ther·a·py
self–en·grossed	self–ne·gat·ing	self–tor·ment
self–en·hance·ment	self–ob·sessed	self–tor·men·tor
self–eval·u·ate	self–op·er·at·ing	self–tor·ture
self–eval·u·a·tion	self–or·dained	self–tran·scen·dence
self–ex·clu·sion	self–ori·ent·ed	self–trans·for·ma·tion
self–ex·cul·pa·tion	self–par·o·dist	self–un·der·stand·ing
self–ex·hi·bi·tion	self–par·o·dy	self–val·i·dat·ing
self–ex·is·tence	self–penned	self–wor·ship
self–ex·is·tent		self–wor·ship·er

self–aban·doned \,self-ə-'ban-dənd\ *adj* (1791) : abandoned by oneself; *esp* : given up to one's impulses
self–aban·don·ment \-dən-mənt\ *n* (1818) **1** : a surrender of one's selfish interests or desires **2** : a lack of self-restraint
self–ab·sorbed \-əb-'sórbd, -'zórbd\ *adj* (1847) : absorbed in one's own thoughts, activities, or interests
self–ab·sorp·tion \-'sórp-shən, -'zórp-\ *n* (1862) : preoccupation with oneself
self–abuse \-ə-'byüs\ *n* (1605) **1** : reproach of oneself **2** : MASTURBATION **3** : abuse of one's body or health
self–act·ing \-'ak-tiŋ\ *adj* (ca. 1680) : acting or capable of acting of or by itself : AUTOMATIC
self–ac·tiv·i·ty \-,ak-'ti-və-tē\ *n* (1644) : independent and esp. self-determined activity
self–ac·tu·al·ize \-'ak-ch(ə-w)ə-,līz, -sh(ə-w)ə-,līz\ *vi* (1874) : to realize fully one's potential — **self–ac·tu·al·i·za·tion** \-,ak-ch(ə-w)ə-lə-'zā-shən, -sh(ə-w)ə-lə-\ *n*
self–ad·dressed \-ə-'drest, -'a-,drest\ *adj* (1904) : addressed for return to the sender ⟨a ~ envelope⟩
self–ad·he·sive \-əd-'hē-siv, -ziv\ *adj* (1958) : having a side coated with an adhesive that sticks without wetting ⟨~ labels⟩
self–ad·just·ment \-ə-'jəs(t)-mənt\ *n* (1848) : adjustment to oneself or one's environment
self–ad·mi·ra·tion \-,ad-mə-'rā-shən\ *n* (1661) : SELF-CONCEIT
self–af·fect·ed \-ə-'fek-təd\ *adj* (1606) : CONCEITED, SELF-LOVING
self–anal·y·sis \-ə-'na-lə-səs\ *n* (1860) : a systematic attempt by an individual to understand his or her own personality without the aid of another person
self–an·a·lyt·i·cal \-,a-nᵊl-'i-ti-kəl\ *also* **self–an·a·lyt·ic** *adj* (1943) : using self-analysis
self–an·ni·hi·la·tion \-ə-,nī-ə-'lā-shən\ *n* (1647) : annihilation of the self (as in mystical contemplation of God)
self–ap·plaud·ing \-ə-'plò-diŋ\ *adj* (1654) : marked by self-applause
self–ap·plause \-'plòz\ *n* (1678) : an expression or feeling of approval of oneself
self–ap·point·ed \-ə-'póin-təd\ *adj* (1799) : appointed by oneself : SELF-STYLED
self–as·sem·bly \-ə-'sem-blē\ *n* (1966) : the process by which a complex macromolecule (as collagen) or a supramolecular system (as a

\a\ abut \ᵊ\ kitten, F table \ər\ further \a\ ash \ā\ ace \ä\ mop, mar \aú\ out \ch\ chin \e\ bet \ē\ easy \g\ go \i\ hit \ī\ ice \j\ job \ŋ\ sing \ō\ go \ò\ law \òi\ boy \th\ thin \t̶h̶\ the \ü\ loot \ù\ foot \y\ yet \zh\ vision \ȧ, k̲, ⁿ, œ, œ̄, ᵫ, ᵫ̄, ᵋ\ *see* Guide to Pronunciation virus) spontaneously assembles itself from its components — **self–as-sem·ble** \-ə-'sem-bəl\ *vi*

self–as·sert·ing \-ə-'sər-tiŋ\ *adj* (1837) **1** : asserting oneself or one's own rights, claims, or opinions **2 a** : SELF-ASSURED, CONFIDENT **b** : ARROGANT — **self–as·sert·ing·ly** \-tiŋ-lē\ *adv*

self–as·ser·tion \-ə-'sər-shən\ *n* (1806) **1** : the act of asserting oneself or one's own rights, claims, or opinions **2** : the act of asserting one's superiority over others

self–as·ser·tive \-'sər-tiv\ *adj* (1865) : given to or characterized by self-assertion *syn* see AGGRESSIVE — **self–as·ser·tive·ly** *adv* — **self–as·ser·tive·ness** *n*

self–as·sump·tion \-'səm(p)-shən\ *n* (1606) : SELF-CONCEIT

self–as·sur·ance \-ə-'shùr-ən(t)s\ *n* (1594) : SELF-CONFIDENCE

self–as·sured \-'shùrd\ *adj* (1711) : sure of oneself : SELF-CONFIDENT — **self–as·sured·ly** \-'shùr-əd-lē, -'shùrd-\ *adv* — **self–as·sured·ness** \-'shùr-əd-nəs, -'shùrd-\ *n*

self–aware \-ə-'war, -'wer\ *adj* (ca. 1934) : characterized by self-awareness

self–aware·ness *n* (1880) : an awareness of one's own personality or individuality

self–belt \'self-'belt\ *n* (1965) : a belt made of the same material as the garment with which it is worn — **self–belt·ed** \-'bel-təd\ *adj*

self–be·tray·al \-self-bi-'trā(-ə)l\ *n* (1857) : SELF-REVELATION

self–born \-'bòrn\ *adj* (1587) **1** : arising within the self (~ sorrows) **2** : springing from a prior self (phoenix rising ~ from the fire)

self–ca·ter·ing \-'kā-tər-iŋ\ *adj* (1970) *Brit* : provided with lodging and cooking facilities but not meals (~ holiday cottages)

self–cen·tered \-'sen-tərd\ *adj* (ca. 1764) **1** : independent of outside force or influence : SELF-SUFFICIENT **2** : concerned solely with one's own desires, needs, or interests — **self–cen·tered·ly** *adv* — **self–cen·tered·ness** *n*

self–clos·ing \-'klō-ziŋ\ *adj* (ca. 1875) : closing or shutting automatically after being opened

self–cock·ing \-'kä-kiŋ\ *adj* (1862) *of a firearm* : cocked by the operation of some part of the action (~ on pushing the bolt forward)

self–col·lect·ed \-'lek-təd\ *adj* (ca. 1711) : SELF-POSSESSED

self–col·ored \-'kə-lərd\ *adj* (1759) : of a single color (a ~ flower)

self–com·pat·i·ble \-kəm-'pa-tə-bəl\ *adj* (1922) : capable of effective self-pollination that results in the production of seeds and fruits — **self–com·pat·i·bil·i·ty** \-,pa-tə-'bi-lə-tē\ *n*

self–com·posed \-kəm-'pōzd\ *adj* (ca. 1934) : having control over one's emotions : CALM — **self–com·pos·ed·ly** \-'pō-zəd-lē\ *adv* — **self–com·posed·ness** \-'pō-zəd-nəs, -'pōz(d)-nəs\ *n*

self–con·ceit \-kən-'sēt\ *n* (ca. 1589) : an exaggerated opinion of one's own qualities or abilities : VANITY — **self–con·ceit·ed** \-'sē-təd\ *adj*

self–con·cept \'self-'kän-,sept\ *n* (1925) : the mental image one has of oneself

self–con·cep·tion \,self-kən-'sep-shən\ *n* (1950) : SELF-CONCEPT

self–con·cern \-'sərn\ *n* (1681) : a selfish or morbid concern for oneself — **self–con·cerned** \-'sərnd\ *adj*

self–con·fessed \-'fest\ *adj* (ca. 1900) : openly acknowledged by oneself : AVOWED — **self–con·fess·ed·ly** \-'fe-səd-lē, -'fest-lē\ *adv*

self–con·fes·sion \-'fe-shən\ *n* (ca. 1961) : open acknowledgment : AVOWAL

self–con·fi·dence \-'kän-fə-dən(t)s, -,den(t)s\ *n* (1637) : confidence in oneself and in one's powers and abilities — **self–con·fi·dent** \-fə-dənt, -,dent\ *adj* — **self–con·fi·dent·ly** *adv*

self–con·fron·ta·tion \-,kän-(,)frən-'tā-shən\ *n* (1961) : SELF-ANALYSIS

self–con·grat·u·la·tion \-kən-,gra-chə-'lā-shən, -,gra-jə-\ *n* (1712) : congratulation of oneself; *esp* : a complacent acknowledgment of one's own superiority or good fortune

self–con·grat·u·la·to·ry \-'gra-chə-lə-,tōr-ē, -,gra-jə-, -,tòr-\ *adj* (1877) : expressive of self-congratulation (~ memoirs)

self–con·scious \-'kän(t)-shəs\ *adj* (ca. 1680) **1 a** : conscious of one's own acts or states as belonging to or originating in oneself : aware of oneself as an individual **b** : intensely aware of oneself : CONSCIOUS (a rising and ~ social class); *also* : produced or done with such awareness (~ art) **2** : uncomfortably conscious of oneself as an object of the observation of others : ILL AT EASE — **self–con·scious·ly** *adv* — **self–con·scious·ness** *n*

self–con·se·quence \-'kän(t)-sə-,kwen(t)s, -si-kwən(t)s\ *n* (1778) : SELF-IMPORTANCE

self–con·sis·ten·cy \-kən-'sis-tən(t)-sē\ *n* (1692) : the quality or state of being self-consistent

self–con·sis·tent \-tənt\ *adj* (1683) : having each part logically consistent with the rest

self–con·tained \-kən-'tānd\ *adj* (1591) **1 a** : complete in itself : INDEPENDENT (a ~ machine) (a ~ program of study) **b** : BUILT-IN (a lectern with a ~ light fixture) **2 a** : showing self-control **b** : formal and reserved in manner — **self–con·tained·ly** \-'tā-nəd-lē, -'tānd-lē\ *adv* — **self–con·tained·ness** \-'tä-nəd-nəs, -'tän(d)-nəs\ *n* — **self–con·tain·ment** \-'tān-mənt\ *n*

self–con·tam·i·na·tion \-kən-,ta-mə-'nā-shən\ *n* (1955) **1** : contamination by oneself **2** : contamination from within

self–con·tent \-kən-'tent\ *n* (1654) : SELF-SATISFACTION

self–con·tent·ed \-'ten-təd\ *adj* (1818) : SELF-SATISFIED — **self–con·tent·ed·ly** *adv* — **self–con·tent·ed·ness** *n*

self–con·tent·ment \-'tent-mənt\ *n* (1815) : SELF-SATISFACTION

self–con·tra·dic·tion \-,kän-trə-'dik-shən\ *n* (1658) **1** : contradiction of oneself **2** : a self-contradictory statement or proposition

self–con·tra·dic·to·ry \-'dik-t(ə-)rē\ *adj* (1657) : consisting of two contradictory members or parts

self–con·trol \-kən-'trōl\ *n* (1711) : restraint exercised over one's own impulses, emotions, or desires — **self–con·trolled** \-'trōld\ *adj*

self–cor·rect·ing \-kə-'rek-tiŋ\ *adj* (1939) : correcting or compensating for one's own errors or weaknesses

self–cor·rec·tive \-'rek-tiv\ *adj* (ca. 1925) : SELF-CORRECTING

self–deal·ing \'self-'dē-liŋ\ *n* (1940) : financial dealing that is not at arm's length; *esp* : borrowing from or lending to a company by a controlling individual primarily to the individual's own advantage

self–de·fense \-di-'fen(t)s\ *n* (1651) **1** : a plea of justification for the use of force or for homicide **2** : the act of defending oneself, one's property, or a close relative

self–de·fen·sive \-'fen(t)-siv\ *adj* (1828) : of, relating to, or given to self-defense (a ~ person) (a ~ attitude)

self–def·i·ni·tion \-,de-fə-'ni-shən\ *n* (1957) : the evaluation by oneself of one's worth as an individual in distinction from one's interpersonal or social roles

self–de·ni·al \-di-'nī(-ə)l\ *n* (1642) : a restraint or limitation of one's own desires or interests

self–de·ny·ing \-'nī-iŋ\ *adj* (1632) : showing self-denial — **self–de·ny·ing·ly** \-iŋ-lē\ *adv*

self–de·spair \-di-'spar, -'sper\ *n* (1677) : despair of oneself : HOPE-LESSNESS

self–de·stroy·er \-di-'stròi(-ə)r\ *n* (1654) : one who destroys oneself

self–de·stroy·ing \-di-'stròi-iŋ\ *adj* (1645) : SELF-DESTRUCTIVE

self–de·struct \-di-'strəkt\ *vi* (1968) : to destroy oneself or itself — **self–destruct** *adj*

self–de·struc·tion \-'strək-shən\ *n* (ca. 1586) : destruction of oneself; *esp* : SUICIDE

self–de·struc·tive \-'strək-tiv\ *adj* (1654) : acting or tending to harm or destroy oneself; *also* : SUICIDAL — **self–de·struc·tive·ness** *n*

self–de·ter·mi·na·tion \-di-,tər-mə-'nā-shən\ *n* (ca. 1670) **1** : free choice of one's own acts or states without external compulsion **2** : determination by the people of a territorial unit of their own future political status

self–de·ter·mined \-'tər-mənd\ *adj* (ca. 1670) : determined by oneself

self–de·ter·min·ing \-'tər-mə-niŋ, -'tərm-niŋ\ *adj* (1662) : capable of determining one's or its own acts

self–de·ter·min·ism \-'tər-mə-,ni-zəm\ *n* (1936) : a doctrine that the actions of a self are determined by itself

self–de·vot·ed \-di-'vō-təd\ *adj* (1713) : characterized by total devotion of oneself (as to a cause) — **self–de·vot·ed·ness** *n*

self–dis·ci·pline \-'di-sə-plən\ *n* (1838) : correction or regulation of oneself for the sake of improvement

self–dis·ci·plined \-plənd\ *adj* (1932) : capable of or subject to self-discipline

self–dis·cov·ery \-dis-'kə-v(ə-)rē\ *n* (1924) : the act or process of achieving self-knowledge

self–dis·trust \-'trəst\ *n* (1789) : a lack of confidence in oneself : DIF-FIDENCE — **self–dis·trust·ful** \-fəl\ *adj*

self–dra·ma·ti·za·tion \-self-,dra-mə-tə-'zā-shən, -,drä-\ *n* (1937) : the act or an instance of dramatizing oneself

self–dra·ma·tiz·ing \-'dra-mə-,tī-ziŋ, -'drä-\ *adj* (1938) : seeing and presenting oneself as an important or dramatic figure

self–drive \-'drīv\ *adj* (1929) *chiefly Brit* : being a rental car

self–elect·ed \,self-ə-'lek-təd\ *adj* (1818) : SELF-APPOINTED

self–em·ployed \-im-'plòid\ *adj* (1946) : earning income directly from one's own business, trade, or profession rather than as a specified salary or wages from an employer — **self–employed** *n*

self–em·ploy·ment \-'plòi-mənt\ *n* (1745) : the state of being self-employed

self–en·er·giz·ing \-'e-nər-,jī-ziŋ\ *adj* (1931) : containing means for augmentation of power within itself (a ~ brake)

self–en·forc·ing \-in-'fòr-siŋ, -'fòr-\ *adj* (1952) : containing in itself the authority or means that provide for its enforcement

self–en·rich·ment \-in-'rich-mənt\ *n* (1920) : the act or process of increasing one's intellectual or spiritual resources

self–es·teem \-ə-'stēm\ *n* (1657) **1** : a confidence and satisfaction in oneself : SELF-RESPECT **2** : SELF-CONCEIT

self–ev·i·dence \-'e-və-dən(t)s, -,den(t)s\ *n* (1671) : the quality or state of being self-evident

self–ev·i·dent \-dənt, -,dent\ *adj* (1671) : evident without proof or reasoning — **self–ev·i·dent·ly** *adv*

self–ex·am·i·na·tion \-ig-,za-mə-'nā-shən\ *n* (1647) **1** : a reflective examination (as of one's beliefs or motives) : INTROSPECTION **2** : examination of one's body esp. for evidence of disease

self–ex·cit·ed \-ik-'si-təd\ *adj* (ca. 1896) : excited by a current produced by the generator itself (~ generators)

self–ex·e·cut·ing \-'ek-sə-,kyü-tiŋ\ *adj* (1868) : taking effect immediately without implementing legislation (a ~ treaty)

self–ex·iled \-'eg-,zīld, -'ek-,sīld\ *adj* (1737) : exiled by one's own wish or decision

self–ex·plan·a·to·ry \ik-'spla-nə-,tōr-ē, -,tòr-\ *adj* (1898) : explaining itself : capable of being understood without explanation

self–ex·plo·ra·tion \-,ek-splə-'rā-shən, -,splō-\ *n* (1959) : the examination and analysis of one's own unrealized spiritual or intellectual capacities

self–ex·pres·sion \-ik-'spre-shən\ *n* (1892) : the expression of one's own personality : assertion of one's individual traits — **self–ex·pres·sive** \-'spre-siv\ *adj*

self–feed \'self-'fēd\ *vt* **-fed** \-'fed\; **-feed·ing** (ca. 1924) : to provide rations to (animals) in bulk so as to permit feeding as wanted

self–feed·er \-'fē-dər\ *n* (1924) : a device for providing feed to livestock that is equipped with a feed hopper that automatically supplies a trough below

self–feel·ing \'self-'fē-liŋ\ *n* (1879) : self-centered emotion

self–fer·tile \,self-'fər-t³l\ *adj* (1865) : fertile by means of its own pollen or sperm — **self–fer·til·i·ty** \-(,)fər-'ti-lə-tē\ *n*

self–fer·til·i·za·tion \-,fər-t³l-ə-'zā-shən\ *n* (1859) : fertilization effected by union of ova with pollen or sperm from the same individual

self–fer·til·ized \-'fər-t³l-,īzd\ *adj* (1871) : fertilized by one's own pollen or sperm

self–fer·til·iz·ing \-,ī-ziŋ\ *adj* (1859) : SELF-FERTILIZED

self–flag·el·la·tion \-,fla-jə-'lā-shən\ *n* (1845) : extreme criticism of oneself

self–flat·ter·ing \-'fla-tə-riŋ\ *adj* (ca. 1586) : given to self-flattery

self–flat·tery \-'la-tə-rē\ *n* (1680) : the glossing over of one's own weaknesses or mistakes and the exaggeration of one's own good qualities and achievements

self–for·get·ful \-fər-'get-fəl\ *adj* (1848) : having or showing no thought of self or selfish interests — **self–for·get·ful·ly** \-fə-lē\ *adv* — **self–for·get·ful·ness** *n*

self–for·get·ting \-'ge-tiŋ\ *adj* (1847) : SELF-FORGETFUL — **self–for·get·ting·ly** \-tiŋ-lē\ *adv*

self–fruit·ful \'self-'früt-fəl\ *adj* (1940) : capable of setting a crop of self-pollinated fruit — **self–fruit·ful·ness** *n*

self·ful·fill·ing \ˌself-fu̇l-'fi-liŋ\ *adj* (1949) **1** : marked by or achieving self-fulfillment **2** : becoming real or true by virtue of having been predicted or expected ⟨a ~ prophecy⟩

self·ful·fill·ment \-'fil-mənt\ *n* (ca. 1864) : fulfillment of oneself

self-giv·en \'gi-vən\ *adj* (1742) **1** : derived from itself ⟨a ~ entity⟩ **2** : given by oneself ⟨~ authority⟩

self·glo·ri·fi·ca·tion \-ˌglȯr-ə-fə-'kā-shən, -ˌglȯr-\ *n* (1838) : a feeling or expression of one's own superiority

self·glo·ri·fy·ing \-'glȯr-ə-ˌfī-iŋ, -'glȯr-\ *adj* (1860) : given to or marked by boasting : BOASTFUL

self·glo·ry \-'glȯr-ē, -'glȯr-ē\ *n* (1647) : personal vanity : PRIDE

self·gov·er·nance \-'gə-vər-nən(t)s\ *n* (1964) : SELF-GOVERNMENT 2

self·gov·erned \-'gə-vərnd\ *adj* (1709) **1** : not influenced or controlled by others **2** : exercising self-control

self·gov·ern·ing \-'gə-vər-niŋ\ *adj* (1845) : having control or rule over oneself; *specif* : having self-government : AUTONOMOUS

self·gov·ern·ment \-'gə-vər(n)-mənt, -'gə-vᵊm-ənt\ *n* (1734) **1** : SELF-COMMAND, SELF-CONTROL **2** : government under the control and direction of the inhabitants of a political unit rather than by an outside authority; *broadly* : control of one's own affairs

self·grat·i·fi·ca·tion \-ˌgra-tə-fə-'kā-shən\ *n* (1677) : the act of pleasing oneself or of satisfying one's desires; *esp* : the satisfying of one's own sexual urges

self·grat·u·la·tion \-ˌgra-chə-'lā-shən\ *n* (1802) : SELF-CONGRATULATION

self·grat·u·la·to·ry \-'gra-chə-lə-ˌtȯr-ē, -ˌtȯr-\ *adj* (1859) : SELF-CONGRATULATORY

self·heal \-ˌhēl\ *n* (14c) : a blue-flowered Eurasian mint (*Prunella vulgaris*) naturalized throughout No. America and formerly considered to have medicinal properties

self·hood \-ˌhu̇d\ *n* (1649) **1** : INDIVIDUALITY **2** : the quality or state of being selfish

self·iden·ti·cal \ˌself-ī-'den-ti-kəl, -ə-'den-\ *adj* (1877) : having self-identity

self·iden·ti·fi·ca·tion \-ˌden-tə-fə-'kā-shən\ *n* (1941) : identification with someone or something outside oneself

self·iden·ti·ty \-'den-tə-tē, -'de-nə-tē\ *n* (1866) **1** : sameness of a thing with itself **2** : INDIVIDUALITY ⟨self-understanding is the necessary condition of a sense of ~ —J. C. Murray⟩

self·ig·nite \-ig-'nīt\ *vi* (1943) : to become ignited without flame or spark (as under high compression)

self·ig·ni·tion \-'ni-shən\ *n* (1903) : ignition without flame or spark

self·im·age \'self-'i-mij\ *n* (1939) : one's conception of oneself or of one's role

self·im·mo·la·tion \ˌself-ˌi-mə-'lā-shən\ *n* (1817) : a deliberate and willing sacrifice of oneself often by fire — **self·im·mo·late** \-'i-mə-ˌlāt\ *vb*

self·im·por·tance \-im-'pȯr-tᵊn(t)s, -tᵊn(t)s\ *n* (ca. 1775) **1** : an exaggerated estimate of one's own importance : SELF-CONCEIT **2** : arrogant or pompous behavior

self·important \-t²nt, -tənt\ *adj* (ca. 1775) : having or showing self-importance — **self·im·por·tant·ly** *adv*

self·in·clu·sive \-in-'klü-siv, -ziv\ *adj* (ca. 1909) **1** : enclosing itself **2** : complete in itself

self·in·com·pat·i·ble \-ˌin-kəm-'pa-tə-bəl\ *adj* (1922) : incapable of effective self-pollination — **self·in·com·pat·i·bil·i·ty** \-ˌpa-tə-'bi-lə-tē\ *n*

self·in·crim·i·nat·ing \-in-'kri-mə-ˌnā-tiŋ\ *adj* (1931) : serving or tending to incriminate oneself

self·in·crim·i·na·tion \-ˌkri-mə-'nā-shən\ *n* (1911) : incrimination of oneself; *specif* : the giving of testimony which will likely subject one to criminal prosecution

self·in·duc·tance \-'dək-tən(t)s\ *n* (1865) : inductance in which an electromotive force is produced by self-induction

self·in·duc·tion \-'dək-shən\ *n* (1873) : induction of an electromotive force in a circuit by a varying current in the same circuit

self·in·dul·gence \-'dəl-jən(t)s\ *n* (1753) : excessive or unrestrained gratification of one's own appetites, desires, or whims — **self·in·dul·gent** \-jənt\ *adj* — **self·in·dul·gent·ly** *adv*

self·in·sur·ance \in-'shu̇r-ən(t)s, -'in-ˌ\ *n* (ca. 1897) : insurance of oneself or of one's own interests by the setting aside of money at regular intervals to provide a fund to cover possible losses

self·insure \-in-'shu̇r\ *vb* (1932) : to insure oneself; *esp* : to practice self-insurance — **self·insurer** \-'shu̇r-ər\ *n*

self·in·ter·est \-'in-t(ə-)rəst; -'in-tə-ˌrest, -ˌtrest; -'in-tərst\ *n* (1649) **1** : a concern for one's own advantage and well-being ⟨acted out of ~ and fear⟩ **2** : one's own interest or advantage ⟨~ requires that we be generous in foreign aid⟩ — **self·in·ter·est·ed** *adj* — **self·in·ter·est·ed·ness** *n*

self·in·volved \-in-'välvd, -'vȯlvd *also* -'vävd *or* 'vȯvd\ *adj* (1842) : SELF-ABSORBED

self·ish \'sel-fish\ *adj* (1640) **1** : concerned excessively or exclusively with oneself : seeking or concentrating on one's own advantage, pleasure, or well-being without regard for others **2** : arising from concern with one's own welfare or advantage in disregard of others ⟨a ~ act⟩ — **self·ish·ly** *adv* — **self·ish·ness** *n*

self·jus·ti·fi·ca·tion \ˌself-ˌjəs-tə-fə-'kā-shən\ *n* (ca. 1775) : the act or an instance of making excuses for oneself

self·jus·ti·fy·ing \-'jəs-tə-ˌfī-iŋ\ *adj* (1740) : seeking to justify oneself

self·know·ing \-'nō-iŋ\ *adj* (1667) : having self-knowledge

self·knowl·edge \-'nä-lij\ *n* (ca. 1613) : knowledge or understanding of one's own capabilities, character, feelings, or motivations

self·less \'sel-fləs\ *adj* (1825) : having no concern for self : UNSELFISH — **self·less·ly** *adv* — **self·less·ness** *n*

self·lim·it·ed \ˌself-'li-mə-təd\ *adj* (1845) : limited by one's or its own nature; *specif* : running a definite and limited course ⟨a ~ disease⟩

self·lim·it·ing \-tiŋ\ *adj* (1863) : limiting oneself or itself; *esp, of a disease* : SELF-LIMITED

self·liq·ui·dat·ing \-'li-kwə-ˌdā-tiŋ\ *adj* (1915) **1** : of or relating to a commercial transaction in which goods are converted into cash in a short time **2** : generating funds from its own operations to repay the investment made to create it ⟨a ~ housing project⟩

self·load·er \-'lō-dər\ *n* (ca. 1936) : a semiautomatic firearm

self·load·ing \-diŋ\ *adj* (1899) *of a firearm* : SEMIAUTOMATIC

self·love \'self-'ləv\ *n* (1563) : love of self: **a** : CONCEIT **b** : regard for one's own happiness or advantage — **self·lov·ing** \-'lə-viŋ\ *adj*

self·made \'self-'mād\ *adj* (1615) : made such by one's own actions; *esp* : having achieved success or prominence by one's own efforts ⟨a ~ man⟩

self·mail·er \-'mā-lər\ *n* (ca. 1942) : a folder that can be sent by mail without enclosure in an envelope by use of a gummed sticker or a precanceled stamp to hold the leaves together

self·mail·ing \-liŋ\ *adj* (ca. 1948) : capable of being mailed without being enclosed in an envelope

self·moved \'self-'müvd\ *adj* (ca. 1670) : moved by inherent power

self·mur·der \-'mər-dər\ *n* (1563) : SELF-DESTRUCTION, SUICIDE

self·ness \'self-nəs\ *n* (ca. 1586) **1** : EGOISM, SELFISHNESS **2** : PERSONALITY, SELFHOOD

self·ob·ser·va·tion \ˌself-ˌäb-sər-'vā-shən, -zər-\ *n* (1832) **1** : INTROSPECTION **2** : observation of one's own appearance

self·opin·ion \-ə-'pin-yən\ *n* (ca. 1580) : high or exaggerated opinion of oneself : SELF-CONCEIT

self·opin·ion·at·ed \-yə-ˌnā-təd\ *adj* (1671) **1** : CONCEITED **2** : stubbornly holding to one's own opinion : OPINIONATED — **self·opin·ion·at·ed·ness** *n*

self·or·ga·ni·za·tion \-ˌȯr-gə-nə-'zā-shən, -ˌȯrg-nə-\ *n* (1898) : organization of oneself or itself; *specif* : the act or process of forming or joining a labor union

self·paced \'self-'pāst\ *adj* (1962) : designed to permit learning at the student's own pace ⟨~ math course⟩

self·par·tial·i·ty \ˌself-ˌpär-shē-'a-lə-tē, -ˌpär-'sha-\ *n* (1628) **1** : an excessive estimate of oneself as compared with others **2** : a prejudice in favor of one's own claims or interests

self·per·cep·tion \-pər-'sep-shən\ *n* (1678) : perception of oneself; *esp* : SELF-CONCEPT

self·pity \'self-'pi-tē\ *n* (1621) : pity for oneself; *esp* : a self-indulgent dwelling on one's own sorrows or misfortunes — **self·pity·ing** \-tē-iŋ\ *adj* — **self·pity·ing·ly** \-iŋ-lē\ *adv*

self·pleased \-'plēzd\ *adj* (1748) : SELF-SATISFIED

self·poise \-'pȯiz\ *n* (1854) : the quality or state of being self-poised

self·poised \-'pȯizd\ *adj* (1621) : having poise through self-command

self·pol·li·nate \'self-'pä-lə-ˌnāt\ *vt* (1890) : SELF 2 ~ *vi* : to undergo self-pollination

self·pol·li·na·tion \ˌself-ˌpä-lə-'nā-shən\ *n* (1872) : the transfer of pollen from the anther of a flower to the stigma of the same flower or sometimes to that of a genetically identical flower (as of the same plant or clone)

self·por·trait \-'pȯr-trət, -'pȯr-, -ˌtrāt\ *n* (1831) : a portrait of oneself done by oneself

self·pos·sessed \-pə-'zest *also* -'sest\ *adj* (1818) : having or showing self-possession : composed in mind or manner : CALM — **self·pos·sessed·ly** \-'ze-səd-lē, -'se-; -'zest-lē, -'sest-\ *adv*

self·pos·ses·sion \-pə-'ze-shən *also* -'se-\ *n* (1745) : control of one's emotions or reactions esp. when under stress : PRESENCE OF MIND, COMPOSURE **syn** see CONFIDENCE

self·pres·er·va·tion \-ˌpre-zər-'vā-shən\ *n* (ca. 1614) **1** : preservation of oneself from destruction or harm **2** : a natural or instinctive tendency to act so as to preserve one's own existence

self·pride \'self-'prīd\ *n* (ca. 1586) : pride in oneself or in that which relates to oneself

self·pro·pelled \ˌself-prə-'peld\ *adj* (1899) **1** : containing within itself the means for its own propulsion ⟨a ~ vehicle⟩ **2** : mounted on or fired from a moving vehicle ⟨a ~ gun⟩

self·pro·pel·ling \-'pe-liŋ\ *adj* (1862) : SELF-PROPELLED 1

self·pro·pul·sion \-'pəl-shən\ *n* (ca. 1934) : propulsion by one's own power

self·pub·lished \-'pə-blisht\ *adj* (1975) : published by the author ⟨~ book⟩

self·pu·ri·fi·ca·tion \-ˌpyu̇r-ə-fə-'kā-shən\ *n* (1919) **1** : purification by natural process ⟨~ of water⟩ **2** : purification of oneself

self·ques·tion \'self-'kwes-chən, -'kwesh-\ *n* (1917) : a question asked of oneself by oneself

self·ques·tion·ing \-chə-niŋ\ *n* (1856) : examination of one's own actions and motives

self·rat·ing \-'rā-tiŋ\ *n* (1925) : determination of one's own rating with reference to a standard scale

self·re·al·i·za·tion \-ˌrē-ə-lə-'zā-shən, -ˌri-ə-\ *n* (1874) : fulfillment by oneself of the possibilities of one's character or personality

self·re·al·i·za·tion·ism \-shə-ˌni-zəm\ *n* (ca. 1874) : the ethical theory that the highest good for a person consists in realizing or fulfilling oneself usu. on the assumption that one has certain inborn abilities constituting one's real or ideal self — **self·re·al·i·za·tion·ist** \-sh(ə-)nist\ *n*

self·rec·og·ni·tion \-ˌre-kig-'ni-shən, -kəg-\ *n* (1946) **1** : recognition of one's own self **2** : the process by which the immune system of an organism distinguishes between the body's own chemicals, cells, and tissues and those of foreign organisms and agents

self·re·cord·ing \-ri-'kȯr-diŋ\ *adj* (1875) : making an automatic record ⟨~ instruments⟩

self·re·flec·tion \-ri-'flek-shən\ *n* (1652) : SELF-EXAMINATION 1

self·re·flec·tive \-ri-'flek-tiv\ *adj* (1875) : marked by or engaging in self-reflection

self·re·gard \-ri-'gärd\ *n* (1595) : regard for or consideration of oneself or one's own interests

self·re·gard·ing \-ri-'gär-diŋ\ *adj* (1789) : concerned with oneself or one's own interests

self·reg·u·lat·ing \-'re-gyə-ˌlā-tiŋ\ *adj* (1837) : regulating oneself or itself; *esp* : AUTOMATIC ⟨a ~ mechanism⟩

self·re·li·ance \-ri-'lī-ən(t)s\ *n* (1833) : reliance on one's own efforts and abilities

---

\ə\ abut \ᵊ\ kitten, F table \ər\ further \a\ ash \ā\ ace \ä\ mop, mar
\au̇\ out \ch\ chin \e\ bet \ē\ easy \g\ go \i\ hit \ī\ ice \j\ job
\ŋ\ sing \ō\ go \ȯ\ law \ȯi\ boy \th\ thin \t͟h\ the \ü\ loot \u̇\ foot
\y\ yet \zh\ vision \á, k̲, ⁿ, œ, œ̄, ᵫ, ᵭ, ᵞ\ see Guide to Pronunciation

self-re-li-ant \-ənt\ *adj* (1848) : having confidence in and exercising one's own powers or judgment

self-rep-li-cat-ing \-'re-plə-ˌkā-tiŋ\ *adj* (1946) : reproducing itself autonomously ⟨DNA is a ∼ molecule⟩ — **self-rep-li-ca-tion** \-ˌre-plə-'kā-shən\ *n*

self-re-spect \-ri-'spekt\ *n* (ca. 1814) **1 :** a proper respect for oneself as a human being **2 :** regard for one's own standing or position

self-re-spect-ing \-ri-'spek-tiŋ\ *adj* (1786) : having or characterized by self-respect

self-re-veal-ing \-ri-'vē-liŋ\ *adj* (1839) : marked by self-revelation

self-rev-e-la-tion \-ˌre-və-'lā-shən\ *n* (1852) : revelation of one's own thoughts, feelings, and attitudes esp. without deliberate intent

self-re-ward-ing \-ri-'wȯr-diŋ\ *adj* (1740) : containing or producing its own reward ⟨virtue is ∼⟩

self-right-teous \-'rī-chəs\ *adj* (ca. 1680) : convinced of one's own righteousness esp. in contrast with the actions and beliefs of others : narrow-mindedly moralistic — **self-right-teous-ly** *adv* — **self-right-teous-ness** *n*

self-ris-ing flour \'self-'rī-ziŋ-\ *n* (1854) : a commercially prepared mixture of flour, salt, and a leavening agent

self-rule \'self-'rül\ *n* (ca. 1855) : SELF-GOVERNMENT

self-rul-ing \-'rü-liŋ\ *adj* (ca. 1680) : SELF-GOVERNING

self-sac-ri-fice \'self-'sa-krə-ˌfīs *also* -fəs *or* -ˌfīz\ *n* (1805) : sacrifice of oneself or one's interest for others or for a cause or ideal

self-sac-ri-fic-er \-ˌfī-sər *also* -fə- *or* -ˌfī-\ *n* (1668) : one that practices self-sacrifice

self-sa-cri-fic-ing \-ˌfīs-iŋ *also* -fə- *or* -ˌfī-\ *adj* (1817) : sacrificing oneself for others — **self-sac-ri-fic-ing-ly** \-siŋ-lē\ *adv*

self-same \'self-ˌsām\ *adj* (15c) : being the one mentioned or in question : IDENTICAL ⟨left the ∼ day⟩ *syn* see SAME — **self-same-ness** \-ˌsām-nəs, -'sām-\ *n*

self-sat-is-fac-tion \ˌself-ˌsa-təs-'fak-shən\ *n* (1739) : a usu. smug satisfaction with oneself or one's position or achievements

self-sat-is-fied \'self-'sa-təs-ˌfīd\ *adj* (1734) : feeling or showing self-satisfaction

self-scru-ti-ny \'self-'skrü-t²n-ē, -'skrüt-nē\ *n* (ca. 1711) : SELF-EXAMINATION

self-seal-ing \'self-'sē-liŋ\ *adj* (1924) **1 :** capable of sealing itself (as after puncture) ⟨a ∼ tire⟩ **2 :** capable of being sealed by pressure without the addition of moisture ⟨∼ envelopes⟩

self-search-ing \-sər-chiŋ\ *n* (1687) : SELF-QUESTIONING

self-seek-er \-'sē-kər\ *n* (1632) : a self-seeking person

¹self-seek-ing \-kiŋ\ *n* (ca. 1586) : the act or practice of selfishly advancing one's own ends

²self-seeking *adj* (ca. 1628) : seeking only to further one's own interests

self-serve \'self-'sərv\ *adj* (1926) : permitting self-service

self-ser-vice \'self-'sər-vəs\ *n* (1919) : the serving of oneself (as in a restaurant or service station) with goods or services to be paid for at a cashier's desk or by means of a coin-operated mechanism — **self-service** *adj*

self-serv-ing \-'sər-viŋ\ *adj* (1827) : serving one's own interests often in disregard of the truth or the interests of others — **self-serv-ing-ly** *adv*

self-slaugh-ter \-'slȯ-tər\ *n* (1602) : SUICIDE 1a

self-slaugh-tered \-tərd\ *adj* (1593) : killed by oneself

self-sow \'self-'sō\ *vi* -sowed \-'sōd\; -sown \-'sōn\ *or* -sowed; -sow-ing (1608) : to sow itself by dropping seeds or by natural action (as of wind or water)

self-start-er \ˌself-'stär-tər\ *n* (1894) **1 :** STARTER 3a **2 :** a person who has initiative

self-start-ing \-'stär-tiŋ\ *adj* (1866) : capable of starting by oneself or itself

self-ster-ile \-'ster-əl\ *adj* (1876) : sterile to its own pollen or sperm — **self-ste-ril-i-ty** \-stə-'ri-lə-tē\ *n*

self-stick \'self-'stik\ *adj* (1947) : capable of adhering to a surface by application of pressure without the addition of moisture

self-stim-u-la-tion \ˌself-ˌstim-yə-'lā-shən\ *n* (1947) : stimulation of oneself as a result of one's own activity or behavior ⟨electrical ∼ of the brain⟩; *esp* : MASTURBATION — **self-stim-u-la-to-ry** \-'stim-yə-lə-ˌtȯr-ē, -ˌtȯr-\ *adj*

self-study \'self-'stə-dē\ *n* (1683) : study of oneself; *also* : a record of observations from such study

self-styled \-'stī(ə)ld\ *adj* (1823) : called by oneself ⟨∼ experts⟩

self-sub-sis-tent \ˌself-səb-'sis-tənt\ *adj* (1647) : subsisting independently of anything external to itself — **self-sub-sis-tence** \-tən(t)s\ *n*

self-sub-sist-ing \-'sis-tiŋ\ *adj* (1654) : SELF-SUBSISTENT

self-suf-fi-cien-cy \-sə-'fi-shən(t)-sē\ *n* (1623) : the quality or state of being self-sufficient

self-suf-fi-cient \-'fi-shənt\ *adj* (1589) **1 :** able to maintain oneself or itself without outside aid : capable of providing for one's own needs **2 :** having an extreme confidence in one's own ability or worth : HAUGHTY, OVERBEARING

self-suf-fic-ing \-'fi-siŋ *also* -ziŋ\ *adj* (1687) : SELF-SUFFICIENT — **self-suf-fic-ing-ly** *adv* — **self-suf-fic-ing-ness** *n*

self-sug-ges-tion \ˌself-səg-'jes-chən, -sə-, -'jesh-\ *n* (1892) : AUTOSUGGESTION

self-sup-port \ˌself-sə-'pȯrt, -'pȯrt\ *n* (1774) : independent support of oneself or itself — **self-sup-port-ed** *adj*

self-supporting *adj* (1829) : characterized by self-support: as **a** : meeting one's needs by one's own efforts or output **b :** supporting itself or its own weight ⟨a ∼ wall⟩

self-sus-tain-ing \-sə-'stā-niŋ\ *adj* (1844) **1 :** maintaining or able to maintain oneself or itself by independent effort **2 :** maintaining or able to maintain itself once commenced ⟨a ∼ nuclear reaction⟩

self-taught \'self-'tȯt\ *adj* (1725) **1 :** having knowledge or skills acquired by one's own efforts without formal instruction ⟨a ∼ musician⟩ **2 :** learned by oneself ⟨∼ knowledge⟩

self-tol-er-ance \-'tä-lə-rən(t)s, -'täl-rən(t)s\ *n* (1964) : the physiological state that exists in an organism when its immune system has proceeded far enough in the process of self-recognition to lose the capacity to attack and destroy its own bodily constituents

self-treat-ment \-'trēt-mənt\ *n* (1886) : medication of oneself or treatment of one's own disease or condition without medical supervision or prescription

self-trust \-'trəst\ *n* (1583) : SELF-CONFIDENCE

self-will \-'wil\ *n* (14c) : stubborn or willful adherence to one's own desires or ideas : OBSTINACY

self-willed \-'wild\ *adj* (14c) : governed by one's own will : not yielding to the wishes of others : OBSTINATE — **self-willed-ly** \-'wild-lē\ *adv* — **self-willed-ness** \-'wild-nəs\ *n*

self-wind-ing \-'wīn-diŋ\ *adj* (1825) : not needing to be wound by hand ⟨a ∼ watch⟩

self-worth \-'wərth\ *n* (1944) : SELF-ESTEEM

Sel-juk \'sel-ˌjük, sel-'\ *or* **Sel-ju-ki-an** \sel-'jü-kē-ən\ *adj* [Turk *Selçuk*, eponymous ancestor of the dynasties] (1834) **1 :** of or relating to any of several Turkish dynasties ruling over a great part of western Asia in the 11th, 12th, and 13th centuries **2 :** of, relating to, or characteristic of a Turkish people ruled over by a Seljuk dynasty — **Seljuk** *or* **Seljukian** *n*

¹sell \'sel\ *vb* **sold** \'sōld\; **sell-ing** [ME, fr. OE *sellan*; akin to OHG *sellen* to sell, ON *sala* sale, Gk *helein* to take] *vt* (bef. 12c) **1 :** to deliver or give up in violation of duty, trust, or loyalty : BETRAY — often used with *out* **2 a** (1) : to give up (property) to another for something of value (as money) (2) : to offer for sale **b :** to give up in return for something else esp. foolishly or dishonorably ⟨*sold* his birthright for a mess of pottage⟩ **c :** to exact a price for ⟨*sold* their lives dearly⟩ **3 a :** to deliver into slavery for money **b :** to give into the power of another ⟨*sold* his soul to the devil⟩ **c :** to deliver the personal services of for money **4 :** to dispose of or manage for profit instead of in accordance with conscience, justice, or duty ⟨*sold* their votes⟩ **5 a :** to develop a belief in the truth, value, or desirability of : gain acceptance for ⟨trying to ∼ a program to the Congress⟩ **b :** to persuade or influence to a course of action or to the acceptance of something ⟨∼ children on reading⟩ **6 :** to impose on : CHEAT **7 a :** to cause or promote the sale of ⟨using television advertising to ∼ cereal⟩ **b :** to make or attempt to make sales to **c :** to influence or induce to make a purchase **8 :** to achieve a sale of ⟨*sold* a million copies⟩ ∼ *vi* **1 :** to dispose of something by sale **2 :** to achieve a sale; *also* : to achieve satisfactory sales ⟨hoped that the new line would ∼⟩ **3 :** to have a specified price — **sell-able** \'se-lə-bəl\ *adj* — **sell down the river :** to betray the faith of — **sell short 1 :** to make a short sale **2 :** to fail to value properly : UNDERESTIMATE

²sell *n* (1838) **1 :** a deliberate deception : HOAX **2 :** the act or an instance of selling

³sell *or* **selle** \'sel\ *n* [ME *selle*, fr. MF, fr. L *sella* — more at SETTLE] (15c) *archaic* : SADDLE

⁴sell *chiefly Scot var of* SELL

sell-er \'se-lər\ *n* (13c) **1 :** one that offers for sale **2 :** a product offered for sale and selling well, to a specified extent, or in a specified manner ⟨a million-copy ∼⟩ ⟨a poor ∼⟩

seller's market *n* (1932) : a market in which goods are scarce, buyers have a limited range of choice, and prices are high — compare BUYER'S MARKET

selling climax *n* (ca. 1949) : a sharp decline in stock prices for a short time on very heavy trading volume followed by a rally

sell-ing-plat-er \'se-liŋ-ˌplā-tər\ *n* (1886) : a horse that runs in selling races

selling point *n* (1923) : an aspect or detail of something that is emphasized (as in selling or promoting)

selling race *n* (1898) : a claiming race in which the winning horse is put up for auction

sell-off \-ˌȯf\ *n* (1937) : a usu. sudden sharp decline in security prices accompanied by increased volume of trading

sell off *vi* (ca. 1700) : to suffer a drop in prices

sell-out \'sel-ˌaut\ *n* (1859) **1 :** the act or an instance of selling out **2 :** something sold out; *esp* : something (as a concert or contest) for which all tickets are sold **3 :** one who sells out

sell out *vt* (1796) **1 :** to sell the goods of (a debtor) in order to satisfy creditors **2 :** to sell security or commodity holdings of his. to satisfy an uncovered margin **3 a :** to sell all the available tickets for **b :** to sell all of ⟨the merchandise was quickly *sold out*⟩ ∼ *vi* **1 :** to dispose of one's goods by sale; *esp* : to sell one's business **2 :** to betray one's cause or associates **3 :** to be or achieve a sellout

sel-syn \'sel-ˌsin\ *n* [*self-synchronizing*] (1926) : a system comprising a generator and a motor so connected by wire that angular rotation or position in the generator is reproduced simultaneously in the motor — called also *synchro*

selt-zer \'selt-sər\ *n* [modif. of G *Selterser* (*Wasser*) water of Selters, fr. Nieder *Selters*, Germany] (1775) : artificially carbonated water

sel-vage *or* **sel-vedge** \'sel-vij\ *n* [ME *selvage*, prob. fr. MD *selvegge*, *selvage*, fr. *selv* self + *egge* edge; akin to OE *self* and to OE *ecg* edge — more at EDGE] (15c) **1 a :** the edge on either side of a woven or flat-knitted fabric so finished as to prevent raveling; *specif* : a narrow border often of different or heavier threads than the fabric and sometimes in a different weave **b :** an edge (as of fabric or paper) meant to be cut off and discarded **2 :** an outer or peripheral part : BORDER, EDGE — **sel-vaged** *or* **sel-vedged** \-vijd\ *adj*

selves *pl of* SELF

se-man-tic \si-'man-tik\ *also* **se-man-ti-cal** \-ti-kəl\ *adj* [Gk *sēmantikos* significant, fr. *sēmainein* to signify, mean, fr. *sēma* sign, token] (1894) **1 :** of or relating to meaning in language **2 :** of or relating to semantics — **se-man-ti-cal-ly** \-ti-k(ə-)lē\ *adv*

se-man-ti-cist \-'man-tə-sist\ *n* (1902) : a specialist in semantics

se-man-tics \si-'man-tiks\ *n pl but sing or pl in constr* (1893) **1 :** the study of meanings: **a :** the historical and psychological study and the classification of changes in the signification of words or forms viewed as factors in linguistic development **b** (1) : SEMIOTIC (2) : a branch of semiotic dealing with the relations between signs and what they refer to and including theories of denotation, extension, naming, and truth **2 :** GENERAL SEMANTICS **3 a :** the meaning or relationship of meanings of a sign or set of signs; *esp* : connotative meaning **b :** the language used (as in advertising or political propaganda) to achieve a desired effect on an audience esp. through the use of words with novel or dual meanings

¹sem-a-phore \'se-mə-ˌfōr, -ˌfȯr\ *n* [Gk *sēma* sign, signal + ISV *-phore*]

semaphore 2: alphabet; 3 positions following Z: error, end of word, numerals follow; numerals 1, 2, 3, 4, 5, 6, 7, 8, 9, 0 same as A through J

(1816) **1** : an apparatus for visual signaling (as by the position of one or more movable arms) **2** : a system of visual signaling by two flags held one in each hand

²**semaphore** *vb* **-phored; -phor·ing** *vt* (1893) : to convey (information) by or as if by semaphore ~ *vi* : to send signals by or as if by semaphore

se·ma·si·ol·o·gy \si-ˌmä-sē-ˈä-lə-jē, -ˌmä-zē-\ *n* [ISV, fr. Gk *sēmasia* meaning, fr. *sēmainein* to mean] (1857) : SEMANTICS 1 — **se·ma·si·o·log·i·cal** \-sē-ə-ˈlä-ji-kəl, -zē-\ *adj*

¹**sem·bla·ble** \ˈsem-blə-bəl\ *adj* [ME, fr. MF, fr. OF, fr. *sembler* to be like, seem] (14c) **1** : SIMILAR **2** : SUITABLE **3** : APPARENT, SEEMING — **sem·bla·bly** \-blə-blē\ *adv*

²**semblable** *n* (15c) **1** *archaic* : something similar : LIKE **2** : one that is like oneself : one's fellow

sem·blance \ˈsem-blən(t)s\ *n* [ME, fr. MF, fr. OF *sembler* to be like, seem — more at RESEMBLE] (14c) **1 a** : outward and often specious appearance or show : FORM ⟨wrapped in a ~ of composure —Harry Hervey⟩ **b** : MODICUM ⟨has been struggling to get some ~ of justice for his people —Bayard Rustin⟩ **2** : ASPECT, COUNTENANCE **3 a** : a phantasmal form : APPARITION **b** : IMAGE, LIKENESS **4** : actual or apparent resemblance

seme \ˈsēm\ *n* [Gk *sēma* sign] (ca. 1866) **1** : a linguistic sign **2** : any of the basic components of the meaning of a morpheme

se·mei·ol·o·gy *var of* SEMIOLOGY

se·mei·ot·ic *var of* SEMIOTIC

Sem·e·le \ˈse-mə-ˌlē\ *n* [L, fr. Gk *Semelē*] : a daughter of Cadmus consumed by flames when visited by Zeus in his divine splendor

sem·eme \ˈse-ˌmēm\ *n* [ISV, fr. Gk *sēma* + ISV *-eme*] (1913) **1** : the meaning of a morpheme **2 a** : SEME 2 **b** : a class of related semes — **se·me·mic** \sə-ˈmē-mik\ *adj*

se·men \ˈsē-mən\ *n* [ME, fr. L, seed, semen; akin to OHG *sāmo* seed, L *serere* to sow — more at SOW] (14c) : a viscid whitish fluid of the male reproductive tract consisting of spermatozoa suspended in secretions of accessory glands

se·mes·ter \sə-ˈmes-tər\ *n* [G, fr. L *semestris* half-yearly, fr. *sex* six + *mensis* month — more at SIX, MOON] (1827) **1** : either of the two usu. 18-week periods of instruction into which an academic year is often divided **2** : a period of six months — **se·mes·tral** \-trəl\ *or* **se·mes·tri·al** \-trē-əl\ *adj*

semester hour *n* (1922) : a unit of academic credit representing an hour of class (as lecture class) or three hours of laboratory work each week for an academic semester

¹**semi** \ˈse-mē *also* -ˌmī\ *n, pl* **sem·is** [short for *semidetached*] (1912) *chiefly Brit* : a semidetached house

²**semi** \ˈse-ˌmī *also* -mē\ *n, pl* **sem·is** (1942) : SEMITRAILER

³**semi** *same as* ²\ *n, pl* **sem·is** (1942) : SEMIFINAL — often used in pl.

semi- \ˌse-mē-, -ˌmī-, -mi-\ *prefix* [ME, fr. L; akin to OHG *sāmi-* half, Gk *hēmi-*] **1 a** : precisely half of: (1) : forming a bisection of ⟨*semi*diameter⟩ (2) : being a usu. vertically bisected form of ⟨a specified architectural feature⟩ ⟨*semi*dome⟩ **b** : half in quantity or value : half of or occurring halfway through a specified period of time ⟨*semi*annual⟩ ⟨*semi*monthly⟩ — compare BI- **2** : to some extent : partly : incompletely ⟨*semi*civilized⟩ ⟨*semi*-independent⟩ ⟨*semi*dry⟩ — compare DEMI-, HEMI- **3 a** : partial : incomplete ⟨*semi*consciousness⟩ ⟨*semi*darkness⟩ **b** : having some of the characteristics of ⟨*semi*porcelain⟩ **c** : QUASI- ⟨*semi*governmental⟩ ⟨*semi*monastic⟩

semi·ab·stract \-ab-ˈstrakt, -ˈab-ˌ\ *adj* (1871) : having subject matter that is easily recognizable although the form is stylized ⟨~ art⟩ — **semi·ab·strac·tion** \-ab-ˈstrak-shən\ *n*

semi·an·nu·al \-ˈan-yə-(wə)l\ *adj* (1794) : occurring every six months or twice a year — **semi·an·nu·al·ly** *adv*

semi—an·tique \-an-ˈtēk\ *adj* (ca. 1930) : being approximately 50 to 100 years old ⟨a ~ carpet⟩ — **semi—antique** *n*

semi·aquat·ic \-ə-ˈkwä-tik, -ˈkwa-\ *adj* (1833) : growing equally well in or adjacent to water; *also* : frequenting but not living wholly in water

semi·ar·bo·re·al \-är-ˈbōr-ē-əl, -ˈbor-\ *adj* (1938) : often inhabiting and frequenting trees but not completely arboreal

semi·ar·id \-ˈar-əd\ *adj* (1898) : characterized by light rainfall; *esp* : having from about 10 to 20 inches (25 to 51 centimeters) of annual precipitation — **semi·arid·i·ty** \-ə-ˈri-də-tē, -a-ˈri-\ *n*

semi·au·to·bio·graph·i·cal \-ˌȯ-tə-ˌbī-ə-ˈgra-fi-kəl\ *adj* (1939) : partly autobiographical ⟨a ~ comedy⟩

semi·au·to·mat·ic \-ˌȯ-tə-ˈma-tik\ *adj* (1890) : not fully automatic: as **a** : operated partly automatically and partly by hand **b** *of a firearm* : employing gas pressure or force of recoil and mechanical spring action to eject the empty cartridge case after the first shot and load the next cartridge from the magazine but requiring release and another pressure of the trigger for each successive shot — **semiautomatic** *n* — **semi·au·to·mat·i·cal·ly** \-ti-k(ə-)lē\ *adv*

semi·au·ton·o·mous \-ˌȯ-ˈtä-nə-məs\ *adj* (1915) : largely self-governing within a larger political or organizational entity

semi·breve \ˈse-mē-ˌbrēv, ˈse-ˌmī-, -mi-, -ˌbrev\ *n* (15c) : WHOLE NOTE

semi·cen·ten·ni·al \-ˌsen-ˈte-nē-əl\ *n* (1859) : a 50th anniversary or its celebration — **semicentennial** *adj*

semi·cir·cle \ˈse-mē-ˌsər-kəl, ˈse-ˌmī-, -mi-\ *n* [L *semicirculus*, fr. *semi-* + *circulus* circle] (1526) **1** : a half of a circle **2** : an object or arrangement of objects in the form of a half circle — **semi·cir·cu·lar** \ˌse-mē-ˈsər-kyə-lər\ *adj*

semicircular canal *n* (1748) : any of the loop-shaped tubular parts of the labyrinth of the ear that together constitute a sensory organ associated with the maintenance of bodily equilibrium — see EAR illustration

semi·civ·i·lized \ˌse-mē-ˈsi-və-ˌlīzd, ˌse-ˌmī-, -mi-\ *adj* (1836) : partly civilized

semi·clas·sic \-ˈkla-sik\ *n* (1843) : a semiclassical work (as of music)

semi·clas·si·cal \-si-kəl\ *adj* (1904) : having some of the characteristics of the classical: as **a** : of, relating to, or being a musical composition that acts as a bridge between classical and popular music **b** : of, relating to, or being a classical composition that has developed popular appeal

semi·co·lon \ˈse-mē-ˌkō-lən, ˈse-ˌmī-, -mi-\ *n* (1644) : a punctuation mark ; used chiefly in a coordinating function between major sentence elements (as independent clauses of a compound sentence)

semi·co·lo·nial \ˌse-mē-kə-ˈlō-nyəl, ˌse-ˌmī-, -mi-, -nē-əl\ *adj* (1932) **1** : nominally independent but actually under foreign domination **2** : dependent on foreign nations as suppliers of manufactured goods and as purchasers of raw materials — **semi·co·lo·nial·ism** \-nyə-ˌli-zəm, -nē-ə-\ *n*

semi·col·o·ny \-ˈkä-lə-nē\ *n* (1945) : a semicolonial state

semi·com·mer·cial \-kə-ˈmər-shəl\ *adj* (1926) : of, relating to, adapted to, or characterized by limited marketing of an experimental product

semi·con·duct·ing \ˌse-mē-kən-ˈdək-tiŋ, ˌse-ˌmī-, -mi-\ *adj* (1782) : of, relating to, or having the characteristics of a semiconductor

semi·con·duc·tor \-ˈdək-tər\ *n* (1838) : any of a class of solids (as germanium or silicon) whose electrical conductivity is between that of a conductor and that of an insulator in being nearly as great as that of a metal at high temperatures and nearly absent at low temperatures

semi·con·scious \-ˈkän(t)-shəs\ *adj* (1839) : incompletely conscious : imperfectly aware or responsive — **semi·con·scious·ness** *n*

semi·con·ser·va·tive \-kən-ˈsər-və-tiv\ *adj* (1957) : relating to or being genetic replication in which a double-stranded molecule of nucleic acid separates into two single strands each of which serves as a template for the formation of a complementary strand that together with the template forms a complete molecule — **semi·con·ser·va·tive·ly** *adv*

semi·crys·tal·line \-ˈkris-tə-lən\ *adj* (1816) : incompletely or imperfectly crystalline

semi·cy·lin·dri·cal \-sə-ˈlin-dri-kəl\ *adj* (ca. 1731) : having the shape of a longitudinal half of a cylinder

semi·dark·ness \-ˈdärk-nəs\ *n* (1849) : partial darkness

semi·de·ify \-ˈdē-ə-ˌfī, -ˈdā-\ *vt* (1953) : to regard as somewhat godlike

semi·des·ert \-ˈde-zərt\ *n* (1849) : an arid area that has some of the characteristics of a desert but has greater annual precipitation

semi·de·tached \-di-ˈtacht\ *adj* (1859) : forming one of a pair of residences joined into one building by a common sidewall

semi·di·am·e·ter \-dī-ˈa-mə-tər\ *n* (14c) : RADIUS; *specif* : the apparent radius of a generally spherical celestial body

semi·di·ur·nal \-dī-ˈər-nᵊl\ *adj* (1594) **1** : relating to or accomplished in half a day **2** : occurring twice a day **3** : occurring approximately every half day ⟨the ~ tides⟩

semi·di·vine \-də-ˈvīn\ *adj* (1600) : more than mortal but not fully divine

semi·doc·u·men·ta·ry \-ˌdä-kyə-ˈmen-tə-rē, -ˈmen-ˌtrē\ *n* (1939) : a motion picture that uses many details taken from actual events or situations in presenting a fictional story — **semidocumentary** *adj*

semi·dome \ˈse-mē-ˌdōm, ˈse-ˌmī-, -mi-\ *n* (1788) : a roof or ceiling covering a semicircular or nearly semicircular room or recess — **semi·domed** \-ˌdōmd\ *adj*

semi·do·mes·ti·ca·tion \ˌse-mē-də-ˌmes-ti-ˈkā-shən, ˌse-ˌmī-, -mi-\ *n* (ca. 1835) : a captive state of a wild animal in which its living conditions and often its breeding are controlled by humans — **semi·do·mes·ti·cat·ed** \-də-ˈmes-ti-ˌkā-təd\ *adj*

semi·dom·i·nant \-ˈdä-mə-nənt, -ˈdäm-nənt\ *adj* (1942) : producing an intermediate phenotype in the heterozygous condition ⟨a ~ mutant gene⟩

semi·dry \-ˈdrī\ *adj* (1878) : moderately dry

semi·dry·ing \-ˈdrī-iŋ\ *adj* (1905) : that dries imperfectly or slowly — used of some oils (as cottonseed oil)

semi·dwarf \-ˈdwȯrf\ *adj* (1959) : of or being a plant of a variety that is undersized but larger than a dwarf ⟨~ wheats⟩ — **semidwarf** *n*

semi·em·pir·i·cal \-im-ˈpir-ə-kəl, -em-\ *adj* (1935) : partly empirical; *esp* : involving assumptions, approximations, or generalizations designed to simplify calculation or to yield a result in accord with observation

semi·erect \-ə-ˈrekt\ *adj* (1822) **1** : incompletely upright in bodily posture ⟨~ primates⟩ **2** : erect for half the length ⟨~ stems⟩

semi·ev·er·green \-ˈe-vər-ˌgrēn\ *adj* (1901) **1** : having functional and persistent foliage during part of the winter or dry season **2** : tending to be evergreen in a mild climate but deciduous in a rigorous climate

---

\ə\ abut \ᵊ\ kitten, F table \ər\ further \a\ ash \ā\ ace \ä\ mop, mar \aú\ out \ch\ chin \e\ bet \ē\ easy \g\ go \i\ hit \ī\ ice \j\ job \ŋ\ sing \ō\ go \ȯ\ law \ȯi\ boy \th\ thin \t̲h̲\ the \ü\ loot \ú\ foot \y\ yet \zh\ vision \ȧ, k̲, ⁿ, œ, œ̄, ᵫ, ᵫ̄, ᵊ\ *see* Guide to Pronunciation

semi·feu·dal \-'fyü-d⁰l\ *adj* (1898) : having some characteristics of feudalism

¹**semi·fi·nal** \-'fī-n⁰l\ *adj* (1884) **1** : being next to the last in an elimination tournament **2** : of or participating in a semifinal

²**semi·fi·nal** \'se-mē-,fī-n⁰l, 'se-,mī-, -mi-\ *n* (1895) **1** : a semifinal match **2** : a semifinal round — **semi·fi·nal·ist** \,se-mē-'fī-n⁰l-ist, ,se-,mī-, -mi-\ *n*

semi·fin·ished \,se-mē-'fi-nisht, ,se-,mī-, -mi-\ *adj* (1902) : partially finished or processed; *esp, of steel* : rolled from raw ingots into shapes (as bars, billets, or plates) suitable for further processing

semi·fit·ted \-'fi-təd\ *adj* (ca. 1950) : conforming somewhat to the lines of the body

semi·flex·i·ble \-'flek-sə-bəl\ *adj* (1925) **1** : somewhat flexible **2** *of a book cover* : having a thin board stiffener under the covering material

semi·flu·id \-'flü-əd\ *adj* (ca. 1735) : having the qualities of both a fluid and a solid : VISCOUS ⟨fluid and ~ lubricants⟩ — **semifluid** *n*

semi·for·mal \-'fòr-mal\ *adj* (1906) : being or suitable for an occasion of moderate formality ⟨a ~ dinner⟩ ⟨~ gowns⟩

semi·gloss \'se-mē-,gläs, 'se-,mī-, -mi-, -,glós\ *adj* (1937) : having a low luster; *specif* : producing a finish midway between gloss and flat

semi·gov·ern·men·tal \,se-mē-,gəv-ər(n)-'men-t⁰l, ,se-,mī-, -mi-, -,gə-v⁰m-'en-\ *adj* (1919) : having some governmental functions and powers

semi·group \'se-mē-,grüp, 'se-,mī-, -mi-\ *n* (1904) : a mathematical set that is closed under an associative binary operation

semi–in·de·pen·dent \-,in-də-'pen-dənt\ *adj* (1860) : partially independent; *specif* : SEMIAUTONOMOUS

semi·leg·end·ary \-'le-jən-,der-ē\ *adj* (1878) : having historical foundation but elaborated in legend

semi·le·thal \-'lē-thəl\ *n* (1919) : a mutation that in the homozygous condition produces more than 50 percent mortality but not complete mortality — **semilethal** *adj*

semi·liq·uid \-'li-kwəd\ *adj* (1684) : having the qualities of both a liquid and a solid ⟨~ manure⟩ — **semiliquid** *n*

semi·lit·er·ate \-'li-tə-rət *also* -'li-trət\ *adj* (1927) **1 a** : able to read and write on an elementary level **b** : able to read but unable to write **2** : having limited knowledge or understanding : not well-versed — **semiliterate** *n*

semi·log \-'lòg, -'läg\ *adj* (1921) : SEMILOGARITHMIC

semi·log·a·rith·mic \-,lò-gə-'rith-mik, -,lä-\ *adj* (1919) : having one scale logarithmic and the other arithmetic — used of graph paper or of a graph on such paper

semi·lu·nar \-'lü-nər\ *adj* [NL *semilunaris*, fr. L *semi-* + *lunaris* lunar] (1597) : shaped like a crescent

semilunar valve *n* (ca. 1719) : any of the crescent-shaped cusps that occur as a set of three between the heart and the aorta and another of three between the heart and the pulmonary artery, are forced apart by pressure in the ventricles during systole and pushed together by pressure in the arteries during diastole, and prevent regurgitation of blood into the ventricles; *also* : either set of three cusps

semi·lus·trous \-'ləs-trəs\ *adj* (1953) : slightly lustrous

semi·ma·jor axis \-'mā-jər\ *n* (1899) : one half of the major axis of an ellipse (as that formed by the orbit of a planet)

semi·matte *also* **semi·mat** *or* **semi·matt** \-'mat\ *adj* [*semi-* + ²*matte*] (1937) : having a slight luster

semi·met·al \-'me-t⁰l\ *n* (1661) : an element (as arsenic) possessing metallic properties in an inferior degree and not malleable — **semi·me·tal·lic** \,se-mə-'ta-lik\ *adj*

semi·mi·cro \-'mī-(,)krō\ *adj* (1935) : of, relating to, or dealing with quantities intermediate between those treated as micro and macro ⟨~ analysis for chlorine⟩ ⟨a ~ balance⟩

semi·mi·nor axis \-'mī-nər-\ *n* (1909) : one half of the minor axis of an ellipse (as that formed by the orbit of a planet)

semi·moist \-'mòist\ *adj* (1903) : slightly moist

semi·mo·nas·tic \-mə-'nas-tik\ *adj* (1911) : having some features characteristic of a monastic order

¹**semi·month·ly** \-'mən(t)th-lē\ *n* (1851) : a semimonthly publication

²**semimonthly** *adj* (1860) : occurring twice a month

³**semimonthly** *adv* (ca. 1890) : twice a month

semi·mys·ti·cal \-'mis-ti-kəl\ *adj* (1890) : having some of the qualities of mysticism

sem·i·nal \'se-mə-n⁰l\ *adj* [ME, fr. MF, fr. L *seminalis*, fr. *semin-*, *semen* seed — more at SEMEN] (14c) **1** : of, relating to, or consisting of seed or semen **2** : containing or contributing the seeds of later development : CREATIVE, ORIGINAL ⟨a ~ book⟩ ⟨one of the most ~ of the great poets⟩ — **sem·i·nal·ly** \-n⁰l-ē\ *adv*

seminal duct *n* (ca. 1909) : a tube or passage serving esp. or exclusively as an efferent duct of the testis and in the human male being made up of the tubules of the epididymis, the vas deferens, and the ejaculatory duct

seminal fluid *n* (ca. 1929) **1** : SEMEN **2** : the part of the semen that is produced by various accessory glands : semen excepting the spermatozoa

seminal vesicle *n* (ca. 1890) : either of a pair of glandular pouches that lie one on either side of the male reproductive tract and in the human male secrete a sugar- and protein-containing fluid into the ejaculatory duct

sem·i·nar \'se-mə-,när\ *n* [G, fr. L *seminarium* nursery] (1889) **1** : a group of advanced students studying under a professor with each doing original research and all exchanging results through reports and discussions **2 a** (1) : a course of study pursued by a seminar (2) : an advanced or graduate course often featuring informality and discussion **b** : a scheduled meeting of a seminar or a room for such meetings **3** : a meeting for giving and discussing information

sem·i·nar·i·an \,se-mə-'ner-ē-ən\ *n* (1794) : a student in a seminary esp. of the Roman Catholic Church

sem·i·na·rist \'se-mə-nə-rist\ *n* (1835) : SEMINARIAN

sem·i·nary \'se-mə-,ner-ē\ *n, pl* **-nar·ies** [ME, seedbed, nursery, fr. L *seminarium*, fr. *semin-*, *semen* seed] (1542) **1** : an environment in which something originates and from which it is propagated ⟨a ~ of vice and crime⟩ **2 a** : an institution of secondary or higher education **b** : an institution for the training of candidates for the priesthood, ministry, or rabbinate

semi·nat·u·ral \,se-mē-'na-chə-rəl, ,se-,mī-, -mi-, -'nach-rəl\ *adj* (ca. 1962) : modified by human influence but retaining many natural features ⟨a ~ park⟩

sem·i·nif·er·ous \,se-mə-'ni-f(ə-)rəs\ *adj* [L *semin-*, *semen* seed + E *-iferous*] (1692) : producing or bearing seed or semen

seminiferous tubule *n* (1860) : any of the coiled threadlike tubules that make up the bulk of the testis and are lined with a layer of epithelial cells from which the spermatozoa are produced

Sem·i·nole \'se-mə-,nōl\ *n, pl* **Seminoles** *or* **Seminole** [Creek *simanóli* fugitive, wild, alter. of *simalóni*, fr. AmerSp *cimarrón* wild] (1771) : a member of any of the groups of American Indians that emigrated to Florida from Georgia and Alabama in the 18th century and that are now located in southern Florida and Oklahoma

semi·no·mad \-'nō-,mad, ,se-,mī-, -mi-\ *n* (ca. 1934) : a member of a people living usu. in portable or temporary dwellings and practicing seasonal migration but having a base camp at which some crops are cultivated — **semi·no·mad·ic** \-nō-'ma-dik\ *adj*

semi·nude \-'nüd, -'nyüd\ *adj* (1849) : partially nude — **semi·nu·di·ty** \-'nü-də-tē, -'nyü-\ *n*

semi·of·fi·cial \-ə-'fi-shəl\ *adj* (1806) : having some official authority or standing — **semi·of·fi·cial·ly** \-'fi-sh(ə-)lē\ *adv*

se·mi·ol·o·gy \,sē-mē-'ä-lə-jē, ,se-mē-, ,sē-,mī-\ *n* [Gk *sēmeion* sign] (ca. 1890) : the study of signs; *esp* : SEMIOTIC — **se·mi·o·log·i·cal** \-(,)sē-,mī-ə-'lä-ji-kəl, ,se-mē-ə-\ *adj* — **se·mi·o·log·i·cal·ly** \-ə-'lä-ji-k(ə-)lē\ *adv* — **se·mi·ol·o·gist** \-'ä-lə-jist\ *n*

semi·opaque \,se-mē-ō-'pāk, ,se-,mī-, -mi-\ *adj* (1691) : nearly opaque

se·mi·o·sis \,sē-mē-'ō-səs, ,se-mē-, ,sē-,mī-\ *n* [NL, fr. Gk *sēmeiōsis* observation of signs, fr. *sēmeioun* to observe signs, fr. *sēmeion*] (ca. 1907) : a process in which something functions as a sign to an organism

se·mi·ot·ic \-'ä-tik\ *or* **se·mi·ot·ics** \-tiks\ *n, pl* **semiotics** [Gk *sēmeiōtikos* observant of signs, fr. *sēmeiousthai* to interpret signs, fr. *sēmeion* sign, fr. *sēma* sign] (1880) : a general philosophical theory of signs and symbols that deals esp. with their function in both artificially constructed and natural languages and comprises syntactics, semantics, and pragmatics — **semiotic** *adj* — **se·mi·o·ti·cian** \-ə-'ti-shən\ *n* — **se·mi·ot·i·cist** \-'ä-tə-sist\ *n*

semi·pal·mat·ed \,se-mē-'pal-,mā-təd, ,se-,mī-, -mi-, -'pāl-, -'pä-\ *adj* (1785) : having the toes joined only part way down with a web ⟨a plover with ~ feet⟩

semi·par·a·sit·ic \-,par-ə-'si-tik\ *adj* (ca. 1880) : of, relating to, or being a parasitic plant that contains some chlorophyll and is capable of photo·synthesis — **semi·par·a·site** \-'par-ə-,sīt\ *n*

semi·per·ma·nent \-'pər-mə-nənt, -'pərm-nənt\ *adj* (ca. 1890) : lasting or intended to last for a long time but not permanent

semi·per·me·able \-'pər-mē-ə-bəl\ *adj* (1888) : partially but not freely or wholly permeable; *specif* : permeable to some usu. small molecules but not to other usu. larger particles ⟨a ~ membrane⟩ — **semi·per·me·abil·i·ty** \-,pər-mē-ə-'bi-lə-tē\ *n*

semi·po·lit·i·cal \-pə-'li-ti-kəl\ *adj* (1857) : of, relating to, or involving some political features or activity

semi·pop·u·lar \-'pä-pyə-lər\ *adj* (1860) : somewhat popular

semi·por·ce·lain \-'pòr-s(ə-)lən, -'pòr-\ *n* (1880) : any of several ceramic wares resembling or imitative of porcelain; *esp* : a relatively high-fired and hard-glazed white earthenware widely used for tableware

semi·por·no·graph·ic \-,pòr-nə-'gra-fik\ *adj* (1964) : somewhat pornographic — **semi·por·nog·ra·phy** \-,pòr-'nä-grə-fē\ *n*

semi·post·al \-'pōs-t⁰l\ *n* (1927) : a postage stamp sold at a premium over its postal value esp. for a humanitarian purpose

semi·pre·cious \-'pre-shəs\ *adj* (ca. 1890) *of a gemstone* : of less commercial value than a precious stone

semi·pri·vate \-'prī-vət\ *adj* (1876) : of, receiving, or associated with hospital service giving a patient more privileges than a ward patient but fewer than a private patient

semi·pro \'se-mē-,prō, 'se-,mī-, -mi-\ *adj or n* (1908) : SEMIPROFESSIONAL

¹**semi·pro·fes·sion·al** \,se-mē-prə-'fesh-nəl, ,se-,mī-, -mi-, -'fe-shə-n⁰l\ *adj* (1897) : one who engages in an activity (as a sport) semiprofessionally

²**semiprofessional** *adj* (1900) **1** : engaging in an activity for pay or gain but not as a full-time occupation **2** : engaged in by semiprofessional players ⟨~ baseball⟩ — **semi·pro·fes·sion·al·ly** *adv*

semi·pub·lic \-'pə-blik\ *adj* (1804) **1** : open to some persons outside the regular constituency **2** : having some features of a public institution; *specif* : maintained as a public service by a private nonprofit organization

semi·quan·ti·ta·tive \-'kwän-tə-,tā-tiv\ *adj* (1927) : constituting or involving less than quantitative precision — **semi·quan·ti·ta·tive·ly** *adv*

semi·qua·ver \'se-mē-,kwā-vər, 'se-,mī-, -mi-\ *n* (1576) : SIXTEENTH NOTE

semi·re·li·gious \,se-mē-ri-'li-jəs, ,se-,mī-, -mi-\ *adj* (1864) : somewhat religious

semi·re·tired \-ri-'tīrd\ *adj* (1937) : working only part-time esp. because of age or ill health

semi·re·tire·ment \-'tīr-mənt\ *n* (1923) : the state or condition of being semiretired

semi·rig·id \-'ri-jəd\ *adj* (1908) **1** : rigid to some degree or in some parts **2** *of an airship* : having a flexible cylindrical gas container with an attached stiffening keel that carries the load

semi·rur·al \-'rür-əl\ *adj* (1835) : somewhat rural

semi·sa·cred \-'sā-krəd\ *adj* (1898) : SEMIRELIGIOUS

semi·se·cret \-'sē-krət\ *adj* (1917) : not publicly announced but widely known nevertheless

semi·sed·en·tary \-'se-d⁰n-,ter-ē\ *adj* (ca. 1930) : sedentary during part of the year and nomadic otherwise ⟨~ tribes⟩

semi·shrub·by \'se-mē-,shrə-bē, 'se-,mī-, -mi-, *esp Southern* -,srə-\ *adj* (1930) : resembling or being a subshrub

semi·skilled \,se-mē-'skild, ,se-,mī-, -mi-\ *adj* (1916) : having or requiring less training than skilled labor and more than unskilled labor

semi·soft \-'sòft\ *adj* (ca. 1903) : moderately soft; *specif* : firm but easily cut ⟨~ cheese⟩

semi·sol·id \-'sä-ləd\ *adj* (1834) : having the qualities of both a solid and a liquid : highly viscous — **semisolid** *n*

semi·sub·mers·ible \-səb-'mər-sə-bəl\ *adj* (1962) : being a floating deepwater drilling platform that is towed to a desired location and then partially flooded for stabilization and usu. anchored — **semisubmersible** *n*

semi·sweet \-'swēt\ *adj* (1943) : slightly sweetened ⟨~ chocolate⟩

semi·syn·thet·ic \-sin-'the-tik\ *adj* (1937) **1 :** produced by chemical alteration of a natural starting material ⟨~ penicillins⟩ **2 :** containing both chemically identified and complex natural ingredients ⟨a ~ diet⟩

Sem·ite \'se-,mīt, *esp Brit* 'sē-,mīt\ *n* [F *sémite*, fr. *Sem* Shem, fr. LL, fr. Gk *Sēm*, fr. Heb *Shēm*] (1848) **1 a :** a member of any of a number of peoples of ancient southwestern Asia including the Akkadians, Phoenicians, Hebrews, and Arabs **b :** a descendant of these peoples **2 :** a member of a modern people speaking a Semitic language

semi·ter·res·tri·al \,se-mē-tə-'res-trē-əl, ,se-,mī-, -mi-, -'res-chəl, -'resh-\ *adj* (1919) **1 :** growing on boggy ground **2 :** frequenting but not living wholly on land

¹**Se·mit·ic** \sə-'mi-tik *also* -'me-\ *adj* [G *semitisch*, fr. *Semit*, *Semite* Semite, prob. fr. NL *Semita*, fr. LL *Sem* Shem] (1813) **1 :** of, relating to, or constituting a subfamily of the Afro-Asiatic language family that includes Hebrew, Aramaic, Arabic, and Amharic **2 :** of, relating to, or characteristic of the Semites **3 :** JEWISH

²**Semitic** *n* (1875) : any or all of the Semitic languages

Se·mit·i·cist \sə-'mi-tə-sist\ *n* (1956) : SEMITIST

Se·mit·ics \-'mi-tiks\ *n pl but sing in constr* (1895) : the study of the language, literature, and history of Semitic peoples; *specif* : Semitic philology

Sem·i·tism \'se-mə-,ti-zəm\ *n* (1851) **1 a :** Semitic character or qualities **b :** a characteristic feature of a Semitic language occurring in another language **2 :** policy favorable to Jews : predisposition in favor of Jews

Sem·i·tist \-tist\ *n* (1885) **1 :** a scholar of the Semitic languages, cultures, or histories **2** *often not cap* : a person favoring or disposed to favor the Jews

semi·ton·al \,se-mē-'tō-nᵊl, ,se-,mī-, -mi-\ *adj* (1863) : CHROMATIC 3a, SEMITONIC — **semi·ton·al·ly** *adv*

semi·tone \'se-mē-,tōn, 'se-,mī-, -mi-\ *n* (15c) : the tone at a half step; *also* : HALF STEP — **semi·ton·ic** \,se-mē-'tä-nik, ,se-,mī-, -mi-\ *adj* — **semi·ton·i·cal·ly** \-ni-k(ə-)lē\ *adv*

semi·trail·er \'se-,mī-,trā-lər, 'se-mē-, -mi-\ *n* (1919) **1 :** a freight trailer that when attached is supported at its forward end by the fifth wheel device of the truck tractor **2 :** a trucking rig made up of a tractor and a semitrailer

semi·trans·lu·cent \,se-mē-,tran(t)s-'lü-sᵊnt, ,se-,mī-, -mi-, -,tranz-\ *adj* (1832) : somewhat translucent

semi·trans·par·ent \-,tran(t)s-'par-ənt, -'per-\ *adj* (ca. 1793) : imperfectly transparent

semi·trop·i·cal \-'trä-pi-kəl\ *also* **semi·trop·ic** \-pik\ *adj* (1853) : SUBTROPICAL

semi·trop·ics \-piks\ *n pl* (1908) : SUBTROPICS

semi·vow·el \'se-mē-,vaū(-ə)l, 'se-,mī-, -mi-\ *n* (1530) **1 :** a speech sound (as \y\, \w\, or \r\) that has the articulation of a vowel but that is shorter in duration and is treated as a consonant in syllabication **2** : a letter representing a semivowel

¹**semi·week·ly** \,se-mē-'wē-klē, ,se-,mī-, -mi-\ *adj* (1791) : occurring twice a week — **semiweekly** *adv*

²**semiweekly** *n* (1833) : a semiweekly publication

semi·works \'se-mē-,works, 'se-,mī-, -mi-\ *n pl, often attrib* (1926) : a manufacturing plant operating on a limited commercial scale to provide final tests of a new product or process

semi·year·ly \,se-mē-'yir-lē, ,se-,mī-, -mi-\ *adj* (ca. 1928) : occurring twice a year

sem·o·li·na \,se-mə-'lē-nə\ *n* [It *semolino*, dim. of *semola* bran, fr. L *simila* wheat flour] (1797) : the purified middlings of hard wheat (as durum) used esp. for pasta (as macaroni or spaghetti)

sem·per·vi·vum \,sem-pər-'vī-vəm\ *n* [NL, fr. L, neuter of *sempervivus* ever-living, fr. *semper* ever + *vivus* living — more at QUICK] (1591) : any of a large genus (*Sempervivum*) of Old World fleshy herbs of the orpine family often grown as ornamentals

sem·pi·ter·nal \,sem-pi-'tər-nᵊl\ *adj* [ME, fr. LL *sempiternalis*, fr. L *sempiternus*, fr. *semper* ever, always, fr. *sem-* one, same (akin to ON *samr* same) + *per* through — more at SAME, FOR] (15c) : of neverending duration : ETERNAL — **sem·pi·ter·nal·ly** *adv*

sem·pi·ter·ni·ty \-'tər-nə-tē\ *n* (1599) : ETERNITY

sem·ple \'sem-pəl\ *adj* [alter. of *simple*] (1759) *Scot* : of humble birth

sem·pli·ce \'sem-pli-,chā\ *adj or adv* [It, fr. L *simplic-*, *simplex* — more at SIMPLE] (ca. 1740) : SIMPLE — used as a direction in music

sem·pre \'sem-(,)prā\ *adv* [It, fr. L *semper*] (ca. 1801) : ALWAYS — used in music directions ⟨~ legato⟩

semp·stress \'sem(p)-strəs\ *var of* SEAMSTRESS

¹**sen** \'sen\ *n, pl* **sen** [Jp] (1875) — see *yen* at MONEY table

²**sen** *n, pl* **sen** [Malay, prob. fr. E *cent*] (1952) — see *dollar, ringgit, rupiah* at MONEY table

³**sen** *n, pl* **sen** [Khmer *sein*, prob. fr. F *cent*, abbr. of *centime* centime] (1964) — see *riel* at MONEY table

se·nar·i·us \si-'nar-ē-əs, -'ner-\ *n, pl* **se·nar·ii** \-ē-,ī, -ē-,ē\ [L, fr. *senarius* consisting of six each, fr. *seni* six each, fr. *sex* six — more at SIX] (1540) : a verse consisting of six feet esp. in Latin prosody

se·na·ry \'se-nə-rē, 'sē-\ *adj* [L *senarius* consisting of six] (1661) : of, based on, or characterized by six : compounded of six things or six parts ⟨~ scale⟩ ⟨~ division⟩

sen·ate \'se-nət\ *n* [ME *senat*, fr. OF, fr. L *senatus*, fr. *sen-*, *senex* old, old man — more at SENIOR] (13c) **1 :** an assembly or council usu. possessing high deliberative and legislative functions: as **a :** the supreme council of the ancient Roman republic and empire **b :** the second chamber in the bicameral legislature of a major political unit (as a nation, state, or province) **2 :** the hall or chamber in which a senate meets **3 :** a governing body of some universities charged with maintaining academic standards and regulations and usu. composed of the principal or representative members of the faculty

sen·a·tor \'se-nə-tər\ *n* [ME *senatour*, fr. OF *senateur*, fr. L *senator*, fr. *senatus*] (13c) : a member of a senate — **sen·a·tor·ship** \-,ship\ *n*

sen·a·to·ri·al \,se-nə-'tōr-ē-əl, -'tòr-\ *adj* (1740) : of, relating to, or befitting a senator or a senate ⟨~ office⟩ ⟨~ rank⟩

senatorial courtesy *n* (1884) : a custom of the U.S. Senate of refusing to confirm a presidential appointment of an official in or from a state when the appointment is opposed by the senators or senior senator of the president's party from that state

senatorial district *n* (1785) : a territorial division from which a senator is elected — compare CONGRESSIONAL DISTRICT

sen·a·to·ri·an \,se-nə-'tōr-ē-ən, -'tòr-\ *adj* (1614) : SENATORIAL; *specif* : of or relating to the ancient Roman senate

se·na·tus con·sul·tum \sə-,nä-təs-kən-'səl-təm, -'sùl-təm\ *n, pl* **senatus con·sul·ta** \-tə\ [L, decree of the senate] (1696) : a decree of the ancient Roman senate

¹**send** \'send\ *vb* **sent** \'sent\; **send·ing** [ME, fr. OE *sendan*; akin to OHG *sendan* to send, OE *sith* road, journey, OIr *sét* path, way] *vt* (bef. 12c) **1 a :** to cause to go: as **a :** to propel or throw in a particular direction **b :** DELIVER ⟨*sent* a blow to the chin⟩ **c :** DRIVE ⟨*sent* the ball between the goalposts⟩ **2 :** to cause to happen ⟨whatever fate may ~⟩ **3 :** to dispatch by a means of communication **4 a :** to direct, order, or request to go **b :** to permit or enable to attend a term or session ⟨~ a daughter to college⟩ **c :** to direct by advice or reference **d :** to cause or order to depart : DISMISS **5 a :** to force to go : drive away **b** : to cause to assume a specified state ⟨*sent* them into a rage⟩ **6 :** to cause to issue: as **a :** to pour out : DISCHARGE ⟨clouds ~*ing* forth rain⟩ **b :** UTTER ⟨~ forth a cry⟩ **c :** EMIT ⟨*sent* out waves of perfume⟩ **d :** to grow out (parts) in the course of development ⟨a plant ~*ing* forth shoots⟩ **7 :** to cause to be carried to a destination; *esp* : to consign to death or a place of punishment **8 :** to convey or cause to be conveyed or transmitted by an agent ⟨~ a package by mail⟩ ⟨*sent* out invitations⟩ **9 :** to strike or thrust so as to impel violently ⟨*sent* him sprawling⟩ **10 :** DELIGHT, THRILL ~ *vi* **1 a :** to dispatch someone to convey a message or do an errand — often used with ⟨~ out for pizza⟩ **b :** to dispatch a request or order — often used with *away* **2** : SCEND **3 :** TRANSMIT — **send·er** *n* — **send for :** to request by message to come : SUMMON — **send packing :** to send off or dismiss roughly or in disgrace

²**send** *n* (1726) : the lift of a wave

send down *vt* (1853) *Brit* : to suspend or expel from a university

send in *vt* (1715) **1 :** to cause to be delivered ⟨*send in* a letter of complaint⟩ **2 :** to give (one's name or card) to a servant when making a call **3 :** to send (a player) into an athletic contest

send–off \'send-,òf\ *n* (1872) : a demonstration of goodwill and enthusiasm for the beginning of a new venture (as a trip)

send–up \-,əp\ *n* (1958) : PARODY, TAKEOFF

send up *vt* (1852) **1 :** to sentence to imprisonment : send to jail **2** : to make fun of : SATIRIZE, PARODY

se·ne \'sä-(,)nā\ *n, pl* **sene** [Samoan, fr. E *cent*] (1967) — see *tala* at MONEY table

Sen·e·ca \'se-ni-kə\ *n, pl* **Seneca** *or* **Senecas** [D *Sennecaas*, pl., the Iroquois living west of the Mohawks] (ca. 1616) **1 :** a member of an American Indian people of what is now western New York **2 :** the Iroquoian language of the Seneca people

seneca snakeroot *n* (1789) : a milkwort (*Polygala senega*) of eastern No. America having racemes of small white flowers — called also *rattlesnake root*, *senega root;* compare SENEGA

se·ne·cio \si-'nē-sh(ē-,)ō\ *n, pl* **-cios** [NL, fr. L, old man, groundsel (fr. its hoary pappus), fr. *sen-*, *senic-*, *senex* old man] (ca. 1890) : any of a genus (*Senecio*) of widely distributed composite plants that have alternate or basal leaves and flower heads usu. with yellow ray flowers

se·nec·ti·tude \si-'nek-tə-,tüd, -,tyüd\ *n* [ML *senectitudo*, alter. of L *senectus* old age, fr. *sen-*, *senic-*, *senex* old, old man — more at SENIOR] (1796) : the final stage of the normal life span

sen·e·ga \'se-ni-gə\ *n* (1748) : the dried root of seneca snakeroot that contains an irritating saponin and is used medicinally

senega root *n* [alter. of *Seneca* root; fr. its use by the Seneca as a remedy for snakebite] (ca. 1846) **1** : SENECA SNAKEROOT **2 :** SENEGA

seneca snakeroot

se·nes·cence \si-'ne-sᵊn(t)s\ *n* [*senescent*, fr. L *senescent-*, *senescens*, prp. of *senescere* to grow old, fr. *sen-*, *senex* old] (1695) **1 :** the state of being old : the process of becoming old **2 :** the growth phase in a plant or plant part (as a leaf) from full maturity to death — **se·nes·cent** \-sᵊnt\ *adj*

sen·e·schal \'se-nə-shəl\ *n* [ME, fr. MF, of Gmc origin; akin to Goth *sineigs* old and to OHG *scalc* servant — more at SENIOR] (14c) : an agent or steward in charge of a lord's estate in feudal times

se·nhor \si-'nyōr, -'nyòr\ *n, pl* **senhors** *or* **se·nho·res** \-'nyòr-ēsh, -'nyòr-, -ēzh, -ēs, -ēz\ [Pg, fr. ML *senior* superior, lord, fr. L, adj., elder] (1795) : a Portuguese or Brazilian man — used as a title equivalent to *Mr.*

se·nho·ra \-'nyòr-ə, -'nyòr-\ *n* [Pg, fem. of *senhor*] (1802) : a married Portuguese or Brazilian woman — used as a title equivalent to *Mrs.*

se·nho·ri·ta \,se-nyə-'rē-tə\ *n* [Pg, fr. dim. of *senhora*] (1874) : an unmarried Portuguese or Brazilian girl or woman — used as a title equivalent to *Miss*

se·nile \'sē-,nīl *also* 'se-\ *adj* [L *senilis*, fr. *sen-*, *senex* old, old man] (1661) **1 :** of, relating to, exhibiting, or characteristic of old age ⟨~ weakness⟩; *esp* : exhibiting a loss of mental faculties associated with old age **2 :** approaching the end of a geological cycle of erosion — **se·nile·ly** \-,nīl-lē\ *adv*

senile dementia *n* (ca. 1851) : a mental disorder of old age esp. of the degenerative type associated with Alzheimer's disease

se·nil·i·ty \si-'ni-lə-tē *also* se-\ *n* (1791) : the quality or state of being senile; *specif* : the physical and mental infirmity of old age

¹**se·nior** \'sē-nyər\ *n* [ME, fr. L, fr. *senior*, adj.] (14c) **1 :** a person older than another ⟨five years my ~⟩ **2 a :** a person with higher

\ə\ abut \ᵊ\ kitten, F table \ər\ further \a\ ash \ā\ ace \ä\ mop, mar \aù\ out \ch\ chin \e\ bet \ē\ easy \g\ go \i\ hit \ī\ ice \j\ job \ŋ\ sing \ō\ go \ò\ law \òi\ boy \th\ thin \th\ the \ü\ loot \ù\ foot \y\ yet \zh\ vision \à, k̲, ⁿ, œ, œ̄, ᵫ, ᵫ̄, ᵞ\ *see* Guide to Pronunciation standing or rank **b** : a senior fellow of a college at an English university **c** : a student in the year preceding graduation from a school of secondary or higher level **3** *cap* : a member of a program of the Girl Scouts for girls in the ninth through twelfth grades in school **4** : SENIOR CITIZEN

²senior *adj* [ME, fr. L, older, elder, compar. of *sen-*, *senex* old; akin to Goth *sineigs* old, Gk *henos*] (14c) **1** : of prior birth, establishment, or enrollment — often used to distinguish a father with the same given name as his son **2** : higher ranking : SUPERIOR ⟨~ officers⟩ **3** : of or relating to seniors ⟨the ~ class⟩ **4** : having a claim on corporate assets and income prior to other securities

senior airman *n* (ca. 1977) : an enlisted man in the air force who ranks above an airman first class but who has not been made sergeant

senior chief petty officer *n* (ca. 1960) : an enlisted man in the navy or coast guard ranking above a chief petty officer and below a master chief petty officer

senior citizen *n* (1938) : an elderly person; *esp* : one who has retired

senior high school *n* (1909) : a school usu. including grades 10 to 12

se·nior·i·ty \sēn-'yȯr-ə-tē, -'yär-\ *n* (15c) **1** : the quality or state of being senior : PRIORITY **2** : a privileged status attained by length of continuous service (as in a company)

senior master sergeant *n* (ca. 1962) : a noncommissioned officer in the air force ranking above a master sergeant and below a chief master sergeant

sen·i·ti \'se-nə-tē\ *n, pl* **seniti** [Tongan, modif. of E *cent*] (1967) — see *pa'anga* at MONEY table

sen·na \'se-nə\ *n* [NL, fr. Ar *sanā*] (1543) **1** : any of a genus (*Cassia*) of leguminous herbs, shrubs, and trees native to warm regions; *esp* : one used medicinally **2** : the dried leaflets or pods of various sennas (esp. *Cassia acutifolia* and *C. angustifolia*) used as a purgative

sen·net \'se-nət\ *n* [prob. alter. of obs. *signet* signal] (ca. 1590) : a signal call on a trumpet or cornet for entrance or exit on the stage

sen·night *also* **se'n·night** \'se-,nīt\ *n* [ME, fr. OE *seofon nihta* seven nights] (15c) *archaic* : the space of seven nights and days : WEEK

sen·nit \'se-nət\ *n* [origin unknown] (ca. 1769) **1** : a braided cord or fabric (as of plaited rope yarns) **2** : a straw or grass braid for hats

se·nor *or* **se·ñor** \sān-'yȯr\ *n, pl* **senors** *or* **se·ño·res** \-'yȯr-(,)ās, -'yȯr-\ [Sp *señor*, fr. ML *senior* superior, lord, fr. L, adj., elder] (1622) : a Spanish or Spanish-speaking man — used as a title equivalent to *Mr.*

se·no·ra *or* **se·ño·ra** \sān-'yȯr-ə, -'yȯr-\ *n* [Sp *señora*, fem. of *señor*] (1579) : a married Spanish or Spanish-speaking woman — used as a title equivalent to *Mrs.*

se·no·ri·ta *or* **se·ño·ri·ta** \,sān-yə-'rē-tə\ *n* [Sp *señorita*, fr. dim. of *señora*] (1823) : an unmarried Spanish or Spanish-speaking girl or woman — used as a title equivalent to *Miss*

sen·ryu \'sen-rē-(,)ü\ *n, pl* **senryu** [Jp] (1938) : a 3-line unrhymed Japanese poem structurally similar to haiku but treating human nature usu. in an ironic or satiric vein

sensa *pl of* SENSUM

sen·sate \'sen-,sāt\ *adj* [ME *sensat*, fr. ML *sensatus*, fr. LL, endowed with sense, fr. L *sensus* sense] (15c) **1** : relating to or apprehending or apprehended through the senses **2** : preoccupied with things that can be experienced through a sense modality — **sen·sate·ly** *adv*

sen·sa·tion \sen-'sā-shən, sən-\ *n* [ML *sensation-*, *sensatio*, fr. LL, understanding, idea, fr. L *sensus*] (1615) **1 a** : a mental process (as seeing, hearing, or smelling) due to immediate bodily stimulation often as distinguished from awareness of the process — compare PERCEPTION **b** : awareness (as of heat or pain) due to stimulation of a sense organ **c** : a state of consciousness of a kind usu. due to physical objects or internal bodily changes ⟨a burning ~ in his chest⟩ **d** : an indefinite bodily feeling ⟨a ~ of buoyancy⟩ **2** : something (as a physical object, sense-datum, pain, or afterimage) that causes or is the object of sensation **3 a** : a state of excited interest or feeling ⟨their elopement caused a ~⟩ **b** : a cause of such excitement ⟨the show was the musical ~ of the season⟩; *esp* : one (as a person) in some respect exceptional or outstanding ⟨the rookie hitting ~ of the American League⟩

sen·sa·tion·al \-shnəl, -shə-nᵊl\ *adj* (1840) **1** : of or relating to sensation or the senses **2** : arousing or tending to arouse (as by lurid details) a quick, intense, and usu. superficial interest, curiosity, or emotional reaction **3** : exceedingly or unexpectedly excellent or great — **sen·sa·tion·al·ly** *adv*

sen·sa·tion·al·ise *Brit var of* SENSATIONALIZE

sen·sa·tion·al·ism \-shnə-,li-zəm, -shə-nᵊl-,i-zəm\ *n* (1846) **1** : empiricism that limits experience as a source of knowledge to sensation or sense perceptions **2** : the use or effect of sensational subject matter or treatment — **sen·sa·tion·al·ist** \-list, -ist\ *adj or n* — **sen·sa·tion·al·is·tic** \-,sā-shnə-'lis-tik, -shən-ᵊl-'is-tik\ *adj*

sen·sa·tion·al·ize \-,līz, -,īz\ *vt* **-ized; -iz·ing** (1869) : to present in a sensational manner

¹sense \'sen(t)s\ *n* [ME, fr. MF or L; MF *sens* sensation, feeling, mechanism of perception, meaning, fr. L *sensus*, fr. *sentire* to perceive, feel; perh. akin to OHG *sinnan* to go, strive, OE *sith* journey — more at SEND] (14c) **1** : a meaning conveyed or intended : IMPORT, SIGNIFICATION; *esp* : one of a set of meanings a word or phrase may bear esp. as segregated in a dictionary entry **2 a** : the faculty of perceiving by means of sense organs **b** : a specialized animal function or mechanism (as sight, hearing, smell, taste, or touch) basically involving a stimulus and a sense organ **c** : the sensory mechanisms constituting a unit distinct from other functions (as movement or thought) **3** : conscious awareness or rationality — usu. used in pl. ⟨finally came to his ~s⟩ **4 a** : a particular sensation or kind or quality of sensation ⟨a good ~ of balance⟩ **b** : a definite but often vague awareness or impression ⟨felt a ~ of insecurity⟩ ⟨a ~ of danger⟩ **c** : a motivating awareness ⟨a ~ of shame⟩ **d** : a discerning awareness and appreciation ⟨her ~ of humor⟩ **5** : CONSENSUS ⟨the ~ of the meeting⟩ **6 a** : capacity for effective application of the powers of the mind as a basis for action or response : INTELLIGENCE **b** : sound mental capacity and understanding typically marked by shrewdness and practicality; *also* : agreement with or satisfaction of such power ⟨this decision makes ~⟩ **7** : one of two opposite directions esp. of motion (as of a point, line, or surface)

syn SENSE, COMMON SENSE, JUDGMENT, WISDOM mean ability to reach intelligent conclusions. SENSE implies a reliable ability to judge and decide with soundness, prudence, and intelligence ⟨a choice showing good *sense*⟩. COMMON SENSE suggests an average degree of such ability without sophistication or special knowledge ⟨*common sense* tells me it's wrong⟩. JUDGMENT implies sense tempered and refined by experience, training, and maturity ⟨they relied on her *judgment* for guidance⟩. WISDOM implies sense and judgment far above average ⟨a leader of rare *wisdom*⟩.

²sense *vt* **sensed; sens·ing** (ca. 1531) **1 a** : to perceive by the senses **b** : to be or become conscious of ⟨~ danger⟩ **2** : GRASP, COMPREHEND **3** : to detect automatically esp. in response to a physical stimulus (as light or movement)

sense–datum *n, pl* **sense–data** (1882) : an immediate unanalyzable private object of sensation

sense·ful \'sen(t)s-fəl\ *adj* (1591) : REASONABLE, JUDICIOUS

sense·less \'sen(t)s-ləs\ *adj* (1557) : destitute of, deficient in, or contrary to sense: as **a** : UNCONSCIOUS ⟨knocked ~⟩ **b** : FOOLISH, STUPID ⟨it was some ~ practical joke —A. Conan Doyle⟩ **c** : MEANINGLESS, PURPOSELESS ⟨a ~ murder⟩ — **sense·less·ly** *adv* — **sense·less·ness** *n*

sense organ *n* (1854) : a bodily structure that receives a stimulus (as heat or sound waves) and is affected in such a manner as to initiate a wave of excitation in associated sensory nerve fibers which convey specific impulses to the central nervous system where they are interpreted as corresponding sensations : RECEPTOR

sen·si·bil·ia \,sen(t)-sə-'bi-lē-ə, -'bil-yə\ *n pl* [LL, fr. neut. pl. of L *sensibilis* sensible] (1856) : what may be sensed

sen·si·bil·i·ty \,sen(t)-sə-'bi-lə-tē\ *n, pl* **-ties** (15c) **1** : ability to receive sensations : SENSITIVENESS ⟨tactile ~⟩ **2** : peculiar susceptibility to a pleasurable or painful impression (as from praise or a slight) — often used in pl. **3** : awareness of and responsiveness toward something (as emotion in another) **4** : refined or excessive sensitiveness in emotion and taste with especial responsiveness to the pathetic

¹sen·si·ble \'sen(t)-sə-bəl\ *adj* [ME, fr. MF, fr. L *sensibilis*, fr. *sensus*, pp. of *sentire* to feel] (14c) **1** : of a kind to be felt or perceived: as **a** : perceptible to the senses or to reason or understanding ⟨felt a ~ chill⟩ ⟨her distress was ~ from her manner⟩ **b** *archaic* : perceptibly large : CONSIDERABLE **c** (1) : perceptible as real or material : SUBSTANTIAL ⟨the ~ world in which we live⟩ (2) : of a kind to arouse emotional response ⟨his whipping was a ~ expression of his father's anger⟩ **2 a** : capable of receiving sensory impressions ⟨~ to pain⟩ **b** : receptive to external influences : SENSITIVE ⟨the most ~ reaches of the spirit⟩ **3 a** : perceiving through the senses or mind : COGNIZANT ⟨~ of the increasing heat⟩; *also* : convinced by perceived evidence : SATISFIED ⟨~ of my error⟩ **b** : emotionally aware and responsive ⟨we are ~ of your problems⟩ **c** : CONSCIOUS **4** : having, containing, or indicative of good sense or reason : RATIONAL, REASONABLE ⟨~ people⟩ ⟨made a ~ answer⟩ *syn* see MATERIAL, PERCEPTIBLE, AWARE, WISE — **sen·si·ble·ness** *n* — **sen·si·bly** \-blē\ *adv*

²sensible *n* (1589) : something that can be sensed

sen·sil·lum \sen-'si-ləm\ *also* **sen·sil·la** \-'si-lə\ *n, pl* **-sil·la** \-'si-lə\ *also* **-sil·lae** \-'si-(,)lē\ [NL *sensillum*, dim. of ML *sensus* sense organ, fr. L, sense] (1925) : a simple epithelial sense organ of an invertebrate (as an insect) usu. in the form of a spine, plate, rod, cone, or peg that is composed of one or a few cells with a nerve connection

sen·si·ti·sa·tion, sen·si·tise *Brit var of* SENSITIZATION, SENSITIZE

¹sen·si·tive \'sen(t)-sə-tiv, 'sen(t)s-təv\ *adj* [ME, fr. MF *sensitif*, fr. ML *sensitivus*, prob. alter. of *sensativus*, fr. *sensatus* sensate] (15c) **1** : SENSORY **2** : receptive to sense impressions **b** : capable of being stimulated or excited by external agents (as light, gravity, or contact) ⟨a photographic emulsion ~ to red light⟩ ⟨~ protoplasm⟩ **3** : highly responsive or susceptible: as **a** (1) : easily hurt or damaged; *esp* : easily hurt emotionally (2) : delicately aware of the attitudes and feelings of others **b** : excessively or abnormally susceptible : HYPERSENSITIVE ⟨~ to egg protein⟩ **c** : readily fluctuating in price or demand ⟨~ commodities⟩ **d** : capable of indicating minute differences : DELICATE ⟨~ scales⟩ **e** : readily affected or changed by various agents (as light or mechanical shock) **f** : highly radiosensitive **4 a** : concerned with highly classified government information or involving discretionary authority over important policy matters ⟨~ documents⟩ **b** : calling for tact, care, or caution in treatment : TOUCHY ⟨a ~ issue like race relations⟩ *syn* see LIABLE — **sen·si·tive·ly** *adv* — **sen·si·tive·ness** *n*

²sensitive *n* (1850) **1** : a person having occult or psychical abilities **2** : a sensitive person

sensitive plant *n* (1659) : any of several mimosas (esp. *Mimosa pudica*) with leaves that fold or droop when touched; *broadly* : a plant responding to touch with movement

sen·si·tiv·i·ty \,sen(t)-sə-'ti-və-tē\ *n, pl* **-ties** (1803) : the quality or state of being sensitive: as **a** : the capacity of an organism or sense organ to respond to stimulation : IRRITABILITY **b** : the quality or state of being hypersensitive **c** : the degree to which a radio receiving set responds to incoming waves **d** : the capacity of being easily hurt **e** : awareness of the needs and emotions of others ⟨a book written with just the right mix of empathy and ~ —L.C. Brown⟩

sen·si·ti·za·tion \,sen(t)-sə-tə-'zā-shən, ,sen(t)s-tə-'zā-\ *n* (1887) **1** : the action or process of sensitizing **2** : the quality or state of being sensitized (as to an antigen)

sen·si·tize \'sen(t)-sə-,tīz\ *vb* **-tized; -tiz·ing** ⟨*sensitive* + *-ize*⟩ *vt* (ca. 1859) : to make sensitive or hypersensitive ~ *vi* : to become sensitive — **sen·si·tiz·er** *n*

sen·si·tom·e·ter \,sen(t)-sə-'tä-mə-tər\ *n* [ISV *sensitive* + *-o-* + *-meter*] (1880) : an instrument for measuring sensitivity of photographic material — **sen·si·to·met·ric** \,sen(t)-sə-tə-'me-trik\ *adj* — **sen·si·tom·e·try** \-sə-'tä-mə-trē\ *n*

sen·sor \'sen-,sȯr, 'sen(t)-sər\ *n* [L *sentire* to perceive + E ¹*-or* — more at SENSE] (ca. 1928) : a device that responds to a physical stimulus (as heat, light, sound, pressure, magnetism, or a particular motion) and transmits a resulting impulse (as for measurement or operating a control); *also* : SENSE ORGAN

sen·so·ri·al \sen-'sȯr-ē-əl, -'sȯr-\ *adj* (1768) : SENSORY — **sen·so·ri·al·ly** \-ə-lē\ *adv*

sen·so·ri·mo·tor \,sen(t)s-rē-'mō-tər, ,sen(t)s-rə-\ *adj* [*sensory* + *motor*] (1855) : of, relating to, or functioning in both sensory and motor aspects of bodily activity

sen·so·ri·neu·ral \-'nȯr-əl, -'nyu̇r-\ *adj* (ca. 1977) : of, relating to, or involving the aspects of sense perception mediated by nerves 〈~ hearing loss〉

sen·so·ri·um \sen-'sōr-ē-əm, -'sȯr-\ *n, pl* **-ri·ums** *or* **-ria** \-ē-ə\ [LL, sense organ, fr. L *sentire*] (1647) : the parts of the brain or the mind concerned with the reception and interpretation of sensory stimuli; *broadly* : the entire sensory apparatus

sen·so·ry \'sen(t)s-rē, 'sen(t)-sə-rē\ *adj* (1749) **1** : of or relating to sensation or to the senses **2** : conveying nerve impulses from the sense organs to the nerve centers : AFFERENT

sensory area *n* (1896) : an area of the cerebral cortex that receives afferent nerve fibers from lower sensory or motor areas

sen·su·al \'sen(t)-sh(ə-)wəl, -shəl\ *adj* [ME, fr. LL *sensualis*, fr. L *sensus* sense] (15c) **1** : relating to or consisting in the gratification of the senses or the indulgence of appetite : FLESHLY **2** : SENSORY **3 a** : devoted to or preoccupied with the senses or appetites **b** : VOLUPTUOUS **c** : deficient in moral, spiritual, or intellectual interests : WORLDLY; *esp* : IRRELIGIOUS *syn* see CARNAL, SENSUOUS — **sen·su·al·i·ty** \,sen(t)-shə-'wa-lə-tē\ *n* — **sen·su·al·ly** \'sen(t)-sh(ə-)wə-lē, 'sen-shə-lē\ *adv*

sen·su·al·ism \'sen(t)-sh(ə-)wə-,li-zəm, 'sen-shə-,li-\ *n* (1813) : persistent or excessive pursuit of sensual pleasures and interests — **sen·su·al·ist** \-list\ *n* — **sen·su·al·is·tic** \,sen(t)-sh(ə-)wə-'lis-tik, ,sen-shə-'lis-\ *adj*

sen·su·al·ize \'sen(t)-sh(ə-)wə-,līz, 'sen-shə-,līz\ *vt* -ized; -iz·ing (ca. 1687) : to make sensual — **sen·su·al·i·za·tion** \,sen(t)-sh(ə-)wə-lə-'zā-shən, ,sen-shə-lə-\ *n*

sen·sum \'sen(t)-səm\ *n, pl* **sen·sa** \-sə\ [ML, fr. L, neut. of *sensus*, pp. of *sentire* to feel — more at SENSE] (1868) : SENSE-DATUM

sen·su·ous \'sen(t)-sh(ə-)wəs\ *adj* [L *sensus* sense + E *-ous*] (1640) **1 a** : of or relating to the senses or sensible objects **b** : producing or characterized by gratification of the senses : having strong sensory appeal 〈~ pleasure〉 **2** : characterized by sense impressions or imagery aimed at the senses 〈~ verse〉 **3** : highly susceptible to influence through the senses — **sen·su·os·i·ty** \,sen(t)-shə-'wä-sə-tē\ *n* — **sen·su·ous·ly** \'sen(t)-shə-wəs-lē\ *adv* — **sen·su·ous·ness** *n*

syn SENSUOUS, SENSUAL, LUXURIOUS, VOLUPTUOUS mean relating to or providing pleasure through gratification of the senses. SENSUOUS implies gratification of the senses for the sake of aesthetic pleasure 〈the *sensuous* delights of great music〉. SENSUAL tends to imply the gratification of the senses or the indulgence of the physical appetites as ends in themselves 〈a life devoted to *sensual* pleasures〉. LUXURIOUS suggests the providing of or indulgence of sensuous pleasure inducing bodily ease and languor 〈a *luxurious* hotel〉. VOLUPTUOUS implies more strongly an abandonment esp. to sensual pleasure 〈a *voluptuous* feast〉.

sen·su stric·to \'sen-(,)sü-'strik-(,)tō\ *adv* [NL] (1902) : in a narrow or strict sense

sent *past and past part of* SEND

sen·te \'sen-tē\ *n, pl* **li·cen·te** *or* **li·sen·te** \li-'sen-tē\ [Sesotho, fr. E *cent*] (1966) — see *loti* at MONEY table

¹sen·tence \'sen-t⁹n(t)s, -t⁹nz\ *n* [ME, fr. MF, fr. L *sententia* feeling, opinion, fr. (assumed) *sentent-, sentens*, irreg. prp. of *sentire* to feel — more at SENSE] (14c) **1 a** *obs* : OPINION; *esp* : a conclusion given on request or reached after deliberation **2 a** : JUDGMENT 2a; *specif* : one formally pronounced by a court or judge in a criminal proceeding and specifying the punishment to be inflicted upon the convict **b** : the punishment so imposed 〈serve out a ~〉 **3** *archaic* : MAXIM, SAW **4 a** : a word, clause, or phrase or a group of clauses or phrases forming a syntactic unit which expresses an assertion, a question, a command, a wish, an exclamation, or the performance of an action, that in writing usu. begins with a capital letter and concludes with appropriate end punctuation, and that in speaking is distinguished by characteristic patterns of stress, pitch, and pauses **b** : a mathematical or logical statement (as an equation or a proposition) in words or symbols **5** : PERIOD 2b

²sentence *vt* **sen·tenced; sen·tenc·ing** (1592) **1** : to impose a sentence on **2** : to cause to suffer something 〈*sentenced* these most primitive cultures to extinction —E. W. Count〉

sentence fragment *n* (1947) : a word, phrase, or clause that usu. has in speech the intonation of a sentence but lacks the grammatical structure usu. found in the sentences of formal and esp. written composition

sentence stress *n* (1884) : the manner in which stresses are distributed on the syllables of words assembled into sentences — called also *sentence accent*

sen·ten·tia \sen-'ten(t)-sh(ē-)ə\ *n, pl* **-ti·ae** \-shē-,ē\ [L, lit., feeling, opinion] (1917) : APHORISM — usu. used in pl.

sen·ten·tial \sen-'ten(t)-shəl\ *adj* (1646) **1** : of or relating to a sentence 〈a relative clause with a ~ antecedent〉 **2** : of, relating to, or involving a proposition in logic 〈~ connective〉

sentential calculus *n* (1937) : PROPOSITIONAL CALCULUS

sentential function *n* (1937) : an expression that contains one or more variables and becomes a declarative sentence when constants are substituted for the variables

sen·ten·tious \sen-'ten(t)-shəs\ *adj* [ME, full of meaning, fr. L *sententiosus*, fr. *sententia* sentence, maxim] (1509) **1 a** : given to or abounding in aphoristic expression **b** : given to or abounding in excessive moralizing **2** : terse, aphoristic, or moralistic in expression : PITHY, EPIGRAMMATIC — **sen·ten·tious·ly** *adv* — **sen·ten·tious·ness** *n*

sen·tience \'sen(t)-sh(ē-)ən(t)s, 'sen-tē-ən(t)s\ *n* (1839) **1** : a sentient quality or state **2** : feeling or sensation as distinguished from perception and thought

sen·tient \'sen(t)-sh(ē-)ənt, 'sen-tē-ənt\ *adj* [L *sentient-, sentiens*, prp. of *sentire* to perceive, feel] (1632) **1** : responsive to or conscious of sense impressions **2** : AWARE **3** : finely sensitive in perception or feeling — **sen·tient·ly** *adv*

sen·ti·ment \'sen-tə-mənt\ *n* [F or ML; F, fr. ML *sentimentum*, fr. L *sentire*] (1639) **1 a** : an attitude, thought, or judgment prompted by feeling : PREDILECTION **b** : a specific view or notion : OPINION **2 a** : EMOTION **b** : refined feeling : delicate sensibility esp. as expressed in a work of art **c** : emotional idealism **d** : a romantic or nostalgic feeling verging on sentimentality **3 a** : an idea colored by emotion **b** : the emotional significance of a passage or expression as distinguished from its verbal context *syn* see FEELING, OPINION

sen·ti·men·tal \,sen-tə-'men-t⁹l\ *adj* (1749) **1 a** : marked or governed by feeling, sensibility, or emotional idealism **b** : resulting from feeling rather than reason or thought **2** : having an excess of sentiment or sensibility — **sen·ti·men·tal·ly** *adv*

sen·ti·men·tal·ise *Brit var of* SENTIMENTALIZE

sen·ti·men·tal·ism \,sen-tə-'men-t⁹l-,i-zəm\ *n* (1817) **1** : the disposition to favor or indulge in sentimentality **2** : an excessively sentimental conception or statement **c** : SENTIMENT — **sen·ti·men·tal·ist** \-t⁹l-ist\ *n*

sen·ti·men·tal·i·ty \,sen-tə-,men-'ta-lə-tē, -mən-\ *n, pl* **-ties** (1770) **1** : the quality or state of being sentimental esp. to excess or in affectation **2** : a sentimental idea or its expression

sen·ti·men·tal·ize \-'men-t⁹l-,īz\ *vb* **-ized; -iz·ing** *vi* (1788) : to indulge in sentiment 〈~ *vt* : to look upon or imbue with sentiment — **sen·ti·men·tal·i·za·tion** \-,men-t⁹l-ə-'zā-shən\ *n*

sen·ti·mo \sen-'tē-(,)mō\ *n, pl* **-mos** [Tag, fr. Sp *céntimo*] (1968) — see *peso* at MONEY table

¹sen·ti·nel \'sent-nəl, 'sen-t⁹n-əl\ *n* [MF *sentinelle*, fr. OIt *sentinella*, fr. *sentina* vigilance, fr. *sentire* to perceive, fr. L] (1579) : SENTRY

²sentinel *vt* **-neled** *or* **-nelled; -nel·ing** *or* **-nel·ling** (1593) **1** : to watch over as a sentinel **2** : to furnish with a sentinel **3** : to post as sentinel

sen·try \'sen-trē\ *n, pl* **sentries** [perh. fr. obs. *sentry* sanctuary, watch-tower] (1632) : GUARD, WATCH; *esp* : a soldier standing guard at a point of passage (as a gate)

sentry box *n* (ca. 1728) : a shelter for a sentry on his post

se·pal \'sē-pəl, 'se-\ *n* [NL *sepalum*, fr. *sep-* (irreg. fr. Gk *skepē* covering) + *-alum* (as in *petalum* petal)] (1821) : one of the modified leaves comprising a calyx — see FLOWER illustration

se·pal·oid \-pə-,lȯid\ *adj* (1830) : resembling or functioning as a sepal

sep·a·ra·ble \'se-p(ə-)rə-bəl\ *adj* [ME, fr. L *separabilis*, fr. *separare*] (14c) **1** : capable of being separated or dissociated **2** *obs* : causing separation — **sep·a·ra·bil·i·ty** \,se-p(ə-)rə-'bi-lə-tē\ *n* — **sep·a·ra·ble·ness** *n*

¹sep·a·rate \'se-p(ə-),rāt\ *vb* **-rat·ed; -rat·ing** [ME, fr. L *separatus*, pp. of *separare*, fr. *se-* apart + *parare* to prepare, procure — more at SECEDE, PARE] *vt* (15c) **1 a** : to set or keep apart : DISCONNECT, SEVER **b** : to make a distinction between : DISCRIMINATE, DISTINGUISH 〈~ religion from magic〉 **c** : SORT 〈~ mail〉 **d** : to disperse in space or time : SCATTER 〈widely *separated* homesteads〉 **2** *archaic* : to set aside for a special purpose : CHOOSE, DEDICATE **3** : to part by a legal separation: **a** : to sever conjugal ties with **b** : to sever contractual relations with : DISCHARGE 〈*separated* from the army〉 **4** : to block off : SEGREGATE **5 a** : to isolate from a mixture : EXTRACT 〈~ cream from milk〉 **b** : to divide into constituent parts **6** : to dislocate (as a shoulder) esp. in sports 〈~ *vi* **1** : to become divided or detached **2 a** : to sever an association : WITHDRAW **b** : to cease to live together as a married couple **3** : to go in different directions **4** : to become isolated from a mixture

syn SEPARATE, PART, DIVIDE, SEVER, SUNDER, DIVORCE mean to become or cause to become disunited or disjointed. SEPARATE may imply any of several causes such as dispersion, removal of one from others, or presence of an intervening thing 〈*separated* her personal life from her career〉. PART implies the separating of things or persons in close union or association 〈vowed never to *part*〉. DIVIDE implies separating into pieces or sections by cutting or breaking 〈civil war *divided* the nation〉. SEVER implies violence esp. in the removal of a part or member 〈a *severed* limb〉. SUNDER suggests violent rending or wrenching apart 〈a city *sundered* by racial conflict〉. DIVORCE implies separating two things that commonly interact and belong together 〈cannot *divorce* scientific research from moral responsibility〉.

²sep·a·rate \'se-p(ə-)rət\ *adj* (15c) **1 a** : set or kept apart : DETACHED **b** *archaic* : SOLITARY, SECLUDED **c** : IMMATERIAL, DISEMBODIED **2 a** : not shared with another : INDIVIDUAL 〈~ rooms〉 **b** *often cap* : estranged from a parent body 〈~ churches〉 **3 a** : existing by itself : AUTONOMOUS **b** : dissimilar in nature or identity *syn* see DISTINCT — **sep·a·rate·ly** \-p(ə-)rət-lē, 'se-pərt-lē\ *adv* — **sep·a·rate·ness** \-nəs\ *n*

³sep·a·rate \'se-p(ə-)rət\ *n* (1886) **1** : OFFPRINT **2** : an article of dress designed to be worn interchangeably with others to form various costume combinations — usu. used in pl.

sep·a·ra·tion \,se-pə-'rā-shən\ *n* (14c) **1** : the act or process of separating : the state of being separated **2 a** : a point, line, or means of division **b** : an intervening space : GAP **3 a** : cessation of cohabitation between a married couple by mutual agreement or judicial decree **b** : termination of a contractual relationship (as employment or military service)

sep·a·ra·tion·ist \-sh(ə-)nist\ *n* (1831) : SEPARATIST

sep·a·rat·ism \'se-p(ə-)rə-,ti-zəm\ *n* (1628) : a belief in, movement for, or state of separation (as schism, secession, or segregation)

sep·a·rat·ist \'se-p(ə-)rə-tist, 'se-pə-,ra-\ *n* (1608) : one that favors separatism: as **a** *cap* : one of a group of 16th and 17th century English Protestants preferring to separate from rather than to reform the Church of England **b** : an advocate of independence or autonomy for a part of a political unit (as a nation) **c** : an advocate of racial or cultural separation — **separatist** *adj* — **sep·a·ra·tis·tic** \,se-p(ə-)rə-'tis-tik\ *adj*

sep·a·ra·tive \'se-pə-,rā-tiv, 'se-p(ə-)rə-\ *adj* (1592) : tending toward, causing, or expressing separation

sep·a·ra·tor \'se-p(ə-),rā-tər\ *n* (1607) : one that separates; *esp* : a device for separating liquids of different specific gravities (as cream from milk) or liquids from solids

Se·phar·di \sə-'fär-dē\ *n, pl* **Se·phar·dim** \-'fär-dəm\ [LHeb *sĕphāradhī*, fr. *sĕphāradh* Spain, fr. Heb, region where Jews were once exiled (Obad 1:20)] (1851) : a member of the occidental branch of European Jews settling in Spain and Portugal and later in the Balkans, the Levant, England, the Netherlands, and the Americas; *also* : one of their descendants — compare ASHKENAZI — **Se·phar·dic** \-'fär-dik\ *adj*

¹se·pia \'sē-pē-ə\ *n* [L, cuttlefish, ink, fr. Gk *sēpia*] (1821) **1 a** : the

\ə\ abut \⁹\ kitten, F table \ər\ further \a\ ash \ā\ ace \ä\ mop, mar \au̇\ out \ch\ chin \e\ bet \ē\ easy \g\ go \i\ hit \ī\ ice \j\ job \ŋ\ sing \ō\ go \ȯ\ law \ȯi\ boy \th\ thin \t̲h̲\ the \ü\ loot \u̇\ foot \y\ yet \zh\ vision \á, k, ⁿ, œ, œ̄, ᴜ, ᵫ, ʸ\ see Guide to Pronunciation inky secretion of a cuttlefish **b** : a brown melanin-containing pigment from the ink of cuttlefishes **2** : a print or photograph of a brown color resembling sepia **3** : a brownish gray to dark olive brown color

²**sepia** *adj* (1827) **1** : made of or done in sepia **2** : of the color sepia

se·pi·o·lite \'sē-pē-ə-,līt\ *n* [G *Sepiolith*, fr. Gk *sēpion* cuttlebone (fr. *sēpia*) + G -*lith* -lite] (1854) : MEERSCHAUM 1

se·poy \'sē-,pȯi\ *n* [Pg *sipai*, fr. Hindi *sipāhī*, fr. Per, cavalryman] (ca. 1718) : a native of India employed as a soldier by a European power

sep·pu·ku \se-'pü-(,)kü, 'se-pə-,kü\ *n* [Jp] (1871) : HARA-KIRI 1

sep·sis \'sep-səs\ *n, pl* **sep·ses** \'sep-,sēz\ [NL, fr. Gk *sēpsis* decay, fr. *sēpein* to putrefy] (1876) : a toxic condition resulting from the spread of bacteria or their products from a focus of infection; *esp* : SEPTICEMIA

sept \'sept\ *n* [perh. fr. L *septum, saeptum* enclosure, fold — more at SEPTUM] (1517) : a branch of a family; *esp* : CLAN

sep·tal \'sep-t²l\ *adj* (ca. 1847) : of or relating to a septum

sep·tate \'sep-,tāt\ *adj* (1846) : divided by or having a septum

Sep·tem·ber \sep-'tem-bər, səp-\ *n* [ME *Septembre*, fr. OF & OE, both fr. L *September* (seventh month), fr. *septem* seven — more at SEVEN] (bef. 12c) : the 9th month of the Gregorian calendar

sep·te·nar·i·us \,sep-tə-'nar-ē-əs, -'ner-\ *n, pl* **-nar·ii** \-ē-,ī, -ē-,ē\ [L, fr. *septenarius* of seven, fr. *septeni* seven each, fr. *septem* seven] (1819) : a verse consisting of seven feet esp. in Latin prosody

sep·ten·de·cil·lion \(,)sep-,ten-di-'sil-yən\ *n, often attrib* [L *septendecim* seventeen (fr. *septem* seven + *decem* ten) + E -*illion* (as in *million*) — more at TEN] (ca. 1938) — see NUMBER table

sep·ten·ni·al \sep-'te-nē-əl\ *adj* [LL *septennium* period of seven years, fr. L *septem* + -*ennium* (as in *biennium*)] (1640) **1** : occurring or being done every seven years **2** : consisting of or lasting for seven years — **sep·ten·ni·al·ly** \-ə-lē\ *adv*

sep·ten·tri·on \sep-'ten-trē-,än, -trē-ən\ *n* [ME, fr. MF, fr. L *septentriones*, pl., the seven stars of Ursa Major or Ursa Minor, fr. *septem* seven + *triones* plowing oxen] (14c) *obs* : the northern regions : NORTH

sep·ten·tri·o·nal \-trē-ə-n²l\ *adj* (14c) : NORTHERN

sep·tet \sep-'tet\ *n* [G, fr. L *septem*] (1828) **1** : a musical composition for seven instruments or voices **2** : a group or set of seven; *esp* : the performers of a septet

sep·tic \'sep-tik\ *adj* [L *septicus*, fr. Gk *sēptikos*, fr. *sēpein* to putrefy] (1605) **1** : of, relating to, or causing putrefaction **2** : relating to, involving, or characteristic of sepsis

sep·ti·ce·mia \,sep-tə-'sē-mē-ə\ *n* [NL, fr. L *septicus* + NL -*emia*] (ca. 1860) : invasion of the bloodstream by virulent microorganisms from a local seat of infection accompanied esp. by chills, fever, and prostration — called also *blood poisoning;* compare SEPSIS — **sep·ti·ce·mic** \-'sē-mik\ *adj*

sep·ti·ci·dal \,sep-tə-'sī-d²l\ *adj* [NL *septum* + L -*cidere* to cut, fr. *caedere*] (1819) : dehiscent longitudinally at or along a septum ⟨a ~ fruit⟩

septic sore throat *n* (1924) : STREP THROAT

septic tank *n* (ca. 1902) : a tank in which the solid matter of continuously flowing sewage is disintegrated by bacteria

sep·til·lion \sep-'til-yən\ *n, often attrib* [F, fr. L *septem* + F -*illion* (as in *million*) — more at SEVEN] (1690) — see NUMBER table

sep·tu·a·ge·nar·i·an \(,)sep-,tü-ə-jə-'ner-ē-ən, -,tyü-, -,chü-\ *n* [LL *septuagenarius* seventy years old, fr. L, of or containing seventy, fr. *septuageni* seventy each, fr. *septuaginta*] (1805) : a person whose age is in the seventies — **septuagenarian** *adj*

Sep·tu·a·ge·si·ma \,sep-tə-wə-'je-sə-mə, -'jä-zə-\ *n* [ME, fr. LL, fr. L, fem. of *septuagesimus* seventieth, fr. *septuaginta* seventy; fr. its being approximately seventy days before Easter] (14c) : the third Sunday before Lent

Sep·tu·a·gint \sep-'tü-ə-jənt, -'tyü-; 'sep-tə-wə-,jint\ *n* [LL *Septuaginta*, fr. L, seventy, irreg. fr. *septem* seven + -*ginta* (akin to L *viginti* twenty); fr. the approximate number of its translators — more at SEVEN, VIGESIMAL] (1633) : a Greek version of the Jewish Scriptures redacted in the 3d and 2d centuries B.C. by Jewish scholars and adopted by Greek-speaking Christians — **Sep·tu·a·gin·tal** \(,)sep-,tü-ə-'jin-t²l, -,tyü-; ,sep-tə-wə-\ *adj*

sep·tum \'sep-təm\ *n, pl* **sep·ta** \-tə\ [NL, fr. L *saeptum* enclosure, fence, wall, fr. *saepire* to fence in, fr. *saepes* fence, hedge] (1698) : a dividing wall or membrane esp. between bodily spaces or masses of soft tissue — compare DISSEPIMENT

se·pul·chral \sə-'pəl-krəl *also* -'pul-\ *adj* (1615) : suited to or suggestive of a sepulchre : FUNEREAL, MORTUARY — **se·pul·chral·ly** \-krə-lē\ *adv*

¹**se·pul·chre** *or* **sep·ul·cher** \'se-pəl-kər\ *n* [ME *sepulcre*, fr. OF, fr. L *sepulcrum, sepulchrum,* fr. *sepelire* to bury; akin to Gk *hepein* to care for, Skt *saparyati* he honors] (13c) **1** : a place of burial : TOMB **2** : a receptacle for religious relics esp. in an altar

²**sepulchre** *or* **sepulcher** *vt* **-chred** *or* **-chered; -chring** *or* **-chering** \-k(ə-)riŋ\ (1591) **1** *archaic* : to place in or as if in a sepulchre : BURY **2** *archaic* : to serve as a sepulchre for

sep·ul·ture \'se-pəl-,chu̇r\ *n* [ME, fr. OF, fr. L *sepultura,* fr. *sepultus,* pp. of *sepelire*] (14c) **1** : BURIAL **2** : SEPULCHRE

se·qua·cious \si-'kwā-shəs\ *adj* [L *sequac-, sequax* inclined to follow, fr. *sequi*] (1643) **1** *archaic* : SUBSERVIENT, TRACTABLE **2** : intellectually servile — **se·qua·cious·ly** *adv* — **se·quac·i·ty** \-'kwa-sə-tē\ *n*

se·quel \'sē-kwəl *also* -,kwel\ *n* [ME, fr. MF *sequelle,* fr. L *sequela,* fr. *sequi* to follow — more at SUE] (15c) **1** : CONSEQUENCE, RESULT **2 a** : subsequent development **b** : the next installment (as of a speech or story); *esp* : a literary or cinematic work continuing the course of a story begun in a preceding one

se·quela \si-'kwe-lə\ *n, pl* **se·quel·ae** \-'kwe-(,)lē\ [NL, fr. L, sequel] (ca. 1793) **1** : an aftereffect of disease or injury **2** : a secondary result

¹**se·quence** \'sē-kwən(t)s, -,kwen(t)s\ *n* [ME, fr. ML *sequentia,* fr. LL, sequel, lit., act of following, fr. L *sequent-, sequens,* prp. of *sequi*] (14c) **1** : a hymn in irregular meter between the gradual and Gospel in masses for special occasions (as Easter) **2** : a continuous or connected series: as **a** : an extended series of poems united by a single theme ⟨a sonnet ~⟩ **b** : three or more playing cards usu. of the same suit in consecutive order of rank **c** : a succession of repetitions of a melodic phrase or harmonic pattern each in a new position **d** : a set of elements ordered so that each may be labeled with the positive integers **e** (1) : a succession of related shots or scenes developing a single subject

or phase of a film story (2) : EPISODE **3 a** : order of succession **b** : an arrangement of the tenses of successive verbs in a sentence designed to express a coherent relationship esp. between main and subordinate parts **4 a** : CONSEQUENCE, RESULT **b** : a subsequent development **5** : continuity of progression

²**sequence** *vt* **se·quenced; se·quenc·ing** (1941) **1** : to arrange in a sequence **2** : to determine the sequence of chemical constituents (as amino-acid residues) in ⟨*sequenced* biological macromolecules⟩

se·quenc·er \'sē-kwən(t)-sər, -,kwen(t)-\ *n* (1949) : one that sequences: as **a** : a device for arranging (as events in the ignition of a rocket) in a sequence **b** : a device for determining the order of occurrence of amino acids in a protein

se·quen·cy \'sē-kwən(t)-sē\ *n* [LL *sequentia*] (1818) : SEQUENCE 3a, 5

se·quent \'sē-kwənt\ *adj* [L *sequent-, sequens,* prp.] (1601) **1** : CONSECUTIVE, SUCCEEDING **2** : CONSEQUENT, RESULTANT

se·quen·tial \si-'kwen(t)-shəl\ *adj* (1854) **1** : of, relating to, or arranged in a sequence : SERIAL ⟨~ file systems⟩ **2** : following in sequence **3** : relating to or based on a method of testing a statistical hypothesis that involves examination of a sequence of samples for each of which the decision is made to accept or reject the hypothesis or to continue sampling — **se·quen·tial·ly** \-'kwen(t)-sh(ə-)lē\ *adv*

¹**se·ques·ter** \si-'kwes-tər\ *vt* **-tered; -ter·ing** \-t(ə-)riŋ\ [ME *sequestren,* fr. MF *sequestrer,* fr. L *sequestrare* to hand over to a trustee, fr. *sequester* third party to whom disputed property is entrusted, agent, fr. *secus* beside, otherwise; akin to L *sequi* to follow] (14c) **1 a** : to set apart : SEGREGATE **b** : SECLUDE, WITHDRAW **2 a** : to seize esp. by a writ of sequestration **b** : to place (property) in custody esp. in sequestration **3** : to hold (as a metallic ion) in solution usu. by inclusion in an appropriate coordination complex

²**sequester** *n* (1604) *obs* : SEPARATION, ISOLATION

se·ques·trate \'sē-kwəs-,trāt, 'se-; si-'kwes-\ *vt* **-trat·ed; -trat·ing** [L *sequestratus,* pp. of *sequestrare*] (15c) : SEQUESTER

se·ques·tra·tion \,sē-kwəs-'trā-shən, ,se-; (,)sē-,kwes-\ *n* (15c) **1** : the act of sequestering : the state of being sequestered **2 a** : a legal writ authorizing a sheriff or commissioner to take into custody the property of a defendant who is in contempt until the orders of a court are complied with **b** : a deposit whereby a neutral depositary agrees to hold property in litigation and to restore it to the party to whom it is adjudged to belong

se·ques·trum \si-'kwes-trəm\ *n, pl* **-trums** *also* **-tra** \-trə\ [NL, fr. L, legal sequestration, fr. *sequester*] (1831) : a fragment of dead bone detached from adjoining sound bone

se·quin \'sē-kwən\ *n* [F, fr. It *zecchino,* fr. *zecca* mint, fr. Ar *sikkah* die, coin] (1617) **1** : an old gold coin of Italy and Turkey **2** : a small plate of shining metal or plastic used for ornamentation esp. on clothing

se·quined *or* **se·quinned** \-kwənd\ *adj* (1894) : ornamented with or as if with sequins

se·qui·tur \'se-kwə-tər, -,tu̇r\ *n* [L, it follows, 3d pers. sing. pres. indic. of *sequi* to follow — more at SUE] (1836) : the conclusion of an inference : CONSEQUENCE

se·quoia \si-'kwȯi-ə\ *n* [NL, genus name, fr. *Sequoya* (George Guess)] (ca. 1866) : either of two huge coniferous California trees of the bald cypress family that may reach a height of over 300 feet (90 meters): **a** : BIG TREE **b** : REDWOOD 3a

sera *pl of* SERUM

se·rac \sə-'rak, sā-\ *n* [F *sérac,* lit., a kind of white cheese, fr. ML *seracium* whey, fr. L *serum* whey — more at SERUM] (1860) : a pinnacle, sharp ridge, or block of ice among the crevasses of a glacier

se·ra·glio \sə-'ral-(,)yō, -'räl-\ *n, pl* **-glios** [It *serraglio,* modif. of Turk *saray* palace] (1581) **1** : HAREM 1a **2** : a palace of a sultan

se·rai \sə-'rī\ *n* [Turk & Per; Turk *saray* mansion, palace, fr. Per *sarāī* mansion, inn] (1609) **1** : CARAVANSARY **2** : SERAGLIO 2

ser·al \'sir-əl\ *adj* (1916) : of, relating to, or constituting an ecological sere

se·ra·pe \sə-'rä-pē, -'ra-\ *n* [MexSp *sarape*] (1834) : a colorful woolen shawl worn over the shoulders esp. by Mexican men

ser·aph \'ser-əf\ *n, pl* **ser·a·phim** \-ə-,fim, -,fēm\ *or* **seraphs** [assumed sing. of Heb *śērāphīm*] (1667) : SERAPHIM 2

ser·a·phim \'ser-ə-,fim, -,fēm\ *n pl* [LL *seraphim,* pl., seraphs, fr. Heb *śērāphīm*] (12c) **1** : an order of angels — see CELESTIAL HIERARCHY **2** *sing, pl* **seraphim** : one of the 6-winged angels standing in the presence of God — **se·raph·ic** \sə-'ra-fik\ *adj* — **se·raph·i·cal·ly** \-fi-k(ə-)lē\ *adv*

Se·ra·pis \sə-'rā-pəs\ *n* [L, fr. Gk *Sarapis*] : an Egyptian god combining attributes of Osiris and Apis and having a widespread cult in Ptolemaic Egypt and ancient Greece

Serb \'sərb\ *n* [ultim. fr. Serbo-Croatian *srb*] (1860) **1** : a native or inhabitant of Serbia **2** : SERBIAN 2 — **Serb** *adj*

Ser·bi·an \'sər-bē-ən\ *n* (1848) **1** : SERB 1 **2 a** : the Serbo-Croatian language as spoken in Serbia **b** : a literary form of Serbo-Croatian using the Cyrillic alphabet — **Serbian** *adj*

Ser·bo-Cro·a·tian \,sər-(,)bō-krō-'ā-shən\ *n* (1883) **1** : a Slavic language spoken in Croatia, Bosnia and Herzegovina, Serbia, and Montenegro **2** : a person whose native language is Serbo-Croatian — **Serbo-Croatian** *adj*

¹**sere** \'sir\ *adj* [ME, fr. OE *sēar* dry; akin to OHG *sōrēn* to wither, Gk *hauos* dry, Lith *sausas*] (bef. 12c) **1** : being dried and withered **2** *archaic* : THREADBARE

²**sere** *n* [L *series* series] (1916) : a series of ecological communities formed in ecological succession

¹**ser·e·nade** \,ser-ə-'nād\ *n* [F *sérénade,* fr. It *serenata,* fr. *sereno* clear, calm (of weather), fr. L *serenus* serene] (1649) **1 a** : a complimentary vocal or instrumental performance; *esp* : one given outdoors at night for a woman being courted **b** : a work so performed **2 a** : an instrumental composition in several movements, written for a small ensemble, and midway between the suite and the symphony in style

²**serenade** *vb* **-nad·ed; -nad·ing** *vi* (1668) : to play a serenade ~ *vt* : to perform a serenade in honor of — **ser·e·nad·er** *n*

ser·e·na·ta \,ser-ə-'nä-tə\ *n* [It, serenade] (ca. 1724) : an 18th century secular cantata of a dramatic character usu. composed in honor of an individual or event

ser·en·dip·i·tous \,ser-ən-'di-pə-təs\ *adj* (1943) : obtained or characterized by serendipity ⟨~ discoveries⟩ — **ser·en·dip·i·tous·ly** *adv*

ser·en·dip·i·ty \-'di-pə-tē\ *n* [fr. its possession by the heroes of the Persian fairy tale *The Three Princes of Serendip*] (1754) : the faculty or phenomenon of finding valuable or agreeable things not sought for

¹se·rene \sə-'rēn\ *adj* [L *serenus* clear, cloudless, untroubled] (15c) **1 a** : clear and free of storms or unpleasant change ⟨~ skies⟩ **b** : shining bright and steady ⟨the moon, ~ in glory —Alexander Pope⟩ **2** : AUGUST — used as part of a title ⟨His *Serene* Highness⟩ **3** : marked by or suggestive of utter calm and unruffled repose or quietude ⟨a ~ smile⟩ *syn* see CALM — **se·rene·ly** *adv* — **se·rene·ness** \-'rēn-nəs\ *n*

²serene *n* (1644) **1** *archaic* : a serene condition or expanse (as of sky, sea, or light) **2** *archaic* : SERENITY, TRANQUILLITY

se·ren·i·ty \sə-'re-nə-tē\ *n* (15c) : the quality or state of being serene

serf \'sərf\ *n* [F, fr. OF, fr. L *servus* slave] (1611) : a member of a servile feudal class bound to the soil and subject to the will of his lord — **serf·age** \'sər-fij\ *n* — **serf·dom** \-'sərf-dəm, -təm\ *n*

serge \'sərj\ *n* [ME *sarge*, fr. MF, fr. (assumed) VL *sarica*, alter. of L *serica*, fem. of *sericus* silken — more at SERICEOUS] (14c) : a durable twilled fabric having a smooth clear face and a pronounced diagonal rib on the front and the back

ser·gean·cy \'sär-jən(t)-sē\ *n* (ca. 1670) : the function, office, or rank of a sergeant

ser·geant \'sär-jənt\ *n* [ME, servant, attendant, sergeant, fr. MF *sergent, serjant*, fr. L *servient-, serviens*, prp. of *servire* to serve] (13c) **1** : SERGEANT AT ARMS **2** *obs* : an officer who enforces the judgments of a court or the commands of one in authority **3** : a noncommissioned officer ranking in the army and marine corps above a corporal and below a staff sergeant and in the air force above an airman first class or senior airman and below a staff sergeant; *broadly* : NONCOMMISSIONED OFFICER **4** : an officer in a police force ranking in the U.S. just below captain or sometimes lieutenant and in England just below inspector

sergeant at arms (14c) : an officer of an organization (as a legislative body or court of law) who preserves order and executes commands

sergeant first class *n* (1948) : a noncommissioned officer in the army ranking above a staff sergeant and below a master sergeant

sergeant fish *n* (1873) **1** : COBIA **2** : SNOOK 1

sergeant major *n, pl* **sergeants major** *or* **sergeant majors** (1802) **1** : a noncommissioned officer in the army, air force, or marine corps serving as chief administrative assistant in a headquarters **2** : a noncommissioned officer in the marine corps ranking above a first sergeant **3** : a bluish green to yellow bony fish (*Abudefduf saxatilis* of the family Pomacentridae) with black vertical stripes on the sides that is widely distributed in the western tropical Atlantic Ocean

sergeant major of the army (1966) : the ranking noncommissioned officer of the army serving as adviser to the chief of staff

sergeant major of the marine corps (ca. 1971) : the ranking noncommissioned officer of the marine corps serving as adviser to the commandant

ser·geanty \'sär-jən-tē\ *n, pl* **-geant·ies** [ME *sergeantie*, fr. MF *sergentie*, fr. *sergent* sergeant] (15c) : any of numerous feudal services of a personal nature by which an estate is held of the king or other lord distinct from military tenure and from socage tenure

serg·ing \'sər-jiŋ\ *n* [*serge*] (ca. 1909) : the process of overcasting the raw edges of a piece of fabric (as a carpet) to prevent raveling

¹se·ri·al \'sir-ē-əl\ *adj* (1840) **1** : of, relating to, consisting of, or arranged in a series, rank, or row ⟨~ order⟩ **2** : appearing in successive parts or numbers ⟨a ~ story⟩ **3** : belonging to a series maturing periodically rather than on a single date ⟨~ bonds⟩ **4** : of, relating to, or being music based on a series of tones in a chosen pattern without regard for traditional tonality **5 a** : effecting a series of similar acts over a period of time ⟨a ~ killer⟩ **b** : occurring in such a series ⟨a ~ murder⟩ **6** : relating to or being a connection in a computer system in which the bits of a byte are transmitted sequentially over a single wire — compare PARALLEL — **se·ri·al·ly** \-ə-lē\ *adv*

²serial *n* (1846) **1 a** : a work appearing (as in a magazine or on television) in parts at intervals **b** : one part of a serial work : INSTALLMENT **2** : a publication (as a newspaper or journal) issued as one of a consecutively numbered and indefinitely continued series

se·ri·al·ise *Brit var of* SERIALIZE

se·ri·al·ism \'sir-ē-ə-ˌli-zəm\ *n* (1958) : serial music; *also* : the theory or practice of composing serial music

se·ri·al·ist \-list\ *n* (1846) **1** : a writer of serials **2** : a composer of serial music

se·ri·al·ize \-ˌlīz\ *vt* **-ized; -iz·ing** (1857) : to arrange or publish in serial form — **se·ri·al·i·za·tion** \ˌsir-ē-ə-lə-'zā-shən\ *n*

serial number *n* (1896) : a number indicating place in a series and used as a means of identification

¹se·ri·ate \'sir-ē-ˌāt, -ē-ət\ *adj* [L *series*] (1846) : arranged in a series or succession — **se·ri·ate·ly** *adv*

²se·ri·ate \sir-ē-ˌāt\ *vt* **-at·ed; -at·ing** (ca. 1899) : to arrange in a series

¹se·ri·a·tim \ˌsir-ē-'ā-təm, -'a-\ *adv* [ML, fr. L *series*] (1680) : in a series

²seriatim *adj* (1871) : following seriatim

se·ri·ceous \sə-'ri-shəs\ *adj* [LL *sericeus* silken, fr. L *sericum* silk garment, silk, fr. neut. of *sericus* silken, fr. Gk *sērikos*, fr. *Sēres*, an eastern Asian people, prob. the Chinese] (ca. 1777) : covered with fine silky hair ⟨~ leaf⟩

ser·i·cin \'ser-ə-sən\ *n* [ISV, fr. L *sericum* silk] (ca. 1868) : a gelatinous protein that cements the two fibroin filaments in a silk fiber

seri·cul·ture \'ser-ə-ˌkəl-chər\ *n* [L *sericum* silk + E *culture*] (ca. 1854) : the production of raw silk by raising silkworms — **seri·cul·tur·al** \-ˌkəl-chə-rəl, -ˈkəlch-rəl\ *adj* — **seri·cul·tur·ist** \-rist\ *n*

se·ries \'sir-(ˌ)ēz\ *n, pl* **series** *often attrib* [L, fr. *serere* to join, link together; akin to Gk *eirein* to string together, *hormos* chain, necklace, and perh. to L *sort-, sors* lot] (1611) **1 a** : a number of things or events of the same class coming one after another in spatial or temporal succession ⟨a concert ~⟩ ⟨the hall opened into a ~ of small rooms⟩ **b** : a set of regularly presented television programs each of which is complete in itself **2** : the indicated sum of a usu. infinite sequence of numbers **3 a** : the coins or currency of a particular country and period **b** : a group of postage stamps in different denominations **4** : a succession of volumes or issues published with related subjects or authors, similar format and price, or continuous numbering **5** : a division of rock formations that is smaller than a system and comprises rocks deposited during an epoch **6** : a group of chemical compounds related in composition and structure **7** : an arrangement of the parts of or elements

in an electric circuit whereby the whole current passes through each part or element without branching — compare PARALLEL **8** : a set of vowels connected by ablaut (as *i, a, u* in *ring, rang, rung*) **9** : a number of games (as of baseball) played usu. on consecutive days between two teams ⟨in town for a 3-game ~⟩ **10** : a group of successive coordinate sentence elements joined together **11** : SOIL SERIES **12** : three consecutive games in bowling — **in series** : in a serial arrangement

ser·if \'ser-əf\ *n* [prob. fr. D *schreef* stroke, line, fr. MD, fr. *schriven* to write, fr. L *scribere* — more at SCRIBE] (1841) : any of the short lines stemming from and at an angle to the upper and lower ends of the strokes of a letter — **ser·ifed** *or* **ser·iffed** \-əft\ *adj*

seri·graph \'ser-ə-ˌgraf\ *n* [L *sericum* silk + Gk *graphein* to write, draw — more at CARVE] (1940) : an original silk-screen color print — **se·rig·ra·pher** \sə-'ri-grə-fər\ *n* — **se·rig·ra·phy** \-fē\ *n*

se·rin \sə-'ran\ *n* [F] (1530) : a small yellow and grayish Old World finch (*Serinus serinus*) that is related to the canary

ser·ine \'ser-ˌēn\ *n* [ISV *sericin* + ²*-ine*] (1880) : a crystalline nonessential amino acid $C_3H_7NO_3$ that occurs esp. as a structural part of many proteins

1 serif

se·rio·com·ic \ˌsir-ē-ō-'kä-mik\ *adj* [*serious* + *-o-* + *comic*] (1783) : having a mixture of the serious and the comic ⟨a ~ novel⟩ — **se·rio·com·i·cal·ly** \-mi-k(ə-)lē\ *adv*

se·ri·ous \'sir-ē-əs\ *adj* [ME *seryows*, fr. MF or LL; MF *serieux*, fr. LL *seriosus*, alter. of L *serius* weighty, serious; prob. akin to OE *swær* heavy, sad] (15c) **1** : thoughtful or subdued in appearance or manner : SOBER **2 a** : requiring much thought or work ⟨~ study⟩ **b** : of or relating to a matter of importance ⟨a ~ play⟩ **3 a** : not joking or trifling : being in earnest **b** *archaic* : PIOUS **c** : deeply interested : DEVOTED ⟨a ~ musician⟩ **4 a** : not easily answered or solved ⟨~ objections⟩ **b** : having important or dangerous possible consequences ⟨a ~ injury⟩ **5** : excessive or impressive in quantity, extent, or degree : CONSIDERABLE ⟨making ~ money⟩ ⟨~ drinking⟩ — **se·ri·ous·ness** *n*
syn SERIOUS, GRAVE, SOLEMN, SEDATE, STAID, SOBER, EARNEST mean not light or frivolous. SERIOUS implies a concern for what really matters ⟨a *serious* play about social injustice⟩. GRAVE implies both seriousness and dignity in expression or attitude ⟨read the proclamation in a *grave* voice⟩. SOLEMN suggests an impressive gravity utterly free from levity ⟨a sad and *solemn* occasion⟩. SEDATE implies a composed and decorous seriousness ⟨remained *sedate* amid the commotion⟩. STAID suggests a settled, accustomed sedateness and prim self-restraint ⟨a quiet and *staid* community⟩. SOBER stresses seriousness of purpose and absence of levity or frivolity ⟨a *sober* look at the state of our schools⟩. EARNEST suggests sincerity or often zealousness of purpose ⟨an *earnest* reformer⟩.

se·ri·ous·ly *adv* (1509) **1** : in a sincere manner : EARNESTLY **2** : to a serious extent : SEVERELY

se·ri·ous–mind·ed \ˌsir-ē-əs-'mīn-dəd\ *adj* (1845) : having a serious disposition or trend of thought — **se·ri·ous–mind·ed·ly** *adv* — **se·ri·ous–mind·ed·ness** *n*

ser·jeant, ser·jeanty *var of* SERGEANT, SERGEANTY

ser·jeant–at–law \ˌsär-jənt-ət-'lò\ *n, pl* **ser·jeants–at–law** (1503) : a member of a former class of barristers of the highest rank

ser·mon \'sər-mən\ *n* [ME, fr. OF, fr. ML *sermon-, sermo*, fr. L, speech, conversation, fr. *serere* to link together — more at SERIES] (13c) **1** : a religious discourse delivered in public usu. by a clergyman as a part of a worship service **2** : a speech on conduct or duty — **ser·mon·ic** \ˌsər-'mä-nik\ *adj*

ser·mon·ette \ˌsər-mə-'net\ *n* (1814) : a short sermon

ser·mon·ize \'sər-mə-ˌnīz\ *vb* **-ized; -iz·ing** *vi* (1635) **1** : to compose or deliver a sermon **2** : to speak didactically or dogmatically ~ *vt* : to preach to or on at length — **ser·mon·iz·er** *n*

Sermon on the Mount : an ethical discourse delivered by Jesus and recorded in Matthew 5–7 and paralleled briefly in Luke 6:20–49

sero- *comb form* [L *serum*] : serum ⟨*serology*⟩

se·ro·con·ver·sion \ˌsir-ō-kən-'vər-zhən, -shən\ *n* (1963) : the production of antibodies in response to an antigen

se·ro·di·ag·no·sis \-ˌdī-ig-'nō-səs\ *n* [NL] (1896) : diagnosis by the use of serum (as in the Wassermann test) — **se·ro·di·ag·nos·tic** \-'näs-tik\ *adj*

se·rol·o·gy \sə-'rä-lə-jē, si-\ *n* [ISV] (1909) : a science dealing with serums and esp. their reactions and properties — **se·ro·log·i·cal** \ˌsir-ə-'lä-ji-kəl\ *or* **se·ro·log·ic** \-jik\ *adj* — **se·ro·log·i·cal·ly** \-ji-k(ə-)lē\ *adv* — **se·rol·o·gist** \sə-'rä-lə-jist, si-\ *n*

se·ro·neg·a·tive \ˌsir-ō-'ne-gə-tiv\ *adj* (1927) : having or being a negative serum reaction esp. in a test for the presence of an antibody — **se·ro·neg·a·tiv·i·ty** \-ˌne-gə-'ti-və-tē\ *n*

se·ro·pos·i·tive \-'pä-zə-tiv, -'päz-tiv\ *adj* (ca. 1930) : having or being a positive serum reaction esp. in a test for the presence of an antibody — **se·ro·pos·i·tiv·i·ty** \-ˌpä-zə-'ti-və-tē\ *n*

se·ro·pu·ru·lent \-'pyùr-ə-lənt, ˌser-, -'pyùr-yə-\ *adj* (ca. 1836) : consisting of a mixture of serum and pus ⟨a ~ exudate⟩

se·ro·sa \sə-'rō-zə\ *n* [NL, fr. fem. of *serosus* serous, fr. L *serum*] (ca. 1890) : a usu. enclosing serous membrane — **se·ro·sal** \-zəl\ *adj*

se·ro·ti·nal \sə-'rät-nəl, -'rä-tⁿn-əl; ˌser-ə-'tī-nⁿl\ *adj* [L *serotinus* coming late] (1889) : of or relating to the latter and usu. drier part of summer

se·rot·i·nous \sə-'rät-nəs, -'rä-tⁿn-əs; ˌser-ə-'tī-nəs\ *adj* [L *serotinus* coming late, fr. *sero* late — more at SOIREE] (ca. 1656) : remaining closed on the tree with seed dissemination delayed or occurring gradually ⟨~ cones⟩

se·ro·to·ner·gic \ˌsir-ə-tō-'nər-jik\ *also* **se·ro·to·nin·er·gic** \ˌsir-ə-ˌtō-nə-'nər-jik\ *adj* [*serotonin* + *-ergic*] (1957) : liberating, activated by, or

\ə\ abut \ʼ\ kitten, F table \ər\ further \a\ ash \ā\ ace \ä\ mop, mar \aù\ out \ch\ chin \e\ bet \ē\ easy \g\ go \i\ hit \ī\ ice \j\ job \ŋ\ sing \ō\ go \ò\ law \òi\ boy \th\ thin \t̷h\ the \ü\ loot \ù\ foot \y\ yet \zh\ vision \à, k̲, ⁿ, œ, œ̄, ɶ, ɶ̄, ᐟ\ *see* Guide to Pronunciation involving serotonin in the transmission of nerve impulses ⟨~ path-ways⟩

se·ro·to·nin \ˌsir-ə-'tō-nən, ˌser-\ n [sero- + tonic + [1]-in] (1948) : a phenolic amine neurotransmitter $C_{10}H_{12}N_2O$ that is a powerful vaso-constrictor and is found esp. in the brain, blood serum, and gastric mucosa of mammals

se·ro·type \'sir-ə-ˌtīp, 'ser-\ n (1946) : a group of intimately related microorganisms distinguished by a common set of antigens; also : the set of antigens characteristic of such a group

se·rous \'sir-əs\ adj [ME, fr. ML serosus, fr. L serum] (15c) : of, relat-ing to, or resembling serum; esp : of thin watery constitution ⟨a ~ exudate⟩

serous membrane n (ca. 1852) : a thin membrane (as the peritoneum) with cells that secrete a serous fluid; esp : SEROSA

se·row \sə-'rō\ n [Lepcha sā-ro long-haired Tibetan goat] (1847) : any of several artiodactyl mammals (genus Capricornis) of eastern Asia that are usu. rather dark and heavily built and some of which have distinct manes

ser·pent \'sər-pənt\ n [ME, fr. MF, fr. L serpent-, serpens, fr. prp. of serpere to creep; akin to Gk herpein to creep, Skt sarpati he creeps] (13c) 1 a archaic : a noxious creature that creeps, hisses, or stings b : SNAKE 2 : DEVIL 1 3 : a treacherous person

[1]ser·pen·tine \'sər-pən-ˌtēn, -ˌtīn\ adj [ME, fr. MF serpentin, fr. LL serpentinus, fr. L serpent-, serpens] (15c) 1 : of or resembling a serpent (as in form or movement) 2 : subtly wily or tempting 3 a : winding or turning one way and another b : having a compound curve whose central curve is convex — **ser·pen·tine·ly** adv

[2]serpentine n (1519) : something that winds sinuously

[3]ser·pen·tine \-ˌtēn\ n [ME, fr. ML serpentina, serpentinum, fr. LL, fem. & neut. of serpentinus resembling a serpent] (15c) : a mineral or rock consisting essentially of a hydrous magnesium silicate usu. having a dull green color and often a mottled appearance

ser·pig·i·nous \(ˌ)sər-'pij-ə-nəs\ adj [ME serpiginose, fr. ML ser-piginosus, fr. serpigin-, serpigo creeping skin disease, fr. L serpere to creep] (15c) : CREEPING, SPREADING; esp : healing over in one portion while continuing to advance in another ⟨~ ulcer⟩ — **ser·pig·i·nous·ly** adv

ser·ra·nid \sə-'ra-nəd, 'ser-ə-nəd\ n [ultim. fr. L serra saw] (ca. 1900) : any of a large family (Serranidae) of carnivorous marine bony fishes which have an oblong compressed body covered with usu. ctenoid scales and many of which are important food and sport fishes (as the sea basses) esp. of warm seas — **serranid** adj

ser·ra·no \sə-'rä-(ˌ)nō, si-\ n, pl **-nos** [prob. fr. MexSp, fr. Sp serrano, adj., montane, highland, fr. sierra mountain range — more at SIERRA] (ca. 1972) : a small Mexican hot pepper

[1]ser·rate \'ser-ˌāt, sə-'rāt\ adj [L serratus, fr. serra saw] (1668) : notched or toothed on the edge; specif : having marginal teeth point-ing forward or toward the apex ⟨a ~ leaf⟩

[2]ser·rate \sə-'rāt, 'ser-ˌāt\ vt **ser·rat·ed; ser·rat·ing** [LL serratus, pp. of serrare to saw, fr. L serra] (1750) : to mark or make with serrations ⟨a serrated knife⟩

ser·ra·tion \sə-'rā-shən, se-\ n (1842) 1 : the condition of being ser-rate 2 : a formation resembling the toothed edge of a saw 3 : one of the teeth in a serrate margin

ser·ried \'ser-ēd\ adj (1667) 1 : crowded or pressed together : COM-PACT ⟨the crowd collected in a ~ mass —W. S. Maugham⟩ 2 [by al-ter.] : marked by ridges : SERRATE ⟨the ~ contours of the . . . moun-tains —Amer. Guide Series: Oregon⟩ — **ser·ried·ly** adv — **ser·ried·ness** n

ser·ry \'ser-ē\ vb **ser·ried; ser·ry·ing** [MF serré, pp. of serrer to press, crowd — more at SEAR] vi (1581) archaic : to press together esp. in ranks ~ vt : to crowd together

Ser·to·li cell \ˌsər-'tō-lē-\ n [Enrico Sertoli †1910 Ital. histologist] (1888) : one of the elongated striated cells lining the seminiferous tubules that support and apparently nourish the spermatids

Ser·to·man \(ˌ)sər-'tō-mən\ n [Sertoma (Club)] (1956) : a member of a major international service club

se·rum \'sir-əm\ n, pl **serums** or **se·ra** \-ə\ [L, whey, wheylike fluid; akin to Gk oros whey] (1665) 1 : the watery portion of an animal fluid remaining after coagulation: a (1) : BLOOD SERUM (2) : ANTISERUM b : WHEY c : a normal or pathological serous fluid (as in a blister) 2 : the watery part of a plant fluid

serum albumin n (1879) : a crystallizable albumin or mixture of albu-mins that normally constitutes more than half of the protein in blood serum and serves to maintain the osmotic pressure of the blood

serum globulin n (ca. 1890) : a globulin or mixture of globulins occur-ring in blood serum and containing most of the antibodies of the blood

serum hepatitis n (1932) : HEPATITIS B

serum sickness n (ca. 1913) : an allergic reaction to the injection of foreign serum manifested by urticaria, swelling, eruption, arthritis, and fever

ser·val \'sər-vəl, (ˌ)sər-'val\ n [F, fr. Pg lobo cerval lynx, fr. ML lupus cervalis, lit., deerlike wolf] (1771) : a long-legged African wildcat (Felis serval) having large ears and a tawny black-spotted coat

ser·vant \'sər-vənt\ n [ME, fr. OF, fr. prp. of servir] (13c) : one that serves others ⟨a public ~⟩; esp : one that performs duties about the person or home of a master or personal employer — **ser·vant·hood** \-ˌhu̇d\ n — **ser·vant·less** adj

[1]serve \'sərv\ vb **served; serv·ing** [ME, fr. MF servir, fr. OF, fr. L servire to be a slave, serve, fr. servus slave, servant] vi (13c) 1 a : to be a servant b : to do military or naval service 2 : to assist a cele-brant as server at mass 3 : to be of use ⟨in a day when few people could write, seals served as signatures —Elizabeth W. King⟩ b : to be favorable, opportune, or convenient c : to be worthy of reliance or trust ⟨if memory ~s⟩ d : to hold an office : discharge a duty or func-tion ⟨~ on a jury⟩ 4 : to prove adequate or satisfactory : SUFFICE 5 : to help persons to food: as a : to wait at table b : to set out por-tions of food or drink 6 : to wait on customers 7 : to put the ball or shuttlecock in play in various games (as tennis, volleyball, or badmin-ton) ~ vt 1 a : to be a servant to : ATTEND b : to give the service and respect due to (a superior) c : to comply with the commands or demands of : GRATIFY d : to give military or naval service to e : to perform the duties of (an office or post) 2 : to act as server at (mass) 3 archaic : to pay a lover's or suitor's court to (a lady) ⟨that gentle

lady, whom I love and ~ —Edmund Spenser⟩ 4 a : to work through (a term of service) b : to put in (a term of imprisonment) 5 a : to wait on at table b : to bring (food) to a diner c : PRESENT, PROVIDE — usu. used with up ⟨the novel served up many laughs⟩ 6 a : to furnish or supply with something needed or desired b : to wait on (a cus-tomer) in a store c : to furnish professional service to 7 a : to an-swer the needs of b : to be enough for : SUFFICE c : to contribute or conduce to : PROMOTE 8 : to treat or act toward in a specified way ⟨he served me ill⟩ 9 a : to bring to notice, deliver, or execute as required by law b : to make legal service upon (a person named in a process) 10 of a male animal : to copulate with 11 : to wind yarn or wire tightly around (a rope or stay) for protection 12 : to provide services that benefit or help 13 : to put (the ball or shuttlecock) in play (as in tennis or badminton) — **serve one right** : to be deserved

[2]serve n (1688) : the act or action of putting the ball or shuttlecock in play in various games (as volleyball, badminton, or tennis); also : a turn to serve

serv·er \'sər-vər\ n (15c) 1 : one that serves food or drink 2 : the player who serves (as in tennis) 3 : something used in serving food or drink 4 : one that serves legal processes upon another 5 : the cele-brant's assistant at low mass 6 : a computer in a network that is used to provide services (as access to files or shared peripherals or the rout-ing of electronic mail) to other computers in the network

[1]ser·vice \'sər-vəs\ n [ME, fr. MF, fr. L servitium condition of a slave, body of slaves, fr. servus slave] (13c) 1 a : the occupation or function of serving ⟨in active ~⟩ b : employment as a servant ⟨entered his ~⟩ 2 a : the work performed by one that serves ⟨good ~⟩ b : HELP, USE, BENEFIT ⟨glad to be of ~⟩ c : contribution to the welfare of others d : disposal for use ⟨I'm entirely at your ~⟩ 3 a : a form followed in worship or in a religious ceremony ⟨the burial ~⟩ b : a meeting for worship — often used in pl. ⟨held evening ~s⟩ 4 : the act of serving: as a : a helpful act ⟨did him a ~⟩ b : useful labor that does not produce a tangible commodity — usu. used in pl. ⟨charge for profes-sional ~s⟩ c : SERVE 2 : a set of articles for a particular use ⟨a silver tea ~⟩ 6 a : an administrative division (as of a government or busi-ness) ⟨the consular ~⟩ b : one of a nation's military forces (as the army or navy) 7 a : a facility supplying some public demand ⟨tele-phone ~⟩ ⟨bus ~⟩ b : a facility providing maintenance and repair ⟨television ~⟩ 8 : the materials (as spun yarn, small lines, or canvas) used for serving a rope 9 : the act of bringing a legal writ, process, or summons to notice as prescribed by law 10 : the act of copulating with a female animal 11 : a branch of a hospital medical staff devoted to a particular specialty ⟨obstetrical ~⟩

[2]service vt **ser·viced; ser·vic·ing** (1528) : to perform services for: as a : to repair or provide maintenance for b : to meet interest and sink-ing fund payments on (as government debt) c : to perform any of the business functions auxiliary to production or distribution of d of a male animal : SERVE 10 — **ser·vic·er** n

[3]service adj (1837) 1 : of or relating to the armed services 2 : used in serving or supplying ⟨delivery men use the ~ entrance⟩ 3 : intended for hard or everyday use 4 a : providing services ⟨the ~ trades— from filling stations to universities —John Fischer⟩ b : offering re-pair, maintenance, or incidental services

[4]service n [ME serves, pl. of serve fruit of the service tree, service tree, fr. OE syrfe, fr. (assumed) VL sorbea, fr. L sorbus service tree] (1530) : an Old World tree (Sorbus domestica) resembling the related mountain ashes but having larger flowers and larger edible fruit; also : a related Old World tree (S. torminalis) with bitter fruits

ser·vice·able \'sər-və-sə-bəl\ adj (14c) 1 : HELPFUL, USEFUL 2 : fit for use ⟨her ~ but not exceptional voice —Irving Kolodin⟩ — **ser·vice·abil·i·ty** \ˌsər-və-sə-'bil-ə-tē\ n — **ser·vice·able·ness** \'sər-və-sə-bəl-nəs\ n — **ser·vice·ably** \-blē\ adv

ser·vice·ber·ry \'sər-vəs-ˌber-ē also 'sär-\ n [[4]service] (1784) 1 : the edible purple or red fruit of any of various No. American trees or shrubs (genus Amelanchier) of the rose family 2 : a tree or shrub that produces serviceberries and has showy white flowers in the spring — called also Juneberry, shadblow, shadbush

service book n (1580) : a book setting forth forms of worship used in religious services

service box n (ca. 1898) : the area in which a player stands while serv-ing in various court games (as squash or handball)

service cap n (ca. 1908) : a flat-topped visor cap worn as part of a military uniform — compare GARRISON CAP

service ceiling n (1920) : the altitude at which under standard air conditions a particular airplane can no longer rise at a rate greater than a small designated rate (as 100 feet per minute)

service charge n (1917) : a fee charged for a particular service often in addition to a standard or basic fee — called also service fee

service club n (1926) 1 : a club of business or professional men or women organized for their common benefit and active in community service 2 : a recreation center for enlisted personnel provided by one of the armed services

service court n (ca. 1878) : a part of the court into which the ball or shuttlecock must be served

service line n (1875) : a line marked on a court in various games (as handball or tennis) parallel to the front wall or to the net to mark a boundary of the service area or service court

ser·vice·man \'sər-vəs-ˌman, -mən\ n (1899) 1 : a male member of the armed forces 2 : a man employed to repair or maintain equipment 3 : a service station attendant

service mark n (1945) : a mark or device used to identify a service (as transportation or insurance) offered to customers

service medal n (ca. 1934) : a medal awarded to an individual for military service in a specified war or campaign

service module n (1961) : a space vehicle module that contains oxy-gen, water, fuel cells, propellant tanks, and the main rocket engine

service road n (1921) : FRONTAGE ROAD

service station n (1916) 1 : a retail station for servicing motor vehi-cles esp. with gasoline and oil 2 : a place at which some service is offered

service stripe n (ca. 1920) : a stripe worn on an enlisted man's left sleeve to indicate three years of service in the army or four years in the navy

service tree n (1600) : [4]SERVICE

ser·vice·wom·an \'sər-vəs-ˌwu̇-mən\ n (1943) : a female member of the armed forces

ser·vi·ette \ˌsər-vē-'et\ n [F, fr. MF, fr. servir to serve] (1818) chiefly Brit : a table napkin

ser·vile \'sər-vəl, -ˌvīl\ adj [ME, fr. L servilis, fr. servus slave] (15c) 1 : of or befitting a slave or a menial position 2 : meanly or cravenly submissive : ABJECT syn see SUBSERVIENT — **ser·vile·ly** \-və(l)-lē, -ˌvīl-lē\ adv — **ser·vile·ness** \-vəl-nəs, -ˌvīl-\ n — **ser·vil·i·ty** \(ˌ)sər-'vi-lə-tē\ n

serv·ing \'sər-viŋ\ n (1864) : a helping of food or drink

Ser·vite \'sər-ˌvīt\ n [ML Servitae, pl., Servites, fr. L servus] (ca. 1550) : a member of the mendicant Order of Servants of Mary founded in Florence, Italy, in 1233 — **Servite** adj

ser·vi·tor \'sər-və-tər, -ˌtȯr\ n [ME servitour, fr. MF, fr. LL servitor, fr. L servire to serve] (14c) : a male servant

ser·vi·tude \'sər-və-ˌtüd, -ˌtyüd\ n [ME, fr. MF, fr. L servitudo slavery, fr. servus slave] (15c) 1 : a condition in which one lacks liberty esp. to determine one's course of action or way of life 2 : a right by which something (as a piece of land) owned by one person is subject to a specified use or enjoyment by another

ser·vo \'sər-(ˌ)vō\ n, pl **servos** (1947) 1 : SERVOMOTOR 2 : SERVOMECHANISM

ser·vo·mech·a·nism \'sər-vō-ˌme-kə-ˌni-zəm\ n [servo- (as in servomotor) + mechanism] (1926) : an automatic device for controlling large amounts of power by means of very small amounts of power and automatically correcting the operation of a mechanism

ser·vo·mo·tor \'sər-vō-ˌmō-tər\ n [F servo-moteur, fr. L servus slave, servant + F -o- + moteur motor, fr. L motor one that moves — more at MOTOR] (1889) : a power-driven mechanism that supplements a primary control operated by a comparatively feeble force (as in a servomechanism)

-ses pl of -SIS

ses·a·me \'se-sə-mē also 'se-zə-\ n [alter. of earlier sesam, sesama, fr. L sesamum, sesama, fr. Gk sēsamon, sēsamē, of Sem origin; akin to Akkadian šamaššamu sesame] (1682) 1 : a widely cultivated chiefly tropical or subtropical annual erect herb (Sesamum indicum of the family Pedaliaceae); also : its small seeds used esp. as a source of oil and a flavoring agent 2 : OPEN SESAME

sesame oil n (1870) : a pale yellow bland semi-drying fatty oil obtained from sesame seeds and used chiefly as an edible oil, as a vehicle for various pharmaceuticals, and in cosmetics and soaps

ses·a·moid \'se-sə-ˌmȯid\ n [Gk sēsamoeidēs, lit., resembling sesame seed, fr. sēsamon] (ca. 1696) : a nodular mass of bone (as the patella) or cartilage in a tendon esp. at a joint or bony prominence — **sesamoid** adj

sesame 1

Se·so·tho \se-'sō-(ˌ)thō, -ˌ)tȯ\ n [Sesotho] (1846) : the Bantu language of the Basotho people

sesqui- comb form [L, one and a half, half again, lit., and a half, fr. semis half of an as, one half (prob. fr. semi- + as as) + -que (enclitic) and; akin to Gk te and, Skt ca, Goth -h, -uh] 1 : one and a half times (sesquicentennial) 2 : containing half again as many atoms (sesquiterpene) 3 : intermediate : combination (sesquicarbonate)

ses·qui·car·bon·ate \ˌses-kwi-'kär-bə-ˌnāt, -nət\ n (1825) : a salt that is neither a simple normal carbonate nor a simple bicarbonate but often (as Na₂CO₃·NaHCO₃·2H₂O) a combination of the two

ses·qui·cen·te·na·ry \-kwi-sen-'te-nə-rē, -'sen-t²n-ˌer-ē, -sen-'tē-nə-rē\ n (1954) : SESQUICENTENNIAL

ses·qui·cen·ten·ni·al \-sen-'te-nē-əl\ n (1880) : a 150th anniversary or its celebration — **sesquicentennial** adj

ses·qui·pe·da·lian \ˌses-kwə-pə-'dāl-yən\ adj [L sesquipedalis, lit., a foot and a half long, fr. sesqui- + ped-, pes foot — more at FOOT] (1656) 1 : having many syllables : LONG (~ terms) 2 : given to or characterized by the use of long words (a ~ television commentator)

ses·qui·ter·pene \ˌses-kwə-'tər-ˌpēn\ n (ca. 1888) : any of a class of terpenes C₁₅H₂₄; also : a derivative of such a terpene

ses·sile \'se-ˌsil, -səl\ adj [L sessilis of or fit for sitting, low, dwarf (of plants), fr. sessus, pp. of sedēre] (1753) 1 : attached directly by the base : not raised upon a stalk or peduncle (a ~ leaf) (~ bubbles) 2 : permanently attached or established : not free to move about (~ polyps)

ses·sion \'se-shən\ n [ME, fr. MF, fr. L session-, sessio, lit., act of sitting, fr. sedēre to sit — more at SIT] (14c) 1 : a meeting or series of meetings of a body (as a court or legislature) for the transaction of business (morning ~) 2 pl a (1) : a sitting of English justices of peace in execution of the powers conferred by their commissions (2) : an English court holding such sessions b : any of various courts similar to the English sessions 3 : the period between the first meeting of a legislative or judicial body and the prorogation or final adjournment 4 : the ruling body of a Presbyterian congregation consisting of the elders in active service 5 : the period during the year or day in which a school conducts classes 6 : a meeting or period devoted to a particular activity (a recording ~) — **ses·sion·al** \'sesh-nəl, 'se-shə-n²l\ adj

session man n (1958) : a studio musician who backs up a performer at a recording session

ses·terce \'ses-ˌtərs\ n [L sestertius, fr. sestertius two and a half times as great (fr. its being equal orig. to two and a half asses), fr. semis half of an as, one half + tertius third — more at SESQUI-, THIRD] (1598) : an ancient Roman coin equal to ¼ denarius

ses·ter·tium \se-'stər-sh(ē-)əm\ n, pl -tia \-sh(ē-)ə\ [L, fr. gen. pl. of sestertius (in the phrase milia sestertium thousands of sesterces)] (ca. 1541) : a unit of value in ancient Rome equal to 1000 sesterces

ses·tet \ses-'tet\ n [It sestetto, fr. sesto sixth, fr. L sextus — more at SEXT] (1859) : a stanza or a poem of six lines; specif : the last six lines of an Italian sonnet

ses·ti·na \se-'stē-nə\ n [It, fr. sesto sixth] (ca. 1586) : a lyrical fixed form consisting of six 6-line usu. unrhymed stanzas in which the end words of the first stanza recur as end words of the following five stan-

zas in a successively rotating order and as the middle and end words of the three verses of the concluding tercet

¹set \'set\ vb **set; set·ting** [ME setten, fr. OE settan; akin to OHG sezzen to set, OE sittan to sit] vt (bef. 12c) 1 : to cause to sit : place in or on a seat 2 a : to put (a fowl) on eggs to hatch them b : to put (eggs) for hatching under a fowl or into an incubator 3 : to place (oneself) in position to start running in a race 4 a : to place with care or deliberate purpose and with relative stability (~ a ladder against the wall) (~ a stone on the grave) b : TRANSPLANT 1 (~ seedlings) c (1) : to make (as a trap) ready to catch prey (2) : to fix (a hook) firmly into the jaw of a fish d : to put aside (as dough containing yeast) for fermenting 5 : to direct with fixed attention (~ your mind to it) 6 a : to cause to assume a specified condition, relation, or occupation (slaves were ~ free) (~ the house on fire) b : to cause the start of (~ a fire) 7 a : to appoint or assign to an office or duty b : POST, STATION 8 : to cause to assume a specified posture or position (~ the door ajar) 9 a : to fix as a distinguishing imprint, sign, or appearance (the years have ~ their mark on him) b : AFFIX c : APPLY (~ a match to kindling) 10 : to fix or decide on as a time, limit, or regulation : PRESCRIBE (~ a wedding day) (~ the rules for the game) 11 a : to establish as the highest level or best performance (~ a record for the half mile) b : to furnish as a pattern or model (~ an example of generosity) c : to allot as a task (setting lessons for the children to work upon at home —Manchester Examiner) 12 a : to adjust (a device and esp. a measuring device) to a desired position (~ the alarm for 7:00) (~ a thermostat at 68); also : to adjust (as a clock) in conformity with a standard b : to restore to normal position or connection when dislocated or fractured (~ a broken bone) c : to spread to the wind (~ the sails) 13 a : to put in order for use (~ a place for a guest) b : to make scenically ready for a performance (~ the stage) c (1) : to arrange (type) for printing (~ type by hand) (2) : to put into type or its equivalent (as on film) (~ the first word in italic) 14 a : to put a fine edge on by grinding or honing (~ a razor) b : to bend slightly the tooth points of (a saw) alternately in opposite directions c : to sink (the head of a nail) below the surface 15 : to fix in a desired position (as by heating or stretching) 16 : to arrange (hair) in a desired style by using implements (as curlers, rollers, or clips) and gels or lotions 17 a : to adorn with something affixed or infixed : STUD, DOT (clear sky ~ with stars) b : to fix (as a precious stone) in a border of metal : place in a setting 18 a : to hold something in regard or esteem at the rate of (~s a great deal by daily exercise) b : to place in a relative rank or category (~ duty before pleasure) c : to fix at a certain amount (~ bail at $500) d : VALUE, RATE (their promises were ~ at naught) e : to place as an estimate of worth (~ a high value on life) 19 : to place in relation for comparison or balance (theory ~ against practice) 20 a : to direct to action b : to incite to attack or antagonism (war ~s brother against brother) 21 a : to place by transporting (was ~ ashore on the island) b : to put in motion c : to put and fix in a direction (~ our faces toward home once more) d of a dog : to point out the position of (game) by holding a fixed attitude 22 : to defeat (an opponent or a contract) in bridge 23 a : to fix firmly : make immobile : give rigid form or condition to (~ her jaw in determination) b : to make unyielding or obstinate 24 : to cause to become firm or solid (~ milk for cheese) 25 : to cause (as fruit) to develop ~ vi 1 chiefly dial : SIT 2 : to be becoming : be suitable : FIT (the coat ~s well) 3 : to cover and warm eggs to hatch them 4 a : to become lodged or fixed (the pudding ~ heavily on my stomach) b : to place oneself in position in preparation for an action (as running) 5 of a plant part : to undergo development usu. as a result of pollination 6 a : to pass below the horizon : go down (the sun ~s) b : to come to an end (this century ~s with little mirth —Thomas Fuller) 7 : to apply oneself to some activity (~ to work) 8 : to have a specified direction in motion : FLOW, TEND (the wind was setting from Pine Hill to the farm —Esther Forbes) 9 of a dog : to indicate the position of game by crouching or pointing 10 : to dance face to face with another in a square dance (~ to your partner and turn) 11 a : to become solid or thickened by chemical or physical alteration (the cement ~s rapidly) b of a dye or color : to become permanent c of a bone : to become whole by knitting d of metal : to acquire a permanent twist or bend from strain — **set about** : to begin to do — **set apart** 1 : to reserve to a particular use 2 : to make noticeable or outstanding — **set aside** 1 : to put to one side : DISCARD 2 : to reserve for a purpose : SAVE 3 : DISMISS 4 : ANNUL, OVERRULE — **set at** : to mount an attack on : ASSAIL (would go although . . . devils should set at me —Charlotte Yonge) — **set eyes on** : to catch sight of — **set foot in** : ENTER — **set foot on** : to step onto — **set forth** 1 : to give an account or statement of 2 : to start out on a journey — **set forward** 1 : FURTHER 2 : to start out on a journey — **set in motion** : to give impulse to (sets the story in motion vividly —Howard Thompson) — **set one's hand to** : to become engaged in — **set one's heart on** : RESOLVE vt 5 (she set her heart on going to medical school) — **set one's house in order** : to organize one's affairs — **set one's sights on** : to determine to pursue — **set one's teeth on edge** : IRRITATE, ANNOY — **set one straight** : to correct someone by providing accurate information — **set sail** : to start out on a course; esp : to begin a voyage (set sail for Bermuda) — **set store by** or **set store on** : to consider valuable, trustworthy, or worthwhile — **set the stage** : to provide the basis or background (this trend will set the stage for higher earnings) — **set to music** : to provide music or instrumental accompaniment for (a text) — **set upon** : to attack usu. with violence (the dogs set upon the trespassers)

²set n (14c) 1 a : the act or action of setting b : the condition of being set 2 : a number of things of the same kind that belong or are used together (an electric train ~) 3 a : mental inclination, tendency, or habit : BENT (a ~ toward mathematics) b : a state of psychological preparedness usu. of limited duration for action in response to an anticipated stimulus or situation (the influence of mental ~ on

---

\ə\ abut \²\ kitten, F table \ər\ further \a\ ash \ā\ ace \ä\ mop, mar \au̇\ out \ch\ chin \e\ bet \ē\ easy \g\ go \i\ hit \ī\ ice \j\ job \ŋ\ sing \ō\ go \ȯ\ law \ȯi\ boy \th\ thin \t̲h̲\ the \ü\ loot \u̇\ foot \y\ yet \zh\ vision \à, k̲, ⁿ, œ, œ̄, ue, ūe, ᵞ\ see Guide to Pronunciation the effect experienced with marijuana⟩ **4** : direction of flow ⟨the ~ of the wind⟩ **5** : form or carriage of the body or of its parts ⟨her face took on a cynical ~ —Raymond Kennedy⟩ **6** : the manner of fitting or of being placed or suspended ⟨in order to give the skirt a pretty ~ —Mary J. Howell⟩ **7** : amount of deflection from a straight line ⟨~ of a saw's teeth⟩ **8** : permanent change of form (as of metal) due to repeated or excessive stress **9** : the act or result of arranging hair by curling or waving **10** *also* **sett** \'set\ **a** : a young plant or rooted cutting ready for transplanting **b** : a small bulb, corm, or tuber or a piece of tuber used for propagation ⟨onion ~s⟩ **11** *or* **sett** : the burrow of a badger **12** : the width of the body of a piece of type **13** : an artificial setting for a scene of a theatrical or film production **14** *also* **sett** : a rectangular paving stone of sandstone or granite **15** : a division of a tennis match won by the side that wins at least six games beating the opponent by two games or by winning a tiebreaker **16** : a collection of books or periodicals forming a unit **17** : a clutch of eggs **18** : the basic formation in a country-dance or square dance **19** : a session of music (as jazz or dance music) usu. followed by an intermission; *also* : the music played at one session **20** : a group of persons associated by common interests **21** : a collection of elements and esp. mathematical ones (as numbers or points) — called also *class* **22** : an apparatus of electronic components assembled so as to function as a unit ⟨a television ~⟩ **23** : a usu. offensive formation in football or basketball **24** : a group of a specific number of repetitions of a particular exercise

³**set** *adj* [ME *sett*, fr. OE *gesett*, pp. of *settan*] (14c) **1** : INTENT, DETERMINED ⟨~ upon going⟩ **2** : INTENTIONAL, PREMEDITATED ⟨did it of ~ purpose⟩ **3** : fixed by authority or appointment : PRESCRIBED, SPECIFIED ⟨~ hours of study⟩ **4** : reluctant to change ⟨~ in their ways⟩ **5 a** : IMMOVABLE, RIGID ⟨~ frown⟩ **b** : BUILT-IN ⟨a ~ tub⟩ **6** : SETTLED, PERSISTENT ⟨~ defiance⟩ **7** : being in readiness : PREPARED ⟨~ for an early morning start⟩

se·ta \'sē-tə\ *n, pl* **se·tae** \'sē-,tē\ [NL, fr. L *saeta, seta* bristle] (ca. 1793) : a slender usu. rigid or bristly and springy organ or part of an animal or plant — **se·tal** \'sē-t²l\ *adj*

se·ta·ceous \si-'tā-shəs\ *adj* [L *saeta, seta*] (1664) **1** : set with or consisting of bristles **2** : resembling a bristle in form or texture

set–aside \'set-ə-,sīd\ *n* (1943) : something (as a portion of receipts or production) that is set aside for a specified purpose

set·back \'set-,bak\ *n* (1674) **1** : a checking of progress **2** : DEFEAT, REVERSE **3** : ⁴PITCH 7 **4** : a placing of the face of a building on a line some distance to the rear of the building line or of the wall below; *also* : the rooftop area produced by a setback **5** : automatic scheduled adjustment to a lower temperature setting of a thermostat

set back *vt* (1600) **1** : to slow the progress of : HINDER, DELAY **2** : COST ⟨a new suit will *set you back* $200⟩

set by *vt* (1595) : to set apart for future use

set down *vt* (15c) **1** : to cause to sit down : SEAT **2** : to place at rest on a surface or on the ground **3** : to suspend (a jockey) from racing **4** : to cause or allow to get off a vehicle : DELIVER **5** : to land (an airplane) on the ground or water **6 a** : ORDAIN, ESTABLISH **b** : to put in writing **7 a** : REGARD, CONSIDER ⟨set him *down* as a liar⟩ **b** : ATTRIBUTE

se te·nant \sə-'te-nənt, sē-; ,se-tə-'näⁿ\ *adj* [F, lit., holding one another] (ca. 1911) *of postage stamps* : joined together as in the original sheet but differing in design, overprint, color, or perforation

Seth \'seth\ *n* [Heb *Shēth*] : a son of Adam and Eve

¹**set–in** \'set-'in\ *adj* (1534) **1** : placed, located, or built as a part of some other construction ⟨a ~ bookcase⟩ ⟨a ~ washbasin⟩ **2** : cut separately and stitched in ⟨~ sleeves⟩

²**set–in** \'set-,in\ *n* (1953) : INSERT

set in *vt* (15c) **1** : INSERT; *esp* : to stitch (a small part) within a large article ⟨*set in* a sleeve of a dress⟩ ~ *vi* : to become established

set·line \'set-,līn\ *n* (1865) : a long heavy fishing line to which several hooks are attached in series

set·off \'set-,óf\ *n* (1621) **1** : something that is set off against another thing: **a** : DECORATION, ORNAMENT **b** : COMPENSATION, COUNTERBALANCE **2** : the discharge of a debt by setting against it a distinct claim in favor of the debtor; *also* : the claim itself **3** : OFFSET 7a

set off *vt* (1596) **1 a** : to put in relief : show up by contrast **b** : ADORN, EMBELLISH **c** : to set apart : make distinct or outstanding **2 a** : OFFSET, COMPENSATE ⟨more variety in the Lancashire weather to *set off* its most disagreeable phases —Geog. Jour.⟩ **b** : to make a setoff of ⟨the respective totals shall be *set off* against one another —O. R. Hobson⟩ **3 a** : to set in motion : cause to begin **b** : to cause to explode **4** : to measure off on a surface ~ *vi* : to start out on a course or a journey ⟨*set off* for home⟩

set on *vt* (14c) **1** : ATTACK **2 a** *obs* : PROMOTE **b** : to urge (as a dog) to attack or pursue **c** : to incite to action : INSTIGATE **d** : to set to work ~ *vi* : GO ON, ADVANCE

se·tose \'sē-,tōs\ *adj* [L *saetosus*, fr. *saeta*] (1661) : SETACEOUS, BRISTLY

set·out \'set-,aút\ *n* (1537) **1 a** (1) : ARRAY, DISPLAY (2) : ARRANGEMENT, LAYOUT **b** : BUFFET, SPREAD **c** : TURNOUT 5 **2** : PARTY, ENTERTAINMENT **3** : BEGINNING, OUTSET

set out *vt* (14c) **1 a** : to arrange and present graphically or systematically **b** : to mark out (as a design) : lay out the plan of **2** : to state, describe, or recite at length ⟨distributed copies of a pamphlet *setting out* his ideas in full —S. F. Mason⟩ **3** : to begin with a definite purpose : INTEND, UNDERTAKE ~ *vi* : to start out on a course, a journey, or a career

set piece *n* (ca. 1909) **1** : a realistic piece of stage scenery standing by itself **2 a** : a composition (as in literature, art, or music) executed in a fixed or ideal form often with studied artistry and brilliant effect **b** : a scene, depiction, speech, or event that is obviously designed to have an imposing effect **3** : a precisely planned and conducted military operation — **set–piece** *adj*

set point *n* (1928) : a situation (as in tennis) in which one player will win the set by winning the next point; *also* : the point won

set·screw \'set-,skrü\ *n* (ca. 1855) **1** : a screw screwed through one part tightly upon or into another part to prevent relative movement **2** : a screw for regulating a valve opening or a spring tension

set shot *n* (1937) : a two-handed shot in basketball taken from a stationary position

sett *var of* SET

set·tee \se-'tē\ *n* [alter. of *settle*] (1716) **1** : a long seat with a back **2** : a medium-sized sofa with arms and a back

set·ter \'se-tər\ *n* (15c) **1** : one that sets **2** : a large bird dog of a type trained to point on finding game

set theory *n* (1936) : a branch of mathematics or of symbolic logic that deals with the nature and relations of sets — **set theoretic** *adj*

set·ting \'se-tiŋ\ *n* (14c) **1** : the manner, position, or direction in which something is set **2** : the frame or bed in which a gem is set; *also* : style of mounting **3 a** : the time, place, and circumstances in which something occurs or develops **b** : the time and place of the action of a literary, dramatic, or cinematic work **c** : the scenery used in a theatrical or film production **4** : the music composed for a text (as a poem) **5** : the articles of tableware for setting a place at table ⟨two ~s of sterling silver⟩ **6** : a batch of eggs for incubation *syn* see BACKGROUND

setting circle *n* (ca. 1891) : a graduated scale or wheel on the mounting of an equatorial telescope for indicating right ascension or declination

setting–up exercise *n* (ca. 1900) : any of a series of gymnastic exercises used to give an erect carriage, supple muscles, and easy control of the limbs

¹**set·tle** \'se-t²l\ *vb* **set·tled; set·tling** \'set-liŋ, 'se-t²l-iŋ\ [ME, to seat, bring to rest, come to rest, fr. OE *setlan*, fr. *setl* seat] *vt* (1515) **1** : to place so as to stay **2 a** : to establish in residence **b** : to furnish with inhabitants : COLONIZE **3 a** : to cause to pack down **b** : to clarify by causing dregs or impurities to sink **4** : to make quiet or orderly **5 a** : to fix or resolve conclusively ⟨~ the question⟩ **b** : to establish or secure permanently ⟨~ the order of royal succession⟩ **c** : to conclude (a lawsuit) by agreement between parties usu. out of court **d** : to close (as an account) by payment often of less than is due **6** : to arrange in a desired position **7** : to make or arrange for final disposition of ⟨*settled* his affairs⟩ **8** *of an animal* : IMPREGNATE ~ *vi* **1** : to come to rest **2 a** : to sink gradually or to the bottom **b** : to become clear by the deposit of sediment or scum **c** : to become compact by sinking **3 a** : to become fixed, resolved, or established ⟨a cold *settled* in his chest⟩ **b** : to establish a residence or colony ⟨*settled* in Wisconsin⟩ — often used with *down* **4 a** : to become quiet or orderly **b** : to take up an ordered or stable life — often used with *down* ⟨marry and ~ down⟩ **5 a** : to adjust differences or accounts **b** : to come to a decision — used with *on* or *upon* ⟨~ed on a new plan⟩ **c** : to conclude a lawsuit by agreement out of court **6** *of an animal* : CONCEIVE *syn* see DECIDE — **set·tle·able** \'se-t²l-ə-bəl, 'set-lə-bəl\ *adj* — **settle for** : to be content with — **settle one's hash** : to silence or subdue someone by decisive action — **settle the stomach** : to remove or relieve the distress or nausea of indigestion

²**set·tle** *n* [ME, place for sitting, seat, chair, fr. OE *setl;* akin to OHG *sezzal* seat, L *sella* seat, chair, OE *sittan* to sit] (1553) : a wooden bench with arms, a high solid back, and an enclosed foundation which can be used as a chest

settle

set·tle·ment \'se-t²l-mənt\ *n* (1648) **1** : the act or process of settling **2 a** : an act of bestowing or giving possession under legal sanction **b** : the sum, estate, or income secured to one by such a settlement **3 a** : occupation by settlers **b** : a place or region newly settled **c** : a small village **4** : SETTLEMENT HOUSE **5** : an agreement composing differences **6** : payment or adjustment of an account

settlement house *n* (1907) : an institution providing various community services esp. to large city populations

set·tler \'set-lər, 'se-t²l-ər\ *n* (1696) : one that settles (as a new region)

set·tling \'set-liŋ, 'se-t²l-iŋ\ *n* (1594) : SEDIMENT, DREGS — usu. used in pl.

set·tlor \'set-lər, 'se-t²l-,ór\ *n* (1818) : one that makes a settlement or creates a trust of property

set–to \'set-,tü\ *n, pl* **set–tos** (1743) : a usu. brief and vigorous fight or debate

set to *vi* (ca. 1525) **1** : to begin actively and earnestly **2** : to begin fighting

set·up \'set-,əp\ *n* (1890) **1 a** : carriage of the body; *esp* : erect and soldierly bearing **b** : CONSTITUTION, MAKEUP **2 a** : the assembly and arrangement of the tools and apparatus required for the performance of an operation **b** : the preparation and adjustment of machines for an assigned task **3 a** : a table setting **b** : glass, ice, and mixer served to patrons who supply their own liquor **4 a** : a camera position from which a scene is filmed; *also* : the footage taken from one camera position **b** : the final arrangement of the scenery and properties for a scene of a theatrical or cinematic production **5 a** : a position of the balls in billiards or pool from which it is easy to score **b** : a task or contest purposely made easy **c** : something easy to get or accomplish **d** : something (as a plot) that has been constructed or contrived **e** : the execution of a planned scoring play in sports **6 a** : the manner in which the elements or components of a machine, apparatus, or mechanical, electrical, or hydraulic system are arranged, designed, or assembled **b** : the patterns within which political, social, or administrative forces operate : customary or established practice **7** : PROJECT, PLAN **8** : something done by deceit or trickery in order to compromise or frame someone

set up *vt* (13c) **1 a** : to raise to and place in a high position **b** : to place in view : POST **c** : to put forward (as a plan) for acceptance **2 a** : to place upright : ERECT ⟨*set up* a statue⟩ **b** : to assemble the parts of and erect in position ⟨*set up* a printing press⟩ **c** : to put (a machine) in readiness or adjustment for a tooling operation **3 a** : CAUSE, CREATE ⟨*set up* a clamor⟩ **b** : BRING ABOUT **4** : to place in power or in office ⟨*set up* the general as dictator⟩ **5 a** : to raise from depression : ELATE, GRATIFY **b** : to make proud or vain **6 a** : to put forward or extol as a model **b** : to claim oneself to be ⟨*sets* himself *up* as an authority⟩ **7** : FOUND, INAUGURATE ⟨*set up* a home for orphans⟩ **8 a** : to provide with means of making a living ⟨*set* him *up* in business⟩ **b** : to bring or restore to normal health **c** : to cause (one) to take on a soldierly or athletic appearance esp. through drill **9** : to erect (as a perpendicular or a figure) on a base in drawing **10 a** : to make taut (a stay or hawser) **b** : to tighten firmly **11** : to make carefully worked out plans for ⟨*set up* a bank robbery⟩ **12 a :** to pay for (drinks) **b** : to treat (someone) to something **13 a :** to put in a compromising or dangerous position usu. by trickery or deceit **b :** FRAME 3 **14 :** to execute one or more plays in preparation for scoring ∼ *vi* **1 :** to come into active operation or use **2 :** to begin business **3 :** to make pretensions ⟨has never *set up* to be a wise man —Thomas Rogers⟩ **4** : to become firm or consolidated : HARDEN — **set up housekeeping** : to establish one's living quarters — **set up shop :** to establish one's business

sev·en \'se-vən, 'se-bᵊm\ *n* [ME, fr. *seven,* adj., fr. OE *seofon;* akin to OHG *sibun* seven, L *septem,* Gk *hepta*] (bef. 12c) **1** — see NUMBER table **2 :** the seventh in a set or series ⟨the ∼ of diamonds⟩ **3 :** something having seven units or members — **seven** *adj* — **seven** *pron, pl in constr*

sev·en·fold \-ˌfōld\ *adj* (bef. 12c) **1 :** having seven units or members **2 :** being seven times as great or as many — **sevenfold** *adv*

seven seas *n pl* (1872) **:** all the waters or oceans of the world

sev·en·teen \ˌse-vən-'tēn, ˌse-bᵊm-\ *n* [*seventeen,* adj., fr. ME *seventene,* fr. OE *seofontēne;* akin to OE *tien* ten] (14c) — see NUMBER table — **seventeen** *adj* — **seventeen** *pron, pl in constr* — **sev·en·teenth** \-'tēn(t)th\ *adj or n*

seventeen–year locust *n* (1817) **:** a cicada (*Magicicada septendecim*) of the U.S. that has in the North a life of seventeen years and in the South of thirteen years of which most is spent underground as a nymph and only a few weeks as a winged adult

sev·enth \'se-vən(t)th, 'se-bᵊm(t)th\ *n, pl* **sevenths** \'se-vən(t)s, -vən(t)ths; 'se-bᵊm(t)s, -bᵊm(t)ths\ (12c) **1** — see NUMBER table **2 a** : a musical interval embracing seven diatonic degrees **b :** a tone at this interval; *specif* **:** LEADING TONE **c :** the harmonic combination of two tones a seventh apart — **seventh** *adj or adv*

seventh chord *n* (ca. 1909) **:** a chord comprising a fundamental tone with its third, fifth, and seventh

Seventh–Day *adj* (1684) **:** advocating or practicing observance of Saturday as the Sabbath

seventh heaven *n* [fr. the seventh being the highest of the seven heavens of Islamic and cabalist doctrine] (1818) **:** a state of extreme joy

sev·en·ty \'se-vən-tē, 'se-bᵊm-, -dē\ *n, pl* **-ties** [*seventy,* adj., fr. ME, fr. OE *seofontig,* short for *hundseofontig,* fr. *hundseofontig,* n., group of seventy, fr. *hund* hundred + *seofon* seven + *-tig* group of ten; akin to OE *tien* ten] (13c) **1** — see NUMBER table **2** *pl* **:** the numbers 70 to 79; *specif* **:** the years 70 to 79 in a lifetime or century **3** *cap* **:** a Mormon elder ordained for missionary work under the apostles — **sev·en·ti·eth** \-tē-əth, -dē-\ *adj or n* — **seventy** *adj* — **seventy** *pron, pl in constr*

sev·en·ty–eight \ˌse-vən-tē-'āt, ˌse-bᵊm-, -dē-'āt\ *n* (ca. 1934) **1** — see NUMBER table **2 :** a phonograph record designed to be played at 78 revolutions per minute — usu. written 78 — **seventy–eight** *adj* — **seventy–eight** *pron, pl in constr*

sev·en–up \ˌse-və-'nəp, ˌse-bᵊm-'əp\ *n* (1830) **:** an American variety of all fours in which a total of seven points constitutes game

sev·er \'se-vər\ *vb* **sev·ered; sev·er·ing** \'sev-riŋ, 'se-və-\ [ME, fr. MF *severer,* fr. L *separare* — more at SEPARATE] *vt* (14c) **:** to put or keep apart : DIVIDE; *esp* **:** to remove (as a part) by or as if by cutting ∼ *vi* **:** to become separated **syn** see SEPARATE

sev·er·able \'sev-rə-bəl, 'se-və-\ *adj* (1548) **:** capable of being severed; *esp* **:** capable of being divided into legally independent rights or obligations — **sev·er·abil·i·ty** \ˌsev-rə-'bi-lə-tē, ˌse-və-\ *n*

¹sev·er·al \'sev-rəl, 'se-və-\ *adj* [ME, fr. AF, fr. ML *separalis,* fr. L *separ* separate, back-formation fr. *separare* to separate] (15c) **1 a :** separate or distinct from one another ⟨federal union of the ∼ states⟩ **b** (1) **:** individually owned or controlled : EXCLUSIVE ⟨a ∼ fishery⟩ — compare COMMON (2) **:** of or relating separately to each individual involved ⟨a ∼ judgment⟩ **c :** being separate and distinctive : RESPECTIVE ⟨specialists in their ∼ fields⟩ **2 a :** more than one ⟨∼ pleas⟩ **b** : more than two but fewer than many ⟨moved ∼ inches⟩ **c** *chiefly dial* : being a great many

²several *pron, pl in constr* (1686) **:** an indefinite number more than two and fewer than many ⟨∼ of the guests⟩

sev·er·al·fold \ˌsev-rəl-'fōld, ˌse-və-\ *adj* (1738) **1 :** having several parts or aspects **2 :** being several times as large, as great, or as many as some understood size, degree, or amount — **severalfold** *adv*

sev·er·al·ly \'sev-rə-lē, 'se-və-\ *adv* (14c) **1 :** one at a time : each by itself : SEPARATELY **2 :** apart from others : INDEPENDENTLY

sev·er·al·ty \'sev-rəl-tē, 'se-və-\ *n* [ME *severalte,* fr. AF *severalté,* fr. *several*] (15c) **1 :** the quality or state of being several : DISTINCTNESS, SEPARATENESS **2 a :** a sole, separate, and exclusive possession, dominion, or ownership : one's own right without a joint interest in any other person ⟨tenants in ∼⟩ **b :** the quality or state of being individual or particular **3 a :** land owned in severalty **b :** the quality or state of being held in severalty

sev·er·ance \'sev-rən(t)s, 'se-və-\ *n* (15c) **:** the act or process of severing : the state of being severed

severance pay *n* (1943) **:** an allowance usu. based on length of service that is payable to an employee on termination of employment

severance tax *n* (1928) **:** a tax levied by a state on the extractor of oil, gas, or minerals intended for consumption in other states — compare ROYALTY 5a

se·vere \sə-'vir\ *adj* **se·ver·er; -est** [MF or L; MF, fr. L *severus*] (1548) **1 a :** strict in judgment, discipline, or government **b :** of a strict or stern bearing or manner : AUSTERE **2 :** rigorous in restraint, punishment, or requirement : STRINGENT, RESTRICTIVE **3 :** strongly critical or condemnatory : CENSORIOUS ⟨a ∼ critic⟩ **4 a :** maintaining a scrupulously exacting standard of behavior or self-discipline **b :** establishing exacting standards of accuracy and integrity in intellectual processes ⟨a ∼ logician⟩ **5 :** sober or restrained in decoration or manner : PLAIN **6 a :** inflicting physical discomfort or hardship : HARSH ⟨∼ winters⟩ **b** : inflicting pain or distress : GRIEVOUS ⟨a ∼ wound⟩ **7 :** requiring great effort : ARDUOUS ⟨a ∼ test⟩ **8 :** of a great degree : SERIOUS ⟨∼ depression⟩ — **se·vere·ly** *adv* — **se·vere·ness** *n* — **se·ver·i·ty** \sə-'ver-ə-tē\ *n*

syn SEVERE, STERN, AUSTERE, ASCETIC mean given to or marked by strict discipline and firm restraint. SEVERE implies standards enforced without indulgence or laxity and may suggest harshness ⟨*severe* military discipline⟩. STERN stresses inflexibility and inexorability of temper or character ⟨*stern* arbiters of public morality⟩. AUSTERE stresses absence

of warmth, color, or feeling and may apply to rigorous restraint, simplicity, or self-denial ⟨living an *austere* life in the country⟩. ASCETIC implies abstention from pleasure and comfort or self-indulgence as spiritual discipline ⟨the *ascetic* life of the monastic orders⟩.

severe combined immunodeficiency *n* (1974) **:** a rare congenital disorder of the immune system that is characterized by inability to produce a normal complement of antibodies and T cells and that usu. results in early death — called also *severe combined immune deficiency*

se·vi·che \sə-'vē-(ˌ)chā, -chē\ *n* [AmerSp] (1952) **:** a dish of raw fish marinated in lime or lemon juice often with oil, onions, peppers, and seasonings and served esp. as an appetizer

Sevres *or* **Sèvres** \'sev-rə, 'sev(r²)\ *n* [*Sèvres,* France] (1786) **:** an often elaborately decorated French porcelain

sev·ru·ga \sə-'vrü-gə, se-\ *n* [Russ *sevryuga,* a species of sturgeon] (1591) **:** a light to dark gray caviar from a sturgeon (*Acipenser sevru*) of the Caspian Sea that has very small roe; *also* **:** the fish

sew \'sō\ *vb* **sewed;** **sewn** \'sōn\ *or* **sewed; sew·ing** [ME, fr. OE *siwian;* akin to OHG *siuwen* to sew, L *suere*] *vt* (bef. 12c) **1 :** to unite or fasten by stitches **2 :** to close or enclose by sewing ⟨∼ the money in a bag⟩ ∼ *vi* **:** to practice or engage in sewing — **sew·abil·i·ty** \ˌsō-ə-'bi-lə-tē\ *n* — **sew·able** \'sō-ə-bəl\ *adj*

sew·age \'sü-ij\ *n* [³*sewer*] (1834) **:** refuse liquids or waste matter carried off by sewers

¹sew·er \'sü-ər, 'sú(-ə)r\ *n* [ME, fr. AF *asseour,* lit., seater, fr. OF *asseoir* to seat — more at ASSIZE] (14c) **:** a medieval household officer often of high rank in charge of serving the dishes at table and sometimes of seating and tasting

²sew·er \'sō(-ə)r\ *n* (14c) **:** one that sews

³sew·er \'sü-ər, 'sú(-ə)r\ *n* [ME *esseweur, seweur,* fr. *essewer* to drain, fr. (assumed) VL *exaquare,* fr. L *ex-* + *aqua* water — more at ISLAND] (15c) **:** an artificial usu. subterranean conduit to carry off sewage and sometimes surface water (as from rainfall)

sew·er·age \'sü-ə-rij, 'sü(-ə)r-ij\ *n* (1834) **1 :** the removal and disposal of sewage and surface water by sewers **2 :** a system of sewers **3** : SEWAGE

sew·ing \'sō-iŋ\ *n* (14c) **1 :** the act, method, or occupation of one that sews **2 :** material that has been or is to be sewed

sew up *vt* (15c) **1 :** to mend completely by sewing **2 :** to get exclusive use or control of **3 :** to make certain of : ASSURE

¹sex \'seks\ *n* [ME, fr. L *sexus*] (14c) **1 :** either of the two major forms of individuals that occur in many species and that are distinguished respectively as female or male **2 :** the sum of the structural, functional, and behavioral characteristics of living things that are involved in reproduction by two interacting parents and that distinguish males and females **3 a :** sexually motivated phenomena or behavior **b** : SEXUAL INTERCOURSE **4 :** GENITALIA

²sex *vt* (1884) **1 :** to identify the sex of ⟨∼ chicks⟩ **2 a :** to increase the sexual appeal of — often used with *up* **b :** to arouse the sexual desires of

sex·a·ge·nar·i·an \ˌsek-sə-jə-'ner-ē-ən\ *n* [L *sexagenarius* of or containing sixty, sixty years old, fr. *sexageni* sixty each, fr. *sexaginta* sixty, fr. *sex* six + *-ginta* (akin to L *viginti* twenty) — more at SIX, VIGESIMAL] (1738) **:** a person whose age is in the sixties — **sexagenarian** *adj*

¹sex·a·ges·i·mal \-'je-sə-məl\ *adj* [L *sexagesimus* sixtieth, fr. *sexaginta* sixty] (1685) **:** of, relating to, or based on the number 60

²sexagesimal *n* (1685) **:** a sexagesimal fraction

sex appeal *n* (1924) **1 :** personal appeal or physical attractiveness for members of the opposite sex **2 :** general attractiveness

sex cell *n* (1889) **:** GAMETE; *also* **:** its cellular precursor

sex chromatin *n* (1952) **:** BARR BODY

sex chromosome *n* (1906) **:** a chromosome that is inherited differently in the two sexes, that is concerned directly with the inheritance of sex, and that is the seat of factors governing the inheritance of various sex-linked and sex-limited characters

sex·de·cil·lion \ˌseks-di-'sil-yən\ *n, often attrib* [L *sedecim, sexdecim* sixteen (fr. *sex* six + *decem* ten) + E *-illion* (as in *million*) — more at TEN] (ca. 1934) — see NUMBER table

sexed \'sekst\ *adj* (ca. 1891) **1 :** having sex or sexual instincts **2** : having sex appeal

sex gland *n* (1935) **:** GONAD

sex hormone *n* (1917) **:** a hormone (as from the gonads or adrenal cortex) that affects the growth or function of the reproductive organs or the development of secondary sex characteristics

sex·ism \'sek-ˌsi-zəm\ *n* [¹*sex* + *-ism* (as in *racism*)] (1968) **1 :** prejudice or discrimination based on sex; *esp* **:** discrimination against women **2 :** behavior, conditions, or attitudes that foster stereotypes of social roles based on sex — **sex·ist** \'sek-sist\ *adj or n*

sex kitten *n* (1958) **:** a young woman with conspicuous sex appeal

sex·less \'seks-ləs\ *adj* (1598) **1 :** lacking sex : NEUTER **2 :** devoid of sexual interest or activity ⟨a ∼ relationship⟩ — **sex·less·ly** *adv* — **sex·less·ness** *n*

sex·lim·it·ed \'seks-'li-mə-təd\ *adj* (1923) **:** expressed in the phenotype of only one sex

sex–link·age \-ˌliŋ-kij\ *n* (1912) **:** the quality or state of being sex-linked

sex–linked \-ˌliŋ(k)t\ *adj* (1912) **1 :** located on a sex chromosome ⟨a ∼ gene⟩ **2 :** mediated by a sex-linked gene ⟨a ∼ character⟩

sex object *n* (1911) **:** a person regarded esp. exclusively as an object of sexual interest

sex·ol·o·gy \sek-'sä-lə-jē\ *n* (1902) **:** the study of sex or of the interaction of the sexes esp. among human beings — **sex·ol·o·gist** \-jist\ *n*

sex·ploi·ta·tion \ˌseks-ˌplȯi-'tā-shən\ *n* [blend of *sex* and *exploitation*] (ca. 1942) **:** the exploitation of sex in the media and esp. in film

sex·pot \'seks-ˌpät\ *n* (1948) **:** a conspicuously sexy woman

sex symbol *n* (ca. 1911) **:** a usu. renowned person (as an entertainer) noted and admired for conspicuous sex appeal

---

\ə\ abut \ᵊ\ kitten, F table \ər\ further \a\ ash \ā\ ace \ä\ mop, mar \au̇\ out \ch\ chin \e\ bet \ē\ easy \g\ go \i\ hit \ī\ ice \j\ job \ŋ\ sing \ō\ go \ȯ\ law \ȯi\ boy \th\ thin \t̲h̲\ the \ü\ loot \u̇\ foot \y\ yet \zh\ vision \à, ᴋ, ⁿ, œ, œ̄, ᴜᴇ, ᵫ, ʸ\ *see* Guide to Pronunciation

sext \'sekst\ *n, often cap* [ME *sexte*, fr. LL *sexta*, fr. L, sixth hour of the day, fr. fem. of *sextus* sixth, fr. *sex* six] (15c) : the fourth of the canonical hours

Sex·tans \'seks-ˌtanz\ *n* [NL (gen. *Sextantis*), lit., sextant] : a constellation on the equator south of Leo

sex·tant \'seks-tənt\ *n* [NL *sextant-, sextans* sixth part of a circle, fr. L, sixth part, fr. *sextus* sixth] (1628) : an instrument for measuring angular distances used esp. in navigation to observe altitudes of celestial bodies (as in ascertaining latitude and longitude)

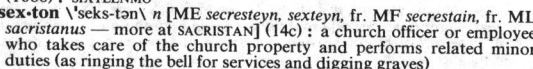

sextant

sex·tet \seks-'tet\ *n* [alter. of *sestet*] (1841) **1** : a musical composition for six instruments or voices **2** : a group or set of six: as **a** : the performers of a sextet **b** : a hockey team

sex·til·lion \seks-'til-yən\ *n, often attrib* [F, irreg. fr. *sex-* (fr. L *sex*) + *-illion* (as in *million*)] (1690) — see NUMBER table

sex·to \'seks-(ˌ)tō\ *n, pl* **sextos** [L *sexto,* abl. of *sextus* sixth] (1847) : SIXMO

sex·to·dec·i·mo \ˌseks-tə-'de-sə-ˌmō\ *n, pl* **-mos** [L, abl. of *sextus decimus* sixteenth, fr. *sextus* sixth + *decimus* tenth — more at DIME] (1688) : SIXTEENMO

sex·ton \'seks-tən\ *n* [ME *secresteyn, sexteyn,* fr. MF *secrestain,* fr. ML *sacristanus* — more at SACRISTAN] (14c) : a church officer or employee who takes care of the church property and performs related minor duties (as ringing the bell for services and digging graves)

¹sex·tu·ple \seks-'tü-pəl, -'tyü-, -'tə-; 'seks-tə-\ *adj* [prob. fr. ML *sextuplus,* fr. L *sextus* sixth + *-plus* multiplied by; akin to L *-plex -plex* — more at -FOLD] (1626) **1** : having six units or members **2** : being six times as great or as many **3** : marked by six beats per measure of music (~ time) — **sextuple** *n*

²sextuple *vb* **sex·tu·pled; sex·tu·pling** \-p(ə-)liŋ\ *vt* (1632) : to make six times as much or as many ~ *vi* : to become six times as much or as numerous

sex·tu·plet \seks-'tə-plət, -'tü-, -'tyü-; 'seks-t(y)ə-\ *n* (1852) **1** : a combination of six of a kind **2** : one of six offspring born at one birth **3** : a group of six equal musical notes performed in the time ordinarily given to four of the same value

¹sex·tu·pli·cate \seks-'tü-pli-kət, -'tyü-\ *adj* [blend of *sextuple* and *-plicate* (as in *duplicate*)] (1657) **1** : repeated six times **2** : SIXTH ⟨file the ~ copy⟩ — **sextuplicate** *n*

²sex·tu·pli·cate \-plə-ˌkāt\ *vt* **-cat·ed; -cat·ing** (ca. 1934) **1** : SEXTUPLE **2** : to provide in sextuplicate

sex·u·al \'sek-sh(ə-)wəl, 'sek-shəl\ *adj* [LL *sexualis,* fr. L *sexus* sex] (1651) **1** : of, relating to, or associated with sex or the sexes ⟨~ differentiation⟩ ⟨~ conflict⟩ **2** : having or involving sex ⟨~ reproduction⟩ — **sex·u·al·ly** \'sek-sh(ə-)wə-lē, 'sek-sh(ə-)lē\ *adv*

sexual generation *n* (1880) : the generation of an organism with alternation of generations that reproduces sexually

sexual harassment *n* (1975) : uninvited and unwelcome verbal or physical conduct directed at an employee because of his or her sex

sexual intercourse *n* (1799) **1** : heterosexual intercourse involving penetration of the vagina by the penis : COITUS **2** : intercourse involving genital contact between individuals other than penetration of the vagina by the penis

sex·u·al·i·ty \ˌsek-shə-'wa-lə-tē\ *n* (ca. 1800) : the quality or state of being sexual: **a** : the condition of having sex **b** : sexual activity **c** : expression of sexual receptivity or interest esp. when excessive

sex·u·al·ize \'sek-sh(ə-)wə-ˌlīz, 'sek-shə-ˌlīz\ *vt* **-ized; -iz·ing** (1839) : to make sexual : endow with a sexual character or cast

sexual relations *n pl* (1950) : COITUS

sexual selection *n* (1859) : natural selection for characters that confer success in competition for a mate as distinguished from competition with other species; *also* : the choice of a mate based on a preference for certain characteristics (as color or bird song)

sexy \'sek-sē\ *adj* **sex·i·er; -est** (1925) **1** : sexually suggestive or stimulating : EROTIC **2** : generally attractive or interesting : APPEALING ⟨a ~ stock⟩ — **sex·i·ly** \-sə-lē\ *adv* — **sex·i·ness** \-sē-nəs\ *n*

Sey·fert galaxy \'sē-fərt- *also* 'sī-\ *n* [Carl K. *Seyfert* †1960 Am. astronomer] (1959) : any of a class of spiral galaxies that have small compact bright nuclei characterized by variability in light intensity, emission of radio waves, and spectra which indicate hot gases in rapid motion — called also *Seyfert*

sfer·ics \'sfir-iks, 'sfer-\ *n pl* [by shortening & alter.] (1945) : ATMOSPHERICS

¹sfor·zan·do \sfȯrt-'sän-(ˌ)dō, -'san-\ *adj or adv* [It, verbal of *sforzare* to force] (ca. 1801) : played with prominent stress or accent — used as a direction in music

²sforzando *n, pl* **-dos** *or* **-di** \-(ˌ)dē\ (1890) : an accented tone or chord

sfu·ma·to \sfü-'mä-(ˌ)tō\ *n* [It, fr. pp. of *sfumare* to evaporate] (1909) : the definition of form in painting without abrupt outline by the blending of one tone into another

sgraf·fi·to \zgra-'fē-(ˌ)tō, skra-\ *n, pl* **-ti** \-(ˌ)tē\ [It, fr. pp. of *sgraffire* to scratch, produce sgraffito] (ca. 1730) **1** : decoration by cutting away parts of a surface layer (as of plaster or clay) to expose a different colored ground — compare GRAFFITO **2** : something (as traditional Pennsylvania Dutch pottery) decorated with sgraffito

sh \sh *often prolonged*\ *interj* (1847) — used often in prolonged or rapidly repeated form to urge or command silence or less noise

Sha·ban \shə-'bän\ *n* [Ar *sha'bān*] (ca. 1771) : the 8th month of the Islamic year — see MONTH table

Shab·bat \shə-'bät, 'shä-bəs\ *n* [Heb *shabbāth*] (ca. 1905) : the Jewish Sabbath

shab·by \'sha-bē\ *adj* **shab·bi·er; -est** [obs. E *shab* a low fellow] (1669) **1** : clothed with worn or seedy garments ⟨a ~ hobo⟩ **2 a** : threadbare and faded from wear ⟨a ~ sofa⟩ **b** : ill-kept : DILAPIDATED ⟨a ~ neighborhood⟩ **3 a** : MEAN, DESPICABLE, CONTEMPTIBLE ⟨must feel ~ . . . because of his compromises —Nat Hentoff⟩ **b** : UNGENEROUS, UNFAIR ⟨laments the ~ way in which this country often treated a poet —Paul Engle⟩ **c** : inferior in quality ⟨~ reasoning⟩ — **shab·bi·ly** \'sha-bə-lē\ *adv* — **shab·bi·ness** \'sha-bē-nəs\ *n*

Sha·bu·oth \shə-'vü-ˌōt, -ˌōth, -ˌōs, -əs\ *n* [Heb *shābhū'ōth,* lit., weeks]

(ca. 1903) : a Jewish holiday observed on the 6th and 7th of Sivan in commemoration of the revelation of the Ten Commandments at Mt. Sinai — called also *Pentecost*

shack \'shak\ *n* [prob. back-formation fr. E dial. *shackly* rickety] (1878) **1** : HUT, SHANTY **2** : a room or similar enclosed structure for a particular person or use ⟨a guard ~⟩

¹shack·le \'sha-kəl\ *n* [ME *schakel,* fr. OE *sceacul;* akin to ON *skǫkull* pole of a cart] (bef. 12c) **1** : something (as a manacle or fetter) that confines the legs or arms **2** : something that checks or prevents free action as if by fetters — usu. used in pl. **3** : a usu. U-shaped fastening device secured by a bolt or pin through holes in the end of the two arms **4** : a length of cable or anchor chain of usu. 15 fathoms

²shackle *vt* **shack·led; shack·ling** \-k(ə-)liŋ\ (15c) **1 a** : to bind with shackles : FETTER **b** : to make fast with or as if with a shackle **2** : to deprive of freedom esp. of action by means of restrictions or handicaps : IMPEDE *syn* see HAMPER — **shack·ler** \-k(ə-)lər\ *n*

shack·le·bone \'sha-kəl-ˌbōn, 'shä-\ *n* (1571) *Scot* : WRIST

shack up *vi* (1935) : to sleep or live together as unmarried sexual partners

shad \'shad\ *n, pl* **shad** [(assumed) ME, fr. OE *sceadd*] (bef. 12c) : any of several clupeid fishes (esp. genus *Alosa*) that differ from the typical herrings in having a relatively deep body and in being anadromous and that include some important food fishes of Europe and No. America

shad·ber·ry \-ˌber-ē\ *n* (1847) : SERVICEBERRY

shad·blow \'shad-ˌblō\ *n* (1846) : SERVICEBERRY 2

shad·bush \-ˌbu̇sh\ *n* (ca. 1818) : SERVICEBERRY 2

shad·dock \'sha-dək\ *n* [Captain *Shaddock,* 17th cent. Eng. ship commander] (1696) : a very large thick-rinded usu. pear-shaped citrus fruit differing from the closely related grapefruit esp. in its loose rind and often coarse dry pulp; *also* : the tree (*Citrus maxima* syn. *C. grandis*) that bears it

¹shade \'shād\ *n* [ME, fr. OE *sceadu;* akin to OHG *scato* shadow, Gk *skotos* darkness] (bef. 12c) **1 a** : comparative darkness or obscurity owing to interception of the rays of light **b** : relative obscurity or retirement **2 a** : shelter (as by foliage) from the heat and glare of sunlight **b** : a place sheltered from the sun **3** : an evanescent or unreal appearance **4** *pl* **a** : the shadows that gather as darkness comes on **b** : NETHERWORLD, HADES **5 a** : a disembodied spirit : GHOST **b** — used to signal the similarity between a previously encountered person or situation and one at hand; usu. used in pl. ⟨~s of my childhood⟩ **6** : something that intercepts or shelters from light, sun, or heat: as **a** : a device partially covering a lamp so as to reduce glare **b** : a flexible screen usu. mounted on a roller for regulating the light or the view through a window **c** *pl* : SUNGLASSES **7 a** : the reproduction of the effect of shade in painting or drawing **b** : a subdued or somber feature **8 a** : a color produced by a pigment or dye mixture having some black in it **b** : a color slightly different from the one under consideration **9 a** : a minute difference or variation : NUANCE **b** : a minute degree or quantity **10** : a facial expression of sadness or displeasure — **shade·less** \-ləs\ *adj*

²shade *vb* **shad·ed; shad·ing** *vt* (14c) **1 a** : to shelter or screen by intercepting radiated light or heat **b** : to cover with a shade **2** : to hide partly by or as if by a shadow **3** : to darken with or as if with a shadow **4** : to better or exceed by a shade : SURPASS, ECLIPSE **5 a** : to represent the effect of shade or shadow on **b** : to add shading to **c** : to color so that the shades pass gradually from one to another **6** : to change by gradual transition or qualification **7** : to reduce slightly (as a price) **8** : SLANT, BIAS ~ *vi* **1** : to pass by slight changes or imperceptible degrees **2** : to undergo or exhibit minute difference or variation — **shad·er** *n*

shade–grown \'shād-ˌgrōn\ *adj* (1922) : grown in the shade; *specif* : grown under cloth ⟨~ tobacco⟩

shade tree *n* (1806) : a tree grown primarily to produce shade

shad·ing \'shā-diŋ\ *n* (1663) **1** : the use of marking made within outlines to suggest three-dimensionality, shadow, or degrees of light and dark in a picture or drawing **2** : an interpretative effect in music gained esp. by subtle changes in dynamics

sha·doof *also* **sha·duf** \shə-'düf, sha-\ *n* [Ar *shādūf*] (1836) : a counterbalanced sweep used since ancient times esp. in Egypt for raising water (as for irrigation)

¹shad·ow \'sha-(ˌ)dō\ *n* [ME *shadwe,* fr. OE *sceaduw-, sceadu* shade] (bef. 12c) **1** : partial darkness or obscurity within a part of space from which rays from a source of light are cut off by an interposed opaque body **2** : a reflected image **3** : shelter from danger or observation **4 a** : an imperfect and faint representation **b** : an imitation of something : COPY **5** : the dark figure cast upon a surface by a body intercepting the rays from a source of light **6** : PHANTOM **7** *pl* : DARK 1a **8** : a shaded or darker portion of a picture **9** : an attenuated form or a vestigial remnant **10 a** : an inseparable companion or follower **b** : one (as a spy or detective) that shadows **11** : a small degree or portion : TRACE **12** : a source of gloom or unhappiness **13 a** : an area near an object : VICINITY **b** : pervasive and dominant influence **14** : a state of ignominy or obscurity — **shad·ow·less** \'sha-dō-ləs, -də-ləs\ *adj* — **shad·ow·like** \-ˌlīk\ *adj*

²shadow *vt* (bef. 12c) **1** *archaic* : SHELTER, PROTECT **2** : to cast a shadow upon : CLOUD **3** *obs* : to shelter from the sun **4** *obs* : CONCEAL **5** : to represent or indicate obscurely or faintly — often used with *forth* or *out* **6** : to follow esp. secretly : TRAIL **7** *archaic* : SHADE **5** ~ *vi* **1** : to pass gradually or by degrees **2** : to become overcast with or as if with shadows — **shad·ow·er** \-dō-ər, -də-wər\ *n*

³shadow *adj* (1906) **1** : of, relating to, or resembling a shadow cabinet ⟨~ minister of defense⟩ **2 a** : having an indistinct pattern ⟨~ plaid⟩ **b** : having darker sections of design ⟨~ lace⟩

shadow band *n* (1900) : one of a series of dark narrow parallel bands that appear to rush swiftly across the landscape just before or after totality in a solar eclipse

shad·ow-box \'sha-dō-ˌbäks, -də-ˌbäks\ *vi* (1919) : to box with an imaginary opponent esp. as a form of training

shadow box *n* (ca. 1909) : a shallow enclosing case usu. with a glass front in which something is set for protection and display

shadow cabinet *n* (1906) : a group of leaders of a parliamentary opposition who constitute the probable membership of the cabinet when their party is returned to power

shadow dance n (ca. 1909) : a dance shown by throwing the shadows of dancers on a screen
shad·ow·graph \'sha-dō-₁graf, -də-₁graf\ n (1888) 1 : SHADOW PLAY 2 : a photographic image resembling a shadow — **shad·ow·graphy** \-₁gra-fē\ n
shadow mask n (1951) : a metal plate in a color television tube that contains minute apertures permitting passage of electron beams to specific phosphors on the screen during a scan
shadow play n (1895) : a drama exhibited by throwing shadows of puppets or actors on a screen — called also *shadow show*
shad·owy \'sha-dō-ē, -də-wē\ adj (14c) 1 a : of the nature of or resembling a shadow : UNSUBSTANTIAL b : faintly perceptible : INDISTINCT, VAGUE 2 : being in or obscured by shadow ⟨deep ~ interiors⟩ 3 : SHADY 1, 3 — **shad·ow·i·ly** \-wə-lē\ adv — **shad·ow·i·ness** \-wē-nəs\ n
shady \'shā-dē\ adj **shad·i·er; -est** (1579) 1 : producing or affording shade 2 : sheltered from the sun's rays 3 a : of questionable merit : UNCERTAIN, UNRELIABLE b : DISREPUTABLE — **shad·i·ly** \'shā-dᵊl-ē\ adv — **shad·i·ness** \'shā-dē-nəs\ n
¹**shaft** \'shaft\ n, pl **shafts** \'shaf(t)s, for 1b usu 'shavz\ [ME, fr. OE sceaft; akin to OHG scaft shaft, L scapus shaft, stalk, Gk skēptesthai to prop oneself, lean] (bef. 12c) 1 a (1) : the long handle of a spear or similar weapon (2) : SPEAR, LANCE b or pl **shaves** \'shavz\ : POLE; specif : either of two long pieces of wood between which a horse is hitched to a vehicle c (1) : an arrow esp. for a longbow (2) : the body or stem of an arrow extending from the nock to the head 2 : a sharply delineated beam of light shining through an opening 3 : something suggestive of the shaft of a spear or arrow esp. in long slender cylindrical form: as a : the trunk of a tree b : the cylindrical pillar between the capital and the base c : the handle of a tool or instrument (as a golf club) d : a commonly cylindrical bar used to support rotating pieces or to transmit power or motion by rotation e : the stem or central axis of a feather f : the upright member of a cross esp. below the arms g : a small architectural column (as at each side of a doorway) h : a column, obelisk, or other spire-shaped or columnar monument i : a vertical or inclined opening of uniform and limited cross section for finding or mining ore, raising water, or ventilating underground workings (as in a cave) j : a vertical opening or passage through the floors of a building 4 a : a projectile thrown like a spear or shot like an arrow b : a scornful, satirical, or pithy critical remark or attack c : harsh or unfair treatment — usu. used with *the*
²**shaft** vt (1611) 1 : to fit with a shaft 2 : to treat unfairly or harshly
shaft horsepower n (1908) : horsepower transmitted by an engine shaft
shaft·ing \'shaf-tiŋ\ n (1825) : shafts or material for shafts
¹**shag** \'shag\ n [(assumed) ME shagge, fr. OE sceacga; akin to ON skegg beard, skaga to project] (bef. 12c) 1 a : a shaggy tangled mass or covering (as of hair) b : long coarse or matted fiber, nap, or pile 2 : tobacco cut into fine shreds : CORMORANT 1
²**shag** adj (1592) : SHAGGY
³**shag** vb **shagged; shag·ging** vi (1596) : to fall or hang in shaggy masses ~ vt : to make rough or shaggy
⁴**shag** vt **shagged; shag·ging** [origin unknown] (1904) 1 a : to chase after; esp : to chase after and return (a ball) hit usu. out of play b : to catch (a fly) in baseball practice 2 : to chase away
⁵**shag** vi **shagged; shag·ging** [perh. alter. of shack to lumber along] (1914) 1 : to move or lope along 2 : to dance the shag
⁶**shag** n (1932) : a dance step executed by hopping livelily on each foot in turn
shag·bark \'shag-₁bärk\ n (1777) : SHAGBARK HICKORY
shagbark hickory n (1751) : a hickory (*Carya ovata*) with sweet edible nuts and a gray shaggy outer bark that peels off in long strips; also : its wood
shag·gy \'sha-gē\ adj **shag·gi·er; -est** (ca. 1590) 1 a : covered with or consisting of long, coarse, or matted hair b : covered with or consisting of thick, tangled, or unkempt vegetation c : having a rough nap, texture, or surface d : having hairlike processes 2 a : UNKEMPT b : confused or unclear in conception or thinking — **shag·gi·ly** \'sha-gə-lē\ adv — **shag·gi·ness** \'sha-gē-nəs\ n
shag·gy–dog story \₁sha-gē-'dóg-\ n (1946) : a long-drawn-out circumstantial story concerning an inconsequential happening that impresses the teller as humorous but the hearer as boring and pointless; also : a similar humorous story whose humor lies in the pointlessness or irrelevance of the punch line
shag·gy·mane \'sha-gē-₁mān\ n (ca. 1909) : a common edible mushroom (*Coprinus comatus*) having an elongated shaggy white pileus with deliquescing gills and black spores — called also *shaggy cap*

shaggymane

sha·green \sha-'grēn, shə-\ n [by folk etymology fr. F chagrin, modif. of Turk sağrı] (1677) 1 : an untanned leather covered with small round granulations and usu. dyed green 2 : the rough skin of various sharks and rays when covered with small close-set tubercles — **shagreen** adj
shah \'shä, 'shó\ n, often cap [Per shāh king — more at CHECK] (1566) : a sovereign of Iran — **shah·dom** \'shä-dəm, 'shó-\ n
Sha·hap·ti·an \shə-'hap-tē-ən\ n, pl **Shahaptian** or **Shahaptians** (1836) 1 : a member of a group of American Indian peoples who formerly inhabited a large territory along the Columbia River and its tributaries 2 : the language of the Shahaptian people including Nez Percé and Yakima
shai·tan \shä-'tän, shī-\ n [Ar shaytān] (1638) : an evil spirit; specif : an evil jinni
¹**shake** \'shāk\ vb **shook** \'shuk\; **shak·en** \'shā-kən\; **shak·ing** [ME, fr. OE sceacan; akin to ON skaka to shake] vi (bef. 12c) 1 : to move irregularly to and fro 2 : to vibrate esp. as the result of a blow or shock 3 : to tremble as a result of physical or emotional disturbance 4 : to experience a state of instability : TOTTER 5 : to briskly move something to and fro or up and down esp. in order to mix 6 : to clasp hands 7 : ³TRILL ~ vt 1 : to brandish, wave, or flourish often in a

threatening manner 2 : to cause to move in a usu. quick jerky manner 3 : to cause to quake, quiver, or tremble 4 a : to free oneself from ⟨~ a habit⟩ ⟨~ off a cold⟩ b : to get away from : get rid of ⟨can you ~ your friend? I want to talk to you alone —Elmer Davis 5 : to lessen the stability of : WEAKEN ⟨~ one's faith⟩ 6 : to bring to a specified condition by or as if by repeated quick jerky movements ⟨shook himself loose from the man's grasp⟩ 7 : to dislodge or eject by quick jerky movements of the support or container ⟨shook the dust from the cloth⟩ 8 : to clasp (hands) in greeting or farewell or as a sign of goodwill or agreement 9 : to stir the feelings of : UPSET ⟨shook her up⟩ 10 : ³TRILL — **shak·able** or **shake·able** \'shā-kə-bəl\ adj — **shake a leg** 1 : DANCE 2 : to hurry up
syn SHAKE, AGITATE, ROCK, CONVULSE mean to move up and down or to and fro with some violence. SHAKE often carries a further implication of a particular purpose ⟨shake well before using⟩. AGITATE suggests a violent and prolonged tossing or stirring ⟨an ocean agitated by storms⟩. ROCK suggests a swinging or swaying motion resulting from violent impact or upheaval ⟨the whole city was rocked by the explosion⟩. CONVULSE suggests a violent pulling or wrenching as of a body in a paroxysm ⟨spectators were convulsed with laughter⟩.
²**shake** n (1581) 1 a : an act of shaking: as a : an act of shaking hands b : an act of shaking oneself 2 a : a blow or shock that upsets the equilibrium or disturbs the balance of something b : EARTHQUAKE 3 pl a : a condition of trembling or nervousness; specif : DELIRIUM TREMENS b : MALARIA 2a 4 : something produced by shaking: as a : a fissure separating annual rings of growth in timber b (1) : MILK SHAKE (2) : a beverage resembling a milk shake but made without milk 5 : a wavering, quivering, or alternating motion caused by a blow or shock 6 : ³TRILL 7 : a very brief period of time 8 pl : one that is exceptional esp. in importance, ability, or merit — usu. used in the phrase no great shakes 9 : a shingle split from a piece of log usu. three or four feet (about one meter) long 10 : ³DEAL 3 ⟨a fair ~⟩
shake–down \'shāk-₁daun\ n (ca. 1730) 1 : an improvised bed (as one made up on the floor) 2 : a boisterous dance 3 : an act or instance of shaking someone down; esp : EXTORTION 4 : a thorough search 5 : a process or period of adjustment 6 : a testing under operating conditions of something new (as a ship) for possible faults and defects and for familiarizing the operators with it
shake down vi (ca. 1859) 1 a : to take up temporary quarters b : to occupy an improvised or makeshift bed 2 a : to become accustomed esp. to new surroundings or duties b : to settle down ~ vt 1 : to obtain money from in a deceitful or illegal manner 2 : to make a thorough search of 3 : to bring about a reduction of 4 : to give a shakedown test to
shake-out \'shā-₁kaut\ n (1895) 1 : the failure or retrenchment of a significant number of firms in the economy or a sector or an industry that usu. results in a depressed market 2 : a period or process in which the relatively weak or unessential are eliminated
shak·er \'shā-kər\ n (15c) 1 : one that shakes: as a : a utensil or machine used in shaking ⟨cocktail ~⟩ b : one that incites, promotes, or directs action ⟨a mover and ~⟩ 2 cap [fr. a dance with shaking movements performed as part of worship] : a member of a millenarian sect originating in England in 1747 and practicing celibacy and an ascetic communal life — **Shaker** adj — **Shak·er·ism** \-kə-₁ri-zəm\ n
¹**Shake·spear·ean** or **Shake·spear·ian** also **Shak·sper·ean** or **Shak·sper·ian** \shāk-'spir-ē-ən\ adj (1755) 1 : of, relating to, or having the characteristics of Shakespeare or his writings 2 : evocative of a theme, setting, or event from a work of Shakespeare ⟨~ pageantry⟩
²**Shakespearean** or **Shakespearian** also **Shaksperean** or **Shaksperian** n (1837) : an authority on or devotee of Shakespeare
Shake·spear·eana or **Shake·spear·iana** \(₁)shāk-₁spir-ē-'a-nə, -'ä-, -'ā-\ n pl (1718) : collected items by, about, or relating to Shakespeare
Shakespearean sonnet n (1903) : ENGLISH SONNET
shake–up \'shā-₁kəp\ n (1847) : an act or instance of shaking up; specif : an extensive and often drastic reorganization
shake up vt (1538) 1 : CHIDE, SCOLD 2 : to jar by or as if by a physical shock ⟨the collision shook up both drivers⟩ 3 : to effect an extensive and often drastic reorganization of
shaking palsy n (1615) : PARKINSON'S DISEASE
sha·ko \'sha-(₁)kō, 'shā-, 'shä-\ n, pl **shakos** or **shakoes** [F, fr. Hung csákó] (1815) : a stiff military hat with a high crown and plume
Shak·ta \'shäk-tə, 'säk-\ n or adj [Skt śākta, fr. Śakti] (1810) : an adherent of Shaktism
Shak·ti \-tē\ n [Skt Śakti] (1810) : the dynamic energy of a Hindu god personified as his female consort; broadly : cosmic energy as conceived in Hindu thought
Shak·tism \-₁ti-zəm\ n (1877) : a Hindu sect worshiping Shakti under various names (as Kali or Durga) in a cult of devotion to the female principle often with magical or orgiastic rites
shaky \'shā-kē\ adj **shak·i·er; -est** (1703) 1 : characterized by shakes ⟨~ timber⟩ 2 : lacking stability : PRECARIOUS b : lacking in firmness (as of beliefs or principles) c : lacking in authority or reliability : QUESTIONABLE 3 a : somewhat unsound in health b : characterized by shaking 4 : likely to give way or break down — **shak·i·ly** \-kə-lē\ adv — **shak·i·ness** \-kē-nəs\ n
shale \'shā(ə)l\ n [prob. fr. obs. or dial. shale scale, shell, fr. ME, fr. OE scealu — more at SHELL] (1747) : a fissile rock that is formed by the consolidation of clay, mud, or silt, has a finely stratified or laminated structure, and is composed of minerals essentially unaltered since deposition — **shal·ey** \'shā-lē\ adj
shale oil n (1857) : a crude dark oil obtained from oil shale by heating
shall \shəl, 'shal\ vb, past **should** \shəd, 'shúd\; pres sing & pl **shall** [ME shal (1st & 3d sing. pres. indic.), fr. OE sceal; akin to OHG scal (1st & 3d sing. pres. indic.) ought to, must, Lith skola debt] (bef. 12c) verbal auxiliary 1 archaic a : will have to : MUST b : will be able to : CAN 2 a — used to express a command or exhortation ⟨you ~ go⟩ b — used in laws, regulations, or directives to express what is manda-

\ə\ abut \ᵊ\ kitten, F table \ər\ further \a\ ash \ā\ ace \ä\ mop, mar \aú\ out \ch\ chin \e\ bet \ē\ easy \g\ go \i\ hit \ī\ ice \j\ job \ŋ\ sing \ō\ go \ó\ law \ói\ boy \th\ thin \t̲h̲\ the \ü\ loot \ú\ foot \y\ yet \zh\ vision \a, k̲, ⁿ, œ, œ̄, ᵫ, ᵫ̄, ᶣ\ see Guide to Pronunciation

tory ⟨it ∼ be unlawful to carry firearms⟩ **3 a** — used to express what is inevitable or seems likely to happen in the future ⟨we ∼ have to be ready⟩ ⟨we ∼ see⟩ **b** — used to express simple futurity ⟨when ∼ we expect you⟩ **4** — used to express determination ⟨they ∼ not pass⟩ ∼ *vi, archaic* : will go ⟨he to England ∼ along with you —Shak.⟩
usage From the reams of pronouncements written about the distinction between *shall* and *will*—dating back as far as the 17th century—it is clear that the rules laid down have never very accurately reflected actual usage. The nationalistic statements of 18th and 19th century British grammarians, who commonly cited the misuses of the Irish, the Scots, and occas. the Americans, suggest that the traditional rules may have come closest to the usage of southern England. Some modern commentators believe that English usage is still the closest to the traditionally prescribed norms. Most modern commentators allow that *will* is more common in nearly all uses. The entries for *shall* and *will* in this dictionary show current usage.
shal·loon \shə-'lün, sha-\ *n* [*Châlons*-sur-Marne, France] (1678) : a lightweight twilled fabric of wool or worsted used chiefly for the linings of coats and uniforms
shal·lop \'sha-ləp\ *n* [MF *chaloupe*] (ca. 1578) **1 a** : a usu. 2-masted ship with lugsails **b** : a small open boat propelled by oars or sails and used chiefly in shallow waters
shal·lot \shə-'lät *also* 'sha-lət\ *n* [modif. of F *échalote*, alter. of *escaloigne*, fr. (assumed) VL *escalonia* — more at SCALLION] (1664) **1** : a bulbous perennial herb (*Allium cepa aggregatum*) that resembles an onion and produces small clustered bulbs used in seasoning **2** : GREEN ONION
¹shal·low \'sha-(ˌ)lō\ *adj* [ME *schalowe*; prob. akin to OE *sceald* shallow — more at SKELETON] (14c) **1** : having little depth ⟨∼ water⟩ **2** : having little extension inward or backward ⟨office buildings have taken the form of ∼ slabs —Lewis Mumford⟩ **3 a** : penetrating only the easily or quickly perceived ⟨∼ generalizations⟩ **b** : lacking in depth of knowledge, thought, or feeling ⟨a ∼ demagogue⟩ **4** : displacing comparatively little air : WEAK ⟨∼ breathing⟩ *syn* see SUPERFICIAL — **shal·low·ly** \-lō-lē, -lə-lē\ *adv* — **shal·low·ness** *n*
²shallow *vt* (1510) : to make shallow ∼ *vi* : to become shallow
³shallow *n* (1571) : a shallow place or area in a body of water — usu. used in pl. but sing. or pl. in constr.
sha·lom \shä-'lōm, shə-\ *interj* [Heb *shālōm* peace] (1904) — used as a Jewish greeting and farewell
sha·lom alei·chem \-,shō-ləm-ə-'lä-kəm, ,shō-, -kəm\ *interj* [Heb *shālōm 'alēkhem* peace unto you] (1881) — used as a traditional Jewish greeting
shalt \'shalt, 'shält\ *archaic pres 2d sing of* SHALL
¹sham \'sham\ *n* [perh. fr. E dial. *sham* shame, alter. of E *shame*] (1677) **1** : a trick that deludes : HOAX **2** : cheap falseness : HYPOCRISY **3** : an ornamental covering for a pillow **4** : an imitation or counterfeit purporting to be genuine **5** : a person who shams *syn* see IMPOSTURE
²sham *adj* (1681) **1** : not genuine : FALSE, FEIGNED **2** : having such poor quality as to seem false
³sham *vb* **shammed; sham·ming** *vt* (1755) : to go through the external motions necessary to counterfeit ∼ *vi* : to act intentionally so as to give a false impression : FEIGN — **sham·mer** \'sha-mər\ *n syn* see ASSUME
sha·man \'shä-mən, 'shā- *also* shə-'män\ *n, pl* **shamans** [ultim. fr. Evenki (Tungusic language of Siberia) *šamān*] (1698) **1** : a priest or priestess who uses magic for the purpose of curing the sick, divining the hidden, and controlling events **2** : one who resembles a shaman; *esp* : HIGH PRIEST **3** — **sha·man·ic** \shə-'ma-nik, -'mä-\ *adj*
sha·man·ism \-,ni-zəm\ *n* (1780) : a religion practiced by indigenous peoples of far northern Europe and Siberia that is characterized by belief in an unseen world of gods, demons, and ancestral spirits responsive only to the shamans; *also* : any similar religion — **sha·man·ist** \-nist\ *n* — **sha·man·is·tic** \,shä-mə-'nis-tik, shā-mə-\ *adj*
sham·ble \'sham-bəl\ *vi* **sham·bled; sham·bling** \-b(ə-)liŋ\ [*shamble* bowed, malformed] (1681) : to walk awkwardly with dragging feet : SHUFFLE — **shamble** *n*
sham·bles \'sham-bəlz\ *n pl but sing or pl in constr* [ME *shameles*, pl. of *schamel* vendor's table, footstool, fr. OE *sceamol* stool, fr. L *scamillum*, dim. of *scamnum* stool, bench; perh. akin to Skt *skambha* pillar] (15c) **1** *archaic* : a meat market : SLAUGHTERHOUSE **3 a** : a place of mass slaughter or bloodshed **b** : a scene or a state of great destruction : WRECKAGE **c** (1) : a scene or a state of great disorder or confusion (2) : great confusion : MESS
sham·bling *adj* (1592) : characterized by slow awkward movement
sham·bol·ic \sham-'bä-lik\ *adj* [prob. fr. *shambles*] (1970) *chiefly Brit* : obviously disorganized or confused
¹shame \'shām\ *n* [ME, fr. OE *scamu*; akin to OHG *scama* shame] (bef. 12c) **1 a** : a painful emotion caused by consciousness of guilt, shortcoming, or impropriety **b** : the susceptibility to such emotion **2 a** : a condition of humiliating disgrace or disrepute : IGNOMINY **3 a** : something that brings censure or reproach; *also* : something to be regretted : PITY ⟨it's a ∼ you can't go⟩ **b** : a cause of feeling shame
²shame *vt* **shamed; sham·ing** (13c) **1** : to bring shame to : DISGRACE **2** : to put to shame by outdoing **3** : to cause to feel shame **4** : to force by causing to feel guilty ⟨*shamed* into confessing⟩
shame·faced \'shām-,fāst\ *adj* [alter. of *shamefast*] (1593) **1** : showing modesty : BASHFUL **2** : showing shame : ASHAMED — **shame·faced·ly** \-,fā-səd-lē, -,fāst-lē\ *adv* — **shame·faced·ness** \-,fā-səd-nəs, -,fās(t)-nəs\ *n*
shame·fast \'shām-,fast\ *adj* [ME, fr. OE *scamfæst*, fr. *scamu* + *fæst* fixed, fast] (bef. 12c) *archaic* : SHAMEFACED
shame·ful \'shām-fəl\ *adj* (13c) **1 a** : bringing shame : DISGRACEFUL **b** : arousing the feeling of shame **2** *archaic* : full of the feeling of shame : ASHAMED — **shame·ful·ly** \-fə-lē\ *adv* — **shame·ful·ness** *n*
shame·less \'shām-ləs\ *adj* (bef. 12c) **1** : having no shame : insensible to disgrace **2** : showing lack of shame : DISGRACEFUL — **shame·less·ly** *adv* — **shame·less·ness** *n*
sham·mes \'shä-məs\ *n, pl* **sham·mo·sim** \shä-'mò-səm\ [Yiddish *shames*, fr. LHeb *shammāsh*] (1650) **1** : the sexton of a synagogue **2** : the candle or taper used to light the other candles in a Hanukkah menorah
sham·my \'sha-mē\ *var of* CHAMOIS
¹sham·poo \sham-'pü\ *vt* [Hindi *cãpo*, imper. of *cãpnā* to press, sham-

poo] (1762) **1** *archaic* : MASSAGE **2 a** : to wash (as the hair) with soap and water or with a special preparation **b** : to wash the hair of — **sham·poo·er** *n*
²shampoo *n, pl* **shampoos** (1838) **1** : an act or instance of shampooing **2** : a preparation used in shampooing
sham·rock \'sham-,räk\ *n* [Ir *seamróg*, dim. of *seamar* clover] (1577) : a trifoliolate plant used as a floral emblem by the Irish: as **a** : a yellow-flowered clover (*Trifolium dubium*) often regarded as the true shamrock **b** : WOOD SORREL **c** : WHITE CLOVER
sha·mus \'shä-məs, 'shā-\ *n* [perh. fr. Yiddish *shames* shammes; fr. a jocular comparison of the duties of a sexton and those of a store detective] (1925) *slang* : POLICE OFFICER **2** *slang* : PRIVATE INVESTIGATOR
Shan \'shän, 'shan\ *n, pl* **Shan** *or* **Shans** (1795) **1** : a member of a people living primarily in Myanmar and southern China **2** : the Thai language of the Shan
shan·dy \'shan-dē\ *n, pl* **shandies** (1888) **1** : SHANDYGAFF **2** : a drink consisting of beer and lemonade
shan·dy·gaff \'shan-dē-,gaf\ *n* [origin unknown] (1853) : beer diluted with a nonalcoholic drink (as ginger beer)
Shang \'shäŋ\ *n* [Chin (Beijing) *Shāng*] (1669) : a Chinese dynasty traditionally dated 1766–1122 B.C. and known esp. for bronze work
shang·hai \shaŋ-'hī\ *vt* **shang·haied; shang·hai·ing** [*Shanghai*, China; fr. the formerly widespread use of this method to secure sailors for voyages to the Orient] (1871) **1 a** : to put aboard a ship by force often with the help of liquor or a drug **b** : to put by force or threat of force into or as if into a place of detention **2** : to put by trickery into an undesirable position — **shang·hai·er** \-'hī(-ə)r\ *n*
Shan·gri–la \,shaŋ-gri-'lä\ *n* [*Shangri-La*, imaginary land depicted in the novel *Lost Horizon* (1933) by James Hilton] (1940) **1** : a remote beautiful imaginary place where life approaches perfection : UTOPIA **2** : a remote usu. idyllic hideaway
¹shank \'shaŋk\ *n* [ME *shanke*, fr. OE *scanca*; akin to ON *skakkr* crooked, Gk *skazein* to limp] (bef. 12c) **1 a** : the part of the leg between the knee and the ankle in humans or the corresponding part in various other vertebrates **b** : LEG **c** : a cut of beef, veal, mutton, or lamb from the upper or the lower part of the leg : SHIN — see BEEF illustration **2** : a straight narrow usu. essential part of an object: as **a** : the straight part of a nail or pin **b** : a straight part of a plant : STEM, STALK **c** : the part of an anchor between the ring and the crown — see ANCHOR illustration **d** : the part of a fishhook between the eye and the bend **e** : the part of a key between the handle and the bit **f** : the stem of a tobacco pipe or the part between the stem and the bowl **g** : TANG 1 **h** (1) : the narrow part of the sole of a shoe beneath the instep (2) : SHANKPIECE **3** : a part of an object by which it can be attached: as **a** (1) : a projection on the back of a solid button (2) : a short stem of thread that holds a sewn button away from the cloth **b** : the end (as of a drill bit) that is gripped in a chuck **4 a** : the latter part of a period of time **b** : the early or main part of a period of time **5** *slang* : an often homemade knife — **shanked** \'shaŋ(k)t\ *adj*
²shank *vt* (1927) : to hit (a golf ball or shot) with the extreme heel of the club so that the ball goes off in an unintended direction; *also* : to kick (a football) in an unintended direction
shank·piece \'shaŋk-,pēs\ *n* (1885) : a support for the arch of the foot inserted in the shank of a shoe
shank's mare *n* (ca. 1795) : one's own legs ⟨traveling by *shank's mare*⟩
shan't \'shant, 'shänt\ (1664) : shall not
shan·tung \(ˌ)shan-'təŋ\ *n* [*Shantung* (Shandong), China] (ca. 1882) : a fabric in plain weave having a slightly irregular surface due to uneven slubbed filling yarns
¹shan·ty \'shan-tē\ *var of* CHANTEY
²shanty *n, pl* **shanties** [prob. fr. CanF *chantier* lumber camp, hut, fr. F, gantry, fr. L *cantherius* rafter, trellis] (1820) : a small crudely built dwelling or shelter usu. of wood
shan·ty·man \-mən, -,man\ *n* (ca. 1858) : one who lives in a shanty
shan·ty·town \-,taùn\ *n* (1876) : a usu. poor town or section of a town consisting mostly of shanties
shap·able *or* **shape·able** \'shā-pə-bəl\ *adj* (1647) **1** : capable of being shaped **2** : SHAPELY
¹shape \'shāp\ *vb* **shaped; shap·ing** [ME, alter. of OE *scieppan*; akin to OHG *skepfen* to shape] *vt* (bef. 12c) **1** : FORM, CREATE; *esp* : to give a particular form or shape to **2** *obs* : ORDAIN, DECREE **3** : to adapt in shape so as to fit neatly and closely ⟨a dress *shaped* to her figure⟩ **4 a** : DEVISE, PLAN **b** : to embody in definite form ⟨*shaping* a folktale into an epic⟩ **5 a** : to make fit for (as a particular use or purpose) : ADAPT **b** : to determine or direct the course or character of (as life) **c** : to modify (behavior) by rewarding changes that tend toward a desired response ∼ *vi* **1** : HAPPEN, BEFALL **2** : to take on or approach a mature or definite form — often used with *up* — **shap·er** *n*
²shape *n* (bef. 12c) **1 a** : the visible makeup characteristic of a particular item or kind of item **b** (1) : spatial form or contour (2) : a standard or universally recognized spatial form **2** : the appearance of the body as distinguished from that of the face : FIGURE **3 a** : PHANTOM, APPARITION **b** : assumed appearance : GUISE **4** : form of embodiment **5** : a mode of existence or form of being having identifying features **6** : something having a particular form **7** : the condition in which someone or something exists at a particular time ⟨the car was in fine ∼⟩ — **shaped** \'shāpt\ *adj* — **in shape** : in an original, normal, or fit condition ⟨exercises to keep *in shape*⟩
shape·less \'shā-pləs\ *adj* (14c) **1** : having no definite shape **2 a** : deprived of usual or normal shape : MISSHAPEN ⟨a ∼ old hat⟩ **b** : not shapely — **shape·less·ly** *adv* — **shape·less·ness** *n*
shape·ly \'shā-plē\ *adj* **shape·li·er; -est** (14c) **1** : having a regular or pleasing shape **2** : orderly and consistent in arrangement or plan — **shape·li·ness** *n*
shap·en \'shā-pən\ *adj* [ME, fr. pp. of *shapen* to shape] (14c) : fashioned in or provided with a definite shape — usu. used in combination ⟨an ill-*shapen* body⟩
shape note (1932) : one of a system of seven notes showing the musical scale degree by the shape of the note head
shape–shift·er \'shāp-,shif-tər\ *n* (1887) : one that seems able to change form at will
shape–up \'shāp-,əp\ *n* (1940) : a system of hiring workers and esp. longshoremen by the day or shift by having applicants gather for each day's selection; *also* : an instance of such hiring practice

shape up *vi* (ca. 1920) : to improve to a good or acceptable condition or standard of behavior ∼ *vt* : to bring to a good or acceptable condition or standard of behavior

shard \'shärd\ *also* **sherd** \'shərd\ *n* [ME, fr. OE *sceard;* akin to OE *scieran* to cut — more at SHEAR] (bef. 12c) **1 a :** a piece or fragment of a brittle substance; *broadly* : a small piece or part **b :** SHELL, SCALE; *esp* : ELYTRON **2** *usu* **sherd :** fragments of pottery vessels found on sites and in refuse deposits where pottery-making peoples have lived **3** : highly angular curved glass fragments of tuffaceous sediments

¹share \'shar, 'sher\ *n* [ME *schare,* fr. OE *scear;* akin to OHG *scaro* plowshare, OE *scieran* to cut — more at SHEAR] (bef. 12c) : PLOWSHARE

²share *n* [ME, fr. OE *scearu* cutting, tonsure; akin to OE *scieran* to cut] (14c) **1 a :** a portion belonging to, due to, or contributed by an individual or group **b :** one's full or fair portion **2 a :** the part allotted or belonging to one of a number owning together property or interest **b :** any of the equal portions into which property or invested capital is divided; *specif* : any of the equal interests or rights into which the entire capital stock of a corporation is divided and ownership of which is regularly evidenced by one or more certificates **c** *pl, chiefly Brit* : STOCK 7c(1)

³share *vb* **shared; shar·ing** *vt* (1590) **1 :** to divide and distribute in shares : APPORTION — usu. used with *out* or *with* **2 :** to partake of, use, experience, occupy, or enjoy with others **b :** to have in common **3 :** to grant or give a share in ∼ *vi* **1 :** to have a share — used with *in* **2 :** to apportion and take shares of something — **shar·er** *n*

syn SHARE, PARTICIPATE, PARTAKE mean to have, get, or use in common with another or others. SHARE usu. implies that one as the original holder grants to another the partial use, enjoyment, or possession of a thing ⟨*shared* my toys with the others⟩. PARTICIPATE implies a having or taking part in an undertaking, activity, or discussion ⟨*participated* in sports⟩. PARTAKE implies accepting or acquiring a share esp. of food or drink ⟨*partook* freely of the refreshments⟩.

share·able *or* **shar·able** \'shar-ə-bəl, 'shar-\ *adj* (1920) : capable of being shared — **share·abil·i·ty** \,sher-ə-'bi-lə-tē, ,shar-\ *n*

share·crop \'sher-,kräp, 'shar-\ *vb* [back-formation fr. *sharecropper*] *vi* (ca. 1930) : to farm as a sharecropper ∼ *vt* : to farm (land) or produce (a crop) as a sharecropper

share·crop·per \-,krä-pər\ *n* (1923) : a tenant farmer esp. in the southern U.S. who is provided with credit for seed, tools, living quarters, and food, who works the land, and who receives an agreed share of the value of the crop minus charges

share·hold·er \-,hōl-dər\ *n* (ca. 1828) : one that holds or owns a share in property; *esp* : STOCKHOLDER

share·ware \-,war, -,wer\ *n* (1983) : software with usu. limited capability or incomplete documentation which is available for trial use at little or no cost but which can be upgraded upon payment of a fee to the author

sha·rif \shə-'rēf\ *n* [Ar *sharif,* lit., illustrious] (1599) : a descendant of the prophet Muhammad through his daughter Fatima; *broadly* : one of noble ancestry or political preeminence in predominantly Islamic countries — **sha·rif·ian** \-'rē-fē-ən\ *adj*

¹shark \'shärk\ *n* [ME] (15c) : any of numerous mostly marine cartilaginous fishes of medium to large size that have a fusiform body, lateral branchial clefts, and a tough usu. dull gray skin roughened by minute tubercles and are typically active predators sometimes dangerous to humans — **shark·like** \'shärk-,līk\ *adj*

shark: *1* mako, *2* tiger, *3* thresher, *4* hammerhead, *5* great white

²shark *n* [prob. modif. of G *Schurke* scoundrel] (1599) **1 :** a rapacious crafty person who preys upon others through usury, extortion, or trickery **2 :** one who excels greatly esp. in a particular field

³shark *vt* (1602) **1** *archaic* : to gather hastily **2** *archaic* : to obtain by some irregular means ∼ *vi* **1** *archaic* : to practice fraud or trickery **2** *archaic* : SNEAK

shark·skin \'shärk-,skin\ *n* (1851) **1 :** the hide of a shark or leather made from it **2 a :** a smooth durable woolen or worsted suiting in twill or basket weave with small woven designs **b :** a smooth crisp fabric with a dull finish made usu. of rayon in basket weave

shark sucker *n* (ca. 1850) : REMORA 1

¹sharp \'shärp\ *adj* [ME, fr. OE *scearp;* akin to OHG *scarf* sharp and perh. to OE *scrapian* to scrape — more at SCRAPE] (bef. 12c) **1** : adapted to cutting or piercing: as **a :** having a thin keen edge or fine point **b :** briskly or bitingly cold : NIPPING ⟨a ∼ wind⟩ **2 a :** keen in intellect : QUICK-WITTED **b :** keen in perception : ACUTE ⟨∼ sight⟩

c : keen in attention : VIGILANT ⟨keep a ∼ lookout⟩ **d :** keen in attention to one's own interest sometimes to the point of being unethical ⟨a ∼ trader⟩ **3 :** keen in spirit or action: as **a :** full of activity or energy : BRISK ⟨∼ blows⟩ **b :** capable of acting or reacting strongly; *esp* : CAUSTIC **4 :** SEVERE, HARSH: as **a :** inclined to or marked by irritability or anger ⟨a ∼ temper⟩ **b :** causing intense mental or physical distress ⟨a ∼ pain⟩ **c :** cutting in language or import ⟨a ∼ rebuke⟩ **5** : affecting the senses or sense organs intensely: as **a** (1) : having a strong odor or flavor ⟨∼ cheese⟩ (2) : ACRID **b :** having a strong piercing sound **c :** having the effect of or involving a sudden brilliant display of light ⟨a ∼ flash⟩ **6 a :** terminating in a point or edge ⟨∼ features⟩ **b :** involving an abrupt or marked change esp. in direction ⟨a ∼ turn⟩ **c :** clear in outline or detail : DISTINCT ⟨a ∼ image⟩ **d** : set forth with clarity and distinctness ⟨∼ contrast⟩ **7** *a of a tone* : raised a half step in pitch **b :** higher than the proper pitch **c :** MAJOR, AUGMENTED — used of an interval in music **8 :** STYLISH, DRESSY — **sharp·ly** *adv* — **sharp·ness** *n*

syn SHARP, KEEN, ACUTE mean having or showing alert competence and clear understanding. SHARP implies quick perception, clever resourcefulness, or sometimes questionable trickiness ⟨*sharp* enough to spot a confidence game⟩. KEEN suggests quickness, enthusiasm, and a penetrating mind ⟨a *keen* observer of the political scene⟩. ACUTE implies a power to penetrate and may suggest subtlety and sharpness of discrimination ⟨an *acute* sense of style⟩.

²sharp *adv* (bef. 12c) **1 :** in a sharp manner **2 :** EXACTLY ⟨1:15 ∼⟩

³sharp *n* (14c) **1 :** one that is sharp: as **a :** a sharp edge or point **b** (1) : a musical note or tone one half step higher than a note or tone named (2) : a character # on a line or space of the musical staff indicating a pitch a half step higher than the degree would indicate without it **c :** a needle with a small eye for sewing by hand **d :** a real or self-styled expert; *also* : SHARPER

⁴sharp *vt* (1662) : to raise (as a musical tone) in pitch; *esp* : to raise in pitch by a half step ∼ *vi* : to sing or play above the proper pitch

shar–pei \,shä-'pā, ,shär-\ *n, pl* **shar–peis** [Chin (Guangdong) *sà* sand + *péi* fur] (1975) : any of an ancient breed of dogs originating in China that have loose wrinkled skin esp. when young, a short bristly coat, blue-black tongue, and wide blunt muzzle

sharp·en \'shär-pən\ *vb* **sharp·ened; sharp·en·ing** \'shärp-niŋ, 'shär-pə-\ *vt* (15c) : to make sharp or sharper; *esp* : HONE ∼ *vi* : to become sharp or sharper — **sharp·en·er** \'shärp-nər, 'shär-pə-\ *n*

sharp·er \'shär-pər\ *n* (1681) : CHEAT, SWINDLER; *esp* : a cheating gambler

sharp–eyed \'shärp-'īd\ *adj* (1670) : having keen sight; *also* : keen in observing or penetrating

sharp·ie *or* **sharpy** \'shär-pē\ *n, pl* **sharp·ies** (ca. 1859) **1 :** a long narrow shallow-draft boat with flat or slightly V-shaped bottom and one or two masts each carrying a triangular sail **2 a :** SHARPER **b** : an exceptionally keen or alert person

sharp–nosed \'shärp-'nōzd\ *adj* (1561) **1 :** keen in smelling **2 :** having a pointed nose or snout

sharp practice *n* (1845) : the act of dealing in which advantage is taken or sought unscrupulously

sharp–set \'shärp-'set\ *adj* (1540) : eager in appetite or desire

sharp–shinned hawk \'shärp-'shind-\ *n* (ca. 1812) : a common widely distributed American accipiter (*Accipiter striatus*) that is grayish above, has a chestnut breast, short rounded wings, and a tail with a notched or square tip when folded — called also *sharp-shin*

sharp–shoot·er \'shärp-,shü-tər\ *n* (1802) : a good marksman

sharp–shoot·ing \-,shü-tiŋ\ *n* (1806) **1 :** shooting with great precision **2 :** accurate and usu. unexpected attack (as in words)

sharp–sight·ed \-'sī-təd\ *adj* (1571) **1 :** having acute sight **2 :** mentally keen or alert — **sharp–sight·ed·ly** *adv* — **sharp–sight·ed·ness** *n*

sharp–tongued \-'təŋd\ *adj* (1837) : having a sharp tongue : harsh or bitter in speech or language

sharp–wit·ted \-'wi-təd\ *adj* (ca. 1586) : having an acute mind

shash·lik *also* **shash·lick** *or* **shas·lik** \shäsh-'lik, 'shäsh-lik\ *n* [Russ *shashlyk,* prob. modif. of Crimean Tatar *šišlik,* fr. *šiš* skewer] (1926) : KABOB

Shas·ta daisy \'shas-tə-\ *n* [Mount *Shasta,* California] (ca. 1893) : a large-flowered garden daisy (*Chrysanthemum superbum* syn. *C. maximum*) that resembles the oxeye daisy

shat *past and past part of* SHIT

¹shat·ter \'sha-tər\ *vb* [ME *schateren*] *vt* (14c) **1 :** to cause to drop or be dispersed **2 a :** to break at once into pieces **b :** to damage badly : RUIN **3 :** to cause the disruption or annihilation of : DEMOLISH ∼ *vi* **1 :** to break apart : DISINTEGRATE **2 :** to drop off parts (as leaves, petals, or fruit) — **shat·ter·ing·ly** \-tə-riŋ-lē\ *adv*

²shatter *n* (ca. 1640) **1 :** FRAGMENT, SHRED — usu. used in pl. ⟨the broken vase lay in ∼s⟩ **2 :** an act of shattering : the state of being shattered **3 :** a result of shattering : SHOWER

shatter cone *n* (1933) : a conical fragment of rock that has striations radiating from the apex and that is formed by high pressure (as from volcanism or meteorite impact)

shat·ter·proof \'sha-tər-,prüf\ *adj* (1930) : proof against shattering

¹shave \'shāv\ *vb* **shaved; shaved** *or* **shav·en** \'shā-vən\; **shav·ing** [ME, fr. OE *scafan;* akin to Lith *skobti* to scoop, L *scabere* to scratch, and perh. to Gk *koptein* to cut — more at CAPON] *vt* (bef. 12c) **1 a** : to remove a thin layer from **b :** to cut off in thin layers or shreds : SLICE **c :** to cut off closely **2 a :** to sever the hair from (the head or another part of the body) close to the roots **b :** to cut off (hair or beard) close to the skin **3 a :** to discount (a note) at an exorbitant rate **b :** DEDUCT, REDUCE **4 :** to come close to or touch lightly in passing ∼ *vi* **1 :** to cut off hair or beard close to the skin **2 :** to proceed with difficulty : SCRAPE

²shave *n* (bef. 12c) **1 :** SHAVER 3 **2 :** a thin slice : SHAVING **3 :** an act or the process of shaving

\ə\ abut \ʼ\ kitten, F table \ər\ further \a\ ash \ā\ ace \ä\ mop, mar
\aů\ out \ch\ chin \e\ bet \ē\ easy \g\ go \i\ hit \ī\ ice \j\ job
\ŋ\ sing \ō\ go \ô\ law \ôi\ boy \th\ thin \t̶h̶\ the \ü\ loot \ů\ foot
\y\ yet \zh\ vision \ä, k̲, ⁿ, œ, œ̄, ɶ, ū̄, ᵞ\ *see* Guide to Pronunciation

shave·ling \'shāv-liŋ\ *n* (1529) **1** : a tonsured clergyman : PRIEST — usu. used disparagingly **2** : YOUTH, STRIPLING

shav·er \'shā-vər\ *n* (15c) **1** : a person who shaves **2** *archaic* : one who swindles **3** : a tool or machine for shaving; *esp* : an electric razor **4** : BOY, YOUNGSTER

shaves *pl of* SHAFT

shave·tail \'shāv-,tāl\ *n* [fr. the practice of shaving the tails of newly broken mules to distinguish them from seasoned ones] (1846) **1** : a pack mule esp. when newly broken in **2** : SECOND LIEUTENANT — usu. used disparagingly

Sha·vi·an \'shā-vē-ən\ *n* [NL *Shavius*, Latinized form of George Bernard *Shaw*] (1905) : an admirer or devotee of G. B. Shaw, his writings, or his social and political theories — **Shavian** *adj*

shav·ie \'shā-vē\ *n* [*shave* (swindle) + *-ie*] (1737) *Scot* : PRANK

shav·ing \'shā-viŋ\ *n* (14c) **1** : the act of one that shaves **2** : something shaved off ⟨wood ~s⟩

¹shaw \'shȯ\ *n* [ME, fr. OE *sceaga*; akin to ON *skegg* beard — more at SHAG] (bef. 12c) *dial* : COPPICE, THICKET

²shaw *n* [prob. alter. of *show*] (1726) *chiefly Brit* : the tops and stalks of a cultivated crop (as potatoes or turnips)

¹shawl \'shȯl\ *n* [Per *shāl*] (1662) : a square or oblong usu. fabric garment or wrapper used esp. as a covering for the head or shoulders

²shawl *vt* (1812) : to wrap in or as if in a shawl

shawl collar *n* (ca. 1908) : a turned-over collar of a garment that combines with lapels forming an unbroken curving line

shawm \'shȯm\ *n* [ME *schalme*, fr. MF *chalemie*, fr. OF, alter. of *chalemel*, fr. LL *calamellus*, dim. of L *calamus* reed — more at CALAMUS] (14c) : an early double-reed woodwind instrument

Shaw·nee \shȯ-'nē, shä-\ *n, pl* **Shawnee** *or* **Shawnees** [back-formation fr. obs. E *Shawnese*, ultim. fr. Shawnee *ša·wano·ki*, lit., southerners] (1769) **1** : a member of an American Indian people orig. of the central Ohio valley **2** : the Algonquian language of the Shawnee people

Shaw·wal \shä-'wäl\ *n* [Ar *shawwāl*] (ca. 1771) : the 10th month of the Islamic year — see MONTH table

shay \'shā\ *n* [back-formation fr. *chaise*, taken as pl.] (1717) *chiefly dial* : CHAISE 1

she \'shē\ *pron* [ME, prob. alter. of *hye*, alter. of OE *hēo* she — more at HE] (12c) **1** : that female one who is neither speaker nor the one addressed ⟨~ is my wife⟩ — compare HE, HER, HERS, IT, THEY **2** — used to refer to one regarded as feminine (as by personification) ⟨~ was a fine ship⟩

²she *n* (14c) : a female person or animal — often used in combination ⟨*she*-cat⟩ ⟨*she*-cousin⟩

s/he \'shē-'hē; 'shē-ər-'hē; 'shē-,slash-'hē\ *pron* (1973) : she or he — used in writing as a pronoun of common gender

shea butter \'shē-, 'shā-\ *n* (1847) : a pale solid fat from the seeds of the shea tree used in food, soap, and candles

sheaf \'shēf\ *n, pl* **sheaves** \'shēvz\ [ME *sheef*, fr. OE *scēaf*; akin to OHG *scoub* sheaf, Russ *chub* forelock] (bef. 12c) **1** : a quantity of the stalks and ears of a cereal grass or sometimes other plant material bound together **2** : something resembling a sheaf of grain ⟨a ~ of papers⟩ — **sheaf·like** \'shēf-,līk\ *adj*

shea nut *n* (1919) : the seed of the shea tree

¹shear \'shir\ *vb* **sheared**; **sheared** *or* **shorn** \'shȯrn, 'shȯrn\; **shear·ing** [ME *sheren*, fr. OE *scieran*; akin to ON *skera* to cut, L *curtus* shortened, Gk *keirein* to cut, shear, Skt *kṛṇāti* he injures] *vt* (bef. 12c) **1** : to cut off the hair from ⟨with crown *shorn*⟩ **b** : to cut or clip (as hair or wool) from someone or something; *also* : to cut something from ⟨~ a lawn⟩ **c** *chiefly Scot* : to reap with a sickle **d** : to cut or trim with shears or a similar instrument **2** : to cut with something sharp **3** : to deprive of something as if by cutting **4** **a** : to subject to a shear force **b** : to cause (as a rock mass) to move along the plane of contact ~ *vi* **1** : to cut through something with or as if with a sharp instrument **2** *chiefly Scot* : to reap crops with a sickle **3** : to become divided under the action of a shear ⟨the bolt may ~ off⟩ — **shear·er** *n*

²shear *n* (bef. 12c) **1** **a** (1) : a cutting implement similar or identical to a pair of scissors but typically larger — usu. used in pl. (2) : one blade of a pair of shears **b** : any of various cutting tools or machines operating by the action of opposed cutting edges of metal — usu. used in pl. **c** (1) : something resembling a shear or a pair of shears (2) : a hoisting apparatus consisting of two or sometimes more upright spars fastened together at their upper ends and having tackle for masting or dismasting ships or lifting heavy loads (as guns) — usu. used in pl. but sing. or pl. in constr. **2** *chiefly Brit* : the action or process or an instance of shearing — used in combination to indicate the approximate age of sheep in terms of shearings undergone **3** **a** : internal force tangential to the section on which it acts — called also *shearing force* **b** : an action or stress resulting from applied forces that causes or tends to cause two contiguous parts of a body to slide relatively to each other in a direction parallel to their plane of contact

sheared *adj* (1616) : formed or finished by shearing; *esp* : cut to uniform length ⟨a ~ rug⟩

shear·ling \'shir-liŋ\ *n* (14c) : skin from a recently sheared sheep or lamb that has been tanned and dressed with the wool left on

shear pin *n* (ca. 1931) : an easily replaceable pin inserted at a critical point in a machine and designed to break when subjected to excess stress

shear·wa·ter \'shir-,wȯ-tər, -,wä-\ *n* (ca. 1671) : any of numerous oceanic birds (esp. genus *Puffinus*) that are related to the petrels and usu. skim close to the waves in flight

sheath \'shēth\ *n, pl* **sheaths** \'shēthz, 'shēths\ [ME *shethe*, fr. OE *scēath*; akin to OHG *sceida* sheath and perh. to L *scindere* to split — more at SHED] (bef. 12c) **1** : a case for a blade (as of a knife) **2** : an investing cover or case of a plant or animal body or body part: as **a** : the tubular fold of skin into which the penis of many mammals is retracted **b** (1) : the lower part of a leaf (as of a grass) when surrounding the stem (2) : an ensheathing spathe **3** : any of various covering or supporting structures that are applied like or resemble in appearance or function the sheath of a blade: as **a** : SHEATHING 2 **b**

: a woman's close-fitting dress usu. worn without a belt **c** *Brit* : CONDOM

sheath·bill \'shēth-,bil\ *n* (ca. 1781) : either of two white shorebirds (*Chionis alba* and *C. minor* of the family Chionididae) of colder parts of the southern hemisphere that have a horny sheath over the base of the upper mandible and suggest the pigeons in general appearance

sheathe \'shēth\ *also* **sheath** \'shēth\ *vt* **sheathed; sheath·ing** [ME *shethen*, fr. *shethe* sheath] (15c) **1** : to put into or furnish with a sheath **2** : to plunge or bury (as a sword) in flesh **3** : to withdraw (a claw) into a sheath **4** : to case or cover with something (as sheets of metal) that protects — **sheath·er** \'shē-thər, -thər\ *n*

sheath·ing \'shē-thiŋ, -thiŋ\ *n* (15c) **1** : the action of one that sheathes something **2** : material used to sheathe something; *esp* : the first covering of boards or of waterproof material on the outside wall of a frame house or on a timber roof

sheath knife *n* (1837) : a knife having a fixed blade and designed to be carried in a sheath

shea tree \'shē-, 'shā-\ *n* [Bambara *si*] (1799) : a tropical African tree (*Vitellaria paradoxa* syn. *Butyrospermum parkii*) of the sapodilla family with fatty nuts that yield shea butter

¹sheave \'shiv, 'shēv\ *n* [ME *sheve*; akin to OHG *sciba* disk] (14c) : a grooved wheel or pulley (as of a pulley block)

²sheave \'shēv\ *vt* **sheaved; sheav·ing** [*sheaf*] (1598) : to gather and bind into a sheaf

she·bang \shi-'baŋ\ *n* [origin unknown] (1869) : everything involved in what is under consideration — usu. used in the phrase *the whole shebang*

She·bat \shə-'bät, -'vät\ *n* [Heb *shēbhāṭ*] (1535) : the 5th month of the civil year or the 11th month of the ecclesiastical year in the Jewish calendar — see MONTH table

she·been \shə-'bēn\ *n* [Ir *síbín* illicit whiskey, shebeen] (ca. 1787) *chiefly Irish* : an unlicensed or illegally operated drinking establishment

She·chi·nah \shə-'kē-nə, -'kē-nə, -'kī-nə\ *n* [Heb *shēkhīnāh*] (1663) : the presence of God in the world as conceived in Jewish theology

¹shed \'shed\ *vb* **shed; shed·ding** [ME, to divide, separate, fr. OE *scēadan*; akin to OHG *skeidan* to separate, L *scindere* to split, cleave, Gk *schizein* to split] *vt* (bef. 12c) **1** *chiefly dial* : to set apart : SEGREGATE **2** : to cause to be dispersed without penetrating ⟨duck's plumage ~s water⟩ **3** **a** : to cause (blood) to flow by cutting or wounding **b** : to pour forth in drops ⟨~ tears⟩ **c** : to give off in a stream ⟨fish *shedding* their eggs in spawning⟩ **d** : to give off or out ⟨~s some light on the subject⟩ **4** **a** (1) : to cast off (as a body covering) : MOLT (2) : to let fall (as leaves) (3) : to eject (as seed or spores) from a natural receptacle **b** : to rid oneself of temporarily or permanently as superfluous or unwanted ⟨~ her inhibitions⟩ ⟨the company ~ 100 jobs⟩ ~ *vi* **1** : to pour out : SPILL **2** : to become dispersed : SCATTER **3** : to cast off some natural covering (as fur or skin) ⟨the cat is *shedding*⟩ *syn* see DISCARD — **shed blood** : to cause death by violence

²shed *n* (12c) **1** *obs* : DISTINCTION, DIFFERENCE **2** : something (as the skin of a snake) that is discarded in shedding **3** : a divide of land

³shed *n* [alter. of earlier *shadde*, prob. fr. ME *shade* shed] (1557) **1** **a** : a slight structure built for shelter or storage; *esp* : a single-storied building with one or more sides unenclosed **b** : a building that resembles a shed **2** *archaic* : HUT — **shed·like** \-,līk\ *adj*

⁴shed *vt* **shed·ded; shed·ding** (1850) : to put or house in a shed

she'd \'shēd\ (1609) : she had : she would

shed·der \'she-dər\ *n* (14c) : one that sheds something: as **a** : a crab or lobster about to molt **b** : a newly molted crab

shed dormer *n* (1948) : a dormer with a roof sloping in the same direction as the roof from which the dormer projects

¹sheen \'shēn\ *adj* [ME *shene*, fr. OE *scīene*; akin to OE *scēawian* to look — more at SHOW] (bef. 12c) **1** *archaic* : BEAUTIFUL **2** *archaic* : SHINING, RESPLENDENT

²sheen *vi* (14c) : to be bright : show a sheen

³sheen *n* (1602) **1** **a** : a bright or shining condition : BRIGHTNESS **b** : a subdued glitter approaching but short of optical reflection **c** : a lustrous surface imparted to textiles through finishing processes or use of shiny yarns **2** : a textile finishing notable sheen — **sheeny** \'shē-nē\ *adj*

sheep \'shēp\ *n, pl* **sheep** *often attrib* [ME, fr. OE *scēap* also OHG *scāf* sheep] (bef. 12c) **1** : any of various ruminant mammals (genus *Ovis*) related to the goats but stockier and lacking a beard in the male; *specif* : one (*O. aries*) long domesticated esp. for its flesh and wool **2** **a** : a timid defenseless creature **b** : a timid docile person; *esp* : one easily influenced or led **3** : leather prepared from the skins of sheep : SHEEPSKIN

sheep·ber·ry \-,ber-ē\ *n* (ca. 1818) : an often shrubby No. American viburnum (*Viburnum lentago*) with white flowers in flat cymes

sheep·cote \-,kōt, -,kät\ *n* (15c) *chiefly Brit* : SHEEPFOLD

sheep·dip \-,dip\ *n* (1865) : a liquid preparation of usu. toxic chemicals into which sheep are plunged esp. to destroy parasitic arthropods

sheep·dog \-,dȯg\ *n* (ca. 1774) : a dog (as a Border collie) used to tend, drive, or guard sheep

sheep fescue *n* (1945) : a hardy fine-foliaged perennial grass (*Festuca ovina*) widely used as a pasture grass — called also *sheep's fescue*

sheep·fold \'shēp-,fōld\ *n* (15c) : a pen or shelter for sheep

sheep·herd·er \'shēp-,hər-dər\ *n* (1871) : a worker in charge of sheep esp. on open range

sheep·herd·ing \-,hər-diŋ\ *n* (1891) : the activities of a worker engaged in tending sheep

sheep·ish \'shē-pish\ *adj* (13c) **1** : resembling a sheep in meekness, stupidity, or timidity **2** : affected by or showing embarrassment caused by consciousness of a fault ⟨a ~ grin⟩ — **sheep·ish·ly** *adv* — **sheep·ish·ness** *n*

sheep ked \'shēp-,ked\ *n* [*sheep* + *ked* sheep ked, of unknown origin] (1925) : a wingless bloodsucking dipteran fly (*Melophagus ovinus*) that feeds chiefly on sheep and is a vector of sheep trypanosomiasis — called also *sheep tick*

sheep laurel *n* (1810) : a dwarf shrub (*Kalmia angustifolia*) of the eastern U.S. that is poisonous to young stock and resembles mountain laurel but has narrower leaves and smaller bright red flowers — called also *lambkill*

sheep's eye *n* (ca. 1529) : a shy longing usu. amorous glance — usu. used in pl.

sheep·shank \'shēp-,shaŋk\ *n* (1627) 1 : a knot for shortening a line — see KNOT illustration 2 *Scot* : something of no worth or importance

sheeps·head \'shēps-,hed\ *n* (1643) 1 : a marine bony fish (*Archosargus probatocephalus* of the family Sparidae) of the Atlantic and Gulf coasts of the U.S. that has broad incisor teeth and is used for food 2 : FRESHWATER DRUM 3 : a largely red or rose California wrasse (*Semicossyphus pulcher*)

sheep·shear·er \'shēp-,shir-ər\ *n* (1539) : one that shears sheep

sheep·shear·ing \'shēp-,shir-iŋ\ *n* (1586) 1 : the act of shearing sheep 2 : the time or season for shearing sheep

sheep·skin \-,skin\ *n* (13c) 1 a : the skin of a sheep; *also* : leather prepared from it b : PARCHMENT c : a garment made of or lined with sheepskin 2 : DIPLOMA

sheep sorrel *n* (1806) : a small dock (*Rumex acetosella*) of acidic soils

sheep walk *n* (1586) *chiefly Brit* : a pasture or range for sheep

¹**sheer** \'shir\ *vb* [perh. alter. of ¹*shear*] *vi* (1539) : to deviate from a course : SWERVE ~ *vt* : to cause to sheer

²**sheer** *n* (1670) 1 : a turn, deviation, or change in a course (as of a ship) 2 : the position of a ship riding to a single anchor and heading toward it

³**sheer** *adj* [ME *schere* freed from guilt, prob. alter. of *skere*, fr. ON *skærr* pure; akin to OE *scinan* to shine] (ca. 1568) 1 *obs* : BRIGHT, SHINING 2 : of very thin or transparent texture : DIAPHANOUS 3 a : UNQUALIFIED, UTTER ⟨~ folly⟩ ⟨~ ignorance⟩ b : being free from an adulterant : PURE, UNMIXED c : viewed or acting in dissociation from all else ⟨in terms of ~ numbers⟩ 4 : marked by great and continuous steepness *syn* see STEEP — **sheer·ly** *adv* — **sheer·ness** *n*

⁴**sheer** *adv* (ca. 1600) 1 : in a complete manner : ALTOGETHER 2 : straight up or down without a break : PERPENDICULARLY

⁵**sheer** *n* (ca. 1920) : a sheer fabric; *also* : an article of such a fabric

⁶**sheer** *n* [perh. alter. of ²*shear*] (1691) : the fore-and-aft curvature from bow to stern of a ship's deck as shown in side elevation

sheer·legs \'shir-,legz, -,lāgz\ *n pl but sing or pl in constr* (ca. 1860) : SHEAR 1c(2)

¹**sheet** \'shēt\ *n* [ME *shete*, fr. OE *scȳte*; akin to OE *scēat* edge, OHG *scōz* flap, skirt] (bef. 12c) 1 a : a broad piece of cloth; *esp* : BEDSHEET b : SAIL 1a(1) 2 a (1) : a usu. rectangular piece of paper; *esp* : one manufactured for printing (2) : a rectangular piece of heavy paper with a plant specimen mounted on it ⟨an herbarium of 100,000 ~s⟩ b : a printed signature for a book esp. before it has been folded, cut, or bound — usu. used in pl. c : a newspaper, periodical, or occasional publication ⟨a gossip ~⟩ d : the unseparated postage stamps printed by one impression of a plate on a single piece of paper; *also* : a pane of stamps 3 : a broad stretch or surface of something ⟨a ~ of ice⟩ 4 : a suspended or moving expanse (as of fire or rain) 5 a : a portion of something that is thin in comparison to its length and breadth b : a flat baking pan of tinned metal ⟨a cookie ~⟩ 6 : a surface or part of a surface in which it is possible to pass from any one point of it to any other without leaving the surface ⟨a hyperboloid of two ~s⟩ — **sheet·like** \-,līk\ *adj*

²**sheet** *adj* (1582) 1 : rolled or spread out in a sheet 2 : of, relating to, or concerned with the making of sheet metal

³**sheet** *vt* (1606) 1 : to cover with a sheet : SHROUD 2 : to furnish with sheets 3 : to form into sheets ~ *vi* : to fall, spread, or flow in a sheet ⟨the rain ~ed against the windows⟩ — **sheet·er** *n* — **sheet home** 1 : to extend (a sail) and set as flat as possible by hauling upon the sheets 2 : to fix the responsibility for : bring home to one

⁴**sheet** *n* [ME *shete*, fr. OE *scēata* lower corner of a sail; akin to OE *scȳte* sheet] (13c) 1 : a rope or chain that regulates the angle at which a sail is set in relation to the wind 2 *pl* : the spaces at either end of an open boat not occupied by thwarts : foresheets and stern sheets together — **three sheets in the wind** *or* **three sheets to the wind** : DRUNK 1a

sheet anchor *n* (15c) 1 : a large strong anchor formerly carried in the waist of a ship and used as a spare in an emergency 2 : something that constitutes a main support or dependence esp. in danger

sheet bend *n* (ca. 1823) : a bend or hitch used for temporarily fastening a rope to the bight of another rope or to an eye — see KNOT illustration

sheet·fed \'shēt-,fed\ *adj* (1926) : of, relating to, being, or printed by a press that prints on paper in sheet form

sheet glass *n* (1805) : glass made in large sheets directly from the furnace or by making a cylinder and then flattening it

sheet·ing \'shē-tiŋ\ *n* (1711) 1 : material in the form of sheets or suitable for forming into sheets 2 : a lining (as wood or steel) used to support an embankment or the walls of an excavation

sheet lightning *n* (1794) : lightning in diffused or sheet form due to reflection and diffusion by the clouds and sky

sheet metal *n* (ca. 1909) : metal in the form of a sheet

sheet music *n* (1857) : music printed on unbound sheets of paper

Sheet·rock \'shēt-,räk\ *trademark* — used for plasterboard

sheikh *or* **sheik** \'shēk, *also* 'shāk *for 1*\ *n* [Ar *shaykh*] (1577) 1 : an Arab chief 2 *usu* sheik : a man held to be irresistibly attractive to romantic young women

sheikh·dom *or* **sheik·dom** \-dəm, -,təm\ *n* (1860) : a region under the rule of a sheikh

shei·la \'shē-lə\ *n* [prob. fr. *Sheila*, female given name] (ca. 1919) *Austral & NewZeal* : a girl or young woman

shek·el \'she-kəl\ *n* [Heb *sheqel*] (15c) 1 a : any of various ancient units of weight; *esp* : a Hebrew unit equal to about 252 grains troy b : a unit of value based on a shekel weight of gold or silver 2 : a coin weighing one shekel 3 *pl* : MONEY 4 — see MONEY table

Shekinah *var of* SHECHINAH

shel·drake \'shel-,drāk\ *n* [ME, fr. *sheld*- (akin to MD *schillede* parti-colored) + *drake*] (14c) 1 : SHELDUCK 2 : MERGANSER

shel·duck \-,dək\ *n* [*shel*- (as in *sheldrake*) + *duck*] (1707) : any of various Old World ducks (genus *Tadorna*); *esp* : a common mostly black-and-white duck (*T. tadorna*) slightly larger than the mallard

shelduck

shelf \'shelf\ *n, pl* **shelves** \'shelvz\ [ME, prob. fr. OE *scylfe*; akin to ON hlith*skjalf* Odin's seat] (14c) 1 a : a thin flat usu. long and narrow piece of material (as wood) fastened horizontally (as on a wall) at a distance from the floor to hold objects b : one of several similar pieces in a closet, bookcase, or similar structure c : the contents of a shelf 2 : something resembling a shelf in form or position: as a : a sandbank or ledge of rocks usu. partially submerged b : a flat projecting layer of rock c : the submerged gradually sloping border of a continent or island : CONTINENTAL SHELF — **shelf·ful** \'shelf-,fúl\ *n* — **shelf·like** \'shelf-,līk\ *adj* — **off the shelf** : available from stock : not made to order ⟨*off the shelf* equipment⟩ — **on the shelf** : in a state of inactivity or uselessness

shelf fungus *n* (ca. 1903) : BRACKET FUNGUS

shelf ice *n* (1910) : an extensive ice sheet originating on land but continuing out to sea beyond the depths at which it rests on the sea bottom

shelf life *n* (1927) : the period of time during which a material may be stored and remain suitable for use; *broadly* : the period of time during which something lasts or remains popular

¹**shell** \'shel\ *n* [ME, fr. OE *sciell*; akin to OE *scealu* shell, ON *skel*, Lith *skelti* to split, Gk *skallein* to hoe] (bef. 12c) 1 a : a hard rigid usu. largely calcareous covering or support of an animal b : the hard or tough often thin outer covering of an egg (as of a bird or reptile) — see EGG illustration 2 : the covering or outside part of a fruit or seed esp. when hard or fibrous 3 : shell material (as of mollusks or turtles) or their substance 4 : something that resembles a shell: as a : a framework or exterior structure; *esp* : a building with an unfinished interior b (1) : an external case or outside covering ⟨the ~ of a ship⟩ (2) : a thin usu. spherical layer or surface enclosing a space or surrounding an object ⟨an expanding ~ of gas around a neutron star⟩ c : a casing without substance ⟨mere effigies and ~s of men —Thomas Carlyle⟩ d : an edible crust for holding a filling ⟨a pastry ~⟩ e : BAND SHELL f : a small beer glass g : an unlined article of outerwear 5 : a shell-bearing mollusk 6 : an impersonal attitude or manner that conceals the presence or absence of feeling ⟨he retreated into his ~⟩ 7 : a narrow light racing boat propelled by one or more persons pulling oars or sculls 8 : any of the spaces occupied by the orbits of a group of electrons of approximately equal energy surrounding the nucleus of an atom 9 a : a projectile for cannon containing an explosive bursting charge b : a metal or paper case which holds the charge of powder and shot or bullet used with breech-loading small arms 10 : a plain usu. sleeveless blouse or sweater 11 : a company or corporation that exists without assets or independent operations as a legal entity through which another company or corporation can conduct various dealings — **shell** *adj*

²**shell** *vt* (1562) 1 a : to take out of a natural enclosing cover (as a shell, husk, pod, or capsule) ⟨~ peanuts⟩ b : to separate the kernels of (as an ear of Indian corn, wheat, or oats) from the cob, ear, or husk 2 : to throw shells at, upon, or into : BOMBARD 3 : to score heavily against (as an opposing pitcher in baseball) ~ *vi* 1 : to fall or scale off in thin pieces 2 : to cast the shell or exterior covering : fall out of the pod or husk ⟨nuts which ~ in falling⟩ 3 : to gather shells (as from a beach) : collect shells

she'll \'shē(ə)l, shil\ (ca. 1590) : she will : she shall

¹**shel·lac** \shə-'lak\ *n* [¹*shell* + *lac*] (1713) 1 : purified lac usu. prepared in thin orange or yellow flakes by heating and filtering and often bleached white 2 : a preparation of lac dissolved usu. in alcohol and used chiefly as a wood filler and finish 3 : a composition containing shellac formerly used for making phonograph records b : an old 78 rpm phonograph record

²**shellac** *vt* **shel·lacked; shel·lack·ing** (1876) 1 : to coat or otherwise treat with shellac or a shellac varnish 2 : to defeat decisively

shellacking *n* (1931) : a decisive defeat : DRUBBING

shell·back \'shel-,bak\ *n* (1853) 1 : an old or veteran sailor 2 : a person who has crossed the equator and been initiated in the traditional ceremony

shell bean *n* (1868) 1 : a bean grown primarily for its edible seeds — compare SNAP BEAN 2 : the edible seed of a bean

shell-crack·er \'shel-,kra-kər\ *n* (ca. 1890) : REDEAR

shelled \'sheld\ *adj* (15c) 1 : having a shell esp. of a specified kind — often used in combination ⟨pink-*shelled*⟩ ⟨thick-*shelled*⟩ 2 a : having the shell removed ⟨~ oysters⟩ ⟨~ nuts⟩ b : removed from the cob ⟨~ corn⟩

shell·er \'she-lər\ *n* (1694) 1 : one that shells ⟨a peanut ~⟩ 2 : a person who collects seashells

shell·fish \-,fish\ *n* (bef. 12c) : an aquatic invertebrate animal with a shell; *esp* : an edible mollusk or crustacean

shell·fish·ery \-,fi-shə-rē, -,fish-rē\ *n* (1885) : a commercially exploited population of shellfish

shell game *n* (1890) 1 : thimblerig played esp. with three walnut shells 2 : FRAUD; *esp* : a swindle involving the substitution of something of little or no value for a valuable item

shell jacket *n* (1840) 1 : a short tight military jacket worn buttoned up the front 2 : MESS JACKET

shell out *vb* (1801) : PAY

shell pink *n* (1887) : a light yellowish pink

shell-proof \'shel-'prüf\ *adj* (ca. 1859) : capable of resisting shells or bombs

shell shock *n* (1915) : post-traumatic stress disorder in soldiers as a result of combat experience

shell-shocked *adj* (1918) 1 : affected with shell shock 2 : mentally confused, upset, or exhausted as a result of excessive stress

shell steak *n* (ca. 1968) : the part of a short loin of beef that contains no tenderloin

shell·work \'shel-,wərk\ *n* (1611) : work adorned with shells or composed of a pattern of shells

---

\ə\ abut \ᵊ\ kitten, F table \ər\ further \a\ ash \ā\ ace \ä\ mop, mar \aú\ out \ch\ chin \e\ bet \ē\ easy \g\ go \i\ hit \ī\ ice \j\ job \ŋ\ sing \ō\ go \ó\ law \ói\ boy \th\ thin \th\ the \ü\ loot \ú\ foot \y\ yet \zh\ vision \à, k, ⁿ, œ, œ̄, ue, ūe, ʸ\ see Guide to Pronunciation

shelly \'she-lē\ *adj* **shell·i·er; -est** (1555) **1** : abounding in or covered with shells ⟨a ~ shore⟩ **2** : of, relating to, or resembling a shell

¹shel·ter \'shel-tər\ *n* [origin unknown] (1585) **1 a** : something that covers or affords protection ⟨a bomb ~⟩ **b** : an establishment providing food and shelter (as to the homeless) **c** : an establishment that houses and feeds stray animals **2** : a position or the state of being covered and protected ⟨took ~⟩ — **shel·ter·less** \-ləs\ *adj*

²shelter *vb* **shel·tered; shel·ter·ing** \-t(ə-)riŋ\ *vt* (1590) **1** : to constitute or provide a shelter for : PROTECT ⟨has led a ~ed life⟩ **2** : to place under shelter or protection ⟨~ed himself in a mountain cave⟩ **3** : to protect (income) from taxation ~ *vi* : to take shelter — **shel·ter·er** \-tər-ər\ *n*

shel·ter·belt \'shel-tər-,belt\ *n* (1868) : a barrier of trees and shrubs that protects (as crops) from wind and storm and lessens erosion

shelter half *n* (1911) : one of the halves of a shelter tent

shelter tent *n* (1862) : a small tent usu. consisting of two interchangeable pieces : PUP TENT

shel·tie *or* **shel·ty** \'shel-tē\ *n, pl* **shelties** [prob. fr. ON *Hjalti* Shetlander] (1650) **1** : SHETLAND PONY **2** : SHETLAND SHEEPDOG

shelve \'shelv\ *vb* **shelved; shelv·ing** [*shelf*] *vt* (1598) **1** : to furnish with shelves **2** : to place on a shelf **3 a** : to remove from active service **b** : to put off or aside ⟨~ a project⟩ ~ *vi* : to slope in a formation like a shelf — **shelv·er** *n*

¹shelv·ing \'shel-viŋ\ *n* (1687) **1** : the state or degree of sloping **2 a** : a sloping surface or place

²shelving *n* (1817) **1** : material for shelves **2** : SHELVES

Shem \'shem\ *n* [Heb *Shēm*] : the eldest son of Noah held to be the progenitor of the Semitic peoples

She·ma \shə-'mä\ *n* [Heb *shēma'* hear, first word of Deut 6:4] (1706) : the Jewish confession of faith made up of Deut 6:4–9 and 11:13–21 and Num 15:37–41

She·mi·ni Atze·reth \shə-'mē-nē-ät-'ser-ət, -əth, -əs\ *n* [LHeb *shēmīnī 'ăsereth*, fr. Heb *shēmīnī* eighth + *'ăsereth* assembly] (ca. 1905) : a Jewish festival following the seventh day of Sukkoth and marked by a special prayer for seasonal rain

Shem·ite \'she-,mīt\ *n* [*Shem*] (1659) *archaic* : SEMITE — **She·mit·ic** \shə-'mi-tik\ *or* **Shem·it·ish** \'she-,mī-tish\ *adj, archaic*

she·nan·i·gan \shə-'na-ni-gən\ *n* [origin unknown] (1855) **1** : a devious trick used esp. for an underhand purpose **2 a** : tricky or questionable practices or conduct — usu. used in pl. **b** : high-spirited or mischievous activity — usu. used in pl.

shend \'shend\ *vt* **shent** \'shent\; **shend·ing** [ME, fr. OE *scendan*; akin to OE *scamu* shame — more at SHAME] (bef. 12c) **1** *archaic* : to put to shame or confusion **2** *archaic* : REPROVE, REVILE **3** *chiefly dial* **a** : INJURE, MAR **b** : RUIN, DESTROY

she-oak \'shē-,ōk\ *n* (1792) : any of several casuarinas

She·ol \'shē-ōl, 'shē-,\ *n* [Heb *Shĕ'ōl*] (1599) : the abode of the dead in early Hebrew thought

¹shep·herd \'she-pərd\ *n* [ME *sheepherde*, fr. OE *scēaphyrde*, fr. *scēap* sheep + *hierde* herdsman; akin to OE *heord* herd] (bef. 12c) **1** : one who tends sheep **2** : PASTOR **3** : GERMAN SHEPHERD

²shepherd *vt* (1790) **1** : to tend as a shepherd **2** : to guide or guard in the manner of a shepherd ⟨~ed the bill through Congress⟩

shepherd dog *n* (15c) : SHEEPDOG

shep·herd·ess \'she-pər-dəs\ *n* (14c) : a woman or girl who tends sheep; *also* : a rural girl or woman

shepherd's check *n* (1896) : a pattern of small even black-and-white checks; *also* : a fabric woven in this pattern — called also *shepherd's plaid*

shepherd's pie *n* (1877) : a meat pie with a mashed potato crust

shepherd's purse *n* (15c) : a white-flowered weedy annual herb (*Capsella bursa-pastoris*) of the mustard family with flat heart-shaped pods

sheq·el \'she-kəl\ *n, pl* **sheq·a·lim** \she-kä-lim\ *var of* SHEKEL

Sher·a·ton \'sher-ə-t°n\ *adj* [Thomas *Sheraton*] (1883) : of, relating to, or being a style of furniture that originated in England around 1800 and is characterized by straight lines and graceful proportions

shepherd's check

sher·bet \'shər-bət\ *also* **sher·bert** \-bərt\ *n* [Turk & Per; Turk *şerbet*, fr. Per *sharbat*, fr. Ar *sharbah* drink] (1603) **1** : a cold drink of sweetened and diluted fruit juice **2** : an ice with milk, egg white, or gelatin added

sherd *var of* SHARD

sher·got·tite \'shər-gə-,tīt\ *n* [*Shergotty* (Sherghati), town in India] (ca. 1911) : any of a class of rare achondritic geologically young meteorites that are apparently composed of solidified lava from celestial bodies other than earth

she·rif \shə-'rēf\ *var of* SHARIF

sher·iff \'sher-əf\ *n* [ME *shirreve*, fr. OE *scirgerēfa*, fr. *scir* shire + *gerēfa* reeve — more at SHIRE, REEVE] (bef. 12c) : an important official of a shire or county charged primarily with judicial duties (as executing the processes and orders of courts and judges) — **sher·iff·dom** \-əf-dəm, -təm\ *n*

sher·lock \'shər-,läk, -lək\ *n, often cap* [*Sherlock* Holmes, detective in stories by Sir Arthur Conan Doyle] (1903) : DETECTIVE

Sher·pa \'sher-pə, 'shər-\ *n* (1847) : a member of a Tibetan people living on the high southern slopes of the Himalayas in eastern Nepal who provide support for foreign trekkers and mountain climbers

sher·ris \'sher-is\ *archaic var of* SHERRY

sher·ry \'sher-ē\ *n, pl* **sherries** [alter. of earlier *sherris* (taken as pl.), fr. *Xeres* (now *Jerez*), Spain] (1597) : a Spanish fortified wine with a distinctive nutty flavor; *also* : a similar wine produced elsewhere

she's \'shēz\ (ca. 1592) : she is : she has

Shet·land \'shet-lənd\ *n* (1836) **1 a** : SHETLAND PONY **b** : SHETLAND SHEEPDOG *often not cap* **a** : a lightweight loosely twisted yarn of Shetland wool used for knitting and weaving **b** : a fabric or a garment made from Shetland wool

Shetland pony *n* (1801) : any of a breed of small stocky hardy ponies that originated in the Shetland Islands

Shetland sheepdog *n* (1909) : any of a breed of small heavy-coated dogs developed in the Shetland Islands that resemble miniature collies

Shetland wool *n* (1790) : fine wool from sheep raised in the Shetland Islands; *also* : yarn spun from this

sheugh \'shük\ *n* [ME *sogh* swamp; akin to MLG *sō* gutter] (1501) *chiefly Scot* : DITCH, TRENCH

shew \'shō\ *Brit var of* SHOW

shew·bread \'shō-,bred\ *n* [trans. of G *Schaubrot*] (1530) : consecrated unleavened bread ritually placed by the Jewish priests of ancient Israel on a table in the sanctuary of the Tabernacle on the Sabbath

Shia \'shē-(,)ä\ *n* [Ar *shī'ah* sect] (1626) **1** : the Muslims of the branch of Islam comprising sects believing in Ali and the Imams as the only rightful successors of Muhammad and in the concealment and messianic return of the last recognized Imam — compare SUNNI **2** : SHIITE **3** : the branch of Islam formed by the Shia

shi·at·su *also* **shi·at·zu** \shē-'ät-(,)sü\ *n, often cap* [short for Jp *shiatsuryōhō*, fr. *shi-* finger + *-atsu* pressure + *ryōhō* treatment] (1967) : a massage with the fingers applied to those specific areas of the body used in acupuncture

shib·bo·leth \'shi-bə-ləth *also* -,leth\ *n* [Heb *shibbōleth* stream; fr. the use of this word in Judg 12:6 as a test to distinguish Gileadites from Ephraimites, who pronounced it *sibbōleth*] (1638) **1 a** : a word or saying used by adherents of a party, sect, or belief and usu. regarded by others as empty of real meaning ⟨the old ~s come rolling off their lips —Joseph Epstein⟩ **b** : a widely held belief ⟨today this book publishing ~ is a myth —L. A. Wood⟩ **c** : TRUISM, PLATITUDE ⟨some truth in the ~ that crime does not pay —Lee Rogow⟩ **2 a** : a use of language regarded as distinctive of a particular group ⟨accent was . . . a ~ of social class —Vivian Ducat⟩ **b** : a custom or usage regarded as distinguishing one group from others ⟨for most of the well-to-do in the town, dinner was a ~, its hour ordained by the Shia —Osbert Sitwell⟩

shiel \'shē(ə)l\ *n* [ME (northern dial.) *schele*] (13c) *chiefly Scot* : SHIELING

¹shield \'shē(ə)ld\ *n* [ME *sheld*, fr. OE *scield*; akin to OHG *scilt* shield and prob. to OE *sciell* shell] (bef. 12c) **1** : a broad piece of defensive armor carried on the arm **2** : one that protects or defends : DEFENSE **3** : DRESS SHIELD **4 a** : a device or part that serves as a protective cover or barrier **b** : a protective structure (as a carapace, scale, or plate) of some animals **5** : ESCUTCHEON; *esp* : one that is wide at the top and rounds to a point at the bottom **6** : the Precambrian nuclear mass of a continent that is surrounded and sometimes covered by sedimentary rocks **7** : something resembling a shield: as **a** : APOTHECIUM **b** : a police officer's badge **c** : a decorative or identifying emblem

²shield *vt* (bef. 12c) **1 a** : to protect with or as if with a shield : provide with a protective cover or shelter **b** : to cut off from observation : HIDE **2** *obs* : FORBID *syn* see DEFEND — **shield·er** *n*

shield law *n* (1971) : a law that protects journalists from forced disclosure of confidential news sources

shield volcano *n* (1911) : a broad rounded volcano that is built up by successive outpourings of very fluid lava

shiel·ing \'shē-liŋ, -liŋ\ *n* (1568) **1** *Brit* : a mountain hut used as a shelter by shepherds **2** *dial Brit* : a summer pasture in the mountains

shier *comparative of* SHY

shiest *superlative of* SHY

¹shift \'shift\ *vb* [ME, fr. OE *sciftan* to divide, arrange; akin to ON *skipa* to arrange, assign] *vt* (13c) **1** : to exchange for or replace by another : CHANGE **2 a** : to change the place, position, or direction of : MOVE **b** : to make a change in (place) **3** : to change phonetically ~ *vi* **1** : to change place or position **2** : to change direction ⟨the wind ~ed⟩ **c** : to change gears **d** : to depress the shift key (as on a typewriter) **2 a** : to assume responsibility ⟨had to ~ for themselves⟩ **b** : to resort to expedients **3 a** : to go through a change **b** : to change one's clothes **c** : to become changed phonetically — **shift·able** \'shif-tə-bəl\ *adj* — **shift·er** *n* — **shift gears** : to make a change

²shift *n* (1523) **1 a** : a means or device for effecting an end **b** (1) : a deceitful or underhand scheme : DODGE (2) : an expedient tried in difficult circumstances : EXTREMITY **2 a** *chiefly dial* : a change of clothes **b** (1) *chiefly dial* : SHIRT (2) : a woman's slip or chemise (3) : a usu. loose-fitting or semifitted dress **3 a** : a change in direction ⟨a ~ in the wind⟩ **b** : a change in emphasis, judgment, or attitude **4 a** : a group of people who work or occupy themselves in turn with other groups **b** (1) : a change of one group of people (as workers) for another in regular alternation (2) : a scheduled period of work or duty **5** : a change in place or position: as **a** : a change in the position of the hand on a fingerboard (as of a violin) **b** (1) : FAULT 5 (2) : the relative displacement of rock masses on opposite sides of a fault or fault zone **c** (1) : a simultaneous change of position in football by two or more players from one side of the line to the other (2) : a change of positions made by one or more players in baseball to provide better defense against a particular hitter **d** : a change in frequency resulting in a change in position of a spectral line or band — compare DOPPLER EFFECT **e** : a movement of bits in a computer register a specified number of places to the right or left **6** : a removal from one person or thing to another : TRANSFER **7** : CONSONANT SHIFT **8** : a bid in bridge in a suit other than the suit one's partner has bid — compare JUMP **9** : GEARSHIFT *syn* see RESOURCE

shift key *n* (1893) : a key on a keyboard (as of a typewriter) that when pressed enables an alternate set of characters to be printed

shift·less \'shif(t)-ləs\ *adj* [*shift* (resourcefulness)] (1584) **1** : lacking in resourcefulness : INEFFICIENT **2** : lacking in ambition or incentive : LAZY — **shift·less·ly** *adv* — **shift·less·ness** *n*

shifty \'shif-tē\ *adj* **shift·i·er; -est** (ca. 1570) **1** : full of or ready with expedients : RESOURCEFUL **2 a** : given to deception, evasion, or fraud : TRICKY **b** : capable of evasive movement : ELUSIVE ⟨a ~ boxer⟩ **3** : indicative of a tricky nature ⟨~ eyes⟩ — **shift·i·ly** \-tə-lē\ *adv* — **shift·i·ness** \-tē-nəs\ *n*

shi·gel·la \shi-'ge-lə\ *n, pl* **-gel·lae** \-'ge-(,)lē, -(,)lī\ *also* **-gellas** [NL, fr. Kiyoshi *Shiga* †1957 Jp. bacteriologist] (1937) : any of a genus (*Shigella*) of nonmotile rod-shaped bacteria that cause dysenteries in animals and esp. humans

shig·el·lo·sis \,shi-gə-'lō-səs\ *n, pl* **-lo·ses** \-'lō-,sēz\ [NL] (1944) : dysentery caused by shigellae

shih tzu \'shēd-zü, 'shēt-'sü\ *n, pl* **shih tzus** *also* **shih tzu** *often cap* S&T [Chin (Beijing) *shīzi* (gǒu), fr. *shīzi* lion + *gǒu* dog] (1921) : any of a breed of small short-legged dogs of Chinese origin that have a short muzzle and a long dense coat

Shi·ism \'shē-ˌi-zəm\ n (ca. 1883) : Islam as taught by the Shia

shii·ta·ke \shē-'tä-kē\ n [Jp, fr. *shii*, the Japanese chinquapin + *take* mushroom] (1877) : a dark Oriental mushroom (*Lentinus edodes* of the family Agaricaceae) widely cultivated esp. on woods of the beech family for its edible flavorful cap

Shi·ite \'shē-ˌīt\ n (1728) : a Muslim of the Shia branch of Islam

¹**shi·kar** \shi-'kär\ n [Hindi *shikār*, fr. Per] (ca. 1610) *India* : HUNTING

²**shikar** vb **shi·karred; shi·kar·ring** (1872) *India* : HUNT

shi·ka·ri \shi-'kär-ē, -'kär-\ n [Hindi *shikārī*, fr. Per, fr. *shikār*] (1827) *India* : a big game hunter; *esp* : a professional hunter or guide

shik·sa or **shik·se** \'shik-sə\ n [Yiddish *shikse*, fem. of *sheygets* non≠ Jewish boy, fr. Heb *sheqeṣ* blemish, abomination] (1892) **1 :** a non≠ Jewish girl or woman — often used disparagingly **2 :** a Jewish girl or woman who does not observe Jewish precepts — used esp. by Orthodox Jews

¹**shill** \'shil\ vi [²*shill*] (ca. 1914) **1 :** to act as a shill **2 :** to act as a spokesperson or promoter ⟨the eminent Shakespearean producer, director, actor and star . . . is now ∼*ing* for a brokerage house —Andy Rooney⟩

²**shill** n [perh. short for *shillaber*, of unknown origin] (ca. 1916) **1 :** one who acts as a decoy (as for a pitchman or gambler); *also* : one who makes a sales pitch **2 :** PITCH 8a

shil·le·lagh also **shil·la·lah** \shə-'lā-lē\ n [*Shillelagh*, town in Ireland] (1772) : CUDGEL

shil·ling \'shi-liŋ\ n [ME, fr. OE *scilling*; akin to OHG *skilling*, a gold coin] (bef. 12c) **1 a :** a former monetary unit of the United Kingdom equal to 12 pence or ¹/₂₀ pound **b :** a former monetary unit equal to ¹/₂₀ pound of any of various countries in or formerly in the Commonwealth **2 :** a coin representing one shilling **3 :** any of several early American coins **4 —** see MONEY table

Shil·luk \shi-'lük\ n, pl **Shilluk** or **Shilluks** (1790) **1 :** a member of a Nilotic people of the Sudan dwelling mainly on the west bank of the White Nile **2 :** the language of the Shilluk people

¹**shil·ly–shal·ly** \'shi-lē-ˌsha-lē\ adv [irreg. redupl. of *shall* I] (1700) : in an irresolute, undecided, or hesitating manner

²**shil·ly–shal·ly** adj (1734) : IRRESOLUTE, VACILLATING

³**shil·ly–shal·ly** n (1755) : INDECISION, IRRESOLUTION

⁴**shil·ly–shal·ly** vi **shil·ly–shal·lied; shil·ly–shal·ly·ing** (1782) **1 :** to show hesitation or lack of decisiveness or resolution **2 :** DAWDLE

shil·pit \'shil-pət\ adj [origin unknown] (1812) **1** *Scot* : pinched and starved in appearance **2** *Scot* : WEAK, INSIPID — used of drink

¹**shim** \'shim\ n [origin unknown] (1860) : a thin often tapered piece of material (as wood, metal, or stone) used to fill in space between things (as for support, leveling, or adjustment of fit)

²**shim** vt **shimmed; shim·ming** (ca. 1890) : to fill out or level up by the use of a shim

¹**shim·mer** \'shi-mər\ vb **shim·mered; shim·mer·ing** \'shi-mə-riŋ, 'shim-riŋ\ [ME *schimeren*, fr. OE *scimerian*; akin to OE *scinan* to shine — more at SHINE] vi (bef. 12c) **1 :** to shine with a soft tremulous or fitful light : GLIMMER **2 :** to reflect a wavering sometimes distorted visual image ∼ vt : to cause to shimmer **syn** see FLASH

²**shimmer** n (1821) **1 :** a light that shimmers : subdued sparkle or sheen : GLIMMER **2 :** a wavering sometimes distorted visual image usu. resulting from heat-induced changes in atmospheric refraction — **shim·mery** \'shi-mə-rē, 'shim-rē\ adj

¹**shim·my** \'shi-mē\ n, pl **shimmies** (1837) **1** [by alter.] : CHEMISE **2** [short for *shimmy-shake*] : a jazz dance characterized by a shaking of the body from the shoulders down **3 :** an abnormal vibration esp. in the front wheels of a motor vehicle

²**shimmy** vi **shim·mied; shim·my·ing** (1919) **1 :** to shake, quiver, or tremble in or as if in dancing a shimmy **2 :** to vibrate abnormally — used esp. of automobiles

¹**shin** \'shin\ n [ME *shine*, fr. OE *scinu*; akin to OHG *scina* shin, OE *scia* shin, leg] (bef. 12c) : the front part of the vertebrate leg below the knee

²**shin** vb **shinned; shin·ning** vi (1829) **1 :** to move oneself up or down something vertical (as a pole) esp. by alternately hugging it with the arms or hands and the legs **2 :** to move forward rapidly on foot ∼ vt **1 :** to kick or strike on the shins **2 :** to climb by shinning

³**shin** \'shēn, 'shin\ n [Heb *shīn*] (ca. 1823) : the 22d letter of the Hebrew alphabet — see ALPHABET table

Shin \'shin, 'shēn\ n [Jp, lit., truth] (1877) : a major Japanese Buddhist sect that emphasizes salvation by faith in exclusive worship of Amida Buddha

Shi·na \'shē-nə\ n (1854) : an Indo-Aryan language spoken in Gilgit in northern Kashmir

shin·bone \'shin-ˌbōn\ n (bef. 12c) : TIBIA 1

shin·dig \'shin-ˌdig\ n [prob. alter. of *shindy*] (1871) **1 a :** a social gathering with dancing **b :** a usu. large or lavish party **2 :** SHINDY 2

shin·dy \'shin-dē\ n, pl **shindys** or **shindies** [prob. alter. of ¹*shinny*] (1821) **1 :** SHINDIG 1 **2 :** FRACAS, UPROAR

¹**shine** \'shīn\ vb **shone** \'shōn, *esp Canad & Brit* 'shän\ or **shined; shin·ing** [ME, fr. OE *scinan*; akin to OHG *skinan* to shine and perh. to Gk *skia* shadow] vi (bef. 12c) **1 :** to emit rays of light **2 :** to be bright by reflection of light **3 :** to be eminent, conspicuous, or distinguished ⟨∼s in math⟩ **4 :** to have a bright glowing appearance ⟨his face *shone* with enthusiasm⟩ **5 :** to be conspicuously evident or clear ∼ vt **1 a :** to cause to emit light **b :** to throw or direct the light of **2** *past & past part* **shined** : to make bright by polishing ⟨*shined* his shoes⟩

²**shine** n (15c) **1 :** brightness caused by the emission of light **2** : brightness caused by the reflection of light : LUSTER **3 :** BRILLIANCE, SPLENDOR **4 :** fair weather : SUNSHINE ⟨rain or ∼⟩ **5 :** TRICK, CAPER — usu. used in pl. **6 :** LIKING, FANCY ⟨took a ∼ to him⟩ **7 a :** a polish or gloss given to shoes **b :** a single polishing of a pair of shoes

shin·er \'shi-nər\ n (14c) **1 :** one that shines **2 :** a silvery fish; *esp* : any of numerous small freshwater American cyprinid fishes (esp. genus *Notropis*) — compare GOLDEN SHINER **3 :** BLACK EYE 1

¹**shin·gle** \'shiŋ-gəl\ n [ME *schingel*] (13c) **1 :** a small thin piece of building material often with one end thicker than the other for laying in overlapping rows as a covering for the roof or sides of a building **2** : a small signboard esp. designating a professional office — used

chiefly in the phrase *hang out one's shingle* **3 :** a woman's haircut with the hair trimmed short from the back of the head to the nape

²**shingle** vt **shin·gled; shin·gling** \-g(ə-)liŋ\ (1562) **1 :** to cover with or as if with shingles **2 :** to bob and shape (the hair) in a shingle **3** : to lay out or arrange so as to overlap — **shin·gler** \-g(ə-)lər\ n

³**shingle** n [prob. of Scand origin; akin to Norw *singel* coarse gravel] (15c) **1 :** coarse rounded detritus or alluvial material esp. on the seashore that differs from ordinary gravel only in the larger size of the stones **2 :** a place strewn with shingle — **shin·gly** \-g(ə-)lē\ adj

shin·gles \'shiŋ-gəlz\ n pl but sing in constr [ME *schingles*, by folk etymology fr. ML *cingulus*, fr. L *cingulum* girdle — more at CINGULUM] (14c) : HERPES ZOSTER

Shin·gon \'shin-ˌgän, 'shēn-\ n [Jp] (1727) : an esoteric Japanese Buddhist sect claiming the achievement of Buddhahood in this life through prescribed rituals

shin·ing \'shī-niŋ\ adj (bef. 12c) **1 :** emitting or reflecting light **2** : bright and often splendid in appearance : RESPLENDENT **3 :** possessing a distinguished quality : ILLUSTRIOUS **4 :** full of sunshine

shin·leaf \'shin-ˌlēf\ n, pl **shinleafs** (ca. 1818) : any of several wintergreens (esp. *Pyrola elliptica*) with lustrous evergreen basal leaves and racemose white or pinkish flowers

shin·nery \'shi-nə-rē\ n, pl **-ner·ies** [modif. of LaF *chênière*, fr. F *chêne* oak] (1901) : a dense growth of small trees or an area of such growth; *esp* : one of scrub oak in the West and Southwest

¹**shin·ny** also **shin·ney** \'shi-nē\ n [perh. fr. ¹*shin*] (1672) : a variation of hockey played by children with a curved stick and a ball or block of wood; *also* : the stick used

²**shinny** vi **shin·nied; shin·ny·ing** [alter. of ²*shin*] (1851) : SHIN 1

shin·plas·ter \'shin-ˌplas-tər\ n (1824) **1 :** a piece of privately-issued paper currency; *esp* : one poorly secured and depreciated in value **2** : a piece of fractional currency

shin·splints \'shin-ˌsplin(t)s\ n pl but sing or pl in constr (ca. 1930) : injury to and inflammation of the tibial and toe extensor muscles or their fasciae caused by repeated minimal traumas (as by running)

Shin·to \'shin-(ˌ)tō\ n [Jp *shintō*] (1727) : the indigenous religion of Japan consisting chiefly in the cultic devotion to deities of natural forces and veneration of the Emperor as a descendant of the sun goddess — **Shinto** adj — **Shin·to·ism** \-(ˌ)tō-ˌi-zəm\ n — **Shin·to·ist** \-ˌtō-ist\ n or adj — **Shin·to·is·tic** \ˌshin-tō-'is-tik\ adj

shiny \'shī-nē\ adj **shin·i·er; -est** (1590) **1 a :** bright with the rays of the sun : SUNSHINY **b :** filled with light **2 :** bright in appearance : POLISHED ⟨∼ new shoes⟩ **3 :** rubbed or worn smooth **4 :** lustrous with natural secretions ⟨a ∼ nose⟩ — **shin·i·ness** n

¹**ship** \'ship\ n, often attrib [ME, fr. OE *scip*; akin to OHG *skif* ship] (bef. 12c) **1 a :** a large seagoing vessel **b :** a sailing vessel having a bowsprit and usu. three masts each composed of a lower mast, a topmast, and a topgallant mast **2 :** BOAT; *esp* : one propelled by power or sail **3 :** a ship's crew **4 :** FORTUNE 3 ⟨when their ∼ comes in they'll be able to live in better style⟩ **5 :** AIRSHIP, AIRPLANE, SPACECRAFT

²**ship** vb **shipped; ship·ping** vt (14c) **1 a :** to place or receive on board a ship for transportation by water **b :** to cause to be transported ⟨*shipped* him off to prep school⟩ **2** *obs* : to provide with a ship **3 :** to put in place for use ⟨∼ the tiller⟩ **4 :** to take into a ship or boat ⟨∼ the gangplank⟩ **5 :** to engage for service on a ship **6 :** to take (as water) over the side — used of a boat or a ship ∼ vi **1 :** to embark on a ship **2 a :** to go or travel by ship — often used with *out* **b :** to proceed by ship or other means under military orders — often used with *out* **3 :** to engage to serve on shipboard — **ship·pa·ble** \'shi-pə-bəl\ adj

-ship n suffix [ME, fr. OE *-scipe*; akin to OHG *-scaft* -ship, OE *scieppan* to shape — more at SHAPE] **1 :** state : condition : quality ⟨friend*ship*⟩ **2 :** office : dignity : profession ⟨clerk*ship*⟩ **3 :** art : skill ⟨horseman*ship*⟩ **4 :** something showing, exhibiting, or embodying a quality or state ⟨town*ship*⟩ **5 :** one entitled to a (specified) rank, title, or appellation ⟨his Lord*ship*⟩ **6 :** the body of persons participating in a specified activity ⟨reader*ship*⟩ ⟨listener*ship*⟩

ship biscuit n (1799) : HARDTACK — called also *ship bread*

¹**ship·board** \'ship-ˌbōrd, -ˌbȯrd\ n (13c) **1 :** the side of a ship **2** : SHIP ⟨met on ∼⟩

²**shipboard** adj (1857) : existing or taking place on board a ship

ship·borne \'ship-ˌbȯrn, -ˌbōrn\ adj (ca. 1835) : transported or designed to be transported by ship ⟨∼ aircraft⟩

ship·build·er \'ship-ˌbil-dər\ n (ca. 1700) : one who designs or constructs ships — **ship·build·ing** \-diŋ\ n

ship·fit·ter \'ship-ˌfi-tər\ n (1941) **1 :** one that fits together the structural members of ships and puts them into position for riveting or welding **2 :** a naval enlisted man who works in sheet metal and performs the work of a plumber aboard ship

ship·lap \-ˌlap\ n (1895) : wooden sheathing in which the boards are rabbeted so that the edges of each board lap over the edges of adjacent boards to make a flush joint

ship·load \-ˈlōd, -ˌlōd\ n (1639) **1 :** as much or as many as will fill or load a ship **2 :** an indefinitely large amount or number

ship·man \-mən\ n (bef. 12c) **1 :** SAILOR, SEAMAN **2 :** SHIPMASTER

ship·mas·ter \-ˌmas-tər\ n (14c) : the master or commander of a ship other than a warship

ship·mate \-ˌmāt\ n (1748) : a fellow sailor

ship·ment \-mənt\ n (1802) **1 :** the act or process of shipping **2 :** the goods shipped

ship of state n (1847) : the affairs of a state symbolized as a ship on a course

ship of the line (1706) : a warship large enough to have a place in the line of battle

ship·own·er \'ship-ˌō-nər\ n (ca. 1530) : the owner of a ship or of a share in a ship

ship·per \'shi-pər\ n (1755) : one that sends goods by any form of conveyance

\ə\ abut \ᵊ\ kitten, F table \ər\ further \a\ ash \ā\ ace \ä\ mop, mar \au̇\ out \ch\ chin \e\ bet \ē\ easy \g\ go \i\ hit \ī\ ice \j\ job \ŋ\ sing \ō\ go \ȯ\ law \ȯi\ boy \th\ thin \th̲\ the \ü\ loot \u̇\ foot \y\ yet \zh\ vision \ä, k̲, ⁿ, œ, œ̄, ᵫ, ᵫ̄, ᵜ\ see Guide to Pronunciation

ship·ping \'ship-pin\ n (14c) **1 a :** passage on a ship **b :** SHIPS **c :** the body of ships in one place or belonging to one port or country **2 :** the act or business of one that ships

shipping clerk n (ca. 1858) **:** one who is employed in a shipping room to assemble, pack, and send out or receive goods

ship·shape \'ship-ˌshāp, 'ship-ˌ\ adj [short for earlier shipshapen, fr. ship + shapen, archaic pp. of shape] (1644) **:** TRIM, TIDY

ship·side \'ship-ˌsīd\ n (15c) **:** the area adjacent to a ship; specif **:** a dock at which a ship loads or unloads passengers and freight

ship's papers n pl **:** the papers a ship is legally required to carry for due inspection to show the character of the ship and cargo

ship·way \'ship-ˌwā\ n (1834) **:** the ways on which a ship is built

ship·worm \-ˌwərm\ n (ca. 1778) **:** any of various elongated marine clams (esp. family Teredinidae) that resemble worms, burrow in submerged wood, and damage wharf piles and wooden ships

¹ship·wreck \-ˌrek\ n [alter. of earlier shipwrack, fr. ME schipwrak, fr. OE scipwræc, fr. scip ship + wræc something driven by the sea — more at WRACK] (12c) **1 :** a wrecked ship or its parts **2 :** the destruction or loss of a ship **3 :** an irretrievable loss or failure

²shipwreck vt (1589) **1 a :** to cause to experience shipwreck **b :** RUIN **2 :** to destroy (a ship) by grounding or foundering

ship·wright \'ship-ˌrīt\ n (bef. 12c) **:** a carpenter skilled in ship construction and repair

ship·yard \-ˌyärd\ n (ca. 1700) **:** a yard, place, or enclosure where ships are built or repaired

shire \'shīr, in place-name compounds ˌshir, shər\ n [ME, fr. OE scir office, shire; akin to OHG scira care] (bef. 12c) **1 :** an administrative subdivision; esp **:** a county in England **2 :** any of a breed of large heavy draft horses of British origin that have heavily feathered legs

shire town n (15c) **1** Brit **:** a town that is the seat of the government of a shire **2** NewEng **:** a town where a court of superior jurisdiction (as a circuit court or a court with a jury) sits

shirk \'shərk\ vb [origin unknown] vi (15c) **1 :** to go stealthily **:** SNEAK **2 :** to evade the performance of an obligation ~ vt **:** AVOID, EVADE ⟨~ one's duty⟩ — **shirk·er** n

shirr \'shər\ vt [origin unknown] (1891) **1 :** to draw (as cloth) together in a shirring **2 :** to bake (eggs removed from the shell) until set

shirr·ing \'shər-in\ n (ca. 1882) **:** a decorative gathering (as of cloth) made by drawing up the material along two or more parallel lines of stitching

shirring

shirt \'shərt\ n [ME shirte, fr. OE scyrte; akin to ON skyrta shirt, OE scort short] (bef. 12c) **1 :** a garment for the upper part of the body: as **a :** a cloth garment usu. having a collar, sleeves, a front opening, and a tail long enough to be tucked inside trousers or a skirt **b :** UNDERSHIRT **2 :** all or a large part of one's money or resources ⟨lost his ~ on that business deal⟩ — **shirt·less** \-ləs\ adj

shirt·dress \-ˌdres\ n (1943) **:** a tailored dress patterned after a shirt and having buttons down the front

shirt·front \-ˌfrənt\ n (1838) **:** the front of a shirt; also **:** the part of a man's shirt not covered by coat or vest

shirt·ing \'shər-tin\ n (1604) **:** fabric suitable for shirts

shirt jacket n (1879) **:** a jacket designed in the style of a shirt — called also shirt-jac

shirt·mak·er \'shərt-ˌmā-kər\ n (ca. 1858) **:** one that makes shirts

¹shirt·sleeve \-ˌslēv\ n (ca. 1566) **:** the sleeve of a shirt — **in shirtsleeves :** wearing a shirt but no coat

²shirtsleeve also **shirt·sleeves** \-ˌslēvz\ or **shirt·sleeved** \-ˌslēvd\ adj (1864) **1 a :** being without a coat ⟨a ~ spectator⟩ **b :** calling for the removal of coats for the sake of comfort or efficiency ⟨~ weather⟩ **2 :** marked by informality and directness ⟨~ diplomacy⟩

¹shirt·tail \'shərt-ˌtāl\ adj (1845) **1 :** very young **:** IMMATURE ⟨~ boys fishing in the creek⟩ **2 :** distantly and indefinitely related ⟨a ~ cousin on her father's side⟩ **3 :** small, trivial, or short typically to the point of inadequacy ⟨has a gullied ~ ranch in the hills⟩

²shirttail n (1873) **1 :** the part of a shirt that reaches below the waist esp. in the back **2 :** something small or inadequate

shirt·waist \'shərt-ˌwāst\ n (1879) **:** a woman's tailored garment (as a blouse or dress) with details copied from men's shirts

shirty \'shər-tē\ adj (1846) chiefly Brit **:** ANGRY, IRRITATED

shish ke·bab \'shish-kə-ˌbäb\ n [Turk şişkebabı, fr. şiş spit + kebap roast meat] (1914) **:** kabob cooked on skewers

¹shit \'shit, interjectionally also 'shē-ət\ n [(assumed) ME, fr. OE scite; akin to OE -scitan to defecate] (ca. 1585) **1 :** EXCREMENT — usu. considered vulgar **2 :** an act of defecation — usu. considered vulgar **3 :** NONSENSE, CRAP — usu. considered vulgar **4 :** any of several intoxicating or narcotic drugs; esp **:** HEROIN — usu. considered vulgar **5 :** DAMN **2** — usu. considered vulgar **6 :** a worthless, offensive, or detestable person — usu. considered vulgar — **shit·ty** \'shi-tē\ adj

²shit \'shit vb shit or shat \'shat\; **shit·ting** [alter. of earlier shite, fr. ME shiten, fr. OE -scitan; akin to OHG scizan to defecate and prob. to OE scēadan to separate — more at SHED] vi (ca. 1720) **:** DEFECATE — usu. considered vulgar ~ vt **1 :** to defecate in — usu. considered vulgar **2 :** to attempt to deceive **:** BULLSHIT — usu. considered vulgar

shi·ta·ke var of SHIITAKE

shit·tah \'shi-tə\ n, pl **shittahs** or **shit·tim** \'shi-təm\ [Heb shittāh] (1611) **:** a tree of uncertain identity but prob. an acacia (as Acacia seyal) from the wood of which the ark and fittings of the Hebrew tabernacle were made

shit·tim·wood \'shi-təm-ˌwüd\ n [Heb shittīm (pl. of shittāh) + E wood] (1588) **1 :** the wood of the shittah tree **2 :** any of several trees (genus Bumelia, esp. B. lanuginosa) of the sapodilla family of the southern U.S.; also **:** their hard heavy dense wood

shiv \'shiv\ n [alter. of chiv, of unknown origin] (1674) slang **:** KNIFE

Shi·va \'shi-və, 'shē-\ var of SIVA

shi·vah or **shi·va** also **shi·ve** \'shi-və\ n [Heb shibh'āh seven (days)] (1892) **:** a traditional seven-day period of mourning the dead that is observed in Jewish homes — often used in the phrase sit shivah

shiv·a·ree \ˌshi-və-'rē, 'shi-və-ˌ\ n [modif. of F charivari — more at CHARIVARI] (1843) **:** a noisy mock serenade to a newly married couple — **shivaree** vt

¹shiv·er \'shi-vər\ n [ME; akin to OHG scivaro splinter] (13c) **:** one of the small pieces into which a brittle thing is broken by sudden violence

²shiver vb **shiv·ered; shiv·er·ing** \'shi-və-rin, 'shiv-rin\ (13c) **:** to break into many small pieces **:** SHATTER

³shiver vb **shiv·ered; shiv·er·ing** \'shi-və-rin, 'shiv-rin\ [ME, alter. of chiveren] vi (15c) **1 :** to undergo trembling **:** QUIVER **2 :** to tremble in the wind as it strikes first one and then the other side (of a sail) ~ vt **:** to cause (a sail) to shiver by steering close to the wind

⁴shiver n (1727) **1 :** an instance of shivering **:** TREMBLE **2 :** an intense shivery sensation esp. of fear — often used in pl. with the ⟨horror movies give him the ~s⟩

¹shiv·ery \'shi-və-rē, 'shiv-rē\ adj (1683) **:** easily broken into shivers

²shivery adj (1747) **1 :** characterized by shivers **2 :** causing shivers

shle·miehl var of SCHLEMIEL

shlep, shlepp var of SCHLEPP

shlock var of SCHLOCK

shm- — see SCHM-

¹shoal \'shōl\ adj [alter. of ME shold, fr. OE sceald — more at SKELETON] (1554) **:** SHALLOW

²shoal n (1555) **1 :** SHALLOW **2 :** a sandbank or sandbar that makes the water shallow; specif **:** an elevation which is not rocky and on which there is a depth of water of six fathoms (11 meters) or less

³shoal vi (1574) **:** to become shallow ~ vt **1 :** to come to a shallow or less deep part of **2 :** to cause to become shallow or less deep

⁴shoal n [(assumed) ME shole, fr. OE scolu multitude — more at SCHOOL] (1579) **:** a large group or number **:** CROWD ⟨a ~ of fish⟩

⁵shoal vi (1610) **:** THRONG, SCHOOL

shoat \'shōt\ n [ME shote; akin to Flem schote shoat] (15c) **:** a young hog usu. less than one year old

¹shock \'shäk\ n [ME; akin to MHG schoc heap] (14c) **:** a pile of sheaves of grain or stalks of Indian corn set up in a field with the butt ends down

²shock vt (15c) **:** to collect into shocks

³shock n, often attrib [MF choc, fr. choquer to strike against, fr. OF choquier, prob. of Gmc origin; akin to MD schocken to jolt] (1565) **1 :** the impact or encounter of individuals or groups in combat **2 a :** violent shake or jar **:** CONCUSSION **b :** an effect of such violence **3 a** (1) **:** a disturbance in the equilibrium or permanence of something (2) **:** a sudden or violent mental or emotional disturbance **b :** something that causes such disturbance **c :** a state of being so disturbed **4 :** a state of profound depression of the vital processes associated with reduced blood volume and pressure and caused usu. by severe esp. crushing injuries, hemorrhage, or burns **5 :** sudden stimulation of the nerves and convulsive contraction of the muscles caused by the discharge of electricity through the animal body **6 a :** STROKE **5 b :** CORONARY THROMBOSIS **7 :** SHOCK ABSORBER

⁴shock vt (1576) **1 a :** to strike with surprise, terror, horror, or disgust **b :** to cause to undergo a physical or nervous shock **c :** to subject to the action of an electrical discharge **2 :** to drive by or as if by a shock ~ vi **1 :** to meet with a shock **:** COLLIDE **2 :** to cause surprise or shock — **shock·able** \'shä-kə-bəl\ adj

⁵shock adj [perh. fr. ¹shock] (1681) **:** BUSHY, SHAGGY

⁶shock n (1819) **:** a thick bushy mass (as of hair)

shock absorber n (1906) **:** any of several devices for absorbing the energy of sudden impulses or shocks in machinery or structures

shock·er \'shä-kər\ n (ca. 1824) **:** one that shocks; esp **:** something horrifying or offensive (as a sensational film or work of fiction)

shock front n (1949) **:** the advancing edge of a shock wave

shock·ing \'shä-kin\ adj (1703) **:** extremely startling, distressing, or offensive — **shock·ing·ly** \-kin-lē\ adv

shocking pink n (1938) **:** a striking, vivid, bright, or intense pink

shock·proof \'shäk-ˌprüf\ adj (1911) **1 :** incapable of being shocked **2 a :** resistant to damage by shock **b :** unlikely to cause shock: protectively insulated ⟨a ~ switch⟩

shock therapy n (1917) **:** the treatment of mental disorder by the artificial induction of coma or convulsions through use of drugs or electric current — called also shock treatment

shock troops n pl (1917) **1 :** troops esp. suited and chosen for offensive work because of their high morale, training, and discipline **2 :** a group of people militant in pressing for a cause

shock tube n (1949) **:** a usu. enclosed tube in which experimental shock waves are produced as a result of the rupturing of a diaphragm separating two chambers containing a gas or gases at differential pressure

shock wave n (1907) **1 :** a compressional wave of high amplitude caused by a shock (as from an earthquake or explosion) to the medium through which the wave travels **2 :** a violent often pulsating disturbance or reaction ⟨shock waves of rebellion⟩

shod \'shäd\ adj [ME, fr. pp. of shoen to shoe, fr. OE scōgan, fr. scōh shoe — more at SHOE] (13c) **1 a :** wearing footgear (as shoes) **b :** equipped with tires **2 :** furnished or equipped with a shoe

¹shod·dy \'shä-dē\ n [origin unknown] (1832) **1 a :** a reclaimed wool from materials that are not felted that is of better quality and longer staple than mungo **b :** a fabric often of inferior quality manufactured wholly or partly from reclaimed wool **2 a :** inferior, imitative, or pretentious articles or matter **b :** pretentious vulgarity

²shoddy adj **shod·di·er; -est** (1847) **1 :** made wholly or partly of shoddy **2 a :** cheaply imitative **:** vulgarly pretentious **b :** hastily or poorly done **:** INFERIOR **c :** SHABBY — **shod·di·ly** \'shä-dᵊl-ē\ adv — **shod·di·ness** \'shä-dē-nəs\ n

¹shoe \'shü\ n [ME shoo, fr. OE scōh; akin to OHG scuoh shoe] (bef. 12c) **1 a :** an outer covering for the human foot typically having a thick or stiff sole with an attached heel and an upper part of lighter material (as leather) **b :** a metal plate or rim for the hoof of an animal **2 :** something resembling a shoe in function or placement **3** pl **:** another's place, function, or viewpoint ⟨steps from assistant stage manager into the star's ~s —Steven Fuller⟩ **4 :** a device that retards, stops, or controls the motion of an object; esp **:** the part of a brake that presses on the brake drum **5 a :** any of various devices that are inserted in or run along a track or groove to guide a movement, provide a contact or friction grip, or protect against wear, damage, or slipping **b**

: a device (as a clip or track) on a camera that permits attachment of an accessory item (as a flash unit) **6** : a dealing box designed to hold several decks of playing cards — **shoe·less** *adj*
²**shoe** *vt* **shod** \'shäd\ *also* **shoed** \'shüd\; **shoe·ing** \'shü-iŋ\ (bef. 12c) **1** : to furnish with a shoe **2** : to cover for protection, strength, or ornament
shoe·bill \'shü-ˌbil\ *n* (1874) : a large broad-billed wading bird (*Balaeniceps rex*) of the valley of the White Nile that is related to the storks and herons
shoe·black \-ˌblak\ *n* (1778) : BOOTBLACK
¹**shoe·horn** \-ˌhȯrn\ *n* (1589) : a curved piece (as of horn, wood, or metal) used in putting on a shoe
²**shoehorn** *vt* (1926) : to force into a small, narrow, or insufficient space : SQUEEZE ⟨~ the past, present, and future into about 500 pages —Otis Port⟩
shoe·lace \'shü-ˌlās\ *n* (ca. 1647) : a lace or string for fastening a shoe
shoe·mak·er \-ˌmā-kər\ *n* (14c) : one whose occupation is making or repairing shoes
shoe·pac *or* **shoe·pack** \'shü-ˌpak\ *n* [by folk etymology fr. Delaware Jargon (Delaware-based pidgin) *seppock* shoe, fr. Delaware (Unami dial.) *cípahkʌ* shoes] (1755) : a waterproof laced boot worn esp. over heavy socks in cold weather
¹**shoe·string** \'shü-ˌstriŋ\ *n* (1616) **1** : SHOELACE **2** [fr. shoestrings being a typical item sold by itinerant vendors] : a small sum of money : capital inadequate or barely adequate to the needs of a transaction ⟨started the business on a ~⟩
²**shoestring** *adj* (1878) **1** : narrow and long like a shoestring ⟨a ~ tie⟩ **2** : operating on, accomplished by, or consisting of a small amount of money or capital ⟨a ~ budget⟩
shoestring catch *n* (1926) : a catch (as in baseball) made very close to the feet
shoe tree *n* (1827) : a foot-shaped device for inserting in a shoe to preserve its shape
sho·far \'shō-ˌfär, -fər\ *n, pl* **sho·froth** \shō-ˈfrōt, -'frōth, -'frōs\ [Heb *shōphār*] (1833) : a ram's-horn trumpet blown by the ancient Hebrews in battle and high religious observances and used in synagogues before and during Rosh Hashanah and at the conclusion of Yom Kippur

shofar

¹**shog** \'shäg\ *vi* **shogged**; **shog·ging** [ME *shoggen*] (15c) *chiefly dial* : to move along
²**shog** *n* (1611) *chiefly dial* : SHAKE, JOLT
sho·gun \'shō-gən\ *n* [Jp *shōgun* general] (1727) : one of a line of military governors ruling Japan until the revolution of 1867–68 — **sho·gun·al** \'shō-gə-nəl\ *adj* — **sho·gun·ate** \'shō-gə-nət, -ˌnāt\ *n*
sho·ji \'shō-(ˌ)jē\ *n, pl* **shoji** *also* **shojis** [Jp *shōji*] (1880) : a paper screen serving as a wall, partition, or sliding door
sho·lom \shä-'lōm, shə-\ *var of* SHALOM
Sho·na \'shō-nə\ *n, pl* **Shona** *or* **Shonas** (ca. 1895) **1** : a member of any of a group of Bantu peoples of Zimbabwe and southern Mozambique **2** : the group of languages spoken by the Shona
shone *past and past part of* SHINE
¹**shoo** \'shü\ *interj* [ME *schowe*] (15c) — used esp. in driving away an unwanted animal
²**shoo** *vt* (ca. 1798) : to scare, drive, or send away by or as if by crying *shoo*
shoo·fly \'shü-ˌflī\ *n* [¹*shoo* + *fly*] (1887) **1** : a child's rocker having the seat built on or usu. between supports representing an animal figure **2** : any of several plants held to repel flies
shoofly pie *n* (1926) : a rich pie of Pennsylvania-Dutch origin made of molasses or brown sugar sprinkled with a crumbly mixture of flour, sugar, and butter
shoo-in \'shü-ˌin\ *n* (1937) : one that is a certain and easy winner
¹**shook** *past or chiefly dial past part of* SHAKE
²**shook** \'shu̇k\ *n* [origin unknown] (1796) **1 a** : a set of staves and headings for one hogshead, cask, or barrel **b** : a bundle of parts (as of boxes) ready to be put together **2** : ¹SHOCK
shook-up \ˌshu̇k-'əp\ *adj* (1897) : nervously upset : AGITATED
shoon \'shün, 'shȯn\ *chiefly dial pl of* SHOE
¹**shoot** \'shüt\ *vb* **shot** \'shät\; **shoot·ing** [ME *sheten, shuten*, fr. OE *scēotan*; akin to ON *skjōta* to shoot] *vt* (bef. 12c) **1 a** (1) : to eject or impel or cause to be ejected or impelled by a sudden release of tension (as of a bowstring or slingshot or by a flick of a finger) ⟨~ an arrow⟩ ⟨~ a spitball⟩ ⟨~ a marble⟩ (2) : to drive forth or cause to be driven forth by an explosion (as of a powder charge in a firearm or of ignited fuel in a rocket) (3) : to drive forth or cause to be driven forth by a sudden release of gas or air ⟨~ darts from a blowgun⟩ ⟨a steam catapult ~s planes from a carrier⟩ (4) : to propel (as a ball or puck) toward a goal by striking or pushing with part of the body (as the hand or foot) or with an implement; *also* : to score by so doing ⟨~ the winning goal⟩ ⟨~ a basket⟩ (5) : to throw or cast off or out often with force ⟨~ dice⟩ ⟨the horse *shot* his rider out of the saddle⟩ **b** : to cause (as a gun or bow) to propel a missile **c** (1) : to utter (as words or sounds) rapidly or suddenly or with force ⟨~ out a stream of invective⟩ (2) : to emit (as light, flame, or fumes) suddenly and rapidly (3) : to send forth with suddenness or intensity ⟨*shot* a look of anger at them⟩ **d** : to discharge, dump, or empty esp. by overturning, upending, or directing into a slide **2** (1) : to affect by shooting: as **a** : to strike with a missile esp. from a bow or gun; *esp* : to wound or kill with a missile discharged from a bow or firearm **b** : to remove or destroy by use of firearms ⟨*shot* out the light⟩; *also* : WRECK, EXPLODE **3 a** : to push or slide (as the bolt of a door or lock) into or out of a fastening **b** : to push or thrust forward : stick out ⟨toads ~*ing* out their tongues⟩ **c** : to put forth in growing **d** : to place, send, or bring into position abruptly **4 a** : to engage in (a sport or game or a portion of a game that involves shooting) : PLAY ⟨~ pool⟩ ⟨~ a round of golf⟩ ⟨~ craps⟩ **b** (1) : to place or offer (a bet) on the result of casting dice ⟨~ $5⟩ (2) : to use up by or as if by betting : EXHAUST ⟨*shot* his whole wad on a shady deal⟩ **5 a** : to engage in the hunting and killing of (as game)

with firearms esp. as a sport ⟨~ woodcock⟩ **b** : to hunt over ⟨~ a tract of woodland⟩ **6 a** : to cause to move suddenly or swiftly forward ⟨*shot* the car onto the highway⟩ **b** : to send or carry quickly : DISPATCH ⟨~ the letter on to me as soon as you receive it⟩ **7** : to variegate as if by sprinkling color in streaks, flecks, or patches **8** : to pass swiftly by, past, or along ⟨~*ing* rapids⟩ **9** : to plane (as the edge of a board) straight or true **10 a** : SET OFF, DETONATE, IGNITE ⟨~ a charge of dynamite⟩ **b** : to effect by blasting **11** : to determine the altitude of **12** : to take a picture or series of pictures or television images of : PHOTOGRAPH, FILM **13 a** : to give an injection to **b** : to inject (an illicit drug) esp. into the bloodstream ~ *vi* **1 a** : to go or pass rapidly and precipitately ⟨sparks ~*ing* all over⟩ ⟨his feet *shot* out from under him⟩ **b** : to move ahead by force of momentum **c** : to stream out suddenly : SPURT **d** : to dart in or as if in rays from a source of light **e** : to dart with a piercing sensation ⟨pain *shot* up my arm⟩ **2 a** : to cause an engine or weapon to discharge a missile **b** : to use a firearm or bow (as in hunting) **3** : to propel a missile ⟨guns that ~ many miles⟩ **4** : PROTRUDE, PROJECT **5 a** : to grow or sprout by or as if by putting forth shoots **b** : DEVELOP, MATURE **c** : to spring or rise rapidly or suddenly — often used with *up* ⟨in a burst of growth he *shot* up to six feet tall⟩ ⟨prices *shot up*⟩ **6 a** : to propel an object (as a ball) in a particular way **b** : to drive the ball or puck toward a goal **7** : to cast dice **8** : to slide into or out of a fastening ⟨a bolt that ~s in either direction⟩ **9** : to record something (as on film or videotape) with a camera **10** : to begin to speak — usu. used as an imperative ⟨OK, ~, what do you have to say⟩ — **shoot at** *or* **shoot for** : to aim at : strive for — **shoot from the hip** : to act or speak hastily without consideration of the consequences — **shoot one's bolt** : to exhaust one's capabilities and resources — **shoot oneself in the foot** : to act against one's own best interests — **shoot the breeze** : to converse idly : GOSSIP — **shoot the works** : to venture all one's capital on one play **2** : to put forth all one's efforts
²**shoot** *n* (15c) **1** : a sending out of new growth or the growth sent out: as **a** : a stem or branch with its leaves and appendages esp. when not yet mature **b** : OFFSHOOT **2 a** : an act of shooting (as with a bow or a firearm): (1) : SHOT (2) : the firing of a missile esp. by artillery **b** (1) : a hunting trip or party (2) : the right to shoot game in a particular area or land over which it is held **c** (1) : a shooting match ⟨skeet ~⟩ (2) : a round of shots in a shooting match **d** : the action or an instance of shooting with a camera : a session or a series of sessions of photographing or filming ⟨a movie ~⟩ **3 a** : a motion or movement of rapid thrusting: as (1) : a sudden or rapid advance (2) : a momentary darting sensation : TWINGE (3) : THRUST 2b (4) : the pace between strokes in rowing **b** : a bar of rays : BEAM ⟨a ~ of sunlight⟩ **4** [prob. by folk etymology fr. F *chute* — more at CHUTE] **a** : a rush of water down a steep or rapid **b** : a place where a stream runs or descends swiftly
³**shoot** *interj* [euphemism for *shit*] (1876) — used to express annoyance or surprise
shoot down *vt* (1845) **1** : to cause to fall by shooting ⟨enemy aircraft *shot down* the helicopter⟩; *esp* : to kill in this way ⟨was *shot down* in cold blood⟩ **2** : to put an end to : DEFEAT **3** : DEFLATE, RIDICULE **4** : DISCREDIT **2** ⟨*shoot down* a theory⟩
shoot-'em-up \'shüt-əm-ˌəp\ *n* (1947) : a movie or television show with much shooting and bloodshed
shoot·er \'shü-tər\ *n* (13c) **1** : one that shoots: as **a** : a person who fires a missile-discharging device (as a rifle or bow) **b** : the person who is shooting or whose turn it is to shoot **2** : something that is used in shooting: as **a** : a marble shot from the hand **b** : REVOLVER — usu. used in combination ⟨six-*shooter*⟩ **3** : a shot of whiskey or whiskey diluted with something (as soda); *also* : a shot glass containing a bit of food (as a raw oyster)
shooting gallery *n* (1836) **1** : a usu. covered range equipped with targets for practice with firearms **2** *slang* : a place where one can obtain narcotics and shoot up
shooting iron *n* (1775) : FIREARM
shooting script *n* (1929) **1** : the final completely detailed version of a motion-picture script in which scenes are grouped in the order most convenient for shooting **2** : the final version of a television script used in the production of a program
shooting star *n* (1593) **1** : a visual meteor appearing as a temporary streak of light in the night sky **2** : any of several No. American perennial herbs (genus *Dodecatheon*, esp. *D. meadia*) of the primrose family that have entire oblong leaves and showy flowers with reflexed petals
shooting stick *n* (1926) : a spiked stick with a top that opens into a seat
shoot-out \'shüt-ˌau̇t\ *n* (1948) **1** : a battle fought with handguns or rifles **2** : something resembling a shoot-out; *broadly* : SHOWDOWN
shoot-the-chutes \ˌshüt-thə-'shüts\ *n pl but sing in constr* (1920) : an amusement ride consisting of a steep incline down which boats slide into a pool at the bottom
shoot up *vt* (1890) **1** : to shoot or shoot at esp. indiscriminately or recklessly ⟨cowboys *shooting up* the town⟩ **2** : to inject (a narcotic drug) into a vein ~ *vi* : to inject a narcotic into a vein — **shoot-up** \'shüt-ˌəp\ *n*
¹**shop** \'shäp\ *n, often attrib* [ME *shoppe*, fr. OE *sceoppa* booth; akin to OHG *scopf* shed] (14c) **1** : a handicraft establishment : ATELIER **2 a** : a building or room stocked with merchandise for sale : STORE **b** *or* **shoppe** \'shäp\ : a small retail establishment or a department in a large one offering a specified line of goods or services ⟨a millinery ~⟩ ⟨a sandwich ~⟩ **3** : a commercial establishment for the making or repair of goods or machinery ⟨machine ~⟩ ⟨repair ~⟩ **4 a** : a school laboratory equipped for manual training **b** : the art or science of working with tools and machinery **5 a** : a business establishment : OFFICE **b** : SHOPTALK
²**shop** *vb* **shopped**; **shop·ping** *vi* (1764) **1 a** : to examine goods or services with intent to buy **b** : to hunt through a market in search of

\ə\ abut \ᵊ\ kitten, F table \ər\ further \a\ ash \ā\ ace \ä\ mop, mar \au̇\ out \ch\ chin \e\ bet \ē\ easy \g\ go \i\ hit \ī\ ice \j\ job \ŋ\ sing \ō\ go \ȯ\ law \ȯi\ boy \th\ thin \t̲h̲\ the \ü\ loot \u̇\ foot \y\ yet \zh\ vision \ȧ, k̲, ⁿ, œ, œ̄, ue, ᵫ, ᵊ\ *see* Guide to Pronunciation

the best buy 2 : to make a search : HUNT ~ *vt* : to examine the stock or offerings of ⟨~ the stores for Christmas gift ideas⟩

shop·keep·er \'shäp-ˌkē-pər\ *n* (1530) : STOREKEEPER 2

shop·lift \-ˌlift\ *vb* [back-formation fr. *shoplifter*] *vi* (1820) : to steal displayed goods from a store ~ *vt* : to steal (displayed goods) from a store

shop·lift·er \-ˌlif-tər\ *n* (1680) : one who shoplifts

shop·per \'shä-pər\ *n* (1860) **1 :** one that shops **2 :** one whose occupation is shopping as an agent for customers or for an employer **3 :** a usu. free paper carrying advertising and sometimes local news

shopping bag *n* (1886) : a bag (as of strong paper) that has handles and is intended for carrying purchases

shopping center *n* (1898) : a group of retail stores and service establishments usu. with ample parking facilities and usu. designed to serve a community or neighborhood — called also *shopping plaza*

shopping list *n* (1913) : a list of items to be purchased; *broadly* : a list of related items ⟨the biggest possible *shopping list* of budget cuts — Leonard Silk⟩

shopping mall *n* (1959) : MALL 3

shop steward *n* (1904) : a union member elected as the union representative of a shop or department in dealings with the management

shop·talk \'shäp-ˌtök\ *n* (1881) : the jargon or subject matter peculiar to an occupation or a special area of interest

shop·win·dow \-ˌwin-(ˌ)dō\ *n* (15c) : a display window of a store

shop·worn \-ˌwörn, -ˌwórn\ *adj* (1838) **1 :** faded, soiled, or otherwise impaired by remaining too long in a store **2 :** stale from excessive use or familiarity ⟨~ clichés⟩ **3 :** WORN-OUT ⟨think of himself as a ~ Hollywood cynic —A. H. Johnston⟩

¹shore \'shōr, 'shór\ *n*, *often attrib* [ME, fr. (assumed) OE *scor*; akin to MLG *schōr* foreland and perh. to OE *scieran* to cut — more at SHEAR] (14c) **1 :** the land bordering a usu. large body of water; *specif* : COAST **2 :** a boundary or the country or place that it bounds ⟨hold him accountable for difficulties beyond our ~s that he could do nothing about —Dorothy Fosdick⟩ **3 :** land as distinguished from the sea ⟨shipboard and ~ duty⟩

²shore *vt* **shored; shor·ing** [ME; akin to ON *skortha* to prop] (14c) **1 :** to support by a shore : PROP **2 :** to give support to : BRACE — usu. used with *up*

³shore *n* (14c) : a prop for preventing sinking or sagging

shore·bird \'shōr-ˌbərd, 'shór-\ *n* (ca. 1672) : any of a suborder (Charadrii) of birds (as a plover or snipe) that frequent the seashore

shore dinner *n* (1892) : a dinner consisting chiefly of seafoods

shore·front \-ˌfrənt\ *n* (1919) : land along a shore; *specif* : BEACHFRONT

shore leave *n* (1888) : a leave of absence to go on shore granted to a sailor or naval officer

shore·line \-ˌlīn\ *n* (1852) **1 :** the line where a body of water and the shore meet **2 :** the strip of land along the shoreline

shore patrol *n* (1917) **1 :** a branch of a navy that exercises guard and police functions — compare MILITARY POLICE **2 :** petty officers detailed to perform police duty while a ship is in port

shore·side \-ˌsīd\ *adj* (1883) : situated at or near a shore

shore·ward \-wərd\ *or* **shore·wards** \-wərdz\ *adv* (ca. 1691) : toward the shore

shor·ing \'shōr-iŋ, 'shór-\ *n* (15c) **1 :** the act of supporting with or as if with a prop **2 :** a system or group of shores

shorn *past part of* SHEAR

¹short \'shórt\ *adj* [ME, fr. OE *sceort*; akin to OHG *scurz* short, ON *skortr* lack] (bef. 12c) **1 a :** having little length **b :** not tall or high : LOW **2 a :** not extended in time : BRIEF ⟨a ~ vacation⟩ **b :** not retentive ⟨a ~ memory⟩ **c :** EXPEDITIOUS, QUICK ⟨made ~ work of the problem⟩ **d :** seeming to pass quickly ⟨made great progress in just a few ~ years⟩ **3 a** *of a speech sound* : having a relatively short duration **b :** being the member of a pair of similarly spelled vowel or vowel-containing sounds that is descended from a vowel that was short in duration but is no longer so and that does not necessarily have duration as its chief distinguishing feature ⟨~ *i* in *sin*⟩ **c** *of a syllable in prosody* (1) : of relatively brief duration (2) : UNSTRESSED **4 :** limited in distance ⟨a ~ trip⟩ **5 a :** not coming up to a measure or requirement : INSUFFICIENT ⟨in ~ supply⟩ **b :** not reaching far enough ⟨the throw to first was ~⟩ **c :** enduring privation **d :** insufficiently supplied ⟨~ of cash⟩ ⟨~ on brains⟩ **6 a :** ABRUPT, CURT **b :** quickly provoked **7 :** CHOPPY 2 **8 :** payable at an early date **9 a :** containing or cooked with shortening; *also* : FLAKY ⟨~ pastry⟩ **b** *of metal* : brittle under certain conditions **10 a :** not lengthy or drawn out **b :** made briefer : ABBREVIATED **11 a :** not having goods or property that one has sold in anticipation of a fall in prices **b :** consisting of or relating to a sale of securities or commodities that the seller does not possess or has not contracted for at the time of the sale ⟨~ sale⟩ **12 :** near the end of a tour of duty — **short·ish** \'shór-tish\ *adj* — **in short order :** with dispatch : QUICKLY

²short *adv* (14c) **1 :** in a curt manner **2 :** for or during a brief time ⟨*short*-lasting⟩ **3 :** at a disadvantage : UNAWARES ⟨caught ~⟩ **4 :** in an abrupt manner : SUDDENLY ⟨the car stopped ~⟩ **5 :** at some point or degree before a goal or limit aimed at or under consideration ⟨the shells fell ~⟩ ⟨quit a month ~ of graduation⟩ **6 :** clean across ⟨the axle was snapped ~⟩ **7 :** by or as if by a short sale

³short *n* (ca. 1586) **1 :** the sum and substance : UPSHOT **2 a :** a short syllable **b :** a short sound or signal **3** *pl* **a :** a by-product of wheat milling that includes the germ, fine bran, and some flour **b :** refuse, clippings, or trimmings discarded in various manufacturing processes **4 a :** knee-length or less than knee-length trousers — usu. used in pl. **b** *pl* : short drawers **c :** a size in clothing for short men **5 a :** one who operates on the short side of the market **b** *pl* : short-term bonds **6** *pl* : DEFICIENCIES **7 :** SHORT CIRCUIT **8 :** SHORTSTOP **9 a :** SHORT SUBJECT **b :** a brief story or article (as in a newspaper) — **for short** : as an abbreviation ⟨named Katherine or Kate *for short*⟩ — **in short** : by way of summary : BRIEFLY

⁴short *vt* (1904) **1 :** SHORT-CIRCUIT **2 :** SHORTCHANGE, CHEAT

short account *n* (ca. 1902) : the total of open short sales in a given subject of trade or in the market as a whole

short·age \'shór-tij\ *n* (1868) : LACK, DEFICIT

short ballot *n* (1909) : a ballot limiting the number of elective offices to the most important legislative and executive posts and leaving minor positions to be filled by appointment

short·bread \'shórt-ˌbred\ *n* (1801) : a thick cookie made of flour, sugar, and a large amount of shortening

short·cake \-ˌkāk\ *n* (1594) **1 :** a crisp and often unsweetened biscuit or cookie **2 a :** a dessert made typically of very short baking powder-biscuit dough spread with sweetened fruit **b :** a dish consisting of a rich biscuit split and covered with a meat mixture

short·change \-'chānj\ *vt* (1903) **1 :** to give less than the correct amount of change to **2 :** to deprive of or give less than something due : CHEAT — **short·chang·er** *n*

short–cir·cuit *vt* (1867) **1 :** to apply a short circuit to or establish a short circuit in **2 :** BYPASS **3 :** FRUSTRATE, IMPEDE

short circuit *n* (1854) : a connection of comparatively low resistance accidentally or intentionally made between points on a circuit between which the resistance is normally much greater

short–com·ing \'shórt-ˌkə-miŋ, ˌshórt-\ *n* (15c) : DEFICIENCY, DEFECT

¹short–cut \'shórt-ˌkət *also* -'kət\ *n* (1637) **1 :** a route more direct than the one ordinarily taken **2 :** a method of doing something more directly and quickly than and often not so thoroughly as by ordinary procedure

²shortcut *vb* **-cut; -cut·ting** *vt* (1915) : to shorten (as a route or procedure) by use of a shortcut; *also* : CIRCUMVENT ~ *vi* : to take or use a shortcut

short–day \'shórt-ˌdā\ *adj* (1920) : responding to or relating to a short photoperiod — used esp. of a plant; compare DAY-NEUTRAL, LONG-DAY

short division *n* (ca. 1890) : mathematical division in which the successive steps are performed without writing out the remainders

short–eared owl \'shórt-ˌird-\ *n* (1766) : a medium-sized nearly cosmopolitan owl (*Asio flammeus*) that has very short ear tufts and usu. nests on the ground

short·en \'shórt-°n\ *vb* **short·ened; short·en·ing** \'shórt-niŋ, -°n-iŋ\ *vt* (14c) **1 a :** to reduce the length or duration of **b :** to cause to seem short **2 a :** to reduce in power or efficiency ⟨is my hand ~ed, that it cannot redeem —Isa 50:2 (RSV)⟩ **b :** to deprive of effect **3 :** to add fat to (as pastry dough) in order to make tender and flaky ~ *vi* : to become short or shorter — **short·en·er** \'shórt-nər, 'shór-t°n-ər\ *n*

syn SHORTEN, CURTAIL, ABBREVIATE, ABRIDGE, RETRENCH mean to reduce in extent. SHORTEN implies reduction in length or duration ⟨*shorten* a speech⟩. CURTAIL adds an implication of cutting that in some way deprives of completeness or adequacy ⟨ceremonies *curtailed* because of rain⟩. ABBREVIATE implies a making shorter usu. by omitting some part ⟨using an *abbreviated* title⟩. ABRIDGE implies a reduction in compass or scope with retention of essential elements and a relative completeness in the result ⟨the *abridged* version of the novel⟩. RETRENCH suggests a reduction in extent or costs of something felt to be excessive ⟨declining business forced the company to *retrench*⟩.

short·en·ing \'shórt-niŋ, 'shór-t°n-iŋ\ *n* (1538) **1 :** the action or process of making or becoming short; *specif* : the dropping of the latter part of a word so as to produce a new and shorter word of the same meaning **2 :** an edible fat used to shorten baked goods

short·fall \'shórt-ˌfól\ *n* (1895) : a failure to come up to expectation or need; *also* : the amount of such failure

short–grass prairie \'shórt-ˌgras-\ *n* (1844) : PRAIRIE 2b

short·hair \-ˌhar, -ˌher\ *n* (1903) : a domestic cat with a short thick coat; *esp* : a member of any of several breeds of muscular medium- to large-sized cats with a short plushy coat — **short–haired** *adj*

short·hand \-ˌhand\ *n* (1636) **1 :** a method of writing rapidly by substituting characters, abbreviations, or symbols for letters, sounds, words, or phrases : STENOGRAPHY **2 :** a system or instance of rapid or abbreviated communication or representation — **shorthand** *adj*

short·hand·ed \ˌshórt-'han-dəd\ *adj* (1794) : having, working with, or done with fewer than the regular or necessary number of people

short–haul \'shórt-ˌhól\ *adj* (1895) : traveling or involving a short distance ⟨~ flights⟩

short·horn \-ˌhórn\ *n*, *often cap* (1847) : any of a breed of red, roan, or white beef cattle originating in the north of England and including good milk-producing strains — called also *Durham*

short–horned grasshopper \'shórt-ˌhórn(d)-\ *n* (ca. 1890) : any of a family (Acrididae) of grasshoppers with short antennae

short hundredweight *n* (1924) : HUNDREDWEIGHT 1

short–leaf pine \'shórt-ˌlēf-\ *n* (1796) : a pine (*Pinus echinata*) of the southeastern U.S. that has short flexible needles usu. in clusters of two and reddish brown bark; *also* : its yellow wood

short line *n* (ca. 1917) : a transportation system (as a railroad) operating over a relatively short distance

short·list \'shórt-ˌlist\ *n* (1927) : a list of candidates for final consideration (as for a position or a prize) — **short list** *vt*, *chiefly Brit*

short–lived \'shórt-'livd *also* -'līvd\ *adj* (1588) : not living or lasting long ⟨~ insects⟩ ⟨~ joy⟩

short loin *n* (ca. 1923) : a portion of the hindquarter of beef immediately behind the ribs that is usu. cut into steaks — see BEEF illustration

short·ly \'shórt-lē\ *adv* (bef. 12c) **1 a :** in a few words : BRIEFLY **b :** in an abrupt manner **2 a :** in a short time ⟨we will be there ~⟩ **b :** at a short interval ⟨~ after sunset⟩

short·ness \-nəs\ *n* (bef. 12c) : the quality or state of being short

short–nosed cattle louse \'shórt-ˌnōz(d)-\ *n* (1942) : a large bluish sucking louse (*Haematopinus eurysternus*) that attacks domestic cattle

short–order \'shórt-ˌór-dər, -ˌór-\ *adj* (1920) : preparing or serving food that can be cooked quickly to a customer's order ⟨a ~ cook⟩

short–range \'shórt-'rānj\ *adj* (1869) **1 :** involving or taking into account a short period of time ⟨~ plans⟩ **2 :** relating to or fit for short distances

short ribs *n pl* (1912) : a cut of beef consisting of rib ends between the rib roast and the plate — see BEEF illustration

short run *n* (1879) : a relatively brief period of time — often used in the phrase *in the short run* — **short–run** *adj*

short shrift *n* (1594) **1 :** barely adequate time for confession before execution **2 a :** little or no attention or consideration **b :** quick work — usu. used in the phrase *make short shrift of*

short sight *n* (ca. 1829) : MYOPIA

short·sight·ed \'shȯrt-ˌsī-təd\ *adj* (ca. 1649) **1** : NEARSIGHTED **2** : lacking foresight — **short·sight·ed·ly** *adv* — **short·sight·ed·ness** *n*
short–spo·ken \-ˌspō-kən\ *adj* (1865) : CURT
short·stop \-ˌstäp\ *n* (1857) **1** : the player position in baseball for defending the infield area on the third-base side of second base **2** : the player stationed in the shortstop position
short–stop \-ˌstäp\ *n* (1936) : STOP BATH
short story *n* (1877) : an invented prose narrative shorter than a novel usu. dealing with a few characters and aiming at unity of effect and often concentrating on the creation of mood rather than plot
short subject *n* (1944) : a brief often documentary or educational film
short–tem·pered \ˌshȯrt-'tem-pərd\ *adj* (1900) : having a quick temper
short–term \'shȯrt-ˌtərm\ *adj* (1901) **1** : occurring over or involving a relatively short period of time **2 a** : of, relating to, or constituting a financial operation or obligation based on a brief term and esp. one of less than a year **b** : generated by assets held for less than six months
short ton *n* (1881) — see WEIGHT table
short·wave \'shȯrt-ˌwāv\ *n, often attrib* (1902) **1** : a radio wave having a wavelength between 10 and 100 meters **2** : a radio transmitter using shortwaves **3** : electromagnetic radiation having a wavelength equal to or less than that of visible light
short–weight \'shȯrt-'wāt\ *vt* (1926) : to defraud with short weight
short weight \'shȯrt-'wāt\ *n* (1789) : weight less than the stated weight or less than one is charged for
short–wind·ed \ˌshȯrt-'win-dəd\ *adj* (15c) **1** : affected with or characterized by shortness of breath **2 a** : BRIEF **b** : broken up into short units
shorty *or* **short·ie** \'shȯr-tē\ *n, pl* **short·ies** (1888) : one that is short
Sho·sho·ne \shə-'shōn, -'shō-nē; 'shō-ˌshōn\ *or* **Sho·sho·ni** \shə-'shō-nē\ *n, pl* **Shoshones** *or* **Shoshoni** *also* **Shoshone** *or* **Shoshonis** (1805) **1** : a member of a group of American Indian peoples orig. ranging through California, Idaho, Nevada, Utah, and Wyoming **2** : the Uto-Aztecan language of the Shoshones
¹**shot** \'shät\ *n* [ME, fr. OE *scot*; akin to ON *skot* shot, OHG *scuz*, OE *scēotan* to shoot — more at SHOOT] (bef. 12c) **1 a** : an action of shooting **b** : a directed propelling of a missile; *specif* : a directed discharge of a firearm **c** : a stroke or throw in an attempt to score points in a game (as tennis, pool, or basketball); *also* : HOME RUN **d** : BLAST **2** : a medical or narcotics injection **2 a** *pl* **shot** : something propelled by shooting; *esp* : small lead or steel pellets esp. forming a charge for a shotgun **b** : a metal sphere of iron or brass that is heaved in the shot put **3 a** : the distance that a missile is or can be thrown **b** : RANGE, REACH **4** : a charge to be paid : SCOT **5** : one that shoots; *esp* : MARKSMAN **6 a** : ATTEMPT, TRY **b** : GUESS, CONJECTURE **c** : CHANCE **d** : a single appearance as an entertainer (did a guest ~ for the program) **7** : an effective remark **8 a** : a single photographic exposure; *esp* : SNAPSHOT **b** : a single sequence of a motion picture or a television program shot by one camera without interruption **9** : a charge of explosives **10 a** : a small measure or serving (as one ounce) of undiluted liquor **b** : a small amount applied at one time : DOSE **11 shot** *pl* : SPRINKLES, JIMMIES — **a shot** : for each one : APIECE — **like a shot** : very rapidly — **shot in the arm** : STIMULUS, BOOST — **shot in the dark 1** : a wild guess **2** : an attempt that has little chance of success
²**shot** *past and past part of* SHOOT
³**shot** *adj* (1763) **1 a** *of a fabric* : having contrasting and changeable color effects : IRIDESCENT **b** : suffused or streaked with a color (hair ~ with gray) **c** : infused or permeated with a quality or element (~ through with wit) **2** : having the form of pellets resembling shot **3** : reduced to a state of ruin, prostration, or uselessness (his nerves are ~)
¹**shot·gun** \'shät-ˌgən\ *n* (1776) **1** : a smoothbore shoulder weapon for firing shot at short ranges **2** : an offensive football formation in which the quarterback plays a few yards behind the line of scrimmage and the other backs are scattered as flankers or slotbacks — **shotgun** *vt* — **shot·gun·ner** \-ˌgə-nər\ *n*
²**shotgun** *adj* (1892) **1** : of, relating to, or using a shotgun **2** : involving coercion **3** : covering a wide field with hit-or-miss effectiveness
shotgun house *n* (1940) : a house in which all the rooms are in direct line with each other usu. front to back — called also *shotgun cottage;* compare RAILROAD FLAT
shotgun marriage *n* (1929) **1** : a marriage forced or required because of pregnancy — called also *shotgun wedding* **2** : a forced union (a spate of brokerage mergers ... hastily arranged *shotgun marriages* — John Brooks)
shot hole *n* (1875) **1** : a drilled hole in which a charge of dynamite is exploded **2** : the dropping out of small rounded fragments of leaves that produces a shot-riddled appearance and is caused esp. by parasitic action
shot put *n* (1894) : a field event in which a shot is heaved for distance — **shot–put·ter** \'shät-ˌpu̇-tər\ *n*
shot·ten \'shä-t³n\ *adj* [ME *shotyn*, fr. pp. of *shuten* to shoot] (15c) : having ejected the spawn and so of inferior food value (~ herring)
should \shəd, 'shu̇d\ [ME *sholde*, fr. OE *sceolde* owed, was obliged to, ought to] (bef. 12c) *past of* SHALL **1** — used in auxiliary function to express condition (if he ~ leave his father, his father would die —Gen 44:22 (RSV)) **2** — used in auxiliary function to express obligation, propriety, or expediency ('tis commanded I ~ do so —Shak.) (this is as it ~ be —H. L. Savage) (you ~ brush your teeth after each meal) **3** — used in auxiliary function to express futurity from a point of view in the past (realized that she ~ have to do most of her farm work before sunrise —Ellen Glasgow) **4** — used in auxiliary function to express what is probable or expected (with an early start, they ~ be here by noon) **5** — used in auxiliary function to express a request in a polite manner or to soften direct statement (I ~ suggest that a guide ... is the first essential —L. D. Reddick)
¹**shoul·der** \'shōl-dər\ *n* [ME *sholder*, fr. OE *sculdor*; akin to OHG *scultra* shoulder] (bef. 12c) **1 a** : the laterally projecting part of the human body formed of the bones and joints with their covering tissue by which the arm is connected with the trunk **b** : the region of the body of nonhuman vertebrates that corresponds to the shoulder but is less projecting **2 a** : the two shoulders and the upper part of the back — usu. used in pl. **b** *pl* : capacity for bearing a task or blame

(placed the guilt squarely on his ~s) **3** : a cut of meat including the upper joint of the foreleg and adjacent parts — see LAMB illustration **4** : the part of a garment at the wearer's shoulder **5** : an area adjacent to or along the edge of a higher, more prominent, or more important part: as **a** (1) : the part of a hill or mountain near the top (2) : a lateral protrusion or extension of a hill or mountain **b** : either edge of a roadway; *specif* : the part of a roadway outside of the traveled way **6** : a rounded or sloping part (as of a stringed instrument or a bottle) where the neck joins the body — **shoul·dered** \-dərd\ *adj*
²**shoulder** *vb* **shoul·dered; shoul·der·ing** \-d(ə-)riŋ\ *vt* (14c) **1** : to push or thrust with or as if with the shoulder : JOSTLE (~ed his way through the crowd) **2 a** : to place or bear on the shoulder (~ed her knapsack and took off) **b** : to assume the burden or responsibility of (~ the blame) ~ *vi* : to push with or as if with the shoulders aggressively
shoulder bag *n* (1912) : a handbag looped over the shoulder by a strap
shoulder belt *n* (1967) : an automobile safety belt worn across the torso and over the shoulder — called also *shoulder harness*
shoulder blade *n* (14c) : SCAPULA
shoulder board *n* (1945) : one of a pair of broad pieces of stiffened cloth worn on the shoulders of a military uniform and carrying insignia
shoulder girdle *n* (1868) : PECTORAL GIRDLE
shoulder knot *n* (1676) **1** : an ornamental knot of ribbon or lace worn on the shoulder in the 17th and 18th centuries **2** : a detachable ornament of braided wire cord worn on ceremonial occasions on the shoulders of a uniform by a commissioned officer
shoulder patch *n* (1945) : a cloth patch bearing an identifying mark and worn on one sleeve of a uniform below the shoulder
shoulder strap *n* (1688) : a strap that passes across the shoulder and holds up an article or garment
should·est \'shu̇-dəst\ *archaic past 2d sing of* SHALL
shouldn't \'shu̇-d³nt, -d³n, *dial also* 'shu̇-t³n(t) *or* 'shu̇nt\ (1848) : should not
shouldst \shədst, 'shu̇dst, shətst, 'shu̇tst\ *archaic past 2d sing of* SHALL
¹**shout** \'shau̇t\ *vb* [ME] *vi* (14c) **1** : to utter a sudden loud cry **2** : to command attention as if by shouting (a quality that ~s from good novels —John Gardner) ~ *vt* **1** : to utter in a loud voice **2** : to cause to be, come, or stop by or as if by shouting (~ himself hoarse) (the proponents ~ed down the opposition) — **shout·er** *n*
²**shout** *n* (14c) : a loud cry or call
shouting distance *n* (1930) : a short distance : easy reach — usu. used with *within* (lived within *shouting distance* of her cousins)
shout song *n* (1925) : a rhythmic song sung at religious services esp. by black Americans and characterized by responsive singing or shouting between leader and congregation
¹**shove** \'shəv\ *vb* **shoved; shov·ing** [ME, fr. OE *scūfan* to thrust away; akin to OHG *scioban* to push and prob. to Lith *skubti* to hurry] *vt* (bef. 12c) **1** : to push along **2** : to push or put in a rough, careless, or hasty manner : THRUST **3** : to force by other than physical means : COMPEL (~ a bill through the legislature) ~ *vi* **1** : to move by forcing a way (bargain hunters *shoving* up to the counter) **2 a** : to move something by exerting force **b** : LEAVE — usu. used with *off* (shoved off for home) — **shov·er** *n*
²**shove** *n* (14c) : an act or instance of shoving : a forcible push
¹**shov·el** \'shə-vəl\ *n* [ME, fr. OE *scofl;* akin to OHG *scūfla* shovel, OE *scūfan* to thrust away] (bef. 12c) **1 a** : a hand implement consisting of a broad scoop or a more or less hollowed out blade with a handle used to lift and throw material **b** : something that resembles a shovel **c** : an excavating machine; *esp* : an hydraulic diesel-engine driven power shovel **2** : SHOVELFUL
²**shovel** *vb* **-eled** *or* **-elled; -el·ing** *or* **-el·ling** \'shə-və-liŋ, 'shəv-liŋ\ *vt* (15c) **1** : to take up and throw with a shovel **2** : to dig or clean out with a shovel **3** : to throw or convey roughly or in a mass as if with a shovel (~ed his food into his mouth) ~ *vi* : to use a shovel
shov·el·er *or* **shov·el·ler** \'shə-və-lər, 'shəv-lər\ *n* (15c) **1** : one that shovels **2** : any of several river ducks (genus *Anas*) having a large and very broad bill
shov·el·ful \'shə-vəl-ˌfu̇l\ *n, pl* **shovelfuls** \-ˌfu̇lz\ *also* **shov·els·ful** \-vəlz-ˌfu̇l\ (1533) : as much as a shovel will hold
shovel hat *n* (1829) : a shallow-crowned hat with a wide brim curved up at the sides that is worn by some clergymen
shov·el·nose \-ˌnōz\ *n* (1709) : a shovel-nosed animal and esp. a fish
shov·el·nosed \'shə-vəl-ˌnōzd\ *adj* (1707) : having a broad flat head, nose, or beak
¹**show** \'shō\ *vb* **showed** \'shōd\; **shown** \'shōn\ *or* **showed; show·ing** [ME *shewen, showen,* OE *scēawian* to look, look at, see; akin to OHG *scouwōn* to look, look at, and prob. to L *cavēre* to be on one's guard] *vt* (12c) **1** : to cause or permit to be seen : EXHIBIT (~ed pictures of the baby) **2** : to offer for sale (stores were ~ing new spring suits) **3** : to present as a public spectacle : PERFORM **4** : to reveal by one's condition, nature, or behavior (~ed themselves to be cowards) **5** : to give indication or record of (an anemometer ~s wind speed) **6 a** : to point out : direct attention to (~ed the view from the terrace) **b** : CONDUCT, USHER (~ed me to an aisle seat) **7** : ACCORD, BESTOW (~s them no mercy) **8 a** : to set forth : DECLARE **b** : ALLEGE, PLEAD — used esp. in law (~ cause) **9 a** : to demonstrate or establish by argument or reasoning (~ a plan to be faulty) **b** : INFORM, INSTRUCT (~ed me how to solve the problem) **10** : to present (an animal) for judging in a show ~ *vi* **1 a** : to be or come in view (3:15 ~ed on the clock) **b** : to put in an appearance (failed to ~) **2 a** : to appear in a particular way (anger ~ed in their faces) **b** : SEEM, APPEAR **3 a** : to give a theatrical performance **b** : to be staged or presented **4 a** : to appear as a contestant **b** : to present an animal in a show **5** : to finish third or at least third (as in a horse race) **6** : to exhibit one's artistic work — **show·able** \'shō-ə-bəl\ *adj* — **show one's hand 1** : to display one's cards faceup **2** : to declare one's intentions or reveal one's resources — **show one the door** : to tell someone to get out

\ə\ abut \ᵊ\ kitten, F table \ər\ further \a\ ash \ā\ ace \ä\ mop, mar \au̇\ out \ch\ chin \e\ bet \ē\ easy \g\ go \i\ hit \ī\ ice \j\ job \ŋ\ sing \ō\ go \ȯ\ law \ȯi\ boy \th\ thin \th\ the \ü\ loot \u̇\ foot \y\ yet \zh\ vision \ä, k̲, ⁿ, œ, œ̄, ue, ū̄, ᵞ\ see Guide to Pronunciation

syn SHOW, EXHIBIT, DISPLAY, EXPOSE, PARADE, FLAUNT mean to present so as to invite notice or attention. SHOW implies no more than enabling another to see or examine ⟨*showed* her snapshots to the whole group⟩. EXHIBIT stresses putting forward prominently or openly ⟨*exhibit* paintings at a gallery⟩. DISPLAY emphasizes putting in a position where others may see to advantage ⟨*display* sale items⟩. EXPOSE suggests bringing forth from concealment and displaying ⟨sought to *expose* the hypocrisy of the town fathers⟩. PARADE implies an ostentatious or arrogant displaying ⟨*parading* their piety for all to see⟩. FLAUNT suggests a shameless, boastful, often offensive parading ⟨nouveaux riches *flaunting* their wealth⟩.

syn SHOW, MANIFEST, EVIDENCE, EVINCE, DEMONSTRATE mean to reveal outwardly or make apparent. SHOW is the general term but sometimes implies that what is revealed must be gained by inference from acts, looks, or words ⟨careful not to *show* his true feelings⟩. MANIFEST implies a plainer, more immediate revelation ⟨*manifested* musical ability at an early age⟩. EVIDENCE suggests serving as proof of the actuality or existence of something ⟨a commitment *evidenced* by years of loyal service⟩. EVINCE implies a showing by outward marks or signs ⟨*evinced* not the slightest fear⟩. DEMONSTRATE implies showing by action or by display of feeling ⟨*demonstrated* their approval by loud applause⟩.

²show *n, often attrib* (13c) **1 :** a demonstrative display ⟨a ~ of strength⟩ **2 a** *archaic* **:** outward appearance **b :** a false semblance **: PRETENSE** ⟨made a ~ of friendship⟩ **c :** a more or less true appearance of something **: SIGN** **d :** an impressive display ⟨his role as househusband . . . was purely for ~ —John Lahr⟩ **e :** OSTENTATION **3 :** CHANCE ⟨gave him a ~ in spite of his background⟩ **4 :** something exhibited esp. for wonder or ridicule **: SPECTACLE 5 a :** a large display or exhibition arranged to arouse interest or stimulate sales ⟨the national auto ~⟩ **b :** a competitive exhibition of animals (as dogs) to demonstrate quality in breeding **6 a :** a theatrical presentation **b :** a radio or television program **c :** ENTERTAINMENT 3a **7 :** ENTERPRISE, AFFAIR ⟨they ran the whole ~⟩ **8 :** an indication of metal in a mine or of gas or oil in a well **9 :** third place at the finish (as of a horse race)

show–and–tell \'shō-ən(d)-'tel\ *n* (1950) **1 :** a classroom exercise in which children display an item and talk about it **2 :** a public display or demonstration

show bill *n* (1801) **:** an advertising poster

show-biz \'shō-,biz\ *n, often attrib* [by shortening & alter.] (1945) **: SHOW BUSINESS;** *also* **:** RAZZLE-DAZZLE 3 — **show-biz-zy** \-,bi-zē\ *adj*

¹show-boat \'shō-,bōt\ *n* (1869) **1 :** a river steamboat containing a theater and carrying a troupe of actors to give plays at river communities **2 :** one who tries to attract attention by conspicuous behavior

²showboat *vi* (1951) **:** to behave in a conspicuous or ostentatious manner **:** SHOW OFF

showbread *var of* SHEWBREAD

show business *n* (1850) **:** the arts, occupations, and businesses (as theater, motion pictures, and television) that comprise the entertainment industry

¹show-case \'shō-,kās\ *n* (1835) **1 :** a glazed case, box, or cabinet for displaying and protecting wares in a store or articles in a museum **2 :** a setting, occasion, or medium for exhibiting something or someone esp. in an attractive or favorable aspect

²showcase *vt* **show-cased; show-cas-ing** (1945) **:** to exhibit esp. in an attractive or favorable aspect ⟨~ new talent⟩

show-down \'shō-,daùn\ *n* (1884) **1 :** the placing of poker hands faceup on the table to determine the winner of a pot **2 :** a decisive confrontation or contest

¹show-er \'shaù(-ə)r\ *n* [ME *shour,* fr. OE *scūr;* akin to OHG *scūr* shower, storm, L *caurus* northwest wind] (bef. 12c) **1 a :** a fall of rain of short duration **b :** a similar fall of sleet, hail, or snow **2 :** something resembling a rain shower ⟨a ~ of statistics⟩; *esp* **:** a fall of meteors which belong to a single group and whose trails appear to originate at the same point in space **3 :** a party given by friends who bring gifts often of a particular kind **4 :** a bath in which water is showered on the body; *also* **:** the apparatus that provides a shower — **show-er-less** \-ləs\ *adj* — **show-ery** \'shaù(-ə)-rē\ *adj* — **to the showers :** out of the ball game

²shower *vi* (15c) **1 :** to rain or fall in or as if in a shower ⟨letters ~ed on him in praise and protest⟩ **2 :** to bathe in a shower ~ *vt* **1 a :** to wet (as with water) in a spray, fine stream, or drops **b** (1) **:** to cause to fall in a shower ⟨factory chimneys ~ed soot on the district⟩ (2) **:** to cause a shower to fall on ⟨~ed the newlyweds with rice⟩ **2 :** to give in abundance ⟨~ed the writer with honors⟩ — **show-er-er** \'shaù(-ə)r-ər\ *n*

³show-er \'shō(-ə)r\ *n* (14c) **:** one that shows **:** EXHIBITOR

shower bath *n* (1785) **:** SHOWER 4

show-er-head \'shaù(-ə)r-,hed\ *n* (1925) **:** a fixture for directing the spray of water in a bathroom shower

show-girl \'shō-,gər(-ə)l\ *n* (1836) **:** a chorus girl in a musical comedy or nightclub show

show-ing \'shō-iŋ\ *n* (bef. 12c) **1 :** an act or an instance of putting something (as an artist's work) on view **:** DISPLAY **2 :** PERFORMANCE, RECORD ⟨made a good ~ in competition⟩ **3 a :** a statement or presentation of a case **b :** APPEARANCE, EVIDENCE

show jumping *n* (1929) **:** the competitive riding of horses one at a time over a set course of obstacles in which the winner is judged according to ability and speed — **show jumper** *n*

show-man \'shō-mən\ *n* (ca. 1734) **1 :** the producer of a play or theatrical show **2 :** an individual having a sense or knack for dramatically effective presentation — **show-man-ship** \-,ship\ *n*

show-me \'shō-mē\ *adj* (1909) **:** insistent on proof or evidence

show-off \'shō-,óf\ *n, often attrib* (1843) **1 :** the act of showing off **2 :** one that shows off **:** EXHIBITIONIST — **show-offy** \-,ó-fē\ *adj*

show off *vt* (ca. 1793) **:** to display proudly ⟨wanted to *show* our new car *off*⟩ ~ *vi* **:** to seek to attract attention by conspicuous behavior ⟨boys *showing off* for the girls⟩

show-piece \'shō-,pēs\ *n* (1885) **:** a prime or outstanding example used for exhibition

show-place \-,plās\ *n* (1794) **:** a place (as an estate or building) that is regarded as an example of beauty or excellence

show-ring \-,riŋ\ *n* (1926) **:** a ring (as at a cattle show) where animals are displayed

show-room \-,rüm, -,rùm\ *n* (1616) **:** a room where merchandise is exhibited for sale or where samples are displayed

show-stop-per \-,stä-pər\ *n* (1926) **1 :** an act, song, or performer that wins applause so prolonged as to interrupt a performance **2 :** something or someone exceptionally arresting or attractive ⟨the gold crown was the ~ of the exhibition⟩ — **show-stop-ping** \-,stä-piŋ\ *adj*

show trial *n* (1937) **:** a trial (as of political opponents) in which the verdict is rigged and a public confession is often extracted

show up *vt* (1826) **1 :** to expose or discredit esp. by revealing faults ⟨*showed* them *up* as frauds⟩ **2 :** to embarrass or cause to look bad esp. by comparison ⟨trying to *show up* the boss⟩ **3 :** REVEAL ⟨*showed up* my ignorance⟩ ~ *vi* **1 :** ARRIVE, APPEAR ⟨*showed up* late for his own wedding⟩ **2 :** to be plainly evident

show window *n* (1826) **1 :** an outside display window in which a store exhibits merchandise **2 :** a sample or setting used to exhibit or illustrate something at its best

showy \'shō-ē\ *adj* **show-i-er; -est** (1712) **1 :** making an attractive show **:** STRIKING ⟨a ~ orchid⟩ **2 :** given to or marked by a flashy often tasteless display — **show-i-ly** \'shō-ə-lē\ *adv* — **show-i-ness** \'shō-ē-nəs\ *n*

syn SHOWY, PRETENTIOUS, OSTENTATIOUS mean given to excessive outward display. SHOWY implies an imposing or striking appearance but usu. suggests cheapness or poor taste ⟨the performers' *showy* costumes⟩. PRETENTIOUS implies an appearance of importance not justified by the thing's value or the person's standing ⟨a *pretentious* parade of hard words⟩. OSTENTATIOUS stresses vainglorious display or parade ⟨the *ostentatious* summer homes of the rich⟩.

sho-yu \'shō-(,)yü\ *n* [Jp *shōyu*] (1727) **:** SOY 1

shrank *past of* SHRINK

shrap-nel \'shrap-n²l\ *n, pl* **shrapnel** [Henry *Shrapnel* †1842 Eng. artillery officer] (1806) **1 :** a projectile that consists of a case provided with a powder charge and a large number of usu. lead balls and that is exploded in flight **2 :** bomb, mine, or shell fragments

¹shred \'shred, *esp Southern* 'sred\ *n* [ME *shrede,* fr. OE *scrēade;* akin to OHG *scrōt* piece cut off] (bef. 12c) **1 a :** a long narrow strip cut or torn off **b :** a shredded, damaged, disrupted, or ruined condition ⟨torn to ~s by an air attack⟩ **2 :** PARTICLE, SCRAP ⟨not a ~ of evidence⟩

²shred *vb* **shred-ded; shred-ding** *vt* (bef. 12c) **1** *archaic* **:** to cut off **2 :** to cut or tear into shreds ⟨*shredded* the documents⟩ **3 :** DEMOLISH **2** ⟨sharp lawyers *shredding* hapless witnesses —Charles Krauthammer⟩ ~ *vi* **:** to come apart in or break up into shreds — **shred-der** *n*

shredded wheat *n* (1898) **:** a breakfast cereal made from cooked partially dried wheat that is shredded and molded into biscuits which are then oven-baked and toasted

¹shrew \'shrü, *esp Southern* 'srü\ *n* [ME *shrewe* evil or scolding person, fr. OE *scrēawa* shrew (animal)] (bef. 12c) **1 :** any of a family (Soricidae) of small chiefly nocturnal insectivores related to the moles and distinguished by a long pointed snout, very small eyes, and velvety fur **2 :** an ill-tempered scolding woman — **shrew-like** \-,līk\ *adj*

²shrew *vt* (14c) *obs* **:** CURSE

shrewd \'shrüd, *esp Southern* 'srüd\ *adj* [ME *shrewed,* fr. *shrewe +* ¹-ed] (13c) **1** *archaic* **:** MISCHIEVOUS **2** *obs* **:** ABUSIVE, SHREWISH **3** *obs* **:** OMINOUS, DANGEROUS **4 a :** SEVERE, HARD ⟨a ~ knock⟩ **b :** SHARP, PIERCING ⟨a ~ wind⟩ **5 a :** marked by clever discerning awareness and hardheaded acumen ⟨~ common sense⟩ **b :** given to wily and artful ways or dealing ⟨a ~ operator⟩ — **shrewd-ly** *adv* — **shrewd-ness** *n*

syn SHREWD, SAGACIOUS, PERSPICACIOUS, ASTUTE mean acute in perception and sound in judgment. SHREWD stresses practical, hardheaded cleverness and judgment ⟨a *shrewd* judge of character⟩. SAGACIOUS suggests wisdom, penetration, and farsightedness ⟨*sagacious* investors got in on the ground floor⟩. PERSPICACIOUS implies unusual power to see through and understand what is puzzling or hidden ⟨a *perspicacious* counselor saw through the child's facade⟩. ASTUTE suggests shrewdness, perspicacity, and diplomatic skill ⟨an *astute* player of party politics⟩.

shrew-ish \'shrü-ish, *esp Southern* 'srü-\ *adj* (1565) **:** ILL-NATURED, INTRACTABLE — **shrew-ish-ly** *adv* — **shrew-ish-ness** *n*

shri \'shrē, 'srē\ *var of* SRI

¹shriek \'shrēk, *esp Southern* 'srēk\ *vb* [ME *shreken,* prob. irreg. fr. *shriken* to shriek; akin to ON *skrækja* to shriek] *vi* (15c) **1 :** to utter a sharp shrill sound **2 a :** to cry out in a high-pitched voice **:** SCREECH **b :** to suggest such a cry (as by vividness of expression) ⟨neon colors ~ed for attention —Calvin Tomkins⟩ ~ *vt* **1 :** to utter with a shriek or sharply and shrilly ⟨~ an alarm⟩ **2 :** to express in a manner suggestive of a shriek

²shriek *n* (1590) **1 :** a shrill usu. wild or involuntary cry **2 :** a sound resembling a shriek ⟨the ~ of chalk on the blackboard⟩

shrie-val \'shrē-vəl, *esp Southern* 'srē-\ *adj* [obs. *shrieve* sheriff, fr. ME *shirreve* — more at SHERIFF] (1681) *chiefly Brit* **:** of or relating to a sheriff

shrie-val-ty \-vəl-tē\ *n* (1502) *chiefly Brit* **:** the office, term of office, or jurisdiction of a sheriff

shrieve \'shrēv, *esp Southern* 'srēv\ *archaic var of* SHRIVE

shrift \'shrift, *esp Southern* 'srift\ *n* [ME, fr. OE *scrift,* fr. *scrīfan* to shrive — more at SHRIVE] (bef. 12c) **1** *archaic* **:** a remission of sins pronounced by a priest in the sacrament of reconciliation **b :** the act of shriving **:** CONFESSION **2** *obs* **:** CONFESSIONAL

shrike \'shrīk, *esp Southern* 'srīk\ *n* [perh. fr. (assumed) ME *shrik,* fr. OE *scrīc* thrush; akin to ME *shriken* to shriek] (1544) **:** any of numerous usu. gray or brownish oscine birds (family Laniidae) that have a hooked bill, feed chiefly on insects, and often impale their prey on thorns

¹shrill \'shril, *esp Southern* 'sril\ *vb* [ME; prob. akin to OE *scrallettan* to resound loudly — more at SKIRL] *vt* (13c) **:** SCREAM ~ *vi* **:** to utter or emit an acute piercing sound

²shrill *adj* (14c) **1 a :** having or emitting a sharp high-pitched tone or sound **:** PIERCING **b :** accompanied by sharp high-pitched sounds or cries ⟨~ gaiety⟩ **2 :** having a sharp or vivid effect on the senses ⟨~ light⟩ **3 :** STRIDENT, INTEMPERATE ⟨~ anger⟩ ⟨~ criticism⟩ — **shrill** *adv* — **shrill-ness** *n* — **shril-ly** \'shril-lē, *esp Southern* 'sril-\ *adv*

³shrill *n* (1591) **:** a shrill sound ⟨the ~ of the ship's whistle⟩

¹**shrimp** \'shrimp, *esp Southern* 'srimp\ *n, pl* **shrimps** *or* **shrimp** [ME *shrimpe;* akin to MLG *schrempen* to contract, wrinkle, ON *skorpna* to shrivel up] (14c) **1 :** any of numerous mostly small and marine decapod crustaceans (suborders Dendrobranchiata and Pleocyemata) having a slender elongated body, a compressed abdomen, and a long spiny rostrum; *also* **:** a small crustacean (as an amphipod or a branchiopod) resembling the true shrimps **2 :** a very small or puny person or thing — **shrimp-like** \-,līk\ *adj* — **shrimpy** \'shrim-pē, 'srim-\ *adj*

²**shrimp** *vi* (ca. 1859) **:** to fish for or catch shrimps

shrimp-er \'shrim-pər, *esp Southern* 'srim-\ *n* (1851) **1 :** a shrimp fisherman **2 :** a boat engaged in shrimping

shrimp pink *n* (1882) **:** a deep pink

¹**shrine** \'shrīn, *esp Southern* 'srīn\ *n* [ME, fr. OE *scrīn,* fr. L *scrinium* case, chest] (bef. 12c) **1 a :** a case, box, or receptacle; *esp* **:** one in which sacred relics (as the bones of a saint) are deposited **b :** a place in which devotion is paid to a saint or deity **:** SANCTUARY **c :** a niche containing a religious image **2 :** a receptacle (as a tomb) for the dead **3 :** a place or object hallowed by its associations

²**shrine** *vt* **shrined; shrin-ing** (14c) **:** ENSHRINE

Shrin-er \'shrī-nər, *esp Southern* 'srī-\ *n* [Ancient Arabic Order of Nobles of the Mystic *Shrine*] (1886) **:** a member of a secret fraternal society that is non-Masonic but admits only Knights Templars and 32d-degree Masons to membership

¹**shrink** \'shriŋk, *esp Southern* 'sriŋk\ *vb* **shrank** \'shraŋk, 'sraŋk\ *also* **shrunk** \'shrəŋk, 'srəŋk\; **shrunk** *or* **shrunk-en** \'shrəŋ-kən, 'srəŋ-\; **shrink-ing** [ME, fr. OE *scrincan;* akin to MD *schrinken* to draw back] *vi* (bef. 12c) **1 :** to contract or curl up the body or part of it **:** HUDDLE, COWER **2 a :** to contract to less extent or compass **b :** to become smaller or more compacted **c :** to lose substance or weight **d :** to lessen in value **:** DWINDLE **3 :** to recoil instinctively (as from something painful or horrible) ⟨*shrank* from the challenge⟩ ~ *vt* **:** to cause to contract or shrink; *specif* **:** to compact (cloth) by causing to contract when subjected to washing, boiling, steaming, or other processes *syn* see CONTRACT, RECOIL — **shrink-able** \'shriŋ-kə-bəl, 'sriŋ-\ *adj* — **shrink-er** *n*

²**shrink** *n* (1590) **1 :** the act of shrinking **2 :** SHRINKAGE **3** [short for *headshrinker*] **:** a clinical psychiatrist or psychologist ⟨regaling us with all the stories he never told his ~ —*Rolling Stone*⟩

shrink-age \'shriŋ-kij, *esp Southern* 'sriŋ-\ *n* (1800) **1 :** the act or process of shrinking **2 :** the loss in weight of livestock during shipment and in the process of preparing the meat for consumption **3 :** the amount lost by shrinkage

shrinking violet *n* (1915) **:** a bashful or retiring person

shrink–wrap \'shriŋk-,rap, *esp Southern* 'sriŋk-\ *vt* (1966) **:** to wrap (as a book or meat) in tough clear plastic film that is then shrunk (as by heating) to form a tightly fitting package — **shrink–wrap** *n*

shrive \'shrīv, *esp Southern* 'srīv\ *vb* **shrived** *or* **shrove** \'shrōv, 'srōv\; **shriv-en** \'shri-vən, 'sri-\ *or* **shrived; shriv-ing** [ME *scrifan* to shrive, prescribe (akin to OHG *scriban* to write), fr. L *scribere* to write — more at SCRIBE] *vt* (bef. 12c) **1 :** to administer the sacrament of reconciliation to **2 :** to free from guilt ~ *vi, archaic* **:** to confess one's sins *esp.* to a priest

shriv-el \'shri-vəl, *esp Southern* 'sri-\ *vb* **-eled** *or* **-elled; -el-ing** *or* **-el-ling** \'shri-və-liŋ, 'sri-; 'shriv-liŋ, 'sriv-\ [origin unknown] *vi* (1588) **1 :** to draw into wrinkles esp. with a loss of moisture **2 a :** to become reduced to inanition, helplessness, or inefficiency **b :** DWINDLE ~ *vt* **:** to cause to shrivel

shroff \'shräf, 'shröf, *esp Southern* 'sräf, 'sröf\ *n* [Hindi *śarāf,* fr. Ar *ṣarrāf*] (1618) **:** a banker or money changer in the Far East; *esp* **:** one who tests and evaluates coin

Shrop-shire \'shräp-,shir, -shər, *esp US* -,shīr, *esp Southern* 'sräp-\ *n* [*Shropshire,* England] (1803) **:** any of a breed of dark-faced hornless sheep of English origin that are raised for both mutton and wool

¹**shroud** \'shraůd, *esp Southern* 'sraůd\ *n* [ME, garment, fr. OE *scrūd;* akin to OE *scrēade* shred — more at SHRED] (14c) **1** *obs* **:** SHELTER, PROTECTION **2 :** something that covers, screens, or guards: as **a :** one of two flanges that give peripheral support to turbine or fan bedding **b :** a usu. fiberglass guard that protects a spacecraft from the heat of launching **3 :** burial garment **:** WINDING-SHEET, CEREMENT **4 a :** one of the ropes leading usu. in pairs from a ship's mastheads to give lateral support to the masts **b :** one of the cords that suspend the harness of a parachute from the canopy

²**shroud** *vt* (14c) **1 a** *archaic* **:** to cover for protection **b** *obs* **:** CONCEAL **2 a :** to cut off from view **:** OBSCURE ⟨trees ~ed by a heavy fog⟩ **b :** to veil under another appearance (as by obscuring or disguising) ⟨~ed the decision in a series of formalities⟩ **3 :** to dress for burial ~ *vi, archaic* **:** to seek shelter

1 shroud 4a

Shrove-tide \'shrōv-,tīd, *esp Southern* 'srōv-\ *n* [ME *schroftide,* fr. *schrof-* (fr. *shriven* to shrive) + *tide*] (15c) **:** the period usu. of three days immediately preceding Ash Wednesday

Shrove Tuesday \'shrōv-, *esp Southern* 'srōv-\ *n* [ME *schroftewesday,* fr. *schrof-* (as in *schroftide*) + *tewesday* Tuesday] (15c) **:** the Tuesday before Ash Wednesday

¹**shrub** \'shrəb, *esp Southern* 'srəb\ *n* [ME *schrobbe,* fr. OE *scrybb* brushwood; akin to Norw *skrubbebær* a cornel of a dwarf species] (bef. 12c) **:** a low usu. several-stemmed woody plant

²**shrub** *n* [Ar *sharāb* beverage] (1747) **1 :** an aged blend of fruit juice, sugar, and spirits served chilled and diluted with water **2 :** a beverage made by adding acidulated fruit juice to iced water

shrub-bery \'shrə-b(ə-)rē, *esp Southern* 'srə-\ *n, pl* **-ber-ies** (1748) **:** a planting or growth of shrubs

shrub-by \'shrə-bē, *esp Southern* 'srə-\ *adj* **shrub-bi-er; -est** (1540) **1 :** consisting of or covered with shrubs **2 :** resembling a shrub

¹**shrug** \'shrəg, *esp Southern* 'srəg\ *vb* **shrugged; shrug-ging** [ME *schruggen*] *vi* (14c) **:** to raise or draw up the shoulders esp. to express aloofness, indifference, or uncertainty ~ *vt* **:** to lift or contract (the shoulders) esp. to express aloofness, indifference, or uncertainty

²**shrug** *n* (1594) **1 :** an act of shrugging **2 :** a woman's small waist-length or shorter jacket

shrug off *vt* (1904) **1 :** to brush aside **:** MINIMIZE ⟨*shrugs off* the problem⟩ **2 :** to shake off ⟨*shrugging off* sleep⟩ **3 :** to remove (a garment) by wriggling out

shtetl *also* **shte-tel** \'shte-t³l, 'shtä-\ *n, pl* **shtet-lach** \'shtet-,läk, 'shtät-\ *also* **shtetels** [Yiddish *shtetl,* fr. MHG *stetel,* dim. of *stat* place, town, city, fr. OHG, place — more at STEAD] (1949) **:** a small Jewish town or village formerly found in Eastern Europe

shtick *also* **shtik** \'shtik\ *n* [Yiddish *shtik* pranks, lit., piece, fr. MHG *stücke,* fr. OHG *stucki;* akin to OE *stycce* piece, OHG *stoc* stick — more at STOCK] (1959) **1 :** a show-business routine, gimmick, or gag **: BIT 2 :** one's special trait, interest, or activity **:** BAG ⟨he's alive and well and now doing his ~ out in Hollywood —Robert Daley⟩

¹**shuck** \'shək\ *n* [origin unknown] (ca. 1674) **1 :** SHELL, HUSK: as **a :** the outer covering of a nut or of Indian corn **b :** the shell of an oyster or clam **2 :** something of little value — usu. used in pl. often interjectionally ⟨not worth ~s⟩ ⟨~s, it was nothing⟩

²**shuck** *vt* (1772) **1 :** to strip of shucks **2 a :** to peel off (as clothing) — often used with *off* **b :** to lay aside — often used with *off* ⟨bad habits are being ~ed off —A. W. Smith⟩ — **shuck-er** *n*

¹**shud-der** \'shə-dər\ *vi* **shud-dered; shud-der-ing** \-d(ə-)riŋ\ [ME *shoddren;* akin to OHG *skutten* to shake and perh. to Lith *kutéti* to shake up] (13c) **1 :** to tremble convulsively **:** SHIVER **2 :** to shake (as with cold) — **shud-dery** \-d(ə-)rē\ *adj*

²**shudder** *n* (1607) **:** an act of shuddering

¹**shuf-fle** \'shə-fəl\ *vb* **shuf-fled; shuf-fling** \-f(ə-)liŋ\ [perh. irreg. fr. ¹*shove*] *vt* (1570) **1 :** to mix in a mass confusedly **:** JUMBLE **2 :** to put or thrust aside or under cover ⟨*shuffled* the whole matter out of his mind⟩ **3 a :** to rearrange (as playing cards, dominoes, or tiles) to produce a random order **b :** to move about, back and forth, or from one place to another **:** SHIFT ⟨~ funds among various accounts⟩ **4 a :** to move (as the feet) by sliding along or back and forth without lifting **b :** to perform (as a dance) with a dragging, sliding step ~ *vi* **1 :** to work into or out of trickily ⟨*shuffled* out of the difficulty⟩ **2 :** to act or speak in a shifty or evasive manner **3 a :** to move or walk in a sliding dragging manner without lifting the feet **b :** to dance in a lazy nonchalant manner with sliding and tapping motions of the feet **c :** to execute in a perfunctory or clumsy manner **4 :** to mix playing cards or counters by shuffling — **shuf-fler** \-f(ə-)lər\ *n*

²**shuffle** *n* (1628) **1 :** an evasion of the issue **:** EQUIVOCATION **2 a :** an act of shuffling (as of cards) **b :** a right or turn to shuffle ⟨was reminded that it was his ~⟩ **c :** JUMBLE ⟨lost in the ~ of papers⟩ **3 a :** a dragging sliding movement; *specif* **:** a sliding or scraping step in dancing **b :** a dance characterized by such a step

shuf-fle-board \'shə-fəl-,bōrd, -,bȯrd\ *n* [alter. of obs. E *shove-board*] (1836) **1 :** a game in which players use long-handled cues to shove disks into scoring areas of a diagram marked on a smooth surface **2 :** a diagram on which shuffleboard is played

shul \'shůl\ *n* [Yiddish, school, synagogue, fr. MHG *schuol* school] (ca. 1874) **:** SYNAGOGUE

shun \'shən\ *vt* **shunned; shun-ning** [ME *shunnen,* fr. OE *scunian*] (bef. 12c) **:** to avoid deliberately and esp. habitually *syn* see ESCAPE — **shun-ner** *n*

shun-pike \'shən-,pīk\ *n* (1862) **:** a side road used to avoid the toll on or the speed and traffic of a superhighway — **shun-pik-er** \-,pī-kər\ *n* — **shun-pik-ing** \-kiŋ\ *n*

¹**shunt** \'shənt\ *vb* [ME, to flinch] *vt* (13c) **1 a :** to turn off to one side **:** SHIFT ⟨was ~ed aside⟩ **b :** to switch (as a train) from one track to another **2 :** to provide with or divert by means of an electrical shunt **3 :** to divert (blood) from one part to another by a surgical shunt **4 :** SHUTTLE ⟨~ed the missiles from shelter to shelter⟩ ~ *vi* **1 :** to move to the side **2 :** to travel back and forth ⟨~ed between the two towns⟩ — **shunt-er** *n*

²**shunt** *n* (ca. 1859) **1 :** a means or mechanism for turning or thrusting aside: as **a** *chiefly Brit* **:** a railroad switch **b :** a conductor joining two points in an electrical circuit so as to form a parallel or alternative path through which a portion of the current may pass (as for regulating the amount passing in the main circuit) **c :** a surgical passage created between two blood vessels to divert blood from one part to another **2 :** an accident (as a collision between two cars) esp. in auto racing

shush \'shəsh, 'shùsh\ *vt* [imit.] (1925) **:** to urge to be quiet **:** HUSH — **shush** *n*

¹**shut** \'shət\ *vb* **shut; shut-ting** [ME *shutten,* fr. OE *scyttan;* akin to MD *schutten* to shut in, OE *scēotan* to shoot — more at SHOOT] (bef. 12c) **1 a :** to move into position to close an opening ⟨~ the lid⟩ **b :** to prevent entrance to or passage to or from **2 :** to confine by or as if by enclosure ⟨~ herself in her study⟩ **3 :** to fasten with a lock or bolt **4 :** to close by bringing enclosing or covering parts together ⟨~ the eyes⟩ **5 :** to cause to cease or suspend an operation or activity — often used with *down* ~ *vi* **1 :** to close itself or become closed ⟨flowers that ~ at night⟩ **2 :** to cease or suspend an operation or activity — often used with *down*

²**shut** *adj* (15c) **1 :** closed, fastened, or folded together **2 :** RID, CLEAR, FREE — usu. used with *of*

³**shut** *n* (1667) **:** the act of shutting

shut-down \'shət-,daůn\ *n* (1888) **:** the cessation or suspension of an operation or activity

shut down *vi* (1779) **:** to settle so as to obscure vision **:** CLOSE IN ⟨the night *shut down* early⟩

shute *var of* CHUTE

shut–eye \'shət-,ī\ *n* (1899) **:** SLEEP ⟨get some ~⟩

¹**shut–in** \'shət-,in\ *n* (1903) **1 :** an invalid confined to home, a room, or bed **2 :** a narrow gorge-shaped part of an otherwise wide valley **3 :** available oil or gas which is not being produced from an existing well

²**shut–in** \'shət-'in\ *adj* (1909) **1 :** confined to one's home or an institution by illness or incapacity **2 a :** SECRETIVE, BROODING ⟨a bitter, ~

\ə\ abut \³\ kitten, F table \ər\ further \a\ ash \ā\ ace \ä\ mop, mar \aů\ out \ch\ chin \e\ bet \ē\ easy \g\ go \i\ hit \ī\ ice \j\ job \ŋ\ sing \ō\ go \ȯ\ law \ȯi\ boy \th\ thin \th\ the \ü\ loot \ů\ foot \y\ yet \zh\ vision \ȧ, k̲, ⁿ, œ, œ̄, ue, ūe, ᵉ\ see Guide to Pronunciation

face —Claudia Cassidy⟩ **b :** tending to avoid social contact **:** WITH-DRAWN ⟨the ~ personality type —S. K. Weinberg⟩
shut in *vt* (14c) **1 :** CONFINE, ENCLOSE **2 :** to prevent production of (oil or gas) by closing down a well
shut-off \'shət-ˌȯf\ *n* (1869) **1 :** something (as a valve) that shuts off **2 :** STOPPAGE, INTERRUPTION
shut off *vt* (1824) **1 a :** to cut off (as flow or passage) **:** STOP ⟨*shuts off* the oxygen supply⟩ **b :** to stop the operation of (as a machine) ⟨*shut* the motor *off*⟩ **2 :** to close off **:** SEPARATE — usu. used with *from* ⟨*shut off* from the rest of the world⟩ ~ *vi* **:** to cease operating **:** STOP ⟨*shuts off* automatically⟩
shut-out \'shət-ˌau̇t\ *n* (1889) **1 :** a game or contest in which one side fails to score **2 :** a preemptive bid in bridge
shut out *vt* (14c) **1 :** EXCLUDE **2 :** to prevent (an opponent) from scoring in a game or contest **3 :** to forestall the bidding of (bridge opponents) by making a high or preemptive bid
¹shut-ter \'shət-ər\ *n* (1542) **1 :** one that shuts **2 :** a usu. movable cover or screen for a window or door **3 :** a mechanical device that limits the passage of light; *esp* **:** a camera attachment that exposes the film or plate by opening and closing an aperture **4 :** the movable louvers in a pipe organ by which the swell box is opened — **shut-ter-less** \-ləs\ *adj*
²shutter *vt* (1826) **1 :** to close by or as if by shutters **2 :** to furnish with shutters
shut-ter-bug \'shə-tər-ˌbəg\ *n* (1940) **:** a photography enthusiast
¹shut-tle \'shə-tᵊl\ *n* [ME *shittle*, prob. fr. OE *scytel* bar, bolt; akin to ON *skutill* bolt, OE *scēotan* to shoot — more at SHOOT] (14c) **1 a :** a device used in weaving for passing the thread of the weft between the threads of the warp **b :** a spindle-shaped device holding the thread in tatting, knotting, or netting **c :** a sliding thread holder for the lower thread of a sewing machine that carries the lower thread through a loop of the upper thread to make a stitch **2 :** SHUTTLECOCK **3 a :** a going back and forth regularly over an often short route by a vehicle **b :** an established route used in a shuttle; *also* **:** a vehicle used in a shuttle **c :** SPACE SHUTTLE — **shut-tle-less** *adj*
²shuttle *vb* **shut-tled; shut-tling** \'shət-liŋ, 'shə-tᵊl-iŋ\ *vt* (1550) **1 :** to cause to move or travel back and forth frequently **2 :** to transport in, by, or as if by a shuttle ~ *vi* **1 :** to move or travel back and forth frequently **2 :** to move by or as if by a shuttle
¹shut-tle-cock \'shə-tᵊl-ˌkäk\ *n* (1522) **:** a lightweight conical object with a rounded often rubber-covered nose that is used in badminton
²shuttlecock *vt* (1687) **:** to send or toss to and fro **:** BANDY
shuttle diplomacy *n* (1974) **:** negotiations esp. between nations carried on by an intermediary who shuttles back and forth between the disputants
shut up *vt* (1814) **:** to cause (a person) to stop talking ~ *vi* **:** to cease writing or speaking
¹shy \'shī\ *adj* **shi-er** *or* **shy-er** \'shī(-ə)r\; **shi-est** *or* **shy-est** \'shī-əst\ [ME *schey*, fr. OE *scēoh*; akin to OHG *sciuhen* to frighten off] (bef. 12c) **1 :** easily frightened **:** TIMID **2 :** disposed to avoid a person or thing ⟨publicity ~⟩ ⟨book-*shy* children⟩ **3 :** hesitant in committing oneself **:** CIRCUMSPECT **4 :** sensitively diffident or retiring **:** RESERVED ⟨a ~ seclusive person⟩; *also* **:** expressive of such a state or nature ⟨spoke in a ~ voice⟩ **5 :** SECLUDED, HIDDEN **6 :** having less than the full or specified amount or number **:** SHORT ⟨just ~ of six feet tall⟩ ⟨the stew is a little ~ of seasoning⟩ **7 :** DISREPUTABLE ⟨gambling hells and ~ saloons —*Blackwood's*⟩ — **shy-ly** *adv* — **shy-ness** *n*
syn SHY, BASHFUL, DIFFIDENT, MODEST, COY mean not inclined to be forward. SHY implies a timid reserve and a shrinking from familiarity or contact with others ⟨*shy* with strangers⟩. BASHFUL implies a frightened shyness characteristic of childhood and adolescence ⟨a *bashful* boy out on his first date⟩. DIFFIDENT stresses a distrust of one's own ability or opinion that causes hesitation in acting or speaking ⟨felt *diffident* about raising an objection⟩. MODEST suggests absence of undue confidence or conceit ⟨very *modest* about her achievements⟩. COY implies an assumed or affected shyness ⟨put off by her *coy* manner⟩.
²shy *vi* **shied; shy-ing** (1650) **1 :** to develop or show a dislike or distaste — usu. used with *from* or *away from* ⟨an author who *shies* away from publicity⟩ **2 :** to start suddenly aside through fright or alarm
³shy *n, pl* **shies** (1791) **:** a sudden start aside (as from fright)
⁴shy *vb* **shied; shy-ing** [perh. fr. ¹*shy*] *vi* (1787) **:** to make a sudden throw ~ *vt* **:** to throw (an object) with a jerk **:** FLING
⁵shy *n, pl* **shies** (1791) **1 :** the act of shying **:** TOSS, THROW **2 :** a verbal fling or attack **3 :** COCKSHY
¹shy-lock \'shī-ˌläk\ *n* **1** *cap* **:** the Jewish usurer and antagonist of Antonio in Shakespeare's *The Merchant of Venice* **2 :** an extortionate creditor **:** LOAN SHARK
²shylock *vi* (ca. 1934) **:** to lend money at high rates of interest ⟨exposé of systematic thievery . . . —*ing*, and murder —*Current Biog.*⟩
shy-ster \'shīs-tər\ *n* [prob. fr. G *Scheisser*, lit., defecator] (1844) **:** one who is professionally unscrupulous esp. in the practice of law or politics **:** PETTIFOGGER
si \'sē\ *n* [It] (1728) **:** ²TI
si-a-gogue \sī-ˈa-lə-ˌgäg\ *n* [NL *sialagogus* promoting the expulsion of saliva, fr. Gk *sialon* saliva + NL *-agogus* -agogue] (ca. 1783) **:** an agent that promotes the flow of saliva
si-al-ic \sī-ˈa-lik\ *adj* [ISV *s*ilicon + *al*uminum] (1924) **:** of, relating to, or being relatively light rock that is rich in silica and alumina and is typical of the outer layers of the earth
sialic acid *n* [Gk *sialon* saliva] (1952) **:** any of a group of reducing amido acids that are essentially carbohydrates and are found esp. as components of blood glycoproteins and mucoproteins
si-a-mang \'sē-ə-ˌmäŋ, 'sī-\ *n* [Malay] (1822) **:** a black gibbon (*Hylobates syndactylus*) of Sumatra and the Malay Peninsula that is the largest of the gibbons
¹Si-a-mese \ˌsī-ə-ˈmēz, -ˈmēs\ *adj* [*Siam* (Thailand); in senses 2 & 3, fr. *Siamese twin*] (1693) **1 :** of, relating to, or characteristic of Thailand, the Thais, or their language **2 :** exhibiting great resemblance **:** very like **3** *not cap* **:** connecting two or more pipes or hoses so as to permit discharge in a single stream
²Siamese *n, pl* **Siamese** (1693) **1 :** THAI 2 **2 :** THAI 3 **3 :** SIAMESE CAT

Siamese cat *n* (1871) **:** any of a breed of slender blue-eyed shorthaired domestic cats of oriental origin with pale fawn or gray body and darker ears, paws, tail, and face
Siamese fighting fish *n* (1933) **:** a brightly colored betta (*Betta splendens*) that has highly aggressive males and is a popular aquarium fish

Siamese twin *n* [fr. Chang †1874 and Eng †1874 congenitally united twins born in Siam] (1829) **:** one of a pair of congenitally united twins in humans or other vertebrates

Siamese fighting fish

¹sib \'sib\ *adj* [ME, fr. OE *sibb*, fr. *sibb* kinship; akin to OHG *sippa* kinship, family, L *sodalis* comrade, Gk *ēthos* custom, character, L *suus* one's own — more at SUICIDE] (bef. 12c) **:** related by blood **:** AKIN
²sib *n* (bef. 12c) **1 a :** KINDRED, RELATIVES **b :** a blood relation **:** KINSMAN **2 :** a brother or sister considered irrespective of sex; *broadly* **:** any plant or animal of a group sharing a degree of genetic relationship corresponding to that of human sibs **3 :** a group of persons unilaterally descended from a real or supposed ancestor
Si-be-ri-an husky \sī-ˈbir-ē-ən-\ *n* (1930) **:** any of a breed of medium-sized thick-coated compact dogs that were developed in Siberia for use as sled dogs and that have erect ears and a bushy tail
sib-i-lance \'si-bə-lən(t)s\ *n* (1823) **:** a sibilant quality or sound
¹sib-i-lant \'si-bə-lənt\ *adj* [L *sibilant-, sibilans*, prp. of *sibilare* to hiss, whistle, of imit. origin] (1669) **:** having, containing, or producing the sound of or a sound resembling that of the *s* or the *sh* in *sash* ⟨a ~ affricate⟩ ⟨a ~ snake⟩ — **sib-i-lant-ly** *adv*
²sibilant *n* (1788) **:** a sibilant speech sound (as English \s\, \z\, \sh\, \zh\, \ch⟨=tsh)\, or \j⟨=dzh)\)
sib-i-late \'si-bə-ˌlāt\ *vb* **-lat-ed; -lat-ing** [L *sibilatus*, pp. of *sibilare*] *vi* (ca. 1656) **1 :** HISS **2 :** to utter an initial sibilant **:** prefix an \s\-sound ~ *vt* **1 :** HISS **2 :** to pronounce with an initial sibilant **:** prefix an \s\-sound to — **sib-i-la-tion** \ˌsi-bə-ˈlā-shən\ *n*
sib-ling \'si-bliŋ\ *n* (bef. 12c) **1 :** SIB 2; *also* **:** one of two or more individuals having one common parent **2 :** one of two or more things related by a common tie or characteristic
sibling species *n* (1940) **:** one of two or more species that are nearly indistinguishable morphologically
sib-yl \'si-bəl\ *n, often cap* [ME *sibile, sybylle*, fr. MF & L; MF *sibile*, L *sibylla*, fr. Gk] (14c) **1 :** any of several prophetesses usu. accepted as 10 in number and credited to widely separate parts of the ancient world (as Babylonia, Egypt, Greece, and Italy) **2 a :** a female prophet **b :** FORTUNE-TELLER — **si-byl-ic** *or* **si-byl-lic** \sə-ˈbi-lik\ *adj* — **sib-yl-line** \'si-bə-ˌlīn, -ˌlēn\ *adj*
¹sic \'sik\ *chiefly Scot var of* SUCH
²sic *also* **sick** \'sik\ *vt* **sicced** *also* **sicked** \'sikt\; **sic-cing** *also* **sick-ing** [alter. of *seek*] (1845) **1 :** CHASE, ATTACK — usu. used as a command esp. to a dog ⟨~ 'em⟩ **2 :** to incite or urge to an attack, pursuit, or harassment **:** SET
³sic \'sik, 'sēk\ *adv* [L, so, thus — more at SO] (ca. 1859) **:** intentionally so written — used after a printed word or passage to indicate that it is intended exactly as printed or to indicate that it exactly reproduces an original ⟨said he seed [~] it all⟩
Sichuan *var of* SZECHUAN
sick \'sik\ *adj* [ME *sek, sik*, fr. OE *sēoc*; akin to OHG *sioh* sick] (bef. 12c) **1 a** (1) **:** affected with disease or ill health **:** AILING (2) **:** of, relating to, or intended for use in sickness ⟨~ pay⟩ ⟨a ~ ward⟩ **b :** QUEASY, NAUSEATED ⟨~ to one's stomach⟩ ⟨was ~ in the car⟩ **c :** undergoing menstruation **2 :** spiritually or morally unsound or corrupt **3 a :** sickened by strong emotion ⟨~ with fear⟩ ⟨worried ~⟩ **b :** having a strong distaste from surfeit ⟨SATIATED ⟨~ of flattery⟩ **c :** filled with disgust or chagrin ⟨gossip makes me ~⟩ **d :** depressed and longing for something ⟨~ for one's home⟩ **4 a :** mentally or emotionally unsound or disordered **:** MORBID ⟨~ thoughts⟩ **b :** MACABRE, SADISTIC ⟨~ jokes⟩ **5 :** lacking vigor **:** SICKLY: as **a :** badly outclassed ⟨looked ~ in the contest⟩ **b :** incapable of yielding a profitable crop esp. because of buildup of disease organisms ⟨clover-*sick* soils⟩
sick and tired *adj* (1783) **:** thoroughly fatigued or bored; *also* **:** FED UP
sick bay *n* (1813) **:** a compartment in a ship used as a dispensary and hospital; *broadly* **:** a place for the care of the sick or injured
sick-bed \'sik-ˌbed\ *n* (14c) **:** the bed on which one lies sick
sick call *n* (1836) **:** a scheduled time at which individuals (as soldiers) may report as sick to the medical officer
sick day *n* (1968) **:** a paid day of sick leave
sick-en \'si-kən\ *vb* **sick-ened; sick-en-ing** \'si-kə-niŋ, 'sik-niŋ\ *vi* (13c) **1 :** to become sick **2 :** to become weary or satiated ~ *vt* **1 :** to make sick **2 :** to cause revulsion in as a result of weariness or satiety — **sick-en-er** \'si-kə-nər, 'sik-nər\ *n*
sick-en-ing \-niŋ\ *adj* (1789) **:** causing sickness or disgust ⟨a ~ odor⟩ ⟨a ~ display⟩ — **sick-en-ing-ly** \-niŋ-lē\ *adv*
sick-er \'si-kər\ *adj* [ME *siker*, fr. OE *sicor*, fr. L *securus* secure] (bef. 12c) *chiefly Scot* **:** SECURE, SAFE; *also* **:** DEPENDABLE — **sicker** *adv, chiefly Scot* — **sick-er-ly** *adv, chiefly Scot*
sick headache *n* (1778) **:** MIGRAINE
sick-ie \'si-kē\ *n* (1967) **:** a person who is mentally or morally sick
sick-ish \'si-kish\ *adj* (1581) **1** *archaic* **:** somewhat ill **:** SICKLY **2 :** somewhat nauseated **:** QUEASY **3 :** somewhat sickening ⟨a ~ odor⟩ — **sick-ish-ly** *adv* — **sick-ish-ness** *n*

¹sick-le \'si-kəl\ *n* [ME *sikel*, fr. OE *sicol*, fr. L *secula* sickle, fr. *secare* to cut — more at SAW] (bef. 12c) **1 :** an agricultural implement consisting of a curved metal blade with a short handle fitted on a tang **2 :** the cutting mechanism (as of a reaper, combine, or mower) consisting of a bar with a series of cutting elements
²sickle *adj* (1688) **:** having the form of a sickle blade **:** having a curve similar to that of a sickle blade ⟨the ~ moon⟩
³sickle *vb* **sick-led; sick-ling** \'si-k(ə-)liŋ\ *vt* (1922) **1 :** to mow or reap with a sickle **2 :** to change (a red

¹sickle 1

blood cell) into a sickle cell ~ *vi* : to change into a sickle cell ⟨the ability of red blood cells to ~⟩

sick leave *n* (1840) **1** : an absence from work permitted because of illness **2** : the number of days per year for which an employer agrees to pay employees who are sick

sickle cell *n* (1923) : an abnormal red blood cell of crescent shape

sickle–cell anemia *n* (1922) : a chronic inherited anemia in which a large proportion or the majority of the red blood cells tend to sickle, which occurs primarily in individuals of African, Mediterranean, or southwest Asian ancestry, and which results from homozygosity for a semidominant gene — called also *sickle-cell disease*

sickle–cell trait *n* (1928) : an inherited blood condition in which some red blood cells tend to sickle but usu. not enough to produce anemia, which occurs primarily in individuals of African, Mediterranean, or southwest Asian ancestry, and which results from heterozygosity for a semidominant gene

sick·le·mia \ˌsi-kə-ˈlē-mē-ə\ *n* [NL, fr. E *sickle* (cell) + NL *-emia*] (1932) : SICKLE-CELL TRAIT

¹sick·ly \ˈsi-klē\ *adj* (14c) **1** : somewhat unwell; *also* : habitually ailing **2** : produced by or associated with sickness ⟨a ~ complexion⟩ ⟨a ~ appetite⟩ **3** : producing or tending to produce disease : UNWHOLESOME ⟨a ~ climate⟩ **4 a** : appearing as if sick **b** : lacking in vigor : WEAK ⟨a ~ plant⟩ **5** : SICKENING ⟨a ~ odor⟩ ⟨a ~ green⟩ — **sick·li·ness** — **sickly** *adv*

²sickly *vt* **sick·lied; sick·ly·ing** (1763) : to make sick or sickly

sick·ness \ˈsik-nəs\ *n* (bef. 12c) **1 a** : ill health : ILLNESS **b** : a disordered, weakened, or unsound condition **2** : a specific disease **3** : NAUSEA, QUEASINESS

sicko \ˈsi-(ˌ)kō\ *n*, *pl* **sick·os** (1963) : SICKIE

sick–out \ˈsik-ˌaút\ *n* (1951) : an organized absence from work by workers on the pretext of sickness

sick pay *n* (1887) : salary or wages paid to an employee while on sick leave

sick·room \ˈsik-ˌrüm, -ˌrûm\ *n* (1749) : a room in which a person is confined by sickness

sic pas·sim \ˈsik-ˈpa-səm, ˈsēk-ˈpä-sim\ *adv* [L] (1921) : so throughout — used of a word or idea to be found throughout a book or a writer's work

sid·dur \ˈsi-dər, -ˌdûr\ *n*, *pl* **sid·du·rim** \sə-ˈdúr-əm\ [LHeb *siddūr*, lit., order, arrangement] (1864) : a Jewish prayer book containing liturgies for daily, Sabbath, and holiday observances

¹side \ˈsīd\ *n* [ME, fr. OE *sīde*; akin to OHG *sīta* side, OE *sīd* ample, wide] (bef. 12c) **1 a** : the right or left part of the wall or trunk of the body ⟨a pain in the ~⟩ **b** (1) : one of the halves of the animal body on either side of the mesial plane (2) : a cut of meat including that about the ribs of one half of the body — used chiefly of smoked pork products **c** : one longitudinal half of a hide **2 a** : a place, space, or direction with respect to a center or to a line of division (as of an aisle, river, or street) **3 a** : one of the longer bounding surfaces or lines of an object esp. contrasted with the ends ⟨the ~ of a barn⟩ **b** : a line or surface forming a border or face of an object ⟨a die has six ~s⟩ ⟨the back ~ of the moon⟩ **c** : either surface of a thin object ⟨one ~ of a record⟩ ⟨right ~ of the cloth⟩ **d** : a bounding line of a geometric figure ⟨~ of a triangle⟩ **4 a** : the space beside one ⟨stood by my ~⟩ **b** : an area next to something — usu. used in combination ⟨a poolside interview⟩ **5** : a slope (as of a hill) considered as opposed to another slope ⟨the far ~ of the hill⟩ **6 a** : the attitude or activity of one person or group with respect to another : PART ⟨there was no malice on my ~⟩ **b** : a position that is opposite to or contrasted with another ⟨two ~s to every question⟩ ⟨came down on the ~ of law and order⟩ **c** : a body of partisans or contestants ⟨victory for neither ~⟩ **d** : TEAM ⟨11 players on each ~⟩ **7 a** : a line of descent traced through one's parent ⟨grandfather on his mother's ~⟩ **8** : an aspect or part of something contrasted with some other real or implied aspect or part ⟨the better ~ of his nature⟩ ⟨the sales ~ of the business⟩ ⟨the seasoning is a bit on the heavy ~⟩ **9** *Brit* : sideways spin imparted to a billiard or snooker ball **10** : a sheet containing the lines and cues for a single theatrical role **11** : a recording of music **12** : a side order or dish ⟨a ~ of fries⟩ — **on the side 1** : in addition to the main portion **2** : in addition to a principal occupation — **this side of** : short of : ALMOST ⟨an attitude just *this side of* scandalous⟩

²side *adj* (14c) **1 a** : situated on the side ⟨~ window⟩ **b** : of or relating to the side **2 a** : directed toward or from the side ⟨~ thrust⟩ ⟨~ wind⟩ **b** : INCIDENTAL, INDIRECT ⟨~ issue⟩ ⟨~ remark⟩ **c** : made on the side ⟨~ payment⟩ **d** : additional to the main portion ⟨~ order of french fries⟩

³side *vb* **sid·ed; sid·ing** *vt* (1591) **1** : to agree with : SUPPORT **2** : to be side by side with **3** : to set or put aside : clear away ⟨~ the dishes⟩ **4** : to furnish with sides or siding ⟨~ a house⟩ ~ *vi* : to take sides : join or form sides ⟨*sided* with the rebels⟩

⁴side *n* [obs. E *side* proud, boastful] (1878) *chiefly Brit* : swaggering or arrogant manner : PRETENTIOUSNESS

side–arm \ˈsīd-ˌärm\ *adj* (1908) : of, relating to, using, or being a baseball pitching style in which the arm is not raised above the shoulder and the ball is thrown with a sideways sweep of the arm between shoulder and hip ⟨~ delivery⟩ — **sidearm** *adv*

side arm *n* (1689) : a weapon (as a sword, revolver, or bayonet) worn at the side or in the belt

side·band \-ˌband\ *n* (1922) : the band of frequencies (as of radio waves) on either side of the carrier frequency produced by modulation

side·bar \-ˌbär\ *n* (1945) : a short news story accompanying and presenting sidelights of a major story

side bearing *n* (ca. 1894) : the space provided at each side of a typeset letter to prevent its touching adjoining letters

side·board \ˈsīd-ˌbōrd, -ˌbȯrd\ *n* (1671) : a piece of dining-room furniture having compartments and shelves for holding articles of table service

side·burns \-ˌbərnz\ *n pl* [anagram of *burnsides*] (1887) **1** : SIDE-WHISKERS **2** : continuations of the hairline in front of the ears — **side·burned** \-ˌbȯrnd\ *adj*

side by side *adv* (13c) **1** : beside one another **2** : in the same place, time, or circumstance ⟨lived peacefully *side by side* for many years⟩ — **side–by–side** *adj*

side·car \ˈsīd-ˌkär\ *n* (1904) **1** : a car attached to the side of a motorcycle for a passenger **2** : a cocktail consisting of a liqueur with lemon juice and brandy

side chain *n* (1886) : a shorter chain or group of atoms attached to a principal chain or to a ring in a molecule

side chair *n* (1925) : a chair without arms used usu. in a dining room

sid·ed \ˈsī-dəd\ *adj* (15c) : having sides often of a specified number or kind ⟨one-*sided*⟩ ⟨glass-*sided*⟩ — **sid·ed·ness** *n*

side dish *n* (1725) : a food served separately along with the main course

side–dress \ˈsīd-ˌdres\ *n* (1966) : SIDE-DRESSING — **side–dress** \ˈsīd-ˌdres\ *vt*

side–dress·ing \-ˌdre-siŋ\ *n* (1935) **1** : plant nutrients placed on or in the soil near the roots of a growing crop often by means of a cultivator having a fertilizer-distributing attachment **2** : the act or process of applying side-dressing to a crop

side drum *n* (ca. 1800) : SNARE DRUM

side effect *n* (1884) : a secondary and usu. adverse effect (as of a drug) ⟨toxic *side effects*⟩ — called also *side reaction*

side–glance \ˈsīd-ˌglan(t)s\ *n* (1611) **1** : a glance directed to the side **2** : a passing allusion : an indirect or slight reference

side·hill \-ˌhil\ *n* (1674) : HILLSIDE — **sidehill** *adj*

side horse *n* (ca. 1934) : POMMEL HORSE

side·kick \ˈsīd-ˌkik\ *n* (1906) : a person closely associated with another as subordinate or partner

side·light \-ˌlīt\ *n* (1610) **1 a** : light coming or produced from the side **b** : incidental light or information **2** : the red light on the port bow or the green light on the starboard bow carried by ships under way at night

¹side·line \-ˌlīn\ *n* (1862) **1** : a line at right angles to a goal line or end line and marking a side of a court or field of play for athletic games **2 a** : a line of goods sold in addition to one's principal line **b** : a business or activity pursued in addition to one's regular occupation **3 a** : the space immediately outside the lines along either side of an athletic field or court **b** : a sphere of little or no participation or activity — usu. used in pl.

²sideline *vt* (1943) : to put out of action : put on the sidelines

side·lin·er \ˈsīd-ˌlī-nər\ *n* (1947) : one that remains on the sidelines during an activity : one that does not participate

¹side·ling \ˈsīd-liŋ\ *adv* [ME *sidling*, fr. ¹*side* + ²*-ling*] (14c) *archaic* : in a sidelong direction : SIDEWAYS

²sideling *adj* (1611) **1** *archaic* : directed toward one side : OBLIQUE **2** *archaic* : having an inclination : SLOPING ⟨~ ground⟩

¹side·long \ˈsīd-ˌlȯŋ\ *adv* [alter. of ¹*sideling*] (14c) **1** : SIDEWAYS, OBLIQUELY **2** *archaic* : on the side

²sidelong *adj* (1597) **1** : lying or inclining to one side : SLANTING **2 a** : directed to one side ⟨~ looks⟩ **b** : indirect rather than straightforward

side·man \ˈsīd-ˌman\ *n* (1936) : a member of a band or orchestra and esp. of a jazz or swing orchestra

side·piece \-ˌpēs\ *n* (1802) : a piece forming or contained in the side of something ⟨the ~ of a carriage⟩

sider- or **sidero-** *comb form* [MF, fr. L, fr. Gk *sidēr-, sidēro-, fr. sidēros*] : iron ⟨*hemosiderin*⟩ ⟨*siderolite*⟩

-sid·er \ˈsīd-ər\ *comb form* : one placed or living in a usu. specified side (as a section of the city) ⟨an east-*sider*⟩

si·de·re·al \sī-ˈdir-ē-əl, sə-\ *adj* [L *sidereus*, fr. *sider-, sidus* star, constellation] (1647) : of, relating to, or expressed in relation to stars or constellations : ASTRAL

sidereal day *n* (1794) : the interval between two successive transits of a point on the celestial sphere (as the vernal equinox) over the upper meridian of a place : 23 hours, 56 minutes, 4.1 seconds of mean time

sidereal hour *n* (ca. 1891) : the 24th part of a sidereal day

sidereal minute *n* (ca. 1909) : the 60th part of a sidereal hour

sidereal month *n* (1868) : the mean time of the moon's revolution in its orbit with reference to a star's position : 27 days, 7 hours, 43 minutes, 11.5 seconds of mean time

sidereal second *n* (ca. 1909) : the 60th part of a sidereal minute

sidereal time *n* (1812) **1** : time based on the sidereal day **2** : the hour angle of the vernal equinox at a place

sidereal year *n* (1681) : the time in which the earth completes one revolution in its orbit around the sun measured with respect to the fixed stars : 365 days, 6 hours, 9 minutes, and 9.5 seconds of mean time

¹sid·er·ite \ˈsi-də-ˌrīt\ *n* [G *Siderit*, fr. Gk *sidēros* iron] (1850) : a native ferrous carbonate FeCO₃ that is a valuable iron ore

²siderite *n* (1875) : a nickel-iron meteorite

side road *n* (1854) : a smaller road off a main road

si·de·ro·lite \ˈsī-dir-ə-ˌlīt, ˈsi-də-rə-\ *n* (1863) : a stony iron meteorite

side·sad·dle \ˈsīd-ˌsa-dᵊl\ *n* (15c) : a saddle for women in which the rider sits with both legs on the same side of the horse — **sidesaddle** *adv*

side–scan sonar \-ˌskan-\ *n* (1967) : a sonar that scans the ocean floor to the side of a ship's track and is used esp. for mapping the ocean bottom

side·show \-ˌshō\ *n* (1846) **1** : a minor show offered in addition to a main exhibition (as of a circus) **2** : an incidental diversion or spectacle

side·slip \-ˌslip\ *vi* (1887) **1** : to skid or slide sideways **2** : to slide sideways through the air in a downward direction in an airplane along an inclined lateral axis — **sideslip** *n*

side·spin \-ˌspin\ *n* (1926) : a rotary motion that causes a ball to revolve horizontally

side·split·ting \-ˌspli-tiŋ\ *adj* (1856) : extremely funny — **side·split·ting·ly** *adv*

side·step \ˈsīd-ˌstep\ *vi* (1901) **1** : to take a side step **2** : to avoid an issue or decision ~ *vt* **1** : to move out of the way of : AVOID ⟨~ a blow⟩ **2** : BYPASS, EVADE ⟨~ a question⟩ — **side·step·per** *n*

\ə\ abut \ᵊ\ kitten, F table \ər\ further \a\ ash \ā\ ace \ä\ mop, mar
\aú\ out \ch\ chin \e\ bet \ē\ easy \g\ go \i\ hit \ī\ ice \j\ job
\ŋ\ sing \ō\ go \ȯ\ law \ȯi\ boy \th\ thin \t̲h̲\ the \ü\ loot \ú\ foot
\y\ yet \zh\ vision \ä, k̲, ⁿ, œ, œ̄, ᵫ, ᵫ̄, ᶦ\ see Guide to Pronunciation

side step n (1789) **1** : a step aside (as in boxing to avoid a blow) **2** : a step taken sideways (as when climbing on skis)

side-strad-dle hop \'sīd-₁stra-d³l-\ n (1952) : JUMPING JACK 2

side-stream \-₁strēm\ adj (1951) : relating to or being tobacco smoke that is emitted from the lighted end of a cigarette or cigar

side street n (1617) : a street joining and often terminated by a main thoroughfare

side-stroke \'sīd-₁strōk\ n (1867) : a swimming stroke which is executed on the side and in which the arms are swept in separate strokes towards the feet and downward and the legs do a scissors kick

¹**side-swipe** \-₁swīp\ vt (1904) : to strike with a glancing blow along the side ⟨sideswiped a parked car⟩

²**sideswipe** n (1917) **1 a** : the action of sideswiping **b** : an instance of sideswiping : a glancing blow **2** : an incidental deprecatory remark, allusion, or reference

side table n (14c) : a table designed to be placed against a wall

¹**side-track** \'sīd-₁trak\ n (1835) **1** : SIDING 2 **2** : a position or condition of secondary importance to which one may be diverted

²**sidetrack** vt (1880) **1** : to shunt aside (as to a railroad siding) **2 a** : to turn aside from a purpose : DEFLECT **b** : to prevent action on by diversionary tactics ⟨~ an issue⟩

side-walk \'sīd-₁wȯk\ n (1739) : a usu. paved walk for pedestrians at the side of a street

sidewalk superintendent n (1940) : a spectator at a building or demolition job

side-wall \'sīd-₁wȯl\ n (14c) **1** : a wall forming the side of something **2** : the side of an automotive tire between the tread shoulder and the rim bead

side-ward \'sīd-wərd\ or **side-wards** \-wərdz\ adv (15c) : toward a side

side-way \'sīd-₁wā\ adv or adj (1612) : SIDEWAYS

side-ways \-₁wāz\ adv or adj (1577) **1** : from one side **2** : with one side forward ⟨turn ~⟩ **3 a** : in a lateral direction or downward to one side ⟨hopped ~⟩ ⟨slump ~⟩ **b** : ASKANCE ⟨look ~ at someone⟩

side-wheel \'sīd-₁hwēl, -₁wēl\ adj (1857) : of or being a steamer having a paddle wheel on each side — **side-wheel-er** \-₁hwē-lər, -₁wē-\ n

side-whis-kers \'sīd-₁hwis-kərz, -₁wis-\ n pl (1888) : whiskers on the side of the face usu. worn long — **side-whis-kered** \-kərd\ adj

side-wind-er \'sīd-₁wīn-dər\ n (1840) **1** : a heavy swinging blow from the side **2** : a small pale-colored desert rattlesnake (Crotalus cerastes) of the southwestern U.S. that moves by thrusting its body diagonally forward in a series of flat S-shaped curves

side-wise \'sīd-₁wīz\ adv (1571) : SIDEWAYS

sid-ing \'sī-diŋ\ n (1603) **1** archaic : the taking of sides : PARTISANSHIP **2** : a short railroad track connected with the main track **3** : material (as boards or metal pieces) forming the exposed surface of outside walls of frame buildings

si-dle \'sī-d³l\ vb **si-dled; si-dling** \'sīd-liŋ, 'sī-d³l-iŋ\ [prob. backformation fr. sideling] vi (1697) : to go or move with one side foremost esp. in a furtive advance ~ vt : to cause to move or turn sideways — **sidle** n

siege \'sēj\ also \'sēzh\ n [ME sege, fr. OF, seat, blockade, fr. siegier to seat, settle, fr. (assumed) VL sedicare, fr. L sedēre to sit — more at SIT] (13c) **1** obs : a seat of distinction : THRONE **2 a** : a military blockade of a city or fortified place to compel it to surrender **b** : a persistent or serious attack (as of illness) — **siege** vt — **lay siege to 1** : to besiege militarily **2** : to pursue diligently or persistently

siege mentality n (1953) : a defensive or overly fearful attitude

Siege Perilous n : a seat at King Arthur's Round Table reserved for the knight destined to achieve the quest of the Holy Grail and fatal to any other occupying it

Sieg-fried \'sig-₁frēd, 'sēg-\ n [G] : a hero in Germanic legend who slays a dragon guarding a gold hoard and wakes Brunhild from her enchanted sleep

Siegfried line n [Siegfried] (1918) : a line of German defensive fortifications facing the Maginot Line

sie-mens \'sē-mənz, 'zē-\ n, pl **siemens** [Werner von Siemens †1892 Ger. electrical engineer] (ca. 1933) : a unit of conductance in the meter-kilogram-second system equivalent to one ampere per volt

si-en-na \sē-'e-nə\ n [It terra di Siena, lit., Siena earth, fr. Siena, Italy] (1787) : an earthy substance containing oxides of iron and usu. of manganese that is brownish yellow when raw and orange red or reddish brown when burnt and is used as a pigment

si-er-o-zem \sē-'er-ə-₁zem, sē-₁er-ə-'zyȯm\ n [Russ serozem, fr. seryĭ gray + zemlya earth; akin to L humus earth — more at HUMBLE] (1934) : any of a group of zonal soils brownish gray at the surface and lighter below, based in a carbonate or hardpan layer, and characteristic of temperate to cool arid regions

si-er-ra \sē-'er-ə\ n [Sp, lit., saw, fr. L serra] (1600) **1 a** : a range of mountains esp. with a serrated or irregular outline **b** : the country about a sierra **2** : any of several large fishes (genus Scomberomorus) related to the mackerel

Sierra (1952) — a communications code word for the letter s

si-er-ran \sē-'er-ən\ adj (1873) **1** : of or relating to a sierra ⟨~ foothills⟩ **2** cap : of or relating to the Sierra Nevada Mountains of the western U.S.

Sierran n (1906) : a native or inhabitant of the region around the Sierra Nevada Mountains

si-es-ta \sē-'es-tə\ n [Sp, fr. L sexta (hora) noon, lit., sixth hour — more at SEXT] (1655) : an afternoon nap or rest

sie-va bean \'sē-və-, 'si-vē-\ n [origin unknown] (1888) : a bean plant (Phaseolus lunatus) of tropical America that is closely related to and sometimes classified with the lima bean; also : its flat edible seed

¹**sieve** \'siv\ n [ME sive, fr. OE sife; akin to OHG sib sieve] (bef. 12c) : a device with meshes or perforations through which finer particles of a mixture (as of ashes, flour, or sand) of various sizes may be passed to separate them from coarser ones, through which the liquid may be drained from liquid-containing material, or through which soft materials may be forced for reduction to fine particles

²**sieve** vb **sieved; siev-ing** (15c) : SIFT

sieve of Er-a-tos-the-nes \-₁er-ə-'täs-thə-₁nēz\ (1803) : a procedure for finding prime numbers that involves writing down the odd numbers from 2 up in succession and lining out every third number after 3, every fifth after 5 including those already lined out, every seventh after 7, and

so on with each successive number which has not been lined out with every number that is not lined out being prime

sieve plate n (1875) : a perforated wall or part of a wall at the end of one of the individual cells making up a sieve tube

sieve tube n (1875) : a tube consisting of an end-to-end series of thin-walled living plant cells characteristic of the phloem and held to function chiefly in translocation of organic solutes

si-faka \sə-'fä-kə\ n [Malagasy] (1845) : any of several diurnal mostly black and white lemurs (genus Propithecus) with a long tail and silky fur

sift \'sift\ vb [ME, fr. OE siftan; akin to OE sife sieve] vt (bef. 12c) **1 a** : to put through a sieve ⟨~ flour⟩ **b** : to separate or separate out by or as if by putting through a sieve **2 a** : to go through esp. to sort out what is useful or valuable ⟨~ed the evidence⟩ — often used with through ⟨~ through a pile of old letters⟩ **3** : to scatter by or as if by sifting ⟨~ sugar on a cake⟩ ~ vi **1** : to use a sieve **2** : to pass or fall as if through a sieve — **sift-er** n

sift-ing n (15c) **1** : the act or process of sifting **2** pl : sifted material

¹**sigh** \'sī\ vb [ME sihen, alter. of sichen, fr. OE sican; akin to MD versiken to sigh] vi (13c) **1** : to take a deep audible breath (as in weariness or relief) **2** : to make a sound like sighing ⟨wind ~ing in the branches⟩ **3** GRIEVE, YEARN ⟨~ing for days gone by⟩ ~ vt **1** : to express by sighs **2** archaic : to utter sighs over : MOURN — **sigh-er** \'sī-(-ə)r\ n

²**sigh** n (14c) **1** : an often involuntary act of sighing esp. when expressing an emotion or feeling (as weariness or relief) **2** : the sound of gently moving or escaping air ⟨~s of the summer breeze⟩

¹**sight** \'sīt\ n [ME, fr. OE gesiht faculty or act of sight, thing seen; akin to OHG gisiht sight, OE sēon to see] (bef. 12c) **1** : something that is seen : SPECTACLE **2 a** : a thing regarded as worth seeing — usu. used in pl. ⟨the ~s of the city⟩ **b** : something ludicrous or disorderly in appearance ⟨you look a ~⟩ **3** a chiefly dial : a great number or quantity ⟨a good deal : LOT ⟨a far ~ better⟩ ⟨not by a damn ~⟩ **4 a** : the process, power, or function of seeing; specif : the animal sense of which the end organ is the eye and by which the position, shape, and color of objects are perceived **b** : mental or spiritual perception ⟨a : mental view; specif : JUDGMENT **5 a** : the act of looking at or beholding **b** : INSPECTION, PERUSAL **c** : VIEW, GLIMPSE **d** : an observation to determine direction or position (as by a navigator) **6 a** : a perception of an object by or as if by the eye ⟨never lost ~ of the objective⟩ **b** : the range of vision ⟨was nowhere in ~⟩ **7** : presentation of a note or draft to the maker or draftee : DEMAND **8 a** : a device that aids the eye in aiming or in finding the direction of an object **b** pl : ASPIRATION ⟨set her ~s on a medical career⟩ — **in sight** : at or within a reasonable distance or time — **on sight** : as soon as seen ⟨ordered to shoot on sight⟩ — **out of sight 1** : beyond comparison **2** : beyond all expectation or reason **3** — used as a generalized expression of approval — **sight for sore eyes** : one whose appearance or arrival is an occasion for joy or relief

²**sight** vt (1602) **1** : to get or catch sight of ⟨several whales were ~ed⟩ **2** : to look at through or as if through a sight; esp : to test for straightness **3** : to aim by means of sights **4 a** : to equip with sights **b** : to adjust the sights of ~ vi **1** : to take aim **2** : to look carefully in a particular direction

³**sight** adj (1801) **1** : based on recognition or comprehension without previous study ⟨~ translation⟩ **2** : payable on presentation ⟨a ~ draft⟩

sight-ed \'sī-təd\ adj (1552) : having sight ⟨clear-sighted⟩ ⟨a ~ person⟩

sight gag n (1949) : a comic bit or episode whose effect is produced by pantomime or camera shot rather than by words

sight-less \'sīt-ləs\ adj (13c) **1** : lacking sight : BLIND **2** : INVISIBLE 1 — **sight-less-ly** adv — **sight-less-ness** n

sight line n (1859) : a line extending from an observer's eye to a viewed object or area (as a stage) ⟨a theater with excellent sight lines⟩

sight-ly \-lē\ adj (1534) **1** : pleasing to the sight : ATTRACTIVE **2** : affording a fine view — **sight-li-ness** n — **sightly** adv

sight—read \-₁rēd\ vb **-read** \-₁red\; **-read-ing** \-₁rē-diŋ\ [back-formation fr. sight reader] vt (1903) : to read (as a foreign language) or perform (music) without previous preparation or study ~ vi : to read at sight; esp : to perform music at sight — **sight reader** n

sight rhyme n (ca. 1936) : EYE RHYME

sight-see \'sīt-₁sē\ vi, past **-saw**; pres part **-see-ing** [back-formation fr. sight-seeing] (1824) : to go about seeing sights of interest — **sight-seer** \-₁sē-ər, -₁sir\ n

sight-see-ing \'sīt-₁sē-iŋ\ adj (1827) : devoted to or used for seeing sights — **sight-seeing** n

sight unseen adv (1892) : without inspection or appraisal

sig-il \'si-jil\ n [ME sigulle, fr. L sigillum — more at SEAL] (15c) **1** : SEAL, SIGNET **2** : a sign, word, or device held to have occult power in astrology or magic

sig-ma \'sig-mə\ n [Gk] (1607) **1** : the 18th letter of the Greek alphabet — see ALPHABET table **2** : STANDARD DEVIATION

sig-moid \'sig-₁mȯid\ also **sig-moi-dal** \sig-'mȯi-d³l\ adj [Gk sigmoeidēs, fr. sigma; fr. a common form of sigma shaped like the Roman letter C] (1670) **1 a** : curved like the letter C **b** : curved in two directions like the letter S **2** : of, relating to, or being the sigmoid flexure of the intestine — **sig-moi-dal-ly** \sig-'mȯi-d³l-ē\ adv

sigmoid flexure n (1786) : the contracted and crooked part of the colon immediately above the rectum — called also sigmoid colon

sig-moid-os-co-py \₁sig-₁mȯi-'däs-kə-pē\ n (ca. 1900) : the process of using a long hollow tubular instrument passed through the anus for inspection, diagnosis, treatment, and photography esp. of the sigmoid flexure

¹**sign** \'sīn\ n [ME signe, fr. OF, fr. L signum mark, token, sign, image, seal; perh. akin to L secare to cut — more at SAW] (13c) **1 a** : a motion or gesture by which a thought is expressed or a command or wish made known **b** : SIGNAL 2a **c** : a fundamental linguistic unit that designates an object or relation or has a purely syntactic function ⟨a : one of a set of gestures used to represent language; also : SIGN LANGUAGE **2** : a mark having a conventional meaning and used in place of words or to represent a complex notion **3** : one of the 12 divisions of the zodiac **4 a** (1) : a character (as a flat or sharp) used in musical notation (2) : SEGNO **b** : a character (as ÷) indicating a mathematical operation; also : one of two characters + and — that form part of

the symbol of a number and characterize it as positive or negative **5 a** : a display (as a lettered board or a configuration of neon tubing) used to identify or advertise a place of business or a product **b** : a posted command, warning, or direction **c** : SIGNBOARD **6 a** : something material or external that stands for or signifies something spiritual **b** : something indicating the presence or existence of something else ⟨~s of success⟩ ⟨a ~ of the times⟩ **c** : PRESAGE, PORTENT ⟨~s of an early spring⟩ **d** : an objective evidence of plant or animal disease **7** *pl usu* **sign** : traces of a usu. wild animal ⟨red fox ~⟩ — **signed** *adj*
syn SIGN, MARK, TOKEN, NOTE, SYMPTOM mean a discernible indication of what is not itself directly perceptible. SIGN applies to any indication to be perceived by the senses or the reason ⟨encouraging *signs* for the economy⟩. MARK suggests something impressed on or inherently characteristic of a thing often in contrast to general outward appearance ⟨a *mark* of a good upbringing⟩. TOKEN applies to something that serves as a proof of something intangible ⟨this gift is a *token* of our esteem⟩. NOTE suggests a distinguishing mark or characteristic ⟨a *note* of irony in her writing⟩. SYMPTOM suggests an outward indication of an internal change or condition ⟨rampant crime is a *symptom* of that city's decay⟩.
²**sign** *vb* [ME, fr. MF *signer*, fr. L *signare* to mark, sign, seal, fr. *signum*] *vt* (13c) **1 a** : CROSS **2 b** : to place a sign on **c** : to represent or indicate by a sign **2 a** : to affix a signature to : ratify or attest by hand or seal ⟨~ a bill into law⟩ ⟨the prisoner ~ed a confession⟩ **b** : to assign or convey formally ⟨~ed over his property to his brother⟩ **c** : to write down (one's name) **3** : to communicate by making a sign or by sign language **4** : to engage or hire by securing the signature of on a contract of employment — often used with *up* or *on* ~ *vi* **1** : to write one's name in token of assent, responsibility, or obligation **2 a** : to make a sign or signal **b** : to use sign language — **sign•ee** \ˌsī-ˈnē\ *n* — **sign•er** \ˈsī-nər\ *n*
sign•age \ˈsī-nij\ *n* (1976) : signs (as of identification, warning, or direction) or a system of such signs
¹**sig•nal** \ˈsig-nᵊl\ *n* [ME, fr. MF, fr. ML *signale*, fr. LL, neut. of *signalis* of a sign, fr. L *signum*] (14c) **1** : SIGN, INDICATION **2 a** : an act, event, or watchword that has been agreed on as the occasion of concerted action **b** : something that incites to action **3** : something (as a sound, gesture, or object) that conveys notice or warning **4 a** : an object used to transmit or convey information beyond the range of human voice **b** : the sound or image conveyed in telegraphy, telephony, radio, radar, or television **c** : a detectable physical quantity or impulse (as a voltage, current, or magnetic field strength) by which messages or information can be transmitted
²**signal** *vb* **sig•naled** *or* **sig•nalled; sig•nal•ing** *or* **sig•nal•ling** \-nə-liŋ\ *vt* (1805) **1** : to notify by a signal ⟨~ the fleet to turn back⟩ **2 a** : to communicate or indicate by or as if by signals ⟨~ed the end of an era⟩ **b** : to constitute a characteristic feature of (a meaningful linguistic form) ~ *vi* : to make or send a signal — **sig•nal•er** *or* **sig•nal•ler** *n*
³**signal** *adj* [modif. of F *signalé*, pp. of *signaler* to distinguish, fr. OIt *segnalare* to signal, distinguish, fr. *segnale* signal, fr. ML *signale*] (1641) : distinguished from the ordinary ⟨~ achievement⟩
sig•nal•ise *Brit var of* SIGNALIZE
sig•nal•ize \ˈsig-nə-ˌlīz\ *vt* **-ized; -iz•ing** (1654) **1** : to make conspicuous : DISTINGUISH **2** : to point out carefully or distinctly **3** : to make signals to : SIGNAL; *also* : INDICATE **4** : to place traffic signals at or on — **sig•nal•i•za•tion** \ˌsig-nə-lə-ˈzā-shən\ *n*
sig•nal•ly \ˈsig-nə-lē\ *adv* (1641) : in a signal manner : NOTABLY
sig•nal•man \ˈsig-nᵊl-mən, -ˌman\ *n* (1737) : a person who signals or works with signals (as on a railway)
sig•nal•ment \-mənt\ *n* [F *signalement*, fr. *signaler*] (1778) : description by peculiar, appropriate, or characteristic marks; *specif* : the systematic description of a person for purposes of identification
sig•na•to•ry \ˈsig-nə-ˌtōr-ē, -ˌtȯr-\ *n, pl* **-ries** [L *signatorius* of sealing, fr. *signare*] (1866) : a signer with another or others ⟨signatories to a petition⟩; *esp* : a government bound with others by a signed convention — **signatory** *adj*
sig•na•ture \ˈsig-nə-ˌchùr, -chər, -ˌtyùr, -ˌtùr\ *n* [MF or ML; MF, fr. ML *signatura*, fr. L *signatus*, pp. of *signare* to sign, seal] (1536) **1 a** : the act of signing one's name **b** : the name of a person written with his or her own hand **2** : a feature in the appearance or qualities of a natural object formerly held to indicate its utility in medicine **3 a** : a letter or figure placed usu. at the bottom of the first page on each sheet of printed pages (as of a book) as a direction to the binder in arranging and gathering the sheets **b** : a folded sheet that is one unit of a book **4 a** : KEY SIGNATURE **b** : TIME SIGNATURE **5** : the part of a medical prescription that contains the directions to the patient **6** : something (as a tune, style, or logo) that serves to identify; *also* : a characteristic mark
sign•board \ˈsīn-ˌbȯrd, -ˌbȯrd\ *n* (1632) : a board bearing a notice or sign
signed \ˈsīnd\ *adj* (1873) : having a sign and esp. a plus or minus sign ⟨~ numbers like +6 and −4⟩
¹**sig•net** \ˈsig-nət\ *n* [ME, fr. MF, dim. of *signe* sign, seal] (14c) **1** : a seal used officially to give personal authority to a document in lieu of signature **2** : the impression made by or as if by a signet **3** : a small intaglio seal (as in a finger ring)
²**signet** *vt* (15c) : to stamp or authenticate with a signet
signet ring *n* (1681) : a finger ring engraved with a signet, seal, or monogram : SEAL RING
sig•nif•i•cance \sig-ˈni-fi-kən(t)s\ *n* (13c) **1 a** : something that is conveyed as a meaning often obscurely or indirectly **b** : the quality of conveying or implying **2 a** : the quality of being important : MOMENT **b** : the quality of being statistically significant *syn* see IMPORTANCE
significance level *n* (1947) : LEVEL OF SIGNIFICANCE
sig•nif•i•can•cy \sig-ˈni-fi-kən(t)-sē\ *n* (ca. 1595) : SIGNIFICANCE
sig•nif•i•cant \-kənt\ *adj* [L *significant-, significans*, prp. of *significare* to signify] (1579) **1** : having meaning; *esp* : SUGGESTIVE ⟨a ~ glance⟩ **2 a** : having or likely to have influence or effect : IMPORTANT ⟨a ~ piece of legislation⟩; *also* : of a noticeably or measurably large amount ⟨a ~ number of layoffs⟩ ⟨producing ~ profits⟩ **b** : probably caused by something other than mere chance ⟨statistically ~ correlation between vitamin deficiency and disease⟩

significant digit *n* (1923) : one of the digits of a number beginning with the digit farthest to the left that is not zero and ending with the last digit farthest to the right that is not zero or is a zero considered to be exact — called also *significant figure*
sig•nif•i•cant•ly \sig-ˈni-fi-kənt-lē\ *adv* (1577) **1** : in a significant manner : to a significant degree **2** : it is significant
significant other *n* (1953) : a person who is important to one's well-being; *esp* : a spouse or one in a similar relationship
sig•nif•i•ca•tion \ˌsig-nə-fə-ˈkā-shən\ *n* (14c) **1 a** : the act or process of signifying by signs or other symbolic means **b** : a formal notification **2** : PURPORT; *esp* : the meaning that a term, symbol, or character regularly conveys or is intended to convey **3** *chiefly dial* : IMPORTANCE, CONSEQUENCE
sig•nif•i•ca•tive \sig-ˈni-fi-ˌkā-tiv\ *adj* (15c) **1** : SIGNIFICANT, SUGGESTIVE **2** : INDICATIVE ⟨symptoms ~ of malaria⟩
sig•nif•ics \sig-ˈni-fiks\ *n pl but sing or pl in constr* [*signify*] (1896) : SEMIOTIC, SEMANTICS
signified *n* (1939) : a concept or meaning as distinguished from the sign through which it is communicated — compare SIGNIFIER 2
sig•nif•i•er \ˈsig-nə-ˌfī(-ə)r\ *n* (1532) **1** : one that signifies **2** : a symbol, sound, or image (as a word) that represents an underlying concept or meaning — compare SIGNIFIED
sig•ni•fy \ˈsig-nə-ˌfī\ *vb* **-fied; -fy•ing** [ME *signifien*, fr. OF *signifier*, fr. L *significare* to indicate, signify, fr. *signum* sign] *vt* (13c) **1 a** : to be a sign of : MEAN **b** : IMPLY **2** : to show esp. by a conventional token (as word, signal, or gesture) ~ *vi* **1** : to have significance : MATTER **2** : to engage in signifying
sig•ni•fy•ing \ˈsig-nə-ˌfī-iŋ\ *n* (1959) : a good-natured needling or goading esp. among urban blacks by means of indirect gibes and clever often preposterous put-downs; *also* : DOZENS
sign in *vi* (1930) : to make a record of arrival by signing a register or punching a time clock ~ *vt* : to record arrival of (a person) or receipt of (an article) by signing
sign language *n* (1847) **1** : a formal language employing a system of hand gestures for communication (as by the deaf) **2** : an unsystematic method of communicating chiefly by manual gestures used by people speaking different languages
sign of aggregation *n* (ca. 1942) : any of various conventional devices (as braces, brackets, parentheses, or vinculums) used in mathematics to indicate that two or more terms are to be treated as one quantity
sign off *vi* (1926) **1** : to announce the end of something (as a message or broadcast) **2** : to approve or acknowledge something by or as if by a signature ⟨*sign off* on a memo⟩ — **sign–off** \ˈsī-ˌnȯf\ *n*
sign of the cross (14c) : a gesture of the hand forming a cross esp. on forehead, breast, and shoulders to profess Christian faith or invoke divine protection or blessing
sign on *vi* (1885) **1** : to engage oneself by or as if by a signature **2** : to announce the start of broadcasting for the day — **sign–on** \ˈsī-ˌnȯn, -ˌnän\ *n*
si•gnor *also* **si•gnior** \sēn-ˈyȯr, -ˈyȯr\ *n, pl* **signors** *or* **si•gno•ri** \sēn-ˈyȯr-(ˌ)ē, -ˈyȯr\ *also* **signiors** [It *signore, signor*, fr. ML *senior* superior, lord — more at SENOR] (ca. 1580) : an Italian man usu. of rank or gentility — used as a title equivalent to *Mister*
si•gno•ra \sēn-ˈyȯr-ə, -ˈyȯr-\ *n, pl* **signoras** *or* **si•gno•re** \-ˈyȯr-(ˌ)ä, -ˈyȯr-\ [It, fem. of *signore, signor*] (1763) : a married Italian woman usu. of rank or gentility — used as a title equivalent to *Mrs.*
si•gno•re \sēn-ˈyȯr-(ˌ)ä, -ˈyȯr-\ *n, pl* **si•gno•ri** \-ˈyȯr-(ˌ)ē, -ˈyȯr-\ [It] (1594) : SIGNOR
si•gno•ri•na \ˌsē-nyə-ˈrē-nə\ *n, pl* **-nas** *or* **-ne** \-(ˌ)nä\ [It, fr. dim. of *signora*] (1820) : an unmarried Italian woman — used as a title equivalent to *Miss*
si•gno•ry *or* **si•gnio•ry** \ˈsē-nyə-rē\ *n, pl* **si•gno•ries** *or* **si•gnior•ies** [ME *signorie*, fr. MF *seigneurie*] (14c) : SEIGNIORY
sign out *vi* (1948) : to indicate departure by signing a register ~ *vt* : to record or approve the release or departure of — **sign–out** \ˈsī-ˌnaùt\ *n or adj*
¹**sign•post** \ˈsīn-ˌpōst\ *n* (1620) **1** : a post (as at the fork of a road) with signs on it to direct travelers **2** : GUIDE, BEACON
²**signpost** *vt* (1895) : to provide with signposts or guides
sign up *vi* (1903) : to sign one's name (as to a contract) in order to obtain, do, or join something ⟨*sign up* for insurance⟩ ⟨*sign up* for classes⟩ — **sign–up** \ˈsī-ˌnəp\ *n or adj*
Sig•urd \ˈsi-gùrd, -gərd\ *n* [ON *Sigurthr*] : a hero in Norse mythology who slays the dragon Fafnir
sike \ˈsīk\ *n* [ME, fr. OE *sīc*; akin to ON *sik* slow stream, OE *sicerian* to trickle] (bef. 12c) **1** *dial chiefly Brit* : a small stream; *esp* : one that dries up in summer **2** *dial chiefly Brit* : DITCH
¹**Sikh** \ˈsēk\ *n* [Hindi, lit., disciple] (1756) : an adherent of a monotheistic religion of India founded about 1500 by Guru Nānak and marked by rejection of idolatry and caste — **Sikh•ism** \ˈsē-ˌki-zəm\ *n*
²**Sikh** *adj* (1845) : of or relating to Sikhs or Sikhism
si•lage \ˈsī-lij\ *n* [short for *ensilage*] (1884) : fodder converted into succulent feed for livestock through processes of anaerobic acid fermentation (as in a silo)
si•lane \ˈsi-ˌlān, ˈsī-\ *n* [ISV *silicon* + *methane*] (1916) : any of various compounds of hydrogen and silicon that have the general formula Si_nH_{2n+2} and are analogous to alkanes
Si•las•tic \sə-ˈlas-tik, sī-\ *trademark* — used for a soft pliable plastic
sild \ˈsil(d)\ *n, pl* **sild** *or* **silds** [Norw] (1921) : a young herring other than a brisling that is canned as a sardine in Norway
¹**si•lence** \ˈsī-lən(t)s\ *n* [ME, fr. OF, fr. L *silentium*, fr. *silent-, silens*] (13c) **1** : forbearance from speech or noise : MUTENESS **2** : absence of sound or noise : STILLNESS **3** : absence of mention: **a** : OBLIVION, OBSCURITY **b** : SECRECY ⟨weapons research was conducted in ~⟩

\ə\ abut \ᵊ\ kitten, F table \ər\ further \a\ ash \ā\ ace \ä\ mop, mar
\aù\ out \ch\ chin \e\ bet \ē\ easy \g\ go \i\ hit \ī\ ice \j\ job
\ŋ\ sing \ō\ go \ȯ\ law \ȯi\ boy \th\ thin \t̲h̲\ the \ü\ loot \ù\ foot
\y\ yet \zh\ vision \à, k̲, ⁿ, œ, œ̄, ᵫ, ᵫ̄, ᵞ\ *see* Guide to Pronunciation

²**silence** *vt* **si·lenced; si·lenc·ing** (1597) **1** : to compel or reduce to silence : STILL **2** : to restrain from expression : SUPPRESS **3** : to cause to cease hostile firing or criticism

si·lenc·er \'sī-lən(t)-sər\ *n* (1600) : one that silences: as **a** *chiefly Brit* : the muffler of an internal combustion engine **b** : a silencing device for small arms

¹**si·lent** \'sī-lənt\ *adj* [ME *sylent*, fr. L *silent-, silens*, fr. prp. of *silēre* to be silent; akin to Goth ana*silan* to cease, grow calm] (15c) **1 a** : making no utterance : MUTE, SPEECHLESS **b** : indisposed to speak : not loquacious **2** : free from sound or noise : STILL **3** : performed or borne without utterance : UNSPOKEN ⟨~ prayer⟩ ⟨~ grief⟩ **4 a** : making no mention ⟨history is ~ about this person⟩ **b** : not widely or generally known or appreciated ⟨the ~ pressures on a person in public office⟩ **c** : making no protest or outcry ⟨the ~ majority⟩ **5** : UNPRONOUNCED ⟨~ *b* in *doubt*⟩ **6** : not exhibiting the usual signs or symptoms of presence ⟨a ~ infection⟩ **7 a** : made without spoken dialogue ⟨~ movies⟩ **b** : of or relating to silent movies — **si·lent·ly** *adv* — **si·lent·ness** *n*

syn SILENT, TACITURN, RETICENT, RESERVED, SECRETIVE mean showing restraint in speaking. SILENT implies a habit of saying no more than is needed ⟨the strong, *silent* type⟩. TACITURN implies a temperamental disinclination to speech and usu. connotes unsociability ⟨*taciturn* villagers⟩. RETICENT implies a reluctance to speak out or at length, esp. about one's own affairs ⟨was *reticent* about his plans⟩. RESERVED implies reticence and suggests the restraining influence of caution or formality in checking easy informal conversational exchange ⟨greetings were brief, formal, and *reserved*⟩. SECRETIVE, too, implies reticence but usu. carries a suggestion of deviousness and lack of frankness or of an often ostentatious will to conceal ⟨the *secretive* research and development division⟩.

²**silent** *n* (1929) : a motion picture made without spoken dialogue — usu. used in pl.

silent auction *n* (1952) : an auction in which sealed bids are submitted beforehand

silent butler *n* (1937) : a receptacle with hinged lid for collecting table crumbs and the contents of ashtrays

silent partner *n* (1828) **1** : a partner who is known to the public but has no voice in the conduct of a firm's business **2** : SECRET PARTNER

silent service *n* (ca. 1929) **1** : NAVY — used with *the* **2** : the submarine service — used with the

silent treatment *n* (1947) : an act of completely ignoring a person or thing by resort to silence esp. as a means of expressing contempt or disapproval

si·le·nus \sī-'lē-nəs\ *n, pl* **-ni** \-,nī\ *often cap* [L, fr. Gk *silēnos*, fr. *Silēnos* foster father of Dionysus] : a minor woodland deity and companion of Dionysus in Greek mythology with a horse's ears and tail

si·lex \'sī-,leks\ *n* [L *silic-, silex* hard stone, flint] (ca. 1592) : silica or a siliceous material (as powdered tripoli) esp. for use as a filler in paints or wood

¹**sil·hou·ette** \,si-lə-'wet\ *n* [F, fr. Étienne de *Silhouette* †1767 Fr. controller general of finances; perh. fr. his ephemeral tenure] (1783) **1** : a likeness cut from dark material and mounted on a light ground or one sketched in outline and solidly colored in **2** : the outline of a body viewed as circumscribing a mass ⟨the ~ of a bird⟩ **syn** see OUTLINE

²**silhouette** *vt* **-ett·ed; -ett·ing** (1876) : to represent by a silhouette; *also* : to project on a background like a silhouette — **sil·hou·et·tist** \-'we-tist\ *n*

sil·i·ca \'si-li-kə\ *n* [NL, fr. L *silic-, silex* hard stone, flint] (ca. 1801) : silicon dioxide SiO₂ occurring in crystalline, amorphous, and impure forms (as in quartz, opal, and sand respectively)

silica gel *n* (1919) : colloidal silica resembling coarse white sand in appearance but possessing many fine pores and therefore extremely adsorbent

sil·i·cate \'si-lə-,kāt, -kət\ *n* [*silicic (acid)*] (1811) : a salt or ester derived from a silicic acid; *esp* : any of numerous insoluble often complex metal salts that contain silicon and oxygen in the anion, constitute the largest class of minerals, and are used in building materials (as cement, bricks, and glass)

si·li·ceous *or* **si·li·cious** \sə-'li-shəs\ *adj* [L *siliceus* of flint, fr. *silic-, silex* hard stone, flint] (ca. 1656) : of, relating to, or containing silica or a silicate ⟨~ limestone⟩

si·lic·ic \sə-'li-sik\ *adj* [NL *silica* & NL *silicium* silicon (fr. *silica*)] (1817) : of, relating to, or derived from silica or silicon

silicic acid *n* (1817) : any of various weakly acid substances obtained as gelatinous masses by treating silicates with acids

sil·i·cide \'si-lə-,sīd\ *n* [ISV *silicon* + *-ide*] (ca. 1868) : a binary compound of silicon with a more electropositive element or group

si·lic·i·fi·ca·tion \sə-,li-sə-fə-'kā-shən\ *n* (1830) : the action or process of silicifying : the state of being silicified

si·lic·i·fy \sə-'li-sə-,fī\ *vb* **-fied; -fy·ing** *vt* (ca. 1828) : to convert into or impregnate with silica ~ *vi* : to become silicified

sil·i·con \'si-li-kən, 'si-lə-,kän\ *n* [NL *silica* + E *-on* (as in *carbon*)] (1817) : a tetravalent nonmetallic element that occurs combined as the most abundant element next to oxygen in the earth's crust and is used esp. in alloys and electronic devices — see ELEMENT table

silicon carbide *n* (1893) : a very hard dark crystalline compound SiC of silicon and carbon that is used as an abrasive and as a refractory and in electric resistors

sil·i·cone \'si-lə-,kōn\ *n* [*silicon* + *-one*] (1943) : any of various polymeric organic silicon compounds obtained as oils, greases, or plastics and used esp. for water-resistant and heat-resistant lubricants, varnishes, binders, and electric insulators

silicone rubber *n* (1944) : rubber made from silicone elastomers and noted for its retention of flexibility, resilience, and tensile strength over a wide temperature range

sil·i·con·ized \'si-lə-kə-,nīzd, -,kō-\ *adj* (1949) : treated or coated with a silicone ⟨~ glassware⟩

silicon nitride *n* (1903) : any of several compounds of silicon and nitrogen; *specif* : a compound Si₃N₄ that is a hard ceramic used in high-temperature applications and in composites

sil·i·co·sis \,si-lə-'kō-səs\ *n* [NL, fr. *silica* + *-osis*] (1881) : pneumoconiosis characterized by massive fibrosis of the lungs resulting in shortness of breath and caused by prolonged inhalation of silica dusts — **sil·i·cot·ic** \-'kä-tik\ *adj or n*

si·lique \sə-'lēk\ *n* [F, fr. NL *siliqua*, fr. L, pod, husk] (1785) : a narrow elongated two-valved usu. many-seeded capsule that is characteristic of the mustard family, opens by sutures at either margin, and has two parietal placentas

¹**silk** \'silk\ *n, often attrib* [ME, fr. OE *seolc*, prob. ultim. fr. Gk *sērikos* silken — more at SERICEOUS] (bef. 12c) **1** : a fine continuous protein fiber produced by various insect larvae usu. for cocoons; *esp* : a lustrous tough elastic fiber produced by silkworms and used for textiles **2** : thread, yarn, or fabric made from silk filaments **3 a** : a garment of silk **b** (1) : a distinctive silk gown worn by a King's or Queen's Counsel (2) : a King's or Queen's Counsel **c** *pl* : the colored cap and blouse of a jockey or harness horse driver made in the registered racing color of the employing stable **4 a** : a filament resembling silk; *esp* : one produced by a spider **b** : silky material ⟨milkweed ~⟩; *esp* : the styles of an ear of Indian corn **5** : PARACHUTE — **silk·like** \-,līk\ *adj*

²**silk** *vi* (1783) *of corn* : to develop the silk

silk·a·line *or* **silk·o·line** \,sil-kə-'lēn\ *n* [¹*silk* + *-oline* (as in *crinoline*)] (1896) : a soft light cotton fabric with a smooth lustrous finish like that of silk

silk cotton *n* (1697) : the silky or cottony covering of seeds of various silk-cotton trees; *esp* : KAPOK

silk–cotton tree *n* (1712) : any of various tropical trees (family Bombacaceae, the silk-cotton family) with palmate leaves and large fruits with the seeds enveloped by silk cotton; *esp* : CEIBA 1

silk·en \'sil-kən\ *adj* (bef. 12c) **1** : made or consisting of silk **2** : resembling silk: as **a** : SOFT, LUSTROUS **b** (1) : agreeably smooth : HARMONIOUS (2) : SUAVE, INGRATIATING **3 a** : dressed in silk ⟨~ ankles⟩ **b** : LUXURIOUS 2, 3

silk gland *n* (1870) : a gland that produces a viscid fluid which is extruded in filaments and hardens into silk on exposure to air: as **a** : either of a pair of greatly enlarged and modified salivary glands of an insect larva that produce a compound filament from which a larval or pupal cover (as a cocoon) is spun **b** : any of two or more abdominal glands of a spider that open through spinnerets and produce a filament used chiefly in the spinning of webs

silk hat *n* (1834) : a hat with a tall cylindrical crown and a silk-plush finish worn by men as a dress hat

silk oak *n* (1866) : any of various Australian timber trees (esp. genus *Grevillea*) of the protea family that have mottled wood used in cabinet-making and veneering — called also *silky oak*

silk screen *n* (1930) : a stencil process in which coloring matter is forced onto the material to be printed through the meshes of a silk or organdy screen so prepared as to have pervious printing areas and impervious nonprinting areas; *also* : a print made by this process — **silk–screen** *vt*

silk–stock·ing \'silk-'stä-kiŋ\ *adj* (1798) **1** : ARISTOCRATIC, WEALTHY ⟨a ~ district⟩ **2** : fashionably dressed ⟨a ~ audience⟩ **3** : of or relating to the American Federalist party

silk stocking *n* (1891) **1** : an aristocratic or wealthy person **2** : a fashionably dressed person **3** : FEDERALIST 2

silk tree *n* (ca. 1852) : a leguminous Asian tree (*Albizia julibrissin*) having pink flowers with long silky stamens — called also *mimosa*

silk·weed \'silk-,wēd\ *n* (1784) : MILKWEED

silk·worm \-,wərm\ *n* (bef. 12c) : a moth whose larva spins a large amount of strong silk in constructing its cocoon; *esp* : an Asian moth (*Bombyx mori* of the family Bombycidae) whose rough wrinkled hairless yellowish caterpillar produces the silk of commerce

silkworm: *1* cocoon, *2* larva, *3* adult female

silky \'sil-kē\ *adj* **silk·i·er; -est** (1611) **1** : SILKEN 1, 2 **2** : having or covered with fine soft hairs, plumes, or scales — **silk·i·ly** \-kə-lē\ *adv* — **silk·i·ness** \-kē-nəs\ *n*

silky terrier *n* (1959) : any of a breed of low-set toy terriers of Australian origin that have a flat silky glossy coat colored blue with tan on the head, chest, and legs — called also *silky*

sill \'sil\ *n* [ME *sille*, fr. OE *syll*; akin to OHG *swelli* beam, threshold] (bef. 12c) **1** : a horizontal piece (as a timber) that forms the lowest member or one of the lowest members of a framework or supporting structure: as **a** : the horizontal member at the base of a window **b** : the threshold of a door **2** : a tabular body of igneous rock injected while molten between sedimentary or volcanic beds or along foliation planes of metamorphic rocks **3** : a submerged ridge at relatively shallow depth between the basins of two bodies of water

sillabub *var of* SYLLABUB

sil·li·man·ite \'si-lə-mə-,nīt\ *n* [Benjamin *Silliman* †1864 Am. geologist] (ca. 1830) : a brown, grayish, or pale green mineral that consists of an aluminum silicate in orthorhombic crystals often occurring in fibrous or columnar forms

sil·ly \'si-lē\ *adj* **sil·li·er; -est** [ME *sely, silly* happy, innocent, pitiable, feeble, fr. OE *sǣlig*, fr. OE *sǣl* happiness; akin to OHG *sālig* happy] (14c) **1** *archaic* : HELPLESS, WEAK **2 a** : RUSTIC, PLAIN **b** *obs* : lowly in station : HUMBLE **3 a** : weak in intellect : FOOLISH **b** : exhibiting or indicative of a lack of common sense or sound judgment ⟨a very ~ mistake⟩ **c** : TRIFLING, FRIVOLOUS **4** : being stunned or dazed ⟨scared ~⟩ ⟨knocked me ~⟩ **syn** see SIMPLE — **sil·li·ly** \'si-lə-lē\ *adv* — **sil·li·ness** \'si-lē-nəs\ *n* — **silly** *n or adv*

silly season *n* (1861) **1** : a period (as late summer) when newspapers often resort to trivial or frivolous matters for lack of major news stories

2 : a period marked by frivolous, outlandish, or illogical activity or behavior

si·lo \'sī-(ˌ)lō\ *n, pl* **silos** [Sp] (1881) **1 :** a trench, pit, or esp. a tall cylinder (as of wood or concrete) usu. sealed to exclude air and used for making and storing silage **2 a :** a deep bin for storing material (as cement or coal) **b :** an underground structure for housing a guided missile

si·lox·ane \sə-'läk-ˌsān, sī-\ *n* [*sil*icon + *ox*ygen + meth*ane*] (1917) **:** any of various compounds containing alternate silicon and oxygen atoms in either a linear or cyclic arrangement usu. with one or two organic groups attached to each silicon atom

¹silt \'silt\ *n* [ME *cylte*, prob. of Scand origin; akin to Dan *sylt* salt marsh; akin to OHG *sulza* salt marsh, OE *sealt* salt] (15c) **1 :** loose sedimentary material with rock particles usu. ¹/₂₀ millimeter or less in diameter; *also* **:** soil containing 80 percent or more of such silt and less than 12 percent of clay **2 :** a deposit of sediment (as by a river) — **silty** \'sil-tē\ *adj*

²silt *vi* (1799) **:** to become choked or obstructed with silt — often used with *up* ⟨the channel ∼*ed up*⟩ ∼ *vt* **:** to choke, fill, cover, or obstruct with silt or mud ⟨the beaver had ∼*ed* the creek —Hugh Fosburgh⟩ — **sil·ta·tion** \sil-'tā-shən\ *n*

silt·stone \'silt-ˌstōn\ *n* (ca. 1920) **:** a rock composed chiefly of indurated silt

Sil·u·res \'sil-yə-ˌrēz\ *n* [L] (ca. 1895) **:** a people of ancient Britain described by Tacitus as occupying chiefly southern Wales

Si·lu·ri·an \si-'lùr-ē-ən, sə-\ *adj* [L *Silures*] (1708) **1 :** of or relating to the Silures or their place of habitation **2 :** of, relating to, or being a period of the Paleozoic era between the Ordovician and Devonian or the corresponding system of rocks marked by numerous eurypterid crustaceans and the appearance of the first land plants — see GEOLOGIC TIME table — **Silurian** *n*

sil·va \'sil-və\ *n* [NL, fr. L, wood, forest] (ca. 1848) **:** the forest trees of a region or country

silvan *var of* SYLVAN

¹sil·ver \'sil-vər\ *n* [ME, fr. OE *seolfor*; akin to OHG *silbar* silver, Lith *sidabras*] (bef. 12c) **1 :** a white metallic element that is sonorous, ductile, very malleable, capable of a high degree of polish, and chiefly univalent in compounds, and that has the highest thermal and electric conductivity of any substance — see ELEMENT table **2 :** silver as a commodity ⟨the value of ∼ has risen⟩ **3 :** coin made of silver **4 :** articles (as hollowware or table flatware) made of or plated with silver; *also* **:** similar articles esp. flatware of other metals (as stainless steel) **5 :** a nearly neutral slightly brownish medium gray

²silver *adj* (bef. 12c) **1 :** made of silver **2 :** resembling silver: as **a :** having a white lustrous sheen **b :** giving a soft resonant sound **:** dulcet in tone **c :** eloquently persuasive **3 :** consisting of or yielding silver **4 :** of, relating to, or characteristic of silver **5 :** advocating the use of silver as a standard of currency **6 :** of, relating to, or being a 25th anniversary or its celebration

³silver *vt* **sil·vered; sil·ver·ing** \'sil-v(ə-)riŋ\ (14c) **1 a :** to cover with silver (as by electroplating) **b :** to coat with a substance (as a metal) resembling silver **2 :** to give a silvery luster to **b :** to make white like silver — **sil·ver·er** \'sil-vər-ər\ *n*

silver age *n* (1565) **:** an historical period of achievement secondary to that of a golden age

sil·ver·back \'sil-vər-ˌbak\ *n* (1963) **:** an older adult usu. dominant male gorilla having gray or whitish hair on the back

silver bell *n* (1785) **:** any of a genus (*Halesia*) of trees and shrubs of the storax family; *esp* **:** one (*H. carolina*) of the southeastern U.S. cultivated for its bell-shaped white flowers

sil·ver·ber·ry \'sil-vər-ˌber-ē\ *n* (1856) **:** a silvery No. American shrub (*Elaeagnus commutata*) of the oleaster family

silver bromide *n* (1885) **:** a compound AgBr that is extremely sensitive to light and is much used in the preparation of sensitive emulsion coatings for photographic materials

silver bullet *n* (1935) **:** something that acts as a magical weapon; *esp* **:** one that instantly solves a long-standing problem

silver certificate *n* (1882) **:** a certificate formerly issued against the deposit of silver coin as legal tender in the U.S. and its possessions

silver chloride *n* (1885) **:** a compound AgCl sensitive to light and used esp. for photographic materials

silver cord *n* [*The Silver Cord* (1926), play by Sidney Howard] (1942) **:** the emotional tie between mother and child and esp. son

silver fir *n* (1707) **:** any of various firs (genus *Abies*) with leaves that are white or silvery white beneath; *esp* **:** a valuable European timber tree (*A. alba*)

sil·ver·fish \'sil-vər-ˌfish\ *n* (1703) **1 :** any of various silvery fishes (as a tarpon or silversides) **2 :** any of various small wingless insects (order Thysanura); *esp* **:** one (*Lepisma saccharina*) found in houses and sometimes injurious esp. to sized papers or starched clothes

silver fox *n* (ca. 1792) **:** a genetically determined color phase of the common red fox in which the fur is black tipped with white

silver hake *n* (1884) **:** a common hake (*Merluccius bilinearis*) of the northern Atlantic coast of the U.S. that is an important food fish

silver iodide *n* (1885) **:** a compound AgI that darkens on exposure to light and is used in photography, rainmaking, and medicine

silver lining *n* [fr. the phrase "every cloud has a *silver lining*"] (1871) **:** a consoling or hopeful prospect

sil·ver·ly \'sil-vər-lē\ *adv* (1595) **:** with silvery appearance or sound

silver maple *n* (1765) **1 :** a common maple (*Acer saccharinum*) of eastern No. America with deeply cut leaves that are light green above and silvery white below **2 :** the hard close-grained but brittle light brown wood of the silver maple

sil·vern \'sil-vərn\ *adj* (bef. 12c) **1 :** made of silver **2 :** resembling or characteristic of silver **:** SILVERY

silver nitrate *n* (1885) **:** an irritant compound AgNO₃ that in contact with organic matter turns black and is used as a chemical reagent, in photography, and in medicine esp. as an antiseptic and caustic

silver paper *n* (ca. 1875) **:** TIN FOIL

silver perch *n* (1820) **:** any of various somewhat silvery fishes that resemble perch: as **a :** a drum (*Bairdiella chrysoura*) that occurs esp. along the more southern Atlantic coast of the U.S. — called also *mademoiselle, yellowtail* **b :** WHITE PERCH 1

silver plate *n* (1610) **1 :** domestic flatware and hollowware of silver or of a silver-plated base metal **2 :** a plating of silver

sil·ver·point \'sil-vər-ˌpóint\ *n* (1882) **:** a drawing technique utilizing a pencil of silver usu. on specially prepared paper or parchment

silver protein *n* (1928) **:** any of several colloidal light-sensitive preparations of silver and protein used in aqueous solution on mucous membranes as antiseptics

silver salmon *n* (1878) **:** COHO

silver screen *n* (1918) **1 :** a motion-picture screen **2 :** MOTION PICTURES

sil·ver·side \'sil-vər-ˌsīd\ *n* (1820) **:** SILVERSIDES

sil·ver·sides \'sil-vər-ˌsīdz\ *n pl but sing or pl in constr* (1851) **:** any of various small bony fishes (family Atherinidae) with a silvery stripe along each side of the body

sil·ver·smith \-ˌsmith\ *n* (bef. 12c) **:** an artisan who makes articles of silverware — **sil·ver·smith·ing** *n*

silver spoon *n* [fr. the phrase "born with a *silver spoon* in one's mouth" (born wealthy)] (1801) **1 :** WEALTH; *esp* **:** inherited wealth

silver standard *n* (1860) **:** a monetary standard under which the currency unit is defined by a stated quantity of silver

Silver Star Medal *n* (1932) **:** a U.S. military decoration awarded for gallantry in action

sil·ver·tongued \'sil-vər-ˌtəŋd\ *adj* (1592) **:** marked by convincing and eloquent expression

sil·ver·ware \'sil-vər-ˌwar, -ˌwer\ *n* (1860) **1 :** SILVER PLATE 1 **2 :** FLATWARE

sil·ver·weed \-ˌwēd\ *n* (1578) **:** any of several cinquefoils with leaves silvery or white-tomentose beneath; *esp* **:** one (*Potentilla anserina*) with silky hairs over the entire plant

sil·very \'sil-v(ə-)rē\ *adj* (14c) **1 :** having the luster of silver **2 :** having a soft clear musical tone **:** RESONANT ⟨a ∼ voice⟩ **3 :** containing or consisting of silver — **sil·ver·i·ness** *n*

sil·vex \'sil-ˌveks\ *n* [prob. fr. L *silva* wood + E *ex*terminator] (1961) **:** a selective herbicide C₉H₇Cl₃O₃ esp. effective in controlling woody plants but toxic to animals

sil·vi·cul·ture \'sil-və-ˌkəl-chər\ *n* [F, fr. L *silva* + *cultura* culture] (1880) **:** a branch of forestry dealing with the development and care of forests — **sil·vi·cul·tur·al** \ˌsil-və-'kəlch-rəl, -'kəl-chə-\ *adj* — **sil·vi·cul·tur·al·ly** \-rə-lē\ *adv* — **sil·vi·cul·tur·ist** \ˌsil-və-'kəlch-rist, -'kəl-chə-\ *n*

si·ma·zine \'sī-mə-ˌzēn\ *n* [*sim-* (prob. alter. of *sym-* symmetrical, prefix used in names of organic compounds) + *triazine*] (1956) **:** a selective herbicide C₇H₁₂N₅Cl used to control weeds esp. among crop plants

Sim·chas To·rah \ˌsim-kəs-'tōr-ə, -'tór-\ *n* [Heb *simḥath tōrāh* rejoicing of the Torah] (1891) **:** a Jewish holiday observed on the 23d of Tishri in celebration of the completion of the annual reading of the Torah

Sim·e·on \'si-mē-ən\ *n* [LL, fr. Gk *Symeōn*, fr. Heb *Shim'ōn*] **1 :** a son of Jacob and the traditional eponymous ancestor of one of the tribes of Israel **2 :** a devout man of Jerusalem held to have uttered the Nunc Dimittis on seeing the infant Jesus in the temple

¹sim·i·an \'si-mē-ən\ *adj* [L *simia* ape, fr. *simus* snub-nosed, fr. Gk *simos*] (1607) **:** of, relating to, or resembling monkeys or apes

²simian *n* (1880) **:** MONKEY, APE

sim·i·lar \'si-mə-lər, 'sim-lər\ *adj* [F *similaire*, fr. L *similis* like, similar — more at SAME] (1611) **1 :** having characteristics in common **:** strictly comparable **2 :** alike in substance or essentials **:** CORRESPONDING ⟨no two animal habitats are exactly ∼ —W. H. Dowdeswell⟩ **3 :** not differing in shape but only in size or position ⟨∼ triangles⟩ ⟨∼ polygons⟩ — **sim·i·lar·ly** *adv*

syn SIMILAR, ANALOGOUS, PARALLEL mean closely resembling each other. SIMILAR implies the possibility of being mistaken for each other ⟨all the houses in the development are *similar*⟩. ANALOGOUS applies to things belonging in essentially different categories but nevertheless having many similarities ⟨*analogous* political systems⟩. PARALLEL suggests a marked likeness in the development of two things ⟨the *parallel* careers of two movie stars⟩.

sim·i·lar·i·ty \ˌsi-mə-'lar-ə-tē\ *n, pl* **-ties** (1664) **1 :** the quality or state of being similar **:** RESEMBLANCE **2 :** a comparable aspect **:** CORRESPONDENCE **syn** see LIKENESS

sim·i·le \'si-mə-(ˌ)lē\ *n* [ME, fr. L, comparison, fr. neut. of *similis*] (14c) **:** a figure of speech comparing two unlike things that is often introduced by *like* or *as* (as in *cheeks like roses*) — compare METAPHOR

si·mil·i·tude \sə-'mi-lə-ˌtüd, -ˌtyüd\ *n* [ME, fr. MF, resemblance, likeness, fr. L *similitudo*, fr. *similis*] (14c) **1 a :** COUNTERPART, DOUBLE **b :** a visible likeness **:** IMAGE **2 :** an imaginative comparison **:** SIMILE **3 a :** correspondence in kind or quality **b :** a point of comparison **syn** see LIKENESS

Sim·men·tal *also* **Sim·men·thal** \'zi-mən-ˌtäl\ *n* [*Simmental,* valley of the Simme River in Switzerland] (1906) **:** any of a breed of large buff or dull red and white cattle of Swiss origin that are used widely throughout the world for meat and milk

¹sim·mer \'si-mər\ *vb* **sim·mered; sim·mer·ing** \'si-mə-riŋ, 'sim-riŋ\ [alter. of E dial. *simper,* fr. ME *simperen,* of imit. origin] *vi* (1653) **1 :** to stew gently below or just at the boiling point **2 a :** to be in a state of incipient development **:** FERMENT ⟨ideas ∼*ing* in the back of my mind⟩ **b :** to be in inward turmoil **:** SEETHE ∼ *vt* **:** to cook slowly in a liquid just below the boiling point

²simmer *n* (1809) **:** the state of simmering

simmer down *vi* (1871) **1 :** to become calm or peaceful **2 :** to become reduced by or as if by simmering

sim·nel \'sim-nᵊl\ *n* [ME *simenel,* fr. MF, ultim. fr. L *simila* wheat flour] (13c) **1 :** a bun or bread of fine wheat flour **2** *Brit* **:** a rich fruitcake sometimes coated with almond paste and baked for mid-Lent, Easter, and Christmas

si·mo·le·on \sə-'mō-lē-ən\ *n* [origin unknown] (1896) *slang* **:** DOLLAR

Si·mon \'sī-mən\ *n* [Gk *Simōn,* fr. Heb *Shim'ōn*] **1 :** PETER — called

\ə\ abut \ᵊ\ kitten, F table \ər\ further \a\ ash \ā\ ace \ä\ mop, mar \aù\ out \ch\ chin \e\ bet \ē\ easy \g\ go \i\ hit \ī\ ice \j\ job \ŋ\ sing \ō\ go \ò\ law \òi\ boy \th\ thin \t͟h\ the \ü\ loot \ù\ foot \y\ yet \zh\ vision \à, k̲, ⁿ, œ, œ̄, ᴜᴇ, ᵫ, ᵊ\ *see* Guide to Pronunciation also *Simon Peter* **2** : one of the twelve disciples of Jesus — called also *Simon the Zealot* **3** : a kinsman of Jesus **4** : a Cyrenian constrained to help Jesus bear his cross to his place of crucifixion — called also *Simon the Cyrenian* **5** : SIMON MAGUS

si·mo·ni·ac \sī-'mō-nē-,ak, sə-\ *n* [ME, fr. MF or ML; MF *simoniaque*, fr. ML *simoniacus*, fr. LL *simonia* simony] (14c) : one who practices simony — **simoniac** *or* **si·mo·ni·a·cal** \,sī-mə-'nī-ə-kəl, ,si-\ *adj* — **si·mo·ni·a·cal·ly** \-k(ə-)lē\ *adv*

si·mo·nize \'sī-mə-,nīz\ *vt* **-nized; -niz·ing** [fr. *Simoniz*, a trademark] (1934) : to polish with or as if with wax

Si·mon Le·gree \,sī-mən-lə-'grē\ *n* : a slave owner who has Tom flogged to death in Harriet B. Stowe's novel *Uncle Tom's Cabin*

Simon Ma·gus \-'mā-gəs\ *n* : a Samaritan sorcerer converted by the apostle Philip and severely rebuked by Peter for offering money for the gifts of the Holy Ghost

si·mon–pure \,sī-mən-'pyùr\ *adj* [fr. *the real Simon Pure*, alluding to a character impersonated by another in the play *A Bold Stroke for a Wife* (1718) by Susannah Centlivre †1723 Eng. dramatist and actress] (1840) : of untainted purity or integrity; *also* : pretentiously or hypocritically pure

si·mo·ny \'sī-mə-nē, 'si-\ *n* [ME *symonie*, fr. LL *simonia*, fr. *Simon Magus*, Samaritan sorcerer in Acts 8: 9–24] (13c) : the buying or selling of a church office or ecclesiastical preferment

si·moom \sə-'müm, si-\ *or* **si·moon** \-'mün\ *n* [Ar *samūm*] (1790) : a hot dry violent dust-laden wind from Asian and African deserts

simp \'simp\ *n* (1903) : SIMPLETON

sim·pa·ti·co \sim-'pä-ti-,kō, -'pa-\ *adj* [It *simpatico* & Sp *simpático*, ultim. fr. L *sympathia* sympathy] (1864) **1** : AGREEABLE, LIKABLE **2** : being on the same wavelength : CONGENIAL, SYMPATHETIC

¹sim·per \'sim-pər\ *vb* **sim·pered; sim·per·ing** \-p(ə-)riŋ\ [perh. of Scand origin; akin to Dan dial. *simper* affected, coy] *vi* (ca. 1563) : to smile in a silly manner ~ *vt* : to say with a simper ⟨~ed an apology⟩ — **sim·per·er** \-pər-ər\ *n*

²simper *n* (1599) : a silly smile : SMIRK

¹sim·ple \'sim-pəl\ *adj* **sim·pler** \-p(ə-)lər\; **sim·plest** \-p(ə-)ləst\ [ME, fr. OF, plain, uncomplicated, artless, fr. L *simplus, simplex*, lit., single; L *simplus* fr. *sem-, sim-* one + *-plus* multiplied by; L *simplic-, simplex* fr. *sem-, sim-* + *-plic-, -plex* -fold — more at SAME, -FOLD] (13c) **1** : free from guile : INNOCENT **2 a** : free from vanity : MODEST **b** : free from ostentation or display **3** : of humble origin or modest position ⟨a ~ farmer⟩ **4 a** : lacking in knowledge or expertise ⟨a ~ amateur of the arts⟩ **b** : STUPID; *esp* : mentally retarded **c** : not socially or culturally sophisticated : NAIVE; *also* : CREDULOUS **5 a** : SHEER, UNMIXED ⟨~ honesty⟩ **b** : free of secondary complications ⟨a ~ vitamin deficiency⟩ **c** (1) : having only one main clause and no subordinate clauses ⟨a ~ sentence⟩ (2) *of a subject or predicate* : having no modifiers, complements, or objects **d** : constituting a basic element : FUNDAMENTAL **e** : not made up of many like units ⟨a ~ eye⟩ **6** : free from elaboration or figuration ⟨~ harmony⟩ **7 a** (1) : not subdivided into branches or leaflets ⟨a ~ stem⟩ ⟨a ~ leaf⟩ (2) : consisting of a single carpel (3) : developing from a single ovary ⟨a ~ fruit⟩ **b** : controlled by a single gene ⟨~ inherited characters⟩ **8** : not limited or restricted : UNCONDITIONAL ⟨a ~ obligation⟩ **9** : readily understood or performed ⟨~ directions⟩ ⟨the adjustment was ~ to make⟩ **10** *of a statistical hypothesis* : specifying exact values for one or more statistical parameters — compare COMPOSITE 3 — **sim·ple·ness** \-pəl-nəs\ *n*

syn SIMPLE, FOOLISH, SILLY, FATUOUS, ASININE mean actually or apparently deficient in intelligence. SIMPLE implies a degree of intelligence inadequate to cope with anything complex or involving mental effort ⟨considered people *simple* who had trouble with computers⟩. FOOLISH implies the character of being or seeming unable to use judgment, discretion, or good sense ⟨*foolish* stunts⟩. SILLY suggests failure to act as a rational being esp. by ridiculous behavior ⟨the *silly* antics of revelers⟩. FATUOUS implies foolishness, inanity, and disregard of reality ⟨*fatuous* conspiracy theories⟩. ASININE suggests utter and contemptible failure to use normal rationality or perception ⟨an *asinine* plot⟩. *syn* see in addition EASY

²simple *n* (14c) **1 a** : a person of humble birth : COMMONER ⟨thought very little of anybody, ~s or gentry —Virginia Woolf⟩ **b** (1) : a rude or credulous person : IGNORAMUS (2) : a mentally retarded person **2 a** : a medicinal plant **b** : a vegetable drug having only one ingredient **3** : one component of a complex; *specif* : an unanalyzable constituent

simple closed curve *n* (1919) : a closed plane curve (as a circle or an ellipse) that does not intersect itself — called also *Jordan curve*

simple equation *n* (1798) : a linear equation

simple fraction *n* (1910) : a fraction having whole numbers for the numerator and denominator — compare COMPLEX FRACTION

simple fracture *n* (1685) : a bone fracture that does not form an open wound in the skin — compare COMPOUND FRACTURE

simple interest *n* (1798) : interest paid or computed on the original principal only of a loan or on the amount of an account

simple machine *n* (1704) : any of various elementary mechanisms formerly considered as the elements of which all machines are composed and including the lever, the wheel and axle, the pulley, the inclined plane, the wedge, and the screw

sim·ple–mind·ed \,sim-pəl-'mīn-dəd, 'sim-pəl-,\ *adj* (1744) : devoid of subtlety : UNSOPHISTICATED; *also* : FOOLISH — **sim·ple·mind·ed·ly** *adv* — **sim·ple·mind·ed·ness** *n*

simple protein *n* (ca. 1909) : a protein (as a globulin) that yields amino acids as the chief or only products of complete hydrolysis — compare CONJUGATED PROTEIN

simple sugar *n* (1942) : MONOSACCHARIDE

sim·ple·ton \'sim-pəl-tən\ *n* [¹*simple* + *-ton* (as in surnames such as *Washington*)] (1650) : a person lacking in common sense

simple vow *n* (1759) : a public vow taken by a religious in the Roman Catholic Church under which retention of property by the individual is permitted and marriage though illicit is valid under canon law

¹sim·plex \'sim-,pleks\ *adj* [L *simplic-, simplex* — more at SIMPLE] (1594) **1** : SIMPLE, SINGLE **2** : allowing telecommunication in only one direction at a time ⟨~ system⟩

²simplex *n, pl* **sim·plex·es** \-plə-,sēz\ *or* **sim·pli·ces** \-plə-,sēz\ : a simple word **2** : a spatial configuration of *n* dimensions determined by *n* + 1 points in a space of dimen-

sion equal to or greater than *n* ⟨a triangle together with its interior determined by its three vertices is a two-dimensional ~ in the plane or any space of higher dimension⟩

sim·pli·cial \sim-'pli-shəl\ *adj* (1926) : of or relating to simplexes — **sim·pli·cial·ly** \-shə-lē\ *adv*

sim·plic·i·ty \sim-'pli-sə-tē, -'plis-tē\ *n* [ME *simplicite*, fr. MF *simplicité*, fr. L *simplicitat-, simplicitas*, fr. *simplic-, simplex*] (14c) **1** : the state of being simple, uncomplicated, or uncompounded **2** : lack of subtlety or penetration : INNOCENCE, NAIVETÉ **b** : FOLLY, SILLINESS **3** : freedom from pretense or guile : CANDOR **4 a** : directness of expression : CLARITY **b** : restraint in ornamentation : AUSTERITY

sim·pli·fy \'sim-plə-,fī\ *vt* **-fied; -fy·ing** [F *simplifier*, fr. ML *simplificare*, fr. L *simplus* simple] (1759) : to make simple or simpler: as **a** : to reduce to basic essentials **b** : to diminish in scope or complexity : STREAMLINE ⟨was urged to ~ management procedures⟩ **c** : to make more intelligible : CLARIFY — **sim·pli·fi·ca·tion** \,sim-plə-fə-'kā-shən\ *n* — **sim·pli·fi·er** \'sim-plə-,fī(-ə)r\ *n*

sim·plism \'sim-,pli-zəm\ *n* (ca. 1882) : the act or an instance of oversimplifying; *esp* : the reduction of a problem to a false simplicity by ignoring complicating factors

sim·plis·tic \sim-'plis-tik\ *adj* (ca. 1881) **1** : SIMPLE **2** : of, relating to, or characterized by simplism : OVERSIMPLE ⟨adequate, if occasionally ~, historical background —Harlow Robinson⟩ — **sim·plis·ti·cal·ly** \-ti-k(ə-)lē\ *adv*

sim·ply \'sim-plē, *for 1 also* -pə-lē\ *adv* (14c) **1 a** : without ambiguity : CLEARLY **b** : without embellishment : PLAINLY **c** : DIRECTLY, CANDIDLY **2 a** : SOLELY, MERELY ⟨eats ~ to keep alive⟩ ⟨~ cleaned it up and went to bed —Garrison Keillor⟩ **b** : REALLY, LITERALLY ⟨the concert was ~ marvelous⟩ — often used as an intensive ⟨~ crawling with geniuses —F. Scott Fitzgerald⟩

simply connected *adj* (1893) : being or characterized by a surface that is divided into two separate parts by every closed curve it contains

simply ordered *adj* (ca. 1909) : having any two elements connected by a relationship that is reflexive, antisymmetric, and transitive

Simp·son's rule \'sim(p)-sənz-\ *n* [Thomas *Simpson* †1761 Eng. mathematician] (1875) : a method for approximating the area under a curve over a given interval that involves partitioning the interval by an odd number *n* + 1 of equally spaced ordinates and adding the areas of the *n*/2 figures formed by pairs of successive odd-numbered ordinates and the parabolas which they determine with their included even-numbered ordinates

sim·u·la·cre \'sim-yə-,lā-kər, -,la-\ *n* [ME, fr. MF, fr. L *simulacrum*] (14c) *archaic* : SIMULACRUM

sim·u·la·crum \,sim-yə-'la-krəm, -'lā-\ *n, pl* **-cra** \-krə\ *also* **-crums** [ME, fr. L, fr. *simulare*] (15c) **1** : IMAGE, REPRESENTATION ⟨a reasonable ~ of reality —Martin Mayer⟩ **2** : an insubstantial form or semblance of something : TRACE

¹sim·u·lar \'sim-yə-lər, -,lär\ *n* [irreg. fr. L *simulare* to simulate] (1526) *archaic* : one that simulates : DISSEMBLER

²simular *adj* (1611) *archaic* : COUNTERFEIT, PRETENDED

sim·u·late \'sim-yə-,lāt\ *vt* **-lat·ed; -lat·ing** [L *simulatus*, pp. of *simulare* to copy, represent, feign, fr. *similis* like — more at SAME] (1652) **1** : to give or assume the appearance or effect of often with the intent to deceive : IMITATE **2** : to make a simulation of (as a physical system) — *syn* see ASSUME — **sim·u·la·tive** \-,lā-tiv\ *adj*

simulated *adj* (1622) : made to look genuine : FAKE ⟨~ pearls⟩

sim·u·la·tion \,sim-yə-'lā-shən\ *n* [ME *simulacion*, fr. MF, fr. L *simulation-, simulatio*, fr. *simulare*] (14c) **1** : the act or process of simulating **2** : a sham object : COUNTERFEIT **3 a** : the imitative representation of the functioning of one system or process by means of the functioning of another ⟨a computer ~ of an industrial process⟩ **b** : examination of a problem often not subject to direct experimentation by means of a simulating device

sim·u·la·tor \'sim-yə-,lā-tər\ *n* (1835) : one that simulates; *esp* : a device that enables the operator to reproduce or represent under test conditions phenomena likely to occur in actual performance

si·mul·cast \'sī-məl-,kast *also* 'si-\ *vb* [*simul*taneous broad*cast*] *vi* (1948) : to broadcast simultaneously (as by radio and television) ~ *vt* : to broadcast (a program) by simulcasting — **simulcast** *n*

si·mul·ta·neous \,sī-məl-'tā-nē-əs, -nyəs *also* ,si-\ *adj* [L *simul* at the same time + E *-taneous* (as in *instantaneous*) — more at SAME] (ca. 1660) **1** : existing or occurring at the same time : exactly coincident **2** : satisfied by the same values of the variables ⟨~ equations⟩ *syn* see CONTEMPORARY — **si·mul·ta·ne·ity** \-tə-'nē-ə-tē, -'nā-\ *n* — **si·mul·ta·neous·ly** \-'tā-nē-əs-lē, -nyəs-\ *adv* — **si·mul·ta·neous·ness** *n*

¹sin \'sin\ *n* [ME *sinne*, fr. OE *synn*; akin to OHG *sunta* sin; prob. akin to L *sont-, sons* guilty, *est* is — more at IS] (bef. 12c) **1 a** : an offense against religious or moral law **b** : an action that is or is felt to be highly reprehensible ⟨it's a ~ to waste food⟩ **c** : an often serious shortcoming : FAULT **2 a** : transgression of the law of God **b** : a vitiated state of human nature in which the self is estranged from God *syn* see OFFENSE

²sin *vi* **sinned; sin·ning** (bef. 12c) **1** : to commit a sin **2** : to commit an offense or fault

³sin \'sēn, 'sin\ *n* [Heb *śīn*] (ca. 1823) : the 21st letter of the Hebrew alphabet — called *also* ALPHABET table

Sin·an·thro·pus \sī-'nan(t)-thrə-pəs, sə-; ,sī-,nan-'thrō-, ,si-\ *n* [NL, fr. LL *Sinae*, pl., Chinese + Gk *anthropos* man — more at SINO-] (1928) : PEKING MAN

Sin·bad *or* **Sind·bad** \'sin-,bad\ *n* : a citizen of Baghdad whose adventures at sea are told in the *Arabian Nights' Entertainments*

¹since \'sin(t)s\ *adv* [ME *sins*, contr. of *sithens*, fr. *sithen*, fr. OE *siththan*, fr. *sith tham* after that, fr. *sith* after, late + *tham*, dat. of *thæt* that; akin to OHG *sid* later and perh. to L *setius* to a lesser degree] (bef. 12c) **1** : from a definite past time until now ⟨has stayed there ever ~⟩ **2** : before the present time : AGO ⟨long ~ dead⟩ **3** : after a time in the past : SUBSEQUENTLY ⟨has ~ become rich⟩

²since *conj* (15c) **1** : at a time in the past after or later than ⟨has held two jobs ~ he graduated⟩ : from the time in the past when ⟨ever ~ I was a child⟩ **2** *obs* : WHEN **3** : in view of the fact that : BECAUSE ⟨~ it was raining she took an umbrella⟩

³since *prep* (ca. 1530) : in the period after a specified time in the past : from a specified time in the past

sin·cere \sin-'sir, sən-\ **sin·cer·er; sin·cer·est** *adj* [MF, fr. L *sincerus* whole, pure, genuine, prob. fr. *sem*- one + *-cerus* (akin to L *crescere* to grow) — more at SAME, CRESCENT] (1533) **1 a :** free of dissimulation **: HONEST** ⟨~ interest⟩ **b :** free from adulteration **: PURE** ⟨a ~ doctrine⟩ ⟨~ wine⟩ **2 :** marked by genuineness **: TRUE** — **sin·cere·ly** *adv* — **sin·cere·ness** *n*
syn SINCERE, WHOLEHEARTED, HEARTFELT, HEARTY, UNFEIGNED mean genuine in feeling. SINCERE stresses absence of hypocrisy, feigning, or any falsifying embellishment or exaggeration ⟨a *sincere* apology⟩. WHOLEHEARTED suggests sincerity and earnest devotion without reservation or misgiving ⟨promised our *wholehearted* support⟩. HEARTFELT suggests depth of genuine feeling outwardly expressed ⟨expresses our *heartfelt* gratitude⟩. HEARTY suggests honesty, warmth, and exuberance in displaying feeling ⟨received a *hearty* welcome⟩. UNFEIGNED stresses spontaneity and absence of pretense ⟨her *unfeigned* delight at receiving the award⟩.
sin·cer·i·ty \-'ser-ə-tē, -'sir-\ *n* (15c) **:** the quality or state of being sincere : honesty of mind : freedom from hypocrisy
sin·cip·i·tal \sin-'si-pə-t²l\ *adj* (1653) **:** of or relating to the sinciput
sin·ci·put \'sin(t)-sə-(ˌ)pət\ *n, pl* **sinciputs** *or* **sin·cip·i·ta** \sin-'si-pə-tə\ [L *sinciput*, *sinciput*, fr. *semi*- + *caput* head — more at HEAD] (1578) **1 :** FOREHEAD **2 :** the upper half of the skull
Sind·hi \'sin-dē\ *n, pl* **Sindhi** *or* **Sindhis** [Ar *Sindī*] (1815) **1 :** a member of a mostly Muslim people of Sind **2 :** the Indo-Aryan language of the Sindhi people
sine \'sīn\ *n* [ML *sinus*, fr. L, curve] (1593) **1 :** the trigonometric function that for an acute angle is the ratio between the leg opposite the angle when it is considered part of a right triangle and the hypotenuse **2 :** a trigonometric function sin θ that for all real numbers θ is exactly equal to the sine of an angle of measure θ in radians and that is given by the sum of the alternating series

$$\sin\theta = \theta - \frac{\theta^3}{3!} + \frac{\theta^5}{5!} - \frac{\theta^7}{7!} + \frac{\theta^9}{9!} - \cdots$$

si·ne·cure \'sī-ni-ˌkyùr, 'si-\ *n* [ML *sine cura* without cure (of souls)] (1662) **1** *archaic* **:** an ecclesiastical benefice without cure of souls **2 :** an office or position that requires little or no work and that usu. provides an income
sine curve *n* (1902) **:** the graph in rectangular coordinates of the equation *y*=*a* sin *bx* where *a* and *b* are constants
si·ne die \ˌsī-ni-'dī(-ˌē), ˌsi-nā-'dē-ˌā\ *adv* [L, without day] (1607) **:** without any future date being designated (as for resumption) **:** INDEFINITELY ⟨the meeting adjourned *sine die*⟩

sine curve: graph of *y*=*a* sin *bx* where *a*=1, *b*=1

si·ne qua non \ˌsi-ni-ˌkwä-'nän, -'nōn *also* ˌsē-; *also* ˌsi-ni-ˌkwä-'nän\ *n, pl* **sine qua nons** *also* **sine qui·bus non** \-ˌkwi-(ˌ)bùs- *also* -ˌkwī-\ [LL, without which not] (1602) **:** something absolutely indispensable or essential
¹sin·ew \'sin-(ˌ)yü *also* 'si-(ˌ)nü\ *n* [ME *sinewe*, fr. OE *seono;* akin to OHG *senawa* sinew, Skt *syati* he binds] (bef. 12c) **1 :** TENDON; *esp* **:** one dressed for use as a cord or thread **2** *obs* **:** NERVE **3 a :** solid resilient strength **:** POWER ⟨astonishing intellectual ~ and clarity — Reynolds Price⟩ **b :** the chief supporting force **:** MAINSTAY — usu. used in pl. ⟨providing the ~s of better living —Sam Pollock⟩
²sinew *vt* (ca. 1614) **:** to strengthen as if with sinews
sine wave *n* (1893) **:** a waveform that represents periodic oscillations in which the amplitude of displacement at each point is proportional to the sine of the phase angle of the displacement and that is visualized as a sine curve **:** SINE CURVE; *also* **:** a wave so represented
sin·ewy \'sin-yə-wē *also* \si-nə-\ *adj* (14c) **1 :** full of sinews: as **a :** TOUGH, STRINGY ⟨~ meat⟩ **b :** STRONG ⟨~ arms⟩ **2 :** marked by the strength of sinews ⟨a demanding ~ intelligence —Helen Dudar⟩
sin·fo·nia \ˌsin-fə-'nē-ə\ *n, pl* **-nie** \-'nē-ˌā\ [It, fr. L *symphonia* symphony] (1773) **1 :** an orchestral musical composition serving as an introduction to choral works (as opera) esp. in the 18th century — OVERTURE **2 :** RITORNELLO 1, SYMPHONY 2c
sinfonia con·cer·tante \-ˌkän(t)-sər-'tän-tē, -shər-, -ˌtä\ *n* [It, lit., symphony in concerto style] (ca. 1903) **:** a concerto for more than one solo instrument
sin·fo·niet·ta \ˌsin-fən-'ye-tə, -fōn-\ *n* [It, dim. of *sinfonia*] (ca. 1907) **1 :** a symphony of less than standard length or for fewer instruments **2 :** a small symphony orchestra; *esp* **:** an orchestra of strings only
sin·ful \'sin-fəl\ *adj* (bef. 12c) **1 :** tainted with, marked by, or full of sin **:** WICKED **2 :** such as to make one feel guilty ⟨a ~ chocolate cake⟩ — **sin·ful·ly** \-fə-lē\ *adv* — **sin·ful·ness** *n*
¹sing \'siŋ\ *vb* **sang** \'saŋ\ *or* **sung** \'səŋ\; **sung; sing·ing** \'siŋ-iŋ\ [ME, fr. OE *singan;* akin to OHG *singan* to sing, Gk *omphē* voice] *vi* (bef. 12c) **1 a :** to produce musical tones by means of the voice **b :** to utter words in musical tones and with musical inflections and modulations **c :** to deliver songs as a trained or professional singer **2 :** to make a shrill whining or whistling sound **3 a :** to relate or celebrate something in verse **b :** to compose poetry **c :** to create in or through words a feeling or sense of song ⟨prose that ~s⟩ **4 :** to produce musical or harmonious sounds **5 :** BUZZ, RING **6 :** to make a cry **:** CALL **7 :** to give information or evidence ~ *vt* **1 :** to utter with musical inflections; *esp* **:** to interpret in musical tones produced by the voice **2 :** to relate or celebrate in verse **3 :** CHANT, INTONE **4 :** to bring or accompany to a state or place by singing ⟨~s the child to sleep⟩ — **sing·able** \'siŋ-ə-bəl\ *adj*
²sing *n* (1850) **:** a session of group singing
¹singe \'sinj\ *vt* **singed; singe·ing** \'sin-jiŋ\ [ME *sengen*, fr. OE *sengan;* akin to OHG *bisengan* to singe, OCS *isęknǫti* to dry up] (bef. 12c) **:** to burn superficially or lightly **:** SCORCH; *esp* **:** to remove the hair, down, or fuzz from usu. by passing rapidly over a flame
²singe *n* (1658) **:** a slight burn **:** SCORCH
¹sing·er \'siŋ-ər\ *n* (14c) **:** one that sings
²sing·er \'sin-jər\ *n* (ca. 1875) **:** one that singes

singing game *n* (1881) **:** a children's game in which the players accompany their actions with the singing of a narrative song
¹sin·gle \'siŋ-gəl\ *adj* [ME, fr. MF, fr. L *singulus*] (14c) **1 a :** not married **b :** of or relating to celibacy **2 :** unaccompanied by others **:** LONE, SOLE ⟨the ~ survivor of the disaster⟩ **3 a** (1) **:** consisting of or having only one part, feature, or portion ⟨~ consonants⟩ (2) **:** consisting of one as opposed to or in contrast with many ⟨~ standard for men and women⟩ (3) **:** consisting of only one in number ⟨holds to a ~ ideal⟩ **b :** having but one whorl of petals or ray flowers ⟨a ~ rose⟩ **4 a :** consisting of a separate unique whole **:** INDIVIDUAL ⟨every ~ citizen⟩ **b :** of, relating to, or involving only one person ⟨a ~ FRANK, HONEST ⟨a ~ devotion⟩ **b :** exclusively attentive ⟨an eye ~ to the truth⟩ **6 :** UNBROKEN, UNDIVIDED **7 :** having no equal or like **:** SINGULAR **8 :** designed for the use of one person only ⟨a ~ room⟩ ⟨~ bed⟩
²single *vb* **sin·gled; sin·gling** \-g(ə-)liŋ\ *vt* (1628) **1 :** to select or distinguish from a number or group — usu. used with *out* **2 a :** to advance or score (a base runner) by a single **b :** to bring about the scoring of (a run) by a single ~ *vi* **:** to make a single in baseball
³single *n* (1646) **1 a :** a separate individual person or thing **b :** an unmarried person and esp. one young and socially active — usu. used in pl. **c :** a recording having one short tune on each side **2 :** a base hit that allows the batter to reach first base **3 a** *pl* **:** a tennis match or similar game with one player on each side **b :** a golf match between two players — usu. used in pl. **4 :** a room (as in a hotel) for one guest — compare DOUBLE 7
sin·gle–ac·tion \'siŋ-gəl-'ak-shən\ *adj* (1900) *of a revolver* **:** that can be cocked only by manually retracting the hammer
sin·gle–blind \'siŋ-gəl-ˌblīnd\ *adj* (1963) **:** of, relating to, or being an experimental procedure in which the experimenters but not the subjects know the makeup of the test and control groups during the actual course of the experiments — compare DOUBLE-BLIND
single bond *n* (1903) **:** a chemical bond in which one pair of electrons is shared by two atoms in a molecule esp. when the atoms can share more than one pair of electrons — compare DOUBLE BOND, TRIPLE BOND
sin·gle–breast·ed \'siŋ-gəl-'bres-təd\ *adj* (1796) **:** having a center closing with one row of buttons and no lap ⟨a ~ coat⟩
single combat *n* (1610) **:** combat between two persons
single cross *n* (1940) **:** a first-generation hybrid between two selected and usu. inbred lines — compare DOUBLE CROSS 2
single entry *n* (1826) **:** a method of bookkeeping that recognizes only one side of a business transaction and usu. consists only of a record of cash and personal accounts with debtors and creditors
single file *n* (1670) **:** ⁶FILE 1 — **single file** *adv*
¹sin·gle–foot \'siŋ-gəl-ˌfút\ *n, pl* **single–foots** (1867) **:** ⁷RACK b
²single–foot *vi* (1890) *of a horse* **:** to go at a rack — **sin·gle–foot·er** *n*
¹sin·gle–hand·ed \ˌsiŋ-gəl-'han-dəd\ *adj* (1709) **1 :** managed or done by one person or with one on a side **2 :** working alone or unassisted by others — **sin·gle–hand·ed·ly** *adv*
²single–handed *adv* (1815) **:** in a single-handed manner
sin·gle–hand·er \-'han-dər\ *n* (1946) **:** a person who sails single-handed
sin·gle–heart·ed \ˌsiŋ-gəl-'här-təd\ *adj* (1577) **:** characterized by sincerity and unity of purpose or dedication — **sin·gle–heart·ed·ly** *adv* — **sin·gle–heart·ed·ness** *n*
single knot *n* (ca. 1930) **:** OVERHAND KNOT
single–lens reflex \'siŋ-gəl-'lenz-\ *n* (1940) **:** a camera having a single lens that forms an image which is reflected to the viewfinder or recorded on film
sin·gle–mind·ed \ˌsiŋ-gəl-'mīn-dəd, 'siŋ-gəl-ˌ\ *adj* (1860) **:** having one driving purpose or resolve **:** DETERMINED, DEDICATED — **sin·gle–mind·ed·ly** *adv* — **sin·gle–mind·ed·ness** *n*
sin·gle–ness \'siŋ-gəl-nəs\ *n* (1560) **:** the quality or state of being single
sin·gle–phase \'siŋ-gəl-'fāz\ *adj* (1900) **:** of or relating to a circuit energized by a single alternating electromotive force
sin·gle–space \-'spās\ *vt* (1928) **:** to type or print with no blank lines between lines of text
sin·gle·stick \-ˌstik\ *n* (1771) **:** fighting or fencing with a wooden stick or sword held in one hand; *also* **:** the weapon used
sin·glet \'siŋ-glət\ *n* (ca. 1746) **1** [fr. its having only one thickness of cloth] *chiefly Brit* **:** an athletic jersey **:** UNDERSHIRT **2 :** an atom or molecule that has no net electronic magnetic moment; *also* **:** an excited state of an atom or molecule that is a singlet
single tax *n* (1853) **:** a tax to be levied on a single item (as real estate) as the sole source of public revenue
sin·gle·ton \'siŋ-gəl-tən\ *n* [F, fr. E *single*] (1876) **1 :** a card that is the only one of its suit orig. dealt to a player **2 a :** an individual member or thing distinct from others grouped with it **b :** an offspring born singly ⟨~s are more common than twins⟩
sin·gle–track \'siŋ-gəl-'trak\ *adj* (1849) **1 :** having only one track **2 :** lacking intellectual range, receptiveness, or flexibility **:** ONE-TRACK
sin·gle·tree \'siŋ-gəl-(ˌ)trē\ *n* (ca. 1841) **:** WHIFFLETREE
sin·gle–val·ued \ˌsiŋ-gəl-'val-(ˌ)yüd\ *adj* (1879) **:** having one and only one value of the range associated with each value of the domain ⟨a ~ function⟩ — compare MULTIPLE-VALUED
single wing *n* (1945) **:** an offensive football formation in which one back plays as a flanker and two backs line up four or five yards behind the line in position to receive a direct snap from center
sin·gly \'siŋ-g(ə-)lē\ *adv* (14c) **1 :** without the company of others **:** INDIVIDUALLY **2 :** SINGLE-HANDED
¹sing·song \'siŋ-ˌsóŋ\ *n* (1609) **1 :** verse with marked and regular rhythm and rhyme **2 :** a voice delivery marked by a narrow range or monotonous pattern of pitch **3** *Brit* **:** SONGFEST — **sing·songy** \-ˌsòŋ-ē\ *adj*
²singsong *adj* (1734) **:** having a monotonous cadence or rhythm
sing·spiel \'siŋ-ˌspēl, 'ziŋ-ˌspēl\ *n* [G, fr. *singen* to sing + *Spiel* play] (1876) **:** a musical work popular in Germany esp. in the latter part of

\ə\ abut \ᵊ\ kitten, F table \ər\ further \a\ ash \ā\ ace \ä\ mop, mar \aú\ out \ch\ chin \e\ bet \ē\ easy \g\ go \i\ hit \ī\ ice \j\ job \ŋ\ sing \ō\ go \ò\ law \òi\ boy \th\ thin \tẖ\ the \ü\ loot \ù\ foot \y\ yet \zh\ vision \á, k̲, ⁿ, œ, œ̄, ᵾ, ᵫ, ᵊ\ see Guide to Pronunciation the 18th century characterized by spoken dialogue interspersed with popular or folk songs

¹**sin·gu·lar** \'siŋ-gyə-lər\ *adj* [ME *singuler*, fr. MF, fr. L *singularis*, fr. *singulus* only one — more at SINGLE] (14c) **1 a :** of or relating to a separate person or thing : INDIVIDUAL **b :** of, relating to, or being a word form denoting one person, thing, or instance **c :** of or relating to a single instance or to something considered by itself **2 :** distinguished by superiority : EXCEPTIONAL ⟨an artist of ~ attainments⟩ **3 :** being out of the ordinary : UNUSUAL ⟨on the way home we had a ~ adventure⟩ **4 :** departing from general usage or expectation : PECULIAR, ODD ⟨the air had a ~ chill⟩ **5 a** *of a matrix* : having a determinant equal to zero **b** *of a linear transformation* : having the property that the matrix of coefficients of the new variables has a determinant equal to zero — **syn** see STRANGE — **sin·gu·lar·ly** *adv*

²**singular** *n* (14c) **1 :** the singular number, the inflectional form denoting it, or a word in that form **2 :** a singular term

sin·gu·lar·i·ty \ˌsiŋ-gyə-'lar-ə-tē\ *n, pl* **-ties** (14c) **1 :** something that is singular: as **a :** a separate unit **b :** unusual or distinctive manner or behavior : PECULIARITY **2 :** the quality or state of being singular **3 :** a point at which the derivative of a given function of a complex variable does not exist but every neighborhood of which contains points for which the derivative exists **4 :** a point or region of infinite mass density at which space and time are infinitely distorted by gravitational forces and which is held to be the final state of matter falling into a black hole

sin·gu·lar·ize \'siŋ-gyə-lə-ˌrīz\ *vt* **-ized; -iz·ing** (1589) : to make singular

singular point *n* (ca. 1856) : SINGULARITY 3

Sin·ha·la \sin-'hä-lä, siŋ-\ *n* [Skt *Siṃhala* Sri Lanka] (ca. 1954) : SINHALESE 2

Sin·ha·lese *or* **Sin·gha·lese** \ˌsiŋ-gə-'lēz, ˌsin-(h)ə-, -'lēs\ *n, pl* **Sinhalese** *or* **Singhalese** (1598) **1 :** a member of a people that inhabit Sri Lanka and form a major part of its population **2 :** the Indo-Aryan language of the Sinhalese people — **Sinhalese** *or* **Sin·ghalese** *adj*

si·ni·cize \'si-nə-ˌsiz, 'si-\ *vt* **-cized; -ciz·ing** *often cap* [ML *sinicus* Chinese, fr. LL *Sinae*, pl., Chinese — more at SINO-] (1889) : to modify by Chinese influence

sin·is·ter \'si-nəs-tər, *archaic* sə-'nis-\ *adj* [ME *sinistre*, fr. L *sinistr-, sinister* on the left side, unlucky, inauspicious] (15c) **1** *archaic* : UNFAVORABLE, UNLUCKY **2** *archaic* : FRAUDULENT **3 :** singularly evil or productive of evil **4 a :** of, relating to, or situated to the left or on the left side of something; *esp* : being or relating to the side of a heraldic shield at the left of the person bearing it **b :** of ill omen by reason of being on the left **5 :** presaging ill fortune or trouble **6 :** accompanied by or leading to disaster — **sin·is·ter·ly** *adv* — **sin·is·ter·ness** *n*

syn SINISTER, BALEFUL, MALIGN mean seriously threatening evil or disaster. SINISTER suggests a general or vague feeling of fear or apprehension on the part of the observer ⟨a *sinister* aura haunts the place⟩. BALEFUL imputes perniciousness or destructiveness to something whether working openly or covertly ⟨exerting a corrupt and *baleful* influence⟩. MALIGN applies to what is inherently evil or harmful ⟨the *malign* effects of racism⟩.

si·nis·tral \'si-nəs-trəl, sə-'nis-\ *adj* (1803) : of, relating to, or inclined to the left: as **a :** LEFT-HANDED **b** *of a gastropod shell* : having the whorls coiling counterclockwise down the spire when viewed with the apex toward the observer and having the aperture situated on the left of the axis when held with the spire uppermost and with the aperture opening toward the observer — compare DEXTRAL b

si·nis·trous \'si-nəs-trəs, sə-'nis-\ *adj* (ca. 1575) *archaic* : SINISTER

Si·nit·ic \si-'ni-tik, sə-\ *adj* [LL *Sinae*, pl., Chinese + E *-itic* (as in *Semitic*) — more at SINO-] (ca. 1895) : of or relating to the Chinese, their language, or their culture

¹**sink** \'siŋk\ *vb* **sank** \'saŋk\ *or* **sunk** \'səŋk\; **sunk; sink·ing** [ME, fr. OE *sincan*; akin to OHG *sinkan* to sink] *vi* (bef. 12c) **1 a :** to go to the bottom : SUBMERGE **b :** to become partly buried (as in mud) **c :** to become engulfed **2 a** (1) **:** to fall or drop to a lower place or level (2) **:** to flow at a lower depth or level (3) **:** to burn with lower intensity (4) **:** to fall to a lower pitch or volume ⟨his voice *sank* to a whisper⟩ **b :** to subside gradually : SETTLE **c :** to disappear from view **d :** to slope gradually : DIP **3 a :** to soak or become absorbed : PENETRATE **b :** to become impressively known or felt ⟨the lesson had *sunk* in⟩ **4 :** to become deeply absorbed ⟨*sank* into reverie⟩ **5 a :** to go downward in quality, state, or condition **b :** to grow less in amount or worth **6 a :** to fall or drop slowly for lack of strength **b :** to become depressed **c :** to fail in health or strength ~ *vt* **1 a :** to cause to sink ⟨~ a battleship⟩ **b :** to force down esp. below the earth's surface **c :** to cause (something) to penetrate **2 :** to engage deeply the attention of : IMMERSE **3 a :** to dig or bore (a well or shaft) in the earth : EXCAVATE **b :** to form by cutting or excising ⟨~ words in stone⟩ **4 :** to cast down or bring to a low condition or state : OVERWHELM, DEFEAT **5 :** to lower in standing or reputation : ABASE **6 a :** to lessen in value or amount **b :** to lower or soften (the voice) in speaking **7 :** RESTRAIN, SUPPRESS ⟨~s her pride and approaches the despised neighbor —Richard Harrison⟩ **8 :** to pay off (as a debt) : LIQUIDATE **9 :** INVEST **10 :** DROP 7c ⟨~ a putt⟩ — **sink·able** \'siŋ-kə-bəl\ *adj*

²**sink** *n* (15c) **1 a :** a pool or pit for the deposit of waste or sewage : CESSPOOL **b :** a ditch or tunnel for carrying off sewage : SEWER **c :** a stationary basin connected with a drain and usu. a water supply for washing and drainage **2 :** a place where vice, corruption, or evil collects **3 :** SUMP 3 **4 a :** a depression in the land surface; *esp* : one having a saline lake with no outlet **b :** SINKHOLE **5 :** a body or process that acts as a storage device or disposal mechanism: as **a :** HEAT SINK; *broadly* : a device that collects or dissipates energy (as radiation) **b :** a reactant with or absorber of a substance

sink·age \'siŋ-kij\ *n* (1883) **1 :** the process or degree of sinking **2 :** DEPRESSION, INDENTATION **3 :** the distance from the top line of a full page to the first line of sunk matter

sink·er \'siŋ-kər\ *n* (1708) **1 :** one that sinks; *specif* : a weight for sinking a fishing line, seine, or sounding line **2 :** DOUGHNUT **3 :** a fastball that sinks as it reaches the plate — called also *sinker ball*

sink·hole \'siŋk-ˌhōl\ *n* (15c) **1 :** a hollow place or depression in which drainage collects **2 :** a hollow in a limestone region that communicates with a cavern or passage **3 :** SINK 2

sinking fund *n* (1724) : a fund set up and accumulated by usu. regular deposits for paying off the principal of a debt when it falls due

sin·less \'sin-ləs\ *adj* (bef. 12c) : free from sin : IMPECCABLE — **sin·less·ly** *adv* — **sin·less·ness** *n*

sin·ner \'si-nər\ *n* (14c) : one that sins **2 :** REPROBATE, SCAMP

Si·no- \ˌsī-(ˌ)nō, 'si-, -nə\ *comb form* [F, fr. LL *Sinae*, pl., Chinese, fr. Gk *Sinai*, prob. of Indo-Aryan origin; akin to Skt *Cīnā*, pl., Chinese] **1 :** Chinese ⟨*sinology*⟩ **2 :** Chinese and ⟨*Sino*-Tibetan⟩

si·no·atri·al \ˌsī-nō-'ā-trē-əl\ *adj* [NL *sinus* + *atrium*] (1913) : of, involving, or being the sinoatrial node ⟨~ block⟩

sinoatrial node *n* (1913) : a small mass of tissue that is embedded in the musculature of the right atrium of higher vertebrates and that originates the impulses stimulating the heartbeat

si·no·logue \'sī-nᵊl-ˌȯg, 'si-, -ˌäg\ *n* [F, fr. LL *Sinae* + F *-logue*] (1853) : a specialist in sinology

si·nol·o·gy \si-'nä-lə-jē, sə-\ *n* [prob. fr. F *sinologie*, fr. *sino-* + *-logie* *-logy*] (ca. 1882) : the study of the Chinese and esp. their language, literature, history, and culture — **si·no·log·i·cal** \ˌsī-nᵊl-'ä-ji-kəl, ˌsi-\ *adj* — **si·nol·o·gist** \sī-'nä-lə-jist, sə-\ *n*

si·no·pia \sə-'nō-pē-ə\ *n, pl* **-pi·as** *or* **-pie** \-pē-ˌā\ [It, fr. L *sinopis*, fr. Gk *sinōpis*, fr. *Sinōpē* Sinop, ancient seaport in Asia Minor] (1844) **1 :** a red to reddish brown earth pigment used by the ancients that depends for its color on its content of red ferric oxide **2 :** a preliminary drawing for a fresco done in sinopia

Si·no-Ti·bet·an \ˌsī-nō-tə-'be-tᵊn, 'si-\ *n* (1920) : a language family comprising Tibeto-Burman and Chinese

sin·se·mil·la \ˌsin-sə-'mē-lə, -'mi-; -'mē-yə, -'mēl-\ *n* [AmerSp, fr. *sin* without + *semilla* seed] (1975) : highly potent marijuana from female plants that are specially tended and kept seedless by preventing pollination in order to induce a high resin content; *also* : a female hemp plant grown to produce sinsemilla

sin·syne \'sin-ˌsin\ *adv* [ME (Sc) *sensyne*, fr. *sen* since (contr. of ME *sithen*) + *syne* since — more at SINCE, SYNE] (14c) *chiefly Scot* : since that time

sin tax *n* (1964) : a tax on substances or activities considered sinful or harmful (as tobacco, alcohol, or gambling)

sin·ter \'sin-tər\ *vb* [G *Sinter* slag, cinder, fr. OHG *sintar* — more at CINDER] *vt* (1871) : to cause to become a coherent mass by heating without melting ~ *vi* : to undergo sintering — **sinter** *n* — **sin·ter·abil·i·ty** \ˌsin-tə-rə-'bi-lə-tē\ *n*

sin·u·ate \'sin-yə-wət, -ˌwāt\ *adj* [L *sinuatus*, pp. of *sinuare* to bend, fr. *sinus* curve] (1688) : having the margin wavy with strong indentations ⟨~ leaves⟩

sin·u·os·i·ty \ˌsin-yə-'wä-sə-tē\ *n, pl* **-ties** (1598) **1 :** the quality or state of being sinuous **2 :** something that is sinuous

sin·u·ous \'sin-yə-wəs\ *adj* [L *sinuosus*, fr. *sinus*] (1578) **1 a :** of a serpentine or wavy form : WINDING **b :** marked by strong lithe movements **2 :** INTRICATE, COMPLEX — **sin·u·ous·ly** *adv* — **sin·u·ous·ness** *n*

si·nus \'sī-nəs\ *n* [ME, fr. ML, fr. L, curve, fold, hollow] (15c) : CAVITY, HOLLOW: as **a :** a narrow elongated tract extending from a focus of suppuration and serving for the discharge of pus **b** (1) **:** a cavity in the substance of a bone of the skull that usu. communicates with the nostrils and contains air (2) **:** a channel for venous blood (3) **:** a dilatation in a bodily canal or vessel **c :** a cleft or indentation between adjoining lobes (as of a leaf or corolla)

si·nus·itis \ˌsīn-yə-'sī-təs, ˌsī-nə-\ *n* (1896) : inflammation of a sinus of the skull

si·nu·soid \'sīn-yə-ˌsȯid, 'sī-nə-\ *n* [ML *sinus* sine] (1823) **1 :** SINE CURVE, SINE WAVE **2** [NL *sinus*] : a minute endothelium-lined space or passage for blood in the tissues of an organ (as the liver)

si·nu·soi·dal \ˌsīn-yə-'sȯi-dᵊl, ˌsī-nə-\ *adj* (1878) : of, relating to, shaped like, or varying according to a sine curve or sine wave ⟨~ motion⟩ ⟨~ alternating current⟩ ⟨~ grooves⟩ — **si·nu·soi·dal·ly** \-dᵊl-ē\ *adv*

sinusoidal projection *n* (1944) : an equal-area map projection capable of showing the entire surface of the earth with all parallels as straight lines evenly spaced, the central meridian as one half the length of the equator, and all other meridians as curved lines

si·nus ve·no·sus \'sī-nəs-vi-'nō-səs\ *n* [NL, venous sinus] (ca. 1839) : an enlarged pouch that adjoins the heart, is formed by the union of the large systemic veins, and is the passage through which venous blood enters the heart in lower vertebrates and in embryos of higher forms

Si·on \'sī-ən\ *var of* ZION

Siou·an \'sü-ən\ *n* (1889) **1 :** an American Indian language family of central and southeastern No. America **2 :** a member of any of the peoples speaking Siouan languages

Sioux \'sü\ *n, pl* **Sioux** \'sü, 'süz\ [F, short for *Nadouessioux*, fr. Ojibwa *na·towe·ssiw-*] (1712) **1 :** DAKOTA **2 :** SIOUAN

¹**sip** \'sip\ *vb* **sipped; sip·ping** [ME *sippen;* akin to LG *sippen* to sip] *vi* (14c) : to take a sip of something esp. repeatedly ~ *vt* **1 :** to drink in small quantities **2 :** to take sips from — **sip·per** *n*

²**sip** *n* (15c) **1 :** a small draft taken with the lips **2 :** the act of sipping

¹**si·phon** \'sī-fən\ *n* [F *siphon*, fr. L *siphon-, sipho* tube, pipe, siphon, fr. Gk *siphōn*] (1659) **1 a :** a tube bent to form two legs of unequal length by which a liquid can be transferred to a lower level over an intermediate elevation by the pressure of the atmosphere in forcing the liquid up the shorter branch of the tube immersed in it while the excess of weight of the liquid in the longer branch when once filled causes a continuous flow **b** *usu* **syphon :** a bottle for holding aerated water that is driven out through a bent tube in its neck by the pressure of the gas when a valve in the tube is opened **2 :** any of various tubular organs in animals and esp. mollusks or arthropods that are used for drawing in or ejecting fluids — see CLAM illustration

siphon 1a

²**siphon** vb **si·phoned; si·phon·ing** \'sī-fə-niŋ, 'sīf-niŋ\ vt (1859) : to convey, draw off, or empty by or as if by a siphon — often used with *off* ~ vi : to pass by or as if by a siphon

si·pho·no·phore \sī-'fä-nə-ˌfōr, 'sī-fə-nə-, -ˌfȯr\ n [ultim. fr. Gk *siphōn* + *pherein* to carry — more at BEAR] (1883) : any of an order (Siphonophora) of compound free-swimming or floating pelagic hydrozoans that are mostly delicate, transparent, and colored and have specialized zooids

si·pho·no·stele \sī-'fä-nə-ˌstēl, ˌsī-fə-nə-'stē-lē\ n [Gk *siphōn* tube, siphon] (1902) : a stele consisting of vascular tissue surrounding a central core of pith parenchyma

sip·pet \'si-pət\ n [alter. of *sop*] (1530) *chiefly Brit* : a small bit of toast or fried bread esp. for garnishing

sir \'sər\ n [ME, fr. *sire*] (13c) **1 a** : a man entitled to be addressed as *sir* — used as a title before the given name of a knight or baronet and formerly sometimes before the given name of a priest **b** : a man of rank or position **2 a** — used as a usu. respectful form of address **b** *cap* — used as a conventional form of address in the salutation of a letter

Si·rach \'sī-rak *also* sə-'räk\ n [Gk *Seirach*] : a didactic book of the Roman Catholic canon of the Old Testament

sir·dar \'sər-ˌdär, sər-'\ n [Hindi *sardār*, fr. Per] (1595) **1 a** : a person of high rank (as an hereditary noble) esp. in India **b** : the commander of the Anglo-Egyptian army **2** : one (as a foreman) holding a responsible position esp. in India

¹**sire** \'sīr\ n [ME, fr. OF, fr. L *senior* older — more at SENIOR] (13c) **1 a** : FATHER **b** *archaic* : male ancestor : FOREFATHER **c** : AUTHOR, ORIGINATOR **2 a** *archaic* : a man of rank or authority; *esp* : LORD — used formerly as a form of address and as a title **b** *obs* : an elderly man : SENIOR **3** : the male parent of an animal and esp. of a domestic animal

²**sire** vt **sired; sir·ing** (1611) **1** : BEGET — used esp. of male domestic animals **2** : to bring into being : ORIGINATE

¹**si·ren** \'sī-rən, *for 3 also* sī-'rēn\ n [ME, fr. MF & L; MF *sereine*, fr. LL *sirena*, fr. L *siren*, fr. Gk *seirēn*] (14c) **1** *often cap* : any of a group of female and partly human creatures in Greek mythology that lured mariners to destruction by their singing **2 a** : a woman who sings with bewitching sweetness **b** : TEMPTRESS **3 a** : an apparatus producing musical tones esp. in acoustical studies by the rapid interruption of a current of air, steam, or fluid by a perforated rotating disk **b** : a device often electrically operated for producing a penetrating warning sound ⟨ambulance ~⟩ ⟨air-raid ~⟩ **4** [NL, fr. L] : either of two No. American eel-shaped amphibians that constitute a genus (*Siren*) and have small forelimbs but neither hind legs nor pelvis and have permanent external gills as well as lungs

²**si·ren** \'sī-rən\ adj (1568) : resembling that of a siren : ENTICING

si·re·ni·an \sī-'rē-nē-ən\ n [NL *Sirenia*, fr. L *siren*] (1883) : any of an order (Sirenia) of aquatic herbivorous mammals including the manatee, dugong, and Steller's sea cow

siren song n (1568) : an alluring utterance or appeal; *esp* : one that is seductive or deceptive

Sir·i·us \'sir-ē-əs\ n [ME, fr. L, fr. Gk *Seirios*] : a star of the constellation Canis Major that is the brightest star in the heavens — called also *Dog Star*

sir·loin \'sər-ˌlȯin\ n [alter. of earlier *surloin*, modif. of MF *surlonge*, fr. *sur* over (fr. L *super*) + *loigne*, *longe* loin — more at OVER, LOIN] (1554) : a cut of meat and esp. of beef from the part of the hindquarter just in front of the round — see BEEF illustration

si·roc·co \sə-'rä-(ˌ)kō, shə-\ n, pl **-cos** [It *scirocco, sirocco*, fr. Ar *sharq* east] (1617) **1 a** : a hot dust-laden wind from the Libyan deserts that blows on the northern Mediterranean coast chiefly in Italy, Malta, and Sicily **b** : a warm moist oppressive southeast wind in the same regions **2** : a hot or warm wind of cyclonic origin from an arid or heated region

sir·rah *also* **sir·ra** \'sir-ə\ n [alter. of *sir*] (1526) *obs* — used as a form of address implying inferiority in the person addressed

sir·ree *also* **sir·ee** \(ˌ)sər-'ē\ n [by alter.] (1823) : SIR — used as an emphatic form usu. after *yes* or *no*

sir–reverence n [prob. alter. of *save-reverence*, trans. of ML *salva reverentia* saving (your) reverence] (1575) **1** *obs* — used as an expression of apology before a statement that might be taken as offensive **2** *obs* : human feces; *also* : a lump of human feces

Sir Rog·er de Cov·er·ley \sə(r)-ˌrä-jər-di-'kə-vər-lē\ n [alter. of *roger of coverley*, prob. fr. *Roger*, male given name + *of* + *Coverley*, a fictitious place name] (1804) : an English country-dance that resembles the Virginia reel

sirup *var of* SYRUP

sir·vente \sir-'vänt\ *or* **sir·ven·tes** \-'ven-təs\ n, pl **sir·ventes** \-'vänt, -'vän(t)s, -'ven-təs\ [F, fr. Prov *sirventes*, lit., servant's song, fr. *sirvent* servant, fr. L *servient-, serviens*, prp. of *servire* to serve] (1819) : a usu. moral or religious song of the Provençal troubadours satirizing social vices

sis \'sis\ n (1656) : SISTER — usu. used in direct address

-sis n suffix, pl **-ses** [L, fr. Gk, fem. suffix of action] : process : action ⟨peristalsis⟩

si·sal \'sī-səl, -zəl\ n [*Sisal*, port in Yucatán, Mexico] (1843) **1 a** : a strong durable white fiber used esp. for hard fiber cordage and twine — called also *sisal hemp* **b** : a widely cultivated Mexican agave (*Agave sisalana*) whose leaves yield sisal **2** : any of several fibers similar to true sisal

sis·kin \'sis-kən\ n [G dial. *Sisschen*, dim. of MHG *zīse* siskin, of Slav origin; akin to Czech *čížek* siskin] (1562) : a small chiefly greenish and yellowish finch (*Carduelis spinus*) of Europe, Asia, and northern Africa that is related to the goldfinch — compare PINE SISKIN, RED SISKIN

sis·si·fied \'si-si-ˌfīd\ adj (ca. 1903) : of, relating to, or having the characteristics of a sissy

sis·sy \'si-sē\ n, pl **sissies** [*sis*] (1891) : an effeminate man or boy; *also* : a timid or cowardly person — **sissy** adj

sis·ter \'sis-tər\ n [ME *suster, sister*, partly fr. OE *sweostor* and partly of Scand origin; akin to ON *systir* sister; akin to L *soror* sister, Skt *svasr*] (bef. 12c) **1** : a female who has one or both parents in common with another **2** *often cap* : a member of a women's religious order (as of nuns or deaconesses); *esp* : one of a Roman Catholic congregation under simple vows **b** : a woman or girl who is a member of a Christian church **3** : a woman regarded as a comrade ⟨my Korean ~s —

Alice Walker⟩ **4** : one that is closely similar to or associated with another ⟨~ schools⟩ ⟨~ cities⟩ **5** *chiefly Brit* : NURSE **6 a** : GIRL, WOMAN; *esp* : a girl or woman who is black **b** : PERSON — usu. used in the phrase *weak sister* **7** : a member of a sorority

sis·ter·hood \-ˌhu̇d\ n (1609) **1 a** : the state of being a sister **b** : sisterly relationship **2** : a community or society of sisters; *esp* : a society of women religious **3** : the solidarity of women based on shared conditions, experiences, or concerns

sis·ter–in–law \'sis-t(ə-)rən-ˌlȯ, -tərn-ˌlȯ\ n, pl **sis·ters–in–law** \-tər-zən-\ (15c) **1** : the sister of one's spouse **2 a** : the wife of one's brother **b** : the wife of one's spouse's brother

sis·ter·ly \'sis-tər-lē\ adj (ca. 1570) : of, relating to, or having the characteristics of a sister — **sisterly** adv

Sis·tine \'sis-ˌtēn, sis-\ adj [It *sistino*, fr. NL *sixtinus*, fr. *Sixtus*, name of some popes] (ca. 1864) **1** : of or relating to any of the popes named Sixtus **2** [fr. Pope *Sixtus* IV †1484] : of or relating to the Sistine chapel in the Vatican

Sis·y·phe·an \ˌsi-sə-'fē-ən\ *or* **Si·syph·i·an** \sī-'si-fē-ən\ adj (1635) : of, relating to, or suggestive of the labors of Sisyphus

Sis·y·phus \'si-sə-fəs\ n [L, fr. Gk *Sisyphos*] : a legendary king of Corinth condemned eternally to repeat the cycle of rolling a heavy rock up a hill in Hades only to have it roll down again as it nears the top

¹**sit** \'sit\ vb **sat** \'sat\; **sit·ting** [ME *sitten*, fr. OE *sittan*; akin to OHG *sizzen* to sit, L *sedēre*, Gk *hezesthai* to sit, *hedra* seat] (bef. 12c) **1 a** : to rest on the buttocks or haunches ⟨~ in a chair⟩ — often used with *down* **b** : PERCH, ROOST **2** : to occupy a place as a member of an official body ⟨~ in Congress⟩ **3** : to hold a session : be in session for official business **4** : to cover eggs for hatching : BROOD **5 a** : to take a position for having one's portrait painted or for being photographed **b** : to serve as a model **6** *archaic* : to have one's dwelling place : DWELL **7 a** : to lie or hang relative to a wearer ⟨the collar ~s awkwardly⟩ **b** : to affect one with or as if with weight ⟨the food *sat* heavily on his stomach⟩ **8** : LIE, REST ⟨a kettle *sitting* on the stove⟩ **9 a** : to have a location ⟨the house ~s well back from the road⟩ **b** *of wind* : to blow from a certain direction **10** : to remain inactive or quiescent ⟨the car ~s in the garage⟩ **11** : to take an examination **12** : BABY-SIT **13** : to please or agree with one — used with *with* and an adverb ⟨the decision did not ~ well with me⟩ ~ vt **1** : to cause to be seated : place on or in a seat — often used with *down* **2** : to sit on ⟨eggs⟩ **3** : to keep one's seat on ⟨a horse⟩ **4** : to provide seats or seating room for ⟨the car will ~ six people⟩ — **sit on 1** : to hold deliberations concerning **2** : REPRESS, SQUELCH **3** : to delay action or decision concerning — **sit pretty** : to be in a highly favorable situation — **sit tight 1** : to maintain one's position without change **2** : to remain quiet in or as if in hiding — **sit under** : to attend religious service under the instruction or ministrations of; *also* : to attend the classes or lectures of

²**sit** n (1776) **1** : the manner in which a garment fits **2** : an act or period of sitting

si·tar \si-'tär, 'si-ˌ\ n [Hindi *sitār*, fr. Per, a three-stringed lute, fr. *sih* three + *tār* string, thread] (1845) : an Indian lute with a long neck and a varying number of strings — **si·tar·ist** \-ist\ n

sit·com \'sit-ˌkäm\ n [*situation comedy*] (1964) : SITUATION COMEDY

¹**sit–down** \'sit-ˌdau̇n\ adj (ca. 1837) : served to seated diners ⟨a ~ dinner⟩; *also* : of, relating to, or serving sit-down meals ⟨a ~ restaurant⟩

²**sit–down** \'sit-ˌdau̇n\ n (1936) **1** : a cessation of work by employees while maintaining continuous occupation of their place of employment as a protest and means toward forcing compliance with demands **2** : a mass obstruction of an activity by sitting down to demonstrate a grievance or to get the activity modified or halted

sitar

¹**site** \'sīt\ n [ME, place, position, fr. MF or L; MF, fr. L *situs*, fr. *sinere* to leave, allow] (14c) **1 a** : the spatial location of an actual or planned structure or set of structures (as a building, town, or monuments) **b** : a space of ground occupied or to be occupied by a building **2** : the place, scene, or point of something

²**site** vt **sit·ed; sit·ing** (15c) : to place on a site or in position : LOCATE

sith \'sith\ *or* **sith·ence** \'si-thən(t)s\ *or* **sith·ens** \'si-thənz\ *archaic var of* SINCE

sit–in \'sit-ˌin\ n (1937) **1** : SIT-DOWN 1 **2 a** : an act of occupying seats in a racially segregated establishment in organized protest against discrimination **b** : an act of sitting in the seats or on the floor of an establishment as a means of organized protest

sit in vi (1868) **1** : to take part in or be present at a session of music or discussion as a visitor **2** : to participate in a sit-in

Sit·ka spruce \'sit-kə-\ n [*Sitka*, Alaska] (1895) : a tall spruce (*Picea sitchensis*) of the northern Pacific coast that has thin reddish brown bark, flat needles, and cones with slightly toothed scales

si·tos·ter·ol \sī-'täs-tə-ˌrȯl, sə-, -ˌrōl\ n [Gk *sitos* grain + E *sterol*] (1898) : any of several sterols that are widespread esp. in plant products (as wheat germ or soy bean oil) and are used as starting materials for the synthesis of steroid hormones

sit out vt (1659) : to refrain from participating in ⟨*sit out* the next dance⟩

sit·ter \'si-tər\ n (14c) : one that sits; *esp* : one who baby-sits children

¹**sit·ting** \'si-tiŋ\ n (13c) **1 a** : the act of one that sits **b** : a single occasion of continuous sitting (as for a portrait or meal) **2** **a** : a brooding over eggs for hatching **b** : SETTING 6 **3** : SESSION ⟨a ~ of the legislature⟩

²**sitting** adj (15c) **1** : that is setting ⟨a ~ hen⟩ **2** : occupying a judi-

\ə\ abut \ᵊ\ kitten, F table \ər\ further \a\ ash \ā\ ace \ä\ mop, mar
\au̇\ out \ch\ chin \e\ bet \ē\ easy \g\ go \i\ hit \ī\ ice \j\ job
\ŋ\ sing \ō\ go \ȯ\ law \ȯi\ boy \th\ thin \t͟h\ the \ü\ loot \u̇\ foot
\y\ yet \zh\ vision \á, �, ⁿ, œ, œ̄, ᵫ, ᵫ̄, ᵉ\ see Guide to Pronunciation

cial, legislative, or executive seat : being in office   **3** : easily hit or played ⟨a ~ target⟩   **4   a** : used in or for sitting ⟨a ~ position⟩   **b** : performed while sitting ⟨a ~ shot⟩
sitting duck *n* (1942) : an easy or defenseless target for attack or criticism or unscrupulous dealings
sitting room *n* (1771) : LIVING ROOM 1
¹sit·u·ate \'si-chə-wət, -wāt; 'sich-wət\ *adj* [ME, fr. LL *situatus*, fr. L *situs*] (15c) : having a site : LOCATED
²sit·u·ate \'si-chə-,wāt\ *vt* **-at·ed; -at·ing** (ca. 1532) : to place in a site, situation, context, or category : LOCATE
situated *adj* (15c)   **1** : having a site, situation, or location : LOCATED   **2** : provided with money or possessions ⟨comfortably ~⟩
sit·u·a·tion \,si-chə-'wā-shən\ *n* (15c)   **1   a** : the way in which something is placed in relation to its surroundings   **b** : SITE   **c** *archaic* : LOCALITY   **2** *archaic* : state of health   **3   a** : position or place of employment : POST, JOB   **b** : position in life : STATUS   **4** : position with respect to conditions and circumstances ⟨the military ~ remains obscure⟩   **5   a** : relative position or combination of circumstances at a certain moment   **b** : a critical, trying, or unusual state of affairs : PROBLEM   **c** : a particular or striking complex of affairs at a stage in the action of a narrative or drama
sit·u·a·tion·al \-shnəl, -shə-ⁿl\ *adj* (1903)   **1** : of, relating to, or appropriate to a situation   **2** : of or relating to situation ethics — **sit·u·a·tion·al·ly** *adv*
situation comedy *n* (1946) : a radio or television comedy series that involves a continuing cast of characters in a succession of episodes
situation ethics *n* (1955) : a system of ethics by which acts are judged within their contexts instead of by categorical principles
sit–up \'sit-,əp\ *n* (1938) : a conditioning exercise performed from a supine position by raising the trunk to a sitting position without lifting the feet and returning to the original position
sit up *vi* (13c)   **1   a** : to rise from a lying to a sitting position   **b** : to sit with the back erect   **2** : to show interest, alertness, or surprise ⟨*sit up* and take notice⟩   **3** : to stay up after the usual time for going to bed ⟨*sat up* late to watch the movie⟩
si·tus \'sī-təs\ *n* [L — more at SITE] (1701) : the place where something exists or originates; *specif* : the place where something (as a right) is held to be located in law
sitz bath \'sits-\ *n* [part trans. of G *Sitzbad*, fr. *Sitz* act of sitting + *Bad* bath] (1849) : a tub in which one bathes in a sitting posture; *also* : a bath so taken esp. therapeutically
sitz·mark \'sits-,märk, -\ *n* [part trans. of G *Sitzmarke*, fr. *Sitz* + *Marke* mark] (1935) : a depression left in the snow by a skier falling backward
Si·va \'si-və, 'shi-, 'sē-, 'shē-\ *n* [Skt *Śiva*] (1788) : the god of destruction and regeneration in the Hindu sacred triad — compare BRAHMA, VISHNU
Si·van \'si-vən\ *n* [Heb *Sīwān*] (1535) : the 9th month of the civil year or the 3d month of the ecclesiastical year in the Jewish calendar — see MONTH table
Si·wash \'sī-,wȯsh, -,wäsh\ *n* [*Siwash*, fictional college in stories by George Fitch †1915 Am. author] (1936) : a small usu. inland college that is notably provincial in outlook ⟨cheer for dear old *Siwash*⟩
six \'siks\ *n* [ME, fr. *six*, adj., fr. OE *siex*; akin to OHG *sehs* six, L *sex*, Gk *hex*] (bef. 12c)   **1** — see NUMBER table   **2** : the sixth in a set or series ⟨the ~ of spades⟩   **3** : something having six units or members: as   **a** : an ice-hockey team   **b** : a 6-cylinder engine or automobile — **six** *adj* — **six** *pron, pl in constr* — **at sixes and sevens** : being in disorder
six·fold \'siks-,fōld, -'fōld\ *adj* (bef. 12c)   **1** : having six units or members   **2** : being six times as great or as many — **six·fold** \-'fōld\ *adv*
six–gun \'siks-,gən\ *n* (1912) : a 6-chambered revolver
six–mo \'siks-(,)mō\ *n, pl* **sixmos** (1924) : the size of a piece of paper cut six from a sheet; *also* : a book, a page, or paper of this size
six–o–six *or* **606** \,siks-,ō-'siks\ *n* [fr. its having been the 606th compound tested and introduced by Paul Ehrlich †1915] (1910) : ARSPHENAMINE
six–pack \'siks-,pak\ *n* (1952)   **1** : six bottles or cans (as of beer) packaged and purchased as a unit   **2** : the contents of a six-pack
six·pence \'siks-pən(t)s, *US also* -,pen(t)s\ *n* (14c)   **1** : a former British monetary unit equal to six pennies   **2** *pl* **sixpence** *or* **six·penc·es** : a coin worth sixpence
six·pen·ny \'siks-pə-nē, *US also* -,pe-nē\ *adj* (15c) : costing or worth sixpence
sixpenny bit *n* (ca. 1887) : SIXPENCE 2
six·pen·ny nail \'siks-,pe-nē-\ *n* (15c) : a nail about two inches long
six–shoot·er \'sik(s)-,shü-tər\ *n* (1844) : SIX-GUN
six·teen \,sik-'stēn, 'siks-,tēn\ *n* [ME *sixtene*, fr. OE *sixtȳne*, adj., fr. *six* six + *-tȳne* (akin to OE *tien* ten) — more at TEN] (bef. 12c) — see NUMBER table — **sixteen** *adj* — **sixteen** *pron, pl in constr* — **six·teenth** \-'stēn(t)th, -,tēn(t)th\ *adj or n*
six·teen·mo \'siks-,tēn-(,)mō\ *n, pl* **-mos** (1847) : the size of a piece of paper cut 16 from a sheet; *also* : a book, a page, or paper of this size
sixteenth note *n* (ca. 1861) : a musical note with the time value of ¹/₁₆ of a whole note — see NOTE illustration
sixteenth rest *n* (ca. 1890) : a musical rest corresponding in time value to a sixteenth note — see REST illustration
sixth \'siks(t)th, 'siks(t)\ *n, pl* **sixths** \'siks(t)ths, \'siks(t)ths\ (12c)   **1** — see NUMBER table   **2   a** : a musical interval embracing six diatonic degrees   **b** : a tone at this interval; *specif* : SUBMEDIANT   **c** : the harmonic combination of two tones a sixth apart — **sixth** *adj or adv* — **sixth·ly** \'siksth-lē, 'sikst-\ *adv*
sixth chord *n* (ca. 1903) : a musical chord consisting of a tone with its third and its sixth above and usu. being the first inversion of a triad
sixth sense *n* (1761) : a power of perception like but not one of the five senses : a keen intuitive power
Six·tine \'sik-,stīn, -,stēn\ *var of* SISTINE
six·ty \'siks-tē\ *n, pl* **sixties** [ME, fr. *sixty*, adj., fr. OE *siextig*, n., group of sixty, fr. *siex* six + *-tig* group of ten; akin to OE *tien* ten] (14c)   **1** — see NUMBER table   **2** *pl* : the numbers 60 to 69; *specif* : the years 60 to 69 in a lifetime or century — **six·ti·eth** \'siks-tē-əth\ *adj or n* — **sixty** *adj* — **sixty** *pron, pl in constr* — **six·ty·ish** \'siks-tē-ish\ *adj*
sixty–fourth note \,siks-tē-'fȯrth-, -'fȯrth-\ *n* (ca. 1890) : a musical note with the time value of ¹/₆₄ of a whole note — see NOTE illustration

sixty–fourth rest *n* (ca. 1903) : a musical rest corresponding in time value to a sixty-fourth note
six·ty–nine \,siks-tē-'nīn\ *n* (1924)   **1** — see NUMBER table   **2** : mutual cunnilingus and fellatio : mutual fellatio : mutual cunnilingus
siz·able *or* **size·able** \'sī-zə-bəl\ *adj* (1613) : fairly large : CONSIDER-ABLE — **siz·able·ness** *n* — **siz·ably** \-blē\ *adv*
siz·ar *also* **siz·er** \'sī-zər\ *n* [*sizar* alter. of *sizer*, fr. ¹*size*] (1588) : a student (as in the university of Cambridge) who receives an allowance toward college expenses and who orig. acted as a servant to other students in return for this allowance
¹size \'sīz\ *n* [ME *sise* assize, fr. MF, fr. OF, short for *assise* — more at ASSIZE] (13c)   **1** *dial Brit* : ASSIZE 2a — usu. used in pl.   **2** *obs* : a fixed portion of food or drink   **3   a** : physical magnitude, extent, or bulk : relative or proportionate dimensions   **b** : relative aggregate amount or number   **c** : considerable proportions : BIGNESS   **4** : one of a series of graduated measures esp. of manufactured articles (as of clothing) conventionally identified by numbers or letters ⟨a ~ 7 hat⟩   **5** : character, quality, or status of a person or thing esp. with reference to importance, relative merit, or correspondence to needs ⟨try this idea on for ~⟩   **6** : actual state of affairs ⟨that's about the ~ of it⟩
²size *vb* **sized; siz·ing** *vt* (1609)   **1** : to make a particular size : bring to proper or suitable size   **2** : to arrange, grade, or classify according to size or bulk   ~ *vi* : to equal in size or other particular characteristic : COMPARE — usu. used with *up* and often with *to* or *with*
³size \'sīz, ,sīz\ *adj* (1924) : SIZED — usu. used in combination ⟨bite= size⟩
⁴size \'sīz\ *n* [ME *sise*] (15c) : any of various glutinous materials (as preparations of glue, flour, varnish, or resins) used for filling the pores in surfaces (as of paper, textiles, leather, or plaster) or for applying color or metal leaf (as to book edges or covers)
⁵size *vt* **sized; siz·ing** (1667) : to cover, stiffen, or glaze with or as if with size
sized \'sīzd, ,sīzd\ *adj* (1582)   **1** : having a specified size or bulk — usu. used in combination ⟨a small-*sized* house⟩   **2** : arranged or adjusted according to size
size up *vt* (1884) : to form a judgment of
siz·ing \'sī-ziŋ\ *n* (1825) : ⁴SIZE
¹siz·zle \'si-zəl\ *vb* **siz·zled; siz·zling** \'si-zə-liŋ, 'siz-liŋ\ [perh. freq. of *siss* to hiss] *vt* (1603)   **1** : to burn up or sear with or as if with a hissing sound   ~ *vi*   **1** : to make a hissing sound in or as if in burning or frying   **2** : to seethe with deep anger or resentment
²sizzle *n* (ca. 1823) : a hissing sound (as of something frying over a fire)
siz·zler \'si-zə-lər, 'siz-lər\ *n* (1848) : one that sizzles; *esp* : SCORCHER
ska \'skä\ *n* [origin unknown] (1969) : popular music of Jamaican origin that combines elements of traditional Caribbean rhythms and jazz
skag *var of* SCAG
skald \'skȯld, 'skäld\ *n* [ON *skáld*] (1780) : an ancient Scandinavian poet; *broadly* : BARD — **skald·ic** \'skȯl-dik, 'skäl-\ *adj*
skat \'skät, 'skat\ *n* [G, modif. of It *scarto* discard, fr. *scartare* to discard, fr. *s-* (fr. L *ex-*) + *carta* card — more at CARD] (1864)   **1** : a three-handed card game played with 32 cards in which players bid for the privilege of attempting any of several contracts   **2** : a widow of two cards in skat that may be used by the winner of the bid
¹skate \'skāt\ *n, pl* **skates** *also* **skate** [ME *scate*, fr. ON *skata*] (14c) : any of a family (Rajidae, esp. genus *Raja*) of rays with the pectoral fins greatly developed giving the fish a flat diamond shape
²skate *n* [modif. of D *schaats* stilt, skate, fr. ONF *escache* stilt, prob. of Gmc origin; akin to OE *sceacan* to shake — more at SHAKE] (1684)   **1   a** : a metal frame that can be fitted to the sole of a shoe and to which is attached a runner or a set of wheels for gliding over ice or a surface other than ice   **b** : ROLLER SKATE : ICE SKATE   **2** : a period of skating
³skate *vb* **skat·ed; skat·ing** *vi* (1696)   **1** : to glide along on skates propelled by the alternate action of the legs   **2** : to slip or glide as if on skates   **3** : to proceed in a superficial or blithe manner   ~ *vt* : to go along or through by skating
⁴skate *n* [prob. alter. of E dial. *skite* an offensive person] (1894)   **1** : a thin awkward-looking or decrepit horse : NAG   **2** : FELLOW 4c
skate·board \'skāt-,bȯrd, -,bȯrd\ *n* (1964) : a short board mounted on small wheels that is used for coasting and often for performing athletic stunts — **skate·board·er** \-,bȯr-dər, -,bȯr-\ *n* — **skate·board·ing** \-diŋ\ *n*
skat·er \'skā-tər\ *n* (1700)   **1** : one that skates   **2** : WATER STRIDER
skat·ing \'skā-tiŋ\ *n* (1723) : the act, art, or sport of gliding on skates
ska·tole \'ska-,tōl, 'skä-\ *also* **ska·tol** \-,tȯl, -,tōl, -,tōl\ *n* [ISV, fr. Gk *skat-, skōr* excrement — more at SCATOLOGY] (1879) : a foul-smelling compound C₉H₉N found in the intestines and feces, in civet, and in several plants or made synthetically and used in perfumes as a fixative
¹skean *or* **skeane** *var of* SKENE
²skean *or* **skene** \'skē-(ə)n\ *n* [ME *skene*, fr. Ir *scian* & ScGael *sgian*, fr. OIr *scían*; prob. akin to Skt *chyati* he cuts off — more at SCIENCE] (15c) : DAGGER, DIRK
ske·dad·dle \ski-'da-dᵊl\ *vi* **ske·dad·dled; ske·dad·dling** \-'dad-liŋ, -'da-dᵊl-iŋ\ [origin unknown] (1861) : RUN AWAY, SCRAM; *esp* : to flee in a panic — **ske·dad·dler** \-'dad-lər, -'da-dᵊl-ər\ *n*
skeet \'skēt\ *n* [perh. fr. Norw *skyte* to shoot] (1926) : trapshooting in which clay targets are thrown in such a way as to simulate the angles of flight of birds
¹skee·ter \'skē-tər\ *n* [by shortening & alter.] (1839)   **1** : MOSQUITO   **2** : an iceboat 16 feet (5 meters) or more in length equipped with a single sail
²skeet·er \'skē-tər\ *n* (1926) : a skeet shooter
skeg \'skeg\ *also* **skag** \'skag\ *n* [ME *skegge*, fr. ON *skegg* cutwater, lit., beard — more at SHAG] (13c)   **1** : the stern of the keel of a ship near the sternpost; *esp* : the part connecting the keel with the bottom of the rudderpost in a single-screw ship   **2** : a fin situated on the rear bottom of a surfboard that is used for steering and stability
skeigh \'skē\ *adj* [perh. of Scand origin; akin to Sw *skygg* shy; akin to OE *scēoh* shy — more at SHY] (1508) *chiefly Scot* : proudly spirited : SKITTISH
¹skein \'skān\ *n* [ME *skeyne*, fr. MF *escaigne*] (14c)   **1** *or* **skean** *or* **skeane** \'skān\ : a loosely coiled length of yarn or thread wound on a reel   **2** : something suggesting the twists or coils of a skein : TANGLE   **3** : a flock of wildfowl (as geese or ducks) in flight

²**skein** vt (ca. 1775) : to wind into skeins ⟨~ yarn⟩
skel·e·tal \'ske-lə-t²l\ adj (1854) : of, relating to, forming, attached to, or resembling a skeleton — **skel·e·tal·ly** \-t²l-ē\ adv
skeletal muscle n (1877) : striated muscle that is usu. attached to the skeleton and is usu. under voluntary control
¹**skel·e·ton** \'ske-lə-t²n\ n [NL, fr. Gk, neut. of skeletos dried up; akin to Gk skellein to dry up, sklēros hard and perh. to OE sceald shallow] (1578) **1** : a usu. rigid supportive or protective structure or framework of an organism; esp : the bony or more or less cartilaginous framework supporting the soft tissues and protecting the internal organs of a vertebrate **2** : something reduced to its minimum form or essential parts **3** : an emaciated person or animal **4 a** : something forming a structural framework **b** : the straight or branched chain or ring of atoms that forms the basic structure of an organic molecule **5** : something shameful and kept secret (as in a family) — often used in the phrase skeleton in the closet — **ske·le·ton·ic** \,ske-lə-'tä-nik\ adj
²**skeleton** adj (1778) : of, consisting of, or resembling a skeleton
skel·e·ton·ise Brit var of SKELETONIZE
skel·e·ton·ize \-,īz\ vt **-ized; -iz·ing** (1644) : to produce in or reduce to skeleton form ⟨~ a leaf⟩ ⟨~ a news story⟩ ⟨~ a regiment⟩
skel·e·ton·iz·er \-,ī-zər\ n (ca. 1891) : any of various lepidopterous larvae that eat the parenchyma of leaves reducing them to a skeleton of veins
skeleton key n (1810) : a key with a large part of the bit filed away to enable it to open low quality locks as a master key

skeleton 1: 1 skull, 2 clavicle, 3 scapula, 4 sternum, 5 humerus, 6 rib, 7 pelvis, 8 radius, 9 ulna, 10 carpus, 11 metacarpal bones, 12 phalanges (fingers), 13 femur, 14 patella, 15 tibia, 16 fibula, 17 tarsus, 18 metatarsal bones, 19 phalanges (toes), 20 spinal column

skel·lum \'ske-ləm\ n [D schelm, fr. LG; akin to OHG skelmo person deserving death] (1611) chiefly Scot : SCOUNDREL, RASCAL
¹**skelp** \'skelp\ vb **skelped** \'skelpt\ also **skel·pit** \'skel-pət\; **skelp·ing** [ME] vt (15c) dial Brit : STRIKE, SLAP, BEAT ~ vi : to step lively : HUSTLE
²**skelp** n (15c) dial Brit : a smart blow : SLAP
skel·ter \'skel-tər\ vi **skel·tered; skel·ter·ing** \-t(ə-)riŋ\ [fr. -skelter (in helter-skelter)] (1852) : SCURRY
Skel·ton·ics \skel-'tä-niks\ n pl [John Skelton] (1898) : short verses of an irregular meter with two or three stresses sometimes in falling and sometimes in rising rhythm and usu. with rhymed couplets
skep \'skep\ n [ME skeppe basket, beehive, fr. OE sceppe basket, fr. ON skeppa bushel; akin to OHG sceffil bushel, scaf tub] (15c) : BEEHIVE; esp : a domed hive made of twisted straw
skep·sis \'skep-səs\ n [NL, fr. Gk skepsis examination, doubt, skeptical philosophy, fr. skeptesthai] (ca. 1864) : philosophic doubt as to the objective reality of phenomena; broadly : a skeptical outlook or attitude
skep·tic \'skep-tik\ n [L or Gk; L scepticus, fr. Gk skeptikos, fr. skeptesthai to look, consider — more at SPY] (1587) **1** : an adherent or advocate of skepticism **2** : a person disposed to skepticism esp. regarding religion or religious principles
skep·ti·cal \-ti-kəl\ adj (1639) : relating to, characteristic of, or marked by skepticism ⟨a ~ listener⟩ — **skep·ti·cal·ly** \-k(ə-)lē\ adv
skep·ti·cism \'skep-tə-,si-zəm\ n (1646) **1** : an attitude of doubt or a disposition to incredulity either in general or toward a particular object **2 a** : the doctrine that true knowledge or knowledge in a particular area is uncertain **b** : the method of suspended judgment, systematic doubt, or criticism characteristic of skeptics **3** : doubt concerning basic religious principles (as immortality, providence, and revelation) syn see UNCERTAINTY
sker·ry \'sker-ē\ n, pl **skerries** [of Scand origin; akin to ON sker skerry and to ON ey island; akin to L aqua water — more at SCAR, ISLAND] (1612) : a rocky isle : REEF
¹**sketch** \'skech\ n [D schets, fr. It schizzo, lit., splash, fr. schizzare to splash, of imit. origin] (1668) **1 a** : a rough drawing representing the chief features of an object or scene and often made as a preliminary study **b** : a tentative draft (as for a literary work) **2** : a brief description (as of a person) or outline **3 a** : a short literary composition somewhat resembling the short story and the essay but intentionally slight in treatment, discursive in style, and familiar in tone **b** : a short instrumental composition usu. for piano **c** : a slight theatrical piece having a single scene; esp : a comic variety act
²**sketch** vt (1694) : to make a sketch, rough draft, or outline of ~ vi : to draw or paint a sketch — **sketch·er** n
sketch·book \'skech-,buk\ n (1820) : a book of or for sketches
sketchy \'ske-chē\ adj **sketch·i·er; -est** (1805) **1** : of the nature of a sketch : roughly outlined **2** : wanting in completeness, clearness, or substance : SLIGHT, SUPERFICIAL — **sketch·i·ly** \'ske-chə-lē\ adv — **sketch·i·ness** \'ske-chē-nəs\ n
¹**skew** \'skyü\ vb [ME, to escape, skew, fr. ONF escuer to shun, fr. Gmc origin; akin to OHG sciuhen to frighten off — more at SHY] vi (15c) **1** : to take an oblique course **2** : to look askance ~ vt **1** : to make, set, or cut on the skew **2** : to distort esp. from a true value or symmetrical form ⟨~ed statistical data⟩

²**skew** adj (1609) **1** : set, placed, or running obliquely : SLANTING **2** : more developed on one side or in one direction than another : not symmetrical
³**skew** n (1688) : a deviation from a straight line : SLANT
skew·back \'skyü-,bak\ n (1703) : a course of masonry, a stone, or an iron plate having an inclined face against which the voussoirs of an arch abut
¹**skew·bald** \-,bȯld\ adj [skewed (skewbald) + bald] (1654) of an animal : marked with patches of white and any other color but black
²**skewbald** n (1863) : a skewbald horse
skew curve n (ca. 1889) : a curve in three-dimensional space that does not lie in a single plane
skew distribution n (ca. 1931) : an unsymmetrical frequency distribution having the mode at a different value from the mean
¹**skew·er** \'skyü-ər, 'skyü(-ə)r\ n [ME skeuier] (15c) **1** : a pin of wood or metal for fastening meat to keep it in form while roasting or to hold small pieces of meat or vegetables for broiling **2** : any of various things shaped or used like a meat skewer
²**skewer** vt (1701) **1** : to fasten or pierce with or as if with a skewer **2** : to criticize or ridicule sharply and effectively
skew lines n pl (1952) : straight lines that do not intersect and are not in the same plane
skew·ness \'skyü-nəs\ n (1894) : lack of straightness or symmetry : DISTORTION; esp : lack of symmetry in a frequency distribution
¹**ski** \'skē, Brit sometimes 'shē\ n, pl **skis** also **ski** [Norw, fr. ON skith stick of wood, ski; akin to OE scīd board, sceadan to divide — more at SHED] (1755) **1 a** : one of a pair of narrow strips of wood, metal, or plastic curving upward in front that are used esp. for gliding over snow **b** : WATER SKI **2** : a piece of material that resembles a ski and is used as a runner on a vehicle
²**ski** vb **skied** \'skēd, 'shēd\; **ski·ing** vi (ca. 1890) : to glide on skis in travel or as a sport ~ vt : to travel or pass over on skis — **ski·able** \'skē-ə-bəl\ adj — **ski·er** n
skia·gram \'skī-ə-,gram\ n [ISV, fr. Gk skia shadow + ISV -gram — more at SCENE] (1801) **1** : a figure formed by shading in the outline of a shadow **2** : RADIOGRAPH
ski·bob \'skē-,bäb\ n [¹ski + ⁷bob] (1966) : a vehicle that resembles a bicycle with two short skis in place of wheels and that is used for gliding downhill over snow by a rider wearing miniature skis for balance — **ski·bob·ber** \-,bä-bər\ n — **ski·bob·bing** \-,bä-biŋ\ n
ski boot n (1907) : a rigid padded shoe that extends just above the ankle, is securely fastened to the foot (as with laces, buckles, or clasps), and is locked into position in a ski binding
¹**skid** \'skid\ n [perh. of Scand origin; akin to ON skith stick of wood — more at SKI] (ca. 1610) **1** : one of a group of objects (as planks or logs) used to support or elevate a structure or object **2** : a wooden fender hung over a ship's side to protect it in handling cargo **3** : a usu. iron shoe or clog attached to a chain and placed under a wheel to prevent its turning when descending a steep hill : DRAG **4** : a timber, bar, rail, pole, or log used in pairs or sets to form a slideway (as for an incline from a truck to the sidewalk) **5** : the act of skidding : SLIP, SIDESLIP **6** : a runner used as a member of the landing gear of an airplane or helicopter **7 a** pl : a route to defeat or downfall ⟨on the ~s⟩ ⟨his career hit the ~s⟩ **b** : a losing streak ⟨a five-game ~⟩ **8** : a low platform mounted (as on wheels) on which material is set for handling and moving; also : PALLET 3 — **skidproof** adj
²**skid** vb **skid·ded; skid·ding** vt (1674) **1** : to apply a brake or skid to : slow or halt by a skid **2 a** : to haul (as logs) by dragging ⟨cutting and skidding firewood⟩ **b** : to haul along, slide, hoist, or store on skids ~ vi **1** : to slide without rotating (as a wheel held from turning while a vehicle moves onward) **2 a** : to fail to grip the roadway; esp : to slip sideways on the road **b** of an airplane : to slide sideways away from the center of curvature when turning **c** : SLIDE, SLIP **3** : to fall rapidly, steeply, or far
skid·der \'ski-dər\ n (1870) **1** : one that skids or uses a skid **2** : a tractor used esp. for hauling logs
skid·doo or **ski·doo** \ski-'dü, skē-\ vi [prob. alter. of skedaddle] (1903) : to go away : DEPART
skid·dy \'ski-dē\ adj **skid·di·er; -est** (1902) : likely to skid or cause skidding ⟨a wet ~ road⟩
skid road n (1880) **1** : a road along which logs are skidded **2** a West : the part of a town frequented by loggers **b** : SKID ROW
skid row \-'rō\ n [alter. of skid road] (ca. 1931) : a district of cheap saloons and flophouses frequented by vagrants and alcoholics
ski·ey var of SKYEY
skiff \'skif\ n [ME skif, fr. MF or OIt; MF esquif, fr. OIt schifo, of Gmc origin; akin to OE scip ship] (15c) : any of various small boats; esp : a flat-bottomed rowboat
skif·fle \'ski-fəl\ n [origin unknown] (1926) : American jazz or folk music played entirely or in part on nonstandard instruments (as jugs, washboards, or Jew's harps); also : a derivative form of music formerly popular in Great Britain featuring vocals with a simple instrumental accompaniment
ski·ing n (1893) : the art or sport of sliding and jumping on skis
ski·jor·ing \'skē-,jōr-iŋ, -,jȯr-, (,)skē-'\ n [modif. of Norw skikjøring, fr. ski + kjøring driving] (1910) : a winter sport in which a person wearing skis is drawn over snow or ice (as by a horse or vehicle)
ski jump n (1907) : a jump made by a person wearing skis; also : a course or track esp. prepared for such jumping — **ski jump** vi — **ski jumper** n
skil·ful chiefly Brit var of SKILLFUL
ski lift n (1939) : a motor-driven conveyer consisting usu. of a series of bars or seats suspended from an overhead moving cable and used for transporting skiers or sightseers up a long slope
¹**skill** \'skil\ vi [ME skilen, fr. ON skilja to separate, divide; akin to ON skil distinction] (13c) archaic : to make a difference : MATTER, AVAIL
²**skill** n [ME skil, fr. ON, distinction, knowledge; prob. akin to OE

\a\ abut \²\ kitten, F table \ər\ further \a\ ash \ā\ ace \ä\ mop, mar \aù\ out \ch\ chin \e\ bet \ē\ easy \g\ go \i\ hit \ī\ ice \j\ job \ŋ\ sing \ō\ go \ȯ\ law \ȯi\ boy \th\ thin \ṯh\ the \ü\ loot \u̇\ foot \y\ yet \zh\ vision \à, k̲, ⁿ, œ, œ̄, ue, ūe, ᵞ\ see Guide to Pronunciation *scylian* to separate, *sciell* shell — more at SHELL] (13c) **1** *obs* : CAUSE, REASON **2 a** : the ability to use one's knowledge effectively and readily in execution or performance **b** : dexterity or coordination esp. in the execution of learned physical tasks **3** : a learned power of doing something competently : a developed aptitude or ability (language *~s*) *syn* see ART — **skill–less** *or* **skil·less** \'skil-ləs\ *adj* — **skill–less·ness** *or* **skil·less·ness** *n*

skilled \'skild\ *adj* (1552) **1** : having acquired mastery of or skill in something (as a technique or a trade) **2** : of, relating to, or requiring workers or labor with skill and training in a particular occupation, craft, or trade *syn* see PROFICIENT

skil·let \'ski-lət\ *n* [ME *skelet*] (15c) **1** *chiefly Brit* : a small kettle or pot usu. having three or four often long feet and used for cooking on the hearth **2** : FRYING PAN

skill·ful \'skil-fəl\ *adj* (14c) **1** : possessed of or displaying skill : EXPERT **2** : accomplished with skill *syn* see PROFICIENT — **skill·ful·ly** \-fə-lē\ *adv* — **skill·ful·ness** *n*

skil·ling \'ski-liŋ, 'shi-\ *n* [Sw, Norw, & Dan, fr. ON *skillingr*, a gold coin; akin to OE *scilling* shilling] (1793) : any of various old Scandinavian units of value or the coins representing them

¹**skim** \'skim\ *vb* **skimmed; skim·ming** [ME *skymmen*] *vt* (14c) **1 a** : to clear (a liquid) of scum or floating substance (*~* boiling syrup) **b** : to remove (as film or scum) from the surface of a liquid **c** : to remove cream from by skimming **d** : to remove the best or most easily obtainable contents from **2** : to read, study, or examine superficially and rapidly; *esp* : to glance through (as a book) for the chief ideas or the plot **3** : to throw in a gliding path; *esp* : to throw so as to ricochet along the surface of water **4** : to cover with or as if with a film, scum, or coat **5** : to pass swiftly or lightly over **6** : to remove or conceal (as a portion of casino profits) to avoid payment of taxes *~ vi* **1 a** : to pass lightly or hastily : glide or skip along, above, or near a surface **b** : to give a cursory glance, consideration, or reading **2** : to become coated with a thin layer of film or scum **3** : to put on a finishing coat of plaster

²**skim** *n* (14c) **1** : a thin layer, coating, or film **2** : the act of skimming **3** : something skimmed; *specif* : SKIM MILK

³**skim** *adj* (1794) **1** : having the cream removed by skimming **2** : made of skim milk (*~* cheese)

ski mask *n* (1966) : a knit fabric mask that covers the head, has openings for the eyes, mouth, and sometimes the nose, and is worn esp. by skiers for protection from the cold

skim·ble–skam·ble \,skim-bəl-'skam-bəl\ *adj* [redupl. of E dial. *scamble* to stumble along] (1596) : rambling and confused : SENSELESS

skim·mer \'ski-mər\ *n* (14c) **1** : one that skims; *specif* : a flat perforated scoop or spoon used for skimming **2** : any of a small genus (*Rynchops*) of long-winged marine birds that have the lower mandible longer than the upper **3** : a usu. straw flat-crowned hat with a wide straight brim **4** : a fitted sleeveless dress with a usu. flaring skirt

skim milk *n* (1596) : milk from which the cream has been taken — called also *skimmed milk*

skimming *n* (15c) : that which is skimmed from a liquid

ski·mo·bile \'skē-mō-,bēl\ *n* (1944) : SNOWMOBILE

¹**skimp** \'skimp\ *adj* [perh. alter. of *scrimp*] (1775) : SKIMPY

²**skimp** *vt* (ca. 1879) : to give insufficient or barely sufficient attention or effort to or funds for *~ vi* : to save by or as if by skimping

skimpy \'skim-pē\ *adj* **skimp·i·er; -est** (1842) : deficient in supply or execution esp. through skimping : SCANTY *syn* see MEAGER — **skimp·i·ly** \-pə-lē\ *adv* — **skimp·i·ness** \-pē-nəs\ *n*

¹**skin** \'skin\ *n, often attrib* [ME, fr. ON *skinn;* akin to OE *scinn* skin, MHG *schint* fruit peel] (13c) **1 a** (1) : the integument of an animal (as a fur-bearing mammal or a bird) separated from the body usu. with its hair or feathers (2) : a usu. unmounted specimen of a vertebrate (as in a museum) **b** : the hide or pelt of a game or domestic animal **c** (1) : the pelt of an animal prepared for use as a trimming or in a garment — compare ⁴HIDE (2) : a sheet of parchment or vellum made from a hide (3) : BOTTLE 1b **2 a** : the external limiting tissue layer of an animal body esp. when forming a tough but flexible cover relatively impermeable from without while intact **b** : any of various outer or surface layers (as a rind, husk, or pellicle) **3** : the life or physical well-being of a person (saved his own *~*) **4** : a sheathing or casing forming the outside surface of a structure (as a ship or airplane) — **skin·less** \-ləs\ *adj* — **by the skin of one's teeth** : by a very narrow margin — **under one's skin** : so deeply penetrative as to irritate, stimulate, provoke thought, or otherwise excite — **under the skin** : beneath apparent or surface differences : at heart

²**skin** *vb* **skinned; skin·ning** *vt* (14c) **1 a** : to strip, scrape, or rub off an outer covering (as the skin or rind) of **b** : to strip or peel off **c** : to cut, chip, or damage the surface of (fell and *skinned* my knee) **2 a** : to cover with or as if with skin **b** : to heal over with skin **3 a** : to strip of money or property : FLEECE **b** : to defeat badly **c** : CENSURE, CASTIGATE **4** : to urge on and direct the course of (as a draft animal) *~ vi* **1** : to become covered with or as if with skin **2 a** : SHIN 1 **b** : to pass or get by with scant room to spare

³**skin** *adj* (ca. 1935) : involving subjects who are nude (expected to conduct *~* searches for weapons —Diane K. Shah); *esp* : devoted to showing nudes (*~* magazines)

skin–deep \'skin-'dēp\ *adj* (1613) **1** : as deep as the skin **2** : not thorough or lasting in impression : SUPERFICIAL

skin diving *n* (1938) : the sport of swimming under water with a face mask and flippers and esp. without a portable breathing device — **skin–dive** *vi* — **skin diver** *n*

skin effect *n* (1891) : an effect characteristic of current distribution in a conductor at high frequencies by virtue of which the current density is greater near the surface of the conductor than in its interior

skin·flint \'skin-,flint\ *n* (ca. 1700) : a person who would save, gain, or extort money by any means : MISER, NIGGARD

skin·ful \-,fûl\ *n* (1788) **1** : a large or satisfying quantity esp. of liquor **2** : the contents of a skin bottle

skin game *n* (1868) : a swindling game or trick

skin graft *n* (1871) : a piece of skin that is taken from a donor area to replace skin in a defective or denuded area (as one that has been burned) — **skin grafting** *n*

skin·head \'skin-,hed\ *n* (ca. 1953) **1** : a person whose hair is cut very short **2** : a usu. white male belonging to any of various sometimes violent youth gangs whose members have close-shaven hair and often espouse white-supremacist beliefs

¹**skink** \'skiŋk\ *vt* [ME, fr. MD *schenken;* akin to OE *scencan* to pour out drink and prob. to *scanca* shank] (15c) *chiefly dial* : to draw, pour out, or serve (drink)

²**skink** *n* [L *scincus,* fr. Gk *skinkos*] (1590) : any of a family (Scincidae) of typically small insectivorous lizards with long tapering bodies

skink·er \'skiŋ-kər\ *n* (1586) : one that serves liquor : BARTENDER

skinned \'skind\ *adj* (15c) : having skin esp. of a specified kind — usu. used in combination (dark-*skinned*)

skin·ner \'ski-nər\ *n* (14c) **1 a** : one that deals in skins, pelts, or hides **b** : one that removes, cures, or dresses skins **2** : SHARPER **3 a** : driver of draft animals : TEAMSTER

Skin·ner box \'ski-nər-,bäks\ *n* [B. F. Skinner] (1940) : a laboratory apparatus in which an animal is caged for experiments in operant conditioning and which typically contains a lever that must be pressed by the animal to gain reward or avoid punishment

¹**skin·ny** \'ski-nē\ *adj* **skin·ni·er; -est** (1573) **1** : resembling skin : MEMBRANOUS **2 a** : lacking sufficient flesh : very thin : EMACIATED **b** : lacking usual or desirable bulk, quantity, qualities, or significance *syn* see LEAN — **skin·ni·ness** *n*

²**skinny** *n* [perh. fr. ¹*skin* + ⁴*-y*] (1938) *slang* : inside information : DOPE (the straight *~* on what's going on —John Geary)

skin·ny–dip \'ski-nē-,dip\ *vi* (1964) : to swim in the nude — **skinny–dip** *n* — **skin·ny–dip·per** \-,di-pər\ *n*

skin–pop \'skin-'päp\ *vi* (ca. 1952) : to inject a drug subcutaneously rather than into a vein *~ vt* : to inject (a drug) by skin-popping — **skin–pop·per** \-,pä-pər\ *n*

skint \'skint\ *adj* [alter. of *skinned,* pp. of ²*skin*] (ca. 1925) *chiefly Brit* : PENNILESS

skin test *n* (1925) : a test (as a scratch test) performed on the skin and used in detecting allergic hypersensitivity

skin·tight \'skin-'tīt\ *adj* (1885) : closely fitted to the figure

¹**skip** \'skip\ *vb* **skipped; skip·ping** [ME *skippen,* perh. of Scand origin; akin to Sw dial. *skopa* to hop] *vi* (14c) **1 a** : to move or proceed with leaps and bounds or with a skip **b** : to bound off one point after another : RICOCHET **2** : to leave hurriedly or secretly (*skipped* out without paying their bill) **3 a** : to pass over or omit an interval, item, or step **b** : to omit a grade in school in advancing to the next **c** : MISFIRE 1 *~ vt* **1 a** : to pass over without notice or mention : OMIT **b** : to pass by or leave out (a step in a progression or series) **2 a** : to cause to skip (a grade in school) **b** : to cause to bound or skim over a surface (*~* a stone across a pond) **3** : to leap over lightly and nimbly **4 a** : to depart from quickly and secretly (*skipped* town) **b** : to fail to attend or participate in (*~* the tournament) (*~* the meeting) — **skip·pa·ble** \'ski-pə-bəl\ *adj* — **skip bail** : to jump bail — **skip rope** : to use a jump rope (as for exercise or a game)

²**skip** *n* (15c) **1 a** : a light bounding step **b** : a gait composed of alternating hops and steps **2** : an act of omission or the thing omitted

³**skip** *n* [short for ²*skipper*] (1830) **1** : the captain of a side in a game (as curling or lawn bowling) who advises the team as to the play and controls the action **2** : ²SKIPPER

⁴**skip** *vt* **skipped; skip·ping** (1900) : to act as skipper of

skip bomb *vt* (1943) : to attack by releasing delayed-action bombs from a low-flying airplane so that they skip along a land or water surface and strike a target

skip·jack \'skip-,jak\ *n, pl* **skipjacks** *or* **skipjack** (1703) **1** : any of various fishes (as a ladyfish or bluefish) that jump above or are active at the surface of the water; *esp* : SKIPJACK TUNA **2** : a sailboat with vertical sides and a bottom similar to a flat V

skipjack tuna *n* (1950) : a relatively small scombroid food and sport fish (*Katsuwonus pelamis* syn. *Euthynnus pelamis*) that is bluish above and silvery below with oblique dark stripes on the sides and belly

ski pole *n* (1920) : one of a pair of lightweight poles used in skiing that have a handgrip and usu. a wrist strap at one end and an encircling disk set above the point at the other end

¹**skip·per** \'ski-pər\ *n* (13c) **1** : any of various erratically active insects (as a click beetle or a water strider) **2** : one that skips **3** : SAURY **4** : any of a superfamily (Hesperioidea, esp. family Hesperiidae) of stoutbodied lepidopterous insects that differ from the typical butterflies esp. in wing venation and the form of the antennae

²**skipper** *n* [ME, fr. MD *schipper,* fr. *schip* ship; akin to OE *scip* ship — more at SHIP] (14c) **1** : the master of a ship; *esp* : the master of a fishing, small trading, or pleasure boat **2** : the captain or first pilot of an airplane **3** : a person in a position of leadership; *esp* : a baseball team's manager

³**skip·per** *vt* **skip·pered; skip·per·ing** \'ski-p(ə-)riŋ\ (1893) **1** : to act as skipper of (as a boat) **2** : to act as coach of (as a team)

¹**skirl** \'skər(-ə)l, 'skir(-ə)l\ *vb* [ME (Sc) *skrillen, skirlen* to scream, shriek, of Scand origin; akin to OSw *skrælla* to rattle; akin to OE *scrallettan* to resound loudly] *vi* (ca. 1665) *of a bagpipe* : to emit the high shrill tone of the chanter; *also* : to give forth music *~ vt* : to play (music) on the bagpipe

²**skirl** *n* (1856) : a high shrill sound produced by the chanter of a bagpipe

¹**skir·mish** \'skər-mish\ *n* [ME *skyrmissh,* alter. of *skarmish,* fr. MF *escarmouche,* fr. OIt *scaramuccia*] (14c) **1** : a minor fight in war usu. incidental to larger movements **2 a** : a brisk preliminary verbal conflict **b** : a minor dispute or contest between opposing parties

²**skirmish** *vi* (14c) **1** : to engage in a skirmish **2** : to search about (as for supplies) : scout around — **skir·mish·er** *n*

¹**skirr** \'skər, 'skir\ *vb* [perh. alter. of ³*scour*] *vi* (ca. 1548) **1** : to leave hastily : FLEE (birds *~ed* off from the bushes —D. H. Lawrence) **2** : to run, fly, sail, or move along rapidly *~ vt* **1** : to search about in (*~* the country round —Shak.) **2 a** : to pass rapidly over : SKIM **b** *dial* : to cause to skim

²**skirr** *n* [prob. imit.] (ca. 1870) : WHIR, ROAR

¹**skirt** \'skərt\ *n* [ME, fr. ON *skyrta* shirt, kirtle — more at SHIRT] (14c) **1 a** (1) : a free-hanging part of an outer garment or undergarment extending from the waist down (2) : a separate free-hanging outer garment or undergarment usu. worn by women and girls covering some or all of the body from the waist down **b** : either of two usu. leather flaps on a saddle covering the bars on which the stirrups are hung **c** : a cloth facing that hangs loosely and usu. in folds or pleats

from the bottom edge or across the front of a piece of furniture **d :** the lower branches of a tree when near the ground **2 a :** the rim, periphery, or environs of an area **b** *pl :* outlying parts (as of a town or city) **3 :** a part or attachment serving as a rim, border, or edging **4 :** a girl or woman — **skirt·ed** *adj*

²**skirt** *vt* (1602) **1 :** to form or run along the border or edge of : BORDER **2 a :** to provide a skirt for **b :** to furnish a border or shield for **3 a :** to go or pass around or about; *specif :* to go around or keep away from in order to avoid danger or discovery **b :** to avoid esp. because of difficulty or fear of controversy ⟨~*ed* the issue⟩ **c :** to evade or miss by a narrow margin ⟨having ~*ed* disaster —Edith Wharton⟩ ~ *vi :* to be, lie, or move along an edge or border — **skirt·er** *n*

skirt·ing \'skər-tiŋ\ *n* (1764) **1 :** something that skirts: as **a :** BORDER, EDGING **b** *chiefly Brit :* BASEBOARD **2 :** fabric suitable for skirts

skirt steak *n* (ca. 1909) **:** a boneless strip of beef cut from the plate

ski run *n* (1924) **:** a slope or trail suitable for skiing

skit \'skit\ *n* [origin unknown] (ca. 1727) **1 :** a jeering or satirical remark : TAUNT **2 a :** a satirical or humorous story or sketch **b** (1) **:** a brief burlesque or comic sketch included in a dramatic performance (as a revue) (2) **:** a short serious dramatic piece; *esp :* one done by amateurs

ski touring *n* (1935) **:** cross-country skiing for pleasure

ski tow *n* (1935) **1 :** a motor-driven conveyor that is used for pulling skiers up a slope and that consists usu. of an endless moving rope which a skier grasps **2 :** SKI LIFT

skit·ter \'ski-tər\ *vb* [prob. freq. of E dial. *skite* to move quickly] *vi* (1845) **1 :** to glide or skip lightly or quickly **2 :** to twitch the hook of a fishing line through or along the surface of water ~ *vt :* to cause to skitter

skit·tery \'ski-tə-rē\ *adj* (1941) **:** SKITTISH

skit·tish \'ski-tish\ *adj* [ME] (15c) **1 a :** lively or frisky in action : CAPRICIOUS **b :** VARIABLE, FLUCTUATING **2 :** easily frightened : RESTIVE ⟨a ~ horse⟩ **3 a :** COY, BASHFUL **b :** marked by extreme caution : WARY — **skit·tish·ly** *adv* — **skit·tish·ness** *n*

skit·tle \'ski-t²l\ *n* [perh. of Scand origin; akin to ON *skutill* bolt — more at SHUTTLE] (1634) **1** *pl but sing in constr :* English ninepins played with a wooden disk or ball **2 :** one of the pins used in skittles

skive \'skīv\ *vt skived; skiv·ing* [prob. of Scand origin; akin to ON *skifa* to slice] (ca. 1825) **:** to cut off (as leather or rubber) in thin layers or pieces : PARE

skiv·er \'skī-vər\ *n* (1800) **1 :** a thin soft leather made of the grain side of a split sheepskin, usu. tanned in sumac and dyed **2 :** one that skives something (as leather)

Skiv·vies \'ski-vēz\ *trademark* — used for men's underwear

skiv·vy \'ski-vē\ *n, pl* **skivvies** [origin unknown] (ca. 1902) *Brit :* a female domestic servant

ski·wear \'skē-,war, -,wer\ *n* (1961) **:** clothing suitable for wear while skiing

sklent \'sklent\ *vb* [ME *sclenten* to strike obliquely, alter. of *slenten* — more at SLANT] *vi* (1805) **1** *chiefly Scot :* to look askance **2** *chiefly Scot :* to cast aspersions ~ *vt, Scot :* to direct sideways : SLANT

skoal \'skōl\ *n* [Dan *skaal*, lit., cup; akin to ON *skāl* bowl — more at SCALE] (1600) **:** TOAST, HEALTH — often used interjectionally

skosh \'skōsh\ *n* [Jp *sukoshi*] (1952) **:** a small amount : BIT, SMIDGEN — used adverbially with *a* ⟨just a ~ bit shook —Josiah Bunting⟩

skua \'skyü-ə\ *n* [NL, fr. Faeroese *skūgvur*; akin to ON *skūfr* tassel, skua, OE *scēaf* sheaf — more at SHEAF] (1678) **:** either of two seabirds related to the jaegers: **a :** GREAT SKUA **b :** a bird (*Catharacta maccormicki*) that resembles but is slightly smaller than the great skua and that breeds in the Antarctic

skul·dug·gery *or* **skull·dug·gery** \,skəl-'də-g(ə-)rē, 'skəl-\ *n, pl* **-ger·ies** [origin unknown] (1867) **:** a devious device or trick; *also :* underhanded or unscrupulous behavior

¹**skulk** \'skəlk\ *vi* [ME, of Scand origin; akin to Dan *skulke* to shirk, play truant] (13c) **1 :** to move in a stealthy or furtive manner **2 a :** to hide or conceal something (as oneself) often out of cowardice or fear or with sinister intent **b** *chiefly Brit :* MALINGER *syn* see LURK — **skulk·er** *n*

²**skulk** *n* (14c) **1 :** one that skulks **2 :** a group of foxes

skull \'skəl\ *n* [ME *skulle*, of Scand origin; akin to Sw *skulle* skull] (13c) **:** the skeleton of the head of a vertebrate forming a bony or cartilaginous case that encloses and protects the brain and chief sense organs and supports the jaws **2 :** the seat of understanding or intelligence : MIND — **skulled** \'skəld\ *adj*

skull and cross·bones \-'krós-,bōnz\ *n, pl* **skulls and crossbones** (1826) **:** a representation of a human skull over crossbones usu. used as a warning of danger to life

skull·cap \'skəl-,kap\ *n* (1682) **1 :** a close-fitting cap; *esp :* a light cap without brim for indoor wear **2 :** any of various mints (genus *Scutellaria*) having a calyx that when inverted resembles a helmet **3 :** the upper portion of the skull : CALVARIUM

skull session *n* (1937) **1 :** a strategy class for an athletic team **2 :** a meeting for consultation, discussion, or the interchange of ideas or information — called also *skull practice*

¹**skunk** \'skəŋk\ *n, pl* **skunks** *also* **skunk** [of Algonquian origin; akin to Eastern Abenaki *segañk8* skunk] (1634) **1 a :** any of various common omnivorous black-and-white New World mammals (esp. genus *Mephitis*) of the weasel family that have a pair of perineal glands from which a secretion of pungent and offensive odor is ejected **b :** the fur of a skunk **2 :** an obnoxious or disliked person

²**skunk** *vt* (1843) **1 a :** DEFEAT **b :** to shut out in a game **2 :** to fail to pay; *also :* CHEAT

skunk cabbage *n* (1751) **:** either of two No. American perennial herbs of the arum family that occur in shaded wet to swampy areas and have a fetid

skunk cabbage

odor suggestive of a skunk: **a :** one (*Symplocarpus foetidus*) of eastern No. America that sends up in spring a cowl-shaped brownish purple spathe **b :** one (*Lysichitum americana*) chiefly of the Pacific coast region that has a large yellow spathe

skunk works *n pl but sing or pl in constr* [fr. the *Skonk Works*, illicit distillery in the comic strip *Li'l Abner* by Al Capp] (ca. 1974) **:** a usu. small and often isolated department or facility (as for engineering research and development) that functions with minimal supervision within a company or corporation

¹**sky** \'skī\ *n, pl* **skies** [ME, cloud, sky, fr. ON *skȳ* cloud; akin to OE *scēo* cloud] (13c) **1 :** the upper atmosphere or expanse of space that constitutes an apparent great vault or arch over the earth **2 :** HEAVEN **3 a :** weather in the upper atmosphere **b :** CLIMATE ⟨temperate English skies —G. G. Coulton⟩

²**sky** *vt* **skied** *or* **skyed; sky·ing** (1802) **1** *chiefly Brit :* to throw or toss up : FLIP **2 :** to hang (as a painting) above the line of vision **3 :** to hit (a ball) high into the air

sky blue *n* (1738) **:** a pale to light blue color

sky·borne \'skī-,bōrn, -,bórn\ *adj* (1589) **:** AIRBORNE ⟨~ troops⟩

sky·box \-,bäks\ *n* (1974) **:** a roofed enclosure of private seats situated high in a sports stadium and typically featuring luxurious amenities

sky·cap \-,kap\ *n* [¹*sky* + -*cap* (as in *redcap*)] (1941) **:** one employed to carry hand luggage at an airport — compare REDCAP

sky·div·ing \-,dī-viŋ\ *n* (1957) **:** the sport of jumping from an airplane at a moderate altitude (as 6000 feet) and executing various body maneuvers before pulling the rip cord of a parachute — **sky diver** *n*

Skye terrier \'skī-\ *n* [*Skye*, Scotland] (1847) **:** any of a Scottish breed of terriers with a long low body and long straight coat

sky·ey \'skī-ē\ *adj* (1603) **:** of or resembling the sky : ETHEREAL

¹**sky–high** \'skī-'hī\ *adv* (1818) **1 a :** high into the air **b :** to a high or exorbitant level or degree **2 :** in an enthusiastic manner **3 :** to bits : APART ⟨blown ~⟩

²**sky–high** *adj* (1945) **:** excessively expensive : EXORBITANT

sky·hook \-,húk\ *n* (1915) **:** a hook conceived as being suspended from the sky

sky·jack \'skī-,jak\ *vt* [¹*sky* + -*jack* (as in *hijack*)] (1961) **:** to commandeer (an airplane in flight) by the threat of violence — **sky·jack·er** \-,ja-kər\ *n* — **sky·jack·ing** \-,kiŋ\ *n*

¹**sky·lark** \'skī-,lärk\ *n* (1686) **1 :** a common largely brown Old World lark (*Alauda arvensis*) noted for its song esp. as uttered in flight **2 :** any of various birds resembling the skylark

²**skylark** *vi* (1809) **1 :** to run up and down the rigging of a ship in sport **2 :** FROLIC, SPORT — **sky·lark·er** *n*

sky·light \'skī-,līt\ *n* (1679) **1 :** the diffused and reflected light of the sky **2 :** an opening in a house roof or ship's deck that is covered with translucent or transparent material and that is designed to admit light — **sky·light·ed** \-,lī-təd\ *also* **sky–lit** \-,lit\ *adj* (1849) **:** having a skylight

sky·line \-,līn\ *n* (1824) **1 :** the apparent juncture of earth and sky : HORIZON **2 :** an outline (as of buildings or a mountain range) against the background of the sky

sky marshal *n* (1968) **:** an armed federal plainclothesman assigned to prevent skyjackings

sky pilot *n* (1883) **:** CLERGYMAN; *specif :* CHAPLAIN

¹**sky·rock·et** \'skī-,rä-kət\ *n* (1688) **:** ²ROCKET 1a

²**skyrocket** *vt* (1851) **1 :** to cause to rise or increase abruptly and rapidly **2 :** CATAPULT ~ *vi :* to shoot up abruptly ⟨prices are ~*ing*⟩

sky·sail \'skī-,sāl, -səl\ *n* (1829) **:** the sail above the royal

sky·scrap·er \-,skrā-pər\ *n* (1883) **:** a very tall building

sky·walk \-,wók\ *n* (1953) **:** a usu. enclosed aerial walkway connecting two buildings

sky·ward \-wərd\ *adv* (1582) **1 :** toward the sky **2 :** UPWARD

sky wave *n* (1928) **:** a radio wave that is propagated by means of the ionosphere

sky·way \'skī-,wā\ *n* (1919) **1 :** a route used by airplanes : AIR LANE **2 :** an elevated highway **3 :** SKYWALK

sky·write \-,rīt\ *vb* **-wrote** \-,rōt\; **-writ·ten** \-,ri-t²n\; **-writ·ing** \-,rī-tiŋ\ [back-formation from *skywriting*] *vt* (1926) **:** to letter by skywriting ~ *vi :* to do skywriting — **sky·writ·er** *n*

sky·writ·ing \-,rī-tiŋ\ *n* (1922) **:** writing formed in the sky by means of a visible substance (as smoke) emitted from an airplane

¹**slab** \'slab\ *n* [ME *slabbe*] (14c) **1 :** a thick plate or slice (as of stone, wood, or bread): as **a :** the outside piece cut from a log in squaring it **b :** concrete pavement (as of a road); *specif :* a strip of concrete pavement laid as a single unjointed piece **c** (1) **:** a flat rectangular architectural element that is usu. formed of a single piece or mass (a concrete foundation ~) (2) **:** a rectangular building having little width with respect to its length and usu. height **2 :** something that resembles a slab (as in size) ⟨backed up by a solid ~ of reference material —*Times Lit. Supp.*⟩ — **slab·like** \-,līk\ *adj*

²**slab** *vt* **slabbed; slab·bing** (1703) **1 a :** to remove an outer slab from (as a log) **b :** to divide or form into slabs **2 :** to cover or support (as a roadbed or roof) with slabs **3 :** to put on thickly

³**slab** *adj* [prob. of Scand origin; akin to obs. Dan *slab* slippery] (1605) *dial chiefly Eng :* THICK, VISCOUS

¹**slab·ber** \'sla-bər\ *vb* **slab·bered; slab·ber·ing** \-b(ə-)riŋ\ [prob. fr. D *slabberen*, freq. of *slabben* to slaver — more at SLAVER] (1542) **:** SLOBBER, DROOL

²**slabber** *n* (1718) **:** SLOBBER, SLAVER

slab–sid·ed \'slab-'sī-dəd\ *adj* (1817) **:** having flat sides; *also :* being tall or long and lank

¹**slack** \'slak\ *adj* [ME *slak*, fr. OE *sleac*; akin to OHG *slah* slack, L *laxus* slack, loose, *languēre* to languish, Gk *lagnos* lustful and perh. to Gk *lēgein* to stop] (bef. 12c) **1 :** not using due diligence, care, or dispatch : NEGLIGENT **2 a :** characterized by slowness, sluggishness, or lack of energy ⟨a ~ pace⟩ **b :** moderate in some quality; *esp :* moderately warm ⟨a ~ oven⟩ **c :** blowing or flowing at low speed ⟨the tide was ~⟩ **3 a :** not tight or taut ⟨a ~ rope⟩ **b :** lacking in usual or

\ə\ abut \ᵊ\ kitten, F table \ər\ further \a\ ash \ā\ ace \ä\ mop, mar \aú\ out \ch\ chin \e\ bet \ē\ easy \g\ go \i\ hit \ī\ ice \j\ job \ŋ\ sing \ō\ go \ó\ law \ói\ boy \th\ thin \t̲h̲\ the \ü\ loot \ú\ foot \y\ yet \zh\ vision \à, k̲, ⁿ, œ, œ̄, ɯ, ɯ̄, ʸ\ see Guide to Pronunciation normal firmness and steadiness : WEAK ⟨~ muscles⟩ ⟨~ supervision⟩ 4 : wanting in activity : DULL ⟨a ~ market⟩ 5 : lacking in completeness, finish, or perfection ⟨a very ~ piece of work⟩ *syn* see NEGLIGENT — **slack·ly** *adv* — **slack·ness** *n*

²**slack** *vi* (13c) 1 : to be or become slack 2 : to shirk or evade work or duty ~ *vt* 1 a : to be slack or negligent in performing or doing b : LESSEN, MODERATE 2 : to release tension on : LOOSEN 3 a : to cause to abate b : SLAKE 3

³**slack** *n* (1756) 1 : cessation in movement or flow 2 : a part of something that hangs loose without strain ⟨take up the ~ of a rope⟩ 3 : trousers esp. for casual wear — usu. used in pl. 4 : a dull season or period 5 a : a part that is available but not used ⟨some ~ in the budget⟩ b : a part that is wanted but not supplied : SHORTFALL ⟨take up the ~ in supplying oil⟩

⁴**slack** *n* [ME *slak*, fr. ON *slakki*] (14c) *dial Eng* : a pass between hills

⁵**slack** *n* [ME *sleck*] (15c) : the finest screenings of coal produced at a mine unusable as fuel unless cleaned

slack·en \'sla-kən\ *vb* **slack·ened; slack·en·ing** \'sla-kᵉn-iŋ\ *vt* (15c) 1 : to make less active : slow up ⟨~ speed at a crossing⟩ 2 : to make slack (as by lessening tension or firmness) ⟨~ sail⟩ ~ *vi* 1 : to become slack or slow or negligent : slow down 2 : to become less active : SLACK *syn* see DELAY

slack·er \'sla-kər\ *n* (1898) : a person who shirks work or obligation; *esp* : one who evades military service in time of war

slack water *n* (ca. 1769) : the period at the turn of the tide when there is little or no horizontal motion of tidal water — called also *slack tide*

slag \'slag\ *n* [MLG *slagge*] (1552) : the dross or scoria of a metal

slain *past part of* SLAY

slake \'slāk, *vi* 2 & *vt* 3 *are also* 'slak\ *vb* **slaked; slak·ing** [ME, fr. OE *slacian*, fr. *sleac* slack] *vi* (14c) 1 *archaic* : SUBSIDE, ABATE 2 : to become slaked : CRUMBLE ⟨lime may ~ spontaneously in moist air⟩ ~ *vt* 1 *archaic* : to lessen the force of : MODERATE 2 : SATISFY, QUENCH ⟨~ your thirst⟩ ⟨will ~ your curiosity⟩ 3 : to cause (as lime) to heat and crumble by treatment with water : HYDRATE

¹**sla·lom** \'slä-ləm\ *n, often attrib* [Norw *slalåm*, lit., sloping track] (1921) 1 : skiing in a zigzag or wavy course between upright obstacles (as flags) 2 : a timed race (as on skis or in an automobile or kayak) over a winding or zigzag course past a series of flags or markers; *broadly* : movement over a zigzag course

²**slalom** *vi* (1932) : to move over a zigzag course in or as if in a slalom

¹**slam** \'slam\ *n* [origin unknown] (1660) 1 : GRAND SLAM 2 : LITTLE SLAM

²**slam** *n* [prob. of Scand origin; akin to Icel *slæma* to slam] (1672) 1 : a heavy blow or impact 2 a : a noisy violent closing b : a banging noise; *esp* : one made by the slam of a door 3 : a cutting or violent criticism 4 : SLAMMER

³**slam** *vb* **slammed; slam·ming** *vt* (ca. 1691) 1 : to strike or beat hard : KNOCK 2 : to shut forcibly and noisily : BANG 3 a : to set or slap down violently or noisily ⟨slammed down the phone⟩ b : to propel, thrust, or produce by or as if by striking hard ⟨~ on the brakes⟩ ⟨slammed the car into a wall⟩ 4 : to criticize harshly ~ *vi* 1 : to make a banging noise 2 : to function (as in moving) with emphatic and usu. noisy vigor ⟨the hurricane slammed into the coast⟩ ⟨slammed out of the room⟩ 3 : to utter verbal abuse or harsh criticism

slam–bang \'slam-'baŋ\ *adj* (ca. 1823) 1 : unduly loud or violent ⟨a ~ clatter⟩ 2 : having fast-paced often nonstop action ⟨a ~ adventure novel⟩ 3 : vigorously enthusiastic ⟨made a ~ effort to win⟩

slam dunk *n* (1972) : DUNK SHOT — **slam–dunk** *vb*

slam·mer \'sla-mər\ *n* (1952) : JAIL, PRISON

¹**slan·der** \'slan-dər\ *vt* **slan·dered; slan·der·ing** \-d(ə-)riŋ\ (13c) : to utter slander against : DEFAME *syn* see MALIGN — **slan·der·er** \-dər-ər\ *n*

²**slander** *n* [ME *sclaundre, slaundre*, fr. OF *esclandre*, fr. LL *scandalum* stumbling block, offense — more at SCANDAL] (14c) 1 : the utterance of false charges or misrepresentations which defame and damage another's reputation 2 : a false and defamatory oral statement about a person — compare LIBEL — **slan·der·ous** \-d(ə-)rəs\ *adj* — **slan·der·ous·ly** *adv* — **slan·der·ous·ness** *n*

¹**slang** \'slaŋ\ *n* [origin unknown] (1756) 1 : language peculiar to a particular group: as a : ARGOT b : JARGON 2 : an informal nonstandard vocabulary composed typically of coinages, arbitrarily changed words, and extravagant, forced, or facetious figures of speech — **slang** *adj* — **slang·i·ly** \'slaŋ-ə-lē\ *adv* — **slang·i·ness** \'slaŋ-ē-nəs\ *n* — **slangy** \'slaŋ-ē\ *adj*

²**slang** *vi* (1828) : to use slang or vulgar abuse ~ *vt* : to abuse with harsh or coarse language

slanging match *n* (1896) *chiefly Brit* : a heated exchange of abuse

slan·guage \'slaŋ-gwij\ *n* [blend of *slang* and *language*] (1879) : slangy speech or writing

¹**slant** \'slant\ *n* (1655) 1 : a slanting direction, line, or plane : SLOPE 2 a : something that slants b : DIAGONAL 3 c : a football running play in which the ballcarrier runs obliquely toward the line of scrimmage 3 a : a peculiar or personal point of view, attitude, or opinion b : a slanting view : GLANCE — **slant** *adj* — **slant·ways** \-,wāz\ *adv* — **slant·wise** \-,wīz\ *adv or adj* — **slanty** \'slan-tē\ *adj*

²**slant** *vb* [ME *slenten* to fall obliquely, of Scand origin; akin to Sw *slinta* to slide] *vi* (1692) 1 : to take a diagonal course, direction, or path 2 : to turn or incline from a right line or a level : SLOPE ~ *vt* 1 : to give an oblique or sloping direction to 2 : to interpret or present in line with a special interest : ANGLE ⟨stories ~ed toward youth⟩; *esp* : to maliciously or dishonestly distort or falsify — **slant·ing·ly** \'slan-tiŋ-lē\ *adv*

slant height *n* (1798) 1 : the length of an element of a right circular cone 2 : the altitude of a side of a regular pyramid

¹**slap** \'slap\ *n* [ME *slop*, fr. MD; akin to MD *slippen* to slip] (14c) *dial Brit* : OPENING, BREACH

²**slap** *vt* **slapped; slap·ping** [akin to LG *slapp*, n. blow] (15c) 1 a : to strike sharply with or as if with the open hand b : to cause to strike with a motion or sound like that of a blow with the open hand 2 : to put, place, or throw with careless haste or force ⟨slapped on a coat of paint⟩ 3 : to assail verbally : INSULT 4 : to subject to a penalty — usu. used with *with* ⟨slapped him with a $10 fine⟩

³**slap** *n* (1648) 1 a : a blow with the open hand b : a quick sharp blow 2 : a noise like that of a slap 3 : REBUFF, INSULT — **slap on the wrist** : a gentle usu. ineffectual reprimand

⁴**slap** *adv* [prob. fr. LG *slapp*, fr. *slapp*, n.] (1672) : DIRECTLY, SMACK

slap-dash \'slap-'dash, -,dash\ *adj* (ca. 1792) : HAPHAZARD, SLIPSHOD

slap down *vt* (1842) 1 : to prohibit or restrain usu. abruptly and with censure from acting in a specified way : SQUELCH 2 : to put an abrupt stop to : SUPPRESS

slap-hap-py \'slap-,ha-pē\ *adj* (1936) 1 : PUNCH-DRUNK 2 : buoyantly or recklessly carefree or foolish : HAPPY-GO-LUCKY

slap·jack \-,jak\ *n* [²*slap* + *-jack* (as in *flapjack*)] (1796) 1 : PANCAKE 2 : a card game in which each player tries to be the first to slap a hand on any jack that appears faceup

slap shot *n* (1942) : a shot in ice hockey made with a swinging stroke

slap·stick \'slap-,stik\ *n* (1896) 1 : a device made of two flat pieces of wood fastened at one end so as to make a loud noise when used by an actor to strike a person 2 : comedy stressing farce and horseplay; *also* : activity resembling slapstick — **slapstick** *adj*

slap–up \'slap-,əp\ *adj* (ca. 1823) *chiefly Brit* : FIRST-RATE, BANG-UP

¹**slash** \'slash\ *vb* [origin unknown] *vi* (1548) : to lash out, cut, or thrash about with or as if with an edged blade ~ *vt* 1 : to cut with or as if with rough sweeping strokes : CANE, LASH 2 : to cut slits in (as a garment) so as to reveal a color beneath 3 : to criticize cuttingly 5 : to reduce sharply : CUT — **slash·er** *n*

²**slash** *n* (1576) 1 : the act of slashing; *also* : a long cut or stroke made by or as if by slashing 2 : an ornamental slit in a garment 3 a : an open tract in a forest strewn with debris (as from logging) b : the debris in such a tract 4 : DIAGONAL 3 — called also *slash mark*

³**slash** *n* [origin unknown] (1652) : a low swampy area often overgrown with brush

slash–and–burn *adj* (1939) : characterized or developed by felling and burning trees to clear land esp. for temporary agriculture

¹**slash·ing** \'sla-shiŋ\ *adj* (1593) 1 : incisively satiric or critical 2 : DRIVING, PELTING 3 : VIVID, BRILLIANT — **slash·ing·ly** \-shiŋ-lē\ *adv*

²**slashing** *n* (1596) 1 : the act or process of slashing 2 : an insert or layer of contrasting color revealed by a slash (as in a garment) 3 : SLASH 3

slash pine *n* [³*slash*] (1882) : a pine (*Pinus elliottii*) of the southeastern U.S. that has two or three needles in a cluster and is a source of turpentine and lumber

slash pocket *n* (1799) : a pocket suspended on the wrong side of a garment from a finished slit on the right side that serves as its opening

¹**slat** \'slat\ *vt* **slat·ted; slat·ting** [prob. of Scand origin; akin to ON *sletta* to slap, throw] (1611) 1 : to hurl or throw smartly 2 : STRIKE, PUMMEL

²**slat** *n* [ME, slate, fr. MF *esclat* splinter, fr. OF, fr. *esclater* to burst, splinter] (1764) 1 : a thin narrow flat strip esp. of wood or metal 2 *pl, slang* : RIBS 3 : an auxiliary airfoil at the leading edge of the wing of an airplane — **slat** *adj* — **slat·ted** \'sla-təd\ *adj*

³**slat** *vt* **slat·ted; slat·ting** (1886) : to make or equip with slats

¹**slate** \'slāt\ *n* [ME, fr. MF *esclat* splinter] (14c) 1 : a piece of construction material (as laminated rock) prepared as a shingle for roofing and siding 2 : a dense fine-grained metamorphic rock produced by the compression of various sediments (as clay or shale) so as to develop a characteristic cleavage 3 : a tablet (as of slate) used for writing on 4 a : a written or unwritten record (as of deeds) ⟨started with a clean ~⟩ b : a list of candidates for nomination or election 5 a : a dark purplish gray b : any of various grays similar in color to common roofing slates — **slate** *adj* — **slate·like** \-,līk\ *adj*

²**slate** *vt* **slat·ed; slat·ing** (15c) 1 : to cover with slate or a slatelike substance ⟨~ a roof⟩ 2 : to designate for a specified purpose or action : SCHEDULE ⟨was *slated* to direct the play⟩

³**slate** *vt* **slat·ed; slat·ing** [prob. alter. of ¹*slat*] (1825) 1 : to thrash or pummel severely 2 *chiefly Brit* : to criticize or censure severely

slate black *n* (ca. 1890) : a nearly neutral slightly purplish black

slate blue *n* (1796) : a grayish blue color

slat·er \'slā-tər\ *n* (14c) 1 : one that slates 2 [¹*slate*; fr. its color] a : WOOD LOUSE b : any of various marine isopods

¹**slath·er** \'sla-thər\ *n* [origin unknown] (1857) : a great quantity — often used in pl.

²**slather** *vt* **slath·ered; slath·er·ing** \'sla-thə-riŋ, 'slath-riŋ\ (1866) 1 : to use or spend in a wasteful or lavish manner : SQUANDER 2 a : to spread thickly or lavishly b : to spread something thickly or lavishly on

slat·ing \'slā-tiŋ\ *n* (15c) : the work of a slater

¹**slat·tern** \'sla-tərn\ *n* [prob. fr. G *schlottern* to hang loosely, slouch; akin to D *sloddern* to hang loosely, *slodder* slut] (ca. 1639) : an untidy slovenly woman; *also* : SLUT, PROSTITUTE

²**slattern** *adj* (1716) : SLATTERNLY

slat·tern·ly \'sla-tərn-lē\ *adj* (ca. 1680) 1 : untidy and dirty through habitual neglect; *also* : CARELESS, DISORDERLY 2 : of, relating to, or characteristic of a slut or prostitute — **slat·tern·li·ness** *n*

slaty *also* **slat·ey** \'slā-tē\ *adj* (ca. 1529) : of, containing, or characteristic of slate; *also* : gray like slate

¹**slaugh·ter** \'slȯ-tər\ *n* [ME, of Scand origin; akin to ON *slātra* to slaughter; akin to OE *sleaht* slaughter, *slēan* to slay — more at SLAY] (14c) 1 : the act of killing; *specif* : the butchering of livestock for market 2 : killing of great numbers of human beings (as in battle or a massacre) : CARNAGE

²**slaughter** *vt* (1535) 1 : to kill (animals) for food : BUTCHER 2 a : to kill in a bloody or violent manner : SLAY b : to kill in large numbers : MASSACRE 3 : to discredit or demolish completely — **slaugh·ter·er** \-tər-ər\ *n*

slaugh·ter·house \'slȯ-tər-,hau̇s\ *n* (14c) : an establishment where animals are butchered

slaugh·ter·ous \'slȯ-tə-rəs\ *adj* (1582) : of or relating to slaughter : MURDEROUS — **slaugh·ter·ous·ly** *adv*

Slav \'släv, 'slav\ *n* [ME *Sclav*, fr. ML *Sclavus*, fr. LGk *Sklabos*, fr. *Sklabēnoi* Slavs, of Slav origin; akin to ORuss *Slovēne*, an East Slavic tribe] (14c) : a person whose native tongue is a Slavic language — **Slav** *adj*

¹**slave** \'slāv\ *n* [ME *sclave*, fr. OF or ML; OF *esclave*, fr. ML *sclavus* Slav; fr. the frequent enslavement of Slavs in central Europe] (14c) 1 : a person held in servitude as the chattel of another 2 : one

that is completely subservient to a dominating influence **3** : a device (as the printer of a computer) that is directly responsive to another **4** : DRUDGE, TOILER — **slave** *adj*

²**slave** *vb* **slaved; slav·ing** *vt* (1602) **1** *archaic* : ENSLAVE **2** : to make directly responsive to another mechanism ~ *vi* **1** : to work like a slave : DRUDGE **2** : to traffic in slaves

slave driver *n* (1807) **1** : a supervisor of slaves at work **2** : a harsh taskmaster

slave·hold·er \'slāv-ˌhōl-dər\ *n* (1776) : an owner of slaves — **slave-hold·ing** \-diŋ\ *adj or n*

slave—mak·ing ant \'slāv-ˌmā-kiŋ-\ *n* (1817) : an ant that attacks the colonies of ants of other species and carries off the larvae and pupae to be reared in its own nest as slaves

¹**sla·ver** \'sla-vər, 'slā-, 'slä-\ *vb* **sla·vered; sla·ver·ing** \-v(ə-)riŋ\ [ME, of Scand origin; akin to ON *slafra* to slaver; akin to MD *slabben* to slaver] *vi* (14c) : DROOL, SLOBBER ~ *vt, archaic* : to smear with or as if with saliva

²**slaver** *n* (14c) : saliva dribbling from the mouth

³**slav·er** \'slā-vər\ *n* [¹*slave*] (1827) **1 a** : a person engaged in the slave trade **b** : a ship used in the slave trade **2** : WHITE SLAVER

slav·ery \'slā-v(ə-)rē\ *n* (1551) **1** : DRUDGERY, TOIL **2** : submission to a dominating influence **3 a** : the state of a person who is a chattel of another **b** : the practice of slaveholding

slave state *n* (1810) **1** : a state of the U.S. in which slavery was legal until the Civil War **2** : a nation subjected to totalitarian rule

slave trade *n* (1734) : traffic in slaves; *esp* : the buying and selling of blacks for profit prior to the American Civil War

slav·ey \'slā-vē\ *n, pl* **slaveys** (ca. 1812) : DRUDGE; *esp* : a household servant who does general housework

¹**Slav·ic** \'slä-vik, 'sla-\ *n* (1812) : a branch of the Indo-European language family containing Belorussian, Bulgarian, Czech, Polish, Serbo-Croatian, Slovene, Russian, and Ukrainian — see INDO-EUROPEAN LANGUAGES table

²**Slavic** *adj* (1813) : of, relating to, or characteristic of the Slavs or their languages

Slav·i·cist \'slä-və-sist, 'sla-\ *n* (1930) : a specialist in the Slavic languages or literatures

slav·ish \'slā-vish *sometimes* 'sla-\ *adj* (1565) **1 a** : of or characteristic of a slave; *esp* : basely or abjectly servile **b** *archaic* : DESPICABLE, LOW **2** *archaic* : OPPRESSIVE, TYRANNICAL **3** : copying obsequiously or without originality : IMITATIVE — **syn** see SUBSERVIENT — **slav·ish·ly** *adv* — **slav·ish·ness** *n*

Slav·ist \'slä-vist, 'sla-\ *n* (1863) : SLAVICIST

slav·oc·ra·cy \slä-'vä-krə-sē\ *n* (1840) : a faction of slaveholders and advocates of slavery in the South before the Civil War

¹**Sla·von·ic** \slə-'vä-nik\ *adj* [NL *Sclavonia, Slavonia,* the Slavic-speaking countries, fr. *Sclavus* Slav] (ca. 1645) : SLAVIC

²**Slavonic** *n* (1668) **1** : SLAVIC **2** : OLD CHURCH SLAVONIC

Slav·o·phile \'slä-və-ˌfīl, 'sla-\ *or* **Slav·o·phil** \-ˌfil\ *n* (1877) : an admirer of the Slavs : an advocate of Slavophilism

Slav·oph·i·lism \slä-'vä-fə-ˌli-zəm; 'sla-və-ˌfī-ˌli-, 'slä-\ *n* (1877) : advocacy of Slavic and specif. Russian culture over western European culture esp. as practiced among some members of the Russian intelligentsia in the middle 19th century

slaw \'slò\ *n* (1861) : COLESLAW

slay \'slā\ *vb* **slew** \'slü\ *also esp in sense 2* **slayed; slain** \'slān\; **slay·ing** [ME *slen,* fr. OE *slēan* to strike, slay; akin to OHG *slahan* to strike, MIr *slachta* stricken] *vt* (bef. 12c) **1** : to kill violently, wantonly, or in great numbers; *broadly* : to strike down : KILL **2** : to delight or amuse immensely ⟨~ed the audience⟩ ~ *vi* : KILL, MURDER **syn** see KILL — **slay·er** *n*

¹**sleave** \'slēv\ *n* [²*sleave*] (1591) *archaic* : SKEIN ⟨sleep that knits up the raveled ~ of care —Shak.⟩

²**sleave** *vt* [(assumed) ME *sleven,* fr. OE *-slǣfan* to cut] (ca. 1628) *obs* : to separate (silk thread) into filaments

sleave silk *n* (1588) *obs* : floss silk that is easily separated into filaments for embroidery

sleaze \'slēz *also* 'slāz\ *n* [back-formation fr. *sleazy*] (1954) **1** : sleazy quality, appearance, or behavior; *also* : sleazy material **2** : a sleazy person

sleaze·bag \-ˌbag *also* -ˌbäg\ *n* (1983) *slang* : a sleazy person

sleaze·ball \-ˌból\ *n* (1981) *slang* : a sleazy person

sleazo \'slē-(ˌ)zō\ *adj* (1972) *slang* : SLEAZY

slea·zy \'slē-zē *also* 'slā-\ *adj* **slea·zi·er; -est** [origin unknown] (ca. 1645) **1 a** : lacking firmness of texture : FLIMSY **b** : carelessly made of inferior materials : SHODDY **2 a** : marked by low character or quality ⟨~ tabloids⟩ **b** : SQUALID, DILAPIDATED ⟨~ bars⟩ — **slea·zi·ly** \-zə-lē\ *adv* — **slea·zi·ness** \-zē-nəs\ *n*

¹**sled** \'sled\ *n* [ME *sledde,* fr. MD; akin to OE *slīdan* to slide] (14c) **1** : a vehicle with runners for transportation esp. on snow or ice; *esp* : a small steerable one used esp. by children for coasting down snow-covered hills **2** : ROCKET SLED

²**sled** *vb* **sled·ded; sled·ding** *vt* (1706) : SLEDGE ~ *vi* : to ride on a sled or sleigh — **sled·der** *n*

sled·ding *n* (15c) **1 a** : the use of a sled **b** : the conditions under which one may use a sled **2** : GOING 4 ⟨tough ~⟩

sled dog *n* (1692) : a dog trained to draw a sledge esp. in the Arctic regions — called also *sledge dog*

¹**sledge** \'slej\ *n* [ME *slegge,* fr. OE *slecg;* akin to ON *sleggja* sledgehammer, OE *slēan* to strike — more at SLAY] (bef. 12c) : SLEDGEHAMMER

²**sledge** *vb* **sledged; sledg·ing** (1654) : SLEDGEHAMMER

³**sledge** *n* [D dial. *sleedse;* akin to MD *sledde* sled] (1617) **1** *Brit* : SLEIGH **2** : a strong heavy sled

⁴**sledge** *vb* **sledged; sledg·ing** *vi* (1853) **1** : to travel with a sledge **2** *Brit* : to ride in a sleigh ~ *vt* : to transport on a sledge

¹**sledge·ham·mer** \'slej-ˌha-mər\ *n* (15c) : a large heavy hammer that is wielded with both hands; *also* : something that resembles a sledgehammer in action

²**sledgehammer** *vt* (1834) : to strike with or as if with a sledgehammer ~ *vi* : to strike blows with or as if with a sledgehammer

³**sledgehammer** *adj* (1843) : marked by heavy-handed directness or hard-hitting force ⟨trusting in ~ warfare —C. J. Rolo⟩

¹**sleek** \'slēk\ *vb* [ME *sleken,* alter. of *sliken* — more at SLICK] *vt* (15c) **1** : SLICK ⟨grooms ~ing cooled horses —*Sunset*⟩ **2** : to cover up : gloss over ~ *vi* : SLICK

²**sleek** *adj* [alter. of ²*slick*] (1589) **1 a** : smooth and glossy as if polished ⟨~ dark hair⟩ **b** : having a smooth well-groomed look ⟨~ cattle⟩ **c** : healthy-looking **2** : smooth in speech or manner; *also* : UNCTUOUS **3 a** : having a prosperous air ⟨a ~ apartment building with a pool on the roof⟩ **b** : having trim graceful lines ⟨a ~ car⟩ **c** : ELEGANT, STYLISH ⟨~ restaurants⟩ — **sleek·ly** *adv* — **sleek·ness** *n*
syn SLEEK, SLICK, GLOSSY mean having a smooth bright surface or appearance. SLEEK suggests a smoothness or brightness resulting from attentive grooming or physical conditioning ⟨a *sleek* racehorse⟩. SLICK suggests extreme smoothness that results in a slippery surface ⟨slipped and fell on the *slick* floor⟩. GLOSSY suggests a highly reflective surface ⟨photographs having a *glossy* finish⟩.

sleek·en \'slē-kən\ *vt* **sleek·ened; sleek·en·ing** \'slē-kə-niŋ, 'slēk-niŋ\ (1621) : to make sleek

sleek·it \'slē-kət\ *adj* [Sc, fr. pp. of ¹*sleek*] (1513) **1** *chiefly Scot* : SLEEK, SMOOTH **2** *chiefly Scot* : CRAFTY, DECEITFUL

¹**sleep** \'slēp\ *n* [ME *slepe,* fr. OE *slǣp;* akin to OHG *slāf* sleep and perh. to L *labi* to slip, slide] (bef. 12c) **1** : the natural periodic suspension of consciousness during which the powers of the body are restored **2** : a state resembling sleep: as **a** : a state of torpid inactivity **b** : DEATH ⟨put a pet cat to ~⟩; *also* : TRANCE, COMA **c** : the closing of leaves or petals esp. at night **d** : a state marked by a diminution of feeling followed by tingling ⟨my foot's gone to ~⟩ **e** : the state of an animal during hibernation **3 a** : a period spent sleeping **b** : NIGHT **c** : a day's journey — **sleep·like** \-ˌlīk\ *adj*

²**sleep** *vb* **slept** \'slept\; **sleep·ing** (bef. 12c) **1** : to rest in a state of sleep **2** : to be in a state (as of quiescence or death) resembling sleep **3** : to have sexual relations — usu. used *with* ~ *vt* **1** : to be slumbering in ⟨*slept* the sleep of the dead⟩ **2** : to get rid of or spend in or by sleep ⟨~ away the hours⟩ ⟨~ off a drunk⟩ **3** : to provide sleeping accommodations for ⟨the boat ~s six⟩

sleep around *vi* (1928) : to engage in sex promiscuously

sleep·er \'slē-pər\ *n* (12c) **1** : one that sleeps **2** : a piece of timber, stone, or steel on or near the ground to support a superstructure, keep railroad rails in place, or receive floor joists : STRINGPIECE **3** : SLEEPING CAR **4** : someone or something unpromising or unnoticed that suddenly attains prominence or value ⟨the low-budget film became the summer's ~⟩ **5** : children's pajamas usu. with feet — usu. used in pl. **6** *chiefly Brit* : a small earring or stud worn to keep the hole of a pierced ear from closing **7** : MOLE 4

sleep—in \'slēp-ˌin\ *adj* (1951) : that lives at the place of employment ⟨a ~ maid⟩

sleep in *vi* (1827) **1** : to sleep where one is employed **2 a** : OVERSLEEP **b** : to sleep late intentionally

sleeping bag *n* (1850) : a bag that is warmly lined or padded for sleeping outdoors or in a camp or tent

Sleeping Beauty *n* : a princess of a fairy tale who is wakened from an enchanted sleep by the kiss of a prince

sleeping car *n* (1839) : a railroad passenger car having berths for sleeping

sleeping partner *n* (ca. 1785) *chiefly Brit* : SILENT PARTNER

sleeping pill *n* (1664) : a drug and esp. a barbiturate that is taken as a tablet or capsule to induce sleep — called also *sleeping tablet*

sleeping porch *n* (1915) : a porch or room having open sides or many windows arranged to permit sleeping in the open air

sleeping sickness *n* (1875) **1** : a serious disease that is prevalent in much of tropical Africa, is marked by fever, protracted lethargy, tremors, and loss of weight, is caused by either of two trypanosomes (*Trypanosoma brucei gambiense* and *T. b. rhodesiense*), and is transmitted by tsetse flies **2** : any of various viral encephalitides or encephalomyelitides of which lethargy or somnolence is a prominent feature

sleep·less \'slēp-ləs\ *adj* (15c) **1** : not able to sleep ⟨lay ~ with fever⟩ **2** : affording no sleep ⟨~ nights⟩ **3** : unceasingly active or operative ⟨~ casinos⟩ — **sleep·less·ly** *adv* — **sleep·less·ness** *n*

sleep out *vi* (1908) : to sleep outdoors

sleep·over \'slēp-ō-vər\ *n* (1965) **1** : an overnight stay (as at another's home) **2** : an instance of hosting a sleepover in one's home

sleep·walk·er \'slēp-ˌwó-kər\ *n* (1747) : one that walks while or as if while asleep : SOMNAMBULIST — **sleep·walk** \-ˌwók\ *vi or n*

sleep·wear \-ˌwar, -ˌwer\ *n* (1935) : NIGHTCLOTHES

sleepy \'slē-pē\ *adj* **sleep·i·er; -est** (13c) **1** : ready to fall asleep **b** : of, relating to, or characteristic of sleep **2** : sluggish as if from sleep : LETHARGIC; *also* : having little activity ⟨a ~ coastal village⟩ **3** : sleep-inducing — **sleep·i·ly** \-pə-lē\ *adv* — **sleep·i·ness** \-pē-nəs\ *n*

sleepy·head \'slē-pē-ˌhed\ *n* (1577) : a sleepy person

¹**sleet** \'slēt\ *n* [ME *slete;* akin to MHG *slōz* hailstone] (13c) : frozen or partly frozen rain — **sleety** \'slē-tē\ *adj*

²**sleet** *vi* (14c) : to shower sleet

sleeve \'slēv\ *n* [ME *sleve,* fr. OE *slīefe;* perh. akin to OE *slēfan* to slip (clothes) on, *slūpan* to slip, OHG *sliofan,* L *lubricus* slippery] (bef. 12c) **1 a** : a part of a garment covering an arm **b** : SLEEVELET **2 a** : a tubular part (as a hollow axle or a bushing) designed to fit over another part **b** : an open-ended flat or tubular packaging or cover; *esp* : JACKET 3c(2) — **sleeved** \'slēvd\ *adj* — **sleeve·less** \'slēv-ləs\ *adj* — **up one's sleeve** : held secretly in reserve

sleeve·let \'slēv-lət\ *n* (1889) : a covering for the forearm to protect clothing from wear or dirt

¹**sleigh** \'slā\ *n* [D dial. *slede,* alter. of *sledde;* akin to MD *sledde* sled] (1703) : an open usu. horse-drawn vehicle with runners for use on snow or ice

sleigh

\ə\ abut \ᵊ\ kitten, F table \ər\ further \a\ ash \ā\ ace \ä\ mop, mar \aù\ out \ch\ chin \e\ bet \ē\ easy \g\ go \i\ hit \ī\ ice \j\ job \ŋ\ sing \ō\ go \ò\ law \òi\ boy \th\ thin \th\ the \ü\ loot \ù\ foot \y\ yet \zh\ vision \à, ḵ, ⁿ, œ, œ̄, ue, uē, ᵞ\ *see* Guide to Pronunciation

²**sleigh** vi (ca. 1729) : to drive or travel in a sleigh

sleigh bed n (1902) : a bed common esp. in the first half of the 19th century having a solid headboard and footboard that roll outward at the top

sleigh bell n (1772) : any of various bells commonly attached to a sleigh or to the harness of a horse drawing a sleigh: as **a** : CASCABEL 2 **b** : a hemispherical bell with an attached clapper

sleight \'slit\ n [ME, fr. ON slœgth, fr. slœgr sly — more at SLY] (14c) **1** : deceitful craftiness; also : STRATAGEM **2** : DEXTERITY, SKILL

sleight of hand (ca. 1605) **1 a** : a conjuring trick requiring manual dexterity **b** : a cleverly executed trick or deception **2 a** : skill and dexterity in conjuring tricks **b** : adroitness in deception

slen·der \'slen-dər\ adj [ME sclendre, slendre] (14c) **1 a** : spare in frame or flesh; esp : gracefully slight **b** : small or narrow in circumference or width in proportion to length or height **2** : limited or inadequate in amount or scope : MEAGER ⟨people of ~ means⟩ **syn** see THIN — **slen·der·ly** adv — **slen·der·ness** n

slen·der·ize \-də-,riz\ vt -ized; -iz·ing (1923) : to make slender

¹**sleuth** \'slüth\ n [short for sleuthhound] (1872) : DETECTIVE

²**sleuth** vi (1900) : to act as a detective : search for information ~ vt : to search for and discover

sleuth·hound \'slüth-,haúnd\ n [ME sleuth hund, a kind of bloodhound, fr. sleuth track of an animal or person (fr. ON slōth) + hund hound] (1856) : DETECTIVE

S level n (1951) **1** : the highest of three standardized British examinations in a secondary school subject used as a qualification for university entrance; also : successful completion of an S-level examination in a particular subject — called also Scholarship level; compare A LEVEL, O LEVEL **2 a** : the level of education required to pass an S-level examination **b** : a course leading to an S-level examination

¹**slew** \'slü\ past of SLAY

²**slew** var of SLOUGH

³**slew** vb [origin unknown] vt (ca. 1769) **1** : to turn (as a telescope or a ship's spar) about a fixed point that is usu. the axis **2** : to cause to skid : VEER ⟨~ a car around a turn⟩ ~ vi **1** : to turn, twist, or swing about : PIVOT **2** : SKID

⁴**slew** n [perh. fr. Ir slua army, host, throng, fr. OIr slúag; akin to Lith slaugyti to tend] (1839) : a large number ⟨a ~ of books⟩

¹**slice** \'slis\ vb sliced; slic·ing [ME sklicen, fr. MF esclicier to splinter, fr. OF, of Gmc origin; akin to OHG slizan to tear apart — more at SLIT] vt (1551) **1** : to cut with or as if with a knife **2** : to stir or spread with a slice **3** : to hit (a ball) so that a slice results ~ vi **1** : to slice something **2** : to move with a cutting action ⟨the ship sliced through the waves⟩ — **slice·able** \'sli-sə-bəl\ adj — **slic·er** n

²**slice** n [ME sklice, fr. MF esclice splinter, fr. OF, fr. esclicier] (1613) **1 a** : a thin flat piece cut from something **b** : a wedge-shaped piece (as of pie or cake) **2** : a spatula for spreading paint or ink **3** : a serving knife with wedge-shaped blade ⟨a fish ~⟩ **4** : a flight of a ball that deviates from a straight course in the direction of the dominant hand of the player propelling it; also : a ball following such a course — compare HOOK **5** : PORTION, SHARE ⟨a ~ of the profits⟩

slice–of–life adj (1895) : of, relating to, or marked by the accurate transcription (as into drama) of a segment of actual life experience

¹**slick** \'slik\ vb [ME sliken; akin to OHG slīhhan to glide] vt (14c) : to make sleek or smooth ~ vi : SPRUCE — usu. used with up

²**slick** adj (14c) **1 a** : having a smooth surface : SLIPPERY ⟨~ wet leaves⟩ **b** : having surface plausibility or appeal : GLIB, GLOSSY ⟨~ advertising⟩ **c** : based on stereotype : TRITE ⟨~ stories soon forgotten⟩ **2** archaic : SLEEK 1 **3 a** : characterized by subtlety or nimble wit : CLEVER; esp : WILY ⟨a reputation as a ~ operator⟩ **b** : DEFT, SKILLFUL ⟨a ~ ballplayer⟩ **4** : extremely good : FIRST-RATE **syn** see SLEEK, SLY — **slick** adv — **slick·ly** adv — **slick·ness** n

³**slick** n (1849) **1 a** : something that is smooth or slippery; esp : a smooth patch of water covered with a film of oil **b** : a film of oil **2** : an implement for producing a slick surface: as **a** : a flat paddle usu. of steel for smoothing a sample of flour **b** : a foundry tool for smoothing the surface of a sand mold or unbaked core **3** : a shrewd untrustworthy person **4** : a popular magazine printed on coated stock and intended to appeal to sophisticated readers **5** : an automobile tire made without a tread for maximum traction (as in drag racing)

slick–ear \'slik-,ir\ n (1914) : a range animal lacking an earmark

slick·en·side \'sli-kən-,sid\ n [E dial. slicken smooth (alter. of E ²slick) + E side] (1822) : a smooth often striated surface produced on rock by movement along a fault or a subsidiary fracture — usu. used in pl.

slick·er \'sli-kər\ n (1881) 1 [²slick] **a** : OILSKIN; broadly : RAINCOAT **2** [slick to defraud cleverly] **a** : a clever crook : SWINDLER **b** : a city dweller esp. of natty appearance or sophisticated mannerisms

slick·rock \'slik-,räk\ n (1925) : smooth wind-polished rock

¹**slide** \'slid\ vb slid \'slid\; slid·ing \'sli-diŋ\ [ME, fr. OE slidan; akin to MHG sliten to slide] vi (bef. 12c) **1 a** : to move smoothly along a surface : SLIP **b** : to coast over snow or ice **c** of a base runner in baseball : to fall or dive feetfirst or headfirst when approaching a base **2 a** : to slip or fall by loss of footing **b** : to change position or become dislocated : SHIFT **3 a** : to slither along the ground : CRAWL **b** : to stream along : FLOW **4 a** : to move or pass smoothly or easily ⟨slid into the prepared speech⟩ **b** : to pass unnoticed or unremarked ⟨could have responded but let it ~⟩ **5 a** : to pass unobtrusively : STEAL **b** : to pass by gradations esp. downward ⟨the economy slid from recession to depression⟩ ~ vt **1** : to cause to glide or slip **2** : to traverse in a sliding manner ⟨slid the bill into his hand⟩

²**slide** n (1570) **1 a** : an act or instance of sliding **b** (1) : a musical grace of two or more small notes (2) : PORTAMENTO **2** : a sliding part or mechanism: as **a** (1) : a U-shaped section of tube in the trombone that is pushed out and in to produce the tones between the fundamental and its harmonics (2) : a short U-shaped section of tube in a brass instrument that is used to adjust the pitch of the instrument or of individual valves **b** (1) : a moving piece (as the ram of a punch press) that is guided by a part along which it slides (2) : a guiding surface (as a feeding mechanism) along which something slides **c** : SLIDING SEAT **3 a** : the descent of a mass of earth, rock, or snow down a hill or mountainside **b** : a dislocation in which one rock mass in a mining lode has slid on another : FAULT **4 a** (1) : a slippery surface for coasting (2) : a chute with a slippery bed down which children slide

in play **b** : a channel or track on which something is slid **c** : a sloping trough down which objects are carried by gravity ⟨a log ~⟩ **5 a** : a flat piece of glass on which an object is mounted for microscopic examination **b** : a photographic transparency on a small plate or film mounted for projection **6** : BOTTLENECK 3

slide fastener n (1934) : ZIPPER

slid·er \'sli-dər\ n (1530) **1** : one that slides **2** : a fast baseball pitch that breaks slightly in the same direction as a curve

slide rule n (1663) : a manual device used for calculation that consists in its simple form of a ruler and a movable middle piece which are graduated with similar logarithmic scales

slide valve n (1802) : a valve that opens and closes a passageway by sliding over a port; specif : such a valve often used in steam engines for admitting steam to the piston and releasing it

slide·way \'slid-,wa\ n (1856) : a way along which something slides

sliding scale n (1842) **1** : a wage scale geared to the selling price of the product or to the consumer price index but usu. guaranteeing a minimum below which the wage will not fall **2 a** : a system for raising or lowering tariffs in accord with price changes **b** : a flexible scale (as of fees or subsidies) adjusted to the needs or income of individuals ⟨the sliding scale of medical fees⟩

sliding seat n (1874) : a rower's seat (as in a racing shell) that slides fore and aft — called also slide

slier comparative of SLY

sliest superlative of SLY

¹**slight** \'slit\ adj [ME, smooth, slight, prob. fr. MD slicht; akin to OHG slihhan to glide — more at SLICK] (14c) **1 a** : having a slim or delicate build : not stout or massive in body **b** : lacking in strength or substance : FLIMSY, FRAIL **c** : deficient in weight, solidity, or importance : TRIVIAL **2** : small of its kind or in amount : SCANTY, MEAGER **syn** see THIN — **slight·ly** adv — **slight·ness** n

²**slight** vt (1597) **1** : to treat as slight or unimportant : make light of **2** : to treat with disdain or indifference **3** : to perform or attend to carelessly and inadequately **4** : ³SLUR 3 **syn** see NEGLECT

³**slight** n (1701) **1** : an act or an instance of slighting **2** : an instance of being slighted : a humiliating discourtesy

slight·ing adj (1632) : characterized by disregard or disrespect : DISPARAGING ⟨a ~ remark⟩ — **slight·ing·ly** \'sli-tiŋ-le\ adv

sli·ly var of SLYLY

¹**slim** \'slim\ adj slim·mer; slim·mest [D, bad, inferior, fr. MD slimp crooked, bad; akin to MHG slimp awry] (1657) **1** : of small diameter or thickness in proportion to the height or length : SLENDER **2 a** : MEAN, WORTHLESS **b** : ADROIT, CRAFTY **3 a** : inferior in quality or amount : SLIGHT **b** : SCANTY, SMALL ⟨a ~ chance⟩ **syn** see THIN — **slim·ly** adv — **slim·ness** n

²**slim** vb slimmed; slim·ming vt (1862) : to make slender : decrease the size of ~ vi : to become slender

¹**slime** \'slim\ n [ME, fr. OE slim; akin to MHG slīm slime, L limus mud — more at LIME] (bef. 12c) **1** : soft moist earth or clay; esp : viscous mud **2** : a viscous or glutinous substance: as **a** : a mucous or mucoid secretion of various animals (as slugs and catfishes) **b** : a product of wet crushing consisting of ore ground so fine as to pass a 200-mesh screen **3** : a repulsive or odious person

²**slime** vb slimed; slim·ing vt (1628) **1** : to smear or cover with slime **2** : to remove slime from (as fish for canning) ~ vi : to become slimy

slime·ball \'slim-,ból\ n (1986) slang : SLIME 3

slime mold n (1880) : any of a group (Myxomycetes or Mycetozoa) of organisms usu. held to be lower fungi but sometimes considered protozoans that exist vegetatively as mobile plasmodia and reproduce by spores

slim–jim \'slim-'jim, -,jim\ adj [¹slim + Jim, nickname for James] (1889) : notably slender

slim·mer \'slim-ər\ n (1967) chiefly Brit : a person dieting to lose weight : DIETER

slim·nas·tics \,slim-'nas-tiks\ n pl but sing in constr [¹slim + gymnastics] (1967) : exercises designed to reduce one's weight

slim·sy or **slimp·sy** \'slim-ze, 'slim(p)-se\ adj [blend of slim and flimsy] (1845) : FLIMSY, FRAIL

slimy \'sli-me\ adj slim·i·er; -est (14c) **1** : of, relating to, or resembling slime : VISCOUS; also : covered with or yielding slime **2** : VILE, OFFENSIVE — **slim·i·ly** \-mə-le\ adv — **slim·i·ness** \-me-nəs\ n

¹**sling** \'sliŋ\ vt slung \'sləŋ\; sling·ing \'sliŋ-iŋ\ [ME, prob. fr. ON slyngva to hurl; akin to OE & OHG slingan to worm, twist, Lith slinkti] (14c) **1** : to cast with a sudden and usu. sweeping or swirling motion ⟨slung the sack over my shoulder⟩ **2** : to throw with or as if with a sling ⟨~ing punches⟩ ⟨~ mud⟩ **syn** see THROW — **sling·er** \'sliŋ-ər\ n

²**sling** n (14c) **1 a** : an instrument for throwing stones that usu. consists of a short strap with strings fastened to its ends and is whirled round to discharge its missile by centrifugal force **b** : SLINGSHOT 1 **2 a** : a usu. looped line (as of strap, chain, or rope) used to hoist, lower, or carry something; esp : a hanging bandage suspended from the neck to support an arm or hand **b** : a chain or rope attached to a lower yard at the middle and passing around a mast near the masthead to support a yard **c** : a chain hooked at the bow and stern of a boat for lowering or hoisting **d** : a device (as a rope net) for enclosing material to be hoisted by a tackle or crane **3** : a slinging or hurling of or as if of a missile

³**sling** vt slung \'sləŋ\; sling·ing \'sliŋ-iŋ\ (1522) **1** : to place in a sling for hoisting or lowering **2** : to suspend by or as if by a sling

⁴**sling** n [origin unknown] (1768) : an alcoholic drink that is served hot or cold and that usu. consists of liquor, sugar, lemon juice, and plain or carbonated water ⟨gin ~⟩ ⟨rum ~⟩

slings and arrows n pl [fr. the phrase "the slings and arrows of outrageous fortune" in Shakespeare's Hamlet] (1963) : pointed often acerbic critical attacks ⟨has suffered the slings and arrows of detractors —Roland Gelatt⟩

sling·shot \'sliŋ-,shät\ n (1849) **1** : a forked stick with an elastic band attached for shooting small stones **2 a** : a maneuver in auto racing in which a drafting car accelerates past the car in front by taking advantage of reserve power **b** : a dragster in which the driver sits behind the rear wheels

¹**slink** \'sliŋk\ vb slunk \'sləŋk\ also slinked \'sliŋ(k)t\; slink·ing [ME, fr. OE slincan to creep; akin to OE slingan to worm, twist] vi

(14c)   **1** : to go or move stealthily or furtively (as in fear or shame) : STEAL   **2** : to move in a sinuous provocative manner ~ *vt* : to give premature birth to — used esp. of a domestic animal ⟨a cow that ~s her calf⟩ *syn* see LURK

²**slink** *n* (1607) : the young of an animal (as a calf) brought forth prematurely; *also* : the flesh or skin of such an animal

³**slink** *adj* (1750) : born prematurely or abortively ⟨a ~ calf⟩

slinky \'sliŋ-kē\ *adj* **slink·i·er; -est** (1918)   **1** : characterized by slinking : stealthily quiet ⟨~ movements⟩   **2** : sleek and sinuous in movement or outline; *esp* : following the lines of the figure in a gracefully flowing manner ⟨a ~ evening gown⟩ — **slink·i·ly** \-kə-lē\ *adv* — **slink·i·ness** \-kē-nəs\ *n*

¹**slip** \'slip\ *vb* **slipped; slip·ping** [ME *slippen*, fr. MD or MLG; akin to MHG *slipfen* to slide, OHG *slīfan* to smooth, and perh. to Gk *olibros* slippery] *vi* (14c)   **1 a** : to move with a smooth sliding motion   **b** : to move quietly and cautiously : STEAL   **c** : ELAPSE, PASS   **2 a** (1) : to escape from memory or consciousness   (2) : to become uttered through inadvertence   **b** : to pass quickly or easily away : become lost ⟨let an opportunity ~⟩   **3** : to fall into error or fault : LAPSE   **4 a** : to slide out of place or away from a support or one's grasp   **b** : to slide on or down a slippery surface ⟨~ on the stairs⟩   **c** : to flow smoothly   **5** : to get speedily into or out of clothing ⟨slipped into his coat⟩   **6** : to fall off from a standard or accustomed level by degrees : DECLINE   **7** : SIDESLIP ~ *vt*   **1** : to cause to move easily and smoothly : SLIDE   **2 a** : to get away from : ELUDE, EVADE ⟨slipped his pursuers⟩   **b** : to free oneself from ⟨the dog *slipped* its collar⟩   **c** : to escape from ⟨one's memory or notice⟩ ⟨their names ~ my mind⟩   **3** : SHED, CAST ⟨the snake *slipped* its skin⟩   **4** : to put on (a garment) quickly — usu. used with *on* ⟨~ on a coat⟩   **5 a** : to let loose from a restraining leash or grasp   **b** : to cause to slip open : RELEASE, UNDO ⟨~ a lock⟩   **c** : to let go of   **d** : to disengage from (an anchor) instead of hauling   **6 a** : to insert, place, or pass quietly or secretly   **b** : to give or pay on the sly   **7** : SLINK, ABORT   **8** : DISLOCATE ⟨*slipped* his shoulder⟩   **9** : to transfer (a stitch) from one needle to another without working a stitch   **10** : to avoid (a punch) by moving the body or head quickly to one side

²**slip** *n* (15c)   **1 a** : a sloping ramp extending out into the water to serve as a place for landing or repairing ships   **b** : a ship's or boat's berth between two piers   **2** : the act or an instance of departing secretly or hurriedly ⟨gave his pursuer the ~⟩   **3 a** : a mistake in judgment, policy, or procedure   **b** : an unintentional and trivial mistake or fault : LAPSE ⟨a ~ of the tongue⟩   **4** : a leash so made that it can be quickly slipped   **5 a** : the act or an instance of slipping down or out of a place ⟨a ~ on the ice⟩; *also* : a sudden mishap   **b** : a movement dislocating parts (as of a rock or soil mass); *also* : the result of such movement   **c** : a fall from some level or standard : DECLINE ⟨a ~ in stock prices⟩   **6 a** : an undergarment made in dress length with shoulder straps; *also* : HALF-SLIP   **b** : a case into which something is slipped; *specif* : PILLOWCASE   **7 a** : the motion of the center of resistance of the float of a paddle wheel or the blade of an oar through the water horizontally   **b** : retrograde movement of a turn on a pulley   **c** : the amount of leakage past the piston of a pump or the impellers of a blower   **8** : a disposition or tendency to slip easily   **9** : the action of sideslipping : an instance of sideslipping *syn* see ERROR

³**slip** *n* [ME *slippe*, prob. fr. MD or MLG, split, slit, flap] (15c)   **1 a** : a small shoot or twig cut for planting or grafting : SCION   **b** : DESCENDANT, OFFSPRING   **2 a** : a long narrow strip of material   **b** : a small piece of paper   **3** : a young and slender person ⟨a ~ of a girl⟩   **4** : a long seat or narrow pew

⁴**slip** *vt* **slipped; slip·ping** (1530) : to take cuttings from (a plant) : divide into slips ⟨~ a geranium⟩

⁵**slip** *n* [ME *slyp* slime, fr. OE *slypa* slime, paste; akin to OE *slūpan* to slip — more at SLEEVE] (1640) : a mixture of finely divided clay and water used by potters (as for casting or decorating wares or in cementing separately formed parts)

slip·case \'slip-ˌkās\ *n* (ca. 1925) : a protective container with one open end for books — **slip·cased** \-ˌkāst\ *adj*

slip·cov·er \'slip-ˌkə-vər\ *n* (1886) : a cover that may be slipped off and on; *specif* : a removable covering for an article of furniture

slip·form \'slip-ˌfȯrm\ *vt* (1962) : to construct with the use of a slip form

slip form *n* (1949) : a form that is moved slowly as concrete is placed during construction (as of a building or pavement)

slip·knot \'slip-ˌnät\ *n* (1659) : a knot that slips along the rope or line around which it is made; *esp* : one made by tying an overhand knot around the standing part of a rope — see KNOT illustration

slip noose *n* (1847) : a noose with a slipknot

slip-on \'slip-ˌȯn, -ˌän\ *n* (1815) : an article of clothing that is easily slipped on or off: as   **a** : a glove or shoe without fastenings   **b** : a garment (as a girdle) that one steps into and pulls up   **c** : PULLOVER

slip·over \-ˌō-vər\ *n* (1917) : a garment or cover that slips on and off easily; *specif* : a pullover sweater

slip·page \'sli-pij\ *n* (1850)   **1** : an act, instance, or process of slipping   **2** : a loss in transmission of power; *also* : the difference between theoretical and actual output (as of power)

slipped disk *n* (1942) : a protrusion of one of the cartilage disks between vertebrae with pressure on spinal nerves resulting in low back pain or sciatic pain

¹**slip·per** \'sli-pər\ *adj* [ME, fr. OE *slipor*; akin to MLG *slipper* slippery, *slippen* to slip] (bef. 12c) *chiefly dial* : SLIPPERY

²**slipper** *n* [ME, fr. *slippen* to slip] (15c) : a light low-cut shoe that is easily slipped on the foot — **slip·pered** \-pərd\ *adj*

slip·pery \'sli-p(ə-)rē\ *adj* **slip·per·i·er; -est** [alter. of ME *slipper*] (ca. 1500)   **1 a** : causing or tending to cause something to slide or fall ⟨~ roads⟩   **b** : tending to slip from the grasp   **2** : not firmly fixed : UNSTABLE   **3** : not to be trusted : TRICKY — **slip·per·i·ness** *n*

slippery elm *n* (1748) : a large-leaved elm ⟨*Ulmus fulva*⟩ syn. *U. fulva*⟩ of eastern No. America that has hard wood and fragrant mucilaginous inner bark; *also* : the bark

slip·py \'sli-pē\ *adj* **slip·pi·er; -est** (1548) : SLIPPERY

slip ring *n* [²*slip*] (1898) : one of two or more continuous conducting rings from which the brushes take or to which they deliver current in a generator or motor

¹**slip–sheet** \'slip-ˌshēt\ *vt* (ca. 1909) : to insert slip sheets between (newly printed sheets)

slip sheet *n* [¹*slip*] (1903) : a sheet of paper placed between newly printed sheets to prevent offsetting

slip·shod \'slip-ˈshäd\ *adj* [¹*slip*] (1580)   **1 a** : wearing loose shoes or slippers   **b** : down at the heel : SHABBY   **2** : CARELESS, SLOVENLY

slip-slop \-ˌsläp\ *n* [redupl. of ²*slop*] (1675)   **1** *archaic* : watery food : SLOPS   **2** *archaic* : shallow talk or writing — **slip–slop** *adj*

slip·sole \-ˌsōl\ *n* (ca. 1908)   **1** : a thin insole   **2** : a half sole inserted between the insole or welt and the outsole of a shoe to give additional height — called also *slip tap*

slip stitch *n* (ca. 1882)   **1** : a concealed stitch for sewing folded edges (as hems) made by alternately running the needle inside the fold and picking up a thread or two from the body of the article   **2** : an unworked stitch; *esp* : a knitting stitch that is shifted from one needle to another without knitting it

¹**slip·stream** \'slip-ˌstrēm\ *n* (1913)   **1** : a stream of fluid (as air or water) driven aft by a propeller   **2** : an area of reduced air pressure and forward suction immediately behind a rapidly moving vehicle

²**slipstream** *vi* (1957) : to drive in the slipstream of a vehicle

slip-up \'slip-ˌəp\ *n* (1854)   **1** : MISTAKE   **2** : MISCHANCE

slip up *vi* (1909) : to make a mistake : BLUNDER

slip·ware \'slip-ˌwar, -ˌwer\ *n* (1883) : pottery coated with slip to improve or decorate the surface

slip·way \-ˌwā\ *n* (1840) : an inclined usu. concrete surface for a ship being built or repaired

¹**slit** \'slit\ *n* [ME, fr. *slitten*] (12c) : a long narrow cut or opening — **slit** *adj* — **slit·less** \'slit-ləs\ *adj*

²**slit** *vt* **slit·ting** [ME *slitten*; akin to MHG *slitzen* to slit, OHG *slīzan* to tear apart, OE *sciell* shell — more at SHELL] (14c)   **1 a** : to make a slit in   **b** : to cut off or away : SEVER   **c** : to form into a slit   **2** : to cut into long narrow strips — **slit·ter** *n*

slith·er \'sli-thər\ *vb* [ME *slideren*, fr. OE *slidrian*, freq. of *slīdan* to slide] *vi* (bef. 12c)   **1** : to slide on or as if on a loose gravelly surface   **2** : to slip or slide like a snake ~ *vt* : to cause to slide

slith·ery \'sli-thə-rē\ *adj* (ca. 1825) : having a slippery surface, texture, or quality

slit trench *n* (1942) : a narrow trench esp. for shelter in battle from bomb and shell fragments

¹**sliv·er** \'sli-vər, 2 is usu 'slī-\ *n* [ME *slivere*, fr. *sliven* to slice off, fr. OE *-slīfan*; akin to OE *-slǣfan* to cut] (14c)   **1 a** : a long slender piece cut or torn off : SPLINTER   **b** : a small and narrow portion ⟨a ~ of land⟩ : PARTICLE, SCRAP ⟨not a ~ of evidence⟩   **2** : an untwisted strand or rope of textile fiber produced by a carding or combing machine and ready for drawing, roving, or spinning

²**sliv·er** \'sli-vər\ *vb* **sliv·ered; sliv·er·ing** \'sli-və-riŋ, 'sliv-riŋ\ *vt* (1605) : to cut into slivers : SPLINTER ~ *vi* : to become split into slivers

sliv·o·vitz \'sli-və-ˌvits, 'slē-, -ˌwits\ *n* [Serbo-Croatian *šljivovica*, fr. *šljiva, sliva* plum; akin to Russ *sliva* plum — more at LIVID] (1885) : a dry usu. colorless plum brandy made esp. in the Balkan countries

slob \'släb\ *n* [Ir *slab* mud, ooze, slovenly person] (1861) : a slovenly or boorish person — **slob·bish** \'slä-bish\ *adj* — **slob·by** \-bē\ *adj*

¹**slob·ber** \'slä-bər\ *vb* **slob·bered; slob·ber·ing** \-b(ə-)riŋ\ [ME *sloberen* to eat in a slovenly manner; akin to LG *slubberen* to sip] *vi* (1733)   **1** : to let saliva dribble from the mouth : DROOL   **2** : to indulge the feelings effusively and without restraint ~ *vt* : to smear with or as if with dribbling saliva or food — **slob·ber·er** \-bər-ər\ *n*

²**slobber** *n* (ca. 1755)   **1** : saliva drooled from the mouth   **2** : driveling, sloppy, or incoherent utterance — **slob·bery** \'slä-b(ə-)rē\ *adj*

sloe \'slō\ *n* [ME *slo*, fr. OE *slāh*; akin to OHG *slēha* sloe and prob. to Russ *sliva* plum — more at LIVID] (bef. 12c) : the small dark globose astringent fruit of the blackthorn; *also* : BLACKTHORN

sloe–eyed \'slō-ˌīd\ *adj* (1867)   **1** : having soft dark bluish or purplish black eyes   **2** : having slanted eyes

sloe gin *n* (1895) : a sweet reddish liqueur consisting of grain spirits flavored chiefly with sloes

¹**slog** \'släg\ *vb* **slogged; slog·ging** [origin unknown] *vt* (1824)   **1** : to hit hard : BEAT   **2** : to plod (one's way) perseveringly esp. against difficulty ~ *vi*   **1** : to plod heavily : TRAMP ⟨*slogged* through the snow⟩   **2** : to work hard and steadily : PLUG — **slog·ger** *n*

²**slog** *n* (1888)   **1** : hard persistent work   **2** : a hard dogged march or tramp

slo·gan \'slō-gən\ *n* [alter. of earlier *slogorn*, fr. ScGael *sluagh-ghairm*, fr. *sluagh* army, host + *gairm* cry] (1513)   **1 a** : a war cry or rallying cry esp. of a Scottish clan   **b** : a word or phrase used to express a characteristic position or stand or a goal to be achieved   **2** : a brief attention-getting phrase used in advertising or promotion

slo·gan·eer \ˌslō-gə-ˈnir\ *n* (1922) : a maker or user of slogans — **slo·ganeer** *vi*

slo·gan·ize \'slō-gə-ˌnīz\ *vt* **-ized; -iz·ing** (1926) : to express as a slogan

sloop \'slüp\ *n* [D *sloep*] (1629) : a fore-and-aft rigged boat with one mast and a single jib

sloop of war *n* (1704) : a small warship with guns on only one deck

¹**slop** \'släp\ *n* [ME *sloppe*, prob. fr. MD *slop*; akin to OE *oferslop* surplice] (14c)   **1** : a loose smock or overall   **2** *pl* : short full breeches worn by men in the 16th century   **3** *pl* : articles (as clothing) sold to sailors

²**slop** *n* [ME *sloppe*] (15c)   **1** : soft mud : SLUSH   **2** : thin tasteless drink or liquid food — usu. used in pl.   **3** : liquid spilled or splashed   **4 a** : food waste (as garbage) fed to animals : SWILL 2a   **b** : excreted body waste — usu. used in pl.   **5** : sentimental effusiveness in speech or writing : GUSH

³**slop** *vb* **slopped; slop·ping** *vt* (1557)   **1 a** : to spill from a container   **b** : to splash or spill liquid on   **c** : to cause (a liquid) to splash   **2** : to dish out messily   **3** : to eat or drink greedily or noisily   **4** : to feed slop to ⟨~ the hogs⟩ ~ *vi*   **1** : to tramp in mud and slush   **2** : to be-

\ə\ abut \ᵊ\ kitten, F table \ər\ further \a\ ash \ā\ ace \ä\ mop, mar
\au̇\ out \ch\ chin \e\ bet \ē\ easy \g\ go \i\ hit \ī\ ice \j\ job
\ŋ\ sing \ō\ go \ȯ\ law \ȯi\ boy \th\ thin \ṯẖ\ the \ü\ loot \u̇\ foot
\y\ yet \zh\ vision \ä, k̲, ⁿ, œ, œ̄, ᴜᴇ, ᵫ, ᴊ\ see Guide to Pronunciation

come spilled or splashed **3 :** to be effusive : GUSH **4 :** to pass beyond or exceed a boundary or limit

slop basin n (1731) Brit : SLOP BOWL

slop bowl n (1810) **:** a bowl for receiving the leavings of tea or coffee cups at table

slop chest n [¹slop] (1840) **:** a store of clothing and personal requisites (as tobacco) carried on merchant ships for issue to the crew usu. as a charge against their wages

¹slope \'slōp\ adj [ME slope, adv., obliquely] (1502) **:** that slants : SLOPING — often used in combination ⟨slope-sided⟩

²slope vb sloped; slop·ing vi (1591) **1 a :** to take an oblique course **2 :** to lie or fall in a slant : INCLINE **3 :** GO, TRAVEL ⟨~s off into the night —Wolcott Gibbs⟩ ~ vt **:** to cause to incline or slant — slop·er n

³slope n (ca. 1611) **1 :** upward or downward slant or inclination or degree of slant **2 :** ground that forms a natural or artificial incline **3 :** the part of a continent draining to a particular ocean ⟨Alaska's North Slope⟩ **4 a :** the tangent of the angle made by a straight line with the x-axis **b :** the slope of the line tangent to a plane curve at a point

slope–intercept form n (ca. 1942) **:** the equation of a straight line in the form $y = mx + b$ where m is the slope of the line and b is the point on the y-axis through which the line passes

slo–pitch \'slō-ˌpich, -ˌpich\ n [alter. of slow pitch] (1967) **:** SLOW-PITCH

slop jar n (1855) **:** a large pail used as a chamber pot or to receive waste water from a washbowl or the contents of chamber pots

slop pail n (1864) **:** a pail for toilet or household slops

slop·py \'slä-pē\ adj slop·pi·er; -est (1707) **1 a :** wet so as to spatter easily : SLUSHY ⟨a ~ racetrack⟩ **b :** wet or smeared with or as if with something slopped over **2 :** SLOVENLY, CARELESS ⟨a ~ dresser⟩ ⟨did ~ work⟩ **3 :** disagreeably effusive ⟨~ sentimentalism⟩ — slop·pi·ly \'slä-pə-lē\ adv — slop·pi·ness n

sloppy joe \-'jō\ n [prob. fr. the name Joe, nickname for Joseph] (1961) **:** ground beef cooked in a thick spicy sauce and usu. served on a bun

slop·work \'släp-ˌwərk\ n (1849) **1 :** the manufacture of cheap ready-made clothing **2 :** hasty slovenly work

¹slosh \'släsh, 'slȯsh\ n [prob. blend of slop and slush] (1814) **1 :** SLUSH **2 :** the slap or splash of liquid

²slosh vi (1844) **1 :** to flounder or splash through water, mud, or slush **2 :** to move with a splashing motion ⟨the water ~ed around him —Bill Alcine⟩ ~ vt **1 :** to splash about in liquid **2 :** to splash (a liquid) about or on something **3 :** to splash with liquid

sloshed \'släsht, 'slȯsht\ adj (ca. 1946) slang **:** DRUNK, INTOXICATED

¹slot \'slät\ n [ME, the hollow running down the middle of the breast, fr. MF esclot] (1523) **1 a :** a narrow opening or groove : SLIT, NOTCH ⟨a mail ~ in a door⟩ **b :** a narrow passage or enclosure **c :** a passage through the wing of an airplane or of a missile that is located usu. near the leading edge and formed between a main and an auxiliary airfoil for improving flow conditions over the wing so as to increase lift and delay stalling of the wing **2 :** a place or position in an organization or sequence : NICHE **3 :** SLOT MACHINE **4 :** a gap between an end and a tackle in an offensive football line

²slot vt slot·ted; slot·ting (1747) **1 :** to cut a slot in **2 :** to place in or assign to a slot

³slot n, pl slot [MF esclot track] (1575) **:** the track of an animal (as a deer)

slot·back \'slät-ˌbak\ n (1959) **:** an offensive football halfback who lines up just behind the slot between an offensive end and tackle

slot car n (1966) **:** an electric toy racing car with a pin underneath that fits into a groove on a track for guidance

sloth \'slȯth, 'släth also 'slōth\ n, pl **sloths** \with ths or thz\ [ME slouthe, fr. slow] (12c) **1 a :** disinclination to action or labor : INDOLENCE **b :** spiritual apathy and inactivity (the deadly sin of ~) **2 :** any of the slow-moving arboreal edentate mammals that comprise two genera (Bradypus and Choloepus), inhabit tropical forests of So. and Central America, hang from the branches back downward, and feed on leaves, shoots, and fruits — compare THREE-TOED SLOTH, TWO-TOED SLOTH

sloth·ful \'slȯth-fəl, 'släth- also 'slōth-\ adj (15c) **:** inclined to sloth : INDOLENT syn see LAZY — sloth·ful·ly \-fə-lē\ adv — sloth·ful·ness n

sloth 2

slot machine n (1891) **1 :** a machine whose operation is begun by dropping a coin into a slot **2 :** a coin-operated gambling machine that pays off according to the matching of symbols on wheels spun by a handle — called also one-armed bandit

slot racing n (1965) **:** the racing of slot cars — slot racer n

¹slouch \'slau̇ch\ n [origin unknown] (1515) **1 a :** an awkward fellow : LOUT **b :** one that is unimpressive; esp **:** a lazy or incompetent person — used in negative constructions ⟨was no ~ at cooking⟩ **2 a :** a gait or posture characterized by an ungainly stooping of the head and shoulders or excessive relaxation of body muscles

²slouch vi (1754) **1 :** to walk, stand, or sit with a slouch : assume a slouch **2 :** DROOP ~ vt **:** to cause to droop ⟨~ed his shoulders⟩ — slouch·er n

slouch hat n (1837) **:** a soft usu. felt hat with a wide flexible brim

slouchy \'slau̇-chē\ adj slouch·i·er; -est (ca. 1693) **:** lacking erectness or stiffness (in form or posture) ⟨a ~ sweater⟩ ⟨~ figures waiting in line⟩ — slouch·i·ly \-chə-lē\ adv — slouch·i·ness \-chē-nəs\ n

¹slough \'slü, 'slau̇; in the US (exc NewEng) 'slü is usual for sense 1 with those to whom the sense is familiar; Brit usu 'slau̇ for both senses\ n [ME slogh, fr. OE slōh; akin to MHG slouche ditch] (bef. 12c) **1 a :** a place of deep mud or mire **b** (1) **:** SWAMP (2) **:** an inlet on a river; also **:** BACKWATER (3) **:** a creek in a marsh or tide flat **2 :** a state of moral degradation or spiritual dejection — sloughy \-ē\ adj

²slough vt (1846) **:** to engulf in a slough ~ vi **:** to plod through or as if through mud : SLOG

³slough \'sləf\ also **sluff** n [ME slughe; akin to MHG slüch snakeskin] (14c) **1 :** the cast-off skin of a snake **2 :** a mass of dead tissue separating from an ulcer **3 :** something that may be shed or cast off

⁴slough \'sləf\ also **sluff** vi (1720) **1 a :** to become shed or cast off **b**

: to cast off one's skin **c :** to separate in the form of dead tissue from living tissue **2 :** to crumble slowly and fall away ~ vt **1 :** to cast off **2 a :** to get rid of or discard as irksome, objectionable, or disadvantageous — usu. used with off **b :** to dispose of (a losing card in bridge) by discarding syn see DISCARD

slough of de·spond \ˌslau̇-əv-di-'spänd, ˌslü-\ [fr. the Slough of Despond, deep bog into which Christian falls on the way from the City of Destruction and from which Help saves him in the allegory Pilgrim's Progress (1678) by John Bunyan] (1776) **:** a state of extreme depression

Slo·vak \'slō-ˌvak, -vak\ n [Slovak slovák] (1829) **1 :** a member of a Slavic people of Slovakia **2 :** the Slavic language of the Slovak people — Slovak adj — Slo·va·ki·an \slō-'vä-kē-ən, -'va-\ adj or n

¹slov·en \'slə-vən\ n [ME sloveyn rascal, perh. fr. Flem sloovin woman of low character] (15c) **:** one habitually negligent of neatness or cleanliness esp. in personal appearance

²sloven adj (1815) **:** SLOVENLY

Slo·vene \'slō-ˌvēn\ n [G Slowene fr. Slovene Slovenec] (1883) **1 :** a member of a Slavic people living largely in Slovenia **2 :** the language of the Slovenes — Slovene adj — Slo·ve·nian \slō-'vē-nē-ən, -nyən\ adj or n

slov·en·ly \'slə-vən-lē\ adj (ca. 1568) **1 a :** untidy esp. in personal appearance **b :** lazily slipshod ⟨~ in thought⟩ **2 :** characteristic of a sloven ⟨~ habits⟩ — slov·en·li·ness n — slovenly adv

¹slow \'slō\ adj [ME, fr. OE slāw; akin to OHG slēo dull] (bef. 12c) **1 a :** mentally dull : STUPID ⟨a ~ student⟩ **b :** naturally inert or sluggish **2 a :** lacking in readiness, promptness, or willingness **b :** not hasty or precipitate ⟨was ~ to anger⟩ **3 a :** moving, flowing, or proceeding without speed or at less than usual speed ⟨traffic was ~⟩ **b :** exhibiting or marked by low speed ⟨he moved with ~ deliberation⟩ **c :** not acute ⟨a ~ disease⟩ **d :** LOW, GENTLE ⟨~ fire⟩ **4 :** requiring a long time : GRADUAL ⟨a ~ recovery⟩ **5 :** having qualities that hinder rapid progress or action ⟨a ~ track⟩ **6 a :** registering behind or below what is correct ⟨the clock is ~⟩ **b :** less than the time indicated by another method of reckoning **c :** that is behind the time at a specified time or place **7 a :** lacking in life, animation, or gaiety : BORING **b :** marked by reduced sales or patronage ⟨business was ~⟩ — slow·ish \'slō-ish\ adj — slow·ness n

²slow adv (15c) **:** SLOWLY

usage Some commentators claim that careful writers avoid the adverb slow, in spite of the fact that it has had over four centuries of usage ⟨have a continent forbearance till the speed of his rage goes slower —Shak.⟩. In actual practice, slow and slowly are not used in quite the same way. Slow is almost always used with verbs that denote movement or action, and it regularly follows the verb it modifies ⟨beans . . . are best cooked long and slow —Louise Prothro⟩. Slowly is used before the verb ⟨a sense of outrage, which slowly changed to shame —Paul Horgan⟩ and with participial adjectives ⟨a slowly dawning awareness . . . of the problem —Amer. Labor⟩. Slowly is used after verbs where slow might also be used ⟨burn slow or slowly⟩ and after verbs where slow would be unidiomatic ⟨the leadership turned slowly toward bombing as a means of striking back —David Halberstam⟩.

³slow vt (1557) **:** to make slow or slower : slacken the speed of ⟨~ a car⟩ — often used with down or up ~ vi **:** to go or become slower ⟨production of new cars ~ed sharply⟩ syn see DELAY

slow·down \'slō-ˌdau̇n\ n (1897) **:** a slowing down ⟨a business ~⟩

slow–foot·ed \-ˌfu̇-təd\ adj (1642) **:** moving at a very slow pace : PLODDING ⟨a ~ novel⟩ ⟨a ~ ship⟩ — slow–foot·ed·ness n

slow·ly \-lē\ adv (13c) **:** in a slow manner : not quickly, fast, early, rashly, or readily usage see SLOW

slow match n (ca. 1802) **:** a match or fuse made so as to burn slowly and evenly and used for firing (as of blasting charges)

slow–motion \'slō-'mō-shən\ adj (1923) **:** of, relating to, or being motion-picture or video photography in which the action that has been photographed is made to appear to occur slower than it actually occurred ⟨a ~ replay⟩; also **:** slowly moving ⟨a ~ dance⟩

slow motion n (1924) **:** slow-motion photography

slow–pitch \'slō-ˌpich\ n (1967) **:** softball which is played with 10 players on each side and in which each pitch must have an arc 3 to 10 feet high and base stealing is not allowed

slow·poke \'slō-ˌpōk\ n [¹slow + poke annoyingly stupid person] (1848) **:** a very slow person

slow–twitch \'slō-ˌtwich\ adj (1971) **:** of, relating to, or being muscle fiber that contracts slowly esp. during sustained physical activity requiring endurance — compare FAST-TWITCH

slow virus n (1954) **:** any of various viruses with a long incubation period between infection and development of a degenerative disease (as kuru or Creutzfeldt-Jakob disease)

slow–wit·ted \-'wi-təd\ adj (1571) **:** mentally slow : DULL

slow·worm \'slō-ˌwərm\ n [ME sloworm, fr. OE slāwyrm, fr. slā- (akin to Sw slå earthworm) + wyrm worm] (bef. 12c) **:** a burrowing limbless European lizard (Anguis fragilis) with small eyes — called also blindworm

¹slub \'sləb\ vt slubbed; slub·bing [back-formation fr. slubbing] (1834) **:** to draw out and twist (as slivers of wool) slightly

²slub n (1851) **:** a soft thick uneven section in a yarn or thread

slub·ber \'slə-bər\ vt slub·bered; slub·ber·ing \-b(ə-)riŋ\ [prob. fr. obs. D slubberen] (1530) **1** dial chiefly Eng **:** STAIN, SULLY **2 :** to perform in a slipshod fashion

slub·bing \'slə-biŋ\ n [origin unknown] (1786) **:** ROVING

sludge \'sləj\ n [ME slugge, perh. alter. of slicche mud, slush; akin to OHG slīh mire] (15c) **1 :** MUD, MIRE; esp **:** a muddy deposit (as on a riverbed) : OOZE **2 :** a muddy or slushy mass, deposit, or sediment: as **a :** precipitated solid matter produced by water and sewage treatment processes **b :** muddy sediment in a steam boiler **c :** a precipitate or settling (as a mixture of impurities and acid) from a mineral oil **3 :** SLUSH **5** — sludgy \'slə-jē\ adj

¹slue \'slü\ var of ¹SLOUGH

²slue var of ³SLEW

³slue n [²slue] (ca. 1860) **1 :** position or inclination after slewing **2 :** SKID **5**

slug \'sləg\ n [ME slugge, of Scand origin; akin to Norw dial. slugga to walk sluggishly] (15c) **1 :** SLUGGARD **2 :** a lump, disk, or cylinder of material (as plastic or metal): as **a** (1) **:** a musket ball (2) **:** BULLET **b :** a piece of metal roughly shaped for subsequent processing **c :** a

$50 gold piece   **d** : a disk for insertion in a slot machine; *esp* : one used illegally instead of a coin   **3** : any of numerous chiefly terrestrial pulmonate gastropods (order Stylommatophora) that are found in most parts of the world where there is a reasonable supply of moisture and are closely related to the land snails but are long and wormlike and have only a rudimentary shell often buried in the mantle or entirely absent   **4** : a smooth soft larva of a sawfly or moth that creeps like a mollusk   **5 a** : a quantity of liquor drunk in one swallow   **b** : a detached mass of fluid (as water vapor or oil) that causes impact (as in a circulating system)   **6 a** : a metal thicker than a printer's lead   **b** : a line of type cast as one piece   **c** : a usu. temporary type line serving to instruct or identify   **7** : the gravitational unit of mass in the foot-pound-second system to which a pound force can impart an acceleration of one foot per second per second and which is equal to the mass of an object weighing 32 pounds

²**slug** *vt* **slugged; slug·ging** (1912)   **1** : to add a printer's slug to   **2** : to drink in gulps — often used with *down*

³**slug** *n* [perh. fr. *slug* to load with slugs] (1830) : a heavy blow esp. with the fist

⁴**slug** *vt* **slugged; slug·ging** (ca. 1861)   **1** : to strike heavily with or as if with the fist or a bat   **2** : FIGHT 4b — usu. used in the phrase *slug it out*

slug·a·bed \'slə-gə-ˌbed\ *n* (1592) : a person who stays in bed after the usual or proper time to get up; *broadly* : SLUGGARD

slug·fest \'sləg-ˌfest\ *n* (1916) : a fight marked by the exchange of heavy blows; *also* : a heated dispute ⟨a vocal ~⟩

¹**slug·gard** \'slə-gərd\ *n* [ME *sluggart*] (14c) : an habitually lazy person

²**sluggard** *adj* (1593) : SLUGGARDLY — **slug·gard·ness** *n*

slug·gard·ly \'slə-gərd-lē\ *adj* (1865) : lazily inactive

slug·ger \'slə-gər\ *n* (1877) : one that strikes hard or with heavy blows: as   **a** : a prizefighter who punches hard but has usu. little defensive skill   **b** : a hard-hitting batter in baseball

slugging percentage *n* (ca. 1949) : the ratio (as a rate per thousand) of the total number of bases reached on base hits to official times at bat for a baseball player — called also *slugging average*

slug·gish \'slə-gish\ *adj* (15c)   **1** : averse to activity or exertion : INDOLENT; *also* : TORPID   **2** : slow to respond (as to stimulation or treatment)   **3 a** : markedly slow in movement, flow, or growth   **b** : economically inactive or slow — **slug·gish·ly** *adv* — **slug·gish·ness** *n*

¹**sluice** \'slüs\ *n* [ME *sluse*, alter. of *scluse*, fr. MF *escluse*, fr. LL *exclusa*, fr. L, fem. of *exclusus*, pp. of *excludere* to exclude] (15c)   **1 a** : an artificial passage for water (as in a millstream) fitted with a valve or gate for stopping or regulating flow   **b** : a body of water pent up behind a floodgate   **2** : a dock gate : FLOODGATE   **3 a** : a stream flowing through a floodgate   **b** : a channel to drain or carry off surplus water   **4** : a long inclined trough usu. on the ground; *esp* : such a contrivance paved usu. with riffles to hold quicksilver for catching gold

²**sluice** *vb* **sluiced; sluic·ing** *vt* (1593)   **1 a** : to draw off by or through a sluice   **2 a** : to wash with or in water running through or from a sluice   **b** : to drench with a sudden flow : FLUSH   **3** : to transport (as logs) in a sluice ~ *vi* : to pour as if from a sluice

sluice·way \'slüs-ˌwā\ *n* (1779) : an artificial channel into which water is let by a sluice

sluicy \'slü-sē\ *adj* (1697) : falling copiously or in streams : STREAMING

¹**slum** \'sləm\ *n, often attrib* [origin unknown] (1825) : a densely populated usu. urban area marked by crowding, dirty run-down housing, poverty, and social disorganization

²**slum** *vi* **slummed; slum·ming** (1884) : to visit slums esp. out of curiosity; *broadly* : to go somewhere or do something that might be considered beneath one's station — sometimes used with *it* ⟨*slumming* it in a cabin without plumbing⟩ — **slum·mer** *n*

¹**slum·ber** \'sləm-bər\ *vi* **slum·bered; slum·ber·ing** \-b(ə-)riŋ\ [ME, freq. of *slumen* to doze, prob. fr. *slume* slumber, fr. OE *slūma*; akin to MHG *slumen* to slumber] (13c)   **1 a** : to sleep lightly : DOZE   **b** : SLEEP   **2 a** : to be in a torpid, slothful, or negligent state   **b** : to lie dormant or latent — **slum·ber·er** \-bər-ər\ *n*

²**slumber** *n* (14c)   **1 a** : SLEEP   **b** : a light sleep   **2** : LETHARGY, TORPOR

slum·ber·ous *or* **slum·brous** \'sləm-b(ə-)rəs\ *adj* (15c)   **1** : heavy with sleep : SLEEPY   **2** : inducing slumber : SOPORIFIC   **3** : marked by or suggestive of a state of sleep or lethargy ⟨a ~ state of peace⟩

slumber party *n* (1925) : an overnight gathering esp. of teenage girls usu. at one of their homes

slum·bery \'sləm-b(ə-)rē\ *adj* (14c) *archaic* : SLUMBEROUS

slum·gul·lion \'sləm-ˌgəl-yən, ˌsləm-'\ *n* [perh. fr. *slum* slime + E dial. *gullion* mud, cesspool] (1902) : a meat stew

slum·lord \'sləm-ˌlȯrd\ *n* [¹*slum* + land*lord*] (1953) : a landlord who receives unusually large profits from substandard properties

slum·my \'slə-mē\ *adj* **slum·mi·er; -est** (1873) : of, relating to, or suggestive of a slum ⟨~ streets⟩

¹**slump** \'sləmp\ *vi* [prob. of Scand origin; akin to Norw *slumpa* to fall] (ca. 1677)   **1 a** : to fall or sink suddenly   **b** : to drop or slide down suddenly : COLLAPSE ⟨~*ed* to the floor⟩   **2** : to assume a drooping posture or carriage : SLOUCH   **3** : to go into a slump ⟨sales ~*ed*⟩

²**slump** *n* (1887)   **1 a** : a marked or sustained decline esp. in economic activity or prices ⟨a post-election ~⟩   **b** : a period of poor or losing play by a team or individual ⟨one spring I was in a batting ~ —Ted Williams⟩   **2** : a downward slide of a mass of rock or land

slump·fla·tion \ˌsləmp-'flā-shən\ *n* [²*slump* + in*flation*] (1974) : a state or period of combined economic decline and rising inflation

slung *past and past part of* SLING

slung·shot \'sləŋ-ˌshät\ *n* (1842) : a striking weapon consisting of a small mass of metal or stone fixed on a flexible handle or strap

slunk *past and past part of* SLINK

¹**slur** \'slər\ *n* [obs. E dial. *slur* thin mud, fr. ME *sloor*; akin to MHG *slier* mud] (1609)   **1 a** : an insulting or disparaging remark or innuendo : ASPERSION   **b** : a shaming or degrading effect : STAIN, STIGMA   **2** : a blurred spot in printed matter : SMUDGE

²**slur** *vb* **slurred; slur·ring** *vt* (1660)   **1** : to cast aspersions on : DISPARAGE   **2** : to make indistinct : OBSCURE ~ *vi* : to slip so as to cause a slur — used of a sheet being printed

³**slur** *vb* **slurred; slur·ring** [prob. fr. LG *slurrn* to shuffle; akin to ME *sloor* mud] *vt* (1660)   **1 a** : to slide or slip over without due mention, consideration, or emphasis ⟨*slurred* over certain facts⟩   **b** : to perform hurriedly : SKIMP ⟨let him not ~ his lesson —R. W. Emerson⟩   **2** : to perform (successive tones of different pitch) in a smooth or connected manner   **3 a** : to reduce, make a substitution for, or omit (sounds that would normally occur in an utterance)   **b** : to utter with such reduction, substitution, or omission of sounds ⟨his speech was *slurred*⟩ ~ *vi*   **1** *dial chiefly Eng* : SLIP, SLIDE   **2** : DRAG, SHUFFLE

⁴**slur** *n* (ca. 1801)   **1 a** : a curved line connecting notes to be sung to the same syllable or performed without a break   **b** : the combination of two or more slurred tones   **2** : a slurring manner of speech

slurp \'slərp\ *vb* [D *slurpen*; akin to MLG *slorpen* to slurp] *vi* (1648) : to make a sucking noise while eating or drinking ~ *vt* : to eat or drink noisily or with a sucking sound — **slurp** *n*

¹**slur·ry** \'slər-ē, 'slə-rē\ *n, pl* **slur·ries** [ME *slory*] (15c) : a watery mixture of insoluble matter (as mud, lime, or plaster of paris)

²**slurry** *vt* **slur·ried; slur·ry·ing** (1947) : to convert into a slurry

¹**slush** \'sləsh\ *n* [perh. of Scand origin; akin to Norw *slusk* slush] (1641)   **1 a** : partly melted or watery snow   **b** : loose ice crystals formed during the early stages of freezing of salt water   **2** : soft mud : MIRE   **3** : refuse grease and fat from cooking esp. on shipboard   **4** : paper pulp in water suspension   **5** : trashy and usu. cheaply sentimental material   **6** : unsolicited writings submitted (as to a magazine) for publication

²**slush** *vt* (1807) : to wet, splash, or paint with slush ~ *vi*   **1** : to make one's way through slush   **2** : to make a splashing sound

slush fund *n* (1864)   **1** : a fund raised from the sale of refuse to obtain small luxuries or pleasures for a warship's crew   **2** : a fund for bribing public officials or carrying on corruptive propaganda

slushy \'slə-shē\ *adj* **slush·i·er; -est** (1791) : being, involving, or resembling slush: as   **a** : full of or covered with slush ⟨~ streets⟩   **b** : made up of or having the consistency of slush ⟨~ snow⟩ ⟨a ~ mixture⟩   **c** : having a cheaply sentimental quality : TRASHY ⟨a ~ novel⟩ — **slush·i·ness** *n*

slut \'slət\ *n* [ME *slutte*] (15c)   **1** *chiefly Brit* : a slovenly woman   **2 a** : a promiscuous woman; *esp* : PROSTITUTE   **b** : a saucy girl : MINX — **slut·tish** \'slə-tish\ *adj* — **slut·tish·ly** *adv* — **slut·tish·ness** *n* — **slut·ty** \'slə-tē\ *adj*

sly \'slī\ *adj* **sli·er** *or* **sly·er** \'slī(-ə)r\; **sli·est** *or* **sly·est** \'slī-əst\ [ME *sli*, fr. ON *slœgr*; akin to OE *slēan* to strike — more at SLAY] (13c)   **1** *chiefly dial* : wise in practical affairs   **b** : displaying cleverness : INGENIOUS   **2 a** : clever in concealing one's aims or ends : FURTIVE ⟨the ~ fox⟩   **b** : lacking in straightforwardness and candor : DISSEMBLING ⟨a ~ scheme⟩   **3** : lightly mischievous : ROGUISH ⟨a ~ jest⟩ ⟨a ~ smile⟩ — **sly·ly** *adv* — **sly·ness** *n* — **on the sly** : in a manner intended to avoid notice

   syn SLY, CUNNING, CRAFTY, WILY, TRICKY, FOXY, ARTFUL, SLICK mean attaining or seeking to attain one's ends by guileful or devious means. SLY implies furtiveness, lack of candor, and skill in concealing one's aims and methods ⟨a *sly* corporate raider⟩. CUNNING suggests the inventive use of sometimes limited intelligence in overreaching or circumventing ⟨the *cunning* fox avoided the trap⟩. CRAFTY implies cleverness and subtlety of method ⟨a *crafty* lefthander⟩. WILY implies skill and deception in maneuvering ⟨the *wily* fugitive escaped the posse⟩. TRICKY is more likely to suggest shiftiness and unreliability than skill in deception and maneuvering ⟨a *tricky* political operative⟩. FOXY implies a shrewd and wary craftiness usu. involving devious dealing ⟨a *foxy* publicity man planting stories⟩. ARTFUL implies indirectness in dealing and often connotes sophistication or cleverness ⟨elicited the information by *artful* questioning⟩. SLICK emphasizes smoothness and guile ⟨*slick* operators selling time-sharing⟩.

sly·boots \'slī-ˌbüts\ *n pl but sing in constr* (ca. 1700) : a sly tricky person; *esp* : one who is cunning or mischievous in an engaging way

¹**smack** \'smak\ *n* [ME, fr. OE *smæc*; akin to OHG *smac* taste and prob. to Lith *smaguris* sweet tooth] (bef. 12c)   **1** : characteristic taste or flavor; *also* : a perceptible taste or tincture   **2** : a small quantity

²**smack** *vi* (13c)   **1** : to have a taste or flavor   **2** : to have a trace, vestige, or suggestion ⟨a proposal that ~*s* of treason⟩

³**smack** *n* [D *smak* or LG *smack*] (1533) : a sailing ship (as a sloop or cutter) used chiefly in coasting and fishing

⁴**smack** *vb* [akin to MD *smacken* to strike] *vt* (1557)   **1** : to close and open (lips) noisily and in rapid succession esp. in eating   **2 a** : to kiss with or as if with a smack   **b** : to strike so as to produce a smack ~ *vi* : to make or give a smack

⁵**smack** *n* (1570)   **1** : a quick sharp noise made by rapidly compressing and opening the lips   **2** : a loud kiss   **3** : a sharp slap or blow

⁶**smack** *adv* (1782) : squarely and sharply : DIRECTLY ⟨~ in the middle⟩

⁷**smack** *n* [perh. fr. Yiddish *shmek* sniff, whiff, pinch (of snuff)] (ca. 1960) *slang* : HEROIN

smack–dab \'smak-'dab\ *adv* (1892) : EXACTLY, SQUARELY

smack·er \'sma-kər\ *n* (1611)   **1** : one that smacks   **2** *slang* : DOLLAR

smack·ing \'sma-kin\ *adj* (1820) : BRISK, LIVELY ⟨a ~ breeze⟩

¹**small** \'smȯl\ *adj* [ME *smal*, fr. OE *smæl*; akin to OHG *smal* small, Gk *mēlon* small domestic animal] (bef. 12c)   **1 a** : having comparatively little size or slight dimensions   **b** : LOWERCASE   **2** : minor in influence, power, or rank   **b** : operating on a limited scale   **3** : lacking in strength ⟨a ~ voice⟩   **4 a** : little or close to zero in an objectively measurable aspect (as quantity, amount, or value)   **b** : made up of few or little units   **5 a** : of little consequence : TRIVIAL, INSIGNIFICANT   **b** : HUMBLE, MODEST ⟨a ~ beginning⟩   **6** : limited in degree   **7 a** : MEAN, PETTY   **b** : reduced to a humiliating position — **small·ish** \'smȯ-lish\ *adj* — **small·ness** \'smȯl-nəs\ *n*

   syn SMALL, LITTLE, DIMINUTIVE, MINUTE, TINY, MINIATURE mean noticeably below average in size. SMALL and LITTLE are often interchangeable, but SMALL applies more to relative size determined by capacity, value, number ⟨a relatively *small* backyard⟩. LITTLE is more absolute in implication often carrying the idea of petiteness, pettiness, insignificance, or immaturity ⟨your pathetic *little* smile⟩. DIMINUTIVE implies abnormal smallness ⟨*diminutive* bonsai plants⟩. MINUTE implies extreme smallness ⟨a *minute* amount of caffeine in the soda⟩. TINY is an

\ə\ abut \ᵊ\ kitten, F table \ər\ further \a\ ash \ā\ ace \ä\ mop, mar
\aú\ out \ch\ chin \e\ bet \ē\ easy \g\ go \i\ hit \ī\ ice \j\ job
\ŋ\ sing \ō\ go \ȯ\ law \ȯi\ boy \th\ thin \t̷h\ the \ü\ loot \ú\ foot
\y\ yet \zh\ vision \à, ᶄ, ⁿ, œ, œ̄, ue, uē, ᵞ\ *see* Guide to Pronunciation

informal equivalent to MINUTE ⟨tiny cracks formed in the painting⟩.
MINIATURE applies to an exactly proportioned reproduction on a
very small scale ⟨a dollhouse complete with miniature furnishings⟩.

²**small** adv (bef. 12c) **1** : in or into small pieces **2** : without force or
loudness ⟨speak as ∼ as you will —Shak.⟩ **3** : in a small manner

³**small** n (14c) **1** : a part smaller than and esp. narrower than the remainder
⟨the ∼ of the back⟩ **2** a pl : small-sized products **b** pl, chiefly Brit
: SMALLCLOTHES; esp : UNDERWEAR

small arm n (1689) : a handheld firearm (as a handgun or shoulder
arm) — usu. used in pl.

small beer n (1568) **1** : weak or inferior beer **2** : something of small
importance — **small–beer** adj

small calorie n (ca. 1889) : CALORIE 1a

small capital n (1770) : a letter having the form of but smaller than a
capital letter (as in THESE WORDS) — called also small cap

small change n (1819) **1** : coins of low denomination **2** : something
trifling or petty

small–claims court n (1925) : a special court intended to simplify and
expedite the handling of small claims on debts — called also small≠
debts court

small–clothes \'smȯl-ˌklō(th)z\ n pl (1796) **1** : close-fitting knee
breeches worn in the 18th century **2** : small articles of clothing (as
underclothing or handkerchiefs)

smaller European elm bark beetle n (ca. 1945) : ELM BARK BEETLE b

small–fry \'smȯl-ˌfrī\ adj(1817) **1** : MINOR, UNIMPORTANT ⟨a ∼ politi-
cian⟩ **2** : of, relating to, or intended for children : CHILDISH

small–hold·ing \-ˌhōl-diŋ\ n (1892) chiefly Brit : a small farm —
small–hold·er \-dər\ n

small hours n pl (ca. 1837) : the early morning hours

small intestine n (1767) : the part of the intestine that lies between the
stomach and colon, consists of duodenum, jejunum, and ileum, secretes digestive enzymes, and is the chief site of the absorption of digested nutrients

small–mind·ed \'smȯl-'mīn-dəd\ adj (1847) **1** : having narrow interests, sympathies, or outlook **2** : typical of a small-minded person
: marked by pettiness, narrowness, or meanness ⟨∼ conduct⟩ —
small–mind·ed·ly adv — **small–mind·ed·ness** n

small·mouth bass \'smȯl-
ˌmau̇th-\ n (1938) : a black bass
(Micropterus dolomieu) of clear
rivers and lakes that is bronzy
green above and lighter below and
has the vertex of the angle of the
jaw falling below the eye — called
also smallmouth, smallmouth
black bass

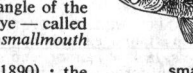
smallmouth bass

small octave n (ca. 1890) : the
musical octave that begins on the
first C below middle C — see PITCH illustration

small potato n (1831) : one that is of trivial importance or worth —
usu. used in pl. but sing. or pl. in constr.

small–pox \'smȯl-ˌpäks\ n (1518) : an acute contagious febrile disease
caused by a poxvirus and characterized by skin eruption with pustules,
sloughing, and scar formation

small–scale \-'skā(ə)l\ adj (1852) **1** : small in scope; esp : small in
output or operation **2** of a map : having a scale (as one inch to 25
miles) that permits plotting of comparatively little detail and shows
mainly large features

small screen n (1956) : TELEVISION

small stuff n (ca. 1857) : small rope (as spun yarn or marline) usu.
identified by the number of threads or yarns which it contains

small·sword \'smȯl-ˌsȯrd, -ˌsȯrd\ n (1687) : a light tapering sword for
thrusting used chiefly in dueling and fencing

small talk n (1751) : light or casual conversation : CHITCHAT

small–time \'smȯl-ˈtīm\ adj (1910) : insignificant in performance,
scope, or standing : PETTY ⟨∼ thieves⟩ — **small–tim·er** \-ˈtī-mər\ n

smalt \'smȯlt\ n [MF, fr. OIt smalto, of Gmc origin; akin to OHG
smelzan to melt — more at SMELT] (1558) : a deep blue pigment used
esp. as a ceramic color and prepared by fusing together silica, potash,
and oxide of cobalt and grinding to powder the resultant glass

smalt·ite \'smȯl-ˌtīt\ n [alter. of smaltine, fr. F, fr. smalt, fr. MF] (1868)
: a bluish white or gray isometric mineral of metallic luster that is
essentially an arsenide of cobalt and nickel

smal·to \'smäl-(ˌ)tō, 'smȯl-\ n, pl **smal·ti** \-(ˌ)tē\ [It, smalt, smalto]
(1705) : colored glass or enamel or a piece of either used in mosaic
work

sma·ragd \smə-'ragd, 'smar-ˌagd\ n [ME smaragde, fr. L smaragdus]
(13c) : EMERALD — **sma·rag·dine** \smə-'rag-dən, 'smar-əg-ˌdīn\ adj

sma·rag·dite \smə-'rag-ˌdīt, 'smar-əg-ˌdīt\ n [F, fr. L smaragdus emerald — more at EMERALD] (1804) : a green foliated amphibole

smarm \'smärm\ n [back-formation fr. smarmy] (1937) : smarmy language or behavior

smarmy \'smär-mē\ adj [smarm to gush, slobber] (1924) **1** : revealing
or marked by a smug, ingratiating, or false earnestness ⟨a tone of ∼
self-satisfaction —New Yorker⟩ **2** : of low sleazy taste or quality ⟨∼
eroticism⟩ — **smarm·i·ly** \-mə-lē\ adv — **smarm·i·ness** \-mē-nəs\ n

¹**smart** \'smärt\ adj (bef. 12c) **1** : making one smart : causing a sharp
stinging **2** : marked by often sharp forceful activity or vigorous
strength ⟨a ∼ pull of the starter cord⟩ **3** : BRISK, SPIRITED **4** a : mentally alert : BRIGHT **b** : KNOWLEDGEABLE **c** : SHREWD ⟨a ∼ investment⟩
5 a : WITTY, CLEVER **b** : PERT, SAUCY ⟨don't get ∼ with me⟩ **6** a
: NEAT, TRIM **b** : stylish or elegant in dress or appearance **c** (1) : SO-
PHISTICATED (2) : characteristic of or patronized by fashionable society
7 a : being a guided missile ⟨a laser-guided ∼ bomb⟩ **b** : operating
by automation ⟨a ∼ machine tool⟩ **c** : INTELLIGENT **3** — **smart·ly** adv
— **smart·ness** n

²**smart** vi [ME smerten, fr. OE smeortan; akin to OHG smerzan to pain]
(13c) **1** : to cause or be the cause or seat of a sharp poignant pain; also
: to feel or have such a pain **2** a : to feel or endure distress, remorse,
or embarrassment ⟨∼ing from wounded vanity —W. L. Shirer⟩ **b** : to
pay a heavy or stinging penalty ⟨would have to ∼ for this foolishness⟩

³**smart** n (13c) **1** : a smarting pain; esp : a stinging local pain **2** : poi-
gnant grief or remorse ⟨was not the sort to get over ∼s —Sir Winston
Churchill⟩ **3** : an affectedly witty or fashionable person **4** pl, slang
: INTELLIGENCE, KNOW-HOW

⁴**smart** adv (13c) : in a smart manner : SMARTLY

smart al·eck also **smart al·ec** \'smärt-ˌa-lik, -ˌe-\ n [Aleck, nickname
for Alexander] (1865) : an obnoxiously conceited and self-assertive
person with pretensions to smartness or cleverness — **smart–aleck**
adj — **smart–al·ecky** \-ˌa-lə-kē, -ˌe-\ adj

smart–ass \-ˌas\ n (1964) : SMART ALECK — **smart–ass** adj — **smart–
assed** \-ˌast\ adj

smart card n (1980) : a small plastic card that has a built-in microprocessor to store and process data and records

smart·en \'smärt-ˀn\ vb **smart·ened;** **smart·en·ing** \'smärt-ˀn-iŋ,
'smär-t°n-iŋ\ vt (1815) : to make smart or smarter; esp : SPRUCE — usu.
used with up ∼ vi : to smarten oneself — used with up

¹**smart money** \'smärt-ˌmə-nē\ n [³smart] (1693) : PUNITIVE DAMAGES

²**smart money** n \-'mə-nē, -ˌmə-nē\ n [¹smart] (1926) **1** : money ventured by one having inside information or much experience **2** : well-
informed bettors or speculators

smart·weed \'smärt-ˌwēd\ n (ca. 1787) : any of various polygonums
with strong acid juice

smarty or **smart·ie** \'smär-tē\ n, pl **smart·ies** (1861) : SMART ALECK

smarty–pants \-ˌpan(t)s\ n pl but sing in constr (1941) : SMART ALECK
— **smarty–pants** adj

¹**smash** \'smash\ n [perh. blend of ⁴smack and ²mash] (1725) **1** a : a
smashing blow or attack **b** : a hard overhand stroke (as in tennis or
badminton) **2** a : the action or sound of smashing; esp : a wreck due
to collision : CRASH **b** : utter collapse : RUIN **3** : a striking success

²**smash** vt (1778) **1** : to break or crush by violence **2** a : to drive or
throw violently esp. with a shattering or battering effect; also : to effect
in this way **b** : to hit violently : BATTER **c** (1) : to hit (as a tennis
ball) with a hard overhand stroke (2) : to drive (a ball) with a forceful
stroke **3** : to destroy utterly : WRECK ∼ vi **1** : to move or become
propelled with violence or crashing effect ⟨∼ed into a tree⟩ **2** : to
become wrecked **3** : to go to pieces suddenly under collision or pressure — **smash·er** n

³**smash** adj (1923) : being a smash : OUTSTANDING ⟨a ∼ hit⟩

smashed \'smasht\ adj (ca. 1959) slang : DRUNK, INTOXICATED

smash·ing \'sma-shiŋ\ adj (1833) **1** : that smashes : CRUSHING ⟨a ∼
defeat⟩ **2** : extraordinarily impressive or effective ⟨a ∼ performance⟩
— **smash·ing·ly** \-shiŋ-lē\ adv

smash–up \'smash-ˌəp\ n (1856) **1** : a collision between vehicles **2** : a
complete collapse

¹**smat·ter** \'sma-tər\ vb [ME smateren] vi (15c) : to talk superficially
: BABBLE ∼ vt **1** : to speak with spotty or superficial knowledge ⟨∼s
French⟩ **2** : to dabble in — **smat·ter·er** \-tər-ər\ n

²**smatter** n (1668) : SMATTERING

smat·ter·ing \'sma-tə-riŋ\ n (1538) **1** : superficial piecemeal knowledge ⟨a ∼ of carpentry, house painting, bricklaying —Alva Johnston⟩
2 : a small scattered number or amount ⟨a ∼ of spectators⟩

¹**smear** \'smir\ n [ME smere, fr. OE smeoru; akin to OHG smero grease
and prob. to OIr smiur marrow] (bef. 12c) **1** a : a viscous or sticky
substance **b** : a spot made by or as if by an unctuous or adhesive substance **2** : material smeared on a surface (as of a microscopic slide);
also : a preparation made by smearing material on a surface ⟨a vaginal
∼⟩ **3** : a usu. unsubstantiated charge or accusation against a person
or organization

²**smear** vt (bef. 12c) **1** a : to overspread with something unctuous,
viscous, or adhesive : DAUB **b** : to spread over a surface **2** a : to
stain, smudge, or dirty by or as if by smearing **b** : SULLY, BESMIRCH;
specif : to vilify esp. by secretly and maliciously spreading grave
charges and imputations **3** : to obliterate, smear, blur, blend, wipe
out, or defeat by or as if by smearing — **smear·er** n

smear–case also **smier·case** \'smir-ˌkäs\ n [modif. of G Schmierkäse,
fr. schmieren to smear + Käse cheese] (1829) chiefly Midland : COT-
TAGE CHEESE

smeary \'smir-ē\ adj (ca. 1529) **1** : marked by or covered with smears
2 : liable to cause smears ⟨∼ lipstick⟩

smec·tic \'smek-tik\ adj [L smecticus cleansing, having the properties
of soap, fr. Gk smēktikos, fr. smēchein to clean] (1923) : of, relating to,
or being the phase of a liquid crystal characterized by arrangement of
molecules in layers with the long molecular axes in a given layer being
parallel to one another and those of other layers and perpendicular or
slightly inclined to the plane of the layer — compare CHOLESTERIC,
NEMATIC

smec·tite \'smek-ˌtīt\ n [smectis fuller's earth, modif. of Gk smēktris
kind of fuller's earth, fr. smēchein to clean] (1811) : MONTMORILLONITE
— **smec·tit·ic** \(ˌ)smek-'ti-tik\ adj

smeg·ma \'smeg-mə\ n [NL, fr. L, detergent, soap, fr. Gk smēgma, fr.
smēchein to wash off, clean] (ca. 1819) : the secretion of a sebaceous
gland; specif : the cheesy sebaceous matter that collects between the
glans penis and the foreskin or around the clitoris and labia minora

¹**smell** \'smel\ vb **smelled** \'smeld\ or **smelt** \'smelt\; **smell·ing** [ME]
vt (12c) **1** : to perceive the odor or scent of through stimuli affecting
the olfactory nerves : get the odor or scent of with the nose **2** : to
detect or become aware of as if by the sense of smell **3** : to emit the
odor of ∼ vi **1** : to exercise the sense of smell **2** a (1) : to have an
odor or scent (2) : to have a characteristic aura or atmosphere
: SMACK ⟨the accounts . . . seemed to me to ∼ of truth —R. S. Bourne⟩;
also : SEEM, APPEAR ⟨the story didn't ∼ right⟩ **b** (1) : to have an
offensive odor : STINK (2) : to be of bad or questionable quality ⟨all
this from the moral point of view ∼s —A. F. Wills⟩ — **smell·er** n —
smell a rat : to have a suspicion of something wrong

²**smell** n (12c) **1** : the property of a thing that affects the olfactory
organs : ODOR **2** a : the process, function, or power of smelling **b**
: the special sense concerned with the perception of odor **3** a : a
very small amount : TRACE ⟨add only a ∼ of garlic⟩ **b** : a pervading
or characteristic quality : AURA ⟨the ∼ of affluence, of power —Harry
Hervey⟩ **4** : an act or instance of smelling

syn SMELL, SCENT, ODOR, AROMA mean the quality that makes a thing
perceptible to the olfactory sense. SMELL implies solely the sensation
without suggestion of quality or character ⟨an odd smell permeated
the room⟩. SCENT applies to the characteristic smell given off by a
substance, an animal, or a plant ⟨the scent of lilacs⟩. ODOR may imply a
stronger or more readily distinguished scent or it may be equivalent to

SMELL ⟨a cheese with a strong *odor*⟩. AROMA suggests a somewhat penetrating usu. pleasant odor ⟨the *aroma* of freshly ground coffee⟩.

smelling salts *n pl but sing or pl in constr* (1840) : a usu. scented aromatic preparation of ammonium carbonate and ammonia water used as a stimulant and restorative

smelly \'sme-lē\ *adj* **smell·i·er; -est** (1862) : having a smell; *esp* : MALODOROUS

¹smelt \'smelt\ *n, pl* **smelts** *or* **smelt** [ME, fr. OE; akin to Norw *smelte* whiting] (bef. 12c) : any of a family (Osmeridae) of small salmonoid fishes that closely resemble the trouts in general structure, live along coasts and ascend rivers to spawn or are landlocked, and have delicate oily flesh with a distinctive odor and taste

²smelt *vt* [D or LG *smelten;* akin to OHG *smelzan* to melt, OE *meltan* — more at MELT] (1543) **1** : to melt or fuse (as ore) often with an accompanying chemical change usu. to separate the metal **2** : REFINE, REDUCE

smelt·er \'smel-tər\ *n* (15c) : one that smelts: **a** : a worker who smelts ore **b** : an owner or operator of a smeltery **c** *or* **smelt·ery** \-t(ə-)rē\ : an establishment for smelting

smew \'smyü\ *n* [akin to MHG *smiehe* smew] (1674) : a small Eurasian merganser (*Mergus albellus*) with the male being white, gray, and black and the female chiefly gray but with a chestnut and white head

smid·gen *also* **smid·geon** *or* **smid·gin** \'smi-jən\ *or* **smidge** \'smij\ *n* [prob. alter. of E dial. *smitch* soiling mark] (1845) : a small amount : BIT

smi·lax \'smī-,laks\ *n* [L, bindweed, yew, fr. Gk] (1601) **1** : GREENBRIER **2** : a tender twining plant (*Asparagus asparagoides*) of the lily family that has ovate bright green cladophylls and is often grown in greenhouses

¹smile \'smī(ə)l\ *vb* **smiled; smil·ing** [ME; akin to OE *smerian* to laugh, Skt *smayate* he smiles] (14c) **1** : to have, produce, or exhibit a smile **2 a** : to look or regard with amusement or ridicule ⟨*smiled* at his own folly —Martin Gardner⟩ **b** : to bestow approval ⟨feeling that Heaven *smiled* on his labors —Sheila Rowlands⟩ **c** : to appear pleasant or agreeable ∼ *vt* **1** : to affect with or by smiling **2** : to express by a smile — **smil·er** *n* — **smil·ey** \'smī-lē\ *adj* — **smil·ing·ly** \'smī-liŋ-lē\ *adv*

²smile *n* (15c) **1** : a facial expression in which the eyes brighten and the corners of the mouth curve slightly upward and which expresses esp. amusement, pleasure, approval, or sometimes scorn **2** : a pleasant or encouraging appearance — **smile·less** \'smī(ə)l-ləs\ *adj*

smirch \'smərch\ *vt* [ME *smorchen*] (15c) **1 a** : to make dirty, stained, or discolored : SULLY **b** : to smear with something that stains or dirties **2** : to bring discredit or disgrace on — **smirch** *n*

smirk \'smərk\ *vi* [ME, fr. OE *smearcian* to smile; akin to OE *smerian* to laugh] (bef. 12c) : to smile in an affected or smug manner : SIMPER — **smirk** *n*

smirky \'smər-kē\ *adj* (1728) : that smirks : SMIRKING

smite \'smīt\ *vb* **smote** \'smōt\; **smit·ten** \'smi-tᵊn\ *or* **smote; smit·ing** \'smī-tiŋ\ [ME, fr. OE *smitan* to smear, defile; akin to OHG *bismīzan* to defile] *vt* (12c) **1** : to strike sharply or heavily esp. with the hand or an implement held in the hand **2 a** : to kill or severely injure by smiting **b** : to attack or afflict suddenly and injuriously ⟨*smitten* by disease⟩ **3** : to cause to strike **4** : to affect as if by striking ⟨children *smitten* with the fear of hell —V. L. Parrington⟩ **5** : CAPTIVATE, TAKE ⟨*smitten* with her beauty⟩ ∼ *vi* : to deliver or deal a blow with or as if with the hand or something held — **smit·er** \'smī-tər\ *n*

smith \'smith\ *n* [ME, fr. OE; akin to OHG *smid* smith and prob. to Gk *smīle* wood-carving knife] (bef. 12c) **1** : a worker in metals : BLACKSMITH **2** : MAKER — often used in combination ⟨gun*smith*⟩ ⟨tune*smith*⟩

smith·er·eens \,smi-thə-'rēnz\ *n pl* [perh. fr. Ir *smidiríní*] (1829) : FRAGMENTS, BITS ⟨the house was blown to ∼ by the explosion⟩

smith·ery \'smi-thə-rē\ *n, pl* **-er·ies** (1625) **1** : the work, art, or trade of a smith **2** : SMITHY 1

Smith·field ham \'smith-,fēld-\ *n* (1908) : a Virginia ham produced in or near Smithfield, Va.

smith·son·ite \'smith-sə-,nīt\ *n* [James *Smithson*] (1856) : a mineral that is a carbonate of zinc and constitutes an important ore of zinc

smithy \'smi-thē *also* -thē\ *n, pl* **smith·ies** (13c) **1** : the workshop of a smith **2** : BLACKSMITH

¹smock \'smäk\ *n* [ME *smok*, fr. OE *smoc;* akin to OHG *smocco* adornment] (bef. 12c) **1** *archaic* : a woman's undergarment; *esp* : CHEMISE **2** : a light loose garment worn esp. for protection of clothing while working

²smock *vt* (1888) : to embroider or shirr with smocking

smock frock *n* (ca. 1800) : a loose outer garment worn by workmen esp. in Europe

smock·ing \'smä-kiŋ\ *n* (1888) : a decorative embroidery or shirring made by gathering cloth in regularly spaced round tucks

smog \'smäg, 'smȯg\ *n* [*smoke* + *fog*] (1905) : a fog made heavier and darker by smoke and chemical fumes; *also* : a photochemical haze caused by the action of solar ultraviolet radiation on atmosphere polluted with hydrocarbons and oxides of nitrogen from automobile exhaust — **smog·less** \'smä-gləs, 'smȯ-\ *adj*

smog·gy \'smä-gē, 'smȯ-\ *adj* **smog·gi·er; -est** (1905) : characterized by or abounding in smog

smok·able *or* **smoke·able** \'smō-kə-bəl\ *adj* (1839) : fit for smoking

¹smoke \'smōk\ *n* [ME, fr. OE *smoca;* akin to OE *smēocan* to emit smoke, MHG *smouch* smoke, and prob. to Gk *smychein* to smolder] (bef. 12c) **1 a** : the gaseous products of burning materials esp. of organic origin made visible by the presence of small particles of carbon **b** : a suspension of particles in a gas **2 a** : a mass or column of smoke **b** : SMUDGE **3** : fume or vapor often resulting from the action of heat on moisture **4** : something of little substance, permanence, or value **5** : something that obscures **6 a** (1) : something (as a cigarette) to smoke (2) : MARIJUANA **2 b** : an act or spell of smoking tobacco **7 a** : a pale blue **b** : any of the colors of smoke **8** : pitches that are fastballs ⟨if a guy's going to hit you . . . he certainly isn't going to throw a spitter—he gives you ∼ —Tony Conigliaro⟩ — **smoke·less** \'smō-kləs\ *adj* — **smoke·like** \'smōk-,līk\ *adj*

²smoke *vb* **smoked; smok·ing** *vi* (bef. 12c) **1 a** : to emit or exhale smoke **b** : to emit excessive smoke **2** *archaic* : to undergo punishment : SUFFER **3** : to spread or rise like smoke **4** : to inhale and ex-

hale the fumes of burning plant material and esp. tobacco; *esp* : to smoke tobacco habitually ∼ *vt* **1 a** : FUMIGATE **b** : to drive (as mosquitoes) away by smoke **c** : to blacken or discolor with smoke ⟨*smoked* glasses⟩ **d** : to cure by exposure to smoke **e** : to stupefy (as bees) by smoke **2** *archaic* : SUSPECT **3** : to inhale and exhale the smoke of **4** *archaic* : RIDICULE

smoke and mirrors *n pl* (1982) : something intended to disguise or draw attention away esp. from an embarrassing or unpleasant issue — usu. hyphenated when used attributively

smoke detector *n* (ca. 1927) : an alarm that activates automatically when it detects smoke

smoke–filled room \'smōk-'fild-\ *n* (1920) : a room (as in a hotel) in which a small group of politicians carry on negotiations

smoke·house \'smōk-,hau̇s\ *n* (1746) : a building where meat or fish is cured by means of dense smoke

smoke·jack \-,jak\ *n* (1675) : a device for turning a spit by a fly or wheel moved by rising gases in a chimney

smoke jumper *n* (1927) : a forest firefighter who parachutes to locations otherwise difficult to reach

smokeless powder *n* (1890) : any of a class of explosive propellants that produce comparatively little smoke on explosion and consist mostly of gelatinized nitrocellulose

smokeless tobacco *n* (1981) : pulverized or shredded tobacco chewed or placed between cheek and gum

smoke out *vt* (1593) **1** : to drive out by or as if by smoke **2** : to cause to be made public

smok·er \'smō-kər\ *n* (1599) **1** : one that smokes **2** : a railroad car or compartment in which smoking is allowed **3** : an informal social gathering for men

smoke screen *n* (1915) **1** : a screen of smoke to hinder enemy observation of a military force, area, or activity **2** : something designed to obscure, confuse, or mislead

¹smoke·stack \'smōk-,stak\ *n* (1859) : a pipe or funnel through which smoke and gases are discharged

²smokestack *adj* (1926) : of, relating to, being, or characterized by manufacturing and esp. heavy industry ⟨∼ industries⟩

smoke tree *n* (1846) : either of two small shrubby trees (genus *Cotinus*) of the cashew family with large panicles of minute flowers that suggest a cloud of smoke: **a** : one (*C. coggygria*) of the Old World that is widely planted in the eastern U.S. **b** : one (*C. obovatus*) of the southeastern U.S. and Texas

smoking gun *n* (1974) : something that serves as conclusive evidence or proof esp. of a crime

smoking jacket *n* (1878) : a loose-fitting jacket or short robe for wear at home

smoking lamp *n* (ca. 1881) : a lamp on a ship kept lighted during the hours when smoking is allowed

smoking room *n* (1689) : a room (as in a hotel or club) set apart for smokers

smoky *also* **smok·ey** \'smō-kē\ *adj* **smok·i·er; -est** (14c) **1** : emitting smoke esp. in large quantities **2 a** : having the characteristics of or resembling smoke **b** : suggestive of smoke esp. in flavor or odor **3 a** : filled with smoke **b** : made dark or black by or as if by smoke — **smok·i·ly** \-kə-lē\ *adv* — **smok·i·ness** \-kē-nəs\ *n*

smoky quartz *n* (1837) : CAIRNGORM

smoky topaz *n* (1797) : CAIRNGORM

smol·der *or* **smoul·der** \'smōl-dər\ *vi* **smol·dered** *or* **smoul·dered; smol·der·ing** *or* **smoul·der·ing** \-d(ə-)riŋ\ [ME *smolderen* to smother, fr. *smolder* smoke, smudge; akin to MD *smōlen* to smolder] (1529) **1 a** : to burn sluggishly, without flame, and often with much smoke **b** : to be consumed by smoldering — often used with *out* **2** : to exist in a state of suppressed activity ⟨hostilities ∼*ed* for years⟩ **3** : to show suppressed anger, hate, or jealousy ⟨eyes ∼*ing* with hate⟩

smolt \'smōlt\ *n* [ME (Sc)] (15c) : a young salmon or sea trout about two years old that is at the stage of development when it assumes the silvery color of the adult and is ready to migrate to the sea

¹smooch \'müch\ *n* (1578) : KISS

²smooch *vi* [alter. of *smouch* to kiss loudly] (1588) : KISS, PET

³smooch *vt* [prob. alter. of *smutch,* vb.] (1631) : SMUDGE, SMEAR

⁴smooch *n* (1825) : SMUDGE, SMEAR — **smoochy** \'smü-chē\ *adj*

¹smooth \'smüth\ *adj* [ME *smothe,* fr. OE *smōth;* akin to OS *smōthi* smooth] (bef. 12c) **1 a** (1) : having a continuous even surface (2) *of a curve* : being the representation of a function with a continuous first derivative (3) : having or being a short even coat of hair ⟨a ∼ collie⟩ — compare ROUGH, WIREHAIRED **b** : being without hair **c** : GLABROUS ⟨a ∼ leaf⟩ **d** : causing no resistance to sliding **2** : free from difficulties or impediments ⟨the ∼ course of his life⟩ **3** : even and uninterrupted in flow or flight **4** : excessively and often artfully suave : INGRATIATING ⟨a ∼ operator⟩ **5 a** : SERENE, EQUABLE ⟨a ∼ disposition⟩ **b** : AMIABLE, COURTEOUS **6 a** : not sharp or harsh ⟨a ∼ sherry⟩ **b** : free from lumps *syn* see LEVEL, EASY, SUAVE — **smooth** *adv* — **smooth·ly** *adv* — **smooth·ness** *n*

²smooth *vb* **smoothed; smooth·ing; smooths** *also* **smoothes** *vt* (15c) **1** : to make smooth **2 a** : to free from what is harsh or disagreeable : POLISH ⟨∼*ed* out his style⟩ **b** : to minimize (as a fault) esp. in order to allay anger or ill will ⟨his main job is to ∼ over the friction that so often arises —Brian Crozier⟩ **4** : to free from obstruction or difficulty **5 a** : to press flat **b** : to remove expression from (one's face) : COMPOSE **6** : to cause to lie evenly and in order : PREEN **7** : to free (as a graph or data) from irregularities ∼ *vi* : to become smooth — **smooth·er** *n*

³smooth *n* (15c) **1** : a smooth part **2** : the act of smoothing **3** : a smoothing implement

smooth·bore \'smüth-'bȯr, -'bȯr\ *adj* (1799) *of a firearm* : having a barrel with an unrifled bore — **smoothbore** \-,bȯr, -,bȯr\ *n*

\ə\ abut \ᵊ\ kitten, F table \ər\ further \a\ ash \ā\ ace \ä\ mop, mar
\au̇\ out \ch\ chin \e\ bet \ē\ easy \g\ go \i\ hit \ī\ ice \j\ job
\ŋ\ sing \ō\ go \ȯ\ law \ȯi\ boy \th\ thin \t͟h\ the \ü\ loot \u̇\ foot
\y\ yet \zh\ vision \ȧ, k̲, ⁿ, œ, œ̄, ᵫ, ᵫ̄, ᵊ\ *see* Guide to Pronunciation

smooth breathing n (ca. 1888) **1** : a mark ' placed over some initial vowels in Greek to show that they are not aspirated (as in ἐκεῖ pronounced \e-'kā\) **2** : the absence of aspiration indicated by a mark '
smooth·en \'smü-<u>th</u>ən\ vb **smooth·ened; smooth·en·ing** \'smü-<u>th</u>ə-niŋ, 'smü<u>th</u>-niŋ\ vt (1635) : to make smooth ~ vi : to become smooth
smooth hound n [fr. the absence of a spine in front of the dorsal fin] (1603) : any of several dogfishes (genus *Mustelus*) closely related to or included with the requiem sharks
smooth muscle n (ca. 1890) : muscle tissue that lacks cross striations, that is made up of elongated spindle-shaped cells having a central nucleus, and that is found in vertebrate visceral structures (as the stomach and bladder) as thin sheets performing functions not subject to conscious control by the mind and in all or most of the musculature of invertebrates other than arthropods — compare STRIATED MUSCLE
smooth–tongued \'smü<u>th</u>-'təŋd\ adj (1592) : ingratiating in speech
smoothy or **smooth·ie** \'smü-<u>th</u>ē\ n, pl **smooth·ies** (1904) **1** : a smooth-tongued person **2 a** : a person with polished manners **b** : one who behaves or performs with deftness, assurance, and easy competence; esp : a man with an ingratiating manner toward women
smor·gas·bord \'smȯr-gəs-,bȯrd, -,bȯrd\ n [Sw *smörgåsbord*, fr. *smörgås* open sandwich + *bord* table] (1893) **1** : a luncheon or supper buffet offering a variety of foods and dishes (as hors d'oeuvres, hot and cold meats, smoked and pickled fish, cheeses, salads, and relishes) **2** : a heterogeneous mixture : MÉLANGE
smote past of SMITE
¹smoth·er \'smə-<u>th</u>ər\ n [ME, alter. of *smorther*, fr. *smoren* to smother, fr. OE *smorian* to suffocate; akin to MD *smoren* to suffocate] (13c) **1 a** : thick stifling smoke or smudge **b** : a state of being stifled or suppressed **2** : a dense cloud (as of fog, spray, or dust) **3** : a confused multitude of things : WELTER — **smoth·ery** \'smə-<u>th</u>ə-rē, 'smə<u>th</u>-rē\ adj
²smother vb **smoth·ered; smoth·er·ing** \'smə-<u>th</u>ə-riŋ, 'smə<u>th</u>-riŋ\ vi (ca. 1520) : to be overcome or killed through or as if through lack of air ~ vt **1** : to overcome or kill with smoke or fumes **2 a** : to destroy the life of by depriving of air **b** : to overcome or discomfit through or as if through lack of air **c** : to suppress (a fire) by excluding oxygen **3 a** : to cause to smolder **b** : to suppress expression or knowledge of (~ed his rage) **c** : to stop or prevent the growth or activity of (~ a child with too much care); also : OVERWHELM **d** : to cover thickly : BLANKET (snow ~ed the trails) **e** : to overcome or vanquish quickly or decisively **4** : to cook in a covered pan or pot with little liquid over low heat
¹smudge \'sməj\ vb **smudged; smudg·ing** [ME *smogen*] vt (15c) **1 a** : to make a smudge on **b** : to soil as if by smudging **2 a** : to rub, daub, or wipe in a smeary manner **b** : to make indistinct : BLUR **3** : to smoke or protect by means of a smudge ~ vi **1** : to make a smudge **2** : to become smudged
²smudge n (ca. 1774) **1 a** : a blurry spot or streak **b** : an immaterial stain (cleanse him of every last ~ of impropriety —Richard Hanser) **c** : an indistinct mass : BLUR **2** : a smoldering mass placed on the windward side (as to protect from frost) **3** : a bid of 4 in pitch that if made wins the game — **smudg·i·ly** \'smə-jə-lē\ adv — **smudg·i·ness** \'smə-jē-nəs\ n — **smudgy** \-jē\ adj
smug \'sməg\ adj **smug·ger; smug·gest** [prob. modif. of LG *smuck* neat, fr. MLG, fr. *smucken* to dress; akin to OE *smoc* smock] (1551) **1** : trim or smart in dress : SPRUCE **2** : scrupulously clean, neat, or correct : TIDY **3** : highly self-satisfied — **smug·ly** adv — **smug·ness** n
smug·gle \'smə-gəl\ vb **smug·gled; smug·gling** \-g(ə-)liŋ\ [LG *smuggeln* & D *smokkelen*] vt (1687) **1** : to import or export secretly contrary to the law and esp. without paying duties imposed by law **2** : to convey or introduce surreptitiously ~ vi : to import or export something in violation of the customs laws — **smug·gler** \'smə-glər\ n
¹smut \'smət\ vb **smut·ted; smut·ting** [prob. alter. of earlier *smot* to stain, fr. ME *smotten*; akin to MHG *smutzen* to stain] vt (1587) **1** : to stain or taint with smut **2** : to affect (a crop or plant) with smut ~ vi : to become affected by smut
²smut n (1664) **1** : matter that soils or blackens; specif : a particle of soot **2** : any of various destructive diseases esp. of cereal grasses caused by parasitic fungi (order Ustilaginales) and marked by transformation of plant organs into dark masses of spores; also : a fungus causing a smut **3** : obscene language or matter
smutch \'sməch\ n [akin to ME *smogen* to smudge] (1530) : a dark stain : SMUDGE — **smutch** vt — **smutchy** \'smə-chē\ adj
smut·ty \'smə-tē\ adj **smut·ti·er; -est** (1597) **1** : soiled or tainted with smut; esp : affected with smut fungus **2** : OBSCENE, INDECENT **3** : resembling smut in appearance : SOOTY — **smut·ti·ly** \'smə-t²l-ē\ adv — **smut·ti·ness** \'smə-tē-nəs\ n
¹snack \'snak\ n [ME *snak* bite, fr. *snaken* to bite, perh. fr. MD *snacken* to snap at — more at SNATCH] (1757) : a light meal : food eaten between regular meals; also : food suitable for snacking
²snack vi (1807) : to eat a snack
snack bar n (1930) : a public eating place where snacks are served usu. at a counter
¹snaf·fle \'sna-fəl\ n [origin unknown] (1533) : a simple usu. jointed bit for a bridle
²snaffle vt **snaf·fled; snaf·fling** \'sna-f(ə-)liŋ\ [origin unknown] (1724) : to obtain esp. by devious or irregular means
¹sna·fu \sna-'fü, 'sna-,fü\ n [situation normal all fucked up (fouled up)] (ca. 1941) : CONFUSION, MUDDLE
²snafu adj (1943) : snarled or stalled in confusion : AWRY
³snafu vt (1943) : to bring into a state of confusion
¹snag \'snag\ n [of Scand origin; akin to ON *snagi* clothes peg] (ca. 1587) **1 a** : a tree or branch embedded in a lake or stream bed and constituting a hazard to navigation **b** : a standing dead tree **2 a** : rough sharp or jagged projecting part : PROTUBERANCE: as **a** : a projecting tooth **b** : one of the secondary branches of an antler **3** : a concealed or unexpected difficulty or obstacle **4** : a jagged tear made by or as if by catching on a snag (a ~ in her stocking) — **snag·gy** \'sna-gē\ adj
²snag vt **snagged; snag·ging** (1807) **1 a** : to catch and usu. damage on or as if on a snag **b** : to halt or impede as if by catching on a snag **2** : to hew, trim, or cut roughly or jaggedly **3** : to clear (as a river) of snags **4** : to catch or obtain by quick action or good fortune

snag·gle·tooth \'sna-gəl-,tüth\ n [E dial. *snaggle* irregularly shaped tooth + E *tooth*] (ca. 1825) : an irregular, broken, or projecting tooth — **snag·gle-toothed** \-,tütht\ adj
¹snail \'snā(ə)l\ n [ME, fr. OE *snægl*; akin to OHG *snecko* snail, *snahhan* to creep] (bef. 12c) **1** : a gastropod mollusk esp. when having an external enclosing spiral shell **2** : a slow-moving or sluggish person or thing — **snail·like** \'snā(ə)l-,līk\ adj
²snail vi (1582) : to move, act, or go slowly or lazily
snail darter n (1975) : a darter (*Percina tanasi*) of the Tennessee River drainage system of eastern Tennessee and northern Georgia
snail fever n [fr. the snails which serve as intermediate hosts to the schistosomes causing the disease] (1947) : SCHISTOSOMIASIS
snail–paced \'snā(ə)l-'pāst\ adj (1594) : moving very slowly
snail's pace n (15c) : an extremely slow pace
¹snake \'snāk\ n [ME, fr. OE *snaca*; akin to ON *snakr* snake, OHG *snahhan* to crawl] (bef. 12c) **1** : any of numerous limbless scaled reptiles (suborder Serpentes syn. Ophidia) with a long tapering body and with salivary glands often modified to produce venom which is injected through grooved or tubular fangs **2** : a worthless or treacherous fellow **3** : something (as a plumber's snake) resembling a snake — **snake·like** \-,līk\ adj
²snake vb **snaked; snak·ing** vt (1653) **1** : to wind (as one's way) in the manner of a snake **2** : to move (as logs) by dragging ~ vi : to crawl, move, or extend silently, secretly, or sinuously
snake·bird \'snāk-,bərd\ n (1791) : ANHINGA
snake·bit \-,bit\ or **snake·bit·ten** \-,bi-t²n\ adj (1957) : UNLUCKY 1, 3
snake·bite \-,bit\ n (1839) : the bite of a snake and esp. a venomous snake
snake charmer n (1836) : an entertainer who exhibits a professed power to charm or fascinate venomous snakes
snake–dance vi (1922) : to engage in a snake dance
snake dance n (1772) **1** : a ceremonial dance in which snakes or their images are handled, invoked, or symbolically imitated by individual sinuous actions **2** : a group progression in a single-file serpentine path (as in celebration of an athletic victory)
snake doctor n (1862) **1** : DRAGONFLY **2** : HELLGRAMMITE
snake fence n (1805) : WORM FENCE
snake in the grass (1696) : a secretly faithless friend
snake oil n (1927) **1** : any of various substances or mixtures sold (as by a traveling medicine show) as medicine usu. without regard to their medical worth or properties **2** : POPPYCOCK, BUNKUM
snake pit n (1946) **1** : a hospital for mental diseases **2** : a place or state of chaotic disorder and distress
snake·root \'snāk-,rüt, -,rút\ n (1635) : any of numerous plants (as seneca snakeroot) most of which have roots sometimes believed to cure snakebites; also : the root of such a plant
snake·skin \'snāk-,skin\ n (1825) : leather prepared from the skin of a snake
snake·weed \-,wēd\ n (1597) : any of various plants popularly associated with snakes (as in appearance, habitat, or the treatment of snakebite); esp : any of an American genus (*Gutierrezia*) of composite herbs or low shrubs with clustered yellow flower heads
snaky also **snak·ey** \'snā-kē\ adj (1567) **1** : of, formed of, or entwined with snakes (the Gorgon with ~ hair —Joseph Addison) **2** : SERPENTINE, SNAKELIKE (~ coils) **3** : suggestive of a snake (the oiliness and ~ insinuation of his demeanor —Thomas DeQuincy) **4** : abounding in snakes — **snak·i·ly** \-kə-lē\ adv
¹snap \'snap\ vb **snapped; snap·ping** [D or LG *snappen*; akin to MHG *snappen* to snap] vi (1530) **1 a** : to make a sudden closing of the jaws : seize something sharply with the mouth (fish *snapping* at the bait) **b** : to grasp at something eagerly : make a pounce or snatch (~ at any chance) **2** : to utter sharp biting words : bark out irritable or peevish retorts **3 a** : to break suddenly with a sharp sound (the twig *snapped*) **b** : to give way suddenly under strain **4** : to make a sharp or crackling sound **5** : to close or fit in place with an abrupt movement or sharp sound (the lock *snapped* shut) **6 a** : to move briskly or sharply (~s to attention) **b** : to undergo a sudden and rapid change (as from one condition to another) (~ out of it) (*snapped* awake) **7** : SPARKLE, FLASH (eyes *snapping* with fury) ~ vt **1** : to seize with or as if with a snap of the jaws **2** : to take possession or advantage of suddenly or eagerly — usu. used with *up* (shoppers *snapping* up bargains) **3 a** : to retort to or interrupt curtly and irritably **b** : to utter curtly or abruptly **4** : to break suddenly : break short or in two **5 a** : to cause to make a snapping sound (~ a whip) **b** : to put into or remove from a particular position by a sudden movement or with a sharp sound (~ the lock shut) **6 a** : to project with a snap **b** : to put (a football) in play with a snap **c** (1) : to take photographically (*snapping* exclusive news pictures —Current Biog.) (2) : to take a snapshot of
²snap n (1555) **1** : an abrupt closing (as of the mouth in biting or of scissors in cutting) **2 a** archaic : a share of profits or booty **b** : something that brings quick and easy profit or advantage **c** : something that is easy and presents no problems : CINCH **3** : a small amount : BIT **4 a** : an act or instance of seizing abruptly : a sudden snatching at something **b** : a quick short movement (lithe ~s of its body —Barbara Taylor) **c** : a sudden sharp breaking **5 a** : a sound made by snapping something (shut the book with a ~) **b** : a brief sharp and usu. irritable speech or retort **6** : a sudden spell of weather (a cold ~) **7** : a catch or fastening that closes or locks with a click (the ~ of a bracelet) **8** : a flat brittle cookie — compare GINGERSNAP **9** : SNAPSHOT **10** : the condition of being vigorous in body, mind, or spirit : ALERTNESS, ENERGY **b** : a pleasing vigorous quality **11** : the act of a center's putting the football in play from its position on the ground by quickly passing it between his legs to a teammate (as a quarterback) standing behind him
³snap adv (1583) : with a snap
⁴snap adj (1739) **1** : done, made, or carried through suddenly or without deliberation (a ~ judgment) **2** : called or taken without prior warning (a ~ election) **3** : fastening with a snap (a ~ lock) **4** : unusually easy or simple (a ~ course)
snap–back \'snap-,bak\ n (1887) **1** : a football snap **2** : a sudden rebound or recovery (a ~ of prices on the stock exchange)
snap back vi (1945) : to make a quick or vigorous recovery

snap bean *n* (1770) : a bean grown primarily for its pods that are usu. broken in pieces and cooked as a vegetable while young and tender and before the seeds have become enlarged — compare SHELL BEAN

snap-brim \'snap-ˌbrim\ *n, often attrib* (ca. 1908) : a usu. felt hat with brim turned up in back and down in front and with a dented crown

snap-drag-on \'snap-ˌdra-gən\ *n* [fr. the fancied resemblance of the flowers to the face of a dragon] (1593) : any of a genus (*Antirrhinum* esp. *A. majus* of the family Scrophulariaceae, the snapdragon family) of herbs having showy white, crimson, or yellow bilabiate flowers

snap-on \'snap-ˌȯn, -ˌän\ *adj* (1925) : designed to snap into position and fit tightly ⟨~ cuffs⟩

snap pea *n* (1980) : a cultivated pea that has edible usu. round pods easily snapped like beans and that is classified with the snow pea as a variety (*Pisum sativum macrocarpon*) — called also *sugar snap pea*

snap-per \'sna-pər\ *n, pl* **snappers** (ca. 1587) 1 : one that snaps: as **a** : something (as a remark) that gives new orientation to a situation or utterance **b** (1) : SNAPPING TURTLE (2) : CLICK BEETLE 2 *pl also* **snapper a** : any of numerous active carnivorous fishes (family Lutjanidae) of warm seas important as food and often as sport fishes **b** : any of several immature fishes (as the young of the bluefish) that resemble a snapper

snap-per-back \-ˌbak\ *n* (1887) : a football center

snapping turtle *n* (1784) : either of two large American aquatic turtles (family Chelydridae) with powerful jaws and a strong musky odor: **a** : one (*Chelydra serpentina*) that has the head covered with smooth skin, has large plates in a double row on the underside of the tail, and is distributed from eastern Canada to Central America **b** : ALLIGATOR SNAPPER

snap-pish \'sna-pish\ *adj* (1542) 1 **a** : given to curt irritable speech **b** : arising from annoyance or irascibility 2 : inclined to bite ⟨a ~ dog⟩ — **snap-pish-ly** *adv* — **snap-pish-ness** *n*

snap-py \'sna-pē\ *adj* **snap-pi-er; -est** (1746) 1 : SNAPPISH 1 2 **a** : quickly made or done **b** : marked by vigor or liveliness **c** : briskly cold **d** : STYLISH, SMART ⟨a ~ dresser⟩ — **snap-pi-ly** \'sna-pə-lē\ *adv* — **snap-pi-ness** \'sna-pē-nəs\ *n*

snap roll *n* (ca. 1934) : an airplane maneuver in which a rapid full revolution is completed about the plane's longitudinal axis while an approximately level line of flight is maintained

snap-shoot-er \'snap-ˌshü-tər\ *n* (1896) : a person who takes snapshots

snap-shot \'snap-ˌshät\ *n* (1890) 1 : a casual photograph made typically by an amateur with a small handheld camera 2 : an impression or view of something brief or transitory

¹**snare** \'snar, 'sner\ *n* [ME, fr. OE *sneare*, fr. ON *snara*; akin to OHG *snuor* cord and perh. to Gk *narkē* numbness] (bef. 12c) 1 **a** (1) : a contrivance often consisting of a noose for entangling birds or mammals (2) : TRAP, GIN **b** (1) : something by which one is entangled, involved in difficulties, or impeded (2) : something deceptively attractive 2 [prob. fr. D *snaar*, lit., cord; akin to OHG *snuor*] **a** : one of the catgut strings or metal spirals of a snare drum **b** : SNARE DRUM 3 : a surgical instrument consisting usu. of a wire loop constricted by a mechanism in the handle and used for removing tissue masses (as tonsils)

²**snare** *vt* **snared; snar-ing** (14c) 1 **a** : to capture by or as if by use of a snare **b** : to win or attain by artful or skillful maneuvers 2 : to entangle or hold as if in a snare ⟨any object that *snared* his eye —*Current Biog.*⟩ *syn* see CATCH — **snar-er** *n*

snare drum *n* (ca. 1859) : a small double-headed drum with one or more snares stretched across its lower head — see DRUM illustration

snarky \'snär-kē\ *adj* [dial. *snark* to annoy, perh. alter. of *nark* to irritate] (1906) : CROTCHETY, SNAPPISH

¹**snarl** \'snär(-ə)l\ *vb* [²*snarl*] *vt* (14c) 1 : to cause to become knotted and intertwined : TANGLE 2 : to make excessively complicated ~ *vi* : to become snarled — **snarl-er** *n*

²**snarl** *n* [ME *snarle*, prob. dim. of *snare*] (1609) 1 : a tangle esp. of hairs or thread : KNOT 2 : a tangled situation ⟨traffic ~s⟩ — **snarly** \'snär-lē\ *adj*

³**snarl** *vb* [freq. of obs. E *snar* to growl] (1589) 1 : to growl with a snapping or gnashing of teeth 2 : to give vent to anger in surly language ~ *vt* : to utter or express with a snarl or by snarling — **snarl-er** *n*

⁴**snarl** *n* (1613) : a surly angry growl — **snarly** \'snär-lē\ *adj*

¹**snatch** \'snach\ *vb* [ME *snacchen* to give a sudden snap, seize; akin to MD *snacken* to snap at] *vi* (13c) : to attempt to seize something suddenly ~ *vt* : to take or grasp abruptly or hastily; *also* : to seize or grab suddenly without permission, ceremony, or right *syn* see TAKE — **snatch-er** *n*

²**snatch** *n* (1563) 1 **a** : a brief period ⟨caught ~es of sleep⟩ **b** : a brief, fragmentary, or hurried part : BIT ⟨caught ~es of the conversation⟩ 2 **a** : a snatching at or of something **b** *slang* : an act or instance of kidnapping 3 : a lift in weight lifting in which the weight is raised from the floor directly to an overhead position in a single motion — compare CLEAN AND JERK, PRESS 4 : the female pudenda — usu. considered vulgar

snatch block *n* (ca. 1625) : a block that can be opened on one side to receive the bight of a rope

snath \'snath, 'sneth\ *or* **snathe** \'snāth, 'snath\ *n* [ME *snede*, fr. OE *snæd*] (1574) : the handle of a scythe

snaz-zy \'sna-zē\ *adj* **snaz-zi-er; -est** [origin unknown] (ca. 1932) : conspicuously or flashily attractive : FANCY

¹**sneak** \'snēk\ *vb* **sneaked** \'snēkt\ *or* **snuck** \'snək\; **sneak-ing** [akin to OE *snican* to sneak along, ON *snikja*] *vi* (1596) 1 : to go stealthily or furtively : SLINK 2 : to act in or as if in a furtive manner 3 : to carry the football on a quarterback sneak ~ *vt* : to put, bring, or take in a furtive or artful manner ⟨~ a smoke⟩ *syn* see LURK — **sneak up on** : to approach or act on stealthily

usage From its earliest appearance in print in the late 19th century as a dialectal and prob. uneducated form, the past and past participle *snuck* has risen to the status of standard and to approximate equality with *sneaked*. Indications are that it is continuing to grow in frequency. It is most common in the U.S. and Canada, but has also been spotted in British and Australian English.

²**sneak** *n* (ca. 1643) 1 : a person who acts in a stealthy, furtive, or shifty manner 2 **a** : a stealthy or furtive move **b** : an unobserved departure or escape 3 : SNEAKER 2 4 : QUARTERBACK SNEAK

³**sneak** *adj* (ca. 1859) 1 : carried on secretly : CLANDESTINE 2 : occurring without warning : SURPRISE ⟨a ~ attack⟩

sneak-er \'snē-kər\ *n* (1598) 1 : one that sneaks 2 : a usu. canvas sports shoe with a pliable rubber sole — **sneak-ered** \-kərd\ *adj*

sneak-ing \'snē-kiŋ\ *adj* (1582) 1 : MEAN, CONTEMPTIBLE 2 : characteristic of a sneak : FURTIVE, UNDERHANDED 3 **a** : not openly expressed or acknowledged ⟨he has a ~ respect for culture —H. A. Burton⟩ **b** : that is a persistent conjecture ⟨a ~ suspicion⟩ — **sneak-ing-ly** \-kiŋ-lē\ *adv*

sneak preview *n* (ca. 1937) : a special advance showing of a motion picture usu. announced but not named

sneak thief *n* (ca. 1859) : a thief who steals whatever is readily available without using violence or forcibly breaking into buildings

sneaky \'snē-kē\ *adj* **sneak-i-er; -est** (1833) : marked by stealth, furtiveness, or shiftiness — **sneak-i-ly** \-kə-lē\ *adv* — **sneak-i-ness** \-kē-nəs\ *n*

¹**sneap** \'snēp\ *vt* [ME *snaipen*, prob. of Scand origin; akin to Icel *sneypa* to scold — more at SNUB] (14c) 1 *archaic* : to blast or blight with cold : NIP 2 *dial Eng* : CHIDE

²**sneap** *n* (1597) *archaic* : REBUKE, SNUB

sneck \'snek\ *n* [ME *snekke*] (14c) *chiefly dial* : LATCH

¹**sneer** \'snir\ *vb* [prob. akin to MHG *snerren* to chatter, gossip — more at SNORE] *vi* (1680) 1 : to smile or laugh with facial contortions that express scorn or contempt 2 : to speak or write in a scornfully jeering manner ~ *vt* : to utter with a sneer *syn* see SCOFF — **sneer-er** *n*

²**sneer** *n* (1707) : the act of sneering; *also* : a sneering expression or remark

¹**sneeze** \'snēz\ *vi* **sneezed; sneez-ing** [ME *snesen*, alter. of *fnesen*, fr. OE *fnēosan*; akin to MHG *pfnüsen* to snort, sneeze, Gk *pnein* to breathe] (14c) : to make a sudden violent spasmodic audible expiration of breath through the nose and mouth esp. as a reflex act — **sneez-er** *n* — **sneeze at** : to make light of

²**sneeze** *n* (1646) : an act or instance of sneezing

sneeze-weed \'snēz-ˌwēd\ *n* (ca. 1837) : any of several composite plants; *esp* : a No. American perennial herb (*Helenium autumnale*) with yellow ray flowers and a darker globose disk

sneezy \'snē-zē\ *adj* (1839) : given to or causing sneezing

¹**snell** \'snel\ *adj* [ME, fr. OE; akin to OHG *snel* bold, agile] (bef. 12c) 1 *chiefly Scot* : QUICK, ACUTE 2 *chiefly Scot* : KEEN, PIERCING ⟨a ~ wind smote us —*Scotsman*⟩ 3 *chiefly Scot* : GRIEVOUS, SEVERE

²**snell** *n* [origin unknown] (1846) : a short line (as of gut) by which a fishhook is attached to a longer line

¹**snick** \'snik\ *vb* [prob. fr. obs. *snick or snee* to engage in cut-and-thrust fighting — more at SNICKERSNEE] *vt* (ca. 1700) 1 *archaic* : to cut through 2 : to cut slightly : NICK ~ *vi* : to perform a light cutting action

²**snick** *n* (ca. 1775) : a small cut : NICK

³**snick** *vb* [imit.] (1828) : CLICK

⁴**snick** *n* (ca. 1886) : a slight often metallic sound : CLICK

¹**snick-er** \'sni-kər\ *vi* **snick-ered; snick-er-ing** \-k(ə-)riŋ\ [origin unknown] (1694) : to laugh in a covert or partly suppressed manner : TITTER — **snick-er-er** \-kər-ər\ *n* — **snick-ery** \-k(ə-)rē\ *adj*

²**snicker** *n* (1835) : an act or sound of snickering

snick-er-snee \'sni-kə(r)-ˌsnē\ *n* [obs. *snick or snee* to engage in cut-and-thrust fighting, alter. of earlier *steake or snye*, fr. D *steken of snijden* to thrust or cut] (ca. 1775) : a large knife

snide \'snīd\ *adj* [origin unknown] (ca. 1859) 1 **a** : FALSE, COUNTERFEIT **b** : practicing deception : DISHONEST ⟨a ~ merchant⟩ 2 : unworthy of esteem : LOW ⟨a ~ trick⟩ 3 : slyly disparaging : INSINUATING ⟨~ remarks⟩ — **snide-ly** *adv* — **snide-ness** *n*

¹**sniff** \'snif\ *vb* [ME] *vi* (14c) 1 : to draw air audibly up the nose esp. for smelling ⟨~ed at the flowers⟩ 2 : to show or express disdain or scorn ~ *vt* 1 : to smell or take by inhalation through the nose 2 : to utter contemptuously 3 : to recognize or detect by or as if by smelling ⟨~ out trouble⟩

²**sniff** *n* (1767) 1 : an act or sound of sniffing 2 : a quantity that is sniffed

sniff-er *n* (1864) : one that sniffs esp : one who takes drugs illicitly by sniffing

sniff-ish \'sni-fish\ *adj* (1923) : having or expressing a haughty attitude : DISDAINFUL, SUPERCILIOUS — **sniff-ish-ly** *adv* — **sniff-ish-ness** *n*

¹**snif-fle** \'sni-fəl\ *vi* **snif-fled; snif-fling** \-f(ə-)liŋ\ [freq. of *sniff*] (1632) 1 : to sniff repeatedly : SNUFFLE 2 : to speak with or as if with sniffling — **snif-fler** \-f(ə-)lər\ *n*

²**sniffle** *n* (ca. 1825) 1 *pl* : a head cold marked by nasal discharge 2 : an act or sound of sniffling

sniffy \'sni-fē\ *adj* **sniff-i-er; -est** (1871) : SNIFFISH, SUPERCILIOUS — **sniff-i-ly** \'sni-fə-lē\ *adv* — **sniff-i-ness** \'sni-fē-nəs\ *n*

snif-ter \'snif-tər\ *n* [E dial., sniff, snort, fr. ME, to sniff, snort] (1844) 1 : a small drink of distilled liquor 2 : a short-stemmed goblet with a bowl narrowing toward the top

¹**snig-ger** \'sni-gər\ *vi* **snig-gered; snig-ger-ing** \-g(ə-)riŋ\ [by alter.] (ca. 1706) : SNICKER — **snig-ger-er** \-gər-ər\ *n*

²**snigger** *n* (ca. 1823) : SNICKER

snig-gle \'sni-gəl\ *vb* **snig-gled; snig-gling** \-g(ə-)liŋ\ [E dial. *snig* small eel, fr. ME *snygge*] *vi* (1653) : to fish for eels by thrusting a baited hook or needle into their hiding places ~ *vt* : to catch (an eel) by sniggling

¹**snip** \'snip\ *n* [fr. or akin to D & LG *snip*; akin to MHG *snipfen* to snap the fingers] (1558) 1 **a** : a small piece that is snipped off; *also* : FRAGMENT, BIT **b** : a cut or notch made by snipping **c** : an act or sound of snipping 2 : a white or light mark; *esp* : a white spot be-

\a\ abut \ᵊ\ kitten, F table \ər\ further \a\ ash \ā\ ace \ä\ mop, mar \aú\ out \ch\ chin \e\ bet \ē\ easy \g\ go \i\ hit \ī\ ice \j\ job \ŋ\ sing \ō\ go \ó\ law \ói\ boy \th\ thin \tẖ\ the \ü\ loot \ú\ foot \y\ yet \zh\ vision \ā, k̲, ⁿ, œ, œ̄, ᵫ, ᵫ̄, ᵊ\ *see* Guide to Pronunciation

tween the nostrils of a horse **3** : a presumptuous or impertinent person; *esp* : an impertinent or saucy girl **4** *Brit* : BARGAIN, BUY
²**snip** *vb* **snipped; snip·ping** *vt* (1586) : to cut or cut off with or as if with shears or scissors; *specif* : to clip suddenly or by bits ~ *vi* : to make a short quick cut with or as if with shears or scissors — **snip·per** *n*
¹**snipe** \'snīp\ *n, pl* **snipes** [ME, of Scand origin; akin to ON *snipa* snipe; akin to OHG *snepfa* snipe] (14c) **1** *or pl* **snipe** : any of various usu. slender-billed birds of the same family as the sandpipers; *esp* : any of several game birds (esp. genus *Gallinago*) esp. of marshy areas **2** : a contemptible person
²**snipe** *vi* **sniped; snip·ing** (1832) **1** : to shoot at exposed individuals (as of an enemy's forces) from a usu. concealed point of vantage **2** : to aim a carping or snide attack — **snip·er** *n*
snip·er·scope \'snī-pər-ˌskōp\ *n* (1941) : an optical device for use esp. with a rifle that allows a person to see targets better in the dark
snip·per·snap·per \'sni-pər-ˌsna-pər\ *n* [origin unknown] (ca. 1590) : WHIPPERSNAPPER
snip·pet \'sni-pət\ *n* [¹snip] (1664) : a small part, piece, or thing; *esp* : a brief quotable passage
snip·pety \'sni-pə-tē\ *adj* (1864) **1** : made up of snippets **2** [prob. fr. ²*snip* + -*ety* (as in *pernickety*)] : SNIPPY
snip·py \'sni-pē\ *adj* **snip·pi·er; -est** [²*snip*] (ca. 1848) **1** : SHORT-TEMPERED, SNAPPISH **2** : unduly brief or curt **3** : putting on airs : SNIFFY — **snip·pi·ly** \'sni-pə-lē\ *adv*
snips \'snips\ *n pl but sing or pl in constr* (ca. 1846) : hand shears used esp. for cutting sheet metal
snit \'snit\ *n* [origin unknown] (1939) : a state of agitation
¹**snitch** \'snich\ *n* [origin unknown] (ca. 1785) : one that snitches : TATTLETALE
²**snitch** *vi* (1801) : INFORM, TATTLE — **snitch·er** *n*
³**snitch** *vt* [prob. alter. of *snatch*] (1904) : to take by stealth : PILFER
¹**sniv·el** \'sni-vəl\ *vi* -**eled** *or* -**elled;** -**el·ing** *or* -**el·ling** \'sni-və-liŋ, 'sniv-liŋ\ [ME, fr. (assumed) OE *snyflan*; akin to D *snuffelen* to snuffle, *snuffen* to sniff] (14c) **1** : to run at the nose **2** : to snuff mucus up the nose audibly : SNUFFLE **3** : to cry or whine with snuffling **4** : to speak or act in a whining, sniffling, tearful, or weakly emotional manner — **sniv·el·er** \'sni-və-lər, 'sniv-lər\ *n*
²**snivel** *n* (1600) **1** *pl, dial* : HEAD COLD **2** : an act or instance of sniveling
snob \'snäb\ *n* [origin unknown] (1781) **1** *Brit* : COBBLER **2** : one who blatantly imitates, fawningly admires, or vulgarly seeks association with those regarded as social superiors **3 a** : one who tends to rebuff, avoid, or ignore those regarded as inferior **b** : one who has an offensive air of superiority in matters of knowledge or taste
snob appeal *n* (1933) : qualities in a product that appeal to the snobbery in a purchaser
snob·bery \'snä-b(ə-)rē\ *n, pl* -**ber·ies** (1843) **1** : snobbish conduct or character : SNOBBISHNESS **2** : an instance of snobbery
snob·bish \'snä-bish\ *adj* (1840) : being, characteristic of, or befitting a snob — **snob·bish·ly** *adv* — **snob·bish·ness** *n*
snob·bism \'snä-ˌbi-zəm\ *n* (1855) : SNOBBERY
snob·by \'snä-bē\ *adj* **snob·bi·er; -est** (1846) : characterized by snobbery
sno–cone *var of* SNOW CONE
snol·ly·gos·ter \'snä-lē-ˌgäs-tər\ *n* [prob. alter. of *snallygaster* a mythical creature that preys on poultry and children] (ca. 1860) : a shrewd unprincipled person
¹**snood** \'snüd\ *n* [(assumed) ME, fr. OE *snōd*] (bef. 12c) **1** *a Scot* : a fillet or band for a woman's hair **b** : a net or fabric bag pinned or tied on at the back of a woman's head for holding the hair **2** : SNELL
²**snood** *vt* (1714) : to secure with a snood
¹**snook** \'snuk, 'snük\ *n, pl* **snook** *or* **snooks** [D *snoek* pike, snook] (1697) **1** : a large vigorous bony fish (*Centropomus undecimalis* of the family Centropomidae) of warm seas and rivers that is a prized food and sport fish **2** : any of various marine fishes of the same family as the snook
²**snook** *n* [origin unknown] (1879) : a gesture of derision made by thumbing the nose
¹**snook·er** \'snu̇-kər\ *n* [origin unknown] (1889) : a variation of pool played with 15 red balls and 6 variously colored balls
²**snooker** *vt* (1925) : to make a dupe of : HOODWINK
¹**snoop** \'snüp\ *vi* [D *snoepen* to buy or eat on the sly; akin to D *snappen* to snap] (1832) : to look or pry esp. in a sneaking or meddlesome manner — **snoop·er** *n*
²**snoop** *n* (ca. 1890) : one that snoops
snoopy \'snü-pē\ *adj* (ca. 1895) : given to snooping esp. for personal information about others — **snoop·i·ly** \-pə-lē\ *adv*
¹**snoot** \'snüt\ *n* [ME *snute*] (1861) **1 a** : SNOUT **b** : NOSE **2** : a grimace expressive of contempt : a snooty person : SNOB
²**snoot** *vt* (1928) : to treat with disdain : look down one's nose at
snooty \'snü-tē\ *adj* **snoot·i·er; -est** (1919) **1** : looking down the nose : showing disdain ⟨~ people who won't speak to their neighbors⟩ **2** : characterized by snobbery ⟨a ~ store⟩ — **snoot·i·ly** \'snü-t³l-ē\ *adv* — **snoot·i·ness** \'snü-tē-nəs\ *n*
¹**snooze** \'snüz\ *vi* **snoozed; snooz·ing** [origin unknown] (1788) : to take a nap : DOZE — **snooz·er** *n*
²**snooze** *n* (1793) : NAP
snoo·zle \'snü-zəl\ *vb* **snoo·zled; snoo·zling** \'snü-zə-liŋ, 'snüz-liŋ\ [perh. blend of *snooze* and *nuzzle*] (1831) *chiefly dial* : NUZZLE
¹**snore** \'snōr, 'snȯr\ *vb* **snored; snor·ing** [ME; akin to MLG *snorren* to drone, MHG *snerren* to chatter] *vi* (15c) : to breathe during sleep with a rough hoarse noise due to vibration of the soft palate ~ *vt* : to spend (time) in snoring or sleeping — **snor·er** *n*
²**snore** *n* (1605) **1** : an act of snoring **2** : a noise of or as if of snoring
¹**snor·kel** \'snȯr-kəl\ *n* [G *Schnorchel*] (1944) **1** : a tube housing air intake and exhaust pipes for a submarine's diesel engine that can be extended above the water's surface so that the engines can be operated while the submarine is submerged **2** : any of various devices (as for an underwater swimmer) resembling a snorkel in function

²**snorkel** *vi* **snor·keled; snor·kel·ing** \-k(ə-)liŋ\ (1949) : to operate or swim submerged with only a snorkel above water — **snor·kel·er** \-k(ə-)lər\ *n*
¹**snort** \'snȯrt\ *vb* [ME] *vi* (14c) **1 a** : to force air violently through the nose with a rough harsh sound **b** : to express scorn, anger, indignation, or surprise by a snort **2** : to emit explosive sounds resembling snorts **3** : to take in a drug by inhalation ~ *vt* **1** : to utter with or express by a snort **2** : to expel or emit with or as if with snorts **3** : to take in (a drug) by inhalation
²**snort** *n* (1808) **1** : an act or sound of snorting **2** : a drink of usu. straight liquor taken in one draft
snort·er \'snȯr-tər\ *n* (1601) **1** : one that snorts **2** : something that is extraordinary or prominent : HUMDINGER **3** : SNORT 2
snot \'snät\ *n* [ME, fr. OE *gesnot*; akin to OHG *snuzza* nasal mucus] (15c) **1** : nasal mucus **2** : a snotty person
snot·ty \'snä-tē\ *adj* **snot·ti·er; -est** (ca. 1570) **1** : foul with nasal mucus **2** : annoyingly or spitefully unpleasant — **snot·ti·ly** \'snä-t³l-ē\ *adv* — **snot·ti·ness** \'snä-tē-nəs\ *n*
snout \'snau̇t\ *n* [ME *snute*; akin to MD *snūt* snout, G *Schnauze*] (13c) **1 a** (1) : a long projecting nose (as of a swine) (2) : an anterior prolongation of the head of various animals (as a weevil) : ROSTRUM **b** : the human nose esp. when large or grotesque **2** : something resembling an animal's snout in position, function, or shape: as **a** : PROW **b** : NOZZLE **c** : the terminal face of a glacier — **snout·ed** \'snau̇-təd\ *adj* — **snout·ish** \-tish\ *adj* — **snouty** \-tē\ *adj*
snout beetle *n* (1862) : WEEVIL
¹**snow** \'snō\ *n, often attrib* [ME, fr. OE *snāw*; akin to OHG *snēo* snow, L *niv-, nix,* Gk *nipha* (acc.)] (bef. 12c) **1 a** : precipitation in the form of small white ice crystals formed directly from the water vapor of the air at a temperature of less than 32°F (0°C) **b** (1) : a descent or shower of snow crystals (2) : a mass of fallen snow crystals **2** : something resembling snow: as **a** : a dessert made of stiffly beaten whites of eggs, sugar, and fruit pulp (apple ~) **b** : a usu. white crystalline substance that condenses from a fluid phase as snow does ⟨ammonia ~⟩ **c** *slang* (1) : COCAINE (2) : HEROIN **d** : small transient light or dark spots on a television screen — **snow·less** \-ləs\ *adj*
²**snow** *vi* (14c) : to fall in or as snow ~ *vt* **1** : to cause to fall like or as snow **2 a** : to cover, shut in, or imprison with or as if with snow **b** : to deceive, persuade, or charm glibly **3** : to whiten like snow
¹**snow·ball** \'snō-ˌbȯl\ *n* (15c) **1 a** : a round mass of snow pressed or rolled together **b** : shaved ice molded into a ball and flavored with a syrup **2** : any of several cultivated shrubs (genus *Viburnum*) with clusters of white sterile flowers — called also *snowball bush*
²**snowball** *vt* (1854) **1** : to throw snowballs at **2** : to cause to increase or multiply at a rapidly accelerating rate ~ *vi* **1** : to engage in throwing snowballs **2** : to increase, accumulate, expand, or multiply at a rapidly accelerating rate
snow·bank \'snō-ˌbaŋk\ *n* (1779) : a mound or slope of snow
snow·belt \-ˌbelt\ *n, often cap* (1874) : a region that receives an appreciable amount of annual snowfall
snow·ber·ry \-ˌber-ē\ *n* (1760) : any of several white-berried shrubs (esp. genus *Symphoricarpos* of the honeysuckle family); *esp* : a low-growing No. American shrub (*S. albus*) with pink flowers in small axillary clusters
snow·bird \-ˌbərd\ *n* (1674) **1** : any of several birds (as a junco or fieldfare) seen chiefly in winter **2** : one who travels to warm climes for the winter
snow blindness *n* (1748) : inflammation and photophobia caused by exposure of the eyes to ultraviolet rays reflected from snow or ice — **snow–blind** \'snō-ˌblīnd\ *or* **snow–blind·ed** \-ˌblīn-dəd\ *adj*
snow·blow·er \'snō-ˌblō-(ə)r\ *n* (1950) : SNOW THROWER
snow·board \-ˌbȯrd, -ˌbȯrd\ *n* (1981) : a board like a wide ski ridden in a surfing position downhill over snow — **snow·boarder** *n* — **snow·board·ing** *n*
snow·bound \-ˌbau̇nd\ *adj* (1814) : shut in or blockaded by snow
snow·brush \-ˌbrəsh\ *n* (ca. 1923) : a spreading white-flowered western No. American shrub (*Ceanothus velutinus*) of the buckthorn family with scented leaves and panicles of small flowers
snow·cap \-ˌkap\ *n* (1871) : a covering cap of snow (as on a mountain peak) — **snow·capped** \-ˌkapt\ *adj*
snow cone *n* (1964) : SNOWBALL 1b
snow crab *n* (1974) : either of two crabs (*Chionoecetes opilio* and *C. bairdi*) of the northern Pacific Ocean and esp. Alaska marketed for food
snow·drift \'snō-ˌdrift\ *n* (14c) : a bank of drifted snow
snow·drop \-ˌdräp\ *n* (1664) : a bulbous European herb (*Galanthus nivalis*) of the amaryllis family bearing nodding white flowers that often appear while the snow is on the ground
snow·fall \-ˌfȯl\ *n* (1821) : a fall of snow; *specif* : the amount of snow that falls in a single storm or in a given period
snow fence *n* (1872) : a usu. slatted fence placed across the path of prevailing winds to protect (as a building, road, or railroad track) from drifting snow by disrupting the flow of wind and causing the snow to be deposited on the lee side of the fence
snow·field \'snō-ˌfēld\ *n* (1845) : a broad level expanse of snow; *esp* : a mass of perennial snow at the head of a glacier
snow·flake \-ˌflāk\ *n* (1734) **1** : a flake or crystal of snow **2** : any of a genus (*Leucojum*) of bulbous plants of the amaryllis family; *esp* : one (*L. vernum*) resembling the snowdrop
snow goose *n* (1771) : a wild goose (*Anser caerulescens* syn. *Chen caerulescens*) that has a pinkish bill and exists either as a white form with black primaries or as a grayish black form with a white head
snow job *n* (1943) : an intensive effort at persuasion or deception
snow leopard *n* (1866) : a large cat (*Panthera uncia*) of upland central Asia with long heavy grayish white fur irregularly marked with brownish black spots, rosettes, and rings
snow line *n* (ca. 1835) : the lower margin of a perennial snowfield
snow·mak·er \'snō-ˌmā-kər\ *n* (1954) : a device for making snow artificially
snow·mak·ing \-ˌmā-kiŋ\ *adj* (1953) : used for the production of artificial snow usu. for ski slopes ⟨~ machines⟩
snow·man \-ˌman\ *n* (1827) : snow shaped to resemble a human figure
snow·melt \-ˌmelt\ *n* (ca. 1946) : runoff produced by the melting of snow

snood 1b

snow·mo·bile \'snō-mō-ˌbēl\ n (1923) : any of various automotive vehicles for travel on snow; *specif* : an open vehicle for usu. one or two persons with steerable skis on the front and an endless belt at the rear

snow·mo·bil·ing \-ˌbē-liŋ\ n (1964) : the sport of driving a snowmobile — **snow·mo·bil·er** \-lər\ *also* **snow·mo·bil·ist** \-list\ n

snow–on–the–mountain n (1873) : a spurge (*Euphorbia marginata*) of the central and western U.S. that has showy white-bracted flower clusters and is grown as an ornamental

snow·pack \'snō-ˌpak\ n (ca. 1946) : a seasonal accumulation of slow-melting packed snow

snow pea n (1949) : a cultivated pea with flat edible pods that is classified with the snap pea as a variety (*Pisum sativum macrocarpon*)

snow plant n (1846) : a fleshy bright-red saprophytic chiefly California herb (*Sarcodes sanguinea*) of the wintergreen family that grows in high-altitude coniferous woods and often appears before the snow melts

¹snow·plow \'snō-ˌplaù\ n (1792) **1** : any of various devices used for clearing away snow **2** : a stemming with both skis used for coming to a stop, slowing down, or descending slowly

²snowplow vi (1904) : to execute a snowplow ⟨~ed to a stop⟩

snow pudding n (1876) : a pudding made very fluffy and light by the addition of whipped egg whites and gelatin

snow·scape \'snō-ˌskāp\ n (1886) : a landscape covered with snow

snow·shed \-ˌshed\ n (1868) : a shelter against snowslides

¹snow·shoe \-ˌshü\ n (1666) : a light oval frame that is strengthened by two crosspieces, strung with thongs, and attached to the foot and that is used to enable a person to walk on soft snow without sinking

²snowshoe vi **snow·shoed; snow·shoe·ing** (1880) : to travel on snowshoes — **snow·sho·er** \-ˌshü-ər\ n

snowshoe hare n (ca. 1890) : a hare (*Lepus americanus*) of northern No. America with heavy fur on the hind feet and a coat that in most populations is brown in the summer but usu. white in the winter — called also **snowshoe rabbit, varying hare**

snow·slide \'snō-ˌslīd\ n (1841) : an avalanche of snow

snow·storm \-ˌstòrm\ n (1771) **1** : a storm of or with snow **2** : something that resembles a snowstorm

snow·suit \-ˌsüt\ n (1937) : a one-piece or two-piece lined garment for winter wear by children

snow thrower n (1954) : a machine for removing snow (as from a driveway or sidewalk) in which a rotating spiral blade picks up and propels the snow aside

snow tire n (1943) : an automotive tire with a tread designed to give added traction on snow

snow under vt (1880) **1** : to overwhelm esp. in excess of capacity to absorb or deal with something **2** : to defeat by a large margin

snow–white \'snō-'hwīt, -'wīt\ adj (bef. 12c) : white as snow

snowy \'snō-ē\ adj **snow·i·er; -est** (bef. 12c) **1 a** : composed of snow or melted snow **b** : marked by or covered with snow **2 a** : whitened by snow **b** : SNOW-WHITE — **snow·i·ly** \'snō-ə-lē\ adv — **snow·i·ness** \'snō-ē-nəs\ n

snowy egret n (1869) : a white American egret (*Egretta thula*) having a slender black bill, black legs, and yellow feet

snowy owl n (1781) : a large ground-nesting diurnal arctic owl (*Nyctea scandiaca*) that enters the chiefly northern parts of the U.S. in winter and has plumage that is sometimes nearly pure white but usu. with brownish spots or bars

¹snub \'snəb\ vt **snubbed; snub·bing** [ME *snubben*, of Scand origin; akin to ON *snubba* to scold; akin to Icel *sneypa* to scold] (13c) **1** : to check or stop with a cutting retort : REBUKE **2 a** : to check (as a line) suddenly while running out esp. by turning around a fixed object (as a post); *also* : to check the motion of by snubbing a line ⟨~ a horse to a tree⟩ **b** : to restrain the action of : SUPPRESS ⟨~ a vibration⟩ **3** : to treat with contempt or neglect **4** : to extinguish by stubbing ⟨~ out a cigarette⟩

²snub n (14c) : an act or an instance of snubbing; *esp* : SLIGHT

³snub adj (1724) **1 or snubbed** \'snəbd\ : BLUNT, STUBBY ⟨a ~ nose⟩ **2** : used in snubbing ⟨~ line⟩ — **snub·ness** n

snub·ber \'snə-bər\ n (1853) **1** : one that snubs **2** : SHOCK ABSORBER

snub·by \'snə-bē\ adj (1828) **1** : SNUB **2** : SNUB-NOSED — **snub·bi·ness** n

snub–nosed \'snəb-ˌnōzd\ adj (1725) **1** : having a stubby and usu. slightly turned-up nose **2** : having a very short barrel ⟨a ~ revolver⟩

snuck past and past part of SNEAK

¹snuff \'snəf\ n [ME *snoffe*] (14c) **1** : the charred part of a candlewick **2 a** *obs* : UMBRAGE, OFFENSE **b** *chiefly Scot* : HUFF

²snuff vt (15c) **1** : to crop the snuff of (a candle) by pinching or by the use of snuffers so as to brighten the light **2 a** : to extinguish by or as if by the use of a snuffer — often used with *out* **b** : to make extinct : put an end to — usu. used with *out* ⟨an accident that ~ed out a life⟩

³snuff adj (1975) : characterized by the sensationalistic depiction of violence; *esp* : featuring a real rather than a staged murder ⟨~ movies⟩

⁴snuff vb [akin to D *snuffen* to sniff, snuff — more at SNIVEL] vt (1527) **1** : to draw forcibly through or into the nostrils **2** : SCENT, SMELL **3** : to sniff at in order to examine — used of an animal ~ vi **1** : to inhale through the nose noisily and forcibly; *also* : to sniff or smell inquiringly **2** *obs* : to sniff loudly in or as if in disgust **3** : to take snuff

⁵snuff n (1570) : the act of snuffing : SNIFF

⁶snuff n [D *snuf*, short for *snuftabak*, fr. *snuffen* to snuff + *tabak* tobacco] (1683) **1** : a preparation of pulverized tobacco to be inhaled through the nostrils, chewed, or placed against the gums **2** : the amount of snuff taken at one time — **up to snuff** : of sufficient quality : meeting an applicable standard

snuff–box \'snəf-ˌbäks\ n (ca. 1687) : a small box for holding snuff usu. carried about the person

¹snuff·er \'snə-fər\ n (15c) **1** : a device similar to a pair of scissors for cropping and holding the snuff of a candle — usu. used in pl. but sing. or pl. in constr. **2** : a device for extinguishing candles

²snuffer n (ca. 1610) : one that snuffs or sniffs

¹snuf·fle \'snə-fəl\ vb **snuf·fled; snuf·fling** \-f(ə-)liŋ\ [akin to D *snuffelen* to snuffle — more at SNIVEL] vi (ca. 1600) **1** : to snuff or sniff usu. audibly and repeatedly **2** : to breathe through an obstructed nose with a sniffing sound **3** : to speak through or as if through the nose : WHINE ~ vt : to seek or test by or as if by repeated sniffs — **snuf·fler** \-f(ə-)lər\ n

²snuffle n (ca. 1764) **1** : the act or sound of snuffling **2** : a nasal twang **3** *pl* : SNIFFLES

¹snuffy \'snə-fē\ adj [⁴*snuff*] (1678) **1** : quick to become annoyed or take offense **2** : marked by snobbery

²snuffy adj [⁶*snuff*] (1787) **1** : resembling snuff **2 a** : addicted to the use of snuff **b** : having unpleasant habits **3** : soiled with snuff

¹snug \'snəg\ vb **snugged; snug·ging** [²*snug*] vi (1583) : SNUGGLE ~ vt **1** : to cause to fit closely **2** : to make snug **3** : HIDE **4** : to secure by fastening or lashing down

²snug adj **snug·ger; snug·gest** [perh. of Scand origin; akin to Sw *snygg* tidy] (ca. 1595) **1 a** *of a ship* : manifesting seaworthiness : TAUT **b** : TRIM, NEAT **c** : fitting closely and comfortably ⟨a ~ coat⟩ **2 a** : enjoying or affording warm secure shelter or cover and opportunity for ease and contentment **b** : marked by cordiality and secure privacy **3** : affording a degree of comfort and ease **4** : offering safe concealment ⟨a ~ hideout⟩ *syn* see COMFORTABLE — **snug** adv — **snug·ly** adv — **snug·ness** n

³snug n [short for *snuggery*] (1860) *Brit* : a small private room or compartment in a pub

snug·gery \'snə-g(ə-)rē\ n, pl **-ger·ies** (1812) *chiefly Brit* : a snug cozy place; *esp* : a small room

snug·gle \'snə-gəl\ vb **snug·gled; snug·gling** \-g(ə-)liŋ\ [freq. of ¹*snug*] vi (1687) : to curl up comfortably or cozily ~ vt **1** : to draw close esp. for comfort or in affection **2** : to make snug — **snuggle** n

¹so \'sō, esp before adj or adv followed by "that" sə\ adv [ME, fr. OE *swā*; akin to OHG *sō* so, L *sīc* so, thus, si if, Gk *hōs* so, thus, L *suus* one's own — more at SUICIDE] (bef. 12c) **1 a** : in a manner or way indicated or suggested ⟨do you really think ~⟩ — often used as a substitute for a preceding clause ⟨are you ready? I think ~⟩ ⟨I didn't like it and I told her ~⟩ **b** : in the same manner or way : ALSO ⟨worked hard and ~ did she⟩ **c** : THUS ⟨for the Lord said —Isa 18:4 (AV)⟩ **d** : THEN, SUBSEQUENTLY ⟨and ~ home and to bed⟩ **2 a** : to an indicated or suggested extent or degree ⟨had never been ~ happy⟩ **b** : to a great extent or degree : VERY, EXTREMELY ⟨loves her ~⟩ **c** : to a definite but unspecified extent or degree ⟨can only do ~ much in a day⟩ **d** : most certainly : INDEED ⟨you did ~ do it⟩ **3** : THEREFORE, CONSEQUENTLY ⟨the witness is biased and ~ unreliable⟩

usage The intensive use of *so* (sense 2b) is widely condemned in college handbooks but is nonetheless standard ⟨why is American television *so* shallow?—Anthony Lewis⟩ ⟨the cephalopod eye is an example of a remarkable evolutionary parallel because it is *so* like the eye of a vertebrate —Sarah F. Robbins⟩ ⟨the kind of sterile over-ingenuity which afflicts *so* many academic efforts —*Times Lit. Supp.*⟩. There is no stigma attached to its use in negative contexts and when qualified by a dependent clause ⟨not *so* long ago⟩ ⟨was *so* good in mathematics that he began to consider engineering —*Current Biog.*⟩. The denotation in these uses is, of course, slightly different (see sense 2a).

²so conj (bef. 12c) **1 a** : with the result that ⟨the acoustics are good, ~ every note is clear⟩ **b** : in order that ⟨be quiet ~ he can sleep⟩ **2** *archaic* : provided that **3 a** : for that reason : THEREFORE ⟨don't want to go, ~ I won't⟩ **b** (1) — used as an introductory particle ⟨~ here we are⟩ often to belittle a point under discussion ⟨~ what?⟩ (2) — used interjectionally to indicate awareness of a discovery ⟨~, that's who did it⟩ or surprised dissent

usage Although occas. condemned, use of *so* to introduce clauses of result (sense 1a) and purpose (sense 1b) is standard. In sense 1b *so that* is more common in formal contexts than *so* alone.

³so adj (bef. 12c) **1** : conforming with actual facts : TRUE ⟨said things that were not ~⟩ **2** : marked by a desired order ⟨his books are always just ~⟩ **3** — used to replace a preceding adjective ⟨was witty by adult standards and of course doubly ~ by mine —Sally Kempton⟩

⁴so pron (bef. 12c) **1** : such as has been specified or suggested : the same ⟨if you have to file a claim, do ~ as soon as possible⟩ **2** — used in the phrase *or so* to indicate an estimate, approximation, or conjecture ⟨stayed a week or ~⟩ ⟨cost $15 or ~⟩

⁵so var of SOL

¹soak \'sōk\ vb [ME *soken*, fr. OE *socian*; akin to OE *sūcan* to suck] vi (bef. 12c) **1** : to lie immersed in liquid (as water) : become saturated by or as if by immersion **2 a** : to enter or pass through something by or as if by pores or interstices : PERMEATE **b** : to penetrate or affect the mind or feelings — usu. used with *in* or *into* **3** : to drink alcoholic beverages intemperately ~ vt **1** : to permeate so as to wet, soften, or fill thoroughly **2** : to place in a surrounding element (as liquid) to wet or permeate thoroughly **3** : to extract by or as if by steeping ⟨~ the dirt out⟩ **4 a** : to draw in by or as if by suction or absorption ⟨~ed up the sunshine⟩ **b** : to intoxicate (oneself) by drinking alcoholic beverages **5** : to cause to pay an exorbitant amount — **soak·er** n

syn SOAK, SATURATE, DRENCH, STEEP, IMPREGNATE mean to permeate or be permeated with a liquid. SOAK implies usu. prolonged immersion as for softening or cleansing ⟨*soak* the garment in soapy water⟩. SATURATE implies a resulting effect of complete absorption until no more liquid can be held ⟨a *saturated* sponge⟩. DRENCH implies a thorough wetting by something that pours down or is poured ⟨clothes *drenched* by a cloudburst⟩. STEEP suggests either the extraction of an essence (as of tea leaves) by the liquid or the imparting of a quality (as a color) to the thing immersed ⟨*steep* the tea for five minutes⟩. IMPREGNATE implies a thorough interpenetration of one thing by another ⟨a cake strongly *impregnated* with brandy⟩.

²soak n (15c) **1 a** : the act or process of soaking : the state of being soaked **b** : that (as liquid) in which something is soaked **2** : DRUNKARD **3** *slang* : PAWN 2

so–and–so \'sō-ən-ˌsō\ n, pl **so–and–sos** *or* **so–and–so's** \-ˌsōz\ (1596) **1** : an unnamed or unspecified person, thing, or action **2** : BASTARD 3

²so–and–so adv (1631) **1** : to an unspecified amount or degree **2** : in an unspecified manner or fashion

¹soap \'sōp\ n [ME *sope*, fr. OE *sāpe*; akin to OHG *seifa* soap] (bef. 12c)

\ə\ abut \ᵊ\ kitten, F table \ər\ further \a\ ash \ā\ ace \ä\ mop, mar \aù\ out \ch\ chin \e\ bet \ē\ easy \g\ go \i\ hit \ī\ ice \j\ job \ŋ\ sing \ō\ go \ò\ law \òi\ boy \th\ thin \t̲h̲\ the \ü\ loot \ù\ foot \y\ yet \zh\ vision \à, k̲, ⁿ, œ, œ̄, ᵫ, ᵫ̄, ʸ\ see Guide to Pronunciation

1 a : a cleansing and emulsifying agent made usu. by action of alkali on fat or fatty acids and consisting essentially of sodium or potassium salts of such acids   **b** : a salt of a fatty acid and a metal   **2** : SOAP OPERA

²soap vt (1585)   **1** : to rub soap over or into   **2** : FLATTER

soap·bark \'sōp-,bärk\ n (1861) : a Chilean tree (*Quillaja saponaria*) of the rose family with glossy leaves and terminal white flowers; *also* : its saponin-rich bark used in cleaning and in emulsifying oils

soap·ber·ry \-,ber-ē\ n (1693) : any of a genus (*Sapindus* of the family Sapindaceae, the soapberry family) of chiefly tropical woody plants; *also* : the fruit of a soapberry and esp. of a tree (*S. saponaria*) that is saponin-rich and used as a soap substitute

soap·box \-,bäks\ n (1907) : an improvised platform used by a self-appointed, spontaneous, or informal orator; *broadly* : something that provides an outlet for delivering opinions — **soapbox** adj

soap bubble n (1800) : a hollow iridescent globe formed by blowing a film of soapsuds (as from a pipe)

soap·er \'sō-pər\ n (1946) : SOAP OPERA

soap opera n [fr. its sponsorship by soap manufacturers] (1939)   **1 a** : a serial drama performed orig. on a daytime radio or television program and chiefly characterized by tangled interpersonal situations and melodramatic or sentimental treatment   **b** : a series of real-life events resembling a soap opera   **2** : the melodrama and sentimentality characteristic of a soap opera ⟨even cops need a little *soap opera* in their lives —Joseph Wambaugh⟩; *also* : something (as a novel) having such qualities

soap plant n (1844) : a plant having a part (as a root or fruit) that may be used in place of soap; *esp* : a California plant (*Chlorogalum pomeridianum*) of the lily family

soap·stone \'sōp-,stōn\ n (ca. 1681) : a soft stone having a soapy feel and composed essentially of talc, chlorite, and often some magnetite

soap·suds \-,sədz\ n pl (1611) : SUDS 1

soap·wort \-,wərt, -,wȯrt\ n (1548) : BOUNCING BET

soapy \'sō-pē\ adj **soap·i·er; -est** (1610)   **1** : smeared with soap : LATHERED   **2** : containing or combined with soap or saponin   **3 a** : resembling or having the qualities of soap; *esp* : being smooth and slippery   **b** : UNCTUOUS, SUAVE   **4** : of, relating to, or having the characteristics of soap opera — **soap·i·ly** \-pə-lē\ adv — **soap·i·ness** \-pē-nəs\ n

¹soar \'sōr, 'sȯr\ vi [ME soren, fr. MF essorer, fr. (assumed) VL ex-aurare, fr. L ex- + aura air — more at AURA] (14c)   **1 a** : to fly aloft or about   **b** (1) : to sail or hover in the air often at a great height : GLIDE   (2) of a glider : to fly without engine power and without loss of altitude   **2** : to rise or increase dramatically (as in position, value, or price)   **3** : to ascend to a higher or more exalted level   **4** : to rise to majestic stature — **soar·er** n

²soar n (1596)   **1** : the range, distance, or height attained in soaring   **2** : the act of soaring : upward flight

soar·ing n (15c) : the act or process of soaring; *specif* : the act or sport of flying a heavier-than-air craft without power by utilizing ascending air currents

Soa·ve \'swä-(,)vā\ n [*Soave*, village near Verona, Italy] (1935) : a dry white Italian wine

¹sob \'säb\ vb **sobbed; sob·bing** [ME sobben] vi (13c)   **1 a** : to catch the breath audibly in a spasmodic contraction of the throat   **b** : to cry or weep with convulsive catching of the breath   **2** : to make a sound like that of a sob or sobbing ~ vt   **1** : to bring (as oneself) to a specified state by sobbing ⟨*sobbed* himself to sleep⟩   **2** : to utter with sobs ⟨*sobbed* out her grief⟩

²sob n (14c)   **1** : an act of sobbing   **2** : a sound like that of a sob

SOB \,es-,ō-'bē\ n [son of a bitch] (1918) : BASTARD 3, SON OF A BITCH

¹so·ber \'sō-bər\ adj **so·ber·er** \-bər-ər\; **so·ber·est** \-b(ə-)rəst\ [ME sobre, fr. MF, fr. L sobrius; akin to L ebrius drunk] (14c)   **1 a** : sparing in the use of food and drink : ABSTEMIOUS   **b** : not addicted to intoxicating drink   **c** : not drunk   **2** : marked by sedate or gravely or earnestly thoughtful character or demeanor   **3** : UNHURRIED, CALM   **4** : marked by temperance, moderation, or seriousness   **5** : subdued in tone or color   **6** : showing no excessive or extreme qualities of fancy, emotion, or prejudice   syn see SERIOUS — **so·ber·ly** \-bər-lē\ adv — **so·ber·ness** n

²sober vb **so·bered; so·ber·ing** \-b(ə-)riŋ\ vt (14c) : to make sober ~ vi : to become sober — usu. used with *up*

so·ber·ing adj (1816) : tending to make one thoughtful or sober

so·ber·ize \'sō-bə-,rīz\ vt -ized; -iz·ing (1706) archaic : to make sober

so·ber·sid·ed \,sō-bər-'sī-dəd\ adj (1847) : solemn or serious in nature or appearance — **so·ber·sid·ed·ness** \-nəs\ n

so·ber·sides \'sō-bər-,sīdz\ n pl but sing or pl in constr (1705) : a sober-sided person

so·bri·ety \sə-'brī-ə-tē, sō-\ n [ME sobrietie, fr. MF sobrieté, fr. L sobrietat-, sobrietas, fr. sobrius] (15c) : the quality or state of being sober

so·bri·quet \'sō-bri-,kā, -,ket, ,sō-bri-'\ n [F] (1646) : a descriptive name or epithet : NICKNAME

sob sister n (1912)   **1** : a journalist who specializes in writing or editing sob stories or other material of a sentimental type   **2** : a sentimental and often impractical person usu. engaged in good works

sob story n (1913) : a sentimental story or account intended chiefly to evoke sympathy or sadness

so·cage \'sä-kij, 'sō-\ also **soc·cage** \'sä-\ n [ME, fr. soc soke] (14c) : a tenure of land by agricultural service fixed in amount and kind or by payment of money rent only and not burdened with any military service — **so·cag·er** \-ki-jər\ n

so–called \'sō-'kȯld\ adj (15c)   **1** : commonly named : popularly so termed ⟨the ~ pocket veto⟩   **2** : falsely or improperly so named ⟨deceived by a ~ friend⟩

soc·cer \'sä-kər\ n [by shortening & alter. fr. association football] (1889) : a game played on a field between two teams of 11 players each with the object to propel a round ball into the opponent's goal by kicking or by hitting it with any part of the body except the hands and arms — called also *association football*

so·cia·bil·i·ty \,sō-shə-'bi-lə-tē\ n, pl -ties (15c) : the quality or state of being sociable; *also* : the act or an instance of being sociable

¹so·cia·ble \'sō-shə-bəl\ adj [MF or L; MF, fr. L sociabilis, fr. sociare to join, associate, fr. socius] (1553)   **1** : inclined by nature to companionship with others of the same species : SOCIAL   **2 a** : inclined to seek or

enjoy companionship   **b** : marked by or conducive to friendliness or pleasant social relations   syn see GRACIOUS — **so·cia·ble·ness** n — **so·cia·bly** \-blē\ adv

²sociable n (1750) : an informal social gathering frequently involving a special activity or interest

¹so·cial \'sō-shəl\ adj [ME, fr. L socialis, fr. socius companion, ally, associate; akin to OE secg man, companion, L sequi to follow — more at SUE] (14c)   **1** : involving allies or confederates ⟨the *Social* War between the Athenians and their allies⟩   **2 a** : marked by or passed in pleasant companionship with one's friends or associates ⟨leads a very full ~ life⟩   **b** : SOCIABLE   **c** : of, relating to, or designed for sociability ⟨a ~ club⟩   **3** : of or relating to human society, the interaction of the individual and the group, or the welfare of human beings as members of society ⟨~ institutions⟩   **4 a** : tending to form cooperative and interdependent relationships with others of one's kind : GREGARIOUS   **b** : living and breeding in more or less organized communities ⟨~ insects⟩   **c** of a plant : tending to grow in groups or masses so as to form a pure stand   **5 a** : of, relating to, or based on rank or status in a particular society ⟨a member of our ~ set⟩   **b** : of, relating to, or characteristic of the upper classes   **c** : FORMAL

²social n (1870) : SOCIABLE

social climber n (1924) : one who attempts to gain a higher social position or acceptance in fashionable society — **social climbing** n

social contract n (ca. 1850) : an actual or hypothetical agreement among individuals forming an organized society or between the community and the ruler that defines and limits the rights and duties of each

social Darwinism n (1887) : an extension of Darwinism to social phenomena; *specif* : a theory in sociology: sociocultural advance is the product of intergroup conflict and competition and the socially elite classes (as those possessing wealth and power) possess biological superiority in the struggle for existence — **social Darwinist** n or adj

social democracy n (1888) : a political movement advocating a gradual and peaceful transition from capitalism to socialism by democratic means — **social democrat** n — **social democratic** adj

social disease n (1891)   **1** : VENEREAL DISEASE   **2** : a disease (as tuberculosis) whose incidence is directly related to social and economic factors

social drinker n (ca. 1949) : a person who drinks alcoholic beverages in moderation at social gatherings esp. as distinguished from one who drinks habitually or to excess

social engineering n (1925) : management of human beings in accordance with their place and function in society : applied social science — **social engineer** n

social gospel n (1890)   **1** : the application of Christian principles to social problems   **2** cap S&G : a movement in American Protestant Christianity esp. in the first part of the 20th century to bring the social order into conformity with Christian principles

social insurance n (1909) : protection of the individual against economic hazards (as unemployment, old age, or disability) in which the government participates or enforces the participation of employers and affected individuals

so·cial·ise Brit var of SOCIALIZE

so·cial·ism \'sō-shə-,li-zəm\ n (1837)   **1** : any of various economic and political theories advocating collective or governmental ownership and administration of the means of production and distribution of goods   **2 a** : a system of society or group living in which there is no private property   **b** : a system or condition of society in which the means of production are owned and controlled by the state   **3** : a stage of society in Marxist theory transitional between capitalism and communism and distinguished by unequal distribution of goods and pay according to work done

so·cial·ist \'sō-shə-list\ n (1827)   **1** : one who advocates or practices socialism   **2** cap : a member of a party or political group advocating socialism — **socialist** adj, often cap — **so·cial·is·tic** \,sō-shə-'lis-tik\ adj — **so·cial·is·ti·cal·ly** \-ti-k(ə-)lē\ adv

socialist realism n (1934) : a Marxist aesthetic theory calling for the didactic use of literature, art, and music to develop social consciousness in an evolving socialist state — **socialist realist** n or adj

so·cial·ite \'sō-shə-,līt\ n (1928) : a socially prominent person

so·ci·al·i·ty \,sō-shē-'a-lə-tē\ n, pl -ties (ca. 1649)   **1 a** : SOCIABILITY   **b** : an instance of social intercourse or sociability   **2** : the tendency to associate in or form social groups

so·cial·ize \'sō-shə-,līz\ vb -ized; -iz·ing vt (1828)   **1** : to make social; *esp* : to fit or train for a social environment   **2 a** : to constitute on a socialistic basis ⟨~ industry⟩   **b** : to adapt to social needs or uses ⟨~ science⟩   **3** : to organize group participation in ⟨~ a recitation⟩ ~ vi : to participate actively in a social group — **so·cial·i·za·tion** \,sō-sh(ə-)lə-'zā-shən\ n — **so·cial·iz·er** \'sō-shə-,lī-zər\ n

socialized medicine n (1938) : medical and hospital services for the members of a class or population administered by an organized group (as a state agency) and paid for from funds obtained usu. by assessments, philanthropy, or taxation

so·cial·ly \'sō-sh(ə-)lē\ adv (ca. 1763)   **1** : in a social manner   **2** : with respect to society   **3** : by or through society

so·cial–mind·ed \,sō-shəl-'mīn-dəd\ adj (1927) : having an interest in society; *specif* : actively interested in social welfare or the well-being of society as a whole

social psychology n (1891) : the study of the manner in which the personality, attitudes, motivations, and behavior of the individual influence and are influenced by social groups — **social psychologist** n

social science n (1811)   **1** : a branch of science that deals with the institutions and functioning of human society and with the interpersonal relationships of individuals as members of society   **2** : a science (as economics or political science) dealing with a particular phase or aspect of human society — **social scientist** n

social secretary n (1903) : a personal secretary employed to handle social correspondence and appointments

social security n (1908)   **1** : the principle or practice or a program of public provision (as through social insurance or assistance) for the economic security and social welfare of the individual and his or her family; *esp, often cap both Ss* : a U.S. government program established in 1935 to include old-age and survivors insurance, contributions to state unemployment insurance, and old-age assistance   **2** : money paid out through a social security program ⟨began collecting *social security*⟩

social service *n* (1851) : an activity designed to promote social well-being; *specif* : organized philanthropic assistance of the sick, destitute, or unfortunate : WELFARE WORK

social studies *n pl* (1926) : a part of a school or college curriculum concerned with the study of social relationships and the functioning of society and usu. made up of courses in history, government, economics, civics, sociology, geography, and anthropology

social welfare *n* (1917) : organized public or private social services for the assistance of disadvantaged groups; *specif* : SOCIAL WORK

social work *n* (1890) : any of various professional activities or methods concretely concerned with providing social services and esp. with the investigation, treatment, and material aid of the economically underprivileged and socially maladjusted — **social worker** *n*

so·ci·e·tal \sə-ˈsī-ə-tˀl\ *adj* (1898) : of or relating to society : SOCIAL ⟨~ forces⟩ — **so·ci·e·tal·ly** \-tˀl-ē\ *adv*

¹so·ci·e·ty \sə-ˈsī-ə-tē\ *n, pl* **-ties** [MF *societé*, fr. L *societat-, societas*, fr. *socius* companion — more at SOCIAL] (1531) **1** : companionship or association with one's fellows : friendly or intimate intercourse : COMPANY **2** : a voluntary association of individuals for common ends; *esp* : an organized group working together or periodically meeting because of common interests, beliefs, or profession **3 a** : an enduring and cooperating social group whose members have developed organized patterns of relationships through interaction with one another **b** : a community, nation, or broad grouping of people having common traditions, institutions, and collective activities and interests **4 a** : a part of a community that is a unit distinguishable by particular aims or standards of living or conduct : a social circle or a group of social circles having a clearly marked identity ⟨move in polite ~⟩ ⟨literary ~⟩ **b** : a part of the community that sets itself apart as a leisure class and that regards itself as the arbiter of fashion and manners **5 a** : a natural group of plants usu. of a single species or habit within an association **b** : the progeny of a pair of insects when constituting a social unit (as a hive of bees); *broadly* : an interdependent system of organisms or biological units

²society *adj* (1693) : of, relating to, or characteristic of fashionable society

So·cin·i·an \sə-ˈsi-nē-ən, sō-\ *n* [NL *socinianus*, fr. Faustus *Socinus*] (1645) : an adherent of a 16th and 17th century theological movement professing belief in God and adherence to the Christian Scriptures but denying the divinity of Christ and consequently denying the Trinity — **Socinian** *adj* — **So·cin·i·an·ism** \-nē-ə-ˌni-zəm\ *n*

socio- *comb form* [F, fr. L *socius* companion] **1** : society : social ⟨*sociogram*⟩ **2** : social and ⟨*sociopolitical*⟩

so·cio·bi·ol·o·gy \ˌsō-sē-ō-bī-ˈä-lə-jē, ˌsō-shē-\ *n* (1946) : the comparative study of social organization in animals including humans esp. with regard to its genetic basis and evolutionary history — **so·cio·bio·log·i·cal** \-ˌbī-ə-ˈlä-ji-kəl\ *adj* — **so·cio·bi·ol·o·gist** \-bī-ˈä-lə-jist\ *n*

so·cio·cul·tur·al \-ˈkəlch-rəl, -ˈkəl-chə-\ *adj* (1928) : of, relating to, or involving a combination of social and cultural factors — **so·cio·cul·tur·al·ly** \-ē\ *adv*

so·cio·eco·nom·ic \-ˌe-kə-ˈnä-mik, -ˌē-kə-\ *adj* (1883) : of, relating to, or involving a combination of social and economic factors — **so·cio·eco·nom·i·cal·ly** \-mi-k(ə-)lē\ *adv*

so·cio·gram \ˈsō-sē-ə-ˌgram, ˈsō-shē-\ *n* (1933) : a sociometric chart plotting the structure of interpersonal relations in a group situation

so·cio·his·tor·i·cal \ˌsō-sē-ō-his-ˈtȯr-i-kəl, ˌsō-shē-, -ˈtär-\ *adj* (1949) : of, relating to, or involving social history or a combination of social and historical factors

so·cio·lin·guist \-ˈliŋ-gwist\ *n* (1960) : a linguist specializing in sociolinguistics

so·cio·lin·guis·tic \-liŋ-ˈgwis-tik\ *adj* (1949) **1** : of or relating to the social aspects of language **2** : of or relating to sociolinguistics

so·cio·lin·guis·tics \-tiks\ *n pl but sing in constr* (1938) : the study of linguistic behavior as determined by sociocultural factors

so·ci·ol·o·gese \ˌsō-sē-ˌä-lə-ˈjēz, ˌsō-shē-, -ˈjēs\ *n* [*sociology* + *²-ese*] (1952) : a style of writing held to be characteristic of sociologists

so·cio·log·i·cal \ˌsō-sē-ə-ˈlä-ji-kəl, ˌsō-shē(-ē-)ə-\ *also* **so·cio·log·ic** \-jik\ *adj* (1843) **1** : of or relating to sociology or to the methodological approach of sociology **2** : oriented or directed toward social needs and problems — **so·cio·log·i·cal·ly** \-ji-k(ə-)lē\ *adv*

so·ci·ol·o·gy \ˌsō-sē-ˈä-lə-jē, ˌsō-shē-\ *n* [F *sociologie*, fr. *socio-* + *-logie* -logy] (1843) **1** : the science of society, social institutions, and social relationships; *specif* : the systematic study of the development, structure, interaction, and collective behavior of organized groups of human beings **2** : the scientific analysis of a social institution as a functioning whole and as it relates to the rest of society **3** : SYNECOLOGY — **so·ci·ol·o·gist** \-jist\ *n*

so·ci·om·e·try \-ˈä-mə-trē\ *n* [ISV] (1908) : the study and measurement of interpersonal relationships in a group of people — **so·cio·met·ric** \ˌsō-sē-ə-ˈme-trik, ˌsō-shē-\ *adj*

so·cio·path \ˈsō-sē-ə-ˌpath, ˈsō-sh(ē-)ə-\ *n* (1930) : PSYCHOPATH

so·cio·path·ic \ˌsō-sē-ə-ˈpa-thik, ˌsō-sh(ē-)ə-\ *adj* (1930) : of, relating to, or characterized by asocial or antisocial behavior or a psychopathic personality

so·cio·po·lit·i·cal \ˌsō-sē-ō-pə-ˈli-ti-kəl, ˌsō-shē-\ *adj* (1884) : of, relating to, or involving a combination of social and political factors

so·cio·psy·cho·log·i·cal \-ˌsī-kə-ˈlä-ji-kəl\ *adj* (1899) **1** : of, relating to, or involving a combination of social and psychological factors **2** : of or relating to social psychology

so·cio·re·li·gious \-ri-ˈli-jəs\ *adj* (1871) : involving a combination of social and religious factors

so·cio·sex·u·al \-ˈsek-sh(ə-)wəl, -ˈsek-shəl\ *adj* (1932) : of or relating to the interpersonal aspects of sexuality

¹sock \ˈsäk\ *n, pl* **socks** [ME *socke*, fr. OE *socc*, fr. L *soccus*] (bef. 12c) **1** *archaic* : a low shoe or slipper **2** *also pl* **sox** \ˈsäks\ : a knitted or woven covering for the foot usu. extending above the ankle and sometimes to the knee **3 a** : a shoe worn by actors in Greek and Roman comedy **b** : comic drama — **sock·less** *adj*

²sock *vb* [origin unknown] *vt* (ca. 1700) : to hit, strike, or apply forcefully ⟨~ a home run⟩ ⟨an area ~ed by a blizzard⟩ **~** *vi* : to deliver a blow : HIT — **sock it to** *slang* : to subject to or as if to a vigorous

assault ⟨they may let you off the first time . . . but the second time they'll *sock it to* you —James Jones⟩

³sock *n* (ca. 1700) : a vigorous or violent blow; *also* : ²PUNCH 3

sock away *vt* [fr. the practice of concealing savings in the toe of a sock] (ca. 1942) : to put away (money) as savings or investment

sock·dol·a·ger *or* **sock·dol·o·ger** \säk-ˈdä-li-jər\ *n* [origin unknown] (ca. 1830) **1** : something that settles a matter : a decisive blow or answer : FINISHER **2** : something outstanding or exceptional

¹sock·et \ˈsä-kət\ *n* [ME *soket*, fr. AF, dim. of OF *soc* plowshare, of Celt origin; akin to MIr *soc* plowshare, snout; akin to OE *sugu* sow — more at SOW] (15c) : an opening or hollow that forms a holder for something ⟨an electric bulb ~⟩ ⟨the eye ~⟩

²socket *vt* (1533) : to provide with or support in or by a socket

socket wrench *n* (ca. 1890) : a wrench usu. in the form of a bar and removable socket made to fit a bolt or nut

sock·eye \ˈsäk-ˌī\ *n* [by folk etymology fr. Northern Straits (Salishan language of southern Vancouver Island and nearby islands) *s̓qəy̓*] (1869) : a small but commercially important Pacific salmon (*Oncorhynchus nerka*) that ascends rivers chiefly from the Columbia northward to spawn in late summer or fall — called also *red salmon*

socket wrenches

sock in *vt* [*(wind) sock*] (1944) **1** : to close to takeoffs or landings by aircraft ⟨an airport *socked in* by fog⟩ **2** : to restrict from flying

socko \ˈsä-(ˌ)kō\ *adj* [²*sock*] (1938) : strikingly impressive, effective, or successful : OUTSTANDING

so·cle \ˈsō-kəl, ˈsä-\ *n* [F, fr. It *zoccolo* socle, fr. L *socculus*, dim. of *soccus* sock] (ca. 1704) : a projecting usu. molded member at the foot of a wall or pier or beneath the base of a column, pedestal, or superstructure

¹So·crat·ic \sə-ˈkra-tik, sō-\ *adj* (1628) : of or relating to Socrates, his followers, or his philosophical method of systematic doubt and questioning of another to elicit a clear expression of a truth supposed to be implicitly known by all rational beings — **So·crat·i·cal·ly** \-ti-k(ə-)lē\ *adv*

²Socratic *n* (1678) : a follower of Socrates

Socratic irony *n* (ca. 1871) : IRONY 1

¹sod \ˈsäd\ *n* [ME, fr. MD or MLG *sode*; akin to OFris *sātha* sod] (15c) **1** : TURF 1; *also* : the grass- and forb-covered surface of the ground **2** : one's native land

²sod *vt* **sod·ded; sod·ding** (1653) : to cover with sod or turfs

³sod *n* [short for *sodomite*] (1818) *chiefly Brit* : BUGGER ⟨if I ever find the ~ I'll kill him —John Le Carré⟩ ⟨he's not a bad little ~ taken by and large —Noel Coward⟩

⁴sod *vt* (1904) *chiefly Brit* : DAMN 2

so·da \ˈsō-də\ *n* [It, fr. Ar *suwwād*, any of several saltworts from the ashes of which sodium carbonate is obtained] (1558) **1 a** : SODIUM CARBONATE **b** : SODIUM BICARBONATE **c** : SODIUM — used in combination ⟨~ alum⟩ **2 a** : SODA WATER 2a **b** : SODA POP **c** : a sweet drink consisting of soda water, flavoring, and often ice cream **3** : the faro card that shows faceup in the dealing box before play begins

soda ash *n* (1839) : commercial anhydrous sodium carbonate

soda biscuit *n* (1830) **1** : a biscuit leavened with baking soda and sour milk or buttermilk **2** : SODA CRACKER

soda bread *n* (1850) : a quick bread made esp. with buttermilk and leavened with baking soda

soda cracker *n* (1830) : a cracker leavened with bicarbonate of soda and cream of tartar

soda fountain *n* (1824) **1** : an apparatus with delivery tube and faucets for drawing soda water **2** : the equipment and counter for the preparation and serving of sodas, sundaes, and ice cream

soda jerk *n* \-ˌjərk\ *n* (1922) : a person who dispenses carbonated drinks and ice cream at a soda fountain — called also *soda jerker*

soda lime *n* (1862) : a mixture of sodium hydroxide and slaked lime used esp. to absorb moisture and gases

so·da·list \ˈsō-dˀl-ist, sō-ˈda-list\ *n* (1794) : a member of a sodality

so·da·lite \ˈsō-dˀl-ˌīt\ *n* [*soda*] (1810) : a transparent to translucent mineral that consists of a silicate of sodium and aluminum with some chlorine, has a vitreous or greasy luster, and is found in various igneous rocks

so·dal·i·ty \sō-ˈda-lə-tē\ *n, pl* **-ties** [L *sodalitat-, sodalitas* comradeship, club, fr. *sodalis* comrade — more at SIB] (1600) **1** : BROTHERHOOD, COMMUNITY **2** : an organized society or fellowship; *specif* : a devotional or charitable association of Roman Catholic laity

soda pop *n* (1863) : a beverage consisting of soda water, flavoring, and a sweet syrup

soda water *n* (1802) **1** : a weak solution of sodium bicarbonate with some acid added to cause effervescence **2 a** : a beverage consisting of water highly charged with carbon dioxide **b** : SODA POP

sod·bust·er \ˈsäd-ˌbəs-tər\ *n* (ca. 1918) : one (as a farmer or a plow) that breaks the sod

¹sod·den \ˈsä-dˀn\ *adj* [ME *soden*, fr. pp. of *sethen* to seethe] (1589) **1 a** : dull or expressionless esp. from continued indulgence in alcoholic beverages ⟨~ features⟩ **b** : TORPID, SLUGGISH ⟨~ minds⟩ **2 a** : heavy with or as if with moisture or water ⟨the ~ ground⟩ **b** : heavy or doughy because of imperfect cooking ⟨~ biscuits⟩ — **sod·den·ly** *adv* — **sod·den·ness** \-dˀn-(n)əs\ *n*

²sodden *vb* **sod·dened; sod·den·ing** \ˈsäd-niŋ, ˈsä-dˀn-iŋ\ *vt* (1812) : to make sodden **~** *vi* : to become soaked or saturated

so·dic \ˈsō-dik\ *adj* (1859) : of, relating to, or containing sodium

so·di·um \ˈsō-dē-əm\ *n* [NL, fr. E *soda*] (1807) : a silver white soft waxy ductile element of the alkali metal group that occurs abundantly

\ə\ abut \ˀ\ kitten, F table \ər\ further \a\ ash \ā\ ace \ä\ mop, mar \aů\ out \ch\ chin \e\ bet \ē\ easy \g\ go \i\ hit \ī\ ice \j\ job \ŋ\ sing \ō\ go \ȯ\ law \ȯi\ boy \th\ thin \t͟h\ the \ü\ loot \ů\ foot \y\ yet \zh\ vision \à, ḵ, ⁿ, œ, œ̄, ư, ư̄, ʸ\ see Guide to Pronunciation in nature in combined form and is very active chemically — see ELEMENT table

sodium azide *n* (ca. 1937) : a poisonous crystalline salt NaN_3 used esp. to make lead azide

sodium benzoate *n* (ca. 1900) : a crystalline or granular salt $C_7H_5O_2Na$ used chiefly as a food preservative

sodium bicarbonate *n* (1885) : a white crystalline weakly alkaline salt $NaHCO_3$ used esp. in baking powders, fire extinguishers, and medicine — called also *baking soda, bicarbonate of soda*

sodium bo·ro·hy·dride \-ˌbŏr-ō-ˈhī-ˌdrīd, -ˌbŏr-\ *n* [*sodium* + *boron* + *hydride*] (1946) : a crystalline compound $NaBH_4$ used in various industrial applications and as a reducing agent in organic chemistry

sodium carbonate *n* (1868) : a sodium salt of carbonic acid used esp. in making soaps and chemicals, in water softening, in cleaning and bleaching, and in photography: as **a** : a hygroscopic crystalline anhydrous strongly alkaline salt Na_2CO_3 **b** : WASHING SODA

sodium chlorate *n* (1885) : a colorless crystalline salt $NaClO_3$ used esp. as an oxidizing agent and weed killer

sodium chloride *n* (1868) : an ionic crystalline chemical compound consisting of equal numbers of sodium and chlorine atoms : SALT 1a

sodium citrate *n* (1919) : a crystalline salt $Na_3C_6H_5O_7$ used chiefly as a buffering agent, as an emulsifier, as an alkalizer and cathartic in pharmaceuticals, and as a blood anticoagulant

sodium cyanide *n* (1885) : a white deliquescent poisonous salt NaCN used esp. in electroplating, in fumigating, and in treating steel

sodium dichromate *n* (ca. 1903) : a red crystalline salt $Na_2Cr_2O_7$ used esp. in tanning leather, in cleaning metals, and as an oxidizing agent

sodium fluoride *n* (ca. 1903) : a poisonous crystalline salt NaF that is used in trace amounts in the fluoridation of water, in metallurgy, as a flux, and as a pesticide

sodium fluo·ro·ac·e·tate \-ˌflùr-ō-ˈa-sə-ˌtāt, -ˌflŏr-, -ˌflŏr-\ *n* (1945) : a poisonous powdery compound $C_2H_2FNaO_2$ — compare 1080

sodium hydroxide *n* (1885) : a white brittle solid NaOH that is a strong caustic base used esp. in making soap, rayon, and paper

sodium hypochlorite *n* (1885) : an unstable salt NaOCl produced usu. in aqueous solution and used as a bleaching and disinfecting agent

sodium meta·sil·i·cate \-ˌme-tə-ˈsi-lə-ˌkāt, -ˈsi-li-kət\ *n* (ca. 1926) : a toxic corrosive crystalline salt Na_2SiO_3 used esp. as a detergent or as a substitute for phosphates in detergent formulations

sodium nitrate *n* (1885) : a deliquescent crystalline salt $NaNO_3$ used as a fertilizer and an oxidizing agent and in curing meat

sodium nitrite *n* (ca. 1903) : a salt $NaNO_2$ used esp. in dye manufacture and as a meat preservative

sodium pump *n* (1951) : a molecular mechanism by which sodium ions are actively transported across a cell membrane; *esp* : the one by which the appropriate internal and external concentrations of sodium and potassium ions are maintained in a nerve fiber and which involves the active transport of sodium ions outward with movement of potassium ions to the interior

sodium salicylate *n* (ca. 1904) : a crystalline salt $NaC_7H_5O_3$ that has a sweetish saline taste and is used chiefly as an analgesic, antipyretic, and antirheumatic

sodium sulfate *n* (1885) : a bitter salt Na_2SO_4 used esp. in detergents, in the manufacture of wood pulp and rayon, in dyeing and finishing textiles, and in its hydrated form as a cathartic — compare GLAUBER'S SALT

sodium thiosulfate *n* (1885) : a hygroscopic crystalline salt $Na_2S_2O_3$ used esp. as a photographic fixing agent and a reducing or bleaching agent — called also *hypo*

sodium tri·poly·phos·phate \-ˌtrī-ˌpä-li-ˈfäs-ˌfāt\ *n* (1945) : a crystalline salt $Na_5P_3O_{10}$ that is used as a food additive and as a component in some detergents and is suspected of contributing to water pollution

sodium–vapor lamp *n* (1936) : an electric lamp that contains sodium vapor and electrodes between which a luminous discharge takes place and that is used esp. for lighting highways

sod off *vi* [4*sod*] (1960) *Brit* : SCRAM — usu. used as a command

Sod·om \ˈsä-dəm\ *n* [*Sodom*, ancient city destroyed by God for its wickedness in Gen 19] (1598) : a place notorious for vice or corruption

sod·om·ist \ˈsä-də-mist\ *n* (1891) : SODOMITE

sod·om·ite \-ˌmīt\ *n* (14c) : one who practices sodomy

sod·om·ize \-ˌmīz\ *vt* **-ized; -iz·ing** (1868) : to perform sodomy on

sod·omy \ˈsä-də-mē\ *n* [ME, fr. OF *sodomie*, fr. LL *Sodoma* Sodom; fr. the homosexual proclivities of the men of the city in Gen 19:1–11] (13c) **1** : copulation with a member of the same sex or with an animal **2** : noncoital and esp. anal or oral copulation with a member of the opposite sex — **sod·om·it·ic** \ˌsä-də-ˈmi-tik\ *or* **sod·om·it·i·cal** \-ti-kəl\ *adj*

so·ev·er \sō-ˈe-vər\ *adv* [-*soever* (as in *howsoever*)] (12c) **1** : to any possible or known extent — used after an adjective preceded by *how* or a superlative preceded by *the* ⟨how fair ∼ she may be⟩ ⟨the most selfish ∼ in this world⟩ **2** : of any or every kind that may be specified — used after a noun modified esp. by *any, no,* or *what* ⟨gives no information ∼⟩

so·fa \ˈsō-fə\ *n* [Ar *ṣuffah* long bench] (1717) : a long upholstered seat usu. with arms and a back and often convertible into a bed

sofa bed *n* (1816) : a sofa that can be made to serve as a bed by lowering its hinged upholstered back to horizontal position or by pulling out a concealed mattress

so·far \ˈsō-ˌfär\ *n* [*so*und *f*ixing *a*nd *r*anging] (1946) : a system for locating an underwater explosion at sea by triangulation based on the reception of the sound by three widely separated stations

so far as *conj* (1565) : INSOFAR AS

sof·fit \ˈsä-fət\ *n* [F *soffite*, fr. It *soffitto*, fr. (assumed) VL *suffictus*, pp. of L *suffigere* to fasten underneath — more at SUFFIX] (1592) : the underside of a part or member of a building (as of an overhang or staircase); *esp* : the intrados of an arch

¹soft \ˈsȯft\ *adj* [ME, fr. OE *sōfte*, alter. of *sēfte*; akin to OHG *semfti* soft] (bef. 12c) **1 a** : pleasing or agreeable to the senses : bringing ease, comfort, or quiet ⟨the ∼ influences of home⟩ **b** : having a bland or mellow rather than a sharp or acid taste **c** (1) : not bright or glaring : SUBDUED (2) : having or producing little contrast or a relatively short range of tones ⟨a ∼ photographic print⟩ **d** : quiet in pitch or volume **e** *of the eyes* : having a liquid or gentle appearance **f** : smooth or delicate in texture, grain, or fiber ⟨∼ cashmere⟩ ⟨∼ fur⟩ **g**

(1) : balmy, mild, or clement in weather or temperature (2) : moving or falling with slight force or impact : not violent ⟨∼ breezes⟩ **2** : demanding little work or effort : EASY ⟨a ∼ job⟩ **3 a** : sounding as in *ace* and *gem* respectively — used of *c* and *g* or their sound **b** *of a consonant* : VOICED **c** : constituting a vowel before which there is a \y\ sound or a \y\-like modification of a consonant or constituting a consonant in whose articulation there is a \y\-like modification or which is followed by a \y\ sound (as in Russian) **4** *archaic* : moving in a leisurely manner **5** : rising gradually ⟨a ∼ slope⟩ **6** : having curved or rounded outline : not harsh or jagged ⟨∼ hills against the horizon⟩ **7** : marked by a gentleness, kindness, or tenderness: as **a** (1) : not harsh or onerous in character ⟨a policy of ∼ competition⟩ (2) : based on negotiation, conciliation, or flexibility rather than on force, threats, or intransigence ⟨took a ∼ line during the crisis⟩ (3) : tending to take a soft line — usu. used with *on* ⟨∼ on dictators⟩ ⟨∼ on law and order⟩ **b** : tending to ingratiate or disarm : ENGAGING, KIND ⟨a ∼ answer turns away wrath —Prov 15:1 (RSV)⟩ **c** : marked by mildness : UNASSUMING, LOW-KEY **8 a** : emotionally suggestible or responsive : IMPRESSIONABLE **b** : unduly susceptible to influence : COMPLIANT **c** : lacking firmness or strength of character : FEEBLE, UNMANLY **d** : amorously attracted or emotionally involved — used with *on* ⟨has been ∼ on her for years⟩ **9 a** : lacking robust strength, stamina, or endurance esp. because of living in ease or luxury ⟨grown ∼ and indolent⟩ **b** : weak or deficient mentally ⟨∼ in the head⟩ **10 a** : yielding to physical pressure **b** : permitting someone or something to sink in — used of wet ground **c** (1) : of a consistency that may be shaped or molded (2) : capable of being spread **d** : easily magnetized and demagnetized **e** : lacking relatively or comparatively in hardness ⟨∼ iron⟩ **11** : deficient in or free from substances (as calcium and magnesium salts) that prevent lathering of soap ⟨∼ water⟩ **12** : having relatively low energy ⟨∼ X rays⟩ **13** *of news* : relatively less serious or significant **14** : occurring at such a speed and under such circumstances as to avoid destructive impact ⟨∼ landing of a spacecraft on the moon⟩ **15** : not protected against enemy attack ⟨a ∼ aboveground launching site⟩ ⟨∼ targets⟩ **16** : BIODEGRADABLE ⟨a ∼ detergent⟩ ⟨∼ pesticides⟩ **17** *of a drug* : considered less detrimental than a hard narcotic **18** : easily polarized — used of acids and bases **19 a** *of currency* : not readily convertible **b** *of a loan* : not secured by collateral **20 a** : being rare due to sluggish market conditions ⟨∼ prices⟩ **b** : SLUGGISH, SLOW ⟨a ∼ market⟩ **21** : not firmly committed ⟨∼ unreliable political support⟩ **22** : SOFT-CORE ⟨∼ porn⟩ **23 a** : being or based on interpretive or speculative data ⟨∼ evidence⟩ **b** : utilizing or based on soft data ⟨∼ science⟩ **24** : being or using renewable sources of energy (as solar radiation, wind, or tides) ⟨∼ technologies⟩ — **soft·ish** \ˈsȯf-tish\ *adj* — **soft·ly** \ˈsȯf(t)-lē\ *adv* — **soft·ness** \ˈsȯf(t)-nəs\ *n*

²soft *adv* (bef. 12c) : in a soft or gentle manner : SOFTLY

³soft *n* (15c) : a soft object, material, or part ⟨the ∼ of the thumb⟩

soft·back \ˈsȯf(t)-ˌbak\ *adj* (1958) : SOFTCOVER — **softback** *n*

soft·ball \-ˌbȯl\ *n* (1926) : baseball played on a small diamond with a ball that is larger than a baseball and that is pitched underhand; *also* : the ball used in this game — **soft·ball·er** \-ˌbȯ-lər\ *n*

soft–boiled \-ˈbȯi(ə)ld\ *adj* (ca. 1902) **1** *of an egg* : boiled to a soft consistency **2** : SENTIMENTAL

soft–bound \-ˌbau̇nd\ *adj* (1953) : SOFTCOVER

soft chancre *n* (1859) : CHANCROID

soft coal *n* (1789) : BITUMINOUS COAL

soft–coated wheaten terrier *n* (1948) : any of a breed of compact medium-sized terriers developed in Ireland and having a soft abundant light fawn coat

soft–core \ˈsȯf(t)-ˈkȯr, -ˈkȯr\ *adj* [¹*soft* + *hard-core*] (1966) *of pornography* : containing descriptions or scenes of sex acts that are less explicit than hard-core material

soft·cov·er \-ˌkə-vər\ *adj* (1952) : bound in flexible covers : not bound in hard covers; *specif* : PAPERBACK ⟨∼ books⟩ — **softcover** *n*

soft drink *n* (1880) : a usu. carbonated nonalcoholic beverage; *esp* : SODA POP

soft·en \ˈsȯ-fən\ *vb* **soft·ened; soft·en·ing** \ˈsȯ-fə-niŋ, ˈsȯf-niŋ\ *vt* (14c) **1** : to make soft or softer **2 a** : to weaken the military resistance or the morale of esp. by harassment (as preliminary bombardment) — often used with *up* **b** : to impair the strength or resistance of — often used with *up* ⟨∼ up a sales prospect⟩ ∼ *vi* : to become soft or softer — **soft·en·er** \ˈsȯ-fə-nər, ˈsȯf-nər\ *n*

soft–fo·cus \ˈsȯf(t)-ˈfō-kəs\ *adj* (1916) **1** *of a photographic image* : having unsharp outlines **2** *of a lens* : producing an image having unsharp outlines

soft goods *n pl* (1894) : goods that are not durable — used esp. of textile products

soft hail *n* (1894) : GRAUPEL

soft·head \ˈsȯft-ˌhed\ *n* (1650) : a silly or feebleminded person

soft·head·ed \-ˈhe-dəd\ *adj* (1667) : having or indicative of a weak, unrealistic, or uncritical mind — **soft·head·ed·ly** *adv* — **soft·head·ed·ness** *n*

soft·heart·ed \-ˈhär-təd\ *adj* (1593) : emotionally responsive : SYMPATHETIC — **soft·heart·ed·ly** *adv* — **soft·heart·ed·ness** *n*

soft–land \-ˈland\ *vb* [back-formation fr. *soft landing*] *vt* (1960) : to cause to make a soft landing on a celestial body (as the moon) ∼ *vi* : to make a soft landing — **soft–lander** *n*

soft–line \-ˈlīn\ *adj* (1949) : advocating or involving a conciliatory or flexible course of action — **soft–lin·er** \-ˈlī-nər\ *n*

soft palate *n* (ca. 1811) : the fold at the back of the hard palate that partially separates the mouth and pharynx

soft–ped·al \ˈsȯf(t)-ˈpe-dᵊl\ *vt* (1925) **1** : PLAY DOWN, DE-EMPHASIZE ⟨∼ the issue⟩ **2** : to use the soft pedal in playing

soft pedal *n* (1854) **1** : a foot pedal on a piano that reduces the volume of sound **2** : something that muffles, deadens, or reduces effect

soft rock *n* (1967) : rock music that is less driving and gentler sounding than hard rock

soft rot *n* (1901) : a mushy, watery, or slimy decay of plants or their parts caused by bacteria or fungi

soft sell *n* (1954) : the use of suggestion or gentle persuasion in selling rather than aggressive pressure — compare HARD SELL

soft·shell \ˈsȯf(t)-ˌshel\ *n* (1771) : any of a family (Trionychidae) of aquatic turtles that have sharp claws and mandibles and a flat shell covered with soft leathery skin instead of with horny plates — called also *soft-shelled turtle*

soft–shell \'sȯf(t)-ˌshel\ *or* **soft–shelled** \-'sheld\ *adj* (1805) : having a soft or fragile shell esp. as a result of recent shedding ⟨~ crabs⟩

soft–shell clam *n* (1796) : an elongated clam (*Mya arenaria*) of the east coast of No. America that has a thin friable shell and long siphons and is used esp. for steaming — called also *soft= shelled clam, steamer*

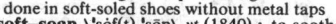

softshell

soft–shoe \'sȯf(t)-'shü\ *adj* (1920) : of or relating to tap dancing done in soft-soled shoes without metal taps

soft–soap \'sȯf(t)-'sōp\ *vt* (1840) : to soothe or persuade with flattery or blarney — **soft–soap·er** \-ˌsō-pər\ *n*

soft soap *n* (1634)   **1** : a semifluid soap made esp. from potassium hydroxide   **2** : FLATTERY

soft–spo·ken \-'spō-kən\ *adj* (1609) : having a mild or gentle voice; *also* : SUAVE

soft spot *n* (1845)   **1** : a sentimental weakness ⟨has a *soft spot* for him⟩   **2** : a vulnerable point ⟨a *soft spot* in the defense system⟩

soft touch *n* (1939) : one who is easily imposed on or taken advantage of

soft·ware \'sȯft-ˌwar, -ˌwer\ *n* (1960) : something used or associated with and usu. contrasted with hardware: as   **a** : the entire set of programs, procedures, and related documentation associated with a system and esp. a computer system; *specif* : computer programs   **b** : materials for use with audiovisual equipment

soft wheat *n* (1812) : a wheat with soft starchy kernels high in starch but usu. low in gluten

¹soft·wood \'sȯft-ˌwu̇d\ *n* (1832)   **1** : the wood of a coniferous tree (as a fir or pine) whether hard or soft as distinguished from that of an angiospermous tree   **2** : a tree that yields softwood

²softwood *adj* (1905) : having or made of softwood

soft–wood·ed \'sȯft-ˌwu̇-dəd\ *adj* (1827)   **1** : having soft wood that is easy to work or finish   **2** : SOFTWOOD

softy *or* **soft·ie** \'sȯf-tē\ *n, pl* **soft·ies** [¹*soft*] (1863)   **1** : a weak or foolish person   **2** : a softhearted or sentimental person

Sog·di·an \'säg-dē-ən\ *n* [L *Sogdiani*, pl., fr. Gk *Sogdianoi*, fr. OPers *Suguda* Sogdiana] (1553)   **1** : a native or inhabitant of Sogdiana   **2** : an Iranian language of the Sogdians — see INDO-EUROPEAN LANGUAGES table — **Sogdian** *adj*

sog·gy \'sä-gē, 'sȯ-\ *adj* **sog·gi·er; -est** [E dial. *sog* to soak] (1599)   **1** : saturated or heavy with water or moisture: as   **a** : WATERLOGGED, SOAKED ⟨a ~ lawn⟩   **b** : heavy or doughy because of imperfect cooking ⟨~ bread⟩   **2** : heavily dull : SPIRITLESS ⟨~ prose⟩ — **sog·gi·ly** \'sä-gə-lē, 'sȯ-\ *adv* — **sog·gi·ness** \'sä-gē-nəs, 'sȯ-\ *n*

soi–di·sant \ˌswä-dē-'zäⁿ\ *adj* [F, lit., saying oneself] (1752) : SELF= STYLED, SO-CALLED — usu. used disparagingly ⟨a ~ artist⟩

soi·gné *or* **soi·gnée** \swän-'yā\ *adj* [F, fr. pp. of *soigner* to take care of] (1821)   **1** : WELL-GROOMED, SLEEK   **2** : elegantly maintained or designed ⟨a ~ restaurant⟩ ⟨a ~ black dress⟩

¹soil \'sȯi(ə)l\ *vb* [ME, fr. OF *souillier* to wallow, soil, fr. *soil* abyss, pigpen, prob. fr. L *solium* chair, bathtub; akin to L *sedēre* to sit — more at SIT] *vt* (13c)   **1** : to stain or defile morally : CORRUPT, POLLUTE   **2** : to make unclean esp. superficially : DIRTY   **3** : to blacken or besmirch (as a person's reputation) by word or deed   ~ *vi* : to become soiled or dirty

²soil *n* (1501)   **1 a** : SOILAGE, STAIN ⟨protect a dress from ~⟩   **b** : moral defilement : CORRUPTION   **2** : something that spoils or pollutes: as   **a** : REFUSE   **b** : SEWAGE   **c** : DUNG, EXCREMENT

³soil *n* [ME, fr. AF, prob. fr. L *solium* chair] (14c)   **1** : firm land : EARTH   **2 a** : the upper layer of earth that may be dug or plowed and in which plants grow   **b** : the superficial unconsolidated and usu. weathered part of the mantle of a planet and esp. of the earth   **3** : COUNTRY, LAND ⟨our native ~⟩   **4** : the agricultural life or calling   **5** : a medium in which something takes hold and develops

⁴soil *vt* [origin unknown] (1605) : to feed (livestock) in the barn or an enclosure with fresh grass or green food; *also* : to purge (livestock) by feeding on green food

¹soil·age \'sȯi-lij\ *n* [¹*soil*] (1926) : the act of soiling : the condition of being soiled

²soilage *n* [⁴*soil*] (1928) : green crops for feeding confined animals

soil bank *n* (1955) : acreage retired from crop cultivation and planted with soil-building plants under a plan sponsored by the U.S. government that provides subsidies to farmers for the retired land

soil·borne \'sȯil-ˌbȯrn, -ˌbórn\ *adj* (1944) : transmitted by or in soil ⟨~ fungi⟩ ⟨~ diseases⟩

soil·less \'sȯi(ə)l-ləs\ *adj* (1938) : having, containing, or utilizing no soil ⟨~ agriculture⟩

soil pipe *n* (1833) : a pipe for carrying off wastes from toilets

soil science *n* (1915) : a science dealing with soils — called also *pedology* — **soil scientist** *n*

soil series *n* (1905) : a group of soils with similar profiles developed from similar parent materials under comparable climatic and vegetational conditions

soil·ure \'sȯil-yər\ *n* [ME, fr. OF *soilleure*, fr. *souillier* to soil] (13c)   **1** : the act of soiling : the condition of being soiled   **2** : STAIN, SMUDGE

soi·ree *or* **soi·rée** \swä-'rā\ *n* [F *soirée* evening period, evening party, fr. MF, fr. *soir* evening, fr. L *sero* at a late hour, fr. *serus* late; akin to OIr *sír* long, lasting and perh. to OE *sīth* late — more at SINCE] (1802) : a party or reception held in the evening

soi·xante–neuf \ˌswä-säⁿt-nœf\ *n* [F] (1888) : SIXTY-NINE 2

¹so·journ \'sō-ˌjərn, sō-'\ *n* [ME *sojorn*, fr. OF, fr. *sojorner*] (13c) : a temporary stay ⟨a ~ in the country⟩

²sojourn *vi* [ME *sojornen*, fr. OF *sojorner*, fr. (assumed) VL *subdiurnare*, fr. L *sub* under, during + LL *diurnum* day — more at UP, JOURNEY] (14c) : to stay as a temporary resident : STOP ⟨~ed for a month at a resort⟩ — **so·journ·er** *n*

soke \'sōk\ *n* [ME *soc, soke*, fr. OE *soka*, fr. ML *soca*, fr. OE *sōcn* inquiry, jurisdiction; akin to OE *sēcan* to seek] (12c)   **1** : the right in Anglo-Saxon and early English law to hold court and administer justice with the franchise to receive certain fees or fines arising from it : jurisdiction over a territory or over people   **2** : the district included in a soke jurisdiction or franchise

soke·man \'sōk-mən\ *n* (1579) : a man who is under the soke of another

¹sol \'sōl\ *also* **so** \'sō\ *n* [ML *sol*; fr. the syllable sung to this note in a medieval hymn to St. John the Baptist] (14c) : the 5th tone of the diatonic scale in solmization

²sol \'sōl\ *n* [MF — more at SOU] (1583) : an old French coin equal to 12 deniers; *also* : a corresponding unit of value

³sol \'säl, 'sȯl\ *n, pl* **so·les** \'sō-(ˌ)lās\ [AmerSp, fr. Sp, sun, fr. L] (ca. 1883) : the basic monetary unit of Peru before 1985 and since 1990 — see MONEY table

⁴sol \'säl, 'sȯl\ *n* [-*sol* (as in *hydrosol*), fr. *solution*] (1899) : a fluid colloidal system; *esp* : one in which the continuous phase is a liquid

Sol \'säl\ *n* [ME, fr. L]   **1** : the Roman god of the sun — compare HELIOS   **2** : SUN

sola *pl of* SOLUM

¹so·lace \'sä-ləs *also* 'sō-\ *vt* **so·laced; so·lac·ing** (13c)   **1** : to give solace to : CONSOLE   **2 a** : to make cheerful   **b** : AMUSE   **3** : ALLAY, SOOTHE ⟨~ grief⟩ — **so·lace·ment** \-mənt\ *n* — **so·lac·er** *n*

²solace *n* [ME *solas*, fr. OF, fr. L *solacium*, fr. *solari* to console] (14c)   **1** : alleviation of grief or anxiety   **2** : a source of relief or consolation

so·la·na·ceous \ˌsō-lə-'nā-shəs\ *adj* [NL *Solanaceae*, family name, fr. *Solanum*] (1804) : of or relating to the nightshade family of plants

so·la·nine *also* **so·la·nin** \'sō-lə-ˌnēn, -nən\ *n* [F *solanine*, fr. L *solanum*] (1838) : a bitter poisonous crystalline alkaloid $C_{45}H_{73}NO_{15}$ from several plants (as some potatoes or tomatoes) of the nightshade family

so·la·num \sə-'lā-nəm, -'lä-, -'la-\ *n* [NL, fr. L, nightshade] (ca. 1652) : any of a genus (*Solanum*) chiefly of herbs and shrubs of the nightshade family that have often prickly-veined leaves, cymose white, purple, or yellow flowers, and a fruit that is a berry

so·lar \'sō-lər, -ˌlär\ *adj* [ME, fr. L *solaris*, fr. *sol* sun; akin to OE & ON *sōl* sun, Lith *saulė*, Gk *hēlios*] (15c)   **1** : of, derived from, or relating to the sun esp. as affecting the earth   **2** : measured by the earth's course in relation to the sun ⟨~ time⟩ ⟨~ year⟩; *also* : relating to or reckoned by solar time   **3 a** : produced or operated by the action of the sun's light or heat ⟨~ energy⟩ ⟨~ cooker⟩   **b** : utilizing the sun's rays esp. to produce heat or electricity ⟨a ~ house⟩; *also* : of or relating to such utilization ⟨~ design⟩ ⟨~ subsidies⟩

solar battery *n* (1954) : an array of solar cells

solar cell *n* (1955) : a photovoltaic cell (as one including a junction between two types of silicon semiconductors) that is able to convert light into electrical energy and is used as a power source

solar collector *n* (1955) : any of various devices for the absorption of solar radiation for the heating of water or buildings or the production of electricity

solar constant *n* (1869) : the quantity of radiant solar energy received at the outer layer of the earth's atmosphere that has a mean value of 1370 watts per square meter

solar day *n* (1764) : the interval between transits of the apparent or mean sun across the meridian at any place

solar eclipse *n* (ca. 1890) : an eclipse of the sun by the moon — see ECLIPSE illustration

solar flare *n* (1938) : a sudden temporary outburst of energy from a small area of the sun's surface — called also *flare*

so·lar·i·um \sō-'lar-ē-əm, sə-, -'ler-\ *n, pl* **-ia** \-ē-ə\ *also* **-ums** [L, porch exposed to the sun, fr. *sol*] (ca. 1823) : a glass-enclosed porch or room; *also* : a room (as in a hospital) used esp. for sunbathing or therapeutic exposure to light

so·lar·i·za·tion \ˌsō-lə-rə-'zā-shən\ *n* (1853)   **1** : a reversal of gradation in a photographic image obtained by intense or continued exposure   **2** : an act or process of solarizing

so·lar·ize \'sō-lə-ˌrīz\ *vt* **-ized; -iz·ing** (1853)   **1 a** : to affect by the action of the sun's rays   **b** : to expose to sunlight   **2** : to subject (photographic materials) to solarization

solar panel *n* (1961) : a battery of solar cells (as in a spacecraft)

so·lar plexus \'sō-lər-\ *n* [fr. the radiating nerve fibers] (1771)   **1** : a nerve plexus in the abdomen that is situated behind the stomach and in front of the aorta and the crura of the diaphragm and contains several ganglia distributing nerve fibers to the viscera   **2** : the pit of the stomach

solar pond *n* (1961) : a pool of salt water heated by the sun and used either as a direct source of heat or to provide power for an electric generator

solar sail *n* (1958) : a propulsive device for a spacecraft that consists of a flat material (as aluminized plastic) designed to receive thrust from solar radiation pressure

solar system *n* (ca. 1704) : the sun together with the group of celestial bodies that are held by its attraction and revolve around it; *also* : a similar system centered on another star

solar wind *n* (1958) : plasma continuously ejected from the sun's surface into and through interplanetary space

sol·ation \sä-'lā-shən, sō-\ *n* (1915) : the process of changing to a sol

so·la·ti·um \sō-'lā-shē-əm\ *n, pl* **-tia** \-shē-ə\ [LL *solacium, solatium*, fr. L, solace] (1817) : a compensation (as money) given as solace for suffering, loss, or injured feelings

sold *past and past part of* SELL

sol·dan \'säl-dən, 'sȯl-\ *n* [ME, fr. OF, fr. Ar *sulṭān*] (14c) *archaic* : SULTAN; *esp* : the sultan of Egypt

¹sol·der \'sä-dər, 'sȯ-, *Brit also* 'säl-dər, 'sȯl-\ *n* [ME *soudure*, fr. MF, fr. *souder* to solder, fr. L *solidare* to make solid, fr. *solidus* solid] (14c)   **1** : a metal or metallic alloy used when melted to join metallic surfaces; *esp* : an alloy of lead and tin so used   **2** : something that unites

---

\ə\ abut \ᵊ\ kitten, F table \ər\ further \a\ ash \ā\ ace \ä\ mop, mar
\au̇\ out \ch\ chin \e\ bet \ē\ easy \g\ go \i\ hit \ī\ ice \j\ job
\ŋ\ sing \ō\ go \ȯ\ law \ȯi\ boy \th\ thin \tẖ\ the \ü\ loot \u̇\ foot
\y\ yet \zh\ vision \à, k̲, ⁿ, œ, œ̄, ᵫ, ᵧ\ *see* Guide to Pronunciation

²**solder** vb **sol·dered; sol·der·ing** \-d(ə-)riŋ\ vt (15c) **1 :** to unite or make whole by solder **2 :** to bring into or restore to firm union ⟨a friendship ~ed by common interests⟩ ~ vi **1 :** to use solder **2 :** to become united or repaired by or as if by solder — **sol·der·abil·i·ty** \ˌsä-də-rə-'bi-lə-tē, ˌsò-\ n — **sol·der·er** \'sä-dər-ər, 'sò-\ n

soldering iron n (1688) **:** a pointed or wedge-shaped device that is usu. electrically heated and that is used for soldering

¹**sol·dier** \'sōl-jər\ n [ME soudier, fr. MF, fr. soulde pay, fr. LL solidus solidus] (14c) **1 a :** one engaged in military service and esp. in the army **b :** an enlisted man or woman **c :** a skilled warrior **2 :** a militant leader, follower, or worker **3 :** one of a caste of wingless sterile termites usu. differing from workers in larger size and head and long jaws **b :** one of a type of worker ants distinguished by exceptionally large head and jaws **4** \'sō-jər, 'sòl-\ **:** one who shirks work — **sol·dier·ly** \-lē\ adj or adv — **sol·dier·ship** \-ˌship\ n

²**soldier** vi **sol·diered; sol·dier·ing** \'sōl-jə-riŋ, 'sòlj-riŋ\ (1647) **1 a :** to serve as a soldier **b :** to behave in a soldierly manner **c :** to push doggedly forward — usu. used with on ⟨~ed on to the end⟩ **2 :** to make a pretense of working while really loafing

soldiering n (1643) **:** the life, service, or practice of one who soldiers

soldier of fortune (1661) **:** one who follows a military career wherever there is promise of profit, adventure, or pleasure

soldiers' home n (1860) **:** an institution maintained (as by the federal or a state government) for the care and relief of military veterans

soldier's medal n (ca. 1930) **:** a U.S. military decoration awarded for heroism not involving combat

sol·diery \'sōl-jə-rē, 'sòlj-rē\ n (ca. 1570) **1 a :** a body of soldiers **b :** SOLDIERS, MILITARY **2 :** the profession or technique of soldiering

sol·do \'sòl-(ˌ)dō\ n, pl **sol·di** \-(ˌ)dē\ [It, fr. LL solidus solidus] (1599) **:** an old Italian coin worth five centesimi

sold–out \'sōld-'aut\ adj (1907) **:** having all available tickets or accommodations sold completely and esp. in advance

¹**sole** \'sōl\ n [ME, fr. MF, fr. L solea sandal, a flatfish] (13c) **:** any of various flatfishes (family Soleidae) having a small mouth, small or rudimentary fins, and small eyes placed close together and including superior food fishes (as the European Dover sole); also **:** any of various mostly market flatfishes (as lemon sole) of other families (as Pleuronectidae)

²**sole** n [ME, fr. MF, fr. L solea sandal; akin to L solum base, ground, soil] (14c) **1 a :** the undersurface of a foot **b :** the part of an item of footwear on which the sole rests and upon which the wearer treads **2 :** the usu. flat or flattened bottom or lower part of something or the base on which something rests — **soled** \'sōld\ adj

³**sole** vt **soled; sol·ing** (1570) **1 :** to furnish with a sole ⟨~ a shoe⟩ **2 :** to place the sole of (a golf club) on the ground

⁴**sole** adj [ME, alone, fr. MF seul, fr. L solus] (14c) **1 :** not married — used chiefly of women **2** archaic **:** having no companion **: SOLITARY 3 a :** having no sharer **b :** being the only one ⟨she was her mother's ~ support⟩ **4 :** functioning independently and without assistance or interference ⟨let conscience be the ~ judge⟩ **5 :** belonging exclusively or otherwise limited to one usu. specified individual, unit, or group — **sole·ness** \'sōl-nəs\ n

so·le·cism \'sä-lə-ˌsi-zəm, 'sō-\ n [L soloecismus, fr. Gk soloikismos, fr. soloikos speaking incorrectly, lit., inhabitant of Soloi, fr. Soloi, city in ancient Cilicia where a substandard form of Attic was spoken] (ca. 1555) **1 :** an ungrammatical combination of words in a sentence; also **:** a minor blunder in speech **2 :** something deviating from the proper, normal, or accepted order **3 :** a breach of etiquette or decorum — **so·le·cis·tic** \ˌsä-lə-'sis-tik, ˌsō-\ adj

sole·ly \'sō(l)-lē\ adv (15c) **1 :** without another **: SINGLY** ⟨went ~ on her way⟩ **2 :** to the exclusion of all else ⟨done ~ for money⟩

sol·emn \'sä-ləm\ adj [ME solemne, fr. MF, fr. L sollemnis regularly appointed, solemn] (14c) **1 :** marked by the invocation of a religious sanction ⟨a ~ oath⟩ **2 :** marked by the observance of established form or ceremony; specif **:** celebrated with full liturgical ceremony **3 a :** awe-inspiring **: SUBLIME b :** marked by grave sedateness and earnest sobriety **c :** SOMBER, GLOOMY syn see SERIOUS — **sol·emn·ly** adv — **sol·emn·ness** n

so·lem·ni·fy \sə-'lem-nə-ˌfī\ vt-fied; -fy·ing (1780) **:** to make solemn

so·lem·ni·ty \sə-'lem-nə-tē\ n, pl **-ties** (14c) **1 :** formal or ceremonious observance of an occasion or event **2 :** a solemn event or occasion **3 :** a solemn condition or quality ⟨the ~ of his words⟩

sol·em·nize \'sä-ləm-ˌnīz\ vb **-nized; -niz·ing** vt (14c) **1 :** to observe or honor with solemnity **2 :** to perform with pomp or ceremony; esp **:** to celebrate (a marriage) with religious rites **3 :** to make solemn **: DIGNIFY** ~ vi **:** to speak or act with solemnity — **sol·em·ni·za·tion** \ˌsä-ləm-nə-'zā-shən\ n

solemn mass n (15c) **:** a mass marked by the use of incense and by the presence of a deacon and a subdeacon in attendance on the celebrant

solemn vow n (14c) **:** an absolute and irrevocable public vow taken by a religious in the Roman Catholic Church under which ownership of property by the individual is prohibited and marriage is invalid under canon law

so·le·noid \'sō-lə-ˌnòid, 'sä-\ n [F solénoïde, fr. Gk sōlēnoeidēs pipeshaped, fr. Gk sōlēn pipe] (1827) **:** a coil of wire usu. in cylindrical form that when carrying a current acts like a magnet so that a movable core is drawn into the coil when a current flows and that is used esp. as a switch or control for a mechanical device (as a valve) — **so·le·noi·dal** \ˌsō-lə-'nòi-dᵊl, ˌsä-\ adj

sole·plate \'sōl-ˌplāt\ n (1741) **1 :** the lower plate of a studded partition on which the bases of the studs butt **2 :** the undersurface of a flatiron

soles pl of SOL

so·le·us \'sō-lē-əs\ n, pl **so·lei** \-lē-ˌī\ [NL, fr. L solea sandal — more at SOLE] (1676) **:** a broad flat muscle of the calf of the leg lying immediately below the gastrocnemius

¹**sol–fa** \ˌsōl-'fä, 'sōl-\ vi (ca. 1529) **1 :** to sing the sol-fa syllables ~ vt **:** to sing (as a melody) to sol-fa syllables

²**sol–fa** n (1548) **1 : SOL-FA SYLLABLES 2 : SOLMIZATION;** also **:** an exercise thus sung **3 : TONIC SOL-FA** — **sol–fa·ist** \-'fä(-)ist, -'fä-ˌist\ n

sol–fa syllables n pl (1913) **:** the syllables do, re, mi, fa, sol, la, ti, used in singing the tones of the scale

sol·fa·ta·ra \ˌsōl-fə-'tär-ə\ n [It, sulfur mine, fr. solfo sulfur, fr. L sulfur] (1777) **:** a volcanic area or vent that yields only hot vapors and sulfurous gases

sol·fège \säl-'fezh\ n [F, fr. It solfeggio] (ca. 1903) **1 :** the application of the sol-fa syllables to a musical scale or to a melody **2 :** a singing exercise esp. using sol-fa syllables; also **:** practice in sight-reading vocal music using the sol-fa syllables

sol·feg·gio \säl-'fe-j(ē-ˌ)ō\ n [It, fr. sol-fa] (1774) **: SOLFÈGE**

sol–gel \säl-ˌjel, 'sòl-\ adj (1915) **:** involving alternation between sol and gel states

soli pl of SOLO

so·lic·it \sə-'li-sət\ vb [ME, to disturb, take charge of, fr. MF solliciter, fr. L sollicitare to disturb, fr. sollicitus anxious, fr. sollus whole (fr. Oscan; akin to Gk holos whole) + citus, pp. of ciēre to move — more at SAFE, ·KINESIS] vt (15c) **1 a :** to make petition to **: ENTREAT b :** to approach with a request or plea **2 :** to urge (as one's cause) strongly **3 a :** to entice or lure esp. into evil **b :** to proposition (someone) esp. as or in the character of a prostitute **4 :** to try to obtain by usu. urgent requests or pleas ~ vi **1 :** to make solicitation **: IMPORTUNE 2** of a prostitute **:** to offer to have sexual relations with someone for money syn see ASK

so·lic·i·tant \sə-'li-sə-tənt\ n (ca. 1812) **:** one who solicits

so·lic·i·ta·tion \sə-ˌli-sə-'tā-shən\ n (ca. 1520) **1 :** the practice or act or an instance of soliciting; esp **: ENTREATY, IMPORTUNITY 2 :** a moving or drawing force **: INCITEMENT, ALLUREMENT**

so·lic·i·tor \sə-'li-sə-tər, -'lis-tər\ n (15c) **1 :** one that solicits; esp **:** an agent that solicits (as contributions to charity) **2 :** a British lawyer who advises clients, represents them in the lower courts, and prepares cases for barristers to try in higher courts **3 :** the chief law officer of a municipality, county, or government department — **so·lic·i·tor·ship** \-ˌship\ n

solicitor general n, pl **solicitors general** (1647) **:** a law officer appointed primarily to assist an attorney general

so·lic·i·tous \sə-'li-sə-təs, -'lis-təs\ adj [L sollicitus] (1563) **1 :** manifesting or expressing solicitude ⟨a ~ inquiry about his health⟩ **2 :** full of concern or fears **: APPREHENSIVE** ⟨~ about the future⟩ **3 :** meticulously careful ⟨~ in matters of dress⟩ **4 :** full of desire **: EAGER** — **so·lic·i·tous·ly** adv — **so·lic·i·tous·ness** n

so·lic·i·tude \sə-'li-sə-ˌtüd, -ˌtyüd\ n (15c) **1 a :** the state of being solicitous **: ANXIETY b :** attentive care and protectiveness; also **:** an attitude of solicitous concern or attention **2 :** a cause of care or concern — usu. used in pl.

¹**sol·id** \'sä-ləd\ adj [ME solide, fr. MF, fr. L solidus; akin to Gk holos whole — more at SAFE] (14c) **1 a :** being without an internal cavity ⟨a ~ ball of rubber⟩ **b** (1) **:** printed with minimum space between lines (2) **:** joined without a hyphen ⟨a ~ compound⟩ **c :** not interrupted by a break or opening ⟨a ~ wall⟩ **2 :** having, involving, or dealing with three dimensions or with solids ⟨~ configuration⟩ **3 a :** of uniformly close and coherent texture **:** not loose or spongy **: COMPACT b :** possessing or characterized by the properties of a solid **:** neither gaseous nor liquid **4 :** of good substantial quality or kind ⟨~ comfort⟩: as **a : SOUND** ⟨~ reasons⟩ **b :** made firmly and well ⟨~ furniture⟩ **5 a :** having no break or interruption ⟨waited three ~ hours⟩ **b : UNANIMOUS** ⟨had the ~ support of the party⟩ **c :** intimately friendly or associated ⟨~ with the boss⟩ **6 a : PRUDENT;** also **:** well-established financially **b :** serious in purpose or character **7 :** of one substance or character: as **a :** entirely of one metal or containing the minimum of alloy necessary to impart hardness ⟨~ gold⟩ **b :** of a single color — **sol·id·ly** adv — **sol·id·ness** n

²**solid** n (15c) **1 :** a geometrical figure or element (as a cube or sphere) having three dimensions — see VOLUME table **2 a :** a substance that does not flow perceptibly under moderate stress, has a definite capacity for resisting forces (as compression or tension) which tend to deform it, and under ordinary conditions retains a definite size and shape **b :** the part of a solution or suspension that when freed from solvent or suspending medium has the qualities of a solid — usu. used in pl. ⟨milk ~s⟩ **3 :** something that is solid: as **a :** a solid color **b :** a compound word whose members are joined together without a hyphen

³**solid** adv (1651) **:** in a solid manner; also **: UNANIMOUSLY**

sol·i·da·go \ˌsä-lə-'dā-(ˌ)gō, -'dä-\ n, pl **-gos** [NL, fr. ML soldago, an herb reputed to heal wounds, fr. soldare to make whole, fr. L solidare, fr. solidus solid] (ca. 1771) **:** any of a genus (Solidago) of chiefly No. American composite herbs including the typical goldenrods

solid angle n (ca. 1704) **:** the three-dimensional angular spread at the vertex of a cone measured by the area intercepted by the cone on a unit sphere whose center is the vertex of the cone

sol·i·da·rism \'sä-lə-də-ˌri-zəm\ n (1906) **: SOLIDARITY — sol·i·da·rist** \-rist\ n — **sol·i·da·ris·tic** \ˌsä-lə-də-'ris-tik\ adj

sol·i·dar·i·ty \ˌsä-lə-'dar-ə-tē\ n [F solidarité, fr. solidaire characterized by solidarity, fr. L solidum whole sum, fr. neut. of solidus solid] (1841) **:** unity (as of a group or class) that produces or is based on community of interests, objectives, and standards

solid geometry n (1733) **:** a branch of geometry that deals with figures of three-dimensional space

so·lid·i·fy \sə-'li-də-ˌfī\ vb **-fied; -fy·ing** vt (1799) **1 :** to make solid, compact, or hard **2 :** to make secure, substantial, or firmly fixed ⟨factors that ~ public opinion⟩ ~ vi **:** to become solid, compact, or hard — **so·lid·i·fi·ca·tion** \-ˌli-də-fə-'kā-shən\ n

so·lid·i·ty \sə-'li-də-tē\ n, pl **-ties** (14c) **1 :** the quality or state of being solid **2 :** something solid

sol·id–look·ing \ˌsä-ləd-'lük-iŋ\ adj (1840) **:** giving an impression of solid worth or substance ⟨~ citizens⟩

solid of revolution (1816) **:** a mathematical solid conceived as formed by the revolution of a plane figure about an axis in its plane

solid–state adj (ca. 1951) **1 :** relating to the properties, structure, or reactivity of solid material; esp **:** relating to the arrangement or behavior of ions, molecules, nucleons, electrons, and holes in the crystals of a substance (as a semiconductor) or to the effect of crystal imperfections on the properties of a solid substance ⟨~ physics⟩ **2 a :** utilizing the electric, magnetic, or optical properties of solid materials ⟨~ circuitry⟩ **b :** using semiconductor devices rather than electron tubes ⟨a ~ stereo system⟩

sol·i·dus \'sä-lə-dəs\ n, pl **-i·di** \-lə-ˌdī, -ˌdē\ [ME, fr. LL, fr. L, solid] (14c) **1 :** an ancient Roman gold coin introduced by Constantine and used to the fall of the Byzantine Empire 2 [ML, shilling, fr. LL; fr. its use as a symbol for shillings] : DIAGONAL 3

so·li·fluc·tion \'sō-lə-,flək-shən\ *n* [L *solum* soil + *-i-* + *fluction-, fluctio* act of flowing, fr. *fluere* to flow — more at FLUID] (1906) : the slow creeping of saturated fragmental material (as soil) down a slope that usu. occurs in regions of perennial frost

so·lil·o·quist \sə-'li-lə-kwist\ *n* (1804) : one who soliloquizes

so·lil·o·quise *Brit var of* SOLILOQUIZE

so·lil·o·quize \-,kwīz\ *vi* **-quized; -quiz·ing** (1759) : to utter a soliloquy : talk to oneself — **so·lil·o·quiz·er** *n*

so·lil·o·quy \sə-'li-lə-kwē\ *n, pl* **-quies** [LL *soliloquium*, fr. L *solus* alone + *loqui* to speak] (ca. 1613) 1 : the act of talking to oneself 2 : a dramatic monologue that gives the illusion of being a series of unspoken reflections

so·lip·sism \'sō-ləp-,si-zəm, 'sä-\ *n* [L *solus* alone + *ipse* self] (1874) : a theory holding that the self can know nothing but its own modifications and that the self is the only existent thing — **so·lip·sist** \'sō-ləp-sist, 'sä-ləp-, sə-'lip-\ *n* — **so·lip·sis·tic** \,sō-ləp-'sis-tik, ,sä-\ *adj* — **so·lip·sis·ti·cal·ly** \-ti-k(ə-)lē\ *adv*

sol·i·taire \'sä-lə-,tar, -,ter\ *n* [F, fr. *solitaire*, adj., solitary, fr. L *solitarius*] (ca. 1727) 1 : a single gem (as a diamond) set alone 2 : any of various card games that can be played by one person

¹sol·i·tary \'sä-lə-,ter-ē\ *adj* [ME, fr. L *solitarius*, fr. *solitas* aloneness, fr. *solus* alone] (14c) 1 a : being, living, or going alone or without companions b : saddened by isolation 2 : UNFREQUENTED, DESOLATE 3 a : taken, passed, or performed without companions ⟨a ~ ramble⟩ b : keeping a prisoner apart from others ⟨~ confinement⟩ 4 : being at once single and isolated ⟨a ~ example⟩ 5 a : occurring singly and not as part of a group or cluster ⟨flowers terminal and ~⟩ b : not gregarious, colonial, social, or compound ⟨~ bees⟩ *syn* see ALONE — **sol·i·tar·i·ly** \,sä-lə-'ter-ə-lē\ *adv* — **sol·i·tar·i·ness** \'sä-lə-,ter-ē-nəs\ *n*

²solitary *n, pl* **-tar·ies** (15c) 1 : one who lives or seeks to live a solitary life : RECLUSE 2 : solitary confinement in prison

sol·i·ton \'sä-lə-,tän\ *n* [*solitary* + *²-on*] (1965) : a solitary wave (as in a gaseous plasma) that propagates with little loss of energy and retains its shape and speed after colliding with another such wave

sol·i·tude \'sä-lə-,tüd, -,tyüd\ *n* [ME, fr. MF, fr. L *solitudin-, solitudo*, fr. *solus*] (14c) 1 : the quality or state of being alone or remote from society : SECLUSION 2 : a lonely place (as a desert)
syn SOLITUDE, ISOLATION, SECLUSION mean the state of one who is alone. SOLITUDE may imply a condition of being apart from all human beings or of being cut off by wish or circumstances from one's usual associates ⟨a few quiet hours of *solitude*⟩. ISOLATION stresses detachment from others often involuntarily ⟨the *isolation* of the village in winter⟩. SECLUSION suggests a shutting away or keeping apart from others often connoting deliberate withdrawal from the world or retirement to a quiet life ⟨lived in pastoral *seclusion*⟩.

sol·i·tu·di·nar·i·an \,sä-lə-,tü-d⁹n-'er-ē-ən, -,tyü-\ *n* [L *solitudin-, solitudo* + E *-arian*] (1691) : RECLUSE

sol·ler·et \,sä-lə-'ret\ *n* [F] (1826) : a flexible steel shoe forming part of a medieval suit of armor — see ARMOR illustration

sol·mi·za·tion \,säl-mə-'zā-shən\ *n* [F *solmisation*, fr. *solmiser* to sol-fa, fr. *sol* (fr. ML) + *mi* (fr. ML) + *-iser -ize*] (1730) : the act, practice, or system of using syllables to denote the tones of a musical scale

¹so·lo \'sō-(,)lō\ *n, pl* **solos** [It, fr. *solo* alone, fr. L *solus*] (1695) 1 *or pl* **so·li** \'sō-(,)lē\ a : a musical composition for a single voice or instrument with or without accompaniment b : the featured part of a concerto or similar work 2 : a performance in which the performer has no partner or associate 3 : any of several card games in which a player elects to play without a partner against the other players

²solo *adv* (1712) : without a companion : ALONE ⟨fly ~⟩

³solo *adj* (1774) : of, relating to, or being a solo ⟨a ~ performance⟩

⁴solo *vi* **so·loed; so·lo·ing** \-(,)lō-iŋ, -lə-wiŋ\ (1886) : to perform by oneself; *esp* : to fly an airplane without one's instructor on board

so·lo·ist \'sō-lə-wist, -(,)lō-ist\ *n* (1864) : one who performs a solo

Sol·o·mon \'sä-lə-mən\ *n* [LL, fr. Heb *Shĕlōmōh*] : a son of David and 10th century B.C. king of Israel proverbial for his wisdom

Sol·o·mon·ic \,sä-lə-'mä-nik\ *adj* (1857) : marked by notable wisdom, reasonableness, or discretion esp. under trying circumstances

Solomon's seal *n* (1543) 1 : any of a genus (*Polygonatum*) of perennial herbs of the lily family with tubular flowers and gnarled rhizomes — called also *Solomonseal* 2 : an emblem consisting of two interlaced triangles forming a 6-pointed star and formerly used as an amulet esp. against fevers — compare HEXAGRAM

so·lon \'sō-lən, -,län\ *n* [*Solon*] (1625) 1 : a wise and skillful lawgiver 2 : a member of a legislative body

sol·on·chak \,sä-lən-'chak\ *n* [Russ, salt marsh] (1925) : any of a group of intrazonal strongly saline usu. pale soils found esp. in poorly drained arid or semiarid areas

sol·o·netz \,sä-lə-'nets\ *n* [Russ *solonets* salt not extracted by decoction] (1924) : any of a group of intrazonal dark hard alkaline soils evolved by leaching and alkalizing from solonchak — **sol·o·netz·ic** \-'net-sik\ *adj*

so long \sō-'lóŋ, sə-\ *interj* [origin unknown] (ca. 1861) — used to express farewell

so long as *conj* (14c) 1 : during and up to the end of the time that : WHILE 2 : provided that

sol·stice \'säl-stəs, 'sōl-, 'sòl-\ *n* [ME, fr. OF, fr. L *solstitium*, fr. *sol* sun + *-stit-, -stes* standing; akin to L *stare* to stand — more at SOLAR, STAND] (13c) 1 : either of the two points on the ecliptic at which its distance from the celestial equator is greatest and which is reached by the sun each year about June 22d and December 22d 2 : the time of the sun's passing a solstice which occurs about June 22d to begin summer in the northern hemisphere and about December 22d to begin winter in the northern hemisphere

sol·sti·tial \säl-'sti-shəl, sōl-, sòl-\ *adj* [ME *solsticial*, fr. OF & L; OF, fr. L *solstitialis*, fr. *solstitium*] (14c) 1 : of, relating to, or characteristic of a solstice and esp. the summer solstice 2 : happening or appearing at or associated with a solstice

sol·u·bi·lise *Brit var of* SOLUBILIZE

sol·u·bil·i·ty \,säl-yə-'bi-lə-tē\ *n* (1661) 1 : the quality or state of being soluble 2 : the amount of a substance that will dissolve in a given amount of another substance

sol·u·bi·lize \'säl-yə-bə-,līz\ *vt* **-lized; -liz·ing** (ca. 1926) : to make soluble or increase the solubility of — **sol·u·bi·li·za·tion** \,säl-yə-bə-lə-'zā-shən\ *n*

sol·u·ble \'säl-yə-bəl\ *adj* [ME, fr. MF, capable of being loosened or dissolved, fr. LL *solubilis*, fr. L *solvere* to loosen, dissolve — more at SOLVE] (15c) 1 : susceptible of being dissolved in or as if in a liquid and esp. water 2 : subject to being solved or explained ⟨~ questions⟩

so·lum \'sō-ləm\ *n, pl* **so·la** \-lə\ *or* **solums** [NL, fr. L, ground, soil] (1928) : the altered layer of soil above the parent material that includes the A and B horizons

so·lus \'sō-ləs\ *adv or adj* [L] (1599) : ALONE — often used in stage directions

sol·ute \'säl-,yüt\ *n* [L *solutus*, pp. of *solvere*] (1893) : a dissolved substance

so·lu·tion \sə-'lü-shən\ *n* [ME, fr. MF, fr. L *solution-, solutio*, fr. *solvere* to loosen, solve] (14c) 1 a : an action or process of solving a problem b : an answer to a problem : EXPLANATION; *specif* : a set of values of the variables that satisfies an equation 2 a : an act or the process by which a solid, liquid, or gaseous substance is homogeneously mixed with a liquid or sometimes a gas or solid b : a homogeneous mixture formed by this process; *esp* : a single-phase liquid system c : the condition of being dissolved 3 : a bringing or coming to an end or into a state of discontinuity

solution set *n* (1959) : the set of values that satisfy an equation; *also* : TRUTH SET

So·lu·tre·an \sə-'lü-trē-ən\ *adj* [*Solutré*, village in France] (1888) : of or relating to an upper Paleolithic culture characterized by leaf-shaped finely flaked stone implements

solv·able \'säl-və-bəl, 'sòl-\ *adj* (ca. 1676) : susceptible of solution or of being solved, resolved, or explained — **solv·abil·i·ty** \,säl-və-'bi-lə-tē, ,sòl-\ *n*

¹sol·vate \'säl-,vāt, 'sòl-\ *n* [*solvent* + *¹-ate*] (1904) : an aggregate that consists of a solute ion or molecule with one or more solvent molecules; *also* : a substance (as a hydrate) containing such ions

²solvate *vt* **sol·vat·ed; sol·vat·ing** (1909) : to make part of a solvate — **sol·va·tion** \säl-'vā-shən, sòl-\ *n*

Sol·vay process \'säl-,vā-\ *n* [Ernest *Solvay* †1922 Belg. chemist] (1884) : a process for making soda from common salt by passing carbon dioxide into ammoniacal brine resulting in precipitation of sodium bicarbonate which is then calcined to carbonate

solve \'sälv, 'sòlv\ *vb* **solved; solv·ing** [ME, to loosen, fr. L *solvere* to loosen, solve, dissolve, fr. *sed-, se-* apart + *luere* to release — more at SECEDE, LOSE] *vt* (ca. 1533) 1 : to find a solution, explanation, or answer for ⟨~ a problem⟩ ⟨*solved* the crime⟩ 2 : to pay (as a debt) in full ~ *vi* : to solve something ⟨substitute the known values of the constants and ~ for *x*⟩ — **solv·er** *n*

sol·ven·cy \'säl-vən(t)-sē, 'sòl-\ *n* (ca. 1727) : the quality or state of being solvent

¹sol·vent \-vənt\ *adj* [L *solvent-, solvens*, prp. of *solvere* to dissolve, pay] (1630) 1 : able to pay all legal debts 2 : that dissolves or can dissolve ⟨~ action of water⟩ — **sol·vent·ly** *adv*

²solvent *n* (1671) 1 : a usu. liquid substance capable of dissolving or dispersing one or more other substances 2 : something that provides a solution 3 : something that eliminates or attenuates something esp. unwanted — **sol·vent·less** \-ləs\ *adj*

sol·vol·y·sis \säl-'vä-lə-səs, sòl-\ *n* [NL, fr. E *solvent* + NL *-o-* + *-lysis*] (1916) : a chemical reaction (as hydrolysis) of a solvent and solute that results in the formation of new compounds — **sol·vo·lyt·ic** \,säl-və-'li-tik, ,sòl-\ *adj*

¹so·ma \'sō-mə\ *n* [Skt; akin to Av *haoma*, a Zoroastrian ritual drink, Skt *sunoti* he presses out] (1827) : an intoxicating plant juice prob. from a leafless vine (*Sarcostemma intermedium*) of the milkweed family used in ancient India as an offering to the gods and as a drink of immortality by worshipers in Vedic ritual and worshiped as a Vedic god

²soma *n, pl* **so·ma·ta** \'sō-mə-tə\ *or* **somas** [NL *somat-, soma*, fr. Gk *sōmat-, sōma* body] (ca. 1885) 1 : the body of an organism 2 : all of an organism except the germ cells 3 : CELL BODY

So·ma·li \sō-'mä-lē, sə-\ *n, pl* **Somali** *or* **Somalis** (1814) 1 : a member of a people of Somaliland 2 : the Cushitic language of the Somali

so many *adj* (1533) 1 : constituting an unspecified number ⟨read *so many* chapters each night⟩ 2 : constituting a group or pack ⟨behaved like *so many* animals⟩

somat- *or* **somato-** *comb form* [NL, fr. Gk *sōmat-, sōmato-*, fr. *sōmat-, sōma* body] : body ⟨*somatology*⟩

so·mat·ic \sō-'ma-tik, sə-\ *adj* [Gk *sōmatikos*, fr. *sōmat-, sōma*] (ca. 1775) 1 : of, relating to, or affecting the body esp. as distinguished from the germ plasm or the psyche 2 : of or relating to the wall of the body : PARIETAL — **so·mat·i·cal·ly** \-ti-k(ə-)lē\ *adv*

somatic cell *n* (1888) : one of the cells of the body that compose the tissues, organs, and parts of that individual other than the germ cells

so·ma·tol·o·gy \,sō-mə-'tä-lə-jē\ *n* [NL *somatologia*, fr. *somat-* + *-logia -logy*] (ca. 1878) : a branch of anthropology primarily concerned with the comparative study of human evolution, variation, and classification esp. through measurement and observation — **so·ma·to·log·i·cal** \,sō-mə-t⁹l-'ä-ji-kəl, sō-,ma-tə-\ *adj*

so·ma·to·me·din \,sō-mə-tō-'mē-d⁹n, sō-,ma-tə-\ *n* [*somat-* + *intermediary* + *¹-in*] (1971) : any of several endogenous peptides produced esp. in the liver that are dependent on and prob. mediate growth hormone activity (as in sulfate uptake by epiphyseal cartilage)

so·ma·to·pleure \sō-'ma-tə-,plùr\ *n* [NL *somatopleura*, fr. *somat-* + Gk *pleura* side] (1874) : a complex fold of tissue in the embryo of a craniate vertebrate consisting of an outer layer of mesoderm together with the ectoderm that sheathes it and giving rise to the amnion and chorion

so·ma·to·sen·so·ry \sō-,ma-tə-'sen(t)s-rē, -'sen(t)-sə-rē\ *adj* (1952) : of, relating to, or being sensory activity having its origin elsewhere than in the special sense organs (as eyes and ears) and conveying information about the state of the body proper and its immediate environment

---

\ə\ abut \ᵊ\ kitten, F table \ər\ further \a\ ash \ā\ ace \ä\ mop, mar \aú\ out \ch\ chin \e\ bet \ē\ easy \g\ go \i\ hit \ī\ ice \j\ job \ŋ\ sing \ō\ go \ò\ law \òi\ boy \th\ thin \th\ the \ü\ loot \ù\ foot \y\ yet \zh\ vision \à, k̩, ⁿ, œ, œ̄, ᵫ, ᵫ̄, ᵊ\ *see* Guide to Pronunciation

so·mato·stat·in \sō-,ma-tə-'sta-t²n\ *n* [*somat-* + L *status* (pp. of *sistere* to halt, cause to stand) + E ¹-*in;* akin to L *stare* to stand — more at STAND] (1973) : a polypeptide neurohormone that is found esp. in the hypothalamus and inhibits the secretion of several other hormones (as growth hormone, insulin, and gastrin)

so·mato·tro·pic hormone \-'trō-pik-\ *n* [*somat-* + -*tropic*] (1938) : GROWTH HORMONE 1

so·mato·tro·pin \-'trō-pən\ *also* **so·mato·tro·phin** \-fən\ *n* [*somato-tropic* + ¹-*in*] (1941) : GROWTH HORMONE 1

so·mato·type \'sō-'ma-tə-,tīp\ *n* (1940) : body type : PHYSIQUE

som·ber *or* **som·bre** \'säm-bər\ *adj* [F *sombre*] (1760) **1** : so shaded as to be dark and gloomy **2 a** : of a serious mien : GRAVE **b** : of a dismal or depressing character : MELANCHOLY **c** : conveying gloomy suggestions or ideas **3** : of a dull or heavy cast or shade : dark colored — **som·ber·ly** *adv* — **som·ber·ness** *n*

som·bre·ro \səm-'brer-(,)ō, säm-\ *n, pl* **-ros** [Sp, fr. *sombra* shade] (1599) : a high=crowned hat of felt or straw with a very wide brim worn esp. in the Southwest and Mexico

sombrero

som·brous \'säm-brəs\ *adj* [F *sombre*] (1730) *archaic* : SOMBER

¹some \'səm, *for 2 without stress*\ *adj* [ME *som,* adj. & pron., fr. OE *sum;* akin to OHG *sum* some, Gk *hamē* somehow, *homos* same — more at SAME] (bef. 12c) **1** : being an unknown, undetermined, or unspecified unit or thing ⟨~ person knocked⟩ **2 a** : being one, a part, or an unspecified number of something (as a class or group) named or implied ⟨~ gems are hard⟩ **b** : being of an unspecified amount or number ⟨give me ~ water⟩ ⟨have ~ apples⟩ **3** : REMARKABLE, STRIKING ⟨that was ~ party⟩ **4** : being at least one — used to indicate that a logical proposition is asserted only of a subclass or certain members of the class denoted by the term which it modifies

²some \'səm\ *pron, sing or pl in constr* (bef. 12c) **1** : one indeterminate quantity, portion, or number as distinguished from the rest **2** : an indefinite additional amount ⟨ran a mile and then ~⟩

³some \'səm, ,səm\ *adv* (bef. 12c) **1** : ABOUT ⟨~ 80 houses⟩ ⟨twenty=*some* people⟩ **2 a** : in some degree : SOMEWHAT ⟨felt ~ better⟩ **b** : to some degree or extent : a little ⟨the cut bled ~⟩ ⟨I need to work on it ~ more⟩ **c** — used as a mild intensive ⟨that's going ~⟩

usage When *some* is used to modify a number, it is almost always a round number ⟨a community of *some* 150,000 inhabitants⟩ but because *some* is slightly more emphatic than *about* or *approximately* it is occas. used with a more exact number in an intensive function ⟨an expert parachutist, he has *some* 115 jumps to his credit —*Current Biog.*⟩. When *some* is used without a number, most commentators feel that *somewhat* is to be preferred. Their advice is an oversimplification, however; only when *some* modifies an adjective, usu. a comparative, will *somewhat* always substitute smoothly. When *some* modifies a verb or adverb, and esp. when it follows a verb, substitution of *somewhat* may prove awkward ⟨Italy forced me to grow up *some* —E. W. Brooke⟩ ⟨I'm not a prude; I've been around *some* in my day —Roy Rogers⟩ ⟨here in Newport, both Southern Cross and Courageous practiced *some* more —W. N. Wallace⟩.

¹-some *adj suffix* [ME -*som,* fr. OE -*sum;* akin to OHG -*sam* -some, OE *sum* some] : characterized by a (specified) thing, quality, state, or action ⟨awesome⟩ ⟨burdensome⟩ ⟨cuddlesome⟩

²-some *n suffix* [ME (northern dial.) -*sum,* fr. ME *sam,* pron., one, some] : group of (so many) members and esp. persons ⟨foursome⟩

³-some *n comb form* [NL -*somat-,* -*soma,* fr. Gk *sōmat-, sōma*] **1** : body ⟨chromosome⟩ **2** : chromosome ⟨monosome⟩

¹some·body \'səm-(,)bə-dē, -,bä-\ *pron* (14c) : one or some person of unspecified or indefinite identity ⟨~ will come in⟩

²somebody *n* (ca. 1566) : a person of position or importance

some·day \'səm-,dā\ *adv* (14c) : at some future time

some·deal \'səm-,dēl\ *adv* (bef. 12c) *archaic* : SOMEWHAT

some·how \'səm-,haù\ *adv* (1664) : in one way or another not known or designated : by some means

some·one \-(,)wən\ *pron* (14c) : some person : SOMEBODY

some·place \-,plās\ *adv* (1880) : SOMEWHERE

som·er·sault \'sə-mər-,sòlt\ *n* [MF *sombresaut* leap, ultim. fr. L *super* over + *saltus* leap, fr. *salire* to jump — more at OVER, SALLY] (ca. 1530) : a leap or roll in which a person turns forward or backward in a complete revolution bringing the feet over the head and finally landing on the feet; *also* : a falling or tumbling head over heels — **somersault** *vi*

som·er·set \-,set\ *n or vi* [by alter.] (1591) : SOMERSAULT

¹some·thing \'səm(p)-thiŋ, *esp in rapid speech or for 2* 'səm-p²m\ *pron* (bef. 12c) **1** : some indeterminate or unspecified thing **2** : a person or thing of consequence **3** : one having more or less the character, qualities, or nature of something different ⟨is ~ of a bore⟩ — **some-thing else** : something or someone special or extraordinary

²something *adv* (13c) **1** : in some degree : SOMEWHAT **2** — used as an intensive giving adverbial force to an adjective ⟨swears ~ awful⟩

¹some·time \'səm-,tīm\ *adv* (14c) **1** *archaic* : in the past : FORMERLY **2** *archaic* : once in a while : OCCASIONALLY **3** : at some time in the future ⟨I'll do it ~⟩ **4** : at some not specified or definitely known point of time ⟨~ last night⟩

²sometime *adj* (14c) **1** : having been formerly : FORMER, LATE **2** : being so occasionally or in only some respects ⟨a ~ . . . father who appears and disappears —Evelyn Shelby⟩

¹some·times \'səm-,tīmz *also* (,)səm-\ *adv* (14c) : at times : now and then : OCCASIONALLY

²sometimes *adj* (1593) : SOMETIME

some·way \'səm-,wā\ *also* **some·ways** \-,wāz\ *adv* (15c) : SOMEHOW

¹some·what \-,(h)wät, -,(h)wət, (,)səm-\ *pron* (13c) : SOMETHING

²somewhat *adv* (13c) : in some degree or measure : SLIGHTLY

some·when \'səm-,(h)wen\ *adv* (1833) : SOMETIME

¹some·where \-,(h)wer, -,(h)war, -,(h)wər\ *adv* (13c) **1** : in, at, from, or to a place unknown or unspecified ⟨mentions it ~⟩ **2** : to a place symbolizing positive accomplishment or progress ⟨now we're getting ~⟩ **3** : in the vicinity of : APPROXIMATELY ⟨~ about nine o'clock⟩

²somewhere *n* (1647) : an undetermined or unnamed place

some·wheres \-,(h)werz, -,(h)warz, -,(h)wərz\ *adv* (1815) : SOMEWHERE

some·whith·er \-,(h)wi-thər\ *adv* (1530) *archaic* : to some place : SOMEWHERE

-somic *adj comb form* [ISV ³-*some* + -*ic*] : having or being a chromosome complement of which one or more but not all members exhibit (such) a degree of reduplication of chromosomes or genomes ⟨monosomic⟩

so·mite \'sō-,mīt\ *n* [ISV, fr. Gk *sōma* body] (1869) : one of the longitudinal series of segments into which the body of many animals (as articulate animals and vertebrates) is divided : METAMERE

som·me·lier \,sə-məl-'yā\ *n, pl* **sommeliers** \-'yā(z)\ [F, fr. MF, court official charged with transportation of supplies, pack animal driver, fr. OProv *saumalier* pack animal driver, fr. *sauma* pack animal, load of a pack animal, fr. LL *sagma* packsaddle — more at SUMPTER] (1829) : a waiter in a restaurant who has charge of wines and their service : a wine steward

somnambul- *comb form* [NL, fr. *somnambulus* somnambulist, fr. L *somnus* sleep + -*ambulus* (as in *funambulus* funambulist) — more at SOMNOLENT] : somnambulism : somnambulist ⟨*somnambulant*⟩

som·nam·bu·lant \säm-'nam-byə-lənt\ *adj* (1866) : walking or addicted to walking while asleep

som·nam·bu·late \-,lāt\ *vi* **-lat·ed; -lat·ing** (1833) : to walk when asleep — **som·nam·bu·la·tion** \(,)säm-,nam-byə-'lā-shən\ *n*

som·nam·bu·lism \säm-'nam-byə-,li-zəm\ *n* (1797) **1** : an abnormal condition of sleep in which motor acts (as walking) are performed **2** : actions characteristic of somnambulism — **som·nam·bu·list** \-list\ *n* — **som·nam·bu·lis·tic** \(,)säm-,nam-byə-'lis-tik\ *adj* — **som·nam-bu·lis·ti·cal·ly** \-ti-k(ə-)lē\ *adv*

som·ni·fa·cient \,säm-nə-'fā-shənt\ *adj* [L *somnus* sleep + E -*facient*] (ca. 1890) : HYPNOTIC 1 — **somnifacient** *n*

som·nif·er·ous \säm-'ni-f(ə-)rəs\ *adj* [L *somnifer* somniferous, fr. *somnus* + -*fer* -ferous] (1602) : SOPORIFIC

som·no·lence \'säm-nə-lən(t)s\ *n* (14c) : the quality or state of being drowsy : SLEEPINESS

som·no·lent \-lənt\ *adj* [ME *sompnolent,* fr. MF, fr. L *somnolentus,* fr. *somnus* sleep; akin to OE *swefn* sleep, Gk *hypnos*] (15c) **1** : of a kind likely to induce sleep ⟨a ~ sermon⟩ **2 a** : inclined to or heavy with sleep : DROWSY **b** : SLEEPY 2 ⟨~ rivers⟩ — **som·no·lent·ly** *adv*

¹so much *adv* (13c) : by the amount indicated or suggested ⟨if they lose their way, *so much* the better for us⟩

²so much *pron* (14c) **1** : something (as an amount or price) unspecified or undetermined ⟨charge *so much* a mile⟩ **2** : all that can be or is to be said or done ⟨*so much* for the history of the case⟩

³so much *adj* (1557) — used as an intensive ⟨the house burned like *so much* paper⟩ ⟨sounded like *so much* nonsense⟩

so much as *adv* (15c) : EVEN 3d

son \'sən\ *n* [ME *sone,* fr. OE *sunu;* akin to OHG *sun* son, Gk *hyios*] (bef. 12c) **1 a** : a male offspring esp. of human beings **b** : a male adopted child **c** : a male descendant **2** *cap* : the second person of the Trinity **3** : a person closely associated with or deriving from a formative agent (as a nation, school, or race) — **son·hood** \-,hùd\ *n*

son- *or* **sono-** *comb form* [L *sonus* sound] : sound ⟨sonic⟩ ⟨sonogram⟩

so·nant \'sō-nənt\ *adj* [L *sonant-, sonans,* prp. of *sonare* to sound — more at SOUND] (1846) **1** : VOICED **2** : SYLLABIC 1a — **sonant** *n*

so·nar \'sō-,när\ *n* [*sound navigation ranging*] (1945) : a method or device for detecting and locating objects esp. underwater by means of sound waves sent out to be reflected by the objects; *also* : a device for detecting the presence of a vessel (as a submarine) by the sound it emits in water

so·na·ta \sə-'nä-tə\ *n* [It, fr. *sonare* to sound, fr. L] (1694) : an instrumental musical composition typically of three or four movements in contrasting forms and keys

sonata form *n* (1873) : a musical form that consists basically of an exposition, a development, and a recapitulation and that is used esp. for the first movement of a sonata

son·a·ti·na \,sä-nə-'tē-nə\ *n* [It, dim. of *sonata*] (ca. 1801) : a short usu. simplified sonata

sonde \'sänd\ *n* [F, lit., sounding line — more at SOUND] (1901) : any of various devices for testing physical conditions (as at high altitudes, below the earth's surface, or inside the body)

sone \'sōn\ *n* [ISV, fr. L *sonus* sound — more at SOUND] (1948) : a subjective unit of loudness for an average listener equal to the loudness of a 1000-hertz sound that has an intensity 40 decibels above the listener's own threshold of hearing

son et lu·mière \,sōⁿ-(n)ä-lüm-'yer\ *n* [F, lit., sound and light] (1957) : an outdoor spectacle at an historic site consisting of recorded narration with light and sound effects

song \'sòŋ\ *n* [ME, fr. OE *sang;* akin to OE *singan* to sing] (bef. 12c) **1** : the act or art of singing **2** : poetical composition **3 a** : a short musical composition of words and music **b** : a collection of such compositions **4** : a distinctive or characteristic sound or series of sounds (as of a bird or insect) **5 a** : a melody for a lyric poem or ballad **b** : a poem easily set to music **6 a** : a habitual or characteristic manner **b** : a violent, abusive, or noisy reaction ⟨put up quite a ~⟩ **7** : a small amount ⟨sold for a ~⟩ — **song·like** \-,līk\ *adj*

song and dance *n* (1872) **1** : a theatrical performance (as a vaudeville performance) combining singing and dancing **2** : a long and often familiar statement or explanation that is usu. not true or pertinent

song·bird \'sòŋ-,bərd\ *n* (1774) **1 a** : a bird that utters a succession of musical tones **b** : an oscine bird **2** : a female singer

song·book \-'bùk\ *n* (bef. 12c) : a collection of songs; *specif* : a book containing vocal music (as hymns)

song cycle *n* (1899) : a group of related songs designed to form a musical entity

song·fest \'sòŋ-,fest\ *n* (ca. 1912) : an informal session of group singing of popular or folk songs

song·ful \'sòŋ-fəl\ *adj* (14c) : given to or suggestive of singing : MELODIOUS — **song·ful·ly** \-fə-lē\ *adv* — **song·ful·ness** *n*

song·less \-ləs\ *adj* (ca. 1805) : lacking in, incapable of, or not given to song — **song·less·ly** *adv*

Song of Sol·o·mon \'sä-lə-mən\ *n* [fr. the opening verse: "The song of songs, which is Solomon's"] : a collection of love poems forming a book in the Protestant canon of the Old Testament — see BIBLE table

Song of Songs [trans. of Heb *shīr hashshīrīm*] : a collection of love poems forming a book in the canonical Jewish Scriptures and in the Roman Catholic canon of the Old Testament and corresponding to the Song of Solomon in the Protestant canon of the Old Testament — see BIBLE table

song-smith \'sȯŋ-,smith\ *n* (1795) : a composer of songs

song sparrow *n* (1810) : a common No. American sparrow (*Melospiza melodia*) that is brownish above and white below with brownish streaks on the breast and that is noted for its melodious song

song-ster \'sȯŋ(k)-stər\ *n* (14c) **1** : one that sings with skill **2** : SONG-BOOK

song-stress \'sȯŋ(k)-strəs\ *n* (1703) : a female singer

song thrush *n* (1668) : an Old World thrush (*Turdus philomelos*) that is largely brown above with brown-spotted white underparts — called also *mavis, throstle*

song-writ-er \'sȯŋ-,rī-tər\ *n* (1821) : a person who composes words or music or both esp. for popular songs — **song-writ-ing** \-,rī-tiŋ\ *n*

son-ic \'sä-nik\ *adj* (1923) **1** : utilizing, produced by, or relating to sound waves (~ altimeter); *broadly* : of or involving sound (~ pollution) **2** : having a frequency within the audibility range of the human ear — used of waves and vibrations **3** : of, relating to, or being the speed of sound in air or about 761 miles per hour (1224 kilometers per hour) at sea level at 59°F (15°C) **4** : capable of uttering sounds — **son-i-cal-ly** \-ni-k(ə-)lē\ *adv*

son-i-cate \'sä-nə-,kāt\ *vt* **-cat-ed; -cat-ing** [*sonic* + [4]-*ate*] (1960) : to disrupt (as bacteria) by treatment with high-frequency sound waves — **son-i-ca-tion** \,sä-nə-'kā-shən\ *n*

sonic barrier *n* (1946) : SOUND BARRIER

sonic boom *n* (1952) : a sound resembling an explosion produced when a shock wave formed at the nose of an aircraft traveling at supersonic speed reaches the ground — called also *sonic bang*

son–in–law \'sən-ən-,lȯ\ *n, pl* **sons–in–law** (14c) : the husband of one's daughter

son-less \'sən-ləs\ *adj* (14c) : not possessing or never having had a son

son-ly \-lē\ *adj* (15c) : FILIAL

son-net \'sä-nət\ *n* [It *sonetto*, fr. OProv *sonet* little song, fr. *son* sound, song, fr. L *sonus* sound] (1557) : a fixed verse form of Italian origin consisting of fourteen lines that are typically five-foot iambics rhyming according to a prescribed scheme; *also* : a poem in this pattern

son-ne-teer \,sä-nə-'tir\ *n* (1665) **1** : a composer of sonnets **2** : a minor or insignificant poet — **son-ne-teer-ing** \-iŋ\ *n*

sonnet sequence *n* (1881) : a series of sonnets often having a unifying theme

son-ny \'sə-nē\ *n* (1850) : a young boy — usu. used in address

so-no-buoy \'sä-nə-,bȯi, -,bü-ē\ *n* (1945) : a buoy equipped for detecting underwater sounds and transmitting them by radio

son of a bitch \'sən-ə-və-,bich *also* 'səm-,bich; *as an interj* ,sən-ə-və-'bich\ *n, pl* **sons of bitch-es** \,sən-zə-'bi-chəz\ (1671) : BASTARD 2 — sometimes considered vulgar; sometimes used interjectionally to express surprise or disappointment

son of a gun \'sən-ə-və-,gən; *as an interj* ,sən-ə-və-'gən\ *n, pl* **sons of guns** (1708) — usu. used as a mild or euphemistic alternative to *son of a bitch*; sometimes used interjectionally to express surprise or disappointment

son of God (14c) **1** *often cap S* : a superhuman or divine being (as an angel) **2** *cap S* : MESSIAH 1 **3** : a person established in the love of God by divine promise

son of man (14c) **1** : a human being **2** *often cap S* : God's messiah destined to preside over the final judgment of mankind

sono-gram \'sä-nə-,gram\ *n* (1956) : an image produced by ultrasound

so-nog-ra-phy \sō-'nä-grə-fē\ *n* (1977) : ULTRASOUND 2

so-nor-i-ty \sə-'nȯr-ə-tē, -'när-\ *n, pl* **-ties** (ca. 1623) **1** : the quality or state of being sonorous : RESONANCE **2** : a sonorous tone or speech

so-no-rous \sə-'nȯr-əs, -'nȯr-; 'sä-nə-rəs\ *adj* [L *sonorus*; akin to L *sonus* sound] (1611) **1** : producing sound (as when struck) **2** : full or loud in sound **3** : imposing or impressive in effect or style **4** : having a high or an indicated degree of sonority (~ sounds such as \ä\ and \ȯ\) — **so-no-rous-ly** *adv* — **so-no-rous-ness** *n*

son-ship \'sən-,ship\ *n* (1587) : the relationship of son to father

son-sy *or* **son-sie** \'sän(t)-sē\ *adj* [Sc *sons* health] (1725) *chiefly dial* : BUXOM, COMELY

soon \'sün, *esp* NewEng 'sȯn\ *adv* [ME *soone*, fr. OE *sōna*; akin to OHG *sān* immediately] (bef. 12c) **1 a** *obs* : at once : IMMEDIATELY **b** : before long : without undue time lapse (~ after sunrise) **2** : in a prompt manner : SPEEDILY (as ~ as possible) (the ~er the better) **3** *archaic* : before the usual time **4** : in agreement with one's choice or preference : WILLINGLY (I'd just as ~ walk as drive)

soon-er \'sü-nər\ *n* [*sooner*, compar. of *soon*] (1890) **1** : a person settling on land in the early West before its official opening to settlement in order to gain the prior claim allowed by law to the first settler after official opening **2** *cap* : a native or resident of Oklahoma — used as a nickname

sooner or later *adv* (1577) : at some uncertain future time : SOMETIME

[1]**soot** \'sut, 'sȯt, 'süt\ *n* [ME, fr. OE *sōt*; akin to OIr *suide* soot, OE *sittan* to sit] (bef. 12c) : a black substance formed by combustion or separated from fuel during combustion, rising in fine particles, and adhering to the sides of the chimney or pipe conveying the smoke; *esp* : the fine powder consisting chiefly of carbon that colors smoke

[2]**soot** *vt* (1602) : to coat or cover with soot

[1]**sooth** \'süth\ *adj* [ME, fr. OE *sōth*; akin to OHG *sand* true, L *esse* to be] (bef. 12c) **1** *archaic* : TRUE **2** *archaic* : SOFT, SWEET

[2]**sooth** *n* (bef. 12c) **1** : TRUTH, REALITY **2** *obs* : BLANDISHMENT

soothe \'süth\ *vb* **soothed; sooth-ing** [ME *sothen* to verify, fr. OE *sōthian*, fr. *sōth*] *vt* (1697) **1** : to please by or as if by attention or concern : PLACATE **2** : RELIEVE, ALLEVIATE **3** : to bring comfort, solace, or reassurance to ~ *vi* : to bring peace, composure, or quietude — **sooth-er** *n*

sooth-fast \'süth-,fast\ *adj* (bef. 12c) **1** *archaic* : TRUE **2** *archaic* : TRUTHFUL

sooth-ing \'sü-thiŋ\ *adj* (1749) : tending to soothe; *also* : having a sedative effect (~ syrup) — **sooth-ing-ly** \-thiŋ-lē\ *adv* — **sooth-ing-ness** *n*

sooth-ly \'süth-lē\ *adv* (bef. 12c) *archaic* : in truth : TRULY

sooth-say-er \-,sā-ər, -,se(-ə)r\ *n* (14c) : a person who predicts the future by magical, intuitive, or more rational means : PROGNOSTICATOR

sooth-say-ing \-,sā-iŋ\ *n* (15c) **1** : the act of foretelling events **2** : PREDICTION, PROPHECY — **sooth-say** \-,sā\ *vi*

sooty \'su-tē, 'sȯ-, 'sü-\ *adj* **soot-i-er; -est** (13c) **1 a** : of, relating to, or producing soot **b** : soiled with soot **2** : of the color of soot — **soot-i-ly** \-t[e]l-ē\ *adv* — **soot-i-ness** \-tē-nəs\ *n*

sooty mold *n* (1901) : a dark growth of fungus mycelium growing in insect honeydew on plants; *also* : a fungus producing such growth

sooty tern *n* (1785) : a widely distributed tern (*Sterna fuscata*) of tropical oceans that is blackish above and white below — called also *wideawake*

[1]**sop** \'säp\ *n* [ME *soppe*, fr. OE *sopp*; akin to OE *sūpan* to swallow — more at SUP] (bef. 12c) **1** *chiefly dial* : a piece of food dipped or steeped in a liquid **2** : a conciliatory or propitiatory bribe, gift, or gesture

[2]**sop** *vt* **sopped; sop-ping** (ca. 1529) **1 a** : to steep or dip in or as if in liquid **b** : to wet thoroughly : SOAK **2** : MOP a **3** : to give a bribe or conciliatory gift to

so-pai-pil-la \,sō-pī-'pē-yə, -'pēl-yə\ *or* **so-pa-pil-la** \'sō-pə-\ *n* [AmerSp *sopaipilla*, dim. of Sp *sopaipa* fritter soaked in honey, fr. *sopa* food soaked in milk, of Gmc origin; akin to OE *sūpan* to swallow] (ca. 1940) : a square of deep-fried dough often sweetened and eaten as dessert

soph-ism \'sä-,fi-zəm\ *n* (15c) **1** : an argument apparently correct in form but actually invalid; *esp* : such an argument used to deceive **2** : SOPHISTRY 1

soph-ist \'sä-fist\ *n* [L *sophista*, fr. Gk *sophistēs*, lit., expert, wise man, fr. *sophizesthai* to become wise, deceive, fr. *sophos* clever, wise] (1542) **1** *cap* : any of a class of ancient Greek teachers of rhetoric, philosophy, and the art of successful living prominent about the middle of the 5th century B.C. for their adroit subtle and allegedly often specious reasoning **2** : PHILOSOPHER, THINKER **3** : a captious or fallacious reasoner

so-phis-tic \sä-'fis-tik, sə-\ *or* **so-phis-ti-cal** \-ti-kəl\ *adj* (15c) **1** : of or relating to sophists, sophistry, or the ancient Sophists (~ rhetoric) (~ subtleties) **2** : plausible but fallacious (~ reasoning) — **so-phis-ti-cal-ly** \-ti-k(ə-)lē\ *adv*

[1]**so-phis-ti-cate** \sə-'fis-tə-,kāt\ *vt* **-cat-ed; -cat-ing** [ME, fr. ML *sophisticatus*, pp. of *sophisticare*, fr. L *sophisticus* sophistic, fr. Gk *sophistikos*, fr. *sophistēs* sophist] (15c) **1** : to alter deceptively; *esp* : ADULTERATE **2** : to deprive of genuineness, naturalness, or simplicity; *esp* : to deprive of naïveté and make worldly-wise : DISILLUSION **3** : to make complicated or complex

[2]**so-phis-ti-cate** \-ti-kət, -tə-,kāt\ *n* (1923) : a sophisticated person

so-phis-ti-cat-ed \-tə-,kā-təd\ *adj* [ML *sophisticatus*] (1601) **1** : not in a natural, pure, or original state : ADULTERATED (a ~ oil) **2** : deprived of native or original simplicity: as **a** : highly complicated or developed : COMPLEX (~ electronic devices) **b** : having a refined knowledge of the ways of the world cultivated esp. through wide experience (a ~ lady) **3** : devoid of grossness: as **a** : finely experienced and aware (a ~ columnist) **b** : intellectually appealing (a ~ novel) — **so-phis-ti-cat-ed-ly** *adv*

syn SOPHISTICATED, WORLDLY-WISE, BLASÉ mean experienced in the ways of the world. SOPHISTICATED often implies refinement, urbanity, cleverness, and cultivation (guests at her salon were usually rich and *sophisticated*). WORLDLY-WISE suggests a close and practical knowledge of the affairs and manners of society and an inclination toward materialism (a *worldly-wise* woman with a philosophy of personal independence). BLASÉ implies a lack of responsiveness to common joys as a result of a real or affected surfeit of experience and cultivation (*blasé* travelers who claimed to have been everywhere).

so-phis-ti-ca-tion \sə-,fis-tə-'kā-shən\ *n* (15c) **1 a** : the use of sophistry : sophistic reasoning **b** : SOPHISM, QUIBBLE **2** : the process of making impure or weak : ADULTERATION **3** : the process or result of becoming cultured, knowledgeable, or disillusioned; *esp* : CULTIVATION, URBANITY **4** : the process or result of becoming more complex, developed, or subtle

soph-ist-ry \'sä-fi-strē\ *n* (14c) **1** : subtly deceptive reasoning or argumentation **2** : SOPHISM 1

soph-o-more \'säf-,mȯr, -,mȯr *also* 'sȯf- *or* 'sä-fə- *or* 'sȯ-fə-\ *n* [perh. fr. Gk *sophos* wise + *mōros* foolish] (1688) : a student in the second year at college or a 4-year secondary school

soph-o-mor-ic \,säf-'mȯr-ik, -'mȯr-, -'mär- *also* ,sȯf- *or* ,sä-fə- *or* ,sȯ-fə-\ *adj* (1813) **1** : conceited and overconfident of knowledge but poorly informed and immature **2** : of, relating to, or characteristic of a sophomore (a ~ prank)

So-pho-ni-as \,sä-fə-'nī-əs, ,sō-\ *n* [LL, fr. Gk, fr. Heb *Sěphanyāh*] : ZEPHANIAH

so-phy \'sō-fē\ *n* [Per *Safī*] (1534) *archaic* : a sovereign of Persia

-sophy *n comb form* [ME -*sophie*, fr. OF, fr. L -*sophia*, fr. Gk, fr. *sophia* wisdom, fr. *sophos*] : knowledge : wisdom : science (anthropo*sophy*)

so-pite \sō-'pīt\ *vt* **so-pit-ed; so-pit-ing** [L *sopitus*, pp. of *sopire* to put to sleep; akin to L *sopor* deep sleep] (1542) **1** *archaic* : to put to sleep : LULL **2** *archaic* : to put an end to (as a claim) : SETTLE

sop-o-rif-er-ous \,sä-pə-'ri-f(ə-)rəs\ *adj* [L *soporifer* soporiferous, fr. *sopor* + -*fer* -ferous] (1590) : SOPORIFIC — **sop-o-rif-er-ous-ness** *n*

[1]**sop-o-rif-ic** \-'ri-fik\ *adj* [prob. fr. F *soporifique*, fr. L *sopor* deep sleep; akin to L *somnus* sleep — more at SOMNOLENT] (1665) **1 a** : causing or tending to cause sleep **b** : tending to dull awareness or alertness **2** : of, relating to, or marked by sleepiness or lethargy

[2]**soporific** *n* (ca. 1727) : a soporific agent; *specif* : HYPNOTIC 1

sop-ping \'sä-piŋ\ *adj* (1877) : wet through : SOAKING

sop-py \'sä-pē\ *adj* **sop-pi-er; -est** (1823) **1 a** : soaked through : SATURATED **b** : very wet **2** : SENTIMENTAL, MAWKISH — **sop-pi-ness** \-nəs\ *n*

\ə\ abut \ᵊ\ kitten, F table \ər\ further \a\ ash \ā\ ace \ä\ mop, mar \au̇\ out \ch\ chin \e\ bet \ē\ easy \g\ go \i\ hit \ī\ ice \j\ job \ŋ\ sing \ō\ go \ȯ\ law \ȯi\ boy \th\ thin \t͟h\ the \ü\ loot \u̇\ foot \y\ yet \zh\ vision \à, k̲, ⁿ, œ, œ̄, ue, ᵫ, ᵊ\ *see* Guide to Pronunciation

so·pra·ni·no \,sō-prə-'nē-(,)nō, ,sä-\ n, pl **-nos** [It, dim. of *soprano*] (1905) : a musical instrument (as a recorder or saxophone) higher in pitch than the soprano

¹so·pra·no \sə-'pra-(,)nō, -'prä-\ adj [It, adj. & n., fr. *sopra* above, fr. L *supra* — more at SUPRA-] (1730) : relating to or having the range or part of a soprano

²soprano n, pl **-nos** (1738) **1** : the highest singing voice of women, boys, or castrati; *also* : a person having this voice **2** : the highest voice part in a 4-part chorus **3** : a member of a family of instruments having the highest range

so·ra \'sōr-ə, 'sȯr-\ n [origin unknown] (1705) : a small short-billed No. American rail (*Porzana carolina*) common in marshes

sorb \'sȯrb\ vt [back-formation fr. *absorb* & *adsorb*] (1909) : to take up and hold by either adsorption or absorption — **sorb·abil·i·ty** \,sȯr-bə-'bi-lə-tē\ n — **sorb·able** \'sȯr-bə-bəl\ adj

Sorb \'sȯrb\ n [G *Sorbe*, fr. Sorbian *serbje*] (1843) **1** : WEND **2** : WENDISH — **Sor·bi·an** \'sȯr-bē-ən\ adj or n

sor·bate \'sȯr-,bāt, 'sȯr-bət\ n (ca. 1823) : a salt or ester of sorbic acid — compare POTASSIUM SORBATE

sor·bent \'sȯr-bənt\ n [L *sorbent-, sorbens*, prp. of *sorbēre* to suck up — more at ABSORB] (ca. 1856) : a substance that sorbs

sor·bet \sȯr-'bā also 'sȯr-bət\ n [MF, fr. OIt *sorbetto*, fr. Turk *şerbet* — more at SHERBET] (1864) : a fruit-flavored ice served as a dessert or between courses as a palate refresher

sor·bic acid \'sȯr-bik-\ n [*sorb* fruit of the service or related trees, fr. F *sorbe*, fr. L *sorbum*] (1815) : a crystalline acid $C_6H_8O_2$ obtained from the unripe fruits of the mountain ash or synthesized and used esp. as a fungicide and food preservative

sor·bi·tol \'sȯr-bə-,tȯl, -,tōl\ n [*sorb* fruit of the service or related trees + *-itol*] (1895) : a faintly sweet alcohol $C_6H_{14}O_6$ that occurs in some fruits, is made synthetically, and is used esp. as a humectant and softener and in making ascorbic acid

sor·cer·er \'sȯr-sə-rər, 'sȯrs-rər\ n (15c) : a person who practices sorcery : WIZARD

sor·cer·ess \-rəs\ n (14c) : a woman who is a sorcerer

sor·cer·ous \-rəs\ adj (1546) : of or relating to sorcery : MAGICAL

sor·cery \-rē\ n [ME *sorcerie*, fr. MF, fr. *sorcier* sorcerer, fr. (assumed) VL *sortiarius*, fr. L *sort-, sors* chance, lot — more at SERIES] (14c) **1** : the use of power gained from the assistance or control of evil spirits esp. for divining : NECROMANCY **2** : MAGIC 2a

sor·did \'sȯr-dəd\ adj [L *sordidus*, fr. *sordes* dirt — more at SWART] (1609) **1** : marked by baseness or grossness : VILE 〈~ motives〉 **2 a** : DIRTY, FILTHY **b** : WRETCHED, SQUALID **3** : meanly avaricious : COVETOUS **4** : of a dull or muddy color *syn* see MEAN — **sor·did·ly** adv — **sor·did·ness** n

sor·di·no \sȯr-'dē-(,)nō\ n, pl **-di·ni** \-(,)nē\ [It, fr. *sordo* silent, fr. L *surdus*] (ca. 1801) : MUTE 3

¹sore \'sōr, 'sȯr\ adj **sor·er; sor·est** [ME *sor*, fr. OE *sār*; akin to OHG *sēr* sore and prob. to OIr *saeth* distress] (bef. 12c) **1 a** : causing pain or distress **b** : painfully sensitive : TENDER 〈~ muscles〉 **c** : hurt or inflamed so as to be or seem painful 〈~ runny eyes〉 〈a dog limping on a ~ leg〉 **2** : attended by difficulties, hardship, or exertion **3** : ANGRY, IRKED 〈a ~ loser〉 — **sore·ness** n

²sore n (bef. 12c) **1** : a localized sore spot on the body; *esp* : one (as an ulcer) with the tissues ruptured or abraded and usu. with infection **2** : a source of pain or vexation : AFFLICTION

³sore adv (bef. 12c) : SORELY

sore·head \'sōr-,hed, 'sȯr-\ n (1848) : a person easily angered or disgruntled — **sorehead** or **sore·head·ed** \-'he-dəd\ adj

sore·ly \'sōr-lē, 'sȯr-\ adv (bef. 12c) **1** : in a sore manner : PAINFULLY **2** : VERY, EXTREMELY 〈~ needed changes〉

sore throat n (1686) : pain in the throat due to inflammation of the fauces and pharynx

sor·ghum \'sȯr-gəm\ n [NL, fr. It *sorgo*, fr. (assumed) VL *Syricum* (*granum*), lit., Syrian grain] (1597) **1** : any of an economically important genus (*Sorghum*) of Old World tropical grasses similar to Indian corn in habit but with the spikelets in pairs on a hairy rachis; *esp* : any of various cultivars (as grain sorghum or sorgo) derived from a wild form (*S. bicolor* syn. *S. vulgare*) **2** : syrup from the juice of a sorgo that resembles cane syrup **3** : something cloyingly sentimental

sor·go \'sȯr-(,)gō\ n [It] (ca. 1760) : a sorghum cultivated primarily for the sweet juice in its stems from which sugar and syrup are made but also used for fodder and silage — called also *sweet sorghum*

so·ri·tes \sə-'rī-(,)tēz\ n, pl **sorites** [L, fr. Gk *sōritēs*, fr. *sōros* heap] (1551) : an argument consisting of propositions so arranged that the predicate of any one forms the subject of the next and the conclusion unites the subject of the first proposition with the predicate of the last

Sor·op·ti·mist \sə-'räp-tə-mist, sȯ-\ n [*Soroptimist* (Club)] (1924) : a member of a service club composed of professional women and women business executives

so·ro·ral \sə-'rōr-əl, -'rȯr-\ adj [L *soror* sister — more at SISTER] (1858) : of, relating to, or characteristic of a sister : SISTERLY

so·ro·rate \sə-'rōr-ət, -'rȯr-\ n [L *soror*] (1910) : the marriage of one man to two or more sisters usu. successively and after the first wife has been found to be barren or after her death

so·ror·i·ty \sə-'rȯr-ə-tē, -'rär-\ n, pl **-ties** [ML *sororitas* sisterhood, fr. L *soror* sister] (1900) : a club of women; *specif* : a women's student organization (as at a college) that is formed chiefly for social purposes and has a name consisting of Greek letters

sorp·tion \'sȯrp-shən\ n [back-formation fr. *absorption* & *adsorption*] (1909) : the process of sorbing : the state of being sorbed — **sorp·tive** \'sȯrp-tiv\ adj

¹sor·rel \'sȯr-əl, 'sär-\ n [ME *sorelle*, fr. MF *sorel*, n. & adj., fr. *sor* reddish brown] (15c) **1** : a sorrel-colored animal; *esp* : a light bright chestnut horse often with white mane and tail — compare ¹CHESTNUT 4, ²BAY 1 **2** : a brownish orange to light brown

²sorrel n [ME *sorel*, fr. MF *surele*, fr. OF, fr. *sur* sour, of Gmc origin; akin to OHG *sūr* sour — more at SOUR] (15c) : any of various plants or plant parts with sour juice: as **a** : any of various docks (as *Rumex*

acetosa and *R. acetosella*); *also* : the leaves used as a potherb **b** : WOOD SORREL

sorrel tree n (1687) : SOURWOOD

¹sor·row \'sär-(,)ō, 'sȯr-\ n [ME *sorow*, fr. OE *sorg*; akin to OHG *sorga* sorrow] (bef. 12c) **1 a** : deep distress, sadness, or regret esp. for the loss of someone or something loved **b** : resultant unhappy or unpleasant state 〈to his ~ he lost his temper〉 **2** : a cause of grief or sadness **3** : a display of grief or sadness

syn SORROW, GRIEF, ANGUISH, WOE, REGRET mean distress of mind. SORROW implies a sense of loss or a sense of guilt and remorse 〈a family united in *sorrow* upon the patriarch's death〉. GRIEF implies poignant sorrow for an immediate cause 〈the inexpressible *grief* of the bereaved parents〉. ANGUISH suggests torturing grief or dread 〈the *anguish* felt by the parents of the kidnapped child〉. WOE is deep or inconsolable grief or misery 〈cries of *woe* echoed throughout the bombed city〉. REGRET implies pain caused by deep disappointment, fruitless longing, or unavailing remorse 〈nagging *regret* for missed opportunities〉.

²sorrow vi (bef. 12c) : to feel or express sorrow — **sor·row·er** \'sär-ə-wər, 'sȯr-\ n

sor·row·ful \-ō-fəl, -ə-fəl\ adj (bef. 12c) **1** : full of or marked by sorrow **2** : expressive of or inducing sorrow — **sor·row·ful·ly** \-f(ə-)lē\ adv — **sor·row·ful·ness** \-fəl-nəs\ n

sor·ry \'sär-ē, 'sȯr-\ adj **sor·ri·er; -est** [ME *sory*, fr. OE *sārig*, fr. *sār* sore] (bef. 12c) **1** : feeling sorrow, regret, or penitence **2** : MOURNFUL, SAD **3** : inspiring sorrow, pity, scorn, or ridicule : CONTEMPTIBLE — **sor·ri·ly** \-ə-lē\ adv — **sor·ri·ness** \-ē-nəs\ n

¹sort \'sȯrt\ n [ME, fr. MF *sorte*, prob. fr. ML *sort-, sors*, fr. L, chance, lot — more at SERIES] (14c) **1 a** : a group set up on the basis of any characteristic in common : CLASS, KIND **b** : an instance of a kind 〈a ~ of black Paul Bunyan, towering 6'10" —Jack Olsen〉 **c** : PERSON, INDIVIDUAL 〈he's not a bad ~〉 **2** *archaic* : GROUP, COMPANY **3 a** : method or manner of acting : WAY, MANNER **b** : CHARACTER, NATURE 〈people of an evil ~〉 **4 a** : a letter or character that is one element of a font **b** : a character or piece of type that is not part of a regular font **5** : an instance of sorting 〈a numeric ~ of a data file〉 *syn* see TYPE — **after a sort** : in a rough or haphazard way — **of sorts** or **of a sort** : of an inconsequential or mediocre quality 〈a poet *of sorts*〉 — **out of sorts** **1** : somewhat ill **2** : GROUCHY, IRRITABLE

²sort vt (14c) **1 a** : to put in a certain place or rank according to kind, class, or nature 〈~ apples〉 〈~ mail〉 **b** : to arrange according to characteristics : CLASSIFY 〈~ out colors〉 **2** *chiefly Scot* : to put to rights : put in order **3 a** : to examine in order to clarify 〈~ing out his problems〉 **b** : to free of confusion : CLARIFY 〈waited until things ~ed themselves out〉 ~ vi **1** : to join or associate with others esp. of the same kind 〈~ with thieves〉 **2** : SUIT, AGREE — **sort·able** \'sȯr-tə-bəl\ adj — **sort·er** n

sor·tie \'sȯr-tē, sȯr-'tē\ n [F, fr. MF, fr. *sortir* to escape] (1778) **1** : a sudden issuing of troops from a defensive position against the enemy **2** : one mission or attack by a single plane **3** : FORAY, RAID — **sortie** vi

sor·ti·lege \'sȯr-t⁹l-ij, -,ej\ n [ME, fr. ML *sortilegium*, fr. L *sortilegus* foretelling, fr. *sort-, sors* lot + *-i-* + *legere* to gather — more at LEGEND] (14c) **1** : divination by lots **2** : SORCERY

sor·ti·tion \sȯr-'ti-shən\ n [L *sortition-, sortitio*, fr. *sortiri* to cast or draw lots, fr. *sort-, sors* lot] (1597) : the act or an instance of casting lots

sort of \'sȯr-dəv, -dər\ adv (1790) : to a moderate degree : RATHER

so·rus \'sōr-əs, 'sȯr-\ n, pl **so·ri** \'sōr-,ī, 'sȯr-, -,ē\ [NL, fr. Gk *sōros* heap] (1832) : a cluster of plant reproductive bodies: as **a** : one of the dots on the underside of a fertile fern frond consisting of a cluster of sporangia **b** : a mass of spores bursting through the epidermis of the host plant of a parasitic fungus **c** : a cluster of gemmae on the thallus of a lichen

SOS \,es-(,)ō-'es\ n (1910) **1** : an internationally recognized signal of distress in radio code · · · · · · · · · used esp. by ships calling for help **2** : a call or request for help or rescue

¹so–so \'sō-'sō\ adv (ca. 1530) : moderately well : TOLERABLY, PASSABLY

²so–so adj (1542) : neither very good nor very bad : MIDDLING

¹so·ste·nu·to \,sōs-tə-'nü-(,)tō, ,sȯs-\ adj or adv [It, fr. pp. of *sostenere* to sustain, fr. L *sustinēre*] (ca. 1724) : sustained to or beyond the note's full value — used as a direction in music

²sostenuto n (1757) : a movement or passage whose notes are markedly prolonged

sot \'sät\ n [ME, fool, fr. OE *sott*] (1592) : a habitual drunkard

so·te·ri·ol·o·gy \sō-,tir-ē-'ä-lə-jē\ n [Gk *sōtērion* salvation (fr. *sōtēr* savior, preserver) + E *-logy* — more at CREOSOTE] (ca. 1774) : theology dealing with salvation esp. as effected by Jesus Christ — **so·te·ri·o·log·i·cal** \-ē-ə-'lä-ji-kəl\ adj

so that conj (bef. 12c) : THAT 2a(1)

So·tho \'sō-(,)tō\ n (1928) **1** : any one of the Sotho languages and esp. Sesotho **2** : a group of closely related Bantu languages of Lesotho, Botswana, and northern So. Africa

so·tol \'sō-,tōl\ n [AmerSp, fr. Nahuatl *zōtōlin* palm tree] (1881) : any of several plants (genus *Dasylirion*) of the agave family of the southwestern U.S. and Mexico that resemble a yucca

sot·tish \'sä-tish\ adj (1583) : resembling a sot : DRUNKEN; *also* : DOLTISH, STUPID — **sot·tish·ly** adv — **sot·tish·ness** n

sot·to vo·ce \,sä-tō-'vō-chē\ adv or adj [It *sottovoce*, lit., under the voice] (1737) **1** : under the breath : in an undertone; *also* : in a private manner **2** : very softly — used as a direction in music

sou \'sü\ n, pl **sous** \'süz\ [F, fr. OF *sol*, fr. LL *solidus* solidus] (1814) **1** : ²SOL **2** : a 5-centime piece

sou·bise \sü-'bēz\ n [F, fr. Charles de Rohan, Prince de *Soubise* †1787 Fr. nobleman] (1822) : a garnish or white sauce containing onions or onion purée

sou·brette \sü-'bret\ n [F, fr. Prov *soubreto*, fem. of *soubret* coy, fr. *soubra* to surmount, exceed, fr. L *superare* — more at INSUPERABLE] (1753) **1 a** : a coquettish maid or frivolous young woman in comedies **b** : an actress who plays such a part **2** : a soprano who sings supporting roles in comic opera

sou·bri·quet \'sü-,brā-, ,sō-, 'sü-, ,sü-\ var of SOBRIQUET

sou·chong \'sü-,chȯn, -,shȯn\ n [of Chin origin; akin to Chin (Beijing) *xiāozhŏng*, lit., small sort] (1760) : a tea made from the larger leaves of the shoot

sorghum 1

¹souf·flé \sü-'flā, 'sü-,\ n [F, fr. *soufflé*, pp. of *souffler* to blow, puff up, fr. L *sufflare*, fr. *sub-* + *flare* to blow — more at BLOW] (1813) : a dish that is made from a sauce, egg yolks, beaten egg whites, and a flavoring or purée (as of seafood, fruit, or vegetables) and baked until puffed up

²soufflé *or* souf·fléed \-'flād, -,flād\ *adj* (1888) : puffed up by or in cooking

sough \saù, 'səf\ *vi* [ME *swoughen*, fr. OE *swōgan*; akin to Goth ga-*swogjan* to groan, Lith *svagéti* to sound] (bef. 12c) : to make a moaning or sighing sound — **sough** *n*

sought *past and past part of* SEEK

souk \'sük\ *n* [Ar *sūq* market] (1826) : a marketplace in northern Africa or the Middle East; *also* : a stall in such a marketplace

¹soul \'sōl\ *n* [ME *soule*, fr. OE *sāwol*; akin to OHG *sēula* soul] (bef. 12c) **1** : the immaterial essence, animating principle, or actuating cause of an individual life **2 a** : the spiritual principle embodied in human beings, all rational and spiritual beings, or the universe **b** *cap, Christian Science* : GOD 1b **3** : a person's total self **4 a** : an active or essential part **b** : a moving spirit : LEADER **5 a** : the moral and emotional nature of human beings **b** : the quality that arouses emotion and sentiment **c** : spiritual or moral force : FERVOR **6** : PERSON **7** : EXEMPLIFICATION, PERSONIFICATION ⟨she is the ~ of integrity⟩ **8 a** : a strong positive feeling (as of intense sensitivity and emotional fervor) conveyed esp. by black American performers **b** : NEGRITUDE **c** : SOUL MUSIC **d** : SOUL FOOD **e** : SOUL BROTHER

²soul *adj* (1958) **1** : of, relating to, or characteristic of black Americans or their culture **2** : designed for or controlled by blacks ⟨~ radio stations⟩

soul brother *n* (1959) : a black male

souled \'sōld\ *adj* (15c) : having a soul : possessing soul and feeling — usu. used in combination ⟨whole-*souled* repentance⟩

soul food *n* (1964) : food (as chitterlings, ham hocks, and collard greens) traditionally eaten by southern black Americans

soul·ful \'sōl-fəl\ *adj* (1860) : full of or expressing feeling or emotion — soul·ful·ly \-fə-lē\ *adv* — soul·ful·ness *n*

soul kiss *n* (ca. 1948) : FRENCH KISS

soul·less \'sōl-ləs\ *adj* (15c) : having no soul or no greatness or warmth of mind or feeling — soul·less·ly *adv* — soul·less·ness *n*

soul mate *n* (1822) : a person temperamentally suited to another

soul music *n* (1961) : music that originated in black American gospel singing, is closely related to rhythm and blues, and is characterized by intensity of feeling and earthiness

soul–search·ing \'sōl-,sər-chiŋ\ *n* (1924) : examination of one's conscience esp. with regard to motives and values

¹sound \'saùnd\ *adj* [ME, fr. OE *gesund*; akin to OHG *gisunt* healthy] (13c) **1 a** : free from injury or disease : exhibiting normal health **b** : free from flaw, defect, or decay ⟨~ timber⟩ **2** : SOLID, FIRM; *also* : STABLE **3** : free from error, fallacy, or misapprehension ⟨~ reasoning⟩ **b** : exhibiting or based on thorough knowledge and experience ⟨~ scholarship⟩ **c** : legally valid ⟨a ~ title⟩ **d** : logically valid and having true premises **e** : agreeing with accepted views : ORTHODOX **4 a** : THOROUGH **b** : deep and undisturbed ⟨a ~ sleep⟩ **c** : HARD, SEVERE ⟨a ~ whipping⟩ **5** : showing good judgment or sense *syn* see HEALTHY, VALID — **sound·ly** \'saùn(d)-lē\ *adv* — **sound·ness** \'saùn(d)-nəs\ *n*

²sound *adv* (14c) : to the full extent : THOROUGHLY ⟨~ asleep⟩

³sound *n* [ME *soun*, fr. OF *son*, fr. L *sonus*, fr. *sonare* to sound; akin to OE *swinn* melody, Skt *svanati* it sounds] (13c) **1 a** : a particular auditory impression : TONE **b** : the sensation perceived by the sense of hearing **c** : mechanical radiant energy that is transmitted by longitudinal pressure waves in a material medium (as air) and is the objective cause of hearing **2 a** : a speech sound ⟨a peculiar *r-sound*⟩ **b** : value in terms of speech sounds ⟨-*cher* of *teacher* and -*ture* of *creature* have the same ~⟩ **3** *archaic* : RUMOR, FAME **4 a** : meaningless noise **b** *obs* : MEANING **c** : the impression conveyed : IMPORT **5** : hearing distance : EARSHOT **6** : recorded auditory material **7** : a particular musical style characteristic of an individual, a group, or an area ⟨the Nashville ~⟩

⁴sound *vb* (13c) **1 a** : to cause to sound ⟨~ a trumpet⟩ **b** : PRONOUNCE 3a **2** : to put into words : VOICE **3 a** : to make known : PROCLAIM **b** : to order, signal, or indicate by a sound ⟨~ the alarm⟩ **4** : to examine by causing to emit sounds ⟨~ the lungs⟩ **5** *chiefly Brit* : to convey the impression of : sound like ⟨that ~s a logical use of resources —*Economist*⟩ ~ *vi* **1 a** : to make a sound **b** : RESOUND **c** : to give a summons by sound ⟨the bugle ~s to battle⟩ **2** : to make or convey an impression esp. when heard ⟨it ~s good to me⟩ ⟨you ~ just like your mother⟩ — **sound·able** \'saùn-də-bəl\ *adj*

⁵sound *n* [ME, fr. OE *sund* swimming, sea & ON *sund* swimming, strait; akin to OE *swimman* to swim] (14c) **1 a** : a long broad inlet of the ocean generally parallel to the coast **b** : a long passage of water connecting two larger bodies (as a sea with the ocean) or separating a mainland and an island **2** : the air bladder of a fish

⁶sound *vb* [ME, fr. MF *sonder*, fr. *sonde* sounding line, prob. of Gmc origin; akin to OE *sundline* sounding line, *sund* sea] *vt* (15c) **1 a** : to measure the depth of : FATHOM **2** : to try to find out the views or intentions of : PROBE — often used with *out* **3** : to explore or examine (a body cavity) with a sound ~ *vi* **1 a** : to ascertain the depth of water esp. with a sounding line **b** : to look into or investigate the possibility ⟨sent commissioners . . . to ~ for peace —Thomas Jefferson⟩ **2** : to dive down suddenly — used of a fish or whale

⁷sound *n* [F *sonde*, fr. MF, lit., sounding line] (1739) : an elongated instrument for exploring or sounding body cavities

sound·alike \'saùn-də-,līk\ *n* (1970) : one that sounds like another

sound–and–light show *n* (1967) : SON ET LUMIÈRE

sound barrier *n* (1939) : a sudden large increase in aerodynamic drag that occurs as the speed of an aircraft approaches the speed of sound

sound bite *n* (1972) : a brief recorded statement (as by a public figure) broadcast esp. on a television news program; *also* : a brief catchy comment suitable for use as a sound bite

sound·board \'saùn(d)-,bōrd, -,bòrd\ *n* (1504) **1** : a thin resonant board (as the belly of a violin) so placed in an instrument as to reinforce its tones by sympathetic vibration — see VIOLIN illustration **2** : SOUNDING BOARD 1a

sound bow *n* (1688) : the thick part of a bell against which the clapper strikes

sound box *n* (ca. 1875) **1** : a device in an early phonograph for producing sound from a record by using the vibration of a needle to move a diaphragm **2** : a hollow chamber in a musical instrument for increasing its sonority

sound effects *n pl* (1909) : effects that are imitative of sounds called for in the script of a dramatic production (as a radio show) and that enhance the production's illusion of reality

sound·er \'saùn-dər\ *n* (1575) : one that sounds; *specif* : a device for making soundings

sound hole *n* (1611) : an opening in the top surface of a stringed instrument (as a violin) to enhance vibration and resonance — see VIOLIN illustration

¹sound·ing \'saùn-diŋ\ *adj* (14c) **1** : RESONANT, SONOROUS **2 a** : POMPOUS **b** : IMPOSING — **sound·ing·ly** \-diŋ-lē\ *adv*

²sounding *n* (15c) **1** : measurement of depth esp. with a sounding line **b** : the depth so ascertained **c** *pl* : a place or part of a body of water where a hand sounding line will reach bottom **2** : measurement of atmospheric conditions at various heights **3** : a probe, test, or sampling of opinion or intention

sounding board *n* (1729) **1 a** : a structure behind or over a pulpit, rostrum, or platform to give distinctness and sonority to sound **b** : a device or agency that helps propagate opinions or utterances **c** : a person or group on whom one tries out an idea or opinion as a means of evaluating it **2** : SOUNDBOARD 1

sounding line *n* (14c) : a line or wire weighted at one end for sounding

sounding rocket *n* (ca. 1945) : a rocket used to obtain information concerning atmospheric conditions at various altitudes

¹sound·less \'saùn(d)-ləs\ *adj* [⁶sound] (1586) : incapable of being sounded : UNFATHOMABLE

²soundless *adj* [³sound] (1601) : making no sound : SILENT — **sound·less·ly** *adv*

sound·man \'saùn(d)-,man\ *n* (1929) : a person who controls the volume and tone of sound picked up by a microphone (as in a recording studio or on a motion-picture set) for recording

sound off *vi* (1909) **1** : to play three chords before and after marching up and down a line of troops during a ceremonial parade or formal guard mount **2** : to count cadence while marching **3 a** : to speak up in a loud voice **b** : to voice one's opinions freely and vigorously

sound pressure *n* (1893) : the difference between the actual pressure at any point in the field of a sound wave at any instant and the average pressure at that point

¹sound·proof \'saùn(d)-,prüf\ *adj* (ca. 1878) : impervious to sound

²soundproof *vt* (1919) : to insulate so as to obstruct the passage of sound

sound·stage \'saùn(d)-,stāj\ *n* (1931) : the part of a motion-picture studio in which a production is filmed

sound track *n* (ca. 1929) **1** : the area on a motion-picture film or television videotape that carries the sound record **2** : the sound recorded on a sound track; *esp* : the music on a sound track

sound truck *n* (1936) : a truck equipped with a loudspeaker

sound wave *n* (1848) **1** : ³SOUND 1a **2** *pl* : longitudinal pressure waves in any material medium regardless of whether they constitute audible sound ⟨earthquake waves and ultrasonic waves are sometimes called *sound waves*⟩

soup \'süp\ *n* [ME *soupe*, fr. MF, sop, soup, of Gmc origin; akin to ON *soppa* soup, OE *sopp* sop — more at SUP] (14c) **1** : a liquid food esp. with a meat, fish, or vegetable stock as a base and often containing pieces of solid food **2** : something (as a heavy fog or nitroglycerine) having or suggesting the consistency or nutrient qualities of soup **3** : an unfortunate predicament

soup·con \süp-'sō⁰, 'süp-,sän\ *n* [F, lit., suspicion, fr. (assumed) VL *suspection-, suspectio*, fr. L *suspicere* to suspect — more at SUSPECT] (1766) : a little bit : TRACE

soup du jour \,süp-də-'zhùr\ *n* [part trans. of F *soupe du jour* soup of the day] (ca. 1945) : a soup that is offered by a restaurant on a particular day

soup kitchen *n* (1839) : an establishment dispensing minimum dietary essentials (as soup and bread) to the needy

soup·spoon \'süp-,spün\ *n* (1705) : a spoon with a large or rounded bowl for eating soup

soup up *vt* [soup (drug injected into a racehorse to improve its performance)] (ca. 1933) : to increase the power or efficiency of ⟨soup up an engine⟩

soupy \'sü-pē\ *adj* soup·i·er; -est (1869) **1** : having the consistency of soup **2** : densely foggy or cloudy **3** : overly sentimental

¹sour \'saù(-ə)r\ *adj* [ME, fr. OE *sūr*; akin to OHG *sūr* sour, Lith *sūrus* salty] (bef. 12c) **1** : causing or characterized by the one of the four basic taste sensations that is produced chiefly by acids ⟨~ pickles⟩ — compare BITTER, SALT, SWEET **2 a** (1) : having the acid taste or smell of or as if of fermentation : TURNED ⟨~ milk⟩ (2) : of or relating to fermentation **b** : smelling or tasting of decay : RANCID, ROTTEN ⟨~ breath⟩ **c** (1) : BAD, WRONG ⟨a project gone ~⟩ (2) : HOSTILE, DISENCHANTED ⟨went ~ on Marxism⟩ **3 a** : UNPLEASANT, DISTASTEFUL **b** : CROSS, SULLEN **c** : not up to the usual, expected, or standard quality or pitch **4** : acid in reaction — used esp. of soil **5** : containing malodorous sulfur compounds — used esp. of petroleum products — **sour·ish** \'saù(-ə)r-ish\ *adj* — **sour·ly** *adv* — **sour·ness** *n*

²sour *n* (bef. 12c) **1 a** : something sour **b** : the primary taste sensation produced by acid stimuli **2** : a cocktail consisting of a liquor (as whiskey), lemon or lime juice, sugar, and sometimes ice

³sour *vi* (14c) : to become sour ~ *vt* : to make sour

sour ball *n* (ca. 1909) : a spherical hard candy having a tart flavor

¹source \'sōrs, 'sòrs\ *n* [ME *sours*, fr. MF *sors, sourse*, fr. OF, fr. pp. of *sourdre* to rise, spring forth, fr. L *surgere* — more at SURGE] (14c) **1 a** : a generative force : CAUSE **b** (1) : a point of origin or procurement : BEGINNING (2) : one that initiates : AUTHOR; *also* : PROTOTYPE, MODEL (3) : one that supplies information **2 a** : the point of origin of a

---

\ə\ abut \ᵊ\ kitten, F table \ər\ further \a\ ash \ā\ ace \ä\ mop, mar \aù\ out \ch\ chin \e\ bet \ē\ easy \g\ go \i\ hit \ī\ ice \j\ job \ŋ\ sing \ō\ go \ò\ law \òi\ boy \th\ thin \t̲h̲\ the \ü\ loot \ù\ foot \y\ yet \zh\ vision \à, k̲, ⁿ, œ, œ̄, ue̱, ūe, ᵞ\ see Guide to Pronunciation stream of water : FOUNTAINHEAD **b** *archaic* : SPRING, FOUNT **3** : a firsthand document or primary reference work **4** : an electrode in a field-effect transistor that supplies the charge carriers for current flow — compare DRAIN, GATE *syn* see ORIGIN — **source-less** \-ləs\ *adj*

²source *vt* **sourced; sourc-ing** (1957) **1** : to specify the source of (as quoted material) **2** : to obtain from a source ⟨metals *sourced* from abroad⟩

³source *adj* (1959) : of, relating to, or being a computer program in its original programming language ⟨~ listing⟩ ⟨~ code⟩

source-book \-ˌbûk\ *n* (1899) : a fundamental document or record (as of history, literature, art, or religion) on which subsequent writings, compositions, opinions, beliefs, or practices are based; *also* : a collection of such documents

source language *n* (1953) : a language which is to be translated into another language — compare TARGET LANGUAGE

sour cherry *n* (ca. 1884) : a widely cultivated cherry (*Prunus cerasus*) that has a round crown and bright red to almost black soft-fleshed acid fruits; *also* : the fruit

sour cream *n* (1885) : a soured cream product produced by the action of lactobacilli

sour-dough \'saú(-ə)r-ˌdō, *1 is also* -'dō\ *n* (14c) **1** : a leaven consisting of dough in which fermentation is active **2** [fr. the use of sourdough for making bread in prospectors' camps] : a veteran inhabitant and esp. an old-time prospector of Alaska or northwestern Canada

sour grapes *n pl* [fr. the fable ascribed to Aesop of the fox who after finding himself unable to reach some grapes he had desired disparaged them as sour] (1760) : disparagement of something that has proven unattainable

sour gum *n* (1785) : BLACK GUM

sour mash *n* (1885) : grain mash for brewing or distilling whose initial acidity has been adjusted to optimum condition for yeast fermentation by mash from a previous run

sour orange *n* (1748) : a citrus tree (*Citrus aurantium*) that is used esp. as a stock in grafting citrus; *also* : its bitter fruit

sour-puss \'saú(-ə)r-ˌpús\ *n* [²puss] (1937) : GROUCH, KILLJOY

sour-sop \'saú(-ə)r-ˌsäp\ *n* (1667) : a small tropical American tree (*Annona muricata*) of the custard-apple family that has spicy odoriferous leaves; *also* : its large edible fruit that has fleshy spines and a slightly acid fibrous pulp

sour-wood \-ˌwúd\ *n* (1709) : a small U.S. tree (*Oxydendrum arboreum*) of the heath family with white flowers and sour-tasting leaves

sous \'sü\ *adj* [F, prep., lit., under, fr. L *subtus*, adv., below, under; akin to L *sub* under — more at UP] (1687) : being an assistant — used chiefly in titles ⟨a *sous-chef*⟩

sou-sa-phone \'sü-zə-ˌfōn, -sə-\ *n* [John Philip *Sousa*] (1925) : a large circular tuba that has a flared adjustable bell — compare HELICON

¹souse \'saús\ *vb* **soused; sous-ing** [ME, fr. MF *souz, souce* pickling solution, of Gmc origin; akin to OHG *sulza* brine, OE *sealt* salt] *vt* (14c) **1** : PICKLE **2 a** : to plunge in liquid : IMMERSE **b** : DRENCH, SATURATE **3** : to make drunk : INEBRIATE ~ *vi* : to become immersed or drenched

²souse *n* (14c) **1** : something pickled; *esp* : seasoned and chopped pork trimmings, fish, or shellfish **2** : an act of sousing : WETTING **3 a** : a habitual drunkard **b** : a drinking spree : BINGE

³souse *vb* **soused; sous-ing** [ME *souce, n.,* start of a bird's flight, alter. of *sours,* fr. MF *sourse* source — more at SOURCE] *vi* (1583) *archaic* : to swoop down : PLUNGE ~ *vt, archaic* : to swoop down on

sou-tache \sü-'tash\ *n* [F, fr. Hung *sujtás*] (ca. 1856) : a narrow braid with herringbone pattern used as trimming

sou-tane \sü-'tän, -'tan\ *n* [F, fr. It *sottana,* lit., undergarment, fr. fem. of *sottano* being underneath, fr. ML *subtanus,* fr. L *subtus* underneath — more at SOUS] (1838) : CASSOCK

sou-ter \'sü-tər\ *n* [ME, fr. OE *sūtere,* fr. L *sutor,* fr. *suere* to sew — more at SEW] (bef. 12c) *chiefly Scot* : SHOEMAKER

¹south \'saúth\ *adv* [ME, fr. OE *sūth;* akin to OHG *sund-* south and prob. to OE *sunne* sun] (bef. 12c) **1** : to, toward, or in the south **2** : into a state of decline or ruin ⟨causes the sluggish economy to go ~ —G. F. Will⟩

²south *adj* (12c) **1** : situated toward or at the south ⟨the ~ entrance⟩ **2** : coming from the south ⟨a ~ wind⟩

³south *n* (13c) **1 a** : the direction of the south terrestrial pole : the direction to the right of one facing east **b** : the compass point directly opposite to north **2** *cap* : regions or countries lying to the south of a specified or implied point of orientation; *esp* : the southeastern part of the U.S. **3** : the right side of a church looking toward the altar from the nave **4** *often cap* **a** : the one of four positions at 90-degree intervals that lies to the south or at the bottom of a diagram **b** : a person (as a bridge player) occupying this position in the course of a specified activity; *specif* : the declarer in bridge **5** *often cap* : the developing nations of the world : THIRD WORLD 3 — compare NORTH 2b

South African *n* (1806) : a native or inhabitant of the Republic of South Africa; *esp* : AFRIKANER — **South African** *adj*

south-bound \'saúth-ˌbaúnd\ *adj* (1885) : traveling or heading south

south by east (ca. 1771) : a compass point that is one point east of due south : S11°15′E

south by west (ca. 1743) : a compass point that is one point west of due south : S11°15′W

South Dev-on \-'de-vən\ *n* [*Devon,* England] (1897) : any of a breed of large red dual-purpose cattle of English origin

South-down \'saúth-ˌdaún\ *n* [*South Downs,* England] (1787) : any of a breed of small medium-wooled hornless sheep of English origin

¹south-east \saú-'thēst, *naut* saú-'ēst\ *adv* (bef. 12c) : to, toward, or in the southeast

²southeast *n* (14c) **1 a** : the general direction between south and east **b** : the point midway between the south and east compass points **2** *cap* : regions or countries lying to the southeast of a specified or implied point of orientation

³southeast *adj* (14c) **1** : coming from the southeast ⟨a ~ wind⟩ **2** : situated toward or at the southeast ⟨the ~ corner⟩

southeast by east (ca. 1771) : a compass point that is one point east of due southeast : S56°15′E

southeast by south (1682) : a compass point that is one point south of due southeast : S33°45′E

south-east-er \saú-'thē-stər, saú-'ē-\ *n* (1797) **1** : a strong southeast wind **2** : a storm with southeast winds

south-east-er-ly \-stər-lē\ *adv or adj* [²southeast + -erly (as in *easterly*)] (1708) **1** : from the southeast **2** : toward the southeast

south-east-ern \-stərn\ *adj* [²southeast + -ern (as in *eastern*)] (1577) **1** *often cap* : of, relating to, or characteristic of a region conventionally designated southeast **2** : lying toward or coming from the southeast — **south-east-ern-most** \-ˌmōst\ *adj*

South-east-ern-er \-stə(r)-nər\ *n* (1919) : a native or inhabitant of the Southeast; *esp* : a native or resident of the southeastern part of the U.S.

¹south-east-ward \saú-'thēs-twərd, saú-'ēs-\ *adv or adj* (1528) : toward the southeast — **south-east-wards** \-twərdz\ *adv*

²southeastward *n* (1555) : SOUTHEAST

¹south-er-ly \'sə-thər-lē\ *adj or adv* [³south + -erly (as in *easterly*)] (1551) **1** : situated toward or belonging to the south ⟨the ~ shore of the lake⟩ **2** : coming from the south ⟨a ~ wind⟩

²southerly *n, pl* **-lies** (1943) : a wind from the south

south-ern \'sə-thərn\ *adj* [ME *southern, southren,* fr. OE *sūtherne;* akin to OHG *sundrōni* southern, OE *sūth* south] (bef. 12c) **1** *cap* : of, relating to, or characteristic of a region conventionally designated South **2 a** : lying toward the south **b** : coming from the south ⟨a ~ breeze⟩ — **south-ern-most** \-ˌmōst\ — **south-ern-ness** \-thərn-nəs\ *n, often cap*

Southern *n* (1935) : the dialect of English spoken in most of the Chesapeake Bay area, the coastal plain and the greater part of the upland plateau in Virginia, No. Carolina, So. Carolina, and Georgia, and the Gulf states at least as far west as the valley of the Brazos in Texas and sometimes taken to include the south Midland area

Southern blot *n* [Edwin M. *Southern* 20th-cent. Brit. biologist] (1981) : a blot consisting of a nitrocellulose sheet containing spots of DNA for identification by a suitable molecular probe — compare WESTERN BLOT — **Southern blotting** *n*

southern corn rootworm *n* (1914) : SPOTTED CUCUMBER BEETLE

Southern Cross *n* : four bright stars in the southern hemisphere, situated as if at the extremities of a Latin cross; *also* : the constellation of which these four stars are the brightest

Southern Crown *n* : CORONA AUSTRALIS

Southern English *n* (14c) **1** : the English spoken esp. by cultivated people native to or educated in the South of England **2** : SOUTHERN

South-ern-er \'sə-thə(r)-nər\ *n* (1828) : a native or inhabitant of the South; *esp* : a native or resident of the southern part of the U.S.

southern hemisphere *n, often cap S&H* (ca. 1771) : the part of the earth that lies south of the equator

South-ern-ism \'sə-thər-ˌni-zəm\ *n* (1861) **1** : an attitude or trait characteristic of the South or Southerners esp. in the U.S. **2** : a locution or pronunciation characteristic of the southern U.S.

southern lights *n pl* (1775) : AURORA AUSTRALIS

south-ern-wood \'sə-thərn-ˌwúd\ *n* (bef. 12c) : a shrubby fragrant European wormwood (*Artemisia abrotanum*) with bitter foliage

south-ing \'saú-thiŋ, -thiŋ\ *n* (1669) **1** : difference in latitude to the south from the last preceding point of reckoning **2** : southerly progress

south-land \'saúth-ˌland, -lənd\ *n, often cap* (bef. 12c) : land in the south : the south of a country

south-paw \-ˌpò\ *n* (1891) : LEFT-HANDER; *esp* : a left-handed baseball pitcher — **southpaw** *adj*

south pole *n* (14c) **1 a** *often cap S&P* : the southernmost point of the earth **b** : the zenith of the heavens as viewed from the south terrestrial pole **2** *of a magnet* : the pole that points toward the south

¹South-ron \'sə-thrən\ *adj* [ME (Sc)] (15c) *chiefly Scot* : SOUTHERN, *specif* : ENGLISH

²Southron *n* (15c) : SOUTHERNER: as **a** *chiefly Scot* : ENGLISHMAN **b** *chiefly Southern* : a native or inhabitant of the southern U.S.

south–seek-ing pole *n* (ca. 1922) : SOUTH POLE 2

south–southeast *n* (15c) : a compass point that is two points east of due south : S22°30′E

south–southwest *n* (1513) : a compass point that is two points west of due south : S22°30′W

¹south-ward \'saúth-wərd\ *adv or adj* (bef. 12c) : toward the south — **south-wards** \-wərdz\ *adv*

²southward *n* (14c) : southward direction or part ⟨sail to the ~⟩

¹south-west \saúth-'west, *naut* saú-'west\ *adv* (bef. 12c) : to, toward, or in the southwest

²southwest *n* (12c) **1 a** : the general direction between south and west **b** : the point midway between the south and west compass points **2** *cap* : regions or countries lying to the southwest of a specified or implied point of orientation

³southwest *adj* (14c) **1** : coming from the southwest ⟨a ~ wind⟩ **2** : situated toward or at the southwest ⟨the ~ corner⟩

southwest by south (1725) : a compass point that is one point south of due southwest : S33°45′W

southwest by west (ca. 1771) : a compass point that is one point west of due southwest : S56°15′W

south-west-er \saú(th)-'wes-tər\ *n* (1833) **1** : a strong southwest wind **2** : a storm with southwest winds

south-west-er-ly \-tər-lē\ *adv or adj* [²southwest + -erly (as in *westerly*)] (1708) **1** : from the southwest **2** : toward the southwest

south-west-ern \-tərn\ *adj* [ME, fr. OE *sūth-westerne,* fr. *sūth* south + *westerne* western] (bef. 12c) **1** : lying toward or coming from the southwest **2** *often cap* : of, relating to, or characteristic of a region conventionally designated Southwest — **south-west-ern-most** \-ˌmōst\ *adj*

sousaphone

southwestern corn borer *n* (1943) : a pyralid moth (*Diatraea grandiosella*) whose larva causes serious damage esp. to corn crops by boring in the stalks

South·west·ern·er \saù(th)-'wes-tə(r)-nər\ *n* (1860) : a native or inhabitant of the Southwest; *esp* : a native or resident of the southwestern U.S.

¹south·west·ward \saù(th)-'wes-tword\ *adv or adj* (1548) : toward the southwest — **south·west·wards** \-twərdz\ *adv*

²southwestward *n* (1775) : SOUTHWEST

sou·ve·nir \,sü-və-'nir, ,sü-və-'\ *n* [F, lit., act of remembering, fr. MF, fr. (*se*) *souvenir* to remember, fr. L *subvenire* to come up, come to mind — more at SUBVENTION] (1782) : something that serves as a reminder : MEMENTO

souvenir sheet *n* (1940) : a block or set of postage stamps or a single stamp printed on a single sheet of paper often without gum or perforations and with margins containing lettering or design that identifies some notable event being commemorated

sou·vla·kia \süv-'lä-kē-ə\ *or* **sou·vla·ki** \-'lä-kē\ *n* [NGk *soublakia*, pl. of *soublaki*, fr. dim. of *soubla* skewer, fr. MGk, fr. L *subula* awl, fr. *suere* to sew — more at SEW] (1950) : SHISH KEBAB

sou'·west·er \saù-'wes-tər\ *n* (1837) **1 a** : a long oilskin coat worn esp. at sea during stormy weather **2** : a waterproof hat with wide slanting brim longer in back than in front

¹sov·er·eign *also* **sov·ran** \'sä-v(ə-)rən, -vərn *also* 'sə-\ *n* [ME *soverain*, fr. OF, fr. *soverain*, adj.] (13c) **1 a** : one possessing or held to possess sovereignty **b** : one that exercises supreme authority within a limited sphere **c** : an acknowledged leader : ARBITER **2 a** : any of various gold coins of the United Kingdom

²sovereign *also* **sovran** *adj* [ME *soverain*, fr. MF, fr. OF, fr. (assumed) VL *superanus*, fr. L *super* over, above — more at OVER] (14c) **1 a** : superlative in quality : EXCELLENT **b** : of the most exalted kind : SUPREME ⟨~ virtue⟩ **c** : having generalized curative powers ⟨a ~ remedy⟩ **d** : of an unqualified nature : UNMITIGATED ⟨~ contempt⟩ **e** : having undisputed ascendancy : PARAMOUNT **2 a** : possessed of supreme power ⟨~ ruler⟩ **b** : unlimited in extent : ABSOLUTE **c** : enjoying autonomy : INDEPENDENT ⟨~ state⟩ **3** : relating to, characteristic of, or befitting a sovereign *syn* see FREE — **sov·er·eign·ly** *adv*

sov·er·eign·ty *also* **sov·ran·ty** \-tē\ *n, pl* **-ties** [ME *soverainte*, fr. MF *soveraineté*, fr. OF, fr. *soverain*] (14c) **1** *obs* : supreme excellence or an example of it **2 a** : supreme power esp. over a body politic **b** : freedom from external control : AUTONOMY **c** : controlling influence **3** : one that is sovereign; *esp* : an autonomous state

so·vi·et \'sō-vē-,et, 'sä-, -vē-ət\ *n* [Russ *sovet* council, soviet] (1917) **1** : an elected governmental council in a Communist country **2** *pl, cap* **a** : BOLSHEVIKS **b** : the people and esp. the political and military leaders of the U.S.S.R. — **soviet** *adj, often cap* — **so·vi·et·ism** \-vē-ə-,ti-zəm\ *n, often cap*

so·vi·et·ize \'sō-vē-,e-,tīz, 'sä-, -vē-ə-\ *vt* **-ized; -iz·ing** *often cap* (1919) **1** : to bring under Soviet control **2** : to force into conformity with Soviet cultural patterns or governmental policies — **so·vi·et·i·za·tion** \,sō-vē-,e-tə-'zā-shən, -vē-ə-\ *n, often cap*

So·vi·et·ol·o·gist \,sō-vē-ə-'tä-lə-jist, ,sä-, -vē-ə-\ *n* (1955) : one who studies or is knowledgeable about the policies and practices of the Soviet government : KREMLINOLOGIST

sov·khoz \säf-'kòz, -'kós\ *n, pl* **sov·kho·zy** \-'kò-zē\ *or* **sov·khoz·es** [Russ, short for *sovetskoe khozyaistvo* soviet farm] (1921) : a state-owned farm of the U.S.S.R. paying wages to the workers

¹sow \'saù\ *n* [ME *sowe*, fr. OE *sugu*; akin to OE & OHG *sū* sow, L *sus* pig, swine, hog, Gk *hys*] (bef. 12c) **1** : an adult female swine; *also* : the adult female of various other animals (as a bear) **2 a** : a channel that conducts molten metal to molds **b** : a mass of metal solidified in such a mold : INGOT

²sow \'sō\ *vb* **sowed; sown** \'sōn\ *or* **sowed; sow·ing** [ME, fr. OE *sāwan*; akin to OHG *sāwen* to sow, L *serere*, Lith *sėti*] *vi* (bef. 12c) **1** : to plant seed for growth esp. by scattering **2** : to set something in motion : begin an enterprise ~ *vt* **1 a** : to scatter (as seed) upon the earth for growth; *broadly* : PLANT 1a **b** : to strew with or as if with seed **c** : to introduce into a selected environment : IMPLANT **2** : to set in motion : FOMENT ⟨~ suspicion⟩ **3** : to spread abroad : DISPERSE — **sow·er** \'sō(-ə)r\ *n*

sow·bel·ly \'saù-,be-lē\ *n* (1867) : fat salt pork or bacon

sow bug \'saù-\ *n* (1750) : WOOD LOUSE

sow·ens \'saù-ənz, 'sō-\ *n pl but sing or pl in constr* [ScGael *sùghan*] (1582) : porridge from oat husks and siftings

sow thistle \'saù-\ *n* (15c) : any of a genus (*Sonchus*) of spiny weedy European composite herbs widely naturalized in No. America

sox *pl of* SOCK

soy \'sòi\ *n* [Jp *shōyu*] (1679) **1** : a brown liquid sauce made by subjecting beans (as soybeans) to long fermentation and to digestion in brine **2** *also* **soya** \'sòi-ə\ : SOYBEAN

soy·bean \'sòi-,bēn\ *also* **soya bean** \'sòi-ə-\ *n* (1802) : a hairy annual Asian legume (*Glycine max*) widely grown for its oil-rich proteinaceous seeds and for soil improvement; *also* : its seed

soybean oil *n* (ca. 1916) : a pale yellow drying or semidrying oil that is obtained from soybeans and is used chiefly as a food, in paints, varnishes, linoleum, printing ink, and soap, and as a source of phospholipids, fatty acids, and sterols — called *also soya oil*

soz·zled \'sä-zəld\ *adj* [*sozzle* to splash, intoxicate, alter. of *sossle*, prob. freq. of Brit. dial. *soss* to mess] (ca. 1880) : DRUNK, INTOXICATED

spa \'spä, 'spó\ *n* [*Spa*, watering place in Belgium] (1610) **1 a** : a mineral spring **b** : a resort with mineral springs **2** : a fashionable resort or hotel **3** *NewEng* : SODA FOUNTAIN **4** : HEALTH SPA **5** : a hot tub with a whirlpool device

¹space \'spās\ *n, often attrib* [ME, fr. OF *espace*, fr. L *spatium* area, room, interval of space or time] (14c) **1** : a period of time; *also* : its duration **2 a** : a limited extent in one, two, or three dimensions : DISTANCE, AREA, VOLUME **b** : an extent set apart or available ⟨parking ~⟩ ⟨floor ~⟩ **3** : one of the degrees between or above or below the lines of a musical staff — compare LINE **4 a** : a boundless three-dimensional extent in which objects and events occur and have relative position and direction **b** : physical space independent of what occupies it — called *also absolute space* **5** : the region beyond the earth's atmosphere or beyond the solar system **6 a** : a blank area separating words or lines **b** : material used to produce such blank area; *esp* : a

piece of type less than one en in width **7** : a set of mathematical elements and esp. of abstractions of all the points on a line, in a plane, or in physical space; *esp* : a set of mathematical entities with a set of axioms of geometric character — compare METRIC SPACE, TOPOLOGICAL SPACE, VECTOR SPACE **8** : an interval in operation during which a telegraph key is not in contact **9 a** : LINAGE **b** : broadcast time available esp. to advertisers **10** : accommodations on a public vehicle **11** : the opportunity to assert or experience one's identity or needs freely

²space *vb* **spaced; spac·ing** *vt* (1703) : to place at intervals or arrange with space between — often used with *out* ~ *vi* : to leave one or more blank spaces (as in a line of typing) — **spac·er** *n*

space–age \'spās-'āj\ *adj* (1946) : of, relating to, or befitting the age of space exploration; *esp* : MODERN ⟨~ technology⟩

space·band \-,band\ *n* (1904) : a device on a linecaster that provides variable but even spacing between words in a justified line

space cadet *n* (1979) : a flaky, lightheaded, or forgetful person

space charge *n* (1913) : an electric charge distributed throughout a three-dimensional region

space·craft \'spās-,kraft\ *n* (1930) : a vehicle or device designed for travel or operation outside the earth's atmosphere

spaced–out \,spāst-'aùt\ *adj* (1937) **1** *or* **spaced** \'spāst\ : dazed or stupefied by or as if by a narcotic substance : HIGH **2** : of very strange character : WEIRD ⟨a ~ fantasy⟩

space·flight \'spās-,flīt\ *n* (1931) : flight beyond the earth's atmosphere

space frame *n* (1912) : a usu. open three-dimensional framework of struts and braces (as in buildings and racing cars) which defines a structure and in which the weight of the structure is evenly distributed in all directions

space heater *n* (1925) : a usu. portable appliance for heating a relatively small area

space heating *n* (1934) : heating of spaces esp. for human comfort by any means (as fuel, electricity, or solar radiation) with the heater either within the space or external to it

space lattice *n* (1895) : LATTICE 2

space·less \'spās-ləs\ *adj* (1606) **1** : having no limits : BOUNDLESS **2** : occupying no space

space·man \'spās-,man, -mən\ *n* (1938) **1** : one who travels outside the earth's atmosphere **2** : a visitor to earth from outer space

space mark *n* (ca. 1890) : the symbol #

space medicine *n* (1949) : a branch of medicine that deals with the physiological and biological effects on the human body of rocket or jet flight beyond the earth's atmosphere

space opera *n* (1949) : a futuristic melodramatic fantasy involving space travelers and extraterrestrial beings

space·port \'spās-,pōrt, -,pòrt\ *n* (1935) : an installation for testing and launching spacecraft

space·ship \-,ship\ *n* (1894) : a vehicle used for space travel

space shuttle *n* (1969) : a reusable spacecraft designed to transport people and cargo between earth and space

space station *n* (1936) : a large artificial satellite designed to be occupied for long periods and to serve as a base (as for scientific observation) — called *also space platform*

space suit *n* (1929) **1** : a suit equipped with life supporting provisions to make life in space possible for its wearer **2** : G SUIT

space–time \'spās-'tim, 'spās-,\ *n* (1915) **1** : a system of one temporal and three spatial coordinates by which any physical object or event can be located — called *also space-time continuum* **2** : the whole or a portion of physical reality determinable by a usu. four-dimensional coordinate system; *also* : the properties characteristic of such an order

space walk *n* (1965) : a period of activity spent outside a spacecraft by an astronaut in space — **space·walk** \'spās-,wòk\ *vi* — **space·walk·er** \-,wò-kər\ *n*

space·ward \'spās-wərd\ *adv* (1958) : toward space

spac·ey *also* **spacy** \'spā-sē\ *adj* **spac·i·er; -est** (1970) : SPACED-OUT

spa·cial *var of* SPATIAL

spac·ing \'spā-siŋ\ *n* (1683) **1 a** : the act of providing with spaces or placing at intervals **b** : an arrangement in space **2 a** : a limited extent : SPACE **b** : the distance between any two objects in a usu. regularly arranged series

spa·cious \'spā-shəs\ *adj* [ME, fr. MF *spacieux*, fr. L *spatiosus*, fr. *spatium* space, room] (14c) **1** : vast or ample in extent : ROOMY ⟨a ~ residence⟩ **2** : large or magnificent in scale : EXPANSIVE ⟨a more ~ and stimulating existence than the farm could offer —H. L. Mencken⟩ — **spa·cious·ly** *adv* — **spa·cious·ness** *n*

syn SPACIOUS, COMMODIOUS, CAPACIOUS, AMPLE mean larger in extent or capacity than the average. SPACIOUS implies great length and breadth ⟨a *spacious* front lawn⟩. COMMODIOUS stresses roominess and comfortableness ⟨a *commodious* and airy penthouse apartment⟩. CAPACIOUS stresses the ability to hold, contain, or retain more than the average ⟨a *capacious* suitcase⟩. AMPLE implies having a greater size, expanse, or amount than that deemed adequate ⟨*ample* closet space⟩.

spack·le \'spa-kəl\ *vt* **spack·led; spack·ling** \-k(ə-)liŋ\ [*Spackle*] (1940) : to apply Spackle paste to

Spackle *trademark* — used for a powder mixed with water to form a paste and used as a filler for cracks in a surface before painting

¹spade \'spād\ *n* [ME, fr. OE *spadu*; akin to Gk *spathē* blade of a sword or oar] (bef. 12c) **1** : a digging implement adapted for being pushed into the ground with the foot **2** : a spade-shaped instrument — **spade·ful** \-,fùl\ *n* — **call a spade a spade 1** : to call a thing by its right name however coarse **2** : to speak frankly

²spade *vb* **spad·ed; spad·ing** *vt* (1647) : to dig up or out or shape with or as if with a spade ~ *vi* : to use a spade — **spad·er** *n*

³spade *n* [It *spada* or Sp *espada* broadsword; both fr. L *spatha*, fr. Gk *spathē* blade] (1598) **1 a** : a black figure that resembles a stylized spearhead on each playing card of one of the four suits; *also* : a card marked with this figure **b** *pl but sing or pl in constr* : the suit compris-

\ə\ abut \ᵊ\ kitten, F table \ər\ further \a\ ash \ā\ ace \ä\ mop, mar \aù\ out \ch\ chin \e\ bet \ē\ easy \g\ go \i\ hit \ī\ ice \j\ job \ŋ\ sing \ō\ go \ò\ law \òi\ boy \th\ thin \t͟h\ the \ü\ loot \ù\ foot \y\ yet \zh\ vision \á, k̲, ⁿ, œ, œ̄, ᵫ, ᵫ̄, ᵞ\ see Guide to Pronunciation

ing cards marked spades **2** : BLACK 4 — usu. taken to be offensive —
in spades : to an unusually great degree : in the extreme
spade beard *n* [¹*spade*] (1598) **1** : an oblong beard with square ends **2** : a beard rounded off at the top and pointed at the bottom — **spade–beard·ed** \'spād-'bir-dəd\ *adj*
spade·fish \'spād-,fish\ *n* (1704) : a deep-bodied bony fish (*Chaetodipterus faber* of the family Ephippidae) that resembles the angelfishes and is found in the warmer parts of the western Atlantic
spade-foot toad \'spād-,fút-\ *n* (1867) : any of a family (Pelobatidae) of burrowing toads having the inner bone of the tarsus edged with a strong horny sheath with which they dig
spade·work \-,wərk\ *n* (1778) **1** : work done with a spade **2** : the hard plain preliminary drudgery in an undertaking
spa·dille \spə-'dil, -'dē\ *n* [F, fr. Sp *espadilla*, dim. of *espada* broadsword, spade (in cards) — more at SPADE] (1728) : the highest trump in various card games (as ombre)
spa·dix \'spā-diks\ *n, pl* **spa·di·ces** \'spā-d-,sēz\ [NL *spadic-, spadix*, fr. L, frond torn from a palm tree, fr. Gk *spadic-, spadix*, fr. *span* to draw, pull] (ca. 1760) : a floral spike with a fleshy or succulent axis usu. enclosed in a spathe
spae \'spā\ *vt* **spaed; spae·ing** [ME *span*, fr. ON *spā*; akin to OHG *spehōn* to watch, spy — more at SPY] (14c) *chiefly Scot* : FORETELL
spaetz·le \'shpet-slə, -s°l, -slē *also* 'shpät-\ *n, pl* **spaetzle** *or* **spaetzles** [G *Spätzle*, fr. G dial., dim. of *Spatz* sparrow, dumpling] (1933) : a small dumpling cooked by running batter through a colander into boiling water
spa·ghet·ti \spə-'ge-tē\ *n* [It, fr. pl. of *spaghetto*, dim. of *spago* cord, string, fr. LL *spacus*] (1888) **1** : pasta made in thin solid strings **2** : insulating tubing typically of varnished cloth or of plastic for covering bare wire or holding insulated wires together — **spa·ghet·ti·like** \-,līk\ *adj*
spa·ghet·ti·ni \spə-ge-'tē-nē\ *n* [It, dim. of *spaghetti*] (1923) : a pasta thinner than spaghetti but thicker than vermicelli

1 spadix

spaghetti squash *n* (1975) : an oval winter squash with flesh that once cooked is similar in texture to spaghetti
spaghetti western *n, often cap W* (1969) : a western motion picture produced in Italy
spa·hi \'spä-,hē\ *n* [MF, fr. Turk *sipahi*, fr. Per *sipāhī* cavalryman] (1562) **1** : one of a former corps of irregular Turkish cavalry **2** : one of a former corps of Algerian native cavalry in the French army
spake \'spāk\ *archaic past of* SPEAK
¹spall \'spól\ *n* [ME *spalle*] (15c) : a small fragment or chip esp. of stone
²spall *vt* (1758) : to break up or reduce by or as if by chipping with a hammer ~ *vi* **1** : to break off chips, scales, or slabs : EXFOLIATE **2** : to undergo spallation — **spall·able** \'spó-lə-bəl\ *adj*
spall·ation \spó-'lā-shən\ *n* (1947) **1** : a nuclear reaction in which light particles are ejected as the result of bombardment (as by high-energy protons) **2** : the process of spalling
spal·peen \spal-'pēn, spöl-\ *n* [Ir *spailpín* seasonal laborer, rascal] (1815) *chiefly Irish* : RASCAL
¹span \'span\ *archaic past of* SPIN
²span *n* [ME, fr. OE *spann*; akin to OHG *spanna* span, MD *spannen* to stretch, hitch up] (bef. 12c) **1** : the distance from the end of the thumb to the end of the little finger of a spread hand; *also* : an English unit of length equal to 9 inches (22.9 centimeters) **2** : an extent, stretch, reach, or spread between two limits: as **a** : a limited space (as of time); *esp* : an individual's lifetime **b** : the spread or extent between abutments or supports (as of a bridge); *also* : a portion thus supported **c** : the maximum distance laterally from tip to tip of an airplane
³span *vt* **spanned; span·ning** (1560) **1 a** : to measure by or as if by the hand with fingers and thumb extended **b** : MEASURE **2 a** : to extend across (a career that *spanned* four decades) **b** : to form an arch over (a small bridge *spanned* the pond) **c** : to place or construct a span over **3** : to be capable of expressing any element of under given operations (a set of vectors that ~s a vector space)
⁴span *n* [D, fr. MD, fr. *spannen* to hitch up] (1769) : a pair of animals (as mules) usu. matched in appearance and action and driven together
spa·na·ko·pi·ta *also* **spa·no·ko·pi·ta** \,spä-nə-'kō-pē-tə, -pi-tə\ *n* [NGk *spanakopēta*, fr. *spanaki* spinach + *pēta, pita* pie] (1950) : a traditional Greek pie of spinach, feta cheese, and seasonings baked in phyllo
span·dex \'span-,deks\ *n* [anagram of *expands*] (1959) : any of various elastic textile fibers made chiefly of polyurethane; *also* : clothing made of this material
span·drel *also* **span·dril** \'span-drəl\ *n* [ME *spandrell*, fr. AF *spaundre*, fr. OF *espandre* to spread out — more at SPAWN] (15c) **1** : the sometimes ornamented space between the right or left exterior curve of an arch and an enclosing right angle **2** : the triangular space beneath the string of a stair
spang \'spaŋ\ *adv* [Sc *spang* to leap, cast, bang] (1843) **1** : to a complete degree **2** : in an exact or direct manner : SQUARELY
¹span·gle \'spaŋ-gəl\ *n* [ME *spangel*, dim. of *spang* shiny ornament, prob. of Scand origin; akin to ON *spong* spangle; akin to OE *spang* buckle, MD *spannen* to stretch] (15c) **1** : a small plate of shining metal or plastic used for ornamentation esp. on clothing **2** : a small glittering object or particle
²spangle *vb* **span·gled; span·gling** \'spaŋ-g(ə-)liŋ\ *vt* (1598) : to set or sprinkle with or as if with spangles ~ *vi* : to glitter as if covered with spangles : SPARKLE
Span·glish \'spaŋ-glish, -lish\ *n* [blend of *Spanish* and *English*] (1965) : Spanish marked by numerous borrowings from English; *broadly* : any of various combinations of Spanish and English
Span·iard \'span-yərd\ *n* [ME *Spaignart*, fr. MF *Espaignart*, fr. *Espaigne* Spain, fr. L *Hispania*] (15c) : a native or inhabitant of Spain
span·iel \'span-yəl *also* 'spa-n°l\ *n* [ME *spaniell*, fr. MF *espaignol*, lit., Spaniard, fr. (assumed) VL *Hispaniolus*, fr. L *Hispania* Spain] (14c) **1** : a member of any of several breeds of small or medium-sized mostly

short-legged dogs usu. having long wavy hair, feathered legs and tail, and large drooping ears **2** : a fawning servile person
Span·ish \'spa-nish\ *n* [*Spanish*, adj., fr. ME *Spainish*, fr. *Spain*] (15c) **1** : the Romance language of the largest part of Spain and of the countries colonized by Spaniards **2** *pl in constr* : the people of Spain — **Spanish** *adj* — **Span·ish·ness** *n*
Spanish American *n* (1811) **1** : a resident of the U.S. whose native language is Spanish and whose culture is of Spanish origin **2** : a native or inhabitant of one of the countries of America in which Spanish is the national language — **Spanish–American** *adj*
Spanish bayonet *n* (1843) : any of several yuccas; *esp* : one (*Yucca aloifolia*) with a short trunk and rigid spine-tipped leaves
Spanish chestnut *n* (1699) : MARRON
Spanish fly *n* (1634) **1** : a green blister beetle (*Lytta vesicatoria*) of southern Europe **2** : CANTHARIS 2
Spanish mackerel *n* (1666) : a large scombroid food and game fish (*Scomberomorus maculatus*) that is bluish above with oval brown spots on the sides and is found off the American Atlantic coast from Cape Ann to Brazil
Spanish moss *n* (1823) : an epiphytic plant (*Tillandsia usneoides*) of the pineapple family forming pendent tufts of grayish green filaments on trees from the southern U.S. to Argentina
Spanish needles *n pl but sing or pl in constr* (1743) : any of several bur marigolds; *esp* : an annual (*Bidens bipinnata*) of No. America and Asia having yellow flowers and dissected leaves
Spanish omelet *n* (ca. 1886) : an omelet served with a sauce containing chopped green pepper, onion, and tomato
Spanish rice *n* (1928) : rice cooked with onions, green pepper, and tomatoes
¹spank \'spaŋk\ *vt* [imit.] (ca. 1727) : to strike esp. on the buttocks with the open hand — **spank** *n*
²spank *vi* [back-formation fr. *spanking*] (ca. 1810) : to move quickly, dashingly, or spiritedly (~*ing* along in his new car)
span·ker \'spaŋ-kər\ *n* [origin unknown] (1794) **1** : the fore-and-aft sail on the mast nearest the stern of a square-rigged ship **2** : the sail on the sternmost mast in a schooner of four or more masts
¹spank·ing \'spaŋ-kiŋ\ *adj* [origin unknown] (1666) **1** : remarkable of its kind : being fresh and strong : BRISK
²spanking *adv* (1886) : VERY (a ~ clean floor) (~ new)
span·ner \'spa-nər\ *n* [G, instrument for winding springs, fr. *spannen* to stretch; akin to MD *spannen* to stretch — more at SPAN] (ca. 1790) **1** *chiefly Brit* : WRENCH **2** : a wrench that has a hole, projection, or hook at one or both ends of the head for engaging with a corresponding device on the object that is to be turned

spanner 2

span–new \'span-'nü, -'nyü\ *adj* [ME, part trans. of ON *spānnȳr*, fr. *spānn* chip of wood + *nȳr* new] (14c) : BRAND-NEW
span·worm \'span-,wərm\ *n* [³*span*] (1820) : LOOPER 1
¹spar \'spär\ *n* [ME *sparre*; akin to OE *spere* spear — more at SPEAR] (14c) **1** : a stout pole **2 a** : a stout rounded wood or metal piece (as a mast, boom, gaff, or yard) used to support rigging **b** : any of the main longitudinal members of the wing of an airplane that carry the ribs
²spar *vi* **sparred; spar·ring** [prob. alter. of ²*spur*] (1537) **1 a** : BOX; *esp* : to gesture without landing a blow to draw one's opponent or create an opening **b** : to engage in a practice or exhibition bout of boxing **2** : SKIRMISH, WRANGLE **3** : to strike or fight with feet or spurs in the manner of a gamecock
³spar *n* (1814) **1** : a movement of offense or defense in boxing **2** : a sparring match or session
⁴spar *n* [LG; akin to OE *spærstān* gypsum, *spæren* of plaster] (1581) : any of various nonmetallic usu. cleavable and lustrous minerals
SPAR \'spär\ *n* [Semper *Paratus*, motto of the U.S. Coast Guard, fr. NL, always ready] (1942) : a member of the women's reserve of the U.S. Coast Guard
¹spare \'spar, 'sper\ *vb* **spared; spar·ing** [ME, fr. OE *spare*; akin to OHG *sparōn* to spare, OE *spær*, adj., scant] *vt* (bef. 12c) **1** : to forbear to destroy, punish, or harm **2** : to refrain from attacking or reprimanding with necessary or salutary severity **3** : to relieve of the necessity of doing or undergoing something (~ yourself the trouble) **4** : to refrain from : AVOID (*spared* no expense) **5** : to use or dispense frugally — used chiefly in the negative (don't ~ the syrup) **6 a** : to give up as not strictly needed (do you have any cash to ~) **b** : to have left over or as margin (time to ~) ~ *vi* **1** : to be frugal **2** : to refrain from doing harm : be lenient — **spare·able** \-ə-bəl\ *adj* — **spar·er** *n*
²spare *adj* **spar·er; spar·est** [ME, fr. OE *spær* sparing, scant; akin to OHG *spar* spare] (14c) **1** : not being used; *esp* : held for emergency use (a ~ tire) **2** : being over and above what is needed : SUPERFLUOUS (~ time) **3** : not liberal or profuse : SPARING (a ~ prose style) **4** : healthily lean **5** : not abundant or plentiful *syn* see LEAN, MEAGER — **spare·ly** *adv* — **spare·ness** *n*
³spare *n* (1642) **1 a** : a spare tire **b** : a duplicate (as a key or a machine part) kept in reserve **2** : the knocking down of all 10 pins with the first 2 balls in a frame in bowling
spare·ribs \'spar-,(r)ibz, 'sper-, -əbz\ *n pl* [by folk etymology fr. LG *ribbesper* pickled pork ribs roasted on a spit, fr. MLG, fr. *ribbe* rib + *sper* spear, spit] (1596) : a cut of pork ribs separated from the bacon strip
sparge \'spärj\ *vt* **sparged; sparg·ing** [prob. fr. MF *espargier*, fr. L *spargere* to scatter] (1785) **1** : SPRINKLE, BESPATTER; *esp* : SPRAY **2** : to agitate (a liquid) by means of compressed air or gas entering through a pipe — **sparge** *n* — **sparg·er** *n*
spar·ing \'spar-iŋ, 'sper-\ *adj* (14c) **1** : marked by or practicing careful restraint (as in the use of resources) **2** : MEAGER, BARE (the map is ~ of information) — **spar·ing·ly** \-iŋ-lē\ *adv*
  syn SPARING, FRUGAL, THRIFTY, ECONOMICAL mean careful in the use of one's money or resources. SPARING stresses abstention and restraint (*sparing* in the offering of advice). FRUGAL implies absence of luxury and simplicity of lifestyle (ran a *frugal* household). THRIFTY stresses

good management and industry ⟨*thrifty* use of nonrenewable resources⟩. ECONOMICAL stresses prudent management, lack of wastefulness, and use of things to their best advantage ⟨an *economical* health care plan⟩.

¹spark \'spärk\ n [ME *sparke*, fr. OE *spearca*; akin to MD *sparke* spark and perh. to L *spargere* to scatter] (bef. 12c) 1 a : a small particle of a burning substance thrown out by a body in combustion or remaining when combustion is nearly completed b : a hot glowing particle struck from a larger mass; *esp* : one heated by friction 2 a : a luminous disruptive electrical discharge of very short duration between two conductors separated by a gas (as air) b : the discharge in a spark plug c : the mechanism controlling the discharge in a spark plug 3 : SPARKLE, FLASH 4 : something that sets off a sudden force ⟨provided the ∼ that helped the team to rally⟩ 5 : a latent particle capable of growth or developing : GERM ⟨still retains a ∼ of decency⟩ 6 *pl but sing in constr* : a radio operator on a ship

²spark vi (13c) 1 a : to throw out sparks b : to flash or fall like sparks 2 : to produce sparks; *specif* : to have the electric ignition working 3 : to respond with enthusiasm ∼ vt 1 : to set off in a burst of activity : ACTIVATE ⟨the question ∼*ed* a lively discussion⟩ — often used with *off* 2 : to stir to activity : INCITE ⟨∼*ed* her team to victory⟩ — **spark·er** n

³spark n [perh. of Scand origin; akin to ON *sparkr* sprightly] (ca. 1600) 1 : a foppish young man 2 : LOVER, BEAU — **spark·ish** \'spär-kish\ adj

⁴spark vb (1787) : WOO, COURT — **spark·er** n

spark chamber n (1961) : a device usu. used to detect the path of a high-energy particle that consists of a series of charged metal plates or wires separated by a gas (as neon) in which observable electric discharges follow the path of the particle

spark coil n (1896) : an induction coil for producing the spark for an internal combustion engine

spark gap n (1889) : a space between two high-potential terminals (as of an induction coil) through which pass discharges of electricity; *also* : a device having a spark gap

sparking plug n (1902) *Brit* : SPARK PLUG

¹spar·kle \'spär-kəl\ vb spar·kled; spar·kling \-k(ə-)liŋ\ [ME, freq. of *sparken* to spark] vi (13c) 1 a : to throw out sparks b : to give off or reflect bright moving points of light c : to perform brilliantly 2 : EFFERVESCE ⟨wine that ∼*s*⟩ 3 : to become lively or animated ⟨the dialogue ∼*s* with wit⟩ ⟨eyes *sparkling* with anger⟩ ∼ vt 1 : to cause to glitter or shine syn see FLASH — **spar·kly** \-k(ə-)lē\ adj

²sparkle n [ME, dim. of *sparke*] (14c) 1 : a little spark : SCINTILLATION 2 : the quality of sparkling 3 a : ANIMATION, LIVELINESS b : the quality or state of being effervescent

spar·kler \'spär-klər\ n (1713) : one that sparkles: as a : DIAMOND b : a firework that throws off brilliant sparks on burning c : SPARKLING WINE

sparkling wine n (1697) : an effervescent table wine

spark plug n (1903) 1 : a part that fits into the cylinder head of an internal combustion engine and carries two electrodes separated by an air gap across which the current from the ignition system discharges to form the spark for combustion 2 : one that initiates or gives impetus to an undertaking — **spark·plug** \'spärk-,pləg\ vt

sparky \'spär-kē\ adj spark·i·er; -est (ca. 1865) : marked by animation : LIVELY — **spark·i·ly** \-kə-lē\ adv

spar·row \'spar-(,)ō\ n [ME *sparowe*, fr. OE *spearwa*; akin to OHG *sparo* sparrow] (bef. 12c) 1 : any of a genus (*Passer* of the family Ploceidae) of small chiefly brownish or grayish Old World oscine songbirds that include some which have been widely introduced; *esp* : HOUSE SPARROW 2 : any of various finches (as the song sparrow or tree sparrow) resembling the true sparrows — **spar·row·like** \-ō-,lik, -ə-,lik\ adj

sparrow hawk n (15c) : any of various small hawks: as a : an Old World accipiter (*Accipiter nisus*) that is dark gray to blackish above with the female having a grayish brown barred underside and the male having a chestnut barred underside b : KESTREL b

sparse \'spärs\ adj spars·er; spars·est [L *sparsus* spread out, fr. pp. of *spargere* to scatter — more at SPARK] (1753) : of few and scattered elements; *esp* : not thickly grown or settled syn see MEAGER — **sparse·ly** adv — **sparse·ness** n — **spar·si·ty** \'spär-sə-tē, -stē\ n

Spar·ta·cist \'spär-tə-sist\ n [G *Spartakist*, fr. *Spartakusbund*, lit., league of Spartakus, a revolutionary organization, fr. *Spartakus*, pen name of Karl Liebknecht, its cofounder] (1919) : a member of a revolutionary political group organized in Germany in 1918 and advocating extreme socialistic doctrines

¹Spar·tan \'spär-tᵊn\ n (15c) 1 : a native or inhabitant of ancient Sparta 2 : a person of great courage and self-discipline — **Spar·tan·ism** \-,i-zəm\ n

²Spartan adj (1582) 1 : of or relating to Sparta in ancient Greece 2 a *often not cap* : marked by strict self-discipline or self-denial ⟨a ∼ athlete⟩ b *often not cap* : marked by simplicity, frugality, or avoidance of luxury and comfort ⟨a ∼ room⟩ c : LACONIC d : undaunted by pain or danger — **Spar·tan·ly** adv

spar·te·ine \'spär-tē-ən, 'spär-,tēn\ n [L *spartum* esparto, broom + ISV -*eine* — more at ESPARTO] (1851) : a liquid alkaloid $C_{15}H_{26}N_2$ extracted from the Scotch broom and used in medicine in the form of its sulfate

spar varnish n [¹*spar*] (ca. 1909) : an exterior waterproof varnish

spasm \'spa-zəm\ n [ME *spasme*, fr. MF, fr. L *spasmus*, fr. Gk *spasmos*, fr. *span* to draw, pull] (14c) 1 : an involuntary and abnormal muscular contraction 2 : a sudden violent and temporary effort or emotion ⟨a ∼ of creativity⟩

spas·mod·ic \spaz-'mä-dik\ adj [NL *spasmodicus*, fr. Gk *spasmōdēs*, fr. *spasmos*] (ca. 1681) 1 a : relating to or affected or characterized by spasm b : resembling a spasm esp. in sudden violence ⟨a ∼ jerk⟩ 2 : acting or proceeding fitfully : INTERMITTENT 3 : subject to outbursts of emotional excitement : EXCITABLE syn see FITFUL — **spas·mod·i·cal·ly** \-di-k(ə-)lē\ adv

spas·mo·lyt·ic \,spaz-mə-'li-tik\ adj [ISV *spasmo*- (fr. Gk *spasmos* spasm) + -*lytic*] (ca. 1935) : tending or having the power to relieve spasms or convulsions — **spasmolytic** n

¹spas·tic \'spas-tik\ adj [L *spasticus*, fr. Gk *spastikos* drawing in, fr. *span*] (1753) 1 : of, relating to, characterized by, or affected with

spasm ⟨a ∼ colon⟩ ⟨a ∼ patient⟩ 2 : SPASMODIC 2 ⟨a ∼ influx of data⟩ — **spas·ti·cal·ly** \-ti-k(ə-)lē\ adv

²spastic n (1896) : one suffering from spastic paralysis

spas·tic·i·ty \spa-'sti-sə-tē\ n (ca. 1827) : a spastic state or condition; *esp* : muscular hypertonicity with increased tendon reflexes

spastic paralysis n (1879) : paralysis with tonic spasm of the affected muscles and with increased tendon reflexes — compare CEREBRAL PALSY

¹spat \'spat\ *past and past part of* SPIT

²spat n, pl spat or spats [origin unknown] (1667) : a young bivalve (as an oyster)

³spat n [short for *spatterdash* legging] (ca. 1802) : a cloth or leather gaiter covering the instep and ankle

⁴spat n [origin unknown] (1804) 1 : a brief petty quarrel or angry outburst 2 *chiefly dial* : SLAP 3 : a sound like that of rain falling in large drops

⁵spat vb spat·ted; spat·ting vt (ca. 1832) *chiefly dial* : SLAP ∼ vi 1 : to quarrel pettily or briefly 2 : to strike with a sound like that of rain falling in large drops

spate \'spāt\ n [ME] (15c) 1 : FRESHET, FLOOD 2 a : a large number or amount ⟨a ∼ of books on gardening⟩ b : a sudden or strong outburst : RUSH ⟨a ∼ of anger⟩

spathe \'spāth\ n [NL *spatha*, fr. L, broadsword — more at SPADE] (1785) : a sheathing bract or pair of bracts partly enclosing an inflorescence and esp. a spadix on the same axis ⟨the ∼ of the calla lily⟩

spath·u·late \'spath-yə-lət\ adj [LL *spathula*, spatula spatula] (1821) : SPATULATE ⟨∼ petals of a flower⟩

spa·tial \'spā-shəl\ adj [L *spatium* space] (1847) : relating to, occupying, or having the character of space — **spa·ti·al·i·ty** \,spā-shē-'a-lə-tē\ n — **spa·tial·ly** \'spā-sh(ə-)lē\ adv

spatial summation n (1968) : sensory summation that involves stimulation of several spatially separated neurons at the same time

spa·tio·tem·po·ral \,spā-shē-ō-'tem-p(ə-)rəl\ adj [L *spatium* + *tempor*-, *tempus* time] (1900) 1 : having both spatial and temporal qualities 2 : of or relating to space-time — **spa·tio·tem·po·ral·ly** \-p(ə-)rə-lē\ adv

¹spat·ter \'spa-tər\ vb [akin to Flem *spetteren* to spatter] vi (1600) 1 : to spurt forth in scattered drops ⟨blood ∼*ing* everywhere⟩ ∼ vt 1 : to splash with or as if with a liquid; *also* : to soil in this way ⟨his coat was ∼*ed* with mud⟩ 2 : to scatter by or as if by splashing ⟨∼ water⟩ 3 : to cover with or as if with splashes or spots 4 : to injure by aspersion : DEFAME ⟨∼*ed* my reputation⟩

²spatter n (1797) 1 a : the act or process of spattering : the state of being spattered b : the noise of spattering 2 a : a drop or splash spattered on something or a spot or stain due to spattering b : a small amount or number : SPRINKLE ⟨a ∼ of applause⟩

spat·ter·dock \'spa-tər-,däk\ n (1813) : a common yellow No. American water lily (*Nuphar advena*); *also* : a congeneric plant

spat·u·la \'spa-chə-lə, 'spach-lə\ n [LL, spoon, spatula — more at EPAULET] (1525) : a flat thin usu. metal implement used esp. for spreading or mixing soft substances, scooping, or lifting

spat·u·late \'spa-chə-lət\ adj (1760) : shaped like a spatula ⟨a ∼ leaf⟩ ⟨∼ spines of a caterpillar⟩ ⟨a ∼ tool⟩ — see LEAF illustration

spätz·le var of SPAETZLE

spav·in \'spa-vən\ n [ME *spavayne*, fr. MF *espavain*] (15c) : SWELLING; *esp* : a bony enlargement of the hock of a horse associated with strain

spav·ined \-vənd\ adj (15c) 1 : affected with spavin 2 : old and decrepit : OVER-THE-HILL

¹spawn \'spón, 'spän\ vb [ME, fr. AF *espaundre*, fr. OF *espandre* to spread out, expand, fr. L *expandere*] vi (15c) 1 : to deposit spawn 2 : to produce young esp. in large numbers ∼ vt 1 a : to produce or deposit (eggs) — used of an aquatic animal b : to induce (fish) to spawn c : to plant with mushroom spawn 2 : BRING FORTH, GENERATE — **spawn·er** n

²spawn n (15c) 1 : the eggs of aquatic animals (as fishes or oysters) that lay many small eggs 2 : PRODUCT, OFFSPRING; *also* : numerous issue 3 : the seed, germ, or source of something 4 : mycelium esp. prepared (as in bricks) for propagating mushrooms

spay \'spā, nonstand 'späd\ vt spayed \'spād, nonstand 'spä-dəd\; spay·ing \'spā-iŋ, nonstand 'spä-diŋ\ [ME, fr. MF *espeer* to cut with a sword, fr. OF, fr. *espee* sword, fr. L *spatha* sword — more at SPADE] (15c) : to remove the ovaries of (a female animal)

spaz \'spaz\ n, pl spaz·zes [by shortening & alter. fr. *spastic*] (1965) *slang* : one who is inept : KLUTZ

speak \'spēk\ vb spoke \'spōk\; spo·ken \'spō-kən\; speak·ing [ME *speken*, fr. OE *sprecan*, *specan*; akin to OHG *sprehhan* to speak, Gk *spharageisthai* to crackle] vi (bef. 12c) 1 a : to utter words or articulate sounds with the ordinary voice : TALK b (1) : to express thoughts, opinions, or feelings orally (2) : to extend a greeting (3) : to be on speaking terms ⟨still were not ∼*ing* after the dispute⟩ c (1) : to express oneself before a group (2) : to address one's remarks ⟨∼ to the issue⟩ 2 a : to make a written statement ⟨his diaries . . . *spoke* . . . of his entrancement with death —Sy Kahn⟩ b : to use such an expression — often used in the phrase *so to speak* ⟨was at the enemy's gates, so to ∼ —C. S. Forester⟩ c : to serve as spokesman ⟨spoke for the whole group⟩ 3 a : to express feelings by other than verbal means ⟨actions ∼ louder than words⟩ b : SIGNAL c : to be interesting or attractive : APPEAL ⟨great music . . . ∼*s* directly to the emotions — A. N. Whitehead⟩ 4 a : to make a request : ASK ⟨*spoke* for the remaining piece of pie⟩ 5 : to make a characteristic or natural sound ⟨all at once the thunder *spoke* —George Meredith⟩ 6 a : TESTIFY b : to be indicative or suggestive ⟨his gold . . . *spoke* of riches in the land —Julian Dana⟩ ∼ vt 1 (1) : to utter with the speaking voice : PRONOUNCE (2) : to give a recitation of : DECLAIM b : to express orally : DECLARE ⟨free to ∼ their minds⟩ c : ADDRESS, ACCOST; *esp* : HAIL 2 : to make known in writing : STATE 3 : to use or be able to use in speaking ⟨∼*s* Spanish⟩ 4 : to indicate by other than verbal means 5

\ə\ abut \ᵊ\ kitten, F table \ər\ further \a\ ash \ā\ ace \ä\ mop, mar \aů\ out \ch\ chin \e\ bet \ē\ easy \g\ go \i\ hit \ī\ ice \j\ job \ŋ\ sing \ō\ go \ó\ law \ói\ boy \th\ thin \t̲h̲\ the \ü\ loot \ů\ foot \y\ yet \zh\ vision \ā, k̲, ⁿ, œ, œ̄, ue, ūe, ʸ\ see Guide to Pronunciation archaic : DESCRIBE, DEPICT — **speak·able** \'spē-kə-bəl\ *adj* — **to speak of** : worthy of mention or notice — usu. used in negative constructions

-speak \-ˌspēk\ *n comb form* [*newspeak*] — used to form esp. nonce words denoting a particular kind of jargon ⟨architect*speak*⟩ ⟨California*speak*⟩

speak·easy \'spēk-ˌē-zē\ *n, pl* **-eas·ies** (1889) : a place where alcoholic beverages are illegally sold; *specif* : such a place during the period of prohibition in the U.S.

speak·er \'spē-kər\ *n* (14c) **1 a** : one that speaks; *esp* : one who uses a language ⟨native ∼s of French⟩ **b** : one who makes a public speech **c** : one who acts as a spokesman **2** : the presiding officer of a deliberative assembly ⟨*Speaker* of the House of Representatives⟩ **3** : LOUDSPEAKER — **speak·er·ship** \-ˌship\ *n*

speak·er·phone \'spē-kər-ˌfōn\ *n* (1955) : a combination microphone and loudspeaker device for two-way communication by telephone lines

speak·ing \'spē-kiŋ\ *adj* (13c) **1 a** : that speaks : capable of speech **b** : having a population that speaks a specified language — usu. used in combination ⟨English-*speaking* countries⟩ **c** : that involves talking or giving speeches ⟨a ∼ role⟩ ⟨a ∼ tour⟩ **2** : highly significant or expressive : ELOQUENT **3** : resembling a living being or a real object

speaking tube *n* (1833) : a pipe through which conversation may be conducted (as between different parts of a building)

speak-out \'spēk-ˌaut\ *n* (1968) : an event in which people publicly share their experiences of or views on an issue

speak out *vi* (1530) **1** : to speak loud enough to be heard **2** : to speak boldly : express an opinion frankly ⟨*spoke out* on the issues⟩

speak up *vi* (1705) **1** : to express an opinion freely ⟨*speak up* for truth and justice —Clive Bell⟩ **2** : to speak loudly and distinctly

spean \'spēn\ *vt* [MD *spenen*] (1595) *chiefly Scot* : WEAN

¹spear \'spir\ *n* [ME *spere*, fr. OE; akin to OHG *sper* spear, L *sparus* hunting spear] (bef. 12c) **1 a** : a thrusting or throwing weapon with long shaft and sharp head or blade **2** : a sharp-pointed instrument with barbs used in spearing fish **3** : SPEARMAN

²spear *vt* (15c) **1** : to pierce, strike, or take with or as if with a spear ⟨∼ salmon⟩ ⟨∼ed a chop from the platter⟩ **2** : to catch (as a baseball) with a sudden thrust of the arm ∼ *vi* : to thrust at or wound something with or as if with a spear — **spear·er** *n*

³spear *adj* (1861) : PATERNAL, MALE ⟨the ∼ side of the family⟩ — compare DISTAFF

⁴spear *vi* [⁵*spear*] (1573) *of a plant* : to thrust a spear upward

⁵spear *n* [alter. of ¹*spire*] (1647) : a usu. young blade, shoot, or sprout (as of grass)

spear–car·ri·er \'spir-ˌkar-ē-ər\ *n* (1953) **1 a** : a member of an opera chorus **b** : a bit actor in a play **2** : a person whose actions are of little significance or value in an event or organization

¹spear·fish \-ˌfish\ *n* (ca. 1882) : any of several billfishes (genus *Tetrapturus*) having the anterior part of the first dorsal fin about as high as the body is deep

²spearfish *vi* (ca. 1949) : to fish with a spear

spear·gun \'spir-ˌgən\ *n* (1951) : a gun that shoots a spear and is used in spearfishing

¹spear·head \-ˌhed\ *n* (14c) **1** : the sharp-pointed head of a spear **2** : a leading element, force, or influence in an undertaking or development

²spearhead *vt* (1937) : to serve as leader or leading element of

spear·man \'spir-mən\ *n* (14c) : one armed with a spear

spear·mint \-ˌmint, -mənt\ *n* (1562) : a common mint (*Mentha spicata*) grown for flavoring and esp. for its aromatic oil

spear–throw·er \-ˌthrō(-ə)r\ *n* (1871) : ATLATL

spear·wort \-ˌwort, -ˌwört\ *n* (14c) : any of several buttercups (esp. *Ranunculus flammula*) with spear-shaped leaves

spec \'spek\ *vt* **specced** or **spec'd** \'spekt\; **spec·cing** [²*specs*] (1965) : to write specifications for

¹spe·cial \'spe-shəl\ *adj* [ME, fr. OF or L; OF *especial*, fr. L *specialis* individual, particular, fr. *species* species] (13c) **1** : distinguished by some unusual quality; *esp* : being in some way superior ⟨our ∼ blend⟩ **2** : held in particular esteem ⟨a ∼ friend⟩ **3 a** : readily distinguishable from others of the same category : UNIQUE ⟨they set it apart as a ∼ day of thanksgiving⟩ **b** : of, relating to, or constituting a species : SPECIFIC **4** : being other than the usual : ADDITIONAL, EXTRA **5** : designed for a particular purpose or occasion — **spe·cial·ness** *n*

syn SPECIAL, ESPECIAL, SPECIFIC, PARTICULAR, INDIVIDUAL mean of or relating to one thing or class. SPECIAL stresses having a quality, character, identity, or use of its own ⟨*special* ingredients⟩. ESPECIAL may add implications of preeminence or preference ⟨a matter of *especial* importance⟩. SPECIFIC implies a quality or character distinguishing a kind or a species ⟨children with *specific* nutritional needs⟩. PARTICULAR stresses the distinctness of something as an individual ⟨a ballet step of *particular* difficulty⟩. INDIVIDUAL implies unequivocal reference to one of a class or group ⟨valued each *individual* opinion⟩.

²special *n* (1866) **1** : one that is used for a special service or occasion ⟨caught the commuter ∼ to work⟩ **2** : something (as a television program) that is not part of a regular series

special assessment *n* (1875) : a specific tax levied on private property to meet the cost of public improvements that enhance the value of the property

special delivery *n* (1886) : expedited messenger delivery of mail matter for an extra fee

special district *n* (1950) : a political subdivision of a state established to provide a single public service (as water supply or sanitation) within a specific geographical area

special drawing rights *n* (1967) : a means of exchange used by governments to settle their international indebtedness

special education *n* (1921) : classes for students (as the handicapped) with special educational needs

special effects *n pl* (1937) : visual or sound effects introduced into a motion picture or a taped television production

spearmint

Special Forces *n pl* (1962) : a branch of the army composed of soldiers specially trained in guerrilla warfare

special handling *n* (1928) : the handling of parcel-post or fourth-class mail as first-class but not as special-delivery matter for an extra fee

special interest *n* (1910) : a person or group seeking to influence legislative or government policy to further often narrowly defined interests; *esp* : LOBBY

spe·cial·i·sa·tion, spe·cial·ise, specialised *Brit var of* SPECIALIZATION, SPECIALIZE, SPECIALIZED

spe·cial·ism \'spe-shə-ˌli-zəm\ *n* (1856) **1** : specialization in an occupation or branch of learning **2** : a field of specialization : SPECIALTY

spe·cial·ist \'spe-sh(ə-)list\ *n* (1856) **1** : one who specializes in a particular occupation, practice, or branch of learning **2** : any of four enlisted ranks in the army corresponding to the grades of corporal through sergeant first class — **specialist** or **spe·cial·is·tic** \ˌspe-shə-'lis-tik\ *adj*

spe·ci·al·i·ty \ˌspe-shē-'a-lə-tē\ *n, pl* **-ties** (15c) **1** : a special mark or quality **2** : a special object or class of objects **3 a** : a special aptitude or skill **b** : SPECIALTY 3

spe·cial·i·za·tion \ˌspe-sh(ə-)lə-'zā-shən\ *n* (1843) **1** : a making or becoming specialized **2 a** : structural adaptation of a body part to a particular function or of an organism for life in a particular environment **b** : a body part or an organism adapted by specialization

spe·cial·ize \'spe-shə-ˌlīz\ *vb* **-ized**; **-iz·ing** *vt* (1613) **1** : to make particular mention of : PARTICULARIZE **2** : to apply or direct to a specific end or use ⟨*specialized* their study⟩ ∼ *vi* **1** : to concentrate one's efforts in a special activity, field, or practice **2** : to undergo specialization; *esp* : to change adaptively

specialized *adj* (1853) **1** : characterized by or exhibiting biological specialization; *esp* : highly differentiated esp. in a particular direction or for a particular end **2** : designed or fitted for one particular purpose or occupation ⟨∼ personnel⟩

spe·cial·ly \'spe-sh(ə-)lē\ *adv* (14c) **1** : in a special manner ⟨treated her friends ∼⟩ **2 a** : for a special purpose ⟨dresses made ∼ for the occasion⟩ ⟨wines ∼ selected to match each course⟩ **b** : in particular : SPECIFICALLY ⟨made ∼ for you⟩ **3** : ESPECIALLY 2 ⟨makes a ∼ fine curry⟩ ⟨was ∼ pleased with the gift⟩

special pleading *n* (1684) **1** : the allegation of special or new matter to offset the effect of matter pleaded by the opposite side and admitted, as distinguished from a direct denial of the matter pleaded **2** : misleading argument that presents one point or phase as if it covered the entire question at issue

special relativity *n* (1941) : RELATIVITY 3a

special theory of relativity *n* (1941) : RELATIVITY 3a

spe·cial·ty \'spe-shəl-tē\ *n, pl* **-ties** [ME *specialte*, fr. MF *especialté*, fr. LL *specialitat-, specialitas*, fr. L *specialis* special] (15c) **1** : a distinctive mark or quality **2 a** : a special object or class of objects: *esp* (1) : a legal agreement embodied in a sealed instrument (2) : a product of a special kind or of special excellence ⟨fried chicken is my ∼⟩ **b** : the state of being special, distinctive, or peculiar **3** : something in which one specializes

spe·ci·a·tion \ˌspē-shē-'ā-shən, -sē-\ *n* (1906) : the process of biological species formation — **spe·ci·ate** \'spē-shē-ˌāt, -sē-\ *vi* — **spe·ci·a·tion·al** \ˌspē-shē-'ā-shnəl, -sē-, -shə-nᵊl\ *adj*

¹spe·cie \'spē-shē, -sē\ *n* [fr. *in specie*, fr. L, in kind] (1617) : money in coin — **in specie** **1** : in the same or like form or kind ⟨ready to return insult *in specie*⟩; *also* : in coin

²specie *n* [back-formation fr. *species* (taken as a pl.)] (1711) *nonstand* : SPECIES

¹spe·cies \'spē-(ˌ)shēz, -(ˌ)sēz\ *n, pl* **species** [ME, fr. L, appearance, kind, species, fr. *specere* to look — more at SPY] (14c) **1 a** : KIND, SORT **b** : a class of individuals having common attributes and designated by a common name; *specif* : a logical division of a genus or more comprehensive class **c** : the human race : human beings — often used with *the* ⟨survival of the ∼ in the nuclear age⟩ **d** (1) : a category of biological classification ranking immediately below the genus or subgenus, comprising related organisms or populations potentially capable of interbreeding, and being designated by a binomial that consists of the name of a genus followed by a Latin or latinized uncapitalized noun or adjective agreeing grammatically with the genus name (2) : an individual or kind belonging to a biological species **e** : a particular kind of atomic nucleus, atom, molecule, or ion **2** : the consecrated eucharistic elements of the Roman Catholic or Eastern Orthodox Eucharist **3 a** : a mental image; *also* : a sensible object **b** : an object of thought correlative with a natural object

²species *adj* (1899) : belonging to a biological species as distinguished from a horticultural variety ⟨a ∼ rose⟩

spe·cies·ism \'spē-shēz-ˌi-zəm, -sē-\ *n* (1973) **1** : prejudice or discrimination based on species; *esp* : discrimination against animals **2** : the assumption of human superiority on which speciesism is based

¹spe·cif·ic \spi-'si-fik\ *adj* [LL *specificus*, fr. L *species*] (ca. 1631) **1 a** : constituting or falling into a specifiable category **b** : sharing or being those properties of something that allow it to be referred to a particular category **2 a** : restricted to a particular individual, situation, relation, or effect ⟨a disease ∼ to horses⟩ **b** : exerting a distinctive influence (as on a body part or a disease) ⟨∼ antibodies⟩ **3** : free from ambiguity : ACCURATE ⟨a ∼ statement of faith⟩ **4** : of, relating to, or constituting a species and esp. a biologic species **5 a** : being any of various arbitrary physical constants and esp. one relating a quantitative attribute to unit mass, volume, or area **b** : imposed at a fixed rate per unit (as of weight or count) ⟨∼ import duties⟩ — compare AD VALOREM **syn** see SPECIAL, EXPLICIT — **spe·cif·i·cal·ly** \-fi-k(ə-)lē\ *adv*

²specific *n* (1661) **1 a** : something peculiarly adapted to a purpose or use **b** : a drug or remedy having a specific mitigating effect on a disease **2 a** : a characteristic quality or trait **b** : DETAILS, PARTICULARS — usu. used in pl. ⟨haggling over the legal and financial ∼s of independence —*Time*⟩ *c pl* : SPECIFICATION 2

spec·i·fi·ca·tion \ˌspe-sə-fə-'kā-shən, ˌspes-fə-\ *n* (1633) **1** : the act or process of specifying **2 a** : a detailed precise presentation of something or of a plan or proposal for something — usu. used in pl. **b** : a statement of legal particulars (as of charges or of contract terms); *also* : a single item of such statement **c** : a written description of an invention for which a patent is sought

specific epithet _n_ (1906) : the Latin or latinized noun or adjective that follows the genus name in a taxonomic binomial

specific gravity _n_ (1666) : the ratio of the density of a substance to the density of some substance (as pure water) taken as a standard when both densities are obtained by weighing in air

specific heat _n_ (1832) : the heat in calories required to raise the temperature of one gram of a substance one degree Celsius

specific impulse _n_ (1947) : the thrust produced per unit rate of consumption of the propellant that is usu. expressed in pounds of thrust per pound of propellant used per second and that is a measure of the efficiency of a rocket engine

spec·i·fic·i·ty \ˌspe-sə-ˈfi-sə-tē\ _n_ (1876) : the quality or condition of being specific: as **a** : the condition of being peculiar to a particular individual or group of organisms ⟨host ~ of a parasite⟩ **b** : the condition of participating in or catalyzing only one or a few chemical reactions ⟨the ~ of an enzyme⟩

specific performance _n_ (ca. 1876) **1** : the performance of a legal contract strictly or substantially according to its terms **2** : an equitable remedy enjoining specific performance

spec·i·fy \ˈspe-sə-ˌfī\ _vt_ **-fied; -fy·ing** [ME _specifien_, fr. MF _specifier_, fr. LL _specificare_, fr. _specificus_] (14c) **1** : to name or state explicitly or in detail **2** : to include as an item in a specification — **spec·i·fi·able** \ˌspe-sə-ˈfī-ə-bəl\ _adj_ — **spec·i·fi·er** \ˈspe-sə-ˌfī(-ə)r\ _n_

spec·i·men \ˈspes-mən, ˈspe-sə-\ _n_ [L, fr. _specere_ to look at, look — more at SPY] (1610) **1 a** : an individual, item, or part considered typical of a group, class, or whole **b** : a portion or quantity of material for use in testing, examination, or study ⟨a urine ~⟩ **2 a** : something that obviously belongs to a particular category but is noticed by reason of an individual distinguishing characteristic **b** : PERSON, INDIVIDUAL ⟨he's a tough ~⟩ **3** : a plant grown for exhibition or in the open to display its full development ⟨~ trees⟩ ⟨~ plantings⟩ _syn_ see INSTANCE

spe·ci·os·i·ty \ˌspē-shē-ˈä-sə-tē\ _n_ (1608) : the quality or state of being specious : SPECIOUSNESS

spe·cious \ˈspē-shəs\ _adj_ [ME, visually pleasing, fr. L _speciosus_ beautiful, plausible, fr. _species_] (1513) **1** _obs_ : SHOWY **2** : having deceptive attraction or allure **3** : having a false look of truth or genuineness : SOPHISTIC — **spe·cious·ly** _adv_ — **spe·cious·ness** _n_

¹speck \ˈspek\ _n_ [ME _specke_, fr. OE _specca_] (bef. 12c) **1** : a small discoloration or spot esp. from stain or decay **2** : a very small amount : BIT **3** : something marked or marred with specks — **specked** \ˈspekt\ _adj_

²speck _vt_ (1580) : to produce specks on or in

¹speck·le \ˈspe-kəl\ _n_ [ME; akin to OE _specca_] (15c) : a little speck (as of color)

²speckle _vt_ **speck·led; speck·ling** \-k(ə-)liŋ\ (ca. 1570) **1** : to mark with speckles **2** : to be distributed in or on like speckles

speckled perch _n_ (1877) : BLACK CRAPPIE

speckled trout _n_ (1805) **1** : BROOK TROUT **2** : SPOTTED SEA TROUT

speckle interferometry _n_ (1970) : a technique for generating a clear composite image of a celestial object blurred by atmospheric turbulence in which a large number of short-exposure photographs are mathematically correlated by a computer

¹specs \ˈspeks\ _n pl_ [contr. of _spectacles_] (1807) : GLASSES

²specs _n pl_ [by contr.] (1942) : SPECIFICATIONS

spec·ta·cle \ˈspek-ti-kəl _also_ -ˌti-kəl\ _n_ [ME, fr. MF, fr. L _spectaculum_, fr. _spectare_ to watch, freq. of _specere_ to look, look at — more at SPY] (14c) **1 a** : something exhibited to view as unusual, notable, or entertaining; _esp_ : an eye-catching or dramatic public display **b** : an object of curiosity or contempt ⟨made a ~ of herself⟩ **2** _pl_ : GLASSES **3** : something (as natural markings on an animal) suggesting a pair of glasses

spec·ta·cled \-kəld\ _adj_ (1607) **1** : having or wearing spectacles **2** : having markings suggesting a pair of spectacles ⟨a ~ alligator⟩

¹spec·tac·u·lar \spek-ˈta-kyə-lər, spak-\ _adj_ [L _spectaculum_] (1682) : of, relating to, or being a spectacle : STRIKING, SENSATIONAL ⟨a ~ display of fireworks⟩ — **spec·tac·u·lar·ly** _adv_

²spectacular _n_ (1890) : something that is spectacular; _esp_ : an elaborate film, television, or theatrical production

spec·tate \ˈspek-ˌtāt\ _vi_ **spec·tat·ed; spec·tat·ing** [back-formation fr. _spectator_] (1858) : to be present as a spectator (as at a sports event)

spec·ta·tor \ˈspek-ˌtā-tər, spek-ˈ\ _n_ [L, fr. _spectare_ to watch] (ca. 1586) **1** : one who looks on or watches **2** : a woman's pump usu. having contrasting colors with a perforated design at the toe and sometimes heel — **spectator** _adj_ — **spec·ta·to·ri·al** \ˌspek-tə-ˈtōr-ē-əl, -ˈtȯr-\ _adj_ — **spec·ta·tor·ship** \ˈspek-ˌtā-tər-ˌship, spek-ˈ\ _n_

spec·ter _or_ **spec·tre** \ˈspek-tər\ _n_ [F _spectre_, fr. L _spectrum_ appearance, specter, fr. _specere_ to look, look at — more at SPY] (1605) **1** : a visible disembodied spirit : GHOST **2** : something that haunts or perturbs the mind : PHANTASM ⟨the ~ of hunger⟩

spec·ti·no·my·cin \ˌspek-tə-nō-ˈmī-sⁿn\ _n_ [_spect-_ (fr. NL _spectabilis_, specific epithet of _Streptomyces spectabilis_) + _actinomycin_] (1964) : a white crystalline broad-spectrum antibiotic $C_{14}H_{24}N_2O_7$ produced by a bacterium (_Streptomyces spectabilis_) that used clinically esp. in the form of its hydrochloride to treat gonorrhea

spec·tral \ˈspek-trəl\ _adj_ (1815) **1** : of, relating to, or suggesting a specter : GHOSTLY **2** : of, relating to, or made by a spectrum — **spec·tral·ly** \ˈspek-trə-lē\ _adv_

spectral line _n_ (1866) : one of a series of linear images of the narrow slit of a spectrograph or similar instrument corresponding to a component of the spectrum of the radiation emitted by a particular source

spectro- _comb form_ [NL _spectrum_] : spectrum ⟨_spectroscope_⟩

spec·tro·flu·o·rom·e·ter \ˈspek-(ˌ)trō-ˌflü-ˈrä-mə-tər, -flō-, -flō-\ _also_ **spec·tro·flu·o·rim·e·ter** \-ˈri-\ _n_ (1957) : a device for measuring and recording fluorescence spectra — **spec·tro·flu·o·ro·met·ric** \-ˌflür-ə-ˈme-trik, -ˌflō-, -ˌflō-\ _adj_ — **spec·tro·flu·o·rom·e·try** \-ˌflü-ˈrä-mə-trē, -ˌflō-, -ˌflō-\ _n_

spec·tro·gram \ˈspek-t(r)ə-ˌgram\ _n_ [ISV] (1892) : a photograph or diagram of a spectrum

spec·tro·graph \-ˌgraf\ _n_ [ISV] (1884) : an instrument for dispersing radiation (as electromagnetic radiation or sound waves) into a spectrum and photographing or mapping the spectrum — **spec·tro·graph·ic** \ˌspek-t(r)ə-ˈgra-fik\ _adj_ — **spec·tro·graph·i·cal·ly** \-fi-k(ə-)lē\ _adv_ — **spec·trog·ra·phy** \spek-ˈträ-grə-fē\ _n_

spec·tro·he·lio·gram \ˌspek-trō-ˈhē-lē-ə-ˌgram\ _n_ (1905) : a photograph of the sun that is made by monochromatic light and shows the sun's faculae and prominences

spec·tro·he·lio·graph \-ˌgraf\ _n_ [ISV] (1892) : an apparatus for making spectroheliograms — **spec·tro·he·li·og·ra·phy** \-ˌhē-lē-ˈä-grə-fē\ _n_

spec·tro·he·lio·scope \-ˈhē-lē-ə-ˌskōp\ _n_ [ISV] (1906) **1** : SPECTROHELIOGRAPH **2** : an instrument similar to a spectroheliograph used for visual as distinguished from photographic observations

spec·trom·e·ter \spek-ˈträ-mə-tər\ _n_ [ISV] (1874) **1** : an instrument used for measuring wavelengths of light spectra **2** : any of various analytical instruments in which an emission (as of particles or radiation) is dispersed according to some property (as mass or energy) of the emission and the amount of dispersion is measured ⟨nuclear magnetic resonance ~⟩ — **spec·tro·met·ric** \ˌspek-trə-ˈme-trik\ _adj_ — **spec·trom·e·try** \spek-ˈträ-mə-trē\ _n_

spec·tro·pho·tom·e·ter \ˌspek-trō-fə-ˈtä-mə-tər\ _n_ [ISV] (1881) : a photometer for measuring the relative intensities of the light in different parts of a spectrum — **spec·tro·pho·to·met·ric** \-ˌtrō-ˌfō-tə-ˈme-trik\ _also_ **spec·tro·pho·to·met·ri·cal** \-ˌtri-kəl\ _adj_ — **spec·tro·pho·to·met·ri·cal·ly** \-ˌtri-k(ə-)lē\ _adv_ — **spec·tro·pho·tom·e·try** \ˌspek-(ˌ)trō-fə-ˈtä-mə-trē\ _n_

spec·tro·scope \ˈspek-trə-ˌskōp\ _n_ [ISV] (1861) : an instrument for forming and examining spectra esp. in the visible region of the electromagnetic spectrum — **spec·tro·scop·ic** \ˌspek-trə-ˈskä-pik\ _adj_ — **spec·tro·scop·i·cal·ly** \-pi-k(ə-)lē\ _adv_ — **spec·tros·co·pist** \spek-ˈträs-kə-pist\ _n_

spec·tros·co·py \spek-ˈträs-kə-pē\ _n_ (1870) **1** : the production and investigation of spectra **2** : the process or technique of using a spectroscope or spectrometer

spec·trum \ˈspek-trəm\ _n, pl_ **spec·tra** \-trə\ _or_ **spectrums** [NL, fr. L, appearance — more at SPECTER] (1671) **1 a** : a continuum of color formed when a beam of white light is dispersed (as by passage through a prism) so that its component wavelengths are arranged in order **b** : any of various continua that resemble a spectrum in consisting of an ordered arrangement by a particular characteristic (as frequency or energy): as (1) : ELECTROMAGNETIC SPECTRUM (2) : RADIO SPECTRUM (3) : the range of frequencies of sound waves (4) : MASS SPECTRUM **c** : the representation (as a plot) of a spectrum **2 a** : a continuous sequence or range ⟨a wide ~ of interests⟩ **b** : kinds of organisms associated with a particular situation (as an environment) or susceptible to an agent (as an antibiotic)

spec·u·lar \ˈspe-kyə-lər\ _adj_ [L _specularis_ of a mirror, fr. _speculum_] (1661) : of, relating to, or having the qualities of a mirror — **spec·u·lar·i·ty** \ˌspe-kyə-ˈlar-ə-tē\ _n_ — **spec·u·lar·ly** \ˈspe-kyə-lər-lē\ _adv_

spec·u·late \ˈspe-kyə-ˌlāt\ _vb_ **-lat·ed; -lat·ing** [L _speculatus_, pp. of _speculari_ to spy out, examine, fr. _specula_ watchtower, fr. _specere_ to look, look at — more at SPY] _vi_ (1599) **1 a** : to meditate on or ponder a subject : REFLECT **b** : to review something idly or casually and often inconclusively **2** : to assume a business risk in hope of gain; _esp_ : to buy or sell in expectation of profiting from market fluctuations ~ _vt_ **1** : to take to be true on the basis of insufficient evidence : THEORIZE ⟨_speculated_ that a virus caused the disease⟩ **2** : to be curious or doubtful about : WONDER ⟨~s whether it will rain all vacation⟩ _syn_ see THINK — **spec·u·la·tor** \-ˌlā-tər\ _n_

spec·u·la·tion \ˌspe-kyə-ˈlā-shən\ _n_ (14c) : an act or instance of speculating: as **a** : assumption of unusual business risk in hopes of obtaining commensurate gain **b** : a transaction involving such speculation

spec·u·la·tive \ˈspe-kyə-lə-tiv, -ˌlā-\ _adj_ (14c) **1** : involving, based on, or constituting intellectual speculation; _also_ : theoretical rather than demonstrable ⟨~ knowledge⟩ **2** : marked by questioning curiosity ⟨gave him a ~ glance⟩ **3** : of, relating to, or being a financial speculation ⟨~ stocks⟩ ⟨~ venture⟩ — **spec·u·la·tive·ly** _adv_

spec·u·lum \ˈspe-kyə-ləm\ _n, pl_ **-la** \-lə\ _also_ **-lums** [ME, fr. L, mirror, fr. _specere_] (15c) **1** : an instrument inserted into a body passage for inspection or medication **2** : a drawing or table showing the relative positions of all the planets (as in an astrological nativity) **3** : a patch of color on the secondaries of most ducks and some other birds

speech \ˈspēch\ _n_ [ME _speche_, fr. OE _sprǣc, spǣc_; akin to OE _sprecan_ to speak — more at SPEAK] (bef. 12c) **1 a** : the communication or expression of thoughts in spoken words **b** : exchange of spoken words : CONVERSATION **2 a** : something that is spoken : UTTERANCE **b** : a usu. public discourse : ADDRESS **3 a** : LANGUAGE, DIALECT **b** : an individual manner or style of speaking **4** : the power of expressing or communicating thoughts by speaking

speech community _n_ (1894) : a group of people sharing characteristic patterns of vocabulary, grammar, and pronunciation

speech form _n_ (1863) : LINGUISTIC FORM

speech·i·fy \ˈspē-chə-ˌfī\ _vi_ **-fied; -fy·ing** (1723) : to make a speech

speech·less \ˈspēch-ləs\ _adj_ (bef. 12c) **1** : unable to speak : DUMB **2** : not speaking : SILENT **3** : not capable of being expressed in words — **speech·less·ly** _adv_ — **speech·less·ness** _n_

speech·writ·er \-ˌrī-tər\ _n_ (1834) : a person who writes speeches (as for a politician)

¹speed \ˈspēd\ _n_ [ME _spede_, fr. OE _spēd_; akin to OHG _spuot_ prosperity, speed, OE _spōwan_ to succeed, L _spes_ hope, L _spéti_ to be in time] (bef. 12c) **1** _archaic_ : prosperity in an undertaking : SUCCESS **2 a** : the act or state of moving swiftly : SWIFTNESS **b** : rate of motion: as (1) : VELOCITY 1, 3a (2) : the magnitude of a velocity irrespective of direction **c** : IMPETUS **3** : swiftness or rate of performance or action **4 a** : the sensitivity of a photographic film, plate, or paper expressed numerically **b** : the light-gathering power of a lens or optical system ~ **c** : the time during which a camera shutter is open **5** : a transmission gear in automotive vehicles or bicycles — usu. used in combination ⟨a ten-_speed_ bicycle⟩ **6** : someone or something that appeals to one's taste **7** : METHAMPHETAMINE; _also_ : a related stimulant drug and esp. an amphetamine _syn_ see HASTE — **speed·ster** \ˈspēd-stər\ _n_ — **at speed**

\ə\ abut \ⁿ\ kitten, F table \ər\ further \a\ ash \ā\ ace \ä\ mop, mar \au̇\ out \ch\ chin \e\ bet \ē\ easy \g\ go \i\ hit \ī\ ice \j\ job \ŋ\ sing \ō\ go \ȯ\ law \ȯi\ boy \th\ thin \t̲h̲\ the \ü\ loot \u̇\ foot \y\ yet \zh\ vision \á, k̲, ⁿ, œ, œ̄, ue, ūe, ᵞ\ see Guide to Pronunciation *chiefly Brit* : FAST, RAPIDLY — **up to speed** : operating at full effectiveness or potential

²speed *vb* **sped** \'sped\ *or* **speed·ed; speed·ing** *vi* (bef. 12c) **1 a** *archaic* : to prosper in an undertaking **b** *archaic* : GET ALONG, FARE **2 a** : to make haste ⟨*sped* to her bedside⟩ **b** : to go or drive at excessive or illegal speed **3** : to move, work, or take place faster : ACCELERATE ⟨the heart ~s up⟩ ~ *vt* **1 a** *archaic* : to cause or help to prosper : AID **b** : to further the success of **2 a** : to cause to move quickly : HASTEN **b** : to wish Godspeed to **c** : to increase the speed of : ACCELERATE **3** : to send out ⟨~ an arrow⟩ — **speed·er** *n*

¹speed·ball \'sped-,bol\ *n* (1905) **1** *slang* : a dose of cocaine mixed with heroin or morphine or an amphetamine and usu. taken by injection **2** : a game which resembles soccer but in which a ball caught in the air may be passed with the hands and in which a score is made by kicking or heading the ball between the goalposts or by a successful forward pass over the goal line **3** : one that is outstandingly fast

²speedball *vi* (1970) *slang* : to take a speedball esp. by injection

speed·boat \-,bot\ *n* (1911) : a fast launch or motorboat — **speed·boat·ing** \-,bo-tiŋ\ *n*

speed bump *n* (1972) : a low raised ridge across a roadway (as in a parking lot) to limit vehicle speed

speed freak *n* (1967) : one who habitually misuses amphetamines and esp. methamphetamine

speed limit *n* (1902) : the maximum or minimum speed permitted by law in a given area under specified circumstances

speedo \'spe-(,)do\ *n, pl* **speed·os** [by shortening] (1934) *chiefly Brit* : SPEEDOMETER

speed of light (1823) : a fundamental physical constant that is the speed at which electromagnetic radiation propagates in a vacuum and that has a value fixed by international convention of 299,792,458 meters per second — symbol *c*

speed·om·e·ter \spi-'dä-mə-tər\ *n* (1903) **1** : an instrument for indicating speed : TACHOMETER **2** : an instrument for indicating distance traversed as well as speed of travel; *also* : ODOMETER

speed–read·ing \'sped-,re-diŋ\ *n* (1962) : a method of reading rapidly by skimming — **speed–read** *vt*

speed shop *n* (1953) : a shop that sells custom automotive equipment esp. to hot-rodders

speed skating *n* (1885) : the sport of racing on skates — **speed skater** *n*

speed trap *n* (1925) : a stretch of road policed by often concealed officers or devices (as radar) so as to catch speeders

speed-up \'sped-,əp\ *n* (1921) **1** : ACCELERATION **2** : an employer's demand for accelerated output without increased pay

speed·way \'sped-,wa\ *n* (1894) **1** : a public road on which fast driving is allowed; *specif* : EXPRESSWAY **2** : a racecourse for automobiles or motorcycles **3** : a sprint race for motorcycles

speed·well \'sped-,wel\ *n* (1578) : a perennial European herb (*Veronica officinalis*) of the snapdragon family that is naturalized in No. America and has small bluish flowers in axillary racemes; *also* : any plant of the same genus

speedy \'spe-de\ *adj* **speed·i·er; -est** (14c) : marked by swiftness of motion or action; *also* : PROMPT **2** *syn* see FAST — **speed·i·ly** \'spe-d²l-e\ *adv* — **speed·i·ness** \'spe-de-nəs\ *n*

speel \'spe(ə)l\ *vb* [origin unknown] (1513) *chiefly Scot* : CLIMB

speer *or* **speir** \'spir\ *vb* [ME (Sc) *speren*, fr. OE *spyrian* to seek after; akin to OE *spor* spoor] (bef. 12c) *chiefly Scot* : ASK, INQUIRE

spe·le·ol·o·gy \,spe-le-'ä-lə-je, ,spe-\ *n* [L *speleum* cave (fr. Gk *spelaion*) + ISV -o- + -*logy* — more at SPELUNKER] (1895) : the scientific study or exploration of caves — **spe·le·o·log·i·cal** \,spe-le-ə-'lä-ji-kəl, ,spe-\ *adj* — **spe·le·ol·o·gist** \,spe-le-'ä-lə-jist, ,spe-\ *n*

¹spell \'spel\ *vb* **spelled** \'speld, 'spelt\; **spell·ing** [ME, fr. MF *espeller*, of Gmc origin; akin to OE *spell* talk] *vt* (14c) **1** : to read slowly and with difficulty — often used with *out* **2** : to find out by study : come to understand — often used with *out* ⟨it requires some pains to ~ out those decorations —F. J. Mather⟩ **3 a** (1) : to name the letters of in order; *also* : to write or print the letters of in order (2) : to write or print the letters of in a particular way ⟨you can ~ it either way⟩ ⟨I ~ed it wrong⟩ **b** : to make up (a word) ⟨what word do these letters ~⟩ **c** : WRITE 1b ⟨catnip is ~ed as one word⟩ **4** : to add up to : MEAN ⟨crop failure was likely to ~ stark famine —Stringfellow Barr⟩ ~ *vi* : to form words with letters ⟨teach children to ~⟩; *also* : to spell words in a certain way ⟨~s the way he speaks⟩

²spell *n* [ME, tale, tale, fr. OE; akin to OHG *spel* talk, tale] (1579) **1 a** : a spoken word or form of words held to have magic power : INCANTATION **b** : a state of enchantment **2** : a strong compelling influence or attraction

³spell \'spel\ *vt* **spelled** \'speld\; **spell·ing** (ca. 1623) : to put under a spell

⁴spell *n* [prob. alter. of ME *spale* substitute, fr. OE *spala*] (1593) **1 a** *archaic* : a shift of workers **b** : one's turn at work **2 a** : a period spent in a job or occupation **b** *chiefly Austral* : a period of rest from work, activity, or use **3 a** : an indeterminate period of time ⟨waited a ~ before advancing⟩; *also* : a continuous period of time ⟨did a ~ in prison⟩ **b** : a stretch of a specified type of weather **4** : a period of bodily or mental distress or disorder ⟨a ~ of coughing⟩ ⟨fainting ~s⟩

⁵spell *vb* **spelled** \'speld\; **spell·ing** [ME *spelen*, fr. OE *spelian*; akin to OE *spala* substitute] *vt* (1595) **1** : to take the place of for a time : RELIEVE ⟨he and the other assistant . . . ~ed each other —Mary McCarthy⟩ **2** : REST ~ *vi* **1** : to work in turns **2** *chiefly Austral* : to rest from work or activity for a time

spell·bind \'spel-,bind\ *vt* **-bound** \-,baund\; **-bind·ing** [backformation fr. *spellbound*] (1808) : to bind or hold by or as if by a spell or charm : FASCINATE

spell·bind·er \-,bin-dər\ *n* (1888) : a speaker of compelling eloquence; *also* : one that compels attention

spell·bind·ing \-,bin-diŋ\ *adj* (ca. 1934) : holding the attention as if by a spell — **spell·bind·ing·ly** \-,diŋ-le\ *adv*

spell·bound \-,baund\ *adj* (1799) : held by or as if by a spell

spell·er \'spe-lər\ *n* (15c) **1** : a person who spells words esp. in a certain way ⟨a poor ~⟩ **2** : a book with exercises for teaching spelling

spell·ing \'spe-liŋ\ *n* (15c) **1** : the forming of words from letters according to accepted usage : ORTHOGRAPHY **2 a** : a sequence of letters composing a word **b** : the way in which a word is spelled

spelling bee *n* (1872) : a spelling contest in which contestants are eliminated as soon as they misspell a word

spelling pronunciation *n* (1901) : a pronunciation of a word based on its spelling alone

spell out *vt* (1940) **1** : to make plain ⟨*spelled out* the orders in detail⟩ **2** : to write or print in letters and in full ⟨numbers are to be *spelled out*⟩

¹spelt \'spelt\ *n* [ME, fr. OE, fr. LL *spelta*, of Gmc origin; perh. akin to MHG *spelte* split piece of wood, OHG *spaltan* to split — more at SPLIT] (bef. 12c) : a wheat (*Triticum aestivum spelta*) with lax spikes and spikelets containing two light red kernels

²spelt \'spelt\ *chiefly Brit past and past part of* SPELL

spel·ter \'spel-tər\ *n* [prob. alter. of MD *speauter*] (1661) : ZINC; *esp* : zinc cast in slabs for commercial use

spe·lunk·er \spi-'ləŋ-kər, 'spe-,\ *n* [L *spelunca* cave, fr. Gk *spelynx*; akin to Gk *spelaion* cave] (1944) : one who makes a hobby of exploring and studying caves

spe·lunk·ing \-kiŋ\ *n* (1944) : the hobby or practice of exploring caves

spence \'spen(t)s\ *n* [ME, fr. MF *despense*, fr. ML *dispensa*, fr. L, fem. of *dispensus*, pp. of *dispendere* to weigh out — more at DISPENSE] (14c) *chiefly dial Brit* : PANTRY

¹spen·cer \'spen(t)-sər\ *n* [George John, 2d earl *Spencer* †1834 Eng. politician] (1795) : a short waist-length jacket

²spencer *n* [prob. fr. the name *Spencer*] (1840) : a trysail abaft the foremast or mainmast

Spen·ce·ri·an \spen-'sir-e-ən\ *adj* [Platt R. *Spencer* †1864 Am. calligrapher] (1863) : of or relating to a form of slanting handwriting

Spen·ce·ri·an·ism \spen-'sir-e-ə-,ni-zəm\ *n* (1881) : the synthetic philosophy of Herbert Spencer that has as its central idea the mechanistic evolution of the cosmos from relative simplicity to relative complexity

spend \'spend\ *vb* **spent** \'spent\; **spend·ing** [ME, fr. OE & OF; OE *spendan*, fr. L *expendere* to expend; OF *despendre*, fr. L *dispendere* to weigh out — more at DISPENSE] *vt* (13c) **1** : to use up or pay out : EXPEND **2 a** : EXHAUST, WEAR OUT ⟨the hurricane gradually *spent* itself⟩ **b** : to consume wastefully : SQUANDER ⟨the waters are not ours to ~ —J. R. Ellis⟩ **3** : to cause or permit to elapse : PASS ⟨~ the night⟩ **4** : GIVE UP, SACRIFICE ~ *vi* **1** : to expend or waste wealth or strength **2** : to become expended or consumed **3** : to have an orgasm — **spend·able** \'spen-də-bəl\ *adj* — **spend·er** *n*

spending money *n* (15c) : POCKET MONEY

spend·thrift \'spen(d)-,thrift\ *n* (1601) : a person who spends improvidently or wastefully — **spendthrift** *adj*

Spen·gle·ri·an \,shpeŋ-'glir-e-ən, ,speŋ-, -'lir-\ *adj* (1922) : of or relating to the theory of world history developed by Oswald Spengler which holds that all major cultures undergo similar cyclical developments from birth to maturity to decay — **Spenglerism** *n*

Spen·se·ri·an stanza \spen-'sir-e-ən-\ *n* [Edmund *Spenser*] (1817) : a stanza consisting of eight verses of iambic pentameter and an alexandrine with a rhyme scheme *ababbcbcc*

spent \'spent\ *adj* [ME, fr. pp. of *spenden* to spend] (15c) **1 a** : used up : CONSUMED **b** : exhausted of active or required components or qualities often for a particular purpose ⟨~ nuclear fuel⟩ **2** : drained of energy or effectiveness : EXHAUSTED **3** : exhausted of spawn or sperm ⟨a ~ salmon⟩

sperm \'spərm\ *n, pl* **sperm** *or* **sperms** [ME, fr. MF *esperme*, fr. LL *spermat-, sperma*, fr. Gk, lit., seed, fr. *speirein* to sow; prob. akin to Arm *p'aratem* I dispense] (14c) **1 a** : the male fecundating fluid : SEMEN **b** : a male gamete **2** : a product (as spermaceti or oil) of the sperm whale

sperm- *or* **spermo-** *or* **sperma-** *or* **spermi-** *comb form* [Gk *sperm-, spermo-*, fr. *sperma*] : seed : germ : sperm ⟨*spermatheca*⟩ ⟨*spermicide*⟩

sper·ma·ce·ti \,spər-mə-'se-te, -'se-\ *n* [ME *sperma cete*, fr. ML *sperma ceti* whale sperm] (15c) : a waxy solid obtained from the oil of cetaceans and esp. sperm whales and used in ointments, cosmetics, and candles

sper·ma·go·ni·um \,spər-mə-'go-ne-əm\ *n, pl* **-nia** \-ne-ə\ [NL] (1861) : a flask-shaped or depressed receptacle in which spermatia are produced in some fungi and lichens

sper·ma·ry \'spər-mə-re, 'spərm-re\ *n, pl* **-ries** [NL *spermarium*, fr. Gk *sperma*] (ca. 1859) : an organ in which male gametes are developed

spermat- *or* **spermato-** *comb form* [MF, fr. Gk, fr. *spermat-, sperma*] : seed : spermatozoon ⟨*spermatid*⟩ ⟨*spermatocyte*⟩

sper·ma·the·ca \,spər-mə-'the-kə\ *n* [NL] (1826) : a sac for sperm storage in the female reproductive tract of various lower animals and esp. insects

sper·mat·ic \(,)spər-'ma-tik\ *adj* (15c) **1** : relating to sperm or a spermary **2** : resembling, carrying, or full of sperm

spermatic cord *n* (1797) : a cord that suspends the testis within the scrotum and contains the vas deferens and vessels and nerves of the testis

sper·ma·tid \'spər-mə-təd\ *n* (1889) : one of the haploid cells that are formed by division of the secondary spermatocytes and that differentiate into spermatozoa

sper·ma·ti·um \(,)spər-'mä-sh(e-)əm\ *n, pl* **-tia** \-sh(e-)ə\ [NL, fr. Gk *spermation*, dim. of *spermat-, sperma*] (1856) : a nonmotile cell functioning as a male gamete in some lower plants (as red algae) — **sper·ma·tial** \-sh(e-)əl\ *adj*

sper·ma·to·cyte \(,)spər-'ma-tə-,sit\ *n* (1886) : a cell giving rise to sperm cells; *esp* : a cell that is derived from a spermatogonium and ultimately gives rise to four haploid spermatids

sper·ma·to·gen·e·sis \(,)spər-,ma-tə-'je-nə-səs\ *n* [NL] (1881) : the process of male gamete formation including formation of a primary spermatocyte from a spermatogonium, meiotic division of the spermatocyte, and transformation of the four resulting spermatids into spermatozoa — **sper·ma·to·gen·ic** \-'je-nik\ *adj*

sper·ma·to·go·ni·um \-'go-ne-əm\ *n, pl* **-nia** \-ne-ə\ [NL] (1861) : a primitive male germ cell — **sper·ma·to·go·ni·al** \-ne-əl\ *adj*

sper·ma·to·phore \(,)spər-'ma-tə-,for, -,for\ *n* [ISV] (ca. 1849) : a capsule, packet, or mass enclosing spermatozoa extruded by the male and conveyed to the female in the insemination of various lower animals (as insects)

sper·ma·to·phyte \-,fit\ *n* [ultim. fr. NL *spermat-* + Gk *phyton* plant — more at PHYT-] (1897) : any of a group (Spermatophyta) of higher plants comprising those that produce seeds and including the gymnosperms and angiosperms — **sper·ma·to·phyt·ic** \-,ma-tə-'fi-tik\ *adj*

sper·ma·to·zo·an \(ˌ)spər-ˌma-tə-ˈzō-ən, ˌspər-mə-tə-\ *n* (ca. 1900) : SPERMATOZOON — **spermatozoan** *adj*

sper·ma·to·zo·id \-ˈzō-əd\ *n* [ISV, fr. NL *spermatozoon*] (1857) : a male gamete of a plant motile by anterior cilia and usu. produced in an antheridium

sper·ma·to·zo·on \-ˈzō-ˌän, -ˈzō-ən\ *n, pl* **-zoa** \-ˈzō-ə\ [NL] (ca. 1839) **1** : a motile male gamete of an animal usu. with rounded or elongate head and a long posterior flagellum **2** : SPERMATOZOID — **sper·ma·to·zo·al** \-ˈzō-əl\ *adj*

sperm cell *n* (1851) : a male gamete : a male germ cell

sper·mi·cide \ˈspər-mə-ˌsīd\ *n* (1929) : a preparation or substance (as nonoxynol-9) used to kill sperm — **sper·mi·cid·al** \ˌspər-mə-ˈsī-dəl\ *adj*

sper·mio·gen·e·sis \ˌspər-mē-ō-ˈje-nə-səs\ *n* [NL, fr. *spermium* spermatozoon + *-o-* + L *genesis*] (1916) : SPERMATOGENESIS; *specif* : transformation of a spermatid into a spermatozoon

sperm nucleus *n* (1887) : either of two nuclei that derive from the generative nucleus of a pollen grain and function in the fertilization of a seed plant

sperm oil *n* (1839) : a pale yellow oil from the sperm whale

sper·mo·phile \ˈspər-mə-ˌfil\ *n* [ultim. fr. Gk *sperma* seed + *philos* loving] (1824) : GROUND SQUIRREL

sperm whale \ˈspərm-\ *n* [short for *spermaceti whale*] (1834) : a large toothed whale (*Physeter macrocephalus* syn. *P. catodon*) with a large closed cavity in the head containing a fluid mixture of spermaceti and oil

-spermy *n comb form* [Gk *sperma* seed, sperm] : state of exhibiting or resulting from (such) a fertilization ⟨agamo*spermy*⟩

sper·ry·lite \ˈsper-i-ˌlīt\ *n* [Francis L. *Sperry*, 19th cent. Canad. chemist + E *-lite*] (1889) : a mineral consisting of an arsenide of platinum that is found near Sudbury, Ontario, and occurs in grains and minute isometric crystals of a bluish white color

spes·sar·tite \ˈspe-sar-ˌtīt\ *or* **spes·sar·tine** \-ˌtēn\ *n* [F, fr. *Spessart* mountain range, Germany] (1868) : a manganese aluminum garnet usu. containing other elements (as iron and magnesium) in minor amounts

¹spew \ˈspyü\ *vb* [ME, fr. OE *spīwan*; akin to OHG *spīwan* to spit, L *spuere*, Gk *ptyein*] *vi* (bef. 12c) **1** : VOMIT **2** : to come forth in a flood or gush **3** : to ooze out as if under pressure : EXUDE ∼ *vt* **1** : VOMIT **2** : to send or cast forth with vigor or violence or in great quantity — often used with *out* — **spew·er** *n*

²spew *n* (15c) **1** : matter that is vomited : VOMIT **2** : material that exudes or is extruded

sphag·nous \ˈsfag-nəs\ *adj* (ca. 1828) : of, relating to, or abounding in sphagnum

sphag·num \ˈsfag-nəm\ *n* [NL, fr. L *sphagnos*, a moss, fr. Gk] (1741) **1** : any of an order (Sphagnales, containing a single genus *Sphagnum*) of atypical mosses that grow only in wet acid areas where their remains become compacted with other plant debris to form peat **2** : a mass of sphagnum plants

sphal·er·ite \ˈsfa-lə-ˌrīt\ *n* [G *Sphalerit*, fr. Gk *sphaleros* deceitful, fr. *sphallein* to cause to fall; fr. its often being mistaken for galena — more at SPILL] (ca. 1868) : a widely distributed ore of zinc composed essentially of zinc sulfide

S phase *n* [synthesis] (1945) : the period in the cell cycle during which DNA replication takes place — compare G₁ PHASE, G₂ PHASE, M PHASE

sphene \ˈsfēn\ *n* [F *sphène*, fr. Gk *sphēn* wedge] (1815) : a mineral that is a silicate of calcium and titanium and often contains other elements

sphen·odon \ˈsfē-nə-ˌdän, ˈsfe-\ *n* [NL, genus name, fr. Gk *sphēn* wedge + *odōn, odous* tooth — more at TOOTH] (1878) : TUATARA — **sphenodont** \-ˌdänt\ *adj*

¹sphe·noid \ˈsfē-ˌnȯid\ *or* **sphe·noi·dal** \sfi-ˈnȯi-dᵊl\ *adj* [NL *sphenoides*, fr. Gk *sphēnoeidēs* wedge-shaped, fr. *sphēn* wedge] (1732) **1** : of, relating to, or having a winged compound bone of the base of the cranium **2** *usu* **sphenoidal** : having a wedged shape

²sphenoid *n* (1828) : a sphenoid bone

sphe·nop·sid \sfi-ˈnäp-səd\ *n* [ultim. fr. Gk *sphēn* wedge + NL *-opsis*] (1957) : any of a class (Sphenopsida or Sphenophyta) of the tracheophytes characterized by jointed ribbed stems, small leaves usu. in whorls at distinct stem nodes, and sporangia in sporangiophores and made up of the equisetums and extinct related forms

spher- *or* **sphero-** *also* **sphaer-** *or* **sphaero-** *comb form* [L *sphaer-*, fr. Gk *sphair-, sphairo-*, fr. *sphaira* sphere] : sphere ⟨*spher*ule⟩ ⟨*sphero*meter⟩

spher·al \ˈsfir-əl\ *adj* (1545) **1** : SPHERICAL **2** : of or relating to the spheres of ancient astronomy

¹sphere \ˈsfir\ *n* [ME *spere* globe, celestial sphere, fr. MF *espere*, fr. L *sphaera*, fr. Gk *sphaira*, lit., ball; perh. akin to Gk *spairein* to quiver — more at SPURN] (14c) **1 a** (1) : the apparent surface of the heavens of which half forms the dome of the visible sky (2) : any of the concentric and eccentric revolving spherical transparent shells in which according to ancient astronomy stars, planets, and moon are set **b** : a globe depicting such a sphere; *broadly* : GLOBE **2 a** : a globular body : BALL **b** : PLANET, STAR **c** (1) : a solid that is bounded by a surface consisting of all points at a given distance from a point constituting its center — see VOLUME table (2) : the bounding surface of a sphere **3** : natural, normal, or proper place; *esp* : social order or rank **4 a** *obs* : ORBIT **b** : an area or range over or within which someone or something acts, exists, or has influence or significance — **spher·ic** \ˈsfir-ik, ˈsfer-\ *adj, archaic* — **sphe·ric·i·ty** \sfir-ˈi-sə-tē\ *n*

²sphere *vt* **sphered; spher·ing** (1607) **1** : to place in a sphere or among the spheres : ENSPHERE **2** : to form into a sphere

sphere of influence (1885) : a territorial area within which the political influence or the interests of one nation are held to be more or less paramount

spher·i·cal \ˈsfir-i-kəl, ˈsfer-\ *adj* (15c) **1** : having the form of a sphere or of one of its segments **2** : relating to or dealing with a sphere or its properties — **spher·i·cal·ly** \-k(ə-)lē\ *adv*

spherical aberration *n* (1868) : aberration that is caused by the spherical form of a lens or mirror and that gives different foci for central and marginal rays

spherical angle *n* (1678) : the angle between two intersecting arcs of great circles of a sphere measured by the plane angle formed by the tangents to the arcs at the point of intersection

spherical coordinate *n* (ca. 1864) : one of three coordinates that are used to locate a point in space and that comprise the radius of the sphere on which the point lies in a system of concentric spheres, the angle formed by the point, the center, and a given axis of the sphere, and the angle between the plane of the first angle and a reference plane through the given axis of the sphere

spherical geometry *n* (1728) : the geometry of figures on a sphere

spherical polygon *n* (ca. 1825) : a figure analogous to a plane polygon that is formed on a sphere by arcs of great circles

spherical triangle *n* (1585) : a spherical polygon of three sides

spherical trigonometry *n* (1728) : trigonometry applied to spherical triangles and polygons

spher·oid \ˈsfir-ˌȯid, ˈsfer-\ *n* (1570) : a figure resembling a sphere; *also* : an object of approximately spherical shape — **sphe·roi·dal** \sfi-ˈrȯi-dᵊl\ *also* **spheroid** \-ˈd⁹l-ē\ *adv*

sphe·rom·e·ter \sfir-ˈä-mə-tər\ *n* [ISV] (ca. 1828) : an instrument for measuring the curvature of a surface

sphe·ro·plast \ˈsfir-ə-ˌplast, ˈsfer-\ *n* (ca. 1920) : a bacterium or yeast cell that is modified by nutritional or environmental factors or by artificial means (as the use of a lysozyme) and that is characterized by partial loss of the cell wall and by increased osmotic sensitivity

spher·ule \ˈsfir-ü(ə)l, ˈsfer-, -ˌyü(ə)l\ *n* (1665) : a little sphere or spherical body

spher·u·lite \ˈsfir-yə-ˌlīt, ˈsfer-, -ə-ˌlīt\ *n* (1823) : a usu. spherical crystalline body of radiating crystal fibers often found in vitreous volcanic rocks — **spher·u·lit·ic** \ˌsfir-yə-ˈli-tik, ˌsfer-, -ə-ˌli-\ *adj*

sphery \ˈsfir-ē\ *adj* (1590) **1** : of, relating to, or suggestive of the celestial bodies **2** : ROUND, SPHERICAL

sphinc·ter \ˈsfiŋ(k)-tər\ *n* [LL, fr. Gk *sphinktēr*, lit., band, fr. *sphingein* to bind tight] (1578) : an annular muscle surrounding and able to contract or close a bodily opening — **sphinc·ter·ic** \sfiŋ(k)-ˈter-ik\ *adj*

sphin·gid \ˈsfin-jəd\ *n* [ultim. fr. Gk *sphing-, sphinx* sphinx] (ca. 1909) : HAWKMOTH

sphin·go·sine \ˈsfiŋ-gə-ˌsēn\ *n* [Gk *sphingos* (gen. of *sphinx*) + E *-ine*; fr. riddles it posed to its first investigators] (1884) : a long-chain unsaturated amino alcohol $C_{18}H_{37}O_2N$ found esp. in nervous tissue and cell membranes

sphinx \ˈsfiŋ(k)s\ *n, pl* **sphinx·es** *or* **sphin·ges** \ˈsfin-ˌjēz\ [L, fr. Gk *Sphinx, Sphix*] **1 a** *cap* : a winged female monster in Greek mythology having a woman's head and a lion's body and noted for killing anyone unable to answer its riddle **b** : an enigmatic or mysterious person **2** : an ancient Egyptian image in the form of a recumbent lion having a man's head, a ram's head, or a hawk's head **3** : HAWKMOTH — **sphinx·like** \-ˌlīk\ *adj*

sphyg·mo·graph \ˈsfig-mə-ˌgraf\ *n* [Gk *sphygmos* pulse + ISV *-graph*] (ca. 1859) : an instrument that records graphically the movements or character of the pulse

sphyg·mo·ma·nom·e·ter \ˌsfig-mō-mə-ˈnä-mə-tər\ *n* [Gk *sphygmos* pulse (fr. *sphyzein* to throb) + ISV *manometer*] (ca. 1891) : an instrument for measuring blood pressure and esp. arterial blood pressure — **sphyg·mo·ma·nom·e·try** \-mə-ˈnä-mə-trē\ *n*

spi·ca \ˈspī-kə\ *n, pl* **spi·cae** \-ˌkē\ *or* **spicas** [L, ear of grain — more at SPINE] (ca. 1731) : a bandage that is applied in successive V-shaped crossings and is used to immobilize a limb esp. at a joint

Spi·ca \ˈspī-kə\ *n* [L, lit., ear of grain] : a star of the first magnitude in the constellation Virgo

spi·cate \ˈspī-ˌkāt\ *adj* [L *spicatus*, pp. of *spicare* to arrange in the shape of heads of grain, fr. *spica*] (1668) : arranged in the form of a spike ⟨a ∼ inflorescence⟩

¹spic·ca·to \spi-ˈkä-(ˌ)tō\ *adj* [It, pp. of *spiccare* to detach, pick off] (ca. 1724) : performed with a slight lifting of the bow after each note — used as a direction in music

²spiccato *n, pl* **-tos** (ca. 1903) : a spiccato technique, performance, or passage

¹spice \ˈspīs\ *n* [ME, fr. OF *espice*, fr. LL *species* spices, fr. L, species, fr. *specere* to look — more at SPY] (13c) **1** : any of various aromatic vegetable products (as pepper or nutmeg) used to season or flavor foods **2 a** *archaic* : a small portion, quantity, or admixture : DASH **b** : something that gives zest or relish ⟨variety's the very ∼ of life —William Cowper⟩ **3** : a pungent or fragrant odor : PERFUME — **spice·less** \-ləs\ *adj*

²spice *vt* **spiced; spic·ing** (14c) **1** : to season with spices **2** : to add zest or relish to ⟨cynicism *spiced* with humor —J. W. Dawson⟩ — often used with *up*

spice·bush \ˈspīs-ˌbúsh\ *n* (1770) : an aromatic shrub (*Lindera benzoin*) of the laurel family that bears dense clusters of small yellow flowers followed by scarlet or yellow berries

spic·ery \ˈspī-sə-rē, ˈspīs-rē\ *n, pl* **-er·ies** (13c) **1** : SPICES **2** *archaic* : a repository of spices **3** : a spicy quality

spick *or* **spic** *or* **spik** \ˈspik\ *n* [by shortening & alter. fr. *spiggoty*, of unknown origin] (1916) : SPANISH AMERICAN — usu. taken to be offensive

spick–and–span *or* **spic–and–span** \ˌspik-ən(d)-ˈspan, ˌspik-ᵊŋ-\ *adj* [short for *spick-and-span-new*, fr. obs. E *spick* spike + E *and* + *span= new* brand-new] (1665) **1** : FRESH, BRAND-NEW **2** : spotlessly clean

spic·ule \ˈspi-(ˌ)kyü(ə)l\ *n* [NL *spicula* & L *spiculum*; NL *spicula*, alter. of L *spiculum* head of a spear or arrow, dim. of *spicum, spica* ear of grain] (1785) **1** : a slender pointed usu. hard body; *esp* : one of the minute calcareous or siliceous bodies that support the tissue of various invertebrates (as a sponge) **2** : a spikelike short-lived prominence appearing close to the chromosphere of the solar atmosphere — **spic·u·lar** \ˈspi-kyə-lər\, *also* **spic·u·la·tion** \ˌspi-kyə-ˈlā-shən\ *n*

spicy \ˈspī-sē\ *adj* **spic·i·er; -est** (1562) **1** : having the quality, flavor, or fragrance of spice **2** : producing or abounding in spices **3** : LIVELY, SPIRITED **4** : PIQUANT, RACY; *esp* : somewhat scandalous or salacious ⟨∼ gossip⟩ — **spic·i·ly** \-sə-lē\ *adv* — **spic·i·ness** \-sē-nəs\ *n*

\ə\ abut \ᵊ\ kitten, F table \ər\ further \a\ ash \ā\ ace \ä\ mop, mar \aú\ out \ch\ chin \e\ bet \ē\ easy \g\ go \i\ hit \ī\ ice \j\ job \ŋ\ sing \ō\ go \ó\ law \ói\ boy \th\ thin \th\ the \ü\ loot \ú\ foot \y\ yet \zh\ vision \ä, k̲, ⁿ, œ, œ̄, ue, ūe, ʸ\ see Guide to Pronunciation

spi·der \'spī-dər\ *n* [ME *spyder*, alter. of *spithre;* akin to OE *spinnan* to spin] (15c) **1 :** any of an order (Araneae syn. Araneida) of arachnids having the abdomen usu. unsegmented and constricted at the base, chelicerae modified into poison fangs, and two or more pairs of abdominal spinnerets for spinning threads of silk used in making cocoons for their eggs, nests for themselves, or webs to catch prey **2 :** a cast-iron frying pan orig. made with short feet to stand among coals on the hearth **3 :** any of various devices consisting of a frame or skeleton with radiating arms or members — **spi·der·ish** \-də-rish\ *adj* — **spi·der·like** \-,līk\ *adj*

spider crab *n* (ca. 1710) **:** any of a family (Majidae) of crabs with extremely long legs and nearly triangular bodies which they often cover with kelp

spider mite *n* (1870) **:** any of several small web-spinning mites (family Tetranychidae) that attack forage and crop plants — called also *red spider*

spider monkey *n* (1764) **:** any of a genus (*Ateles*) of New World monkeys with long slender limbs, the thumb absent or rudimentary, and a very long prehensile tail

spider plant *n* (1944) **:** a widely grown houseplant (*Chlorophytum comosum* var. *variegatum*) of the lily family having long narrow green leaves usu. striped with white or ivory and producing white flowers and tufts of plantlets on long hanging stems

spi·der·web \'spī-dər-,web\ *n* (ca. 1649) **1 :** the network of silken thread spun by most spiders and used as a resting place and as a trap for small prey **2 :** something that resembles or suggests a spiderweb

spi·der·wort \-,wərt, -,wȯrt\ *n* (1629) **:** any of a genus (*Tradescantia* of the family Commelinaceae, the spiderwort family) of American monocotyledonous plants with ephemeral often blue or violet flowers

spi·dery \'spī-də-rē\ *adj* (1837) **1** **a :** resembling a spider in form or manner **b :** resembling a spiderweb; *esp* **:** composed of fine threads or lines in a weblike arrangement ⟨~ lace⟩ **2 :** infested with spiders

spie·gel·ei·sen \'spē-gə-,lī-z'n\ *also* **spie·gel** \'spē-gəl\ *n* [G *Spiegeleisen,* fr. *Spiegel* mirror + *Eisen* iron] (1868) **:** a composition of iron that contains 15 to 30 percent manganese and 4.5 to 6.5 percent carbon

¹spiel \'spē(ə)l\ *vb* [G *spielen* to play, fr. OHG *spilōn;* akin to OE *spilian* to revel] (1870) **1 :** to play music **2 :** to talk volubly or extravagantly ~ *vt* **:** to utter, express, or describe volubly or extravagantly — **spiel·er** \'spē-lər\ *n*

²spiel *n* (1896) **:** a voluble line of often extravagant talk **:** PITCH

¹spi·er \'spī(-ə)r\ *n* (13c) **:** SPY

²spier \'spir\ *chiefly Scot var of* SPEER

spiff \'spif\ *vb* [E dial. spiff *dandified*] (1877) **:** SPRUCE — usu. used with *up* ⟨~ up your wardrobe⟩ — **spiffed–up** \'spift-'əp\ *adj*

spiffy \'spi-fē\ *adj* **spiff·i·er; -est** (1853) **:** fine looking **:** SMART ⟨a ~ sports jacket⟩ — **spiff·i·ly** \-fə-lē\ *adv* — **spiff·i·ness** \-fē-nəs\ *n*

spig·ot \'spi-gət, -kət\ *n* [ME] (14c) **1** **a :** SPILE 2 **b :** the plug of a faucet or cock **c :** FAUCET 2 **2 :** something resembling a spigot esp. in regulating availability or flow (as of money)

¹spike \'spīk\ *n* [ME, prob. fr. MD; akin to MHG *spicher* spike] (13c) **1 :** a very large nail **2** **a :** one of a row of pointed irons placed (as on the top of a wall) to prevent passage **b** (1) **:** one of several metal projections set in the sole and heel of a shoe to improve traction (2) *pl* **:** a pair of shoes having spikes attached to the soles or soles and heels **c :** SPINDLE 1e **3 :** something resembling a spike: as **a :** a young mackerel not over six inches (15.2 centimeters) long **b :** an unbranched antler of a young deer **4** *pl* **:** shoes with spike heels **5 :** the act or an instance of spiking (as in volleyball) **6** **a :** a pointed element in a graph or tracing **b :** an unusually high and sharply defined maximum (as of amplitude in a wave train) **7** *slang* **:** HYPODERMIC NEEDLE **8 :** a momentary sharp increase and fall in the record of an electric potential; *also* **:** ACTION POTENTIAL **9 :** an abrupt sharp increase in prices or rates — **spike·like** \-,līk\ *adj*

²spike *vt* **spiked; spik·ing** (1624) **1 :** to fasten or furnish with spikes **2** **a :** to disable (a muzzle-loading cannon) temporarily by driving a spike into the vent **b :** to suppress or block completely ⟨spiked the rumor⟩ **3** **a :** to pierce or impale with or on a spike **b :** to reject (as a story) for publication or broadcast for editorial reasons **4** **a :** to add an alcoholic beverage to (a drink) **b :** to add something highly reactive (as a radioactive tracer) to **c :** to add vitality, zest, or spice to **:** LIVEN ⟨spiked the speech with humor⟩ ⟨~ the broth with peppers⟩ **5 :** to drive (as a volleyball) sharply downward with a hard blow; *also* **:** to throw down sharply ⟨spiked the ball in the end zone⟩ **6 :** to undergo a sudden sharp increase in (temperature or fever) ⟨the patient *spiked* a fever of 103°⟩ — **spik·er** *n*

³spike *n* [ME *spik,* fr. L *spica* — more at SPINE] (14c) **1 :** an ear of grain **2 :** an elongated inflorescence similar to a raceme but having the flowers sessile on the main axis — see INFLORESCENCE illustration

spiked \'spīkt, 'spī-kəd\ *adj* (1601) **1 :** having an inflorescence that is a spike **2 :** having a sharp projecting point

spike heel *n* (1926) **:** a very high tapering heel used on women's shoes

spike lavender \'spīk-\ *n* [alter. of E dial. *spick* lavender] (1607) **:** a European mint (*Lavandula latifolia*) related to true lavender

spike·let \'spīk-klət\ *n* (1851) **:** a small or secondary spike; *specif* **:** one of the small few-flowered bracted spikes that make up the compound inflorescence of a grass or sedge

spike·nard \'spīk-,närd\ *n* [ME, fr. MF or ML; MF *spicanarde,* fr. ML *spica nardi,* lit., spike of nard] (14c) **1** **a :** a fragrant ointment of the ancients **b :** a Himalayan aromatic plant (*Nardostachys jatamansi*) of the valerian family from which spikenard is believed to have been derived **2 :** an American herb (*Aralia racemosa*) of the ginseng family with aromatic root and panicled umbels

spike–tooth harrow \'spīk-'tüth-\ *n* (1926) **:** a harrow with straight steel teeth set in horizontal bars

spiky \'spī-kē\ *adj* **spik·i·er; -est** (1720) **1 :** of, relating to, or characterized by spikes **2 :** sharply irritating or acerbic (as in temper or manner) **3** [fr. the alleged harshness of such views] *Brit* **:** strongly favoring Anglo-Catholic teaching or practice — **spik·i·ly** \-kə-lē\ *adv* — **spik·i·ness** \-kē-nəs\ *n*

¹spile \'spī(ə)l\ *n* [prob. fr. D *spijl* stake] (1513) **1 :** ¹PILE 1 **2 :** a small plug used to stop the vent of a cask **:** BUNG **3 :** a spout inserted in a tree to draw off sap

²spile *vt* **spiled; spil·ing** (1691) **1 :** to plug with a spile **2 :** to supply with a spile

¹spill \'spil\ *vb* **spilled** \'spild, 'spilt\ *also* **spilt** \'spilt\; **spill·ing** [ME, fr. OE *spillan;* akin to OE *spildan* to destroy and perh. to L *spolium* animal skin, Gk *sphallein* to cause to fall] *vt* (bef. 12c) **1** **a** *archaic* **:** KILL, DESTROY **b :** to cause (blood) to flow **2 :** to cause or allow esp. accidentally or unintentionally to fall, flow, or run out so as to be lost or wasted **3** **a :** to relieve (a sail) from the pressure of the wind so as to reef or furl it **b :** to relieve the pressure of (wind) on a sail by coming about or by adjusting the sail with lines **4 :** to throw off or out ⟨a horse ~ed him⟩ **5 :** to let out: DIVULGE ⟨~ a secret⟩ ~ *vi* **1** **a :** to flow, run, or fall out, over, or off and become wasted, scattered, or lost **b :** to cause or allow something to spill **2 :** to spread profusely or beyond bounds ⟨crowds ~ed into the streets⟩ **3 :** to fall from one's place (as on a horse) — **spill·able** \'spi-lə-bəl\ *adj* — **spill·er** *n* — **spill the beans :** to divulge secret or hidden information

²spill *n* (ca. 1845) **1 :** the act or an instance of spilling; *esp* **:** a fall from a horse or vehicle or an erect position **2 :** something spilled

³spill *n* [ME *spille*] (14c) **1 :** a wooden splinter **2 :** a slender piece: as **a :** a metallic rod or pin **b** (1) **:** a small roll or twist of paper or slip of wood for lighting a fire (2) **:** a roll or cone of paper serving as a container **c :** a peg or pin for plugging a hole **:** SPILE

spill·age \'spi-lij\ *n* (1924) **1 :** the act or process of spilling **2 :** the quantity that spills **:** material lost or scattered by spilling

spil·li·kin \'spi-li-kən\ *n* [prob. alter. of obs. D *spelleken* small peg] (1734) **1 :** JACKSTRAW 2 **2** *pl* **:** JACKSTRAW 1

spill·over \'spil-,ō-vər\ *n, often attrib* (1920) **1 :** the act or an instance of spilling over **2 :** a quantity that spills over **3 :** an extension of something esp. when due to an excess

spill·way \-,wā\ *n* (1889) **:** a passage for surplus water to run over or around an obstruction (as a dam)

spilth \'spilth\ *n* (1607) **1 :** the act or an instance of spilling **2** **a :** something spilled **b :** REFUSE, RUBBISH

¹spin \'spin\ *vb* **spun** \'spən\; **spin·ning** [ME *spinnen,* fr. OE *spinnan;* akin to OHG *spinnan* to spin and perh. to Lith *spesti* to set (a trap)] *vi* (bef. 12c) **1 :** to draw out and twist fiber into yarn or thread **2 :** to form a thread by extruding a viscous rapidly hardening fluid — used esp. of a spider or insect **3** **a :** to revolve rapidly **:** GYRATE **b :** to feel as if in a whirl **:** REEL ⟨my head is *spinning*⟩ **4 :** to move swiftly esp. on or as if on wheels or in a vehicle **5 :** to fish with spinning bait **:** TROLL **6** **a** *of an airplane* **:** to fall in a spin **b :** to plunge helplessly and out of control ~ *vt* **1** **a :** to draw out and twist into yarns or threads **b :** to produce by drawing out and twisting a fibrous material **2 :** to form (as a web or cocoon) by spinning **3** **a :** to stretch out or extend (as a story) lengthily **:** PROTRACT — usu. used with *out* **b :** to evolve, express, or fabricate by processes of mind or imagination ⟨~ a yarn⟩ **4 :** to cause to whirl **:** impart spin to ⟨~ a top⟩ **5 :** to shape into threadlike form in manufacture; *also* **:** to manufacture by a whirling process

²spin *n* (1831) **1** **a :** the act of spinning or twirling something; *also* **:** an instance of spinning or of spinning something ⟨doing axels and ~s⟩ ⟨an assortment of ~s and lobs⟩ **b :** the whirling motion imparted (as to a ball or top) by spinning **c :** an excursion or ride in a vehicle esp. on wheels ⟨go for a ~⟩ **2** **a :** an aerial maneuver or flight condition consisting of a combination of roll and yaw with the longitudinal axis of the airplane inclined steeply downward **b :** a plunging descent or downward spiral **c :** a state of mental confusion ⟨in a ~⟩ **3** **a :** a quantum characteristic of an elementary particle that is visualized as the rotation of the particle on its axis and that is responsible for measurable angular momentum and magnetic moment **b :** the angular momentum associated with such rotation whose magnitude is quantized and which may assume either of two possible directions; *also* **:** the angular momentum of a system of such particles derived from the spins and orbital motions of the particles **4 :** a special point of view, emphasis, or interpretation ⟨put the most favorable ~ on the findings⟩ — **spin·less** \'spin-ləs\ *adj*

spi·na bi·fi·da \,spī-nə-'bi-fə-də\ *n* [NL, lit., spine split in two] (1720) **:** a congenital cleft of the vertebral column with hernial protrusion of the meninges and sometimes the spinal cord

spin·ach \'spi-nich\ *n* [ME *spynache,* fr. MF *espinache, espinage,* fr. OSp *espinaca,* fr. Ar *isfānākh,* fr. Per] (15c) **1 :** an Asian herb (*Spinacia oleracea*) of the goosefoot family cultivated for its edible leaves which form in a dense basal rosette **2** **a :** something unwanted, pretentious, or spurious **b :** an untidy overgrowth — **spin·ach·like** \-nich-,līk\ *adj* — **spin·achy** \-ni-chē\ *adj*

¹spi·nal \'spī-n⁰l\ *adj* (1578) **1 :** of, relating to, or situated near the backbone **2** **a :** of, relating to, or affecting the spinal cord ⟨~ reflexes⟩ **b :** having the spinal cord functionally isolated (as by surgical section) from the brain ⟨experiments on ~ animals⟩ **3 :** of, relating to, or resembling a spine

²spinal *n* (1944) **:** a spinal anesthetic

spinal canal *n* (1845) **:** VERTEBRAL CANAL

spinal column *n* (1836) **:** the axial skeleton of the trunk and tail of a vertebrate consisting of an articulated series of vertebrae and protecting the spinal cord — called also *backbone*

spinal cord *n* (1836) **:** the cord of nervous tissue that extends from the brain lengthwise along the back in the vertebral canal, gives off the pairs of spinal nerves, carries impulses to and from the brain, and serves as a center for initiating and coordinating many reflex acts — see BRAIN illustration

spinal ganglion *n* (ca. 1860) **:** a ganglion on the dorsal root of each spinal nerve that is one of a series of ganglia lodging cell bodies of sensory neurons

spi·nal·ly \'spī-n⁰l-ē\ *adv* (1885) **:** with respect to or along the spine

spinal nerve *n* (ca. 1793) **:** any of the paired nerves which leave the spinal cord of a craniate vertebrate, supply muscles of the trunk and limbs, and connect with the nerves of the sympathetic nervous system, which arise by a short motor ventral root and a short sensory dorsal root, and of which there are 31 pairs in humans classified according to the part of the spinal cord from which they arise into 8 cervical pairs, 12 thoracic pairs, 5 lumbar pairs, 5 sacral pairs, and one coccygeal pair

¹spin·dle \'spin-d⁰l\ *n* [ME *spindel,* fr. OE *spinel;* akin to OE *spinnan* to spin] (12c) **1** **a :** a round stick with tapered ends used to form and twist the yarn in hand spinning **b :** the long slender pin by which the thread is twisted in a spinning wheel **c :** any of various rods or pins holding a bobbin in a textile machine (as a spinning frame) **d :** the pin in a loom shuttle   **e** : a device usu. consisting of a long upright pin in a base on which papers can be stuck for filing — called also *spindle file*   **2** : something shaped like a spindle: as   **a** : a spindle-shaped network of chiefly microtubular fibers along which the chromosomes are distributed during mitosis and meiosis   **b** : MUSCLE SPINDLE   **3**   **a** : the bar or shaft usu. of square section that carries the knobs and actuates the latch or bolt of a lock   **b** (1) : a turned often decorative piece (as in a baluster) (2) : NEWEL   **c** (1) : a revolving piece esp. when thinner than a shaft (2) : a horizontal or vertical axle revolving on pin or pivot ends   **d** : the part of an axle on which a vehicle wheel turns

²**spindle** *vb* **spin·dled; spin·dling** \'spin(d)-liŋ, 'spin-d²l-iŋ\ *vi* (1577)   **1** : to shoot or grow into a long slender stalk   **2** : to grow to stalk or stem rather than to flower or fruit ∼ *vt*   **1** : to impale, thrust, or perforate on the spike of a spindle file   **2** : to make or equip (as a piece of furniture) with spindles — **spin·dler** \'spin(d)-lər, 'spin-d²l-ər\ *n*

spindle cell *n* (1878) : a fusiform cell (as in some tumors)

spin·dle–legged \'spin-d²l-,(l)egd *also* -,(l)lā- *or* -,(l)egd\ *adj* (1710) : having long slender legs

spin·dle–shanked \-,shaŋ(k)t\ *adj* (ca. 1600) : SPINDLE-LEGGED

spindle tree *n* (1548) : any of various often evergreen shrubs, small trees, or vines (genus *Euonymus*) of the staff-tree family

spin·dling \'spin(d)-liŋ, -lən; 'spin-d²l-iŋ, -ən\ *adj* (1750) : SPINDLY

spin·dly \'spin(d)-lē, 'spin-d²l-ē\ *adj* **spin·dli·er; -est** (1651)   **1** : of a disproportionately tall or long and thin appearance that often suggests physical weakness ⟨∼ legs⟩   **2** : frail or flimsy in appearance or structure

spin doctor *n* (1984) : a person (as a political aide) responsible for ensuring that others interpret an event from a particular point of view

spin·drift \'spin-,drift\ *n* [alter. of Sc *speendrift*, fr. *speen* to drive before a strong wind + E *drift*] (1823)   **1** : sea spray; *esp* : spray blown from waves during a gale   **2** : fine wind-borne snow or sand

spine \'spīn\ *n* [ME, thorn, spinal column, fr. L *spina*; perh. akin to L *spica* ear of grain] (15c)   **1**   **a** : SPINAL COLUMN   **b** : something resembling a spinal column or constituting a central axis or chief support   **c** : the part of a book to which the pages are attached and on the cover of which usu. appear the title and author's and publisher's names   **2** : a stiff pointed plant process; *esp* : one that is a modified leaf or leaf part   **3** : a sharp rigid process on an animal: as   **a** : SPICULE   **b** : a stiff unsegmented fin ray of a fish   **c** : a pointed prominence on a bone — **spined** \'spīnd\ *adj* — **spine·like** \-,līk\ *adj*

spine–chill·ing \-,chi-liŋ\ *adj* (1946) : alarmingly or eerily frightening

spi·nel *or* **spi·nelle** \spə-'nel\ *n* [It *spinella*, dim. of *spina* thorn, fr. L] (1528)   **1** : a hard crystalline mineral consisting of an oxide of magnesium and aluminum that varies from colorless to ruby-red to black and is used as a gem   **2** : any of a group of minerals that are essentially oxides of magnesium, ferrous iron, zinc, or manganese

spine·less \'spīn-ləs\ *adj* (1827)   **1** : free from spines, thorns, or prickles   **2** : having no spinal column : INVERTEBRATE   **b** : lacking strength of character — **spine·less·ly** *adv* — **spine·less·ness** *n*

spin·et \'spi-nət *also* spi-'net\ *n* [It *spinetta*, perh. fr. dim. of *spina* thorn, fr. L; fr. the manner of plucking its strings] (1664)   **1** : an early harpsichord having a single keyboard and only one string for each note   **2**   **a** : a compactly built small upright piano   **b** : a small electronic organ

spin fishing *n* (1950) : SPINNING

spi·ni·fex \'spī-nə-,feks\ *n* [NL, fr. L *spina* + *facere* to make — more at DO] (1846) : any of several Australian grasses (genera *Spinifex* and *Triodia*) with spiny seeds or stiff sharp leaves

spin·na·ker \'spi-ni-kər\ *n* [origin unknown] (1866) : a large triangular sail set on a long light pole and used when running before the wind

spin·ner \'spi-nər\ *n* (13c)   **1** : one that spins   **2** : a fisherman's lure consisting of a spoon, blade, or set of wings that revolves when drawn through the water   **3** : a conical sheet metal fairing that is attached to an airplane propeller boss and revolves with it   **4** : a movable arrow that is spun on its dial to indicate the number or kind of moves a player may make in a board game

spin·ner·et \,spi-nə-'ret\ *n* (1826)   **1** : an organ (as of a spider or caterpillar) for producing threads of silk from the secretion of silk glands   **2** *or* **spin·ner·ette** : a small metal plate, thimble, or cap with fine holes through which a chemical solution (as of cellulose) is forced in the spinning of man-made filaments (as of rayon or nylon)

spin·ney \'spi-nē\ *n, pl* **spinneys** [MF *espinaye* thorny thicket, fr. *es-pine* thorn, fr. L *spina*] (1597) *chiefly Brit* : a small wood with undergrowth

spin·ning \'spi-niŋ\ *n* (1855) : a method of fishing in which a lure is cast by use of a light flexible rod, a spinning reel, and a light line

spinning frame *n* (1825) : a machine that draws, twists, and winds yarn

spinning jen·ny \-,je-nē\ *n* [*Jenny*, nickname for *Jane*] (1783) : an early multiple-spindle machine for spinning wool or cotton

spinning reel *n* (1950) : a fishing reel with a nonmoving spool on which the line is wound by means of a revolving arm which can be disengaged to allow the line to spiral freely off the spool during casting

spinning rod *n* (1870) : a light flexible fishing rod used with a spinning reel

spinning wheel *n* (15c) : a small domestic hand-driven or foot-driven machine for spinning yarn or thread

spin–off \'spin-,óf\ *n* (1950)   **1** : the distribution by a business to its stockholders of particular assets and esp. of stock of another company; *also* : the new company created by such a distribution   **2** : a collateral or derived product or effect : BY-PRODUCT; *also* : a number of such products ⟨the ∼ from the space program⟩   **3** : something that is imitative or derivative of an earlier work; *esp* : a television show starring a character popular in a secondary role of an earlier show

spin off *vt* (1950) : to establish or produce as a spin-off ⟨the company *spun off* its computer division⟩ ⟨*spin off* a new TV series⟩ ∼ *vi* : to establish or become a spin-off

spin·or \'spi-nər, -,nór\ *n* [ISV *spin* + -*or* (as in *vector*)] (1931) : a vector whose components are complex numbers in a two-dimensional or four-dimensional space and which is used esp. in the mathematics of the theory of relativity

spi·nose \'spī-,nōs\ *adj* (1660) : SPINY 1 ⟨a fly with black ∼ legs⟩ — **spi·nos·i·ty** \spī-'nä-sə-tē\ *n*

spi·nous \'spī-nəs\ *adj* (15c)   **1** : SPINY 1, 3 ⟨∼ appendages⟩ ⟨a ∼ larva⟩   **2** : difficult or unpleasant to handle or meet : THORNY

spin·out \'spin-,aút\ *n* (1955) : a rotational skid by an automobile that usu. causes it to leave the roadway

spin out *vi* (1951) : to make a rotational skid in an automobile

Spi·no·zism \spi-'nō-,zi-zəm\ *n* (1728) : the philosophy of Baruch Spinoza who taught that reality is one substance with an infinite number of attributes of which only thought and extension are capable of being apprehended by the human mind — **Spi·no·zist** \-zist\ *n* — **Spi·no·zis·tic** \,spi-nō-'zis-tik\ *adj*

spin·ster \'spin(t)-stər\ *n* (14c)   **1** : a woman whose occupation is to spin   **2**   **a** *archaic* : an unmarried woman of gentle family   **b** : an unmarried woman and esp. one past the common age for marrying   **3** : a woman who seems unlikely to marry — **spin·ster·hood** \-,húd\ *n* — **spin·ster·ish** \-st(ə-)rish\ *adj* — **spin·ster·ly** *adj*

spin·thar·i·scope \spin-'thar-ə-,skōp\ *n* [Gk *spintharis* spark + E -*scope*] (1903) : an instrument for visual detection of alpha particles that consists of a fluorescent screen and a magnifying lens system

spin the bottle *n* (1955) : a kissing game in which one has as a partner the person a bottle points to when it stops spinning

spin·to \'spēn-(,)tō, 'spin-\ *n, pl* **spin·tos** [It, lit., pushed, fr. pp. of *spingere* to push, fr. (assumed) VL *expingere*, fr. L *ex-* + *pangere* to fasten — more at PACT] (1944) : a singing voice having both lyric and dramatic qualities — **spinto** *adj*

spi·nule \'spī-(,)nyü(ə)l\ *n* [L *spinula*, dim. of *spina* thorn — more at SPINE] (1752) : a minute spine — **spi·nu·lose** \'spī-nyə-,lōs\ *adj*

spiny \'spī-nē\ *adj* **spin·i·er; -est** (1586)   **1** : covered or armed with spines; *broadly* : bearing spines, prickles, or thorns   **2** : abounding with difficulties, obstacles, or annoyances : THORNY ⟨∼ problems⟩   **3** : slender and pointed like a spine — **spin·i·ness** *n*

spiny anteater *n* (1827) : ECHIDNA

spiny–head·ed worm \'spī-nē-,he-dəd-\ *n* (1946) : any of a small phylum (Acanthocephala) of unsegmented parasitic worms that have a proboscis bearing hooks by which attachment is made to the intestinal wall of the host

spiny lobster *n* (1819) : any of several edible crustaceans (family Palinuridae and esp. genus *Panulirus*) distinguished from the true lobsters by the simple unenlarged first pair of legs and claws and the spiny carapace

spi·ra·cle \'spir-i-kəl, 'spī-ri-\ *n* [ME, fr. L *spiraculum*, fr. *spirare* to breathe] (15c)   **1** : a breathing hole : VENT   **2** : a breathing orifice: as   **a** : BLOWHOLE 2   **b** : an external tracheal aperture of a terrestrial arthropod that in an insect is usu. one of a series of small apertures located along each side of the thorax and abdomen — see INSECT illustration — **spi·rac·u·lar** \spə-'ra-kyə-lər, spī-\ *adj*

¹**spi·ral** \'spī-rəl\ *adj* [ML *spiralis*, fr. L *spira* coil — more at SPIRE] (1551)   **1**   **a** : winding around a center or pole and gradually receding from or approaching it ⟨the ∼ curve of a watch spring⟩   **b** : HELICAL   **c** : SPIRAL-BOUND ⟨a ∼ notebook⟩   **2** : of or relating to the advancement to higher levels through a series of cyclical movements — **spi·ral·ly** \-rə-lē\ *adv*

²**spiral** *n* (1656)   **1**   **a** : the path of a point in a plane moving around a central point while continuously receding from or approaching it   **b** : a three-dimensional curve (as a helix) with one or more turns about an axis   **2** : a single turn or coil in a spiral object   **3**   **a** : something having a spiral form   **b** (1) : a spiral flight (2) : a kick or pass in which a football rotates on its long axis while moving through the air   **4** : a continuously spreading and accelerating increase or decrease ⟨wage ∼s⟩

³**spiral** *vb* **-raled** *or* **-ralled; -ral·ing** *or* **-ral·ling** *vi* (1834) : to go and esp. to rise or fall in a spiral course ⟨costs ∼ed upward⟩ ∼ *vt*   **1** : to form into a spiral   **2** : to cause to spiral

spiral binding *n* (1944) : a book or notebook binding in which a continuous spiral wire or plastic strip is passed through holes along one edge

spi·ral–bound \'spī-rəl-,baúnd\ *adj* (1941) : having a spiral binding

spiral cleavage *n* (1892) : holoblastic cleavage that is typical of protostomes and that is characterized by arrangement of the blastomeres of each upper tier over the cell junctions of the next lower tier so that the blastomeres spiral around the pole to pole axis of the embryo — compare RADIAL CLEAVAGE

spiral galaxy *n* (1913) : a galaxy exhibiting a central nucleus or barred structure from which extend concentrations of matter forming curved arms — called also *spiral nebula*

spiral of Ar·chi·me·des \-,är-kə-'mē-dēz\ [*Archimedes*] (ca. 1856) : a plane curve that is generated by a point moving away from or toward a fixed point at a constant rate while the radius vector from the fixed point rotates at a constant rate and that has the equation $\rho = a\,\theta$ in polar coordinates

spiral spring *n* (1690) : a spring consisting of a wire coiled usu. in a flat spiral or in a helix

spi·rant \'spī-rənt\ *n* [ISV, fr. L *spirant-, spirans*, prp. of *spirare* to breathe] (1862) : a consonant (as \f\, \s\, \sh\) uttered with friction of the breath against some part of the oral passage : FRICATIVE — **spirant** *adj*

¹**spire** \'spīr\ *n* [ME, fr. OE *spīr*; akin to MD *spier* blade of grass] (bef. 12c)   **1** : a slender tapering blade or stalk (as of grass)   **2** : the upper tapering part of something (as a tree or antler) : PINNACLE   **3**   **a** : a tapering roof or analogous pyramidal construction surmounting a tower : STEEPLE

²**spire** *vi* **spired; spir·ing** (14c) : to rise like a spire

1 spinnaker

\ə\ abut   \²\ kitten, F table   \ər\ further   \a\ ash   \ā\ ace   \ä\ mop, mar
\aú\ out   \ch\ chin   \e\ bet   \ē\ easy   \g\ go   \i\ hit   \ī\ ice   \j\ job
\ŋ\ sing   \ō\ go   \ó\ law   \ói\ boy   \th\ thin   \t̲h̲\ the   \ü\ loot   \ú\ foot
\y\ yet   \zh\ vision   \ȧ, k̲, ⁿ, œ, œ̄, ᵾ, ᵫ, ʸ\ see Guide to Pronunciation

³**spire** n [L *spira* coil, fr. Gk *speira*; perh. akin to Gk *sparton* rope, esparto] (1545) **1 a :** SPIRAL **b :** COIL **2 :** the inner or upper part of a spiral gastropod shell consisting of all the whorls except the whorl in contact with the body

⁴**spire** vi **spired; spir·ing** (1591) : to rise in or as if in a spiral

spi·rea or **spi·raea** \spī-'rē-ə\ n [NL *Spiraea*, fr. L, a plant, fr. Gk *speiraia*] (1669) **1 :** any of a genus (*Spiraea*) of shrubs of the rose family with small perfect usu. white or pink flowers in dense racemes, corymbs, cymes, or panicles **2 :** any of several garden plants resembling spireas; *esp* : a shrub (*Astilbe japonica*) of the saxifrage family

spired \'spīrd\ adj (1610) **1 :** having a spire ⟨a ~ church⟩ **2 :** tapering usu. to a sharp point ⟨~ cedars⟩

spi·ril·lum \spi-'ri-ləm\ n, pl **-ril·la** \-'ri-lə\ [NL, fr. dim. of L *spira* coil] (ca. 1875) : any of a genus (*Spirillum*) of long curved bacteria having tufts of flagella; *broadly* : a spiral filamentous bacterium (as a spirochete)

¹**spir·it** \'spir-ət\ n [ME, fr. OF or L; OF, fr. L *spiritus*, lit., breath, fr. *spirare* to blow, breathe] (13c) **1 :** an animating or vital principle held to give life to physical organisms **2 :** a supernatural being or essence: as **a** cap : HOLY SPIRIT **b :** SOUL 2a **c :** an often malevolent being that is bodiless but can become visible; *specif* : GHOST 2 **d :** a malevolent being that enters and possesses a human being **3 :** temper or disposition of mind or outlook esp. when vigorous or animated ⟨in high ~s⟩ **4 :** the immaterial intelligent or sentient part of a person **5 a :** the activating or essential principle influencing a person ⟨acted in a ~ of helpfulness⟩ **b :** an inclination, impulse, or tendency of a specified kind : MOOD **6 a :** a special attitude or frame of mind ⟨the money-making ~ was for a time driven back —J. A. Froude⟩ **b :** the feeling, quality, or disposition characterizing something ⟨undertaken in a ~ of fun⟩ **7 :** a lively or brisk quality in a person or a person's actions **8 :** a person having a character or disposition of a specified nature **9 :** a mental disposition characterized by firmness or assertiveness ⟨denied the charge with ~⟩ **10 a :** DISTILLATE 1: as (1) : the liquid containing ethyl alcohol and water that is distilled from an alcoholic liquid or mash — often used in pl. (2) : any of various volatile liquids obtained by distillation or cracking (as of petroleum, shale, or wood) — often used in pl. **b :** a usu. volatile organic solvent (as an alcohol, ester, or hydrocarbon) **11 a :** prevailing tone or tendency ⟨~ of the age⟩ **b :** general intent or real meaning ⟨~ of the law⟩ **12 :** an alcoholic solution of a volatile substance ⟨~ of camphor⟩ **13 :** enthusiastic loyalty ⟨school ~⟩ **14** cap, Christian Science : GOD 1b **syn** see COURAGE

²**spirit** vt (1608) **1 :** to infuse with spirit; *esp* : ANIMATE ⟨hope and apprehension of feasibleness ~s all industry —John Goodman⟩ **2 :** to carry off usu. secretly or mysteriously ⟨was hustled into a . . . motorcar and ~ed off to the country —W. L. Shirer⟩

spir·it·ed \'spir-ə-təd\ adj (1592) : full of energy, animation, or courage ⟨a ~ discussion⟩ — **spir·it·ed·ly** adv — **spir·it·ed·ness** n

spirit gum n (1886) : a solution (as of gum arabic in ether) used esp. for attaching false hair to the skin

spir·it·ism \'spir-ə-ˌti-zəm\ n (1856) : SPIRITUALISM 2a — **spir·it·ist** \-tist\ n — **spir·it·is·tic** \ˌspir-ə-'tis-tik\ adj

spir·it·less \'spir-ət-ləs\ adj (1597) : lacking animation, cheerfulness, or courage — **spir·it·less·ly** adv — **spir·it·less·ness** n

spirit level n (1768) : LEVEL 1

spirit of hartshorn (ca. 1684) : AMMONIA WATER

spirit of wine (1753) : ALCOHOL 1c

spir·i·to·so \ˌspir-ə-'tō-(ˌ)sō, -(ˌ)zō\ adj [It, fr. *spirito* spirit, fr. L *spiritus*] (ca. 1724) : ANIMATED — used as a direction in music

spir·it·ous \'spir-ə-təs\ adj (1605) **1** archaic : PURE, REFINED **2 :** SPIRITUOUS

spirit rapping n (1852) : communication by raps held to be from the spirits of the dead

spirits of hartshorn (ca. 1909) : AMMONIA WATER

spirits of turpentine (ca. 1792) : TURPENTINE 2a

spirits of wine (1710) : rectified spirit : ALCOHOL 1c

¹**spir·i·tu·al** \'spir-i-chə-wəl, -chəl, -ich-wəl\ adj [ME, fr. MF & LL; MF *spirituel*, fr. LL *spiritualis*, fr. L, of breathing, of wind, fr. *spiritus*] (14c) **1 :** of, relating to, consisting of, or affecting the spirit : INCORPOREAL ⟨man's ~ needs⟩ **2 a :** of or relating to sacred matters ⟨~ songs⟩ **b :** ecclesiastical rather than lay or temporal ⟨~ authority⟩ ⟨lords ~⟩ **3 :** concerned with religious values **4 :** related or joined in spirit ⟨our ~ home⟩ ⟨his ~ heir⟩ **5 a :** of or relating to supernatural beings or phenomena **b :** of, relating to, or involving spiritualism : SPIRITUALISTIC — **spir·i·tu·al·ly** adv — **spir·i·tu·al·ness** n

²**spiritual** n (1582) **1** pl : things of a spiritual, ecclesiastical, or religious nature **2 :** a religious song usu. of a deeply emotional character that was developed esp. among blacks in the southern U.S. **3** cap : any of a party of 13th and 14th century Franciscans advocating strict observance of a rule of poverty for their order

spiritual bouquet n (1926) : a card notifying the recipient of a number of devotional acts performed by a Roman Catholic on behalf of a person on special occasions (as name days or anniversaries) or for the soul of someone recently deceased esp. as an expression of sympathy

spir·i·tu·al·ism \'spir-i-chə-wə-ˌli-zəm, -i-chə-ˌli-, -ich-wə-ˌli-\ n (1796) **1 :** the view that spirit is a prime element of reality **2 a :** a belief that spirits of the dead communicate with the living usu. through a medium **b** cap : a movement comprising religious organizations emphasizing spiritualism — **spir·i·tu·al·ist** \-list\ n, often cap — **spir·i·tu·al·is·tic** \ˌspir-i-chə-wə-'lis-tik, -i-chə-'lis-, -ich-wə-'lis-\ adj

spir·i·tu·al·i·ty \ˌspir-i-chə-'wa-lə-tē\ n, pl **-ties** (15c) **1 :** something that in ecclesiastical law belongs to the church or to a cleric as such **2 :** CLERGY **3 :** sensitivity or attachment to religious values **4 :** the quality or state of being spiritual

spir·i·tu·al·ize \'spir-i-chə-wə-ˌliz, -i-chə-ˌliz, -ich-wə-ˌliz\ vt **-ized; -iz·ing** (1631) **1 :** to make spiritual; *esp* : to purify from the corrupting influences of the world **2 :** to give a spiritual meaning to or understand in a spiritual sense — **spir·i·tu·al·i·za·tion** \ˌspir-i-chə-wə-lə-'zā-shən, -i-chə-lə-, -ich-wə-lə-\ n

spir·i·tu·al·ty \'spir-i-chə-wəl-tē, -i-chəl-tē, -ich-wəl-tē\ n [ME *spiritualte*, fr. MF *spiritualté*, fr. ML *spiritualitat-*, *spiritualitas*, fr. LL *spiritualis* spiritual] (14c) **1 :** SPIRITUALITY 1 **2 :** CLERGY

spi·ri·tu·el or **spi·ri·tu·elle** \ˌspir-i-chə-'wel, spē-rē-tw(ʸ)el\ adj [spirituel fr. F, lit., spiritual; spirituelle fr. F, fem. of spirituel] (1673) : having or marked by a refined and esp. sprightly or witty nature

spir·i·tu·ous \'spir-i-chə-wəs, -ich-wəs\ adj [prob. fr. F *spiritueux*, fr. L *spiritus* spirit] (1681) : containing or impregnated with alcohol obtained by distillation ⟨~ liquors⟩

spirit varnish n (1850) : a varnish in which a volatile liquid (as alcohol) is the solvent

spirit writing n (1864) : automatic writing held to be produced under the influence of spirits

spi·ro·chet·al \ˌspī-rə-'kē-t³l\ adj (1915) : caused by spirochetes

spi·ro·chete also **spi·ro·chaete** \'spī-rə-ˌkēt\ n [NL *Spirochaeta*, genus of bacteria, fr. L *spira* coil + Gk *chaitē* long hair — more at SPIRE] (ca. 1877) : any of an order (Spirochaetales) of slender spirally undulating bacteria including those causing syphilis and relapsing fever

spi·ro·chet·osis \ˌspī-rə-ˌkē-'tō-səs\ n, pl **-oses** \-ˌsēz\ [NL] (1906) : infection with or a disease caused by spirochetes

spi·ro·gy·ra \ˌspī-rə-'ji-rə\ n [NL, fr. L *spira* + Gk *gyros* ring, circle] (1875) : any of a genus (*Spirogyra*) of freshwater green algae with spiral chloroplasts

spi·rom·e·ter \spī-'rä-mə-tər\ n [ISV spiro- (fr. L *spirare* to breathe) + -meter] (1846) : an instrument for measuring the air entering and leaving the lungs — **spi·ro·met·ric** \ˌspī-rə-'me-trik\ adj — **spi·rom·e·try** \spī-'rä-mə-trē\ n

spirt var of SPURT

spiry \'spī-rē\ adj (1602) : resembling a spire; *esp* : being tall, slender, and tapering ⟨~ trees⟩

¹**spit** \'spit\ n [ME, fr. OE *spitu*; akin to OHG *spiz* spit, *spizzi* pointed] (bef. 12c) **1 :** a slender pointed rod for holding meat over a fire **2 :** a small point of land esp. of sand or gravel running into a body of water

²**spit** vt **spit·ed; spit·ing** (13c) : to fix on or as if on a spit : IMPALE

³**spit** vb **spit** or **spat** \'spat\; **spit·ting** [ME *spitten*, fr. OE *spittan*; akin to MHG *spiutzen* to spit] vt (bef. 12c) **1 a :** to eject (as saliva) from the mouth : EXPECTORATE **b** (1) : to express (unpleasant or malicious feelings) by or as if by spitting (2) : to utter with a spitting sound or scornful expression ⟨spat out his words⟩ **c :** to emit as if by spitting; *esp* : to emit (precipitation) in driving particles or in flurries ⟨~ rain⟩ **2 :** to set to burning ⟨~ a fuse⟩ ~ vi **1 a** (1) : to eject saliva as an expression of aversion or contempt (2) : to exhibit contempt **b :** to eject matter (as saliva) from the mouth : EXPECTORATE **2 :** to emit rain or snow slightly or in flurries **3 :** to make a noise suggesting expectoration : SPUTTER — **spit it out** : to say what is in the mind without further delay

⁴**spit** n (14c) **1 a** (1) : SPITTLE, SALIVA (2) : the act or an instance of spitting **b** (1) : a frothy secretion exuded by spittlebugs (2) : SPITTLEBUG **2 :** perfect likeness **3 :** a sprinkle of rain or flurry of snow

spit·al \'spi-t³l\ n [ME *spitel*, modif. of ML *hospitale* — more at HOSPITAL] (14c) archaic : LAZARETTO, HOSPITAL

spit and polish n [fr. the practice of polishing objects such as shoes by spitting on them and then rubbing them with a cloth] (1895) : extreme attention to cleanliness, orderliness, smartness of appearance, and ceremony often at the expense of operational efficiency — **spit–and–polish** adj

spit·ball \'spit-ˌbȯl\ n (1846) **1 :** paper chewed and rolled into a ball to be thrown or shot as a missile **2 :** a baseball pitch delivered after the ball has been moistened with saliva or sweat

spit curl n [prob. fr. its being sometimes plastered down with saliva] (1831) : a spiral curl that is usu. plastered on the forehead, temple, or cheek

¹**spite** \'spit\ n [ME, short for *despite*] (14c) **1 :** petty ill will or hatred with the disposition to irritate, annoy, or thwart **2 :** an instance of spite **syn** see MALICE — **in spite of** : in defiance or contempt of : without being prevented by

²**spite** vt **spit·ed; spit·ing** (ca. 1555) **1 a :** ANNOY, OFFEND **b :** to fill with spite **2 :** to treat maliciously (as by shaming or thwarting)

spite·ful \'spit-fəl\ adj (15c) : filled with or showing spite : MALICIOUS — **spite·ful·ly** \-fə-lē\ adv — **spite·ful·ness** n

spit·fire \'spit-ˌfir\ n (1680) : a quick-tempered or highly emotional person

¹**spit·ter** \'spi-tər\ n (14c) : one that spits

²**spitter** n (1908) : SPITBALL 2

spitting cobra n (1910) : either of two African cobras (*Naja nigricollis* and *Hemachatus haemachatus*) that in defense typically eject their venom toward the victim without striking

spitting image n [alter. of *spit and image*] (1901) : IMAGE 3b

spit·tle \'spi-t³l\ n [ME *spetil*, fr. OE *spætl*; akin to OE *spittan* to spit] (bef. 12c) **1 :** SALIVA **2 :** SPIT 1b(1)

spit·tle·bug \-ˌbəg\ n (1882) : any of a family (Cercopidae) of leaping homopterous insects whose larvae secrete froth — called also *froghopper*

spittle insect n (1891) : SPITTLEBUG

spit·toon \spi-'tün, spə-\ n [⁴spit + -oon (as in *balloon*)] (1823) : a receptacle for spit — called also *cuspidor*

spit up vb (1779) : REGURGITATE, VOMIT

spitz \'spits\ n [G, fr. *spitz* pointed, fr. OHG *spizzi*; fr. the shape of its ears and muzzle — more at SPIT] (1842) : a member of any of several breeds of stocky heavy-coated dogs of northern origin with erect ears and usu. a heavily furred tail carried over the back

spiv \'spiv\ n [alter. of E dial. *spiff* flashy dresser, fr. *spiff* dandified] (ca. 1934) **1** Brit : one who lives by his wits without regular employment **2** Brit : SLACKER

splanch·nic \'splaŋk-nik\ adj [NL *splanchnicus*, fr. Gk *splanchnikos*, fr. *splanchna*, pl., viscera; akin to Gk *splēn* spleen] (1681) : of or relating to the viscera : VISCERAL

¹**splash** \'splash\ vb [alter. of *plash*] vt (ca. 1727) **1 a** (1) : to dash a liquid or thinly viscous substance upon or against (2) : to soil or stain with splashed liquid **b :** to mark or overlay with patches of contrast-

spitz

ing color or texture   **c** : to display prominently   **2 a** : to cause (a liquid or thinly viscous substance) to spatter about esp. with force   **b** : to scatter in the manner of a splashed liquid ~ *vi* **1 a** : to strike and dash about a liquid or semiliquid substance   **b** : to move in or into a liquid or semiliquid substance and cause it to spatter   **2 a** (1) : to become spattered about   (2) : to spread or scatter in the manner of splashed liquid   **b** : to fall, strike, or move with a splashing sound ⟨a brook ~*ing* over rocks⟩ — **splash·er** *n*

²**splash** *n* (1736)   **1 a** (1) : splashed liquid or semiliquid substance; *also* : impounded water released suddenly   (2) : a spot or daub from or as if from splashed liquid ⟨a mud ~ on the fender⟩   **b** : a colored patch   **2 a** : the action of splashing   **b** : a short plunge   **3** : a sound produced by or as if by a liquid falling, moving, being hurled, or oscillating   **4 a** : a vivid impression created esp. by ostentatious activity or appearance   **b** : ostentatious display   **5** : a small amount : SPRINKLING

splash·board \'splash-,bōrd, -,bȯrd\ *n* (1826)   **1** : DASHBOARD 1   **2** : a panel to protect against splashes

splash·down \'splash-,daủn\ *n* (1959) : the landing of a manned spacecraft in the ocean — **splash down** *vi*

splash guard *n* (1926) : a flap suspended behind a rear wheel to prevent tire splash from muddying windshields of following vehicles

splashy \'spla-shē\ *adj* **splash·i·er; -est** (1856)   **1** : that can be easily splashed about   **2** : moving or being moved with a splash or splashing sounds   **3** : tending to or exhibiting ostentatious display   **4** : consisting of, being, or covered with colored splashes — **splash·i·ly** \'spla-shə-lē\ *adv* — **splash·i·ness** \'spla-shē-nəs\ *n*

¹**splat** \'splat\ *n* [obs. *splat* to spread flat] (1833) : a single flat thin often ornamental member of a back of a chair

²**splat** *n* [imit.] (1897) : a spattering or slapping sound

¹**splat·ter** \'spla-tər\ *vb* [prob. blend of *splash* and *spatter*] *vt* (1785) : SPATTER ~ *vi* : to scatter or fall in or as if in drops

²**splatter** *n* (1819) : SPLATTER, SPLASH

¹**splay** \'splā\ *vb* [ME, short for *displayen* — more at DISPLAY] *vt* (15c)   **1** : to cause to spread outward   **2** : to make oblique : BEVEL ~ *vi* **1** : to extend apart or outward esp. in an awkward manner   **2** : SLOPE, SLANT

²**splay** *n* (ca. 1508)   **1** : a slope or bevel esp. of the sides of a door or window   **2** : SPREAD, EXPANSION

³**splay** *adj* (1767)   **1** : turned outward ⟨~ knees⟩   **2** : AWKWARD, UNGAINLY

splay·foot \'splā-,fủt\ *n* (1548)   **1** : a foot abnormally flattened and spread out; *specif* : FLATFOOT — **splay·foot·ed** \-,fủ-təd\ *adj*

spleen \'splēn\ *n* [ME *splen*, fr. MF or L; MF *esplen*, fr. L *splen*, fr. Gk *splēn*; akin to L *lien* spleen, Skt *plīhan*] (14c)   **1** : a highly vascular ductless organ that is located in the left abdominal region near the stomach or intestine of most vertebrates and is concerned with final destruction of red blood cells, filtration and storage of blood, and production of lymphocytes   **2** *obs* : the seat of emotions or passions   **3** *archaic* : MELANCHOLY   **4** : feelings of anger or ill will often suppressed   **5** *obs* : a sudden impulse or whim : CAPRICE   *syn* see MALICE

spleen·ful \-fəl\ *adj* (1588) : full of or affected with spleen : SPLENETIC

spleen·wort \-,wərt, -,wȯrt\ *n* [fr. the belief in its power to cure disorders of the spleen] (1578) : any of a large genus (*Asplenium*) of chiefly evergreen ferns having linear or oblong sori

spleeny \'splē-nē\ *adj* (1604)   **1** : full of or displaying spleen   **2** *NewEng* : peevish and irritable with hypochondriac inclinations

splen- or **spleno-** *comb form* [L, fr. Gk *splēn-*, *splēno-*, fr. *splēn*] : spleen ⟨*splenectomy*⟩ ⟨*splenomegaly*⟩

splen·dent \'splen-dənt\ *adj* [ME, fr. LL *splendent-*, *splendens*, fr. L, prp. of *splendēre*] (15c)   **1** : SHINING, GLOSSY ⟨~ luster⟩   **2** : ILLUSTRIOUS, BRILLIANT ⟨~ genius⟩

splen·did \'splen-dəd\ *adj* [L *splendidus*, fr. *splendēre* to shine; perh. akin to MIr *lainn* bright] (1634)   **1** : possessing or displaying splendor: as   **a** : SHINING, BRILLIANT   **b** : marked by showy magnificence   **2** : ILLUSTRIOUS, GRAND   **3** : EXCELLENT ⟨a ~ opportunity⟩   **4** : being out of the ordinary : SINGULAR — **splen·did·ly** *adv* — **splen·did·ness** *n*

syn SPLENDID, RESPLENDENT, GORGEOUS, GLORIOUS, SUBLIME, SUPERB mean extraordinarily or transcendently impressive. SPLENDID implies outshining the usual or customary ⟨the wedding was a *splendid* occasion⟩. RESPLENDENT suggests a glowing or blazing splendor ⟨*resplendent* in her jewelry⟩. GORGEOUS implies a rich splendor esp. in display of color ⟨a *gorgeous* red dress⟩. GLORIOUS suggests radiance that heightens beauty or distinction ⟨a *glorious* sunset⟩. SUBLIME implies an exaltation or elevation almost beyond human comprehension ⟨a vision of *sublime* beauty⟩. SUPERB suggests a magnificence or excellence reaching the highest conceivable degree ⟨her singing was *superb*⟩.

splen·dif·er·ous \splen-'di-f(ə-)rəs\ *adj* [*splendor* + *-i-* + *-ferous*] (1843) : extraordinarily or showily impressive — **splen·dif·er·ous·ly** *adv* — **splen·dif·er·ous·ness** *n*

splen·dor \'splen-dər\ *n* [ME *splendure*, fr. AF *splendur*, fr. L *splendor*, fr. *splendēre*] (15c)   **1 a** : great brightness or luster : BRILLIANCY   **b** : MAGNIFICENCE, POMP   **2** : something splendid — **splen·dor·ous** *also* **splen·drous** \-d(ə-)rəs\ *adj*

splen·dour \-dər\ *chiefly Brit var of* SPLENDOR

sple·nec·to·my \spli-'nek-tə-mē\ *n, pl* **-mies** [ISV] (ca. 1859) : surgical removal of the spleen — **sple·nec·to·mize** \-,mīz\ *vt*

sple·net·ic \spli-'ne-tik\ *adj* [LL *spleneticus*, fr. L *splen* spleen] (1697)   **1** *archaic* : given to melancholy   **2** : marked by bad temper, malevolence, or spite — **splenetic** *n* — **sple·net·i·cal·ly** \spli-'ne-ti-k(ə-)lē\ *adv*

splen·ic \'sple-nik\ *adj* [L *splenicus*, fr. Gk *splēnikos*, fr. *splēn* spleen] (1619) : of, relating to, or located in the spleen ⟨~ blood flow⟩

sple·ni·us \'splē-nē-əs\ *n, pl* **-nii** \-nē-,ī\ [NL, fr. L *splenium* plaster, compress, fr. Gk *splēnion*, fr. *splēn*] (1732) : either of two flat oblique muscles on each side of the back of the neck and upper thoracic region

sple·no·meg·a·ly \,splē-nō-'me-gə-lē\ *n, pl* **-lies** [ISV] (ca. 1900) : enlargement of the spleen

spleu·chan \'splü-kən, 'splyü-\ *n* [ScGael *spliùcan* & Ir *spliúchán*] (1785) *Scot & Irish* : a pouch esp. for tobacco or money

¹**splice** \'splīs\ *vt* **spliced; splic·ing** [obs. D *splissen*; akin to MD *splitten* to split] (ca. 1525)   **1 a** : to unite (as two ropes) by interweaving the strands   **b** : to unite (as lengths of magnetic tape) by lapping two

ends together or by applying a piece that laps upon two ends and making fast   **2** : to unite, link, or insert as if by splicing   **3** : to combine (genetic material) from either the same organism or different organisms ⟨use enzymes to cut and ~ genes⟩ — **splic·er** *n*

²**splice** *n* (1627)   **1** : a joining or joint made by splicing something   **2** : MARRIAGE, WEDDING

spliff \'splif\ *n* [origin unknown] (1936) : JOINT 4

spline \'splīn\ *n* [origin unknown] (1756)   **1** : a thin wood or metal strip used in building construction   **2** : a key that is fixed to one of two connected mechanical parts and fits into a keyway in the other; *also* : a keyway for such a key   **3** : a function that is defined on an interval, is used to approximate a given function, and is composed of pieces of simple functions defined on subintervals and joined at their endpoints with a suitable degree of smoothness

splice 1

¹**splint** \'splint\ *also* **splent** \'splent\ *n* [ME, fr. MLG *splinte*, *splente*; prob. akin to MD *splitten* to split] (14c)   **1** : a small plate or strip of metal used in making armor   **2 a** : a thin strip of wood suitable for interweaving (as into baskets)   **b** : SPLINTER   **c** : material or a device used to protect and immobilize a body part (as a broken arm)   **3 a** : a bony enlargement on the upper part of the cannon bone of a horse usu. on the inside of the leg

²**splint** *vt* (15c)   **1** : to support and immobilize (as a broken bone) with a splint   **2** : to brace with or as if with splints

splint bone *n* (1704) : one of the slender rudimentary metacarpal or metatarsal bones on either side of the cannon bone in the limbs of the horse and related animals

¹**splin·ter** \'splin-tər\ *n* [ME, fr. MD; akin to MLG *splinte* splint] (14c)   **1 a** : a thin piece split or broken off lengthwise : SLIVER   **b** : a small needlelike particle   **2** : a group or faction broken away from a parent body — **splinter** *adj* — **splin·tery** \'splin-tə-rē, -trē\ *adj*

²**splinter** *vb* **splin·tered; splin·ter·ing** \'splin-tə-riŋ, -triŋ\ *vt* (1582)   **1** : to split or rend into long thin pieces : SHIVER   **2** : to split into fragments, parts, or factions ~ *vi* : to become splintered

¹**split** \'split\ *vb* **split; split·ting** [D *splitten*, fr. MD; akin to MHG *splizen* to split and prob. to OHG *spaltan* to split] *vt* (1593)   **1 a** : to divide lengthwise usu. along a grain or seam or by layers   **b** : to affect as if by cleaving or forcing apart ⟨the river ~s the town in two⟩   **2 a** (1) : to tear or rend apart   (2) : to subject (an atom or atomic nucleus) to artificial disintegration by fission   **b** : to affect as if by breaking up or tearing apart : SHATTER ⟨a roar that ~ the air⟩   **3** : to divide into parts or portions: as   **a** : to divide between persons : SHARE   **b** : to divide into factions, parties, or groups   **c** : to mark (a ballot) or cast or register (a vote) so as to vote for candidates of different parties   **d** (1) : to divide or break down (a chemical compound) into constituents ⟨~ a fat into glycerol and fatty acids⟩   (2) : to remove by such separation ⟨~ off carbon dioxide⟩   **e** : to divide (stock) by issuing a larger number of shares to existing shareholders usu. without increase in total par value   **4** : to separate (the parts of a whole) by interposing something ⟨~ an infinitive⟩   **5** : LEAVE ⟨~ the party⟩ ⟨~ town⟩ ~ *vi* **1 a** : to become split lengthwise or into layers   **b** : to break apart : BURST   **2 a** : to become divided up or separated off ⟨~ into factions⟩   **b** : to sever relations or connections   **c** : LEAVE; *esp* : to leave without delay   **3** *Brit* : to betray confidence : act as an informer — usu. used with *on*   **4** : to apportion shares   *syn* see TEAR — **split hairs** : to make oversubtle or trivial distinctions — **split one's sides** : to laugh heartily

²**split** *n* (1597)   **1 a** : a narrow break made by or as if by splitting   **b** : an arrangement of bowling pins left standing with space for pins between them   **2** : a piece split off or made thin by splitting   **3 a** : a division into or between divergent or antagonistic elements or forces   **b** : a faction formed in this way   **4 a** : the act or process of splitting (as the stock of a corporation)   **b** : the act of lowering oneself to the floor or leaping into the air with legs extended at right angles to the trunk   **5** : a product of division by or as if by splitting   **6** : a whole bottle holding one quarter the usual amount or about .1875 liters (6 to 6.5 ounces); *also* : the quantity held by a split   **7** : an ice cream sundae served over slices of fruit (as banana)   **8** : the recorded time at or for a specific part of a race

³**split** *adj* (1648)   **1** : DIVIDED, FRACTURED   **2** : prepared for use by splitting ⟨~ bamboo⟩ ⟨~ hides⟩   **3** : HETEROZYGOUS — used esp. by breeders of cage birds sometimes with *for*   **4** : widely spaced

split–brain \'split-'brān\ *adj* (1958) : having the optic chiasma and corpus callosum severed ⟨behavior in ~ animals⟩

split decision *n* (1952) : a decision in a boxing match reflecting a division of opinion among the referee and judges

split end *n* (1955) : an offensive football end who lines up usu. several yards to the side of the formation

split–fingered fastball \'split-'fiŋ-gərd-\ *n* (1979) : a fast baseball pitch thrown with the ball gripped as for a forkball

split infinitive *n* (1897) : an infinitive with *to* having a modifier between the *to* and the verbal (as in "to really start")

usage The split infinitive was discovered and named in the 19th century. 19th century writers seem to have made greater use of this construction than earlier writers; the frequency of occurrence attracted the disapproving attention of grammarians, many of whom thought it to be a modern corruption. The construction had in fact been in occasional use since the 14th century; only its frequency had changed. Even though there has never been a rational basis for objecting to the split infinitive, the subject has become a fixture of folk belief about grammar. You can hardly publish a sentence containing one without hearing about it from somebody. Modern commentators know the split infinitive is not a vice, but they are loath to drop such a popular subject. They usu. say it's all right to split an infinitive in the interest

---

\ə\ abut   \ᵊ\ kitten, F table   \ər\ further   \a\ ash   \ā\ ace   \ä\ mop, mar   \aủ\ out   \ch\ chin   \e\ bet   \ē\ easy   \g\ go   \i\ hit   \ī\ ice   \j\ job   \ŋ\ sing   \ō\ go   \ȯ\ law   \ȯi\ boy   \th\ thin   \t͟h\ the   \ü\ loot   \ủ\ foot   \y\ yet   \zh\ vision   \á, k̇, ⁿ, œ, œ̄, ue, ū̃, ᵊ\ *see* Guide to Pronunciation of clarity. Since clarity is the usual reason for splitting, this advice means merely that you can split them whenever you need to.

split–lev·el \'split-'le-vəl\ *adj* (1946) : divided vertically so that the floor level of rooms in one part is approximately midway between the levels of two successive stories in an adjoining part ⟨a ∼ house⟩ — **split–lev·el** \-,le-vəl\ *n*

split pea *n* (1736) : a dried hulled pea in which the cotyledons usu. split apart

split personality *n* (1927) : SCHIZOPHRENIA; *also* : MULTIPLE PERSONALITY

split rail *n* (1826) : a fence rail split from a log

split screen *n* (1944) : a film or video technique in which the frame is divided into discrete nonoverlapping images; *also* : the visual composition based on this technique

split second *n* (1912) : a fractional part of a second : FLASH

split shift *n* (1943) : a shift of working hours divided into two or more working periods at times (as morning and evening) separated by more than normal periods of time off (as for lunch or rest)

split·ter \'spli-tər\ *n* (1648) **1** : one that splits **2** : one who classifies organisms into numerous named groups based on relatively minor variations or characters — compare LUMPER **3** : SPLIT-FINGERED FASTBALL

split ticket *n* (1836) : a ballot cast by a voter who votes for candidates of more than one party

split·ting \'spli-tiŋ\ *adj* (1593) : that splits or causes to split: as **a** : causing a piercing sensation ⟨a ∼ headache⟩ **b** : very fast or quick **c** : SIDESPLITTING ⟨a ∼ laugh⟩

splore \'splōr, 'splȯr\ *n* [origin unknown] (1785) **1** *Scot* : FROLIC, CAROUSAL **2** *Scot* : COMMOTION

¹splotch \'spläch\ *n* [perh. blend of *spot* and *blotch*] (1601) : SPOT, BLOTCH — **splotchy** \'splä-chē\ *adj*

²splotch *vt* (1654) : to mark with a splotch : cover with splotches

¹splurge \'splərj\ *n* [perh. blend of *splash* and *surge*] (1830) : an ostentatious effort, display, or expenditure

²splurge *vb* **splurged; splurg·ing** *vi* (1843) **1** : to make a splurge **2** : to indulge oneself extravagantly — often used with *on* ⟨∼ on a new dress⟩ ∼ *vt* : to spend extravagantly or ostentatiously

¹splut·ter \'splə-tər\ *n* [prob. alter. of *sputter*] (1677) **1** : a confused noise (as of hasty speaking) : a splashing or sputtering sound

²splutter *vi* (1818) **1** : to make a noise as if spitting **2** : to speak hastily and confusedly ∼ *vt* : to utter hastily or confusedly — STAMMER — **splut·ter·er** \-tər-ər\ *n*

splut·tery \'splə-tə-rē\ *adj* (1866) : marked by spluttering

Spode \'spōd\ *n* (1869) : ceramic ware (as bone china, stone china, or Parian ware) made at the works established by Josiah Spode in 1770 at Stoke in Staffordshire, England

spod·u·mene \'späd-jə-,mēn\ *n* [prob. fr. F *spodumène*, fr. G *Spodumen*, fr. Gk *spodoumenos*, prp. of *spodousthai* to be burnt to ashes, fr. *spodos* ashes] (1893) : a white to yellowish, purplish, or emerald-green monoclinic mineral that is a silicate of lithium and aluminum and occurs in prismatic crystals often of great size

¹spoil \'spȯi(ə)l\ *n* [ME *spoile*, fr. MF *espoille*, fr. L *spolia*, pl. of *spolium* animal skin — more at SPILL] (14c) **1 a** : plunder taken from an enemy in war or a victim in robbery : LOOT **b** : public offices made the property of a successful party — usu. used in pl. **c** : something valuable or desirable gained through special effort or opportunism or in return for a favor — usu. used in pl. **2 a** : SPOLIATION, PLUNDERING **b** : the act of damaging : HARM, IMPAIRMENT **3** : an object of plundering : PREY **4** : earth and rock excavated or dredged **5** : an object damaged or flawed in the making

syn SPOIL, PLUNDER, BOOTY, PRIZE, LOOT mean something taken from another by force or craft. SPOIL, more commonly SPOILS, applies to what belongs by right or custom to the victor in war or political contest ⟨the *spoils* of political victory⟩. PLUNDER applies to what is taken not only in war but in robbery, banditry, grafting, or swindling ⟨a bootlegger's *plunder*⟩. BOOTY implies plunder to be shared among confederates ⟨thieves dividing up their *booty*⟩. PRIZE applies to spoils captured on the high seas or territorial waters of the enemy ⟨the wartime right of seizing *prizes* at sea⟩. LOOT applies esp. to what is taken from victims of a catastrophe ⟨picked through the ruins for *loot*⟩.

²spoil *vb* **spoiled** \'spȯi(ə)ld, 'spȯi(ə)lt\ *also* **spoilt** \'spȯi(ə)lt\; **spoil·ing** [ME, fr. MF *espoillier*, fr. L *spoliare*, fr. *spolium*] *vt* (14c) **1 a** *archaic* : DESPOIL, STRIP **b** : PILLAGE, ROB **2** *archaic* : to seize by force **3 a** : to damage seriously : RUIN **b** : to impair the quality or effect of ⟨a quarrel ∼ed the celebration⟩ **4 a** : to impair the disposition or character of by overindulgence or excessive praise **b** : to pamper excessively : CODDLE ∼ *vi* **1** : to practice plunder and robbery **2** : to lose valuable or useful qualities usu. as a result of decay **3** : to have an eager desire ⟨∼ing for a fight⟩ *syn* see DECAY, INDULGE — **spoil·able** \'spȯi-lə-bəl\ *adj*

spoil·age \'spȯi-lij\ *n* (1597) **1** : the act or process of spoiling; *esp* : the process of decay in foodstuffs **2** : something spoiled or wasted **3** : loss by spoilage

spoil·er \'spȯi-lər\ *n* (15c) **1 a** : one that spoils **b** : one (as a political candidate) having little or no chance of winning but capable of depriving a rival of success **2 a** : a long narrow plate along the upper surface of an airplane wing that may be raised for reducing lift and increasing drag — see AIRPLANE illustration **b** : an air deflector on an automobile to reduce the tendency to lift off the road at high speeds

spoils·man \'spȯi(ə)lz-mən\ *n* (1846) : one who serves a party for a share of the spoils; *also* : one who sanctions such practice

spoil·sport \'spȯi(ə)l-,spōrt, -,spȯrt\ *n* (1821) : one who spoils the sport or pleasure of others

spoils system *n* (1838) : a practice of regarding public offices and their emoluments as plunder to be distributed to members of the victorious party

¹spoke \'spōk\ *past & archaic past part of* SPEAK

²spoke *n* [ME, fr. OE *spāca*; akin to MD *spike* spike — more at SPIKE] (bef. 12c) **1 a** : any of the small radiating bars inserted in the hub of a wheel to support the rim **b** : something resembling the spoke of a wheel **2** : any of the projecting handles of a steering wheel of a boat

³spoke *vt* **spoked; spok·ing** (bef. 12c) : to furnish with or as if with spokes

spo·ken \'spō-kən\ *adj* [pp. of *speak*] (1595) **1** : delivered by word of mouth : ORAL **2** : characterized by speaking in (such) a manner — used in combination ⟨soft-*spoken*⟩ ⟨plain*spoken*⟩

spoke·shave \'spōk-,shāv\ *n* [²*spoke*] (1510) : a drawknife or small transverse plane with end handles for planing convex or concave surfaces

spokes·man \'spōks-mən\ *n* [prob. irreg. fr. *spoke*, obs. pp. of *speak*] (1537) : a person who speaks as the representative of another or others often in a professional capacity — **spokes·man·ship** \-,ship\ *n*

spokes·peo·ple \-,pē-pəl\ *n pl* (1972) : people serving as spokesmen or spokeswomen

spokes·per·son \-,pər-s³n\ *n* (1972) : SPOKESMAN

spokes·wom·an \-,wu̇-mən\ *n* (1654) : a woman who speaks as the representative of another or others often in a professional capacity

spo·li·ate \'spō-lē-,āt\ *vt* **-at·ed; -at·ing** [L *spoliatus*, pp. of *spoliare*] (ca. 1727) : DESPOIL — **spo·li·a·tor** \-,ā-tər\ *n*

spo·li·a·tion \,spō-lē-'ā-shən\ *n* [ME, fr. L *spoliation-, spoliatio*, fr. *spoliare* to plunder — more at SPOIL] (15c) **1 a** : the act of plundering **b** : the state of having been plundered esp. in war **2** : the act of injuring esp. beyond reclaim

spon·dee \'spän-,dē\ *n* [ME *sponde*, fr. MF or L; MF *spondee*, fr. L *spondeum*, fr. Gk *spondeios*, fr. *spondeios* of a libation, fr. *spondē* libation, fr. *spendein* to make a libation; fr. its use in music accompanying libations — more at SPOUSE] (14c) : a metrical foot consisting of two long or stressed syllables — **spon·da·ic** \spän-'dā-ik\ *adj or n*

spon·dy·li·tis \,spän-də-'lī-təs\ *n* [NL, fr. Gk *sphondylos, spondylos* vertebra] (ca. 1849) : inflammation of the vertebrae

¹sponge \'spənj\ *n* [ME, fr. OE, fr. L *spongia*, fr. Gk] (bef. 12c) **1 a** (1) : an elastic porous mass of interlacing horny fibers that forms the internal skeleton of various marine animals (phylum Porifera) and is able when wetted to absorb water (2) : a piece of sponge (as for scrubbing and cleaning) (3) : a porous rubber or cellulose product used similarly to a sponge **b** : any of a phylum (Porifera) of aquatic chiefly marine lower invertebrate animals that are essentially double-walled cell colonies that are permanently attached as adults **2** : a pad (as of folded gauze) used in surgery and medicine (as to remove discharge or apply medication) **3** : one who lives on others : SPONGER **4 a** : raised dough (as for yeast bread) **b** : a whipped dessert usu. containing whites of eggs or gelatin **c** : a metal (as platinum) obtained in porous form usu. by reduction without fusion ⟨titanium ∼⟩ **d** : the egg mass of a crab **5** : an absorbent contraceptive device that is impregnated with spermicide and inserted into the vagina before sexual intercourse to cover the cervix *syn* see PARASITE

²sponge *vb* **sponged; spong·ing** *vt* (14c) **1** : to cleanse, wipe, or moisten with or as if with a sponge **2** : to erase or destroy with or as if with a sponge — often used with *out* **3** : to get by sponging on another **4** : to absorb with or as if with or in the manner of a sponge ∼ *vi* **1** : to absorb, soak up, or imbibe like a sponge **2** : to get something from or live on another by imposing on hospitality or good nature **3** : to dive or dredge for sponges — **spong·er** *n*

sponge cake *n* (1805) : a light cake made without shortening

sponge cloth *n* (1862) : any of various soft porous fabrics esp. in a loose honeycomb weave

sponge rubber *n* (1886) : cellular rubber resembling a natural sponge in structure used esp. for cushions, vibration dampeners, weather stripping, and gaskets

sponge·ware \'spənj-,war, -,wer\ *n* (1943) : a typically 19th century earthenware with background color spattered or dabbed (as with a sponge) and usu. a freehand central design

spon·gin \'spən-jən\ *n* [G, fr. L *spongia* sponge] (ca. 1868) : a scleroprotein that is the chief constituent of fibers in sponge skeletons

spongy \'spən-jē\ *adj* **spong·i·er; -est** (14c) **1** : resembling a sponge: **a** : soft and full of cavities ⟨∼ ice⟩ **b** : elastic, porous, and absorbent **2 a** : not firm or solid **b** : being in the form of a metallic sponge ⟨∼ iron⟩ **3** : moist and soft like a sponge full of water ⟨a ∼ moor⟩ — **spong·i·ness** *n*

spongy parenchyma *n* (1884) : a spongy layer of irregular chlorophyll-bearing cells interspersed with air spaces that fills the interior part of a leaf below the palisade layer — called also *spongy layer, spongy tissue*

spon·son \'spän(t)-sən\ *n* [perh. by shortening & alter. fr. *expansion*] (1835) **1 a** : a projection (as a gun platform) from the side of a ship or a tank **b** : an air chamber along a canoe to increase stability and buoyancy **2** : a light air-filled structure or a winglike part protruding from the hull of a seaplane to steady it in water

¹spon·sor \'spän(t)-sər\ *n* [LL, fr. L, guarantor, surety, fr. *spondēre* to promise — more at SPOUSE] (1651) **1** : one who presents a candidate for baptism or confirmation and undertakes responsibility for the person's religious education or spiritual welfare **2** : one who assumes responsibility for some other person or thing **3** : a person or an organization that pays for or plans and carries out a project or activity; *esp* : one that pays the cost of a radio or television program usu. in return for advertising time during its course — **spon·so·ri·al** \spän-'sȯr-ē-əl, -'sȯr-\ *adj* — **spon·sor·ship** \'spän(t)s-ər-,ship\ *n*

²sponsor *vt* **spon·sored; spon·sor·ing** \'spän(t)s-(ə-)riŋ\ (1884) : to be or stand sponsor for

spon·ta·ne·i·ty \,spän-tə-'nē-ə-tē, -'nā-; -t³n-'ē-, -'ā-\ *n* (1651) **1** : the quality or state of being spontaneous **2** : voluntary or undetermined action or movement; *also* : its source

spon·ta·ne·ous \spän-'tā-nē-əs\ *adj* [LL *spontaneus*, fr. L *sponte* of one's free will, voluntarily] (1656) **1** : proceeding from natural feeling or native tendency without external constraint **2** : arising from a momentary impulse **3** : controlled and directed internally : SELF-ACTING ⟨∼ movement characteristic of living things⟩ **4** : produced without being planted or without human labor : INDIGENOUS **5** : developing without apparent external influence, force, cause, or treatment **6** : not apparently contrived or manipulated : NATURAL — **spon·ta·ne·ous·ly** *adv* — **spon·ta·ne·ous·ness** *n*

syn SPONTANEOUS, IMPULSIVE, INSTINCTIVE, AUTOMATIC, MECHANICAL mean acting or activated without deliberation. SPONTANEOUS implies lack of prompting and connotes naturalness ⟨a *spontaneous* burst of applause⟩. IMPULSIVE implies acting under stress of emotion or spirit of the moment ⟨*impulsive* acts of violence⟩. INSTINCTIVE stresses spontaneous action involving neither judgment nor will ⟨blinking is an *in-*

stinctive reaction⟩. AUTOMATIC implies action engaging neither the mind nor the emotions and connotes a predictable response ⟨his denial was *automatic*⟩. MECHANICAL stresses the lifeless, often perfunctory character of the response ⟨a *mechanical* teaching method⟩.

spontaneous combustion *n* (1795) : self-ignition of combustible material through chemical action (as oxidation) of its constituents — called also *spontaneous ignition*

spontaneous generation *n* (1665) : ABIOGENESIS

spontaneous recovery *n* (1943) : reappearance of an extinguished conditioned response without positive reinforcement

spon·toon \spän-'tün\ *n* [F *sponton*, fr. It *spuntone*, fr. *punta* sharp point, fr. (assumed) VL *puncta* — more at POINT] (1598) : a short pike formerly borne by subordinate officers of infantry

¹spoof \'spüf\ *vt* [*Spoof*, a hoaxing game invented by Arthur Roberts †1933 Eng. comedian] (1889) **1** : DECEIVE, HOAX **2** : to make good-natured fun of

²spoof *n* (1889) **1** : HOAX, DECEPTION **2** : a light humorous parody — **spoof·ery** \'spü-f(ə-)rē\ *n* — **spoofy** \'spü-fē\ *adj*

¹spook \'spük\ *n* [D; akin to MLG *spōk* ghost] (1801) **1** : GHOST, SPECTER **2** : an undercover agent : SPY — **spook·ish** \'spü-kish\ *adj*

²spook *vt* (1883) **1** : HAUNT 3 **2** : to make frightened or frantic : SCARE; *esp* : to startle into violent activity (as stampeding) ~ *vi* : to become spooked ⟨cattle ~*ing* at shadows⟩

spook·ery \'spü-k(ə-)rē\ *n, pl* **-er·ies** (1893) : the quality of being spooky; *also* : something (as a story) that involves spooks

spooky \'spü-kē\ *adj* **spook·i·er; -est** (1854) **1** : relating to, resembling, or suggesting spooks **2** : NERVOUS, SKITTISH ⟨a ~ horse⟩ — **spook·i·ly** \-kə-lē\ *adv* — **spook·i·ness** \-kē-nəs\ *n*

¹spool \'spül\ *n* [ME *spole*, fr. MF or MD; MF *espole*, fr. MD *spoele*; akin to OHG *spuola* spool] (14c) **1** : a cylindrical device which has a rim or ridge at each end and an axial hole for a pin or spindle and on which material (as thread, wire, or tape) is wound **2** : material or the amount of material wound on a spool

²spool *vt* (1603) **1** : to wind on a spool **2** : WIND ⟨~ the thread off the bobbin⟩ ~ *vi* **1** : to wind itself on a spool **2** : WIND

¹spoon \'spün\ *n* [ME, fr. OE *spōn* splinter, chip; akin to OHG *spān* splinter, chip] (14c) **1** : an eating or cooking implement consisting of a small shallow bowl with a relatively long handle **2** : something (as a tool or fishing lure) that resembles a spoon in shape

²spoon *vt* (1715) : to take up and usu. transfer in a spoon ~ *vi* [perh. fr. the Welsh custom of an engaged man's presenting his fiancée with an elaborately carved wooden spoon] : to make love by caressing, kissing, and talking amorously : NECK

spoon·bill \'spün-,bil\ *n* (ca. 1678) **1** : any of several wading birds (family Threskiornithidae) related to the ibises that have an expanded bill that is flattened and rounded at the tip **2** : any of several broad-billed ducks (as the shoveler)

spoonbill cat *n* (ca. 1882) : a paddlefish (*Polyodon spathula*)

spoon–billed \'spün-,bild\ *adj* (1668) : having the bill or snout expanded and spatulate at the end

spoon bread *n* (1916) : soft bread made of cornmeal mixed with milk, eggs, and shortening and served with a spoon

spoo·ner·ism \'spü-nə-,ri-zəm\ *n* [William A. *Spooner* †1930 Eng. clergyman & educator] (1900) : a transposition of usu. initial sounds of two or more words (as in *tons of soil* for *sons of toil*)

spoon–feed \'spün-,fēd\ *vt* **-fed** \-,fed\; **-feed·ing** (1615) **1** : to feed by means of a spoon **2 a** : to present (information) so completely as to preclude independent thought ⟨~ material to students⟩ **b** : to present information to in this manner

spoon·ful \'spün-,ful\ *n, pl* **spoonfuls** \-,fülz\ *also* **spoons·ful** \'spünz-,ful\ (14c) : as much as a spoon will hold; *specif* : TEASPOONFUL

spoony *or* **spoon·ey** \'spü-nē\ *adj* **spoon·i·er; -est** [E slang *spoon* simpleton] (ca. 1812) **1** : SILLY, FOOLISH; *esp* : unduly sentimental **2** : being sentimentally in love

¹spoor \'spur, 'spōr, 'spȯr\ *n, pl* **spoor** *or* **spoors** [Afrik, fr. D; akin to OE *spor* footprint, *spoor*, *spurnan* to kick — more at SPURN] (1823) **1** : a track, a trail, a scent, or droppings esp. of a wild animal **2** : a trace by which the progress of someone or something may be followed

²spoor *vt* (1850) : to track by a spoor ~ *vi* : to track something by its spoor

spor- *or* **spori-** *or* **sporo-** *comb form* [NL *spora*] : seed : spore ⟨*sporocyst*⟩ ⟨*sporangium*⟩ ⟨*sporicidal*⟩

spo·rad·ic \spə-'ra-dik\ *adj* [ML *sporadicus*, fr. Gk *sporadikos*, fr. *sporadēn* here and there, fr. *sporad-, sporas* scattered; akin to Gk *speirein* to sow — more at SPERM] (ca. 1689) : occurring occasionally, singly, or in scattered instances **syn** see INFREQUENT — **spo·rad·i·cal·ly** \-di-k(ə-)lē\ *adv*

sporadic E layer *n* (1949) : a layer of ionization occurring irregularly within the E region of the ionosphere

spo·ran·gio·phore \spə-'ran-jē-ə-,fōr, -,fȯr\ *n* (1875) : a stalk or similar structure bearing sporangia

spo·ran·gi·um \spə-'ran-jē-əm\ *n, pl* **-gia** \-jē-ə\ [NL, fr. *spor-* + Gk *angeion* vessel — more at ANGI-] (1821) : a structure within which spores are produced — **spo·ran·gial** \-jē-əl\ *adj*

¹spore \'spōr, 'spȯr\ *n* [NL *spora* seed, spore, fr. Gk, act of sowing, seed, fr. *speirein* to sow — more at SPERM] (1836) : a primitive usu. unicellular often environmentally resistant dormant or reproductive body produced by plants and some microorganisms and capable of development into a new individual either directly or after fusion with another spore — **spored** \'spōrd, 'spȯrd\ *adj*

²spore *vi* **spored; spor·ing** (1903) : to produce or reproduce by spores

spore case *n* (1836) : a case containing spores : SPORANGIUM

spo·ri·cid·al \,spōr-ə-'sī-d³l, ,spȯr-\ *adj* (1939) : tending to kill spores — **spo·ri·cide** \'spōr-ə-,sīd, 'spȯr-\ *n*

spo·ro·carp \'spōr-ə-,kärp, 'spȯr-\ *n* [ISV] (1849) : a structure (as in red algae, fungi, or mosses) in or on which spores are produced

spo·ro·cyst \-,sist\ *n* [ISV] (1861) **1** : a case or cyst secreted by some sporozoans preliminary to sporogony; *also* : a sporozoan encysted in such a case **2** : a saccular body that is the first asexual reproductive form of a digenetic trematode, develops from a miracidium, and buds off cells from its inner surface which develop into rediae

spo·ro·gen·e·sis \,spōr-ə-'je-nə-səs, ,spȯr-\ *n* [NL] (ca. 1890) **1** : reproduction by spores **2** : spore formation — **spo·rog·e·nous** \spə-'rä-jə-nəs, spō-\ *also* **spo·ro·gen·ic** \,spōr-ə-'je-nik, ,spȯr-\ *adj*

spo·ro·go·ni·um \,spōr-ə-'gō-nē-əm, ,spȯr-\ *n, pl* **-nia** \-nē-ə\ [NL, fr. *spor-* + *-gonium* (as in *archegonium*)] (1875) : the sporophyte of a moss or liverwort consisting typically of a stalk bearing a spore-producing capsule which remains permanently attached to the gametophyte

spo·rog·o·ny \spə-'rä-gə-nē, spō-\ *n* [ISV] (1888) : reproduction by spores; *specif* : formation of spores typically containing sporozoites that is characteristic of some sporozoans and that results from the encystment and subsequent division of a zygote — **spo·ro·gon·ic** \,spōr-ə-'gä-nik, ,spȯr-\ *adj*

spo·ro·phore \'spōr-ə-,fōr, 'spȯr-ə-,fȯr\ *n* [ISV] (1849) : the spore-producing organ of a fungus or slime mold

spo·ro·phyll \-,fil\ *n* [ISV] (1888) : a spore-bearing and usu. greatly modified leaf

spo·ro·phyte \-,fīt\ *n* [ISV] (1886) : the individual or generation of a plant exhibiting alternation of generations that bears asexual spores — compare GAMETOPHYTE — **spo·ro·phyt·ic** \,spōr-ə-'fi-tik, ,spȯr-\ *adj*

spo·ro·pol·len·in \,spōr-ə-'pä-lə-nən, ,spȯr-\ *n* [ISV *spor-* + *pollen* + ¹*-in*] (1931) : a relatively chemically inert polymer that makes up the outer layer of pollen grains and some spores

spo·ro·tri·cho·sis \spə-,rä-tri-'kō-səs, ,spōr-ə-tri-, ,spȯr-\ *n* [NL, fr. *Sporotrich-, Sporothrix*, genus name, fr. *spor-* + Gk *trich-, thrix* hair] (1908) : infection with or disease caused by a fungus (*Sporothrix schenckii*) that is characterized by nodules and abscesses in the superficial lymph nodes, skin, and subcutaneous tissues and that is usu. transmitted by entry of the fungus through a skin abrasion or wound

-sporous *adj comb form* [NL *spora* spore] : having (such or so many) spores ⟨homo*sporous*⟩

spo·ro·zo·an \,spōr-ə-'zō-ən, ,spȯr-\ *n* [NL *Sporozoa*, fr. *spor-* + *-zoa*] (1888) : any of a large class (Sporozoa) of strictly parasitic protozoans that have a complicated life cycle usu. involving both asexual and sexual generations in different hosts and include important pathogens (as malaria parasites and babesias) — **sporozoan** *adj*

spo·ro·zo·ite \-'zō-,īt\ *n* [NL *Sporozoa* + ISV *-ite*] (1888) : a usu. motile infective form of some sporozoans that is a product of sporogony and initiates an asexual cycle in the new host

spor·ran \'spȯr-ən, 'spär-\ *n* [ScGael *sporan* purse] (1752) : a pouch usu. of skin with the hair or fur on that is worn in front of the kilt with Scots Highland dress

1 sporran

¹sport \'spōrt, 'spȯrt\ *vb* [ME, to divert, disport, short for *disporten*] *vi* (15c) **1 a** : to amuse oneself : FROLIC ⟨lambs ~*ing* in the meadow⟩ **b** : to engage in a sport **2 a** : to mock or ridicule something **b** : to speak or act in jest : TRIFLE **3** [²*sport*] : to deviate or vary abruptly from type (as by bud variation) : MUTATE ~ *vt* **1** : to display or wear usu. ostentatiously : BOAST **2** [²*sport*] : to put forth as a sport or bud variation

²sport *n* (15c) **1 a** : a source of diversion : RECREATION **b** : sexual play **c** (1) : physical activity engaged in for pleasure (2) : a particular activity (as an athletic game) so engaged in **2 a** : PLEASANTRY, JEST **b** : often mean-spirited jesting : MOCKERY, DERISION **3** : something tossed or driven about in or as if in play **b** : LAUGHINGSTOCK **4 a** : SPORTSMAN **b** : a person considered with respect to living up to the ideals of sportsmanship ⟨a good ~⟩ ⟨a poor ~⟩ **c** : a companionable person **5** : an individual exhibiting a sudden deviation from type beyond the normal limits of individual variation usu. as a result of mutation esp. of somatic tissue **syn** see FUN

³sport *or* **sports** *adj* (1582) : of, relating to, or suitable for sports; *esp* : styled in a manner suitable for casual or informal wear ⟨~ coats⟩

sport fish *n* (1944) : a fish important for the sport it affords anglers

sport·fish·er·man \'spōrt-,fi-shər-mən, 'spȯrt-\ *n* (1954) : a motorboat equipped for sportfishing

sport·fish·ing \-,fi-shiŋ\ *n* (1910) : fishing done with a rod and reel for sport or recreation

sport·ful \-fəl\ *adj* (15c) **1 a** : productive of sport or amusement : ENTERTAINING, DIVERTING **b** : PLAYFUL, FROLICSOME **2** : done in sport — **sport·ful·ly** \-fə-lē\ *adv* — **sport·ful·ness** *n*

spor·tif \'spȯr-tif, 'spȯr-\ *adj* [F, sporting, of sports, fr. *sport* sports, fr. E] (1920) : SPORTY

sport·ing \'spȯr-tiŋ, 'spȯr-\ *adj* (1799) **1 a** : of, relating to, used, or suitable for sport **b** : marked by or calling for sportsmanship **c** : involving such risk as a sports contender may expect to take or encounter ⟨a ~ chance⟩ **2** : of or relating to dissipation and esp. gambling **3** : tending to mutate freely — **sport·ing·ly** \-tiŋ-lē\ *adv*

sporting house *n* (1894) : BORDELLO

sport·ive \'spȯr-tiv, 'spȯr-\ *adj* (1590) **1 a** : FROLICSOME, PLAYFUL **b** : ARDENT, WANTON **2** : of or relating to sports and esp. field sports — **sport·ive·ly** *adv* — **sport·ive·ness** *n*

sports car *n* (1928) : a low small usu. 2-passenger automobile designed for quick response, easy maneuverability, and high-speed driving

sports·cast \'spȯrts-,kast, 'spȯrts-\ *n* [*sport* + *broadcast*] (1941) : a radio or television broadcast of a sports event or of information about sports — **sports·cast·er** \-,kas-tər\ *n*

sports·man \'spȯrts-mən, 'spȯrts-\ *n* (ca. 1707) **1** : a person who engages in sports (as in hunting or fishing) **2** : a person who shows sportsmanship — **sports·man·like** \-,līk\ *adj* — **sports·man·ly** \-lē\ *adj*

sports·man·ship \-,ship\ *n* (1745) : conduct (as fairness, respect for one's opponent, and graciousness in winning or losing) becoming to one participating in a sport

---

\ə\ abut \ʾ\ kitten, F table \ər\ further \a\ ash \ā\ ace \ä\ mop, mar
\au̇\ out \ch\ chin \e\ bet \ē\ easy \g\ go \i\ hit \ī\ ice \j\ job
\ŋ\ sing \ō\ go \ȯ\ law \ȯi\ boy \th\ thin \t̲h̲\ the \ü\ loot \u̇\ foot
\y\ yet \zh\ vision \á, k̲, ⁿ, œ, œ̄, ᵫ, ᵫ̄, ᵊ\ *see* Guide to Pronunciation

sports-wear \'spȯrts-,war, 'spȯrts-, -,wer\ *n* (1912) : clothing suitable for recreation; *broadly* : clothing designed for casual or informal wear

sports-wom-an \-,wu̇-mən\ *n* (1754) : a woman who engages in sports

sports-writ-er \'spȯrts-,rī-tər, 'spȯrts-\ *n* (1927) : one who writes about sports esp. for a newspaper — **sports-writ-ing** \-tiŋ\ *n*

sporty \'spȯr-tē, 'spȯr-\ *adj* **sport-i-er; -est** (1889) **1** : of, relating to, or typical of sports, sportsmen, sportswomen, or sportswear ⟨a ∼ life⟩ ⟨clothes of a ∼ cut⟩ **2** *of an automobile* : resembling a sports car in styling or performance — **sport-i-ly** \'spȯr-t'l-ē, 'spȯr-\ *adv* — **sport-i-ness** \'spȯr-tē-nəs\ *n*

spor-u-late \'spȯr-yə-,lāt, 'spȯr-, -ə-,lāt\ *vi* **-lat-ed; -lat-ing** [back-formation fr. *sporulation*] (ca. 1891) : to undergo sporulation

spor-u-la-tion \,spȯr-yə-'lā-shən, ,spȯr-, -ə-'lā-\ *n* [ISV, fr. NL *sporula*, dim. of *spora* spore] (1876) : the formation of spores; *esp* : division into many small spores (as after encystment) — **spor-u-la-tive** \'spȯr-yə-,lā-tiv, 'spȯr-, -ə-,lā-\ *adj*

-spory *n comb form* [-*sporous* + 2-*y*] : quality or state of having (such) spores ⟨homo*spory*⟩

1spot \'spät\ *n* [ME; akin to MD *spotte* stain, speck, ON *spotti* small piece] (13c) **1** : a taint on character or reputation : FAULT ⟨the only ∼ on the family name⟩ **2 a** : a small area visibly different (as in color, finish, or material) from the surrounding area **b** (1) : an area marred or marked (as by dirt) (2) : a circumscribed surface lesion of disease (as measles) or decay ⟨∼*s* of rot⟩ ⟨*rust* ∼*s* on a leaf⟩ **c** : a conventionalized design used on playing cards to distinguish the suits and indicate values **3** : an object having a specified number of spots or a specified numeral on its surface **4** : a small quantity or amount : BIT **5 a** : a particular place, area, or part **b** : a small extent of space **6** *pl usu* **spot** : a small croaker (*Leiostomus xanthurus*) of the Atlantic coast with a black spot behind the opercula **7 a** : a particular position (as in an organization or a hierarchy) **b** : a place or appearance on an entertainment program **8** : SPOTLIGHT **9** : a position usu. of difficulty or embarrassment **10** : a brief announcement or advertisement broadcast between scheduled radio or television programs **11** : a brief segment or report on a broadcast esp. of news — **on the spot 1** : at once : IMMEDIATELY **2** : at the place of action **3 a** : in a responsible or accountable position **b** : in a difficult or trying situation

2spot *vb* **spot-ed; spot-ting** *vt* (14c) **1** : to stain the character or reputation of : DISGRACE **2** : to mark in or with a spot : STAIN **3** : to locate or identify by a spot **4 a** : to single out : IDENTIFY; *esp* : to note as a known criminal or a suspicious person **b** : DETECT, NOTICE ⟨∼ a mistake⟩ **c** (1) : to locate accurately ⟨∼ an enemy position⟩ (2) : to cause to strike accurately ⟨∼ the battery's fire⟩ **5 a** : to lie at intervals in or over : STUD **b** : to place at intervals or in a desired spot ⟨∼ field telephones⟩ **c** : to fix in or as if in the beam of a spotlight **d** : to schedule in a particular spot or at a particular time **6** : to remove a spot from **7** : to allow as a handicap ∼ *vi* **1** : to become stained or discolored in spots **2** : to cause a spot **3** : to act as a spotter; *esp* : to locate targets **4** : to experience abnormal and sporadic bleeding in small amounts from the uterus — **spot-ta-ble** \'spä-tə-bəl\ *adj*

3spot *adj* (1881) **1 a** : being, originating, or done on the spot or in or for a particular spot ⟨∼ coverage of the news⟩ **b** : available for immediate delivery after sale ⟨∼ commodities⟩ **c** (1) : paid out upon delivery ⟨∼ cash⟩ (2) : involving immediate cash payment ⟨∼ transaction⟩ **d** (1) : broadcast between scheduled programs ⟨∼ announcements⟩ (2) : originating in a local station for a national advertiser **e** : performing occasionally when needed ⟨chance of making the ... varsity as a ∼ starter and relief pitcher —*N. Y. Times*⟩ **2** : made at random or restricted to a few places or instances ⟨a ∼ check⟩; *also* : selected at random or as a sample

spot–check \'spät-,chek\ *vt* (1943) : to sample or investigate quickly or at random ∼ *vi* : to make a spot check

spot-less \'spät-ləs\ *adj* (14c) : having no spot: **a** : free from impurity : IMMACULATE ⟨∼ kitchens⟩ **b** : PURE, UNBLEMISHED ⟨∼ reputation⟩ — **spot-less-ly** *adv* — **spot-less-ness** *n*

1spot-light \'spät-,līt\ *n* (1904) **1 a** : a projected spot of light used to illuminate brilliantly a person, object, or group on a stage **b** : conspicuous public notice ⟨held the political ∼⟩ **2 a** : a light designed to direct a narrow intense beam of light on a small area **b** : something that illuminates brilliantly

2spotlight *vt* **-light-ed** *or* **-lit; -light-ing** (1922) : to illuminate with or as if with a spotlight

spot pass *n* (1948) : a pass (as in football or basketball) made to a predetermined spot on the field or court rather than directly to a player

spot-ted \'spä-təd\ *adj* (13c) **1** : marked with spots **2** : being sullied : TARNISHED **3** : characterized by the appearance of spots

spotted alfalfa aphid *n* (1958) : a highly destructive Old World aphid (*Therioaphis maculata*) that is established in the U.S. in warmer areas and causes yellowing and stunting of affected plants

spotted cucumber beetle *n* (1923) : a rather slender greenish yellow beetle (*Diabrotica undecimpunctata howardi*) that feeds as an adult on various ornamental and crop plants and is a vector of wilt disease esp. of cucumbers and melons

spotted fever *n* (1650) : any of various eruptive fevers: as **a** : TYPHUS **b** : ROCKY MOUNTAIN SPOTTED FEVER

spotted owl *n* (1910) : a rare large dark brown dark-eyed owl (*Strix occidentalis*) that has barred and spotted underparts and is found in humid old growth forests and thickly wooded canyons from British Columbia to southern California and central Mexico

spotted salamander *n* (1922) : a common salamander (*Ambystoma maculatum*) of eastern No. America with glossy black skin spotted with yellow or orange on the back

spotted sea trout *n* (1902) : a weakfish (*Cynoscion nebulosus*) that is a valuable food and sport fish of the southern Atlantic and Gulf coasts of the U.S. — called also *sea trout, speckled trout, spotted weakfish*

spotted turtle *n* (ca. 1909) : a freshwater turtle (*Clemmys guttata*) of the eastern U.S. that has a blackish carapace with round yellow spots

spot-ter \'spä-tər\ *n* (1611) **1** : one that makes or applies a spot (as for identification) **2** : one that looks or keeps watch: as **a** : one that locates enemy targets **b** : a civilian who watches for approaching airplanes **3** : one that removes spots **4** : one that places something on or in a desired spot

spot test *n* (1922) **1** : a test limited to a few key or sample points or a relatively small percentage of random spots **2** : a test conducted on the spot to yield immediate results

spot-ty \'spä-tē\ *adj* **spot-ti-er; -est** (14c) **1** : marked with spots : SPOTTED **2** : lacking uniformity esp. in quality ⟨the performance was ∼⟩; *also* : irregularly or sparsely distributed ⟨∼ attendance⟩ ⟨∼ data⟩ — **spot-ti-ly** \'spä-t'l-ē\ *adv* — **spot-ti-ness** \'spä-tē-nəs\ *n*

spou-sal \'spau̇-zəl, -səl\ *n* [ME *spousaille*, fr. MF *espousailles* espousal] (14c) : NUPTIALS — usu. used in pl.

1spouse \'spau̇s *also* 'spau̇z\ *n* [ME, fr. OF *espous* (masc.) & *espouse* (fem.), fr. L *sponsus* betrothed man, groom & *sponsa* betrothed woman, bride, both fr. *sponsus*, pp. of *spondēre* to promise, betroth; akin to Gk *spendein* to pour a libation, Hitt *šipant*-] (13c) : married person : HUSBAND, WIFE — **spou-sal** \'spau̇-zəl, -səl\ *adj*

2spouse \'spau̇z, 'spau̇s\ *vt* **spoused; spous-ing** (13c) *archaic* : WED

1spout \'spau̇t\ *vb* [ME; akin to MD *spoiten* to spout, OE *spīwan* to spew] *vt* (14c) **1** : to eject (as liquid) in a stream ⟨wells ∼*ing* oil⟩ **2 a** : to speak or utter readily, volubly, and at length **b** : to speak or utter in a pompous or oratorical manner : DECLAIM ∼ *vi* **1** : to issue with force or in a jet : SPURT **2** : to eject material (as liquid) in a jet **3** : DECLAIM — **spout-er** *n*

2spout *n* (14c) **1** : a pipe or conductor through which a liquid is discharged or conveyed in a stream: as **a** : a pipe for carrying rainwater from a roof **b** : a projecting tube or lip from which a liquid (as water) issues **2** : a discharge or jet of liquid from or as if from a pipe; *esp* : WATERSPOUT **3** *archaic* : PAWNSHOP — **spout-ed** \'spau̇-təd\ *adj*

sprach-ge-fühl \'shpräk-gə-,fȳel\ *n* [G, fr. *Sprache* language + *Gefühl* feeling] (1894) **1** : the character of a language **2** : an intuitive sense of what is linguistically appropriate

sprad-dle \'spra-d'l\ *vb* **sprad-dled; sprad-dling** \'sprad-liŋ, 'spra-d'l-iŋ\ [perh. blend of *straddle* and *sprawl*] (1674) **1** : SPRAWL **2** : to go or walk with a straddling gait : STRADDLE ∼ *vt* **1** : SPRAWL **2** : to spread (the legs) in walking : STRADDLE

sprag \'sprag\ *n* [origin unknown] (1878) : a pointed stake or steel bar let down from a halted vehicle (as a wagon) to prevent it from rolling

1sprain \'sprān\ *n* [origin unknown] (1601) **1** : a sudden or violent twist or wrench of a joint with stretching or tearing of ligaments **2** : a sprained condition

2sprain *vt* (1622) : to injure by a sudden or severe twist

1sprang \'spraŋ\ *past of* SPRING

2sprang *n* [prob. fr. Norw, a kind of embroidery] (1951) : a weaving technique in which threads or cords are intertwined and twisted over one another to form an openwork mesh

sprat \'sprat\ *n* [alter. of ME *sprot*, fr. OE *sprott*] (1537) **1 a** : a small European herring (*Sprattus sprattus*) related to the common herring — called also *brisling* **b** : a small or young herring or similar fish (as an anchovy) **2** : a young, small, or insignificant person

sprawl \'sprȯl\ *vb* [ME, fr. OE *sprēawlian*] *vi* (bef. 12c) **1 a** *archaic* : to lie thrashing or tossing about **b** : to creep or clamber awkwardly **2** : to lie or sit with arms and legs spread out **3** : to spread or develop irregularly ∼ *vt* : to cause to spread out carelessly or awkwardly — **sprawl** *n*

1spray \'sprā\ *n* [ME] (13c) **1** : a usu. flowering branch or shoot **2** : a decorative flat arrangement of flowers and foliage (as on a coffin) **3** : something (as a jeweled pin) resembling a spray

2spray *n* [obs. E *spray* to sprinkle, fr. MD *sprayen*] (1621) **1** : water flying in small drops or particles blown from waves or thrown up by a waterfall **2 a** : a jet of vapor or finely divided liquid **b** : a device (as an atomizer or sprayer) by which a spray is dispersed or applied **c** (1) : an application of a spray or by spraying (2) : a substance (as paint) so applied

3spray *vt* (1829) **1** : to disperse or apply as a spray **2** : to project spray on or into ∼ *vi* **1** : to break up into spray **2** : to disperse or apply a spray **3** : to emit a stream or spray of urine ⟨a cat may ∼ to mark its territory⟩ — **spray-er** *n*

spray can *n* (1958) : a pressurized container from which aerosols are dispensed

spray gun *n* (1920) : an apparatus resembling a gun for applying a substance (as paint or insecticide) in the form of a spray

1spread \'spred\ *vb* **spread; spread-ing** [ME *spreden*, fr. OE *sprǣdan*; akin to OHG *spreiten* to spread] *vt* (13c) **1 a** : to open or expand over a larger area ⟨∼ out the map⟩ **b** : to stretch out : EXTEND ⟨∼ its wings for flight⟩ **2 a** : to distribute over an area ⟨∼ fertilizer⟩ **b** : to distribute over a period or among a group ⟨∼ the work over a few weeks⟩ **c** : to apply on a surface ⟨∼ butter on bread⟩ **d** (1) : to cover or overlay something with ⟨∼ the cloth on the table⟩ (2) *archaic* : to cover completely ⟨∼ 1) : to prepare or furnish for dining : SET ⟨∼ the table⟩ (2) : SERVE ⟨∼ the afternoon tea⟩ **3 a** : to make widely known ⟨∼ the news⟩ **b** : to extend the range or incidence of ⟨∼ a disease⟩ **c** : DIFFUSE, EMIT ⟨flowers ∼*ing* their fragrance⟩ **4** : to push apart by weight or force ∼ *vi* **1 a** : to become dispersed, distributed, or scattered **b** : to become known or disseminated ⟨panic ∼ rapidly⟩ **2** : to grow in length or breadth : EXPAND **3** : to move apart (as from pressure or weight) : SEPARATE — **spread-abil-i-ty** \,spre-də-'bi-lə-tē\ *n* — **spread-able** \'spre-də-bəl\ *adj*

2spread *n* (1626) **1 a** : the act or process of spreading **b** : extent of spreading **2** : something spread out: as **a** : a surface area : EXPANSE **b** *West* (1) : RANCH (2) : a herd of animals **c** (1) : a prominent display in a periodical (2) : two facing pages (as of a newspaper) usu. with matter running across the fold; *also* : the matter occupying these pages **3** : something spread on or over a surface: as **a** : a food to be spread (as on bread or crackers) ⟨a cheese ∼⟩ **b** : a sumptuous meal : FEAST **c** : a cloth cover for a table or bed **4** : distance between two points : GAP **5** : a commodities market transaction in which a participant hedges with simultaneous long and short options in different commodities or different delivery dates in the same commodity

1spread–ea-gle \'spred-,ē-gəl\ *vb* **-ea-gled; -ea-gling** \-,ē-g(ə-)liŋ\ *vi* (1826) **1** : to execute a spread eagle (as in skating) **2** : to stand or move with arms and legs stretched out : SPRAWL ∼ *vt* **1** : to stretch out into the position of a spread eagle **2** : to spread over

2spread–eagle *adj* [fr. the spread eagle on the Great Seal of the U.S.] (1858) : marked by bombast and boastful exaggeration esp. of the greatness of the U.S. ⟨∼ oratory⟩

spread eagle *n* (1570) **1** : a representation of an eagle with wings raised and legs extended 2 : something resembling or suggestive of a spread eagle; *specif* : a skating figure executed with the skates heel to heel in a straight line

spread·er \'spre-dər\ *n* (15c) : one that spreads: as a : an implement for scattering material b : a small knife for spreading butter c : a device (as a bar) holding two linear elements (as lines, guys, rails) apart and usu. taut

spread formation *n* (ca. 1949) : an offensive football formation in which the pass receivers are spread out across the field

spreading factor *n* (1932) : HYALURONIDASE

spread·sheet \'spred-,shēt\ *n* (1982) : an accounting program for a computer; *also* : the ledger layout modeled by such a program

spree \'sprē\ *n* [origin unknown] (1804) : an unrestrained indulgence in or outburst of an activity ⟨went on a buying ∼⟩; *esp* : BINGE, CAROUSAL

sprent \'sprent\ *adj* [ME *spreynt*, fr. pp. of *sprengen* to sprinkle] (14c) *archaic* : sprinkled over

sprier *comparative of* SPRY

spriest *superlative of* SPRY

¹sprig \'sprig\ *n* [ME *sprigge*] (14c) 1 a : a small shoot : TWIG ⟨a ∼ of parsley⟩ b : a small division of grass used for propagation 2 a : HEIR b : YOUTH c : a small specimen 3 : an ornament resembling a sprig, stemmed flower, or leaf 4 : a small headless nail : BRAD

²sprig *vt* **sprigged; sprig·ging** (1713) 1 : to drive sprigs or brads into 2 : to mark or adorn with the representation of plant sprigs 3 : to propagate (a grass) by means of stolons or small divisions

spright·ful \'sprīt-fəl\ *adj* [obs. *spright*] (1595) *archaic* : full of life or spirit : SPRIGHTLY — **spright·ful·ly** \-fə-lē\ *adv* — **spright·ful·ness** *n*

spright·ly \-lē\ *adj* **spright·li·er; -est** [obs. *spright* (sprite), alter. of *sprite*] (1596) : marked by a gay lightness and vivacity : SPIRITED *syn* see LIVELY — **spright·li·ness** *n* — **sprightly** *adv*

¹spring \'spriŋ\ *vb* **sprang** \'spraŋ\ *or* **sprung** \'sprəŋ\; **sprung; spring·ing** \'spriŋ-iŋ\ [ME, fr. OE *springan*; akin to OHG *springan* to jump and perh. to Gk *sperchesthai* to hasten] *vi* (bef. 12c) 1 a (1) : DART, SHOOT (2) : to be resilient or elastic; *also* : to move by elastic force ⟨the lid *sprang* shut⟩ b : to become warped 2 : to issue with speed and force or as a stream 3 a : to grow as a plant b : to issue by birth or descent c : to come into being : ARISE ⟨towns *sprang* up across the plains⟩ d *archaic* : DAWN c : to begin to blow — used with *up* ⟨a breeze quickly *sprang* up⟩ 4 a : to make a leap or series of leaps b : to leap or jump up suddenly 5 : to stretch out in height : RISE 6 : PAY — used with *for* ⟨I'll ∼ for the drinks⟩, ∼ *vt* 1 : to cause to spring 2 a : to undergo or bring about the splitting or cracking of ⟨wind *sprang* the mast⟩ b : to undergo the opening of (a leak) 3 a : to cause to operate suddenly ⟨∼ a trap⟩ b : to apply or insert by bending c : to bend by force 4 : to leap over 5 : to produce or disclose suddenly or unexpectedly 6 : to make lame 7 : to release or cause to be released from confinement or custody

syn SPRING, ARISE, RISE, ORIGINATE, DERIVE, FLOW, ISSUE, EMANATE, PROCEED, STEM mean to come up or out of something into existence. SPRING implies rapid or sudden emerging ⟨an idea that *springs* to mind⟩. ARISE and RISE may both convey the fact of coming into existence or notice but RISE often stresses gradual growth or ascent ⟨new questions have *arisen*⟩ ⟨slowly *rose* to prominence⟩. ORIGINATE implies a definite source or starting point ⟨the fire *originated* in the basement⟩. DERIVE implies a prior existence in another form ⟨the holiday *derives* from an ancient Roman feast⟩. FLOW adds to SPRING a suggestion of abundance or ease of inception ⟨words *flowed* easily from her pen⟩. ISSUE suggests emerging from confinement through an outlet ⟨blood *issued* from the cut⟩. EMANATE applies to the coming of something immaterial (as a thought) from a source ⟨reports *emanating* from the capital⟩. PROCEED stresses place of origin, derivation, parentage, or logical cause ⟨advice that *proceeds* from the best of intentions⟩. STEM implies originating by dividing or branching off from something as an outgrowth or subordinate development ⟨industries *stemming* from space research⟩.

²spring *n, often attrib* (bef. 12c) 1 a : a source of supply; *esp* : a source of water issuing from the ground b : an ultimate source esp. of action or motion 2 : SPRING TIDE 3 : a time or season of growth or development; *specif* : the season between winter and summer comprising in the northern hemisphere usu. the months of March, April, and May or as reckoned astronomically extending from the March equinox to the June solstice 4 : an elastic body or device that recovers its original shape when released after being distorted 5 a : the act or an instance of leaping up or forward : BOUND b (1) : capacity for springing : RESILIENCE (2) : ENERGY, BOUNCE 6 : the point or plane at which an arch or vault curve springs from its impost — **spring·like** \-,līk\ *adj*

³spring *vt* **sprung** \'sprəŋ\; **spring·ing** \'spriŋ-iŋ\ (1884) : to fit with springs

spring·ald \'spriŋ-əld\ *or* **spring·al** \-əl\ *n* [prob. fr. ME, a kind of catapult, fr. MF *espringale*] (1501) : a young man : STRIPLING

spring beauty *n* (1821) : any of a genus (*Claytonia*) of herbs of the purslane family; *esp* : one (*C. virginica*) that sends up in early spring a 2-leaved stem bearing delicate pink flowers

spring·board \'spriŋ-,bōrd, -,bȯrd\ *n* (1799) 1 : a flexible board usu. secured at one end and used for gymnastic stunts or diving 2 : a point of departure : JUMPING-OFF PLACE

spring·bok \'spriŋ-,bäk\ *n, pl* **springbok** *or* **springboks** [Afrik. fr. *spring* to jump + *bok* male goat] (1775) : a swift and graceful southern African gazelle (*Antidorcas marsupialis*) noted for its habit of springing lightly and suddenly into the air

spring bolt *n* (1634) : a bolt retracted by pressure and shot by a spring when the pressure is released

spring chicken *n* (1879) : a young person ⟨is no *spring chicken*⟩

spring–clean·ing \'spriŋ-'klē-niŋ\ *n* [²*spring*] (1857) : the act or process of giving a thorough cleaning of a place

springe \'sprinj\ *n* [ME *sprenge, springe*; akin to OE *springan* to spring] (13c) : a noose fastened to an elastic body to catch small game 2 : SNARE, TRAP

spring·er \'spriŋ-ər\ *n* (1611) 1 : a stone or other solid laid at the impost of an arch — see ARCH illustration 2 : one that springs 3 : SPRINGER SPANIEL 4 : a cow nearly ready to calve

springer spaniel *n* (1885) : a medium-sized sporting dog of either of two breeds that is often used for finding and flushing small game: a : ENGLISH SPRINGER SPANIEL b : WELSH SPRINGER SPANIEL

spring fever *n* (1843) : a lazy or restless feeling often associated with the onset of spring

Spring·field rifle \'spriŋ-,fēld-\ *n* [*Springfield*, Mass.] (1888) : a .30 caliber bolt-action rifle used by U.S. troops esp. in World War I

spring-form pan \'spriŋ-,fȯrm-\ *n* (1927) : a pan or mold with an upright detachable rim fastened to the bottom of the pan with a clamp or spring

spring·head \'spriŋ-,hed\ *n* (1561) : FOUNTAINHEAD

spring·house \-,haús\ *n* (1755) : a small building situated over a spring and used for cool storage (as of dairy products or meat)

spring·ing \'spriŋ-iŋ\ *n* (1590) 1 : SPRING 5 2 : a point where an arch rises from its support

spring-load \'spriŋ-'lōd\ *vt* (1944) : to load or secure by means of spring tension or compression

spring peeper *n* (1906) : a small brown tree frog (*Hyla crucifer*) of the eastern U.S. and Canada that has a shrill piping call and breeds in ponds and streams in the spring

spring peeper

spring roll *n* (1943) : EGG ROLL; *also* : any of various similar appetizers in oriental cuisine

spring·tail \'spriŋ-,tāl\ *n* (ca. 1797) : any of an order (Collembola) of small primitive wingless insects usu. with a forked structure on the fourth or fifth abdominal segment that is used for jumping — called also *collembolan*

spring·tide \-,tīd\ *n* (1530) : SPRINGTIME

spring tide *n* (1548) : a tide of greater-than-average range around the times of new and full moon

spring·time \'spriŋ-,tīm\ *n* (15c) 1 : the season of spring 2 : YOUTH 1a 3 : an early or flourishing stage of development

spring wagon *n* (1794) : a light farm wagon equipped with springs

spring-wa·ter \'spriŋ-,wȯ-tər, -,wä-\ *n* (15c) : water from a spring

spring·wood \-,wúd\ *n* (1884) : the softer more porous portion of an annual ring of wood that develops early in the growing season — compare SUMMERWOOD

springy \'spriŋ-ē\ *adj* **spring·i·er; -est** (1641) 1 : having an elastic quality : RESILIENT 2 : having or showing a lively and energetic movement ⟨walks with a ∼ step⟩ *syn* see ELASTIC — **spring·i·ly** \'spriŋ-ə-lē\ *adv* — **spring·i·ness** \'spriŋ-ē-nəs\ *n*

¹sprin·kle \'spriŋ-kəl\ *vb* **sprin·kled; sprin·kling** \-k(ə-)liŋ\ [ME *sprenklen, sprinclen*; akin to MHG *spreckel, sprenkel* spot] *vt* (14c) 1 : to scatter in drops or particles 2 a : to scatter over b : to scatter at intervals in or among : DOT ⟨*sprinkled* the speech with quips⟩ c : to wet lightly ∼ *vi* 1 : to scatter a liquid in fine drops 2 : to rain lightly in scattered drops — **sprin·kler** \-k(ə-)lər\ *n*

²sprinkle *n* (1641) 1 : the act or an instance of sprinkling; *esp* : a light rain 2 : SPRINKLING 3 *pl* : small particles of candy used as a topping (as on ice cream) : JIMMIES

sprin·klered \'spriŋ-klərd\ *adj* (1927) : having a sprinkler system

sprinkler system *n* (ca. 1909) : a system for protecting a building against fire by means of overhead pipes which convey an extinguishing fluid (as water) to heat-activated outlets

sprin·kling \'spriŋ-kliŋ\ *n* (1594) 1 : a limited quantity or amount : MODICUM 2 : a small quantity falling in scattered drops or particles 3 : a small number distributed at random : SCATTERING

¹sprint \'sprint\ *vi* [of Scand origin; akin to Sw dial. *sprinta* to jump, hop; akin to OHG *sprinzan* to jump up] (ca. 1864) : to run or go at top speed esp. for a short distance — **sprint·er** *n*

²sprint *n* (ca. 1865) 1 : the act or an instance of sprinting 2 a : DASH 6b b : a burst of speed

sprint car *n* (ca. 1965) : a rugged racing automobile that is midway in size between midget racers and ordinary racers, has about the same horsepower as the larger racers, and is usu. raced on a dirt track

sprit \'sprit\ *n* [ME *spret, sprit*, fr. OE *sprēot* pole, spear; akin to OE *-sprūtan* to sprout] (14c) : a spar that crosses a fore-and-aft sail diagonally

sprite \'sprīt\ *n* [ME *sprit*, fr. MF *esprit*, fr. L *spiritus* spirit — more at SPIRIT] (14c) 1 a *archaic* : SOUL b : a disembodied spirit : GHOST 2 a : ELF, FAIRY b : an elfish person

sprit·sail \'sprit-,sāl, -səl\ *n* (15c) 1 : a sail extended by a sprit 2 : a sail formerly set on a yard beneath the bowsprit

spritz \'sprits, 'shprits\ *vb* [G *spritzen* to squirt, spray] *vt* (1902) : SPRAY ∼ *vi* : to disperse or apply a spray — **spritz** *n*

spritz·er \'sprit-sər, 'shprit-\ *n* [G, fr. *spritzen*] (1945) : a beverage of usu. white wine and soda water

sprock·et \'sprä-kət\ *n* [origin unknown] (1750) 1 : a toothed wheel whose teeth engage the links of a chain 2 : a cylinder with teeth around the circumference at either end that project through perforations in something (as motion-picture film) to move it through a mechanism (as a projector)

¹sprout \'spraùt\ *vb* [ME *spruten*, fr. OE *-sprūtan*; akin to OHG *spriozan* to sprout, Lith *sprausti* to squeeze, thrust] *vi* (13c) 1 : to grow, spring up, or come forth as or as if a sprout 2 : to send out new growth ∼ *vt* : to send forth or up : cause to develop : GROW

²sprout *n* (13c) 1 a : SHOOT 1a; *esp* : a young shoot (as from a seed or root) b *pl* (1) *chiefly Brit* : BRUSSELS SPROUT 2 (2) : edible sprouts esp. from recently germinated seeds (as of alfalfa or mung beans) 2 : something resembling a sprout: as a : a young person b : SCION

sprouting broccoli *n* (1852) : BROCCOLI 2a(2)

\ə\ abut \ᵊ\ kitten, F table \ər\ further \a\ ash \ā\ ace \ä\ mop, mar \aú\ out \ch\ chin \e\ bet \ē\ easy \g\ go \i\ hit \ī\ ice \j\ job \ŋ\ sing \ō\ go \ȯ\ law \ȯi\ boy \th\ thin \t̲h̲\ the \ü\ loot \ú\ foot \y\ yet \zh\ vision \à, k̲, ⁿ, œ, œ̄, ᵫ, ᵬ̄, ʸ\ *see* Guide to Pronunciation

¹spruce \'sprüs\ *vb* **spruced; spruc·ing** *vt* (1594) : to make spruce — often used with *up* ~ *vi* : to make oneself spruce ⟨~ up a bit⟩
²spruce *adj* **spruc·er; spruc·est** [perh. fr. obs. E *Spruce leather* leather imported from Prussia] (1599) : neat or smart in appearance : TRIM — **spruce·ly** *adv* — **spruce·ness** *n*
³spruce *n* [obs. *Spruce* Prussia, fr. ME, alter. of *Pruce*, fr. OF] (1670) **1 a** : any of a genus (*Picea*) of evergreen trees of the pine family with a conical head of dense foliage and soft light wood **b** : any of several coniferous trees (as Douglas fir) of similar habit **2** : the wood of a spruce
spruce beer *n* (1500) : a beverage flavored with spruce; *esp* : one made from spruce twigs and leaves boiled with molasses or sugar and fermented with yeast
spruce budworm *n* (1884) : a tortricid moth (*Choristoneura fumiferana*) whose larva feeds on evergreen trees (as spruce and balsam fir) in the northern U.S. and Canada
spruce pine *n* (1684) : an American tree (as some pines and spruces or the common eastern hemlock) of the pine family with light, soft, or weak wood
sprucy \'sprü-sē\ *adj* **spruc·i·er; -est** (1774) : SPRUCE
¹sprue \'sprü\ *n* [origin unknown] (1880) **1** : the hole through which metal or plastic is poured into the gate and thence into a mold **2** : the waste piece cast in a sprue
²sprue *n* [D *spruw*; akin to MLG *sprüwe*, a kind of tumor] (1888) **1** : CELIAC DISEASE **2** : a disease of tropical regions that is of unknown cause and is characterized by fatty diarrhea and malabsorption of nutrients — called also *tropical sprue*
sprung *past and past part of* SPRING
sprung rhythm *n* (1877) : a poetic rhythm designed to approximate the natural rhythm of speech and characterized by the frequent juxtaposition of single accented syllables and the occurrence of mixed types of feet
spry \'sprī\ *adj* **spri·er** *or* **spry·er** \'sprī(-ə)r\; **spri·est** *or* **spry·est** \'sprī-əst\ [perh. of Scand origin; akin to Sw dial. *sprygg* spry] (1746) : NIMBLE 1 ⟨a ~ 75-year-old⟩ — **spry·ly** *adv* — **spry·ness** *n*
¹spud \'spəd\ *vb* **spud·ded; spud·ding** *vt* (1652) **1** : to dig with a spud **2** : to begin to drill (an oil well) ~ *vi* : to use a spud
²spud *n* [ME *spudde* dagger] (1667) **1** : a tool or device (as for digging, lifting, or cutting) having the characteristics of a spade and a chisel **2** : POTATO
¹spume \'spyüm\ *n* [ME, fr. MF, fr. L *spuma* — more at FOAM] (14c) : frothy matter on liquids : FOAM, SCUM — **spu·mous** \'spyü-məs\ *adj* — **spumy** \-mē\ *adj*
²spume *vi* **spumed; spum·ing** (14c) : FROTH, FOAM
spu·mo·ni *or* **spu·mo·ne** \spü-'mō-nē\ *n* [It *spumone*, aug. of *spuma* foam, fr. L] (1924) : ice cream in layers of different colors, flavors, and textures often with candied fruits and nuts
spun *past and past part of* SPIN
spun·bond·ed \'spən-,bän-dəd\ *adj* (1961) : of or relating to a nonwoven polymeric material that resembles cloth or fabric
spun glass *n* (1779) **1** : blown glass that has slender threads of glass incorporated in it **2** : FIBERGLASS
¹spunk \'spəŋk\ *n* [ScGael *spong* sponge, tinder, fr. L *spongia* sponge] (1582) **1 a** : a woody tinder : PUNK **b** : any of various fungi used to make tinder **2** : METTLE, PLUCK **3** : SPIRIT, LIVELINESS
²spunk *vi* (1840) *dial* : to show spirit — usu. used with *up*
spunk·ie \'spəŋ-kē\ *n* (1727) *Scot* : IGNIS FATUUS 1
spunky \'spəŋ-kē\ *adj* **spunk·i·er; -est** (1786) : full of spunk : SPIRITED — **spunk·i·ly** \-kə-lē\ *adv* — **spunk·i·ness** \-kē-nəs\ *n*
spun sugar *n* (1846) : sugar boiled to long threads and gathered up and shaped or heaped on a stick as a candy
spun yarn *n* (14c) **1** : a textile yarn spun from staple-length fiber **2** : a small rope or stuff formed of two or more rope yarns loosely twisted and used for seizings esp. on board ship
¹spur \'spər\ *n* [ME, fr. OE *spura*; akin to OE *spurnan* to kick — more at SPURN] (bef. 12c) **1 a** : a pointed device secured to a rider's heel and used to urge on the horse **b** *pl* [fr. the acquisition of spurs by a person achieving knighthood] : recognition and reward for achievement ⟨won his academic ~s as the holder of a chair in a university — James Mountford⟩ **2** : a goad to action : STIMULUS **3** : something projecting like or suggesting a spur: as **a** : a projecting root or branch of a tree, shrub, or vine **b** (1) : a stiff sharp spine (as on the wings or legs of a bird or insect); *esp* : one on a cock's leg (2) : a gaff for a gamecock **c** : a hollow projecting appendage of a corolla or calyx (as in larkspur or columbine) **d** : a bony outgrowth (as on the heel of the foot) : CLIMBING IRON **4 a** : an angular projection, offshoot, or branch extending out beyond or away from a main body or formation; *esp* : a ridge or lesser elevation that extends laterally from a mountain or mountain range **b** : a railroad track that branches off from a main line **5** : a reinforcing buttress of masonry in a fortification *syn* see MOTIVE — **on the spur of the moment** : on impulse : SUDDENLY
²spur *vb* **spurred; spur·ring** (13c) **1** : to urge (a horse) on with spurs **2** : to incite to action or accelerated growth or development : STIMULATE **3** : to put spurs on ~ *vi* : to spur one's horse on
spurge \'spərj\ *n* [ME, fr. MF, purge, spurge, fr. *espurgier* to purge, fr. L *expurgare* — more at EXPURGATE] (14c) : any of a genus (*Euphorbia* of the family Euphorbiaceae, the spurge family) of chiefly herbs and shrubs with a bitter milky juice
spur gear *n* (1823) : a gear wheel with radial teeth parallel to its axis — called also *spur wheel*
spurge laurel *n* (1597) : a low Eurasian shrub (*Daphne laureola*) with oblong evergreen leaves and axillary racemes of yellowish flowers
spu·ri·ous \'spyür-ē-əs\ *adj* [LL & L; LL *spurius* false, fr. L, of illegitimate birth, fr. *spurius*, n., bastard] (1598) **1** : of illegitimate birth : BASTARD **2** : outwardly similar or corresponding to something without having its genuine qualities : FALSE **3 a** : of falsified or erroneously attributed origin : FORGED **b** : of a deceitful nature or quality — **spu·ri·ous·ly** *adv* — **spu·ri·ous·ness** *n*
¹spurn \'spərn\ *vb* [ME, fr. OE *spurnan*; akin to OHG *spurnan* to kick, L *spernere* to spurn, Gk *spairein* to quiver] *vi* (bef. 12c) **1** *obs* **a** : STUMBLE **b** : KICK **2** *archaic* : to reject something disdainfully ~ *vt*

[spur gear illustration]
spur gear

1 : to tread sharply or heavily upon : TRAMPLE **2** : to reject with disdain or contempt : SCORN *syn* see DECLINE — **spurn·er** *n*
²spurn *n* (14c) **1 a** : KICK **b** *obs* : STUMBLE **2 a** : disdainful rejection **b** : contemptuous treatment
spur-of-the-moment *adj* (1948) : occurring or developing without premeditation : hastily extemporized ⟨a ~ decision⟩
spurred \'spərd\ *adj* (15c) **1** : wearing spurs **2** : having one or more spurs ⟨a ~ violet⟩
spur·rey *or* **spur·ry** \'spər-ē, 'spə-rē\ *n, pl* **spurreys** *or* **spurries** [D *spurrie*, fr. ML *spergula*] (1577) : a small white-flowered European weed (*Spergula arvensis*) of the pink family with whorled filiform leaves; *also* : any of several related and similar herbs
¹spurt \'spərt\ *vb* [perh. akin to MHG *spürzen* to spit, OE *-sprūtan* to sprout — more at SPROUT] *vi* (1570) : to gush forth : SPOUT ~ *vt* : to expel in a stream or jet : SQUIRT
²spurt *n* (ca. 1775) : a sudden gush : JET
³spurt *n* [origin unknown] (ca. 1591) **1** : a short period of time : MOMENT **2 a** : a sudden brief burst of effort or activity **b** : a sharp or sudden increase in business activity
⁴spurt *vi* (1664) : to make a spurt
spur·tle \'spər-t⁾l\ *n* [origin unknown] (1756) *chiefly Scot* : a wooden stick for stirring porridge
sput·nik \'sput-nik, 'spət-, 'spüt-\ *n* [Russ, lit., traveling companion, fr. *s, so* with + *put'* path] (1957) : SATELLITE 2b
¹sput·ter \'spə-tər\ *vb* [akin to D *sputteren* to sputter] *vt* (1598) **1** : to spit or squirt from the mouth with explosive sounds **2** : to utter hastily or explosively in confusion or excitement **3** : to dislodge (atoms) from the surface of a material by collision with high energy particles; *also* : to deposit (a metallic film) by such a process ~ *vi* **1** : to spit or squirt particles of food or saliva noisily from the mouth **2** : to speak explosively or confusedly in anger or excitement **3** : to make explosive popping sounds — **sput·ter·er** *n*
²sputter *n* (1673) **1** : confused and excited speech or discussion **2** : the act or sound of sputtering
spu·tum \'spyü-təm, 'spü-\ *n, pl* **spu·ta** \-tə\ [L, fr. neut. of *sputus*, pp. of *spuere* to spit — more at SPEW] (ca. 1693) : expectorated matter made up of saliva and often discharges from the respiratory passages
¹spy \'spī\ *vb* **spied; spy·ing** [ME *spien*, fr. OF *espier*, fr. Gmc origin; akin to OHG *spehōn* to spy; akin to L *specere* to look, look at, Gk *skeptesthai & skopein* to watch, look at, consider] *vt* (13c) **1** : to watch secretly usu. for hostile purposes **2** : to catch sight of : SEE **3** : to search or look for intensively ~ *vi* **1** : to observe or search for something : LOOK **2** : to watch secretly as a spy
²spy *n, pl* **spies** (13c) **1** : one that spies: **a** : one who keeps secret watch on a person or thing to obtain information **b** : a person employed by one nation to secretly convey classified information of strategic importance to another nation; *also* : a person who conveys the trade secrets of one company to another **2** : an act of spying
spy·glass \'spī-,glas\ *n* (1706) : a small telescope
spy·mas·ter \'spī-,mas-tər\ *n* (1938) : the head of a ring of spies : a director of intelligence
squab \'skwäb\ *n, pl* **squabs** [prob. of Scand origin; akin to Sw dial. *skvabb* anything soft and thick] (1664) **1 a** : COUCH **b** : a cushion for a chair or couch **2** *or pl* **squab** : a fledgling bird; *specif* : a fledgling pigeon about four weeks old **3** : a short fat person — **squab** *adj*
¹squab·ble \'skwä-bəl\ *vb* [prob. of Scand origin; akin to Sw dial. *skvabbel* dispute] (1602) : a noisy altercation or quarrel usu. over trifles
²squabble *vi* **squab·bled; squab·bling** \-b(ə-)liŋ\ (1604) : to quarrel noisily and usu. over trifles — **squab·bler** \-b(ə-)lər\ *n*
¹squad \'skwäd\ *n* [MF *esquade*, fr. OSp & OIt; OSp *escuadra* & OIt *squadra*, ultim. fr. (assumed) VL *exquadrare* to make square — more at SQUARE] (1649) **1** : a small organized group of military personnel; *esp* : a tactical unit that can be easily directed in the field **2** : a small group engaged in a common effort or occupation
²squad *vt* **squad·ded; squad·ding** (ca. 1802) : to arrange in squads
squad car *n* (1938) : a police automobile connected by a two-way radio with headquarters — called also *cruiser, prowl car*
squad·ron \'skwä-drən\ *n* [It *squadrone*, aug. of *squadra* squad, fr. OIt] (1562) : a unit of military organization : **a** : a cavalry unit higher than a troop and lower than a regiment **b** : a naval unit consisting of two or more divisions and sometimes additional vessels **c** (1) : a unit of the U.S. Air Force higher than a flight and lower than a group (2) : a military flight formation
squadron leader *n* (1919) : a commissioned officer in the British air force who ranks with a major in the army
squad room *n* (1943) **1** : a room in a barracks used to billet soldiers **2** : a room in a police station where members of the force assemble
squa·lene \'skwä-,lēn\ *n* [ISV, fr. L *squalus*, a sea fish — more at WHALE] (1916) : an acyclic hydrocarbon $C_{30}H_{50}$ that is widely distributed in nature (as a major component of sebum and in shark-liver oils) and is a precursor of sterols (as cholesterol)
squal·id \'skwä-ləd\ *adj* [L *squalidus* rough, dirty, fr. *squalēre* to be covered with scales or dirt, fr. *squalus* dirty; perh. akin to *squama* scale] (1596) **1** : marked by filthiness and degradation from neglect or poverty **2** : SORDID *syn* see DIRTY — **squal·id·ly** *adv* — **squal·id·ness** *n*
¹squall \'skwȯl\ *vb* [prob. of Scand origin; akin to ON *skval* useless chatter] *vi* (ca. 1631) : to cry out raucously : SCREAM ~ *vt* : to utter in a strident voice — **squall·er** *n*
²squall *n* (1709) : a raucous cry
³squall *n* [prob. of Scand origin; akin to Sw *skval* rushing water] (1699) **1** : a sudden violent wind often with rain or snow **2** : a short-lived commotion
⁴squall *vi* (ca. 1890) : to blow a squall
squally \'skwȯ-lē\ *adj* **squall·i·er; -est** (1719) **1** : marked by squalls **2** : GUSTY
squa·lor \'skwä-lər *also* 'skwā- *or* 'skwȯ-\ *n* [L, fr. *squalēre*] (1621) : the quality or state of being squalid
squa·ma \'skwā-mə, 'skwä-\ *n, pl* **squa·mae** \'skwā-,mē, 'skwä-,mī\ [L] (ca. 1706) : SCALE; *also* : a structure resembling a scale
squa·mate \-,māt\ *adj* (1826) : SCALY ⟨~ reptiles⟩
squa·ma·tion \skwə-'mā-shən\ *n* (1881) **1** : the state of being scaly **2** : the arrangement of scales on an animal
¹squa·mo·sal \skwə-'mō-səl, -zəl\ *n* (1848) : a squamosal bone

²**squamosal** *adj* (ca. 1852) **1** : SQUAMOUS **2** : of, relating to, or being a bone of the skull of many vertebrates corresponding to the squamous portion of the temporal bone of most mammals including humans

squa·mous \'skwā-məs *also* 'skwä-\ *adj* [ME, fr. L *squamosus*, fr. *squama* scale] (15c) **1 a** : covered with or consisting of scales : SCALY **b** : of, relating to, or being a stratified epithelium that consists at least in its outer layers of small scalelike cells **2** : of, relating to, or being the anterior upper portion of the temporal bone of most mammals including humans

squamous cell *n* (ca. 1947) : a cell of or derived from squamous epithelium

squa·mu·lose \'skwā-myə-ˌlōs, 'skwä-\ *adj* [L *squamula*, dim. of *squama*] (1846) : being or having a thallus made up of small leafy lobes ⟨a ~ lichen⟩

¹**squan·der** \'skwän-dər\ *vb* **squan·dered; squan·der·ing** \-d(ə-)riŋ\ [origin unknown] *vt* (1536) **1** : to spend extravagantly or foolishly : DISSIPATE **2** : to cause to disperse : SCATTER **3** : to lose (as an advantage or opportunity) through negligence or inaction ~ *vi* : DISPERSE, SCATTER — **squan·der·er** \-dər-ər\ *n*

²**squander** *n* (1709) : an act of squandering

¹**square** \'skwar, 'skwer\ *n* [ME, fr. MF *esquarre*, fr. (assumed) VL *exquadra*, fr. *exquadrare* to square, fr. L *ex-* + *quadrare* to square — more at QUADRATE] (13c) **1** : an instrument having at least one right angle and two straight edges used esp. to lay out or test right angles **2** : a rectangle with all four sides equal **3** : any of the quadrilateral spaces marked out on a board for playing games **4** : the product of a number multiplied by itself **5 a** : an open place or area formed at the meeting of two or more streets **b** : BLOCK 6a **6** : a solid object or piece approximating a cube or having a square as its largest face **7** : an unopened cotton flower with its enclosing bracts **8** : a person who is conventional or conservative in taste or way of life — **on the square 1** : at right angles **2** : in a fair open manner : HONESTLY — **out of square** : not at an exact right angle

²**square** *adj* **squar·er; squar·est** (14c) **1 a** : having four equal sides and four right angles **b** : forming a right angle ⟨~ corner⟩ **c** : having a square base ⟨a ~ pyramid⟩ **2** : raised to the second power **3 a** : being approximately a cube ⟨~ cabinet⟩ **b** : having a shape that is broad for the height and rectangular rather than curving in outline ⟨~ shoulders⟩ ⟨a ~, thick, hard-working man —Maria Edgeworth⟩ **c** : rectangular and equilateral in section ⟨~ tower⟩ **4 a** : being or converted to a unit of area equal in measure to a square each side of which measures one unit of a specified unit of length ⟨a ~ foot⟩ — see METRIC SYSTEM table, WEIGHT table **b** : being of a specified length in each of two equal dimensions ⟨10 feet ~⟩ **5 a** : exactly adjusted : precisely constructed or aligned **b** : JUST, FAIR ⟨a ~ deal⟩ ⟨~ in all his dealings⟩ **c** : leaving no balance : SETTLED **d** : EVEN, TIED **e** : SUBSTANTIAL, SATISFYING ⟨~ meal⟩ **f** : being unsophisticated, conservative, or conventional **6** : set at right angles with the mast and keel — used of the yards of a square-rigged ship — **square·ness** *n*

³**square** *vb* **squared; squar·ing** *vt* (14c) **1 a** : to make square or rectangular ⟨~ a building stone⟩ **b** : to test for deviation from a right angle, straight line, or plane surface **2** : to bring approximately to a right angle ⟨*squared* his shoulders⟩ **3 a** : to multiply (a number) by itself : raise to the second power **b** : to find a square equal in area to ⟨~ a circle⟩ **4** : to regulate or adjust by or to some standard or principle ⟨~ our actions by the opinions of others —John Milton⟩ **5 a** : BALANCE, SETTLE ⟨~ an account⟩ **b** : to even the score of ⟨~ mark off into squares **7 a** : to set right : bring into agreement **b** : BRIBE, FIX ~ *vi* **1** : to agree precisely : CORRESPOND ⟨your actions should ~ with your words⟩ **2** : to settle matters; *esp* : to pay the bill — **squar·er** *n*

⁴**square** *adv* (ca. 1582) **1** : in a straightforward or honest manner **2 a** : so as to face or be face to face **b** : at right angles **3** : with nothing intervening : DIRECTLY ⟨ran ~ into it⟩ **4** : in a firm manner ⟨looked her ~ in the eye⟩ **5** : in a square shape

square away *vi* (1849) **1** : to square the yards so as to sail before the wind **2** : to put everything in order or in readiness **3** : to take up a fighting stance ~ *vt* : to put in order or in readiness

square bracket *n* (ca. 1888) : BRACKET 3a

square dance *n* (1870) : a dance for four couples who form the sides of a square — **square–dance** *vi* — **square dancer** *n* — **square dancing** *n*

square knot *n* (ca. 1867) : a knot made of two reverse half-knots and typically used to join the ends of two cords — see KNOT illustration

square·ly \'skwar-lē, 'skwer-\ *adv* (1564) **1** : in a straightforward or honest manner ⟨we must ~ face the issue⟩ **2 a** : EXACTLY, PRECISELY ⟨~ in the middle⟩ **b** : so as to make solid contact ⟨hit the ball ~⟩ ⟨feet ~ planted⟩ **3** : in a square form or manner : so as to be square ⟨a ~ cut dress⟩ **4** : in a plain or unequivocal manner ⟨the responsibility lies ~ with us⟩ ⟨align ourselves ~ with our allies⟩

square matrix *n* (1858) : a mathematical matrix with the same number of rows and columns

square measure *n* (1728) : a unit or system of units for measuring area — see METRIC SYSTEM table, WEIGHT table

square off *vi* (1837) : to take a fighting stance : prepare to fight; *also* : FIGHT

square of opposition (1864) : a square figure on which may be demonstrated the logical relationships of contraries, contradictories, subcontraries, and subalterns and superalterns

square one *n* [fr. the use of numbered squares in some board games] (1960) : the initial stage or starting point ⟨the failure set us back to *square one*⟩

square rig *n* (ca. 1875) : a sailing ship rig in which the principal sails are extended on yards fastened to the masts horizontally and at their center

square–rigged \'skwar-ˌrigd, 'skwer-\ *adj* (1769) : having or equipped with a square rig

square–rig·ger \-ˌri-gər\ *n* (1855) : a square-rigged craft

square-rigger

square root *n* (1557) : a factor of a number that when squared gives the number ⟨the *square root* of 9 is +3⟩

square sail \'skwar-ˌsāl, 'skwer-, -səl\ *n* (1600) : a 4-sided sail extended on a yard suspended at the middle from a mast

square shooter *n* (ca. 1914) : a just or honest person

square–shoul·dered \'skwar-ˌshōl-dərd, 'skwer-\ *adj* (1825) : having shoulders of a rectangular outline that are straight across the back

square–toed \-ˌtōd\ *adj* (1785) **1** : having a toe that is square **2** : OLD-FASHIONED, CONSERVATIVE

square wave *n* (1932) : the rectangular waveform of a quantity that varies periodically and abruptly from one to the other of two uniform values

squar·ish \'skwar-ish, 'skwer-\ *adj* (1742) : somewhat square in form or appearance — **squar·ish·ly** *adv* — **squar·ish·ness** *n*

¹**squash** \'skwäsh, 'skwȯsh\ *vb* [MF *esquasser*, fr. (assumed) VL *exquassare*, fr. L *ex-* + *quassare* to shake — more at QUASH] *vt* (1565) **1** : to press or beat into a pulp or a flat mass : CRUSH **2** : PUT DOWN, SUPPRESS ⟨~ a revolt⟩ ~ *vi* **1** : to flatten out under pressure or impact **2** : to proceed with a splashing or squelching sound **3** : SQUEEZE, PRESS — **squash·er** *n*

²**squash** *n* (1590) **1** *obs* : something soft and easily crushed; *specif* : an unripe pod of peas **2** : the sudden fall of a heavy soft body or the sound of such a fall **3** : a squelching sound made by walking on oozy ground or in water-soaked boots **4** : a crushed mass **5** *Brit* : sweetened citrus fruit juice often served with added soda water **6** : a singles or doubles game played in a 4-wall court with a long-handled racket and a rubber ball that can be hit off any number of walls

³**squash** *adv* (1766) : with a squash or a squashing sound

⁴**squash** *n, pl* **squash·es** *or* **squash** [by shortening & alter. fr. earlier *isquoutersquash*, fr. Narraganset *askútasquash*] (1634) : any of various fruits of plants (genus *Cucurbita*) of the gourd family widely cultivated as vegetables; *also* : a plant and esp. a vine that bears squashes — compare SUMMER SQUASH, WINTER SQUASH

squash bug *n* (ca. 1846) : a large black American bug (*Anasa tristis* of the family Coreidae) injurious to plants of the gourd family

squash racquets *n pl but sing in constr* (1886) : SQUASH 6

squash tennis *n* (1901) : a singles racket game resembling squash played with an inflated ball the size of a tennis ball

squashy \'skwä-shē, 'skwȯ-\ *adj* **squash·i·er; -est** (1698) **1** : easily squashed : very soft ⟨~ cushions⟩ **2** : softly wet : BOGGY **3** : soft because overripe ⟨~ melons⟩ — **squash·i·ly** \-shə-lē\ *adv* — **squash·i·ness** \-shē-nəs\ *n*

¹**squat** \'skwät\ *vb* **squat·ted; squat·ting** [ME *squatten*, fr. MF *esquatir* fr. es- ex- (fr. L *ex-*) + *quatir* to press, fr. (assumed) VL *coactire* to press together, fr. L *coactus*, pp. of *cogere* to drive together — more at COGENT] *vt* (15c) **1** : to cause (oneself) to crouch or sit on the ground **2** : to occupy as a squatter ~ *vi* **1** : to crouch close to the ground as if to escape observation ⟨a hare *squatting* in the grass⟩ **2** : to assume or maintain a position in which the body is supported on the feet and the knees are bent so that the buttocks rest on or near the heels **3** : to be or become a squatter

²**squat** *adj* **squat·ter; squat·test** (15c) **1** : sitting with the haunches close above the heels **2 a** : low to the ground **b** : marked by disproportionate shortness or thickness — **squat·ly** *adv* — **squat·ness** *n*

³**squat** *n* (1580) **1 a** : the act of squatting **b** : the posture of one that squats **2 a** : a place where one squats **b** : the lair of a small animal ⟨~ of a hare⟩ **3** : a lift in weight lifting in which the lifter performs a knee bend while holding a barbell on the shoulders; *also* : a competitive event involving this lift **4** *chiefly Brit* : an empty house or building that is occupied by squatters **5** *slang* : DIDDLY-SQUAT

¹**squat·ter** \'skwä-tər\ *vi* [imit.] (1785) : to go along through or as if through water

²**squatter** *n* (1788) : one that squats: as **a** : one that settles on property without right or title or payment of rent **b** : one that settles on public land under government regulation with the purpose of acquiring title

squatter sovereignty *n* (1854) : POPULAR SOVEREIGNTY 2

squat·ty \'skwä-tē\ *adj* **squat·ti·er; -est** (1881) **1** : low to the ground **2** : DUMPY, THICKSET

squaw \'skwȯ\ *n* [Massachuset *squa, ussqua* woman] (1634) **1** : an American Indian woman **2** : WOMAN, WIFE — usu. used disparagingly

squaw·fish \-ˌfish\ *n* (1881) : any of several large cyprinid fishes (genus *Ptychocheilus*) of western No. America

¹**squawk** \'skwȯk\ *vi* [prob. blend of *squall* and *squeak*] (1821) **1** : to utter a harsh abrupt scream **2** : to complain or protest loudly or vehemently — **squawk·er** *n*

²**squawk** *n* (1850) **1** : a harsh abrupt scream **2** : a noisy complaint

squawk box *n* (1945) : an intercom speaker

squaw man *n* (1866) : a white man married to an Indian woman and usu. living as one of her tribe

squaw·root \'skwȯ-ˌrüt, -ˌrut\ *n* (ca. 1848) : a No. American scaly herb (*Conopholis americana*) of the broomrape family parasitic on oak and hemlock roots

¹**squeak** \'skwēk\ *vb* **squeaked** *vi* (14c) **1** : to utter or make a short shrill cry or noise **2** : SQUEAL 2a **3** : to pass, succeed, or win by a narrow margin ⟨just ~ed by in the election⟩ ~ *vt* : to utter in a shrill piping tone

²**squeak** *n* (1700) **1** : a sharp shrill cry or sound **2** : ESCAPE ⟨a close ~⟩ — **squeaky** \'skwē-kē\ *adj*

squeak·er \'skwē-kər\ *n* (1671) **1** : one that squeaks **2** : a contest (as a game or an election) won by a small margin

squeaky–clean *adj* (1968) **1** : completely clean ⟨~ hair⟩ **2** : completely free from moral taint of any kind ⟨a ~ reputation⟩

¹**squeal** \'skwē(ə)l\ *vb* [ME *squelen*] *vi* (14c) **1** : to make a shrill cry or noise **2 a** : to turn informer **b** : COMPLAIN, PROTEST ~ *vt* **1** : to utter or express with or as if with a squeal **2** : to cause to make a loud shrill noise ⟨~ing the tires⟩ — **squeal·er** *n*

\ə\ abut \ᵊ\ kitten, F table \ər\ further \a\ ash \ā\ ace \ä\ mop, mar \aú\ out \ch\ chin \e\ bet \ē\ easy \g\ go \i\ hit \ī\ ice \j\ job \ŋ\ sing \ō\ go \ȯ\ law \ȯi\ boy \th\ thin \t͟h\ the \ü\ loot \u̇\ foot \y\ yet \zh\ vision \á, k̲, ⁿ, œ, œ̄, ue, ūe, ᵊ\ *see* Guide to Pronunciation

²**squeal** *n* (1747) : a shrill sharp cry or noise

squea·mish \'skwē-mish\ *adj* [ME *squaymisch*, modif. of AF *escoymous*] (15c) **1 a :** easily nauseated : QUEASY **b :** affected with nausea **2 a :** excessively fastidious or scrupulous in conduct or belief **b :** easily offended or disgusted — **squea·mish·ly** *adv* — **squea·mish·ness** *n*

¹**squee·gee** \'skwē-jē\ *n* [origin unknown] (1844) : a blade of leather or rubber set on a handle and used for spreading, pushing, or wiping liquid material on, across, or off a surface (as a window); *also* : a smaller similar device or a small rubber roller with handle used by a photographer or lithographer

²**squeegee** *vt* **squee-geed; squee-gee-ing** (1883) : to smooth, wipe, or treat with a squeegee

¹**squeeze** \'skwēz\ *vb* **squeezed; squeez·ing** [alter. of obs. E *quease*, fr. ME *queysen*, fr. OE *cwȳsan*; akin to Icel *kveisa* stomach cramps] *vt* (ca. 1601) **1 a :** to exert pressure esp. on opposite sides of : COMPRESS **b :** to extract or emit under pressure **c :** to force or thrust by compression **2 a** (1) : to get by extortion (2) : to deprive by extortion **b :** to cause economic hardship to **c :** to reduce the amount of ⟨~*s* profits⟩ **3 :** to crowd into a limited area **4 :** to gain or win by a narrow margin **5 :** to force (another player) to discard in bridge so as to unguard a suit **6 :** to score by means of a squeeze play ~ *vi* **1 :** to give way before pressure **2 :** to exert pressure; *also* : to practice extortion or oppression **3 :** to force one's way ⟨~ through a door⟩ **4 :** to pass, win, or get by narrowly — **squeez·abil·i·ty** \,skwē-zə-'bi-lə-tē\ *n* — **squeez·able** \'skwē-zə-bəl\ *adj* — **squeez·er** *n*

²**squeeze** *n* (1611) **1 a :** an act or instance of squeezing : COMPRESSION **b :** HANDCLASP; *also* : EMBRACE **2 a :** a quantity squeezed out from something ⟨a ~ of lemon⟩ **b :** a group crowded together : CROWD **3 :** a profit taken by a middleman on goods or transactions **4 :** a financial pressure caused by narrowing margins or by shortages **5 :** a forced discard in bridge **6 :** SQUEEZE PLAY **7** *slang* : MAIN SQUEEZE

squeeze bottle *n* (1950) : a bottle of flexible plastic that dispenses its contents when it is squeezed

squeeze off *vt* (ca. 1949) : to fire (a round) by squeezing the trigger ~ *vi* : to fire a weapon by squeezing the trigger

squeeze play *n* (1905) **1 :** a baseball play in which a runner on third base starts for home plate as the ball is being pitched and the batter attempts to bunt to give the runner a chance to score **2 :** the exertion of pressure in order to extort a concession or gain a goal

¹**squelch** \'skwelch\ *vb* [origin unknown] *vt* (1624) **1 a :** to fall or stamp on so as to crush **b** (1) : to completely suppress : QUELL (2) : SILENCE **2 :** to emit or move with a sucking sound ~ *vi* **1 :** to emit a sucking sound **2 :** to splash through water, slush, or mire — **squelch·er** *n*

²**squelch** *n* (1895) **1 :** a sound of or as if of semiliquid matter under suction ⟨the ~ of mud⟩ **2 :** the act of suppressing; *esp* : a retort that silences an opponent — **squelchy** *adj*

sque·teague \skwi-'tēg\ *n, pl* **squeteague** [of Algonquian origin; akin to Mohegan *cheegut* weakfish] (1803) : any of several weakfishes (esp. *Cynoscion regalis*)

¹**squib** \'skwib\ *n* [origin unknown] (ca. 1525) **1 a :** a short humorous or satiric writing or speech **b :** a short news item; *esp* : FILLER **2 a :** a small firecracker **b :** a broken firecracker in which the powder burns with a fizz **2 :** a small electric or pyrotechnic device used to ignite a charge

²**squib** *vb* **squibbed; squib·bing** *vi* (ca. 1580) **1 :** to speak, write, or publish squibs **2 :** to fire a squib ~ *vt* **1 a :** to utter in an offhand manner **b :** to make squibs against : LAMPOON **2 :** to shoot off : FIRE **3 :** to kick (a football) just far enough on a kickoff to be legally recoverable by the kicking team

squib kick *n* (ca. 1956) : ONSIDE KICK

¹**squid** \'skwid\ *n, pl* **squid** *or* **squids** [origin unknown] (1613) : any of an order (Teuthoidea) of cephalopods having eight short arms and two usu. longer tentacles, a long tapered body, a caudal fin on each side, and usu. a slender internal chitinous support

²**squid** *vi* **squid·ded; squid·ding** (ca. 1859) : to fish with or for squid

SQUID \'skwid\ *n* [*s*uperconducting *qu*antum *i*nterference *d*evice] (1967) : an instrument for detecting and measuring very weak magnetic fields

squiffed \'skwift\ *or* **squif·fy** \'skwi-fē\ *adj* [origin unknown] (ca. 1855) : INTOXICATED, DRUNK

¹**squig·gle** \'skwi-gəl\ *vb* **squig·gled; squig·gling** \-g(ə-)liŋ\ [blend of *squirm* and *wriggle*] *vi* (ca. 1816) **1 :** SQUIRM, WRIGGLE **2 :** to write or paint hastily : SCRIBBLE ~ *vt* **1 :** SCRIBBLE **2 :** to form or cause to form in squiggles

²**squiggle** *n* (1900) : a short wavy twist or line : CURLICUE; *esp* : an illegible scrawl — **squig·gly** \-g(ə-)lē\ *adj*

squil·gee \'skwē-jē, 'skwil-jē\ *var of* SQUEEGEE

¹**squill** \'skwil\ *n* [ME, fr. L *squilla, scilla*, fr. Gk *skilla*] (14c) **1 a :** a Mediterranean bulbous herb (*Urginea maritima*) of the lily family — called also *sea onion*; compare RED SQUILL 1 **b** (1) : the dried sliced bulb scales of a squill used as an expectorant, cardiac stimulant, and diuretic (2) : RED SQUILL 2 **2 :** SCILLA

squil·la \'skwi-lə\ *n, pl* **squillas** *or* **squil·lae** \'skwi-,lē, -,lī\ [NL, fr. L *squilla*] (1658) : any of various stomatopod crustaceans (esp. genus *Squilla*) that burrow in mud or beneath stones in shallow water along the seashore

¹**squinch** \'skwinch\ *vb* [prob. blend of *squint* and *pinch*] *vt* (1835) **1 :** to screw up (the eyes or face) : SQUINT **2 a :** to make more compact **b :** to cause to crouch down or draw together ~ *vi* **1 :** FLINCH **2 :** to crouch down or draw together **3 :** SQUINT

²**squinch** *n* [alter. of earlier *scunch* back part of the side of an opening] (ca. 1840) : a support (as an arch, lintel, or corbeling) carried across the corner of a room under a superimposed mass

¹**squin·ny** \'skwi-nē\ *vb* **squin·nied; squin·ny·ing** [prob. fr. obs. E *squin* asquint, fr. ME *skuin*] (1605) : SQUINT

²**squinny** *n* (ca. 1881) : SQUINT — **squinny** *adj*

¹**squint** \'skwint\ *adj* [ME *asquint*] (1579) **1** *of an eye* : looking or tending to look obliquely or askance (as with envy or disdain) **2** *of the eyes* : not having the visual axes parallel : CROSSED

²**squint** *vi* (1599) **1 a :** to have an indirect bearing, reference, or aim **b :** to deviate from a true line **2 a :** to look in a squint-eyed manner

b : to be cross-eyed **c :** to look or peer with eyes partly closed ~ *vt* : to cause (an eye) to squint — **squint·er** *n* — **squint·ing·ly** \'skwin-tiŋ-lē\ *adv*

³**squint** *n* (ca. 1652) **1 :** STRABISMUS **2 :** an instance of squinting **3 :** HAGIOSCOPE — **squinty** \'skwin-tē\ *adj*

squint–eyed \'skwint-,īd\ *adj* (1589) **1 :** having eyes that squint; *specif* : affected with cross-eye **2 :** looking askance (as in envy)

squinting modifier *n* (1924) : a modifier (as often in "getting dressed often is a nuisance") so placed in a sentence that it can be interpreted as modifying either what precedes or what follows

¹**squire** \'skwir\ *n* [ME *squier*, fr. OF *esquier* — more at ESQUIRE] (13c) **1 :** a shield bearer or armor bearer of a knight **2 a :** a male attendant esp. on a great personage **b :** a man who devotedly attends a lady : GALLANT **3 a :** a member of the British gentry ranking below a knight and above a gentleman **b :** an owner of a country estate; *esp* : the principal landowner in a village or district **c** (1) : JUSTICE OF THE PEACE (2) : LAWYER (3) : JUDGE — **squir·ish** \'skwir-ish\ *adj*

²**squire** *vt* **squired; squir·ing** (14c) : to attend as a squire : ESCORT

squir·ar·chy *also* **squir·ar·chy** \'skwīr-,är-kē\ *n, pl* **-chies** (1796) : the class of landed gentry or landed proprietors

squirm \'skwərm\ *vi* [origin unknown] (ca. 1691) : to twist about like a worm : FIDGET — **squirm** *n* — **squirmy** \'skwər-mē\ *adj*

¹**squir·rel** \'skwər(-ə)l, 'skwə-rəl, *chiefly Brit* 'skwir-əl\ *n, pl* **squirrels** *also* **squirrel** [ME *squirel*, fr. MF *esquireul*, fr. (assumed) VL *scuriolus*, dim. of *scurius*, alter. of L *sciurus*, fr. Gk *skiouros*, prob. fr. *skia* shadow + *oura* tail — more at SHINE, ASS] (14c) **1 :** any of various small or medium-sized rodents (family Sciuridae, the squirrel family): as **a :** any of numerous New or Old World arboreal forms having a long bushy tail and strong hind legs **b :** GROUND SQUIRREL **2 :** the fur of a squirrel

²**squirrel** *vt* **-reled** *or* **-relled; -rel·ing** *or* **-rel·ling** [fr. the squirrel's habit of storing up gathered nuts and seeds for winter use] (1925) : to store up for future use — often used with *away*

squirrel cage *n* (1821) **1 :** a cage for a small animal (as a squirrel) that contains a rotatable cylinder for exercising **2 :** something resembling the working of a squirrel cage in repetitiveness or endlessness

squirrel corn *n* (1843) : a No. American herb (*Dicentra canadensis*) of the fumitory family with much-divided leaves and a scapose raceme of cream-colored flowers

squir·rel·ly \'skwər(-ə)-lē, 'skwə-rə-\ *adj* (1928) : NUTTY 3

squirrel monkey *n* (1773) : a small soft-haired So. American monkey (*Saimiri sciureus*) that has a long tail not used for grasping and is colored chiefly yellowish gray with a white face and black muzzle

squirrel rifle *n* [fr. its being suitable only for small game] (1834) : a small-caliber rifle — called also *squirrel gun*

¹**squirt** \'skwərt\ *vb* [ME; akin to LG *swirtjen* to squirt] *vi* (15c) : to come forth in a sudden rapid stream from a narrow opening : SPURT ~ *vt* : to cause to squirt — **squirt·er** *n*

²**squirt** *n* (15c) **1 a :** an instrument (as a syringe) for squirting a liquid **b :** a small quick stream : JET **c :** the action or an instance of squirting **2 a :** an impudent youngster **b :** KID

squirt gun *n* (1803) : WATER PISTOL

squirting cucumber *n* (1802) : a Mediterranean plant (*Ecballium elaterium*) of the gourd family with oblong fruit that bursts from the peduncle when ripe and forcibly ejects the seeds

squish \'skwish\ *vb* [alter. of *squash*] *vt* (ca. 1647) **1 :** SQUASH **2 :** SQUELCH, SUCK ~ *vi* : SQUELCH, SUCK ⟨their wet tennis shoes ~*ed* — Frank Noel⟩ — **squish** *n*

squishy \'skwi-shē\ *adj* **squish·i·er; -est** (ca. 1847) : being soft, yielding, and damp — **squish·i·ness** *n*

squoosh \'skwüsh, 'skwüish\ *vb* [by alter.] (1942) : SQUASH

squush \'skwəsh\ *vb* [by alter.] (1837) : SQUASH

Sra·nan \'srä-nən\ *n* [Sranan, short for *Sranan Tongo*, lit., Suriname tongue] (1953) : an English-based creole widely spoken in Suriname

sri \'srē, 'shrē\ *n* [Skt *śrī*, lit., beauty, majesty; akin to Gk *kreiōn* ruler, master] (1799) — used as a conventional title of respect when addressing or speaking of a distinguished Indian

sRNA \,es-,är-,en-'ā\ *n* [*soluble RNA*] (1957) : TRANSFER RNA

SRO \,es-(,)är-'ō\ *n* [*single-room occupancy*] (1941) : a house, apartment building, or residential hotel in which low-income or welfare tenants live in single rooms

SS \,es-'es\ *n* [G, abbr. for *Schutzstaffel*, lit., protection echelon] (1932) : a unit of Nazis created to serve as bodyguard to Hitler and later expanded to take charge of intelligence, central security, policing action, and the mass extermination of those they considered inferior or undesirable

SST \,es-,es-'tē\ *n* [*supersonic transport*] (1961) : SUPERSONIC TRANSPORT

¹**-st** — see -EST

²**-st** *symbol* — used after the figure 1 to indicate the ordinal number *first* ⟨1*st*⟩ ⟨91*st*⟩

¹**stab** \'stab\ *n* [ME *stabbe*] (15c) **1 :** a wound produced by a pointed weapon **2 a :** a thrust of a pointed weapon **b :** a jerky thrust **3 :** EFFORT, TRY

²**stab** *vb* **stabbed; stab·bing** *vt* (1530) **1 :** to wound or pierce by the thrust of a pointed weapon **2 :** THRUST, DRIVE ~ *vi* **1 :** to thrust or give a wound with or as if with a pointed weapon — **stab·ber** *n*

¹**sta·bile** \'stā-,bil, -,bil\ *adj* [L *stabilis* — more at STABLE] (1896) : STATIONARY, STABLE

²**sta·bile** \-,bēl\ *n* [prob. fr. F, fr. L *stabilis*, adj.] (1937) : an abstract sculpture or construction similar in appearance to a mobile but made to be stationary

sta·bil·i·ty \stə-'bi-lə-tē\ *n, pl* **-ties** (14c) **1 :** the quality, state, or degree of being stable: as **a :** the strength to stand or endure : FIRMNESS **b :** the property of a body that causes it when disturbed from a condition of equilibrium or steady motion to develop forces or moments that restore the original condition **c :** resistance to chemical change or to physical disintegration **2 :** residence for life in one monastery

sta·bi·lize \'stā-bə-,līz\ *vb* **-lized; -liz·ing** *vt* (1861) **1 :** to make stable, steadfast, or firm **2 :** to hold steady: as **a :** to maintain the stability of (as an airplane) by means of a stabilizer **b :** to limit fluctuations of (as prices) **c :** to establish a minimum price for ~ *vi* : to become stable, firm, or steadfast — **sta·bi·li·za·tion** \ˌstā-bə-lə-'zā-shən\ *n*

sta·bi·liz·er \'stā-bə-ˌlī-zər\ *n* (ca. 1909) : one that stabilizes something: as **a** : a substance added to another substance (as an explosive or plastic) or to a system (as an emulsion) to prevent or retard an unwanted alteration of physical state **b** : a gyroscope device to keep ships steady in a heavy sea **c** : an airfoil providing stability for an airplane; *specif* : the fixed horizontal member of the tail assembly — see AIRPLANE illustration

¹sta·ble \'stā-bəl\ *n* [ME, fr. OF *estable*, fr. L *stabulum*, fr. *stare* to stand — more at STAND] (13c) **1** : a building in which domestic animals are sheltered and fed; *esp* : such a building having stalls or compartments ⟨horse ∼⟩ **2 a** : the racehorses of one owner **b** : a group of athletes (as boxers) or performers under one management **c** : the racing cars of one owner **:** GROUP, COLLECTION — **sta·ble·man** \-mən, -ˌman\ *n*

²stable *vb* **sta·bled; sta·bling** \-b(ə-)liŋ\ *vt* (14c) : to put or keep in a stable ∼ *vi* : to dwell in or as if in a stable

³stable *adj* **sta·bler** \-b(ə-)lər\; **sta·blest** \-b(ə-)ləst\ [ME, fr. MF *estable*, fr. L *stabilis*, fr. *stare* to stand] (13c) **1 a** : firmly established **:** FIXED, STEADFAST **b** : not changing or fluctuating **:** UNVARYING **c** : PERMANENT, ENDURING **2 a** : steady in purpose : firm in resolution **b** : not subject to insecurity or emotional illness **:** SANE, RATIONAL ⟨a ∼ personality⟩ **3 a** (1) : placed so as to resist forces tending to cause motion or change of motion (2) : designed so as to develop forces that restore the original condition when disturbed from a condition of equilibrium or steady motion **b** (1) : not readily altering in chemical makeup or physical state ⟨∼ emulsions⟩ (2) : not spontaneously radioactive *syn* see LASTING — **sta·ble·ness** \-bəl-nəs\ *n* — **sta·bly** \-b(ə-)lē\ *adv*

stable fly *n* (1862) : a biting dipteran fly (*Stomoxys calcitrans*) that resembles the common housefly and is abundant about stables

sta·ble·mate \'stā-bəl-ˌmāt\ *n* (1926) **1** : an animal stabled with another **2** : a member of a stable

sta·bler \-b(ə-)lər\ *n* (15c) : one who keeps a stable

sta·bling \-b(ə-)liŋ\ *n* (15c) : accommodation for animals in a building; *also* : the building for this

stab·lish \'sta-blish\ *vb* [ME, short for *establissen*] (14c) *archaic* **:** ESTABLISH — **stab·lish·ment** \-mənt\ *n, archaic*

stac·ca·to \stə-'kä-(ˌ)tō\ *adj* [It, fr. pp. of *staccare* to detach, fr. s- ex- (fr. L *ex-*) + at*taccare* to attach, attach, perh. fr. OF *estachier* — more at ATTACH] (ca. 1724) **1 a** : cut short or apart in performing **:** DISCONNECTED ⟨∼ notes⟩ **b** : marked by short clear-cut playing or singing of tones or chords ⟨a ∼ style⟩ **2** : ABRUPT, DISJOINTED — **staccato** *adv* — **staccato** *n*

staccato mark *n* (ca. 1903) : a pointed vertical stroke or a dot placed over or under a musical note to be produced staccato

¹stack \'stak\ *n* [ME *stak*, fr. ON *stakkr*; akin to Russ *stog* stack and prob. to OE *staca* stake] (14c) **1 a** : a large usu. conical pile (as of hay, straw, or grain in the sheaf) left standing in the field for storage **2 a** : an orderly pile or heap **b** : a large quantity or number **3** : an English unit of measure esp. for firewood that is equal to 108 cubic feet **4 a** : a number of flues embodied in one structure rising above a roof **b** : a vertical pipe (as to carry off smoke) **c** : the exhaust pipe of an internal combustion engine **5** : a structure of bookshelves for compact storage of books — usu. used in pl. **6** : a pile of chips sold to or won by a poker player **7 a** : a memory or a section of memory in a computer for temporary storage in which the last item stored is the first retrieved; *also* : a data structure that simulates a stack ⟨a push-down ∼⟩ **b** : a computer memory consisting of arrays of memory elements stacked one on top of another

²stack *vt* (14c) **1 a** : to arrange in a stack **:** PILE **b** : to pile in or on ⟨∼ed the table with books⟩ ⟨∼ the dishwasher⟩ **2 a** : to arrange secretly for cheating ⟨∼ a deck of cards⟩ **b** : to arrange or fix so as to make a particular result likely ⟨the odds are ∼ed against us⟩ ⟨will ∼ juries to suit themselves —Patrice Horn⟩ **3 a** : to assign (an airplane) by radio to a particular altitude and position within a group circling before landing **b** : to put into a waiting line ⟨another dozen rigs are ∼ed up and waiting —P. H. Hutchins, Jr.⟩ **4** : COMPARE — used with *against* ⟨such a crime is nothing when ∼ed against a murder —Pete Censky⟩ ∼ *vi* : to form a stack — **stack·er** *n*

stack·able \'sta-kə-bəl\ *adj* (1958) : easily arranged in a stack

stacked \'stakt\ *adj* (1942) of *a woman* : being shapely and having large breasts

stack up *vi* (1896) **1** : to add up **:** TOTAL **2** : MEASURE UP, COMPARE — usu. used with *against*

stac·te \'stak-tē\ *n* [ME *stacten*, fr. L *stacte*, fr. Gk *staktē*, fr. fem. of *staktos* oozing out in drops, fr. *stazein* to drip] (1535) : a sweet spice used by the ancient Jews in preparing incense

stad·dle \'sta-dᵊl\ *n* [ME *stathel* base, support, bottom of a stack, fr. OE *statho* base; akin to OHG *stan* to stand — more at STAND] (15c) : a base (as of piling) for a stack of hay or straw

stade \'städ\ *n* [MF *estade*, fr. L *stadium*] (1537) : STADIUM 1a

sta·dia \'stā-dē-ə\ *n* [It, prob. fr. L, pl. of *stadium*] (1865) : a surveying method for determination of distances and differences of elevation by means of a telescopic instrument having two horizontal lines through which the marks on a graduated rod are observed; *also* : the instrument or rod

sta·di·um \'stā-dē-əm\ *n, pl* **-dia** \-dē-ə\ *or* **-di·ums** [ME, fr. L, fr. Gk *stadion*] (14c) **1 a** : any of various ancient Greek units of length ranging in value from 607 to 738 feet ⟨about 185 to 225 meters⟩ **b** : an ancient Roman unit of length equal to 607 feet (185 meters) **2 a** : a course for footraces in ancient Greece orig. one stadium in length **b** : a tiered structure with seats for spectators surrounding an ancient Greek running track **c** : a large usu. unroofed building with tiers of seats for spectators at sports events **3** [NL, fr. L] : a stage in a life history; *esp* : one between successive molts

stadt·hold·er \'stat-ˌhōl-dər\ *n* [part trans. of D *stadhouder*, fr. *stad* place + *houder* holder] (1668) **1** : a viceroy in a province of the Netherlands **2** : a chief executive officer of the provinces that formed a union leading to establishment of the Netherlands — **stadt·hold·er·ate** \-ˌāt\ *n* — **stadt·hold·er·ship** \-dər-ˌship\ *n*

¹staff \'staf\ *n, pl* **staffs** \'stafs, 'stavz\ *or* **staves** \'stavz, 'stāvz\ [ME *staf*, fr. OE *stæf*; akin to OHG *stab* staff, Skt *stabhnāti* he supports]

(bef. 12c) **1 a** : a long stick carried in the hand for support in walking **b** : a supporting rod: as (1) *archaic* **:** SHAFT 1a(1) (2) : a crosspiece in a ladder or chair **:** RUNG (3) : FLAGSTAFF (4) : a pivoted arbor **c** : CLUB, CUDGEL **2 a** : CROSIER **b** : a rod carried as a symbol of office or authority **3** : the horizontal lines with their spaces on which music is written — called also *stave* **4** : any of various graduated sticks or rules used for measuring **:** ROD **5** *pl* **staffs a** : the officers chiefly responsible for the internal operations of an institution or business **b** : a group of officers appointed to assist a civil executive or commanding officer **c** : military or naval officers not eligible for operational command **d** : the personnel who assist a director in carrying out an assigned task **e** *pl* **staff** : a member of a staff — **staff** *adj*

²staff *vt* (1859) **1** : to supply with a staff or with workers **2** : to serve as a staff member of

³staff *n* [prob. fr. G *staffieren* to trim] (1892) : a building material having a plaster of Paris base and used in exterior wall coverings of temporary buildings

staff·er \'sta-fər\ *n* (1941) : a member of a staff (as of a newspaper)

staff officer *n* (1777) : a commissioned officer assigned to a military commander's staff — compare LINE OFFICER

staff of life (1638) : a staple of diet; *esp* : BREAD

Staf·ford·shire bull terrier \'sta-fərd-ˌshir-, -shər-\ *n* [*Staffordshire*, England] (1901) : any of a breed of compact muscular terriers that have a short stiff glossy coat

staff sergeant *n* (1851) : a noncommissioned officer ranking in the army above a sergeant and below a platoon sergeant or sergeant first class, in the air force above a sergeant and below a technical sergeant, and in the marine corps above a sergeant and below a gunnery sergeant

staff sergeant major *n* (1967) : a noncommissioned officer in the army ranking above a master sergeant

staff tree *n* (ca. 1633) : any of a genus (*Celastrus* of the family Celastraceae, the staff-tree family) of mostly twining shrubby plants including the common bittersweet

¹stag \'stag\ *n, pl* **stags** [ME *stagge*, fr. OE *stagga*; akin to ON *andarsteggi* drake] (12c) **1** *or pl* **stag** : an adult male red deer; *also* : the male of various other deer (esp. genus *Cervus*) **2** *chiefly Scot* : a young horse; *esp* : a young unbroken stallion **3** : a male animal castrated after maturity — compare STEER 1 **4** : a young adult male domestic fowl **5 a** : a social gathering of men only **b** : one who attends a dance or party without a companion

²stag *vb* **stagged; stag·ging** [*stag* (informer)] *vt* (ca. 1823) *Brit* : to spy on ∼ *vi* : to attend a dance or party without a companion

³stag *adj* (1843) **1 a** : restricted to men ⟨a ∼ party⟩ **b** : intended or suitable for a gathering of men only; *esp* : PORNOGRAPHIC ⟨∼ movies⟩ **2** : unaccompanied by someone of the opposite sex ⟨∼ women⟩ — **stag** *adv*

stag beetle *n* (1681) : any of a family (Lucanidae) of mostly large lamellicorn beetles having males with long and often branched mandibles suggesting the antlers of a stag

¹stage \'stāj\ *n* [ME, fr. MF *estage*, fr. (assumed) VL *staticum*, fr. L *stare* to stand — more at STAND] (14c) **1 a** : one of a series of positions or stations one above the other **:** STEP **b** : the height of the surface of a river above an arbitrary zero point ⟨flood ∼⟩ **2 a** (1) : a raised platform (2) : the part of a theater on which the acting takes place and which often includes the wings (3) : the acting profession **:** the theater as an occupation or activity ⟨∼ SOUNDSTAGE **b** : a center of attention or scene of action **3 a** : a scaffold for workmen **b** : the small platform of a microscope on which an object is placed for examination **4 a** : a place of rest formerly provided for those traveling by stagecoach **:** STATION **b** : the distance between two stopping places on a road **:** STAGECOACH **5 a** : a period or step in a progress, activity, or development; *esp* : one of the distinguishable periods of growth and development of a plant or animal ⟨the larval ∼ of an insect⟩ **b** : one passing through a (specified) stage **6** : an element or part of an electronic device (as an amplifier) **7** : one of two or more sections of a rocket that have their own fuel and engine — **stage·ful** \-ˌful\ *n* — **stage·like** \-ˌlīk\ *adj* — **on the stage** : in or into the acting profession

²stage *vt* **staged; stag·ing** (1879) **1** : to produce (as a play) on a stage **2** : to produce or cause to happen for public view or public effect ⟨∼ a track meet⟩ ⟨∼ a hunger strike⟩ — **stage·able** \'stā-jə-bəl\ *adj*

³stage *adj* (1824) : intended to represent a type or stereotype ⟨a ∼ Irishman⟩ ⟨a ∼ French accent⟩

stage business *n* (1825) : BUSINESS 6

stage·coach \'stāj-ˌkōch\ *n* (1658) : a horse-drawn passenger and mail coach running on a regular schedule between established stops

stage·craft \-ˌkraft\ *n* (1882) : the effective management of theatrical devices or techniques

stage direction *n* (1790) : a description (as of a character or setting) or direction (as to indicate stage business) provided in the text of a play

stage director *n* (1782) **1** : DIRECTOR c **2** : STAGE MANAGER

stage fright *n* (1878) : nervousness felt at appearing before an audience

stage·hand \'stāj-ˌhand\ *n* (ca. 1902) : a stage worker who handles scenery, properties, or lights

stage left *n* (1931) : the left part of a stage from the viewpoint of one who faces the audience

stage–man·age \-ˌma-nij\ *vt* [back-formation fr. *stage manager*] (1879) **1 a** : to arrange or exhibit so as to achieve a desired effect **b** : to arrange or direct from behind the scenes **2** : to act as stage manager for — **stage management** *n*

stage manager *n* (1805) : one who supervises the physical aspects of a stage production, assists the director during rehearsals, and is in charge of the stage during a performance

stag·er \'stā-jər\ *n* (1570) : an experienced person **:** VETERAN

stage right *n* (1931) : the right part of a stage from the viewpoint of one who faces the audience

---

\ə\ abut \ᵊ\ kitten, F table \ər\ further \a\ ash \ā\ ace \ä\ mop, mar
\aù\ out \ch\ chin \e\ bet \ē\ easy \g\ go \i\ hit \ī\ ice \j\ job
\ŋ\ sing \ō\ go \ò\ law \òi\ boy \th\ thin \t̲h̲\ the \ü\ loot \ù\ foot
\y\ yet \zh\ vision \ä, k̲, ⁿ, œ, œ̄, ᵫ, ᵫ̄, ʸ\ see Guide to Pronunciation

stage set *n* (1861) : scenery and properties designed and arranged for a particular scene in a play
stage-struck \'stāj-,strək\ *adj* (1813) : fascinated by the stage; *esp* : having an ardent desire to become an actor
stage whisper *n* (ca. 1865) **1** : a loud whisper by an actor that is audible to the spectators but is supposed for dramatic effect not to be heard by one or more of the actors **2** : an audible whisper — **stage-whisper** *vb*
stag-fla-tion \stag-'flā-shən\ *n* [blend of *stagnation* and *inflation*] (1965) : persistent inflation combined with stagnant consumer demand and relatively high unemployment — **stag-fla-tion-ary** \-shə-,ner-ē\ *adj*
¹stag-ger \'sta-gər\ *vb* **stag-gered; stag-ger-ing** \-g(ə-)riŋ\ [alter. of earlier *stacker*, fr. ME *stakeren*, fr. ON *stakra*, freq. of *staka* to push; perh. akin to OE *staca* stake — more at STAKE] *vi* (15c) **1 a** : to reel from side to side : TOTTER **b** : to move on unsteadily **2** : to waver in purpose or action : HESITATE **3** : to rock violently ⟨the ship ~ed⟩ ~ *vt* **1** : to cause to doubt or hesitate : PERPLEX **2** : to cause to reel or totter **3** : to arrange in any of various zigzags, alternations, or overlappings of position or time ⟨~ work shifts⟩ ⟨~ teeth on a cutter⟩ — **stag-ger-er** \-gər-ər\ *n*
²stagger *n* (1577) **1** *pl but sing or pl in constr* : an abnormal condition of domestic mammals and birds associated with damage to the central nervous system and marked by incoordination and a reeling unsteady gait **2** : a reeling or unsteady gait or stance **3** : an arrangement in which the leading edge of the upper wing of a biplane is advanced over that of the lower
³stagger *adj* (1875) : marked by an alternating or overlapping pattern
stag-ger-bush \'sta-gər-,bush\ *n* (1847) : a shrubby heath (*Lyonia mariana*) of the eastern U.S. that is poisonous to livestock
staggering *adj* (1530) : so great as to cause one to stagger : ASTONISHING, OVERWHELMING ⟨a ~ feat⟩ ⟨~ medical bills⟩ — **stag-ger-ing-ly** \-g(ə-)riŋ-lē\ *adv*
stag-gery \'sta-g(ə-)rē\ *adj* (1778) : UNSTEADY
stag-gy \'sta-gē\ *adj* (1918) : having the appearance of a mature male — used of female or castrated male domestic animals
stag-horn coral \'stag-,hȯrn-\ *n* (1884) : any of several large branching corals (genus *Acropora* and esp. *A. cervicornis*) that somewhat resemble antlers
staghorn sumac *n* (ca. 1868) : a sumac (*Rhus typhina*) of eastern No. America that is a shrub or small tree with velvety-pubescent branches and flower stalks, leaves turning brilliant red in fall, and dense panicles of greenish yellow flowers followed by hairy crimson fruits

staghorn sumac

stag-hound \'stag-,haůnd\ *n* (1707) : a hound formerly used in hunting the stag and other large animals; *specif* : a large heavy hound resembling the English foxhound
stag-ing \'stā-jiŋ\ *n* (14c) **1** : SCAFFOLDING **2 a** : the business of running stagecoaches **b** : the act of journeying in stagecoaches **3** : the putting of a play on the stage **4 a** : the moving of troops or matériel forward in several stages **b** : the assembling of troops or matériel in transit in a particular place
staging area *n* (1943) : an area in which participants in a new operation or mission are assembled and readied
Stag-i-rite \'sta-jə-,rīt\ *n* [Gk *Stagirītēs*, fr. *Stagira*, city in ancient Macedonia] (ca. 1620) : a native or resident of Stagira ⟨Aristotle the ~⟩
stag-nant \'stag-nənt\ *adj* (1666) **1 a** : not flowing in a current or stream ⟨~ water⟩ **b** : STALE ⟨long disuse had made the air ~ and foul —Bram Stoker⟩ **2** : not advancing or developing — **stag-nan-cy** \-nən(t)-sē\ *n* — **stag-nant-ly** *adv*
stag-nate \'stag-,nāt\ *vi* **stag-nat-ed; stag-nat-ing** [L *stagnatus*, pp. of *stagnare*, fr. *stagnum* body of standing water] (1669) : to become or remain stagnant — **stag-na-tion** \stag-'nā-shən\ *n*
stagy \'stā-jē\ *or* **stag-ey** *adj* **stag-i-er; -est** (1860) : of or characteristic of the stage; *esp* : marked by pretense or artificiality : THEATRICAL — **stag-i-ly** \-jə-lē\ *adv* — **stag-i-ness** \-jē-nəs\ *n*
¹staid \'stād\ *adj* [fr. pp. of ³stay] (1557) : marked by settled sedateness and often prim self-restraint : SOBER, GRAVE **syn** see SERIOUS — **staid-ly** *adv* — **staid-ness** *n*
²staid *past and past part of* STAY
¹stain \'stān\ *vb* [ME *steynen*, partly fr. MF *desteindre* to discolor & partly of Scand origin; akin to ON *steina* to paint — more at DISTAIN] *vt* (14c) **1** : to suffuse with color **2** : DISCOLOR, SOIL **3 a** : to taint with guilt, vice, or corruption **b** : to bring reproach on **4** : to color (as wood, glass, or cloth) by processes affecting chemically or otherwise the material itself ~ *vi* : to receive a stain — **stain-able** \'stā-nə-bəl\ *adj* — **stain-er** \'stā-nər\ *n*
²stain *n* (1583) **1 a** : a soiled or discolored spot **b** : a natural spot of color contrasting with the ground **2** : a taint of guilt : STIGMA **3 a** : a preparation (as of dye or pigment) used in staining; *esp* : one capable of penetrating the pores of wood **b** : a dye or mixture of dyes used in microscopy to make visible minute and transparent structures, to differentiate tissue elements, or to produce specific chemical reactions — **stain-proof** \-,prüf\ *adj*
stain-abil-i-ty \,stā-nə-'bi-lə-tē\ *n* (1890) : the capacity of cells and cell parts to stain specifically and consistently with particular dyes and stains
stained glass *n* (1791) : glass colored or stained (as by fusing metallic oxides into it) for decorative applications (as in windows)
¹stain-less \'stān-ləs\ *adj* (1586) **1 a** : free from stain or stigma **b** : highly resistant to stain or corrosion **2** : made from materials resistant to stain — **stain-less-ly** *adv*
²stainless *n* (1945) : tableware made of stainless steel

stainless steel *n* (1920) : an alloy of steel with chromium and sometimes another element (as nickel or molybdenum) that is practically immune to rusting and ordinary corrosion
stair \'star, 'ster\ *n* [ME *steir*, fr. OE *stæger*; akin to OE & OHG *stīgan* to rise, Gk *steichein* to walk] (bef. 12c) **1 a** : a series of steps or flights of steps for passing from one level to another — often used in pl. but sing. or pl. in constr. ⟨a narrow private ~s —Lewis Mumford⟩ **2 a** : a single step of a stairway
stair-case \-,kās\ *n* (1624) **1** : the structure containing a stairway **2** : a flight of stairs with the supporting framework, casing, and balusters
stair-way \-,wā\ *n* (1767) : one or more flights of stairs usu. with landings to pass from one level to another
stair-well \-,wel\ *n* (1920) : a vertical shaft in which stairs are located
¹stake \'stāk\ *n* [ME, fr. OE *staca*; akin to MLG *stake* stake and perh. to L *tignum* beam] (bef. 12c) **1** : a pointed piece of wood or other material driven or to be driven into the ground as a marker or support **2 a** : a post to which a person is bound for execution by burning **b** : execution by burning at a stake **3 a** : something that is staked for gain or loss **b** : the prize in a contest **c** : an interest or share in an undertaking (as a commercial venture) **4** : a Mormon territorial jurisdiction comprising a group of wards **5** : an upright stick at the side or end of a vehicle to retain the load **6** : GRUBSTAKE — **at stake** : at issue : in jeopardy
²stake *vt* **staked; stak-ing** (14c) **1** : to mark the limits of by or as if by stakes **2** : to tether to a stake **3** : BET, WAGER **4** : to fasten up or support (as plants) with stakes **5** : to back financially **6** : GRUBSTAKE — **stake a claim** : to assert a title or right to something by or as if by placing stakes to satisfy a legal requirement
stake body *n* (1907) : an open motortruck body consisting of a platform with stakes inserted along the outside edges to retain a load
stake-hold-er \'stāk-,hōl-dər\ *n* (1708) : a person entrusted with the stakes of bettors
stake-out \'stā-,kaůt\ *n* (ca. 1942) : a surveillance maintained by the police of an area or a person suspected of criminal activity
stake out *vt* (1951) **1** : to assign (as a police officer) to an area usu. to conduct a surveillance **2** : to maintain a stakeout of
stake race *n* (1896) : a horse race in which the prize offered is made up at least in part of money (as entry fees) put up by the owners of the horses entered
stake truck *n* (1907) : a truck having a stake body
Sta-kha-nov-ite \stə-'kä-nə-,vīt\ *n* [trans. of Russ *stakhanovets*, fr. Alexei G. *Stakhanov* †1977 Russ. miner] (1935) : a Soviet industrial worker awarded recognition and special privileges for output beyond production norms — **Sta-kha-nov-ism** \-,vi-zəm\ *n*
sta-lac-tite \stə-'lak-,tīt *also* 'sta-lək-\ *n* [NL *stalactites*, fr. Gk *stalaktos* dripping, fr. *stalassein* to let drip] (1677) : a deposit of calcium carbonate (as calcite) resembling an icicle hanging from the roof or sides of a cavern — **sta-lac-tit-ic** \,sta-(,)lak-'ti-tik, stə-,\ *adj*
sta-lag \'stä-,läg\ *n* [G, short for *Stammlager* base camp, fr. *Stamm* base + *Lager* camp] (1940) : a German prison camp for noncommissioned officers or enlisted men; *broadly* : PRISON CAMP 2
sta-lag-mite \stə-'lag-,mīt *also* 'sta-ləg-\ *n* [NL *stalagmites*, fr. Gk *stalagma* drop or *stalagmos* dripping, fr. *stalassein* to let drip] (1681) : a deposit of calcium carbonate like an inverted stalactite formed on the floor of a cave by the drip of calcareous water — **sta-lag-mit-ic** \,sta-(,)lag-'mi-tik, stə-,\ *adj*
¹stale \'stā(ə)l\ *adj* **stal-er; stal-est** [ME, aged (of ale), not fresh; akin to MD *stel* stale] (15c) **1** : tasteless or unpalatable from age **2** : tedious from familiarity **3** : impaired in legal force or effect by reason of being allowed to rest without timely use, action, or demand ⟨a ~ affidavit⟩ ⟨a ~ debt⟩ **4** : impaired in vigor or effectiveness — **stale-ly** \'stā(ə)l-lē\ *adv* — **stale-ness** *n*
²stale *vb* **staled; stal-ing** (1599) **1** : to make stale **2** *archaic* : to make common : CHEAPEN ~ *vi* : to become stale
³stale *vi* **staled; stal-ing** [ME; akin to MLG *stallen* to urinate, *stal* urine of horses] (15c) : URINATE — used chiefly of camels and horses
⁴stale *n* (1548) : urine of a domestic animal (as a horse)
¹stale-mate \'stā(ə)l-,māt\ *n* [obs. E *stale* stalemate + E ¹*mate*] (1765) **1** : a drawing position in chess in which only the king can move and although not in check can move only into check **2** : a drawn contest : DEADLOCK; *also* : the state of being stalemated
²stalemate *vt* (1765) : to bring into a stalemate
Sta-lin-ism \'stä-lə-,ni-zəm, 'sta-\ *n* (1927) : the political, economic, and social principles and policies associated with Stalin; *esp* : the theory and practice of communism developed by Stalin from Marxism-Leninism and marked esp. by rigid authoritarianism, widespread use of terror, and often emphasis on Russian nationalism — **Sta-lin-ist** \-nist\ *n or adj* — **Sta-lin-ize** \-,nīz\ *vt* — **Sta-lin-oid** \-,nȯid\ *n or adj*
¹stalk \'stȯk\ *n* [ME *stalke*; akin to OE *stela* stalk, support] (14c) **1** : a slender upright object or supporting or connecting part; *esp* : PEDUNCLE ⟨the ~ of a crinoid⟩ **2 a** : the main stem of an herbaceous plant often with its dependent parts **b** : a part of a plant (as a petiole, stipe, or peduncle) that supports another — **stalked** \'stȯkt\ *adj* — **stalk-less** \'stȯ-kləs\ *adj* — **stalky** \'stȯ-kē\ *adj*
²stalk *vb* [ME, fr. OE *bestealcian*; akin to OE *stelan* to steal — more at STEAL] *vi* (14c) **1** : to pursue quarry or prey stealthily **2** : to walk stiffly or haughtily ~ *vt* **1** : to pursue by stalking **2** : to go through (an area) in search of prey or quarry ⟨~ the woods for deer⟩ — **stalk-er** *n*
³stalk *n* (14c) **1** : the act of stalking **2** : a stalking gait
stalk-ing-horse \'stȯ-kiŋ-,hȯrs\ *n* (1519) **1** : a horse or a figure like a horse behind which a hunter stalks game **2** : something used to mask a purpose **3** : a candidate put forward to divide the opposition or to conceal someone's real candidacy
¹stall \'stȯl\ *n* [ME, fr. OE *steall*; akin to OHG *stal* place, stall and perh. to L *locus* (OL *stlocus*) place] (bef. 12c) **1 a** : a compartment for a domestic animal in a stable or barn **b** : a space marked off for parking a motor vehicle **2 a** : a seat in the chancel of a church with back and sides wholly or partly enclosed **b** : a church pew **c** *chiefly Brit* : a front orchestra seat in a theater — usu. used in pl. **3 a** : a booth, stand, or counter at which articles are displayed for sale **4** : a protective sheath for a finger or toe **5** : a small compartment ⟨a shower ~⟩

²**stall** vt (14c) **1** : to put into or keep in a stall **2** obs : to install in office **3 a** : to bring to a standstill : BLOCK; esp : MIRE **b** : to cause (an engine) to stop usu. inadvertently **c** : to cause (an aircraft or airfoil) to go into a stall ~ vi **1** : to come to a standstill (as from mired wheels or engine failure) **2** : to experience a stall in flying
³**stall** n (1916) : the condition of an airfoil or aircraft in which excessive angle of attack causes disruption of airflow with attendant loss of lift
⁴**stall** n [alter. of stale lure] (1903) : a ruse to deceive or delay
⁵**stall** vi (1903) : to play for time : DELAY ~ vt : to hold off, divert, or delay by evasion or deception
stall–feed \'stȯl-ˌfēd\ vt **-fed** \-ˌfed\; **-feed·ing** (1554) : to feed in a stall esp. so as to fatten ⟨~ an ox⟩
stall·hold·er \-ˌhōl-dər\ n (1881) chiefly Brit : one who manages a stall at which articles are sold
stal·lion \'stal-yən\ n [ME stalion, fr. MF estalon, of Gmc origin; akin to OHG stal stall] (14c) : an uncastrated male horse : a male horse kept for breeding; also : a male animal (as a dog or a sheep) kept primarily as a stud
¹**stal·wart** \'stȯl-wərt\ adj [ME, alter. of stalworth, fr. OE stǣlwierthe serviceable] (15c) : marked by outstanding strength and vigor of body, mind, or spirit ⟨~ common sense⟩ syn see STRONG — **stal·wart·ly** adv — **stal·wart·ness** n
²**stalwart** n (15c) **1** : a stalwart person **2** : an unwavering partisan
stal·worth \'stȯl-(ˌ)wərth\ adj archaic var of STALWART
sta·men \'stā-mən\ n, pl stamens also sta·mi·na \'stā-mə-nə, 'sta-\ [L, warp, thread, fr. stare to stand — more at STAND] (1668) **1** : a microsporophyll of a seed plant; specif : the pollen-producing male organ of a flower that consists of an anther and a filament — see FLOWER illustration
stamin- comb form [L stamin-, stamen] : stamen ⟨staminodium⟩
stam·i·na \'sta-mə-nə\ n [L, pl. of stamen warp, thread of life spun by the Fates] (1726) : STAYING POWER, ENDURANCE
sta·mi·nate \'sta-mə-nət, -ˌnāt\ adj (ca. 1850) **1** : having or producing stamens **2** of a diclinous flower : having stamens but no pistils
sta·mi·no·di·um \ˌstā-mə-ˈnō-dē-əm, ˌsta-\ n, pl **-dia** \-dē-ə\ [NL, fr. stamin- + -odium thing resembling, fr. Gk -ōdēs like] (ca. 1821) : an abortive or sterile stamen
stam·mel \'sta-məl\ n [prob. fr. stamin a woolen fabric] (1530) **1** obs : a coarse woolen clothing fabric usu. dyed red and used sometimes for undershirts of penitents **2** archaic : the bright red color of stammel
stam·mer \'sta-mər\ vb **stam·mered; stam·mer·ing** \'sta-mə-riŋ, 'stam-riŋ\ [ME stameren, fr. OE stamerian; akin to OHG stamalōn to stammer, ON stemma to hinder, damn up — more at STEM] vi (bef. 12c) : to make involuntary stops and repetitions in speaking : HALT — compare STUTTER ~ vt : to utter with involuntary stops or repetitions — **stammer** n — **stam·mer·er** \-mər-ər\ n
¹**stamp** \'stamp; vt2a & vi2 are also 'stämp or 'stȯmp\ vb [ME; akin to OHG stampfōn to stamp and perh. to Gk stembein to shake up] vt (13c) **1** : to pound or crush with a pestle or a heavy instrument **2 a** (1) : to strike or beat forcibly with the bottom of the foot (2) : to bring down (the foot) forcibly **b** : to extinguish or destroy by or as if by stamping with the foot — usu. used with out ⟨~ out cancer⟩ **3 a** : IMPRESS, IMPRINT ⟨~ "paid" on the bill⟩ **b** : to attach a stamp to **4** : to cut out, bend, or form with a stamp or die **5 a** : to provide with a distinctive character ⟨~ed with a dreary, institutionalized look — Bernard Taper⟩ **b** : CHARACTERIZE ~ vi **1** : POUND 1 **2** : to strike or thrust the foot forcibly or noisily downward
²**stamp** n (15c) **1** : a device or instrument for stamping **2** : the impression or mark made by stamping or imprinting **3 a** : a distinctive character, indication, or mark **b** : a lasting imprint **4** : the act of stamping **5** : a stamped or printed paper affixed in evidence that a tax has been paid; also : POSTAGE STAMP — **stamp·less** adj
¹**stam·pede** \(ˌ)stam-ˈpēd\ n [AmerSp estampida, fr. Sp, crash, fr. estampar to stamp, of Gmc origin; akin to OHG stampfōn to stamp] (1828) **1** : a wild headlong rush or flight of frightened animals **2** : a mass movement of people at a common impulse **3** : an extended festival combining a rodeo with exhibitions, contests, and social events
²**stampede** vb **stam·ped·ed; stam·ped·ing** vt (1838) **1** : to cause to run away in headlong panic **2** : to cause (as a group of people) to act on sudden or rash impulse ~ vi **1** : to flee headlong in panic **2** : to act on mass impulse — **stam·ped·er** n
stamp·er \'stam-pər, 'stäm-, 'stȯm-\ compare ¹STAMP\ n (14c) : one that stamps: as **a** : a worker who performs an industrial stamping operation **b** : an implement for pounding or stamping **c** : any of various stamping machines
stamping ground \'stam-piŋ, 'stäm-, 'stȯm-\ n (1786) : a favorite or habitual resort; also : familiar territory
stamp·ing mill \'stam-piŋ-\ n (1552) : STAMP MILL
stamp mill \'stamp-\ n (1749) : a mill in which ore is crushed with stamps; also : a machine for stamping ore
stamp tax n (1797) : a tax collected by means of a stamp purchased and affixed (as to a deck of playing cards); specif : such a tax on a document (as a deed or promissory note) — called also stamp duty
stance \'stan(t)s\ n [MF estance position, posture, stay, fr. (assumed) VL stantia, fr. L stant-, stans, prp. of stare to stand] (14c) **1** chiefly Scot **a** : STATION **b** : SITE **2 a** : a way of standing or being placed : POSTURE **b** : intellectual or emotional attitude ⟨took an antiwar ~⟩ **3 a** : the position of the feet of a golfer or batter preparatory to making a swing **b** : the position of both body and feet from which an athlete starts or operates
¹**stanch** \'stȯnch, 'stänch, 'stanch\ vt [ME staunchen, fr. MF estancher, perh. fr. (assumed) VL stanticare, fr. L stant-, stans, prp.] (14c) **1** : to check or stop the flowing of ⟨~ed her tears⟩; also : to stop the flow of blood from (a wound) **2** archaic : ALLAY, EXTINGUISH **3 a** : to stop or check in its course ⟨trying to ~ the crime wave⟩ **b** : to make watertight : stop up — **stanch·er** n
²**stanch** var of STAUNCH
stan·chion \'stan-chən\ n [ME stanchon, fr. MF estanchon, fr. OF, dim. of estance stay, prop] (15c) **1** : an upright bar, post, or support (as for a roof) **2 a** : a device that fits loosely around the neck of an animal (as a cow) and limits forward and backward motion (as in a stall) — **stanchioned** \-chənd\ adj
¹**stand** \'stand\ vb **stood** \'stu̇d\; **stand·ing** [ME, fr. OE standan; akin

to OHG stantan, stān to stand, L stare, Gk histanai to cause to stand, set, histasthai to stand, be standing] vi (bef. 12c) **1 a** : to support oneself on the feet in an erect position **b** : to be a specified height when fully erect ⟨~s six feet two⟩ **c** : to rise to an erect position **2 a** : to take up or maintain a specified position or posture ⟨~ aside⟩ ⟨can you ~ on your head⟩ **b** : to maintain one's position ⟨~ firm⟩ **3** : to be in a particular state or situation ⟨~s accused⟩ **4** : to hold a course at sea **5** obs : HESITATE **6 a** : to have or maintain a relative position in or as if in a graded scale ⟨~s first in the class⟩ **b** : to be in a position to gain or lose because of an action taken or a commitment made ⟨~s to make quite a profit⟩ **7** chiefly Brit : to be a candidate : RUN **8 a** : to rest or remain upright on a base or lower end ⟨a clock stood on the mantle⟩ **b** : to occupy a place or location ⟨the house ~s on a knoll⟩ **9 a** : to remain stationary or inactive ⟨the car stood in the garage for a week⟩ **b** : to gather slowly and remain ⟨tears ~ing in her eyes⟩ **10** : AGREE, ACCORD — used chiefly in the expression it stands to reason **11 a** : to exist in a definite written or printed form ⟨copy a passage exactly as it ~s⟩ **b** : to remain valid or efficacious ⟨the order given last week still ~s⟩ **12** of a male animal : to be available as a sire — used esp. of horses ~ vt **1 a** : to endure or undergo successfully ⟨this book will ~ the test of time⟩ **b** : to tolerate without flinching : bear courageously ⟨~s pain well⟩ **c** : to endure the presence or personality of ⟨can't ~ the boss⟩ **d** : to derive benefit or enjoyment from ⟨you look like you could ~ a drink⟩ **2** : to remain firm in the face of ⟨~ a siege⟩ **3** : to submit to ⟨~ trial⟩ **4 a** : to perform the duty of ⟨~ guard⟩ **b** : to participate in (a military formation) **5** : to pay the cost of (a treat) : pay for ⟨I'll ~ you a dinner⟩ ⟨~ drinks⟩ **6** : to cause to stand : set upright **7** : to make available for breeding ⟨~ a stallion⟩ syn see BEAR — **stand·er** n — **stand a chance** : to have a chance — **stand for 1** : to be a symbol for : REPRESENT **2** : to put up with : PERMIT — **stand on 1** : to depend on **2** : to insist on ⟨never stands on ceremony⟩ — **stand one's ground** : to maintain one's position — **stand on one's own feet** : to think or act independently — **stand treat** : to pay the cost of food, drink, or entertainment for others in a group
²**stand** n (1592) **1** : an act of stopping or staying in one place **2 a** : a halt for defense or resistance **b** : an often defensive effort of some duration or degree of success ⟨a goal-line ~⟩ **c** (1) : a stop made to give a performance ⟨a 6-game ~ at home⟩ (2) : a town where such a stop is made **3 a** : a place or post where one stands **b** : a strongly or aggressively held position esp. on a debatable issue **4 a** : the place taken by a witness for testifying in court **b** pl (1) : a section of the tiered seats for spectators of a sport or spectacle (2) : the occupants of such seats **c** : a raised platform (as for a speaker) serving as a point of vantage **5 a** : a small often open-air structure for a small retail business ⟨a vegetable ~⟩ ⟨a hot dog ~⟩ **b** : a site fit for business opportunity **6** : a place where a passenger vehicle stops or parks ⟨a taxi ~⟩ **7** : HIVE 2 **8** : a frame on or in which something may be placed for support **9** : a group of plants growing in a continuous area **10** : a standing posture
stand–alone \'stan-də-ˈlōn\ adj (1966) : SELF-CONTAINED; esp : operating or capable of operating independently of a computer system ⟨a ~ word processor⟩
¹**stan·dard** \'stan-dərd\ n [ME, fr. OF estandard rallying point, standard, of Gmc origin; akin to OE standan to stand and to OE ord point — more at ODD] (12c) **1** : a conspicuous object (as a banner) formerly carried at the top of a pole and used to mark a rallying point esp. in battle or to serve as an emblem **2 a** : a long narrow tapering flag that is personal to an individual or corporation and bears heraldic devices **b** : the personal flag of the head of a state or of a member of a royal family **c** : an organization flag carried by a mounted or motorized military unit **d** : BANNER **3** : something established by authority, custom, or general consent as a model or example : CRITERION **4** : something set up and established by authority as a rule for the measure of quantity, weight, extent, value, or quality **5 a** : the fineness and legally fixed weight of the metal used in coins **b** : the basis of value in a monetary system **6** : a structure built for or serving as a base or support **7 a** : a shrub or herb grown with an erect main stem so that it forms or resembles a tree **b** : a fruit tree grafted on a stock that does not induce dwarfing **8 a** : the large odd upper petal of a papilionaceous flower (as the pea) **b** : one of the three inner usu. erect and incurved petals of an iris **9** : a musical composition (as a song) that has become a part of the standard repertoire — **stan·dard·less** adj
syn STANDARD, CRITERION, GAUGE, YARDSTICK, TOUCHSTONE mean a means of determining what a thing should be. STANDARD applies to any definite rule, principle, or measure established by authority ⟨standards of behavior⟩. CRITERION may apply to anything used as a test of quality whether formulated as a rule or principle or not ⟨questioned the critic's criteria for excellence⟩. GAUGE applies to a means of testing a particular dimension (as thickness, depth, diameter) or figuratively a particular quality or aspect ⟨polls as a gauge of voter dissatisfaction⟩. YARDSTICK is an informal substitute for CRITERION that suggests quantity more often than quality ⟨housing construction as a yardstick of economic growth⟩. TOUCHSTONE suggests a simple test of the authenticity or value of something intangible ⟨fine service is one touchstone of a first-class restaurant⟩.
²**standard** adj (1622) **1 a** : constituting or conforming to a standard esp. as established by law or custom ⟨~ weight⟩ **b** : sound and usable but not of top quality ⟨~ beef⟩ **2 a** : regularly and widely used, available, or supplied ⟨~ automobile equipment⟩ **b** : well-established and very familiar ⟨the ~ opera⟩ **3** : having recognized and permanent value ⟨a ~ reference work⟩ **b** : substantially uniform and well established by usage in the speech and writing of the educated and widely recognized as acceptable ⟨~ pronunciation is subject to regional variations⟩ — **stan·dard·ly** adv

\ə\ abut \ˈə\ kitten, F table \ər\ further \a\ ash \ā\ ace \ä\ mop, mar \au̇\ out \ch\ chin \e\ bet \ē\ easy \g\ go \i\ hit \ī\ ice \j\ job \ŋ\ sing \ō\ go \ȯ\ law \ȯi\ boy \th\ thin \t͟h\ the \ü\ loot \u̇\ foot \y\ yet \zh\ vision \ä, k̲, ⁿ, œ, œ̅, ue, ue̅, ᵜ\ see Guide to Pronunciation

stan·dard–bear·er \'stan-dərd-,bar-ər, -,ber-\ *n* (15c) **1** : one that bears a standard or banner **2** : the leader of an organization, movement, or party

stan·dard·bred \-,bred\ *n, often cap* (1921) : any of a breed of trotting and pacing horses developed in the U.S., noted for speed and stamina, and used esp. in harness racing

standard candle *n* (1879) : CANDELA

standard deviation *n* (1894) **1** : a measure of the dispersion of a frequency distribution that is the square root of the arithmetic mean of the squares of the deviation of each of the class frequencies from the arithmetic mean of the frequency distribution; *also* : a similar quantity found by dividing by one less than the number of squares in the sum of squares instead of taking the arithmetic mean **2** : a parameter that indicates the way in which a probability function or a probability density function is centered around its mean and that is equal to the square root of the moment in which the deviation from the mean is squared

standardbred

Standard English *n* (1836) : the English that with respect to spelling, grammar, pronunciation, and vocabulary is substantially uniform though not devoid of regional differences, that is well established by usage in the formal and informal speech and writing of the educated, and that is widely recognized as acceptable wherever English is spoken and understood

standard error *n* (1897) : the standard deviation of the probability function or probability density function of a random variable and esp. of a statistic; *specif* : the standard error of the mean of a sample from a population with a normal distribution that is equal to the standard deviation of the normal distribution divided by the square root of the sample size

standard gauge *n* (1871) : a railroad gauge of 4 feet 8½ inches

stan·dard·ise *Brit var of* STANDARDIZE

stan·dard·ize \'stan-dər-,dīz\ *vt* **-ized; -iz·ing** (1873) **1** : to compare with a standard **2** : to bring into conformity with a standard — **stan·dard·i·za·tion** \,stan-dər-də-'zā-shən\ *n*

standard of living (1902) **1** : the necessities, comforts, and luxuries enjoyed or aspired to by an individual or group **2** : a minimum of necessities, comforts, or luxuries held essential to maintaining a person or group in customary or proper status or circumstances

standard operating procedure *n* (1952) : established or prescribed methods to be followed routinely for the performance of designated operations or in designated situations — called also *standing operating procedure*

standard position *n* (1950) : the position of an angle with its vertex at the origin of a rectangular-coordinate system and its initial side coinciding with the positive x-axis

standard schnauzer *n* (ca. 1934) : any of a breed of medium-sized schnauzers that attain a height at the highest point of the shoulder blades of 18 to 20 inches (46 to 51 centimeters) and have a pepper-and-salt or black coat

standard score *n* (1928) : an individual test score expressed as the deviation from the mean score of the group in units of standard deviation

standard time *n* (1879) : the time of a region or country that is established by law or general usage as civil time; *specif* : the mean solar time of a meridian that is a multiple of 15 arbitrarily applied to a local area or to one of the 24 time zones and designated as a number of hours earlier or later than Greenwich time

stand·away \'stan-də-,wā\ *adj* (1948) : standing out from the body ⟨a ~ skirt⟩

¹stand·by \'stan(d)-,bī\ *n, pl* **stand·bys** \-,bīz\ (1796) **1 a** : one to be relied on esp. in emergencies **b** : a favorite or reliable choice or resource **2** : one that is held in reserve ready for use : SUBSTITUTE — **on standby** : ready or available for immediate action or use

²standby *adj* (1921) **1** : held near at hand and ready for use ⟨a ~ power plant⟩ ⟨~ equipment⟩ **2** : relating to the act or condition of standing by ⟨~ duty⟩ ⟨a ~ period⟩ **3** : of, relating to, or traveling by an airline service in which the passenger must wait for an available unreserved seat ⟨~ passengers⟩ ⟨a ~ ticket⟩

³standby *adv* (1971) : on a standby basis ⟨fly ~⟩

stand by *vi* (13c) **1** : to be present; *also* : to remain apart or aloof **2** : to be or to get ready to act ~ *vt* : to remain loyal or faithful to : DEFEND

stand–down \'stan(d)-,daún\ *n* (ca. 1919) : a relaxation of status of a military unit or force from an alert or operational posture

stand down *vi* (1681) **1** : to leave the witness stand **2** *chiefly Brit* **a** : to go off duty **b** : to withdraw from a contest or from a position of leadership

stand·ee \stan-'dē\ *n* (1856) : one who occupies standing room

stand–in \'stan-,din\ *n* (ca. 1928) **1** : someone employed to occupy an actor's place while lights and camera are readied **2** : SUBSTITUTE

stand in *vi* (1904) : to act as a stand-in — **stand in with** : to be in a specially favored position with

¹stand·ing \'stan-din\ *adj* (14c) **1 a** : not yet cut or harvested ⟨~ timber⟩ ⟨~ grain⟩ **b** : upright on the feet or base : ERECT ⟨the ~ audience⟩ **2 a** : not being used or operated ⟨a ~ factory⟩ **b** : not flowing : STAGNANT ⟨~ water⟩ **3 a** : remaining at the same level, degree, or amount for an indeterminate period ⟨a ~ offer⟩ **b** : continuing in existence or use indefinitely **4** : established by law or custom **5** : not movable **6** : done from a standing position ⟨a ~ jump⟩ ⟨a ~ ovation⟩

²standing *n* (15c) **1 a** : a place to stand in : LOCATION **b** : a position from which one may assert or enforce legal rights and duties **2 a** : length of service or experience esp. as determining rank, pay, or privilege **b** : position or condition in society or in a profession; *esp* : good reputation **c** : position relative to a standard of achievement or to

achievements of competitors **3** : maintenance of position or condition : DURATION ⟨a custom of long ~⟩

standing army *n* (1603) : a permanent army of paid soldiers

standing committee *n* (ca. 1636) : a permanent committee esp. of a legislative body

standing crop *n* (1861) : the total amount or number of living things or of one kind of living thing (as an uncut farm crop, the fish in a pond, or organisms in an ecosystem) in a particular situation at any given time

standing O \-'ō\ *n* [*ovation*] (1975) : a standing ovation

standing order *n* (1737) : an instruction or prescribed procedure in force permanently or until changed or canceled; *esp* : any of the rules for the guidance and government of parliamentary procedure which endure through successive sessions until vacated or repealed

standing room *n* (1603) : space for standing; *esp* : accommodation available for spectators or passengers after all seats are filled

standing wave *n* (1896) : a single-frequency mode of vibration of a body or physical system in which the amplitude varies from place to place, is constantly zero at fixed points, and has maxima at other points

stan·dish \'stan-dish\ *n* [ME *standyshe*] (14c) : a stand for writing materials : INKSTAND

¹stand·off \'stan-,dȯf\ *adj* (1837) **1** : STANDOFFISH **2** : used for holding something at a distance from a surface ⟨a ~ insulator⟩

²standoff *n* (1843) **1 a** : TIE, DEADLOCK ⟨the two teams played to a ~⟩ **b** : a counterbalancing effect **2** : the act of standing off

stand off *vi* (1601) **1** : to stay at a distance from something **2** : to sail away from the shore ~ *vt* **1** : to keep from advancing : REPEL **2** : PUT OFF, STALL

stand·off·ish \stan-'dȯ-fish\ *adj* (1860) : somewhat cold and reserved — **stand·off·ish·ly** *adv* — **stand·off·ish·ness** *n*

stand oil *n* (1908) : a thickened drying oil; *esp* : linseed oil heated to about 600° F (315° C)

stand·out \'stan-,daút\ *n, often attrib* (1928) : one that is prominent or conspicuous esp. because of excellence

stand out *vi* (15c) **1 a** : to appear as if in relief : PROJECT **b** : to be prominent or conspicuous **2** : to steer away from shore **3** : to be stubborn in resolution or resistance

stand·pat \'stan(d)-'pat\ *adj* (1904) : stubbornly conservative : resisting or opposing change

stand pat *vi* [*¹pat*] (1882) **1** : to play one's hand as dealt in draw poker without drawing **2** : to oppose or resist change — **stand·pat·ter** \'stan(d)-,pa-tər, -'pa-tər\ *n* — **stand·pat·tism** \-,pa-,ti-zəm\ *n*

stand·pipe \'stan(d)-,pīp\ *n* (ca. 1850) : a high vertical pipe or reservoir that is used to secure a uniform pressure in a water-supply system

stand·point \-,pȯint\ *n* (1829) : a position from which objects or principles are viewed and according to which they are compared and judged

stand·still \-,stil\ *n* (1702) : a state characterized by absence of motion or of progress : STOP

¹stand–up \'stan-,dəp\ *adj* (1812) **1 a** : ERECT, UPRIGHT **b** : stiffened to stay upright without folding over ⟨a ~ collar⟩ **2** : performed in, performing in, or requiring a standing position ⟨a ~ bar⟩; *esp* : of, relating to, performing, or being a monologue of jokes, gags, or satirical comments delivered usu. while standing alone on a stage or in front of a camera ⟨~ comedy⟩ ⟨a ~ comedian⟩

²stand–up *n* (1971) : stand-up comedy

stand up *vi* (bef. 12c) **1** : to rise to a standing position **2** : to remain sound and intact under stress, attack, or close scrutiny ~ *vt* : to fail to keep an appointment with — **stand up for** : to defend against attack or criticism — **stand up to** : to meet fairly and fully **2** : to face boldly — **stand up with** : to be best man or maid of honor for at a wedding ceremony

stand–up·per \'stan-'də-pər\ *n* (1973) : a television news report or interview by an on-camera reporter standing usu. at the scene of an occurrence

stane \'stān\ *Scot var of* STONE

Stan·ford–Bi·net test \,stan-fərd-bi-'nā-\ *n* [*Stanford* University + Alfred *Binet* †1911 Fr. psychologist] (1918) : an intelligence test prepared at Stanford University as a revision of the Binet-Simon scale and commonly used with children — called also *Stanford-Binet*

¹stang \'stan\ *vt* [ME, fr. ON *stanga* to prick; akin to ON *stinga* to sting] (14c) *chiefly Scot* : STING

²stang *n* (1513) *chiefly Scot* : PANG

³stang *var of* SATANG

stan·hope \'sta-nəp\ *n* [Fitzroy *Stanhope* †1864 Brit. clergyman] (1825) : a gig, buggy, or phaeton typically having a high seat and closed back

sta·nine \'stā-,nīn\ *n* [*sta*ndard (score) + *nine*] (1944) : any of the nine classes into which a set of normalized standard scores arranged according to rank in educational testing are divided, which include the bottom 4% and the top 4% of the scores in the first and ninth classes and the middle 20% in the fifth, and which have a standard deviation of 2 and a mean of 5

Sta·ni·slav·ski method \,sta-nə-'slaf-ski-, -'slav-\ *n* [Konstantin *Stanislavsky*] (1941) : a technique in acting by which an actor strives to empathize with the character being portrayed so as to effect a realistic interpretation

¹stank \'stank\ *past of* STINK

²stank *n* [ME, fr. MF *estanc*, fr. *estancher* to dam up, stanch — more at STANCH] (14c) **1** *dial Brit* **a** : POND, POOL **b** : a ditch containing water **2** *Brit* : a small dam : WEIR

stan·na·ry \'sta-nə-rē\ *n, pl* **-ries** [ME *stannarie*, fr. ML *stannaria* tin mine, fr. LL *stannum* tin] (15c) : any of the regions in England containing establishments for the working of tin — usu. used in pl.

stan·nic \'sta-nik\ *adj* [prob. fr. F *stannique*, fr. LL *stannum* tin, fr. L *stagnum*, an alloy of silver and lead] (1790) : of, relating to, or containing tin esp. with a valence of four

stan·nite \'sta-,nīt\ *n* [LL *stannum*] (1868) : a mineral that is a steel-gray or iron-black sulfide of copper, iron, and tin with a metallic luster and occurs in granular masses

stan·nous \'sta-nəs\ *adj* [ISV, fr. LL *stannum*] (1849) : of, relating to, or containing tin esp. with a valence of two

stan·za \'stan-zə\ *n* [It, stay, abode, room, stanza, fr. (assumed) VL *stantia* stay — more at STANCE] (1588) : a division of a poem consisting of a series of lines arranged together in a usu. recurring pattern of meter and rhyme : STROPHE — **stan·za·ic** \stan-'zā-ik\ *adj*

sta·pe·dec·to·my \ˌstā-pi-'dek-tə-mē\ *n, pl* **-mies** [ISV, fr. NL *staped-, stapes*] (1894) : surgical removal and prosthetic replacement of part or all of the stapes to relieve deafness

sta·pe·di·al \stā-'pē-dē-əl, stə-\ *adj* (ca. 1859) : of, relating to, or located near the stapes

sta·pe·lia \stə-'pēl-yə\ *n* [NL, fr. J. B. van *Stapel* †1636 Du. botanist] (ca. 1785) : any of a genus (*Stapelia*) of African perennial herbs of the milkweed family with succulent typically leafless toothed stems like cactus joints and showy but usu. putrid-smelling flowers

sta·pes \'stā-(ˌ)pēz\ *n, pl* **stapes** *or* **sta·pe·des** \'stā-pə-ˌdēz\ [NL *staped-, stapes*, fr. ML, stirrup, alter. of LL *stapia*] (1670) : the innermost ossicle of the ear of mammals — called also *stirrup*; see EAR illustration

staph \'staf\ *n* (ca. 1933) : STAPHYLOCOCCUS

staph·y·li·nid \ˌsta-fə-'li-nəd\ *n* [NL *Staphylinidae*, ultim. fr. Gk *staphylē* bunch of grapes] (1911) : ROVE BEETLE — **staphylinid** *adj*

staph·y·lo·coc·cal \ˌsta-f(ə-)lō-'kä-kəl\ *also* **staph·y·lo·coc·cic** \-'kä-kik, -'käk-sik\ *adj* (1900) : of, relating to, caused by, or being a staphylococcus

staph·y·lo·coc·cus \-'kä-kəs\ *n, pl* **-coc·ci** \-'kä-ˌkī, -(ˌ)kē, -'käk-ˌsī, -(ˌ)sē\ [NL, fr. Gk *staphylē* bunch of grapes + NL *-coccus*] (1887) : any of various nonmotile gram-positive spherical bacteria (esp. genus *Staphylococcus*) that occur singly, in pairs or tetrads, or in irregular clusters and include pathogens which infect skin and mucous membranes

¹sta·ple \'stā-pəl\ *n* [ME *stapel* post, staple, fr. OE *stapol* post; akin to MD *stapel* step, heap, emporium, OE *steppan* to step] (13c) **1** : a U= shaped metal loop both ends of which are driven into a surface to hold the hook, hasp, or bolt of a lock, secure a rope, or fix a wire in place **2** : a small U-shaped wire both ends of which are driven through layers of thin and easily penetrable material (as paper) and usu. clinched to hold the layers together

²staple *vt* **sta·pled; sta·pling** \-p(ə-)liŋ\ (14c) : to provide with or secure by staples

³staple *n* [ME, fr. MF *estaple*, fr. MD *stapel* emporium] (14c) **1** : a town used as a center for the sale or exportation of commodities in bulk **2** : a place of supply : SOURCE **3** : a chief commodity or production of a place **4** : a commodity for which the demand is constant **b** : something having widespread and constant use or appeal **c** : the sustaining or principal element : SUBSTANCE **5** : RAW MATERIAL **6 a** : textile fiber (as wool and rayon) of relatively short length that when spun and twisted forms a yarn rather than a filament **b** : the length of a piece of such textile fiber

⁴staple *adj* (1615) **1** : used, needed, or enjoyed constantly usu. by many individuals **2** : produced regularly or in large quantities ⟨~ crops such as wheat and rice⟩ **3** : PRINCIPAL, CHIEF

¹sta·pler \'stā-p(ə-)lər\ *n* (ca. 1513) : one that deals in staple goods or in staple fiber

²stapler *n* (ca. 1909) : one that inserts staples; *esp* : a small usu. hand-operated device for inserting wire staples

¹star \'stär\ *n, often attrib* [ME *sterre*, fr. OE *steorra*; akin to OHG *sterno* star, L *stella*, Gk *astēr, astron*] (bef. 12c) **1 a** : a natural luminous body visible in the sky esp. at night **b** : a self-luminous gaseous celestial body of great mass which produces energy by means of nuclear fusion reactions, whose shape is usu. spheroidal, and whose size may be as small as the earth or larger than the earth's orbit **2 a** (1) : a planet or a configuration of the planets that is held in astrology to influence one's destiny or fortune — used in pl. (2) : a waxing or waning fortune or fame ⟨her ~ was rising⟩ **b** *obs* : DESTINY **3 a** : a conventional figure with five or more points that represents a star; *esp* : ASTERISK **b** : an often star-shaped ornament or medal worn as a badge of honor, authority, or rank or as the insignia of an order **c** : one of a group of conventional stars used to place something in a scale of value **4** : something resembling a star ⟨was hit on the head and saw ~s⟩ **5 a** : the principal member of a theatrical or operatic company who usu. plays the chief roles **b** : a highly publicized theatrical or motion-picture performer **c** : an outstandingly talented performer ⟨a track ~⟩ **d** : a person who is preeminent in a particular field — **star·less** \-ləs\ *adj* — **star·like** \-ˌlīk\ *adj*

²star *vb* **starred; star·ring** *vt* (1718) **1** : to sprinkle or adorn with stars **2 a** : to mark with a star as being preeminent **b** : to mark with an asterisk **3** : to advertise or display prominently : FEATURE ⟨the movie ~s a famous stage personality⟩ ~ *vi* **1** : to play the most prominent or important role **2** : to perform outstandingly

³star *adj* (1832) **1** : of, relating to, or being a star ⟨received ~ billing⟩ **2** : of outstanding excellence : PREEMINENT ⟨a ~ athlete⟩

star apple *n* (1683) : a tropical American tree (*Chrysophyllum cainito*) of the sapodilla family grown in warm regions for ornament or fruit; *also* : its usu. green to purple apple-shaped edible fruit

¹star·board \'stär-bərd\ *n* [ME *sterbord*, fr. OE *stēorbord*, fr. *stēor-* steering oar + *bord* ship's side — more at STEER, BOARD] (bef. 12c) : the right side of a ship or aircraft looking forward — compare PORT

²starboard *adj* (15c) : of, relating to, or situated on starboard

³starboard *vt* (1598) : to turn or put (a helm or rudder) to the right

¹starch \'stärch\ *vt* [ME *sterchen*, prob. fr. (assumed) OE *stercan* to stiffen; akin to OE *stearc* stiff — more at STARK] (15c) : to stiffen with or as if with starch

²starch *n* (15c) **1** : a white odorless tasteless granular or powdery complex carbohydrate ($C_6H_{10}O_5$)$_x$ that is the chief storage form of carbohydrate in plants, is an important foodstuff, and is used also in adhesives and sizes, in laundering, and in pharmacy and medicine **2** : a stiff formal manner : FORMALITY **3** : resolute vigor

star–cham·ber \'stär-'chäm-bər\ *adj* [*Star Chamber*, a court existing in England from the 15th century until 1641] (1800) : characterized by secrecy and often being irresponsibly arbitrary and oppressive

starchy \'stär-chē\ *adj* **starch·i·er; -est** (1802) **1** : containing, consisting of, or resembling starch **2** : consisting of or marked by formality or stiffness — **starch·i·ly** \-chə-lē\ *adv* — **starch·i·ness** \-chē-nəs\ *n*

star–crossed \'stär-ˌkrȯst\ *adj* (1592) : not favored by the stars : ILL-FATED ⟨a pair of ~ lovers take their life —Shak.⟩

star·dom \'stär-dəm\ *n* (1865) : the status or position of a star

star·dust \'stär-ˌdəst\ *n* (1927) : a feeling or impression of romance, magic, or ethereality

¹stare \'star, 'ster\ *vb* **stared; star·ing** [ME, fr. OE *starian*; akin to OHG *starēn* to stare, Gk *stereos* solid, Lith *starinti* to stiffen] (bef. 12c) **1** : to look fixedly often with wide-open eyes **2** : to show oneself conspicuously ⟨the error *stared* from the page⟩ **3** *of hair* : to stand on end : BRISTLE; *also* : to appear rough and lusterless ~ *vt* **1** : to have an effect on by staring **2** : to look at with a searching or earnest gaze — **star·er** *n* — **stare one in the face** : to be undeniably and forcefully evident or apparent

²stare *n* (15c) : the act or an instance of staring ⟨a blank ~⟩

sta·re de·ci·sis \ˌster-ē-di-'sī-səs, ˌstar-, ˌstär-\ [L, to stand by decided matters] (1782) : a doctrine or policy of following rules or principles laid down in previous judicial decisions unless they contravene the ordinary principles of justice

stare down *vt* (1925) : to cause to waver or submit by or as if by staring

sta·rets \'stär-əts, -yəts\ *n, pl* **star·tsy** \'stärt-sē\ [Russ., fr. *staryĭ* old — more at STOUR] (1917) : a spiritual director or religious teacher in the Eastern Orthodox Church; *specif* : a spiritual adviser who is not necessarily a priest, who is recognized for his piety, and who is turned to by monks or laymen for spiritual guidance

star facet *n* (1751) : one of the eight small triangular facets which abut on the table in the bezel of a brilliant

star·fish \'stär-ˌfish\ *n* (1538) : any of a class (Asteroidea) of echinoderms having a body of usu. five radially disposed arms about a central disk and feeding largely on mollusks (as oysters) — called also *sea star*

star-flow·er \-ˌflau̇(-ə)r\ *n* (1629) : any of several plants having star-shaped pentamerous flowers; *esp* : any of a genus (*Trientalis*, esp. *T. borealis*) of perennial herbs of the primrose family

star fruit *n* (1974) : CARAMBOLA 1

star·gaze \-ˌgāz\ *vi* [back-formation fr. *stargazer*] (1626) **1** : to gaze at stars **2** : to gaze raptly or contemplatively

star·gaz·er \-ˌgā-zər\ *n* (1560) **1** : one who gazes at the stars: as **a** : ASTROLOGER **b** : ASTRONOMER **2** : any of various marine bony fishes (families Uranoscopidae and Dactyloscopidae) with the eyes on top of a blocky or conical head

star·gaz·ing \-ˌgā-ziŋ\ *n* (1576) **1** : the act or practice of a stargazer **2 a** : absorption in chimerical or impractical ideas : WOOLGATHERING **b** : the quality or state of being absentminded

star grass *n* (1687) : any of various grassy plants with stellate flowers or arrangement of leaves: as **a** : any of a genus (*Hypoxis*) of herbs of the amaryllis family **b** : either of two colicroots (*Aletris farinosa* and *A. aurea*)

¹stark \'stärk\ *adj* [ME, stiff, strong, fr. OE *stearc*; akin to OHG *starc* strong, Lith *starinti* to stiffen — more at STARE] (bef. 12c) **1 a** : rigid in or as if in death **b** : rigidly conforming (as to a pattern or doctrine) : ABSOLUTE ⟨~ discipline⟩ **2** *archaic* : STRONG, ROBUST **3** : UTTER, SHEER ⟨~ nonsense⟩ **4 a** : BARREN, DESOLATE **b** (1) : having few or no ornaments : BARE ⟨a ~ white room⟩ (2) : HARSH, BLUNT ⟨the ~ realities of death⟩ **5** : sharply delineated ⟨a ~ contrast⟩ — **stark·ly** *adv* — **stark·ness** *n*

²stark *adv* (13c) **1** : in a stark manner **2** : to an absolute or complete degree : WHOLLY ⟨~ naked⟩ ⟨~ mad⟩

stark·ers \'stär-kərz\ *adj* [alter. of ¹*stark*] (ca. 1923) *chiefly Brit* : completely unclothed : NAKED

star·let \'stär-lət\ *n* (1920) : a young movie actress being coached and publicized for starring roles

star·light \-ˌlīt\ *n* (14c) : the light given by the stars

star·ling \'stär-liŋ\ *n* [ME, fr. OE *stærlinc*, fr. *stær* starling + *-ling, -linc* -ling; akin to OHG *stara* starling, L *sturnus*] (bef. 12c) : any of a family (Sturnidae, esp. genus *Sturnus*) of usu. dark gregarious oscine birds; *esp* : a dark brown or in summer glossy greenish black European bird (*S. vulgaris*) naturalized nearly worldwide and often considered a pest

star·lit \'stär-ˌlit\ *adj* (ca. 1835) : lighted by the stars

star–nosed mole \'stär-ˌnōz(d)-\ *n* (1826) : a common black long-tailed semiaquatic mole (*Condylura cristata*) of the northeastern U.S. and adjacent Canada that has a series of pink fleshy projections surrounding the nostrils

star-of–Beth·le·hem \-'beth-li-ˌhem, -lē-(h)əm\ *n* (1573) : any of various Old World bulbous herbs (genus *Ornithogalum*) of the lily family with basal leaves resembling grass; *esp* : one (*O. umbellatum*) with white flowers that is naturalized in the eastern U.S.

star of Bethlehem : a star which according to Christian tradition guided the Magi to the infant Jesus in Bethlehem

Star of Da·vid \-'dā-vəd\ *n* (ca. 1936) : MAGEN DAVID

star route *n* [so called fr. the asterisk used to designate such routes in postal publications] (1880) : a mail-delivery route in a rural or thinly populated area served by a private carrier under contract who takes mail from one post office to another or from a railroad station to a post office and usu. also delivers mail to private mailboxes along the route

star·ry \'stär-ē\ *adj* **star·ri·er; -est** (14c) **1 a** : adorned with stars; *esp* : STAR-STUDDED **b** : of, relating to, or consisting of stars : STELLAR **c** : shining like stars : SPARKLING **d** : having parts arranged like the rays of a star : STELLATE **2** : as high as or seemingly as high as the stars ⟨~ speculations⟩ **3** : STARRY-EYED

star·ry–eyed \'stär-ē-ˌīd\ *adj* (1904) : regarding an object or a prospect in an overly favorable light; *specif* : characterized by dreamy, impracticable, or utopian thinking : VISIONARY

Stars and Bars *n pl but sing in constr* (1861) : the first flag of the Confederate States of America having three bars of red, white, and red respectively and a blue union with white stars in a circle representing the seceded states

Stars and Stripes *n pl but sing in constr* (1777) : the flag of the United States having 13 alternately red and white horizontal stripes and a blue union with white stars representing the states

---

\ə\ abut \ᵊ\ kitten, F table \ər\ further \a\ ash \ā\ ace \ä\ mop, mar
\au̇\ out \ch\ chin \e\ bet \ē\ easy \g\ go \i\ hit \ī\ ice \j\ job
\ŋ\ sing \ō\ go \ȯ\ law \ȯi\ boy \th\ thin \t͟h\ the \ü\ loot \u̇\ foot
\y\ yet \zh\ vision \ȧ, k̲, ⁿ, œ, œ̄, ᵫ, ᵫ̄, ᵞ\ *see* Guide to Pronunciation

star sapphire n (ca. 1817) : a sapphire that when cut with a convex surface and polished exhibits asterism

star shell n (ca. 1876) **1** : a shell that on bursting releases a shower of brilliant stars and is used for signaling **2** : a shell with an illuminating projectile

star-ship \'stär-,ship\ n (1934) : a spacecraft designed for interstellar travel

star–span-gled \'stär-,span-gəld\ adj (1591) : STAR-STUDDED

star-struck \-,strək\ adj (1968) : particularly taken with celebrities (as movie stars)

star-stud-ded \'stär-,stə-dəd\ adj (1955) : abounding in or covered with stars ⟨a ~ cast⟩ ⟨a ~ uniform⟩

star system n (1902) : the practice of casting famous performers in principal roles (as in motion pictures or the theater) esp. in order to capitalize on their popular appeal

¹start \'stärt\ vb [ME sterten; akin to MHG sterzen to stand up stiffly, move quickly] vi (14c) **1 a** : to move suddenly and violently : SPRING ⟨~ed angrily to his feet⟩ **b** : to react with a sudden brief involuntary movement ⟨~ed when a shot rang out⟩ **2 a** : to issue with sudden force ⟨blood ~ing from the wound⟩ **b** : to come into being, activity, or operation ⟨when does the movie ~⟩ ⟨the rain ~ed up again⟩ **3** : to protrude or seem to protrude ⟨eyes ~ing from their sockets⟩ **4** : to become loosened or forced out of place ⟨one of the planks has ~ed⟩ **5 a** : to begin a course or journey ⟨~ed toward the door⟩ ⟨just ~ing out⟩ **b** : to range from a specified initial point ⟨the rates ~ at $10⟩ **6** : to begin an activity or undertaking; esp : to begin work **7 a** : to be a participant in a game or contest; esp : to be in the starting lineup ~ vt **1** : to cause to leave a place of concealment : FLUSH ⟨~ a rabbit⟩ **2** archaic : STARTLE, ALARM **3** : to bring up for consideration or discussion **4** : to bring into being ⟨~ a rumor⟩ **5** : to cause to become loosened or displaced **6** : to begin the use of ⟨~ a fresh loaf of bread⟩ **7 a** : to cause to move, act, or operate ⟨~ the motor⟩ **b** : to cause to enter a game or contest; esp : to put in the starting lineup **c** : to care for or train during the early stages of growth and development ⟨~ed plants⟩ ⟨a well-started cohound⟩ **8** : to do or experience the first stages or actions of ⟨~ed studying music at the age of five⟩ **syn** see BEGIN — **start something** also **start anything** : to make trouble ⟨always trying to start something⟩ ⟨don't start anything⟩ — **to start with 1** : at the beginning : INITIALLY **2** : in any event

²start n (14c) **1 a** : a sudden involuntary bodily movement or reaction ⟨woke with a ~⟩ **b** : a brief and sudden action or movement **c** : a sudden capricious impulse or outburst **2** : a beginning of movement, activity, or development ⟨a false ~⟩ ⟨housing ~s⟩ **3** : HEAD START **4** : a place of beginning **5** : the act or an instance of being a competitor in a race or a member of a starting lineup ⟨undefeated in six ~s —Current Biog.⟩

start-er \'stär-tər\ n (1622) **1** : a person who initiates or sets going: as **a** : an official who gives the signal to begin a race **b** : one who dispatches vehicles **2 a** : one that engages in a competition; esp : a member of a starting lineup **b** : one that begins to engage in an activity or process **3** : one that causes something to begin operating: as **a** : a device for starting an engine; esp : an electric motor used to start an internal combustion engine **b** : material containing microorganisms used to induce a desired fermentation **4** : something that is the beginning of a process, activity, or series; esp : APPETIZER — **for starters** : to begin with

star thistle n (1578) **1** : a widely naturalized spiny European knapweed (Centaurea calcitrapa) with purple flowers — called also caltrops **2** : any of various knapweeds related to the star thistle

starting block n (1937) : a device that consists of two blocks mounted on either side of an adjustable frame which is usu. anchored to the ground and that provides a runner with a rigid surface against which to brace the feet at the start of a race

starting gate n (1898) **1** : a mechanically operated barrier used as a starting device for a race **2** : a barrier that when knocked aside by a competitor (as a skier) starts an electronic timing device

¹star-tle \'stär-t⁰l\ vb star-tled; star-tling \'stärt-liŋ, 'stär-t⁰l-iŋ\ [ME stertlen, freq. of sterten to start] vi (1530) : to move or jump suddenly (as in surprise or alarm) ⟨the baby ~s easily⟩ ~ vt : to frighten or surprise suddenly and not seriously — **star-tle-ment** \-mənt\ n

²startle n (1714) : a sudden mild shock (as of surprise or alarm)

star-tling adj (1714) : causing momentary fright, surprise, or astonishment — **star-tling-ly** \'stärt-liŋ-lē, 'stär-t⁰l-iŋ-\ adv

start–up \'stärt-,əp\ n, often attrib (1845) **1** : the act or an instance of setting in operation or motion **2** : a fledgling business enterprise

star turn n (1898) chiefly Brit : the featured skit or number in a theatrical production; broadly : the most widely publicized person or item in a group

star-va-tion \stär-'vā-shən\ n (1778) **1** : the act or an instance of starving **2** : the state of being starved

starvation wages n (1898) : wages insufficient to provide the ordinary necessities of life

starve \'stärv\ vb starved; starv-ing [ME sterven to die, starve, fr. OE steorfan to die; akin to OHG sterban to die, Lith starinti to stiffen — more at STARE] vi (15c) **1 a** : to perish from lack of food **b** : to suffer extreme hunger **2** archaic : to die of cold **b** Brit : to suffer greatly from cold **3** : to suffer or perish from deprivation ⟨starved for affection⟩ ~ vt **1 a** : to kill with hunger **b** : to deprive of nourishment **c** : to cause to capitulate by or as if by depriving of nourishment **2** : to destroy or cause to suffer from deprivation **3** archaic : to kill with cold

¹starve-ling \'stärv-liŋ\ n (1546) : one that is thin from or as if from lack of food

²starveling adj (1597) : being a starveling; also : marked by poverty or inadequacy ⟨~ wages⟩

¹stash \'stash\ vt [origin unknown] (1785) : to store in a usu. secret place for future use — often used with away

²stash n (ca. 1914) **1** : hiding place : CACHE **2** : something stored or hidden away ⟨a ~ of narcotics⟩

sta-sis \'stā-səs, 'sta-\ n, pl sta-ses \-,sēz, 'sta-\ [NL, fr. Gk, act or condition of standing, stopping, fr. histasthai to stand — more at STAND] (1745) **1 a** : a slowing or stoppage of the normal flow of a bodily fluid or semifluid: as **a** : slowing of the current of circulating blood **b** : reduced motility of the intestines with retention of feces **2** : a state of static balance or equilibrium : STAGNATION

-stasis n comb form, pl **-stases** [NL, fr. Gk stasis] **1** : stoppage : slowing ⟨hemostasis⟩ **2** : stable state ⟨homeostasis⟩

stat \'stat\ n (ca. 1961) : STATISTIC

-stat n comb form [NL -stata, fr. Gk -states one that stops or steadies, fr. histanai to cause to stand — more at STAND] **1** : stabilizing agent or device ⟨thermostat⟩ **2** : instrument for reflecting (something specified) constantly in one direction ⟨heliostat⟩ **3** : agent causing inhibition of growth without destruction ⟨bacteriostat⟩

sta-tant \'stā-t⁰nt\ adj [L status, pp. + E -ant] (ca. 1500) : standing in profile with all feet on the ground — used of a heraldic animal

¹state \'stāt\ n, often attrib [ME stat, fr. OF & L; OF estat, fr. L status, fr. stare to stand — more at STAND] (13c) **1 a** : mode or condition of being ⟨a ~ of readiness⟩ **b** (1) : condition of mind or temperament ⟨in a highly nervous ~⟩ (2) : a condition of abnormal tension or excitement **2 a** : a condition or stage in the physical being of something ⟨insects in the larval ~⟩ ⟨the gaseous ~ of water⟩ **b** : any of various conditions characterized by definite quantities (as of energy, angular momentum, or magnetic moment) in which an atomic system may exist **3 a** : social position; esp : high rank **b** (1) : elaborate or luxurious style of living (2) : formal dignity : POMP — usu. used with in **4 a** : a body of persons constituting a special class in a society : ESTATE **3 b** pl : the members or representatives of the governing classes assembled in a legislative body **c** obs : a person of high rank (as a noble) **5 a** : a politically organized body of people usu. occupying a definite territory; esp : one that is sovereign **b** : the political organization of such a body of people **c** : a government or politically organized society having a particular character ⟨a police ~⟩ ⟨the welfare ~⟩ **6** : the operations or concerns of the government of a country **7 a** : one of the constituent units of a nation having a federal government ⟨the fifty ~s⟩ **b** pl, cap : The United States of America **8** : the territory of a state

²state vt stat-ed; stat-ing (1647) **1** : to set by regulation or authority **2** : to express the particulars of esp. in words : REPORT; broadly : to express in words — **stat-able** or **state-able** \'stā-tə-bəl\ adj

state aid n (1856) : public monies appropriated by a state government for the partial support or improvement of a public local institution

state bank n (1815) **1** : CENTRAL BANK **2** : a bank chartered by and operating under the laws of a state of the U.S.

state bird n (1910) : a bird selected (as by the legislature) as an emblem of a state of the U.S.

state capitalism n (1903) : an economic system in which private capitalism is modified by a varying degree of government ownership and control

state church n, often cap S&C (1726) : ESTABLISHED CHURCH

state college n (1831) : a college that is financially supported by a state government, often specializes in a branch of technical or professional education, and often forms part of the state university

state-craft \'stāt-,kraft\ n (1642) : the art of conducting state affairs

stat-ed \'stā-təd\ adj (ca. 1641) **1** : FIXED, REGULAR ⟨the president shall, at ~ times, receive . . . a compensation —U.S. Constitution⟩ **2** : set down explicitly : DECLARED ⟨our ~ intention⟩ — **stat-ed-ly** adv

stated clerk n (ca. 1909) : an executive officer of a Presbyterian general assembly, synod, or presbytery ranking below the moderator

state flower n (1898) : a flowering plant selected (as by the legislature) as an emblem of a state of the U.S.

state-hood \'stāt-,hud\ n (1868) : the condition of being a state; esp : the status of being one of the states of the U.S.

state-house \-,haus\ n (1638) : the building in which a state legislature sits

state-less \-ləs\ adj (1609) **1** : having no state **2** : lacking the status of a national ⟨a ~ refugee⟩ — **state-less-ness** n

state-ly \-lē\ adj state-li-er; -est (14c) **1 a** : marked by lofty or imposing dignity **b** : HAUGHTY, UNAPPROACHABLE **2** : impressive in size or proportions **syn** see GRAND — **state-li-ness** n — **stately** adv

state-ment \'stāt-mənt\ n (ca. 1775) **1** : something stated: as **a** : a single declaration or remark : ASSERTION **b** : a report of facts or opinions **2** : the act or process of stating or presenting orally or on paper **3** : PROPOSITION 2a **4** : the presentation of a theme in a musical composition **5** : a summary of a financial account showing the balance due **6** : an opinion, comment, or message conveyed indirectly usu. by nonverbal means ⟨monuments are ~s in form and space —O. B. Hardison, Jr.⟩ **7** : an instruction in a computer program

state of the art (1910) : the level of development (as of a device, procedure, process, technique, or science) reached at any particular time usu. as a result of modern methods — **state-of-the-art** adj

state of war (1880) **1 a** : a state of actual armed hostilities regardless of a formal declaration of war **b** : a legal state created and ended by official declaration regardless of actual armed hostilities and usu. characterized by operation of the rules of war **2** : the period of time during which a state of war is in effect

sta-ter \'stā-tər, stä-'ter\ n [ME, fr. LL, fr. Gk statēr, lit., a unit of weight, fr. histanai to cause to stand, weigh — more at STAND] (14c) : an ancient gold or silver coin of the Greek city-states

state-room \'stāt-,rüm, -,rum\ n (1660) **1** : CABIN 1a(1) **2** : a private room on a railroad car with one or more berths and a toilet

state's attorney n (1809) : a legal officer (as a district attorney) appointed or elected to represent a state in court proceedings within a district — called also state attorney

state's evidence n, often cap S (1827) : a participant in a crime or an accomplice who gives evidence for the prosecution esp. in return for a reduced sentence; also : the evidence given — used chiefly in the phrase turn state's evidence

starting block

States General *n pl* (1585) **1** : the assembly of the three orders of clergy, nobility, and third estate in France before the Revolution **2** : the legislature of the Netherlands from the 15th century to 1796

¹state·side \'stāt-₁sīd\ *adj, often cap* [(*United*) *States* + *side*] (1944) : being in, going to, coming from, or characteristic of the 48 conterminous states of the U.S. ⟨transferred from Europe to ~ duty⟩

²stateside *adv, often cap* (1945) : in or to the continental U.S.

states·man \'stāts-mən\ *n* (1592) **1** : one versed in the principles or art of government; *esp* : one actively engaged in conducting the business of a government or in shaping its policies **2** : one who exercises political leadership wisely and without narrow partisanship — **states·man-like** \-₁līk\ *adj* — **states·man·ly** \-lē\ *adj* — **states·man·ship** \-₁ship\ *n*

state socialism *n* (1879) : an economic system with limited socialist characteristics introduced by usu. gradual political action

states' right·er \'stāts-'rī-tər\ *n* (1945) : one who advocates strict interpretation of the U.S. constitutional guarantee of states' rights

states' rights *n pl* (1858) : all rights not vested by the Constitution of the U.S. in the federal government nor forbidden by it to the separate states

state tree *n* (1917) : a tree selected (as by the legislature) as an emblem of a state of the U.S.

state university *n* (1831) : a university maintained and administered by one of the states of the U.S. as part of the state public educational system

¹state·wide \'stāt-'wīd\ *adj* (1911) : affecting or extending throughout all parts of a state

²statewide *adv* (ca. 1934) : throughout the state

¹stat·ic \'sta-tik\ *adj* [NL *staticus*, fr. Gk *statikos* causing to stand, skilled in weighing, fr. *histanai* to cause to stand, weigh — more at STAND] (1638) **1** : exerting force by reason of weight alone without motion **2** : of or relating to bodies at rest or forces in equilibrium **3** : showing little change ⟨a ~ population⟩ **4 a** : characterized by a lack of movement, animation, or progression **b** : producing an effect of repose or quiescence ⟨a ~ design⟩ **5 a** : standing or fixed in one place : STATIONARY **b** *of water* : stored in a tank but not under pressure **6** : of, relating to, or producing stationary charges of electricity : ELECTROSTATIC **7** : of, relating to, or caused by radio static — **stat·i-cal** \-ti-kəl\ *adj* — **stat·i·cal·ly** \-ti-k(ə-)lē\ *adv*

²static *n* [*static electricity*] (1913) **1** : noise produced in a radio or television receiver by atmospheric or various natural or man-made electrical disturbances; *also* : the electrical disturbances producing this noise **2** : heated opposition or criticism — **stat·icky** \'sta-ti-kē\ *adj*

-static *adj comb form* [NL *-staticus*, fr. *staticus*] **1** : of or relating to a position or state ⟨ortho*static*⟩ **2** : inhibiting the growth of ⟨fungi*static*⟩

stat·i·ce \'sta-tə-(₁)sē\ *n* [NL, genus of herbs, fr. L, an astringent plant, fr. Gk *statikē*, fr. fem. of *statikos* causing to stand, astringent] (1745) : SEA LAVENDER

static electricity *n* (1876) : electricity that consists of isolated motionless charges (as those produced by friction)

static line *n* (1930) : a cord attached to a parachute pack and to an airplane to open the parachute after a jumper clears the plane

stat·ics \'sta-tiks\ *n pl but sing or pl in constr* (1837) : mechanics dealing with the relations of forces that produce equilibrium among material bodies

static tube *n* (1923) : a tube used for indicating static as distinct from impact pressure in a stream of fluid

¹sta·tion \'stā-shən\ *n* [ME *stacioun*, fr. MF *station*, fr. L *station-, statio*, fr. *stare* to stand — more at STAND] (14c) **1 a** : the place or position in which something or someone stands or is assigned to stand or remain **b** : any of the places in a manufacturing operation at which one part of the work is done **c** : equipment used usu. by one person for performing a particular job **2** : the act or manner of standing : POSTURE **3** : a stopping place: as **a** (1) : a regular stopping place in a transportation route (2) : the building connected with such a stopping place : DEPOT **3 b** : one of the stations of the cross **4 a** : a post or sphere of duty or occupation **b** : a stock farm or ranch esp. of Australia or New Zealand **5** : STANDING, RANK ⟨a woman of high ~⟩ **6** : a place for specialized observation and study of scientific phenomena ⟨a seismological ~⟩ ⟨a marine biological ~⟩ **7** : a place established to provide a public service: as **a** (1) : FIRE STATION (2) : POLICE STATION **b** : a branch post office **8** : SERVICE STATION 1 **9 a** : a complete assemblage of radio or television equipment for transmitting or receiving **b** : the place in which such a station is located

²station *vt* **sta·tioned; sta·tion·ing** \'stā-sh(ə-)niŋ\ (1748) : to assign to or set in a station or position : POST

sta·tion·al \'stā-shnəl, -shə-nᵊl\ *adj* (1902) : of, relating to, or being a mass formerly celebrated by the pope at designated churches in Rome on appointed holy days

sta·tion·ary \'stā-shə-₁ner-ē\ *adj* (1626) **1** : fixed in a station, course, or mode : IMMOBILE **2** : unchanging in condition

stationary bicycle *n* (1962) : an exercise apparatus that can be pedaled like a bicycle — called also *stationary bike*

stationary front *n* (ca. 1940) : the boundary between two air masses neither of which is replacing the other

stationary wave *n* (1856) : STANDING WAVE

station break *n* (1937) : a pause in a radio or television broadcast for announcement of the identity of the network or station; *also* : an announcement or advertisement during this pause

sta·tio·ner \'stā-sh(ə-)nər\ *n* [ME *staciouner*, fr. ML *stationarius*, fr. *station-, statio* shop, fr. L, station] (14c) **1** *archaic* **a** : BOOKSELLER **b** : PUBLISHER **2** : one that sells stationery

sta·tio·nery \'stā-shə-₁ner-ē\ *n* [*stationer*] (ca. 1688) **1** : materials (as paper, pens, and ink) for writing or typing **2** : letter paper usu. accompanied with matching envelopes

station house *n* (1833) : a house at a post or station; *esp* : POLICE STATION

sta·tion·mas·ter \'stā-shən-₁mas-tər\ *n* (1856) : an official in charge of the operation of a railroad station

stations of the cross *often cap S&C* (ca. 1890) **1** : a series of usu. 14 images or pictures esp. in a church that represent the stages of Christ's passion and death **2** : a devotion involving commemorative meditation before the stations of the cross

station wagon *n* (1904) : an automobile that has a passenger compartment which extends to the back of the vehicle, that has no trunk, that has one or more rear seats which can be folded down to make space for light cargo, and that has a tailgate or liftgate

stat·ism \'stā-₁ti-zəm\ *n* (1880) : concentration of economic controls and planning in the hands of a highly centralized government

stat·ist \'stā-tist\ *n* (1946) : an advocate of statism — **statist** *adj*

sta·tis·tic \stə-'tis-tik\ *n* [sing. of *statistics*] (1880) **1** : a single term or datum in a collection of statistics **2 a** : a quantity (as the mean of a sample) that is computed from a sample; *specif* : ESTIMATE 3b **b** : a random variable that takes on the possible values of a statistic

sta·tis·ti·cal \-ti-kəl\ *adj* (1787) : of, relating to, based on, or employing the principles of statistics — **sta·tis·ti·cal·ly** \-k(ə-)lē\ *adv*

statistical mechanics *n pl but usu sing in constr* (1885) : a branch of mechanics dealing with the application of the principles of statistics to the mechanics of a system consisting of a large number of parts having motions that differ by small steps over a large range

stat·is·ti·cian \₁sta-tə-'sti-shən\ *n* (1825) : one versed in or engaged in compiling statistics

sta·tis·tics \stə-'tis-tiks\ *n pl but sing or pl in constr* [G *Statistik* study of political facts and figures, fr. NL *statisticus* of politics, fr. L *status* state] (1770) **1** : a branch of mathematics dealing with the collection, analysis, interpretation, and presentation of masses of numerical data **2** : a collection of quantitative data

sta·tive \'stā-tiv\ *adj* (1874) : expressing a state, condition, or relation — compare ACTIVE 3b

stato- *comb form* [ISV, fr. Gk *statos* stationary, fr. *histasthai* to stand — more at STAND] **1** : resting ⟨*stato*blast⟩ **2** : equilibrium ⟨*stato*cyst⟩

stato·blast \'sta-tə-₁blast\ *n* [ISV] (1855) **1** : a bud in a freshwater bryozoan that overwinters in a chitinous envelope and develops into a new individual in spring **2** : GEMMULE b

stato·cyst \-₁sist\ *n* [ISV] (1902) : an organ of equilibrium occurring esp. among invertebrate animals and consisting usu. of a fluid-filled vesicle in which are suspended statoliths

stato·lith \'sta-tᵊl-₁ith\ *n* [ISV] (1900) **1** : any of the usu. calcareous bodies suspended in a statocyst **2** : any of various starch grains or other solid bodies in the plant cytoplasm that are held to be responsible by changes in their position for changes in orientation of a part or organ

sta·tor \'stā-tər\ *n* [NL, fr. L, one that stands, fr. *stare* to stand — more at STAND] (1902) : a stationary part in a machine in or about which a rotor revolves

stato·scope \'sta-tə-₁skōp\ *n* [ISV] (ca. 1900) : a sensitive aneroid barometer for recording small changes in atmospheric pressure; *esp* : one used for indicating small changes in the altitude of an aircraft

¹stat·u·ary \'sta-chə-₁wer-ē\ *n, pl* **-ar·ies** (1542) **1** : SCULPTOR **2 a** : the art of making statues **b** : a collection of statues : STATUES

²statuary *adj* (1627) : of, relating to, or suitable for statues

stat·ue \'sta-(₁)chü\ *n* [ME, fr. MF, fr. L *statua*, fr. *statuere* to set up — more at STATUTE] (14c) : a three-dimensional representation usu. of a person, animal, or mythical being that is produced by sculpturing, modeling, or casting

Statue of Liberty (ca. 1900) **1** : a large copper statue of a woman holding a torch aloft in her right hand located on Liberty Island in New York harbor **2** : a trick played in football in which the ballcarrier takes the ball from the raised hand of a teammate who is faking a pass

stat·u·esque \₁sta-chə-'wesk\ *adj* (1834) : resembling a statue esp. in dignity, shapeliness, or stillness; *esp* : tall and shapely — **stat·u·esque·ly** *adv*

stat·u·ette \₁sta-chə-'wet\ *n* (1843) : a small statue

stat·ure \'sta-chər\ *n* [ME, fr. MF, fr. L *statura*, fr. *status*, pp. of *stare* to stand — more at STAND] (14c) **1** : natural height (as of a person) in an upright position **2** : quality or status gained by growth, development, or achievement

sta·tus \'stā-təs, 'sta-\ *n, pl* **sta·tus·es** *often attrib* [L — more at STATE] (1791) **1** : the condition of a person or thing in the eyes of the law **2 a** : position or rank in relation to others ⟨the ~ of a father⟩ **b** : relative rank in a hierarchy of prestige; *esp* : high prestige **3** : state of affairs

status offender *n* (ca. 1976) : a young offender (as a runaway or a truant) who is under the jurisdiction of a court for repeated offenses that are not crimes

status quo \-'kwō\ *n* [L, state in which] (1833) : the existing state of affairs ⟨seeks to preserve the *status quo*⟩

status quo an·te \-'an-tē\ *n* [L, state in which previously] (1877) : the state of affairs that existed previously

sta·tusy \'stā-tə-sē, 'sta-\ *adj* (1962) : having, showing, or conferring prestige

stat·ut·able \'sta-chə-tə-bəl, 'sta-₁chü-\ *adj* (1636) : made, regulated, or imposed by or in conformity to statute : STATUTORY ⟨~ tonnage⟩

stat·ute \'sta-(₁)chüt, -chət\ *n* [ME, fr. OF *statut*, fr. LL *statutum* law, regulation, fr. L, neut. of *statutus*, pp. of *statuere* to set up, station, fr. *status* position, state] (14c) **1** : a law enacted by the legislative branch of a government **2** : an act of a corporation or of its founder intended as a permanent rule **3** : an international instrument setting up an agency and regulating its scope or authority *syn* see LAW

statute book *n* (1593) : the whole body of legislation of a given jurisdiction whether or not published as a whole — usu. used in pl.

statute mile *n* (1862) : MILE 1a

statute of limitations (1768) : a statute assigning a certain time after which rights cannot be enforced by legal action or offenses cannot be punished

stat·u·to·ry \'sta-chə-₁tōr-ē, -₁tòr-\ *adj* (1766) **1** : of or relating to statutes **2** : enacted, created, or regulated by statute ⟨a ~ age limit⟩ — **stat·u·to·ri·ly** \₁sta-chə-'tōr-ə-lē, -'tòr-\ *adv*

statutory rape *n* (1898) : sexual intercourse with a person who is below the statutory age of consent

---

\ə\ abut \ᵊ\ kitten, F table \ər\ further \a\ ash \ā\ ace \ä\ mop, mar
\aᵘ\ out \ch\ chin \e\ bet \ē\ easy \g\ go \i\ hit \ī\ ice \j\ job
\ŋ\ sing \ō\ go \ò\ law \òi\ boy \th\ thin \t̲h̲\ the \ü\ loot \u̇\ foot
\y\ yet \zh\ vision \à, k̲, ⁿ, œ, œ̄, ᵫ, ᵫ̄, �окь\ *see* Guide to Pronunciation

¹**staunch** \'stònch, 'stänch\ *var of* STANCH

²**staunch** *adj* [ME, fr. MF *estanche*, fem. of *estanc*, fr. OF, fr. *estancher* to stanch — more at STANCH] (15c) **1 a** : WATERTIGHT, SOUND **b** : strongly built : SUBSTANTIAL **2** : steadfast in loyalty or principle *syn* see FAITHFUL — **staunch·ly** *adv* — **staunch·ness** *n*

stau·ro·lite \'stòr-ə-‚līt\ *n* [F, fr. Gk *stauros* cross + F *-lite* — more at STEER] (ca. 1815) : a mineral consisting of a basic silicate of iron and aluminum in prismatic orthorhombic crystals often twinned so as to resemble a cross — **stau·ro·lit·ic** \‚stòr-ə-'li-tik\ *adj*

¹**stave** \'stāv\ *n* [ME, back-formation fr. *staves*, pl. of *staf* staff] (13c) **1** : ¹STAFF 1, 2 **2** : any of the narrow strips of wood or narrow iron plates placed edge to edge to form the sides, covering, or lining of a vessel (as a barrel) or structure **3** : STANZA **4** : ¹STAFF 3

²**stave** *vb* **staved** *or* **stove** \'stōv\; **stav·ing** *vt* (ca. 1595) **1** : to break in the staves of (a cask) **2** : to smash a hole in ⟨*stove* in the boat⟩; *also* : to crush or break inward ⟨*staved* in several ribs⟩ **3** : to drive or thrust away ~ *vi* **1** *archaic* : to become stove in — used of a boat or ship **2** : to walk or move rapidly

stave off *vt* (1624) **1** : to fend off ⟨*staving off* creditors⟩ **2** : to ward off (as something adverse) : FORESTALL ⟨trying to *stave off* disaster⟩

staves *pl of* STAFF

staves·acre \'stāv-‚zā-kər\ *n* [by folk etymology fr. ME *staphisagre*, fr. ML *staphis agria*, fr. Gk, lit., wild raisin] (15c) : a Eurasian delphinium (*Delphinium staphisagria*); *also* : its violently emetic and cathartic seeds

¹**stay** \'stā\ *n* [ME, fr. OE *stæg*; akin to ON *stag* stay, OE *stēle* steel] (bef. 12c) **1** : a large strong rope usu. of wire used to support a mast **2** : ¹GUY

²**stay** *vt* (1627) **1** : to secure upright with or as if with stays **2** : to incline (a mast) forward, aft, or to one side by the stays ~ *vi* : to go about : TACK

³**stay** *vb* **stayed** \'stād\ *also* **staid** \'stād\; **stay·ing** [ME, fr. MF *ester* to stand, stay, fr. L *stare* — more at STAND] *vi* (15c) **1** : to stop going forward : PAUSE **2** : to stop doing something : CEASE **3** : to continue in a place or condition : REMAIN ⟨~ed up all night⟩ ⟨went for a short vacation but ~ed on for weeks⟩ ⟨~ put till I come back⟩ **4** : to stand firm **5** : to take up residence : LODGE **6** : to keep even in a contest or rivalry ⟨~ with the leaders⟩ **7** : to call a poker bet without raising **8** *obs* : to be in waiting or attendance ~ *vt* **1** : to wait for : AWAIT **2** : to stick or remain with (as a race or trial of endurance) to the end — usu. used in the phrase *stay the course* **3** : to remain during ⟨~ed the whole time⟩ **4 a** : to stop or delay the proceeding or advance of by or as if by interposing an obstacle : HALT ⟨~ an execution⟩ **b** : to check the course of (as a disease) **c** : ALLAY, PACIFY ⟨~ed tempers⟩ **d** : to quiet the hunger of temporarily *syn* see DEFER

⁴**stay** *n* (1536) **1 a** : the action of halting : the state of being stopped **b** : a stopping or suspension of procedure or execution by judicial or executive order **2** *obs* : SELF-CONTROL, MODERATION **3** : a residence or sojourn in a place **4** : capacity for endurance

⁵**stay** *n* [MF *estaie*, of Gmc origin; akin to OHG *stān* to stand — more at STAND] (1515) **1** : one that serves as a prop : SUPPORT **2** : a corset stiffened with bones — usu. used in pl.

⁶**stay** *vt* (1548) **1** : to provide physical or moral support for : SUSTAIN **2** : to fix on something as a foundation

stay-at–home \'stā-ət-‚hōm\ *adj* (1806) : remaining habitually in one's residence, locality, or country — **stay–at–home** *n*

stay·er \'stā-ər\ *n* (ca. 1580) : one that stays; *esp* : one that upholds or supports

staying power *n* (1859) : capacity for endurance : STAMINA

stay·sail \'stā-‚sāl, -səl\ *n* (1669) : a fore-and-aft sail hoisted on a stay — see SAIL illustration

STD \‚es-(‚)tē-'dē\ *n* [sexually transmitted disease] (1976) : any of various diseases transmitted by direct sexual contact that include the classic venereal diseases (as syphilis, gonorrhea, and chancroid) and other diseases (as hepatitis A, hepatitis B, giardiasis, and AIDS) that are often or sometimes contracted by other than sexual means

¹**stead** \'sted\ *n* [ME *stede*, fr. OE; akin to OHG *stat* place, OE *standan* to stand — more at STAND] (bef. 12c) **1** : LOCALITY, PLACE **2** : AD-VANTAGE — used chiefly in the phrase *to stand one in good stead* **3** : the office, place, or function ordinarily occupied or carried out by someone or something else ⟨acted in his brother's ~⟩

²**stead** *vt* (13c) : to be of avail to : HELP

stead·fast \'sted-‚fast *also* -fəst\ *adj* [ME *stedefast*, fr. OE *stedefæst*, fr. *stede* + *fæst* fixed, fast] (bef. 12c) **1 a** : firmly fixed in place : IMMOV-ABLE **b** : not subject to change ⟨the ~ doctrine of original sin —Ellen Glasgow⟩ **2** : firm in belief, determination, or adherence : LOYAL *syn* see FAITHFUL — **stead·fast·ly** *adv* — **stead·fast·ness** \-‚fas(t)-nəs, -fəs(t)-\ *n*

stead·ing \'ste-dⁿn, 'ste-, -diŋ\ *n* [ME *steding*, fr. *stede* place, farm] (15c) **1** : a small farm **2** *chiefly Scot* : the service buildings or area of a farm

¹**steady** \'ste-dē\ *adj* **steadi·er; -est** [ME *stedy*, fr. *stede*] (14c) **1 a** : direct or sure in movement : UNFALTERING **b** : firm in position : FIXED **c** : keeping nearly upright in a seaway ⟨~ a ship⟩ **2 a** : showing little variation or fluctuation : STABLE, UNIFORM ⟨a ~ breeze⟩ ⟨~ prices⟩ **3 a** : not easily disturbed or upset ⟨~ nerves⟩ **b** (1) : constant in feeling, principle, purpose, or attachment (2) : DEPENDABLE **c** : not given to dissipation : SOBER — **steadi·ly** \'ste-d³l-ē\ *adv* — **stea·di·ness** \'ste-dē-nəs\ *n*
syn STEADY, EVEN, EQUABLE mean not varying throughout a course or extent. STEADY implies lack of fluctuation or interruption of movement ⟨*steady* progress⟩. EVEN suggests a lack of variation in quality or character ⟨an *even* distribution⟩. EQUABLE implies lack of extremes or of sudden sharp changes ⟨maintain an *equable* temper⟩.

²**steady** *vb* **stead·ied; steady·ing** *vt* (1530) **1** : to make or keep steady ~ *vi* : to become steady — **steadi·er** *n*

³**steady** *adv* (ca. 1605) **1** : in a steady manner : STEADILY **2** : on the course set — used as a direction to the helmsman of a ship

⁴**steady** *n, pl* **stead·ies** (1792) : one that is steady; *specif* : a boyfriend or girlfriend with whom one goes steady

steady state *n* (1885) : a state or condition of a system or process (as one of the energy states of an atom) that does not change in time; *broadly* : a condition that changes only negligibly over a specified time

steady state theory *n* (1948) : a theory in astronomy: the universe has always existed and has always been expanding with hydrogen being created continuously — compare BIG BANG THEORY

steak \'stāk\ *n* [ME *steke*, fr. ON *steik*; akin to ON *steikja* to roast on a stake, *stik* stick, stake — more at STICK] (15c) **1 a** : a slice of meat cut from a fleshy part of a beef carcass **b** : a similar slice of a specified meat other than beef ⟨ham ~⟩ **c** : a cross-section slice of a large fish ⟨swordfish ~⟩ **2** : ground beef prepared for cooking or for serving in the manner of a steak ⟨hamburger ~⟩

steak house *n* (1762) : a restaurant whose specialty is beefsteak

steak knife *n* (1895) : a table knife with a sharp often serrated blade

steak tar·tare \-tär-'tär\ *n* [F *tartare* Tartar] (1911) : highly seasoned ground beef eaten raw

¹**steal** \'stē(ə)l\ *vb* **stole** \'stōl\; **sto·len** \'stō-lən\; **steal·ing** [ME *stelen*, fr. OE *stelan*; akin to OHG *stelan* to steal] (bef. 12c) **1** : to take the property of another wrongfully and esp. as an habitual or regular practice **2** : to come or go secretly, unobtrusively, gradually, or unexpectedly **3** : to steal or attempt to steal a base ~ *vt* **1 a** : to take or appropriate without right or leave and with intent to keep or make use of wrongfully ⟨*stole* a car⟩ **b** : to take away by force or unjust means ⟨they've *stolen* our liberty⟩ **c** : to take surreptitiously or without permission ⟨~ a kiss⟩ **d** : to appropriate to oneself or beyond one's proper share : make oneself the focus of ⟨~ the show⟩ **2 a** : to move, convey, or introduce secretly : SMUGGLE **b** : to accomplish in a concealed or unobserved manner ⟨~ a visit⟩ **3 a** : to seize, gain, or win by trickery, skill, or daring ⟨a basketball player adept at ~ing the ball⟩ ⟨*stole* the election⟩ **b** *of a base runner* : to reach (a base) safely solely by running and usu. catching the opposing team off guard — **steal·able** \'stē-lə-bəl\ *adj* — **steal·er** *n* — **steal a march on** : to gain an advantage on unobserved — **steal one's thunder** : to grab attention from another esp. by anticipating an idea, plan, or presentation; *also* : to claim credit for another's idea
syn STEAL, PILFER, FILCH, PURLOIN mean to take from another without right or without detection. STEAL may apply to any surreptitious taking of something and differs from the other terms by commonly applying to intangibles as well as material things ⟨*steal* jewels⟩ ⟨*stole* a look at the gifts⟩. PILFER implies stealing repeatedly in small amounts ⟨*pilfered* from his employer⟩. FILCH adds a suggestion of snatching quickly and surreptitiously ⟨*filched* an apple from the tray⟩. PURLOIN stresses removing or carrying off for one's own use or purposes ⟨printed a *purloined* document⟩.

²**steal** *n* (ca. 1825) **1** : the act or an instance of stealing **2** : a fraudulent or questionable political deal **3** : BARGAIN 2 ⟨it's a ~ at that price⟩

stealth \'stelth\ *n* [ME *stelthe*; akin to OE *stelan* to steal] (13c) **1 a** *archaic* : THEFT **b** *obs* : something stolen **2** : the act or action of proceeding furtively, secretly, or imperceptibly ⟨the state moves by ~ to gather information —Nat Hentoff⟩ **3** : the state of being furtive or unobtrusive **4** : an aircraft-design characteristic consisting of oblique angular construction and avoidance of vertical surfaces that is intended to produce a very weak radar return

stealthy \'stel-thē\ *adj* **stealth·i·er; -est** (1605) **1** : slow, deliberate, and secret in action or character **2** : intended to escape observation : FURTIVE *syn* see SECRET — **stealth·i·ly** \-thə-lē\ *adv* — **stealth·i·ness** \-thē-nəs\ *n*

¹**steam** \'stēm\ *n* [ME *stem*, fr. OE *stēam*; akin to D *stoom* steam] (bef. 12c) **1** : a vapor arising from a heated substance **2 a** : the invisible vapor into which water is converted when heated to the boiling point **b** : the mist formed by the condensation on cooling of water vapor **3 a** : water vapor kept under pressure so as to supply energy for heating, cooking, or mechanical work; *also* : the power so generated **b** : active force : POWER, MOMENTUM ⟨got there under his own ~⟩ ⟨sales began to pick up ~⟩; *also* : normal force ⟨at full ~⟩ **c** : pent-up emotional tension ⟨needed to let off a little ~⟩ **4 a** : STEAMER 2a **b** : travel by or a trip in a steamer

²**steam** *vt* (15c) **1** : to give out as fumes : EXHALE **2** : to apply steam to; *esp* : to expose to the action of steam (as for softening or cooking) ~ *vi* **1** : to rise or pass off as vapor **2** : to give off steam or vapor **3 a** : to move or travel by the agency of steam **b** : to move or proceed with energy or force **4** : to be angry : BOIL ⟨~ing over the insult⟩

steam·boat \'stēm-‚bōt\ *n* (1785) : a boat driven by steam power; *specif* : a shallow-draft vessel used on inland waterways

steamboat Gothic *n* [fr. its use in homes of retired steamboat captains in imitation of the style of river steamboats] (1941) : an elaborately ornamented architectural style used in homes built in the middle 19th century in the Ohio and Mississippi river valleys

steam boiler *n* (1805) : a boiler for producing steam

steam chest *n* (1797) : the chamber from which steam is distributed to a cylinder of a steam engine

steamed \'stēmd\ *adj* (1802) **1** : cooked by steam **2** : ANGRY 1 — often used with *up*

steam engine *n* (1751) : an engine driven or worked by steam; *specif* : a reciprocating engine having a piston driven in a closed cylinder by steam

steam·er \'stē-mər\ *n* (1814) **1** : a vessel in which articles are subjected to steam **2 a** : a ship propelled by steam **b** : an engine, machine, or vehicle operated or propelled by steam **3** : one that steams **4** : SOFT-SHELL CLAM

steamer rug *n* (1890) : a warm covering for the lap and feet esp. of a person sitting on a ship's deck

steamer trunk *n* (1886) : a trunk suitable for use in a stateroom of a steamer; *esp* : a shallow trunk that may be stowed beneath a berth

steam-fit·ter \'stēm-‚fi-tər\ *n* (ca. 1890) : one that installs or repairs equipment (as steam pipes) for heating, ventilating, or refrigerating systems — **steam fitting** *n*

steam iron *n* (ca. 1943) : a pressing iron with a compartment holding water that is converted to steam by the iron's heat and emitted through the soleplate onto the fabric being pressed

¹**steam·roll·er** \'stēm-‚rō-lər\ *n* (1866) **1** : a steam-driven road roller; *broadly* : ROAD ROLLER **2** : a crushing force esp. when ruthlessly applied to overcome opposition

²**steamroller** *or* **steam-roll** \-‚rōl\ *vt* (1879) **1** : to overwhelm usu. by greatly superior force ⟨~ the opposition⟩ **2** : to bring or advance by

overwhelming force or pressure ⟨∼ed the bill through the legislature⟩ ∼ *vi* : to move or proceed with irresistible force

steam·ship \'stēm-ˌship\ *n* (1790) : STEAMER 2a

steamship round *n* (1964) : a large beef roast consisting of the whole round with rump and heel

steam shovel *n* (1879) : a power shovel operated by steam; *broadly* : POWER SHOVEL

steam table *n* (1861) : a table having openings to hold containers of cooked food over steam or hot water circulating beneath them

steam turbine *n* (1900) : a turbine that is driven by the pressure of steam discharged at high velocity against the turbine vanes

steam up *vt* (1860) : to make angry or excited : AROUSE

steamy \'stē-mē\ *adj* **steam·i·er; -est** (1644) **1** : consisting of, characterized by, or full of steam **2** : intensely or uncomfortably hot: as **a** : hot and humid ⟨a ∼ afternoon⟩ **b** : sensually hot : EROTIC ⟨a ∼ love scene⟩ — **steam·i·ly** \-mə-lē\ *adv* — **steam·i·ness** \-mē-nəs\ *n*

ste·ap·sin \stē-'ap-sən\ *n* [Gk *stear* hard fat + E *-psin* (as in *pepsin*)] (1896) : the lipase in pancreatic juice

stea·rate \'stē-ə-ˌrāt, 'sti(-ə)r-ˌāt\ *n* (1841) : a salt or ester of stearic acid

stea·ric acid \stē-'ar-ik-, 'sti(ə)r-ik-\ *n* (1831) : a white crystalline fatty acid $C_{18}H_{36}O_2$ obtained by saponifying tallow or other hard fats containing stearin; *also* : a commercial mixture of stearic and palmitic acids

stea·rin \'stē-ə-rən, 'stir-ən\ *n* [F *stéarine*, fr. Gk *stear*] (1817) : an ester of glycerol and stearic acid

ste·a·tite \'stē-ə-ˌtīt\ *n* [L *steatitis*, a precious stone, fr. Gk, fr. *steat-, stear*] (1758) **1** : a massive talc having a grayish green or brown color : SOAPSTONE **2** : an electrically insulating porcelain composed largely of steatite — **ste·a·tit·ic** \ˌstē-ə-'ti-tik\ *adj*

steato- *comb form* [Gk, fr. *steat-, stear;* perh. akin to Skt *styāyate* it hardens] : fat ⟨*steatorrhea*⟩

ste·a·to·py·gia \ˌstē-a-tə-'pi-j(ē-)ə, -'pī-\ *n* [NL, fr. *steat-, stear* + Gk *pygē* buttocks] (1879) : an excessive development of fat on the buttocks that occurs esp. among women of the Hottentots and some black peoples — **ste·a·to·py·gous** \-gəs\ *or* **ste·a·to·py·gic** \ˌstē-ə-'tä-pə-jik, -tə-'pī-jik\ *adj*

ste·at·or·rhea \(ˌ)stē-ˌa-tə-'rē-ə\ *n* [NL] (ca. 1859) : an excess of fat in the stools

stedfast *var of* STEADFAST

steed \'stēd\ *n* [ME *stede*, fr. OE *stēda* stallion; akin to OE *stōd* stud — more at STUD] (bef. 12c) : HORSE; *esp* : a spirited horse (as for war)

steek \'stēk\ *vb* [ME *steken* to pierce, fix, enclose; akin to OE *stician* to pierce — more at STICK] (13c) *chiefly Scot* : SHUT, CLOSE

¹steel \'stē(ə)l\ *n* [ME *stele*, fr. OE *stȳle, stēle;* akin to OHG *stahal* steel and perh. to Skt *stakati* he resists] (bef. 12c) **1** : commercial iron that contains carbon in any amount up to about 1.7 percent as an essential alloying constituent, is malleable when under suitable conditions, and is distinguished from cast iron by its malleability and lower carbon content **2** : an instrument or implement of or characteristically of steel: as **a** : a thrusting or cutting weapon **b** : an instrument (as a fluted round rod with a handle) for sharpening knives **c** : a piece of steel for striking sparks from flint **3** : a quality (as hardness of mind or spirit) that suggests steel ⟨nerves of ∼⟩ **4 a** : the steel manufacturing industry **b** *pl* : shares of stock in steel companies

²steel *vt* (13c) **1** : to overlay, point, or edge with steel **2 a** : to cause to resemble steel (as in looks or hardness) **b** : to fill with resolution or determination

³steel *adj* (13c) **1** : made of steel **2** : of or relating to the production of steel **3** : resembling steel

steel band *n* (1949) : a band of steel drums

steel blue *n* (1817) **1** : a grayish blue **2** : any of the blue colors assumed by steel at various temperatures in tempering

steel drum *n* (1952) : a musical instrument orig. developed in Trinidad that is played by hammering raised and tuned portions of the bottom of an oil drum

steel engraving *n* (1824) **1** : the art or process of engraving on steel **2** : an impression taken from an engraved steel plate

steel guitar *n* (1925) **1** : HAWAIIAN GUITAR **2** : PEDAL STEEL — **steel guitarist** *n*

steel·head \'stē(ə)l-ˌhed\ *n, pl* **steelhead** *also* **steelheads** (ca. 1882) : an anadromous rainbow trout

steel·ie *also* **steely** \'stē-lē\ *n, pl* **steel·ies** (1922) : a steel playing marble

steel·mak·er \'stē(ə)l-ˌmā-kər\ *n* (1839) : a manufacturer of steel — **steel·mak·ing** \-kiŋ\ *n*

steel–trap \'stē(ə)l-'trap\ *adj* (1945) : QUICK, INCISIVE ⟨a ∼ mind⟩

steel wool *n* (1896) : an abrasive material composed of long fine steel shavings and used esp. for scouring and burnishing

steel·work \'stē(ə)l-ˌwərk\ *n* (1681) **1** : work in steel **2** *pl but sing or pl in constr* : an establishment where steel is made

steel·work·er \-ˌwər-kər\ *n* (1884) : one who works in steel and esp. in the manufacturing of it

steely \'stē-lē\ *adj* **steel·i·er; -est** (1509) **1** : resembling or suggesting steel (as in hardness, color, strength, or coldness) ⟨∼ determination⟩ ⟨∼ blue⟩ **2** : made of steel — **steel·i·ness** *n*

steel·yard \'stē(ə)l-ˌyärd, 'stil-yərd\ *n* [prob. fr. ³steel + ⁴yard (rod)] (1639) : a balance in which an object to be weighed is suspended from the shorter arm of a lever and the weight determined by moving a counterpoise along a graduated scale on the longer arm until equilibrium is attained

steelyard

steen·bok \'stēn-ˌbäk, 'stän-\ *or* **stein·bok** \'stīn-, 'stän-\ *n* [Afrik *steenbok;* akin to OE *stānbucca* ibex, fr. *stān* stone, *bucca* buck] (1775) : a small slender antelope (*Raphicerus campestris*) with long legs that inhabits chiefly grasslands of eastern and southern Africa

¹steep \'stēp\ *adj* [ME *stepe*, fr. OE *stēap* high, steep, deep; akin to MHG *stief* steep] (bef. 12c) **1** : LOFTY, HIGH — used chiefly of a sea **2** : making a large angle with the plane of the horizon **3 a** : mounting

or falling precipitously ⟨the stairs were very ∼⟩ **b** : being or characterized by a rapid and intensive decline or increase **4** : extremely or excessively high ⟨∼ prices⟩ — **steep·ish** \'stē-pish\ *adj* — **steep·ly** *adv* — **steep·ness** *n*

syn STEEP, ABRUPT, PRECIPITOUS, SHEER mean having an incline approaching the perpendicular. STEEP implies such sharpness of pitch that ascent or descent is very difficult ⟨a *steep* hill⟩ ⟨a *steep* dive⟩. ABRUPT implies a sharper pitch and a sudden break in the level ⟨a beach with an *abrupt* drop-off⟩. PRECIPITOUS applies to an incline approaching the vertical ⟨the river winds through a *precipitous* gorge⟩. SHEER suggests an unbroken perpendicular expanse ⟨*sheer* cliffs that daunted the climbers⟩.

²steep *n* (1555) : a precipitous place

³steep *vb* [ME *stepen;* akin to Sw *stöpa* to steep] *vt* (14c) **1** : to soak in a liquid at a temperature under the boiling point (as for softening, bleaching, or extracting an essence) **2** : to cover with or plunge into a liquid (as in bathing, rinsing, or soaking) **3** : to saturate with or subject thoroughly to (some strong or pervading influence) ⟨practices ∼ed in tradition⟩ ∼ *vi* : to undergo the process of soaking in a liquid **syn** *see* SOAK — **steep·er** *n*

⁴steep *n* (15c) **1** : the state or process of being steeped **2** : a bath or solution in which something is steeped

steep·en \'stē-pən, -pᵊm\ *vb* **steep·ened; steep·en·ing** \'stē-pə-niŋ, 'stēp-niŋ\ *vi* (1847) : to become steeper ∼ *vt* : to make steeper

stee·ple \'stē-pəl\ *n* [ME *stepel*, fr. OE *stēpel* tower; akin to OE *stēap* steep] (bef. 12c) : a tall structure usu. having a small spire at the top and surmounting a church tower; *broadly* : a whole church tower — **stee·pled** \-pəld\ *adj*

stee·ple·bush \'stē-pəl-ˌbush\ *n* (ca. 1818) : HARDHACK

stee·ple·chase \-ˌchās\ *n* [fr. the use of church steeples as landmarks to guide the riders] (1793) **1 a** : a horse race across country **b** : a horse race over a closed course with obstacles (as hedges and walls) **2** : a footrace of usu. 3000 meters over hurdles and a water jump — **stee·ple·chas·er** \-ˌchā-sər\ *n* — **stee·ple·chas·ing** \-siŋ\ *n*

stee·ple·jack \-ˌjak\ *n* (1881) : one whose work is building smokestacks, towers, or steeples or climbing up the outside of such structures to paint and make repairs

¹steer \'stir\ *n* [ME, fr. OE *stēor* young ox; akin to OHG *stior* young ox] (bef. 12c) **1** : a male bovine animal castrated before sexual maturity — compare STAG 3 **2** : an ox less than four years old

²steer *vb* [ME *steren*, fr. OE *stīeran;* akin to OE *stēor-* steering oar, Gk *stauros* stake, cross, *stylos* pillar, Skt *sthavira, sthūra* stout, thick] *vt* (12c) **1** : to control the course of : DIRECT; *esp* : to guide by mechanical means (as a rudder) **2** : to set and hold to (a course) ∼ *vi* **1** : to direct the course (as of a ship or automobile) **2** : to pursue a course of action **3** : to be subject to guidance or direction ⟨an automobile that ∼s well⟩ **syn** *see* GUIDE — **steer·able** \'stir-ə-bəl\ *adj* — **steer·er** *n* — **steer clear** : to keep entirely away — often used with *of* ⟨trying to *steer clear* of controversy⟩

³steer *n* (1894) : a hint as to procedure : TIP

⁴steer *dial Brit var of* STIR

steer·age \'stir-ij\ *n* (15c) **1** : the act or practice of steering; *broadly* : DIRECTION **2** [fr. its orig. being located near the rudder] : a section of inferior accommodations in a passenger ship for passengers paying the lowest fares

steer·age·way \-ˌwā\ *n* (1769) : a rate of motion sufficient to make a ship or boat respond to movements of the rudder

steering column *n* (1903) : the column that encloses the connections to the steering gear of a vehicle (as an automobile)

steering committee *n* (1887) : a managing or directing committee; *specif* : a committee that determines the order in which business will be taken up in a U.S. legislative body

steering gear *n* (1869) : a mechanism by which something is steered

steering wheel *n* (1750) : a handwheel by means of which one steers

steers·man \'stirz-mən\ *n* (bef. 12c) : one who steers : HELMSMAN

¹steeve \'stēv\ *n* [ME *steven*, prob. fr. Sp *estibar* or Pg *estivar* to pack tightly, fr. L *stipare* to press together — more at STIFF] (15c) *archaic* : to stow esp. in a ship's hold

²steeve *vb* **steeved; steev·ing** [origin unknown] *vi* (ca. 1644) *of a bowsprit* : to incline upward at an angle with the horizon or the line of the keel ∼ *vt* : to set (a bowsprit) at an upward inclination

stego·saur \'ste-gə-ˌsȯr\ *n* [NL *Stegosauria*, fr. *Stegosaurus*] (1901) : any of a suborder (Stegosauria) of quadrupedal ornithischian dinosaurs with strongly developed dorsal plates and spikes

stego·sau·rus \ˌste-gə-'sȯr-əs\ *n* [NL, fr. Gk *stegos* roof + *sauros* lizard — more at THATCH] (1892) : any of a genus (*Stegosaurus*) of stegosaurs known from the Upper Jurassic rocks esp. of Colorado and Wyoming

stein \'stīn\ *n* [prob. fr. G *Steingut* stoneware, fr. *Stein* stone + *Gut* goods] (1855) : a large mug (as of earthenware) used esp. for beer; *also* : the quantity of beer that a stein holds

ste·la \'stē-lə\ *or* **ste·le** \'stē-lē\ *n, pl* **ste·lae** \-(ˌ)lē\ [L & Gk; L *stela*, fr. Gk *stēlē;* akin to OHG *stollo* pillar, Gk *stellein* to set up] (1776) : a usu. carved or inscribed stone slab or pillar used for commemorative purposes

ste·lar \'stē-lər, -ˌlär\ *adj* (1901) : of, relating to, or constituting a stele

stele \'stē(ə)l, 'stē-lē\ *n* [NL, fr. Gk *stēlē* stela, pillar] (1895) : the usu. cylindrical central vascular portion of the axis of a vascular plant

stel·la \'ste-lə\ *n* [L, star; fr. the star on the reverse] (1879) : an experimental international coin based on the metric system that was issued by the U.S. in 1879 and 1880 and was worth about four dollars

stel·lar \'ste-lər\ *adj* [LL *stellaris*, fr. L *stella* star — more at STAR] (ca. 1656) **1 a** : of or relating to the stars ⟨∼ astronomy⟩ **b** : composed of stars **2** : of or relating to a theatrical or film star ⟨∼ names⟩ **3 a** : PRINCIPAL, LEADING ⟨a ∼ role⟩ **b** : OUTSTANDING ⟨a ∼ student⟩ ⟨a ∼ performance⟩

stellar wind *n* (1965) : plasma continuously ejected from a star's surface into surrounding space

---

\ə\ abut \ᵊ\ kitten, F table \ər\ further \a\ ash \ā\ ace \ä\ mop, mar \au̇\ out \ch\ chin \e\ bet \ē\ easy \g\ go \i\ hit \ī\ ice \j\ job \ŋ\ sing \ō\ go \ȯ\ law \ȯi\ boy \th\ thin \t͟h\ the \ü\ loot \u̇\ foot \y\ yet \zh\ vision \á, ḵ, ⁿ, œ, œ̄, ue, ūe, ᵞ\ *see* Guide to Pronunciation

stel·late \'ste-,lāt\ *adj* [L *stella*] (1661) : resembling a star (as in shape) ⟨a ~ leaf⟩

Stel·ler's jay \'ste-lərz, 'shte-\ *n* [Georg W. *Steller* †1746 Ger. naturalist] (1828) : a jay (*Cyanocitta stelleri*) of western No. America with a high crest and black and dark blue plumage

Steller's sea cow *n* (1814) : an extinct very large aquatic sirenian (*Hydrodamalis gigas*) formerly common near the Asian coast of the Bering Sea

¹**stem** \'stem\ *n* [ME, fr. OE *stefn, stemn* stem of a plant or ship; akin to OHG *stam* plant stem and prob. to Gk *stamnos* wine jar, *histanai* to set — more at STAND] (bef. 12c) **1 a** : the main trunk of a plant; *specif* : a primary plant axis that develops buds and shoots instead of roots **b** : a plant part (as a branch, petiole, or stipe) that supports another (as a leaf or fruit) **c** : the complete fruiting stalk of a banana plant with its bananas **2 a** : the main upright member at the bow of a ship **b** : the bow or prow of a ship — compare STERN **3** : a line of ancestry : STOCK; *esp* : a fundamental line from which others have arisen **4** : the part of an inflected word that remains unchanged except by phonetic changes or variations throughout an inflection **5** : something held to resemble a plant stem: as **a** : a main or heavy stroke of a letter **b** : the short perpendicular line extending from the head of a musical note **c** : the part of a tobacco pipe from the bowl outward **d** : the cylindrical support of a piece of stemware (as a goblet) **e** : a shaft of a watch used for winding — **from stem to stern** : THROUGHOUT, THOROUGHLY

²**stem** *vt* **stemmed; stem·ming** [ME (Sc) *stemmen* to keep a course, fr. ¹*stem* (of a ship)] (1593) **1** : to make headway against (as an adverse tide, current, or wind) **2** : to check or go counter to (something adverse) — **stem·mer** *n*

³**stem** *vb* **stemmed; stem·ming** [¹*stem* (of a plant)] *vt* (1724) **1** : to remove the stem from **2** : to make stems for (as artificial flowers) ~ *vi* : to occur or develop as a consequence : have or trace an origin ⟨her success ~s from hard work⟩ *syn* see SPRING — **stem·mer** *n*

⁴**stem** *vb* **stemmed; stem·ming** [ME *stemmen* to dam up, fr. ON *stemma;* akin to MHG *stemmen* to dam up and prob. to Lith *stumti* to shove] *vt* (14c) **1 a** : to stop or dam up (as a river) **b** : to stop or check by or as if by damming; *esp* : STANCH ⟨~ a flow of blood⟩ **2** : to turn (a ski) in stemming ~ *vi* **1** : to restrain or check oneself; *also* : to become checked or stanched **2** : to slide the heel of one ski or of both skis outward usu. in making or preparing to make a turn

⁵**stem** *n* (ca. 1700) **1** : CHECK, DAM **2** : an act or instance of stemming on skis

stem cell *n* (1885) : an unspecialized cell that gives rise to differentiated cells ⟨hematopoietic *stem cells* in bone marrow⟩

stem christie *n, often cap* C (1936) : a turn in skiing begun by stemming a ski and completed by bringing the skis parallel into a christie

stem·less \'stem-ləs\ *adj* (1796) : having no stem : ACAULESCENT

stem·ma \'ste-mə\ *n, pl* **stem·ma·ta** \-mə-tə\ [L, wreath, pedigree (fr. the wreaths placed on ancestral images), fr. Gk, wreath, fr. *stephein* to crown, enwreathe] (1826) **1** : a simple eye present in some insects **2** : a scroll (as among the ancient Romans) containing a genealogical list **3** : a tree showing the relationships of the manuscripts of a literary work — **stem·mat·ic** \ste-'ma-tik, stə-\ *adj*

stemmed \'stemd\ *adj* (1576) : having a stem — usu. used in combination ⟨long-*stemmed* roses⟩

stem·my \'ste-mē\ *adj* **stem·mi·er; -est** (1863) : abounding in stems

stem rust *n* (1899) **1** : a rust attacking the stem of a plant; *esp* : a destructive disease esp. of wheat caused by a rust fungus (*Puccinia graminis*) which produces reddish brown lesions in the uredospore stage and black lesions in the teliospore stage and has any of several plants of the barberry family as an intermediate host **2** : the fungus causing stem rust

stem turn *n* (1922) : a skiing turn executed by stemming an outside ski

stem·ware \'stem-,war, -,wer\ *n* (1926) : glass hollowware mounted on a stem

stem–wind·er \-,wīn-dər\ *n* (1875) **1** : a stem-winding watch **2** [fr. the superiority of the stem-winding watch over the older key-wound watch] : one that is first-rate of its kind; *esp* : a stirring speech

stem–wind·ing \-diŋ\ *adj* (1867) : wound by an inside mechanism turned by the knurled knob at the outside end of the stem ⟨a ~ watch⟩

Sten \'sten\ *n* [R. V. *Sheppard*, 20th cent. Eng. army officer + H. J. *Turpin*, 20th cent. Eng. civil servant + *England*] (1942) : a light simple 9-millimeter British submachine gun

sten- *or* **steno-** *comb form* [Gk, fr. *stenos*] : close : narrow : little ⟨*steno*bathic⟩

stench \'stench\ *n* [ME, fr. OE *stenc*; akin to OE *stincan* to emit a smell — more at STINK] (bef. 12c) : STINK — **stench·ful** \-fəl\ *adj* — **stenchy** \'sten-chē\ *adj*

¹**sten·cil** \'sten(t)-səl\ *n* [ME *stanselen* to ornament with sparkling colors, fr. MF *estanceler*, fr. *estancele* spark, fr. (assumed) VL *stincilla*, alter. of L *scintilla*] (1707) **1** : an impervious material (as a sheet of paper, thin wax, or woven fabric) perforated with lettering or a design through which a substance (as ink, paint, or metallic powder) is forced onto a surface to be printed **2** : something (as a pattern, design, or print) that is produced by means of a stencil **3** : a printing process that uses a stencil

²**stencil** *vt* **sten·ciled** *or* **sten·cilled; sten·cil·ing** *or* **sten·cil·ling** \-s(ə-)liŋ\ (ca. 1828) **1** : to mark or paint with a stencil **2** : to produce by stencil — **sten·cil·er** *or* **sten·cil·ler** \-s(ə-)lər\ *n*

steno \'ste-(,)nō\ *n, pl* **sten·os** (1913) **1** : STENOGRAPHER **2** : STENOGRAPHY

steno·bath·ic \,ste-nə-'ba-thik\ *adj* [*sten-* + Gk *bathos* depth] (1902) *of a pelagic organism* : living within narrow limits of depth

ste·nog·ra·pher \stə-'nä-grə-fər\ *n* (1809) **1** : a writer of shorthand **2** : a person employed chiefly to take and transcribe dictation

ste·nog·ra·phy \-fē\ *n* (1602) **1** : the art or process of writing in shorthand **2** : shorthand esp. written from dictation or oral discourse **3** : the making of shorthand notes and subsequent transcription of them — **steno·graph·ic** \,ste-nə-'gra-fik\ *adj* — **steno·graph·i·cal·ly** \-fi-k(ə-)lē\ *adv*

steno·ha·line \,ste-nō-'hā-,līn, -'ha-,līn\ *adj* [ISV *sten-* + Gk *halinos* of salt, fr. *hals* salt — more at SALT] (ca. 1920) *of an aquatic organism* : unable to withstand wide variation in salinity of the surrounding water

ste·nosed \stə-'nōzd, -'nōst\ *adj* [fr. pp. of *stenose* to affect with stenosis] (1897) : affected with stenosis

ste·no·sis \stə-'nō-səs\ *n, pl* **-no·ses** \-,sēz\ [NL, fr. Gk *stenōsis* act of narrowing, fr. *stenoun* to narrow, fr. *stenos* narrow] (ca. 1860) : a narrowing or constriction of the diameter of a bodily passage or orifice — **ste·not·ic** \-'nä-tik\ *adj*

steno·ther·mal \,ste-nə-'thər-məl\ *adj* (1881) : capable of surviving over only a narrow range of temperatures ⟨~ fish⟩ — **steno·therm** \'ste-nə-,thərm\ *n*

steno·top·ic \,ste-nə-'tä-pik\ *adj* [prob. fr. G *stenotop* stenotopic, fr. *sten-* + Gk *topos* place] (1945) : having a narrow range of adaptability to changes in environmental conditions

steno·type \'ste-nə-,tīp\ *n* [*steno-* (as in *stenography*) + *type*] (1922) : a small machine somewhat like a typewriter used to record speech by means of phonograms — **stenotype** *vt* — **steno·typ·ist** \-,tī-pist\ *n* — **steno·ty·py** \-,tī-pē\ *n*

sten·tor \'sten-,tōr, -tər\ *n* [L, fr. Gk *Stentōr* Stentor, a Greek herald in the Trojan War noted for his loud voice] (1609) **1** : a person having a loud voice **2** : any of a widely distributed genus (*Stentor*) of ciliate protozoans having a trumpet-shaped body with the mouth at the broad end and with the narrow end often attached to the substrate

sten·to·ri·an \sten-'tōr-ē-ən, -'tor-\ *adj* (1605) : extremely loud *syn* see LOUD

¹**step** \'step\ *n* [ME, fr. OE *stæpe*; akin to OHG *stapfo* step, *stampfōn* to stamp] (bef. 12c) **1** : a rest for the foot in ascending or descending: as **a** : one of a series of structures consisting of a riser and a tread **b** : a ladder rung **2 a** (1) : an advance or movement made by raising the foot and bringing it down elsewhere (2) : a combination of foot or foot and body movements constituting a unit or a repeated pattern ⟨a dance ~⟩ (3) : manner of walking : STRIDE **b** : FOOTPRINT 1 **c** : the sound of a footstep ⟨heard ~s in the hall⟩ **3 a** : the space passed over in one step **b** : a short distance ⟨just a ~ away from the bank⟩ **c** : the height of one stair **4** *pl* : COURSE, WAY ⟨directed his ~s toward the river⟩ **5 a** : a degree, grade, or rank in a scale **b** : a stage in a process ⟨was guided through every ~ of my career⟩ **6** : a frame on a ship designed to receive an upright shaft; *esp* : a block supporting the heel of a mast **7** : an action, proceeding, or measure often occurring as one in a series ⟨taking ~s to improve the situation⟩ **8** : a steplike offset or part usu. occurring in a series **9** : an interval in a musical scale — **step·like** \-,līk\ *adj* — **stepped** \'stept\ *adj* — **in step 1** : with each foot moving to the same time as the corresponding foot of others or in time to music **2** : in harmony or agreement — **out of step** : not in step ⟨out of step with the times⟩

²**step** *vb* **stepped; step·ping** *vi* (bef. 12c) **1 a** : to move by raising the foot and bringing it down elsewhere or by moving each foot in succession **b** : DANCE **2 a** : to go on foot : WALK **b** *obs* : ADVANCE, PROCEED **c** : to be on one's way : LEAVE — often used with *along* ⟨~ along⟩ **3** : to press down with the foot ⟨~ on the brake⟩ **4** : to come as if at a single step ⟨*stepped* into a good job⟩ ~ *vt* **1** : to take by moving the feet in succession ⟨~ three paces⟩ **2 a** : to move (the foot) in any direction : SET ⟨the first man to ~ foot on the moon⟩ **b** : to traverse on foot **3** : to go through the steps of : PERFORM ⟨~ a minuet⟩ **4** : to make erect by fixing the lower end in a step ⟨~ the mast⟩ **5** : to measure by steps ⟨~ off 50 yards⟩ **6 a** : to provide with steps **b** : to make steps in ⟨~ a key⟩ **7** : to construct or arrange in or as if in steps ⟨craggy peaks with terraces *stepped* up the sides — *Time*⟩ — **step on it** : to increase one's speed : hurry up

step- *comb form* [ME, fr. OE *stēop-;* akin to OHG *stiof-* step, OE *astēpan* to deprive, bereave] : related by virtue of a remarriage (as of a parent) and not by blood ⟨*step*parent⟩ ⟨*step*sister⟩

step·broth·er \'step-,brə-thər\ *n* (13c) : a son of one's stepparent by a former marriage

step–by–step \,step-bī-'step\ *adj or adv* (1701) : marked by successive degrees usu. of limited extent : GRADUAL

step·child \'step-,chīld\ *n* (bef. 12c) **1** : a child of one's wife or husband by a former marriage **2** : one that fails to receive proper care or attention ⟨no longer a ~ in the family of nations —F. R. Smith⟩

step dance *n* (1887) : a dance in which steps are emphasized rather than gesture or posture

step·daugh·ter \'step-,do-tər\ *n* (bef. 12c) : a daughter of one's wife or husband by a former marriage

step–down \'step-,daun\ *n* (1922) : a decrease or reduction in size or amount ⟨a ~ in dosage⟩

step down *vi* (1890) : RETIRE, RESIGN ~ *vt* **1** : to lower (a voltage) by means of a transformer **2** : to decrease or reduce esp. by one or more steps — **step–down** \'step-,daun\ *adj*

step·fam·i·ly \'step-,fam-lē, -,fa-mə-\ *n* (1966) : a family in which there is a stepparent

step·fa·ther \'step-,fä-thər\ *n* (bef. 12c) : the husband of one's mother by a subsequent marriage

step function *n* (ca. 1929) : a mathematical function of a single real variable that remains constant within each of a series of adjacent intervals but changes in value from one interval to the next

steph·a·no·tis \,ste-fə-'nō-təs\ *n* [NL, fr. Gk *stephanōtis* fit for a crown, fr. *stephanos* crown, fr. *stephein* to crown] (1843) : any of a genus (*Stephanotis* and esp. *S. floribunda*) of Old World tropical woody vines of the milkweed family with fragrant white flowers the corolla of which has a cylindrical dilated tube and spreading limb

stephanotis

step–in \'step-,in\ *n* (1921) : an article of clothing put on by being stepped into: as **a** : a shoe resembling but usu. having a higher vamp than a pump and concealed elastic to adjust the fit **b** : short panties for women — usu. used in pl. — **step–in** *adj*

step in *vi* (15c) **1** : to intervene in an affair or dispute **2** : to make a brief informal visit

step·lad·der \'step-,la-dər\ *n* (1751) : a ladder that has broad flat steps and two pairs of legs connected by a hinge at the top and that opens at the bottom to become freestanding

step·moth·er \-,mə-thər\ *n* (bef. 12c) : the wife of one's father by a subsequent marriage

step out *vi* (ca. 1533) **1** : to go away from a place usu. for a short distance and for a short time **2** : to go or march at a vigorous or increased pace **3** : DIE **4** : to lead an active social life **5** : to be unfaithful — usu. used with *on*

step·par·ent \'step-,par-ǝnt, -,per-\ *n* (ca. 1890) : the spouse of one's mother or father by a subsequent marriage

step·par·ent·ing *n* (1979) : the raising of a child by a stepparent

steppe \'step\ *n* [Russ *step'*] (1671) **1** : one of the vast usu. level and treeless tracts in southeastern Europe or Asia **2** : arid land with xerophilous vegetation found usu. in regions of extreme temperature range and loess soil

stepped–up \'stept-'ǝp\ *adj* (1902) : increased in intensity : ACCELERATED, INTENSIFIED ⟨~ security⟩

step·per \'ste-pǝr\ *n* (1835) : one (as a fast horse or a dancer) that steps

stepper motor *n* (1961) : a motor whose driveshaft rotates in small steps rather than continuously — called also *stepping motor*

step·ping–stone \'ste-piŋ-,stōn\ *n* (14c) **1** : a stone on which to step (as in crossing a stream) **2** : a means of progress or advancement

step·sis·ter \'step-,sis-tǝr\ *n* (15c) : a daughter of one's stepparent by a former marriage

step·son \-,sǝn\ *n* (bef. 12c) : a son of one's husband or wife by a former marriage

step stool *n* (1946) : a stool with one or two steps that often fold away beneath the seat

step turn *n* (1941) : a skiing turn executed in a downhill traverse by lifting the upper ski from the ground, placing it in the desired direction, weighting it, and bringing the other ski parallel

step–up \'step-,ǝp\ *n* (1922) : an increase or advance in size or amount

step up *vt* (1902) **1** : to increase (a voltage) by means of a transformer **2** : to increase, augment, or advance esp. by one or more steps ⟨*step up* production⟩ ~ *vi* **1** : to come forward **2** : to undergo an increase ⟨business is *stepping up*⟩ **3** : to receive a promotion — **step–up** \'step-,ǝp\ *adj*

step·wise \-,wīz\ *adj* (1902) **1** : marked by or proceeding in steps **2** : moving by step to adjacent musical tones

-ster *n comb form* [ME, fr. OE *-estre* female agent; akin to MD *-ster*] **1** : one that does or handles or operates ⟨spin*ster*⟩ ⟨tap*ster*⟩ ⟨team*ster*⟩ **2** : one that makes or uses ⟨song*ster*⟩ ⟨pun*ster*⟩ **3** : one that is associated with or participates in ⟨game*ster*⟩ ⟨gang*ster*⟩ **4** : one that is ⟨young*ster*⟩

ster·co·ra·ceous \,stǝr-kǝ-'rā-shǝs\ *adj* [L *stercor-, stercus* excrement] (1731) : relating to, being, or containing feces

ster·cu·lia gum \,stǝr-'k(y)ü-lē-ǝ-\ *n* [NL *Sterculia*, genus of trees] (ca. 1943) : KARAYA GUM

stere- *or* **stereo-** *comb form* [NL, fr. Gk, fr. *stereos* solid — more at STARE] **1** : solid : solid body ⟨*stereogram*⟩ **2 a** : stereoscopic ⟨*stereopsis*⟩ **b** : having or dealing with three dimensions of space ⟨*stereochemistry*⟩

¹ste·reo \'ster-ē-,ō, 'stir-\ *n, pl* **ste·re·os** (ca. 1823) **1** : STEREOTYPE **2** [by shortening] **a** : stereophonic reproduction **b** : a stereophonic sound system

²stereo *adj* (1876) **1 a** : STEREOSCOPIC **b** : produced by or as if by means of a stereotype **2** : STEREOPHONIC

ste·reo·chem·is·try \,ster-ē-ō-'ke-mǝ-strē, ,stir-\ *n* [ISV] (1890) **1** : a branch of chemistry that deals with the spatial arrangement of atoms and groups in molecules **2** : the spatial arrangement of atoms and groups in a compound and its relation to the properties of the compound — **ste·reo·chem·i·cal** \-'ke-mi-kǝl\ *adj*

ste·reo·gram \'ster-ē-ǝ-,gram, 'stir-\ *n* [ISV] (1868) **1** : a diagram or picture representing objects with an impression of solidity or relief **2** : STEREOGRAPH

ste·reo·graph \-,graf\ *n* [ISV] (1859) : a pair of stereoscopic pictures or a picture composed of two superposed stereoscopic images that gives a three-dimensional effect when viewed with a stereoscope or special spectacles — **stereograph** *vt*

ste·reo·graph·ic \,ster-ē-ǝ-'gra-fik\ *adj* (1704) : of, relating to, or being a delineation of the form of a solid body (as the earth) on a plane ⟨~ projection⟩ — **ste·re·og·ra·phy** \,ster-ē-'ä-grǝ-fē\ *n*

ste·reo·iso·mer \,ster-ē-ō-'ī-sǝ-mǝr, ,stir-\ *n* [ISV] (1894) : any of a group of isomers in which atoms are linked in the same order but differ in their spatial arrangement — **ste·reo·iso·mer·ic** \-,ī-sǝ-'mer-ik\ *adj* — **ste·reo·isom·er·ism** \-ī-'sä-mǝ-,ri-zǝm\ *n*

ste·re·ol·o·gy \,ster-ē-'ä-lǝ-jē, ,stir-\ *n* [ISV] (1963) : a branch of science concerned with inferring the three-dimensional properties of objects or matter ordinarily observed two-dimensionally — **ste·reo·log·i·cal** \-ē-ǝ-'lä-ji-kǝl\ *adj* — **ste·reo·log·i·cal·ly** \-k(ǝ-)lē\ *adv*

ste·reo·mi·cro·scope \-'mī-krǝ-,skōp\ *n* (1948) : a microscope having a set of optics for each eye to make an object appear in three dimensions — **ste·reo·mi·cro·scop·ic** \-,mī-krǝ-'skä-pik\ *adj* — **ste·reo·mi·cro·scop·i·cal·ly** \-pi-k(ǝ-)lē\ *adv*

ste·reo·phon·ic \,ster-ē-ǝ-'fä-nik, ,stir-\ *adj* [ISV] (1927) : of, relating to, or constituting sound reproduction involving the use of separated microphones and two transmission channels to achieve the sound separation of a live hearing — **ste·reo·phon·i·cal·ly** \-ni-k(ǝ-)lē\ *adv* — **ste·reo·pho·ny** \,ster-ē-'ä-fǝ-nē, 'ster-ē-ǝ-,fō-nē; 'stir-\ *n*

ste·reo·pho·tog·ra·phy \,ster-ē-ō-fǝ-'tä-grǝ-fē, ,stir-\ *n* [ISV] (1903) : stereoscopic photography — **ste·reo·pho·to·graph·ic** \-,fō-tǝ-'gra-fik\ *adj*

ste·re·op·sis \,ster-ē-'äp-sǝs, ,stir-\ *n* [NL, fr. *stere-* + Gk *opsis* vision, appearance — more at OPTIC] (ca. 1911) : stereoscopic vision

ste·re·op·ti·con \,ster-ē-'äp-ti-kǝn\ *n* [NL, fr. *stere-* + Gk *optikon*, neut. of *optikos* optic] (1863) **1** : a projector for transparent slides often made double so as to produce dissolving views — **2** : STEREOSCOPE

ste·reo·reg·u·lar \,ster-ē-ō-'re-gyǝ-lǝr, ,stir-\ *adj* (1958) : of, relating to, or involving stereochemical regularity in the repeating units of a polymeric structure — **ste·reo·reg·u·lar·i·ty** \-,re-gyǝ-'lar-ǝ-tē\ *n*

ste·reo·scope \'ster-ē-ǝ-,skōp, 'stir-\ *n* (1838) : an optical instrument with two eyeglasses for helping the observer to combine the images of two pictures taken from points of view a little way apart and thus to get the effect of solidity or depth

ste·reo·scop·ic \,ster-ē-ǝ-'skä-pik, ,stir-\ *adj* (1855) **1** : of or relating to stereoscopy or the stereoscope **2** : characterized by stereoscopy ⟨~ vision⟩ — **ste·reo·scop·i·cal·ly** \-pi-k(ǝ-)lē\ *adv*

ste·re·os·co·py \,ster-ē-'äs-kǝ-pē, ,stir-; 'ster-ē-ǝ-,skō-pē, 'stir-\ *n* [ISV] (ca. 1859) **1** : a science that deals with stereoscopic effects and methods **2** : the seeing of objects in three dimensions

ste·reo·spe·cif·ic \,ster-ē-ō-spi-'si-fik, ,stir-\ *adj* (1949) : being, produced by, or involved in a stereochemically specific process ⟨many enzymes act as ~ catalysts⟩ ⟨plastics⟩ — **ste·reo·spec·if·i·cal·ly** \-fi-k(ǝ-)lē\ *adv* — **ste·reo·spec·i·fic·i·ty** \-,spe-sǝ-'fi-sǝ-tē\ *n*

ste·reo·tac·tic \,ster-ē-ǝ-'tak-tik, ,stir-\ *adj* (1950) : STEREOTAXIC

ste·reo·tax·ic \,ster-ē-ǝ-'tak-sik, ,stir-\ *adj* [NL *stereotaxis* stereotaxic technique, fr. *stere-* + *-taxis*] (1908) : of, relating to, or being a technique or apparatus used in neurological research or surgery for directing the tip of a delicate instrument (as a needle or an electrode) in three planes in attempting to reach a specific locus in the brain — **ste·reo·tax·i·cal·ly** \-si-k(ǝ-)lē\ *adv*

¹ste·reo·type \'ster-ē-ǝ-,tīp, 'stir-\ *vt* (1804) **1** : to make a stereotype from **2 a** : to repeat without variation : make hackneyed **b** : to develop a mental stereotype about — **ste·reo·typ·er** *n*

²stereotype *n* [F *stéréotype*, fr. *stéré-* stere- + *type*] (1817) **1** : a plate cast from a printing surface **2** : something conforming to a fixed or general pattern; *esp* : a standardized mental picture that is held in common by members of a group and that represents an oversimplified opinion, prejudiced attitude, or uncritical judgment — **ste·reo·typ·i·cal** \,ster-ē-ǝ-'ti-pi-kǝl\ *also* **ste·reo·typ·ic** \-'pik\ *adj* — **ste·reo·typ·i·cal·ly** \-pi-k(ǝ-)lē\ *adv*

ste·reo·typed *adj* (1849) : lacking originality or individuality *syn* see TRITE

ste·reo·ty·py \'ster-ē-ǝ-,tī-pē, 'stir-\ *n, pl* **-pies** (ca. 1889) : frequent almost mechanical repetition of the same posture, movement, or form of speech (as in schizophrenia)

ste·ric \'ster-ik, 'stir-\ *adj* [ISV *stere-* + ¹*-ic*] (1898) : relating to or involving the arrangement of atoms in space : SPATIAL — **ste·ri·cal·ly** \'ster-i-k(ǝ-)lē, 'stir-\ *adv*

ste·rig·ma \stǝ-'rig-mǝ\ *n, pl* **-ma·ta** \-mǝ-tǝ\ *also* **-mas** [NL, fr. Gk *stērigma* support, fr. *stērizein* to prop; perh. akin to Gk *stereos* solid — more at STARE] (ca. 1866) : one of the slender stalks at the top of the basidium of some fungi from the tips of which the basidiospores are formed; *broadly* : a stalk or filament that bears conidia or spermatia

ster·il·ant \'ster-ǝ-lǝnt\ *n* (1941) : a sterilizing agent

ster·ile \'ster-ǝl, *chiefly Brit* -,īl\ *adj* [ME *steryle*, fr. L *sterilis*; akin to Goth *stairo* barren animal, Skt *starī* sterile cow] (15c) **1 a** : failing to bear or incapable of producing fruit or spores **b** : failing to produce or incapable of producing offspring ⟨a ~ hybrid⟩ **c** : incapable of germinating ⟨~ spores⟩ **d** *of a flower* : neither perfect nor pistillate **2 a** : unproductive of vegetation ⟨a ~ arid region⟩ **b** : free from living organisms and esp. microorganisms **c** : lacking in stimulating emotional or intellectual quality : LIFELESS ⟨a ~ work of art⟩ — **ster·ile·ly** \-ǝ(l)-lē\ *adv* — **ste·ril·i·ty** \stǝ-'ri-lǝ-tē\ *n*

ster·il·ize \'ster-ǝ-,līz\ *vt* **-ized; -iz·ing** (1695) : to make sterile: as **a** : to cause (land) to become unfruitful **b** (1) : to deprive of the power of reproducing (2) : to make incapable of germination **c** : to make powerless or useless usu. by restraining from a normal function, relation, or participation **d** : to free from living microorganisms — **ster·il·i·za·tion** \,ster-ǝ-lǝ-'zā-shǝn\ *n* — **ster·il·iz·er** \'ster-ǝ-,lī-zǝr\ *n*

¹ster·ling \'stǝr-liŋ\ *n* [ME, silver penny, prob. fr. (assumed) OE *steorling*, fr. OE *steorra* star + ¹*-ling* — more at STAR] (14c) **1** : British money **2** : sterling silver or articles of it

²sterling *adj* (15c) **1 a** : of, relating to, or calculated in terms of British sterling **b** : payable in sterling **2 a** *of silver* : having a fixed standard of purity usu. defined legally as represented by an alloy of 925 parts of silver with 75 parts of copper **b** : made of sterling silver **3** : conforming to the highest standard ⟨~ character⟩ — **ster·ling·ly** \-liŋ-lē\ *adv* — **ster·ling·ness** *n*

sterling area *n* (1932) : a former group of countries with currencies tied to the British pound sterling

¹stern \'stǝrn\ *adj* [ME *sterne*, fr. OE *styrne*; akin to OE *starian* to stare — more at STARE] (bef. 12c) **1 a** : having a definite hardness or severity of nature or manner : AUSTERE **b** : expressive of severe displeasure : HARSH **2** : forbidding or gloomy in appearance **3** : INEXORABLE ⟨~ necessity⟩ **4** : STURDY, STOUT ⟨a ~ resolve⟩ *syn* see SEVERE — **stern·ly** *adv* — **stern·ness** \'stǝrn-nǝs\ *n*

²stern *n* [ME, rudder, prob. fr. Scand origin; akin to ON *stjörn* act of steering; akin to OE *stieran* to steer — more at STEER] (14c) **1** : the rear end of a boat **2** : a hinder or rear part : the last or latter part

ster·nal \'stǝr-n²l\ *adj* (1756) : of or relating to the sternum

stern chase *n* [²*stern*] (1627) : a chase in which a pursuing ship follows in the path of another

stern chaser *n* (1815) : a gun so placed as to be able to fire astern at a pursuing ship

stern·fore·most \'stǝrn-'fōr-,mōst, -'fȯr-\ *adv* (1840) : with the stern in advance : BACKWARD

ster·nite \'stǝr-,nīt\ *n* [ISV, fr. Gk *sternon* chest] (1868) : the ventral part or shield of a somite of an arthropod; *esp* : the chitinous plate that forms the ventral surface of an abdominal or occas. a thoracic segment of an insect

stern·most \'stǝrn-,mōst\ *adj* (1622) : farthest astern

ster·no·cos·tal \,stǝr-nō-'käs-t²l\ *adj* [NL *sternum* + E *-o-* + *costal*] (1785) : of, relating to, or situated between the sternum and ribs

stern·post \'stǝrn-,pōst\ *n* (15c) : the principal member at the stern of a ship extending from keel to deck

stern sheets *n pl* (15c) : the space in the stern of an open boat not occupied by the thwarts

ster·num \'stǝr-nǝm\ *n, pl* **sternums** *or* **ster·na** \-nǝ\ [NL, fr. Gk *sternon* chest, breastbone; akin to OHG *stirna* forehead, L *sternere* to spread out — more at STREW] (1667) : a compound ventral bone or cartilage of most vertebrates other than fishes that connects the ribs or the shoulder girdle or both and in humans consists of the manubrium, gladiolus, and xiphoid process — called also *breastbone*

\ǝ\ abut \ʾ\ kitten, F table \ǝr\ further \a\ ash \ā\ ace \ä\ mop, mar \au̇\ out \ch\ chin \e\ bet \ē\ easy \g\ go \i\ hit \ī\ ice \j\ job \ŋ\ sing \ō\ go \ȯ\ law \ȯi\ boy \th\ thin \t̲h̲\ the \ü\ loot \u̇\ foot \y\ yet \zh\ vision \à, k̲, ⁿ, œ, œ̄, ᵫ, ᵫ̄, ᵫ\ *see* Guide to Pronunciation

ster·nu·ta·tion \,stər-nyə-'tā-shən\ *n* [ME *sternutacion*, fr. L *sternuta-tion-*, *sternutatio*, fr. *sternutare* to sneeze, freq. of *sternuere* to sneeze; akin to Gk *ptarnysthai* to sneeze] (15c) : the act, fact, or noise of sneezing

ster·nu·ta·tor \'stər-nyə-,tā-tər\ *n* (1922) : an agent that induces sneezing and often lacrimation and vomiting

stern·ward \'stərn-wərd\ *or* **stern·wards** \-wərdz\ *adv* (1832) : AFT

stern·way \'stərn-,wā\ *n* (1769) : movement of a ship backward or with stern foremost

stern–wheel·er \-'hwē-lər, -'wē-\ *n* (1855) : a steamboat driven by a single paddle wheel at the stern

ste·roid \'stir-,öid *also* 'ster-\ *n* [ISV *sterol* + *-oid*] (1926) : any of numerous compounds containing a 17-carbon 4-ring system and including the sterols and various hormones and glycosides — **steroid** *or* **ste·roi·dal** \stə-'rȯi-dᵊl\ *adj*

ste·roi·do·gen·e·sis \stə-,rȯi-də-'je-nə-səs, ,stir-,ȯid- *also* ,ster-\ *n* [NL] (1951) : synthesis of steroids — **ste·roi·do·gen·ic** \-'je-nik\ *adj*

ste·rol \'stir-,ȯl, 'ster-, -,ōl\ *n* [ISV, fr. *-sterol* (as in *cholesterol*)] (1913) : any of various solid steroid alcohols (as cholesterol) widely distributed in animal and plant lipids

-sterone *comb form* [*sterol* + *-one*] : steroid hormone ⟨*androsterone*⟩

ster·tor \'stər-tər, -,tȯr\ *n* [NL, fr. L *stertere* to snore; akin to *sternuere* to sneeze] (1804) : the act or fact of producing a snoring sound : SNORING

ster·to·rous \'stər-tə-rəs\ *adj* (1802) : characterized by a harsh snoring or gasping sound — **ster·to·rous·ly** *adv*

stet \'stet\ *vt* **stet·ted; stet·ting** [L, let it stand, fr. *stare* to stand — more at STAND] (1755) : to direct retention of (a word or passage previously ordered to be deleted or omitted from a manuscript or printer's proof) by annotating usu. with the word *stet*

stetho·scope \'ste-thə-,skōp *also* -thə-\ *n* [F *stéthoscope*, fr. Gk *stēthos* chest + F *-scope*] (1820) : an instrument used to detect and study sounds produced in the body — **stetho·scop·ic** \,ste-thə-'skä-pik *also* -thə-\ *adj*

Stet·son \'stet-sən\ *trademark* — used for a broad-brimmed high-crowned felt hat

¹ste·ve·dore \'stē-və-,dȯr, -,dōr *also* 'stēv-,\ *n* [Sp *estibador*, fr. *estibar* to pack, fr. L *stipare* to press together — more at STIFF] (1788) : one who works at or is responsible for loading and unloading ships in port

²stevedore *vb* **-dored; -dor·ing** *vt* (1862) : to handle (cargo) as a stevedore; *also* : to load or unload the cargo of (a ship) in port ∼ *vi* : to work as a stevedore

stevedore knot *n* (ca. 1863) : a stopper knot similar to a figure eight knot but with one or more extra turns — called also *stevedore's knot;* see KNOT illustration

Ste·ven·graph \'stē-vən-,graf\ *or* **Ste·vens·graph** \-vənz-\ *n* [Thomas *Stevens*, 19th cent. Am. weaver] (1879) : a woven silk picture

¹stew \'stü, 'styü\ *n* [ME *stewe* heated room for a steam bath, fr. MF *estuve*, fr. (assumed) VL *extufa* — more at STOVE] (13c) **1** *obs* : a utensil used for boiling **2** : a hot bath **3** a : WHOREHOUSE **b** : a district of bordellos — usu. used in pl. **4** a : fish or meat usu. with vegetables prepared by stewing **b** (1) : a heterogeneous mixture (2) : a state of heat and congestion **5** : a state of excitement, worry, or confusion

²stew *vt* (14c) : to boil slowly or with simmering heat ∼ *vi* **1** : to become cooked by stewing **2** : to swelter esp. from confinement in a hot or stuffy atmosphere **3** : to be in a state of suppressed agitation, worry, or resentment

³stew *n* [short for *stewardess*] (1970) : FLIGHT ATTENDANT

¹stew·ard \'stü-ərd, 'styü-;, 'st(y)ü(-ə)rd\ *n* [ME, fr. OE *stīweard*, fr. *stī, stig* hall, sty + *weard* ward — more at STY, WARD] (bef. 12c) **1** : one employed in a large household or estate to manage domestic concerns (as the supervision of servants, collection of rents, and keeping of accounts) **2** : SHOP STEWARD **3** : a fiscal agent **4** a : an employee on a ship, airplane, bus, or train who manages the provisioning of food and attends passengers **b** : one appointed to supervise the provision and distribution of food and drink in an institution **5** : one who actively directs affairs : MANAGER

²steward *vt* (1621) : to act as a steward for : MANAGE ∼ *vi* : to perform the duties of a steward

stew·ard·ess \'stü-ər-dəs, 'styü-;, 'st(y)ü(-ə)r-dəs\ *n* (1631) : a woman who performs the duties of a steward; *esp* : one who attends passengers (as on an airplane)

stew·ard·ship \'stü-ərd-,ship, 'styü-;, 'st(y)ü(-ə)rd-\ *n* (15c) **1** : the office, duties, and obligations of a steward **2** : the conducting, supervising, or managing of something; *esp* : the careful and responsible management of something entrusted to one's care ⟨∼ of our natural resources⟩

stewed *adj* (ca. 1737) : DRUNK 1a

stew·pan \'stü-,pan, 'styü-\ *n* (1651) : a pan used for stewing

stib·nite \'stib-,nīt\ *n* [alter. of obs. E *stibine* stibnite, fr. F, fr. L *stibium* antimony, fr. Gk *stibi*, fr. Egypt *stm*] (ca. 1854) : a mineral that consists of the trisulfide of antimony and occurs in orthorhombic lead-gray crystals of metallic luster or in massive form

sticho·myth·ia \,sti-kə-'mi-thē-ə\ *also* **sti·chom·y·thy** \,sti-'kä-mə-thē\ *n* [Gk *stichomythia*, fr. *stichomythein* to speak dialogue in alternate lines, fr. *stichos* row, verse + *mythos* speech, myth; akin to Gk *steichein* to walk, go — more at STAIR] (1861) : dialogue esp. of altercation or dispute delivered by two actors in alternating lines (as in classical Greek drama) — **sticho·myth·ic** \,sti-kə-'mi-thik\ *adj*

¹stick \'stik\ *n* [ME *stik*, fr. OE *sticca*; akin to ON *stik* stick, OE *stician* to stick] (bef. 12c) **1** : a woody piece or part of a tree or shrub: as **a** : a usu. dry or dead severed shoot, twig, or slender branch **b** : a cut or broken branch or piece of wood gathered for fuel or construction material **2** a : a long slender piece of wood or metal: as (1) : a club or staff used as a weapon (2) : WALKING STICK **b** : an

stick 2b: *a* lacrosse, *b* ice hockey, *c* field hockey

implement used for striking or propelling an object in a game **c** : something used to force compliance **d** : a baton symbolizing an office or dignity; *also* : a person entitled to bear such a baton **3** : a piece of the materials composing something (as a building) **4** a : any of various implements resembling a stick in shape, origin, or use: as (1) : COMPOSING STICK (2) : an airplane lever operating the elevators and ailerons (3) : the gearshift lever of an automobile **b** : STICKFUL **5** : something prepared (as by cutting, molding, or rolling) in a relatively long and slender often cylindrical form ⟨a ∼ of candy⟩ ⟨a ∼ of butter⟩ **6** a : PERSON, CHAP **b** : a dull, inert, stiff, or spiritless person **7** *pl* : remote usu. rural districts regarded esp. as backward, dull, or unsophisticated : BOONDOCKS **8** a : an herbaceous stalk resembling a woody stick ⟨celery ∼s⟩ **9** : ¹MAST 1; *also* : ¹YARD 4 **10** : a piece of furniture **11** a : a number of bombs arranged for release from a bombing plane in a series across a target **b** : a number of parachutists dropping together **12** *slang* : a marijuana cigarette **13** a : punishment or the threat of punishment used to force compliance or cooperation ⟨choosing between the carrot and the ∼⟩ **b** *Brit* : CRITICISM, ABUSE — **stick·like** \-,līk\ *adj*

²stick *vt* (1573) **1** : to arrange (lumber) in stacks **2** : to provide a stick as a support for

³stick *vb* **stuck** \'stək\; **stick·ing** [ME *stikken*, fr. OE *stician;* akin to OHG *sticken* to prick, L in*stigare* to urge on, goad, Gk *stizein* to tattoo] *vt* (bef. 12c) **1** a : to pierce with something pointed : STAB **b** : to kill by piercing **2** : to push or thrust so as or as if to pierce **3** a : to fasten by thrusting in : IMPALE **c** : PUSH, THRUST **4** : to put or set in a specified place or position **5** : to furnish with things fastened by or as if by piercing **6** : to attach by or as if by causing to adhere to a surface **7** a : to compel to pay esp. by trickery ⟨got *stuck* with the bar bill⟩ **b** : OVERCHARGE **8** a : to halt the movement or action of **b** : BAFFLE, STUMP **9** a : CHEAT, DEFRAUD **b** : to saddle with something disadvantageous or disagreeable ⟨is still *stuck* with that lousy car⟩ ∼ *vi* **1** : to hold to something firmly by or as if by adhesion: **a** : to become fixed in place by means of a pointed end **b** : to become fast by or as if by miring or by gluing or plastering ⟨*stuck* in the mud⟩ **2** a : to remain in a place, situation, or environment **b** : to hold fast or adhere resolutely : CLING **c** : to remain effective **d** : to keep close in a chase or competition **3** : to become blocked, wedged, or jammed **4** a : BALK, SCRUPLE **b** : to find oneself baffled **c** : to be unable to proceed **5** : PROJECT, PROTRUDE — **stick in one's craw** : to irritate, nag at, or obsess one — **stick it to** : to treat harshly or unfairly — **stick one's neck out** : to make oneself vulnerable by taking a risk — **stick to one's guns** : to maintain one's position esp. in face of opposition — **stuck on** : infatuated with

syn STICK, ADHERE, COHERE, CLING, CLEAVE mean to become closely attached. STICK implies attachment by affixing or by being glued together ⟨couldn't get the label to *stick*⟩. ADHERE is often interchangeable with *stick* but sometimes implies a growing together ⟨antibodies *adhering* to a virus⟩. COHERE suggests a sticking together of parts so that they form a unified mass ⟨eggs will make the mixture *cohere*⟩. CLING implies attachment by hanging on with arms or tendrils ⟨*clinging* to a capsized boat⟩. CLEAVE stresses strength of attachment ⟨the wet shirt *cleaved* to his back⟩.

⁴stick *n* (1633) **1** : a thrust with a pointed instrument : STAB **2** a : DELAY, STOP **b** : IMPEDIMENT **3** : adhesive quality or substance

stick around *vi* (ca. 1912) : to stay or wait about : LINGER

stick·ball \'stik-,bȯl\ *n* (1934) : baseball adapted for play in streets or small areas and using a broomstick and a lightweight ball

stick·er \'sti-kər\ *n* (15c) **1** : one that pierces with a point **2** a : one that adheres or causes adhesion **b** : a slip of paper with adhesive back that can be fastened to a surface

sticker price *n* (1969) : a manufacturer's suggested retail price that is printed on a sticker and affixed to a new automobile

stick figure *n* (1949) **1** : a drawing showing the head of a human being or animal as a circle and all other parts as straight lines **2** : a fictional character lacking depth and believability

stick·ful \'stik-,fu̇l\ *n* (1683) : as much set type as fills a composing stick

stick·han·dle \'stik-,han-dᵊl\ *vi* (1929) : to maneuver a puck (as in hockey) or a ball (as in lacrosse) with a stick — **stick·han·dler** \-,han(d)-lər, -,han-dᵊl-ər\ *n*

sticking plaster *n* (1655) *chiefly Brit* : an adhesive plaster esp. for closing superficial wounds

sticking point *n* (1946) : an item (as in negotiations) resulting or likely to result in an impasse

stick insect *n* (1854) : any of various usu. wingless insects (esp. family Phasmatidae) with a long cylindrical body resembling a stick

stick–in–the–mud \'stik-ən-thə-,məd\ *n* (1733) : one who is slow, old-fashioned, or unprogressive; *esp* : an old fogy

stick·it \'sti-kət\ *adj* [Sc, fr. pp. of E ³*stick*] (1787) **1** *Scot* : UNFINISHED **2** *chiefly Scot* : having failed esp. in an intended profession

stick·le \'sti-kəl\ *vi* **stick·led; stick·ling** \-k(ə-)liŋ\ [alter. of ME *stightlen*, freq. of *stighten* to arrange, fr. OE *stihtan;* akin to ON *stētta* to found, support] (1642) **1** : to contend esp. stubbornly and usu. on insufficient grounds **2** : to feel scruples : SCRUPLE

stick·le·back \'sti-kəl-,bak\ *n* [ME *stykylbak*, fr. OE *sticel* goad + ME *bak* back; akin to OE *stician* to stick] (15c) : any of a family (Gasterosteidae) of small scaleless bony fishes having two or more free spines in front of the dorsal fin and including marine, anadromous, and freshwater forms

stick·ler \'sti-k(ə-)lər\ *n* (1644) **1** : one who insists on exactness or completeness in the observance of something ⟨a ∼ for the rules⟩ **2** : something that baffles or puzzles : POSER, STICKER

stick·man \'stik-,man, -mən\ *n* (ca. 1931) : one who handles a stick: as **a** : one who supervises the play at a dice table, calls the decisions, and retrieves the dice **b** : a player in any of various games (as hockey or lacrosse) played with a stick

stick out *vi* (1567) **1** : to jut out : PROJECT **b** : to be prominent or conspicuous **2** : to be persistent (as in a demand or an opinion) ∼ *vt* : ENDURE, LAST — often used with *it* ⟨*stuck* it *out* to the end⟩

stick·pin \'stik-,pin\ *n* (1895) : an ornamental pin; *esp* : one worn in a necktie

stick·seed \-,sēd\ *n* (1843) : any of various weedy herbs (genera *Lappula* and *Hackelia*) of the borage family with bristly adhesive fruit

stick shift n (1959) : a manually operated gearshift for a motor vehicle usu. mounted on the floor

stick-tight \'stik-,tīt\ n (ca. 1884) : BUR MARIGOLD

stick-to-it-ive-ness \stik-'tü-ə-tiv-nəs\ n [fr. the phrase *stick to it*] (1867) : dogged perseverance : TENACITY

stick-um \'sti-kəm\ n [³*stick* + *-um* (prob. alter. of *'em* them)] (ca. 1909) : a substance that adheres or causes adhesion

stick-up \'stik-,əp\ n (1904) : a robbery at gunpoint : HOLDUP

stick up vi (15c) : to stand upright or on end : PROTRUDE ~ vt : to rob at gunpoint — **stick up for** : to speak or act in defense of : SUPPORT

stick-weed \'stik-,wēd\ n (1743) : any of several plants (as a beggar's-lice) with adhesive seeds

stick-work \-,wərk\ n (1903) : the use of one's stick in offensive and defensive techniques (as in hockey)

sticky \'sti-kē\ adj **stick-i-er; -est** (ca. 1735) 1 a : ADHESIVE b (1) : VISCOUS, GLUEY (2) : coated with a sticky substance 2 : HUMID, MUGGY; also : CLAMMY 3 : tending to stick 4 a : DISAGREEABLE, UNPLEASANT b : AWKWARD, STIFF c : DIFFICULT, PROBLEMATIC 5 : excessively sentimental : CLOYING — **stick-i-ly** \'sti-kə-lē\ adv — **stick-i-ness** \'sti-kē-nəs\ n

sticky wicket n (1926) : a difficult or delicate problem or situation

stic-tion \'stik-shən\ n [*static* + *fr*iction] (1946) : the force required to cause one body in contact with another to begin to move

¹**stiff** \'stif\ adj [ME *stif*, fr. OE *stif*; akin to MD *stijf* stiff, L *stipare* to press together, Gk *steibein* to tread on] (bef. 12c) 1 a : not easily bent : RIGID b : lacking in suppleness or responsiveness (~ muscles) c : impeded in movement — used of a mechanism (~ DRUNK 1a 2 a : FIRM, RESOLUTE b : STUBBORN, UNYIELDING c : PROUD d (1) : marked by reserve or decorum (2) : lacking in ease or grace : STILTED 3 : hard fought : PUGNACIOUS, SHARP 4 a (1) : exerting great force (a ~ wind) (2) : FORCEFUL, VIGOROUS b : POTENT (a ~ dose) b : of a dense or glutinous consistency : THICK 6 a : HARSH, SEVERE (a ~ penalty) b : ARDUOUS, RUGGED (~ terrain) 7 : not easily heeled over by an external force (as the wind) (a ~ ship) 8 : EXPENSIVE, STEEP (paid a ~ price) — **stiff-ish** \'sti-fish\ adj — **stiff-ly** adv — **stiff-ness** n

syn STIFF, RIGID, INFLEXIBLE mean difficult to bend. STIFF may apply to any degree of this condition (stretching will prevent your muscles from becoming *stiff*). RIGID applies to something so stiff that it cannot be bent without breaking (a *rigid* surfboard). INFLEXIBLE stresses lack of suppleness or pliability (ski boots with *inflexible* soles).

²**stiff** adv (13c) 1 : in a stiff manner : STIFFLY 2 : to an extreme degree : SEVERELY (scared ~) (bored ~)

³**stiff** n (ca. 1859) 1 : CORPSE 2 a : TRAMP, BUM b : HAND, LABORER c : PERSON (a lucky ~) 3 : FLOP, FAILURE

⁴**stiff** vt (1950) 1 a : to refuse to pay or tip (~ed the doctor for the fee) (~ed the waiter) b : CHEAT (~ed him in a business deal) c : STICK 7a (~ed us with the bar bill) 2 : SNUB 3 (~ed sportswriters after the game)

stiff-arm \'stif-,ärm\ vb or n (1909) : STRAIGHT-ARM

stiff-en \'sti-fən\ vb **stiff-ened; stiff-en-ing** \'sti-fə-niŋ, 'stif-niŋ\ vt (15c) : to make stiff or stiffer ~ vi : to become stiffer — **stiff-en-er** \'sti-fə-nər, 'stif-nər\ n

stiff-necked \'stif-'nekt\ adj (1526) 1 : HAUGHTY, STUBBORN 2 : STILTED

stiff upper lip n [fr. the phrase *keep a stiff upper lip*] (1815) : a steady and determined attitude or manner in the face of trouble — **stiff-upper-lip** adj

¹**sti-fle** \'stī-fəl\ n [ME] (14c) : the joint next above the hock in the hind leg of a quadruped (as a horse or dog) corresponding to the human knee — see HORSE illustration

²**stifle** vb **sti-fled; sti-fling** \-f(ə-)liŋ\ [alter. of ME *stuflen*] vt (1513) 1 a : to kill by depriving of oxygen : SUFFOCATE b (1) : SMOTHER (2) : MUFFLE 2 a : to cut off (as the voice or breath) b : to withhold from circulation or expression : REPRESS (~ed our anger) c : DETER, DISCOURAGE ~ vi : to become suffocated by or as if by lack of oxygen : SMOTHER — **sti-fler** \-f(ə-)lər\ n — **sti-fling-ly** \-f(ə-)liŋ-lē\ adv

stig-ma \'stig-mə\ n, pl **stig-ma-ta** \stig-'mä-tə, 'stig-mə-tə\ or **stigmas** [L *stigmat-*, *stigma* mark, brand, fr. Gk, fr. *stizein* to puncture — more at STICK] (ca. 1593) 1 a archaic : a scar left by a hot iron : BRAND b : a mark of shame or discredit : STAIN c : an identifying mark or characteristic; specif : a specific diagnostic sign of a disease 2 a **stigmata** pl : bodily marks or pains resembling the wounds of the crucified Christ and sometimes accompanying religious ecstasy b : PETECHIA 2 a : a small spot, scar, or opening on a plant or animal b : the usu. apical part of the pistil of a flower which receives the pollen grains and on which they germinate — see FLOWER illustration — **stigmal** \'stig-məl\ adj

stig-mas-ter-ol \stig-'mas-tə-,ròl, -,rōl\ n [NL Physo*stigma* (genus including the Calabar bean) + ISV *sterol*] (1907) : a crystalline sterol $C_{29}H_{48}O$ obtained esp. from the oils of Calabar beans and soybeans

¹**stig-mat-ic** \stig-'ma-tik\ n (1594) : one marked with stigmata

²**stigmatic** adj (1607) 1 : having or conveying a social stigma 2 : of or relating to supernatural stigmata 3 : ANASTIGMATIC — used esp. of a bundle of light rays intersecting at a single point — **stig-mat-i-cal-ly** \-ti-k(ə-)lē\ adv

stig-ma-tist \'stig-mə-tist, stig-'mä-\ n (1607) : STIGMATIC

stig-ma-tize \'stig-mə-,tīz\ vt **-tized; -tiz-ing** (1585) 1 a archaic : BRAND b : to describe or identify in opprobrious terms 2 : to mark with stigmata — **stig-ma-ti-za-tion** \,stig-mə-tə-'zā-shən\ n

stil-bene \'stil-,bēn\ n [ISV, fr. Gk *stilbein* to glitter] (ca. 1868) : an aromatic hydrocarbon $C_{14}H_{12}$ used as a phosphor and in making dyes; also : a compound derived from stilbene

stil-bes-trol \stil-'bes-,tròl, -,trōl\ n [*stilbene* + *estrus* + ¹-*ol*] (1938) 1 : a crystalline synthetic derivative $C_{14}H_{12}O_2$ of stilbene that differs from the related diethylstilbestrol in lack of the ethyl groups and in possession of but weak estrogenic activity 2 : DIETHYLSTILBESTROL

stil-bite \'stil-,bīt\ n [F, fr. Gk *stilbein*] (1815) : a mineral consisting of a hydrous silicate of aluminum, calcium, and sodium and often occurring in sheaflike aggregations of crystals

¹**stile** \'stī(ə)l\ n [ME, fr. OE *stigel*; akin to OE *stīeger* stair — more at STAIR] (bef. 12c) : a step or set of steps for passing over a fence or wall; also : TURNSTILE

²**stile** n [prob. fr. D *stijl* post] (1678) : one of the vertical members in a frame or panel into which the secondary members are fitted

sti-let-to \stə-'le-(,)tō\ n, pl **-tos** or **-toes** [It, dim. of *stilo* stylus, dagger, fr. L *stilus* stylus — more at STYLE] (1611) 1 : a slender dagger with a blade thick in proportion to its breadth 2 : a pointed instrument for piercing holes for eyelets or embroidery 3 : STILETTO HEEL

stiletto heel n (1953) : a high thin heel on women's shoes that is narrower than a spike heel

¹**still** \'stil\ adj [ME *stille*, fr. OE; akin to OHG *stilli* still and perh. to OE *steall* stall — more at STALL] (bef. 12c) 1 a : devoid of or abstaining from motion b archaic : SEDENTARY c : not effervescent (~ wine) d (1) : of, relating to, or being a static photograph as contrasted with a motion picture (2) : designed for taking still photographs (a ~ camera) (3) : engaged in taking still photographs (a ~ photographer) 2 a : uttering no sound : QUIET b : SUBDUED, MUTED 3 a : CALM, TRANQUIL b : free from noise or turbulence — **still-ness** n

²**still** vt (bef. 12c) : to become motionless or silent : QUIET ~ vt 1 a : ALLAY, CALM b : to put an end to : SETTLE 2 : to arrest the motion of 3 : SILENCE

³**still** adv (bef. 12c) 1 : without motion (sit ~) 2 archaic a : ALWAYS, CONTINUALLY b : in a progressive manner : INCREASINGLY 3 — used as a function word to indicate the continuance of an action or condition (~ lives there) (drink it while it's ~ hot) 4 : in spite of that : NEVERTHELESS (those who take the greatest care ~ make mistakes) 5 a : EVEN 2c (a ~ more difficult problem) b : YET 1a

⁴**still** n (13c) 1 : QUIET, SILENCE 2 : a static photograph; specif : a photograph of actors or scenes of a motion picture for publicity or documentary purposes

⁵**still** vb [ME *stillen*, short for *distillen* to distill] (13c) : DISTILL

⁶**still** n (1533) 1 : DISTILLERY 2 : apparatus used in distillation comprising either the chamber in which the vaporization is carried out or the entire equipment

still alarm n (1875) : a fire alarm transmitted (as by telephone call) without sounding the signal apparatus

still and all adv (1829) : NEVERTHELESS, STILL

still-birth \'stil-,bərth, -'bərth\ n (1785) : the birth of a dead fetus

still-born \-'bòrn\ adj (1593) 1 : dead at birth 2 : failing from the start : ABORTIVE (a ~ plan) — **still-born** \-,bòrn\ n

still-hunt \-,hənt\ vi (1858) : to ambush or stalk a quarry; esp : to pursue game noiselessly usu. without a dog ~ vt : to lie in wait for : approach by stealth

still hunt n (1828) : a quiet pursuing or ambushing of game

still life n, pl **still lifes** (1695) 1 : a picture consisting predominantly of inanimate objects 2 : the category of graphic arts concerned with inanimate subject matter

still-man \'stil-mən\ n (ca. 1864) : one who owns or operates a still

still-room \'stil-,rüm, -,rům\ n [⁶*still*] (ca. 1710) Brit : a room connected with the kitchen where liqueurs, preserves, and cakes are kept and beverages (as tea) are prepared

still water n (1832) : a part of a stream where no current is visible

¹**stil-ly** \'stil-lē\ adv (bef. 12c) : in a calm manner : QUIETLY

²**stilly** \'sti-lē\ adj [⁴*still* + ¹-*y*] (1776) : STILL, QUIET

¹**stilt** \'stilt\ n [ME *stilte*; akin to OHG *stelza* stilt] (15c) 1 a : one of two poles each with a rest or strap for the foot used to elevate the wearer above the ground in walking 2 a : a pile or post serving as one of the supports of a structure above ground or water level 2 pl also **stilt** : any of various notably long-legged 3-toed shorebirds (genera *Himantopus* and *Cladorhynchus*) that are related to the avocets, frequent inland ponds and marshes, and nest in small colonies

²**stilt** vt (1649) : to raise on or as if on stilts

stilt-ed \'stil-təd\ adj (1820) 1 a : POMPOUS, LOFTY b : FORMAL, STIFF 2 : having the curve beginning at some distance above the impost (a ~ arch) — **stilt-ed-ly** adv — **stilt-ed-ness** n

Stil-ton \'stil-tⁿn\ n [*Stilton*, Huntingdon, England] (1826) : a blue-veined cheese with wrinkled rind made of whole cows' milk enriched with cream

stime \'stīm\ n [ME (northern dial.)] (14c) chiefly Scot & Irish : GLIMMER; also : GLIMPSE

stim-u-lant \'stim-yə-lənt\ n (ca. 1728) 1 : an agent (as a drug) that produces a temporary increase of the functional activity or efficiency of an organism or any of its parts 2 : STIMULUS 3 : an alcoholic beverage — not used technically — **stimulant** adj

stim-u-late \-,lāt\ vb **-lat-ed; -lat-ing** [L *stimulatus*, pp. of *stimulare*, fr. *stimulus* goad; perh. akin to L *stilus* stem, stylus — more at STYLE] vt (1619) 1 : to excite to activity or growth or to greater activity : ANIMATE, AROUSE 2 a : to function as a physiological stimulus to b : to arouse or affect by a stimulant (as a drug) ~ vi : to act as a stimulant or stimulus syn see PROVOKE — **stim-u-la-tion** \,stim-yə-'lā-shən\ n — **stim-u-la-tive** \'stim-yə-,lā-tiv\ adj — **stim-u-la-tor** \-,lā-tər\ n — **stim-u-la-to-ry** \-lə-,tōr-ē, -,tòr-\ adj

stim-u-lus \'stim-yə-ləs\ n, pl **-li** \-,lī, -,lē\ [L] (1684) : something that rouses or incites to activity: as a : INCENTIVE b : STIMULANT 1 c : an agent (as an environmental change) that directly influences the activity of a living organism or one of its parts (as by exciting a sensory organ or evoking muscular contraction or glandular secretion)

¹**sting** \'stiŋ\ vb **stung** \'stəŋ\; **sting-ing** \'stiŋ-iŋ\ [ME, fr. OE *stingan*; akin to ON *stinga* to sting and prob. to Gk *stachys* spike of grain, *stochos* target, aim] vt (bef. 12c) 1 : to prick painfully: as a : to pierce or wound with a poisonous or irritating process b : to affect with sharp quick pain or smart (hail *stung* their faces) 2 : to cause to suffer acutely (*stung* with remorse) 3 : OVERCHARGE, CHEAT ~ vi 1 : to wound one with or as if with a sting 2 : to feel a keen burning pain or smart; also : to cause such pain — **sting-ing-ly** \-iŋ-lē\ adv

²**sting** n (bef. 12c) 1 a : the act of stinging; specif : the thrust of a stinger into the flesh b : a wound or pain caused by or as if by stinging 2 : STINGER 2 3 : a sharp or stinging element, force, or quality 4

\ə\ abut \ⁿ\ kitten, F table \ər\ further \a\ ash \ā\ ace \ä\ mop, mar \aů\ out \ch\ chin \e\ bet \ē\ easy \g\ go \i\ hit \ī\ ice \j\ job \ŋ\ sing \ō\ go \ò\ law \òi\ boy \th\ thin \t̶h̶\ the \ü\ loot \ů\ foot \y\ yet \zh\ vision \ä, k̲, ⁿ, œ, œ̄, ue, ūe, ʸ\ see Guide to Pronunciation

: an elaborate confidence game; *specif* : such a game worked by under-cover police in order to trap criminals

sting·a·ree \'stiŋ-ə-rē *also* 'stiŋ-rē\ *n* [by alter.] (1836) : STINGRAY

sting·er \'stiŋ-ər\ *n* (ca. 1552) **1** : one that stings; *specif* : a sharp blow or remark **2** : a sharp organ (as of a bee, scorpion, or stingray) that is usu. connected with a poison gland or otherwise adapted to wound by piercing and injecting a poison **3** : a cocktail usu. consisting of brandy and white crème de menthe

stinging nettle *n* (1525) **1** : NETTLE 1; *esp* : one (*Urtica dioica*) established in No. America that has broad coarsely toothed leaves

sting·less \'stiŋ-ləs\ *adj* (1554) : having no sting or stinger

sting·ray \-,rā\ *n* (1624) : any of numerous rays (as of the family Dasyatidae) with one or more large sharp barbed dorsal spines near the base of the whiplike tail capable of inflicting severe wounds

stin·gy \'stin-jē\ *adj* **stin·gi·er; -est** [perh. fr. (assumed) E dial. *stinge,* n., sting; akin to OE *stingan* to sting] (1659) **1** : not generous or liberal : sparing or scant in giving or spending **2** : meanly scanty or small — **stin·gi·ly** \-jə-lē\ *adv* — **stin·gi·ness** \-jē-nəs\ *n*

syn STINGY, CLOSE, NIGGARDLY, PARSIMONIOUS, PENURIOUS, MISERLY mean being unwilling or showing unwillingness to share with others. STINGY implies a marked lack of generosity ⟨a *stingy* child, not given to sharing⟩. CLOSE suggests keeping a tight grip on one's money and possessions ⟨folks who are very *close* when charity calls⟩. NIGGARDLY implies giving or spending the very smallest amount possible ⟨the *niggardly* amount budgeted for the town library⟩. PARSIMONIOUS suggests a frugality so extreme as to lead to stinginess ⟨a *parsimonious* life-style notably lacking in luxuries⟩. PENURIOUS implies niggardliness that gives an appearance of actual poverty ⟨the *penurious* eccentric bequeathed a fortune⟩. MISERLY suggests a sordid avariciousness and a morbid pleasure in hoarding ⟨a *miserly* couple devoid of social conscience⟩.

¹stink \'stiŋk\ *vi* **stank** \'staŋk\ *or* **stunk** \'stəŋk\; **stunk; stink·ing** [ME, fr. OE *stincan;* akin to OHG *stinkan* to emit a smell] (bef. 12c) **1** : to emit a strong offensive odor **2** : to be offensive; *also* : to be in bad repute **3** : to possess something to an offensive degree ⟨∼*ing* with wealth⟩ **4** : to be extremely bad in quality — **stinky** \'stiŋ-kē\ *adj*

²stink *n* (13c) **1** : a strong offensive odor : STENCH **2** : a public outcry against something

stink·ard \'stiŋ-kərd\ *n* (ca. 1600) : a mean or contemptible person

stink bomb *n* (1915) : a small bomb charged usu. with chemicals that gives off a foul odor on bursting

stink·bug \'stiŋk-,bəg\ *n* (1877) : any of various hemipterous bugs (esp. family Pentatomidae) that emit a disagreeable odor

stink·er \'stiŋ-kər\ *n* (1607) **1 a** : one that stinks **b** : an offensive or contemptible person **c** : something of very poor quality **2** : any of several large petrels that have an offensive odor **3** *slang* : something extremely difficult ⟨the examination was a real ∼⟩

stink·horn \'stiŋk-,hȯrn\ *n* (1724) : any of various fetid basidiomycetous fungi (order Phallales, esp. *Phallus impudicus*) having spores dispersed by insects

¹stink·ing *adj* (bef. 12c) **1** : strong and offensive to the sense of smell **2** *slang* : offensively drunk **syn** see MALODOROUS — **stink·ing·ly** \'stiŋ-kiŋ-lē\ *adv*

²stinking *adv* (1887) : to an extreme degree ⟨got ∼ drunk⟩

stinking smut *n* (ca. 1891) : ⁴BUNT

stink·pot \'stiŋk-,pät\ *n* (1669) **1** : an earthen jar filled with fetid material and formerly sometimes thrown as a stink bomb on an enemy's deck **2** : MUSK TURTLE **3** : STINKER 1 **4** *slang* : MOTORBOAT

stink up *vt* (1941) : to cause to stink or be filled with a stench

stink·weed \'stiŋk-,wēd\ *n* (1753) : any of various strong-scented or fetid plants; *esp* : PENNYCRESS

stink·wood \-,wůd\ *n* (1731) **1** : any of several trees with a wood of unpleasant odor; *esp* : a southern African tree (*Ocotea bullata*) of the laurel family yielding a valued cabinet wood **2** : the wood of a stinkwood

¹stint \'stint\ *vb* [ME, fr. OE *styntan* to blunt, dull; akin to ON *stuttr* scant] *vi* (13c) **1** *archaic* : STOP, DESIST **2** : to be sparing or frugal ∼ *vt* **1** *archaic* : to put an end to : STOP **2 a** : to restrain within certain limits : CONFINE **b** : to restrict with respect to a share or allowance **3** : to assign a task to (a person) — **stint·er** *n*

²stint *n* (ca. 1530) **1 a** : a definite quantity of work assigned **b** : a period of time spent at a particular activity ⟨served a brief ∼ as a waiter⟩ **2** : RESTRAINT, LIMITATION **syn** see TASK

³stint *n, pl* **stints** *also* **stint** [ME *stynte*] (15c) : any of several small sandpipers

stipe \'stīp\ *n* [NL *stipes,* fr. L, tree trunk; akin to L *stipare* to press together — more at STIFF] (1785) : a usu. short plant stalk: as **a** : the stem supporting the cap of a fungus **b** : a part that is similar to a stipe and connects the holdfast and blade of a frondose alga **c** : the petiole of a fern frond **d** : a prolongation of the receptacle beneath the ovary of a seed plant — **stiped** \'stīpt\ *adj*

sti·pend \'stī-,pend, -pənd\ *n* [ME, alter. of *stipendy,* fr. L *stipendium,* fr. *stip-, stips* gift + *pendere* to weigh, pay] (15c) : a fixed sum of money paid periodically for services or to defray expenses

¹sti·pen·di·ary \stī-'pen-dē-,er-ē\ *n, pl* **-ar·ies** (15c) : one who receives a stipend

²stipendiary *adj* (ca. 1545) **1** : receiving or compensated by wages or salary ⟨a ∼ curate⟩ **2** : of or relating to a stipend

sti·pes \'stī-,pēz\ *n, pl* **stip·i·tes** \'sti-pə-,tēz\ [NL *stipit-, stipes,* fr. L, tree trunk] (1760) : PEDUNCLE; *esp* : the second basal segment of a maxilla of an insect or crustacean

¹stip·ple \'sti-pəl\ *vt* **stip·pled; stip·pling** \-p(ə-)liŋ\ [D *stippelen* to spot, dot] (ca. 1762) **1** : to engrave by means of dots and flicks **2 a** : to make by small short touches (as of paint or ink) that together

produce an even or softly graded shadow **b** : to apply (as paint) by repeated small touches **3** : SPECKLE, FLECK — **stip·pler** \-p(ə-)lər\ *n*

²stipple *n* (1837) **1** : production of gradation of light and shade in graphic art by stippling small points, larger dots, or longer strokes; *also* : an effect produced in this way

stip·u·lar \'sti-pyə-lər\ *adj* (1793) : of, resembling, or provided with stipules ⟨∼ glands⟩

¹stip·u·late \'sti-pyə-,lāt\ *vb* **-lat·ed; -lat·ing** [L *stipulatus,* pp. of *stipulari* to demand some term in an agreement] *vi* (ca. 1624) **1** : to make an agreement or covenant to do or forbear something : CONTRACT **2** : to demand an express term in an agreement — used with *for* ∼ *vt* **1** : to specify as a condition or requirement of an agreement or offer **2** : to give a guarantee of — **stip·u·la·tor** \-,lā-tər\ *n*

²stip·u·late \'sti-pyə-lət\ *adj* [NL *stipula*] (1776) : having stipules

stip·u·la·tion \,sti-pyə-'lā-shən\ *n* (ca. 1552) **1** : an act of stipulating **2** : something stipulated; *esp* : a condition, requirement, or item specified in a legal instrument — **stip·u·la·to·ry** \'sti-pyə-lə-,tōr-ē, -,tȯr-\ *adj*

stip·ule \'sti-(,)pyü(ə)l\ *n* [NL *stipula,* fr. L, stalk; akin to L *stipes* tree trunk] (1793) : either of a pair of appendages borne at the base of the leaf in many plants

¹stir \'stər\ *vb* **stirred; stir·ring** [ME, fr. OE *styrian;* akin to OHG *stōren* to scatter] *vt* (bef. 12c) **1 a** : to cause an esp. slight movement or change of position of **b** : to disturb the quiet of : AGITATE **2 a** : to disturb the relative position of the particles or parts of esp. by a continued circular movement **b** : to mix by or as if by stirring **3** : BESTIR, EXERT **4** : to bring into notice or debate : RAISE **5 a** : to rouse to activity : evoke strong feelings in **b** : to call forth (as a memory) : EVOKE **c** : PROVOKE ∼ *vi* **1 a** : to make a slight movement **b** : to begin to move (as in rousing) **2** : to begin to be active **3** : to be active or busy **4** : to pass an implement through a substance with a circular movement **5** : to be able to be stirred — **stir·rer** *n*

²stir *n* (14c) **1 a** : a state of disturbance, agitation, or brisk activity **b** : widespread notice and discussion : IMPRESSION ⟨the book caused quite a ∼⟩ **2** : a slight movement **3** : a stirring movement

³stir *n* [origin unknown] (1851) *slang* : PRISON

stir·about \'stər-ə-,baůt\ *n* (1682) : a porridge of Irish origin consisting of oatmeal or cornmeal boiled in water or milk and stirred

stir–cra·zy \'stər-'krā-zē\ *adj* [³*stir*] (ca. 1908) *slang* : distraught because of prolonged confinement

¹stir–fry \-'frī\ *vt* (1958) : to fry quickly over high heat in a lightly oiled pan (as a wok) while stirring continuously

²stir–fry \-,frī\ *n* (1959) : a dish of something stir-fried

stirk \'stərk\ *n* [ME, fr. OE *stirc;* akin to MLG *sterke* young cow and perh. to Goth *stairo* sterile animal — more at STERILE] (bef. 12c) *Brit* : a young bull or cow esp. between one and two years old

Stir·ling engine \'stər-liŋ-\ *n* [Robert *Stirling* †1878 Scot. engineer] (1896) : an external combustion engine having an enclosed working fluid (as helium) that is alternately compressed and expanded to operate a piston

Stir·ling's formula \'stər-liŋz-\ *n* [James *Stirling* †1770 Scot. mathematician] (1926) : a formula

$$\sqrt{2\pi n}\, n^n e^{-n}$$

that approximates the value of the factorial of a very large number *n*

stirp \'stərp\ *n* [L *stirp-, stirps*] (1502) : a line descending from a common ancestor : STOCK, LINEAGE

stirps \'stirps, 'stərps\ *n, pl* **stir·pes** \'stir-,pās, 'stər-(,)pēz\ [L, lit., stem, stock] (1681) **1** : a branch of a family; *also* : the person from whom it is descended **2 a** : a group of animals equivalent to a superfamily **b** : a race or fixed variety of plants

stir·ring \'stər-iŋ\ *adj* (bef. 12c) **1** : ACTIVE, BUSTLING **2** : ROUSING, INSPIRING ⟨a ∼ speech⟩

stir·rup \'stər-əp *also* 'stir-əp *or* 'stə-rəp\ *n* [ME *stirop,* fr. OE *stigrāp,* fr. *stig-* (akin to OHG *stigan* to go up) + *rāp* rope — more at STAIR, ROPE] (bef. 12c) **1** : either of a pair of small light frames or rings for receiving the foot of a rider that are attached by a strap to a saddle and used to aid in mounting and as a support while riding **2** : a piece resembling a stirrup (as a support or clamp in carpentry and machinery) **3** : a rope secured to a yard and attached to a thimble in its lower end for supporting a footrope **4** : STAPES

stirrup cup *n* (1681) **1** : a small serving of drink (as wine) taken by a rider about to depart; *also* : the vessel in which it is served **2** : a farewell cup

stirrup leather *n* (14c) : the looped strap suspending a stirrup

stirrup pump *n* (1939) : a portable hand pump held in position by a foot bracket and used for throwing a jet or spray of liquid

¹stitch \'stich\ *n* [ME *stiche,* fr. OE *stice;* akin to OE *stician* to stick] (bef. 12c) **1** : a local sharp and sudden pain esp. in the side **2 a** : one in-and-out movement of a threaded needle in sewing, embroidering, or suturing **b** : a portion of thread left in the material or suture left in the tissue after one stitch **3** : a least part esp. of clothing **4** : a single loop of thread or yarn around an implement (as a knitting needle or crochet hook) **5** : a stitch or series of stitches formed in a particular way ⟨a basting ∼⟩ — **in stitches** : in a state of uncontrollable laughter

²stitch *vt* (13c) **1 a** : to fasten, join, or close with or as if with stitches **b** : to make, mend, or decorate with or as if with stitches **2** : to unite by means of staples ∼ *vi* : SEW — **stitch·er** *n*

stitch·ery \'stich-rē, 'sti-chə-\ *n* (1607) : NEEDLEWORK

stitch·wort \'stich-,wərt, -,wȯrt\ *n* (13c) : any of several chickweeds (genus *Stellaria*)

stithy \'sti-thē, -thē\ *n, pl* **stith·ies** [ME, fr. ON *stethi;* akin to OE *stede* stead] (13c) **1** *archaic* : ANVIL **2** *archaic* : SMITHY 1

sti·ver \'stī-vər\ *n* [D *stuiver*] (1502) **1** : a unit of value and coin of the Netherlands equal to ¹/₂₀ gulden **2** : something of little value

stoa \'stō-ə\ *n* [Gk; akin to Gk *stylos* pillar — more at STEER] (1603) : an ancient Greek portico usu. walled at the back with a front colonnade designed to afford a sheltered promenade

stoat \'stōt\ *n, pl* **stoats** *also* **stoat** [ME *stote*] (15c) : the common Holarctic ermine (*Mustela erminea*) esp. in its brown summer coat

stob \'stäb\ *n* [ME, stump; akin to ME *stubb* stub] (15c) *chiefly dial* : STAKE, POST

stingray

stoc·ca·do \stə-'kä-(ˌ)dō\ *n, pl* **-dos** [It *stoccata*] (1582) *archaic* : a thrust with a rapier

sto·chas·tic \stə-'kas-tik, stō-\ *adj* [Gk *stochastikos* skillful in aiming, fr. *stochazesthai* to aim at, guess at, fr. *stochos* target, aim, guess — more at STING] (1923) **1** : RANDOM; *specif* : involving a random variable (a ~ process)   **2** : involving chance or probability : PROBABILISTIC (a ~ model of radiation-induced mutation) — **sto·chas·ti·cal·ly** \-ti-k(ə-)lē\ *adv*

¹stock \'stäk\ *n* [ME *stok*, fr. OE *stocc;* akin to OHG *stoc* stick] (bef. 12c)   **1 a** *archaic* : STUMP   **b** *archaic* : a log or block of wood   **c** (1) *archaic* : something without life or consciousness   (2) : a dull, stupid, or lifeless person   **2** : a supporting framework or structure: as   **a** *pl* : the frame or timbers holding a ship during construction   **b** *pl* : a device for publicly punishing offenders consisting of a wooden frame with holes in which the feet or feet and hands can be locked   **c** (1) : the wooden part by which a shoulder arm is held during firing   (2) : the butt of an implement (as a whip or fishing rod)   (3) : BITSTOCK, BRACE   **d** : a long beam on a field gun forming the third support point in firing   **3 a** : the main stem of a plant : TRUNK   **b** (1) : a plant or plant part united with a scion in grafting and supplying mostly underground parts to a graft   (2) : a plant from which slips or cuttings are taken   **4** : the crosspiece of an anchor — see ANCHOR illustration   **5 a** : the original (as a person, race, or language) from which others derive : SOURCE   **b** (1) : the descendants of one individual : FAMILY, LINEAGE   (2) : a compound organism — compare CLONE   **c** : an infraspecific group usu. having unity of descent   **d** (1) : a related group of languages   (2) : a language family   **6 a** (1) : the equipment, materials, or supplies of an establishment   (2) : LIVESTOCK   **b** : a store or supply accumulated; *esp* : the inventory of goods of a merchant or manufacturer   **7 a** *archaic* : a supply of capital : FUNDS; *esp* : money or capital invested or available for investment or trading   **b** (1) : the part of a tally formerly given to the creditor in a transaction   (2) : a debt or fund due (as from a government) for money loaned at interest; *also, Brit* : capital or a debt or fund bearing interest in perpetuity and not ordinarily redeemable as to principal   **c** (1) : the proprietorship element in a corporation usu. divided into shares and represented by transferable certificates   (2) : a portion of such stock of one or more companies   (3) : STOCK CERTIFICATE   **8** : any of a genus (Matthiola) of Old World herbs or subshrubs of the mustard family with racemes of usu. sweet-scented flowers   **9** : a wide band or scarf worn about the neck esp. by some clergymen   **10 a** : liquid in which meat, fish, or vegetables have been simmered that is used as a basis for soup, gravy, or sauce   **b** (1) : raw material from which something is manufactured   (2) : paper used for printing   **c** : the portion of a pack of cards not distributed to the players at the beginning of a game   **11 a** (1) : an estimate or evaluation of something (take ~ of the situation)   (2) : the estimation in which someone or something is held (his ~ with the electorate remains high —*Newsweek*)   **b** : confidence or faith placed in someone or something (put little ~ in his testimony)   **12** : the production and presentation of plays by a stock company : STOCK CAR 1 — **in stock** : on hand : in the store and ready for delivery — **out of stock** : having no more on hand : completely sold out

²stock *vt* (15c)   **1** : to make (a domestic animal) pregnant   **2** : to fit to or with a stock   **3** : to provide with stock or a stock : SUPPLY (~ a stream with trout)   **4** : to procure or keep a stock of   **5** : to graze (livestock) on land   ~ *vi*   **1** : to send out new shoots   **2** : to put in stock or supplies (~ up on canned goods)

³stock *adj* (1625)   **1 a** : kept regularly in stock (comes in ~ sizes) (a ~ model)   **b** : commonly used or brought forward : STANDARD (the ~ answer)   **2 a** : kept for breeding purposes : BROOD (a ~ mare)   **b** : devoted to the breeding and rearing of livestock (a ~ farm)   **c** : used or intended for livestock (a ~ train)   **d** : used in herding livestock (a ~ horse) (a ~ dog)   **3** : of or relating to a stock company   **4** : employed in handling, checking, or taking care of the stock of merchandise on hand (a ~ clerk)

¹stock·ade \stä-'kād\ *n* [Sp *estacada*, fr. *estaca* stake, pale, of Gmc origin; akin to OE *staca* stake] (1614)   **1** : a line of stout posts set firmly to form a defense   **2** : an enclosure or pen made with posts and stakes   **b** : an enclosure in which prisoners are kept

²stockade *vt* **stock·ad·ed; stock·ad·ing** (1677) : to fortify or surround with a stockade

stockade fence (1985) : a solid fence of half-round boards pointed at the top

stock·breed·er \'stäk-ˌbrē-dər\ *n* (1815) : a person engaged in the breeding and care of livestock for the market, for show purposes, or for racing

stock·bro·ker \-ˌbrō-kər\ *n* (ca. 1706) : a broker who executes orders to buy and sell securities and often also acts as a securities dealer — **stock·bro·ker·age** \-k(ə-)rij\ *n* — **stock·brok·ing** \-ˌbrō-kiŋ\ *n*

stock car *n* (1858)   **1** : a latticed railroad boxcar for carrying livestock   **2** : a racing car having the basic chassis of a commercially produced assembly-line model

stock certificate *n* (1863) : an instrument evidencing ownership of one or more shares of the capital stock of a corporation

stock company *n* (1827)   **1** : a corporation or joint-stock company of which the capital is represented by stock   **2** : a theatrical company attached to a repertory theater; *esp* : one without outstanding stars

stock dividend *n* (ca. 1902)   **1** : the payment by a corporation of a dividend in the form of shares usu. of its own stock without change in par value — compare STOCK SPLIT   **2** : the stock distributed in a stock dividend

stock·er \'stä-kər\ *n* (1881)   **1** : a young animal (as a steer or heifer) suitable for being fed and fattened for market   **2** : an animal (as a heifer) suitable for use in a breeding establishment   **3** : STOCK CAR 2

stock exchange *n* (1773)   **1** : a place where security trading is conducted on an organized system   **2** : an association of people organized to provide an auction market among themselves for the purchase and sale of securities

stock·fish \-ˌfish\ *n* [ME *stokfish*, fr. MD *stocvisch*, fr. *stoc* stick + *visch* fish] (13c) : fish (as cod, haddock, or hake) dried hard in the open air without salt

stock·hold·er \'stäk-ˌhōl-dər\ *n* (ca. 1776) : an owner of corporate stock

stock·i·nette *or* **stock·i·net** \ˌstä-kə-'net\ *n* [alter. of earlier *stocking net*] (1784) : a soft elastic usu. cotton fabric used esp. for bandages and infants' wear

stock·ing \'stä-kiŋ\ *n* [obs. *stock* to cover with a stocking] (1583)   **1 a** : a usu. knit close-fitting covering for the foot and leg   **b** : SOCK 2   **2** : something resembling a stocking; *esp* : a ring of distinctive color on the lower part of the leg of an animal — **stock·inged** \-kiŋd\ *adj* — **in one's stocking feet** : having on stockings but no shoes

stocking cap *n* (ca. 1897) : a long knitted cone-shaped cap with a tassel or pom-pom worn esp. for winter sports or play

stocking stuffer *n* (1948) : a small gift suitable for placing in a Christmas stocking

stock–in–trade \ˌstäk-ən-'trād, 'stäk-ən-ˌ\ *n* (ca. 1771)   **1** : the equipment, merchandise, or materials necessary to or used in a trade or business   **2** : something that resembles the standard equipment of a tradesman or business (humor was her ~ as a writer)

stock·ish \'stä-kish\ *adj* (1596) : like a stock : STUPID

stock·ist \'stä-kist\ *n* (1910) *Brit* : one (as a retailer) that stocks goods

stock·job·ber \'stäk-ˌjä-bər\ *n* (ca. 1626) : one who deals in stocks: as   **a** : a member of the London Stock Exchange who deals speculatively with brokers or other jobbers and usu. specializes in one class of securities — called also *jobber*   **b** : STOCKBROKER — usu. used disparagingly — **stock·job·bing** \-ˌjä-biŋ\ *n* (1692) : speculative exchange dealings

stock·keep·er \'stäk-ˌkē-pər\ *n* (ca. 1786)   **1** : one (as a herdsman or shepherd) having the charge or care of livestock   **2** : one that keeps and records stock (as in a warehouse) : one that keeps an inventory of goods on hand, shipped, or received

stock·man \-mən, -ˌman\ *n* (1806) : one occupied as an owner or worker in the raising of livestock (as cattle or sheep)

stock market *n* (1809)   **1** : STOCK EXCHANGE 1   **2 a** : a market for particular stocks   **b** : the market for stocks throughout a country

stock option *n* (1945)   **1** : an option contract involving stock   **2** : a right granted by a corporation to officers or employees as a form of compensation that allows purchase of corporate stock at a fixed price at a specified time with reimbursement derived from the difference between purchase and market prices

¹stock·pile \'stäk-ˌpīl\ *n* (1872) : a storage pile: as   **a** : a reserve supply of something essential accumulated within a country for use during a shortage   **b** : a gradually accumulated reserve of something (avert ~s of unsold cars —Bert Pierce)

²stockpile *vt* (1921)   **1** : to place or store in or on a stockpile   **2** : to accumulate a stockpile of (~ war materials in Europe —A. O. Wolfers) — **stock·pil·er** *n*

stock·pot \'stäk-ˌpät\ *n* (1853)   **1** : a pot in which soup stock is prepared   **2** : an abundant supply : REPOSITORY

stock·room \-ˌrüm, -ˌrum\ *n* (1825) : a storage place for supplies or goods used in a business

stock saddle *n* (1886) : WESTERN SADDLE

stock split *n* (1950) : a division of corporate stock by the issuance to existing shareholders of a specified number of new shares with a corresponding lowering of par value for each outstanding share — compare STOCK DIVIDEND

stock–still \'stäk-'stil\ *adj* (15c) : very still : MOTIONLESS (stood ~)

stock·tak·ing \'stäk-ˌtā-kiŋ\ *n* (ca. 1858)   **1** : INVENTORY 3   **2** : the action of estimating a situation at a given moment

stocky \'stä-kē\ *adj* **stock·i·er; -est** (1622) : compact, sturdy, and relatively thick in build — **stock·i·ly** \'stä-kə-lē\ *adv* — **stock·i·ness** \'stä-kē-nəs\ *n*

stock·yard \'stäk-ˌyärd\ *n* (1802) : a yard for stock; *specif* : one in which transient cattle, sheep, swine, or horses are kept temporarily for slaughter, market, or shipping

¹stodge \'stäj\ *vt* **stodged; stodg·ing** [origin unknown] (1674) *Brit* : to stuff full esp. with food

²stodge *n* (1825) *Brit* : something or someone stodgy

stodgy \'stä-jē\ *adj* **stodg·i·er; -est** (1858)   **1** : having a rich filling quality : HEAVY (~ bread)   **2** : moving in a slow plodding way esp. as a result of physical bulkiness   **3** : BORING, DULL (out on a peaceful rather ~ Sunday boat trip —Edna Ferber)   **4** : extremely old-fashioned : HIDEBOUND (received a pompously Victorian letter from his ~ father —E. E. S. Montagu)   **5 a** : DRAB   **b** : DOWDY — **stodg·i·ly** \'stä-jə-lē\ *adv* — **stodg·i·ness** \'stä-jē-nəs\ *n*

sto·gie *or* **sto·gy** \'stō-gē\ *n, pl* **stogies** [*Conestoga*, Pa.] (1853)   **1** : a stout coarse shoe : BROGAN   **2** : an inexpensive slender cylindrical cigar; *broadly* : CIGAR

¹sto·ic \'stō-ik\ *n* [ME, fr. L *stoicus*, fr. Gk *stōïkos*, lit., of the portico, fr. *Stoa* (*Poikilē*) the Painted Portico, portico at Athens where Zeno taught] (14c)   **1** *cap* : a member of a school of philosophy founded by Zeno of Citium about 300 B.C. holding that the wise man should be free from passion, unmoved by joy or grief, and submissive to natural law   **2** : one apparently or professedly indifferent to pleasure or pain

²stoic *or* **sto·i·cal** \-i-kəl\ *adj* (15c)   **1** *cap* : of, relating to, or resembling the Stoics or their doctrines (*Stoic* logic)   **2** : not affected by or showing passion or feeling; *esp* : firmly restraining response to pain or distress (a ~ indifference to cold) **syn** see IMPASSIVE — **sto·ical·ly** \-i-k(ə-)lē\ *adv*

stoi·chio·met·ric \ˌstöi-kē-ō-'me-trik\ *adj* (1892) : of, relating to, used in, or marked by stoichiometry — **stoi·chio·met·ri·cal·ly** \-tri-k(ə-)lē\ *adv*

stoi·chi·om·e·try \ˌstöi-kē-'ä-mə-trē\ *n* [Gk *stoicheion* element (fr. *stoichos* row) + E *-metry*; akin to Gk *steichein* to walk, go — more at STAIR] (1807)   **1** : a branch of chemistry that deals with the application of the laws of definite proportions and of the conservation of mass and energy to chemical activity   **2 a** : the quantitative relationship between constituents in a chemical substance   **b** : the quantitative relationship between two or more substances esp. in processes involving physical or chemical change

---

\ə\ abut \ᵊ\ kitten, F table \ər\ further \a\ ash \ā\ ace \ä\ mop, mar \aú\ out \ch\ chin \e\ bet \ē\ easy \g\ go \i\ hit \ī\ ice \j\ job \ŋ\ sing \ō\ go \ó\ law \ói\ boy \th\ thin \t͟h\ the \ü\ loot \ú\ foot \y\ yet \zh\ vision \ä, k̲, ⁿ, œ, œ̄, ue, ūe, ᵊ\ *see* Guide to Pronunciation

sto·i·cism \'stō-ə-ˌsi-zəm\ *n* (1626) **1** *cap* : the philosophy of the Stoics **2** : indifference to pleasure or pain : IMPASSIVENESS

stoke \'stōk\ *vb* **stoked; stok·ing** [D *stoken;* akin to MD *stuken* to push] *vt* (1683) **1** : to poke or stir up (as a fire) : supply with fuel **2** : to feed abundantly ∼ *vi* : to stir up or tend a fire (as in a furnace) : supply a furnace with fuel

stoked \'stōkt\ *adj* (1965) *slang* : being in an enthusiastic or exhilarated state

stoke-hold \'stōk-ˌhōld\ *n* (1887) : the boiler room of a ship

stok·er \'stō-kər\ *n* (1660) **1** : one employed to tend a furnace and supply it with fuel; *specif* : one that tends a marine steam boiler **2** : a machine for feeding a fire

Stokes' aster \'stōks-\ *n* [Jonathan *Stokes* †1831 Eng. botanist] (ca. 1890) : a perennial composite herb (*Stokesia laevis*) of the southern U.S. often grown for its large showy heads of usu. blue flowers — called also **sto·ke·sia** \stō-ˈkē-zh(ē-)ə, -zē-ə\

¹stole \'stōl\ *past of* STEAL

²stole *n* [ME, fr. OE, fr. L *stola*, fr. Gk *stolē* equipment, robe, fr. *stellein* to set up, make ready] (bef. 12c) **1** : a long loose garment : ROBE **2** : an ecclesiastical vestment consisting of a long usu. silk band worn traditionally around the neck by bishops and priests and over the left shoulder by deacons **3** : a long wide scarf or similar covering worn by women usu. across the shoulders

stolen *past part of* STEAL

stol·id \'stä-ləd\ *adj* [L *stolidus* dull, stupid] (ca. 1600) : having or expressing little or no sensibility : UNEMOTIONAL *syn* see IMPASSIVE — **sto·lid·i·ty** \stä-ˈli-də-tē, stə-\ *n* — **stol·id·ly** \'stä-ləd-lē\ *adv*

stol·len \'shtō-lən, 'shtȯ-, 'shtä-, *or with* s *for* sh\ *n, pl* **stollen** *or* **stollens** [G, lit., post, support, fr. OHG *stollo* — more at STELA] (1906) : a sweet yeast bread of German origin containing fruit and nuts

sto·lon \'stō-lən, -ˌlän\ *n* [NL *stolon-, stolo,* fr. L, branch, sucker; akin to OE *stela* stalk, Arm *stełn* branch] (1601) **1 a** : a horizontal branch from the base of a plant that produces new plants from buds at its tip or nodes (as in the strawberry) — called also *runner* **b** : a hypha (as of rhizopus) produced on the surface and connecting a group of conidiophores **2** : an extension of the body wall (as of a hydrozoan or bryozoan) that develops buds giving rise to new zooids which usu. remain united by the stolon

s stolon 1a

sto·lon·if·er·ous \ˌstō-lə-ˈni-f(ə-)rəs\ *adj* (ca. 1777) : bearing or developing stolons

sto·ma \'stō-mə\ *n, pl* **sto·ma·ta** \-mə-tə\ *also* **stomas** [NL, fr. Gk *stomat-, stoma* mouth] (ca. 1684) **1** : any of various small simple bodily openings esp. in a lower animal **2** : one of the minute openings in the epidermis of a plant organ (as a leaf) through which gaseous interchange takes place; *also* : the opening with its associated cellular structures **3** : an artificial permanent opening esp. in the abdominal wall made in surgical procedures

¹stom·ach \'stə-mək, -mik\ *n* [ME *stomak,* fr. MF *estomac,* fr. L *stomachus* gullet, esophagus, stomach, fr. Gk *stomachos,* fr. *stoma* mouth; akin to MBret *staffn* mouth, Av *staman*-] (14c) **1 a** (1) : a dilatation of the alimentary canal of a vertebrate communicating anteriorly with the esophagus and posteriorly with the duodenum (2) : one of the compartments of a ruminant stomach ⟨the abomasum is the fourth ∼ of a ruminant⟩ **b** : a cavity in an invertebrate animal that is analogous to a stomach **c** : the part of the body that contains the stomach : BELLY, ABDOMEN **2 a** : desire for food caused by hunger : APPETITE **b** : INCLINATION, DESIRE ⟨had no ∼ for an argument⟩; *also* : COURAGE, GUTS **3** *obs* **a** : SPIRIT, VALOR **b** : PRIDE **c** : SPLEEN, RESENTMENT

²stomach *vt* (1523) **1** *archaic* : to take offense at **2** : to bear without overt reaction or resentment : put up with ⟨couldn't ∼ office politics⟩

stom·ach·ache \-ˌāk\ *n* (1763) : pain in or in the region of the stomach

stom·ach·er \'stə-mi-kər, -chər\ *n* (15c) : the center front section of a waist or underwaist or a usu. heavily embroidered or jeweled separate piece for the center front of a bodice worn by men and women in the 15th and 16th centuries and later by women only

¹sto·mach·ic \stə-ˈma-kik\ *adj* (ca. 1656) : of or relating to the stomach ⟨∼ vessels⟩

²stomachic *n* : a stimulant or tonic for the stomach

stom·achy \'stə-mə-kē, -mi-\ *adj* (ca. 1825) **1** *dial Brit* : IRASCIBLE, IRRITABLE **2** : having a large stomach

sto·mal \'stō-məl\ *adj* (ca. 1941) : of, relating to, or situated near a surgical stoma ⟨a ∼ ulcer⟩

stomat- *or* **stomato-** *comb form* [NL, fr. Gk, fr. *stomat-, stoma*] : mouth : stoma ⟨*stoma*titis⟩

sto·ma·tal \'stō-mə-t³l\ *adj* (1861) : of, relating to, or constituting plant stomata ⟨∼ openings⟩ ⟨∼ transpiration⟩

sto·mate \'stō-ˌmāt\ *n* [irreg. fr. NL *stomat-, stoma*] (1835) : STOMA 2

sto·ma·ti·tis \ˌstō-mə-ˈtī-təs\ *n, pl* **-tit·i·des** \-'ti-tə-ˌdēz\ *or* **-ti·tis·es** \-'ti-tə-səz\ [NL] (1859) : any of numerous inflammatory diseases of the mouth

sto·mato·pod \stō-ˈma-tə-ˌpäd\ *n* [NL *Stomatopoda,* fr. *stomat-* + Gk *pod-, pous* foot — more at FOOT] (1877) : any of an order (Stomatopoda) of marine crustaceans (as a squilla) that have gills on the abdominal appendages — **stomatopod** *adj*

sto·mo·de·um *or* **sto·mo·dae·um** \ˌstō-mə-ˈdē-əm\ *n, pl* **-dea** \-'dē-ə\ *or* **-daea** \-'dē-ə\ *also* **-deums** *or* **-daeums** [NL, fr. Gk *stoma* mouth + *hodaion,* neut. of *hodaios* being on the way, fr. *hodos* way] (1876) : the embryonic anterior ectodermal part of the alimentary canal or tract — **sto·mo·de·al** *or* **sto·mo·dae·al** \-'dē-əl\ *adj*

¹stomp \'stämp, 'stȯmp\ *vb* [by alter.] (1803) : STAMP 1, 2

²stomp *n* (ca. 1899) **1** : STAMP 4 **2** : a jazz dance marked by heavy stamping

stomping ground *n* (1854) : STAMPING GROUND

-stomy *n comb form* [ISV, fr. Gk *stoma* mouth, opening] : surgical operation establishing a usu. permanent opening into (such) a part ⟨entero*stomy*⟩

¹stone \'stōn\ *n* [ME, fr. OE *stān;* akin to OHG *stein* stone, OCS *stěna* wall, and perh. to Skt *styāyate* it hardens — more at STEATO-] (bef. 12c) **1** : a concretion of earthy or mineral matter: **a** (1) : such a concretion of indeterminate size or shape (2) : ROCK **b** : a piece of rock for a specified function: as (1) : a building block (2) : a paving block (3) : a precious stone : GEM (4) : GRAVESTONE (5) : GRINDSTONE (6) : WHETSTONE (7) : a surface upon which a drawing, text, or design to be lithographed is drawn or transferred **2** : something resembling a small stone: as **a** : CALCULUS 3a **b** : the hard central portion of a drupaceous fruit (as a peach) **c** : a hard stony seed (as of a date) **3** *pl usu* **stone** : any of various units of weight; *esp* : an official British unit equal to 14 pounds (6.3 kilograms) **4 a** : CURLING STONE **b** : a round playing piece used in various games (as backgammon or go) **5** : a stand or table with a smooth flat top on which to impose or set type

²stone *vt* **stoned; ston·ing** (13c) **1** : to hurl stones at; *esp* : to kill by pelting with stones **2** *archaic* : to make hard or insensitive to feeling **3** : to face, pave, or fortify with stones **4** : to remove the stones or seeds of (a fruit) **5 a** : to rub, scour, or polish with a stone **b** : to sharpen with a whetstone — **ston·er** *n*

³stone *adv* (13c) : ENTIRELY, UTTERLY — used as an intensive; often used in combination ⟨*stone*-broke⟩ ⟨*stone*-cold soup⟩ ⟨*stone*-dead⟩

⁴stone *adj* (14c) **1** : of, relating to, or made of stone **2** : ABSOLUTE, UTTER ⟨pure ∼ craziness —Edwin Shrake⟩

Stone Age *n* (1864) : the first known period of prehistoric human culture characterized by the use of stone tools

stone-blind \'stōn-'blīnd\ *adj* (14c) : totally blind

stone-boat \-ˌbōt\ *n* (1859) : a flat sledge or drag for transporting heavy articles (as stones)

stone canal *n* (1887) : a tube in many echinoderms that contains calcareous deposits and leads from the madreporite to the ring of the water-vascular system surrounding the mouth

stone cell *n* (1875) : SCLEREID

stone·chat \-ˌchat\ *n* [²*chat*] (ca. 1783) : an Old World oscine songbird (*Saxicola torquata*) related to the thrushes; *also* : any of various related birds (genus *Saxicola*)

stone china *n* (1823) : a hard dense opaque feldspathic pottery developed in England; *broadly* : IRONSTONE CHINA

stone-cold \'stōn-'kōld\ *adv* (1592) : ABSOLUTELY ⟨∼ sober⟩

stone crab *n* (1709) : a large brownish edible crab (*Menippe mercenaria*) found on the southern coast of the U.S. and in the Caribbean area

stone·crop \'stōn-ˌkräp\ *n* (bef. 12c) **1** : SEDUM; *esp* : an Old World creeping evergreen sedum (*Sedum acre*) with pungent fleshy leaves and yellow flowers **2** : any of various plants of the orpine family related to the sedums

stone·cut·ter \-ˌkə-tər\ *n* (1540) **1** : one that cuts, carves, or dresses stone **2** : a machine for dressing stone — **stone·cut·ting** \-ˌkə-tiŋ\ *n*

stoned \'stōnd\ *adj* (1952) **1** : DRUNK 1a **2** : being under the influence of a drug (as marijuana) taken esp. for pleasure : HIGH

stone-deaf \-'def\ *adj* (1837) : totally deaf

stone-faced \-ˌfāst\ *adj* (1932) : showing no emotion : EXPRESSIONLESS

stone·fish \'stōn-ˌfish\ *n* (1896) : any of several small spiny venomous scorpion fishes (esp. genus *Synanceja*) common about coral reefs of the tropical Indo-Pacific

stone fly *n* (15c) : any of an order (Plecoptera) of insects with an aquatic carnivorous nymph having gills and an adult having long antennae, two pairs of membranous wings, and usu. long cerci

stone fruit *n* (ca. 1534) : a fruit with a stony endocarp : DRUPE

stone-ground \'stōn-'graùnd\ *adj* (1905) : ground in a buhrstone mill ⟨∼ flour⟩

stone·ma·son \'stōn-ˌmā-s³n\ *n* (1758) : a mason who builds with stone — **stone·ma·son·ry** \-rē\ *n*

stone roller *n* (1878) **1** : HOG SUCKER **2** : a common cyprinid fish (*Campostoma anomalum*) found esp. in clear streams of the central U.S.

stone's throw *n* (1581) : a short distance ⟨lives within a *stone's throw* of town⟩

stone·wall \'stōn-ˌwȯl\ *vi* (1880) **1** *chiefly Brit* : to engage in obstructive parliamentary debate or delaying tactics **2** : to be uncooperative, obstructive, or evasive ∼ *vt* : to refuse to comply or cooperate with — **stone·wall·er** *n*

stone wall *n* (bef. 12c) **1** : a fence made of stones; *esp* : one built of rough stones without mortar to enclose a field **2** : an immovable block or obstruction (as in public affairs)

stone·ware \-ˌwar, -ˌwer\ *n* (1683) : a strong opaque ceramic ware that is high-fired, well vitrified, and nonporous

stone·washed \-ˌwȯsht, -ˌwäsht *also* -ˌwȯrsht *or* -ˌwärsht\ *adj* (1982) : subjected to a washing process during manufacture that includes the use of abrasive stones esp. to create a softer fabric ⟨∼ denim jeans⟩

stone·work \-ˌwərk\ *n* (bef. 12c) **1** : a structure or part built of stone : MASONRY **2** : the shaping, preparation, or setting of stone

stone·wort \-ˌwərt, -ˌwȯrt\ *n* (1816) : any of various freshwater green algae (order Charales) that have a thallus differentiated into rhizoids and stems with whorls of branchlets and that are often encrusted with calcareous deposits

stony *also* **ston·ey** \'stō-nē\ *adj* **ston·i·er; -est** (bef. 12c) **1** : abounding in or having the nature of stone : ROCKY **2 a** : insensitive to pity or human feeling : OBDURATE **b** : manifesting no movement or reaction : DUMB, EXPRESSIONLESS **c** : fearfully gripping : PETRIFYING **3** *archaic* : consisting of or made of stones **4** *Brit* : stone-broke — **ston·i·ly** \'stō-n³l-ē\ *adv* — **ston·i·ness** \'stō-nē-nəs\ *n*

stony·heart·ed \'stō-nē-ˌhär-təd\ *adj* (1569) : UNFEELING, CRUEL

stood *past and past part of* STAND

¹stooge \'stüj\ *n* [origin unknown] (1913) **1 a** : one who plays a subordinate or compliant role to a principal **b** : PUPPET 3 **2** : STRAIGHT MAN **3** : STOOL PIGEON

²stooge *vi* **stooged; stoog·ing** (1939) : to act as a stooge ⟨congressmen who ∼ for the oil and mineral interests —*New Republic*⟩

stook \'stùk, 'stük\ *n* [ME *stouk;* akin to OE *stocc* stock — more at STOCK] (15c) *chiefly Brit* : SHOCK — **stook** *vt, chiefly Brit*

¹stool \'stül\ *n* [ME, fr. OE *stōl;* akin to OHG *stuol* chair, OCS *stolŭ* seat, throne] (bef. 12c) **1 a** : a seat usu. without back or arms supported by three or four legs or by a central pedestal **b** : a low bench or portable support for the feet or knees : FOOTSTOOL **2** : a seat used as

a symbol of office or authority; *also* : the rank, dignity, office, or rule of a chieftain **3 a :** a seat used while defecating or urinating **b :** a discharge of fecal matter **4 a :** a stump or group of stumps of a tree esp. when producing suckers **b :** a plant crown from which shoots grow out **c :** a shoot or growth from a stool **5 :** STOOL PIGEON
²**stool** *vi* (1770) : to throw out shoots in the manner of a stool
stool·ie \'stü-lē\ *n* (1924) : STOOL PIGEON 2
stool pigeon *n* [prob. fr. the early practice of fastening the decoy bird to a stool] (1836) **1 :** a pigeon used as a decoy to draw others within a net **2 :** a person acting as a decoy or informer; *esp* : a spy sent into a group to report (as to the police) on its activities
¹**stoop** \'stüp\ *vb* [ME *stoupen*, fr. OE *stūpian*; akin to OE *stēap* steep, deep — more at STEEP] *vi* (bef. 12c) **1 a :** to bend the body or a part of the body forward and downward sometimes simultaneously bending the knees **b :** to stand or walk with a forward inclination of the head, body, or shoulders **2 :** YIELD, SUBMIT **3 a :** to descend from a superior rank, dignity, or status **b :** to lower oneself morally **4 a** *archaic* : to move down from a height : ALIGHT **b :** to fly or dive down swiftly usu. to attack prey ~ *vt* **1 :** DEBASE, DEGRADE **2 :** to bend (a part of the body) forward and downward
²**stoop** *n* (1571) **1 a :** an act of bending the body forward **b :** a temporary or habitual forward bend of the back and shoulders **2 :** the descent of a bird esp. on its prey **3 :** a lowering of oneself
³**stoop** *n* [D *stoep*; akin to OE *stæpe* step — more at STEP] (1755) : a porch, platform, entrance stairway, or small veranda at a house door
stoop-ball \'stüp-,bȯl\ *n* (1941) : a variation of baseball in which a player throws a ball against a stoop or building and runs to base while other players attempt to retrieve the rebound and put the runner out
stoop labor *n* (1949) : the hard labor done or required to plant, cultivate, and harvest a crop and esp. a crop of vegetables
¹**stop** \'stäp\ *vb* **stopped; stop·ping** [ME *stoppen*, fr. OE *-stoppian*, fr. (assumed) VL *stuppare* to stop with tow, fr. L *stuppa* tow, fr. Gk *styppē*] *vt* (13c) **1 a :** to close by filling or obstructing **b :** to hinder or prevent the passage of **c :** to get in the way of : be wounded or killed by ⟨easy to ~ a bullet along a lonely . . . road —Harvey Fergusson⟩ **2 a** : to close up or block off (an opening) : PLUG **b :** to make impassable : CHOKE, OBSTRUCT **c :** to cover over or fill in (a hole or crevice) **3 a** : to cause to give up or change a course of action **b :** to keep from carrying out a proposed action : RESTRAIN, PREVENT **4 a :** to cause to cease : CHECK, SUPPRESS **b :** DISCONTINUE **5 a :** to deduct or withhold (a sum due) **b :** to instruct one's bank to refuse (payment) or refuse payment of (as a check) **6 a :** to arrest the progress or motion of : cause to halt ⟨*stopped* the car⟩ **b :** PARRY **c :** to check by means of a weapon : BRING DOWN, KILL **d :** to beat in a boxing match by a knockout; *broadly* : DEFEAT **e :** BAFFLE, NONPLUS **7 :** to change the pitch of (as a violin string) by pressing with the finger or (as a wind instrument) by closing one or more finger holes or by thrusting the hand or a mute into the bell **8 :** to hold an honor card and enough protecting cards to be able to block (a bridge suit) before an opponent can run many tricks ~ *vi* **1 a :** to cease activity or operation **b :** to come to an end esp. suddenly : CLOSE, FINISH **2 a :** to cease to move on : HALT **b :** PAUSE, HESITATE **3 a :** to break one's journey : STAY **b** *chiefly Brit* : REMAIN **c :** to make a brief call : drop in **4 :** to become choked : CLOG — **stop·pa·ble** \'stä-pə-bəl\ *adj*
syn STOP, CEASE, QUIT, DISCONTINUE, DESIST mean to suspend or cause to suspend activity. STOP applies to action or progress or to what is operating or progressing and may imply suddenness or definiteness ⟨*stopped* at the red light⟩. CEASE applies to states, conditions, or existence and may add a suggestion of gradualness and a degree of finality ⟨by nightfall the fighting had *ceased*⟩. QUIT may stress either finality or abruptness in stopping or ceasing ⟨the engine faltered, sputtered, then *quit* altogether⟩. DISCONTINUE applies to the stopping of an accustomed activity or practice ⟨we have *discontinued* the manufacture of that item⟩. DESIST implies forbearance or restraint as a motive for stopping or ceasing ⟨*desisted* from further efforts to persuade them⟩.
²**stop** *n* (15c) **1 a :** CESSATION, END **b :** a pause or breaking off in speech **2 a** (1) : a graduated set of organ pipes of similar design and tone quality (2) : a corresponding set of vibrators or reeds of a reed organ (3) : STOP KNOB — often used figuratively in phrases like *pull out all the stops* to suggest holding nothing back **b :** a means of regulating the pitch of a musical instrument **3 :** something that impedes, obstructs, or brings to a halt : IMPEDIMENT, OBSTACLE **b :** the aperture of a camera lens; *also* : a marking of a series (as of f-numbers) on a camera for indicating settings of the diaphragm **c :** a drain plug : STOPPER **4 :** a device for arresting or limiting motion **5 :** the act of stopping : the state of being stopped : CHECK **6 a :** a halt in a journey : STAY ⟨made a brief ~ to refuel⟩ **b :** a stopping place ⟨a bus ~⟩ **7 a** *chiefly Brit* : any of several punctuation marks **b :** used in telegrams and cables to indicate a period **c :** a pause or break in a verse that marks the end of a grammatical unit **8 a :** an order stopping payment (as of a check or note) by a bank **b :** STOP ORDER **9 :** a consonant characterized by complete closure of the breath passage in the course of articulation — compare CONTINUANT **10 :** a depression in the face of an animal at the junction of forehead and muzzle
³**stop** *adj* (1594) : serving to stop : designed to stop ⟨~ line⟩ ⟨~ signal⟩
stop-and-go \,stäp-ən-'gō, -'m-, attributively -,gō\ *adj* (1925) : of, relating to, or involving frequent stops; *esp* : controlled or regulated by traffic lights ⟨~ driving⟩
stop bath *n* (1898) : an acid bath used to check photographic development of a negative or print
stop-cock \'stäp-,käk\ *n* (1584) : a cock for stopping or regulating flow (as through a pipe)
stop down *vt* (ca. 1891) : to reduce the effective aperture of (a lens) by means of a diaphragm
stope \'stōp\ *n* [prob. fr. LG *Stope*, lit., step; akin to OE *stæpe* step — more at STEP] (1747) : a usu. steplike excavation underground for the removal of ore that is formed as the ore is mined in successive layers
stop-gap \'stäp-,gap\ *n, often attrib* (1684) : something that serves as a temporary expedient : MAKESHIFT ⟨~ measures⟩ **syn** see RESOURCE
stop knob *n* (1887) : one of the handles by which an organist draws or shuts off a particular stop
stop-light \'stäp-,līt\ *n* (1926) **1 :** a light on the rear of a motor vehicle that is illuminated when the driver presses the brake pedal **2** : TRAFFIC SIGNAL

stop order *n* (ca. 1891) : an order to a broker to buy or sell respectively at the market when the price of a security advances or declines to a designated level
stop out *vi* [after *drop out*] (1973) : to withdraw temporarily from enrollment at a college or university — **stop–out** \'stäp-,aut\ *n*
stop-over \'stäp-,ō-vər\ *n* (1885) **1 :** a stop at an intermediate point in one's journey **2 :** a stopping place on a journey
stop·page \'stä-pij\ *n* (15c) : the act of stopping : the state of being stopped : HALT, OBSTRUCTION
stop payment *n* (ca. 1919) : a depositor's order to a bank to refuse to honor a specified check drawn by him or her
¹**stop·per** \'stä-pər\ *n* (15c) **1 :** one that brings to a halt or causes to stop operating or functioning : CHECK: as **a :** a playing card that will stop the running of a suit **b :** a baseball pitcher depended on to win important games or to stop a losing streak; *also* : an effective relief pitcher **2 :** one that closes, shuts, or fills up; *specif* : something (as a bung or cork) used to plug an opening
²**stopper** *vt* **stop·pered; stop·per·ing** \-p(ə-)riŋ\ (ca. 1769) : to close or secure with or as if with a stopper
stopper knot *n* (1860) : a knot used to prevent a rope from passing through a hole or opening
¹**stop·ple** \'stä-pəl\ *n* [ME *stoppell*, fr. *stoppen* to stop] (14c) : something that closes an aperture : STOPPER, PLUG
²**stopple** *vt* **stop·pled; stop·pling** \-p(ə-)liŋ\ (1795) : STOPPER
stop-watch \'stäp-,wäch\ *n* (1737) : a watch with a hand or a digital display that can be started and stopped at will for exact timing (as of a race)
stor·age \'stȯr-ij, 'stȯr-\ *n* (ca. 1613) **1 a :** space or a place for storing **b :** an amount stored **c :** MEMORY 4 **2 a :** the act of storing : the state of being stored; *esp* : the safekeeping of goods in a depository (as a warehouse) **b :** the price charged for keeping goods in a storehouse **3 :** the production by means of electric energy of chemical reactions that when allowed to reverse themselves generate electricity again without serious loss
storage battery *n* (1881) : a cell or connected group of cells that converts chemical energy into electrical energy by reversible chemical reactions and that may be recharged by passing a current through it in the direction opposite to that of its discharge — called also *storage cell*
sto·rax \'stȯr-,aks, 'stȯr-\ *n* [ME, fr. LL, alter. of L *styrax*, fr. Gk] (14c) **1 a :** a fragrant balsam obtained from the bark of an Asian tree (*Liquidambar orientalis*) of the witch-hazel family that is used as an expectorant and sometimes in perfumery — called also *Levant storax* **b :** a balsam from the sweet gum that is similar to storax **2 :** any of a genus (*Styrax* of the family Styracaceae, the storax family) of trees or shrubs with usu. hairy leaves and white flowers in drooping racemes — compare BENZOIN
¹**store** \'stȯr, 'stȯr\ *vt* **stored; stor·ing** [ME, fr. OF *estorer* to construct, restore, store, fr. L *instaurare* to renew, restore] (13c) **1 :** LAY AWAY, ACCUMULATE ⟨~ vegetables for winter use⟩ ⟨an organism that absorbs and ~s DDT⟩ **2 :** FURNISH, SUPPLY; *esp* : to stock against a future time ⟨~ a ship with provisions⟩ **3 :** to place or leave in a location (as a warehouse, library, or computer memory) for preservation or later use or disposal **4 :** to provide storage room for : HOLD ⟨elevators for *storing* surplus wheat⟩ — **stor·able** \'stȯr-ə-bəl, 'stȯr-\ *adj*
²**store** *n* (13c) **1 a :** something that is stored or kept for future use **b** *pl* : articles (as of food) accumulated for some specific object and drawn upon as needed : STOCK, SUPPLIES **c :** something that is accumulated **d :** a source from which things may be drawn as needed : a reserve fund **2 :** STORAGE — usu. used with *in* ⟨when placing eggs in ~ —*Dublin Sunday Independent*⟩ **3 :** VALUE, IMPORTANCE ⟨set great ~ by a partner's opinion⟩ **4 :** a large quantity, supply, or number : ABUNDANCE **5 a :** STOREHOUSE, WAREHOUSE **b** *chiefly Brit* : MEMORY 4 **6 :** a business establishment where usu. diversified goods are kept for retail sale ⟨grocery ~⟩ — compare SHOP — **in store :** in readiness : in preparation ⟨there's a surprise *in store* for you⟩
³**store** *adj* (1602) **1** *or* **stores :** of, relating to, kept in, or used for a store **2 :** purchased from a store as opposed to being natural or home-made : MANUFACTURED, READY-MADE ⟨~ clothes⟩ ⟨~ bread⟩
store–bought \'stȯr-,bȯt, 'stȯr-\ *adj* (1905) : STORE 2
store cheese *n* [fr. its being a staple article stocked in grocery stores] (1863) : CHEDDAR
¹**store·front** \'stȯr-,frənt, 'stȯr-\ *n* (1880) **1 :** the front side of a store or store building facing a street **2 :** a building, room, or suite of rooms having a storefront
²**storefront** *adj* (1937) **1 :** of, relating to, or characteristic of a storefront church ⟨a ~ evangelist⟩ **2 :** occupying a room or suite of rooms in a store building at street level and immediately behind a storefront ⟨a ~ school⟩ **3 :** of, relating to, or being outreach professional services ⟨~ lawyers⟩ ⟨a ~ clinic⟩
storefront church *n* (1937) : a city church that utilizes storefront quarters as a meeting place
store·house \'stȯr-,haus, 'stȯr-\ *n* (14c) **1 :** a building for storing goods (as provisions) : MAGAZINE, WAREHOUSE **2 :** an abundant supply or source : REPOSITORY
store·keep·er \-,kē-pər\ *n* (1618) **1 :** one that has charge of supplies (as military stores) **2 :** one that operates a retail store
store·room \-,rüm, -,rum\ *n* (1746) **1 :** a room or space for the storing of goods or supplies **2 :** STOREHOUSE 2
store·ship \-,ship\ *n* (1693) : a ship used to carry supplies
store·wide \-'wid\ *adj* (ca. 1937) : including all or most merchandise in a store ⟨a ~ sale⟩
¹**sto·ried** \'stȯr-ēd, 'stȯr-\ *adj* (14c) **1 :** decorated with designs representing scenes from story or history ⟨a ~ tapestry⟩ **2 :** having an interesting history : celebrated in story or history ⟨a ~ institution⟩
²**storied** *or* **sto·reyed** \'stȯr-ēd, 'stȯr-\ *adj* (1624) : having stories — used in combination ⟨a two-*storied* house⟩
stork \'stȯrk\ *n* [ME, fr. OE *storc*; akin to OHG *storah* stork and prob.

\ə\ abut \ᵊ\ kitten, F table \ər\ further \a\ ash \ā\ ace \ä\ mop, mar
\au\ out \ch\ chin \e\ bet \ē\ easy \g\ go \i\ hit \ī\ ice \j\ job
\ŋ\ sing \ō\ go \o\ law \oi\ boy \th\ thin \th\ the \ü\ loot \u\ foot
\y\ yet \zh\ vision \ā, k̲, ⁿ, œ, œ̄, ᵫ, ᵫ̄, � y\ *see* Guide to Pronunciation

to OE *stearc* stiff — more at STARK] (bef. 12c) : any of various large mostly Old World wading birds (family Ciconiidae) that have long stout bills and are related to the ibises and herons

storks·bill \'storks-,bil\ *n* (1562) : any of several plants of the geranium family with elongate beaked fruits: **a** : PELARGONIUM **b** : ALFILARIA; *also* : any of several related plants (genus *Erodium*)

¹storm \'storm\ *n, often attrib* [ME, fr. OE; akin to OHG *sturm* storm, OE *styrian* to stir] (bef. 12c) **1 a** : a disturbance of the atmosphere marked by wind and usu. by rain, snow, hail, sleet, or thunder and lightning **b** : a heavy fall of rain, snow, or hail **c** (1) : wind having a speed of 64 to 72 miles (103 to 116 kilometers) per hour (2) : WHOLE GALE — see BEAUFORT SCALE table **2** : a serious disturbance of any element of nature **2** : a disturbed or agitated state : a sudden or violent commotion **3** : a heavy discharge of objects (as missiles) **4** : a tumultuous outburst **5 a** : PAROXYSM, CRISIS **b** : a sudden heavy influx or onset **6** : a violent assault on a defended position **7** *pl* : STORM WINDOW — **by storm** : by or as if by employing a bold swift frontal movement esp. with the intent of defeating or winning over quickly ⟨took the literary world *by storm*⟩ — **up a storm** : in a remarkable or energetic fashion — used as an intensifier ⟨dancing *up a storm*⟩ ⟨can write *up a storm*⟩

²storm *vi* (15c) **1 a** : to blow with violence **b** : to rain, hail, snow, or sleet vigorously **2** : to attack by storm ⟨*~ed* ashore at zero hour⟩ **3** : to be in or to exhibit a violent passion : RAGE ⟨*~ing* at the unusual delay⟩ **4** : to rush about or move impetuously, violently, or angrily ⟨the mob *~ed* through the streets⟩ ~ *vt* : to attack, take, or win over by storm ⟨*~* a fort⟩ *syn* see ATTACK

storm and stress *n, often cap both Ss* (1855) : STURM UND DRANG

storm·bound \'storm-'baund\ *adj* (1830) : cut off from outside communication by a storm or its effects : stopped or delayed by storms

storm cellar *n* (ca. 1902) : a cellar or covered excavation designed for protection from dangerous windstorms (as tornadoes)

storm door *n* (1878) : an additional door placed outside an ordinary outside door for protection against severe weather

storm petrel *n* (ca. 1833) : any of various small petrels (family Hydrobatidae); *esp* : a small sooty black white-marked petrel (*Hydrobates pelagicus*) frequenting the north Atlantic and Mediterranean

storm trooper *n* (1933) **1** : a member of a private Nazi army notorious for aggressiveness, violence, and brutality **2** : one that resembles a Nazi storm trooper

storm window *n* (ca. 1888) : a sash placed outside an ordinary window as a protection against severe weather — called also *storm sash*

stormy \'stor-me\ *adj* **storm·i·er; -est** (12c) **1** : relating to, characterized by, or indicative of a storm ⟨a *~* day⟩ ⟨a *~* autumn⟩ **2** : marked by turmoil or fury ⟨a *~* life⟩ ⟨a *~* conference⟩ — **storm·i·ly** \'stor-mə-le\ *adv* — **storm·i·ness** \-me-nəs\ *n*

stormy petrel *n* (ca. 1776) **1** : STORM PETREL **2 a** : one fond of strife **b** : a harbinger of trouble

¹sto·ry \'stor-e, 'stor-\ *n, pl* **stories** [ME *storie*, fr. OF *estorie*, fr. L *historia* — more at HISTORY] (13c) **1** *archaic* : HISTORY 1, 3 **2 a** : an account of incidents or events **b** : a statement regarding the facts pertinent to a situation in question **c** : ANECDOTE; *esp* : an amusing one **3 a** : a fictional narrative shorter than a novel; *specif* : SHORT STORY **b** : the intrigue or plot of a narrative or dramatic work **4 a** : a widely circulated rumor **5** : LIE, FALSEHOOD **6** : LEGEND, ROMANCE **7** : a news article or broadcast **8** : MATTER, SITUATION

²story *vt* **sto·ried; sto·ry·ing** (15c) **1** *archaic* : to narrate or describe in story **2** : to adorn with a story or a scene from history

³story *also* **sto·rey** \'stor-e, 'stor-e\ *n, pl* **stories** *also* **storeys** [ME *storie*, fr. ML *historia* picture, story of a building, fr. L, history, tale; prob. fr. pictures adorning the windows of medieval buildings] (14c) **1 a** : the space in a building between two adjacent floor levels or between a floor and the roof **b** : a set of rooms in such a space **c** : a unit of measure equal to the height of the story of a building ⟨one *~* high⟩ **2** : a horizontal division of a building's exterior not necessarily corresponding exactly with the stories within

sto·ry·board \-,bord, -,bord\ *n* (1942) : a panel or series of panels on which a set of sketches is arranged depicting consecutively the important changes of scene and action in a series of shots (as for a film, television show, or commercial) — **storyboard** *vt*

¹sto·ry·book \-,buk\ *n* (1711) : a book of stories ⟨*~s* for children⟩

²storybook *adj* (1844) : FAIRY-TALE

story line *n* (1941) : the plot of a story or drama

sto·ry·tell·er \'stor-e-,te-lər, 'stor-\ *n* (1709) : a teller of stories: as **a** : a relater of anecdotes **b** : a reciter of tales (as in a children's library) **c** : LIAR, FIBBER **d** : a writer of stories — **sto·ry·tell·ing** *n*

stoss \'stäs, 'stos, 'stōs, 'shtōs\ *adj* [G *stoss-*, fr. *stossen* to push, fr. OHG *stōzen*; akin to Goth *stautan* to strike — more at CONTUSION] (1878) : facing toward the direction from which an overriding glacier impinges ⟨the *~* slope of a hill⟩

sto·tin·ka \stō-'tin-kə, stə-\ *n, pl* **-tin·ki** \-ke\ [Bulg] (ca. 1892) — see *lev* at MONEY table

stound \'staund, 'stünd\ *n* [ME, fr. OE *stund;* akin to OHG *stunta* time, hour] (bef. 12c) *archaic* : TIME, WHILE

stoup \'stüp\ *n* [ME *stowp*, prob. of Scand origin; akin to ON *staup* cup] (14c) **1 a** : a beverage container (as a glass or tankard) **b** : FLAGON **2** : a basin for holy water at the entrance of a church

¹stour \'stur\ *adj* [ME *stor*, fr. OE *stōr;* akin to OHG *stuori* large, Russ *staryi* old, OE *standan* to stand] (bef. 12c) **1** *chiefly Scot* : STRONG, HARDY **2** *chiefly Scot* : STERN, HARSH

²stour *n* [ME, fr. MF *estour*, of Gmc origin; akin to OHG *sturm* storm, battle — more at STORM] (14c) **1 a** *archaic* : BATTLE, CONFLICT **b** *dial Brit* : TUMULT, UPROAR **2** *chiefly Scot* : DUST, POWDER

¹stout \'staut\ *adj* [ME, fr. MF *estout*, of Gmc origin; akin to OHG *stolz* proud; perh. akin to OHG *stelza* stilt — more at STILT] (14c) **1**

: strong of character: as **a** : BRAVE, BOLD **b** : FIRM, DETERMINED; *also* : OBSTINATE, UNCOMPROMISING **2** : physically or materially strong: **a** : STURDY, VIGOROUS **b** : STAUNCH, ENDURING **c** : sturdily constructed **d** : SUBSTANTIAL **3** : FORCEFUL ⟨a *~* attack⟩; *also* : VIOLENT ⟨a *~* wind⟩ **4** : bulky in body : FAT *syn* see STRONG — **stout·ish** \'staù-tish\ *adj* — **stout·ly** *adv* — **stout·ness** *n*

²stout *n* (1677) **1** : a very dark full-bodied ale with a distinctive malty flavor **2 a** : a fat person **b** : a clothing size designed for the large figure

stout·en \'staut-ᵊn\ *vb* **stout·ened; stout·en·ing** \'staut-niŋ, 'staù-tᵊn-iŋ\ *vt* (1834) : to make stout ⟨*~* a resolve⟩ ~ *vi* : to become stout

stout·heart·ed \'staut-,här-təd\ *adj* (1552) : having a stout heart or spirit: **a** : COURAGEOUS **b** : STUBBORN — **stout·heart·ed·ly** *adv* — **stout·heart·ed·ness** *n*

¹stove \'stov\ *n* [ME, heated room, steam room, fr. MD or MLG, fr. (assumed) VL *extufa*, ultim. fr. L *ex-* + Gk *typhein* to smoke — more at DEAF] (1591) **1 a** : a portable or fixed apparatus that burns fuel or uses electricity to provide heat (as for cooking or heating) **b** : a device that generates heat for special purposes (as for heating tools or heating air for a hot blast) **c** : KILN **2** *chiefly Brit* : a hothouse esp. for the cultivation of tropical exotics; *broadly* : GREENHOUSE

²stove *past and past part of* STAVE

stove·pipe \'stov-,pip\ *n* (1699) **1** : pipe of large diameter usu. of sheet steel used as a stove chimney or to connect a stove with a flue **2** : SILK HAT

sto·ver \'stō-vər\ *n* [ME, modif. of AF *estovers* necessary supplies, fr. OF *estoveir* to be necessary, ultim. fr. L *est opus* there is need] (14c) **1** *chiefly dial Eng* : FODDER **2** : mature cured stalks of grain with the ears removed that are used as feed for livestock

stow \'stō\ *vt* [ME, to place, fr. *stowe* place, fr. OE *stōw;* akin to OFris *stō* place, Gk *stylos* pillar — more at STEER] (14c) **1** : HOUSE, LODGE **2 a** : to put away for future use : STORE **b** *obs* : to lock up for safekeeping : CONFINE **3 a** : to dispose in an orderly fashion : ARRANGE, PACK **b** : LOAD 4 *slang* : to put aside : STOP **5 a** *archaic* : CROWD **b** : to eat or drink up : CONSUME — usu. used with *away* ⟨*~ed* away a huge dinner⟩

stow·age \-ij\ *n* (14c) **1 a** : an act or process of stowing **b** : goods in storage or to be stowed **2 a** : storage capacity **b** : a place or receptacle for storage **3** : the state of being stored

stow·away \'stō-ə-,wā\ *n* (1850) : one that stows away

stow away *vi* (1879) : to secrete oneself aboard a vehicle as a means of obtaining transportation

STP \,es-,tē-'pē\ *n* [prob. fr. *STP*, a trademark for a motor fuel additive] (1967) : a psychedelic drug chemically related to mescaline and amphetamine

stra·bis·mus \strə-'biz-məs\ *n* [NL, fr. Gk *strabismos* condition of squinting, fr. *strabizein* to squint, fr. *strabos* squint-eyed; akin to Gk *strephein* to twist] (ca. 1684) : inability of one eye to attain binocular vision with the other because of imbalance of the muscles of the eyeball — called also *squint* — **stra·bis·mic** \-mik\ *adj*

¹strad·dle \'stra-dᵊl\ *vb* **strad·dled; strad·dling** \'strad-liŋ, 'stra-dᵊl-iŋ\ [irreg. fr. *stride*] *vi* (1565) **1** : to stand, sit, or walk with the legs wide apart; *esp* : to sit astride **2** : to spread out irregularly : SPRAWL **3** : to favor or seem to favor two apparently opposite sides **4** : to execute a commodities market spread ~ *vt* **1** : to stand, sit, or be astride of ⟨*~* a horse⟩ **2** : to be noncommittal in regard to ⟨*~* an issue⟩ — **strad·dler** \'strad-lər, 'stra-dᵊl-ər\ *n* — **straddle the fence** : to be in a position of neutrality or indecision

²straddle *n* (1611) **1** : the act or position of one who straddles **2** : a noncommittal or equivocal position **3** : SPREAD 5

Stra·di·va·ri \,stra-də-'vär-ē, -'var-, -'ver-\ *n* (ca. 1903) : STRADIVARIUS

Strad·i·var·i·us \,stra-də-'var-ē-əs, -'ver-\ *n, pl* **-var·ii** \-ē-,i\ [Latinized form of *Stradivari*] (1833) : a stringed instrument (as a violin) made by Antonio Stradivari of Cremona

strafe \'sträf, *esp Brit* 'sträf\ *vt* **strafed; straf·ing** [G *Gott strafe England* God punish England, German propaganda slogan during World War I] (1915) : to rake (as ground troops) with fire at close range and esp. with machine-gun fire from low-flying aircraft — **strafe** *n* — **straf·er** *n*

¹strag·gle \'stra-gəl\ *vi* **strag·gled; strag·gling** \-g(ə-)liŋ\ [ME *straglen*] (15c) **1** : to wander from the direct course or way : ROVE, STRAY **2** : to trail off from others of its kind ⟨little cabins *straggling* off into the woods⟩ — **strag·gler** \-g(ə-)lər\ *n*

²straggle *n* (1865) : a straggling group (as of persons or objects)

strag·gly \'stra-g(ə-)lē\ *adj* **strag·gli·er; -est** (1862) : spread out or scattered irregularly ⟨a *~* beard⟩

¹straight \'strāt\ *adj* [ME *streght, straight*, fr. pp. of *strecchen* to stretch — more at STRETCH] (14c) **1 a** : free from curves, bends, angles, or irregularities ⟨*~* hair⟩ ⟨*~* timber⟩ **b** : generated by a point moving continuously in the same direction and expressed by a linear equation ⟨a *~* line⟩ ⟨the *~* segment of a curve⟩ **2 a** : lying along or holding to a direct or proper course or method ⟨a *~* thinker⟩ **b** : CANDID, FRANK ⟨a *~* answer⟩ **c** : coming directly from a trustworthy source ⟨a *~* tip on the horses⟩ **d** (1) : having the elements in an order ⟨the *~* sequence of events⟩ (2) : CONSECUTIVE ⟨12 *~* days⟩ **e** : having the cylinders arranged in a single straight line ⟨a *~* 8-cylinder engine⟩ **f** : PLUMB, VERTICAL ⟨the picture isn't quite *~*⟩ **3 a** : exhibiting honesty and fairness ⟨*~* dealing⟩ **b** : properly ordered or arranged ⟨set the kitchen *~*⟩; *also* : CORRECT ⟨get the facts *~*⟩ **c** : free from extraneous matter : UNMIXED ⟨*~* whiskey⟩ **d** : marked by no exceptions or deviations in support of a principle or party ⟨votes a *~* Democratic ticket⟩ **e** : having a fixed price for each regardless of the number sold **f** : not deviating from an indicated pattern ⟨writes *~* humor⟩ ⟨a *straight*-A student⟩ **g** (1) : exhibiting no deviation from what is established or accepted as usual, normal, or proper : CONVENTIONAL; *also* : SQUARE 5f (2) : not using or under the influence of drugs or alcohol **h** : HETEROSEXUAL **4** : being the only form of remuneration ⟨on *~* commission⟩ — **straight·ish** \'strā-tish\ *adj* — **straight·ly** *adv* — **straight·ness** *n*

²straight *adv* (14c) : in a straight manner

³straight *vt* (15c) *chiefly Scot* : STRAIGHTEN

⁴straight *n* (1645) **1** : something that is straight: as **a** : a straight line or arrangement **b** : STRAIGHTAWAY; *esp* : HOMESTRETCH **c** : a true or honest report or course **2 a** : a sequence (as of shots, strokes, or

storm petrel

moves) resulting in a perfect score in a game or contest **b** : first place at the finish of a horse race : WIN **3** : a poker hand containing five cards in sequence but not of the same suit — see POKER illustration **4** : a person who adheres to conventional attitudes and mores

straight-ahead \'strāt-ə-'hed\ *adj* (1836) : relating to or being music performed in an unembellished manner typical of a given idiom or performer; *broadly* : STRAIGHTFORWARD

straight and narrow *n* [prob. alter. of *strait and narrow;* fr. the admonition of Mt 7:14 (AV), "strait is the gate and narrow is the way which leadeth unto life"] (1930) : the way of propriety and rectitude — used with *the*

straight angle *n* (1601) : an angle whose sides lie in opposite directions from the vertex in the same straight line and which equals two right angles

straight-arm \'strāt-,ärm\ *n* (1903) : an act or instance of warding off a football tackler with the arm fully extended from the shoulder, elbow locked, and the palm of the hand placed firmly against any part of his body — called also *stiff-arm* — **straight-arm** *vb*

straight-arrow \-'ar-(,)ō\ *adj* [fr. the expression *straight as an arrow*] (ca. 1969) : rigidly proper and conventional

¹**straight-away** \,strāt-ə-'wā\ *adv* (1662) : without hesitation or delay

²**straight-away** \'strāt-ə-,wā\ *adj* (1874) **1** : proceeding in a straight line : continuous in direction **2** : IMMEDIATE

³**straight-away** \'strā-tə-,wā\ *n* (1878) : a straight course: as **a** : the straight part of a closed racecourse : STRETCH **b** : a straight and unimpeded stretch of road or way

straight-bred \'strāt-'bred\ *adj* (1898) : produced by breeding a single breed, strain, or type ⟨~ cattle⟩ — **straight-bred** \-,bred\ *n*

straight chain *n* (1890) : an open chain of atoms having no side chains — usu. hyphenated when used attributively

straight-edge \'strāt-,ej\ *n* (1812) : a bar or piece of material (as of wood, metal, or plastic) with a straight edge for testing straight lines and surfaces or drawing straight lines

straight-en \'strā-t°n\ *vb* **straight-ened; straight-en-ing** \'strāt-niŋ, 'strā-t°n-iŋ\ *vt* (1542) : to make straight — usu. used with *up* or *out* ~ *vi* : to become straight — usu. used with *up* or *out* — **straight-en-er** \'strāt-nər, 'strā-t°n-ər\ *n*

straight face *n* (ca. 1890) : a face giving no evidence of emotion and esp. of merriment — **straight-faced** \'strāt-'fāst\ *adj* — **straight-faced-ly** \-'fā-səd-lē, -'fāst-lē\ *adv*

straight flush *n* (1864) : a poker hand containing five cards of the same suit in sequence — see POKER illustration

¹**straight-for-ward** \,strāt-'fór-wərd, 'strāt-,\ *adj* (1806) **1 a** : free from evasiveness or obscurity : EXACT, CANDID ⟨a ~ account⟩ **b** : CLEAR-CUT, PRECISE **2** : proceeding in a straight course or manner : DIRECT, UNDEVIATING — **straight-for-ward-ly** *adv* — **straight-for-ward-ness** *n*

²**straightforward** *also* **straight-for-wards** \-wərdz\ *adv* (1809) : in a straightforward manner

straight-line \'strāt-'lin\ *adj* (1843) **1** : being a mechanical linkage or equivalent device designed to produce or copy motion in a straight line **2** : having the principal parts arranged in a straight line **3** : marked by a uniform spread and esp. in equal segments over a given term ⟨~ amortization⟩ ⟨~ depreciation⟩ **4** : occurring, measured, or made in or along a straight line ⟨~ motion⟩ ⟨~ extrapolation⟩

straight man *n* (1923) : a member of a comedy team who feeds lines to his partner who in turn replies with usu. humorous quips

straight off *adv* (1873) : at once : IMMEDIATELY

straight-out \'strāt-'aút\ *adj* (1848) **1** : FORTHRIGHT, BLUNT ⟨gave him a ~ answer⟩ **2** : OUTRIGHT, THOROUGHGOING — **straight-out** *adv*

straight poker *n* (1864) : poker in which the players bet on the five cards dealt to them and then have a showdown without drawing — compare DRAW POKER, STUD POKER

straight razor *n* (1938) : a razor with a rigid steel cutting blade hinged to a case that forms a handle when the razor is open for use

straight-way \'strāt-'wā, -,wā\ *adv* (15c) **1** : in a direct course : DIRECTLY ⟨fell ~ down the stairs⟩ **2** : RIGHT AWAY, IMMEDIATELY, STRAIGHTAWAY ⟨~ the clouds began to part⟩

¹**strain** \'strān\ *n* [ME *streen* progeny, lineage, fr. OE *strēon* gain, acquisition; akin to OHG *gistriuni* gain, L *struere* to heap up — more at STREW] (13c) **1 a** : LINEAGE, ANCESTRY **b** : a group of presumed common ancestry with clear-cut physiological but usu. not morphological distinctions ⟨a high-yielding ~ of winter wheat⟩; *broadly* : a specified infraspecific group (as a stock, line, or ecotype) **c** : KIND, SORT ⟨discussions of a lofty ~⟩ **2 a** : inherited or inherent character, quality, or disposition ⟨a ~ of madness in the family⟩ **b** : TRACE, STREAK ⟨a ~ of fanaticism⟩ **3 a** : TUNE, AIR **b** : a passage of verbal or musical expression **c** : a stream or outburst of forceful or impassioned speech **4 a** : the tenor, pervading note, burden, or tone of an utterance or of a course of action or conduct **b** : MOOD, TEMPER

²**strain** *vb* [ME, fr. MF *estraindre*, fr. L *stringere* to bind or draw tight, press together; akin to Gk *strang-, stranx* drop squeezed out, *strangalē* halter] *vt* (14c) **1 a** : to draw tight : cause to fit firmly ⟨~ the bandage over the wound⟩ **b** : to stretch to maximum extension and tautness ⟨~ a canvas over a frame⟩ **2 a** : to exert (as oneself) to the utmost **b** : to injure by overuse, misuse, or excessive pressure ⟨~ed his back⟩ **c** : to cause a change of form or size in (a body) by application of external force **3** : to squeeze or clasp tightly: as **a** : HUG **b** : to compress painfully : CONSTRICT **4 a** : to cause to pass through a strainer : FILTER **b** : to remove by straining ⟨~ lumps out of the gravy⟩ **5** : to stretch beyond a proper limit ⟨that story ~s my credulity⟩ **6** *obs* : to squeeze out : EXTORT ~ *vi* **1** : to make violent efforts : STRIVE ⟨has to ~ to reach the high notes⟩ **b** : to pull against resistance ⟨a dog ~ing at its leash⟩ **c** : to contract the muscles forcefully in attempting to defecate — often used in the phrase *strain at stool* **2** : to pass through or as if through a strainer ⟨the liquid ~s readily⟩ **3** : to make great difficulty or resistance : BALK — **strain a point** : to go beyond a usual, accepted, or proper limit or rule

³**strain** *n* (1558) **1** : an act of straining or the condition of being strained: as **a** : bodily injury from excessive tension, effort, or use ⟨heart ~⟩; *esp* : one resulting from a wrench or twist and involving undue stretching of muscles or ligaments ⟨back ~⟩ **b** : excessive or difficult exertion or labor **c** : excessive physical or mental tension; *also* : a force, influence, or factor causing such tension ⟨her responsibil-

ities were a constant ~⟩ **d** : deformation of a material body under the action of applied forces **2** : an unusual reach, degree, or intensity : PITCH **3** *archaic* : a strained interpretation of something said or written

strained \'strānd\ *adj* (ca. 1542) **1** : done or produced with excessive effort **2** : pushed by antagonism near to open conflict ⟨~ relations⟩

strain-er \'strā-nər\ *n* (14c) : one that strains: as **a** : a device (as a sieve) to retain solid pieces while a liquid passes through **b** : any of various devices for stretching or tightening something

strain gauge *n* (1910) : EXTENSOMETER

¹**strait** \'strāt\ *adj* [ME, fr. OF *estreit*, fr. L *strictus* strait, strict, fr. pp. of *stringere*] (13c) **1** *archaic* : STRICT, RIGOROUS **2** *archaic* **a** : NARROW **b** : limited in space or time **c** : closely fitting : CONSTRICTED, TIGHT **3 a** : causing distress : DIFFICULT **b** : limited as to means or resources — **strait-ly** *adv* — **strait-ness** *n*

²**strait** *adv* (13c) *obs* : in a close or tight manner

³**strait** *n* (14c) **1 a** *archaic* : a narrow space or passage **b** : a comparatively narrow passageway connecting two large bodies of water — often used in pl. but sing. in constr. **c** : ISTHMUS **2** : a situation of perplexity or distress — often used in pl. ⟨in dire ~s⟩ *syn* see JUNCTURE

strait-en \'strā-t°n\ *vt* **strait-ened; strait-en-ing** \'strāt-niŋ, 'strā-t°n-iŋ\ (ca. 1552) **1 a** : to make strait or narrow **b** : to hem in : CONFINE **2** *archaic* : to restrict in freedom or scope : HAMPER **3** : to subject to distress, privation, or deficiency ⟨in ~ed circumstances⟩

¹**strait-jack-et** *also* **straight-jack-et** \'strāt-,ja-kət\ *n* (1814) **1** : a cover or overgarment of strong material (as canvas) used to bind the body and esp. the arms closely in restraining a violent prisoner or patient **2** : something that restricts or confines like a strait jacket

²**straitjacket** *also* **straightjacket** *vt* (1863) : to confine in or as if in a straitjacket

strait-laced *or* **straight-laced** \'strāt-'lāst\ *adj* (1554) **1** : excessively strict in manners, morals, or opinion **2** : wearing or having a bodice or stays tightly laced — **strait-laced-ly** \-'lā-səd-lē, -'lāst-lē\ *adv* — **strait-laced-ness** \-'lās(t)-nəs, -'lā-səd-nəs\ *n*

Straits dollar \'strāts-\ *n* [*Straits* Settlements, former British crown colony] (1908) : a dollar formerly issued by British Malaya and used in much of southern and eastern Asia and the East Indies

strake \'strāk\ *n* [ME; akin to OE *streccan* to stretch — more at STRETCH] (14c) **1** : a continuous band of hull planking or plates on a ship; *also* : the width of such a band **2** : STREAK, STRIPE

stra-mash \strə-'mash\ *n* [origin unknown] (1803) *chiefly Scot* **1** : DISTURBANCE, RACKET **2** : CRASH, SMASHUP

stra-mo-ni-um \strə-'mō-nē-əm\ *n* [NL] (1663) **1** : the dried leaves of the jimsonweed or of a related plant (genus *Datura*) that contain toxic alkaloids (as atropine) and are used in medicine similarly to belladonna **2** : JIMSONWEED

¹**strand** \'strand\ *n* [ME, fr. OE; akin to ON *strǫnd* shore] (bef. 12c) : the land bordering a body of water : SHORE, BEACH

²**strand** *vt* (1621) **1** : to run, drive, or cause to drift onto a strand : run aground **2** : to leave in a strange or an unfavorable place esp. without funds or means to depart **3** : to leave (a base runner) on base at the end of an inning in baseball ~ *vi* : to become stranded

³**strand** *n* [ME *stronde, strande*] (13c) **1** *Scot & dial Eng* : STREAM **2** *Scot & dial Eng* : SEA

⁴**strand** *n* [ME *strond*] (15c) **1 a** : fibers or filaments twisted, plaited, or laid parallel to form a unit for further twisting or plaiting into yarn, thread, rope, or cordage **b** : one of the wires twisted together or laid parallel to form a wire rope or cable **c** : something (as a molecular chain) resembling a strand **2** : an element (as a yarn or thread) of a woven or plaited material **3** : an elongated or twisted and plaited body resembling a rope ⟨a ~ of pearls⟩ **4** : one of the elements interwoven in a complex whole

⁵**strand** *vt* (1841) **1** : to break a strand of (a rope) accidentally **2 a** : to form (as a rope) from strands **b** : to play out, twist, or arrange in a strand

strand-ed \'stran-dəd\ *adj* (1875) : having a strand or strands esp. of a specified kind or number — usu. used in combination ⟨the double-*stranded* molecule of DNA⟩ — **strand-ed-ness** *n*

strand-line \'strand-,lin\ *n* (1903) : SHORELINE; *esp* : a shoreline above the present water level

strange \'strānj\ *adj* **strang-er; strang-est** [ME, fr. OF *estrange*, fr. L *extraneus*, lit., external, fr. *extra* outside — more at EXTRA-] (13c) **1 a** *archaic* : of, relating to, or characteristic of another country : FOREIGN **b** : not native to or naturally belonging in a place : of external origin, kind, or character **2 a** : not before known, heard, or seen : UNFAMILIAR **b** : exciting wonder or awe : EXTRAORDINARY **3 a** : discouraging familiarities : RESERVED, DISTANT **b** : ILL AT EASE **4** : UNACCUSTOMED **2** ⟨she was ~ to his ways⟩ **5** : having the quantum characteristic of strangeness ⟨~ quark⟩ ⟨~ particle⟩ — **strange-ly** *adv*

syn STRANGE, SINGULAR, UNIQUE, PECULIAR, ECCENTRIC, ERRATIC, ODD, QUEER, QUAINT, OUTLANDISH mean departing from what is ordinary, usual, or to be expected. STRANGE stresses unfamiliarity and may apply to the foreign, the unnatural, the unaccountable ⟨a journey filled with *strange* sights⟩. SINGULAR suggests individuality or puzzling strangeness ⟨a *singular* feeling of impending disaster⟩. UNIQUE implies singularity and the fact of being without a known parallel ⟨a career *unique* in the annals of science⟩. PECULIAR implies a marked distinctiveness ⟨the *peculiar* status of America's first lady⟩. ECCENTRIC suggests a wide divergence from the usual or normal esp. in behavior ⟨the *eccentric* eating habits of preschoolers⟩. ERRATIC stresses a capricious and unpredictable wandering or deviating ⟨a friend's suddenly *erratic* behavior⟩. ODD applies to a departure from the regular or expected ⟨an *odd* sense of humor⟩. QUEER suggests a dubious sometimes sinister oddness ⟨*queer* happenings offering no ready explanation⟩. QUAINT suggests an old-fashioned but pleasant oddness ⟨a *quaint* fishing vil-

\ə\ abut \'ə\ kitten, F table \ər\ further \a\ ash \ā\ ace \ä\ mop, mar \aú\ out \ch\ chin \e\ bet \ē\ easy \g\ go \i\ hit \ī\ ice \j\ job \ŋ\ sing \ō\ go \ò\ law \òi\ boy \th\ thin \t͟h\ the \ü\ loot \ú\ foot \y\ yet \zh\ vision \ä, ᵏ, ⁿ, œ, œ̄, ᵫ, ᵫ̄, ᵫᵉ, ʳ\ see Guide to Pronunciation lage). OUTLANDISH applies to what is uncouth, bizarre, or barbaric ⟨the *outlandish* getups of heavy metal bands⟩

strange-ness \'strānj-nəs\ *n* (14c) **1** : the quality or state of being strange **2** : a quantum characteristic of subatomic particles that accounts for the relatively long lifetime of certain particles, is conserved in interactions involving electromagnetism or the strong force, and has a value of zero for most known particles

¹**strang-er** \'strān-jər\ *n* [ME, fr. MF *estrangier* foreign, foreigner, fr. *estrange*] (14c) **1** : one who is strange: as **a** (1) : FOREIGNER (2) : a resident alien **b** : one in the house of another as a guest, visitor, or intruder **c** : a person or thing that is unknown or with whom one is unacquainted **d** : one who does not belong to or is kept from the activities of a group **e** : one not privy or party to an act, contract, or title : one that interferes without right **2** : one ignorant of or unacquainted with someone or something

²**stranger** *adj* (15c) : of, relating to, or being a stranger : FOREIGN

³**stranger** *vt* (1605) *obs* : ESTRANGE, ALIENATE

strange woman *n* [fr. the expression frequently used in Prov (AV)] (1535) : PROSTITUTE

stran-gle \'straŋ-gəl\ *vb* **stran-gled**; **stran-gling** \-g(ə-)liŋ\ [ME, fr. MF *estrangler*, fr. L *strangulare*, fr. Gk *strangalan*, fr. *strangalē* halter — more at STRAIN] *vt* (14c) **1 a** : to choke to death by compressing the throat with something (as a hand or rope) : THROTTLE **b** : to obstruct seriously or fatally the normal breathing of **c** : to suppress or hinder the rise, expression, or growth of ~ *vi* **1** : to become strangled **2** : to die from or as if from interference with breathing — **stran-gler** \-g(ə-)lər\ *n*

stran-gle-hold \'straŋ-gəl-ˌhōld\ *n* (1893) **1** : an illegal wrestling hold by which one's opponent is choked **2** : a force or influence that chokes or suppresses freedom of movement or expression

strangler fig *n* (1933) : any of various vines and trees esp. of the mulberry family (as *Ficus aurea* of the southeastern U.S.) and Saint-John's-wort family (as *Clusia rosea* of tropical America) that start as epiphytes but send down roots to the ground around the host tree

stran-gles \'straŋ-gəlz\ *n pl but sing or pl in constr* [pl. of obs. *strangle* act of strangling] (ca. 1706) : an infectious febrile disease of horses caused by a bacterium (*Streptococcus equi*) and marked by inflammation and congestion of mucous membranes

stran-gu-late \'straŋ-gyə-ˌlāt\ *vb* **-lat-ed**; **-lat-ing** [L *strangulatus*, pp. of *strangulare*] *vt* (1665) : STRANGLE, CONSTRICT ~ *vi* : to become constricted so as to stop circulation ⟨the hernia will ~⟩

stran-gu-la-tion \ˌstraŋ-gyə-'lā-shən\ *n* (1542) **1** : the action or process of strangling or strangulating **2** : the state of being strangled or strangulated; *esp* : excessive or pathological constriction or compression of a bodily tube (as a blood vessel or a loop of intestine) that interrupts its ability to act as a passage

stran-gu-ry \'straŋ-gyə-rē, -ˌgyur-ē\ *n, pl* **-ries** [ME, fr. L *stranguria*, fr. Gk *strangouria*, fr. *strang-, stranx* drop squeezed out + *ourein* to urinate, fr. *ouron* urine — more at STRAIN, URINE] (14c) : a slow and painful spasmodic discharge of urine drop by drop

¹**strap** \'strap\ *n* [alter. of *strop*, fr. ME, band or loop of leather or rope, fr. OE, thong for securing an oar, fr. L *struppus* band, strap, fr. Gk *strophos* twisted band, fr. *strephein* to twist] (1601) **1 a** : a narrow usu. flat strip or thong of a flexible material and esp. leather used for securing, holding together, or wrapping **b** : something made of a strap forming a loop ⟨a boot ~⟩ **c** : a strip of leather used for flogging **d** : STROP **2** : a band, plate, or loop of metal for binding objects together or for clamping an object in position **3** : a shoe fastened with a usu. buckled strap **4** *Irish* : TROLLOP 2

²**strap** *vt* **strapped**; **strap-ping** (1711) **1 a** (1) : to secure with or attach by means of a strap (2) : to support (as a sprained joint) with overlapping strips of adhesive plaster **b** : BIND, CONSTRICT **2** : to beat or punish with a strap **3** : STROP **4** : to cause to suffer from an extreme scarcity ⟨is often *strapped* for cash⟩

strap-hang-er \'strap-ˌhaŋ-ər\ *n* (1905) : a standing passenger in a subway, streetcar, bus, or train who clings for support to one of the short straps or similar devices placed along the aisle — **strap-hang** \-ˌhaŋ\ *vi*

strap-less \-ləs\ *adj* (1846) : having no strap; *specif* : made or worn without shoulder straps ⟨a ~ evening gown⟩ — **strapless** *n*

strap-pa-do \stra-'pā-(ˌ)dō, -'pä-\ *n* [modif. of It *strappata*, lit., sharp pull] (1560) : a punishment or torture in which the subject is hoisted by rope and allowed to fall its full length; *also* : a machine used to inflict this torture

strap-per \'stra-pər\ *n* (1675) : one that is unusually large or robust

¹**strap-ping** \'stra-piŋ\ *adj* (1657) : having a vigorously sturdy constitution

²**strapping** *n* (1818) **1** : material for a strap **2** : STRAPS

strass \'stras\ *n* [F *stras, strass*] (1820) : PASTE 3

strat-a-gem \'stra-tə-jəm, -ˌjem\ *n* [It *stratagemma*, fr. L *strategema*, fr. Gk *stratēgēma*, fr. *stratēgein* to be a general, maneuver, fr. *stratēgos* general, fr. *stratos* camp, army (akin to L *stratus*, pp., spread out) + *agein* to lead — more at STRATUM, AGENT] (15c) **1** : an artifice or trick in war for deceiving and outwitting the enemy **b** : a cleverly contrived trick or scheme for gaining an end **2** : skill in ruses or trickery *syn* see TRICK

stra-te-gic \strə-'tē-jik\ *adj* (1825) **1** : of, relating to, or marked by strategy ⟨a ~ retreat⟩ **2 a** : necessary to or important in the initiation, conduct, or completion of a strategic plan **b** : required for the conduct of war and not available in adequate quantities domestically ⟨~ materials⟩ **c** : of great importance within an integrated whole or to a planned effect ⟨emphasized ~ points⟩ **3** : designed or trained to strike an enemy at the sources of his military, economic, or political power ⟨a ~ bomber⟩ — **stra-te-gi-cal** \-ji-kəl\ *adj* — **stra-te-gi-cal-ly** \-ji-k(ə-)lē\ *adv*

strat-e-gist \'stra-tə-jist\ *n* (1838) : one skilled in strategy

strat-e-gize \-ˌjīz\ *vi* **-gized**; **-giz-ing** (1921) : to devise a strategy or course of action

strat-e-gy \-jē\ *n, pl* **-gies** [Gk *stratēgia* generalship, fr. *stratēgos*] (1810) **1 a** (1) : the science and art of employing the political, economic, psychological, and military forces of a nation or group of nations to afford the maximum support to adopted policies in peace or war (2) : the science and art of military command exercised to meet the enemy in combat under advantageous conditions **b** : a variety of

or instance of the use of strategy **2 a** : a careful plan or method : a clever stratagem **b** : the art of devising or employing plans or stratagems toward a goal **3** : an adaptation or complex of adaptations (as of behavior, metabolism, or structure) that serves or appears to serve an important function in achieving evolutionary success ⟨foraging *strategies* of insects⟩

strath \'strath\ *n* [ScGael *srath*] (1540) : a flat wide river valley or the low-lying grassland along it

strath-spey \ˌstrath-'spā\ *n, pl* **strathspeys** [*Strath Spey*, district of Scotland] (ca. 1653) : a Scottish dance that is similar to but slower than the reel; *also* : the music for this dance

strati- *comb form* [NL *stratum*] : stratum ⟨*strati*form⟩

strat-i-fi-ca-tion \ˌstra-tə-fə-'kā-shən\ *n* (ca. 1617) **1 a** : the act or process of stratifying **b** : the state of being stratified **2** : a stratified formation

strat-i-fi-ca-tion-al grammar \ˌstra-tə-fə-'kā-shnəl-, -shə-n°l-\ *n* (1962) : a grammar based on the theory that language consists of a series of hierarchically related strata linked together by representational rules

stratified charge engine *n* (1962) : an internal-combustion engine in whose cylinders the combustion of fuel in a layer of rich fuel-air mixture promotes ignition in a greater volume of lean mixture

strat-i-form \'stra-tə-ˌfȯrm\ *adj* (1805) : having a stratified formation

strat-i-fy \'stra-tə-ˌfī\ *vb* **-fied**; **-fy-ing** [NL *stratificare*, fr. *stratum* + L *-ificare* -ify] *vt* (1661) **1** : to form, deposit, or arrange in strata **2 a** : to divide or arrange into classes, castes, or social strata **b** : to divide into a series of graded statuses ~ *vi* : to become arranged in strata

strati-graph-ic \ˌstra-tə-'gra-fik\ *adj* (1877) : of, relating to, or determined by stratigraphy

stra-tig-ra-phy \strə-'ti-grə-fē\ *n* [ISV] (1865) **1** : geology that deals with the origin, composition, distribution, and succession of strata **2** : the arrangement of strata

strato- *comb form* [NL *stratus*] : stratus and ⟨*strato*cumulus⟩

stra-toc-ra-cy \strə-'tä-krə-sē\ *n, pl* **-cies** [Gk *stratos* army — more at STRATAGEM] (1652) : a military government

stra-to-cu-mu-lus \ˌstra-tō-'kyü-myə-ləs, ˌstra-\ *n* [NL] (ca. 1891) : stratified cumulus consisting of large balls or rolls of dark cloud which often cover the whole sky esp. in winter — see CLOUD illustration

strato-sphere \'stra-tə-ˌsfir\ *n* [F *stratosphère*, fr. NL *stratum* + -o- + F *sphère* sphere, fr. L *sphaera*] (1909) **1** : the part of the earth's atmosphere which extends from about 7 miles (11 kilometers) above the surface to 31 miles (50 kilometers) and in which temperature increases gradually to about 32° F (0° C) and clouds rarely form **2** : a very high or the highest region on or as if on a graded scale ⟨construction costs in the ~⟩ ⟨the celebrity ~⟩ — **strato-spher-ic** \ˌstra-tə-'sfir-ik, -'sfer-\ *adj*

stra-to-vol-ca-no \ˌstra-tō-väl-'kā-(ˌ)nō, ˌstra-, -vȯl-\ *n* [NL *stratum* + E -o- + *volcano*] (1937) : a volcano composed of explosively erupted cinders and ash with occasional lava flows

stra-tum \'strā-təm, 'stra-\ *n, pl* **stra-ta** \'strā-tə, 'stra-\ [NL, fr. L, spread, bed, fr. neut. of *stratus*, pp. of *sternere* to spread out — more at STREW] (1599) **1** : a bed or layer artificially made **2 a** : a sheetlike mass of sedimentary rock or earth of one kind lying between beds of other kinds **b** : a region of the sea or atmosphere that is analogous to a stratum of the earth **c** : a layer of tissue ⟨deep ~ of the skin⟩ **d** : a layer in which archaeological material (as artifacts, skeletons, and dwelling remains) is found on excavation **3 a** : a part of a historical or sociological series representing a period or a stage of development **b** : a socioeconomic level of society comprising persons of the same or similar status esp. with regard to education or culture **4** : one of a series of layers, levels, or gradations in an ordered system ⟨*strata* of thought⟩ **5** : a statistical subpopulation

usage The plural *strata* has occas. been used as a singular since the 18th century and is sometimes given the plural *stratas* ⟨there was a *strata* of Paris which mere criticism of books fails to get hold of — Ezra Pound⟩ ⟨a Roman burial ground suggests *stratas* of corruption and decay —Connie Fletcher, *Booklist*⟩. Current evidence shows senses 2, 3b, and 4 so used, with 3b the most common. Singular *strata* is persistent but not frequent. It may someday establish itself as a singular like *agenda*, but its current status is something less than established.

stra-tus \'strā-təs, 'stra-\ *n, pl* **stra-ti** \'strā-ˌtī, 'stra-\ [NL, fr. L, pp. of *sternere*] (ca. 1803) : a cloud form extending over a large area at altitudes of usu. 2000 to 7000 feet (600 to 2100 meters) — see CLOUD illustration

stra-vage *or* **stra-vaig** \strə-'vāg\ *vi* [prob. by shortening & alter. fr. *extravagate*] (1773) *chiefly Scot* : ROAM

¹**straw** \'strȯ\ *n* [ME, fr. OE *strēaw*; akin to OHG *strō* straw, OE *strewian* to strew] (bef. 12c) **1 a** : stalks of grain after threshing; *broadly* : dry stalky plant residue used like grain straw (as for bedding or packing) **b** : a natural or artificial heavy fiber used for weaving, plaiting, or braiding **2** : a dry coarse stem esp. of a cereal grass **3 a** (1) : something of small worth or significance (2) : something too insubstantial to provide support or help in a desperate situation ⟨clutching at ~s⟩ **b** : CHAFF 2 **4** : something (as a hat) made of straw **b** : a tube (as of paper, plastic, or glass) for sucking up a beverage — **strawy** \'strȯ-ē\ *adj* — **straw in the wind** : a slight fact that is an indication of a coming event

²**straw** *adj* (15c) **1** : made of straw ⟨a ~ rug⟩ **2** : of, relating to, or used for straw ⟨a ~ barn⟩ **3** : of the color of straw ⟨~ hair⟩ **4** : of little or no value : WORTHLESS **5** : of, relating to, resembling, or being a straw man **6** : of, relating to, or concerned with the discovery of preferences by means of a straw vote

straw-ber-ry \'strȯ-ˌber-ē, -b(ə-)rē\ *n, often attrib* [ME, fr. OE *strēawberige*, fr. *strēaw* straw + *berige* berry; perh. fr. the appearance of the achenes on the surface] (bef. 12c) : the juicy edible usu. red fruit of any of several low-growing temperate herbs (genus *Fragaria*) of the rose family that is technically an enlarged pulpy receptacle bearing numerous achenes; *also* : a plant whose fruits are strawberries

strawberry bush *n* (ca. 1856) **1** : a shrubby No. American spindle tree (*Euonymus americanus*) with crimson pods and seeds with a scarlet aril **2** : ²WAHOO

strawberry mark *n* (1847) : a tumor of the skin filled with small blood vessels and appearing usu. as a red and elevated birthmark

strawberry roan *n* (1955) : a roan horse with a light red ground color

strawberry shrub *n* (ca. 1890) : any of a genus (*Calycanthus* of the family Calycanthaceae, the strawberry-shrub family) of shrubs with fragrant brownish red flowers

strawberry tomato *n* (ca. 1847) : GROUND-CHERRY; *esp* : a stout hairy annual herb (*Physalis pruinosa*) of eastern No. America with sweet globular yellow fruits

strawberry tree *n* (15c) : a small European evergreen tree (*Arbutus unedo*) of the heath family with racemose white flowers and fruits like strawberries

straw boss *n* (1894) **1** : an assistant to a foreman in charge of supervising and expediting the work of a small gang of workers **2** : a member of a group of workers who supervises the work of the others in addition to doing his or her own job

straw-flow·er \'strȯ-ˌflau̇(-ə)r\ *n* (ca. 1922) : any of several everlasting flowers; *esp* : an Australian perennial composite herb (*Helichrysum bracteatum*) that is widely cultivated for its heads of chaffy brightly colored long-keeping flowers

straw-hat \ˌstrȯ-ˌhat\ *adj* [fr. the former fashion of wearing straw hats in summer] (1935) : of, relating to, or being summer theater

straw man *n* (1896) **1** : a weak or imaginary opposition (as an argument or adversary) set up only to be easily confuted **2** : a person set up to serve as a cover for a usu. questionable transaction

straw vote *n* (1866) : an unofficial vote taken (as at a chance gathering) to indicate the relative strength of opposing candidates or issues — called also *straw poll*

straw wine *n* (1824) : a sweet wine produced by partially drying the grapes on beds of straw prior to vinification

straw yellow *n* (ca. 1796) : a pale yellow

¹stray \'strā\ *n* [ME, fr. OF *estraié*, pp. of *estraier*] (13c) **1 a** : a domestic animal that is wandering at large or is lost **b** : a person or thing that strays **2** [ME, fr. *straien* to stray] *archaic* : the act of going astray

²stray *vi* [ME *straien*, fr. MF *estraier*, fr. (assumed) VL *extravagare*, fr. L *extra-* outside + *vagari* to wander — more at EXTRA-] (14c) : WANDER: as **a** : to wander from company, restraint, or proper limits **b** : to roam about without fixed direction or purpose **c** : to move in a winding course : MEANDER **d** : to move without conscious or intentional effort ⟨eyes ~*ing* absently around the room⟩ **e** : to become distracted from an argument or chain of thought ⟨~*ed* from the point⟩ **f** : to wander accidentally from a fixed or chosen route **g** : ERR, SIN — **stray·er** *n*

³stray *adj* (1607) **1** : having strayed or escaped from a proper or intended place ⟨a ~ cow⟩ ⟨hit by a ~ bullet⟩ ⟨fixed a few ~ hairs⟩ **2** : occurring at random or sporadically ⟨a few ~ thoughts⟩ **3** : not serving any useful purpose : UNWANTED ⟨~ light⟩

¹streak \'strēk\ *n* [ME *streke*, fr. OE *strica*; akin to OHG *strich* line, L *striga* row — more at STRIKE] (bef. 12c) **1** : a line or mark of a different color or texture from the ground : STRIPE **2 a** : the color of the fine powder of a mineral obtained by scratching or rubbing against a hard white surface and constituting an important distinguishing character **b** : inoculum implanted in a line on a solid medium **c** : any of several virus diseases of plants (as the potato, tomato, or raspberry) resembling mosaic but usu. producing at least some linear markings **3 a** : a narrow band of light **b** : a lightning bolt **4 a** : a slight admixture : TRACE ⟨had a mean ~ in him⟩ **b** : a brief run (as of luck) **c** : a consecutive series ⟨was on a winning ~⟩ **5** : a narrow layer (as of ore) **6** : an act or instance of streaking

²streak *vt* (1595) : to make streaks on or in ⟨tears ~*ing* her face⟩ ~ *vi* **1** : to move swiftly : RUSH ⟨a jet ~*ing* across the sky⟩ **2** : to have a streak (as of winning or outstanding performances) **3** : to run naked through a public place — **streak·er** *n*

streak camera *n* (1959) : a camera for recording very fast or short-lived phenomena (as fluorescence or shock waves)

streaked \'strēkt, 'strē-kəd\ *adj* (1596) **1** : marked with stripes or linear discolorations **2** : physically or mentally disturbed : UPSET

streak·ing \'strē-kiŋ\ *n* (ca. 1964) : the lightening (as by chemicals) of a few long strands of hair to produce a streaked effect

streaky \'strē-kē\ *adj* **streak·i·er; -est** (1745) **1** : marked with streaks ⟨~ bacon⟩ **2** : APPREHENSIVE ⟨nervous and ~⟩ **3** : apt to vary (as in effectiveness) : UNRELIABLE — **streak·i·ness** *n*

¹stream \'strēm\ *n* [ME *streme*, fr. OE *strēam*; akin to OHG *stroum* stream, Gk *rhein* to flow] (bef. 12c) **1** : a body of running water (as a river or brook) flowing on the earth; *also* : any body of flowing fluid (as water or gas) **2 a** : a steady succession of words or events ⟨kept up an endless ~ of chatter⟩ **b** : a constantly renewed supply **c** : a continuous moving procession ⟨a ~ of traffic⟩ **3** : an unbroken flow (as of gas or particles of matter) **4** : a ray of light **5 a** : a prevailing attitude or group ⟨has always run against the ~ of current fashion⟩ **b** : a dominant influence or line of development **6** *Brit* : TRACK 3c

²stream *vi* (13c) **1 a** : to flow in or as if in a stream **b** : to leave a bright trail ⟨a meteor ~*ed* through the sky⟩ **2 a** : to exude a bodily fluid profusely ⟨her eyes were ~*ing*⟩ **b** : to become wet with a discharge of bodily fluid ⟨~*ing* with perspiration⟩ **3** : to trail out at full length ⟨her hair ~*ing* back as she ran⟩ **4** : to pour in large numbers ⟨complaints came ~*ing* in⟩ ~ *vt* **1** : to emit freely or in a stream ⟨his eyes ~*ed* tears⟩ **2** : to display (as a flag) by waving

stream-bed \'strēm-ˌbed\ *n* (1857) : the channel occupied or formerly occupied by a stream

stream·er \'strē-mər\ *n* (13c) **1 a** : a flag that streams in the wind; *esp* : PENNANT **b** : any long narrow wavy strip resembling or suggesting a banner floating in the wind **c** : BANNER 2 **2 a** : a long extension of the solar corona visible only during a total solar eclipse **b** *pl* : AURORA BOREALIS

stream·ing \'strē-miŋ\ *n* (14c) **1** : an act or instance of flowing; *specif* : CYCLOSIS **2** *Brit* : TRACKING

stream·let \'strēm-lət\ *n* (ca. 1552) : a small stream

¹stream·line \'strēm-ˌlīn\ *n* (1868) **1** : the path of a particle in a fluid relative to a solid body past which the fluid is moving in smooth flow without turbulence **2 a** : a contour designed to minimize resistance to motion through a fluid (as air) **b** : a smooth or flowing line designed as if for decreasing air resistance

²streamline *vt* (1913) **1** : to design or construct with a streamline **2** : to bring up to date : MODERNIZE **3 a** : to put in order : ORGANIZE **b** : to make simpler or more efficient

stream·lined \-ˌlīnd\ *adj* (1913) **1 a** : contoured to reduce resistance to motion through a fluid (as air) **b** : stripped of nonessentials : COMPACT **c** : effectively integrated : ORGANIZED **2** : having flowing lines **3** : brought up to date : MODERNIZED **4** : of or relating to streamline flow

streamline flow *n* (ca. 1918) : an uninterrupted flow (as of air) past a solid body in which the direction at every point remains unchanged with the passage of time

stream·lin·er \'strēm-ˌlī-nər\ *n* (1934) : one that is streamlined; *esp* : a streamlined train

stream of consciousness (1855) **1** : the continuous unedited chronological flow of conscious experience through the mind **2** : INTERIOR MONOLOGUE

stream·side \'strēm-ˌsīd\ *n* (1844) : the land bordering on a stream

streek \'strēk\ *vt* [ME (northern dial.) *streken*; akin to OE *streccan* to stretch] (13c) **1** *chiefly Scot* : STRETCH, EXTEND **2** *chiefly Scot* : to lay out (a dead body)

¹streel \'strē(ə)l\ *vi* [Ir *straoill-*, *sraoill-* to tear apart, trail, trudge, fr. OIr *sroiglid* he scourges, fr. *sroigell* scourge, fr. L *flagellum* — more at FLAGELLATE] (1805) **1** *chiefly Irish* : to saunter idly and aimlessly **2** *chiefly Irish* : to trail or float in the manner of a streamer

²streel *n* [Ir *straoill*, *sraoill*, fr. *straoill-*, v.] (1842) *chiefly Irish* : an untidy slovenly person

¹street \'strēt\ *n* [ME *strete*, fr. OE *strǣt*, fr. LL *strata* paved road, fr. L, fem. of *stratus*, pp. — more at STRATUM] (bef. 12c) **1 a** : a thoroughfare esp. in a city, town, or village that is wider than an alley or lane and that usu. includes sidewalks **b** : the part of a street reserved for vehicles **c** : a thoroughfare with abutting property ⟨lives on a fashionable ~⟩ **2** : the people occupying property on a street ⟨the whole ~ knew about the accident⟩ **3** : a promising line of development or a channeling of effort **4** *cap* : a district (as Wall Street or Fleet Street) identified with a particular profession **5** : an environment (as in a depressed neighborhood or section of a city) of prostitution, poverty, dereliction, or crime — **on the street** *or* **in the street** **1** : idle, homeless, or out of a job **2** : out of prison : at liberty — **up one's street** *or* **down one's street** : suited to one's abilities or taste

²street *adj* (15c) : of or relating to the streets: as **a** : adjoining or giving access to a street ⟨the ~ door⟩ **b** : carried on or taking place in the street ⟨~ fighting⟩ **c** : living or working on the streets ⟨a ~ peddler⟩ ⟨~ people⟩ **d** : located in, used for, or serving as a guide to the streets ⟨a ~ map⟩ **e** : performing in or heard on the street ⟨a ~ band⟩ **f** (1) : suitable for wear or use on the street ⟨~ clothes⟩ (2) : not touching the ground — used of a woman's dress in lengths reaching the knee, calf, or ankle **g** : of or relating to the street environment ⟨~ drugs⟩

street arab \-'ar-əb, -'ä-ˌrab\ *n, often cap A* (1859) : a homeless vagabond and esp. an outcast boy or girl in the streets of a city : GAMIN

street·car \'strēt-ˌkär\ *n* (1862) : a vehicle on rails used primarily for transporting passengers and typically operating on city streets

street·light \-ˌlīt\ *n* (1906) : a light usu. mounted on a pole and constituting one of a series spaced at intervals along a public street or highway — called also *streetlamp*

street railway *n* (1861) : a line operating streetcars or buses

streets \'strēts\ *adv* (1898) *chiefly Brit* : by a considerable margin ⟨a nice woman, ~ above these other callers —Katherine Mansfield⟩

street·scape \'strēt-ˌskāp\ *n* (1924) **1** : the appearance or view of a street **2** : a work of art depicting a view of a street

street–smart \-ˌsmärt\ *adj* (1974) : STREETWISE

street smarts *n pl* (1972) : the quality of being streetwise

street theater *n* (1967) : drama dealing with controversial social and political issues that is usu. performed outdoors

street virus *n* (ca. 1911) : a naturally occurring rabies virus as distinguished from virus attenuated in the laboratory

street·walk·er \'strēt-ˌwȯ-kər\ *n* (1592) : PROSTITUTE; *esp* : one who solicits in the streets — compare CALL GIRL — **street·walk·ing** \-kiŋ\ *n*

street·wise \-ˌwīz\ *adj* (1965) : possessing the skills and attitudes necessary to survive in an often violent urban environment

strength \'streŋ(k)th, 'streŋ(t)th\ *n, pl* **strengths** \'streŋ(k)ths, 'streŋ(t)ths, 'streŋks\ [ME *strengthe*, fr. OE *strengthu*; akin to OHG *strengi* strong — more at STRONG] (bef. 12c) **1** : the quality or state of being strong : capacity for exertion or endurance **2** : power to resist force : SOLIDITY, TOUGHNESS **3** : power of resisting attack : IMPREGNABILITY **4** : legal, logical, or moral force : a strong attribute or inherent asset ⟨the ~s and the weaknesses of the book are evident⟩ **5 a** : degree of potency of effect or of concentration **b** : intensity of light, color, sound, or odor **c** : vigor of expression **6** : force as measured in numbers : effective numbers of any body or organization ⟨an army at full ~⟩ **7** : one regarded as embodying or affording force or firmness : SUPPORT **8** : maintenance of or a rising tendency in a price level : firmness of prices **9** : BASIS — used in the phrase *on the strength of* *syn* see POWER — **from strength to strength** : vigorously forward : from one high point to the next

strength·en \'streŋ(k)-thən, 'streŋ(t)-\ *vb* **strength·ened; strength·en·ing** \'streŋ(k)th-niŋ, 'streŋ(t)th-; 'streŋ(k)th-thə-, 'streŋ(t)th-\ *vt* (15c) : to make stronger ~ *vi* : to become stronger — **strength·en·er** \'streŋ(k)th-nər, 'streŋ(t)th-; 'streŋ(k)th-thə-, 'streŋ(t)th-\ *n*

stren·u·ous \'stren-yə-wəs\ *adj* [L *strenuus*] (1599) **1 a** : vigorously active : ENERGETIC **b** : FERVENT, ZEALOUS **2** : marked by or calling for energy or stamina : ARDUOUS *syn* see VIGOROUS — **stren·u·os·i·ty** \ˌstren-yə-'wä-sə-tē\ *n* — **stren·u·ous·ly** \'stren-yə-wəs-lē\ *adv* — **stren·u·ous·ness** *n*

strep \'strep\ *n, often attrib* (1927) : STREPTOCOCCUS

---

strep throat *n* (ca. 1927) : an inflammatory sore throat caused by hemolytic streptococci and marked by fever, prostration, and toxemia — called also *septic sore throat*

strepto- *comb form* [NL, fr. Gk, fr. *streptos* twisted, fr. *strephein* to twist] **1** : twisted : twisted chain ⟨*streptococcus*⟩ **2** : streptococcus ⟨*strepto*kinase⟩

strep·to·ba·cil·lus \,strep-tō-bə-'si-ləs\ *n* [NL] (1897) : any of a genus (*Streptobacillus*) of nonmotile gram-negative rod-shaped bacteria in which the individual cells are often joined in a chain; *esp* : one (*S. moniliformis*) that is the causative agent of one form of rat-bite fever

strep·to·coc·cal \,strep-tə-'kä-kəl\ *also* **strep·to·coc·cic** \-'kä-kik, -'käk-sik\ *adj* (1877) : of, relating to, caused by, or being streptococcus ⟨a ~ sore throat⟩ ⟨~ organisms⟩

strep·to·coc·cus \-'kä-kəs\ *n, pl* **-coc·ci** \-'kä-,kī, -,(,)kē; -'käk-,sī, -,(,)sē\ [NL] (1877) : any of a genus (*Streptococcus*) of spherical or ovoid chiefly nonmotile and parasitic gram-positive bacteria that divide only in one plane, occur in pairs or chains, and include important pathogens of humans and domestic animals; *broadly* : a coccus occurring in chains

strep·to·ki·nase \,strep-tō-'kī-,nās, -,nāz\ *n* (1944) : a proteolytic enzyme from hemolytic streptococci active in promoting dissolution of blood clots

strep·to·ly·sin \,strep-tə-'lī-s³n\ *n* (1904) : an antigenic hemolysin produced by streptococci

strep·to·my·ces \-'mī-,sēz\ *n, pl* **streptomyces** [NL, fr. *strepto-* + Gk *mykēs* fungus — more at MYC-] (1951) : any of a genus (*Streptomyces*) of mostly soil streptomycetes including some that form antibiotics as by-products of their metabolism

strep·to·my·cete \-'mī-,sēt, -,mī-'sēt\ *n* [NL *Streptomycet-, Streptomyces,* genus name] (1948) : any of a family (Streptomycetaceae) of actinomycetes (as a streptomyces) that form vegetative mycelia which rarely break up into bacillary forms, have conidia borne on sporophores, and are typically aerobic soil saprophytes but include a few parasites of plants and animals

strep·to·my·cin \-'mī-s³n\ *n* (1944) : an antibiotic organic base $C_{21}H_{39}N_7O_{12}$ produced by a soil actinomycete (*Streptomyces griseus*), active against many bacteria, and used esp. in the treatment of infections (as tuberculosis) by gram-negative bacteria

strep·to·thri·cin \-'thrī-s³n, -'thri-\ *n* [NL *Streptothric-, Streptothrix,* genus of bacteria, fr. *strepto-* + Gk *trich-, thrix* hair] (1926) : any of a group of related basic antibiotics produced by a soil actinomycete (*Streptomyces lavendulae*) and active against bacteria and to some degree against fungi

¹stress \'stres\ *n* [ME *stresse* stress, distress, short for *destresse* — more at DISTRESS] (14c) **1** : constraining force or influence: as **a** : a force exerted when one body or body part presses on, pulls on, pushes against, or tends to compress or twist another body or body part; *esp* : the intensity of this mutual force commonly expressed in pounds per square inch **b** : the deformation caused in a body by such a force **c** : a physical, chemical, or emotional factor that causes bodily or mental tension and may be a factor in disease causation **d** : a state resulting from a stress; *esp* : one of bodily or mental tension resulting from factors that tend to alter an existent equilibrium **e** : STRAIN, PRESSURE ⟨the environment is under ~ to the point of collapse —Joseph Shoben⟩ **2** : EMPHASIS, WEIGHT ⟨lay ~ on a point⟩ **3** *archaic* : intense effort or exertion **4** : intensity of utterance given to a speech sound, syllable, or word producing relative loudness **5 a** : relative force or prominence of sound in verse **b** : a syllable having relative force or prominence **6** : ACCENT 6a

²stress *vt* (1545) **1** : to subject to physical or psychological stress **2** : to subject to phonetic stress : ACCENT **3** : to lay stress on : EMPHASIZE

stressed–out \'strest-'aút\ *adj* (1983) : suffering from high levels of physical or esp. psychological stress

stress fracture *n* (1952) : a usu. hairline fracture of a bone that has been subjected to repeated stress

stress·ful \'stres-fəl\ *adj* (1853) : full of or tending to induce stress — **stress·ful·ly** \-fə-lē\ *adv*

stress·less \-ləs\ *adj* (1885) : having no stress; *specif* : having no accent ⟨a ~ syllable⟩ — **stress·less·ness** *n*

stress mark *n* (1888) : a mark used with (as before, after, or over) a written syllable in the respelling of a word to show that this syllable is to be stressed when spoken : ACCENT MARK

stress·or \'stre-sər, -,sòr\ *n* (1952) : a stimulus that causes stress

stress test *n* (1975) : an electrocardiographic test of heart function before, during, and after a controlled period of increasingly strenuous exercise (as on a treadmill)

¹stretch \'strech\ *vb* [ME *strecchen,* fr. OE *streccan;* akin to OHG *strecchan* to stretch, OE *stræc* firm, severe] *vt* (bef. 12c) **1** : to extend (as one's limbs or body) in a reclining position **2** : to reach out : EXTEND ⟨~ed out her arms⟩ **3** : to extend in length ⟨~ed his neck to see what was going on⟩ **4** : to fell with or as if with a blow **5** : to cause the limbs of (a person) to be pulled esp. in torture **6** : to draw up (one's body) from a cramped, stooping, or relaxed position **7** : to pull taut ⟨canvas ~ed on a frame⟩ **8 a** : to enlarge or distend esp. by force **b** : to extend or expand as if by physical force ⟨~ one's mind with a good book⟩ **c** : STRAIN ⟨~ed his already thin patience⟩ **9** : to cause to reach or continue (as from one point to another or across a space) ⟨~ a wire between two posts⟩ **10 a** : to amplify or enlarge beyond natural or proper limits ⟨the rules can be ~ed this once⟩ **b** : to expand (as by improvisation) to fulfill a larger function ⟨~ing a dollar⟩ **11** : to extend (a hit) to an extra base usu. by fast or daring running ⟨~ a single into a double⟩ ~ *vi* **1 a** : to become extended in length or breadth or both : SPREAD ⟨broad plains ~ing to the sea⟩ **b** : to extend over a continuous period **2** : to become extended without breaking **3 a** : to extend one's body or limbs **b** : to lie down at full length — **stretch·abil·i·ty** \,stre-chə-'bi-lə-tē\ *n* — **stretch·able** \'stre-chə-bəl\ *adj* — **stretchy** \-chē\ *adj* — **stretch a point** : to go beyond what is strictly warranted in making a claim or concession — **stretch one's legs 1** : to extend the legs **2** : to take a walk in order to relieve stiffness caused by prolonged sitting

²stretch *n* (1541) **1 a** : an exercise of something (as the understanding or the imagination) beyond ordinary or normal limits **b** : an extension of the scope or application of something ⟨a ~ of language⟩ **2** : the extent to which something may be stretched **3** : the act of stretching : the state of being stretched **4 a** : an extent in length or area ⟨a ~ of woods⟩ **b** : a continuous period of time ⟨can write for eight hours at a ~⟩ **5** : a walk to relieve fatigue **6** : a term of imprisonment **7 a** : either of the straight sides of a racecourse; *esp* : HOMESTRETCH **b** : a final stage **8** : the capacity for being stretched : ELASTICITY **9** : STRETCH LIMO

³stretch *adj* (1954) : easily stretched : ELASTIC ⟨a ~ wig⟩

stretch·er \'stre-chər\ *n* (15c) **1 a** : one that stretches; *esp* : a device or machine for stretching or expanding something **b** : an exaggerated story : a tall tale **2 a** : a brick or stone laid with its length parallel to the face of the wall **b** : a timber or rod used esp. when horizontal as a tie in framed work **3** : a device for carrying a sick, injured, or dead person **4** : a rod or bar extending between two legs of a chair or table

stretch limo *n* (1971) : a long limousine that is luxuriously furnished (as with a TV or bar) — called also *stretch limousine*

stretch marks *n pl* (1956) : striae on the skin (as of the hips, abdomen, and breasts) from excessive stretching and rupture of elastic fibers esp. due to pregnancy or obesity

stretch–out \'strech-,aút\ *n* (1930) **1** : a system of industrial operation in which workers are required to do extra work with slight or with no additional pay **2** : the act of stretching out : the state of being stretched out **3** : an economizing measure that spreads a limited quantity over a larger field than orig. intended: as **a** : a slackening of production schedules so that a quantity of goods will be produced over a longer period than initially planned **b** : a restructuring of a loan repayment schedule over an extended period of time

stretch receptor *n* (1936) : MUSCLE SPINDLE

stretch runner *n* (1922) : a racehorse that makes a strong bid in the homestretch

stret·to \'stre-(,)tō\ *also* **stret·ta** \-tə\ *n, pl* **stret·ti** \-(,)tē\ *or* **strettos** [stretto fr. It, fr. *stretto* narrow, close, fr. L *strictus,* pp.; stretta fr. It, fr. fem. of *stretto* — more at STRICT] (ca. 1740) **1 a** : the overlapping of answer with subject in a musical fugue **b** : the part of a fugue characterized by this overlapping **2** : a concluding passage performed in a quicker tempo

streu·sel \'strü-səl, -zəl, 'stroi-, 'shtroi-\ *n* [G, lit., something strewn, fr. MHG *ströusel,* fr. *ströuwen* to strew, fr. OHG *strewen*] (1909) : a crumbly mixture of fat, sugar, and flour and sometimes nuts and spices that is used as topping or filling for cake

strew \'strü\ *vt* **strewed; strewed** *or* **strewn** \'strün\; **strew·ing** [ME *strewen, strowen,* fr. OE *strewian;* akin to OHG *strewen* to strew, L *struere* to heap up, *sternere* to spread out, Gk *stornynai*] (bef. 12c) **1** : to spread by scattering **2** : to cover by or as if by scattering something ⟨~ing the highways with litter⟩ **3** : to become dispersed over as if scattered **4** : to spread abroad : DISSEMINATE

strew·ment \'strü-mənt\ *n* (1602) *archaic* : something (as flowers) strewed or designed for strewing

stria \'strī-ə\ *n, pl* **striae** \'strī-,ē\ [L, furrow, channel — more at STRIKE] (1563) **1** : STRIATION **2** : a stripe or line (as in the skin) distinguished from the surrounding area by color, texture, or elevation — compare STRETCH MARKS

¹stri·ate \'strī-ət, -,āt\ *adj* (1670) : STRIATED

²stri·ate \-,āt\ *vt* **stri·at·ed; stri·at·ing** (1709) : to mark with striations or striae

stri·at·ed \'strī-,ā-təd\ *adj* (1646) **1** : marked with striations or striae **2** : of, relating to, or being striated muscle

striated muscle *n* (1866) : muscle tissue that is marked by transverse dark and light bands, that is made up of elongated multinuclear fibers, and that includes skeletal muscle, cardiac muscle, and most muscle of arthropods — compare SMOOTH MUSCLE, VOLUNTARY MUSCLE

stri·a·tion \strī-'ā-shən\ *n* (ca. 1847) **1 a** : the fact or state of being striated **b** : arrangement of striations or striae **2** : a minute groove, scratch, or channel esp. when one of a parallel series **3** : any of the alternate dark and light cross bands of a myofibril of striated muscle

strick \'strik\ *n* [ME *stric, strik,* prob. of LG or D origin; akin to MLG *strik* rope, MD *stric*] (14c) : a bunch of hackled flax, jute, or hemp

strick·en \'stri-kən\ *adj* [ME *striken,* fr. pp. of *striken* to strike] (14c) **1 a** : afflicted or overwhelmed by or as if by disease, misfortune, or sorrow **b** : made incapable or unfit **2** : hit or wounded by or as if by a missile

strick·le \'stri-kəl\ *n* [ME *strikell* a piece of wood for leveling a measure of grain; akin to OE *strican* to stroke — more at STRIKE] (1688) : a foundry tool for smoothing the surface of a core or mold — **strickle** *vt*

strict \'strikt\ *adj* [ME *stricte,* fr. L *strictus,* fr. pp. of *stringere* to bind tight — more at STRAIN] (15c) **1** *archaic* **a** : TIGHT, CLOSE; *also* : INTIMATE **b** : NARROW **2 a** : stringent in requirement or control ⟨under ~ orders⟩ **b** : severe in discipline ⟨a ~ teacher⟩ **3 a** : inflexibly maintained or adhered to ⟨~ secrecy⟩ **b** : rigorously conforming to principle or a norm or condition **4** : EXACT, PRECISE ⟨in the ~ sense of the word⟩ **5** : of narrow erect habit of growth ⟨a ~ inflorescence⟩ *syn* see RIGID — **strict·ly** \'strik(t)-lē\ *adv* — **strict·ness** \-nəs\ *n*

strict liability *n* (1896) : liability imposed without regard to fault

stric·ture \'strik-chər\ *n* [ME, fr. LL *strictura,* fr. L *strictus,* pp.] (14c) **1 a** : an abnormal narrowing of a bodily passage; *also* : the narrowed part **b** : a constriction of the breath passage in the production of a speech sound **2** : something that closely restrains or limits : RESTRICTION ⟨moral ~s⟩ **3** : an adverse criticism : CENSURE

¹stride \'strīd\ *vb* **strode** \'strōd\; **strid·den** \'stri-d²n\; **strid·ing** \'strī-diŋ\ [ME, fr. OE *strīdan;* akin to MLG *striden* to straddle, OHG *strītan* to quarrel] *vi* (bef. 12c) **1** : to stand astride **2** : to move with or as if with long steps **3** : to take a very long step ~ *vt* **1** : BESTRIDE, STRADDLE **2** : to step over **3** : to move over or along with or as if with long measured steps — **strid·er** \'strī-dər\ *n*

²stride *n* (bef. 12c) **1 a** : a cycle of locomotor movements (as of a horse) completed when the feet regain the initial relative positions; *also* : the distance traversed in a stride **b** : the most effective natural pace : maximum competence or capability — often used in the phrase *hit one's stride* **2** : a long step **3** : an act of striding **4** : a stage of progress : ADVANCE **5** : a manner of striding **6** : STRIDE PIANO — **in stride 1** : without interference with regular activities **2** : without emotional reaction ⟨took the news *in stride*⟩

stri·dence \'strī-d²n(t)s\ *n* (1890) : STRIDENCY

stri·den·cy \'strī-d²n(t)-sē\ n (1865) : the quality or state of being strident

stri·dent \'strī-d²nt\ adj [L strident-, stridens, prp. of stridere, stridēre to make a harsh noise] (ca. 1656) : characterized by harsh, insistent, and discordant sound ⟨a ~ voice⟩; also : commanding attention by a loud or obtrusive quality ⟨~ slogans⟩ syn see LOUD, VOCIFEROUS — **stri·dent·ly** adv

stride piano n [fr. stride bass left hand part consisting of large skips] (1952) : a style of jazz piano playing in which the right hand plays the melody while the left hand alternates between a single note and a chord played an octave or more higher

stri·dor \'strī-dər, -ˌdȯr\ n [L, fr. stridere, stridēre] (1632) 1 : a harsh, shrill, or creaking noise 2 : a harsh vibrating sound heard during respiration in cases of obstruction of the air passages

strid·u·late \'stri-jə-ˌlāt\ vi -lat·ed; -lat·ing [back-formation fr. stridulation, fr. F, high-pitched sound, fr. L stridulus shrill] (1838) : to make a shrill creaking noise by rubbing together special bodily structures — used esp. of male insects (as crickets or grasshoppers) — **strid·u·la·tion** \ˌstri-jə-'lā-shən\ n — **strid·u·la·to·ry** \'stri-jə-lə-ˌtōr-ē, -ˌtȯr-\ adj

strid·u·lous \'stri-jə-ləs\ adj [L stridulus, fr. stridere, stridēre] (1611) : making a shrill creaking sound — **strid·u·lous·ly** adv

strife \'strīf\ n [ME strif, fr. OF estrif, prob. fr. estriver to struggle — more at STRIVE] (13c) 1 a : bitter sometimes violent conflict or dissension ⟨political ~⟩ b : an act of contention : FIGHT, STRUGGLE 2 : exertion or contention for superiority 3 archaic : earnest endeavor syn see DISCORD — **strife·less** \'strī-fləs\ adj

strig·il \'stri-jəl\ n [L strigilis; akin to L stringere to touch lightly] (1581) : an instrument used by ancient Greeks and Romans for scraping moisture off the skin after bathing or exercising

stri·gose \'strī-ˌgōs\ adj [NL strigosus, fr. striga row of bristles, fr. L, furrow] (1793) : having appressed bristles or scales ⟨a ~ leaf⟩

¹**strike** \'strīk\ vb struck \'strək\; struck or strick·en \'stri-kən\; strik·ing \'strī-kiŋ\ [ME, fr. OE strican to stroke, go; akin to OHG strīhhan to stroke, L stringere to touch lightly, striga, stria furrow] vi (bef. 12c) 1 : to take a course : GO ⟨struck off through the brush⟩ 2 a : to aim and usu. deliver a blow, stroke, or thrust (as with the hand, a weapon, or a tool) b : to arrive with detrimental effect ⟨disaster struck⟩ c : to attempt to undermine or harm something as if by a blow ⟨struck at . . . cherished notions —R. P. Warren⟩ 3 : to come into contact forcefully ⟨two ships struck in mid channel⟩ 4 : to delete something 5 : to lower a flag usu. in surrender 6 a : to become indicated by a clock, bell, or chime ⟨the hour had just struck⟩ b : to make known the time by sounding ⟨the clock struck as they entered⟩ 7 : PIERCE, PENETRATE ⟨the wind seemed to ~ through our clothes⟩ 8 a : to engage in battle b : to make a military attack 9 : to become ignited 10 : to discover something ⟨struck on a new plan of attack⟩ 11 a : to pull on a fishing rod in order to set the hook b of a fish : to seize the bait 12 : DART, SHOOT 13 a of a plant cutting : to take root b of a seed : GERMINATE 14 : to make an impression 15 : to stop work in order to force an employer to comply with demands 16 : to make a beginning ⟨the need to ~ vigorously for success⟩ 17 : to thrust oneself forward ⟨he struck into the midst of the argument⟩ 18 : to work diligently : STRIVE ~ vt 1 : to strike at : HIT b : to drive or remove by or as if by a blow c : to attack or seize with a sharp blow ⟨struck by a snake⟩ d : INFLICT ⟨~ a blow⟩ e : to produce by or as if by a blow or stroke ⟨Moses struck water from the rock⟩ f : to separate by a sharp blow ⟨~ off flints⟩ 2 a : to haul down : LOWER ⟨~ the sails⟩ b : to dismantle and take away c : to strike the tents of (a camp) 3 : to afflict suddenly ⟨stricken by a heart attack⟩ 4 a : to engage in (a battle) : FIGHT b : to make a military attack on 5 : DELETE, CANCEL ⟨~ the last paragraph⟩ 6 a : to penetrate painfully : PIERCE b : to cause to penetrate c : to send down or out ⟨trees struck roots deep into the soil⟩ 7 a : to level (as a measure of grain) by scraping off what is above the rim b : to smooth or form with a strickle 8 : to indicate by sounding 9 a (1) : to bring into forceful contact (2) : to shake (hands) in confirming an agreement (3) : to thrust suddenly b : to come into contact or collision with c of light : to fall on d of a sound : to become audible to 10 a : to affect with a mental or emotional state or a strong emotion ⟨struck with horror at the sight⟩ b : to affect a person with (a strong emotion) ⟨words that struck fear in the listeners⟩ c : to cause to become by or as if by a sudden blow ⟨struck him dead⟩ 11 a : to produce by stamping b (1) : to produce (as fire) by or as if by striking (2) : to cause to ignite by friction 12 : to make and ratify the terms of ⟨~ a bargain⟩ 13 a : to play or produce by stroking keys or strings ⟨struck a series of chords on the piano⟩ b : to produce as if by playing an instrument ⟨his voice struck a note of concern⟩ 14 a : to hook (a fish) by a sharp pull on the line b of a fish : to snatch at (a bait) 15 a : to occur to ⟨the answer struck me suddenly⟩ b : to appear to esp. as a revelation or as remarkable : IMPRESS 16 : BEWITCH 17 : to arrive at by or as if by computation ⟨~ a balance⟩ 18 a : to come to : ATTAIN b : to come upon : DISCOVER ⟨~ gold⟩ 19 : to engage in a strike against (an employer) 20 : TAKE ON, ASSUME ⟨~ a pose⟩ 21 a : to place (a plant cutting) in a medium for growth and rooting b : to so propagate (a plant) 22 : to make one's way along 23 : to cause (an arc) to form (as between electrodes of an arc lamp) 24 of an insect : to oviposit on or in syn see AFFECT — **strike it rich** : to become rich usu. suddenly

²**strike** n (15c) 1 : STRICKLE 2 : an act or instance of striking 3 a : a work stoppage by a body of workers to enforce compliance with demands made on an employer b : a temporary stoppage of activities in protest against an act or condition 4 : the direction of the line of intersection of a horizontal plane with an uptilted geological stratum 5 a : a pull on a fishing rod to strike a fish b : a pull on a line by a fish in striking 6 : a stroke of good luck; esp : a discovery of a valuable mineral deposit 7 a : a pitched ball that is in the strike zone or is swung at and is not hit fair b : a perfectly thrown ball or pass 8 : DISADVANTAGE, HANDICAP 9 : an act or instance of knocking down

strigil

all the bowling pins with the first bowl 10 : establishment of roots and plant growth 11 : cutaneous myiasis (as of sheep) 12 a : a military attack; esp : an air attack on a single objective b : a group of airplanes taking part in such an attack

strike·bound \'strīk-ˌbau̇nd\ adj (1943) : subjected to a strike

strike·break·er \-ˌbrā-kər\ n (1904) : a person hired to replace a striking worker

strike·break·ing \-kiŋ\ n (1905) : action designed to break up a strike

strike force n (1968) : a team of federal agents assigned to investigate organized crime in a specific area

strike off vt (1821) 1 : to produce in an effortless manner 2 : to depict clearly and exactly

strike·out \'strīk-ˌau̇t\ n (1887) : an out in baseball resulting from a batter's being charged with three strikes

strike out vi (1712) 1 : to enter upon a course of action 2 : to set out vigorously 3 : to make an out in baseball by a strikeout 4 : to finish bowling a string with consecutive strikes; specif : to bowl three strikes in the last frame 5 : FAIL 2c ~ vt, of a baseball pitcher : to retire (as a batter) by a strikeout

strike·over \'strīk-ˌō-vər\ n (1938) : an act or instance of striking a typewriter character on a spot occupied by another character

strik·er \'strī-kər\ n (1581) 1 : one that strikes: as a : a player in any of several games who is striking or attempting to strike a ball b : the hammer of the striking mechanism of a clock or watch c : a blacksmith's helper who swings the sledgehammer d : a worker on strike 2 : a junior enlisted man in the U.S. Navy who has declared an occupational specialty

strike up vi (ca. 1562) : to begin to sing or play or to be sung or played ~ vt 1 : to cause to begin singing or playing ⟨strike up the band⟩ 2 : to cause to begin ⟨strike up a conversation⟩

strike zone n (1948) : the area over home plate through which a pitched baseball must pass to be called a strike

strik·ing \'strī-kiŋ\ adj (1752) : attracting attention or notice through unusual or conspicuous qualities ⟨a place of ~ beauty⟩ syn see NOTICEABLE — **strik·ing·ly** \-kiŋ-lē\ adv

striking distance n (1751) : a distance from which something can be easily reached or attained ⟨almost within striking distance of their goal⟩

striking price n (1961) : an agreed-upon price at which an option contract can be exercised — called also strike price

¹**string** \'striŋ\ n [ME, fr. OE streng; akin to OHG strang rope, L stringere to bind tight — more at STRAIN] (bef. 12c) 1 : a small cord used to bind, fasten, or tie 2 a archaic : a cord (as a tendon or ligament) of an animal body b : a plant fiber (as a leaf vein) 3 a : the gut, wire, or nylon cord of a musical instrument b pl (1) : the stringed instruments of an orchestra (2) : the players of such instruments 4 a : a group of objects threaded on a string ⟨a ~ of fish⟩ ⟨a ~ of pearls⟩ b (1) : a series of things arranged in or as if in a line ⟨a ~ of cars⟩ ⟨a ~ of names⟩ (2) : a sequence of like items (as bits, characters, or words) c : a group of business properties scattered geographically ⟨a ~ of newspapers⟩ d : the animals and esp. horses belonging to or used by one individual 5 a : a means of recourse : EXPEDIENT b : a group of players ranked according to skill or proficiency 6 : SUCCESSION 3a ⟨a ~ of successes⟩ 7 a : one of the inclined sides of a stair supporting the treads and risers b : STRINGCOURSE 8 a : BALKLINE 1 b : the action of lagging for break in billiards 9 : LINE 13 10 pl : contingent conditions or obligations b : CONTROL, DOMINATION 11 : a scanty bikini — called also string bikini 12 : a hypothetical one-dimensional object that is infinitely thin but has a length of 10⁻³³ centimeters, that vibrates as it moves through space, and whose mode of vibration manifests itself as a subatomic particle — **string·less** \'striŋ-ləs\ adj — **on the string** : subject to one's influence

²**string** vb strung \'strəŋ\; string·ing \'striŋ-iŋ\ vt (15c) 1 a : to equip with strings b : to tune the strings of 2 : to make tense : key up 3 a : to thread on or as if on a string b : to thread with objects c : to tie, hang, or fasten with string d : to put together (as words or ideas) like objects threaded on a string 4 : to hang by the neck — used with up 5 : to remove the strings of ⟨~ beans⟩ 6 a : to extend or stretch like a string ⟨~ wires from tree to tree⟩ b : to set out in a line or series — often used with out 7 : FOOL, HOAX ⟨cowboys ~ing tenderfeet with tall tales —Carl Van Doren⟩ — often used with along ~ vi 1 : to move, progress, or lie in a string 2 : to form into strings 3 : LAG 3

³**string** adj (1712) : of or relating to stringed musical instruments ⟨the ~ section⟩

string along vt (1914) : to keep waiting ~ vi : GO ALONG, AGREE

string bass n (ca. 1927) : DOUBLE BASS

string bean n (1759) 1 : a bean of one of the older varieties of kidney bean that have stringy fibers on the lines of separation of the pods; broadly : SNAP BEAN 2 : a very tall thin person

string·course \-ˌkōrs, -ˌkȯrs\ n (1825) : a horizontal band (as of bricks) in a building forming a part of the design

stri·nged \'striŋd\ adj (bef. 12c) 1 : having strings ⟨~ instruments⟩ 2 : produced by strings

strin·gen·cy \'strin-jən(t)-sē\ n (1844) : the quality or state of being stringent

strin·gen·do \strin-'jen-(ˌ)dō\ adv [It, verbal of stringere to press, fr. L, to bind tight — more at STRAIN] (1853) : with quickening of tempo ⟨as to a climax⟩ — used as a direction in music

strin·gent \'strin-jənt\ adj [L stringent-, stringens, prp. of stringere] (1736) 1 : TIGHT, CONSTRICTED 2 : marked by rigor, strictness, or severity esp. with regard to rule or standard 3 : marked by money scarcity and credit strictness syn see RIGID — **strin·gent·ly** adv

string·er \'striŋ-ər\ n (14c) 1 : one that strings 2 : a string, wire, or chain often with snaps on which fish are strung by a fisherman 3 : a narrow vein or irregular filament of mineral traversing a rock mass of different material 4 a : a long horizontal timber to connect uprights in a frame or to support a floor b : STRING 7a c : a tie in a truss 5

\ə\ abut \²\ kitten, F table \ər\ further \a\ ash \ā\ ace \ä\ mop, mar \au̇\ out \ch\ chin \e\ bet \ē\ easy \g\ go \i\ hit \ī\ ice \j\ job \ŋ\ sing \ō\ go \ȯ\ law \ȯi\ boy \th\ thin \t̲h̲\ the \ü\ loot \u̇\ foot \y\ yet \zh\ vision \à, ᵏ, ⁿ, œ, œ̄, ᵫ, ᵫ̄, ᵊ\ see Guide to Pronunciation a : a longitudinal member extending from bent to bent of a railroad bridge and carrying the track **b** : a longitudinal member (as in an airplane fuselage or wing) to reinforce the skin **6 a** : a news correspondent who is paid space rates **b** : a reporter who works for a publication or news agency on a part-time basis; *broadly* : CORRESPONDENT **7** : one estimated to be of specified excellence or efficiency — used in combination ⟨first-*stringer*⟩ ⟨second-*stringer*⟩

string·halt \'striŋ-ˌhȯlt\ *n* (ca. 1534) : a condition of lameness in a horse's hind legs caused by muscular spasms — **string·halt·ed** \-ˌhȯl-təd\ *adj*

string·ing \'striŋ-iŋ\ *n* (1812) **1** : lines of inlay in furniture decoration **2** : the material with which a racket is strung

string line *n* (1867) : BALKLINE 1

string·piece \'striŋ-ˌpēs\ *n* (1769) : the heavy squared timber lying along the top of the piles forming a dock front or pier

string quartet *n* (1875) **1** : a composition for string quartet **2** : a quartet of performers on stringed instruments usu. including a first and second violin, a viola, and a cello

string tie *n* (1895) : a narrow necktie

stringy \'striŋ-ē\ *adj* **string·i·er; -est** (1669) **1 a** : containing, consisting of, or resembling fibrous matter or string ⟨~ hair⟩ **b** : lean and sinewy in build : WIRY **2** : capable of being drawn out to form a string : ROPY ⟨a ~ precipitate⟩ — **string·i·ness** *n*

stringy·bark \'striŋ-ē-ˌbärk\ *n* (1799) **1** : any of several Australian eucalypti with fibrous inner bark **2** : the bark of a stringybark

¹strip \'strip\ *vb* **stripped** \'stript\ *also* **stript; strip·ping** [ME *strippen,* fr. OE *-striepan;* akin to OHG *stroufen* to strip] *vt* (13c) **1 a** : to remove clothing, covering, or surface matter from **b** : to deprive of possessions **c** : to divest of honors, privileges, or functions **2 a** : to remove extraneous or superficial matter from ⟨a prose style *stripped* to the bones⟩ **b** : to remove furniture, equipment, or accessories from ⟨~ a ship for action⟩ **3** : to make bare or clear (as by cutting or grazing) **4** : to finish a milking of by pressing the last available milk from the teats ⟨~ a cow⟩ **5 a** : to remove cured leaves from the stalks of (tobacco) **b** : to remove the midrib from (tobacco leaves) **6** : to tear or damage the thread of (a separable part or fitting) **7** : to separate (components) from a mixture or solution **8** : to press eggs or milt out of (a fish) ~ *vi* **1 a** : to take off clothes **b** : to perform a striptease **2** : PEEL 1 — **strip·pa·ble** \'stri-pə-bəl\ *adj*

²strip *n* [ME, perh. fr. MLG *strippe* strap] (15c) **1 a** : a long narrow piece of a material **b** : a long narrow area of land or water **2** : AIR-STRIP **3** : a commercially developed area esp. along a highway **4** : COMIC STRIP **5** : STRIPTEASE

strip–chart recorder \'strip-ˌchärt-\ *n* (1950) : a device used for the continuous graphic recording of time-dependent data — **strip–chart recording** *n*

strip–crop·ping \'strip-ˌkrä-piŋ\ *n* (1936) : the growing of a cultivated crop (as corn) in strips alternating with strips of a sod-forming crop (as hay) arranged to follow an approximate contour of the land and minimize erosion — **strip–crop** \'strip-ˌkräp\ *vb*

¹stripe \'strīp\ *n* [ME; akin to MD *stripe* strip, stripe] (15c) : a stroke or blow with a rod or lash

²stripe *vt* **striped** \'stript\; **strip·ing** [prob. fr. MD; akin to MHG *strīfe* stripe] (15c) : to make stripes on or variegate with stripes

³stripe *n* (1626) **1 a** : a line or long narrow section differing in color or texture from parts adjoining **b** (1) : a textile design consisting of lines or bands against a plain background (2) : a fabric with a striped design **2** : a narrow strip of braid or embroidery usu. in the shape of a bar, arc, or chevron that is worn (as on the sleeve of a military uniform) to indicate rank or length of service **3** : a distinct variety or sort : TYPE ⟨persons of the same political ~⟩ — **stripe·less** \'strī-pləs\ *adj*

striped \'stript, 'strī-pəd\ *adj* (1616) : having stripes or streaks

striped bass *n* (1818) : a large anadromous food and sport fish (*Morone saxatilis* of the family Percichthyidae) that occurs along the Atlantic coast of the U.S. and has been introduced along the Pacific coast — called also *rockfish*

striped skunk *n* (1882) : a common No. American skunk (*Mephitis mephitis*) usu. with white on the top of the head that extends posteriorly in two narrowly separated stripes

strip·er \'strī-pər\ *n* (1937) : STRIPED BASS

strip·ing \'strī-piŋ\ *n* (1677) **1 a** : the stripes marked or painted on something **b** : a design of stripes **2** : the act or process of marking with stripes

strip·ling \'stri-pliŋ\ *n* [ME] (14c) : YOUTH 2a

strip mine *n* (1926) : a mine that is worked from the earth's surface by the stripping of overburden; *esp* : a coal mine situated along the outcrop of a flat dipping bed — **strip–mine** *vb* — **strip miner** *n*

stripped–down \'strip(t)-ˈdau̇n\ *adj* (1928) : lacking any extra features : SIMPLE 2b

strip·per \'stri-pər\ *n* (1581) **1** : one that strips **2** : STRIPTEASER **3** : a machine that separates a desired part of an agricultural crop **4** : an oil well that produces 10 barrels or less per day

strip poker *n* (1919) : a poker game in which players pay their losses by removing articles of clothing

strip search *n* (1947) : a search for something concealed on a person made after removal of the person's clothing — **strip–search** *vb*

strip·tease \'strip-ˌtēz\ *n* (1936) : a burlesque act in which a performer removes clothing piece by piece

strip·teas·er \-ˌtē-zər\ *n* (1930) : one who performs a striptease

stripy \'strī-pē\ *adj* **strip·i·er; -est** (1513) : marked by stripes or streaks

strive \'strīv\ *vi* **strove** \'strōv\ *also* **strived** \'strīvd\; **striv·en** \'stri-vən\ *or* **strived; striv·ing** \'strī-viŋ\ [ME, fr. OF *estriver,* of Gmc origin; akin to MHG *strēben* to endeavor] (13c) **1** : to devote serious effort or energy : ENDEAVOR **2** : to struggle in opposition : CONTEND *syn* see ATTEMPT — **striv·er** \'strī-vər\ *n*

strobe \'strōb\ *n* [by shortening & alter.] (1942) **1** : STROBOSCOPE **2** : a device that utilizes a flashtube for high-speed illumination (as in photography) **3** : STROBOTRON

strobe light *n* (1947) : STROBE

stro·bi·la \strō-ˈbī-lə, ˈstrō-bə-\ *n, pl* **-lae** \-(ˌ)lē\ [NL, fr. Gk *strobilē* plug of lint shaped like a pinecone, fr. *strobilos* pinecone] (1864) : a linear series of similar animal structures (as the proglottids of a tapeworm) produced by budding

stro·bi·la·tion \ˌstrō-bə-ˈlā-shən\ *n* [NL *strobila*] (1878) : asexual reproduction (as in various coelenterates and tapeworms) by transverse division of the body into segments which develop into separate individuals, zooids, or proglottids

stro·bi·lus \strō-ˈbī-ləs, ˈstrō-bə-\ *n, pl* **-li** \-ˌlī\ [NL, fr. LL, pinecone, fr. Gk *strobilos* twisted object, top, pinecone, fr. *strobos* action of whirling; akin to *strephein* to twist] (ca. 1753) **1** : an aggregation of sporophylls resembling a cone (as in the club mosses and horsetails) **2** : the cone of a gymnosperm

stro·bo·scope \'strō-bə-ˌskōp\ *n* [Gk *strobos* whirling + ISV *-scope*] (1896) : an instrument for determining the speed of cyclic motion (as rotation or vibration) that causes the motion to appear slowed or stopped: as **a** : a revolving disk with holes around the edge through which an object is viewed **b** : a device that uses a flashtube to intermittently illuminate a moving object **c** : a cardboard disk with marks to be viewed under intermittent light

stro·bo·scop·ic \ˌstrō-bə-ˈskä-pik\ *adj* (ca. 1846) : of, utilizing, or relating to a stroboscope or a strobe — **stro·bo·scop·i·cal·ly** \-pi-k(ə-)lē\ *adv*

stro·bo·tron \'strō-bə-ˌträn\ *n* [*stroboscope* + *-tron*] (1937) : a gas-filled electron tube used esp. as a source of bright flashes of light for a stroboscope

strode *past of* STRIDE

¹stroke \'strōk\ *vt* **stroked; strok·ing** [ME, fr. OE *strācian;* akin to OHG *strīhhan* to stroke — more at STRIKE] (bef. 12c) **1** : to rub gently in one direction; *also* : CARESS **2** : to flatter or pay attention to in a manner designed to reassure or persuade — **strok·er** *n*

²stroke *n* [ME; akin to OE *strīcan* to stroke — more at STRIKE] (13c) **1** : the act of striking; *esp* : a blow with a weapon or implement **2** : a single unbroken movement; *esp* : one of a series of repeated or to-and-fro movements **3 a** : a controlled swing intended to hit a ball or shuttlecock; *also* : a striking of the ball **b** : such a stroke charged to a player as a unit of scoring in golf **4 a** : a sudden action or process producing an impact ⟨~ of lightning⟩ **b** : an unexpected result ⟨~ of luck⟩ **5** : sudden diminution or loss of consciousness, sensation, and voluntary motion caused by rupture or obstruction (as by a clot) of an artery of the brain — called also *apoplexy* **6 a** : one of a series of propelling beats or movements against a resisting medium ⟨a ~ of the oar⟩ **b** : a rower who sets the pace for a crew **7 a** : a vigorous or energetic effort ⟨a ~ of genius⟩ **b** : a delicate or clever touch in a narrative, description, or construction **8** : HEARTBEAT **9** : the movement or the distance of the movement in either direction of a mechanical part (as a piston) having a reciprocating motion **10** : the sound of a bell being struck ⟨at the ~ of twelve⟩ **11** [¹STROKE] : an act of stroking or caressing **12 a** : a mark or dash made by a single movement of an implement **b** : one of the lines of a letter of the alphabet

³stroke *vb* **stroked; strok·ing** *vt* (1597) **1 a** : to mark with a short line ⟨~ the *t*'s⟩ **b** : to cancel by drawing a line through ⟨*stroked* out his name⟩ **2** : to set the stroke for (a rowing crew); *also* : to set the stroke for the crew of (a rowing boat) **3** : HIT; *esp* : to propel (a ball) with a controlled swinging blow ~ *vi* **1** : to execute a stroke **2** : to row at a certain number of strokes a minute

stroke play *n* (1905) : golf competition scored by total number of strokes

stroll \'strōl\ *vb* [prob. fr. G dial. *strollen*] *vi* (1680) **1** : to walk in a leisurely or idle manner : RAMBLE **2** : to go from place to place in search of work or profit ⟨~ing players⟩ ⟨~ing musicians⟩ ~ *vt* : to walk at leisure along or about — **stroll** *n*

stroll·er \'strō-lər\ *n* (1608) **1 a** : an itinerant actor **b** : VAGRANT, TRAMP **2** : one that strolls **3** : a collapsible carriage designed as a chair in which a small child may be pushed

stro·ma \'strō-mə\ *n, pl* **stro·ma·ta** \-mə-tə\ [NL *stromat-, stroma,* fr. L, bed covering, fr. Gk *strōmat-, strōma,* fr. *stornynai* to spread out — more at STREW] (1832) **1 a** : a compact mass of fungal hyphae producing perithecia or pycnidia **b** : the colorless proteinaceous matrix of a chloroplast in which the chlorophyll-containing lamellae are embedded **2 a** : the supporting framework of an animal organ typically consisting of connective tissue **b** : the spongy protoplasmic framework of some cells (as a red blood cell) — **stro·mal** \-məl\ *adj*

stro·mat·o·lite \strō-ˈma-tᵊl-ˌīt\ *n* [L *stromat-, stroma* bed covering + E *-o-* + *-lite*] (1930) : a laminated sedimentary fossil formed from layers of blue-green algae — **stro·mat·o·lit·ic** \-ˌma-tᵊl-ˈi-tik\ *adj*

strong \'strȯŋ\ *adj* **stron·ger** \'strȯŋ-gər *also* -ər\; **stron·gest** \'strȯŋ-gəst *also* -əst\ [ME, fr. OE *strang;* akin to OHG *strengi* strong, L *stringere* to bind tight — more at STRAIN] (bef. 12c) **1** : having or marked by great physical power **2** : having moral or intellectual power **3** : having great resources (as of wealth or talent) **4** : of a specified number ⟨an army ten thousand ~⟩ **5 a** : striking or superior of its kind ⟨a ~ resemblance⟩ **b** : effective or efficient esp. in a specified direction ⟨~ on watching other people work —A. Alvarez⟩ **6** : FORCEFUL, COGENT ⟨~ evidence⟩ ⟨~ talk⟩ **7** : not mild or weak : EXTREME, INTENSE: as **a** : rich in some active agent ⟨~ beer⟩ **b** *of a color* : high in chroma **c** : ionizing freely in solution ⟨~ acids and bases⟩ **d** : magnifying by refracting greatly ⟨~ lens⟩ **8** *obs* : FLAGRANT **9** : moving with rapidity or force ⟨~ wind⟩ **10** : ARDENT, ZEALOUS ⟨a ~ supporter⟩ **11 a** : not easily injured or disturbed : SOLID **b** : not easily subdued or taken ⟨a ~ fort⟩ **12** : well established : FIRM ⟨~ beliefs⟩ **13** : not easily upset or nauseated ⟨a ~ stomach⟩ **14** : having an offensive or intense odor or flavor : RANK **15** : tending to steady or higher prices ⟨a ~ market⟩ **16** : of, relating to, or being a verb that is inflected by a change in the root vowel (as *strive, strove, striven*) rather than by regular affixation — **strong** *adv* — **strong·ish** \'strȯŋ-ish\ *adj* — **strong·ly** \'strȯŋ-lē\ *adv*

syn STRONG, STOUT, STURDY, STALWART, TOUGH, TENACIOUS mean showing power to resist or to endure. STRONG may imply power derived from muscular vigor, large size, structural soundness, intellectual or spiritual resources ⟨*strong* arms⟩ ⟨the defense has a *strong* case⟩. STOUT suggests an ability to endure stress, pain, or hard use without giving way ⟨*stout* hiking boots⟩. STURDY implies strength derived from vigorous growth, determination of spirit, solidity of construction ⟨a *sturdy* table⟩ ⟨people of *sturdy* independence⟩. STALWART suggests an unshakable dependability ⟨*stalwart* environmentalists⟩. TOUGH implies great firmness and resiliency ⟨a *tough* political opponent⟩. TENACIOUS suggests strength in seizing, retaining, clinging to, or holding together ⟨*tenacious* farmers clinging to an age-old way of life⟩.

strong anthropic principle *n* (1985) : ANTHROPIC PRINCIPLE b

¹**strong–arm** \'stróŋ-,ärm\ *adj* (1897) : having or using undue force

²**strong–arm** *vt* (1903) **1 a** : to use force on : ASSAULT **b** : BULLY, INTIMIDATE **2** : to rob by force

strong-box \'stróŋ-,bäks\ *n* (1684) : a strongly made chest or case for money or valuables

strong breeze *n* (1867) : wind having a speed of 25 to 31 miles (40 to 50 kilometers) per hour — see BEAUFORT SCALE table

strong drink *n* (14c) : intoxicating liquor

strong force *n* (1969) : a fundamental physical force that acts on hadrons and is responsible for the binding together of protons and neutrons in the atomic nucleus and for processes of particle creation in high-energy collisions and that is the strongest known fundamental physical force but acts only over distances comparable to those between nucleons in an atomic nucleus — called also *strong interaction, strong nuclear force;* compare ELECTROMAGNETISM 2a, GRAVITY 3a(2), WEAK FORCE

strong gale *n* (ca. 1867) : wind having a speed of 47 to 54 miles (76 to 87 kilometers) per hour — see BEAUFORT SCALE table

strong-hold \'stróŋ-,hōld\ *n* (15c) **1** : a fortified place **2 a** : a place of security or survival ⟨one of the last ∼s of the ancient Gaelic language —George Holmes⟩ **b** : a place dominated by a particular group or marked by a particular characteristic ⟨a Republican ∼⟩ ⟨∼s of snobbery —Lionel Trilling⟩

strong-man \'stróŋ-,man\ *n* (1859) : one who leads or controls by force of will and character or by military methods

strong–mind-ed \'stróŋ-'mīn-dəd\ *adj* (1791) : having a vigorous mind; *esp* : marked by independence of thought and judgment — **strong–mind-ed-ly** *adv* — **strong–mind-ed-ness** *n*

strong room *n* (1761) : a room for money or valuables specially constructed to be fireproof and burglarproof

strong safety *n* (1970) : a safety in football who plays opposite the strong side of an offensive formation

strong side *n* (ca. 1951) : the side of a football formation having the greater number of players; *specif* : the side on which the tight end plays

strong suit *n* (1857) **1** : a long suit containing high cards **2** : something in which one excels : FORTE ⟨details of legislation have never been my *strong suit* —Tip O'Neill⟩

stron-gyle \'strän-,jil, -jəl\ *n* [NL *Strongylus*, genus of worms, fr. Gk *strongylos* round, compact; akin to Gk *stranx* drop squeezed out — more at STRAIN] (1847) : any of various nematode worms (family Strongylidae) related to the hookworms and parasitic esp. in the alimentary tract and tissues of horses

stron-gy-loi-di-a-sis \,strän-jə-,lói-'dī-ə-səs\ *also* **stron-gy-loi-do-sis** \-'dō-səs\ *n* [NL, fr. *Strongyloides*, genus name, fr. *Strongylus*] (1905) : infestation with or disease caused by any of a genus (*Strongyloides*) of strongyles that sometimes parasitize the intestines of vertebrates including humans

stron-tian-ite \'strän(t)-shə-,nīt\ *n* (1794) : a mineral consisting of a carbonate of strontium and occurring in various forms and colors

stron-tium \'strän(t)-sh(ē-)əm, 'strän-tē-əm\ *n* [NL, fr. *strontia* strontium oxide, fr. obs. E *strontian*, fr. *Strontian*, village in Scotland] (1808) : a soft malleable ductile metallic element of the alkaline-earth group occurring only in combination and used esp. in color TV tubes, in crimson fireworks, and in the production of some ferrites — see ELEMENT table

strontium 90 *n* (1952) : a heavy radioactive isotope of strontium of mass number 90 that has a half-life of 29 years and that is present in the fallout from nuclear explosions and is hazardous because like calcium it can be assimilated in biological processes and deposited in the bones of human beings and animals — called also *radiostrontium*

¹**strop** \'sträp\ *n* [ME — more at STRAP] (bef. 12c) : STRAP **a** : a short rope with its ends spliced to form a circle **b** : a usu. leather band for sharpening a razor

²**strop** *vt* **stropped; strop-ping** (1841) : to sharpen (a razor) on a strop

stro-phan-thin \strō-'fan(t)-thən\ *n* [ISV, fr. NL *Strophanthus*, fr. Gk *strophos* twisted band (fr. *strephein* to twist) + *anthos* flower — more at ANTHOLOGY] (1873) : any of several glycosides (as ouabain) or mixtures of glycosides from African plants (genera *Strophanthus* and *Acokanthera*) of the dogbane family; *esp* : a bitter toxic glycoside $C_{36}H_{54}O_{14}$ from a woody vine (*Strophanthus kombé*) used similarly to digitalis

stro-phe \'strō-(,)fē\ *n* [Gk *strophē*, lit., act of turning, fr. *strephein* to turn, twist] (1603) **1 a** : a rhythmic system composed of two or more lines repeated as a unit; *esp* : such a unit recurring in a series of strophic units **b** : STANZA **2 a** : the movement of the classical Greek chorus while turning from one side to the other of the orchestra **b** : the part of a Greek choral ode sung during the strophe of the dance

stro-phic \'strō-fik, 'strä-\ *adj* (1848) **1** : relating to, containing, or consisting of strophes **2** *of a song* : using the same music for successive stanzas — compare THROUGH-COMPOSED

strop-py \'strä-pē\ *adj* [perh. by shortening & alter. fr. *obstreperous*] (1951) *Brit* : TOUCHY, BELLIGERENT

stroud \'straúd\ *n* [prob. fr. *Stroud*, town in England] (1683) **1** *also* **stroud-ing** \'straú-diŋ\ : a coarse woolen cloth formerly used in trade with No. American Indians **2** : a blanket or garment of stroud

strove *past & chiefly dial past part of* STRIVE

strow \'strō\ *vt* **strowed; strown** \'strōn\ *or* **strowed; strow-ing** [ME — more at STREW] (14c) *archaic* : SCATTER

stroy *vb* [ME *stroyen*, short for *destroyen*] (13c) *obs* : DESTROY

¹**struck** \'strək\ *past and past part of* STRIKE

²**struck** *adj* (1894) : closed by or subjected to a labor strike ⟨a ∼ factory⟩ ⟨a ∼ employer⟩

struc-tur-al \'strək-chə-rəl, 'strək-shrəl\ *adj* (1835) **1** : of or relating to the physical makeup of a plant or animal body **2 a** : of, relating to, or affecting structure ⟨∼ stability⟩ **b** : used in building structures ⟨∼ clay⟩ **c** : involved in or caused by structure esp. of the economy ⟨∼ unemployment⟩ **3** : of, relating to, or resulting from the effects of folding or faulting of the earth's crust : TECTONIC **4** : concerned with or relating to structure rather than history or comparison ⟨∼ linguistics⟩ — **struc-tur-al-ly** *adv*

structural formula *n* (1872) : an expanded molecular formula showing the arrangement within the molecule of atoms and of bonds

structural gene *n* (1959) : a gene that codes for the amino acid sequence of a protein (as an enzyme) or for a ribosomal RNA or transfer RNA

struc-tur-al-ism \'strək-chə-rə-,li-zəm, 'strək-shrə-\ *n* (1907) **1** : psychology concerned esp. with resolution of the mind into structural elements **2** : structural linguistics **3** : an anthropological movement associated esp. with Claude Lévi-Strauss that seeks to analyze social relationships in terms of highly abstract relational structures often expressed in a logical symbolism **4** : a method of analysis (as of a literary text or a political system) that is related to cultural anthropology and that focuses on recurring patterns of thought and behavior — **struc-tur-al-ist** \-list\ *n or adj*

structural isomer *n* (1926) : one of two or more compounds that contain the same number and kinds of atoms but that differ significantly in their geometric arrangement

struc-tur-al-ize \'strək-chə-rə-,līz, 'strək-shrə-,līz\ *vt* **-ized; -iz-ing** (ca. 1931) : to organize or incorporate into a structure — **struc-tur-al-i-za-tion** \,strək-chə-rə-lə-'zā-shən, ,strək-shrə-\ *n*

structural steel *n* (1895) **1** : rolled steel in structural shapes **2** : steel suitable for structural shapes

struc-tur-a-tion \,strək-chə-rə-'shən, -shə-'rā-\ *n* (1925) : the interrelation of parts in an organized whole

¹**struc-ture** \'strək-chər\ *n* [ME, fr. L *structura*, fr. *structus*, pp. of *struere* to heap up, build — more at STREW] (15c) **1** : the action of building : CONSTRUCTION **2 a** : something (as a building) that is constructed **b** : something arranged in a definite pattern of organization ⟨a rigid totalitarian ∼ —J. L. Hess⟩ ⟨leaves and other plant ∼s⟩ **3** : manner of construction : MAKEUP ⟨Gothic in ∼⟩ **4 a** : the arrangement of particles or parts in a substance or body ⟨soil ∼⟩ ⟨molecular ∼⟩ **b** : organization of parts as dominated by the general character of the whole ⟨economic ∼⟩ ⟨personality ∼⟩ **5** : the aggregate of elements of an entity in their relationships to each other — **struc-ture-less** \-ləs\ *adj* — **struc-ture-less-ness** \-nəs\ *n*

²**structure** *vt* **struc-tured; struc-tur-ing** \'strək-chə-riŋ, 'strək-shriŋ\ (ca. 1693) **1** : to form into or according to a structure **2** : CONSTRUCT

struc-tured *adj* (1966) : of, relating to, or being a method of computer programming in which each step of the solution to a problem is contained in a separate subprogram

stru-del \'strü-d'l, 'shtrü-\ *n* [G, lit., whirlpool] (ca. 1893) : a pastry made from a thin sheet of dough rolled up with filling and baked ⟨apple ∼⟩

¹**strug-gle** \'strə-gəl\ *vi* **strug-gled; strug-gling** \-g(ə-)liŋ\ [ME *struglen*] (14c) **1** : to make strenuous or violent efforts against opposition : CONTEND **2** : to proceed with difficulty or with great effort ⟨*struggled* through the high grass⟩ ⟨*struggling* to make a living⟩ — **strug-gler** \-g(ə-)lər\ *n*

²**struggle** *n* (1692) **1** : CONTEST, STRIFE ⟨armed ∼⟩ ⟨a power ∼⟩ **2** : a violent effort or exertion : an act of strongly motivated striving

struggle for existence (1832) : the automatic competition (as for food, space, or light) of members of a natural population that tends to eliminate less efficient individuals and thereby increase the chance of the more efficient to pass on inherited adaptive traits

¹**strum** \'strəm\ *vb* **strummed; strum-ming** [imit.] *vt* (1777) **1 a** : to brush the fingers over the strings of (a musical instrument) in playing ⟨∼ a guitar⟩; *also* : ³THRUM 1 **b** : to play (music) on a stringed instrument ⟨∼ a tune⟩ **2** : to cause to sound vibrantly ⟨winds *strummed* the rigging —H. A. Chippendale⟩ ∼ *vi* **1** : to strum a stringed instrument **2** : to sound vibrantly — **strum-mer** *n*

²**strum** *n* (ca. 1793) : an act, instance, or sound of strumming

stru-ma \'strü-mə\ *n, pl* **stru-mae** \-(,)mē, -,mī\ *or* **strumas** [L, swelling of the lymph glands] (1565) : GOITER

strum-pet \'strəm-pət\ *n* [ME] (14c) : PROSTITUTE 1a

strung \'strəŋ\ *past and past part of* STRING

strung out *adj* (ca. 1959) **1** : physically debilitated (as from long-term drug addiction) **2** : addicted to a drug **3** : intoxicated or stupefied from drug use

strunt \'strənt\ *vi* [by alter.] (1786) *Scot* : STRUT

¹**strut** \'strət\ *vb* **strut-ted; strut-ting** [ME *strouten*, fr. OE *strūtian* to exert oneself; akin to MHG *strozzen* to be swollen] *vi* (13c) **1** : to become turgid : SWELL **2 a** : to walk with a proud gait **b** : to walk with a pompous and affected air ∼ *vt* : to parade (as clothes) with a show of pride — **strut-ter** *n* — **strut one's stuff** : to display one's best work : SHOW OFF

²**strut** *n* (1587) **1** : a structural piece designed to resist pressure in the direction of its length **2** : a pompous step or walk **3** : arrogant behavior : SWAGGER

³**strut** *vt* **strut-ted; strut-ting** (ca. 1828) : to provide, stiffen, support, or hold apart with or as if with a strut

stru-thi-ous \'strü-thē-əs, -thē-\ *adj* [LL *struthio* ostrich, irreg. fr. Gk *strouthos*] (1773) : of or relating to the ostriches and related birds

strych-nine \'strik-,nīn, -nən, -,nēn\ *n* [F, fr. NL *Strychnos*, fr. L, nightshade, fr. Gk] (1819) : a bitter poisonous alkaloid $C_{21}H_{22}N_2O_2$ that is obtained from nux vomica and related plants (genus *Strychnos*) and is used as a poison (as for rodents) and medicinally as a stimulant to the central nervous system

Stu-art \'stü-ərt, 'styü-, 'st(y)ù(-ə)rt\ *adj* [Robert *Stewart* (Robert II of Scotland) †1390] (1873) : of or relating to the Scottish royal house to which belonged the rulers of Scotland from 1371 to 1603 and of Great Britain from 1603 to 1649 and from 1660 to 1714 — **Stuart** *n*

¹**stub** \'stəb\ *n* [ME *stubbe*, fr. OE *stybb*; akin to ON *stūfr* stump, Gk *stypos* stem, *typtein* to beat — more at TYPE] (bef. 12c) **1 a** : STUMP 2 **b** : a short piece remaining on a stem or trunk where a branch has been lost **2** : something made or worn to a short or blunt shape; *esp* : a pen with a short blunt nib **3** : a short blunt part left after a larger part has been broken off or used up ⟨pencil ∼⟩ **4** : something cut short or stunted **5 a** : a small part of a leaf (as of a checkbook) attached to

---

\ə\ abut \'ᵊ\ kitten, F table \ər\ further \a\ ash \ā\ ace \ä\ mop, mar \aú\ out \ch\ chin \e\ bet \ē\ easy \g\ go \i\ hit \ī\ ice \j\ job \ŋ\ sing \ō\ go \ó\ law \ói\ boy \th\ thin \t̲h̲\ the \ü\ loot \ù\ foot \y\ yet \zh\ vision \à, k̲, ⁿ, œ, œ̄, ue, ūe, ᵞ\ *see* Guide to Pronunciation the backbone for memoranda of the contents of the part torn away **b** : the part of a ticket returned to the user

²**stub** *vt* **stubbed; stub·bing** (15c) **1 a** : to grub up by the roots **b** : to clear (land) by grubbing out rooted growth **c** : to hew or cut down (a tree) close to the ground **2** : to extinguish (as a cigarette) by crushing **3** : to strike (one's foot or toe) against an object

stub·ble \'stə-bəl\ *n, often attrib* [ME *stuble*, fr. OF *estuble*, fr. L *stupula* stalk, straw, alter. of *stipula* — more at STIPULE] (14c) **1** : the basal part of herbaceous plants and esp. cereal grasses remaining attached to the soil after harvest **2** : a rough surface or growth resembling stubble; *esp* : a short growth of beard — **stub·bled** \-bəld\ *adj* — **stub·bly** \-b(ə-)lē\ *adj*

stubble mulch *n* (1942) : a lightly tilled mulch of plant residue used to prevent erosion, conserve moisture, and add organic matter to the soil

stub·born \'stə-bərn\ *adj* [ME *stuborn*] (14c) **1 a (1)** : unreasonably or perversely unyielding : MULISH **(2)** : justifiably unyielding : RESOLUTE **b** : suggestive or typical of a strong stubborn nature ⟨a ~ jaw⟩ **2** : performed or carried on in an unyielding, obstinate, or persistent manner ⟨~ effort⟩ **3** : difficult to handle, manage, or treat ⟨a ~ cold⟩ **4** : LASTING ⟨~ facts⟩ *syn* see OBSTINATE — **stub·born·ly** *adv* — **stub·born·ness** \-bər(n)-nəs\ *n*

stub·by \'stə-bē\ *adj* **stub·bi·er; -est** (15c) **1** : abounding with stubs **2 a** : resembling a stub : being short and thick ⟨~ fingers⟩ **b** : being short and thickset : SQUAT **c** : being short, broad, or blunt (as from use or wear)

stuc·co \'stə-(,)kō\ *n, pl* **stuccos** *or* **stuccoes** [It, of Gmc origin; akin to OHG *stucki* piece, crust, OE *stocc* stock — more at STOCK] (1598) **1 a** : a fine plaster used in decoration and ornamentation (as of interior walls) **b** : a material usu. made of portland cement, sand, and a small percentage of lime and applied in a plastic state to form a hard covering for exterior walls **2** : STUCCOWORK — **stuc·coed** \-(,)kōd\ *adj*

stuc·co·work \'stə-kō-,wərk\ *n* (1686) : work done in stucco

stuck *past and past part of* STICK

stuck–up \'stək-'əp\ *adj* (1829) : superciliously self-important : CONCEITED

¹**stud** \'stəd\ *n, often attrib* [ME *stod*, fr. OE *stōd*; akin to OCS *stado* flock and prob. to OHG *stān* to stand — more at STAND] (bef. 12c) **1 a** : a group of animals and esp. horses kept primarily for breeding **b** : a place (as a farm) where a stud is kept **2** : STUDHORSE; *broadly* : a male animal kept for breeding **3 a** : a young man : GUY; *esp* : one who is virile and promiscuous **b** : a tough person **c** : HUNK **2** — **at stud** : for breeding as a stud ⟨retired racehorses *at stud*⟩

²**stud** *n* [ME *stode*, fr. OE *studu*; akin to MHG *stud* prop, OE *stōw* place — more at STOW] (bef. 12c) **1 a** : one of the smaller uprights in the framing of the walls of a building to which sheathing, paneling, or laths are fastened : SCANTLING **b** : height from floor to ceiling **2 a** : a boss, rivet, or nail with a large head used (as on a shield or belt) for ornament or protection **b** : a solid button with a shank or eye on the back inserted (as through an eyelet in a garment) as a fastener or ornament **c** : a small often round earring made for a pierced ear **3 a** : any of various infixed pieces (as a rod or pin) projecting from a machine and serving chiefly as a support or axis **b** : one of the metal cleats inserted in a snow tire to increase traction

³**stud** *vt* **stud·ded; stud·ding** (ca. 1506) **1** : to furnish (as a building or wall) with studs **2** : to adorn, cover, or protect with studs **3** : to set, mark, or decorate conspicuously often at intervals ⟨a sky *studded* with stars⟩ ⟨a career *studded* with honors⟩

stud·book \'stəd-,buk\ *n* (1803) : an official record (as in a book) of the pedigree of purebred animals (as horses or dogs)

stud·ding \'stə-diŋ\ *n* (1588) : the studs of a building or wall

stud·ding sail \'stə-diŋ-,sāl, 'stən(t)-səl\ *n* [origin unknown] (1549) : a light sail set at the side of a principal square sail of a ship in free winds

stu·dent \'stü-dᵊnt, 'styü-\ *n, chiefly Southern* -dənt\ *n, often attrib* [ME, fr. L *student-, studens*, fr. prp. of *studēre* to study — more at STUDY] (14c) **1** : SCHOLAR, LEARNER; *esp* : one who attends a school **2** : one who studies : an attentive and systematic observer

student body *n* (1906) : the students at an educational institution

student government *n* (1948) : the organization and management of student life by various student organizations

student lamp *n* (1873) : a desk reading lamp with a tubular shaft, one or two arms for a shaded light, and orig. an oil reservoir

stu·dent·ship \'stü-dᵊnt-,ship, 'styü-, -dənt-\ *n* (ca. 1782) **1** *Brit* : a grant for university study **2** : the state of being a student

stu·dent's t distribution \'stü-dᵊn(t)s-, -dən(t)s-\ *n, often cap S* [*Student*, pen name of W. S. Gossett †1937 Brit. statistician] (1929) : T DISTRIBUTION

Student's t–test *n* (1935) : T-TEST

student teacher *n* (1909) : a student who is engaged in practice teaching

student teaching *n* (1929) : PRACTICE TEACHING

student union *n* (1949) : a building on a college campus that is devoted to student activities and that usu. contains lounges, auditoriums, offices, and game rooms

stud·horse \'stəd-,hȯrs\ *n* (bef. 12c) : a stallion kept esp. for breeding

stud·ied \'stə-dēd\ *adj* (15c) **1** : carefully considered or prepared : THOUGHTFUL **2** : KNOWLEDGEABLE, LEARNED **3** : produced or marked by conscious design or premeditation : CALCULATED ⟨~ indifference⟩ — **stud·ied·ly** *adv* — **stud·ied·ness** *n*

stu·dio \'stü-dē-(,)ō, 'styü-\ *n, pl* **-dios** [It, lit., study, fr. L *studium*] (1819) **1 a** : the working place of a painter, sculptor, or photographer **b** : a place for the study of an art (as dancing, singing, or acting) **2** : a place where motion pictures are made **3** : a place maintained and equipped for the transmission of radio or television programs **4** : a place where audio recordings are made **5** : STUDIO APARTMENT

studio apartment *n* (1903) : a small apartment consisting typically of a main room, kitchenette, and bathroom

studio couch *n* (1931) : an upholstered usu. backless couch that can be made to serve as a double bed by sliding from underneath it the frame of a single cot

stu·di·ous \'stü-dē-əs, 'styü-\ *adj* (14c) **1** : assiduous in the pursuit of learning **2** : of, relating to, or concerned with study **b** : favorable to study ⟨a ~ environment⟩ **3** : diligent or earnest in intent ⟨made a ~ effort⟩ **b** : marked by or suggesting purposefulness or diligence ⟨a

~ expression on his face⟩ **c** : deliberately or consciously planned ⟨spoke with a ~ accent⟩ — **stu·di·ous·ly** *adv* — **stu·di·ous·ness** *n*

stud·ly \'stəd-lē\ *adj* [¹*stud*] (1972) *slang* : HUNKY

stud poker *n* [¹*stud*] (1864) : poker in which each player is dealt the first card facedown and the other four cards faceup with a round of betting taking place after each of the last four rounds of dealing

¹**study** \'stə-dē\ *n, pl* **stud·ies** [ME *studie*, fr. OF *estudie*, fr. L *studium*, fr. *studēre* to devote oneself, study; prob. akin to L *tundere* to beat — more at CONTUSION] (14c) **1** : a state of contemplation : REVERIE **2 a** : application of the mental faculties to the acquisition of knowledge ⟨years of ~⟩ **b** : such application in a particular field or to a specific subject ⟨the ~ of Latin⟩ **c** : careful or extended consideration ⟨the proposal is under ~⟩ **d (1)** : a careful examination or analysis of a phenomenon, development, or question **(2)** : the published report of such a study **3** : a building or room devoted to study or literary pursuits **4** : PURPOSE, INTENT **5 a** : a branch or department of learning : SUBJECT **b** : the activity or work of a student ⟨returning to her *studies* after vacation⟩ **c** : an object of study or deliberation ⟨every gesture a careful ~ —Marcia Davenport⟩ **d** : something attracting close attention or examination **6** : a person who learns or memorizes something (as a part in a play) — usu. used with a qualifying adjective ⟨he's a fast ~⟩ **7** : a literary or artistic production intended as a preliminary outline, an experimental interpretation, or an exploratory analysis of specific features or characteristics **8** : a musical composition for the practice of a point of technique

²**study** *vb* **stud·ied; study·ing** *vi* (14c) **1 a** : to engage in study **b** : to undertake formal study of a subject **2** *dial* : MEDITATE, REFLECT **3** : ENDEAVOR, TRY ~ *vt* **1** : to read in detail esp. with the intention of learning **2** : to engage in the study of ⟨~ biology⟩ **3** : PLOT, DESIGN **4** : to consider attentively or in detail *syn* see CONSIDER — **studi·er** \'stə-dē-ər\ *n*

study hall *n* (1846) **1** : a room in a school set aside for study **2** : a period in a student's day set aside for study and homework

¹**stuff** \'stəf\ *n* [ME, fr. MF *estoffe*, fr. OF, fr. *estoffer* to equip, stock, of Gmc origin; akin to OHG *stopfōn* to stop up, fr. (assumed) VL *stuppare* — more at STOP] (14c) **1** : materials, supplies, or equipment used in various activities: as **a** *obs* : military baggage **b** : PERSONAL PROPERTY **2** : material to be manufactured, wrought, or used in construction ⟨clear half-inch pine ~ —Emily Holt⟩ **3** : a finished textile suitable for clothing; *esp* : wool or worsted material **4 a** : literary or artistic production **b** : writing, discourse, talk, or ideas of little value : TRASH **5 a** : an unspecified material substance or aggregate of matter ⟨volcanic rock is curious ~⟩ **b** : something (as a drug or food) consumed or introduced into the body by humans **c** : a matter to be considered ⟨the truth was heady ~⟩ ⟨long-term policy ~⟩ **d** : a group or scattering of miscellaneous objects or articles ⟨pick that ~ up off the floor⟩; *also* : nonphysical miscellaneous material **6 a** : fundamental material : SUBSTANCE ⟨~ of greatness⟩ **b** : subject matter ⟨a teacher who knows her ~⟩ **7** : special knowledge or capability ⟨showing their ~⟩ **8 a** : spin imparted to a thrown or hit ball to make it curve or change course **b** : the movement of a baseball pitch out of its apparent line of flight : the liveliness of a pitch ⟨greatest pitcher of my time . . . had tremendous ~ —Ted Williams⟩ **9** : DUNK SHOT — **stuff·less** *adj*

²**stuff** *vt* (15c) **1 a** : to fill by packing things in : CRAM ⟨the boy ~ed his pockets with candy⟩ **b** : to fill to satiety : SURFEIT ⟨~ed themselves with turkey⟩ **c** : to prepare (meat or vegetables) by filling or lining with a stuffing **d** : to fill (as a cushion) with a soft material **e** : to fill out the skin of (an animal) for mounting **2 a** : to fill by intellectual effort ⟨~ing their heads with facts⟩ **b** : to pack full of something immaterial ⟨a book ~ed with information⟩ **3** : to fill or block up (as nasal passages) **4 a** : to cause to enter or fill : THRUST ⟨~ed a lot of clothing into a laundry bag⟩ **b** : to put (as a ball or puck) into a goal forcefully from close range **5** — used in the imperative to express contempt (if they didn't like it, ~ 'em —Eric Clapton); often used in the phrases *stuff it* and *get stuffed* **6** : to stop abruptly in a football game ⟨~ the run⟩

stuffed shirt *n* (1913) : a smug, conceited, and usu. pompous person often with an inflexibly conservative or reactionary attitude

stuff·er \'stə-fər\ *n* (1611) **1** : one that stuffs **2** : an enclosure (as a leaflet) inserted in an envelope in addition to a bill, statement, or notice **3** : a series of extra threads or yarn running lengthwise in a fabric to add weight and bulk and to form a backing esp. for carpets

stuff·ing \'stə-fiŋ\ *n* (15c) : material used to stuff; *esp* : a seasoned mixture used to stuff food (as meat, vegetables, or eggs)

stuffing box *n* (1798) : a device that prevents leakage along a moving part (as a connecting rod) passing through a hole in a vessel (as a cylinder) containing steam, water, or oil and that consists of a box or chamber made by enlarging the hole and a gland to compress the contained packing

stuffy \'stə-fē\ *adj* **stuff·i·er; -est** (1813) **1** : lacking in vitality or interest : STODGY, DULL **2** : ILL-NATURED, ILL-HUMORED **3 a** : oppressive to the breathing : CLOSE **b** : stuffed up ⟨a ~ nose⟩ **4** : narrowly inflexible in standards of conduct : SELF-RIGHTEOUS — **stuff·i·ly** \'stə-fə-lē\ *adv* — **stuff·i·ness** \'stə-fē-nəs\ *n*

stul·ti·fy \'stəl-tə-,fī\ *vt* **-fied; -fy·ing** [LL *stultificare* to make foolish, fr. L *stultus* foolish; akin to L *stolidus* stolid] (1766) **1** : to allege or prove to be of unsound mind and hence not responsible **2** : to cause to appear or be stupid, foolish, or absurdly illogical **3 a** : to impair, invalidate, or make ineffective : NEGATE **b** : to have a dulling or inhibiting effect on — **stul·ti·fi·ca·tion** \,stəl-tə-fə-'kā-shən\ *n*

¹**stum·ble** \'stəm-bəl\ *vb* **stum·bled; stum·bling** \-b(ə-)liŋ\ [ME, prob. of Scand origin; akin to Norw dial. *stumla* to stumble; akin to ON *stemma* to hinder — more at STEM] *vi* (14c) **1 a** : to fall into sin or waywardness **b** : to make an error : BLUNDER **c** : to come to an obstacle to belief **2** : to trip in walking or running **3 a** : to walk unsteadily or clumsily **b** : to speak or act in a hesitant or faltering manner **4 a** : to come unexpectedly or by chance ⟨~ onto the truth⟩ **b** : to fall or move carelessly ~ *vt* **1** : to cause to stumble : TRIP **2** : BEWILDER, CONFOUND — **stum·bler** \-b(ə-)lər\ *n* — **stum·bling·ly** \-b(ə-)liŋ-lē\ *adv*

²**stumble** *n* (1547) : an act or instance of stumbling

stum·ble·bum \'stəm-bəl-,bəm\ *n* (1932) : a clumsy or inept person; *esp* : an inept boxer

stum·bling block \'stəm-bliŋ-\ *n* (1588) **1** : an obstacle to progress **2** : an impediment to belief or understanding : PERPLEXITY

¹**stump** \'stəmp\ *n* [ME *stumpe*; akin to OHG *stumpf* stump and perh. to ME *stampen* to stamp] (14c) **1 a** : the basal portion of a bodily part remaining after the rest is removed **b** : a rudimentary or vestigial bodily part **2** : the part of a plant and esp. a tree remaining attached to the root after the trunk is cut **3** : a remaining part : STUB **4** : one of the pointed rods stuck in the ground to form a cricket wicket **5** : a place or occasion for public speaking (as for a cause or candidate); *also* : the circuit followed by a maker of such speeches — used esp. in the phrase *on the stump*

²**stump** *vt* (1596) **1** : to reduce to a stump : TRIM **2 a** : DARE, CHALLENGE **b** : to frustrate the progress or efforts of : BAFFLE **3** : to clear (land) of stumps **4** : to travel over (a region) making political speeches or supporting a cause **5 a** : to walk over heavily or clumsily **b** : STUB **3** ~ *vi* **1** : to walk heavily or clumsily **2** : to go about making political speeches or supporting a cause — **stump·er** *n*

³**stump** *n* [F or Flem; F *estompe*, fr. Flem *stomp*, lit., stub, fr. MD; akin to OHG *stumpf* stump] (1778) : a short thick roll of leather, felt, or paper usu. pointed at both ends and used for shading or blending a drawing in crayon, pencil, charcoal, pastel, or chalk

⁴**stump** *vt* (1807) : to tone or treat (a drawing) with a stump

stump·age \'stəm-pij\ *n* (1835) **1** : the value of standing timber **2** : uncut marketable timber; *also* : the right to cut it

stump–tailed macaque \'stəmp-'tāl(d)-\ *n* (1938) : a dark reddish brown naked-faced short-tailed macaque (*Macaca arctoides* syn. *M. speciosa*) that is found in eastern Asia — called also *stump-tailed monkey*

stump work *n* (1904) : embroidery with intricate padded designs or scenes in high relief popular esp. in the 17th century

stumpy \'stəm-pē\ *adj* (1600) **1** : being short and thick : STUBBY **2** : full of stumps

¹**stun** \'stən\ *vt* **stunned; stun·ning** [ME, modif. of MF *estoner* — more at ASTONISH] (14c) **1** : to make senseless, groggy, or dizzy by or as if by a blow : DAZE **2** : to shock with noise **3** : to overcome esp. with paralyzing astonishment or disbelief

²**stun** *n* (1727) : the effect of something that stuns : SHOCK

stung *past and past part of* STING

stun gun *n* (1967) : a weapon designed to stun or immobilize (as by electric shock) rather than kill or injure the one affected

stunk *past and past part of* STINK

stun·ner \'stə-nər\ *n* (1829) : one that stuns or is stunning

stun·ning \'stə-niŋ\ *adj* (1667) **1** : causing astonishment or disbelief **2** : strikingly impressive esp. in beauty or excellence — **stun·ning·ly** \-niŋ-lē\ *adv*

¹**stunt** \'stənt\ *vt* [E dial. *stunt* stubborn, stunted, abrupt, prob. of Scand origin; akin to ON *stuttr* scant — more at STINT] (1659) : to hinder the normal growth, development, or progress of — **stunt·ed·ness** *n*

²**stunt** *n* (1725) **1** : one (as an animal) that is stunted **2** : a check in growth **3** : a plant disease in which dwarfing occurs

³**stunt** *n* [origin unknown] (1878) **1** : an unusual or difficult feat requiring great skill or daring : *esp* : one performed or undertaken chiefly to gain attention or publicity **2** : a shifting or switching of the positions by defensive players at the line of scrimmage in football to disrupt the opponent's blocking efforts

⁴**stunt** *vi* (1917) : to perform or engage in a stunt

stunt·man \'stənt-,man\ *n* (1927) : a man who performs stunts; *esp* : one who doubles for an actor during the filming of stunts and dangerous scenes

stunt·wom·an \-,wù-mən\ *n* (1948) : a woman who doubles for an actress during the filming of stunts and dangerous scenes

stu·pa \'stü-pə\ *n* [Skt *stūpa*] (1876) : a usu. dome-shaped structure (as a mound) serving as a Buddhist shrine

¹**stupe** \'stüp, 'styüp\ *n* [ME, fr. L *stuppa* coarse part of flax, tow, fr. Gk *styppē*] (14c) : a hot wet often medicated cloth applied externally (as to stimulate circulation)

²**stupe** *n* [short for *stupid*] (1762) : a stupid person : DOLT

stu·pe·fac·tion \,stü-pə-'fak-shən, ,styü-\ *n* [ME *stupefaccioun*, fr. ML *stupefaction-, stupefactio*, fr. L *stupefacere*] (15c) : the act of stupefying : the state of being stupefied

stu·pe·fy \'stü-pə-,fī, 'styü-\ *vt* **-fied; -fy·ing** [ME *stupifien*, fr. MF *stupefier*, modif. of L *stupefacere*, fr. *stupēre* to be astonished + *facere* to make, do — more at DO] (15c) **1** : to make stupid, groggy, or insensible **2** : ASTONISH, ASTOUND — **stu·pe·fy·ing·ly** \-iŋ-lē\ *adv*

stu·pen·dous \stù-'pen-dəs, styù-\ *adj* [L *stupendus*, gerundive of *stupēre*] (1666) **1** : causing astonishment or wonder : AWESOME, MARVELOUS **2** : of amazing size or greatness : TREMENDOUS *syn* see MONSTROUS — **stu·pen·dous·ly** *adv* — **stu·pen·dous·ness** *n*

¹**stu·pid** \'stü-pəd, 'styü-\ *adj* [MF *stupide*, fr. L *stupidus*, fr. *stupēre* to be numb, be astonished — more at TYPE] (1541) **1 a** : slow of mind : OBTUSE **b** : given to unintelligent decisions or acts : acting in an unintelligent or careless manner **c** : lacking intelligence or reason : BRUTISH **2** : dulled in feeling or sensation : TORPID (still ~ from the sedative) **3** : marked by or resulting from unreasoned thinking or acting : SENSELESS **4 a** : lacking interest or point **b** : VEXATIOUS, EXASPERATING (this ~ flashlight won't work) — **stu·pid·ly** *adv* — **stu·pid·ness** *n*

syn STUPID, DULL, DENSE, CRASS, DUMB mean lacking in power to absorb ideas or impressions. STUPID implies a slow-witted or dazed state of mind that may be either congenital or temporary (*stupid* students just keeping the seats warm) (*stupid* with drink). DULL suggests a slow or sluggish mind such as results from disease, depression, or shock (monotonous work that leaves the mind *dull*). DENSE implies a thick-headed imperviousness to ideas (too *dense* to take a hint). CRASS suggests a grossness of mind precluding discrimination or delicacy (a *crass*, materialistic people). DUMB applies to an exasperating obtuse-

ness or lack of comprehension (too *dumb* to figure out what's going on).

²**stupid** *n* (1712) : a stupid person

stu·pid·i·ty \stü-'pi-də-tē, styü-\ *n, pl* **-ties** (1541) **1** : the quality or state of being stupid **2** : a stupid idea or act

stu·por \'stü-pər, 'styü-\ *n* [ME, fr. L, fr. *stupēre*] (14c) **1** : a condition of greatly dulled or completely suspended sense or sensibility (drunken ~) **2** : a state of extreme apathy or torpor resulting often from stress or shock : DAZE *syn* see LETHARGY

stu·por·ous \'stü-p(ə-)rəs, 'styü-\ *adj* (1892) : marked or affected by or as if by stupor

stur·dy \'stər-dē\ *adj* **stur·di·er; -est** [ME, brave, stubborn, fr. MF *estourdi* stunned, fr. pp. of *estourdir* to stun, fr. (assumed) VL *exturdire*, fr. L *ex-* + (assumed) VL *turdus* simpleton, fr. L, thrush — more at THRUSH] (14c) **1 a** : firmly built or constituted : STOUT **b** : HARDY **c** : sound in design or execution : SUBSTANTIAL **2 a** : marked by or reflecting physical strength or vigor **b** : FIRM, RESOLUTE **c** : RUGGED, STABLE *syn* see STRONG — **stur·di·ly** \'stər-dᵊl-ē\ *adv* — **stur·di·ness** \'stər-dē-nəs\ *n*

stur·geon \'stər-jən\ *n* [ME, fr. MF *estourjon*, of Gmc origin; akin to OE *styria* sturgeon] (13c) : any of a family (Acipenseridae) of usu. large elongate anadromous or freshwater bony fishes which are widely distributed in the north temperate zone and whose roe is made into caviar

Sturm und Drang \,shtùrm-ùnt-'dräŋ, ,stùr-, -ənt-\ *n* [G, lit., storm and stress, fr. *Sturm und Drang* (1776), drama by Friedrich von Klinger †1831 Ger. novelist and dramatist] (1845) **1** : a late 18th century German literary movement characterized by works containing rousing action and high emotionalism that often deal with the individual's revolt against society **2** : TURMOIL

sturt \'stərt\ *n* [ME, contention, alter. of *strut*; akin to OE *strūtian* to exert oneself — more at STRUT] (14c) *chiefly Scot* : CONTENTION

¹**stut·ter** \'stə-tər\ *vb* [freq. of E dial. *stut* to stutter, fr. ME *stutten*; akin to D *stotteren* to stutter, Goth *stautan* to strike — more at CONTUSION] *vi* (ca. 1570) **1** : to speak with involuntary disruption or blocking of speech (as by spasmodic repetition or prolongation of vocal sounds) **2** : to move or act in a halting or spasmodic manner (the old jalopy bucks and ~s uphill —William Cleary) ~ *vt* : to say, speak, or sound with or as if with a stutter — **stut·ter·er** \-tər-ər\ *n*

²**stutter** *n* (ca. 1847) **1** : an act or instance of stuttering **2** : a speech disorder involving stuttering accompanied by fear and anxiety

¹**sty** \'stī\ *n, pl* **sties** *also* **styes** [ME, fr. OE *stig*; akin to ON *-stī* sty] (bef. 12c) **1** : a pen or enclosed housing for swine **2** : an unkempt filthy place (this house is a ~)

²**sty** *vb* **stied** *or* **styed; sty·ing** *vt* (bef. 12c) : to lodge or keep in a sty ~ *vi* : to live in a sty

³**sty** *or* **stye** \'stī\ *n, pl* **sties** *or* **styes** [short for obs. E *styan*, fr. (assumed) ME, alter. of OE *stigend*, fr. *stigan* to go up, rise — more at STAIR] (1617) : an inflamed swelling of a sebaceous gland at the margin of an eyelid

sty·gian \'sti-j(ē-)ən\ *adj, often cap* [L *stygius*, fr. Gk *stygios*, fr. *Styg-, Styx* Styx] (1566) **1** : of or relating to the river Styx **2** : extremely dark, gloomy, or forbidding

styl- *or* **styli-** *or* **stylo-** *comb form* [L *stilus* spike, stem — more at STYLE] : style : styloid process (*stylopodium*) (*stylography*)

sty·lar \'stī-lər, -,lär\ *adj* [¹*style*] (ca. 1928) : of or relating to the style of a plant ovary

¹**style** \'stī(ə)l\ *n* [ME *stile, style*, fr. L *stilus* spike, stem, stylus, style of writing; perh. akin to L in*stigare* to goad — more at STICK] (14c) **1** : DESIGNATION, TITLE **2 a** : a distinctive manner of expression (as in writing or speech) (writes with more attention to ~ than to content) (the flowery ~ of 18th century prose) **b** : a distinctive manner or custom of behaving or conducting oneself (the formal ~ of the court) (his ~ is abrasive); *also* : a particular mode of living (in high ~) **c** : a particular manner or technique by which something is done, created, or performed (a unique ~ of horseback riding) (the classical ~ of dance) **3 a** : STYLUS **b** : GNOMON 1b **c** : a filiform prolongation of a plant ovary bearing a stigma at its apex — see FLOWER illustration **d** : a slender elongated process (as a bristle) on an animal **4 a** : distinctive quality, form, or type of something (a new dress ~) (the Greek ~ of architecture) **5 a** : the state of being popular : FASHION (clothes that are always in ~) **b** : fashionable elegance **c** : beauty, grace, or ease of manner or technique (an awkward moment she handled with ~) **6** : a convention with respect to spelling, punctuation, capitalization, and typographic arrangement and display followed in writing or printing *syn* see FASHION — **style·less** \'stī(ə)l-ləs\ *adj* — **style·less·ness** *n*

²**style** *vt* **styled; styl·ing** (ca. 1580) **1** : to call or designate by an identifying term : NAME **2** : to give a particular style to **b** : to design, make, or arrange in accord with the prevailing mode — **styl·er** *n*

-style *adj or adv comb form* : being in the style of (a Beaujolais-*style* wine)

style·book *n* (1708) : a book explaining, describing, or illustrating a prevailing, accepted, or authorized style

sty·let \stī-'let, 'stī-lət\ *n* [F, fr. MF *stilet* stiletto, fr. OIt *stiletto* — more at STILETTO] (1697) **1 a** : a slender surgical probe **b** : a thin wire inserted into a catheter to maintain rigidity or into a hollow needle to maintain patency **c** : a pointed instrument (as for graving) **2** : a relatively rigid elongated organ or appendage (as a piercing mouthpart) of an animal **3** : STILETTO

sty·li·form \'sti-lə-,fòrm\ *adj* [NL *stiliformis*, fr. L *stilus* + *-formis* -form] (1578) : resembling a style : bristle-shaped (a ~ copulatory organ)

styl·ing \'stī-liŋ\ *n* (1928) : the way in which something is styled

styl·ise *Brit var of* STYLIZE

\ə\ abut \ᵊ\ kitten, F table \ər\ further \a\ ash \ā\ ace \ä\ mop, mar \aù\ out \ch\ chin \e\ bet \ē\ easy \g\ go \i\ hit \ī\ ice \j\ job \ŋ\ sing \ō\ go \ò\ law \òi\ boy \th\ thin \th\ the \ü\ loot \ù\ foot \y\ yet \zh\ vision \à, k̟, ⁿ, œ, œ̄, ᴜᴇ, ᵾᴇ, ʸ\ *see* Guide to Pronunciation

styl·ish \'stī-lish\ *adj* (1785) : having style; *specif* : conforming to current fashion — **styl·ish·ly** *adv* — **styl·ish·ness** *n*

styl·ist \'stī-list\ *n* (1795) **1 a** : a master or model of style; *esp* : a writer or speaker who is eminent in matters of style **b** : one (as a writer or singer) noted for a distinctive style **2 a** : one who develops, designs, or advises on styles **b** : HAIRSTYLIST

sty·lis·tic \stī-'lis-tik\ *adj* (1860) : of or relating esp. to literary or artistic style — **sty·lis·ti·cal·ly** \-ti-k(ə-)lē\ *adv*

sty·lis·tics \stī-'lis-tiks\ *n pl but sing or pl in constr* (ca. 1883) **1** : an aspect of literary study that emphasizes the analysis of various elements of style (as metaphor and diction) **2** : the study of the devices in a language that produce expressive value

sty·lite \'stī-‚līt\ *n* [LGk *stylitēs*, fr. Gk *stylos* pillar — more at STEER] (ca. 1638) : a Christian ascetic living atop a pillar — **sty·lit·ic** \stī-'li-tik\ *adj*

styl·ize \'stī(-ə)-‚līz\ *vt* **styl·ized; styl·iz·ing** (1898) : to conform to a conventional style; *specif* : to represent or design according to a style or stylistic pattern rather than according to nature or tradition — **styl·i·za·tion** \‚stī-lə-'zā-shən\ *n*

sty·lo·bate \'stī-lə-‚bāt\ *n* [L *stylobates*, fr. Gk, *stylobatēs*, fr. *stylos* pillar + *bainein* to walk, go — more at COME] (1694) : a continuous flat coping or pavement supporting a row of architectural columns

sty·log·ra·phy \stī-'lä-grə-fē\ *n* (ca. 1840) : a mode of writing or tracing lines by means of a style or similar instrument

sty·loid \'stī(-ə)-‚lȯid\ *adj* (1709) : resembling a style : STYLIFORM — used esp. of slender pointed skeletal processes (as on the ulna)

sty·lo·po·di·um \‚stī-lə-'pō-dē-əm\ *n, pl* **-dia** \-dē-ə\ [NL, fr. *styl-* + Gk *podion* small foot, base — more at PEW] (ca. 1832) : a disk-shaped or conical expansion at the base of the style in plants of the carrot family

sty·lus \'stī-ləs\ *n, pl* **sty·li** \'stī(-ə)-‚lī\ *also* **sty·lus·es** \'stī-lə-səz\ [L *stylus, stilus* spike, stylus — more at STYLE] (1807) : an instrument for writing, marking, or incising: as **a** : an instrument used by the ancients in writing on clay or waxed tablets **b** : a hard-pointed pen-shaped instrument for marking on stencils used in a reproducing machine **c** (1) : NEEDLE 3c (2) : a cutting tool used to produce an original record groove during disc recording **d** : a pen-shaped pointing device used for entering positional information (as from a graphics tablet) into a computer

sty·mie \'stī-mē\ *vt* **sty·mied; sty·mie·ing** [Sc *stimie, stymie* to obstruct a golf shot by interposition of the opponent's ball] (1902) : to present an obstacle to : stand in the way of

styp·tic \'stip-tik\ *adj* [ME *stiptik*, fr. L *stypticus*, fr. Gk *styptikos*, fr. *styphein* to contract] (14c) : tending to contract or bind : ASTRINGENT; *esp* : tending to check bleeding — **styptic** *n*

styptic pencil *n* (1908) : a stick of a medicated styptic substance for use esp. in shaving to stop the bleeding from small cuts

sty·rax \'stī-‚raks\ *n* [L — more at STORAX] (1558) : STORAX

sty·rene \'stī-‚rēn\ *n* [ISV, fr. L *styrax*] (1885) : a fragrant liquid unsaturated hydrocarbon C_8H_8 used chiefly in making synthetic rubber, resins, and plastics and in improving drying oils; *also* : any of various synthetic plastics made from styrene by polymerization or copolymerization

Sty·ro·foam \'stī-rə-‚fōm\ *trademark* — used for an expanded rigid polystyrene plastic

Styx \'stiks\ *n* [L *Styg-, Styx*, fr. Gk] : the principal river of the underworld in Greek mythology

su·able \'sü-ə-bəl\ *adj* (ca. 1623) : liable to be sued in court — **su·abil·i·ty** \‚sü-ə-'bi-lə-tē\ *n* — **su·ably** \-blē\ *adv*

sua·sion \'swā-zhən\ *n* [ME, fr. L *suasion-, suasio*, fr. *suadēre* to urge, persuade — more at SWEET] (14c) : the act of influencing or persuading — **sua·sive** \'swā-siv, -ziv\ *adj* — **sua·sive·ly** *adv* — **sua·sive·ness** *n*

suave \'swäv\ *adj* **suav·er; -est** [MF, pleasant, sweet, fr. L *suavis* — more at SWEET] (1847) **1** : smoothly though often superficially gracious and sophisticated **2** : smooth in texture, performance, or style — **suave·ly** *adv* — **suave·ness** *n* — **sua·vi·ty** \'swä-və-tē\ *n*

syn SUAVE, URBANE, DIPLOMATIC, BLAND, SMOOTH, POLITIC mean pleasantly tactful and well-mannered. SUAVE suggests a specific ability to deal with others easily and without friction ⟨a *suave* public relations coordinator⟩. URBANE implies high cultivation and poise coming from wide social experience ⟨an *urbane* traveler⟩. DIPLOMATIC stresses an ability to deal with ticklish situations tactfully ⟨a *diplomatic* negotiator⟩. BLAND emphasizes mildness of manner and absence of irritating qualities ⟨a *bland* master of ceremonies⟩. SMOOTH suggests often a deliberately assumed suavity ⟨a *smooth* salesman⟩. POLITIC implies shrewd as well as tactful and suave handling of people ⟨a cunningly *politic* manager⟩.

¹sub \'səb\ *n* (1830) : SUBSTITUTE

²sub *vb* **subbed; sub·bing** *vi* (1853) : to act as a substitute ~ *vt* **1** *Brit* : to read and edit as a copy editor : SUBEDIT **2** : SUBCONTRACT 1

³sub *n* (1916) : SUBMARINE

sub- *prefix* [ME, fr. L, under, below, secretly, from below, up, near, fr. *sub* under, close to — more at UP] **1** : under : beneath : below ⟨*sub*soil⟩ ⟨*sub*aqueous⟩ **2 a** : subordinate : secondary : next lower than or inferior to ⟨*sub*station⟩ ⟨*sub*editor⟩ **b** : subordinate portion of : subdivision of ⟨*sub*committee⟩ ⟨*sub*species⟩ **c** : with repetition (as of a process) so as to form, stress, or deal with subordinate parts or relations ⟨*sub*let⟩ ⟨*sub*contract⟩ **3** : less than completely, perfectly, or normally : somewhat ⟨*sub*acute⟩ ⟨*sub*clinical⟩ **4 a** : almost : nearly ⟨*sub*erect⟩ **b** : falling nearly in the category of and often adjoining : bordering on ⟨*sub*arctic⟩

sub·ad·o·les·cent	sub·cat·e·go·ri·za·tion	sub·col·le·giate
sub·agen·cy	sub·cat·e·go·rize	sub·col·o·ny
sub·agent	sub·cat·e·go·ry	sub·com·mis·sion
sub·al·lo·ca·tion	sub·ceil·ing	sub·com·po·nent
sub·ar·ea	sub·cel·lar	sub·cor·date
sub·au·di·ble	sub·chap·ter	sub·co·ri·a·ceous
sub·av·er·age	sub·chief	sub·coun·ty
sub·base·ment	sub·clan	sub·cult
sub·ba·sin	sub·clus·ter	sub·cu·ra·tive
sub·block	sub·code	sub·dean
sub·branch	sub·col·lec·tion	sub·de·ci·sion
sub·caste	sub·col·lege	sub·de·part·ment

sub·de·vel·op·ment	sub·net·work	sub·sense
sub·di·a·lect	sub·niche	sub·sen·tence
sub·di·rec·tor	sub·op·ti·mal	sub·se·ries
sub·dis·ci·pline	sub·op·ti·mi·za·tion	sub·site
sub·dis·trict	sub·op·ti·mize	sub·skill
sub·econ·o·my	sub·op·ti·mum	sub·so·ci·ety
sub·erect	sub·or·bic·u·lar	sub·spe·cial·ist
sub·file	sub·or·ga·ni·za·tion	sub·spe·cial·ize
sub·frame	sub·pan·el	sub·spe·cial·ty
sub·gen·er·a·tion	sub·par	sub·state
sub·genre	sub·para·graph	sub·sys·tem
sub·goal	sub·par·al·lel	sub·task
sub·gov·ern·ment	sub·part	sub·tax·on
sub·hu·mid	sub·pe·ri·od	sub·test
sub·in·dus·try	sub·phase	sub·theme
sub·in·hib·i·to·ry	sub·pri·mate	sub·ther·a·peu·tic
sub·lan·guage	sub·pro·cess	sub·top·ic
sub·lev·el	sub·prod·uct	sub·trea·sury
sub·li·brar·i·an	sub·proj·ect	sub·trend
sub·li·cense	sub·pro·le·tar·i·at	sub·tribe
sub·lit·er·a·cy	sub·ra·tio·nal	sub·type
sub·lit·er·ate	sub·sat·u·rat·ed	sub·unit
sub·lot	sub·sat·u·ra·tion	sub·va·ri·ety
sub·man·ag·er	sub·scale	sub·vas·sal
sub·mar·ket	sub·science	sub·vis·i·ble
sub·max·i·mal	sub·sea	sub·vi·su·al
sub·menu	sub·sec·re·tary	sub·world
sub·min·i·mal	sub·sec·tor	sub·writ·er
sub·min·is·ter	sub·seg·ment	sub·ze·ro
sub·na·tion·al	sub·sei·zure	sub·zone

sub·ac·id \‚səb-'a-səd\ *adj* [L *subacidus*, fr. *sub-* + *acidus* acid] (1765) : somewhat acrimonious : CUTTING ⟨~ comments⟩ — **sub·ac·id·ly** *adv* — **sub·ac·id·ness** *n*

sub·acute \-ə-'kyüt\ *adj* (1822) **1** : having a tapered but not sharply pointed form ⟨~ leaves⟩ **2 a** : falling between acute and chronic in character esp. when closer to acute ⟨~ endocarditis⟩ **b** : less marked in severity or duration than a corresponding acute state ⟨~ pain⟩ — **sub·acute·ly** *adv*

subacute sclerosing pan·en·ceph·a·li·tis \-‚pan-in-‚se-fə-'lī-təs\ *n* [*panencephalitis* fr. NL, fr. *pan-* + *encephalitis*] (1950) : a central nervous system disease of children and young adults caused by infection of the brain by measles virus or a closely related virus and marked by intellectual deterioration, convulsions, and paralysis

sub·adult \‚səb-ə-'dəlt; ‚səb-'a-‚dəlt\ *n* (1923) : an individual that has passed through the juvenile period but not yet attained typical adult characteristics — **subadult** *adj*

sub·aer·i·al \-'ar-ē-əl, -'er-; -ā-'ir-ē-əl\ *adj* (1833) : situated, formed, or occurring on or immediately adjacent to the surface of the earth ⟨~ erosion⟩ ⟨~ roots⟩ — **sub·aer·i·al·ly** \-ē-ə-lē\ *adv*

su·bah·dar *or* **su·ba·dar** \‚sü-bə-'där\ *n* [Per *sūbadār*] (1698) **1** : a governor of a province **2** : the chief Indian officer of a company of Indian troops in the British army of India

sub·al·pine \‚səb-'al-‚pīn\ *adj* (ca. 1656) **1** : of or relating to the region about the foot and lower slopes of the Alps **2** : of, relating to, or inhabiting high upland slopes and esp. the zone just below the timberline

¹sub·al·tern \sə-'bȯl-tərn, *esp Brit* 'sə-bəl-tərn\ *adj* [LL *subalternus*, fr. L *sub-* + *alternus* alternate, fr. *alter* other (of two) — more at ALTER] (1570) **1** : particular with reference to a related universal proposition ⟨"some S is P" as a ~ proposition to "all S is P"⟩ **2** : SUBORDINATE

²subaltern *n* (1605) **1** : a person holding a subordinate position; *specif* : a junior officer (as in the British army) **2** : a particular proposition that follows immediately from a universal

sub·ant·arc·tic \‚səb-ant-'ärk-tik, -'är-tik\ *adj* (1875) : of, relating to, or characteristic of, or being a region just outside the antarctic circle

sub·api·cal \-'ā-pi-kəl *also* -'a-\ *adj* (1846) : situated below or near an apex

sub·aquat·ic \-ə-'kwä-tik, -'kwa-\ *adj* [ISV] (1844) : somewhat aquatic ⟨a marginal ~ flora⟩

sub·aque·ous \-'ā-kwē-əs, -'a-\ *adj* (1677) : existing, formed, or taking place in or under water

sub·arach·noid \-ə-'rak-‚nȯid\ *also* **sub·arach·noid·al** \-rak-'nȯi-d³l\ *adj* (1843) : of, relating to, occurring, or situated under the arachnoid membrane ⟨~ hemorrhage⟩

sub·arc·tic \-'ärk-tik, -'är-tik\ *adj* [ISV] (1854) : of, relating to, or being regions immediately outside of the arctic circle or regions similar to these in climate or conditions of life — **subarctic** *n*

sub·as·sem·bly \-ə-'sem-blē\ *n* (1919) : an assembled unit designed to be incorporated with other units in a finished product

sub·at·mo·spher·ic \-‚at-mə-'sfir-ik, -'sfer-\ *adj* (1941) : less or lower than that of the atmosphere ⟨~ pressure⟩

sub·atom·ic \-ə-'tä-mik\ *adj* (1903) **1** : of or relating to the inside of the atom **2** : of, relating to, or being particles smaller than atoms

sub·au·di·tion \-ȯ-'di-shən\ *n* [LL *subauditon-, subauditio*, fr. *subaudire* to understand, fr. L *sub-* + *audire* to hear — more at AUDIBLE] (1798) : the act of understanding or supplying something not expressed : a reading between the lines

sub·base \'səb-‚bās\ *n* (1826) : underlying support placed below what is normally construed as a base: as **a** : the lowest member horizontally of an architectural base or of a baseboard or pedestal **b** : pervious fill (as crushed stone) placed under a roadbed

sub·bi·tu·mi·nous \‚səb-bə-'tü-mə-nəs, -bī-, -'tyü-\ *adj* (1908) : of, relating to, or being coal of lower rank than bituminous coal but higher than lignite

sub·cab·i·net \-'kab-nit, -'ka-bə-\ *adj* (1954) : of, relating to, or being a high administrative position in the U.S. government that ranks below the cabinet level

sub·cap·su·lar \-'kap-sə-lər\ *adj* (1889) : situated or occurring beneath or within a capsule ⟨~ cataracts⟩

sub·cel·lu·lar \-'sel-yə-lər\ *adj* (1948) : of less than cellular scope or level of organization ⟨~ particles⟩ ⟨~ studies⟩

sub·cen·ter \-'sen-tər\ *n* (ca. 1925) : a secondary center; *esp* : a center (as for shopping) located outside the main business area of a city

sub·cen·tral \-trəl\ *adj* (1822) **1** : nearly but not quite central **2** : located under a center — **sub·cen·tral·ly** \-trə-lē\ *adv*

sub·chas·er \'səb-ˌchā-sər\ *n* (ca. 1918) : a small maneuverable patrol or escort vessel used for antisubmarine warfare

sub·class \'səb-ˌklas\ *n* (1819) : a primary division of a class: as **a** : a category in biological classification ranking below a class and above an order **b** : SUBSET

sub·clas·si·fi·ca·tion \ˌsəb-ˌkla-sə-fə-'kā-shən\ *n* (1873) **1** : a primary division of a classification **2** : arrangement into or assignment to subclassifications — **sub·clas·si·fy** \'-'kla-sə-ˌfi\ *vt*

¹sub·cla·vi·an \-'klā-vē-ən\ *adj* [NL *subclavius*, fr. *sub-* + *clavicula* clavicle] (1646) : of, relating to, being, or performed on a part (as an artery, vein, or nerve) located under the clavicle ⟨~ angioplasty⟩

²subclavian *n* (1719) : a subclavian part (as an artery, vein, or nerve)

subclavian artery *n* (1688) : the proximal part of the main artery of the arm or forelimb

subclavian vein *n* (1770) : the proximal part of the main vein of the arm or forelimb

sub·cli·max \ˌsəb-'klī-ˌmaks\ *n* (1916) : a stage or community in an ecological succession immediately preceding a climax; *esp* : one held in relative stability throughout edaphic or biotic influences or by fire

sub·clin·i·cal \-'kli-ni-kəl\ *adj* (ca. 1935) : not detectable or producing effects that are not detectable by the usual clinical tests ⟨a ~ infection⟩ ⟨~ cancer⟩ — **sub·clin·i·cal·ly** \-k(ə-)lē\ *adv*

sub·com·mit·tee \'səb-kə-ˌmi-tē, ˌsəb-kə-'\ *n* (ca. 1607) : a subdivision of a committee usu. organized for a specific purpose

sub·com·mu·ni·ty \ˌsəb-kə-'myü-nə-tē\ *n* (1966) : a distinct grouping within a community

sub·com·pact \'səb-'käm-ˌpakt\ *n* (1967) : an automobile smaller than a compact

¹sub·con·scious \ˌsəb-'kän(t)-shəs, 'səb-\ *adj* (ca. 1834) : existing in the mind but not immediately available to consciousness ⟨a ~ motive⟩ — **sub·con·scious·ly** *adv* — **sub·con·scious·ness** *n*

²subconscious *n* (1886) : the mental activities just below the threshold of consciousness

sub·con·ti·nent \ˌsəb-'kän-t⁹n-ənt, -'känt-nənt\ *n* (1863) : a large land-mass smaller than a continent; *esp* : a major subdivision of a continent ⟨the Indian ~⟩ — **sub·con·ti·nen·tal** \ˌsəb-ˌkän-t⁹n-'en-t⁹l\ *adj*

¹sub·con·tract \ˌsəb-'kän-ˌtrakt\ *n* (1817) : a contract between a party to an original contract and a third party; *esp* : one to provide all or a specified part of the work or materials required in the original contract

²sub·con·tract \ˌsəb-'kän-ˌtrakt, ˌsəb-kən-'\ *vi* (1842) : to let out or undertake work under a subcontract ~ *vt* **1** : to engage a third party to perform under a subcontract all or part of (work included in an original contract) — sometimes used with *out* **2** : to undertake (work) under a subcontract

sub·con·trac·tor \ˌsəb-'kän-ˌtrak-tər, ˌsəb-kən-'\ *n* (1842) : an individual or business firm contracting to perform part or all of another's contract

sub·con·tra·oc·tave \ˌsəb-ˌkän-trə-'äk-tiv, -təv, -ˌtäv\ *n* (ca. 1901) : the musical octave that begins on the fourth C below middle C — see PITCH illustration

sub·con·trary \ˌsəb-'kän-ˌtrer-ē\ *n* (1685) : a proposition so related to another that though both may be true they cannot both be false — **subcontrary** *adj*

sub·cool \-'kül\ *vt* (1916) : SUPERCOOL

sub·cor·ti·cal \-'kȯr-ti-kəl\ *adj* (1887) : of, relating to, involving, or being nerve centers below the cerebral cortex ⟨~ lesions⟩

sub·crit·i·cal \-'kri-ti-kəl\ *adj* (1930) **1** : less or lower than critical in respect to a specified factor **2 a** : of insufficient size to sustain a chain reaction ⟨a ~ mass of fissionable material⟩ **b** : designed for use with fissionable material of subcritical mass ⟨a ~ reactor⟩

sub·crust·al \-'krəs-t⁹l\ *adj* (1897) : situated or occurring below a crust and esp. the crust of the earth

sub·cul·ture \'səb-ˌkəl-chər\ *n* (1886) **1 a** : a culture (as of bacteria) derived from another culture **b** : an act or instance of producing a subculture **2** : an ethnic, regional, economic, or social group exhibiting characteristic patterns of behavior sufficient to distinguish it from others within an embracing culture or society ⟨a criminal ~⟩ — **sub·cul·tur·al** \'-ˈkəlch-rəl, -ˈkəl-chə-\ *adj* — **sub·cul·tur·al·ly** *adv* — **subculture** *vt*

sub·cu·ta·ne·ous \ˌsəb-kyü-'tā-nē-əs\ *adj* [LL *subcutaneus*, fr. L *sub-* + *cutis* skin — more at HIDE] (1651) : being, living, used, or made under the skin ⟨~ parasites⟩ — **sub·cu·ta·ne·ous·ly** *adv*

sub·cu·tis \ˌsəb-'kyü-təs\ *n* [NL, fr. LL, beneath the skin, fr. L *sub-* + *cutis*] (1900) : the deeper part of the dermis

sub·dea·con \-'dē-kən\ *n* [ME *subdecon*, fr. LL *subdiaconus*, fr. L *sub-* + LL *diaconus* deacon — more at DEACON] (14c) : a cleric ranking below a deacon: as **a** : a cleric in the lowest of the former major orders of the Roman Catholic Church **b** : an Eastern Orthodox or Armenian cleric in minor orders **c** : a clergyman performing the liturgical duties of a subdeacon

sub·deb \'səb-ˌdeb\ *n* (1917) : SUBDEBUTANTE

sub·deb·u·tante \ˌsəb-'de-byü-ˌtänt\ *n* (1919) : a young girl who is about to become a debutante; *broadly* : a girl in her middle teens

sub·der·mal \-'dər-məl\ *adj* (1887) : SUBCUTANEOUS — **sub·der·mal·ly** \-mə-lē\ *adv*

sub·di·vide \ˌsəb-də-'vīd, 'səb-də-ˌ\ *vb* [ME, fr. LL *subdividere*, fr. L *sub-* + *dividere* to divide] *vt* (15c) **1** : to divide the parts of into more parts **2** : to divide into several parts; *esp* : to divide (a tract of land) into building lots ~ *vi* : to separate or become separated into subdivisions — **sub·di·vid·able** \-'vi-də-bəl, -ˌvi-\ *adj* — **sub·di·vid·er** *n*

sub·di·vi·sion \'səb-də-ˌvi-zhən\ *n* (15c) **1** : an act or instance of subdividing **2** : something produced by subdividing; *esp* : a tract of land surveyed and divided into lots for purposes of sale **3** : a category in botanical classification ranking below a division and above a class

sub·dom·i·nant \ˌsəb-'däm-nənt, -'dä-mə-\ *n* (1793) **1** : the fourth tone of a diatonic scale **2** : something partly but incompletely dominant; *esp* : an ecologically important life form subordinate in influence to the dominants of a community — **subdominant** *adj*

sub·duc·tion \(ˌ)səb-'dək-shən\ *n* [LL *subduction-, subductio* withdrawal, fr. L *subducere* to withdraw, fr. *sub-* + *ducere* to draw — more at TOW] (1970) : the action or process of the edge of one crustal plate descending below the edge of another — **sub·duct** \(ˌ)səb-'dəkt\ *vb*

sub·due \səb-'dü, -'dyü\ *vt* **sub·dued; sub·du·ing** [ME *sodewen, subduen* (influenced in form and meaning by L *subdere* to subject), fr. MF *soduire* to seduce (influenced in meaning by L *seducere* to seduce), fr. L *subducere*] (14c) **1** : to conquer and bring into subjection : VANQUISH **2** : to bring under control esp. by an exertion of the will : CURB ⟨subdued my foolish fears⟩ **3** : to bring under cultivation **4** : to reduce the intensity or degree of : tone down *syn* see CONQUER — **sub·du·er** *n*

sub·dued \-'düd, -'dyüd\ *adj* (1591) : lacking in vitality, intensity, or strength ⟨~ colors⟩ — **sub·dued·ly** \-'dü(-ə)d-lē, -'dyü(-ə)d-\ *adv*

sub·dur·al \ˌsəb-'dúr-əl, -'dyúr-; 'səb-ˌ\ *adj* [*sub-* + *dura (mater)*] (1875) : situated or occurring beneath the dura mater or between the dura mater and the arachnoid membrane ⟨~ space⟩ ⟨~ hematomas⟩

sub·ed·i·tor \-'e-də-tər\ *n* (1835) *chiefly Brit* : COPY EDITOR — **sub·ed·it** \-'e-dət\ *vt, chiefly Brit* — **sub·ed·i·to·ri·al** \ˌsəb-ˌe-də-'tȯr-ē-əl, -ˌtȯr-\ *adj, chiefly Brit*

sub·em·ployed \ˌsəb-im-'plȯid\ *adj* (1967) : UNDEREMPLOYED

sub·em·ploy·ment \-'plȯi-mənt\ *n* (1967) : a condition of inadequate employment in a labor force including unemployment and underemployment

sub·en·try \'səb-ˌen-trē\ *n* (ca. 1891) : an entry (as in a catalog or an account) made under a more general entry

sub·epi·der·mal \ˌsəb-ˌe-pə-'dər-məl\ *adj* (1853) : lying beneath or constituting the innermost part of the epidermis

su·ber·in \'sü-bə-rən\ *n* [F *subérine*, fr. L *suber* cork tree, cork] (1830) : a complex fatty substance found esp. in the cell walls of cork

su·ber·i·za·tion \ˌsü-bə-rə-'zā-shən\ *n* (1882) : conversion of the cell walls into corky tissue by infiltration with suberin — **su·ber·ized** \'sü-bə-ˌrizd\ *adj*

sub·fam·i·ly \'səb-ˌfam-lē, -ˌfa-mə-\ *n* [ISV] (1833) **1** : a category in biological classification ranking below a family and above a genus **2** : a subgroup of languages within a language family

sub·field \-ˌfēld\ *n* (ca. 1949) **1** : a subset of a mathematical field that is itself a field **2** : a subdivision of a field (as of study)

sub·floor \-ˌflȯr, -ˌflȯr\ *n* (1893) : a rough floor laid as a base for a finished floor

sub·fos·sil \-ˌfä-səl\ *adj* [ISV] (1832) : of less than typical fossil age but partially fossilized — **subfossil** *n*

sub·freez·ing \-'frē-ziŋ\ *adj* (1949) : being or marked by temperature below the freezing point (as of water) ⟨~ weather⟩

sub·fusc \(ˌ)səb-'fəsk, 'səb-ˌ\ *adj* [L *subfuscus* brownish, dusky, fr. *sub-* + *fuscus* dark brown — more at DUSK] (1710) *chiefly Brit* : DRAB, DUSKY

sub·ge·nus \'səb-ˌjē-nəs\ *n* [NL] (1813) : a category in biological classification ranking below a genus and above a species

sub·gla·cial \ˌsəb-'glā-shəl\ *adj* (1820) : of or relating to the bottom of a glacier or the area immediately underlying a glacier — **sub·gla·cial·ly** \-shə-lē\ *adv*

sub·grade \'səb-ˌgrād\ *n* (1898) : a surface of earth or rock leveled off to receive a foundation (as of a road)

sub·graph \'səb-ˌgraf\ *n* (1963) : a graph all of whose points and lines are contained in a larger graph

sub·group \-ˌgrüp\ *n* (1845) **1** : a subordinate group whose members usu. share some common differential quality **2** : a subset of a mathematical group that is itself a group

sub·gum \'səb-'gəm\ *n* [Chin (Guangdong) *sahp-gám*, lit., assorted, mixed] (1938) : a dish of Chinese origin prepared with a mixture of vegetables (as peppers, water chestnuts, and mushrooms)

sub·head \-ˌhed\ *n* (1673) **1** : a heading of a subdivision (as in an outline) **2** : a subordinate caption, title, or headline

sub·head·ing \-ˌhe-diŋ\ *n* (1889) : SUBHEAD

¹sub·hu·man \ˌsəb-'hyü-mən, -'yü-\ *adj* (1793) : less than human: as **a** : failing to attain the level (as of morality or intelligence) associated with normal human beings **b** : unsuitable to or unfit for human beings ⟨~ living conditions⟩ **c** : of or relating to an infrahuman taxonomic group ⟨the ~ primates⟩

²subhuman *n* (1937) : a subhuman being

sub·in·dex \ˌsəb-'in-ˌdeks\ *n* (1923) : an index to a division of a main classification

sub·in·feu·da·tion \ˌsəb-ˌin-fyü-'dā-shən\ *n* [*sub-* + *infeudation* enfeoffment] (ca. 1730) : the subdivision of a feudal estate by a vassal who in turn becomes feudal lord over his tenants — **sub·in·feu·date** *vt*

sub·in·ter·val \ˌsəb-'in-tər-vəl\ *n* (1927) : an interval that is a subdivision or a subset of an interval

sub·ir·ri·ga·tion \ˌ-ir-ə-'gā-shən\ *n* (1880) : irrigation below the surface (as by a periodic rise of the water table or by a system of underground porous pipes) — **sub·ir·ri·gate** \'-ir-ə-ˌgāt\ *vt*

su·bi·to \'sü-bi-ˌtō\ *adv* [It, fr. L, suddenly, fr. *subitus* sudden — more at SUDDEN] (ca. 1724) : IMMEDIATELY, SUDDENLY — used as a direction in music

sub·ja·cen·cy \ˌsəb-'jā-s⁹n(t)-sē\ *n* (ca. 1891) : the quality or state of being subjacent

sub·ja·cent \-s⁹nt\ *adj* [L *subjacent-, subjacens*, prp. of *subjacēre* to lie under, fr. *sub-* + *jacēre* to lie — more at ADJACENT] (1597) : lying under or below; *also* : lower than though not directly below ⟨hills and ~ valleys⟩ — **sub·ja·cent·ly** *adv*

¹sub·ject \'səb-jikt, -(ˌ)jekt\ *n* [ME, fr. MF, fr. L *subjectus* one under authority & *subjectum* subject of a proposition, fr. masc. & neut. respectively of *subjectus*, pp. of *subicere* to subject, fr. L *sub-* + *jacere* to throw — more at JET] (14c) **1** : one that is placed under authority or control: as **a** : VASSAL **b** (1) : one subject to a monarch and governed by the monarch's law (2) : one who lives in the territory of, enjoys the protection of, and owes allegiance to a sovereign power or state **2 a** : that of which a quality, attribute, or relation may be affirmed or in which it may inhere **b** : SUBSTRATUM; *esp* : material or essential substance **c** : the mind, ego, or agent of whatever sort that sustains or assumes the form of thought or consciousness

---

\ə\ abut \ᵊ\ kitten, F table \ər\ further \a\ ash \ā\ ace \ä\ mop, mar \au̇\ out \ch\ chin \e\ bet \ē\ easy \g\ go \i\ hit \ī\ ice \j\ job \ŋ\ sing \ō\ go \ȯ\ law \ȯi\ boy \th\ thin \t͟h\ the \ü\ loot \u̇\ foot \y\ yet \zh\ vision \ȧ, k̟, ⁿ, œ, œ̄, ᵫ, ᵫ̄, ʸ\ see Guide to Pronunciation

3 a : a department of knowledge or learning **b :** MOTIVE, CAUSE **c (1) :** one that is acted on ⟨the helpless ∼ of their cruelty⟩ **(2) :** an individual whose reactions or responses are studied **(3) :** a dead body for anatomical study and dissection **d (1) :** something concerning which something is said or done ⟨the ∼ of the essay⟩ **(2) :** something represented or indicated in a work of art **e (1) :** the term of a logical proposition that denotes the entity of which something is affirmed or denied; *also* **:** the entity denoted **(2) :** a word or word group denoting that of which something is predicated **f :** the principal melodic phrase on which a musical composition or movement is based *syn* see CITIZEN — **sub·ject·less** \-ləs\ *adj*

²subject *adj* (14c) **1 :** owing obedience or allegiance to the power or dominion of another **2 :** suffering a particular liability or exposure ⟨∼ to temptation⟩ **b :** having a tendency or inclination : PRONE ⟨∼ to colds⟩ **3 :** contingent on or under the influence of some later action ⟨the plan is ∼ to discussion⟩ *syn* see LIABLE

³sub·ject \səb-'jekt, 'səb-jekt\ *vt* (14c) **1 a :** to bring under control or dominion : SUBJUGATE **b :** to make (as oneself) amenable to the discipline and control of a superior **2 :** to make liable : PREDISPOSE **3 :** to cause or force to undergo or endure (something unpleasant, inconvenient, or trying) ⟨was ∼ed to constant verbal abuse⟩ — **sub·jec·tion** \səb-'jek-shən\ *n*

¹sub·jec·tive \(,)səb-'jek-tiv\ *adj* (15c) **1 :** of, relating to, or constituting a subject: as **a** *obs* **:** of, relating to, or characteristic of one that is a subject esp. in lack of freedom of action or in submissiveness **b :** being or relating to a grammatical subject; *esp* **:** NOMINATIVE **2 :** of or relating to the essential being of that which has substance, qualities, attributes, or relations **3 a :** characteristic of or belonging to reality as perceived rather than as independent of mind : PHENOMENAL — compare OBJECTIVE 1b **b :** relating to or being experience or knowledge as conditioned by personal mental characteristics or states **4 a (1) :** peculiar to a particular individual : PERSONAL ⟨∼ judgments⟩ **(2) :** modified or affected by personal views, experience, or background ⟨a ∼ account of the incident⟩ **b :** arising from conditions within the brain or sense organs and not directly caused by external stimuli ⟨∼ sensations⟩ **c :** arising out of or identified by means of one's perception of one's own states and processes ⟨a ∼ symptom of disease⟩ — compare OBJECTIVE 1c **5 :** lacking in reality or substance : ILLUSORY — **sub·jec·tive·ly** *adv* — **sub·jec·tive·ness** *n* — **sub·jec·tiv·i·ty** \-jek-'ti-və-tē\ *n*

²subjective *n* (1817) **:** something that is subjective; *also* **:** NOMINATIVE

subjective complement *n* (1923) **:** a grammatical complement relating to the subject of an intransitive verb (as *sick* in "he had fallen sick")

sub·jec·tiv·ise *Brit var of* SUBJECTIVIZE

sub·jec·tiv·ism \(,)səb-'jek-ti-,vi-zəm\ *n* (ca. 1857) **1 a :** a theory that limits knowledge to subjective experience **b :** a theory that stresses the subjective elements in experience **2 a :** a doctrine that the supreme good is the realization of a subjective experience or feeling (as pleasure) **b :** a doctrine that individual feeling or apprehension is the ultimate criterion of the good and the right — **sub·jec·tiv·ist** \-vist\ *n* — **sub·jec·tiv·is·tic** \-,jek-ti-'vis-tik\ *adj*

sub·jec·tiv·ize \-ti-,vīz\ *vt* **-ized; -iz·ing** (1868) **:** to make subjective — **sub·jec·tiv·i·za·tion** \-jek-ti-və-'zā-shən\ *n*

subject matter *n* (1598) **:** matter presented for consideration in discussion, thought, or study

sub·join \(,)səb-'jóin\ *vt* [MF *subjoindre*, fr. L *subjungere* to join beneath, add, fr. *sub-* + *jungere* to join — more at YOKE] (1573) **:** ANNEX, APPEND ⟨∼ed a statement of expenses to her report⟩

sub ju·di·ce \,süb-'yü-di-,kā, 'səb-'jü-də-(,)sē\ *adv* [L] (1613) **:** before a judge or court : not yet judicially decided

sub·ju·gate \'səb-ji-,gāt\ *vt* **-gat·ed; -gat·ing** [ME, fr. L *subjugatus*, pp. of *subjugare*, fr. *sub-* + *jugum* yoke — more at YOKE] (15c) **1 :** to bring under control and governance as a subject : CONQUER **2 :** to make submissive : SUBDUE — **sub·ju·ga·tion** \,səb-ji-'gā-shən\ *n* — **sub·ju·ga·tor** \'səb-ji-,gā-tər\ *n*

sub·junc·tion \(,)səb-'jəŋ(k)-shən\ *n* (1633) **1 :** an act of subjoining or the state of being subjoined **2 :** something subjoined

¹sub·junc·tive \səb-'jəŋ(k)-tiv\ *adj* [LL *subjunctivus*, fr. L *subjunctus*, pp. of *subjungere* to join beneath, subordinate] (1530) **:** of, relating to, or constituting a verb form or set of verb forms that represents a denoted act or state not as fact but as contingent or possible or viewed emotionally (as with doubt or desire) ⟨the ∼ mood⟩

²subjunctive *n* (1622) **1 :** the subjunctive mood of a language **2 :** a form of verb or verbal in the subjunctive mood

sub·king·dom \'səb-,kiŋ-dəm\ *n* (1825) **:** a category in biological classification ranking below a kingdom and above a phylum

sub·late \,sə-'blāt\ *vt* **sub·lat·ed; sub·lat·ing** [L *sublatus* (pp. of *tollere* to take away, lift up), fr. *sub-* up + *latus*, pp. of *ferre* to carry — more at SUB-, TOLERATE, BEAR] (1838) **1 :** NEGATE, DENY **2 :** to negate or eliminate (as an element in a dialectic process) but preserve as a partial element in a synthesis — **sub·la·tion** \-'blā-shən\ *n*

¹sub·lease \'səb-,lēs, -,lēs\ *n* (1826) **:** a lease by a tenant or lessee of part or all of leased premises to another person but with the original tenant retaining some right or interest under the original lease

²sublease *vt* (ca. 1843) **:** to make or obtain a sublease of

¹sub·let \'səb-'let\ *vb* **-let; -let·ting** *vt* (1766) **1 :** SUBLEASE **2 :** SUBCONTRACT 1 ∼ *vi* **:** to lease or rent all or part of a leased or rented property

²sub·let \-,let\ *n* (1906) **:** property and esp. housing obtained by or available through a sublease

sub·le·thal \,səb-'lē-thəl\ *adj* (1895) **:** less than but usu. only slightly less than lethal ⟨a ∼ dose⟩ — **sub·le·thal·ly** \-thə-lē\ *adv*

sub·lieu·ten·ant \,səb-lü-'te-nənt, *Brit* -le(f)-'ten-\ *n* (1804) **:** a commissioned officer in the British navy ranking immediately below lieutenant

¹sub·li·mate \'sə-blə-,māt\ *vt* **-mat·ed; -mat·ing** [ME, fr. ML *sublimatus*, pp. of *sublimare*] (15c) **1 a :** SUBLIME 1 **b** *archaic* **:** to improve or refine as if by subliming **2 :** to divert the expression of (an instinctual desire or impulse) from its primitive form to one that is considered more socially or culturally acceptable — **sub·li·ma·tion** \,sə-blə-'mā-shən\ *n*

²sub·li·mate \'sə-blə-,māt, -mət\ *n* (ca. 1626) **:** a chemical product obtained by sublimation

¹sub·lime \sə-'blīm\ *vb* **sub·limed; sub·lim·ing** [ME, fr. MF *sublimer*,

fr. ML *sublimare* to refine, sublime, fr. L, to elevate, fr. *sublimis*] *vt* (14c) **1 :** to cause to pass directly from the solid to the vapor state and condense back to solid form **2** [F *sublimer*, fr. L *sublimare*] **a (1) :** to elevate or exalt esp. in dignity or honor **(2) :** to render finer (as in purity or excellence) **b :** to convert (something inferior) into something of higher worth ∼ *vi* **:** to pass directly from the solid to the vapor state — **sub·lim·able** \-'blī-mə-bəl\ *adj* — **sub·lim·er** *n*

²sublime *adj* **sub·lim·er; -est** [L *sublimis*, lit., high, elevated] (1586) **1 a :** lofty, grand, or exalted in thought, expression, or manner **b :** of outstanding spiritual, intellectual, or moral worth **c :** tending to inspire awe usu. because of elevated quality (as of beauty, nobility, or grandeur) or transcendent excellence **2 a** *archaic* **:** high in place **b** *obs* **:** lofty of mien : HAUGHTY **c** *cap* **:** SUPREME — used in a style of address **d :** COMPLETE, UTTER ⟨∼ ignorance⟩ *syn* see SPLENDID — **sub·lime·ly** *adv* — **sub·lime·ness** *n*

sub·lim·i·nal \(,)sə-'bli-mə-n°l\ *adj* [*sub-* + L *limin-, limen* threshold] (1886) **1 :** inadequate to produce a sensation or a perception **2 :** existing or functioning below the threshold of consciousness ⟨the ∼ mind⟩ ⟨∼ advertising⟩ — **sub·lim·i·nal·ly** *adv*

sub·lim·i·ty \sə-'bli-mə-tē\ *n, pl* **-ties** (15c) **1 :** the quality or state of being sublime **2 :** something sublime or exalted

sub·line \'səb-,līn\ *n* (1942) **:** an inbred or selectively cultured line (as of cells) within a strain

sub·lin·gual \,səb-'liŋ-gwəl, -gyə-wəl\ *adj* [NL *sublingualis*, fr. L *sub-* + *lingua* tongue — more at TONGUE] (1661) **:** situated or administered under the tongue ⟨∼ tablets⟩ ⟨∼ glands⟩

sub·lit·er·ary \-'li-tə-,rer-ē\ *adj* (1936) **:** relating to or being subliterature

sub·lit·er·a·ture \-'li-tə-rə-,chùr, -'li-trə-,chùr, -'li-tə(r)-,chùr, -chər, -,tyùr, -,tùr\ *n* (1952) **:** popular writing (as mystery or adventure stories) considered inferior to standard literature

¹sub·lit·to·ral \-'li-tə-rəl, ,səb-,li-tə-'ral, -'räl\ *adj* (1846) **1 :** situated, occurring, or formed on the aquatic side of a shoreline or littoral zone **2 :** constituting the sublittoral

²sublittoral *n* (ca. 1935) **:** the deeper part of the littoral portion of a body of water: **a :** the region in a lake between the deepest-growing rooted vegetation and the part of the lake below the thermocline **b :** the region in an ocean between the lowest point exposed by a low tide and the margin of the continental shelf

sub·lu·na·ry \,səb-'lü-nə-rē, 'səb-lü-,ner-ē\ *also* **sub·lu·nar** \,səb-'lü-nər *also* -,när\ *adj* [modif. of LL *sublunaris*, fr. L *sub-* + *luna* moon — more at LUNAR] (1592) **:** of, relating to, or characteristic of the terrestrial world ⟨dull ∼ lovers —John Donne⟩

sub·lux·a·tion \,sə-,blək-'sā-shən\ *n* (ca. 1688) **:** partial dislocation (as of one of the bones in a joint)

sub·ma·chine gun \,səb-mə-'shēn-,gən\ *n* (1920) **:** a portable automatic firearm that uses pistol-type ammunition and is fired from the shoulder or hip

¹sub·man·dib·u·lar \,səb-man-'di-byə-lər\ *adj* (1875) **1 :** of, relating to, situated in, or performed in the region below the lower jaw **2 :** of, relating to, or associated with the salivary glands inside of and near the lower edge of the mandible on each side

²submandibular *n* (1974) **:** a submandibular part (as an artery or bone)

sub·mar·gin·al \,səb-'märj-nəl, -'mär-jə-n°l\ *adj* (1829) **1 :** adjacent to a margin or a marginal part or structure ⟨∼ spots on an insect wing⟩ **2 :** falling below a necessary minimum ⟨∼ economic conditions⟩

¹sub·ma·rine \'səb-mə-,rēn, ,səb-mə-'\ *adj* (1648) **:** UNDERWATER; *esp* **:** UNDERSEA ⟨∼ plants⟩ ⟨∼ minerals⟩

²submarine *n* (1703) **1 :** something that functions or operates underwater; *specif* **:** a naval vessel designed to operate underwater **2 :** a large sandwich on a long split roll with any of a variety of fillings (as meatballs or cold cuts, cheese, lettuce, and tomato) — called also **grinder, hero, hoagie, Italian sandwich, poor boy, sub, torpedo**

³submarine *vb* **-rined; -rin·ing** *vt* (1914) **:** to attack by or as if by a submarine : attack from beneath ∼ *vi* **:** to dive or slide under something

sub·ma·ri·ner \,səb-mə-'rē-nər, -'mar-ə-nər\ *n* (1914) **:** a member of a submarine crew

sub·max·il·lary \,səb-'mak-sə-,ler-ē, 'səb-, *chiefly Brit* ,səb-mak-'si-lə-rē\ *adj or n* (1787) **:** SUBMANDIBULAR

sub·me·di·ant \,səb-'mē-dē-ənt\ *n* (1806) **:** the sixth tone of a diatonic scale

sub·merge \səb-'mərj\ *vb* **sub·merged; sub·merg·ing** [L *submergere*, fr. *sub-* + *mergere* to plunge — more at MERGE] *vt* (1611) **1 :** to put under water **2 :** to cover or overflow with water **3 :** to make obscure or subordinate : SUPPRESS ⟨personal lives *submerged* by professional responsibilities⟩ ∼ *vi* **:** to go under water — **sub·mer·gence** \-'mər-jən(t)s\ *n* — **sub·merg·ible** \-'mər-jə-bəl\ *adj*

submerged *adj* (1799) **1 :** covered with water **2 :** SUBMERSED **3 :** sunk in poverty and misery ⟨the ∼ masses⟩ ⟨the ∼ tenth of the population⟩ **4 :** HIDDEN, SUPPRESSED ⟨∼ emotions⟩

sub·merse \səb-'mərs\ *vt* **sub·mersed; sub·mers·ing** [L *submersus*, pp. of *submergere*] (1837) **:** SUBMERGE — **sub·mer·sion** \-'mər-zhən, -shən\ *n*

submersed *adj* (ca. 1727) **:** SUBMERGED: as **a :** covered with water **b :** growing or adapted to grow underwater ⟨∼ weeds⟩

¹sub·mers·ible \səb-'mər-sə-bəl\ *adj* (1866) **:** capable of being submerged

²submersible *n* (1900) **:** something that is submersible; *esp* **:** a usu. small underwater craft used esp. for deep-sea research

sub·meta·cen·tric \,səb-,me-tə-'sen-trik\ *adj* (1962) **:** having the centromere situated so that one chromosome is somewhat shorter than the other — **submetacentric** *n*

sub·mi·cro·gram \,səb-'mī-krə-,gram\ *adj* (1946) **:** relating to or having a mass of less than one microgram ⟨∼ quantities of a chemical⟩

sub·mi·cron \-'krän\ *adj* (1948) **1 :** being less than a micron in a (specified) measurement and esp. in diameter ⟨a ∼ particle⟩ **2 :** having or consisting of submicron particles ⟨a ∼ metal powder⟩

sub·mi·cro·scop·ic \,səb-,mī-krə-'skä-pik\ *adj* [ISV] (1912) **1 :** too small to be seen in an ordinary light microscope **2 :** of, relating to, or dealing with the very minute ⟨the ∼ world⟩ — **sub·mi·cro·scop·i·cal·ly** \-pi-k(ə-)lē\ *adv*

sub·mil·li·me·ter \'səb-ˌmil-ə-ˌmē-tər\ *adj* (1955) : being less than a millimeter in diameter or wavelength ⟨a ~ particle⟩ ⟨a ~ radio wave⟩

sub·min·i·a·ture \ˌsəb-'mi-nē-ə-ˌchu̇r, -'mi-ni-ˌchu̇r, -'min-yə-, -chər, -ˌtyu̇r, -ˌtu̇r\ *adj* [ISV] (1947) : very small — used esp. of a very compact assembly of electronic equipment

sub·miss \səb-'mis\ *adj* [L *submissus*, fr. pp. of *submittere*] (1570) *archaic* : SUBMISSIVE, HUMBLE

sub·mis·sion \səb-'mi-shən\ *n* [ME, fr. MF, fr. L *submission-, submissio* act of lowering, fr. *submittere*] (14c) **1 a** : a legal agreement to submit to the decision of arbitrators **b** : an act of submitting something (as for consideration or inspection); *also* : something submitted (as a manuscript) **2** : the condition of being submissive, humble, or compliant **3** : an act of submitting to the authority or control of another

sub·mis·sive \-'mi-siv\ *adj* (ca. 1586) : submitting to others — **sub·mis·sive·ly** *adv* — **sub·mis·sive·ness** *n*

sub·mit \səb-'mit\ *vb* **sub·mit·ted; sub·mit·ting** [ME *submitten*, fr. L *submittere* to lower, submit, fr. *sub-* + *mittere* to send] *vt* (14c) **1 a** : to yield to governance or authority **b** : to subject to a condition, treatment, or operation (the metal was *submitted* to analysis) **2** : to present or propose to another for review, consideration, or decision ⟨~ a question to the court⟩ ⟨~ a bid on a contract⟩ ⟨~ a report⟩; *also* : to deliver formally ⟨*submitted* my resignation⟩ **3** : to put forward as an opinion or contention ⟨we ~ that the charge is not proved⟩ ~ *vi* **1 a** : to yield oneself to the authority or will of another : SURRENDER **b** : to permit oneself to be subjected to something ⟨had to ~ to surgery⟩ **2** : to defer to or consent to abide by the opinion or authority of another *syn* see YIELD — **sub·mit·tal** \-'mi-t²l\ *n*

sub·mi·to·chon·dri·al \ˌsəb-ˌmī-tə-'kän-drē-əl\ *adj* (1963) : relating to, composed of, or being parts and esp. fragments of mitochondria ⟨~ membranes⟩ ⟨~ particles⟩

sub·mu·co·sa \ˌsəb-myü-'kō-zə\ *n* [NL] (1885) : a supporting layer of loose connective tissue directly under a mucous membrane — **sub·mu·co·sal** \-zəl\ *adj*

sub·mul·ti·ple \'məl-tə-pəl\ *n* (1758) : an exact divisor of a number ⟨8 is a ~ of 72⟩

sub·mu·ni·tion \ˌsəb-myü-'ni-shən\ *n* (1975) : any of a group of smaller weapons carried as a warhead by a missile or projectile and expelled as the carrier approaches its target

sub·nor·mal \-'nȯr-məl\ *adj* [ISV] (ca. 1890) **1** : lower or smaller than normal **2** : having less of something and esp. of intelligence than is normal — **sub·nor·mal·i·ty** \ˌsəb-nȯr-'ma-lə-tē\ *n* — **sub·nor·mal·ly** \-'nȯr-mə-lē\ *adv*

sub·nu·cle·ar \ˌsəb-'nü-klē-ər, -'nyü-, -÷-kyə-lər\ *adj* (1937) : of, relating to, or being a particle smaller than the atomic nucleus

sub·oce·an·ic \ˌsəb-ˌō-shē-'a-nik\ *adj* (1858) : situated, taking place, or formed beneath the ocean or its bottom ⟨~ oil resources⟩

sub·or·bit·al \ˌsəb-'ȯr-bə-t²l\ *adj* (ca. 1827) **1** : situated beneath the eye or the orbit of the eye **2** : being or involving less than one orbit (as of the earth or moon) ⟨a spacecraft's ~ flight⟩; *also* : intended for suborbital flight ⟨a ~ rocket⟩

sub·or·der \'səb-ˌȯr-dər\ *n* (1826) : a subdivision of an order ⟨a soil ~⟩; *esp* : a taxonomic category ranking between an order and a family

¹sub·or·di·nate \sə-'bȯr-d²n-ət, -'bȯrd-nət\ *adj* [ME *subordinat*, fr. ML *subordinatus*, pp. of *subordinare* to subordinate, fr. L *sub-* + *ordinare* to order — more at ORDAIN] (15c) **1** : placed in or occupying a lower class, rank, or position : INFERIOR **2** : submissive to or controlled by authority **3 a** : of, relating to, or constituting a clause that functions as a noun, adjective, or adverb **b** : SUBORDINATING — **sub·or·di·nate·ly** *adv* — **sub·or·di·nate·ness** *n*

²subordinate *n* (1640) : one that is subordinate

³sub·or·di·nate \sə-'bȯr-d²n-ˌāt\ *vt* **-nat·ed; -nat·ing** [ML *subordinatus*] (1597) **1** : to make subject or subservient **2** : to treat as of less value or importance ⟨stylist . . . whose crystalline prose ~s content to form —Susan Heath⟩ — **sub·or·di·na·tion** \-ˌbȯr-d²n-'ā-shən\ *n* — **sub·or·di·na·tive** \-'bȯr-d²n-ˌā-tiv\ *adj*

subordinating *adj* (1857) : introducing and linking a subordinate clause to a main clause ⟨~ conjunction⟩

sub·or·di·na·tor \-ˌā-tər\ *n* (1959) : one that subordinates; *esp* : a subordinating conjunction

sub·orn \sə-'bȯrn\ *vt* [MF *suborner*, fr. L *subornare*, fr. *sub-* secretly + *ornare* to furnish, equip — more at ORNATE] (1534) **1** : to induce secretly to do an unlawful thing **2** : to induce to commit perjury; *also* : to obtain (perjured testimony) from a witness — **sub·or·na·tion** \ˌsə-ˌbȯr-'nā-shən\ *n* — **sub·orn·er** *n*

sub·phy·lum \'səb-ˌfī-ləm\ *n* [NL] (ca. 1934) : a category in biological classification ranking below a phylum and above a class

sub·plot \'səb-ˌplät\ *n* (1916) **1** : a subordinate plot in fiction or drama **2** : a subdivision of an experimental plot of land

¹sub·poe·na \sə-'pē-nə, ÷-'nē\ *n* [ME *suppena*, fr. L *sub poena* under penalty] (15c) : a writ commanding a person designated in it to appear in court under a penalty for failure

²subpoena *vt* **-naed; -na·ing** (1640) : to serve or summon with a writ of subpoena

subpoena ad tes·ti·fi·can·dum \-ˌad-ˌtes-tə-fi-'kan-dəm\ *n* [NL, under penalty to give testimony] (ca. 1769) : a writ commanding a person to appear in court to testify as a witness

subpoena du·ces te·cum \-ˌdü-səs-'tē-kəm\ *n* [NL, under penalty you shall bring with you] (1768) : a writ commanding a person to produce in court certain designated documents or evidence

sub·po·lar \ˌsəb-'pō-lər\ *adj* (1826) : SUBANTARCTIC, SUBARCTIC

sub·pop·u·la·tion \'səb-ˌpä-pyə-'lā-shən\ *n* (1944) : an identifiable fraction or subdivision of a population

sub·po·tent \ˌsəb-'pō-t²nt\ *adj* (ca. 1909) : less potent than normal ⟨~ drugs⟩ — **sub·po·ten·cy** \-'pō-t²n(t)-sē\ *n*

sub·prin·ci·pal \-'prin(t)-s(ə-)pəl, -sə-bəl\ *n* (1597) **1** : an assistant principal (as of a school) **2** : a secondary or bracing rafter

sub·prob·lem \'səb-ˌprä-bləm\ *n* (1906) : a problem that is contingent on or forms a part of another more inclusive problem

sub·pro·fes·sion·al \ˌsəb-prə-'fesh-nəl, -'fe-shə-n²l\ *adj* (1941) : functioning or qualified to function below the professional level but distinctly above the clerical or labor level and usu. under the supervision of a professionally trained person — **subprofessional** *n*

sub·pro·gram \'səb-ˌprō-ˌgram, -grəm\ *n* (1947) : a semi-independent portion of a program (as for a computer)

sub·re·gion \'səb-ˌrē-jən\ *n* [ISV] (1864) **1** : a subdivision of a region **2** : one of the primary divisions of a biogeographic region — **sub·re·gion·al** \-ˌrēj-nəl, -ˌrē-jə-n²l\ *adj*

sub·rep·tion \ˌsəb-'rep-shən\ *n* [LL *subreption-, subreptio*, fr. L, act of stealing, fr. *subripere, surripere* to take away secretly — more at SURREPTITIOUS] (1600) : a deliberate misrepresentation; *also* : an inference drawn from it — **sub·rep·ti·tious** \ˌsəb-ˌrep-'ti-shəs\ *adj* — **sub·rep·ti·tious·ly** *adv*

sub·ring \'səb-ˌriŋ\ *n* (1937) : a subset of a mathematical ring which is itself a ring

sub·ro·gate \'sə-brō-ˌgāt\ *vt* **-gat·ed; -gat·ing** [ME, fr. L *subrogatus*, pp. of *subrogare, surrogare* — more at SURROGATE] (15c) : to put in the place of another; *esp* : to substitute (as a second creditor) for another with regard to a legal right or claim

sub·ro·ga·tion \ˌsə-brō-'gā-shən\ *n* (15c) : the act of subrogating; *specif* : the assumption by a third party (as a second creditor or an insurance company) of another's legal right to collect a debt or damages

sub-rosa *adj* (1923) : SECRETIVE, PRIVATE

sub rosa \ˌsəb-'rō-zə\ *adv* [NL, lit., under the rose; fr. the ancient association of the rose with secrecy] (1654) : in confidence : SECRETLY

sub·rou·tine \'səb-ˌrü-ˌtēn\ *n* [ISV] (ca. 1946) : a subordinate routine; *specif* : a sequence of computer instructions for performing a specified task that can be used repeatedly

sub–Sa·ha·ran \ˌsəb-sə-'har-ən, -'her-, -'här-\ *adj* (1955) : of, relating to, or being the part of Africa south of the Sahara

¹sub·sam·ple \'səb-ˌsam-pəl, ˌsəb-'sam-\ *vt* (ca. 1899) : to draw samples from (a previously selected group or population) : sample a sample of

²subsample *n* (ca. 1899) : a sample or specimen obtained by subsampling

sub·sat·el·lite \ˌsəb-'sa-t²l-ˌīt\ *n* (1956) : an object carried into orbit in and subsequently released from a satellite or spacecraft

sub·scribe \səb-'skrīb\ *vb* **sub·scribed; sub·scrib·ing** [ME, fr. L *subscribere*, lit., to write beneath, fr. *sub-* + *scribere* to write — more at SCRIBE] *vt* (15c) **1** : to write (one's name) underneath : SIGN **2 a** : to sign (as a document) with one's own hand in token of consent or obligation **b** : to attest by signing **c** : to pledge (a gift or contribution) by writing one's name with the amount **3** : to assent to : SUPPORT ~ *vi* **1** : to sign one's name to a document **2 a** : to give consent or approval to something written by signing ⟨unwilling to ~ to the agreement⟩ **b** : to set one's name to a paper in token of promise to give something (as a sum of money); *also* : to give something in accordance with such a promise **c** : to enter one's name for a publication or service; *also* : to receive a periodical or service regularly on order **d** : to agree to purchase and pay for securities esp. of a new offering ⟨*subscribed* for 1000 shares⟩ **3** : to feel favorably disposed ⟨I ~ to your sentiments⟩ *syn* see ASSENT — **sub·scrib·er** *n*

sub·script \'səb-ˌskript\ *n* [L *subscriptus*, pp. of *subscribere*] (1895) : a distinguishing symbol (as a letter or numeral) written immediately below or below and to the right or left of another character — **subscript** *adj*

sub·scrip·tion \səb-'skrip-shən\ *n* [ME *subscripcioun* signature, fr. L *subscription-, subscriptio*, fr. *subscribere*] (15c) **1 a** : the act of signing one's name (as in attesting or witnessing a document) **b** : the acceptance (as of ecclesiastical articles of faith) attested by the signing of one's name **2** : something that is subscribed: as **a** : an autograph signature; *also* : a paper to which a signature is attached **b** : a sum subscribed or pledged **3** : an arrangement for providing, receiving, or making use of something of a continuing or periodic nature on a prepayment plan: as **a** : a purchase by prepayment for a certain number of issues (as of a periodical) **b** : application to purchase securities of a new issue **c** : a method of offering or presenting a series of public performances **d** *Brit* : membership dues

subscription TV *n* (1953) : pay-TV that broadcasts programs directly over the air to customers provided with a special receiver — called also *subscription television*; compare PAY-CABLE, PAY-TV

sub·sec·tion \'səb-ˌsek-shən\ *n* (1621) **1** : a subdivision or a subordinate division of a section **2** : a subordinate part or branch

¹sub·se·quence \'səb-sə-ˌkwen(t)s, -si-kwən(t)s\ *n* (ca. 1500) : the quality or state of being subsequent; *also* : a subsequent event

²sub·se·quence \'səb-ˌsē-kwən(t)s, -ˌkwen(t)s\ *n* (1908) : a mathematical sequence that is part of another sequence

sub·se·quent \'səb-si-kwənt, -sə-ˌkwent\ *adj* [ME, fr. L *subsequent-, subsequens*, prp. of *subsequi* to follow close, fr. *sub-* near + *sequi* to follow — more at SUB, SUE] (15c) : following in time, order, or place — **subsequent** *n* — **sub·se·quent·ly** \-ˌkwent-lē, -kwənt-\ *adv*

subsequent to *prep* (1647) : at a time later or more recent than : SINCE

sub·serve \(ˌ)səb-'sərv\ *vt* [L *subservire* to serve, be subservient, fr. *sub-* + *servire* to serve] (1661) **1** : to promote the welfare or purposes of **2** : to serve as an instrument or means in carrying out

sub·ser·vi·ence \səb-'sər-vē-ən(t)s\ *n* (ca. 1676) **1** : a subservient or subordinate place or function **2** : obsequious servility

sub·ser·vi·en·cy \-ən(t)-sē\ *n* (1651) : SUBSERVIENCE

sub·ser·vi·ent \-ənt\ *adj* [L *subservient-, subserviens*, prp. of *subservire*] (1632) **1** : serving to promote some end **2** : useful in an inferior capacity : SUBORDINATE **3** : obsequiously submissive : TRUCKLING — **sub·ser·vi·ent·ly** *adv*

syn SUBSERVIENT, SERVILE, SLAVISH, OBSEQUIOUS mean showing or characterized by extreme compliance or abject obedience. SUBSERVIENT implies the cringing manner of one very conscious of a subordinate position ⟨domestic help was expected to be properly *subservient*⟩. SERVILE suggests the mean or fawning behavior of a slave ⟨a political boss and his entourage of *servile* hangers-on⟩. SLAVISH suggests abject or debased servility ⟨the *slavish* status of migrant farm workers⟩. OBSE-

\ə\ abut \²\ kitten, F table \ər\ further \a\ ash \ā\ ace \ä\ mop, mar \au̇\ out \ch\ chin \e\ bet \ē\ easy \g\ go \i\ hit \ī\ ice \j\ job \ŋ\ sing \ō\ go \ȯ\ law \ȯi\ boy \th\ thin \t̲h̲\ the \ü\ loot \u̇\ foot \y\ yet \zh\ vision \à, k̲, ⁿ, œ, œ̄, ᵫ, ᵫ̄, ᵞ\ see Guide to Pronunciation

QUIOUS implies fawning or sycophantic compliance and exaggerated deference of manner ⟨waiters who are *obsequious* in the presence of celebrities⟩.

sub·set \'səb-ˌset\ *n* (1902) : a set each of whose elements is an element of an inclusive set

sub·shrub \ˌ-shrəb, *esp Southern* -ˌsrəb\ *n* (1851) : a perennial plant having woody stems except for the terminal part of the new growth which is killed back annually; *also* : a low shrub

sub·side \səb-'sīd\ *vi* **sub·sid·ed; sub·sid·ing** [L *subsidere*, fr. *sub-* + *sidere* to sit down, sink; akin to L *sedēre* to sit — more at SIT] (1607) **1** : to sink or fall to the bottom : SETTLE **2** : to tend downward : DESCEND; *esp* : to flatten out so as to form a depression **3** : to let oneself settle down : SINK ⟨*subsided* into a chair⟩ **4** : to become quiet or less ⟨as the fever ~s⟩ ⟨my anger *subsided*⟩ *syn* see ABATE — **sub·si·dence** \səb-'sī-dᵊn(t)s, 'səb-sə-dən(t)s\ *n*

sub·sid·i·ar·i·ty \ˌsəb-si-dē-'er-ə-tē, səb-ˌsi-\ *n* (1936) **1** : the quality or state of being subsidiary **2** : a principle in social organization: functions which subordinate or local organizations perform effectively belong more properly to them than to a dominant central organization

¹sub·sid·i·ary \səb-'si-dē-ˌer-ē, -'si-də-rē\ *adj* [L *subsidiarius*, fr. *subsidium* reserve troops] (1543) **1 a** : furnishing aid or support : AUXILIARY ⟨~ details⟩ **b** : of secondary importance ⟨a ~ stream⟩ **2** : of, relating to, or constituting a subsidy ⟨a ~ payment to an ally⟩ — **sub·sid·i·ari·ly** \ˌsi-dē-'er-ə-lē\ *adv*

²subsidiary *n, pl* **-ar·ies** (1603) : one that is subsidiary; *esp* : a company wholly controlled by another

sub·si·dise *Brit var of* SUBSIDIZE

sub·si·dize \'səb-sə-ˌdīz, -zə-\ *vt* **-dized; -diz·ing** (1795) : to furnish with a subsidy: as **a** : to purchase the assistance of by payment of a subsidy **b** : to aid or promote (as a private enterprise) with public money ⟨~ soybean farmers⟩ ⟨~ public transportation⟩ — **sub·si·di·za·tion** \ˌsəb-sə-də-'zā-shən, -zə-\ *n* — **sub·si·diz·er** *n*

sub·si·dy \'səb-sə-dē, -zə-\ *n, pl* **-dies** [ME, fr. L *subsidium* reserve troops, support, assistance, fr. *sub-* near + *sedēre* to sit — more at SUB-, SIT] (14c) : a grant or gift of money: as **a** : a sum of money formerly granted by the British Parliament to the crown and raised by special taxation **b** : money granted by one state to another **c** : a grant by a government to a private person or company to assist an enterprise deemed advantageous to the public

sub·sist \səb-'sist\ *vb* [LL *subsistere* to exist, fr. L, to come to a halt, remain, fr. *sub-* + *sistere* to come to a stand; akin to L *stare* to stand — more at STAND] *vi* (1549) **1 a** : to have existence : BE **b** : PERSIST, CONTINUE **2** : to have or acquire the necessities of life (as food and clothing); *esp* : to nourish oneself ⟨~*ing* on roots, berries and grubs⟩ **3 a** : to hold true **b** : to be logically conceivable as the subject of true statements ~ *vt* : to support with provisions

sub·sis·tence \səb-'sis-tən(t)s\ *n* [ME, fr. LL *subsistentia*, fr. *subsistent-, subsistens*, prp. of *subsistere*] (15c) **1 a** (1) : real being : EXISTENCE (2) : the condition of remaining in existence : CONTINUATION, PERSISTENCE **b** : an essential characteristic quality of something that exists **c** : the character possessed by whatever is logically conceivable **2** : means of subsisting: as **a** : the minimum (as of food and shelter) necessary to support life **b** : a source or means of obtaining the necessities of life — **sub·sis·tent** \-tənt\ *adj*

subsistence farming *n* (1939) **1** : farming or a system of farming that provides all or almost all the goods required by the farm family usu. without any significant surplus for sale **2** : farming or a system of farming that produces a minimum and often inadequate return to the farmer — called also *subsistence agriculture* — **subsistence farmer** *n*

sub·so·cial \ˌsəb-'sō-shəl\ *adj* (ca. 1909) : incompletely social; *esp* : tending to associate gregariously but lacking fixed or complex social organization ⟨~ insects⟩

¹sub·soil \'səb-ˌsȯil\ *n* (1799) : the stratum of weathered material that underlies the surface soil

²subsoil *vt* (1840) : to turn, break, or stir the subsoil of — **sub·soil·er** *n*

sub·so·lar point \ˌsəb-'sō-lər-\ *n* (ca. 1908) : the point on the surface of the earth or a planet at which the sun is at the zenith

sub·son·ic \ˌsəb-'sä-nik\ *adj* [ISV] (1937) **1** : of, relating to, or being a speed less than that of sound in air **2** : moving, capable of moving, or utilizing air currents moving at a subsonic speed **3** : INFRASONIC 1 — **sub·son·i·cal·ly** \-ni-k(ə-)lē\ *adv*

sub·space \'səb-ˌspās\ *n* (1927) : a subset of a space; *esp* : one that has the essential properties (as those of a vector space or topological space) of the including space

sub spe·cie ae·ter·ni·ta·tis \ˌsùb-'spe-kē-ˌā-ˌī-ˌter-nə-'tä-təs\ *adv* [NL, lit., under the aspect of eternity] (1895) : in its essential or universal form or nature

sub·spe·cies \'səb-ˌspē-shēz, -sēz\ *n* [NL] (1699) : a subdivision of a species: as **a** : a category in biological classification that ranks immediately below a species and designates a population of a particular geographical region genetically distinguishable from other such populations of the same species and capable of interbreeding successfully with them where its range overlaps theirs **b** : a named subdivision (as a race or variety) of a taxonomic species ⟨~ SUBGROUP 1 ⟨~ of economy fares —Michael DiPaola⟩ — **sub·spe·cif·ic** \ˌsəb-spi-'si-fik\ *adj*

sub·stage \'səb-ˌstāj\ *n* (1888) : an attachment to a microscope by means of which accessories (as mirrors, diaphragms, or condensers) are held in place beneath the stage of the instrument

sub·stance \'səb-stən(t)s\ *n* [ME, fr. MF, fr. L *substantia*, fr. *substant-, substans*, prp. of *substare* to stand under, fr. *sub-* + *stare* to stand — more at STAND] (14c) **1 a** : essential nature : ESSENCE **b** : a fundamental or characteristic part or quality **c** *Christian Science* : GOD 1b **2 a** : ultimate reality that underlies all outward manifestations and change **b** : practical importance : MEANING, USEFULNESS ⟨the . . . bill—which will be without ~ in the sense that it will authorize nothing more than a set of ideas —Richard Reeves⟩ **3 a** : physical material from which something is made or which has discrete existence **b** : matter of particular or definite chemical constitution **c** : something (as drugs or alcoholic beverages) deemed harmful and usu. subject to legal restriction ⟨possession of a controlled ~⟩ ⟨has a ~ problem⟩ **4** : material possessions : PROPERTY ⟨a family of ~⟩ — **sub·stance·less** \-ləs\ *adj* — **in substance** : in respect to essentials : FUNDAMENTALLY

substance abuse *n* (1982) : excessive use of a drug (as alcohol, narcotics, or cocaine) : use of a drug without medical justification — **substance abuser** *n*

substance P *n* (1934) : a neuropeptide that consists of 11 amino-acid residues, that is widely distributed in the brain, spinal cord, and peripheral nervous system, and that acts across nerve synapses to produce prolonged postsynaptic excitation

sub·stan·dard \ˌsəb-'stan-dərd\ *adj* (1897) : deviating from or falling short of a standard or norm: as **a** : of a quality lower than that prescribed by law **b** : conforming to a pattern of linguistic usage existing within a speech community but not that of the prestige group in that community **c** : constituting a greater than normal risk to an insurer

sub·stan·tial \səb-'stan(t)-shəl\ *adj* (14c) **1 a** : consisting of or relating to substance **b** : not imaginary or illusory : REAL, TRUE **c** : IMPORTANT, ESSENTIAL **2** : ample to satisfy and nourish : FULL ⟨a ~ meal⟩ **3 a** : possessed of means : WELL-TO-DO **b** : considerable in quantity : significantly great ⟨earned a ~ wage⟩ **4** : firmly constructed : STURDY **5** : being largely but not wholly that which is specified ⟨a ~ lie⟩ — **substantial** *n* — **sub·stan·ti·al·i·ty** \-ˌstan(t)-shē-'a-lə-tē\ *n* — **sub·stan·tial·ly** \-'stan(t)-sh(ə-)lē\ *adv* — **sub·stan·tial·ness** \-'stan(t)-shəl-nəs\ *n*

sub·stan·tia ni·gra \səb-ˌstan(t)-shē-ə-'nī-grə, -'ni-\ *n, pl* **sub·stan·ti·ae ni·grae** \-chē-ˌē-'nī-(ˌ)grē, -'ni-\ [NL, lit., black substance] (1882) : a layer of deeply pigmented gray matter situated in the midbrain and containing the cell bodies of a tract of dopamine-producing nerve cells whose secretion tends to be deficient in Parkinson's disease

sub·stan·ti·ate \səb-'stan(t)-shē-ˌāt\ *vt* **-at·ed; -at·ing** (1657) **1** : to give substance or form to : EMBODY **2** : to establish by proof or competent evidence : VERIFY ⟨~ a charge⟩ *syn* see CONFIRM — **sub·stan·ti·a·tion** \-ˌstan(t)-shē-'ā-shən\ *n* — **sub·stan·ti·a·tive** \-'stan(t)-shē-ˌā-tiv\ *adj*

sub·stan·ti·val \ˌsəb-stən-'tī-vəl\ *adj* (ca. 1832) : of, relating to, or serving as a substantive — **sub·stan·ti·val·ly** \-və-lē\ *adv*

¹sub·stan·tive \'səb-stən-tiv\ *n* [ME *substantif*, fr. MF, fr. *substantif*, adj., having or expressing substance, fr. LL *substantivus*] (14c) : NOUN; *broadly* : a word or word group functioning syntactically as a noun — **sub·stan·tiv·ize** \-ti-ˌvīz\ *vt*

²sub·stan·tive \'səb-stən-tiv; *2c & 3 also* səb-'stan-tiv\ *adj* [ME, fr. LL *substantivus* having substance, fr. L *substantia*] (14c) **1** : being a totally independent entity **2 a** : real rather than apparent : FIRM; *also* : PERMANENT, ENDURING **b** : belonging to the substance of a thing : ESSENTIAL **c** : expressing existence ⟨the ~ verb is the verb *to be*⟩ **d** : requiring or involving no mordant ⟨a ~ dyeing process⟩ **3 a** : having the nature or function of a grammatical substantive ⟨a ~ phrase⟩ **b** : relating to or having the character of a noun or pronominal term in logic **4** : considerable in amount or numbers : SUBSTANTIAL **5** : creating and defining rights and duties ⟨~ law⟩ — compare PROCEDURAL **6** : having substance : involving matters of major or practical importance to all concerned ⟨~ discussions among world leaders⟩ — **sub·stan·tive·ly** *adv* — **sub·stan·tive·ness** *n*

substantive due process *n* (1954) : DUE PROCESS 2

substantive right *n* (1939) : a right (as of life, liberty, property, or reputation) held to exist for its own sake and to constitute part of the normal legal order of society

sub·sta·tion \'səb-ˌstā-shən\ *n* (1881) : a subordinate or subsidiary station: as **a** : a branch post office **b** : a subsidiary station in which electric current is transformed **c** : a police station serving a particular area

sub·stit·u·ent \səb-'sti-chə-wənt, -'stich-wənt\ *n* [L *substituent-, substituens*, prp. of *substituere*] (ca. 1896) : an atom or group that replaces another atom or group in a molecule — **substituent** *adj*

sub·sti·tut·able \'səb-stə-ˌtü-tə-bəl, -ˌtyü-\ *adj* (1805) : capable of being substituted — **sub·sti·tut·abil·i·ty** \ˌsəb-stə-ˌtü-tə-'bi-lə-tē, -ˌtyü-\ *n*

¹sub·sti·tute \'səb-stə-ˌtüt, -ˌtyüt\ *n* [ME, fr. L *substitutus*, pp. of *substituere* to put in place of, fr. *sub-* + *statuere* to set up, place — more at STATUTE] (15c) : a person or thing that takes the place or function of another — **substitute** *adj*

²substitute *vb* **-tut·ed; -tut·ing** *vt* (1588) **1 a** : to put or use in the place of another **b** : to introduce (an atom or group) as a substituent; *also* : to alter (as a compound) by introduction of a substituent ⟨a *substituted* benzene ring⟩ **2** : to take the place of : REPLACE ~ *vi* : to serve as a substitute

sub·sti·tu·tion \ˌsəb-stə-'tü-shən, -'tyü-\ *n* [ME *substitucion*, fr. MF *substitution*, fr. LL *substitution-, substitutio*, fr. L *substituere*] (14c) **1 a** : the act, process, or result of substituting one thing for another **b** : replacement of one mathematical entity by another of equal value **2** : one that is substituted for another — **sub·sti·tu·tion·al** \-shnəl, -shə-nᵊl\ *adj* — **sub·sti·tu·tion·al·ly** *adv* — **sub·sti·tu·tion·ary** \-shə-ˌner-ē\ *adj*

substitution cipher *n* (1936) : a cipher in which the letters of the plaintext are systematically replaced by substitute letters — compare TRANSPOSITION CIPHER

sub·sti·tu·tive \'səb-stə-ˌtü-tiv, -ˌtyü-\ *adj* (1668) : serving or suitable as a substitute — **sub·sti·tu·tive·ly** *adv*

sub·strate \'səb-ˌstrāt\ *n* [ML *substratum*] (1807) **1** : SUBSTRATUM 2 : the base on which an organism lives ⟨the soil is the ~ of most weed plants⟩ **3** : a substance acted upon (as by an enzyme)

sub·stra·tum \'səb-ˌstrā-təm, -ˌstra-, -ˌsäb-ˌ\ *n, pl* **-stra·ta** \-tə\ [ML, fr. L, neut. of *substratus*, pp. of *substernere* to spread under, fr. *sub-* + *sternere* to spread — more at STREW] (1631) : an underlying support : FOUNDATION: as **a** : substance that is a permanent subject of qualities or phenomena **b** : the material of which something is made and from which it derives its special qualities **c** : a layer beneath the surface soil; *specif* : SUBSOIL **d** : SUBSTRATE 2

sub·struc·ture \'səb-ˌstrək-chər\ *n* (1726) : an underlying or supporting part of a structure — **sub·struc·tur·al** \-chə-rəl, -shrəl\ *adj*

sub·sume \səb-'süm\ *vt* **sub·sumed; sub·sum·ing** [NL *subsumere*, fr. L *sub-* + *sumere* to take up — more at CONSUME] (1825) : to include or place within something larger or more comprehensive : encompass as a subordinate or component element ⟨red, green, and yellow are *subsumed* under the term "color"⟩ — **sub·sum·able** \-'sü-mə-bəl\ *adj*

sub·sump·tion \səb-'səm(p)-shən\ *n* [NL *subsumption-, subsumptio*, fr. *subsumere*] (1651) : the act or process of subsuming

¹**sub·sur·face** \'səb-ˌsər-fəs\ n (1778) : earth material (as rock) near but not exposed at the surface of the ground

²**sub·sur·face** \ˌsəb-'sər-fəs\ adj (1875) : of, relating to, or being something located beneath a surface and esp. underground

sub·teen \'səb-ˌtēn\ n (1951) : a preadolescent child

sub·tem·per·ate \ˌsəb-'tem-p(ə-)rət\ adj (1852) : of or occurring in the colder parts of the temperate zones

sub·ten·an·cy \-'te-nən(t)-sē\ n (ca. 1861) : the state of being a subtenant

sub·ten·ant \-'te-nənt\ n (15c) : one who rents from a tenant

sub·tend \səb-'tend\ vt [L subtendere to stretch beneath, fr. sub- + tendere to stretch — more at THIN] (1570) 1 a : to be opposite to and extend from one side to the other of ⟨a hypotenuse ~s a right angle⟩ b : to fix the angular extent of with respect to a fixed point or object taken as the vertex ⟨the angle ~ed at the eye by an object of given width and a fixed distance away⟩ ⟨a central angle ~ed by an arc⟩ c : to determine the measure of by marking off the endpoints of ⟨a chord ~s an arc⟩ 2 a : to underlie so as to include b : to occupy an adjacent and usu. lower position to and often so as to embrace or enclose ⟨a bract that ~s a flower⟩

sub·ter·fuge \'səb-tər-ˌfyüj\ n [LL subterfugium, fr. L subterfugere to escape, evade, fr. subter- secretly (fr. subter underneath; akin to L sub under) + fugere to flee — more at UP, FUGITIVE] (1573) 1 : deception by artifice or stratagem in order to conceal, escape, or evade 2 : a deceptive device or stratagem **syn** see DECEPTION

sub·ter·mi·nal \ˌsəb-'tərm-nəl, -'tər-mə-n³l\ adj (1828) : situated or occurring near but not precisely at an end ⟨a ~ band of color on the tail feathers⟩

sub·ter·ra·nean \ˌsəb-tə-'rā-nē-ən, -nyən\ also **sub·ter·ra·neous** \-nē-əs, -nyəs\ adj [L subterraneus, fr. sub- + terra earth — more at THIRST] (1603) 1 : being, lying, or operating under the surface of the earth 2 : existing or working in secret : HIDDEN — **sub·ter·ra·nean·ly** also **sub·ter·ra·neous·ly** adv

sub·text \'səb-ˌtekst\ n (1950) : the implicit or metaphorical meaning (as of a literary text) — **sub·tex·tu·al** \ˌsəb-'teks-chə-wəl, -chəl\ adj

sub·thresh·old \ˌsəb-'thre-ˌshōld, -'thresh-ˌhōld\ adj (1942) : inadequate to produce a response ⟨~ dosage⟩ ⟨a ~ stimulus⟩

sub·tile \'sə-t³l, 'səb-t³l\ adj [ME subtil, fr. L subtilis] (14c) 1 : SUBTLE, ELUSIVE ⟨a ~ aroma⟩ 2 a : CUNNING, CRAFTY b : SAGACIOUS, DISCERNING — **sub·tile·ly** \'sət-lē, 'sə-t³l-(l)ē; 'səb-tə-lē\ adv — **sub·tile·ness** \'sə-t³l-nəs, 'səb-t³l-\ n

sub·til·i·sin \ˌsəb-'ti-lə-sən\ n [NL subtilis, specific epithet of Bacillus subtilis, species to which Bacillus amyloliquefaciens was once thought to belong] (1953) : an extracellular protease produced by a soil bacillus (Bacillus amyloliquefaciens)

sub·til·ize \'sə-t³l-ˌīz, 'səb-tə-ˌlīz\ vb **-ized**; **-iz·ing** vi (1592) : to act or think subtly ~ vt : to make subtile — **sub·til·i·za·tion** \ˌsə-t³l-ə-'zā-shən, ˌsəb-tə-lə-\ n

sub·til·ty \'sə-t³l-tē, 'səb-t³l-\ n, pl **-ties** (14c) : SUBTLETY

¹**sub·ti·tle** \'səb-ˌti-t³l\ n (1825) 1 : a secondary or explanatory title 2 : a printed statement or fragment of dialogue appearing on the screen between the scenes of a silent motion picture or appearing as a translation at the bottom of the screen during the scenes of a motion picture or television show in a foreign language

²**subtitle** vt (1891) : to give a subtitle to

sub·tle \'sə-t³l\ adj **sub·tler** \'sə-t³l-ər, 'sə-t³l-ər\; **sub·tlest** \'sət-ləst, 'sə-t³l-əst\ [ME sutil, sotil, fr. MF soutil, fr. L subtilis, lit., finely textured, fr. sub- + tela cloth on a loom; akin to L texere to weave — more at TECHNICAL] (14c) 1 a : DELICATE, ELUSIVE ⟨a ~ fragrance⟩ b : difficult to understand or perceive : OBSCURE ⟨~ differences in sound⟩ 2 a : PERCEPTIVE, REFINED ⟨a writer's sharp and ~ moral sense⟩ b : having or marked by keen insight and ability to penetrate deeply and thoroughly ⟨a ~ scholar⟩ 3 a : highly skillful : EXPERT ⟨a ~ craftsman⟩ b : cunningly made or contrived : INGENIOUS 4 : ARTFUL, CRAFTY ⟨a ~ rogue⟩ 5 : operating insidiously ⟨~ poisons⟩ — **sub·tle·ness** \'sə-t³l-nəs\ n — **subt·ly** \'sət-lē, 'sə-t³l-(l)ē\ adv

sub·tle·ty \'sə-t³l-tē\ n, pl **-ties** [ME subtilte, fr. MF sutilté, fr. L subtilitat-, subtilitas, fr. subtilis] (14c) 1 : the quality or state of being subtle 2 : something subtle

sub·ton·ic \ˌsəb-'tä-nik\ n [fr. its being a half tone below the upper tonic] (ca. 1854) : LEADING TONE

¹**sub·to·tal** \ˌsəb-ˌtō-t³l\ n (1906) : the sum of part of a series of figures

²**sub·to·tal** \ˌsəb-'tō-t³l\ adj (1908) : somewhat less than complete : nearly total ⟨~ thyroidectomy⟩ — **sub·to·tal·ly** adv

sub·tract \səb-'trakt\ vb [L subtractus, pp. of subtrahere to draw from beneath, withdraw, fr. sub- + trahere to draw] vt (1557) : to take away by or as if by deducting ⟨~ 5 from 9⟩ ⟨~ funds from the project⟩ ~ vi : to perform a subtraction — **sub·tract·er** n

sub·trac·tion \səb-'trak-shən\ n [ME subtraccion, fr. LL subtraction-, subtractio, fr. L subtrahere] (15c) : an act, operation, or instance of subtracting: as a : the withdrawing or withholding of a right to which an individual is entitled b : the operation of deducting one number from another

sub·trac·tive \-'trak-tiv\ adj (1690) 1 : tending to subtract 2 : constituting or involving subtraction

sub·tra·hend \'səb-trə-ˌhend\ n [L subtrahendus, gerundive of subtrahere] (1674) : a number that is to be subtracted from a minuend

sub·trop·i·cal \ˌsəb-'trä-pi-kəl\ also **sub·trop·ic** \-pik\ adj [ISV] (1842) : of, relating to, or being the regions bordering on the tropical zone ⟨~ environment⟩ ⟨~ grasses⟩

sub·trop·ics \-piks\ n pl (1886) : subtropical regions

su·bu·late \'sü-byə-lət, 'sə-, -ˌlāt\ adj [NL subulatus, fr. L subula awl, fr. suere to sew — more at SEW] (ca. 1760) : linear and tapering to a fine point ⟨a ~ leaf⟩

sub·um·brel·la \ˌsəb-(ˌ)əm-'bre-lə\ n (1878) : the concave undersurface of a jellyfish

sub·urb \'sə-ˌbərb\ n [ME, fr. MF, fr. L suburbium, fr. sub- near + urbs city — more at SUB-] (14c) 1 a : an outlying part of a city or town b : a smaller community adjacent to or within commuting distance of a city c pl : the residential area on the outskirts of a city or large town 2 pl : the near vicinity : ENVIRONS — **sub·ur·ban** \sə-'bər-bən\ adj or n — **sub·ur·ban·ite** \-bə-ˌnīt\ n

sub·ur·ban·ise Brit var of SUBURBANIZE

sub·ur·ban·ize \sə-'bər-bə-ˌnīz\ vt **-ized**; **-iz·ing** (1893) : to make suburban : give a suburban character to — **sub·ur·ban·i·za·tion** \-ˌbər-bə-nə-'zā-shən\ n

sub·ur·bia \sə-'bər-bē-ə\ n [NL, fr. E suburb] (1895) 1 : the suburbs of a city 2 : people who live in the suburbs 3 : suburban life

sub·ven·tion \səb-'ven(t)-shən\ n [ME subvencion, fr. OF & LL; OF subvención, fr. LL subvention-, subventio assistance, fr. L subvenire to come up, come to the rescue, fr. sub- up + venire to come — more at SUB-, COME] (15c) : the provision of assistance or financial support: as a : ENDOWMENT b : a subsidy from a government or foundation — **sub·ven·tion·ary** \-shə-ˌner-ē\ adj

sub·ver·sion \səb-'vər-zhən, -shən\ n [ME, fr. MF, fr. LL subversion-, subversio, fr. L subvertere] (14c) 1 : the act of subverting : the state of being subverted; esp : a systematic attempt to overthrow or undermine a government or political system by persons working secretly from within 2 obs : a cause of overthrow or destruction — **sub·ver·sion·ary** \-zhə-ˌner-ē, -shə-\ adj — **sub·ver·sive** \-'vər-siv, -ziv\ adj or n — **sub·ver·sive·ly** adv — **sub·ver·sive·ness** n

sub·vert \səb-'vərt\ vt [ME, fr. MF subvertir, fr. L subvertere, lit., to turn from beneath, fr. sub- + vertere to turn — more at WORTH] (14c) 1 : to overturn or overthrow from the foundation : RUIN 2 : to pervert or corrupt by an undermining of morals, allegiance, or faith — **sub·vert·er** n

sub·vi·ral \ˌsəb-'vī-rəl\ adj (1963) : relating to, being, or caused by a piece or a structural part (as a protein) of a virus ⟨~ infection⟩

sub·vo·cal \ˌsəb-'vō-kəl\ adj (1924) : characterized by the occurrence in the mind of words in speech order with or without inaudible articulation of the speech organs — **sub·vo·cal·ly** \-kə-lē\ adv

sub·vo·cal·i·za·tion \ˌsəb-ˌvō-kə-lə-'zā-shən\ n (1947) : the act or process of inaudibly articulating speech with the speech organs — **sub·vo·cal·ize** \ˌsəb-'vō-kə-ˌlīz\ vb

sub·way \'səb-ˌwā\ n (1825) : an underground way: as a : a passage under a street (as for pedestrians, power cables, or water or gas mains) b : a usu. electric underground railway c : UNDERPASS — **subway** vi

suc·ce·da·ne·um \ˌsək-sə-'dā-nē-əm\ n, pl **-ne·ums** or **-nea** \-nē-ə\ [NL, fr. L, neut. of succedaneus substituted, fr. succedere to follow after] (1641) : SUBSTITUTE — **suc·ce·da·ne·ous** \-nē-əs\ adj

suc·ce·dent \sək-'sē-d³nt\ adj [ME, fr. L succedent-, succedens, prp. of succedere] (15c) : coming next : SUCCEEDING, SUCCESSIVE

suc·ceed \sək-'sēd\ vb [ME succeden, fr. L succedere to go up, follow after, succeed, fr. sub- near + cedere to go — more at SUB-] vi (14c) 1 a : to come next after another in office or position or in possession of an estate; esp : to inherit sovereignty, rank, or title b : to follow after another in order 2 a : to turn out well b : to attain a desired object or end 3 obs : to pass to a person by inheritance ~ vt 1 : to follow in sequence and esp. immediately 2 : to come after as heir or successor **syn** see FOLLOW — **suc·ceed·er** n

suc·cès de scan·dale \sək-ˌsā-də-skän-'däl, (ˌ)sük-\ n [F, lit., success of scandal] (1896) : something (as a work of art) that wins popularity or notoriety because of its scandalous nature; also : the reception accorded such a piece

suc·cès d'es·time \-ˌdes-'tēm\ n [F, lit., success of esteem] (1859) : something (as a work of art) that wins critical respect but not popular success; also : the reception accorded such a piece

suc·cès fou \-'fü\ n [F, lit., mad success] (1878) : an extraordinary success

suc·cess \sək-'ses\ n [L successus, fr. succedere] (1537) 1 obs : OUTCOME, RESULT 2 a : degree or measure of succeeding b : favorable or desired outcome; also : the attainment of wealth, favor, or eminence 3 : one that succeeds

suc·cess·ful \-fəl\ adj (1588) 1 : resulting or terminating in success 2 : gaining or having gained success — **suc·cess·ful·ly** \-fə-lē\ adv — **suc·cess·ful·ness** n

suc·ces·sion \sək-'se-shən\ n [ME, fr. MF or L; MF, fr. L succession-, successio, fr. succedere] (14c) 1 a : the order in which or the conditions under which one person after another succeeds to a property, dignity, title, or throne b : the right of a person or line to succeed c : the line having such a right 2 a : the act or process of following in order : SEQUENCE b (1) : the act or process of one person's taking the place of another in the enjoyment of or liability for rights or duties or both (2) : the act or process of a person's becoming beneficially entitled to a property or property interest of a deceased person c : the continuance of corporate personality 3 : unidirectional change in the composition of an ecosystem as the available competing organisms and esp. the plants respond to and modify the environment 3 a : a number of persons or things that follow each other in sequence b : a group, type, or series that succeeds or displaces another — **suc·ces·sion·al** \-'sesh-nəl, -'se-shə-n³l\ adj — **suc·ces·sion·al·ly** adv

succession duty n (1853) chiefly Brit : INHERITANCE TAX

suc·ces·sive \sək-'se-siv\ adj (15c) 1 : following in order : following each other without interruption 2 : characterized by or produced in succession — **suc·ces·sive·ly** adv — **suc·ces·sive·ness** n

suc·ces·sor \sək-'se-sər\ n [ME successour, fr. OF, fr. L successor, fr. succedere] (14c) : one that follows; esp : one who succeeds to a throne, title, estate, or office

suc·ci·nate \'sək-sə-ˌnāt\ n (1790) : a salt or ester of succinic acid

succinate dehydrogenase n (1962) : an iron-containing flavoprotein enzyme that catalyzes often reversibly the dehydrogenation of succinic acid to fumaric acid in the Krebs cycle and that is widely distributed esp. in animal tissues, bacteria, and yeast — called also succinic dehydrogenase

suc·cinct \(ˌ)sək-'siŋ(k)t, sə-'siŋ(k)t\ adj [ME, fr. L succinctus, pp. of succingere to gird from below, tuck up, fr. sub- + cingere to gird — more at CINCTURE] (15c) 1 archaic a : being girded b : close-fitting 2 : marked by compact precise expression without wasted words **syn** see CONCISE — **suc·cinct·ly** \-'siŋ(k)t-lē, -'siŋ-klē\ adv — **suc·cinct·ness** \-'siŋt-nəs, -'siŋk-nəs\ n

---

\ə\ abut \ᵊ\ kitten, F table \ər\ further \a\ ash \ā\ ace \ä\ mop, mar \aù\ out \ch\ chin \e\ bet \ē\ easy \g\ go \i\ hit \ī\ ice \j\ job \ŋ\ sing \ō\ go \ò\ law \òi\ boy \th\ thin \ṯẖ\ the \ü\ loot \ù\ foot \y\ yet \zh\ vision \à, ḵ, ⁿ, œ, œ̄, ᴜᴇ, ᵒ\ see Guide to Pronunciation

suc·cin·ic acid \(.)sək-'si-nik-\ *n* [F *succinique*, fr. L *succinum* amber] (ca. 1790) : a crystalline dicarboxylic acid $C_4H_6O_4$ found widely in nature and active in energy-yielding metabolic reactions

suc·ci·nyl \'sək-sə-n²l, -.nil\ *n* [ISV] (ca. 1868) : either of two groups of succinic acid: **a** : a bivalent group $OCCH_2CH_2CO$ **b** : a univalent group $HOOCCH_2CH_2CO$

suc·ci·nyl·cho·line \.sək-sə-n²l-'kō-.lēn, -.nil-\ *n* (1950) : a basic compound that is used intravenously chiefly in the form of a hydrated chloride $C_{14}H_{30}Cl_2N_2O_4\cdot2H_2O$ as a muscle relaxant in surgery

¹suc·cor \'sə-kər\ *n* [ME *succur*, fr. earlier *sucurs*, taken as pl., fr. OF *sucors*, fr. ML *succursus*, fr. L *succurrere* to run up, run to help, fr. *sub*-up + *currere* to run — more at CAR] (13c) **1** : RELIEF; *also* : AID, HELP **2** : something that furnishes relief

²succor *vt* **suc·cored; suc·cor·ing** \'sə-k(ə-)riŋ\ (13c) : to go to the aid of : RELIEVE — **suc·cor·er** \'sə-kər-ər\ *n*

suc·co·ry \'sə-k(ə-)rē\ *n* [alter. of ME *cicoree*] (1533) : CHICORY

suc·co·tash \'sə-kə-.tash\ *n* [Narraganset *msíckquatash* boiled corn kernels] (1751) : lima or shell beans and green corn cooked together

suc·cour \'sə-kər\ *chiefly Brit var of* SUCCOR

suc·cu·ba \'sə-kyə-bə\ *n, pl* **-bae** \-.bē, -.bī\ [L, paramour] (1559) : SUCCUBUS

suc·cu·bus \-bəs\ *n, pl* **-bi** \-.bī, -.bē\ [ME, fr. ML, alter. of L *succuba* paramour, fr. *succubare* to lie under, fr. *sub*- + *cubare* to lie, recline] (14c) : a demon assuming female form to have sexual intercourse with men in their sleep — compare INCUBUS

suc·cu·lence \'sə-kyə-lən(t)s\ *n* (1787) **1** : the state of being succulent **2** : succulent feed ⟨wild game subsisting on ~⟩

¹suc·cu·lent \-lənt\ *adj* [L *suculentus*, fr. *sucus* juice, sap; perh. akin to L *sugere* to suck — more at SUCK] (1601) **1 a** : full of juice : JUICY **b** : moist and tasty : TOOTHSOME **c** *of a plant* : having fleshy tissues that conserve moisture **2** : rich in interest — **suc·cu·lent·ly** *adv*

²succulent *n* (1825) : a succulent plant (as a cactus)

suc·cumb \sə-'kəm\ *vi* [F & L; F *succomber*, fr. L *succumbere*, fr. *sub*- + *-cumbere* to lie down; akin to L *cubare* to lie] (1604) **1** : to yield to superior strength or force or overpowering appeal or desire **2** : to be brought to an end (as death) by the effect of destructive or disruptive forces *syn* see YIELD

¹such \'səch, 'sich\ *adj* [ME, fr. OE *swilc*; akin to OHG *sulih* such, OE *swā* so, *gelik* like — more at SO, LIKE] (bef. 12c) **1 a** : of a kind or character to be indicated or suggested ⟨a bag ~ as a doctor carries⟩ **b** : having a quality to a degree to be indicated ⟨his excitement was ~ that he shouted⟩ **2** : of the character, quality, or extent previously indicated or implied ⟨in the past few years many ~ women have shifted to full-time jobs⟩ **3** : of so extreme a degree or quality ⟨never heard ~ a hubbub⟩ **4** : of the same class, type, or sort ⟨other ~ clinics throughout the state⟩ **5** : not specified

²such *pron* (bef. 12c) **1** : such a person or thing **2** : someone or something stated, implied, or exemplified ⟨~ was the result⟩ **3** : someone or something similar : similar persons or things ⟨tin and glass and ~⟩ — **as such** : intrinsically considered : in itself ⟨as such the gift was worth little⟩

usage For reasons that are hard to understand, commentators on usage disapprove of *such* used as a pronoun. Dictionaries, however, recognize it as standard; all of the citations upon which our definitions of this word are based are clearly standard.

³such *adv* (bef. 12c) **1 a** : to such a degree : SO ⟨~ tall buildings⟩ ⟨~ a fine person⟩ **b** : VERY, ESPECIALLY ⟨hasn't been in ~ good spirits lately⟩ **2** : in such a way ⟨related ~ that each excludes the other⟩

¹such and such *adj* (13c) : not named or specified

²such and such *pron* (15c) : something not specified

¹such·like \'səch-.līk\ *adj* (15c) : of like kind : SIMILAR

²suchlike *pron* (15c) : SUCH 3

¹suck \'sək\ *vb* [ME *suken*, fr. OE *sūcan*; akin to OHG *sūgan* to suck, L *sugere*] *vt* (bef. 12c) **1 a** : to draw (as liquid) into the mouth through a suction force produced by movements of the lips and tongue ⟨~ed milk from his mother's breast⟩ **b** : to draw something from or consume by such movements ⟨~ an orange⟩ ⟨~ a lollipop⟩ **c** : to apply the mouth to in order to or as if to suck out a liquid ⟨~ed his burned finger⟩ **2 a** : to draw by or as if by suction ⟨when a receding wave ~s the sand from under your feet —Kenneth Brower⟩ ⟨inadvertently ~ed into the . . . intrigue —Martin Levin⟩ **b** : to take in and consume by or as if by suction ⟨a vacuum cleaner ~ing up dirt⟩ ⟨~ up a few beers⟩ ⟨opponents say that malls ~ the life out of downtown areas —Michael Knight⟩ ~ *vi* **1** : to draw something in by or as if by exerting a suction force; *esp* : to draw milk from a breast or udder with the mouth **2** : to make a sound or motion associated with or caused by suction ⟨his pipe ~ed wetly⟩ ⟨flanks ~ed in and out, the long nose resting on his paws —Virginia Woolf⟩ **3** : to act in an obsequious manner ⟨when they want votes . . . the candidates come ~ing around —W. G. Hardy⟩ ⟨~ed up to the boss⟩ **4** *slang* : to be objectionable or inadequate ⟨our lifestyle ~s —*Playboy*⟩ ⟨people who went said it ~ed —H. S. Thompson⟩

²suck *n* (13c) **1** : a sucking movement or force **2** : the act of sucking

¹suck·er \'sə-kər\ *n* (14c) **1 a** : one that sucks esp. a breast or udder : SUCKLING **b** : a device for creating or regulating suction (as a piston or valve in a pump) **c** : a pipe or tube through which something is drawn by suction **d** (1) : an organ in various animals for adhering or holding (2) : a mouth (as of a leech) adapted for sucking or adhering **2** : a shoot from the roots or lower part of the stem of a plant **3** : any of numerous chiefly No. American freshwater bony fishes (family Catostomidae) closely related to the carps but distinguished from them esp. by the structure of the mouth which usu. has thick soft lips : LOLLIPOP 1 **5 a** : a person easily cheated or deceived **b** : a person irresistibly attracted by something specified ⟨a ~ for ghost stories⟩ **c** — used as generalized term of reference ⟨see if you can get that ~ working again⟩

²sucker *vb* **suck·ered; suck·er·ing** \'sə-k(ə-)riŋ\ *vt* (ca. 1661) **1** : to remove suckers from ⟨~ tobacco⟩ **2** : HOODWINK ~ *vi* : to send out suckers

sucker punch *vt* (1964) : to punch (a person) suddenly without warning and often without apparent provocation — **sucker punch** *n*

suck in *vt* (1840) **1** : DUPE, HOODWINK **2** : to contract, flatten, and tighten (the abdomen) esp. by inhaling deeply

suck·ing *adj* (bef. 12c) : not yet weaned; *broadly* : very young

sucking louse *n* (ca. 1907) : any of an order (Anoplura) of wingless insects comprising the true lice with mouthparts adapted to sucking body fluids

suck·le \'sə-kəl\ *vb* **suck·led; suck·ling** \-k(ə-)liŋ\ [ME *suklen*, prob. back-formation fr. *suklyng*] *vt* (14c) **1 a** : to give milk to from the breast or udder ⟨a mother *suckling* her child⟩ **b** : to nurture as if by giving milk from the breast ⟨was *suckled* on pulp magazines⟩ **2** : to draw milk from the breast or udder of ⟨lambs *suckling* the ewes⟩ ~ *vi* : to draw milk from the breast or udder

suck·ling \'sə-kliŋ\ *n* [ME *suklyng*, fr. *suken* to suck] (13c) : a young unweaned animal

su·crase \'sü-.krās, -.krāz\ *n* [ISV, fr. F *sucre* sugar, fr. MF — more at SUGAR] (ca. 1900) : INVERTASE

su·cre \'sü-(.)krā\ *n* [Sp, fr. Antonio José de *Sucre*] (1886) — see MONEY table

su·crose \'sü-.krōs, -.krōz\ *n* [ISV, fr. F *sucre* sugar] (1857) : a sweet crystalline dextrorotatory disaccharide sugar $C_{12}H_{22}O_{11}$ that occurs naturally in most plants and is obtained commercially esp. from sugarcane or sugar beets

¹suc·tion \'sək-shən\ *n* [LL *suction-, suctio*, fr. L *sugere* to suck — more at SUCK] (1626) **1** : the act or process of sucking **2 a** : the act or process of exerting a force upon a solid, liquid, or gaseous body by reason of reduced air pressure over part of its surface **b** : force so exerted **3** : a device (as a pipe or fitting) used in a machine that operates by suction — **suc·tion·al** \-shə-n²l, -shnəl\ *adj*

²suction *vt* (1954) : to remove (as from a body cavity or passage) by suction

suction cup *n* (1942) : a cup-shaped device in which a partial vacuum can be produced when applied to a surface

suction pump *n* (1825) : a common pump in which the liquid to be raised is pushed by atmospheric pressure into the partial vacuum under a retreating valved piston on the upstroke and reflux is prevented by a check valve in the pipe

suction stop *n* (1887) : a voice stop in the formation of which air behind the articulation is rarefied with consequent inrush of air when articulation is broken

suc·to·ri·al \.sək-'tōr-ē-əl, -'tor-\ *adj* [NL *suctorius*, fr. L *sugere*] (1833) : adapted for sucking; *esp* : serving to draw up fluid or to adhere by suction ⟨~ mouths⟩

suc·to·ri·an \-ē-ən\ *n* [NL *Suctoria*, fr. neut. pl. of *suctorius* suctorial] (ca. 1842) : any of a class or subclass (Suctoria) of complex protozoans which are ciliated only early in development and in which the mature form is fixed to the substrate, lacks locomotor organelles or a mouth, and obtains food through specialized suctorial tentacles

Su·dan grass \sü-'dan-, -'dän-\ *n* [the *Sudan*, region in Africa] (1911) : a vigorous tall-growing annual sorghum grass (*Sorghum bicolor sudanese*) widely grown for hay and fodder

Su·dan·ic \sü-'da-nik\ *n* [the *Sudan* region] (1912) : a group of languages neither Bantu nor Afro-Asiatic spoken in central and western Africa that were formerly considered a residual category and are now divided among the Niger-Congo and other families — **Sudanic** *adj*

su·da·to·ri·um \.sü-də-'tōr-ē-əm, -'tor-\ *n* [L, fr. *sudare* to sweat — more at SWEAT] (ca. 1757) : a sweat room in a bath

su·da·to·ry \'sü-də-.tōr-ē, -.tor-\ *n, pl* **-ries** (1615) : SUDATORIUM

sudd \'səd\ *n* [Ar, lit., obstruction] (1874) : floating vegetable matter that forms obstructive masses esp. in the upper White Nile

¹sud·den \'sə-d²n\ *adj* [ME *sodain*, fr. MF, fr. L *subitaneus*, fr. *subitus* sudden, fr. pp. of *subire* to come up, fr. *sub*-up + *ire* to go — more at SUB-, ISSUE] (14c) **1 a** : happening or coming unexpectedly ⟨a ~ shower⟩ **b** : changing angle or character all at once **2** : marked by or manifesting abruptness or haste **3** : made or brought about in a short time : PROMPT *syn* see PRECIPITATE — **sud·den·ly** *adv* — **sud·den·ness** \'sə-d²n-(n)əs\ *n*

²sudden *n* (1559) *obs* : an unexpected occurrence : EMERGENCY — **all of a sudden** *or* **on a sudden** : sooner than was expected : at once

sudden death *n* (14c) **1** : unexpected death that is instantaneous or occurs within minutes from any cause other than violence ⟨*sudden death* following coronary occlusion⟩ **2** : extra play to break a tie in a sports contest in which the first to go ahead wins

sudden infant death syndrome *n* (1970) : death of an apparently healthy infant usu. before one year of age that is of unknown cause and occurs esp. during sleep — called also *crib death*; *abbr. SIDS*

su·do·rif·er·ous \.sü-də-'ri-f(ə-)rəs\ *adj* [LL *sudorifer*, fr. L *sudor* sweat (fr. *sudare* to sweat) + *-ifer* -iferous — more at SWEAT] (1597) : producing or conveying sweat ⟨~ glands⟩ ⟨a ~ duct⟩

su·do·rif·ic \-'ri-fik\ *adj* [NL *sudorificus*, fr. L *sudor*] (1626) : causing or inducing sweat : DIAPHORETIC ⟨~ herbs⟩ — **sudorific** *n*

Su·dra \'sü-drə, 'shü-\ *n* [Skt *śūdra*] (1630) : a Hindu of a lower caste traditionally assigned to menial occupations — **Sudra** *adj*

¹suds \'sədz\ *n pl but sing or pl in constr* [prob. fr. MD *sudse* marsh; akin to OE *sēothan* to seethe — more at SEETHE] (1581) **1** : water impregnated with soap or a synthetic detergent compound and worked up into froth; *also* : the lather or froth on such water **2 a** : FOAM, FROTH **b** : BEER — **suds·less** \-ləs\ *adj*

²suds *vt* (1834) : to wash in suds ~ *vi* : to form suds

suds·er \'səd-zər\ *n* (1967) : SOAP OPERA

sud·sy \'səd-zē\ *adj* **suds·i·er; -est** (1866) **1** : full of suds : FROTHY, FOAMY **2** : SOAPY 4

sue \'sü\ *vb* **sued; su·ing** [ME, fr. MF *suivre*, fr. (assumed) VL *sequere*, fr. L *sequi* to follow, come or go after; akin to Gk *hepesthai* to follow, Skt *sacate* he accompanies] *vt* (14c) **1** *obs* : to make petition to or for **2** *archaic* : to pay court or suit to : WOO **3 a** : to seek justice or right from (a person) by legal process; *specif* : to bring an action against **b** : to proceed with and follow up (a legal action) to proper termination ~ *vi* **1** : to make a request or application : PLEAD — usu. used with *for* or *to* **2** : to pay court : WOO **3** : to take legal proceedings in court — **su·er** *n*

¹suede *or* **suède** \'swād\ *n* [F *gants de Suède* Swedish gloves] (1884) **1** : leather with a napped surface **2** : a fabric finished with a nap to simulate suede

²suede *vb* **sued·ed; sued·ing** *vt* (1921) : to give a suede finish or nap to (a fabric or leather) ~ *vi* : to give cloth or leather a suede finish

su·et \'sü-ət\ n [ME sewet, fr. (assumed) AF, dim. of AF sue, fr. L sebum tallow] (14c) : the hard fat about the kidneys and loins in beef and mutton that yields tallow

suf·fer \'sə-fər\ vb **suf·fered**; **suf·fer·ing** \-f(ə-)riŋ\ [ME suffren, fr. OF souffrir, fr. (assumed) VL sufferire, fr. L sufferre, fr. sub- up + ferre to bear — more at SUB-, BEAR] vt (13c) **1 a :** to submit to or be forced to endure ⟨~ martyrdom⟩ **b :** to feel keenly : labor under ⟨~ thirst⟩ **2 :** UNDERGO, EXPERIENCE **3 :** to put up with esp. as inevitable or unavoidable **4 :** to allow esp. by reason of indifference ⟨the eagle ~s little birds to sing —Shak.⟩ ~ vi **1 :** to endure death, pain, or distress **2 :** to sustain loss or damage **3 :** to be subject to disability or handicap *syn* see BEAR — **suf·fer·able** \'sə-f(ə-)rə-bəl\ adj — **suf·fer·able·ness** n — **suf·fer·ably** \-blē\ adv — **suf·fer·er** \'sə-fər-ər\ n

suf·fer·ance \'sə-f(ə-)rən(t)s\ n (14c) **1 :** patient endurance : LONGSUFFERING **2 :** PAIN, MISERY **3 :** consent or sanction implied by a lack of interference or failure to enforce a prohibition **4 :** power or ability to withstand : ENDURANCE

suffering n (14c) **1 :** the state or experience of one that suffers **2 :** PAIN *syn* see DISTRESS

suf·fice \sə-'fīs also -'fīz\ vb **suf·ficed**; **suf·fic·ing** [ME, fr. MF suffis-, stem of suffire, fr. L sufficere to provide, be adequate, fr. sub- + facere to make, do — more at DO] vi (14c) **1 :** to meet or satisfy a need : be sufficient ⟨a brief note will ~⟩ — often used with an impersonal it ⟨~ it to say that they are dedicated, serious personalities —Cheryl Aldridge⟩ **2 :** to be competent or capable ~ vt : to be enough for — **suf·fic·er** n

suf·fi·cien·cy \sə-'fi-shən(t)-sē\ n (15c) **1 :** sufficient means to meet one's needs : COMPETENCY; also : a modest but adequate scale of living **2 :** the quality or state of being sufficient : ADEQUACY

suf·fi·cient \sə-'fi-shənt\ adj [ME, fr. L sufficient-, sufficiens, fr. prp. of sufficere] (14c) **1 a :** enough to meet the needs of a situation or a proposed end ⟨~ provisions for a month⟩ **b :** being a sufficient condition **2** archaic : QUALIFIED, COMPETENT — **suf·fi·cient·ly** adv
syn SUFFICIENT, ENOUGH, ADEQUATE, COMPETENT mean being what is necessary or desirable. SUFFICIENT suggests a close meeting of a need ⟨sufficient savings⟩. ENOUGH is less exact in suggestion than SUFFICIENT ⟨do you have enough food?⟩. ADEQUATE may imply barely meeting a requirement ⟨the service was adequate⟩. COMPETENT suggests measuring up to all requirements without question or being adequately adapted to an end ⟨had no competent notion of what was going on⟩.

sufficient condition n (1914) **1 :** a proposition whose truth assures the truth of another proposition **2 :** a state of affairs whose existence assures the existence of another state of affairs

¹suf·fix \'sə-fiks\ n [NL suffixum, fr. L, neut. of suffixus, pp. of suffigere to fasten underneath, fr. sub- + figere to fasten — more at FIX] (1778) : an affix occurring at the end of a word, base, or phrase — compare PREFIX — **suf·fix·al** \'sə-fik-səl\, (,)sə-'fik-səl\ adj

²suf·fix \sə-fiks, (,)sə-'fiks\ vt (1778) : to attach as a suffix — **suf·fix·a·tion** \,sə-fik-'sā-shən\ n

suf·fo·cate \'sə-fə-,kāt\ vb **-cat·ed**; **-cat·ing** [ME, fr. L suffocatus, pp. of suffocare to choke, stifle, fr. sub- + fauces throat] vt (15c) **1 a :** to stop the respiration of (as by strangling or asphyxiation) **b :** to deprive of oxygen **c :** to make uncomfortable by want of cool fresh air **2 :** to impede or stop the development of ~ vi **1 :** to become suffocated: **a :** to die from being unable to breathe **b :** to be uncomfortable through lack of air **2 :** to become checked in development — **suf·fo·cat·ing·ly** \-,kā-tiŋ-lē\ adv — **suf·fo·ca·tion** \,sə-fə-'kā-shən\ n — **suf·fo·ca·tive** \'sə-fə-,kā-tiv\ adj

Suf·folk \'sə-fək, -,fōk\ n [Suffolk, England] (1831) **1 :** any of a breed of chestnut-colored draft horses of English origin — called also Suffolk punch **2 :** any of a breed of large hornless black-faced sheep of English origin raised chiefly for mutton

¹suf·fra·gan \'sə-fri-gən, -jən\ n [ME, fr. MF, fr. ML suffraganeus, fr. suffragium support, prayer] (14c) **1 :** a diocesan bishop (as in the Roman Catholic Church and the Church of England) subordinate to a metropolitan **2 :** an Anglican or Episcopal bishop assisting a diocesan bishop and not having the right of succession

²suffragan adj (15c) **1 :** of or being a suffragan **2 :** subordinate to a metropolitan or archiepiscopal see

suf·frage \'sə-frij, sometimes -fə-rij\ n [in sense 1, fr. ME, fr. MF, fr. ML suffragium, fr. L, vote, political support; in other senses, fr. L suffragari to support with one's vote; in other senses, fr. L suffragium] (14c) **1 :** a short intercessory prayer usu. in a series **2 :** a vote given in deciding a controverted question or in the choice of a person for an office or trust **3 :** the right of voting : FRANCHISE; also : the exercise of such right

suf·frag·ette \,sə-fri-'jet\ n (1906) : a woman who advocates suffrage for women

suf·frag·ist \'sə-fri-jist\ n (1822) : one who advocates extension of suffrage esp. to women

suf·fuse \sə-'fyüz\ vt **suf·fused**; **suf·fus·ing** [L suffusus, pp. of suffundere, lit., to pour beneath, fr. sub- + fundere to pour — more at FOUND] (1590) : to spread over or through in the manner of fluid or light : FLUSH, FILL *syn* see INFUSE — **suf·fu·sion** \-'fyü-zhən\ n — **suf·fu·sive** \-'fyü-siv, -ziv\ adj

Su·fi \'sü-(,)fē\ n [Ar ṣūfiy, perh. fr. ṣūf wool] (1653) : a Muslim mystic — **Sufi** adj — **Su·fic** \-fik\ adj — **Su·fism** \-,fi-zəm\ n

¹sug·ar \'shu̇-gər\ n [ME sugre, sucre, fr. MF sucre, fr. ML zuccarum, fr. Olt zucchero, fr. Ar sukkar, fr. Per shakar, fr. Skt śarkarā; akin to Skt śarkarā pebble — more at CROCODILE] (14c) **1 a :** a sweet crystallizable material that consists wholly or essentially of sucrose, is colorless or white when pure tending to brown when less refined, is obtained commercially from sugarcane or sugar beet and less extensively from sorghum, maples, and palms, and is important as a source of dietary carbohydrate and as a sweetener and preservative of other foods **b :** any of various water-soluble compounds that vary widely in sweetness and include the oligosaccharides (as sucrose) **2 :** a unit (as a spoonful, cube, or lump) of sugar **3 :** a sugar bowl — **sug·ar·less** \-ləs\ adj

²sugar vb **sug·ared**; **sug·ar·ing** \'shu̇-g(ə-)riŋ\ vt (15c) **1 :** to make palatable or attractive : SWEETEN **2 :** to sprinkle or mix with sugar ~ vi **1 :** to form or be converted into sugar **2 :** to become granular : GRANULATE **3 :** to make maple syrup or maple sugar

sugar apple n (1738) : a tropical American tree (Annona squamosa) of the custard apple family; also : its edible sweet pulpy fruit with thick green scaly rind and shining black seeds

sugar beet n (1817) : a white-rooted beet grown for the sugar in its roots

sug·ar·ber·ry \'shu̇-gər-,ber-ē\ n (ca. 1818) : any of several hackberries (esp. Celtis laevigata and C. occidentalis) with sweet edible fruits

sugar bush n (1823) : a woods in which sugar maples predominate

sug·ar·cane \'shu̇-gər-,kān\ n (15c) : a stout tall perennial grass (Saccharum officinarum) that has a large terminal panicle and is widely grown in warm regions as a source of sugar

sugarcane

sug·ar·coat \'shu̇-gər-,kōt\ vt [back-formation fr. sugarcoated] (1870) **1 :** to coat with sugar **2 :** to make superficially attractive or palatable ⟨tried to ~ an unpleasant truth⟩

sugar daddy n (1926) **1 :** a well-to-do usu. older man who supports or spends lavishly on a mistress or girlfriend **2 :** a generous benefactor of a cause

sug·ar·house \'shu̇-gər-,hau̇s\ n (1600) : a building where sugar is made or refined; specif : one where maple sap is boiled and maple syrup and maple sugar are made

sugaring off n (1836) **1 :** the act or process of converting maple syrup into sugar **2 :** a party held at the time of sugaring off

sug·ar·loaf \'shu̇-gər-,lōf\ n (15c) **1 :** refined sugar molded into a cone **2 :** a hill or mountain shaped like a sugarloaf — **sugar–loaf** adj

sugar maple n (1731) **1 :** a maple (Acer saccharum) of eastern No. America with 3- to 5-lobed leaves, hard close-grained wood much used for cabinetwork, and sap that is the chief source of maple syrup and maple sugar — called also rock maple, hard maple **2 :** any of several maples (esp. Acer nigrum and A. grandidentatum) sometimes considered subspecies of the sugar maple

sugar off vi (1836) **1 :** to complete the process of boiling down the syrup in making maple sugar until it is thick enough to crystallize **2 :** to approach or reach the state of granulation

sugar orchard n (1833) chiefly NewEng : SUGAR BUSH

sugar pea n (1707) : SNOW PEA

sugar pine n (1846) : a very tall pine (Pinus lambertiana) found from Oregon to Baja California and having needles in clusters of five, cones up to 18 inches (46 cm) long, and soft reddish brown wood; also : its wood

sug·ar·plum \'shu̇-gər-,pləm\ n (ca. 1668) : a small candy in the shape of a ball or disk : SWEETMEAT

sugar snap pea n (1979) : SNAP PEA

sug·ary \'shu̇-g(ə-)rē\ adj (1591) **1 a :** exaggeratedly sweet : HONEYED ⟨his ~ deprecating voice —D. H. Lawrence⟩ **b :** cloyingly sweet : SENTIMENTAL **2 :** containing, resembling, or tasting of sugar

sug·gest \səg-'jest, sə-'jest\ vt [L suggestus, pp. of suggerere to pile up, furnish, suggest, fr. sub- + gerere to carry] (1526) **1 a** obs : to seek to influence : SEDUCE **b :** to call forth : EVOKE **c :** to mention or imply as a possibility ⟨~ed that he might bring his family⟩ **d :** to propose as desirable or fitting ⟨~ a stroll⟩ **e :** to offer for consideration or as a hypothesis ⟨~ a solution to a problem⟩ **2 :** to call to mind by thought or association ⟨the explosion . . . ~ed sabotage —F. L. Paxson⟩ **b :** to serve as a motive or inspiration for ⟨a play ~ed by a historic incident⟩ — **sug·gest·er** n
syn SUGGEST, IMPLY, HINT, INTIMATE, INSINUATE mean to convey an idea indirectly. SUGGEST may stress putting into the mind by association of ideas, awakening of a desire, or initiating a train of thought ⟨a film title that suggests its subject matter⟩. IMPLY is close to SUGGEST but may indicate a more definite or logical relation of the unexpressed idea to the expressed ⟨measures implying that bankruptcy was imminent⟩. HINT implies the use of slight or remote suggestion with a minimum of overt statement ⟨hinted that she might have a job lined up⟩. INTIMATE stresses delicacy of suggestion without connoting any lack of candor ⟨intimates that there is more to the situation than meets the eye⟩. INSINUATE applies to the conveying of a usually unpleasant idea in a sly underhanded manner ⟨insinuated that there were shady dealings⟩.

sug·gest·ible \səg-'jes-tə-bəl, sə-'jes-\ adj (1890) : easily influenced by suggestion — **sug·gest·ibil·i·ty** \-,jes-tə-'bi-lə-tē\ n

sug·ges·tion \səg-'jes-chən, sə-'jes-, -'jesh-\ n (14c) **1 a :** the act or process of suggesting **b :** something suggested **2 a :** the process by which a physical or mental state is influenced by a thought or idea ⟨the power of ~⟩ **b :** the process by which one thought leads to another esp. through association of ideas **3 :** a slight indication : TRACE ⟨a ~ of a smile⟩

sug·ges·tive \səg-'jes-tiv, sə-'jes-\ adj (1631) **1 a :** giving a suggestion : INDICATIVE ⟨~ of a past era⟩ **b :** full of suggestions : stimulating thought ⟨provided a ~ . . . commentary on the era —Lloyd Morris⟩ **c :** stirring mental associations : EVOCATIVE **2 :** suggesting or tending to suggest something improper or indecent : RISQUÉ — **sug·ges·tive·ly** adv — **sug·ges·tive·ness** n

sui·cid·al \,sü-ə-'sī-dᵊl\ adj (1777) **1 a :** dangerous esp. to life **b :** destructive to one's own interests **2 :** relating to or of the nature of suicide **3 :** marked by an impulse to commit suicide — **sui·cid·al·ly** adv

¹sui·cide \'sü-ə-,sīd\ n [L sui (gen.) of oneself + E -cide; akin to OE & OHG sīn his, L suus one's own, sed, se without, Skt sva oneself, one's own] (1643) **1 a :** the act or an instance of taking one's own life voluntarily and intentionally esp. by a person of years of discretion and of sound mind **b :** ruin of one's own interests ⟨political ~⟩ **2 :** one that commits or attempts suicide

²suicide vb **sui·cid·ed**; **sui·cid·ing** vi (1841) : to commit suicide ~ vt : to put (oneself) to death

---

\ə\ abut \ᵊ\ kitten, F table \ər\ further \a\ ash \ā\ ace \ä\ mop, mar \au̇\ out \ch\ chin \e\ bet \ē\ easy \g\ go \i\ hit \ī\ ice \j\ job \ŋ\ sing \ō\ go \ȯ\ law \ȯi\ boy \th\ thin \t̲h̲\ the \ü\ loot \u̇\ foot \y\ yet \zh\ vision \à, k̲, ⁿ, œ, œ̄, ue, ūe, ᵞ\ see Guide to Pronunciation

suicide squad *n* [fr. the fact that kickoffs are more dangerous than other plays] (ca. 1966) : a special squad used on kickoffs in football

suicide squeeze *n* (1955) : a squeeze play in which the runner runs all out at the pitch without knowing whether the batter will contact the ball

sui ge·ner·is \ˌsü-ˌī-ˈje-nə-rəs; ˌsü-ē-ˈje-, -ˈge-\ *adj* [L, of its own kind] (1787) : constituting a class alone : UNIQUE, PECULIAR

sui ju·ris \ˌsü-ˌī-ˈjùr-əs, ˌsü-ē-ˈyùr-\ *adj* [L, of one's own right] (1675) : having full legal rights or capacity

su·int \ˈsü-ənt, ˈswint\ *n* [F, fr. MF, fr. *suer* to sweat, fr. L *sudare* — more at SWEAT] (1791) : dried perspiration of sheep deposited in the wool and rich in potassium salts

¹suit \ˈsüt\ *n* [ME *siute* act of following, retinue, sequence, set, fr. OF, act of following, retinue, fr. (assumed) VL *sequita*, fr. fem. of *sequitus*, pp. of *sequere* to follow — more at SUE] (14c) **1** *archaic* : SUITE 1 **2 a** : recourse or appeal to a feudal superior for justice or redress **b** : an action or process in a court for the recovery of a right or claim **3** : an act or instance of suing or seeking by entreaty : APPEAL; *specif* : COURTSHIP **4** : SUITE 2 — used chiefly of armor, sails, and counters in games **5** : a set of garments: as **a** : an outer costume of two or more pieces **b** : a costume to be worn for a special purpose or under particular conditions ⟨gym ~⟩ **6 a** : all the playing cards in a pack bearing the same symbol **b** : all the dominoes bearing the same number **c** : all the cards or counters in a particular suit held by one player ⟨a 5-card ~⟩ **d** : the suit led ⟨follow ~⟩ **7** *slang* : a business executive — usu. used in pl.

²suit *vt* (14c) **1 a** : to be becoming to **b** : to be proper for : BEFIT **2** : to outfit with clothes **3** : ACCOMMODATE, ADAPT ⟨~ the action to the word⟩ **4** : to meet the needs or desires of : PLEASE ⟨~s me fine⟩ — *vi* **1** : to be in accordance : AGREE ⟨the position ~s with your abilities⟩ **2** : to be appropriate or satisfactory ⟨these prices don't ~⟩ **3** : to put on specially required clothing (as a uniform or protective garb) — usu. used with *up*

suit·able \ˈsü-tə-bəl\ *adj* (1582) **1** *obs* : SIMILAR, MATCHING **2 a** : adapted to a use or purpose **b** : satisfying propriety : PROPER **c** : ABLE, QUALIFIED **syn** see FIT — **suit·abil·i·ty** \ˌsü-tə-ˈbi-lə-tē\ *n* — **suit·able·ness** *n* — **suit·ably** \-blē\ *adv*

suit·case \ˈsüt-ˌkās\ *n* (1897) : a bag or case carried by hand and designed to hold a traveler's clothing and personal articles

suite \ˈswēt, *2d is also* ˈsüt\ *n* [F, alter. of OF *siute* — more at SUIT] (1673) **1** : RETINUE; *esp* : the personal staff accompanying a ruler, diplomat, or dignitary on official business **2** : a group of things forming a unit or constituting a collection : SET: as **a** : a group of rooms occupied as a unit **b** (1) : a 17th and 18th century instrumental musical form consisting of a series of dances in the same or related keys (2) : a modern instrumental composition in several movements of different character (3) : a long orchestral concert arrangement in suite form of material drawn from a longer work (as a ballet) **c** : a collection of minerals or rocks having some characteristic in common (as type or origin) **d** : a set of matched furniture

suit·er \ˈsü-tər\ *n* (1952) : a suitcase for holding a specified number of suits — usu. used in combination ⟨a two-*suiter*⟩

suit·ing \ˈsü-tiŋ\ *n* (1883) **1** : fabric for suits **2** : a suit of clothes

suit·or \ˈsü-tər\ *n* [ME, follower, pleader, fr. AF, fr. L *secutor* follower, fr. *sequi* to follow — more at SUE] (15c) **1** : one that petitions or entreats **2** : a party to a suit at law **3** : one who courts a woman or seeks to marry her **4** : one who seeks to take over a business

su·ki·ya·ki \ˌskē-ˈyä-kē; ˌsü-kē-ˈ, ˌsù-kē-ˈ, ˌsü-\ *n* [Jp, fr. *suki-* slice + *yaki* broil] (1920) : a dish consisting of thin slices of meat, bean curd, and vegetables cooked in soy sauce and sugar

suk·kah \ˈsù-kə\ *n* [Heb *sukkāh*] (1875) : a booth or shelter with a roof of branches and leaves that is used esp. for meals during the Sukkoth

Suk·koth *or* **Suk·kot** \ˈsù-kəs, -ˌkōt, -ˌkōth, -ˌkōs\ *n* [Heb *sukkōth,* pl. of *sukkāh*] (1882) : a Jewish harvest festival beginning on the 15th of Tishri and commemorating the temporary shelters used by the Jews during their wandering in the wilderness

sul·cate \ˈsəl-ˌkāt\ *adj* [L *sulcatus,* pp. of *sulcare* to furrow, fr. *sulcus*] (1760) : scored with usu. longitudinal furrows ⟨a ~ seedpod⟩

sul·cus \ˈsəl-kəs\ *n, pl* **sul·ci** \-ˌkī, -ˌkē, -ˌsī\ [L; akin to OE *sulh* plow, Gk *holkos* furrow, *helkein* to pull] (1662) : FURROW, GROOVE; *esp* : a shallow furrow on the surface of the brain separating adjacent convolutions

sulf- *or* **sulfo-** *comb form* [F *sulf-, sulfo-,* fr. L *sulfur*] : sulfur : containing sulfur ⟨*sulfide*⟩

sul·fa \ˈsəl-fə\ *adj* [short for *sulfanilamide*] (1940) **1** : related chemically to sulfanilamide **2** : of, relating to, or containing sulfa drugs

sul·fa·di·a·zine \ˌsəl-fə-ˈdī-ə-ˌzēn\ *n* [*sulfa* + *diazine* (C₄H₄N₂)] (1940) : a sulfa drug C₁₀H₁₀N₄O₂S that is used esp. in the treatment of meningitis, pneumonia, and intestinal infections

sulfa drug *n* (1940) : any of various synthetic organic bacteria-inhibiting drugs that are sulfonamides closely related chemically to sulfanilamide

sul·fa·nil·amide \ˌsəl-fə-ˈni-lə-ˌmīd, -məd\ *n* [*sulfanilic* + *amide*] (1937) : a crystalline sulfonamide C₆H₈N₂O₂S that is the amide of sulfanilic acid and the parent compound of most of the sulfa drugs

sul·fa·nil·ic acid \ˌsəl-fə-ˈni-lik-\ *n* [ISV *sulf-* + *aniline* + *-ic*] (1856) : a crystalline acid C₆H₇NO₃S obtained from aniline

sul·fa·tase \ˈsəl-fə-ˌtās, -ˌtāz\ *n* [¹*sulfate*] (1924) : any of various enzymes that accelerate the hydrolysis of sulfuric esters and that are found in animal tissues and in microorganisms

¹sul·fate \ˈsəl-ˌfāt\ *n* [F, fr. L *sulfur*] (1790) **1** : a salt or ester of sulfuric acid **2** : a bivalent group or anion SO₄ characteristic of sulfuric acid and the sulfates

²sulfate *vt* **sul·fat·ed; sul·fat·ing** (1802) : to treat or combine with sulfuric acid or a sulfate

sulf·hy·dryl \ˌsəlf-ˈ(h)ī-drəl\ *n* [ISV] (ca. 1901) : THIOL 2 — used chiefly in molecular biology

sul·fide \ˈsəl-ˌfīd\ *n* (1836) **1** : any of various organic compounds characterized by a sulfur atom attached to two carbon atoms **2** : a binary compound (as CuS) of sulfur usu. with a more electropositive element or group : a salt of hydrogen sulfide

sul·fin·py·ra·zone \ˌsəl-fən-ˈpī-rə-ˌzōn\ *n* [*sulfinic* acid (RSO₂H) + *pyr-* + *azole* + *-one*] (1958) : a uricosuric drug C₂₃H₂₀N₂O₃S used in long-term treatment of chronic gout

sul·fite \ˈsəl-ˌfīt\ *n* [F *sulfite,* alter. of *sulfate*] (1790) : a salt or ester of sulfurous acid — **sul·fit·ic** \ˌsəl-ˈfi-tik\ *adj*

sulfon- *comb form* [ISV *sulfonic*] : sulfonic ⟨*sulfo*namide⟩

sul·fon·amide \ˌsəl-ˈfä-nə-ˌmīd, -məd; -ˈfō-nə-ˌmīd\ *n* (1881) : any of various amides (as sulfanilamide) of a sulfonic acid; *also* : SULFA DRUG

¹sul·fo·nate \ˈsəl-fə-ˌnāt\ *n* (1876) : a salt or ester of a sulfonic acid

²sulfonate *vt* **-nat·ed; -nat·ing** (1882) : to introduce the SO₃H group into; *broadly* : to treat (an organic substance) with sulfuric acid — **sul·fo·na·tion** \ˌsəl-fə-ˈnā-shən\ *n*

sul·fone \ˈsəl-ˌfōn\ *n* (1872) : any of various compounds containing the sulfonyl group with its sulfur atom having two bonds with carbon

sul·fon·ic \ˌsəl-ˈfä-nik, -ˈfō-\ *adj* (ca. 1891) : of, relating to, being, or derived from the univalent acid group SO₃H

sulfonic acid *n* (1873) : any of numerous acids that contain the SO₃H group and may be derived from sulfuric acid by replacement of a hydroxyl group by either an inorganic anion or a univalent organic group

sul·fo·ni·um \ˌsəl-ˈfō-nē-əm\ *n* [NL, fr. *sulf-* + *-onium*] (1885) : a univalent group or cation SH₃ or derivative SR₃

sul·fo·nyl \ˈsəl-fə-ˌnil\ *n* (1920) : the bivalent group SO₂

sul·fo·nyl·urea \ˌsəl-fə-ˌnil-ˈyùr-ē-ə\ *n* [NL, fr. ISV *sulfonyl* + NL *urea*] (1956) : any of several hypoglycemic compounds related to the sulfonamides and used in the oral treatment of diabetes

sulf·ox·ide \ˌsəl-ˈfäk-ˌsīd\ *n* [ISV] (ca. 1894) : any of a class of organic compounds characterized by an SO group with its sulfur atom having two bonds with carbon

sul·fur *also* **sul·phur** \ˈsəl-fər\ *n* [ME *sulphur* brimstone, fr. L *sulpur, sulphur, sulfur*] (14c) **1** : a nonmetallic element that occurs either free or combined esp. in sulfides and sulfates, is a constituent of proteins, exists in several allotropic forms including yellow orthorhombic crystals, resembles oxygen chemically but is less active and more acidic, and is used esp. in the chemical and paper industries, in rubber vulcanization, and in medicine for treating skin diseases — see ELEMENT table **2** : something (as scathing language) that suggests sulfur — **sul·fury** *or* **sul·phury** \-ē\ *adj*

usage The spelling *sulfur* predominates in U.S. technical usage, while both *sulfur* and *sulphur* are common in general usage. British usage tends to favor *sulphur* for all applications. The same pattern is seen in most of the words derived from *sulfur.*

sulfur bacterium *n* (1891) : any of various bacteria (esp. genus *Thiobacillus*) capable of metabolizing sulfur compounds

sulfur dioxide *n* (1869) : a heavy pungent toxic gas SO₂ that is easily condensed to a colorless liquid, is used esp. in making sulfuric acid, in bleaching, as a preservative, and as a refrigerant, and is a major air pollutant esp. in industrial areas

sul·fu·ric \ˌsəl-ˈfyùr-ik\ *adj* (1790) : of, relating to, or containing sulfur esp. with a higher valence than sulfurous compounds ⟨~ esters⟩

sulfuric acid *or* **sul·phu·ric acid** \ˌsəl-ˈfyùr-ik-\ *n* (1790) : a heavy corrosive oily dibasic strong acid H₂SO₄ that is colorless when pure and is a vigorous oxidizing and dehydrating agent *usage* see SULFUR

sul·fu·rize \ˈsəl-fə-ˌrīz, -fyə-\ *vt* **-rized; -riz·ing** (1794) : to treat with sulfur or a sulfur compound

sul·fu·rous *also* **sul·phu·rous** \ˈsəl-fə-rəs, -fyə- *also esp for 1b* ˌsəl-ˈfyùr-əs\ *adj* (1530) **1 a** : of, relating to, or containing sulfur esp. with a lower valence than sulfuric compounds ⟨~ esters⟩ **b** : resembling or emanating from sulfur and esp. burning sulfur **2 a** : of, relating to, or dealing with the fire of hell : INFERNAL **b** : SCATHING, VIRULENT ⟨~ denunciations⟩ **c** : PROFANE, BLASPHEMOUS ⟨~ language⟩ *usage* see SULFUR — **sul·fu·rous·ly** *adv* — **sul·fu·rous·ness** *n*

sulfurous acid *n* (1790) : a weak unstable dibasic acid H₂SO₃ known in solution and through its salts and used as a reducing and bleaching agent

sul·fu·ryl \ˈsəl-fə-ˌril, -fyə-\ *n* [ISV] (1867) : SULFONYL — used esp. in names of inorganic compounds

¹sulk \ˈsəlk\ *vi* [back-formation fr. *sulky*] (1781) : to be moodily silent

²sulk *n* (1804) **1** : the state of one sulking — often used in pl. ⟨had a case of the ~s⟩ **2** : a sulky mood or spell ⟨in a ~⟩

¹sulky \ˈsəl-kē\ *adj* [prob. alter. of obs. *sulke* sluggish] (1744) **1 a** : sulking or given to spells of sulking **b** : relating to or indicating a sulk ⟨a ~ expression⟩ **2** [²*sulky*]: having wheels and usu. a seat for the driver ⟨a ~ plow⟩ **syn** see SULLEN — **sulk·i·ly** \-kə-lē\ *adv* — **sulk·i·ness** \-kē-nəs\ *n*

²sulky *n, pl* **sulkies** [prob. fr. ¹*sulky*; fr. its having room for only one person] (1756) : a light 2-wheeled vehicle (as for harness racing) having a seat for the driver only and usu. no body

sul·lage \ˈsə-lij\ *n* [prob. fr. MF *soiller, souiller* to soil — more at SOIL] (1553) : REFUSE, SEWAGE

sul·len \ˈsə-lən\ *adj* [ME *solain* solitary, prob. fr. (assumed) AF *solein,* alter. of OF *soltain,* fr. LL *solitaneus* private, ultim. fr. L *solus* alone] (14c) **1 a** : gloomily or resentfully silent or repressed **b** : suggesting a sullen state : LOWERING **2** : dull or somber in sound or color **3** : DISMAL, GLOOMY **4** : moving sluggishly — **sul·len·ly** *adv* — **sul·len·ness** \ˈsə-lə(n)-nəs\ *n*

syn SULLEN, GLUM, MOROSE, SURLY, SULKY, CRABBED, SATURNINE, GLOOMY mean showing a forbidding or disagreeable mood. SULLEN implies a silent ill humor and a refusal to be sociable ⟨remained *sullen* amid the festivities⟩. GLUM suggests a silent dispiritedness ⟨a *glum* candidate left to ponder a stunning defeat⟩. MOROSE adds to GLUM an element of bitterness or misanthropy ⟨*morose* job seekers who are inured to rejection⟩. SURLY implies gruffness and sullenness of speech or manner ⟨a typical *surly* teenager⟩. SULKY suggests childish resentment expressed in peevish sullenness ⟨grew *sulky* after every spat⟩. CRABBED applies to a forbidding morose harshness of manner ⟨the school's notoriously *crabbed* headmaster⟩. SATURNINE describes a heavy forbidding aspect or suggests a bitter disposition ⟨a *saturnine* cynic always finding fault⟩. GLOOMY implies a depression in mood making for seeming sullenness or glumness ⟨a *gloomy* mood ushered in by bad news⟩.

¹sul·ly \ˈsə-lē\ *vt* **sul·lied; sul·ly·ing** [ME *sollyen,* prob. fr. MF *soiller* to soil] (15c) : to make soiled or tarnished : DEFILE

²sully *n, pl* **sullies** (1602) *archaic* : SOIL, STAIN

sulph- *or* **sulpho-** *chiefly Brit var of* SULF-

sul·phate, sul·phide *chiefly Brit var of* SULFATE, SULFIDE

sulphur butterfly *n* (1879) : any of numerous butterflies (esp. *Colias* and related genera of the family Pieridae) having the wings usu. yellow or orange with a black border — called also *sulphur*

sul·phu·re·ous *adj* (ca. 1552) : SULFUROUS
sul·phu·rise *Brit var of* SULFURIZE
sulphur yellow *n* (1816) : a brilliant greenish yellow
Sul·pi·cian \ˌsəl-ˈpi-shən\ *n* [F *sulpicien*, fr. Compagnie de Saint⹀
Sulpice Society of St. Sulpice] (1786) : a member of the Society of
Priests of St. Sulpice founded by Jean Jacques Olier in Paris, France, in
1642 and dedicated to the teaching of seminarians
sul·tan \ˈsəl-tˀn\ *n* [MF, fr. Ar *sulṭān*] (1555) : a king or sovereign esp.
of a Muslim state — **sul·tan·ic** \ˌsəl-ˈta-nik\ *adj*
sul·ta·na \ˌ(ˌ)səl-ˈta-nə\ *n* [It, fem. of *sultano* sultan, fr. Ar *sulṭān*]
(1585) **1 a** : a female member of a sultan's family; *esp* : a sultan's wife
2 a : a pale yellow seedless grape grown for raisins and wine **b** : the
raisin of a sultana
sul·tan·ate \ˈsəl-tˀn-ˌāt\ *n* (1822) **1** : a state or country governed by a
sultan **2** : the office, dignity, or power of a sultan
sul·tan·ess \ˈsəl-tˀn-əs\ *n* (1611) *archaic* : SULTANA 1
sul·try \ˈsəl-trē\ *adj* **sul·tri·er; -est** [obs. E *sulter* to swelter, alter. of E
swelter] (1594) **1 a** : very hot and humid : SWELTERING ⟨a ~ day⟩ **b**
: burning hot : TORRID **2 a** : hot with passion or anger **b** : exciting
or capable of exciting strong sexual desire ⟨~ glances⟩ — **sul·tri·ly**
\-trə-lē\ *adv* — **sul·tri·ness** \-trē-nəs\ *n*
¹sum \ˈsəm\ *n* [ME *summe*, fr. OF, fr. L *summa*, fr. fem. of *summus*
highest; akin to L *super* over — more at OVER] (14c) **1** : an indefinite
or specified amount of money ⟨a ~⟩ **2** : the whole amount : AGGREGATE **3**
: the utmost degree : SUMMIT ⟨reached the ~ of human happiness⟩ **4**
a : a summary of the chief points or thoughts : SUMMATION ⟨the ~ of
this criticism follows —C. W. Hendel⟩ **b** : GIST ⟨the ~ and substance
of an argument⟩ **5 a** (1) : the result of adding numbers ⟨~ of 5 and
7 is 12⟩ (2) : the limit of the sum of the first *n* terms of an infinite
series as *n* increases indefinitely **b** : numbers to be added; *broadly* : a
problem in arithmetic **c** (1) : DISJUNCTION 2 (2) : UNION 2d — **sum·
ma·bil·i·ty** \ˌsə-mə-ˈbi-lə-tē\ *n* — **sum·ma·ble** \ˈsə-mə-bəl\ *adj* — **in
sum** : in short : BRIEFLY
²sum *vb* **summed; sum·ming** *vt* (14c) **1** : to calculate the sum of
: TOTAL **2** : SUMMARIZE ~ *vi* : to reach a sum : AMOUNT
su·mac *also* **su·mach** \ˈshü-ˌmak, ˈsü-\ *n* [ME *sumac*, fr. MF, fr. Ar
summāq] (14c) **1** : a material used in tanning and dyeing that consists
of dried powdered leaves and flowers of various sumacs **2** : any of a
genus (*Rhus*) of trees, shrubs, and woody vines of the cashew family
that have pinnately compound leaves turning to brilliant colors in the
autumn, dioecious flowers, spikes or loose clusters of red or whitish
berries, and in some cases foliage poisonous to the touch — compare
POISON IVY, POISON OAK
Su·me·ri·an \sü-ˈmer-ē-ən, -ˈmir-\ *n* (1878) **1** : a native of Sumer **2**
: the language of the Sumerians that has no known linguistic affinities
— **Sumerian** *adj*
Su·me·rol·o·gy \ˌsü-mə-ˈrä-lə-jē\ *n* (1897) : the study of Sumerian
culture, language, and history — **Su·me·rol·o·gist** \-jist\ *n*
sum·ma \ˈsü-mə, ˈsü-\ *n, pl* **sum·mae** \ˈsü-ˌmī, ˈsü-, -ˌmā; ˈsə-ˌmē,
-ˌmī\ [ML, fr. L, sum] (1725) : a comprehensive treatise; *esp* : one by a
scholastic philosopher
sum·ma cum lau·de \ˌsu̇-mə-(ˌ)ku̇m-ˈlau̇-də, ˌsü-, -ˈlau̇-dē; ˌsə-mə-
ˌkəm-ˈlȯ-dē\ *adv or adj* [L, with highest praise] (1900) : with highest
distinction ⟨graduated *summa cum laude*⟩ — compare CUM LAUDE,
MAGNA CUM LAUDE
sum·mand \ˈsə-ˌmand, ˌsə-ˈmand\ *n* [ML *summandus*, gerund of *sum·
mare* to sum, fr. *summa*] (1893) : a term in a summation : ADDEND
sum·ma·rise *Brit var of* SUMMARIZE
sum·ma·ri·za·tion \ˌsə-mə-rə-ˈzā-shən, ˌsəm-rə-\ *n* (1865) **1** : the act
of summarizing **2** : SUMMARY
sum·ma·rize \ˈsə-mə-ˌrīz\ *vt* (1871) : to tell in or
reduce to a summary ~ *vi* : to make a summary — **sum·ma·riz·able**
\ˌsə-mə-ˈrī-zə-bəl\ *adj* — **sum·ma·riz·er** *n*
¹sum·ma·ry \ˈsə-mə-rē *also* ˈsəm-rē *or* -ˌmer-ē\ *adj* [ME, fr. ML *sum·
marius*, fr. L *summa* sum] (15c) **1** : COMPREHENSIVE; *esp* : covering the
main points succinctly ⟨a ~ account⟩ **2 a** : done without delay or formality
: quickly executed ⟨a ~ dismissal⟩ **b** : of, relating to, or using a sum·
mary proceeding ⟨a ~ trial⟩ *syn* see CONCISE — **sum·mar·i·ly** \(ˌ)sə-
ˈmer-ə-lē\ *adv*
²sum·ma·ry \ˈsə-mə-rē *also* ˈsəm-rē\ *n, pl* **-ries** (1509) : an abstract,
abridgment, or compendium esp. of a preceding discourse
sum·mate \ˈsə-ˌmāt\ *vb* **sum·mat·ed; sum·mat·ing** [back-formation
fr. *summation*] *vt* (1900) : to add together : SUM UP ~ *vi* : to form a
sum or cumulative effect
sum·ma·tion \(ˌ)sə-ˈmā-shən\ *n* (1760) **1** : the act or process of form-
ing a sum : ADDITION **2** : SUM, TOTAL **3** : cumulative action or effect;
esp : the process by which a sequence of stimuli that are individually
inadequate to produce a response are cumulatively able to induce a
nerve impulse **4** : a final part of an argument reviewing points made
and expressing conclusions — **sum·ma·tion·al** \-shnəl, -shə-nˀl\ *adj*
sum·ma·tive \ˈsə-mə-tiv, -ˌmā-\ *adj* (1881) : ADDITIVE, CUMULATIVE
¹sum·mer \ˈsə-mər\ *n* [ME *sumer*, fr. OE *sumor*; akin to OHG & ON
sumer summer, Skt *samā* year, season] (bef. 12c) **1** : the season between spring and autumn comprising in the northern hemisphere usu.
the months of June, July, and August or as reckoned astronomically
extending from the June solstice to the September equinox **2** : the
warmer half of the year **3** : YEAR ⟨a girl of seventeen ~s⟩ **4** : a period
of maturing powers — **sum·mer·like** \-ˌlīk\ *adj*
²summer *adj* (14c) **1** : of, relating to, or suitable for summer ⟨~ vaca-
tion⟩ ⟨a ~ home⟩ **2** : sown in the spring and harvested in the same
year as sown ⟨~ wheat⟩ — compare WINTER
³summer *vb* **sum·mered; sum·mer·ing** \ˈsə-mə-riŋ, ˈsəm-riŋ\ *vi* (15c)
: to pass the summer ~ *vt* : to keep or carry through the summer; *esp*
: to provide ⟨as cattle or sheep⟩ with pasture during the summer
summer cypress *n* (1767) : a densely branched Eurasian herb (*Kochia
scoparia*) of the goosefoot family grown for its foliage which turns red
in autumn
sum·mer·house \ˈsə-mər-ˌhau̇s\ *n* (bef. 12c) **1** : a country house for
summer residence **2** : a covered structure in a garden or park designed to provide a shady resting place in summer
summer kitchen *n* (1874) : a small building or shed that is usu. adjacent to a house and is used as a kitchen in warm weather
sum·mer·long \-ˌlȯŋ, -ˈlȯŋ\ *adj* (1960) : lasting through the summer

sum·mers \ˈsə-mərz\ *adv* (1907) : during the summers ⟨worked ~ as a
waiter⟩
sum·mer·sault *var of* SOMERSAULT
summer savory *n* (ca. 1573) : an annual European mint (*Satureja
hortensis*) used in cookery — compare WINTER SAVORY
summer school *n* (1860) : a school or school session conducted in
summer enabling students to accelerate progress toward a degree, to
make up credits lost through absence or failure, or to round out professional education
summer squash *n* (1815) : any of various garden squashes derived
from a variety (*Cucurbita pepo* var. *melopepo*) and used as a vegetable
while immature and before hardening of the seeds and rind
summer stock *n* (1927) : theatrical productions of stock companies
presented during the summer
summer theater *n* (1801) : a theater that presents several different
plays or musicals during the summer
sum·mer·time \ˈsə-mər-ˌtīm\ *n* (14c) : the summer season or a period
like summer
summer time *n* (1916) *chiefly Brit* : DAYLIGHT SAVING TIME
sum·mer·wood \ˈsə-mər-ˌwu̇d\ *n* (1902) : the harder less porous portion of an annual ring of wood that develops late in the growing season
— compare SPRINGWOOD
sum·mery \ˈsə-mə-rē, -mə-rē\ *adj* (1824) : of, resembling, or fit for
summer
sum·ming-up \ˌsə-miŋ-ˈəp\ *n, pl* **sum·mings-up** \-miŋz-\ (1790) : the
act or statement of one who sums up
¹sum·mit \ˈsə-mət\ *n* [ME *somete*, fr. MF, fr. OF, dim. of *sum* top, fr. L
summum, neut. of *summus* highest — more at SUM] (15c) **1** : TOP,
APEX; *esp* : the highest point : PEAK **2** : the topmost level attainable
⟨the ~ of human fame⟩ **3 a** : the highest level of officials; *esp* : the
diplomatic level of heads of government **b** : a conference of highest⹀
level officials ⟨as heads of government⟩ ⟨an economic ~⟩
syn SUMMIT, PEAK, PINNACLE, CLIMAX, APEX, ACME, CULMINATION mean
the highest point attained or attainable. SUMMIT implies the topmost
level attainable ⟨at the *summit* of the Victorian social scene⟩. PEAK
suggests the highest among other high points ⟨an artist working at the
peak of her powers⟩. PINNACLE suggests a dizzying and often insecure
height ⟨the *pinnacle* of worldly success⟩. CLIMAX implies the highest
point in an ascending series ⟨the war was the *climax* to a series of
hostile actions⟩. APEX implies the point where all ascending lines converge ⟨the *apex* of Dutch culture⟩. ACME implies a level of quality representing the perfection of a thing ⟨a statue that was once deemed the
acme of beauty⟩. CULMINATION suggests the outcome of a growth or
development representing an attained objective ⟨the *culmination* of
years of effort⟩.
²summit *vi* (1972) : to participate in a summit conference
sum·mit·eer \ˌsə-mə-ˈtir\ *n* (1957) : one who takes part in a summit
sum·mit·ry \ˈsə-mə-trē\ *n* (1958) : the use of a summit conference for
international negotiation
sum·mon \ˈsə-mən\ *vt* **sum·moned; sum·mon·ing** \ˈsə-mə-niŋ, ˈsəm-
niŋ\ [ME *somonen*, fr. OF *somondre*, fr. (assumed) VL *summonere*,
alter. of L *summonēre* to remind secretly, fr. *sub-* secretly + *monēre* to
warn — more at SUB, MIND] (13c) **1** : to issue a call to convene : CON-
VOKE **2** : to command by service of a summons to appear in court
: to call upon for specified action **4** : to bid to come : send for ⟨~ a
physician⟩ **5** : to call forth : EVOKE — often used with *up* — **sum·
mon·able** \ˈsə-mə-nə-bəl\ *adj* — **sum·mon·er** \ˈsə-mə-nər, ˈsəm-nər\
n
syn SUMMON, CALL, CITE, CONVOKE, CONVENE, MUSTER mean to demand
the presence of. SUMMON implies the exercise of authority ⟨was *summoned* to answer charges⟩. CALL may be used less formally for SUMMON
⟨*called* the legislature into special session⟩. CITE implies a summoning
to court usu. to answer a charge ⟨*cited* for drunken driving⟩. CONVOKE
implies a summons to assemble for deliberative or legislative purposes
⟨*convoked* a Vatican council⟩. CONVENE is somewhat less formal than
CONVOKE ⟨*convened* the students⟩. MUSTER suggests a calling up of a
number of things that form a group in order that they may be exhibited, displayed, or utilized as a whole ⟨*mustered* the troops⟩.
¹sum·mons \ˈsə-mənz\ *n, pl* **sum·mons·es** [ME *somouns*, fr. OF *so-
monse*, fr. pp. of *somondre*] (13c) **1** : the act of summoning; *esp* : a
call by authority to appear at a place named or to attend to a duty **2**
: a warning or citation to appear in court: as **a** : a written notification
to be served on a person as a warning to appear in court at a day specified to answer to the plaintiff **b** : a subpoena to appear as a witness **3**
: something ⟨as a call⟩ that summons
²summons *vt* (1683) : SUMMON 2
sum·mum bo·num \ˌsu̇-məm-ˈbō-nəm, ˌsü-, ˌsə-\ *n* [L] (1563) : the
supreme good from which all others are derived
su·mo \ˈsü-(ˌ)mō\ *n* [Jp *sumō*] (1880) : a Japanese form of wrestling in
which a contestant loses if he is forced out of the ring or if any part of
his body except the soles of his feet touches the ground
sump \ˈsəmp\ *n* [ME *sompe* swamp — more at SWAMP] (1653) **1** : a pit
or reservoir serving as a drain or receptacle for liquids: as **a** : CESS-
POOL **b** : a pit at the lowest point in a circulating or drainage system
⟨as the oil-circulating system of an internal combustion engine⟩ **c**
chiefly Brit : OIL PAN **2** *Brit* : CRANKCASE **3** [G *Sumpf*, lit., marsh, fr.
MHG — more at SWAMP] **a** : the lowest part of a mine shaft into
which water drains **b** : an excavation ahead of regular work in driving
a mine tunnel or sinking a mine shaft **4** : something resembling a
sump : SINK 2
sump pump *n* (ca. 1899) : a pump ⟨as in a basement⟩ to remove accumulations of liquid from a sump pit
sump·ter \ˈsəm(p)-tər\ *n* [ME, short for *sumpter horse*, fr. *sumpter*
driver of a packhorse, fr. MF *sometier*, fr. (assumed) VL *sagmatarius*,
fr. LL *sagmat-, sagma* packsaddle, fr. Gk; akin to Gk *sattein* to pack,
stuff] (15c) : a pack animal
sump·tu·ary \ˈsəm(p)-chə-ˌwer-ē\ *adj* [L *sumptuarius*, fr. *sumptus* ex-

\ə\ abut \ˀ\ kitten, F table \ər\ further \a\ ash \ā\ ace \ä\ mop, mar
\au̇\ out \ch\ chin \e\ bet \ē\ easy \g\ go \i\ hit \ī\ ice \j\ job
\ŋ\ sing \ō\ go \ȯ\ law \ȯi\ boy \th\ thin \t̲h̲\ the \ü\ loot \u̇\ foot
\y\ yet \zh\ vision \à, k̲, ⁿ, œ, œ̄, ᵫ, ᵫ̄, ᵻ\ see Guide to Pronunciation

pense, fr. *sumere* to take, spend — more at CONSUME] (1600) **1** : relating to personal expenditures and esp. to prevent extravagance and luxury ⟨conservative ~ tastes —John Cheever⟩ **2** : designed to regulate extravagant expenditures or habits esp. on moral or religious grounds ⟨~ laws⟩ ⟨~ tax⟩

sump·tu·ous \'səm(p)(t)-shə-wəs, -shəs, -shwəs\ *adj* [ME, fr. MF *sumptueux*, fr. L *sumptuosus*, fr. *sumptus*] (15c) : extremely costly, rich, luxurious, or magnificent ⟨~ banquets⟩ ⟨a ~ residence⟩; *also* : MAGNIFICENT 4 — **sump·tu·ous·ly** *adv* — **sump·tu·ous·ness** *n*

sum total *n* (14c) **1** : a total arrived at through the counting of sums **2** : total result : TOTALITY

sum–up \'səm-,əp\ *n* (1894) : SUMMARY

sum up *vt* (15c) **1** : to be the sum of : bring to a total ⟨10 victories *summed up* his record⟩ **2 a** : to present or show succinctly : SUMMARIZE ⟨*sum up* the evidence presented⟩ **b** : to assess and then describe briefly : size up ~ *vi* : to present a summary or recapitulation

¹**sun** \'sən\ *n* [ME *sunne*, fr. OE; akin to OHG *sunna* sun, L *sol* — more at SOLAR] (bef. 12c) **1 a** *often cap* : the luminous celestial body around which the earth and other planets revolve, from which they receive heat and light, and which has a mean distance from earth of 93,000,000 miles (150,000,000 kilometers), a linear diameter of 864,000 miles (1,390,000 kilometers), a mass 332,000 times greater than earth, and a mean density about one fourth that of earth **b** : a celestial body like the sun **2** : the heat or light radiated from the sun **3** : one resembling the sun (as in warmth or brilliance) **4** : the rising or setting of the sun ⟨from ~ to ~⟩ **5** : GLORY, SPLENDOR — **in the sun** : in the public eye — **under the sun** : in the world : on earth

²**sun** *vb* **sunned; sun·ning** *vt* (15c) : to expose to or as if to the rays of the sun ~ *vi* : to sun oneself

sun-baked \'sən-,bākt\ *adj* (1628) **1** : heated, parched, or compacted esp. by excessive sunlight **2** : baked by exposure to sunshine

sun-bath \'sən-,bath, -,bȧth\ *n* (1866) : an exposure to sunlight or a sunlamp

sun-bathe \-,bāth\ *vi* [back-formation fr. *sunbather*] (1600) : to take a sunbath — **sun-bath-er** \-,bā-thər\ *n*

sun-beam \-,bēm\ *n* (bef. 12c) : a ray of sunlight

sun bear *n* (1842) : a small forest-dwelling bear (*Ursus malayanus* syn. *Helarctos malayanus*) that is found from Myanmar to Borneo and has short glossy black fur with a lighter muzzle and often an orange or white breast mark

sun-bird \-,bərd\ *n* (1826) : any of numerous small brilliantly colored oscine birds (family Nectariniidae) of the tropical Old World somewhat resembling hummingbirds

sun-block \-,bläk\ *n* (1972) : a preparation designed to block out more of the sun's rays than a sunscreen; *also* : its active ingredient (as para-aminobenzoic acid)

sun-bon·net \-,bä-nət\ *n* (1824) : a woman's bonnet with a wide brim framing the face and usu. having a ruffle at the back to protect the neck from the sun

sun-bow \-,bō\ *n* (1816) : an arch resembling a rainbow made by the sun shining through vapor or mist

¹**sun-burn** \-,bərn\ *vb* **-burned** \-,bərnd\ *or* **-burnt** \-,bərnt\; **-burning** [back-formation fr. *sunburned*, fr. *sun* + *burned*] *vt* (1530) : to burn or discolor by the sun ~ *vi* : to become sunburned

²**sunburn** *n* (1652) : inflammation of the skin caused by overexposure to sunlight

sun-burst \'sən-,bərst\ *n, often attrib* (1816) **1** : a flash of sunlight esp. through a break in clouds **2 a** : a jeweled brooch representing a sun surrounded by rays **b** : a design in the form of rays diverging from a central point

sun-choke \-,chōk\ *n* (1980) : JERUSALEM ARTICHOKE

sun-dae \'sən-dē, -(,)dā\ *n* [prob. alter. of *Sunday*] (1897) : ice cream served with topping (as crushed fruit, syrup, nuts, or whipped cream)

sun dance *n, often cap S&D* (1849) : a solo or group solstice rite of American Indians

¹**Sun-day** \'sən-dē, -(,)dā\ *n* [ME, fr. OE *sunnandæg* (akin to OHG *sunnūntag*), fr. *sunne* sun + *dæg* day] (bef. 12c) : the first day of the week : the Christian analogue of the Jewish Sabbath — **Sun-days** \-dēz, -(,)dāz\ *adv*

²**Sunday** *adj* (14c) **1** : of, relating to, or associated with Sunday **2** [fr. the practice of wearing one's best clothes on Sunday to attend church] : BEST ⟨~ suit⟩ **3** : AMATEUR ⟨~ painters⟩

Sun-day–go–to–meet·ing \'sən-dē-,gō-tə-'mē-tiŋ\ *adj* (1831) : appropriate for Sunday churchgoing

Sunday punch *n* (1929) **1** : a powerful or devastating blow; *esp* : a knockout punch **2** : something capable of delivering a powerful or devastating blow to the opposition ⟨saving his *Sunday punch* for the end of the campaign —*Newsweek*⟩

Sunday school *n* (1783) : a school held on Sunday for religious education; *also* : the teachers and pupils of such a school

sun-deck \'sən-,dek\ *n* (1897) **1** : the usu. upper deck of a ship that is exposed to the most sun **2** : a roof, deck, or terrace for sunning

sun-der \'sən-dər\ *vb* **sun-dered; sun-der-ing** \-d(ə-)riŋ\ [ME, fr. OE *gesundrian, syndrian*; akin to OHG *suntarōn* to sunder, OE *sundor* apart, L *sine* without, Skt *sanutar* away] *vt* (bef. 12c) : to break apart or in two : separate by or as if by violence or by intervening time or space ~ *vi* : to become parted, disunited, or severed **syn** see SEPARATE

sun-dew \'sən-(,)dü, -(,)dyü\ *n* (1578) : any of a genus (*Drosera* of the family Droseraceae, the sundew family) of bog-inhabiting insectivorous herbs having viscid glands on the leaves

sun-di·al \-,dī(-ə)l\ *n* (1599) : an instrument to show the time of day by the shadow of a gnomon on a usu. horizontal plate or on a cylindrical surface

sun disk *n* (1877) : an ancient Near Eastern symbol consisting of a disk with conventionalized wings emblematic of the sun-god (as Ra in Egypt)

sun disk

sun dog *n* (1635) **1** : PARHELION **2** : a small nearly round halo on the parhelic circle most frequently just outside the halo of 22 degrees

sun-down \'sən-,daun\ *n* (1620) : SUNSET 2

sun-down·er \-,daù-nər\ *n* (1868) **1** [fr. his habit of arriving at a place where he hopes to obtain food and lodging too late to do any work] : *Austral* : HOBO, TRAMP **2** *chiefly Brit* : a drink taken at sundown

sun-dress \-,dres\ *n* (1942) : a dress with an abbreviated bodice usu. exposing the shoulders, arms, and back

sun-dries \'sən-drēz\ *n pl* [¹*sundry*] (1755) : miscellaneous small articles, details, or items

sun-drops \'sən-,dräps\ *n pl but sing or pl in constr* (1784) : any of several day-flowering herbs (genus *Oenothera*) of the evening-primrose family

¹**sun-dry** \'sən-drē\ *adj* [ME, different for each, fr. OE *syndrig*, fr. *sundor* apart — more at SUNDER] (13c) : MISCELLANEOUS, VARIOUS ⟨~ articles⟩

²**sundry** *pron, pl in constr* (15c) : an indeterminate number ⟨recommended for reading by all and ~ —Edward Huberman⟩

sun-fish \-,fish\ *n* (1629) **1** : OCEAN SUNFISH **2** : any of numerous American freshwater bony fishes (family Centrarchidae, esp. genus *Lepomis*) usu. with a deep compressed body and metallic luster

Sunfish *trademark* — used for a light sailboat that has one sail and is designed for use by no more than two people

sun-flow·er \-,flaù(-ə)r\ *n* (1597) : any of a genus (*Helianthus*) of New World composite plants with large yellow-rayed flower heads bearing edible seeds that yield an edible oil

sung \'səŋ\ *past and past part of* SING

Sung \'sùŋ\ *n* [Chin (Beijing) *Sòng*] (1673) : a Chinese dynasty dated A.D. 960–1280 and marked by cultural refinement and achievements in philosophy, literature, and art — **Sung** *adj*

sun-glass \'sən-,glas\ *n* (1804) **1** : a convex lens for converging the sun's rays **2** *pl* : glasses to protect the eyes from the sun

sung mass *n* (1931) : HIGH MASS

sun god *n, often cap* (1592) : a god that represents or personifies the sun in various religions

sun goddess *n, often cap* (1861) : a goddess that represents or personifies the sun in various religions

sun–grebe \'sən-,grēb\ *n* (ca. 1889) : any of a small family (Heliornithidae) of African, Asian, and American tropical birds related to the rails

¹**sunk** \'səŋk\ *past and past part of* SINK

²**sunk** *adj* (1719) **1** : depressed in spirits **2** : DONE FOR, RUINED

sunk·en \'səŋ-kən\ *adj* [ME *sonkyn*, pp. of *sinken* to sink] (14c) **1** : SUBMERGED; *esp* : lying at the bottom of a body of water **2 a** : HOLLOW, RECESSED ⟨~ cheeks⟩ **b** : lying in a depression ⟨a ~ garden⟩ **c** : settled below the normal level **d** : constructed below the normal floor level ⟨a ~ living room⟩

sunk fence *n* (ca. 1771) : a ditch with a retaining wall used to divide lands without defacing a landscape — called also *ha-ha*

sun-lamp \'sən-,lamp\ *n* (1885) : an electric lamp designed to emit radiation of wavelengths from ultraviolet to infrared

sun-less \-ləs\ *adj* (1589) : lacking sunshine : DARK, CHEERLESS

sun-light \-,līt\ *n* (13c) : the light of the sun : SUNSHINE

sun-lit \-,lit\ *adj* (1822) : lighted by or as if by the sun

sunn \'sən\ *n* [Hindi *san*, fr. Skt *śaṇa*] (1774) : an East Indian leguminous plant (*Crotalaria juncea*) with slender branches, simple leaves, and yellow flowers; *also* : its valuable fiber resembling hemp that is lighter and stronger than jute

sun-na *also* **sun-nah** \'sù(n)-(,)nə, 'sə(n)-\ *n, often cap* [Ar *sunnah*] (1728) : the body of Islamic custom and practice based on Muhammad's words and deeds

sunn hemp *n* (1849) : SUNN

Sun-ni \'sù(n)-(,)nē\ *n* [Ar *sunniy*, fr. *sunnah*] (1595) **1** : the Muslims of the branch of Islam that adheres to the orthodox tradition and acknowledges the first four caliphs as rightful successors of Muhammad — compare SHIA **2** : a Sunni Muslim — **Sunni** *adj*

Sun-nism \'sù(n)-,ni-zəm\ *n* (1892) : the religious system or distinctive tenets of the Sunni

Sun-nite \-,nīt\ *n* (1718) : SUNNI 2 — **Sun-nite** \'sù(n)-,nīt\ *adj*

sun-ny \'sə-nē\ *adj* **sun-ni-er; -est** (14c) **1** : marked by brilliant sunlight : full of sunshine **2** : CHEERFUL, OPTIMISTIC ⟨a ~ disposition⟩ **3** : exposed to, brightened, or warmed by the sun ⟨a ~ room⟩ — **sun-ni-ly** \'sə-nᵊl-ē\ *adv* — **sun-ni-ness** \'sə-nē-nəs\ *n*

sun-ny–side up \,sə-nē-,sīd-'əp\ *adj* (ca. 1901) *of an egg* : fried on one side only

sun-porch \-,pōrch, -,pȯrch\ *n* (1918) : a screened-in or glassed-in porch with a sunny exposure

sun-rise \'sən-,rīz\ *n* (15c) **1** : the apparent rising of the sun above the horizon; *also* : the accompanying atmospheric effects **2** : the time when the upper limb of the sun appears above the horizon as a result of the diurnal rotation of the earth

sun-roof \-,rüf, -,rȯf\ *n* (1952) : a panel in an automobile roof that can be opened

sun-room \-,rüm, -,rùm\ *n* (1917) : a glass-enclosed porch or living room with a sunny exposure — called also *sun parlor*

sun-scald \-,skȯld\ *n* (1855) : an injury of woody plants (as fruit or forest trees) characterized by localized death of the tissues and sometimes by cankers and caused when it occurs in the summer by the combined action of both the heat and light of the sun and in the winter by the combined action of sun and low temperature to produce freezing of bark and underlying tissues

sun-screen \-,skrēn\ *n* (1738) : a screen to protect against sun; *esp* : a substance (as para-aminobenzoic acid) used in suntan preparations to protect the skin from excessive ultraviolet radiation — **sun-screen-ing** *adj*

sun-seek·er \-,sē-kər\ *n* (1954) : a person who travels to an area of warmth and sun esp. in winter

¹**sun-set** \-,set\ *n* (14c) **1** : the apparent descent of the sun below the horizon; *also* : the accompanying atmospheric effects **2** : the time when the upper limb of the sun disappears below the horizon as a result of the diurnal rotation of the earth **3** : a period of decline; *esp* : old age

²**sunset** *adj* (1976) : stipulating the periodic review of government agencies and programs in order to continue their existence ⟨~ law⟩

sun-shade \'sən-,shād\ *n* (1842) : something used as a protection from the sun's rays: as **a** : PARASOL **b** : AWNING

¹**sun-shine** \-,shīn\ *n* (13c) **1 a** : the sun's light or direct rays **b**

' : the warmth and light given by the sun's rays **c** : a spot or surface on which the sun's light shines **2** : something (as a person, condition, or influence) that radiates warmth, cheer, or happiness — **sun·shiny** \-ˌshī-nē\ *adj*

²**sunshine** *adj* (1972) : forbidding or restricting closed meetings of legislative or executive bodies and sometimes providing for public access to records ⟨~ law⟩

sun·spot \ˈsən-ˌspät\ *n* (1868) : any of the dark spots that appear from time to time on the sun's surface and are usu. visible only through a telescope

sun·stroke \-ˌstrōk\ *n* (1851) : heatstroke caused by direct exposure to the sun

sun·struck \-ˌstrək\ *adj* (1794) : affected or touched by the sun

sun·suit \-ˌsüt\ *n* (1929) : an outfit worn usu. for sunbathing and play

sun·tan \-ˌtan\ *n* (1904) **1** : a browning of the skin from exposure to the rays of the sun **2** *pl* : a tan-colored summer uniform — **sun·tanned** \-ˌtand\ *adj*

sun-up \-ˌəp\ *n* (1712) : SUNRISE

¹**sun·ward** \ˈsən-wərd\ *or* **sun·wards** \-wərdz\ *adv* (1611) : toward the sun

²**sunward** *adj* (1769) : facing the sun

sun·wise \ˈsən-ˌwīz\ *adv* (ca. 1864) : CLOCKWISE

¹**sup** \ˈsəp\ *vb* **supped; sup·ping** [ME *suppen*, fr. OE *sūpan, suppan;* akin to OHG *sūfan* to drink, sip, OE *sopp* sop] *vt* (bef. 12c) : to take or drink in swallows or gulps ~ *vi, chiefly dial* : to take food and esp. liquid food into the mouth a little at a time

²**sup** *n* (ca. 1570) : a mouthful esp. of liquor or broth : SIP; *also* : a small quantity of liquid ⟨pour me just a ~ of tea⟩

³**sup** *vi* **supped; sup·ping** [ME *soupen, suppen,* fr. OF *souper,* fr. *soupe* sop, soup — more at SOUP] (14c) **1** : to eat the evening meal **2** : to make one's supper — used with *on* or *off* ⟨~ on roast beef⟩

¹**su·per** \ˈsü-pər\ *adj* [*super-*] (1837) **1 a** — used as a generalized term of approval ⟨a ~ cook⟩ **b** : of high grade or quality **2** : very large or powerful ⟨a ~ atomic bomb⟩ **3** : exhibiting the characteristics of its type to an extreme or excessive degree ⟨~ secrecy⟩

²**super** *n* (1838) **1** [by shortening] **a** : SUPERNUMERARY; *esp* : a supernumerary actor **b** : SUPERINTENDENT, SUPERVISOR; *esp* : the superintendent of an apartment building **2** [short for obs. *superhive*] : a removable upper story of a beehive **3** [¹*super*] : a superfine grade or extra large size **4** [origin unknown] : a thin loosely woven open-meshed starched cotton fabric used esp. for reinforcing books

³**super** *adv* [*super-*] (1946) **1** : VERY, EXTREMELY ⟨a ~ fast car⟩ **2** : to an excessive degree

super- *prefix* [L, over, above, in addition, fr. *super* over, above, on top of — more at OVER] **1 a** (1) : over and above : higher in quantity, quality, or degree than : more than ⟨*super*human⟩ (2) : in addition : extra ⟨*super*tax⟩ **b** (1) : exceeding or so as to exceed a norm ⟨*super*heat⟩ (2) : in or to an extreme or excessive degree or intensity ⟨*super*subtle⟩ **c** : surpassing all or most others of its kind ⟨*super*highway⟩ **2 a** : situated or placed above, on, or at the top of ⟨*super*lunary⟩; *specif* : situated on the dorsal side of **b** : next above or higher ⟨*super*tonic⟩ **3** : having the (specified) ingredient present in a large or unusually large proportion ⟨*super*phosphate⟩ **4** : constituting a more inclusive category than that specified ⟨*super*family⟩ **5** : superior in status, title, or position ⟨*super*power⟩

su·per·ab·sor·bent
su·per·achiev·er
su·per·ac·tiv·i·ty
su·per·ad·di·tion
su·per·agent
su·per·am·bi·tious
su·per·ath·lete
su·per·bad
su·per·bank
su·per·bil·lion·aire
su·per·bitch
su·per·board
su·per·bomb
su·per·bright
su·per·bu·reau·crat
su·per·cab·i·net
su·per·car
su·per·car·ri·er
su·per·cau·tious
su·per·cen·ter
su·per·chic
su·per·church
su·per·civ·i·li·za·tion
su·per·civ·i·lized
su·per·clean
su·per·club
su·per·co·los·sal
su·per·com·fort·able
su·per·com·pet·i·tive
su·per·con·fi·dent
su·per·con·glom·er·ate
su·per·con·ser·va·tive
su·per·con·ve·nient
su·per·cop
su·per·cor·po·ra·tion
su·per·crim·i·nal
su·per·cute
su·per·de·luxe
su·per·dip·lo·mat
su·per·ef·fec·tive
su·per·ef·fi·cien·cy
su·per·ef·fi·cient
su·per·ego·ist
su·per·elite
su·per·em·i·nence
su·per·em·i·nent

su·per·em·i·nent·ly
su·per·ex·pen·sive
su·per·ex·press
su·per·fan
su·per·farm
su·per·fast
su·per·firm
su·per·flack
su·per·fund
su·per·good
su·per·gov·ern·ment
su·per·growth
su·per·hard·en
su·per·heavy
su·per·her·o·ine
su·per·hit
su·per·hot
su·per·hype
su·per·in·su·lat·ed
su·per·in·tel·lec·tu·al
su·per·in·tel·li·gence
su·per·in·tel·li·gent
su·per·in·ten·si·ty
su·per·jock
su·per·jum·bo
su·per·large
su·per·law·yer
su·per·light
su·per·lob·by·ist
su·per·loy·al·ist
su·per·lux·u·ri·ous
su·per·lux·u·ry
su·per·ma·cho
su·per·ma·jor·i·ty
su·per·male
su·per·mas·cu·line
su·per·mas·sive
su·per·mil·i·tant
su·per·mil·lion·aire
su·per·mind
su·per·min·is·ter
su·per·mod·el
su·per·mod·ern
su·per·mom
su·per·na·tion
su·per·na·tion·al
su·per·nu·tri·tion
su·per·or·gan·ic

su·per·or·gasm
su·per·pa·tri·ot
su·per·pa·tri·ot·ic
su·per·pa·tri·o·tism
su·per·per·son
su·per·per·son·al
su·per·phe·nom·e·non
su·per·pimp
su·per·plane
su·per·play·er
su·per·po·lite
su·per·port
su·per·pow·er·ful
su·per·pre·mi·um
su·per·pro
su·per·prof·it
su·per·qual·i·ty
su·per·race
su·per·real
su·per·re·al·ism
su·per·re·gion·al
su·per·rich
su·per·road
su·per·ro·man·tic
su·per·ro·man·ti·cism
su·per·safe
su·per·sale
su·per·sales·man
su·per·scale
su·per·school
su·per·scout
su·per·se·cre·cy
su·per·se·cret
su·per·sell
su·per·sell·er
su·per·sex·u·al·i·ty
su·per·sharp
su·per·show
su·per·sing·er
su·per·size
su·per·sized
su·per·sleuth
su·per·slick
su·per·smart
su·per·smooth
su·per·soft
su·per·so·phis·ti·cat·ed
su·per·spe·cial

su·per·spe·cial·ist
su·per·spe·cial·i·za·tion
su·per·spe·cial·ized
su·per·spec·ta·cle
su·per·spec·tac·u·lar
su·per·spec·u·la·tion
su·per·spy
su·per·state
su·per·sta·tion
su·per·stim·u·late
su·per·stock

su·per·stra·tum
su·per·strength
su·per·strike
su·per·strong
su·per·stud
su·per·sub·tle
su·per·sub·tle·ty
su·per·sur·geon
su·per·sweet
su·per·tank·er
su·per·ter·rif·ic

su·per·thick
su·per·thin
su·per·thril·ler
su·per·tight
su·per·vir·ile
su·per·vir·tu·o·so
su·per·wave
su·per·weap·on
su·per·wide
su·per·wife

su·per·a·ble \ˈsü-p(ə-)rə-bəl\ *adj* [L *superabilis,* fr. *superare* to surmount — more at INSUPERABLE] (1629) : capable of being overcome or conquered — **su·per·a·ble·ness** *n* — **su·per·a·bly** \-blē\ *adv*

su·per·abound \ˌsü-pər-ə-ˈbau̇nd\ *vi* [ME, fr. LL *superabundare,* fr. L *super-* + *abundare* to abound] (14c) : to abound or prevail in greater measure or to excess

su·per·abun·dant \-ˈbən-dənt\ *adj* [ME, fr. LL *superabundant-, superabundans,* fr. prp. of *superabundare*] (15c) : more than ample : EXCESSIVE — **su·per·abun·dance** \-dən(t)s\ *n* — **su·per·abun·dant·ly** *adv*

su·per·add \ˌsü-pər-ˈad\ *vt* [ME, fr. L *superaddere,* fr. *super-* + *addere* to add] (15c) : to add esp. in a way that compounds an effect ⟨the loss of his job was ~ed to the loss of his house⟩

su·per·agen·cy \ˈsü-pər-ˌā-jən(t)-sē\ *n* (1943) : a large complex governmental agency esp. when set up to supervise other agencies

su·per·al·loy \ˌsü-pər-ˈa-ˌlȯi, -ə-ˈlȯi\ *n* (1948) : any of various high-strength often complex alloys resistant to high temperature

su·per·al·tern \ˌsü-pər-ˈȯl-tərn\ *n* [*super-* + *subaltern*] (1921) : a universal proposition in traditional logic that is a ground for the immediate inference of a corresponding subaltern

su·per·an·nu·ate \ˌsü-pər-ˈan-yə-ˌwāt\ *vb* **-at·ed; -at·ing** [back-formation fr. *superannuated*] *vt* (1649) **1** : to make, declare, or prove obsolete or out-of-date **2** : to retire and pension because of age or infirmity ~ *vi* **1** : to become retired **2** : to become antiquated — **su·per·an·nu·a·tion** \-ˌan-yə-ˈwā-shən\ *n*

superannuated *adj* [ML *superannuatus,* pp. of *superannuari* to be too old, fr. L *super-* + *annus* year — more at ANNUAL] (1740) : incapacitated or disqualified for active duty by advanced age

su·perb \su̇-ˈpərb\ *adj* [L *superbus* excellent, proud, fr. *super* above + *-bus* (akin to OE *bēon* to be) — more at OVER, BE] (1549) : marked to the highest degree by grandeur, excellence, brilliance, or competence *syn* see SPLENDID — **su·perb·ly** *adv* — **su·perb·ness** *n*

Su·per·ball \ˈsü-pər-ˌbȯl\ *trademark* — used for a toy rubber ball with a high bounce

su·per·block \-ˌbläk\ *n* (1928) : a very large commercial or residential block barred to through traffic, crossed by pedestrian walks and sometimes access roads, and often spotted with grassed malls

Super Bowl *n* [fr. the *Super Bowl,* annual championship game of the National Football League] (1969) : a contest or event that is the most important or prestigious of its kind ⟨the 2,500-mile, 24-day *Super Bowl* of bicycle racing —John Krakauer⟩

¹**su·per·cal·en·der** \ˈsü-pər-ˌka-lən-dər\ *vt* (1888) : to process (paper) in a supercalender

²**supercalender** *n* (1894) : a stack of highly polished calender rolls used to give an extra finish to paper

su·per·car·go \ˌsü-pər-ˈkär-(ˌ)gō, ˈsü-pər-ˌ\ *n* [Sp *sobrecargo,* fr. *sobre-* over (fr. L *super-*) + *cargo* cargo] (1697) : an officer on a merchant ship in charge of the commercial concerns of the voyage

supercede *var of* SUPERSEDE

su·per·charge \ˈsü-pər-ˌchärj\ *vt* (1876) **1** : to charge greatly or excessively (as with vigor or tension) **2** : to supply a charge to the intake of (as an engine) at a pressure higher than that of the surrounding atmosphere **3** : PRESSURIZE 1 — **supercharge** *n*

su·per·charg·er \-ˌchär-jər\ *n* (1921) : a device (as a blower or compressor) for pressurizing the cabin of an airplane or for increasing the volume air charge of an internal combustion engine over that which would normally be drawn in through the pumping action of the pistons

su·per·cil·i·ary \ˌsü-pər-ˈsi-lē-ˌer-ē\ *adj* [NL *superciliaris,* fr. L *supercilium*] (1732) : of, relating to, or adjoining the eyebrow : SUPRAORBITAL

su·per·cil·ious \-ˈsi-lē-əs, -ˈsil-yəs\ *adj* [L *superciliosus,* fr. *supercilium* eyebrow, haughtiness, fr. *super-* + *-cilium* eyelid (akin to *celare* to hide) — more at HELL] (1598) : coolly and patronizingly haughty *syn* see PROUD — **su·per·cil·ious·ly** *adv* — **su·per·cil·ious·ness** *n*

su·per·city \ˈsü-pər-ˌsi-tē\ *n* (1925) : MEGALOPOLIS

su·per·class \-ˌklas\ *n* (ca. 1891) : a category in biological classification ranking below a phylum or division and above a class

su·per·clus·ter \ˈsü-pər-ˌkləs-tər\ *n* (1926) : a group of gravitationally associated clusters of galaxies

su·per·coil \-ˌkȯi(ə)l\ *n* (1960) : SUPERHELIX — **supercoil** *vb*

su·per·col·lid·er \-kə-ˌlī-dər\ *n* (1984) : a very large collider capable of accelerating particles to very high energies

su·per·com·put·er \-kəm-ˌpyü-tər\ *n* (1968) : a large very fast mainframe used esp. for scientific computations

su·per·con·duct \-kən-ˈdəkt\ *vi* (1952) : to exhibit superconductivity — **su·per·con·duc·tive** \-ˈdək-tiv\ *adj*

su·per·con·duc·tiv·i·ty \-ˌkän-ˌdək-ˈti-və-tē, -kən-ˌ\ *n* (1913) : a complete disappearance of electrical resistance in a substance esp. at very low temperatures — **su·per·con·duc·tor** \-ˈkən-ˈdək-tər\ *n*

su·per·con·ti·nent \ˈsü-pər-ˌkän-tᵊn-ənt, -ˌkänt-nənt\ *n* (1960) : a former large continent from which other continents are held to have broken off and drifted away

su·per·cool \ˌsü-pər-ˈkül\ *vt* (1906) : to cool below the freezing point without solidification or crystallization ~ *vi* : to become supercooled

\ə\ abut \ᵊ\ kitten, F table \ər\ further \a\ ash \ā\ ace \ä\ mop, mar \au̇\ out \ch\ chin \e\ bet \ē\ easy \g\ go \i\ hit \ī\ ice \j\ job \ŋ\ sing \ō\ go \ȯ\ law \ȯi\ boy \th\ thin \t̲h̲\ the \ü\ loot \u̇\ foot \y\ yet \zh\ vision \á, k̲, ⁿ, œ, œ̄, ᵫ, ᵾ̄, ᵊ\ see Guide to Pronunciation

su·per·crit·i·cal \-'kri-ti-kəl\ *adj* (1934) : being or having a temperature above a critical temperature ⟨~ fluid⟩

su·per·cur·rent \'sü-pər-ˌkər-ənt, -ˌkə-rənt\ *n* (1940) : a current of electricity flowing in a superconductor

su·per–du·per \'sü-pər-'dü-pər\ *adj* [redupl. of ¹*super*] (1940) : of the greatest excellence, size, effectiveness, or impressiveness

su·per·ego \ˌsü-pər-'ē-(ˌ)gō *also* -'e-(ˌ)gō\ *n* [NL, trans. of G *Über-ich,* fr. *über* over + *ich* I] (1919) : the one of the three divisions of the psyche in psychoanalytic theory that is only partly conscious, represents internalization of parental conscience and the rules of society, and functions to reward and punish through a system of moral attitudes, conscience, and a sense of guilt — compare EGO, ID

su·per·el·e·vate \-'e-lə-ˌvāt\ *vt* (ca. 1945) : BANK 1c

su·per·el·e·va·tion \-ˌe-lə-'vā-shən\ *n* (1889) **1** : the vertical distance between the heights of inner and outer edges of highway pavement or railroad rails **2** : additional elevation

su·per·er·o·ga·tion \ˌsü-pə-ˌrer-ə-'gā-shən\ *n* [ML *supererogation-, supererogatio,* fr. *supererogare* to perform beyond the call of duty, fr. LL, to expend in addition, fr. L *super-* + *erogare* to expend public funds after asking the consent of the people, fr. *e-* + *rogare* to ask — more at RIGHT] (1526) : the act of performing more than is required by duty, obligation, or need

su·per·erog·a·to·ry \ˌsü-pə-ri-'rä-gə-ˌtōr-ē, -ˌtȯr-\ *adj* (1593) **1** : observed or performed to an extent not enjoined or required **2** : exceeding what is needed : SUPERFLUOUS

su·per·fam·i·ly \'sü-pər-ˌfam-lē, -'fa-mə-\ *n* (ca. 1890) : a category of biological classification ranking below an order and above a family

su·per·fat·ted \-ˌfa-təd\ *adj* (1891) : containing extra oil or fat ⟨~ soap⟩

su·per·fe·cun·da·tion \ˌsü-pər-ˌfe-kən-'dā-shən, -ˌfē-\ *n* (ca. 1855) **1** : successive fertilization of two or more ova from the same ovulation esp. by different sires **2** : fertilization at one time of a number of ova excessive for the species

su·per·fe·ta·tion \-fē-'tā-shən\ *n* [ML *superfetation-, superfetatio,* fr. L *superfetare* to conceive while already pregnant, fr. *super-* + *fetus* act of bearing young, offspring — more at FETUS] (1603) : a progressive accumulation or accretion reaching an extreme or excessive degree

su·per·fi·cial \ˌsü-pər-'fi-shəl\ *adj* [ME, fr. LL *superficialis,* fr. L *superficies*] (15c) **1 a** (1) : of or relating to a surface (2) : lying on, not penetrating below, or affecting only the surface ⟨~ wounds⟩ **b** *Brit, of a unit of measure* : SQUARE ⟨~ foot⟩ **2 a** : concerned only with the obvious or apparent : SHALLOW **b** : lying on the surface : EXTERNAL **c** : presenting only an appearance without substance or significance — **su·per·fi·cial·ly** \-'fi-sh(ə-)lē\ *adv*

syn SUPERFICIAL, SHALLOW, CURSORY mean lacking in depth or solidity. SUPERFICIAL implies a concern only with surface aspects or obvious features ⟨a *superficial* analysis of the problem⟩. SHALLOW is more generally derogatory in implying lack of depth in knowledge, reasoning, emotions, or character ⟨a light, *shallow,* and frivolous review⟩. CURSORY suggests a lack of thoroughness or a neglect of details ⟨gave the letter only a *cursory* reading⟩.

superficial fascia *n* (1876) : the thin layer of loose fatty connective tissue underlying the skin and binding it to the parts beneath — called also *hypodermis*

su·per·fi·ci·al·i·ty \ˌsü-pər-ˌfi-shē-'a-lə-tē\ *n, pl* **-ties** (1530) **1** : the quality or state of being superficial **2** : something superficial

su·per·fi·cies \-'fi-(ˌ)shēz, -shē-ˌēz\ *n, pl* **superficies** [L, surface, fr. *super-* + *facies* face, aspect — more at FACE] (1530) **1** : a surface of a body or a region of space **2** : the external aspects or appearance of a thing

su·per·fine \ˌsü-pər-'fīn\ *adj* (1575) **1** : overly refined or nice **2** : of extremely fine size or texture ⟨~ toothbrush bristles⟩ ⟨~ sugar⟩ **3** : of high quality or grade — used esp. of merchandise

su·per·fix \'sü-pər-ˌfiks\ *n* [*super-* + *-fix* (as in *prefix*)] (ca. 1948) : a morpheme consisting of a pattern of stress, intonation, or juncture features that are associated with the syllables of a word or phrase (as the distinctive stress patterns of the noun *subject* and the verb *subject*)

su·per·flu·id \ˌsü-pər-'flü-əd\ *n* (1938) : an unusual state of matter noted only in liquid helium cooled to near absolute zero and characterized by apparently frictionless flow (as through fine holes) — **superfluid** *adj* — **su·per·flu·id·i·ty** \-flü-'i-də-tē\ *n*

su·per·flu·i·ty \ˌsü-pər-'flü-ə-tē\ *n, pl* **-ties** [ME *superfluitee,* fr. MF *superfluité,* fr. LL *superfluitat-, superfluitas,* fr. L *superfluus*] (14c) **1 a** : EXCESS, OVERSUPPLY **b** : something unnecessary or superfluous **2** : immoderate and esp. luxurious living, habits, or desires

su·per·flu·ous \sü-'pər-flü-əs\ *adj* [ME, fr. L *superfluus,* lit., running over, fr. *superfluere* to overflow, fr. *super-* + *fluere* to flow — more at FLUID] (15c) **1 a** : exceeding what is sufficient or necessary : EXTRA **b** : not needed : UNNECESSARY **2** *obs* : marked by wastefulness : EXTRAVAGANT — **su·per·flu·ous·ly** *adv* — **su·per·flu·ous·ness** *n*

su·per·gene \'sü-pər-ˌjēn\ *n* (ca. 1949) : a group of linked genes acting as an allelic unit esp. when due to the suppression of crossing-over

su·per·gi·ant \-ˌjī-ənt\ *n* (1926) : something that is extremely large; *esp* : a star of very great intrinsic luminosity and enormous size — **supergiant** *adj*

su·per·glue *n* (1946) : a very strong glue; *specif* : a glue whose chief ingredient is a cyanoacrylate that becomes adhesive through polymerization rather than evaporation of a solvent

su·per·graph·ics \-ˌgra-fiks\ *n pl but sing or pl in constr* (1969) : billboard-sized graphic shapes usu. of bright color and simple design

su·per·grav·i·ty \ˌsü-pər-'gra-və-tē\ *n* (1976) : any of various theories in physics that are based on supersymmetry and attempt to unify general relativity and quantum theory and that state that the principle transmitter of gravity is the graviton

su·per·group \'sü-pər-ˌgrüp\ *n* (1968) : a rock group made up of prominent former members of other rock groups; *also* : an extremely successful rock group

¹su·per·heat \ˌsü-pər-'hēt\ *vt* (1859) **1** : to heat (a vapor not in contact with its own liquid) so as to cause to remain free from suspended liquid droplets ⟨~ed steam⟩ **2** : to heat (a liquid) above the boiling point without converting into vapor — **su·per·heat·er** *n*

²su·per·heat \-ˌhēt, ˌsü-pər-'\ *n* (1884) : the extra heat imparted to a vapor in superheating it from a dry and saturated condition; *also* : the corresponding rise of temperature

su·per·heat·ed \-ˌhē-təd, -'hē-\ *adj* (1857) : very hot; *also* : exceedingly emotional or intense

su·per·hea·vy·weight \ˌsü-pər-'he-vē-ˌwāt\ *n* (1971) : an athlete (as an Olympic weightlifter, boxer, or wrestler) who competes in the heaviest class or division

su·per·he·lix \'sü-pər-ˌhē-liks\ *n* (1964) : a helix (as of DNA) which has its axis arranged in a helical coil — **su·per·he·li·cal** \ˌsü-pər-'he-li-kəl, -'hē-\ *adj*

su·per·hero \-ˌhir-(ˌ)ō, -ˌhē-(ˌ)rō\ *n* (1917) : a fictional hero having extraordinary or superhuman powers; *also* : an exceptionally skillful or successful person

su·per·het·ero·dyne \ˌsü-pər-'he-tə-rə-ˌdīn, -'he-trə-\ *adj* [*super*sonic + *heterodyne*] (1922) : used in or being a radio receiver in which an incoming signal is mixed with a locally generated frequency to produce an ultrasonic signal at a fixed frequency that is then rectified, amplified, and rectified again to reproduce the sound — **superheterodyne** *n*

su·per·high frequency \'sü-pər-ˌhī-\ *n* (ca. 1945) : a radio frequency in the next to the highest range of the radio spectrum — see RADIO FREQUENCY table

su·per·high·way \ˌsü-pər-'hī-ˌwā, 'sü-pər-ˌ\ *n* (1925) : a multilane highway (as an expressway or turnpike) designed for high-speed traffic

su·per·hu·man \ˌsü-pər-'hyü-mən, -'yü-\ *adj* (1633) **1** : being above the human : DIVINE ⟨~ beings⟩ **2** : exceeding normal human power, size, or capability : HERCULEAN ⟨a ~ effort⟩; *also* : having such power, size, or capability — **su·per·hu·man·i·ty** \-hyü-'ma-nə-tē, -yü-\ *n* — **su·per·hu·man·ly** \-'hyü-mən-lē, -'yü-\ *adv* — **su·per·hu·man·ness** \-mən-nəs\ *n*

su·per·im·pose \ˌsü-pər-im-'pōz\ *vt* (1794) : to place or lay over or above something ⟨*superimposed* images⟩ ⟨*superimposed* a formula on the stories⟩ — **su·per·im·pos·able** \-'pō-zə-bəl\ *adj* — **su·per·im·po·si·tion** \-ˌim-pə-'zi-shən\ *n*

su·per·in·cum·bent \-in-'kəm-bənt\ *adj* [L *superincumbent-, superincumbens,* prp. of *superincumbere* to lie on top of, fr. *super-* + *incumbere* to lie down on — more at INCUMBENT] (1664) : lying or resting and usu. exerting pressure on something else — **su·per·in·cum·bent·ly** *adv*

su·per·in·di·vid·u·al \ˌsü-pər-ˌin-də-'vij-wəl, -'vi-jə-wəl, -'vi-jəl\ *adj* (1916) : of, relating to, or being an organism, entity, or complex of more than individual complexity or nature

su·per·in·duce \-in-'düs, -'dyüs\ *vt* [L *superinducere,* fr. *super-* + *inducere* to lead in — more at INDUCE] (ca. 1555) **1** : to introduce as an addition over or above something already existing **2** : BRING ON, INDUCE — **su·per·in·duc·tion** \-'dək-shən\ *n*

su·per·in·fec·tion \-in-'fek-shən\ *n* (ca. 1922) : reinfection or a second infection with a microbial agent (as a bacterium, fungus, or virus) — **su·per·in·fect** \-'fekt\ *vt*

su·per·in·tend \ˌsü-p(ə-)rin-'tend, ˌsü-pərn-\ *vt* [LL *superintendere,* fr. L *super-* + *intendere* to stretch out, direct — more at INTEND] (ca. 1615) : to have or exercise the charge and oversight of : DIRECT

su·per·in·ten·dence \-'ten-dən(t)s\ *n* (1603) : the act or function of superintending or directing : SUPERVISION

su·per·in·ten·den·cy \-dən(t)-sē\ *n, pl* **-cies** (1598) : the office, post, or jurisdiction of a superintendent; *also* : SUPERINTENDENCE

su·per·in·ten·dent \-dənt\ *n* [ML *superintendent-, superintendens,* fr. LL, prp. of *superintendere*] (1554) : one who has executive oversight and charge — **superintendent** *adj*

¹su·pe·ri·or \sü-'pir-ē-ər\ *adj* [ME, fr. MF *superieur,* fr. L *superior,* compar. of *superus* upper, fr. *super* over, above — more at OVER] (14c) **1** : situated higher up **2** : of higher rank, quality, or importance **3** : courageously or serenely indifferent (as to something painful or disheartening) **4 a** : greater in quantity or numbers ⟨escaped by ~ speed⟩ **b** : excellent of its kind : BETTER ⟨her ~ memory⟩ **5** : being a superscript **6 a** *of an animal structure* : situated above or anterior or dorsal to another and esp. a corresponding part ⟨a ~ artery⟩ **b** *of a plant structure* : situated above or near the top of another part: as (1) *of a calyx* : attached to and apparently arising from the ovary (2) *of an ovary* : free from the calyx or other floral envelope **7** : more comprehensive ⟨a genus is ~ to a species⟩ **8** : affecting or assuming an air of superiority : SUPERCILIOUS — **su·pe·ri·or·ly** *adv*

²superior *n* (15c) **1** : one who is above another in rank, station, or office; *esp* : the head of a religious house or order **2** : one that surpasses another in quality or merit **3** : SUPERSCRIPT

superior conjunction *n* (1833) : a conjunction in which the primary of an orbiting celestial body is aligned between the celestial body and an observer

superior court *n* (1686) **1** : a court of general jurisdiction intermediate between the inferior courts (as a justice of the peace court) and the higher appellate courts **2** : a court with juries having original jurisdiction

superior general *n, pl* **superiors general** (1775) : the superior of a religious order or congregation

su·pe·ri·or·i·ty \sü-ˌpir-ē-'ȯr-ə-tē, ˌsü-, -'är-\ *n, pl* **-ties** (15c) : the quality or state of being superior; *also* : a superior characteristic

superiority complex *n* (ca. 1924) : an exaggerated opinion of oneself

superior planet *n* (1583) : a planet whose orbit lies outside that of the earth

superior vena cava *n* (1901) : the branch of the vena cava of a vertebrate that brings blood back from the head and anterior part of the body to the heart

su·per·ja·cent \ˌsü-pər-'jā-sənt\ *adj* [L *superjacent-, superjacens,* prp. of *superjacēre* to lie over or upon, fr. *super-* + *jacēre* to lie; akin to L *jacere* to throw — more at JET] (1610) : lying above or upon : OVERLYING ⟨~ rocks⟩

su·per·jet \'sü-pər-ˌjet\ *n* (1958) : a very large jet airplane

¹su·per·la·tive \sü-'pər-lə-tiv\ *adj* [ME *superlatif,* fr. MF, fr. LL *superlativus,* fr. L *superlatus* (pp. of *superferre* to carry over, raise high), fr. *super-* + *latus,* pp. of *ferre* to carry — more at TOLERATE, BEAR] (14c) **1** : of, relating to, or constituting the degree of grammatical comparison that denotes an extreme or unsurpassed level or extent **2 a** : surpassing all others : SUPREME **b** : of very high quality : EXCELLENT **3** : EXCESSIVE, EXAGGERATED — **su·per·la·tive·ly** *adv* — **su·per·la·tive·ness** *n*

²superlative *n* (15c) **1 a** : the superlative degree of comparison in a

language b : a superlative form of an adjective or adverb **2 :** the superlative or utmost degree of something : ACME **3 : a** a superlative person or thing **4 :** an admiring sometimes exaggerated expression esp. of praise

su·per·lin·er \'sü-pər-,li-nər\ *n* (1919) : a fast luxurious passenger liner of great size

su·per·lu·na·ry \,sü-pər-'lü-nə-rē\ *or* **su·per·lu·nar** \-nər, -,när\ *adj* [L *super-* + *luna* moon — more at LUNAR] (1614) *archaic* : being above the moon : CELESTIAL

su·per·man \'sü-pər-,man\ *n* [trans. of G *Übermensch*, fr. *über* over, *super-* + *Mensch* man] (1903) **1 :** a superior man that according to Nietzsche has learned to forgo fleeting pleasures and attain happiness and dominance through the exercise of creative power **2 :** a person of extraordinary or superhuman power or achievements

su·per·mar·ket \-,mär-kət\ *n, often attrib* (1933) **1 :** a self-service retail market selling esp. foods and household merchandise **2 :** something resembling a supermarket esp. in the variety or volume of its goods or services

su·per·mi·cro \-,mī-(,)krō\ *n* (1982) : a very fast and powerful microcomputer

su·per·mini·com·put·er \-'mi-nē-kəm-,pyü-tər\ *n* (1980) : a very fast and powerful minicomputer — called also *supermini*

su·per·nal \su-'pər-n²l\ *adj* [ME, fr. MF, fr. L *supernus*, fr. *super* over, above — more at OVER] (15c) **1 a :** being or coming from on high **b :** HEAVENLY, ETHEREAL ⟨∼ melodies⟩ **c :** superlatively good ⟨∼ trumpet playing⟩ **2 :** located in or belonging to the sky — **su·per·nal·ly** \-n²l-ē\ *adv*

su·per·na·tant \,sü-pər-'nā-t²nt\ *n* [L *supernatant-, supernatans*, prp. of *supernatare* to float, fr. *super-* + *natare* to swim — more at NATANT] (1922) : the usu. clear liquid overlying material deposited by settling, precipitation, or centrifugation — **supernatant** *adj*

su·per·nat·u·ral \,sü-pər-'na-chə-rəl, -'nach-rəl\ *adj* [ML *supernaturalis*, fr. L *super-* + *natura* nature] (15c) **1 :** of or relating to an order of existence beyond the visible observable universe; *esp* : of or relating to God or a god, demigod, spirit, or devil **2 a :** departing from what is usual or normal esp. so as to appear to transcend the laws of nature **b :** attributed to an invisible agent (as a ghost or spirit) — **supernatural** *n* — **su·per·nat·u·ral·ly** \-'na-chər-ə-lē, -'nach-rə-, -'na-chər-lē\ *adv* — **su·per·nat·u·ral·ness** *n*

su·per·nat·u·ral·ism \,sü-pər-'na-chə-rə-,li-zəm, -'nach-rə-\ *n* (1799) **1 :** the quality or state of being supernatural **2 :** belief in a supernatural power and order of existence — **su·per·nat·u·ral·ist** \-list\ *n or adj* — **su·per·nat·u·ral·is·tic** \-,na-chə-rə-'lis-tik, -,nach-rə-\ *adj*

su·per·na·ture \'sü-pər-,nā-chər\ *n* [back-formation fr. *supernatural*] (1844) : the realm of the supernatural

su·per·nor·mal \,sü-pər-'nor-məl\ *adj* (1868) **1 :** exceeding the normal or average **2 :** being beyond normal human powers : PARANORMAL — **su·per·nor·mal·i·ty** \-nor-'ma-lə-tē\ *n* — **su·per·nor·mal·ly** \-'nor-mə-lē\ *adv*

su·per·no·va \,sü-pər-'nō-və\ *n* [NL] (1926) **1 :** the explosion of a very large star in which the star may reach a maximum intrinsic luminosity one billion times that of the sun **2 :** one that explodes into prominence or popularity; *also* : SUPERSTAR

¹su·per·nu·mer·ary \,sü-pər-'nü-mə-,rer-ē, -'nyü-, -mə-rē\ *adj* [LL *supernumerarius*, fr. L *super-* + *numerus* number] (1605) **1 a :** exceeding the usual, stated, or prescribed number ⟨a ∼ tooth⟩ **b :** not enumerated among the regular components of a group and esp. of a military organization **2 :** exceeding what is necessary, required, or desired **3 :** more numerous

²supernumerary *n, pl* **-ar·ies** (1639) **1 :** a supernumerary person or thing **2 :** an actor employed to play a walk-on

su·per·or·der \'sü-pər-,or-dər\ *n* (ca. 1890) : a category of biological classification ranking below a class and above an order

su·per·or·di·nate \,sü-pər-'ord-nət, -'or-d²n-ət, -'or-d²n-,āt\ *adj* [*super-* + *subordinate*] (1620) : superior in rank, class, or status

su·per·or·gan·ism \-'or-gə-,ni-zəm\ *n* (ca. 1899) : an organized society (as of a social insect) that functions as an organic whole

su·per·ovu·la·tion \-,äv-yə-'lā-shən, -,ōv-\ *n* (1927) : production of exceptional numbers of ova at one time — **su·per·ovu·late** \-'äv-yə-,lāt, -'ōv-\ *vb*

su·per·ox·ide \-'äk-,sīd\ *n* (ca. 1847) : the univalent anion O⁻₂ or a compound containing it ⟨potassium ∼ KO_2⟩

superoxide dis·mut·ase \-dis-'myü-,tās, -,tāz\ *n* [*dismutation* (simultaneous oxidation and reduction) + *-ase*] (1969) : a metal-containing enzyme that reduces potentially harmful free radicals of oxygen formed during normal metabolic cell processes to oxygen and hydrogen peroxide

su·per·par·a·sit·ism \,sü-pər-'par-ə-,sī-,ti-zəm, -sə-\ *n* (ca. 1899) : parasitization of a host by more than one parasitic individual usu. of a kind — used esp. of parasitic insects

su·per·phos·phate \,sü-pər-'fäs-,fāt\ *n* (1797) **1 :** an acid phosphate **2 :** a soluble mixture of phosphates used as fertilizer and made from insoluble mineral phosphates by treatment with sulfuric acid

su·per·phys·i·cal \-'fi-zi-kəl\ *adj* (ca. 1603) : being above or beyond the physical world or explanation on physical principles

su·per·plas·tic \-'plas-tik\ *adj* (1947) **1 :** capable of plastic deformation under low stress at an elevated temperature — used of metals and alloys **2 :** of or relating to superplastic materials ⟨∼ forming⟩ — **su·per·plas·tic·i·ty** \-pla-'sti-sə-tē\ *n*

su·per·pose \,sü-pər-'pōz\ *vt* **-posed; -pos·ing** [prob. fr. F *superposer*, back-formation fr. *superposition*, fr. LL *superposition-, superpositio*, fr. L *superponere* to superpose, fr. *super-* + *ponere* to place — more at POSITION] (1823) **1 :** to place or lay over or above whether in or not in contact : SUPERIMPOSE **2 :** to lay (as a geometric figure) upon another so as to make all like parts coincide — **su·per·pos·able** \-'pō-zə-bəl\ *adj* — **su·per·po·si·tion** \-pə-'zi-shən\ *n*

su·per·posed \-'pōzd\ *adj* (1823) : situated vertically over another layer or part

su·per·pow·er \'sü-pər-,pau̇(-ə)r\ *n* (1922) **1 :** excessive or superior power **2 a :** an extremely powerful nation; *specif* : one of a very few dominant states in an era when the world is divided politically into these states and their satellites **b :** an international governing body able to enforce its will upon the most powerful states — **su·per·pow·ered** \-,pau̇(-ə)rd\ *adj*

su·per·sat·u·rate \,sü-pər-'sa-chə-,rāt\ *vt* (1788) : to add to (a solution) beyond saturation

su·per·sat·u·rat·ed *adj* (1854) : containing an amount of a substance greater than that required for saturation as a result of having been cooled from a higher temperature to a temperature below that at which saturation occurs ⟨a ∼ solution⟩ ⟨air ∼ with water vapor⟩ — **su·per·sat·u·ra·tion** \-,sa-chə-'rā-shən\ *n* (1836) : the state of being supersaturated

su·per·scribe \'sü-pər-,skrīb, ,sü-pər-'\ *vt* **-scribed; -scrib·ing** [ME, fr. L *superscribere*, fr. *super-* + *scribere* to write — more at SCRIBE] (15c) **1 :** to write (as a name or address) on the outside or cover of : ADDRESS **2 :** to write or engrave on the top or outside

su·per·script \'sü-pər-,skript\ *n* [L *superscriptus*, pp. of *superscribere*] (1901) : a distinguishing symbol (as a numeral or letter) written immediately above or above and to the right or left of another character — **superscript** *adj*

su·per·scrip·tion \,sü-pər-'skrip-shən\ *n* [ME, fr. MF, fr. LL *superscription-, superscriptio*, fr. L *superscribere*] (14c) **1 :** something written or engraved on the surface of, outside, or above something else : INSCRIPTION; *also* : ADDRESS **2 :** the act of superscribing

su·per·sede \,sü-pər-'sēd\ *vt* **-sed·ed; -sed·ing** [ME *superceden*, fr. MF *superseder* to refrain from, fr. L *supersedēre* to be superior to, refrain from, fr. *super-* + *sedēre* to sit — more at SIT] (15c) **1 a :** to cause to be set aside **b :** to force out of use as inferior **2 :** to take the place, room, or position of **3 :** to displace in favor of another : SUPPLANT *syn* see REPLACE — **su·per·sed·er** *n*

su·per·se·de·as \,sü-pər-'sē-dē-əs\ *n, pl* **supersedeas** [ME, fr. L, you shall refrain, fr. *supersedēre*] (14c) **1 :** a common-law writ commanding a stay of legal proceedings that is issued under various conditions and esp. to stay an officer from proceeding under another writ **2 :** an order staying proceedings of an inferior court

su·per·se·dure \-'sē-jər\ *n* (1788) : the act or process of superseding; *esp* : the replacement of an old or inferior queen bee by a young or superior queen

su·per·sen·si·ble \,sü-pər-'sen(t)-sə-bəl\ *adj* (1798) : being above or beyond that which is apparent to the senses : SPIRITUAL

su·per·sen·si·tive \-'sen(t)-sə-tiv, -'sen(t)-stiv\ *adj* (1839) : HYPERSENSITIVE ⟨a ∼ palate⟩ — **su·per·sen·si·tive·ly** *adv* — **su·per·sen·si·tiv·i·ty** \-,sen(t)-sə-'ti-və-tē\ *n*

su·per·so·ry \,sü-pər-'sō-rē, -'sen(t)-sə-rē\ *adj* (1883) : SUPERSENSIBLE

su·per·ser·vice·able \-'sər-və-sə-bəl\ *adj* (1605) : offering unwanted services : OFFICIOUS

su·per·ses·sion \,sü-pər-'se-shən\ *n* [ML *supersession-, supersessio*, fr. L *supersedēre*] (1790) : the act of superseding : the state of being superseded

¹su·per·son·ic \-'sä-nik\ *adj* [L *super-* + *sonus* sound — more at SOUND] (1919) **1 :** ULTRASONIC **2 :** of, being, or relating to speeds from one to five times the speed of sound in air — compare SONIC **3 :** moving, capable of moving, or utilizing air currents moving at supersonic speed **4 :** relating to supersonic airplanes or missiles ⟨the ∼ age⟩ — **su·per·son·i·cal·ly** \-ni-k(ə-)lē\ *adv*

²supersonic *n* (ca. 1924) **1 :** a supersonic wave or frequency **2 :** a supersonic airplane

su·per·son·ics \,sü-pər-'sä-niks\ *n pl but sing in constr* (1925) : the science of supersonic phenomena

supersonic transport *n* (1961) : a supersonic transport airplane

su·per·star \'sü-pər-,stär\ *n* (1924) **1 :** a star (as in sports or the movies) who is considered extremely talented, has great public appeal, and can usu. command a high salary **2 :** one that is very prominent or is a prime attraction — **su·per·star·dom** \-dəm\ *n*

su·per·sti·tion \,sü-pər-'sti-shən\ *n* [ME *supersticion*, fr. MF, fr. L *superstition-, superstitio*, fr. *superstit-, superstes* standing over (as witness or survivor), fr. *super-* + *stare* to stand — more at STAND] (13c) **1 a :** a belief or practice resulting from ignorance, fear of the unknown, trust in magic or chance, or a false conception of causation **b :** an irrational abject attitude of mind toward the supernatural, nature, or God resulting from superstition **2 :** a notion maintained despite evidence to the contrary

su·per·sti·tious \-'sti-shəs\ *adj* [ME *supersticious*, fr. MF *supersticieux*, fr. L *superstitiosus*, fr. *superstitio*] (14c) : of, relating to, or swayed by superstition — **su·per·sti·tious·ly** *adv*

su·per·store \'sü-pər-,stōr, -,stȯr\ *n* (1943) : a very large store offering a wide variety of merchandise for sale

su·per·string \-,striŋ\ *n* (1983) : a hypothetical string obeying the rules of supersymmetry whose vibrations manifest themselves as particles existing in ten dimensions of which only four are evident

su·per·struc·ture \-,strək-chər\ *n* (1641) **1 a :** an entity, concept, or complex based on a more fundamental one **b :** social institutions (as the law or politics) that are in Marxist theory erected upon the economic base **2 :** a structure built as a vertical extension of something else: as **a :** all of a building above the basement **b :** the structural part of a ship above the main deck — **su·per·struc·tur·al** \,sü-pər-'strək-chə-rəl, -'strək-shrəl\ *adj*

su·per·stan·tial \,sü-pər-səb-'stan(t)-shəl\ *adj* [LL *supersubstantialis*, fr. L *super-* + *substantia* substance] (1534) : being above material substance : of a transcending substance

su·per·sym·me·try \-'si-mə-trē\ *n* (1974) : the correspondence between fermions and bosons of identical mass that is postulated to have existed during the opening moments of the big bang and that relates gravity to the other forces of nature — **su·per·sym·met·ric** \-sə-'me-trik\ *adj*

su·per·sys·tem \'sü-pər-,sis-təm\ *n* (ca. 1928) : a system that is made up of systems

su·per·tax \-,taks\ *n* (1906) : SURTAX

su·per·ton·ic \,sü-pər-'tä-nik\ *n* (1806) : the second tone of a diatonic scale

su·per·vene \,sü-pər-'vēn\ *vi* **-vened; -ven·ing** [L *supervenire*, fr. *super-* + *venire* to come — more at COME] (ca. 1648) : to follow or result

---

\ə\ abut \'ə\ kitten, F table \ər\ further \a\ ash \ā\ ace \ä\ mop, mar \au̇\ out \ch\ chin \e\ bet \ē\ easy \g\ go \i\ hit \ī\ ice \j\ job \ŋ\ sing \ō\ go \ȯ\ law \ȯi\ boy \th\ thin \th\ the \ü\ loot \u̇\ foot \y\ yet \zh\ vision \ä, k̲, ⁿ, œ, œ̄, ūe, ᵊ\ *see* Guide to Pronunciation as an additional, adventitious, or unlooked-for development *syn* see FOLLOW — **su·per·ven·tion** \-'ven(t)-shən\ *n*

su·per·ve·nient \-'vē-nyənt\ *adj* [L *supervenient-, superveniens,* prp. of *supervenire*] (1594) : coming or occurring as something additional, extraneous, or unexpected

su·per·vise \'sü-pər-ˌvīz\ *vt* **-vised; -vis·ing** [ML *supervisus,* pp. of *supervidēre,* fr. L *super-* + *vidēre* to see — more at WIT] (1588) : SUPER-INTEND, OVERSEE

su·per·vi·sion \ˌsü-pər-'vi-zhən\ *n* (1640) : the action, process, or occupation of supervising; *esp* : a critical watching and directing (as of activities or a course of action)

su·per·vi·sor \'sü-pər-ˌvī-zər\ *n* (15c) : one that supervises; *esp* : an administrative officer in charge of a business, government, or school unit or operation — **su·per·vi·so·ry** \ˌsü-pər-'vī-zə-rē, -'vīz-rē\ *adj*

su·per·wom·an \'sü-pər-ˌwu̇-mən\ *n* (1906) : an exceptional woman; *esp* : a woman who succeeds in having a career and raising a family

su·pi·nate \'sü-pə-ˌnāt\ *vb* **-nat·ed; -nat·ing** [L *supinatus,* pp. of *supinare* to lay backward or on the back, fr. *supinus*] *vt* (1831) : to cause to undergo supination ~ *vi* : to undergo supination

su·pi·na·tion \ˌsü-pə-'nā-shən\ *n* (1666) **1** : rotation of the forearm and hand so that the palm faces forward or upward and the radius lies parallel to the ulna; *also* : a corresponding movement of the foot and leg **2** : the position resulting from supination

su·pi·na·tor \'sü-pə-ˌnā-tər\ *n* [NL, fr. L *supinare*] (1615) : a muscle that produces the motion of supination

¹su·pine \'sü-ˌpīn\ *n* [ME *supyn,* fr. LL *supinum,* fr. L, neut. of *supinus,* adj.] (15c) **1** : a Latin verbal noun having an accusative of purpose in *-um* and an ablative of specification in *-u* **2** : an English infinitive with *to*

²su·pine \sü-'pīn, *attrib usu* 'sü-ˌpīn\ *adj* [ME *suppyne,* fr. L *supinus;* akin to L *sub* under, up to — more at UP] (15c) **1 a** : lying on the back or with the face upward **b** : marked by supination **2** : exhibiting indolent or apathetic inertia or passivity; *esp* : mentally or morally slack **3** *archaic* : leaning or sloping backward *syn* see PRONE, INACTIVE — **su·pine·ly** \sü-'pīn-lē\ *adv* — **su·pine·ness** \-'pīn-nəs\ *n*

sup·per \'sə-pər\ *n* [ME, fr. OF *souper,* fr. *souper* to sup — more at SUP] (13c) **1 a** : the evening meal esp. when dinner is taken at midday **b** : a social affair featuring a supper; *esp* : an evening social esp. for raising funds (a church ~) **2** : the food served as a supper (eat your ~) **3** : a light meal served late in the evening

supper club *n* (1925) : NIGHTCLUB

sup·plant \sə-'plant\ *vt* [ME, fr. MF *supplanter,* fr. L *supplantare* to overthrow by tripping up, fr. *sub-* + *planta* sole of the foot — more at PLACE] (14c) **1** : to supersede (another) esp. by force or treachery **2 a** (1) *obs* : UPROOT (2) : to eradicate and supply a substitute for (efforts to ~ the vernacular) **b** : to take the place of and serve as a substitute for esp. by reason of superior excellence or power *syn* see REPLACE — **sup·plan·ta·tion** \ˌ(ˌ)sə-ˌplan-'tā-shən\ *n* — **sup·plant·er** \sə-'plan-tər\ *n*

¹sup·ple \'sə-pəl *also* 'sü-\ *adj* **sup·pler** \-p(ə-)lər\; **sup·plest** \-p(ə-)ləst\ [ME *souple,* fr. MF, fr. L *supplic-, supplex* entreating for mercy, suppliant, perh. fr. *sub-* + *-plic-* (akin to *plicare* to fold) — more at PLY] (14c) **1 a** : compliant often to the point of obsequiousness **b** : readily adaptable or responsive to new situations **2 a** : capable of being bent or folded without creases, cracks, or breaks : PLIANT (~ leather) **b** : able to perform bending or twisting movements with ease and grace : LIMBER (~ legs of a dancer) **c** : easy and fluent without stiffness or awkwardness (sang with a lively, ~ voice —Douglas Watt) *syn* see ELASTIC — **sup·ple·ly** \-p(ə)l-lē\ *or* **sup·ply** \-p(ə-)lē\ *adv* — **sup·ple·ness** \-pəl-nəs\ *n*

²sup·ple *vb* **sup·pled; sup·pling** \-p(ə-)liŋ\ *vt* (14c) **1** : to make pacific or complaisant (~ the tempers of your race —Laurence Sterne) **2** : to alleviate with a salve **3** : to make flexible or pliant ~ *vi* : to become soft and pliant

sup·ple·jack \'sə-pəl-ˌjak *also* 'sü-\ *n* (ca. 1725) : any of various woody climbers having tough pliant stems; *esp* : a southern U.S. vine (*Berchemia scandens*) of the buckthorn family

¹sup·ple·ment \'sə-plə-mənt\ *n* [ME, fr. L *supplementum,* fr. *supplēre* to fill up, complete — more at SUPPLY] (14c) **1** : something that completes or makes an addition (dietary ~s) **2** : a part added to or issued as a continuation of a book or periodical to correct errors or make additions **3** : an angle or arc that when added to a given angle or arc equals 180°

²sup·ple·ment \'sə-plə-ˌment\ *vt* (1829) : to add or serve as a supplement to (does odd jobs to ~ his income) — **sup·ple·men·ta·tion** \ˌsə-plə-ˌmen-'tā-shən, -mən-\ *n* — **sup·ple·ment·er** \'sə-plə-ˌmen-tər\ *n*

sup·ple·men·tal \ˌsə-plə-'men-t�ᵊl\ *adj* (1605) **1** : serving to supplement **2** : NONSCHEDULED (an ~ airline) — **supplemental** *n*

sup·ple·men·ta·ry \ˌsə-plə-'men-tə-rē, -'men-trē\ *adj* (1667) **1** : added or serving as a supplement : ADDITIONAL (~ reading) **2** : being or relating to a supplement or a supplementary angle

supplementary angle *n* (ca. 1924) : one of two angles or arcs whose sum is 180° — usu. used in pl.

sup·ple·tion \sə-'plē-shən\ *n* [ML *suppletion-, suppletio* act of supplementing, fr. L *supplēre*] (1914) : the occurrence of phonemically unrelated allomorphs of the same morpheme (as *went* as the past tense of *go* or *better* as the comparative form of *good*) — **sup·ple·tive** \sə-'plē-tiv, 'sə-plə-\ *adj*

sup·ple·to·ry \sə-'plē-tə-rē; 'sə-plə-ˌtōr-ē, -ˌtȯr-\ *adj* [L *supplēre*] (1628) : supplying deficiencies : SUPPLEMENTARY

sup·pli·ance \sə-'plē-ən(t)s\ *n* (ca. 1611) : ENTREATY, SUPPLICATION

¹sup·pli·ant \-ənt\ *n* [ME, fr. MF, fr. prp. of *supplier* to supplicate, fr. L *supplicare*] (15c) : one who supplicates

²suppliant *adj* [MF, prp.] (ca. 1586) **1** : humbly imploring : ENTREATING (a ~ sinner seeking forgiveness —O. J. Baab) **2** : expressing supplication (upraised to the heavens . . . ~ arms —William Styron) — **sup·pli·ant·ly** *adv*

¹sup·pli·cant \'sə-pli-kənt\ *adj* (1597) : SUPPLIANT

²supplicant *n* (1597) : SUPPLIANT

sup·pli·cate \'sə-plə-ˌkāt\ *vb* **-cat·ed; -cat·ing** [ME, fr. L *supplicatus,* pp. of *supplicare,* fr. *supplic-, supplex* suppliant — more at SUPPLE] *vi* (15c) : to make a humble entreaty; *esp* : to pray to God ~ *vt* **1** : to

ask humbly and earnestly of **2** : to ask for earnestly and humbly *syn* see BEG — **sup·pli·ca·tion** \ˌsə-plə-'kā-shən\ *n*

sup·pli·ca·to·ry \'sə-pli-kə-ˌtōr-ē, -ˌtȯr-\ *adj* (15c) : expressing supplication : SUPPLIANT (a ~ prayer)

¹sup·ply \sə-'plī\ *vb* **sup·plied; sup·ply·ing** [ME *supplien,* fr. MF *soupleier,* fr. L *supplēre* to fill up, supplement, supply, fr. *sub-* up + *plēre* to fill — more at SUB, FULL] *vt* (14c) **1** : to add as a supplement **2 a** : to provide for : SATISFY (laws by which the material wants of men are supplied —*Bull. of Bates Coll.*) **b** : to make available for use : PROVIDE (supplied the necessary funds) **c** : to satisfy the needs or wishes of **d** : to furnish (organs, tissues, or cells) with a vital element (as blood or nerve fibers) **3** : to substitute for another in; *specif* : to serve as a supply in (a church or pulpit) ~ *vi* : to serve as a supply or substitute — **sup·pli·er** \-'plī(-ə)r\ *n*

²supply *n, pl* **supplies** (15c) **1** *obs* : ASSISTANCE, SUCCOR **2 a** *obs* : REINFORCEMENTS — often used in pl. **b** : a clergyman filling a vacant pulpit temporarily **c** : the quantity or amount (as of a commodity) needed or available (beer was in short ~ in that hot weather —Nevil Shute) **d** : PROVISIONS, STORES — usu. used in pl. **3** : the act or process of filling a want or need (engaged in the ~ of raw materials to industry) **4** : the quantities of goods or services offered for sale at a particular time or at one price **5** : something that maintains or constitutes a supply

sup·ply–side \sə-'plī-ˌsīd\ *adj* (1976) : of, relating to, or being an economic theory that reduction of tax rates encourages more earnings, savings, and investment and thereby expands economic activity and the total taxable national income — **sup·ply–sid·er** \-'sī-dər\ *n*

¹sup·port \sə-'pōrt, -'pȯrt\ *vt* [ME, fr. MF *supporter,* fr. L *supportare,* fr. L, to carry, fr. *sub-* + *portare* to carry — more at FARE] (14c) **1** : to endure bravely or quietly : BEAR **2 a** (1) : to promote the interests or cause of (2) : to uphold or defend as valid or right : ADVOCATE (3) : to argue or vote for **b** (1) : ASSIST, HELP (2) : to act with (a star actor) (3) : to bid in bridge so as to show support for **c** : to provide with substantiation : CORROBORATE (~ an alibi) **3 a** : to pay the costs of : MAINTAIN **b** : to provide a basis for the existence or subsistence of (the island could probably ~ three —A. B. C. Whipple) **4 a** : to hold up or serve as a foundation or prop for **b** : to maintain (a price) at a desired level by purchases or loans; *also* : to maintain the price of by purchases or loans **5** : to keep from fainting, yielding, or losing courage : COMFORT **6** : to keep (something) going — **sup·port·abil·i·ty** \sə-ˌpōr-tə-'bi-lə-tē, -ˌpȯr-\ *n* — **sup·port·able** \-'pōr-tə-bəl, -'pȯr-\ *adj* — **sup·port·ive** \-'pōr-tiv, -'pȯr-\ *adj* — **sup·port·ive·ness** \-nəs\ *n*

syn SUPPORT, UPHOLD, ADVOCATE, BACK, CHAMPION mean to favor actively one that meets opposition. SUPPORT is least explicit about the nature of the assistance given (supports waterfront development). UPHOLD implies extended support given to something attacked (upheld the legitimacy of the military action). ADVOCATE stresses urging or pleading (advocated prison reform). BACK suggests supporting by lending assistance to one failing or falling (refusing to *back* the call for sanctions). CHAMPION suggests publicly defending one unjustly attacked or too weak to advocate his or her own cause (championed the rights of children).

²support *n* (14c) **1** : the act or process of supporting : the condition of being supported **2** : one that supports **3** : sufficient strength in a suit bid by one's partner in bridge to justify raising the suit

sup·port·er *n* (15c) : one that supports or acts as a support: as **a** : ADHERENT, PARTISAN **b** : one of two figures (as of men or animals) placed one on each side of an escutcheon and exterior to it **c** : GARTER **1 d** : ATHLETIC SUPPORTER

support group *n* (1969) : a group of people with common experiences and concerns who provide emotional and moral support for one another

support hose *n* (1963) : elastic stockings

support level *n* (1953) : a price level on a declining market at which a security resists further decline due to increased attractiveness to traders and investors — called *also support area*

support system *n* (1980) : a network of people who provide an individual with practical or emotional support

sup·pos·able \sə-'pō-zə-bəl\ *adj* (1643) : capable of being supposed : CONCEIVABLE — **sup·pos·ably** \-blē\ *adv*

sup·pos·al \-'pō-zəl\ *n* (14c) **1** : the act or process of supposing **2** : something supposed : HYPOTHESIS, SUPPOSITION

sup·pose \sə-'pōz, *oftenest after "I"* 'spōz\ *vb* **sup·posed; sup·pos·ing** [ME, fr. MF *supposer,* fr. ML *supponere* (perf. indic. *supposui*), fr. L, to put under, substitute, fr. *sub-* + *ponere* to put — more at POSITION] *vt* (14c) **1 a** : to lay down tentatively as a hypothesis, assumption, or proposal (~ a fire broke out) (~ you bring the salad) **b** (1) : to hold as an opinion : BELIEVE (they supposed they were early) (2) : to think probable or in keeping with the facts (seems reasonable to ~ that he would profit) **2 a** : CONCEIVE, IMAGINE **b** : to have a suspicion of **3** : PRESUPPOSE ~ *vi* : CONJECTURE, OPINE

sup·posed \sə-'pōzd; *1b & 2a usu* -'pōst, *3 & 4 often* -'pōst\ *adj* (1566) **1 a** : PRETENDED (twelve hours are ~ to elapse between Acts I and II —A. S. Sullivan) **b** : ALLEGED (trusted my ~ friends) **2 a** : held as an opinion : BELIEVED; *also* : mistakenly believed : IMAGINED (the sight which makes ~ terror true —Shak.) **b** : considered probable or certain : EXPECTED (it was not ~ that everybody could master the technical aspects —J. C. Murray) **c** : UNDERSTOOD (you will be ~ to refer to my grandaunt —G. B. Shaw) **3** : made or fashioned by intent or design (what's that button ~ to do) **4 a** : required by or as if by authority (soldiers are ~ to obey their commanding officers) **b** : given permission : PERMITTED (was not ~ to have visitors) — **sup·pos·ed·ly** \-'pō-zəd-lē *also* -'pōzd-lē\ *adv*

sup·pos·ing \sə-'pō-ziŋ\ *conj* (ca. 1843) : if by way of hypothesis : on the assumption that

sup·po·si·tion \ˌsə-pə-'zi-shən\ *n* [ME, fr. ML *supposition-, suppositio,* fr. L, act of placing beneath, fr. *supponere*] (15c) **1** : something that is supposed : HYPOTHESIS **2** : the act of supposing — **sup·po·si·tion·al** \-'zish-nəl, -'zi-shə-n⁷l\ *adj*

sup·po·si·tious \-'zi-shəs\ *adj* [by contr.] (1624) : SUPPOSITITIOUS

sup·pos·i·ti·tious \sə-ˌpä-zə-'ti-shəs\ *adj* [L *supposititius,* fr. *suppositus,* pp. of *supponere* to substitute] (1611) **1 a** : fraudulently substituted : SPURIOUS **b** *of a child* (1) : falsely presented as a genuine heir (2)

: ILLEGITIMATE **2** [influenced in meaning by *supposition*] **a** : IMAGINARY **b** : of the nature of or based on a supposition : HYPOTHETICAL — **sup·pos·i·ti·tious·ly** *adv*

sup·pos·i·to·ry \sə-'pä-zə-ˌtōr-ē, -ˌtòr-\ *n, pl* **-ries** [ME, fr. ML *suppositorium*, fr. LL, neut. of *suppositorius* placed beneath, fr. L *supponere* to put under] (14c) : a solid but readily meltable cone or cylinder of usu. medicated material for insertion into a bodily passage or cavity (as the rectum)

sup·press \sə-'pres\ *vt* [ME, fr. L *suppressus*, pp. of *supprimere*, fr. *sub-* + *premere* to press — more at PRESS] (14c) **1** : to put down by authority or force : SUBDUE **2** : to keep from public knowledge: as **a** : to keep secret **b** : to stop or prohibit the publication or revelation of **3 a** : to exclude from consciousness **b** : to keep from giving vent to : CHECK **4** *obs* : to press down **5 a** : to restrain from a usual course or action : ARREST ⟨~ a cough⟩ **b** : to inhibit the growth or development of : STUNT **6** : to inhibit the genetic expression of ⟨~ a mutation⟩ — **sup·press·ibil·i·ty** \-ˌpre-sə-'bi-lə-tē\ *n* — **sup·press·ible** \-'pre-sə-bəl\ *adj* — **sup·pres·sive** \-'pre-siv\ *adj* — **sup·pres·sive·ness** \-nəs\ *n*

sup·pres·sant \sə-'pre-sᵊnt\ *n* (1942) : an agent (as a drug) that tends to suppress or reduce in intensity rather than eliminate something (as appetite)

sup·pres·sion \sə-'pre-shən\ *n* (15c) **1** : an act or instance of suppressing : the state of being suppressed **2** : the conscious intentional exclusion from consciousness of a thought or feeling

sup·pres·sor \sə-'pre-sər\ *n* (1560) : one that suppresses; *esp* : a mutant gene that suppresses the expression of another nonallelic mutant gene when both are present

suppressor T cell *n* (1972) : a T cell that suppresses the immune response of B cells and other T cells to an antigen — called also *suppressor cell*

sup·pu·rate \'sə-pyə-ˌrāt\ *vi* **-rat·ed; -rat·ing** [L *suppuratus*, pp. of *suppurare*, fr. *sub-* + *pur-, pus* pus — more at FOUL] (1656) : to form or discharge pus — **sup·pu·ra·tion** \ˌsə-pyə-'rā-shən\ *n* — **sup·pu·ra·tive** \'sə-pyə-rə-tiv, -ˌrā-\ *adj*

su·pra \'sü-prə, -ˌprä\ *adv* [L] (1526) : earlier in this writing : ABOVE

supra- *prefix* [L, fr. *supra* above, beyond, earlier; akin to L *super* over — more at OVER] **1** : SUPER- 2a ⟨*supra*orbital⟩ **2** : transcending ⟨*supra*molecular⟩

su·pra·lim·i·nal \ˌsü-prə-'li-mə-nᵊl, -ˌprä-\ *adj* [*supra-* + L *limin-, limen* threshold] (1892) **1** : existing above the threshold of consciousness **2** : adequate to evoke a response or induce a sensation ⟨~ stimulus⟩

su·pra·mo·lec·u·lar \-mə-'le-kyə-lər\ *adj* (ca. 1909) : more complex than a molecule; *also* : composed of many molecules

su·pra·na·tion·al \-'nash-nəl, -'na-shə-nᵊl\ *adj* (1908) : transcending national boundaries, authority, or interests ⟨a ~ authority, regulating ocean usage —N. H. Jacoby⟩ — **su·pra·na·tion·al·ism** \-'nash-nə-ˌli-zəm, -'na-shə-nᵊl-ˌi-\ *n* — **su·pra·na·tion·al·ist** \-list, -ist\ *n* — **su·pra·na·tion·al·i·ty** \-ˌna-shə-'na-lə-tē\ *n*

su·pra·op·tic \-'äp-tik\ *adj* (1921) : situated above the optic chiasma; *also* : being a small nucleus of closely packed neurons overlying the optic chiasma and intimately connected with the neurohypophysis

su·pra·or·bit·al \-'òr-bə-tᵊl\ *adj* [NL *supraorbitalis*, fr. L *supra-* + ML *orbita* orbit] (1828) : situated or occurring above the orbit of the eye

su·pra·ra·tio·nal \-'rash-nəl, -'ra-shə-nᵊl\ *adj* (1894) : transcending the rational : based on or involving factors not to be comprehended by reason alone ⟨the stars inspire ~ dreams —R. J. Dubos⟩

¹su·pra·re·nal \-'rē-nᵊl\ *adj* [NL *suprarenalis*, fr. L *supra-* + *renes* kidneys] (1828) : situated above or anterior to the kidneys

²suprarenal *n* (1841) : a suprarenal part; *esp* : ADRENAL GLAND

suprarenal gland *n* (1876) : ADRENAL GLAND

su·pra·seg·men·tal \ˌsü-prə-seg-'men-tᵊl, -ˌprä-\ *adj* (1941) : of or relating to significant features (as stress, pitch, or juncture) that occur simultaneously with vowels and consonants in an utterance

sup·ra·ven·tric·u·lar \-ven-'tri-kyə-lər, -vən-\ *adj* (1951) : relating to or being a rhythmic abnormality of the heart caused by impulses originating above the ventricles ⟨~ tachycardia⟩

su·pra·vi·tal \-'vi-tᵊl\ *adj* [ISV] (1919) : constituting or relating to the staining of living tissues or cells surviving after removal from a living body by dyes that penetrate living substance but induce more or less rapid degenerative changes — compare INTRAVITAL 2 — **su·pra·vi·tal·ly** \-tᵊl-ē\ *adv*

su·prem·a·cist \sə-'pre-mə-sist, sü-\ *n* (1949) **1** : an advocate or adherent of group supremacy **2** : WHITE SUPREMACIST

su·prem·a·cy \sə-'pre-mə-sē, sü- *also* -'prē-\ *n, pl* **-cies** [*supreme* + *-acy* (as in *primacy*)] (1537) : the quality or state of being supreme; *also* : supreme authority or power

su·prem·a·tism \sə-'pre-mə-ˌti-zəm\ *n, often cap* [Russ *suprematizm*, fr. F *suprématie* supremacy + Russ *-izm* -ism] (1933) : an early 20th-century art movement in Russia producing abstract works featuring flat geometric forms — **su·prem·a·tist** \-tist\ *adj or n, often cap*

su·preme \sə-'prēm, sü-\ *adj* [L *supremus*, superl. of *superus* upper — more at SUPERIOR] (ca. 1533) **1** : highest in rank or authority ⟨the ~ commander⟩ **2** : highest in degree or quality ⟨~ endurance in war and in labour —R. W. Emerson⟩ **3** : ULTIMATE, FINAL ⟨the ~ sacrifice⟩ — **su·preme·ly** *adv* — **su·preme·ness** *n*

Supreme Being *n* (1699) : GOD 1

supreme court *n, often cap S&C* (1709) **1** : the highest judicial tribunal in a political unit (as a nation or state) **2** : a court of original jurisdiction in New York state subordinate to a final court of appeals

Supreme Soviet *n* (1936) : the highest legislative body of a nation (as Russia or the former Soviet Union)

su·pre·mo \sə-'prē-(ˌ)mō, sü-\ *n, pl* **-mos** [Sp & It, fr. *supremo*, adj., supreme, fr. L *supremus*] (1937) *Brit* : one who is highest in rank or authority

suq \'sük\ *var of* SOUK

sur- *prefix* [ME, fr. OF, fr. L *super-*] **1** : over : SUPER- ⟨*sur*print⟩ ⟨*sur*tax⟩ **2** : above : up ⟨*sur*base⟩

su·ra \'sur-ə\ *n* [Ar *sūrah*, lit., row] (1661) : a chapter of the Koran

su·rah \'sur-ə\ *n* [prob. alter. of *surat*, a cotton produced in Surat, India] (1873) : a soft twilled fabric of silk or rayon

sur·base \'sər-ˌbās\ *n* (1678) : a molding just above the base of a wall, pedestal, or podium

---

¹sur·cease \(ˌ)sər-'sēs, 'sər-ˌ\ *vb* **sur·ceased; sur·ceas·ing** [ME *sursesen, surcesen*, fr. MF *sursis*, pp. of *surseoir*, fr. L *supersedēre* — more at SUPERSEDE] *vi* (15c) : to desist from action; *also* : to come to an end : CEASE ~ *vt* : to put an end to : DISCONTINUE

²sur·cease \'sər-ˌsēs, (ˌ)sər-'\ *n* (1586) : CESSATION; *esp* : a temporary respite or end ⟨to borrow from my books ~ of sorrow —E. A. Poe⟩

¹sur·charge \'sər-ˌchärj\ *vt* [ME, fr. MF *surchargier*, fr. *sur-* + *chargier* to charge, fr. OF — more at CHARGE] (15c) **1 a** : OVERCHARGE **b** : to charge an extra fee **c** : to show an omission in (an account) for which credit ought to have been given **2** *Brit* : OVERSTOCK **3** : to fill or load to excess ⟨the atmosphere . . . was *surcharged* with war hysteria —H. A. Chippendale⟩ **4 a** : to mark a surcharge on (a stamp) **b** : OVERPRINT ⟨~ a banknote⟩

²surcharge *n* (15c) **1 a** : an additional tax, cost, or impost **b** : an extra fare ⟨a sleeping car ~⟩ **c** : an instance of surcharging an account **2** : an excessive load or burden **3** : the action of surcharging : the state of being surcharged **4 a** (1) : an overprint on a stamp; *specif* : one that alters the denomination (2) : a stamp bearing such an overprint **b** : a surcharge on a currency note

sur·cin·gle \'sər-ˌsiŋ-gəl\ *n* [ME *sursengle*, fr. MF *surcengle*, fr. *sur-* + *cengle* girdle, fr. L *cingulum* — more at CINGULUM] (14c) **1** : a belt, band, or girth passing around the body of a horse to bind a saddle or pack fast to the horse's back **2** *archaic* : the cincture of a cassock

sur·coat \'sər-ˌkōt\ *n* [ME *surcote*, fr. MF, fr. *sur-* + *cote* coat] (13c) : an outer coat or cloak; *specif* : a tunic worn over armor

¹surd \'sərd\ *adj* [L *surdus* deaf, silent, stupid] (1551) **1** : lacking sense : IRRATIONAL ⟨the ~ mystery and the strange forces of existence —D. C. Williams⟩ **2** : VOICELESS — used of speech sounds

²surd *n* (1557) **1 a** : an irrational root (as √3) **b** : IRRATIONAL NUMBER **2** : a surd speech sound

¹sure \'shur, *esp Southern* 'shòr\ *adj* **sur·er; sur·est** [ME, fr. MF *sur*, fr. L *securus* secure] (13c) **1** *obs* : safe from danger or harm **2** : firmly established : STEADFAST ⟨a ~ hold⟩ **3** : RELIABLE, TRUSTWORTHY **4** : marked by or given to feelings of confident certainty ⟨I'm ~ I'm right⟩ **5** : admitting of no doubt : INDISPUTABLE ⟨spoke from ~ knowledge⟩ **6 a** : bound to happen : INEVITABLE ⟨~ disaster⟩ **b** : BOUND, DESTINED ⟨is ~ to win⟩ **7** : careful to remember, attend to, or find out something ⟨be ~ to lock the door⟩ — **sure·ness** *n* — **for sure** : without doubt or question : CERTAINLY — **to be sure** : it must be acknowledged : ADMITTEDLY

syn SURE, CERTAIN, POSITIVE, COCKSURE mean having no doubt or uncertainty. SURE usu. stresses the subjective or intuitive feeling of assurance ⟨felt *sure* that I had forgotten something⟩. CERTAIN may apply to a basing of a conclusion or conviction on definite grounds or indubitable evidence ⟨police are *certain* about the cause of the fire⟩. POSITIVE intensifies sureness or certainty and may imply opinionated conviction or forceful expression of it ⟨I'm *positive* that's the person I saw⟩. COCKSURE implies presumptuous or careless positiveness ⟨you're always so *cocksure* about everything⟩.

²sure *adv* (14c) : SURELY

usage Most commentators consider the adverb *sure* to be something less than completely standard; *surely* is usu. recommended as a substitute. Our current evidence shows, however, that *sure* and *surely* have become differentiated in use. *Sure* is used in much more informal contexts than *surely*. It is used as a simple intensive ⟨I can never know how much I bored her, but, be certain, she *sure* amused me —Norman Mailer⟩ and, because it connotes strong affirmation, it is used when the speaker or writer expects to be agreed with ⟨it's a moot point whether politicians are less venal than in Twain's day. But they're *sure* as the devil more intrusive —Alan Abelson⟩ ⟨he *sure* gets them to play —D. S. Looney⟩. *Surely*, like *sure*, is used as a simple intensive ⟨I *surely* don't want to leave the impression that I had an unhappy childhood —E. C. Welsh⟩ but it occurs in more formal contexts than *sure*. Unlike *sure* it may be used neutrally ⟨the reader or hearer may or may not agree ⟨it would *surely* be possible, within a few years, to program a computer to construct a grammar —Noam Chomsky⟩ and it is often used when the writer is trying to persuade ⟨*surely* a book on the avant-garde cannot be so conventional —Karl Shapiro⟩.

sure—enough \'shur-ə-ˌnəf\ *adj* (ca. 1846) : ACTUAL, GENUINE, REAL

sure enough *adv* (ca. 1545) : as one might expect : CERTAINLY

sure-fire \'shur-ˌfir\ *adj* (ca. 1909) : certain to get successful or expected results ⟨a ~ recipe⟩

sure-foot·ed \-'fu-təd\ *adj* (1633) : not liable to stumble, fall, or err — **sure-foot·ed·ly** *adv* — **sure-foot·ed·ness** *n*

sure-hand·ed \-'han-dəd\ *adj* (1930) : proficient and confident in performance esp. using the hands — **sure-hand·ed·ness** *n*

sure·ly \'shur-lē\ *adv* (14c) **1** : in a sure manner: **a** *archaic* : without danger or risk of injury or loss : SAFELY **b** (1) : with assurance : CONFIDENTLY ⟨answered quickly and ~⟩ (2) : without doubt : CERTAINLY ⟨they will ~ be heard from in the future —R. J. Lifton⟩ **2** : INDEED, REALLY — often used as an intensive ⟨you ~ don't believe that⟩ **usage** see SURE

sure thing *n* (1836) : one that is certain to succeed : a sure bet

sure·ty \'shur(-ə)-tē\ *n, pl* **-ties** [ME *surte*, fr. MF *surté*, fr. L *securitat-, securitas* security, fr. *securus*] (14c) **1** : the state of being sure: as **a** : sure knowledge : CERTAINTY **b** : confidence in manner or behavior : ASSURANCE **2 a** : a formal engagement (as a pledge) given for the fulfillment of an undertaking : GUARANTEE **b** : ground of confidence or security **3** : one who has become legally liable for the debt, default, or failure in duty of another — **sure·ty·ship** \-ˌship\ *n*

surety bond *n* (1911) : a bond guaranteeing performance of a contract or obligation

¹surf \'sərf\ *n* [origin unknown] (1685) **1** : the swell of the sea that breaks upon the shore **2** : the foam, splash, and sound of breaking waves

²surf *vi* (1926) : to ride the surf (as on a surfboard) — **surf·er** *n*

¹sur·face \'sər-fəs\ *n* [F, fr. *sur-* + *face* face, fr. OF — more at FACE]

\ə\ abut \ᵊ\ kitten, F table \ər\ further \a\ ash \ā\ ace \ä\ mop, mar
\aú\ out \ch\ chin \e\ bet \ē\ easy \g\ go \i\ hit \ī\ ice \j\ job
\ŋ\ sing \ō\ go \ò\ law \òi\ boy \th\ thin \t͟h\ the \ü\ loot \ú\ foot
\y\ yet \zh\ vision \ä, k̲, ⁿ, œ, œ̄, ɶ, ue̅, ʸ\ *see* Guide to Pronunciation

(ca. 1604) **1** : the exterior or upper boundary of an object or body **2** : a plane or curved two-dimensional locus of points (as the boundary of a three-dimensional region) ⟨plane ∼⟩ ⟨∼ of a sphere⟩ **3 a** : the external or superficial aspect of something **b** : an external part or layer — **on the surface** : to all outward appearances

²**surface** adj (1664) **1 a** : of, located on, or designed for use at the surface of something **b** : situated, transported, or employed on the surface of the earth ⟨∼ mail⟩ ⟨∼ vehicles⟩ **2** : appearing to be such on the surface only : SUPERFICIAL ⟨∼ friendships⟩

³**surface** vb **sur·faced; sur·fac·ing** vt (1778) **1** : to give a surface to: as **a** : to plane or make smooth **b** : to apply the surface layer to ⟨∼ a highway⟩ **2** : to bring to the surface ∼ vi **1** : to work on or at the surface **2** : to come to the surface **3** : to come into public view : SHOW UP — **sur·fac·er** n

surface–active adj (1920) : altering the properties and esp. lowering the tension at the surface of contact between phases ⟨soaps and wetting agents are typical ∼ substances⟩

surface of revolution (1840) : a surface formed by the revolution of a plane curve about a line in its plane

sur·face–rip·ened \'sər-fəs-ˌrī-pənd, -ˌrī-p² md\ adj (1945) of cheese : ripened by the action of microorganisms (as molds) on the surface

surface structure n (1964) : a formal representation of the phonetic form of a sentence; also : the structure which such a representation describes

surface tension n (1876) : the attractive force exerted upon the surface molecules of a liquid by the molecules beneath that tends to draw the surface molecules into the bulk of the liquid and makes the liquid assume the shape having the least surface area

surface–to–air adj (1949) : launched from the ground against a target in the air

surfacing n (1882) : material forming or used to form a surface

sur·fac·tant \(ˌ)sər-'fak-tənt, 'sər-ˌ\ n [surface-active + -ant] (1950) : a surface-active substance (as a detergent) — **surfactant** adj

surf and turf n (1973) : seafood and steak served as a single course

surf·bird \'sərf-ˌbərd\ n (1839) : a shorebird (Aphriza virgata) of the Pacific coasts of America that has a black-tipped white tail

surf·board \-ˌbōrd, -ˌbȯrd\ n (ca. 1826) : a long narrow buoyant board (as of lightweight wood or fiberglass-covered foam) used in the sport of surfing — **surfboard** vi — **surf·board·er** n

surf·boat \-ˌbōt\ n (1847) : a boat for use in heavy surf

surf casting n (1928) : a method of fishing in which artificial or natural bait is cast into the open ocean or in a bay where waves break on a beach — **surf caster** n

surf clam n (1884) : any of various typically rather large surf-dwelling edible clams (family Mactridae); esp : a common clam (Spisula solidissima) of the Atlantic coast chiefly from Nova Scotia to So. Carolina

¹**sur·feit** \'sər-fət\ n [ME surfait, fr. MF, fr. surfaire to overdo, fr. sur- + faire to do, fr. L facere — more at DO] (14c) **1** : an overabundant supply : EXCESS **2** : an intemperate or immoderate indulgence in something (as food or drink) **3** : disgust caused by excess

²**surfeit** vt (14c) : to feed, supply, or give to surfeit ∼ vi, archaic : to indulge to satiety in a gratification (as indulgence of the appetite or senses) syn see SATIATE — **sur·feit·er** n

surf fish n (1882) : SURFPERCH

sur·fi·cial \ˌsər-'fi-shəl\ adj [surface + -icial (as in superficial)] (1892) : of or relating to a surface ⟨∼ geologic processes⟩

surf·ing \'sər-fiŋ\ n (1926) : the sport of riding the surf esp. on a surfboard

surf·perch \'sərf-ˌpərch\ n (1885) : any of a family (Embiotocidae) of small or medium-sized viviparous bony fishes chiefly of shallow water along the Pacific coast of No. America that resemble the perches

¹**surge** \'sərj\ vb **surged; surg·ing** [MF sourge-, stem of sourdre to rise, surge, fr. L surgere to go straight up, rise, fr. sub- up + regere to lead straight — more at SUB-, RIGHT] vi (1511) **1** : to rise and fall actively : TOSS ⟨a ship surging in heavy seas⟩ **2** : to rise and move in waves or billows : SWELL **3** : to slip around a windlass, capstan, or bitts — used esp. of a rope **4** : to rise suddenly to an excessive or abnormal value ⟨the stock market ∼ed to a record high⟩ **5** : to move with a surge or in surges ⟨felt the blood surging into his face—Harry Hervey⟩ ∼ vt : to let go or slacken gradually (as a rope)

²**surge** n (1520) **1** : a swelling, rolling, or sweeping forward like that of a wave or series of waves ⟨a ∼ of interest⟩ **2 a** : a large wave or billow : SWELL **b** (1) : a series of such swells or billows (2) : the resulting elevation of water level **3** : the tapered part of a windlass barrel or a capstan **4 a** : a movement (as a slipping or slackening) of a rope or cable **b** : a sudden jerk or strain caused by such a movement **5** : a transient sudden rise of current or voltage in an electrical circuit

sur·geon \'sər-jən\ n [ME surgien, fr. AF, fr. OF cirurgien, fr. cirurgie surgery] (14c) : a medical specialist who practices surgery

sur·geon·fish \-ˌfish\ n (1871) : any of a family (Acanthuridae) of tropical bony fishes that have toxic flesh and typically a movable spine on each side of the body near the base of the tail capable of inflicting a painful wound

surgeon general n, pl **surgeons general** (1706) : the chief medical officer of a branch of the armed services or of a public health service

surgeon's knot n (1733) : any of several knots used in tying ligatures or surgical stitches; esp : a reef knot in which the first knot has two turns — see KNOT illustration

sur·gery \'sərj-rē, 'sər-jə-\ n, pl **-ger·ies** [ME surgerie, fr. MF cirurgie, surgerie, fr. L chirurgia, fr. Gk cheirourgia, fr. cheirourgos surgeon, fr. cheirourgos doing by hand, fr. cheir hand + ergon work — more at CHIR-, WORK] (14c) **1** : a branch of medicine concerned with diseases and conditions requiring or amenable to operative or manual procedures **2** : alterations made as if by surgery ⟨literary ∼⟩ **3** Brit : a physician's or dentist's office **b** : a room or area where surgery is performed **4 a** : the work done by a surgeon **b** : OPERATION

sur·gi·cal \'sər-ji-kəl\ adj [surgeon + -ical] (1770) **1 a** : of or relating to surgeons or surgery ⟨∼ skills⟩ **b** : used in or in connection with surgery **c** : characteristic of or resembling surgery or a surgeon esp. in control or incisiveness ⟨∼ precision⟩ **2** : following or resulting from surgery ⟨∼ fevers⟩ — **sur·gi·cal·ly** \-k(ə-)lē\ adv

su·ri·mi \sú-'rē-mē\ n [Jp, chopped meat or fish] (1976) : a fish product made from inexpensive whitefish and often processed to resemble more expensive seafood (as crabmeat)

sur·jec·tion \(ˌ)sər-'jek-shən\ n [prob. fr. sur- + -jection (as in projection)] (1964) : a mathematical function that is an onto mapping — compare BIJECTION, INJECTION 3

sur·jec·tive \-'jek-tiv\ adj (1964) : ONTO ⟨a set of ∼ functions⟩

sur·ly \'sər-lē\ adj **sur·li·er; -est** [alter. of ME sirly lordly, imperious, fr. sir] (ca. 1572) **1** obs : ARROGANT, IMPERIOUS **2** : irritably sullen and churlish in mood or manner : CRABBED **3** : menacing or threatening in appearance ⟨∼ weather⟩ syn see SULLEN — **sur·li·ly** \-lə-lē\ adv — **sur·li·ness** \-lē-nəs\ n — **surly** adv

¹**sur·mise** \sər-'mīz, 'sər-ˌ\ n (1569) : a thought or idea based on scanty evidence : CONJECTURE

²**sur·mise** \sər-'mīz\ vt **sur·mised; sur·mis·ing** [ME, to accuse, fr. MF surmis, pp. of surmettre, fr. L supermittere to throw on, fr. super- + mittere to send] (1700) : to imagine or infer on slight grounds

sur·mount \sər-'maúnt\ vt [ME, fr. MF surmonter, fr. sur- + monter to mount] (14c) **1** obs : to surpass in quality or attainment : EXCEL **2** : to prevail over : OVERCOME ⟨∼ an obstacle⟩ **3** : to get to the top of : CLIMB **4** : to stand or lie at the top of — **sur·mount·able** \-'maúntə-bəl\ adj

¹**sur·name** \'sər-ˌnām\ n (14c) **1** : an added name derived from occupation or other circumstance : NICKNAME 1 **2** : the name borne in common by members of a family

²**surname** vt (15c) : to give a surname to

sur·pass \sər-'pas\ vt [MF surpasser, fr. sur- + passer to pass] (1555) **1** : to become better, greater, or stronger than : EXCEED **2** : to go beyond : OVERSTEP **3** : to transcend the reach, capacity, or powers of syn see EXCEED — **sur·pass·able** \-'pa-sə-bəl\ adj

sur·pass·ing adj (ca. 1580) : greatly exceeding others : of a very high degree — **sur·pass·ing·ly** \-'pa-siŋ-lē\ adv

¹**sur·plice** \'sər-pləs\ n [ME surplis, fr. OF surpliz, fr. ML superpellicium, fr. super- + pellicium coat of skins, fr. L, neut. of pellicius made of skins, fr. pellis skin — more at FELL] (13c) : a loose white outer ecclesiastical vestment usu. of knee length with large open sleeves

²**surplice** adj (1845) : having a diagonally overlapping neckline or closing ⟨a ∼ collar⟩ ⟨∼ sweaters⟩

sur·plus \'sər-(ˌ)pləs\ n [ME, fr. MF, fr. ML superplus, fr. L super- + plus more — more at PLUS] (14c) **1 a** : the amount that remains when use or need is satisfied **b** : an excess of receipts over disbursements **2** : the excess of a corporation's net worth over the par or stated value of its capital stock — **surplus** adj

sur·plus·age \-(ˌ)plə-sij\ n (15c) **1** : SURPLUS 1a **2 a** : excessive or nonessential matter **b** : matter introduced in legal pleading which is not necessary or relevant to the case

surplus value n (1887) : the difference in Marxist theory between the value of work done or of commodities produced by labor and the usu. subsistence wages paid by the employer

sur·print \'sər-ˌprint\ vt or n (1917) : OVERPRINT

sur·pris·al \sə(r)-'prī-zəl\ n (1591) : the action of surprising : the state of being surprised

¹**sur·prise** also **sur·prize** \sə(r)-'prīz\ n [ME, fr. MF, fr. fem. of surpris, pp. of surprendre to take over, surprise, fr. sur- + prendre to take — more at PRIZE] (15c) **1 a** : an attack made without warning **b** : a taking unawares **2** : something that surprises **3** : the state of being surprised : ASTONISHMENT

²**surprise** also **surprize** vb **sur·prised; sur·pris·ing** vt (15c) **1** : to attack unexpectedly; also : to capture by an unexpected attack **2 a** : to take unawares **b** : to detect or elicit by a taking unawares **3** : to strike with wonder or amazement esp. because unexpected ∼ vi : to cause astonishment or surprise ⟨her success didn't ∼⟩ — **sur·pris·er** n syn SURPRISE, ASTONISH, ASTOUND, AMAZE, FLABBERGAST mean to impress forcibly through unexpectedness. SURPRISE stresses causing an effect through being unexpected at a particular time or place rather than by being essentially unusual or novel ⟨surprised to find them at home⟩. ASTONISH implies surprising so greatly as to seem incredible ⟨a discovery that astonished the world⟩. ASTOUND stresses the shock of astonishment ⟨too astounded to respond⟩. AMAZE suggests an effect of bewilderment ⟨amazed by the immense size of the place⟩. FLABBERGAST may suggest thorough astonishment and bewilderment or dismay ⟨flabbergasted by his angry refusal⟩.

sur·pris·ing adj (1645) : of a nature that excites surprise

sur·pris·ing·ly \sə(r)-'prī-ziŋ-lē\ adv (1661) **1** : in a surprising manner : to a surprising degree ⟨a ∼ fast runner⟩ **2** : it is surprising that ⟨∼, voter turnout was high⟩

sur·ra \'súr-ə\ n [Marathi sūra wheezing sound] (1883) : a severe Old World febrile and hemorrhagic disease of domestic animals that is caused by a flagellate protozoan (Trypanosoma evansi) and is transmitted by biting insects

sur·re·al \sə-'rē(-ə)l, -'rī-əl also -'rā-əl\ adj [back-formation fr. surrealism] (1937) **1** : having the intense irrational reality of a dream **2** : SURREALISTIC — **sur·re·al·ly** adv

sur·re·al·ism \sə-'rē-ə-ˌli-zəm, -'rī- also -'rā-\ n [F surréalisme, fr. sur- + réalisme realism] (1925) : the principles, ideals, or practice of producing fantastic or incongruous imagery or effects in art, literature, film, or theater by means of unnatural juxtapositions and combinations — **sur·re·al·ist** \-list\ n or adj

sur·re·al·is·tic \-ˌrē-ə-'lis-tik, -ˌrī- also -ˌrā-\ adj (1925) **1** : of or relating to surrealism **2** : having a strange dreamlike atmosphere or quality like that of a surrealist painting — **sur·re·al·is·ti·cal·ly** \-ti-k(ə-)lē\ adv

sur·re·but·ter \ˌsər-ri-'bə-tər\ n (ca. 1601) : the reply in common law pleading of a plaintiff to a defendant's rebutter

sur·re·join·der \-(r)i-'jȯin-dər\ n (ca. 1543) : the reply in common law pleading of a plaintiff to a defendant's rejoinder

¹**sur·ren·der** \sə-'ren-dər\ vb **-dered; -der·ing** \-d(ə-)riŋ\ [ME, fr. MF surrendre, fr. sur- + rendre to give back, yield — more at RENDER] vt (15c) **1** : to yield to the power, control, or possession of another upon compulsion or demand ⟨∼ed the fort⟩ **b** : to give up completely or agree to forgo esp. in favor of another **2 a** : to give (oneself) up into the power of another esp. as a prisoner **b** : to give (oneself) over to something (as an influence) ∼ vi : to give oneself up into the power of another : YIELD syn see RELINQUISH

²**surrender** n (15c) **1 a** : the action of yielding one's person or giving up the possession of something esp. into the power of another **b** : the relinquishment by a patentee of rights or claims under a patent **c** : the

delivery of a principal into lawful custody by bail — called also *surrender by bail*   **d** : the voluntary cancellation of the legal liability of an insurance company by the insured and beneficiary for a consideration   **e** : the delivery of a fugitive from justice by one government to another   **2** : an instance of surrendering

sur·rep·ti·tious \ˌsər-əp-'ti-shəs, ˌsə-rəp-, sə-ˌrep-\ *adj* [ME, fr. L *surrepticius*, fr. *surreptus*, pp. of *surripere* to snatch secretly, fr. *sub-* + *rapere* to seize — more at RAPID] (15c)   **1** : done, made, or acquired by stealth : CLANDESTINE   **2** : acting or doing something clandestinely : STEALTHY   *syn* see SECRET — **sur·rep·ti·tious·ly** *adv*

sur·rey \'sər-ē, 'sə-rē\ *n, pl* **surreys** [*Surrey*, England] (ca. 1891) : a four-wheel two-seated horse-drawn pleasure carriage

sur·ro·ga·cy \'sər-ə-gə-sē\ *n* (1984) : the practice of serving as a surrogate mother

surrey

¹sur·ro·gate \'sər-ə-ˌgāt, 'sə-rə-\ *vt* **-gat·ed; -gat·ing** [L *surrogatus*, pp. of *surrogare* to choose in place of another, substitute, fr. *sub-* + *rogare* to ask — more at RIGHT] (1533) : to put in the place of another: **a** : to appoint as successor, deputy, or substitute for oneself   **b** : SUBSTITUTE

²sur·ro·gate \ˌ-gāt, -gət\ *n, often attrib* (1603)   **1 a** : one appointed to act in place of another : DEPUTY   **b** : a local judicial officer in some states (as New York) who has jurisdiction over the probate of wills, the settlement of estates, and the appointment and supervision of guardians   **2** : one that serves as a substitute   **3** : SURROGATE MOTHER

surrogate mother *n* (1978) : a woman who becomes pregnant usu. by artificial insemination or surgical implantation of a fertilized egg for the purpose of carrying the fetus to term for another woman — **surrogate motherhood** *n*

¹sur·round \sə-'raund\ *vt* [ME, to overflow, fr. MF *suronder*, fr. LL *superundare*, fr. L *super-* + *unda* wave; influenced in meaning by **⁵round** — more at WATER] (ca. 1616)   **1 a** (1) : to enclose on all sides : ENVELOP ⟨the crowd ∼ed her⟩   (2) : to enclose so as to cut off communication or retreat : INVEST   **b** : to form or be a member of the entourage of (flatterers who ∼ the king)   **c** : to constitute part of the environment of (∼ed by poverty)   **d** : to extend around the margin or edge of : ENCIRCLE ⟨a wall ∼s the old city⟩   **2** : to cause to be surrounded by something ⟨∼ed himself with friends⟩

²surround *n* (1825) : something (as a border or ambient environment) that surrounds ⟨from urban centre to rural ∼ —Emrys Jones⟩

sur·round·ings \sə-'raun-dinz\ *n pl* (1861) : the circumstances, conditions, or objects by which one is surrounded : ENVIRONMENT

sur·roy·al \'sər-ˌroi(-ə)l\ *n* [ME *surryal*, fr. *sur-* + *ryall* royal antler] (15c) : one of the terminal tines above the royal antler of a large deer (as a stag) usu. grown by four years of age

sur·sum cor·da \ˌsür-səm-'kór-də, -ˌdä\ *n* [LL, (lift) up (your) hearts; fr. the opening words] (1537)   **1** *often cap S&C* : a versicle that in traditional eucharistic liturgies exhorts the faithful to enthusiastic worship   **2** : something inspiriting

sur·tax \'sər-ˌtaks\ *n* (1881)   **1** : an extra tax or charge   **2** : a graduated income tax in addition to the normal income tax imposed on the amount by which one's net income exceeds a specified sum

sur·tout \(ˌ)sər-'tü, 'sər-ˌ\ *n* [F, fr. *sur* over (fr. L *super*) + *tout* all, fr. L *totus* whole — more at OVER] (1686) : a man's long close-fitting overcoat

sur·veil \sər-'vā(ə)l\ *vt* **sur·veilled; sur·veil·ling** [back-formation fr. *surveillance*] (1949) : to subject to surveillance

sur·veil·lance \sər-'vā-lən(t)s *also* -'väl-yən(t)s *or* -'vā-ən(t)s\ *n* [F, fr. *surveiller* to watch over, fr. *sur-* + *veiller* to watch, fr. L *vigilare*, fr. *vigil* watchful — more at VIGIL] (1802) : close watch kept over someone or something (as by a detective) : SUPERVISION

sur·veil·lant \-'vā-lənt *also* -'väl-yənt *or* -'vā-ənt\ *n* (1819) : one that exercises surveillance

¹sur·vey \sər-'vā, 'sər-ˌ\ *vb* **sur·veyed; sur·vey·ing** [ME, fr. MF *surveir* to look over, fr. *sur-* + *veeir* to see — more at VIEW] *vt* (15c)   **1 a** : to examine as to condition, situation, or value : APPRAISE   **b** : to query (someone) in order to collect data for the analysis of some aspect of a group or area   **2** : to determine and delineate the form, extent, and position of (as a tract of land) by taking linear and angular measurements and by applying the principles of geometry and trigonometry   **3** : to view or consider comprehensively   **4** : INSPECT, SCRUTINIZE ⟨he ∼ed us in a lordly way —Alan Harrington⟩   ∼ *vi* : to make a survey

²sur·vey \'sər-ˌvā, sər-'\ *n, pl* **surveys** (1548)   **1** : the act or an instance of surveying: as **a** : a broad treatment of a subject   **b** : POLL 5a   **2** : something that is surveyed

survey course \'sər-ˌvā-\ *n* (1916) : a course treating briefly the chief topics of a broad field of knowledge

sur·vey·ing \sər-'vā-iŋ\ *n* (1682) : a branch of applied mathematics that teaches the art of determining the area of any portion of the earth's surface, the lengths and directions of the bounding lines, and the contour of the surface and of accurately delineating the whole on paper

sur·vey·or \sər-'vā-ər\ *n* (15c) : one that surveys; *esp* : one whose occupation is surveying land

sur·viv·able \sər-'vī-və-bəl\ *adj* (1955) : resulting in or permitting survival — **sur·viv·abil·i·ty** \-ˌvī-və-'bi-lə-tē\ *n*

sur·viv·al \sər-'vī-vəl\ *n, often attrib* (1598)   **1 a** : a living or continuing longer than another person or thing   **b** : the continuation of life or existence ⟨problems of ∼ in arctic conditions⟩   **2** : one that survives

sur·viv·al·ist \-və-list\ *n* (1970) : one who views survival as a primary objective; *esp* : one who has prepared to survive in the anarchy of an anticipated breakdown of society — **survivalist** *adj*

survival of the fittest (1864) : NATURAL SELECTION

sur·viv·ance \sər-'vī-vən(t)s\ *n* (ca. 1623) : SURVIVAL

sur·vive \sər-'vīv\ *vb* **sur·vived; sur·viv·ing** [ME, fr. MF *survivre* to outlive, fr. L *supervivere*, fr. *super-* + *vivere* to live — more at QUICK] *vi* (15c)   **1** : to remain alive or in existence : live on   **2** : to continue to function or prosper ∼ *vt*   **1** : to remain alive after the death of ⟨he is survived by his wife⟩   **2** : to continue to exist or live after ⟨survived the

earthquake⟩   **3** : to continue to function or prosper despite : WITHSTAND — **sur·vi·vor** \-'vī-vər\ *n*

sur·vi·vor \-'vī-vər\ *n* (1602) *archaic* : one that survives : SURVIVOR

sur·vi·vor·ship \-'vī-vər-ˌship\ *n* (ca. 1625)   **1** : the legal right of the survivor of persons having joint interests in property to take the interest of the person who has died   **2** : the state of being a survivor   **3** : the probability of surviving to a particular age; *also* : the number or proportion of survivors (as of an age group)

Su·san B. An·tho·ny Day \'sü-z²n-ˌbē-'an(t)-thə-nē-\ *n* (ca. 1951) : February 15 observed to commemorate the birth of Susan B. Anthony

sus·cep·ti·bil·i·ty \sə-ˌsep-tə-'bi-lə-tē\ *n, pl* **-ties** (1644)   **1** : the quality or state of being susceptible; *esp* : lack of ability to resist some extraneous agent (as a pathogen or drug) : SENSITIVITY   **2 a** : a susceptible temperament or constitution   **b** *pl* : FEELINGS, SENSIBILITIES   **3 a** : the ratio of the magnetization in a substance to the corresponding magnetizing force   **b** : the ratio of the electric polarization to the electric intensity in a polarized dielectric

sus·cep·ti·ble \sə-'sep-tə-bəl\ *adj* [LL *susceptibilis*, fr. L *susceptus*, pp. of *suscipere* to take up, admit, fr. *sub-*, *sus-* up + *capere* to take — more at SUB-, HEAVE] (1605)   **1** : capable of submitting to an action, process, or operation ⟨a theory ∼ to proof⟩   **2** : open, subject, or unresistant to some stimulus, influence, or agency   **3** : IMPRESSIONABLE, RESPONSIVE   *syn* see LIABLE — **sus·cep·ti·ble·ness** *n* — **sus·cep·ti·bly** \-blē\ *adv*

sus·cep·tive \-tiv\ *adj* (15c)   **1** : RECEPTIVE   **2** : SUSCEPTIBLE — **sus·cep·tive·ness** *n* — **sus·cep·tiv·i·ty** \ˌsə-ˌsep-'ti-və-tē\ *n*

su·shi \'sü-shē *also* 'sü-\ *n* [Jp] (1893) : cold rice dressed with vinegar, formed into any of various shapes, and garnished esp. with bits of raw fish or shellfish

su·slik \'sü-slik\ *n* [Russ] (1774)   **1** : any of several rather large short-tailed ground squirrels (genus *Citellus*) of eastern Europe or northern Asia   **2** : the mottled grayish black fur of a suslik

¹sus·pect \'səs-ˌpekt, sə-'spekt\ *adj* [ME, fr. MF, fr. L *suspectus*, fr. pp. of *suspicere*] (14c)   **1** : regarded or deserving to be regarded with suspicion : SUSPECTED ⟨investigates ∼ employees⟩   **2** : DOUBTFUL, QUESTIONABLE ⟨whose skills are ∼ —Peter Vecsey⟩

²sus·pect \'səs-ˌpekt\ *n* (1591) : one who is suspected; *esp* : one suspected of a crime

³sus·pect \sə-'spekt\ *vb* [ME, fr. L *suspectare*, freq. of *suspicere* to look up at, regard with awe, suspect, fr. *sub-*, *sus-* up, secretly + *specere* to look at — more at SUB-, SPY] *vt* (15c)   **1** : to imagine (one) to be guilty or culpable on slight evidence or without proof ⟨∼ him of giving false information⟩   **2** : to have doubts of : DISTRUST   **3** : to imagine to exist or be true, likely, or probable ∼ *vi* : to imagine something to be true or likely

sus·pend \sə-'spend\ *vb* [ME, fr. OF *suspendre* to hang up, interrupt, fr. L *suspendere*, fr. *sub-*, *sus-* up + *pendere* to cause to hang, weigh] *vt* (14c)   **1** : to debar temporarily from a privilege, office, or function ⟨∼ a student from school⟩   **2 a** : to cause to stop temporarily ⟨∼ bus service⟩   **b** : to set aside or make temporarily inoperative ⟨∼ the rules⟩   **3** : to defer to a later time on specified conditions ⟨∼ sentence⟩   **4** : to hold in an undetermined or undecided state awaiting further information ⟨∼ judgment⟩ ⟨∼ disbelief⟩   **5 a** : HANG; *esp* : to hang so as to be free on all sides except at the point of support ⟨∼ a ball by a thread⟩   **b** : to keep from falling or sinking by some invisible support (as buoyancy) ⟨dust ∼ed in the air⟩   **6 a** : to keep fixed or lost (as in wonder or contemplation)   **b** : to keep waiting in suspense or indecision   **7** : to hold (a musical note) over into the following chord ∼ *vi*   **1** : to cease operation temporarily   **2** : to stop payment or fail to meet obligations   **3** : HANG   *syn* see DEFER

suspended animation *n* (1795) : temporary suspension of the vital functions (as in persons nearly drowned)

sus·pend·er \sə-'spen-dər\ *n* (1524)   **1** : one that suspends   **2** : a device by which something may be suspended: as **a** : one of two supporting bands worn across the shoulders to support trousers, skirt, or belt — usu. used in pl. and often with *pair*   **b** *Brit* : a fastener attached to a garment or garter to hold up a stocking or sock; *also* : a device consisting of garter and fastener — **sus·pend·ered** \-dərd\ *adj*

sus·pense \sə-'spen(t)s\ *n* [ME, fr. MF, fr. *suspendre*] (15c)   **1** : the state of being suspended : SUSPENSION   **2 a** : mental uncertainty : ANXIETY   **b** : pleasant excitement as to a decision or outcome ⟨a novel of ∼⟩   **3** : the state or character of being undecided or doubtful : INDECISIVENESS — **sus·pense·ful** \-fəl\ *adj* — **sus·pense·ful·ly** \-fə-lē\ *adv* — **sus·pense·ful·ness** \-fəl-nəs\ *n* — **sus·pense·less** \-ləs\ *adj*

suspense account *n* (1869) : an account for the temporary entry of charges or credits or esp. of doubtful accounts receivable pending determination of their ultimate disposition

sus·pens·er \sə-'spen(t)-sər\ *n* (ca. 1960) : a suspenseful film

sus·pen·sion \sə-'spen(t)-shən\ *n* [ME *suspensyon*, fr. MF *suspension*, fr. LL *suspension-*, *suspensio*, fr. L *suspendere*] (15c)   **1** : the act of suspending : the state or period of being suspended: as **a** : temporary removal from office or privileges   **b** : temporary withholding (as of belief or decision)   **c** : temporary abrogation of a law or rule   **d** (1) : the holding over of one or more musical tones of a chord into the following chord producing a momentary discord and suspending the concord which the ear expects; *specif* : such a dissonance which resolves downward — compare ANTICIPATION, RETARDATION   (2) : the tone thus held over   **e** : stoppage of payment of business obligations : FAILURE — used esp. of a business or a bank   **f** : a rhetorical device whereby the principal idea is deferred to the end of a sentence or longer unit   **2 a** : the act of hanging : the state of being hung   **b** (1) : the state of a substance when its particles are mixed with but undissolved in a fluid or solid   (2) : a substance in this state   **3** : a system consisting of a solid dispersed in a solid, liquid, or gas usu. in particles of larger than colloidal size — compare EMULSION   **3** : something suspended   **4 a** : a device by which something (as a magnetic needle) is suspended   **b** : the system of devices (as springs) supporting the upper

---

\ə\ abut \ᵊ\ kitten, F table \ər\ further \a\ ash \ā\ ace \ä\ mop, mar
\aù\ out \ch\ chin \e\ bet \ē\ easy \g\ go \i\ hit \ī\ ice \j\ job
\ŋ\ sing \ō\ go \ò\ law \òi\ boy \th\ thin \t̲h̲\ the \ü\ loot \ù\ foot
\y\ yet \zh\ vision \à, k̲, ⁿ, œ, œ̄, ᵫ, ᵫ̄, ʸ\ see Guide to Pronunciation

part of a vehicle on the axles   **c** : the act, process, or manner in which the pendulum of a timepiece is suspended

suspension bridge n (1821) : a bridge that has its roadway suspended from two or more cables usu. passing over towers and securely anchored at the ends — see BRIDGE illustration

suspension points n pl (1919) : usu. three spaced periods used to show the omission of a word or word group from a written context

sus·pen·sive \sə-'spen(t)-siv\ adj (15c)   **1** : stopping temporarily : SUSPENDING ⟨a ~ veto⟩   **2** : characterized by suspense, suspended judgment, or indecisiveness   **3** : characterized by suspension — **sus·pen·sive·ly** adv

sus·pen·sor \sə-'spen(t)-sər\ n [NL, fr. L suspendere] (1832) : a suspending part or structure: as   **a** : a group or chain of cells that is produced from the zygote of a heterosporous plant and serves to push the embryo which arises at its extremity deeper into the embryo sac and into contact with the food supply of the megaspore   **b** : either of a pair of gametangia-bearing hyphal outgrowths in fungi (order Mucorales) that extend from two sexually compatible hyphae and support the resulting zygospore

¹sus·pen·so·ry \sə-'spen(t)-sə-rē, -'spen(t)s-rē\ adj (15c)   **1** : held in suspension; also : fitted or serving to suspend   **2** : temporarily leaving undetermined : SUSPENSIVE 1

²suspensory n, pl **-ries** (15c) : something that suspends or holds up; esp : a fabric supporter for the scrotum

suspensory ligament n (1831) : a ligament or fibrous membrane suspending an organ or part; esp : a ringlike fibrous membrane connecting the ciliary body and the lens of the eye and holding the lens in place — see EYE illustration

¹sus·pi·cion \sə-'spi-shən\ n [ME, fr. L suspicion-, suspicio, fr. suspicere to suspect — more at SUSPECT] (14c)   **1 a** : the act or an instance of suspecting something wrong without proof or on slight evidence : MISTRUST   **b** : a state of mental uneasiness and uncertainty : DOUBT   **2** : a barely detectable amount : TRACE ⟨just a ~ of garlic⟩   syn see UNCERTAINTY

²suspicion vt **sus·pi·cioned; sus·pi·cion·ing** \-'spi-sh(ə-)niŋ\ (ca. 1637) chiefly dial : SUSPECT

sus·pi·cious \sə-'spi-shəs\ adj (14c)   **1** : tending to arouse suspicion : QUESTIONABLE   **2** : disposed to suspect : DISTRUSTFUL ⟨~ of strangers⟩   **3** : expressing or indicative of suspicion ⟨a ~ glance⟩ — **sus·pi·cious·ly** adv — **sus·pi·cious·ness** n

sus·pi·ra·tion \ˌsəs-pə-'rā-shən\ n (15c) : a long deep breath : SIGH

sus·pire \sə-'spīr\ vi **sus·pired; sus·pir·ing** [ME, fr. L suspirare, fr. sub- + spirare to breathe] (15c) : to draw a long deep breath : SIGH

suss \'səs\ vt [by shortening & alter. fr. suspect] (1966)   **1** chiefly Brit : to inspect or investigate so as to gain more knowledge — usu. used with out   **2** chiefly Brit : FIGURE OUT — usu. used with out

Sus·sex spaniel \'sə-siks-, -ˌseks-\ n [Sussex, England] (1856) : any of a breed of short-legged short-necked long-bodied spaniels of English origin with a flat or slightly wavy golden liver-colored coat

sus·tain \sə-'stān\ vt [ME sustenen, fr. OF sustenir, fr. L sustinēre to hold up, sustain, fr. sub-, sus- up + tenēre to hold — more at SUB-, THIN] (13c)   **1** : to give support or relief to   **2** : to supply with sustenance : NOURISH   **3** : KEEP UP, PROLONG   **4** : to support the weight of : PROP; also : to carry or withstand (a weight or pressure)   **5** : to buoy up ⟨~ed by hope⟩   **6 a** : to bear up under   **b** : SUFFER, UNDERGO ⟨~ed heavy losses⟩   **7 a** : to support as true, legal, or just   **b** : to allow or admit as valid ⟨the court ~ed the motion⟩   **8** : to support by adequate proof : CONFIRM ⟨testimony that ~s our contention⟩ — **sus·tained·ly** \-'stā-nəd-lē, -'stānd-lē\ adv — **sus·tain·er** n

sus·tain·able \sə-'stā-nə-bəl\ adj (ca. 1727)   **1** : capable of being sustained   **2 a** : of, relating to, or being a method of harvesting or using a resource so that the resource is not depleted or permanently damaged ⟨~ techniques⟩ ⟨~ agriculture⟩   **b** : of or relating to a lifestyle involving the use of sustainable methods ⟨~ society⟩ — **sus·tain·abil·i·ty** \-ˌstā-nə-'bi-lə-tē\ n

sustained yield n (ca. 1905) : production of a biological resource (as timber or fish) under management procedures which insure replacement of the part harvested by regrowth or reproduction before another harvest occurs — **sustained-yield** adj

sus·tain·ing adj (1605)   **1** : serving to sustain   **2** : aiding in the support of an organization through a special fee ⟨a ~ member⟩

sus·te·nance \'səs-tə-nən(t)s\ n [ME, fr. OF, fr. sustenir] (14c)   **1 a** : means of support, maintenance, or subsistence : LIVING   **b** : FOOD, PROVISIONS; also : NOURISHMENT   **2 a** : the act of sustaining : the state of being sustained   **b** : a supplying or being supplied with the necessaries of life   **3** : something that gives support, endurance, or strength

sus·ten·tac·u·lar cell \ˌsəs-tən-'ta-kyə-lər-, -ˌten-\ n [NL sustentaculum supporting part, fr. L, prop, fr. sustentare] (1901) : a supporting epithelial cell (as a Sertoli cell or a cell of the olfactory epithelium) that lacks a specialized function (as nerve-impulse conduction)

sus·ten·ta·tion \-'tā-shən\ n [ME, fr. MF, fr. L sustentation-, sustentatio act of holding up, fr. sustentare to hold up, freq. of sustinēre to sustain] (14c)   **1** : the act of sustaining : the state of being sustained: as   **a** : MAINTENANCE, UPKEEP   **b** : PRESERVATION, CONSERVATION   **c** : maintenance of life, growth, or morale   **d** : provision with sustenance   **2** : something that sustains : SUPPORT — **sus·ten·ta·tive** \'səs-tən-ˌtā-tiv, sə-'sten-tə-tiv\ adj

Su·su \'sü-(ˌ)sü\ n, pl **Susu** or **Susus** (1786)   **1** : a member of a West African people of Mali, Guinea, and the area along the northern border of Sierra Leone   **2** : the Mande language of the Susu people

su·sur·ra·tion \ˌsü-sə-'rā-shən\ n (14c) : a whispering sound : MURMUR

su·sur·rous \su̇-'sər-əs, -'sə-rəs\ adj (1859) : full of whispering sounds

su·sur·rus \su̇-'sər-əs, -'sə-rəs\ n [L, hum, whisper — more at SWARM] (1826) : a whispering or rustling sound — **su·sur·rant** \-'sər-ənt, -'sə-rənt\ adj

sut·ler \'sət-lər\ n [obs. D soeteler, fr. LG suteler sloppy worker, camp cook] (1599) : a civilian provisioner to an army post often with a shop on the post

su·tra \'sü-trə\ n [Skt sūtra precept, lit., thread; akin to L suere to sew — more at SEW] (1801)   **1** : a precept summarizing Vedic teaching; also : a collection of these precepts   **2** : a discourse of the Buddha

sut·tee \(ˌ)sə-'tē, 'sə-ˌtē\ n [Skt satī wife who performs suttee, lit., devoted woman, fr. fem. of sat true, good; akin to OE sōth true — more at SOOTH] (1786) : the act or custom of a Hindu widow willingly being cremated on the funeral pyre of her husband as an indication of her devotion to him; also : a woman cremated in this way

su·ture \'sü-chər\ n [MF & L; MF, fr. L sutura seam, suture, fr. sutus, pp. of suere to sew — more at SEW] (1541)   **1 a** : a strand or fiber used to sew parts of the living body; also : a stitch made with a suture   **b** : the act or process of sewing with sutures   **2 a** : a uniting of parts   **b** : the seam or seamlike line along which two things or parts are sewed or united   **3 a** : the line of union in an immovable articulation (as between the bones of the skull); also : such an articulation   **b** : a furrow at the junction of adjacent bodily parts; esp : a line of dehiscence (as on a fruit) — **su·tur·al** \'sü-chə-rəl, 'süch-rəl\ adj — **su·tur·al·ly** \-rə-lē\ adv

²suture vt **su·tured; su·tur·ing** \'sü-chə-riŋ, 'süch-riŋ\ (1777) : to unite, close, or secure with sutures ⟨~ a wound⟩

su·zer·ain \'sü-zə-rən, -ˌrān; 'süz-rən\ n [F, fr. (assumed) MF suserain, fr. MF sus up (fr. L sursum, fr. sub- up + versum -ward, fr. neut. of versus, pp. of vertere to turn) + -erain (as in soverain sovereign) — more at SUB-, WORTH] (1807)   **1** : a superior feudal lord to whom fealty is due : OVERLORD   **2** : a dominant state controlling the foreign relations of a vassal state but allowing it sovereign authority in its internal affairs

su·zer·ain·ty \-tē\ n [F suzeraineté, fr. MF susereneté, fr. (assumed) MF suserain] (1823) : the dominion of a suzerain : OVERLORDSHIP

sved·berg \'sved-ˌbərg, 'sfed-, -ˌber-ē\ n [The Svedberg] (1939) : a unit of time amounting to 10^{-13} second that is used to measure the sedimentation velocity of a colloidal solution (as of a protein) in an ultracentrifuge and to determine molecular weight by substitution in an equation — called also svedberg unit

svelte \'svelt, 'sfelt\ adj [F, fr. It svelto, fr. pp. of svellere to pluck out, modif. of L evellere, fr. e- + vellere to pluck — more at VULNERABLE] (ca. 1817)   **1 a** : SLENDER, LITHE   **b** : having clean lines : SLEEK   **2** : URBANE, SUAVE — **svelte·ly** adv — **svelte·ness** n

Sven·ga·li \sven-'gä-lē, sfen-\ n [Svengali, maleficent hypnotist in the novel Trilby (1894) by George du Maurier] (1919) : one who attempts usu. with evil intentions to persuade or force another to do his bidding

¹swab \'swäb\ n [prob. fr. obs. D swabbe; akin to LG swabber mop] (1653)   **1 a** : MOP; esp : a yarn mop   **b** (1) : a wad of absorbent material usu. wound around one end of a small stick and used for applying medication or for removing material from an area   (2) : a specimen taken with a swab   **c** : a sponge or cloth patch attached to a long handle and used to clean the bore of a firearm   **2 a** : a useless or contemptible person   **b** : SAILOR, GOB

²swab vt **swabbed; swab·bing** [back-formation fr. swabber] (1719)   **1** : to clean with or as if with a swab   **2** : to apply medication to with a swab ⟨swabbed the wound with iodine⟩

swab·ber \'swä-bər\ n [akin to LG swabber mop, ME swabben to sway] (1592)   **1** : one that swabs   **2** : SWAB 2a

swab·bie also **swab·by** \'swä-bē\ n, pl **swabbies** (1944) slang : SWAB 2b

swad·dle \'swä-dᵊl\ vt **swad·dled; swad·dling** \'swäd-liŋ, 'swä-dᵊl-iŋ\ [ME swadelen, swathelen, prob. alter. of swedelen, swethelen, fr. swethel swaddling band, fr. OE; akin to OE swathian to swathe] (14c)   **1 a** : to wrap (an infant) with swaddling clothes   **b** : ENVELOP, SWATHE ⟨swaddled ourselves in sleeping bags⟩   **2** : RESTRAIN, RESTRICT ⟨marriage . . . swaddled him in a domesticity he came to loathe —Nina Auerbach⟩

swaddling clothes n pl (1535)   **1** : narrow strips of cloth wrapped around an infant to restrict movement   **2** : limitations or restrictions imposed on the immature or inexperienced

¹swag \'swag\ vb **swagged; swag·ging** [prob. of Scand origin; akin to ON sveggja to cause to sway; akin to OHG swingan to swing] vi (1530)   **1** : SWAY, LURCH   **2** : SAG   ~ vt   **1** : to adorn with swags   **2** : to arrange (as drapery) in swags

²swag n (1660)   **1** : SWAY   **2 a** : something (as a decoration) hanging in a curve between two points : FESTOON   **b** : a suspended cluster (as of evergreen branches)   **3 a** : goods acquired by unlawful means : LOOT   **b** : SPOILS, PROFITS   **4** : a depression in the earth   **5** chiefly Austral : a pack of personal belongings

¹swage \'swāj, 'swej\ n [ME, ornamental border, fr. MF souage] (ca. 1812) : a tool used by metalworkers for shaping their work by holding it on the work or the work on it and striking with a hammer or sledge

²swage vt **swaged; swag·ing** (1831) : to shape by or as if by means of a swage

swage block n (1843) : a perforated cast-iron or steel block with grooved sides that is used in heading bolts and swaging bars by hand

¹swag·ger \'swa-gər\ vb **swag·gered; swag·ger·ing** \-g(ə-)riŋ\ [prob. fr. ¹swag + -er (as in chatter)] vi (1590)   **1** : to conduct oneself in an arrogant or superciliously pompous manner; esp : to walk with an air of overbearing self-confidence   **2** : BOAST, BRAG   ~ vt : to force by argument or threat : BULLY — **swag·ger·er** \-gər-ər\ n — **swag·ger·ing·ly** \-g(ə-)riŋ-lē\ adv

²swagger n (1725)   **1 a** : an act or instance of swaggering   **b** : arrogant or conceitedly self-assured behavior   **c** : ostentatious display or bravado   **2** : a self-confident outlook : COCKINESS

³swagger adj (1879) : marked by elegance or showiness : POSH

swagger stick n (1887) : a short light stick usu. covered with leather and tipped with metal at each end and intended for carrying in the hand (as by military officers)

swag·gie \'swa-gē\ n [by shortening & alter.] (1891) chiefly Austral : SWAGMAN

swag·man \'swag-mən\ n (1851) chiefly Austral : DRIFTER; esp : one who carries a swag when traveling

Swa·hi·li \swä-'hē-lē\ n, pl **Swahili** or **Swahilis** [Ar sawāḥil, pl. of sāḥil coast] (1814)   **1** : a member of a Bantu-speaking people of Zanzibar and the adjacent coast   **2** : a Bantu language that is a trade and governmental language over much of East Africa and in the Congo region

swain \'swān\ n [ME swein boy, servant, fr. ON sveinn; akin to OE swān swain, L suus one's own — more at SUICIDE] (14c)   **1** : RUSTIC, PEASANT; specif : SHEPHERD   **2** : a male admirer or suitor — **swain·ish** \'swā-nish\ adj — **swain·ish·ness** n

Swain·son's hawk \'swān(t)-sənz-\ n [William *Swainson* †1855 Eng. naturalist] (1895) : a buteo (*Buteo swainsonii*) chiefly of western No. America and So. America having pointed wings and usu. a dark breast

swale \'swā(ə)l\ n [origin unknown] (1584) : a low-lying or depressed and often wet stretch of land; *also* : a shallow depression on a golf fairway or green

¹swal·low \'swä-(,)lō\ n [ME *swalowe*, fr. OE *swealwe*; akin to OHG *swalawa* swallow] (bef. 12c) : any of numerous small widely distributed oscine birds (family Hirundinidae) that have a short bill, long pointed wings, and often a deeply forked tail and that feed on insects caught on the wing 2 : any of several swifts that superficially resemble swallows

²swallow vb [ME *swalowen*, fr. OE *swelgan*; akin to OHG *swelgan* to swallow] vt (bef. 12c) 1 : to take through the mouth and esophagus into the stomach 2 : to envelop or take in as if by swallowing : ABSORB 3 : to accept without question, protest, or resentment ⟨~ an insult⟩ ⟨a hard story to ~⟩ 4 : TAKE BACK, RETRACT ⟨~ my words⟩ 5 : to keep from expressing or showing : REPRESS ⟨~ed my anger⟩ 6 : to utter (as words) indistinctly ~ vi 1 : to receive something into the body through the mouth and esophagus 2 : to perform the action characteristic of swallowing something esp. under emotional stress — **swal·low·able** \'swä-lō-ə-bəl\ adj — **swal·low·er** \'swä-lə-wər\ n

³swallow n (14c) 1 : the passage connecting the mouth to the stomach 2 : a capacity for swallowing 3 a : an act of swallowing b : an amount that can be swallowed at one time 4 : an aperture in a block on a ship between the sheave and frame through which the rope reeves

swal·low·tail \'swä-lō-,tāl, -lə-\ n (1703) 1 : a deeply forked and tapering tail (as of a swallow) 2 : TAILCOAT 3 : any of various large butterflies (family Papilionidae and esp. genus *Papilio*) with each hind wing usu. having an elongated process — **swal·low–tailed** \-,tāld\ adj

swam *past of* SWIM

swa·mi \'swä-mē\ n [Hindi *svāmī*, fr. Skt *svāmin* owner, lord, fr. *sva* one's own — more at SUICIDE] (1895) 1 : a Hindu ascetic or religious teacher; *specif* : a senior member of a religious order — used as a title 2 : one that resembles or emulates a swami : PUNDIT, SEER

swallowtail 3

¹swamp \'swämp, 'swömp\ n [perh. alter. of ME *sompe*, fr. MD *somp* morass; akin to MHG *sumpf* marsh, Gk *somphos* spongy] (1624) 1 : a wetland often partially or intermittently covered with water; *esp* : one dominated by woody vegetation 2 : a tract of swamp 3 : a difficult or troublesome situation or subject — **swamp** adj

²swamp vt (1784) 1 a : to fill with or as if with water : INUNDATE, SUBMERGE b : to overwhelm numerically or by an excess of something : FLOOD ⟨~ed with work⟩ 2 : to open by removing underbrush and debris ~ vi : to become submerged

swamp buggy n (1941) : a vehicle designed to travel over swampy terrain; *esp* : a four-wheel motor vehicle with oversize tires

swamp·er \'swäm-pər, 'swöm-\ n (1775) 1 a : an inhabitant of swamps or lowlands b : one familiar with swampy terrain 2 : a general assistant : HANDYMAN, HELPER

swamp·land \'swämp-,land, 'swömp-\ n (1662) : SWAMP 1

swampy \'swäm-pē, 'swöm-\ adj **swamp·i·er; -est** (1649) : consisting of, suggestive of, or resembling swamp : MARSHY — **swamp·i·ness** n

¹swan \'swän\ n, pl **swans** [ME, fr. OE *swan*; akin to L *sonus* sound — more at SOUND] (bef. 12c) 1 pl also **swan** : any of various large heavy-bodied long-necked mostly pure white aquatic birds (family Anatidae and esp. genus *Cygnus*) that are related to but larger than the geese 2 : one that resembles or is likened to a swan 3 cap : the constellation Cygnus

²swan vi **swanned; swan·ning** (1942) : to wander aimlessly or idly : DALLY

³swan vi **swanned; swan·ning** [perh. euphemism for *swear*] (1784) dial : DECLARE, SWEAR

swan boat n (1953) : a small boat usu. for children or sightseers pedaled by an operator who sits aft in a large model of a swan

swan dive n (1898) : a front dive executed with the head back, back arched, and arms spread sideways and then brought together above the head to form a straight line with the body as the diver enters the water

¹swank \'swaŋk\ adj [MLG or MD *swanc* supple; akin to OHG *swingan* to swing] (1773) *Scot* : full of life or energy : ACTIVE

²swank vi [perh. akin to MHG *swanken* to sway; akin to MD *swanc* supple] (ca. 1809) : SHOW OFF, SWAGGER; *also* : BOAST 1

³swank *or* **swanky** \'swaŋ-kē\ adj **swank·er** *or* **swank·i·er; -est** (ca. 1842) 1 : characterized by showy display : OSTENTATIOUS ⟨a ~ limousine⟩ 2 : fashionably elegant : SMART ⟨a ~ restaurant⟩ — **swank·i·ly** \-kə-lē\ adv — **swank·i·ness** \-kē-nəs\ n

⁴swank n (ca. 1854) 1 : arrogance or ostentation of dress or manner : PRETENTIOUSNESS, SWAGGER 2 : ELEGANCE, FASHIONABLENESS

swan·nery \'swä-nə-rē, 'swän-rē\ n, pl **-ner·ies** (1754) : a place where swans are bred or kept

swans–down \'swänz-,daun\ n (1606) 1 : the soft downy feathers of the swan often used as trimming on articles of dress 2 : a heavy cotton flannel that has a thick nap on the face and is made with sateen weave

swan·skin \'swän-,skin\ n (1610) 1 : the skin of a swan with the down or feathers on it 2 : fabric resembling flannel and having a soft nap or surface

swan song n (1831) 1 : a song of great sweetness said to be sung by a dying swan 2 : a farewell appearance or final act or pronouncement

¹swap \'swäp\ vb **swapped; swap·ping** [ME *swappen* to strike; fr. the practice of striking hands in closing a business deal] vt (14c) 1 a : to give in trade : BARTER b : EXCHANGE 2 2 : to take turns in telling ⟨~ stories⟩ ~ vi : to make an exchange — **swap·per** n

²swap n (1625) : an act, instance, or process of exchanging one thing for another

swap meet n (1965) : a gathering for the sale or barter of usu. secondhand objects

swa·raj \swə-'räj\ n [Hindi *svarāj*, fr. Skt *sva* own + Hindi *rāj* rule — more at SUICIDE, RAJ] (1908) : national or local self-government in India — **swa·raj·ist** \-'rä-jist\ n

sward \'swörd\ n [ME, fr. OE *sweard, swearth* skin, rind; akin to MHG *swart* skin, hide] (15c) 1 : a portion of ground covered with grass 2 : the grassy surface of land — **sward·ed** \'swör-dəd\ adj

swarf \'swörf\ n [of Scand origin; akin to ON *svarf* file dust; akin to OE *sweorfan* to file away — more at SWERVE] (1587) : material (as metallic particles and abrasive fragments) removed by a cutting or grinding tool

¹swarm \'swörm\ n [ME, fr. OE *swearm*; akin to OHG *swaram* swarm and prob. to L *susurrus* hum] (bef. 12c) 1 a (1) : a great number of honeybees emigrating together from a hive in company with a queen to start a new colony elsewhere (2) : a colony of honeybees settled in a hive b : an aggregation of free-floating or free-swimming unicellular organisms — usu. used of zoospores 2 a : a large number of animate or inanimate things massed together and usu. in motion : THRONG ⟨~s of sightseers⟩ ⟨a ~ of locusts⟩ ⟨a ~ of meteors⟩ b : a number of similar geological features or phenomena close together in space or time ⟨a ~ of dikes⟩ ⟨an earthquake ~⟩

²swarm vi (14c) 1 : to form and depart from a hive in a swarm 2 a : to move or assemble in a crowd : THRONG b : to hover about in the manner of a bee in a swarm 3 : to contain a swarm : TEEM ~ vt 1 : to fill with a swarm 2 : to beset or surround in a swarm ⟨players ~ing the quarterback⟩ — **swarm·er** n

³swarm vb [origin unknown] vi (14c) : to climb with the hands and feet; *specif* : SHIN ⟨~ up a pole⟩ ~ vt : to climb up : MOUNT

swarm spore n (1859) : any of various minute motile sexual or asexual spores; *esp* : ZOOSPORE

swart \'swört\ adj [ME, fr. OE *sweart*; akin to OHG *swarz* black, L *sordes* dirt] (bef. 12c) 1 a : SWARTHY b archaic : producing a swarthy complexion 2 : BANEFUL, MALIGNANT — **swart·ness** n

swar·thy \'swör-thē, -thē\ adj **swar·thi·er; -est** [alter. of obs. *swarty*, fr. *swart*] (1587) : of a dark color, complexion, or cast — **swar·thi·ness** n

¹swash \'swäsh, 'swösh\ vb [prob. imit.] vi (1556) 1 : BLUSTER, SWAGGER 2 : to make violent noisy movements 3 : to move with a splashing sound ~ vt : to cause to splash

²swash n (1593) 1 : SWAGGER 2 : a narrow channel of water lying within a sandbank and the shore 3 : a dashing of water against or on something; *esp* : the rush of water up a beach from a breaking wave

³swash n [obs. E *swash* slanting] (1683) : an extended flourish on a printed character

⁴swash adj (1683) : having one or more swashes ⟨~ capitals⟩

swash·buck·le \'swäsh-,bə-kəl, 'swösh-\ vi **-led; -ling** \-,bə-k(ə-)liŋ\ [back-formation fr. *swashbuckler*] (1897) : to act the part of a swashbuckler

swash·buck·ler \-,bə-klər\ n [¹*swash* + *buckler*] (1560) 1 : a swaggering or daring soldier or adventurer 2 : a novel or drama dealing with a swashbuckler

swash·buck·ling \-,bə-k(ə-)liŋ\ adj [*swashbuckler*] (ca. 1693) 1 : acting in the manner of a swashbuckler 2 : characteristic of, marked by, or done by swashbucklers

swash·er \'swä-shər, 'swö-\ n (1589) : SWASHBUCKLER

swas·ti·ka \'swäs-ti-kə *also* swä-'stē-\ n [Skt *svastika*, fr. *svasti* well-being, fr. *su-* well + *as-* to be; akin to Skt *asti* he is, OE *is*; fr. its being regarded as a good luck symbol] (1871) 1 : a symbol or ornament in the form of a Greek cross with the ends of the arms extended at right angles all in the same rotary direction 2 : a swastika used as a symbol of anti-Semitism or of Nazism

¹swat \'swät\ vt **swat·ted; swat·ting** [E dial., to squat, alter. of E *squat*] (ca. 1796) : to hit with a sharp slapping blow usu. with an instrument (as a bat or swatter)

²swat n (ca. 1800) 1 : a powerful or crushing blow 2 : a long hit in baseball; *esp* : HOME RUN

swatch \'swäch\ n [origin unknown] (1647) 1 a : a sample piece (as of fabric) or a collection of samples b : a characteristic specimen 2 : PATCH 3 : a small collection 4 : SWATCH 2

swath \'swäth, 'swöth\ *or* **swathe** \'swäth, 'swöth, 'swäth\ n [ME, fr. OE *swæth* footstep, trace; akin to MHG *swade* swath] (14c) 1 a : the row of cut grain or grass left by a scythe or mowing machine b : the sweep of a scythe or a machine in mowing or the path cut in one course 2 : a long broad strip or belt 3 : a stroke of or as if of a scythe 4 : a space devastated as if by a scythe

¹swathe \'swäth, 'swöth, 'swäth\ *or* **swath** \'swäth, 'swöth, 'swöth\ n [ME, fr. (assumed) OE *swæth*; akin to OE *swathian* to swathe] (bef. 12c) 1 : a band used in swathing 2 : an enveloping medium

²swathe \'swäth, 'swöth, 'swäth\ vt **swathed; swath·ing** [ME, fr. OE *swathian*] (12c) 1 : to bind, wrap, or swaddle with or as if with a bandage 2 : ENVELOP

swath·er \'swä-thər, -thər\ n (ca. 1875) : a harvesting machine that cuts and windrows grain and seed crops; *also* : a mower attachment that windrows the swath

swathing clothes n pl [ME] (14c) obs : SWADDLING CLOTHES

swats \'swäts\ n pl [prob. fr. OE *swätan*, pl., beer] (1508) *Scot* : DRINK; *esp* : new ale

swat·ter \'swä-tər\ n (1912) : one that swats; *esp* : FLYSWATTER

S wave n [*secondary*] (1937) : a wave (as from an earthquake) in which the propagated disturbance is a shear in an elastic medium (as the earth) — compare PRESSURE WAVE

¹sway \'swā\ n (14c) 1 : the action or an instance of swaying or of being swayed : an oscillating, fluctuating, or sweeping motion 2 : an inclination or deflection caused by or as if by swaying 3 a : a controlling influence b : sovereign power : DOMINION c : the ability to exercise influence or authority : DOMINANCE *syn* see POWER

²sway vb [alter. of earlier *swey* to fall, swoon, fr. ME *sweyen*, prob. of

---

\ə\ abut \ᵊ\ kitten, F table \ər\ further \a\ ash \ā\ ace \ä\ mop, mar \au̇\ out \ch\ chin \e\ bet \ē\ easy \g\ go \i\ hit \ī\ ice \j\ job \ŋ\ sing \ō\ go \ȯ\ law \ȯi\ boy \th\ thin \t͟h\ the \ü\ loot \u̇\ foot \y\ yet \zh\ vision \a, k̲, ⁿ, œ, œ̄, ᵫ, ᵾ, ᵊ\ *see* Guide to Pronunciation

Scand origin; akin to ON *sveigja* to sway; akin to Lith *svaigti* to become dizzy] *vi* (ca. 1500)   **1 a** : to swing slowly and rhythmically back and forth from a base or pivot   **b** : to move gently from an upright to a leaning position   **2** : to hold sway : act as ruler or governor   **3** : to fluctuate or veer between one point, position, or opinion and another ~ *vt*   **1 a** : to cause to sway : set to swinging, rocking, or oscillating   **b** : to cause to bend downward to one side   **c** : to cause to turn aside : DEFLECT, DIVERT   **2** *archaic* **a** : WIELD   **b** : GOVERN, RULE   **3 a** : to cause to vacillate   **b** : to exert a guiding or controlling influence on   **4** : to hoist in place ⟨~ up a mast⟩   *syn* see SWING, AFFECT — **sway·er** *n*
sway-backed \'swā-,bakt\ *also* **sway-back** \-,bak\ *adj* (1680) : having an abnormally hollow or sagging back ⟨a ~ mare⟩ — **sway-back** *n*
sway bar *n* (1949) : a bar that torsionally couples the right and left front-wheel suspensions of an automobile to reduce roll and sway
Swa-zi \'swä-zē\ *n*, *pl* **Swazi** or **Swazis** (1878)   **1** : a member of a Bantu people of southeastern Africa   **2** : a Bantu language of the Swazi people
¹swear \'swar, 'swer\ *vb* **swore** \'swōr, 'swȯr\; **sworn** \'swōrn, 'swȯrn\; **swear-ing** [ME *sweren*, fr. OE *swerian*; akin to OHG *swerien* to swear and perh. to OCS *svarŭ* quarrel] *vt* (bef. 12c)   **1** : to utter or take solemnly (an oath)   **2 a** : to assert as true or promise under oath ⟨a *sworn* affidavit⟩   **b** : to assert or promise emphatically or earnestly ⟨*swore* to uphold the Constitution⟩   **3 a** : to put to an oath : administer an oath to   **b** : to bind by an oath ⟨*swore* them to secrecy⟩   **4** *obs* : to invoke the name of (a sacred being) in an oath   **5** : to bring into a specified state by swearing ⟨*swore* his life away⟩ ~ *vi*   **1** : to take an oath   **2** : to use profane or obscene language : CURSE — **swear·er** *n* — **swear by** : to place great confidence in — **swear for** : to give assurance for : GUARANTEE — **swear off** : to vow to abstain from : RENOUNCE ⟨*swear off* smoking⟩
²swear *n* (14c) : OATH, SWEARWORD
swear in *vt* (1536) : to induct into office by administration of an oath
swear out *vt* (1895) : to procure (a warrant for arrest) by making a sworn accusation
swear·word \'swar-,wərd, 'swer-\ *n* (1883) : a profane or obscene oath or word
¹sweat \'swet\ *vb* **sweat** *or* **sweat·ed**; **sweat·ing** [ME *sweten*, fr. OE *swǣtan*, fr. *swāt* sweat; akin to OHG *sweiz* sweat, L *sudare* to sweat, Gk *hidrōs* sweat] *vi* (bef. 12c)   **1 a** : to excrete moisture in visible quantities through the openings of the sweat glands : PERSPIRE   **b** : to labor or exert oneself so as to cause perspiration   **2 a** : to emit or exude moisture ⟨cheese ~s in ripening⟩   **b** : to gather surface moisture in beads as a result of condensation ⟨stones ~ at night⟩   **c** (1) : FERMENT (2) : PUTREFY   **3** : to undergo anxiety or mental or emotional distress   **4** : to become exuded through pores or a porous surface : OOZE ~ *vt*   **1** : to emit or seem to emit from pores : EXUDE   **2** : to manipulate or produce by hard work or drudgery   **3** : to get rid of or lose (weight) by or as if by sweating or being sweated   **4** : to make wet with perspiration   **5 a** : to cause to excrete moisture from the skin   **b** : to drive hard : OVERWORK   **c** : to exact work from at low wages and under unfair or unhealthful conditions   **d** *slang* : to give the third degree to   **6** : to cause to exude or lose moisture; *esp* : to subject (as tobacco leaves) to fermentation   **7 a** : to extract something valuable from by unfair or dishonest means : FLEECE   **b** : to remove particles of metal from (a coin) by abrasion   **8 a** : to heat (as solder) so as to melt and cause to run esp. between surfaces to unite them; *also* : to unite by such means ⟨~ a pipe joint⟩   **b** : to heat so as to extract an easily fusible constituent ⟨~ bismuth ore⟩   **c** : to sauté in a covered vessel until natural juices are exuded   **9** *slang* : to worry about ⟨doesn't ~ the small stuff —Barry McDermott⟩ — **sweat blood** : to work or worry intensely ⟨in preparing speeches each *sweats blood* in his own way — Stewart Cockburn⟩
²sweat *n* (13c)   **1** : hard work : DRUDGERY   **2** : the fluid excreted from the sweat glands of the skin : PERSPIRATION   **3** : moisture issuing from or gathering in drops on a surface   **4 a** : the condition of one sweating or sweated   **b** : a spell of sweating   **5** : a state of anxiety or impatience   **6** *pl* **a** : SWEAT SUIT   **b** : SWEATPANTS — **no sweat** *slang* : with little or no difficulty : EASILY; *also* : EASY — often used interjectionally
sweat·band \'swet-,band\ *n* (1891)   **1** : a usu. leather band lining the inner edge of a hat or cap to prevent sweat damage   **2** : a band of material worn around the head or wrist to absorb sweat
sweat bee *n* (1894) : any of various small black or brownish bees (family Halictidae) that are attracted to perspiration
sweat-box \-,bäks\ *n* (1864)   **1** : a place in which one is made to sweat; *esp* : a narrow box or cell in which a prisoner is placed for punishment   **2** : a device for sweating something (as hides in tanning or dried figs)
sweat·ed \'swe-təd\ *adj* (1882) : of, subjected to, or produced under sweatshop conditions ⟨~ labor⟩ ⟨~ goods⟩
sweat equity *n* (1966) : equity in a property resulting from labor invested in improvements that increase its value; *also* : the labor so invested
sweat·er \'swe-tər\ *n* (15c)   **1** : one that sweats or causes sweating   **2** : a knitted or crocheted jacket or pullover
sweat·er·dress \-,dres\ *n* (1952) : a knitted or crocheted dress
sweater girl *n* (1940) : a woman with a shapely bust
sweat·er·vest \'swe-tər-,vest\ *n* (1952) : a sleeveless pullover or buttoned sweater
sweat gland *n* (1845) : a simple tubular gland of the skin that secretes perspiration, is widely distributed in nearly all parts of the human skin, and consists typically of an epithelial tube extending spirally from a minute pore on the surface of the skin into the dermis or subcutaneous tissues where it ends in a convoluted tuft
sweat lodge *n* (1850) : a hut, lodge, or cavern heated by steam from water poured on hot stones and used esp. by American Indians for ritual or therapeutic sweating
sweat out *vt* (1589)   **1** : to work one's way painfully through or to   **2** : to endure or wait through the course of
sweat·pants \'swet-,pan(t)s\ *n pl* (1925) : pants having a drawstring or elastic waist and elastic cuffs at the ankle that are worn esp. by athletes in warming up
sweat·shirt \-,shərt\ *n* (1925) : a loose collarless pullover usu. of heavy cotton jersey

sweat·shop \-,shäp\ *n* (1892) : a shop or factory in which workers are employed for long hours at low wages and under unhealthy conditions
sweat suit *n* (1930) : a suit worn usu. for exercise that consists of a sweatshirt and sweatpants
sweat test *n* (1978) : a test for cystic fibrosis that involves measuring the subject's sweat for abnormally high sodium chloride content
sweaty \'swe-tē\ *adj* **sweat·i·er**; **-est** (14c)   **1** : causing sweat ⟨a ~ day⟩ ⟨~ work⟩   **2** : wet or stained with or smelling of sweat — **sweat·i·ly** \'swe-t°l-ē\ *adv* — **sweat·i·ness** \'swe-tē-nəs\ *n*
swede \'swēd\ *n* [LG or obs. D] (1589)   **1** *cap* **a** : a native or inhabitant of Sweden   **b** : a person of Swedish descent   **2** *chiefly Brit* : RUTABAGA
Swe·den·bor·gian \,swē-d°n-'bȯr-j(ē-)ən, -'bȯr-gē-ən\ *adj* (1807) : of or relating to the teachings of Emanuel Swedenborg or the Church of the New Jerusalem based on his teachings — **Swedenborgian** *n* — **Swe·den·bor·gian·ism** \-j(ē-)ə-,ni-zəm, -gē-ə-\ *n*
Swed·ish \'swē-dish\ *n* (1605)   **1** : the North Germanic language spoken in Sweden and a part of Finland   **2** *pl in constr* : the people of Sweden — **Swedish** *adj*
Swedish massage *n* (1911) : massage involving a system of active and passive exercise of muscles and joints
¹sweep \'swēp\ *vb* **swept** \'swept\; **sweep·ing** [ME *swepen*; akin to OE *swāpan* to sweep, OHG *sweifen* to wander] *vt* (14c)   **1 a** : to remove from a surface with or as if with a broom or brush ⟨*swept* the crumbs from the table⟩   **b** : to destroy completely : WIPE OUT — usu. used with *away* ⟨everything she cherished, might be *swept* away overnight — Louis Bromfield⟩   **c** : to remove or take with a single continuous forceful action ⟨*swept* the books off the desk⟩   **d** : to remove from sight or consideration ⟨the problem can't be *swept* under the rug⟩   **e** : to drive or carry along with irresistible force ⟨a wave of protest that *swept* the opposition into office⟩   **2 a** : to clean with or as if with a broom or brush   **b** : to clear by repeated and forcible action   **c** : to move across or along swiftly, violently, or overwhelmingly ⟨fire *swept* the business district —Amer. Guide Series: Md.⟩   **d** : to win an overwhelming victory in or on ⟨~ the elections⟩   **e** : to win all the games or contests of ⟨~ a double-header⟩ ⟨~ a series⟩   **3** : to touch in passing with a swift continuous movement   **4** : to trace or describe the locus or extent of (as a line, circle, or angle)   **5** : to cover the entire range of ⟨his eyes *swept* the horizon⟩ ~ *vi*   **1 a** : to clean a surface with or as if with a broom   **b** : to move swiftly, forcefully, or devastatingly ⟨the wind *swept* through the treetops⟩   **2** : to go with stately or sweeping movements ⟨proudly *swept* into the room⟩   **3** : to move or extend in a wide curve or range — **sweep one off one's feet** : to gain immediate and unquestioning support, approval, or acceptance by a person — **sweep the board** *or* **sweep the table**   **1** : to win all the bets on the table   **2** : to win everything : beat all competitors
²sweep *n* (1548)   **1** : something that sweeps or works with a sweeping motion: as   **a** : a long pole or timber pivoted on a tall post and used to raise and lower a bucket in a well   **b** : a triangular cultivator blade that cuts off weeds under the soil surface   **c** : a windmill sail   **2** : an instance of sweeping; *esp* : a clearing out or away with or as if with a broom   **b** : the removal from the table in one play in casino of all the cards by pairing or combining   **c** : an overwhelming victory   **d** : a winning of all the contests or prizes in a competition   **e** : a wide-ranging search of an area (as by police)   **3 a** : a movement of great range and force   **b** : a curving or circular course or line   **c** : the compass of a sweeping movement : SCOPE   **d** : a broad unbroken area or extent   **e** : an end run in football in which one or more linemen pull back and run interference for the ballcarrier   **4** : CHIMNEY SWEEP   **5** : SWEEPSTAKES   **6** : obliquity with respect to a reference line ⟨~ of an airplane wing⟩; *esp* : SWEEPBACK   **7** : a television ratings period during which surveys are taken to determine advertising rates   *syn* see RANGE
sweep·back \'swēp-,bak\ *n* (1914) : the backward slant of an airplane wing in which the outer portion of the wing is downstream from the inner portion
sweep·er \'swē-pər\ *n* (15c)   **1** : one that sweeps   **2** : a lone back in soccer who plays between the line of the defenders and the goal
sweep hand *n* (1943) : SWEEP-SECOND HAND
¹sweep·ing *n* (14c)   **1** : the act or action of one that sweeps ⟨gave the room a good ~⟩   **2** *pl* : things collected by sweeping : REFUSE
²sweeping *adj* (1610)   **1 a** : moving or extending in a wide curve or over a wide area   **b** : having a curving line or form   **2 a** : EXTENSIVE ⟨~ reforms⟩   **b** : marked by wholesale and indiscriminate inclusion ⟨~ generalities⟩ — **sweep·ing·ly** \'swē-piŋ-lē\ *adv* — **sweep·ing·ness** *n*
sweep-sec·ond hand \'swēp-,se-kənd-, -kənt-\ *n* (ca. 1940) : a hand marking seconds on a timepiece mounted concentrically with the other hands and read from the same dial as the minute hand
sweep·stakes \-,stāks\ *n pl but sing or pl in constr*, *also* **sweep-stake** \-,stāk\ [ME *swepestake* one who wins all the stakes in a game, fr. *swepen* to sweep + *stake*] (1785)   **1 a** : a race or contest in which the entire prize may be awarded to the winner; *specif* : STAKE RACE   **b** : CONTEST, COMPETITION   **2** : any of various lotteries
sweepy \'swē-pē\ *adj* **sweep·i·er**; **-est** (1697) : sweeping in motion, line, or force
¹sweet \'swēt\ *adj* [ME *swete*, fr. OE *swēte*; akin to OHG *suozi* sweet, L *suadēre* to urge, *suavis* sweet, Gk *hēdys*] (bef. 12c)   **1 a** (1) : pleasing to the taste   (2) : being or inducing the one of the four basic taste sensations that is typically induced by disaccharides and is mediated esp. by receptors in taste buds at the front of the tongue — compare BITTER, SALT, SOUR   **b** (1) *of a beverage* : containing a sweetening ingredient : not dry   (2) *of wine* : retaining a portion of natural sugar   **2 a** : pleasing to the mind or feelings : AGREEABLE, GRATIFYING — often used as a generalized term of approval ⟨how ~ it is⟩   **b** : marked by gentle good humor or kindliness   **c** : FRAGRANT   **d** (1) : delicately pleasing to the ear or eye   (2) : played in a straightforward melodic style ⟨~ jazz⟩   **e** : SACCHARINE, CLOYING   **3** : much loved : DEAR   **4 a** : not sour, rancid, decaying, or stale : WHOLESOME ⟨~ milk⟩   **b** : not salt or salted : FRESH ⟨~ butter⟩   **c** *of land* : free from excessive acidity   **d** : free from noxious gases and odors   **e** : free from excess of acid, sulfur, or corrosive salts ⟨~ crude oil⟩   **5** : SKILLFUL, PROFICIENT ⟨a ~ golf swing⟩   **6** — used as an intensive ⟨take your own ~ time⟩ — **sweet·ly** *adv* — **sweet·ness** *n* — **sweet on** : having a crush on

²**sweet** adv (13c) : in a sweet manner
³**sweet** n (14c) **1** : something that is sweet to the taste: as **a** : a food (as a candy or preserve) having a high sugar content ⟨fill up on ~s⟩ **b** Brit : DESSERT **c** Brit : HARD CANDY **2** : a sweet taste sensation **3** : a pleasant or gratifying experience, possession, or state **4** : DARLING, SWEETHEART **5** **a** archaic : FRAGRANCE **b** pl, archaic : things having a sweet smell

sweet alyssum n (1822) : a widely cultivated perennial European herb (Lobularia maritima) of the mustard family having narrow leaves and clusters of small fragrant usu. white or pink flowers

sweet–and–sour \‚swē-t²n-'saú(ə)r\ adj (1928) : seasoned with a sauce containing sugar and vinegar or lemon juice ⟨~ shrimp⟩

sweet basil n (ca. 1647) : a basil (Ocimum basilicum) with whitish or purple flowers that includes several cultivars (as bush basil)

sweet bay n (1716) **1** : LAUREL 1 **2** : a magnolia (Magnolia virginiana) of the eastern U.S. that has fragrant white flowers and leaves with glaucous undersides

sweet birch n (1785) : a common birch (Betula lenta) of the eastern U.S. that has spicy brown bark when young, hard dark-colored wood, and a volatile oil in its bark resembling wintergreen — called also black birch

sweet-bread \'swēt-‚bred\ n (1565) : the thymus or pancreas of a young animal (as a calf) used for food

sweet-bri-er also **sweet-bri-ar** \-‚brī(-ə)r\ n (1538) : an Old World rose (esp. Rosa eglanteria) with stout recurved prickles and white to deep rosy pink single flowers — called also eglantine

sweet cherry n (ca. 1901) : a white-flowered Eurasian cherry (Prunus avium) widely grown for its large sweet-flavored fruits; also : its fruit

sweet chocolate n (1897) : chocolate that contains added sugar

sweet cic-e-ly \-'si-s(ə-)lē\ n [cicely fr. L seselis, fr. Gk] (1668) : any of a genus (Osmorhiza) of American and eastern Asian herbs of the carrot family that typically have thick fleshy roots and grow in moist woodlands

sweet clover n (1868) : any of a genus (Melilotus) of Old World legumes that have trifoliolate leaves and are widely grown for soil improvement or hay

sweet corn n (1646) : an Indian corn (esp. Zea mays rugosa) with kernels containing a high percentage of sugar and adapted for table use when the kernels are unripe

sweet-en \'swē-t²n\ vb **sweet-ened**; **sweet-en-ing** \'swēt-niŋ, 'swē-t²n-iŋ\ vt (ca. 1552) **1** : to make sweet **2** : to soften the mood or attitude of **3** : to make less painful or trying **4** : to free from a harmful or undesirable quality or substance; esp : to remove sulfur compounds from ⟨~ natural gas⟩ **5** : to make more valuable or attractive: as **a** : to increase (a pot not won on the previous deal) by anteing prior to another deal **b** : to place additional securities as collateral for (a loan) ~ vi : to become sweet — **sweet-en-er** \'swēt-nər, 'swē-t²n-ər\ n

sweetening n (1819) : something that sweetens

sweet fern n (1654) : a small No. American shrub (Comptonia peregrina) of the wax-myrtle family with aromatic leaves

sweet flag n (1784) : a perennial marsh herb (Acorus calamus) of the arum family with long narrow leaves and an aromatic rootstock — called also calamus

sweet gum n (1700) **1** : a No. American tree (Liquidambar styraciflua) of the witch-hazel family with palmately lobed leaves, corky branches, and hard wood **2** : heartwood of the sweet gum or reddish brown lumber sawed from it

¹**sweet-heart** \'swēt-‚härt\ n (14c) **1** : DARLING **2** : one who is loved **3** : a generally likable person **4** : a remarkable one of its kind

²**sweetheart** adj (1942) : of or relating to an agreement between an employer and a labor union official arranged privately for their benefit usu. at the expense of the workers ⟨a ~ contract⟩; broadly : arranged in private for the benefit of a few at the expense of many ⟨a ~ deal⟩

sweetheart neckline n (1941) : a neckline for women's clothing that is high in back and low in front where it is scalloped to resemble the top of a heart

sweet-ie \'swē-tē\ n (1705) **1** pl, Brit : SWEET 1a **2** : SWEETHEART

sweetie pie n (1928) : SWEETHEART

sweet-ing \'swē-tiŋ\ n (13c) **1** archaic : SWEETHEART **2** : a sweet apple

sweet-ish \-tish\ adj (1580) **1** : somewhat sweet **2** : unpleasantly sweet — **sweet-ish-ly** adv

sweet marjoram n (1565) : a perennial marjoram (Origanum majorana syn. Majorana hortensis) with dense spikelike flower clusters

sweet-meat \'swēt-‚mēt\ n (14c) **1** : a food rich in sugar: as **a** : a candied or crystallized fruit **b** : CANDY, CONFECTION

sweetness and light n (1704) **1** : a harmonious combination of beauty and enlightenment viewed as a hallmark of culture **2** **a** : amiable reasonableness of disposition (they were all sweetness and light) **b** : an untroubled or harmonious state or condition ⟨but all was not sweetness and light⟩

sweet orange n (1538) **1** **a** : an orange (Citrus sinensis) that is prob. native to southeastern Asia, has a fruit with a pithy central axis, and is the source of the widely cultivated oranges of commerce **b** : a cultivated orange derived from the sweet orange and usu. having fruit with a relatively thin skin and sweet juicy edible pulp **2** : the fruit of a sweet orange

sweet pea n (1732) **1** : a widely cultivated Italian legume (Lathyrus odoratus) having slender usu. climbing stems, ovate leaves, and large fragrant flowers **2** : the flower of a sweet pea

sweet pepper n (1814) : a large mild thick-walled capsicum fruit; also : a pepper plant bearing this fruit

sweet potato n (1750) **1** : a tropical vine (Ipomoea batatas) related to the morning glory with variously shaped leaves and purplish flowers; also : its large thick sweet and nutritious tuberous root that is cooked and eaten as a vegetable — compare YAM 2 **2** : OCARINA

sweet–shop \'swēt-‚shäp\ n (1879) chiefly Brit : a candy store

sweet-sop \-‚säp\ n (1696) : SUGAR APPLE

sweet sorghum n (1867) : SORGO

sweet spot n (ca. 1949) : the area around the center of mass of a bat, racket, or head of a club that is the most effective part with which to hit a ball

sweet–talk \'swēt-‚tók\ vt (1928) : CAJOLE, COAX ~ vi : to use flattery

sweet talk n (1926) : FLATTERY

sweet tooth n (14c) : a craving or fondness for sweet food

sweet wil-liam \‚swēt-'wil-yəm\ n, often cap W [fr. the name William] (1573) : a widely cultivated Old World pink (Dianthus barbatus) with small white to deep red or purple flowers often showily spotted, banded, or mottled and borne in flat bracteate heads on erect stalks

sweet william

¹**swell** \'swel\ vb **swelled**; **swelled** or **swol-len** \'swō-lən\; **swell-ing** [ME, fr. OE swellan; akin to OHG swellan to swell] vi (bef. 12c) **1** **a** : to expand (as in size, volume, or numbers) gradually beyond a normal or original limit ⟨the population ~ed⟩ **b** : to become distended or puffed up ⟨her ankle is badly swollen⟩ **c** : to form a bulge or rounded elevation **2** **a** : to become filled with pride and arrogance **b** : to behave or speak in a pompous, blustering, or self-important manner **c** : to play the swell **3** : to become distended with emotion ~ vt **1** : to affect with a powerful or expansive emotion **2** : to increase the size, number, or intensity of syn see EXPAND

²**swell** n (1606) **1** : a long often massive and crestless wave or succession of waves often continuing beyond or after its cause (as a gale) **2** **a** : the condition of being protuberant **b** : a rounded elevation **3** **a** : the act or process of swelling **b** (1) : a gradual increase and decrease of the loudness of a musical sound; also : a sign indicating a swell (2) : a device used in an organ for governing loudness **4** **a** archaic : an impressive, pompous, or fashionable air or display **b** : a person dressed in the height of fashion **c** : a person of high social position or outstanding competence

³**swell** adj (1785) **1** : STYLISH **b** : socially prominent **2** : EXCELLENT — used as a generalized term of enthusiasm

swell box n (ca. 1801) : a chamber in an organ containing a set of pipes and having shutters that open or shut to regulate the volume of tone

swelled head n (1891) : an exaggerated opinion of oneself : SELF-CONCEIT — **swelled–head-ed** \'sweld-‚he-dəd\ adj — **swelled–head-ed-ness** n

swell-fish \'swel-‚fish\ n (1807) : PUFFER 2a

swell–front \'swel-‚frənt\ adj (1914) : BOWFRONT 1

swell-head \-‚hed\ n (1845) : one who has a swelled head — **swell-head-ed** \-‚he-dəd\ adj — **swell-head-ed-ness** n

swell-ing \'swe-liŋ\ n (bef. 12c) **1** : something that is swollen; specif : an abnormal bodily protuberance or localized enlargement **2** : the condition of being swollen

¹**swel-ter** \'swel-tər\ vb **swel-tered**; **swel-ter-ing** \-t(ə-)riŋ\ [ME sweltren, freq. of swelten to die, be overcome by heat, fr. OE sweltan to die; akin to Goth swiltan to die] vi (14c) **1** : to suffer, sweat, or be faint from heat **2** : to become exceedingly hot ⟨in summer, the place ~s⟩ ~ vt **1** : to oppress with heat **2** archaic : EXUDE ⟨~ed venom —Shak.⟩

²**swelter** n (1851) **1** : a state of oppressive heat **2** : WELTER **3** : an excited or overwrought state of mind : SWEAT ⟨in a ~⟩

swel-ter-ing adj (1586) : oppressively hot — **swel-ter-ing-ly** \-t(ə-)riŋ-lē\ adv

swept \'swept\ adj [swept, pp. of sweep] (1903) : slanted backward

swept–back \'swep(t)-'bak\ adj (1914) : possessing sweepback

swerve \'swərv\ vb **swerved**; **swerv-ing** [ME, fr. OE sweorfan to wipe, file away; akin to OHG swerban to wipe off, W chwerfu to whirl] vi (14c) **1** : to turn aside abruptly from a straight line or course : DEVIATE ~ vt : to cause to turn aside or deviate — **swerve** n

syn SWERVE, VEER, DEVIATE, DEPART, DIGRESS, DIVERGE mean to turn aside from a straight course. SWERVE may suggest a physical, mental, or moral turning away from a given course, often with abruptness ⟨swerved to avoid hitting the dog⟩. VEER implies a major change in direction ⟨at that point the path veers to the right⟩. DEVIATE implies a turning from a customary or prescribed course ⟨never deviated from her daily routine⟩. DEPART suggests a deviation from a traditional or conventional course or type ⟨occasionally departs from his own guidelines⟩. DIGRESS applies to a departing from the subject of one's discourse ⟨a professor prone to digress⟩. DIVERGE may equal DEPART but usu. suggests a branching of a main path into two or more leading in different directions ⟨after school their paths diverged⟩.

swev-en \'swe-vən\ n [ME, fr. OE swefn sleep, dream, vision — more at SOMNOLENT] (bef. 12c) archaic : DREAM, VISION

swid-den \'swi-d²n\ n, often attrib [E dial., burned clearing, prob. fr. ON svithinn, pp. of svitha to burn, singe] (ca. 1868) : a temporary agricultural plot produced by cutting back and burning off vegetative cover

¹**swift** \'swift\ adj [ME, fr. OE; akin to OE swīfan to revolve — more at SWIVEL] (bef. 12c) **1** : moving or capable of moving with great speed **2** : occurring suddenly or within a very short time **3** : quick to respond : READY syn see FAST

²**swift** adv (14c) : SWIFTLY ⟨swift-flowing⟩

³**swift** n (15c) **1** : any of several lizards (esp. of the genus Sceloporus) that run swiftly **2** : a reel for winding yarn or thread **3** : any of numerous small plainly colored birds (family Apodidae) that are related to the hummingbirds but superficially much resemble swallows

swift fox n (1869) : a small fox (Vulpes velox) with large ears that occurs on the plains of western No. America

swift-let \'swift(t)-lət\ n (ca. 1890) : any of various cave-dwelling swifts (genus Collocalia) of Asia including one (C. unicolor) that produces the nest used in bird's nest soup

swift-ly adv (bef. 12c) : in a swift manner : with speed : QUICKLY

swift-ness \'swift-nəs\ n (bef. 12c) **1** : the quality or state of being swift : CELERITY **2** : the fact of being swift

¹**swig** \'swig\ n [origin unknown] (ca. 1623) : a quantity drunk at one time

\ə\ abut \²\ kitten, F table \ər\ further \a\ ash \ā\ ace \ä\ mop, mar
\aú\ out \ch\ chin \e\ bet \ē\ easy \g\ go \i\ hit \ī\ ice \j\ job
\ŋ\ sing \ō\ go \ó\ law \ói\ boy \th\ thin \t̲h̲\ the \ü\ loot \ú\ foot
\y\ yet \zh\ vision \à, k̲, ⁿ, œ, œ̄, ue, ūe, ʸ\ see Guide to Pronunciation

²**swig** *vb* **swigged; swig·ging** *vt* (ca. 1650) : to drink in long drafts ⟨~ cider⟩ ~ *vi* : to take a swig : DRINK — **swig·ger** *n*

¹**swill** \'swil\ *vb* [ME *swilen*, fr. OE *swillan*] *vt* (bef. 12c) **1** : WASH, DRENCH **2** : to drink great drafts of : GUZZLE **3** : to feed (as a pig) with swill ~ *vi* **1** : to drink or eat freely, greedily, or to excess **2** : SWASH — **swill·er** *n*

²**swill** *n* (1553) **1** : something suggestive of slop or garbage : REFUSE **2 a** : a semiliquid food for animals (as swine) composed of edible refuse mixed with water or skimmed or sour milk **b** : GARBAGE

¹**swim** \'swim\ *vb* **swam** \'swam\; **swum** \'swəm\; **swim·ming** [ME *swimmen*, fr. OE *swimman* to swim] *vi* (bef. 12c) **1 a** : to propel oneself in water by natural means (as movements of the limbs, fins, or tail) **b** : to play in the water (as at a beach or swimming pool) **2** : to move with a motion like that of swimming : GLIDE ⟨a cloud *swam* slowly across the moon⟩ **3 a** : to float on a liquid : not sink **b** : to surmount difficulties : not go under ⟨sink or ~, live or die, survive or perish —Daniel Webster⟩ **4** : to become immersed in or flooded with or as if with a liquid ⟨potatoes *swimming* in gravy⟩ **5** : to have a floating or reeling appearance or sensation ~ *vt* **1 a** : to cross by propelling oneself through water ⟨~ a stream⟩ **b** : to execute in swimming **2** : to cause to swim or float — **swim·mer** *n*

²**swim** *n* (1599) **1** : a smooth gliding motion **2** : an act or period of swimming **3 a** : a temporary dizziness or unconsciousness **4 a** : an area frequented by fish **b** : the main current of activity ⟨in the ~⟩

³**swim** *adj* (1924) : of, relating to, or used in or for swimming ⟨a ~ meet⟩

swim bladder *n* (1837) : the air bladder of a fish

swim fin *n* (1947) : FLIPPER 1b

swim·ma·ble \'swi-mə-bəl\ *adj* (1852) : that can be swum

swim·mer·et \,swi-mə-'ret, 'swi-mə-,\ *n* (1840) : one of a series of small unspecialized appendages under the abdomen of many crustaceans that are best developed in some decapods (as a lobster) and usu. function in locomotion or reproduction

swimmer's itch *n* (1928) : a severe urticarial reaction to the presence in the skin of larval schistosomes that are not normally human parasites

¹**swimming** *adj* (bef. 12c) **1** [prp. of *swim*] : that swims ⟨a ~ bird⟩ **2** [gerund of *swim*] : adapted to or used in or for swimming

²**swimming** *n* (14c) : the act, art, or sport of one that swims and dives

swim·ming·ly \'swi-miŋ-lē\ *adv* (1622) : very well : SPLENDIDLY

swimming pool *n* (1899) : a pool suitable for swimming; *esp* : a tank (as of concrete or plastic) made for swimming

swim·my \'swi-mē\ *adj* **swim·mi·er; -est** (1836) **1** : verging on, causing, or affected by dizziness or giddiness **2** *of vision* : UNSTEADY, BLURRED — **swim·mi·ly** \'swi-mə-lē\ *adv*

swim·suit \'swim-,süt\ *n* (1926) : a suit for swimming or bathing

swim·wear \-,war, -,wer\ *n* (1935) : clothing suitable for wear while swimming or bathing

¹**swin·dle** \'swin-d⁹l\ *vb* **swin·dled; swin·dling** \'swin(d)-liŋ, 'swin-d⁹l-iŋ\ [back-formation fr. *swindler*, fr. G *Schwindler* giddy person, fr. *schwindeln* to be dizzy, fr. OHG *swintilōn*, freq. of *swintan* to diminish, vanish; akin to OE *swindan* to vanish] *vi* (ca. 1782) : to obtain money or property by fraud or deceit ~ *vt* : to take money or property from by fraud or deceit *syn* see CHEAT — **swin·dler** \'swin(d)-lər, 'swin-d⁹l-ər\ *n*

²**swindle** *n* (1833) : an act or instance of swindling : FRAUD

swine \'swin\ *n, pl* **swine** [ME, fr. OE *swin;* akin to OHG *swin* swine, L *sus* — more at SOW] (bef. 12c) **1** : any of various stout-bodied short-legged omnivorous mammals (family Suidae) with a thick bristly skin and a long mobile snout; *esp* : a domesticated member of the species (*Sus scrofa*) that includes the European wild boar **2** : a contemptible person

swine·herd \-,hərd\ *n* (bef. 12c) : one who tends swine

¹**swing** \'swiŋ\ *vb* **swung** \'swəŋ\; **swing·ing** \'swiŋ-iŋ\ [ME, to beat, fling, hurl, rush, fr. OE *swingan* to beat, fling oneself, rush; akin to OHG *swingan* to fling, rush] *vt* (13c) **1 a** : to cause to move vigorously through a wide arc or circle ⟨~ an ax⟩ **b** : to cause to sway to and fro **c** (1) : to cause to turn on an axis (2) : to cause to face or move in another direction ⟨~ the car into a side road⟩ **2** : to suspend so as to permit swaying or turning **3** : to convey by suspension ⟨cranes ~*ing* cargo into the ship's hold⟩ **4 a** (1) : to influence decisively ⟨~ a lot of votes⟩ (2) : to bring around by influence **b** : to handle successfully : MANAGE ⟨wasn't able to ~ a new car on his income⟩ ⟨~ a deal⟩ **5** : to play or sing (as a melody) in the style of swing music ~ *vi* **1** : to move freely to and fro esp. in suspension from an overhead support **2 a** : to die by hanging **b** : to hang freely from a support **3** : to move in or describe a circle or arc : to turn on a hinge or pivot **b** : to turn in place **c** : to convey oneself by grasping a fixed support ⟨~ aboard the train⟩ **4 a** : to have a steady pulsing rhythm **b** : to play or sing with a lively compelling rhythm; *specif* : to play swing music **5** : to shift or fluctuate from one condition, form, position, or object of attention or favor to another ⟨~ constantly from optimism to pessimism and back —Sinclair Lewis⟩ **6 a** : to move along rhythmically **b** : to start up in a smooth vigorous manner ⟨ready to ~ into action⟩ **7** : to hit or aim at something with a sweeping arm movement **8 a** : to be lively and up-to-date **b** : to engage freely in sex

syn SWING, WAVE, FLOURISH, BRANDISH, THRASH mean to wield or cause to move to and fro or up and down. SWING implies regular or uniform movement ⟨*swing* the rope back and forth⟩. WAVE usu. implies smooth or continuous motion ⟨*waving* the flag⟩. FLOURISH suggests vigorous, ostentatious, graceful movement ⟨*flourished* the winning lottery ticket⟩. BRANDISH implies threatening or menacing motion ⟨*brandishing* a knife⟩. THRASH suggests vigorous, abrupt, violent movement ⟨an infant *thrashing* his arms about⟩.

syn SWING, SWAY, OSCILLATE, VIBRATE, FLUCTUATE, WAVER, UNDULATE mean to move from one direction to its opposite. SWING implies a movement of something attached at one end or one side ⟨the door suddenly *swung* open⟩. SWAY implies a slow swinging or teetering movement ⟨trees *swaying* in the breeze⟩. OSCILLATE stresses a usu. regular alternation of direction ⟨an *oscillating* fan⟩. VIBRATE suggests the rapid oscillation of an elastic body under stress or impact ⟨the *vibrating* strings of a piano⟩. FLUCTUATE suggests constant irregular changes

of level, intensity, or value ⟨*fluctuating* interest rates⟩. WAVER stresses irregular motion suggestive of reeling or tottering ⟨the exhausted runner *wavered* before collapsing⟩. UNDULATE suggests a gentle wave-like motion ⟨an *undulating* sea of grass⟩.

²**swing** *n* (14c) **1** : an act or instance of swinging : swinging movement: as **a** (1) : a stroke or blow delivered with a sweeping arm movement ⟨a batter with a powerful ~⟩ (2) : a sweeping or rhythmic movement of the body or a bodily part (3) : a dance figure in which two dancers revolve with joined arms or hands (4) : jazz dancing in moderate tempo with a lilting syncopation **b** (1) : the regular movement of a freely suspended object (as a pendulum) along an arc and back (2) : back and forth sweep ⟨the ~ of the tides⟩ **c** (1) : steady pulsing rhythm (as in poetry or music) (2) : a steady vigorous movement characterizing an activity or creative work **d** (1) : a trend toward a high or low point in a fluctuating cycle (as of business activity) (2) : an often periodic shift from one condition, form, position, or object of attention or favor to another **2 a** : liberty of action **b** (1) : the driving power of something swung or hurled (2) : steady vigorous advance : driving speed ⟨a train approaching at full ~⟩ **3** : the progression of an activity, process, or phase of existence ⟨the work is in full ~⟩ **4** : the arc or range through which something swings **5** : something that swings freely from or on a support; *esp* : a seat suspended by a rope or chains for swinging to and fro on for pleasure **6 a** : a curving course and back to a point **b** : a course from and back to a point : a circular tour **7** : jazz played usu. by a large dance band and characterized by a steady lively rhythm, simple harmony, and a basic melody often submerged in improvisation **8** : a short pass in football thrown to a back running to the outside

³**swing** *adj* (1934) **1** : of or relating to musical swing ⟨a ~ band⟩ ⟨~ music⟩ **2** : that may swing often decisively either way on an issue or in an election ⟨~ voters⟩ ⟨a ~ state⟩

¹**swinge** \'swinj\ *vt* **swinged; swinge·ing** [ME *swengen* to shake, fr. OE *swengan;* akin to OE *swingan*] (12c) *chiefly dial* : BEAT, SCOURGE

²**swinge** *vt* **swinged; swinge·ing** [alter. of *singe*] (1590) *dial* : SINGE, SCORCH

swinge·ing *also* **swing·ing** \'swin-jiŋ\ *adj* [fr. prp. of ¹*swinge*] (ca. 1590) *chiefly Brit* : very large, high, or severe ⟨~ fines⟩ ⟨~ taxes⟩

swingeing *or* **swinging** *adv* (1690) *chiefly Brit* : VERY, SUPERLATIVELY

¹**swing·er** \'swiŋ-ər\ *n* (1543) : one that swings: as **a** : a lively up-to-date person who indulges in what is considered fashionable **b** : one who engages freely in sex

²**swing·er** \'swiŋ-jər\ *n* [¹*swinge*] (1599) : WHOPPER 1

swing·ing \'swiŋ-iŋ\ *adj* [prp. of ¹*swing*] (1956) : being lively and up-to-date; *also* : abounding in swingers and swinging entertainment ⟨a ~ coffeehouse⟩

¹**swing·ing·ly** \'swin-jiŋ-lē\ *adv* (1672) *chiefly Brit* : VERY, EXTREMELY

²**swing·ing·ly** \'swiŋ-iŋ-lē\ *adv* (1882) : in a swinging manner : with a swinging movement

swin·gle·tree \'swiŋ-gəl-(,)trē\ *n* [ME *swyngyll tre*, fr. *swyngyll* rod for beating flax (fr. MD *swengel*) + *tre* tree] (15c) : WHIFFLETREE

swing·man \'swiŋ-,man, -mən\ *n* (1965) : a player capable of playing effectively in two different positions and esp. of playing both guard and forward on a basketball team

swing shift *n* (1940) **1** : the work shift between the day and night shifts (as from 4 P.M. to midnight) **2** : a group of workers in a factory operating seven days a week that work as needed to permit the regular shift workers to have one or more free days per week

swingy \'swiŋ-ē\ *adj* **swing·i·er; -est** (1915) : marked by swing

swin·ish \'swī-nish\ *adj* (13c) : of, suggesting, or characteristic of swine : BEASTLY — **swin·ish·ly** *adv* — **swin·ish·ness** *n*

¹**swink** \'swiŋk\ *vi* [ME, fr. OE *swincan;* akin to OHG *swingan* to rush — more at SWING] (bef. 12c) *archaic* : TOIL, SLAVE

²**swink** *n* (12c) *archaic* : LABOR, DRUDGERY

¹**swipe** \'swīp\ *n* [prob. alter. of *sweep*] (1739) **1** : a strong sweeping blow **2** : a sharp often critical remark ⟨took a parting ~ at management⟩

²**swipe** *vb* **swiped; swip·ing** *vi* (ca. 1825) : to strike or move with a sweeping motion ~ *vt* **1** : to strike or wipe with a sweeping motion **2** : STEAL, PILFER

swipes \'swīps\ *n pl* [origin unknown] (ca. 1796) *Brit* : poor, thin, or spoiled beer; *also* : BEER

¹**swirl** \'swər(-ə)l\ *vb* [ME] *vi* (14c) **1 a** : to move with an eddying or whirling motion **b** : to pass in whirling confusion **2** : to have a twist or convolution ~ *vt* : to cause to swirl — **swirl·ing·ly** \'swər-liŋ-lē\ *adv*

²**swirl** *n* (15c) **1 a** : a whirling mass or motion : EDDY **b** : whirling confusion ⟨a ~ of events⟩ **2** : a twisting shape, mark, or pattern **3** : an act or instance of swirling

swirly \'swər-lē\ *adj* **swirl·i·er; -est** (1785) **1** *Scot* : KNOTTED, TWISTED **2** : that swirls : SWIRLING ⟨the ~ water of the rapids⟩

¹**swish** \'swish\ *vb* [imit.] *vi* (1756) : to move, pass, swing, or whirl with the sound of a swish ~ *vt* **1** : to move, cut, or strike with a swish ⟨the horse ~ed its tail⟩ **2** : to make (a basketball shot) so that the ball falls through the rim without touching it ⟨~ed a three-point jumper⟩ — **swish·er** *n* — **swish·ing·ly** \'swi-shiŋ-lē\ *adv*

²**swish** *n* (1820) **1 a** : a prolonged hissing sound (as of a whip cutting the air) **b** : a light sweeping or brushing sound (as of a full silk skirt in motion) **2** : a swishing movement **3** : an effeminate homosexual — usu. used disparagingly

³**swish** *adj* [origin unknown] (1879) : SMART, FASHIONABLE

swishy \'swi-shē\ *adj* **swish·i·er; -est** (1828) **1** : producing a swishing sound **2** : characterized by effeminate behavior

¹**Swiss** \'swis\ *n* [MF *Suisse*, fr. MHG *Swizer*, fr. *Swiz* Switzerland] (1515) **1** *pl* **Swiss a** : a native or inhabitant of Switzerland **b** : one that is of Swiss descent **2** *often not cap* : any of various fine sheer fabrics of cotton orig. made in Switzerland; *esp* : DOTTED SWISS **3** : SWISS CHEESE

²**Swiss** *adj* (1530) : of, relating to, or characteristic of Switzerland or the Swiss

Swiss chard *n* (1832) : a beet (*Beta vulgaris cicla*) having large leaves and succulent stalks often cooked as a vegetable — called also *chard*

Swiss cheese *n* (1822) : a hard cheese characterized by elastic texture, mild nutlike flavor, and large holes that form during ripening

Swiss steak *n* (1924) : a slice of steak pounded with flour and braised usu. with vegetables and seasonings

¹**switch** \'swich\ *n* [perh. fr. MD *swijch* twig] (1592)   **1 a** : a slender flexible whip, rod, or twig ⟨a riding ∼⟩   **2** : an act of switching: as   **a** : a blow with a switch   **b** : a shift from one to another   **c** : a change from the usual   **3** : a tuft of long hairs at the end of the tail of an animal (as a cow) — see COW illustration   **4 a** : a device made usu. of two movable rails and necessary connections and designed to turn a locomotive or train from one track to another   **b** : a railroad siding   **5** : a device for making, breaking, or changing the connections in an electrical circuit   **6** : a heavy strand of hair used in addition to a person's own hair for some coiffures

²**switch** *vt* (ca. 1611)   **1** : to strike or beat with or as if with a switch   **2** : WHISK, LASH ⟨a cat ∼ing its tail⟩   **3 a** (1) : to turn from one railroad track to another : SHUNT   (2) : to move (cars) to different positions on the same track within terminal areas   **b** : to make a shift in or exchange of ⟨∼ seats⟩   **4 a** : to shift to another electrical circuit by means of a switch   **b** : to operate an electrical switch so as to turn (as a light) off or on   ∼ *vi*   **1** : to lash from side to side   **2** : to make a shift or exchange — **switch·able** \'swi-chə-bəl\ *adj* — **switch·er** *n*

¹**switch·back** \'swich-,bak\ *n* (1863) : a zigzag road, trail, or section of railroad tracks for climbing a steep hill

²**switchback** *adj* (1887) : resembling a switchback (as in taking a zigzag course) ⟨a ∼ career⟩

³**switchback** *vi* (1903) : to follow a zigzag course esp. in ascending or descending

switch·blade \-,blād\ *n* (1932) : a pocketknife having the blade spring-operated so that pressure on a release catch causes it to fly open — called also *switchblade knife*

switch·board \-,bȯrd, -,bōrd\ *n* (1873) : an apparatus (as in a telephone exchange) consisting of a panel on which are mounted electric switches so arranged that a number of circuits may be connected, combined, and controlled

switch engine *n* (1867) : a railroad engine used in switching cars

switch·er·oo \,swi-chə-'rü\ *n*, *pl* **-oos** [alter. of *switch*] (1933) *slang* : a surprising variation : REVERSAL

switch·grass \'swich-,gras\ *n* (1840) : a panic grass (*Panicum virgatum*) of the western U.S. that is used for hay

switch–hit \-'hit\ *vi* **-hit; -hit·ting** [back-formation fr. *switch-hitter*] (1938) : to bat right-handed against a left-hander and left-handed against a right-hander in baseball

switch–hit·ter \-'hi-tər\ *n* (1948)   **1** : a baseball player who switch-hits   **2** *slang* : BISEXUAL

switch knife *n* (1950) : SWITCHBLADE

switch·man \'swich-mən\ *n* (1843) : one who attends a switch (as in a railroad yard)

switch·yard \-,yärd\ *n* (1943) : a usu. enclosed area for the switching facilities of a power station

swith \'swith\ *adv* [ME, strongly, quickly, fr. OE *swithe* strongly, fr. *swith* strong; akin to Goth *swinths* strong, OE *gesund* sound — more at SOUND] (13c) *chiefly dial* : INSTANTLY, QUICKLY

swith·er \'swi-thər\ *vi* [origin unknown] (1501) *dial chiefly Brit* : DOUBT, WAVER — **swither** *n*, *dial chiefly Brit*

Swit·zer \'swit-sər\ *n* [MHG *Swizer*] (1549) : SWISS

¹**swiv·el** \'swi-vəl\ *n*, *often attrib* [ME; akin to OE *swifan* to revolve, OHG *swebōn* to roll, heave] (14c) : a device joining two parts so that one or both can pivot freely (as on a bolt or pin)

²**swivel** *vb* **-eled** *or* **-elled; -el·ing** *or* **-el·ling** \'swi-və-liŋ, 'swiv-liŋ\ *vt* (1794) : to turn on or as if on a swivel ⟨∼ed his eyes in various directions⟩   ∼ *vi* : to swing or turn on or as if on a swivel

swivel chair *n* (1860) : a chair that swivels on its base

swiv·el–hipped \'swi-vəl-,hipt\ *adj* (1947) : moving with or characterized by movement with a twisting motion of the hips

swiv·et \'swi-vət\ *n* [origin unknown] (ca. 1892) : a state of extreme agitation

¹**swiz·zle** \'swi-zəl\ *n* [origin unknown] (1813) : an iced whiskey sour churned with a swizzle stick until the glass or pitcher becomes frosted

²**swizzle** *vb* **swiz·zled; swiz·zling** \'swi-zə-liŋ, 'swiz-liŋ\ *vi* (ca. 1847) : to drink esp. to excess : GUZZLE   ∼ *vt* : to mix or stir with or as if with a swizzle stick — **swiz·zler** \'swi-zə-lər, 'swiz-lər\ *n*

swizzle stick *n* (1879) : a stick used to stir mixed drinks

swob *archaic var of* SWAB

swollen *past part of* SWELL

¹**swoon** \'swün\ *vi* [ME *swounen*] (13c)   **1 a** : FAINT   **b** : to become enraptured ⟨∼ing with joy⟩   **2** : DROOP, FADE — **swoon·er** *n* — **swoon·ing·ly** \'swü-niŋ-lē\ *adv*

²**swoon** *n* (13c)   **1 a** : a partial or total loss of consciousness   **b** : a state of bewilderment or ecstasy : DAZE, RAPTURE   **2** : a state of suspended animation : TORPOR

¹**swoop** \'swüp\ *vb* [alter. of ME *swopen* to sweep, fr. OE *swāpan* — more at SWEEP] *vi* (1566) : to move with a sweep ⟨the eagle ∼ed down on its prey⟩   ∼ *vt* : to gain or carry off in or as if in a swoop — usu. used with *up* — **swoop·er** *n*

²**swoop** *n* (1605) : an act or instance of swooping

swoop–stake \'swüp-,stāk\ *adv* [fr. alter. of *sweepstake*] (1602) *obs* : in an indiscriminate manner

¹**swoosh** \'swüsh, 'wüsh\ *vb* [imit.] *vi* (1867)   **1** : to make or move with a rushing sound ⟨a car ∼ed by⟩   **2** : GUSH, SWIRL   ∼ *vt* : to discharge or transport with a rushing sound

²**swoosh** *n* (1885) : an act or instance of swooshing

swop *chiefly Brit var of* SWAP

sword \'sȯrd, 'sōrd\ *n*, *often attrib* [ME, fr. OE *sweord*; akin to OHG *swert* sword] (bef. 12c)   **1** : a weapon (as a cutlass or rapier) with a long blade for cutting or thrusting that is often used as a symbol of honor or authority   **2 a** : an agency or instrument of destruction or combat   **b** : the use of force ⟨the pen is mightier than the ∼ —E. G. Bulwer-Lytton⟩   **3** : coercive power   **4** : something that resembles a sword — **sword·like** \-,līk\ *adj* — **at swords' points** : mutually antagonistic : ready to fight

sword cane *n* (1837) : a cane in which a sword blade is concealed

sword dance *n* (1604)   **1** : a dance performed by men in a circle holding a sword in the right hand and grasping the tip of a neighbor's sword in the left hand   **2** : a dance performed over or around swords — **sword dancer** *n*

sword fern *n* (ca. 1829) : any of several ferns with long narrow more or less sword-shaped fronds: as   **a** : a tropical fern (*Nephrolepis exaltata*) from which the Boston fern has been developed   **b** : a fern (*Polystichum munitum*) of western No. America with a large fleshy rhizome

sword·fish \'sȯrd-,fish, 'sōrd-\ *n* (15c) : a very large oceanic bony fish (*Xiphias gladius* of the family Xiphiidae) that has a long swordlike beak formed by the bones of the upper jaw and is an important food and game fish

swordfish

sword grass *n* (1598) : any of various grasses or sedges having leaves with a sharp or toothed edge

sword knot *n* (1694) : an ornamental cord or tassel tied to the hilt of a sword

sword of Dam·o·cles \-'da-mə-,klēz\ *often cap S* (1820) : an impending disaster

sword·play \'sȯrd-,plā, 'sōrd-\ *n* (1627)   **1** : the art or skill of wielding a sword esp. in fencing   **2** : an exhibition of swordplay — **sword·play·er** *n*

swords·man \'sȯrdz-mən, 'sōrdz-\ *n* (ca. 1680)   **1** : one skilled in swordplay; *esp* : a saber fencer   **2** *archaic* : a soldier armed with a sword

swords·man·ship \-,ship\ *n* (ca. 1852) : SWORDPLAY

sword·tail \'sȯrd-,tāl, 'sōrd-\ *n* (ca. 1928) : a small brightly marked Central American live-bearer (*Xiphophorus helleri* of the family Poeciliidae) often kept in tropical aquariums and bred in many colors

swore *past of* SWEAR

sworn *past part of* SWEAR

¹**swot** \'swät\ *n* [E dial., sweat, fr. ME *swot*, fr. OE *swāt* — more at SWEAT] (1850) *Brit* : GRIND 2b

²**swot** *vi* **swot·ted; swot·ting** (ca. 1860) *Brit* : GRIND 4

¹**swound** \'swaùnd, 'swünd\ *n* [ME, alter. of *swoun* swoon, fr. *swounen* to swoon] (15c) *archaic* : SWOON 1a

²**swound** *vi* (1530) *archaic* : SWOON

swum *past part of* SWIM

swung *past and past part of* SWING

swung dash *n* (1951) : a character ∼ used in printing to conserve space by representing part or all of a previously spelled-out word

syb·a·rite \'si-bə-,rīt\ *n* (ca. 1555)   **1** [fr. the notorious luxury of the Sybarites] : VOLUPTUARY, SENSUALIST   **2** *cap* : a native or resident of the ancient city of Sybaris — **syb·a·rit·ic** \,si-bə-'ri-tik\ *adj* — **syb·a·rit·i·cal·ly** \-ti-k(ə-)lē\ *adv* — **syb·a·rit·ism** \'si-bə-,rī-,tī-zəm\ *n*

syc·a·mine \'si-kə-,mīn, -mən\ *n* [L *sycaminus*, fr. Gk *sykaminos*, of Sem origin; akin to Heb *shiqmāh* mulberry tree, sycamore] (1526) : a tree of the Bible that is usu. considered a mulberry (*Morus nigra*)

syc·a·more \'si-kə-,mȯr, -,mōr\ *n* [ME *sicamour*, fr. MF *sicamor*, fr. L *sycomorus*, fr. Gk *sykomoros*, prob. modif. of a Sem word akin to Heb *shiqmāh* sycamore] (14c)   **1** *also* **syc·o·more** \'si-kə-\ : a fig tree (*Ficus sycomorus*) of Africa and the Middle East that is the sycamore of Scripture and has sweet and edible fruit similar but inferior to the common fig   **2** : a Eurasian maple (*Acer pseudoplatanus*) with long racemes of showy yellowish green flowers that is widely planted as a shade tree   **3** : ²PLANE; *esp* : a very large spreading tree (*Platanus occidentalis*) of eastern and central No. America with 3- to 5-lobed broadly ovate leaves

syce \'sīs\ *n* [Hindi *sāīs*, fr. Ar *sā'is*] (1653) : an attendant (as a groom) esp. in India

sy·cee \'sī-,sē\ *n* [Chin (Guangdong) *sai-sì*, lit., fine silk] (1711) : silver money made in the form of ingots and formerly used in China

sy·co·ni·um \sī-'kō-nē-əm\ *n*, *pl* **-nia** \-nē-ə\ [NL, fr. Gk *sykon* fig + NL *-ium*] (ca. 1856) : the multiple fleshy fruit of a fig in which the ovaries are borne within an enlarged succulent concave or hollow receptacle

sy·co·phan·cy \'si-kə-fən(t)-sē *also* 'sī- & -,fan(t)-sē\ *n* (1672) : obsequious flattery; *also* : the character or behavior of a sycophant

sy·co·phant \-fənt *also* -,fant\ *n* [L *sycophanta* slanderer, swindler, fr. Gk *sykophantēs* slanderer, fr. *sykon* fig + *phainein* to show — more at FANCY] (1575) : a servile self-seeking flatterer — **syn** see PARASITE — **sycophant** *adj*

sy·co·phan·tic \,si-kə-'fan-tik *also* ,sī-\ *adj* (1676) : of, relating to, or characteristic of a sycophant : FAWNING, OBSEQUIOUS — **sy·co·phan·ti·cal·ly** \-'fan-ti-k(ə-)lē\ *adv*

sy·co·phan·tish \'si-kə-,fan-tish *also* ,sī-\ *adj* (1794) : SYCOPHANTIC — **sy·co·phant·ish·ly** *adv*

sy·co·phan·tism \'si-kə-fən-,ti-zəm *also* 'sī- & -,fan-\ *n* (1821) : SYCOPHANCY

sy·co·phant·ly \-lē\ *adv* (1672) : in a sycophantic manner

sy·co·sis \sī-'kō-səs\ *n* [NL, fr. Gk *sykōsis*, fr. *sykon* fig] (ca. 1827) : a chronic inflammatory disorder of the hair follicles marked by papules, pustules, and tubercles with crusting

sy·e·nite \'sī-ə-,nīt\ *n* [L *Syenites* (*lapis*) stone of Syene, fr. *Syene*, ancient city in Egypt] (ca. 1796) : an igneous rock composed chiefly of feldspar — **sy·e·nit·ic** \,sī-ə-'ni-tik\ *adj*

\ə\ abut \ᵊ\ kitten, F table \ər\ further \a\ ash \ā\ ace \ä\ mop, mar
\aù\ out \ch\ chin \e\ bet \ē\ easy \g\ go \i\ hit \ī\ ice \j\ job
\ŋ\ sing \ō\ go \ȯ\ law \ȯi\ boy \th\ thin \t̲h̲\ the \ü\ loot \ù\ foot
\y\ yet \zh\ vision \ä, k̲, ⁿ, œ, œ̄, ue, ūe, ᵜ\ see Guide to Pronunciation

sy·li \'sē-lē\ *n, pl* **sylis** [Susu *síli*, lit., elephant] (1974) : the monetary unit of Guinea from 1972 to 1986

syl·la·bary \'sil-ə-,ber-ē\ *n, pl* **-bar·ies** [NL *syllabarium*, fr. L *syllaba* syllable] (1586) : a table or listing of syllables; *specif* : a series or set of written characters each one of which is used to represent a syllable

¹syl·lab·ic \sə-'la-bik\ *adj* [LL *syllabicus*, fr. Gk *syllabikos*, fr. *syllabē* syllable] (1728) **1** : constituting a syllable or the nucleus of a syllable: **a** : not accompanied in the same syllable by a vowel ⟨a ~ consonant⟩ **b** : having vowel quality more prominent than that of another vowel in the syllable ⟨the first vowel of a falling diphthong, as \ȯ\ in \ȯi\, is ~⟩ **2** : of, relating to, or denoting syllables ⟨~ accent⟩ **3** : characterized by distinct enunciation or separation of syllables **4** : of, relating to, or constituting a type of verse distinguished primarily by count of syllables rather than by rhythmical arrangement of accents or quantities — **syl·lab·i·cal·ly** \-bi-k(ə-)lē\ *adv*

²syllabic *n* (1880) : a syllabic character or sound

syl·lab·i·cate \sə-'la-bə-,kāt\ *vt* **-cat·ed; -cat·ing** (ca. 1654) : SYLLABIFY

syl·lab·i·ca·tion \sə-,la-bə-'kā-shən\ *n* (15c) : the act, process, or method of forming or dividing words into syllables

syl·la·bic·i·ty \,sil-ə-'bi-sə-tē\ *n* (1933) : the state of being or the power of forming a syllable

syl·lab·i·fi·ca·tion \sə-,la-bə-fə-'kā-shən\ *n* (1838) : SYLLABICATION

syl·lab·i·fy \sə-'la-bə-,fī\ *vt* **-fied; -fy·ing** [L *syllaba* syllable] (ca. 1859) : to form or divide into syllables

¹syl·la·ble \'si-lə-bəl\ *n* [ME, fr. MF *sillabe*, fr. L *syllaba*, fr. Gk *syllabē*, fr. *syllambanein* to gather together, fr. *syn-* + *lambanein* to take — more at LATCH] (14c) **1** : a unit of spoken language that is next bigger than a speech sound and consists of one or more vowel sounds alone or of a syllabic consonant alone or of either with one or more consonant sounds preceding or following **2** : one or more letters (as *syl*, *la*, and *ble*) in a word (as *syl·la·ble*) usu. set off from the rest of the word by a centered dot or a hyphen and roughly corresponding to the syllables of spoken language and treated as helps to pronunciation or as guides to placing hyphens at the end of a line **3** : the smallest conceivable expression or unit of something : JOT **4** : SOL-FA SYLLABLES

²syllable *vt* **syl·la·bled; syl·la·bling** \-b(ə-)liŋ\ (15c) **1** : to give a number or arrangement of syllables to (a word or verse) **2** : to express or utter in or as if in syllables

syl·la·bub \'si-lə-,bəb\ *n* [origin unknown] (ca. 1537) **1** : a drink made by curdling milk or cream with an acid beverage (as wine or cider) **2** : a sweetened drink or topping made of milk or cream beaten with wine or liquor and sometimes further thickened with gelatin and served as a dessert

syl·la·bus \-bəs\ *n, pl* **-bi** \-,bī, -,bē\ *or* **-bus·es** [LL, alter. of L *sillybus* label for a book, fr. Gk *sillybos*] (ca. 1656) **1** : a summary outline of a discourse, treatise, or course of study or of examination requirements **2** : HEADNOTE 2

syl·lep·sis \sə-'lep-səs\ *n, pl* **-lep·ses** \-,sēz\ [L, fr. Gk *syllēpsis*, fr. *syllambanein*] (ca. 1550) **1** : the use of a word to modify or govern syntactically two or sometimes more words with only one of which it formally agrees in gender, number, or case **2** : the use of a word in the same grammatical relation to two adjacent words in the context with one literal and the other metaphorical in sense — **syl·lep·tic** \si-lə-'jis-tik\ *adj*

syl·lo·gism \'si-lə-,ji-zəm\ *n* [ME *silogisme*, fr. MF, fr. L *syllogismus*, fr. Gk *syllogismos*, fr. *syllogizesthai* to syllogize, fr. *syn-* + *logizesthai* to calculate, fr. *logos* reckoning, word — more at LEGEND] (14c) **1** : a deductive scheme of a formal argument consisting of a major and a minor premise and a conclusion (as in "every virtue is laudable; kindness is a virtue; therefore kindness is laudable") **2** : a subtle, specious, or crafty argument **3** : deductive reasoning — **syl·lo·gis·tic** \,si-lə-'jis-tik\ *adj* — **syl·lo·gis·ti·cal·ly** \-ti-k(ə-)lē\ *adv*

syl·lo·gist \'si-lə-jist\ *n* (1799) : one who applies or is skilled in syllogistic reasoning

syl·lo·gize \'si-lə-,jīz\ *vb* **-gized; -giz·ing** [ME *sylogysen*, fr. LL *syllogizare*, fr. Gk *syllogizesthai*] *vi* (15c) : to reason by means of syllogisms ~ *vt* : to deduce by syllogism ⟨~s moral laws⟩

sylph \'silf\ *n* [NL *sylphus*] (1657) **1** : an elemental being in the theory of Paracelsus that inhabits air **2** : a slender graceful woman or girl — **sylph·like** \'sil-,flīk\ *adj*

sylph·id \'sil-fəd\ *n* (1680) : a young or diminutive sylph

sylva, sylviculture *var of* SILVA, SILVICULTURE

¹syl·van \'sil-vən\ *n* (1565) : one that frequents groves or woods

²sylvan *adj* [ML *silvanus, sylvanus*, fr. L *silva, sylva* wood] (ca. 1583) **1 a** : living or located in the woods or forest **b** : of, relating to, or characteristic of the woods or forest **2 a** : made, shaped, or formed of woods or trees **b** : abounding in woods, groves, or trees : WOODED

syl·va·nite \'sil-və-,nīt\ *n* [F *sylvanite*, fr. NL *sylvanium* tellurium, fr. *Transylvania*, region in Romania] (1796) : a mineral that is a gold silver telluride and often occurs in crystals resembling written characters

syl·vat·ic \sil-'va-tik\ *adj* [L *silvaticus* of the woods, wild — more at SAVAGE] (1661) **1** : SYLVAN ⟨~ rodents⟩ **2** : occurring in or affecting wild animals ⟨~ diseases⟩

syl·vite \'sil-,vīt\ *also* **syl·vine** \-,vēn\ *n* [alter. of *sylvine*, fr. F, fr. NL *sal digestivus Sylvii* digestive salt of Sylvius, fr. *Sylvius* latinized name of Jacques Dubois †1555 Fr. physician] (1868) : a mineral that is a natural potassium chloride and occurs in colorless cubes or crystalline masses

sym- — see SYN-

sym·bi·ont \'sim-bē-,änt\ *n* [prob. fr. G, modif. of Gk *symbiount-, symbiōn*, prp. of *symbioun*] (1887) : an organism living in symbiosis; *esp* : the smaller member of a symbiotic pair

sym·bi·o·sis \,sim-bē-'ō-səs, -,bī-\ *n, pl* **-bi·o·ses** \-,sēz\ [NL, fr. G *Symbiose*, fr. Gk *symbiōsis* state of living together, fr. *symbioun* to live together, fr. *symbios* living together, fr. *sym-* + *bios* life — more at QUICK] (1622) **1** : the living together in more or less intimate association or close union of two dissimilar organisms **2** : the intimate living together of two dissimilar organisms in a mutually beneficial relationship; *esp* : MUTUALISM **3** : a cooperative relationship (as between two persons or groups) ⟨the ~ . . . between the resident population and the immigrants —John Geipel⟩ — **sym·bi·ot·ic** \-'ä-tik\ *adj* — **sym·bi·ot·i·cal·ly** \-ti-k(ə-)lē\ *adv*

sym·bi·ote \'sim-bē-,ōt, -,bī-\ *n* [F, fr. Gk *symbiōtēs* companion, fr. *symbioun* to live together] (ca. 1909) : SYMBIONT

¹sym·bol \'sim-bəl\ *n* [in sense 1, fr. LL *symbolum*, fr. LGk *symbolon*, fr. Gk, token, sign; in other senses fr. L *symbolum* token, sign, symbol, fr. Gk *symbolon*, lit., token of identity verified by comparing its other half, fr. *symballein* to throw together, compare, fr. *syn-* + *ballein* to throw — more at DEVIL] (15c) **1** : an authoritative summary of faith or doctrine : CREED **2** : something that stands for or suggests something else by reason of relationship, association, convention, or accidental resemblance; *esp* : a visible sign of something invisible ⟨the lion is a ~ of courage⟩ **3** : an arbitrary or conventional sign used in writing or printing relating to a particular field to represent operations, quantities, elements, relations, or qualities **4** : an object or act representing something in the unconscious mind that has been repressed ⟨phallic ~s⟩ **5** : an act, sound, or object having cultural significance and the capacity to excite or objectify a response

²symbol *vb* **-boled** *or* **-bolled; -bol·ing** *or* **-bol·ling** (1832) : SYMBOLIZE

sym·bol·ic \sim-'bä-lik\ *also* **sym·bol·i·cal** \-li-kəl\ *adj* (1610) **1 a** : using, employing, or exhibiting a symbol **b** : consisting of or proceeding by means of symbols **2** : of, relating to, or constituting a symbol **3** : characterized by or terminating in symbols ⟨~ thinking⟩ **4** : characterized by symbolism ⟨a ~ dance⟩ — **sym·bol·i·cal·ly** \-li-k(ə-)lē\ *adv*

symbolic logic *n* (1856) : a science of developing and representing logical principles by means of a formalized system consisting of primitive symbols, combinations of these symbols, axioms, and rules of inference

sym·bol·ise *Brit var of* SYMBOLIZE

sym·bol·ism \'sim-bə-,li-zəm\ *n* (1654) **1** : the art or practice of using symbols esp. by investing things with a symbolic meaning or by expressing the invisible or intangible by means of visible or sensuous representations: as **a** : artistic imitation or invention that is a method of revealing or suggesting immaterial, ideal, or otherwise intangible truth or states **b** : the use of conventional or traditional signs in the representation of divine beings and spirits **2** : a system of symbols or representations

sym·bol·ist \'sim-bə-list\ *n* (1812) **1** : one who employs symbols or symbolism **2** : one skilled in the interpretation or explication of symbols **3** : one of a group of writers and artists in France after 1880 reacting against realism, concerning themselves with general truths instead of actualities, exalting the metaphysical and the mysterious, and aiming to unify and blend the arts and the functions of the senses — **symbolist** *adj*

sym·bol·is·tic \,sim-bə-'lis-tik\ *adj* (ca. 1864) : SYMBOLIC

sym·bol·i·za·tion \,sim-bə-lə-'zā-shən\ *n* (1603) **1** : an act or instance of symbolizing **2** : the human capacity to develop a system of meaningful symbols

sym·bol·ize \'sim-bə-,līz\ *vb* **-ized; -iz·ing** *vt* (1603) **1** : to serve as a symbol of **2** : to represent, express, or identify by a symbol ~ *vi* : to use symbols or symbolism — **sym·bol·iz·er** *n*

sym·bol·o·gy \sim-'bä-lə-jē\ *n, pl* **-gies** [*symbol* + *-logy*] (1840) **1** : the art of expression by symbols **2** : the study or interpretation of symbols **3** : a system of symbols

sym·met·al·lism \(,)si(m)-'me-t⁵l-,i-zəm\ *n* [*syn-* + *-metallism* (as in *bimetallism*)] (ca. 1895) : a system of coinage in which the unit of currency consists of a particular weight of an alloy of two or more metals

sym·met·ri·cal \sə-'me-tri-kəl\ *or* **sym·met·ric** \-trik\ *adj* (1751) **1** : having, involving, or exhibiting symmetry **2** : having corresponding points whose connecting lines are bisected by a given point or perpendicularly bisected by a given line or plane ⟨~ curves⟩ **3** *symmetric* : being such that the terms or variables may be interchanged without altering the value, character, or truth ⟨*symmetric* equations⟩ ⟨R is a *symmetric* relation if *aRb* implies *bRa*⟩ **4 a** : capable of division by a longitudinal plane into similar halves ⟨~ plant parts⟩ **b** : having the same number of members in each whorl of floral leaves ⟨~ flowers⟩ **5** : affecting corresponding parts simultaneously and similarly ⟨~ rash⟩ **6** : exhibiting symmetry in a structural formula; *esp* : being a derivative with groups substituted symmetrically in the molecule — **sym·met·ri·cal·ly** \-tri-k(ə-)lē\ *adv* — **sym·met·ri·cal·ness** \-kəl-nəs\ *n*

symmetric group *n* (1897) : a permutation group that is composed of all of the permutations of *n* things

symmetric matrix *n* (ca. 1949) : a matrix that is its own transpose

sym·me·trize \'si-mə-,trīz\ *vt* **-trized; -triz·ing** (1796) : to make symmetrical — **sym·me·tri·za·tion** \,si-mə-trə-'zā-shən\ *n*

sym·me·try \'si-mə-trē\ *n, pl* **-tries** [L *symmetria*, fr. Gk, fr. *symmetros* symmetrical, fr. *syn-* + *metron* measure — more at MEASURE] (1541) **1** : balanced proportions; *also* : beauty of form arising from balanced proportions **2** : the property of being symmetrical; *esp* : correspondence in size, shape, and relative position of parts on opposite sides of a dividing line or median plane or about a center or axis — compare BILATERAL SYMMETRY, RADIAL SYMMETRY **3** : a rigid motion of a geometric figure that determines a one-to-one mapping onto itself **4** : the property of remaining invariant under certain changes (as of orientation in space, of the sign of the electric charge, of parity, or of the direction of time flow) — used of physical phenomena and of equations describing them

sympath- *or* **sympatho-** *comb form* [ISV, fr. *sympathetic*] : sympathetic nerve ⟨*sympatho*lytic⟩

sym·pa·thec·to·my \,sim-pə-'thek-tə-mē\ *n, pl* **-mies** [ISV] (1900) : surgical interruption of sympathetic nerve pathways — **sym·pa·thec·to·mized** \-,mīzd\ *adj*

¹sym·pa·thet·ic \,sim-pə-'the-tik\ *adj* [NL *sympatheticus*, fr. L *sympathia* sympathy] (1644) **1** : existing or operating through an affinity, interdependence, or mutual association **2 a** : not discordant or antagonistic **b** : appropriate to one's mood, inclinations, or disposition **c** : marked by kindly or pleased appreciation **3** : given to, marked by, or arising from sympathy, compassion, friendliness, and sensitivity to others' emotions ⟨a ~ gesture⟩ **4** : favorably inclined : APPROVING ⟨not ~ to the idea⟩ **5 a** : showing empathy **b** : arousing sympathy or compassion ⟨a ~ role in the play⟩ **6 a** : of or relating to the sympathetic nervous system **b** : mediated by or acting on the sympathetic nerves **7** : relating to musical tones produced by sympathetic vibra-

tion or to strings so tuned as to sound by sympathetic vibration —
sym·pa·thet·i·cal·ly \-ti-k(ə-)lē\ *adv*
²**sympathetic** *n* (1808) : a sympathetic structure; *esp* : SYMPATHETIC NERVOUS SYSTEM
sympathetic magic *n* (1905) : magic based on the assumption that a person or thing can be supernaturally affected through its name or an object representing it
sympathetic nervous system *n* (ca. 1891) : the part of the autonomic nervous system that contains chiefly adrenergic fibers and tends to depress secretion, decrease the tone and contractility of smooth muscle, and increase heart rate — compare PARASYMPATHETIC NERVOUS SYSTEM
sympathetic strike *n* (1895) : SYMPATHY STRIKE
sympathetic vibration *n* (1898) : a vibration produced in one body by the vibrations of exactly the same period in a neighboring body
sym·pa·thin \'sim-pə-thən\ *n* [ISV] (1931) : a substance (as norepinephrine) that is secreted by sympathetic nerve endings and acts as a chemical mediator
sym·pa·thise *chiefly Brit var of* SYMPATHIZE
sym·pa·thize \'sim-pə-,thīz\ *vi* **-thized; -thiz·ing** (1591) 1 : to be in keeping, accord, or harmony 2 : to react or respond in sympathy 3 : to share in suffering or grief : COMMISERATE ⟨~ with a friend in trouble⟩; *also* : to express such sympathy 4 : to be in sympathy intellectually ⟨~ with a proposal⟩ — **sym·pa·thiz·er** *n*
sym·pa·tho·lyt·ic \,sim-pə-thō-'li-tik\ *adj* [ISV] (1943) : tending to oppose the physiological results of sympathetic nervous activity or of sympathomimetic drugs — **sympatholytic** *n*
sym·pa·tho·mi·met·ic \-mə-'me-tik, -,(,)mī-\ *adj* [ISV] (1910) : simulating sympathetic nervous action in physiological effect — **sympathomimetic** *n*
sym·pa·thy \'sim-pə-thē\ *n, pl* **-thies** [L *sympathia*, fr. Gk *sympatheia*, fr. *sympathēs* having common feelings, sympathetic, fr. *syn-* + *pathos* feelings, emotion, experience — more at PATHOS] (1579) 1 a : an affinity, association, or relationship between persons or things wherein whatever affects one similarly affects the other b : mutual or parallel susceptibility or a condition brought about by it c : unity or harmony in action or effect 2 a : inclination to think or feel alike : emotional or intellectual accord b : feeling of loyalty : tendency to favor or support ⟨republican *sympathies*⟩ 3 a : the act or capacity of entering into or sharing the feelings or interests of another b : the feeling or mental state brought about by such sensitivity ⟨have ~ for the poor⟩ 4 : the correlation existing between bodies capable of communicating their physical energy to one another through some medium **syn** *see* ATTRACTION, PITY
sympathy strike *n* (1912) : a strike in which the strikers have no direct grievance against their own employer but attempt to support or aid usu. another group of workers on strike
sym·pat·ric \sim-'pa-trik\ *adj* [*syn-* + Gk *patra* fatherland, fr. *patēr* father — more at FATHER] (ca. 1904) : occurring in the same area; *specif* : occupying the same range without loss of identity from interbreeding ⟨~ species⟩ — compare ALLOPATRIC — **sym·pat·ri·cal·ly** \-tri-k(ə-)lē\ *adv* — **sym·pat·ry** \'sim-,pa-trē\ *n*
sym·pet·al·ous \(,)sim-'pe-tᵊl-əs\ *adj* (ca. 1877) : GAMOPETALOUS — **sym·pet·aly** \-tᵊl-ē, 'sim-,\ *n*
sym·phon·ic \sim-'fä-nik\ *adj* (1856) 1 : HARMONIOUS, SYMPHONIOUS 2 : relating to or having the form or character of a symphony ⟨~ music⟩ 3 : suggestive of a symphony esp. in form, interweaving of themes, or harmonious arrangement ⟨a ~ drama⟩ — **sym·phon·i·cal·ly** \-ni-k(ə-)lē\ *adv*
symphonic poem *n* (1873) : an extended programmatic composition for symphony orchestra usu. freer in form than a symphony
sym·pho·ni·ous \sim-'fō-nē-əs\ *adj* (1652) : agreeing esp. in sound : HARMONIOUS — **sym·pho·ni·ous·ly** *adv*
sym·pho·nist \'sim(p)-fə-nist\ *n* (1767) 1 : a member of a symphony orchestra 2 : a composer of symphonies
sym·pho·ny \-nē\ *n, pl* **-nies** [ME *symphonie*, fr. MF, fr. L *symphonia*, fr. Gk *symphōnia*, fr. *symphōnos* concordant in sound, fr. *syn-* + *phōnē* voice, sound — more at BAN] (15c) 1 : consonance of sounds 2 a : RITORNELLO 1 b : SINFONIA 1 c (1) : a usu. long and complex sonata for symphony orchestra (2) : a musical composition (as for organ) resembling such a symphony in complexity or variety 3 : consonance or harmony of color (as in a painting) 4 a : SYMPHONY ORCHESTRA b : a symphony orchestra concert 5 : something that in its harmonious complexity or variety suggests a symphonic composition
symphony orchestra *n* (ca. 1881) : a large orchestra of winds, strings, and percussion that plays symphonic works
sym·phy·se·al \,sim(p)-fə-'sē-əl\ *also* **sym·phys·i·al** \sim-'fi-zē-əl\ *adj* [Gk *symphyse-, symphysis* symphysis] (ca. 1836) : of, relating to, or constituting a symphysis
sym·phy·sis \'sim(p)-fə-səs\ *n, pl* **-phy·ses** \-,sēz\ [NL, fr. Gk, state of growing together, fr. *symphyesthai* to grow together, fr. *syn-* + *phyein* to make grow, bring forth — more at BE] (ca. 1578) 1 : an immovable or more or less movable articulation of various bones in the median plane of the body 2 : an articulation in which the bony surfaces are connected by pads of fibrous cartilage without a synovial membrane
sym·po·di·al \sim-'pō-dē-əl\ *adj* [NL *sympodium* apparent main axis formed from secondary axes, fr. Gk *syn-* + *podion* base — more at ·PODIUM] (1875) : having or involving the formation of an apparent main axis from successive secondary axes ⟨~ branching of a cyme⟩
sym·po·si·arch \sim-'pō-zē-,ärk\ *n* [Gk *symposiarchos*, fr. *symposion* symposium + *-archos* -arch] (1603) : one who presides over a symposium
sym·po·si·ast \-zē-,ast, -əst\ *n* [Gk *symposiazein* to take part in a symposium, fr. *symposion*] (ca. 1656) : a contributor to a symposium
sym·po·si·um \sim-'pō-zē-əm *also* -zh(ē-)əm\ *n, pl* **-sia** \-zē-ə, -zh(ē-)ə\ *or* **-siums** [L, fr. Gk *symposion*, fr. *sympinein* to drink together, fr. *syn-* + *pinein* to drink — more at POTABLE] (1711) 1 a : a convivial party (as after a banquet in ancient Greece) with music and conversation b : a social gathering at which there is free interchange of ideas 2 a : a formal meeting at which several specialists deliver short addresses on a topic or on related subjects — compare COLLOQUIUM b : a collection of opinions on a subject; *esp* : one published by a periodical : DISCUSSION
symp·tom \'sim(p)-təm\ *n* [LL *symptomat-, symptoma*, fr. Gk *symptōmat-, symptōma* happening, attribute, symptom, fr. *sympiptein* to

happen, fr. *syn-* + *piptein* to fall — more at FEATHER] (1541) 1 a : subjective evidence of disease or physical disturbance; *broadly* : something that indicates the presence of bodily disorder b : an evident reaction by a plant to a pathogen 2 a : something that indicates the existence of something else ⟨~s of the time⟩ b : a slight indication : TRACE *syn* see SIGN — **symp·tom·less** \-ləs\ *adj*
symp·tom·at·ic \,sim(p)-tə-'ma-tik\ *adj* (1698) 1 a : being a symptom of a disease b : having the characteristics of a particular disease but arising from another cause 2 : concerned with or affecting symptoms 3 : CHARACTERISTIC, INDICATIVE ⟨his behavior was ~ of his character⟩ — **symp·tom·at·i·cal·ly** \-ti-k(ə-)lē\ *adv*
symp·tom·atol·o·gy \,sim(p)-tə-mə-'tä-lə-jē\ *n* (1798) 1 : the symptom complex of a disease 2 : a branch of medical science concerned with symptoms of diseases — **symp·tom·at·o·log·i·cal** \-,ma-tᵊl-'ä-ji-kəl\ *or* **symp·tom·at·o·log·ic** \-'ä-jik\ *adj* — **symp·tom·at·o·log·i·cal·ly** \-ji-k(ə-)lē\ *adv*
syn- *or* **sym-** *prefix* [ME, fr. OF, fr. L, fr. Gk, fr. *syn* with, together with] 1 : with : along with : together ⟨synclinal⟩ ⟨sympetalous⟩ 2 : at the same time ⟨synesthesia⟩
syn·ae·re·sis *var of* SYNERESIS
syn·aes·the·sia *var of* SYNESTHESIA
syn·aes·the·sis \,si-nəs-'thē-səs\ *n* [Gk *synaisthēsis* joint perception, fr. *synaisthanesthai* to perceive simultaneously, fr. *syn-* + *aisthanesthai* to perceive — more at AUDIBLE] (1922) : harmony of different or opposing impulses produced by a work of art
syn·a·gogue *or* **syn·a·gog** \'si-nə-,gäg\ *n* [ME *synagoge*, fr. OF, fr. LL *synagoga*, fr. Gk *synagōgē* assembly, synagogue, fr. *synagein* to bring together, fr. *syn-* + *agein* to lead — more at AGENT] (13c) 1 : a Jewish congregation 2 : the house of worship and communal center of a Jewish congregation — **syn·a·gog·al** \,si-nə-'gä-gəl\ *adj*
syn·a·loe·pha *or* **syn·a·le·pha** \,si-nə-'lē-fə\ *n* [NL, fr. Gk *synaloiphē*, fr. *synaleiphein* to clog up, coalesce, unite two syllables into one, fr. *syn-* + *aleiphein* to anoint — more at ALIPHATIC] (1540) : the reduction to one syllable of two vowels of adjacent syllables (as in *th' army* for *the army*)
¹**syn·apse** \'si-,naps, sə-'naps\ *n* [NL *synapsis*, fr. Gk, juncture, fr. *synaptein* to fasten together, fr. *syn-* + *haptein* to fasten] (1899) : the point at which a nervous impulse passes from one neuron to another
²**synapse** *vi* **syn·apsed; syn·aps·ing** (1910) 1 : to form a synapse 2 : to come together in synapsis
syn·ap·sid \sə-'nap-səd\ *n* [NL *Synapsida*, fr. Gk *syn-* + *apsid-, apsis* arch, vault — more at APSIS] (1956) : any of a subclass (Synapsida) of extinct reptiles existing during the Pennsylvanian, Permian, and Jurassic, having a single pair of lateral temporal openings in the skull, and usu. held to be ancestral to mammals — **synapsid** *adj*
syn·ap·sis \sə-'nap-səs\ *n, pl* **-ap·ses** \-,sēz\ [NL] (ca. 1892) : the association of homologous chromosomes that is characteristic of the first meiotic prophase
syn·ap·tic \sə-'nap-tik\ *adj* [NL *synapsis*] (1895) 1 : of or relating to a synapsis 2 : of or relating to a synapse — **syn·ap·ti·cal·ly** \-ti-k(ə-)lē\ *adv*
syn·ap·to·ne·mal complex \sə-,nap-tə-'nē-məl-\ *n* [*synaptic* + *-o-* or *-i-* + Gk *nēma* thread — more at NEMAT-] (1958) : a complex tripartite protein structure that spans the region between synapsed chromosomes in meiotic prophase — called also *syn·ap·ti·ne·mal complex* \sə-,nap-tə-'nē-məl-\
syn·ap·to·some \sə-'nap-tə-,sōm\ *n* [*synaptic* + *-o-* + ³*-some*] (1964) : a nerve ending that is isolated from homogenized nerve tissue — **syn·ap·to·som·al** \-,nap-tə-'sō-məl\ *adj*
syn·ar·thro·di·al \,sin-är-'thrō-dē-əl\ *adj* [NL *synarthrodia* synarthrosis] (1830) : of, relating to, or being a synarthrosis
syn·ar·thro·sis \-'thrō-səs\ *n, pl* **-thro·ses** \-,sēz\ [Gk *synarthrōsis*, fr. *syn-* + *arthrōsis* arthrosis] (1578) : an immovable articulation in which the bones are united by intervening fibrous connective tissues
¹**sync** *also* **synch** \'siŋk\ *vt* **synced** *also* **synched** \'siŋ(k)t\; **sync·ing** *also* **synch·ing** \'siŋ-kiŋ\ (1929) : SYNCHRONIZE
²**sync** *also* **synch** *n* (1937) : SYNCHRONIZATION, SYNCHRONISM — **sync** *adj*
syn·car·pous \(,)sin-'kär-pəs\ *adj* (ca. 1830) : having the carpels of the gynoecium united in a compound ovary — **syn·car·py** \'sin-,kär-pē\ *n*
syn·cat·e·gor·e·mat·ic \,sin-,ka-tə-,gór-ə-'ma-tik, -,gór-ē-\ *adj* [LL *syncategoremat-, syncategorema* syncategorematic term, fr. Gk *synkatēgorēma*, fr. *synkatēgorein* to predicate jointly, fr. *syn-* + *katēgorein* to predicate — more at CATEGORY] (1827) : forming a meaningful expression only in conjunction with a denotative expression (as a content word) ⟨logical operators and function words are ~⟩ — **syn·cat·e·gor·e·mat·i·cal·ly** \-ti-k(ə-)lē\ *adv*
¹**syn·chro** \'siŋ-(,)krō, 'sin-\ *n, pl* **synchros** [*synchronous*] (1943) : SELSYN
²**synchro** *adj* [*synchro-*] (1947) : adapted to synchronization
synchro- *comb form* [*synchronized & synchronous*] : synchronized : synchronous ⟨*synchromesh*⟩
syn·chro·cy·clo·tron \,siŋ-(,)krō-'sī-klə-,trän, ,sin-\ *n* (1947) : a modified cyclotron that achieves greater energies for the charged particles by compensating for the variation in mass that the particles experience with increasing velocity
syn·chro·mesh \'siŋ-krō-,mesh, 'sin-\ *adj* (1928) : designed for effecting synchronized shifting of gears — **synchromesh** *n*
syn·chro·nal \'siŋ-krə-nᵊl, 'sin-\ *adj* (1660) : SYNCHRONOUS
syn·chro·ne·ity \,siŋ-krə-'nē-ə-tē, ,sin-, -'nā-\ *n* [*synchronous* + *-eity* (as in *spontaneity*)] (ca. 1909) : the state of being synchronous
syn·chron·ic \sin-'krä-nik, siŋ-\ *adj* (1833) 1 : SYNCHRONOUS 2 a : DESCRIPTIVE 4 ⟨~ linguistics⟩ b : concerned with events existing in a limited time period and ignoring historical antecedents — **syn·chron·i·cal** \-ni-kəl\ *adj* — **syn·chron·i·cal·ly** \-ni-k(ə-)lē\ *adv*
syn·chro·nic·i·ty \,siŋ-krə-'ni-sə-tē, ,sin-\ *n* (ca. 1889) 1 : the quality or fact of being synchronous 2 : the coincidental occurrence of events

---

\ə\ abut \ᵊ\ kitten, F table \ər\ further \a\ ash \ā\ ace \ä\ mop, mar \au̇\ out \ch\ chin \e\ bet \ē\ easy \g\ go \i\ hit \ī\ ice \j\ job \ŋ\ sing \ō\ go \ȯ\ law \ȯi\ boy \th\ thin \t͟h\ the \ü\ loot \u̇\ foot \y\ yet \zh\ vision \ā, k̲, ⁿ, œ, œ̄, ᵫ, ᵫ̄, ᵜ\ *see* Guide to Pronunciation and esp. psychic events (as similar thoughts in widely separated persons or a mental image of an unexpected event before it happens) that seem related but are not explained by conventional mechanisms of causality — used esp. in the psychology of C. G. Jung

syn·chro·ni·sa·tion, syn·chro·nise *Brit var of* SYNCHRONIZATION, SYNCHRONIZE

syn·chro·nism \'siŋ-krə-,ni-zəm, 'sin-\ *n* (1588) **1** : the quality or state of being synchronous : SIMULTANEOUSNESS **2** : chronological arrangement of historical events and personages so as to indicate coincidence or coexistence; *also* : a table showing such concurrences — **syn·chro·nis·tic** \,siŋ-krə-'nis-tik, ,sin-\ *adj*

syn·chro·ni·za·tion \,siŋ-krə-nə-'zā-shən, ,sin-\ *n* (1828) **1** : the act or result of synchronizing **2** : the state of being synchronous

syn·chro·nize \'siŋ-krə-,nīz, 'sin-\ *vb* **-nized; -niz·ing** *vi* (ca. 1624) : to happen at the same time ~ *vt* **1** : to represent or arrange (events) to indicate coincidence or coexistence **2** : to make synchronous in operation **3** : to make (motion picture sound) exactly simultaneous with the action — **syn·chro·niz·er** *n*

synchronized swimming *n* (1950) : swimming in which the movements of one or more swimmers are synchronized with a musical accompaniment so as to form changing patterns

syn·chro·nous \'siŋ-krə-nəs, 'sin-\ *adj* [LL *synchronos,* fr. Gk, fr. *syn-* + *chronos* time] (1669) **1** : happening, existing, or arising at precisely the same time **2** : recurring or operating at exactly the same periods **3** : involving or indicating synchronism **4 a** : having the same period; *also* : having the same period and phase **b** : GEOSTATIONARY **5** : of, used in, or being digital communication (as between computers) in which a common timing signal is established that dictates when individual bits can be transmitted, in which characters are not individually delimited, and which allows for very high rates of data transfer *syn* see CONTEMPORARY — **syn·chro·nous·ly** *adv* — **syn·chro·nous·ness** *n*

synchronous motor *n* (1897) : an electric motor having a speed strictly proportional to the frequency of the operating current

syn·chro·ny \'siŋ-krə-nē, 'sin-\ *n, pl* **-nies** (1848) : synchronistic occurrence, arrangement, or treatment

syn·chro·scope \-,skōp\ *n* (1907) : any of several devices for showing whether two associated machines or moving parts are operating in synchronism with each other

syn·chro·tron \'siŋ-krə-,trän, 'sin-\ *n* (1945) **1** : an apparatus for imparting very high speeds to charged particles by means of a combination of a high-frequency electric field and a low-frequency magnetic field **2** : SYNCHROTRON RADIATION

synchrotron radiation *n* [fr. its having been first observed in a synchrotron] (1956) : radiation emitted by high-energy charged relativistic particles (as electrons) when they are accelerated by a magnetic field (as in a nebula)

syn·cli·nal \(,)sin-'klī-nᵊl\ *adj* [Gk *syn-* + *klinein* to lean — more at LEAN] (1833) **1** : inclined down from opposite directions so as to meet **2** : having or relating to a folded rock structure in which the sides dip toward a common line or plane

syn·cline \'sin-,klīn\ *n* [back-formation fr. *synclinal*] (1873) : a trough of stratified rock in which the beds dip toward each other from either side — compare ANTICLINE

cross section of strata showing syncline

syn·co·pate \'siŋ-kə-,pāt, 'sin-\ *vt* **-pat·ed; -pat·ing** (1605) **1 a** : to shorten or produce by syncope (~ *suppose* to *s'pose*) **b** : to cut short : CLIP, ABBREVIATE **2** : to modify or affect (musical rhythm) by syncopation — **syn·co·pa·tor** \-,pā-tər\ *n*

syncopated *adj* (1665) **1** : cut short : ABBREVIATED **2** : marked by or exhibiting syncopation (~ rhythm)

syn·co·pa·tion \,siŋ-kə-'pā-shən, ,sin-\ *n* (1597) **1** : a temporary displacement of the regular metrical accent in music caused typically by stressing the weak beat **2** : a syncopated rhythm, passage, or dance step — **syn·co·pa·tive** \'siŋ-kə-,pā-tiv, 'sin-\ *adj*

syn·co·pe \'siŋ-kə-(,)pē, 'sin-\ *n* [LL, fr. Gk *synkopē,* lit., cutting short, fr. *synkoptein* to cut short, fr. *syn-* + *koptein* to cut — more at CAPON] (ca. 1550) **1** : loss of consciousness resulting from insufficient blood flow to the brain : FAINT **2** : the loss of one or more sounds or letters in the interior of a word (as in *fo'c'sle* for *forecastle*) — **syn·co·pal** \-kə-pəl\ *adj*

syn·cret·ic \sin-'kre-tik, siŋ-\ *adj* (1840) : characterized or brought about by syncretism : SYNCRETISTIC

syn·cre·tise *Brit var of* SYNCRETIZE

syn·cre·tism \'siŋ-krə-,ti-zəm, 'sin-\ *n* [NL *syncretismus,* fr. Gk *synkrētismos* federation of Cretan cities, fr. *syn-* + *Krēt-, Krēs* Cretan] (1618) **1** : the combination of different forms of belief or practice **2** : the fusion of two or more orig. different inflectional forms — **syn·cre·tist** \-tist\ *n or adj* — **syn·cre·tis·tic** \,siŋ-krə-'tis-tik, ,sin-\ *adj*

syn·cre·tize \'siŋ-krə-,tīz, 'sin-\ *vt* **-tized; -tiz·ing** (ca. 1891) : to attempt to unite and harmonize esp. without critical examination or logical unity

syn·cy·tium \sin-'si-sh(ē-)əm\ *n, pl* **-tia** \-sh(ē-)ə\ [NL, fr. *syn-* + *cyt-*] (1877) **1** : a multinucleate mass of protoplasm (as in the plasmodium of a slime mold) resulting from fusion of cells **2** : COENOCYTE 1 — **syn·cy·tial** \-'si-sh(ē-)əl\ *adj*

syn·dac·ty·lism \(,)sin-'dak-tə-,li-zəm\ *n* (1889) : SYNDACTYLY

syn·dac·ty·ly \-lē\ *n* [NL *syndactylia,* fr. *syn-* + Gk *daktylos* finger] (1864) : a union of two or more digits that is normal in some animals (as various marsupials) and occurs as a human hereditary disorder marked by webbing of two or more fingers or toes

syn·des·mo·sis \,sin-,dez-'mō-səs, -,des-\ *n, pl* **-mo·ses** \-,sēz\ [NL, fr. Gk *syndesmos* fastening, ligament, fr. *syndein*] (1726) : an articulation in which the contiguous surfaces of the bones are rough and are bound together by a ligament

syn·det·ic \sin-'de-tik\ *adj* [Gk *syndetikos,* fr. *syndein* to bind together — more at ASYNDETON] (1621) : CONNECTIVE, CONNECTING (~ pronoun); *also* : marked by a conjunctive (~ relative clause) — **syn·det·i·cal·ly** \-ti-k(ə-)lē\ *adv*

syn·dic \'sin-dik\ *n* [F, fr. LL *syndicus* representative of a corporation, fr. Gk *syndikos* assistant at law, advocate, representative of a state, fr. *syn-* + *dikē* judgment, case at law — more at DICTION] (1601) **1** : a municipal magistrate in some countries **2** : an agent of a university or corporation

syn·di·cal \-di-kəl\ *adj* (1864) **1** : of or relating to a syndic or to a committee that assumes the powers of a syndic **2** : of or relating to syndicalism

syn·di·cal·ism \'sin-di-kə-,li-zəm\ *n* [F *syndicalisme,* fr. *chambre syndicale* trade union] (1907) **1** : a revolutionary doctrine by which workers seize control of the economy and the government by direct means (as a general strike) **2** : a system of economic organization in which industries are owned and managed by the workers **3** : a theory of government based on functional rather than territorial representation — **syn·di·cal·ist** \-list\ *adj or n*

¹syn·di·cate \'sin-di-kət\ *n* [F *syndicat,* fr. *syndic*] (1624) **1 a** : a council or body of syndics **b** : the office or jurisdiction of a syndic **2** : an association of persons officially authorized to undertake a duty or negotiate business **3 a** : a group of persons or concerns who combine to carry out a particular transaction **b** : CARTEL 2 **c** : a loose association of racketeers in control of organized crime **4** : a business concern that sells materials for publication in a number of newspapers or periodicals simultaneously **5** : a group of newspapers under one management

²syn·di·cate \'sin-də-,kāt\ *vb* **-cat·ed; -cat·ing** *vt* (1882) **1** : to subject to or manage as a syndicate **2 a** : to sell (as a cartoon) to a syndicate or for publication in many newspapers or periodicals at once **b** : to sell (as a series of television programs) directly to local stations ~ *vi* : to unite to form a syndicate — **syn·di·ca·tion** \,sin-də-'kā-shən\ *n* — **syn·di·ca·tor** \'sin-də-,kā-tər\ *n*

syn·drome \'sin-,drōm *also* -drəm\ *n* [NL, fr. Gk *syndromē* combination, syndrome, fr. *syn-* + *dramein* to run — more at DROMEDARY] (1541) **1** : a group of signs and symptoms that occur together and characterize a particular abnormality **2** : a set of concurrent things (as emotions or actions) that usu. form an identifiable pattern

syn·ec·do·che \sə-'nek-də-(,)kē\ *n* [L, fr. Gk *synekdochē,* fr. *syn-* + *ekdochē* sense, interpretation, fr. *ekdechesthai* to receive, understand, fr. *ex* from + *dechesthai* to receive; akin to Gk *dokein* to seem good — more at EX-, DECENT] (15c) : a figure of speech by which a part is put for the whole (as *fifty sail* for *fifty ships*), the whole for a part (as *society* for *high society*), the species for the genus (as *cutthroat* for *assassin*), the genus for the species (as *a creature* for *a man*), or the name of the material for the thing made (as *boards* for *stage*) — **syn·ec·doch·ic** \,si-,nek-'dä-kik\ *adj* — **syn·ec·doch·i·cal** \-'dä-ki-kəl\ *adj* — **syn·ec·doch·i·cal·ly** \-ki-k(ə-)lē\ *adv*

syn·ecol·o·gy \,si-ni-'kä-lə-jē, ,si-ne-\ *n* [G *Synökologie,* fr. *syn-* syn- + *Ökologie* ecology] (1910) : a branch of ecology that deals with the structure, development, and distribution of ecological communities — **syn·eco·log·i·cal** \,si-,ne-kə-'lä-ji-kəl, ,si-,ne-\ *adj*

syn·er·e·sis \sə-'ner-ə-səs, -'nir-, *esp for 2* ,si-nə-'rē-\ *n* [LL *synaeresis,* fr. Gk *synairesis,* fr. *synairein* to contract, fr. *syn-* + *hairein* to take] (ca. 1577) **1** : SYNIZESIS **2** : the separation of liquid from a gel caused by contraction

syn·er·get·ic \,si-nər-'je-tik\ *adj* [Gk *synergētikos,* fr. *synergein* to work with, cooperate, fr. *synergos* working together, fr. *syn-* + *ergon* work — more at WORK] (ca. 1836) : SYNERGIC

syn·er·gic \sə-'nər-jik\ *adj* (ca. 1859) : working together : COOPERATING — **syn·er·gi·cal·ly** \-ji-k(ə-)lē\ *adv*

syn·er·gid \sə-'nər-jəd, 'si-nər-\ *n* [NL *synergida,* fr. Gk *synergos* working together] (1898) : one of two small cells lying near the micropyle of the embryo sac of an angiosperm

syn·er·gism \'si-nər-,ji-zəm\ *n* [NL *synergismus,* fr. Gk *synergos*] (1910) : interaction of discrete agencies (as industrial firms), agents (as drugs), or conditions such that the total effect is greater than the sum of the individual effects

syn·er·gist \-jist\ *n* (1876) : something (as a chemical or a muscle) that enhances the effectiveness of an active agent; *broadly* : either member of a synergistic pair

syn·er·gis·tic \,si-nər-'jis-tik\ *adj* (ca. 1847) **1** : having the capacity to act in synergism (~ drugs) **2** : of, relating to, or resembling synergism (a ~ reaction) — **syn·er·gis·ti·cal·ly** \-ti-k(ə-)lē\ *adv*

syn·er·gy \'si-nər-jē\ *n* [NL *synergia,* fr. Gk *synergos* working together] (1660) : SYNERGISM; *broadly* : combined action or operation

syn·e·sis \'si-nə-səs\ *n* [NL, fr. Gk, understanding, sense, fr. *synienai* to bring together, understand, fr. *syn-* + *hienai* to send — more at JET] (ca. 1891) : a grammatical construction in which agreement or reference is according to sense rather than strict syntax (as *anyone* and *them* in "if anyone calls, tell them I am out")

syn·es·the·sia \,si-nəs-'thē-zh(ē-)ə\ *n* [NL, fr. *syn-* + *-esthesia* (as in *anesthesia*)] (ca. 1891) : a concomitant sensation; *esp* : a subjective sensation or image of a sense (as of color) other than the one (as of sound) being stimulated — **syn·es·thet·ic** \-'the-tik\ *adj*

syn·fu·el \'sin-,fyü(-ə)l\ *n* [synthetic + fuel] (1976) : a liquid or gaseous fuel derived esp. from a fossil fuel that is a solid (as coal) or part of a solid (as tar sand or oil shale)

syn·ga·my \'siŋ-gə-mē\ *n* [ISV] (1904) : sexual reproduction by union of gametes

syn·gas \'sin-,gas\ *n* (1975) : SYNTHESIS GAS

syn·ge·ne·ic \,sin-jə-'nē-ik\ *adj* [syn- + -geneic (as in *isogeneic*)] (1961) : genetically identical or similar esp. with respect to antigens or immunological reactions (~ tumor cells) (grafts between ~ mice) — compare ALLOGENEIC, XENOGENEIC

syn·i·ze·sis \,si-nə-'zē-səs\ *n* [LL, fr. Gk *synizēsis,* fr. *synizein* to sit down together, collapse, blend, fr. *syn-* + *hizein* to sit down; akin to L *sidere* to sit down — more at SUBSIDE] (1846) : contraction of two syllables into one by uniting in pronunciation two adjacent vowels

syn·kary·on \sin-'kar-ē-,än, -ē-ən\ *n* [NL, fr. Gk *syn-* + *karyon* nut — more at CAREEN] (1905) : a cell nucleus formed by the fusion of two preexisting nuclei

syn·od \'si-nəd *also* -,äd\ *n* [ME *sinod,* fr. LL *synodus,* fr. LGk *synodos,* fr. Gk, meeting, assembly, fr. *syn-* + *hodos* way, journey] (14c) **1** : an ecclesiastical governing or advisory council: as 'a : the governing assembly of an Episcopal province b : a Presbyterian governing body ranking between the presbytery and the general assembly c : a regional or national organization of Lutheran congregations 2 : the ecclesiastical district governed by a synod — **syn·od·al** \'si-nə-dªl, -,nä-; sə-'nä-dªl\ *adj*

syn·od·ic \sə-'nä-dik\ *or* **syn·od·i·cal** \-di-kəl\ *adj* (1561) 1 : of or relating to a synod : SYNODAL 2 *usu* synodic [Gk *synodikos*, fr. *synodos* meeting, conjunction] : relating to conjunction; *esp* : relating to the period between two successive conjunctions of the same celestial bodies (as the moon and the sun)

synodic month *n* (1654) : a lunar month

syn·o·nym \'si-nə-,nim\ *n* [ME *sinonyme*, fr. L *synonymum*, fr. Gk *synōnymon*, fr. neut. of *synōnymos* synonymous, fr. *syn-* + *onyma* name — more at NAME] (15c) 1 : one of two or more words or expressions of the same language that have the same or nearly the same meaning in some or all senses 2 : a symbolic or figurative name : METONYM 3 : a taxonomic name rejected as being incorrectly applied or incorrect in form — compare HOMONYM — **syn·o·nym·ic** \,si-nə-'ni-mik\ *also* **syn·o·nym·i·cal** \-mi-kəl\ *adj* — **syn·o·nym·i·ty** \-'ni-mə-tē\ *n*

syn·on·y·mist \sə-'nä-nə-mist\ *n* (ca. 1753) : one who lists, studies, or discriminates synonyms

syn·on·y·mize \-,mīz\ *vt* **-mized; -miz·ing** (ca. 1595) 1 a : to give or analyze the synonyms of (a word) b : to provide (as a dictionary) with synonymies 2 : to demonstrate (a taxonomic name) to be a synonym

syn·on·y·mous \-məs\ *adj* (1610) 1 : having the character of a synonym; *also* : alike in meaning or significance 2 : having the same connotations, implications, or reference (to runners, Boston is ~ with marathon —*Runners World*) — **syn·on·y·mous·ly** *adv*

syn·on·y·my \-mē\ *n, pl* **-mies** (1683) 1 a : a list or collection of synonyms often defined and discriminated from each other b : the study or discrimination of synonyms 2 : the scientific names that have been used in different publications to designate a taxonomic group (as a species); *also* : a list of these 3 : the quality or state of being synonymous

syn·op·sis \sə-'näp-səs\ *n, pl* **-op·ses** \-,sēz\ [LL, fr. Gk, lit., comprehensive view, fr. *synopsesthai* to be going to see together, fr. *syn-* + *opsesthai* to be going to see — more at OPTIC] (1611) 1 : a condensed statement or outline (as of a narrative or treatise) : ABSTRACT 2 : the abbreviated conjugation of a verb in one person only

syn·op·size \-,sīz\ *vt* **-sized; -siz·ing** (1882) 1 : EPITOMIZE 2 : to make a synopsis of (as a novel)

syn·op·tic \sə-'näp-tik\ *also* **syn·op·ti·cal** \-ti-kəl\ *adj* [Gk *synoptikos*, fr. *synopsesthai*] (1763) 1 : affording a general view of a whole 2 : manifesting or characterized by comprehensiveness or breadth of view 3 : presenting or taking the same or common view; *specif, often cap* : of or relating to the first three Gospels of the New Testament 4 : relating to or displaying conditions (as of the atmosphere or weather) as they exist simultaneously over a broad area — **syn·op·ti·cal·ly** \-ti-k(ə-)lē\ *adv*

syn·os·to·sis \,si-,näs-'tō-səs\ *n, pl* **-to·ses** \-,sēz\ [NL] (ca. 1848) : union of two or more separate bones to form a single bone

sy·no·via \sə-'nō-vē-ə, sī-\ *n* [NL] (1726) : a transparent viscid lubricating fluid secreted by a membrane of an articulation, bursa, or tendon sheath

sy·no·vi·al \-vē-əl\ *adj* (1756) : of, relating to, secreting, or being synovia (~ membranes) (~ fluid)

sy·no·vi·tis \,si-nə-'vī-təs\ *n* (ca. 1836) : inflammation of a synovial membrane

syn·tac·tic \sin-'tak-tik\ *or* **syn·tac·ti·cal** \-ti-kəl\ *adj* [NL *syntacticus*, fr. Gk *syntaktikos* arranging together, fr. *syntassein*] (1577) : of, relating to, or according to the rules of syntax or syntactics — **syn·tac·ti·cal·ly** \-ti-k(ə-)lē\ *adv*

syn·tac·tics \-tiks\ *n pl but sing or pl in constr* (1937) : a branch of semiotic that deals with the formal relations between signs or expressions in abstraction from their signification and their interpreters

syn·tag·ma \sin-'tag-mə\ *n, pl* **-mas** *or* **-ma·ta** \-mə-tə\ [Gk, fr. *syntassein*] (1937) : a syntactic element — **syn·tag·mat·ic** \,sin-,tag-'ma-tik\ *adj*

syn·tax \'sin-,taks\ *n* [F or LL; F *syntaxe*, fr. LL *syntaxis*, fr. Gk, fr. *syntassein* to arrange together, fr. *syn-* + *tassein* to arrange] (1574) 1 a : the way in which linguistic elements (as words) are put together to form constituents (as phrases or clauses) b : the part of grammar dealing with this 2 : a connected or orderly system : harmonious arrangement of parts or elements 3 : syntactics esp. as dealing with the formal properties of languages or calculi

synth \'sin(t)th\ *n, often attrib* (1976) : SYNTHESIZER 2

syn·the·sis \'sin(t)-thə-səs\ *n, pl* **-the·ses** \-,sēz\ [Gk, fr. *syntithenai* to put together, fr. *syn-* + *tithenai* to put, place — more at DO] (1589) 1 a : the composition or combination of parts or elements so as to form a whole b : the production of a substance by the union of chemical elements, groups, or simpler compounds or by the degradation of a complex compound c : the combining of often diverse conceptions into a coherent whole; *also* : the complex so formed 2 a : deductive reasoning b : the dialectic combination of thesis and antithesis into a higher stage of truth 3 : the frequent and systematic use of inflected forms as a characteristic device of a language — **syn·the·sist** \-sist\ *n*

synthesis gas *n* (ca. 1941) : a mixture of carbon monoxide and hydrogen used esp. in chemical synthesis

syn·the·size \-,sīz\ *vb* **-sized; -siz·ing** *vt* (1830) 1 : to combine or produce by synthesis 2 : to make a synthesis of ~ *vi* : to make a synthesis

syn·the·siz·er \-,sī-zər\ *n* (1869) 1 : one that synthesizes (an expert ~ of diverse views) 2 : a usu. computerized electronic apparatus for the production and control of sound (as for producing music)

syn·the·tase \'sin-thə-,tās, -,tāz\ *n* [*synthetic* + *-ase*] (1947) : an enzyme that catalyzes the linking together of two molecules usu. using the energy derived from the concurrent splitting off of a pyrophosphate group from a triphosphate (as ATP) — called also *ligase*

¹syn·thet·ic \sin-'the-tik\ *adj* [Gk *synthetikos* of composition, component, fr. *syntithenai* to put together] (1697) 1 : relating to or involving synthesis : not analytic 2 : attributing to a subject something determined by observation rather than analysis of the nature of the subject

and not resulting in self-contradiction if negated — compare ANALYTIC 3 : characterized by frequent and systematic use of inflected forms to express grammatical relationships 4 a (1) : of, relating to, or produced by chemical or biochemical synthesis; *esp* : produced artificially (~ drugs) (~ silk) (2) : of or relating to a synfuel b : devised, arranged, or fabricated for special situations to imitate or replace usual realities c : FACTITIOUS, BOGUS — **syn·thet·i·cal·ly** \-ti-k(ə-)lē\ *adv*

²synthetic *n* (1946) : something resulting from synthesis rather than occurring naturally; *esp* : a product (as a drug or plastic) of chemical synthesis

synthetic division *n* (1904) : a simplified method for dividing a polynomial by another polynomial of the first degree by writing down only the coefficients of the several powers of the variable and changing the sign of the constant term in the divisor so as to replace the usual subtractions by additions

synthetic geometry *n* (1889) : elementary euclidean geometry or projective geometry as distinguished from analytic geometry

synthetic resin *n* (1907) : RESIN 2

syph \'sif\ *n* (ca. 1914) *slang* : SYPHILIS

syph·i·lis \'si-f(ə-)ləs\ *n* [NL, fr. *Syphilus*, hero of the poem *Syphilis sive Morbus Gallicus* (*Syphilis or the French disease*) (1530) by Girolamo Fracastoro †1553 Ital. poet, physician, and astronomer] (1718) : a chronic contagious usu. venereal and often congenital disease caused by a spirochete (*Treponema pallidum*) and if left untreated producing chancres, rashes, and systemic lesions in a clinical course with three stages continued over many years — compare PRIMARY SYPHILIS, SECONDARY SYPHILIS, TERTIARY SYPHILIS — **syph·i·lit·ic** \,si-fə-'li-tik\ *adj or n*

sy·phon *var of* SIPHON

Sy·rette \sə-'ret\ *trademark* — used for a small collapsible tube fitted with a hypodermic needle for injecting a single dose of a medicinal agent

Syr·i·ac \'sir-ē-,ak\ *n* [L *syriacus* Syrian, fr. Gk *syriakos*, fr. *Syria*, ancient country in Asia] (1605) 1 : a literary language based on an eastern Aramaic dialect and used as the literary and liturgical language by several eastern Christian churches 2 : Aramaic spoken by Christian communities — **Syriac** *adj*

Syr·i·an hamster \'sir-ē-ən-\ *n* [*Syria*, Asia] (ca. 1949) : GOLDEN HAMSTER

sy·rin·ga \sə-'riŋ-gə\ *n* [NL, genus name, fr. Gk *syring-, syrinx* panpipe] (1664) : MOCK ORANGE 1

¹sy·ringe \sə-'rinj *also* 'sir-inj\ *n* [ME *syring*, fr. ML *syringa*, fr. LL, injection, fr. Gk *syring-, syrinx* panpipe, tube] (14c) : a device used to inject fluids into or withdraw them from something (as the body or its cavities): as a : a device that consists of a nozzle of varying length and a compressible rubber bulb and is used for injection or irrigation b : an instrument (as for the injection of medicine or the withdrawal of bodily fluids) that consists of a hollow barrel fitted with a plunger and a hollow needle c : a gravity device consisting of a reservoir fitted with a long rubber tube ending with an exchangeable nozzle that is used for irrigation of the vagina or bowel

²syringe *vt* **sy·ringed; sy·ring·ing** (1610) : to irrigate or spray with or as if with a syringe

sy·rin·go·my·e·lia \sə-,riŋ-gō-mī-'ē-lē-ə\ *n* [NL, fr. Gk *syring-, syrinx* tube, fistula + NL *myel-* + *-ia*] (1897) : a chronic progressive disease of the spinal cord associated with sensory disturbances, muscle atrophy, and spasticity — **sy·rin·go·my·el·ic** \-'e-lik\ *adj*

syr·inx \'sir-in(k)s\ *n, pl* **sy·rin·ges** \sə-'rin-jēz, -'rin-jēz\ *or* **syr·inx·es** (1606) 1 [LL, fr. Gk] : PANPIPE 2 [NL, fr. Gk] : the vocal organ of birds that is a special modification of the lower part of the trachea or of the bronchi or of both

syr·phid fly \'sər-fəd-, 'sir-\ *n* [NL *Syrphidae*, fr. *Syrphus*, genus of flies, fr. Gk *syrphos* gnat] (ca. 1891) : any of a family (Syrphidae) of dipteran flies which frequent flowers and some of whose larvae prey on plant lice — called also *syrphid* — **syrphid** *adj*

syr·up \'sər-əp, 'sir-əp, 'sə-rəp\ *n* [ME *sirup*, fr. MF *sirop*, fr. ML *syrupus*, fr. Ar *sharāb*] (14c) 1 a : a thick sticky solution of sugar and water often flavored or medicated b : the concentrated juice of a fruit or plant 2 : cloying sweetness or sentimentality — **syr·upy** *adj*

sys·op \'sis-,äp\ *n* [*system operator*] (1983) : the administrator of a computer bulletin board

sys·tal·tic \sis-'tȯl-tik, -'tal-\ *adj* [LL *systalticus*, fr. Gk *systaltikos*, fr. *systellein* to contract — more at SYSTOLE] (1676) : marked by regular contraction and dilatation : PULSING

sys·tem \'sis-təm\ *n* [LL *systemat-, systema*, fr. Gk *systēmat-, systēma*, fr. *synistanai* to combine, fr. *syn-* + *histanai* to cause to stand — more at STAND] (1603) 1 : a regularly interacting or interdependent group of items forming a unified whole (a number ~): as a (1) : a group of interacting bodies under the influence of related forces (a gravitational ~) (2) : an assemblage of substances that is in or tends to equilibrium (a thermodynamic ~) b (1) : a group of body organs that together perform one or more vital functions (the digestive ~) (2) : the body considered as a functional unit c : a group of related natural objects or forces (a river ~) d : a group of devices or artificial objects or an organization forming a network esp. for distributing something or serving a common purpose (a telephone ~) (a heating ~) (a highway ~) (a data processing ~) e : a major division of rocks usu. larger than a series and including all formed during a period or era f : a form of social, economic, or political organization or practice (the capitalist ~) 2 : an organized set of doctrines, ideas, or principles usu. intended to explain the arrangement or working of a systematic whole (the Newtonian ~ of mechanics) 3 a : an organized or established procedure (the touch ~ of typing) b : a manner of classifying, symbolizing, or schematizing (a taxonomic ~) (the decimal ~) 4 : harmonious arrangement or pattern : ORDER (bring ~ out of confusion —Ellen Glasgow) 5 : an organized society or social situation

---

\ə\ abut \ª\ kitten, F table \ər\ further \a\ ash \ā\ ace \ä\ mop, mar \au̇\ out \ch\ chin \e\ bet \ē\ easy \g\ go \i\ hit \ī\ ice \j\ job \ŋ\ sing \ō\ go \ȯ\ law \ȯi\ boy \th\ thin \t̲h̲\ the \ü\ loot \u̇\ foot \y\ yet \zh\ vision \á, k̲, ⁿ, œ, œ̄, ᵫ, ᵫ̄, ᵞ\ see Guide to Pronunciation regarded as stultifying : ESTABLISHMENT 2 — usu. used with *the* **syn** see METHOD — **sys·tem·less** \-ləs\ *adj*

sys·tem·at·ic \,sis-tə-'ma-tik\ *adj* [LL *systematicus*, fr. Gk *systēmatikos*, fr. *systēmat-, systēma*] (ca. 1680) **1** : relating to or consisting of a system **2** : presented or formulated as a coherent body of ideas or principles ⟨~ thought⟩ **3 a** : methodical in procedure or plan ⟨a ~ approach⟩ ⟨a ~ scholar⟩ **b** : marked by thoroughness and regularity ⟨~ efforts⟩ **4** : of, relating to, or concerned with classification; *specif* : TAXONOMIC — **sys·tem·at·i·cal·ly** \-ti-k(ə-)lē\ *adv* — **sys·tem·at·ic·ness** \-tik-nəs\ *n*

systematic error *n* (1891) : an error that is not determined by chance but is introduced by an inaccuracy (as of observation or measurement) inherent in the system

sys·tem·at·ics \,sis-tə-'ma-tiks\ *n pl but sing in constr* (1888) **1** : the science of classification **2 a** : a system of classification **b** : the classification and study of organisms with regard to their natural relationships : TAXONOMY

systematic theology *n* (1836) : a branch of theology concerned with summarizing the doctrinal traditions of a religion (as Christianity) esp. with a view to relating the traditions convincingly to the religion's present-day setting

sys·tem·a·tise *Brit var of* SYSTEMATIZE

sys·tem·a·tism \'sis-tə-mə-,ti-zəm, sis-'te-mə-\ *n* (1846) : the practice of forming intellectual systems

sys·tem·a·tist \'sis-tə-mə-tist, sis-'te-mə-\ *n* (1700) **1** : a maker or follower of a system **2** : a specialist in taxonomy : TAXONOMIST

sys·tem·a·tize \'sis-tə-mə-,tīz\ *vt* **-tized; -tiz·ing** (ca. 1767) : to arrange in accord with a definite plan or scheme : order systematically ⟨the need to ~ their work⟩ *syn* see ORDER — **sys·tem·a·ti·za·tion** \,sis-tə-mə-tə-'zā-shən, sis-,te-mə-\ *n* — **sys·tem·a·tiz·er** *n*

¹sys·tem·ic \sis-'te-mik\ *adj* (1803) **1** : of, relating to, or common to a system: as **a** : affecting the body generally **b** : supplying those parts of the body that receive blood through the aorta rather than through the pulmonary artery **c** : of, relating to, or being a pesticide that as used is harmless to the plant or higher animal but when absorbed into its sap or bloodstream makes the entire organism toxic to pests (as an insect or fungus) — **sys·tem·i·cal·ly** \-mi-k(ə-)lē\ *adv*

²systemic *n* (1951) : a systemic pesticide

systemic lupus er·y·the·ma·to·sus \-,er-ə-,thē-mə-'tō-səs\ *n* (1951) : an inflammatory connective tissue disease of unknown cause that occurs chiefly in women, is characterized esp. by fever, skin rash, and arthritis, often by acute hemolytic anemia, by small hemorrhages in the skin and mucous membranes, by inflammation of the pericardium, and in serious cases by involvement of the kidneys and central nervous system

sys·tem·ize \'sis-tə-,mīz\ *vt* **-ized; -iz·ing** (1778) : SYSTEMATIZE — **sys·tem·i·za·tion** \,sis-tə-mə-'zā-shən\ *n*

systems analysis *n* (1950) : the act, process, or profession of studying an activity (as a procedure, a business, or a physiological function) typically by mathematical means in order to define its goals or purposes and to discover operations and procedures for accomplishing them most efficiently — **systems analyst** *n*

sys·to·le \'sis-tə-(,)lē\ *n* [Gk *systolē,* fr. *systellein* to contract, fr. *syn-* + *stellein* to send] (1578) : a rhythmically recurrent contraction; *esp* : the contraction of the heart by which the blood is forced onward and the circulation kept up — **sys·tol·ic** \sis-'tä-lik\ *adj*

syz·y·gy \'si-zə-jē\ *n, pl* **-gies** [LL *syzygia* conjunction, fr. Gk, fr. *syzygos* yoked together, fr. *syn-* + *zygon* yoke — more at YOKE] (ca. 1847) : the nearly straight-line configuration of three celestial bodies (as the sun, moon, and earth during a solar or lunar eclipse) in a gravitational system

Szech·uan *or* **Szech·wan** \'sech-,wän, 'sesh-\ *adj* [*Szechwan or Szechuan* (Sichuan), province in China] (1956) : of, relating to, or being a style of Chinese cooking that is spicy, oily, and esp. peppery

---

T

t \'tē\ *n, pl* **t's** *or* **ts** \'tēz\ *often cap, often attrib* (bef. 12c) **1 a** : the 20th letter of the English alphabet **b** : a graphic representation of this letter **c** : a speech counterpart of orthographic *t* **2** : a graphic device for reproducing the letter *t* **3** : one designated *t* esp. as the 20th in order or class **4** : something shaped like the letter T **5** : T FORMATION **6** : TECHNICAL FOUL — **to a T** [short for *to a tittle*] : to perfection

't \t\ *pron* : IT ⟨my country, 'tis of thee —S. F. Smith⟩

ta \'tä\ *n* [baby talk] (1772) *Brit* : THANKS

Taal \'täl\ *n* [Afrik, fr. D, language; akin to OE *talu* talk — more at TALE] (1896) : AFRIKAANS — usu. used with *the*

¹tab \'tab\ *n, often attrib* [origin unknown] (1607) **1 a** : a short projecting device: as (1) : a small flap or loop by which something may be grasped or pulled (2) : a projection from a card used as an aid in filing **b** : a small insert, addition, or remnant **c** : APPENDAGE, EXTENSION; *esp* : one of a series of small pendants forming a decorative border or edge of a garment **d** : a small auxiliary airfoil hinged to a control surface (as a trailing edge) to help stabilize an airplane in flight — see AIRPLANE illustration **2** [partly short for ¹*table*; partly fr. sense 1] **a** : close surveillance : WATCH ⟨keep ~*s* on trends⟩ **b** : a creditor's statement : BILL, CHECK ⟨~ : COST ⟨the ~ for the new program⟩ **3** [by shortening] **a** : TABLOID **b** : TABLET **4** [short for *tabulator*] : a device (as on a typewriter) for arranging data in columns

²tab *vt* **tabbed; tab·bing** (1872) **1** : to furnish or ornament with tabs **2** : to single out : DESIGNATE **3** : TABULATE

ta·ba·nid \tə-'bā-nəd, -'ba-\ *n* [ultim. fr. L *tabanus* horsefly] (ca. 1891) : HORSEFLY

tab·ard \'ta-bərd *also* -,bärd\ *n* [ME, fr. MF *tabart*] (14c) : a short loose-fitting sleeveless or short-sleeved coat or cape: as **a** : a tunic worn by a knight over his armor and emblazoned with his arms **b** : a herald's official cape or coat emblazoned with his lord's arms **c** : a woman's sleeveless outer garment often worn with side slits

Ta·bas·co \tə-'bas-(,)kō\ *trademark* — used for a pungent condiment sauce made from hot peppers

tab·bou·leh \tə-'bü-lə, -,lē\ *n* [Ar *tabbūla*] (1955) : a salad of Lebanese origin consisting chiefly of cracked wheat, tomatoes, parsley, mint, onions, lemon juice, and olive oil

¹tab·by \'ta-bē\ *n, pl* **tabbies** [F *tabis*, fr. ML *attabi*, fr. Ar *'attābī*, fr. Al-'*Attābiya*, quarter in Baghdad] (1638) **1 a** : a plain silk taffeta esp. with moiré finish **b** : a plain-woven fabric **2** [²*tabby*] **a** : a domestic cat with a striped and mottled coat **b** : a domestic cat; *esp* : a female cat

²tabby *adj* (1661) **1** : of, relating to, or made of tabby **2** : striped and mottled with darker color : BRINDLED ⟨a ~ cat⟩

³tabby *n* [Gullah *tabi*, ultim. fr. Sp *tapia* adobe wall] (1775) : a cement made of lime, sand or gravel, and oyster shells and used chiefly along the coast of Georgia and So. Carolina in the 17th and 18th centuries

¹tab·er·na·cle \'ta-bər-,na-kəl\ *n* [ME, fr. OF, fr. LL *tabernaculum*, fr. L, tent, fr. *taberna* hut] (13c) **1 a** *often cap* : a tent sanctuary used by the Israelites during the Exodus **b** *archaic* : a dwelling place **c** *archaic* : a temporary shelter : TENT **2** : a receptacle for the consecrated elements of the Eucharist; *esp* : an ornamental locked box used for reserving the Communion hosts **3** : a house of worship; *specif* : a large building or tent used for evangelistic services — **tab·er·nac·u·lar** \,ta-bər-'na-kyə-lər\ *adj*

²tabernacle *vi* **tab·er·na·cled; tab·er·na·cling** \-,na-k(ə-)liŋ\ (1653) : to take up temporary residence; *also* : to inhabit a physical body

ta·bes \'tā-(,)bēz\ *n, pl* **tabes** [L, wasting disease, decay, fr. *tabēre* to decay — more at THAW] (1651) : wasting accompanying a chronic disease — **ta·bet·ic** \tə-'be-tik\ *adj or n*

tabes dor·sa·lis \-,dor-'sa-ləs, -'sä-, -'sä-\ *n* [NL, dorsal tabes] (ca. 1681) : a syphilitic disorder of the nervous system marked by wasting, pain, lack of coordination of voluntary movements and reflexes, and disorders of sensation, nutrition, and vision — called also *locomotor ataxia*

ta·bla \'tä-blə\ *n* [Hindi *tablā*, fr. Ar *tabla*] (1865) : a pair of small different-sized hand drums used esp. in music of India

tab·la·ture \'ta-blə-,chúr, -chər, -,tyúr, -,túr\ *n* [MF, fr. ML *tabulatus* tablet, fr. L *tabula*] (1574) : an instrumental notation indicating the string, fret, key, or finger to be used instead of the tone to be sounded

¹ta·ble \'tā-bəl\ *n, often attrib* [ME, fr. OE *tabule* & OF *table*; both fr. L *tabula* board, tablet, list] (bef. 12c) **1** : TABLET 1a **2 a** *pl* : BACKGAMMON **b** : one of the two leaves of a backgammon board or either half of a leaf **3 a** : a piece of furniture consisting of a smooth flat slab fixed on legs **b** (1) : a supply or source of food (2) : an act or instance of assembling to eat : MEAL ⟨sit down to ~⟩ **c** (1) : a group of people assembled at or as if at a table (2) : a legislative or negotiating session ⟨the bargaining ~⟩ **4** : STRINGCOURSE **5 a** : a systematic arrangement of data usu. in rows and columns for ready reference **b** : a condensed enumeration : LIST ⟨a ~ of contents⟩ **6** : something that resembles a table esp. in having a plane surface: as **a** : the upper flat surface of a cut precious stone — see BRILLIANT illustration **b** (1) : TABLELAND (2) : a horizontal stratum ⟨water ~⟩ — **under the table** **1** : into a stupor ⟨can drink you *under the table*⟩ **2** : in a covert manner ⟨took money *under the table*⟩

²table *vt* **ta·bled; ta·bling** \-b(ə-)liŋ\ (15c) **1** : to enter in a table **2** *a Brit* : to place on the agenda **b** : to remove (as a parliamentary motion) from consideration indefinitely **c** : to put on a table

³table *adj* (1547) **1** : suitable for a table or for use at a table ⟨a ~ lamp⟩ **2** : suitable for serving at a table ⟨~ grapes⟩ **3** : proper for conduct at a table ⟨~ manners⟩

tab·leau \'ta-,blō, ta-'blō\ *n, pl* **tab·leaux** \-,blōz, -'blōz\ *also* **tableaus** [F, fr. MF *tablel*, dim. of *table*, fr. OF] (1699) **1** : a graphic description or representation : PICTURE ⟨winsome *tableaux* of old-fashioned literary days —J. D. Hart⟩ **2** : a striking or artistic grouping **3** [short for *tableau vivant* (fr. F, lit., living picture)] : a depiction of a scene usu. presented on a stage by silent and motionless costumed participants

tableau curtain *n* (1881) : a stage curtain that opens in the center and has its sections drawn upward as well as to the side

ta·ble·cloth \'tā-bəl-,klóth\ *n* (15c) : a covering spread over a dining table before the tableware is set

ta·ble d'hôte \,tä-bəl-'dōt, ,ta-\ *n* [F, lit., host's table] (1617) **1** : a meal served to all guests at a stated hour and fixed price **2** : a complete meal of several courses offered at a fixed price

ta·ble·ful \'tā-bəl-,fúl\ *n* (1535) : as much or as many as a table can hold or accommodate

ta·ble–hop \'tā-bəl-ˌhäp\ vi (1942) : to move from table to table (as in a restaurant) in order to chat with friends — **ta·ble–hop·per** n
ta·ble·land \-bə(l)-ˌland\ n (1697) : a broad level elevated area : PLATEAU
table linen n (1629) : linen (as tablecloths and napkins) for the table
ta·ble·mate \'tā-bəl-ˌmāt\ n (1624) : a dining companion
table of organization (ca. 1918) : a table listing the number and duties of personnel and the major items of equipment authorized for a military unit
table salt n (1878) : salt suitable for use at the table and in cooking
ta·ble·spoon \'tā-bəl-ˌspün\ n (1763) 1 : a large spoon used for serving 2 : a unit of measure used esp. in cookery equal to ½ fluid ounce (15 milliliters)
ta·ble·spoon·ful \ˌtā-bəl-'spün-ˌfûl, 'tā-bəl-ˌ\ n, pl **tablespoonfuls** \-ˌfûlz\ also **ta·ble·spoons·ful** \-'spünz-ˌfûl, -ˌspünz-\ (1772) 1 : enough to fill a tablespoon 2 : TABLESPOON 2
table sugar n (1958) : SUGAR 1a; esp : granulated white sugar
tab·let \'ta-blət\ n [ME tablett, fr. MF tablete, dim. of table table] (14c) 1 a : a flat slab or plaque suited for or bearing an inscription b : a thin slab or one of a set of portable sheets used for writing ⟨~ PAD 4⟩ 2 a : a compressed or molded block of a solid material b : a small mass of medicated material ⟨an aspirin ~⟩ 3 : GRAPHICS TABLET
table talk n (1569) : informal conversation at or as if at a dining table; esp : the social talk of a celebrity recorded for publication
table tennis n (1901) : a game resembling tennis that is played on a tabletop with wooden paddles and a small hollow plastic ball
ta·ble·top \'tā-bəl-ˌtäp\ n (1807) 1 : the top of a table 2 : a photograph of small objects or a miniature scene arranged on a table — **table·top** adj
ta·ble·ware \-ˌwar, -ˌwer\ n (1832) : utensils (as of china, glass, or silver) for table use
table wine n (ca. 1827) : an unfortified wine averaging 12 percent alcohol by volume and esp. suitable for serving with food
¹**tab·loid** \'ta-ˌblòid\ adj [fr. Tabloid, a trademark] (1901) 1 : compressed or condensed into small scope ⟨~ criticism⟩ 2 : of, relating to, or characteristic of tabloids; esp : featuring stories of violence, crime, or scandal presented in a sensational manner
²**tabloid** n (1906) 1 : DIGEST, SUMMARY 2 : a newspaper that is about half the page size of an ordinary newspaper and that contains news in condensed form and much photographic matter
¹**ta·boo** also **ta·bu** \tə-'bü, ta-\ adj [Tongan tabu] (1777) 1 : forbidden to profane use or contact because of what are held to be dangerous supernatural powers 2 a : banned on grounds of morality or taste ⟨the subject is ~⟩ b : banned as constituting a risk ⟨the area beyond is ~, still alive with explosives —Robert Leckie⟩
²**taboo** also **tabu** n, pl **taboos** also **tabus** (1777) 1 : a prohibition against touching, saying, or doing something for fear of immediate harm from a supernatural force 2 : a prohibition imposed by social custom or as a protective measure 3 : belief in taboos
³**taboo** also **tabu** vt (1777) 1 : to set apart as taboo esp. by marking with a ritualistic symbol 2 : to avoid or ban as taboo
ta·bor also **ta·bour** \'tā-bər\ n [ME, fr. OF] (14c) : a small drum with one head of soft calfskin used to accompany a pipe or fife played by the same person
ta·bor·er also **ta·bour·er** \-bər-ər\ n (15c) : one that plays on the tabor
tab·o·ret or **tab·ou·ret** \ˌta-bə-'ret, -'rä\ n [F tabouret, lit., small drum, fr. MF, dim. of tabor, tabour drum] (1630) 1 : a cylindrical seat or stool without arms or back 2 : a small portable stand or cabinet
ta·bou·li var of TABBOULEH
Ta·briz \tə-'brēz\ n, pl **Tabriz** [Tabriz, Iran] (1904) : a Persian rug usu. having a cotton warp, firm wool pile, and a medallion design
tab·u·lar \'ta-byə-lər\ adj [L tabularis of boards, fr. tabula board, table] (ca. 1656) 1 : having a flat surface : LAMINAR ⟨a ~ crystal⟩ 2 a : of, relating to, or arranged in a table; specif : set up in rows and columns b : computed by means of a table

tabor

ta·bu·la ra·sa \ˌta-byə-lə-'rä-zə, -sə\ n, pl **ta·bu·lae ra·sae** \-ˌli-'rä-ˌzī, -ˌsi\ [L, smoothed or erased tablet] (1607) 1 : the mind in its hypothetical primary blank or empty state before receiving outside impressions 2 : something existing in its original pristine state
tab·u·late \'ta-byə-ˌlāt\ vt **-lat·ed; -lat·ing** [L tabula tablet] (1734) 1 : to put into tabular form 2 : to count, record, or list systematically — **tab·u·la·tion** \ˌta-byə-'lā-shən\ n — **tab·u·la·tor** \'ta-byə-ˌlā-tər\ n
ta·bun \'tä-ˌbün\ n [G] (1948) : a liquid organophosphate C₅H₁₁N₂O₂P that acts as a nerve gas
tac·a·ma·hac \'ta-kə-mə-ˌhak\ n [Sp tacamahaca, fr. Nahuatl tecamac] (1739) : BALSAM POPLAR
TACAN \'ta-ˌkan\ n, often attrib [tactical air navigation] (1955) : a system of navigation that uses ultrahigh frequency signals to determine the distance and bearing of an aircraft from a transmitting station
ta·cet \'tä-ˌket; 'tä-sət, 'ta-sət\ [L, lit., (it) is silent, fr. tacēre to be silent — more at TACIT] (ca. 1724) — used as a direction in music to indicate that an instrument is not to play during a movement or long section
tach \'tak\ n (ca. 1930) : TACHOMETER
tach·i·nid \'ta-kə-nəd, -ˌnid\ n [NL Tachinidae, fr. Tachina, genus of flies, fr. Gk tachinos fleet, fr. tachys swift] (1888) : any of a family (Tachinidae) of bristly usu. grayish or black dipteran flies whose parasitic larvae are often used in the biological control of insect pests — **tachinid** adj
tach·ism \'ta-ˌshi-zəm\ n, often cap [F tachisme, fr. tache stain, spot, blob, fr. MF teche, tache, of Gmc origin; akin to OS tēkan sign, OHG zeihhan — more at TOKEN] (1955) : ACTION PAINTING — **tach·ist** \'ta-shist\ also **ta·chiste** \tä-'shēst\ adj or n, often cap
ta·chis·to·scope \tə-'kis-tə-ˌskōp, ta-\ n [Gk tachistos (superl. of tachys swift) + ISV -scope] (ca. 1890) : an apparatus for the brief exposure of visual stimuli that is used in the study of learning, attention, and perception — **ta·chis·to·scop·ic** \-ˌkis-tə-'skä-pik\ adj — **ta·chis·to·scop·i·cal·ly** \-pi-k(ə-)lē\ adv
ta·chom·e·ter \ta-'kä-mə-tər, tə-\ n [Gk tachos speed + E -meter] (1810) : a device for indicating speed of rotation
tachy- comb form [Gk, fr. tachys] : rapid : accelerated ⟨tachycardia⟩

tachy·ar·rhyth·mia \ˌta-kē-ā-'rith-mē-ə\ n [NL] (1926) : arrhythmia characterized by a rapid irregular heartbeat
tachy·car·dia \ˌta-ki-'kär-dē-ə\ n [NL] (1889) : relatively rapid heart action whether physiological (as after exercise) or pathological — compare BRADYCARDIA
tachy·on \'ta-kē-ˌän\ n [tachy- + ²-on] (1967) : a hypothetical particle held to travel only faster than light
tac·it \'ta-sət\ adj [F or L; F tacite, fr. L tacitus silent, fr. pp. of tacēre to be silent; akin to OHG dagēn to be silent] (ca. 1604) 1 : expressed or carried on without words or speech 2 a : implied or indicated but not actually expressed ⟨~ consent⟩ b (1) : arising without express contract or agreement (2) : arising by operation of law ⟨~ mortgage⟩ — **tac·it·ly** adv — **tac·it·ness** n
tac·i·turn \'ta-sə-ˌtərn\ adj [F or L; F taciturne, fr. L taciturnus, fr. tacitus] (1771) : temperamentally disinclined to talk syn see SILENT — **tac·i·tur·ni·ty** \ˌta-sə-'tər-nə-tē\ n
¹**tack** \'tak\ vb [ME takken, fr. tak] vt (14c) 1 : ATTACH; esp : to fasten or affix with tacks 2 : to join in a slight or hasty manner 3 a : to add as a supplement b : to add (a rider) to a parliamentary bill 4 : to change the direction of (a sailing ship) when sailing close-hauled by turning the bow to the wind and shifting the sails so as to fall off on the other side at about the same angle as before ~ vi 1 a : to tack a sailing ship b of a ship : to change to an opposite tack by turning the bow to the wind c : to follow a course against the wind by a series of tacks 2 a : to follow a zigzag course b : to modify one's policy or attitude abruptly — **tack·er** n
²**tack** n [ME tak something that attaches; akin to MD tac sharp point] (1574) 1 : a small short sharp-pointed nail usu. having a broad flat head 2 a : the direction of a ship with respect to the trim of her sails ⟨starboard ~⟩ b : the run of a sailing ship on one tack c : a change when close-hauled from the starboard to the port tack or vice versa d : a zigzag movement on land e : a course or method of action; esp : one sharply divergent from that previously followed 3 : any of various usu. temporary stitches 4 : the lower forward corner of a fore-and-aft sail 5 : a sticky or adhesive quality or condition
³**tack** n [origin unknown] (1841) : HARDTACK 1
⁴**tack** n [perh. short for tackle] (1924) : stable gear; esp : articles of harness (as saddle and bridle) for use on a saddle horse
tack·board \'tak-ˌbörd, -ˌbórd\ n (ca. 1927) : a board (as of cork) for tacking up notices and display materials
tack claw n (ca. 1876) : a small hand tool for removing tacks
tack·i·fy \'ta-kə-ˌfī\ vt **-fied; -fy·ing** (1942) : to make (as a resin adhesive) tacky or more tacky — **tack·i·fi·er** \-ˌfi(-ə)r\ n
tack·i·ly \'ta-kə-lē\ adv (1903) : in a tacky manner : so as to be tacky
tack·i·ness \'ta-kē-nəs\ n (1883) : the quality or state of being tacky
¹**tack·le** \'ta-kəl, naut often 'tā-\ n [ME takel; akin to MD takel ship's rigging] (13c) 1 : a set of the equipment used in a particular activity : GEAR ⟨fishing ~⟩ 2 a : a ship's rigging b : an assemblage of ropes and pulleys arranged to gain mechanical advantage for hoisting and pulling 3 a : the act or an instance of tackling b (1) : either of two offensive football players positioned on each side of the center and between guard and end (2) : either of two football players positioned on the inside of a defensive line
²**tackle** vb **tack·led; tack·ling** \-k(ə-)liŋ\ vt (1714) 1 : to attach or secure with or as if with tackle 2 a : to seize, take hold of, or grapple with esp. with the intention of stopping or subduing b : to seize and throw down or stop (an opposing player with the ball) in football 3 : to set about dealing with ⟨~ the problem⟩ ~ vi : to tackle an opposing player in football — **tack·ler** \-k(ə-)lər\ n
tack·ling \'ta-kliŋ, naut often 'tā-\ n (15c) : TACKLE, GEAR
¹**tacky** \'ta-kē\ adj **tack·i·er; -est** [²tack] (1788) : somewhat sticky to the touch ⟨~ varnish⟩; also : characterized by tack : ADHESIVE
²**tacky** adj **tack·i·er; -est** [tacky a low-class person] (1862) 1 a : characterized by lack of good breeding : COMMON ⟨couldn't run around downtown . . . in a bikini, which was ~ —Cyra McFadden⟩ b : SHABBY, SEEDY ⟨a ~ town whose citrus groves were blighted by smoke —Bryce Nelson⟩ 2 : not having or exhibiting good taste ⟨hopelessly ~ bric-a-brac —T. C. Boyle⟩: as a : marked by lack of style : DOWDY b : marked by cheap showiness : GAUDY
ta·co \'tä-(ˌ)kō\ n, pl **tacos** \-(ˌ)kōz\ [MexSp] (1934) : a usu. fried tortilla that is folded or rolled and stuffed with a mixture (as of seasoned meat, cheese, and lettuce)
tac·o·nite \'ta-kə-ˌnīt\ n [Taconic Range, mountains in U.S.] (1892) : a flintlike rock high enough in iron content to constitute a low-grade iron ore
tact \'takt\ n [F, sense of touch, fr. L tactus, fr. tangere to touch — more at TANGENT] (1797) 1 : sensitive mental or aesthetic perception ⟨converted the novel into a play with remarkable skill and ~⟩ 2 : a keen sense of what to do or say in order to maintain good relations with others or avoid offense

syn TACT, ADDRESS, POISE, SAVOIR FAIRE mean skill and grace in dealing with others. TACT implies delicate and considerate perception of what is appropriate ⟨questions showing a lack of tact⟩. ADDRESS stresses dexterity and grace in dealing with new and trying situations and may imply success in attaining one's ends ⟨brought it off with remarkable address⟩. POISE may imply both tact and address but stresses self-possession and ease in meeting difficult situations ⟨answered the accusations with unruffled poise⟩. SAVOIR FAIRE is likely to stress worldly experience and a sure awareness of what is proper or expedient ⟨the savoir faire of a seasoned traveler⟩.

tact·ful \'takt-fəl\ adj (1864) : having or showing tact — **tact·ful·ly** \-fə-lē\ adv — **tact·ful·ness** n

\ə\ abut \ˌ\ kitten, F table \ər\ further \a\ ash \ā\ ace \ä\ mop, mar \aù\ out \ch\ chin \e\ bet \ē\ easy \g\ go \i\ hit \ī\ ice \j\ job \ŋ\ sing \ō\ go \ò\ law \òi\ boy \th\ thin \th\ the \ü\ loot \ù\ foot \y\ yet \zh\ vision \à, k, ⁿ, œ, œ̄, ue, ūe, ᵊ\ see Guide to Pronunciation

¹**tac·tic** \'tak-tik\ *n* [NL *tactica,* fr. Gk *taktikē,* fr. fem. of *taktikos*] (1640) **1** : a device for accomplishing an end **2** : a method of employing forces in combat

²**tactic** *adj* [NL *tacticus,* fr. Gk *taktikos*] (1871) : of or relating to arrangement or order

-tactic *adj comb form* [Gk *taktikos*] **1** : of, relating to, or having (such) an arrangement or pattern ⟨para*tactic*⟩ **2** : showing orientation or movement directed by a (specified) force or agent ⟨geo*tactic*⟩

tac·ti·cal \'tak-ti-kəl\ *adj* (1570) **1** : of or relating to combat tactics: as **a** (1) : of or occurring at the battlefront ⟨~ defense⟩ ⟨~ first strike⟩ (2) : using or being weapons or forces employed at the battlefront ⟨~ missiles⟩ **b** *of an air force* : of, relating to, or designed for air attack in close support of friendly ground forces **2 a** : of or relating to tactics: as (1) : of or relating to small-scale actions serving a larger purpose (2) : made or carried out with only a limited or immediate end in view **b** : adroit in planning or maneuvering to accomplish a purpose — **tac·ti·cal·ly** \-k(ə-)lē\ *adv*

tac·ti·cian \tak-'ti-shən\ *n* (1798) : one versed in tactics

tac·tics \'tak-tiks\ *n pl but sing or pl in constr* [NL *tactica,* pl., fr. Gk *taktika,* fr. neut. pl. of *taktikos* of order, of tactics, fit for arranging, fr. *tassein* to arrange, place in battle formation] (1626) **1 a** : the science and art of disposing and maneuvering forces in combat **b** : the art or skill of employing available means to accomplish an end **2** : a system or mode of procedure **3** : the study of the grammatical relations within a language including morphology and syntax

tac·tile \'tak-t²l, -,tīl\ *adj* [F or L; F, fr. L *tactilis,* fr. *tangere* to touch — more at TANGENT] (1615) **1** : perceptible by touch : TANGIBLE **2** : of or relating to the sense of touch — **tac·tile·ly** \-tə-lē, -,tīl-lē\ *adv*

tactile corpuscle *n* (1873) : an end organ of touch

tac·til·i·ty \tak-'ti-lə-tē\ *n* (1659) **1** : the capability of being felt or touched **2** : responsiveness to stimulation of the sense of touch

tac·tion \'tak-shən\ *n* [L *taction-, tactio,* fr. *tangere*] (ca. 1623) : TOUCH

tact·less \'takt-ləs\ *adj* (ca. 1847) : marked by lack of tact — **tact·less·ly** *adv* — **tact·less·ness** *n*

tac·tu·al \'tak-chə-wəl, -chəl\ *adj* [L *tactus* sense of touch — more at TACT] (1642) : TACTILE 2 — **tac·tu·al·ly** *adv*

tad \'tad\ *n* [prob. fr. E dial., toad, fr. ME *tode* — more at TOAD] (ca. 1877) **1** : a small child; *esp* : BOY **2** : a small or insignificant amount or degree : BIT ⟨might give him some water and a ~ to eat —C. T. Walker⟩ — **a tad** : SOMEWHAT, RATHER ⟨looked *a tad* bigger than me —Larry Hodgson⟩

tad·pole \'tad-,pōl\ *n* [ME *taddepol,* fr. *tode* toad + *polle* head] (15c) : a larval amphibian; *specif* : a frog or toad larva that has a rounded body with a long tail bordered by fins and external gills soon replaced by internal gills and that undergoes a metamorphosis to the adult

Ta·dzhik *var of* TAJIK

tae·di·um vi·tae \,tē-dē-əm-'vī-,tē, ,tī-dē-əm-'wē-,tī\ *n* [L] (1759) : weariness or loathing of life

tae kwon do \'tī-'kwän-'dō\ *n, often cap T&K&D* [Korean *t'aekwŏndo,* fr. *t'ae-* to trample + *kwŏn* fist + *to* way] (1967) : a Korean martial art resembling karate

tael \'tā(ə)l\ *n* [Pg, fr. Malay *tahil*] (1588) **1** : any of various Chinese units of value based on the value of a tael weight of silver **2** : any of various units of weight of eastern Asia

tae·nia \'tē-nē-ə\ *n, pl* -**ni·ae** \-nē-,ī, -,ē\ *or* -**nias** [L, ribbon, fillet, fr. Gk *tainia;* akin to Gk *teinein* to stretch — more at THIN] (1563) **1** : a band on a Doric order separating the frieze from the architrave **2** : TAPEWORM **3** : an ancient Greek fillet **4** [NL, fr. L, fillet, band] : a band of nervous tissue or muscle

tae·ni·a·sis \tē-'nī-ə-səs\ *n* [NL, fr. L *taenia* tapeworm] (ca. 1890) : infestation with or disease caused by tapeworms

taf·fe·ta \'ta-fə-tə\ *n* [ME, fr. MF *taffetas,* fr. OIt *taffettà,* fr. Turk *tafta,* fr. Per *tāftah* woven] (14c) : a crisp plain-woven lustrous fabric of various fibers used esp. for women's clothing

taf·fe·tized \'ta-fə-,tīzd\ *adj* (1949) *of cloth* : having a crisp finish

taff·rail \'taf-,rāl, -rəl\ *n* [modif. of D *tafereel,* fr. MD, panel, fr. OF *tablel* — more at TABLEAU] (ca. 1704) **1** : the upper part of the stern of a wooden ship **2** : a rail around the stern of a ship

taf·fy \'ta-fē\ *n, pl* **taffies** [origin unknown] (ca. 1817) **1** : a boiled candy usu. of molasses or brown sugar that is pulled until porous and light-colored **2** : insincere flattery

¹**tag** \'tag\ *n* [ME *tagge,* prob. of Scand origin; akin to Sw *tagg* barb] (15c) **1** : a loose hanging piece of cloth : TATTER **2** : a metal or plastic binding on an end of a shoelace **3** : a piece of hanging or attached material; *specif* : a loop, knot, or tassel on a garment **4 a** : a brief quotation used for rhetorical emphasis or sententious effect **b** : a recurrent or characteristic verbal expression **c** : TAG LINE 1 **5 a** : a cardboard, plastic, or metal marker used for identification or classification ⟨license ~s⟩ **b** : a descriptive or identifying epithet **c** : something used for identification or location : FLAG **d** : LABEL 3d **e** : PRICE TAG **6** : a detached fragmentary piece : BIT

²**tag** *vb* **tagged; tag·ging** *vt* (15c) **1** : to provide or mark with or as if with a tag: as **a** : to supply with an identifying marker or price ⟨*tagged* every item in the store⟩ ⟨was *tagged* at $4.95⟩ **b** : to provide with a name or epithet : LABEL, BRAND ⟨*tagged* him a has-been⟩ **c** : to put a ticket on (a motor vehicle) for a traffic violation **2** : to attach as an addition : APPEND **3** : to follow closely and persistently **4** : to hold to account; *esp* : to charge with violating the law ⟨was *tagged* for . . . assault —Burt Woolis⟩ **5** : LABEL 2 ~ *vi* : to keep close ⟨*tagging* at their heels —Corey Ford⟩

³**tag** *n* [origin unknown] (1738) **1** : a game in which the player who is it chases others and tries to touch one of them who then becomes it **2** : an act or instance of tagging a runner in baseball

⁴**tag** *vt* **tagged; tag·ging** (1878) **1 a** : to touch in or as if in a game of tag **b** : to put out (a runner) in baseball by a touch with the ball or the gloved hand containing the ball **2** : to hit solidly **3** : to choose usu. for a special purpose : SELECT **4** : to make a hit or run off (a pitcher) in baseball

Ta·ga·log \tə-'gä-,lóg\ *n, pl* **Tagalog** *or* **Tagalogs** [Tag] (ca. 1808) **1** : a member of a people of central Luzon **2** : an Austronesian language of the Tagalog people — compare PILIPINO

tag·along \'ta-gə-,lón\ *n* (1935) : one that persistently and often annoyingly follows the lead of another

tag along *vi* (1900) : to follow another's lead esp. in going from one place to another

tag·board \'tag-,bórd, -,bórd\ *n* (1904) : strong cardboard used esp. for making shipping tags

tag end *n* (1807) **1** : the last part **2** : a miscellaneous or random bit

ta·glia·tel·le \,täl-yä-'te-(,)lā\ *n* [It, fr. *tagliare* to cut, fr. LL *taliare* — more at TAILOR] (1899) : FETTUCCINE

tag line *n* (1926) **1** : a final line (as in a play or joke); *esp* : one that serves to clarify a point or create a dramatic effect **2** : a reiterated phrase identified with an individual, group, or product : SLOGAN

tag question *n* (1933) : a question (as *isn't it* in "it's fine, isn't it?") added to a statement or command (as to gain the assent of or challenge the person addressed); *also* : a sentence ending in a tag question

tag, rag, and bobtail *or* **tagrag and bobtail** \,tag-,rag-ən-'bäb-,tāl, -,rag-²n-\ *n* (1645) : RABBLE

tag sale *n* [fr. the price tag on each item] (1955) : GARAGE SALE

tag team *n* [⁴*tag*] (1952) : a team of two or more professional wrestlers who spell each other during a match

tag up *vi* (1942) : to touch a base before running in baseball after a fly ball is caught

ta·hi·ni \tə-'hē-nē, tä-\ *n* [Ar dial. *ṭaḥīna,* fr. *ṭaḥana* to grind] (1950) : a smooth paste of sesame seeds

Ta·hi·tian \tə-'hē-shən\ *n* (1825) **1** : a native or inhabitant of Tahiti **2** : the Polynesian language of the Tahitians — **Tahitian** *adj*

tahr \'tär\ *n* [Nepali *thār*] (1835) : any of a genus (*Hemitragus*) of wild Asian goats; *esp* : one (*H. jemlahicus*) of the Himalayas having a reddish brown to dark brown coat and a long shaggy mane

tah·sil \tä-'sē(ə)l\ *n* [Urdu *taḥsīl,* fr. Ar, collection of revenue] (1846) : a district administration or revenue subdivision in India

Tai \'tī\ *n, pl* **Tai** (1693) : a widespread group of peoples in southeast Asia associated ethnically with valley paddy-rice culture

tai chi chuan *or* **t'ai chi ch'uan** \'tī-'jē-chü-'än, 'tī-'chē-\ *n, often cap T & both Cs* [Chin (Beijing) *tàijíquán,* fr. *tàijí* the Absolute in Chinese cosmology + *quán* fist, boxing] (1954) : an ancient Chinese discipline of meditative movements practiced as a system of exercises — called also *tai chi, t'ai chi*

tai·ga \'tī-gə\ *n* [Russ *taĭga*] (1888) : a moist subarctic forest dominated by conifers (as spruce and fir) that begins where the tundra ends

¹**tail** \'tā(ə)l\ *n, often attrib* [ME, fr. OE *tægl;* akin to OHG *zagal* tail, MIr *dúal* lock of hair] (bef. 12c) **1** : the rear end or a process or prolongation of the rear end of the body of an animal **2** : something resembling an animal's tail in shape or position: as **a** : the luminous train of a comet **b** : the rear part of an airplane consisting usu. of horizontal and vertical stabilizing surfaces with attached control surfaces **3** : RETINUE **4** *pl* **a** : TAILCOAT **b** : full evening dress for men **5 a** : BUTTOCKS, BUTT **b** : a female sexual partner — usu. considered vulgar **6** : the back, last, lower, or inferior part of something **7** : TAILING 1 — usu. used in pl. **8** : the reverse of a coin — usu. used in pl. ⟨~*s,* I win⟩ **9** : one (as a detective) who follows or keeps watch on someone **10** : the blank space at the bottom of a page **11** : a location immediately or not far behind ⟨had a posse on his ~⟩ — **tailed** \'tā(ə)ld\ *adj* — **tail·less** \'tā(ə)l-ləs\ *adj* — **tail·like** \-,līk\ *adj*

²**tail** *vt* (1523) **1** : to connect end to end **2 a** : to remove the tail of (an animal) : DOCK **b** : to remove the stem or bottom part of ⟨topping and ~*ing* gooseberries⟩ **3 a** : to make or furnish with a tail **b** : to follow or be drawn behind like a tail **4** : to follow for purposes of surveillance ~ *vi* **1** : to form or move in a straggling line **2** : to grow progressively smaller, fainter, or more scattered : ABATE — usu. used with *off* ⟨productivity is ~*ing* off —Tom Nicholson⟩ **3** : to swing or lie with the stern in a named direction — used of a ship at anchor **4** : ²TAG — **tail·er** *n*

³**tail** *n* [ME, fr. MF, fr. OF, fr. *taillier*] (14c) : ENTAIL 1a

⁴**tail** *adj* [ME *taille,* fr. AF *taylé,* fr. OF *taillié,* pp. of *taillier* to cut, limit — more at TAILOR] (15c) : limited as to tenure : ENTAILED

tail·back \'tā(ə)l-,bak\ *n* (1930) : the offensive football back farthest from the line of scrimmage

tail·board \-,bōrd, -,bórd\ *n* (1805) *chiefly Brit* : TAILGATE 1

tail·bone \-,bōn\ *n* (ca. 1577) **1** : a caudal vertebra **2** : COCCYX

tail·coat \-,kōt\ *n* (1847) : a coat with tails; *esp* : a man's full-dress coat with two long tapering skirts at the back — **tail·coat·ed** \-,kō-təd\ *adj*

tail covert *n* (1815) : one of the coverts of the tail quills

tail end *n* (14c) **1** : BUTTOCKS, RUMP **2** : the hindmost end **3** : the concluding period ⟨the *tail end* of the session⟩

tail·end·er \'tā(ə)l-,en-dər\ *n* (1885) : one positioned at the end or in last place ⟨the ~*s* in a race⟩

tail fin *n* (1681) **1** : the terminal fin of a fish or cetacean **2** : FIN 2b

¹**tail·gate** \'tā(ə)l-,gāt\ *n* (1868) **1** : a board or gate at the rear of a vehicle that can be removed or let down (as for loading) **2** [fr. the custom of seating trombonists at the rear of trucks carrying jazz bands in parades] : a jazz trombone style marked by much use of slides and from long sustained tones

²**tailgate** *vb* **tail·gat·ed; tail·gat·ing** *vi* (1949) **1** : to drive dangerously close behind another vehicle **2** : to hold a tailgate picnic ~ *vt* : to drive dangerously close behind — **tail·gat·er** *n*

³**tailgate** *adj* (1965) : relating to or being a picnic set up on the tailgate esp. of a station wagon

tail·ing \'tā-liŋ\ *n* (1764) **1** : residue separated in the preparation of various products (as grain or ores) — usu. used in pl. **2** : the part of a projecting stone or brick inserted in a wall

taille \'tä-yə, 'tī-, 'tä(ə)l\ *n* [MF, fr. OF, fr. *taillier* to cut, tax] (ca. 1533) : a tax formerly levied by a French king or seigneur on his subjects or on lands held of him

tail·light \'tā(ə)l-,līt\ *n* (1844) : a usu. red warning light mounted at the rear of a vehicle — called also *taillamp*

¹**tai·lor** \'tā-lər\ *n* [ME *taillour,* fr. OF *tailleur,* fr. *taillier* to cut, fr. LL *taliare,* fr. L *talea* twig, cutting] (14c) : a person whose occupation is making or altering outer garments

²**tailor** *vi* (1719) : to do the work of a tailor ~ *vt* **1 a** : to make or fashion as the work of a tailor **b** : to make or adapt to suit a special need or purpose **2** : to fit with clothes **3** : to style with trim straight lines and finished handwork

tai·lor·bird \'tā-lər-ˌbərd\ *n* (1769) : any of a genus (*Orthotomus* of the family Sylviidae) of chiefly Asian warblers that stitch leaves together to support and hide their nests

tai·lored \'tā-lərd\ *adj* (1862) **1** : fashioned or fitted to resemble a tailor's work **2** : CUSTOM-MADE **3** : having the look of one fitted by a custom tailor

tai·lor·ing \'tā-lə-riŋ\ *n* (1662) **1 a** : the business or occupation of a tailor **b** : the work or workmanship of a tailor **2** : the making or adapting of something to suit a particular purpose

¹tai·lor–made \ˌtā-lər-'mād\ *adj* (1832) **1** : made by a tailor or with a tailor's care and style **2** : made or fitted esp. to a particular use or purpose **3** : factory made rather than hand-rolled 〈~ cigarettes〉

²tailor–made *n* (1892) : one that is tailor-made; *specif* : a woman's garment styled for a trim fit and with stiff straight lines

tail·piece \'tā(ə)l-ˌpēs\ *n* (1601) **1** : a piece added at the end **2** : a device from which the strings of a stringed instrument are stretched to the pegs — see VIOLIN illustration **3** : an ornament placed below the text matter of a page

tail·pipe \-ˌpīp\ *n* (1922) : an outlet by which the exhaust gases are removed from an engine (as of an automobile or jet aircraft)

tail·plane \-ˌplān\ *n* (1909) : the horizontal tail surfaces of an airplane including the stabilizer and the elevator

tail·race \'tā(ə)l-ˌrās\ *n* (1776) : a race for conveying water away from a point of industrial application (as a waterwheel or turbine) after use

tail·slide \-ˌslīd\ *n* (1916) : an aerobatic maneuver in which an aircraft that has been pulled into a steep climb stalls and then loses altitude by dropping backward

tail·spin \-ˌspin\ *n* (ca. 1917) **1** : SPIN 2a **2** : a mental or emotional letdown or collapse **3** : a sustained and usu. severe decline or downturn 〈stock prices in a ~〉

tail·wa·ter \-ˌwȯ-tər, -ˌwä-\ *n* (1759) **1** : water below a dam or water-power development **2** : excess surface water draining esp. from a field under cultivation

tail·wind \-ˌwind\ *n* (1897) : a wind having the same general direction as a course of movement (as of an aircraft)

Tai·no \'tī-(ˌ)nō\ *n, pl* **Taino** *or* **Tainos** [Sp] (ca. 1895) **1** : a member of an aboriginal Arawakan people of the Greater Antilles and the Bahamas **2** : the extinct language of the Taino people

¹taint \'tānt\ *vb* [ME *tainten* to color & *taynten* to attaint; ME *tainten*, fr. AF *teinter*, fr. MF *teint*, pp. of *teindre*, fr. L *tingere*; ME *taynten*, fr. MF *ataint*, pp. of *ataindre* — more at TINGE, ATTAIN] *vt* (1573) **1** : to contaminate morally : CORRUPT 〈scholarship ~ed by envy〉 **2** : to affect with putrefaction : SPOIL **3** : to touch or affect slightly with something bad 〈persons ~ed with prejudice〉 ~ *vi* **1** *obs* : to become weak **2** : to become affected with putrefaction : SPOIL *syn* see CONTAMINATE

²taint *n* (1601) : a contaminating mark or influence — **taint·less** \-ləs\ *adj*

'tain't \'tānt\ (1818) : it ain't

¹tai·pan \'tī-ˌpan, 'ti-'pän\ *n* [Chin (Guangdong) *daaih-bāan*, fr. *daaih* big + *bāan* class] (1834) : a powerful businessman and esp. formerly a foreigner living and operating in Hong Kong or China

²tai·pan \'tī-ˌpan\ *n* [Wik Munkan (Australian aboriginal language of northern Queensland) *dhayban*] (1933) : an exceedingly venomous elapid snake (*Oxyuranus scutellatus*) of northern Australia and New Guinea

Ta·jik \tä-'jik, tə-, -'jēk\ *n* (1815) **1** : a member of a Persian-speaking ethnic group living in Tajikistan, Afghanistan, and adjacent areas of central Asia **2** : the form of Persian spoken by the Tajiks

ta·ka \'tä-kə, -(ˌ)kä\ *n* [Bengali *tākā* rupee, taka, fr. Skt *ṭaṅka* stamped coin] (1972) — see MONEY table

ta·ka·he \tä-'kä-(ˌ)hä\ *n* [Maori] (1851) : a flightless bird (*Notornis mantelli* syn. *Porphyrio mantelli*) of New Zealand that is related to the gallinules

¹take \'tāk\ *vb* **took** \'tủk\; **tak·en** \'tā-kən\; **tak·ing** [ME, fr. OE *tacan*, fr. ON *taka*; akin to MD *taken* to take] *vt* (bef. 12c) **1 a** : to get into one's hands or into one's possession, power, or control: as **a** : to seize or capture physically 〈took them as prisoners〉 **b** : to get possession of (as fish or game) by killing or capturing **c** (1) : to move against (as an opponent's piece in chess) and remove from play (2) : to win in a card game 〈able to ~ 12 tricks〉 **d** : to acquire by eminent domain **2** : GRASP, GRIP 〈~ the ax by the handle〉 **3 a** : to catch or attack through the effect of a sudden force or influence 〈taken with a fit of laughing〉 〈taken ill〉 **b** : to catch or come upon in a particular situation or action 〈was taken unawares〉 **c** : to gain the approval or liking of : CAPTIVATE, DELIGHT 〈was quite taken with her at their first meeting〉 **4 a** : to receive into one's body (as by swallowing, drinking, or inhaling) 〈~ a pill〉 **b** : to expose oneself to (as sun or air) for pleasure or physical benefit **c** : to partake of : EAT 〈~s dinner about seven〉 **5 a** : to bring or receive into a relation or connection 〈~s just four students a year〉 〈it's time he took a wife〉 **b** : to copulate with **6** : to transfer into one's own keeping: **a** : APPROPRIATE **b** : to obtain or secure for use (as by lease, subscription, or purchase) 〈~ a cottage for the summer〉 〈I'll ~ the red one〉 〈took an ad in the paper〉 **7 a** : ASSUME 〈gods often took the likeness of a human being〉 〈when the college took its present form〉 **b** (1) : to enter into or undertake the duties of 〈~ a job〉 〈~ office〉 〈took command of the fleet〉 (2) : to move onto or into : move into position on 〈the home team took the field〉 **c** (1) : to bind oneself by 〈~ the oath of office〉 (2) : to make (a decision) esp. with finality or authority **d** : to impose upon oneself 〈~ the trouble to do good work〉 **e** (1) : to adopt as one's own 〈~ a stand on the issue〉 〈~ an interest〉 (2) : to align or ally oneself with 〈mother took his side〉 **f** : to assume as if rightfully one's own or as if granted 〈~ the credit〉 **g** : to have or assume a proper part of or accompaniment to itself 〈transitive verbs ~ an object〉 **8** : to secure by winning in competition 〈took first place〉 **b** : DEFEAT **9** : to pick out : CHOOSE, SELECT **10** : to adopt, choose, or avail oneself of for use: as **a** : to have recourse to as an instrument for doing something 〈~ a scythe to the weeds〉 **b** : to use as a means of transportation or progression 〈~ the bus〉 **c** : to have recourse to for safety or refuge 〈~ shelter〉 **d** : to go along, into, or through 〈took a different route〉 (1) : to proceed to occupy 〈~ a seat in the rear〉 (2) : to use up (as space or time) 〈~s a long time to dry〉 (3) : NEED, REQUIRE 〈~s a size nine shoe〉 〈it ~s two to start a fight〉 **11 a** : to

obtain by deriving from a source : DRAW 〈~s its title from the name of the hero〉 **b** (1) : to obtain as the result of a special procedure : ASCERTAIN 〈~ the temperature〉 〈~ a census〉 (2) : to get in or as if in writing 〈~ notes〉 〈~ an inventory〉 (3) : to get by drawing or painting or by photography 〈~ a snapshot〉 (4) : to get by transference from one surface to another 〈~ a proof〉 〈~ fingerprints〉 **12** : to receive or accept whether willingly or reluctantly 〈~ a bribe〉 〈will you ~ this call〉 〈~ a bet〉: as **a** (1) : to submit to : ENDURE 〈~ a cut in pay〉 (2) : WITHSTAND 〈it will ~ a lot of punishment〉 (3) : SUFFER 〈took a direct hit〉 **b** (1) : to accept as true : BELIEVE 〈I'll ~ your word for it〉 (2) : FOLLOW 〈~ my advice〉 (3) : to accept with the mind in a specified way 〈took the news hard〉 **c** : to indulge in and enjoy 〈was taking his ease on the porch〉 **d** : to receive or accept as a return (as in payment, compensation, or reparation) **e** : to accept in a usu. professional relationship — often used with *on* 〈agreed to ~ him on as a client〉 **f** : to refrain from hitting at 〈a pitched ball〉 **13 a** (1) : to let in : ADMIT 〈the boat was ~*ing* water fast〉 (2) : ACCOMMODATE 〈the suitcase wouldn't ~ another thing〉 **b** : to be affected injuriously (as by a disease) : CONTRACT 〈~ cold〉; *also* : to be seized by 〈~ a fit〉 〈~ fright〉 **c** : to absorb or become impregnated with (as dye); *also* : to be effectively treated by 〈a surface that ~s a fine polish〉 **14 a** : APPREHEND, UNDERSTAND 〈how should I ~ your remark〉 **b** : CONSIDER, SUPPOSE 〈I ~ it you're not going〉 **c** : RECKON, ACCEPT 〈taking a stride at 30 inches〉 **d** : FEEL, EXPERIENCE 〈~ pleasure〉 〈~ an instant dislike to someone〉 〈~ offense〉 **15** : to lead, carry, or cause to go along to another place 〈this bus will ~ you into town〉 〈took an umbrella with her〉 **16 a** : REMOVE 〈~ eggs from a nest〉 **b** (1) : to put an end to (life) (2) : to remove by death 〈was taken in his prime〉 **c** : SUBTRACT 〈~ two from four〉 **d** : EXACT 〈the weather took its toll〉 **17 a** : to undertake and make, do, or perform 〈~ a walk〉 〈~ aim〉 〈~ legal action〉 〈~ a test〉 〈~ a look〉 **b** : to participate in 〈~ a meeting〉 **18 a** : to deal with 〈~ first things first〉 **b** : to consider or view in a particular relation 〈taken together, the details were significant〉; *esp* : to consider as an example 〈~ style, for instance〉 **c** (1) : to apply oneself to the study of 〈~ music lessons〉 〈~ French〉 (2) : to study for esp. successfully 〈taking a degree in engineering〉 〈took holy orders〉 **19** : to obtain money from esp. fraudulently 〈took me for all I had〉 **20** : to pass or attempt to pass through, along, or over 〈took the curve too fast〉 ~ *vi* **1** : to obtain possession: as **a** : CAPTURE **b** : to receive property under law as one's own **2** : to lay hold : CATCH, HOLD **3** : to establish a take esp. by uniting or growing 〈90 percent of the grafts ~〉 **4 a** : to betake oneself : set out : GO 〈~ after a purse snatcher〉 **b** *chiefly dial* — used as an intensifier or redundantly with a following verb 〈took and swung at the ball〉 **5 a** : to take effect : ACT, OPERATE 〈hoped the lesson he taught would ~〉 **b** : to show the natural or intended effect 〈dry fuel ~s readily〉 **6** : CHARM, CAPTIVATE 〈a taking smile〉 **7** : DETRACT **8** : to be seized or attacked in a specified way : BECOME 〈took sick〉 — **tak·er** *n* — **take a back seat** : to have or assume a secondary position or status — **take a bath** : to suffer a heavy financial loss — **take account of** : to take into account — **take advantage of 1** : to use to advantage : profit by **2** : to impose on : EXPLOIT — **take after** : to resemble in features, build, character, or disposition — **take apart 1** : to disconnect the pieces of : DISASSEMBLE **2** : to treat roughly or harshly : tear into — **take a powder** : to leave hurriedly — **take care** : to be careful or watchful : exercise caution or prudence — **take care of** : to attend to or provide for the needs, operation, or treatment of — **take charge** : to assume care, custody, command, or control — **take effect 1** : to become operative **2** : to be effective — **take exception** : OBJECT 〈took exception to the remark〉 — **take five** *or* **take ten** : to take a break esp. from work — **take for** : to suppose to be; *esp* : to suppose mistakenly to be — **take for granted 1** : to assume as true, real, or expected **2** : to value too lightly — **take heart** : to gain courage or confidence — **take hold 1** : GRASP, GRIP, SEIZE **2** : to become attached or established : take effect — **take into account** : to make allowance for — **take in vain** : to use (a name) profanely or without proper respect — **take issue** : DISAGREE — **take it on the chin** : to suffer from the results of a situation — **take kindly to** : to show an inclination to accept or approve — **take notice of** : to observe or treat with special attention — **take one's time** : to be leisurely about doing something — **take part** : JOIN, PARTICIPATE, SHARE — **take place** : HAPPEN, OCCUR — **take root 1** : to become rooted **2** : to become fixed or established — **take shape** : to assume a definite or distinctive form — **take stock** : to make an assessment — **take the cake** : to carry off the prize : rank first — **take the count 1** *of a boxer* : to be counted out **2** : to go down in defeat — **take the floor** : to rise (as in a meeting or a legislative assembly) to make a formal address — **take to 1** : to go to or into 〈take to the woods〉 **2** : to apply or devote oneself to (as a practice, habit, or occupation) 〈take to begging〉 **3** : to adapt oneself to : respond to 〈takes to water like a duck〉 **4** : to conceive a liking for — **take to task** : to call to account for a shortcoming : CRITICIZE — **take turns** : ALTERNATE

syn TAKE, SEIZE, GRASP, CLUTCH, SNATCH, GRAB mean to get hold of by or as if by catching up with the hand. TAKE is a general term applicable to any manner of getting something into one's possession or control 〈take some salad from the bowl〉. SEIZE implies a sudden and forcible movement in getting hold of something tangible or an apprehending of something fleeting or elusive when intangible 〈seized the suspect〉. GRASP stresses a laying hold so as to have firmly in possession 〈grasp the handle and pull〉. CLUTCH suggests avidity or anxiety in seizing or grasping and may imply less success in holding 〈clutching her purse〉. SNATCH suggests more suddenness or quickness but less force than SEIZE 〈snatched a doughnut and ran〉. GRAB implies more roughness or rudeness than SNATCH 〈grabbed roughly by the arm〉.

²take *n* (1654) **1** : something that is taken: **a** : the amount of money received : PROCEEDS, RECEIPTS, INCOME **b** : SHARE, CUT 〈wanted a bigger ~〉 **c** : the number or quantity (as of animals, fish, or pelts) taken at one time : CATCH, HAUL **d** : a section or installment done as a unit or at one time **e** (1) : a scene filmed or televised at one time without stopping the camera (2) : a sound recording made during a single recording period; *esp* : a trial recording **2** : an act or the action of taking: as **a** : the action of killing, capturing, or catching (as game or fish) **b** (1) : the uninterrupted photographing or televising of a scene (2) : the making of a sound recording **3 a** : a local or systemic reaction indicative of successful vaccination (as against smallpox) **b** : a successful union (as of a graft) **4** : a visible response or reaction (as to something unexpected) ⟨a delayed ~⟩ **5** : a distinct or personal point of view, outlook, or assessment ⟨was asked for her ~ on recent developments⟩; *also* : a distinct treatment or variation ⟨a new ~ on an old style⟩ — **on the take** : illegally paid for favors

take–away \'tāk-ə-ˌwā\ *adj* (1964) *Brit* : TAKE-OUT — **take–away** *n*
take back *vt* (1775) : to make a retraction of : WITHDRAW
take–charge \'tāk-ˈchärj\ *adj* (1954) : having the qualities of a forceful leader ⟨a ~ executive⟩
¹**take–down** \'tāk-ˌdau̇n\ *n* (1893) **1** : the action or an act of taking down **2** : something (as a rifle) having takedown construction
²**take–down** \'tāk-'dau̇n\ *adj* (1907) : constructed so as to be readily taken apart ⟨a ~ rifle⟩
take down *vt* (15c) **1** : to lower without removing ⟨took down his pants⟩ **2 a** : to pull to pieces ⟨take down a building⟩ **b** : DISASSEMBLE ⟨take a rifle down⟩ **3** : to lower the spirit or vanity of **4 a** : to write down **b** : to record by mechanical means **~** *vi* : to become seized or attacked esp. by illness
take–home pay \'tāk-ˌhōm-\ *n* (1943) : income remaining from salary or wages after deductions (as for income-tax withholding)
take–in \'tā-ˌkin\ *n* (1778) : an act of taking in esp. by deceiving
take in *vt* (ca. 1515) **1** : to draw into a smaller compass ⟨*take in* the slack of a line⟩: **a** : FURL **b** : to make (a garment) smaller by enlarging seams or tucks **2 a** : to receive as a guest or lodger **b** : to give shelter to **c** : to take to a police station as a prisoner **3** : to receive as payment or proceeds **4** : to receive (work) into one's house to be done for pay ⟨*take in* washing⟩ **5** : to encompass within its limits **6 a** : to include in an itinerary **b** : ATTEND ⟨*take in* a movie⟩ **7** : to receive into the mind : PERCEIVE **8** : DECEIVE, DUPE
taken *past part of* TAKE
take–off \'tā-ˌkȯf\ *n* (1846) **1** : an imitation esp. in the way of caricature **2 a** : a spot at which one takes off **b** : a starting point : point of departure **3** : a rise or leap from a surface in making a jump or flight or an ascent in an aircraft or in the launching of a rocket **b** : an action of starting out **c** : a rapid rise in activity, growth, or popularity ⟨an economic ~⟩ **4** : an action of removing something **5** : a mechanism for transmission of the power of an engine or vehicle to operate some other mechanism
take off *vt* (14c) **1** : REMOVE ⟨take your shoes off⟩ **2 a** : RELEASE ⟨take the brake off⟩ **b** : DISCONTINUE, WITHDRAW ⟨took off the morning train⟩ **c** : to take or allow as a discount : DEDUCT ⟨took 10 percent off⟩ **d** : to spend (a period of time) away from a usual occupation or activity ⟨took two weeks off⟩ **3** *slang* : ROB **~** *vi* **1** : to take away : DETRACT **2 a** : to start off or away : SET OUT, DEPART **b** (1) : to branch off (as from a main stream or stem) (2) : to take a point of origin **c** : to leap a leap or spring **d** : to leave the surface : begin flight **e** : to embark on rapid activity, development, or growth **f** : to spring into wide use or popularity
take on *vt* (15c) **1 a** : to begin to perform or deal with : UNDERTAKE ⟨took on new responsibilities⟩ **b** : to contend with as an opponent ⟨took on the neighborhood bully⟩ **2** : ENGAGE, HIRE **3 a** : to assume or acquire as or as if one's own ⟨the city's plaza takes on a carnival air —W. T. LeViness⟩ **b** : to have as a mathematical domain or range ⟨what values does the function take on⟩ **~** *vi* **1** : to show one's feelings esp. of grief or anger in a demonstrative way ⟨they cried and took on something terrible —Bob Hope⟩
take–out \'tā-ˌkau̇t\ *n* (ca. 1917) **1** : the action or an act of taking out **2 a** : something taken out or prepared to be taken out **b** (1) : an article (as in a newspaper) printed on consecutive pages so as to be conveniently removed (2) : an intensive study or report **3** : CARRY-OUT 1
take–out \'tā-ˌkau̇t\ *adj* (1965) : of, relating to, selling, or being food not to be consumed on the premises ⟨~ counter⟩ ⟨a ~ supper⟩
take out *vt* (13c) **1 a** (1) : DEDUCT, SEPARATE (2) : EXCLUDE, OMIT (3) : WITHDRAW, WITHHOLD **b** : to find release for : VENT ⟨take out their resentments on one another —J. W. Aldridge⟩ **c** (1) : ELIMINATE (2) : KILL, DESTROY (3) : KNOCK OUT **2** : to take as an equivalent in another form ⟨took the debt out in trade⟩ **3 a** : to obtain from the proper authority ⟨take out a charter⟩ **b** : to arrange for (insurance) **4** : to overcall (a bridge partner) in a different suit **~** *vi* : to start on a course : SET OUT — **take it out on** : to expend anger, vexation, or frustration in harassment of
take–out double \'tā-ˌkau̇t-\ *n* (ca. 1944) : a double made in bridge to convey information to and request a bid from one's partner
take–over \'tā-ˌkō-vər\ *n* (ca. 1917) : the action or an act of taking over
take over *vt* (1884) : to assume control or possession of or responsibility for ⟨military leaders took over the government⟩ **~** *vi* **1** : to assume control or possession **2** : to become dominant
take–up \'tā-ˌkəp\ *n* (1838) : the action of taking up
take up *vt* (14c) **1** : PICK UP, LIFT **2 a** : to begin to occupy (land) **b** : to gather from a number of sources ⟨took up a collection⟩ **3 a** : to accept or adopt for the purpose of assisting **b** : to accept or adopt as one's own ⟨took up the life of a farmer⟩ ⟨took up Irish citizenship⟩ **c** : to absorb or incorporate into itself ⟨plants taking up nutrients⟩ **4 a** : to enter upon (as a business, hobby, or subject of study) ⟨take up skiing⟩ ⟨took up the trumpet⟩ ⟨had taken up Marxism⟩ **b** : to proceed to consider or deal with ⟨take up one problem at a time⟩ **5** : to establish oneself in or at ⟨take up residence in town⟩ **6** : to occupy entirely or exclusively : fill up ⟨the meeting was taken up with old business⟩ **7** : to make tighter or shorter ⟨take up the slack⟩ **8** : to respond favorably to (as a person offering a bet, challenge, or proposal) ⟨took me up on it⟩ **9** : to begin again or take over from another ⟨we must take the good work up again⟩ **~** *vi* **1** : to make a beginning where another has left off **2** : to become shortened : draw together : SHRINK — **take up the cudgels** : to engage vigorously in a defense or dispute — **take up**

with **1** : to become interested or absorbed in **2** : to begin to associate or consort with
ta·kin \'tä-ˌkēn\ *n* [Mishmi (Tibeto-Burman language of northeast India)] (1850) : a large heavily built ruminant (*Budorcas taxicolor*) of Tibet and adjacent areas of Asia that is related to the goats but in some respects resembles the antelopes

takin

tak·ings \'tā-kiŋz\ *n pl* (1632) *chiefly Brit* : receipts esp. of money
¹**ta·la** \'tä-lə\ *n* [Skt *tāla*, lit., handclapping] (1891) : one of the ancient traditional rhythmic patterns of Indian music — compare RAGA
²**ta·la** \'tä-lə, -(ˌ)lä\ *n, pl* **tala** [Samoan, fr. E *dollar*] (1967) — see MONEY table
Tal·bot \'tȯl-bət, 'tal-\ *n* [prob. fr. *Talbot*, name of a Norman family in England] (1562) : a large heavy mostly white hound with pendulous ears and drooping flews held to be ancestral to the bloodhound
talc \'talk\ *n* [MF *talc* mica, fr. ML *talk*, fr. Ar *talq*] (1610) **1** : a very soft mineral that is a basic silicate of magnesium, has a soapy feel, and is used esp. in making talcum powder **2** : TALCUM POWDER — **talc·ose** \'tal-ˌkōs\ *adj*
tal·cum powder \'tal-kəm-\ *n* [ML *talcum* mica, alter. of earlier *talk*] (ca. 1890) **1** : powdered talc **2** : a toilet powder composed of perfumed talc or talc and a mild antiseptic
tale \'tā(ə)l\ *n* [ME, fr. OE *talu*; akin to ON *tala* talk] (bef. 12c) **1** *obs* : DISCOURSE, TALK **2 a** : a series of facts or events told or presented : ACCOUNT **b** (1) : a report of a private or confidential matter ⟨dead men tell no ~s⟩ (2) : a libelous report or piece of gossip **3 a** : a usu. imaginative narrative of an event : STORY **b** : an intentionally untrue report : FALSEHOOD ⟨always preferred the ~ to the truth —Sir Winston Churchill⟩ **4 a** : COUNT, TALLY **b** : TOTAL
tale·bear·er \-ˌbar-ər, -ˌber-\ *n* (15c) : one that spreads gossip or rumors; *also* : TATTLETALE — **tale·bear·ing** \-iŋ\ *adj or n*
tal·ent \'ta-lənt\ *n* [ME, fr. OE *talente*, fr. L *talenta*, pl. of *talentum* unit of weight or money, fr. Gk *talanton* pan of a scale, weight; akin to Gk *tlēnai* to bear; in senses 2–5, fr. the parable of the talents in Mt 25:14–30 — more at TOLERATE] (bef. 12c) **1 a** : any of several ancient units of weight **b** : a unit of value equal to the value of a talent of gold or silver **2** *archaic* : a characteristic feature, aptitude, or disposition of a person or animal **3** : the natural endowments of a person **4 a** : a special often creative or artistic aptitude **b** : general intelligence or mental power : ABILITY **5** : a person of talent or a group of persons of talent in a field or activity *syn* see GIFT — **tal·ent·ed** \-lən-təd\ *adj* — **tal·ent·less** \-lənt-ləs\ *adj*
talent scout *n* (1936) : a person engaged in discovering and recruiting people of talent for a specialized field or activity
talent show *n* (1953) : a show consisting of a series of individual performances (as singing) by amateurs who may be selected for special recognition as performing talent
ta·ler \'tä-lər\ *n* [G — more at DOLLAR] (ca. 1905) : any of numerous silver coins issued by various German states from the 15th to the 19th centuries
tales·man \'tā(ə)lz-mən, 'tā-lēz-\ *n* [ME *tales* talesmen, fr. ML *tales de circumstantibus* such (persons) of the bystanders; fr. the wording of the writ summoning them] (1679) **1** : a person added to a jury usu. from among bystanders to make up a deficiency in the available number of jurors **2** : a member of a large pool of persons called for jury duty from which jurors are selected
tale–tell·er \'tā(ə)l-ˌtel-ər\ *n* (14c) **1** : one who tells tales or stories **2** : TALEBEARER — **tale–tell·ing** \-ˌte-liŋ\ *adj or n*
tali *pl of* TALUS
tal·i·pes \'ta-lə-ˌpēz\ *n* [NL, fr. L *talus* ankle + *pes* foot — more at FOOT] (ca. 1841) : CLUBFOOT
tal·is·man \'ta-ləs-mən, -ləz-\ *n, pl* **-mans** [F *talisman* or Sp *talismán* or It *talismano*; all fr. Ar *tilsam*, fr. MGk *telesma*, fr. Gk, consecration, fr. *telein* to initiate into the mysteries, complete, fr. *telos* end — more at TELOS] (1638) **1** : an object held to act as a charm to avert evil and bring good fortune **2** : something producing apparently magical or miraculous effects — **tal·is·man·ic** \ˌta-ləs-'ma-nik, -ləz-\ *adj* — **tal·is·man·i·cal·ly** \-ni-k(ə-)lē\ *adv*
¹**talk** \'tȯk\ *vb* [ME; akin to OE *talu* tale] *vt* (13c) **1** : to deliver or express in speech : UTTER **2** : to make the subject of conversation or discourse : DISCUSS ⟨~ business⟩ **3** : to influence, affect, or cause by talking ⟨~ed them into going⟩ **4** : to use (a language) for conversing or communicating : SPEAK **~** *vi* **1** : to express or exchange ideas by means of spoken words **b** : to convey information or communicate in any way (as with signs or sounds) ⟨can make a trumpet ~⟩ **2** : to use speech : SPEAK **3 a** : to speak idly : PRATE **b** : GOSSIP **c** : to reveal secret or confidential information **4** : to give a talk : LECTURE — **talk·er** *n* — **talk back** : to answer impertinently — **talk sense** : to voice rational, logical, or sensible thoughts — **talk through one's hat** : to voice irrational, illogical, or erroneous ideas — **talk turkey** : to speak frankly or bluntly
²**talk** *n* (15c) **1** : the act or an instance of talking : SPEECH **2** : a way of speaking : LANGUAGE **3** : pointless or fruitless discussion : VERBIAGE **4** : a formal discussion, negotiation, or exchange of views — often used in pl. **5 a** : MENTION, REPORT **b** : RUMOR, GOSSIP **6** : the topic of interested comment, conversation, or gossip ⟨it's the ~ of the town⟩ **7 a** : ADDRESS, LECTURE **b** : written analysis or discussion presented in an informal or conversational manner **8** : communicative sounds or signs resembling or functioning as talk ⟨bird ~⟩
talk·a·thon \'tȯ-kə-ˌthän\ *n* (1934) : a long session of discussion or speech-making
talk·a·tive \'tȯ-kə-tiv\ *adj* (15c) : given to talking; *also* : full of talk — **talk·a·tive·ly** *adv* — **talk·a·tive·ness** *n*
syn TALKATIVE, LOQUACIOUS, GARRULOUS, VOLUBLE mean given to talk or talking. TALKATIVE may imply a readiness to engage in talk or a disposition to enjoy conversation ⟨a *talkative* neighbor⟩. LOQUACIOUS suggests the power of expressing oneself articulately, fluently, or glibly ⟨a *loquacious* spokesperson⟩. GARRULOUS implies prosy, ram-

bling, or tedious loquacity ⟨*garrulous* traveling companions⟩. VOLUBLE suggests a free, easy, and unending loquacity ⟨a *voluble* raconteur⟩.

talk down *vi* (1901) : to speak in a condescending or oversimplified fashion ~ *vt* : to disparage or belittle by talking

talk·ie \'tȯ-kē\ *n* (1913) : a motion picture with a synchronized sound track

talking book *n* (1932) : a phonograph or tape recording of a reading of a book or magazine designed chiefly for the use of the blind

talking head *n* (1968) : the televised head and shoulders shot of a person talking; *also* : a television personality who appears in such shots

talking machine *n* (1890) : an early phonograph

talking point *n* (ca. 1914) : something that lends support to an argument; *also* : a subject of discussion

talk·ing-to \'tȯ-kiŋ-,tü\ *n* (1884) : REPRIMAND, LECTURE

talk out *vt* (1954) : to clarify or settle by oral discussion

talk over *vt* (1734) : to review or consider in conversation : DISCUSS

talk radio *n* (1972) : radio programming consisting of call-in shows

talk show *n* (1965) : a radio or television program in which usu. well-known persons engage in discussions or are interviewed

talk up *vt* (1722) : to discuss favorably : ADVOCATE, PROMOTE ~ *vi* : to speak up plainly or directly

talky \'tȯ-kē\ *adj* **talk·i·er; -est** (1815) 1 : TALKATIVE 2 : containing too much talk — **talk·i·ness** \-nəs\ *n*

tall \'tȯl\ *adj* ME, prob. fr. OE *getæl* quick, ready; akin to OHG *gizal* quick] (15c) 1 *obs* : BRAVE, COURAGEOUS 2 a : high in stature b : of a specified height ⟨five feet ~⟩ 3 a : of considerable height ⟨~ trees⟩ b : long from bottom to top ⟨a ~ book⟩ c : of a higher growing variety or species of plant 4 a : large or formidable in amount, extent, or degree ⟨a ~ order to fill⟩ b : POMPOUS, HIGH-FLOWN ⟨~ talk about the vast mysteries of life —W. A. White⟩ c : highly exaggerated : INCREDIBLE, IMPROBABLE ⟨a ~ story⟩ *syn* see HIGH — **tall** *adv* — **tall·ish** \'tȯ-lish\ *adj* — **tall·ness** \'tȯl-nəs\ *n*

tal·lage \'ta-lij\ *n* [ME *taillage, tallage,* fr. OF *taillage,* fr. *taillier* to cut, limit, tax — more at TAILOR] (14c) : an impost or due levied by a lord upon his tenants

tall·boy \'tȯl-,bȯi\ *n* (1769) 1 a : HIGHBOY b : a double chest of drawers usu. with the upper section slightly smaller than the lower 2 *Brit* : CLOTHESPRESS

tall fescue *n* (ca. 1762) : a European fescue (*Festuca elatior*) with erect smooth stems 3 to 4 feet (about 1 meter) high that has been introduced into No. America — called also *tall fescue grass;* compare FESCUE FOOT

tall-grass prairie \'tȯl-,gras-\ *n* (1920) : PRAIRIE 2a

tal·lith \'tä-ləs, 'ta-, -lət, -ləth\ or **tal·lis** \-ləs\ *n* [Heb *ṭallīth* cover, cloak] (1613) : a shawl with fringed corners worn over the head or shoulders by Jewish men esp. during morning prayers

tall oil \'tȧl-, 'tȯl-\ *n* [part trans. of G *Tallöl,* part trans. of Sw *tallolja,* fr. *tall* pine + *olja* oil] (ca. 1926) : a resinous by-product from the manufacture of chemical wood pulp used esp. in making soaps, coatings, and oils

¹**tal·low** \'ta-(,)lō\ *n* [ME *talgh, talow;* akin to MD *talch* tallow] (14c) : the white nearly tasteless solid rendered fat of cattle and sheep used chiefly in soap, candles, and lubricants — **tal·lowy** \'ta-lə-wē\ *adj*

²**tallow** *vt* (15c) : to grease or smear with tallow

tall ship *n* (ca. 1548) : a sailing vessel with at least two masts; *esp* : SQUARE-RIGGER

¹**tal·ly** \'ta-lē\ *n, pl* **tallies** [ME *talye,* fr. ML *talea, tallia,* fr. L *talea* twig, cutting] (15c) 1 : a device (as a notched rod or mechanical counter) for visibly recording or accounting esp. business transactions 2 a : a recorded reckoning or account (as of items or charges) ⟨keep a daily ~ of accidents⟩ b : a score or point made (as in a game) 3 a : a part that corresponds to or is opposite or companion member : COMPLEMENT b : a state of correspondence or agreement

²**tally** *vb* **tal·lied; tal·ly·ing** *vt* (15c) 1 a : to record on or as if on a tally : TABULATE b : to list or check off (as a cargo) by items c : to register (as a score) in a contest 2 a : to make a count of : RECKON 3 : to cause to correspond ~ *vi* 1 a : to make a tally by or as if by tabulating b : to register a point in a contest : SCORE 2 : CORRESPOND, MATCH

tal·ly·ho \,ta-lē-'hō\ *n, pl* **-hos** [prob. fr. F *taïaut,* a cry used to excite hounds in deer hunting] (1772) 1 : a call of a huntsman at sight of the fox 2 [*Tally-ho,* name of a coach formerly plying between London and Birmingham] : a four-in-hand coach

tal·ly·man \'ta-lē-mən, -,man\ *n* (1654) 1 *Brit* : one who sells goods on the installment plan 2 : one who tallies, checks, or keeps an account or record (as of receipt of goods)

Tal·mud \'täl-,mùd, 'tal-məd\ *n* [LHeb *talmūdh,* lit., instruction] (1532) : the authoritative body of Jewish tradition comprising the Mishnah and Gemara — **Tal·mu·dic** \tal-'mü-dik, -'myü-, -'mə-; täl-'mù-\ *adj* — **Tal·mud·ism** \'täl-,mù-,di-zəm, 'tal-, -mə-\ *n, often cap* **Tal·mud·ist** \-mù-dist, 'tal-, -mə-\ *n* (1569) : a specialist in Talmudic studies

tal·on \'ta-lən\ *n* [ME, fr. MF, heel, spur, fr. (assumed) VL *talon-, talo,* fr. L *talus* ankle, anklebone] (15c) 1 a : the claw of an animal and esp. of a bird of prey b : a finger or hand of a human being 2 a : a part or object shaped like or suggestive of a heel or claw: as a : an ogee molding b : the shoulder of the bolt of a lock on which the key acts to shoot the bolt 3 a : cards laid aside in a pile in solitaire b : STOCK 10c — **tal·oned** \-lənd\ *adj*

¹**ta·lus** \'tā-ləs, 'ta-\ *n* [F, fr. L *talutium* slope indicating presence of gold under the soil] (1645) 1 : a slope formed esp. by an accumulation of rock debris 2 : rock debris at the base of a cliff

²**ta·lus** \'tā-ləs\ *n, pl* **ta·li** \'tā-,lī\ [NL, fr. L] (ca. 1693) 1 : the human tarsal bone that bears the weight of the body and that together with the tibia and fibula forms the ankle joint 2 : the entire ankle

tam \'tam\ *n* (1895) : TAM-O'-SHANTER

ta·ma·le \tə-'mä-lē\ *n* [MexSp *tamales,* pl. of *tamal* tamale, fr. Nahuatl *tamalli* steamed cornmeal dough] (1854) : ground meat seasoned usu. with chili, rolled in cornmeal dough, wrapped in corn husks, and steamed

ta·man·dua \tə-'man-də-wə, -,man-də-'wä\ *n* [Pg *tamanduá,* fr. Tupi] (1834) : either of two arboreal anteaters (*Tamandua mexicana* and *T. tetradactyla*) of Central and So. America having a nearly hairless tail

tam·a·rack \'ta-mə-,rak, 'tam-rak\ *n* [origin unknown] (1805) 1 : any of several American larches; *esp* : a larch (*Larix laricina*) of northern No. America that inhabits usu. moist or wet areas 2 : the wood of a tamarack

tam·a·rau \,ta-mə-'raù\ *n* [Tag *tamaráw*] (1898) : a small dark sturdily built buffalo (*Bubalus mindorensis*) native to Mindoro

ta·ma·ri \tə-'mär-ē\ *n* [Jp] (1965) : an aged soy sauce prepared with little or no added wheat

tam·a·ril·lo \,ta-mə-'ri-(,)lō\ *n* [alter. of *tomatillo*] (1966) : the reddish edible fruit of an arborescent shrub (*Cyphomandra betacea*) of the nightshade family that is native to So. America but is grown commercially elsewhere; *also* : the shrub itself

tam·a·rin \'ta-mə-rən, -,ran\ *n* [F, fr. Carib] (1780) : any of numerous small chiefly So. American monkeys (genera *Saguinus* and *Leontopithecus*) that are related to the marmosets and have silky fur, a long tail, and lower canine teeth that are longer than the incisors

tam·a·rind \'ta-mə-rənd, -,rind\ *n* [Sp & Pg *tamarindo,* fr. Ar *tamr hindī,* lit., Indian date] (1533) : a tropical Old World leguminous tree (*Tamarindus indica*) with hard yellowish wood, pinnate leaves, and red-striped yellow flowers; *also* : its fruit which has an acid pulp often used for preserves or in a cooling laxative drink

tam·a·risk \'ta-mə-,risk\ *n* [ME *tamarisc,* fr. LL *tamariscus,* fr. L *tamaric-, tamarix*] (14c) : any of a genus (*Tamarix* of the family Tamaricaceae, the tamarisk family) of chiefly Old World desert shrubs and trees having tiny narrow leaves and masses of minute flowers with five stamens and a one-celled ovary

tam·ba·la \täm-'bä-lə\ *n, pl* **-la** or **-las** [Nyanja (Bantu language of Malawi), lit., cockerel] (1970) — see *kwacha* at MONEY table

¹**tam·bour** \'tam-,bùr, tam-'\ *n* [MF, drum, fr. Ar *tanbūr,* modif. of Per *tabīr*] (15c) 1 : ¹DRUM 1 2 a : an embroidery frame; *esp* : a set of two interlocking hoops between which cloth is stretched before stitching b : embroidery made on a tambour frame 3 : a shallow metallic cup or drum with a thin elastic membrane supporting a writing lever used to transmit and register slight motions (as arterial pulsations) 4 : a rolling top or front (as of a rolltop desk) of narrow strips of wood glued on canvas

²**tambour** *vt* (1774) : to embroider (cloth) with tambour ~ *vi* : to work at a tambour frame — **tam·bour·er** *n*

tam·bou·ra or **tam·bu·ra** \tam-'bùr-ə\ *n* [Per *ṭambūra*] (1585) : an Asian musical instrument resembling a lute in construction but without frets and used to produce a drone accompaniment to singing

tam·bou·rine \,tam-bə-'rēn\ *n* [MF *tambourin,* dim. of *tambour*] (1579) : a small drum; *esp* : a shallow one-headed drum with loose metallic disks at the sides played esp. by shaking or striking with the hand

¹**tame** \'tām\ *adj* **tam·er; tam·est** [ME, fr. OE *tam;* akin to OHG *zam* tame, L *domare* to tame, Gk *damnanai*] (bef. 12c) 1 : reduced from a state of native wildness esp. so as to be tractable and useful to humans : DOMESTICATED ⟨~ animals⟩ 2 : made docile and submissive : SUBDUED 3 : lacking spirit, zest, interest, or the capacity to excite : INSIPID ⟨a ~ campaign⟩ — **tame·ly** *adv* — **tame·ness** *n*

²**tame** *vb* **tamed; tam·ing** *vt* (14c) 1 a : to reduce from a wild to a domestic state b : to subject to cultivation c : to bring under control : HARNESS 2 : to deprive of spirit : HUMBLE, SUBDUE ⟨the once revolutionary . . . party, long since *tamed* —*Times Lit. Supp.*⟩ 3 : to tone down : SOFTEN ⟨*tamed* the language in the play⟩ ~ *vi* : to become tame — **tam·able** or **tame·able** \'tā-mə-bəl\ *adj* — **tam·er** *n*

tame·less \'tām-ləs\ *adj* (ca. 1598) : not tamed or not capable of being tamed

Tam·il \'ta-məl, 'tä-\ *n* (1734) 1 : a Dravidian language of Tamil Nadu state, India, and of northern and eastern Sri Lanka 2 : a Tamil-speaking person or a descendant of Tamil-speaking ancestors

Tam·ma·ny \'ta-mə-nē\ *adj* [*Tammany Hall,* headquarters of the Tammany Society, political organization in New York City] (1872) : of, relating to, or constituting a group or organization exercising or seeking municipal political control by methods often associated with corruption and bossism — **Tam·ma·ny·ism** \-,i-zəm\ *n*

Tam·muz \'tä-,mùz\ *n* [Heb *Tammūz*] (1614) : the 10th month of the civil year or the 4th month of the ecclesiastical year in the Jewish calendar — see MONTH table

Tam o' Shan·ter *n* 1 \,ta-mə-'shan-tər\ : the hero of Burns's poem *Tam o' Shanter* 2 *usu* **tam–o'–shanter** \,ta-mə-'\ : a woolen cap of Scottish origin with a tight headband, wide flat circular crown, and usu. a pompon in the center

ta·mox·i·fen \tə-'mäk-sə-,fen\ *n* [perh. fr. trans- + *amine* + *oxi-* (alter. of *oxy*) + *-fen* (alter. of *phenyl*)] (1972) : an estrogen antagonist $C_{26}H_{29}NO$ used esp. to treat postmenopausal breast cancer

¹**tamp** \'tamp\ *vt* [prob. back-formation fr. obs. *tampion, tampin* plug, fr. ME, fr. MF *tapon, tampon,* fr. (assumed) OF *taper* to plug, of Gmc origin; akin to OE *tæppa* tap] (1834) 1 : to drive in or down by a succession of light or medium blows ⟨~ wet concrete⟩ 2 : to put a check on : REDUCE, LESSEN — **tamp·er** *n*

²**tamp** *n* (1920) : a tool for tamping

tam·per \'tam-pər\ *vi* **tam·pered; tam·per·ing** \-p(ə-)riŋ\ [prob. fr. MF *temperer* to temper, mix, meddle — more at TEMPER] (1567) 1 : to carry on underhand or improper negotiations (as by bribery) 2 a : to interfere so as to weaken or change for the worse — used with *with* b : to try foolish or dangerous experiments — used with *with* — **tam·per·er** \-pər-ər\ *n* — **tam·per-proof** \'tam-pər-,prüf\ *adj*

tam·pi·on \'tam-pē-ən, 'täm-\ *n* [obs. *tampion, tampin* plug — more at TAMP] (ca. 1625) : a wooden plug or a metal or canvas cover for the muzzle of a gun

---

\ə\ abut \ᵊ\ kitten, F table \ər\ further \a\ ash \ā\ ace \ä\ mop, mar
\aú\ out \ch\ chin \e\ bet \ē\ easy \g\ go \i\ hit \ī\ ice \j\ job
\ŋ\ sing \ō\ go \ó\ law \ói\ boy \th\ thin \t͟h\ the \ü\ loot \ú\ foot
\y\ yet \zh\ vision \à, ᴷ, œ, œ̄, ᴜᴇ, ᴜ̄ᴇ, ᵞ\ *see* Guide to Pronunciation

¹tam·pon \'tam-ˌpän\ n [F, lit., plug, fr. MF — more at TAMP] (1848) : a plug (as of cotton) introduced into a body cavity usu. to absorb secretions (as from menstruation) or to arrest hemorrhaging

²tampon vt (1860) : to plug with a tampon

tam–tam \'tam-ˌtam, 'täm-ˌtäm\ n [Hindi ṭamṭam] (1782) **1** : TOM-TOM **2** : GONG; esp : one of a tuned set in a gamelan orchestra

Tam·worth \'tam-(ˌ)wərth\ n [Tamworth, borough in Staffordshire, England] (1860) : any of a breed of large long-bodied red swine developed in England esp. for the production of bacon

¹tan \'tan\ vb tanned; tan·ning [ME tannen, fr. MF tanner, fr. ML tannare, fr. tanum, tannum tanbark] vt (14c) **1 a** : to convert (hide) into leather by treatment with an infusion of tannin-rich bark or other agent of similar effect **b** : to convert (protein) to leather or a similar substance **2** : to make (skin) tan esp. by exposure to the sun **3** : THRASH, WHIP ~ vi : to get or become tanned

²tan adj tan·ner; tan·nest (1586) **1** : of, relating to, or used for tan or tanning **2** : of the color tan

³tan n [F, tanbark, fr. OF, fr. ML tanum] (1674) **1** : a tanning material or its active agent (as tannin) **2** : a brown color imparted to the skin by exposure to the sun or wind **3** : a light yellowish brown **4** pl : tan-colored articles of clothing

tan·a·ger \'ta-ni-jər\ n [NL tanagra, fr. Pg tangará, fr. Tupi] (1688) : any of numerous chiefly tropical American oscine birds (family Thraupidae) that are often brightly colored and usu. unmusical and inhabit mostly woodlands

tan·bark \'tan-ˌbärk\ n (1799) **1** : a bark rich in tannin bruised or cut into small pieces and used in tanning **2** : a surface (as a circus ring) covered with spent tanbark

¹tan·dem \'tan-dəm\ n [L, at last, at length (taken to mean "lengthwise"), fr. tam so; akin to OE thæt that] (ca. 1785) **1 a** (1) : a 2-seated carriage drawn by horses harnessed one before the other (2) : a team so harnessed **b** : TANDEM BICYCLE **c** : a vehicle (as a motor-truck) having close-coupled pairs of axles **2** : a group of two or more arranged one behind the other or used or acting in conjunction — **in tandem** **1** : in a tandem arrangement **2** : in partnership or conjunction

²tandem adv (ca. 1795) : one after or behind another ⟨ride ~⟩

³tandem adj (1801) **1** : consisting of things or having parts arranged one behind the other **2** : working or occurring in conjunction with each other

tandem bicycle n (ca. 1890) : a bicycle for usu. two persons sitting tandem

tan·door \tän-'du̇r\ n [Hindi tandūr, tannūr, fr. Per tanūr, fr. Ar tannūr] (1840) : a cylindrical clay oven in which food is cooked over charcoal

tan·doori \tän-'du̇r-ē\ adj [Hindi tandurī, fr. tandūr] (ca. 1968) : cooked in a tandoor ⟨~ chicken⟩ — **tandoori** n

¹tang \'taŋ\ n [ME, of Scand origin; akin to ON tangi point of land, tang] (15c) **1** : a projecting shank, prong, fang, or tongue (as on a knife, file, or sword) to connect with the handle **2 a** : a sharp distinctive often lingering flavor **b** : a pungent odor **c** : something having the effect of a tang (as in stimulation of the senses) **3 a** : a faint suggestion : TRACE **b** : a distinguishing characteristic that sets apart or gives a special individuality — **tanged** \'taŋd\ adj

²tang vt (1566) **1** : to furnish with a tang **2** : to affect with a tang

³tang vb [imit.] (1556) : CLANG, RING

⁴tang n (ca. 1625) : a sharp twanging sound

Tang or **T'ang** \'täŋ\ n [Chin (Beijing) Táng] (1669) : a Chinese dynasty dated A.D. 618–907 and marked by wide contacts with other cultures and by the development of printing and the flourishing of poetry and art

tan·ge·lo \'tan-jə-ˌlō\ n, pl **-los** [tangerine + pomelo] (1904) : the fruit of a hybrid (Citrus tangelo) between a tangerine or mandarin orange and a grapefruit; also : the tree

tan·gen·cy \'tan-jən(t)-sē\ n (1819) : the quality or state of being tangent

¹tan·gent \-jənt\ adj [L tangent-, tangens, prp. of tangere to touch; perh. akin to OE thaccian to touch gently, stroke] (1594) **1 a** : meeting a curve or surface in a single point if a sufficiently small interval is considered ⟨straight line ~ to a curve⟩ **b** (1) : having a common tangent line at a point ⟨~ curves⟩ (2) : having a common tangent plane at a point ⟨~ surfaces⟩ **2** : diverging from an original purpose or course : IRRELEVANT ⟨~ remarks⟩

²tangent n [NL tangent-, tangens, fr. linea tangens tangent line] (1594) **1 a** : the trigonometric function that for an acute angle is the ratio between the leg opposite to the angle when it is considered part of a right triangle and the leg adjacent **b** : a trigonometric function that is equal to the sine divided by the cosine for all real numbers θ for which the cosine is not equal to zero and is exactly equal to the tangent of an angle of measure θ in radians **2** : a line that is tangent; specif : a straight line that is the limiting position of a secant of a curve through a fixed point and a variable point on the curve as the variable point approaches the fixed point — see CIRCLE illustration **3** : an abrupt change of course : DIGRESSION ⟨the speaker went off on a ~⟩ **4** : a small upright flat-ended metal pin at the inner end of a clavichord key that strikes the string to produce the tone

tan·gen·tial \tan-'jen(t)-shəl\ adj (1630) **1** : of, relating to, or of the nature of a tangent **2** : acting along or lying in a tangent ⟨~ forces⟩ **3 a** : DIVERGENT, DIGRESSIVE **b** : touching lightly : INCIDENTAL, PERIPHERAL ⟨~ involvement⟩ — **tan·gen·tial·ly** \-'jen(t)-sh(ə-)lē\ adv

tangent plane n (1856) : the plane through a point of a surface that contains the tangent lines to all the curves on the surface through the same point

tan·ger·ine \'tan-jə-ˌrēn, ˌtan-jə-'-\ n [F Tanger Tangier, Morocco] (1842) **1 a** : any of various mandarins that have usu. deep orange skin and pulp; broadly : MANDARIN 3b **b** : a tree producing tangerines **2** : a moderate to strong reddish orange

¹tan·gi·ble \'tan-jə-bəl\ adj [LL tangibilis, fr. L tangere to touch] (1589) **1 a** : capable of being perceived esp. by the sense of touch : PALPABLE **b** : substantially real : MATERIAL **2** : capable of being precisely identified or realized by the mind ⟨her grief was ~⟩ **3** : capable of being appraised at an actual or approximate value ⟨~ assets⟩ syn see PERCEPTIBLE — **tan·gi·bil·i·ty** \ˌtan-jə-'bi-lə-tē\ n — **tan·gi·ble·ness** \'tan-jə-bəl-nəs\ n — **tan·gi·bly** \-blē\ adv

²tangible n (1890) : something tangible; esp : a tangible asset

¹tan·gle \'taŋ-gəl\ vb tan·gled; tan·gling \-g(ə-)liŋ\ [ME tangilen, prob. of Scand origin; akin to Sw dial. taggla to tangle] vt (14c) **1** : to involve so as to hamper, obstruct, or embarrass **2** : to seize and hold in or as if in a snare : ENTRAP **3** : to unite or knit together in intricate confusion ~ vi **1** : to interact in a contentious or conflicting way **2** : to become entangled

²tangle n (1615) **1** : a tangled twisted mass : SNARL **2 a** : a complicated or confused state or condition **b** : a state of perplexity or complete bewilderment **3** : a serious altercation : DISPUTE

³tangle n [of Scand origin; akin to ON thongull tangle, thang kelp] (1536) : a large seaweed

tan·gled \'taŋ-gəld\ adj (1590) **1** : existing in or giving the appearance of a state of utter disorder **2** : very involved : exceedingly complex

tan·gle·ment \-gəl-mənt\ n (1831) : ENTANGLEMENT

tan·gly \'taŋ-g(ə-)lē\ adj (1813) : full of tangles or knots : INTRICATE

tan·go \'taŋ-(ˌ)gō\ n, pl **tangos** [AmerSp] (1913) : a ballroom dance of Latin-American origin in 4/4 time with a basic pattern of step-step-close and characterized by long pauses and stylized body positions; also : the music for this dance

²tango vi (1913) : to dance the tango

Tan·go (1952) — a communications code word for the letter t

tan·gram \'taŋ-grəm, 'tan-\ n [perh. fr. Chin (Beijing) táng Chinese + E -gram] (ca. 1864) : a Chinese puzzle made by cutting a square of thin material into five triangles, a square, and a rhomboid which are capable of being recombined in many different figures

tangram

tangy \'taŋ-ē\ adj tang·i·er; -est (1875) : having or suggestive of a tang

¹tank \'taŋk\ n [Pg tanque, alter. of estanque, fr. estancar to stanch, perh. fr. (assumed) VL stanticare — more at STANCH] (ca. 1616) **1** dial : POND, POOL; esp : one built as a water supply **2 a** : usu. large receptacle for holding, transporting, or storing liquids (as water or fuel) **3** : an enclosed heavily armed and armored combat vehicle that moves on tracks **4** : a prison cell or enclosure used esp. for receiving prisoners **5** : TANK TOP — **tank·ful** \-ˌfu̇l\ n — **tank·like** \-ˌlīk\ adj

²tank vt (1863) **1** : to place, store, or treat in a tank **2** : to make no effort to win : lose intentionally ⟨~ed the match⟩ ~ vi : to lose intentionally : give up in competition

tan·ka \'täŋ-kə\ n [Jp] (ca. 1877) : an unrhymed Japanese verse form of five lines containing 5, 7, 5, 7, and 7 syllables respectively; also : a poem in this form — compare HAIKU

tank·age \'taŋ-kij\ n (1866) **1 a** : the aggregate of tanks required for a purpose **b** : the capacity or contents of a tank **2** : dried animal residues usu. freed from the fat and gelatin and used as fertilizer and feedstuff **3** : the act or process of putting or storing in tanks

tan·kard \'taŋ-kərd\ n [ME] (15c) : a tall one-handled drinking vessel; esp : a silver or pewter mug with a lid

tank destroyer n (1941) : a highly mobile lightly armored vehicle usu. on a half-track or a tank chassis and mounting a cannon

tanked \'taŋ(k)t\ adj (1893) slang : DRUNK 1a — often used with up

tank·er \'taŋ-kər\ n (1900) **1 a** : a cargo ship fitted with tanks for carrying liquid in bulk **b** : a vehicle on which a tank is mounted to carry fluids; also : a cargo airplane for transporting fuel **2** : a member of a military tank crew

tank suit n (1940) : a one-piece bathing suit with usu. wide shoulder straps

tank top n (1950) : a sleeveless collarless shirt with usu. wide shoulder straps and no front opening

tank town n [fr. the fact that formerly trains stopped at such towns only to take on water] (1906) : a small town

tan·nage \'ta-nij\ n (1662) : the act, process, or result of tanning

tan·nate \'ta-ˌnāt\ n [F, fr. tannin] (1802) : a compound of a tannin

¹tan·ner \'ta-nər\ n (bef. 12c) **1** : one that tans hides **2** : one who acquires or seeks to acquire a suntan

²tanner n [origin unknown] (ca. 1811) Brit : SIXPENCE

tanner crab n [prob. fr. NL tanneri, specific epithet of Chionoecetes tanneri, fr. Zera L. Tanner †1906 Am. naval officer] (1947) : any of several spider crabs (genus Chionoecetes); esp : SNOW CRAB

tan·nery \'ta-nə-rē, 'tan-rē\ n, pl **-ner·ies** (1736) : a place where tanning is carried on

tan·nic \'ta-nik\ adj [F tannique, fr. tannin] (ca. 1859) **1** : of, resembling, or derived from tan or a tannin **2** of wine : containing an abundance of tannins : markedly astringent

tannic acid n (1836) : TANNIN 1

tan·nin \'ta-nən\ n [F, fr. tanner to tan] (1802) **1** : any of various soluble astringent complex phenolic substances of plant origin used esp. in tanning, dyeing, the making of ink, and in medicine **2** : a substance that has a tanning effect

tan·ning \'ta-niŋ\ n (15c) **1** : the art or process by which a skin is tanned **2** : a browning of the skin esp. by exposure to sun **3** : a sound spanking **4** : a natural darkening and hardening of the cuticle of an insect immediately after molting

tan·nish \'ta-nish\ adj (1935) : somewhat tan

tan oak n (ca. 1925) : a U.S. Pacific coast evergreen tree (Lithocarpus densiflora) of the beech family that has erect staminate catkins and is rich in tannins

Ta·no·an \tə-'nō-ən, 'tä-nō-wən\ n [Tano, a group of former pueblos in New Mexico] (1891) : a family of American Indian languages spoken in New Mexico and Arizona — **Tanoan** adj

tan·sy \'tan-zē\ n, pl **tansies** [ME tanesey, fr. MF tanesie, fr. ML athanasia, fr. Gk, immortality, fr. athanatos immortal, fr. a- + thanatos death — more at THANATOS] (15c) : a common aromatic Old World composite herb (Tanacetum vulgare) that is naturalized in No. America and has bitter-tasting finely divided leaves; broadly : a plant of the same genus

tansy ragwort n (ca. 1900) : an Old World yellow-flowered senecio (Senecio jacobaea) that is naturalized in No. America and is toxic to livestock

tan·ta·late \'tan-t⁹l-ˌāt\ n (1849) : a salt containing tantalum in combination with oxygen

tan·ta·lise Brit var of TANTALIZE

tan·ta·lite \'tan-t⁹l-ˌīt\ n (1805) : a mineral consisting of a heavy dark lustrous oxide of tantalum and usu. other metals (as iron or manganese)

tan·ta·lize \'tan-t⁹l-ˌīz\ vb **-lized; -liz·ing** [Tantalus] vt (1597) : to tease or torment by or as if by presenting something desirable to the view but continually keeping it out of reach ~ vi : to cause one to be tantalized — **tan·ta·liz·er** n

tantalizing adj (ca. 1683) : possessing a quality that arouses or stimulates desire or interest; also : mockingly or teasingly out of reach — **tan·ta·liz·ing·ly** \-ˌī-zin-lē\ adv

tan·ta·lum \'tan-t⁹l-əm\ n [NL, fr. L Tantalus; fr. its inability to absorb acid] (1802) : a hard ductile gray-white acid-resisting metallic element of the vanadium family found combined in rare minerals (as tantalite and columbite) — see ELEMENT table

Tan·ta·lus \'tan-t⁹l-əs\ n [L, fr. Gk Tantalos] 1 : a legendary king of Lydia condemned to stand up to the chin in a pool of water in Hades and beneath fruit-laden boughs only to have the water or fruit recede at each attempt to drink or eat 2 not cap : a locked cellarette with contents visible but not obtainable without a key

tan·ta·mount \'tan-tə-ˌmaunt\ adj [obs. tantamount, n., equivalent, fr. AF tant amunter to amount to as much] (1641) : equivalent in value, significance, or effect

tan·ta·ra \tan-'tar-ə, -'tär-\ n [L taratantara, of imit. origin] (1584) : the blare of a trumpet or horn

tan·tivy \tan-'ti-vē\ adv [origin unknown] (1641) : at a gallop

²**tantivy** n, pl **-tiv·ies** (ca. 1658) 1 : a rapid gallop or ride 2 : TANTARA

tan·tra \'tən-trə, 'tän-, 'tan-\ n, often cap [Skt, lit., warp, fr. tanoti he stretches, weaves; akin to Gk teinein to stretch — more at THIN] (1799) : one of the later Hindu or Buddhist scriptures dealing esp. with techniques and rituals including meditative and sexual practices; also : the rituals or practices outlined in the tantra — **tan·tric** \-trik\ adj, often cap — **Tan·trism** \-ˌtri-zəm\ n — **Tan·trist** \-trist\ n

tan·trum \'tan-trəm\ n [origin unknown] (1714) : a fit of bad temper

ta·nu·ki \tä-'nü-kē\ n [Jp, raccoon dog] (ca. 1929) : the fur of a raccoon dog; also : RACCOON DOG

tan·yard \'tan-ˌyärd\ n (1666) : the section or part of a tannery housing tanning vats

tan·za·nite \'tan-zə-ˌnīt\ n [Tanzania, Africa] (1968) : a mineral that is a deep blue variety of zoisite and is used as a gemstone

Tao \'dau, 'tau\ n [Chin (Beijing) dào, lit., way] (1736) 1 a : the unconditional and unknowable source and guiding principle of all reality as conceived by Taoists b : the process of nature by which all things change and which is to be followed for a life of harmony 2 often not cap : the path of virtuous conduct as conceived by Confucians 3 often not cap : the art or skill of doing something in harmony with the essential nature of the thing ⟨the ~ of archery⟩

Tao·ism \-ˌi-zəm\ n [Tao] 1 : a Chinese mystical philosophy traditionally founded by Lao-tzu in the 6th century B.C. that teaches conformity to the Tao by unassertive action and simplicity 2 : a religion developed from Taoist philosophy and folk and Buddhist religion and concerned with obtaining long life and good fortune often by magical means — **Tao·ist** \-ist\ adj or n — **Tao·is·tic** \dau-'is-tik, tau-\ adj

¹**tap** \'tap\ n [ME tappe, fr. OE tæppa; akin to OHG zapho tap] (bef. 12c) 1 a : a plug for a hole (as in a cask) : SPIGOT b : a device consisting of a spout and valve attached to the end of a pipe to control the flow of a fluid : FAUCET 2 a : a liquor drawn through a tap b : the procedure of removing fluid (as from a body cavity) 3 : a tool for forming an internal screw thread 4 : an intermediate point in an electric circuit where a connection may be made 5 : WIRETAP — **on tap** 1 : ready to be drawn from a large container (as a cask or keg) ⟨ale on tap⟩ 2 : broached or furnished with a tap 3 : on hand : AVAILABLE ⟨services instantly on tap —Hugh Dwan⟩ 4 : coming up ⟨other matches on tap —H. W. Wind⟩

²**tap** vt **tapped; tap·ping** (15c) 1 : to let out or cause to flow by piercing or by drawing a plug from the containing vessel ⟨~ wine from a cask⟩ 2 a : to pierce so as to let out or draw off a fluid ⟨~ maple trees⟩ b : to draw out, from, or upon ⟨~ new sources of revenue⟩ 3 a : to cut in on (a telephone or telegraph wire) to get information b : to cut in (an electrical circuit) on another circuit 4 : to form an internal screw thread in by means of a tap 5 : to get money from as a loan or gift 6 : to connect (a street gas or water main) with a local supply — **tap·per** n — **tap into** : to make a usu. advantageous connection with ⟨clothing that . . . taps into the currents of popular culture —John Duka⟩

³**tap** vb **tapped; tap·ping** [ME tappen, fr. MF taper to strike with the flat of the hand, of Gmc origin; akin to MHG tāpe paw, blow dealt with the paw] vt (13c) 1 : to strike lightly esp. with a slight sound 2 : to give a light blow with ⟨~ a pencil on the table⟩ 3 : to bring about by repeated light blows ⟨~ out a story on the typewriter⟩ 4 : to repair by putting a tap on 5 : SELECT, DESIGNATE ⟨was tapped for police commissioner⟩; specif : to elect to membership (as in a fraternity) ~ vi 1 : to strike a light audible blow : RAP 2 : to walk with light audible steps 3 : TAP-DANCE — **tap·per** n

⁴**tap** n (14c) 1 a : a light usu. audible blow; also : its sound b : one of several usu. rapid drumbeats on a snare drum 2 : HALF SOLE 3 : a small metal plate for the sole or heel of a shoe 4 : TAP DANCE 1 5 : FLAP 7

¹**ta·pa** \'tä-pə, 'tä-\ n [Marquesan & Tahitian] (1823) : a coarse cloth made in the Pacific islands from the pounded bark esp. of the paper mulberry and usu. decorated with geometric patterns

²**tapa** n [Sp, lit., cover, lid, prob. of Gmc origin; akin to OE tæppa tap] (1953) : an hors d'oeuvre served with drinks in Spanish bars — usu. used in pl.

tap dance n (1928) 1 : a step dance tapped out audibly by means of shoes with hard soles or soles and heels to which taps have been added 2 : something suggesting a tap dance; esp : an action or discourse intended to rationalize or distract ⟨does a clever tap dance to explain —Campbell Geeslin⟩ — **tap–dance** vi — **tap dancer** n — **tap dancing** n

¹**tape** \'tāp\ n [ME, fr. OE tæppe] (bef. 12c) 1 : a narrow woven fabric 2 : a string or ribbon stretched breast-high above the finish line of a race 3 : a narrow flexible strip or band: as a : ADHESIVE TAPE b : MAGNETIC TAPE 4 : TAPE RECORDING

²**tape** vb **taped; tap·ing** vt (1609) 1 : to fasten, tie, bind, cover, or support with tape 2 : to record on tape and esp. magnetic tape ⟨~ an interview⟩ ~ vi : to record something on tape and esp. magnetic tape

³**tape** adj (1947) 1 : recorded on tape ⟨~ music⟩ 2 : intended for use with recording (as magnetic) tape ⟨a ~ cartridge⟩

tape deck n (1949) : a device used to play back and often to record on magnetic tape that usu. has to be connected to an audio system

tape grass n (ca. 1818) : any of several submerged aquatic monocotyledonous plants (genus Vallisneria of the family Hydrocharitaceae) with long ribbonlike leaves — called also eelgrass, wild celery

tape measure n (1845) : a narrow strip (as of a limp cloth or steel tape) marked off in units (as inches or centimeters) for measuring

¹**ta·per** \'tā-pər\ n [ME, fr. OE tapor candle, wick, perh. modif. of L papyrus papyrus] (bef. 12c) 1 a : a slender candle b : a long waxed wick used esp. for lighting candles, lamps, pipes, or fires c : a feeble light 2 a : a tapering form or figure b : gradual diminution of thickness, diameter, or width in an elongated object c : a gradual decrease

²**taper** adj (15c) 1 : progressively narrowed toward one end 2 : furnished with or adjusted to a scale : GRADUATED ⟨~ freight rates⟩

³**taper** vb **ta·pered; ta·per·ing** \'tā-p(ə-)riŋ\ vi (1610) 1 : to become progressively smaller toward one end 2 : to diminish gradually ~ vt : to cause to taper

⁴**taper** n \'tā-pər\ n [¹tape] (ca. 1920) : one that applies or dispenses tape

tape–re·cord \ˌtā-pri-'kord, 'tā-pri-ˌ\ vt [back-formation fr. tape recording] (1950) : to make a recording of on magnetic tape

tape recorder n (1932) : a device for recording on and playing back magnetic tape

tape recording n (1940) : magnetic recording on magnetic tape; also : a recording made by this process

ta·per·er \'tā-pər-ər\ n (15c) : one who bears a taper in a religious procession

taper off vb (1848) : TAPER ⟨business growth had tapered off seriously while the unemployment rate had climbed —Current Biog.⟩

ta·per·stick \'tā-pər-ˌstik\ n (1546) : a candlestick that holds tapers

tap·es·tried \'ta-pə-strēd\ adj (1769) 1 : covered or decorated with or as if with tapestry 2 : woven or depicted in tapestry

tap·es·try \'ta-pə-strē\ n, pl **-tries** [ME tapistry, modif. of MF tapisserie, fr. tapisser to carpet, cover with tapestry, fr. OF tapis carpet, fr. Gk tapēt-, tapēs rug, carpet] (15c) 1 a : a heavy handwoven reversible textile used for hangings, curtains, and upholstery and characterized by complicated pictorial designs b : a nonreversible imitation of tapestry used chiefly for upholstery c : embroidery on canvas resembling woven tapestry ⟨needlepoint ~⟩ 2 : something resembling tapestry (as in complexity or richness of design)

tapestry carpet n (1852) : a carpet in which the designs are printed in colors on the threads before the fabric is woven

ta·pe·tum \tə-'pē-təm\ n, pl **ta·pe·ta** \-'pē-tə\ [NL, fr. L tapete carpet, tapestry, fr. Gk tapēt-, tapēs rug, carpet] (1713) 1 : any of various membranous layers or areas esp. of the choroid coat and retina of the eye 2 : a layer of nutritive cells that invests the sporogenous tissue in the sporangium of higher plants

tape·worm \'tāp-ˌwərm\ n [fr. its shape] (1752) : any of a class (Cestoda) of platyhelminthic worms parasitic esp. in the intestines of vertebrates — called also cestode

tap·hole \'tap-ˌhōl\ n (1594) : a hole for a tap; specif : a hole at or near the bottom of a furnace or ladle through which molten metal, matte, or slag can be tapped

ta·phon·o·my \tə-'fä-nə-mē, ta-\ n [Gk taphē burial + E -nomy] (1940) : the study of the processes (as burial, decay, and preservation) that affect animal and plant remains as they become fossilized — **taph·o·nom·ic** \ˌta-fə-'nä-mik\ adj — **ta·phon·o·mist** \tə-'fä-nə-mist, ta-\ n

tap–in \'tap-ˌin\ n (1948) 1 : TIP-IN 2 : a short putt in golf

tap·i·o·ca \ˌta-pē-'ō-kə\ n [Sp & Pg, fr. Tupi tipióka] (1707) 1 : a usu. granular preparation of cassava starch used esp. in puddings and as a thickening in liquid food; also : a dish (as pudding) containing tapioca 2 : CASSAVA

ta·pir \'tā-pər also 'tä-ˌpir or tə-'pir\ n, pl **tapir** or **tapirs** [Pg tapira, fr. Tupi tapiíra] (1774) : any of a genus (Tapirus) of chiefly nocturnal perissodactyl ungulates of tropical America and Myanmar to Sumatra that have the snout and upper lip prolonged into a short flexible proboscis

tap·is \'ta-ˌpē, ta-'pē\ n [ME, fr. MF — more at TAPESTRY] (15c) archaic : a small tapestry used for hangings and floor and table coverings — **on the tapis** : under consideration

tapir

tap–off \'tap-ˌof\ n (ca. 1932) : ²TIP-OFF

tap out vi (1939) : to run out of money by betting

tap pants n pl (1977) : a loose-fitting woman's undergarment of a style similar to shorts formerly worn for tap dancing

tapped out adj (1950) : out of money : BROKE

tap·pet \'ta-pət\ n [irreg. fr. ³tap] (1745) : a lever or projection moved by some other piece (as a cam) or intended to tap or touch something else to cause a particular motion

tapping n (1597) : the act, process, or means by which something is tapped

---

\ə\ abut \ᵊ\ kitten, F table \ər\ further \a\ ash \ā\ ace \ä\ mop, mar \aú\ out \ch\ chin \e\ bet \ē\ easy \g\ go \i\ hit \ī\ ice \j\ job \ŋ\ sing \ō\ go \ò\ law \òi\ boy \th\ thin \th\ the \ü\ loot \ù\ foot \y\ yet \zh\ vision \à, ḵ, ⁿ, œ, œ̄, ue, ūe, ᵋ\ see Guide to Pronunciation

tap·pit hen \'ta-pət-\ n [Sc tappit, alter. of E topped] (1721) Scot : a drinking vessel with a knob on the lid

tap·room \'tap-‚rüm, -‚rùm\ n (1807) : BARROOM

tap·root \-‚rüt, -‚rút\ n [¹tap] (1601) 1 : a primary root that grows vertically downward and gives off small lateral roots 2 : the central element or position in a line of growth or development

taps \'taps\ n pl but sing or pl in constr [prob. alter. of earlier taptoo tattoo — more at TATTOO] (1824) : the last bugle call at night blown as a signal that lights are to be put out; also : a similar call blown at military funerals and memorial services

tap·sal–tee·rie \‚tap-səl-'tē-rē\ adv [by alter.] (1784) Scot : TOPSY-TURVY

tap·ster \'tap-stər\ n (bef. 12c) : BARTENDER

tap water n (1881) : water as it comes from a tap (as in a home)

¹tar \'tär\ n [ME terr, tarr, fr. OE teoru; akin to OE trēow tree — more at TREE] (bef. 12c) 1 a : a dark brown or black bituminous usu. odorous viscous liquid obtained by destructive distillation of organic material (as wood, coal, or peat) b : a substance in some respects resembling tar; esp : a condensable residue present in smoke from burning tobacco that contains combustion by-products (as resins, acids, phenols, and essential oils) 2 [short for tarpaulin] : SAILOR

²tar vt tarred; tar·ring (13c) 1 : to cover with tar 2 : to defile as if with tar ⟨least tarred by the scandal —Newsweek⟩ — tar and feather : to smear (a person) with tar and cover with feathers as a punishment or indignity — tar with the same brush : to mark or stain with the same fault or characteristic

³tar or tarre \'tär\ vt tarred; tar·ring; tars or tarres [ME terren, tarren, fr. OE tyrwan] (bef. 12c) : to urge to action — usu. used with on

tar·a·did·dle or **tar·ra·did·dle** \‚tar-ə-'di-d²l, 'tar-ə-‚\ n [origin unknown] (ca. 1796) 1 : FIB 2 : pretentious nonsense

Tar·a·hu·ma·ra \‚tär-ə-hü-'mär-ə\ n, pl **Tarahumara** or **Tarahuma·ras** [Sp] (1874) 1 : a member of an American Indian people living in the state of Chihuahua, Mexico 2 : the Uto-Aztecan language of the Tarahumara people

tar·an·tel·la \‚tär-ən-'te-lə\ n [It, fr. Taranto, Italy] (1782) : a lively folk dance of southern Italy in ⁶/₈ time

tar·an·tism \'tar-ən-‚ti-zəm\ n [NL tarantismus, fr. Taranto, Italy] (ca. 1656) : a dancing mania or malady of late medieval Europe

ta·ran·tu·la \tə-'ran-chə-lə, -tə-lə; -'ranch-lə, -'rant-\ n, pl **ta·ran·tu·las** also **ta·ran·tu·lae** \-‚lē\ [ML, fr. OIt tarantola, fr. Taranto] (1561) 1 : a European wolf spider (Lycosa tarentula) popularly held to be the cause of tarantism 2 : any of a family (Theraphosidae) of large hairy American spiders that are typically rather sluggish and capable of biting sharply though most forms are not significantly poisonous to humans

Ta·ras·can \tə-'ras-kən, -'räs-\ n [Sp tarasco] (1922) 1 : a member of an American Indian people of the state of Michoacán, Mexico 2 : the language of the Tarascan people

tar baby n [fr. the tar baby that trapped Brer Rabbit in an Uncle Remus story by Joel Chandler Harris] (1924) : something from which it is nearly impossible to extricate oneself

tar·boosh also **tar·bush** \tär-'büsh, 'tär-‚\ n [Ar ṭarbūsh] (1702) : a red hat similar to the fez worn esp. by Muslim men

tar·di·grade \'tär-də-‚grād\ n [ultim. fr. L tardigradus slow-moving, fr. tardus slow + gradi to step, go — more at GRADE] (1860) : any of a phylum (Tardigrada) of microscopic arthropods with four pairs of stout legs that usu. in water or damp moss — called also water bear

tar·di·ly \'tär-d²l-ē\ adv (1597) 1 : at a slow pace 2 : LATE

tar·dive dyskinesia \'tär-div-\ n [tardive tending toward late development (fr. F, fem. of tardif, fr. MF) + dyskinesia] (1964) : a central nervous system disorder characterized by twitching of the face and tongue and involuntary motor movements of the trunk and limbs and occurring esp. as a side effect of prolonged use of antipsychotic drugs (as phenothiazine)

tar·do \'tär-(‚)dō\ adj [It, fr. L tardus] (ca. 1843) : SLOW — used as a direction in music

¹tar·dy \'tär-dē\ adj tar·di·er; -est [alter. of earlier tardif, fr. MF, fr. (assumed) VL tardivus, fr. L tardus] (15c) 1 : moving slowly : SLUGGISH 2 : delayed beyond the expected or proper time : LATE — tar·di·ness \'tär-dē-nəs\ n

²tardy n, pl tardies (1960) : an instance of being tardy (as to a class)

¹tare \'tar, 'ter\ n [ME; prob. akin to MD tarwe wheat] (14c) 1 a : the seed of a vetch b : any of several vetches (esp. Vicia sativa and V. hirsuta) 2 : a weed of grainfields usu. held to be the darnel 3 pl : an undesirable element

²tare n [ME, fr. MF, fr. OIt tara, fr. Ar ṭarḥa, lit., that which is removed] (15c) 1 : a deduction from the gross weight of a substance and its container made in allowance for the weight of the container; also : the weight of the container 2 : COUNTERWEIGHT

³tare vt tared; tar·ing (1812) : to ascertain or mark the tare of; esp : to weigh so as to determine the tare

targe \'tärj\ n [ME, fr. OF] (14c) : a light shield used esp. by the Scots

¹tar·get \'tär-gət\ n, often attrib [ME, fr. MF targette, dim. of targe light shield, of Gmc origin; akin to ON targa shield] (15c) 1 a : a small round shield 2 a : a mark to shoot at b : a target marked by shots fired at it c : something or someone fired at or marked for attack d : a goal to be achieved 3 a : an object of ridicule or criticism b : something or someone to be affected by an action or development 4 a : a railroad day signal that is attached to a switch stand and indicates whether the switch is open or closed b : a sliding sight on a surveyor's leveling rod 5 a : the metallic surface (as of platinum or tungsten) upon which the stream of electrons within an X-ray tube is focused and from which the X rays are emitted b : a body, surface, or material bombarded with nuclear particles or electrons; esp : fluorescent material on which desired visual effects are produced in electronic devices (as in radar) — off target : not valid : INACCURATE — on target : precisely correct or valid esp. in interpreting or addressing a problem or vital issue

²target vt (1837) 1 : to make a target of; esp : to set as a goal 2 : to direct or use toward a target

tar·get·able \'tär-gə-tə-bəl\ adj (1964) : capable of being aimed at a target ⟨missiles with ~ warheads⟩

target date n (1945) : the date set for an event or for the completion of a project, goal, or quota

target language n (1953) 1 : a language into which another language is to be translated — compare SOURCE LANGUAGE 2 : a language other than one's native language that is being learned

Tar·gum \'tär-‚gúm, -‚güm\ n [LHeb targūm, fr. Aram, translation] (1587) : an Aramaic translation or paraphrase of a portion of the Old Testament

Tar·heel \'tär-‚hēl\ n (1864) : a native or resident of North Carolina — used as a nickname

¹tar·iff \'tar-əf\ n [It tariffa, fr. Ar ta'rīf notification] (1592) 1 a : a schedule of duties imposed by a government on imported or in some countries exported goods b : a duty or rate of duty imposed in such a schedule 2 : a schedule of rates or charges of a business or a public utility 3 : PRICE, CHARGE

²tariff vt (ca. 1828) : to subject to a tariff

tar·la·tan \'tär-lə-t²n\ n [F tarlatane] (ca. 1741) : a sheer cotton fabric in open plain weave usu. heavily sized for stiffness

tar·mac \'tär-‚mak\ n [fr. Tarmac, a trademark] (1919) : a tarmacadam road, apron, or runway

Tarmac trademark — used for a bituminous binder for roads

tar·mac·ad·am \‚tär-mə-'ka-dəm\ n (1882) 1 : a pavement constructed by spraying or pouring a tar binder over layers of crushed stone and then rolling 2 : a material of tar and aggregates mixed in a plant and shaped on the roadway

tarn \'tärn\ n [ME tarne, of Scand origin; akin to ON tjǫrn small lake] (14c) : a small steep-banked mountain lake or pool

tar·na·tion \tär-'nā-shən\ n [alter. of darnation, euphemism for damnation] (1790) : DAMNATION — often used as an interjection or intensive; often used with in ⟨~ strike me —James Joyce⟩ ⟨where in ~ you from? —Jessamyn West⟩

¹tar·nish \'tär-nish\ vb [MF terniss-, stem of ternir, prob. of Gmc origin; akin to OHG ternen to hide] vt (1598) 1 : to dull or destroy the luster of by or as if by air, dust, or dirt : SOIL, STAIN 2 a : to detract from the good quality of : VITIATE ⟨his fine dreams now slightly ~ed⟩ b : to bring disgrace on : SULLY ~ vi : to become tarnished — tar·nish·able \-ni-shə-bəl\ adj

²tarnish n (1713) : something that tarnishes; esp : a film of chemically altered material on the surface of a metal (as silver)

tarnished plant bug n (ca. 1890) : a common hemipterous bug (Lygus lineolaris) of eastern No. America that causes injury to plants by sucking sap from buds, leaves, and fruits and that carries plant diseases

ta·ro \'tär-(‚)ō, 'tar-, 'ter-\ n, pl **taros** [Tahitian & Maori] (1769) : a plant (Colocasia esculenta) of the arum family grown throughout the tropics for its edible starchy tuberous rootstocks and in temperate regions for ornament; also : its rootstock

tar·ok \'tar-‚äk\ n [It tarocchi tarots] (1739) : an old card game popular in central Europe and played with a pack containing 40, 52, or 56 cards equivalent to modern playing cards plus the 22 tarots

tar·ot \'tar-(‚)ō\ n [MF, fr. It tarocchi (pl.)] (ca. 1623) : any of a set of usu. 78 playing cards including 22 pictorial cards used for fortune-telling; also : the 22 pictorial cards serving as trumps in tarok

tarp \'tärp\ n (1906) : TARPAULIN

tar paper n (1891) : a heavy paper coated or impregnated with tar for use esp. in building

tar·pau·lin \tär-'pȯ-lən, 'tär-pə-‚; ÷tär-'pȯl-yən\ n [prob. fr. ¹tar + -palling, -pauling (fr. pall)] (1605) 1 : a piece of material (as durable plastic) used for protecting exposed objects or areas 2 : SAILOR

tar pit n (1839) : an area in which natural bitumens collect and are exposed at the earth's surface and which tends to trap animals and preserve their hard parts (as bones or teeth)

tar·pon \'tär-pən\ n, pl **tarpon** or **tarpons** [origin unknown] (1685) : a large silvery elongate anadromous bony fish (Megalops atlanticus of the family Elopidae) that occurs esp. in the Gulf of Mexico, Caribbean, and warm coastal waters of the Atlantic, reaches a length of about six feet (two meters), and is often caught for sport

tar·ra·gon \'tar-ə-gən\ n [MF targon, fr. ML tarchon, fr. Ar ṭarkhūn] (1538) : a small widely cultivated perennial artemisia (Artemisia dracunculus) having pungent narrow usu. entire leaves; also : its leaves used as a flavoring

tarre var of TAR

tar·ri·ance \'tar-ē-ən(t)s\ n (15c) : the act or an instance of tarrying

¹tar·ry \'tar-ē\ vi tar·ried; tar·ry·ing [ME tarien] (14c) 1 a : to delay or be tardy in acting or doing b : to linger in expectation : WAIT 2 : to abide or stay in or at a place

²tarry n, pl tarries (14c) : STAY, SOJOURN

³tar·ry \'tär-ē\ adj (1552) : of, resembling, or covered with tar

¹tar·sal \'tär-səl\ adj (1817) 1 : of or relating to the tarsus 2 : being or relating to plates of dense connective tissue that serve to stiffen the eyelids

²tarsal n (1881) : a tarsal part (as a bone or cartilage)

tar sand n (1899) : a natural impregnation of sand or sandstone with petroleum from which the lighter portions have escaped

tar·si·er \'tär-sē-ər, -sē-‚ā\ n [F, fr. tarse tarsus, fr. NL tarsus] (1774) : any of a family (Tarsiidae) of small chiefly nocturnal and arboreal carnivorous primates of the Malay Archipelago that have large round eyes, long legs, and a long nearly hairless tail

tar·so·meta·tar·sus \‚tär-(‚)sō-'me-tə-‚tär-səs\ n [NL, fr. tarsus + -o- + metatarsus] (1854) : the large compound bone of the tarsus of a bird; also : the segment of the limb it supports

tar·sus \'tär-səs\ n, pl **tar·si** \-‚sī, -‚sē\ [NL, fr. Gk tarsos wickerwork mat, flat of the foot, ankle, edge of the eyelid; akin to Gk tersesthai to become dry — more at THIRST] (1676) 1 : the part of the foot of a vertebrate between the metatarsus and the leg; also : the small bones that support this part of the limb 2 : the tarsal plate of the eyelid 3 : the distal part of the limb of an arthropod 4 : TARSOMETATARSUS

¹tart \'tärt\ adj [ME, fr. OE teart sharp, severe; akin to MHG traz spite] (14c) 1 : agreeably sharp or acid to the taste 2 : marked by a biting, acrimonious, or cutting quality — tart·ish \'tär-tish\ adj — tart·ly adv — tart·ness n

²tart n [ME tarte, fr. MF] (15c) 1 : dish baked in a pastry shell : PIE: as a : a small pie or pastry shell without a top containing jelly, custard, or fruit b : a small pie made of pastry folded over a filling 2 : PROSTITUTE

tar·tan \'tär-t²n\ n [prob. fr. MF tiretaine linsey-woolsey] (ca. 1500) 1 : a plaid textile design of Scottish origin consisting of stripes of varying width and color usu. patterned to designate a distinctive clan **2 a** : a twilled woolen fabric with tartan design **b** : a fabric with tartan design **3** : a garment of tartan design

¹tar·tar \'tär-tər\ *n* [ME, fr. ML *tartarum*] (14c) **1** : a substance consisting essentially of cream of tartar that is derived from the juice of grapes and deposited in wine casks together with yeast and other suspended matters as a pale or dark reddish crust or sediment; *esp* : a recrystallized product yielding cream of tartar on further purification **2** : an incrustation on the teeth consisting of salivary secretion, food residue, and various salts (as calcium carbonate)

²tartar *n* [ME *Tartre*, fr. MF *Tartare*, prob. fr. ML *Tartarus*, modif. of Per *Tātār* — more at TATAR] (14c) **1** *cap* : a native or inhabitant of Tatary **2** *cap* : TATAR 2 **3** *often cap* : a person of irritable or violent temper **4** : one that proves to be unexpectedly formidable — **Tartar** *adj* — **Tar·tar·i·an** \tär-'tar-ē-ən, -'ter-\ *adj*

Tar·tar·e·an \tär-'tar-ē-ən, -'ter-\ *adj* [L *tartareus*, fr. Gk *tartareios*, fr. *Tartaros* Tartarus] (ca. 1623) : of, relating to, or resembling Tartarus : INFERNAL

tartar emetic *n* (1704) : a poisonous efflorescent crystalline salt KSbOC₄H₄O₆·½H₂O of sweetish metallic taste that is used in dyeing as a mordant and in medicine esp. in the treatment of amebiasis

tar·tar·ic acid \(ˌ)tär-'tar-ik-\ *n* (1810) : a strong dicarboxylic acid C₄H₆O₆ of plant origin that occurs in three optically isomeric forms, is usu. obtained from tartar, and is used esp. in food and medicines, in photography, and in making salts and esters

tar·tar sauce *or* **tar·tare sauce** \'tär-tər-\ *n* [F *sauce tartare*] (1855) : a sauce made principally of mayonnaise and chopped pickles

Tar·ta·rus \'tär-tə-rəs\ *n* [L, fr. Gk *Tartaros*] : a section of Hades reserved for punishment of the wicked

tart·let \'tärt-lət\ *n* (15c) : a small tart

tar·trate \'tär-ˌtrāt\ *n* [ISV, fr. F *tartre* tartar, fr. ML *tartarum*] (1794) : a salt or ester of tartaric acid

Tar·tuffe \tär-'tüf, -'tüf\ *n* [F *Tartufe*] : a religious hypocrite and protagonist in Molière's play *Tartuffe*

tart up *vt* (1938) : DRESS UP, FANCY UP ⟨*tarted up* pubs and restaurants for the spenders —Arnold Ehrlich⟩

tarty \'tär-(ˌ)tē\ *adj* [²*tart*] (1918) : resembling or suggestive of a prostitute (as in clothing or manner)

¹task \'task\ *n* [ME *taske*, fr. ONF *tasque*, fr. ML *tasca* tax or service imposed by a feudal superior, fr. *taxare* to tax] (14c) **1 a** : a usu. assigned piece of work often to be finished within a certain time **b** : something hard or unpleasant that has to be done **c** : DUTY, FUNCTION **2** : subjection to adverse criticism : REPRIMAND — used in the expressions *to take, call,* or *bring to task*
syn TASK, DUTY, JOB, CHORE, STINT, ASSIGNMENT mean a piece of work to be done. TASK implies work imposed by a person in authority or an employer or by circumstance ⟨charged with a variety of *tasks*⟩. DUTY implies an obligation to perform or responsibility for performance ⟨the *duties* of a lifeguard⟩. JOB applies to a piece of work voluntarily performed; it may sometimes suggest difficulty or importance ⟨the *job* of turning the company around⟩. CHORE implies a minor routine activity necessary for maintaining a household or farm ⟨every child was assigned *chores*⟩. STINT implies a carefully allotted or measured quantity of assigned work or service ⟨a two-month *stint* as a reporter⟩. ASSIGNMENT implies a definite limited task assigned by one in authority ⟨a reporter's *assignment*⟩.

²task *vt* (15c) **1** *obs* : to impose a tax on **2** : to assign a task to **3** : to oppress with great labor ⟨~s his mind with petty details⟩

task force *n* (1941) : a temporary grouping under one leader for the purpose of accomplishing a definite objective

task·mas·ter \'task-ˌmas-tər\ *n* (1530) : one that imposes a task or burdens another with labor

task·mis·tress \-ˌmis-trəs\ *n* (1603) : a woman who is a taskmaster

Tas·ma·nian devil \(ˌ)taz-ˈmā-nē-ən-, -nyən-\ *n* (1867) : a powerful heavily built carnivorous terrestrial Tasmanian marsupial (*Sarcophilus harrisii*) that is about the size of a badger and has a chiefly black coat marked with white on the chest

Tasmanian wolf *n* (ca. 1890) : a somewhat doglike carnivorous marsupial (*Thylacinus cynocephalus*) that formerly inhabited Tasmania but is now considered extinct — called also *Tasmanian tiger*

tasse \'tas\ *n* [perh. fr. MF *tasse* purse, pouch] (ca. 1548) : one of a series of overlapping metal plates in a suit of armor that form a short skirt over the body below the waist — see ARMOR illustration

¹tas·sel \'ta-səl, *oftenest of corn* 'tä-, 'tȯ-\ *n* [ME, clasp, tassel, fr. MF, fr. (assumed) VL *tassellus*, alter. of L *taxillus* small die; akin to L *talus* anklebone, die] (14c) **1** : a dangling ornament made by laying parallel a bunch of cords or threads of even length and fastening them at one end **2** : something resembling a tassel; *esp* : the terminal male inflorescence of some plants esp. Indian corn

²tassel *vb* **-seled** *or* **-selled; -sel·ing** *or* **-sel·ling** \-s(ə-)liŋ\ *vt* (14c) : to adorn with tassels ~ *vi* : to put forth tassel inflorescences

¹taste \'tāst\ *vb* **tast·ed; tast·ing** [ME, to touch, test, taste, fr. MF *taster*, fr. (assumed) VL *taxitare*, freq. of L *taxare* to touch, feel — more at TAX] *vt* (14c) **1** : to become acquainted with by experience ⟨has *tasted* the frustration of defeat⟩ **2** : to ascertain the flavor of by taking a little into the mouth **3** : to eat or drink esp. in small quantities **4** : to perceive or recognize as if by the sense of taste **5** *archaic* : APPRECIATE, ENJOY ~ *vi* **1** : to eat or drink a little **2** : to test the flavor of something by taking a small part into the mouth **3** : to have perception, experience, or enjoyment : PARTAKE — often used with *of* **4** : to have a specific flavor ⟨the apple ~s sour⟩

²taste *n* (14c) **1** *obs* : TEST **2** *obs* : the act of tasting **b** : a small amount **c** : a small amount : BIT; *esp* : a sample of experience ⟨first ~ of success⟩ **3** : the one of the special senses that perceives and distinguishes the sweet, sour, bitter, or salty quality of a dissolved substance and is mediated by taste buds on the tongue **4** : the objective sweet, sour, bitter, or salty quality of a dissolved substance as perceived by the sense of taste **5 a** : a sensation obtained from a substance in the mouth that is typically produced by the stimulation of the sense of taste combined with those of touch and smell : FLAVOR **b** : the distinctive quality of an experience ⟨that gruesome scene left a bad ~ in my mouth⟩ **6** : individual preference : INCLINATION **7 a** : critical judgment, discernment, or appreciation **b** : manner or aesthetic quality indicative of such discernment or appreciation

taste bud *n* (1879) : an end organ mediating the sensation of taste and lying chiefly in the epithelium of the tongue

taste·ful \'tāst-fəl\ *adj* (1611) **1** : TASTY 1a **2** : having, exhibiting, or conforming to good taste — **taste·ful·ly** \-fə-lē\ *adv* — **taste·ful·ness** *n*

taste·less \'tāst-ləs\ *adj* (1603) **1 a** : having no taste : INSIPID ⟨~ vegetables⟩ **b** : arousing no interest : DULL ⟨the tale comes to a flat and ~ end —R. C. Carpenter⟩ **2** : not having or exhibiting good taste — **taste·less·ly** *adv* — **taste·less·ness** *n*

taste·mak·er \-ˌmā-kər\ *n* (1954) : one who sets the standards of what is currently popular or fashionable

tast·er \'tā-stər\ *n* (15c) **1** : one that tastes: as **a** : one that tests (as tea) for quality by tasting **b** : a person who is able to taste the chemical phenylthiocarbamide **2** : a device for tasting or sampling

tasty \'tā-stē\ *adj* **tast·i·er; -est** (1617) **1 a** : having a marked and appetizing flavor **b** : strikingly attractive or interesting ⟨a ~ bit of gossip⟩ **2** : TASTEFUL **syn** see PALATABLE — **tast·i·ly** \-stə-lē\ *adv* — **tast·i·ness** \-stē-nəs\ *n*

tat \'tat\ *vb* **tat·ted; tat·ting** [back-formation fr. *tatting*] *vi* (1882) : to work at tatting ~ *vt* : to make by tatting

ta·ta·mi \tä-'tä-mē, tä-\ *n, pl* **-mi** *or* **-mis** [Jp] (1614) : straw matting used as a floor covering in a Japanese home

Ta·tar \'tä-tər\ *n* [Per *Tātār*, of Turkic origin; akin to Turk *Tatar* Tatar] (1811) **1** : a member of any of a group of Turkic peoples found mainly in the Tatar Republic of Russia and parts of Siberia and central Asia **2** : any of the Turkic languages spoken by the Tatar peoples

ta·ter \'tā-tər\ *n* [by shortening & alter.] (1759) *dial* : POTATO

¹tat·ter \'ta-tər\ *vt* (14c) : to make ragged ~ *vi* : to become ragged

²tatter *n* [ME, of Scand origin; akin to ON *tǫturr* tatter; akin to OE *tætteca* rag, OHG *zotta* matted hair, tuft] (15c) **1** : a part torn and left hanging : SHRED **2** *pl* : tattered clothing : RAGS

¹tat·ter·de·ma·lion \ˌta-tər-di-'māl-yən, -'mal-, -'ma-lē-ən\ *n* [origin unknown] (1611) : a person dressed in ragged clothing : RAGAMUFFIN

²tatterdemalion *adj* (1614) **1** : ragged or disreputable in appearance **b** : being in a decayed state or condition : DILAPIDATED **2** : BEGGARLY, DISREPUTABLE

tat·tered \'ta-tərd\ *adj* (14c) **1** : wearing ragged clothes ⟨a ~ barefoot boy⟩ **2** : torn into shreds : RAGGED ⟨a ~ flag⟩ **3** : broken down : DILAPIDATED ⟨decaying houses along ~ paved streets —P. B. Martin⟩ **b** : being in a shattered condition : DISRUPTED ⟨led their ~ party to victory⟩

tat·ter·sall \'ta-tər-ˌsȯl, -səl\ *n* [*Tattersall's* horse market, London, England] (1891) **1** : a pattern of colored lines forming squares of solid background **2** : a fabric woven or printed in a tattersall pattern

tat·tie \'ta-tē\ *n* [by shortening & alter.] (1788) *Scot* : POTATO

tat·ting \'ta-tiŋ\ *n* [origin unknown] (1842) **1** : a delicate handmade lace formed usu. by looping and knotting with a single cotton thread and a small shuttle **2** : the act or process of making tatting

tatting 1

¹tat·tle \'ta-tᵊl\ *n* (ca. 1529) **1** : idle talk : CHATTER **2** : GOSSIP

²tattle *vb* **tat·tled; tat·tling** \'tat-liŋ, 'ta-tᵊl-iŋ\ [MD *tatelen* to tattle] *vi* (1547) **1** : CHATTER, PRATE **2** : to tell secrets : BLAB ~ *vt* : to utter or disclose in gossip or chatter

tat·tler \'tat-lər, 'ta-tᵊl-ər\ *n* (1550) **1** : TATTLETALE **2** : any of various slender long-legged shorebirds (as the willet, yellowlegs, and redshank) with a loud and frequent call

tat·tle·tale \'ta-tᵊl-ˌtāl\ *n* (1888) : one that tattles : INFORMER

¹tat·too \ta-'tü\ *n, pl* **tattoos** [alter. of earlier *taptoo*, fr. D *taptoe*, fr. the phrase *tap toe!* taps shut!] (ca. 1627) **1 a** : a rapid rhythmic rapping **b** : a call sounded shortly before taps as notice to go to quarters **b** : outdoor military exercise given by troops as evening entertainment

²tattoo *vt* (1780) : to beat or rap rhythmically on : drum on ~ *vi* : to give a series of rhythmic taps

³tattoo *vt* [Tahitian *tatau*, n., tattoo] (1769) **1** : to mark or color (the skin) with tattoos **2** : to mark the skin with (a tattoo) ⟨~ed a flag on his chest⟩ — **tat·too·er** *n* — **tat·too·ist** \-'tü-ist\ *n*

⁴tattoo *n, pl* **tattoos** (1777) **1** : the act of tattooing : the fact of being tattooed **2** : an indelible mark or figure fixed upon the body by insertion of pigment under the skin or by production of scars

tat·ty \'ta-tē\ *adj* **tat·ti·er; -est** [perh. akin to OE *tætteca* rag — more at TATTER] (1513) : rather worn, frayed, or dilapidated : SHABBY — **tat·ti·ness** \-nəs\ *n*

tau \'taů, 'tȯ\ *n* [ME *taw*, fr. L *tau*, fr. Gk, of Sem origin; akin to Heb *tāw* taw] (14c) **1** : the 19th letter of the Greek alphabet — see ALPHABET table **2** : a short-lived elementary particle of the lepton family that exists in positive and negative charge states and has a mass about 3500 times heavier than an electron — called also *tau particle*

tau cross *n* (15c) : a T-shaped cross sometimes having expanded ends and foot — see CROSS illustration

taught *past and past part of* TEACH

¹taunt \'tȯnt, 'tänt\ *n* (ca. 1529) : a sarcastic challenge or insult

²taunt *vt* [perh. fr. MF *tenter* to try, tempt — more at TEMPT] (1539) : to reproach or challenge in a mocking or insulting manner : jeer at **syn** see RIDICULE — **taunt·er** *n* — **taunt·ing·ly** \'tȯn-tiŋ-lē, 'tän-\ *adv*

taupe \'tōp\ *n* [F, lit., mole, fr. L *talpa*] (ca. 1909) : a brownish gray

Tau·re·an \'tȯr-ē-ən\ *n* (1911) : TAURUS 2b

¹tau·rine \'tȯ-ˌrīn\ *adj* [L *taurinus*, fr. *taurus* bull; akin to Gk *tauros* bull, MIr *tarb*] (1613) : of or relating to a bull : BOVINE

²tau·rine \'tȯ-ˌrēn\ *n* [ISV, fr. L *taurus*; fr. its having been discovered in ox bile] (1845) : a colorless crystalline cysteine derivative C₂H₇NO₃S of neutral reaction found in the juices of muscle esp. in invertebrates, nerve tissue, and bile

---

\ə\ abut \ᵊ\ kitten, F table \ər\ further \a\ ash \ā\ ace \ä\ mop, mar \aů\ out \ch\ chin \e\ bet \ē\ easy \g\ go \i\ hit \ī\ ice \j\ job \ŋ\ sing \ō\ go \ȯ\ law \ȯi\ boy \th\ thin \t͟h\ the \ü\ loot \ů\ foot \y\ yet \zh\ vision \á, k̲, ⁿ, œ, œ̄, ᵫ, ᵫ̄, ʸ\ *see* Guide to Pronunciation

tau·ro·cho·lic acid \ˌtȯr-ə-ˈkō-lik-, -ˈkä-\ *n* [L *taurus* + ISV *-o-* + *cholic (acid)*] (1857) : a deliquescent acid $C_{26}H_{45}NO_7S$ occurring as the sodium salt in the bile of the ox, humans, and various carnivores

Tau·rus \ˈtȯr-əs\ *n* [ME, fr. L (gen. *Tauri*, lit., bull] **1** : a zodiacal constellation that contains the Pleiades and Hyades and is represented pictorially by a bull's forequarters **2 a** : the 2d sign of the zodiac in astrology **b** : one born under the sign of Taurus — see ZODIAC table

¹taut \ˈtȯt\ *adj* [ME *tought*] (14c) **1 a** : having no give or slack : tightly drawn **b** : HIGH-STRUNG, TENSE ⟨~ nerves⟩ **2 a** : kept in proper order or condition ⟨a ~ ship⟩ **b** (1) : not loose or flabby (2) : marked by economy of structure and detail ⟨a ~ story⟩ — **taut·ly** *adv* — **taut·ness** *n*

²taut *vt* [origin unknown] (1721) *Scot* : MAT, TANGLE

taut- *or* **tauto-** *comb form* [Gk, fr. *tauto* the same, contr. of *to auto*] : same ⟨*tautomerism*⟩ ⟨*tautonym*⟩

taut·en \ˈtȯt-ᵊn\ *vb* **taut·ened; taut·en·ing** \ˈtȯt-niŋ, ᵊtȯt-ᵊn-iŋ\ *vt* (ca. 1814) : to make taut ~ *vi* : to become taut

tau·tog \ˈtȯ-ˌtȯg, -ˌtäg, tȯ-ˈ\ *n* [Narraganset *tautaūog*, pl.] (1643) : an edible fish (*Tautoga onitis*) of the wrasse family found along the Atlantic coast of the U.S. and adjacent Canada — called also *blackfish*

tau·to·log·i·cal \ˌtȯ-tᵊl-ˈä-ji-kəl\ *adj* (1620) : TAUTOLOGOUS — **tau·to·log·i·cal·ly** \-k(ə-)lē\ *adv*

tau·tol·o·gous \tȯ-ˈtä-lə-gəs\ *adj* [Gk *tautologos*, fr. *taut-* + *legein* to say — more at LEGEND] (1714) **1** : involving or containing rhetorical tautology : REDUNDANT **2** : true by virtue of its logical form alone — **tau·tol·o·gous·ly** *adv*

tau·tol·o·gy \tȯ-ˈtä-lə-jē\ *n, pl* **-gies** [LL *tautologia*, fr. Gk, fr. *tautologos*] (1574) **1 a** : needless repetition of an idea, statement, or word **b** : an instance of tautology **2** : a tautologous statement

tau·to·mer \ˈtȯ-tə-mər\ *n* [ISV, fr. *tautomeric*] (1903) : any of the forms of a tautomeric compound

tau·to·mer·ic \ˌtȯ-tə-ˈmer-ik\ *adj* [ISV] (ca. 1890) : of, relating to, or marked by tautomerism

tau·tom·er·ism \tȯ-ˈtä-mə-ˌri-zəm\ *n* (ca. 1890) : isomerism in which the isomers change into one another with great ease so that they ordinarily exist together in equilibrium

taut·o·nym \ˈtȯ-tə-ˌnim\ *n* (1899) : a taxonomic binomial in which the generic name and specific epithet are alike and which is common in zoology esp. to designate a typical form but is forbidden to botany under the International Code of Botanical Nomenclature — **tau·ton·y·my** \tȯ-ˈtä-nə-mē\ *n*

tav·ern \ˈta-vərn\ *n* [ME *taverne*, fr. OF, fr. L *taberna* hut, shop] (14c) **1** : an establishment where alcoholic beverages are sold to be drunk on the premises **2** : INN

ta·ver·na \tä-ˈver-nə\ *n* [NGk *taberna*, prob. fr. LGk, drinking establishment, fr. L *taberna*] (1914) : a café in Greece

tav·ern·er \ˈtav-ə(r)-nər\ *n* (14c) : one who keeps a tavern

¹taw \ˈtȯ\ *vt* [ME, to prepare for use, fr. OE *tawian*; akin to OHG *zawjan* to hasten, Goth *taujan* to do, make] (bef. 12c) : to dress (skins) usu. by a dry process (as with alum or salt)

²taw \ˈtäf, ˈtȯf, ˈtäv, ˈtȯv\ *n* [Heb *tāw*, lit., mark, cross] (1701) : the 23d letter of the Hebrew alphabet — see ALPHABET table

³taw *n* [origin unknown] (1709) **1 a** : a marble used as a shooter **b** : RINGTAW **2** : the line from which players shoot at marbles **3** : a square-dance partner

⁴taw *vi* (1863) : to shoot a marble

¹taw·dry \ˈtȯ-drē, ˈtä-\ *adj* **taw·dri·er; -est** [*tawdry lace* a tie of lace for the neck, fr. *St. Audrey* (St. Etheldreda) †679 queen of Northumbria] (1676) : cheap and gaudy in appearance or quality; *also* : IGNOBLE *syn* see GAUDY — **taw·dri·ly** \-drə-lē\ *adv* — **taw·dri·ness** \-drē-nəs\ *n*

²tawdry *n* (ca. 1680) : cheap showy finery

¹taw·ny \ˈtȯ-nē, ˈtä-nē\ *adj* **taw·ni·er; -est** [ME, fr. MF *tanné*, pp. of *tanner* to tan] (14c) **1** : of the color tawny **2** : of a warm sandy color like that of well-tanned skin ⟨the lion's ~ coat⟩ — **taw·ni·ness** *n*

²tawny *n, pl* **tawnies** (15c) : a brownish orange to light brown color

taw·pie \ˈtȯ-pē\ *n* [of Scand origin; akin to Norw *tāpe* simpleton] (1728) *chiefly Scot* : a foolish or awkward young person

tawse *also* **taws** \ˈtȯz\ *n pl but sing or pl in constr* [prob. fr. pl. of obs. *taw* tawed leather] (ca. 1585) *Brit* : a leather strap slit into strips at the end and used esp. for disciplining children

¹tax \ˈtaks\ *vt* [ME, to estimate, assess, tax, fr. OF *taxer*, fr. ML *taxare*, fr. L, to feel, estimate, censure, freq. of *tangere* to touch — more at TANGENT] (14c) **1** : to assess or determine judicially the amount of (costs in a court action) **2** : to levy a tax on **3** *obs* : to enter (a name) in a list ⟨there went out a decree . . . that all the world should be ~ed —Lk 2:1 (AV)⟩ **4** : CHARGE, ACCUSE ⟨~ed him with neglect of duty⟩; *also* : CENSURE **5** : to make onerous and rigorous demands on ⟨the job ~ed her strength⟩ — **tax·able** \ˈtak-sə-bəl\ *adj* — **tax·er** *n*

²tax *n, often attrib* (14c) **1 a** : a charge usu. of money imposed by authority on persons or property for public purposes **b** : a sum levied on members of an organization to defray expenses **2** : a heavy demand

tax- *or* **taxo-** *also* **taxi-** *comb form* [Gk *taxi-*, fr. *taxis*] : arrangement ⟨*taxeme*⟩ ⟨*taxidermy*⟩

taxa *pl of* TAXON

tax·a·tion \tak-ˈsā-shən\ *n* (14c) **1** : the action of taxing; *esp* : the imposition of taxes **2** : revenue obtained from taxes **3** : the amount assessed as a tax

tax base *n* (ca. 1943) : the wealth (as real estate or income) within a jurisdiction that is liable to taxation

tax·eme \ˈtak-ˌsēm\ *n* [*tax-*] (1933) : a minimum grammatical feature of selection, order, stress, pitch, or phonetic modification — **tax·e·mic** \tak-ˈsē-mik\ *adj*

tax–ex·empt \ˌtaks-ig-ˈzem(p)t\ *adj* (1923) **1** : exempted from a tax **2** : bearing interest that is free from federal or state income tax

¹taxi \ˈtak-sē\ *n, pl* **tax·is** \-sēz\ *also* **tax·ies** (ca. 1907) : TAXICAB; *also* : a similarly operated boat or aircraft

²taxi *vb* **tax·ied; taxi·ing** *or* **taxy·ing; tax·is** *or* **tax·ies** *vi* (1916) **1 a** *of an aircraft* : to go at low speed along the surface of the ground or water **b** : to operate an aircraft on the ground under its own power **2** : to ride in a taxicab ~ *vt* **1** : to transport by or as if by taxi **2** : to cause (an aircraft) to taxi

taxi·cab \ˈtak-sē-ˌkab\ *n* [*taximeter cab*] (ca. 1907) : an automobile that carries passengers for a fare usu. determined by the distance traveled

taxi dancer *n* (ca. 1927) : a girl employed by a dance hall, café, or cabaret to dance with patrons who pay a certain amount for each dance

taxi·der·my \ˈtak-sə-ˌdər-mē\ *n* [*tax-* + *derm-* + *²-y*] (1820) : the art of preparing, stuffing, and mounting the skins of animals and esp. vertebrates — **taxi·der·mic** \ˌtak-sə-ˈdər-mik\ *adj* — **taxi·der·mist** \ˈtak-sə-ˌdər-mist\ *n*

taxi·man \ˈtak-sē-mən\ *n* (1909) *chiefly Brit* : the operator of a taxi

taxi·me·ter \ˈtak-sē-ˌmē-tər\ *n* [F *taximètre*, modif. of G *Taxameter*, fr. ML *taxa* tax, charge (fr. *taxare* to tax) + G *-meter*] (1894) : an instrument for use in a hired vehicle (as a taxicab) for automatically showing the fare due

tax·ing \ˈtak-siŋ\ *adj* (1841) : ONEROUS, WEARING ⟨a ~ operatic role⟩ — **tax·ing·ly** \-siŋ-lē\ *adv*

tax·is \ˈtak-səs\ *n, pl* **tax·es** \-ˌsēz\ [Gk, lit., arrangement, order, fr. *tassein* to arrange] (1758) **1** : reflex translational or orientational movement by a freely motile and usu. simple organism in relation to a source of stimulation (as a light or a temperature or chemical gradient) **2** : a reflex reaction involving a taxis

-taxis *n comb form, pl* **-taxes** [NL, fr. Gk, fr. *taxis*] **1** : arrangement : ordering ⟨thermo*taxis*⟩ **2** : physiological taxis ⟨chemo*taxis*⟩

taxi stand *n* (1922) : a place where taxis may park while awaiting hire

taxi·way \ˈtak-sē-ˌwā\ *n* (ca. 1933) : a usu. paved strip for taxiing (as from the terminal to a runway) at an airport

tax·on \ˈtak-ˌsän\ *n, pl* **taxa** \-sə\ *also* **tax·ons** [NL, fr. ISV *taxonomy*] (1929) **1** : a taxonomic group or entity **2** : the name applied to a taxonomic group in a formal system of nomenclature

tax·on·o·my \tak-ˈsä-nə-mē\ *n* [F *taxonomie*, fr. *tax-* + *-nomie* -nomy] (ca. 1828) **1** : the study of the general principles of scientific classification : SYSTEMATICS **2** : CLASSIFICATION; *esp* : orderly classification of plants and animals according to their presumed natural relationships — **tax·o·nom·ic** \ˌtak-sə-ˈnä-mik\ *adj* — **tax·o·nom·i·cal·ly** \-mi-k(ə-)lē\ *adv* — **tax·on·o·mist** \tak-ˈsä-nə-mist\ *n*

tax·pay·er \ˈtaks-ˌpā-ər\ *n* (1816) : one that pays or is liable for a tax

tax·pay·ing \-ˌpā-iŋ\ *adj* (1832) : of, relating to, or subject to the paying of a tax

tax selling *n* (1963) : concerted selling of securities late in the year to establish gains and losses for income-tax purposes

tax shelter *n* (1952) : a strategy, investment, or tax code provision that reduces tax liability — **tax–shel·tered** \ˈtaks-ˌshel-tərd\ *adj*

tax stamp *n* (ca. 1929) : a stamp marked on or affixed to a taxable item as evidence that the tax has been paid

tax·us \ˈtak-səs\ *n, pl* **tax·us** \-səs\ [NL, genus comprising the yews, fr. L, yew] (ca. 1945) : YEW 1a

-taxy *n comb form* [Gk *-taxia*, fr. *taktos*, verbal of *tassein* to arrange] : -TAXIS ⟨epi*taxy*⟩

Tay·lor's series \ˈtā-lərz-\ *n* [Brook *Taylor* †1731 Eng. mathematician] (1842) : a power series that gives the expansion of a function $f(x)$ in the neighborhood of a point *a* provided that in the neighborhood the function is continuous, all its derivatives exist, and the series converges to the function in which case it has the form

$$f(x) = f(a) + \frac{f^{[1]}(a)}{1!}(x-a) + \frac{f^{[2]}(a)}{2!}(x-a)^2 + \ldots + \frac{f^{[n]}(a)}{n!}(x-a)^n + \ldots$$

where $f^{[n]}(a)$ is the derivative of nth order of $f(x)$ evaluated at *a* — called also *Taylor series*

Tay–Sachs disease \ˈtā-ˈsaks-\ *n* [Warren *Tay* †1927 Brit. physician & Bernard P. *Sachs* †1944 Am. neurologist] (1907) : a hereditary disorder of lipid metabolism typically affecting individuals of eastern European Jewish ancestry that is characterized by the accumulation of lipids esp. in nervous tissue due to a deficiency of hexosaminidase and causes death in early childhood — called also *Tay-Sachs*

taz·za \ˈtät-sə\ *n* [It, cup, fr. Ar *ṭassah*] (1824) : a shallow cup or vase on a pedestal

TB \ˌtē-ˈbē\ *n* [*TB* (abbr. for *tubercle bacillus*)] (1912) : TUBERCULOSIS

T–ball \ˈtē-ˌbȯl\ *n* [²tee] (1976) : baseball modified for youngsters in which the ball is batted from a tee rather than being pitched

T–bar \ˈtē-ˌbär\ *n* (1948) : a ski lift having a series of T-shaped bars each of which pulls two skiers — called also *T-bar lift*

T–bill \ˈtē-ˌbil\ *n* [Treasury] (1973) : a U.S. treasury note

T–bone \ˈtē-ˌbōn\ *n* (ca. 1916) : a small steak from the thin end of the short loin containing a T-shaped bone and a small piece of tenderloin; *also* : this bone — see BEEF illustration

TCDD \ˌtē-(ˌ)sē-(ˌ)dē-ˈdē\ *n* [tetra- + chlor- + dibenzo- (containing two benzene rings) + dioxin] (1971) : a carcinogenic dioxin $C_{12}H_4O_2Cl_4$ found esp. as a contaminant in 2,4,5-T

T cell *n* [*thymus-derived cell*] (1970) : any of several lymphocytes (as a helper T cell) that differentiate in the thymus, possess highly specific cell-surface antigen receptors, and include some that control the initiation or suppression of cell-mediated and humoral immunity (as by the regulation of T and B cell maturation and proliferation) and others that lyse antigen-bearing cells — called also *T lymphocyte;* compare B CELL

tchotch·ke \ˈchäch-kə, ˈtsäts-\ *n* [Yiddish *tshatshke* trinket, fr. obs. Pol *czaczko*] (1971) : KNICKKNACK, TRINKET

t distribution *n* (ca. 1957) : a probability density function that is used esp. in testing hypotheses concerning means of normal distributions whose standard deviations are unknown and that is the distribution of a random variable

$$t = \frac{u\sqrt{n}}{v}$$

where *u* and *v* are themselves independent random variables and *u* has a normal distribution with mean 0 and a standard deviation of 1 and v^2 has a chi-square distribution with *n* degrees of freedom — called also *student's t distribution*

tea \ˈtē\ *n* [Chin (Xiamen) *t'e*] (ca. 1655) **1 a** : a shrub (*Camellia sinensis* of the family Theaceae, the tea family) cultivated esp. in China, Japan, and the East Indies **b** : the leaves, leaf buds, and internodes of the tea plant prepared and cured for the market, classed according to method of manufacture into one set of types (as green tea, black tea, or oolong), and graded according to leaf size into another (as orange pekoe, pekoe, or souchong) **2** : an aromatic beverage prepared from tea leaves by infusion with boiling water **3** : any of various plants somewhat resembling tea in properties; *also* : an infusion of their leaves used medicinally or as a beverage **4 a** : refreshments usu. including tea with sandwiches, crackers, or cookies served in late afternoon **b** : a reception at which tea is served **5** *slang* : MARIJUANA — **tea·like** \-ˌlīk\ *adj*

tea bag *n* (1935) : a bag usu. of filter paper holding enough tea for an individual serving

tea ball *n* (1895) : a perforated metal ball that holds tea leaves and is used in brewing tea in a pot or cup

tea·ber·ry \ˈtē-ˌber-ē\ *n* [fr. the use of its leaves as a substitute for tea] (1818) : CHECKERBERRY

tea caddy *n* (1790) : CADDY

tea cake *n* (1824) **1** : a small flat cake usu. made with raisins **2** : COOKIE

tea cart *n* (1817) : TEA WAGON

teach \ˈtēch\ *vb* **taught** \ˈtȯt\; **teach·ing** [ME *techen* to show, instruct, fr. OE *tǣcan*; akin to OE *tācn* sign — more at TOKEN] *vt* (bef. 12c) **1 a** : to cause to know something ⟨*taught* them a trade⟩ **b** : to cause to know how ⟨is ∼*ing* me to drive⟩ **c** : to accustom to some action or attitude ⟨∼ students to think for themselves⟩ **d** : to cause to know the disagreeable consequences of some action ⟨I'll ∼ you to come home late⟩ **2** : to guide the studies of **3** : to impart the knowledge of ⟨∼ algebra⟩ **4 a** : to instruct by precept, example, or experience **b** : to make known and accepted ⟨experience ∼*es* us our limitations⟩ **5** : to conduct instruction regularly in ⟨∼ school⟩ ∼ *vi* : to provide instruction : act as a teacher *usage* see LEARN

syn TEACH, INSTRUCT, EDUCATE, TRAIN, DISCIPLINE, SCHOOL mean to cause to acquire knowledge or skill. TEACH applies to any manner of imparting information or skill so that others may learn ⟨*taught* us a lot about our planet⟩. INSTRUCT suggests methodical or formal teaching ⟨*instructs* raw recruits in military drill⟩. EDUCATE implies development of the mind ⟨more things than formal schooling serve to *educate* a person⟩. TRAIN stresses instruction and drill with a specific end in view ⟨*trained* foreign pilots to operate the new aircraft⟩. DISCIPLINE implies training in habits of order and precision ⟨a *disciplined* mind⟩. SCHOOL implies training or disciplining esp. in what is hard to master ⟨*schooled* the horse in five gaits⟩.

teach·able \ˈtē-chə-bəl\ *adj* (15c) **1 a** : capable of being taught **b** : apt and willing to learn **2** : favorable to teaching — **teach·able·ness** *n* — **teach·ably** \-blē\ *adv*

teach·er \ˈtē-chər\ *n* (14c) **1** : one that teaches; *esp* : one whose occupation is to instruct **2** : a Mormon ranking above a deacon in the Aaronic priesthood

teach·er·ly \-lē\ *adj* (ca. 1683) : resembling, characteristic of, or befitting a teacher

teachers college *n* (ca. 1911) : a college for the training of teachers usu. offering a full 4-year course and granting a bachelor's degree

teacher's pet *n* (1914) **1** : a pupil who has won his teacher's special favor **2** : one who has ingratiated himself with an authority

teach-in \ˈtēch-ˌin\ *n* (1965) : an extended meeting usu. held on a college campus for lectures, debates, and discussions to raise awareness of or express a position on a social or political issue

¹teaching *n* (13c) **1** : the act, practice, or profession of a teacher **2** : something taught; *esp* : DOCTRINE ⟨the ∼*s* of Confucius⟩

²teaching *adj* (1642) : of, relating to, used for, or engaged in teaching ⟨a ∼ aid⟩ ⟨the ∼ profession⟩ ⟨a ∼ assistant⟩

teaching hospital *n* (ca. 1951) : a hospital that is affiliated with a medical school and provides means for medical education

tea·cup \ˈtē-ˌkəp\ *n* (1700) : a small cup usu. with a handle used with a saucer for hot beverages — **teacupful** *n*

tea dance *n* (1885) : a dance held in the late afternoon

tea garden *n* (1802) **1** : a public garden where tea and light refreshments are served **2** : a tea plantation

tea gown *n* (1878) : an afternoon gown of fine materials in graceful flowing lines worn esp. for afternoon entertaining at home

tea·house \ˈtē-ˌhau̇s\ *n* (1689) : a public house or restaurant where tea and light refreshments are sold

teak \ˈtēk\ *n* [Pg *teca*, fr. Malayalam *tēkka*] (1698) **1** : a tall East Indian timber tree (*Tectona grandis*) of the vervain family **2** : the hard yellowish brown wood of teak used esp. for furniture and shipbuilding

tea·ket·tle \ˈtē-ˌket-ᵊl\ *n* (1705) : a covered kettle with a handle and spout for boiling water

teak·wood \ˈtēk-ˌwu̇d\ *n* (1783) : TEAK 2

teal \ˈtē(ə)l\ *n, pl* **teal** *or* **teals** [ME *tele*; akin to MD *teling* teal] (14c) **1** : any of various widely distributed small short-necked dabblers (genus *Anas*) — compare GREEN-WINGED TEAL **2** : TEAL BLUE

teal blue *n* (1938) : a dark greenish blue

¹team \ˈtēm\ *n* [ME *teme*, fr. OE *tēam* offspring, lineage, group of draft animals; akin to OHG *zoum* rein, OE *tēon* to draw, pull — more at TOW] (bef. 12c) **1 a** : two or more draft animals harnessed to the same vehicle or implement; *also* : these with their harness and attached vehicle **b** : a draft animal often with harness and vehicle **2** *obs* : LINEAGE, RACE **3** : a group of animals: as **a** : a brood esp. of young pigs or ducks **b** : a matched group of animals for exhibition **4** : a number of persons associated together in work or activity: as **a** : a group on one side (as in football or a debate) **b** : CREW, GANG

²team *vt* (1552) **1** : to yoke or join in a team; *also* : to put together in a coordinated ensemble **2** : to convey or haul with a team ∼ *vi* **1** : to drive a team or motortruck **2** : to form a team or association : COLLABORATE ⟨∼*ed* up to write a book⟩

³team *adj* (1886) : of or performed by a team ⟨a ∼ effort⟩; *also* : marked by devotion to teamwork rather than individual achievement ⟨a ∼ player⟩

team foul *n* (1966) : one of a designated number of personal fouls the players on a basketball team may commit during a given period of play before the opposing team begins receiving bonus free throws

team handball *n* (1970) : a game developed from soccer which is played between two teams of seven players each and in which the ball is thrown, caught, and dribbled with the hands

team·mate \ˈtēm-ˌmāt\ *n* (1915) : a fellow member of a team

team·ster \ˈtēm(p)-stər\ *n* (1777) : one who drives a team or motortruck esp. as an occupation

team·work \ˈtēm-ˌwərk\ *n* (ca. 1828) : work done by several associates with each doing a part but all subordinating personal prominence to the efficiency of the whole

tea party *n* (1778) **1** : an afternoon social gathering at which tea is served **2** [fr. the Boston Tea Party, name applied to the occasion in 1773 when a shipment of tea was thrown into Boston harbor in protest against the tax on imports]: an exciting disturbance or proceeding

tea·pot \ˈtē-ˌpät\ *n* (1705) : a vessel with a spout and a handle in which tea is brewed and from which it is served

tea·poy \ˈtē-ˌpȯi\ *n* [Hindi *tipāī*] (1828) **1** : a 3-legged ornamental stand **2** [influenced by *tea*]: a stand or table containing a tea chest or caddy and used for supporting a tea set; *also* : TEA CADDY

¹tear \ˈtir\ *n* [ME, fr. OE *tæhher, tēar*; akin to OHG *zahar* tear, Gk *dakry*] (bef. 12c) **1 a** : a drop of clear saline fluid secreted by the lacrimal gland and diffused between the eye and eyelids to moisten the parts and facilitate their motion **b** *pl* : a secretion of profuse tears that overflow the eyelids and dampen the face **2** : a transparent drop of fluid or hardened fluid matter (as resin) **3** *pl* : an act of weeping or grieving ⟨broke into ∼*s*⟩ — **tear·less** *adj*

²tear *vi* (bef. 12c) : to fill with tears : shed tears ⟨eyes ∼*ing* in the November wind —Saul Bellow⟩

³tear \ˈtar, ˈter\ *vb* **tore** \ˈtōr, ˈtȯr\; **torn** \ˈtōrn, ˈtȯrn\; **tear·ing** [ME *teren*; akin to OHG *zeran* to destroy, Gk *derein* to skin, Skt *dr̥ṇāti* he bursts, tears] *vt* (bef. 12c) **1 a** : to separate parts of or pull apart by force : REND **b** : to wound by or as if by tearing : LACERATE ⟨∼ the skin⟩ **2** : to divide or disrupt by the pull of contrary forces ⟨a mind *torn* with doubts⟩ **3 a** : to remove by force : WRENCH — often used with *off* ⟨∼ a cover off a box⟩ **b** : to remove as if by wrenching ⟨∼ your thoughts away from the scene⟩ **4** : to make or effect by or as if by tearing ⟨∼ a hole in the wall⟩ ∼ *vi* **1** : to separate on being pulled : REND ⟨this cloth ∼*s* easily⟩ **2 a** : to move or act with violence, haste, or force ⟨went ∼*ing* down the street⟩ **b** : to smash or penetrate something with violent force ⟨the bullet *tore* through his leg⟩ — **tear·able** \ˈtar-ə-bəl, ˈter-\ *adj* — **tear·er** *n* — **tear at** : to cause anguish to : DISTRESS ⟨her grief *tore at* his heart⟩ — **tear into** : to attack without restraint or caution — **tear it** : to cause frustration, defeat, or an end to plans or hopes ⟨that *tears it*⟩ — **tear one's hair** : to pull one's hair as an expression of grief, rage, frustration, desperation, or anxiety

syn TEAR, RIP, REND, SPLIT, CLEAVE, RIVE mean to separate forcibly. TEAR implies pulling apart by force and leaving jagged edges ⟨*tear* up the letter⟩. RIP implies a pulling apart in one rapid uninterrupted motion often along a line or joint ⟨*ripped* the shirt on a nail⟩. REND implies very violent or ruthless severing or sundering ⟨an angry mob *rent* the prisoner's clothes⟩. SPLIT implies a cutting or breaking apart in a continuous, straight, and usu. lengthwise direction or in the direction of grain or layers ⟨*split* logs for firewood⟩. CLEAVE implies very forceful splitting or cutting with a blow ⟨a bolt of lightning *cleaved* the giant oak⟩. RIVE occurs most often in figurative use ⟨a political party *riven* by conflict⟩.

⁴tear \ˈtar, ˈter\ *n* (1611) **1 a** : damage from being torn; *esp* : a hole or flaw made by tearing **b** : the act of tearing **2 a** : a tearing pace : HURRY **b** : SPREE ⟨go on a ∼⟩ **c** : a run of unusual success ⟨the team was on a ∼⟩

tear·away \ˈtar-ə-ˌwā, ˈter-\ *n* (1950) *Brit* : a rebellious and unruly or reckless young person

tear away *vt* (ca. 1699) : to remove (as oneself) reluctantly

tear·down \ˈtar-ˌdau̇n, ˈter-\ *n* (1926) : the act or process of disassembling

tear down *vt* (1614) **1 a** : to cause to decompose or disintegrate **b** : VILIFY, DENIGRATE **2** : to take apart : DISASSEMBLE

tear·drop \ˈtir-ˌdräp\ *n* (1789) **1** : ¹TEAR 1a **2** : something shaped like a dropping tear; *specif* : a pendent gem (as on an earring)

tear·ful \ˈtir-fəl\ *adj* (ca. 1586) **1** : flowing with or accompanied by tears ⟨∼ entreaties⟩ **2** : causing tears : TEARY — **tear·ful·ly** \-fə-lē\ *adv* — **tear·ful·ness** *n*

tear·gas \-ˌgas\ *vt* (1946) : to use tear gas on

tear gas *n* (1917) : a solid, liquid, or gaseous substance that on dispersion in the atmosphere blinds the eyes with tears and is used chiefly in dispelling mobs

tear·ing \ˈtar-iŋ, ˈter-\ *adj* (1606) **1** : causing continued or repeated pain or distress **2** : HASTY, VIOLENT **3** *chiefly Brit* : SPLENDID

tear·jerk·er \ˈtir-ˌjər-kər\ *n* (1912) : an extravagantly pathetic story, song, play, film, or broadcast — **tear·jerk·ing** \-kiŋ\ *adj*

tea·room \ˈtē-ˌrüm, -ˌru̇m\ *n* (1778) : a small restaurant or café with service and decor designed primarily for a female clientele

tea rose *n* (1850) : a garden bush rose (*Rosa odorata*) of Chinese origin that includes several cultivars and is valued esp. for its abundant large usu. tea-scented blossoms — compare HYBRID TEA ROSE

tear sheet *n* (ca. 1924) : a sheet torn from a publication

tear·stain \ˈtir-ˌstān\ *n* (1922) : a spot or streak left by tears — **tear·stained** \-ˌstānd\ *adj*

tear up *vt* (1699) : to damage, remove, or effect an opening in ⟨*tore up* the street to lay a new water main⟩

teary \ˈtir-ē\ *adj* **tear·i·er; -est** (14c) **1 a** : wet or stained with tears : TEARFUL **b** : consisting of tears or drops resembling tears **2** : causing tears : PATHETIC ⟨a ∼ story⟩

¹tease \ˈtēz\ *vt* **teased; teas·ing** [ME *tesen*, fr. OE *tǣsan*; akin to OHG *zeisan* to tease] (bef. 12c) **1 a** : to disentangle and lay parallel by combing or carding ⟨∼ wool⟩ **b** : TEASEL **2** : to tear in pieces; *esp* : to shred (a tissue or specimen) for microscopic examination **3 a** : to

teal 1

\ə\ abut \ᵊ\ kitten, F table \ər\ further \a\ ash \ā\ ace \ä\ mop, mar \au̇\ out \ch\ chin \e\ bet \ē\ easy \g\ go \i\ hit \ī\ ice \j\ job \ŋ\ sing \ō\ go \ȯ\ law \ȯi\ boy \th\ thin \t͟h\ the \ü\ loot \u̇\ foot \y\ yet \zh\ vision \ä, k, ⁿ, œ, ǣ, ūe, ᵊ\ *see* Guide to Pronunciation disturb or annoy by persistent irritating or provoking esp. in a petty or mischievous way **b** : to annoy with petty persistent requests : PESTER; *also* : to obtain by repeated coaxing **c** : to persuade to acquiesce esp. by persistent small efforts : COAX **d** : to manipulate or influence as if by teasing **4** : to comb (hair) by taking hold of a strand and pushing the short hairs toward the scalp with the comb **5** : to tantalize esp. by arousing desire or curiosity without intending to satisfy it *syn* see WORRY — **teas·ing·ly** \'tē-ziŋ-lē\ *adv*

²tease *n* (1693) **1** : the act of teasing : the state of being teased **2** : one that teases

¹tea·sel \'tē-zəl\ *n* [ME *tesel*, fr. OE *tǣsel*; akin to OE *tǣsan* to tease] (bef. 12c) **1 a** : an Old World prickly herb (*Dipsacus fullonum* of the family Dipsacaceae, the teasel family) with flower heads that are covered with stiff hooked bracts and are used in the woolen industry — called also *fuller's teasel* **b** : a plant of the same genus as the teasel **2 a** : a flower head of the fuller's teasel used when dried to raise a nap on woolen cloth **b** : a wire substitute for the teasel

²teasel *vt* **tea·seled** *or* **tea·selled; tea·sel·ing** *or* **tea·sel·ling** \'tēz-liŋ, 'tē-zə-\ (1543) : to nap (cloth) with teasels

tease out *vt* (1828) : to obtain by or as if by disentangling or freeing with a pointed instrument

teas·er \'tē-zər\ *n* (1659) **1** : one that teases **2** : an advertising or promotional device intended to arouse interest or curiosity esp. in something to follow

tea service *n* (1809) : TEA SET

tea set *n* (1849) : a matching set of metalware or china (as a teapot, sugar bowl, creamer, and often plates, cups, and saucers) for serving tea and sometimes coffee at table

tea shop *n* (1856) *chiefly Brit* : a small restaurant or café : TEAROOM

tea·spoon \'tē-,spün, -'spün\ *n* (1686) **1** : a small spoon that is used esp. for eating soft foods and stirring beverages and that holds one third of a tablespoon **2** : a unit of measure esp. in cookery equal to ⅙ fluid ounces or ⅓ tablespoon (5 milliliters)

tea·spoon·ful \-,fúl\ *n, pl* **teaspoonfuls** \-,fúlz\ *also* **tea·spoons·ful** \-,spünz-,fúl, -'spünz-\ (1731) **1** : as much as a teaspoon can hold **2** : TEASPOON 2

teat \'tit, 'tēt\ *n* [ME *tete*, fr. OF, of Gmc origin; akin to OE *tit* teat, MHG *zitze*] (13c) **1** : the protuberance through which milk is drawn from an udder or breast : NIPPLE **2** : a small projection or a nib (as on a mechanical part) — **teat·ed** \'ti-təd, 'tē-\ *adj*

tea table *n* (1688) : a table used or spread for tea; *specif* : a small table for serving afternoon tea

tea-time \'tē-,tīm\ *n* (1741) : the customary time for tea : late afternoon or early evening

tea towel *n* (1871) : a cloth for drying dishes

tea tray *n* (1773) : a tray that accommodates a tea set

tea wagon *n* (1921) : a small table on wheels used in serving tea

Te·bet \tā-'vät, -'väth, 'tä-,ves\ *n* [Heb *Ṭēbhēth*] (14c) : the 4th month of the civil year or the 10th month of the ecclesiastical year in the Jewish calendar — see MONTH table

teched \'techt\ *adj* [alter. of *touched*] (1921) : mentally unbalanced

tech·ie \'te-kē\ *n* [by shortening & alter.] (1982) : TECHNICIAN 1

tech·ne·tium \tek-'nē-sh(ē-)əm\ *n* [NL, fr. Gk *technētos* artificial, fr. *technasthai* to devise by art, fr. *technē*] (ca. 1946) : a metallic element obtained by bombarding molybdenum with deuterons or neutrons and in the fission of uranium — see ELEMENT table

tech·ne·tron·ic \,tek-nə-'trä-nik\ *adj* [*technological* + *electronic*] (1967) : shaped or influenced by the changes wrought by advances in technology and communications ⟨our modern ∼ society⟩

tech·nic \'tek-nik, *for 1 also* tek-'nēk\ *n* (1855) **1** : TECHNIQUE 1 **2** *pl but sing or pl in constr* : TECHNOLOGY 1a

tech·ni·cal \'tek-ni-kəl\ *adj* [Gk *technikos* of art, skillful, fr. *technē* art, craft, skill; akin to Gk *tektōn* builder, carpenter, L *texere* to weave, Skt *takṣati* he fashions] (1617) **1 a** : having special and usu. practical knowledge esp. of a mechanical or scientific subject ⟨a ∼ consultant⟩ **b** : marked by or characteristic of specialization ⟨∼ language⟩ **2 a** : of or relating to a particular subject **b** : of or relating to a practical subject organized on scientific principles ⟨a ∼ school⟩ **c** : TECHNOLOGICAL 1 **3 a** : based on or marked by a strict or legal interpretation **b** : LEGAL 6 **4** : of or relating to technique **5** : of, relating to, or produced by ordinary commercial processes without being subjected to special purification ⟨∼ sulfuric acid⟩ **6** : relating to or caused by the functioning of the market as a discrete mechanism not influenced by macroeconomic factors ⟨∼ rally⟩ ⟨∼ analysis⟩ — **tech·ni·cal·ly** \-k(ə-)lē\ *adv*

technical foul *n* (ca. 1929) : a foul (as in basketball) that involves no physical contact with an opponent and that usu. is incurred by unsportsmanlike conduct — called also *technical*; compare PERSONAL FOUL

tech·ni·cal·i·ty \,tek-nə-'ka-lə-tē\ *n, pl* **-ties** (1814) **1** : something technical; *esp* : a detail meaningful only to a specialist ⟨a legal ∼⟩ **2** : the quality or state of being technical

tech·ni·cal·ize \'tek-ni-kə-,līz\ *vt* **-ized; -iz·ing** (1852) : to give a technical slant to — **tech·ni·cal·i·za·tion** \,tek-ni-kə-lə-'zā-shən\ *n*

technical knockout *n* (1921) : the termination of a boxing match when a boxer is unable or is declared by the referee to be unable (as because of injuries) to continue the fight

technical sergeant *n* (ca. 1956) : a noncommissioned officer in the air force ranking above a staff sergeant and below a master sergeant

tech·ni·cian \tek-'ni-shən\ *n* (1833) **1** : a specialist in the technical details of a subject or occupation ⟨a computer ∼⟩ **2** : one who has acquired the technique of an art or other area of specialization ⟨a superb ∼ and a musician of integrity —Irving Kolodin⟩

Tech·ni·col·or \'tek-ni-,kə-lər\ *trademark* — used for a process of color cinematography

tech·nique \tek-'nēk\ *n* [F, fr. *technique* technical, fr. Gk *technikos*] (1817) **1** : the manner in which technical details are treated (as by a writer) or basic physical movements are used (as by a dancer); *also* : ability to treat such details or use such movements ⟨good piano ∼⟩ **2 a** : a body of technical methods (as in a craft or in scientific research) **b** : a method of accomplishing a desired aim

techno- *comb form* [*technology*] : technical : technological ⟨*technoc*racy⟩

tech·no·bab·ble \'tek-nə-,ba-bəl\ *n* (1981) : technical jargon

tech·noc·ra·cy \tek-'nä-krə-sē\ *n* (ca. 1919) : government by technicians; *specif* : management of society by technical experts

tech·no·crat \'tek-nə-,krat\ *n* (1932) **1** : an adherent of technocracy **2** : a technical expert; *esp* : one exercising managerial authority

tech·no·crat·ic \,tek-nə-'kra-tik\ *adj* (1932) : of, relating to, or suggestive of a technocrat or a technocracy

tech·no·log·i·cal \,tek-nə-'lä-ji-kəl\ *also* **tech·no·log·ic** \-'lä-jik\ *adj* (1800) **1** : of, relating to, or characterized by technology ⟨∼ advances⟩ **2** : resulting from improvements in technical processes that increase productivity of machines and eliminates manual operations or operations done by older machines ⟨∼ unemployment⟩ — **tech·no·log·i·cal·ly** \-ji-k(ə-)lē\ *adv*

tech·nol·o·gize \tek-'nä-lə-,jīz\ *vt* **-gized; -giz·ing** (1954) : to affect or alter by technology

tech·nol·o·gy \-jē\ *n, pl* **-gies** [Gk *technologia* systematic treatment of an art, fr. *technē* art, skill + -*o-* + -*logia* -logy] (1859) **1 a** : the practical application of knowledge esp. in a particular area : ENGINEERING 2 ⟨medical ∼⟩ **b** : a capability given by the practical application of knowledge ⟨a car's fuel-saving ∼⟩ **2** : a manner of accomplishing a task esp. using technical processes, methods, or knowledge ⟨new *technologies* for information storage⟩ **3** : the specialized aspects of a particular field of endeavor ⟨educational ∼⟩ — **tech·nol·o·gist** \-jist\ *n*

tech·no·phile \'tek-nə-,fīl\ *n* (1968) : an enthusiast of technology

tech·no·pho·bia \,tek-nə-'fō-bē-ə\ *n* (1965) : fear or dislike of advanced technology or complex devices and esp. computers — **tech·no·phobe** \'tek-nə-,fōb\ *n* — **tech·no·pho·bic** \,tek-nə-'fō-bik\ *adj*

tech·no·pop \'tek-nə-,(,)nō-,päp\ *n* (1980) : pop music featuring extensive use of synthesizers

tech·no·struc·ture \'tek-nō-,strək-chər\ *n* (1967) : the network of professionally skilled managers (as scientists, engineers, and administrators) that tends to control the economy both within and beyond individual corporate groups

tech·no·thrill·er \'tek-nō-,thri-lər, -nə-\ *n* (1989) : a thriller whose plot relies on modern technology

tec·ton·ic \tek-'tä-nik\ *adj* [LL *tectonicus*, fr. Gk *tektonikos* of a builder, fr. *tektōn* builder — more at TECHNICAL] (1894) : of or relating to tectonics — **tec·ton·i·cal·ly** \-ni-k(ə-)lē\ *adv*

tec·ton·ics \-niks\ *n pl but sing or pl in constr* (1899) **1** : geological structural features as a whole **2 a** : a branch of geology concerned with the structure of the crust of a planet (as earth) or moon and esp. with the formation of folds and faults in it **b** : DIASTROPHISM

tec·to·nism \'tek-tə-,ni-zəm\ *n* [ISV] (1948) : DIASTROPHISM

tec·tum \'tek-təm\ *n, pl* **tec·ta** \-tə\ [NL, fr. L, roof, dwelling, fr. neut. of *tectus*, pp. of *tegere* to cover — more at THATCH] (ca. 1905) : a bodily structure resembling or serving as a roof; *esp* : the dorsal part of the midbrain — **tec·tal** \'tek-t⁷l\ *adj*

ted \'ted\ *vt* **ted·ded; ted·ding** [(assumed) ME *tedden*, prob. fr. ON *tethja* to manure; akin to ON *tath* spread dung, OHG *zetten* to spread] (15c) : to spread or turn from the swath and scatter (as new-mown grass) for drying

ted·der \'te-dər\ *n* (15c) : one that teds; *specif* : a machine for stirring and spreading hay to hasten drying and curing

ted·dy \'te-dē\ *n, pl* **teddies** [origin unknown] (1924) : CHEMISE 1

ted·dy bear \'te-dē-,\ *n* [*Teddy*, nickname of Theodore Roosevelt; fr. a cartoon depicting the president sparing the life of a bear cub while hunting] (1906) : a stuffed toy bear

teddy boy *n* [*Teddy*, nickname for Edward] (1954) : a young British hoodlum affecting Edwardian dress

Te De·um \,tā-'dā-əm, ,tē-'dē-\ *n, pl* **Te Deums** [ME, fr. LL *te deum laudamus* thee, God, we praise; fr. the opening words of the hymn] (bef. 12c) : a liturgical Christian hymn of praise to God

te·dious \'tē-dē-əs, 'tē-jəs\ *adj* [ME, fr. LL *taediosus*, fr. L *taedium*] (15c) : tiresome because of length or dullness : BORING ⟨a ∼ public ceremony⟩ — **te·dious·ly** *adv* — **te·dious·ness** *n*

te·di·um \'tē-dē-əm\ *n* [L *taedium* disgust, irksomeness, fr. *taedēre* to disgust, weary] (1662) **1** : the quality or state of being tedious : TEDIOUSNESS; *also* : BOREDOM **2** : a tedious period of time ⟨long ∼s of strained anxiety —H. G. Wells⟩

¹tee \'tē\ *n* [ME] (15c) **1** : the letter *t* **2** : something shaped like a capital T **3** : a mark aimed at in various games (as curling) — **to a tee** : EXACTLY, PRECISELY

²tee *n* [origin unknown] (1673) **1 a** : a small mound or a peg on which a golf ball is placed before being struck at the beginning of play on a hole **b** : a device for holding a football in position for kicking **2** : the area from which a golf ball is struck at the beginning of play on a hole

³tee *vt* **teed; tee·ing** (1673) : to place (a ball) on a tee — often used with *up*

teed off *adj* [prob. fr. *tee off* (on)] (1951) : ANGRY, ANNOYED

¹teem \'tēm\ *vb* [ME *temen*, fr. OE *tīman, tǣman*; akin to OE *tēam* offspring — more at TEAM] *vt* (bef. 12c) *archaic* : BRING FORTH : give birth to : PRODUCE ∼ *vi* **1** *obs* : to become pregnant : CONCEIVE **2 a** : to become filled to overflowing : ABOUND **b** : to be present in large quantity — **teem·ing·ly** \-lē\ *adv* — **teem·ing·ness** *n*

²teem *vt* [ME *temen*, fr. ON *tœma*; akin to OE *tōm* empty] (14c) : EMPTY, POUR ⟨∼ molten metal into a mold⟩

¹teen \'tēn\ *n* [ME *tene*, fr. OE *tēona* injury, grief; akin to ON *tjōn* loss, damage] (14c) *archaic* : MISERY, AFFLICTION

²teen *n* (1818) : TEENAGER — **teen** *adj*

teen-age \'tē-,nāj\ *or* **teen-aged** \-,nājd\ *adj* (1921) : of, being, or relating to people in their teens — **teen·ag·er** \-,nā-jər\ *n*

teen·er \'tē-nər\ *n* (1894) : a teenage person

teens \'tēnz\ *n pl* [-teen (as in *thirteen*)] (1604) : the numbers 13 to 19 inclusive; *specif* : the years 13 to 19 in a lifetime or century

teen·sy \'tēn(t)-sē\ *adj* **teen·si·er; -est** [baby-talk alter. of *teeny*] (1899) : TINY

teen·sy–ween·sy \,tēn(t)-sē-'wēn(t)-sē\ *adj* [baby-talk alter. of *teeny-weeny*] (ca. 1906) : TINY

tee·ny \'tē-nē\ *adj* **tee·ni·er; -est** [by alter.] (1825) : TINY

teeny·bop \'tē-nē-,bäp\ *adj* [back-formation fr. *teenybopper*] (1967) : of, relating to, or being a teenybopper

teeny·bop·per \-,bä-pər\ *n* [*teeny* teenager + -*bopper*, perh. fr. *⁴bop*] (1966) **1** : a teenage girl **2** : a young teenager who is enthusiastically devoted to pop music and to current fads

tee·ny–wee·ny \ˌtē-nē-ˈwē-nē\ adj [teeny + weeny] (ca. 1879) : TINY
tee off vi (1895) **1** : to drive from a tee **2** : BEGIN, START **3** : to hit hard **4** : to make an angry denunciation — often used with on
tee·pee var of TEPEE
tee shirt var of T-SHIRT
¹tee·ter \ˈtē-tər\ vi [ME titeren to totter, reel; akin to OHG zittarōn to shiver] (1844) **1 a** : to move unsteadily : WOBBLE **b** : WAVER, VACILLATE ⟨~ed on the brink of bankruptcy⟩ **2** : SEESAW
²teeter n (1863) : SEESAW 2b
tee·ter·board \-ˌbȯrd, -ˌbȯrd\ n (1855) **1** : SEESAW 2b **2** : a board placed on a raised support so that a person standing on one end of the board is thrown into the air if another jumps on the opposite end
tee·ter–tot·ter \ˈtē-tər-ˌtä-tər\ n (ca. 1905) : SEESAW 2b
teeth pl of TOOTH
teethe \ˈtēth\ vi teethed; teeth·ing [back-formation fr. teething] (15c) : to cut one's teeth : grow teeth
teeth·er \ˈtē-thər\ n (1946) : an object (as a teething ring) designed for a baby to bite on during teething
teeth·ing \ˈtē-thiŋ\ n [teeth] (1732) **1** : the first growth of teeth **2** : the phenomena accompanying growth of teeth through the gums
teething ring n (1872) : a usu. rubber or plastic ring for a teething infant to bite on
teeth·ridge \ˈtēth-ˌrij\ n (1928) : the inner surface of the gums of the upper front teeth
tee·to·tal \ˈtē-ˈtō-t°l, -ˌtō-\ adj [total + total (abstinence)] (1834) **1** : of, relating to, or practicing teetotalism **2** : TOTAL, COMPLETE — tee·to·tal·ly \-ˈtō-t°l-ē\ adv
tee·to·tal·er or **tee·to·tal·ler** \-ˈtō-t°l-ər\ n (1834) : one who practices or advocates teetotalism
tee·to·tal·ism \-t°l-ˌi-zəm\ n (1834) : the principle or practice of complete abstinence from alcoholic drinks — **tee·to·tal·ist** \-t°l-ist\ n
tee·to·tum \ˈtē-ˈtō-təm\ n [¹tee + L totum all, fr. neut. of totus whole; fr. the letter T inscribed on one side as an abbr. of totum (take) all] (1720) : a small top usu. inscribed with letters and used in put-and-take
teff \ˈtef\ n [Amharic ṭef] (1790) : an economically important African cereal grass (Eragrostis tef syn. E. abyssinica) that is grown for its grain which yields a white flour and as a forage and hay crop
te·fil·lin \tē-ˈfi-lən also -ˌlēm\ n pl but sometimes sing in constr [LHeb tĕphilin, fr. Aram. attachments] (1613) : the phylacteries worn by Jews
Tef·lon \ˈte-ˌflän\ trademark — used for synthetic fluorine-containing resins used esp. for molding articles and for coatings to prevent sticking (as of food in cookware)
teg·men \ˈteg-mən\ n, pl teg·mi·na \-mə-nə\ [NL tegmin-, tegmen, fr. L, covering, fr. tegere to cover — more at THATCH] (1807) : a superficial layer or cover usu. of a plant or animal part
teg·men·tal \teg-ˈmen-t°l\ adj (ca. 1890) : of, relating to, or associated with an integument or a tegmentum
teg·men·tum \teg-ˈmen-təm\ n, pl -men·ta \-ˈmen-tə\ [NL, fr. L tegumentum, tegmentum, covering, fr. tegere] (1832) : an anatomical covering : TEGMEN; esp : the part of the ventral midbrain above the substantia nigra formed of longitudinal white fibers with arched transverse fibers and gray matter
teg·u·ment \ˈte-gyə-mənt\ n [ME, fr. L tegumentum] (15c) : INTEGUMENT
te·iid \ˈtē-əd, ˈtī-\ n [NL Teiidae, fr. Teius, genus of lizards, fr. Pg teiu, a lizard, fr. Tupi tejú] (1956) : any of a family (Teiidae) of mostly tropical American lizards (as the race runner) with a flat elongate scaly forked tongue — **teiid** adj
tek·tite \ˈtek-ˌtīt\ n [ISV, fr. Gk tēktos molten, fr. tēkein to melt — more at THAW] (1909) : a glassy body of probably meteoritic origin and of rounded but indefinite shape — **tek·tit·ic** \tek-ˈti-tik\ adj
tel- or **telo-** comb form [ISV, fr. Gk telos — more at TELOS] : end ⟨tel-angiectasia⟩
tel·a·mon \ˈte-lə-ˌmän\ n, pl tel·a·mo·nes \ˌte-lə-ˈmō-(ˌ)nēz\ [L, fr. Gk telamōn bearer, supporter; akin to Gk tlēnai to bear — more at TOLERATE] (ca. 1706) : ATLAS 5
tel·an·gi·ec·ta·sis \-ˈek-tə-səs\ n, pl -ta·sias or -ta·ses \-tə-ˌsēz\ [NL, fr. tel- + angi- + ectasia, ectasis (as in atelectasis)] (1831) : an abnormal dilatation of capillary vessels and arterioles that often forms an angioma — **tel·an·gi·ec·tat·ic** \-ˌek-ˈta-tik\ adj
tele \ˈte-lē\ n (1936) Brit : TELEVISION
tele- or **tel-** comb form [NL, fr. Gk tēle, tēl-, fr. tēle far off — more at PALE-] **1** : distant : at a distance ⟨over a distance (telegram)⟩ **2 a** : telegraph ⟨teletypewriter⟩ **b** : television ⟨telecast⟩ **c** : telecommunication ⟨telemarketing⟩
tele·cast \ˈte-li-ˌkast\ vb -cast also -cast·ed; -cast·ing [tele- + broadcast] (1937) : to broadcast by television ~ vi : to broadcast a television program — **telecast** n — **tele·cast·er** n
tele·com·mu·ni·ca·tion \ˌte-li-kə-ˌmyü-nə-ˈkā-shən\ n [ISV] (1932) **1** : communication at a distance (as by telephone) **2** : a science that deals with telecommunication — usu. used in pl.
tele·com·mute \ˈte-li-kə-ˌmyüt\ vi (1974) : to work at home by the use of an electronic linkup with a central office — **tele·com·mut·er** n
tele·con·fer·enc·ing \ˈte-li-ˌkän-f(ə-)rən(t)-siŋ, -fərn(t)-\ n (1974) : the holding of a conference among people remote from one another by means of telecommunication devices (as telephones or computer terminals) — **tele·con·fer·ence** \-f(ə-)rən(t)s, -fərn(t)s\ n
Tele·cop·i·er \ˈte-lə-ˌkä-pē-ər\ trademark — used for transmitting and receiving equipment for producing facsimile copies of documents
tele·course \ˈte-li-ˌkȯrs, -ˌkȯrs\ n (1950) : a course of study conducted over television; esp : such a course taken at home for academic credit
tele·fac·sim·i·le \ˌte-li-fak-ˈsi-mə-(ˌ)lē\ n (1952) : FACSIMILE 2
tele·film \ˈte-li-ˌfilm\ n (1939) : a motion picture made to be telecast
tele·gen·ic \ˌte-lə-ˈje-nik, -ˈjē-\ adj (1939) : well-suited to the medium of television; esp : having an appearance and manner that are markedly attractive to television viewers
¹tele·gram \ˈte-lə-ˌgram, Southern also -grəm\ n (ca. 1852) : a telegraphic dispatch
²telegram \-ˌgram\ vt -grammed; -gram·ming (1864) : TELEGRAPH
¹tele·graph \-ˌgraf\ n [F télégraphe, fr. télé- tele- (fr. Gk tēle-) + -graphe -graph] (1794) **1** : an apparatus for communication at a distance by coded signals; esp : an apparatus, system, or process for com-

munication at a distance by electric transmission over wire **2** : TELEGRAM
²telegraph vt (1805) **1 a** : to send or communicate by or as if by telegraph **b** : to send a telegram to **c** : to send by means of a telegraphic order ⟨~ flowers to a sick friend⟩ **2** : to make known by signs esp. unknowingly and in advance ⟨~ a punch⟩ — **te·leg·ra·pher** \tə-ˈle-grə-fər\ n — **te·leg·ra·phist** \-fist\ n
tele·graph·ese \ˌte-lə-gra-ˈfēz, -ˈfēs\ n (1885) : language characterized by the terseness and ellipses that are common in telegrams
tele·graph·ic \ˌte-lə-ˈgra-fik\ adj (1794) **1** : of or relating to the telegraph **2** : CONCISE, TERSE — **tele·graph·i·cal·ly** \-fi-k(ə-)lē\ adv
te·leg·ra·phy \tə-ˈle-grə-fē\ n (1795) : the use or operation of a telegraph apparatus or system for communication
tele·ki·ne·sis \ˌte-li-kə-ˈnē-səs, -kī-\ n [NL] (1890) : the production of motion in objects (as by a spiritualistic medium) without contact or other physical means — **tele·ki·net·ic** \-ˈne-tik\ adj — **tele·ki·net·i·cal·ly** \-ti-k(ə-)lē\ adv
Te·lem·a·chus \tə-ˈle-mə-kəs\ n [L, fr. Gk Tēlemachos] : the son of Odysseus and Penelope who contrives with his father to slay his mother's suitors
tel·e·mark \ˈte-lə-ˌmärk\ n, often cap [Norw., fr. Telemark, region in Norway] (1904) : a turn in skiing in which the outside ski is advanced considerably ahead of the other ski and then turned inward at a steadily widening angle until the turn is completed
tele·mar·ket·ing \ˈte-lə-ˌmär-kə-tiŋ\ n (1980) : the marketing of goods or services by telephone — **tele·mar·ket·er** \-tər\ n
¹tele·me·ter \ˈte-lə-ˌmē-tər\ n [ISV] (1860) **1** : an instrument for measuring the distance of an object from an observer **2** : an electrical apparatus for measuring a quantity (as pressure, speed, or temperature), transmitting the result esp. by radio to a distant station, and there indicating or recording the quantity measured
²telemeter vt (1925) : to transmit (as the measurement of a quantity) by telemeter ~ vi : to telemeter the measurement of a quantity
te·lem·e·try \tə-ˈle-mə-trē\ n (1885) **1** : the science or process of telemetering data **2** : data transmitted by telemetry **3** : BIOTELEMETRY — **tele·met·ric** \ˌte-lə-ˈme-trik\ adj — **tele·met·ri·cal·ly** \-tri-k(ə-)lē\ adv
tel·en·ceph·a·lon \ˌte-len-ˈse-fə-ˌlän, -lən\ n [NL] (1897) : the anterior subdivision of the embryonic forebrain or the corresponding part of the adult forebrain that includes the cerebral hemispheres and associated structures — **tel·en·ce·phal·ic** \-ˌlen(t)-sə-ˈfa-lik\ adj
tel·e·o·log·i·cal \ˌte-lē-ə-ˈlä-ji-kəl, ˌtē-\ also **tel·e·o·log·ic** \-ˈlä-jik\ adj (1798) : exhibiting or relating to design or purpose esp. in nature — **tel·e·o·log·i·cal·ly** \-ji-k(ə-)lē\ adv
tel·e·ol·o·gy \ˌte-lē-ˈä-lə-jē, ˌtē-\ n [NL teleologia, fr. Gk tele-, telos end, purpose + -logia -logy — more at WHEEL] (1740) **1 a** : the study of evidences of design in nature **b** : a doctrine (as in vitalism) that ends are immanent in nature **c** : a doctrine explaining phenomena by final causes **2** : the fact or character attributed to nature or natural processes of being directed toward an end or shaped by a purpose **3** : the use of design or purpose as an explanation of natural phenomena — **tel·e·ol·o·gist** \-jist\ n
tel·e·on·o·my \ˌte-lē-ˈä-nə-mē, ˌtē-\ n [teleo- (as in teleology) + -nomy] (1958) : the quality of apparent purposefulness in living organisms that derives from their evolutionary adaptation — **tel·e·o·nom·ic** \ˌte-lē-ə-ˈnä-mik, ˌtē-\ adj
tel·e·ost \ˈte-lē-ˌäst, ˈtē-\ n [ultim. fr. Gk teleios complete, perfect (fr. telos end) + osteon bone — more at OSSEOUS] (1862) : BONY FISH — **teleost** adj — **tel·e·os·te·an** \ˌte-lē-ˈäs-tē-ən, ˌtē-\ adj
tele·path \ˈte-lə-ˌpath\ n (1904) : one who is able to communicate by telepathy
te·lep·a·thy \tə-ˈle-pə-thē\ n (1882) : communication from one mind to another by extrasensory means — **tele·path·ic** \ˌte-lə-ˈpa-thik\ adj — **tele·path·i·cal·ly** \-thi-k(ə-)lē\ adv
¹tele·phone \ˈte-lə-ˌfōn\ n, often attrib (1849) : an instrument for reproducing sounds at a distance; specif : one in which sound is converted into electrical impulses for transmission by wire
²telephone vb -phoned; -phon·ing vt (1877) **1** : to speak to or attempt to reach by telephone **2** : to send by telephone ~ vi : to communicate by telephone — **tele·phon·er** n
telephone book n (1915) : a book listing the names, addresses, and telephone numbers of telephone customers
telephone booth n (ca. 1895) : an enclosure within which one may stand or sit while making a telephone call
telephone box n (1904) Brit : a public telephone booth
telephone directory n (1907) : TELEPHONE BOOK
telephone number n (1885) : a number assigned to a telephone line for a specific location that is used to call that location
telephone tag n (1980) : telephoning back and forth by parties trying to reach each other without success
tele·phon·ic \ˌte-lə-ˈfä-nik\ adj (1877) : of, relating to, or conveyed by a telephone — **tele·phon·i·cal·ly** \-ni-k(ə-)lē\ adv
te·le·pho·nist \tə-ˈle-fə-nist, ˈte-lə-ˌfō-nist\ n (1880) Brit : a telephone switchboard operator
te·le·pho·ny \tə-ˈle-fə-nē also ˈte-lə-ˌfō-\ n (1835) : the use or operation of an apparatus for transmission of sounds between widely removed points with or without connecting wires
¹tele·pho·to \ˌte-lə-ˈfō-(ˌ)tō\ adj (ca. 1895) : being a camera lens system designed to give a large image of a distant object; also : relating to or being photography in which a telephoto lens is used
²telephoto n, pl -tos (1904) **1** : a telephoto lens **2** : a photograph taken with a camera having a telephoto lens
Telephoto trademark — used for an apparatus for transmitting photographs electrically or for a photograph so transmitted
tele·pho·tog·ra·phy \-fə-ˈtä-grə-fē\ n [ISV] (1892) : the photography of distant objects (as by a camera provided with a telephoto lens)
tele·play \ˈte-li-ˌplā\ n (1952) : a play written for television

\ə\ abut \ˈ, ˌ\ kitten, F table \ər\ further \a\ ash \ā\ ace \ä\ mop, mar \au̇\ out \ch\ chin \e\ bet \ē\ easy \g\ go \i\ hit \ī\ ice \j\ job \ŋ\ sing \ō\ go \ȯ\ law \ȯi\ boy \th\ thin \th\ the \ü\ loot \u̇\ foot \y\ yet \zh\ vision \ȧ, k̯, ⁿ, œ, œ̄, ᴜᴇ, ᵫ, ʸ\ see Guide to Pronunciation

tele·port \'te-lə-ˌpōrt, -ˌpȯrt\ *vt* [back-formation fr. *teleportation*] (1947) : to transfer by teleportation

tele·por·ta·tion \ˌte-lə-ˌpōr-'tā-shən, -ˌpȯr-, -pər-\ *n* [*tele-* + transp*or-tation*] (1931) : the act or process of moving an object or person by psychokinesis

tele·print·er \'te-lə-ˌprin-tər\ *n* (1929) : a device capable of producing hard copy from signals received over a communications circuit; *esp* : TELETYPEWRITER

tele·pro·cess·ing \-'prä-ˌse-siŋ, -'prō-, -sə-siŋ\ *n* (1962) : computer processing via remote terminals

Tele·Promp·Ter \'te-lə-ˌpräm(p)-tər\ *trademark* — used for a device for unrolling a magnified script in front of a speaker on television

¹tele·scope \'te-lə-ˌskōp\ *n, often attrib* [NL *telescopium*, fr. Gk *tēle-skopos* farseeing, fr. *tēle-* tele- + *skopos* watcher; akin to Gk *skopein* to look — more at SPY] (1648) **1 a** : a usu. tubular optical instrument for viewing distant objects by means of the refraction of light rays through a lens or the reflection of light rays by a concave mirror — compare REFLECTOR, REFRACTOR **2** : any of various tubular magnifying optical instruments **3** : RADIO TELESCOPE

²telescope *vb* **-scoped; -scop·ing** *vi* (1867) **1** : to become forced together lengthwise with one part entering another as the result of collision **2** : to slide or pass one within another like the cylindrical sections of a collapsible hand telescope **3** : to become compressed or condensed ~ *vt* **1** : to cause to telescope **2** : COMPRESS, CONDENSE ⟨the book arbitrarily ~s time and space, and as arbitrarily extends them —Phoebe Adams⟩

tele·scop·ic \ˌte-lə-'skä-pik\ *adj* (1705) **1 a** : of, relating to, or performed with a telescope **b** : suitable for seeing or magnifying distant objects **2** : seen or discoverable only by a telescope ⟨~ stars⟩ **3** : able to discern objects at a distance **4** : having parts that telescope — **tele·scop·i·cal·ly** \-pi-k(ə-)lē\ *adv*

tel·e·sis \'te-lə-səs\ *n, pl* **-e·ses** \-ˌsēz\ [NL, fr. Gk, fulfillment, fr. *telein* to complete, fr. *telos* end — more at TELOS] (1896) : progress that is intelligently planned and directed : the attainment of desired ends by the application of intelligent human effort to the means

tele·text \'te-lə-ˌtekst\ *n* (1974) : a system for broadcasting text over an unused portion of a television signal and displaying it on a decoder-equipped television set — compare VIDEOTEX

tele·thon \'te-lə-ˌthän\ *n* [*tele-* + *-thon*] (1949) : a long television program usu. to solicit funds esp. for a charity

Tele·type \'te-lə-ˌtīp\ *trademark* — used for a teletypewriter

Tele·type·set·ter \ˌte-lə-'tīp-ˌse-tər\ *trademark* — used for a telegraphic apparatus for the automatic operation of a keyboard typesetting machine

tele·type·writ·er \-ˌrī-tər\ *n* (1903) : a printing device resembling a typewriter that is used to send and receive telephonic signals

te·leu·to·spore \tə-'lü-tə-ˌspōr, -ˌspȯr\ *n* [Gk *teleutē* end (akin to Gk *telos* end) + ISV *spore* — more at TELOS] (1874) : TELIOSPORE

tel·evan·ge·list \ˌte-li-'van-jə-list\ *n* (1973) : an evangelist who conducts regularly televised religious programs — **tel·evan·ge·lism** \-ˌli-zəm\ *n*

tele·view \'te-li-ˌvyü\ *vi* (1935) : to observe or watch by means of a television receiver — **tele·view·er** *n*

tele·vise \'te-lə-ˌvīz\ *vb* **-vised; -vis·ing** [back-formation fr. *television*] *vt* (1927) : to broadcast (as a baseball game) by television ~ *vi* : to broadcast by television

tele·vi·sion \'te-lə-ˌvi-zhən *esp Brit* ˌte-lə-'\ *n, often attrib* [F *télévision*, fr. *télé-* tele- + *vision* vision] (1907) **1** : an electronic system of transmitting transient images of fixed or moving objects together with sound over a wire or through space by apparatus that converts light and sound into electrical waves and reconverts them into visible light rays and audible sound **2** : a television receiving set **3 a** : the television broadcasting industry **b** : television as a medium of communication

television tube *n* (1937) : PICTURE TUBE

tele·vi·su·al \ˌte-lə-'vi-zhə-wəl, -zhəl; -'vizh-wəl\ *adj* (1926) *chiefly Brit* : of, relating to, or suitable for broadcast by television

¹tel·ex \'te-ˌleks\ *n* [*teleprinter* + *exchange*] (1932) **1** : a communication service involving teletypewriters connected by wire through automatic exchanges; *also* : a teletypewriter used in telex **2** : a message sent by telex

²telex *vt* (1960) **1** : to send (as a message) by telex **2** : to communicate with by telex

te·lic \'te-lik, 'tē-\ *adj* [Gk *telikos*, fr. *telos* end — more at TELOS] (1889) : tending toward an end — **te·li·cal·ly** \-li-k(ə-)lē\ *adv*

te·lio·spore \'tē-lē-ə-ˌspōr, -ˌspȯr\ *n* [Gk *teleios* complete (fr. *telos* end) + E *spore*] (1905) : a chlamydospore that is the final stage in the life cycle of a rust fungus and that after nuclear fusion gives rise to the basidium

te·li·um \'tē-lē-əm\ *n, pl* **-lia** \-lē-ə\ [NL, fr. Gk *teleios* complete] (ca. 1905) : a teliospore-producing sorus or pustule on the host plant of a rust fungus — **te·li·al** \'tē-lē-əl\ *adj*

¹tell \'tel\ *vb* **told** \'tōld\; **tell·ing** [ME, fr. OE *tellan*; akin to OHG *zellen* to count, tell, OE *talu* tale] *vt* (bef. 12c) **1** : COUNT, ENUMERATE **2 a** : to relate in detail : NARRATE **b** : to give utterance to : SAY ⟨who dares think one thing, and another ~ —Alexander Pope⟩ **3 a** : to make known : DIVULGE, REVEAL **b** : to express in words ⟨she never *told* her love —Shak.⟩ **4 a** : to report to : INFORM **b** : to assure emphatically ⟨they did not do it, I ~ you⟩ **5** : ORDER, DIRECT ⟨*told* me to wait⟩ **6** : to find out by observing : RECOGNIZE ⟨you can ~ it's a masterpiece⟩ ~ *vi* **1** : to give an account **2** : to act as an informer — often used with *on* ⟨I'll get even with you if you ever ~ on me —*Inside Detective*⟩ **3** : to have a marked effect **4** : to serve as evidence or indication *syn* see REVEAL

²tell *n* [Ar *tall*] (1864) : HILL, MOUND; *specif* : an ancient mound in the Middle East composed of remains of successive settlements

tell-all \'tel-'ȯl\ *n* (1954) : a written account (as a biography) that contains revealing and often scandalous information — **tell-all** *adj*

tell·er \'te-lər\ *n* (14c) **1** : one that relates or communicates ⟨a ~ of stories⟩ **2** : one that reckons or counts: as **a** : one appointed to count votes **b** : a member of a bank's staff concerned with the direct handling of money received or paid out

tell·ing \'te-liŋ\ *adj* (1851) : carrying great weight and producing a marked effect : EFFECTIVE, EXPRESSIVE ⟨the most ~ evidence⟩ *syn* see VALID — **tell·ing·ly** \-liŋ-lē\ *adv*

tell off *vt* (1804) **1** : to number and set apart; *esp* : to assign to a special duty ⟨*told off* a detail and put them to opening a trench —J. F. Dobie⟩ **2** : REPRIMAND, EXCORIATE ⟨*told* him *off* for his arrogance⟩

tell·tale \'tel-ˌtāl\ *n* (ca. 1548) **1 a** : TALEBEARER, INFORMER **b** : an outward sign : INDICATION **2** : a device for indicating or recording something: as **a** : a wind-direction indicator often in the form of a ribbon **b** : a strip of metal on the front wall of a racquets or squash court above which the ball must be hit — **telltale** *adj*

tellur- *or* **telluro-** *comb form* [L *tellur-, tellus* — more at THILL] **1** : earth ⟨*telluric*⟩ **2** [NL *tellurium*] : tellurium ⟨*telluride*⟩

tel·lu·ric \tə-'lür-ik, te-\ *adj* (1836) **1** : of or relating to the earth : TERRESTRIAL **2** : being or relating to a usu. natural electric current flowing near the earth's surface

tel·lu·ride \'tel-yə-ˌrīd\ *n* [ISV] (1849) : a binary compound of tellurium with a more electropositive element or group

tel·lu·ri·um \tə-'lür-ē-əm, te-\ *n* [NL, fr. L *tellur-, tellus* earth] (1800) : a semimetallic element related to selenium and sulfur that occurs in a silvery white brittle crystalline form of metallic luster, in a dark amorphous form, or combined with metals and that is used esp. in alloys — see ELEMENT table

tel·lu·rom·e·ter \ˌtel-yə-'rä-mə-tər\ *n* (1957) : a device that measures distance by means of microwaves

tel·ly \'te-lē\ *n, pl* **tellys** *also* **tellies** [by shortening & alter.] (1939) *chiefly Brit* : TELEVISION

telo- — see TEL-

telo·cen·tric \ˌte-lə-'sen-trik, ˌtē-\ *adj* [ISV *tel-* + *centromere* + *-ic*] (1939) : having the centromere terminally situated so that there is only one chromosomal arm ⟨a ~ chromosome⟩ — **telocentric** *n*

te·lome \'tē-ˌlōm\ *n* [ISV *tel-* + *-ome*] (1935) : a hypothetical plant structure in a theory of the evolution of leaves and sporophylls in vascular plants that consists of one of the vegetative or reproductive terminal branchlets of a dichotomously branched axis

telo·mere \'te-lə-ˌmir, 'tē-\ *n* [ISV] (1940) : the natural end of a eukaryotic chromosome

telo·phase \'te-lə-ˌfāz, 'tē-\ *n* [ISV] (1895) **1** : the final stage of mitosis and of the second division of meiosis in which the spindle disappears and the nuclear envelope reforms around each set of chromosomes **2** : the final stage in the first division of meiosis that may be missing in some organisms and is characterized by the gathering at opposite poles of the cell of half the original number of chromosomes including one from each homologous pair

te·los \'te-ˌläs, 'tē-\ *n* [Gk; prob. akin to Gk *tellein* to accomplish, *tlēnai* to bear — more at TOLERATE] (1904) : an ultimate end

telo·tax·is \ˌte-lə-'tak-səs, ˌtē-\ *n* [NL] (1934) : a taxis in which an organism orients itself in respect to a stimulus (as a light source) as though that were the only stimulus acting on it

tel·son \'tel-sən\ *n* [NL, fr. Gk, end of a plowed field; perh. akin to Gk *telos* end] (1855) : the terminal segment of the body of an arthropod or segmented worm; *esp* : that of a crustacean forming the middle lobe of the tail

Tel·u·gu \'te-lə-ˌgü\ *n, pl* **Telugu** *or* **Telugus** (1789) **1** : a member of the largest group of people in Andhra Pradesh, India **2** : the Dravidian language of the Telugu people

tem·blor \'tem-blər; 'tem-ˌblȯr, -ˌblōr, tem-'\ *n* [Sp, lit., trembling, fr. *temblar* to tremble, fr. ML *tremulare* — more at TREMBLE] (1876) : EARTHQUAKE

tem·er·ar·i·ous \ˌte-mə-'rer-ē-əs, -'rar-\ *adj* [L *-temerarius*, fr. *temere*] (1532) : marked by temerity : rashly or presumptuously daring — **tem·er·ar·i·ous·ly** *adv* — **tem·er·ar·i·ous·ness** *n*

te·mer·i·ty \tə-'mer-ə-tē\ *n, pl* **-ties** [ME *temeryte*, fr. L *temeritas*, fr. *temere* blindly, recklessly; akin to OHG *demar* darkness, L *tenebrae*, Skt *tamas*] (15c) **1** : unreasonable or foolhardy contempt of danger or opposition : RASHNESS, RECKLESSNESS **2** : an act or instance of temerity *syn* TEMERITY, AUDACITY, HARDIHOOD, EFFRONTERY, NERVE, CHEEK, GALL, CHUTZPAH mean conspicuous or flagrant boldness. TEMERITY suggests boldness arising from rashness and contempt of danger ⟨had the *temerity* to refuse⟩. AUDACITY implies a disregard of restraints commonly imposed by convention or prudence ⟨an entrepreneur with *audacity* and vision⟩. HARDIHOOD suggests firmness in daring and defiance ⟨admired for her *hardihood*⟩. EFFRONTERY implies shameless, insolent disregard of propriety or courtesy ⟨outraged at his *effrontery*⟩. NERVE, CHEEK, GALL, and CHUTZPAH are informal equivalents for EFFRONTERY ⟨the *nerve* of that guy⟩ ⟨has the *cheek* to call herself a singer⟩ ⟨had the *gall* to demand proof⟩ ⟨the *chutzpah* needed for a career in show business⟩.

¹temp \'temp\ *n* (1886) **1** : TEMPERATURE 2a, c **2** : a temporary worker

²temp *vi* (1973) : to work as a temp

tem·peh \'tem-ˌpā\ *n* [Jav *témpé*] (1961) : an Asian food prepared by fermenting soybeans with a rhizopus

¹tem·per \'tem-pər\ *vt* **tem·pered; tem·per·ing** \-p(ə-)riŋ\ [ME, fr. OE & OF; OE *temprian* & OF *temprer*, fr. L *temperare* to moderate, mix, temper; prob. akin to L *tempor-, tempus* time] (bef. 12c) **1** : to dilute, qualify, or soften by the addition or influence of something else : MODERATE ⟨~ justice with mercy⟩ **2** *archaic* : to exercise control over : GOVERN, RESTRAIN **b** : to cause to be well disposed : MOLLIFY ⟨~ed and reconciled them both —Richard Steele⟩ **3** : to bring to a suitable state by mixing in or adding a usu. liquid ingredient: as **a** : to mix (clay) with water or a modifier (as grog) and knead to a uniform texture **b** : to mix oil with (colors) in making paint ready for use **4 a** (1) : to soften (as hardened steel or cast iron) by reheating at a lower temperature (2) : to harden (as steel) by reheating and cooling in oil **b** : to anneal or toughen (glass) by a process of gradually heating and cooling **5** : to make stronger and more resilient through hardship : TOUGHEN ⟨troops ~ed in battle⟩ **6 a** : to put in tune with something : ATTUNE **b** : to adjust the pitch of (a note, chord, or instrument) to a temperament — **tem·per·able** \-p(ə-)rə-bəl\ *adj* — **tem·per·er** \-pər-ər\ *n*

²temper *n* (14c) **1 a** *archaic* : a suitable proportion or balance of qualities : a middle state between extremes : MEAN, MEDIUM ⟨virtue is . . . a just ~ between propensities —T. B. Macaulay⟩ **b** *archaic*

: CHARACTER, QUALITY ⟨the ~ of the land you design to sow —John Mortimer⟩ **c** : characteristic tone : TREND, TENDENCY ⟨the ~ of the times⟩ **d** : high quality of mind or spirit : COURAGE, METTLE **2 a** : the state of a substance with respect to certain desired qualities (as hardness, elasticity, or workability); *esp* : the degree of hardness or resiliency given steel by tempering **b** : the feel and relative solidity of leather **3 a** : a characteristic cast of mind or state of feeling : DISPOSITION **b** : calmness of mind : COMPOSURE, EQUANIMITY **c** : state of feeling or frame of mind at a particular time usu. dominated by a single strong emotion **d** : heat of mind or emotion : proneness to anger : PASSION **4** : a substance (as a metal) added to or mixed with something else (as another metal) to modify the properties of the latter *syn* see DISPOSITION

tem·pera \'tem-pə-rə\ *n* [It *tempera*, lit., temper, fr. *temperare* to temper, fr. L] (1832) **1** : a process of painting in which an albuminous or colloidal medium (as egg yolk) is employed as a vehicle instead of oil; *also* : a painting done in tempera : POSTER COLOR

tem·per·a·ment \'tem-p(ə-)rə-mənt, -pər-mənt\ *n* [ME, fr. L *temperamentum*, fr. *temperare* to mix, temper] (15c) **1** *obs* **a** : constitution of a substance, body, or organism with respect to the mixture or balance of its elements, qualities, or parts : MAKEUP **b** : COMPLEXION 1 **2** *obs* **a** : CLIMATE **b** : TEMPERATURE 2 **3 a** : the peculiar or distinguishing mental or physical character determined by the relative proportions of the humors according to medieval physiology **b** : characteristic or habitual inclination or mode of emotional response ⟨a nervous ~⟩ **c** : extremely high sensibility; *esp* : excessive sensitiveness or irritability **4 a** : the act or process of tempering or modifying : ADJUSTMENT, COMPROMISE **b** : middle course : MEAN **5** : the process of slightly modifying the musical intervals of the pure scale to produce a set of 12 equally spaced tones to the octave which enables a keyboard instrument to play in all keys *syn* see DISPOSITION

tem·per·a·men·tal \,tem-p(ə-)rə-'men-t²l, ,tem-pər-'-\ *adj* (1646) **1** : of, relating to, or arising from temperament : CONSTITUTIONAL ⟨~ peculiarities⟩ **2 a** : marked by excessive sensitivity and impulsive changes of mood ⟨a ~ child⟩ **b** : unpredictable in behavior or performance — **tem·per·a·men·tal·ly** \-t²l-ē\ *adv*

tem·per·ance \'tem-p(ə-)rən(t)s, -pərn(t)s\ *n* [ME, fr. L *temperantia*, fr. *temperant-, temperans*, prp. of *temperare* to moderate, be moderate] (14c) **1** : moderation in action, thought, or feeling : RESTRAINT **2 a** : habitual moderation in the indulgence of the appetites or passions **b** : moderation in or abstinence from the use of intoxicating drink

tem·per·ate \'tem-p(ə-)rət\ *adj* [ME *temperat*, fr. L *temperatus*, fr. pp. of *temperare*] (14c) **1** : marked by moderation: as **a** : keeping or held within limits : not extreme or excessive : MILD **b** : moderate in indulgence of appetite or desire **c** : moderate in the use of intoxicating liquors **d** : marked by an absence or avoidance of extravagance, violence, or extreme partisanship : RESTRAINED **2 a** : having a moderate climate **b** : found in or associated with a moderate climate ⟨~ insects⟩ **3** : existing as a prophage in infected cells and rarely causing lysis ⟨~ bacteriophages⟩ — **tem·per·ate·ly** *adv* — **tem·per·ate·ness** *n*

temperate rain forest *n* (ca. 1930) : woodland of a usu. rather mild climatic area within the temperate zone that receives heavy rainfall, usu. includes numerous kinds of trees, and is distinguished from a tropical rain forest by the presence of a dominant tree

temperate zone *n, often cap T&Z* (1551) : the area or region between the tropic of Cancer and the arctic circle or between the tropic of Capricorn and the antarctic circle

tem·per·a·ture \'tem-pə(r),chùr, -p(ə-)rə-, -chər, -,tyùr, -,tùr\ *n* [L *temperatura* mixture, moderation, fr. *temperatus*, pp. of *temperare*] (1533) **1** *archaic* **a** : COMPLEXION 1 **b** : TEMPERAMENT 3b **2 a** : degree of hotness or coldness measured on a definite scale — compare THERMOMETER **b** : the degree of heat that is natural to the body of a living being **c** : abnormally high body heat **d** : relative state of emotional warmth ⟨aware of a change in the ~ of our friendship —Christopher Isherwood⟩

temperature inversion *n* (1921) : INVERSION 6

tem·pered \'tem-pərd\ *adj* (14c) **1 a** : having the elements mixed in satisfying proportions : TEMPERATE **b** : qualified, lessened, or diluted by the mixture or influence of an additional ingredient : MODERATED ⟨a pale gleam of ~ sunlight fell through the leaves —W. H. Hudson †1922⟩ **2** : treated by tempering; *esp, of glass* : treated so as to impart increased strength and the property of shattering into pellets when broken **3** : having a specified temper — used in combination ⟨short-tempered⟩ **4** : conforming to adjustment by temperament — used of a musical interval, intonation, semitone, or scale

¹tem·pest \'tem-pəst\ *n* [ME, fr. OF *tempeste*, fr. (assumed) VL *tempesta*, alter. of L *tempestas* season, weather, storm, fr. *tempus* time] (13c) **1** : a violent storm **2** : TUMULT, UPROAR

²tempest *vt* (14c) : to raise a tempest in or around

tem·pes·tu·ous \tem-'pes-chə-wəs, -'pesh-\ *adj* [LL *tempestuosus*, fr. OL *tempestus* season, weather, storm, fr. *tempus*] (1509) : of, relating to, or resembling a tempest : TURBULENT, STORMY ⟨a ~ relationship⟩ — **tem·pes·tu·ous·ly** *adv* — **tem·pes·tu·ous·ness** *n*

Tem·plar \'tem-plər\ *n* [ME *templer*, fr. OF *templier*, fr. ML *templarius*, fr. L *templum* temple] (13c) **1** : a knight of a religious military order established in the early 12th century in Jerusalem for the protection of pilgrims and the Holy Sepulcher **2** *not cap* : a barrister or student of law in London **3** : KNIGHT TEMPLAR 2

tem·plate *also* **tem·plet** \'tem-plət\ *n* [prob. fr. F *templet*, dim. of *temple*, part of a loom, prob. fr. L *templum*] (1677) **1** : a short piece or block placed horizontally in a wall under a beam to distribute its weight or pressure (as over a door) **2** (1) : a gauge, pattern, or mold (as a thin plate or board) used as a guide to the form of a piece being made (2) : a molecule (as of DNA) that serves as a pattern for the generation of another macromolecule (as messenger RNA) **b** : OVERLAY **c 3** : something that establishes or serves as a pattern

¹tem·ple \'tem-pəl\ *n* [ME, fr. OE & OF; OE *tempel* & OF *temple*, both fr. L *templum* space marked out for observation of auguries, temple, small timber; prob. akin to Gk *temenos* sacred precinct, *temnein* to cut — more at TOME] (bef. 12c) **1** : an edifice for religious exercises: as **a** *often cap* : one of three successive national sanctuaries in ancient Jerusalem **b** : a building for Mormon sacred ordinances **c** : a Reform or Conservative synagogue **2** : a local lodge of any of various fraternal

---

orders; *also* : the building housing it **3** : a place devoted to a special purpose — **tem·pled** \-pəld\ *adj*

²temple *n* [ME, fr. MF, fr. (assumed) VL *tempula*, alter. of L *tempora* (pl.) temples] (14c) **1** : the flattened space on each side of the forehead of some mammals including humans **2** : one of the side supports of a pair of glasses jointed to the bows and passing on each side of the head

tem·po \'tem-(,)pō\ *n, pl* **tem·pi** \-(,)pē\ *or* **tempos** [It, lit., time, fr. L *tempus*] (ca. 1724) **1** : the rate of speed of a musical piece or passage indicated by one of a series of directions (as largo, presto, or allegro) and often by an exact metronome marking **2** : rate of motion or activity : PACE

¹tem·po·ral \'tem-p(ə-)rəl\ *adj* [ME, fr. L *temporalis*, fr. *tempor-, tempus* time] (14c) **1 a** : of or relating to time as opposed to eternity **b** : of or relating to earthly life **c** : lay or secular rather than clerical or sacred : CIVIL ⟨lords ~⟩ **2** : of or relating to grammatical tense or a distinction of time **3 a** : of or relating to time as distinguished from space **b** : of or relating to the sequence of time or to a particular time : CHRONOLOGICAL — **tem·po·ral·ly** *adv*

²temporal *n* [MF, fr. *temporal, adj.*] (1541) : a temporal part (as a bone or muscle)

³temporal *adj* [ME, fr. LL *temporalis*, fr. L *tempora* temples] (1597) : of or relating to the temples or the sides of the skull behind the orbits

temporal bone *n* (1771) : a compound bone of the side of the skull of some mammals including humans

tem·po·ral·i·ty \,tem-pə-'ra-lə-tē\ *n, pl* **-ties** (14c) **1 a** : civil or political as distinguished from spiritual or ecclesiastical power or authority **b** : an ecclesiastical property or revenue — often used in pl. **2** : the quality or state of being temporal

tem·po·ral·ize \'tem-p(ə-)rə-,līz\ *vt* **-ized; -iz·ing** (1828) **1** : SECULARIZE **2** : to place or define in time relations

temporal lobe *n* (ca. 1891) : a large lobe of each cerebral hemisphere that is situated in front of the occipital lobe and contains a sensory area associated with the organ of hearing

temporal summation *n* (1950) : sensory summation that involves the addition of single stimuli over a short period of time

tem·po·rar·i·ly \,tem-pə-'rer-ə-lē\ *adv* (1534) : during a limited time

¹tem·po·rary \'tem-pə-,rer-ē\ *adj* [L *temporarius*, fr. *tempor-, tempus* time] (ca. 1564) : lasting for a limited time — **tem·po·rar·i·ness** *n*

²temporary *n, pl* **-rar·ies** (1848) : one serving for a limited time ⟨adding several *temporaries* as typists during the summer⟩

temporary duty *n* (1945) : temporary military service away from one's permanent duty station

tem·po·rise *Brit var of* TEMPORIZE

tem·po·rize \'tem-pə-,rīz\ *vi* **-rized; -riz·ing** [MF *temporiser*, fr. ML *temporizare* to pass the time, fr. L *tempor-, tempus*] (1579) **1** : to act to suit the time or occasion : yield to current or dominant opinion : COMPROMISE **2** : to draw out discussions or negotiations so as to gain time ⟨you'd have to ~ until you found out how she wanted to be advised —Mary Austin⟩ — **tem·po·ri·za·tion** \,tem-pə-rə-'zā-shən\ *n* — **tem·po·riz·er** *n*

tem·po·ro·man·dib·u·lar \'tem-pə-rō-man-'di-byə-lər\ *adj* [³*temporal* + *-o-* + *mandibular*] (1889) : of, relating to, being, or affecting the joint between the temporal bone and the mandible ⟨~ dysfunction⟩

tempt \'tem(p)t\ *vt* [ME, fr. OF *tempter, tenter*, fr. L *temptare, tentare* to feel, try] (13c) **1** : to entice to do wrong by promise of pleasure or gain **2** *obs* : to make trial of : TEST **b** : to try presumptuously : PROVOKE **c** : to risk the dangers of **3 a** : to induce to do something **b** : to cause to be strongly inclined ⟨was ~ed to call it quits⟩ *syn* see LURE — **tempt·able** \'tem(p)-tə-bəl\ *adj*

temp·ta·tion \tem(p)-'tā-shən\ *n* (13c) **1** : the act of tempting or the state of being tempted esp. to evil : ENTICEMENT **2** : something tempting : a cause or occasion of enticement

tempt·er \'tem(p)-tər\ *n* (14c) : one that tempts or entices

tempt·ing *adj* (1596) : having an appeal : ENTICING ⟨a ~ offer⟩ — **tempt·ing·ly** \-tiŋ-lē\ *adv*

tempt·ress \'tem(p)-trəs\ *n* (1594) : a woman who tempts or entices

tem·pu·ra \'tem-pə-rə, -,rä; tem-'pùr-ə\ *n* [Jp *tenpura*] (1920) : seafood or vegetables dipped in batter and fried in deep fat

ten \'ten\ *n* [ME, fr. OE *tiene*, fr. *tien*, adj., ten; akin to OHG *zehan* ten, L *decem*, Gk *deka*] (bef. 12c) **1** — see NUMBER table **2** : the 10th in a set or series ⟨wears a ~⟩ **3** : something having 10 units or members **4** : a 10-dollar bill — **ten** *adj* — **ten** *pron, pl in constr*

ten·a·ble \'te-nə-bəl\ *adj* [MF, fr. OF, fr. *tenir* to hold, fr. L *tenēre* — more at THIN] (1579) : capable of being held, maintained, or defended : DEFENSIBLE, REASONABLE — **ten·a·bil·i·ty** \,te-nə-'bi-lə-tē\ *n* — **ten·a·ble·ness** *n* — **ten·a·bly** \'te-nə-blē\ *adv*

ten·ace \'te-,nās, te-'nās, te-'nəs\ *n* [modif. of Sp *tenaza*, lit., forceps, prob. fr. L *tenacia*, neut. pl. of *tenax*] (1655) : a combination of two high or relatively high cards (as ace and queen) of the same suit in one hand with one ranking two degrees below the other

te·na·cious \tə-'nā-shəs\ *adj* [L *tenac-, tenax* tending to hold fast, fr. *tenēre* to hold] (1607) **1 a** : not easily pulled apart : COHESIVE, TOUGH ⟨a ~ metal⟩ **b** : tending to adhere or cling esp. to another substance : STICKY ⟨~ burs⟩ ⟨~ clay⟩ **2 a** : persistent in maintaining or adhering to something valued or habitual ⟨a man very ~ of his rights⟩ **b** : RETENTIVE ⟨a ~ memory⟩ *syn* see STRONG — **te·na·cious·ly** *adv* — **te·na·cious·ness** *n*

te·nac·i·ty \tə-'na-sə-tē\ *n* (1526) : the quality or state of being tenacious *syn* see COURAGE

te·nac·u·lum \tə-'na-kyə-ləm\ *n, pl* **-la** \-lə\ *or* **-lums** [NL, fr. LL, instrument for holding, fr. L *tenēre*] (ca. 1693) **1** : a slender sharp-pointed hook attached to a handle and used mainly in surgery for seizing and holding parts (as arteries) **2** : an adhesive animal structure

ten·an·cy \'te-nən(t)-sē\ *n, pl* **-cies** (1590) : a holding of an estate or a mode of holding an estate : the temporary possession or occupancy of something (as a house) that belongs to another; *also* : the period of a tenant's occupancy or possession

---

\ə\ abut \ᵊ\ kitten, F table \ər\ further \a\ ash \ā\ ace \ä\ mop, mar \aù\ out \ch\ chin \e\ bet \ē\ easy \g\ go \i\ hit \ī\ ice \j\ job \ŋ\ sing \ō\ go \ò\ law \òi\ boy \th\ thin \t̲h̲\ the \ü\ loot \ù\ foot \y\ yet \zh\ vision \â, k̲, ⁿ, œ, œ̄, ᵫ, ūᴇ, ʸ\ see Guide to Pronunciation

¹ten·ant \'te-nənt\ *n* [ME, fr. MF, fr. prp. of *tenir* to hold] (14c) **1 a** : one who holds or possesses real estate or sometimes personal property (as an annuity) by any kind of right **b** : one who has the occupation or temporary possession of lands or tenements of another; *specif* : one who rents or leases (as a house) from a landlord **2** : OCCUPANT, DWELLER — **ten·ant·less** \-ləs\ *adj*

²tenant *vt* (1634) : to hold or occupy as a tenant : INHABIT — **ten·ant·able** \-nən-tə-bəl\ *adj*

tenant farmer *n* (1748) : a farmer who works land owned by another and pays rent either in cash or in shares of produce

ten·ant·ry \'te-nən-trē\ *n, pl* **-ries** (14c) **1** : TENANCY **2** : a body of tenants

ten–cent store \'ten-'sent-\ *n* (1901) : FIVE-AND-TEN

tench \'tench\ *n, pl* **tench** *or* **tench·es** [ME, fr. MF *tenche*, fr. LL *tinca*] (14c) : a cyprinid fish (*Tinca tinca*) native to Eurasia but introduced in the U.S. and noted for its ability to survive outside water

Ten Commandments *n pl* (13c) : the ethical commandments of God given according to biblical accounts to Moses by voice and by writing on stone tablets on Mount Sinai

¹tend \'tend\ *vb* [ME, short for *attenden* to attend] *vi* (14c) **1** *archaic* : LISTEN **2** : to pay attention : apply oneself ⟨~ to your own affairs⟩ **3** : to act as an attendant : SERVE **4** *obs* : AWAIT ~ *vt* **1** *archaic* : to attend as a servant **2 a** : to apply oneself to the care of : watch over **b** : to have or take charge of as a caretaker or overseer **c** : CULTIVATE, FOSTER **d** : to manage the operations of : MIND ⟨~ the store⟩ **3** : to stand by (as a rope) in readiness to prevent mischance (as fouling)

²tend *vi* [ME, fr. MF *tendre* to stretch, fr. L *tendere* — more at THIN] (14c) **1** : to move, direct, or develop one's course in a particular direction ⟨cannot tell where society is ~*ing*⟩ **2** : to exhibit an inclination or tendency : CONDUCE ⟨~*s* to be optimistic⟩

ten·dance \'ten-dən(t)s\ *n* [short for *attendance*] (1573) **1** : watchful care **2** *archaic* : persons in attendance : RETINUE

ten·den·cious *chiefly Brit var of* TENDENTIOUS

ten·den·cy \'ten-dən(t)-sē\ *n, pl* **-cies** [ML *tendentia*, fr. L *tendent-, tendens,* prp. of *tendere*] (1628) **1 a** : direction or approach toward a place, object, effect, or limit **b** : a proneness to a particular kind of thought or action **2 a** : the purposeful trend of something written or said : AIM **b** : deliberate but indirect advocacy

syn TENDENCY, TREND, DRIFT, TENOR, CURRENT mean movement in a particular direction. TENDENCY implies an inclination sometimes amounting to an impelling force ⟨a general *tendency* toward inflation⟩. TREND applies to the general direction maintained by a winding or irregular course ⟨the long-term *trend* of the stock market is upward⟩. DRIFT may apply to a tendency determined by external forces ⟨the *drift* of the population away from large cities⟩ or it may apply to an underlying or obscure trend of meaning or discourse ⟨got the *drift* of her argument⟩. TENOR stresses a clearly perceptible direction and a continuous, undeviating course ⟨the *tenor* of the times⟩. CURRENT implies a clearly defined but not necessarily unalterable course ⟨an encounter that changed the *current* of my life⟩.

ten·den·tious \ten-'den(t)-shəs\ *adj* (1900) : marked by a tendency in favor of a particular point of view : BIASED — **ten·den·tious·ly** *adv* — **ten·den·tious·ness** *n*

¹ten·der \'ten-dər\ *adj* [ME, fr. OF *tendre*, fr. L *tener*; perh. akin to L *tenuis* thin, slight — more at THIN] (13c) **1 a** : having a soft or yielding texture : easily broken, cut, or damaged : DELICATE, FRAGILE ⟨~ feet⟩ **b** : easily chewed : SUCCULENT **2 a** : physically weak : not able to endure hardship **b** : IMMATURE, YOUNG ⟨children of ~ years⟩ **c** : incapable of resisting cold : not hardy **3** : marked by, responding to, or expressing the softer emotions : FOND, LOVING ⟨a ~ lover⟩ **4 a** : showing care : CONSIDERATE, SOLICITOUS ⟨~ regard⟩ **b** : highly susceptible to impressions or emotions : IMPRESSIONABLE ⟨a ~ conscience⟩ **5 a** : appropriate or conducive to a delicate or sensitive constitution or character : GENTLE, MILD ⟨~ breeding⟩ ⟨~ irony⟩ **b** : delicate or soft in quality or tone ⟨never before heard the piano sound so ~ — Elva S. Daniels⟩ **6** *obs* : DEAR, PRECIOUS **7 a** : sensitive to touch or palpation ⟨the bruise was still ~⟩ **b** : sensitive to injury or insult : TOUCHY ⟨~ pride⟩ **c** : demanding careful and sensitive handling : TICKLISH ⟨a ~ situation⟩ **d** *of a ship* : ⁵CRANK — **ten·der·ly** *adv* — **ten·der·ness** *n*

²tender *vb* **ten·dered; ten·der·ing** \-d(ə-)riŋ\ *vt* (14c) **1** : to make tender : SOFTEN, WEAKEN **2** *archaic* : to regard or treat with tenderness ~ *vi* : to become tender

³tender *vb* **ten·dered; ten·der·ing** \-d(ə-)riŋ\ [MF *tendre* to stretch, stretch out, offer — more at TEND] *vt* (1535) **1** : to make a tender of **2** : to present for acceptance : OFFER ⟨~*ed* my resignation⟩ ~ *vi* : to make a bid or tender ⟨~ for a building contract⟩ ⟨~*ed* for 6% of the stock⟩

⁴tender *n, often attrib* (ca. 1543) **1** : an unconditional offer of money or service in satisfaction of a debt or obligation made to save a penalty or forfeiture for nonpayment or nonperformance **2** : an offer or proposal made for acceptance: as **a** : an offer of a bid for a contract **b** : a public expression of willingness to buy not less than a specified number of shares of a stock at a fixed price from stockholders usu. in an attempt to gain control of the issuing company **3** : something that may be offered in payment; *specif* : MONEY

⁵tender *n* [¹*tender*] (1596) *obs* : CONSIDERATION, REGARD

⁶tend·er \'ten-dər\ *n* (1675) : one that tends: as **a** (1) : a ship employed to attend other ships (as to supply provisions) (2) : a boat for communication between shore and a larger ship (3) : a warship that provides logistic support **b** : a car attached to a steam locomotive for carrying a supply of fuel and water

ten·der·foot \'ten-dər-fut\ *n, pl* **ten·der·feet** \-fēt\ *also* **ten·der·foots** \-futs\ (1849) **1** : a newcomer in a comparatively rough or newly settled region; *esp* : one not hardened to frontier or outdoor life **2** : an inexperienced beginner : NOVICE ⟨a political ~⟩

ten·der–heart·ed \'ten-dər-,här-təd\ *adj* (15c) : easily moved to love, pity, or sorrow : COMPASSIONATE, IMPRESSIONABLE — **ten·der·heart·ed·ly** *adv* — **ten·der·heart·ed·ness** *n*

ten·der·ize \'ten-də-,rīz\ *vt* **-ized; -iz·ing** (1930) : to make (meat or meat products) tender by applying a process or substance that breaks down connective tissue — **ten·der·i·za·tion** \,ten-d(ə-)rə-'zā-shən\ *n* — **ten·der·iz·er** \'ten-də-,rī-zər\ *n*

ten·der·loin \'ten-dər-,loin\ *n* (ca. 1828) **1** : a strip of tender meat consisting of a large internal muscle of the loin on each side of the vertebral column **2** [fr. its making possible a luxurious diet for a corrupt police officer] : a district of a city largely devoted to vice

ten·der–mind·ed \'ten-dər-,mīn-dəd\ *adj* (1605) : marked by idealism, optimism, and dogmatism

ten·der·om·e·ter \,ten-də-'rä-mə-tər\ *n* (1938) : a device for determining the maturity and tenderness of samples of fruits and vegetables

ten·di·ni·tis *or* **ten·don·itis** \,ten-də-'nī-təs\ *n* [tendinitis fr. NL, fr. *tendin, tendo* + *-itis*; tendonitis fr. *tendon* + *-itis*] (ca. 1900) : inflammation of a tendon

ten·di·nous \'ten-də-nəs\ *adj* [NL *tendinosus*, fr. *tendin-, tendo* tendon, alter. of ML *tendon-, tendo*] (1658) **1** : consisting of tendons : SINEWY ⟨~ tissue⟩ **2** : of, relating to, or resembling a tendon

ten·don \'ten-dən\ *n* [ML *tendon-, tendo*, fr. L *tendere* to stretch — more at THIN] (1541) : a tough cord or band of dense white fibrous connective tissue that unites a muscle with some other part (as a bone) and transmits the force which the muscle exerts

tendon of Achil·les \-ə-'ki-lēz\ (ca. 1885) : ACHILLES TENDON

ten·dresse \tä⁽ⁿ⁾-dres\ *n* [ME, fr. MF, fr. *tendre* tender] (14c) : FONDNESS

ten·dril \'ten-drəl\ *n* [prob. modif. of MF *tendron, tendrum* bud, cartilage, fr. (assumed) VL *tenerumen*, fr. L *tener* tender — more at TENDER] (1538) **1** : a leaf, stipule, or stem modified into a slender spirally coiling sensitive organ serving to attach a climbing plant to its support **2** : something suggestive of a tendril ⟨hair hanging in ~*s*⟩ ⟨creeping ~*s* of fog⟩ — **ten·driled** *or* **ten·drilled** \-drəld\ *adj* — **ten·dril·ous** \-drə-ləs\ *adj*

¹-tene *adj comb form* [F -*tène*, fr. L *taenia* ribbon, band — more at TAENIA] : having (such or so many) chromosomal filaments ⟨poly*tene*⟩ ⟨pachy*tene*⟩

²-tene *n comb form* : stage of meiotic prophase characterized by (such) chromosomal filaments ⟨diplo*tene*⟩ ⟨pachy*tene*⟩

Ten·e·brae \'te-nə-,brā, -,brī, -,brē\ *n pl but sing or pl in constr* [ML, fr. L, darkness — more at TEMERITY] (1651) : a church service observed during the final part of Holy Week commemorating the sufferings and death of Christ

ten·e·brif·ic \,te-nə-'bri-fik\ *adj* [L *tenebrae* darkness] (1785) **1** : GLOOMY **2** : causing gloom or darkness

te·ne·bri·o·nid \tə-'ne-brē-ə-nəd, ,te-nə-'bri-ə-nəd\ *n* [NL *Tenebrionidae*, fr. *Tenebrion-, Tenebrio*, type genus, fr. L, one that shuns the light, fr. *tenebrae* darkness — more at TEMERITY] (1902) : any of a family (Tenebrionidae) of firm-bodied mostly dark-colored vegetable-feeding beetles which often have vestigial and functionless wings and whose larvae are usu. hard cylindrical worms (as a mealworm) — called also *darkling beetle* — **tenebrionid** *adj*

te·neb·ri·ous \tə-'ne-brē-əs\ *adj* [by alter.] (1594) : TENEBROUS

ten·e·brism \'te-nə-,bri-zəm\ *n, often cap* [L *tenebrae* darkness] (1954) : a style of painting esp. associated with the Italian painter Caravaggio and his followers in which most of the figures are engulfed in shadow but some are dramatically illuminated by a concentrated beam of light usu. from an identifiable source — **ten·e·brist** \-brist\ *n or adj, often cap*

ten·e·brous \'te-nə-brəs\ *adj* [ME, fr. MF *tenebreus*, fr. L *tenebrosus*, fr. *tenebrae*] (15c) **1** : shut off from the light : DARK, MURKY **2** : hard to understand : OBSCURE **3** : causing gloom

1080 *also* **ten–eighty** \(,)ten-'ā-tē\ *n* [fr. its laboratory serial number] (1945) : a poisonous preparation of sodium fluoroacetate used as a rodenticide and pesticide

ten·e·ment \'te-nə-mənt\ *n* [ME, fr. MF, fr. ML *tenementum*, fr. L *tenēre* to hold — more at THIN] (14c) **1** : any of various forms of corporeal property (as land) or incorporeal property that is held by one person from another **2** : DWELLING **3 a** : a house used as a dwelling : RESIDENCE **b** : APARTMENT, FLAT **c** : TENEMENT HOUSE

tenement house *n* (1858) : APARTMENT HOUSE; *esp* : one meeting minimum standards of sanitation, safety, and comfort and usu. located in a city

te·nes·mus \tə-'nez-məs\ *n* [L, fr. Gk *teinesmos*, fr. *teinein* to stretch, strain — more at THIN] (1527) : a distressing but ineffectual urge to evacuate the rectum or bladder

te·net \'te-nət *also* 'tē-nət\ *n* [L, he holds, fr. *tenēre* to hold] (ca. 1600) : a principle, belief, or doctrine generally held to be true; *esp* : one held in common by members of an organization, movement, or profession

ten·fold \'ten-,fōld, -'fōld\ *adj* (bef. 12c) **1** : being 10 times as great or as many **2** : having 10 units or members — **ten·fold** \-'fōld\ *adv*

ten–gallon hat *n* (1927) : COWBOY HAT

te·nia, te·ni·a·sis *var of* TAENIA, TAENIASIS

ten·ner \'te-nər\ *n* (1845) **1** : a 10-pound note **2** : a 10-dollar bill

Ten·nes·see walking horse \'te-nə-,sē-\ *n* [*Tennessee,* state of U.S.] (1938) : any of an American breed of large easy-gaited saddle horses largely of standardbred and Morgan ancestry — called also *Tennessee walker*

ten·nies \'te-nēz\ *n pl* [by shortening & alter.] (1951) : TENNIS SHOES, SNEAKERS

ten·nis \'te-nəs\ *n, often attrib* [ME *tenetz, tenys,* prob. fr. AF *tenetz,* 2d pers. pl. imper. of *tenir* to hold — more at TENABLE] (15c) **1** : COURT TENNIS **2** : an indoor or outdoor game that is played with rackets and a light elastic ball by two players or pairs of players on a level court (as of clay or grass) divided by a low net

Tennessee walking horse

tennis elbow *n* (1883) : inflammation and pain over the outer side of the elbow usu. resulting from excessive strain on and twisting of the forearm

tennis shoe *n* (1886) : a lightweight usu. low-cut sneaker

ten·nist \'te-nist\ *n* [blend of *tennis* and *-ist*] (1932) : a tennis player

¹ten·on \'te-nən\ n [ME, fr. MF, fr. *tenir* to hold — more at TENABLE] (15c) : a projecting member in a piece of wood or other material for insertion into a mortise to form a joint — see DOVETAIL illustration

²tenon vt (1596) **1** : to unite by a tenon **2** : to cut or fit for insertion in a mortise

¹ten·or \'te-nər\ n [ME, fr. MF, fr. L *tenor* uninterrupted course, fr. *tenēre* to hold — more at THIN] (14c) **1 a** : the drift of something spoken or written : PURPORT **b** : an exact copy of a writing : TRANSCRIPT **c** : the concept, object, or person meant in a metaphor **2 a** : the melodic line usu. forming the cantus firmus in medieval music **b** : the voice part next to the lowest in a 4-part chorus **c** : the highest natural adult male singing voice; *also* : a person having this voice **d** : a member of a family of instruments having a range next lower than that of the alto **3** : a continuance in a course, movement, or activity **4** : habitual condition : CHARACTER *syn* see TENDENCY

²tenor adj (1522) : relating to or having the range or part of a tenor

ten·or·ist \'te-nə-rist\ n (1865) : one who sings tenor or plays a tenor instrument

te·no·syn·o·vi·tis \'te-nō-,si-nə-'vī-təs, ,tē-\ n [NL, fr. Gk *tenōn* tendon (akin to Gk *teinein* to stretch) + NL *synovitis* — more at THIN] (ca. 1860) : inflammation of a tendon sheath

ten·our \'te-nər\ *chiefly Brit var of* TENOR

ten·pen·ny \'ten-'pe-nē, *Brit* -pə-nē\ adj (1592) : amounting to, worth, or costing 10 pennies

tenpenny nail n [fr. its original price per hundred] (15c) : a nail three inches (7.6 centimeters) long

ten·pin \'ten-,pin\ n (1807) **1** : a bottle-shaped bowling pin 15 inches high **2** *pl but sing in constr* : a bowling game using 10 tenpins and a large ball 27 inches in circumference and allowing each player to bowl 2 balls in each of 10 frames

ten·pound·er \'ten-'paün-dər\ n (1699) : LADYFISH 2

ten·rec \'ten-,rek\ n [F, fr. Malagasy *tàndraka*] (1785) : any of numerous small often spiny mammalian insectivores (family Tenrecidae) chiefly of Madagascar

¹tense \'ten(t)s\ n [ME *tens* tense, fr. MF, fr. L *tempus*] (14c) **1** : a distinction of form in a verb to express distinctions of time or duration of the action or state it denotes **2 a** : a set of inflectional forms of a verb that express distinctions of time **b** : an inflectional form of a verb expressing a specific time distinction

²tense adj **tens·er; tens·est** [L *tensus*, fr. pp. of *tendere* to stretch — more at THIN] (1670) **1** : stretched tight : made taut : RIGID **2 a** : feeling or showing nervous tension **b** : marked by strain or suspense **3** : produced with the muscles involved in a relatively tense state ⟨the vowels \ē\ and \ü\ in contrast with the vowels \i\ and \u̇\ are ∼⟩ — **tense·ly** adv — **tense·ness** n

³tense vb **tensed; tens·ing** vt (1676) : to make tense ∼ vi : to become tense

ten·sile \'ten(t)-səl *also* 'ten-,sīl\ adj [NL *tensilis*, fr. L *tensus*, pp.] (1626) **1** : capable of tension : DUCTILE **2** : of, relating to, or involving tension ⟨∼ stress⟩ — **ten·sil·i·ty** \ten-'si-lə-tē\ n

tensile strength n (ca. 1864) : the greatest longitudinal stress a substance can bear without tearing apart

ten·si·om·e·ter \,ten(t)-sē-'ä-mə-tər\ n [*tension*] (1912) **1** : a device for measuring tension (as of structural material) **2** : an instrument for determining the moisture content of soil **3** : an instrument for measuring the surface tension of liquids — **ten·sio·met·ric** \-sē-ō-'me-trik\ adj — **ten·si·om·e·try** \-sē-'ä-mə-trē\ n

¹ten·sion \'ten(t)-shən\ n [MF or L; MF, fr. L *tension-, tensio*, fr. *tendere*] (1533) **1 a** : the act or action of stretching or the condition or degree of being stretched to stiffness : TAUTNESS **b** : STRESS 1b **2 a** : either of two balancing forces causing or tending to cause extension **b** : the stress resulting from the elongation of an elastic body **3 a** : inner striving, unrest, or imbalance often with physiological indication of emotion **b** : a state of latent hostility or opposition between individuals or groups **c** : a balance maintained in an artistic work between opposing forces or elements **4** : a device to produce a desired tension (as in a loom) — **ten·sion·al** \'ten(t)-sh(ə-)nəl\ adj — **ten·sion·less** \-shən-ləs\ adj

²tension vt **ten·sioned; ten·sion·ing** \'ten(t)-sh(ə-)niŋ\ (1891) : to subject to tension; *esp* : to tighten to a desired or appropriate degree — **ten·sion·er** \-sh(ə-)nər\ n

ten·si·ty \'ten(t)-sə-tē\ n, pl **-ties** (ca. 1658) : the quality or state of being tense : TENSENESS

ten·sive \'ten(t)-siv\ adj (1702) : of, relating to, or causing tension

ten·sor \'ten(t)-sər, 'ten-,sȯr\ n [NL, fr. L *tendere*] (ca. 1704) **1** : a muscle that stretches a part **2** : a generalized vector with more than three components each of which is a function of the coordinates of an arbitrary point in space of an appropriate number of dimensions

ten–speed \'ten-,spēd\ n (1971) : a bicycle with 10 gear combinations

tens place \'tenz-\ n (1937) : the place two to the left of the decimal point in a number expressed in the Arabic system of writing numbers

ten–strike \'ten-,strīk\ n (1840) **1** : a strike in tenpins **2** : a highly successful stroke or achievement

¹tent \'tent\ n [ME *tente*, fr. OF, fr. L *tenta*, fem. of *tentus*, pp. of *tendere* to stretch — more at THIN] (14c) **1** : a collapsible shelter of fabric (as nylon or canvas) stretched and sustained by poles and used for camping outdoors or as a temporary building **2** : DWELLING **3 a** : something that resembles a tent or that serves as a shelter; *esp* : a canopy or enclosure placed over the head and shoulders to retain vapors or oxygen during medical administration **b** : the web of a tent caterpillar — **tent·less** \'tent-ləs\ adj — **tent·like** \-,līk\ adj

²tent vi (1607) **1** : to reside for the time being : LODGE **2** : to live in a tent ∼ vt **1** : to cover with or as if with a tent **2** : to lodge in tents

³tent vt [ME, fr. *tent* attention, short for *attent*, fr. OF *attente*, fr. *atendre* to attend] (14c) *chiefly Scot* : to attend to

ten·ta·cle \'ten-ti-kəl\ n [NL *tentaculum*, fr. L *tentare* to feel, touch — more at TEMPT] (1762) **1** : any of various elongate flexible usu. tactile or prehensile processes borne by animals and esp. invertebrates chiefly on the head or about the mouth **2 a** : something that resembles a tentacle esp. in or as if in grasping or feeling out **b** : a sensitive hair or emergence on a plant (as the sundew) — **ten·ta·cled** \-kəld\ adj

ten·tac·u·lar \ten-'ta-kyə-lər\ adj [NL *tentaculum*] (1828) **1** : of, relating to, or resembling tentacles **2** : equipped with tentacles

tent·age \'ten-tij\ n (1603) : a collection of tents : tent equipment

ten·ta·tive \'ten-tə-tiv\ adj [ML *tentativus*, fr. L *tentatus*, pp. of *tentare*, *temptare* to feel, try] (1626) **1** : not fully worked out or developed ⟨∼ plans⟩ **2** : HESITANT, UNCERTAIN ⟨a ∼ smile⟩ — **tentative** n — **ten·ta·tive·ly** adv — **ten·ta·tive·ness** n

tent caterpillar n (1854) : any of several destructive gregarious caterpillars (genus *Malacosoma* and esp. *M. americanum* of the family Lasiocampidae) that construct large silken webs on trees

tent·ed \'ten-təd\ adj (1604) **1** : covered with a tent or tents **2** : shaped like a tent

¹ten·ter \'ten-tər\ n [ME *teyntur, tentowre*] (14c) **1** : a frame or endless track with hooks or clips along two sides that is used for drying and stretching cloth **2** *archaic* : TENTERHOOK

²tenter n (1846) : one who lives in or occupies a tent

ten·ter·hook \'ten-tər-,húk\ n (15c) : a sharp hooked nail used esp. for fastening cloth on a tenter — **on tenterhooks** : in a state of uneasiness, strain, or suspense

tenth \'ten(t)th\ n, pl **tenths** \'ten(t)s, 'ten(t)ths\ (15c) **1** — see NUMBER table **2 a** : a musical interval embracing an octave and a third **b** : the tone at this interval — **tenth** adj or adv

tenth–rate \'tenth-'rāt\ adj (1834) : of the lowest character or quality

tent stitch n (1639) : a short stitch slanting to the right that is used in embroidery to form even lines of solid background

ten·ty *also* **tent·ie** \'ten-tē\ adj [³*tent*] (ca. 1555) *Scot* : ATTENTIVE, WATCHFUL

ten·u·is \'ten-yə-wəs\ n, pl **-u·es** \-yə-,wēz, -,wäs\ [ML, fr. L, thin, slight] (1650) : an unaspirated voiceless stop

te·nu·ity \te-'nü-ə-tē, tə-, -'nyü-\ n [L *tenuitas*, fr. *tenuis* thin, tenuous] (ca. 1536) **1** : lack of substance or strength **2** : lack of thickness : SLENDERNESS, THINNESS **3** : lack of density : rarefied quality or state

ten·u·ous \'ten-yə-wəs\ adj [L *tenuis* thin, slight, tenuous — more at THIN] (1597) **1** : not dense : RARE ⟨a ∼ fluid⟩ **2** : not thick : SLENDER ⟨a ∼ rope⟩ **3 a** : having little substance or strength : FLIMSY, WEAK ⟨∼ influences⟩ **b** : SHAKY 2a ⟨∼ reasons⟩ ⟨on grounds that were ∼⟩ *syn* see THIN — **ten·u·ous·ly** adv — **ten·u·ous·ness** n

ten·ure \'ten-yər *also* -,yúr\ n [ME, fr. MF *teneüre, tenure*, fr. ML *tenitura*, fr. (assumed) VL *tenitus*, pp. of L *tenēre* to hold — more at THIN] (15c) **1** : the act, right, manner, or term of holding something (as a landed property, a position, or an office); *esp* : a status granted after a trial period to a teacher that gives protection from summary dismissal **2** : GRASP, HOLD — **ten·ur·able** \-ə-bəl\ adj — **te·nur·ial** \te-'nyúr-ē-əl\ adj — **te·nur·ial·ly** \-ə-lē\ adv

ten·ured \'ten-yərd\ adj (1965) : having tenure ⟨∼ faculty members⟩

ten·ure–track \'ten-yər-,trak *also* -,yúr-\ adj (1976) : relating to or being a teaching position that may lead to a grant of tenure

te·nu·to \tä-'nü-(,)tō\ adv or adj [It, pp. of *tenere* to hold, fr. L *tenēre*] (1762) : in a manner so as to hold a tone or chord to its full value — used as a direction in music

te·o·cal·li \,tē-ə-'ka-lē, ,tā-ə-'kä-\ n [Nahuatl *teōcalli*, fr. *teōtl* god + *calli* house] (1613) : an ancient temple of Mexico or Central America usu. built upon the summit of a truncated pyramidal mound; *also* : the mound itself

te·o·sin·te \,tā-ō-'sin-tē\ n [MexSp, fr. Nahuatl *teōcintli*, fr. *teōtl* god + *cintli* dried ears of maize] (ca. 1877) : a tall annual grass (*Zea mexicana* syn. *Euchlaena mexicana*) of Mexico and Central America that is closely related to and sometimes considered ancestral to maize

te·pa \'tē-pə\ n [*tri-* + *ethylene* + *phosphor-* + *amide*] (1953) : a soluble crystalline compound $C_6H_{12}N_3OP$ that is used esp. as a chemical sterilizing agent of insects, a palliative in some kinds of cancer, and in finishing and flame-proofing textiles

te·pa·ry bean \'te-pə-rē-\ n [origin unknown] (1912) : an annual twining bean (*Phaseolus acutifolius* var. *latifolius*) that is native to the southwestern U.S. and Mexico and is cultivated for its roundish white, yellow, brown, or bluish black edible seeds; *also* : the seed

te·pee \'tē-(,)pē\ n [Dakota *thípi*, fr. *thi-* to dwell] (1743) : a conical tent usu. consisting of skins and used esp. by American Indians of the Plains

tepee

teph·ra \'te-frə\ n [NL, fr. Gk, ashes; akin to Skt *dahati* it burns — more at FOMENT] (1944) : solid material ejected into the air during a volcanic eruption; *esp* : ²ASH 2b

tep·id \'te-pəd\ adj [ME *teped*, fr. L *tepidus*, fr. *tepēre* to be moderately warm; akin to Skt *tapati* it heats, OIr *tess* heat] (14c) **1** : moderately warm : LUKEWARM ⟨a ∼ bath⟩ **2 a** : lacking in passion, force, or zest ⟨a ∼ joke⟩ **b** : marked by an absence of enthusiasm or conviction ⟨a ∼ interest⟩ — **te·pid·i·ty** \tə-'pi-də-tē, te-\ n — **tep·id·ly** \'te-pəd-lē\ adv — **tep·id·ness** n

TEPP \,tē-(,)ē-(,)pē-'pē\ n [*tetra-* + *ethyl* + *pyrophosphate*] (1948) : a mobile hygroscopic corrosive liquid organophosphate $C_8H_{20}O_7P_2$ that is a powerful anticholinesterase and is used esp. as an insecticide

te·qui·la \tə-'kē-lə, tā-\ n [Sp, fr. *Tequila*, town in Jalisco state, Mexico] (1849) : a Mexican liquor distilled from pulque

tequila sunrise n (1965) : a cocktail consisting of tequila, orange juice, and grenadine

ter- *comb form* [L, fr. *ter*; akin to Gk & Skt *tris* three times, L *tres* three — more at THREE] : three times : threefold : three ⟨*tercentenary*⟩

tera- *comb form* [ISV, fr. Gk *terat-, teras* monster] : trillion ⟨*terawatt*⟩

te·rai \tə-'rī\ n [*Tarai*, lowland belt of India] (1888) : a wide-brimmed double felt sun hat worn esp. in subtropical regions

ter·aph \'ter-əf\ n, pl **ter·a·phim** \'ter-ə-,fim\ [Heb *tĕrāphīm* (pl. in form but sing. in meaning)] (14c) : an image of a Semitic household god

\ə\ abut \ᵊ\ kitten, F table \ər\ further \a\ ash \ā\ ace \ä\ mop, mar \aú\ out \ch\ chin \e\ bet \ē\ easy \g\ go \i\ hit \ī\ ice \j\ job \ŋ\ sing \ō\ go \ó\ law \ói\ boy \th\ thin \t̲h̲\ the \ü\ loot \ú\ foot \y\ yet \zh\ vision \á, k̲, ⁿ, œ, œ̄, ᵫ, ᵬ, ᷣ\ *see* Guide to Pronunciation

terat- *or* **terato-** *comb form* [Gk, fr. *terat-*, *teras* marvel, portent, monster] : developmental malformation ⟨*teratogenic*⟩

te·rato·car·ci·no·ma \ˌter-ə-tō-ˌkär-s^ən-ˈō-mə\ *n* (1946) : a malignant teratoma; *esp* : one involving germinal cells of the testis

te·rato·gen \tə-ˈra-tə-jən\ *n* (1959) : a teratogenic agent

ter·a·to·gen·e·sis \ˌter-ə-tə-ˈje-nə-səs\ *n* [NL] (1901) : production of developmental malformations

ter·a·to·gen·ic \-ˈje-nik\ *adj* (1879) : of, relating to, or causing developmental malformations ⟨∼ substances⟩ ⟨∼ effects⟩ — **ter·a·to·ge·nic·i·ty** \-jə-ˈni-sə-tē\ *n*

ter·a·to·log·i·cal \ˌter-ə-t^əl-ˈä-ji-kəl\ *or* **ter·a·to·log·ic** \-jik\ *adj* (1857) **1** : abnormal in growth or structure **2** : of or relating to teratology

ter·a·tol·o·gy \ˌter-ə-ˈtä-lə-jē\ *n* (ca. 1842) : the study of malformations or serious deviations from the normal type in organisms — **ter·a·tol·o·gist** \-jist\ *n*

ter·a·to·ma \ˌter-ə-ˈtō-mə\ *n* [NL] (1879) : a tumor made up of a heterogeneous mixture of tissues

tera·watt \ˈter-ə-ˌwät\ *n* (1970) : a unit of power equal to one trillion watts

ter·bi·um \ˈtər-bē-əm\ *n* [NL, fr. *Ytterby*, Sweden] (1843) : a usu. trivalent metallic element of the rare-earth group — see ELEMENT table

terce \ˈtərs\ *n*, *often cap* [ME, third, terce — more at TIERCE] (14c) : the third of the canonical hours

ter·cel \ˈtər-səl\ *var of* TIERCEL

ter·cen·te·na·ry \ˌtər-(ˌ)sen-ˈte-nə-rē, (ˌ)tər-ˈsen-t^ən-ˌer-ē\ *n*, *pl* **-ries** (1855) : a 300th anniversary or its celebration — **tercentenary** *adj*

ter·cen·ten·ni·al \ˌtər-(ˌ)sen-ˈte-nē-əl\ *adj or n* (1872) : TERCENTENARY

ter·cet \ˈtər-sət\ *n* [It *terzetto*, fr. dim. of *terzo* third, fr. L *tertius* — more at THIRD] (1598) : a unit or group of three lines of verse: **a** : one of the 3-line stanzas in terza rima **b** : one of the two groups of three lines forming the sestet in an Italian sonnet

ter·e·binth \ˈter-ə-ˌbin(t)th\ *n* [ME *terebynt*, fr. MF *terebinthe*, fr. L *terebinthus* — more at TURPENTINE] (14c) : a small European tree (*Pistacia terebinthus*) of the cashew family yielding turpentine

te·re·do \tə-ˈrē-(ˌ)dō, -ˈrā-\ *n*, *pl* **teredos** *or* **te·red·i·nes** \-ˈre-d^ən-ˌēz\ [ME, fr. L *teredin-*, *teredo*, fr. Gk *terēdōn*; akin to Gk *tetrainein* to bore — more at THROW] (14c) : SHIPWORM

tere·phthal·ate \ˌter-ə(f)-ˈtha-ˌlāt\ *n* (1868) : a salt or ester of terephthalic acid; *esp* : a dimethyl-ester that is a major starting material for polyester fibers and coatings

tere·phthal·ic acid \ˌter-ə(f)-ˈtha-lik-\ *n* [ISV *terebene*, mixture of terpenes from distilled turpentine + *phthalic acid*] (1857) : a *p*-dicarboxylic acid C₈H₆O₄ that is obtained esp. by oxidation of xylene and is used chiefly in the synthesis of polyesters

te·rete \tə-ˈrēt, te-\ *adj* [L *teret-*, *teres* well turned, rounded; akin to L *terere* to rub — more at THROW] (ca. 1619) : approximately cylindrical but usu. tapering at both ends ⟨a ∼ seedpod⟩

Te·reus \ˈter-yüs, ˈtē-ˌrüs\ *n* [L, fr. Gk *Tēreus*] : the husband of Procne who rapes his sister-in-law Philomela

ter·gite \ˈtər-ˌgīt\ *n* [NL *tergum*] (1885) : the dorsal plate or dorsal portion of the covering of a metameric segment of an arthropod; *esp* : one on the abdomen

ter·gi·ver·sate \ˈtər-jə-vər-ˌsāt, ˌtər-ˈji-vər-ˌsāt, -ˈgi-; ˌtər-jə-ˈvər-\ *vi* **-sat·ed; -sat·ing** [L *tergiversatus*, pp. of *tergiversari* to show reluctance, fr. *tergum* back + *versare* to turn, freq. of *vertere* to turn — more at WORTH] (1654) : to engage in tergiversation — **ter·gi·ver·sa·tor** \-ˌsā-tər\ *n*

ter·gi·ver·sa·tion \ˌtər-ji-vər-ˈsā-shən, -ˌgi-; ˌtər-ji-(ˌ)vər-\ *n* (1570) **1** : evasion of straightforward action or clear-cut statement : EQUIVOCATION **2** : desertion of a cause, position, party, or faith

ter·gum \ˈtər-gəm\ *n*, *pl* **ter·ga** \-gə\ [NL, fr. L, back] (ca. 1826) : the dorsal part or plate of a segment of an arthropod : TERGITE, NOTUM — **ter·gal** \-gəl\ *adj*

ter·i·ya·ki \ˌter-ē-ˈyä-kē\ *n* [Jp, fr. *teri* glaze + *yaki* broil] (1962) : a Japanese dish of meat or fish that is grilled or broiled after being soaked in a seasoned soy sauce marinade

¹term \ˈtərm\ *n* [ME *terme* boundary, end, fr. OF, fr. L *terminus*; akin to Gk *termōn* boundary, end, Skt *tarman* top of a post] (13c) **1 a** : END, TERMINATION; *also* : a point in time assigned to something (as a payment) **b** : the time at which a pregnancy of normal length terminates ⟨had her baby at full ∼⟩ **2 a** : a limited or definite extent of time; *esp* : the time for which something lasts : DURATION, TENURE ⟨∼ of office⟩ ⟨lost money in the short ∼⟩ **b** : the whole period for which an estate is granted; *also* : the estate or interest held by one for a term **c** : the time during which a court is in session **3** *pl* : provisions that determine the nature and scope of an agreement : CONDITIONS ⟨∼s of sale⟩ ⟨liberal credit ∼s⟩ **4 a** : a word or expression that has a precise meaning in some uses or is peculiar to a science, art, profession, or subject ⟨legal ∼s⟩ **b** *pl* : expression of a specified kind ⟨described in glowing ∼s⟩ **5 a** : a unitary or compound expression connected with another by a plus or minus sign **b** : an element of a fraction or proportion or of a series or sequence **6** *pl* **a** : mutual relationship : FOOTING ⟨on good ∼s⟩ **b** : AGREEMENT, CONCORD ⟨come to ∼s⟩ **7** : any of the three substantive elements of a syllogism **8** : a quadrangular pillar often tapering downward and adorned on the top with the figure of a head or the upper part of the body **9** : division in a school year during which instruction is regularly given to students — **in terms of** : with respect to or in relation to ⟨thinks of everything *in terms of* money⟩ — **on one's own terms** : in accordance with one's wishes : in one's own way ⟨prefers to live *on his own terms*⟩

²term *vt* (ca. 1557) : to apply a term to : CALL, NAME

¹ter·ma·gant \ˈtər-mə-gənt\ *n* [ME] **1** *cap* : a deity erroneously ascribed to Islam by medieval European Christians and represented in early English drama as a violent character **2** : an overbearing or nagging woman : SHREW

²termagant *adj* (1596) : OVERBEARING, SHREWISH

term·er \ˈtər-mər\ *n* (1634) : a person serving for a specified term (as in a political office or in prison) ⟨a first ∼⟩

ter·mi·na·ble \ˈtər-mə-nə-bəl, ˈtərm-nə-\ *adj* [ME, fr. *terminen* to terminate, fr. MF *terminer*, fr. L *terminare*] (15c) : capable of being terminated — **ter·mi·na·ble·ness** *n* — **ter·mi·na·bly** \-blē\ *adv*

¹ter·mi·nal \ˈtərm-nəl, ˈtər-mə-n^əl\ *adj* [L *terminalis*, fr. *terminus*] (1744) **1 a** : of or relating to an end, extremity, boundary, or terminus ⟨a ∼ pillar⟩ **b** : growing at the end of a branch or stem ⟨a ∼ bud⟩ **2 a** : of, relating to, or occurring in a term or each term ⟨∼ payments⟩ **b** : leading ultimately to death : FATAL ⟨∼ cancer⟩ **c** : approaching or close to death : being in the final stages of a fatal disease ⟨a ∼ patient⟩ **d** : extremely or hopelessly severe ⟨∼ boredom⟩ **3 a** : occurring at or constituting the end of a period or series : CONCLUDING ⟨the ∼ moments of life⟩ **b** : not intended as preparation for further academic work ⟨a ∼ curriculum⟩ *syn* see LAST — **ter·mi·nal·ly** *adv*

²terminal *n* (1831) **1** : a part that forms the end : EXTREMITY, TERMINATION **2** : a terminating usu. ornamental detail : FINIAL **3** : a device attached to the end of a wire or cable or to an electrical apparatus for convenience in making connections **4 a** : either end of a carrier line having facilities for the handling of freight and passengers **b** : a freight or passenger station that is central to a considerable area or serves as a junction at any point with other lines **c** : a town or city at the end of a carrier line : TERMINUS **5** : a combination of a keyboard and output device (as a video display unit) by which data can be entered into or output from a computer or electronic communications system

terminal leave *n* (1944) : a final leave consisting of accumulated unused leave granted to a member of the armed forces just prior to separation or discharge from service

terminal side *n* (1927) : a straight line that has been rotated around a point on another line to form an angle measured in a clockwise or counterclockwise direction — compare INITIAL SIDE

¹ter·mi·nate \ˈtər-mə-nət\ *adj* [ME, fr. L *terminatus*, pp. of *terminare*, fr. *terminus*] (15c) : coming to an end or capable of ending

²ter·mi·nate \-ˌnāt\ *vb* **-nat·ed; -nat·ing** *vi* (1610) **1** : to extend only to a limit (as a point or line); *esp* : to reach a terminus **2** : to form an ending **3** : to come to an end in time ∼ *vt* **1 a** : to bring to an end : CLOSE ⟨∼ a marriage by divorce⟩ ⟨∼ a transmission line⟩ **b** : to form the conclusion of ⟨review questions ∼ each chapter⟩ **c** : to discontinue the employment of ⟨workers *terminated* because of slow business⟩ **2** : to serve as an ending, limit, or boundary of *syn* see CLOSE

terminating decimal *n* (ca. 1909) : a decimal which can be expressed in a finite number of figures or for which all figures to the right of some place are zero — compare REPEATING DECIMAL

ter·mi·na·tion \ˌtər-mə-ˈnā-shən\ *n* (ca. 1500) **1** : end in time or existence : CONCLUSION ⟨the ∼ of life⟩ **2** : the last part of a word; *esp* : an inflectional ending **3** : the act of terminating **4** : a limit in space or extent : BOUND **5** : OUTCOME, RESULT — **ter·mi·na·tion·al** \-shnəl, -shə-n^əl\ *adj*

ter·mi·na·tive \ˈtər-mə-ˌnā-tiv\ *adj* (15c) : tending or serving to terminate : ENDING — **ter·mi·na·tive·ly** *adv*

ter·mi·na·tor \-ˌnā-tər\ *n* (1770) **1** : the dividing line between the illuminated and the unilluminated part of the moon's or a planet's disk **2** : one that terminates

ter·mi·nol·o·gy \ˌtər-mə-ˈnä-lə-jē\ *n*, *pl* **-gies** [ML *terminus* term, expression (fr. L, boundary, limit) + E *-o-* + *-logy*] (1801) **1** : the technical or special terms used in a business, art, science, or special subject **2** : nomenclature as a field of study — **ter·mi·no·log·i·cal** \-mə-n^əl-ˈä-ji-kəl\ *adj* — **ter·mi·no·log·i·cal·ly** \-ji-k(ə-)lē\ *adv*

term insurance *n* (1897) : insurance for a specified period that provides for no payment to the insured except on losses during the period and that becomes void upon its expiration

ter·mi·nus \ˈtər-mə-nəs\ *n*, *pl* **-ni** \-ˌnī, -ˌnē\ *or* **-nus·es** [L, boundary, end — more at TERM] (ca. 1617) **1** : a final goal : a finishing point **2** : a post or stone marking a boundary **3** : either end of a transportation line or travel route; *also* : the station, town, or city at such a place : TERMINAL **4** : an extreme point or element : TIP ⟨the ∼ of a glacier⟩

terminus ad quem \-ˌäd-ˈkwem\ *n* [NL, lit., limit to which] (ca. 1555) **1** : a goal, object, or course of action : DESTINATION, PURPOSE **2** : a final limiting point in time

terminus a quo \-ˌä-ˈkwō\ *n* [NL, lit., limit from which] (ca. 1555) **1** : a point of origin **2** : a first limiting point in time

ter·mi·tar·i·um \ˌtər-mə-ˈter-ē-əm, -ˌmī-\ *n*, *pl* **-ia** \-ē-ə\ [NL] (1863) : a termites' nest

ter·mi·tary \ˈtər-mə-ˌter-ē, -ˌmī-ˌter-ē\ *n*, *pl* **-tar·ies** (1826) : TERMITARIUM

ter·mite \ˈtər-ˌmīt\ *n* [NL *Termit-*, *Termes*, genus of termites, fr. LL, a worm that eats wood, alter. of L *tarmit-*, *tarmes*; akin to Gk *tetrainein* to bore — more at THROW] (1781) : any of numerous pale-colored soft-bodied social insects (order Isoptera) that live in colonies consisting usu. of winged sexual forms, wingless sterile workers, and soldiers, feed on wood, and include some which are very destructive to wooden structures and trees — called also *white ant*

term·less \ˈtərm-ləs\ *adj* (ca. 1541) **1** : having no term or end : BOUNDLESS, UNENDING **2** : UNCONDITIONED, UNCONDITIONAL

term paper *n* (1926) : a major written assignment in a school or college course representative of a student's achievement during a term

tern \ˈtərn\ *n* [of Scand origin; akin to Dan *terne* tern] (1678) : any of various chiefly marine birds (subfamily Sterninae of the family Laridae and esp. genus *Sterna*) that differ from the related gulls in usu. smaller size, a more slender build, a sharply pointed bill, narrower wings, and an often forked tail

ter·na·ry \ˈtər-nə-rē\ *adj* [ME, fr. L *ternarius*, fr. *terni* three each; akin to L *tres* three — more at THREE] (15c) **1 a** : of, relating to, or proceeding by threes **b** : having three elements, parts, or divisions : THREEFOLD **c** : arranged in threes ⟨∼ petals⟩ **2** : using three as the base ⟨a ∼ logarithm⟩ **3 a** : being or consisting of an alloy of three elements **b** : of, relating to, or containing three different elements, atoms, radicals, or groups ⟨sulfuric acid is a ∼ acid⟩ **4** : third in order or rank

ter·nate \ˈtər-ˌnāt, -nət\ *adj* [NL *ternatus*, fr. ML, pp. of *ternare* to treble, fr. L *terni*] (1760) : arranged in threes or in subdivisions so arranged ⟨a ∼ leaf⟩ — **ter·nate·ly** *adv*

terne \ˈtərn\ *n* [*terneplate*] (1891) **1** : an alloy of lead and tin typically in a ratio of four to one that is used as a coating in producing terneplate **2** : TERNEPLATE

terne·plate \-ˌplāt\ *n* [prob. fr. F *terne* dull (fr. MF, fr. *ternir* to tarnish) + E *plate*] (ca. 1858) : sheet iron or steel coated with an alloy of about four parts lead to one part tin

ter·pene \ˈtər-ˌpēn\ *n* [ISV *terp-* (fr. G *Terpentin* turpentine, fr. ML terbentina) + -ene — more at TURPENTINE] (1873) : any of various isomeric hydrocarbons $C_{10}H_{16}$ found present in essential oils (as from conifers) and used esp. as solvents and in organic synthesis; *broadly* : any of numerous hydrocarbons $(C_5H_8)_n$ found esp. in essential oils, resins, and balsams — **ter·pene·less** \-ləs\ *adj* — **ter·pe·noid** \'tər-pə-ˌnȯid, ˌtər-'pē-\ *adj or n*

ter·pin·e·ol \ˌtər-'pi-nē-ˌȯl, -ˌōl\ *n* [ISV, fr. *terpine* $(C_{10}H_{18}(OH)_2)$] (1894) : any of three fragrant isomeric alcohols $C_{10}H_{17}OH$ found in essential oils or made artificially and used esp. in perfume or as solvents

ter·poly·mer \ˌtər-'pä-lə-mər\ *n* (1947) : a polymer (as a complex resin) that results from copolymerization of three discrete monomers

Terp·sich·o·re \ˌtərp-'si-kə-(ˌ)rē\ *n* [L, fr. Gk *Terpsichorē*] : the Greek Muse of dancing and choral song

terp·si·cho·re·an \ˌtərp-(ˌ)si-kə-'rē-ən; -sə-'kōr-ē-, -'kȯr-\ *adj* (1825) : of or relating to dancing

ter·ra \'ter-ə\ *n, pl* **ter·rae** \-(ˌ)ē, -ˌī\ [NL, fr. L, land] (1946) : any of the relatively light-colored highland areas on the surface of the moon or a planet

¹**ter·race** \'ter-əs\ *n* [MF, pile of earth, platform, terrace, fr. OProv *terrassa*, fr. *terra* earth, fr. L, earth, land; akin to L *torrēre* to parch — more at THIRST] (1515) **1 a** : a colonnaded porch or promenade **b** : a flat roof or open platform **c** : a relatively level paved or planted area adjoining a building **2 a** : a raised embankment with the top leveled **b** : one of usu. a series of horizontal ridges made in a hillside to increase cultivatable land, conserve moisture, or minimize erosion **3** : a level ordinarily narrow plain usu. with steep front bordering a river, lake, or sea; *also* : a similar undersea feature **4 a** : a row of houses or apartments on raised ground or a sloping site **b** : a group of row houses **c** : a strip of park in the middle of a street often planted with trees or shrubs **d** : STREET **5** : a section of a British soccer stadium set aside for standing spectators

²**terrace** *vt* **ter·raced; ter·rac·ing** (1615) **1** : to provide (as a building or hillside) with a terrace **2** : to make into a terrace

ter·ra-cot·ta \ˌter-ə-'kä-tə\ *n, often attrib* [It *terra cotta*, lit., baked earth] (1722) **1** : a glazed or unglazed fired clay used esp. for statuettes and vases and architectural purposes (as roofing, facing, and relief ornamentation) **2** : a brownish orange

terra fir·ma \-'fər-mə *also* -'fir-\ *n* [NL, lit., solid land] (1693) : dry land : solid ground

ter·rain \tə-'rān *also* te-\ *n* [F, land, ground, fr. (assumed) VL *terranum*, alter. of L *terrenum*, fr. neut. of *terrenus* of earth — more at TERRENE] (1766) **1 a** (1) : a geographical area (2) : a piece of land : GROUND **b** : the physical features of a tract of land **2** : TERRANE 1 **3 a** : a field of knowledge or interest : TERRITORY **b** : ENVIRONMENT, MILIEU

ter·ra in·cog·ni·ta \'ter-ə-ˌin-ˌkäg-'nē-tə, -in-'käg-nə-tə\ *n, pl* **ter·rae in·cog·ni·tae** \'ter-ˌī-ˌin-ˌkäg-'nē-ˌti, -in-'käg-nə-ˌti\ [L] (1616) : unknown territory : an unexplored country or field of knowledge

Ter·ra·my·cin \ˌter-ə-'mī-sᵊn\ *trademark* — used for oxytetracycline

ter·rane \tə-'rān, te-\ *n* [alter. of *terrain*] (1864) **1** : the area or surface over which a particular rock or group of rocks is prevalent **2** : TERRAIN 1a

ter·ra·pin \'ter-ə-pən, 'tar-\ *n* [of Algonquian origin; akin to Delaware (dial. of New York) *tó'lpew*, a kind of turtle] (1613) : any of various aquatic turtles (family Emydidae); *esp* : DIAMONDBACK TERRAPIN

terr·aque·ous \te-'rä-kwē-əs, tə-, -'ra-\ *adj* [L *terra* land + E *aqueous*] (ca. 1658) : consisting of land and water

ter·rar·i·um \tə-'rar-ē-əm, -'rer-\ *n, pl* **-ia** \-ē-ə\ *or* **-i·ums** [NL, fr. L *terra* + -*arium* (as in *vivarium*)] (1890) : a usu. transparent enclosure for keeping or raising plants or usu. small animals (as turtles) indoors

ter·raz·zo \tə-'ra-(ˌ)zō, -'rät-(ˌ)sō\ *n* [It, lit., terrace, perh. fr. OProv *terrassa*] (1897) : a mosaic flooring consisting of small pieces of marble or granite set in mortar and given a high polish

¹**ter·rene** \te-'rēn, tə-; 'ter-ˌēn\ *adj* [ME, fr. L *terrenus* of earth, fr. *terra* earth] (14c) : MUNDANE, EARTHLY

²**terrene** *n* (1667) : a land area : EARTH, TERRAIN

ter·re·plein \'ter-ə-ˌplān\ *n* [MF, fr. OIt *terrapieno*, fr. ML *terraplenum*, fr. *terra plenus* filled with earth] (1591) : the level space behind a parapet of a rampart where guns are mounted

ter·res·tri·al \tə-'res-t(r)ē-əl; -'res-chəl, -'resh-\ *adj* [ME, fr. L *terrestris*, fr. *terra* earth — more at TERRACE] (15c) **1 a** : of or relating to the earth or its inhabitants ⟨~ magnetism⟩ **b** : mundane in scope or character **2 a** : of or relating to land as distinct from air or water ⟨~ transportation⟩ **b** (1) : living on or in or growing from land ⟨~ plants⟩ (2) : of or relating to terrestrial organisms ⟨~ habits⟩ **3** : belonging to the class of planets that are like the earth (as in density and silicate composition) ⟨the ~ planets Mercury, Venus, and Mars⟩ — **terrestrial** *n* — **ter·res·tri·al·ly** *adv*

ter·ret \'ter-ət\ *n* [ME *turette*, alter. of *toret*, fr. MF, fr. OF, dim. of *tour* circuit, ring — more at TURN] (15c) : one of the rings on the top of a harness pad through which the reins pass

ter·ri·ble \'ter-ə-bəl\ *adj* [ME, fr. MF, fr. L *terribilis*, fr. *terrēre* to frighten — more at TERROR] (15c) **1 a** : exciting extreme alarm or intense fear : TERRIFYING **b** : formidable in nature : AWESOME ⟨a ~ responsibility⟩ **c** : DIFFICULT ⟨in a ~ bind⟩ **2** : EXTREME, GREAT ⟨a ~ disappointment⟩ **3** : extremely bad: as **a** : strongly repulsive : OBNOXIOUS ⟨a ~ smell⟩ **b** : notably unattractive or objectionable **c** : of very poor quality ⟨a ~ movie⟩ — **ter·ri·ble·ness** *n* — **ter·ri·bly** \-blē\ *adv*

ter·ric·o·lous \te-'ri-kə-ləs, tə-\ *adj* [L *terricola* earth dweller, fr. *terra* earth + *colere* to inhabit — more at WHEEL] (ca. 1836) : living on or in the ground

ter·ri·er \'ter-ē-ər\ *n* [ME, fr. MF (*chien*) *terrier*, lit., earth dog, fr. *terrier* of earth, fr. ML *terrarius*, fr. L *terra*] (15c) : any of various usu. small dogs orig. used by hunters to dig for small furred game and engage the quarry underground or drive it out

ter·rif·ic \tə-'ri-fik\ *adj* [L *terrificus*, fr. *terrēre* to frighten] (1667) **1 a** : very bad : FRIGHTFUL **b** : exciting or fit to excite fear or awe **2**

: EXTRAORDINARY ⟨~ speed⟩ **3** : unusually fine : MAGNIFICENT ⟨~ weather⟩ — **ter·rif·i·cal·ly** \-fi-k(ə-)lē\ *adv*

ter·ri·fy \'ter-ə-ˌfī\ *vt* **-fied; -fy·ing** [L *terrificare*, fr. *terrificus*] (1575) **1 a** : to drive or impel by menacing : SCARE **b** : DETER, INTIMIDATE **2** : to fill with terror — **ter·ri·fy·ing** \-ˌfī-iŋ\ *adj* (ca. 1586) **1** : causing terror or apprehension **2** : of a formidable nature — **ter·ri·fy·ing·ly** \-iŋ-lē\ *adv*

ter·rig·e·nous \te-'ri-jə-nəs, tə-\ *adj* [L *terrigena* earthborn, fr. *terra* earth + *gignere* to beget — more at KIN] (1882) : being or relating to oceanic sediment derived directly from the destruction of rocks on the earth's surface

ter·rine \tə-'rēn, ter-'ēn\ *n* [F — more at TUREEN] (ca. 1706) **1 a** : TUREEN 1 **b** : a usu. earthenware dish in which foods are cooked and served **2** : a mixture of chopped meat, fish, or vegetables cooked and served in a terrine

¹**ter·ri·to·ri·al** \ˌter-ə-'tȯr-ē-əl, -'tȯr-\ *adj* (1625) **1 a** : NEARBY, LOCAL **b** : serving outlying areas : REGIONAL **2 a** : of or relating to a territory ⟨~ government⟩ **b** : of or relating to or organized chiefly for home defense ⟨a ~ army⟩ **c** : of or relating to private property **3 a** : of or relating to an assigned or preempted area ⟨~ commanders⟩ **b** : exhibiting territoriality ⟨~ birds⟩ — **ter·ri·to·ri·al·ly** \-ē-ə-lē\ *adv*

²**territorial** *n* (1907) : a member of a territorial military unit

territorial court *n* (1857) : a court in a U.S. territory that has jurisdiction over local and federal cases

ter·ri·to·ri·al·ism \ˌter-ə-'tȯr-ē-ə-ˌli-zəm, -'tȯr-\ *n* (1881) **1** : LANDLORDISM **2** : the principle established in 1555 requiring the inhabitants of a territory of the Holy Roman Empire to conform to the religion of their ruler or to emigrate — **ter·ri·to·ri·al·ist** \-list\ *n*

ter·ri·to·ri·al·i·ty \-ˌtȯr-ē-'a-lə-tē, -ˌtȯr-\ *n* (1894) **1** : territorial status **2 a** : persistent attachment to a specific territory **b** : the pattern of behavior associated with the defense of a territory

ter·ri·to·ri·al·ize \-'tȯr-ē-ə-ˌlīz, -'tȯr-\ *vt* **-ized; -iz·ing** (1818) : to organize on a territorial basis — **ter·ri·to·ri·al·i·za·tion** \-ˌtȯr-ē-ə-lə-'zā-shən, -ˌtȯr-\ *n*

territorial waters *n pl* (1841) : the waters under the sovereign jurisdiction of a nation or state including both marginal sea and inland waters

ter·ri·to·ry \'ter-ə-ˌtȯr-ē, -ˌtȯr-\ *n, pl* **-ries** [ME, fr. L *territorium*, lit., land around a town, fr. *terra* land — more at TERRACE] (15c) **1 a** : a geographical area belonging to or under the jurisdiction of a governmental authority **b** : an administrative subdivision of a country **c** : a part of the U.S. not included within any state but organized with a separate legislature **d** : a geographical area (as a colonial possession) dependent on an external government but having some degree of autonomy **2 a** : an indeterminate geographical area **b** : a field of knowledge or interest **3** : an assigned area; *esp* : one in which a sales representative or distributor operates **b** : an area often including a nesting or denning site and a variable foraging range that is occupied and defended by an animal or group of animals — **go with the territory** *or* **come with the territory** : to be a natural or unavoidable aspect or accompaniment of a particular situation, position, or field ⟨criticism *goes with the territory* in this job⟩

ter·ror \'ter-ər\ *n* [ME, fr. MF *terreur*, fr. L *terror*, fr. *terrēre* to frighten; akin to Gk *trein* to be afraid, flee, *tremein* to tremble — more at TREMBLE] (14c) **1** : a state of intense fear : SCOURGE **b** : a frightening aspect ⟨the ~s of invasion⟩ **c** : a cause of anxiety : WORRY **d** : an appalling person or thing; *esp* : BRAT **3** : REIGN OF TERROR **4** : violence (as bombing) committed by groups in order to intimidate a population or government into granting their demands ⟨insurrection and revolutionary ~⟩ *syn* see FEAR — **ter·ror·less** \-ləs\ *adj*

ter·ror·ise *chiefly Brit var of* TERRORIZE

ter·ror·ism \'ter-ər-ˌi-zəm\ *n* (1795) : the systematic use of terror esp. as a means of coercion — **ter·ror·ist** \-ər-ist\ *adj or n* — **ter·ror·is·tic** \ˌter-ər-'is-tik\ *adj*

ter·ror·ize \'ter-ər-ˌīz\ *vt* **-ized; -iz·ing** (1823) **1** : to fill with terror or anxiety : SCARE **2** : to coerce by threat or violence — **ter·ror·i·za·tion** \ˌter-ər-ə-'zā-shən\ *n*

ter·ry \'ter-ē\ *n, pl* **terries** [perh. modif. of F *tiré*, pp. of *tirer* to draw] (1784) **1** : the loop forming the pile in uncut pile fabrics **2** : an absorbent fabric with such loops — called also *terry cloth*

terse \'tərs\ *adj* **ters·er; ters·est** [L *tersus* clean, neat, fr. pp. of *tergēre* to wipe off] (1601) **1** : smoothly elegant : POLISHED **2** : devoid of superfluity ⟨a ~ summary⟩; *also* : SHORT, BRUSQUE ⟨dismissed me with a "no"⟩ *syn* see CONCISE — **terse·ly** *adv* — **terse·ness** *n*

¹**ter·tian** \'tər-shən\ *adj* [ME *tercian*, fr. L *tertianus*, lit., of the third, fr. *tertius* third — more at THIRD] (14c) : recurring at approximately 48-hour intervals — used of malaria

²**tertian** *n* (14c) : a tertian fever (as vivax malaria)

¹**ter·tia·ry** \'tər-shē-ˌer-ē, -shə-rē\ *n, pl* **-ries** (ca. 1550) **1** [ML *tertiarius*, fr. L, of a third] : a member of a monastic third order esp. of lay people **2** *cap* : the Tertiary period or system of rocks

²**tertiary** *adj* [L *tertiarius* of or containing a third, fr. *tertius* third] (ca. 1656) **1 a** : of third rank, importance, or value **b** *chiefly Brit* : of, relating to, or being higher education **c** : of, relating to, or constituting the third strongest of the three or four degrees of stress recognized by most linguists (as the stress of the third syllable of *basketball team*) **2** *cap* : of, relating to, or being the first period of the Cenozoic era or the corresponding system of rocks marked by the formation of high mountains (as the Alps, Caucasus, and Himalayas) and the dominance of mammals on land — see GEOLOGIC TIME table **3 a** : involving or resulting from the substitution of three atoms or groups ⟨a ~ salt⟩ **b** : being or containing a carbon atom having bonds to three other carbon atoms (an acid containing a ~ carbon) ⟨~ alcohols⟩ **4** : occurring in or being a third stage: as **a** : being or relating to the recovery of oil and gas from old wells by means of the underground application of heat and chemicals **b** : being or relating to the purifica-

\ə\ abut \ᵊ\ kitten, F table \ər\ further \a\ ash \ā\ ace \ä\ mop, mar \au̇\ out \ch\ chin \e\ bet \ē\ easy \g\ go \i\ hit \ī\ ice \j\ job \ŋ\ sing \ō\ go \ȯ\ law \ȯi\ boy \th\ thin \t͟h\ the \ü\ loot \u̇\ foot \y\ yet \zh\ vision \à, k̲, ⁿ, œ, œ̄, ᵫ, ᵫ̄, ᵜ\ *see* Guide to Pronunciation

tion of wastewater by removal of fine particles, nitrates, and phosphates

tertiary color n (ca. 1864) **1** : a color produced by mixing two secondary colors **2** : a color produced by an equal mixture of a primary color with a secondary color adjacent to it on the color wheel

tertiary syphilis n (1875) : the third stage of syphilis that develops after the disappearance of the secondary symptoms and is marked by ulcers in and gummas under the skin and commonly by involvement of the skeletel, cardiovascular, and nervous systems

ter·ti·um quid \ˌtər-shē-əm-ˈkwid, ˌtər-tē-\ n [LL, lit., third something; fr. its failing to fit into a dichotomy] (ca. 1724) **1** : a middle course or an intermediate component ⟨where there are two systems of law and two orders of courts, there must . . . be some *tertium quid* to deal with conflicts of law and jurisdiction —Ernest Baker⟩ **2** : a third party of ambiguous status ⟨there was a man and his wife and a *tertium quid* —Rudyard Kipling⟩

ter·va·lent \ˌtər-ˈvā-lənt, ˈtər-\ adj (ca. 1903) : TRIVALENT

ter·za ri·ma \ˌtert-sə-ˈrē-mə\ n [It, lit., third rhyme] (1819) : a verse form consisting of tercets usu. in iambic pentameter in English poetry with an interlaced rhyme scheme (as *aba, bcb, cdc*)

tes·la \ˈtes-lə\ n [Nikola Tesla] (1958) : a unit of magnetic flux density in the meter-kilogram-second system equivalent to one weber per square meter

tes·sel·late \ˈte-sə-ˌlāt\ vt **-lat·ed; -lat·ing** [LL *tessellatus,* pp. of *tessellare* to pave with tesserae, fr. L *tessella,* dim. of *tessera*] (1789) : to form into or adorn with mosaic

tes·sel·lat·ed \-ˌlā-təd\ adj (1695) : having a checkered appearance

tes·sel·la·tion \ˌte-sə-ˈlā-shən\ n (1660) **1** : MOSAIC; esp : a covering of an infinite geometric plane without gaps or overlaps by congruent plane figures of one type or a few types **2** : an act of tessellating : the state of being tessellated

tes·sera \ˈte-sə-rə\ n, pl **-ser·ae** \-ˌrē, -ˌrī\ [L, prob. ultim. fr. Gk *tessares* four; fr. its having four corners — more at FOUR] (ca. 1656) **1** : a small tablet (as of wood, bone, or ivory) used by the ancient Romans as a ticket, tally, voucher, or means of identification **2** : a small piece (as of marble, glass, or tile) used in mosaic work

tes·ser·act \ˈte-sə-ˌrakt\ n [Gk *tessares* four + *aktis* ray — more at ACTIN-] (1888) : the four-dimensional analogue of a cube

tes·si·tu·ra \ˌte-sə-ˈtur-ə\ n [It, lit., texture, fr. L *textura*] (ca. 1891) : the general range of a melody or voice part; specif : the part of the register in which most of the tones of a melody or voice part lie

¹test \ˈtest\ n [ME, vessel in which metals were assayed, cupel, fr. ME, fr. L *testum* earthen vessel; akin to L *testa* earthen pot, shell] (14c) **1 a** chiefly Brit : CUPEL **b** (1) : a critical examination, observation, or evaluation : TRIAL; specif : the procedure of submitting a statement to such conditions or operations as will lead to its proof or disproof or to its acceptance or rejection ⟨a ~ of a statistical hypothesis⟩ (2) : a basis for evaluation : CRITERION **c** : an ordeal or oath required as proof of conformity with a set of beliefs **2 a** : a means of testing: as (1) : a procedure, reaction, or reagent used to identify or characterize a substance or constituent (2) : something (as a series of questions or exercises) for measuring the skill, knowledge, intelligence, capacities, or aptitudes of an individual or group **b** : a positive result in such a test **3** : a result or value determined by testing **4** : TEST MATCH

²test vt (1689) **1 a** : to put to test or proof : TRY **2** : to require a doctrinal oath of ~ vi **1 a** : to undergo a test **b** : to be assigned a standing or evaluation on the basis of tests ⟨~ed positive for cocaine⟩ ⟨the cake ~ed done⟩ **2** : to apply a test as a means of analysis or diagnosis — used with for ⟨~ for mechanical aptitude⟩ — **test·abil·i·ty** \ˌtes-tə-ˈbi-lə-tē\ n — **test·able** \ˈtes-tə-bəl\ adj — **test the waters** also **test the water** : to make a preliminary test or survey (as of reaction or interest) before embarking on a course of action

³test n [L *testa* shell] (ca. 1842) : an external hard or firm covering (as a shell) of many invertebrates (as a foraminifer or a mollusk)

tes·ta \ˈtes-tə\ n, pl **tes·tae** \-ˌtē, -ˌtī\ [NL, fr. L, shell] (1796) : the hard external coating or integument of a seed

tes·ta·ceous \tes-ˈtā-shəs\ adj [L *testaceus,* fr. *testa* shell, earthen pot, brick] (1646) **1** : having a shell ⟨a ~ protozoan⟩ **2** : of any of the several light colors of bricks

tes·ta·cy \ˈtes-tə-sē\ n, pl **-cies** (ca. 1864) : the state of being testate

tes·ta·ment \ˈtes-tə-mənt\ n [ME, fr. LL & L; LL *testamentum* covenant with God, holy scripture, fr. L, last will, fr. *testari* to be a witness, call to witness, make a will, fr. *testis* witness; akin to L *tres* three & to L *stare* to stand; fr. the witness's standing by as a third party in a litigation — more at THREE, STAND] (14c) **1 a** archaic : a covenant between God and the human race **b** cap : either of two main divisions of the Bible **2 a** : a tangible proof or tribute **b** : an expression of conviction : CREDO **3 a** : an act by which a person determines the disposition of his or her property after death **b** : WILL — **tes·ta·men·ta·ry** \ˌtes-tə-ˈmen-tə-rē, -ˈmen-trē\ adj

tes·tate \ˈtes-ˌtāt, -tət\ adj [ME, fr. L *testatus,* pp. of *testari* to make a will] (15c) : having left a valid will ⟨she died ~⟩

tes·ta·tor \ˈtes-ˌtā-tər, tes-ˈ\ n [ME *testatour,* fr. AF, fr. LL *testator,* fr. L *testari*] (15c) : a person who dies leaving a will or testament in force

tes·ta·trix \ˈtes-ˌtā-triks, tes-ˈ\ n [LL, fem. of *testator*] (1591) : a female testator

test ban n (1958) : a self-imposed partial or complete ban on the testing of nuclear weapons that is mutually agreed to by countries possessing such weapons

test bed n (1914) : a vehicle (as an airplane) used for testing new equipment (as engines or weapons systems)

test case n (1894) **1** : a representative case whose outcome is likely to serve as a precedent **2** : a proceeding brought by agreement or on an understanding of the parties to obtain a decision as to the constitutionality of a statute

test·cross \ˈtes(t)-ˌkròs\ n (1934) : a genetic cross between a homozygous recessive individual and a corresponding suspected heterozygote to determine the genotype of the latter — **testcross** vt

test–drive \ˈtes(t)-ˌdrīv\ vt **-drove** \-ˌdrōv\; **-driv·en** \-ˌdri-vən\; **-driv·ing** \-ˌdrī-viŋ\ (1950) : to drive (a motor vehicle) in order to evaluate performance — **test–drive** n

test·ed \ˈtes-təd\ adj (1748) : subjected to or qualified through testing — often used in combination ⟨time-*tested* principles⟩

test·ee \tes-ˈtē\ n (1930) : one who takes an examination

¹tes·ter \ˈtēs-tər, ˈtes-\ n [ME, fr. MF *testiere* headpiece, head covering, fr. *teste* head, fr. LL *testa* skull, fr. L, shell] (14c) : the canopy over a bed, pulpit, or altar

²tes·ter \ˈtes-tər\ n [modif. of MF *testart,* fr. *teston*] (1546) : TESTON

³test·er \ˈtes-tər\ n (1661) : one that tests or is used for testing

test–fly \-ˌflī\ vt **-flew** \-ˌflü\; **-flown** \-ˌflōn\; **-fly·ing** (1936) : to subject to a flight test ⟨~ an experimental plane⟩

tes·ti·cle \ˈtes-ti-kəl\ n [ME *testicule,* fr. L *testiculus,* dim. of *testis*] (15c) : TESTIS; esp : one of a higher mammal usu. with its enclosing structures — **tes·tic·u·lar** \tes-ˈti-kyə-lər\ adj

tes·ti·fy \ˈtes-tə-ˌfī\ vb **-fied; -fy·ing** [ME *testifien,* fr. L *testificari,* fr. *testis* witness] vi (14c) **1 a** : to make a statement based on personal knowledge or belief : bear witness **b** : to serve as evidence or proof **2** : to express a personal conviction **3** : to make a solemn declaration under oath for the purpose of establishing a fact (as in a court) ~ vt **1 a** : to bear witness to : ATTEST **b** : to serve as evidence of : PROVE **2** archaic **a** : to make known (a personal conviction) **b** : to give evidence of : SHOW **3** : to declare under oath before a tribunal or officially constituted public body — **tes·ti·fi·er** \-ˌfī-(-ə)r\ n

¹tes·ti·mo·ni·al \ˌtes-tə-ˈmō-nē-əl, -nyəl\ adj (15c) **1** : of, relating to, or constituting testimony **2** : expressive of appreciation or esteem ⟨a ~ dinner⟩

²testimonial n (15c) **1** : EVIDENCE, TESTIMONY **2 a** : a statement testifying to benefits received **b** : a character reference : letter of recommendation **3** : an expression of appreciation : TRIBUTE

tes·ti·mo·ny \ˈtes-tə-ˌmō-nē\ n, pl **-nies** [ME, fr. LL & L; LL *testimonium* Decalogue, fr. L, evidence, witness, fr. *testis* witness — more at TESTAMENT] (14c) **1 a** (1) : the tablets inscribed with the Mosaic law (2) : the ark containing the tablets **b** : a divine decree attested in the Scriptures **2 a** : firsthand authentication of a fact : EVIDENCE **b** : an outward sign **c** : a solemn declaration usu. made orally by a witness under oath in response to interrogation by a lawyer or authorized public official **3 a** : an open acknowledgment **b** : a public profession of religious experience

test·ing adj (1878) : requiring maximum effort or ability ⟨a most difficult and ~ problem —Ernest Bevin⟩

tes·tis \ˈtes-təs\ n, pl **tes·tes** \ˈtes-ˌtēz\ [L, witness, testis] (ca. 1704) : a typically paired male reproductive gland that produces sperm and that in most mammals is contained within the scrotum at sexual maturity

test–mar·ket \ˈtes(t)-ˌmär-kət\ vt (1953) : to subject (a product) to trial in a limited market

test match n (1862) **1** : any of a series of championship cricket matches played between teams representing Australia and England **2** : a championship game or series (as of cricket) played between teams representing different countries

tes·ton \ˈtes-ˌtän\ or **tes·toon** \tes-ˈtün\ n [MF, fr. OIt *testone,* aug. of *testa* head, fr. LL, skull — more at TESTER] (1536) : any of several old European coins: as **a** : a shilling of Henry VIII of England decreasing in value to ninepence and then to sixpence in Shakespeare's time **b** : a French silver coin of the 16th century worth between 10 and 14½ sous

tes·tos·ter·one \te-ˈstäs-tə-ˌrōn\ n [*testis* + *-o-* + *-sterone*] (1935) : a hormone that is a hydroxy steroid ketone $C_{19}H_{28}O_2$ produced esp. by the testes or made synthetically and that is responsible for inducing and maintaining male secondary sex characters

test pattern n (ca. 1946) : a fixed picture broadcast by a television station to assist viewers in adjusting their receivers

test pilot n (1917) : a pilot who specializes in putting new or experimental airplanes through maneuvers designed to test them (as for strength) by producing strains in excess of normal

test–tube \ˈtes(t)-ˌ\ adj (1935) : produced by fertilization in laboratory apparatus and implantation in the uterus, by fertilization and growth in laboratory apparatus, or sometimes by artificial insemination ⟨~ babies⟩

test tube n (1846) : a plain or lipped tube usu. of thin glass closed at one end and used esp. in chemistry and biology

tes·tu·do \tes-ˈtü-(ˌ)dō, -ˈtyü-\ n, pl **-dos** [L *testudin-, testudo,* lit., tortoise, tortoise shell; akin to L *testa* shell] (1609) : a cover of overlapping shields or a shed wheeled up to a wall used by the ancient Romans to protect an attacking force

tes·ty \ˈtes-tē\ adj **tes·ti·er; -est** [ME *testif,* fr. AF, headstrong, fr. *teste* head — more at TESTER] (15c) **1** : easily annoyed : IRRITABLE **2** : marked by impatience or ill humor ⟨~ remarks⟩ — **tes·ti·ly** \-tə-lē\ adv — **tes·ti·ness** \-tē-nəs\ n

Tet \ˈtet\ n [Vietnamese *têt*] (1885) : the Vietnamese New Year observed for three days beginning at the first new moon after January 20

tet·a·nal \ˈte-tᵊn-əl\ adj (1939) : of, relating to, or derived from tetanus ⟨~ toxin⟩

te·tan·ic \te-ˈta-nik\ adj (ca. 1727) : of, relating to, being, or tending to produce tetany or tetanus — **te·tan·i·cal·ly** \-ni-k(ə-)lē\ adv

tet·a·nize \ˈte-tᵊn-ˌīz\ vt **-nized; -niz·ing** (1849) : to induce tetanus in ⟨~ a muscle⟩ — **tet·a·ni·za·tion** \ˌte-tᵊn-ə-ˈzā-shən, -tet-nə-\ n

tet·a·nus \ˈte-tᵊn-əs, ˈtet-nəs\ n [ME, fr. L, fr. Gk *tetanos,* fr. *tetanos* stretched, rigid; akin to Gk *teinein* to stretch — more at THIN] (14c) **1 a** : an acute infectious disease characterized by tonic spasm of voluntary muscles esp. of the jaw and caused by the specific toxin of a bacterium (*Clostridium tetani*) which is usu. introduced through a wound — compare LOCKJAW **b** : the bacterium that causes tetanus **2** : prolonged contraction of a muscle resulting from rapidly repeated motor impulses

tet·a·ny \ˈte-tᵊn-ē, ˈtet-nē\ n [ISV, fr. L *tetanus*] (ca. 1885) : a condition of physiologic calcium imbalance marked by tonic spasms of muscles and often associated with deficient parathyroid secretion

te·tar·to·he·dral \te-ˌtär-tə-ˈhē-drəl\ adj [Gk *tetartos* fourth; akin to Gk *tettares* four — more at FOUR] (ca. 1858) of a crystal : having one fourth the number of planes required for complete symmetry — compare HEMIHEDRAL, HOLOHEDRAL

tetched var of TECHED

tetchy \ˈte-chē\ adj **tetch·i·er; -est** [perh. fr. obs. *tetch* habit] (1592) : irritably or peevishly sensitive : TOUCHY ⟨the ~ manner of two women living in the same house —Elizabeth Taylor †1975⟩ — **tetch·i·ly** \-chə-lē\ adv — **tetch·i·ness** \-chē-nəs\ n

¹tête–à–tête \ˌtet-ə-ˈtet, ˌtāt-ə-ˈtāt, *2 is also* ˈtet-ə-ˌtet\ n [F, lit., head to head] (1697) **1** : a private conversation between two persons **2** : a short piece of furniture (as a sofa) intended to seat two persons esp. facing each other

tête-à-tête • text   **1219**

²tête–à–tête \ˌtet-ə-'tet, ˌtāt-ə-'tāt\ *adv* (1700) : in private

³tête–à–tête \ˌtet-ə-ˌtet, ˌtāt-ə-ˌtāt\ *adj* (1728) : FACE-TO-FACE, PRIVATE

tête–bêche \'tet-'besh\ *adj* [F, n., pair of inverted stamps, fr. *tête* head + *-bêche*, alter. of MF *bechevet* head against foot] (ca. 1913) : of or relating to a pair of stamps inverted in relation to one another either through a printing error or intentionally

teth \'tāt, 'tāth, 'tās\ *n* [Heb *ṭēth*] (ca. 1823) : the 9th letter of the Hebrew alphabet — see ALPHABET table

¹teth·er \'te-thər\ *n* [ME *tethir*, prob. of Scand origin; akin to ON *tjōthr* tether; akin to OHG *zeotar* pole of a wagon] (14c) 1 : something (as a rope or chain) by which an animal is fastened so that it can range only within a set radius 2 : the limit of one's strength or resources ⟨at the end of my ∼⟩

²tether *vt* teth·ered; teth·er·ing \-th(ə-)riŋ\ (15c) : to fasten or. restrain by or as if by a tether

teth·er·ball \'te-thər-ˌbȯl\ *n* (ca. 1900) : a game played with a ball suspended by a string from an upright pole in which the object for each contestant is to wrap the string around the pole by striking the ball in a direction opposite to that of the other contestant; *also* : the ball used in this game

Te·thys \'tē-thəs\ *n* [L, fr. Gk *Tēthys*] : a Titaness and wife of Oceanus

tet·ra \'te-trə\ *n* [by shortening fr. NL *Tetragonopterus*, former genus name, fr. LL *tetragonum* quadrangle + Gk *pteron* wing — more at TETRAGONAL, FEATHER] (1931) : any of numerous small often brightly colored So. American characin fishes often bred in tropical aquariums

tetra- *or* tetr- *comb form* [ME, fr. L, fr. Gk; akin to Gk *tettares* four — more at FOUR] 1 : four : having four : having four parts ⟨*tetra*valent⟩ 2 : containing four atoms or groups (of a specified kind) ⟨*tetra*chloride⟩

tet·ra·caine \'te-trə-ˌkān\ *n* [*tetra*- + *-caine*] (ca. 1935) : a crystalline basic ester $C_{15}H_{24}N_2O_2$ that is closely related chemically to procaine and is used chiefly in the form of its hydrochloride as a local anesthetic

tet·ra·chlo·ride \ˌte-trə-'klȯr-ˌīd, -'klȯr-\ *n* (1866) : a chloride containing four atoms of chlorine

tet·ra·chord \'te-trə-ˌkȯrd\ *n* [Gk *tetrachordon*, fr. neut. of *tetrachordos* of four strings, fr. *tetra*- + *chordē* string — more at YARN] (1603) : a diatonic series of four tones with an interval of a perfect fourth between the first and last

tet·ra·cy·cline \ˌte-trə-'sī-ˌklēn\ *n* [ISV *tetra*cyclic having four fused hydrocarbon rings + ²-*ine*] (1952) : a yellow crystalline broad-spectrum antibiotic $C_{22}H_{24}N_2O_8$ produced by streptomyces or synthetically

tet·rad \'te-ˌtrad\ *n* [Gk *tetrad-*, *tetras*, fr. *tetra*] (1653) : a group or arrangement of four: as **a** : a group of four cells produced by the successive divisions of a mother cell ⟨a ∼ of spores⟩ **b** : a group of four synapsed chromatids that become visibly evident in the pachytene stage of meiotic prophase — tet·rad·ic \te-'tra-dik\ *adj*

tet·ra·drachm \'te-trə-ˌdram\ *n* [Gk *tetradrachmon*, fr. *tetra*- + *drachmē* drachma] (ca. 1580) : an ancient Greek silver coin worth four drachmas

tet·ra·dy·na·mous \ˌte-trə-'dī-nə-məs\ *adj* [ISV *tetra*- + Gk *dynamis* power — more at DYNAMIC] (1830) : having six stamens four of which are longer than the others ⟨∼ plants of the mustard family⟩

tet·ra·eth·yl lead \ˌte-trə-ˌe-thəl-'led\ *n* (1923) : a heavy oily poisonous liquid $Pb(C_2H_5)_4$ used as an antiknock agent

tet·ra·flu·o·ride \ˌte-trə-'flȯr-ˌīd, -'flu̇r-\ *n* (ca. 1909) : a fluoride containing four atoms of fluorine

te·trag·o·nal \te-'tra-gə-nᵊl\ *adj* [LL *tetragonalis* having four angles and four sides, fr. *tetragonum* quadrangle, fr. Gk *tetragōnos*, fr. neut. of *tetragōnos* tetragonal, fr. *tetra*- + *gōnia* angle — more at -GON] (1868) : of, relating to, or characteristic of the tetragonal system — te·trag·o·nal·ly \-nᵊl-ē\ *adv*

tetragonal system *n* (1879) : a crystal system characterized by three axes at right angles of which only the two lateral axes are equal

tet·ra·gram·ma·ton \ˌte-trə-'gra-mə-ˌtän\ *n* [ME, fr. Gk, fr. neut. of *tetragrammatos* having four letters, fr. *tetra*- + *grammat-*, *gramma* letter — more at GRAM] (15c) : the four Hebrew letters usu. transliterated YHWH or JHVH that form a biblical proper name of God — compare YAHWEH

tet·ra·he·dral \ˌte-trə-'hē-drəl\ *adj* (1794) 1 : being a polyhedral angle with four faces 2 : relating to, forming, or having the form of a tetrahedron — tet·ra·he·dral·ly \-drə-lē\ *adv*

tet·ra·he·drite \-ˌdrīt\ *n* [G *Tetraëdrit*, fr. LGk *tetraedros* having four faces] (1868) : a fine-grained gray mineral that consists of a sulfide of copper, iron, and antimony, often contains other elements (as silver), and occurs in tetrahedral crystals or in massive form

tet·ra·he·dron \ˌte-trə-'hē-drən\ *n, pl* -drons *or* -dra \-drə\ [NL, fr. LGk *tetraedron*, neut. of *tetraedros* having four faces, fr. Gk *tetra*- + *hedra* seat, face — more at SIT] (1570) : a polyhedron that has four faces

tet·ra·hy·dro·can·nab·i·nol \ˌ-ˌhī-drə-kə-'na-bə-ˌnȯl, -ˌnōl\ *n* [*tetrahydro*- (combined with four atoms of hydrogen) + *cannabin* + ¹-*ol*] (1940) : THC

tet·ra·hy·dro·fu·ran \-'fyu̇r-ˌan, -ˌfyu̇-'ran\ *n* [*tetrahydro*- + *furan*] (ca. 1943) : a flammable liquid heterocyclic ether C_4H_8O that is derived from furan and used as a solvent and as an intermediate in organic chemistry

tetrahedron

tet·ra·hy·me·na \ˌte-trə-'hī-mə-nə\ *n* [NL, fr. *tetra*- + Gk *hymēn* membrane] (1962) : any of a genus (*Tetrahymena*) of ciliate protozoans

te·tral·o·gy \te-'trä-lə-jē, -'tra-\ *n, pl* -gies [Gk *tetralogia*, fr. *tetra*- + -*logia* -logy] (1656) 1 : a group of four dramatic pieces presented consecutively on the Attic stage at the Dionysiac festival 2 : a series of four connected works (as operas or novels)

tet·ra·mer \'te-trə-mər\ *n* (1929) : a molecule (as an enzyme or a polymer) that consists of four structural subunits (as peptide chains or condensed monomers) — tet·ra·mer·ic \ˌte-trə-'mer-ik\ *adj*

te·tram·er·ous \te-'tra-mə-rəs\ *adj* [NL *tetramerus*, fr. Gk *tetramerēs*, fr. *tetra*- + *meros* part — more at MERIT] (1826) : having or characterized by the presence of four parts or of parts arranged in sets or multiples of four ⟨∼ flowers⟩

te·tram·e·ter \te-'tra-mə-tər\ *n* [Gk *tetrametron*, fr. neut. of *tetrametros* having four measures, fr. *tetra*- + *metron* measure — more at MEASURE] (1612) : a line of verse consisting either of four dipodies (as in classical iambic, trochaic, and anapestic verse) or four metrical feet (as in modern English verse)

tet·ra·meth·yl·lead \ˌte-trə-ˌme-thəl-'led\ *n* (1964) : a volatile poisonous liquid $Pb(CH_3)_4$ used as an antiknock agent

¹tet·ra·ploid \'te-trə-ˌplȯid\ *adj* [ISV] (1912) : having or being a chromosome number four times the monoploid number ⟨a ∼ cell⟩ — tet·ra·ploi·dy \-ˌplȯi-dē\ *n*

²tetraploid *n* (1921) : a tetraploid individual

tet·ra·pod \'te-trə-ˌpäd\ *n* [NL *tetrapodus*, fr. Gk *tetrapod-*, *tetrapous* four-footed, fr. *tetra*- + *pod-*, *pous* foot — more at FOOT] (ca. 1891) : a vertebrate (as a frog, bird, or cat) with two pairs of limbs

tet·ra·pyr·role \ˌte-trə-'pir-ˌōl\ *n* (ca. 1928) : a chemical group consisting of four pyrrole rings joined either in a straight chain or in a ring (as in chlorophyll)

te·trarch \'te-ˌträrk, 'tē-\ *n* [ME, fr. L *tetrarcha*, fr. Gk *tetrarchēs*, fr. *tetra*- + -*archēs* -arch] (14c) 1 : a governor of the fourth part of a province 2 : a subordinate prince — te·trar·chic \te-'trär-kik, tē-\ *adj*

te·trar·chy \'te-ˌträr-kē, 'tē-\ *n, pl* -chies (ca. 1630) : government by four persons ruling jointly

tet·ra·spore \'te-trə-ˌspȯr, -ˌspȯr\ *n* [ISV] (1857) : one of the haploid asexual spores developed meiotically in the red algae usu. in groups of four — tet·ra·spor·ic \ˌte-trə-'spȯr-ik, -'spȯr-\ *adj*

tet·ra·va·lent \ˌte-trə-'vā-lənt\ *adj* [ISV] (1868) : having a valence of four

te·traz·zi·ni \ˌte-trə-'zē-nē\ *adj, often cap* [Luisa *Tetrazzini* †1940 Ital. opera singer] (1951) : prepared with pasta and a white sauce seasoned with sherry and served au gratin ⟨chicken ∼⟩

tet·ra·zo·li·um \ˌte-trə-'zō-lē-əm\ *n* [NL, fr. ISV *tetrazole* (CH_2N_4)] (1895) : a univalent cation or group CH_3N_4 that is analogous to ammonium; *also* : any of several of its derivatives used esp. as electron acceptors to test for metabolic activity in living cells

tet·rode \'te-ˌtrōd\ *n* (1902) : a vacuum tube with a cathode, an anode, a control grid, and an additional grid or other electrode

te·tro·do·tox·in \te-ˌtrō-də-'täk-sən\ *n* [ISV *tetrodo*- (fr. NL *Tetrodon*, genus of tropical marine fishes) + *toxin*] (1911) : a neurotoxin $C_{11}H_{17}N_3O_8$ found esp. in puffer fish that blocks nerve conduction by suppressing permeability of the nerve fiber to sodium ions

te·trox·ide \te-'träk-ˌsīd\ *n* [ISV] (1866) : a compound of an element or group with four atoms of oxygen

tet·ryl \'te-trəl\ *n* [ISV] (1909) : a pale yellow crystalline explosive $C_7H_5N_5O_8$ used esp. as a detonator

tet·ter \'te-tər\ *n* [ME *teter*, fr. OE; akin to OHG *zittaroh* tetter, Skt *dadru* leprosy, *dṛṇāti* he tears — more at TEAR] (bef. 12c) : any of various vesicular skin diseases (as ringworm, eczema, and herpes)

Teu·ton \'tü-tᵊn, 'tyü-\ *n* [L *Teutoni*, pl.] (ca. 1741) 1 : a member of an ancient prob. Germanic or Celtic people 2 : a member of a people speaking a language of the Germanic branch of the Indo-European language family; *esp* : GERMAN

Teu·ton·ic \tü-'tä-nik, tyü-\ *n* (1612) : GERMANIC

²Teutonic *adj* (1618) : of, relating to, or characteristic of the Teutons — Teu·ton·i·cal·ly \-ni-k(ə-)lē\ *adv*

Teu·ton·ism \'tü-tᵊn-ˌi-zəm, 'tyü-\ *n* (1854) : GERMANISM

Teu·ton·ist \-ist\ *n* (1882) : GERMANIST

teu·ton·ize \-ˌīz\ *vt* -ized; -iz·ing *often cap* (1845) : GERMANIZE

tex·as \'tek-səs, -siz\ *n* [*Texas*, state of U.S.; fr. the naming of cabins on Mississippi steamboats after states, the officers' cabins being the largest] (1857) : a structure on the awning deck of a steamer that contains the officers' cabins and has the pilothouse in front or on top

Texas fever *n* (1866) : an infectious disease of cattle transmitted by the cattle tick and caused by a protozoan (*Babesia bigemina*) that multiplies in the blood and destroys the red blood cells

Texas Independence Day *n* (ca. 1928) : March 2 observed as the anniversary of the declaration of independence of Texas from Mexico in 1836 and also as the birthday of Sam Houston

Texas leaguer *n* [*Texas League*, a baseball minor league] (1905) : a fly in baseball that falls too far out to be caught by an infielder and too close in to be caught by an outfielder

Texas longhorn *n* (1908) 1 : LONGHORN 1a 2 : any of a breed of relatively small cattle developed in the U.S. from descendants of the original longhorns and typically having a 40 inch (one meter) horn spread and a highly variable color pattern

Texas Ranger *n* (1846) : a member of a formerly mounted police force in Texas

Tex–Mex \'teks-'meks\ *adj* [*Tex*as + *Mex*ico] (1949) : of, relating to, or being the Mexican-American culture or cuisine existing or originating in esp. southern Texas ⟨∼ cooking⟩ ⟨∼ music⟩

text \'tekst\ *n* [ME, fr. MF *texte*, fr. ML *textus*, fr. L, texture, context, fr. *texere* to weave — more at TECHNICAL] (14c) 1 **a** (1) : the original words and form of a written or printed work (2) : an edited or emended copy of an original work **b** : a work containing such text 2 **a** : the main body of printed or written matter on a page **b** : the principal part of a book exclusive of front and back matter **c** : the printed score of a musical composition 3 **a** (1) : a verse or passage of Scripture chosen esp. for the subject of a sermon or for authoritative support (as for a doctrine) (2) : a passage from an authoritative source providing an introduction or basis (as for a speech) **b** : a source of information or authority 4 : THEME, TOPIC 5 **a** : the words of something (as a poem) set to music **b** : matter chiefly in the form of words that is treated as data for processing by computerized equipment ⟨a *text*-editing typewriter⟩ 6 : a type suitable for printing running text 7 : TEXTBOOK 8 **a** : something written or spoken considered as an object to be examined, explicated, or deconstructed **b** : something likened to a text ⟨the surfaces of daily life are ∼s to be explicated —Michiko Kakutani⟩ ⟨he ceased to be a teacher and became a ∼ —D. J. Boorstin⟩

\ə\ abut \ᵊ\ kitten, F table \ər\ further \a\ ash \ā\ ace \ä\ mop, mar
\au̇\ out \ch\ chin \e\ bet \ē\ easy \g\ go \i\ hit \ī\ ice \j\ job
\ŋ\ sing \ō\ go \ȯ\ law \ȯi\ boy \th\ thin \t͟h\ the \ü\ loot \u̇\ foot
\y\ yet \zh\ vision \à, k̲, ⁿ, œ, œ̄, ᵫ, ᵫ̄, ᵞ\ *see* Guide to Pronunciation

¹text·book \'teks(t)-ˌbŭk\ *n* (1779) : a book used in the study of a subject: as **a** : one containing a presentation of the principles of a subject **b** : a literary work relevant to the study of a subject

²textbook *adj* (1905) : of, suggesting, or suitable to a textbook; *esp* : CLASSIC ⟨a ~ example of bureaucratic waste⟩

text·book·ish \-ˌbŭ-kish\ *adj* (1914) : of, relating to, or having the characteristics of a textbook ⟨the style is heavy and ~ —*Nation*⟩

text edition *n* (1895) : an edition of a book prepared for use esp. in schools and colleges — compare TRADE EDITION

tex·tile \'tek-ˌstīl, 'teks-t²l\ *n* [L, fr. neut. of *textilis* woven, fr. *texere*] (1626) **1** : CLOTH 1a; *esp* : a woven or knit cloth **2** : a fiber, filament, or yarn used in making cloth

tex·tu·al \'teks-chə-wəl, -chəl\ *adj* [ME, fr. ML *textus* text] (15c) : of, relating to, or based on a text — **tex·tu·al·ly** *adv*

textual critic *n* (1938) : a practitioner of textual criticism

textual criticism *n* (1859) **1** : the study of a literary work that aims to establish the original text **2** : a critical study of literature emphasizing a close reading and analysis of the text

¹tex·tu·ary \'teks-chə-ˌwer-ē\ *n, pl* **-ar·ies** [ML *textus*] (1608) : one who is well informed in the Bible or in biblical scholarship

²textuary *adj* (1646) : TEXTUAL

¹tex·ture \'teks-chər\ *n* [L *textura*, fr. *textus*, pp. of *texere* to weave — more at TECHNICAL] (1578) **1** : something composed of closely interwoven elements; *specif* : a woven cloth **b** : the structure formed by the threads of a fabric **2 a** : essential part : SUBSTANCE **b** : identifying quality : CHARACTER **3 a** : the disposition or manner of union of the particles of a body or substance **b** : the visual or tactile surface characteristics and appearance of something ⟨the ~ of an oil painting⟩ **4 a** : a composite of the elements of prose or poetry ⟨all these words . . . meet violently to form a ~ impressive and exciting —John Berryman⟩ **b** : a pattern of musical sound created by tones or lines played or sung together **5 a** : basic scheme or structure **b** : overall structure — **tex·tur·al** \-chə-rəl\ *adj* — **tex·tur·al·ly** \-rə-lē\ *adv* — **tex·tured** \-chərd\ *adj* — **tex·ture·less** \-chər-ləs\ *adj*

²texture *vt* **tex·tured; tex·tur·ing** (1694) : to give a particular texture to

tex·tur·ize \'teks-chə-ˌrīz\ *vt* **-ized; -iz·ing** (ca. 1950) : TEXTURE ⟨~ a polyester yarn⟩

tex·tus re·cep·tus \ˌtek-stəs-ri-'sep-təs\ *n* [NL, lit., received text] (1856) : the generally accepted text of a literary work (as the Greek New Testament)

T formation *n* (1930) : an offensive football formation in which the fullback lines up behind the center and quarterback with one halfback stationed on each side of the fullback

T4 cell \ˌtē-'fŏr-, -'fôr-\ *n* [*T cell* + *CD4*] (1983) : any of the T cells (as a helper T cell) that bear the CD4 molecular marker and become severely depleted in AIDS — called also *T4 lymphocyte*

T-group \'tē-ˌgrüp\ *n* [*training group*] (1950) : a group of people under the leadership of a trainer who seek to develop self-awareness and sensitivity to others by verbalizing feelings uninhibitedly at group sessions — compare ENCOUNTER GROUP

¹-th — see -ETH

²-th *or* **-eth** *adj suffix* [ME *-the, -te,* fr. OE *-tha, -ta;* akin to OHG *-do* -th, L *-tus,* Gk *-tos,* Skt *-tha*] — used in forming ordinal numbers ⟨hundredth⟩ ⟨fortieth⟩

³-th *n suffix* [ME, fr. OE; akin to OHG *-ida,* suffix forming abstract nouns, L *-ta,* Gk *-tē,* Skt *-tā*] **1** : act or process ⟨spilth⟩ **2** : state or condition ⟨dearth⟩

⁴-th *symbol* [²*-th*] — used with the figures 4, 5, 6, 7, 8, 9, and 0 and related Roman numerals to indicate an ordinal number ⟨25th⟩ ⟨50th wedding anniversary⟩ ⟨XXVth Olympiad⟩

¹Thai \'tī\ *n, pl* **Thai** *or* **Thais** (1808) **1** : a family of languages including Thai and Shan spoken in southeast Asia and China **2 a** : a native or inhabitant of Thailand **b** : one who is descended from a Thai **3** : the official language of Thailand

²Thai *adj* (1808) : of or relating to Thailand, its people, or their language or culture

thal·a·mus \'tha-lə-məs\ *n, pl* **-mi** \-ˌmī, -ˌmē\ [NL, fr. Gk *thalamos* chamber] (1756) : the largest subdivision of the diencephalon that consists chiefly of an ovoid mass of nuclei in each lateral wall of the third ventricle and functions in the integration of sensory information — see BRAIN illustration — **tha·lam·ic** \thə-'la-mik\ *adj*

thal·as·sae·mia *chiefly Brit var of* THALASSEMIA

thal·as·se·mia \ˌtha-lə-'sē-mē-ə\ *n* [NL, fr. Gk *thalassa* sea + NL *-emia*] (1932) : any of a group of inherited disorders of hemoglobin synthesis affecting the globin chain that are characterized usu. by mild to severe hemolytic anemia, are caused by a series of allelic genes, and tend to occur esp. in individuals of Mediterranean, black, or southeast Asian ancestry; *esp* : COOLEY'S ANEMIA — **thal·as·se·mic** \-mik\ *adj or n*

thalassemia major *n* [NL, greater thalassemia] (1944) : COOLEY'S ANEMIA

thalassemia minor *n* [NL, lesser thalassemia] (1944) : a mild form of thalassemia associated with the heterozygous condition for the gene involved

tha·las·sic \thə-'la-sik\ *adj* [F *thalassique,* fr. Gk *thalassa* sea] (1883) : of, relating to, or situated or developed about inland seas ⟨~ civilizations of the Aegean⟩

thal·as·soc·ra·cy \ˌtha-lə-'sä-krə-sē\ *n* [Gk *thalassokratia,* fr. *thalassa* + *-kratia* -cracy] (1846) : maritime supremacy

tha·las·so·crat \thə-'la-sə-ˌkrat\ *n* (1846) : one who has maritime supremacy

tha·ler \'tä-lər\ *var of* TALER

Tha·lia \thə-'lī-ə\ *n* [L, fr. Gk *Thaleia*] **1** : the Greek Muse of comedy **2** : one of the three Graces

tha·lid·o·mide \thə-'li-də-ˌmīd, -məd\ *n* [ph*thal*ic acid + *-id-* (fr. im*ide*) + *-o-* + *imide*] (1958) : a sedative and hypnotic drug C₁₃H₁₀N₂O₄ that has been the cause of malformation of infants born to mothers using it during pregnancy

thal·li·um \'tha-lē-əm\ *n* [NL, fr. Gk *thallos* green shoot; fr. the bright green line in its spectrum] (1861) : a sparsely but widely distributed poisonous metallic element that resembles lead in physical properties and is used chiefly in the form of compounds in photoelectric cells or as a pesticide — see ELEMENT table

thal·loid \'tha-ˌlóid\ *adj* (1857) : of, relating to, resembling, or consisting of a thallus ⟨~ liverworts⟩

thal·lo·phyte \'tha-lə-ˌfīt\ *n* [ultim. fr. Gk *thallos* + *phyton* plant — more at PHYT-] (1854) : any of a primary division (Thallophyta) of the plant kingdom comprising plants with single-celled sex organs or with many-celled sex organs of which all cells give rise to gametes, including the algae, fungi, and lichens, and usu. held to be a heterogeneous assemblage — **thal·lo·phyt·ic** \ˌtha-lə-'fi-tik\ *adj*

thal·lus \'tha-ləs\ *n, pl* **thal·li** \'tha-ˌlī, -ˌlē\ *or* **thal·lus·es** [NL, fr. Gk *thallos,* fr. *thallein* to sprout; akin to Arm *dalar* green, fresh, Alb *dal* I come forth] (1829) : a plant body that is characteristic of thallophytes, lacks differentiation into distinct members (as stem, leaves, and roots), and does not grow from an apical point

¹than \thən, 'than\ *conj* [ME *than, then, then,* than — more at THEN] (bef. 12c) **1 a** — used as a function word to indicate the second member or the member taken as the point of departure in a comparison expressive of inequality; used with comparative adjectives and comparative adverbs ⟨older ~ I am⟩ ⟨easier said ~ done⟩ **b** — used as a function word to indicate difference of kind, manner, or identity; used esp. with some adjectives and adverbs that express diversity ⟨anywhere else ~ at home⟩ **2** : other than — usu. used only after *prefer, preferable,* and *preferably* **3** : other than **4** : WHEN — used esp. after *scarcely* and *hardly*

²than *prep* (1560) : in comparison with ⟨you are older ~ me⟩
   usage After about 200 years of innocent if occasional use, the preposition *than* was called into question by 18th century grammarians. Some 200 years of elaborate and sometimes tortuous reasoning have led to these present-day inconsistent conclusions: *than whom* is standard but clumsy ⟨Beelzebub . . . *than* whom, Satan except, none higher sat —John Milton⟩ ⟨T. S. Eliot, than whom nobody could have been more insularly English —Anthony Burgess⟩; *than me* may be acceptable in speech ⟨a man no mightier *than* thyself or me —Shak.⟩ ⟨why should a man be better *than* me because he's richer *than* me — William Faulkner, in a talk to students⟩; *than* followed by a third-person objective pronoun (*her, him, them*) is usu. frowned upon. Surveyed opinion tends to agree with these conclusions. Our evidence shows that the conjunction is more common than the preposition, that *than whom* is chiefly limited to writing, and that *me* is more common after the preposition than the third-person objective pronouns. You have the same choice Shakespeare had: you can use *than* either as a conjunction or as a preposition.

than·a·tol·o·gy \ˌtha-nə-'tä-lə-jē\ *n* [Gk *thanatos* + E *-logy*] (ca. 1842) : the description or study of the phenomena of death and of psychological mechanisms for coping with them — **than·a·to·log·i·cal** \ˌtha-nə-t²l-'ä-ji-kəl\ *adj* — **than·a·tol·o·gist** \-ə-'tä-lə-jist\ *n*

Than·a·tos \'tha-nə-ˌtäs\ *n* [Gk, death; akin to Skt *adhvanīt* it vanished] (1935) : DEATH INSTINCT

thane \'thān\ *n* [ME *theyn,* fr. OE *thegn;* akin to OHG *thegan* thane and perh. to Gk *tiktein* to bear, beget] (bef. 12c) **1** : a free retainer of an Anglo-Saxon lord; *esp* : one resembling a feudal baron by holding lands of and performing military service for the king **2** : a Scottish feudal lord — **thane·ship** \-ˌship\ *n*

thank \'thaŋk\ *vt* [ME, fr. OE *thancian;* akin to OE *thanc* gratitude — more at THANKS] (bef. 12c) **1** : to express gratitude to ⟨~ed her for the present⟩ — used in the phrase *thank you* usu. without a subject to politely express gratitude ⟨~ you for your consideration⟩; used in such phrases as *thank God, thank goodness* usu. without a subject to express gratitude or more often only the speaker's or writer's pleasure or satisfaction in something **2** : to hold responsible ⟨had only himself to ~ for his loss⟩ — **thank·er** *n*

thank·ful \'thaŋk-fəl\ *adj* (bef. 12c) **1** : conscious of benefit received ⟨for what we are about to receive make us truly ~⟩ **2** : expressive of thanks ⟨~ service⟩ **3** : well pleased : GLAD ⟨was ~ that it didn't rain⟩ — **thank·ful·ness** *n*

thank·ful·ly \-f(ə-)lē\ *adv* (bef. 12c) **1** : in a thankful manner ⟨spoke ~⟩ **2** : as makes one thankful ⟨graceless stadiums . . . ~ going out of fashion —R. G. Echevarría⟩ ⟨~, those opinions are advanced with graceful prose —Ken Auletta⟩

thank·less \'thaŋk-ləs\ *adj* (1536) **1** : not expressing or feeling gratitude : UNGRATEFUL ⟨how sharper than a serpent's tooth it is to have a ~ child —Shak.⟩ **2** : not likely to obtain thanks : UNAPPRECIATED ⟨a ~ task⟩ — **thank·less·ly** *adv* — **thank·less·ness** *n*

thanks \'thaŋ(k)s\ *n pl* [pl. of ME *thank,* fr. OE *thanc* thought, gratitude; akin to OHG *dank* gratitude, L *tongēre* to know] (bef. 12c) **1** : kindly or grateful thoughts : GRATITUDE **2** : an expression of gratitude ⟨return ~ before the meal⟩ — often used in an utterance containing no verb and serving as a courteous and somewhat informal expression of gratitude ⟨many ~⟩ — **no thanks to** : not as a result of any benefit conferred by ⟨he feels better now, *no thanks to you*⟩ — **thanks to** : with the help of ; owing to ⟨arrived early, *thanks to* good weather⟩

thanks·giv·ing \thaŋ(k)s-'gi-viŋ *also* 'thaŋ(k)s-ˌ\ *n* (1533) **1** : the act of giving thanks **2** : a prayer expressing gratitude **3 a** : a public acknowledgment or celebration of divine goodness **b** *cap* : THANKSGIVING DAY

Thanksgiving Day *n* (1674) : a day appointed for giving thanks for divine goodness: as **a** : the fourth Thursday in November observed as a legal holiday in the U.S. **b** : the second Monday in October observed as a legal holiday in Canada

thank·wor·thy \'thaŋk-ˌkwər-thē\ *adj* (14c) : worthy of thanks or gratitude : MERITORIOUS

thank-you \'thaŋ-ˌkyü\ *n* [fr. the phrase *thank you* used in expressing gratitude] (1792) : a polite expression of one's gratitude

thank-you-ma'am \'thaŋk-yü-ˌmam, -(y)ē-\ *n* [prob. fr. its causing a nodding of the head] (1849) : a bump or depression in a road; *esp* : a ridge or hollow made across a road on a hillside to cause water to run off

¹that \'that, thət\ *pron, pl* **those** \'thōz\ [ME, fr. OE *thæt,* neut. demonstrative pron. & definite article; akin to OHG *daz,* neuter demonstrative pron. & definite article, Gk *to,* L *istud,* neut. demonstrative pron.] (bef. 12c) **1 a** : the person, thing, or idea indicated, mentioned, or understood from the situation ⟨~ is my father⟩ **b** : the time, action, or event specified ⟨after ~ I went to bed⟩ **c** : the kind or thing specified as follows ⟨the purest water is ~ produced by distillation⟩ **d** : one or a group of the indicated kind ⟨~'s a cat — quick and agile⟩ **2 a** : the one farther away or less immediately under observation or discussion ⟨*those* are maples and these are elms⟩ **b** : the former one **3 a** — used as a function word after *and* to indicate emphatic repetition of the idea expressed by a previous word or phrase ⟨he was helpful, and ~ to an unusual degree⟩ **b** — used as a function word immediately before or after a word group consisting of a verbal auxiliary or a form of the verb *be* preceded by *there* or a personal pronoun subject to indicate emphatic repetition of the idea expressed by a previous verb or predicate noun or predicate adjective ⟨is she capable? She is ~⟩ **4 a** : the one : the thing : the kind : SOMETHING, ANYTHING ⟨the truth of ~ which is true⟩ ⟨the senses are ~ whereby we experience the world⟩ ⟨what's ~ you say⟩ **b** *pl* : some persons ⟨*those* who think the time has come⟩ — **all that** : everything of the kind indicated ⟨tact, discretion, and *all that*⟩ — **at that** 1 : in spite of what has been said or implied **2** : in addition : ²BESIDES

²**that** \thot, 'that\ *conj* (bef. 12c) **1 a** (1) — used as a function word to introduce a noun clause that is usu. the subject or object of a verb or a predicate nominative ⟨said ~ he was afraid⟩ (2) — used as a function word to introduce a subordinate clause that is anticipated by the expletive *it* occurring as subject of the verb ⟨it is unlikely ~ he'll be in⟩ (3) — used as a function word to introduce a subordinate clause that is joined as complement to a noun or adjective ⟨we are certain ~ this is true⟩ ⟨the fact ~ you are here⟩ (4) — used as a function word to introduce a subordinate clause modifying an adverb or adverbial expression ⟨will go anywhere ~ he is invited⟩ **b** — used as a function word to introduce an exclamatory clause expressing a strong emotion esp. of surprise, sorrow, or indignation ⟨~ it should come to this!⟩ **2 a** (1) — used as a function word to introduce a subordinate clause expressing purpose or desired result ⟨cutting down expenses ~ her son might inherit an unencumbered estate —W. B. Yeats⟩ (2) — used as a function word to introduce a subordinate clause expressing a reason or cause ⟨rejoice ~ you are lightened of a load —Robert Browning⟩ (3) — used as a function word to introduce a subordinate clause expressing consequence, result, or effect ⟨are of sufficient importance ~ they cannot be neglected —Hannah Wormington⟩ **b** — used as a function word to introduce an exclamatory clause expressing a wish ⟨oh, ~ he would come⟩ **3** — used as a function word after a subordinating conjunction without modifying its meaning ⟨if ~ thy bent of love be honorable —Shak.⟩

³**that** *adj, pl* **those** (13c) **1 a** : being the person, thing, or idea specified, mentioned, or understood **b** : being the one specified — usu. used for emphasis ⟨~ rarity among leaders⟩ ⟨~ brother of yours⟩ **c** : so great a : SUCH ⟨~ : the farther away or less immediately under observation or discussion ⟨this chair or ~ one⟩

⁴**that** \thot, 'that\ *pron* [ME, fr. OE *thæt*, neut. rel. pron., fr. *thæt*, neut. demonstrative pron.] (bef. 12c) **1** — used as a function word to introduce a restrictive relative clause and to serve as a substitute within that clause for the substantive modified by the clause ⟨the house ~ Jack built⟩ ⟨I'll make a ghost of him ~ lets me —Shak.⟩ **2 a** : at which : in which : on which : by which : with which : to which ⟨each year ~ the lectures are given⟩ **b** : according to what : to the extent of what — used after a negative ⟨has never been here ~ I know of⟩ **3 a** *archaic* : that which **b** *obs* : the person who

usage That, which, who: In current usage *that* refers to persons or things, *which* chiefly to things and rarely to subhuman entities, *who* chiefly to persons and sometimes to animals. The notion that *that* should not be used to refer to persons is without foundation; such use is entirely standard. Because *that* has no genitive form or construction, *of which* or *whose* must be substituted for it in contexts that call for the genitive.

usage That, which: Although some handbooks say otherwise, *that* and *which* are both regularly used to introduce restrictive clauses in edited prose. *Which* is also used to introduce nonrestrictive clauses. *That* was formerly used to introduce nonrestrictive clauses; such use is virtually nonexistent in present-day edited prose, though it may occas. be found in poetry.

⁵**that** \'that\ *adv* (15c) **1** : to such an extent ⟨a nail about ~ long⟩ **2** : VERY, EXTREMELY — usu. used with the negative ⟨did not take the festival ~ seriously —Eric Goldman⟩

that-away \'tha-də-,wā\ *adv* [alter. of *that way*] (1839) : in that direction

¹**thatch** \'thach\ *vt* [ME *thecchen*, fr. OE *theccan* to cover; akin to OHG *decchen* to cover, L *tegere*, Gk *stegein* to cover, *stegos* roof, Skt *sthagati* he covers] (14c) : to cover with or as if with thatch — **thatch-er** *n*

²**thatch** *n* (14c) **1 a** : a plant material (as straw) used as a sheltering cover esp. of a house **b** : a sheltering cover (as a house roof) made of such material **c** : a mat of undecomposed plant material (as grass clippings) accumulated next to the soil in a grassy area (as a lawn) **2** : something likened to the thatch of a house; *esp* : the hair of one's head

thau-ma-turge \'thȯ-mə-,tərj\ *n* [F, fr. NL *thaumaturgus*, fr. Gk *thaumatourgos* working miracles, fr. *thaumat-, thauma* miracle + *ergon* work — more at THEATER, WORK] (1715) : THAUMATURGIST

thau-ma-tur-gic \,thȯ-mə-'tər-jik\ *adj* (1680) **1** : performing miracles **2** : of, relating to, or dependent on thaumaturgy

thau-ma-tur-gist \'thȯ-mə-,tər-jist\ *n* (1829) : a performer of miracles; *esp* : MAGICIAN

thau-ma-tur-gy \-jē\ *n* (ca. 1727) : the performance of miracles; *specif* : MAGIC

¹**thaw** \'thȯ\ *vb* [ME, fr. OE *thawian*; akin to OHG *douwen* to thaw, Gk *tēkein* to melt, L *tabēre* to waste away] *vt* (bef. 12c) : to cause to thaw ~ *vi* **1 a** : to go from a frozen to a liquid state : MELT **b** : to become free of the effect (as stiffness, numbness, or hardness) of cold as a result of exposure to warmth **2** : to be warm enough to melt ice and snow — used with *it* in reference to the weather **3** : to abandon aloofness, reserve, or hostility : UNBEND **4** : to become mobile, active, or susceptible to change

²**thaw** *n* (15c) **1** : the action, fact, or process of thawing **2** : a period of weather warm enough to thaw ice ⟨the January ~⟩ **3** : the action or process of becoming less aloof, less hostile, or more genial ⟨a ~ in international relations⟩

THC \,tē-(,)āch-'sē\ *n* [tetrahydrocannabinol] (1967) : a physiologically active chemical $C_{21}H_{30}O_2$ from hemp plant resin that is the chief intoxicant in marijuana — called also *tetrahydrocannabinol*

¹**the** \before consonants usu thə, before vowels usu thē, esp Southern before vowels also thə; for emphasis before titles and names or to suggest uniqueness often 'thē\ *definite article* [ME, fr. OE *thē*, masc. demonstrative pron. & definite article, alter. (influenced by oblique cases — as *thæs*, gen. — & neut., *thæt*) of *sē*; akin to Gk *ho*, masc. demonstrative pron. & definite article — more at THAT] (bef. 12c) **1 a** — used as a function word to indicate that a following noun or noun equivalent is definite or has been previously specified by context or by circumstance ⟨put ~ cat out⟩ **b** — used as a function word to indicate that a following noun or noun equivalent is a unique or a particular member of its class ⟨~ President⟩ ⟨~ Lord⟩ **c** — used as a function word before nouns that designate natural phenomena or points of the compass ⟨~ night is cold⟩ **d** — used as a function word before a noun denoting time to indicate reference to what is present or immediate or is under consideration ⟨in ~ future⟩ **e** — used as a function word before names of some parts of the body or of the clothing as an equivalent of a possessive adjective ⟨how's ~ arm today⟩ **f** — used as a function word before the name of a branch of human endeavor or proficiency ⟨~ law⟩ **g** — used as a function word in prepositional phrases to indicate that the noun in the phrase serves as a basis for computation ⟨sold by ~ dozen⟩ **h** — used as a function word before a proper name (as of a ship or a well-known building) ⟨~ Mayflower⟩ **i** — used as a function word before the plural form of a numeral that is a multiple of ten to denote a particular decade of a century or of a person's life ⟨life in ~ twenties⟩ **j** — used as a function word before the name of a commodity or any familiar appurtenance of daily life to indicate reference to the individual thing, part, or supply thought of as at hand ⟨talked on ~ telephone⟩ **k** — used as a function word to designate one of a class as the best, most typical, best known, or most worth singling out ⟨this is ~ life⟩ ⟨~ Pill⟩; sometimes used before a personal name to denote the most prominent bearer of that name **2 a** (1) — used as a function word with a noun modified by an adjective or by an attributive noun to limit the application of the modified noun to that specified by the adjective or by the attributive noun ⟨~ right answer⟩ ⟨Peter ~ Great⟩ (2) — used as a function word before an absolute adjective or an ordinal number ⟨nothing but ~ best⟩ ⟨due on ~ first⟩ **b** (1) — used as a function word before a noun to limit its application to that specified by a succeeding element in the sentence ⟨~ poet Wordsworth⟩ ⟨~ days of our youth⟩ ⟨didn't have ~ time to write⟩ (2) — used as a function word after a person's name to indicate a characteristic trait or notorious activity specified by the succeeding noun ⟨Jack ~ Ripper⟩ **3 a** — used as a function word before a singular noun to indicate that the noun is to be understood generically ⟨~ dog is a domestic animal⟩ **b** — used as a function word before a singular substantivized adjective to indicate an abstract idea ⟨an essay on ~ sublime⟩ **4** — used as a function word before a noun or a substantivized adjective to indicate reference to a group as a whole ⟨~ elite⟩

²**the** *adv* [ME, fr. OE *thȳ* by that, instrumental of *thæt* that] (bef. 12c) **1** : than before : than otherwise — used before a comparative ⟨none ~ wiser for attending⟩ **2 a** : to what extent ⟨~ sooner the better⟩ **b** : to that extent ⟨the sooner ~ better⟩ **3** : beyond all others ⟨likes this ~ best⟩

³**the** *prep* [¹*the*] (15c) : PER 2 ⟨a dollar ~ dozen⟩

the- *or* **theo-** *comb form* [ME *theo-*, fr. L, fr. Gk *the-, theo-*, fr. *theos*] : god : God ⟨*theism*⟩ ⟨*theocentric*⟩

¹**the-ater** *or* **the-atre** \'thē-ə-tər, 'thi-ə-, oftenest in Southern 'thē-,ā- also thē-'ā-\ *n* [ME *theatre*, fr. MF, fr. L *theatrum*, fr. Gk *theatron*, fr. *theasthai* to view, fr. *thea* act of seeing; akin to Gk *thauma* miracle] (14c) **1 a** : an outdoor structure for dramatic performances or spectacles in ancient Greece and Rome **b** : a building for dramatic performances **c** : a building or area for showing motion pictures **2** : a place or sphere of enactment of usu. significant events or action ⟨the ~ of public life⟩ **3 a** : a place rising by steps or gradations ⟨a woody ~ of stateliest view —John Milton⟩ **b** : a room often with rising tiers of seats for assemblies (as for lectures or surgical demonstrations) **4 a** : dramatic literature : PLAYS **b** : dramatic representation as an art or profession : DRAMA **5 a** : dramatic or theatrical quality or effectiveness **b** : SPECTACLE 1a

²**theater** *adj* (1977) : of, relating to, or appropriate for use in a theater of operations ⟨~ nuclear weapons⟩

the-ater-go-er \'thē-ə-tər-,gō(-ə)r\ *n* (1870) : a person who frequently goes to the theater — **the-ater-go-ing** \-,gō-iŋ, -,gȯ(-)iŋ\ *n or adj*

theater-in-the-round *n, pl* **theaters-in-the-round** (1948) : a theater in which the stage is located in the center of the auditorium — called also *arena theater*

theater of operations (ca. 1879) : the part of a theater of war in which active combat operations are conducted

theater of the absurd (1961) : theater that seeks to represent the absurdity of human existence in a meaningless universe by bizarre or fantastic means

theater of war (ca. 1890) : the entire land, sea, and air area that is or may become involved directly in war operations

The-a-tine \'thē-ə-,tīn, -,tēn\ *n* [NL *Theatinus*, fr. L *Teatinus* inhabitant of Chieti, fr. *Teate* Chieti, Italy] (ca. 1598) : a priest of the Order of Clerks Regular founded in 1524 in Italy by St. Cajetan and Gian Pietro Caraffa to reform Catholic morality and combat Lutheranism — **Theatine** *adj*

¹**the-at-ri-cal** \thē-'a-tri-kəl\ *also* **the-at-ric** \-trik\ *adj* (1558) **1** : of or relating to the theater or the presentation of plays ⟨a ~ costume⟩ **2** : marked by pretense or artificiality of emotion **3 a** : HISTRIONIC ⟨a ~ gesture⟩ **b** : marked by extravagant display or exhibitionism *syn* see DRAMATIC — **the-at-ri-cal-ism** \-kə-,li-zəm\ *n* — **the-at-ri-cal-i-ty** \-,a-trə-'ka-lə-tē\ *n* — **the-at-ri-cal-ly** \-'a-tri-k(ə-)lē\ *adv*

²**theatrical** *n* (ca. 1683) **1** *pl* **a** : the performance of plays **b** : DRAMATICS **2** *Brit* : a professional actor **3** *pl* : showy or extravagant gestures

---

\ə\ abut \ᵊ\ kitten, F table \ər\ further \a\ ash \ā\ ace \ä\ mop, mar \aᵫ\ out \ch\ chin \e\ bet \ē\ easy \g\ go \i\ hit \ī\ ice \j\ job \ŋ\ sing \ō\ go \ȯ\ law \ȯi\ boy \th\ thin \th̲\ the \ü\ loot \ᴜ\ foot \y\ yet \zh\ vision \à, ᴋ, ⁿ, œ, œ̄, ᵫ, ᵫ̄, ᵌ\ *see* Guide to Pronunciation

the·at·ri·cal·ize \thē-'a-tri-kə-ˌlīz\ *vt* **-ized; -iz·ing** (1778) **1** : to adapt to the theater : DRAMATIZE **2** : to display in showy fashion — **the·at·ri·cal·i·za·tion** \-ˌa-tri-kə-lə-'zā-shən\ *n*

the·at·rics \thē-'a-triks\ *n pl* (1807) **1** : THEATRICAL 1 **2** : staged or contrived effects

the·be \'thä-(ˌ)bä\ *n, pl* **thebe** [Tswana, lit., shield] (1967) — see *pula* at MONEY table

the·ca \'thē-kə\ *n, pl* **the·cae** \'thē-ˌsē, -ˌkē\ [NL, fr. Gk *thēkē* case — more at TICK] (ca. 1666) : an enveloping sheath or case of an animal or animal part — **the·cal** \'thē-kəl\ *adj*

-thecium *n comb form, pl* **-thecia** [NL, fr. Gk *thēkion*, dim. of *thēkē* case] : small containing structure ⟨endo*thecium*⟩

¹the·co·dont \'thē-kə-ˌdänt\ *adj* [ISV *thec-* (fr. NL *theca*) + *-odont*] (1840) : having the teeth inserted in sockets

²thecodont *n* (1840) : any of an order (Thecodontia) of Triassic diapsid thecodont reptiles that were presumably on the common ancestral line of the dinosaurs, birds, and crocodiles

thé dan·sant \tā-dän-'sän\ *n, pl* **thés dansants** *same*\ [F] (ca. 1845) : TEA DANCE

thee \'thē\ *pron, archaic objective case of* THOU **1 a** — used esp. in ecclesiastical or literary language and by Friends esp. among themselves in contexts where the objective case form would be expected **b** — used by Friends esp. among themselves in contexts where the subjective case form would be expected **2** : THYSELF

thee·lin \'thē-(ə)-lən\ *n* [irreg. fr. Gk *thēlys* female; akin to Gk *thēlē* nipple — more at FEMININE] (1930) : ESTRONE

theft \'theft\ *n* [ME *thiefthe*, fr. OE *thiefth*; akin to OE *thēof* thief] (bef. 12c) **1 a** : the act of stealing; *specif* : the felonious taking and removing of personal property with intent to deprive the rightful owner of it **b** : an unlawful taking (as by embezzlement or burglary) of property **2** *obs* : something stolen **3** : a stolen base in baseball

thegn \'thān\ *n* [OE — more at THANE] (1848) : THANE 1

thegn·ly \-lē\ *adj* (1876) : of, relating to, or befitting a thegn

their \thər, 'ther, 'thar\ *adj* [ME, fr. *their*, pron., fr. ON *theirra*, gen. pl. demonstrative & personal pron.; akin to OE *thæt* that] (13c) **1** : of or relating to them or themselves esp. as possessors, agents, or objects of an action ⟨~ furniture⟩ ⟨~ verses⟩ ⟨~ being seen⟩ **2** : his or her : HIS, HER, ITS — used with an indefinite third person singular antecedent ⟨anyone in ~ senses —W. H. Auden⟩ *usage* see THEY

theirs \'therz, 'tharz\ *pron, sing or pl in constr* (14c) **1** : that which belongs to them — used without a following noun as a pronoun equivalent in meaning to the adjective *their* **2** : his or hers : HIS, HERS — used with an indefinite third person singular antecedent ⟨I will do my part if everybody else will do ~⟩

their·selves \thər-'selvz, (ˌ)ther-, (ˌ)thar-, *Southern also* -'sevz\ *pron pl* (14c) *chiefly dial* : THEMSELVES

the·ism \'thē-ˌi-zəm\ *n* (1678) : belief in the existence of a god or gods; *specif* : belief in the existence of one God viewed as the creative source of man and the world who transcends yet is immanent in the world — **the·ist** \-ist\ *n or adj* — **the·is·tic** \thē-'is-tik\ *also* **the·is·ti·cal** \-kəl\ *adj* — **the·is·ti·cal·ly** \-ti-k(ə-)lē\ *adv*

T–help·er cell \tē-'hel-pər-\ *n* (1980) : HELPER T CELL

¹them \(th)əm, 'them, *after p, b, v, f, also* 'm\ *pron, objective case of* THEY

²them \'them\ *adj* (1594) *nonstand* : THOSE — used chiefly in the speech of less educated people and in the familiar speech of educated people esp. when they are being humorous

the·mat·ic \thi-'ma-tik\ *adj* [Gk *thematikos*, fr. *themat-, thema* theme] (1861) **1 a** : of or relating to the stem of a word **b** *of a vowel* : being the last part of a word stem before an inflectional ending **2** : of, relating to, or constituting a theme — **the·mat·i·cal·ly** \-ti-k(ə-)lē\ *adv*

thematic apperception test *n* (1941) : a projective technique that is widely used in clinical psychology to make personality, psychodynamic, and diagnostic assessments based on the subject's verbal responses to a series of black and white pictures

theme \'thēm\ *n* [ME *teme, theme*, fr. MF & L; MF *teme*, fr. L *thema*, fr. Gk, lit., something laid down, fr. *tithenai* to place — more at DO] (14c) **1 a** : a subject or topic of discourse or of artistic representation **b** : a specific and distinctive quality, characteristic, or concern ⟨the campaign has lacked a ~⟩ **2** : STEM 4 **3** : a written exercise : COMPOSITION ⟨a research ~⟩ **4** : a melodic subject of a musical composition or movement — **themed** \'thēmd\ *adj*

theme park *n* (1960) : an amusement park in which the structures and settings are based on a central theme

theme song *n* (1929) **1** : a melody recurring so often in a musical play that it characterizes the production or one of its characters **2** : a song used as a signature

them·selves \thəm-'selvz, them-\ *pron pl* (14c) **1 a** : those identical ones that are they — compare THEY 1a; used reflexively, for emphasis, or in absolute constructions ⟨nations that govern ~⟩ ⟨they ~ were present⟩ ⟨~ busy, they disliked idleness in others⟩ **b** : himself or herself : HIMSELF, HERSELF — used with an indefinite third person singular antecedent ⟨nobody can call ~ oppressed —Leonard Wibberley⟩ **2** : their normal, healthy, or sane condition ⟨were ~ again after a night's rest⟩ *usage* see THEY

¹then \'then\ *adv* [ME *than, then, then*, than, fr. OE *thonne, thænne*; akin to OHG *denne* then, OE *thæt* that] (bef. 12c) **1** : at that time **2 a** : soon after that : next in order of time ⟨walked to the door, ~ turned⟩ **b** : following next after in order of position, narration, or enumeration : being next in a series ⟨first came the clowns, ~ came the elephants⟩ **c** : in addition : BESIDES ⟨~ there is the interest to be paid⟩ **3 a** (1) : in that case ⟨take it, ~, if you want it so much⟩ (2) — used after *but* to qualify or offset a preceding statement ⟨she lost the race, but ~ she never really expected to win⟩ **b** : according to that : as may be inferred ⟨your mind is made up, ~⟩ **c** : as it appears : by way of summing up ⟨the cause of the accident, ~, is established⟩ **d** : as a necessary consequence ⟨if the angles are equal, ~ the complements are equal⟩ — **and then some** : with much more in addition ⟨would require all his strength *and then some*⟩

²then *n* (14c) : that time ⟨since ~, he's been more cautious⟩

³then *adj* (1584) : existing or acting at or belonging to the time mentioned ⟨the ~ secretary of state⟩

then and there *adv* (15c) : on the spot : IMMEDIATELY ⟨wanted the money right *then and there*⟩

the·nar \'thē-ˌnär, -nər\ *adj* [NL, palm of the hand, fr. Gk; akin to OHG *tenar* palm of the hand] (ca. 1857) : of, relating to, involving, or constituting the ball of the thumb or the intrinsic musculature of the thumb ⟨~ muscles⟩

thence \'then(t)s *also* 'then(t)s\ *adv* [ME *thannes*, fr. *thanne* from that place, fr. OE *thanon*; akin to OHG *thanan* from that place, OE *thænne* then — more at THEN] (14c) **1** : from that place **2** *archaic* : from that time : THENCEFORTH **3** : from that fact or circumstance : THEREFROM — **from thence** : from that place

thence·forth \ˌ-'förth, -'förth\ *adv* (14c) : from that time forward

thence·for·ward \then(t)s-'för-wərd *also* then(t)s-\ *also* **thence·for·wards** \-wərdz\ *adv* (15c) : onward from that place or time

theo- — see THE-

theo·bro·mine \ˌthē-ə-'brō-ˌmēn, -mən\ *n* [NL *Theobroma*, genus that includes the cacao, fr. *the-* + Gk *brōma* food, fr. *bibröskein* to devour — more at VORACIOUS] (1842) : a bitter alkaloid $C_7H_8N_4O_2$ closely related to caffeine that occurs esp. in cacao beans and has stimulant and diuretic properties

theo·cen·tric \ˌ-'sen-trik\ *adj* (1886) : having God as the central interest and ultimate concern ⟨a ~ culture⟩ — **theo·cen·tric·i·ty** \ˌ-'sen-ˌtri-sə-tē\ *n* — **theo·cen·trism** \ˌ-'sen-ˌtri-zəm\ *n*

the·oc·ra·cy \thē-'ä-krə-sē\ *n, pl* **-cies** [Gk *theokratia*, fr. *the-* + *-kratia* -cracy] (1622) **1** : government of a state by immediate divine guidance or by officials who are regarded as divinely guided **2** : a state governed by a theocracy

theo·crat \'thē-ə-ˌkrat\ *n* (1827) **1** : one who rules in or lives under a theocratic form of government **2** : one who favors a theocratic form of government

theo·crat·ic \ˌthē-ə-'kra-tik\ *also* **theo·crat·i·cal** \-ti-kəl\ *adj* (1690) : of, relating to, or being a theocracy — **theo·crat·i·cal·ly** \-ti-k(ə-)lē\ *adv*

the·od·i·cy \thē-'ä-də-sē\ *n, pl* **-cies** [modif. of F *théodicée*, fr. *théothe-* (fr. L *theo-*) + Gk *dikē* judgment, right — more at DICTION] (1797) : defense of God's goodness and omnipotence in view of the existence of evil

the·od·o·lite \thē-'ä-d°l-ˌīt\ *n* [NL *theodelitus*] (1571) : a surveyor's instrument for measuring horizontal and usu. also vertical angles

the·og·o·ny \thē-'ä-gə-nē\ *n, pl* **-nies** [Gk *theogonia*, fr. *the-* + *-gonia* -gony] (1612) : an account of the origin and descent of the gods — **theo·gon·ic** \ˌthē-ə-'gä-nik\ *adj*

theo·lo·gian \ˌthē-ə-'lō-jən\ *n* (15c) : a specialist in theology

theo·log·i·cal \ˌthē-ə-'lä-ji-kəl\ *also* **theo·log·ic** \-jik\ *adj* (15c) **1** : of or relating to theology **2** : preparing for a religious vocation ⟨a ~ student⟩ — **theo·log·i·cal·ly** \-ji-k(ə-)lē\ *adv*

theological virtue *n* (1526) : one of the three spiritual graces faith, hope, and charity drawing the soul to God according to scholastic theology

the·ol·o·gise *Brit var of* THEOLOGIZE

the·ol·o·gize \thē-'ä-lə-ˌjīz\ *vb* **-gized; -giz·ing** *vt* (1649) : to make theological : give a religious significance to ~ *vi* : to theorize theologically — **the·ol·o·giz·er** *n*

theo·logue *also* **theo·log** \'thē-ə-ˌlòg, -ˌläg\ *n* [L *theologus* theologian, fr. Gk *theologos*, fr. *the-* + *legein* to speak — more at LEGEND] (1663) : a theologian or specialist

the·ol·o·gy \thē-'ä-lə-jē\ *n, pl* **-gies** [ME *theologie*, fr. L *theologia*, fr. Gk, fr. *the-* + *-logia* -logy] (14c) **1** : the study of religious faith, practice, and experience; *esp* : the study of God and of God's relation to the world **2 a** : a theological theory or system ⟨Thomist ~⟩ ⟨a ~ of atonement⟩ **b** : a distinctive body of theological opinion ⟨Catholic ~⟩ **3** : a usu. 4-year course of specialized religious training in a Roman Catholic major seminary

the·on·o·mous \thē-'ä-nə-məs\ *adj* [*the-* + *-nomous* (as in *autonomous*)] (1947) : governed by God : subject to God's authority

the·on·o·my \-mē\ *n* [G *theonomie*, fr. *theo-* the- (fr. L) + *-nomie* -nomy] (1890) : the state of being theonomous : government by God

theo·pha·ny \thē-'ä-fə-nē\ *n, pl* **-nies** [ML *theophania*, fr. LGk *theophaneia*, fr. Gk *the-* + *-phaneia* (as in *epiphaneia* appearance) — more at EPIPHANY] (ca. 1633) : a visible manifestation of a deity — **theo·phan·ic** \ˌthē-ə-'fa-nik\ *adj*

theo·phyl·line \thē-'ä-fə-lən\ *n* [ISV *theo-* (fr. NL *thea* tea) + *phyll-* + *²-ine*] (ca. 1894) : a feebly basic bitter crystalline compound $C_7H_8N_4O_2$ from tea leaves that is isomeric with theobromine and is used in medicine esp. as a bronchodilator

the·or·bo \thē-'ör-(ˌ)bō\ *n, pl* **-bos** [modif. of It *tiorba, teorba*] (1605) : a stringed instrument of the 17th century resembling a large lute but having an extra set of long bass strings

the·o·rem \'thē-ə-rəm, 'thi(-ə)r-əm\ *n* [LL *theorema*, fr. Gk *theōrēma*, fr. *theōrein* to look at, fr. *theōros* spectator, fr. *thea* act of seeing — more at THEATER] (1551) **1** : a formula, proposition, or statement in mathematics or logic deduced or to be deduced from other formulas or propositions **2** : an idea accepted or proposed as a demonstrable truth often as a part of a general theory : PROPOSITION ⟨the ~ that the best defense is offense⟩ **3** : STENCIL **4** : a painting produced esp. on velvet by the use of stencils for each color — **the·o·rem·at·ic** \ˌthē-ə-rə-'ma-tik, ˌthi(-ə)r-ə-\ *adj*

the·o·ret·i·cal \ˌthē-ə-'re-ti-kəl, ˌthi(-ə)r-'e-\ *also* **the·o·ret·ic** \-tik\ *adj* [LL *theoreticus*, fr. Gk *theōrētikos*, fr. *theōrein* to look at] (1601) **1 a** : relating to or having the character of theory : ABSTRACT **b** : confined to theory or speculation often in contrast to practical applications : SPECULATIVE ⟨~ physics⟩ **2** : given to or skilled in theorizing ⟨a brilliant ~ physicist⟩ **3** : existing only in theory : HYPOTHETICAL ⟨gave as an example a ~ situation⟩ — **the·o·ret·i·cal·ly** \-ti-k(ə-)lē\ *adv* (1701) **1** : in a theoretical way **2** : according to an ideal or assumed set of facts or principles : in theory

the·o·re·ti·cian \ˌthē-ə-rə-'ti-shən, -re-; ˌthi(-ə)r-ə-\ *n* (1886) : THEORIST

the·o·rise *Brit var of* THEORIZE

the·o·rist \'thē-ə-rist, 'thi(-ə)r-ist\ *n* (1646) : a person who theorizes

the·o·rize \'thē-ə-ˌrīz\ *vb* **-rized; -riz·ing** *vi* (1638) : to form a theory : SPECULATE ~ *vt* **1** : to form a theory about **2** : to propose as a

theorbo

theory — **the·o·ri·za·tion** \ˌthē-ə-rə-'zā-shən, ˌthi(-ə)r-ə-\ *n* — **the·o·riz·er** *n*

the·o·ry \'thē-ə-rē, 'thi(-ə)r-ē\ *n, pl* **-ries** [LL *theoria*, fr. Gk *theōria*, fr. *theōrein*] (1592) **1** : the analysis of a set of facts in their relation to one another **2** : abstract thought : SPECULATION **3** : the general or abstract principles of a body of fact, a science, or an art ⟨music ~⟩ **4 a** : a belief, policy, or procedure proposed or followed as the basis of action ⟨her method is based on the ~ that all children want to learn⟩ **b** : an ideal or hypothetical set of facts, principles, or circumstances — often used in the phrase *in theory* ⟨in ~, we have always advocated freedom for all⟩ **5** : a plausible or scientifically acceptable general principle or body of principles offered to explain phenomena ⟨wave ~ of light⟩ **6 a** : a hypothesis assumed for the sake of argument or investigation **b** : an unproved assumption : CONJECTURE **c** : a body of theorems presenting a concise systematic view of a subject ⟨~ of equations⟩ *syn* see HYPOTHESIS

theory of games (1951) : GAME THEORY

theory of numbers (1811) : NUMBER THEORY

the·os·o·phist \thē-'ä-sə-fist\ *n* (1656) **1** : an adherent of theosophy **2** *cap* : a member of a theosophical society

the·os·o·phy \-fē\ *n* [ML *theosophia*, fr. LGk, fr. Gk *the-* + *sophia* wisdom — more at -SOPHY] (1650) **1** : teaching about God and the world based on mystical insight **2** *often cap* : the teachings of a modern movement originating in the U.S. in 1875 and following chiefly Buddhist and Brahmanic theories esp. of pantheistic evolution and reincarnation — **theo·soph·i·cal** \ˌthē-ə-'sä-fi-kəl\ *adj* — **theo·soph·i·cal·ly** \-k(ə-)lē\ *adv*

Theo·to·kos \ˌthē-ə-'tō-(ˌ)kōs, ˌthä-, -kəs\ *n* [LGk, fr. Gk *the-* + *tokos* childbirth; akin to Gk *tiktein* to beget — more at THANE] : VIRGIN MARY

ther·a·peu·sis \ˌther-ə-'pyü-səs\ *n* [NL, fr. Gk, treatment, fr. *therapeuein*] (ca. 1857) : THERAPEUTICS

ther·a·peu·tic \-'pyü-tik\ *adj* [Gk *therapeutikos*, fr. *therapeuein* to attend, treat, fr. *theraps* attendant] (1646) **1** : of or relating to the treatment of disease or disorders by remedial agents or methods ⟨a ~ rather than a diagnostic specialty⟩ **2** : providing or assisting in a cure : CURATIVE, MEDICINAL ⟨~ diets⟩ ⟨a ~ investigation of government waste⟩ — **ther·a·peu·ti·cal·ly** \-ti-k(ə-)lē\ *adv*

therapeutic index *n* (1926) : a measure of the relative desirability of a drug for the attaining of a particular medical end that is usu. expressed as the ratio of the largest dose producing no toxic symptoms to the smallest dose routinely producing cures

ther·a·peu·tics \ˌther-ə-'pyü-tiks\ *n pl but sing or pl in constr* (1671) : a branch of medical science dealing with the application of remedies to diseases

ther·a·pist \'ther-ə-pist\ *n* (1886) : one specializing in therapy; *esp* : a person trained in methods of treatment and rehabilitation other than the use of drugs or surgery ⟨a speech ~⟩

the·rap·sid \thə-'rap-səd\ *n* [NL *Therapsida*, fr. *ther-* mammal (fr. Gk *thēr* wild animal) + *apsid-, apsis* arch, vault — more at FIERCE, APSIS] (1912) : any of an order (Therapsida) of Permian and Triassic reptiles that are considered ancestors of the mammals — **therapsid** *adj*

ther·a·py \'ther-ə-pē\ *n, pl* **-pies** [NL *therapia*, fr. Gk *therapeia*, fr. *therapeuein*] (ca. 1846) : therapeutic treatment esp. of bodily, mental, or behavioral disorder

Ther·a·va·da \ˌther-ə-'vä-də\ *n* [Pali *theravāda*, lit., doctrine of the elders] (1882) : a conservative branch of Buddhism comprising sects chiefly in Sri Lanka, Myanmar, Thailand, Laos, and Cambodia and adhering to the original Pali scriptures alone and to the nontheistic ideal of nirvana for a limited select number — compare MAHAYANA

¹there \'thar, 'ther\ *adv* [ME, fr. OE *thǣr*; akin to OHG *dār* there, OE *thæt* that] (bef. 12c) **1** : in or at that place ⟨stand over ~⟩ — often used interjectionally **2** : to or into that place : THITHER ⟨went ~ after church⟩ **3** : at that point or stage ⟨stop right ~ before you say something you'll regret⟩ **4** : in that matter, respect, or relation ⟨~ is where I disagree with you⟩ **5** — used interjectionally to express satisfaction, approval, encouragement or sympathy, or defiance ⟨~, it's finished⟩

²there \'thar, 'ther, *1 is also* thər\ *pron* (bef. 12c) **1** — used as a function word to introduce a sentence or clause ⟨~ shall come a time⟩ **2** — used as an indefinite substitute for a name ⟨hi ~⟩

³there *same as* ¹\ (1588) **1** : that place or position ⟨there is no here and no ~ . . . in pure space —James Ward⟩ **2** : that point ⟨you take it from ~⟩

⁴there *same as* ¹\ *adj* (1590) **1** — used for emphasis esp. after a demonstrative pronoun or a noun modified by a demonstrative adjective ⟨those men ~ can tell you⟩ **2** *nonstand* — used for emphasis after a demonstrative adjective but before the noun modified ⟨I bet I cussed that ~ blamed mule five hundred times —Elizabeth M. Roberts⟩ **3** : capable of being relied on for support or aid ⟨she is always ~ for him⟩ **4** : fully conscious, rational, or aware ⟨not all ~⟩

there·abouts *also* **there·about** \ˌthar-ə-'baut(s), 'thar-ə-ˌ, ˌther-ə-'baut(s), 'ther-ə-ˌ\ *adv* (bef. 12c) **1** : near that place or time **2** : near that number, degree, or quantity ⟨a boy of 18 or ~⟩

there·af·ter \tha-'raf-tər, the-\ *adv* (bef. 12c) **1** : after that **2** *archaic* : according to that : ACCORDINGLY

there·at \-'rat\ *adv* (bef. 12c) **1** : at that place **2** : at that occurrence

there·by \thar-'bī, ther-, 'thar-ˌ, 'ther-ˌ\ *adv* (bef. 12c) **1** : by that : by that means ⟨~ lost her chance to win⟩ **2** : connected with or with reference to that ⟨~ hangs a tale —Shak.⟩

there·for \thar-'fȯr, ther-\ *adv* (12c) : for or in return for that ⟨ordered a change and gave his reasons ~⟩

there·fore \'thar-ˌfȯr, 'ther-, -ˌfȯr\ *adv* (14c) **1 a** : for that reason : CONSEQUENTLY **b** : because of that **c** : on that ground **2** : to that end

there·from \thar-'frəm, ther-, -'främ\ *adv* (13c) : from that or it

there·in \tha-'rin, the-\ *adv* (bef. 12c) **1** : in or into that place, time, or thing **2** : in that particular or respect ⟨~ lies the problem⟩

there·in·af·ter \ˌthar-in-'af-tər, ˌther-\ *adv* (1818) : in the following part of that matter (as writing, document, or speech)

there·in·to \tha-'rin-(ˌ)tü, the-\ *adv* (14c) *archaic* : into that or it

the·re·min \'ther-ə-mən\ *n* [Lev Theremin b1896 Russ. engineer & inventor] (1927) : a purely melodic electronic musical instrument typically played by moving a hand between two projecting electrodes

there·of \tha-'rəv, -'räv, the-\ *adv* (bef. 12c) **1** : of that or it **2** : from that cause or particular : THEREFROM

there·on \-'rȯn, -'rän\ *adv* (bef. 12c) **1** : on that ⟨a text with a commentary ~⟩ **2** *archaic* : THEREUPON

there·to \thar-'tü, ther-\ *adv* (bef. 12c) : to that ⟨a text and the notes ~⟩

there·to·fore \'thar-tə-ˌfȯr, 'ther-, -ˌfȯr; ˌthar-tə-', ˌther-\ *adv* (14c) : up to that time ⟨a ~ unknown author⟩

there·un·der \tha-'rən-dər, the-\ *adv* (bef. 12c) : under that

there·un·to \-'rən-(ˌ)tü; ˌthar-ən-'tü, ˌther-\ *adv* (14c) *archaic* : THERETO

there·up·on \'thar-ə-ˌpȯn, 'ther-, -ˌpän; ˌthar-ə-', ˌther-\ *adv* (13c) **1** : on that matter **2** : THEREFORE **3** : immediately after that

there·with \thar-'with, ther-, -'with\ *adv* (bef. 12c) **1** : with that **2** *archaic* : THEREUPON, FORTHWITH

there·with·al \'thar-wi-ˌthȯl, 'ther-, -thȯl\ *adv* (14c) **1** *archaic* : BESIDES **2** : THEREWITH

the·ri·ac \'thir-ē-ˌak\ *n* [NL *theriaca*] (1568) **1** : THERIACA : CURE-ALL

the·ri·a·ca \thi-'rī-ə-kə\ *n* [NL, fr. L, antidote against poison — more at TREACLE] (1562) : a mixture of many drugs and honey formerly held to be an antidote to poison — **the·ri·a·cal** \-kəl\ *adj*

the·rio·mor·phic \ˌthir-ē-ō-'mȯr-fik\ *adj* [Gk *thēriomorphos*, fr. *thērion* beast + *morphē* form — more at TREACLE] (1882) : having an animal form ⟨~ gods⟩

therm \'thərm\ *n* [Gk *thermē* heat, fr. *thermos* hot; akin to L *formus* warm, Skt *gharma* heat] : a unit used to measure quantity of heat that equals 100,000 British thermal units

therm- *or* **thermo-** *comb form* [Gk, fr. *thermē*] **1** : heat ⟨*thermo*stat⟩ **2** : thermoelectric ⟨*thermo*pile⟩

-therm *n comb form* [Gk *thermē* heat] : animal having a (specified) body temperature ⟨ecto*therm*⟩

¹ther·mal \'thər-məl\ *adj* [Gk *thermē*] (1756) **1** [L *thermae* public baths, fr. Gk *thermai*, pl. of *thermē*] : of, relating to, or marked by the presence of hot springs ⟨~ waters⟩ **2 a** : of, relating to, or caused by heat ⟨~ stress⟩ ⟨~ insulation⟩ **b** : being or involving a state of matter dependent upon temperature ⟨~ conductivity⟩ ⟨~ agitation of molecular structure⟩ **3** : designed (as with insulating air spaces) to prevent the dissipation of body heat ⟨~ underwear⟩ **4** : having energies of the order of those due to thermal agitation ⟨~ neutrons⟩ — **ther·mal·ly** \-mə-lē\ *adv*

²thermal *n* (1933) : a rising body of warm air

ther·mal·ize \'thər-mə-ˌlīz\ *vt* **-ized; -iz·ing** (1948) : to change the effective speed of (a particle) to a thermal value ⟨~ a neutron⟩ — **ther·mal·i·za·tion** \ˌthər-mə-lə-'zā-shən\ *n*

thermal pollution (1966) : the discharge of heated liquid (as wastewater from a factory) into natural waters at a temperature harmful to the environment

thermal printer *n* (1966) : a dot matrix printer (as for a computer) in which heat is applied to the pins of the matrix to form dots on usu. heat-sensitive paper

ther·mic \'thər-mik\ *adj* (1842) : ¹THERMAL 2 ⟨~ energy⟩ — **ther·mi·cal·ly** \-mi-k(ə-)lē\ *adv*

therm·ion·ic \ˌthər-(ˌ)mī-'ä-nik\ *adj* [*thermion* charged particle from an incandescent source, fr. *therm-* + *ion*] (1909) : relating to, using, or being the emission of charged particles (as electrons) by an incandescent material

therm·ion·ics \ˌthər-(ˌ)mī-'ä-niks\ *n pl but sing in constr* (1909) : physics dealing with thermionic phenomena

therm·is·tor \'thər-ˌmis-tər\ *n* [*therm*al re*sistor*] (1940) : an electrical resistor making use of a semiconductor whose resistance varies sharply in a known manner with the temperature

Ther·mit \'thər-mət, -ˌmit\ *trademark* — used for thermite

ther·mite \'thər-ˌmīt\ *n* [*therm-* + ¹*-ite*] (1900) : a mixture of aluminum powder and a metal oxide (as iron oxide) that when ignited evolves a great deal of heat and is used in welding and in incendiary bombs

ther·mo·chem·is·try \ˌthər-mō-'ke-mə-strē\ *n* (1844) : a branch of chemistry that deals with the interrelation of heat with chemical reaction or physical change of state — **ther·mo·chem·i·cal** \-'ke-mi-kəl\ *adj* — **ther·mo·chem·ist** \-'ke-mist\ *n*

ther·mo·cline \'thər-mə-ˌklīn\ *n* (1898) : the region in a thermally stratified body of water which separates warmer oxygen-rich surface water from cold oxygen-poor deep water and in which temperature decreases rapidly with depth

ther·mo·cou·ple \'thər-mə-ˌkə-pəl\ *n* (1890) : a device for measuring temperature in which a pair of wires of dissimilar metals (as copper and iron) are joined and the free ends of the wires are connected to an instrument (as a voltmeter) that measures the difference in potential created at the junction of the two metals

ther·mo·du·ric \ˌthər-mō-'dur-ik, -'dyur-\ *adj* [*therm-* + L *durare* to last — more at DURING] (1927) : able to survive high temperatures; *specif* : able to survive pasteurization — used of microorganisms

ther·mo·dy·nam·ic \ˌthər-mō-dī-'na-mik, -də-\ *also* **ther·mo·dy·nam·i·cal** \-mi-kəl\ *adj* (1849) **1** : of or relating to thermodynamics **2** : being or relating to a system of atoms, molecules, colloidal particles, or larger bodies considered as an isolated group in the study of thermodynamic processes — **ther·mo·dy·nam·i·cal·ly** \-mi-k(ə-)lē\ *adv*

ther·mo·dy·nam·ics \-miks\ *n pl but sing or pl in constr* (1854) **1** : physics that deals with the mechanical action or relations of heat **2** : thermodynamic processes and phenomena — **ther·mo·dy·nam·i·cist** \-mə-sist\ *n*

ther·mo·elec·tric \ˌthər-mō-i-'lek-trik\ *adj* (1823) : of, relating to, or dependent on phenomena that involve relations between the temperature and the electrical condition in a metal or in contacting metals

\ə\ abut \ˑ\ kitten, F table \ər\ further \a\ ash \ā\ ace \ä\ mop, mar
\aů\ out \ch\ chin \e\ bet \ē\ easy \g\ go \i\ hit \ī\ ice \j\ job
\ŋ\ sing \ō\ go \ȯ\ law \ȯi\ boy \th\ thin \th̷\ the \ü\ loot \ů\ foot
\y\ yet \zh\ vision \à, ḵ, ⁿ, œ, œ̄, ue, ūe, ᵛ\ *see* Guide to Pronunciation

ther·mo·elec·tric·i·ty \,thər-mō-i-,lek-'tri-sə-tē, -'tris-tē\ n (1823) : electricity produced by the direct action of heat (as by the unequal heating of a circuit composed of two dissimilar metals)

ther·mo·el·e·ment \-'e-lə-mənt\ n (ca. 1888) : a device for measuring small currents consisting of a wire heating element and a thermocouple in electrical contact with it

ther·mo·form \'thər-mə-,fôrm\ vt (1956) : to give a final shape to (as a plastic) with the aid of heat and usu. pressure — **ther·mo·form·able** \-,fôr-mə-bəl\ adj

ther·mo·gram \-,gram\ n (1883) **1** : the record made by a thermograph **2** : a photographic record made by thermography

ther·mo·graph \-,graf\ n [ISV] (1843) **1** : THERMOGRAM **2** : a self= recording thermometer **3** : the apparatus used in thermography

ther·mog·ra·phy \(,)thər-'mä-grə-fē\ n (1840) **1** : a process of writing or printing involving the use of heat; esp : a raised-printing process in which matter printed by letterpress is dusted with powder and heated to make the lettering rise **2** : a technique for detecting and measuring variations in the heat emitted by various regions of the body and transforming them into visible signals that can be recorded photographically (as for diagnosing abnormal or diseased underlying conditions); also : a similar technique used elsewhere (as on buildings) — **ther·mo·graph·ic** \,thər-mə-'gra-fik\ adj — **ther·mo·graph·i·cal·ly** \-fi-k(ə-)lē\ adv

ther·mo·ha·line \,thər-mō-'hā-,lin, -'ha-\ adj [therm- + Gk hal-, hals salt — more at SALT] (1942) : involving or dependent upon the conjoint effect of temperature and salinity (~ circulation in the eastern Pacific)

ther·mo·junc·tion \-'jəŋ(k)-shən\ n (1889) : a junction of two dissimilar conductors used to produce a thermoelectric current

ther·mo·la·bile \-'lā-,bil, -bəl\ adj [ISV] (1904) : unstable when heated; specif : subject to loss of characteristic properties on being heated to or above 55°C (many immune bodies, enzymes, and vitamins are ~) — **ther·mo·la·bil·i·ty** \-lā-'bi-lə-tē\ n

ther·mo·lu·mi·nes·cence \-,lü-mə-'ne-s²n(t)s\ n [ISV] (1897) **1** : phosphorescence developed in a previously excited substance upon gentle heating **2** : the determination of the age of old material (as pottery) by the amount of thermoluminescence it produces — called also thermoluminescence dating — **ther·mo·lu·mi·nes·cent** \-s²nt\ adj

ther·mo·mag·net·ic \-mag-'ne-tik\ adj (1823) : of or relating to the effects of heat upon the magnetic properties of substances or to the effects of a magnetic field upon thermal conduction

ther·mom·e·ter \thə(r)-'mä-mə-tər\ n [F thermomètre, fr. Gk thermē heat + F -o- + -mètre -meter — more at THERM] (1633) : an instrument for determining temperature consisting typically of a glass bulb attached to a fine tube of glass with a numbered scale and containing a liquid (as mercury or colored alcohol) that is sealed in and rises and falls with changes of temperature — **ther·mo·met·ric** \,thər-mə-'me-trik\ adj — **ther·mo·met·ri·cal·ly** \-tri-k(ə-)lē\ adv

ther·mom·e·try \thə(r)-'mä-mə-trē\ n [ISV] (1858) : the measurement of temperature

ther·mo·nu·cle·ar \,thər-mō-'nü-klē-ər, -'nyü-, ÷-'n(y)ü-kyə-lər\ adj [ISV] (1938) **1** : of or relating to the transformations in the nucleus of atoms of low atomic weight (as hydrogen) that require a very high temperature for their inception (as in the hydrogen bomb or in the sun) (~ reaction) (~ weapon) **2** : of, utilizing, or relating to a thermonuclear bomb (~ war) (~ attack)

ther·mo·pe·ri·od·ic·i·ty \-,pir-ē-ə-'di-sə-tē\ n (1944) : THERMOPERIODISM

ther·mo·pe·ri·od·ism \,thər-mō-'pir-ē-ə-,di-zəm\ n (1937) : the sum of the responses of an organism and esp. a plant to appropriately fluctuating temperatures

ther·mo·phil·ic \,thər-mə-'fi-lik\ also **ther·moph·i·lous** \(,)thər-'mä-fə-ləs\ or **ther·mo·phile** \'thər-mə-,fil\ adj (1894) : of, relating to, or being an organism growing at a high temperature (~ fermentation) (~ bacteria) — **thermophile** n

ther·mo·pile \'thər-mə-,pīl\ n [²pile] (1849) : an apparatus that consists of a number of thermocouples combined so as to multiply the effect and is used for generating electric currents or for determining intensities of radiation

ther·mo·plas·tic \,thər-mə-'plas-tik\ adj (1883) : capable of softening or fusing when heated and of hardening again when cooled (~ synthetic resins) — compare THERMOSETTING — **thermoplastic** n — **ther·mo·plas·tic·i·ty** \-,pla-'sti-sə-tē\ n

ther·mo·re·cep·tor \,thər-mō-ri-'sep-tər\ n (1937) : a sensory end organ that is stimulated by heat or cold

ther·mo·reg·u·la·tion \-,re-gyə-'lā-shən\ n [ISV] (1927) : the maintenance or regulation of temperature; specif : the maintenance of a particular temperature of the living body — **ther·mo·reg·u·late** \-'re-gyə-,lāt\ vb

ther·mo·reg·u·la·tor \-'re-gyə-,lā-tər\ n [ISV] (1875) : a device (as a thermostat) for the regulation of temperature

ther·mo·reg·u·la·to·ry \-'re-gyə-lə-,tôr-ē, -,tôr-\ adj (1941) : tending to maintain a body at a particular temperature whatever its environmental temperature (~ adjustments)

ther·mo·rem·a·nent \-'re-mə-nənt\ adj (1951) : being or relating to magnetic remanence (as in a rock cooled from a molten state or in a baked clay object containing magnetic minerals) that indicates the strength and direction of the earth's magnetic field at a former time — **ther·mo·rem·a·nence** \-nən(t)s\ n

ther·mos \'thər-məs\ n [fr. Thermos, a trademark] (1907) : a container (as a bottle or jar) with a vacuum between an inner and outer wall used to keep material and esp. liquids either hot or cold for considerable periods

ther·mo·scope \'thər-mə-,skōp\ n [NL thermoscopium, fr. therm- + -scopium -scope] (1804) : an instrument for indicating changes of temperature by accompanying changes in volume (as of a gas)

ther·mo·set \'thər-mō-,set\ n (1947) : a thermosetting resin or plastic

ther·mo·set·ting \-,se-tiŋ\ adj (ca. 1931) : capable of becoming permanently rigid when heated or cured (a ~ resin) — compare THERMOPLASTIC

ther·mo·sphere \'thər-mə-,sfir\ n [ISV] (1950) : the part of the earth's atmosphere that begins at about 50 miles (80 kilometers) above the earth's surface, extends to outer space, and is characterized by steadily increasing temperature with height — **ther·mo·spher·ic** \,thər-mə-'sfir-ik, -'sfer-\ adj

ther·mo·sta·ble \,thər-mō-'stā-bəl\ adj (1904) : stable when heated; specif : retaining characteristic properties on being moderately heated (a ~ bacterial protease) — **ther·mo·sta·bil·i·ty** \-stə-'bi-lə-tē\ n

¹ther·mo·stat \'thər-mə-,stat\ n (1831) : an automatic device for regulating temperature (as by controlling the supply of gas or electricity to a heating apparatus); also : a similar device for actuating fire alarms or for controlling automatic sprinklers — **ther·mo·stat·ic** \,thər-mə-'stat-ik\ adj — **ther·mo·stat·i·cal·ly** \-ti-k(ə-)lē\ adv

²thermostat vt -stat·ed \-,sta-təd\ also -stat·ted; -stat·ing also -stat·ting (1924) : to provide with or control the temperature of by a thermostat

ther·mo·tac·tic \,thər-mə-'tak-tik\ adj (1839) : of, relating to, or exhibiting thermotaxis

ther·mo·tax·is \-'tak-səs\ n [NL] (ca. 1891) **1** : the regulation of body temperature **2** : a taxis in which a temperature gradient constitutes the directive factor

ther·mo·trop·ic \-'trä-pik\ adj [ISV] (1885) : of, relating to, or exhibiting thermotropism

ther·mot·ro·pism \(,)thər-'mä-trə-,pi-zəm\ n [ISV] (ca. 1890) : a tropism in which a temperature gradient determines the orientation

-ther·my n comb form [NL -thermia, fr. Gk thermē heat — more at THERM] **1** : state of heat (endothermy) **2** : generation of heat (diathermy)

the·ro·pod \'thir-ə-,päd\ n [NL Theropoda, fr. Gk thēr wild animal + pod-, pous foot — more at FIERCE, FOOT] (ca. 1891) : any of a suborder (Theropoda) of carnivorous bipedal saurischian dinosaurs (as a tyrannosaur or allosaurus) usu. having small forelimbs

Ther·si·tes \(,)thər-'si-(,)tēz\ n [L, fr. Gk Thersitēs] : a Greek warrior at Troy known as a carping critic and slain by Achilles for mocking him

the·sau·rus \thi-'sòr-əs\ n, pl **-sau·ri** \-'sòr-,ī, -,ē\ or **-sau·rus·es** \-'sòr-ə-səz\ [NL, fr. L, treasure, collection, fr. Gk thēsauros] (ca. 1823) **1** : TREASURY, STOREHOUSE **2** **a** : a book of words or of information about a particular field or set of concepts; esp : a book of words and their synonyms **b** : a list of subject headings or descriptors usu. with a cross-reference system for use in the organization of a collection of documents for reference and retrieval — **the·sau·ral** \-'sòr-əl\ adj

these pl of THIS

The·seus \'thē-,süs, -sē-əs\ n [L, fr. Gk Thēseus] : a king of Athens in Greek mythology who kills Procrustes and the Minotaur before defeating the Amazons and marrying their queen

the·sis \'thē-səs, Brit esp for 1 'the-sis\ n, pl **the·ses** \'thē-,sēz\ [in sense 1, ME, fr. LL & Gk; LL, lowering of the voice, fr. Gk, downbeat, more important part of a foot, lit., act of laying down; in other senses, L, fr. Gk, lit., act of laying down, fr. tithenai to put, lay down — more at DO] (14c) **1** **a** (1) : the unstressed part of a poetic foot esp. in accentual verse (2) : the longer part of a poetic foot esp. in quantitative verse **b** : the accented part of a musical measure — DOWNBEAT — compare ARSIS **2** **a** : a position or proposition that a person (as a candidate for scholastic honors) advances and offers to maintain by argument **b** : a proposition to be proved or one advanced without proof : HYPOTHESIS **3** : the first and least adequate stage of dialectic — compare SYNTHESIS **4** : a dissertation embodying results of original research and esp. substantiating a specific view; esp : one written by a candidate for an academic degree

¹thes·pi·an \'thes-pē-ən\ adj (1675) **1** cap : of or relating to Thespis **2** often cap [fr. the tradition that Thespis was the originator of the actor's role] : relating to the drama : DRAMATIC

²thespian n (1827) : ACTOR

Thes·sa·lo·nians \,the-sə-'lō-nyənz, -nē-ənz\ n pl but sing in constr [Thessalonian inhabitant of ancient Thessalonica, irreg. fr. Thessalonica] : either of two letters written by St. Paul to the Christians of Thessalonica and included as books in the New Testament — see BIBLE table

the·ta \'thā-tə, chiefly Brit 'thē-tə\ n [Gk thēta, of Sem origin; akin to Heb tēth teth] (1603) **1** : the 8th letter of the Greek alphabet — see ALPHABET table **2** : THETA RHYTHM

theta rhythm n (1944) : a relatively high amplitude brain wave pattern between approximately 4 and 9 hertz that is characteristic esp. of the hippocampus but occurs in many regions of the brain including the cortex — called also theta wave

thet·ic \'the-tik, 'thē-\ adj [Gk thetikos of a proposition, fr. tithenai to lay down — more at DO] (1815) : constituting or beginning with a poetic thesis (a ~ syllable) — **thet·i·cal·ly** \-ti-k(ə-)lē\ adv

The·tis \'thē-təs\ n [L, fr. Gk] : a sea goddess who marries Peleus and becomes the mother of Achilles

the·ur·gist \'thē-(,)ər-jist\ n (1652) : WONDER-WORKER, MAGICIAN

the·ur·gy \'thē-(,)ər-jē\ n [LL theurgia, fr. LGk theourgia, fr. theourgos miracle worker, fr. Gk the- + ergon work — more at WORK] (1569) : the art or technique of compelling or persuading a god or beneficent or supernatural power to do or refrain from doing something — **the·ur·gic** \thē-'ər-jik\ or **the·ur·gi·cal** \-ji-kəl\ adj

thew \'thü, 'thyü\ n [ME, personal quality, virtue, fr. OE thēaw; akin to OHG thau custom] (15c) **1** **a** : muscular power or development **b** : STRENGTH, VITALITY **2** : MUSCLE, SINEW — usu. used in pl.

they \'thā\ pron, pl in constr [ME, fr. ON their, masc. pl. demonstrative & personal pron.; akin to OE thæt that] (13c) **1** **a** : those ones — used as third person pronoun serving as the plural of he, she, or it or referring to a group of two or more individuals not all of the same sex (~ dance well) **b** : ¹HE 2 — often used with an indefinite third person singular antecedent (everyone knew where ~ stood —E. L. Doctorow) (nobody has to go to school if ~ don't want to —N. Y. Times) **2** : PEOPLE 2 — used in a generic sense (as lazy as ~ come)

usage They used as an indefinite subject (sense 2) is sometimes objected to on the grounds that it does not have an antecedent. Not every pronoun requires an antecedent, however. The indefinite they is used in all varieties of contexts and is standard.

usage They, their, them, themselves: English lacks a common-gender third person singular pronoun that can be used to refer to indefinite pronouns (as everyone, anyone, someone). Writers and speakers have supplied this lack by using the plural pronouns (and every one to rest themselves betake —Shak.) (I would have everybody marry if they can do it properly —Jane Austen⟩ ⟨it is too hideous for anyone in *their* senses to buy —W. H. Auden⟩. The plural pronouns have also been put to use as pronouns of indefinite number to refer to singular nouns that stand for many persons ⟨'tis meet that some more audience than a mother, since nature makes *them* partial, should o'erhear the speech —Shak.⟩ ⟨a person can't help *their* birth —W. M. Thackeray⟩ ⟨no man goes to battle to be killed. — But *they* do get killed —G. B. Shaw⟩. The use of *they*, *their*, *them*, and *themselves* as pronouns of indefinite gender and indefinite number is well established in speech and writing, even in literary and formal contexts. This gives you the option of using the plural pronouns where you think they sound best, and of using the singular pronouns (as *he, she, he or she*, and *they* and their inflected forms) where you think they sound best.

they'd \'thād\ (1676) : they had : they would
they'll \'thā(ə)l, thel\ (1607) : they will : they shall
they're \thər, 'ther\ (ca. 1594) : they are
they've \'thāv\ (1611) : they have
thi- *or* **thio-** *comb form* [ISV, fr. Gk *thei-, theio-* sulfur, fr. *theion*] : containing sulfur ⟨*thiamine*⟩ ⟨*thiocyanate*⟩
thia·ben·da·zole \,thī-ə-'ben-də-,zōl\ *n* [*thiazole* + *benz-* + *imide* + *azole*] (1961) : a drug $C_{10}H_7N_3S$ used in the control of parasitic nematode worms, in the treatment of fungus infections, and as an agricultural fungicide
thi·ami·nase \thī-'a-mə-,nās, 'thī-ə-mə-, -,nāz\ *n* [ISV] (1938) : an enzyme that catalyzes the breakdown of thiamine
thi·a·mine \'thī-ə-mən, -,mēn\ *also* **thi·a·min** \-mən\ *n* [*thiamine* alter. of *thiamin*, fr. *thi-* + *-amin* (as in *vitamin*)] (1937) : a vitamin ($C_{12}H_{17}N_4OS)Cl$ of the B complex that is essential to normal metabolism and nerve function and is widespread in plants and animals — called also *vitamin B₁*
thi·a·zide \'thī-ə-,zīd, -zəd\ *n* [*thi-* + diazine + dioxide] (1959) : any of a group of drugs used as oral diuretics esp. in the control of high blood pressure
thi·a·zine \'thī-ə-,zēn\ *n* [ISV] (1900) : any of various compounds that are characterized by a ring composed of four carbon atoms, one sulfur atom, and one nitrogen atom and include some important as dyes and others as tranquilizers — compare PHENOTHIAZINE
thi·a·zole \'thī-ə-,zōl\ *n* [ISV] (1888) **1** : a colorless basic liquid C_3H_3NS consisting of a 5-membered ring and having an odor like pyridine **2** : any of various thiazole derivatives including some used in medicine and others important as chemical accelerators
¹thick \'thik\ *adj* [ME *thikke*, fr. OE *thicce*; akin to OHG *dicki* thick, OIr *tiug*] (bef. 12c) **1 a** : having or being of relatively great depth or extent from one surface to its opposite ⟨a ~ plank⟩ **b** : heavily built : THICKSET **2 a** : close-packed with units or individuals ⟨the air was ~ with snow⟩ **b** : occurring in large numbers : NUMEROUS **c** : viscous in consistency ⟨~ syrup⟩ **d** : SULTRY, STUFFY **e** : marked by haze, fog, or mist ⟨~ weather⟩ **f** : impenetrable to the eye : PROFOUND ⟨~ darkness⟩ **3** : extremely intense ⟨~ silence⟩ **3** : measuring in thickness ⟨12 inches ~⟩ **4 a** : imperfectly articulated : INDISTINCT ⟨~ speech⟩ **b** : plainly apparent : DECIDED ⟨a ~ French accent⟩ **c** : producing inarticulate speech ⟨a ~ tongue⟩ **5** : OBTUSE, STUPID **6** : associated on close terms : INTIMATE ⟨was quite ~ with his pastor⟩ **7** : exceeding bounds of propriety or fitness : EXCESSIVE ⟨called it a bit ~ to be fired without warning⟩ — **thick·ish** \'thi-kish\ *adj* — **thick·ly** *adv*
²thick *adv* (bef. 12c) : in a thick manner : THICKLY
³thick *n* (13c) **1** : the most crowded or active part ⟨in the ~ of the battle⟩ **2** : the part of greatest thickness ⟨the ~ of the thumb⟩
thick and thin *n* (14c) : every difficulty and obstacle — used esp. in the phrase *through thick and thin*
thick·en \'thi-kən\ *vb* **thick·ened; thick·en·ing** \'thik-niŋ, 'thi-kə-\ *vt* (15c) **1 a** : to make thick, dense, or viscous in consistency ⟨~ gravy with flour⟩ **b** : to make close or compact **2** : to increase the depth or diameter of **3** : to make inarticulate : BLUR ⟨alcohol ~*ed* his speech⟩ ~ *vi* **1 a** : to become dense ⟨the mist ~*ed*⟩ **b** : to become concentrated in numbers, mass, or frequency **2** : to grow blurred or obscure **3** : to grow broader or bulkier **4** : to grow complicated or keen ⟨the plot ~*s*⟩ — **thick·en·er** \'thik-nər, 'thi-kə-\ *n*
thickening *n* (ca. 1580) **1** : the act of making or becoming thick **2** : a thickened part or place **3** : something used to thicken
thick·et \'thi-kət\ *n* [assumed] ME *thikket*, fr. OE *thiccet*, fr. *thicce* thick] (bef. 12c) **1** : a dense growth of shrubbery or small trees : COPPICE **2** : something resembling a thicket in density or impenetrability : TANGLE — **thick·ety** \-kə-tē\ *adj*
thick·et·ed \'thi-kə-təd\ *adj* (ca. 1624) : dotted or covered with thickets
thick·head \'thik-,hed\ *n* (1824) : a stupid person : BLOCKHEAD
thick·head·ed \-,he-dəd\ *adj* (1707) **1** : having a thick head **2** : sluggish and obtuse of mind
thick·ness \-nəs\ *n* (bef. 12c) **1** : the smallest of three dimensions ⟨length, width, and ~⟩ **2** : the quality or state of being thick **3 a** : viscous consistency ⟨boiled to the ~ of honey⟩ **b** : the condition of being smoky, foul, or foggy **4** : the thick part of something **5** : CONCENTRATION, DENSITY **6** : STUPIDITY, DULLNESS **7** : LAYER, PLY, SHEET ⟨a single ~ of canvas⟩
thick·set \-,set\ *adj* (14c) **1** : closely placed; *also* : growing thickly ⟨a ~ wood⟩ **2** : having a thick body : BURLY
thick–skinned \-,skind\ *adj* (1545) **1** : having a thick skin : PACHYDERMATOUS **2 a** : CALLOUS, INSENSITIVE **b** : impervious to criticism
thick–wit·ted \-,wi-təd\ *adj* (1634) : dull or slow of mind : STUPID
thief \'thēf\ *n, pl* **thieves** \'thēvz\ [ME *theef*, fr. OE *thēof*; akin to OHG *diob* thief] (bef. 12c) : one that steals esp. stealthily or secretly; *also* : one who commits theft or larceny
thieve \'thēv\ *vb* **thieved; thiev·ing** (bef. 12c) : STEAL, ROB
thiev·ery \'thēv-rē, 'thē-və-\ *n, pl* **-er·ies** (1568) : the act or practice or an instance of stealing : THEFT
thiev·ish \'thē-vish\ *adj* (1538) **1** : given to stealing **2** : of, relating to, or characteristic of a thief — **thiev·ish·ly** *adv* — **thiev·ish·ness** *n*
thigh \'thī\ *n* [ME, fr. OE *thēoh*; akin to OHG *dioh* thigh, Lith *taukai*, pl., fat] (bef. 12c) **1 a** : the proximal segment of the vertebrate hind limb extending from the hip to the knee and supported by a single large bone **b** : the segment of the leg immediately distal to the thigh in a bird or in a quadruped in which the true thigh is obscured **c** : the

femur of an insect **2** : something resembling or covering a thigh — **thighed** \'thīd\ *adj*
thigh·bone \'thī-,bōn\ *n* (15c) : FEMUR 1
thig·mo·tax·is \,thig-mə-'tak-səs\ *n* [NL, fr. Gk *thigma* touch (fr. *thinganein* to touch) + NL *-taxis*; akin to L *fingere* to shape — more at DOUGH] (1903) : a taxis in which contact esp. with a solid body is the directive factor
thig·mot·ro·pism \thig-'mä-trə-,pi-zəm\ *n* [Gk *thigma* + ISV *-o-* + *-tropism*] (ca. 1900) : a tropism in which contact esp. with a solid or a rigid surface is the orienting factor
thill \'thil\ *n* [ME *thille*, perh. fr. OE, plank; akin to OE *thel* board, OHG *dili*, and prob. to L *tellus* earth] (14c) : a shaft of a vehicle
thim·ble \'thim-bəl\ *n* [ME *thymbyl*, prob. alter. of OE *thỹmel* covering for the thumb, fr. *thūma* thumb] (15c) **1** : a pitted cap or cover worn on the finger to push the needle in sewing **2 a** : a grooved ring of thin metal used to fit in a spliced loop in a rope as protection from chafing **b** : a lining (as of metal) for an opening (as in a roof or wall) through which a stovepipe or chimney passes
thim·ble·ber·ry \-,ber-ē\ *n* (1788) : any of several American raspberries or blackberries (esp. *Rubus occidentalis, R. parviflorus*, and *R. odoratus*) having thimble-shaped fruit
thim·ble·ful \-,fūl\ *n* (1607) **1** : as much as a thimble will hold **2** : a very small quantity
¹thim·ble·rig \-,rig\ *n* (1826) **1** : a swindling trick in which a small ball or pea is quickly shifted from under one to another of three small cups to fool the spectator guessing its location **2** : one who manipulates the cup in thimblerig : THIMBLERIGGER
²thimblerig *vt* (1839) **1** : to cheat by trickery **2** : to swindle by thimblerig — **thim·ble·rig·ger** *n*
thim·ble·weed \'thim-bəl-,wēd\ *n* (1833) : any of various anemones (as *Anemone virginiana* and *A. cylindrica*)
thi·mer·o·sal \thī-'mer-ə-,sal\ *n* [prob. fr. *thi-* + mercury + *-o-* + salicylate] (1949) : a crystalline organic mercurial antiseptic $C_9H_9HgNaO_2S$ used esp. for its antifungal and bacteriostatic properties
¹thin \'thin\ *adj* **thin·ner; thin·nest** [ME *thinne*, fr. OE *thynne*; akin to OHG *dunni* thin, L *tenuis* thin, *tenēre* to hold, *tendere* to stretch, Gk *teinein*] (bef. 12c) **1 a** : having little extent from one surface to its opposite ⟨~ paper⟩ **b** : measuring little in cross section or diameter ⟨~ rope⟩ **2** : not dense in arrangement or distribution ⟨~ hair⟩ **3** : not well fleshed : LEAN **4 a** : more fluid or rarefied than normal ⟨~ air⟩ **b** : having less than the usual number : SCANTY ⟨~ attendance⟩ **c** : few in number : SCARCE **d** : scantily supplied **e** : characterized by a paucity of bids or offerings ⟨a ~ market⟩ **5 a** : lacking substance or strength ⟨~ broth⟩ ⟨a ~ plot⟩ **b** *of a soil* : INFERTILE, POOR **6 a** : FLIMSY, UNCONVINCING ⟨a ~ disguise⟩ **b** : disappointingly poor or hard ⟨had a ~ time of it⟩ **7** : somewhat feeble, shrill, and lacking in resonance ⟨a ~ voice⟩ **8** : lacking in intensity or brilliance ⟨~ blue⟩ **9** : lacking sufficient photographic density or contrast — **thin·ly** *adv* — **thin·ness** \'thin-nəs\ *n* — **thin·nish** \'thi-nish\ *adj*
syn THIN, SLENDER, SLIM, SLIGHT, TENUOUS mean not thick, broad, abundant, or dense. THIN implies comparatively little extension between surfaces or in diameter, or it may imply lack of substance, richness, or abundance ⟨*thin* wire⟩ ⟨a *thin* soup⟩. SLENDER implies leanness or spareness often with grace and good proportion ⟨the *slender* legs of a Sheraton chair⟩. SLIM applies to slenderness that suggests fragility or scantiness ⟨a *slim* volume of poetry⟩ ⟨a *slim* chance⟩. SLIGHT implies smallness as well as thinness ⟨a *slight* build⟩. TENUOUS implies extreme thinness, sheerness, or lack of substance and firmness ⟨a *tenuous* thread⟩.
²thin *vb* **thinned; thin·ning** *vt* (bef. 12c) : to make thin or thinner: **a** : to reduce in thickness or depth : ATTENUATE **b** : to make less dense or viscous **c** : DILUTE, WEAKEN **d** : to cause to lose flesh ⟨thinned by weeks of privation⟩ **e** : to reduce in number or bulk ~ *vi* **1** : to become thin or thinner **2** : to become weak
³thin *adv* **thin·ner; thin·nest** (13c) : in a thin manner : THINLY — used esp. in combinations ⟨thin-clad⟩ ⟨thin-flowing⟩
¹thine \'thīn\ *adj* [ME *thin*, fr. OE *thīn*] (bef. 12c) *archaic* : THY — used esp. before a word beginning with a vowel or *h*
²thine *pron, sing or pl in constr* [ME *thin*, fr. OE *thīn*, fr. *thīn* thy — more at THY] (bef. 12c) *archaic* : that which belongs to thee — used without a following noun as a pronoun equivalent in meaning to the adjective *thy*; used esp. in ecclesiastical or literary language and still surviving in the speech of Friends esp. among themselves
thin film *n* (1944) : a very thin layer of a substance on a supporting material; *esp* : a coating (as of a semiconductor) that is deposited in a layer one atom or one molecule thick
thing \'thiŋ\ *n* [ME, fr. OE, thing, assembly; akin to OHG *ding* thing, assembly, Goth *theihs* time] (bef. 12c) **1 a** : a matter of concern : AFFAIR ⟨many ~s to do⟩ **b** *pl* : state of affairs in general or within a specified or implied sphere ⟨~s are improving⟩ **c** : a particular state of affairs : SITUATION ⟨look at this ~ another way⟩ **d** : EVENT, CIRCUMSTANCE ⟨that shooting was a terrible ~⟩ **2 a** : DEED, ACT, ACCOMPLISHMENT ⟨do great ~s⟩ **b** : a product of work or activity ⟨likes to build ~s⟩ **c** : the aim of effort or activity ⟨the ~ is to get well⟩ **3 a** : a separate and distinct individual quality, fact, idea, or usu. entity **b** : the concrete entity as distinguished from its appearances **c** : a spatial entity **d** : an inanimate object distinguished from a living being **4 a** *pl* : POSSESSIONS, EFFECTS ⟨pack your ~s⟩ **b** : whatever may be possessed or owned or be the object of a right **c** : an article of clothing ⟨not a ~ to wear⟩ **d** *pl* : equipment or utensils esp. for a particular purpose ⟨bring the tea ~s⟩ **5** : an object or entity not precisely designated or capable of being designated ⟨use this ~⟩ **6 a** : DETAIL, POINT ⟨checks every little ~⟩ **b** : a material or substance of a specified kind ⟨avoid fatty ~s⟩ **7 a** : a spoken or written observation or point **b** : IDEA, NOTION ⟨says the first ~ he thinks of⟩ **c** : a piece of news or information ⟨couldn't get a ~ out of him⟩ **8** : INDIVIDUAL ⟨not a living ~ in sight⟩ **9** : the proper or fashionable way of behaving, talking, or

\ə\ abut \ᵊ\ kitten, F table \ər\ further \a\ ash \ā\ ace \ä\ mop, mar
\aú\ out \ch\ chin \e\ bet \ē\ easy \g\ go \i\ hit \ī\ ice \j\ job
\ŋ\ sing \ō\ go \ó\ law \ói\ boy \th\ thin \t͟h\ the \ü\ loot \ù\ foot
\y\ yet \zh\ vision \à, k̩, ⁿ, œ, œ̄, ᵫ, ūᵉ, ᵊ\ *see* Guide to Pronunciation

dressing — used with *the* **10 a** : a mild obsession or phobia ⟨has a ~ about driving⟩; *also* : the object of such an obsession or phobia **b** : something (as an activity) that makes a strong appeal to the individual : FORTE, SPECIALTY ⟨letting students do their own ~ —*Newsweek*⟩ ⟨I think travelling is very much a novelist's ~ —Philip Larkin⟩

thing·am·a·bob \'thiŋ-ə-mə-,bäb\ *n* (1832) : THINGAMAJIG

thing·am·a·jig *or* **thing·um·a·jig** \'thiŋ-ə-mə-,jig\ *n* [alter. of earlier *thingum,* fr. *thing*] (1828) : something that is hard to classify or whose name is unknown or forgotten

thing–in–itself *n, pl* **things–in–themselves** [trans. of G *Ding an sich*] (1798) : NOUMENON

thing·ness \'thiŋ-nəs\ *n* (1896) : the quality or state of objective existence or reality

thing·um·my \'thiŋ-ə-mē\ *n, pl* **-mies** [alter. of earlier *thingum*] (1796) : THINGAMAJIG

¹**think** \'thiŋk\ *vb* **thought** \'thȯt\; **think·ing** [ME *thenken,* fr. OE *thencan;* akin to OHG *denken* to think, L *tongēre* to know — more at THANKS] *vt* (bef. 12c) **1** : to form or have in the mind **2** : to have as an intention ⟨*thought* to return early⟩ **3 a** : to have as an opinion ⟨~ it's so⟩ **b** : to regard as : CONSIDER ⟨~ the rule unfair⟩ **4 a** : to reflect on : PONDER ⟨~ the matter over⟩ **b** : to determine by reflecting ⟨~ what to do next⟩ **5** : to call to mind : REMEMBER ⟨he never ~s to ask how we do⟩ **6** : to devise by thinking — usu. used with *up* ⟨*thought* up a plan to escape⟩ **7** : to have as an expectation : ANTICIPATE ⟨we didn't ~ we'd have any trouble⟩ **8 a** : to center one's thoughts on ⟨talks and ~s business⟩ **b** : to form a mental picture of **9** : to subject to the processes of logical thought ⟨~ things out⟩ ~ *vi* **1 a** : to exercise the powers of judgment, conception, or inference : REASON **b** : to have in the mind or call to mind a thought **2 a** : to have the mind engaged in reflection : MEDITATE **b** : to consider the suitability ⟨*thought* of her for president⟩ **3** : to have a view or opinion ⟨~s of himself as a poet⟩ **4** : to have concern — usu. used with *of* ⟨a man must ~ first of his family⟩ **5** : to consider something likely : SUSPECT ⟨may happen sooner than you ~⟩ — **think·er** *n* — **think better of** : to reconsider and make a wiser decision — **think much of** : to view with satisfaction : APPROVE — usu. used in negative constructions ⟨I didn't *think much of* the new car⟩

syn THINK, CONCEIVE, IMAGINE, FANCY, REALIZE, ENVISAGE, ENVISION mean to form an idea of. THINK implies the entrance of an idea into one's mind with or without deliberate consideration or reflection ⟨I just *thought* of a good joke⟩. CONCEIVE suggests the forming and bringing forth and usu. developing of an idea, plan, or design ⟨*conceived* of a new marketing approach⟩. IMAGINE stresses a visualization ⟨*imagine* you're at the beach⟩. FANCY suggests an imagining often unrestrained by reality but spurred by desires ⟨*fancied* himself a super athlete⟩. REALIZE stresses a grasping of the significance of what is conceived or imagined ⟨*realized* the enormity of the task ahead⟩. ENVISAGE and ENVISION imply a conceiving or imagining that is esp. clear or detailed ⟨*envisaged* a totally computerized operation⟩ ⟨*envisioned* a cure for the disease⟩.

syn THINK, COGITATE, REFLECT, REASON, SPECULATE, DELIBERATE mean to use one's powers of conception, judgment, or inference. THINK is general and may apply to any mental activity, but used alone often suggests attainment of clear ideas or conclusions ⟨teaches students how to *think*⟩. COGITATE implies deep or intent thinking ⟨*cogitated* on the mysteries of nature⟩. REFLECT suggests unhurried consideration of something recalled to the mind ⟨*reflecting* on fifty years of married life⟩. REASON stresses consecutive logical thinking ⟨able to *reason* brilliantly in debate⟩. SPECULATE implies reasoning about things theoretical or problematic ⟨*speculated* on the fate of the lost explorers⟩. DELIBERATE suggests slow or careful reasoning before forming an opinion or reaching a conclusion or decision ⟨the jury *deliberated* for five hours⟩.

²**think** *n* (1834) : an act of thinking ⟨has another ~ coming⟩

³**think** *adj* (1906) : relating to, requiring, or stimulating thinking

think·able \'thiŋ-kə-bəl\ *adj* (1854) **1** : capable of being comprehended or reasoned about ⟨the ultimate nature of Deity is scarcely ~⟩ **2** : conceivably possible — **think·able·ness** *n* — **think·ably** \-blē\ *adv*

¹**thinking** *n* (14c) **1** : the action of using one's mind to produce thoughts **2 a** : OPINION, JUDGMENT ⟨I'd like to know your ~ on this⟩ **b** : thought that is characteristic (as of a period, group, or person) ⟨the current student ~ on fraternities⟩

²**thinking** *adj* (1681) : marked by use of the intellect : RATIONAL ⟨~ citizens⟩ — **think·ing·ly** \'thiŋ-kiŋ-lē\ *adv* — **think·ing·ness** *n*

thinking cap *n* (1874) : a state or mood in which one thinks — usu. used in the phrase *put one's thinking cap on*

think piece *n* (1941) : a piece of writing meant to be thought-provoking and speculative that consists chiefly of background material and personal opinion and analysis

think tank *n* (1959) : an institute, corporation, or group organized for interdisciplinary research (as in technological and social problems) — called also *think factory*

thin–layer chromatography *n* (1957) : chromatography in which the stationary phase is an absorbent medium (as alumina or silica gel) arranged as a thin layer on a rigid support (as a glass plate)

thin·ner \'thi-nər\ *n* (1832) : one that thins; *specif* : a volatile liquid (as turpentine) used esp. to thin paint

thin–skinned \'thin-,skind\ *adj* (1598) **1** : having a thin skin or rind **2** : unduly susceptible to criticism or insult : TOUCHY

thio– — see THI-

thio acid \'thī-ō-\ *n* [ISV, fr. *thi-*] (ca. 1891) : an acid in which oxygen is partly or wholly replaced by sulfur

thio·cy·a·nate \,thī-ō-'sī-ə-,nāt, -nət\ *n* [ISV] (1877) : a compound that consists of the chemical group SCN bonded by the sulfur atom to a group or an atom other than a hydrogen atom

thi·ol \'thī-,ȯl, -,ōl\ *n* [ISV *thi-* + ¹*-ol*] (ca. 1890) **1** : any of various compounds having the general formula RSH which are analogous to alcohols but in which sulfur replaces the oxygen of the hydroxyl group and which have disagreeable odors **2** : the functional group —SH characteristic of thiols — **thi·o·lic** \thī-'ō-lik\ *adj*

thion– *comb form* [ISV, fr. Gk *theion*] : sulfur ⟨*methion*ine⟩

thio·pen·tal \,thī-ō-'pen-,tal, -,tȯl\ *n* [*thio-* + *pento*barbi*tal*] (1947) : a barbiturate C₁₁H₁₈N₂O₂S used in the form of its sodium salt esp. as an intravenous anesthetic — compare PENTOTHAL

thio·phene \'thī-ō-,fēn\ *n* [ISV *thi-* + *phene* benzene] (1883) : a heterocyclic liquid C₄H₄S from coal tar that resembles benzene

thi·o·rid·a·zine \,thī-ə-'ri-də-,zēn, -zən\ *n* [*thi-* + piperi*dine* + pheno*thiazine*] (1959) : a phenothiazine tranquilizer used as the hydrochloride C₂₁H₂₆N₂S₂·HCl for relief of anxiety states and in the treatment of schizophrenia

thio·sul·fate \-'səl-,fāt\ *n* [ISV] (1873) : a salt containing the anion S₂O₃²⁻

thio·te·pa \,thī-ə-'tē-pə\ *n* (1953) : a sulfur analogue of tepa C₆H₁₂N₃PS that is used esp. as an antineoplastic agent

thio·ura·cil \,thī-ō-'yuṙ-ə-,sil\ *n* [ISV] (1905) : a bitter crystalline compound C₄H₄N₂OS that depresses the function of the thyroid gland

thio·urea \-yu̇-'rē-ə\ *n* [NL] (1894) : a colorless crystalline bitter compound CS(NH₂)₂ analogous to and resembling urea that is used esp. as a photographic and organic chemical reagent; *also* : a substituted derivative of this compound

thir \thər, 'th(ə)r, 'thu̇r\ *pron or adj* [ME (northern), perh. irreg. fr. ME *this*] (14c) *dial Brit* : THESE

thi·ram \'thī-,ram\ *n* [prob. by alter. fr. *thiuram* the chemical group NH₂CS] (1949) : a compound C₆H₁₂N₂S₄ used as a fungicide and seed disinfectant

¹**third** \'thərd\ *adj* [ME *thridde, thirde,* fr. OE *thridda, thirdda;* akin to L *tertius* third, Gk *tritos, treis* three — more at THREE] (bef. 12c) **1 a** : being next after the second in place or time ⟨the ~ taxi in line⟩ **b** : ranking next after the second of a grade or degree in authority or precedence ⟨~ mate⟩ **c** : being the forward speed or gear next higher than second esp. in a motor vehicle **2 a** : being one of three equal parts into which something is divisible **b** : being the last in each group of three in a series ⟨take out every ~ card⟩ — **third** *or* **third·ly** *adv*

²**third** *n* (14c) **1** : one of three equal parts of something **2 a** — see NUMBER table **b** : one that is next after second in rank, position, authority, or precedence ⟨the ~ in line⟩ **3 a** : the musical interval embracing three diatonic degrees **b** : a tone at this interval; *specif* : MEDIANT **c** : the harmonic combination of two tones a third apart **4** *pl* : merchandise whose quality falls below the manufacturer's standard for seconds **5** : THIRD BASE **6** : the third forward gear or speed esp. of a motor vehicle

third base *n* (1845) **1** : the base that must be touched third by a base runner in baseball **2** : the player position for defending the area around third base — **third baseman** *n*

third–class *adj* (1839) : of or relating to a class, rank, or grade next below the second — **third–class** *adv*

third class *n* (1844) **1** : the third and usu. next below second class in a classification **2** : the least expensive class of accommodations (as on a passenger ship) **3 a** : a class of U.S. mail comprising printed matter exclusive of regularly issued periodicals and merchandise less than 16 ounces (454 grams) in weight that is not sealed against inspection **b** : a similar class of Canadian mail with different weight limits

third degree *n* (1900) : the subjection of a prisoner to mental or physical torture to extract a confession

third–degree burn *n* (1930) : a severe burn characterized by destruction of the skin through its deeper layers and possibly into underlying tissues, loss of fluid, and sometimes shock

third dimension *n* (1858) **1** : THICKNESS, DEPTH; *also* : a dimension that adds the effect of solidity to a two-dimensional system **2** : a quality that confers reality or lifelikeness ⟨night sounds that stick in the mind and give a *third* dimension to the memory —Adie Suehsdorf⟩ — **third–dimensional** *adj*

third estate *n, often cap T&E* (1604) : the third of the traditional political orders; *specif* : the commons

third force *n* [trans. of F *troisième force*] (1936) : a grouping (as of political parties or international powers) intermediate between two opposing political forces

third·hand \'thərd-'hand\ *adj* (1599) **1** : received from or through two intermediaries ⟨~ information⟩ **2 a** : acquired after being used by two previous owners **b** : dealing in thirdhand merchandise

third house *n* (1849) : a legislative lobby

third market *n* (1964) : the over-the-counter market in listed securities

third order *n, often cap T&O* (1629) **1** : an organization composed of lay people living in secular society under a religious rule and directed by a religious order **2** : a congregation esp. of teaching or nursing sisters affiliated with a religious order

third party *n* (1801) **1 a** : a major political party operating over a limited period of time in addition to two other major parties in a nation or state normally characterized by a two-party system **b** : MINOR PARTY **2** : a person other than the principals ⟨a *third party* to a divorce proceeding⟩

third person *n* (ca. 1586) **1 a** : a set of linguistic forms (as verb forms, pronouns, and inflectional affixes) referring to one that is neither the speaker or writer of the utterance in which they occur nor the one to whom that utterance is addressed **b** : a linguistic form belonging to such a set **2** : reference of a linguistic form to one that is neither the speaker or writer of the utterance in which it occurs nor the one to whom that utterance is addressed

third rail *n* (1890) : a metal rail through which electric current is led to the motors of an electric vehicle (as a subway car)

third–rate \'thərd-'rāt\ *adj* (1814) : of third quality or value; *specif* : worse than second-rate — **third–rat·er** \-'rā-tər\ *n*

third reading *n* (ca. 1571) : the final stage of the consideration of a legislative bill before a vote on its final disposition

third–stream *adj* (1962) : of, relating to, or being music that incorporates elements of classical music and jazz

third ventricle *n* (ca. 1860) : the median unpaired ventricle of the brain bounded by parts of the telencephalon and diencephalon

third world *n, often cap T&W* [trans. of F *tiers monde*] (1963) **1** : a group of nations esp. in Africa and Asia not aligned with either the Communist or the non-Communist blocs **2** : an aggregate of minority groups within a larger predominant culture **3** : the aggregate of the underdeveloped nations of the world — **third world·er** \-'wər(-ə)l-dər\ *n, often cap T&W*

¹**thirl** \'thərl\ *n* [ME, fr. OE *thyrel,* fr. *thurh* through — more at THROUGH] (bef. 12c) *dial* : HOLE, PERFORATION, OPENING

²**thirl** *vt* (bef. 12c) *dial Brit* : PIERCE, PERFORATE

¹**thirst** \'thərst\ *n* [ME, fr. OE *thurst;* akin to OHG *durst* thirst, L *torrēre* to dry, parch, Gk *tersesthai* to become dry] (bef. 12c) **1 a :** a sensation of dryness in the mouth and throat associated with a desire for liquids; *also* : the bodily condition (as of dehydration) that induces this sensation **b :** a desire or need to drink **2 :** an ardent desire : CRAVING, LONGING

²**thirst** *vi* (bef. 12c) **1 :** to feel thirsty : suffer thirst **2 :** to crave vehemently and urgently *syn* see LONG — **thirst·er** *n*

thirst·i·ly \'thər-stə-lē\ *adv* (1549) : with or on account of thirst

thirsty \'thər-stē\ *adj* **thirst·i·er; -est** (bef. 12c) **1 a :** feeling thirst **b :** deficient in moisture : PARCHED ⟨~ land⟩ **c :** highly absorbent ⟨~ towels⟩ **d :** having a strong desire : AVID ⟨~ for knowledge⟩ — **thirst·i·ness** \-stē-nəs\ *n*

thir·teen \,thər(t)-'tēn, 'thər(t)-\ *n* [ME *thrittene,* fr. *thrittene,* adj., fr. OE *thrēotīne;* akin to OE *tīen* ten — more at TEN] (14c) — see NUMBER table — **thirteen** *adj* — **thirteen** *pron, pl in constr* — **thir·teenth** \-'tēn(t)th, -,tēn(t)th\ *adj or n*

thir·ty \'thər-tē\ *n, pl* **thirties** [ME *thritty,* fr. *thritty,* adj., fr. OE *thritig,* fr. *thrītig* group of 30, fr. *thrīe* three + *-tig* group; akin to OE *tīen* ten] (bef. 12c) **1** — see NUMBER table **2** *pl* : the numbers 30 to 39; *specif* : the years 30 to 39 in a lifetime or century **3 :** a sign of completion : END — usu. written 30 ⟨wrote ~ on the last page of the story⟩ **4 :** the second point scored by a side in a game of tennis — **thir·ti·eth** \-tē-əth\ *adj or n* — **thirty** *adj* — **thirty** *pron, pl in constr* — **thir·ty·ish** \-ish\ *adj*

thir·ty–eight \,thər-tē-'āt\ *n* (ca. 1934) **1** — see NUMBER table **2 :** a handgun nominally of .38 caliber — usu. written .38 — **thirty–eight** *adj* — **thirty–eight** *pron, pl in constr*

thir·ty–sec·ond note \-'se-kən(d)-,nōt, -kən(t)-\ *n* (ca. 1890) : a musical note with the time value of ¹/₃₂ of a whole note — see NOTE illustration

thirty–second rest *n* (ca. 1903) : a musical rest corresponding in time value to a thirty-second note

thir·ty–thir·ty \,thər-tē-'thər-tē\ *n* (1929) : a rifle that fires a .30 caliber cartridge having a 30 grain powder charge — usu. written .30–30

thir·ty–three \,thər-tē-'thrē\ *n* (1902) **1** — see NUMBER table **2 :** a microgroove phonograph record designed to be played at 33⅓ revolutions per minute — usu. written 33 — **thirty–three** *adj* — **thirty–three** *pron, pl in constr*

thir·ty–two \-'tü\ *n* (1904) **1** — see NUMBER table **2 :** a .32 caliber handgun — usu. written .32 — **thirty–two** *adj* — **thirty–two** *pron, pl in constr*

thir·ty–two–mo \-(,)mō\ *n, pl* **-mos** (ca. 1841) : the size of a piece of paper cut 32 from a sheet; *also* : a book, a page, or paper of this size

¹**this** \'this, thəs\ *pron, pl* **these** \'thēz\ [ME, pron. & adj., fr. OE *thes* (masc.), *this* (neut.); akin to OHG *dese* this, OE *thæt* that] (bef. 12c) **1 a (1) :** the person, thing, or idea that is present or near in place, time, or thought or that has just been mentioned ⟨*these* are my hands⟩ **(2)** : what is stated in the following phrase, clause, or discourse ⟨I can only say ~: it wasn't here yesterday⟩ **b :** this time or place ⟨expected to return before ~⟩ **2 a :** the one nearer or more immediately under observation or discussion ⟨~ is iron and that is tin⟩ **b :** the one more recently referred to

²**this** *adj, pl* **these** (bef. 12c) **1 a :** being the person, thing, or idea that is present or near in place, time, or thought or that has just been mentioned ⟨~ book is mine⟩ ⟨early ~ morning⟩ **b :** constituting the immediately following part of the present discourse **c :** constituting the immediate past or future ⟨friends all *these* years⟩ **d :** being one not previously mentioned — used esp. in narrative to give a sense of immediacy or vividness ⟨then ~ guy runs in⟩ **2 :** being the nearer at hand or more immediately under observation or discussion ⟨~ car or that one⟩

³**this** \'this\ *adv* (15c) : to the degree or extent indicated by something in the immediate context or situation ⟨didn't expect to wait ~ long⟩

This·be \'thiz-bē\ *n* [L, fr. Gk *Thisbē*] : a legendary young woman of Babylon who dies for love of Pyramus

this·tle \'thi-səl\ *n* [ME *thistel,* fr. OE; akin to OHG *distil* thistle] (bef. 12c) : any of various prickly composite plants (esp. genera *Carduus, Cirsium,* and *Onopordum*) with often showy heads of mostly tubular flowers; *also* : any of various other prickly plants — **this·tly** \'thi-s(ə-)lē\ *adj*

this·tle·down \'thi-səl-,daün\ *n* (1561) : the typically plumose pappus from the ripe flower head of a thistle

thistle tube *n* (ca. 1891) : a funnel tube usu. of glass with a bulging top and flaring mouth

this–world·li·ness \'this-'wərld-lē-nəs\ *n* (1887) : interest in, concern with, or devotion to things of this world esp. as opposed to a future stage of existence (as after death)

this–world·ly \-lē\ *adj* (1883) : characterized by or manifesting this-worldliness

¹**thith·er** \'thi-thər *also* 'thi-\ *adv* [ME, fr. OE *thider;* akin to ON *thathra* there, OE *thæt* that] (bef. 12c) : to that place : THERE

²**thither** *adj* (1830) : being on the other and farther side : more remote

thith·er·to \-,tü; ,thi-thər-', ,thi-\ *adv* (15c) : until that time

thith·er·ward \'thi-thər-wərd, 'thi-\ *also* **thith·er·wards** \-wərdz\ *adv* (bef. 12c) : toward that place : THITHER

thix·ot·ro·py \thik-'sä-trə-pē\ *n* [ISV *thixo-* (fr. Gk *thixis* act of touching, fr. *thinganein* to touch) + *-tropy* — more at THIGMOTAXIS] (1927) : the property of various gels of becoming fluid when disturbed (as by shaking) — **thixo·tro·pic** \,thik-sə-'trō-pik, -'trä-\ *adj*

tho *var of* THOUGH

¹**thole** \'thōl\ *vb* **tholed; thol·ing** [ME, fr. OE *tholian* — more at TOLERATE] (bef. 12c) *chiefly dial* : ENDURE

²**thole** *n* [ME *tholle,* fr. OE *thol;* akin to ON *thollr* fir tree, peg, Gk *tylos* knob, callus] (bef. 12c) **1 :** either of a pair of pins set in the gunwale of a boat to hold an oar in place **2 :** PEG, PIN

tho·lei·ite \'thō-lə-,īt, 'thō-\ *n* [G *Tholeiit,* fr. *Tholey,* village in Saarland, Germany + G *-it-* ite] (1866) : a basaltic rock that is rich in aluminum and low in potassium, is found typically in the ocean floor, and is prob. derived from the earth's mantle — **tho·lei·it·ic** \,tō-lə-'i-tik, ,thō-\ *adj*

thole·pin \'thōl-,pin\ *n* (1598) : THOLE 1

Thom·as \'tä-məs\ *n* [Gk *Thomas,* fr. Heb *t'ōm* twin] : an apostle who demanded proof of Christ's resurrection

Thom·as Jef·fer·son's Birthday \'tä-məs-'je-fər-sənz-\ *n* (ca. 1928) : April 13 observed as a legal holiday in Alabama

Tho·mism \'tō-,mi-zəm\ *n* [NL *Thomista* Thomist, fr. St. *Thomas* Aquinas] (ca. 1731) : the scholastic philosophical and theological system of St. Thomas Aquinas — **Tho·mist** \-mist\ *n or adj* — **Tho·mis·tic** \tō-'mis-tik\ *adj*

Thomp·son submachine gun \'täm(p)-sən-\ *n* [John T. *Thompson* †1940 Am. army officer] (1920) : a .45 caliber submachine gun with a drum or stick magazine, a pistol grip, and a detachable buttstock

Thom·son's gazelle \'täm(p)-sənz-\ *n* [Joseph *Thomson* †1895 Scot. explorer] (1897) : a small gazelle (*Gazella thomsoni*) of eastern Africa that is tan above and white below with a broad black stripe on each side

thong \'thȯŋ\ *n* [ME, fr. OE *thwong;* akin ON *thvengr* thong] (bef. 12c) **1 :** a strip esp. of leather or hide **2 :** a sandal held on the foot by a thong fitting between the toes and connected to a strap across the top or around the sides of the foot — **thonged** \'thȯŋd\ *adj*

Thor \'thȯr\ *n* [ON *Thōrr*] : the Norse god of thunder, weather, and crops

tho·rac·ic \thə-'ra-sik\ *adj* (ca. 1658) : of, relating to, located within, or involving the thorax — **tho·rac·i·cal·ly** \-si-k(ə-)lē\ *adv*

thoracic duct *n* (ca. 1741) : the main trunk of the system of lymphatic vessels that lies along the front of the spinal column and opens into the left subclavian vein

tho·ra·cot·o·my \,thȯr-ə-'kä-tə-mē, ,thȯr-\ *n, pl* **-mies** [L *thorac-, thorax* + ISV *-tomy*] (ca. 1857) : surgical incision of the chest wall

tho·rax \'thȯr-,aks, 'thȯr-\ *n, pl* **tho·rax·es** *or* **tho·ra·ces** \'thȯr-ə-,sēz, 'thȯr-\ [ME, fr. L *thorac-, thorax* breastplate, thorax, fr. Gk *thōrak-, thōrax*] (15c) **1 :** the part of the mammalian body between the neck and the abdomen; *also* : its cavity in which the heart and lungs lie **2 :** the middle of the three chief divisions of the body of an insect; *also* : the corresponding part of a crustacean or an arachnid

Tho·ra·zine \'thȯr-ə-,zēn, 'thȯr-\ *trademark* — used for chlorpromazine

tho·ria \'thȯr-ē-ə, 'thȯr-\ *n* [NL, fr. *thorium* + *-a*] (ca. 1841) : a powdery white oxide of thorium ThO₂ used esp. as a catalyst and in crucibles and refractories and optical glass

tho·ri·a·nite \-ē-ə-,nīt\ *n* [irreg. fr. *thoria*] (1904) : a strongly radioactive mineral that is an oxide of thorium and often contains rare-earth metals

tho·rite \'thȯr-,īt, 'thȯr-\ *n* [Sw *thorit,* fr. NL *thorium*] (1832) : a rare mineral that is a brown to black or sometimes orange-yellow silicate of thorium resembling zircon

tho·ri·um \'thȯr-ē-əm, 'thȯr-\ *n* [NL, fr. ON *Thōrr* Thor] (1832) : a radioactive metallic element that occurs combined in minerals and is usu. associated with rare earths — see ELEMENT table

thorn \'thȯrn\ *n, often attrib* [ME, fr. OE; akin to OHG *dorn* thorn, Skt *tṛṇa* grass, blade of grass] (bef. 12c) **1 :** a woody plant bearing sharp impeding processes (as briers, prickles, or spines); *esp* : HAWTHORN **2 a :** a sharp rigid process on a plant; *specif* : a short, indurated, sharp-pointed, and leafless modified branch **b :** any of various sharp spinose structures on an animal **3 :** the runic letter þ used in Old English, Middle English, and Icelandic to represent either of the fricatives \th\ or \th̶\ **4 :** something that causes distress or irritation — often used in the phrase *thorn in one's side* — **thorned** \'thȯrnd\ *adj* — **thorn·less** \'thȯrn-ləs\ *adj* — **thorn·like** \-,līk\ *adj*

thorn apple *n* (1578) **1 :** JIMSONWEED; *also* : any plant of the same genus **2 :** the fruit of a hawthorn; *also* : HAWTHORN

thorn·back \'thȯrn-,bak\ *n* (14c) : any of various rays having spines on the back

thorn·bush \-,büsh\ *n* (1535) **1 :** any of various spiny or thorny shrubs or small trees **2 :** a low growth of thorny shrubs esp. of dry tropical regions

thorny \'thȯr-nē\ *adj* **thorn·i·er; -est** (bef. 12c) **1 :** full of thorns **2 :** full of difficulties or controversial points : TICKLISH ⟨a ~ problem⟩ — **thorn·i·ness** *n*

thoro *nonstand var of* THOROUGH

¹**thor·ough** \'thər-(,)ō, *sometimes* 'thȯr-; 'thə-(,)rō\ *prep* [ME *thorow,* fr. OE *thurh, thuruh,* prep. & adv.] (bef. 12c) *archaic* : THROUGH

²**thorough** *adv* (bef. 12c) *archaic* : THROUGH

³**thorough** *adj* (15c) **1 :** carried through to completion : EXHAUSTIVE ⟨a ~ search⟩ **2 a :** marked by full detail ⟨a ~ description⟩ **b :** careful about detail : PAINSTAKING ⟨a ~ scholar⟩ **c :** complete in all respects ⟨~ pleasure⟩ **d :** having full mastery (as of an art) ⟨a ~ musician⟩ **3 :** passing through — **thor·ough·ly** *adv* — **thor·ough·ness** *n*

thor·ough·bass \'thər-ə-,bās, 'thə-rə-\ *n* (1662) : CONTINUO

thor·ough·brace \-,brās\ *n* (1837) : any of several leather straps supporting the body of a carriage and serving as springs

¹**thor·ough·bred** \-,bred\ *adj* (1701) **1 :** thoroughly trained or skilled **2 :** bred from the best blood through a long line : PUREBRED ⟨~ dogs⟩ **3 a** *cap* : of, relating to, or being a member of the Thoroughbred breed of horses **b :** having characteristics resembling those of a Thoroughbred

²**thoroughbred** *n* (1842) **1** *cap* : any of an English breed of light speedy horses kept chiefly for racing that originated from crosses between English mares of uncertain ancestry and Arabian stallions **2 :** a purebred or pedigreed animal **3 :** one that has

Thoroughbred

\ə\ abut \'ə\ kitten, F table \ər\ further \a\ ash \ā\ ace \ä\ mop, mar \aü\ out \ch\ chin \e\ bet \ē\ easy \g\ go \i\ hit \ī\ ice \j\ job \ŋ\ sing \ō\ go \ȯ\ law \ȯi\ boy \th\ thin \th̶\ the \ü\ loot \ü\ foot \y\ yet \zh\ vision \ä, k̟, ⁿ, œ, œ̄, œ, ᵫ, ᵫ̄, ᵊ\ see Guide to Pronunciation characteristics resembling those of a Thoroughbred

thor·ough·fare \-,far, -,fer\ *n* (14c) **1** : a way or place for passage: as **a** : a street open at both ends **b** : a main road **2 a** : PASSAGE, TRANSIT **b** : the conditions necessary for passing through

thor·ough·go·ing \,thər-ə-'gō-iŋ, ,thə-rə-, -'gō(-)iŋ\ *adj* (1800) : marked by thoroughness or zeal : THOROUGH, COMPLETE

thor·ough–paced \-'pāst\ *adj* (1646) **1** : THOROUGH, COMPLETE **2** : thoroughly trained : ACCOMPLISHED

thor·ough·pin \'thər-ə-,pin, 'thə-rə-\ *n* (1789) : a synovial swelling just above the hock of a horse on both sides of the leg and slightly anterior to the hamstring tendon that is often associated with lameness

thor·ough·wort \-,wərt, -,wórt\ *n* (1814) : BONESET

thorp \'thórp\ *n* [ME, fr. OE, perh. fr. ON; akin to OHG *dorf* village, L *trabs* beam, roof] (bef. 12c) *archaic* : VILLAGE, HAMLET

those [ME, fr. *those* these, fr. OE *thās*, pl. of *thes* this — more at THIS] *pl of* THAT

¹**thou** \'thaù\ *pron* [ME, fr. OE *thū*; akin to OHG *dū* thou, L *tu*, Gk *sy*] (bef. 12c) *archaic* : the one addressed ⟨~ shalt have no other gods before me —Exod 20:3 (AV)⟩ — used esp. in ecclesiastical or literary language and by Friends as the universal form of address to one person; compare THEE, THINE, THY, YE, YOU

²**thou** *vt* (15c) : to address as *thou*

³**thou** \'thaù\ *n, pl* **thou** [short for *thousand*] (1867) : a thousand of something (as dollars)

¹**though** \'thō\ *conj* [ME, adv. & conj., of Scand origin; akin to ON *thō* nevertheless; akin to OE *thēah* nevertheless, OHG *doh*] (bef. 12c) **1** : in spite of the fact that : WHILE ⟨~ they know the war is lost, they continue to fight —Bruce Bliven †1977⟩ **2** : in spite of the possibility that : even if ⟨~ I may fail, I will try⟩

²**though** *adv* (13c) : HOWEVER, NEVERTHELESS ⟨It's hard work. I enjoy it ~⟩

¹**thought** \'thōt\ *past and past part of* THINK

²**thought** *n* [ME, fr. OE *thōht*; akin to OE *thencan* to think — more at THINK] (bef. 12c) **1 a** : the action or process of thinking : COGITATION **b** : serious consideration : REGARD **c** *archaic* : RECOLLECTION, REMEMBRANCE **2 a** : reasoning power : the power to imagine : CONCEPTION **3** : something that is thought: as **a** : an individual act or product of thinking **b** : a developed intention or plan ⟨had no ~ of leaving home⟩ **c** : something (as an opinion or belief) in the mind ⟨he spoke his ~s freely⟩ **d** : the intellectual product or the organized views and principles of a period, place, group, or individual ⟨contemporary Western ~⟩ *syn* see IDEA — **a thought** : a little : SOMEWHAT ⟨a thought too much vinegar in the dressing⟩

thought experiment *n* (1945) : GEDANKENEXPERIMENT

thought·ful \'thōt-fəl\ *adj* (13c) **1 a** : absorbed in thought : MEDITATIVE **b** : characterized by careful reasoned thinking **2 a** : having thoughts : HEEDFUL ⟨became ~ about religion⟩ **b** : given to or chosen or made with heedful anticipation of the needs and wants of others — **thought·ful·ly** \-fə-lē\ *adv* — **thought·ful·ness** *n*

thought·less \-ləs\ *adj* (1592) **1 a** : insufficiently alert : CARELESS **b** : RECKLESS, RASH **2** : devoid of thought : INSENSATE **3** : lacking concern for others : INCONSIDERATE — **thought·less·ly** *adv* — **thought·less·ness** *n*

thought–out \-'aút\ *adj* (1870) : produced or arrived at through mental effort and esp. through careful and thorough consideration

thought·way \-,wā\ *n* (ca. 1944) : a way of thinking that is characteristic of a particular group, time, or culture

thou·sand \'thaù-z³n(d)\ *n, pl* **thousands** *or* **thousand** [ME, fr. OE *thūsend*; akin to OHG *dūsunt* thousand, Lith *tūkstantis*, and prob. to Skt *tavas* strong, L *tumēre* to swell — more at THUMB] (bef. 12c) **1** — see NUMBER table **2** : a very large number ⟨~s of ants⟩ — **thousand** *adj* — **thou·sand·fold** \-z³n(d)-,fōld\ *adj or adv* — **thou·sandth** \-z³n(t)th\ *adj or n*

Thousand Island dressing *n* [*Thousand Islands*, islands in the St. Lawrence River] (1924) : mayonnaise with chili sauce and seasonings (as chopped pimientos, green peppers, and onion)

thousand–leg·ger \,thaù-z³n(d)-'le-gər, -'lā-\ *n* (1914) : MILLIPEDE

thousands place *n* (1937) : the place four to the left of the decimal point in a number expressed in the Arabic system of writing numbers

Thra·cian \'thrā-shən\ *n* (1569) **1** : a native or inhabitant of Thrace **2** : the Indo-European language of the ancient Thracians — see INDO-EUROPEAN LANGUAGES table — **Thracian** *adj*

¹**thrall** \'thról\ *n* [ME *thral*, fr. OE *thrǣl*, fr. ON *thrǣll*] (bef. 12c) **1 a** : a servant slave : BONDMAN; *also* : SERF **b** : a person in moral or mental servitude **2 a** : a state of servitude or submission ⟨in ~ to his emotions⟩ **b** : a state of complete absorption ⟨mountains could hold me in ~ with a subtle attraction of their own —Elyne Mitchell⟩ — **thrall** *adj* — **thrall·dom** *or* **thral·dom** \'thról-dəm\ *n*

²**thrall** *vt* (13c) *archaic* : ENTHRALL, ENSLAVE

¹**thrash** \'thrash\ *vb* [alter. of *thresh*] *vt* (1588) **1** : to separate the seeds of from the husks and straw by beating : THRESH 1 **2 a** : to beat soundly with or as if with a stick or whip : FLOG **b** : to defeat decisively or severely ⟨~ed the visiting team⟩ **3** : to swing, beat, or strike in the manner of a rapidly moving flail ⟨~ing his arms⟩ **4 a** : to go over again and again ⟨~ the matter over inconclusively⟩ **b** : to hammer out : FORGE ⟨~ out a plan⟩ ~ *vi* **1** : THRESH 1 **2** : to deal blows or strokes like one using a flail or whip **3** : to move or stir about violently : toss about ⟨~ in bed with a fever⟩ *syn* see SWING

²**thrash** *n* (1840) : an act of thrashing

¹**thrash·er** \'thra-shər\ *n* (1632) : one that thrashes or threshes

²**thrasher** *n* [perh. alter. of dial. *thresher* thrush] (ca. 1814) : any of various American oscine birds (family Mimidae and esp. genus *Toxostoma*) related to the mockingbird that resemble thrushes but have a curved bill and long tail

thra·son·i·cal \thrā-'sä-ni-kəl, thrə-\ *adj* [L *Thrason-, Thraso* Thraso, braggart soldier in the comedy *Eunuchus* by Terence] (1564) : of, relating to, resembling, or characteristic of Thraso : BRAGGING, BOASTFUL — **thra·son·i·cal·ly** \-k(ə-)lē\ *adv*

¹**thraw** \'thrà\ *vb* [ME — more at THROW] *vt* (bef. 12c) **1** *chiefly Scot* : to cause to twist or turn **2** *chiefly Scot* : CROSS, THWART ~ *vi* **1** *chiefly Scot* : TWIST, TURN **2** *chiefly Scot* : to be in disagreement

²**thraw** *n* (ca. 1585) **1** *chiefly Scot* : TWIST, TURN **2** *chiefly Scot* : ill humor

thra·wart \'thrà-wərt\ *adj* [ME (Sc), alter. of ME *fraward, froward* froward] (15c) *chiefly Scot* : STUBBORN **2** *Scot* : CROOKED

thrawn \'thràn\ *adj* [ME (Sc) *thrawin*, fr. pp. of ME *thrawen* to twist] (15c) *chiefly Scot* : lacking in pleasing or attractive qualities: as **a** : PERVERSE, RECALCITRANT **b** : CROOKED, MISSHAPEN — **thrawn·ly** *adv*, *chiefly Scot*

¹**thread** \'thred\ *n* [ME *thred*, fr. OE *thrǣd*; akin to OHG *drāt* thread, OE *thrāwan* to cause to twist or turn — more at THROW] (bef. 12c) **1 a** : a filament, a group of filaments twisted together, or a filamentous length formed by spinning and twisting short textile fibers into a continuous strand **b** : a piece of thread **2 a** : any of various natural filaments ⟨the ~s of a spiderweb⟩ **b** : a slender stream (as of water) **c** : a streak of light or color **d** : a projecting helical rib (as in a fitting or on a pipe) by which parts can be screwed together : SCREW THREAD **3** : something continuous or drawn out: as **a** : a train of thought **b** : a continuing element ⟨a ~ of melancholy marked all his writing⟩ **4** : a tenuous or feeble support **5** *pl* : CLOTHING — **thread·less** \-ləs\ *adj* — **thread·like** \-,līk\ *adj*

²**thread** *vt* (14c) **1 a** : to pass a thread through the eye of (a needle) **b** : to arrange a thread, yarn, or lead-in piece in working position for use in (a machine) **2 a** (1) : to pass something through in the manner of a thread ⟨~ a pipe with wire⟩ (2) : to pass (as a tape, line, or film) into or through something ⟨~ed a fresh film into the camera⟩ **b** : to make one's way through or between ⟨~ing narrow alleys⟩; *also* : to make (one's way) usu. cautiously through a hazardous situation **3** : to put together on or as if on a thread : STRING ⟨~ beads⟩ **4** : to interweave with or as if with threads : INTERSPERSE ⟨dark hair ~ed with silver⟩ **5** : to form a screw thread on or in ~ *vi* **1** : to make one's way **2** : to form a thread — **thread·er** *n*

thread·bare \'thred-,ber, -,ber\ *adj* (14c) **1** : having the nap worn off so that the thread shows : SHABBY **2** : exhausted of interest or freshness *syn* see TRITE — **thread·bare·ness** *n*

thread·fin \-,fin\ *n* (ca. 1890) : any of various bony fishes (family Polynemidae and esp. genus *Polydactylus*) having filamentous rays on the lower part of the pectoral fin

thread·worm \-,wərm\ *n* (1802) : a long slender nematode worm

thready \'thre-dē\ *adj* (1597) **1** : consisting of or bearing fibers or filaments ⟨a ~ bark⟩ **2 a** : resembling a thread : FILAMENTOUS **b** : tending to form or draw out into strands : ROPY **3** : lacking in fullness, body, or vigor : THIN ⟨a ~ voice⟩ — **thread·i·ness** *n*

threap \'thrēp\ *vt* [ME *threpen*, fr. OE *thrēapian*] (bef. 12c) **1** *chiefly Scot* : SCOLD, CHIDE **2** *chiefly Scot* : to maintain persistently

¹**threat** \'thret\ *n* [ME *thret* coercion, threat, fr. OE *thrēat* coercion; akin to MHG *drōz* annoyance, L *trudere* to push, thrust] (bef. 12c) **1** : an expression of intention to inflict evil, injury, or damage **2** : one that threatens **3** : an indication of something impending ⟨the sky held a ~ of rain⟩

²**threat** *vb* (bef. 12c) *archaic* : THREATEN

threat·en \'thre-t³n\ *vb* **threat·ened; threat·en·ing** \'thret-niŋ, 'thre-t³n-iŋ\ *vt* (13c) **1** : to utter threats against **2 a** : to give signs or warning of : PORTEND ⟨the clouds ~ed rain⟩ **b** : to hang over dangerously : MENACE **3** : to announce as intended or possible ⟨the workers ~ed a strike⟩ ~ *vi* **1** : to utter threats **2** : to portend evil — **threat·en·er** \'thret-nər, 'thre-t³n-ər\ *n* — **threat·en·ing·ly** \'thret-niŋ-lē, 'thre-t³n-iŋ-\ *adv*

threatened *adj* (1960) : having an uncertain chance of continued survival ⟨a ~ species of owls⟩; *specif* : likely to become an endangered species

three \'thrē\ *n* [ME, fr. *three*, adj., fr. OE *thrie* (masc.), *thrēo* (fem. & neut.); akin to OHG *dri* three, L *tres*, Gk *treis*] (bef. 12c) **1** — see NUMBER table **2** : the third in a set or series ⟨the ~ of hearts⟩ **3** : something having three units or members — **three** *adj* — **three** *pron, pl in constr*

three–bag·ger \-'ba-gər\ *n* (1881) : TRIPLE

three–ball \-,ból\ *adj* (ca. 1890) : relating to or being a golf match in which three players compete against one another with each playing a single ball

three–card monte \'thrē-'kärd-\ *n* (1854) : a gambling game in which the dealer shows three cards, shuffles them, places them face down, and invites spectators to bet they can identify the location of a particular card

three–col·or \'thrē-,kə-lər\ *adj* (1893) : being or relating to a printing or photographic process wherein three primary colors are used to reproduce all the colors of the subject

3–D \'thrē-'dē\ *n* [*D*, abbr. of *dimensional*] (1951) : the three-dimensional form; *also* : an image or a picture produced in it — **3–D** *adj*

three–deck·er \'thrē-'de-kər\ *n* (1795) **1** : a wooden warship carrying guns on three decks **2** : TRIPLE-DECKER

three–dimensional *adj* (ca. 1891) **1** : of or relating to three dimensions **2** : giving the illusion of depth or varying distances — used of an image or a pictorial representation esp. when this illusion is enhanced by stereoscopic means **3** : describing or being described in well-rounded completeness ⟨a ~ analysis of multiple historical processes —L. L. Snyder⟩ **4** : true to life : LIFELIKE

three·fold \'thrē-,fōld, -'fōld\ *adj* (bef. 12c) **1** : having three units or members : TRIPLE **2** : being three times as great or as many — **three·fold** \-'fōld\ *adv*

three–gait·ed \-'gā-təd\ *adj* (1948) *of a horse* : trained to use the walk, trot, and canter

three–hand·ed \-'han-dəd\ *adj* (1719) : played by three players ⟨~ bridge⟩

Three Hours *n* (ca. 1891) : a service of devotion between noon and three o'clock on Good Friday

three–legged \'thrē-'legd, -'lāgd; -'le-gəd, -'lā-\ *adj* (1596) : having three legs ⟨a ~ stool⟩

three–legged race *n* (1903) : a race between pairs of competitors with each pair having their adjacent legs bound together

three–line octave *n* (ca. 1931) : the musical octave that begins on the second C above middle C — see PITCH illustration

three–mile limit *n* (ca. 1891) : the limit of the marginal sea of three miles included in the territorial waters of a state

three of a kind *n* (ca. 1897) : three cards of the same rank in one hand — see POKER illustration

three·pence \'thre-pən(t)s, 'thri-, 'thrə-, *US also* 'thrē-pen(t)s\ *n* (1589) **1** *pl* **threepence** *or* **three·penc·es** : a coin worth threepence **2** : the sum of three British pennies

three·pen·ny \'thre-p(ə-)nē, 'thri-, 'thrə-, *US also* 'thrē-ˌpe-nē\ *adj* (15c) **1** : costing or worth threepence **2** : POOR

three–phase *adj* (ca. 1900) : of, relating to, or operating by means of a combination of three circuits energized by alternating electromotive forces that differ in phase by one third of a cycle

three–piece *adj* (ca. 1909) : consisting of or made in three pieces ⟨a ∼ suit⟩

three–point landing *n* (1918) : an airplane landing in which the two main wheels of the landing gear and the tail wheel or skid or nose wheel touch the ground simultaneously

three–quarter *adj* (1677) : extending to three-quarters of the normal full length ⟨a ∼ sleeve⟩

three–quarter–bound *adj* (ca. 1951) *of a book* : bound like a half-bound book but having the material on the spine extended to cover about one third of the boards — **three–quarter binding** *n*

three–ring circus *n* (1904) **1** : a circus with simultaneous performances in three rings **2** : something wild, confusing, engrossing, or entertaining

three R's *n pl* [fr. the facetiously used phrase *reading, 'riting, and 'rithmetic*] (1828) **1** : the fundamentals taught in elementary school; *esp* : reading, writing, and arithmetic **2** : the fundamental skills in a field of endeavor

three·score \'thrē-'skōr, -'skȯr\ *adj* (14c) : being three times twenty : SIXTY

three·some \'thrē-səm\ *n* (14c) **1** : a group of three persons or things : TRIO **2** : a golf match in which one person plays his ball against the ball of two others playing each stroke alternately

three–spined stickleback \'thrē-'spīn(d)-\ *n* (1769) : a stickleback (*Gasterosteus aculeatus*) chiefly of fresh and brackish waters that typically has three dorsal spines

three-spined stickleback

three–toed sloth \'thrē-'tōd-\ *n* (1879) : any of a genus (*Bradypus*) of sloths having three clawed digits on each foot and nine vertebrae in the neck — compare TWO-TOED SLOTH

three–wheel·er \-ˌhwē-lər, -ˌwē-\ *n* (1886) : any of various vehicles having three wheels

thre·node \'thrē-ˌnōd, 'thre-\ *n* (1858) : THRENODY — **thre·nod·ic** \thri-'nä-dik\ *adj* — **thren·o·dist** \'thre-nə-dist\ *n*

thren·o·dy \'thre-nə-dē\ *n, pl* **-dies** [Gk *thrēnōidia*, fr. *thrēnos* dirge + *aeidein* to sing — more at DRONE, ODE] (1634) : a song of lamentation for the dead : ELEGY

thre·o·nine \'thrē-ə-ˌnēn\ *n* [prob. fr. *threonic acid* ($C_4H_8O_5$)] (1936) : a colorless crystalline essential amino acid $C_4H_9NO_3$

thresh \'thrash, 'thresh\ *vb* [ME *thresshen*, fr. OE *threscan;* akin to OHG *dreskan* to thresh] *vt* (bef. 12c) **1** : to separate seed from (a harvested plant) mechanically; *also* : to separate (seed) in this way **2** : THRASH **4 3** : to strike repeatedly ∼ *vi* **1** : to thresh grain **2** : THRASH 2, 3

thresh·er *n* (14c) **1** : one that threshes; *esp* : THRESHING MACHINE **2** : THRESHER SHARK

thresher shark *n* (1888) : a large nearly cosmopolitan shark (*Alopias vulpinus*) having a greatly elongated curved upper lobe of its tail with which it is said to thresh the water to round up the fish on which it feeds — see SHARK illustration

threshing machine *n* (1775) : a machine for separating grain crops into grain or seeds and straw

thresh·old \'thresh-ˌhōld, 'thre-ˌshōld\ *n* [ME *thresshold*, fr. OE *threscwald;* akin to ON *threskjǫldr* threshold, OE *threscan* to thresh] (bef. 12c) **1** : the plank, stone, or piece of timber that lies under a door : SILL **2 a** : GATE, DOOR **b** (1) : END, BOUNDARY; *specif* : the end of a runway (2) : the place or point of entering or beginning : OUTSET ⟨on the ∼ of a new age⟩ **3 a** : the point at which a physiological or psychological effect begins to be produced **b** : a level, point, or value above which something is true or will take place and below which it is not or will not

threw *past of* THROW

thrice \'thrīs\ *adv* [ME *thrie, thries,* fr. OE *thriga;* akin to OFris *thria* three times, OE *thrie* three] (13c) **1** : three times **2 a** : in a threefold manner or degree **b** : to a high degree

thrift \'thrift\ *n* [ME, fr. ON, prosperity, fr. *thrīfask* to thrive] (13c) **1** : healthy and vigorous growth **2** : careful management esp. of money **3** *chiefly Scot* : gainful occupation **4** : any of a genus (*Armeria*) of the plumbago family of perennial evergreen acaulescent herbs; *esp* : a scapose herb (*A. maritima*) with pink or white flower heads **5** : a savings bank or savings and loan association — called also *thrift institution*

thrift·less \'thrift-ləs\ *adj* (1568) **1** : lacking usefulness or worth **2** : careless, wasteful, or incompetent in handling money or resources : IMPROVIDENT — **thrift·less·ly** *adv* — **thrift·less·ness** *n*

thrift shop *n* (1944) : a shop that sells secondhand articles and esp. clothes and is often run for charitable purposes

thrifty \'thrif-tē\ *adj* **thrift·i·er; -est** (15c) **1** : thriving by industry and frugality : PROSPEROUS **2** : growing vigorously **3** : given to or marked by economy and good management **syn** see SPARING — **thrift·i·ly** \-tə-lē\ *adv* — **thrift·i·ness** \-tē-nəs\ *n*

thrill \'thril\ *vb* [ME *thirlen, thrillen* to pierce, fr. OE *thyrlian,* fr. *thyrel* hole, fr. *thurh* through — more at THROUGH] *vt* (1592) **1 a** : to cause to experience a sudden sharp feeling of excitement **b** : to cause to have a shivering or tingling sensation **2** : to cause to vibrate or tremble perceptibly ∼ *vi* **1** : to move or pass so as to cause a sudden wave of emotion **2** : to become thrilled: **a** : to experience a sudden sharp excitement : TINGLE, THROB **3** : TREMBLE, VIBRATE — **thrill** *n* — **thrill·ing·ly** \'thri-lin̠-lē\ *adv*

thril·ler \'thri-lər\ *n* (1889) : one that thrills; *esp* : a work of fiction or drama designed to hold the interest by the use of a high degree of intrigue, adventure, or suspense

thrips \'thrips\ *n, pl* **thrips** [L, woodworm, fr. Gk] (1795) : any of an order (Thysanoptera) of small to minute sucking insects most of which feed often destructively on plant juices

thrive \'thrīv\ *vi* **throve** \'thrōv\ *or* **thrived; thriv·en** \'thri-vən\ *also* **thrived; thriv·ing** \'thrī-vin̠\ [ME, fr. ON *thrīfask,* prob. reflexive of *thrīfa* to grasp] (13c) **1** : to grow vigorously : FLOURISH **2** : to gain in wealth or possessions : PROSPER **3** : to progress toward or realize a goal — **thriv·er** \'thrī-vər\ *n*

thriving *adj* (1607) : characterized by success or prosperity — **thriv·ing·ly** \'thrī-vin̠-lē\ *adv*

thro \'thrü\ *prep* (15c) *archaic* : THROUGH

¹throat \'thrōt\ *n* [ME *throte,* fr. OE; akin to OHG *drozza* throat] (bef. 12c) **1 a** (1) : the part of the neck in front of the spinal column (2) : the passage through the neck to the stomach and lungs **b** (1) : VOICE (2) : the seat of the voice **2** : something resembling the throat esp. in being an entrance, a passageway, a constriction, or a narrowed part: as **a** : the orifice of a tubular organ esp. of a plant **b** : the opening in the vamp of a shoe at the instep **c** : the part of a tennis racket that connects the head with the shaft **3** : the curved part of an anchor's arm where it joins the shank — see ANCHOR illustration — **at each other's throats** : in open and aggressive conflict

²throat *vt* (ca. 1611) **1** : to utter in the throat : MUTTER **2** : to sing or enunciate in a throaty voice

throat·ed \'thrō-təd\ *adj* (ca. 1530) : having a throat esp. of a specified kind — usu. used in combination ⟨white-*throated*⟩

throat·latch \'thrōt-ˌlach\ *n* (1794) **1** : a strap of a bridle or halter passing under a horse's throat **2** : the part of a horse's throat around which the throatlatch passes — see HORSE illustration

throaty \'thrō-tē\ *adj* **throat·i·er; -est** (ca. 1645) **1** : uttered or produced from low in the throat ⟨a ∼ voice⟩ **2** : heavy, thick, and deep as if from the throat ⟨∼ notes of a horn⟩ — **throat·i·ly** \'thrō-t³l-ē\ *adv* — **throat·i·ness** \'thrō-tē-nəs\ *n*

¹throb \'thräb\ *vi* **throbbed; throb·bing** [ME *throbben*] (14c) **1** : to pulsate or pound with abnormal force or rapidity **2** : to beat or vibrate rhythmically — **throb·ber** *n*

²throb *n* (1579) : BEAT, PULSE

throe \'thrō\ *n* [ME *thrawe, throwe,* fr. OE *thrawu, thrēa* threat, pang; akin to OHG *drawa* threat] (13c) **1** : PANG, SPASM ⟨death ∼s⟩ ⟨∼s of childbirth⟩ **2** *pl* : a hard or painful struggle ⟨the ∼s of revolutionary social change⟩ — M. D. Geismar]

thromb- *or* **thrombo-** *comb form* [Gk *thrombos* clot] : blood clot : clotting of blood ⟨*thrombin*⟩ ⟨*thrombo*plastic⟩

throm·bin \'thräm-bən\ *n* [ISV] (1898) : a proteolytic enzyme that is formed from prothrombin and facilitates the clotting of blood by catalyzing conversion of fibrinogen to fibrin

throm·bo·cyte \-bə-ˌsīt\ *n* [ISV] (1893) : BLOOD PLATELET; *also* : an invertebrate cell with similar function — **throm·bo·cyt·ic** \ˌthräm-bə-'si-tik\ *adj*

throm·bo·cy·to·pe·nia \ˌthräm-bə-ˌsī-tə-'pē-nē-ə, -nyə\ *n* [NL, fr. ISV *thrombocyte* + NL -*o*- + -*penia*] (1923) : persistent decrease in the number of blood platelets that is often associated with hemorrhagic conditions — **throm·bo·cy·to·pe·nic** \-nik\ *adj*

throm·bo·em·bo·lism \ˌthräm-bō-'em-bə-ˌli-zəm\ *n* (1907) : the blocking of a blood vessel by a particle that has broken away from a blood clot at its site of formation — **throm·bo·em·bol·ic** \-em-'bä-lik\ *adj*

throm·bo·ki·nase \ˌthräm-bō-'kī-ˌnās, -ˌnāz\ *n* [ISV] (1908) : THROMBOPLASTIN

throm·bo·lyt·ic \ˌthräm-bə-'li-tik\ *adj* (1929) : destroying or breaking up a thrombus ⟨a ∼ agent⟩ ⟨∼ therapy⟩

throm·bo·phle·bi·tis \ˌthräm-bō-fli-'bī-təs\ *n* [NL] (ca. 1890) : inflammation of a vein with formation of a thrombus

throm·bo·plas·tic \-'plas-tik\ *adj* [ISV] (1911) : initiating or accelerating the clotting of blood

throm·bo·plas·tin \-'plas-tən\ *n* [ISV, fr. *thromboplastic*] (1911) : a complex enzyme found esp. in blood platelets that functions in the conversion of prothrombin into thrombin in the clotting of blood

throm·bo·sis \thräm-'bō-səs, thrəm-\ *n, pl* **-bo·ses** \-ˌsēz\ [NL, fr. Gk *thrombōsis* clotting, fr. *thrombousthai* to become clotted, fr. *thrombos* clot] (1866) : the formation or presence of a blood clot within a blood vessel — **throm·bot·ic** \-'bä-tik\ *adj*

throm·box·ane \thräm-'bäk-ˌsān\ *n* [*thromb-* + *ox-* + -*ane*] (1975) : any of several substances that are formed from endoperoxides, cause constriction of vascular and bronchial smooth muscle, and promote blood coagulation

throm·bus \'thräm-bəs\ *n, pl* **throm·bi** \-ˌbī, -ˌbē\ [NL, fr. Gk *thrombos* clot] (ca. 1693) : a clot of blood formed within a blood vessel and remaining attached to its place of origin — compare EMBOLUS

¹throne \'thrōn\ *n* [ME *trone, throne,* fr. OF *trone,* fr. L *thronus,* fr. Gk *thronos* — more at FIRM] (13c) **1 a** : the chair of state of a sovereign or high dignitary (as a bishop) **b** : the seat of a deity **2** : royal power and dignity : SOVEREIGNTY **3** *pl* : an order of angels — see CELESTIAL HIERARCHY

²throne *vb* **throned; thron·ing** *vt* (14c) **1** : to seat on a throne **2** : to invest with kingly rank or power ∼ *vi* **1** : to sit on a throne **2** : to hold kingly power

throne room *n* (1864) : a formal audience room containing the throne of a sovereign

¹throng \'thrȯn̠\ *n* [ME *thrang, throng,* fr. OE *thrang, gethrang;* akin to OE *thringan* to press, crowd, OHG *dringan,* Lith *trenkti* to jolt] (bef. 12c) **1** : a multitude of assembled persons **b** : a large number : HOST **2 a** : a crowding together of many persons **b** : PRESSURE ⟨this ∼ of business —S. R. Crockett⟩ **syn** see CROWD

²throng *vb* **thronged; throng·ing** *vt* (1534) **1** : to crowd upon : PRESS **2** : to crowd into : PACK ⟨shoppers ∼*ing* the streets⟩ ∼ *vi* : to crowd together in great numbers

---

\ə\ abut \ᵊ\ kitten, F table \ər\ further \a\ ash \ā\ ace \ä\ mop, mar \au̇\ out \ch\ chin \e\ bet \ē\ easy \g\ go \i\ hit \ī\ ice \j\ job \n̠\ sing \ō\ go \ȯ\ law \ȯi\ boy \th\ thin \t͟h\ the \ü\ loot \u̇\ foot \y\ yet \zh\ vision \ā, ḵ, ⁿ, œ, œ̄, ᵫ, ᵫ̄, ᵊ\ *see* Guide to Pronunciation

thros·tle \'thrä-səl\ *n* [ME, fr. OE — more at THRUSH] (bef. 12c) : ¹THRUSH 1; *specif* : SONG THRUSH

¹throt·tle \'thrä-t³l\ *vb* **throt·tled; throt·tling** \'thrät-liŋ, 'thrä-t³l-iŋ\ [ME *throtlen*, fr. *throte* throat] *vt* (15c) **1 a** (1) : to compress the throat of : CHOKE (2) : to kill by such action **b** : to prevent or check expression or activity of : SUPPRESS **2 a** : to decrease the flow of (as steam or fuel to an engine) by a valve **b** : to regulate and esp. to reduce the speed of (as an engine) by such means **c** : to vary the thrust of (a rocket engine) during flight ~ *vi* : to throttle something (as an engine) — usu. used with *back* or *down* ⟨the pilot *throttled* back⟩ — **throt·tler** \'thrät-lər, 'thrä-t³l-ər\ *n*

²throttle *n* [perh. fr. (assumed) ME, dim. of ME *throte* throat] (ca. 1547) **1 a** : THROAT 1a **b** : TRACHEA 1 **2 a** : a valve for regulating the supply of a fluid (as steam) to an engine; *esp* : the valve controlling the volume of vaporized fuel charge delivered to the cylinders of an internal combustion engine **b** : the lever controlling this valve **c** : the condition of being throttled — **at full throttle** : at full speed

throt·tle·able \'thrä-t-ə-bəl\ *adj* (1960) : capable of having the thrust varied — used of a rocket engine

throt·tle·hold \'thrä-t³l-,hōld\ *n* (1935) : a vicious, strangling, or stultifying control

¹through \'thrü\ *prep* [ME *thurh, thruh, through,* fr. OE *thurh;* akin to OHG *durh* through, L *trans* across, beyond, Skt *tarati* he crosses over] (bef. 12c) **1 a** (1) — used as a function word to indicate movement into at one side or point and out at another and esp. the opposite side of ⟨drove a nail ~ the board⟩ (2) : by way of ⟨left ~ the door⟩ (3) — used as a function word to indicate passage from one end or boundary to another ⟨a highway ~ the forest⟩ ⟨a road ~ the desert⟩ (4) : without stopping for : PAST ⟨drove ~ a red light⟩ **b** — used as a function word to indicate passage into and out of a treatment, handling, or process ⟨the matter has already passed ~ her hands⟩ **2** — used as a function word to indicate means, agency, or intermediacy: as **a** : by means of : by the agency of **b** : because of ⟨failed ~ ignorance⟩ **c** : by common descent from or relationship with ⟨related ~ their grandfather⟩ **3 a** : over the whole surface or extent of : THROUGHOUT ⟨homes scattered ~ the valley⟩ **b** — used as a function word to indicate movement within a large expanse ⟨flew ~ the air⟩ **c** — used as a function word to indicate exposure to a specified set of conditions ⟨put him ~ hell⟩ **4** — used as a function word to indicate a period of time: as **a** : during the entire period of ⟨all ~ her life⟩ **b** : from the beginning to the end of ⟨the tower stood ~ the earthquake⟩ **c** : to and including ⟨Monday ~ Friday⟩ **5 a** — used as a function word to indicate completion or exhaustion ⟨got ~ the book⟩ ⟨went ~ the money in a year⟩ **b** — used as a function word to indicate acceptance or approval esp. by an official body ⟨got the bill ~ the legislature⟩

²through \'thrü\ *adv* (bef. 12c) **1** : from one end or side to the other **2 a** : from beginning to end **b** : to completion, conclusion, or accomplishment ⟨see it ~⟩ **3** : to the core : COMPLETELY ⟨soaked ~⟩ **4** : into the open : OUT ⟨break ~⟩

³through \'thrü\ *adj* (1523) **1 a** : extending from one surface to another ⟨a ~ mortise⟩ **b** : admitting free or continuous passage : DIRECT ⟨a ~ road⟩ **2 a** (1) : going from point of origin to destination without change or reshipment ⟨a ~ train⟩ (2) : of or relating to such movement ⟨a ~ ticket⟩ **b** : initiated at and destined for points outside a local zone ⟨~ traffic⟩ **3 a** : arrived at completion or accomplishment ⟨is ~ with the job⟩ **b** : WASHED-UP, FINISHED

through and through *adv* (15c) : in every way : THOROUGHLY

through-com·posed \,thrü-kəm-'pōzd\ *adj* [trans. of G *durchkomponiert*] (1884) *of a song* : having new music provided for each stanza — compare STROPHIC

through·ith·er *or* **through·oth·er** \'thrü-(ə-)thər\ *adv* [¹through + other] (1596) *chiefly Scot* : in confusion : PROMISCUOUSLY

through·ly \'thrü-lē\ *adv* (15c) *archaic* : in a thorough manner

¹through·out \thrü-'aut\ *adv* (13c) **1** : in or to every part : EVERYWHERE ⟨of one color ~⟩ **2** : during the whole time or action : from beginning to end ⟨remained loyal ~⟩

²throughout *prep* (13c) **1** : all the way from one end to the other of : in or to every part of ⟨cities ~ the United States⟩ **2** : during the whole course or period of ⟨troubled her ~ her life⟩

through·put \'thrü-,put\ *n* (ca. 1915) : OUTPUT, PRODUCTION ⟨the ~ of a computer⟩

through street *n* (1930) : a street on which the through movement of traffic is given preference

throve *past of* THRIVE

¹throw \'thrō\ *vb* **threw** \'thrü\; **thrown** \'thrōn\; **throw·ing** [ME *thrawen, throwen* to cause to twist, throw, fr. OE *thrāwan* to cause to twist or turn; akin to OHG *drāen* to turn, L *terere* to rub, Gk *tribein* to rub, *tetrainein* to bore, pierce] *vt* (14c) **1** : to propel through the air by a forward motion of the hand and arm ⟨~ a baseball⟩ **b** : to propel through the air in any manner ⟨a rifle that can ~ a bullet a mile⟩ **2 a** : to cause to fall ⟨*threw* his opponent⟩ **b** : to cause to fall off : UNSEAT ⟨the horse *threw* its rider⟩ **c** : to get the better of : OVERCOME ⟨the problem didn't ~ her⟩ **3 a** : to fling (oneself) precipitately ⟨*threw* herself down on the sofa⟩ **b** : to drive or impel violently : DASH ⟨the ship was *thrown* on a reef⟩ **4 a** (1) : to put in a particular position or condition ⟨*threw* her arms around him⟩ (2) : to put on or off hastily or carelessly ⟨*threw* on a coat⟩ **b** : to bring to bear : EXERT ⟨*threw* all his efforts into the boy's defense⟩ **c** : BUILD, CONSTRUCT ⟨*threw* a pontoon bridge over the river⟩ **5** : to form or shape on a potter's wheel **6** : to deliver (a blow) in or as if in boxing **7** : to twist two or more filaments of into a thread or yarn **8 a** : to make a cast of (dice or a specified number on dice) **b** : ROLL 1a ⟨~ a bowling ball⟩ **9** : to give up : ABANDON **10** : to send forth : PROJECT ⟨the setting sun *threw* long shadows⟩ **11** : to make (oneself) dependent : commit (oneself) for help, support, or protection ⟨*threw* himself on the mercy of the court⟩ **12** : to indulge in : give way to ⟨*threw* a temper tantrum⟩ **13** : to bring forth : give birth to : SIRE, PRODUCE ⟨~s a good crop⟩ ⟨*threw* large litters⟩ **14** : to lose intentionally ⟨~ a game⟩ **15** : to move (a lever) so as to connect or disconnect parts of a clutch or switch; *also* : to make or break (a connection) with a lever **16** : to give by way of entertainment ⟨~ a party⟩ ~ *vi* : CAST, HURL — **throw·er** \'thrō-(ə)r\ *n* — **throw one's weight around** *or* **throw one's weight about** : to exercise influence or authority esp. to an excessive degree or in an objectionable manner — **throw together 1** : to put together in a

hurried and usu. careless manner ⟨a bookshelf hastily *thrown together*⟩ **2** : to bring into casual association ⟨different kinds of people are *thrown together* —Richard Sennett⟩

syn THROW, CAST, TOSS, FLING, HURL, PITCH, SLING mean to cause to move swiftly through space by a propulsive movement or a propelling force. THROW is general and interchangeable with the other terms but may specif. imply a distinctive motion with bent arm ⟨can *throw* a fastball and a curve⟩. CAST usu. implies lightness in the thing thrown and sometimes a scattering ⟨*cast* it to the winds⟩. TOSS suggests a light or careless or aimless throwing and may imply an upward motion ⟨*tossed* the coat on the bed⟩. FLING stresses a violent throwing ⟨*flung* the ring back in his face⟩. HURL implies power as in throwing a massive weight ⟨*hurled* himself at the intruder⟩. PITCH suggests throwing carefully at a target ⟨*pitch* horseshoes⟩. SLING stresses either the use of whirling momentum in throwing or directness of aim ⟨*slung* the bag over his shoulder⟩.

²throw *n* (1530) **1 a** : an act of throwing, hurling, or flinging **b** (1) : an act of throwing dice (2) : the number thrown with a cast of dice **c** : a method of throwing an opponent in wrestling or judo **2** : the distance a missile may be thrown or light rays may be projected **3** : an undertaking involving chance or danger : RISK, VENTURE **4** : the amount of vertical displacement produced by a geological fault **5 a** : the extreme movement given to a pivoted or reciprocating piece by a cam, crank, or eccentric : STROKE **b** : the length of the radius of a crank or the virtual crank radius of an eccentric or cam **6 a** : a light coverlet (as for a bed) **b** : a woman's scarf or light wrap — **a throw** : for each one : APIECE ⟨copies are to be sold at $5 *a throw* —Harvey Breit⟩

¹throw·away \'thrō-ə-,wā\ *n* (1903) **1** : one that is or is designed to be thrown away: as **a** : a free handbill or circular **b** : a line of dialogue (as in a play) de-emphasized by casual delivery; *esp* : a joke or witticism delivered casually **2** : something made or done without care or interest

²throwaway *adj* (1928) **1** : designed to be thrown away : DISPOSABLE ⟨~ containers⟩ **2** : written or spoken (as in a play) in a low-key or unemphatic manner ⟨~ lines⟩ **3** : NONCHALANT, CASUAL

throw away *vt* (1530) **1 a** : to get rid of as worthless or unnecessary **b** : DISCARD 2b **2 a** : to use in a foolish or wasteful manner : SQUANDER **b** : to fail to take advantage of : WASTE **3** : to make (as a line in a play) unemphatic by casual delivery

throw·back \'thrō-,bak\ *n* (1888) **1 a** : reversion to an earlier type or phase : ATAVISM **b** : an instance or product of atavistic reversion **2** : one that is suggestive of or suited to an earlier time or style ⟨his manners were a ~ to a more polite era⟩

throw back *vt* (1840) **1** : to delay the progress or advance of : CHECK **2** : to cause to rely : make dependent ⟨they are *thrown back* upon . . . native intelligence —Michael Novak⟩ **3** : REFLECT ~ *vi* : to revert to an earlier type or phase

throw down *vt* (14c) **1** : to cause to fall : OVERTHROW **2** : PRECIPITATE **3** : to cast off : DISCARD

throw-in \'thrō-,in\ *n* (1881) : an act or instance of throwing a ball in: as **a** : a throw made from the touchline in soccer to put the ball back in play after it has gone into touch **b** : a throw from an outfielder to the infield in baseball **c** : an inbounds pass in basketball

throw in *vt* (1678) **1** : to add as a gratuity or supplement **2** : to introduce or interject in the course of something : CONTRIBUTE ⟨they *throw in* some . . . sound effects on several songs —Tom Phillips⟩ **3** : DISTRIBUTE 3b **4** : ENGAGE ⟨*throw in* the clutch⟩ ~ *vi* : to enter into association or partnership : JOIN ⟨agrees to *throw in* with a crooked ex-cop —*Newsweek*⟩ — **throw in the towel** *also* **throw in the sponge** : to abandon a struggle or contest : acknowledge defeat : GIVE UP

throw off *vt* (1618) **1 a** : to free oneself from : get rid of ⟨*threw off* his inhibitions⟩ **b** : to cast off often in a hurried or vigorous manner : ABANDON ⟨*threw off* all restraint⟩ **c** : DISTRACT, DIVERT ⟨dogs *thrown off* by a false scent⟩ **2** : EMIT, GIVE OFF ⟨stacks *throwing off* plumes of smoke⟩ **3** : to produce in an offhand manner : execute with speed or facility ⟨some little . . . tune that the composer had *thrown off* —James Hilton⟩ **4 a** : to cause to depart from an expected or desired course ⟨mistakes *threw* his calculations off a bit⟩ **b** : to cause to make a mistake : MISLEAD ~ *vi* **1** : to begin hunting **2** : to make derogatory comments

throw out *vt* (1526) **1 a** : to remove from a place, office, or employment usu. in a sudden or unexpected manner **b** : to get rid of as worthless or unnecessary **2** : to give expression to : UTTER ⟨*threw out* a remark . . . that utterly confounded him —Jean Stafford⟩ **3** : to dismiss from acceptance or consideration : REJECT ⟨the testimony was *thrown out*⟩ **4** : to make visible or manifest : DISPLAY ⟨the signal was *thrown out* for the . . . fleet to prepare for action —Archibald Duncan⟩ **5** : to leave behind : OUTDISTANCE **6** : to give forth from within : EMIT **7 a** : to send out **b** : to cause to project : EXTEND **8** : CONFUSE, DISCONCERT ⟨automobiles in line blocking the road . . . *threw* the whole schedule *out* —F. D. Roosevelt⟩ **9** : to cause to stand out : make prominent **10** : to make a throw that enables a teammate to put out (a base runner)

throw over *vt* (1835) **1** : to forsake despite bonds of attachment or duty **2** : to refuse to accept : REJECT

throw pillow *n* (1956) : a small pillow used esp. as a decorative accessory

throw rug *n* (1928) : SCATTER RUG

throw·ster \'thrō-stər\ *n* (15c) : one who throws textile filaments

throw up *vt* (15c) **1** : to raise quickly **2** : GIVE UP, QUIT ⟨the urge . . . to *throw up* all intellectual work —Norman Mailer⟩ **3** : to build hurriedly ⟨new houses *thrown up* almost overnight⟩ **4** : VOMIT **5** : to bring forth : PRODUCE **6** : to make distinct esp. by contrast : cause to stand out **7** : to mention repeatedly by way of reproach ~ *vi* : VOMIT — **throw up one's hands** : to admit defeat ⟨in the end *throws up his hands* in despair —Frank Conroy⟩

throw weight *n* (1969) : the maximum payload of an ICBM

thru *var of* THROUGH

¹thrum \'thrəm\ *n* [ME, fr. OE -*thrum* (in *tungethrum* ligament of the tongue); akin to OHG *drum* fragment] (14c) **1 a** (1) : a fringe of warp threads left on the loom after the cloth has been removed (2) : one of these warp threads **b** : a tuft or short piece of rope yarn used in thrumming canvas — usu. used in pl. **c :** BIT, PARTICLE **2 :** a hair, fiber, or threadlike leaf on a plant; *also* : a tuft or fringe of such structures — **thrum** *adj*

²thrum *vt* **thrummed; thrum·ming** (15c) **1 :** to furnish with thrums : FRINGE **2 :** to insert short pieces of rope yarn or spun yarn in (a piece of canvas) to make a rough surface or a mat which can be wrapped about rigging to prevent chafing

³thrum *vb* **thrummed; thrum·ming** [imit.] *vi* (1592) **1 :** to play or pluck a stringed instrument idly : STRUM **2 :** to sound with a monotonous hum ∼ *vt* **1 :** to play (as a stringed instrument) in an idle or relaxed manner **2 :** to recite tiresomely or monotonously

⁴thrum *n* (1798) **:** the monotonous sound of thrumming

¹thrush \'thrəsh\ *n* [ME *thrusche*, fr. OE *thrysce*; akin to OE *throstle* thrush, OHG *droscala*, L *turdus*] (bef. 12c) **1 :** any of numerous small or medium-sized oscine birds (families Turdidae and Muscicapidae) which are mostly of a plain color often with spotted underparts and many of which are excellent singers **2 :** a bird held to resemble a thrush

²thrush *n* [prob. of Scand origin; akin to Dan & Norw *trøske* thrush] (1665) **1 :** a disease that is caused by a fungus (*Candida albicans*), occurs esp. in infants and children, and is marked by white patches in the oral cavity; *broadly* : CANDIDIASIS ⟨vaginal ∼⟩ **2 :** a suppurative disorder of the feet in various animals (as a horse)

¹thrust \'thrəst\ *vb* **thrust; thrust·ing** [ME *thrusten, thristen*, fr. ON *thrȳsta*; prob. akin to ON *thrjōta* to tire, OE *thrēat* coercion — more at THREAT] *vt* (13c) **1 :** to push or drive with force ⟨∼ a dagger into his heart⟩ **3 :** EXTEND, SPREAD **4 :** STAB, PIERCE **5 a :** to put (as an unwilling person) forcibly into a course of action or position ⟨was *thrust* into the job⟩ **b :** to introduce often improperly into a position : INTERPOLATE **6 :** to press, force, or impose the acceptance of upon someone ⟨∼ new responsibilities upon her⟩ ∼ *vi* **1 a :** to force an entrance or passage **b :** to push forward : press onward **c :** to push upward : PROJECT **2 :** to make a thrust, stab, or lunge with or as if with a pointed weapon ⟨∼ at them with a knife⟩

²thrust *n* (ca. 1586) **1 a :** a push or lunge with a pointed weapon **b** (1) **:** a verbal attack (2) **:** a military assault **2 a :** a strong continued pressure **b :** the sideways force or pressure of one part of a structure against another part (as of an arch against an abutment) **c :** the force produced by a propeller or by a jet or rocket engine that drives a vehicle (as an aircraft) forward **d :** a nearly horizontal geological fault **3 a :** a forward or upward push **b :** a movement (as by a group of people) in a specified direction **4 a :** salient or essential element or meaning **b :** principal concern or objective

thrust·er *also* **thrust·or** \'thrəs-tər\ *n* (1597) **:** one that thrusts; *esp* : an engine (as a jet engine) that develops thrust by expelling a jet of fluid or a stream of particles

thrust·ful \'thrəst-fəl\ *adj* (1909) *Brit* : characterized by thrust : AGGRESSIVE ⟨∼ young man on the make —*Current Literature*⟩

thrust stage *n* [*thrust*, pp. of ¹*thrust*] (1965) **:** a stage that projects beyond the proscenium so that the audience sits around the projection; *also* : a forestage that is extended into the auditorium to increase the stage area

thru·way \'thrü-,wā\ *n* (1930) **:** EXPRESSWAY

¹thud \'thəd\ *n* [imit.] (1787) **1 :** BLOW **2 :** a dull sound : THUMP

²thud *vi* **thud·ded; thud·ding** (1796) **:** to move or strike so as to make a thud

thug \'thəg\ *n* [Hindi *thag*, lit., thief] (1810) **:** a brutal ruffian or assassin : GANGSTER, KILLER — **thug·gery** \'thə-g(ə-)rē\ *n* — **thug·gish** \'thə-gish\ *adj*

thu·ja \'thü-jə, 'thyü-\ *n* [NL *Thuja*, fr. ML *thuia*, a cedar, fr. Gk *thyia*, fr. *thyein* to sacrifice — more at THYME] (ca. 1760) **:** any of a genus (*Thuja*) of evergreen shrubs and trees (as an arborvitae) of the cypress family having scalelike closely imbricated or compressed leaves

¹Thu·le \'thü-lē, 'thyü-\ *n* [ME *Tyle*, fr. OE, fr. L *Thule, Thyle*, fr. Gk *Thoulē, Thȳlē*] (bef. 12c) **:** the northernmost part of the habitable ancient world

²Thu·le \'tü-lē\ *adj* [*Thule*, Greenland] (1925) **:** of, relating to, or being the culture existing in the arctic lands from Alaska to Greenland from about 500 A.D. to 1400 A.D.

thu·li·um \'thü-lē-əm, 'thyü-\ *n* [NL, fr. L *Thule*] (1879) **:** a trivalent metallic element of the rare-earth group — see ELEMENT table

¹thumb \'thəm\ *n* [ME *thoume, thoumbe*, fr. OE *thūma*; akin to OHG *thūmo* thumb, L *tumēre* to swell] (bef. 12c) **1 :** the short thick digit of the human hand that is analogous in position to the big toe and differs from the other fingers in having only two phalanges, allowing greater freedom of movement, and being opposable to each of them; *also* : a corresponding digit in lower animals **2 :** the part of a glove or mitten that covers the thumb **3 :** a convex molding : OVOLO — **all thumbs :** extremely awkward or clumsy — **under one's thumb** *or* **under the thumb :** under control : in a state of subservience ⟨her father did not have her that much *under his thumb* —Hamilton Basso⟩

²thumb *vt* (ca. 1647) **1 a :** to leaf through (pages) with the thumb : TURN **b :** to soil or wear by or as if by repeated thumbing ⟨a badly ∼ed book⟩ **2 :** to request or obtain (a ride) in a passing automobile by signaling with the thumb ∼ *vi* **1 :** to turn over pages ⟨∼ through a book⟩ **2 :** to travel by thumbing rides : HITCHHIKE ⟨∼ed across the country⟩ — **thumb one's nose 1 :** to place the thumb at one's nose and extend the fingers as a gesture of scorn or defiance **2 :** to express disdain or defiance ⟨*thumb their nose* at opulence —*Sales Management*⟩

thumb·hole \'thəm-,hōl\ *n* (1859) **1 :** an opening in which to insert the thumb **2 :** a hole in a wind musical instrument opened or closed by the thumb

thumb index *n* (1903) **:** a series of notches cut in the fore edge of a book to facilitate reference

¹thumb·nail \'thəm-,nāl, -'nā(ə)l\ *n* (1604) **:** the nail of the thumb

²thumbnail *adj* (1852) **:** CONCISE, BRIEF ⟨a ∼ sketch⟩

thumb piano *n* (1949) **:** MBIRA

thumb·print \'thəm-,print\ *n* (1900) **:** an impression made by the thumb; *esp* : a print made by the inside of the first joint

thumb·screw \-,skrü\ *n* (1794) **1 :** a screw

having a flat-sided or knurled head so that it may be turned by the thumb and forefinger **2 :** an instrument of torture for compressing the thumb by a screw

thumbs–down \'thəmz-'daún\ *n* (1889) **:** an instance or gesture of rejection, disapproval, or condemnation

thumbs–up \-'əp\ *n* (ca. 1917) **:** an instance or gesture of approval or encouragement

¹thumb·tack \'thəm-,tak\ *n* (1884) **:** a tack with a broad flat head for pressing into a surface with the thumb

²thumbtack *vt* (1914) **:** to fasten with a thumbtack

thumb·wheel \'thəm-,hwēl, -,wēl\ *n* (1903) **:** a control for various devices consisting of a partially exposed wheel that can be turned by moving the exposed edge with a finger

¹thump \'thəmp\ *vb* [imit.] *vt* (1548) **1 :** to strike or beat with or as if with something thick or heavy so as to cause a dull sound **2 :** POUND, KNOCK **3 :** WHIP, THRASH **4 :** to produce (music) mechanically or in a mechanical manner — usu. used with *out* ⟨∼ed out a tune on the piano⟩ ∼ *vi* **a :** to inflict a thump **b :** to make or move with a thumping sound **2 :** to make a vigorous endorsement ⟨got a couple of . . . senators to ∼ for him —*N.Y. Herald Tribune*⟩ — **thump·er** *n*

²thump *n* (1552) **:** a blow or knock with or as if with something blunt or heavy; *also* : the sound made by such a blow

thump·ing *adj* [*thumping*, prp. of ¹*thump*] (1576) **:** impressively large, great, or excellent ⟨a ∼ majority⟩

¹thun·der \'thən-dər\ *n* [ME *thoner, thunder*, fr. OE *thunor*; akin to OHG *thonar* thunder, L *tonare* to thunder] (bef. 12c) **1 :** the sound that follows a flash of lightning and is caused by sudden expansion of the air in the path of the electrical discharge **2 :** a loud utterance or threat **3 :** BANG, RUMBLE ⟨the ∼ of big guns⟩

²thunder *vb* **thun·dered; thun·der·ing** \-d(ə-)riŋ\ *vi* (bef. 12c) **1 a :** to produce thunder — usu. used impersonally ⟨it ∼ed⟩ **b :** to give forth a sound that resembles thunder ⟨horses ∼ed down the road⟩ **2 :** ROAR, SHOUT ∼ *vt* **1 :** to utter loudly : ROAR **2 :** to strike with a sound likened to thunder — **thun·der·er** \-dər-ər\ *n*

thun·der·bird \'thən-dər-,bərd\ *n* (1871) **:** a bird that causes lightning and thunder in American Indian myth

thun·der·bolt \-,bōlt\ *n* (15c) **1 a :** a single discharge of lightning with the accompanying thunder **b :** an imaginary elongated mass cast as a missile to earth in the lightning flash **2 a :** a person or thing that resembles lightning in suddenness, effectiveness, or destructive power **b :** a vehement threat or censure

thun·der·clap \-,klap\ *n* (14c) **1 :** a clap of thunder **2 :** something sharp, loud, or sudden like a clap of thunder

thun·der·cloud \-,klaúd\ *n* (1697) **:** a cloud charged with electricity and producing lightning and thunder

thunder egg *n* (1941) **:** chalcedony in rounded concretionary nodules

thun·der·head \-,hed\ *n* (1853) **:** a rounded mass of cumulus cloud often appearing before a thunderstorm

thun·der·ing *adj* [*thundering*, prp. of ²*thunder*] (1543) **:** awesomely great, intense, or unusual — **thun·der·ing·ly** \-d(ə-)riŋ-lē\ *adv*

thunder lizard *n* [trans. of NL *Brontosaurus*] (1960) **:** BRONTOSAURUS

thun·der·ous \'thən-d(ə-)rəs\ *adj* (1582) **1 a :** producing thunder **b :** making or accompanied by a noise like thunder ⟨∼ applause⟩ **2 :** THUNDERING — **thun·der·ous·ly** *adv*

thun·der·show·er \-,shaú(-ə)r\ *n* (1699) **:** a shower accompanied by lightning and thunder

thun·der·stone \-,stōn\ *n* (1598) **1** *archaic* : THUNDERBOLT 1b **2 :** any of various stones (as a meteorite or an ancient artifact) that are the probable source of the imaginary thunderbolt

thun·der·storm \-,stórm\ *n* (1652) **:** a storm accompanied by lightning and thunder

thun·der·strike \-,strīk\ *vt* **-struck** \-,strək\; **-struck** *also* **-strick·en** \-,stri-kən\; **-strik·ing** \-,strī-kiŋ\ (ca. 1586) **1 :** to strike dumb : ASTONISH ⟨was *thunderstruck* at the news⟩ **2** *archaic* : to strike by or as if by lightning

thun·der·stroke \-,strōk\ *n* (1587) **:** a stroke of or as if of lightning with the attendant thunder

¹thunk \'thəŋk\ *dial* past and past part of THINK

²thunk *n* [imit.] (1947) **:** a flat hollow sound

thu·ri·ble \'thúr-ə-bəl, 'thyúr-\ *n* [ME *turrible*, fr. MF *thurible*, fr. L *thuribulum*, fr. *thur-, thus* incense, fr. Gk *thyos* incense, sacrifice, fr. *thyein* to sacrifice — more at THYME] (15c) **:** CENSER

thu·ri·fer \-ə-fər\ *n* [NL, fr. L *thurifer*, adj., incense-bearing, fr. *thur-, thus* + *-ifer* -iferous] (1853) **:** one who carries a censer in a liturgical service

Thu·rin·ger \'thúr-ən-jər, 'thyúr-\ *n* [G *Thüringerwurst*, fr. *Thüringer* Thuringian + *Wurst* sausage] (ca. 1923) **:** a mildly seasoned fresh or smoked sausage

Thu·rin·gian \thú-'rin-j(ē-)ən, thyúr-\ *n* (1618) **1 :** a member of an ancient Germanic people whose kingdom was overthrown by the Franks in the 6th century **2 :** a native or inhabitant of Thuringia — **Thuringian** *adj*

thurl \'thər(-ə)l\ *n* [perh. fr. E dial., gaunt] **:** the hip joint in cattle — see COW illustration

Thurs·day \'thərz-dē, -(,)dā\ *n* [ME, fr. OE *thursdæg*, fr. ON *thōrsdagr*; akin to OE *thunresdæg* Thursday, ON *Thōrr* Thor, OE *thunor* thunder — more at THUNDER] (bef. 12c) **:** the fifth day of the week — **Thurs·days** \-dēz, -(,)dāz\ *adv*

thus \'thəs\ *adv* [ME, fr. OE; akin to OS *thus* thus] (bef. 12c) **1 :** in this or that manner or way **2 :** to this degree or extent : SO **3 :** because of this or that : HENCE, CONSEQUENTLY **4 :** as an example

thus·ly \-lē\ *adv* (1865) **:** in this manner : THUS

¹thwack \'thwak\ *vt* [imit.] (ca. 1530) **:** to strike with or as if with something that on a flat surface : WHACK

²thwack *n* (1587) **:** a heavy blow : WHACK; *also* : the sound of or as if of such a blow

¹thwart \'thwórt\ *vt* [ME *thwerten*, fr. *thwert*, adv.] (13c) **1 a :** to run

thumbscrew 1

\ə\ abut \ᵊ\ kitten, F table \ər\ further \a\ ash \ā\ ace \ä\ mop, mar \aú\ out \ch\ chin \e\ bet \ē\ easy \g\ go \i\ hit \ī\ ice \j\ job \ŋ\ sing \ō\ go \ó\ law \ói\ boy \th\ thin \th\ the \ü\ loot \ú\ foot \y\ yet \zh\ vision \à, ḵ, ⁿ, œ, œ̄, ᵫ, ūe, ᵞ\ see Guide to Pronunciation counter to so as to effectively oppose or baffle : CONTRAVENE **b** : to oppose successfully : defeat the hopes or aspirations of **2** : to pass through or across *syn* see FRUSTRATE — **thwart·er** *n*

²thwart \'thwȯrt, *naut often* 'thȯrt\ *adv* [ME *thwert*, fr. ON *thvert*, fr. neut. of *thverr* transverse, oblique; akin to OHG *dwerah* transverse, oblique] (14c) : ATHWART

³thwart *adj* (15c) : situated or placed across something else : TRANSVERSE — **thwart·ly** *adv*

⁴thwart *n* [alter. of obs. *thought, thoft,* fr. ME *thoft,* fr. OE *thofte;* akin to OHG *dofta* rower's seat] (ca. 1736) : a rower's seat extending athwart a boat

thwart·wise \-ˌwīz\ *adv or adj* (1589) : CROSSWISE

thy \'thī\ *adj* [ME *thin, thy,* fr. OE *thin,* gen. of *thū* thou — more at THOU] (12c) *archaic* : of or relating to thee or thyself esp. as possessor or agent or as object of an action — used esp. in ecclesiastical or literary language and sometimes by Friends esp. among themselves

Thy·es·te·an \thī-'es-tē-ən\ *adj* [*Thyestes,* brother of Atreus who unwittingly ate the flesh of his children] (1667) : of or relating to the eating of human flesh : CANNIBAL

thy·la·cine \'thī-lə-ˌsīn\ *n* [NL *Thylacinus,* genus of marsupials, fr. Gk *thylakos* sack, pouch] (1838) : TASMANIAN WOLF

thy·la·koid \'thī-lə-ˌkȯid\ *n* [ISV *thylak-* (fr. Gk *thylakos* sack) + *-oid*] (1966) : any of the membranous disks of lamellae within plant chloroplasts that are composed of protein and lipid and are the sites of the photochemical reactions of photosynthesis

thym- *or* **thymo-** *comb form* [NL *thymus*] : thymus ⟨*thymic*⟩ ⟨*thymocyte*⟩

thyme \'tīm *also* 'thīm\ *n* [ME, fr. MF *thym,* fr. L *thymum,* fr. Gk *thymon,* prob. fr. *thyein* to make a burnt offering, sacrifice; akin to L *fumus* smoke — more at FUME] (14c) **1** : any of a genus (*Thymus*) of Eurasian mints with small pungent aromatic leaves; *esp* : a garden herb (*T. vulgaris*) **2** : thyme leaves used as a seasoning

thy·mec·to·my \thī-'mek-tə-mē\ *n, pl* **-mies** (ca. 1905) : excision of the thymus — **thy·mec·to·mize** \-ˌmīz\ *vt*

-thymia *n comb form* [NL, fr. Gk, fr. *thymos* mind] : condition of mind and will ⟨*cyclothymia*⟩

thy·mic \'thī-mik\ *adj* (ca. 1656) : of or relating to the thymus

thy·mi·dine \'thī-mə-ˌdēn\ *n* [*thymine* + *-idine*] (1912) : a nucleoside $C_{10}H_{14}N_2O_5$ that is composed of thymine and deoxyribose and occurs as a structural part of DNA

thy·mine \'thī-ˌmēn\ *n* [ISV, fr. NL *thymus*] (1894) : a pyrimidine base $C_5H_6N_2O_2$ that is one of the four bases coding genetic information in the polynucleotide chain of DNA — compare ADENINE, CYTOSINE, GUANINE, URACIL

thy·mo·cyte \'thī-mə-ˌsīt\ *n* [ISV] (ca. 1923) : a cell of the thymus; *esp* : a thymic lymphocyte

thy·mol \'thī-ˌmȯl, -ˌmōl\ *n* [ISV, fr. L *thymum* thyme] (1857) : a crystalline phenol $C_{10}H_{14}O$ of aromatic odor and antiseptic properties found esp. in thyme oil or made synthetically and used chiefly as a fungicide and preservative

thy·mo·sin \'thī-mə-sən\ *n* [Gk *thymos* thymus + E ¹-*in*] (1966) : a mixture of polypeptides isolated from the thymus; *also* : any of these

thy·mus \'thī-məs\ *n* [NL, fr. Gk *thymos* warty excrescence, thymus] (ca. 1693) : a glandular structure of largely lymphoid tissue that functions esp. in the development of the body's immune system, is present in the young of most vertebrates typically in the upper anterior chest or at the base of the neck, and tends to atrophy in the adult

thymy *or* **thym·ey** \'thī-mē *also* 'thī-\ *adj* (1727) : abounding in or fragrant with thyme

thyr- *or* **thyro-** *comb form* [*thyroid*] : thyroid ⟨*thyrotoxicosis*⟩ ⟨*thyroxine*⟩

thy·ra·tron \'thī-rə-ˌträn\ *n* [fr. *Thyratron,* a trademark] (1929) : a gas-filled hot-cathode electron tube in which the grid controls only the start of a continuous current thus giving the tube a trigger effect

thy·ris·tor \thī-'ris-tər\ *n* [*thyratron* + transistor] (1958) : any of several semiconductor devices that act as switches, rectifiers, or voltage regulators

thy·ro·cal·ci·to·nin \ˌthī-rō-ˌkal-sə-'tō-nən\ *n* (1963) : CALCITONIN

thy·ro·glob·u·lin \-'glä-byə-lən\ *n* [ISV] (ca. 1905) : an iodine-containing protein of the thyroid gland that is the precursor of thyroxine and triiodothyronine

¹thy·roid \'thī-ˌrȯid\ *also* **thy·roi·dal** \thī-'rȯi-d²l\ *adj* [NL *thyroides,* fr. Gk *thyreoeidēs* shield-shaped, thyroid, fr. *thyreos* shield shaped like a door, fr. *thyra* door — more at DOOR] (ca. 1741) **1 a** : of, relating to, or being a large bilobed endocrine gland of craniate vertebrates lying at the base of the neck and producing esp. the hormones thyroxine and triiodothyronine **b** : suggestive of a disordered thyroid ⟨a ~ personality⟩ **2** : of, relating to, or being the chief cartilage of the larynx

²thyroid *n* (1840) **1** : a thyroid gland or cartilage; *also* : a part (as an artery or nerve) associated with either of these **2** : a preparation of mammalian thyroid gland used in treating thyroid disorders

thy·roid·ec·to·my \ˌthī-ˌrȯi-'dek-tə-mē, ˌthī-rə-\ *n, pl* **-mies** (1889) : surgical removal of thyroid gland tissue — **thy·roid·ec·to·mized** \-ˌmīzd\ *adj*

thy·roid·itis \ˌthī-ˌrȯi-'dī-təs, ˌthī-rə-\ *n* [NL] (ca. 1885) : inflammation of the thyroid gland

thyroid–stimulating hormone *n* (1941) : THYROTROPIN

thy·ro·tox·i·co·sis \ˌthī-rō-ˌtäk-sə-'kō-səs\ *n* [NL] (ca. 1911) : HYPERTHYROIDISM

thy·ro·tro·pic \ˌthī-rə-'trō-pik, -'trä-\ *also* **thy·ro·tro·phic** \-'trō-fik\ *adj* (ca. 1923) : exerting or characterized by a direct influence on the secretory activity of the thyroid gland ⟨~ functions⟩

thy·ro·tro·pin \ˌthī-rə-'trō-pən\ *also* **thy·ro·tro·phin** \-fən\ *n* [*thyrotropic, thyrotrophic*] (1939) : a hormone secreted by the anterior pituitary that stimulates the thyroid gland — called also *thyroid-stimulating hormone, thyrotropic hormone*

thyrotropin–releasing hormone *n* (1968) : a tripeptide hormone synthesized in the hypothalamus that stimulates secretion of thyrotropin by the anterior lobe of the pituitary gland — called also *thyrotropin-releasing factor*

thy·rox·ine *or* **thy·rox·in** \thī-'räk-ˌsēn, -sən\ *n* [ISV] (1918) : an iodine-containing hormone $C_{15}H_{11}I_4NO_4$ that is an amino acid produced by the thyroid gland as a product of the cleavage of thyroglobulin, increases metabolic rate, and is used to treat thyroid disorders

thyrse \'thərs\ *n* [NL *thyrsus,* fr. L, thyrsus] (1744) : an inflorescence (as in the lilac and horse chestnut) in which the main axis is racemose and the secondary and later axes are cymose

thyr·sus \'thər-səs\ *n, pl* **thyr·si** \-ˌsī, -ˌsē\ [L, fr. Gk *thyrsos*] (1591) : a staff surmounted by a pinecone or by a bunch of vine or ivy leaves with grapes or berries that is carried by Bacchus and by satyrs and others engaging in bacchic rites

thy·sa·nu·ran \ˌthī-sə-'nu̇r-ən, -'nyu̇r-\ *n* [ultim fr. Gk *thysanos* tassel + *oura* tail — more at ASS] (1835) : BRISTLETAIL — **thysanuran** *adj*

thy·self \thī-'self\ *pron* (bef. 12c) *archaic* : YOURSELF — used esp. in ecclesiastical or literary language and sometimes by Friends esp. among themselves

¹ti \'tē\ *n* [Tahitian, Marquesan, Samoan, & Maori] (1832) : any of several Asian and Pacific trees or shrubs (genus *Cordyline*) of the agave family with leaves in terminal tufts

²ti *n* [alter. of *si*] (1839) : the seventh tone of the diatonic scale in solmization

ti·ara \tē-'ar-ə, -'er-, -'är-\ *n* [L, royal Persian headdress, fr. Gk] (1616) **1** : a 3-tiered crown worn by the pope **2** : a decorative jeweled or flowered headband or semicircle for formal wear by women

Ti·bet·an \tə-'be-t²n\ *n* (1747) **1 a** : a member of the predominant people of Tibet and adjacent areas of Asia **b** : a native or inhabitant of Tibet **2** : the Tibeto-Burman language of the Tibetan people — **Tibetan** *adj*

Tibetan terrier *n* (1905) : any of a breed of terriers resembling Old English sheepdogs but having a curled well-feathered tail

Ti·beto–Bur·man \tə-ˌbe-tō-'bər-mən\ *n* (1901) **1** : a language family that includes Tibetan, Burmese, and related languages of southern and eastern Asia **2** : a member of a people speaking a Tibeto-Burman language

tib·ia \'ti-bē-ə\ *n, pl* **-i·ae** \-bē-ˌē, -bē-ˌī\ *also* **-i·as** [L] (ca. 1706) **1** : the inner and usu. larger of the two bones of the vertebrate hind limb between the knee and ankle **2** : the fourth joint of the leg of an insect between the femur and tarsus — **tib·i·al** \-bē-əl\ *adj*

tib·io·fib·u·la \ˌti-bē-ō-'fi-byə-lə\ *n* [NL] (ca. 1909) : a bone esp. in frogs and toads that is formed by fusion of the tibia and fibula

tic \'tik\ *n* [F] (ca. 1834) **1** : local and habitual spasmodic motion of particular muscles esp. of the face : TWITCHING **2** : a frequent usu. unconscious quirk of behavior or speech ("you know" is a verbal ~)

ti·cal \ti-'käl, 'ti-kəl\ *n, pl* **ticals** *or* **tical** [Thai, fr. Pg, fr. Malay *tikal,* a monetary unit] (1662) : BAHT

tic dou·lou·reux \ˌtik-ˌdü-lə-'rü, -'rə(r)\ *n* [F, painful twitch] (1800) : TRIGEMINAL NEURALGIA

¹tick \'tik\ *n* [ME *tyke, teke;* akin to MHG *zeche* tick, Arm *tiz*] (14c) **1** : any of a superfamily (Ixodoidea of the order Acarina) of bloodsucking arachnids that are larger than the related mites, attach themselves to warm-blooded vertebrates to feed, and include important vectors of infectious diseases **2** : any of various usu. wingless parasitic dipteran flies — compare SHEEP KED

²tick *n* [ME *tike,* prob. fr. MD (akin to OHG *ziahha* tick), fr. L *theca* cover, fr. Gk *thēkē* case; akin to Gk *tithenai* to place — more at DO] (15c) **1** : the fabric case of a mattress, pillow, or bolster; *also* : a mattress consisting of a tick and its filling **2** : TICKING

²tick 1

³tick *n* [ME *tek* pat, light stroke; akin to MHG *zic* light push] (1680) **1 a** : a light rhythmic audible tap or beat; *also* : a series of such ticks **b** *chiefly Brit* : the time taken by the tick of a clock : MOMENT **2** : a small spot or mark; *esp* : one used to direct attention to something, to check an item on a list, or to represent a point on a scale

⁴tick *vi* (1721) **1** : to make the sound of a tick or a series of ticks **2** : to operate as a functioning mechanism : RUN ⟨tried to understand what made him ~⟩ ⟨the motor was ~*ing* over quietly⟩ ~ *vt* **1** : to mark with a written tick : CHECK — usu. used with *off* ⟨~*ed* off each item in the list⟩ **2** : to mark, count, or announce by or as if by ticking beats ⟨a meter ~*ing* off the cab fare⟩ **3** : to touch with a momentary glancing blow ⟨~*ed* the ball⟩

⁵tick *n* [short for ¹*ticket*] (1642) *chiefly Brit* : CREDIT, TRUST; *also* : a credit account

tick–borne \'tik-ˌbȯrn, -ˌbȯrn\ *adj* (1921) : capable of being transmitted by the bites of ticks ⟨~ encephalitis⟩

¹ticked \'tikt\ *adj* (ca. 1688) **1** : marked with ticks : FLECKED **2** : having or made of hair banded with two or more colors ⟨a ~ cat⟩ ⟨a ~ coat⟩

²ticked *adj* [*tick off*] (ca. 1959) : ANGRY, UPSET

tick·er \'ti-kər\ *n* (1828) : something that ticks or produces a ticking sound: as **a** : WATCH **b** : a telegraphic receiving instrument that automatically prints off information (as stock quotations or news) on a paper ribbon **c** *slang* : HEART

ticker tape *n* (1902) : the paper ribbon on which a telegraphic ticker prints off its information

¹tick·et \'ti-kət\ *n* [MF *etiquet, estiquette* notice attached to something, fr. *estiquier* to attach, fr. MD *steken* to stick; akin to OHG *stichen* to prick — more at STICK] (1529) **1 a** : a document that serves as a certificate, license, or permit; *esp* : a mariner's or airman's certificate **b** : TAG, LABEL **2 a** : a certificate or token showing that a fare or admission fee has been paid **b** : a means of access or passage ⟨education is the ~ to a good job⟩ **3** : a list of candidates for nomination or election : SLATE **4** : the correct or desirable thing ⟨cooperation, that's the ~ —K. E. Trombley⟩ **5** : a slip or card recording a transaction or undertaking or giving instructions ⟨a savings deposit ~⟩ **6** : a summons or warning issued to a traffic-law violator — **tick·et·less** \-ləs\ *adj*

²ticket *vt* (1611) **1** : to attach a ticket to : LABEL; *also* : DESIGNATE **2** : to furnish or serve with a ticket ⟨~*ed* for illegal parking⟩

ticket agency *n* (1923) : an agency selling transportation or theater and entertainment tickets

ticket agent *n* (1861) : one who sells transportation or theater and entertainment tickets

ticket office *n* (ca. 1667) : an office of a transportation company, theatrical or entertainment enterprise, or ticket agency where tickets are sold and reservations made

tick·et-of-leave \,ti-kət-ə(v)-'lēv\ *n, pl* **tickets-of-leave** (1732) : a license or permit formerly given in the United Kingdom and the Commonwealth to a convict under imprisonment to go at large and to get work subject to certain specific conditions

tick fever *n* (ca. 1897) **1 :** TEXAS FEVER **2 :** a febrile disease (as Rocky Mountain spotted fever) transmitted by the bites of ticks

¹tick·ing \'ti-kiŋ\ *n* [²*tick*] (1649) : a strong linen or cotton fabric used in upholstering and as a covering for a mattress or pillow

²ticking *n* [³*tick*] (1885) : ticked marking on a bird or mammal or on individual hairs

¹tick·le \'ti-kəl\ *vb* **tick·led; tick·ling** \-k(ə-)liŋ\ [ME *tikelen;* akin to OE *tinclian* to tickle] *vt* (14c) **1 a :** to excite or stir up agreeably : PLEASE ⟨music . . . does more than ~ our sense of rhythm —Edward Sapir⟩ **b :** to provoke to laughter or merriment : AMUSE ⟨were *tickled* by the clown's antics⟩ **2 :** to touch (as a body part) lightly so as to excite the surface nerves and cause uneasiness, laughter, or spasmodic movements ~ *vi* **1 :** to have a tingling or prickling sensation ⟨my back ~s⟩ **2 :** to excite the surface nerves to prickle

²tickle *n* (1801) **1 :** the act of tickling **2 :** a tickling sensation **3 :** something that tickles

tick·ler \'ti-k(ə-)lər\ *n* (1680) **1 :** a person or device that tickles **2 :** a device for jogging the memory; *specif* : a file that serves as a reminder and is arranged to bring matters to timely attention

tick·lish \'ti-k(ə-)lish\ *adj* (1581) **1 a :** TOUCHY, OVERSENSITIVE ⟨~ about his baldness⟩ **b :** easily overturned ⟨a canoe is a ~ craft⟩ **2 :** requiring delicate handling ⟨a ~ subject⟩ **3 :** sensitive to tickling — **tick·lish·ly** *adv* — **tick·lish·ness** *n*

tick off *vt* (1919) **1 :** REPRIMAND, REBUKE ⟨his father *ticked* him *off* for his impudence⟩ **2 :** to make angry or indignant ⟨the cancellation really *ticked* me *off*⟩

tick·seed \'tik-,sēd\ *n* [¹*tick*] (ca. 1562) : COREOPSIS

tick·tack *or* **tic·tac** \'tik-,tak\ *n* [redupl. of *tick*] (1549) **1 :** a ticking or tapping beat like that of a clock or watch **2 :** a contrivance used by children to tap on a window from a distance

tick·tack·toe *also* **tic-tac-toe** \,tik-,tak-'tō\ *n* [*tic-tac-toe,* former game in which players with eyes shut brought a pencil down on a slate marked with numbers and scored the number hit] (ca. 1866) : a game in which two players alternately put Xs and Os in compartments of a figure formed by two vertical lines crossing two horizontal lines and each tries to get a row of three Xs or three Os before the opponent does

tick·tock \'tik-,täk, -,täk\ *n* [imit.] (1848) : the ticking sound of a clock

tick trefoil *n* [¹*tick*] (1857) : any of various leguminous plants (genus *Desmodium*) with trifoliolate leaves and rough sticky loments

¹ticky-tacky \,ti-kē-'ta-kē\ *also* **ticky-tack** \-'tak\ *n, pl* **ticky-tackies** *also* **ticky-tacks** [redupl. of *tacky*] (1962) : sleazy or shoddy material used esp. in the construction of look-alike tract houses; *also* : something built of ticky-tacky

²ticky-tacky *also* **ticky-tack** *adj* (1964) **1 :** of an uninspired or monotonous sameness **2 :** TACKY **3 :** built of ticky-tacky

tid·al \'tī-d²l\ *adj* (1807) **1 a :** of, relating to, caused by, or having tides ⟨~ cycles⟩ ⟨~ erosion⟩ **b :** periodically rising and falling or flowing and ebbing ⟨~ waters⟩ **2 :** dependent (as to the time of arrival or departure) upon the state of the tide ⟨a ~ steamer⟩ — **tid·al·ly** \-d²l-ē\ *adv*

tidal wave *n* (1830) **1 a :** an unusually high sea wave that sometimes follows an earthquake **b :** an unusual rise of water alongshore due to strong winds **2 :** something overwhelming esp. in quantity or volume ⟨a *tidal wave* of tourists⟩

tid·bit \'tid-,bit\ *n* [perh. fr. *tit-* (as in *titmouse*) + *bit*] (ca. 1640) **1 :** a choice morsel of food **2 :** a choice or pleasing bit (as of information)

tid·dle·dy-winks \'ti-d²l-dē-,win(k)s\ *or* **tid·dly-winks** \'ti-d²l-ē-, 'tid-lē-\ *n pl but sing in constr* [prob. fr. E dial. *tiddly* little, alter. of *little*] (1898) : a game whose object is to snap small disks from a flat surface into a small container

tid·dler \'ti-d²l-ər, 'tid-lər\ *n* [prob. fr. E dial. *tiddly* little] (1885) *Brit* : a small fish (as a stickleback or minnow)

tid·dly \'ti-d²l-ē, 'tid-lē\ *adj* [*tiddly* an alcoholic drink, prob. fr. E dial. *tiddly*] (1905) *chiefly Brit* : slightly drunk

¹tide \'tīd\ *n* [ME, time, fr. OE *tīd;* akin to OHG *zīt* time and perh. to Gk *daiesthai* to divide] (bef. 12c) **1 a :** a space of time : PERIOD **b :** a fit or opportune time : OPPORTUNITY **c :** an ecclesiastical anniversary or festival; *also* : its season — usu. used in combination ⟨Eastertide⟩ **2 a** (1) : the alternate rising and falling of the surface of the ocean and of water bodies (as gulfs and bays) connected with the ocean that occurs usu. twice a day and is caused by the gravitational attraction of the sun and moon occurring unequally on different parts of the earth (2) : a less marked rising and falling of an inland body of water (3) : a periodic movement in the earth's crust caused by the same forces that produce ocean tides (4) : a tidal distortion on one celestial body caused by the gravitational attraction of another (5) : one of the tidal movements of the atmosphere resembling those of the ocean and produced by gravitation or diurnal temperature changes **b :** FLOOD TIDE 1 **3 a :** something that fluctuates like the tides of the sea ⟨the ~ of public opinion⟩ **b :** a surging movement of a group ⟨a ~ of opportunists⟩ **4 a :** a flowing stream : CURRENT **b :** the waters of the ocean **c :** the overflow of a flooding stream — **tide·less** \-ləs\ *adj*

²tide *vb* **tid·ed; tid·ing** *vi* (1593) : to flow as or in a tide : SURGE ~ *vt* : to cause to float with or as if with the tide

³tide *vi* **tid·ed; tid·ing** [ME, fr. OE *tīdan;* akin to MD *tiden* to go, come, OE *tīd* time] (bef. 12c) *archaic* : BETIDE, BEFALL

tide·land \'tīd-,land, -lənd\ *n* (1802) **1 :** land overflowed during flood tide **2 :** land underlying the ocean and lying beyond the low-water limit of the tide but being within the territorial waters of a nation — often used in pl.

tide·mark \-,märk\ *n* (1799) **1 a :** a high-water or sometimes low-water mark left by tidal water or a flood **b :** a mark placed to indicate this point **2 :** the point to which something has attained or below which it has receded ⟨the ~ of tolerance has risen —*New Republic*⟩

tide over *vt* [²*tide*] (1821) : to enable to surmount or endure a difficulty ⟨money to *tide* us *over* the emergency⟩

tide table *n* (1594) : a table that indicates the height of the tide at one place at different times of day throughout one year

tide·wa·ter \-,wȯ-tər, -,wä-\ *n* (1772) **1 :** water overflowing land at flood tide; *also* : water affected by the ebb and flow of the tide **2 :** low-lying coastal land

tide·way \-,wā\ *n* (1798) : a channel in which the tide runs

tid·ing \'tī-diŋ\ *n* [ME, fr. OE *tīdung,* fr. *tīdan* to betide] (12c) : a piece of news — usu. used in pl. ⟨good ~s⟩

¹ti·dy \'tī-dē\ *adj* **ti·di·er; -est** [ME, timely, in good condition, fr. *tide* time] (13c) **1 :** properly filled out : PLUMP **2 :** adequately satisfactory : ACCEPTABLE, FAIR ⟨a ~ solution to their problem⟩ **3 a :** neat and orderly in appearance or habits : well ordered and cared for **b :** METHODICAL, PRECISE ⟨a ~ mind⟩ **4 :** LARGE, SUBSTANTIAL ⟨a ~ profit⟩ — **ti·di·ly** \'tī-d²l-ē\ *adv* — **ti·di·ness** \'tī-dē-nəs\ *n*

²tidy *vb* **ti·died; ti·dy·ing** *vt* (1821) : to put in order ⟨~ up a room⟩ ~ *vi* : to make things tidy ⟨~*ing* up after supper⟩ — **ti·di·er** *n*

³tidy *n, pl* **tidies** (ca. 1828) **1 :** a usu. compartmentalized receptacle for various small objects **2 :** a piece of fancywork used to protect the back, arms, or headrest of a chair or sofa from wear or soil

ti·dy-tips \'tī-dē-,tips\ *n pl but sing or pl in constr* (1888) : an annual California composite herb (*Layia platyglossa*) having yellow-rayed flower heads often tipped with white

¹tie \'tī\ *n* [ME *teg, tye,* fr. OE *tēag;* akin to ON *taug* rope, OE *tēon* to pull — more at TOW] (bef. 12c) **1 a :** a line, ribbon, or cord used for fastening, uniting, or drawing something closed; *esp* : SHOELACE **b** (1) : a structural element (as a rod or angle iron) holding two pieces together : a tension member in a construction (2) : any of the transverse supports to which railroad rails are fastened to keep them in line **2 :** something that serves as a connecting link: as **a :** a moral or legal obligation to someone or something typically constituting a restraining power, influence, or duty **b :** a bond of kinship or affection **3 :** a curved line that joins two musical notes of the same pitch to denote a single tone sustained through the time value of the two **4 a :** an equality in number (as of votes or scores) **b :** equality in a contest; *also* : a contest that ends in a draw **5 :** a method or style of tying or knotting **6 :** something that is knotted or is to be knotted when worn: as **a :** NECKTIE **b :** a low laced shoe : OXFORD — **tie·less** \-ləs\ *adj*

²tie *vb* **tied; ty·ing** \'tī-iŋ\ *or* **tie·ing** *vt* (bef. 12c) **1 a :** to fasten, attach, or close by means of a tie **b :** to form a knot or bow in ⟨~ your scarf⟩ **c :** to make by tying constituent elements ⟨*tied* a wreath⟩ ⟨~ a fishing fly⟩ **2 a :** to place or establish in relationship : CONNECT **b :** to unite in marriage **c :** to unite (musical notes) by a tie **d :** to join (power systems) electrically **3 :** to restrain from independence or freedom of action or choice : constrain by or as if by authority, influence, agreement, or obligation **4 a** (1) : to make or have an equal score with in a contest (2) : to equalize (the score) in a game or contest (3) : to equalize the score of (a game) **b :** to provide or offer something equal to : EQUAL ~ *vi* : to make a tie: as **a :** to make a bond or connection **b :** to make an equal score **c :** to become attached **d :** to close by means of a tie — **tie into :** to attack with vigor — **tie one on** *slang* : to get drunk — **tie the knot :** to perform a marriage ceremony; *also* : to get married

tie-and-dye \'tī-ən-,dī\ *n* (1928) : TIE-DYEING

tie·back \'tī-,bak\ *n* (1926) **1 :** a decorative strip or device of cloth, cord, or metal for draping a curtain to the side of a window **2 :** a curtain with a tieback — usu. used in pl.

tie·break·er \'tī-,brā-kər\ *n* (ca. 1932) : a contest used to select a winner from among contestants with tied scores at the end of a previous contest

tied cottage *n* (1899) *Brit* : a cottage or house owned by an employer (as a farmer) and reserved for occupancy by an employee

tie-down \-,daůn\ *n* (ca. 1942) : a fitting or a system of lines and fittings used to secure something (as an aircraft or cargo)

tie-dye \'tī-,dī\ *n* (ca. 1939) **1 :** TIE-DYEING **2 :** a tie-dyed garment or fabric

tie-dyed *adj* (1904) : having patterns produced by tie-dyeing ⟨~ shirts⟩

tie-dye·ing *n* (1904) : a hand method of producing patterns in textiles by tying portions of the fabric or yarn so that they will not absorb the dye

tie-in \'tī-,in\ *n* (1925) **1 :** something that ties in, relates, or connects esp. in a promotional campaign **2 :** a book that inspired or was inspired by a motion picture or television program

tie in *vi* (1793) : to bring into connection with something relevant: as **a :** to make the final connection of ⟨*tied in* the new branch pipeline⟩ **b :** to coordinate in such a manner as to produce balance and unity ⟨the illustrations were *tied in* with the text⟩ **c :** to use as a tie-in esp. in advertising ~ *vi* : to become tied in

tie-line \'tī-,līn\ *n* (1923) : a telephone line that directly connects two or more private branch exchanges

tie·mann·ite \'tē-mə-,nīt\ *n* [G *Tiemannit,* fr. W. *Tiemann* †1899 Ger. scientist] (1868) : a mineral that consists of mercuric selenide and occurs in dark gray or nearly black masses of metallic luster

tie-pin \'tī-,pin\ *n* (1780) : an ornamental straight pin that has usu. a sheath for the point and is used to hold the ends of a necktie in place

tier \'tir\ *n* [MF *tire* rank, fr. OF — more at ATTIRE] (1569) **1 a :** a row, rank, or layer of articles; *esp* : one of two or more rows, levels, or ranks arranged one above another **b :** a group of political or geographical divisions that form a row across the map ⟨the southern ~ of states⟩ **2 :** CLASS, CATEGORY

tier *vt* (ca. 1889) : to place or arrange in tiers ~ *vi* : to rise in tiers

³ti·er \'tī-(ə)r\ *n* (1633) : one that ties

¹tierce \'tirs\ *var of* TERCE

²tierce *n* [ME *terce, tierce,* fr. MF, fr. fem. of *terz,* adj., third, fr. L *tertius* — more at THIRD] (15c) **1** *obs* : THIRD 2 **2 :** a sequence of three playing cards of the same suit

---

\ə\ abut \²\ kitten, F table \ər\ further \a\ ash \ā\ ace \ä\ mop, mar
\aů\ out \ch\ chin \e\ bet \ē\ easy \g\ go \i\ hit \ī\ ice \j\ job
\ŋ\ sing \ō\ go \ȯ\ law \ȯi\ boy \th\ thin \t̲h̲\ the \ü\ loot \ů\ foot
\y\ yet \zh\ vision \á, k̲, ⁿ, œ, œ̄, ɶ, ūe, ᵀ\ *see* Guide to Pronunciation

tier·cel \'tir-səl\ n [ME *tercel*, fr. MF, fr. (assumed) VL *tertiolus*, fr. dim. of L *tertius* third] (14c) : a male hawk

tiered \'tird\ adj (1807) : having or arranged in tiers, rows, or layers — often used in combination ⟨triple-*tiered*⟩

tie-rod \'tī-ˌräd\ n (1839) : a rod (as of steel) used as a connecting member or brace

tie silk n (ca. 1915) : a silk fabric of firm resilient pliable texture used for neckties and for blouses and accessories

tie tack or **tie tac** \-ˌtak\ n (1954) : an ornamented pin with a receiving button or clasp that is used to attach the two parts of a necktie together or to attach a necktie to a shirt

tie-up \'tī-ˌəp\ n (1851) **1 a** : a cow stable; *also* : a space for a single cow in a stable **b** : a mooring place for a boat **2** : a slowdown or stoppage of traffic, business, or operation (as by a mechanical breakdown) **3** : CONNECTION, ASSOCIATION ⟨helpful financial ~s⟩

tie up vt (1530) **1** : to attach, fasten, or bind securely; *also* : to wrap up and fasten **2 a** : to connect closely : JOIN ⟨*tie up* the loose ends⟩ **b** : to cause to be linked so as to depend on or relate to something **3 a** : to place or invest in such a manner as to make unavailable for other purposes ⟨their money was *tied up* in stocks⟩ **b** : to restrain from normal movement, operation, or progress ⟨traffic was *tied up* for miles⟩ **4 a** : to keep busy ⟨was *tied up* in conference all day⟩ **b** : to preempt the use of ⟨*tied up* the phone for an hour⟩ ~ vi **1** : DOCK ⟨the ferry *ties up* at the south slip⟩ **2** : to assume a definite relationship ⟨this *ties up* with what I told you before⟩

¹tiff \'tif\ vi [origin unknown] (1700) : to have a petty quarrel

²tiff n (1754) : a petty quarrel

tif·fa·ny \'ti-fə-nē\ n, pl **-nies** [perh. fr. obs. F *tiphanie* Epiphany, fr. LL *theophania*, fr. LGk, ultim. fr. Gk *theos* god + *phainein* to show] (1601) **1** : a sheer silk gauze formerly used for clothing and trimmings **2** : a plain-woven open-mesh cotton fabric (as cheesecloth)

Tif·fa·ny \'ti-fə-nē\ adj (1936) : being glass or an article of glass made by or in the manner of Louis C. Tiffany; *esp* : made of pieces of stained glass ⟨a *Tiffany*-style lamp⟩ ⟨a ~ window⟩

tif·fin \'ti-fən\ n [prob. alter. of *tiffing*, gerund of obs. E *tiff* to eat between meals] (1800) *chiefly Brit* : a light midday meal : LUNCHEON

ti·ger \'tī-gər\ n, pl **tigers** [ME *tigre*, fr. OE *tigre* & OF *tigre*, both fr. L *tigris*, fr. Gk, prob. of Iranian origin; akin to Av *tighra-* pointed; akin to Gk *stizein* to tattoo — more at STICK] (bef. 12c) **1** *pl also* **tiger a** : a large Asian carnivorous mammal (*Panthera tigris*) of the cat family having a usu. tawny coat transversely striped with black **b** : any of several large wildcats (as the jaguar or cougar) **c** : a domestic cat with striped pattern **d** *Austral* : TASMANIAN WOLF **2 a** : a fierce, daring, or aggressive person or quality ⟨aroused the ~ in him⟩ ⟨a ~ for work⟩ **b** : one (as a situation) that is formidable or impossible to control ⟨how the ~ of inflation can be tamed —J. A. Davenport⟩ — often used in the phrases *ride a tiger* and *have a tiger by the tail* **3** *Brit* : a groom in livery — **ti·ger·ish** \-g(ə-)rish\ adj — **ti·ger·ish·ly** adv — **ti·ger·ish·ness** n — **ti·ger·like** \-gər-ˌlīk\ adj

tiger beetle n (1826) : any of numerous active carnivorous beetles (family Cicindelidae) having larvae that tunnel in the soil

tiger cat n (1699) **1** : any of various wildcats (as the serval, ocelot, or margay) of moderate size and variegated coloration **2** : a striped or sometimes blotched tabby cat

ti·ger-eye \'tī-gər-ˌī\ or **ti·ger's-eye** \-gərz-\ n (ca. 1891) : a usu. yellowish to grayish brown chatoyant stone that is much used for ornament and is a silicified crocidolite

tiger lily n (1824) : a common Asian garden lily (*Lilium lancifolium* syn. *L. tigrinum*) having nodding orange-colored flowers densely spotted with black; *also* : any of various lilies with similar flowers

tiger maple n (1952) : maple lumber having a distinct irregularly striped pattern and much used for furniture

tiger moth n (1816) : any of a family (Arctiidae) of stout-bodied moths usu. with broad striped or spotted wings

tiger salamander n (ca. 1909) : a large widely distributed No. American salamander (*Ambystoma tigrinum*) that is variably colored with contrasting blotches, spots, or bars

tiger lily

tiger shark n (ca. 1785) : a large gray or brown stocky-bodied requiem shark (*Galeocerdo cuvieri*) that is nearly cosmopolitan esp. in warm seas and can be dangerous to humans — see SHARK illustration

tiger shrimp n (1979) : a large shrimp (*Penaeus monodon*) of the Indian and Pacific oceans that is often farmed and widely sold as food

tiger swallowtail n (ca. 1890) : a large widely distributed swallowtail (*Papilio glaucus*) of eastern No. America that in the male is largely yellow with black margins and black stripes on the wings and in the female is usu. similarly marked in the north but is very often all or mostly black in the south; *also* : any of several closely related black and yellow swallowtails (as *P. rutulus* of western No. America)

¹tight \'tīt\ adj [alter. of earlier *thight* close set, dense, of Scand origin; akin to ON *thettr* tight; akin to MHG *dihte* thick, Skt *tanakti* it causes to coagulate] (1507) **1 a** : so close in structure as to prevent passage or escape (as of liquid, gas, or light) ⟨a ~ ship⟩ ⟨a ~ seal⟩ — compare LIGHTPROOF, WATERTIGHT **b** : fitting very close to the body ⟨~ jeans⟩; *also* : too snug ⟨~ shoes⟩ **c** (1) : closely packed : very full ⟨a ~ bale of hay⟩ (2) : barely allowing time for completion ⟨a ~ schedule⟩ ⟨~ deadlines⟩ **d** : having elements close together ⟨a ~ formation⟩ ⟨a ~ line of type⟩ **e** : allowing little or no room for free motion or movement ⟨a ~ connection⟩ ⟨a ~ crawl space⟩; *also* : having a small radius ⟨a ~ turn⟩ **2 a** : strongly fixed or held : SECURE ⟨a ~ jar lid⟩ ⟨a ~ grip on the ladder⟩ **b** (1) : not slack or loose : TAUT ⟨kept the reins ~⟩ ⟨a ~ knot⟩ ⟨a ~ drumhead⟩; *also* : marked by firmness and muscle tone ⟨a ~ stomach⟩ (2) : marked by unusual tension (as in the face or body) ⟨lips ~ with anger⟩ ⟨a family ~ with fear⟩ **3** *chiefly dial* **a** : CAPABLE, COMPETENT **b** : having a graceful or shapely form : COMELY **4 a** : difficult to cope with ⟨in a ~ spot financially⟩ **b** : relatively difficult to obtain ⟨money is ~ just now⟩; *also* : characterized by such difficulty ⟨a ~ job market⟩ **c** : not liberal in giving : STINGY ⟨~ with

a penny⟩ **5** : characterized by little difference in the relative positions of contestants with respect to final outcome : CLOSE ⟨a ~ race for mayor⟩ **6** : somewhat drunk **7 a** : characterized by firmness or strictness in control or application or in attention to details ⟨~ zoning codes⟩ ⟨~ security⟩ ⟨ran a ~ newsroom⟩ ⟨keeps a ~ hand on her investments⟩ **b** : marked by control or discipline in expression or style : having little or no extraneous matter ⟨~ writing⟩ **c** : characterized by a polished style and precise arrangements in music performance **8** : having a close personal or working relationship : INTIMATE ⟨in ~ with the boss⟩ **9** : being such that the subject fills the frame ⟨filming a ~ close-up⟩ — **tight·ly** adv — **tight·ness** n

²tight adv (1680) **1** : FAST, TIGHTLY, FIRMLY ⟨the door was shut ~⟩ **2** : in a sound manner : SOUNDLY ⟨sleep ~⟩

tight·en \'tī-t³n\ vb **tight·ened; tight·en·ing** \'tīt-niŋ, 'tī-t³n-iŋ\ vt (ca. 1727) : to make tight or tighter ~ vi : to become tight or tighter — **tight·en·er** \'tīt-nər, 'tī-t³n-ər\ n — **tighten one's belt** : to practice strict economy

tight end n (1962) : an offensive football end who lines up within two yards of the tackle

tight·fist·ed \'tīt-'fis-təd\ adj (1844) : reluctant to part with money — **tight·fist·ed·ness** \-nəs\ n

tight–knit \-'nit\ adj (1946) : closely integrated and bound in love or friendship ⟨a ~ family⟩

tight–lipped \-'lipt\ adj (1876) **1** : having the lips closed tight (as in determination) **2** : reluctant to speak : TACITURN

tight–mouthed \-'maùthd, -'maùtht\ adj (1926) : CLOSEMOUTHED

tight·rope \'tīt-ˌrōp\ n (1801) **1** : a rope or wire stretched taut for acrobats to perform on **2** : a dangerously precarious situation — usu. used in the phrase *walk a tightrope*

tights \'tīts\ n pl (ca. 1837) : a skintight garment covering the body from the neck down or from the waist down; *also, Brit* : PANTY HOSE

tight·wad \'tīt-ˌwäd\ n (1906) : a close or miserly person

tight·wire \-ˌwir\ n (1928) : a tightrope made of wire

ti·glon \'tī-ˌglän\ n [*tiger* + *lion*] (1942) : a hybrid between a male tiger and a female lion

ti·gon \'tī-ˌgän\ n [*tiger* + *lion*] (1926) : TIGLON

Ti·gre \'ti-(ˌ)grā, 'tē-; tē-'\ n (1878) : a Semitic language of northern Ethiopia

ti·gress \'tī-grəs\ n (1611) : a female tiger; *also* : a tigerish woman

Ti·gri·nya \tə-'grē-nyə\ n (1878) : a Semitic language of northern Ethiopia

tike var of TYKE

ti·ki \'tē-kē\ n [Maori & Marquesan, fr. *Tiki*, first man or creator of first man] (1777) : a wood or stone image of a Polynesian supernatural power

til \'til\ n [Hindi, fr. Skt *tila*] (1840) : SESAME

'til or **til** \'til\ var of ¹TILL 2, ²TILL

ti·la·pia \tə-'lä-pē-ə, -'lā-\ n [NL, genus name] (1849) : any of a genus (*Tilapia*) of African freshwater cichlid fishes often raised for food

til·bury \'til-ˌber-ē, -b(ə-)rē\ n, pl **-bur·ies** [*Tilbury*, 19th cent. Eng. coach builder] (1814) : a light 2-wheeled carriage

til·de \'til-də\ n [Sp, fr. ML *titulus* tittle] (ca. 1864) **1** : a mark ~ placed esp. over the letter *n* (as in Spanish *señor* sir) to denote the sound \nʸ\ or over vowels (as in Portuguese *irmã* sister) to indicate nasality **2** : the mark ~ used to indicate negation in logic and the geometric relation "is similar to" in mathematics

¹tile \'tī(ə)l\ n, often attrib [ME, fr. OE *tigele*, fr. L *tegula* tile; akin to L *tegere* to cover — more at THATCH] (bef. 12c) **1** *pl* **tiles** or **tile a** : a flat or curved piece of fired clay, stone, or concrete used esp. for roofs, floors, or walls and often for ornamental work **b** : a hollow or a semicircular and open earthenware or concrete piece used in constructing a drain **c** : a hollow building unit made of fired clay or of shale or gypsum **2** : TILING **3** : HAT; *esp* : a high silk hat **4** : a thin piece of resilient material (as cork, linoleum, or rubber) used esp. for covering floors or walls **5** : a thin piece resembling a ceramic tile that usu. bears a mark or letter and is used as a playing piece in a board game (as mahjongg) — **on the tiles** *Brit* : engaged in late-night carousing

²tile vt **tiled; til·ing** (14c) **1** : to cover with tiles **2** : to install drainage tile in — **til·er** n

tile·fish \'tī(ə)l-ˌfish\ n [*tile-* modif. of NL *Lopholatilus*] (1881) : any of various marine bony fishes (family Malacanthidae) used as food; *esp* : a large fish (*Lopholatilus chamaeleonticeps*) of deep waters of the Atlantic and Gulf of Mexico with a fleshy appendage on the head and yellow spots on the upper body and some of its fins

til·ing \'tī-liŋ\ n (15c) **1** : the action or work of one who tiles **2 a** : TILES **b** : a surface of tiles

¹till \t³l, təl, 'til\ prep [ME, fr. OE *til*; akin to ON *til* to, till, OE *til* good] (bef. 12c) **1** *chiefly Scot* : TO **2** : UNTIL

²till conj (12c) : UNTIL

³till \'til\ vt [ME *tilien, tillen*, fr. OE *tilian*; akin to OE *til* good, suitable, OHG *zil* goal] (13c) : to work by plowing, sowing, and raising crops : CULTIVATE — **till·able** \'ti-lə-bəl\ adj

⁴till \'til\ n [AF *tylle*] (15c) **1 a** : a box, drawer, or tray in a receptacle (as a cabinet or chest) used esp. for valuables **b** : a money drawer in a store or bank; *also* : CASH REGISTER **2 a** : the money contained in a till **b** : a supply of esp. ready money

⁵till \'til\ n [origin unknown] (1842) : unstratified glacial drift consisting of clay, sand, gravel, and boulders intermingled

till·age \'ti-lij\ n (15c) **1** : the operation of tilling land **2** : cultivated land

til·land·sia \tə-'lan(d)-zē-ə\ n [NL, fr. Elias *Tillands* †1693 Finn. botanist] (1759) : any of a large genus (*Tillandsia*) of chiefly epiphytic plants of the pineapple family native to tropical and subtropical America

¹til·ler \'ti-lər\ n [fr. (assumed) ME, fr. OE *telgor, telgra* twig, shoot; akin to OHG *zelga* twig, OIr *dlongaid* he splits] (bef. 12c) : STALK, SPROUT; *esp* : one from the base of a plant or from the axils of its lower leaves

²til·ler vi **til·lered; til·ler·ing** \'ti-lə-riŋ, 'til-riŋ\ *of a plant* : to put forth tillers

³till·er \'ti-lər\ n (13c) : one that tills : CULTIVATOR

⁴til·ler \'ti-lər\ n [ME *tiler* stock of a crossbow, fr. MF *telier*, lit., beam of a loom, fr. ML *telarium*, fr. L *tela* web — more at TOIL] (ca. 1625)

: a lever used to turn the rudder of a boat from side to side; *broadly* : a device or system that plays a part in steering something

til·ler·man \'ti-lər-mən\ *n* (ca. 1934) : one in charge of a tiller : STEERS-MAN

Til·sit \'til-sət\ *also* **Til·sit·er** \-sə-tər\ *n* [G *Tilsiter*, fr. *Tilsit* (now Sovetsk, Russia] (ca. 1932) : a semisoft porous light yellow cheese with a flavor that ranges from mild to sharp

¹**tilt** \'tilt\ *n* [ME *teld*, *telte* tent, canopy, fr. OE *teld*; akin to OHG *zelt* tent] (15c) : a canopy for a wagon, boat, or stall

²**tilt** *vt* (15c) : to cover or provide with a tilt

³**tilt** *n* [⁴*tilt*] (1511) **1 a** : a contest on horseback in which two combatants charging with lances or similar weapons try to unhorse each other : JOUST **b** : a tournament of tilts **2 a** : DISPUTE, CONTENTION **b** : SPEED — used in the phrase *full tilt* **3 a** : the act of tilting : the state or position of being tilted **b** : a sloping surface **c** : SLANT, BIAS ⟨a ~ toward military involvement⟩ **4** : any of various contests resembling or suggesting tilting with lances — **tilt** *adj*

⁴**tilt** *vb* [ME *tulten*, *tilten* to cause to fall; akin to Sw *tulta* to waddle] *vt* (1594) **1** : to cause to have an inclination **2 a** : to point or thrust in or as if in a tilt ⟨~ a lance⟩ **b** : to charge against ⟨~ an adversary⟩ ~ *vi* **1 a** : to move or shift so as to lean or incline : SLANT **b** : to incline, tend, or become drawn toward an opinion, course of action, or one side of a controversy **2 a** : to engage in a combat with lances : JOUST **b** : to make an impetuous attack ⟨~ at social evils⟩ — **tilt·able** \'til-tə-bəl\ *adj* — **tilt·er** *n*

tilth \'tilth\ *n* [ME, fr. OE, fr. *tilian* to till] (bef. 12c) **1** : cultivated land : TILLAGE **2** : the state of aggregation of a soil esp. in relation to its suitability for crop growth

tilt·me·ter \'tilt-ˌmē-tər\ *n* (1932) : an instrument to measure the tilting of the earth's surface

tilt·ro·tor \-ˌrō-tər\ *n* (1980) : an aircraft that has rotors at the end of each wing which can be oriented vertically for vertical takeoffs and landings, horizontally for forward flight, or to any position in between

tilt·yard \'tilt-ˌyärd\ *n* (1528) : a yard or place for tilting contests

tim·bal \'tim-bəl\ *n* [F *timbale*, fr. MF, alter. of *tamballe*, modif. of OSp *atabal*, fr. Ar *aṭ-ṭabl* the drum] (1680) : KETTLEDRUM

tim·bale \'tim-bəl; tim-'bäl, tam-\ *n* [F, lit., kettledrum] (1824) **1** : a creamy mixture (as of meat or vegetables) baked in a mold; *also* : the mold in which it is baked **2** : a small pastry shell filled with a cooked timbale mixture

¹**tim·ber** \'tim-bər\ *n* [ME, fr. OE, building, wood; akin to OHG *zimbar* wood, room, Gk *demein* to build, *domos* course of stones or bricks] (bef. 12c) **1 a** : growing trees or their wood **b** — used interjectionally to warn of a falling tree **2** : wood suitable for building or for carpentry **3** : MATERIAL, STUFF; *esp* : personal qualification for a particular position or status **4 a** : a large squared or dressed piece of wood ready for use or forming part of a structure **b** *Brit* : LUMBER 2a **c** : a curving frame branching outward from the keel of a ship and bending upward in a vertical direction that is usu. composed of several pieces united : RIB — **tim·ber** *adj*

²**timber** *vt* **tim·bered; tim·ber·ing** \-b(ə-)riŋ\ (bef. 12c) : to frame, cover, or support with timbers

tim·ber·doo·dle \ˌtim-bər-'dü-d°l\ *n* [¹*timber* + *doodle* cock] (1856) : the American woodcock

tim·bered \'tim-bərd\ *adj* (15c) **1** : having walls framed by exposed timbers **2** : having a specified structure or constitution **3** : covered with growing timber : WOODED

tim·ber·head \'tim-bər-ˌhed\ *n* (1794) **1** : the top end of a ship's timber used above the gunwale (as for belaying ropes) **2** : a bollard bolted to the deck where the end of a timber would come

timber hitch *n* (ca. 1815) : a knot used to secure a line to a log or spar — see KNOT illustration

tim·ber·ing \'tim-b(ə-)riŋ\ *n* (15c) : a set or arrangement of timbers

tim·ber·land \-bər-ˌland\ *n* (1654) : wooded land esp. with marketable timber

tim·ber·line \-ˌlīn\ *n* (1867) : the upper limit of arboreal growth in mountains or high latitudes — called also *tree line*

tim·ber·man \-mən\ *n* (1889) : LUMBERMAN

timber rattlesnake *n* (1895) : a widely distributed rattlesnake (*Crotalus horridus*) of the eastern U.S.

timber wolf *n* (1860) : GRAY WOLF

tim·ber·work \'tim-bər-ˌwərk\ *n* (14c) : timber construction

tim·bre *also* **tim·ber** \'tam-bər, 'tim-; 'tam(br³)-\ *n* [F, fr. MF, bell struck by a hammer, fr. OF, drum, fr. MGk *tymbanon* kettledrum, fr. Gk *tympanon* — more at TYMPANUM] (1849) : the quality given to a sound by its overtones: as **a** : the resonance by which the ear recognizes and identifies a voiced speech sound **b** : the quality of tone distinctive of a particular singing voice or musical instrument — **tim·bral** \'tam-brəl, 'tim-\ *adj*

tim·brel \'tim-brəl\ *n* [dim. of obs. E *timbre* tambourine, fr. ME, fr. OF, drum] (ca. 1520) : a small hand drum or tambourine — **tim·brelled** \-brəld\ *adj*

¹**time** \'tīm\ *n* [ME, fr. OE *tīma*; akin to ON *tīmi* time, OE *tīd* — more at TIDE] (bef. 12c) **1 a** : the measured or measurable period during which an action, process, or condition exists or continues : DURATION **b** : a nonspatial continuum that is measured in terms of events which succeed one another from past through present to future **c** : LEISURE ⟨~ for reading⟩ **2** : the point or period when something occurs : OCCASION **3 a** : an appointed, fixed, or customary moment or hour for something to happen, begin, or end ⟨arrived ahead of ~⟩ **b** : an opportune or suitable moment ⟨decided it was ~ to retire⟩ — often used in the phrase *about time* ⟨about ~ for a change⟩ **4 a** : an historical period : AGE **b** : a division of geologic chronology **c** : conditions at present or at some specified period — usu. used in pl. ⟨~s are hard⟩ ⟨move with the ~s⟩ **d** : the present time ⟨issues of the ~⟩ **5 a** : LIFETIME **b** : a period of apprenticeship **c** : a term of military service **d** : a prison sentence **6** : SEASON ⟨very hot for this ~ of year⟩ **7 a** : rate of speed : TEMPO **b** : the grouping of the beats of music : RHYTHM **8 a** : a moment, hour, day, or year as indicated by a clock or calendar ⟨what ~ is it⟩ **b** : any of various systems (as sidereal or solar) of reckoning time **9 a** : one of a series of recurring instances or repeated actions ⟨you've been told many ~s⟩ **b** *pl* (1) : added or accumulated quantities or instances ⟨five ~s greater⟩ (2) : equal fractional parts of which an indicated number equal a comparatively

greater quantity ⟨seven ~s smaller⟩ ⟨three ~s closer⟩ **c** : TURN ⟨three ~s at bat⟩ **10** : finite as contrasted with infinite duration **11** : a person's experience during a specified period or on a particular occasion ⟨a good ~⟩ ⟨a hard ~⟩ **12 a** : the hours or days required to be occupied by one's work ⟨make up ~⟩ ⟨on company ~⟩ **b** : an hourly pay rate ⟨straight ~⟩ **c** : wages paid at discharge or resignation ⟨pick up your ~ and get out⟩ **13 a** : the playing time of a game **b** : TIME-OUT **14** : a period during which something is used or available for use ⟨computer ~⟩ — **at the same time** : NEVERTHELESS, YET ⟨slick and *at the same time* strangely unprofessional —Gerald Weaks⟩ — **at times** : at intervals : OCCASIONALLY — **for the time being** : for the present — **from time to time** : once in a while : OCCASIONALLY — **in no time** : very quickly or soon — **in time** **1** : sufficiently early **2** : EVENTUALLY **3** : in correct tempo ⟨learn to play *in time*⟩ — **on time** **1 a** : at the appointed time **b** : on schedule **2** : on the installment plan — **time and again** : FREQUENTLY, REPEATEDLY

²**time** *vb* **timed; tim·ing** *vt* (14c) **1 a** : to arrange or set the time of : SCHEDULE **b** : to regulate (a watch) to keep correct time **2** : to set the tempo, speed, or duration of ⟨timed his leap perfectly —Neil Amdur⟩ **3** : to cause to keep time with something **4** : to determine or record the time, duration, or rate of ⟨~ a horse⟩ **5** : to dispose (as a mechanical part) so that an action occurs at a desired instant or in a desired way ~ *vi* : to keep or beat time

³**time** *adj* (ca. 1711) **1** : of or relating to time **b** : recording time **2** : timed to ignite or explode at a specific moment ⟨a ~ bomb⟩ **3 a** : payable on a specified future day or a certain length of time after presentation for acceptance ⟨a ~ draft⟩ ⟨~ deposits⟩ **b** : based on installment payments ⟨a ~ sale⟩

time and a half *n* (1888) : payment for work (as overtime or holiday work) at one and a half times the worker's regular wage rate

time bomb *n* (1893) **1** : a bomb so made as to explode at a predetermined time **2** : something with a potentially dangerous or detrimental delayed reaction

time capsule *n* (1938) **1** : a container holding historical records or objects representative of current culture that is deposited (as in a cornerstone) for preservation until discovery by some future age **2** : something resembling a time capsule ⟨sunken vessels are archaeological *time capsules* —Philip Trupp⟩

time card *n* (ca. 1891) : a card used with a time clock to record an employee's starting and quitting times each day or on each job

time chart *n* (ca. 1830) **1** : a chart showing the standard times in various parts of the world with reference to a specified time at a specified place **2** : TIME LINE 1

time clock *n* (1887) : a clock that stamps starting and quitting times on an employee's time card

time–con·sum·ing \'tīm-kən-ˌsü-miŋ\ *adj* (1890) **1** : using or taking up a great deal of time ⟨~ chores⟩ **2** : wasteful of time ⟨~ tactics⟩

timed \'tīmd\ *adj* (ca. 1760) **1** : made to occur at or in a set time ⟨a ~ explosion⟩ **2** : done or taking place at a time of a specified sort ⟨an ill-*timed* arrival⟩

time dilation *n* (1934) : a slowing of time in accordance with the theory of relativity that occurs in a system in motion relative to an outside observer and that becomes apparent esp. as the speed of the system approaches that of light — called also *time dilatation*

timed–re·lease \'tīmd-ri-'lēs\ *or* **time–re·lease** \'tīm-\ *adj* (1966) : consisting of or containing a drug that is released in small amounts over time (as by dissolution of a coating) usu. in the gastrointestinal tract ⟨~ capsules⟩

time exposure *n* (1893) : exposure of a photographic film for a definite time usu. of more than one half second; *also* : a photograph taken by such exposure

time frame *n* (1964) : a period of time esp. with respect to some action or project

time–hon·ored \'tīm-ˌä-nərd\ *adj* (1593) : honored because of age or long usage ⟨~ traditions⟩

time immemorial *n* (1602) **1** : a time antedating a period legally fixed as the basis for a custom or right **2** : time so long past as to be indefinite in history or tradition — called also *time out of mind*

time·keep·er \'tīm-ˌkē-pər\ *n* (1686) **1** : TIMEPIECE **2** : a clerk who keeps records of the time worked by employees **3** : a person appointed to mark and announce the time in an athletic game or contest — **time·keep·ing** \-piŋ\ *n*

time killer *n* (1751) **1** : a person with free time **2** : something that passes the time : DIVERSION

time lag *n* (1892) : an interval of time between two related phenomena (as a cause and its effect)

time–lapse \'tīm-ˌlaps\ *adj* (1927) : of, relating to, or constituting a motion picture made so that when projected a slow action (as the opening of a flower bud) appears to be speeded up

time·less \'tīm-ləs\ *adj* (ca. 1560) **1** *archaic* : PREMATURE, UNTIMELY **2 a** : having no beginning or end : ETERNAL **b** : not restricted to a particular time or date ⟨the ~ themes of love, solitude, joy, and nature —Writer⟩ **3** : not affected by time : AGELESS — **time·less·ly** *adv* — **time·less·ness** *n*

time line *n* (1951) **1** : a table listing important events for successive years within a particular historical period **2** *usu* **time-line** \'tīm-ˌlīn\ : a schedule of events and procedures : TIMETABLE 2

time lock *n* (ca. 1871) : a lock controlled by clockwork to prevent its being opened before a set time

¹**time·ly** \'tīm-lē\ *adv* (bef. 12c) **1** *archaic* : EARLY, SOON **2** : in time : OPPORTUNELY ⟨the question was not . . . ~ raised in the state court —W. O. Douglas⟩

²**timely** *adj* **time·li·er; -est** (13c) **1** : coming early or at the right time : OPPORTUNE **2** : appropriate or adapted to the times or the occasion ⟨a ~ book⟩ — **time·li·ness** *n*

time machine *n* (1895) : a hypothetical device that permits travel into the past and future

---

\ə\ abut \ᵊ\ kitten, F table \ər\ further \a\ ash \ā\ ace \ä\ mop, mar \au̇\ out \ch\ chin \e\ bet \ē\ easy \g\ go \i\ hit \ī\ ice \j\ job \ŋ\ sing \ō\ go \ȯ\ law \ȯi\ boy \th\ thin \t̲h̲\ the \ü\ loot \u̇\ foot \y\ yet \zh\ vision \a̱, k̲, ⁿ, œ, œ̄, ᵫ, ᵫ̄, ᵊ\ see Guide to Pronunciation

time-of-flight \'tīm-ə(v)-'flīt\ *adj* (1945) : of, relating to, being, or done with an instrument (as a mass spectrometer) that separates particles (as ions) according to the time required for them to traverse a tube of a certain length
time-ous \'tī-məs\ *adj* (ca. 1520) *chiefly Brit* : TIMELY — **time-ous-ly** *adv*
time-out \'tī-'aůt\ *n* (1926) : a brief suspension of activity : BREAK; *esp* : a suspension of play in an athletic game
time out of mind (15c) : TIME IMMEMORIAL 2
time-piece \'tīm-,pēs\ *n* (1765) : a device (as a clock or watch) to measure or show progress of time; *esp* : one that does not chime
time-pleas-er \-,plē-zər\ *n* (1601) *obs* : TIMESERVER
tim-er \'tī-mər\ *n* (1841) : one that times: as **a** : TIMEPIECE; *esp* : a stopwatch for timing races **b** : TIMEKEEPER **c** : a device (as a clock) that indicates by a sound the end of an interval of time or that starts or stops a device at predetermined times
time reversal *n* (1955) : a formal operation in mathematical physics that reverses the order in which a sequence of events occurs
times \'tīmz\ *prep* (14c) : multiplied by ⟨two ∼ two is four⟩
time-sav-ing \'tīm-,sā-viŋ\ *adj* (1865) : intended or serving to expedite something ⟨∼ kitchen appliances⟩ — **time-sav-er** \-,sā-vər\ *n*
time-scale \-,skā(ə)l\ *n* (1890) : an arrangement of events used as a measure of the relative or absolute duration or antiquity of a period of history or geologic or cosmic time
time series *n* (1919) : a set of data collected sequentially usu. at fixed intervals of time
time-serv-er \-,sər-vər\ *n* (1584) : a person whose behavior is adjusted to the pattern of the times or to please superiors : TEMPORIZER
¹**time-serv-ing** \-,viŋ\ *n* (1621) : the behavior or practice of a timeserver
²**timeserving** *adj* (1630) : marked by or revealing a lack of independence or integrity ⟨a mean, ∼ little man, grovelling odiously before the wealthy people —Peter Forster⟩
time-shar-ing \'tīm-,sher-iŋ, -,shar-\ *n* (1953) **1** : simultaneous use of a central computer by many users at remote locations **2** *or* **time-share** \-,sher, -,shar\ : joint ownership or rental of a vacation lodging (as a condominium) by several persons with each occupying the premises in turn for short periods — **time-share** *vt*
time sheet *n* (ca. 1909) **1** : a sheet for recording the time of arrival and departure of workers and for recording the amount of time spent on each job **2** : a sheet for summarizing hours worked by each worker during a pay period
time signature *n* (1875) : a sign used in music to indicate meter and usu. written as a fraction with the bottom number indicating the kind of note used as a unit of time and the top number indicating the number of units in each measure
times sign *n* (1948) : the symbol × used to indicate multiplication
time stamp *n* (1892) : a device for recording the date and time of day that letters or papers are received or sent out — **time-stamp** *vt*
time-ta-ble \'tīm-,tā-bəl\ *n* (1838) **1** : a table of departure and arrival times of trains, buses, or airplanes **2** : a schedule showing a planned order or sequence **b** : PROGRAM 3 — **time-table** *vt*
time-test-ed \-,tes-təd\ *adj* (1930) : having effectiveness that has been proved over a long period of time ⟨∼ methods⟩
time trial *n* (ca. 1949) : a competitive event (as in auto racing) in which individuals are successively timed over a set course or distance
time warp *n* (1954) : an anomaly, discontinuity, or suspension held to occur in the progress of time
time-work \'tīm-,wərk\ *n* (1829) : work paid for at a standard rate for the hour or the day — **time-work-er** \-,wər-kər\ *n*
time-worn \-,wōrn, -,wȯrn\ *adj* (1729) **1** : worn or impaired by time ⟨∼ mansions⟩ **2 a** : AGE-OLD, ANCIENT ⟨∼ procedures⟩ **b** : HACKNEYED, STALE ⟨a ∼ joke⟩
time zone *n* (1892) : a geographical region within which the same standard time is used

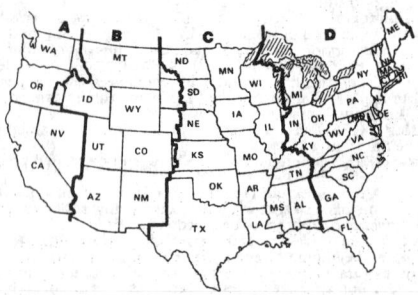

time zones in the conterminous United States: *A* Pacific time, *B* mountain time, *C* central time, *D* eastern time

tim-id \'ti-məd\ *adj* [L *timidus*, fr. *timēre* to fear] (1549) **1** : lacking in courage or self-confidence ⟨a ∼ person⟩ **2** : lacking in boldness or determination ⟨a ∼ policy⟩ — **ti-mid-i-ty** \tə-'mi-də-tē\ *n* — **tim-id-ly** \'ti-məd-lē\ *adv* — **tim-id-ness** *n*
tim-ing \'tī-miŋ\ *n* (1597) **1** : selection or the ability to select for maximum effect of the precise moment for beginning or doing something ⟨haven't got my ∼ down⟩ **2** : observation and recording (as by a stopwatch) of the elapsed time of an act, action, or process
ti-moc-ra-cy \tī-'mä-krə-sē\ *n* [MF *tymocracie*, fr. ML *timocratia*, fr. Gk *timokratia*, fr. *timē* price, value, honor + *-kratia* -cracy; akin to Gk *tiein* to honor, Skt *cāyati* he respects] (1586) **1** : government in which a certain amount of property is necessary for office **2** : government in which love of honor is the ruling principle — **ti-mo-crat-ic** \,tī-mə-'kra-tik\ *or* **ti-mo-crat-i-cal** \-i-kəl\ *adj*
ti-mo-lol \'tī-mə-,lȯl, -,lōl\ *n* [*tim-* (of unknown origin) + *-olol* (as in *propranolol*)] (1973) : a beta-blocker $C_{13}H_{24}N_4O_3S$ used in the form of

its maleate salt to treat glaucoma and to reduce the risk of second heart attacks
tim-o-rous \'ti-mə-rəs, 'tim-rəs\ *adj* [ME, fr. MF *timoureus*, fr. ML *timorosus*, fr. L *timor* fear, fr. *timēre* to fear] (15c) **1** : of a timid disposition : FEARFUL **2** : expressing or suggesting timidity ⟨proceed with doubtful and ∼ steps —Edward Gibbon⟩ — **tim-o-rous-ly** *adv* — **tim-o-rous-ness** *n*
tim-o-thy \'ti-mə-thē\ *n* [prob. after *Timothy* Hanson, 18th cent. Am. farmer said to have introduced it from New England to the southern states] (1747) : a European grass (*Phleum pratense*) that has long cylindrical spikes and is widely grown for hay
Tim-o-thy \'ti-mə-thē\ *n* [L *Timotheus*, fr. Gk *Timotheos*] **1** : a disciple of the apostle Paul **2** : either of two letters written with regard to pastoral care in the early Church and included as books in the New Testament — see BIBLE table
tim-pa-ni \'tim-pə-nē\ *n pl but sing or pl in constr* [It, pl. of *timpano* kettledrum, fr. L *tympanum* drum — more at TYMPANUM] (ca. 1854) : a set of two or more kettledrums played by one performer in an orchestra or band
tim-pa-nist \-nist\ *n* (1906) : one who plays the timpani
¹**tin** \'tin\ *n* [ME, fr. OE; akin to OHG *zin* tin] (bef. 12c) **1** : a soft faintly bluish white lustrous low-melting metallic element that is malleable and ductile at ordinary temperatures and that is used as a protective coating, in tinfoil, and in soft solders and alloys — see ELEMENT table **2 a** : a box, can, pan, vessel, or a sheet made of tinplate; *broadly* : such a container of any metal (as aluminum) **b** : a metal container and its contents ⟨a ∼ of tomatoes⟩ — **tin** *adj* — **tin-ful** \-,fůl\ *n*
²**tin** *vt* **tinned; tin-ning** (14c) **1** : to cover or plate with tin or a tin alloy **2** : to put up or pack in tins : CAN
tin-a-mou \'tin-ə-,mü\ *n* [F, fr. Carib *tinamu*] (ca. 1783) : any of a family (Tinamidae) of So. and Central American game birds that have a deeply keeled sternum and a rudimentary tail and that produce eggs with a surface resembling enamel
tin can *n* (1770) **1** : a can made of tinplate; *broadly* : CAN 1c **2** *slang* : DESTROYER 2
¹**tinct** \'tiŋ(k)t\ *adj* [L *tinctus*, pp.] (1579) : COLORED, TINGED
²**tinct** *n* (1602) : TINCTURE, TINGE
tinc-to-ri-al \tiŋ(k)-'tōr-ē-əl, -'tȯr-\ *adj* [L *tinctorius*, fr. *tingere* to tinge] (1655) : of or relating to colors or to dyeing or staining; *also* : imparting color — **tinc-to-ri-al-ly** \-ē-ə-lē\ *adv*
¹**tinc-ture** \'tiŋ(k)-chər\ *n* [ME, fr. L *tinctura* act of dyeing, fr. *tinctus*, pp. of *tingere* to tinge] (14c) **1 a** *archaic* : a substance that colors, dyes, or stains **b** : COLOR, TINT **2 a** : a characteristic quality : CAST **b** : a slight admixture : TRACE **3** *obs* : an active principle or extract **4** : a heraldic metal, color, or fur **5** : a solution of a medicinal substance in an alcoholic menstruum
²**tincture** *vt* **tinc-tured; tinc-tur-ing** \'tiŋ(k)-chə-riŋ, -shriŋ\ (1616) **1** : to tint or stain with a color : TINGE **2 a** : to infuse or instill with a property or entity : IMPREGNATE **b** : to imbue with a quality : AFFECT ⟨writing *tinctured* with wit and wisdom⟩
tin-der \'tin-dər\ *n* [ME, fr. OE *tynder*; akin to OHG *zuntra* tinder, OE *tendan* to kindle] (bef. 12c) **1** : a very flammable substance adaptable for use as kindling **2** : something that serves to incite or inflame
tin-der-box \'tin-dər-,bäks\ *n* (1530) **1 a** : a metal box for holding tinder and usu. a flint and steel for striking a spark **b** : a highly inflammable object or place **2** : a potentially explosive place or situation
¹**tine** \'tīn\ *n* [ME *tind*, fr. OE; akin to OHG *zint* point, tine] (bef. 12c) **1** : a slender pointed projecting part : PRONG **2** : a pointed branch of an antler — **tined** \'tīnd\ *adj*
²**tine** *vb* **tined** \'tīnd\ *or* **tint** \'tint\; **tin-ing** \'tī-niŋ\ [ME, of Scand origin; akin to ON *tȳna* to lose, destroy, *tjōn* injury, loss — more at TEEN] *vt* (13c) *dial Brit* : LOSE ∼ *vi, dial Brit* : to become lost
tin-ea \'ti-nē-ə\ *n* [ME, fr. ML, fr. L, worm, moth] (14c) : any of several fungal diseases of the skin; *esp* : RINGWORM — **tin-e-al** \-nē-əl\ *adj*
tinea cru-ris \-'krůr-əs\ *n* [NL, lit., tinea of the leg] (ca. 1923) : a fungal infection involving esp. the groin and perineum
tin ear *n* (1935) : a deafened or insensitive ear
tin-foil \'tin-,fȯil\ *n* (15c) : a paper-thin metal sheeting usu. of aluminum or tin-lead alloy
ting *n* [*ting*, vb., fr. ME *tingen*, of imit. origin] (1602) : a high-pitched sound like that made by a light stroke on a crystal goblet — **ting** *vi*
¹**tinge** \'tinj\ *vt* **tinged; tinge-ing** *or* **ting-ing** \'tin-jiŋ\ [ME, fr. L *tingere* to dip, moisten, tinge; akin to Gk *tengein* to moisten and prob. to OHG *dunkōn* to dip] (15c) **1 a** : to color with a slight shade or stain : TINT **b** : to affect or modify with a slight odor or taste **2** : to affect or modify in character
²**tinge** *n* (1752) **1** : a slight staining or suffusing shade or color **2** : an affective or modifying property or influence : TOUCH
tin-gle \'tiŋ-gəl\ *vi* **tin-gled; tin-gling** \-g(ə-)liŋ\ [ME, alter. of *tinklen* to tinkle, tingle] (14c) **1** : to feel a ringing, stinging, prickling, or thrilling sensation **b** : to cause such a sensation **2** : TINKLE — **tingle** *n* —**tin-gling-ly** \-g(ə-)liŋ-lē\ *adv* — **tin-gly** \-g(ə-)lē\ *adj*
tin hat *n* (1903) : a metal helmet
tin-horn \'tin-,hȯrn\ *n* (1885) : one (as a gambler) who pretends to have money, ability, or influence
¹**tin-ker** \'tiŋ-kər\ *n* [ME *tinkere*] (14c) **1 a** : a usu. itinerant mender of household utensils **b** : an unskillful mender : BUNGLER **2** *chiefly Irish* : GYPSY
²**tinker** *vb* **tin-kered; tin-ker-ing** \-k(ə-)riŋ\ *vi* (1592) : to work in the manner of a tinker; *esp* : to repair, adjust, or work with something in an unskilled or experimental manner : FIDDLE ⟨∼ *vt* : to repair, adjust, or experiment with — **tin-ker-er** \-kər-ər\ *n*
tinker's damn *also* **tinker's dam** \-'dam\ *n* [prob. fr. the tinkers' reputation for blasphemy] (1839) : a minimum amount or degree (as of care) ⟨didn't give a *tinker's damn* about poetry —James Blish⟩
Tin-ker-toy \'tiŋ-kər-,tȯi\ *trademark* — used for a construction toy of fitting parts
¹**tin-kle** \'tiŋ-kəl\ *vb* **tin-kled; tin-kling** \-k(ə-)liŋ\ [ME, freq. of *tinken* to tinkle, of imit. origin] *vi* (15c) **1** : to make or emit a tinkle or a sound suggestive of a tinkle **2** : URINATE ∼ *vt* **1** : to sound or make known (the time) by a tinkle **2 a** : to cause to make a tinkle **b** : to produce by tinkling ⟨∼ a tune⟩

²**tinkle** n (1725) **1** : a jingling effect in verse or prose **2** : a series of short high ringing or clinking sounds

tin·kly \'tiŋ-k(ə-)lē\ adj (1892) : that tinkles : TINKLING

tin liz·zie \-'li-zē\ n [fr. *Tin Lizzie*, nickname for the Model T Ford automobile] (1915) : a small inexpensive early automobile

tin·ner \'ti-nər\ n (1512) **1** : a tin miner **2** : TINSMITH

tin·ni·tus \'ti-nə-təs, tə-'nī-təs\ n [L, ringing, tinnitus, fr. *tinnīre* to ring, of imit. origin] (1843) : a sensation of noise (as a ringing or roaring) that is caused by a bodily condition (as a disturbance of the auditory nerve or wax in the ear) and can usu. be heard only by the one affected

tin·ny \'ti-nē\ adj **tin·ni·er; -est** (1552) **1** : of, abounding in, or yielding tin **2 a** : resembling tin **b** : LIGHT, CHEAP **3** : thin in tone ⟨a ~ voice⟩ — **tin·ni·ly** \'ti-nᵊl-ē\ adv — **tin·ni·ness** \'ti-nē-nəs\ n

Tin Pan Alley n (1908) : a district that is a center for composers and publishers of popular music; also : the body of such composers and publishers

tin–plate \'tin-ˌplāt\ n (1677) : thin sheet iron or steel coated with tin

tin–plate vt (1890) : to plate or coat (as a metal sheet) with tin

tin–pot \'tin-ˌpät\ adj (1838) : SMALL-TIME

¹**tin·sel** \'tin(t)-səl also 'tin-zəl\ n [MF *estincelle, estancele, etincelle* spark, glitter, spangle — more at STENCIL] (1538) **1** : a thread, strip, or sheet of metal, paper, or plastic used to produce a glittering and sparkling appearance in fabrics, yarns, or decorations **2** : something superficially attractive or glamorous but of little real worth ⟨disfigured by no gaudy ~ of rhetoric or declamation —Thomas Jefferson⟩

²**tinsel** adj (1575) **1** : made of or covered with tinsel **2 a** : cheaply gaudy : TAWDRY **b** : SPECIOUS ⟨~ promises⟩

³**tinsel** vt **tin·seled** or **tin·selled; tin·sel·ing** or **tin·sel·ling** \'tin(t)-s(ə-)liŋ also 'tin-zə-liŋ\ (1594) **1** : to interweave, overlay, or adorn with or as if with tinsel **2** : to impart a specious brightness to

tin·sel·ly \'tin(t)-s(ə-)lē also 'tin-zə-lē\ adj (1811) : TINSEL

tin·smith \'tin-ˌsmith\ n (1812) : a worker who makes or repairs things of sheet metal (as tinplate) — **tin·smith·ing** \-ˌsmi-thiŋ\ n

tin·stone \'tin-ˌstōn\ n (1602) : CASSITERITE

¹**tint** \'tint\ n [alter. of earlier *tinct*, fr. L *tinctus* act of dyeing, fr. *tingere* to tinge] (1717) **1 a** : a usu. slight or pale coloration : HUE **b** : any of various lighter or darker shades of a color : TINGE **2** : a variation of a color produced by adding white to it and characterized by a low saturation with relatively high lightness **3** : a usu. slight modifying quality or characteristic : TOUCH **4** : a shaded effect in engraving produced by fine parallel lines close together **5** : a panel of light color serving as background **6** : dye for the hair — **tint·er** n

²**tint** vt (1791) : to impart or apply a tint to : COLOR

tint·ing n (ca. 1841) **1** : the act or process of one that tints **2** : the engraved or colored tint produced by tinting

tin·tin·nab·u·lary \ˌtin-tə-'na-byə-ˌler-ē\ adj [L *tintinnabulum* bell] (1787) : of, relating to, or characterized by bells or their sounds

tin·tin·nab·u·la·tion \ˌtin-tə-ˌna-byə-'lā-shən\ n [L *tintinnabulum* bell, fr. *tintinnāre* to ring, jingle, fr. *tinnīre*] (1831) **1** : the ringing or sounding of bells **2** : a jingling or tinkling sound as if of bells

tint·less \'tint-ləs\ adj (1789) archaic : having no tints : lacking color

tin·type \-ˌtīp\ n (1864) : FERROTYPE 1

tin·ware \'tin-ˌwar, -ˌwer\ n (1758) : articles and esp. utensils made of tinplate

tin·work \-ˌwərk\ n (ca. 1934) : work in tin

ti·ny \'tī-nē\ adj **ti·ni·er; -est** [alter. of ME *tine*] (1598) : very small or diminutive : MINUTE syn see SMALL — **ti·ni·ly** \'tī-nᵊl-ē\ adv — **ti·ni·ness** \'tī-nē-nəs\ n

¹**tip** \'tip\ vb **tipped; tip·ping** [ME] vt (14c) **1** : OVERTURN, UPSET — usu. used with *over* **2 a** : CANT, TILT **b** : to raise and tilt forward in salute ⟨*tipped* his hat⟩ ~ vi **1** : to become tipped : TOPPLE **2** : LEAN, SLANT — **tip the scales 1** : to register weight ⟨*tips the scales* at 285 pounds⟩ **2** : to shift the balance of power or influence ⟨*tipped the scales* in favor of a declaration of war —S. F. Bemis⟩

²**tip** n (1673) **1** : the act or an instance of tipping : TILT **2** *chiefly Brit* : a place for depositing something (as rubbish) by dumping

³**tip** vt **tipped; tip·ping** [ME *tipped* having a tip, fr. ⁴*tip*] (14c) **1 a** : to furnish with a tip **b** (1) : to cover or adorn the tip of (2) : to blend (furs) for improved appearance by brushing the tips of the hair with dye **2** : to affix (an insert) in a book — often used with *in* **3** : to remove the ends of ⟨~ raspberries⟩

⁴**tip** n [ME; akin to MHG *zipf* tip, OE *tæppa* tap — more at TAP] (15c) **1** : the usu. pointed end of something **2** : a small piece or part serving as an end, cap, or point — **tipped** \'tipt\ adj — **on the tip of one's tongue 1** : about to be uttered ⟨it was *on the tip of my tongue* to tell him exactly what I thought⟩ **2** : just eluding recall

⁵**tip** n [ME *tippe*; akin to LG *tippen* to tap] (15c) : a light touch or blow

⁶**tip** vb **tipped; tip·ping** vt (1567) **1** : to strike lightly : TAP **2** : to give (a baseball) a glancing blow ~ vi : TIPTOE

⁷**tip** n [origin unknown] (1567) **1** : a piece of advice or expert or authoritative information **2** : a piece of advance or confidential information given by one thought to have access to special or inside sources

⁸**tip** vt **tipped; tip·ping** (1883) **1** : to impart a piece of information or advice about or to — often used with *off* **2** *chiefly Brit* : to mention as a likely candidate, prospective winner, or profitable investment : TOUT **4** — **tip one's hand** also **tip one's mitt 1** : to declare one's intentions or reveal one's opinions or resources ⟨the Justice Department wouldn't *tip its hand* by saying what its next move . . . would be —*Newsweek*⟩

⁹**tip** vb **tipped; tip·ping** [perh. fr. ⁵*tip*] vt (ca. 1610) **1** : GIVE, PRESENT **2** : to give a gratuity to ~ vi : to bestow a gratuity

¹⁰**tip** n (1755) : a gift or a sum of money tendered for a service performed or anticipated : GRATUITY

tip–cart \'tip-ˌkärt\ n (ca. 1877) : a cart whose body can be tipped on the frame to empty its contents

tip–cat \-ˌkat\ n [⁶*tip*] (1676) : a game in which one player using a bat strikes lightly a tapered wooden peg and as it flies up strikes it again to drive it as far as possible while fielders try to recover it; also : the peg used in this game

ti·pi \'tē-(ˌ)pē\ var of TEPEE

tip–in \'tip-ˌin\ n [⁶*tip*] (1948) : a goal in basketball made by deflecting a rebound into the basket with the fingertips

¹**tip–off** \'tip-ˌof\ n [⁸*tip*] (1901) **1** : WARNING, TIP **2** : a telltale sign

²**tip–off** n [⁶*tip*] (1922) : the act or an instance of putting the ball in play in basketball by a jump ball

tip of the iceberg [fr. an iceberg being mostly below the surface] (1969) : the earliest, most obvious, or most superficial manifestation of some phenomenon

tip·per \'ti-pər\ n (1819) : one that tips

tip·pet \'ti-pət\ n [ME *tipet*] (14c) **1** : a long hanging end of cloth attached to a sleeve, cap, or hood **2** : a shoulder cape of fur or cloth often with hanging ends **3** : a long black scarf worn over the robe by Anglican clergymen during morning and evening prayer

¹**tip·ple** \'ti-pəl\ vb **tip·pled; tip·pling** \-p(ə-)liŋ\ [back-formation fr. obs. *tippler* barkeeper] vi (1560) **1** : to drink liquor esp. by habit or to excess ~ vt : to drink (liquor) esp. continuously in small amounts — **tip·pler** \-p(ə-)lər\ n

²**tipple** n (1581) : DRINK 1, 2

³**tipple** n [E dial. *tipple* to tip over, freq. of E ¹*tip*] (1880) **1** : a place where or an apparatus by which cars (as for coal) are loaded or emptied **2** : a coal-screening plant

tip·py \'ti-pē\ adj **tip·pi·er; -est** (1886) : liable to tip ⟨a ~ boat⟩

tip·staff \'tip-ˌstaf\ n, pl **tip·staves** \-ˌstavz, -ˌstāvz\ [obs. *tipstaff* staff tipped with metal] (1535) : an officer (as a constable or bailiff) who bears a staff

tip·ster \'tip-stər\ n (1862) : one who gives or sells tips esp. for gambling or speculation

tip·sy \'tip-sē\ adj **tip·si·er; -est** [¹*tip* + *-sy* (as in *tricksy*)] (1577) **1** : unsteady, staggering, or foolish from the effects of liquor : FUDDLED **2** : UNSTEADY, ASKEW ⟨a ~ angle⟩ — **tip·si·ly** \-sə-lē\ adv — **tip·si·ness** \-sē-nəs\ n

¹**tip·toe** \'tip-ˌtō, -'tō\ n (14c) : the position of being balanced on the balls of the feet and toes with the heels raised — usu. used with *on*; also : the ends of the toes — **on tiptoe 1** : ALERT, AROUSED ⟨the contest of skill that puts one *on tiptoe* to win —*Deerfield (Wisc.) Independent*⟩

²**tiptoe** adv (1592) : on or as if on tiptoe

³**tiptoe** adj (1593) **1** : standing or walking on or as if on tiptoe **2** : CAUTIOUS, STEALTHY

⁴**tiptoe** vi **tip·toed; tip·toe·ing** (ca. 1661) **1** : to stand or raise oneself on tiptoe **2** : to walk or proceed quietly or cautiously on or as if on tiptoe

¹**tip–top** \'tip-ˌtäp, -ˌtäp\ n [⁴*tip* + *top*] (1702) : the highest point

²**tip–top** adj (1722) : EXCELLENT, FIRST-RATE ⟨~ working conditions⟩

³**tip–top** adv (1882) : very well

ti·rade \'tī-ˌrād also ti-'\ n [F, shot, tirade, fr. MF, fr. OIt *tirata*, fr. *tirare* to draw, shoot] (1802) : a protracted speech usu. marked by intemperate, vituperative, or harshly censorious language

tir·a·mi·su \ˌtir-ə-'mē-(ˌ)sü, -'mi-; -mē-'sü\ n [It *tiramisù*, fr. *tirami su*!, lit., pull me up!] (1982) : a dessert made with ladyfingers, mascarpone, chocolate, and espresso

¹**tire** \'tīr\ vb **tired; tir·ing** [ME *tyren*, fr. OE *tēorian, tȳrian*] vi (bef. 12c) : to become weary ~ vt **1** : to exhaust or greatly decrease the physical strength of : FATIGUE **2** : to wear out the patience of : BORE
syn TIRE, WEARY, FATIGUE, EXHAUST, JADE, FAG mean to make or become unable or unwilling to continue. TIRE implies a draining of one's strength or patience ⟨the long ride *tired* us out⟩. WEARY stresses tiring until one is unable to endure more of the same thing ⟨*wearied* of the constant arguing⟩. FATIGUE suggests causing great lassitude through excessive strain or undue effort ⟨*fatigued* by the day's chores⟩. EXHAUST implies complete draining of strength by hard exertion ⟨shoveling snow *exhausted* him⟩. JADE suggests the loss of all freshness and eagerness ⟨*jaded* by overindulgence⟩. FAG implies a drooping with fatigue ⟨shoppers all *fagged* out by the Christmas rush⟩.

²**tire** n [ME, short for *attire*] (14c) **1** obs : ATTIRE **2** archaic : a woman's headband or hair ornament

³**tire** vt **tired; tir·ing** (14c) **1** obs : ATTIRE **2** archaic : to adorn (the hair) with an ornament

⁴**tire** n, often attrib [ME, prob. fr. ²*tire*] (15c) **1** : a metal hoop forming the tread of a wheel **2** : a rubber cushion that fits around a wheel (as of an automobile) and usu. contains compressed air

tired \'tīrd\ adj (15c) **1** : drained of strength and energy : fatigued often to the point of exhaustion **2** : obviously worn by hard use **3** : RUN-DOWN **3** : TRITE, HACKNEYED — **tired·ly** adv — **tired·ness** n

tire·less \'tīr-ləs\ adj (1591) : seemingly incapable of tiring : INDEFATIGABLE — **tire·less·ly** adv — **tire·less·ness** n

Ti·re·si·as \tī-'rē-sē-əs, -zē-\ n [L, fr. Gk *Teiresias*] : a blind seer of Thebes who in one Greek myth is changed into a woman for several years and then changed back to a man

tire·some \'tīr-səm\ adj (ca. 1520) : WEARISOME, TEDIOUS — **tire·some·ly** adv — **tire·some·ness** n

tir·ing–house \'tī-riŋ-ˌhaus\ n [³*tire*] (1590) : a section of a theater reserved for the actors and used esp. for dressing for stage entrances

tir·ing–room \-ˌrüm, -ˌrum\ n [³*tire*] (1623) : a dressing room esp. in a theater

tirl \'tərl\ vb [alter. of ¹*trill*] vi (ca. 1550) *chiefly Scot* : to make a rattling sound (as with a door latch) ~ vt, *chiefly Scot* : TWIRL

tiro *chiefly Brit var of* TYRO

'**tis** \'tiz, (ˌ)tiz, təz\ [contr.] (15c) : it is

ti·sane \ti-'zan, -'zän\ n [ME, fr. MF, fr. L *ptisana*, fr. Gk *ptisanē*, lit., crushed barley, fr. *ptissein* to crush — more at PESTLE] (14c) : an infusion (as of dried herbs) used as a beverage or for medicinal effects

Tish·ah–b'Ab \'ti-shə-ˌbäv, -ˌbov\ n [Heb *tish'āh bĕ Āb* ninth in Ab] (ca. 1902) : a Jewish holiday observed with fasting on the 9th of Ab in commemoration of the destruction of the temples at Jerusalem

Tish·ri \'tish-rē\ n [Heb *tishrī*] (ca. 1771) : the 1st month of the civil year or the 7th month of the ecclesiastical year in the Jewish calendar — see MONTH table

tis·sue \'ti-(ˌ)shü, *chiefly Brit* 'tis-(ˌ)yü\ n [ME *tissu*, a rich fabric, fr. OF, fr. pp. of *tistre* to weave, fr. L *texere* — more at TECHNICAL] (1563) **1 a** : a fine lightweight often sheer fabric **b** : MESH, NETWORK, WEB ⟨a ~ of lies⟩ **2** : a piece of soft absorbent tissue paper used esp. as a handkerchief or for removing cosmetics **3** : an aggregate of cells usu.

\ə\ abut \ᵊ\ kitten, F table \ər\ further \a\ ash \ā\ ace \ä\ mop, mar
\aú\ out \ch\ chin \e\ bet \ē\ easy \g\ go \i\ hit \ī\ ice \j\ job
\ŋ\ sing \ō\ go \o\ law \oi\ boy \th\ thin \th\ the \ü\ loot \u\ foot
\y\ yet \zh\ vision \ə, k, ⁿ, œ, œ̄, ᵫ, ᵫ̄, ᵞ\ see Guide to Pronunciation

of a particular kind together with their intercellular substance that form one of the structural materials of a plant or an animal — **tis·su·ey** \'ti-shə-wē\ adj

tissue culture n (1912) : the process or technique of making body tissue grow in a culture medium outside the organism; also : a culture of tissue (as epithelium)

tissue fluid n (1900) : a fluid that permeates the spaces between individual cells, that is in osmotic contact with the blood and lymph, and that serves in interstitial transport of nutrients and waste

tissue paper n (1777) : a thin gauzy paper used esp. for protecting something (as by covering or wrapping)

tissue plasminogen activator n (1981) : a clot-dissolving enzyme with an affinity for fibrin that is produced naturally in blood vessel linings and is used in a genetically engineered form to prevent damage to heart muscle following a heart attack — abbr. *TPA*

tis·su·lar \'ti-shə-lər\ adj [tissue + -lar (as in cellular)] (ca. 1935) : of, relating to, or affecting organismic tissue ⟨~ grafts⟩ ⟨~ lesions⟩

¹tit \'tit\ n [ME, fr. OE — more at TEAT] (bef. 12c) 1 : TEAT 2 : BREAST — usu. used in pl.; usu. considered vulgar

²tit n (ca. 1706) : TITMOUSE; broadly : any of various small plump often long-tailed birds

ti·tan \'tī-t⁹n\ n [Gk] (ca. 1741) 1 cap : any of a family of giants born of Uranus and Gaea and ruling the earth until overthrown by the Olympian gods 2 : one that is gigantic in size or power : one that stands out for greatness of achievement

titan- or **titani-** comb form [NL titanium] : titanium ⟨titanate⟩

ti·ta·nate \'tī-t⁹n-,āt\ n (1839) 1 : any of various multiple oxides of titanium dioxide with other metallic oxides 2 : a titanium ester of the general formula Ti(OR)₄

ti·tan·ess \'tī-t⁹n-əs\ n, often cap (1596) : a female titan

ti·ta·nia \tī-'tā-nē-ə, tə-, -'tān-yə also -'ta-nē-ə or -'tan-yə\ n [NL] (1922) : TITANIUM DIOXIDE

Ti·ta·nia \tə-'tān-yə, -'tän-; tī-'tān-\ n : the wife of Oberon and queen of the fairies in Shakespeare's *A Midsummer Night's Dream*

ti·tan·ic \tī-'ta-nik also tə-\ adj [Gk titanikos of the Titans] (1709) : having great magnitude, force, or power : COLOSSAL — **ti·tan·i·cal·ly** \-ni-k(ə-)lē\ adv

ti·ta·nif·er·ous \,tī-t⁹n-'i-f(ə-)rəs\ adj (ca. 1828) : containing or yielding titanium ⟨~ minerals⟩

ti·tan·ism \'tī-t⁹n-,i-zəm\ n, often cap [fr. the Titans' rebellion against their father Uranus] (1867) : defiance of and revolt against social or artistic conventions

ti·ta·ni·um \tī-'tā-nē-əm, tə- also -'ta-nē-əm, -'tan-yəm\ n [NL, fr. Gk Titan] (ca. 1796) : a silvery gray light strong metallic element found combined in ilmenite and rutile and used esp. in alloys (as steel) and combined in refractory materials and in coatings — see ELEMENT table

titanium dioxide n (1877) : an oxide TiO₂ of titanium that occurs in rutile, anatase, or ilmenite and is used esp. as a pigment

titanium white n (1920) : TITANIUM DIOXIDE; also : a brilliant white lead-free pigment consisting of titanium dioxide often together with barium sulfate and zinc oxide

tit·bit \'tit-,bit\ var of TIDBIT

ti·ter \'tī-tər\ n [F titre title, proportion of gold or silver in a coin, fr. OF title inscription, title] (1888) : the strength of a solution or the concentration of a substance (as an antibody) in solution as determined by titration

tit·fer \'tit-fər\ n [by shortening & alter. fr. tit for tat, rhyming slang for hat] (ca. 1930) Brit : HAT

tit for tat \,tit-fər-'tat\ [alter. of earlier tip for tap, fr. tip (blow) + for + tap] (1556) : an equivalent given in return (as for an injury) : retaliation in kind — **tit–for–tat** adj

tith·able \'tī-thə-bəl\ adj (15c) : subject or liable to payment of tithes

¹tithe \'tīth\ vb tithed; tith·ing [ME, fr. OE teogotha, fr. teogotha tenth] vt (bef. 12c) 1 : to pay or give a tenth part of esp. for the support of the church 2 : to levy a tithe on ~ vi : to give a tenth of one's income as a tithe

²tithe n [ME, fr. OE teogotha tenth; akin to MLG tegede tenth, OE tīen ten — more at TEN] (bef. 12c) 1 : a tenth part of something paid as a voluntary contribution or as a tax esp. for the support of a religious establishment 2 : the obligation represented by individual tithes 3 : TENTH; broadly : a small part 4 : a small tax or levy

tith·er \'tī-thər\ n (14c) 1 : one that pays tithes 2 : one that collects or advocates the payment of tithes

tith·ing \'tī-thiŋ\ n [ME, fr. OE tēothung, fr. teogothian, tēothian to tithe, take one tenth] (bef. 12c) : a small administrative division preserved in parts of England apparently orig. made up of ten men with their families

ti·tho·nia \tə-'thō-nyə, tī-, -nē-ə\ n [NL, prob. fr. L Tithonia, poetical name of Aurora] (1940) : any of a genus (Tithonia) of tall composite herbs or shrubs of Mexico and Central America that have flower heads resembling sunflowers and that are sometimes grown as ornamentals

¹ti·ti \'ti-,tī\ n [origin unknown] (1827) 1 : a tree (Cliftonia monophylla of the family Cyrillaceae) of the southeastern U.S. with leathery leaves and racemes of fragrant white flowers 2 : LEATHERWOOD 2

²ti·ti \ti-'tē\ n [AmerSp titi] (1832) : any of a genus (Callicebus) of small So. American monkeys having long thick variably colored fur and a tail that is not prehensile

ti·tian \'ti-shən\ adj, often cap [Titian (Tiziano Vecellio)] (1896) : of a brownish orange color

tit·il·late \'ti-t⁹l-,āt\ vb -lat·ed; -lat·ing [L titillatus, pp. of titillare] vt (1620) 1 : to excite pleasurably : arouse by stimulation 2 : TICKLE ~ vi : to act as a stimulant to pleasurable excitement — **tit·il·la·tion** \,ti-t⁹l-'ā-shən\ n — **tit·il·la·tive** \'ti-t⁹l-,ā-tiv\ adj

tit·il·lat·ing \'ti-t⁹l-,ā-tiŋ\ adj (ca. 1714) : pleasantly stimulating or exciting ⟨~ reading⟩; also : EROTIC — **tit·il·lat·ing·ly** \-tiŋ-lē\ adv

tit·i·vate or **tit·ti·vate** \'ti-tə-,vāt\ vb -vat·ed; -vat·ing [perh. fr. ¹tidy + renovate] vt (1824) : to make smart or spruce ~ vi : SMARTEN, SPRUCE — **tit·i·va·tion** \,ti-tə-'vā-shən\ n

tit·lark \'tit-,lärk\ n [tit (as in titmouse) + lark] (1688) : PIPIT

¹ti·tle \'tī-t⁹l\ n [ME, fr. MF, fr. L titulus inscription, title] (14c) 1 a obs : INSCRIPTION b : written material introduced into a motion picture or television program to give credits, explain an action, or represent dialogue — usu. used in pl. 2 a : all the elements constituting legal ownership b : a legally just cause of exclusive possession c

: the instrument (as a deed) that is evidence of a right 3 a : something that justifies or substantiates a claim b : an alleged or recognized right 4 a : a descriptive or general heading (as of a chapter in a book) b : the heading which names an act or statute c : the heading of a legal action or proceeding 5 a : the distinguishing name of a written, printed, or filmed production b : a similar distinguishing name of a musical composition or a work of art 6 : a descriptive name : APPELLATION 7 : a division of an instrument, book, or bill; esp : one larger than a section or article 8 a : an appellation of dignity, honor, distinction, or preeminence attached to a person or family by virtue of rank, office, precedent, privilege, attainment, or lands b : a person holding a title esp. of nobility 9 : a written work as distinguished from a particular copy ⟨published 25 ~s last year⟩ 10 : CHAMPIONSHIP 1 ⟨won the batting ~⟩

²title vt ti·tled; ti·tling \'tī-t⁹l-iŋ, 'tī-t⁹l-iŋ\ (14c) 1 : to provide a title for 2 : to designate or call by a title : TERM, STYLE

³title adj (1886) : of or relating to a title: as a : having the same name as the title of a production ⟨did the ~ role in Hamlet⟩ b : having the same title as or providing the title for the collection or production of which it forms a part ⟨the ~ song⟩ c : of, relating to, or involving a championship ⟨a ~ match⟩ d : of, relating to, or used with the titles that introduce a motion picture or television program ⟨~ music⟩

ti·tled \'tī-t⁹ld\ adj (1593) : having a title esp. of nobility

title deed n (ca. 1768) : the deed constituting the evidence of a person's legal ownership

ti·tle·hold·er \'tī-t⁹l-,hōl-dər\ n (1904) : one that holds a title; specif : CHAMPION

title page n (1594) : a page of a book bearing the title and usu. the names of the author and publisher and the place and sometimes date of publication

ti·tlist \'tī-t⁹l-ist, 'tīt-list\ n (1924) : TITLEHOLDER

tit·mouse \'tit-,maús\ n, pl tit·mice \-,mīs\ [by folk etymology fr. ME titmose, fr. (assumed) ME tit any small object or creature + ME mose titmouse, fr. OE māse; akin to OHG meisa titmouse] (14c) : any of numerous small widely distributed insectivorous oscine birds (family Paridae and esp. genus Parus) that are related to the chickadees and have small bills and relatively long tails

Ti·to·ism \'tē-(,)tō-,i-zəm\ n (1949) : the political, economic, and social policies associated with Tito; specif : nationalistic policies and practices followed by a communist state or group independently of and often in opposition to the U.S.S.R. — **Ti·to·ist** \-,ō-ist\ n or adj

ti·trant \'tī-trənt\ n (1939) : a substance (as a reagent solution of precisely known concentration) that is added in titration

ti·trate \'tī-,trāt\ vb ti·trat·ed; ti·trat·ing [titer] vt (ca. 1859) : to subject to titration ~ vi : to perform titration — **ti·trat·able** \,trā-tə-bəl\ adj — **ti·tra·tor** \-,trā-tər\ n

ti·tra·tion \tī-'trā-shən\ n (ca. 1859) : a method or the process of determining the concentration of a dissolved substance in terms of the smallest amount of a reagent of known concentration required to bring about a given effect in reaction with a known volume of the test solution

ti·tre \'tī-tər\ var of TITER

ti·tri·met·ric \,tī-trə-'me-trik\ adj [titration + -i- + -metric] (1902) : employing or determined by titration

tit–tat–toe \,ti-,ta(t)-'tō\ var of TICKTACKTOE

tit·ter \'ti-tər\ vi [imit.] (ca. 1619) : to laugh in a nervous, affected, or partly suppressed manner : GIGGLE, SNICKER — **titter** n

tit·tie \'ti-tē\ n [prob. baby talk alter. of sister] (ca. 1700) chiefly Scot : SISTER

tit·tle \'ti-t⁹l\ n [ME titel, fr. ML titulus, fr. L, title] (14c) 1 : a point or small sign used as a diacritical mark in writing or printing 2 : a very small part

tit·tle–tat·tle \'ti-t⁹l-,ta-t⁹l\ n [redupl. of ¹tattle] (ca. 1529) : GOSSIP, PRATTLE — **tittle–tattle** vi

¹tit·tup \'ti-təp\ n [imit. of the sound of a horse's hooves] (1703) : lively, gay, or restless behavior

²tittup vi -tupped or -tuped; -tup·ping or -tup·ing (1785) : to move in a lively manner often with an exaggerated or affected action

¹tit·u·lar \'ti-chə-lər, 'tich-lər\ adj [L titulus title] (1611) 1 a : existing in title only; esp : bearing a title derived from a defunct ecclesiastical jurisdiction (as an episcopal see) ⟨a ~ bishop⟩ b : having the title and usu. the honors belonging to an office or dignity without the duties, functions, or responsibilities ⟨the ~ head of a political party⟩ 2 : bearing a title : TITLED 3 : of, relating to, or constituting a title ⟨the ~ hero of the play⟩ — **tit·u·lar·ly** adv

²titular n (1613) : a person holding a title

Ti·tus \'tī-təs\ n [LL, fr. Gk Titos] 1 : an early Christian convert who assisted Paul in his missionary work 2 : a letter written on the subject of pastoral care in the early Church and included as a book in the New Testament — see BIBLE table

Tiu \'tē-(,)ü\ n [OE Tīw — more at DEITY] : an ancient Germanic god of war identified with Tyr

tiz·zy \'ti-zē\ n, pl tizzies [origin unknown] (1935) : a highly excited and distracted state of mind

TKO \,tē-kā-'ō\ n [technical knockout] (1941) : TECHNICAL KNOCKOUT

Tlin·git \'tliŋ-kət, -got also 'kliŋ-\ n, pl Tlingit or Tlingits \-s\ 1 : a member of a group of American Indian peoples of the islands and coast of southern Alaska 2 : the language of the Tlingit peoples — **Tlingit** adj

T lymphocyte n [thymus-derived] (1972) : T CELL

T–man \'tē-,man\ n [Treasury man] (1937) : a special agent of the U.S. Treasury Department

tme·sis \(tə-)'mē-səs\ n [LL, fr. Gk tmēsis act of cutting, fr. temnein to cut — more at TOME] (1550) : separation of parts of a compound word by the intervention of one or more words (as what place soever for whatsoever place)

TNT \,tē-(,)en-'tē\ n [trinitrotoluene] (1915) : a flammable toxic compound C₇H₅N₃O₆ used as a high explosive and in chemical synthesis

¹to \tə, tü, 'tü\ prep [ME, fr. OE tō; akin to OHG zuo to, L donec as long as, until] (bef. 12c) 1 a — used as a function word to indicate movement or an action or condition suggestive of movement toward a place, person, or thing reached ⟨drove ~ the city⟩ ⟨went back ~ the original idea⟩ b — used as a function word to indicate direction ⟨a mile ~ the south⟩ ⟨turned his back ~ the door⟩ ⟨a tendency ~ silli-

ness⟩ **c** — used as a function word to indicate contact or proximity ⟨applied polish ~ the table⟩ ⟨put her hand ~ her heart⟩ **d** (1) — used as a function word to indicate the place or point that is the far limit ⟨100 miles ~ the nearest town⟩ (2) — used as a function word to indicate the limit of extent ⟨stripped ~ the waist⟩ **e** — used as a function word to indicate relative position ⟨perpendicular ~ the floor⟩ **2 a** — used as a function word to indicate purpose, intention, tendency, result, or end ⟨came ~ our aid⟩ ⟨drink ~ his health⟩ **b** — used as a function word to indicate the result of an action or a process ⟨broken all ~ pieces⟩ ⟨go ~ seed⟩ ⟨~ their surprise, the train left on time⟩ **3** — used as a function word to indicate position or relation in time: as **a** : BEFORE ⟨five minutes ~ five⟩ **b** : TILL ⟨from eight ~ five⟩ ⟨up ~ now⟩ **4** — used as a function word to indicate addition, attachment, connection, belonging, possession, accompaniment, or response ⟨the key ~ the door⟩ ⟨danced ~ live music⟩ ⟨comes ~ her call⟩ **5** — used as a function word (1) to indicate the extent or degree (as of completeness or accuracy) ⟨loyal ~ a man⟩ ⟨generous ~ a fault⟩ or the extent and result (as of an action or a condition) ⟨beaten ~ death⟩ (2) to indicate the last or an intermediate point of a series ⟨moderate ~ cool temperatures⟩ **6 a** — used as a function word (1) to indicate a relation to one that serves as a standard ⟨inferior ~ her earlier works⟩ (2) to indicate similarity, correspondence, dissimilarity, or proportion ⟨compared him ~ a god⟩ **b** — used as a function word to indicate agreement or conformity ⟨add salt ~ taste⟩ ⟨~ my knowledge⟩ **c** — used as a function word to indicate a proportion in terms of numbers or quantities ⟨400 ~ the box⟩ ⟨odds of ten ~ one⟩ **7 a** — used as a function word (1) to indicate the application of an adjective or a noun ⟨agreeable ~ everyone⟩ ⟨attitude ~ friends⟩ ⟨title ~ the property⟩ (2) to indicate the relation of a verb to its complement or to a complementary element ⟨refers ~ the traditions⟩ ⟨refers us ~ the traditions⟩ (3) to indicate the receiver of an action or the one for which something is done or exists ⟨spoke ~ his mother⟩ ⟨gives a dollar ~ the man⟩ and often used with a reflexive pronoun to indicate exclusiveness (as of possession) or separateness ⟨had the house ~ themselves⟩ ⟨thought ~ herself⟩ **b** — used as a function word to indicate agency ⟨falls ~ his opponent's blows⟩ **8** — used as a function word to indicate that the following verb is an infinitive ⟨wants ~ go⟩ and often used by itself at the end of a clause in place of an infinitive suggested by the preceding context ⟨knows more than she seems ~⟩
²**to** \'tü\ *adv* (bef. 12c) **1 a** — used as a function word to indicate direction toward ⟨feathers wrong end ~⟩ ⟨run ~ and fro⟩ **b** : close to the wind ⟨the gale having gone over, we came ~ —R. H. Dana⟩ **2 a** : into contact esp. with the frame — used of a door or a window ⟨the door snapped ~⟩ **b** — used as a function word to indicate physical application or attachment ⟨he ... hath set ~ his seal —Jn 3:33 (AV)⟩ **3** — used as a function word to indicate application or attention ⟨will stand ~ —Shak.⟩ **4** : to a state of consciousness or awareness ⟨brings her ~ with smelling salts⟩ **5** : at hand : BY ⟨get to see 'em close ~ —Richard Llewellyn⟩
toad \'tōd\ *n* [ME *tode*, fr. OE *tāde, tādige*] (bef. 12c) **1** : any of numerous anuran amphibians (esp. family Bufonidae) that as compared with the related frogs are generally more terrestrial in habit though returning to water to lay their eggs, squatter and shorter in build and with weaker hind limbs, and rough, dry, and warty rather than smooth and moist of skin **2** : a contemptible person or thing
toad-eat-er \-ˌē-tər\ *n* (ca. 1572) *archaic* : TOADY
toad-fish \-ˌfish\ *n* (1704) : any of a family (Batrachoididae) of chiefly marine bony fishes with jugular pelvic fins, a large thick head, a wide mouth, and usu. scaleless slimy skin
toad-flax \-ˌflaks\ *n* (1578) : BUTTER-AND-EGGS; *also* : any of several related plants (esp. genus *Linaria*) of the snapdragon family
toad-stone \-ˌstōn\ *n* (1558) : a stone or similar object held to have formed in the head or body of a toad and formerly often worn as a charm or antidote to poison
toad-stool \-ˌstül\ *n* (14c) : a fungus having an umbrella-shaped pileus : MUSHROOM; *esp* : a poisonous or inedible one as distinguished from an edible mushroom
¹**toady** \'tō-dē\ *n, pl* **toad-ies** [by shortening & alter. fr. *toadeater*] (1826) : one who flatters in the hope of gaining favors : SYCOPHANT *syn* see PARASITE
²**toady** *vi* **toad-ied; toady-ing** (ca. 1859) : to behave as a toady : engage in sycophancy *syn* see FAWN — **toady-ism** \-ˌē-ˌi-zəm\ *n*
¹**to—and-fro** \ˌtü-ən-ˈfrō\ *adj* (1749) : forward and backward ⟨~ motion⟩
²**to—and-fro** *n* (1847) : activity involving alternating movement in opposite directions ⟨the busy ~ of the holiday shoppers⟩
to and fro *adv* (14c) : from one place to another
¹**toast** \'tōst\ *vb* [ME *tosten*, fr. MF *toster*, fr. LL *tostare* to roast, fr. L *tostus*, pp. of *torrēre* to dry, parch — more at THIRST] *vt* (14c) **1** : to warm thoroughly **2** : to make (as bread) crisp, hot, and brown by heat ~ *vi* : to become toasted; *esp* : to warm thoroughly
²**toast** *n* (15c) **1 a** : sliced bread browned on both sides by heat **b** : food prepared with toasted bread **2** [fr. the use of pieces of spiced toast to flavor drinks] **a** : someone or something in honor of which persons usu. drink **b** : one that is highly admired ⟨she's the ~ of society⟩ **3** [²*toast*] : an act of proposing or of drinking in honor of a toast **4** : a rhyming narrative poem existing in oral tradition among black Americans
³**toast** *vt* (1640) : to propose or drink to as a toast
toast-er \'tō-stər\ *n* (1582) : one that toasts; *esp* : an electrical appliance for toasting
toaster oven *n* (1961) : a portable electrical appliance that can function as an oven or a toaster
toast-mas-ter \'tōs(t)-ˌmas-tər\ *n* (1749) : one who presides at a banquet and introduces the after-dinner speakers
toast-mis-tress \-ˌmis-trəs\ *n* (1921) : a woman who acts as toastmaster
toasty \'tō-stē\ *adj* **toast-i-er; -est** (1953) : pleasantly or comfortably warm ⟨felt snug and ~ by the fire⟩
to-bac-co \tə-ˈba-(ˌ)kō\ *n, pl* **-cos** [Sp *tabaco*, prob. fr. Taino, roll of tobacco leaves] (ca. 1565) **1** : any

of a genus (*Nicotiana*) of chiefly American plants of the nightshade family with viscid foliage and tubular flowers; *esp* : a tall erect annual tropical American herb (*N. tabacum*) cultivated for its leaves **2** : the leaves of cultivated tobacco prepared for use in smoking or chewing or as snuff **3** : manufactured products of tobacco (as cigars or cigarettes); *also* : smoking as a practice ⟨has sworn off ~⟩
tobacco budworm *n* (1918) : a noctuid moth (*Heliothis virescens* syn. *Helicoverpa virescens*) whose small rusty often green-striped caterpillar feeds on buds and young leaves esp. of tobacco and cotton
tobacco hornworm *n* (ca. 1909) : a hawkmoth (*Manduca sexta*) whose large usu. green larva is a hornworm that feeds on plants of the nightshade family
tobacco juice *n* (1833) : saliva colored brown by tobacco or snuff
tobacco mosaic *n* (1914) : any of a complex of virus diseases of plants of the nightshade family and esp. of tobacco
to-bac-co-nist \tə-ˈba-kə-nist\ *n* [irreg. fr. *tobacco* + *-ist*] (1657) : a dealer in tobacco esp. at retail
tobacco road *n, often cap T&R* [fr. *Tobacco Road*, novel (1932) by Erskine Caldwell and play (1933) by Jack Kirkland †1969 Am. playwright] (1937) : a squalid poverty-stricken rural area or community
to—be \tə-ˈbē\ *adj* (ca. 1600) : that is to be : FUTURE — usu. used postpositively and often in combination ⟨a bride-*to-be*⟩
To-bi-as \tə-ˈbī-əs\ *n* [Gk *Tobias*] **1** : a Jewish hero who with divine aid marries his kinswoman Sarah in spite of a jealous evil spirit and restores his father Tobit's sight **2** : TOBIT 2
To-bit \'tō-bət\ *n* [Gk *Tōbit*] **1** : the elderly father of Tobias in a book of Scripture included in the Roman Catholic canon of the Old Testament and in the Protestant Apocrypha — see BIBLE table
¹**to-bog-gan** \tə-ˈbä-gən\ *n* [CanF *tobogan*, fr. Algonquian origin; akin to Micmac *tobâgun* drag made of skin] (ca. 1820) **1** : a long flat-bottomed light sled made usu. of thin boards curved up at one end with usu. low handrails at the sides **2** : a downward course or a sharp decline
²**toboggan** *vi* (1846) **1** : to coast on or as if on a toboggan **2** : to decline suddenly and sharply — **to-bog-gan-er** *n* — **to-bog-gan-ist** \-gə-nist\ *n*
to-bog-gan-ing *n* (1849) : the act, art, or sport of riding a toboggan
to-by jug \ˈtō-bē-\ *n, often cap T* [*Toby*, nickname fr. the name *Tobias*] (1840) : a small jug, pitcher, or mug shaped somewhat like a stout man with a cocked hat for the brim — called also *toby*
toc-ca-ta \tə-ˈkä-tə\ *n* [It, fr. *toccare* to touch, fr. (assumed) VL — more at TOUCH] (ca. 1724) : a musical composition usu. for organ or harpsichord in a free style and characterized by full chords, rapid runs, and high harmonies
To-char-i-an \tō-ˈkar-ē-ən, -ˈker-, -ˈkär-\ *n* [Gk *Tocharoi*] (ca. 1926) **1 a** : a language of central Asia known from documents from the sixth to eighth centuries A.D. **b** : a branch of the Indo-European language family containing Tocharian — see INDO-EUROPEAN LANGUAGES table **2** : a member of a people of presumably European origin dwelling in central Asia during the first millennium of the Christian era
Tocharian A *n* (1926) : the eastern dialect of Tocharian — see INDO-EUROPEAN LANGUAGES table
Tocharian B *n* (1926) : the western dialect of Tocharian — see INDO-EUROPEAN LANGUAGES table
toch-er \'tä-kər\ *n* [ME (Sc) *tochir*, fr. ScGael *tochar*] (15c) *chiefly Scot* : DOWRY 2, 3
to-coph-er-ol \tō-ˈkä-fə-ˌrȯl, -ˌrōl\ *n* [ISV, ultim. fr. Gk *tokos* childbirth, offspring (akin to Gk *tiktein* to beget) + *pherein* to carry, bear — more at THANE, BEAR] (1936) : any of several fat-soluble oily phenolic compounds with varying degrees of antioxidant vitamin E activity; *esp* : one $C_{29}H_{50}O_2$ of high vitamin E potency obtained from germ oils or by synthesis
toc-sin \'täk-sən\ *n* [MF *toquassen*, fr. OProv *tocasenh*, fr. *tocar* to touch, ring a bell (fr. assumed VL *toccare*) + *senh* sign, bell, fr. ML & L *signum*; ML, bell, fr. LL, ringing of a bell, fr. L, mark, sign — more at TOUCH, SIGN] (1586) **1** : an alarm bell or the ringing of it **2** : a warning signal
¹**tod** \'täd\ *n* [ME] (12c) *chiefly Scot* : FOX
²**tod** *n* [ME *todd, todde*; prob. akin to OHG *zotta* tuft of hair] (15c) **1** *archaic* : any of various units of weight for wool; *esp* : one equal to 28 pounds (13 kilograms) **2** *Brit* : a bushy clump (as of ivy)
¹**to-day** \tə-ˈdā\ *adv* (bef. 12c) **1** : on or for this day **2** : at the present time
²**today** *n* (1535) : the present day, time, or age ⟨~'s youth⟩
³**today** *adj* (1966) : of or characteristic of today : NOW
tod-dle \'tä-d⁰l\ *vi* **tod-dled; tod-dling** \'täd-liŋ, 'tä-d⁰l-iŋ\ [origin unknown] (ca. 1600) **1** : to walk with short tottering steps in the manner of a young child **2** : to take a stroll : SAUNTER — **toddle** *n*
tod-dler \'täd-lər, 'tä-d⁰l-ər\ *n* (1793) : one that toddles; *esp* : a young child — **tod-dler-hood** \-ˌhud\ *n*
tod-dy \'tä-dē\ *n, pl* **toddies** [Hindi *tārī* juice of the palmyra palm, fr. *tār* palmyra palm, fr. Skt *tāla*] (ca. 1610) **1** : the fresh or fermented sap of various chiefly East Indian palms **2** : a usu. hot drink consisting of liquor (as rum), water, sugar, and spices
to—do \tə-ˈdü\ *n, pl* **to—dos** \-ˈdüz\ (ca. 1576) : BUSTLE, STIR, FUSS
¹**toe** \'tō\ *n* [ME *to*, fr. OE *tā*; akin to OHG *zēha* toe] (bef. 12c) **1 a** (1) : one of the terminal members of a vertebrate's foot (2) : the fore end of a foot or hoof **b** : a terminal segment of a limb of an invertebrate **c** : the forepart of something worn on the foot ⟨the ~ of a shoe⟩ **2** : a part that by its position or form is felt to resemble a toe ⟨the ~ of Italy⟩: as **a** : a lateral projection at one end or between the ends of a piece (as a rod or bolt) **b** : the lowest part (as of an embankment, dam, or cliff) **3** : TOE DANCE — **toe-less** \-ləs\ *adj* — **on one's toes** : ALERT 1 — **toe to toe** : facing one another
²**toe** *vb* **toed; toe-ing** *vt* (1607) **1** : to furnish with a toe ⟨~ a sock⟩ **2** : to touch, reach, or drive with the toe ⟨~ a football⟩ **3** : to drive (as a nail) obliquely; *also* : to clinch or fasten by or with nails or rods so

tobacco 1

\ə\ abut \ᵊ\ kitten, F table \ər\ further \a\ ash \ā\ ace \ä\ mop, mar \aú\ out \ch\ chin \e\ bet \ē\ easy \g\ go \i\ hit \ī\ ice \j\ job \ŋ\ sing \ō\ go \ȯ\ law \ȯi\ boy \th\ thin \th\ the \ü\ loot \ú\ foot \y\ yet \zh\ vision \à, k̲, ⁿ, œ, œ̄, ᵫ, ᵫ̄, ᷓ\ see Guide to Pronunciation driven ∼ *vi* **1** : TIPTOE **2** : to stand, walk, or be placed so that the toes assume an indicated position or direction ⟨∼ in⟩ — **toe the line** *or* **toe the mark** : to conform rigorously to a rule or standard

toea \'tȯi-ə\ *n, pl* **toea** [Hiri Motu (pidgin of Papua New Guinea based on Motu, an Austronesian language), a kind of shell] (1975) — see *kina* at MONEY table

toe cap *n* (1797) : a piece of leather covering the toe of a shoe and reinforcing or decorating it

toed \'tōd\ *adj* [¹*toe*] (1611) **1** : having a toe or toes esp. of a specified kind or number — usu. used in combination ⟨five-*toed*⟩ ⟨round-*toed* shoes⟩ **2** [fr. pp. of ²*toe*] : driven obliquely ⟨a ∼ nail⟩; *also* : secured by diagonal or oblique nailing

toe dance *n* (1898) : a dance executed on the tips of the toes by means of a ballet slipper with a reinforced toe — **toe–dance** *vi* — **toe dancer** *n* — **toe dancing** *n*

toe·hold \'tō-ˌhōld\ *n* (1880) **1 a** : a hold or place of support for the toes (as in climbing) **b** (1) : a means of progressing (as in surmounting barriers) (2) : a slight footing ⟨used his money to get a ∼, then a foothold, then a near stranglehold on the political economy —R. W. Armstrong⟩ **2** : a wrestling hold in which the aggressor bends or twists his opponent's foot

toe–in \'tō-ˌin\ *n* (1928) **1** : CAMBER 3 **2** : adjustment of the front wheels of an automotive vehicle so that they are closer together at the front than at the back

¹toe-nail \'tō-ˌnāl, -ˌnā(ə)l\ *n* (1841) : a nail of a toe

²toenail *vt* (1900) : to fasten by toed nails : TOE

toe-piece \'tō-ˌpēs\ *n* (1879) : a piece designed to form a toe (as of a shoe) or cover the toes of the foot

toe-plate \-ˌplāt\ *n* (1894) : a tab attached to the toe of a shoe (as to prevent wear due to heavy use)

toe–to–toe *adj or adv* (ca. 1942) : slugging it out at or as if at close range ⟨a ∼ confrontation over the new policy⟩

toff \'täf\ *n* [prob. alter. of *tuft* titled college student] (1851) *chiefly Brit* : DANDY, SWELL

tof·fee *or* **tof·fy** \'tȯ-fē, 'tä-\ *n, pl* **toffees** *or* **toffies** [alter. of *taffy*] (ca. 1825) : candy of brittle but tender texture made by boiling sugar and butter together

tof-fee–nosed \-'nōzd\ *adj* (ca. 1925) *chiefly Brit* : STUCK-UP

toft \'tȯft, 'täft\ *n* [ME, fr. OE, fr. ON *topt*; prob. akin to Gk *dapedon* floor, *demein* to build, *pedon* ground — more at TIMBER, PED] (bef. 12c) *Brit* : a site for a dwelling and its outbuildings; *also* : an entire holding comprising a homestead and additional land

to-fu \'tō-(ˌ)fü\ *n* [Jp *tōfu*] (1771) : BEAN CURD

tog \'täg, 'tȯg\ *vt* **togged; tog·ging** [*togs*] (ca. 1785) : to dress esp. in fine clothing — usu. used with *up* or *out*

to-ga \'tō-gə\ *n* [L; akin to L *tegere* to cover — more at THATCH] (1600) : the loose outer garment worn in public by citizens of ancient Rome; *also* : a similar loose wrap or a professional, official, or academic gown — **to-gaed** \-gəd\ *adj*

to-ga vi·ri·lis \ˌtō-gə-və-'rē-ləs, -'rī-\ *n, pl* **to-gae vi·ri·les** \'tō-ˌgī-və-'rē-ˌlās, -'rī-\ [L, men's toga] (1600) : the white toga of manhood assumed by boys of ancient Rome at age 15

¹to-geth-er \tə-'ge-thər\ *adv* [ME *togedere*, fr. OE *togædere*, fr. *tō* to + *gædere* together; akin to MHG *gater* together, OE *gaderian* to gather] (bef. 12c) **1 a** : in or into one place, mass, collection, or group ⟨the men get ∼ every Thursday for poker⟩ **b** : as a group ⟨students and faculty ∼ presented the petition⟩ **2 a** : in or into contact (as connection, collision, or union) ⟨mix these ingredients ∼⟩ **b** : in or into association or relationship ⟨colors that go well ∼⟩ ⟨went to school ∼⟩ **3 a** : at one time : SIMULTANEOUSLY ⟨events that happened ∼⟩ **b** : in succession : without intermission ⟨was depressed for days ∼⟩ **4 a** : by combined action : JOINTLY ⟨∼ we forced the door⟩ **b** : in or into agreement or harmony ⟨the soloist and the orchestra weren't quite ∼⟩ **c** : in or into a unified or coherent structure or an integrated whole ⟨can't even put a simple sentence ∼⟩ ⟨pull yourself ∼⟩ **5 a** : with each other — used as an intensive after certain verbs ⟨join ∼⟩ ⟨add ∼⟩ **b** : as a unit : in the aggregate ⟨these arguments taken ∼ make a convincing case⟩ **c** : considered as a whole : counted or summed up ⟨all ∼, there were 21 entries⟩ — **to-geth-er-ness** *n* — **together with** : in addition to : in association with

²together *adj* (1963) **1** : appropriately prepared, organized, or balanced **2** : composed in mind or manner : SELF-POSSESSED ⟨a warm, sensitive, reasonably ∼ girl —*East Village Other*⟩

Tog-gen-burg \'tä-gən-ˌbərg\ *n* [*Toggenburg*, district in northeastern Switzerland] (1886) : any of a breed of brown hornless dairy goats of Swiss origin with white stripes on the face

tog-gery \'tä-g(ə-)rē, 'tȯ-\ *n* [*togs*] (ca. 1811) : CLOTHING

¹tog-gle \'tä-gəl\ *n* [origin unknown] (ca. 1775) **1** : a piece or device for holding or securing: as **a** : a pin inserted in a nautical knot to make it more secure or easier to slip **b** : a crosspiece attached to the end of or to a loop in something (as a chain, rope, line, strap, or belt) usu. to prevent slipping, to serve in twisting or tightening, or to hold something attached **2** : a device consisting of two bars jointed together end to end but not in line so that when a force is applied to the joint tending to straighten it pressure will be exerted on the parts adjacent or fixed to the outer ends of the bars; *also* : a device with a joint using a toggle

toggle 2

²toggle *vt* **tog·gled; tog·gling** \-g(ə-)liŋ\ (1836) **1** : to fasten with or as if with a toggle **2** : to furnish with a toggle

toggle bolt *n* (1906) : a bolt that has a nut with wings which close for passage through a small hole and spring open after passing through the hole to keep the bolt from slipping back through

toggle switch *n* (ca. 1924) : an electric switch operated by pushing a projecting lever through a small arc

togs \'tägz, 'tȯgz\ *n pl* [pl. of E slang *tog* coat, short for obs. E cant *togeman, togman*] (1779) : CLOTHING; *esp* : a set of clothes and accessories for a specified use ⟨riding ∼⟩

togue \'tōg\ *n* [CanF] (1839) : LAKE TROUT

¹toil \'tȯi(ə)l\ *n* [ME *toile*, fr. AF *toyl*, fr. OF *toeil* battle, confusion, fr. *toeillier*] (14c) **1** *archaic* **a** : STRUGGLE, BATTLE **b** : laborious effort **2** : long strenuous fatiguing labor *syn* see WORK — **toil·ful** \-fəl\ *adj* — **toil·ful·ly** \-fə-lē\ *adv*

²toil *vb* [ME, to argue, struggle, fr. AF *toiller*, fr. OF *toeillier* to stir, disturb, dispute, fr. L *tudiculare* to crush, grind, fr. *tudicula* machine for crushing olives, dim. of *tudes* hammer; akin to L *tundere* to beat — more at CONTUSION] *vi* (14c) **1** : to work hard and long : LABOR **2** : to proceed with laborious effort : PLOD ⟨∼ing wearily up the hill⟩ ∼ *vt* **1** *archaic* : OVERWORK **2** *archaic* : to get or accomplish with great effort — **toil·er** \'tȯi-lər\ *n*

³toil *n* [MF *toile* cloth, net, fr. L *tela* cloth on a loom — more at SUBTLE] (ca. 1529) **1** : a net to trap game **2** : something by which one is held fast or inextricably involved : SNARE, TRAP — usu. used in pl. ⟨caught in the ∼s of the law⟩

toile \'twäl\ *n* [F, cloth, linen, fr. MF] (1794) **1** : any of many plain or simple twill weave fabrics; *esp* : LINEN **2** : a mock-up model of a garment

toile de Jouy \ˌtwäl-də-'zhwē\ *n* [F, lit., cloth of Jouy, fr. *Jouy-en-Josas*, France] (ca. 1920) : an 18th century French scenic pattern usu. printed on cotton, linen, or silk in one color on a light ground; *broadly* : a similar printed fabric

¹toi-let \'tȯi-lət\ *n* [MF *toilette* cloth put over the shoulders while dressing the hair or shaving, dim. of *toile* cloth] (ca. 1695) **1** *archaic* : DRESSING TABLE **2** : the act or process of dressing and grooming oneself **3 a** (1) : BATHROOM, LAVATORY 2 (2) : PRIVY **b** : a fixture that consists usu. of a water-flushed bowl and seat and is used for defecation and urination **4** : cleansing in preparation for or in association with a medical or surgical procedure ⟨a pharyngeal ∼⟩

²toilet *vi* (1840) **1** : to dress and groom oneself ∼ *vt* **1** : to use the toilet — usu. used of a child ∼ *vt* **1** : DRESS, GARB **2** : to help (as a child or sick person) use the toilet

toilet paper *n* (1884) : a thin sanitary absorbent paper for bathroom use chiefly after defecation and urination

toilet powder *n* (1840) : a fine powder usu. with soothing or antiseptic ingredients for sprinkling or rubbing (as after bathing) over the skin

toi-let-ry \'tȯi-lə-trē\ *n, pl* **-ries** (1892) : an article or preparation (as toothpaste, shaving cream, or cologne) used in making one's toilet — usu. used in pl.

toilet soap *n* (1839) : a mild soap that is often perfumed and colored and stabilized with preservatives

toi-lette \twä-'let\ *n* [F, fr. MF] (1681) **1** : TOILET 2 **2 a** : formal or fashionable attire or style of dressing **b** : a particular costume or outfit

toilet training *n* (1940) : the process of training a child to control bladder and bowel movements and to use the toilet — **toilet train** *vt*

toilet water *n* (1855) : a perfumed liquid containing a high percentage of alcohol for use in or after a bath or as a skin freshener

toil-some \-səm\ *adj* (1581) : marked by or full of toil or fatigue : LABORIOUS — **toil-some·ly** *adv* — **toil-some·ness** *n*

toil-worn \-ˌwȯrn, -ˌwȯrn\ *adj* (1751) : showing the effects of or worn out with toil ⟨∼ hands⟩

to–ing and fro–ing \ˈtü-iŋ-ən(d)-'frō-iŋ\ *n, pl* **to–ings and fro–ings** [*to and fro*] (1847) : a passing back and forth

to-ka-mak *also* **to-ko-mak** \'tō-kə-ˌmak, 'tä-\ *n* [Russ, fr. *toroidal'naya kamera* s *aksial'nym magnitnym polem* (toroidal chamber with an axial magnetic field)] (1965) : a toroidal device for producing controlled nuclear fusion that involves the confining and heating of a gaseous plasma by means of an electric current and magnetic field

To-kay \tō-'kā\ *n* (1710) **1** : a naturally sweet wine from the area around Tokaj, Hungary **2** : a blend of Angelica, port, and sherry made in California

toke \'tōk\ *n* [AmerSp *toque*, fr. Sp, touch, test, fr. *tocar* to touch, fr. VL *toccare* — more at TOUCH] (1968) *slang* : a puff on a marijuana cigarette *or* — **toke** *vi, slang*

¹to-ken \'tō-kən\ *n* [ME, fr. OE *tācen, tācn* sign, token; akin to OHG *zeihhan* sign, Gk *deiknynai* to show — more at DICTION] (bef. 12c) **1** : an outward sign or expression ⟨his tears were ∼s of his grief⟩ **2 a** : SYMBOL, EMBLEM ⟨a white flag is a ∼ of surrender⟩ **b** : an instance of a linguistic expression **3** : a distinguishing feature : CHARACTERISTIC **4 a** : SOUVENIR, KEEPSAKE **b** : a small part representing the whole : INDICATION ⟨this is only a ∼ of what we hope to accomplish⟩ **c** : something given or shown as a guarantee (as of authority, right, or identity) **5 a** : a piece resembling a coin issued as money by some person or body other than a de jure government **b** : a piece resembling a coin issued for use (as for fare on a bus) by a particular group on specified terms **6** : a member of a group (as a minority) that is included within a larger group through tokenism; *esp* : a token employee *syn* see SIGN — **by the same token** : for the same reason

²token *adj* (1547) **1** : done or given as a token esp. in partial fulfillment of an obligation or engagement ⟨a ∼ payment⟩ **2 a** : representing no more than a symbolic effort : MINIMAL, PERFUNCTORY ⟨∼ resistance⟩ ⟨∼ integration⟩ **b** : serving or intended to show absence of discrimination ⟨a ∼ female employee⟩

to-ken-ism \'tō-kə-ˌni-zəm\ *n* (1961) : the policy or practice of making only a symbolic effort (as to desegregate)

token money *n* (1889) : money of regular government issue (as paper currency or coins) having a greater face value than intrinsic value

To-khar-i-an *var of* TOCHARIAN

to-ko-no-ma \ˌtō-kə-'nō-mə\ *n* [Jp] (1871) : a niche or alcove in the wall of a Japanese house for the display of a decorative object

Tok Pis-in \'tōk-'pi-zən, -sən\ *n* [Tok Pisin, lit., pidgin talk] (1974) : an English-based creole that is a national language of Papua New Guinea

tol- *or* **tolu-** *comb form* [ISV, fr. *toluene*] : toluene ⟨*tolyl*⟩

to-la \'tō-lə, tō-'lä\ *n* [Hindi *tolā*, fr. Skt *tulā* weight; akin to L *tollere* to lift up] (1614) : a unit of weight of India equal to 180 grains troy or 0.4114 ounce (11.7 grams)

tol-booth \'tō(l)-ˌbüth, 'täl-, 'tȯl-\ *n* [ME *tolbothe, tollbothe* tollbooth, town hall, jail] (15c) **1** *Scot* : a town or market hall **2** *Scot* : JAIL, PRISON

tol-bu-ta-mide \täl-'byü-tə-ˌmīd\ *n* [*tol-* + *butyric* + *amide*] (1956) : a sulfonylurea $C_{12}H_{18}N_2O_3S$ used in the treatment of diabetes

told *past and past part of* TELL

tole \'tōl\ *n, often attrib* [F *tôle,* fr. MF dial. *taule,* fr. L *tabula* board, tablet] (1927) : sheet metal and esp. tinplate for use in domestic and ornamental wares in which it is usu. japanned or painted and often elaborately decorated; *also* : objects made of tole

To·le·do \tə-'lē-(,)dō\ *n, pl* **-dos** (1596) : a finely tempered sword of a kind made in Toledo, Spain

tol·er·a·ble \'tä-lə-rə-bəl, 'täl-rə-; 'tä-lər-bəl\ *adj* (15c) **1** : capable of being borne or endured ⟨~ pain⟩ **2** : moderately good or agreeable : PASSABLE ⟨a ~ singing voice⟩ — **tol·er·a·bil·i·ty** \,tä-lə-rə-'bi-lə-tē, ,täl-rə-\ *n* — **tol·er·a·bly** \'tä-lə-rə-blē, 'täl-rə-; 'tä-lər-blē\ *adv*

tol·er·ance \'tä-lə-rən(t)s, 'täl-rən(t)s\ *n* (15c) **1** : capacity to endure pain or hardship : ENDURANCE, FORTITUDE, STAMINA **2 a** : sympathy or indulgence for beliefs or practices differing from or conflicting with one's own **b** : the act of allowing something : TOLERATION **3** : the allowable deviation from a standard; *esp* : the range of variation permitted in maintaining a specified dimension in machining a piece **4 a** (1) : the capacity of the body to endure or become less responsive to a substance (as a drug) or a physiological insult with repeated use or exposure ⟨immunological ~ to a virus⟩ ⟨an addict's increasing ~ for a drug⟩ (2) : relative capacity of an organism to grow or thrive when subjected to an unfavorable environmental factor **b** : the maximum amount of a pesticide residue that may lawfully remain on or in food

tol·er·ant \-rənt\ *adj* (1784) **1** : inclined to tolerate; *esp* : marked by forbearance or endurance **2** : exhibiting tolerance (as for a drug or an environmental factor) — **tol·er·ant·ly** *adv*

tol·er·ate \'tä-lə-,rāt\ *vt* **-at·ed; -at·ing** [L *toleratus,* pp. of *tolerare* to endure, put up with; akin to OE *tholian* to bear, L *tollere* to lift up, *latus* carried (suppletive pp. of *ferre*), Gk *tlēnai* to bear] (1531) **1** : to exhibit physiological tolerance for (as a drug) **2 a** : to suffer to be or to be done without prohibition, hindrance, or contradiction **b** : to put up with *syn* see BEAR — **tol·er·a·tive** \-,rā-tiv\ *adj* — **tol·er·a·tor** \-,rā-tər\ *n*

tol·er·a·tion \,tä-lə-'rā-shən\ *n* (1531) **1 a** : the act or practice of tolerating something **b** : a government policy of permitting forms of religious belief and worship not officially established **2** : TOLERANCE 4a(1)

tol·i·dine \'tä-lə-,dēn\ *n* [ISV *tol-* + *-idine*] (1879) : any of several isomeric aromatic diamines $C_{14}H_{16}N_2$ that are homologues of benzidine and used esp. as dye intermediates

¹toll \'tōl\ *n* [ME, fr. OE, fr. (assumed) VL *tolonium,* alter. of LL *telonium* customhouse, fr. Gk *tolōnion,* fr. *telōnēs* collector of tolls, fr. *telos* tax, toll; perh. akin to Gk *tlēnai* to bear] (bef. 12c) **1** : a tax or fee paid for some liberty or privilege (as of passing over a highway or bridge) **2** : compensation for services rendered: as **a** : a charge for transportation **b** : a charge for a long-distance telephone call **3** : a grievous or ruinous price ⟨inflation has taken its ~⟩; *esp* : cost in life or health ⟨the death ~ from the hurricane⟩

²toll *vi* (14c) **1 a** : to take or levy toll ~ *vt* **1 a** : to exact part of as a toll **b** : to take as toll **2** : to exact a toll from (someone)

³toll *or* **tole** \'tōl\ *vt* **tolled** *or* **toled; toll·ing** *or* **tol·ing** [ME *tollen, tolen;* akin to OE *for·tyllan* to seduce] (13c) **1** : ALLURE, ENTICE **2 a** : to entice (game) to approach **b** : to attract (fish) with scattered bait **c** : to lead or attract (domestic animals) to a desired point

⁴toll *vb* [ME, perh. fr. *tollen* to entice] *vt* (15c) **1** : to sound (a bell) by pulling the rope **2 a** : to give signal or announcement of ⟨the clock ~ed each hour⟩ **b** : to announce by tolling ⟨church bells ~ed the death of the bishop⟩ **c** : to call to or from a place or occasion ⟨bells ~ed the congregation to church⟩ ~ *vi* : to sound with slow measured strokes ⟨the bell ~s solemnly⟩

⁵toll *n* (15c) : the sound of a tolling bell

toll-booth \'tōl-,büth\ *n* [ME *tolbothe, tollbothe* tollbooth, town hall, jail, fr. *tol, toll* toll + *bothe* booth] (14c) : a booth (as on a highway or bridge) where tolls are paid

toll call *n* (1928) : a long-distance telephone call at charges above a local rate

toll·gate \'tōl-,gāt\ *n* (1773) : a point where the driver of a vehicle must pay a toll

toll·house \-,haüs\ *n* (15c) : a house or booth where tolls are taken

Toll House *trademark* — used for cookies containing chocolate morsels

toll·way \-,wā\ *n* (1949) : TURNPIKE 2a(1)

Tol·tec \'tōl-,tek, 'täl-\ *n* [Sp *tolteca,* fr. Nahuatl *tōltēcah,* pl. of *tōltēcatl,* lit., person from *Tōllān* (now Tula de Allende, Mexico)] (1787) : a member of a people that dominated central and southern Mexico prior to the Aztecs — **Tol·tec·an** \-ən\ *adj*

tol·u·ene \'täl-yə-,wēn\ *n* [F *toluène,* fr. *tolu* balsam from the tropical American tree *Myroxylon balsamum,* fr. Sp *tolú,* fr. Santiago de *Tolú,* Colombia] (1871) : a liquid aromatic hydrocarbon C_7H_8 that resembles benzene but is less volatile, flammable, and toxic and is used as a solvent, in organic synthesis, and as an antiknock agent for gasoline

to·lu·i·dine \tə-'lü-ə-,dēn\ *n* [ISV] (1850) : any of three isomeric amino derivatives of toluene C_7H_9N that are analogous to aniline and are used as dye intermediates

toluidine blue *n* (1898) : a basic thiazine dye that is related to methylene blue and is used as a biological stain

to·lu·ol \'täl-yə-,wȯl, -,wōl\ *n* (ca. 1848) : toluene esp. of commercial grade

tol·yl \'tä-lil\ *n* [ISV] (ca. 1868) : any of three univalent groups $CH_3C_6H_4$ derived from toluene

tom \'täm\ *n* [*Tom,* nickname for *Thomas*] (1762) **1** : the male of various animals: as **a** : TOMCAT **b** : a male turkey **2** *cap* : UNCLE TOM 2

¹tom·a·hawk \'tä-mi-,hȯk\ *n* [Virginia Algonquian *tomahack*] (ca. 1612) : a light ax used as a missile and as a hand weapon esp. by No. American Indians

²tomahawk *vt* (ca. 1650) : to cut, strike, or kill with a tomahawk

to·mal·ley \tə-'ma-lē; 'tä-,ma-lē, -mə-lē\ *n, pl* **-leys** [Carib *tumali* sauce of lobster livers] (ca. 1666) : the liver of the lobster

Tom and Jer·ry \,täm-ən(d)-'jer-ē\ *n* [Corinthian *Tom & Jerry* Hawthorne, characters in *Life in London* (1821) by Pierce Egan †1849 Eng. sportswriter] (1845) : a hot drink that is a combination of a toddy and an eggnog

to·ma·til·lo \,tō-mə-'tē-(,)yō, -'tēl-(,)yō\ *n, pl* **-los** [Sp, dim. of *tomate*] (ca. 1913) : the small round pale green or yellow or purplish edible viscid fruit of a Mexican ground-cherry (*Physalis ixocarpa*); *also* : the plant

to·ma·to \tə-'mā-(,)tō; *chiefly Brit, eNewEng, neVirginia, and sometimes elsewhere in cultivated speech* -'mä- *or* -'mä-; *chiefly Northern* -'ma-\ *n, pl* **-toes** [alter. of earlier *tomate,* fr. Sp, fr. Nahuatl *tomatl*] (1604) **1** : the usu. large rounded typically red or yellow pulpy berry of a tomato **2** : any of a genus (*Lycopersicon*) of So. American herbs of the nightshade family; *esp* : one (*L. lycopersicum* syn. *L. esculentum*) that is more or less perennial in its native habitat but is widely cultivated as an annual for its edible fruit

to·ma·to·ey \-tə-wē\ *adj* (1972) **1** : of, relating to, or characteristic of a tomato **2** : richly flavored with tomatoes

tomato fruitworm *n* (ca. 1891) : CORN EARWORM

tomato hornworm *n* (1921) : a hawkmoth (*Manduca quinquemaculata*) whose larva is a hornworm feeding on plants of the nightshade family and esp. tobacco and tomato

¹tomb \'tüm\ *n* [ME *tombe,* fr. AF *tumbe,* fr. LL *tumba* sepulchral mound, fr. Gk *tymbos;* perh. akin to L *tumēre* to be swollen — more at THUMB] (13c) **1 a** : an excavation in which a corpse is buried : GRAVE **b** : a place of interment **2** : a house, chamber, or vault for the dead **3** : a building or structure resembling a tomb (as in appearance) — **tomb·less** \-ləs\ *adj*

²tomb *vt* (14c) : BURY, ENTOMB

tom·bac \'täm-,bak\ *n* [F, fr. D *tombak,* fr. Malay *tĕmbaga* copper] (1602) : an alloy essentially of copper and zinc and sometimes tin or arsenic that is used esp. for cheap jewelry and gilding

tom·bo·lo \'tōm-bə-,lō, 'täm-\ *n, pl* **-los** [It, fr. L *tumulus* mound, tumulus] (1899) : a sand or gravel bar connecting an island with the mainland or another island

tom·boy \'täm-,bȯi\ *n* (1592) : a girl who behaves in a manner usu. considered boyish : HOYDEN — **tom·boy·ish** \-ish\ *adj* — **tom·boy·ish·ness** *n*

tomb·stone \'tüm-,stōn\ *n* (1565) : GRAVESTONE

tom·cat \'täm-,kat\ *n* (1789) : a male domestic cat

tom·cod \-,käd\ *n* (1722) : either of two small fishes (*Microgadus tomcod* of the Atlantic and *M. proximus* of the Pacific) of the cod family

Tom Col·lins \'täm-'kä-lənz\ *n* [fr. the name *Tom Collins*] (ca. 1909) : a collins with a base of gin

Tom, Dick, and Har·ry \,täm-,dik-ən(d)-'har-ē\ *n, pl* **Toms, Dicks, and Harrys** (1815) : the common man : ANYONE — often used with *every* ⟨helps every *Tom, Dick, and Harry* in need⟩

tome \'tōm\ *n* [MF *or* L; MF, fr. L *tomus,* fr. Gk *tomos* section, roll of papyrus, tome, fr. *temnein* to cut; akin to MIr *tamnaid* he lops, Pol *ciąć* to cut, and perh. to L *tondēre* to shear] (1519) **1** : a volume forming part of a larger work **2** : BOOK; *esp* : a large or scholarly book

-tome *n comb form* [Gk *tomos*] **1** : part : segment ⟨myo*tome*⟩ **2** : cutting instrument ⟨micro*tome*⟩

to·men·tose \tō-'men-,tōs, 'tō-mən-\ *adj* [NL *tomentosus,* fr. *tomentum*] (1698) : covered with densely matted hairs ⟨a ~ leaf⟩

to·men·tum \tō-'men-təm\ *n, pl* **-ta** \-tə\ [NL, fr. L, cushion stuffing] (1699) : pubescence composed of densely matted woolly hairs

¹tom·fool \'täm-'fül\ *n* (ca. 1709) : a great fool : BLOCKHEAD

²tomfool *adj* (1819) : extremely foolish, stupid, or doltish

tom·fool·ery \,täm-'fül-rē, -'fü-lə-\ *n* (1812) : playful or foolish behavior

Tom·my \'tä-mē\ *n, pl* **Tommies** [*Thomas* Atkins, name used as model in official army forms] (1892) : a British soldier

Tommy At·kins \-'at-kənz\ *n* (1883) : TOMMY

tom·my–gun \'tä-mē-,gən\ *vt* (1942) : to shoot with a tommy gun

tommy gun *n* [by shortening & alter.] (1929) : THOMPSON SUBMACHINE GUN; *broadly* : SUBMACHINE GUN

tom·my·rot \'tä-mē-,rät\ *n* [E dial. *tommy* fool + E *rot*] (1884) : utter foolishness or nonsense

to·mo·gram \'tō-mə-,gram\ *n* (1936) : a roentgenogram made by tomography

to·mog·ra·phy \tō-'mä-grə-fē\ *n* [Gk *tomos* section + ISV *-graphy* — more at TOME] (1935) : a method of producing a three-dimensional image of the internal structures of a solid object (as the human body or the earth) by the observation and recording of the differences in the effects on the passage of waves of energy impinging on those structures — compare COMPUTED TOMOGRAPHY — **to·mo·graph·ic** \,tō-mə-'gra-fik\ *adj*

¹to·mor·row \tə-'mär-(,)ō, -'mȯr-\ *adv* [ME *to morgen,* fr. OE *tō morgen, fr. tō to + morgen* morrow, morning — more at MORN] (13c) : on or for the day after today ⟨will do it ~⟩

²tomorrow *n* (14c) **1** : the day after the present ⟨the court will recess until ~⟩ **2** : FUTURE 1a ⟨the world of ~⟩

tom·pi·on \'täm-pē-ən\ *var of* TAMPION

Tom Thumb \'täm-'thəm\ *n* **1** : a legendary English dwarf **2** : a dwarf type, race, or individual

tom·tit \'täm-,tit, täm-'\ *n* [prob. short for *tomtitmouse,* fr. the name *Tom* + *titmouse*] (1700) : any of various small active birds

tom–tom \'täm-,täm, 'tȧm-,tȧm, 'təm-,təm\ *n* [Hindi *ṭamṭam*] (1693) **1** : a usu. long and narrow small-headed drum commonly beaten with the hands **2** : a monotonous beating, rhythm, or rhythmical sound

-tomy *n comb form* [NL *-tomia,* fr. Gk, fr. *-tomos* that cuts, fr. *temnein* to cut — more at TOME] : incision : section ⟨laparo*tomy*⟩

¹ton \'tən\ *n, pl* **tons** *also* **ton** [ME *tunne* unit of weight or capacity — more at TUN] (14c) **1 a** : a unit of internal capacity for ships equal to 100 cubic feet — called also *register ton* **b** : a unit approximately equal to the volume of a long ton weight of seawater used in reckoning the displacement of ships and equal to 35 cubic feet **c** : a unit of volume for cargo freight usu. reckoned at 40 cubic feet — called also *measurement ton* **2** : any of various units of weight: **a** — see WEIGHT table **b** : METRIC TON **3** : a great quantity : LOT — often used in pl. ⟨ate ~s of hamburgers⟩ ⟨has ~s of money⟩

\ə\ abut \ᵊ\ kitten, F table \ər\ further \a\ ash \ā\ ace \ä\ mop, mar \aü\ out \ch\ chin \e\ bet \ē\ easy \g\ go \i\ hit \ī\ ice \j\ job \ŋ\ sing \ō\ go \ȯ\ law \ȯi\ boy \th\ thin \t̲h̲\ the \ü\ loot \u̇\ foot \y\ yet \zh\ vision \à, k̲, ⁿ, œ, œ̄, ᵫ, ᵫ̄, ʸ\ *see* Guide to Pronunciation

²**ton** \'tōn\ *n* [F, lit., tone, fr. L *tonus*] (1765) **1** : the prevailing fashion : VOGUE **2** : the quality or state of being smart or fashionable

ton·al \'tō-n⁰l\ *adj* (1776) **1** : of or relating to tone, tonality, or tonicity **2** : having tonality — **ton·al·ly** \-n⁰l-ē\ *adv*

to·nal·i·ty \tō-'na-lə-tē\ *n, pl* **-ties** (1838) **1** : tonal quality **2 a** : KEY 7 **b** : the organization of all the tones and harmonies of a piece of music in relation to a tonic **3** : the arrangement or interrelation of the tones of a work of visual art

ton·do \'tän-(,)dō\ *n, pl* **ton·di** \-(,)dē\ [It, fr. *tondo* round, short for *rotondo*, fr. L *rotundus* — more at ROTUND] (1890) **1** : a circular painting **2** : a sculptured medallion

¹**tone** \'tōn\ *n* [ME, fr. L *tonus* tension, tone, fr. Gk *tonos*, lit., act of stretching; akin to Gk *teinein* to stretch — more at THIN] (14c) **1** : vocal or musical sound of a specific quality ⟨spoke in low ~s⟩ ⟨masculine ~s⟩; *esp* : musical sound with respect to timbre and manner of expression **2 a** : a sound of definite pitch and vibration **b** : WHOLE STEP **3** : accent or inflection expressive of a mood or emotion **4** : the pitch of a word often used to express differences of meaning **5** : a particular pitch or change of pitch constituting an element in the intonation of a phrase or sentence ⟨high ~⟩ ⟨low ~⟩ ⟨mid ~⟩ ⟨low-rising ~⟩ ⟨falling ~⟩ **6** : style or manner of expression in speaking or writing ⟨seemed wise to adopt a conciliatory ~⟩ **7 a** (1) : color quality or value (2) : a tint or shade of color **b** : the color that appreciably modifies a hue or white or black ⟨gray walls of greenish ~⟩ **8** : the effect in painting of light and shade together with color **9 a** : the state of a living body or of any of its organs or parts in which the functions are healthy and performed with due vigor **b** : normal tension or responsiveness to stimuli; *specif* : muscular tonus **10 a** : healthy elasticity : RESILIENCY **b** : general character, quality, or trend ⟨a city's upbeat ~⟩ **c** : frame of mind : MOOD

²**tone** *vb* **toned; ton·ing** *vt* (1660) **1** : INTONE **2** : to give a particular intonation or inflection to **3 a** : to impart tone to : STRENGTHEN ⟨medicine to ~ up the system⟩ **b** : to soften or reduce in intensity, color, appearance, or sound : MELLOW — often used with *down* **c** : to change the normal silver image of (as a photographic print) into a colored image ~ *vi* **1** : to assume a pleasing color quality or tint **2** : to blend or harmonize in color

tone·arm \'tōn-,ärm\ *n* (1913) : the movable part of a phonograph or record player that carries the pickup and permits the needle to follow the record groove

tone color *n* (1881) : TIMBRE

toned \'tōnd\ *adj* (15c) **1** : having tone or a specified tone : characterized or distinguished by a tone **2** *of paper* : having a slight tint

tone-deaf \'tōn-,def\ *adj* (1894) : relatively insensitive to differences in musical pitch — **tone deafness** *n*

tone language *n* (ca. 1909) : a language (as Chinese or Zulu) in which variations in tone distinguish words or phrases of different meaning that otherwise would sound alike

tone·less \-ləs\ *adj* (1773) : lacking in tone, modulation, or expression — **tone·less·ly** *adv* — **tone·less·ness** *n*

to·neme \'tō-,nēm\ *n* (1923) : an intonation phoneme in a tone language — **to·ne·mic** \tō-'nē-mik\ *adj*

tone poem *n* (1902) : SYMPHONIC POEM — **tone poet** *n*

ton·er \'tō-nər\ *n* (1888) : one that tones or is a source of tones: as **a** : a solution used to impart color to a silver photographic image **b** : a substance used to develop a latent xerographic image **c** : a liquid cosmetic for cleansing the skin and contracting the pores

tone row *n* (1936) : the chosen sequence of tones that serves as the basis for a work of serial music; *esp* : TWELVE-TONE ROW

to·net·ic \tō-'ne-tik\ *adj* (1922) **1** : relating to linguistic tones or to tone languages **2** : of or relating to intonation ⟨~ notation⟩ — **to·net·i·cal·ly** \-ti-k(ə-)lē\ *adv*

to·net·ics \-tiks\ *n pl but sing in constr* (1921) : the use or study of linguistic tones

to·nette \tō-'net\ *n* [¹tone + -ette] (1939) : a simple fipple flute with a range somewhat larger than an octave that is often used in elementary music education

ton·ey *var of* TONY

¹**tong** \'täŋ, 'tȯŋ\ *n* [Chin (Guangdong) *tòhng*, lit., hall] (1883) : a secret society or fraternal organization esp. of Chinese in the U.S. formerly notorious for gang warfare

²**tong** *vb* [*tongs*] *vt* (1901) : to take, gather, hold, or handle with tongs ⟨~ oysters⟩ ~ *vi* : to use tongs esp. in taking or gathering something — **tong·er** \'täŋ-ər, 'tȯŋ-\ *n*

ton·ga \'täŋ-gə\ *n* [Hindi *tāṅgā*] (1874) : a light 2-wheeled vehicle for two or four persons drawn by one horse and common in India

Ton·gan \'täŋ-gən *also* -ən\ *n* (1853) **1** : a member of a Polynesian people of Tonga **2** : the Polynesian language of the Tongans — **Tongan** *adj*

tongs \'täŋz, 'tȯŋz\ *n pl but sing or pl in constr* [ME *tonges*, pl. of *tonge*, fr. OE *tang*; akin to OHG *zanga* tongs and perh. to Gk *daknein* to bite] (bef. 12c) : any of numerous grasping devices consisting commonly of two pieces joined at one end by a pivot or hinged like scissors

¹**tongue** \'təŋ\ *n* [ME *tunge*, fr. OE; akin to OHG *zunga* tongue, L *lingua*] (bef. 12c) **1 a** : a fleshy movable process of the floor of the mouths of most vertebrates that bears sensory end organs and small glands and functions esp. in taking and swallowing food and in humans as a speech organ **b** : a part of various invertebrate animals that is analogous to the tongue **2** : the flesh of a tongue (as of the ox or sheep) used as food **3** : the power of communication through speech **4 a** : LANGUAGE; *esp* : a spoken language **b** : manner or quality of utterance with respect to tone or sound, the sense of what is expressed, or the intention of the speaker ⟨she has a clever ~⟩ ⟨a sharp ~⟩ **c** : ecstatic usu. unintelligible utterance accompanying religious excitation — usu. used in pl. **d** : the cry of or as if of a hound pursuing or in sight of game — used esp. in the phrase *to give tongue* **5** : a tapering flame ⟨~s of fire⟩ **6** : a long narrow strip of land projecting into a body of water **7** : something resembling an animal's tongue in being elongated and fastened at one end only: as **a** : a movable pin in a buckle **b** : a metal ball suspended inside a bell so as to strike against the sides as the bell is swung **c** : the pole of a vehicle **d** : the flap under the lacing or buckles of a shoe at the throat of the vamp **8 a** : the rib on one edge of a board that fits into a corresponding groove in an edge of another board to make a flush joint **b** : FEATHER 4 — **tongue·like** \-,līk\ *adj*

²**tongue** *vb* **tongued; tongu·ing** \'təŋ-iŋ\ *vt* (14c) **1** *archaic* : SCOLD **2** : to touch or lick with or as if with the tongue **3 a** : to cut a tongue on ⟨~ a board⟩ **b** : to join (as boards) by means of a tongue and groove ⟨~ flooring together⟩ **4** : to articulate (notes) by tonguing ~ *vi* **1** : to project in a tongue **2** : to articulate notes on a wind instrument by successively interrupting the stream of wind with the action of the tongue

tongue and groove *n* (ca. 1876) : a joint made by a tongue on one edge of a board fitting into a corresponding groove on the edge of another board — **tongue-and-groove** *adj*

tongued \'təŋd\ *adj* (14c) : having a tongue esp. of a specified kind — often used in combination ⟨sharp-*tongued*⟩

tongue-in-cheek *adj* (1933) : characterized by insincerity, irony, or whimsical exaggeration

tongue in cheek *adv* (ca. 1934) : with insincerity, irony, or whimsical exaggeration

tongue-lash \'təŋ-,lash\ *vb* [back-formation fr. *tongue-lashing*] (1881) : CHIDE, SCOLD — **tongue-lash·ing** *n*

tongue·less \-ləs\ *adj* (14c) **1** : having no tongue **2** : lacking power of speech : MUTE

¹**tongue-tie** \'təŋ-,tī\ *vt* [back-formation fr. *tongue-tied*] (1555) : to deprive of speech or the power of distinct articulation

²**tongue-tie** *n* (ca. 1852) : limited mobility of the tongue due to shortness of its frenulum

tongue-tied \'təŋ-,tīd\ *adj* (1529) **1** : unable or disinclined to speak freely (as from shyness) **2** : affected with tongue-tie

tongue twister *n* (1904) : a word, phrase, or sentence difficult to articulate because of a succession of similar consonantal sounds (as in "twin-screw steel cruiser")

-tonia *n comb form* [NL, fr. *tonus*] : condition or degree of tonus ⟨myotonia⟩

¹**ton·ic** \'tä-nik\ *adj* [Gk *tonikos*, fr. *tonos* tension, tone] (1649) **1 a** : characterized by tonus ⟨~ contraction of muscle⟩; *also* : marked by prolonged muscular contraction ⟨~ convulsions⟩ **b** : producing or adapted to produce healthy muscular condition and reaction of organs (as muscles) **2 a** : increasing or restoring physical or mental tone : REFRESHING **b** : yielding a tonic substance **3** : relating to or based on the first tone of a scale ⟨~ harmony⟩ **4** *of a syllable* : bearing a principal stress or accent **5** : of or relating to speech tones or to languages using them to distinguish words otherwise identical — **ton·i·cal·ly** \'tä-ni-k(ə-)lē\ *adv*

²**tonic** *n* (1799) **1 a** : an agent (as a drug) that increases body tone **b** : one that invigorates, restores, refreshes, or stimulates ⟨a day in the country was a ~ for him⟩ **c** : a liquid preparation for the scalp or hair **d** *chiefly NewEng* : a carbonated flavored beverage **e** : TONIC WATER **2** : the first tone of a diatonic scale : KEYNOTE **3** : a voiced sound

tonic accent *n* (1867) **1** : relative phonetic prominence (as from greater stress or higher pitch) of a spoken syllable or word **2** : accent depending on pitch rather than stress

to·nic·i·ty \tō-'ni-sə-tē\ *n* (1824) **1** : the property of possessing tone; *esp* : healthy vigor of body or mind **2** : muscular tonus

tonic sol-fa *n* (1852) : a system of solmization based on key relationships that replaces the normal notation with sol-fa syllables or their initials

tonic water *n* (1926) : a carbonated beverage flavored with a small amount of quinine, lemon, and lime

¹**to·night** \tə-'nīt\ *adv* (bef. 12c) : on this present night or the night following this present day ⟨will do it ~⟩

²**tonight** *n* (14c) : the present night or the night following this present day

ton·ka bean \'täŋ-kə-\ *n* [prob. fr. Tupi *tonka*] (1796) : the coumarin-containing seed of any of several tropical American leguminous trees (genus *Dipteryx*) that is used in perfumes and as an artificial vanilla flavoring; *also* : a tree bearing tonka beans

ton·nage \'tə-nij\ *n* [in sense 1, fr. ME, MF, fr. *tonne* tun; in other senses, fr. ¹*ton* — more at TUNNEL] (15c) **1** : duty formerly levied on every tun of wine imported into England **2 a** : a duty or impost on vessels based on cargo capacity **b** : a duty on goods per ton transported **3** : ships in terms of the total number of tons registered or carried or of their carrying capacity **4 a** : the cubical content of a merchant ship in units of 100 cubic feet **b** : the displacement of a warship **5 a** : total weight in tons shipped, carried, or produced **b** : impressively large amount or weight

tonne \'tən\ *n* [F, fr. *tonne* tun, fr. OF — more at TUNNEL] (1877) : METRIC TON

ton·neau \'tä-,nō, tə-'nō\ *n, pl* **tonneaus** [F, lit., tun, fr. OF *tonel* — more at TUNNEL] (1901) **1** : the rear seating compartment of an automobile; *also* : the entire seating compartment **2** : a shape of watch case or dial resembling a barrel in profile

ton·ner \'tə-nər\ *n* (1851) : an object (as a ship) having a specified tonnage — used in combination ⟨a thousand-*tonner*⟩

to·nom·e·ter \tō-'nä-mə-tər\ *n* [Gk *tonos* tone + E *-meter*] (1725) **1** : an instrument or device for determining the exact pitch or the vibration rate of tones **2** : an instrument for measuring tension or pressure and esp. intraocular pressure — **to·nom·e·try** \tō-'nä-mə-trē\ *n*

to·no·plast \'tō-nə-,plast\ *n* [ISV *tono-* (fr. Gk *tonos* tension) + -*plast* — more at TONE] (ca. 1888) : a semipermeable membrane surrounding a plant-cell vacuole

ton·sil \'tän(t)-səl\ *n* [L *tonsillae*, pl., tonsils] (1601) **1** : either of a pair of prominent masses of lymphoid tissue that lie one on each side of the throat between the anterior and posterior pillars of the fauces **2** : any of various masses of lymphoid tissue that are similar to tonsils — **ton·sil·lar** \'tän(t)-s(ə-)lər\ *adj*

tonsill- *comb form* [L *tonsillae*] : tonsil ⟨*tonsillectomy*⟩

ton·sil·lec·to·my \,tän(t)-sə-'lek-tə-mē\ *n, pl* **-mies** (1899) : the surgical removal of the tonsils

ton·sil·li·tis \-'lī-təs\ *n* [NL] (1801) : inflammation of the tonsils

ton·so·ri·al \tän-'sȯr-ē-əl, -'sȯr-\ *adj* [L *tonsorius*, fr. *tondēre*] (1813) : of or relating to a barber or the work of a barber

¹**ton·sure** \'tän(t)-shər\ *n* [ME, fr. ML *tonsura*, fr. L, act of shearing, fr. *tonsus*, pp. of *tondēre* to shear — more at TOME] (14c) **1** : the Roman Catholic or Eastern rite of admission to the clerical state by the clip-

ping or shaving of a portion of the head   **2** : the shaven crown or patch worn by monks and other clerics   **3** : a bald spot resembling a tonsure

²tonsure *vt* **ton·sured; ton·sur·ing** \'tän(t)-sh(ə-)riŋ\ (1706) : to shave the head of; *esp* : to confer the tonsure upon

ton·tine \'tän-,tēn, tän-'\ *n* [F, fr. Lorenzo *Tonti* †1695 Ital. banker] (1765) : a joint financial arrangement whereby the participants usu. contribute equally to a prize that is awarded entirely to the participant who survives all the others

to·nus \'tō-nəs\ *n* [NL, fr. L, tension, tone] (1876) : TONE 9a; *esp* : a state of partial contraction characteristic of normal muscle

tony \'tō-nē\ *adj* **ton·i·er; -est** (1877) : marked by an aristocratic or high-toned manner or style ⟨~ private schools⟩

To·ny \'tō-nē\ *n, pl* **Tonys** [*Tony*, nickname of Antoinette Perry †1946 Am. actress & producer] (1947) : a medallion awarded annually by a professional organization for notable achievement in the theater

too \'tü\ *adv* [ME, fr. OE *tō* to, too — more at TO] (bef. 12c)   **1** : BESIDES, ALSO ⟨sell the house and furniture ~⟩   **2 a** : to an excessive degree : EXCESSIVELY ⟨~ large a house for us⟩   **b** : to such a degree as to be regrettable ⟨this time he has gone ~ far⟩   **c** : VERY ⟨didn't seem ~ interested⟩   **3** : so 2d ("I didn't do it." "You did ~.")

took *past of* TAKE

¹tool \'tül\ *n* [ME, fr. OE *tōl*; akin to OE *tawian* to prepare for use — more at TAW] (bef. 12c)   **1 a** : a handheld device that aids in accomplishing a task   **b** (1) : the cutting or shaping part in a machine or machine tool   (2) : a machine for shaping metal : MACHINE TOOL   **2 a** : something (as an instrument or apparatus) used in performing an operation or necessary in the practice of a vocation or profession ⟨a scholar's books are his ~s⟩   **b** : a means to an end ⟨a book's cover can be a marketing ~⟩   **c** : PENIS — often considered vulgar   **3** : one that is used or manipulated by another   **4** *pl* : natural ability ⟨has all the ~s⟩   *syn* see IMPLEMENT

²tool *vt* (1812)   **1 a** : to cause (a vehicle) to go : DRIVE   **b** : to convey in a vehicle   **2** : to shape, form, or finish with a tool; *esp* : to letter or ornament (as leather or gold) by means of hand tools   **3** : to equip (as a plant or industry) with tools, machines, and instruments for production ~ *vi*   **1** : DRIVE, RIDE   **2** : to equip a plant or industry with the means (as machines, machine tools, and instruments) of production — often used with *up*

³tool *n* (1881) : a design (as on the binding of a book) made by tooling

tool·box \'tül-,bäks\ *n* (1832) : a chest for tools

tool·hold·er \-,hōl-dər\ *n* (ca. 1876) : a short steel bar having a shank at one end by which it is clamped to a machine and a clamp at the other end to hold small interchangeable cutting bits

tool·house \-,haùs\ *n* (1818) : TOOLSHED

tool·mak·er \'tül-,mā-kər\ *n* (1844) : one that makes tools; *esp* : a machinist who specializes in the construction, repair, maintenance, and calibration of the tools, jigs, fixtures, and instruments of a machine shop

tool·mak·ing \-,kiŋ\ *n* (1893) : the action, process, or art of making tools; *also* : the trade of a toolmaker

tool·room \'tül-,rüm, -,rùm\ *n* (1878) : a room where tools are kept; *esp* : a room in a machine shop in which tools are made, stored, and issued for use by workers

tool·shed \-,shed\ *n* (1840) : an outbuilding for storing tools

tools of ignorance [fr. the notion that a smart athlete would not play such a grueling position] (1939) : a baseball catcher's equipment

tool subject *n* (1925) : a subject studied to gain competence in a skill used in other subjects

toom \'tüm\ *adj* [ME, fr. OE *tōm* — more at TEEM] (bef. 12c) *chiefly Scot* : EMPTY

toon \'tün\ *n* [Hindi *tūn*, fr. Skt *tunna*] (1810) : a southeast Asian and Australian tree (*Cedrela toona*) of the mahogany family with fragrant dark red wood and flowers that yield a dye; *also* : its wood

¹toot \'tüt\ *vb* [imit. prob. imit.] *vi* (ca. 1510)   **1 a** : to sound a short blast ⟨the horn ~ed⟩   **b** : to sound a note or call suggesting the short blast of a wind instrument   **2** : to blow or sound an instrument (as a horn) esp. so as to produce short blasts ~ *vt* : to cause to sound ⟨~ a whistle⟩ — **toot·er** *n*

²toot *n* (1641) : a short blast (as on a horn); *also* : a sound resembling such a blast

³toot *n* [Sc *toot* to drink heavily] (ca. 1790) : a drinking bout : SPREE

tooth \'tüth\ *n, pl* **teeth** \'tēth\ [ME, fr. OE *tōth;* akin to OHG *zand* tooth, L *dent-, dens,* Gk *odont-, odous*] (bef. 12c)   **1 a** : one of the hard bony appendages that are borne on the jaws or in many of the lower vertebrates on other bones in the walls of the mouth or pharynx and serve esp. for the prehension and mastication of food and as weapons of offense and defense   **b** : any of various usu. hard and sharp processes esp. about the mouth of an invertebrate   **2** : TASTE, LIKING   **3** : a projection resembling or suggesting the tooth of an animal in shape, arrangement, or action (a saw ~): as   **a** : any of the regular projections on the circumference or sometimes the face of a wheel that engage with corresponding projections on another wheel esp. to transmit force : COG   **b** : a small sharp-pointed marginal lobe or process on a plant   **4 a** : something that injures, tortures, devours, or destroys   **b** *pl* : effective means of enforcement   **5** : a roughness of surface produced by mechanical or artificial means — **tooth·like** \'tüth-,līk\ *adj* — **in the teeth of 1**

tooth 1a: *A* outside of a molar: *1* crown, *2* neck, *3* roots; *B* cross section of a molar: *1* enamel, *2* dentin, *3* pulp, *4* cementum, *5* gum; *C* dentition of adult human, upper; *D* dentition of adult human, lower: *1* incisors, *2* canines, *3* bicuspids, *4* molars

: in or into direct contact or collision with ⟨found themselves sailing *in the teeth of* a hurricane —*Current Biog.*⟩   **2** : in direct opposition to ⟨rule had ... been imposed by conquest *in the teeth of* obstinate resis

tance —A. J. Toynbee⟩ — **to the teeth** : FULLY, COMPLETELY ⟨armed *to the teeth*⟩

tooth·ache \'tüth-,āk\ *n* (14c) : pain in or about a tooth

tooth and nail *adv* (1550) : with every available means : ALL OUT ⟨fight *tooth and nail*⟩

tooth·brush \'tüth-,brəsh\ *n* (1690) : a brush for cleaning the teeth

tooth·brush·ing *n* (1920) : the action of using a toothbrush to clean teeth

toothed \'tütht, *uncompounded also* 'tü-thəd\ *adj* (14c) : having teeth esp. of a specified kind or number — often used in combination ⟨buck*toothed*⟩

toothed whale \'tütht-, 'tü-thəd-\ *n* (1843) : any of a suborder (Odontoceti) of cetaceans (as a dolphin, porpoise, or killer whale) bearing usu. numerous simple conical teeth — compare BALEEN WHALE

tooth fairy *n* (1962) : a fairy believed by children to leave money while they sleep in exchange for a tooth that has come out

tooth·less \'tüth-ləs\ *adj* (14c)   **1** : having no teeth   **2 a** : lacking in sharpness or bite ⟨spoke in ~ generalities —Arthur Hepner⟩   **b** : lacking in means of enforcement or coercion : INEFFECTUAL

tooth·paste \-,pāst\ *n* (1832) : a paste for cleaning the teeth

tooth·pick \-,pik\ *n* (15c) : a pointed instrument (as a slender tapering piece of wood) for removing food particles lodged between the teeth

tooth powder *n* (1542) : a powder for cleaning the teeth

tooth shell *n* (ca. 1711) : any of a class (Scaphopoda) of burrowing marine mollusks with a tapering tubular shell; *also* : this shell

tooth·some \'tüth-səm\ *adj* (1551)   **1 a** : AGREEABLE, ATTRACTIVE   **b** : sexually attractive ⟨a ~ blonde⟩   **2** : of palatable flavor and pleasing texture : DELICIOUS ⟨crisp ~ fried chicken⟩   *syn* see PALATABLE — **tooth·some·ly** *adv* — **tooth·some·ness** *n*

tooth·wort \-,wort, -,wört\ *n* (1597)   **1** : a European parasitic plant (*Lathraea squamaria*) of the broomrape family having a rootstock covered with tooth-shaped scales   **2** : any of various cresses (genus *Dentaria*) including several cultivated for their showy flowers

toothy \'tü-thē\ *adj* **tooth·i·er; -est** (1530)   **1** : having or showing prominent teeth ⟨~ grin⟩   **2** : TOOTHSOME 2 — **tooth·i·ly** \-thə-lē\ *adv*

too·tle \'tü-t³l\ *vb* **too·tled; too·tling** \'tüt-liŋ, 'tü-t³l-iŋ\ [freq. of ¹*toot*] *vi* (1820)   **1** : to toot gently, repeatedly, or continuously   **2** : to drive or move along in a leisurely manner ~ *vt* : to toot continuously on — **tootle** *n* — **too·tler** \'tüt-lər, 'tü-t³l-ər\ *n*

too–too \'tü-'tü\ *adj* (1881)   **1** : going beyond the bounds of convention, good taste, or common sense : EXTREME   **2** : LA-DI-DA

toot·sie \'tùt-sē\ *n* [origin unknown] (1905)   **1** : DEAR, SWEETHEART   **2** : PROSTITUTE

toot·sy *also* **toot·sie** \'tùt-sē\ *n, pl* **tootsies** [baby-talk alter. of *foot*] (1854) : FOOT

¹top \'täp\ *n* [ME, fr. OE; akin to OHG *zopf* tip, tuft of hair] (bef. 12c)   **1 a** (1) : the highest point, level, or part of something : SUMMIT, CROWN   (2) : the head or top of the head — used esp. in the phrase *top to toe*   (3) : the head of a plant and esp. one with edible roots ⟨beet ~s⟩   (4) : a garment worn on the upper body   **b** (1) : the highest or uppermost region or part   (2) : the upper end, edge, or surface   **2** : a fitted, integral, or attached part or unit serving as an upper piece, lid, or covering   **3 a** : a platform surrounding the head of a lower mast that serves to spread the topmast rigging, strengthen the mast, and furnish a standing place for men aloft   **b** : a comparable part of the superstructure; *esp* : such a part on a warship used as a fire-control station or antiaircraft gun platform   **4 a** : the highest degree or pitch conceivable or attained : ACME, PINNACLE   **b** : the loudest or highest range of a sound   **5 a** : the part that is nearest in space or time to the source or beginning   **b** : the first half of an inning in baseball   **6 a** (1) : the highest position (as in rank or achievement)   (2) : a person or thing at the top   **b** *pl* : aces and kings in a hand or the three highest honors in a suit   **7** : the choicest part : CREAM, PICK   **8** : a forward spin given to a ball (as in golf or billiards) by striking it on or near the top or above the center; *also* : the stroke so given — **topped** \'täpt\ *adj* — **off the top of one's head** : in an impromptu manner ⟨sat down and wrote the ... story *off the top of his head* —Jerome Beatty, Jr.⟩ — **on top of 1 a** : in control of ⟨acted like a man *on top of* his job —*Newsweek*⟩   **b** : informed about ⟨tried to keep *on top of* new developments⟩   **2** : in sudden and unexpected proximity to ⟨the deadline was *on top of* them⟩   **3** : in addition to — **on top of the world** : in a position of eminent success, happiness, or fame — **over the top** : beyond the bounds of what is expected, usual, normal, or appropriate

²top *vb* **topped; top·ping** *vt* (1509)   **1** : to remove or cut the top of: as   **a** : to shorten or remove the top of (a plant) : PINCH 1b   **b** : to remove the most volatile parts from (as crude petroleum)   **2 a** : to cover with a top or on the top : provide, form, or serve as a top for   **b** : to supply with a decorative or protective finish or final touch   **c** : to resupply or refill to capacity — usu. used with *off* ⟨*topped* off the tank⟩   **d** : to complete the basic structure of (as a high-rise building) by putting on a cap or uppermost section — usu. used with *out* or *off*   **e** : to bring to an end or climax — usu. used with *off* ⟨the event was *topped* off with a relay race —Paula Rodenas⟩   **3 a** : to be or become higher than : OVERTOP ⟨~s the previous record⟩   **b** : to be superior to : EXCEL, SURPASS   **c** : to gain ascendancy over : DOMINATE   **4 a** : to rise to, reach, or be at the top of   **b** : to go over the top of : CLEAR, SURMOUNT   **5** : to strike (a ball) above the center thereby imparting topspin ~ *vi*   **1** : to make an end, finish, or conclusion   **2** : to reach a summit or crest — usu. used with *off* or *out*

³top *adj* (1593)   **1** : of, relating to, or being at the top : UPPERMOST   **2** : CHIEF, LEADING ⟨one of the world's ~ journalists⟩   **3** : of the highest quality, amount, or degree ⟨~ value⟩ ⟨~ form⟩   **4** : having a quantum characteristic whose existence was postulated on the basis of the discovery of the bottom quark ⟨~ quark⟩

⁴top *n* [ME, fr. OE, plaything] (14c) : a commonly cylindrical or conoidal device that has a tapering usu. steel-shod point on which it is made to spin and that is used esp. as a toy

---

\ə\ abut \ᵊ\ kitten, F table \ər\ further \a\ ash \ā\ ace \ä\ mop, mar \aù\ out \ch\ chin \e\ bet \ē\ easy \g\ go \i\ hit \ī\ ice \j\ job \ŋ\ sing \ō\ go \ò\ law \òi\ boy \th\ thin \t̲h̲\ the \ü\ loot \ù\ foot \y\ yet \zh\ vision \á, k̲, ⁿ, œ, œ̄, ue, ūe, ᵊ\ *see* Guide to Pronunciation

top- or **topo-** comb form [ME, fr. LL, fr. Gk, fr. topos] : place : locality ⟨topology⟩ ⟨toponymy⟩

to·paz \'tō-,paz\ n [ME topace, fr. OF, fr. L topazus, fr. Gk topazos] (13c) **1 a :** a mineral that is essentially a silicate of aluminum and usu. occurs in orthorhombic translucent or transparent crystals or in white translucent masses **b :** a usu. yellow to brownish yellow transparent mineral topaz used as a gem   **c :** a yellow sapphire   **d :** a yellow quartz **2 :** either of two large brilliantly colored So. American hummingbirds (Topaza pella and T. pyra)

top banana n [fr. a burlesque routine involving three comedians in which the one that gets the punch line also gets a banana] (1952) : the leading comedian in a burlesque show; broadly : KINGPIN 2

top billing n (1945) **1 :** prominent emphasis, featuring, or advertising **2 :** the position at the top of a theatrical bill usu. featuring the star's name

top boot n (1768) : a high boot often with light-colored leather bands around the upper part

top·coat \'täp-,kōt\ n (1804) **1 :** a lightweight overcoat **2 :** OVERCOAT 2

top·cross \-,krós\ n (1890) : a cross between a superior or purebred male and inferior female stock to improve the average quality of the progeny; also : the product of such a cross

top dog n (1900) : a person or group in a position of authority esp. through victory in a hard-fought competition

top dollar n (1970) : the highest amount being paid for a commodity or service ⟨willing to pay top dollar to get them —Dean Failey⟩

top–down \'täp-'daún\ adj [fr. the phrase from the top down] (1941) **1 :** controlled, directed, or instituted from the top level ⟨a ~ corporate structure⟩ **2 :** proceeding by breaking large general aspects (as of a problem) into smaller more detailed constituents : working from the general to the specific ⟨~ programming⟩ ⟨~ design⟩

top drawer n (1905) : the highest level of society, authority, or excellence — **top–draw·er** \-'dró(-ə)r\ adj

top–dress \'täp-,dres\ vt (1733) **1 :** to apply material to (as land or a road) without working it in; esp : to scatter fertilizer over (land)

top–dress·ing \-,dre-siŋ\ n (1744) : a material used to top-dress soil

¹tope \'tōp\ vi toped; top·ing [obs. E tope, interj. used to wish good health before drinking] (1667) : to drink liquor to excess

²tope n [origin unknown] (1686) : a small cosmopolitan shark (Galeorhinus galeus) with a liver very rich in vitamin A

³tope n [perh. fr. Panjabi top hat] (1815) : STUPA

to·pee or **to·pi** \tō-'pē, 'tō-(,)pē\ n [Hindi ṭopī] (1835) : a lightweight helmet-shaped hat made of pith or cork

top·er \'tō-pər\ n (1673) : one that topes; esp : DRUNKARD

top–flight \'täp-'flit\ adj (1931) : of, relating to, or being the highest level of achievement, excellence, or eminence — **top flight** n

¹Top 40 n pl (1966) : the forty best-selling phonograph records for a given period

²Top 40 adj (1966) : constituting, playing, listing, or relating to the Top 40 ⟨Top 40 hits⟩ ⟨Top 40 stations⟩ ⟨Top 40 charts⟩

top·ful or **top·full** \'täp-'fúl\ adj (1553) : BRIMFUL

¹top·gal·lant \(,)täp-'ga-lənt, tə-'ga-\ adj [¹top + ²gallant] (1514) : of, relating to, or being a part next above the topmast and below the royal mast ⟨~ sails⟩ ⟨the ~ mast⟩

²topgallant n (1581) **1** archaic : the topmost point : SUMMIT ⟨the high ~ of my joy —Shak.⟩ **2 :** a topgallant mast or sail

top gun n (1976) : one who is at the top (as in ability, rank, or prestige)

top–ham·per \'täp-'ham-pər\ n (1791) **1 :** matter or weight (as spars or rigging) in the upper part of a ship **2 :** unnecessary cumbersome matter

top hat n (1881) : a tall-crowned hat usu. of beaver or silk

top–heavy \'täp-,he-vē\ adj (ca. 1533) **1 :** having the top part too heavy for the lower part **2 :** having too high a proportion of administrators ⟨a ~ bureaucracy⟩ **3 :** oversupplied with one element at the expense of others : lacking balance ⟨a novel ~ with description⟩

To·phet \'tō-fət\ n [ME, shrine south of ancient Jerusalem where human sacrifices were performed to Moloch in Jer 7:31, Gehenna, fr. LL Topheth, fr. Heb tōpheth] (14c) : HELL, GEHENNA

top–hole \'täp-'hōl\ adj (1908) chiefly Brit : EXCELLENT, FIRST-CLASS

to·phus \'tō-fəs\ n, pl to·phi \'tō-,fi, -,fē\ [L, tufa] (1607) : a deposit of urates in tissues (as cartilage) characteristic of gout

to·pi \'tō-pē\ n, pl topi or topis [perh. fr. Swahili] (1894) : a subSaharan antelope (Damaliscus lunatus syn. D. korrigum) having a glossy reddish brown coat with purplish black and yellowish markings

¹to·pi·ary \'tō-pē-,er-ē\ adj [L topiarius, fr. topia ornamental gardening, irreg. fr. Gk topos place] (1592) : of, relating to, or being the practice or art of training, cutting, and trimming trees or shrubs into odd or ornamental shapes; also : characterized by such work

²topiary n, pl -ar·ies (1908) **1 :** topiary art or gardening; also : a topiary garden **2 a :** a plant shaped by topiary art   **b :** topiary plants

top·ic \'tä-pik\ n [L Topica Topics (work by Aristotle), fr. Gk Topika, fr. topika, neut. pl. of topikos of a place, of a topos, fr. topos place, topos] (1603) **1 a :** one of the general forms of argument employed in probable reasoning   **b :** ARGUMENT, REASON **2 a :** a heading in an outlined argument or exposition   **b :** the subject of a discourse or of a section of a discourse

top·i·cal \-pi-kəl\ adj (1588) **1 :** designed for or involving local application and action (as on the body) ⟨a ~ anesthetic⟩ ⟨a ~ remedy⟩ **2 a :** of, relating to, or arranged by topics ⟨set down in ~ form⟩   **b :** referring to the topics of the day or place : of local or temporary interest ⟨a ~ novel⟩ ⟨~ references⟩ — **top·i·cal·ly** \-k(ə-)lē\ adv

top·i·cal·i·ty \,tä-pə-'ka-lə-tē\ n, pl -ties (1904) **1 :** the quality or state of being topical **2 :** an item of topical interest

topic sentence n (1885) : a sentence that states the main thought of a paragraph or of a larger unit of discourse and is usu. placed at or near the beginning

top·kick \'täp-'kik\ n (1918) : FIRST SERGEANT 1

top·knot \-,nät\ n (ca. 1688) **1 :** an ornament (as a knot of ribbons or a pompom) forming a headdress or worn as part of a coiffure **2 :** a crest of feathers or tuft of hair on the top of the head

top·less \-ləs\ adj (1589) **1** archaic : so high as to reach up beyond sight ⟨and burnt the ~ towers of Ilium —Christopher Marlowe⟩ **2 :** being without a top **3 a :** wearing no clothing on the upper body **b :** featuring topless waitresses or entertainers ⟨~ bars⟩   **c :** being a place where topless women are permitted ⟨a ~ beach⟩ — **top·less·ness** \-nəs\ n

top·line \-,līn\ n (ca. 1909) : the outline of the top of the body of an animal (as a dog or horse)

top·lofty \'täp-,lóf-tē\ also **top·loft·i·cal** \täp-'lóf-ti-kəl\ adj [prob. fr. the phrase top loft] (1823) : very superior in air or attitude — **top·loft·i·ly** \täp-'lóf-tə-lē\ adv — **top·loft·i·ness** \'täp-,lóf-tē-nəs\ n

top·mast \'täp-,mast, -məst\ n (15c) : the mast that is next above the lower mast and is topmost in a fore-and-aft rig

top milk n (1891) : the upper layer of milk in a container enriched by whatever cream has risen

top·min·now \'täp-,mi-(,)nō\ n (1884) : any of several live-bearers (family Poeciliidae) or killifish (family Cyprinodontidae)

top·most \'täp-,mōst\ adj (1697) : highest of all : UPPERMOST

top–notch \-'näch\ adj (1900) : of the highest quality : FIRST-RATE — **top–notch·er** \-'nä-chər\ n

to·po·cen·tric \,tä-pə-'sen-trik, ,tō-\ adj (ca. 1942) : relating to, measured from, or as if observed from a particular point on the earth's surface : having or relating to such a point as origin ⟨~ coordinates⟩ — compare GEOCENTRIC

to·pog·ra·pher \tə-'pä-grə-fər\ n (1603) : one skilled in topography

to·po·graph·ic \,tä-pə-'gra-fik, ,tō-\ adj (1632) : of, relating to, or concerned with topography ⟨~ maps⟩

to·po·graph·i·cal \-fi-kəl\ adj (ca. 1576) **1 :** TOPOGRAPHIC **2 :** of, relating to, or concerned with the artistic representation of a particular locality ⟨a ~ poem⟩ ⟨~ painting⟩ — **to·po·graph·i·cal·ly** \-k(ə-)lē\ adv

to·pog·ra·phy \tə-'pä-grə-fē\ n [ME topographie, fr. LL topographia, fr. Gk, fr. topographein to describe a place, fr. topos place + graphein to write — more at CARVE] (15c) **1 a :** the art or practice of graphic delineation in detail usu. on maps or charts of natural and man-made features of a place or region esp. in a way to show their relative positions and elevations   **b :** topographical surveying **2 a :** the configuration of a surface including its relief and the position of its natural and man-made features   **b :** the physical or natural features of an object or entity and their structural relationships

to·po·log·i·cal \,tä-pə-'lä-ji-kəl\ adj (1715) **1 :** of or relating to topology **2 :** being or involving properties unaltered under a homeomorphism ⟨continuity and connectedness are ~ properties⟩ — **to·po·log·i·cal·ly** \-k(ə-)lē\ adv

topological group n (1946) : a mathematical group which is also a topological space, whose multiplicative operation is continuous such that given any neighborhood of a product there exist neighborhoods of the elements composing the product with the property that any pair of elements representing each of these neighborhoods form a product belonging to the given neighborhood, and whose operation of taking inverses is continuous such that for any neighborhood of the inverse of an element there exists a neighborhood of the element itself in which every element has its inverse in the other neighborhood

topologically equivalent adj (1915) : related by a homeomorphism

topological space n (1926) : a set with a collection of subsets satisfying the conditions that both the empty set and the set itself belong to the collection, the union of any number of the subsets is also an element of the collection, and the intersection of any finite number of the subsets is an element of the collection

topological transformation n (1946) : HOMEOMORPHISM

to·pol·o·gy \tə-'pä-lə-jē, tä-\ n, pl -gies (1850) **1 :** topographic study of a particular place; specif : the history of a region as indicated by its topography **2 a** (1) : a branch of mathematics concerned with those properties of geometric configurations (as point sets) which are unaltered by elastic deformations (as a stretching or a twisting) that are homeomorphisms   (2) : the set of all open subsets of a topological space   **b :** CONFIGURATION ⟨~ of a molecule⟩ ⟨~ of a magnetic field⟩ — **to·pol·o·gist** \-jist\ n

top·o·nym \'tä-pə-,nim, 'tō-\ n [ISV, back-formation fr. toponymy] (1899) : PLACE-NAME

top·o·nym·ic \,tä-pə-'ni-mik, ,tō-\ adj (1896) : of or relating to toponyms or toponymy — **top·o·nym·i·cal** \-mi-kəl\ adj

to·pon·y·my \tə-'pä-nə-mē, tō-\ n [ISV, fr. top- + Gk onyma, onoma name — more at NAME] (1876) : the place-names of a region or language or esp. the etymological study of them — **to·pon·y·mist** \-mist\ n

to·pos \'tō-,päs, 'tä-\ n, pl to·poi \-,pói\ [Gk, short for koinos topos, lit., common place] (1936) : a traditional or conventional literary or rhetorical theme or topic

top·per \'tä-pər\ n (1688) **1 :** one that puts on or takes off tops **2 :** one that is at or on the top **3 a :** SILK HAT   **b :** OPERA HAT **4 :** something (as a joke) that caps everything preceding **5 :** a woman's usu. short and loose-fitting lightweight outer coat

¹top·ping \'tä-piŋ\ n (14c) **1 :** something that forms a top; esp : a garnish (as a sauce, bread crumbs, or whipped cream) placed on top of a food for flavor or decoration **2 :** the action of one that tops **3 :** something removed by topping

²topping adj (ca. 1685) **1 :** highest in rank or eminence **2** NewEng : PROUD, ARROGANT **3** chiefly Brit : EXCELLENT

top·ple \'tä-pəl\ vb top·pled; top·pling \-p(ə-)liŋ\ [freq. of ²top] vi (1590) : to fall from or as if from being top-heavy ~ vt **1 :** to cause to topple **2 a :** OVERTHROW 2   **b :** DEFEAT 3

top round n (1903) : meat from the inner part of a round of beef

¹tops \'täps\ adj [pl. of ¹top] (1935) : topmost in quality, ability, popularity, or importance — used predicatively ⟨is ~ in his field⟩

²tops adv (1956) : at the very most ⟨will cost $50, ~⟩

top·sail \'täp-,sāl, -səl\ also **top-s'l** \-səl\ n (14c) **1 :** the sail next above the lowermost sail on a mast in a square-rigged ship **2 :** the sail set above and sometimes on the gaff in a fore-and-aft rigged ship

top secret adj (1944) **1 :** protected by a high degree of secrecy ⟨a top secret weapon⟩ ⟨a top secret meeting⟩ **2 a :** containing or being information whose unauthorized disclosure could result in exceptionally grave danger to the nation ⟨top secret messages⟩ — compare CONFIDENTIAL, SECRET   **b :** of or relating to top secret documents ⟨a top secret clearance⟩

top sergeant n (1898) : FIRST SERGEANT 1

top–shelf \'täp-'shelf\ adj (ca. 1892) : of the best quality

¹**top-side** \'täp-ˌsīd\ n (1815) **1** pl : the top portion of the outer surface of a ship on each side above the waterline **2** : the highest level of authority **3** : the upper portion of the ionosphere

²**topside** adv or adj (1873) **1** : to or on the top or surface **2** : in a position of authority **3** : on deck

Top–Sid·er \'täp-ˌsī-dər\ trademark — used for a low casual shoe having a rubber sole

top-soil \'täp-ˌsȯil\ n (1836) : surface soil usu. including the organic layer in which plants have most of their roots and which the farmer turns over in plowing

top-spin \-ˌspin\ n [¹top] (1902) : a rotary motion imparted to a ball that causes it to rotate forward in the direction it is traveling

top-stitch \'täp-ˌstich\ vt (1934) : to make a line of stitching on the outside of (a garment) close to a seam

top-sy–tur·vi·ness \ˌtäp-sē-'tər-vē-nəs\ n (1842) : the quality or state of being topsy-turvy

¹**top-sy–tur·vy** \ˌtäp-sē-'tər-vē\ adv [prob. ultim. fr. tops (pl. of ¹top) + obs. E terve to turn upside down] (1528) **1** : in utter confusion or disorder **2** : with the top or head downward : UPSIDE DOWN

²**topsy–turvy** adj (1612) : turned topsy-turvy : totally disordered — **top-sy–tur·vi·ly** \-'tər-və-lē\ adv — **top-sy–tur·vy·dom** \-vē-dəm\ n

³**topsy–turvy** n (1655) : TOPSY-TURVINESS

top up vt (1937) Brit : to make up to the full quantity, capacity, or amount ∼ vi, Brit : to replenish a supply — **top–up** \'täp-ˌəp\ n, Brit

top-work \'täp-ˌwərk\ vt (1882) : to graft scions of another variety on the main branches of (an established tree) usu. to obtain more desirable fruit

toque \'tōk\ n [MF, soft hat with a narrow brim worn esp. in the 16th cent., fr. OSp toca headdress] (1505) **1** : a woman's small hat without a brim made in any of various soft close-fitting shapes **2** : TUQUE **3** : a tall brimless hat worn by a chef — called also toque blanche

tor \'tȯr\ n [ME, fr. OE torr] (bef. 12c) : a high craggy hill

To-rah \'tōr-ə, 'tȯr-; 'tȯi-rə\ n [Heb tōrāh] (1577) **1** : the five books of Moses constituting the Pentateuch **2** : the body of wisdom and law contained in Jewish Scripture and other sacred literature and oral tradition **3** : a leather or parchment scroll of the Pentateuch used in a synagogue for liturgical purposes

¹**torch** \'tȯrch\ n, often attrib [ME torche, fr. OF, bundle of twisted straw or tow, torch, fr. (assumed) VL torca; akin to L torquēre to twist — more at TORTURE] (14c) **1** : a burning stick of resinous wood or twist of tow used to give light and usu. carried in the hand : FLAMBEAU **2** : something (as tradition, wisdom, or knowledge) likened to a torch as giving light or guidance **3** : any of various portable devices for emitting an unusually hot flame — compare BLOWTORCH **4** chiefly Brit : FLASHLIGHT **2** 5 INCENDIARY 1a

²**torch** vt (1901) : to set fire to with or as if with a torch

torch-bear·er \-ˌbar-ər, -ˌber-\ n (1538) **1** : one that carries a torch **2** : someone in the forefront of a campaign, crusade, or movement

tor-chère \ˌtȯr-'sher\ n [F, fr. torche torch] (1904) **1** : a tall ornamental stand for a candlestick or candelabra **2** : an electric floor lamp giving indirect light

torch-light \-ˌlīt\ n (15c) **1** : light given by torches **2** : TORCH

tor-chon \'tȯr-ˌshän\ n [F, duster, fr. OF, bundle of twisted straw, fr. torche] (1865) : a coarse bobbin or machine-made lace made with fan≈shaped designs forming a scalloped edge

torch singer n (ca. 1932) : a singer of torch songs

torch song n [fr. the phrase to carry a torch for (to be in love)] (1930) : a popular sentimental song of unrequited love

torch-wood \'tȯrch-ˌwu̇d\ n (1833) **1** : any of a genus (Amyris) of tropical American trees and shrubs of the rue family with hard heavy fragrant resinous streaky yellowish brown wood **2** : the wood of this torchwood

torchy \'tȯr-chē\ adj **torch·i·er; -est** (1941) : of, relating to, or characteristic of a torch song or torch singer

tore past of TEAR

to-re-a-dor \'tȯr-ē-ə-ˌdȯr, 'tȯr-, 'tär-\ n [Sp, fr. torear to fight bulls, fr. toro bull, fr. L taurus — more at TAURINE] (1618) : TORERO, BULLFIGHTER

to-re-ro \tə-'rer-(ˌ)ō\ n, pl -ros [Sp, fr. L taurarius bullfighter, fr. L taurus bull] (1728) : a matador or a member of the attending cuadrilla

to-reu-tics \tə-'rü-tiks\ n pl but sing in constr [toreutic, adj., fr. Gk toreutikos, fr. toreuein to bore through, chase, fr. toreus boring tool; akin to Gk tetrainein to bore — more at THROW] (1847) : the art or process of working in metal esp. by embossing or chasing — **to·reu·tic** \-'rü-tik\ adj

tori pl of TORUS

to-ric \'tȯr-ik, 'tȯr-\ adj (ca. 1898) : of, relating to, or shaped like a torus or segment of a torus (a ∼ lens)

to-rii \'tȯr-ē-ˌē, 'tȯr-\ n, pl torii [Jp] (1727) : a Japanese gateway of light construction commonly built at the approach to a Shinto shrine

¹**tor-ment** \'tȯr-ˌment\ n [ME, fr. OF, fr. L tormentum torture; akin to torquēre to twist — more at TORTURE] (14c) **1** : the infliction of torture (as by rack or wheel) **2** : extreme pain or anguish of body or mind : AGONY **3** : a source of vexation or pain

²**tor-ment** \tȯr-'ment, 'tȯr-\ vt (14c) **1** : to cause severe usu. persistent or recurrent distress of body or mind to (cattle ∼ed by flies) **2** : DISTORT, TWIST **syn** see AFFLICT

tor-men·til \'tȯr-mən-ˌtil\ n [ME turmentill, fr. ML tormentilla, fr. L tormentum; fr. its use in allaying pain] (15c) : a yellow-flowered Eurasian cinquefoil (Potentilla erecta syn. P. tormentilla) with a root sometimes used in tanning and dyeing

tor-men·tor also **tor-ment·er** \tȯr-'men-tər, 'tȯr-\ n (14c) **1** : one that torments **2** : a fixed curtain or flat on each side of a theater stage that prevents the audience from seeing into the wings

torn past part of TEAR

tor-na·dic \tȯr-'nā-dik, -'na-\ adj (1884) : relating to, characteristic of, or constituting a tornado

torii (illustration)

tor-na·do \tȯr-'nā-(ˌ)dō\ n, pl **-does** or **-dos** [modif. of Sp tronada thunderstorm, fr. tronar to thunder, fr. L tonare — more at THUNDER] (1556) **1** archaic : a tropical thunderstorm **2 a** : a squall accompanying a thunderstorm in Africa **b** : a violent destructive whirling wind accompanied by a funnel-shaped cloud that progresses in a narrow path over the land **3** : a violent windstorm : WHIRLWIND

tor-nil·lo \tȯr-'nē-(ˌ)yō, -'ni-(ˌ)lō\ n, pl **-los** [Sp, lit., small lathe, screw, dim. of torno lathe, fr. L tornus — more at TURN] (ca. 1844) : SCREWBEAN 1

to-roid \'tȯr-ˌȯid, 'tȯr-\ n [NL torus] (ca. 1900) **1** : a surface generated by a plane closed curve rotated about a line that lies in the same plane as the curve but does not intersect it **2** : a body whose surface has the form of a toroid

to-roi·dal \tȯ-'rȯi-d²l\ adj (ca. 1889) : of, relating to, or shaped like a torus or toroid : doughnut-shaped (a ∼ resistance coil) — **to-roi·dal·ly** \-d²l-ē\ adv

¹**tor-pe·do** \tȯr-'pē-(ˌ)dō\ n, pl **-does** [L, lit., stiffness, numbness, fr. torpēre to be sluggish or numb — more at TORPID] (ca. 1520) **1** : ELECTRIC RAY **2** : a weapon for destroying ships by rupturing their hulls below the waterline: as **a** : a submarine mine **b** : a thin cylindrical self-propelled underwater projectile **3** : a small firework that explodes when thrown against a hard object **4** : a professional gunman or assassin **5** : SUBMARINE 2

²**torpedo** vt **tor-pe·do·ed; tor-pe·do·ing** \-'pē-də-wiŋ\ (ca. 1879) **1** : to hit or sink (a ship) with a naval torpedo : strike or destroy by torpedo **2** : to destroy or nullify altogether : WRECK (∼ a plan)

torpedo boat n (1810) : a boat designed for launching torpedoes; specif : a small very fast boat with one or more torpedo tubes

torpedo bomber n (1930) : a military airplane designed to carry torpedoes — called also torpedo plane

torpedo tube n (ca. 1891) : a tube from which torpedoes are fired

tor-pid \'tȯr-pəd\ adj [L torpidus, fr. torpēre to be sluggish or numb; akin to Lith tirpti to become numb] (1613) **1 a** : having lost motion or the power of exertion or feeling : DORMANT, NUMB **b** : sluggish in functioning or acting (a ∼ frog) (a ∼ mind) **2** : lacking in energy or vigor : APATHETIC, DULL — **tor-pid·i·ty** \tȯr-'pi-də-tē\ n — **tor-pid·ly** \'tȯr-pəd-lē\ adv

tor-por \'tȯr-pər\ n [L, fr. torpēre] (1607) **1** : APATHY, DULLNESS **2** : a state of mental and motor inactivity with partial or total insensibility : extreme sluggishness or stagnation of function **syn** see LETHARGY

¹**torque** \'tȯrk\ n [F, fr. L torques, fr. torquēre to twist — more at TORTURE] (1695) : a usu. metal collar or neck chain worn by the ancient Gauls, Germans, and Britons

²**torque** n [L torquēre to twist] (ca. 1884) **1** : a force that produces or tends to produce rotation or torsion (an automobile engine delivers ∼ to the drive shaft); also : a measure of the effectiveness of such a force that consists of the product of the force and the perpendicular distance from the line of action of the force to the axis of rotation **2** : a turning or twisting force

³**torque** vt **torqued; torqu·ing** (1959) : to impart torque to : cause to twist (as about an axis) — **torqu·er** n

torque converter n (1927) : a device for transmitting and amplifying torque by hydraulic means

torr \'tȯr\ n, pl torr [Evangelista Torricelli] (1949) : a unit of pressure equal to ¹/₇₆₀ of an atmosphere (about 133.3 pascals)

¹**tor-rent** \'tȯr-ənt, 'tär-\ n [MF, fr. L torrent-, torrens, fr. torrent-, torrens, adj., burning, seething, rushing, fr. prp. of torrēre to parch, burn — more at THIRST] (1582) **1** : a tumultuous outpouring : RUSH **2** : a violent stream of a liquid (as water or lava) **3** : a channel of a mountain stream

²**torrent** adj (1667) : TORRENTIAL

tor-ren·tial \tȯ-'ren(t)-shəl, tə-\ adj (1849) **1 a** : relating to or having the character of a torrent (∼ rains) **b** : caused by or resulting from action of rapid streams (∼ gravel) **2** : resembling a torrent in violence or rapidity of flow — **tor-ren·tial·ly** \-'ren(t)-sh(ə-)lē\ adv

tor-rid \'tȯr-əd, 'tär-\ adj [L torridus, fr. torrēre] (1545) **1 a** : parched with heat esp. of the sun : HOT (∼ sands) **b** : giving off intense heat : SCORCHING **2** : ARDENT, PASSIONATE (∼ love letters) — **tor-rid·i·ty** \tȯ-'ri-də-tē\ n — **tor-rid·ly** \'tȯr-əd-lē, 'tär-\ adv — **tor-rid·ness** n

torrid zone n, often cap T&Z (1586) : the region of the earth between the tropic of Cancer and the tropic of Capricorn

tor-sade \tȯr-'säd, -'sad\ n [F, fr. obs. F tors twisted, fr. (assumed) VL torsus, alter. of L tortus, pp. of torquēre to twist] (1882) : a twisted cord or ribbon used esp. as a hat ornament

tor-sion \'tȯr-shən\ n [LL torsion-, torsio torment, alter. of L tortio, fr. torquēre to twist] (1543) **1** : the twisting or wrenching of a body by the exertion of forces tending to turn one end or part about a longitudinal axis while the other is held fast or turned in the opposite direction; also : the state of being twisted **2** : the twisting of a bodily organ or part on its own axis **3** : the reactive torque that an elastic solid exerts by reason of being under torsion — **tor-sion·al** \'tȯr-shnəl, -shə-n²l\ adj — **tor-sion·al·ly** adv

torsion bar n (1948) : a long metal element in an automobile suspension that has one end held rigidly to the frame and the other twisted and connected to the axle and that acts as a spring

tor-so \'tȯr-(ˌ)sō\ n, pl **torsos** or **tor-si** \'tȯr-ˌsē\ [It, lit., stalk, fr. L thyrsus stalk, thyrsus] (1722) **1** : a sculptured representation of the trunk of a human body **2** : something (as a piece of writing) that is mutilated or left unfinished **3** : the human trunk

tort \'tȯrt\ n [ME, injury, fr. MF, fr. ML tortum, fr. L, neut. of tortus twisted, fr. pp. of torquēre] (1586) : a wrongful act other than a breach of contract for which relief may be obtained in the form of damages or an injunction

torte \'tȯrt-ə, 'tȯrt\ n, pl **tor-ten** \'tȯr-t²n\ or **tortes** [G, prob. fr. It torta cake, fr. LL, round loaf of bread] (1555) : a cake made with many eggs and often grated nuts or dry bread crumbs and usu. covered with a rich frosting

\ə\ abut \'ə\ kitten, F table \ər\ further \a\ ash \ā\ ace \ä\ mop, mar \au̇\ out \ch\ chin \e\ bet \ē\ easy \g\ go \i\ hit \ī\ ice \j\ job \ŋ\ sing \ō\ go \ȯ\ law \ȯi\ boy \th\ thin \th\ the \ü\ loot \u̇\ foot \y\ yet \zh\ vision \ä, k, ⁿ, œ, œ̄, ᴜᴇ, ᴜ̄ᴇ, ᵈ\ see Guide to Pronunciation

tor·tel·li·ni \ˌtȯr-tᵊl-ˈē-nē\ n [It, pl. of *tortellino* pasta round, dim. of *tortello*, fr. *torta* cake] (ca. 1911) : pasta cut in rounds, folded around a filling (as of meat or cheese), formed into rings, and boiled

tor·ti·col·lis \ˌtȯr-tə-ˈkä-ləs\ n [NL, fr. L *tortus* twisted + *-i-* + *collum* neck — more at COLLAR] (ca. 1811) : a twisting of the neck to one side that results in abnormal carriage of the head and is usu. caused by muscle spasms — called also *wryneck*

tor·ti·lla \tȯr-ˈtē-yə\ n [AmerSp, fr. Sp, dim. of *torta* cake, fr. LL, round loaf of bread] (ca. 1699) : a round thin cake of unleavened cornmeal or wheat flour bread usu. eaten hot with a topping or filling (as of ground meat or cheese)

tor·tious \ˈtȯr-shəs\ adj (1544) : implying or involving tort — **tor·tious·ly** adv

tor·toise \ˈtȯr-təs\ n [ME *tortu, tortuce*, fr. MF *tortue* — more at TURTLE] (14c) 1 : any of a family (Testudinidae) of terrestrial turtles; *broadly* : TURTLE 2 : someone or something regarded as slow or laggard

tortoise beetle n (ca. 1711) : any of various chrysomelid beetles (subfamily Cassidinae) with leaf-eating larvae

¹tor·toise·shell \ˈtȯr-tə-ˌshel, -əsh-ˌshel\ n (1632) 1 : the mottled horny substance of the shell of some turtles (as the hawksbill turtle) used in inlaying and in making various ornamental articles 2 : any of several showy nymphalid butterflies (genus *Nymphalis*)

²tortoiseshell adj (1651) 1 : made of or resembling tortoiseshell esp. in mottled brown and yellow coloring 2 : of, relating to, or being a color pattern of the domestic cat consisting of patches of black, orange, and cream

tor·to·ni \tȯr-ˈtō-nē\ n [prob. fr. *Tortoni* 19th cent. Ital. restaurateur in Paris] (1922) : ice cream made of heavy cream often with minced almonds and chopped maraschino cherries and often flavored with rum

tor·tri·cid \ˈtȯr-trə-səd\ n [NL *Tortricidae*, fr. *Tortric-, Tortrix*] (ca. 1891) : any of a family (Tortricidae) of small stout-bodied moths many of whose larvae feed in fruits — **tortricid** adj

tor·trix \ˈtȯr-triks\ n [NL *Tortric-, Tortrix*, genus of moths, fr. L *tortus*, pp. of *torquēre* to twist; fr. the habit of twisting or rolling leaves to make a nest] (ca. 1797) : a tortricid moth

tor·tu·os·i·ty \ˌtȯr-chə-ˈwä-sə-tē\ n, pl **-ties** (1603) 1 : the quality or state of being tortuous 2 : something winding or twisted : BEND

tor·tu·ous \ˈtȯrch-wəs, ˈtȯr-chə-\ adj [ME, fr. MF *tortueux*, fr. L *tortuosus*, fr. *tortus* twist, fr. *torquēre* to twist] (15c) 1 : marked by repeated twists, bends, or turns : WINDING ⟨a ~ path⟩ 2 a : marked by devious or indirect tactics : CROOKED, TRICKY ⟨a ~ conspiracy⟩ b : CIRCUITOUS, INVOLVED ⟨the ~ jargon of legal forms⟩ — **tor·tu·ous·ly** adv — **tor·tu·ous·ness** n

¹tor·ture \ˈtȯr-chər\ n [F, fr. LL *tortura*, fr. L *tortus*, pp. of *torquēre* to twist; prob. akin to OHG *drāhsil* turner, Gk *atraktos* spindle] (1540) 1 a : anguish of body or mind : AGONY b : something that causes agony or pain 2 : the infliction of intense pain (as from burning, crushing, or wounding) to punish, coerce, or afford sadistic pleasure 3 : distortion or overrefinement of a meaning or an argument : STRAINING

²torture vt **tor·tured; tor·tur·ing** \ˈtȯrch-riŋ, ˈtȯr-chə-\ (1588) 1 : to cause intense suffering to : TORMENT 2 : to punish or coerce by inflicting excruciating pain 3 : to twist or wrench out of shape : DISTORT, WARP *syn* see AFFLICT — **tor·tur·er** \ˈtȯr-chər-ər\ n

tor·tur·ous \ˈtȯrch-rəs, ˈtȯr-chə-\ adj (15c) 1 a : causing torture ⟨~ inquisitions⟩ b : very unpleasant or painful ⟨a ~ day⟩ ⟨~ self-doubts⟩ 2 : painfully difficult or slow ⟨the ~ course of the negotiations⟩ — **tor·tur·ous·ly** adv

tor·u·la \ˈtȯr-yə-lə, ˈtär-, -ə-lə\ n, pl **-lae** \-ˌlē, -ˌlī\ *also* **-las** [NL, fr. L *torus* protuberance] (1861) : any of various fungi and esp. yeasts that lack sexual spores, do not produce alcoholic fermentations, and are typically acid formers — called also *torula yeast*

to·rus \ˈtȯr-əs, ˈtōr-\ n, pl **to·ri** \ˈtȯr-ˌī, ˈtȯr-, -ˌē\ [NL, fr. L, protuberance, bulge, *torus* molding] (1563) 1 : a large molding of convex profile commonly occurring as the lowest molding in the base of a column — see BASE illustration 2 : the thickening of a membrane closing a wood-cell pit (as of gymnosperm tracheids) having the secondary cell wall arched over the pit cavity 3 : a doughnut-shaped surface generated by a circle rotated about an axis in its plane that does not intersect the circle; *broadly* : TOROID 4 : a smooth rounded anatomical protuberance (as a bony ridge on the skull)

To·ry \ˈtȯr-ē, ˈtōr-\ n, pl **Tories** [Ir *tóraidhe* outlaw, robber, fr. MIr *tóir* pursuit] (1646) 1 : a dispossessed Irishman subsisting as an outlaw chiefly in the 17th century 2 also : BANDIT, OUTLAW 3 a : a member or supporter of a major British political group of the 18th and early 19th centuries favoring at first the Stuarts and later royal authority and the established church and seeking to preserve the traditional political structure and defeat parliamentary reform — compare WHIG b : CONSERVATIVE 1b 4 : an American upholding the cause of the British Crown against the supporters of colonial independence during the American Revolution : LOYALIST 5 *often not cap* : an extreme conservative esp. in political and economic principles — **Tory** adj

Tory Democracy n (1879) : a political philosophy advocating preservation of established institutions and traditional principles combined with political democracy and a social and economic program designed to benefit the common man

To·ry·ism \ˈtȯr-ē-ˌi-zəm, ˈtōr-\ n (1682) 1 : the principles and practices of or associated with Tories 2 : the British Tory party or its members

tosh \ˈtäsh\ n [origin unknown] (1528) : sheer nonsense : BOSH, TWADDLE

¹toss \ˈtȯs, ˈtäs\ vb [prob. of Scand origin; akin to Sw dial. *tossa* to spread, scatter] vt (1506) 1 a : to fling or heave continuously about, to and fro, or up and down ⟨a ship ~ed by waves⟩ b : BANDY 2b, c, d c : to mix lightly until well coated with a dressing or until the elements are thoroughly combined ⟨~ a salad⟩ 2 : to make uneasy : stir up : DISTURB 3 a : to throw with a quick, light, or careless motion or with a sudden jerk ⟨~ a ball around⟩ b : to throw up in the air ⟨~ed by a bull⟩ c : MATCH 5a d : to send as if by throwing ⟨~ed in jail⟩ ⟨~ed out of the game⟩ e : to get rid of : THROW AWAY 4 a : to fling or lift with a sudden motion ⟨~es her head angrily⟩ b : to tilt suddenly so as to empty by drinking ⟨~ed his glass⟩; *also* : to consume by drinking ⟨~ down a drink⟩ 5 : to accomplish, provide, or produce readily or easily ⟨~ off a few verses⟩ 6 : THROW 16 ⟨~ a party⟩ 7

: VOMIT 1 — often used in the phrase **toss one's cookies** ~ vi 1 a : to move restlessly or turbulently; *esp* : to twist and turn repeatedly ⟨~ed sleeplessly all night⟩ b : to move with a quick or spirited gesture 2 : to decide an issue by flipping a coin *syn* see THROW — **toss·er** n

²toss n (1634) 1 : the state or fact of being tossed 2 : an act or instance of tossing: as a : an abrupt tilting or upward fling b : a deciding by chance and esp. by flipping a coin c : THROW, PITCH

toss·pot \-ˌpät\ n (1568) : DRUNKARD, SOT

toss–up \-ˌəp\ n (1812) 1 : TOSS 2b 2 : an even chance 3 : something that offers no clear basis for choice

tos·ta·da \tō-ˈstä-də\ *also* **tos·ta·do** \-(ˌ)dō\ n [MexSp *tostada*, fr. Sp, fem. of *tostado*, pp. of *tostar* to toast, roast, fr. LL *tostare* — more at TOAST] (1939) : a tortilla fried in deep fat

¹tot \ˈtät\ n [origin unknown] (1725) 1 : a small child : TODDLER 2 : a small drink or allowance of liquor : SHOT

²tot vb **tot·ted; tot·ting** [*tot.*, abbr. of *total*] vt (ca. 1772) : to add together : TOTAL — usu. used with *up* ⟨~s up the score⟩ ~ vi : ADD

¹to·tal \ˈtōt-ᵊl\ adj [ME, fr. MF, fr. ML *totalis*, fr. L *totus* whole, entire] (15c) 1 : comprising or constituting a whole : ENTIRE ⟨the ~ amount⟩ 2 : ABSOLUTE, UTTER ⟨a ~ failure⟩ 3 : involving a complete and unified effort esp. to achieve a desired effect ⟨~ war⟩ ⟨~ theater⟩ *syn* see WHOLE

²total n (1557) 1 : a product of addition : SUM 2 : an entire quantity : AMOUNT

³total adv (1601) : TOTALLY

⁴total vt **to·taled** or **to·talled; to·tal·ing** or **to·tal·ling** (1716) 1 : to add up : COMPUTE 2 : to amount to : NUMBER 3 : to make a total wreck of : DEMOLISH ⟨~ed the car⟩

total depravity n (1794) : a state of corruption due to original sin held in Calvinism to infect every part of man's nature and to make the natural man unable to know or obey God

total eclipse n (1671) : an eclipse in which one celestial body is completely obscured by the shadow or body of another

to·tal·ism \ˈtōt-ᵊl-ˌi-zəm\ n (1941) : TOTALITARIANISM — **to·tal·is·tic** \ˌtō-tᵊl-ˈis-tik\ adj

¹to·tal·i·tar·i·an \(ˌ)tō-ˌta-lə-ˈter-ē-ən\ adj [It *totalitario*, fr. *totalità* totality] (1926) 1 a : of or relating to centralized control by an autocratic leader or hierarchy : AUTHORITARIAN, DICTATORIAL; *esp* : DESPOTIC b : of or relating to a political regime based on subordination of the individual to the state and strict control of all aspects of the life and productive capacity of the nation esp. by coercive measures (as censorship and terrorism) 2 a : advocating or characteristic of totalitarianism b : completely regulated by the state esp. as an aid to national mobilization in an emergency c : exercising autocratic powers : tending toward monopoly

²totalitarian n (ca. 1934) : an advocate or practitioner of totalitarianism

to·tal·i·tar·i·an·ism \(ˌ)tō-ˌta-lə-ˈter-ē-ə-ˌni-zəm\ n (1926) 1 : centralized control by an autocratic authority 2 : the political concept that the citizen should be totally subject to an absolute state authority

to·tal·i·tar·i·an·ize \-ˌnīz\ vt **-ized; -iz·ing** (1935) : to make totalitarian ⟨a society *totalitarianized* by the military-industrial complex —W. F. Buckley *b*1925⟩

to·tal·i·ty \tō-ˈta-lə-tē\ n, pl **-ties** (1598) 1 : an aggregate amount : SUM, WHOLE 2 a : the quality or state of being total : WHOLENESS b : the phase of an eclipse during which it is total : state of total eclipse

to·tal·iza·tor or **to·tal·isa·tor** \ˈtōt-ᵊl-ə-ˌzā-tər\ n (1879) : PARI-MUTUEL 2

to·tal·ize \ˈtōt-ᵊl-ˌīz\ vt **-ized; -iz·ing** (1818) 1 : to add up : TOTAL 2 : to express as a whole

to·tal·iz·er \-ˌī-zər\ n (1887) : one that totalizes: as a : PARI-MUTUEL 2 b : a device (as a meter) that records a remaining total (as of fuel)

to·tal·ly \ˈtōt-ᵊl-ē\ adv (1509) : in a total manner : to a total or complete degree : WHOLLY, ENTIRELY

total recall n (1926) : the faculty of remembering with complete clarity and in complete detail

¹tote \ˈtōt\ vt **tot·ed; tot·ing** [perh. fr. an English-based creole; akin to Gullah & Krio *tot* to carry] (1677) 1 : to carry by hand : bear on the person : LUG, PACK 2 : HAUL, CONVEY — **tot·er** \ˈtō-tər\ n

²tote n (ca. 1772) 1 : BURDEN, LOAD 2 : TOTE BAG

³tote vt **tot·ed; tot·ing** [alter. of *total*] (1888) : ADD, TOTAL — usu. used with *up* ⟨*toted* up his accomplishments —G. P. Morrill⟩

⁴tote n [short for *totalizator*] (1891) : PARI-MUTUEL 2

tote bag n (1900) : a large 2-handled open-topped bag (as of canvas)

tote board n [⁴tote] (ca. 1949) : an electrically operated board (as at a racetrack) on which pertinent information (as betting odds and race results) is posted

to·tem \ˈtō-təm\ n [Ojibwa *ototeman* his totem] (ca. 1776) 1 a : an object (as an animal or plant) serving as the emblem of a family or clan and often as a reminder of its ancestry; *also* : a usu. carved or painted representation of such an object b : a family or clan identified by a common totemic object 2 : something that serves as an emblem or revered symbol

to·tem·ic \tō-ˈte-mik\ adj (1846) 1 : of, relating to, suggestive of, or characteristic of a totem or totemism ⟨a ~ animal⟩ 2 : based on or practicing totemism ⟨~ clan structure⟩

to·tem·ism \ˈtō-tə-ˌmi-zəm\ n (1791) 1 : belief in kinship with or a mystical relationship between a group or an individual and a totem 2 : a system of social organization based on totemic affiliations

to·tem·is·tic \ˌtō-tə-ˈmis-tik\ adj (1873) : TOTEMIC

totem pole n (1897) 1 : a pole or pillar carved and painted with a series of totemic symbols representing family lineage and often mythical or historical incidents and erected before the houses of Indian tribes of the northwest coast of No. America 2 : an order of rank : HIERARCHY

toth·er or **t'oth·er** \ˈtə-thər\ pron or adj [ME *tother*, alter. (resulting from misdivision of *thet other* the other, fr. *thet* the — fr. OE *thæt* — + *other*) of *other* — more at THAT] (13c) *chiefly dial* : the other

totem pole 1

to·ti·po·ten·cy \tō-'ti-pə-tən(t)-sē, ‚tō-tə-'pō-t²n-\ *n* (1909) : ability to generate or regenerate a whole organism from a part

to·ti·po·tent \-tənt, -t²nt\ *adj* [L *totus* whole, entire + E *-i-* + *potent*] (ca. 1899) : capable of developing into a complete organism or differentiating into any of its cells or tissues ⟨~ blastomeres⟩

¹tot·ter \'tä-tər\ *vi* [ME *toteren*] (15c) **1 a** : to tremble or rock as if about to fall : SWAY **b** : to become unstable : threaten to collapse **2** : to move unsteadily : STAGGER, WOBBLE

²totter *n* (1747) : an unsteady gait : WOBBLE

tot·ter·ing *adj* (1534) **1 a** : being in an unstable condition ⟨a ~ building⟩ **b** : walking unsteadily **2** : lacking firmness or stability : INSECURE ⟨a ~ regime⟩ — **tot·ter·ing·ly** \-tə-riŋ-lē\ *adv*

tot·tery \'tä-tə-rē\ *adj* (ca. 1755) : of an infirm or precarious nature

Toua·reg *var of* TUAREG

tou·can \'tü-,kan, -,kän, tü-'\ *n* [F, fr. Pg *tucano*, fr. Tupi *tukána*] (1568) : any of a family (Ramphastidae) of fruit-eating birds of tropical America with brilliant coloring and a very large but light and thin= walled beak

¹touch \'təch\ *vb* [ME, fr. OF *tuchier*, fr. (assumed) VL *toccare* to knock, strike a bell, touch, prob. of imit. origin] *vt* (14c) **1** : to bring a bodily part into contact with esp. so as to perceive through the tactile sense : handle or feel gently usu. with the intent to understand or appreciate ⟨loved to ~ the soft silk⟩ **2** : to strike or push lightly esp. with the hand or foot or an implement **3** : to lay hands upon (one afflicted with scrofula) with intent to heal **4** *archaic* **a** : to play on (a stringed instrument) **b** : to perform (a melody) by playing or singing **5 a** : to take into the hands or mouth ⟨never ~es alcohol⟩ **b** : to put hands upon in any way or degree ⟨don't ~ anything before the police come⟩; *esp* : to commit violence upon ⟨swears he never ~ed the child⟩ **6** : to deal with : become involved with ⟨a sticky situation and I wouldn't ~ it with a 10-foot pole⟩ **7** : to induce to give or lend ⟨~ed him for ten dollars⟩ **8** : to cause to be briefly in contact or conjunction with something ⟨~ed her spurs to the horse⟩ ⟨~ed his hand to his hat⟩ **9 a** (1) : to meet without overlapping or penetrating : ADJOIN (2) : to get to : REACH ⟨the speedometer needle ~ed 80⟩ **b** : to be tangent to **c** : to rival in quality or value ⟨nothing can ~ that cloth for durability⟩ **10** : to speak or tell of esp. in passing ⟨barely ~ed the incident in the speech⟩ **11 a** : to relate to : CONCERN **b** : to have an influence on : AFFECT **12 a** : to leave a mark or impression on ⟨few reagents will ~ gold⟩; *also* : TINGE **b** : to harm slightly by or as if by contact : TAINT, BLEMISH ⟨fruit ~ed by frost⟩ **c** : to give a delicate tint, line, or expression to ⟨a smile ~ed her lips⟩ **13** : to draw or delineate with light strokes **14 a** : to hurt the feelings of : WOUND **b** : to move to sympathetic feeling ~ *vi* **1 a** : to feel something with a body part (as the hand or foot) **b** : to lay hand or finger on a person to cure disease (as scrofula) **2** : to be in contact **3** : to come close : VERGE ⟨your actions ~ on treason⟩ **4** : to have a bearing : RELATE — used with *on* or *upon* **5 a** : to make a brief or incidental stop on shore during a trip by water ⟨~ed at several ports⟩ **b** : to treat a topic in a brief or casual manner — used with *on* or *upon* ⟨~ed upon many points⟩ *syn* see AFFECT — **touch·able** \'tə-chə-bəl\ *adj* — **touch·er** *n* — **touch base** : to come in contact or communication ⟨coming in from the cold to *touch base* with civilization —Carla Hunt⟩

²touch *n* (14c) **1** : a light stroke, tap, or push **2** : the act or fact of touching **3** : the special sense by which pressure or traction exerted on the skin or mucous membrane is perceived **4** : mental or moral sensitiveness, responsiveness, or tact ⟨has a wonderful ~ with children⟩ **5** : a specified sensation that arises in response to stimulation of the tactile receptors : FEEL ⟨the velvety ~ of velour⟩ **6 a** : the act of rubbing gold or silver on a touchstone to test its quality **b** : TEST, TRIAL — used chiefly in the phrase *put to the touch* **7 a** : a visible effect : MARK ⟨a ~ of the tropical sun⟩ **b** : WEAKNESS, DEFECT **8** : something slight of its kind: as **a** : a light attack ⟨a ~ of fever⟩ **b** : a small quantity or indication : HINT ⟨a ~ of spring in the air⟩ **c** : a transient emotion ⟨a momentary ~ of compunction⟩ **d** : a near approach : CLOSE CALL ⟨beaten in the championships by a mere ~⟩ **9 a** *archaic* : the playing of an instrument (as a lute or piano) with the fingers; *also* : musical notes or strains so produced **b** : particular action of a keyboard with reference to the resistance of its keys to pressure ⟨piano with a stiff ~⟩ **10** : control of the hands: as **a** : a manner or method of touching or striking esp. the keys of a keyboard instrument **b** : ability to control the distance something (as a ball) is propelled ⟨developed his putting ~⟩ **11** : a set of changes in change ringing that is less than a peal **12 a** : an effective and subtle detail ⟨applies the finishing ~es to the story⟩ **b** : distinctive and often effective manner or method ⟨the ~ of a master⟩ **c** : a characteristic or distinguishing trait or quality **13** *slang* : an act of soliciting or getting a gift or loan **14** : the state or fact of being in contact or communication or of having awareness ⟨lost ~ with her cousin⟩ ⟨let's keep in ~⟩ ⟨out of ~ with modern times⟩ **15** : the area outside of the touchlines in soccer or outside of and including the touchlines in rugby — **a touch** : SOMEWHAT, RATHER ⟨aimed a *touch* too low and missed⟩

touch–and–go \‚təch-ən(d)-'gō\ *n* (1953) : an airplane landing followed immediately by application of power and a takeoff and usu. executed as one of a series for practice at landings

touch and go *adj* (1815) : unpredictable as to outcome : UNCERTAIN ⟨it was *touch and go* there for a while⟩

touch·back \'təch-‚bak\ *n* (ca. 1890) : a situation in football in which the ball is down behind the goal line after a kick or intercepted forward pass after which it is put in play by the team defending the goal on its own 20-yard line — compare SAFETY

touch·down \'təch-‚daùn\ *n* (1876) **1** : the act of touching a football to the ground behind an opponent's goal; *specif* : the act of scoring six points in American football by being lawfully in possession of the ball on, above, or behind an opponent's goal line when the ball is declared dead **2** : the act or moment of touching down (as with an airplane or spacecraft)

touch down *vt* (1864) : to place (the ball in rugby) by hand on the ground on or over an opponent's goal line in scoring a try or behind one's own goal line as a defensive measure ~ *vi* : to reach the ground : LAND

tou·ché \tü-'shā\ *interj* [F, fr. pp. of *toucher* to touch, fr. OF *tuchier*] (1904) — used to acknowledge a hit in fencing or the success or appropriateness of an argument, an accusation, or a witty point

touched \'təcht\ *adj* (14c) **1** : emotionally stirred (as with gratitude) **2** : slightly unbalanced mentally

touch football *n* (1933) : football played informally and chiefly characterized by the substitution of touching for tackling

touch·hole \'təch-‚hōl\ *n* (1501) : the vent in muzzle-loading guns through which the charge is ignited

¹touch·ing *prep* (14c) : in reference to : CONCERNING

²touching *adj* (1601) : capable of arousing emotions of tenderness or compassion *syn* see MOVING — **touch·ing·ly** \'tə-chiŋ-lē\ *adv*

touch·line \'təch-‚līn\ *n* (1868) : either of the lines that bound the long sides of the field of play in rugby and soccer

touch·mark \-‚märk\ *n* (1904) : an identifying maker's mark impressed on pewter

touch–me–not \'təch-mē-‚nät\ *n* [fr. the bursting of the ripe pods and scattering of their seeds when touched] (1659) : either of two No. American impatiens growing in moist areas: as **a** : one (*Impatiens capensis*) typically having crimson-spotted orange flowers **b** : one (*I. pallida*) having yellow to white flowers sometimes spotted with brownish red

touch off *vt* (ca. 1765) **1** : to describe or characterize with precision **2 a** : to cause to explode by or as if by touching with fire **b** : to provoke or initiate with sudden intensity ⟨the verdict *touched off* local riots⟩

touch pad *n* (1979) : a keypad for an electronic device (as a microwave oven) that consists of a flat surface divided into several differently marked areas which are touched to choose options

touch screen *n* (1974) : a display screen on which the user selects options (as from a menu) by touching the screen

touch·stone \'təch-‚stōn\ *n* (1530) **1** : a black siliceous stone related to flint and formerly used to test the purity of gold and silver by the streak left on the stone when rubbed by the metal **2** : a test or criterion for determining the quality or genuineness of a thing **3** : a fundamental or quintessential part or feature *syn* see STANDARD

touch system *n* (1918) : a method of typing that assigns a particular finger to each key and makes it possible to type without looking at the keyboard

Touch–Tone \'təch-'tōn, -‚tōn\ *trademark* — used for a telephone having push buttons that produce tones corresponding to numbers

touch–type \'təch-‚tīp\ *vi* (1943) : to type by the touch system — **touch typist** *n*

touch–up \'təch-‚əp\ *n* (1885) : an act or instance of touching up

touch up *vt* (1715) **1** : to improve or perfect by small additional strokes or alterations : fix the minor and usu. visible defects or damages of **2** : to stimulate by or as if by a flick of a whip

touch·wood \'təch-‚wùd\ *n* (1579) : ³PUNK

touchy \'tə-chē\ *adj* **touch·i·er; -est** (1605) **1** : marked by readiness to take offense on slight provocation **2 a** *of a body part* : acutely sensitive or irritable **b** *of a chemical* : highly explosive or inflammable **3** : calling for tact, care, or caution in treatment ⟨a ~ subject⟩ — **touch·i·ly** \'tə-chə-lē\ *adv* — **touch·i·ness** \'tə-chē-nəs\ *n*

touchy–feely \‚tə-chē-'fē-lē\ *adj* (1968) : characterized by or encouraging interpersonal touching esp. in the free expression of emotions ⟨~ therapy⟩; *also* : openly or excessively emotional and personal ⟨~ management⟩

¹tough \'təf\ *adj* [ME, fr. OE *tōh*; akin to OHG *zāhi* tough] (bef. 12c) **1 a** : strong or firm in texture but flexible and not brittle **b** : not easily chewed **2** : GLUTINOUS, STICKY **3** : characterized by severity or uncompromising determination **4** : capable of enduring strain, hardship, or severe labor **5** : very hard to influence : STUBBORN **6** : difficult to accomplish, resolve, endure, or deal with ⟨a ~ question⟩ ⟨~ luck⟩ **7** : stubbornly fought ⟨a ~ contest⟩ **8** : UNRULY, ROWDYISH **9** : marked by absence of softness or sentimentality *syn* see STRONG — **tough·ly** *adv* — **tough·ness** *n*

²tough *adv* (14c) : in a tough manner ⟨talks ~ and insensitively —A. E. Stevenson †1965⟩

³tough *vt* (1830) : to bear unflinchingly : ENDURE — usu. used with *out* esp. in the phrase *tough it out*

⁴tough *n* (1866) : a tough person : ROWDY

tough·en \'tə-fən\ *vb* **tough·ened; tough·en·ing** \'tə-fə-niŋ, 'təf-niŋ\ *vt* (1582) : to make tough ~ *vi* : to become tough

tough·ie *also* **toughy** \'tə-fē\ *n, pl* **tough·ies** (1921) : one that is tough: as **a** : a loud rough rowdy person **b** : a difficult problem or question

tough–mind·ed \'təf-‚mīn-dəd\ *adj* (1909) : realistic or unsentimental in temper or outlook — **tough–mind·ed·ness** *n*

tou·pee \tü-'pā\ *n* [F *toupet* forelock, fr. OF, dim. of *top, toup,* of Gmc origin; akin to OHG *zopf* tuft of hair — more at TOP] (1728) **1** : a curl or lock of hair made into a topknot on a periwig or natural coiffure; *also* : a periwig with such a topknot **2** : a wig or section of hair worn to cover a bald spot

¹tour \'tùr, *1 is also* 'taùr\ *n* [ME, fr. MF, fr. OF *tourn, tour* lathe, circuit, turn — more at TURN] (14c) **1 a** : one's turn in an orderly schedule : SHIFT **b** : a period during which an individual or unit is on a specific duty or at one place ⟨a ~ of duty⟩ **2 a** : a journey for business, pleasure, or education often involving a series of stops and ending at the starting point; *also* : something resembling such a tour ⟨a ~ of the history of philosophy⟩ **b** : a brief turn : ROUND **c** : a series of professional tournaments (as in golf or tennis)

²tour *vi* (1789) : to make a tour ~ *vt* **1** : to make a tour of **2** : to present (as a theatrical production) on a tour

tou·ra·co \'tùr-ə-‚kō\ *n, pl* **-cos** [origin unknown] (ca. 1743) : any of a family (Musophagidae) of African birds that are related to the cuckoos and have a long tail, a short stout often colored bill, and red wing feathers

tour·bil·lion \tùr-'bil-yən\ *or* **tour·bil·lon** \tür-bē-yōⁿ\ *n* [ME, fr. MF *tourbillon,* fr. L *turbin-, turbo* — more at TURBINE] (15c) **1** : WHIRLWIND **2** : a vortex esp. of a whirlwind or whirlpool

---

\ə\ abut \ᵊ\ kitten, F table \ər\ further \a\ ash \ā\ ace \ä\ mop, mar
\aù\ out \ch\ chin \e\ bet \ē\ easy \g\ go \i\ hit \ī\ ice \j\ job
\ŋ\ sing \ō\ go \o\ law \oi\ boy \th\ thin \t͟h\ the \ü\ loot \ù\ foot
\y\ yet \zh\ vision \å, k̇, ⁿ, œ, œ̄, ᵫ, ᵫ̄, ᵊ\ see Guide to Pronunciation

tour de force \ˌtu̇r-də-'fōrs, -'fȯrs\ *n, pl* **tours de force** *same*\ [F] (1802) : a feat of strength, skill, or ingenuity

tour·er \'tu̇r-ər\ *n* (1926) **1** : TOURING CAR **2** : one that tours

Tou·rette's syndrome \tu̇-'rets-\ *n* [Georges Gille de la *Tourette* †1904 Fr. physician] (1970) : a rare disease characterized by involuntary tics and by uncontrollable verbalization involving esp. echolalia and the use of obscene language — called also *Tou·rette syndrome* \-'ret-\

tour·ing \'tu̇r-iŋ\ *n* (1794) **1** : participation in a tour **2** : cross-country skiing for pleasure

touring car *n* (1903) : an automobile suitable for distance driving: as **a** : a vintage automobile with two cross seats, usu. four doors, and a folding top : PHAETON **2 b** : a modern usu. 2-door sedan as distinguished from a sports car

touring car a

tour·ism \'tu̇r-ˌi-zəm\ *n* (1811) **1** : the practice of traveling for recreation **2** : the guidance or management of tourists **3 a** : the promotion or encouragement of touring **b** : the accommodation of tourists

tour·ist \'tu̇r-ist\ *n* (1780) **1** : one that makes a tour for pleasure or culture — **tourist** *adj or adv*

tourist card *n* (1948) : a citizenship identity card issued to a tourist usu. for a stated period of time in lieu of a passport or a visa

tourist class *n* (1935) : economy accommodations (as on a ship)

tourist court *n* (1937) : MOTEL

tour·is·tic \tu̇r-'is-tik\ *adj* (1848) : of or relating to a tour, tourism, or tourists — **tour·is·ti·cal·ly** \-ti-k(ə-)lē\ *adv*

tourist trap *n* (1939) : a place that attracts and exploits tourists

tour·isty \'tu̇r-əs-tē\ *adj* (1906) : of or relating to tourists: as **a** : patronized by tourists **b** : of a type appealing to tourists

tour·ma·line \'tu̇r-mə-lən, -ˌlēn\ *n* [Sinhalese *toramalli* carnelian] (1759) : a mineral of variable color that consists of a complex borosilicate and makes a striking gem when transparent and cut

tour·na·ment \'tu̇r-nə-mənt *also* 'tər- *or* 'tȯr-\ *n* [ME *tornement*, fr. OF *torneiement*, fr. *torneier*] (14c) **1 a** : a knightly sport of the middle ages between mounted combatants armed with blunted lances or swords and divided into two parties contesting for a prize or favor bestowed by the lady of the tournament **b** : the whole series of knightly sports, jousts, and tilts occurring at one time and place **2** : a series of games or contests that make up a single unit of competition (as on the professional golf tour), the championship play-offs of a league or conference, or an invitational event

tour·ne·dos \ˌtu̇r-nə-'dō\ *n, pl* **tour·ne·dos** \-'dō(z)\ [F, fr. *tourner* to turn + *dos* back] (1877) : a small fillet of beef usu. cut from the tip of the tenderloin

¹tour·ney \'tu̇r-nē, 'tər- *also* 'tȯr-\ *vi* **tour·neyed; tour·ney·ing** [ME, fr. MF *torneier*, fr. OF, fr. *torn, tourn* lathe, circuit] (14c) : to perform in a tournament

²tourney *n, pl* **tourneys** (14c) : TOURNAMENT

tour·ni·quet \'tu̇r-ni-kət, 'tər-\ *n* [F, turnstile, tourniquet, fr. *tourner* to turn, fr. OF — more at TURN] (1695) : a device (as a bandage twisted tight with a stick) to check bleeding or blood flow

¹touse \'tau̇z\ *vt* **toused; tous·ing** [ME *-tousen;* akin to OHG *zirzūsōn* to pull to pieces] (1598) : RUMPLE, TOUSLE

²touse *n* (1795) : a noisy disturbance

¹tou·sle \'tau̇-zəl, -səl\ *vt* **tou·sled; tou·sling** \'tau̇z-liŋ, 'tau̇s-; 'tau̇-zə-, -sə-\ [ME *touselen*, freq. of *-tousen*] (15c) : DISHEVEL, RUMPLE

²tou·sle \'tau̇-zəl, *1 is also* 'tü-\ *n* (1788) **1** *Scot* : rough dalliance : TUSSLE **2** : a tangled mass (as of hair)

¹tout \'tau̇t, *in sense 4 also* 'tüt\ *vb* [ME *tuten* to peer; prob. akin to OE *tōtian* to stick out, Norw *tyte*] *vt* (ca. 1700) **1** : to spy on : WATCH **2 a** *Brit* : to spy out information about (as a racing stable or horse) **b** : to give a tip or solicit bets on (a racehorse) **3** : to solicit, peddle, or persuade importunately (not meant to ~ you off the movie —Russell Baker) **4** : to praise or publicize loudly or extravagantly (~ed as the . . . most elaborate suburban shopping development —*Wall Street Jour.*) ~ *vi* **1** : to solicit patronage **2 a** *chiefly Brit* : to spy on racehorses in training to gain information for betting **b** : to give a tip or solicit bets on a racehorse

²tout *n* (1853) : one who touts: as **a** : one who solicits patronage **b** *chiefly Brit* : one who spies out racing information for betting purposes **c** : one who gives tips or solicits bets on a racehorse

tout·er \'tau̇-tər\ *n* (ca. 1754) : one that touts

to·va·rich *or* **to·va·rish** \tə-'vär-ish, -ich\ *n* [Russ *tovarishch*] (ca. 1917) : COMRADE

¹tow \'tō\ *vb* [ME, fr. OE *togian;* akin to OE *tēon* to draw, pull, OHG *ziohan* to draw, pull, L *ducere* to draw, lead] *vt* (bef. 12c) : to draw or pull along behind : HAUL ~ *vi* : to move in tow (trailers that ~ behind the family auto —Bob Munger)

²tow *n* (1600) **1** : a rope or chain for towing **2 a** : the act or an instance of towing **b** : the fact or state of being towed **3 a** : something towed (as a boat or car) **b** : a group of barges lashed together and usu. pushed **4** : something (as a tugboat) that tows **5** : SKI TOW — **in tow 1** : under guidance or protection (taken *in tow* by a friendly native) **2** : in the position of a dependent or devoted follower or admirer

³tow *n* [ME, fr. OE *tow-* spinning; akin to ON *tō* tuft of wool for spinning, OE *tawian* to prepare for use — more at TAW] (14c) **1** : short or broken fiber (as of flax, hemp, or synthetic material) that is used esp. for yarn, twine, or stuffing **2 a** : yarn or cloth made of tow **b** : a loose essentially untwisted strand of synthetic fibers

⁴tow *n* [ME (Sc), prob. fr. OE *toh-* (in *tohline* towline); akin to OE *togian* to tow] (15c) *chiefly Scot & dial Eng* : ROPE

tow·age \'tō-ij\ *n* (14c) **1** : the act of towing **2** : a charge for towing

¹to·ward \'tō(-ə)rd, 'tȯ(-ə)rd\ *adj* [ME *toward*, fr. OE *tōweard* facing, imminent, fr. *tō,* prep., to + *-weard* -ward] (bef. 12c) **1** *also* **to·wards** \'tō(-ə)rdz, 'tȯ(-ə)rdz, 'tə-'wȯrdz\ [ME *towardes*, prep., toward, fr. *tōweard,* adj.] **a** : coming soon : IMMINENT **b** : happening at the moment (a ~ breeze) **2** *obs* : quick to learn : APT **b** : PROPITIOUS, FAVORING

²to·ward *or* **to·wards** \'tō(-ə)rd(z), 'tȯ(-ə)rd(z), tə-'wȯrd(z), 'twȯrd(z),

'twȯrd(z)\ *prep* (bef. 12c) **1** : in the direction of (driving ~ town) **2 a** : along a course leading to (a long stride ~ disarmament) **b** : in relation to (an attitude ~ life) **3 a** : at a point in the direction of : NEAR (a cottage somewhere up ~ the lake) **b** : in such a position as to be in the direction of (your back was ~ me) **4** : not long before (~ the end of the afternoon) **5 a** : in the way of help or assistance in (did all he could ~ raising campaign funds) **b** : for the partial payment of (proceeds go ~ the establishment of a scholarship)

to·ward·li·ness \'tȯrd-lē-nəs, 'tȯrd-\ *n* (1566) *archaic* : the quality or state of being toward or towardly

to·ward·ly \'tō(-ə)rd-lē, 'tȯ(-ə)rd-\ *adj* (1513) *archaic* **1** : PLEASANT, AFFABLE **2** : FAVORABLE, PROPITIOUS **3** : developing favorably : PROMISING — **towardly** *adv*

tow·boat \'tō-ˌbōt\ *n* (1815) **1** : TUGBOAT **2** : a compact shallow-draft boat with a squared bow designed and fitted for pushing tows of barges on inland waterways

¹tow·el \'tau̇(-ə)l\ *n* [ME *towaille,* fr. OF *toaille,* of Gmc origin; akin to OHG *dwahila* towel; akin to OHG *dwahan* to wash] (13c) : an absorbent cloth or paper for wiping or drying

²towel *vb* **-eled** *or* **-elled; -el·ing** *or* **-el·ling** *vt* (ca. 1839) : to rub or dry (as the body) with a towel ~ *vi* : to use a towel to dry oneself

tow·el·ette \ˌtau̇(-ə)-'let\ *n* (1902) : a small usu. premoistened piece of material used for personal cleansing (as of the hands)

tow·el·ing *or* **tow·el·ling** \'tau̇(-ə-)liŋ\ *n* (1583) : a cotton or linen fabric often used for making towels

¹tow·er \'tau̇(-ə)r\ *n* [ME *tour, tor,* fr. OE *torr* & OF *tor, tur,* both fr. L *turris,* fr. Gk *tyrris, tyrsis*] (bef. 12c) **1** : a building or structure typically higher than its diameter and high relative to its surroundings that may stand apart (as a campanile), or be attached (as a church belfry) to a larger structure, and that may be fully walled in or of skeleton framework (as an observation or transmission tower) **2** : a towering citadel : FORTRESS **3** : one that provides support or protection : BULWARK (a ~ of strength) — **tow·ered** \'tau̇(-ə)rd\ *adj* — **tow·er·like** \'tau̇(-ə)r-ˌlīk\ *adj*

²tower *vi* (1582) **1** : to reach or rise to a great height **2** : to exhibit superior qualities : SURPASS (her intellect ~ed over the others)

tower block *n* (1966) *chiefly Brit* : a tall building (as a high-rise apartment building)

tower house *n* (1687) : a medieval fortified castle (as in Scotland)

tow·er·ing *adj* (1592) **1** : impressively high or great : IMPOSING (~ pines) **2** : reaching a high point of intensity : OVERWHELMING (a ~ rage) **3** : going beyond proper bounds : EXCESSIVE (~ ambitions) — **tow·er·ing·ly** \'tau̇(-ə)r-iŋ-lē\ *adv*

Tower of Babel (ca. 1887) : BABEL 2

tow·head \'tō-ˌhed\ *n* (1829) **1** : a low alluvial island or shoal in a river : SANDBAR **2** : a head of hair resembling tow esp. in being flaxen or tousled; *also* : a person having such a head of hair — **tow·head·ed** \-ˌhe-dəd\ *adj*

to·whee \'tō-ˌhē, 'tō-(ˌ)ē, tō-'hē\ *n* [imit.] (ca. 1729) **1** : a common finch (*Pipilo erythrophthalmus*) of eastern No. America having the male black, white, and rufous — called also *chewink* **2** : any of the No. American finches belonging to the same genus (*Pipilo*) as the towhee

to wit \tə-'wit\ *adv* [ME *to witen,* lit., to know — more at WIT] (14c) : that is to say : NAMELY

tow·line \'tō-ˌlīn\ *n* (1719) : TOWROPE

tow·mond \'tō-mənd\ *n* [ME *towlmonyth,* fr. OE *twelf mōnath,* fr. *twelf* twelve + *mōnath* month] (15c) *Scot* : YEAR, TWELVEMONTH

town \'tau̇n\ *n* [ME, fr. OE *tūn* enclosure, village, town; akin to OHG *zūn* enclosure, OIr *dún* fortress] (bef. 12c) **1** *dial Eng* : a cluster or aggregation of houses recognized as a distinct place with a place-name : HAMLET **2 a** : a compactly settled area as distinguished from open country **b** : a compactly settled area usu. larger than a village but smaller than a city **c** : a large densely populated urban area : CITY **d** : an English village having a periodic fair or market **3** : a neighboring city, capital city, or metropolis **4** : the city or urban life as contrasted with the country **5** : the inhabitants of a city or town **6** : a New England territorial and political unit usu. containing both rural and unincorporated urban areas under a single town government; *also* : a New England community governed by a town meeting **7** : a group of prairie dog burrows — **town** *adj* — **on the town 1** : in usu. carefree pursuit of entertainment or amusement (as city nightlife) esp. as a relief from routine

town car *n* (1907) : a 4-door automobile with a usu. open driver's compartment and a separate enclosed passenger compartment

town clerk *n* (14c) : a public officer charged with recording the official proceedings and vital statistics of a town

town crier *n* (1602) : a town officer who makes public proclamations

town·ee \tau̇-'nē\ *n* (1897) *chiefly Brit* : TOWNIE

town hall *n* (15c) : a public building used for town-government offices and meetings

town house *n* (1803) **1** : a house in town; *specif* : the city residence of one having a countryseat or having a chief residence elsewhere (stayed at their *town house* during the social season) **2** : a usu. single-family house of two or sometimes three stories that is usu. connected to a similar house by a common sidewall; *also* : ROW HOUSE

town·ie *or* **towny** \'tau̇-nē\ *n, pl* **townies** (1852) : TOWNSMAN; *esp* : a permanent inhabitant of a town as distinguished from a member of another group (as the academic community)

town·let \'tau̇n-lət\ *n* (ca. 1552) : a very small town

town manager *n* (1922) : an official appointed to direct the administration of a town government

town meeting *n* (1636) : a meeting of inhabitants or taxpayers constituting the legislative authority of a town

town·scape \-ˌskāp\ *n* (1880) **1** : a representation of an urban scene **2** : a town or city viewed as a scene

towns·folk \'tau̇nz-ˌfōk\ *n pl* (1737) : TOWNSPEOPLE

town·ship \'tau̇n-ˌship\ *n* (15c) **1** : an ancient unit of administration in England identical in area with or a division of a parish **2 a** : TOWN 6 **b** : a unit of local government in some northeastern and north central states usu. having a chief administrative officer or board **c** : an unorganized subdivision of the county in Maine, New Hampshire, and Vermont **d** : an electoral and administrative district of the county in the southern U.S. **3** : a division of territory in surveys of U.S. public land containing 36 sections or 36 square miles **4** : an area in the Re-

public of South Africa segregated for occupation by persons of non=
European descent

towns·man \'taůnz-mən\ n (bef. 12c) **1 a :** a native or resident of a
town or city **b :** an urban or urbane person **2 :** a fellow citizen of a
town

towns·peo·ple \-ˌpē-pəl\ n pl (1648) **1 :** the inhabitants of a town or
city : TOWNSMEN **2 :** town-dwelling or town-bred persons

towns·wom·an \-ˌwù-mən\ n (1684) **1 :** a woman who is a native or
resident of a town or city **2 :** a woman born or residing in the same
town or city as another

tow·path \'tō-ˌpath, -ˌpáth\ n (1788) **:** a path (as along a canal) traveled esp. by draft animals towing boats — called also *towing path*

tow·rope \-ˌrōp\ n (1743) **:** a line used in towing something (as a boat)

tow sack \'tō-ˌsak\ n [³tow] (1926) *Midland & Southern* **:** GUNNYSACK

tow truck n (1944) **:** a truck with winches and hoist mechanisms for
freeing stuck vehicles and towing wrecked or disabled vehicles

tox- *or* **toxi-** *or* **toxo-** *comb form* [LL, fr. L *toxicum* poison] **:** poisonous : poison ⟨*toxemia*⟩

tox·a·phene \'täk-sə-ˌfēn\ n [fr. *Toxaphene*, a trademark] (1947) **:** an
insecticide with the approximate empirical formula $C_{10}H_{10}Cl_8$ that is a
complex mixture of chlorinated compounds

tox·e·mia \täk-'sē-mē-ə\ n [NL] (ca. 1860) **:** an abnormal condition
associated with the presence of toxic substances in the blood — **tox·e·**
mic \-mik\ *adj*

¹tox·ic \'täk-sik\ *adj* [LL *toxicus*, fr. L *toxicum* poison, fr. Gk *toxikon*
arrow poison, fr. neut. of *toxikos* of a bow, fr. *toxon* bow, arrow] (1664)
1 : of, relating to, or caused by a poison or toxin **2 :** affected by a
poison or toxin ⟨~ pregnant women⟩ **3 :** POISONOUS — **tox·ic·i·ty**
\täk-'si-sə-tē\ n

²toxic n (1890) **:** a toxic substance

toxic- *or* **toxico-** *comb form* [NL, fr. L *toxicum*] **:** poison ⟨*toxicology*⟩

tox·i·cant \'täk-si-kənt\ n [ML *toxicant-, toxicans*, prp. of *toxicare* to
poison, fr. L *toxicum*] (ca. 1882) **:** a toxic agent; *esp* **:** PESTICIDE

tox·i·co·log·i·cal \ˌtäk-si-kə-'lä-ji-kəl\ *or* **tox·i·co·log·ic** \-jik\ *adj*
(1839) **:** of or relating to toxicology or toxins — **tox·i·co·log·i·cal·ly**
\-ji-k(ə-)lē\ *adv*

tox·i·col·o·gy \-'kä-lə-jē\ n (ca. 1799) **:** a science that deals with poisons and their effect and with the problems involved (as clinical, industrial, or legal) — **tox·i·col·o·gist** \-jist\ n

tox·i·co·sis \ˌtäk-sə-'kō-səs\ n, pl **-co·ses** \-ˌsēz\ [NL] (ca. 1857) **:** a
pathological condition caused by the action of a poison or toxin

toxic shock syndrome n (1978) **:** an acute disease that is characterized by fever, diarrhea, nausea, diffuse erythema, and shock, that is
associated esp. with the presence of a bacterium (*Staphylococcus
aureus*), and that occurs esp. in menstruating females using tampons —
called also *toxic shock*

toxi·gen·ic \ˌtäk-sə-'je-nik\ *adj* (ca. 1923) **:** producing toxin ⟨~ bacteria and fungi⟩ — **toxi·ge·nic·i·ty** \ˌtäk-si-jə-'ni-sə-tē\ n

tox·in \'täk-sən\ n [ISV] (1886) **:** a poisonous substance that is a specific product of the metabolic activities of a living organism and is usu.
very unstable, notably toxic when introduced into the tissues, and
typically capable of inducing antibody formation

tox·in–an·ti·tox·in \'täk-sən-'an-ti-ˌtäk-sən\ n (1904) **:** a mixture of
toxin and antitoxin used esp. formerly in immunizing against a disease
(as diphtheria) for which they are specific

tox·oid \'täk-ˌsòid\ n [ISV] (ca. 1894) **:** a toxin of a pathogenic organism treated so as to destroy its toxicity but leave it capable of inducing
the formation of antibodies on injection

tox·oph·i·lite \täk-'sä-fə-ˌlit\ n [Gk *toxon* bow, arrow + *philos* dear,
loving] (1794) **:** a person fond of or expert at archery — **toxophilite**
adj — **tox·oph·i·ly** \-lē\ n

toxo·plas·ma \ˌtäk-sə-'plaz-mə\ n [NL] (1926) **:** any of a genus (*Toxoplasma*) of sporozoans that are typically serious pathogens of vertebrates — **toxo·plas·mic** \-mik\ *adj*

toxo·plas·mo·sis \-ˌplaz-'mō-səs\ n, pl **-mo·ses** \-ˌsēz\ [NL] (1926)
: infection of humans, other mammals, or birds with disease caused by
a toxoplasma (*Toxoplasma gondii*) that invades the tissues and may
seriously damage the central nervous system esp. of infants

¹toy \'tòi\ n [ME *toye*] (15c) **1** *obs* **a :** flirtatious or seductive behavior **b :** PASTIME; *also* **:** a sportive or amusing act **:** ANTIC **2 a :** something (as a preoccupation) that is paltry or trifling **b :** a literary or
musical trifle or diversion **c :** TRINKET, BAUBLE **3 :** something for a
child to play with **4 :** something diminutive; *esp* **:** a diminutive animal (as of a small breed or variety) **5 :** something that can be toyed
with **6** *Scot* **:** a headdress of linen or woolen hanging down over the
shoulders and formerly worn by old women of the lower classes —
toy·like \-ˌlik\ *adj*

²toy *vi* (ca. 1529) **1 :** to act or deal with something lightly or without
vigor or purpose **2 :** to engage in flirtation **3 :** to amuse oneself as if
with a toy **:** PLAY *syn* see TRIFLE — **toy·er** \'tòi-ər\ n

³toy *adj* (1801) **1 :** resembling a toy esp. in diminutive size **2 :** designed or made for use as a toy ⟨a ~ stove⟩

toy Man·ches·ter terrier \-'man-ˌches-tər-, -chə-stər-\ n (1935) **:** any
of a breed of toy dogs developed from the Manchester terrier that have
erect ears of moderate size and weigh not more than 12 pounds (5.4
kilograms) — called also *toy Manchester*

toy·on \'tòi-ˌän\ n [AmerSp *tollon*] (1848) **:** a chiefly Californian ornamental evergreen shrub (*Heteromeles arbutifolia*) of the rose family
having white flowers succeeded by persistent usu. bright red berries

toy poodle n (1935) **:** any of a breed of toy dogs developed from the
standard poodle that are not more than 10 inches (25 centimeters) high
at the withers

TPN \ˌtē-ˌpē-'en\ n [*triphosphopyridine nucleotide*] (1938) **:** NADP

tra·be·at·ed \'trä-bē-ˌā-təd\ *also* **tra·be·ate** \-ˌāt\ *adj* [L *trabs, trabes*
beam — more at THORP] (1843) **:** designed or constructed with horizontal beams or lintels — **tra·be·ation** \ˌträ-bē-'ā-shən\ n

tra·bec·u·la \trə-'be-kyə-lə\ n, pl **-lae** \-ˌlē, -ˌlī\ *also* **-las** [NL, fr. L,
little beam, dim. of *trabs, trabes* beam] (ca. 1866) **1 :** a small bar, rod,
bundle of fibers, or septal membrane in the framework of a body organ
or part **2 :** a fold, ridge, or bar projecting into or extending from a
plant part; *esp* **:** a row of cells bridging an intercellular space — **tra·**
bec·u·lar \-lər\ *adj* — **tra·bec·u·late** \-lət\ *adj*

¹trace \'träs\ n [ME, fr. MF, fr. *tracier* to trace] (14c) **1** *archaic* **a :** a
course or path that one follows **2 a :** a mark or line left by some-

thing that has passed; *also* **:** FOOTPRINT **b :** a path, trail, or road made
by the passage of animals, people, or vehicles **3 a :** a sign or evidence
of some past thing **:** VESTIGE **b :** ENGRAM **4 :** something (as a line)
traced or drawn: *as* **a :** the marking made by a recording instrument
(as a seismograph or kymograph) **b :** the ground plan of a military
installation or position either on a map or on the ground **5 a :** the
intersection of a line or plane with a plane **b :** the usu. bright line or
spot that moves across the screen of a cathode-ray tube; *also* **:** the path
taken by such a line or spot **6 a :** a minute and often barely detectable amount or indication ⟨a ~ of a smile⟩ **b :** an amount of a chemical constituent not always quantitatively determinable because of mi-
nuteness — **trace·less** \-ləs\ *adj*

syn TRACE, VESTIGE, TRACK mean a perceptible sign made by something that has passed. TRACE may suggest any line, mark, or discernible effect ⟨a snowfield pockmarked with the *traces* of caribou⟩. VES-
TIGE applies to a tangible reminder such as a fragment or remnant of
what is past and gone ⟨boulders that are *vestiges* of the last ice age⟩.
TRACK implies a continuous line that can be followed ⟨the fossilized
tracks of dinosaurs⟩.

²trace *vb* **traced; trac·ing** [ME, fr. MF *tracier*, fr. (assumed) VL *trac-
tiare* to drag, fr. L *tractus*, pp. of *trahere* to pull] *vt* (14c) **1 a :** DELIN-
EATE, SKETCH **b :** to form (as letters or figures) carefully or painstak-
ingly **c :** to copy (as a drawing) by following the lines or letters as
seen through a transparent superimposed sheet **d :** to impress or
imprint (as a design or pattern) with a tracer **e :** to record a tracing of
in the form of a curved, wavy, or broken line ⟨~ the heart action⟩ **f**
: to adorn with linear ornamentation (as tracery or chasing) **2** *archaic*
: to travel over **:** TRAVERSE **3 a :** to follow the footprints, track, or
trail of **b :** to follow or study out in detail or step by step ⟨~ the history of the labor movement⟩ **c :** to discover by going backward over
the evidence step by step ⟨~ your ancestry⟩ **d :** to discover signs,
evidence, or remains of **4 :** to lay out the trace of (a military installation) ~ *vi* **1 :** to make one's way; *esp* **:** to follow a track or trail **2**
: to be traceable historically — **trace·abil·i·ty** \ˌtrā-sə-'bi-lə-tē\ n —
trace·able \'trā-sə-bəl\ *adj*

³trace n [ME *trais*, pl., traces, fr. MF, pl. of *trait* pull, draft, trace —
more at TRAIT] (14c) **1 :** either of two straps, chains, or lines of a harness for attaching a draft animal to something (as a vehicle) to be
drawn **2 :** LEADER 1e(2) **3 :** one or more vascular bundles supplying
a leaf or twig **4 :** a connecting bar or rod pivoted at each end to another piece and used for transmitting motion

trace element n (1932) **:** a chemical element present in minute quantities; *esp* **:** one used by organisms and held essential to their physiology

trac·er \'trā-sər\ n (ca. 1552) **1 :** one that traces, tracks down, or
searches out: *as* **a :** a person who traces missing persons or property
and esp. goods lost in transit **b :** an inquiry sent out in tracing a shipment lost in transit **2 :** one who traces designs, patterns, or markings
3 : a device (as a stylus) used in tracing **4 a :** ammunition containing a chemical composition to mark the flight of projectiles by a trail of
smoke or fire **b :** a substance used to trace the course of a chemical or
biological process; *esp* **:** LABEL 3d

trac·ery \'trā-sə-rē, 'träs-rē\ n, pl **-er·ies** (1669) **1**
: architectural ornamental work with branching
lines; *esp* **:** decorative openwork in the head of a
Gothic window **2 :** a decorative interlacing of
lines suggestive of Gothic tracery — **trac·er·ied**
\-rēd\ *adj*

tracery 1

trache- *or* **tracheo-** *comb form* [NL, fr. ML *trachea*] **1 :** trachea ⟨*tracheitis*⟩ ⟨*tracheotomy*⟩ **2**
: tracheal and ⟨*tracheobronchial*⟩

tra·chea \'trā-kē-ə\ n, pl **-che·ae** \-kē-ˌē, -kē-ˌī\
also **-che·as** [ME, fr. ML, fr. LL *trachia*, fr. Gk
tracheia (*artēria*) rough (artery), fr. fem. of *trachys*
rough] (14c) **1 :** the main trunk of the system of
tubes by which air passes to and from the lungs in vertebrates **2** [NL,
fr. ML] **:** VESSEL 3b; *also* **:** one of its constituent cellular elements **3**
[NL] **:** one of the air-conveying tubules forming the respiratory system of most insects and many other arthropods — **tra·che·al** \-kē-əl\
adj

tra·che·ary \'trā-kē-ˌer-ē\ *adj* (1885) **:** of, relating to, or being plant
tracheae ⟨~ elements⟩

tra·che·ate \-kē-ˌāt, -ət\ *or* **tra·che·at·ed** \-ˌā-təd\ *adj* (1877) **:** having
tracheae as breathing organs

tra·cheid \'trā-kē-əd, -ˌkēd\ n [ISV] (1875) **:** a long tubular pitted cell
that is peculiar to xylem, functions in conduction and support, and has
tapering closed ends and thickened lignified walls

tra·che·itis \ˌtrā-kē-'ī-təs\ n [NL] (1859) **:** inflammation of the trachea

tra·cheo·bron·chi·al \ˌtrā-kē-ō-'bräŋ-kē-əl\ *adj* (1896) **:** of or relating
to both trachea and bronchi ⟨~ lesions⟩

tra·che·ole \'trā-kē-ˌōl\ n [NL *tracheola*, dim. of *trachea*] (1901) **:** one
of the minute delicate endings of a branched trachea of an insect —
tra·che·o·lar \trä-'kē-ə-lər\ *adj*

tra·cheo·phyte \'trā-kē-ə-ˌfit\ n [NL *Tracheophyta*, fr. *trache-* + Gk
phyton plant; akin to Gk *phyein* to bring forth — more at BE] (1937)
: any of a division (Tracheophyta) comprising green plants (as ferns
and seed plants) with a vascular system that contains tracheids or tra-
cheary elements

tra·che·os·to·my \ˌtrā-kē-'äs-tə-mē\ n, pl **-mies** (ca. 1923) **:** the surgical formation of an opening into the trachea through the neck esp. to
allow the passage of air

tra·che·ot·o·my \ˌtrā-kē-'ä-tə-mē\ n, pl **-mies** (ca. 1726) **:** the surgical
operation of cutting into the trachea esp. through the skin

tra·cho·ma \trə-'kō-mə\ n [NL, fr. Gk *trachōma*, fr. *trachys* rough] (ca.
1693) **:** a chronic contagious bacterial conjunctivitis marked by inflammatory granulations on the conjunctival surfaces, caused by a chla-

---

\ə\ abut \ʾ\ kitten, F table \ər\ further \a\ ash \ā\ ace \ä\ mop, mar
\aů\ out \ch\ chin \e\ bet \ē\ easy \g\ go \i\ hit \ī\ ice \j\ job
\ŋ\ sing \ō\ go \ò\ law \òi\ boy \th\ thin \t̲h̲\ the \ü\ loot \ů\ foot
\y\ yet \zh\ vision \á, k̲, ⁿ, œ, œ̄, ɶ, ūe, ᵧ\ see Guide to Pronunciation

mydia (*Chlamydia trachomatis*), and commonly resulting in blindness if left untreated

tra·chyte \'trā-,kīt, 'trā-\ *n* [F, fr. Gk *trachys* rough] (1821) : a usu. light-colored volcanic rock consisting chiefly of potash feldspar

tra·chyt·ic \trə-'ki-tik\ *adj* (1827) : of or relating to a texture of igneous rocks in which lath-shaped feldspar crystals are in almost parallel lines

trac·ing \'trā-siŋ\ *n* (15c) **1** : the act of one that traces **2** : something that is traced: as **a** : a copy made on a superimposed transparent sheet **b** : a graphic record made by an instrument (as a seismograph) that registers some movement

tracing paper *n* (1824) : a semitransparent paper for tracing drawings; *also* : a thin paper containing a clothing pattern to be transferred to fabric (as through carbon paper) by tracing

tracing wheel *n* (ca. 1891) : a usu. toothed wheel with a handle that is used on tracing paper to trace a pattern

¹**track** \'trak\ *n* [ME *trak*, fr. MF *trac*, perh. of Gmc origin; akin to MD *tracken*, *trecken* to pull, haul — more at TREK] (15c) **1 a** : detectable evidence (as the wake of a ship, a line of footprints, or a wheel rut) that something has passed **b** : a path made by repeated footfalls : TRAIL **c** : a course laid out esp. for racing **d** : the parallel rails of a railroad **e** (1) : one of a series of parallel or concentric paths along which material (as music or information) is recorded (as on a phonograph record or magnetic tape) (2) : a group of grooves on a phonograph record containing recorded sound (3) : material recorded esp. on a track **f** : a usu. metal wave (as a groove) serving as a guide (as for a movable lighting fixture) **2** : a footprint whether recent or fossil ⟨the huge ~ of a dinosaur⟩ **3 a** : the course along which something moves **b** : a way of life, conduct, or action **c** : one of several curricula of study to which students are assigned according to their needs or levels of ability **d** : the projection on the earth's surface of the path along which something (as a missile or an airplane) has flown **4 a** : a sequence of events : a train of ideas : SUCCESSION **b** : an awareness of a fact, progression, or condition ⟨keep ~ of the costs⟩ ⟨lose ~ of the time⟩ **5 a** : the width of a wheeled vehicle from wheel to wheel and usu. from the outside of the rims **b** : the tread of an automobile tire **c** : either of two endless metal belts on which a tracklaying vehicle travels **6** : track-and-field sports; *esp* : those performed on a running track *syn* see TRACE — **track·less** \'trak-ləs\ *adj* — **in one's tracks** : where one stands or is at the moment : on the spot ⟨was stopped *in his tracks*⟩

²**track** *vt* (1565) **1 a** : to follow the tracks or traces of : TRAIL **b** : to search for by following evidence until found ⟨~ down the source⟩ **2 a** : to follow by vestiges : TRACE **b** : to observe or plot the moving path of (as a spacecraft or missile) instrumentally **3** : to travel over : TRAVERSE ⟨~ a desert⟩ **4 a** : to make tracks upon **b** : to carry (as mud) on the feet and deposit **5** : to keep track of (as a trend) : FOLLOW ~ *vi* **1** : TRAVEL ⟨comet ~s eastward⟩ **2 a** *of a phonograph needle* : to follow the groove undulations of a recording **b** *of a pair of wheels* (1) : to maintain a constant distance apart on the straightaway (2) : to fit a track or rails **c** *of a rear wheel of a vehicle* : to follow accurately the corresponding fore wheel on a straightaway **3** : to leave tracks (as on a floor) — **track·er** *n*

track·age \'trak-kij\ *n* (1880) **1** : lines of railway track **2 a** : a right to use the tracks of another railroad line **b** : the charge for such right

track–and–field \,trak-ən(d)-'fē(ə)ld\ *adj* (1905) : of, relating to, or being any of various competitive athletic events (as running, jumping, and weight throwing) performed on a running track and on the adjacent field

track·ball \'trak-,bȯl\ *n* (1967) : a ball that is mounted usu. in a computer console so as to be only partially exposed and is rotated to control the movement of a cursor on a display

tracked \'trakt\ *adj* (1926) **1** : traveling on endless metal belts instead of wheels **2** : moving along a rail ⟨a ~ air-cushion vehicle⟩

track·ing \'tra-kiŋ\ *n* (ca. 1929) : the assigning of students to a curricular track

tracking shot *n* (ca. 1940) : a scene photographed from a moving dolly

track·lay·er \'trak-,lā-ər, -,le(-ə)r\ *n* (ca. 1861) **1** : a worker engaged in tracklaying **2** : a tracklaying vehicle

¹**track·lay·ing** \-,lā-iŋ\ *n* (1857) : the laying of tracks on a railway line

²**tracklaying** *adj* (1884) : of, relating to, or being a vehicle that travels on two or more endless usu. metal belts

trackless trolley *n* (1921) : TROLLEYBUS

track lighting *n* (1972) : adjustable lamps mounted along an electrified metal track

track·man \'trak-mən, -,man\ *n* (1922) : a runner on a track team

track record *n* [¹track (track-and-field sports)] (1952) : a record of past performance often taken as an indicator of likely future performance

track·side \'trak-,sīd\ *adj* (1886) : of, relating to, or situated in the area immediately adjacent to a track — **trackside** *n*

track·suit \'trak-,süt\ *n* (1922) : a suit of clothing consisting usu. of a jacket and pants that is often worn by athletes when working out

track·walk·er \-,wȯ-kər\ *n* (1872) : a worker employed to walk over and inspect a section of railroad tracks

track·way \-,wā\ *n* (1818) **1** : a beaten or trodden path **2** : a series of fossil footprints of a dinosaur

¹**tract** \'trakt\ *n, often cap* [ME *tracte*, fr. ML *tractus*, fr. L, action of drawing, extension; perh. fr. its being sung without a break by one voice] (14c) : verses of Scripture (as from the Psalms) used between the gradual and the Gospel at some masses (as during penitential seasons)

²**tract** *n* [ME *tracte*, fr. L *tractus* action of drawing, extension, fr. *trahere* to pull, draw] (15c) **1** : extent or lapse of time **2** : an area either large or small: as **a** : an indefinite stretch of land **b** : a defined area of land **3 a** : a system of body parts or organs that act together to perform some function ⟨the digestive ~⟩ **b** : a bundle of nerve fibers having a common origin, termination, and function

³**tract** *n* [ME, treatise, modif. of L *tractatus* tractate] (1760) : a pamphlet or leaflet of political or religious propaganda; *also* : a piece of writing that is suggestive of such a tract

trac·ta·ble \'trak-tə-bəl\ *adj* [L *tractabilis*, fr. *tractare* to handle, treat] (1502) **1** : capable of being easily led, taught, or controlled : DOCILE ⟨a ~ horse⟩ **2** : easily handled, managed, or wrought : MALLEABLE

syn see OBEDIENT — **trac·ta·bil·i·ty** \,trak-tə-'bi-lə-tē\ *n* — **trac·ta·ble·ness** \'trak-tə-bəl-nəs\ *n* — **trac·ta·bly** \-blē\ *adv*

Trac·tar·i·an \trak-'ter-ē-ən\ *n* [fr. *Tracts for the Times*, series of pamphlets expounding the Oxford movement] (ca. 1839) : a promoter or supporter of the Oxford movement

Trac·tar·i·an·ism \-ē-ə-,ni-zəm\ *n* (1840) : a system of High Church principles set forth in a series of tracts at Oxford (1833–41)

trac·tate \'trak-,tāt\ *n* [L *tractatus*, fr. *tractare* to draw out, handle, treat — more at TREAT] (15c) : TREATISE, DISSERTATION

tract house *n* (1956) : any of many similarly designed houses built on a tract of land

trac·tion \'trak-shən\ *n* [ML *traction-, tractio*, fr. L *trahere*] (1615) **1** : the act of drawing : the state of being drawn; *also* : the force exerted in drawing **2** : the drawing of a vehicle by motive power; *also* : the motive power employed **3 a** : the adhesive friction of a body on a surface on which it moves ⟨the ~ of a wheel on a rail⟩ **b** : a pulling force exerted on a skeletal structure (as in a fracture) by means of a special device ⟨a ~ splint⟩; *also* : a state of tension created by such a pulling force ⟨a leg in ~⟩ — **trac·tion·al** \-shnəl, -shə-nᵊl\ *adj*

trac·tive \'trak-tiv\ *adj* [L *tractus*, pp.] (1615) **1** : serving to draw **2** : of or relating to traction : TRACTIONAL

trac·tor \'trak-tər\ *n* [NL, fr. L *trahere*] (1900) **1 a** : a 4-wheeled or tracklaying automotive vehicle used esp. for drawing farm equipment **b** : a smaller 2-wheeled apparatus controlled through handlebars by a walking operator **c** : ³TRUCK 3f **2** : an airplane having the propeller forward of the main supporting surfaces

trad \'trad\ *adj* (1958) *chiefly Brit* : TRADITIONAL

¹**trade** \'trād\ *n* [ME, fr. MLG; akin to OHG *trata* track, course, OE *tredan* to tread] (14c) **1 a** *obs* : a path traversed : WAY **b** *archaic* : a track or trail left by a person or animal : TREAD **1** 2 : a customary course of action : PRACTICE ⟨thy sin's not accidental, but a ~ —Shak.⟩ **3 a** : the business or work in which one engages regularly : OCCUPATION **b** : an occupation requiring manual or mechanical skill : CRAFT **c** : the persons engaged in an occupation, business, or industry **4 a** *obs* : dealings between persons or groups **b** (1) : the business of buying and selling or bartering commodities : COMMERCE (2) : BUSINESS, MARKET ⟨novelties for the tourist ~⟩ ⟨did a good ~ in small appliances⟩ **5 a** : an act or instance of trading : TRANSACTION; *also* : an exchange of property usu. without use of money **b** : a firm's customers : CLIENTELE **c** : the group of firms engaged in a business or industry **6** : TRADE WIND — usu. used in pl. **7** : a publication intended for persons in the entertainment business — usu. used in pl. *syn* see BUSINESS

²**trade** *vb* **trad·ed; trad·ing** *vi* (1553) **1** *obs* : to have dealings : NEGOTIATE **2 a** : to engage in the exchange, purchase, or sale of goods **b** : to make one's purchases : SHOP ⟨~s at his store⟩ **3** : to give one thing in exchange for another : SELL **3** ~ *vt* **1** *archaic* : to do business with **2** : to give in exchange for another commodity : BARTER; *also* : to make an exchange of ⟨traded places⟩ **b** : to engage in frequent buying and selling of (as stocks or commodities) usu. in search of quick profits — **trad·able** *also* **trade·able** \'trā-də-bəl\ *adj* — **trade on** : to take often unscrupulous advantage of : EXPLOIT ⟨traded on their influence . . . in securing special favors —T. C. Pease⟩

³**trade** *adj* (1633) **1** : of, relating to, or used in trade **2** : intended for or limited to persons in a business or industry ⟨a ~ publication⟩ ⟨~ sales⟩ **b** : serving others in the same business rather than the ultimate user or consumer ⟨a ~ printing house⟩ **3** *also* **trades** : of, composed of, or representing the trades or trade unions ⟨a ~ committee⟩ **4** : of a larger softcover format than mass-market paperbacks and usu. sold only in bookstores ⟨~ paperbacks⟩; *also* : of or relating to the publishing of such books

trade acceptance *n* (1916) : a time draft or bill of exchange for the amount of a specific purchase drawn by the seller on the buyer, bearing the buyer's acceptance, and often noting the place of payment (as a bank)

trade agreement *n* (ca. 1921) **1** : an international agreement on conditions of trade in goods and services **2** : an agreement resulting from collective bargaining

trade book *n* (ca. 1945) **1** : a book intended for general readership **2** : TRADE EDITION

trade·craft \'trād-,kraft\ *n* (1961) : the techniques and procedures of espionage

trade discount *n* (1901) : a deduction from the list price of goods allowed by a manufacturer or wholesaler to a retailer

trade dollar *n* (1873) : a U.S. silver dollar weighing 420 grains .900 fine issued 1873–85 for use in oriental trade

trade down *vi* (1942) **1** : to trade something in (as an automobile) for something less expensive or valuable of its kind **2** : to stock or purchase lower-priced items : ECONOMIZE

trade edition *n* (1930) : an edition of a book intended for general distribution — compare TEXT EDITION

trade–in \'trād-,in\ *n* (1917) : an item of merchandise (as an automobile or refrigerator) taken as payment or part payment for a purchase

trade in *vt* (1923) **1** : to turn in as payment or part payment for a purchase or bill ⟨trade the old car in on a new one⟩ **2** : EXCHANGE **2**

trade language *n* (1662) : a restructured language (as a lingua franca or pidgin) used esp. in commercial communication

trade–last \'trād-,last\ *n* (1891) : a complimentary remark by a third person that a hearer offers to repeat to the person complimented if he or she will first report a compliment made about the hearer

¹**trade·mark** \-,märk\ *n* (1838) **1** : a device (as a word) pointing distinctly to the origin or ownership of merchandise to which it is applied and legally reserved to the exclusive use of the owner as maker or seller **2** : a distinguishing characteristic or feature firmly associated with a person or thing ⟨derringers . . . became almost a ~ of gamblers — Elmer Keith⟩ ⟨wearing his ~ bow tie and derby hat⟩

²**trademark** *vt* (1906) : to secure trademark rights for : register the trademark of

¹**trade name** *n* (1861) **1 a** : the name used for an article among traders **b** : an arbitrarily adopted name that is given by a manufacturer or merchant to an article or service to distinguish it as produced or sold by him and that may be used and protected as a trademark **2** : the name or style under which a concern does business

²**trade name** *vt* (1945) : to designate with a trade name

trade–off \'trād-,óf\ n (1961) **1** : a balancing of factors all of which are not attainable at the same time ⟨the education versus experience ∼ which governs personnel practices —H. S. White⟩ **2** : a giving up of one thing in return for another : EXCHANGE — **trade off** vt

trad·er \'trā-dər\ n (1585) **1** : a person whose business is buying and selling or barter: as **a** : MERCHANT **b** : a person who buys and sells (as stocks or commodities futures) in search of short-term profits **2** : a ship engaged in the coastal or foreign trade

trade route n (1876) **1** : a route followed by traders (as in caravans) **2** : one of the sea-lanes ordinarily used by merchant ships

trad·es·can·tia \,trā-də-'skan(t)-sh(ē-)ə\ n [NL, genus name, fr. John Tradescant †1638 Eng. traveler & gardener] (ca. 1909) : SPIDERWORT

trade school n (1889) : a secondary school teaching the skilled trades

trade secret n (1895) : a formula, process, or device used in a business that is not published or divulged and that thereby gives an advantage over competitors

trades·man \'trādz-mən\ n (1597) **1** : a worker in a skilled trade : CRAFTSMAN **2** : one who runs a retail store : SHOPKEEPER

trades·peo·ple \-,pē-pəl\ n pl (1728) : people engaged in trade

trade union also **trades union** n (1835) : LABOR UNION — **trade unionism** n — **trade unionist** n

trade up vi (1926) **1** : to trade something in (as an automobile) for something more expensive or valuable of its kind **2** : to stock or purchase higher-priced items

trade wind n (1650) : a wind blowing almost constantly in one direction; esp : a wind blowing almost continually toward the equator from the northeast in the belt between the northern horse latitudes and the doldrums and from the southeast in the belt between the southern horse latitudes and the doldrums — usu. used in pl.

trading post n (1796) **1** : a station of a trader or trading company established in a sparsely settled region where trade in products of local origin (as furs) is carried on **2** : ⁶POST 3b

trading stamp n (1897) : a printed stamp of value given as a premium to a retail customer to be redeemed in merchandise when accumulated in numbers

tra·di·tion \trə-'di-shən\ n [ME tradicioun, fr. MF & L; MF tradition, fr. L tradition-, traditio action of handing over, tradition — more at TREASON] (14c) **1** : an inherited, established, or customary pattern of thought, action, or behavior (as a religious practice or a social custom) **2** : the handing down of information, beliefs, and customs by word of mouth or by example from one generation to another without written instruction **3** : cultural continuity in social attitudes, customs, and institutions **4** : characteristic manner, method, or style — **tra·di·tion·al** \-'dish-nəl, -'di-shə-n°l\ adj — **tra·di·tion·al·ly** adv — **tra·di·tion·less** \-'di-shən-ləs\ adj

tra·di·tion·al·ism \trə-'dish-nə,li-zəm, -'di-shə-n°l,i-\ n (ca. 1859) **1** : adherence to the doctrines or practices of a tradition **2** : the beliefs of those opposed to modernism, liberalism, or radicalism — **tra·di·tion·al·ist** \-list, -ist\ n or adj — **tra·di·tion·al·is·tic** \-,dish-nə-'lis-tik, -,di-shə-n°l-'is-\ adj

tra·di·tion·al·ize \trə-'dish-nə-,līz, -'di-shə-n°l-,īz\ vt -ized; -iz·ing (1882) : to make traditional : imbue with traditions or traditionalism

tra·di·tion·ary \trə-'di-shə-,ner-ē\ adj (1661) : TRADITIONAL

tra·duce \trə-'düs, -'dyüs\ vt tra·duced; tra·duc·ing [L traducere to lead across, transfer, degrade, fr. tra-, trans- trans- + ducere to lead — more at TOW] (1592) **1** : to expose to shame or blame by means of falsehood and misrepresentation **2** : VIOLATE, BETRAY ⟨∼ a principle of law⟩ syn see MALIGN — **tra·duce·ment** \-mənt\ n — **tra·duc·er** n

¹traf·fic \'tra-fik\ n, often attrib [MF trafique, fr. OIt traffico, fr. trafficare to traffic] (1506) **1 a** : import and export trade **b** : the business of bartering or buying and selling **c** : illegal or disreputable usu. commercial activity ⟨the drug ∼⟩ **2 a** : communication or dealings esp. between individuals or groups **b** : EXCHANGE ⟨a lively ∼ in ideas —F. L. Allen⟩ **3** archaic : WARES, GOODS **4 a** : the movement (as of vehicles or pedestrians) through an area or along a route **b** : the vehicles, pedestrians, ships, or planes moving along a route **c** : the information or signals transmitted over a communications system : MESSAGES **5 a** : the passengers or cargo carried by a transportation system **b** : the business of transporting passengers or freight **6** : the volume of customers visiting a business establishment syn see BUSINESS — **the traffic will bear** : existing conditions will allow or permit ⟨charge what the traffic will bear⟩

²traffic vb **traf·ficked; traf·fick·ing** vi (1540) : to carry on traffic ∼ vt **1** : to travel over ⟨heavily trafficked highways⟩ **2** : TRADE, BARTER — **traf·fick·er** n

traf·fic·abil·i·ty \,tra-fi-kə-'bi-lə-tē\ n (1899) : the quality of a terrain that permits passage (as of vehicles and troops) — **traf·fic·able** \'tra-fi-kə-bəl\ adj

traffic circle n (1942) : ROTARY 2

traffic cone n (1953) : a conical marker used on a road or highway (as for indicating an area under repair)

traffic court n (1919) : a minor court for disposition of petty prosecutions for violations of statutes, ordinances, and local regulations governing the use of highways and motor vehicles

traffic engineering n (1931) : engineering dealing with the design of streets and control of traffic — **traffic engineer** n

traffic island n (1931) : ISLAND 2a

traffic light n (1912) : an electrically operated visual signal (as a system of colored lights) for controlling traffic

traffic manager n (1862) **1** : a supervisor of the traffic functions of a commercial or industrial organization **2** : the director of a large telegraph office

traffic signal n (1917) : a signal (as a traffic light) for controlling traffic

trag·a·canth \'tra-jə-,kan(t)th, 'tra-gə-, -kən(t)th; also 'tra-gə-,san(t)th\ n [MF tragacanthe, fr. L tragacantha, fr. Gk tragakantha, fr. tragos goat + akantha thorn] (1573) : a gum obtained from various Asian or East European leguminous plants (genus Astragalus and esp. A. gummifer) that swells in water and is used chiefly as an emulsifying, suspending, or thickening agent

tra·ge·di·an \trə-'jē-dē-ən\ n [ME tragedien, fr. MF, fr. tragedie] (14c) **1** : a writer of tragedies **2** : an actor specializing in tragic roles

tra·ge·di·enne \trə-,jē-dē-'en\ n [F tragédienne, fr. MF, fr. tragedie] (1851) : an actress who plays tragic roles

trag·e·dy \'tra-jə-dē\ n, pl **-dies** [ME tragedie, fr. MF, fr. L tragoedia, fr. Gk tragōidia, fr. tragos goat (akin to Gk trōgein to gnaw) + aeidein to sing — more at TROGLODYTE, ODE] (14c) **1 a** : a medieval narrative poem or tale typically describing the downfall of a great man **b** : a serious drama typically describing a conflict between the protagonist and a superior force (as destiny) and having a sorrowful or disastrous conclusion that excites pity or terror **c** : the literary genre of tragic dramas **2 a** : a disastrous event : CALAMITY **b** : MISFORTUNE **3** : tragic quality or element

trag·ic \'tra-jik\ also **trag·i·cal** \-ji-kəl\ adj [ME, fr. L tragicus, fr. Gk tragikos, irreg. fr. tragōidia tragedy] (15c) **1** : of, marked by, or expressive of tragedy ⟨the ∼ significance of the atomic bomb —H. S. Truman⟩ **2 a** : dealing with or treated in tragedy ⟨the ∼ hero⟩ **b** : appropriate to or typical of tragedy **3 a** : regrettably serious or unpleasant : DEPLORABLE, LAMENTABLE ⟨a ∼ mistake⟩ **b** : marked by a sense of tragedy — **trag·i·cal·ly** \-ji-k(ə-)lē\ adv

tragic flaw n (1913) : a flaw in character that brings about the downfall of the hero of a tragedy

tragic irony n (1833) : IRONY 3b

tragi·com·e·dy \,tra-ji-'kä-mə-dē\ n [MF tragicomedie, fr. OIt tragicomedia, fr. OSp, fr. L tragicomoedia, fr. tragicus + comoedia comedy] (ca. 1580) : a drama or a situation blending tragic and comic elements — **tragi·com·ic** \-'kä-mik\ also **tragi·com·i·cal** \-mi-kəl\ adj

tra·gus \'trā-gəs\ n, pl **tra·gi** \-,gī, -,jī\ [NL, fr. Gk tragos, a part of the ear, lit., goat] (ca. 1693) : the prominence in front of the external opening of the ear

¹trail \'trā(ə)l\ vb [ME, fr. MF trailler to tow, fr. (assumed) VL tragulare, fr. L tragula sledge, dragnet; akin to L trahere to pull] vi (14c) **1 a** : to hang down so as to drag along or sweep the ground **b** : to extend over a surface in a loose or straggling manner ⟨a vine that ∼s over the ground⟩ **c** : to grow to such length as to droop over toward the ground ⟨∼ing branches of a weeping birch⟩ **2 a** : to walk or proceed draggingly, heavily, or wearily : PLOD, TRUDGE **b** : to lag behind : do poorly in relation to others **3** : to move, flow, or extend slowly in thin streams ⟨smoke ∼ing from chimneys⟩ **4 a** : to extend in an erratic or uneven course or line : STRAGGLE **b** : DWINDLE ⟨voice ∼ing off⟩ **5** : to follow a trail : track game ∼ vt **1 a** : to draw or drag loosely along a surface **b** : HAUL, TOW **2 a** : to drag (as a limb or the body) heavily or wearily **b** : to carry or bring along as an addition, burden, or encumbrance **c** : to draw along in one's wake **3 a** : to follow upon the scent or trace of : TRACK **b** : to follow in the footsteps of : PURSUE **c** : to follow along behind **d** : to lag behind (as a competitor) syn see CHASE

²trail n (14c) **1** : something that trails or is trailed: as **a** : a trailing plant **b** : the train of a gown **c** : a trailing arrangement (as of flowers) : SPRAY **d** : the part of a gun carriage that rests on the ground when the piece is unlimbered **2 a** : something that follows or moves along as if being drawn along : TRAIN ⟨a ∼ of admirers⟩ **b** (1) : the streak produced by a meteor (2) : a continuous line produced photographically by permitting the image of a celestial body (as a star) to move over the plate **c** : a chain of consequences : AFTERMATH ⟨the . . . movement left a ∼ of bitterness and prejudice behind it —Paul Blanshard⟩ **3 a** : a trace or mark left by something that has passed or been drawn along : SCENT, TRACK ⟨a ∼ of blood⟩ **b** (1) : a track made by passage esp. through a wilderness (2) : a marked or established path or route esp. through a forest or mountainous region **c** : a course followed or to be followed ⟨hit the campaign ∼⟩ — **trail·less** \'trā(ə)l-ləs\ adj

trail bike n (1966) : a small motorcycle designed for off-road use

trail·blaz·er \'trā(ə)l-,blā-zər\ n (1908) **1** : one that blazes a trail to guide others : PATHFINDER **2** : PIONEER 2 ⟨a ∼ in astrophysics⟩

trail·blaz·ing \-ziŋ\ adj (1951) : making or pointing a new way ⟨∼ legislation⟩

trail·break·er \-,brā-kər\ n (1925) : TRAILBLAZER

¹trail·er \'trā-lər\ n (1590) **1** : one that trails **2** : a trailing plant **3** : a nonautomotive vehicle designed to be hauled by a truck: as **a** : a vehicle for transporting something ⟨a boat ∼⟩; esp : SEMITRAILER 1 **b** : a vehicle designed to serve wherever parked as a temporary dwelling or place of business **c** : MOBILE HOME **4** : PREVIEW 2 **b** : a short blank strip of film attached to the end of a reel

²trailer vi (1938) **1** : to live or travel in or with a trailer **2** : to be transportable by trailer ⟨a light boat that ∼s easily⟩ ∼ vt : to transport (as a boat) by means of a trailer — **trail·er·able** \-lə-rə-bəl\ adj — **trail·er·ing** n

trail·er·ist \-lə-rist\ n (1950) **1** : a person traveling or vacationing with a trailer **2** : TRAILERITE 1

trail·er·ite \-,rīt\ n (1936) **1** : a person living in a mobile home **2** : TRAILERIST 1

trailer park n (1942) : an area equipped to accommodate mobile homes — called also trailer camp, trailer court

trail·head \'trāl-,hed\ n (1948) : the point at which a trail begins

trailing arbutus n (1785) : ARBUTUS 2

trailing edge n (1909) : the rearmost edge of an object that moves esp. of an airfoil

trail mix n (1979) : a mixture of seeds, nuts, and dried fruits eaten as a snack esp. by hikers

trail·side \'trāl-,sīd\ adj (1923) : of, relating to, or situated in the area immediately adjacent to a trail

¹train \'trān\ n [ME, fr. MF traine, fr. MF, fr. OF, fr. traïr to betray, fr. L tradere — more at TRAITOR] (14c) obs : SCHEME, TRICK

²train n [ME, fr. MF, fr. OF, fr. trainer to draw, drag] (15c) **1** : a part of a gown that trails behind the wearer **2 a** : RETINUE, SUITE **b** : a moving file of persons, vehicles, or animals **3** : the vehicles, personnel, and sometimes animals that furnish supply, maintenance, and evacuation services to a combat unit **4 a** : order of occurrence leading to

\ə\ abut \ᵊ\ kitten, F table \ər\ further \a\ ash \ā\ ace \ä\ mop, mar \au̇\ out \ch\ chin \e\ bet \ē\ easy \g\ go \i\ hit \ī\ ice \j\ job \ŋ\ sing \ō\ go \ȯ\ law \ȯi\ boy \th\ thin \t͟h\ the \ü\ loot \u̇\ foot \y\ yet \zh\ vision \ə, k, ⁿ, œ, œ̄, ᵫ, ᵬ, �478\ see Guide to Pronunciation some result — often used in the phrase *in train* ⟨this humiliating process had been in ~ for decades —Paul Fussell⟩ **b** : an orderly succession ⟨a ~ of thought⟩ **c** : accompanying or resultant circumstances : AFTERMATH ⟨consequences the discovery will bring in its ~⟩ **5** : a line of combustible material laid to lead fire to a charge **6** : a series of moving mechanical parts (as gears) that transmit and modify motion **7 a** : a connected line of railroad cars with or without a locomotive **b** : an automotive tractor with one or more trailer units **8** : a series of parts or elements that together constitute a system for producing a result and esp. for carrying on a process (as of manufacture) automatically — **train·ful** \'trān-ˌfül\ *n*

³**train** *vb* [ME, fr. MF *trainer*, fr. OF, fr. (assumed) VL *traginare*; akin to L *trahere* to draw] *vt* (15c) **1** : TRAIL, DRAG **2** : to direct the growth of (a plant) usu. by bending, pruning, and tying **3 a** : to form by instruction, discipline, or drill **b** : to teach so as to make fit, qualified, or proficient **4** : to make prepared (as by exercise) for a test of skill **5** : to aim at an object or objective : DIRECT ⟨~ed his camera on the deer⟩ ⟨~ing every effort toward success⟩ ~ *vi* **1** : to undergo instruction, discipline, or drill **2** : to go by train *syn* see TEACH — **train·abil·i·ty** \ˌtrā-nə-'bi-lə-tē\ *n* — **train·able** \'trā-nə-bəl\ *adj*

train·band \'trān-ˌband\ *n* [alter. of *trained band*] (1630) : a 17th or 18th century militia company in England or America

train·bear·er \'trān-ˌbar-ər, -ˌber-\ *n* (1722) : an attendant who holds up (as on a ceremonial occasion) the train of a robe or gown

train case *n* (1948) : a small boxlike piece of luggage used esp. for toilet articles

train dispatcher *n* (1857) : a railroad employee who directs the movement of trains within a division and coordinates their movement from one division to another

train·ee \trā-'nē\ *n* (1841) : one that is being trained esp. for a job — **train·ee·ship** \-ˈnē-ˌship\ *n*

train·er \'trā-nər\ *n* (1598) **1** : one that trains **2** : one (as a machine or vehicle) used in training **3** : a person who treats the ailments and minor injuries of the members of an athletic team

train·ing (1548) **1 a** : the act, process, or method of one that trains **b** : the skill, knowledge, or experience acquired by one that trains **2** : the state of being trained

training college *n* (ca. 1829) *Brit* : TEACHERS COLLEGE

training school *n* (1829) **1** : a school preparing students for a particular occupation **2** : a correctional institution for the custody and reeducation of juvenile delinquents

training table *n* (1893) : a table where athletes under a training regimen eat meals planned to help in their conditioning

training wheels *n pl* (1964) : a pair of small wheels connected to the rear axle of a bicycle to help a beginning bicyclist maintain balance

train·load \'trān-ˌlōd\ *n* (1876) : the full freight or passenger capacity of a railroad train; *also* : a load that fills a train

train·man \'trān-mən, -ˌman\ *n* (1877) : a member of a train crew supervised by a conductor

train oil \'trān-\ *n* [obs. *train* train oil, fr. ME *trane*, fr. MD *trane* or MLG *trān*; akin to OHG *trahan* tear] (ca. 1553) : oil from a marine animal (as a whale)

traipse \'trāps\ *vb* **traipsed; traips·ing** [origin unknown] *vi* (1647) : to go on foot : WALK ⟨*traipsed* over to the restaurant⟩ ⟨children *traipsing* at her heels⟩; *also* : to walk or travel about without apparent plan but with or without a purpose ⟨a week *traipsing* through the Ozarks⟩ ⟨*traipsing* from office to office⟩ ~ *vt* : TRAMP, WALK *syn* see WANDER — **traipse** *n*

trait \'trāt, *Brit usu* 'trā\ *n* [MF, lit., act of drawing, fr. L *tractus* — more at TRACT] (1589) **1 a** : a stroke of or as if of a pencil **b** : TOUCH, TRACE **2 a** : a distinguishing quality (as of personal character) : PECULIARITY **b** : an inherited characteristic

trai·tor \'trā-tər\ *n* [ME *traitre*, fr. OF, fr. L *traditor*, fr. *tradere* to hand over, deliver, betray, fr. *trans-, tra-* trans- + *dare* to give — more at DATE] (13c) **1** : one who betrays another's trust or is false to an obligation or duty **2** : one who commits treason

trai·tor·ous \'trā-tə-rəs, 'trā-trəs\ *adj* (14c) **1** : guilty or capable of treason **2** : constituting treason ⟨~ activities⟩ *syn* see FAITHLESS — **trai·tor·ous·ly** *adv*

trai·tress \'trā-trəs\ *or* **trai·tor·ess** \'trā-tə-rəs, 'trā-trəs\ *n* (14c) : a female traitor

tra·ject \trə-'jekt\ *vt* [L *trajectus*, pp. of *traicere*] (1657) : TRANSMIT — **tra·jec·tion** \-'jek-shən\ *n*

tra·jec·to·ry \trə-'jek-t(ə-)rē\ *n, pl* **-ries** [NL *trajectoria*, fr. fem. of *trajectorius* of passing, fr. L *traicere* to cause to cross, cross, fr. *trans-, tra-* trans- + *jacere* to throw — more at JET] (1696) **1** : the curve that a body (as a planet or comet in its orbit or a rocket) describes in space **2** : a path, progression, or line of development resembling a physical trajectory

Tra·keh·ner \trä-'kā-nər\ *n* [G, fr. *Trakehnen*, site of the Prussian royal stud in East Prussia] (1926) : any of a breed of large powerful saddle horses that originated in East Prussia and excel in dressage and jumping

¹**tram** \'tram\ *n* [E dial., shaft of a wheelbarrow, prob. fr. LG *traam*, lit., beam] (ca. 1517) **1** : any of various vehicles: as **a** : a boxlike wagon running on rails (as in a mine) **b** *chiefly Brit* : STREETCAR **c** : a carrier that travels on an overhead cable or rails **2** *pl, chiefly Brit* : a streetcar line

²**tram** *vb* **trammed; tram·ming** (1874) : to haul in a tram or over a tramway

tram·car \'tram-ˌkär\ *n* (1873) *chiefly Brit* : STREETCAR **2** : TRAM 1a

tram·line \-ˌlīn\ *n* (1886) *Brit* : a streetcar line

¹**tram·mel** \'tra-məl\ *n* [ME *tramayle*, a kind of net, fr. MF *tremail*, fr. LL *tremaculum*, fr. L *tres* three + *macula* mesh, spot — more at THREE] (15c) **1** : a net for catching birds or fish; *esp* : one having three layers with the middle one finer-meshed and slack so that fish passing through carry some of the center net through the coarser opposite net and are trapped **2** : an adjustable pothook for a fireplace crane **3** : a shackle used for making a horse amble **4** : something impeding activity, progress, or freedom : RESTRAINT — usu. used in pl. **5 a** : an instrument for drawing ellipses **b** : a compass for drawing large circles that consists of a beam with two sliding parts — usu. used in pl. **c** : any of various gauges used for aligning or adjusting machine parts

²**trammel** *vt* **-meled** *or* **-melled; -mel·ing** *or* **-mel·ling** \'tra-mə-liŋ, 'tram-liŋ\ (1605) **1** : to catch or hold in or as if in a net : ENMESH **2** : to prevent or impede the free play of : CONFINE *syn* see HAMPER

¹**tra·mon·tane** \trə-'män-ˌtān, ˌtra-mən-\ *n* (1593) : one dwelling in a tramontane region; *broadly* : FOREIGNER

²**tramontane** *adj* [It *tramontano*, fr. L *transmontanus*, fr. *trans-* + *mont-, mons* mountain — more at MOUNT] (1596) **1** : TRANSALPINE **2** : lying on or coming from the other side of a mountain range

¹**tramp** \'tramp, *vi 1 & vt 1 are also* 'trämp, 'trômp\ *vb* [ME; akin to MLG *trampen* to stamp] *vi* (14c) **1** : to walk, tread, or step esp. heavily **2 a** : to travel about on foot : HIKE **b** : to journey as a tramp ~ *vt* **1** : to tread on forcibly and repeatedly **2** : to travel or wander through or over on foot ⟨have ~ed all the woods on their property⟩ — **tramp·er** *n*

²**tramp** \'tramp, *3, 4 are also* 'trämp, 'trômp\ *n* (1664) **1 a** : a foot traveler **b** : a begging or thieving vagrant **c** : a woman of loose morals; *specif* : PROSTITUTE **2** : a walking trip : HIKE **3** : the succession of sounds made by the beating of feet on a surface (as a road, pavement, or floor) **4** : an iron plate to protect the sole of a shoe **5** : a ship not making regular trips but taking cargo when and where it offers and to any port — called also *tramp steamer*

³**tramp** \'tramp\ *adj* (1873) : having no fixed abode, connection, or destination ⟨a ~ dog⟩

tramp art *n* (1974) : a style of wood carving flourishing in the U.S. from about 1875 to 1930 that is characterized by ornate layered whittling often of cigar boxes or fruit crates; *also* : an object carved in this style

tram·ple \'tram-pəl\ *vb* **tram·pled; tram·pling** \-p(ə-)liŋ\ [ME, freq. of *trampen* to tramp] *vi* (14c) **1** : TRAMP; *esp* : to tread heavily so as to bruise, crush, or injure **2** : to inflict injury or destruction esp. contemptuously or ruthlessly — usu. used with *on, over,* or *upon* ⟨*trampling* on the rights of others⟩ ~ *vt* : to crush, injure, or destroy by or as if by treading — **trample** *n* — **tram·pler** \-p(ə-)lər\ *n*

tram·po·line \ˌtram-pə-'lēn, 'tram-pə-ˌ\ *n* [It *trampolino* springboard, fr. *trampoli* stilts, of Gmc origin; akin to MLG *trampen* to stamp] (1928) : a resilient sheet or web (as of nylon) supported by springs in a metal frame and used as a springboard and landing area in tumbling — **tram·po·lin·er** \-'lē-nər, -ˌlē-\ *n* — **tram·po·lin·ist** \-nist\ *n*

tram·po·lin·ing *n* (1949) : the sport of jumping and tumbling on a trampoline

tram·way \-ˌwā\ *n* (1825) **1 a** : a railway for trams **b** *Brit* : a streetcar line **2** : an overhead cable for trams

¹**trance** \'tran(t)s\ *n* [ME, fr. MF *transe*, fr. *transir* to pass away, swoon, fr. L *transire* to pass, pass away — more at TRANSIENT] (14c) **1** : a state of partly suspended animation or inability to function **2** : a somnolent state (as of deep hypnosis) **3** : a state of profound abstraction or absorption — **trance·like** \-ˌlīk\ *adj*

²**trance** *vt* **tranced; tranc·ing** (ca. 1598) : ENTRANCE, ENRAPTURE

tranche \'trän(t)sh\ *n* [F, lit., slice, fr. OF, fr. *trenchier, trancher* to cut — more at TRENCH] (1930) : a bond series issued for sale in a foreign country

tran·gam \'traŋ-gəm\ *n* [origin unknown] (ca. 1658) *archaic* : TRINKET, GIMCRACK

tran·quil \'traŋ-kwəl, 'tran-\ *adj* [L *tranquillus*] (1604) **1 a** : free from agitation of mind or spirit ⟨a ~ self-assurance⟩ **b** : free from disturbance or turmoil ⟨a ~ scene⟩ **2** : unvarying in aspect : STEADY, STABLE *syn* see CALM — **tran·quil·ly** \-kwə-lē\ *adv* — **tran·quil·ness** *n*

tran·quil·ize *also* **tran·quil·lize** \'traŋ-kwə-ˌlīz, 'tran-\ *vb* **-ized** *also* **-lized; -iz·ing** *also* **-liz·ing** *vt* (1623) **1** : to make tranquil or calm : PACIFY; *esp* : to relieve of mental tension and anxiety by means of drugs ~ *vi* **1** : to become tranquil : RELAX 1 **2** : to make one tranquil

tran·quil·iz·er *also* **tran·quil·liz·er** \-ˌlī-zər\ *n* (1800) **1** : one that tranquilizes **2** : a drug used to reduce mental disturbance (as anxiety and tension)

tran·quil·li·ty *or* **tran·quil·i·ty** \tran-'kwi-lə-tē, traŋ-\ *n* (14c) : the quality or state of being tranquil

trans \'tran(t)s, 'tranz\ *adj* (1892) : characterized by having certain groups of atoms on opposite sides of the longitudinal axis of a double bond or of the plane of a ring in a molecule

trans- *prefix* [L *trans-, tra-* across, beyond, through, so as to change, fr. *trans* across, beyond — more at THROUGH] **1** : on or to the other side of : across : beyond ⟨*trans*atlantic⟩ **2 a** : beyond ⟨a specified chemical element) in the periodic table ⟨*trans*uranium⟩ **b** *usu ital* : trans ⟨*trans*-dichloro-ethylene⟩ — compare CIS-2 **3** : through ⟨*trans*cutaneous⟩ **4** : so or such as to change or transfer ⟨*trans*literate⟩ ⟨*trans*location⟩ ⟨*trans*amination⟩ ⟨*trans*ship⟩

trans·act \tran-'zakt, tran(t)-'sakt\ *vb* [L *transactus*, pp. of *transigere* to drive through, complete, transact, fr. *trans-* + *agere* to drive, do — more at AGENT] *vi* (ca. 1585) : to carry on business ~ *vt* **1** : to carry to completion ⟨~ a sale⟩ **2** : to carry on the operation or management of : DO ⟨~ business⟩ — **trans·ac·tor** \-'zak-tər, -'sak-tər\ *n*

trans·ac·ti·nide \tran(t)-'sak-tə-ˌnīd, tran-'zak-\ *adj* (1969) : of, relating to, or being actual or hypothetical elements with atomic weights higher than those of the actinide series ⟨~ chemistry⟩

trans·ac·tion \tran-'zak-shən, tran(t)-'sak-\ *n* (1647) **1 a** : something transacted; *esp* : an exchange or transfer of goods, services, or funds ⟨electronic ~s⟩ **b** *pl* : the often published record of the meeting of a society or association **2 a** : an act, process, or instance of transacting **b** : a communicative action or activity involving two parties or things that reciprocally affect or influence each other — **trans·ac·tion·al** \-shnəl, -shə-n²l\ *adj*

transactional analysis *n* (1961) : a system of psychotherapy involving analysis of individual episodes of social interaction for insight that will aid communication

trans·al·pine \tran(t)s-'al-ˌpīn, tranz-\ *adj* [L *transalpinus*, fr. *trans-* + *Alpes* the Alps] (1590) : situated on the north side of the Alps ⟨*Trans*alpine Gaul⟩ — compare CISALPINE

trans·am·i·nase \tran(t)s-'a-mə-ˌnās, tranz-, -ˌnāz\ *n* (1940) : an enzyme promoting transamination — called also *aminotransferase*

trans·am·i·na·tion \ˌtran(t)s-ˌa-mə-'nā-shən, ˌtranz-\ *n* (1939) : a reversible oxidation-reduction reaction in which an amino group is transferred typically from an alpha-amino acid to the carbonyl carbon atom of an alpha-keto acid

trans·at·lan·tic \‚tran(t)s-ət-'lan-tik, ‚tranz-\ *adj* (1779) **1 a** : crossing or extending across the Atlantic Ocean ⟨a ~ cable⟩ **b** : relating to or involving crossing the Atlantic Ocean ⟨~ air fares⟩ **2 a** : situated or originating from beyond the Atlantic Ocean **b** : of, relating to, or involving countries on both sides of the Atlantic Ocean and esp. the U.S. and Great Britain ⟨~ cooperation⟩

trans·ax·le \tran(t)s-'ak-səl, tranz-\ *n* [*trans*mission + *axle*] (1958) : a unit that consists of a combination of transmission and front axle used in front-wheel-drive automobiles

trans·ceiv·er \tran(t)-'sē-vər\ *n* [*trans*mitter + *receiver*] (1934) : a radio transmitter-receiver that uses many of the same components for both transmission and reception

tran·scend \tran(t)-'send\ *vb* [ME, fr. L *transcendere* to climb across, transcend, fr. *trans-* + *scandere* to climb — more at SCAN] *vt* (14c) **1 a** : to rise above or go beyond the limits of **b** : to triumph over the negative or restrictive aspects of : OVERCOME **c** : to be prior to, beyond, and above (the universe or material existence) **2** : to outstrip or outdo in some attribute, quality, or power ~ *vi* : to rise above or extend notably beyond ordinary limits **syn** see EXCEED

tran·scen·dence \-'sen-dən(t)s\ *n* (1601) : the quality or state of being transcendent

tran·scen·den·cy \-dən(t)-sē\ *n* (1615) : TRANSCENDENCE

tran·scen·dent \-dənt\ *adj* [L *transcendent-, transcendens,* prp. of *transcendere*] (1598) **1 a** : exceeding usual limits : SURPASSING **b** : extending or lying beyond the limits of ordinary experience **c** *in Kantian philosophy* : being beyond the limits of all possible experience and knowledge **2** : being beyond comprehension **3** : transcending the universe or material existence — **tran·scen·dent·ly** *adv*

tran·scen·den·tal \‚tran(t)-‚sen-'den-t²l, -sən-\ *adj* (1624) **1 a** : TRANSCENDENT 1b **b** : SUPERNATURAL **c** : ABSTRUSE, ABSTRACT **d** : of or relating to transcendentalism **2 a** : incapable of being the root of an algebraic equation with rational coefficients ⟨π is a ~ number⟩ **b** : being, involving, or representing a function (as sin *x*, log *x*, *e*ˣ) that cannot be expressed by a finite number of algebraic operations ⟨~ curves⟩ **3** *in Kantian philosophy* **a** : of or relating to experience as determined by the mind's makeup **b** : transcending experience but not human knowledge **4** : TRANSCENDENT 1a — **tran·scen·den·tal·ly** \-t²l-ē\ *adv*

tran·scen·den·tal·ism \-t²l-‚i-zəm\ *n* (1803) **1** : a philosophy that emphasizes the a priori conditions of knowledge and experience or the unknowable character of ultimate reality or that emphasizes the transcendent as the fundamental reality **2** : a philosophy that asserts the primacy of the spiritual and transcendental over the material and empirical **3** : the quality or state of being transcendental; *esp* : visionary idealism — **tran·scen·den·tal·ist** \-t²l-ist\ *adj or n*

transcendental meditation *n* (1966) : a technique of meditation in which a mantra is chanted in order to foster calm, creativity, and spiritual well-being

trans·con·ti·nen·tal \‚tran(t)s-‚kän-t²n-'en-t²l, ‚tranz-\ *adj* (1853) : extending or going across a continent ⟨a ~ railroad⟩

tran·scribe \tran(t)-'skrīb\ *vt* **tran·scribed; tran·scrib·ing** [L *transcribere,* fr. *trans-* + *scribere* to write — more at SCRIBE] (1552) **1 a** : to make a written copy of **b** : to make a copy of (dictated or recorded matter) in longhand or on a machine (as a typewriter) **c** : to paraphrase or summarize in writing **d** : WRITE DOWN, RECORD **2 a** : to represent (speech sounds) by means of phonetic symbols **b** : TRANSLATE 2a **c** : to transfer (data) from one recording form to another **d** : to record (as on magnetic tape) for later broadcast **3** : to make a musical transcription of **4** : to cause (as DNA) to undergo genetic transcription — **tran·scrib·er** *n*

tran·script \'tran(t)-‚skript\ *n* [ME, fr. ML *transcriptum,* fr. L, neut. of *transcriptus,* pp. of *transcribere*] (14c) **1 a** : a written, printed, or typed copy; *esp* : a usu. typewritten copy of dictated or recorded material **b** : an official or legal and often published copy ⟨a court reporter's ~⟩; *esp* : an official copy of a student's educational record **2** : a representation (as of experience) in an art form **3** : a sequence of RNA produced by transcription from a DNA template

tran·scrip·tase \tran-'skrip-‚tās, -‚tāz\ *n* [*transcription* + *-ase*] (1963) : RNA POLYMERASE; *also* : REVERSE TRANSCRIPTASE

tran·scrip·tion \tran(t)-'skrip-shən\ *n* (1598) **1** : an act, process, or instance of transcribing : COPY, TRANSCRIPT: as **a** : an arrangement of a musical composition for some instrument or voice other than the original **b** : a recording (as on magnetic tape) made esp. for use in radiobroadcasting **3** : the process of constructing a messenger RNA molecule using a DNA molecule as a template with resulting transfer of genetic information to the messenger RNA — compare TRANSLATION 2, REVERSE TRANSCRIPTION — **tran·scrip·tion·al** \-shnəl, -shə-n²l\ *adj* — **tran·scrip·tion·al·ly** *adv*

tran·scrip·tion·ist \-shə-nist\ *n* (1963) : one that transcribes; *esp* : a typist who transcribes dictated medical reports

trans·cul·tur·al \tran(t)s-'kəl-chə-rəl, tranz-, -'kəlch-rəl\ *adj* (1951) : involving, encompassing, or extending across two or more cultures ⟨~ problems⟩

trans·cu·ta·ne·ous \tran(t)s-kyù-'tā-nē-əs\ *adj* (ca. 1941) : passing, entering, or made by penetration through the skin ⟨~ infection⟩ ⟨~ inoculation⟩

trans·der·mal \tran(t)s-'dər-məl, tranz-\ *adj* (1944) : relating to, being, or supplying a medication in a form for absorption through the skin into the bloodstream ⟨~ drug delivery⟩ ⟨~ nitroglycerin⟩ ⟨~ nicotine patch⟩

trans·dis·ci·plin·ary \-'di-sə-plə-‚ner-ē\ *adj* (1948) : INTERDISCIPLINARY

trans·duce \tran(t)s-'düs, tranz-, -'dyüs\ *vt* **trans·duced; trans·duc·ing** [L *transducere* to lead across, transfer, fr. *trans-* + *ducere* to lead — more at TOW] (1947) **1** : to convert (as energy or a message) into another form ⟨essentially sense organs ~ physical energy into a nervous signal⟩ **2** : to bring about the transfer of (as a gene) from one microorganism to another by means of a viral agent

trans·duc·er \-'dü-sər, -'dyü-\ *n* (1924) : a device that is actuated by power from one system and supplies power usu. in another form to a second system ⟨a loudspeaker is a ~ that transforms electrical signals into sound energy⟩

trans·duc·tion \-'dək-shən\ *n* [L *transducere*] (1947) : the action or process of transducing; *esp* : the transfer of genetic determinants from

one microorganism to another by a viral agent (as a bacteriophage) — **trans·duc·tant** \-tənt\ *n* — **trans·duc·tion·al** \-shnəl, -shə-n²l\ *adj*

¹tran·sect \tran(t)-'sekt\ *vt* [*trans-* + inter*sect*] (1634) : to cut transversely — **tran·sec·tion** \-'sek-shən\ *n*

²tran·sect \'tran(t)-‚sekt\ *n* (1905) : a sample area (as of vegetation) usu. in the form of a long continuous strip

tran·sept \'tran(t)-‚sept\ *n* [NL *transeptum,* fr. L *trans-* + *septum, saeptum* enclosure, wall] (ca. 1542) : the part of a cruciform church that crosses at right angles to the greatest length between the nave and the apse or choir; *also* : either of the projecting ends of a transept — **tran·sep·tal** \tran(t)-'sep-t²l\ *adj*

trans·fec·tion \tran(t)s-'fek-shən, tranz-\ *n* [*trans-* + in*fection*] (1964) : infection of a cell with isolated viral nucleic acid followed by production of the complete virus in the cell; *also* : the incorporation of exogenous DNA into a cell — **trans·fect** \-'fekt\ *vt*

¹trans·fer \tran(t)s-'fər, 'tran(t)s-,\ *vb* **trans·ferred; trans·fer·ring** [ME *transferren,* fr. L *transferre,* fr. *trans-* + *ferre* to carry — more at BEAR] *vt* (14c) **1 a** : to convey from one person, place, or situation to another : TRANSPORT **b** : to cause to pass from one to another : TRANSMIT **c** : TRANSFORM, CHANGE **2** : to make over the possession or control of : CONVEY **3** : to print or otherwise copy from one surface to another by contact ~ *vi* **1** : to move to a different place, region, or situation; *esp* : to withdraw from one educational institution to enroll at another **2** : to change from one vehicle or transportation line to another — **trans·fer·abil·i·ty** \(‚)tran(t)s-‚fər-ə-'bi-lə-tē\ *n* — **trans·fer·able** *also* **trans·fer·ra·ble** \tran(t)s-'fər-ə-bəl\ *adj* — **trans·fer·al** \-əl\ *n* — **trans·fer·rer** \-ər\ *n*

²trans·fer \'tran(t)s-fər\ *n* (1674) **1 a** : conveyance of right, title, or interest in real or personal property from one person to another **b** : removal or acquisition of property by mere delivery with intent to transfer title **2 a** : an act, process, or instance of transferring : TRANSFERENCE **2 b** : the carryover or generalization of learned responses from one type of situation to another **3** : one that transfers or is transferred; *esp* : a graphic image transferred by contact from one surface to another **4** : a place where a transfer is made (as of trains to ferries or as where one form of power is changed to another) **5** : a ticket entitling a passenger on a public conveyance to continue the trip on another route

trans·fer·ase \'tran(t)s-(‚)fər-‚ās, -‚āz\ *n* (1948) : an enzyme that promotes transfer of a group from one molecule to another

trans·fer·ee \‚tran(t)s-(‚)fər-'ē\ *n* (ca. 1736) **1** : a person to whom a conveyance is made **2** : one who is transferred

trans·fer·ence \tran(t)s-'fər-ən(t)s, 'tran(t)s-(‚)\ *n* (1681) **1** : an act, process, or instance of transferring : CONVEYANCE, TRANSFER **2** : the redirection of feelings and desires and esp. of those unconsciously retained from childhood toward a new object (as a psychoanalyst conducting therapy) — **trans·fer·en·tial** \‚tran(t)s-fə-'ren(t)-shəl\ *adj*

transfer factor *n* (1956) : a substance that is produced and secreted by a lymphocyte functioning in cell-mediated immunity and that upon incorporation into a lymphocyte which has not been sensitized confers on it the same immunological specificity as the sensitized cell

trans·fer·or \‚tran(t)s-(‚)fər-'ȯr\ *n* (1875) : one that conveys a title, right, or property

transfer payment *n* (ca. 1945) **1** : a public expenditure made for a purpose (as unemployment compensation) other than procuring goods or services — usu. used in pl. **2** *pl* : money (as welfare payments) that is received by individuals and that is neither compensation for goods or services currently supplied nor income from investments

trans·fer·rin \tran(t)s-'fer-ən\ *n* [*trans-* + L *ferrum* iron] (1947) : a beta globulin in blood plasma capable of combining with ferric ions and transporting iron in the body

transfer RNA \'tran(t)s-‚fər-\ *n* (1961) : a relatively small RNA that transfers a particular amino acid to a growing polypeptide chain at the ribosomal site of protein synthesis during translation — compare MESSENGER RNA

trans·fig·u·ra·tion \(‚)tran(t)s-fi-gyə-'rā-shən, -gə-\ *n* (14c) **1 a** : a change in form or appearance : METAMORPHOSIS **b** : an exalting, glorifying, or spiritual change **2** *cap* : August 6 observed as a Christian feast in commemoration of the transfiguration of Christ on a mountaintop in the presence of three disciples

trans·fig·ure \tran(t)s-'fi-gyər, *esp Brit* -'fi-gər\ *vt* **-ured; -ur·ing** [ME, fr. L *transfigurare,* fr. *trans-* + *figurare* to shape, fashion, fr. *figura* figure] (14c) **1** : to give a new and typically exalted or spiritual appearance to : transform outwardly and usu. for the better **syn** see TRANSFORM

trans·fi·nite \(‚)tran(t)s-'fī-‚nīt\ *adj* [G *transfinit,* fr. *trans-* (fr. L) + *finit* finite, fr. L *finitus*] (1902) **1** : going beyond or surpassing any finite number, group, or magnitude **2** : being or relating to cardinal and ordinal numbers of sets with an infinite number of elements

trans·fix \tran(t)s-'fiks\ *vt* [L *transfixus,* pp. of *transfigere,* fr. *trans-* + *figere* to fasten, pierce — more at FIX] (1590) **1** : to pierce through with or as if with a pointed weapon : IMPALE **2** : to hold motionless by or as if by piercing — **trans·fix·ion** \-'fik-shən\ *n*

¹trans·form \tran(t)s-'fȯrm\ *vb* [ME, fr. L *transformare,* fr. *trans-* + *formare* to form, fr. *forma* form] *vt* (14c) **1 a** : to change in composition or structure **b** : to change the outward form or appearance of **c** : to change in character or condition : CONVERT **2** : to subject to mathematical transformation **3** : to cause (a cell) to undergo genetic transformation ~ *vi* : to become transformed : CHANGE — **trans·form·able** \-'fȯr-mə-bəl\ *adj* — **trans·for·ma·tive** \-'fȯr-mə-tiv\ *adj*
syn TRANSFORM, METAMORPHOSE, TRANSMUTE, CONVERT, TRANSMOGRIFY, TRANSFIGURE mean to change a thing into a different thing. TRANSFORM implies a major change in form, nature, or function ⟨*transformed* a small company into a corporate giant⟩. METAMORPHOSE suggests an abrupt or startling change induced by or as if by magic or a supernatural power ⟨awkward girls *metamorphosed* into graceful ballerinas⟩. TRANSMUTE implies transforming into a higher element or thing ⟨at-

---

\ə\ abut \ᵊ\ kitten, F table \ər\ further \a\ ash \ā\ ace \ä\ mop, mar \aú\ out \ch\ chin \e\ bet \ē\ easy \g\ go \i\ hit \ī\ ice \j\ job \ŋ\ sing \ō\ go \ȯ\ law \ȯi\ boy \th\ thin \t̲h̲\ the \ü\ loot \ù\ foot \y\ yet \zh\ vision \à, k̲, ⁿ, œ, œ̄, ᵫ, ᵫ̄, ᵊ\ *see* Guide to Pronunciation tempted to *transmute* lead into gold⟩. CONVERT implies a change fitting something for a new or different use or function ⟨*converted* the study into a nursery⟩. TRANSMOGRIFY suggests a strange or preposterous metamorphosis ⟨a story in which a frog is *transmogrified* into a prince⟩. TRANSFIGURE implies a change that exalts or glorifies ⟨joy *transfigured* her face⟩.

²**trans·form** \'tran(t)s-ˌfȯrm\ *n* (1853) **1 :** a mathematical element obtained from another by transformation **2 :** TRANSFORMATION 3a(1), (2) **3 :** a linguistic structure (as a sentence) produced by means of a transformation ⟨"the duckling is killed by the farmer" is a ~ of "the farmer kills the duckling"⟩

trans·for·ma·tion \ˌtran(t)s-fər-'mā-shən, -fȯr-\ *n* (15c) **1 :** an act, process, or instance of transforming or being transformed **2 :** false hair worn esp. by a woman to replace or supplement natural hair **3 a** (1) **:** the operation of changing (as by rotation or mapping) one configuration or expression into another in accordance with a mathematical rule; *esp* **:** a change of variables or coordinates in which a function of new variables or coordinates is substituted for each original variable or coordinate (2) **:** the formula that effects a transformation **b :** FUNCTION 5a **c :** an operation that converts (as by insertion, deletion, or permutation) one grammatical string (as a sentence) into another; *also* **:** a formal statement of such an operation **4 a :** genetic modification of a bacterium by incorporation of free DNA from another ruptured bacterial cell — compare TRANSDUCTION **b :** genetic modification of a cell by the uptake and incorporation of exogenous DNA

trans·for·ma·tion·al \-shnəl, -shə-nᵊl\ *adj* (1894) **:** of, relating to, characterized by, or concerned with transformation and esp. linguistic transformation — **trans·for·ma·tion·al·ly** *adv*

transformational grammar *n* (1961) **:** a grammar that generates the deep structures of a language and converts these to the surface structures by means of transformations

trans·for·ma·tion·al·ist \ˌtran(t)s-fər-'mā-shnə-list, -shə-nᵊl-ist\ *n* (1964) **:** an exponent of transformational grammar

trans·form·er \tran(t)s-'fȯr-mər\ *n* (1596) **:** one that transforms; *specif* **:** a device employing the principle of mutual induction to convert variations of current in a primary circuit into variations of voltage and current in a secondary circuit

trans·fuse \tran(t)s-'fyüz\ *vt* **trans·fused; trans·fus·ing** [ME, fr. L *transfusus*, pp. of *transfundere*, fr. *trans-* + *fundere* to pour — more at FOUND] (15c) **1 a :** to cause to pass from one to another **:** TRANSMIT **b :** to diffuse into or through **:** PERMEATE ⟨sunlight ~*s* the bay⟩ **2 a :** to transfer (as blood) into a vein of a person or animal **b :** to subject (a patient) to transfusion — **trans·fus·ible** or **trans·fus·able** \-'fyü-zə-bəl\ *adj*

trans·fu·sion \tran(t)s-'fyü-zhən\ *n* (1578) **1 :** an act, process, or instance of transfusing; *esp* **:** the process of transfusing fluid into a vein or artery **2 :** something transfused — **trans·fu·sion·al** \-'fyüzh-nəl, -'fyü-zhə-nᵊl\ *adj*

trans·gen·ic \tran(t)s-'je-nik\ *adj* (1982) **:** having chromosomes into which one or more heterologous genes have been incorporated either artificially or naturally ⟨~ mice⟩

trans·gress \tran(t)s-'gres, tranz-\ *vb* [MF *transgresser*, fr. L *transgressus*, pp. of *transgredi* to step beyond or across, fr. *trans-* + *gradi* to step — more at GRADE] *vt* (1526) **1 :** to go beyond limits set or prescribed by **:** VIOLATE ⟨~ divine law⟩ **2 :** to pass beyond or go over (a limit or boundary) ~ *vi* **1 :** to violate a command or law **:** SIN **2 :** to go beyond a boundary or limit — **trans·gres·sive** \-'gre-siv\ *adj* — **trans·gres·sor** \-'gre-sər\ *n*

trans·gres·sion \-'gre-shən\ *n* (15c) **:** an act, process, or instance of transgressing: as **a :** infringement or violation of a law, command, or duty **b :** the spread of the sea over land areas and the consequent unconformable deposit of sediments on older rocks

tran·ship *var of* TRANSSHIP

trans·his·tor·i·cal \ˌtran(t)s-(h)is-'tȯr-i-kəl, ˌtranz-, -'tär-\ *adj* (1909) **:** transcending historical bounds

trans·hu·mance \tran(t)s-'hyü-mən(t)s, tranz-, -'yü-\ *n* [F, fr. *transhumer* to practice transhumance, fr. Sp *trashumar*, fr. *tras-* trans- (fr. L *trans-*) + L *humus* earth — more at HUMBLE] (ca. 1901) **:** seasonal movement of livestock and esp. sheep between mountain and lowland pastures either under the care of herders or in company with the owners — **trans·hu·mant** \-mənt\ *adj or n*

tran·sience \'tran(t)-sh(ē-)ən(t)s; 'tran-zē-ən(t)s, 'tran(t)-sē-; 'tran-zhən(t)s, -jən(t)s\ *n* (1745) **:** the quality or state of being transient

tran·sien·cy \-sh(ē-)ən(t)-sē, -zē-ən(t)-, -sē-ən(t)-, -zhən(t)-sē, -jən(t)-\ *n* (1652) **:** TRANSIENCE

¹**tran·sient** \sh(ē-)ənt, -zē-ənt, -sē-; -zhənt, -jənt\ *adj* [L *transeunt-, transiens*, prp. of *transire* to go across, pass, fr. *trans-* + *ire* to go — more at ISSUE] (1599) **1 a :** passing esp. quickly into and out of existence **:** TRANSITORY **b :** passing through or by a place with only a brief stay or sojourn **2 :** affecting something or producing results beyond itself — **tran·sient·ly** *adv*

syn TRANSIENT, TRANSITORY, EPHEMERAL, MOMENTARY, FUGITIVE, FLEETING, EVANESCENT mean lasting or staying only a short time. TRANSIENT applies to what is actually short in its duration or stay ⟨a hotel catering primarily to *transient* guests⟩. TRANSITORY applies to what is by its nature or essence bound to change, pass, or come to an end ⟨fame in the movies is *transitory*⟩. EPHEMERAL implies striking brevity of life or duration ⟨many slang words are *ephemeral*⟩. MOMENTARY suggests coming and going quickly and therefore being merely a brief interruption of a more enduring state ⟨my feelings of guilt were only *momentary*⟩. FUGITIVE and FLEETING imply passing so quickly as to make apprehending difficult ⟨let a *fugitive* smile flit across his face⟩ ⟨*fleeting* moments of joy⟩. EVANESCENT suggests a quick vanishing and an airy or fragile quality ⟨the story has an *evanescent* touch of whimsy that is lost in translation⟩.

²**transient** *n* (1652) **1 :** one that is transient: as **a :** a transient guest **b :** a person traveling about usu. in search of work **2 a :** a temporary oscillation that occurs in a circuit because of a sudden change of voltage or of load **b :** a transient current or voltage

transient ischemic attack *n* (1966) **:** a brief episode of cerebral ischemia that is usu. characterized by temporary blurring of vision, slurring of speech, numbness, paralysis, or syncope and that is often predictive of more serious cerebral accidents — abbr. *TIA*

trans·il·lu·mi·nate \ˌtran(t)s-ə-'lü-mə-ˌnāt, ˌtranz-\ *vt* (1900) **:** to cause

light to pass through; *esp* **:** to pass light through (a body part) for medical examination — **trans·il·lu·mi·na·tion** \-ˌlü-mə-ˌnā-shən\ *n* — **trans·il·lu·mi·na·tor** \-'lü-mə-ˌnā-tər\ *n*

tran·sis·tor \tran-'zis-tər, tran(t)-'sis-\ *n* [¹*transfer* + *resistor*; fr. its transferring an electrical signal across a resistor] (1948) **1 :** a solid-state electronic device that is used to control the flow of electricity in electronic equipment and consists of a small block of a semiconductor (as germanium) with at least three electrodes **2 :** a transistorized radio

tran·sis·tor·ise *Brit var of* TRANSISTORIZE

tran·sis·tor·ize \-tə-ˌrīz\ *vt* **-ized; -iz·ing** (ca. 1952) **:** to equip (a device) with transistors — **tran·sis·tor·i·za·tion** \-ˌzis-tə-rə-'zā-shən\ *n*

¹**tran·sit** \'tran(t)-sət, 'tran-zət\ *n* [ME *transite*, fr. L *transitus*, fr. *transire* to go across, pass] (15c) **1 a :** an act, process, or instance of passing through or over **:** PASSAGE **b :** CHANGE, TRANSITION **c** (1) **:** conveyance of persons or things from one place to another (2) **:** usu. local transportation esp. of people by public conveyance; *also* **:** vehicles or a system engaged in such transportation **2 a :** passage of a celestial body over the meridian of a place or through the field of a telescope **b :** passage of a smaller body (as Venus) across the disk of a larger (as the sun) **3 :** a theodolite with the telescope mounted so that it can be transited

²**transit** *vi* (15c) **:** to make a transit ~ *vt* **1 a :** to pass over or through **:** TRAVERSE **b :** to cause to pass over or through **2 :** to pass across (a meridian, a celestial body, or the field of view of a telescope) **3 :** to turn (a telescope) over about the horizontal transverse axis in surveying

tran·si·tion \tran(t)-'si-shən, tran-'zi-, *chiefly Brit* tran(t)-'si-zhən\ *n* [L *transition-, transitio*, fr. *transire*] (1551) **1 :** passage from one state, stage, subject, or place to another **:** CHANGE **b :** a movement, development, or evolution from one form, stage, or style to another **2 a :** a musical modulation **b :** a musical passage leading from one section of a piece to another **3 :** an abrupt change in energy state or level (as of an atomic nucleus or a molecule) usu. accompanied by loss or gain of a single quantum of energy — **tran·si·tion·al** \-'sish-nəl, -'sizh-, -'zish-; -'si-shə-nᵊl, -'zi-, -zhə-\ *adj* — **tran·si·tion·al·ly** *adv*

transition metal *n* [fr. their being transitional between the more highly electropositive and the less highly electropositive elements] (1940) **:** any of various metallic elements (as chromium, iron, and nickel) that have valence electrons in two shells instead of only one — called also *transition element*

tran·si·tive \'tran(t)-sə-tiv, 'tran-zə-; 'tran(t)s-tiv\ *adj* [LL *transitivus*, fr. L *transitus*, pp. of *transire*] (1590) **1 :** characterized by having or containing a direct object ⟨a ~ verb⟩ ⟨a ~ construction⟩ **2 :** being or relating to a relation with the property that if the relation holds between a first element and a second and between the second element and a third, it holds between the first and third elements ⟨equality is a ~ relation⟩ **3 :** of, relating to, or characterized by transition — **tran·si·tive·ly** *adv* — **tran·si·tive·ness** *n* — **tran·si·tiv·i·ty** \ˌtran(t)-sə-'ti-və-tē, ˌtran-zə-\ *n*

tran·si·to·ry \'tran(t)-sə-ˌtȯr-ē, 'tran-zə-, -ˌtȯr-\ *adj* [ME *transitorie*, fr. MF *transitoire*, fr. LL *transitorius*, fr. L, of or allowing passage, fr. *transire*] (14c) **1 :** tending to pass away **:** not persistent **2 :** of brief duration **:** TEMPORARY ⟨the ~ nature of earthly joy⟩ **syn** see TRANSIENT — **tran·si·to·ri·ly** \ˌtran(t)-sə-'tȯr-ə-lē, ˌtran-zə-, -'tȯr-\ *adv* — **tran·si·to·ri·ness** \'tran(t)-sə-ˌtȯr-ē-nəs, 'tran-zə-, -ˌtȯr-\ *n*

trans·late \tran(t)s-'lāt, tranz-; 'tran(t)s-ˌlāt, 'tranz-\ *vb* **trans·lat·ed; trans·lat·ing** [ME, fr. L *translatus* (pp. of *transferre* to transfer, translate), fr. *trans-* + *latus*, pp. of *ferre* to carry — more at TOLERATE, BEAR] *vt* (14c) **1 a :** to bear, remove, or change from one place, state, form, or appearance to another **:** TRANSFER, TRANSFORM ⟨a country boy *translated* to the city⟩ ⟨~ ideas into action⟩ **b :** to convey to heaven or to a nontemporal condition without death **c :** to transfer (a bishop) from one see to another **2 a :** to turn into one's own or another language **b :** to transfer or turn from one set of symbols into another **:** TRANSCRIBE **c** (1) **:** to express in different terms and esp. different words **:** PARAPHRASE (2) **:** to express in more comprehensible terms **:** EXPLAIN, INTERPRET **3 :** ENRAPTURE **4 :** to subject to mathematical translation **5 :** to subject (as genetic information) to translation in protein synthesis ~ *vi* **1 :** to practice translation or make a translation; *also* **:** to admit of or be adaptable to translation ⟨a word that doesn't ~ easily⟩ **2 :** to undergo a translation **3 :** LEAD, RESULT — usu. used with *into* ⟨tax cuts ~ into bigger savings⟩ — **trans·lat·abil·i·ty** \(ˌ)tran(t)s-ˌlā-tə-'bi-lə-tē, (ˌ)tranz-\ *n* — **trans·lat·able** \tran(t)s-'lā-tə-bəl, tranz-\ *adj* — **trans·la·tor** \-'lā-tər\ *n*

trans·la·tion \tran(t)s-'lā-shən, tranz-\ *n* (14c) **1 :** an act, process, or instance of translating: as **a :** a rendering from one language into another; *also* **:** the product of such a rendering **b :** a change to a different substance, form, or appearance **:** CONVERSION **c** (1) **:** a transformation of coordinates in which the new axes are parallel to the old ones (2) **:** uniform motion of a body in a straight line **2 :** the process of forming a protein molecule at a ribosomal site of protein synthesis from information contained in messenger RNA — compare TRANSCRIPTION 3 — **trans·la·tion·al** \-shnəl, -shə-nᵊl\ *adj*

trans·la·tive \-'lā-tiv\ *adj* (ca. 1682) **1 :** of, relating to, or involving removal or transference from one person or place to another **2 :** of, relating to, or serving to translate from one language or system into another

trans·la·to·ry \'tran(t)s-lə-ˌtȯr-ē, 'tranz-, -ˌtȯr-; tran(t)s-'lā-tə-rē, tranz-\ *adj* (1849) **:** of, relating to, or involving uniform motion in one direction

trans·lit·er·ate \tran(t)s-'li-tə-ˌrāt, tranz-\ *vt* **-at·ed; -at·ing** [*trans-* + L *littera* letter] (1861) **:** to represent or spell in the characters of another alphabet — **trans·lit·er·a·tion** \(ˌ)tran(t)s-ˌli-tə-'rā-shən, (ˌ)tranz-\ *n*

trans·lo·ca·tion \ˌtran(t)s-lō-'kā-shən, ˌtranz-\ *n* (1624) **:** a change of location: DISPLACEMENT: as **a :** the conduction of soluble material (as metabolic products) from one part of a plant to another **b :** transfer of part of a chromosome to a different position esp. on a nonhomologous chromosome; *esp* **:** the exchange of parts between nonhomologous chromosomes — **trans·lo·cate** \'tran(t)s-lō-ˌkāt, 'tranz-; (ˌ)tran(t)s-', (ˌ)tranz-'\ *vb*

trans·lu·cence \tran(t)s-'lü-s³n(t)s, tranz-\ n (1755) : the quality or state of being translucent

trans·lu·cen·cy \-s³n-sē\ n, pl **-cies** (ca. 1610) **1** : TRANSLUCENCE **2** : something that is translucent

trans·lu·cent \-s³nt\ adj [L translucent-, translucens, prp. of translucēre to shine through, fr. trans- + lucēre to shine — more at LIGHT] (1607) **1** : permitting the passage of light: **a** : CLEAR, TRANSPARENT ⟨~ water⟩ **b** : transmitting and diffusing light so that objects beyond cannot be seen clearly **2** : free from disguise or falseness ⟨his ~ patriotism — Newsweek⟩ **syn** see CLEAR — **trans·lu·cent·ly** adv

trans·ma·rine \,tran(t)s-mə-'rēn, ,tranz-\ adj [L transmarinus, fr. trans- + mare sea — more at MARINE] (1583) **1** : being or coming from beyond or across the sea ⟨a ~ people⟩ **2** : passing over or extending across the sea

trans·mem·brane \(,)tran(t)s-'mem-,brān, (,)tranz-\ adj (1944) : taking place or existing across a membrane ⟨a ~ potential⟩

trans·mi·grate \(,)tran(t)s-'mī-,grāt, (,)tranz-, 'tran(t)s-,, 'tranz-\ vb [L transmigratus, pp. of transmigrare to migrate to another place, fr. trans- + migrare to migrate] vt (ca. 1559) : to cause to go from one state of existence or place to another ~ vi **1** of the soul : to pass at death from one body or being to another **2** : MIGRATE — **trans·mi·gra·tion** \,tran(t)s-mī-'grā-shən, ,tranz-\ n — **trans·mi·gra·tor** \(,)tran(t)s-'mī-,grā-tər, (,)tranz-, 'tran(t)s-,, 'tranz-\ n — **trans·mi·gra·to·ry** \tran(t)s-'mī-grə-,tōr-ē, tranz-, -,tòr-\ adj

trans·mis·si·ble \tran(t)s-'mi-sə-bəl, tranz-\ adj (1644) : capable of being transmitted ⟨~ diseases⟩ — **trans·mis·si·bil·i·ty** \(,)tran(t)s-,mi-sə-'bi-lə-tē, (,)tranz-\ n

trans·mis·sion \tran(t)s-'mi-shən, tranz-\ n [L transmission-, transmissio, fr. transmittere to transmit] (1611) **1** : an act, process, or instance of transmitting ⟨~ of a nerve impulse across a synapse⟩ **2** : the passage of radio waves in the space between transmitting and receiving stations; also : the act or process of transmitting by radio or television **3** : an assembly of parts including the speed-changing gears and the propeller shaft by which the power is transmitted from an automobile engine to a live axle; also : the speed-changing gears in such an assembly **4** : something that is transmitted : MESSAGE — **trans·mis·sive** \-'mi-siv\ adj — **trans·mis·siv·i·ty** \,tran(t)s-(,)mi-'si-və-tē, ,tranz-\ n

trans·som·e·ter \tran(t)s-(,)mi-'sä-mə-tər, tranz-\ n (ca. 1931) : an instrument for measuring the transmission of light through a fluid (as the atmosphere)

trans·mit \tran(t)s-'mit, tranz-\ vb **trans·mit·ted; trans·mit·ting** [ME transmitten, fr. L transmittere, fr. trans- + mittere to send] vt (15c) **1 a** : to send or convey from one person or place to another : FORWARD **b** : to cause or allow to spread: as (1) : to convey by or as if by inheritance or heredity : HAND DOWN (2) : to convey (infection) abroad or to another **2 a** (1) : to cause (as light or force) to pass or be conveyed through space or a medium (2) : to admit the passage of : CONDUCT ⟨glass ~s light⟩ **b** : to send out (a signal) either by radio waves or over a wire ~ vi : to send out a signal either by radio waves or over a wire — **trans·mit·ta·ble** \-'mi-tə-bəl\ adj — **trans·mit·tal** \-'mi-t³l\ n

trans·mit·tance \-'mi-t³n(t)s\ n (ca. 1855) **1** : TRANSMISSION **2** : the fraction of radiant energy that having entered a layer of absorbing matter reaches its farther boundary

trans·mit·ter \tran(t)s-'mi-tər, tranz-; 'tran(t)s-,, 'tranz-\ n (1727) : one that transmits: as **a** : an apparatus for transmitting radio or television signals **b** : NEUROTRANSMITTER

trans·mog·ri·fy \tran(t)s-'mä-grə-,fī, tranz-\ vb **-fied; -fy·ing** [origin unknown] vt (1656) : to change or alter greatly and often with grotesque or humorous effect ~ vi : to become transmogrified **syn** see TRANSFORM — **trans·mog·ri·fi·ca·tion** \(,)tran(t)s-,mä-grə-fə-'kā-shən, (,)tranz-\ n

trans·mon·tane \(,)tran(t)s-'män-,tān, (,)tranz-; ,tran(t)s-(,)män-', ,tranz-\ adj [L transmontanus] (1727) : TRAMONTANE

trans·moun·tain \tran(t)s-'maùn-t³n, tranz-\ adj (1929) : crossing or extending over or through a mountain ⟨a ~ road⟩ ⟨a ~ tunnel⟩

trans·mu·ta·tion \,tran(t)s-myù-'tā-shən, ,tranz-\ n [ME transmutacioun, fr. MF or L; MF transmutation, fr. L transmutation-, transmutatio, fr. transmutare] (14c) : an act or instance of transmuting or being transmuted: as **a** : the conversion of base metals into gold or silver **b** : the conversion of one element or nuclide into another either naturally or artificially — **trans·mu·ta·tive** \tran(t)s-'myü-tə-tiv, tranz-\ adj

trans·mute \tran(t)s-'myüt, tranz-\ vb **trans·muted; trans·mut·ing** [ME, fr. L transmutare, fr. trans- + mutare to change — more at MUTABLE] vt (15c) **1** : to change or alter in form, appearance, or nature and esp. to a higher form **2** : to subject (as an element) to transmutation ~ vi : to undergo transmutation **syn** see TRANSFORM — **trans·mut·able** \-'myü-tə-bəl\ adj

trans·na·tion·al \(,)tran(t)s-'nash-nəl, (,)tranz-, -'na-shə-n³l\ adj (1921) : extending or going beyond national boundaries ⟨~ corporations⟩ — **trans·na·tion·al·ism** \-'nash-nə-,li-zəm, -'na-shə-n³l-,i-zəm\ n

trans·nat·u·ral \-'na-chə-rəl, -'nach-rəl\ adj (1569) : being above or beyond nature

trans·oce·an·ic \,tran(t)s-,ō-shē-'a-nik, ,tranz-\ adj (1827) **1** : lying or dwelling beyond the ocean **2** : crossing or extending across the ocean ⟨a ~ telephone cable⟩

tran·som \'tran(t)s-səm\ n [ME traunsom, transyn, prob. alter. of traversayn, fr. MF traversin, fr. traverse traverse] (15c) **1** : a transverse piece in a structure : CROSSPIECE: as **a** : LINTEL **b** : a horizontal crossbar in a window, over a door, or between a door and a window or fanlight above it **c** : the horizontal bar or member of a cross or gallows **d** : any of several transverse timbers or beams secured to the sternpost of a boat; also : the planking forming the stern of a square-ended boat **2** : a window above a door or other window built on and commonly hinged to a transom — **over the transom** : without solicitation or prior arrangement ⟨the manuscript arrived over the transom⟩

tran·son·ic also **trans·son·ic** \tran(t)s-'sä-nik, tran-'sä-\ adj [trans- + supersonic] (1945) **1** : being or relating to speeds near that of sound in air or about 741 miles (1185 kilometers) per hour at sea level and esp. to speeds slightly below the speed of sound at which the speed of airflow varies from subsonic to supersonic at different points along the surface of a body in motion relative to the surrounding air **2** : moving, capable of moving, or utilizing air currents moving at a transonic speed

trans·pa·cif·ic \,tran(t)s-pə-'si-fik\ adj (1891) **1 a** : crossing or extending across the Pacific Ocean ⟨~ airlines⟩ **b** : relating to or involving crossing the Pacific Ocean ⟨~ airfares⟩ **2 a** : situated or occurring beyond the Pacific Ocean **b** : of, relating to, or involving countries on both sides of the Pacific Ocean ⟨the ~ economy⟩

trans·par·ence \tran(t)s-'par-ən(t)s, -'per-\ n (1594) : TRANSPARENCY 1

trans·par·en·cy \-ən(t)-sē\ n, pl **-cies** (1615) **1** : the quality or state of being transparent **2** : something transparent; esp : a picture (as on film) viewed by light shining through it or by projection

trans·par·ent \-ənt\ adj [ME, fr. ML transparent-, transparens, prp. of transparēre to show through, fr. L trans- + parēre to show oneself] (15c) **1 a** (1) : having the property of transmitting light without appreciable scattering so that bodies lying beyond are seen clearly : PELLUCID (2) : allowing the passage of a specified form of radiation (as X rays or ultraviolet light) **b** : fine or sheer enough to be seen through : DIAPHANOUS **2 a** : free from pretense or deceit : FRANK **b** : easily detected or seen through : OBVIOUS **c** : readily understood **syn** see CLEAR — **trans·par·ent·ly** adv — **trans·par·ent·ness** n

trans·par·ent·ize \-ən-,tīz\ vt **-ized; -iz·ing** (1925) : to make transparent or more nearly transparent ⟨~ tracing paper⟩

trans·per·son·al \(,)tran(t)s-'pərs-nəl, -'pər-sə-n³l\ adj (ca. 1906) **1** : extending or going beyond the personal or individual **2** : of, relating to, or being psychology concerned esp. with esoteric mental experience (as mysticism and altered states of consciousness) beyond the usual limits of ego and personality

tran·spic·u·ous \tran(t)s-'pi-kyə-wəs\ adj [NL transpicuus, fr. L transpicere to look through, fr. trans- + specere to look, see — more at SPY] (1638) : clearly seen through or understood

trans·pierce \tran(t)s-'pirs\ vt [MF transpercer, fr. OF, fr. trans- (fr. L) + percer to pierce] (1592) : to pierce through : PENETRATE

tran·spi·ra·tion \,tran(t)s-pə-'rā-shən\ n (1551) : the act or process or an instance of transpiring; esp : the passage of watery vapor from a living body through a membrane or pores — **tran·spi·ra·tion·al** \-shnəl, -shə-n³l\ adj

tran·spire \tran(t)-'spīr\ vb **tran·spired; tran·spir·ing** [MF transpirer, fr. L trans- + spirare to breathe] vt (1597) : to pass off or give passage to (a fluid) through pores or interstices; esp : to excrete (as water) in the form of a vapor through a living membrane (as the skin) ~ vi **1** : to give off vaporous material; specif : to give off or exude watery vapor esp. from the surfaces of leaves **2** : to pass in the form of a vapor from a living body **3 a** : to be revealed : come to light **b** : to become known or apparent : DEVELOP **4** : to take place : GO ON, OCCUR

usage Sense 4 of transpire is the frequent whipping boy of those who suppose sense 3 to be the only meaning of the word. Sense 4 appears to have developed in the late 18th century; it was well enough known to have been used by Abigail Adams in a letter to her husband in 1775 ⟨there is nothing new transpired since I wrote you last —Abigail Adams⟩. Noah Webster recognized the new sense in his dictionary of 1828. Transpire was evidently a popular word with 19th century journalists; sense 4 turns up in such pretentiously worded statements as "The police drill will transpire under shelter to-day in consequence of the moist atmosphere prevailing." Around 1870 the sense began to be attacked as a misuse on the grounds of etymology, and modern critics echo the damnation of 1870. Sense 4 has been in existence for about two centuries; it is firmly established as standard; it occurs now primarily in serious prose, not the ostentatiously flamboyant prose typical of 19th century journalism.

trans·pla·cen·tal \,tran(t)s-plə-'sen-t³l\ adj [ISV] (ca. 1929) : passing through or occurring by way of the placenta ⟨~ immunization⟩ — **trans·pla·cen·tal·ly** \-t³l-ē\ adv

¹**trans·plant** \,tran(t)s-'plant\ vb [ME transplaunten, fr. LL transplantare, fr. L trans- + plantare to plant] vt (15c) **1** : to lift and reset (a plant) in another soil or situation **2** : to remove from one place or context and settle or introduce elsewhere : RELOCATE **3** : to transfer (an organ or tissue) from one part or individual to another ~ vi : to admit of being transplanted — **trans·plant·abil·i·ty** \,tran(t)s-,plan-tə-'bi-lə-tē\ n — **trans·plant·able** \tran(t)s-'plan-tə-bəl\ adj — **trans·plan·ta·tion** \,tran(t)s-,plan-'tā-shən\ n — **trans·plant·er** \tran(t)s-'plan-tər\ n

²**trans·plant** \'tran(t)s-,plant\ n (1756) **1** : a person or thing that is transplanted **2** : the act or process of transplanting

trans·po·lar \(,)tran(t)s-'pō-lər\ adj (1850) : crossing or extending across either of the polar regions

tran·spon·der \tran(t)-'spän-dər\ n [transmitter + responder] (ca. 1944) : a radio or radar set that upon receiving a designated signal emits a radio signal of its own and that is used esp. for the detection, identification, and location of objects

trans·pon·tine \tran(t)s-'pän-,tīn\ adj [trans- + L pont-, pons bridge — more at FIND] (1844) **1** : situated on the farther side of a bridge **2** Brit : situated on the south side of the Thames

¹**trans·port** \tran(t)s-'pōrt, -'pòrt, 'tran(t)s-,\ vt [ME, fr. MF or L; MF transporter, fr. L transportare, fr. trans- + portare to carry — more at FARE] (14c) **1** : to transfer or convey from one place to another ⟨~ing ions across a living membrane⟩ **2** : to carry away with strong and often intensely pleasant emotion **3** : to send to a penal colony overseas ~ syn see BANISH — **trans·port·abil·i·ty** \(,)tran(t)s-,pōr-tə-'bi-lə-tē, -,pòr-\ n — **trans·port·able** \tran(t)s-'pōr-tə-bəl, -'pòr-\ adj

²**trans·port** \'tran(t)s-,pōrt, -,pòrt\ n (1611) **1** : an act or process of transporting : TRANSPORTATION **2** : strong or intensely pleasurable emotion ⟨~s of joy⟩ **3 a** : a ship for carrying soldiers or military equipment **b** : a vehicle (as a truck or airplane) used to transport persons or goods **c** : TRANSPORTATION 3 **4** : a transported convict **5** : a mechanism for moving magnetic tape past a recording head **syn** see ECSTASY

trans·por·ta·tion \,tran(t)s-pər-'tā-shən\ n (1540) **1** : an act, process, or instance of transporting or being transported **2** : banishment to a

\ə\ abut \³\ kitten, F table \ər\ further \a\ ash \ā\ ace \ä\ mop, mar \aů\ out \ch\ chin \e\ bet \ē\ easy \g\ go \i\ hit \ī\ ice \j\ job \ŋ\ sing \ō\ go \ò\ law \òi\ boy \th\ thin \t̲h̲\ the \ü\ loot \ů\ foot \y\ yet \zh\ vision \ä, k̲, ⁿ, œ, œ̄, ᵫ, ᵫ̄, ᵞ\ see Guide to Pronunciation

penal colony **3 a** : means of conveyance or travel from one place to another **b** : public conveyance of passengers or goods esp. as a commercial enterprise — **trans·por·ta·tion·al** \-shnəl, -shə-nᵊl\ *adj*
transport café \-ka-ˈfā, -ˈkaf\ *n* (1938) *Brit* : a roadside restaurant frequented chiefly by truck drivers
trans·port·er \tran(t)s-ˈpȯr-tər, -ˈpȯr-, ˈtran(t)s-,\ *n* (1535) : one that transports; *esp* : a vehicle for transporting large or heavy loads
transposable element *n* (1979) : a segment of genetic material that is capable of changing its location in the genome or in some bacteria of undergoing transfer between an extrachromosomal plasmid and a chromosome
¹trans·pose \tran(t)s-ˈpōz\ *vt* **trans·posed; trans·pos·ing** [ME, fr. MF *transposer*, fr. L *transponere* (perf. indic. *transposui*) to change the position of, fr. *trans-* + *ponere* to put, place — more at POSITION] (14c) **1** : to change in form or nature : TRANSFORM **2** : to render into another language, style, or manner of expression : TRANSLATE **3** : to transfer from one place or period to another : SHIFT **4** : to change the relative place or normal order of : alter the sequence of ⟨~ letters to change the spelling⟩ **5** : to write or perform (a musical composition) in a different key **6** : to bring (a term) from one side of an algebraic equation to the other with change of sign **syn** see REVERSE — **trans·pos·able** \-ˈpō-zə-bəl\ *adj*
²trans·pose \ˈtran(t)s-ˌpōz\ *n* (1937) : a matrix formed from another matrix by interchanging the rows and columns
trans·po·si·tion \ˌtran(t)s-pə-ˈzi-shən\ *n* [ML *transposition-, transpositio*, fr. L *transponere* to transpose] (1538) **1** : an act, process, or instance of transposing or being transposed **2 a** : the transfer of any term of an equation from one side over to the other side with a corresponding change of the sign **b** : a mathematical permutation or interchange of two letters or symbols — **trans·po·si·tion·al** \-ˈzish-nəl, -ˈzi-shə-nᵊl\ *adj*
transposition cipher *n* (1939) : a cipher in which the letters of the plaintext are systematically rearranged into another sequence — compare SUBSTITUTION CIPHER
trans·po·son \tran(t)s-ˈpō-ˌzän\ *n* [*transpose* + *²-on*] (1974) : a transposable element esp. when it contains genetic material controlling functions other than those related to its relocation
trans·sex·u·al \(ˌ)tran(t)s-ˈsek-sh(ə-)wəl, -shəl\ *n* (1957) : a person with a psychological urge to belong to the opposite sex that may be carried to the point of undergoing surgery to modify the sex organs to mimic the opposite sex — **trans·sex·u·al·ism** \-sh(ə-)wə-ˌli-zəm, -shə-ˌli-\ *n* — **trans·sex·u·al·i·ty** \-ˌsek-shə-ˈwa-lə-tē\ *n*
trans·shape \tran(sh)-ˈshāp, tran(t)s-\ *vt* (1575) *archaic* : to change into another shape : TRANSFORM
trans·ship \tran(sh)-ˈship, tran(t)s-\ *vt* (1792) : to transfer for further transportation from one ship or conveyance to another ⟨~ v⟩ : to change from one ship or conveyance to another — **trans·ship·ment** \-mənt\ *n*
trans·tho·rac·ic \ˌtran(t)s-thə-ˈra-sik\ *adj* (1905) : done or made by way of the thoracic cavity — **trans·tho·rac·i·cal·ly** \-si-k(ə-)lē\ *adv*
trans·sub·stan·tial \ˌtran(t)s-səb-ˈstan(t)-shəl\ *adj* (1567) : changed or capable of being changed from one substance to another
trans·sub·stan·ti·ate \ˌtran(t)s-səb-ˈstan(t)-shē-ˌāt\ *vb* **-at·ed; -at·ing** [ML *transubstantiatus*, pp. of *transubstantiare*, fr. L *trans-* + *substantia* substance] *vt* (1533) **1** : to change into another substance : TRANSMUTE **2** : to effect transubstantiation in (sacramental bread and wine) ⟨~ v⟩ : to undergo transubstantiation
trans·sub·stan·ti·a·tion \ˌstan(t)-shē-ˈā-shən\ *n* (14c) **1** : an act or instance of transubstantiating or being transubstantiated **2** : the miraculous change by which according to Roman Catholic and Eastern Orthodox dogma the eucharistic elements at their consecration become the body and blood of Christ while keeping only the appearances of bread and wine
tran·su·date \ˈtran(t)-sü-ˌdāt, -syü-; ˈtran-zü-, -zyü-\ *n* (1876) : a transuded substance
tran·su·da·tion \ˌtran(t)-sü-ˈdā-shən, -syü-; ˌtran-zü-, -zyü-\ *n* (1617) **1** : the act or process of transuding or being transuded **2** : TRANSUDATE
tran·sude \tran(t)-ˈsüd, -ˈsyüd; tran-ˈzüd, -ˈzyüd\ *vb* **tran·sud·ed; tran·sud·ing** [NL *transudare*, fr. L *trans-* + *sudare* to sweat — more at SWEAT] *vi* (1664) : to pass through a membrane or permeable substance : EXUDE ⟨~ v⟩ : to permit passage of
¹trans·ura·nic \ˌtran(t)-syü-ˈra-nik, -shə-, -ˈrā-; ˌtran-zyü-, -zhə-\ *or* **trans·ura·ni·um** \-ˈrä-nē-əm\ *adj* (1935) : of, relating to, or being an element with an atomic number greater than that of uranium
²transuranic *n* (1950) : a transuranic element
trans·val·u·ate \(ˌ)tran(t)s-ˈval-yə-ˌwāt, (ˌ)tranz-\ *vt* **-at·ed; -at·ing** [back-formation fr. *transvaluation*] (1912) : TRANSVALUE
trans·val·u·a·tion \ˌtran(t)s-ˌval-yə-ˈwā-shən, ˌtranz-\ *n* (1898) : the act or process of transvaluing
trans·val·ue \(ˌ)tran(t)s-ˈval-(ˌ)yü, (ˌ)tranz-\ *vt* **-val·ued; -valu·ing** (1911) : to reevaluate esp. on a basis that repudiates accepted standards
trans·ver·sal \tran(t)s-ˈvər-səl, tranz-\ *n* [*transversal*, adj., transverse, fr. ME, fr. ML *transversalis*, fr. L *transversus*] (ca. 1847) : a line that intersects a system of lines
¹trans·verse \tran(t)s-ˈvərs, tranz-, ˈtran(t)s-ˌ, ˈtranz-ˌ\ *adj* [L *transversus*, fr. *trans-* + *-versus* (as in *adversus* adverse)] (1621) **1** : acting, lying, or being across : set crosswise **2** : made at right angles to the anterior-posterior axis of the body ⟨a ~ section⟩ — **trans·verse·ly** *adv*
²trans·verse \ˈtran(t)s-ˌvərs, tranz-\ *n* (ca. 1633) : something (as a piece, section, or part) that is transverse
transverse colon *n* (ca. 1860) : the middle portion of the colon that extends across the abdominal cavity
transverse process *n* (1696) : a lateral process of a vertebra
transverse wave *n* (1922) : a wave in which the vibrating element moves in a direction perpendicular to the direction of advance of the wave
trans·ves·tite \tran(t)s-ˈves-ˌtīt, tranz-\ *n* [G *Transvestit*, fr. L *trans-* + *vestire* to clothe — more at VEST] (ca. 1922) : a person and esp. a male who adopts the dress and often the behavior typical of the opposite sex esp. for purposes of emotional or sexual gratification — **trans·ves·tism** \-ˈves-ˌti-zəm\ *n* — **transvestite** *adj*
¹trap \ˈtrap\ *n* [ME, fr. OE *treppe* & OF *trape* (of Gmc origin); akin to

MD *trappe* trap, stair, OE *treppan* to tread] (bef. 12c) **1** : a device for taking game or other animals; *esp* : one that holds by springing shut suddenly **2 a** : something by which one is caught or stopped unawares; *also* : a position or situation from which it is difficult or impossible to escape **b** : a football play in which a defensive player is allowed to cross the line of scrimmage and then is blocked from the side while the ballcarrier advances through the spot vacated by the defensive player **3 a** : a device for hurling clay pigeons into the air **b** : SAND TRAP **c** : a piece of leather or section of interwoven leather straps between the thumb and forefinger of a baseball glove that forms an extension of the pocket **4** *slang* : MOUTH **5** : a light usu. one-horse carriage with springs **6** : any of various devices for preventing passage of something often while allowing other matter to proceed; *esp* : a device for drains or sewers consisting of a bend or partitioned chamber in which the liquid forms a seal to prevent the passage of sewer gas **7** *pl* : a group of percussion instruments (as a bass drum, snare drums, and cymbals) used esp. in a dance or jazz band **8** : an arrangement of rock strata that favors the accumulation of oil and gas **9** *pl* [*speed trap*] : a measured stretch of a course over which electronic timing devices measure the speed of a vehicle (as a racing car or dragster)
²trap *vb* **trapped; trap·ping** *vt* (14c) **1 a** : to catch or take in or as if in a trap : ENTRAP **b** : to place in a restricted position : CONFINE ⟨*trapped* in the burning wreck⟩ **2** : to provide or set (a place) with traps **3 a** : STOP, HOLD ⟨these mountains ~ rains and fogs generated over the ocean —*Amer. Guide Series: Calif.*⟩ **b** : to separate out (as water from steam) **4 a** : to catch (as a baseball) immediately after a bounce **b** : to block out (a defensive football player) by means of a trap ⟨~ v⟩ *vi* : to engage in trapping animals (as for furs) **syn** see CATCH — **trap·per** *n*
³trap *vt* **trapped; trap·ping** [ME *trappen*, fr. *trappe* cloth, perh. modif. of MF *drap* — more at DRAB] (14c) : to adorn with or as if with trappings
⁴trap *n* [Sw *trapp*, fr. *trappa* stair, fr. MLG *trappe*; akin to MD *trappe* stair] (1794) : TRAPROCK
trap·door \ˈtrap-ˈdȯr, -ˈdȯr\ *n* (14c) : a lifting or sliding door covering an opening (as in a roof, ceiling, or floor)
trap·door spider *n* (1826) : any of various often large burrowing spiders (esp. family Ctenizidae) that construct a tubular subterranean silk-lined nest topped with a hinged lid

trap-door spider

tra·peze \tra-ˈpēz *also* trə-\ *n* [F *trapèze*, fr. NL *trapezium*] (1861) : a gymnastic or acrobatic apparatus consisting of a short horizontal bar suspended by two parallel ropes
tra·pez·ist \-ˈpē-zist\ *n* (1875) : a performer on the trapeze — called also *trapeze artist*
tra·pe·zi·um \trə-ˈpē-zē-əm, tra-\ *n, pl* **-zi·ums** *or* **-zia** \-zē-ə\ [NL, fr. Gk *trapezion*, lit., small table, dim. of *trapeza* table, fr. *tra-* four (akin to *tettares* four) + *peza* foot; akin to Gk *pod-, pous* foot — more at FOUR, FOOT] (1570) **1 a** : a quadrilateral having no two sides parallel **b** *Brit* : TRAPEZOID 1b **2** : a bone in the wrist at the base of the thumb
tra·pe·zi·us \-zē-əs\ *n* [NL, fr. *trapezium*; fr. the pair on the back forming together the figure of a trapezium] (ca. 1704) : a large flat triangular superficial muscle of each side of the upper back
tra·pe·zo·he·dron \ˌtra-pə-ˌpē-zō-ˈhē-drən, ˌtra-pə-\ *n, pl* **-drons** *or* **-dra** \-drə\ [NL, fr. *trapezium* + *-o-* + *-hedron*] (1822) : a crystalline form whose faces are trapeziums
trap·e·zoid \ˈtra-pə-ˌzȯid\ *n* [NL *trapezoïdes*, fr. Gk *trapezoeidēs* trapezium-shaped, fr. *trapeza* table] (ca. 1706) **1 a** *Brit* : TRAPEZIUM 1a **b** : a quadrilateral having only two sides parallel **2** : a bone in the wrist at the base of the forefinger — **trap·e·zoi·dal** \ˌtra-pə-ˈzȯi-dᵊl\ *adj*
trap·line \ˈtrap-ˌlīn\ *n* (1920) : a line or series of traps; *also* : the route along which such a line of traps is set
trap·ping \ˈtra-piŋ\ *n* [ME, fr. gerund of *trappen* to adorn] (14c) **1** : CAPARISON 1 — usu. used in pl. **2** *pl* : outward decoration or dress : ornamental equipment; *also* : outward signs ⟨conventional men with all the ~s . . . of banality —Robert Plank⟩
Trap·pist \ˈtra-pist\ *n* [F *trappiste*, fr. La *Trappe*, France] (1814) : a member of a reformed branch of the Roman Catholic Cistercian Order established by the Abbot de Rancé in 1664 at the monastery of La Trappe in Normandy — **Trappist** *adj*
trap·rock \ˈtrap-ˈräk\ *n* [*⁴trap*] (1813) : any of various dark-colored fine-grained igneous rocks (as basalt) used esp. in road making
traps \ˈtraps\ *n pl* [ME *trappe* cloth — more at TRAP] (1813) : personal belongings : LUGGAGE
trap·shoot·er \ˈtrap-ˌshü-tər\ *n* (1875) : a person who engages in trapshooting
trap·shoot·ing \-ˌshü-tiŋ\ *n* (1875) : shooting at clay pigeons sprung from a trap into the air away from the shooter
tra·pun·to \trə-ˈpün-(ˌ)tō, -ˈpun-\ *n, pl* **-tos** [It, fr. pp. of *trapungere* to embroider, fr. *tra-* across (fr. L *trans-*) + *pungere* to prick, fr. L — more at TRANS-, PUNGENT] (ca. 1924) : a decorative quilted design in high relief worked through at least two layers of cloth by outlining the design in running stitch and padding it from the underside
¹trash \ˈtrash\ *n* [of Scand origin; akin to Norw *trask* trash; akin to ON *tros* fallen leaves and twigs, OE *trus*] (ca. 1518) **1** : something worth little or nothing: as **a** : JUNK, RUBBISH **b** (1) : empty talk : NONSENSE (2) : inferior or worthless writing or artistic matter; *also* : such material intended purely for entertainment **2** : something in a crumbled or broken condition or mass; *esp* : debris from pruning or processing plant material **3** : a worthless person; *also* : such persons as a group : RIFFRAFF
²trash *vt* (ca. 1859) **1** : VANDALIZE, DESTROY **2** : ATTACK, ASSAULT **3** : SPOIL, RUIN ⟨~ing the environment⟩ **4** : to subject to criticism or invective; *esp* : to disparage strongly ⟨a film ~ed by the critics⟩ **5** : THROW AWAY 1 ⟨standards of reality and truth were ~ed —Edwin Diamond⟩ ⟨~ v⟩ *vi* : to trash something or someone

trash fish *n* (1944) **1** : ROUGH FISH **2** : any of various sea fishes that have no market value as human food but are sometimes processed for use in animal feed, fertilizers, and paints

trash·man \'trash-ˌman, -mən\ *n* (1951) : a worker who collects and hauls away trash

trashy \'tra-shē\ *adj* **trash·i·er; -est** (ca. 1620) : resembling or containing trash : of inferior quality — **trash·i·ness** *n*

trat·to·ria \ˌträ-tə-'rē-ə\ *n, pl* **-ri·as** *or* **-rie** \-'rē-ˌā\ [It, fr. *trattore* restaurateur, fr. F *traiteur*, fr. *traiter* to treat, fr. OF *traitier* — more at TREAT] (1832) : RESTAURANT; *specif* : a usu. small modest Italian restaurant

trau·ma \'traù-mə, 'trò-\ *n, pl* **traumas** *also* **trau·ma·ta** \-mə-tə\ [Gk *traumat-, trauma* wound, alter. of *trōma*; akin to Gk *titröskein* to wound, *tetrainein* to pierce — more at THROW] (ca. 1693) **1 a** : an injury (as a wound) to living tissue caused by an extrinsic agent 〈surgical ~〉 **b** : a disordered psychic or behavioral state resulting from mental or emotional stress or physical injury **2** : an agent, force, or mechanism that causes trauma — **trau·mat·ic** \trə-'ma-tik, trò-, traù-\ *adj* — **trau·mat·i·cal·ly** \-ti-k(ə-)lē\ *adv*

trau·ma·tise *Brit var of* TRAUMATIZE

trau·ma·tism \'traù-mə-ˌti-zəm, 'trò-\ *n* (1857) : the development or occurrence of trauma; *also* : TRAUMA

trau·ma·tize \-ˌtiz\ *vt* **-tized; -tiz·ing** (1903) : to inflict a trauma upon — **trau·ma·ti·za·tion** \ˌtraù-mə-ə-'zā-shən, ˌtrò-\ *n*

¹tra·vail \trə-'vā(ə)l, 'tra-ˌvāl\ *n* [ME, fr. OF, fr. *travaillier* to torture, labor, fr. (assumed) VL *trepaliare* to torture, fr. LL *trepalium* instrument of torture, fr. L *tripalis* having three stakes, fr. *tri-* + *palus* stake — more at POLE] (13c) **1 a** : work esp. of a painful or laborious nature : TOIL **b** : a physical or mental exertion or piece of work : TASK, EFFORT **c** : AGONY, TORMENT **2** : LABOR, PARTURITION *syn* see WORK

²travail *same as* ¹; in prayer-book communion service usu 'tra-ˌvāl\ *vi* [ME, fr. OF *travaillier*] (13c) **1** : to labor hard : TOIL **2** : LABOR 3

¹trav·el \'tra-vəl\ *vb* **-eled** *or* **-elled; -el·ing** *or* **-el·ling** \'tra-və-liŋ, 'trav-liŋ\ [ME *travailen* to labor, journey, fr. OF *travaillier* to labor] *vi* (14c) **1 a** : to go on or as if on a trip or tour : JOURNEY **b** (1) : to go as if by traveling : PASS 〈the news ~*ed* fast〉 (2) : ASSOCIATE 〈~*s* with a sophisticated crowd〉 **c** : to go from place to place as a sales representative or business agent **2 a** : to move or undergo transmission from one place to another 〈goods ~*ing* by plane〉 **b** : to move in a given direction or path or through a given distance 〈the stylus ~*s* in a groove〉 **c** : to move rapidly 〈a car that can really ~〉 **3** : to walk or run with a basketball in violation of the rules **~** *vt* **1 a** : to journey through or over **b** : to follow (a course or path) as if by traveling **2** : to traverse (a specified distance) **3** : to cover (a place or region) as a commercial traveler — **travel light** : to travel with a minimum of equipment or baggage

²travel *n* (14c) **1 a** : the act of traveling : PASSAGE **b** : a journey esp. to a distant or unfamiliar place : TOUR, TRIP — often used in pl. **2** *pl* : an account of one's travels **3** : the number traveling : TRAFFIC **4 a** : MOVEMENT, PROGRESSION 〈the ~ of satellites around the earth〉 **b** : the motion of a piece of machinery; *esp* : reciprocating motion

travel agency *n* (1927) : an agency engaged in selling and arranging personal transportation and accommodations for travelers — called also *travel bureau*

travel agent *n* (1925) : a person engaged in selling and arranging transportation, tours, or trips for travelers

trav·eled *or* **trav·elled** \'tra-vəld\ *adj* (15c) **1** : experienced in travel 〈a widely ~ journalist〉 **2** : used by travelers 〈a well-*traveled* highway〉

trav·el·er *or* **trav·el·ler** \'tra-və-lər, 'trav-lər\ *n* (14c) **1** : one that travels: as **a** : one that goes on a trip or journey **b** : TRAVELING SALESMAN **2 a** : an iron ring sliding along a rope, bar, or rod of a ship **b** : a rod on the deck on which such a ring slides **3** : any of various devices for handling something that is being transported laterally

traveler's check *n* (1891) : a draft purchased from a bank or express company and signed by the purchaser at the time of purchase and again at the time of cashing as a precaution against forgery

trav·el·ing *or* **trav·el·ling** \'tra-və-liŋ, 'trav-liŋ\ *adj* (14c) **1** : that travels 〈a ~ opera company〉 〈a ~ executive〉 **2** : carried, used by, or accompanying a traveler 〈a ~ alarm clock〉 〈a ~ companion〉

traveling bag *n* (1838) : SUITCASE

traveling case *n* (1744) : a usu. rigid and box-shaped suitcase

traveling fellowship *n* (1789) : a fellowship whose terms permit or direct the holder to travel or go abroad for study or research

traveling salesman *n* (1885) : a traveling representative of a business concern who solicits orders usu. in an assigned territory

trav·el·ogue *or* **trav·el·og** \'tra-və-ˌlòg, -ˌläg\ *n* [*travel* + *-logue*] (1903) **1** : a talk or lecture on travel usu. accompanied by a film or slides **2** : a narrated motion picture about travel **3** : a piece of writing about travel

travel trailer *n* (1961) : a trailer drawn by a passenger automobile and equipped for use (as while traveling) as a dwelling

tra·vers·al \trə-'vər-səl *also* tra-'\ *or* 'tra-,\ *n* (1897) : the act or an instance of traversing

¹tra·verse \'tra-vərs *also* -ˌvərs, *esp for 6 & 8 also* trə-' *or* 'tra-'\ *n* [ME *travers*, fr. MF *traverse*, fr. *traverser* to cross, fr. LL *transversare*, fr. L *transversus* transverse — more at TRANSVERSE] (14c) **1** : something that crosses or lies across **2** : OBSTACLE, ADVERSITY **3** : a formal denial of a matter of fact alleged by the opposite party in a legal pleading **4 a** : a compartment or recess formed by a partition, curtain, or screen **b** : a gallery or loft of communication from side to side in a large building **5** : a route or way across or over: as **a** : a zigzag course of a sailing ship with contrary winds **b** : a curving or zigzag way up a steep grade **c** : the course followed in traversing **6** : the act or an instance of traversing : CROSSING **7** : a protective projecting wall or bank of earth in a trench **8 a** : a lateral movement (as of the saddle of a lathe carriage); *also* : a device for imparting such movement **b** : the lateral movement of a gun about a pivot or on a carriage to change direction of fire **9** : a line surveyed across a plot of ground

²traverse \trə-'vərs *also* tra-' *or* 'tra-ˌ\ *vb* **tra·versed; tra·vers·ing** *vt* (14c) **1 a** : to go against or act in opposition to : OPPOSE, THWART **b** : to deny (as an allegation of fact or an indictment) formally at law **2 a** : to go or travel across or over **b** : to move or pass along or through 〈light rays *traversing* a crystal〉 **3** : to make a study of : EXAMINE **4**

: to lie or extend across : CROSS 〈the bridge ~*s* a brook〉 **5 a** : to move to and fro over or along **b** : to ascend, descend, or cross (a slope or gap) at an angle **c** : to move (a gun) to right or left on a pivot **6** : to make or carry out a survey of by using traverses **~** *vi* **1** : to move back and forth or from side to side **2** : to move or turn laterally : SWIVEL **3 a** : to climb at an angle or in a zigzag course **b** : to ski across rather than straight down a hill **4** : to make a survey by using traverses — **tra·vers·er** *n*

³tra·verse \'tra-(ˌ)vərs, trə-'\ *adj* (15c) : lying across : TRANSVERSE

trav·erse jury \'trav-ərs-\ *n* (1823) : PETIT JURY

traverse rod *n* (1948) : a metal rod or track with a pulley mechanism for drawing curtains

trav·er·tine \'tra-vər-ˌtēn, -tən\ *n* [F *travertin*, fr. It *travertino, trevertino*, fr. L *tiburtinus*, adj., of travertine, lit., of Tibur (Tivoli)] (1797) : a mineral consisting of a massive usu. layered calcium carbonate (as aragonite or calcite) formed by deposition from spring waters or esp. from hot springs

¹trav·es·ty \'tra-və-stē\ *vt* **-tied; -ty·ing** (1673) : to make a travesty of : PARODY

²travesty *n, pl* **-ties** [obs. E *travesty*, disguised, parodied, fr. F *travesti*, pp. of *travestir* to disguise, fr. It *travestire*, fr. *tra-* across (fr. L *trans-*) + *vestire* to dress, fr. L — more at VEST] (1674) **1** : a burlesque translation or literary or artistic imitation usu. grotesquely incongruous in style, treatment, or subject matter **2** : a debased, distorted, or grossly inferior imitation 〈a ~ of justice〉 *syn* see CARICATURE

tra·vois \trə-'vòi, 'tra-ˌvòi\ *n, pl* **tra·vois** *also* **tra·voises** \-'vòiz, -ˌvòiz\ [AmerF *travail*, fr. CanF, shaft of a cart, fr. MF *traveil* catafalque, prop, fr. LL *trepalium* instrument of torture — more at TRAVAIL] (1847) : a simple vehicle used by Plains Indians consisting of two trailing poles serving as shafts and bearing a platform or net for the load

¹trawl \'tròl\ *vb* [prob. fr. obs. D *tragelen*] *vi* (1561) **1** : to fish with a trawl **2** : TROLL 2 **~** *vt* : to catch (fish) with a trawl

²trawl *n* (1759) **1** : a large conical net dragged along the sea bottom in gathering fish or other marine life **2** : SETLINE

trawl·er \'trò-lər\ *n* (1630) **1** : a person who fishes by trawling **2** : a boat used in trawling

trawl·er·man \-mən\ *n* (1633) : a fisherman who trawls or one who mans a trawler

tray \'trā\ *n* [ME, fr. OE *trīg, trēg;* akin to OSw *trø* wooden grain measure and prob. to OE *trēow* tree — more at TREE] (bef. 12c) : an open receptacle with a flat bottom and a low rim for holding, carrying, or exhibiting articles — **tray·ful** \-ˌfùl\ *n*

treach·er·ous \'tre-chə-rəs, 'trech-rəs\ *adj* (14c) **1** : characterized by or manifesting treachery : PERFIDIOUS **2 a** : likely to betray trust : UNRELIABLE 〈a ~ memory〉 **b** : providing insecure footing or support 〈~ quicksand〉 **c** : marked by hidden dangers, hazards, or perils *syn* see FAITHLESS — **treach·er·ous·ly** *adv* — **treach·er·ous·ness** *n*

treach·ery \-rē\ *n, pl* **-er·ies** [ME *trecherie*, fr. OF, fr. *trechier, trichier* to deceive, fr. (assumed) VL *triccare* — more at TRICK] (13c) **1** : violation of allegiance or of faith and confidence : TREASON **2** : an act of perfidy or treason

trea·cle \'trē-kəl\ *n* [ME *triacle*, fr. MF, fr. L *theriaca*, fr. Gk *thēriakē* antidote against a poisonous bite, fr. fem. of *thēriakos* of a wild animal, fr. *thērion* wild animal, dim. of *thēr* wild animal — more at FIERCE] (14c) **1** : a medicinal compound formerly in wide use as a remedy against poison **2** *chiefly Brit* : MOLASSES **b** : a blend of molasses, invert sugar, and corn syrup used as syrup at the table — called also *golden syrup* **3** : something (as a tone of voice) heavily sweet and cloying

trea·cly \-k(ə-)lē\ *adj* (1733) : resembling treacle (as in quality or appearance) 〈~ sentimentality〉

¹tread \'tred\ *vb* **trod** \'träd\ *also* **tread·ed; trod·den** \'trä-d²n\ *or* **trod; tread·ing** [ME *treden*, fr. OE *tredan;* akin to OHG *tretan* to tread] *vt* (bef. 12c) **1 a** : to step or walk on or over **b** : to walk along : FOLLOW **2 a** : to beat or press with the feet : TRAMPLE **b** : to subdue or repress as if by trampling : CRUSH **3** : to copulate with — used of a male bird **4 a** : to form by treading : BEAT 〈~ a path〉 **b** : to execute by stepping or dancing 〈~ a measure〉 **~** *vi* **1** : to move on foot : WALK **2 a** : to set foot **b** : to put one's foot : STEP **3** : COPULATE — **tread·er** *n* — **tread on one's toes** : to give offense (as by encroaching on one's rights or feelings) — **tread water** : to keep the body nearly upright in the water and the head above water by a treading motion of the feet usu. aided by the hands

²tread *n* (13c) **1** : a mark (as a footprint or the imprint of a tire) made by or as if by treading **2 a** (1) : the action of treading (2) : an act or instance of treading : STEP **b** : manner of stepping **c** : the sound of treading **3 a** : the part of a shoe or boot sole that touches the ground; *also* : the pattern on the bottom of a sole **b** (1) : the part of a wheel or tire that makes contact with a road or rail (2) : the pattern of ridges or grooves made or cut in the face of a tire **4** : the distance between the points of contact with the ground of the two front wheels or the two rear wheels of a vehicle **5 a** : the upper horizontal part of a step **b** : the width of such a tread — **tread·less** \-ləs\ *adj*

¹trea·dle \'tre-d²l\ *n* [ME *tredel* step of a stair, fr. OE, fr. *tredan*] (15c) : a swiveling or lever device pressed by the foot to drive a machine

²treadle *vb* **trea·dled; tread·ling** \'tred-liŋ, 'tre-d²l-iŋ\ *vi* (1891) : to operate a treadle **~** *vt* : to operate (as a machine) by a treadle

tread·mill \'tred-ˌmil\ *n* (1822) **1 a** : a mill worked by persons treading on steps on the periphery of a wide wheel having a horizontal axis and used formerly in prison punishment **b** : a mill worked by an animal treading an endless belt **c** : a device having an endless belt on which an individual walks or runs in place for exercise or physiological testing **2** : a wearisome or monotonous routine resembling continued activity on a treadmill

trea·son \'trē-z²n\ *n* [ME *tresoun*, fr. OF *traison*, fr. L *tradition-, traditio* act of handing over, fr. *tradere* to hand over, betray — more at TRAI-

\ə\ abut \ᵊ\ kitten, F table \ər\ further \a\ ash \ā\ ace \ä\ mop, mar \aù\ out \ch\ chin \e\ bet \ē\ easy \g\ go \i\ hit \ī\ ice \j\ job \ŋ\ sing \ō\ go \ò\ law \òi\ boy \th\ thin \t̲h̲\ the \ü\ loot \ù\ foot \y\ yet \zh\ vision \à, k̲, ⁿ, œ, œ̄, ᵫ, ᵬ, ᵊ\ *see* Guide to Pronunciation

TOR] (13c)   **1** : the betrayal of a trust : TREACHERY   **2** : the offense of attempting by overt acts to overthrow the government of the state to which the offender owes allegiance or to kill or personally injure the sovereign or the sovereign's family

trea·son·able \'trēz-nə-bəl, 'trē-z°n-ə-bəl\ *adj* (14c) : relating to, consisting of, or involving treason — **trea·son·ably** \-blē\ *adv*

trea·son·ous \'trēz-nəs, 'trē-z°n-əs\ *adj* (1593) : TREASONABLE

trea·sur·able \'tre-zhə-rə-bəl, 'trā-; 'trezh-rə-, 'trāzh-rə-\ *adj* (1607) : worthy of being treasured : PRECIOUS

¹treasure \'tre-zhər, 'trā-\ *n* [ME *tresor*, fr. OF, fr. L *thesaurus* — more at THESAURUS] (12c)   **1 a** (1) : wealth (as money, jewels, or precious metals) stored up or hoarded 〈buried ~〉   (2) : wealth of any kind or in any form : RICHES   **b** : a store of money in reserve   **2** : something of great worth or value; *also* : a person esteemed as rare or precious   **3** : a collection of precious things

²treasure *vt* **trea·sured; trea·sur·ing** \-zh(ə-)riŋ\ (14c)   **1** : to collect and store up (something of value) for future use : HOARD   **2** : to hold or keep as precious : CHERISH, PRIZE 〈she *treasured* those memories〉 *syn* see APPRECIATE

trea·sure–house \'tre-zhər-,haus, 'trā-\ *n* (15c)   **1** : a building where treasure is kept : TREASURY   **2** : a place or source (as a collection) where many things of value can be found

trea·sur·er \'tre-zhə-rər, 'trā-; 'trezh-rər, 'trāzh-\ *n* (14c)   **1** : a guardian of a collection of treasures : CURATOR   **2** : an officer entrusted with the receipt, care, and disbursement of funds: as   **a** : a governmental officer charged with receiving, keeping, and disbursing public revenues   **b** : the executive financial officer of a club, society, or business corporation — **trea·sur·er·ship** \-,ship\ *n*

treasure trove \-,trōv\ *n* [AF *tresor trové*, lit., found treasure] (1523)   **1** : treasure that anyone finds; *specif* : gold or silver in the form of money, plate, or bullion which is found hidden and whose ownership is not known   **2** : a valuable discovery, resource, or collection

trea·sury \'tre-zh(ə-)rē, 'trā-\ *n, pl* **-sur·ies** [ME *tresorie*, fr. OF, fr. *tresor* treasure] (14c)   **1 a** : a place in which stores of wealth are kept   **b** : the place of deposit and disbursement of collected funds; *esp* : one where public revenues are deposited, kept, and disbursed   **c** : funds kept in such a depository   **2** *obs* : TREASURE   **3** *cap* : a governmental department in charge of finances and esp. the collection, management, and expenditure of public revenues   **b** : the building in which the business of such a governmental department is transacted   **4** *cap* : a government security (as a note or bill) issued by the Treasury   **5** : a repository for treasures 〈a ~ of poems〉

treasury note *n* (1890)   **1** : a currency note issued by the U.S. Treasury in payment for silver bullion purchased under the Sherman Silver Purchase Act of 1890   **2** : a U.S. government bond usu. with a maturity of not less than one year or more than seven years

treasury of merits (1884) : the superabundant satisfaction of Christ for human sins and the excess of merit of the saints which according to Roman Catholic theology is effective for salvation of others and is available for dispensation through indulgences

treasury stock *n* (1903) : issued stock reacquired by a corporation and held as an asset

¹treat \'trēt\ *vb* [ME *treten*, fr. OF *traitier*, fr. L *tractare* to drag about, handle, deal with, freq. of *trahere* to drag, pull] *vi* (14c)   **1** : to discuss terms of accommodation or settlement : NEGOTIATE   **2** : to deal with a matter esp. in writing : DISCOURSE — usu. used with *of* 〈a book ~*ing* of conservation〉   **3** : to pay another's expenses (as for a meal or drink) esp. as a compliment or as an expression of regard or friendship   ~ *vt*   **1 a** : to deal with in speech or writing : EXPOUND   **b** : to present or represent artistically   **c** : to deal with : HANDLE 〈food is plentiful and ~*ed* with imagination —Cecil Beaton〉   **2 a** : to bear oneself toward : USE 〈~ a horse cruelly〉   **b** : to regard and deal with in a specified manner — usu. used with *as*   **3 a** : to provide with free food, drink, or entertainment   **b** : to provide with enjoyment or gratification   **4** : to care for or deal with medically or surgically 〈~ a disease〉   **5** : to act upon with some agent esp. to improve or alter 〈~ a metal with acid〉 — **treat·er** *n*

²treat *n* (1651)   **1** : an entertainment given without expense to those invited   **2** : an esp. unexpected source of joy, delight, or amusement

treat·able \'trē-tə-bəl\ *adj* (14c) : capable of being treated : yielding or responsive to treatment 〈a ~ disease〉 — **treat·abil·i·ty** \,trē-tə-'bi-lə-tē\ *n*

trea·tise \'trē-təs *also* -təz\ *n* [ME *tretis*, fr. AF *tretiz*, fr. OF *traitier* to treat] (14c)   **1** : a systematic exposition or argument in writing including a methodical discussion of the facts and principles involved and conclusions reached 〈a ~ on higher education〉   **2** *obs* : ACCOUNT, TALE

treat·ment \'trēt-mənt\ *n* (ca. 1560)   **1 a** : the act or manner or an instance of treating someone or something : HANDLING, USAGE   **b** : the techniques or actions customarily applied in a specified situation   **2 a** : a substance or technique used in treating   **b** : an experimental condition

trea·ty \'trē-tē\ *n, pl* **treaties** [ME *tretee*, fr. MF *traité*, fr. ML *tractatus*, fr. L, handling, treatment, fr. *tractare* to treat, handle] (14c)   **1** : the action of treating and esp. of negotiating   **2 a** : an agreement or arrangement made by negotiation: (1) : PRIVATE TREATY   (2) : a contract in writing between two or more political authorities (as states or sovereigns) formally signed by representatives duly authorized and usu. ratified by the lawmaking authority of the state   **b** : a document in which such a contract is set down

treaty port *n* (1863) : any of numerous ports and inland cities in China, Japan, and Korea formerly open by treaty to foreign commerce

¹tre·ble \'tre-bəl\ *n* [ME, perh. fr. MF, trio, fr. *treble*, adj.] (14c)   **1 a** : the highest voice part in harmonic music : SOPRANO   **b** : one that performs a treble part; *also* : a member of a family of instruments having the highest range   **c** : a high-pitched or shrill voice, tone, or sound   **d** : the upper half of the whole vocal or instrumental tonal range — compare BASS   **e** : the higher portion of the audio frequency range in sound recording and broadcasting   **2** : something treble in construction, uses, amount, number, or value

²treble *adj* [ME, fr. MF, fr. L *triplus* — more at TRIPLE] (14c)   **1 a** : having three parts or uses : THREEFOLD   **b** : triple in number or amount   **2 a** : relating to or having the range or part of a treble   **b** : HIGH-PITCHED, SHRILL   **c** : of, relating to, or having the range of treble

in sound recording and broadcasting 〈~ frequencies〉 — **tre·bly** \'tre-b(ə-)lē\ *adv*

³treble *vb* **tre·bled; tre·bling** \'tre-b(ə-)liŋ\ *vt* (14c) : to increase threefold   ~ *vi*   **1** : to sing treble   **2** : to grow to three times the size, amount, or number

treble clef *n* [¹*treble;* fr. its use for the notation of treble parts] (ca. 1854)   **1** : a clef that places G above middle C on the second line of the staff   **2** : TREBLE STAFF

treble staff *n* (ca. 1854) : the musical staff carrying the treble clef

treb·u·chet \'tre-byə-'shet, -bə-, -'chet\ *or* **treb·uc·ket** \-tre-bə-'ket\ *n* [ME *trebochet*, fr. MF *trebuchet*] (15c) : a medieval military engine for hurling heavy missiles (as rocks)

tre·cen·to \trā-'chen-(,)tō\ *n* [It, lit., three hundred, fr. L *tres* three + *centum* hundred — more at THREE, HUNDRED] (1841) : the 14th century; *specif* : the 14th century in Italian literature and art

tre·de·cil·lion \,trē-di-'sil-yən\ *n, often attrib* [L *tredecim* thirteen (fr. *tres* three + *decem* ten) + E *-illion* (as in *million*) — more at THREE, TEN] (ca. 1934) — see NUMBER table

¹tree \'trē\ *n* [ME, fr. OE *trēow;* akin to ON *trē* tree, Gk *drys*, Skt *dāru* wood] (bef. 12c)   **1 a** : a woody perennial plant having a single usu. elongate main stem generally with few or no branches on its lower part   **b** : a shrub or herb of arborescent form 〈rose ~s〉 〈a banana ~〉   **2 a** (1) : a piece of wood (as a post or pole) usu. adapted to a particular use or forming part of a structure or implement   (2) *archaic* : the cross on which Jesus was crucified   **b** *archaic* : GALLOWS   **3** : something in the form of or resembling a tree: as   **a** : a diagram or graph that branches usu. from a simple stem without forming loops or polygons 〈genealogical ~〉   **b** : a much-branched system of channels esp. in an animal body 〈the vascular ~〉   **4** : SADDLETREE — **tree·less** \-ləs\ *adj* — **tree·like** \-,līk\ *adj*

²tree *vt* **treed; tree·ing** (1575)   **1 a** : to drive to or up a tree 〈treed by a bull〉 〈dogs ~*ing* game〉   **b** : to put into a position of extreme disadvantage : CORNER; *esp* : to bring to bay   **2** : to furnish or fit (as a shoe) with a tree

treed \'trēd\ *adj* (1860) : planted or grown with trees : WOODED

tree ear *n* (1967) : any of several brown ear-shaped basidiomycetous fungi (genus *Auricularia*); *esp* : one (*A. polytricha*) used esp. in Chinese cooking

tree farm *n* (1941) : an area of forest land managed to ensure continuous commercial production

tree fern *n* (1832) : any of various ferns (esp. families Cyatheaceae and Marattiaceae) of arborescent habit with a woody stem

tree frog *n* (1738) : any of numerous small anuran amphibians (esp. family Hylidae) of usu. arboreal habits that typically have adhesive suckers on the toes

tree·hop·per \'trē-,hä-pər\ *n* (ca. 1839) : any of a family (Membracidae) of small leaping homopterous insects that feed on the sap esp. of shrubs and trees

tree house *n* (ca. 1899) : a structure (as a playhouse) built among the branches of a tree

tree line *n* (1893) : TIMBERLINE

treen \'trēn\ *n, sing or pl in constr* [*treen* wooden, fr. ME, fr. OE *trēowen*, fr. *treow* tree, wood] (1927) : small woodenware — called also *treenware*

tree·nail *also* **tre·nail** \'trə-n°l\ *n* (13c) : a wooden peg made usu. of dry compressed timber so as to swell in its hole when moistened

tree of heaven (1845) : a Chinese ailanthus (*Ailanthus altissima* syn. *A. glandulosa*) that has foliage similar to that of the sumacs, has illscented staminate flowers, and is grown as a shade and ornamental tree

tree of life (1880) : a conventionalized and often ornate representation of a tree used as a decorative motif

tree peony *n* (ca. 1891) : a shrubby Chinese peony (*Paeonia suffruticosa*) that has large showy flowers and is the source of many horticultural varieties

tree ring *n* (1919) : ANNUAL RING

tree shrew *n* (ca. 1893) : any of an order (Scandentia) of arboreal insectivorous mammals of southeastern Asia often classified as true insectivores or sometimes as primitive primates

tree sparrow *n* (ca. 1770)   **1** : a European sparrow (*Passer montanus*) that has a black spot on the ear coverts   **2** : a No. American sparrow (*Spizella arborea*) that has a single dark spot on the breast and breeds in northern No. America and winters in the U.S.

tree surgeon *n* (1908) : a specialist in tree surgery — compare ARBORIST

tree shrew

tree surgery *n* (1902) : operative treatment of diseased trees esp. for control of decay; *broadly* : practices forming part of the professional care of specimen or shade trees

tree swallow *n* (1873) : an American swallow (*Tachycineta bicolor* syn. *Iridoprocne bicolor*) with iridescent greenish blue upperparts and white underparts

tree toad *n* (1778) : TREE FROG

tree tomato *n* (ca. 1881) : TAMARILLO

tree·top \'trē-,täp\ *n* (1530)   **1** : the topmost part of a tree   **2** *pl* : the height or line marked by the tops of a group of trees

tre·foil \'trē-,fȯil, 'tre-\ *n* [ME, fr. MF *trefeuil*, fr. L *trifolium*, fr. *tri-* + *folium* leaf — more at BLADE] (15c)   **1 a** : CLOVER; *broadly* : any of several trifoliolate leguminous herbs   **b** : a trifoliolate leaf   **2** : an ornament or symbol in the form of a stylized trifoliolate leaf

tre·ha·lose \tri-'hä-,lōs, -,lōz\ *n* [ISV *trehala* (a sweet substance constituting the pupal covering of a beetle) + ²*-ose*] (1862) : a crystalline disaccharide $C_{12}H_{22}O_{11}$ stored instead of starch by many fungi and found in the blood of many insects

treil·lage \tre-'yäzh\ *n* [F, fr. MF, fr. *treille* vine arbor, fr. L *trichila*] (1698) : latticework for vines : TRELLIS

¹trek \'trek\ *vi* **trekked; trek·king** [Afrik, fr. D *trecken* to pull, haul, migrate; akin to OHG *trechan* to pull] (1821)   **1** *chiefly SoAfr*   **a** : to travel by ox wagon   **b** : to migrate by ox wagon or in a train of such

2 : to make one's way arduously; *broadly* : to go on a journey — **trek‑ker** *n*

²trek *n* [Afrik, fr. D *treck* pull, haul, fr. *trecken*] (1835) **1** *chiefly SoAfr* : a journey by ox wagon; *esp* : an organized migration by a group of settlers **2** : a trip or movement esp. when involving difficulties or complex organization

¹trel·lis \'tre‑ləs\ *n* [ME *trelis*, fr. MF *treliz* fabric of coarse weave, trellis, fr. (assumed) VL *trilicius* woven with triple thread, fr. L *tri‑* + *licium* thread] (15c) **1** : a frame of latticework used as a screen or as a support for climbing plants **2** : a construction (as a summerhouse) chiefly of latticework **3** : an arrangement that forms or gives the effect of a lattice ⟨a ~ of interlacing streams⟩ — **trel·lised** \'tre‑ləst\ *adj*

²trellis *vt* (15c) **1** : to provide with a trellis; *esp* : to train (as a vine) on a trellis **2** : to cross or interlace on or through : INTERWEAVE

trel·lis·work \'tre‑ləs‑,wərk\ *n* (1712) : LATTICEWORK

trem·a·tode \'tre‑mə‑,tōd\ *n* [ultim. fr. Gk *trēmatōdēs* pierced with holes, fr. *trēmat‑*, *trēma* hole, fr. *tetrainein* to bore — more at THROW] (ca. 1859) : any of a class (Trematoda) of parasitic platyhelminthic flatworms including the flukes — **trematode** *adj*

¹trem·ble \'trem‑bəl\ *vi* **trem·bled; trem·bling** \‑b(ə‑)liŋ\ [ME, fr. MF *trembler*, fr. ML *tremulare*, fr. L *tremulus* tremulous, fr. *tremere* to tremble; akin to Gk *tremein* to tremble] (14c) **1** : to shake involuntarily (as with fear or cold) : SHIVER **2** : to move, sound, pass, or come to pass as if shaken or tremulous ⟨the building *trembled* from the blast⟩ **3** : to be affected with fear or doubt ⟨~ for the safety of another⟩ — **trem·bler** \‑b(ə‑)lər\ *n*

²tremble *n* (1609) **1** : an act or instance of trembling; *esp* : a fit or spell of involuntary shaking or quivering **2** *pl but sing in constr* : severe poisoning of livestock and esp. cattle by a toxic alcohol present in a snakeroot (*Eupatorium rugosum*) and rayless goldenrod that is characterized by muscular tremors, weakness, and constipation

trem·bly \'trem‑b(ə‑)lē\ *adj* (1848) : marked by trembling : TREMULOUS

tre·men·dous \tri‑'men‑dəs\ *adj* [L *tremendus*, fr. gerundive of *tremere*] (1632) **1** : being such as may excite trembling or arouse dread, awe, or terror **2 a** : notable by reason of extreme size, power, greatness, or excellence — often used as a generalized term of approval **b** : unusually large : HUGE *syn* see MONSTROUS — **tre·men·dous·ly** *adv* — **tre·men·dous·ness** *n*

trem·o·lite \'tre‑mə‑,līt\ *n* [F *trémolite*, fr. *Tremola*, valley in Switzerland] (1799) : a white or gray mineral of the amphibole group that is a silicate of calcium and magnesium — **trem·o·lit·ic** \,tre‑mə‑'li‑tik\ *adj*

trem·o·lo \'tre‑mə‑,lō\ *n*, *pl* **‑los** [It, fr. *tremolo* tremulous, fr. L *tremulus*] (ca. 1801) **1 a** : the rapid reiteration of a musical tone or of alternating tones to produce a tremulous effect **b** : vocal vibrato esp. when prominent or excessive **2** : a mechanical device in an organ for causing a tremulous effect

trem·or \'tre‑mər\ *n* [ME *tremour* terror, fr. MF, fr. L *tremor* trembling, fr. *tremere*] (1615) **1** : a trembling or shaking usu. from physical weakness, emotional stress, or disease **2** : a quivering or vibratory motion; *esp* : a discrete small movement following or preceding a major seismic event **3 a** : a feeling of uncertainty or insecurity **b** : a cause of such a feeling

trem·u·lant \'trem‑yə‑lənt\ *adj* [ML *tremulant‑*, *tremulans*, prp. of *tremulare* — more at TREMBLE] (1837) : TREMULOUS, TREMBLING

trem·u·lous \‑ləs\ *adj* [L *tremulus* — more at TREMBLE] (1611) **1** : characterized by or affected with trembling or tremors **2** : affected with timidity : TIMOROUS **3** : such as is or might be caused by nervousness or shakiness ⟨a ~ smile⟩ ⟨~ handwriting⟩ **4** : exceedingly sensitive : easily shaken or disordered — **trem·u·lous·ly** *adv* — **trem·u·lous·ness** *n*

¹trench \'trench\ *n* [ME *trenche* track cut through a wood, fr. MF, act of cutting, fr. *trenchier* to cut, prob. fr. (assumed) VL *trinicare* to cut in three, fr. L *trini* three each — more at TRINE] (15c) **1 a** : a long cut in the ground : DITCH; *esp* : one used for military defense often with the excavated dirt thrown up in front **b** *pl* : a place, position, or level at which an activity is carried on in a manner likened to trench warfare — often used in the phrase *in the trenches* **2** : a long, narrow, and usu. steep‑sided depression in the ocean floor — compare TROUGH **3** : TRENCH COAT

²trench *vt* (15c) **1** : to make a cut in : CARVE **2 a** : to protect with or as if with a trench **b** : to cut a trench in : DITCH ~ *vi* **1 a** : ENTRENCH, ENCROACH ⟨~*ing* on other domains which were more vital — Sir Winston Churchill⟩ **b** : to come close : VERGE **2** : to dig a trench

tren·chan·cy \'tren‑chən(t)‑sē\ *n* (1866) : the quality or state of being trenchant

tren·chant \'tren‑chənt\ *adj* [ME, fr. MF, prp. of *trenchier*] (14c) **1** : KEEN, SHARP **2** : vigorously effective and articulate ⟨a ~ analysis⟩; *also* : CAUSTIC ⟨~ remarks⟩ **3 a** : sharply perceptive : PENETRATING **b** : CLEAR‑CUT, DISTINCT ⟨the ~ divisions between right and wrong — Edith Wharton⟩ — **tren·chant·ly** *adv*

trench coat *n* (1916) **1** : a waterproof overcoat with a removable lining designed for wear in trenches **2** : a usu. double‑breasted raincoat with deep pockets, wide belt, and often straps on the shoulders

trenched \'trencht\ *adj* (1541) **1** : furrowed or drained by trenches **2** : provided with protective trenches

¹tren·cher \'tren‑chər\ *n* [ME, fr. MF *trencheoir*, fr. *trenchier* to cut] (14c) : a wooden platter for serving food

²trencher *adj* (15c) **1** : of or relating to a trencher or to meals **2** *archaic* : having the nature of a parasite : SYCOPHANTIC

³trench·er \'tren‑chər\ *n* [²*trench*] (ca. 1864) : one that digs trenches; *specif* : a usu. self‑propelled excavating machine typically employing a bucket conveyor and used to dig trenches esp. for pipelines and cables

tren·cher·man \'tren‑chər‑mən\ *n* (1590) **1** : a hearty eater **2** *archaic* : HANGER‑ON, SPONGER

trench fever *n* (1915) : a disease that is marked by fever and pain in muscles, bones, and joints and that is caused by a bacterium (*Rochalimaea quintana*) transmitted by the human body louse (*Pediculus humanus*)

trench foot *n* (1915) : a painful foot disorder resembling frostbite and resulting from exposure to cold and wet

trench mouth *n* (1918) **1** : VINCENT'S ANGINA **2** : VINCENT'S INFECTION

trench warfare *n* (1917) : warfare in which the opposing forces attack and counterattack from a relatively permanent system of trenches protected by barbed‑wire entanglements

¹trend \'trend\ *vi* [ME, to turn, revolve, fr. OE *trendan*; akin to MHG *trendel* disk, spinning top] (1598) **1 a** : to extend in a general direction : follow a general course ⟨mountain ranges ~*ing* north and south⟩ **b** : to veer in a new direction : BEND ⟨coastline that ~*s* westward⟩ **2 a** : to show a tendency : INCLINE ⟨prices ~*ing* upward⟩ **b** : to become deflected : SHIFT ⟨opinions ~*ing* toward conservatism⟩

²trend *n* (1777) **1** : a line of general direction or movement ⟨the ~ of the coast turned toward the west⟩ **2 a** : a prevailing tendency or inclination : DRIFT **b** : a general movement : SWING ⟨the ~ toward suburban living⟩ **c** : a current style or preference : VOGUE ⟨new fashion ~*s*⟩ **d** : a line of development : APPROACH **3** : the general movement in the course of time of a statistically detectable change; *also* : a statistical curve reflecting such a change *syn* see TENDENCY

trend·set·ter \'tren(d)‑,se‑tər\ *n* (1960) : one that sets a trend

trend·set·ting \‑,se‑tiŋ\ *adj* (1960) : that sets a trend ⟨a ~ fashion look⟩

trendy \'tren‑dē\ *adj* **trend·i·er; ‑est** (1962) **1** : very fashionable : UP‑TO‑DATE ⟨he's a ~ dresser —*Sunday Mirror*⟩ **2** : marked by ephemeral, superficial, or faddish appeal or taste ⟨a newspaper of ~ triviality —J.H. Plumb⟩ — **trend·i·ly** \‑də‑lē\ *adv* — **trend·i·ness** \‑dē‑nəs\ *n* — **trendy** \‑dē\ *n*

¹tre·pan \tri‑'pan\ *vt* **tre·panned; tre·pan·ning** [ME, fr. *trepane* trephine] (15c) **1** : to use a trephine on (the skull) **2** : to remove a disk or cylindrical core (as from metal for testing) — **trep·a·na·tion** \,tre‑pə‑'nā‑shən\ *n*

²tre·pan \'trē‑,pan, tri‑'pan\ *n* [ME *trepane* trephine, fr. ML *trepanum*, fr. Gk *trypanon* auger, fr. *trypan* to bore] (ca. 1877) : a heavy tool used in boring mine shafts

³tre·pan \tri‑'pan\ *n* [origin unknown] (1641) **1** *archaic* : TRICKSTER **2** *archaic* : a deceptive device : SNARE

⁴tre·pan \tri‑'pan\ *vt* **tre·panned; tre·pan·ning** (ca. 1656) *archaic* : ENTRAP, LURE

tre·pang \tri‑'paŋ, 'trē‑,\ *n* [Malay *tĕripang*] (1783) : any of several large sea cucumbers (esp. genera *Actinopyga* and *Holothuria*) that are taken mostly in the southwestern Pacific and are boiled, dried, and used esp. by the Chinese for making soup — called also *bêche‑de‑mer*

treph·i·na·tion \,tre‑fə‑'nā‑shən\ *n* (1874) : an act or instance of perforating the skull with a surgical instrument

tre·phine \'trē‑,fīn\ *n* [F *tréphine*, fr. obs. E *trefine*, *trafine*, fr. L *tres fines* three ends, fr. *tres* three + *fines*, pl. of *finis* end — more at THREE] (1628) : a surgical instrument for cutting out circular sections (as of bone or corneal tissue) — **trephine** *vt*

trep·id \'tre‑pəd\ *adj* [L *trepidus*] (1650) : TIMOROUS, FEARFUL

trep·i·dant \'tre‑pə‑dənt\ *adj* [L *trepidant‑*, *trepidans*, prp. of *trepidare*] (1892) : TIMID, TREMBLING

trep·i·da·tion \,tre‑pə‑'dā‑shən\ *n* [L *trepidation‑*, *trepidatio*, fr. *trepidare* to tremble, fr. *trepidus* agitated; prob. akin to OE *thrafian* to urge, push, Gk *trapein* to press grapes] (1605) **1** *archaic* : a tremulous motion : TREMOR **2** : timorous uncertain agitation : APPREHENSION *syn* see FEAR

trep·o·ne·ma \,tre‑pə‑'nē‑mə\ *n*, *pl* **‑ma·ta** \‑mə‑tə\ *or* **‑mas** [NL *Treponemat‑*, *Treponema*, fr. Gk *trepein* to turn + *nēma* thread, fr. *nēn* to spin — more at NEEDLE] (ca. 1908) : any of a genus (*Treponema*) of spirochetes that are pathogenic in humans and other warm‑blooded animals and include organisms causing syphilis and yaws — **trep·o·ne·mal** \‑məl\ *adj*

trep·o·ne·ma·to·sis \‑,nē‑mə‑'tō‑səs, ‑,ne‑\ *n*, *pl* **‑to·ses** \‑,sēz\ [NL] (1927) : infection with or disease caused by treponemata

trep·o·neme \'tre‑pə‑,nēm\ *n* (1919) : TREPONEMA

¹tres·pass \'tres‑pəs, ‑,pas\ *n* [ME *trespas*, fr. OF, crossing, trespass, fr. *trespasser* to go across] (14c) **1 a** : a violation of moral or social ethics : TRANSGRESSION; *esp* : SIN **b** : an unwarranted infringement **2 a** : an unlawful act committed on the person, property, or rights of another; *esp* : a wrongful entry on real property **b** : the legal action for injuries resulting from trespass

²trespass \‑pas *also* ‑pəs\ *vb* [ME, fr. MF *trespasser*, fr. OF, lit., to go across, fr. *tres* across (fr. L *trans*) + *passer* to pass — more at THROUGH, PASS] (14c) **1 a** : ERR, SIN **b** : to make an unwarranted or uninvited incursion **2** : to commit a trespass; *esp* : to enter unlawfully upon the land of another ~ *vt* : VIOLATE ⟨~ the bounds of good taste⟩ — **tres·pass·er** *n*

syn TRESPASS, ENCROACH, INFRINGE, INVADE mean to make inroads upon the property, territory, or rights of another. TRESPASS implies an unwarranted, unlawful, or offensive intrusion ⟨hunters *trespassing* on farmland⟩. ENCROACH suggests gradual or stealthy entrance upon another's territory or usurpation of another's rights or possessions ⟨the *encroaching* settlers gradually displaced the native peoples⟩. INFRINGE implies an encroachment clearly violating a right or prerogative ⟨a product that *infringes* an existing patent⟩. INVADE implies a hostile and injurious entry into the territory or sphere of another ⟨accused of *invading* their privacy⟩.

tress \'tres\ *n* [ME *tresse*, fr. MF *trece*] (14c) **1** : a long lock of hair; *esp* : the long unbound hair of a woman — usu. used in pl. **2** *archaic* : a plait of hair : BRAID

tressed \'trest\ *adj* (14c) **1** *obs* : being braided : PLAITED **2** : having tresses — usu. used in combination ⟨golden‑*tressed*⟩

tres·tle *also* **tres·sel** \'tre‑səl *also* 'trə‑\ *n* [ME *trestel*, fr. MF, fr. (assumed) VL *transtellum*, fr. L *transtillum*, dim. of *transtrum* traverse beam, fr. *trans* across — more at THROUGH] (14c) **1** : HORSE 2b **2** : a braced frame serving as a support **3** : a braced framework of timbers, piles, or steelwork for carrying a road or railroad over a depression

trestle table *n* (ca. 1891) : a table supported on trestles

tres·tle·work \‑,wərk\ *n* (1848) : a system of connected trestles supporting a structure (as a railroad bridge)

\ə\ abut \ᵊ\ kitten, F table \ər\ further \a\ ash \ā\ ace \ä\ mop, mar \au̇\ out \ch\ chin \e\ bet \ē\ easy \g\ go \i\ hit \ī\ ice \j\ job \ŋ\ sing \ō\ go \ȯ\ law \ȯi\ boy \th\ thin \t͟h\ the \ü\ loot \u̇\ foot \y\ yet \zh\ vision \ä, k̟, ⁿ, œ, œ̄, ᵫ, ᵫ̄, ᵊ\ *see* Guide to Pronunciation

tre·tin·o·in \tre-'ti-nə-win\ *n* [perh. fr. trans- + retinoic acid] (1980) : RETINOIC ACID

trews \'trüz\ *n pl* [ScGael *triubhas*] (ca. 1568) **1** *chiefly Brit* : ³PANT 1; *esp* : tight-fitting trousers usu. of tartan **2** : close-cut tartan shorts worn under the kilt in Highland dress

trey \'trā\ *n, pl* **treys** [ME *treye, treis*, fr. MF *treie, treis*, fr. L *tres* three] (14c) **1** : the side of a die or domino that has three spots **2** : a card numbered three or having three main pips

tri- *comb form* [ME, fr. L (fr. *tri-, tres*) & Gk, fr. *tri-, treis* — more at THREE] **1** : three : having three elements or parts ⟨*trigraph*⟩ **2** : into three ⟨*trisect*⟩ **3 a** : thrice ⟨*triweekly*⟩ **b** : every third ⟨*trimonthly*⟩

tri·able \'trī-ə-bəl\ *adj* (15c) : liable or subject to judicial or quasi-judicial examination or trial

tri·ac·e·tate \(,)trī-'a-sə-,tāt\ *n* [ISV] (1885) **1** : an acetate containing three CH₃COO— groups **2** : a textile fiber or fabric consisting of cellulose that is completely or almost completely acetylated

tri·ad \'trī-,ad *also* -əd\ *n* [L *triad-, trias*, fr. Gk, fr. *treis* three] (1546) **1** : a union or group of three : TRINITY **2** : a chord of three tones consisting of a root with its third and fifth and constituting the harmonic basis of tonal music — **tri·ad·ic** \trī-'a-dik\ *adj* — **tri·ad·i·cal·ly** \-di-k(ə-)lē\ *adv*

tri·age \trē-'äzh, 'trē-,\ *n* [F, sorting, sifting, fr. *trier* to sort, fr. OF — more at TRY] (1918) **1** : the sorting and allocation of treatment to patients and esp. battle and disaster victims according to a system of priorities designed to maximize the number of survivors; *broadly* : the assigning of priority order to projects on the basis of where funds and resources can be best used or are most needed — **triage** *vt*

¹tri·al \'trī(-ə)l\ *n* [AF, fr. *trier* to try] (15c) **1 a** : the action or process of trying or putting to the proof : TEST **b** : a preliminary contest (as in a sport) **2** : the formal examination before a competent tribunal of the matter in issue in a civil or criminal cause in order to determine such issue **3** : a test of faith, patience, or stamina through subjection to suffering or temptation; *broadly* : a source of vexation or annoyance **4 a** : a tryout or experiment to test quality, value, or usefulness **b** : one of a number of repetitions of an experiment **5** : ATTEMPT

²trial *adj* (1555) **1** : of, relating to, or used in a trial **2** : made or done as a test or experiment **3** : used or tried out in a test or experiment

trial and error *n* (1806) : a finding out of the best way to reach a desired result or a correct solution by trying out one or more ways or means and by noting and eliminating errors or causes of failure; *also* : the trying of one thing or another until something succeeds

trial balance *n* (1838) : a list of the debit and credit balances of accounts in a double-entry ledger at a given date prepared primarily to test their equality

trial balloon *n* (1935) : a project or scheme tentatively announced in order to test public opinion

trial court *n* (1890) : the court before which issues of fact and law are first determined as distinguished from an appellate court

trial examiner *n* (1949) : a person appointed to hold hearings and to investigate and report facts sometimes with recommendations to an administrative or quasi-judicial agency or tribunal

trial horse *n* (1901) : one set up as an opponent for a champion in trial competitions or workouts

trial jury *n* (1884) : a jury impaneled to try a cause : PETIT JURY

trial lawyer *n* (ca. 1914) : a lawyer who engages chiefly in the trial of cases before courts of original jurisdiction

tri·a·logue \'trī-ə-,lȯg, -,läg\ *n* [*tri-* + *-alogue* (as in *dialogue*)] (1532) : a scene, discourse, or colloquy in which three persons share

trial run *n* (1903) : a testing exercise : EXPERIMENT

tri·am·cin·o·lone \,trī-,am-'si-n°l-,ōn\ *n* [*tri-* + *-amcin-* (alter. of American *Cyanimid* Company) + ¹-*ol* + -*one*] (1957) : a glucocorticoid drug C₂₁H₂₇FO₆ used esp. in treating psoriasis and allergic skin and respiratory disorders

tri·an·gle \'trī-,aŋ-gəl\ *n* [ME, fr. L *triangulum*, fr. neut. of *triangulus* triangular, fr. *tri-* + *angulus* angle] (14c) **1** : a polygon having three sides — compare SPHERICAL TRIANGLE **2 a** : a percussion instrument consisting of a rod of steel bent into the form of a triangle open at one angle and sounded by striking with a small metal rod **b** : a drafting instrument consisting of a thin flat right-angled triangle of wood or plastic with acute angles of 45 degrees or of 30 degrees and 60 degrees **3** : a situation in which one member of a couple is involved in a love affair with a third person

triangle inequality *n* [fr. its application to the distances between three points in a coordinate system] (1941) : an inequality stating that the absolute value of a sum is less than or equal to the sum of the absolute value of the terms

triangle 1: *1* equilateral, *2* acute, *3* obtuse, *4* scalene, *5* isosceles, *6* right triangle

tri·an·gu·lar \trī-'aŋ-gyə-lər\ *adj* [LL *triangularis*, fr. L *triangulum*] (1541) **1 a** : of, relating to, or having the form of a triangle ⟨a ~ plot of land⟩ **b** : having a triangular base or principal surface ⟨a ~ table⟩ ⟨a ~ pyramid⟩ **2 a** (1) : of, relating to, or involving three elements ⟨a ~ agreement⟩ (2) *of a military group* : based primarily on three units **b** : of or relating to a love triangle — **tri·an·gu·lar·i·ty** \(,)trī-,aŋ-gyə-'lar-ə-tē\ *n* — **tri·an·gu·lar·ly** \trī-'aŋ-gyə-lər-lē\ *adv*

triangular number *n* (1796) : any of the numbers (as 1, 3, 6, 10, 15) that represent the number of dots in the figures formed starting with one dot and adding rows one after another to form triangles each row of which has one more dot than the one before and are of the general form

$$\frac{n(n+1)}{2}$$ where *n* = 1, 2, 3, . . .

¹tri·an·gu·late \trī-'aŋ-gyə-lət\ *adj* [ML *triangulatus*, pp. of *triangulare* to make triangles, fr. L *triangulum*] (1766) : consisting of or marked with triangles

²tri·an·gu·late \-,lāt\ *vt* **-lat·ed; -lat·ing** (1833) **1** : to survey, map, or determine by triangulation **2 a** : to divide into triangles **b** : to give triangular form to

tri·an·gu·la·tion \(,)trī-,aŋ-gyə-'lā-shən\ *n* (1818) : the measurement of the elements necessary to determine the network of triangles into which any part of the earth's surface is divided in surveying; *broadly* : any similar trigonometric operation for finding a position or location by means of bearings from two fixed points a known distance apart

tri·ar·chy \'trī-,är-kē\ *n, pl* **-chies** [Gk *triarchia*, fr. *tri-* + -*archia* -archy] (ca. 1656) **1** : government by three persons : TRIUMVIRATE **2** : a country under three rulers

Tri·as·sic \trī-'a-sik\ *adj* [ISV, fr. L *trias* triad; fr. the three subdivisions of the European Triassic — more at TRIAD] (1841) : of, relating to, or being the earliest period of the Mesozoic era or the corresponding system of rocks marked by the first appearance of the dinosaurs — see GEOLOGIC TIME table — **Triassic** *n*

tri·ath·lete \trī-'ath-,lēt, ÷'a-thə-\ *n* (1982) : an athlete who competes in a triathlon

tri·ath·lon \trī-'ath-lən, -,län, ÷-'a-thə-\ *n* [*tri-* + -*athlon* (as in decathlon)] (1978) : an athletic contest that is a long-distance race consisting of three phases (as swimming, bicycling, and running)

tri·atom·ic \,trī-ə-'tä-mik\ *adj* [ISV] (1862) : having three atoms in the molecule ⟨ozone is ~ oxygen⟩

tri·ax·i·al \(,)trī-'ak-sē-əl\ *adj* [ISV] (1886) : having or involving three axes — **tri·ax·i·al·i·ty** \-,ak-sē-'a-lə-tē\ *n*

tri·azine \'trī-ə-,zēn, trī-'a-,zēn\ *n* [ISV] (1894) : any of three compounds C₃H₃N₃ containing a ring composed of three carbon and three nitrogen atoms; *also* : any of various derivatives of these including several used as herbicides

trib·al \'trī-bəl\ *adj* (1632) : of, relating to, or characteristic of a tribe ⟨~ customs⟩ — **trib·al·ly** \-bə-lē\ *adv*

trib·al·ism \-bə-,li-zəm\ *n* (1886) **1** : tribal consciousness and loyalty; *esp* : exaltation of the tribe above other groups **2** : strong in-group loyalty

tri·ba·sic \(,)trī-'bā-sik\ *adj* (1837) : having three replaceable hydrogen atoms — used of acids

tribe \'trīb\ *n* [ME, fr. L *tribus*, a division of the Roman people, tribe] (13c) **1 a** : a social group comprising numerous families, clans, or generations together with slaves, dependents, or adopted strangers **b** : a political division of the Roman people orig. representing one of the three original tribes of ancient Rome **c** : PHYLE **2** : a group of persons having a common character, occupation, or interest **3** : a category of taxonomic classification ranking below a subfamily; *also* : a natural group irrespective of taxonomic rank ⟨the cat ~⟩ ⟨rose ~⟩

tribes·man \'trībz-mən\ *n* (1798) : a member of a tribe

tribes·peo·ple \-,pē-pəl\ *n pl* (1888) : members of a tribe

tribo- *comb form* [F, fr. Gk *tribein* to rub; prob. akin to L *terere* to rub — more at THROW] : friction ⟨*triboluminescence*⟩

tri·bo·elec·tric·i·ty \,trī-bō-i-,lek-'tri-sə-tē, ,tri-, -'tris-tē\ *n* (ca. 1917) : a charge of electricity generated by friction (as by rubbing glass with silk) — **tri·bo·elec·tric** \-'lek-trik\ *adj*

tri·bol·o·gy \trī-'bä-lə-jē, tri-\ *n* (1966) : a study that deals with the design, friction, wear, and lubrication of interacting surfaces in relative motion (as in bearings or gears) — **tri·bo·log·i·cal** \,trī-bə-'lä-ji-kəl, ,tri-\ *adj* — **tri·bol·o·gist** \trī-'bä-lə-jist, tri-\ *n*

tri·bo·lu·mi·nes·cence \,trī-bō-,lü-mə-'ne-s°n(t)s, 'tri-\ *n* [ISV] (1889) : luminescence due to friction — **tri·bo·lu·mi·nes·cent** \-s°nt\ *adj*

tri·brach \'trī-,brak\ *n* [L *tribrachys*, fr. Gk, having three short syllables, fr. *tri-* + *brachys* short — more at BRIEF] (1589) : a metrical foot of three short syllables of which two belong to the thesis and one to the arsis — **tri·brach·ic** \trī-'bra-kik\ *adj*

trib·u·late \'tri-byə-,lāt\ *vt* **-lat·ed; -lat·ing** [LL *tribulatus*, pp. of *tribulare*] (ca. 1637) : to cause to endure tribulation

trib·u·la·tion \,tri-byə-'lā-shən\ *n* [ME *tribulacion*, fr. OF, fr. L *tribulation-, tribulatio*, fr. *tribulare* to press, oppress, fr. *tribulum* drag used in threshing, fr. *terere* to rub — more at THROW] (13c) : distress or suffering resulting from oppression or persecution; *also* : a trying experience

tri·bu·nal \trī-'byü-n°l, tri-\ *n* [L, platform for magistrates, fr. *tribunus* tribune] (1526) **1** : ²TRIBUNE **2** : a court or forum of justice **3** : something that decides or determines ⟨the ~ of public opinion⟩

tri·bu·nate \'tri-byə-,nāt, trī-'byü-nət\ *n* (1546) : the office, function, or term of office of a tribune

¹tri·bune \'tri-,byün, tri-'\ *n* [ME, fr. L *tribunus*, fr. *tribus* tribe] (14c) **1** : a Roman official under the monarchy and the republic with the function of protecting the plebeian citizen from arbitrary action by the patrician magistrates **2** : an unofficial defender of the rights of the individual — **tri·bune·ship** \-,ship\ *n*

²tribune *n* [F, fr. It *tribuna*, fr. L *tribunal*] (ca. 1771) : a dais or platform from which an assembly is addressed

¹trib·u·tary \'tri-byə-,ter-ē\ *adj* (14c) **1** : paying tribute to another to acknowledge submission, to obtain protection, or to purchase peace : SUBJECT **2** : paid or owed as tribute **3** : channeling material or supplies into something more inclusive : CONTRIBUTORY

²tributary *n, pl* **-tar·ies** (15c) **1** : a ruler or state that pays tribute to a conqueror **2** : a stream feeding a larger stream or a lake

trib·ute \'tri-(,)byüt, -byət\ *n* [ME *tribut*, fr. L *tributum*, fr. neut. of *tributus*, pp. of *tribuere* to allot, bestow, grant, pay, fr. *tribus* tribe] (14c) **1 a** : a payment by one ruler or nation to another in acknowledgment of submission or as the price of protection; *also* : the tax levied for such a payment **b** (1) : an excessive tax, rental, or tariff imposed by a government, sovereign, lord, or landlord (2) : an exorbitant charge levied by a person or group having the power of coercion **c** : the liability to pay tribute **2 a** : something given or contributed voluntarily as due or deserved; *esp* : a gift or service showing respect, gratitude, or affection ⟨floral ~⟩ **b** : something (as material evidence or a formal attestation) that indicates the worth, virtue, or effectiveness of the one in question ⟨the product is a ~ to their ingenuity⟩ *syn* see ENCOMIUM

tri·car·box·yl·ic \,trī-,kär-,bäk-'si-lik\ *adj* (1894) : containing three carboxyl groups in the molecule ⟨~ acid⟩

tricarboxylic acid cycle *n* (1945) : KREBS CYCLE

¹trice \'tris\ *vt* **triced; tric·ing** [ME *trisen, tricen* to pull, trice, fr. MD *trisen* to hoist, fr. *trise* windlass] (15c) : to haul up or in and lash or secure (as a sail) with a small rope

²trice *n* [ME *trise*, lit., pull, fr. *trisen*] (15c) : a brief space of time : INSTANT — used chiefly in the phrase *in a trice*

tri·ceps \'trī-,seps\ *n, pl* **triceps** [NL *tricipit-, triceps*, fr. L, three-headed, fr. *tri-* + *capit-, caput* head — more at HEAD] (ca. 1704) : a muscle that arises from three heads; *esp* : the great extensor muscle along the back of the upper arm

tri·cer·a·tops \(ˌ)trī-'ser-ə-ˌtäps\ *n, pl* **-tops** *also* **-tops·es** \-ˌtäp-səz\ [NL, fr. *tri-* + Gk *kerat-, keras* horn + *ōps* face — more at HORN, EYE] (1892) : any of a genus (*Triceratops*) of large herbivorous Cretaceous dinosaurs with three horns, a bony hood or crest on the neck, and hoofed toes

-trices *pl of* -TRIX

trich- *or* **tricho-** *comb form* [NL, fr. Gk, fr. *trich-, thrix* hair] : hair : filament ⟨*trichogyne*⟩

tri·chi·a·sis \tri-'kī-ə-səs\ *n* [LL, fr. Gk, fr. *trich-* + *-iasis*] (1661) : a turning inward of the eyelashes often causing irritation of the eyeball

tri·chi·na \tri-'kī-nə\ *n, pl* **-nae** \-(ˌ)nē\ *also* **-nas** [NL, fr. Gk *trichinos* made of hair, fr. *trich-, thrix* hair] (1857) : a small slender nematode worm (*Trichinella spiralis*) that in the larval state is parasitic in the voluntary muscles of flesh-eating mammals (as humans and swine) — **tri·chi·nal** \-n°l\ *adj*

trich·i·nize \'tri-kə-ˌnīz\ *vt* **-nized; -niz·ing** (1864) : to infest with trichinae ⟨*trichinized* pork⟩

trich·i·no·sis \ˌtri-kə-'nō-səs\ *n* [NL] (1866) : infestation with or disease caused by trichinae and marked esp. by muscular pain, dyspnea, fever, and edema

tri·chi·nous \'tri-kə-nəs, tri-'kī-\ *adj* [ISV] (1857) **1** : infested with trichinae ⟨~ meat⟩ **2** : of, relating to, or involving trichinae or trichinosis ⟨~ infection⟩

tri·chlor·fon *also* **tri·chlor·phon** \(ˌ)trī-'klȯr-ˌfän, -'klȯr-\ *n* [*tri-* + *chlor-* + *-fon* (irreg. fr. *phosphonate* — a salt derived from phosphine)] (1960) : a crystalline compound $C_4H_8Cl_3O_4P$ used esp. as an insecticide

tri·chlo·ro·ace·tic acid \ˌtrī-ˌklȯr-ō-ə-'sē-tik-, -ˌklȯr-\ *n* [ISV] (1885) : a strong vesicant pungent acid $C_2Cl_3HO_2$ used in weed control and in medicine as a caustic and astringent

tri·chlo·ro·eth·y·lene \-'e-thə-ˌlēn\ *n* (ca. 1919) : a nonflammable liquid C_2HCl_3 used esp. as a solvent and in dry cleaning and for the removal of grease from metal

tricho·cyst \'tri-kə-ˌsist\ *n* (1859) : any of the minute lassoing or stinging organelles of protozoans and esp. of many ciliates

tricho·gyne \-ˌjīn, -ˌgīn\ *n* [ISV] (ca. 1875) : a slender terminal prolongation of the ascogonium of a fungus or lichen that may serve as a fertilization tube; *also* : a similar reproductive structure in a red alga

tri·chol·o·gist \tri-'kä-lə-jist\ *n* (1883) : a person who cares for and dresses hair : HAIRDRESSER — **tri·chol·o·gy** \-jē\ *n*

tri·chome \'tri-ˌkōm, 'trī-\ *n* [G *Trichom,* fr. Gk *trichōma* growth of hair, fr. *trichoun* to cover with hair, fr. *trich-, thrix* hair] (1875) : a filamentous outgrowth; *esp* : an epidermal hair structure on a plant

tricho·mo·na·cide \ˌtri-kə-'mō-nə-ˌsīd\ *n* [*trichomonad* + *-cide*] (1949) : an agent used to destroy trichomonads — **tricho·mo·na·cid·al** \-ˌmō-nə-'si-d°l\ *adj*

tricho·mo·nad \ˌtri-kə-'mō-ˌnad, -nəd\ *n* [NL *Trichomonad-, Trichomonas,* fr. *trich-* + LL *monad-, monas* monad] (1861) : any of a genus (*Trichomonas*) of flagellated protozoans parasitic in many animals — **trichomonad** *or* **tricho·mo·nal** \-'mō-n°l\ *adj*

tricho·mo·ni·a·sis \ˌtri-kə-mə-'nī-ə-səs\ *n, pl* **-a·ses** \-ˌsēz\ [NL, fr. *Trichomonas* + *-iasis*] (1915) : infection with or disease caused by trichomonads: as **a** : a human sexually transmitted disease occurring esp. as vaginitis with a persistent discharge and caused by a trichomonad (*Trichomonas vaginalis*) that may also invade the male urethra and bladder **b** : a venereal disease of domestic cattle marked by abortion and sterility **c** : one or more diseases of various birds resembling blackhead — called also *roup*

tri·chop·ter·an \tri-'käp-tə-rən\ *n* [ultim. fr. Gk *trich-, thrix* hair + *pteron* wing — more at FEATHER] (ca. 1842) : CADDIS FLY — **trichopteran** *adj*

tricho·the·cene \ˌtri-kə-'thē-ˌsēn\ *n* [NL *Trichothecium* (fr. *trich-* + *-thecium*) + E *-ene*] (1971) : any of several mycotoxins that are produced by imperfect fungi (genera *Fusarium* and *Trichothecium*) and that include some contaminants of livestock feed and some held to be found in yellow rain

tri·chot·o·mous \trī-'kä-tə-məs\ *adj* [LGk *trichotomein* to trisect, fr. Gk *tricha* in three (akin to *treis* three) + *-tomein* (akin to *temnein* to cut) — more at THREE, TOME] (1800) : divided or dividing into three parts or into threes ⟨~ branching⟩ — **tri·chot·o·mous·ly** *adv*

tri·chot·o·my \-mē\ *n, pl* **-mies** (1610) : division into three parts, elements, or classes

tri·chro·mat \'trī-krō-ˌmat, (ˌ)trī-'\ *n* [back-formation fr. *trichromatic*] (1929) : a person with trichromatism

tri·chro·mat·ic \ˌtrī-krō-'ma-tik\ *adj* (ca. 1890) **1** : of, relating to, or consisting of three colors ⟨~ light⟩ **2 a** : relating to or being the theory that human color vision involves three types of retinal sensory receptors **b** : characterized by trichromatism ⟨~ vision⟩

tri·chro·ma·tism \(ˌ)trī-'krō-mə-ˌti-zəm\ *n* (ca. 1895) : color vision based on the perception of three primary colors and esp. red, green, and blue

¹**trick** \'trik\ *n* [ME *trik,* fr. ONF *trique,* fr. *trikier* to deceive, cheat, fr. (assumed) VL *triccare,* alter. of L *tricari* to behave evasively, shuffle, fr. *tricae* complications, trifles] (15c) **1 a** : a crafty procedure or practice meant to deceive or defraud **b** : a mischievous act : PRANK **c** : an indiscreet or childish action **d** : a deceptive, dexterous, or ingenious feat; *esp* : one designed to puzzle or amuse ⟨a juggler's ~s⟩ **2 a** : a habitual peculiarity of behavior or manner ⟨a horse with the ~ of shying⟩ **b** : a characteristic and identifying feature ⟨a ~ of speech⟩ **c** : a delusive appearance esp. when caused by art or legerdemain ⟨an optical illusion ⟨a mere ~ of the light⟩ **3 a** : a quick or artful way of getting a result : KNACK **b** : a technical device (as of an art or craft) ⟨the ~s of stage technique⟩ **4** : the cards played in one round of a card game often used as a scoring unit **5 a** : a turn of duty at the helm usu. lasting for two hours **b** : SHIFT 4b(1) **c** : a trip taken as part of one's employment **d** : a sexual act performed by a prostitute; *also* : JOHN 2 **6** : an attractive child or woman ⟨a cute little ~⟩
syn TRICK, RUSE, STRATAGEM, MANEUVER, ARTIFICE, WILE, FEINT mean an indirect means to gain an end. TRICK may imply deception, roguishness, illusion, and either an evil or harmless end ⟨the *tricks* of the trade⟩. RUSE stresses an attempt to mislead by a false impression ⟨the

ruses of smugglers⟩. STRATAGEM implies a ruse used to entrap, outwit, circumvent, or surprise an opponent or enemy ⟨the *stratagem*-filled game⟩. MANEUVER suggests adroit and skillful avoidance of difficulty ⟨last-minute *maneuvers* to avert bankruptcy⟩. ARTIFICE implies ingenious contrivance or invention ⟨the clever *artifices* of the stage⟩. WILE suggests an attempt to entrap or deceive with false allurements ⟨used all of his *wiles* to ingratiate himself⟩. FEINT implies a diversion or distraction of attention away from one's real intent ⟨a *feint* toward the enemy's left flank⟩.

²**trick** *vt* (ca. 1511) **1** : to dress or adorn fancifully or ornately : ORNAMENT ⟨~ed out in a gaudy uniform⟩ **2** : to deceive by cunning or artifice : CHEAT *syn* see DUPE

³**trick** *adj* (ca. 1530) **1** : TRIG 2 **a** : of or relating to or involving tricks or trickery ⟨~ photography⟩ ⟨~ dice⟩ **b** : skilled in or used for tricks ⟨a ~ horse⟩ **3 a** : somewhat defective and unreliable ⟨a ~ lock⟩ **b** : inclined to give way unexpectedly ⟨a ~ knee⟩

trick·er \'tri-kər\ *n* (ca. 1553) : one that tricks : TRICKSTER

trick·ery \'tri-k(ə-)rē\ *n* (1800) : the practice of crafty underhanded ingenuity to deceive or cheat *syn* see DECEPTION

trick·ish \'tri-kish\ *adj* (1705) : given to or characterized by tricks or trickery : TRICKY — **trick·ish·ly** *adv* — **trick·ish·ness** *n*

¹**trick·le** \'tri-kəl\ *vi* **trick·led; trick·ling** \-k(ə-)liŋ\ [ME, of imit. origin] (14c) **1 a** : to issue or fall in drops **b** : to flow in a thin gentle stream **2 a** : to move or go one by one or little by little **b** : to dissipate slowly ⟨his enthusiasm *trickled* away⟩

²**trickle** (1580) : a thin, slow, or intermittent stream or movement

trickle–down *adj* (1944) **1** : relating to or working on the principle of trickle-down theory **2** : relating to or being an effect caused gradually by remote or indirect influences

trickle–down theory *n* (1954) : a theory that financial benefits given to big business will in turn pass down to smaller businesses and consumers

trick or treat *n* (ca. 1941) : a children's Halloween practice of asking for treats from door to door under threat of playing tricks on householders who refuse — **trick–or–treat** *vi* — **trick–or–treater** *n*

trick·ster \'trik-stər\ *n* (1711) : one who tricks: as **a** : a dishonest person who defrauds others by trickery **b** : a person (as a stage magician) skilled in the use of tricks and illusion **c** : a deceptive character appearing in various forms in the folklore of many cultures

tricksy \'trik-sē\ *adj* **tricks·i·er; -est** [*tricks,* pl. of *trick*] (1552) **1** *archaic* : smartly attired : SPRUCE **2** : full of tricks : PRANKISH **3 a** *archaic* : having the craftiness of a trickster **b** : difficult to cope with or handle : TRYING ⟨a ~ problem⟩ — **tricks·i·ness** *n*

tricky \'tri-kē\ *adj* **trick·i·er; -est** (1786) **1** : inclined to or marked by trickery **2 a** : giving a deceptive impression of easiness, simplicity, or order : TICKLISH ⟨a ~ path through the swamp⟩ **b** : TRICK 3 **3** : requiring skill, knack, or caution (as in doing or handling) : DIFFICULT; *also* : INGENIOUS ⟨a ~ rhythm⟩ *syn* see SLY — **trick·i·ly** \'tri-kə-lē\ *adv* — **trick·i·ness** \-kē-nəs\ *n*

tri·clad \'trī-ˌklad\ *n* [NL *Tricladida,* fr. *tri-* + Gk *klados* branch — more at CLAD-] (1888) : any of an order (Tricladida) of turbellarian flatworms (as a planarian) that have the intestine composed of a median anterior division and two lateral posterior divisions with side branches — **triclad** *adj*

tri·clin·ic \(ˌ)trī-'kli-nik\ *adj* [ISV] (1854) : having three unequal axes intersecting at oblique angles — used esp. of a crystal

tri·clin·i·um \trī-'kli-nē-əm\ *n, pl* **-ia** \-nē-ə\ [L, fr. Gk *triklinion,* fr. *tri-* + *klinein* to lean, recline — more at LEAN] (1646) **1** : a couch extending round three sides of a table used by the ancient Romans for reclining at meals **2** : a dining room furnished with a triclinium

tric·o·lette \ˌtri-kə-'let\ *n* [*tricot* + *-lette* (as in *flannelette*)] (1919) : a usu. silk or rayon knitted fabric used esp. for women's clothing

¹**tri·col·or** \'trī-ˌkə-lər\ *also* **'trē-,** *esp Brit* **'tri-kə-lər\ *adj* [F *tricolore* three-colored, fr. LL *tricolor,* fr. L *tri-* + *color* color] (1795) **1 a** *or* **tri·col·ored** \'trī-ˌkəl-ərd\ : having, using, or marked with three colors **b** *of a dog* : having a coat of black, tan, and white **2** : of, relating to, or characteristic of a tricolor or a nation whose flag is a tricolor; *esp* : FRENCH

²**tricolor** *n* (1797) **1** : a flag of three colors arranged in equal horizontal or vertical bands ⟨the French ~⟩ **2 a** : a tricolor animal; *esp* : a tricolor dog

tri·corn \'trī-ˌkȯrn\ *adj* [L *tricornis*] (ca. 1844) : having three horns or corners

tri·corne *or* **tri·corn** \'trī-ˌkȯrn\ *n* [F *tricorne,* fr. *tricorne* three-cornered, fr. L *tricornis,* fr. *tri-* + *cornu* horn — more at HORN] (1876) : COCKED HAT 1

tri·cor·nered \'trī-'kȯ(r)-nərd\ *adj* (1819) : having three corners

tri·cot \'trē-(ˌ)kō, 'trī-kət\ *n* [F, fr. *tricoter* to knit, fr. MF, to agitate, hop, ultim. fr. OF *estriquier* to stroke, of Gmc origin; akin to OE *strican* to stroke — more at STRIKE] (1872) **1** : a plain warp-knitted fabric (as of nylon, wool, rayon, silk, or cotton) with a close inelastic knit and used esp. in clothing (as underwear) **2** : a twilled clothing fabric of wool with fine warp ribs or of wool and cotton with fine weft ribs

tri·co·tine \ˌtri-kə-'tēn, ˌtrē-\ *n* [F, fr. *tricot*] (ca. 1899) : a sturdy suiting woven of tightly twisted yarns in a double twill

tric·trac \'trik-ˌtrak\ *n* [F, of imit. origin] (1687) : an old form of backgammon played with pegs

¹**tri·cus·pid** \(ˌ)trī-'kəs-pəd\ *adj* [L *tricuspid-, tricuspis,* fr. *tri-* + *cuspid-, cuspis* point] (1834) : having three cusps ⟨a ~ molar⟩

²**tricuspid** *n* (ca. 1860) : a tricuspid anatomical structure; *esp* : a tooth having three cusps

tricuspid valve *n* (1670) : a valve of three flaps that prevents reflux of blood from the right ventricle to the right atrium

tri·cy·cle \'trī-sə-kəl, -ˌsi-kəl\ *n* [F, fr. *tri-* + Gk *kyklos* wheel — more at WHEEL] (1868) : a 3-wheeled vehicle propelled by pedals or a motor

---

\ə\ abut \ᵊ\ kitten, F table \ər\ further \a\ ash \ā\ ace \ä\ mop, mar \aú\ out \ch\ chin \e\ bet \ē\ easy \g\ go \i\ hit \ī\ ice \j\ job \ŋ\ sing \ō\ go \ȯ\ law \ȯi\ boy \th\ thin \t̲h̲\ the \ü\ loot \ú\ foot \y\ yet \zh\ vision \ä, k̲, ⁿ, œ, œ̄, ue, ue̅, ᵞ\ *see* Guide to Pronunciation

tri·cy·clic \(,)trī-'sī-klik, -'si-klik\ *adj* [*tri-* + *cyclic*] (1891) : being a chemical with three usu. fused rings in the molecular structure and esp. a tricyclic antidepressant

tricyclic antidepressant *n* (1966) : any of a group of antidepressant drugs (as imipramine, amitriptyline, desipramine, and nortriptyline) that potentiate the action of catecholamines and do not inhibit the action of monoamine oxidase — called also *tricyclic*

¹tri·dent \'trī-d°nt\ *adj* [L *trident-, tridens*] (1589) : having three teeth, processes, or points

²trident *n* [L *trident-, tridens*, fr. *trident-, tridens* having three teeth, fr. *tri-* + *dent-, dens* tooth — more at TOOTH] (1599) 1 : a 3-pronged spear serving in classical mythology as the attribute of a sea god (as Neptune) 2 : a 3-pronged spear (as for fishing)

Tri·den·tine \trī-'den-,tin, -,tēn; 'trī-d°n-, trī-\ *adj* [NL *Tridentinus*, fr. L *Tridentum* Trent, Italy] (1561) : of or relating to the Roman Catholic Church council held at Trent from 1545 to 1563

tri·di·men·sion·al \,trī-də-'mench-nəl, -,dī-, -'men(t)-shə-n°l\ *adj* [ISV] (1858) : of, relating to, or concerned with three dimensions ⟨~ space⟩ — **tri·di·men·sion·al·i·ty** \-,men(t)-shə-'na-lə-tē\ *n*

trid·u·um \'tri-jə-wəm, 'tri-dyə-\ *n* [L, space of three days, fr. *tri-* + *-duum* (akin to *dies* day) — more at DEITY] (1873) : a period of three days of prayer usu. preceding a Roman Catholic feast

tried \'trīd\ *adj* [ME, fr. pp. of *trien* to try, test] (15c) 1 : found good, faithful, or trustworthy through experience or testing ⟨a ~ recipe⟩ 2 : subjected to trials or distress ⟨a kind but much-*tried* father⟩

tried–and–true *adj* (1935) : proved good, desirable, or feasible : shown or known to be worthy ⟨a ~ sales technique⟩

tri·ene \'trī-,ēn\ *n* (1917) : a chemical compound containing three double bonds

tri·en·ni·al \(,)trī-'e-nē-əl\ *adj* (1562) 1 : occurring or being done every three years ⟨the ~ convention⟩ 2 : consisting of or lasting for three years ⟨a ~ contract⟩ — **triennial** *n* — **tri·en·ni·al·ly** \-nē-ə-lē\ *adv*

tri·en·ni·um \trī-'e-nē-əm\ *n, pl* **-ni·ums** *or* **-nia** \-nē-ə\ [L, fr. *tri-* + *annus* year — more at ANNUAL] (1847) : a period of three years

tri·er \'trī(-ə)r\ *n* (14c) 1 : someone or something that tries 2 : an implement (as a tapered hollow tube) used in obtaining samples of bulk material for examination and testing

tri·er·arch \'trī(-ə)-,rärk\ *n* [L *trierarchus*, fr. Gk *triērarchos*, fr. *triērēs* trireme (fr. *tri-* + *-ērēs* — akin to L *remus* oar) + *-archos* -arch — more at ROW] (ca. 1656) 1 : the commander of a trireme 2 : an Athenian citizen who had to fit out a trieme for the public service

tri·er·ar·chy \-,rär-kē\ *n* (1837) : the ancient Athenian plan whereby individual citizens furnished and maintained triremes as a civic duty

tri·eth·yl \(,)trī-'e-thəl\ *adj* [ISV] (1858) : containing three ethyl groups in the molecule

tri·fec·ta \trī-'fek-tə, 'trī-,\ *n* [*tri-* + perfecta] (1974) : a variation of the perfecta in which a bettor wins by selecting the first three finishers of a race in the correct order of finish

tri·fid \'trī-,fid, -fəd\ *adj* [L *trifidus* split into three, fr. *tri-* + *findere* to split — more at BITE] (1753) : being deeply and narrowly cleft into three teeth, processes, or points ⟨a spoon with a ~ top⟩

¹tri·fle \'trī-fəl\ *n* [ME *trufle, trifle*, fr. OF *trufe, trufle* mockery] (13c) 1 : something of little value, substance, or importance 2 : a dessert of many varieties typically including plain or sponge cake, sherry, rum, or brandy, jam or jelly, fruit, custard, and whipped cream — **a trifle** : to some small degree : SLIGHTLY ⟨a *trifle* annoyed⟩

²trifle *vb* **tri·fled; tri·fling** \-f(ə-)liŋ\ [ME *truflen, triflen*, fr. OF *trufer, trufler* to mock, trick] *vi* (14c) 1 : to talk in a jesting or mocking manner or with intent to delude or mislead **b** : to treat someone or something as unimportant 2 : to handle something idly ~ *vt* : to spend or waste in trifling or on trifles — **tri·fler** \-f(ə-)lər\ *n*

syn TRIFLE, TOY, DALLY, FLIRT, COQUET mean to deal with or act toward without serious purpose. TRIFLE may imply playfulness, unconcern, indulgent contempt ⟨to *trifle* with a lover's feelings⟩. TOY implies acting without full attention or serious exertion of one's powers ⟨a political novice *toying* with great issues⟩. DALLY suggests indulging in thoughts or plans merely as an amusement ⟨*dallying* with the idea of building a boat someday⟩. FLIRT implies an interest or attention that soon passes to another object ⟨*flirted* with one fashionable ism after another⟩. COQUET implies attracting interest or admiration without serious intention ⟨companies that *coquet* with environmentalism solely for public relations⟩.

tri·fling \'trī-fliŋ\ *adj* (1535) : lacking in significance or solid worth: as **a** : FRIVOLOUS ⟨~ talk⟩ **b** : TRIVIAL ⟨a ~ gift⟩ **c** *chiefly dial* : LAZY, SHIFTLESS ⟨a ~ fellow⟩

tri·fluo·per·a·zine \,trī-,flü-ō-'per-ə-,zēn, -zən\ *n* [*tri-* + *fluor-* + piperazine] (ca. 1957) : a phenothiazine tranquilizer $C_{21}H_{24}F_3N_3S$ used to treat psychotic conditions and esp. schizophrenia

tri·flu·ra·lin \trī-'flur-ə-lən\ *n* [*tri-* + *fluor-* + aniline] (ca. 1961) : an herbicide $C_{13}H_{16}F_3N_3O_4$ used in the control of weeds

¹tri·fo·cal \(,)trī-'fō-kəl\ *adj* (1826) : having three focal lengths

²trifocal *n* (1899) 1 *pl* : eyeglasses with trifocal lenses 2 : a trifocal glass or lens

tri·fo·li·ate \(,)trī-'fō-lē-ət\ *adj* [*tri-* + L *folium* leaf — more at BLADE] (1753) 1 : having three leaves ⟨a ~ plant⟩ 2 : TRIFOLIOLATE

trifoliate orange *n* (ca. 1900) : a Chinese citrus (*Poncirus trifoliata*) with trifoliolate leaves that is widely grown for ornament and esp. as a stock for budding oranges

tri·fo·li·o·late \(,)trī-'fō-lē-ə-,lāt\ *adj* [ISV *tri-* + LL *foliolum* leaflet, dim. of L *folium* leaf] (ca. 1828) : having three leaflets ⟨a ~ leaf⟩ — see LEAF illustration

tri·fo·li·um \trī-'fō-lē-əm\ *n* [NL, fr. L, trefoil — more at TREFOIL] (1541) : CLOVER 1

tri·fo·ri·um \trī-'fōr-ē-əm, -'fòr-\ *n, pl* **-ria** \-ē-ə\ [ML] (1703) : a gallery forming an upper story to the aisle of a church and typically an arcaded story between the nave arches and clerestory

tri·form \'trī-,fòrm\ *adj* [ME *triforme*, fr. L *triformis*, fr. *tri-* + *forma* form] (15c) : having a triple form or nature

tri·fur·cate \(,)trī-'fər-kət, -,kāt; 'trī-(,)fər-,kāt\ *adj* [L *trifurcus*, fr. *tri-* + *furca* fork] (ca. 1831) : having three branches or forks : TRICHOTOMOUS — **tri·fur·cate** \'trī-(,)fər-,kāt, trī-'fər-\ *vi* — **tri·fur·ca·tion** \,trī-(,)fər-'kā-shən\ *n*

¹trig \'trig\ *adj* [ME, trusty, nimble, of Scand origin; akin to ON *tryggr*

faithful; akin to OE *trēowe* faithful — more at TRUE] (1513) 1 : stylishly or jauntily trim 2 : extremely precise : PRIM 3 *dial chiefly Brit* : FIRM, VIGOROUS

²trig *n* [by shortening] (ca. 1895) : TRIGONOMETRY

tri·gem·i·nal \trī-'je-mə-n°l\ *adj* [NL *trigeminus* trigeminal nerve, fr. L, threefold, fr. *tri-* + *geminus* twin] (1872) : of or relating to the trigeminal nerve

trigeminal nerve *n* (1830) : either of a pair or large mixed nerves that are the 5th cranial nerves and supply motor and sensory fibers mostly to the face — called also *trigeminal*

trigeminal neuralgia *n* (1874) : an intense paroxysmal neuralgia involving one or more branches of the trigeminal nerve

¹trig·ger \'tri-gər\ *n* [alter. of earlier *tricker*, fr. D *trekker*, fr. MD *trecker* one that pulls, fr. *trecken* to pull — more at TREK] (1621) 1 **a** : a piece (as a lever) connected with a catch or detent as a means of releasing it; *esp* : the part of the action moved by the finger to fire a gun **b** : a similar movable part by which a mechanism is actuated ⟨~ of a spray gun⟩ 2 : something that acts like a mechanical trigger in initiating a process or reaction — **trigger** *adj* — **trig·gered** \-gərd\ *adj*

²trigger *vb* **trig·gered; trig·ger·ing** \'tri-g(ə-)riŋ\ *vt* (1916) 1 **a** : to release or activate by means of a trigger; *esp* : to fire by pulling a mechanical trigger ⟨~ a rifle⟩ **b** : to cause the explosion of ⟨~ a missile with a proximity fuze⟩ 2 : to initiate, actuate, or set off by a trigger ⟨an indiscreet remark that ~*ed* a fight⟩ ⟨a stimulus that ~*ed* a reflex⟩ ~ *vi* : to release a mechanical trigger

trig·ger·fish \'tri-gər-,fish\ *n* (1849) : any of various deep-bodied bony fishes (family Balistidae, esp. genus *Balistes*) of warm seas having an anterior dorsal fin with two or three stout erectile spines

trig·ger–hap·py \-,ha-pē\ *adj* (1943) 1 : irresponsible in the use of firearms; *esp* : inclined to shoot before clearly identifying the target 2 **a** : inclined to be irresponsible in matters that might precipitate war **b** : aggressively belligerent in attitude

triggerfish

trig·ger·man \-mən, -,man\ *n* (ca. 1930) : a gunman who shoots the victim (as in a gangland murder)

tri·glyc·er·ide \(,)trī-'gli-sə-,rīd\ *n* [ISV] (ca. 1860) : an ester formed from glycerol by reacting all three of its alcohol hydroxy groups with fatty acids

tri·glyph \'trī-,glif\ *n* [L *triglyphus*, fr. Gk *triglyphos*, fr. *tri-* + *glyphein* to carve — more at CLEAVE] (1563) : a slightly projecting rectangular tablet in a Doric frieze with two vertical channels of V section and two corresponding chamfers or half channels on the vertical sides — **tri·glyph·ic** \trī-'gli-fik\ *or* **tri·glyph·i·cal** \-fi-kəl\ *adj*

tri·gon \'trī-,gän\ *n* [L *trigonum*, fr. Gk *trigōnon*, fr. neut. of *trigōnos* triangular, fr. *tri-* + *gōnia* angle — more at -GON] (1563) : TRIPLICITY 1

trig·o·nal \trī-'gō-n°l\ *adj* (1878) : of, relating to, or being the division of the hexagonal crystal system or the forms belonging to it characterized by a vertical axis of threefold symmetry — **tri·go·nal·ly** \-n°l-ē\ *adv*

trig·o·no·met·ric \,tri-gə-nə-'me-trik\ *also* **trig·o·no·met·ri·cal** \-tri-kəl\ *adj* (1690) : of, relating to, or being in accordance with trigonometry — **trig·o·no·met·ri·cal·ly** \-tri-k(ə-)lē\ *adv*

trigonometric function *n* (1909) 1 : a function (as the sine, cosine, tangent, cotangent, secant, or cosecant) of an arc or angle most simply expressed in terms of the ratios of pairs of sides of a right-angled triangle — called also *circular function* 2 : the inverse (as the arcsine, arccosine, or arctangent) of a trigonometric function

trig·o·nom·e·try \,tri-gə-'nä-mə-trē\ *n* [NL *trigonometria*, fr. Gk *trigōnon* + *-metria* -metry] (1614) : the study of the properties of triangles and trigonometric functions and of their applications

tri·gram \'trī-,gram\ *n* (1606) 1 : TRIGRAPH 2 2 : any of the eight possible combinations of three whole or broken lines used esp. in Chinese divination

tri·graph \'trī-,graf\ *n* (ca. 1836) 1 : three letters spelling a single consonant, vowel, or diphthong ⟨*eau* of *beau* is a ~⟩ 2 : a cluster of three successive letters ⟨*the, ion*, and *ing* are high frequency ~s⟩ — **tri·graph·ic** \(,)trī-'gra-fik\ *adj*

tri·halo·meth·ane \,trī-,ha-lō-'me-,thān, *Brit usu* -'mē-\ *n* (1969) : any of various derivatives CHX_3 of methane (as chloroform) that have three halogen atoms per molecule and are formed esp. during the chlorination of drinking water

tri·he·dral \-'hē-drəl\ *adj* (1789) 1 : having three faces ⟨~ angle⟩ 2 : of or relating to a trihedral angle — **trihedral** *n*

tri·hy·brid \-'hī-brəd\ *n* (1903) : an individual or strain that is heterozygous for three pairs of genes — **trihybrid** *adj*

tri·hy·droxy \,trī-hī-'dräk-sē, -hə-\ *adj* [ISV] (1903) : containing three hydroxyl groups in the molecule

tri·io·do·thy·ro·nine \,trī-,ī-ə-dō-'thī-rə-,nēn\ *n* [*tri-* + *iod-* + *thyronine* (an amino acid of which thyroxine is a derivative)] (1952) : an iodine-containing hormone $C_{15}H_{12}I_3NO_4$ that is an amino acid derived from thyroxine

tri·jet \'trī-,jet\ *n* (1967) : an aircraft powered with three jet engines

trike \'trīk\ *n* [by shortening & alter.] (1884) : TRICYCLE

tri·lat·er·al \(,)trī-'la-tə-rəl, -'la-trəl\ *adj* [L *trilaterus*, fr. *tri-* + *later-, latus* side] (1660) : having three sides or parties ⟨~ business ventures⟩ ⟨~ discussions⟩

tril·by \'tril-bē\ *n, pl* **trilbies** [fr. the fact that such a hat was worn in the London stage version of the novel *Trilby* (1894) by George du Maurier] (1897) *chiefly Brit* : a soft felt hat with indented crown

tri·lin·e·ar \(,)trī-'li-nē-ər\ *adj* (1715) : of, relating to, or involving three lines ⟨~ coordinates⟩

tri·lin·gual \-'liŋ-gwəl *also* -'liŋ-gyə-wəl\ *adj* (1834) : consisting of, having, or expressed in three languages; *also* : familiar with or able to use three languages — **tri·lin·gual·ly** *adv*

¹tri·lit·er·al \-'li-t(ə-)rəl\ *adj* [*tri-* + L *littera* letter] (1751) : consisting of three letters and esp. of three consonants ⟨~ roots in Semitic languages⟩ — **tri·lit·er·al·ism** \-t(ə-)rə-,li-zəm\ *n*

²triliteral *n* (ca. 1828) : a root or word that is triliteral

¹trill \'tril\ *vb* [ME, prob. of Scand origin; akin to Sw *trilla* to roll; akin to MD *trillen* to vibrate] *vi* (14c) **1 :** to flow in a small stream or in drops : TRICKLE **2 :** TWIRL, REVOLVE ~ *vt* : to cause to flow in a small stream

²trill *n* [It *trillo* prob. of imit. origin] (1649) **1 a :** the alternation of two musical tones a diatonic second apart — called also *shake* **b :** VIBRATO **c :** a rapid reiteration of the same tone esp. on a percussion instrument **2 :** a sound resembling a musical trill : WARBLE **3 a :** the rapid vibration of one speech organ against another (as of the tip of the tongue against the teethridge) **b :** a speech sound made by a trill

³trill *vi* (ca. 1667): to play or sing with a trill : QUAVER ~ *vt* : to utter as or with or as if with a trill ⟨~ the *r*⟩ — **trill·er** *n*

tril·lion \'tril(l)-yən\ *n* [F, fr. *tri-* + *-illion* (as in *million*)] (ca. 1690) **1** — see NUMBER table **2 :** a very large number — **trillion** *adj* — **trillionth** \-yən(t)th\ *adj or n*

tril·li·um \'tri-lē-əm\ *n* [NL, fr. Sw *trilling* triplet; fr. its three leaves] (ca. 1760): any of a genus (*Trillium*) of herbs of the lily family with an erect stem bearing a whorl of three leaves and a large solitary typically spring-blooming flower

tri·lo·bate \(,)trī-'lō-,bāt\ *adj* (1785): TRILOBED

tri·lobed \'trī-lōbd\ *adj* (1826): having three lobes ⟨a ~ leaf⟩

tri·lo·bite \'trī-lə-,bīt\ *n* [ultim. fr. Gk *trilobos* three-lobed, fr. *tri-* + *lobos* lobe] (1832): any of numerous extinct Paleozoic marine arthropods (group Trilobita) having the segments of the body divided by furrows on the dorsal surface into three lobes

trilobite

tril·o·gy \'tri-lə-jē\ *n, pl* **-gies** [Gk *trilogia*, fr. *tri-* + *-logia* -logy] (ca. 1661): a series of three dramas or literary works or sometimes three musical compositions that are closely related and develop a single theme

¹trim \'trim\ *vb* **trimmed; trim·ming** [prob. fr. (assumed) ME *trimmen* to prepare, put in order, fr. OE *trymian, trymman* to strengthen, arrange, fr. *trum* strong, firm; prob. akin to OE *trēo* tree, wood — more at TREE] *vt* (ca. 1521) **1 :** to embellish with or as if with ribbons, lace, or ornaments ⟨~ the Christmas tree⟩ ⟨the coat was *trimmed* with fur⟩ **2 a :** to administer a beating to : THRASH **b :** DEFEAT ⟨*trimmed* me at chess⟩ **3 a :** to make trim and neat esp. by cutting or clipping ⟨~ the hedges⟩ **b :** to free of excess or extraneous matter by or as if by cutting ⟨~ a budget⟩ ⟨~ down the inventory⟩ **c :** to remove by or as if by cutting ⟨*trimmed* thousands from federal payrolls —*Grit*⟩ **4 a** (1): to cause (as a ship) to assume a desirable position in the water by arrangement of ballast, cargo, or passengers (2): to adjust (as an airplane or submarine) for horizontal movement or for motion upward or downward **b :** to adjust (as cargo or a sail) to a desired position **5 :** to adjust (as one's opinions) for reasons of expediency — often used in the phrase *trim one's sails* ~ *vi* **1 a :** to maintain neutrality between opposing parties or to favor each equally **b :** to change one's views for reasons of expediency **2 :** to assume or cause a boat to assume a desired position in the water ⟨a boat that ~s badly⟩ — **trim one's sails :** to adjust oneself or one's actions to prevailing conditions

²trim *adj* **trim·mer; trim·mest** (ca. 1521) **1** *obs* **:** EXCELLENT, FINE **2 :** ready for service or use; *also* : in good physical condition ⟨keeps ~ by jogging⟩ **3 :** exhibiting neatness, good order, or compactness of line or structure ⟨~ houses⟩ — **trim·ly** *adv* — **trim·ness** *n*

³trim *adv* (1529): in a trim manner : TRIMLY — used chiefly in combination ⟨the *trim*-cut forest vistas —W. M. Thackeray⟩

⁴trim *n* (1590) **1 :** suitable or excellent condition ⟨tries to keep in ~⟩ **2 a :** one's clothing or appearance **b :** material used for ornament or trimming **c :** the lighter woodwork in the finish of a building esp. around openings **d :** the interior furnishings of an automobile **3 a :** the position of a ship or boat esp. with reference to the horizontal; *also* : the difference between the draft of a ship forward and that aft **b :** the relation between the plane of a sail and the direction of the ship **c :** the buoyancy status of a submarine **d :** the attitude of a lighter-than-air craft relative to a fore-and-aft horizontal plane **e :** the attitude with respect to wind axes at which an airplane will continue in level flight with free controls **4 :** something that is trimmed off or cut out **5 :** a haircut that neatens a previous haircut

tri·ma·ran \'trī-mə-,ran, ,trī-mə-'\ *n* [*tri-* + cata*maran*] (1949): a fast pleasure sailboat with three hulls side by side

tri·mer \'trī-mər\ *n* [ISV] (ca. 1930): a polymer formed from three molecules of a monomer — **tri·mer·ic** \trī-'mer-ik\ *adj*

trim·er·ous \'tri-mə-rəs\ *adj* [NL *trimerus*, fr. Gk *tri-* + *meros* part — more at MERIT] (1826): having the parts in threes — used of a flower and often written *3-merous*

tri·mes·ter \(,)trī-'mes-tər, 'trī-,\ *n* [F *trimestre*, fr. L *trimestris* of three months, fr. *tri-* + *mensis* month — more at MOON] (1821) **1 :** a period of three or about three months; *esp* : any of three periods of approximately three months each into which a human pregnancy is divided **2 :** one of three terms into which the academic year is sometimes divided

trim·e·ter \'tri-mə-tər\ *n* [L *trimetrus*, fr. Gk *trimetros* having three measures, fr. *tri-* + *metron* measure — more at MEASURE] (1567): a line of verse consisting of three dipodies or three metrical feet

tri·meth·o·prim \trī-'me-thə-,prim\ *n* [*tri-* + *meth-* + *-prim* (by shortening & alter. fr. *pyrimidine*)] (1964): a synthetic antibacterial and antimalarial drug $C_{14}H_{18}N_4O_3$ often used with a sulfa drug

tri·met·ro·gon \trī-'me-trə-,gän\ *n* [*tri-* + Gk *metron* measure + E *-gon*] (1943): a system of aerial mapping involving the use of sets of one vertical and two oblique aerial photographs taken simultaneously over the area being mapped

trim·mer \'tri-mər\ *n* (1555) **1 a** (1): one that trims articles (2): one that stows coal or freight on a ship so as to distribute the weight properly **b :** an instrument or machine with which trimming is done **c :** a circuit element (as a capacitor) used to tune a circuit to a desired frequency **2 :** a beam that receives the end of a header in floor framing **3 :** a person who modifies a policy, position, or opinion esp. out of expediency

trim·ming *n* (ca. 1518) **1 :** DEFEAT, BEATING **2 :** the act of one who trims **3 a :** a decorative accessory or additional item ⟨~s for a hat⟩ **b :** an additional garnishing ⟨turkey and all the ~s⟩

tri·month·ly \(,)trī-'mən(t)th-lē\ *adj* (1856): occurring every three months

tri·mor·phic \(,)trī-'mór-fik\ *adj* [Gk *trimorphos* having three forms, fr. *tri-* + *-morphos* -morphous] (1866): occurring in or having three distinct forms

tri·mo·tor \'trī-,mō-tər, -'mō-\ *n* (1923): an airplane powered by three engines

trim size *n* (ca. 1929): the actual size (as of a book page) after excess material required in production has been cut off

Tri·mur·ti \tri-'múr-tē\ *n* [Skt *-trimūrti*, fr. *trimūrti* having three forms, fr. *tri-* tri- + *mūrti* body, form] (1810): the great triad of Hindu gods comprising Brahma, Vishnu, and Siva

tri·nal \'trī-nˀl\ *adj* [LL *trinalis*, fr. L *trini* three each] (1590): THREEFOLD

¹trine \'trīn\ *adj* [ME, fr. MF *trin*, fr. L *trinus*, fr. *trini* three each; akin to L *tres* three — more at THREE] (14c) **1 :** THREEFOLD, TRIPLE **2 :** of, relating to, or being the favorable astrological aspect of two celestial bodies 120 degrees apart

²trine *n* (1552) **1 :** a group of three : TRIAD **2 :** the trine astrological aspect of two celestial bodies

trine immersion *n* (1637): the practice of immersing a candidate for baptism three times in the names of the members of the Trinity

trin·i·tar·i·an \,tri-nə-'ter-ē-ən\ *adj* (1628) **1** *cap* **:** of or relating to the Trinity, the doctrine of the Trinity, or adherents to that doctrine **2 :** having three parts or aspects : THREEFOLD

Trinitarian *n* (1628) **1 :** a member of a religious teaching and nursing order for men founded in France in 1198 by John of Matha and Philip of Valois **2 :** one who subscribes to the doctrine of the Trinity — **Trin·i·tar·i·an·ism** \-ē-ə-,ni-zəm\ *n*

tri·ni·tro·tol·u·ene \trī-,nī-trō-'täl-yə-,wēn\ *n* [ISV] (ca. 1900): TNT

Trin·i·ty \'tri-nə-tē\ *n* [ME *trinite*, fr. OF *trinité*, fr. LL *trinitat-, trinitas* state of being threefold, fr. L *trinus* threefold] (13c) **1 :** the unity of Father, Son, and Holy Spirit as three persons in one Godhead according to Christian dogma **2** *not cap* **:** a group of three closely related persons or things **3 :** the Sunday after Whitsunday observed as a feast in honor of the Trinity

Trin·i·ty·tide \-,tīd\ *n* (1511): the season of the church year between Trinity Sunday and Advent

¹trin·ket \'triŋ-kət\ *n* [origin unknown] (ca. 1533) **1 :** a small ornament (as a jewel or ring) **2 :** a small article of equipment **3 :** a thing of little value : TRIFLE

²trinket *vi* [perh. fr. ¹*trinket*] (1646): to deal clandestinely : INTRIGUE — **trin·ket·er** *n*

trin·ket·ry \-kə-trē\ *n* (1810): small items of personal ornament

trin·oc·u·lar \(,)trī-'nä-kyə-lər\ *adj* [*tri-* + *binocular*] (1960): relating to or being a binocular microscope equipped with a lens for photographic recording during direct visual observation

¹tri·no·mi·al \trī-'nō-mē-əl\ *n* [*tri-* + *-nomial* (as in *binomial*)] (1674) **1 :** a polynomial of three terms **2 :** a biological taxonomic name of three terms of which the first designates the genus, the second the species, and the third the subspecies or variety

²trinomial *adj* (ca. 1704) **1 :** consisting of three mathematical terms **2 :** of, relating to, or being a biological trinomial

tri·nu·cle·o·tide \(,)trī-'nü-klē-ə-,tīd, -'nyü-\ *n* (1918): a nucleotide consisting of three mononucleotides in combination : CODON

trio \'trē-(,)ō\ *n, pl* **tri·os** [F, fr. It, fr. *tri-* (fr. L)] (ca. 1724) **1 a :** a musical composition for three voice parts or three instruments **b :** the secondary or episodic division of a minuet or scherzo, a march, or of various dance forms **2 :** the performers of a musical or dance trio **3 :** a group or set of three

tri·ode \'trī-,ōd\ *n* (1922): an electron tube with an anode, a cathode, and a controlling grid

tri·ol \'trē-,ól, -,ōl\ *n* (1936): a chemical compound containing three hydroxyl groups

tri·o·let \'trē-ə-lət, 'trī-\ *n* [F, fr. MF, lit., clover leaf, clover, ultim. fr. Gk *triphyllon*, fr. *tri-* tri- + *phyllon* leaf — more at BLADE] (1651): a poem or stanza of eight lines in which the first line is repeated as the fourth and seventh and the second line as the eighth with a rhyme scheme of *ABaAabAB*

tri·ose \'trī-,ōs, -,ōz\ *n* [ISV] (1894): either of two simple sugars $C_3H_6O_3$ containing three carbon atoms

tri·ox·ide \(,)trī-'äk-,sīd\ *n* [ISV] (ca. 1868): an oxide containing three atoms of oxygen

¹trip \'trip\ *vb* **tripped; trip·ping** [ME *trippen*, fr. MF *triper*, of Gmc origin; akin to OE *treppan* to tread — more at TRAP] *vi* (14c) **1 a :** to dance, skip, or caper with light quick steps **b :** to walk with light quick steps **2 :** to catch the foot against something so as to stumble **3 :** to make a mistake or false step (as in morality or accuracy) **4 :** to stumble in articulation when speaking **5 :** to make a journey **6 :** to run past the pallet of an escapement without previously locking — used of a tooth of the escapement wheel of a watch **7 a :** to actuate a mechanism **b :** to become operative **8 :** to get high on a psychedelic drug (as LSD) : TURN ON — often used with *out* ~ *vt* **1 a :** to cause to stumble — often used with *up* **b :** to cause to fail : OBSTRUCT — often used with *up* **2 :** to detect in a misstep, fault, or blunder; *also* : EXPOSE — usu. used with *up* **3** *archaic* **:** to perform (as a dance) lightly or nimbly **4 :** to raise (an anchor) from the bottom so as to hang free **5 a :** to pull (a yard) into a perpendicular position for lowering **b :** to hoist (a topmast) far enough to enable the fid to be withdrawn preparatory to housing or lowering **6 :** to release or operate (a mechanism) esp. by releasing a catch or detent — **trip the light fantastic :** DANCE

²trip *n* (15c) **1 :** a stroke or catch by which a wrestler is made to lose footing **2 a :** VOYAGE, JOURNEY **b :** a single round or tour on a busi-

\ə\ abut \ᵊ\ kitten, F table \ər\ further \a\ ash \ā\ ace \ä\ mop, mar \aú\ out \ch\ chin \e\ bet \ē\ easy \g\ go \i\ hit \ī\ ice \j\ job \ŋ\ sing \ō\ go \ó\ law \ói\ boy \th\ thin \t̲h̲\ the \ü\ loot \ú\ foot \y\ yet \zh\ vision \ä, k̲, ⁿ, œ, œ̄, ᴜe, ūe, ᵫ\ *see* Guide to Pronunciation ness errand **3** : ERROR, MISSTEP **4** : a quick light step **5** : a faltering step caused by stumbling **6 a** : the action of tripping mechanically **b** (1) : a device for tripping a mechanism (as a catch or detent) (2) : TUP 2 **7** : an intense visionary experience undergone by a person who has taken a psychedelic drug (as LSD) **8** : absorption in or obsession with an interest, attitude, or state of mind ⟨a guilt ∼⟩ ⟨on a nostalgia ∼⟩ **9** : SCENE, LIFESTYLE

tri·pack \'trī-ˌpak\ n (1911) : a combination of three superposed films or emulsions each sensitive to a different primary color for simultaneous exposure in one camera

tri·par·tite \(ˌ)trī-'pär-ˌtīt\ adj [ME, fr. L tripartitus, fr. tri- + partitus divided — more at PARTITE] (15c) **1** : divided into or composed of three parts **2** : having three corresponding parts or copies **3** : made between or involving three parties ⟨a ∼ treaty⟩

tripe \'trīp\ n [ME, fr. MF] (14c) **1** : stomach tissue of a ruminant and esp. of the ox used as food **2** : something poor, worthless, or offensive

¹trip·ham·mer \'trip-ˌha-mər\ n (1781) : a massive power hammer having a head that is tripped and allowed to fall by cam or lever action

²trip–hammer adj (ca. 1864) : suggesting a trip-hammer in loud pounding or persistent action

tri·phe·nyl·meth·ane \ˌtrī-ˌfe-nᵊl-'me-ˌthān, -ˌfē-\ n [ISV] (ca. 1885) : a crystalline hydrocarbon $CH(C_6H_5)_3$ that is the parent compound of many dyes

tri·phos·phate \(ˌ)trī-'fäs-ˌfāt\ n (ca. 1826) : a salt or acid that contains three phosphate groups — compare ATP, GTP

tri·phos·pho·pyr·i·dine nucleotide \ˌtrī-ˌfäs-fō-'pir-ə-ˌdēn-\ n (1937) : NADP

triph·thong \'trif-ˌthȯŋ, 'trip-\ n [tri- + -phthong (as in diphthong)] (ca. 1599) **1** : a phonological unit consisting of three successive vocalic sounds in one syllable **2** : TRIGRAPH — **triph·thon·gal** \trif-'thȯŋ-gəl, trip-, -əl\ adj

tri·pin·nate \(ˌ)trī-'pi-ˌnāt\ adj (ca. 1760) : bipinnate with each division pinnate — **tri·pin·nate·ly** adv

tri·plane \'trī-ˌplān\ n (1909) : an airplane with three main supporting surfaces superposed

¹tri·ple \'tri-pəl\ vb **tri·pled; tri·pling** \-p(ə-)liŋ\ [ME, fr. L triplare, fr. L triplus, adj.] vt (14c) **1** : to make three times as great or as many **2 a** : to score (a base runner) by a triple **b** : to bring about the scoring of (a run) by a triple ∼ vi **1** : to become three times as great or as numerous **2** : to make a triple in baseball

²triple n [ME, fr. L triplus, adj.] (15c) **1 a** : a triple sum, quantity, or number **b** : a combination, group, or series of three **2** : a base hit that allows the batter to reach third base safely **3** : TRIFECTA

³triple adj [MF or L; MF, fr. L triplus, fr. tri- + -plus multiplied by — more at -FOLD] (1550) **1** : being three times as great or as many **2** : having three units or members **3** : having a threefold relation or character ⟨worked as a double or even ∼ agent —Time⟩ **4** : three times repeated : TREBLE **5** : marked by three beats per musical measure ⟨∼ meter⟩ **6 a** : having units of three components ⟨∼ feet⟩ **b** of rhyme : involving correspondence of three syllables (as in unfortunate-importunate)

triple bond n (1889) : a chemical bond in which three pairs of electrons are shared by two atoms in a molecule — compare DOUBLE BOND, SINGLE BOND

triple counterpoint n (ca. 1869) : three-part musical counterpoint so written that any part may be transposed above or below any other

Triple Crown n (ca. 1897) **1** : an unofficial title in horse racing representing the championship achieved by a horse that wins the three classic races for a designated category **2** : the unofficial title signifying the achievement of a baseball player who at the end of a season leads the league in batting average, home runs, and runs batted in

tri·ple–deck·er \ˌtri-pəl-'de-kər\ n, often attrib (1938) : something having three basic components or levels: as **a** : TRILOGY **b** : a sandwich consisting of three pieces of bread and two layers of filling **c** : a 3-story dwelling with an apartment on each floor

tri·ple–head·er \-'he-dər\ n (ca. 1949) : a program consisting of three consecutive games, contests, or events

triple jump n (1964) : a jump for distance in track-and-field athletics usu. from a running start and combining a hop, a stride, and a jump in succession — **triple jumper** n

triple play n (1869) : a play in baseball by which three players are put out

triple point n (1872) : the condition of temperature and pressure under which the gaseous, liquid, and solid phases of a substance can exist in equilibrium

triple sec \-'sek\ n [fr. Triple Sec, a trademark] (1943) : a colorless orange-flavored liqueur

tri·ple–space \ˌtri-pəl-'spās\ vt (ca. 1939) : to type (text) leaving two blank lines between lines of copy ∼ vi : to type on every third line

trip·let \'tri-plət\ n [²triple] (1656) **1** : a unit of three lines of verse **2 a** : a combination, set, or group of three **b** : a group of three elementary particles (as positive, negative, and neutral pions) with different charge states but otherwise similar properties **c** : an atom or molecule with an even number of electrons that have a net magnetic moment **d** : CODON **3** : one of three children or offspring born at one birth **4** : a group of three musical notes or tones performed in the time of two of the same value

tri·ple–tail \'tri-pəl-ˌtāl\ n (ca. 1803) : a large marine bony fish (Lobotes surinamensis of the family Lobotidae) of warm and tropical waters that has long dorsal and anal fins which extend backward and together with the caudal fin appear like a 3-lobed tail

triple threat n (1924) **1** : a football player adept at running, kicking, and passing **2** : a person adept in three different fields of activity — **triple–threat** adj

tri·ple–tongue \ˌtri-pəl-'təŋ\ vi (1879) : to articulate the notes of triplets in fast tempo on a wind instrument by using the tongue positions esp. for t, k, t for the notes of each successive triplet

¹tri·plex \'trī-ˌpleks, 'trī-\ n (1601) : something (as an apartment) that is triplex

²triplex adj [L, fr. tri- + -plex -fold — more at -FOLD] (1655) **1** : THREEFOLD, TRIPLE ⟨∼ windows⟩ **2** : having three apartments, floors, or sections ⟨∼ buildings⟩ ⟨∼ apartments⟩ ⟨a ∼ theater⟩

¹trip·li·cate \'tri-pli-kət\ adj [ME, fr. L triplicatus, pp. of triplicare to triple, fr. triplic-, triplex threefold] (15c) : consisting of or existing in three corresponding or identical parts or examples ⟨∼ invoices⟩

²trip·li·cate \-plə-ˌkāt\ vt **-cat·ed; -cat·ing** (ca. 1623) **1** : to make triple or threefold **2** : to prepare in triplicate — **trip·li·ca·tion** \ˌtri-plə-'kā-shən\ n

³trip·li·cate \-pli-kət\ n (1810) : three copies all alike — used with in ⟨typed in ∼⟩

tri·plic·i·ty \tri-'pli-sə-tē, trī-\ n, pl **-ties** [ME triplicite, fr. LL triplicitas condition of being threefold, fr. L triplic-, triplex] (14c) **1** : one of the groups of three signs each distant 120 degrees from the other two into which the signs of the zodiac are divided — called also trigon **2** : the quality or state of being triple or threefold

trip·lo·blas·tic \ˌtri-plō-'blas-tik\ adj [L triplus + E -o- + -blastic] (ca. 1888) : having three primary germ layers

trip·loid \'tri-ˌplȯid\ adj [ISV, fr. L triplus triple] (1911) : having or being a chromosome number three times the monoploid number — **trip·loid** n — **trip·loi·dy** \-ˌplȯi-dē\ n

tri·ply \'tri-p(ə-)lē\ adv (1660) : in a triple degree, amount, or manner

tri·pod \'trī-ˌpäd\ n [L tripod-, tripus, fr. Gk tripod-, tripous, fr. tripod-, tripous, adj., three-footed, fr. tri- + pod-, pous foot — more at FOOT] (1603) **1** : a vessel (as a cauldron) resting on three legs **2** : a stool, table, or altar with three legs **3** : a three-legged stand (as for a camera) — **tripod** or **tri·po·dal** \'trī-pə-dᵊl, 'trī-ˌpä-\ adj

trip·o·li \'tri-pə-lē\ n [F, fr. Tripoli, region of Africa] (ca. 1601) **1** : an earth consisting of very friable soft schistose deposits of silica and including diatomite and kieselguhr **2** : an earth consisting of friable dustlike silica not of diatomaceous origin

tri·pos \'trī-ˌpäs\ n [modif. of L tripus] (1589) **1** archaic : TRIPOD **2** [fr. the three-legged stool occupied by a participant in a disputation at the degree ceremonies] : a final honors examination at Cambridge university orig. in mathematics

trip·per \'tri-pər\ n (1813) **1** chiefly Brit : one that takes a trip : TOURIST **2** : a tripping device (as for operating a railroad signal)

trip·ping·ly \'tri-piŋ-lē\ adv (1600) : in a nimble or lively manner ⟨the new name . . . may not roll ∼ off the tongue —Paul B. Carroll⟩

trip·py \'tri-pē\ adj (1968) : of, relating to, or suggesting a trip on psychedelic drugs or the culture associated with such drugs

trip·tych \'trip-(ˌ)tik\ n [Gk triptychos having three folds, fr. tri- + ptychē fold] (1731) **1** : an ancient Roman writing tablet with three waxed leaves hinged together **2 a** : a picture (as an altarpiece) or carving in three panels side by side **b** : something composed or presented in three parts or sections; esp : TRILOGY

trip wire n (1916) **1** : a low-placed concealed wire used esp. in warfare to trip an enemy or trespasser and usu. to trigger an alarm or explosive device when moved **2** : something (as a small military force) intended to function like a trip wire (as to set a larger military force in motion)

tri·que·trous \trī-'kwē-trəs, -'kwe-\ adj [L triquetrus three-cornered, fr. tri- + -quetrus; prob. akin to OHG waz sharp — more at WHET] (ca. 1879) : having three acute angles ⟨∼ stem⟩

tri·ra·di·ate \(ˌ)trī-'rā-dē-ət, -dē-ˌāt\ adj (1846) : having three rays or radiating branches ⟨a ∼ sponge spicule⟩

tri·reme \'trī-ˌrēm\ n [L triremis, fr. tri- + remus oar — more at ROW] (1601) : an ancient galley having three banks of oars

tri·sac·cha·ride \(ˌ)trī-'sa-kə-ˌrīd\ n [ISV] (ca. 1899) : a sugar that yields on complete hydrolysis three monosaccharide molecules

tri·sect \'trī-ˌsekt, trī-'\ vt [tri- + intersect] (1695) : to divide into three usu. equal parts — **tri·sec·tion** \ˌtrī-'sek-shən, trī-'\ n — **tri·sec·tor** \'trī-ˌsek-tər, trī-'\ n

tri·shaw \'trī-ˌshȯ\ n [tri- + rickshaw] (1946) : PEDICAB

tris·kai·deka·pho·bia \ˌtris-ˌkī-ˌde-kə-'fō-bē-ə, ˌtris-kə-\ n [NL, fr. Gk treiskaideka thirteen (fr. treis three + kai and + deka ten) + NL phobia — more at THREE, TEN] (ca. 1911) : fear of the number 13

tri·skel·i·on \trī-'ske-lē-ən, trī-\ or **tri·skele** \'trī-ˌskēl, 'trī-\ n [triskelion fr. NL, fr. Gk triskelēs three-legged, fr. tri- + skelos leg; triskele fr. Gk triskelēs — more at ISOSCELES] (1857) : a figure composed of three usu. curved or bent branches radiating from a center

tris·mus \'triz-məs\ n [NL, fr. Gk trismos gnashing (of teeth), fr. trizein to squeak, gnash; akin to L stridēre to creak — more at STRIDENT] (ca. 1693) : spasm of the muscles of mastication : LOCKJAW

tris·oc·ta·he·dron \ˌtri-ˌsäk-tə-'hē-drən\ n [Gk tris thrice + E octahedron — more at TER-] (ca. 1847) : a solid (as a crystal) having 24 congruent faces meeting on the edges of a regular octahedron

triskelion

tri·so·di·um phosphate \ˌtrī-ˌsō-dē-əm-\ n (1923) : a crystalline compound Na_3PO_4 that is used esp. in cleaning compositions

tri·so·my \'trī-ˌsō-mē\ n, pl **-mies** [tri- + ³-some + ²-y] (1930) : the condition (as in Down's syndrome) of having one or a few chromosomes triploid in an otherwise diploid set — **tri·so·mic** \(ˌ)trī-'sō-mik\ adj or n

Tris·tan \'tris-tən, -ˌtän, -ˌtan\ n : TRISTRAM

tri·state \'trī-ˌstāt, -ˌstāt\ adj (1900) : of, relating to, or consisting of three adjoining states ⟨the ∼ area⟩

triste \'trēst\ adj [F, fr. L tristis] (1756) : SAD, MOURNFUL; also : WISTFUL

tri·stea·rin \(ˌ)trī-'stē-ə-rən, -'sti(-ə)r-ən\ n [ISV] (ca. 1856) : the crystallizable triglyceride $C_{57}H_{110}O_6$ of stearic acid that is found esp. in hard fats

tris·te·za \tri-'stā-zə\ n [Pg, lit., sadness, fr. L tristitia, fr. tristis sad] (ca. 1902) : a highly infectious virus disease of citrus trees grafted on sour orange rootstocks that is characterized by rotting of the rootlets and eventually causes the death of the trees

trist·ful \'trist-fəl\ adj [ME trist sad, fr. MF triste] (15c) : SAD, MELANCHOLY — **trist·ful·ly** \-fə-lē\ adv — **trist·ful·ness** n

tri·stim·u·lus \(ˌ)trī-'stim-yə-ləs\ adj (1933) : of or relating to values giving the amounts of the three colored lights red, green, and blue that when combined additively produce a match for the color being considered

Tris·tram \'tris-trəm\ n [ME Tristrem, fr. AF Tristan, fr. OW Trystan] : the lover of Isolde of Ireland and husband of Isolde of Brittany in medieval legend

tri·sub·sti·tut·ed \'trī-'səb-stə-₁tü-təd, -₁tyü-\ *adj* (ca. 1899) : having three substituent atoms or groups in the molecule

tri·sul·fide \-'səl-₁fīd\ *n* (1866) : a compound of an element or radical with three atoms of sulfur

tri·syl·lab·ic \₁trī-sə-'la-bik\ *adj* [L *trisyllabus*, fr. Gk *trisyllabos*, fr. *tri- + syllabē* syllable] (1637) : having three syllables ⟨a ~ word⟩

tri·syl·la·ble \'trī-₁si-lə-bəl, (₁)trī-'\ *n* (1589) : a word of three syllables

trite \'trīt\ *adj* **trit·er; trit·est** [L *tritus*, fr. pp. of *terere* to rub, wear away — more at THROW] (1548) : hackneyed or boring from much use : not fresh or original — **trite·ly** *adv* — **trite·ness** *n*

syn TRITE, HACKNEYED, STEREOTYPED, THREADBARE mean lacking the freshness that evokes attention or interest. TRITE applies to a once effective phrase or idea spoiled from long familiarity ("you win some, you lose some" is a *trite* expression). HACKNEYED stresses being worn out by overuse so as to become dull and meaningless ⟨all of the metaphors and images in the poem are *hackneyed*⟩. STEREOTYPED implies falling invariably into the same pattern or form ⟨views of minorities that are *stereotyped* and out-of-date⟩. THREADBARE applies to what has been used until its possibilities of interest have been totally exhausted ⟨a mystery novel with a *threadbare* plot⟩.

tri·the·ism \'trī-thē-₁i-zəm\ *n* (1678) : the doctrine that the Father, Son, and Holy Spirit are three distinct Gods — **tri·the·ist** \-(₁)thē-ist\ *n or adj* — **tri·the·is·tic** \₁trī-thē-'is-tik\ *or* **tri·the·is·ti·cal** \-'is-ti-kəl\ *adj*

tri·thing \'trī-thin\ *n* [ME, alter. of (assumed) OE *thrithing, thriding*] (13c) *archaic* : ³RIDING 1

tri·ti·at·ed \'tri-tē-₁ā-təd, 'tri-shē-\ *adj* (1953) : containing and esp. labeled with tritium

trit·i·ca·le \₁tri-tə-'kā-lē\ *n* [NL, blend of *Triticum*, genus of wheat, and *Secale*, genus of rye] (1952) : an amphidiploid hybrid between wheat and rye that has a high yield and rich protein content

tri·ti·um \'tri-tē-əm, 'tri-shē-\ *n* [NL, fr. Gk *tritos* third — more at THIRD] (1933) : a radioactive isotope of hydrogen with atoms of three times the mass of ordinary light hydrogen atoms

trit·o·ma \'tri-tə-mə\ *n* [NL, genus name, fr. Gk *tritomos* thrice cut, fr. *tri- + temnein* to cut; fr. their trimerous flowers — more at TOME] (1804) : any of a genus (*Kniphofia*) of African herbs of the lily family that are often grown for their spikes of showy red or yellow flowers

¹tri·ton \'trī-t³n\ *n* [L, fr. Gk *Tritōn*] **1** *cap* : a son of Poseidon described as a demigod of the sea with the lower part of his body like that of a fish **2** [NL, genus name, fr. L *Triton*] : any of various large marine gastropod mollusks (esp. family Ranellidae) with a heavy elongated conical shell; *also* : the shell

²tri·ton \'tri-₁tän\ *n* [*tritium + ²-on*] (1934) : the nucleus of tritium

tri·tone \'trī-₁tōn\ *n* [Gk *tritonon*, fr. *tri- + tonos* tone] (1609) : a musical interval of three whole steps

¹trit·u·rate \'tri-chə-₁rāt\ *vt* **-rat·ed; -rat·ing** [LL *trituratus*, pp. of *triturare* to thresh, fr. L *tritura* act of rubbing, threshing, fr. *tritus*, pp. — more at TRITE] (ca. 1755) **1** : CRUSH, GRIND **2** : to pulverize and comminute thoroughly by rubbing or grinding — **trit·u·ra·ble** \'tri-chə-rə-bəl\ *adj* — **trit·u·ra·tor** \-₁rā-tər\ *n*

²trit·u·rate \-rət\ *n* (ca. 1891) : a triturated substance : TRITURATION 2

trit·u·ra·tion \₁tri-chə-'rā-shən\ *n* (1646) **1** : the act or process of triturating : the state of being triturated : COMMINUTION **2** : a triturated medicinal powder made by triturating a substance with a diluent

¹tri·umph \'trī-əm(p)f\ *n, pl* **tri·umphs** \-əm(p)fs, -əm(p)fts\ [ME *triumphe*, fr. MF, fr. L *triumphus*] (14c) **1** : a ceremony attending the entering of Rome by a general who had won a decisive victory over a foreign enemy — compare OVATION 1 **2** : the joy or exultation of victory or success **3 a** : a victory or conquest by or as if by military force **b** : a notable success — **tri·um·phal** \trī-'əm(p)-fəl\ *adj*

²triumph *vi* (1508) **1** : to obtain victory : PREVAIL **2 a** : to receive the honor of a triumph **b** : to celebrate victory or success boastfully or exultingly

tri·um·phal·ism \trī-'əm(p)-fə-₁li-zəm\ *n* (1964) : the doctrine, attitude, or belief that one religious creed is superior to all others — **tri·um·phal·ist** \-fə-list\ *n or adj*

tri·um·phant \trī-'əm(p)-fənt\ *adj* (15c) **1** : VICTORIOUS, CONQUERING **2** *archaic* : of or relating to a triumph **3** : rejoicing for or celebrating victory **4** : notably successful — **tri·um·phant·ly** *adv*

tri·um·vir \trī-'əm-vər\ *n, pl* **-virs** *also* **-vi·ri** \-və-₁rī, -₁rē\ [L, backformation fr. *triumviri*, pl., commission of three men, fr. *trium virum* of three men] (ca. 1580) : one of a commission or ruling body of three

tri·um·vi·rate \-və-rət\ *n* (1584) **1** : a body of triumvirs **2** : the office or government of triumvirs **3** : a group or association of three

¹tri·une \'trī-₁yün\ *n, often cap* [L *tri- + unus* one — more at ONE] (1605) : TRINITY 1

²triune *adj* (1635) : three in one: **a** *often cap* : of or relating to the Trinity ⟨the ~ God⟩ **b** : consisting of three parts, members, or aspects

tri·va·lent \(₁)trī-'vā-lənt\ *adj* [ISV] (1868) **1** : having a chemical valence of three **2** : reacting immunologically with three different combining sites (as of antigens or antibodies) ⟨~ oral polio vaccine⟩

triv·et \'tri-vət\ *n* [ME *trevet*, fr. OE *trefet*, prob. modif. of LL *triped-, tripes*, fr. L, three-footed, fr. *tri- + ped-, pes* foot — more at FOOT] (bef. 12c) **1** : a three-legged stand : TRIPOD **2** : a usu. metal stand with short feet for use under a hot dish at table

triv·ia \'tri-vē-ə\ *n pl but sing or pl in constr* [(assumed) NL, backformation fr. L *trivialis*] (1920) : unimportant matters : trivial facts or details; *also, sing in constr* : a quizzing game involving obscure facts

triv·i·al \'tri-vē-əl\ *adj* [L *trivialis* found everywhere, commonplace, fr. *trivium* crossroads, fr. *tri- + via* way — more at WAY] (1589) **1** : COMMONPLACE, ORDINARY **2 a** : of little worth or importance **b** : relating to or being the mathematically simplest case; *specif* : characterized by having all variables equal to zero ⟨a ~ solution to a linear equation⟩ **3** : SPECIFIC 4 — **triv·i·al·ist** \-ə-list\ *n* — **triv·i·al·ly** \-ə-lē\ *adv*

triv·i·al·ise *Brit var of* TRIVIALIZE

triv·i·al·i·ty \₁tri-vē-'a-lə-tē\ *n, pl* **-ties** (1598) **1** : the quality or state of being trivial **2** : something trivial : TRIFLE

triv·i·al·ize \'tri-vē-ə-₁līz\ *vt* **-ized; -iz·ing** (1846) : to make trivial : reduce to triviality — **triv·i·al·i·za·tion** \₁tri-vē-ə-lə-'zā-shən\ *n*

trivial name *n* (1759) **1** : SPECIFIC EPITHET **2** : a common or vernacular name of an organism or chemical

triv·i·um \'tri-vē-əm\ *n, pl* **triv·ia** \-vē-ə\ [ML, fr. L, meeting of three ways, crossroads] (1804) : a group of studies consisting of grammar, rhetoric, and logic and forming the lower division of the seven liberal arts in medieval universities — compare QUADRIVIUM

¹tri·week·ly \(₁)trī-'wē-klē\ *adj* (1832) **1** : occurring or appearing three times a week **2** : occurring or appearing every three weeks — **triweekly** *adv*

²triweekly *n, pl* **-lies** (1851) : a triweekly publication

-trix *n suffix, pl* **-trices** *or* **-trixes** [ME, fr. L, fem. of *-tor*, suffix denoting an agent] **1** : female that does or is associated with a (specified) thing ⟨avia*trix*⟩ **2** : geometric line, point, or surface ⟨genera*trix*⟩

tRNA \₁tē-₁är-₁en-'ā, ₁tē-₁är-₁en-₁ā\ *n* (1962) : TRANSFER RNA

tro·car *also* **tro·char** \'trō-₁kär\ *n* [F *trocart*, fr. *trois* three (fr. L *tres*) + *carre* side of a sword blade, fr. *carrer* to make square, fr. L *quadrare* — more at THREE, QUADRATE] (ca. 1706) : a sharp-pointed surgical instrument fitted with a cannula and used esp. to insert the cannula into a body cavity as a drainage outlet

tro·cha·ic \trō-'kā-ik\ *adj* [MF *trochaïque*, fr. L *trochaicus*, fr. Gk *trochaikos*, fr. *trochaios* trochee] (1589) : of, relating to, or consisting of trochees — **trochaic** *n*

tro·chan·ter \trō-'kan-tər\ *n* [Gk *trochantēr*; akin to Gk *trechein* to run] (1615) **1** : a rough prominence at the upper part of the femur of many vertebrates **2** : the second segment counting from the base of the leg of an insect — **tro·chan·ter·al** \-tə-rəl\ *adj* — **tro·chan·ter·ic** \₁trō-kən-'ter-ik, -₁kan-\ *adj*

tro·che \'trō-kē, *Brit usu* 'trōsh\ *n* [alter. of earlier *trochisk*, fr. L *trochiscus*, fr. Gk *trochiskos*, fr. dim. of *trochos* wheel] (1597) : a usu. circular medicinal tablet or lozenge for slow dissolution in the mouth; *esp* : one used as a demulcent

tro·chee \'trō-(₁)kē\ *n* [prob. fr. MF *trochée*, fr. L *trochaeus*, fr. Gk *trochaios*, fr. *trochaios* running, fr. *trochē* run, course, fr. *trechein* to run; akin to Gk *trochos* wheel, OIr *droch*] (1589) : a metrical foot consisting of one long syllable followed by one short syllable or of one stressed syllable followed by one unstressed syllable (as in *apple*)

troch·lea \'trä-klē-ə\ *n* [NL, fr. L, block of pulleys, fr. Gk *trochileia*, fr. *trochilos* sheave, fr. *trochos* wheel] (ca. 1693) : an anatomical structure that is held to resemble a pulley; *esp* : the articular surface on the medial condyle of the humerus that articulates with the ulna

troch·le·ar \-ər\ *adj* (ca. 1681) **1** : of, relating to, or being a trochlea **2** : of, relating to, or being a trochlear nerve

trochlear nerve *n* (ca. 1890) : either of the 4th pair of cranial nerves that supply some of the eye muscles with motor fibers — called also *trochlear*

tro·choid \'trō-₁kȯid, 'trä-₁kȯid\ *n* [Gk *trochoeidēs* like a wheel, fr. *trochos* wheel] (ca. 1704) : the curve generated by a point on the radius of a circle or the radius extended as the circle rolls on a fixed straight line — **tro·choi·dal** \trō-'kȯi-d³l, trä-\ *adj*

trocho·phore \'trä-kə-₁fȯr, -₁fȯr\ *n* [ultim. fr. Gk *trochos* wheel + *pherein* to carry — more at BEAR] (1892) : a free-swimming ciliate larva occurring in several invertebrate groups (as the polychaete worms and mollusks)

trod *past and past part of* TREAD

trodden *past part of* TREAD

trof·fer \'trä-fər, 'trȯ-\ *n* [blend of *trough* and *coffer*] (1942) : an inverted trough serving as a support and reflector usu. for a fluorescent lighting unit

trog·lo·dyte \'trä-glə-₁dīt\ *n* [L *troglodytae*, pl., fr. Gk *trōglodytai*, fr. *trōglē* hole, cave (akin to Gk *trōgein* to gnaw, Arm *aracem* I lead to pasture, graze) + *dyein* to enter] (1558) **1** : a member of a primitive people dwelling in caves **2** : a person resembling a troglodyte (as in reclusive habits or outmoded or reactionary attitudes) — **trog·lo·dyt·ic** \₁trä-glə-'di-tik\ *adj*

tro·gon \'trō-₁gän\ *n* [NL, genus name, fr. Gk *trōgōn*, prp. of *trōgein* to gnaw] (1792) : any of numerous nonpasserine tropical birds (family Trogonidae) with brilliant often iridescent plumage

troi·ka \'trȯi-kə\ *n* [Russ *troĭka*, fr. *troe* three; akin to OE *thrīe* three] (1842) **1** : a Russian vehicle drawn by three horses abreast; *also* : a team for such a vehicle **2** : a group of three; *esp* : an administrative or ruling body of three

troi·lite \'trȯi-ə-₁līt, 'trȯi-₁līt\ *n* [G *Troilit*, fr. Domenico *Troili*, 18th cent. Ital. scientist + G *-it -ite*] (ca. 1868) : a mineral that is a variety of pyrrhotite and that is widely but sparsely distributed (as on earth, in meteorites, and in lunar soil samples)

Troi·lus \'trȯi-ləs, 'trȯi-ə-ləs\ *n* [ME, fr. L, fr. Gk *Trōïlos*] : a son of Priam who in medieval legend loved Cressida and lost her to Diomedes

¹Tro·jan \'trō-jən\ *n* [ME, fr. L *trojanus* of Troy, fr. *Troia, Troja* Troy, fr. Gk *Trōïa*] (14c) **1** : a native or inhabitant of Troy **2** : one who shows qualities (as pluck, endurance, or determined energy) attributed to the defenders of ancient Troy **3** : a gay, irresponsible, or disreputable companion

²Trojan *adj* (14c) **1** : of, relating to, or resembling ancient Troy or its inhabitants **2** : of, relating to, or constituting a Trojan horse

Trojan horse *n* [fr. the large hollow wooden horse filled with Greek soldiers and introduced within the walls of Troy by a stratagem] (1837) **1** : someone or something intended to defeat or subvert from within **2** : a seemingly useful computer program that contains concealed instructions which when activated perform an illicit or malicious action (as destroying data files); *also* : the concealed instructions of such a program — compare VIRUS

Trojan War *n* : a 10-year war between the Greeks and Trojans brought on by the abduction of Helen by Paris and ended with the destruction of Troy

¹troll \'trōl\ *vb* [ME] *vt* (15c) **1** : to cause to move round and round : ROLL **2 a** : to sing the parts of (as a round or catch) in succession **b** : to sing loudly **c** : to celebrate in song **3 a** : to fish for by trolling **b** : to fish by trolling in ⟨~ lakes⟩ **c** : to pull through the water in trolling ⟨~ a lure⟩ ~ *vi* **1** : to move around : RAMBLE **2** : to fish

---

\ə\ abut \'ə\ kitten, F table \ər\ further \a\ ash \ā\ ace \ä\ mop, mar
\au̇\ out \ch\ chin \e\ bet \ē\ easy \g\ go \i\ hit \ī\ ice \j\ job
\ŋ\ sing \ō\ go \ȯ\ law \ȯi\ boy \th\ thin \t̲h̲\ the \ü\ loot \u̇\ foot
\y\ yet \zh\ vision \á, k̲, ⁿ, œ, œ̄, œ̆, ūe, ᵞ\ *see* Guide to Pronunciation

by trailing a lure or baited hook from a moving boat   **3** : to sing or play in a jovial manner   **4** : to speak rapidly — **troll·er** *n*
²troll *n* (1869) : a lure or a line with its lure and hook used in trolling
³troll *n* [Norw *troll* & Dan *trold*, fr. ON *troll* giant, demon; prob. akin to MHG *trolle* lout] (1616) : a dwarf or giant in Scandinavian folklore inhabiting caves or hills
¹trol·ley *also* **trol·ly** \'trä-lē\ *n, pl* **trolleys** *also* **trollies** [prob. fr. ¹*troll*] (1823)   **1** *dial Eng* : a cart of any of various kinds   **2 a** : a device that carries electric current from an overhead wire to an electrically driven vehicle   **b** : a streetcar powered electrically through a trolley — called also **trolley car**   **3** : a wheeled carriage running on an overhead rail or track   **4** *chiefly Brit* : a cart or wheeled stand used for conveying something (as food or books)
²trolley *also* **trolly** *vb* **trol·leyed** *also* **trol·lied; trol·ley·ing** *also* **trol·ly·ing** *vt* (1882) : to convey by a trolley ~ *vi* : to ride on a trolley
trol·ley·bus \'trä-lē-,bəs\ *n* (1921) : a bus powered electrically from two overhead wires
trol·lop \'trä-ləp\ *n* [perh. irreg. fr. *trull*] (1621) : a vulgar or disreputable woman; *esp* : one who engages in sex promiscuously or for money
Trombe wall \'trómb-, 'trämb-, 'trōᵐb-\ [Félix *Trombe* 20th cent. Fr. designer] (1978) : a masonry wall that is usu. separated from the outdoors by a glass wall and is designed to absorb solar heat and release it into the interior of a building
trom·bone \träm-'bōn, (,)trəm-', 'träm-,\ *n* [It, aug. of *tromba* trumpet, of Gmc origin; akin to OHG *trumba, trumpa* trumpet] (ca. 1724?) : a brass instrument consisting of a long cylindrical metal tube with two turns and having a movable slide or valves for varying the tone and a usual range one octave lower than that of the trumpet — **trom·bon·ist** \-'bō-nist, -,bō-\ *n*

trombone

trom·mel \'trä-məl\ *n* [G, drum, fr. MHG *trummel*, dim. of *trumme* drum — more at DRUM] (ca. 1877) : a usu. cylindrical or conical revolving screen used esp. for screening or sizing rock, ore, or coal
tromp \'trämp, 'trómp\ *vb* [by alter.] *vi* (1883)   **1** : TRAMP 1 ⟨a lot of knocking on doors, ~*ing* from room to room —Sara Davidson⟩   **2** : to step hard : STAMP ⟨~*ed* on the brake⟩ ~ *vt*   **1** : TRAMP 2 : STAMP ⟨~*s* the accelerator to the floor —Jim Becker⟩   **3 a** : to give a physical beating to   **b** : to defeat decisively
trompe l'oeil \(,)trómp-'lȯi, trōᵐp-lœ̄i\ *n, often attrib* [F *trompe-l'œil*, lit., deceive the eye] (1889)   **1** : a style of painting in which objects are depicted with photographically realistic detail; *also* : the use of similar technique in interior decorating   **2** : a trompe l'oeil painting or effect
-tron *n suffix* [Gk, suffix denoting an instrument; akin to OE *-thor*, suffix denoting an instrument, L *-trum*]   **1** : vacuum tube ⟨magne*tron*⟩   **2** : device for the manipulation of subatomic particles ⟨cyclo*tron*⟩
tro·na \'trō-nə\ *n* [Sw, prob. fr. Ar *natrūn* natron — more at NATRON] (1799) : a gray-white or yellowish white monoclinic mineral consisting of a hydrous acid sodium carbonate
¹troop \'trüp\ *n* [MF *trope, troupe* company, herd, of Gmc origin; akin to OE *thorp, throp* village — more at THORP] (1545)   **1 a** : a group of soldiers   **b** : a cavalry unit corresponding to an infantry company   **c** *pl* : ARMED FORCES, SOLDIERS   **2** : a collection of people or things : CREW 2   **3** : a flock of mammals or birds   **4** : the basic organizational unit of Boy Scouts or Girl Scouts under an adult leader
²troop *vi* (1565)   **1** : to move or gather in crowds   **2** : to go one's way : WALK   **3** : to spend time together : ASSOCIATE   **4** : to move in large numbers
troop·er \'trü-pər\ *n* (1640)   **1 a** (1) : an enlisted cavalryman   (2) : the horse of a cavalryman   **b** : PARATROOPER   **c** : SOLDIER 2   **2 a** : a mounted police officer   **b** : a state police officer   **3** : TROUPER 2
troop·ship \'trüp-,ship\ *n* (1862) : a ship for carrying troops : TRANSPORT
trop- *or* **tropo-** *comb form* [ISV, fr. Gk *tropos*]   **1** : turn : turning : change ⟨*tropo*sphere⟩   **2** : tropism ⟨*tropic*⟩
trope \'trōp\ *n* [L *tropus*, fr. Gk *tropos* turn, way, manner, style, trope, fr. *trepein* to turn] (1533)   **1** : the use of a word or expression in a figurative sense : FIGURE OF SPEECH   **2** : a phrase or verse added as an embellishment or interpolation to the sung parts of the Mass in the medieval period
troph- *or* **tropho-** *comb form* [F, fr. Gk, fr. *trophē* nourishment] : nutritive ⟨*tropho*blast⟩
troph·al·lax·is \,trō-fə-'lak-səs\ *n* [NL, fr. *troph-* + Gk *allaxis* exchange, fr. *allassein* to change, exchange, fr. *allos* other — more at ELSE] (1918) : exchange of food (as from special glands) between social insects (as ants or termites)
tro·phic \'trō-fik\ *adj* [F *trophique*, fr. Gk *trophikos*, fr. *trophē* nourishment, fr. *trephein* to nourish] (1873)   **1** : of or relating to nutrition : NUTRITIONAL ⟨~ disorders⟩   **2** : ³TROPIC — **tro·phi·cal·ly** \-fi-k(ə-)lē\ *adv*
-trophic *adj comb form* [NL *-trophia* -trophy]   **1 a** : of, relating to, or characterized by (such) nutrition ⟨ecto*trophic*⟩   **b** : requiring or utilizing (such) a kind of nutrition ⟨hetero*trophic*⟩   **2** : -TROPIC 2 ⟨gonado*trophic*⟩
trophic level *n* (1942) : one of the hierarchical strata of a food web characterized by organisms which are the same number of steps removed from the primary producers
tro·pho·blast \'trō-fə-,blast\ *n* [ISV] (1889) : a thin layer of ectoderm that forms the wall of many mammalian blastulas and functions in the nutrition and implantation of the embryo — **tro·pho·blas·tic** \,trō-fə-'blas-tik\ *adj*
tro·pho·zo·ite \,trō-fə-'zō-,īt\ *n* [*troph-* + *zo-* + ¹*-ite*] (ca. 1909) : a protozoan of a vegetative form as distinguished from one of a reproductive or resting form
tro·phy \'trō-fē\ *n, pl* **trophies** [MF *trophee*, fr. L *tropaeum, trophaeum*, fr. Gk *tropaion*, fr. neut. of *tropaios* of a turning, of a rout, fr. *tropē* turn, rout, fr. *trepein* to turn] (15c)   **1** : something gained or given in

victory or conquest esp. when preserved or mounted as a memorial   **2 a** : a memorial of an ancient Greek or Roman victory raised on the field of battle or in case of a naval victory on the nearest land   **b** : a representation of such a victory (as on a medal); *also* : an architectural ornament representing a group of military weapons   **3** : a game animal or fish suitable for mounting as a trophy — usu. used attributively — **trophy** *vt*
-trophy *n comb form* [NL *-trophia*, fr. Gk, fr. *trophos* nourishing, fr. *trephein*] : nutrition : nurture : growth ⟨dys*trophy*⟩
¹trop·ic \'trä-pik\ *n* [ME *tropik*, fr. L *tropicus* of the solstice, fr. Gk *tropikos*, fr. *tropē* turn] (1527)   **1** : either of the two parallels of terrestrial latitude at a distance of about 23½ degrees north or south of the equator where the sun is directly overhead when it reaches its most northerly or southerly point in the sky — compare TROPIC OF CANCER, TROPIC OF CAPRICORN   **2** *pl, often cap* : the region lying between the tropics
²tropic *adj* (1551) : of, relating to, or occurring in the tropics : TROPICAL
³tro·pic \'trō-pik\ *adj* [*trop-*] (1903)   **1** : of, relating to, or characteristic of tropism or of a tropism   **2** *of a hormone* : influencing the activity of a specified gland
-tropic *adj comb form* [F *-tropique*, fr. Gk *-tropos* -tropous]   **1** : turning, changing, or tending to turn or change in a (specified) manner or in response to a (specified) stimulus ⟨geo*tropic*⟩   **2** : attracted to or acting upon (something specified) ⟨neuro*tropic*⟩
trop·i·cal *for 1* 'trä-pi-kəl, *for 2* 'trō- *also* 'trä-\ *adj* (1527)   **1 a** : of, relating to, occurring in, or suitable for use in the tropics   **b** : of, being, or characteristic of a region or climate that is frost-free with temperatures high enough to support year-round plant growth given sufficient moisture ⟨~ Florida⟩   **2** [L *tropicus*, fr. Gk *tropikos*, fr. *tropos* trope] : FIGURATIVE 2 — **trop·i·cal·ly** \-pi-k(ə-)lē\ *adv*
tropical aquarium *n* (ca. 1948) : an aquarium kept at a uniform warmth and used esp. for tropical fish
tropical cyclone *n* (1920) : a cyclone in the tropics characterized by winds rotating at the rate of 74 miles (119 kilometers) an hour or more
tropical fish *n* (1931) : any of various small usu. showy fishes of tropical origin often kept in the tropical aquarium
trop·i·cal·ize \'trä-pi-kə-,līz\ *vt* **-ized; -iz·ing** (1885)   **1** : to make tropical (as in character, conditions, or appearance)   **2** : to fit or adapt for use in a tropical climate esp. by measures designed to combat the effects of fungi and moisture
tropical oil *n* (1988) : any of several oils (as coconut oil and palm oil) that are high in saturated fatty acids
tropical rain forest *n* (1926) : RAIN FOREST 1
tropical sprue *n* (ca. 1955) : SPRUE 2
tropical storm *n* (ca. 1945) : a tropical cyclone with strong winds of less than hurricane intensity
tropic bird *n* (ca. 1681) : any of a genus (*Phaethon* of the family Phaethontidae) of web-footed birds that are related to the pelicans, are found chiefly in tropical seas often far from land, and have mostly white satiny plumage marked with a little black, a greatly elongated central pair of tail feathers, and a bright-colored bill
tropic of Cancer [fr. the sign of the zodiac which its celestial projection intersects] (1555) : the parallel of latitude that is approximately 23½ degrees north of the equator and that is the northernmost latitude reached by the overhead sun
tropic of Capricorn [fr. the sign of the zodiac which its celestial projection intersects] (1545) : the parallel of latitude that is approximately 23½ degrees south of the equator and that is the southernmost latitude reached by the overhead sun

tropic bird

-tropin *or* **-trophin** *n comb form* [*-tropin*, alter. of *-trophin*, fr. *-troph*ic + ¹*-in*] : hormone ⟨gonadotropin⟩ ⟨soma*totropin*⟩
tro·pism \'trō-,pi-zəm\ *n* [ISV *-tropism*] (1899)   **1 a** : involuntary orientation by an organism or one of its parts that involves turning or curving by movement or by differential growth and is a positive or negative response to a source of stimulation   **b** : a reflex reaction involving a tropism   **2** : an innate tendency to react in a definite manner to stimuli; *broadly* : a natural inclination : PROPENSITY — **tro·pis·tic** \trō-'pis-tik\ *adj*
-tropism *n comb form* [ISV, fr. *trop-*] : tropism ⟨helio*tropism*⟩
tropo- *see* TROP-
tro·po·col·la·gen \,trä-pə-'kä-lə-jən, ,trō-\ *n* (1954) : a subunit of collagen fibrils consisting of three polypeptide strands arranged in a helix
tro·po·log·i·cal \,trä-pə-'lä-ji-kəl, ,trä-\ *also* **tro·po·log·ic** \-jik\ *adj* (14c)   **1** : of, relating to, or involving biblical interpretation stressing moral metaphor; *also* : MORAL   **2** : characterized or varied by tropes : FIGURATIVE — **tro·po·log·i·cal·ly** \-ji-k(ə-)lē\ *adv*
tropo·my·o·sin \,trä-pə-'mī-ə-sən, ,trō-\ *n* (1946) : a protein of muscle that forms a complex with troponin regulating the interaction of actin and myosin in muscular contraction
tro·po·nin \'trō-pə-nən, 'trä-, -,nin\ *n* [by shortening & alter. fr. *tropomyosin*] (1966) : a protein of muscle that together with tropomyosin forms a regulatory protein complex controlling the interaction of actin and myosin and that when combined with calcium ions permits muscular contraction
tro·po·pause \'trō-pə-,pȯz, 'trä-\ *n* [ISV *troposphere* + *pause*] (1918) : the region at the top of the troposphere; *also* : a comparable layer of a celestial body
tro·po·sphere \'trō-pə-,sfir, 'trä-\ *n* [ISV] (1909) : the lowest densest part of the earth's atmosphere in which most weather changes occur and temperature generally decreases rapidly with altitude and which extends from the surface to the bottom of the stratosphere — **tro·po·spher·ic** \,trō-pə-'sfir-ik, ,trä-, -'sfer-\ *adj*
tro·po·tax·is \,trō-pə-'tak-səs, ,trä-\ *n* [NL] (1934) : a taxis in which an organism orients itself by the simultaneous comparison of stimuli of different intensity acting on separate end organs

-tropous *adj comb form* [Gk *-tropos,* fr. *trepein* to turn] : turning or curving in (such) a way : exhibiting (such) a tropism ⟨ana*tropous*⟩

-tropy *n comb form* [F *-tropie,* fr. Gk *-tropia,* fr. *-tropos*] **1** : condition of exhibiting (such) a behavior ⟨allo*tropy*⟩ **2** : change in a (specified) way or in response to a (specified) stimulus ⟨thixo*tropy*⟩

¹trot \'trät\ *n* [ME, fr. MF, fr. *troter* to trot, of Gmc origin; akin to OHG *trottōn* to tread, OE *tredan*] (14c) **1 a** (1) : a moderately fast gait of a quadruped (as a horse) in which the legs move in diagonal pairs (2) : a jogging gait of a human that falls between a walk and a run **b** : a ride on horseback **2** : an old woman **3** : a literal translation of a foreign text **4** *pl* : DIARRHEA

²trot *vb* **trot·ted; trot·ting** *vi* **1** : to ride, drive, or proceed at a trot ⟨the fox *trotted* over the knoll⟩ **2** : to proceed briskly : HURRY ~ *vt* **1** : to cause to go at a trot **2** : to traverse at a trot

³trot *n* (1883) : TROTLINE; *also* : one of the short lines with hooks that are attached to it at intervals

¹troth \'träth, 'trȯth, 'trōth, *or with* th\ *n* [ME *trouth,* fr. OE *trēowth* — more at TRUTH] (13c) **1** : loyal or pledged faithfulness : FIDELITY **2** : one's pledged word; *also* : BETROTHAL

²troth *vt* (15c) : PLEDGE, BETROTH

¹troth·plight \'träth-,plīt, 'trȯth-, 'trōth-\ *vt* (15c) : BETROTH

²trothplight *n* (1513) : BETROTHAL

trot·line \'trät-,līn\ *n* [prob. fr. ²*trot*] (1826) : SETLINE; *esp* : a comparatively short setline used near shore or along streams

trot out *vt* (1838) **1** : to lead out and show the paces of (as a horse) **2** : to bring forward for display ⟨always *trots out* some new excuse⟩

Trots·ky·ism \'trät-skē-,i-zəm, 'trȯt-\ *n* (1925) : the political, economic, and social principles advocated by Trotsky; *esp* : the theory and practice of communism developed by or associated with Trotsky and usu. including adherence to the concept of worldwide revolution as opposed to socialism in one country — **Trots·ky·ist** \-skē-ist\ *n or adj* — **Trots·ky·ite** \-skē-,īt\ *n or adj*

trot·ter \'trä-tər\ *n* (14c) **1** : one that trots; *specif* : a standardbred horse trained for harness racing **2** : a pig's foot used as food

trou·ba·dour \'trü-bə-,dȯr, -,dȯr, -,dùr\ *n* [F, fr. OProv *trobador,* fr. *trobar* to compose, prob. fr. (assumed) VL *tropare,* fr. L *tropus* trope] (ca. 1741) : one of a class of lyric poets and poet-musicians often of knightly rank who flourished from the 11th to the end of the 13th century chiefly in the south of France and the north of Italy and whose major theme was courtly love — compare TROUVÈRE

¹trou·ble \'trə-bəl\ *vb* **trou·bled; trou·bling** \'trə-b(ə-)liŋ\ [ME, fr. OF *tourbler, troubler,* fr. (assumed) VL *turbulare,* fr. *turbulus* agitated, alter. of L *turbulentus* — more at TURBULENT] *vt* (13c) **1 a** : to agitate mentally or spiritually : WORRY, DISTURB **b** (1) *archaic* : MISTREAT, OPPRESS (2) : to produce physical disorder in : AFFLICT ⟨*troubled* by a cold⟩ **c** : to put to exertion or inconvenience **2** : to put into confused motion ⟨the wind *troubled* the sea⟩ ~ *vi* **1** : to become mentally agitated : WORRY ⟨refused to ~ over trifles⟩ **2** : to make an effort : be at pains ⟨did not ~ to come⟩ — **trou·bler** \-b(ə-)lər\ *n*

²trouble *n* (13c) **1** : the quality or state of being troubled esp. mentally **2** : public unrest or disturbance ⟨there's ~ brewing downtown⟩ **3** : an instance of trouble ⟨used to disguise her frustrations and despair by making light of her ~s —*Current Biog.*⟩ **4** : a state or condition of distress, annoyance, or difficulty ⟨in ~ with the law⟩ ⟨heading for ~⟩ ⟨got into financial ~⟩: **a** : a condition of physical distress or ill health : AILMENT ⟨back ~⟩ ⟨heart ~⟩ **b** : a condition of mechanical malfunction ⟨engine ~⟩ **c** : a condition of doing something badly or only with great difficulty ⟨has ~ reading⟩ ⟨has ~ breathing⟩ **d** : pregnancy out of wedlock ⟨got a girl in ~⟩ **5** : an effort made : PAINS ⟨took the ~ to do it right⟩ **6 a** : a cause of distress, annoyance, or inconvenience ⟨don't mean to be any ~⟩ ⟨what's the ~?⟩ **b** : a negative feature : DRAWBACK ⟨the ~ with you is you're too honest⟩ ⟨the main ~ with electronic systems is the overreliance on them —John Perham⟩ **c** : the unhappy or sad fact ⟨the ~ is, I need the money⟩

trou·bled \'trə-bəld\ *adj* (14c) **1 a** : CONCERNED, WORRIED ⟨~ feelings about the decision⟩ **b** : emotionally or mentally disturbed ⟨a home for ~ children⟩ **2** : characterized by or indicative of trouble ⟨our ~ cities⟩ ⟨a gray and ~ sky⟩

trou·ble·mak·er \'trə-bəl-,mā-kər\ *n* (ca. 1914) : a person who consciously or unconsciously causes trouble — **trou·ble·mak·ing** \-kiŋ\ *adj or n*

trou·ble·shoot \-,shüt\ *vb* **-shot** \-,shät\; **-shoot·ing** [back-formation fr. *troubleshooter*] *vi* (1918) : to operate or serve as a troubleshooter ⟨is ~ing for an electronics firm⟩ ~ *vt* : to investigate or deal with in the role of troubleshooter ⟨~s TV receivers⟩

trou·ble·shoot·er \-,shü-tər\ *n* (1905) **1** : a skilled worker employed to locate trouble and make repairs in machinery and technical equipment **2** : an expert in resolving diplomatic or political disputes : a mediator of disputes that are at an impasse **3** : a person skilled at solving or anticipating problems or difficulties

trou·ble·some \-səm\ *adj* (1542) **1** : DIFFICULT, BURDENSOME **2** : giving trouble or anxiety : VEXATIOUS — **trou·ble·some·ly** *adv* — **trou·ble·some·ness** *n*

trou·blous \'trə-b(ə-)ləs\ *adj* (15c) **1** : full of trouble : STORMY ⟨these ~ times⟩ **2** : causing trouble : TROUBLESOME ⟨inflation is a ~ matter⟩ — **trou·blous·ly** *adv* — **trou·blous·ness** *n*

trough \'trȯf, 'trȯth, *by bakers often* 'trō\ *n, pl* **troughs** \'trȯfs, 'trȯvz; 'trȯths, 'trō(th)z; 'trōz\ [ME, fr. OE *trog;* akin to OHG *trog* trough, OE *trēow* tree, wood — more at TREE] (bef. 12c) **1 a** : a long shallow often V-shaped receptacle for the drinking water or feed of domestic animals **b** : any of various domestic or industrial containers **2 a** : a conduit, drain, or channel for water; *esp* : a gutter along the eaves of a building **b** : a long and narrow or shallow channel or depression (as between waves or hills); *esp* : a long but shallow depression in the bed of the sea — compare TRENCH **3** : the minimum point of a complete cycle of a periodic function: as **a** : an elongated area of low barometric pressure **b** : the low point in a business cycle

trounce \'traùn(t)s\ *vt* **trounced; trounc·ing** [origin unknown] (1868) **1** : to thrash or punish severely; *esp* : to defeat decisively

¹troupe \'trüp\ *n* [F, fr. MF — more at TROOP] (1825) : COMPANY, TROOP; *esp* : a group of theatrical performers

²troupe *vi* **trouped; troup·ing** (1900) : to travel in a troupe; *also* : to perform as a member of a theatrical troupe

troup·er \'trü-pər\ *n* (1890) **1** : a member of a troupe; *esp* : ACTOR **2** : a person who deals with and persists through difficulty or hardship without complaint ⟨you're a real ~ to wait so long⟩

trou·pi·al \'trü-pē-əl\ *n* [F *troupiale,* fr. *troupe;* fr. its living in flocks] (1825) : a large showy oriole (*Icterus icterus*) of Central and So. America; *also* : any of various related birds (family Icteridae)

¹trou·ser \'traù-zər\ *n* [alter. of earlier *trouse,* fr. ScGael *triubhas*] (1613) : ³PANT 1 — usu. used in pl.

²trouser *adj* (ca. 1771) **1** : of, relating to, or designed for trousers ⟨~ pockets⟩ **2** : of or relating to a male dramatic role played by a woman

trouser suit *n* (1939) *chiefly Brit* : PANTSUIT

trous·seau \'trü-(,)sō, trü-'\ *n, pl* **trous·seaux** \-(,)sōz, -'sōz, -'sōz\ *or* **trous·seaus** [F, fr. OF, dim. of *trousse* bundle, fr. *trousser* to truss] (1833) : the personal possessions of a bride usu. including clothes, accessories, and household linens and wares

trout \'traùt\ *n, pl* **trout** *also* **trouts** [ME, fr. OE *trüht,* fr. LL *trocta, tructa,* a fish with sharp teeth, fr. Gk *trōktēs,* lit., gnawer, fr. *trōgein* to gnaw — more at TROGLODYTE] (bef. 12c) **1** : any of various salmonid food and sport fishes that are mostly smaller than the typical salmons and are anadromous or restricted to cool clear fresh waters: **a** : any of various Old or New World fishes (genera *Salmo* and *Oncorhynchus*) — compare BROWN TROUT, RAINBOW TROUT **b** : ¹CHAR **2** : any of various fishes (as the largemouth bass) held to resemble the true trouts

trout lily *n* [prob. fr. its speckled leaves] (ca. 1898) : DOGTOOTH VIOLET

trout-perch \'traùt-,pərch\ *n* (1883) : a small freshwater fish (*Percopsis omiscomaycus* of the family Percopsidae) chiefly of northern No. America having a scaleless head and large eyes

trouty \'traù-tē\ *adj* **trout·i·er; -est** (1676) : containing or likely to contain abundant trout

trou·vère \trü-'ver\ *n* [F, fr. OF *troveor, troverre,* fr. *trover* to compose, find, fr. (assumed) VL *tropare* — more at TROUBADOUR] (1795) : one of a school of poets who flourished from the 11th to the 14th centuries and who composed mostly narrative works (as chansons de geste and fabliaux) — compare TROUBADOUR

trove \'trōv\ *n* [short for *treasure trove*] (1888) **1** : DISCOVERY, FIND **2** : a valuable collection : TREASURE; *also* : HAUL, COLLECTION

tro·ver \'trō-vər\ *n* [MF *trover* to find, fr. OF] (1594) : a common law action to recover the value of goods wrongfully converted to another's own use

trow \'trō\ *vb* [ME, fr. OE *trēowan;* akin to OE *trēowe* faithful, true — more at TRUE] (bef. 12c) **1** *obs* : BELIEVE **2** *archaic* : THINK

¹trow·el \'traù(-ə)l\ *n* [ME *truel,* fr. MF *truelle,* fr. LL *truella,* fr. L *trulla* ladle] (14c) : any of various hand tools used to apply, spread, shape, or smooth loose or plastic material; *also* : a scoop-shaped or flat-bladed garden tool for taking up and setting small plants

²trowel *vt* **-eled** *or* **-elled; -el·ing** *or* **-el·ling** (ca. 1670) : to smooth, mix, or apply with or as if with a trowel — **trow·el·er** *n*

troy \'troi\ *adj* [ME *troye,* fr. *Troyes,* France] (15c) : expressed in troy weight

troy weight *n* (15c) : a series of units of weight based on a pound of 12 ounces and an ounce of 480 grains — see WEIGHT table

trowel: *1* gardener's, *2* plasterer's, *3* bricklayer's

tru·an·cy \'trü-ən(t)-sē\ *n, pl* **-cies** (1784) : an act or instance of playing truant : the state of being truant

¹tru·ant \'trü-ənt\ *n* [ME, vagabond, idler, fr. OF, vagrant, of Celt origin; akin to OIr *trógán* wretch, *trúag* wretched] (15c) : one who shirks duty; *esp* : one who stays out of school without permission

²truant *adj* (1561) **1** : shirking responsibility **2** : being, resembling or characteristic of a truant

³truant *vi* (1580) : to idle away time esp. while playing truant

truant officer *n* (1872) : ATTENDANCE OFFICER

tru·ant·ry \'trü-ən-trē\ *n, pl* **-ries** (15c) : TRUANCY

¹truce \'trüs\ *n* [ME *trewes,* pl. of *trewe* agreement, fr. OE *trēow* fidelity; akin to OE *trēow* faithful — more at TRUE] (13c) **1** : a suspension of fighting esp. of considerable duration by agreement of opposing forces : ARMISTICE, CEASE-FIRE **2** : a respite esp. from a disagreeable or painful state or action

²truce *vb* **truced; truc·ing** *vi* (1569) : to make a truce ~ *vt* : to end with a truce

¹truck \'trək\ *vb* [ME *trukken,* fr. OF *troquer*] *vt* (13c) **1** : to give in exchange : SWAP **2** : to barter or dispose of by barter ~ *vi* **1** : to exchange commodities : BARTER **2** : to negotiate or traffic esp. in an underhanded way : have dealings

²truck *n* (1553) **1** : BARTER **2** : commodities appropriate for barter or for small trade **3** : close association or connection ⟨will have no ~ with crooks⟩ **4** : payment of wages in goods instead of cash **5** : vegetables grown for market **6** : heterogeneous small articles often of little value; *also* : RUBBISH

³truck *n* [prob. back-formation fr. *truckle* small wheel — more at TRUCKLE BED] (1611) **1 a** : small wheel; *specif* : a small strong wheel for a gun carriage **2 a** : a small wooden cap at the top of a flagstaff or masthead usu. having holes for reeving flag or signal halyards **3 a** : a wheeled vehicle for moving heavy articles: as **a** : a strong horse-drawn or automotive vehicle for hauling **b** : a small barrow consisting of a rectangular frame having at one end a pair of handles and at the other end a pair of small heavy wheels and a projecting edge to slide under a load — called also *hand truck* **c** : a small heavy rectangular frame supported on four wheels for moving heavy objects **d** : a small flat-topped car pushed or pulled by hand **e** : a shelved stand mounted on casters **f** : an automotive vehicle with a short chassis equipped with a swivel for attaching a trailer and used esp. for the highway hauling of freight; *also* : a truck with attached trailer **4 a** *Brit* : an open railroad freight car **b** : a swiveling carriage consisting of a frame with

---

\ə\ abut \ᵊ\ kitten, F table \ər\ further \a\ ash \ā\ ace \ä\ mop, mar \aù\ out \ch\ chin \e\ bet \ē\ easy \g\ go \i\ hit \ī\ ice \j\ job \ŋ\ sing \ō\ go \ò\ law \òi\ boy \th\ thin \th\ the \ü\ loot \ù\ foot \y\ yet \zh\ vision \à, ḵ, ⁿ, œ, œ̄, ᵫ, ᵲ, ᵞ\ *see* Guide to Pronunciation one or more pairs of wheels and springs to carry and guide one end (as of a railroad car) in turning sharp curves — **truck·ful** \-ˌful\ n

⁴truck vt (1748) **1** : to load or transport on a truck ~ vi **1** : to transport goods by truck **2** : to be employed in driving a truck **3** : to roll along esp. in an easy untroubled way

truck·age \ˈtrə-kij\ n (1830) **1** : conveyance by truck **2** : money paid for conveyance on a truck

¹truck·er \ˈtrə-kər\ n [¹truck] (1598) **1** : one that barters **2** Scot : PEDDLER

²trucker n [⁴truck] (1878) **1** : one whose business is transporting goods by truck **2** : a truck driver

truck farm n [²truck] (1866) : a farm devoted to the production of vegetables for the market — **truck farmer** n

truck·ing n (1809) : the process or business of transporting goods on trucks

truck·le \ˈtrə-kəl\ vi **truck·led; truck·ling** \-k(ə-)liŋ\ [fr. the lower position of the truckle bed] (1667) : to act in a subservient manner : SUBMIT syn see FAWN — **truck·ler** \-k(ə-)lər\ n

truckle bed n [truckle small wheel, pulley, fr. ME trocle, fr. L trochlea block of pulleys — more at TROCHLEA] (15c) : TRUNDLE BED

truck·line \ˈtrək-ˌlīn\ n (1924) : a transportation line using trucks

truck·load \-ˈlōd, -ˌlōd\ n (1862) **1** : a load or amount that fills or could fill a truck **2** : the minimum weight required for shipping at truckload rates

truck·man \-mən\ n (1787) **1** : ²TRUCKER **2** : a member of a fire department unit that operates a hook and ladder truck

truck·mas·ter \-ˌmas-tər\ n (1637) archaic : an officer in charge of trade with Indians esp. among the early settlers

truck stop n (ca. 1951) : a facility esp. for truckers that is usu. by a highway and that includes a diner, fuel pumps, and a garage

truck system n (1830) : the system of paying wages in goods instead of cash

tru·cu·lence \ˈtrə-kyə-lən(t)s also ˈtrü-\ n (ca. 1727) : the quality or state of being truculent

tru·cu·len·cy \-lən(t)-sē\ n (1569) : TRUCULENCE

tru·cu·lent \-lənt\ adj [L truculentus, fr. truc-, trux savage; perh. akin to MIr trú doomed person] (ca. 1540) **1** : feeling or displaying ferocity : CRUEL, SAVAGE **2** : DEADLY, DESTRUCTIVE **3** : scathingly harsh : VITRIOLIC **4** : aggressively self-assertive : BELLIGERENT — **tru·cu·lent·ly** adv

¹trudge \ˈtrəj\ vb **trudged; trudg·ing** [origin unknown] vi (1547) : to walk or march steadily and usu. laboriously ⟨trudged through deep snow⟩ ~ vt : to trudge along or over — **trudg·er** n

²trudge n (1835) : a long tiring walk : TRAMP

trud·gen stroke \ˈtrə-jən-\ n [John Trudgen †1902 Eng. swimmer] (1893) : a swimming stroke consisting of alternating overarm strokes and a scissors kick

¹true \ˈtrü\ adj **tru·er; tru·est** [ME trewe, fr. OE trēowe faithful; akin to OHG gitriuwi faithful, OIr derb sure, and prob. to Skt dāruna hard, dāru wood — more at TREE] (bef. 12c) **1** : STEADFAST, LOYAL **b** : HONEST, JUST **c** archaic : TRUTHFUL **2 a** (1) : being in accordance with the actual state of affairs ⟨~ description⟩ (2) : conformable to an essential reality (3) : fully realized or fulfilled ⟨dreams come ~⟩ **b** : IDEAL, ESSENTIAL **c** : being that which is the case rather than what is manifest or assumed ⟨the ~ dimension of the problem⟩ **d** : CONSISTENT ⟨~ to character⟩ **3 a** : properly so called ⟨~ love⟩ ⟨the ~ faith⟩ ⟨the ~ stomach of ruminant mammals⟩ **b** (1) : possessing the basic characters of and belonging to the same natural group as ⟨a whale is a ~ but not a typical mammal⟩ (2) : TYPICAL ⟨the ~ cats⟩ **4** : LEGITIMATE, RIGHTFUL ⟨our ~ and lawful king⟩ **5 a** : that is fitted or formed or that functions accurately **b** : conformable to a standard or pattern : ACCURATE **6** : determined with reference to the earth's axis rather than the magnetic poles ⟨~ north⟩ **7** : logically necessary **8** : NARROW, STRICT ⟨in the truest sense⟩ **9** : corrected for error — **true·ness** n

²true adv (14c) **1** : in accordance with fact or reality **2 a** : without deviation ⟨the bullet flew straight and ~⟩ **b** : without variation from type ⟨breed ~⟩

³true n (1812) **1** : TRUTH, REALITY — usu. used with the **2** : the quality or state of being accurate (as in alignment or adjustment) — used in the phrases in true and out of true

⁴true vt **trued; true·ing** also **tru·ing** (1841) : to make level, square, balanced, or concentric : bring or restore to a desired mechanical accuracy or form ⟨~ up a board⟩ ⟨~ up an engine cylinder⟩

true believer n (ca. 1820) **1** : one who professes absolute belief in something **2** : a zealous supporter of a particular cause

true bill n (1769) : a bill of indictment endorsed by a grand jury as warranting prosecution of the accused

true-blue adj (1674) **1** : marked by unswerving loyalty (as to a party) **2** : GENUINE ⟨~ romantic⟩

true blue n [fr. the association of blue with constancy] (1762) : one who is true-blue

true-born \ˈtrü-ˈbȯrn\ adj (1591) : genuinely such by birth ⟨a ~ Englishman —Shak.⟩

true bug n (1895) : BUG 1c

true-false test \ˈtrü-ˈfȯls-\ n (1924) : a test consisting of a series of statements to be marked as true or false

true-heart·ed \-ˈhär-təd\ adj (15c) : FAITHFUL, LOYAL — **true-heart·ed·ness** n

true-life \ˈtrü-ˈlīf\ adj (1926) : true to life ⟨a ~ story⟩

true-love \ˈtrü-ˌləv\ n (14c) : one truly beloved or loving : SWEETHEART

true lover's knot n (1615) : a complicated ornamental knot not readily untied and symbolic of mutual love — called also truelove knot; see KNOT illustration

true-pen·ny \ˈtrü-ˌpe-nē\ n (1595) : an honest or trusty person

true rib n (1741) : any of the ribs having costal cartilages connected directly with the sternum and in humans constituting the first seven pairs

true seal n (1923) : HAIR SEAL

truf·fle \ˈtrə-fəl, ˈtrü-\ n [modif. of MF truffe, fr. OProv trufa, fr. (assumed) VL tufera; akin to L tuber swelling, truffle — more at TUBER] (1591) **1** : the usu. dark and rugose edible subterranean fruiting body of several European ascomycetous fungi (esp. genus Tuber); also : one

of these fungi **2** : a candy made of chocolate, butter, sugar, and sometimes liqueur shaped into balls and often coated with cocoa

truf·fled \-fəld\ adj (1837) : cooked, stuffed, or garnished with truffles

trug \ˈtrəg\ n [origin unknown] (ca. 1864) chiefly Brit : a shallow rectangular gardening basket

tru·ism \ˈtrü-ˌi-zəm\ n (1708) : an undoubted or self-evident truth; esp : one too obvious for mention — **tru·is·tic** \trü-ˈis-tik\ adj

trull \ˈtrəl\ n [G Trulle, fr. MHG; akin to MHG trolle lout — more at TROLL] (1519) : PROSTITUTE, STRUMPET

tru·ly \ˈtrü-lē\ adv (13c) **1 a** : INDEED — often used as an intensive ⟨~, she is fair⟩ or interjectionally to express astonishment or doubt **b** : without feigning, falsity, or inaccuracy in truth or fact **2 a** : in all sincerity : SINCERELY — often used with yours as a complimentary close **3** : in agreement with fact : TRUTHFULLY **4** : with exactness of construction or operation **5** : in a proper or suitable manner

¹trump \ˈtrəmp\ n [ME trompe, fr. OF, of Gmc origin; akin to OHG trumba, trumpa trumpet] (14c) **1** : TRUMPET **b** chiefly Scot : JEW'S HARP **2** : a sound of or as if of trumpeting ⟨the ~ of doom⟩

²trump n [alter. of ¹triumph] (1529) **1 a** : a card of a suit any of whose cards will win over a card that is not of this suit **b** : the suit whose cards are trumps for a particular hand — often used in pl. **2 a** : a decisive overriding factor or final resource **3** : a dependable and exemplary person

³trump vt (1586) **1** : to get the better of : OUTDO **2** : to play a trump on (a card or trick) when another suit was led ~ vi : to play a trump when another suit was led

trump card n (1822) : ²TRUMP 1a, 2

trumped-up \ˈtrəm(p)t-ˈəp\ adj (1728) : fraudulently concocted : SPURIOUS ⟨~ charges⟩

trum·pery \ˈtrəm-p(ə-)rē\ n [ME tromperie deceit, fr. MF, fr. tromper to deceive] (15c) **1 a** : worthless nonsense **b** : trivial or useless articles : JUNK ⟨a wagon loaded with household ~ —Washington Irving⟩ **2** archaic : tawdry finery — **trumpery** adj

¹trum·pet \ˈtrəm-pət\ n [ME trompette, fr. MF, fr. OF trompe trump] (14c) **1 a** : a wind instrument consisting of a conical or cylindrical usu. metal tube, a cup-shaped mouthpiece, and a flared bell; specif : a valved brass instrument having a cylindrical tube with two turns and a usual range from F sharp below middle C upward for 2½ octaves **b** : a musical instrument (as a cornet) resembling a trumpet **2** : a trumpet player **3** : something that resembles a trumpet or its tonal quality: as **a** : a funnel-shaped instrument (as a megaphone) for collecting, directing, or intensifying sound **b** (1) : a stentorian voice (2) : a penetrating cry (as of an elephant) — **trum·pet·like** adj

²trumpet vi (1530) **1** : to blow a trumpet **2** : to make a sound suggestive of that of a trumpet ~ vt : to sound or proclaim on or as if on a trumpet

trumpet creeper n (1818) : a No. American woody vine (Campsis radicans of the family Bignoniaceae, the trumpet-creeper family) having pinnate leaves and large typically red trumpet-shaped flowers

trum·pet·er \ˈtrəm-pə-tər\ n (15c) **1 a** : a trumpet player; specif : one that gives signals with a trumpet **b** : one that praises or advocates : EULOGIST, SPOKESMAN **2 a** : any of a genus (Psophia of the family Psophiidae) of several large gregarious long-legged long-necked So. American birds related to the cranes **b** : any of an Asian breed of pigeons with a rounded crest and heavily feathered feet

trumpeter swan n (1834) : a rare pure white No. American wild swan (Cygnus buccinator) that is noted for its sonorous voice and is sometimes considered a subspecies (C. cygnus buccinator) of the whooper swan

trumpet creeper

trumpet flower n (ca. 1731) : any of various plants (as a trumpet creeper or a datura) with trumpet-shaped flowers **2** : the flower of a trumpet flower

trumpet honeysuckle n (1731) : a No. American honeysuckle (Lonicera sempervirens) with coral-red or orange flowers having a trumpet-shaped corolla

trumpet vine n (1709) : TRUMPET CREEPER

trump up vt (1695) **1** : to concoct esp. with intent to deceive : FABRICATE, INVENT **2** archaic : to cite as support for an action or claim

¹trun·cate \ˈtrəŋ-ˌkāt, ˈtrən-\ adj [L truncatus, pp. of truncare to shorten, fr. truncus trunk] (1716) : having the end square or even ⟨the ~ leaves of the tulip tree⟩

²truncate vt **trun·cat·ed; trun·cat·ing** (ca. 1727) **1** : to shorten by or as if by cutting off **2** : to replace (an edge or corner of a crystal) by a plane — **trun·ca·tion** \trəŋ-ˈkā-shən, trən-\ n

trun·cat·ed \-ˌkā-təd\ adj (ca. 1704) **1** : having the apex replaced by a plane section and esp. by one parallel to the base ⟨~ cone⟩ **2 a** : cut short : CURTAILED **b** : lacking an expected or normal element (as a syllable) at the beginning or end : CATALECTIC

¹trun·cheon \ˈtrən-chən\ n [ME tronchoun, fr. MF tronchon, fr. (assumed) VL truncion-, truncio, fr. L truncus trunk] (14c) **1** : a shattered spear or lance **2 a** obs : CLUB, BLUDGEON **b** : BATON **2 c** : a police officer's billy club

²truncheon vt (1597) archaic : to beat with a truncheon

¹trun·dle \ˈtrən-d³l\ vb **trun·dled; trun·dling** \ˈtrən(d)-liŋ, ˈtrən-d³l-iŋ\ [²trundle] vt (1598) **1 a** : to propel by causing to rotate : ROLL **b** archaic : to cause to revolve : SPIN **2** : to transport in or as if in a wheeled vehicle : HAUL, WHEEL ~ vi **1** : to progress by revolving **2** : to move on or as if on wheels : ROLL — **trun·dler** \ˈtrən(d)-lər, ˈtrən-d³l-ər\ n

²trundle n [fr. trundle small wheel, alter. of earlier trendle, fr. ME, circle, ring, wheel, fr. OE trendel; akin to OE trendan to revolve — more at TREND] (1851) **1** : TRUNDLE BED **2** : the motion or sound of something rolling **3** : a round or oval wooden tub

trundle bed n (1542) : a low bed usu. on casters that can be rolled or slid under a higher bed when not in use — called also truckle bed

trun·dle-tail \ˈtrən-d³l-ˌtāl\ n (15c) archaic : a curly-tailed dog

trunk \ˈtrəŋk\ n [ME tronke box, trunk, fr. MF tronc, fr. L truncus trunk, torso] (15c) **1 a** : the main stem of a tree apart from limbs and roots — called also *bole* **b** (1) : the human or animal body apart from the head and appendages : TORSO (2) : the thorax of an insect **c** : the central part of anything; *specif* : the shaft of a column or pilaster **2 a** (1) : a large rigid piece of luggage used usu. for transporting clothing and personal effects (2) : the luggage compartment of an automobile **b** (1) : a superstructure over a ship's hatches usu. level with the poop deck (2) : the part of the cabin of a boat projecting above the deck (3) : the housing for a centerboard or rudder **3** : PROBOSCIS; *esp* : the long muscular proboscis of the elephant **4** *pl* : men's shorts worn chiefly for sports **5 a** : a usu. major channel or passage (as a chute or shaft) **b** : a circuit between two telephone exchanges for making connections between subscribers; *broadly* : a central electronic path over which information is transmitted (as between computer memories) **6 a** : the principal channel of a tributary system ⟨an arterial ∼⟩ ⟨∼ of a river⟩ **b** : TRUNK LINE — **trunk·ful** \'trəŋk-,ful\ *n*

trunked \'trəŋ(k)t\ *adj* (1640) : having a trunk esp. of a specified kind — usu. used in combination ⟨a gray-*trunked* tree⟩
trunk·fish \'trəŋk-,fish\ *n* (ca. 1804) : any of numerous small often bright-colored bony fishes (family Ostraciidae) of tropical seas with the body and head enclosed in a bony carapace
trunk hose \'trəŋk-\ *n pl* [prob. fr. obs. E *trunk* to truncate] (1637) : short full breeches reaching about halfway down the thigh that were worn chiefly in the late 16th and early 17th centuries
trunk line *n* (1843) **1** : a transportation system (as an airline, railroad, or highway) handling long-distance traffic **2 a** : a main supply channel (as for gas or oil) **b** : TRUNK 5b
trun·nel \'trə-n²l\ *var of* TREENAIL
trun·nion \'trən-yən\ *n* [F *trognon* core, stump] (ca. 1625) : a pin or pivot on which something can be rotated or tilted; *esp* : either of two opposite gudgeons on which a cannon is swiveled
¹truss \'trəs\ *vt* [ME, fr. OF *trousser, tourser* to bundle, pack, fr. (assumed) VL *torsare*, fr. *torsus* twisted — more at TORSADE] (13c) **1 a** : to secure tightly : BIND **b** : to arrange for cooking by binding close the wings or legs of (a fowl) **2** : to support, strengthen, or stiffen by or as if by a truss — **truss·er** *n*
²truss *n* (13c) **1** : an iron band around a lower mast with an attachment by which a yard is secured to the mast **2 a** : BRACKET 1 **b** : an assemblage of members (as beams) forming a rigid framework **3** : a device worn to reduce a hernia by pressure **4** : a compact flower or fruit cluster
truss bridge *n* (1840) : a bridge supported mainly by trusses — see BRIDGE illustration
truss·ing \'trə-siŋ\ *n* (1840) **1** : the members forming a truss **2** : the trusses and framework of a structure
¹trust \'trəst\ *n* [ME, prob. of Scand origin; akin to ON *traust* trust; akin to OE *trēowe* faithful — more at TRUE] (13c) **1 a** : assured reliance on the character, ability, strength, or truth of someone or something **b** : one in which confidence is placed **2 a** : dependence on something future or contingent : HOPE **b** : reliance on future payment for property (as merchandise) delivered : CREDIT **3 a** : a property interest held by one person for the benefit of another **b** : a combination of firms or corporations formed by a legal agreement; *esp* : one that reduces or threatens to reduce competition **4** *archaic* : TRUSTWORTHINESS **5 a** (1) : a charge or duty imposed in faith or confidence or as a condition of some relationship (2) : something committed or entrusted to one to be used or cared for in the interest of another **b** : responsible charge or office **c** : CARE, CUSTODY ⟨the child committed to her ∼⟩ — **in trust** : in the care or possession of a trustee
²trust *vi* (13c) **1 a** : to place confidence : DEPEND ⟨∼ in God⟩ ⟨∼ to luck⟩ **b** : to be confident : HOPE **2** : to sell or deliver on credit ∼ *vt* **1 a** : to commit or place in one's care or keeping : ENTRUST **b** : to permit to stay or go or to do something without fear or misgiving **2 a** : to rely on the truthfulness or accuracy of : BELIEVE **b** : to place confidence in : rely on **c** : to hope or expect confidently **3** : to extend credit to — **trust·abil·i·ty** \,trəs-tə-'bi-lə-tē\ *n* — **trust·able** \'trəs-tə-bəl\ *adj* — **trust·er** *n* — **trust·ing·ly** \'trəs-tiŋ-lē\ *adv* — **trust·ing·ness** *n*
trust·bust·er \'trəs(t)-,bəs-tər\ *n* (1903) : one who seeks to break up business trusts; *specif* : a federal official who prosecutes trusts under the antitrust laws — **trust·bust·ing** \-,tiŋ\ *n*
trust company *n* (1834) : an incorporated trustee; *broadly* : a corporation that functions as a corporate and personal trustee and usu. also engages in the normal activities of a commercial bank
¹trust·ee \,trəs-'tē\ *n* (1647) **1 a** : one to whom something is entrusted **b** : a country charged with the supervision of a trust territory **2 a** : a natural or legal person to whom property is legally committed to be administered for the benefit of a beneficiary (as a person or a charitable organization) **b** : one (as a corporate director) occupying a position of trust and performing functions comparable to those of a trustee
²trustee *vb* **trust·eed; trust·ee·ing** *vt* (1818) : to commit to the care of a trustee ∼ *vi* : to serve as trustee
trust·ee·ship \,trəs-'tē-,ship\ *n* (ca. 1736) **1** : the office or function of a trustee **2** : supervisory control by one or more countries over a trust territory
trust·ful \'trəst-fəl\ *adj* (1834) : full of trust : CONFIDING — **trust·ful·ly** \-fə-lē\ *adv* — **trust·ful·ness** *n*
trust fund *n* (1780) : property (as money or securities) settled or held in trust
trust·less \'trəst-ləs\ *adj* (ca. 1530) **1** : not deserving of trust : FAITHLESS **2** : DISTRUSTFUL
trust territory *n* (1945) : a non-self-governing territory placed under an administrative authority by the Trusteeship Council of the United Nations
trust·wor·thy \'trəst-,wər-thē\ *adj* (1829) : worthy of confidence : DEPENDABLE — **trust·wor·thi·ly** \-thə-lē\ *adv* — **trust·wor·thi·ness** *n*
¹trusty \'trəs-tē\ *adj* **trust·i·er; -est** (14c) : TRUSTWORTHY, DEPENDABLE — **trust·i·ness** *n*
²trusty \'trəs-tē *also* ,trəs-'tē\ *n, pl* **trust·ies** (1573) : a trusty or trusted person; *specif* : a convict considered trustworthy and allowed special privileges
truth \'trüth\ *n, pl* **truths** \'trüthz, 'trüths\ [ME *trewthe*, fr. OE *trēowth* fidelity; akin to OE *trēowe* faithful — more at TRUE] (bef. 12c)

1 a *archaic* : FIDELITY, CONSTANCY **b** : sincerity in action, character, and utterance **2 a** (1) : the state of being the case : FACT (2) : the body of real things, events, and facts : ACTUALITY (3) *often cap* : a transcendent fundamental or spiritual reality **b** : a judgment, proposition, or idea that is true or accepted as true ⟨∼s of thermodynamics⟩ **c** : the body of true statements and propositions **3 a** : the property (as of a statement) of being in accord with fact or reality **b** *chiefly Brit* : TRUE 2 **c** : fidelity to an original or to a standard **4** *cap, Christian Science* : GOD — **in truth** : in accordance with fact : ACTUALLY
truth·ful \'trüth-fəl\ *adj* (1596) : telling or disposed to tell the truth — **truth·ful·ly** \-fə-lē\ *adv* — **truth·ful·ness** *n*
truth serum *n* (1925) : a hypnotic or anesthetic held to induce a subject under questioning to talk freely
truth set *n* (1940) : a mathematical or logical set containing all the elements that make a given statement of relationships true when substituted in it ⟨the equation $x + 7 = 10$ has as its *truth set* the single number 3⟩
truth table *n* (1921) : a table that shows the truth-value of a compound statement for every truth-value of its component statements; *also* : a similar table (as for a computer logic circuit) showing the value of the output for each value of each input

TRUTH TABLE

a statement	a statement	not *p* denial	*p* and *q* conjunction	*p* or *q* (inclusive) inclusive disjunction	*p* or *q* (exclusive) exclusive disjunction	if *p* then *q* conditional	*p* if and only if *q* biconditional
p	*q*	~*p*	*p* · *q*	*p* ∨ *q*		*p* ⊃ *q*	*p* ≡ *q*
T	T	F	T	T	F	T	T
T	F	F	F	T	T	F	F
F	T	T	F	T	T	T	F
F	F	T	F	F	F	T	T

T = true   F = false

truth–value *n* (1903) : the truth or falsity of a proposition or statement
¹try \'trī\ *vb* **tried; try·ing** [ME *trien*, fr. AF *trier*, fr. OF, to pick out, sift, prob. fr. LL *tritare* to grind, freq. of L *terere* to rub — more at THROW] *vt* (14c) **1 a** : to examine or investigate judicially **b** (1) : to conduct the trial of (2) : to participate as counsel in the judicial examination of **2 a** : to put to test or trial ⟨∼ one's luck⟩ — often used with *out* **b** : to subject to something (as undue strain or excessive hardship or provocation) that tests the powers of endurance **c** : DEMONSTRATE, PROVE **3 a** *obs* : PURIFY, REFINE **b** : to melt down and procure in a pure state : RENDER ⟨∼ out whale oil from blubber⟩ **4** : to fit or finish with accuracy **5** : to make an attempt at — often used with an infinitive ∼ *vi* : to make an attempt *syn* see AFFLICT, ATTEMPT — **try one's hand** : to attempt something for the first time
²try *n, pl* **tries** (1607) **1** : an experimental trial : ATTEMPT **2** : a play in rugby that is similar to a touchdown in football, scores usu. four points, and entitles the scoring side to attempt a placekick at the goal for additional points; *also* : the score made on a try
try for point (1929) : an attempt made after scoring a touchdown in football to score one or two additional points by kicking the ball over the crossbar or again carrying it into the opponents' end zone
try·ing \'trī-iŋ\ *adj* (1718) : severely straining the powers of endurance — **try·ing·ly** \-iŋ-lē\ *adv*
try on *vt* (1693) **1** : to put on (a garment) in order to test the fit **2** : to use or test experimentally — **try–on** \'trī-,ȯn, -,än\ *n*
try·out \'trī-,au̇t\ *n* (1903) : an experimental performance or demonstration: as **a** : a test of the ability (as of an athlete or actor) to fill a part or meet standards **b** : a performance of a play prior to its official opening to determine response and discover weaknesses
try out *vi* (1909) : to compete for a position esp. on an athletic team or for a part in a play
try·pano·some \tri-'pa-nə-,sōm\ *n* [NL *Trypanosoma*, fr. Gk *trypanon* auger + NL *-soma* -some — more at TREPAN] (1903) : any of a genus (*Trypanosoma*) of parasitic flagellate protozoans that infest the blood of various vertebrates including humans, are usu. transmitted by the bite of an insect, and include some that cause serious disease (as sleeping sickness)
try·pano·so·mi·a·sis \tri-,pa-nə-sə-'mī-ə-səs\ *n, pl* **-a·ses** \-,sēz\ [NL] (1902) : infection with or disease caused by trypanosomes
try–pot \'trī-,pät\ *n* (1795) : a metallic pot used on a whaler or on shore to render whale oil from blubber
tryp·sin \'trip-sən\ *n* [perh. fr. Gk *tryein* to wear down + E p*epsin*; akin to L *terere* to rub — more at THROW] (1876) : a proteolytic enzyme from pancreatic juice active in an alkaline medium — compare CHYMOTRYPSIN
tryp·sin·o·gen \trip-'si-nə-jən\ *n* [ISV] (ca. 1890) : the inactive substance released by the pancreas into the duodenum to form trypsin

---

\ə\ abut \ᵊ\ kitten, F table \ər\ further \a\ ash \ā\ ace \ä\ mop, mar \au̇\ out \ch\ chin \e\ bet \ē\ easy \g\ go \i\ hit \ī\ ice \j\ job \ŋ\ sing \ō\ go \ȯ\ law \ȯi\ boy \th\ thin \t̲h̲\ the \ü\ loot \u̇\ foot \y\ yet \zh\ vision \ä, k̲, ⁿ, œ, œ̄, ᵫ, ᵫ̄, ᵜ\ *see* Guide to Pronunciation

trypt·amine \'trip-tə-ˌmēn\ *n* [*tryptophan* + *amine*] (1929) : a crystalline amine $C_{10}H_{12}N_2$ derived from tryptophan

tryp·tic \'trip-tik\ *adj* [ISV, fr. *trypsin*] (1888) : of, relating to, or produced by trypsin or its action

tryp·to·phan \'trip-tə-ˌfan\ *also* **tryp·to·phane** \-ˌfān\ *n* [ISV *tryptic* + *-o-* + *-phane*] (1890) : a crystalline essential amino acid $C_{11}H_{12}N_2O_2$ that is widely distributed in proteins

try·sail \'trī-ˌsāl, -səl\ *n* [obs. *at* try lying to] (1769) : a fore-and-aft sail bent to a gaff and hoisted on a lower mast or a small mast close abaft

try square *n* (ca. 1877) : an instrument consisting of two straightedges fixed at right angles to each other and used for laying off right angles and testing whether work is square

¹**tryst** \'trist, *esp Brit* 'trīst\ *n* [ME, fr. MF *triste* watch post, prob. of Scand origin; akin to ON *traust* trust] (14c) **1** : an agreement (as between lovers) to meet **2** : an appointed meeting or meeting place

²**tryst** *vi* (14c) : to make or keep a tryst — **tryst·er** \'tris-tər, 'trīs-\ *n*

try·works \'trī-ˌwərks\ *n pl* (1792) : a brick furnace in which try-pots are placed; *also* : the furnace with the pots

tsa·de \'(t)sä-də, -dē\ *var of* SADHE

tsar \'zär, '(t)sär\ *var of* CZAR

tset·se fly \'(t)set-sē-, 'tet-, '(t)sēt-, 'tēt-\ *n* [Afrik, fr. Tswana *tsètsè* fly] (1865) : any of several dipteran flies (genus *Glossina*) that occur in Africa south of the Sahara and include vectors of human and animal trypanosomes — called also *tsetse*; compare SLEEPING SICKNESS

Tshi \'chwē, chə-'wē, 'twē, 'chē\ *var of* TWI

Tshi·lu·ba \chi-'lü-bə\ *n* (ca. 1961) : a Bantu language used as a lingua franca in southeastern Zaire

T-shirt \'tē-ˌshərt\ *n* (1920) : a collarless short-sleeved or sleeveless usu. cotton undershirt; *also* : an outer shirt of similar design — **T-shirt·ed** *adj*

T square *n* (1785) : a ruler with a crosspiece or head at one end used in making parallel lines

tsu·na·mi \(t)sü-'nä-mē\ *n, pl* **tsunamis** *also* **tsunami** [Jp, fr. *tsu* harbor + *nami* wave] (1897) : a great sea wave produced by submarine earth movement or volcanic eruption — **tsu·na·mic** \-mik\ *adj*

tsu·tsu·ga·mu·shi disease \ˌ(t)süt-sə-gə-'mü-shē-, ˌtüt-\ *n* [Jp *tsutsugamushi* scrub typhus mite, fr. *tsutsuga* sickness + *mushi* insect] (1906) : an acute febrile bacterial disease that is caused by a rickettsia (*Rickettsia tsutsugamushi*) transmitted by mite larvae, resembles louse-borne typhus, and is widespread in the western Pacific area — called also *scrub typhus, tsutsugamushi*

Tswa·na \'(t)swä-nə\ *n, pl* **Tswana** *or* **Tswanas** (1937) **1** : the language of the Tswana people **2** : a member of a Bantu-speaking people of Botswana and the Republic of South Africa

t-test \'tē-ˈtest\ *n* (1932) : a statistical test involving confidence limits for the random variable *t* of a t distribution and used esp. in testing hypotheses about means of normal distributions when the standard deviations are unknown

T₃ *also* **T-3** \'tē-'thrē\ *n* [*T*, abbr. for *thyronine* + 3, number of iodine atoms attached to the thyronine nucleus] (1956) : TRIIODOTHYRONINE

Tua·reg \'twä-ˌreg\ *n, pl* **Tuareg** *or* **Tuaregs** [Ar *Tawāriq*] (1821) : a member of a nomadic people of the central and western Sahara and along the middle Niger from Tombouctou to Nigeria

tu·a·ta·ra \ˌtü-ə-'tär-ə\ *n* [Maori *tuatàra*] (1890) : a large spiny quadrupedal reptile (*Sphenodon punctatum*) of islands off the coast of New Zealand that has a vestigial third eye in the middle of the forehead representing the pineal gland and that is the only surviving rhynchocephalian

tuatara

¹**tub** \'təb\ *n* [ME *tubbe*, fr. MD; akin to MLG *tubbe* tub] (14c) **1 a** : a wide low vessel orig. formed with wooden staves, round bottom, and hoops **b** : a small round container in which a product is sold ⟨a ~ of oleo⟩ **2** : an old or slow boat **3** : BATHTUB; *also* : BATH **4** : the amount that a tub will hold — **tub·ful** \-ˌfül\ *n* — **tub·like** \-ˌlīk\ *adj*

²**tub** *vb* **tubbed; tub·bing** *vt* (1610) **1** : to wash or bathe in a tub **2** : to put or store in a tub ~ *vi* **1** : BATHE **2** : to undergo washing — **tub·ba·ble** \'tə-bə-bəl\ *adj* — **tub·ber** *n*

tu·ba \'tü-bə, 'tyü-\ *n* [It, fr. L, trumpet] (1852) : a large low-pitched brass instrument usu. oval in shape and having a conical tube, a cup-shaped mouthpiece, and a usual range an octave lower than that of the euphonium — **tu·ba·ist** \-bə(-i)st\ *or* **tub·ist** \-bist\ *n*

tub·al \'tü-bəl, 'tyü-\ *adj* (ca. 1736) : of, relating to, or involving a tube and esp. a fallopian tube ⟨~ infection⟩

tubal ligation *n* (1948) : ligation of the fallopian tubes to prevent passage of ova from the ovaries to the uterus used as a method of female sterilization

tub·by \'tə-bē\ *adj* **tub·bi·er; -est** (ca. 1807) **1** : sounding dull and without proper resonance or freedom of sound ⟨a ~ violin⟩ **2** : PUDGY, FAT

tube \'tüb, 'tyüb\ *n* [F, fr. L *tubus*; akin to L *tuba* trumpet] (1651) **1** : any of various usu. cylindrical structures or devices: as **a** : a hollow elongated cylinder; *esp* : one to convey fluids **b** : a soft tubular container whose contents (as toothpaste) can be removed by squeezing **c** (1) : TUNNEL (2) *Brit* : SUBWAY b **d** : the basically cylindrical section between the mouthpiece and bell that is the fundamental part of a wind instrument **2 a** : a slender channel within a plant or animal body : DUCT — compare FALLOPIAN TUBE **b** : the narrow basal portion of a gamopetalous corolla or a calyx with united sepals **3** : INNER TUBE **4 a** : ELECTRON TUBE; *esp* : VACUUM TUBE **b** : CATHODE-RAY TUBE; *esp* : a television picture tube **c** : TELEVISION **5** : an article of clothing shaped like a tube ⟨~ top⟩ ⟨~ socks⟩ — **tubed** \'tübd, 'tyübd\ *adj* — **tube·like** \'tüb-ˌlīk, 'tyüb-\ *adj* — **down the tube** *or* **down the tubes** : into a state of collapse, deterioration, or ruin

tube foot *n* (1888) : one of the small flexible tubular processes of most echinoderms that are extensions of the water-vascular system and are used esp. in locomotion and grasping

tube·less \'tü-bləs, 'tyü-\ *adj* (1855) : lacking a tube; *specif* : being a pneumatic tire that does not depend on an inner tube for airtightness

tube nucleus *n* (1939) : the one of the two nuclei formed by mitotic division of a microspore during the formation of a pollen grain that is held to control subsequent growth of the pollen tube and that does not divide again — compare GENERATIVE NUCLEUS

tube pan *n* (1926) : a round cake pan having a hollow tube in the center

tu·ber \'tü-bər, 'tyü-\ *n* [L, swelling, truffle; perh. akin to L *tumēre* to swell — more at THUMB] (1668) **1 a** : a short fleshy usu. underground stem bearing minute scale leaves each of which bears a bud in its axil and is potentially able to produce a new plant — compare BULB, CORM **b** : a fleshy root or rhizome resembling a tuber **2** : an anatomical prominence : TUBEROSITY

tu·ber·cle \'tü-bər-kəl, 'tyü-\ *n* [L *tuberculum*, dim. of *tuber*] (1578) **1** : a small knobby prominence or excrescence esp. on a plant or animal : NODULE: as **a** : a protuberance near the head of a rib that articulates with the transverse process of a vertebra **b** : any of several prominences in the central nervous system **c** : NODULE b **2** : a small abnormal discrete lump in the substance of an organ or in the skin; *esp* : the specific lesion of tuberculosis

tubercle bacillus *n* (ca. 1890) : a bacterium (*Mycobacterium tuberculosis*) that is a major cause of tuberculosis

tubercul- *comb form* [NL, fr. L *tuberculum*] **1** : tubercle ⟨*tubercular*⟩ **2** : tubercle bacillus ⟨*tuberculin*⟩ **3** : tuberculosis ⟨*tuberculoid*⟩

¹**tu·ber·cu·lar** \tü-'bər-kyə-lər, tyü-\ *adj* (1799) **1 a** : of, relating to, or affected with tuberculosis : TUBERCULOUS **b** : caused by the tubercle bacillus ⟨~ meningitis⟩ **2** : characterized by lesions that are or resemble tubercles ⟨*tuberculin leprosy*⟩ **3** : relating to, resembling, or constituting a tubercle : TUBERCULATED

²**tubercular** *n* (1925) : a person with tuberculosis

tu·ber·cu·lat·ed \tü-'bər-kyə-ˌlā-təd, tyü-\ *also* **tu·ber·cu·late** \-lət\ *adj* (1771) : having tubercles : characterized by or beset with tubercles

tu·ber·cu·lin \tü-'bər-kyə-lən, tyü-\ *n* [ISV] (ca. 1890) : a sterile liquid containing the growth products of or specific substances extracted from the tubercle bacillus and used in the diagnosis of tuberculosis esp. in children and cattle

tuberculin test *n* (ca. 1900) : a test for hypersensitivity to tuberculin as an indication of past or present tubercular infection

tu·ber·cu·loid \tü-'bər-kyə-ˌlóid, tyü-\ *adj* [ISV] (ca. 1923) : resembling tuberculosis esp. in the presence of tubercles ⟨~ leprosy⟩

tu·ber·cu·lo·sis \tü-ˌbər-kyə-'lō-səs, tyü-\ *n, pl* **-lo·ses** \-ˌsēz\ [NL] (1860) : a highly variable communicable disease of humans and some other vertebrates caused by the tubercle bacillus and rarely in the U.S. by a related mycobacterium (*Mycobacterium bovis*) and characterized by toxic symptoms or allergic manifestations which in humans primarily affect the lungs

tu·ber·cu·lous \tü-'bər-kyə-ləs, tyü-\ *adj* (1891) **1** : constituting or affected with tuberculosis ⟨a ~ process⟩ **2** : caused by or resulting from the presence or products of the tubercle bacillus ⟨~ peritonitis⟩

tube·rose \'tü-ˌbrōz, 'tyü-, *also* -bə-ˌrōz, -bə-ˌrōs\ *n* [NL *tuberosa*, specific epithet, fr. L, fem. of *tuberosus* tuberous, fr. *tuber* tuber] (1664) : a Mexican bulbous herb (*Polianthes tuberosa*) of the agave family cultivated for its spike of fragrant white single or double flowers

tu·ber·os·i·ty \ˌtü-bə-'rä-sə-tē, ˌtyü-\ *n, pl* **-ties** (1611) : a rounded prominence; *esp* : a large prominence on a bone usu. serving for the attachment of muscles or ligaments

tu·ber·ous \'tü-b(ə-)rəs, 'tyü-\ *adj* (1650) **1** : consisting of, bearing, or resembling a tuber **2** : of, relating to, or being a plant tuber or tuberous root of a plant

tuberous root *n* (ca. 1668) : a thick fleshy storage root like a tuber but lacking buds or scale leaves — **tuberous–rooted** *adj*

tube worm *n* (ca. 1819) : a worm that lives in a tube: as **a** : any of various polychaetes or oligochaetes **b** : a pogonophoran and esp. an extremely large one that is found near deep-ocean hydrothermal vents

tu·bi·fex \'tü-bə-ˌfeks, 'tyü-\ *n* [NL *Tubific-, Tubifex*, fr. L *tubus* tube + *facere* to make — more at DO] (1948) : any of a genus (*Tubifex*) of slender reddish oligochaete worms that live in tubes in fresh or brackish water and are widely used as food for aquarium fish

tu·bi·fi·cid \tü-'bi-fə-səd, tyü-; ˌt(y)ü-bə-'fi-səd\ *n* [NL *Tubificidae*, fr. *Tubific-, Tubifex*] (1950) : any of a family (Tubificidae) of aquatic oligochaetes including the tubifex worms — **tubificid** *adj*

tub·ing \'tü-biŋ, 'tyü-\ *n* (1845) **1** : material in the form of a tube; *also* : a length or piece of tube **2** : a series or system of tubes

tu·bo·cu·ra·rine \ˌtü-bō-kyü-'rär-ən, ˌtyü-, -ˌēn\ *n* [ISV *tubo-* (fr. L *tubus* tube) + *curare* + *-ine*; fr. its being shipped in sections of hollow bamboo] (1898) : a toxic alkaloid or its crystalline hydrated hydrochloride salt $C_{37}H_{42}Cl_2N_2O_6 \cdot 5H_2O$ that is obtained chiefly from the bark and stems of a So. American vine (*Chondrodendron tomentosum* of the family Menispermaceae) and in its dextrorotatory form constitutes the chief active constituent of curare and is used esp. as a skeletal muscle relaxant

tub–thump·er \'təb-ˌthəm-pər\ *n* (1662) : a vociferous supporter (as of a cause) — **tub–thump** \-ˌthəmp\ *vb*

tu·bu·lar \'tü-byə-lər, 'tyü-\ *adj* (1673) **1 a** : having the form of or consisting of a tube ⟨a ~ calyx⟩ **b** : made or provided with tubes **2** : of, relating to, or sounding as if produced through tubes

tu·bule \'tü-(ˌ)byü(ə)l, 'tyü-\ *n* [L *tubulus*, dim. of *tubus*] (1677) : a small tube; *esp* : a slender elongated anatomical channel

tu·bu·lin \'tü-byə-lən, 'tyü-\ *n* [*tubule* + ¹*-in*] (1968) : a globular protein that polymerizes to form microtubules

tu·chun \'dü-'jün, -'jüen\ *n* [Chin (Beijing) *dùjūn*] (1917) **1** : a Chinese military governor (as of a province) **2** : a Chinese warlord

¹**tuck** \'tək\ *vb* [ME *tuken* to pull up sharply, scold, fr. OE *tūcian* to ill-treat; akin to OHG *zuhhen* to jerk, OE *togian* to pull — more at TOW] *vt* (15c) **1 a** : to pull up into a fold **b** : to make a tuck in **2** : to put into a snug often concealing or isolating place ⟨cottage ~ed away in the hills⟩ **3 a** : to push in the loose end of so as to hold tightly ⟨~ in your shirt⟩ **b** : to cover by tucking in bedclothes — usu. used with *in* **4** : EAT — usu. used with *away* or *in* ⟨~ed away a big lunch⟩ **5** : to put into a tuck position ~ *vi* **1** : to draw together into tucks or folds **2** : to eat or drink heartily — usu. used with *into* ⟨~ed into their beer and pretzels⟩ **3** : to fit snugly

²**tuck** *n* (1532) **1** : a fold stitched into cloth to shorten, decorate, or control fullness **2** : the part of a vessel where the ends of the lower planks meet under the stern **3 a** : an act or instance of tucking **b** : something tucked or to be tucked in **4 a** : a body position (as in

diving) in which the knees are bent, the thighs drawn tightly to the chest, and the hands clasped around the shins   **b** : a skiing position in which the skier squats forward and holds the ski poles under the arms and parallel to the ground   **5** : a cosmetic surgical operation for the removal of excess skin or fat from a body part ⟨a tummy ∼⟩

³tuck n [ME (Sc) tuicke beat, stroke] (15c) : a sound of or as if of a drumbeat

⁴tuck n [MF estoc, fr. OF, tree trunk, sword point, of Gmc origin; akin to OE stocc stump of a tree — more at STOCK] (1508) archaic : RAPIER

⁵tuck n [prob. fr. ²tuck] (1878) : VIGOR, ENERGY ⟨seemed to kind of take the ∼ all out of me —Mark Twain⟩

tuck·a·hoe \'tə-kə-,hō\ n [Virginia Algonquian tockawhoughe] (1612) **1** : either of two arums (Peltandra virginica and Orontium aquaticum) of the U.S. with rootstocks used as food by American Indians   **2** : the large edible sclerotium of a subterranean fungus (Poria cocos)

¹tuck·er \'tə-kər\ n (1688) **1** : a piece of lace or cloth in the neckline of a dress   **2** : one that tucks

²tucker vt tuck·ered; tuck·er·ing \'tə-k(ə-)riŋ\ [obs. E tucker to reproach + -er (as in ¹batter)] (1833) : EXHAUST — often used with out

tuck·er·bag \'tə-kər-,bag\ n (1885) chiefly Austral : a bag used esp. by travelers in the bush to hold food

tuck·et \'tə-kət\ n [prob. fr. obs. E tuk to beat the drum, sound the trumpet] (1593) : a fanfare on a trumpet

tuck-point \'tək-,point\ vt (1881) : to finish (the mortar joints between bricks or stones) with a narrow ridge of putty or fine lime mortar

tuckshop \-,shäp\ n [Brit tuck food, confectionery] (1857) Brit : a confectioner's shop : CONFECTIONERY

Tu·dor \'tü-dər, 'tyü-\ adj [Henry Tudor (Henry VII of England)] (1779) **1** : of or relating to the English royal house that ruled from 1485 to 1603   **2** : of, relating to, or characteristic of the Tudor period — Tudor n

Tudor arch n (1815) : a low elliptical 3-, 4-, or 5-centered arch; esp : a 4-centered pointed arch — see ARCH illustration

Tues·day \'tüz-dē, 'tyüz-, -(,)dā\ n [ME tiwesday, fr. OE tīwesdæg (akin to OHG ziostag Tuesday), fr. OE Tīw Tiu + dæg day — more at DEITY] (bef. 12c) : the third day of the week — **Tues·days** \-dēz, -(,)dāz\ adv

tu·fa \'tü-fə, 'tyü-\ n [It tufo, fr. L tofus] (1770) **1** : TUFF   **2** : a porous rock forming as a deposit from springs or streams — **tu·fa·ceous** \tü-'fā-shəs, tyü-\ adj

tuff \'təf\ n [MF tuf, fr. OIt tufo] (1683) : a rock composed of the finer kinds of volcanic detritus usu. fused together by heat — **tuff·a·ceous** \,tə-'fā-shəs\ adj

tuf·fet \'tə-fət\ n [alter. of ¹tuft] (1553) **1** : TUFT 1a   **2** : a low seat

¹tuft \'təft\ n [ME, modif. of MF tufe] (14c) **1 a** : a small cluster of elongated flexible outgrowths attached or close together at the base and free at the opposite ends; esp : a growing bunch of grasses or close-set plants   **b** : a bunch of soft fluffy threads cut off short and used as ornament   **2** : CLUMP, CLUSTER   **3** : MOUND   **4** : any of the projections of yarns drawn through a fabric or making up a fabric so as to produce a surface of raised loops or cut pile — **tuft·ed** \'təf-təd\ adj — **tufty** \'təf-tē\ adj

²tuft vt (1535) **1 a** : to provide or adorn with a tuft   **b** : to make (a fabric) of or with tufts   **2** : to make (as a mattress) firm by stitching at intervals and sewing on tufts ∼ vi : to form into or grow in tufts — **tuft·er** n

¹tug \'təg\ vb tugged; tug·ging [ME tuggen; akin to OE togian to pull — more at TOW] (14c) **1** : to pull hard   **2** : to struggle in opposition : CONTEND   **3** : to exert oneself laboriously : LABOR ∼ vt **1** : to pull or strain hard at   **2 a** : to move by pulling hard : HAUL   **b** : to carry with difficulty : LUG   **3** : to tow with a tugboat — **tug·ger** n

²tug n (15c) **1 a** : ³TRACE 1   **b** : a short leather strap or loop   **c** : a rope or chain used for pulling   **2 a** : an act or instance of tugging : PULL   **b** : a strong pulling force   **3 a** : a straining effort   **b** : a struggle between two people or opposite forces   **4** : TUGBOAT

tug·boat \'təg-,bōt\ n (1830) : a strongly built powerful boat used for towing and pushing — called also towboat

tug-of-war \,təg-ə(v)-'wor\ n, pl tugs-of-war (1677) **1** : a struggle for supremacy or control usu. involving two antagonists   **2** : a contest in which two teams pull against each other at opposite ends of a rope with the object of pulling the middle of the rope over a mark on the ground

tu·grik or **tu·ghrik** \'tü-grik\ n [Mongolian tögrig, lit., circle, wheel] (1927) — see MONEY table

tuille \'twē(ə)l\ n [ME toile, fr. MF tuille tile, fr. L tegula — more at TILE] (15c) : one of the hinged plates before the thigh in plate armor — see ARMOR illustration

tu·ition \tə-'wi-shən, tyü-\ n [ME tuicioun protection, fr. OF tuicion, fr. L tuition-, tuitio, fr. tueri to look at, look after] (15c) **1** archaic : CUSTODY, GUARDIANSHIP   **2** : the act or profession of teaching : INSTRUCTION ⟨pursued his studies under private ∼⟩   **3** : the price of or payment for instruction — **tu·ition·al** \-'wish-nəl, -'wi-shə-nᵊl\ adj

tu·la·re·mia \,tü-lə-'rē-mē-ə, ,tyü-\ n [NL, fr. Tulare County, Calif.] (1921) : an infectious disease esp. of wild rabbits, rodents, humans, and some domestic animals that is caused by a bacterium (Francisella tularensis), is transmitted esp. by the bites of insects, and in humans is marked by symptoms (as fever) of toxemia — **tu·la·re·mic** \-mik\ adj

tu·le \'tü-lē\ n [Sp, fr. Nahuatl tōllin] (1837) : either of two large New World bulrushes (Scirpus californicus and S. acutus)

tu·lip \'tü-ləp, 'tyü-\ n [NL tulipa, fr. Turk tülbent turban — more at TURBAN] (1578) : any of a genus (Tulipa) of Eurasian bulbous herbs of the lily family that have linear or broadly lanceolate leaves and are widely grown for their showy flowers; also : the flower or bulb of a tulip

tulip tree n (1705) **1** : a tall No. American timber tree (Liriodendron tulipifera) of the magnolia family having large greenish yellow tulip-shaped flowers and soft white wood used esp. for cabinetwork and woodenware — called also tulip poplar, yellow poplar   **2** : any of various trees other than the tulip tree with tulip-shaped flowers

tu·lip·wood \'tü-ləp-,wud, 'tyü-\ n (1843) **1** : wood of the No. American tulip tree   **2 a** : any of several showily striped or variegated woods; esp : the rose-colored wood of a Brazilian tree (Physocalymma scaberrimum) of the family Lythraceae that is much used by cabinet-makers for inlaying   **b** : a tree that yields tulipwood

tulle \'tül\ n [F, fr. Tulle, France] (ca. 1818) : a sheer often stiffened silk, rayon, or nylon net used chiefly for veils or ballet costumes

¹tum·ble \'təm-bəl\ vb tum·bled; tum·bling \-b(ə-)liŋ\ [ME, freq. of tumben to dance, fr. OE tumbian; akin to OHG tūmōn to reel] vi (14c) **1 a** : to fall suddenly and helplessly   **b** : to suffer a sudden downfall, overthrow, or defeat   **c** : to decline suddenly and sharply (as in price) : DROP ⟨the stock market tumbled⟩   **d** : to fall into ruin : COLLAPSE   **2 a** : to perform gymnastic feats in tumbling   **b** : to turn end over end in falling or flight   **3** : to roll over and over, to and fro, or end over end : TOSS   **4** : to issue forth hurriedly and confusedly   **5** : to come by chance : STUMBLE   **6** : to come to understand : CATCH ON ⟨didn't ∼ to the seriousness of the problem⟩ ∼ vt **1** : to cause to tumble (as by pushing or toppling)   **2 a** : to throw together in a confused mass : RUMPLE, DISORDER   **3** : to whirl in a tumbling barrel

²tumble n (1634) **1 a** : a disordered mass of objects or material   **b** : a disorderly state   **2** : an act or instance of tumbling

tum·ble·bug \'təm-bəl-,bəg\ n (1805) : any of various scarabaeid beetles (esp. genera Scarabaeus, Canthon, Copris, or Phanaeus) that roll dung into small balls, bury them in the ground, and lay eggs in them

tum·ble·down \'təm-bəl-'daun\ adj (1818) : DILAPIDATED, RAMSHACKLE ⟨a ∼ house at the edge of town —Sherwood Anderson⟩

tumble dry vt (1962) : to dry (as clothes) by tumbling in a dryer — **tumble dryer** n — **tumble drying** n

tum·bler \'təm-blər\ n (14c) **1** : one that tumbles: as   **a** : one that performs tumbling feats : ACROBAT   **b** : any of various domestic pigeons that tumble or somersault backward in flight or on the ground   **2** : a drinking glass without foot or stem and orig. with pointed or convex base   **3 a** : a movable obstruction in a lock (as a lever, latch, wheel, slide, or pin) that must be adjusted to a particular position (as by a key) before the bolt can be thrown   **b** : a piece on which the mainspring acts in a gun's lock   **4** : a device or mechanism for tumbling as a revolving cage in which clothes are dried)   **5** : a worker that operates a tumbler — **tum·bler·ful** \-,fùl\ n

tum·ble·weed \'təm-bəl-,wēd\ n (1887) : a plant (as Russian thistle or any of several amaranths) that breaks away from its roots in the autumn and is driven about by the wind as a light rolling mass

¹tum·bling \'təm-b(ə-)liŋ\ n (1604) : the skill, practice, or sport of executing gymnastic feats (as somersaults and handsprings) without the use of apparatus

²tumbling adj (ca. 1916) : tipped or slanted out of the vertical — used esp. of a cattle brand

tumbling barrel n (ca. 1890) : a revolving cask in which objects or materials undergo a process (as drying or polishing) by being whirled about

tumbling verse n (1585) : an early modern English type of verse having four stresses but no prevailing type of foot and no regular number of syllables

tum·brel or **tum·bril** \'təm-brəl\ n [ME tombrel, fr. OF tumberel tipcart, fr. tomber to tumble, of Gmc origin; akin to OHG tūmōn to reel — more at TUMBLE] (15c) **1** : a farm tipcart   **2** : a vehicle carrying condemned persons (as political prisoners during the French Revolution) to a place of execution

tu·me·fac·tion \,tü-mə-'fak-shən, ,tyü-\ n [MF, fr. L tumefacere to cause to swell, fr. tumēre to swell + facere to make, do — more at THUMB, DO] (1597) **1** : an action or process of swelling or becoming tumorous   **2** : SWELLING

tu·mes·cence \tü-'me-sᵊn(t)s, tyü-\ n (1859) : the quality or state of being tumescent; esp : readiness for sexual activity marked esp. by vascular congestion of the sex organs

tu·mes·cent \-sᵊnt\ adj [L tumescent-, tumescens, prp. of tumescere to swell up, incho. of tumēre to swell] (1882) : somewhat swollen ⟨∼ tissue⟩

tu·mid \'tü-məd, 'tyü-\ adj [L tumidus, fr. tumēre] (1541) **1** : marked by swelling : SWOLLEN, ENLARGED ⟨a badly infected ∼ leg⟩   **2** : PROTUBERANT, BULGING ⟨sails ∼ in the breeze⟩   **3** : BOMBASTIC, TURGID

tum·my \'tə-mē\ n, pl tummies [baby-talk alter. of stomach] (1867) : STOMACH 1c

tu·mor \'tü-mər, 'tyü-\ n [L tumor, fr. tumēre] (1597) **1** : a swollen or distended part   **2** : an abnormal benign or malignant mass of tissue that is not inflammatory, arises without obvious cause from cells of preexistent tissue, and possesses no physiologic function — **tu·mor·al** \-mə-rəl\ adj — **tu·mor·like** \-mər-,līk\ adj

tu·mor·i·gen·ic \,tü-mə-rə-'je-nik, ,tyü-\ adj (1941) : producing or tending to produce tumors; also : CARCINOGENIC — **tu·mor·i·gen·e·sis** \-'je-nə-səs\ n — **tu·mor·i·ge·nic·i·ty** \-jə-'ni-sə-tē\ n

tumor necrosis factor n (1975) : a protein that is produced by monocytes and macrophages in response esp. to endotoxins and that activates leukocytes and has antitumor activity

tu·mor·ous \'tü-mə-rəs, 'tyü-; 'tüm-rəs, 'tyüm-\ adj (1547) : of, relating to, or resembling a tumor

tu·mour \'tyü-mər\ chiefly Brit var of TUMOR

¹tump \'təmp\ n [origin unknown] (1589) **1** chiefly dial Eng : MOUND, HUMMOCK   **2** : a clump of vegetation

²tump vb [perh. akin to Brit. dial. tumpoke to fall head over heels] vi (1967) chiefly Southern : to tip or turn over esp. accidentally — usu. used with over ⟨sooner or later everybody ∼s over. Nothing to worry about if you don't get caught under the canoe —Don Kennard⟩ ∼ vt, chiefly Southern : to cause to tip over : OVERTURN, UPSET — usu. used with over

tump·line \'təm-,plīn\ n [tump, of Algonquian origin; akin to Eastern Abenaki mádûmbí pack strap] (1796) : a sling formed by a strap slung over the forehead or chest and used for carrying or helping to support a pack on the back or in hauling loads

tu·mult \'tü-,məlt, 'tyü- also 'tə-\ n [ME tumulte, fr. MF, fr. L tumultus; perh. akin to Skt tumula noisy] (15c) **1** : disorderly agitation or milling about of a crowd usu. with uproar and confusion of voices

\ə\ abut   \ᵊ\ kitten, F table   \ər\ further   \a\ ash   \ā\ ace   \ä\ mop, mar
\aù\ out   \ch\ chin   \e\ bet   \ē\ easy   \g\ go   \i\ hit   \ī\ ice   \j\ job
\ŋ\ sing   \ō\ go   \ò\ law   \òi\ boy   \th\ thin   \t͟h\ the   \ü\ loot   \ù\ foot
\y\ yet   \zh\ vision   \ä, k̲, ⁿ, œ, œ̄, ᵫ, ᵫ̄, ꞏ\ see Guide to Pronunciation

: COMMOTION **b** : a turbulent uprising : RIOT **2** : HUBBUB, DIN **3 a** : violent agitation of mind or feelings **b** : a violent outburst

tu·mul·tu·ary \'tü-ˌməl-chə-ˌwer-ē, tyü-ˌ tə-\ *adj* (1590) : attended or marked by tumult, riot, lawlessness, confusion, or impetuosity

tu·mul·tu·ous \tü-'məl-chə-wəs, tyü-, tə-, -chəs; -'məlch-wəs\ *adj* (ca. 1548) **1** : marked by tumult **2** : tending or disposed to cause or incite a tumult **3** : marked by violent or overwhelming turbulence or upheaval — **tu·mul·tu·ous·ly** *adv* — **tu·mul·tu·ous·ness** *n*

tu·mu·lus \'tü-myə-ləs, 'tyü-, 'tə-\ *n, pl* **-li** \-ˌlī, -ˌlē\ [L; akin to L *tumēre* to swell — more at THUMB] (1686) : an artificial hillock or mound (as over a grave); *esp* : an ancient grave : BARROW

tun \'tən\ *n* [ME *tunne*, fr. OE, fr. ML *tunna*] (bef. 12c) **1** : a large cask esp. for wine **2** : any of various units of liquid capacity; *esp* : one equal to 252 gallons

¹tu·na \'tü-nə\ *n* [Sp, fr. Taino] (ca. 1555) **1** : any of various flat-jointed prickly pears (genus *Opuntia*); *esp* : one (*O. tuna*) of tropical America **2** : the edible fruit of a tuna

²tu·na \'tü-nə, 'tyü-\ *n, pl* **tuna** *or* **tunas** [AmerSp, alter. of Sp *atún*, modif. of Ar *tūn*, fr. L *thunnus*, fr. Gk *thynnos*] (1881) **1** : any of numerous large vigorous scombroid food and sport fishes (as an albacore or a bluefin tuna) **2** : the flesh of a tuna esp. when canned for use as food — called also *tuna fish*

tun·able \'tü-nə-bəl, 'tyü-\ *adj* (ca. 1500) **1** *archaic* : TUNEFUL **b** : sounding in tune : CONCORDANT **2** : capable of being tuned — **tun·abil·i·ty** \ˌtü-nə-bi-lə-tē, ˌtyü-\ *n* — **tun·able·ness** \'tü-nə-bəl-nəs, 'tyü-\ *n* — **tun·ably** \-blē\ *adv*

tun·dish \'tən-ˌdish\ *n* [ME, funnel for filling a tun] (14c) **1** : FUNNEL 1a **2** : a reservoir in the top part of a mold into which molten metal is poured

tun·dra \'tən-drə *also* 'tün-\ *n* [Russ, of Lappish origin; akin to Kola Lappish *tundar* hill] (ca. 1841) : a level or rolling treeless plain that is characteristic of arctic and subarctic regions, consists of black mucky soil with a permanently frozen subsoil, and has a dominant vegetation of mosses, lichens, herbs, and dwarf shrubs; *also* : a similar region confined to mountainous areas above timberline

¹tune \'tün, 'tyün\ *n* [ME, alter. of *tone*] (14c) **1 a** *archaic* : quality of sound : TONE **b** : manner of utterance : INTONATION; *specif* : phonetic modulation **2 a** : a succession of pleasing musical tones : MELODY **b** : a dominant theme **3** : correct musical pitch or consonance — used chiefly in the phrases *in tune* and *out of tune* **4** *archaic* : a frame of mind : MOOD **b** : AGREEMENT, HARMONY ⟨in ∼ with the times⟩ **c** : general attitude : APPROACH ⟨changed his ∼ when the going got rough⟩ **5** : AMOUNT, EXTENT ⟨custom-made to the ∼ of $40 to $50 apiece —*Amer. Fabrics*⟩

²tune *vb* **tuned; tun·ing** *vt* (15c) **1** : to adjust in musical pitch or cause to be in tune ⟨*tuned* her guitar⟩ **2 a** : to bring into harmony : ATTUNE **b** : to adjust for precise functioning — often used with *up* ⟨∼ up an engine⟩ **c** : to make more precise, intense, or effective **3** : to adjust with respect to resonance at a particular frequency: as **a** : to adjust (a radio or television receiver) to respond to waves of a particular frequency — often used with *in* **b** : to establish radio contact with ⟨∼ in a directional beacon⟩ **4** : to adjust the frequency of the output of (a device) to a chosen frequency or range of frequencies; *also* : to alter the frequency of (radiation) ∼ *vi* **1** : to become attuned **2** : to adjust a radio or television receiver to respond to waves of a particular frequency

tuned–in \'tünd-'in, 'tyünd-\ *adj* (1963) : TURNED-ON

tune·ful \'tün-fəl, 'tyün-\ *adj* (1591) : MELODIOUS, MUSICAL — **tune·ful·ly** \-fə-lē\ *adv* — **tune·ful·ness** *n*

tune in *vt* (1913) : to listen to or view a broadcast of ⟨*tuned* in the weather report⟩ ∼ *vi* : to listen to or view a broadcast ⟨*tune* in next week for the conclusion⟩

tune·less \'tün-ləs, 'tyün-\ *adj* (1591) **1** : not tuneful **2** : not producing music — **tune·less·ly** *adv*

tune out *vt* (1910) : to become unresponsive to : IGNORE ∼ *vi* : to dissociate oneself from what is happening or one's surroundings

tun·er \'tü-nər, 'tyü-\ *n* (ca. 1801) **1** : one that tunes ⟨a piano ∼⟩ **2** : something used for tuning; *specif* : the part of a receiving set that converts radio signals into audio or video signals

tune·smith \'tün-ˌsmith, 'tyün-\ *n* (1926) : a composer esp. of popular songs

tune–up \-ˌəp\ *n* (1933) **1** : a general adjustment to insure operation at peak efficiency **2** : a preliminary trial : WARM-UP

tung \'təŋ\ *n* (1914) : TUNG TREE

tung oil *n* [part trans. of Chin (Beijing) *tóngyóu*] (1881) : a pale yellow pungent drying oil obtained from the seeds of tung trees and used chiefly in quick-drying varnishes and paints and as a waterproofing agent

tung·state \'təŋ-ˌstāt\ *n* (1800) : a salt or ester of a tungstic acid esp. of H_2WO_4

tung·sten \'təŋ-stən\ *n* [Sw, fr. *tung* heavy + *sten* stone] (1796) : a gray-white heavy high-melting ductile hard polyvalent metallic element that resembles chromium and molybdenum in many of its properties and is used esp. for electrical purposes and in hardening alloys (as steel) — called also *wolfram*; see ELEMENT table

tung·stic acid \'təŋ-stik-\ *n* [*tungsten*] (1796) : a yellow crystalline powder WO_3 that is the trioxide of tungsten; *also* : an acid (as H_2WO_4) derived from this

tung tree *n* [Chin (Beijing) *tóng*] (1895) : any of several trees (genus *Aleurites*) of the spurge family whose seeds yield tung oil; *esp* : an Asian tree (*A. fordii*) widely grown in warm regions

Tun·gus \tün-'güz, tən-\ *n, pl* **Tungus** *or* **Tun·gus·es** [Russ] (1674) **1** : a member of an indigenous people of central and southeastern Siberia **2** : the Tungusic language of the Tungus people

Tun·gu·sic \-'gü-zik\ *n* (ca. 1867) : a family of Altaic languages spoken in Manchuria and northward — **Tungusic** *adj*

tu·nic \'tü-nik, 'tyü-\ *n* [L *tunica*, of Sem origin; akin to Heb *kuttōneth* coat] (ca. 1609) **1 a** : a simple slip-on garment made with or without sleeves and usu. knee-length or longer, belted at the waist, and worn as an under or outer garment by men and women of ancient Greece and Rome **b** : SURCOAT **2** : an enclosing or covering membrane or tissue ⟨the ∼ of a seed⟩ **3** : a long usu. plain close-fitting jacket with high collar worn esp. as part of a uniform **4** : TUNICLE **5 a** : a short overskirt **b** : a hip-length or longer blouse or jacket

tu·ni·ca \'tü-ni-kə, 'tyü-\ *n, pl* **tu·ni·cae** \-nə-ˌkē, -ˌkī, -ˌsē\ [L, tunic, membrane] (ca. 1828) : an enveloping or lining layer of body tissue

¹tu·ni·cate \'tü-ni-kət, 'tyü-, -nə-ˌkāt\ *also* **tu·ni·cat·ed** \-nə-ˌkā-təd\ *adj* [L *tunicatus*, fr. *tunica*] (ca. 1623) **1 a** : having or covered with a tunic or tunica **b** : having, arranged in, or made up of concentric layers ⟨a ∼ bulb⟩ **2** : of or relating to the tunicates

²tu·ni·cate \-ni-kət, -nə-ˌkāt\ *n* [NL *Tunicata*, fr. neut. pl. of L *tunicatus*] (1889) : any of a subphylum (Urochordata syn. Tunicata) of marine chordate animals that have a thick secreted covering layer, a greatly reduced nervous system, a heart able to reverse the direction of blood flow, and only in the larval stage a notochord

tu·ni·cle \'tü-ni-kəl, 'tyü-\ *n* [ME, fr. L *tunicula*, dim. of *tunica*] (15c) : a short vestment worn by a subdeacon over the alb during mass and by a bishop under the dalmatic at pontifical ceremonies

tuning fork *n* (1799) : a 2-pronged metal implement that gives a fixed tone when struck and is useful for tuning musical instruments and ascertaining standard pitch

tuning pipe *n* (1897) : PITCH PIPE; *specif* : one of a set of pitch pipes used esp. for tuning stringed musical instruments

¹tun·nel \'tə-nᵊl\ *n* [ME *tonel* tube-shaped net, fr. MF, tun, fr. OF, fr. *tonne* tun, fr. ML *tunna*] (1548) **1** : a hollow conduit or recess : TUBE, WELL **2 a** : a covered passageway; *specif* : a horizontal passageway through or under an obstruction **b** : a subterranean gallery (as in a mine) **c** : BURROW — **tun·nel·like** \-nᵊl-ˌ(l)īk\ *adj*

²tunnel *vb* **-neled** *or* **-nelled; -nel·ing** *or* **-nel·ling** \'tən-liŋ, tə-nᵊl-iŋ\ *vi* (1795) **1** : to make or use a tunnel **2** *physics* : to pass through a potential barrier ⟨electrons ∼*ing* through an insulator between semiconductors⟩ ∼ *vt* : to make a tunnel or similar opening through or under; *also* : to make (one's way) by or as if by making a tunnel — **tun·nel·er** \'tən-lər, 'tə-nᵊl-ər\ *n*

tunnel vision *n* (ca. 1942) **1** : constriction of the visual field resulting in loss of peripheral vision **2** : extreme narrowness of viewpoint : NARROWMINDEDNESS; *also* : single-minded concentration on one objective — **tun·nel–vi·sioned** \-'vi-zhənd\ *adj*

tun·ny \'tə-nē\ *n, pl* **tunnies** *also* **tunny** [modif. of MF *thon* or OIt *tonno*; both fr. OProv *ton*, fr. L *thunnus* — more at TUNA] (ca. 1530) : TUNA

¹tup \'təp\ *n* [ME *tupe*] (14c) **1** *chiefly Brit* : RAM 1a **2** : a heavy metal body (as the weight of a pendulum)

²tup *vt* **tupped; tup·ping** (1604) *chiefly Brit* : to copulate with (a ewe)

tu·pe·lo \'tü-pə-ˌlō, 'tyü-\ *n, pl* **-los** [perh. fr. Creek *ito opilwa* swamp tree] (ca. 1730) **1** : any of a genus (*Nyssa* of the family Nyssaceae) of No. American and Asian deciduous trees that have simple alternate leaves, small greenish dioecious stalked flowers, and a rounded drupe; *esp* : BLACK GUM **2** : the pale soft wood of a tupelo

Tu·pi \tü-'pē, 'tü-ˌ(ˌ)\ *n, pl* **Tupi** *or* **Tupis** (1842) **1** : the language of the Tupi people **2** : a member of a group of Tupi-Guaranian peoples of Brazil living esp. in the Amazon valley

Tu·pi·an \tü-'pē-ən, 'tü-ˌ(ˌ)\ *adj* (1902) : of, relating to, or constituting the Tupi or their Tupi-Guaranian peoples or their languages

Tu·pi–Gua·ra·ni \tü-ˌpē-ˌgwär-ə-'nē, ˌtü-ˌ(ˌ)pē-\ *n* (1850) **1** : a member of a group of So. American Indian peoples spread over an area from eastern Brazil to the Peruvian Andes and from the Guianas to Uruguay **2** : TUPI-GUARANIAN

Tupi–Gua·ra·ni·an \-'nē-ən\ *n* (ca. 1902) : a language family widely distributed in tropical So. America

-tu·ple \ˌtə-pəl, ˌtü-\ *n comb form* [quin*tuple*, sex*tuple*] : set of (so many) elements — usu. used of sets with ordered elements ⟨the ordered 2-*tuple* (a, b)⟩

tup·pence *var of* TWOPENCE

tuque \'tük, 'tyük\ *n* [CanF, fr. F *toque* — more at TOQUE] (1871) : a warm knitted usu. pointed stocking cap

tu quo·que \ˌtü-'kwō-kwe, ˌtyü-, -ˌkō-\ *n* [L, you too] (1614) : a retort charging an adversary with being or doing what he criticizes in others

tu·ra·co \'tür-ə-ˌ(ˌ)kō\ *n, pl* **-cos** [origin unknown] (1743) : any of a family (Musophagidae) of African birds that are related to the cuckoos and have a long tail, a short stout often colored bill, and red wing feathers

Tu·ra·ni·an \tü-'rä-nē-ən, tyü-, -'rä-\ *n* [Per *Tūrān* Turkestan, the region north of the Amu Darya] (ca. 1777) **1** : a member of any of various peoples speaking Ural-Altaic languages **2** : URAL-ALTAIC — **Turanian** *adj*

tur·ban \'tər-bən\ *n* [MF *turbant*, fr. It *turbante*, fr. Turk *tülbent*, fr. Per *dulband*] (1588) **1** : a headdress worn chiefly in countries of the eastern Mediterranean and southern Asia esp. by Muslims and made of a cap around which is wound a long cloth **2** : a headdress resembling a turban; *specif* : a woman's close-fitting hat without a brim **3** : a rolled stuffed fillet of fish ⟨∼ of sole⟩ — **tur·baned** *or* **tur·banned** \-bənd\ *adj*

turban 1

tur·bel·lar·i·an \ˌtər-bə-'ler-ē-ən, -'lar-\ *n* [ultim. fr. L *turbellae* (pl.) bustle, stir, dim. of *turba* confusion, crowd; fr. the tiny eddies created in water by the cilia] (1883) : any of a class (Turbellaria) of mostly aquatic and free-living flatworms (as a planarian) — **turbellarian** *adj*

tur·bid \'tər-bəd\ *adj* [L *turbidus* confused, turbid, fr. *turba* confusion, crowd, prob. fr. Gk *tyrbē* confusion] (1626) **1 a** : thick or opaque with or as if with roiled sediment ⟨a ∼ stream⟩ **b** : heavy with smoke or mist **2 a** : deficient in clarity or purity : FOUL, MUDDY ⟨∼ depths of degradation and misery —C. I. Glicksberg⟩ **b** : characterized by or producing obscurity (as of mind or emotions) ⟨an emotionally ∼ response⟩ — **tur·bid·i·ty** \ˌtər-'bi-də-tē\ *n* — **tur·bid·ly** \'tər-bəd-lē\ *adv* — **tur·bid·ness** *n*

tur·bi·dim·e·ter \ˌtər-bə-'di-mə-tər\ *n* [ISV *turbid*ity + *-meter*] (1905) **1** : an instrument for measuring and comparing the turbidity of liquids by viewing light through them and determining how much light is cut off **2** : NEPHELOMETER — **tur·bi·di·met·ric** \ˌtər-bə-də-'me-trik, ˌtər-ˌbi-də-\ *adj* — **tur·bi·di·met·ri·cal·ly** \-tri-k(ə-)lē\ *adv* — **tur·bi·dim·e·try** \ˌtər-bə-'di-mə-trē\ *n*

tur·bi·dite \'tər-bə-ˌdīt\ *n* [*turbid*ity current (a current flowing down a slope and spreading out on the ocean floor) + ¹-*ite*] (1957) : a sedimentary deposit consisting of material that has moved down the steep slope at the edge of a continental shelf; *also* : a rock formed from this deposit

¹**tur·bi·nate** \'tər-bə-nət, -ˌnāt\ *also* **tur·bi·nat·ed** \-ˌnā-təd\ *adj* [L *turbinatus*, fr. *turbin-, turbo*] (1661) **1** : shaped like a top or an inverted cone ⟨~ seed capsule⟩ **2** : relating to or being a turbinate

²**turbinate** *n* (ca. 1803) : one of usu. several thin plicated membrane-covered bony or cartilaginous plates on the walls of the nasal chambers

tur·bine \'tər-bən, -ˌbin\ *n* [F, fr. L *turbin-, turbo* top, whirlwind, whirl, fr. *turba* confusion — more at TURBID] (1842) : a rotary engine actuated by the reaction or impulse or both of a current of fluid (as water, steam, or air) subject to pressure and usu. made with a series of curved vanes on a central rotating spindle

tur·bo \'tər-ˌ)bō\ *n, pl* **turbos** [*turbo-*] (1904) **1** : TURBINE **2** [by shortening]: TURBOCHARGER

turbo- *comb form* [*turbine*] **1** : coupled directly to a driving turbine ⟨*turbo*fan⟩ **2** : consisting of or incorporating a turbine ⟨*turbo*jet engine⟩

tur·bo·car \'tər-ˌ·ō-ˌkär\ *n* (1950) : an automotive vehicle propelled by a gas turbine

tur·bo·charged \-ˌchärjd\ *adj* (1945) : equipped with a turbocharger

tur·bo·charg·er \-ˌchär-jər\ *n* (1934) : a centrifugal blower driven by exhaust gas turbines and used to supercharge an engine

tur·bo·elec·tric \ˌtər-bō-i-'lek-trik\ *adj* (1904) : using or being a turbine generator that produces electricity usu. for motive power

tur·bo·fan \'tər-bō-ˌfan\ *n* (1911) **1** : a fan that is directly connected to and driven by a turbine and is used to supply air for cooling, ventilation, or combustion **2** : a jet engine having a turbofan

tur·bo·gen·er·a·tor \ˌtər-bō-'je-nə-ˌrā-tər\ *n* (1898) : an electric generator driven by a turbine

tur·bo·jet \-ˌjet\ *n* (1945) **1** : an airplane powered by turbojet engines **2** : TURBOJET ENGINE

turbojet engine *n* (1944) : a jet engine in which a turbine drives a compressor that supplies air to a burner and hot gases from the burner drive the turbine before being discharged rearward

tur·bo·ma·chin·ery \ˌtər-bō-mə-'shēn-rē, -'shē-nə-\ *n* (1948) : machinery consisting of, incorporating, or constituting a turbine

tur·bo·prop \'tər-bō-ˌpräp\ *n* (1945) **1** : TURBOPROP ENGINE **2** : an airplane powered by turboprop engines

turboprop engine *n* (1947) : a jet engine designed to produce thrust principally by means of a propeller driven by a turbine with additional thrust usu. obtained by the rearward discharge of hot exhaust gases

tur·bo·shaft \'tər-bō-ˌshaft\ *n* (1958) : a gas turbine engine that is similar in operation to a turboprop engine but instead of being used to power a propeller is used through a transmission system for powering other devices (as helicopter rotors and pumps)

tur·bot \'tər-bət\ *n, pl* **turbot** *also* **turbots** [ME, fr. OF *tourbot*] (14c) **1** : a large European flatfish (*Psetta maxima*) that is a popular food fish and has a brownish upper surface marked with scattered tubercles and a white undersurface **2** : any of various flatfishes resembling the turbot

tur·bu·lence \'tər-byə-lən(t)s\ *n* (1598) : the quality or state of being turbulent: as **a** : wild commotion **b** : irregular atmospheric motion esp. when characterized by up-and-down currents **c** : departure in a fluid from a smooth flow

tur·bu·len·cy \-lən(t)-sē\ *n, pl* **-cies** (1607) *archaic* : TURBULENCE

tur·bu·lent \-lənt\ *adj* [L *turbulentus*, fr. *turba* confusion, crowd — more at TURBID] (1538) **1** : causing unrest, violence, or disturbance **2 a** : characterized by agitation or tumult : TEMPESTUOUS **b** : exhibiting physical turbulence — **tur·bu·lent·ly** *adv*

turbulent flow *n* (1895) : a fluid flow in which the velocity at a given point varies erratically in magnitude and direction — compare LAMINAR FLOW

Tur·co- *or* **Tur·ko-** \'tər-ˌ)kō\ *comb form* [Turco- fr. ML *Turcus* Turk; *Turko-* fr. *Turk*] **1** : Turkic : Turkish : Turk ⟨*Turco*phil⟩ **2** : Turkish and ⟨*Turco*-Greek⟩

turd \'tərd\ *n* [ME *tord, turd*, fr. OE *tord*; akin to MD *tort* dung and prob. to OE *teran* to tear — more at TEAR] (bef. 12c) **1** : a piece of excrement — sometimes considered vulgar **2** : a contemptible person — usu. considered vulgar

tu·reen \tə-'rēn, tyu̇-\ *n* [F *terrine*, fr. MF, fr. fem. of *terrin* of earth, fr. (assumed) VL *terrinus*, fr. L *terra* earth — more at TERRACE] (ca. 1706) **1** : a deep and usu. covered bowl from which foods (as soup) are served **2** : CASSEROLE 1

¹**turf** \'tərf\ *n, pl* **turfs** *also* **turves** \'tərvz\ [ME, fr. OE; akin to OHG *zurba* turf, Skt *darbha* tuft of grass] (bef. 12c) **1 a** : the upper stratum of soil bound by grass and plant roots into a thick mat; *also* : a piece of this **b** : an artificial substitute for this (as on a playing field) **2 a** : PEAT 2 **b** : a piece of peat dried for fuel **3 a** : a track or course for horse racing **b** : the sport or business of horse racing **4 a** : territory considered by a teenage gang to be under its control **b** : TERRITORY ⟨have to play two of the last three games on hostile ~ —Joe Klein⟩ ⟨points toward the biographer's ~, not the critic's —Hugh Kenner⟩; *also* : a sphere of activity or influence ⟨people who could hurt him on his own foreign-policy ~ —*Wall Street Jour.*⟩ — **turfy** \'tər-fē\ *adj*

²**turf** *vt* (15c) **1** : to cover with turf **2** *chiefly Brit* : to eject forcibly : KICK — usu. used with *out*

turf accountant *n* (1915) *Brit* : BOOKMAKER 2

turf·man \'tərf-mən\ *n* (1818) : a devotee of horse racing; *esp* : a person who owns and races horses

turf·ski \-ˌskē\ *n* (1967) : a short ski with rollers on the bottom that can be used to ski down a grassy slope — **turf·ski·ing** *n*

tur·ges·cent \ˌtər-'je-s³nt\ *adj* [L *turgescent-, turgescens,* prp. of *turgescere* to swell, incho. of *turgēre* to be swollen] (ca. 1727) : becoming turgid, distended, or inflated : SWELLING — **tur·ges·cence** \-s³n(t)s\ *n*

tur·gid \'tər-jəd\ *adj* [L *turgidus*, fr. *turgēre* to be swollen] (1620) **1** : being in a state of distension : SWOLLEN, TUMID ⟨~ limbs⟩; *esp* : exhibiting turgor **2** : excessively embellished in style or language : BOMBASTIC, POMPOUS — **tur·gid·i·ty** \ˌtər-'ji-də-tē\ *n* — **tur·gid·ly** \'tər-jəd-lē\ *adv* — **tur·gid·ness** *n*

tur·gor \'tər-gər, -ˌgȯr\ *n* [LL, turgidity, swelling, fr. L *turgēre*] (1876) : the normal state of turgidity and tension in living cells; *esp* : the dis-

tension of the protoplasmic layer and wall of a plant cell by the fluid contents

Tu·ring machine \'tu̇r-iŋ-, 'tyu̇r-\ *n* [A. M. *Turing* †1954 Eng. mathematician] (1937) : a hypothetical computing machine that has an unlimited amount of information storage

tu·ris·ta \tü-'rē-stə\ *n* [Sp, tourist] (1962) : intestinal sickness and diarrhea commonly affecting a tourist in a foreign country; *esp* : MONTEZUMA'S REVENGE

Turk \'tərk\ *n* [ME, fr. MF or Turk; MF *Turc*, fr. ML *Turcus*, fr. Turk *Türk*] (14c) **1** : a member of any of numerous Asian peoples speaking Turkic languages who live in a region extending from the Balkans to eastern Siberia and western China **2** : a native or inhabitant of Turkey **3** *archaic* : one who is cruel or tyrannical **4** : MUSLIM; *specif* : a Muslim subject of the Turkish sultan **5** : a Turkish horse; *specif* : a Turkish strain of Arab and crossbred horses **6** *often not cap* : a usu. young dynamic person eager for change; *esp* : YOUNG TURK

tur·key \'tər-kē\ *n, pl* **turkeys** [*Turkey*, country in western Asia and southeastern Europe; fr. confusion with the guinea fowl, supposed to be imported from Turkish territory] (1555) **1** *pl also* **turkey** : a large No. American gallinaceous bird (*Meleagris gallopavo*) that is domesticated in most parts of the world **2** : FAILURE, FLOP; *esp* : a theatrical production that has failed **3** : three successive strikes in bowling **4** : a stupid, foolish, or inept person

tur·key–cock \'tər-kē-ˌkäk\ *n* (1578) **1** : GOBBLER **2** : a strutting pompous person

turkey oak *n* (1709) : a small oak (*Quercus laevis* syn. *Q. catesbaei*) of the southeastern U.S.; *also* : a Eurasian oak (*Q. cerris*)

Tur·key red \'tər-kē-\ *n* [*Turkey*] (1789) : a brilliant durable red produced on cotton by means of alizarin in connection with an aluminum mordant and fatty matter

tur·key shoot \'tər-kē-\ *n* (1845) : a marksmanship contest using a moving target with a turkey offered as a prize

turkey trot *n* (1908) : a ragtime dance danced with the feet well apart and with a characteristic rise on the ball of the foot followed by a drop upon the heel

turkey vulture *n* (1823) : an American vulture (*Cathartes aura*) with a red head and whitish bill — called also *turkey buzzard*

Turk·ic \'tər-kik\ *adj* (1859) **1 a** : of, relating to, or constituting a family of Altaic languages including Turkish **b** : of or relating to the peoples speaking Turkic **2** : TURKISH 1 — **Turkic** *n*

¹**Turk·ish** \'tər-kish\ *adj* (1545) **1** : of, relating to, or characteristic of Turkey, the Turks, or Turkish **2** : TURKIC 1a

²**Turkish** *n* (1677) : the Turkic language of the Republic of Turkey

Turkish bath *n* (1644) : a bath in which the bather passes through a series of steam rooms of increasing temperature and then receives a rubdown, massage, and cold shower

Turkish coffee *n* (1854) : a sweetened decoction of pulverized coffee

Turkish delight *n* (1877) : a jellylike or gummy confection usu. cut in cubes and dusted with sugar — called also *Turkish paste*

Turkish towel *n* (1862) : a towel made of cotton terry cloth

Turk·ism \'tər-ki-zəm\ *n* (1595) : the customs, beliefs, institutions, and principles of the Turks

Tur·ko·man *or* **Tur·co·man** \'tər-kə-mən\ *n, pl* **Turkomans** *or* **Turcomans** [ML *Turcomannus*, fr. Per *Turkmān*, fr. *turkmān* resembling a Turk, fr. *Turk*] (ca. 1520) : a member of a Turkic-speaking traditionally nomadic people living chiefly in Turkmenistan, Afghanistan, and Iran — **Turkoman** *or* **Turcoman** *adj*

Turk's head *n* (1833) : a turban-shaped knot worked on a rope with a piece of small line — see KNOT illustration

tur·mer·ic \'tər-mə-rik *also* 'tü-mə- *or* 'tyü-\ *n* [modif. of MF *terre merite* saffron, fr. ML *terra merita*, lit., deserving or deserved earth] (1545) **1** : an East Indian perennial herb (*Curcuma domestica* syn. *C. longa*) of the ginger family with a large aromatic yellow rhizome **2** : the cleaned, boiled, dried, and usu. pulverized rhizome of the turmeric plant used as a coloring agent, a flavoring, or a stimulant **3** : a yellow to reddish brown dyestuff obtained from turmeric

tur·moil \'tər-ˌmȯil\ *n* [origin unknown] (1526) : a state or condition of extreme confusion, agitation, or commotion

¹**turn** \'tərn\ *vb* [ME; partly fr. OE *tyrnan & turnian* to turn, fr. ML *tornare* fr. L, to turn on a lathe, fr. *tornus* lathe, fr. Gk *tornos*; partly fr. OF *torner, tourner* to turn, fr. ML *tornare*; akin to L *terere* to rub — more at THROW] *vt* (bef. 12c) **1 a** : to cause to move around an axis or a center : make rotate or revolve ⟨~ a wheel⟩ ⟨~ a crank⟩ **b** (1) : to cause to move around so as to effect a desired end (as of locking, opening, or shutting) ⟨~ed the knob till the door opened⟩ (2) : to affect or alter the functioning of (as a mechanical device) by such movement ⟨~ed the oven to a higher temperature⟩ **c** : to execute or perform by rotating or revolving ⟨~ handsprings⟩ **d** : to twist out of line or shape : WRENCH ⟨had ~ed his ankle⟩ **2 a** (1) : to cause to change position by moving through an arc of a circle ⟨~ed her chair to the fire⟩ (2) : to cause to move around a center so as to show another side of ⟨~ the page⟩ (3) : to cause (as a scale) to move so as to register weight **b** : to revolve mentally : think over : PONDER **3 a** : to reverse the sides or surfaces of : INVERT ⟨~ pancakes⟩ ⟨~ the shirt inside out⟩: as (1) : to dig or plow so as to bring the lower soil to the surface (2) : to make (as a garment) over by reversing the material and resewing ⟨~ a collar⟩ (3) : to invert feet up and face down (as a character, rule, or slug) in setting type **b** : to reverse or upset the order or disposition of ⟨everything was ~ed topsy-turvy⟩ **c** : to disturb or upset the mental balance of : DERANGE, UNSETTLE ⟨a mind ~ed by grief⟩ **d** : to set in another esp. contrary direction **4 a** : to bend or change the course of : DIVERT **b** : to cause to retreat ⟨used fire hoses to ~ the mob⟩ **c** : to alter the drift, tendency, or expected result of **d** : to bend a course around or about : ROUND ⟨~ed the corner at full speed⟩ **5 a** (1) : to direct or point (as the face) in a specified way or direction (2) : to present by a change in direction or position ⟨~ing his back to

\ə\ abut \ᵊ\ kitten, F table \ər\ further \a\ ash \ā\ ace \ä\ mop, mar
\au̇\ out \ch\ chin \e\ bet \ē\ easy \g\ go \i\ hit \ī\ ice \j\ job
\ŋ\ sing \ō\ go \ȯ\ law \ȯi\ boy \th\ thin \t͟h\ the \ü\ loot \u̇\ foot
\y\ yet \zh\ vision \à, ̲k, ⁿ, œ, œ̄, ᵫ, ᵫ̄, ᵊ\ see Guide to Pronunciation

his guests⟩ **b** : to bring to bear (as by aiming, pointing, or focusing) : TRAIN ⟨~ed the light into the dark doorway⟩ ⟨~ed a questioning eye toward her⟩ **c** : to direct (as the attention or mind) toward or away from something **d** : to direct the employment of : APPLY, DEVOTE ⟨~ed his skills to the service of mankind⟩ **e** (1) : to cause to rebound or recoil ⟨~s their argument against them⟩ (2) : to make antagonistic : PREJUDICE ⟨~ a child against its mother⟩ **f** (1) : to cause to go in a particular direction ⟨~ed our steps homeward⟩ (2) : DRIVE, SEND ⟨~ cows to pasture⟩ ⟨~ing hunters off his land⟩ (3) : to convey or direct into or out of a receptacle by inverting **6 a** (1) : to make acid or sour (2) : to change the color (as of foliage) **b** (1) : CONVERT, TRANSFORM ⟨~ defeat into victory⟩ (2) : TRANSLATE, PARAPHRASE **c** : to cause to become of a specified nature or appearance ⟨~ed him into a frog⟩ ⟨illness ~ed her hair white⟩ **d** : to exchange for something else ⟨~ coins into paper money⟩ **e** : to cause to defect to another side **7 a** : to shape esp. in a rounded form by applying a cutting tool while revolving in a lathe **b** : to give a rounded form to by any means ⟨~ the heel of a sock⟩ **c** : to shape or mold artistically, gracefully, or neatly ⟨a well ~ed phrase⟩ **8 a** : to make a fold, bend, or curve in: **a** : to form by bending ⟨~ a lead pipe⟩ **b** : to cause (the edge of a blade) to bend back or over : BLUNT, DULL **9 a** : to keep (as money or goods) moving; *specif* : to dispose of (a stock) to make room for another **b** : to gain in the course of business ⟨~ing a quick profit⟩ **c** : to make use of ⟨~ed her education to advantage⟩ **d** : to carry to completion ⟨~ed a double play⟩ **10** : to engage in (an act of prostitution) ⟨~ tricks⟩ ~ *vi* **1 a** : to move around on an axis or through an arc of a circle : ROTATE **b** : to become giddy or dizzy : SPIN ⟨heights always made his head ~⟩ **c** (1) : to have as a decisive factor : HINGE ⟨the argument ~s on a point of logic⟩ ⟨the outcome of the game ~ed on an interception⟩ (2) : to have a center (as of interest) in something specified **2 a** : to direct one's course **b** (1) : to reverse a course or direction (2) : to have a reactive usu. adverse effect : RECOIL ⟨~ to take a different course or direction ⟨~ed toward home⟩ ⟨the main road ~s sharply to the right⟩ **3 a** : to change position so as to face another way **b** : to face toward or away from someone or something **c** : to change one's attitude or reverse one's course of action to one of opposition or hostility ⟨felt the world had ~ed against him⟩ **d** : to make a sudden violent assault esp. without evident cause ⟨dogs ~ing on their owners⟩ **4 a** : to direct one's attention or thoughts to or away from someone or something **b** (1) : to change one's religion (2) : to go over to another side or party : DEFECT **c** : to have recourse : REFER, RESORT ⟨~ed to a friend for help⟩ ⟨~ed to his notes for the exact figures⟩ **d** : to direct one's efforts or interests : devote or apply oneself ⟨~ed to the study of the law⟩ **5 a** : to become changed, altered, or transformed: as (1) *archaic* : to become different (2) : to change color ⟨the leaves have ~ed⟩ (3) : to become sour, rancid, or tainted ⟨the milk had ~ed⟩ (4) : to be variable or inconstant (5) : to become mentally unbalanced : become deranged **b** (1) : to pass from one state to another : CHANGE ⟨water had ~ed to ice⟩ (2) : BECOME, GROW ⟨his hair had ~ed gray⟩ ⟨the weather ~ed bad⟩ ⟨just ~ed twenty⟩ (3) : to become someone or something specified by change from another state : change into ⟨~ pro⟩ ⟨doctors ~ed authors⟩ **6** : to become curved or bent (as from pressure) *esp* : to become blunted by bending ⟨edge of the knife had ~ed⟩ **7** : to operate a lathe **8** *of merchandise* : to be stocked and disposed of : change hands — **turn-able** \'tər-nə-bəl\ *adj* — **turn a blind eye** : to refuse to see : be oblivious ⟨might *turn a blind eye* to the use of violence —Arthur Krock⟩ — **turn a deaf ear** : to refuse to listen — **turn a hair** : to give a sign of distress or disturbance ⟨did not *turn a hair* when told of the savage murder —*Times Lit. Supp.*⟩ — **turn color 1** : to become of a different color **2 a** : BLUSH, FLUSH **b** : to grow pale — **turn loose 1 a** : to set free ⟨*turned loose* the captured animal⟩ **b** : to free from all restraints ⟨*turned* them *loose* with a pile of theme paper to write whatever they liked —Elizabeth P. Schafer⟩ **2** : to fire off : DISCHARGE **3** : to open fire — **turn one's back on 1** : REJECT, DENY ⟨would be *turning one's back on* history —Pius Walsh⟩ **2** : FORSAKE ⟨*turned his back on* his obligations⟩ — **turn one's hand** *or* **turn a hand** : to set to work : apply oneself — **turn one's head** : to cause to become infatuated or conceited ⟨success had not *turned his head*⟩ — **turn one's stomach** : to disgust completely : SICKEN, NAUSEATE ⟨the foul smell *turned his stomach*⟩ — **turn tail** : to turn away so as to flee ⟨*turned tail* and ran⟩ — **turn the other cheek** : to respond to injury or unkindness with patience : forgo retaliation — **turn the tables** : to bring about a reversal of the relative conditions or fortunes of two contending parties — **turn the trick** : to bring about the desired result or effect — **turn turtle** : CAPSIZE, OVERTURN

²turn *n* [ME; partly fr. OF *tourn, tour* lathe, circuit, turn (partly fr. L *tornus* lathe; partly fr. OF *torner, tourner* to turn); partly fr. ME *turnen* to turn] (13c) **1 a** : the action or an act of turning about a center or axis : REVOLUTION, ROTATION **b** : any of various rotating or pivoting movements in dancing or gymnastics **2 a** : the action or an act of giving or taking a different direction : change of course or posture ⟨illegal left ~⟩: as (1) : a drill maneuver in which troops in mass formation change direction without preserving alignment (2) : any of various shifts of direction in skiing (3) : an interruption of a curve in figure skating **b** : DEFLECTION, DEVIATION **c** : the action or an act of turning so as to face in the opposite direction : reversal of posture or course ⟨an about ~⟩ ⟨~ of the tide⟩ **d** : a change effected by turning over to another side ⟨~ of the cards⟩ **e** : a place at which something turns, turns off, or turns back : BEND, CURVE **3 a** : a short trip out and back or round about ⟨took a ~ through the park⟩ **4** : an act or deed affecting another esp. when incidental or unexpected ⟨one good ~ deserves another⟩ **5 a** : a period of action or activity : GO, SPELL **b** : a place, time, or opportunity accorded an individual or unit of a series in simple succession or in a scheduled order ⟨waiting her ~ in line⟩ **c** : a period or tour of duty : SHIFT **d** : a short act or piece (as for a variety show); *also* : PERFORMANCE **3 e** (1) : an event in any gambling game after which bets are settled (2) : the order of the last three cards in faro — used in the phrase *call the turn* **6** : something that revolves around a center: as **a** (1) : LATHE (2) : a catch or latch for a cupboard or cabinet door operated by turning a handle **b** : a musical ornament consisting of a group of four or more notes that wind about the principal note by including the notes next above and next below **7** : a special purpose or requirement — used chiefly in the phrase *serve*

one's turn **8 a** : an act of changing : ALTERATION, MODIFICATION ⟨a nasty ~ in the weather⟩ **b** : a change in tendency, trend, or drift ⟨hoped for a ~ in his luck⟩ ⟨~ for the better⟩ **c** : the beginning of a new period of time ⟨the ~ of the century⟩ **9 a** : distinctive quality or character **b** (1) : a skillful fashioning of language or arrangement of words (2) : a particular form of expression or peculiarity of phrasing **c** : the shape or mold in which something is fashioned : CAST **10 a** : the state or manner of being coiled or twisted **b** : a single round (as of rope passed about an object or of wire wound on a core) **11** : natural or special ability or aptitude : BENT, INCLINATION ⟨a ~ for logic⟩ ⟨an optimistic ~ of mind⟩ **12** : a special twist, construction, or interpretation ⟨gave the old yarn a new ~⟩ **13 a** : a disordering spell or attack (as of illness, faintness, or dizziness) **b** : a nervous start or shock **14 a** : a complete transaction involving a purchase and sale of securities; *also* : a profit from such a transaction **b** : TURNOVER 7b **15** : something turned or to be turned: as **a** : a character or slug inverted in setting type **b** : a piece of type placed bottom up — **at every turn** : on every occasion : CONTINUALLY ⟨they opposed her *at every turn*⟩ — **by turns 1** : one after another in regular succession **2** : VARIOUSLY, ALTERNATELY ⟨a book that is *by turns* pedantic, delightful, and infuriating⟩ — **in turn** : in due order of succession — **on the turn** : at the point of turning ⟨tide is *on the turn*⟩ — **out of turn 1** : not in due order of succession ⟨play *out of turn*⟩ **2** : at a wrong time or place and usu. imprudently ⟨talking *out of turn*⟩ — **to a turn** : to perfection

turn-about \'tər-nə-,baut\ *n* (1789) **1** : MERRY-GO-ROUND **2 a** : a change or reversal of direction, trend, policy, role, or character **b** : a changing from one allegiance to another **c** : TURNCOAT, RENEGADE **d** : an act or instance of retaliating ⟨~ is fair play⟩

turn-around \-,raund\ *n* (1926) **1 a** : the process of readying a vehicle for departure after its arrival esp. without any intervening delays; *also* : the time spent in this process **b** : the action of receiving, processing, and returning something **2** : a space permitting the turning around of a vehicle **3** : TURNABOUT 2a, b

turn around *vi* (1949) **1** : to act in an abrupt, different, or surprising manner — used with *and* ⟨after three years he just *turned around* and left school⟩ **2** : to become changed for the better ~ *vt* : to change for the better ⟨*turned* her life *around*⟩

turn away *vt* (13c) **1** : DEFLECT, AVERT **2 a** : to send away : REJECT, DISMISS **b** : REPEL **c** : to refuse admittance or acceptance to ~ *vi* : to start to go away : DEPART

turn back *vi* (1535) **1 a** : to go in the reverse direction **b** : to stop going forward **2** : to refer to an earlier time or place ~ *vt* **1** : to drive back or away **2** : to stop the advance of **3** : to fold back **4** : GIVE BACK, RETURN — **turn back the clock** : to revert to or remind of a condition existing in the past

turn-buck-le \'tərn-,bə-kəl\ *n* (ca. 1877) : a device that usu. consists of a link with screw threads at both ends, that is turned to bring the ends closer together, and that is used for tightening a rod or stay

turn-coat \-,kōt\ *n* (1557) : one who switches to an opposing side or party; *specif* : TRAITOR

¹turn-down \'tərn-'daun\ *adj* (1840) : capable of being turned down; *esp* : worn turned down ⟨~ collar⟩

²turn-down \'tərn-,daun\ *n* (1849) **1** : something turned down; *also* : an instance of turning something (as a bed sheet) down ⟨hotel ~ service⟩ **2** : REJECTION **3** : DOWNTURN

turnbuckles

turn down *vt* (1601) **1** : to fold or double down **2** : to turn (a card) face downward **3** : to reduce the height or intensity of by turning a control ⟨*turn down* the radio⟩ **4** : to decline to accept : REJECT ⟨*turned down* the offer⟩ ~ *vi* : to be capable of being folded or doubled down ⟨the collar *turns down*⟩

turned-on \'tərnd-'ȯn, -'än⟩ *adj* (1966) : keenly aware of and responsive to what is new and fashionable : HIP

¹turn-er \'tər-nər\ *n* (15c) : one that turns or is used for turning ⟨a pancake ~⟩; *esp* : a person who forms articles with a lathe

²tur-ner \'tər-nər, 'tur-\ *n* [G, fr. *turnen* to perform gymnastic exercises, fr. OHG *turnēn* to turn, fr. ML *tornare* — more at TURN] (1852) : a member of a turnverein : GYMNAST

Tur-ner's syndrome \'tər-nərz-\ *n* [Henry Hubert *Turner* †1970 Am. physician] (1942) : a genetically determined condition that is associated with the presence of only one complete X chromosome and no Y chromosome and that is characterized by a female phenotype with underdeveloped and infertile ovaries

turn-ery \'tər-nə-rē\ *n, pl* **-er-ies** (1644) : the work, products, or shop of a turner

turn-in \'tər-,nin\ *n* (1902) : something that turns in or is turned in

turn in *vi* (1535) **1** : to make an entrance by turning from a road or path **2** : to go to bed ⟨*turned in* early⟩ ~ *vt* **1** : to deliver up : HAND OVER ⟨*turned in* his badge and quit⟩ **2 a** : to inform on : BETRAY **b** : to deliver to an authority ⟨urged the wanted man to *turn* himself *in*⟩ **3** : to acquit oneself of : PUT ON, PRODUCE ⟨*turned in* a good performance⟩

turn-ing *n* (14c) **1** : the act or course of one that turns **2** : a place of a change in direction **3 a** : a forming by use of a lathe; *broadly* : TURNERY **b** *pl* : waste produced in turning

turning chisel *n* (ca. 1877) : a chisel used for shaping or finishing work in a lathe

turning point *n* (1851) : a point at which a significant change occurs

tur-nip \'tər-nəp\ *n* [prob. fr. *¹turn* + *neep*; fr. the well-rounded root] (1533) **1 a** : either of two biennial herbs of the mustard family with thick edible roots: (1) : one (*Brassica rapa rapifera*) with usu. flattened roots and leaves that are cooked as a vegetable (2) : RUTABAGA **b** : the root of a turnip **2 a** : a large pocket watch

¹turn-key \'tərn-,kē\ *n, pl* **turnkeys** (1654) : one who has charge of a prison's keys

²turnkey *adj* (1927) : built, supplied, or installed complete and ready to operate ⟨a ~ nuclear plant⟩ ⟨a ~ computer system⟩; *also* : of or relating to a turnkey building or installation ⟨a ~ contract⟩ ⟨~ vendors⟩

turn·off \'tər-ˌnȯf\ *n* (ca. 1852) **1** : a turning off **2** : a place where one turns off; *esp* : EXIT 4 **3** : one that causes loss of interest or enthusiasm ⟨the music was a ~⟩

turn off *vt* (1564) **1 a** : DISMISS, DISCHARGE **b** : to dispose of : SELL **2** : DEFLECT, EVADE **3** : PRODUCE, ACCOMPLISH **4** : to stop the flow of or shut off by or as if by turning a control ⟨*turn* the water *off*⟩ **5** : HANG 1b **6 a** : to remove (material) by the process of turning **b** : to shape or produce by turning **7** : to cause to lose interest : BORE ⟨economics *turns* me *off*⟩; *also* : to evoke a negative feeling in ~ *vi* **1** : to deviate from a straight course or from a main road ⟨*turn off* into a side road⟩ **2 a** *Brit* : to turn bad : SPOIL **b** : to change to a specified state : BECOME **3** : to lose interest : WITHDRAW

turn on *vt* (1833) **1** : to activate or cause to flow, operate, or function by or as if by turning a control ⟨*turn* the water *on* full⟩ ⟨*turn on* the power⟩ **2 a** : to cause to undergo an intense often visionary experience by taking a drug; *broadly* : to cause to get high **b** : to move pleasurably ⟨rock music *turns* her *on*⟩; *also* : to excite sexually **c** : to cause to gain knowledge or appreciation of something specified ⟨*turned* her *on* to ballet⟩ ~ *vi* : to become turned on — **turn-on** \'tər-ˌnȯn, -ˌnän\ *n*

turn·out \'tər-ˌnau̇t\ *n* (1688) **1** : an act of turning out **2** *chiefly Brit* **a** : STRIKE 3a **b** : STRIKER 1d **3** : the number of people who participate in or attend an event ⟨a heavy voter ~⟩ **4 a** : a place where something (as a road) turns out or branches off **b** : a space adjacent to a highway in which vehicles may park or pull into to enable others to pass **c** : a railroad siding **5** : a clearing out and cleaning **6 a** : a coach or carriage together with the horses, harness, and attendants **b** : EQUIPMENT, RIG **c** : manner of dress : GETUP **7** : net quantity of produce yielded

turn out *vt* (1546) **1 a** : EXPEL, EVICT **b** : to put (as a horse) to pasture **2 a** : to turn inside out ⟨*turning out* his pockets⟩ **b** : to empty the contents of esp. for cleaning or rearranging; *also* : CLEAN **3** : to produce often rapidly or regularly by or as if by machine ⟨a writer *turning out* stories⟩ **4** : to equip, dress, or finish in a careful or elaborate way **5** : to put out by turning a switch ⟨*turn out* the lights⟩ **6** : to call (as the guard or a company) out from rest or shelter and into formation ~ *vi* **1 a** : to come or go out from home in or as if in answer to a summons ⟨voters *turned out* in droves⟩ **b** : to get out of bed **2 a** : to prove to be in the result or end ⟨the play *turned out* to be a flop⟩ ⟨it *turned out* that we were both wrong⟩ **b** : to become in maturity ⟨nobody thought he'd *turn out* like this⟩ **c** : END ⟨stories that *turn out* happily⟩

¹turn·over \'tər-ˌnō-vər\ *n* (14c) **1** : an act or result of turning over : UPSET **2** : a turning from one side, place, or direction to its opposite : SHIFT, REVERSAL **3** : a reorganization with a view to a shift in personnel : SHAKE-UP **4** : something that is turned over **5** : a filled pastry made by folding half of the crust over the other half **6** : the amount of business done; *esp* : the volume of shares traded on a stock exchange **7 a** : movement (as of goods or people) into, through, and out of a place **b** : a cycle of purchase, sale, and replacement of a stock of goods; *also* : the ratio of sales for a stated period to average inventory **c** : the number of persons hired within a period to replace those leaving or dropped from a workforce; *also* : the ratio of this number to the number in the average force maintained **8** : the act or an instance of a team's losing possession of a ball through error or a minor violation of the rules (as in basketball or football)

²turnover *adj* (ca. 1849) : capable of being turned over

turn over *vt* (14c) **1 a** : to turn from an upright position : OVERTURN **b** : ROTATE ⟨*turn over* a stiff valve with a wrench⟩; *also* : to cause (an internal combustion engine) to begin firing **2** : to search (as clothes or papers) by lifting or moving one by one **3** : to read or examine (as a book) slowly or idly **4** : DELIVER, SURRENDER ⟨I'm *turning* the job *over* to you⟩; *also* : to lose possession of ⟨*turned* the ball *over* three times⟩ **5 a** : to receive and dispose of (a stock of merchandise) **b** : to do business to the amount of ⟨*turning over* $1000 a week⟩ ~ *vi* **1** : UPSET, CAPSIZE **2 a** : ROTATE ⟨of an engine⟩ : to have crankshaft rotation esp. by external means (as by a starter) ⟨the engine *turned over* but didn't start⟩ **3 a** ⟨of one's stomach⟩ : to heave with nausea ⟨something turned my *stomach* over⟩ **b** ⟨of one's *heart*⟩ : to seem to leap or lurch convulsively with sudden fright — **turn over a new leaf** : to make a change for the better esp. in one's way of living

turn·pike \'tərn-ˌpīk\ *n* [ME *turnepike* revolving frame bearing spikes and serving as a barrier, fr. *turnen* to turn + *pike*] (1533) **1** : TOLLGATE **2 a** (1) : a road (as an expressway) for the use of which tolls are collected (2) : a road formerly maintained as a turnpike **b** : a main road; *esp* : a paved highway with crowned surface

turn·sole \'tərn-ˌsōl\ *n* [ME *turnesole*, fr. MF *tournesol*, fr. OIt *tornasole*, fr. *tornare* to turn (fr. ML) + *sole* sun, fr. L *sol* — more at TURN, SOLAR] (14c) **1** : a European herb (*Chrozophora tinctoria*) of the spurge family with juice that is turned blue by ammonia; *also* : a purple dye obtained from it **2** : HELIOTROPE 1

turn·spit \-ˌspit\ *n* (1570) **1 a** : one that turns a spit; *specif* : a small dog formerly used in a treadmill to turn a spit **b** : a roasting jack **2** : a rotatable spit

turn·stile \-ˌstīl\ *n* (1643) : a post with arms pivoted on the top set in a passageway so that persons can pass through only on foot one by one

turn·stone \-ˌstōn\ *n* [fr. a habit of turning over stones to find food] (ca. 1674) : either of two shorebirds (genus *Arenaria*) that resemble the related plovers and sandpipers: **a** : a bird (*A. interpres*) of worldwide distribution that has black and chestnut upperparts and a black breast **b** : a No. American bird (*A. melanocephala*) with black upperparts and breast

turn·ta·ble \-ˌtā-bəl\ *n* (1835) : a revolvable platform: as **a** : a platform with a track for turning wheeled vehicles **b** : LAZY SUSAN **c** : a rotating platform that carries a phonograph record

turn to *vi* (1813) : to apply oneself to work : act vigorously

turnstone

¹turn·up \'tər-ˌnəp\ *adj* (1685) **1** : turned up ⟨a ~ nose⟩ **2** : made or fitted to be turned up ⟨a ~ collar⟩

²turn·up \'tər-ˌnəp\ *n* (1688) : something that is turned up

turn up *vt* (1563) **1** : FIND, DISCOVER **2** : to raise or increase by or as if by turning a control ⟨*turn up* the volume on the radio⟩ **3** *Brit* **a** : to look up (as a word or fact) in a book **b** : to refer to or consult (a book) **4** : to turn (a card) face upward ~ *vi* **1** : to appear or come to light unexpectedly or after being lost ⟨new evidence has *turned up*⟩ **2 a** (1) : to turn out to be ⟨he *turned up* missing at roll call⟩ (2) : APPEAR 4 ⟨her name is always *turning up* in the newspapers⟩ **b** : to arrive or show up at an appointed or expected time or place ⟨*turned up* half an hour late⟩ **3** : to happen or occur unexpectedly ⟨something always *turned up* to prevent their meeting⟩ **4** *of a ship* : TACK 1b — **turn up one's nose** : to show scorn or disdain

turn·ver·ein \'tərn-və-ˌrīn, 'tu̇rn-\ *n* [G, fr. *turnen* to perform gymnastic exercises + *Verein* club] (1852) : an athletic club

tu·ro·phile \'tu̇r-ə-ˌfīl, 'tyu̇r-\ *n* [irreg. fr. Gk *tyros* cheese + E *-phile* — more at BUTTER] (1938) : a connoisseur of cheese : a cheese fancier

¹tur·pen·tine \'tər-pən-ˌtīn, 'tər-pᵊm-\ *n* [ME *terbentyne, turpentyne,* fr. MF & ML; MF *terbentine, tourbentine,* fr. ML *terbentina,* fr. L *terebinthina,* fem. of *terebinthinus* of terebinth, fr. *terebinthus* terebinth, fr. Gk *terebinthos*] (14c) **1 a** : a yellow to brown semifluid oleoresin obtained as an exudate from the terebinth **b** : an oleoresin obtained from various conifers (as some pines and firs) **2 a** : an essential oil obtained from turpentines by distillation and used esp. as a solvent and thinner — called also *gum turpentine* **b** : a similar oil obtained by distillation or carbonization of pinewood — called also *wood turpentine*

²turpentine *vt* **-tined; -tin·ing** (1759) **1** : to apply turpentine to **2** : to extract turpentine from; *also* : to tap (pine trees) in order to obtain turpentine

tur·pi·tude \'tər-pə-ˌtüd, -ˌtyüd\ *n* [MF, fr. L *turpitudo,* fr. *turpis* vile, base] (15c) : inherent baseness : DEPRAVITY ⟨moral ~⟩; *also* : a base act

turps \'tərps\ *n pl but sing in constr* [by shortening & alter.] (ca. 1823) : TURPENTINE

tur·quoise *also* **tur·quois** \'tər-ˌkȯiz, -ˌkwȯiz\ *n* [ME *turkeis, turcas,* fr. MF *turquoyse,* fr. fem. of *turquoys* Turkish, fr. OF, fr. *Turc* Turk] (14c) **1** : a mineral that is a blue, bluish green, or greenish gray hydrous basic phosphate of copper and aluminum, takes a high polish, and is valued as a gem when skyblue **2** : a light greenish blue

turquoise blue *n* (1799) : a light greenish blue that is paler and slightly bluer than average turquoise

turquoise green *n* (1886) : a light bluish green

tur·ret \'tər-ət, 'tə-rət, 'tər-ˌet\ *n* [ME *touret,* fr. MF *torete, tourete,* fr. OF, dim. of *tor, tur* tower — more at TOWER] (14c) **1** : a little tower; *specif* : an ornamental structure at an angle of a larger structure **2 a** : a pivoted and revolvable holder in a machine tool **b** : a device (as on a microscope or a television camera) holding several lenses **3 a** : a tall building usu. moved on wheels and formerly used for carrying soldiers and equipment for breaching or scaling a wall **b** (1) : a gunner's fixed or movable enclosure in an airplane (2) : a revolving armored structure on a warship that protects one or more guns mounted within it (3) : a similar upper structure usu. for one gun on a tank

tur·ret·ed \'tər-ə-təd, 'tə-rə-, 'tu̇r-ə-\ *adj* (1550) : furnished with or as if with turrets

¹tur·tle \'tər-tᵊl\ *n* [ME, fr. OE *turtla,* fr. L *turtur*] (bef. 12c) *archaic* : TURTLEDOVE

²turtle *n, pl* **turtles** *also* **turtle** *often attrib* [modif. of F *tortue,* fr. LL *tartarucha,* fem. of *tartaruchus* of Tartarus, fr. Gk *tartarouchos,* fr. *Tartaros* Tartarus] (1657) : any of an order (Testudines) of terrestrial, freshwater, and marine reptiles that have a toothless horny beak and a shell of bony dermal plates usu. covered with horny shields enclosing the trunk and into which the head, limbs, and tail usu. may be withdrawn

³turtle *n* (1952) : TURTLENECK

tur·tle·back \'tər-tᵊl-ˌbak\ *n* (1881) : a raised convex surface — **turtleback** *or* **tur·tle—backed** \-ˌbakt\ *adj*

tur·tle·dove \-ˌdəv\ *n* (14c) : any of several small wild pigeons (genus *Streptopelia* and esp. *S. turtur*) noted for plaintive cooing

tur·tle·head \-ˌhəd\ *n* (1857) : any of a genus (*Chelone*) of perennial herbs of the snapdragon family with spikes of showy white or purple flowers

tur·tle·neck \-ˌnek\ *n* (1897) **1** : a high close-fitting turnover collar used esp. for sweaters **2** : a sweater with a turtleneck — **tur·tle·necked** \-ˌnekt\ *adj*

tur·tling \'tərt-liŋ, 'tər-tᵊl-iŋ\ *n* (1726) : the action or process of catching turtles

turves *pl of* TURF

¹Tus·can \'təs-kən\ *adj* [L *tuscanus* Etruscan, fr. *Tusci* Etruscans] (1563) **1** : of or relating to one of the five classical orders of architecture that is of Roman origin and plain in style **2** : of, relating to, or characteristic of Tuscany, the Tuscans, or Tuscan

²Tuscan *n* (1568) **1 a** : the Italian language as spoken in Tuscany **b** : the standard literary dialect of Italian **2** : a native or inhabitant of Tuscany

Tus·ca·ro·ra \ˌtəs-kə-ˈrōr-ə, -ˈrȯr-\ *n, pl* **Tuscarora** *or* **Tuscaroras** [Tuscarora *skarò̜rᵊ*] (1650) **1** : a member of an American Indian people orig. of No. Carolina and later of New York and Ontario **2** : the Iroquoian language of the Tuscarora people

tu·sche \'tüsh, 'tu̇-shə\ *n* [G, fr. *tuschen* to lay on color, fr. F *toucher,* lit., to touch, fr. OF *tuchier* — more at TOUCH] (1885) : a black liquid used in lithography for drawing and painting and in etching and the silk-screen process as a resist

¹tush \'təsh\ *n* [ME *tusch,* fr. OE *tūsc*; akin to OFris *tusk* tooth, OE *tōth* tooth] (bef. 12c) : a long pointed tooth; *esp* : a horse's canine

²tush *interj* [ME *tussch*] (15c) — used to express disdain or reproach

---

\ə\ abut \ᵊ\ kitten, F table \ər\ further \a\ ash \ā\ ace \ä\ mop, mar
\au̇\ out \ch\ chin \e\ bet \ē\ easy \g\ go \i\ hit \ī\ ice \j\ job
\ŋ\ sing \ō\ go \ȯ\ law \ȯi\ boy \th\ thin \t̲h̲\ the \ü\ loot \u̇\ foot
\y\ yet \zh\ vision \á, k̲, ⁿ, œ, œ̄, ᵫ, ᵬ, ᵞ\ *see* Guide to Pronunciation

³**tush** \'tŭsh\ *n* [perh. modif. of Yiddish *tokhes*, fr. Heb *taḥath* under, beneath] (1962) *slang* : BUTTOCKS

tusk \'tŭsk\ *n* [ME, alter. of *tux*, fr. OE *tūx*; akin to OE *tūsc* tush] (bef. 12c) **1** : an elongated greatly enlarged tooth (as of an elephant or walrus) that projects when the mouth is closed and serves for digging food or as a weapon; *broadly* : a long protruding tooth **2** : one of the small projections on a tusk tenon — **tusked** \'tŭskt\ *adj* — **tusk-like** \'tŭsk-,līk\ *adj*

²**tusk** *vt* (1629) : to dig up with a tusk; *also* : to gash with a tusk

tusk-er \'tŭs-kər\ *n* (1859) : an animal with tusks; *esp* : a male elephant with two normally developed tusks

tusk tenon *n* (ca. 1825) : a tenon strengthened by one or more smaller tenons underneath forming a steplike outline

tus-sah \'tŭs-ə, -,sȯ\ *or* **tus-sore** \-,sȯr, -,sȯr\ *n* [Hindi *tasar*] (1590) : silk or silk fabric from the brownish fiber produced by larvae of some saturniid moths (as *Antheraea paphia*)

tus-sive \'tə-siv\ *adj* [L *tussis* cough] (ca. 1857) : of, relating to, or involved in coughing

¹**tus-sle** \'tə-səl\ *n* (1629) **1** : a physical contest or struggle : SCUFFLE **2** : an intense argument, controversy, or struggle

²**tussle** *vi* **tus-sled; tus-sling** \-s(ə-)liŋ\ [ME *tussillen*, freq. of ME *-tusen, -tousen* to tousle — more at TOUSE] (1638) : to struggle roughly : SCUFFLE

tus-sock \'tə-sək\ *n* [origin unknown] (1580) : a compact tuft esp. of grass or sedge; *also* : an area of raised solid ground in a marsh or bog that is bound together by roots of low vegetation — **tus-socky** \-sə-kē\ *adj*

tussock grass *n* (1842) : a grass or sedge that typically grows in tussocks

tussock moth *n* (1826) : any of numerous dull-colored moths (family Lymantriidae) that usu. have wingless females and larvae with long tufts of hair

tut \ə t-*sound made by suction rather than explosion; often read as* 'tət\ *interj* (ca. 1529) — used to express disapproval or disbelief

tu-tee \tü-'tē, tyü-\ *n* [*tutor* + *-ee*] (ca. 1927) : one who is being tutored

tu-te-lage \'tü-t³l-ij, 'tyü-\ *n* [L *tutela* protection, guardian (fr. *tutari* to protect, freq. of *tueri* to look at, guard) + *-age*] (1605) **1 a** : an act or process of serving as guardian or protector : GUARDIANSHIP **b** : hegemony over a foreign territory : TRUSTEESHIP **2 2** : the state of being under a guardian or tutor **3 a** : instruction esp. of an individual **b** : a guiding influence

tu-te-lar \'tü-t³l-ər, 'tyü-, -,är\ *adj or n* (1600) : TUTELARY

¹**tu-te-lary** \'tü-t³l-,er-ē, 'tyü-\ *adj* (1611) **1** : having the guardianship of a person or a thing ⟨a ~ goddess⟩ **2** : of or relating to a guardian

²**tutelary** *n, pl* **-lar-ies** (1652) : a tutelary power (as a deity)

¹**tu-tor** \'tü-tər, 'tyü-\ *n* [ME, fr. MF & L; MF *tuteur*, fr. L *tutor*, fr. *tueri*] (14c) : a person charged with the instruction and guidance of another: as **a** : a private teacher **b** : a teacher in a British university who gives individual instruction to undergraduates

²**tutor** *vt* (1592) **1** : to have the guardianship, tutelage, or care of **2** : to teach or guide usu. individually in a special subject or for a particular purpose : COACH ~ *vi* **1** : to do the work of a tutor **2** : to receive instruction esp. privately

tu-tor-age \'tü-tə-rij, 'tyü-\ *n* (1617) : the function or work of a tutor

tu-tor-ess \'tü-tə-rəs, 'tyü-\ *n* (1614) : a woman or girl who is a tutor

¹**tu-to-ri-al** \tü-'tōr-ē-əl, tyü-, -'tȯr-\ *adj* (1822) : of, relating to, or involving a tutor

²**tutorial** *n* (1923) **1** : a class conducted by a tutor for one student or a small number of students **2** : a paper, book, film, or computer program that provides practical information about a specific subject

tu-tor-ship \'tü-tər-,ship, 'tyü-\ *n* (1581) **1** : the office, function, or work of a tutor **2** : TUTELAGE 3

tu-toy-er \tüe-twä-yā\ *vt* [F, to address with the familiar pronoun *tu* thou, fr. MF, fr. *tu* thou (fr. L) + *toi* thee, fr. L *te* (acc. of *tu*) — more at THOU] (1697) : to address familiarly

Tut-si \'tü-sē, 'tüt-\ *n, pl* **Tutsi** *or* **Tutsis** (1950) : a member of a Nilotic people of Rwanda and Burundi

¹**tut-ti** \'tü-tē, 'tü-; 'tü-,tē, 'tü-\ *adj or adv* [It, masc. pl. of *tutto* all, fr. (assumed) VL *tottus*, alter. of L *totus*] (ca. 1724) : with all voices or instruments performing together — used as a direction in music

²**tutti** *n* (1816) : a passage or section performed by all the performers

tut-ti-frut-ti \,tü-ti-'frü-tē, ,tü-\ *n* [It *tutti frutti* all fruits] (1834) : a confection or ice cream containing chopped usu. candied fruits

¹**tut-tut** \two t-*sounds made by suction rather than explosion; often read as* 'tət-'tət\ *interj* (1591) : TUT

²**tut-tut** *vi* **tut-tut-ted; tut-tut-ting** (1873) : to express disapproval or disbelief by or as if by uttering tut ⟨the civilian press corps *tut-tutted* over the officers' equivocation, ignorance and bigotry —M. B. Duberman⟩

tu-tu \'tü-(,)tü\ *n* [F, fr. (baby talk) *tutu* backside] (1913) : a short projecting skirt worn by a ballerina

tu–whit tu–whoo \tə-,(h)wit-tə-'(h)wü\ *n* [imit.] (1588) : the cry of an owl

tux \'təks\ *n* (1922) : TUXEDO

tux-e-do \,tək-'sē-(,)dō\ *n, pl* **-dos** *or* **-does** [Tuxedo Park, N.Y.] (1889) **1 a** : a single-breasted or double-breasted usu. black or blackish blue jacket **2** : semiformal evening clothes for men — **tux-e-doed** \-(,)dōd\ *adj*

tu-yere \twē-'er\ *n* [F *tuyère*, fr. MF, fr. *tuyau* pipe] (1781) : a nozzle through which an air blast is delivered to a forge or blast furnace

TV \'tē-'vē\ *n* [television] (1947) : TELEVISION

TV dinner *n* [fr. its saving the television viewer from having to interrupt viewing to prepare and serve a meal] (1954) : a quick-frozen packaged dinner (as of meat, potatoes, and a vegetable) that requires only heating before it is served

twa \'twä\ *or* **twae** \'twä, 'twē\ *Scot var of* TWO

¹**twad-dle** \'twäd-³l\ *n* [prob. alter. of E dial. *twattle* idle talk] (1782) **1** : silly idle talk : DRIVEL **2** : one that twaddles : TWADDLER

²**twaddle** *vb* **twad-dled; twad-dling** \'twäd-liŋ, 'twä-d³l-iŋ\ (1826) : PRATE, BABBLE — **twad-dler** \'twäd-lər, 'twä-d³l-ər\ *n*

¹**twain** \'twān\ *adj* [ME, fr. OE *twēgen* — more at TWO] (bef. 12c) *archaic* : TWO

²**twain** *pron* (bef. 12c) : TWO; *esp* : two fathoms ⟨mark ~⟩

³**twain** *n* (14c) **1** : TWO **2** : COUPLE, PAIR

¹**twang** \'twaŋ\ *n* [imit.] (ca. 1553) **1** : a harsh quick ringing sound like that of a plucked banjo string **2 a** : nasal speech or resonance **b** : the characteristic speech of a region, locality, or group of people **3 a** : an act of plucking **b** : PANG, TWINGE — **twangy** \'twaŋ-ē\ *adj*

²**twang** *vb* **twanged; twang-ing** \'twaŋ-iŋ\ *vi* (1567) **1** : to sound with a twang ⟨the couch ~*ed* when he sat down⟩ **2** : to speak or sound with a nasal intonation **3** : to throb or twitch with pain or tension ~ *vt* **1** : to cause to sound with a twang **2** : to utter or pronounce with a nasal twang **3** : to pluck the string of — **twang-er** *n*

³**twang** *n* [alter. of *tang*] (1611) **1** : a persisting flavor, taste, or odor : TANG **2** : SUGGESTION, TRACE

'twas \'twəz, 'twäz\ [by contr.] (1588) : it was

twat \'twät\ *n* [origin unknown] (1656) : VULVA — usu. considered vulgar

tway-blade \'twā-,blād\ *n* [E dial. *tway* two] (1578) : any of various orchids (genera *Listera* and *Liparis*) often having two leaves

¹**tweak** \'twēk\ *vb* [prob. alter. of ME *twikken* to pull sharply, fr. OE *twiccian* to pluck — more at TWITCH] *vt* (1601) **1** : to pinch and pull with a sudden jerk and twist : TWITCH ⟨~*ed* a bud from the stem⟩ **2** : to pinch (a person or a body part) lightly or playfully ⟨~*ed* the baby's ear affectionately⟩ **3** : to make small adjustments in or to ⟨~ the controls⟩; *esp* : FINE-TUNE ~ *vi* : PULL 1a, PLUCK

²**tweak** *n* (1609) : an act of tweaking : PINCH

twee \'twē\ *adj* [baby-talk alter. of *sweet*] (1905) *chiefly Brit* : affectedly or excessively dainty, delicate, cute, or quaint ⟨such a theme might sound ~ or corny —*Times Lit. Supp.*⟩

tweed \'twēd\ *n* [prob. short for Sc *tweedling, twidling* twilled cloth] (1841) **1** : a rough woolen fabric made usu. in twill weaves and used esp. for suits and coats **2** *pl* : tweed clothing; *specif* : a tweed suit

Twee-dle-dum and Twee-dle-dee \,twē-d³l-'dəm-ən(d)-,twē-d³l-'dē\ *n* [E *tweedle* to chirp + *dum* (imit. of a low musical note) & *dee* (imit. of a high musical note)] (1725) : two individuals or groups that are practically indistinguishable

tweedy \'twē-dē\ *adj* **tweed-i-er; -est** (1912) **1** : of or resembling tweed **2 a** : given to wearing tweeds **b** : informal or suggestive of the outdoors in taste or habits — **tweed-i-ness** *n*

tween \'twēn\ *prep* [ME *twene*, short for *betwene*] (14c) : BETWEEN

tweet \'twēt\ *n* [imit.] (1845) : a chirping note — **tweet** *vi*

tweet-er \'twē-tər\ *n* (1934) : a small loudspeaker responsive only to the higher acoustic frequencies and reproducing sounds of high pitch — compare WOOFER

tweeze \'twēz\ *vt* **tweezed; tweez-ing** [back-formation fr. *tweezers*] (1932) : to pluck, remove, or handle with tweezers

twee-zer \'twē-zər\ *n* (1904) : TWEEZERS

twee-zers \-zərz\ *n pl but sing or pl in constr* [obs. E *tweeze* n., *etui*, short for obs. E *etweese*, fr. pl. of obs. E *etwee*, fr. F *étui*] (1654) : any of various small metal instruments that are usu. held between the thumb and forefinger, are used for plucking, holding, or manipulating, and consist of two legs joined at one end

Twelfth Day *n* [fr. its being the 12th day after Christmas] (bef. 12c) : EPIPHANY 1

Twelfth Night *n* (bef. 12c) : the evening or sometimes the eve of Epiphany

twelve \'twelv\ *n* [ME, fr. OE *twelf*; akin to OHG *zwelif* twelve, OE *twā* two, *-leofan* (as in *endleofan* eleven) — more at TWO, ELEVEN] (bef. 12c) **1** — see NUMBER table **2** *cap* **a** : the twelve original disciples of Jesus **b** : the books of the Minor Prophets in the Jewish Scriptures **3** : the 12th in a set or series **4** : something having 12 units or members **5** *pl* : TWELVEMO — **twelfth** \'twelf(t)th\ *adj or n* — **twelve** *adj* — **twelve** *pron, pl in constr*

twelve-mo \'twelv-(,)mō\ *n, pl* **-mos** (1819) : the size of a piece of paper cut 12 from a sheet; *also* : a book, a page, or paper of this size

twelve-month \-,mən(t)th\ *n* (13c) : YEAR

twelve-tone \-'tōn\ *adj* (1926) : of, relating to, or being serial music utilizing the 12 chromatic tones

twelve–tone row *n* (1941) : the 12 chromatic tones of the octave placed in a chosen fixed order and constituting with some permitted permutations and derivations the melodic and harmonic material of a serial musical piece

twen-ty \'twen-tē, 'twən-\ *n, pl* **twenties** [ME, fr. *twenty*, adj., fr. OE *twēntig*, n., group of 20, fr. *twēn-* (akin to OE *twā* two) + *-tig* group of 10; akin to OE *tīen* ten — more at TWO, TEN] (15c) **1** — see NUMBER table **2** *pl* : the numbers 20 to 29; *specif* : the years 20 to 29 in a lifetime or century **3** : a 20-dollar bill — **twen-ti-eth** \-tē-əth\ *adj or n* — **twenty** *adj* — **twenty** *pron, pl in constr*

twen-ty–four-mo \,twen-tē-'fȯr-(,)mō, ,twən-, -'fȯr-\ *n, pl* **-mos** (ca. 1841) : the size of a piece of paper cut 24 from a sheet; *also* : a book, a page, or paper of this size

twen-ty–one \,twen-tē-'wən, ,twən-\ *n* (1611) **1** — see NUMBER table **2** [trans. of F *vingt-et-un*] : BLACKJACK — **twenty–one** *adj* — **twenty–one** *pron, pl in constr*

twen-ty–twen-ty *or* **20/20** \-'twen-tē, -'twən-\ *adj* [fr. the testing of vision by reading letters at a distance of 20 feet] (1875) *of the human eye* : meeting a standard of normal visual acuity ⟨~ vision⟩

twen-ty–two \-'tü\ *n* (1526) **1** — see NUMBER table **2** : a .22-caliber firearm; *esp* : one firing rimfire cartridges — usu. written **.22** — **twenty–two** *adj* — **twenty–two** *pron, pl in constr*

'twere \'twər\ [by contr.] (1588) : it were

twerp \'twərp\ *n* [origin unknown] (ca. 1923) : a silly, insignificant, or contemptible person

Twi \'chwē, chə-'wē, 'twē, 'chē\ *n* (1874) **1** : a dialect of Akan **2** : a literary language based on the Twi dialect and used by the Akan-speaking peoples (as the Ashanti)

twi- \'twī\ *prefix* [ME, fr. OE; akin to OHG *zwi-* twi-, L *bi-*, Gk *di-*, OE *twā* two] : two : double : doubly : twice ⟨*twi*-headed⟩

tutu

twice \'twīs\ *adv* [ME *twiges, twies,* fr. OE *twiga;* akin to OE *twi-*] (12c) **1** : on two occasions ⟨~ absent⟩ **2** : two times : in doubled quantity or degree ⟨~ two is four⟩ ⟨~ as much⟩

twice-born \-'bȯrn\ *adj* (15c) **1** : born a second time **2** : having undergone a definite experience of fundamental moral and spiritual renewal : REGENERATE **3** : of or forming one of the three upper Hindu caste groups in which boys undergo an initiation symbolizing spiritual birth

twice-laid \-'lād\ *adj* (ca. 1593) : made from the ends of rope and strands of used rope ⟨~ rope⟩

twice-told \-'tōld\ *adj* (1595) : well known from repeated telling — used chiefly in the phrase *a twice-told tale*

¹twid-dle \'twi-dᵊl\ *vb* **twid-dled; twid-dling** \'twid-liŋ, 'twi-dᵊl-iŋ\ [origin unknown] *vi* (ca. 1540) **1** : to play negligently with something : FIDDLE **2** : to turn or jounce lightly ⟨~s round and round in the water —J. B. S. Haldane⟩ ~ *vt* : to rotate lightly or idly ⟨twiddled his cigar —James Lord⟩ — **twiddle one's thumbs** : to spend time idly : do nothing

²twiddle *n* (1774) : TURN, TWIST

¹twig \'twig\ *n* [ME *twigge,* fr. OE; akin to OHG *zwig* twig, OE *twā* two] (bef. 12c) **1** : a small shoot or branch usu. without its leaves **2** : a minute branch of a nerve or artery — **twigged** \'twigd\ *adj* — **twig-gy** \'twi-gē\ *adj*

²twig *vb* **twigged; twig-ging** [perh. fr. Ir & ScGael *tuig-* understand] *vt* (1764) **1** : NOTICE, OBSERVE **2** : to understand the meaning of : COMPREHEND ~ *vi* : to gain a grasp : UNDERSTAND ⟨twigged instinctively about things —H. E. Bates⟩

³twig *n* [origin unknown] (ca. 1811) *Brit* : FASHION, STYLE

twi-light \'twī-,līt\ *n, often attrib* (15c) **1** : the light from the sky between full night and sunrise or between sunset and full night produced by diffusion of sunlight through the atmosphere and its dust **2 a** : an intermediate state that is not clearly defined ⟨lived in the ~ of neutrality —Newsweek⟩ **b** : a period of decline ⟨the ~ of a great career⟩

twilight glow *n* (1819) : airglow seen at twilight

Twilight of the Gods *n* : RAGNAROK

twilight zone *n* (1909) **1 a** : TWILIGHT 2a **b** : an area just beyond ordinary legal and ethical limits **2** : a world of fantasy, illusion, or unreality

twi-lit \'twī-,lit\ *adj* [*twi*light + *lit*] (1869) : lighted by or as if by twilight

twill \'twil\ *n* [ME *twyll, twylle,* fr. OE *twilic* having a double thread, part trans. of L *bilic-, bilix,* fr. *bi-* + *licium* thread] (14c) **1** : a fabric with a twill weave **2** : a textile weave in which the filling threads pass over one and under two or more warp threads to give an appearance of diagonal lines

twilled \'twild\ *adj* (15c) : made with a twill weave

twill-ing \'twi-liŋ\ *n* (ca. 1859) : twilled fabric; *also* : the process of making it

¹twin \'twin\ *n* [ME, fr. OE *twin* twofold] (14c) **1 a** : either of two offspring produced at a birth **b** *pl, cap* : GEMINI **2** : one of two persons or things closely related to or resembling each other **3** : a compound crystal composed of two adjoining crystals or parts of crystals of the same kind that share a common plane of atoms — **twin-ship** \-,ship\ *n*

²twin *vb* **twinned; twin-ning** *vt* (14c) **1** : to bring together in close association : COUPLE **2** : DUPLICATE, MATCH ~ *vi* **1** : to bring forth twins **2** : to grow as a twin crystal

³twin *adj* [ME, twofold, double, fr. OE *twinn;* akin to ON *tvinnr* two by two, OE *twā* two] (1590) **1** : born with one other or as a pair or one birth ⟨~ brother⟩ ⟨~ girls⟩ **2 a** : made up of two similar, related, or connected members or parts : DOUBLE **b** : paired in a close or necessary relationship : MATCHING **c** : having or consisting of two identical units **d** : being one of a pair

twin bed *n* (1901) : one of a pair of matching single beds

twin-ber-ry \'twin-,ber-ē\ *n* [fr. the occurrence of the berries in pairs] (1821) **1** : a shrubby No. American honeysuckle (*Lonicera involucrata*) with yellowish involucrate flowers **2** : PARTRIDGEBERRY

twin bill *n* (ca. 1939) : DOUBLEHEADER

twin-born \'twin-'bȯrn\ *adj* (1598) : born at the same birth

twin double *n* (1960) : a system of betting (as on horse races) in which the bettor must pick the winners of four stipulated races in order to win — compare DAILY DOUBLE

¹twine \'twīn\ *n* [ME *twin,* fr. OE *twin;* akin to MD *twijn* twine, OE *twā* two] (bef. 12c) **1** : a strong string of two or more strands twisted together **2** : a twined or interlaced part or object **3** : an act of twining, interlacing, or embracing — **twiny** \'twī-nē\ *adj*

²twine *vb* **twined; twin-ing** *vt* (13c) **1 a** : to twist together **b** : to form by twisting : WEAVE **2 a** : INTERLACE ⟨the girl *twined* her hands —John Buchan⟩ **b** : to cause to encircle or enfold something **c** : to cause to be encircled ~ *vi* **1** : to coil about a support **2** : to stretch or move in a sinuous manner : MEANDER ⟨the river ~s through the valley⟩ — **twin-er** *n*

³twine *vb* **twined; twin-ing** [alter. of Sc *twin,* fr. ME *twinnen,* fr. *twin* double] *vt* (1722) *chiefly Scot* : to cause (one) to lose possession : DEPRIVE ⟨*twined* him of his nose —J. C. Ransom⟩ ~ *vi, chiefly Scot* : PART ⟨you and me must ~ —R. L. Stevenson⟩

twin-flow-er \'twin-,flau̇(-ə)r\ *n* (ca. 1818) : a low prostrate subshrub (*Linnaea borealis*) of the honeysuckle family that is found in cool regions of the northern hemisphere and has fragrant usu. pink flowers

¹twinge \'twinj\ *vb* **twinged; twing-ing** \'twin-jiŋ\ *or* **twinge-ing** [ME *twengen,* fr. OE *twengan;* akin to OHG *zwengen* to pinch] *vt* (bef. 12c) **1** *dial* : PLUCK, TWEAK **2** : to affect with a sharp pain or pang ~ *vi* : to feel a sudden sharp local pain

²twinge *n* (1608) **1** : a sudden sharp stab of pain **2** : a moral or emotional pang ⟨a ~ of conscience⟩

twi-night \'twī-,nīt\ *adj* [*twi*light + *night*] (1946) : of, relating to, or being a baseball doubleheader in which the first game is played in the late afternoon and the second continues into the evening

¹twin-kle \'twiŋ-kəl\ *vb* **twin-kled; twin-kling** \-k(ə-)liŋ\ [ME, fr. OE *twinclian;* akin to MHG *zwinken* to blink] *vi* (bef. 12c) **1** : to shine with a flickering or sparkling light : SCINTILLATE **2 a** : to flutter the eyelids **b** : to appear bright esp. with merriment ⟨his eyes *twinkled*⟩ **3** : to flutter or flit rapidly ~ *vt* **1** : to cause to shine with fluctuating light **2** : to flicker or flirt rapidly ⟨*twinkled* the straight, red-lacquered toes —Glenway Wescott⟩ — **twin-kler** \-k(ə-)lər\ *n*

²twinkle *n* (1548) **1** : a wink of the eyelids **2** : the instant's duration of a wink : TWINKLING **3** : an intermittent radiance : FLICKER, SPARKLE **4** : a rapid flashing motion : FLIT — **twin-kly** \-k(ə-)lē\ *adj*

twin-kling \'twin-kliŋ\ *n* (14c) : the time required for a wink : INSTANT ⟨the kettle will boil in a ~ —Punch⟩

twin-set \'twin-'set\ *n* (1937) : a combination of a matching pullover and cardigan worn together

twin-size \'twin-'sīz\ *adj* [*twin bed*] (1926) : having the dimensions 39 inches by 75 inches (about 99 centimeters by 191 centimeters) — used of a bed; compare FULL-SIZE, KING-SIZE, QUEEN-SIZE

¹twirl \'twər(-ə)l\ *vb* [perh. of Scand origin; akin to Norw dial. *tvirla* to twirl; akin to OHG *dweran* to stir] (1598) **1** : to revolve rapidly **2** : to pitch in a baseball game ~ *vt* **1** : to cause to rotate rapidly **2** : PITCH 2a — **twirl-er** \'twər-lər\ *n*

²twirl *n* (1598) **1** : an act of twirling **2** : COIL, WHORL — **twirly** \'twər-lē\ *adj*

twirp *var of* TWERP

¹twist \'twist\ *vb* [ME, fr. OE *-twist* rope; akin to MD *twist* quarrel, twine, OE *twā* two] *vt* (15c) **1 a** : to unite by winding ⟨~ing strands together⟩ **b** : to make by twisting strands together ⟨~ thread from yarn⟩ **c** : to mingle by interlacing **2** : TWINE, COIL **3** : to wring or wrench so as to dislocate or distort; *esp* : SPRAIN ⟨~ed my ankle⟩ **b** : to alter the meaning of : DISTORT, PERVERT ⟨~ed the facts⟩ **c** : CONTORT ⟨~ed his face into a grin⟩ **d** : to pull off, turn, or break by torsion **e** : to cause to move with a turning motion **f** : to form into a spiral shape **g** : to cause to take on moral, mental, or emotional deformity **h** : to make (one's way) in a winding or devious manner to a destination or objective ~ *vi* **1** : to follow a winding course : SNAKE **2 a** : to turn or change shape under torsion **b** : to assume a spiral shape **c** : SQUIRM, WRITHE **d** : to dance the twist **3** *of a ball* : to rotate while taking a curving path or direction **4** : TURN 3a ⟨~ed around to see behind him⟩ — **twist one's arm** : to bring strong pressure to bear on one

²twist *n* (1555) **1** : something formed by twisting or winding: as **a** : a thread, yarn, or cord formed by twisting two or more strands together **b** : a strong tightly twisted sewing silk **c** : a baked piece of twisted dough **d** : tobacco leaves twisted into a thick roll **e** : a strip of citrus peel used to flavor a drink **2 a** : an act of twisting : the state of being twisted **b** : a dance performed with strenuous gyrations esp. of the hips **c** : the spin given the ball in any of various games **d** : a spiral turn or curve **e** (1) : torque or torsional stress applied to a body (as a rod or shaft) (2) : torsional strain (3) : the angle through which a thing is twisted **3 a** : a turning off a straight course **b** : ECCENTRICITY, IDIOSYNCRASY **c** : a distortion of meaning or sense **4 a** : an unexpected turn or development ⟨weird ~s of fate —W. L. Shirer⟩ **b** : a clever device : TRICK ⟨questions demanding special ~s of thinking — New Yorker⟩ **c** : a variant approach or method : GIMMICK ⟨a kind of ~ on the old triangle theme —Dave Fedo⟩ **5** : a front or back dive in which the diver twists sideways a half or full turn before entering the water — **twisty** \'twis-tē\ *adj*

twist drill *n* (ca. 1875) : a drill having deep helical grooves extending from the point to the smooth portion of the shank

twist-ed \'twis-təd\ *adj* (ca. 1890) : mentally or emotionally unsound or disturbed : SICK

twist-er \'twis-tər\ *n* (1579) **1** : one that twists; *esp* : a ball with a forward and spinning motion **2** : a tornado, waterspout, or dust devil in which the rotatory ascending movement of a column of air is esp. apparent

twist-ing \'twis-tiŋ\ *n* (ca. 1905) : the use of misrepresentation or trickery to get someone to lapse a life insurance policy and buy another usu. in another company

¹twit \'twit\ *n* (1528) **1** : an act of twitting : TAUNT **2** : a silly annoying person : FOOL

²twit *vt* **twit-ted; twit-ting** [ME *atwiten* to reproach, fr. OE *ætwītan,* fr. *æt* at + *witan* to reproach; akin to OHG *wizan* to punish, OE *witan* to know] (1530) **1** : to subject to light ridicule or reproach : RALLY **2** : to make fun of as a fault

¹twitch \'twich\ *vb* [ME *twicchen;* akin to OE *twiccian* to pluck, OHG *gizwickan* to pinch] *vt* (14c) **1** : to move or pull with a sudden motion : JERK ~ *vi* **1** : PULL 1a, PLUCK ⟨~ed at my sleeve⟩ **2** : to move jerkily : QUIVER — **twitch-er** *n*

²twitch *n* (1523) **1** : an act of twitching; *esp* : a short sudden pull or jerk **2** : a physical or mental pang **3** : a loop of rope or strap that is tightened over a horse's lip as a restraining device **4 a** : a short spastic contraction of the muscle fibers **b** : a slight jerk of a body part — **twitch-i-ly** \'twi-chə-lē\ *adv* — **twitchy** \'twi-chē\ *adj*

³twitch *n* [alter. of *quitch*] (1597) *dial* : QUACK GRASS

¹twit-ter \'twi-tər\ *vb* [ME *twiteren;* akin to OHG *zwizzirōn* to twitter] *vi* (14c) **1** : to utter successive chirping noises **2 a** : to talk in a chattering fashion : GIGGLE, TITTER **3** : to tremble with agitation : FLUTTER ~ *vt* **1** : to utter in chirps or twitters ⟨the robin ~ed its morning song⟩ **2** : to shake rapidly back and forth : FLUTTER

²twitter *n* (1678) **1** : a trembling agitation : QUIVER **2** : a small tremulous intermittent sound (as of birds) **3 a** : a light chattering **b** : a light silly laugh : GIGGLE — **twit-tery** \'twi-tə-rē\ *adj*

twixt \'twikst\ *or* **'twixt** *prep* [ME *twix,* short for *betwix, betwixt*] (14c) : BETWEEN

¹two \'tü\ *adj* [ME *twa, two,* fr. OE *twā* (fem. & neut.); akin to OE *twēgen* two (masc.), *tū* (neut.), OHG *zwēne,* L *duo,* Gk *dyo*] (bef. 12c) **1** : being one more than one in number **2** : being the second — used postpositively ⟨section ~ of the instructions⟩

²two *pron, pl in constr* (bef. 12c) **1** : two countable individuals not specified ⟨only ~ were found⟩ **2** : a small approximate number of indicated things ⟨only a shot or ~ were fired⟩

³two *n, pl* **twos** (ca. 1585) **1** — see NUMBER table **2** : the second in a set or series ⟨the ~ of spades⟩ **3** : a 2-dollar bill **4** : something having two units or members

---

\ə\ abut \ᵊ\ kitten, F table \ər\ further \a\ ash \ā\ ace \ä\ mop, mar \au̇\ out \ch\ chin \e\ bet \ē\ easy \g\ go \i\ hit \ī\ ice \j\ job \ŋ\ sing \ō\ go \ȯ\ law \ȯi\ boy \th\ thin \t͟h\ the \ü\ loot \u̇\ foot \y\ yet \zh\ vision \á, k̲, ⁿ, œ, œ̄, ue, ūe, ᵜ\ *see* Guide to Pronunciation

two·bag·ger \-'ba-gər\ n (1880) : DOUBLE 1b
two–bit \'tü-'bit\ adj (1802) **1** : of the value of two bits **2** : cheap or trivial of its kind : PETTY, SMALL-TIME
two bits n pl but sing or pl in constr (1730) **1** : the value of a quarter of a dollar **2** : something of small worth or importance
¹**two–by–four** \,tü-bī-'för, -'for\ n (1884) : a piece of lumber approximately 2 by 4 inches as sawed and usu. 1⅝ by 3⅝ inches if dressed
²**two–by–four** adj (1897) **1** : measuring two units (as inches) by four **2** : small or petty of its kind ⟨this house and its ~ garden —Philip Barry⟩
two cents n (1947) **1** : a sum or object of very small value : practically nothing ⟨said angrily that for two cents he'd punch your nose⟩ **2** or **two cents worth** : an opinion offered on a topic under discussion ⟨each speaker . . . is getting in his two cents worth —Dwight Macdonald⟩
two–cycle adj (1902) of an internal combustion engine : having a 2=stroke cycle
two–dimensional adj (1883) **1** : having two dimensions **2** : lacking depth of characterization ⟨~ characters⟩ — **two–dimensionality** n
two–edged sword \'tü-'ejd-, -'e-jəd-\ n (1526) : DOUBLE-EDGED SWORD
two–faced \'tü-'fāst\ adj (1609) **1** : DOUBLE-DEALING, FALSE **2** : having two faces — **two–faced·ness** \-'fāst-nəs, -'fā-səd-nəs\ n
two–fer \'tü-fər\ n [alter. of two for (one)] (1890) **1** : a cheap item of merchandise; esp : a cigar selling at two for a nickel **2** : a free coupon entitling the bearer to purchase two tickets to a specified theatrical production for the price of one **3** : two articles available for the price of one or about the price of one
two–fist·ed \-'fis-təd\ adj (1774) : marked by vigorous often virile energy : HARD-HITTING
two·fold \'tü-,fōld, -'fōld\ adj (1559) **1** : having two parts or aspects **2** : being twice as great or as many — **twofold** \-'fōld\ adv
2,4–D \,tü-,för-'dē, -,for-\ n [di-] (ca. 1945) : a white crystalline irritant compound $C_8H_6Cl_2O_3$ used esp. as a weed killer
2,4,5–T \-,fīv-'tē\ n [tri-] (1946) : an irritant compound $C_8H_5Cl_3O_3$ used esp. as an herbicide and defoliant
two–hand·ed \'tü-'han-dəd\ adj (15c) **1** : used with both hands ⟨a ~ sword⟩ **2** : requiring two persons ⟨a ~ saw⟩ **3** archaic : STOUT, STRONG **4** a : having two hands **b** : efficient with either hand
two–line octave n (ca. 1931) : the musical octave that begins on the first C above middle C — see PITCH illustration
two–party adj (1925) : characterized by two major political parties of comparable strength
two·pence \'tə-pən(t)s, US also 'tü-,pen(t)s\ n (15c) **1** : the sum of two British pennies **2** pl **twopence** or **two·pen·ces** : a coin worth twopence
two·pen·ny \'təp-nē, 'tə-pə-, US also 'tü-,pe-nē\ adj (1532) : costing or worth twopence
two–phase adj (ca. 1896) : DIPHASIC
¹**two–piece** \'tü-'pēs\ adj (1910) : forming a clothing ensemble with matching top and bottom parts
²**two–piece** \'tü-,pēs\ n (1930) : a garment (as a bathing suit) that is two-piece
two–piec·er \'tü-'pē-sər\ n (1943) : TWO-PIECE
two–ply \-'plī\ adj (ca. 1847) **1** : consisting of two thicknesses **2** a : woven with two sets of warp thread and two of filling ⟨a ~ carpet⟩ **b** : consisting of two strands ⟨~ yarn⟩
two–sid·ed \-'sī-dəd\ adj (1884) : having two sides : BILATERAL
two·some \'tü-səm\ n (14c) **1** : a group of two persons or things : COUPLE **2** : a golf singles match
two–spot·ted spider mite \'tü-'spä-təd-\ n (1947) : a widely distributed mite (Tetranychus urticae) that feeds on soft plant parts and is a serious pest in greenhouses and gardens
two–step \'tü-,step\ n (1895) **1** : a ballroom dance in 2/4 or 4/4 time having a basic pattern of step-close-step **2** : a piece of music for the two-step — **two–step** vi
two–suit·er \-'sü-tər\ n (1948) : a man's suitcase designed to hold two suits and accessories
two–tailed \'tü-'tāl(d)\ also **two–tail** \-'tā(ə)l\ adj (1945) : being a statistical test for which the critical region consists of all values of the test statistic greater than a given value plus the values less than another given value — compare ONE-TAILED
two–time \'tü-,tīm\ vt (1924) **1** : DOUBLE-CROSS **2** : to betray (a spouse or lover) by secret lovemaking with another — **two–tim·er** n
two–toed sloth \'tü-'tōd-\ n (1781) : any of a genus (Choloepus) of sloths having two clawed digits on each forefoot, three clawed digits on each hind foot, and usu. six or seven vertebrae in the neck — compare THREE-TOED SLOTH
two–tone \'tü-'tōn\ adj (1906) : colored in two colors or in two shades of one color ⟨~ shoes⟩
two–toned \'tü-'tōnd\ adj (1897) : TWO-TONE
two–way adj (1571) **1** : being a cock or valve that will connect a pipe or channel with either of two others **2** : moving or allowing movement in either direction ⟨a ~ bridge⟩ **3** a : involving or allowing an exchange between two individuals or groups ⟨there must be good ~ communication —Jerrold Orne⟩; esp : designed for both sending and receiving messages ⟨~ radio⟩ **b** : involving mutual responsibility or reciprocal relationships ⟨political alliance is a ~ thing —T. H. White †1986⟩ **4** : involving two participants ⟨a ~ race⟩ **5** : usable in either of two manners ⟨a ~ lamp⟩
two–way street n (1948) : a situation or relationship requiring give= and-take ⟨marriage is a two-way street⟩
two–wheel·er \-'hwē-lər, -'wē-\ n (1861) : a 2-wheeled vehicle (as a bicycle)
two–winged fly \'tü-'wiŋ(d)-\ n (1753) : ⁴FLY 2a
-ty n suffix [ME -te, fr. OF -té, fr. L -tat-, -tas — more at -ITY] : quality : condition : degree ⟨apriority⟩
ty·coon \tī-'kün\ n [Jp taikun] (1857) **1** : SHOGUN **2** a : a top leader (as in politics) **b** : a businessman of exceptional wealth and power : MAGNATE
ty·er \'tī-(ə)r\ n var of ³TIER
tying pres part of TIE
tyke \'tīk\ n [ME tyke, fr. ON tík bitch; akin to MLG tike bitch] (15c) **1** : DOG; esp : an inferior or mongrel dog **2** a chiefly Brit : a clumsy, churlish, or eccentric person **b** : a small child

tym·bal \'tim-bəl\ n [alter. of timbal] (1929) : the vibrating membrane in the shrilling organ of a cicada
tym·pan \'tim-pən\ n [in sense 1, fr. ME, fr. OE timpana, fr. L tympanum; in other senses, fr. ML & L tympanum] (bef. 12c) **1** : DRUM **2** : a sheet (as of paper or cloth) placed between the impression surface of a press and the paper to be printed **3** : TYMPANUM 2
tym·pa·ni, tym·pa·nist var of TIMPANI, TIMPANIST
tym·pan·ic \tim-'pa-nik\ adj [L & NL tympanum] (1808) : of, relating to, or being a tympanum
tympanic membrane n (1860) : a thin membrane that closes externally the cavity of the middle ear and functions in the mechanical reception of sound waves and in their transmission to the site of sensory reception — called also eardrum; see EAR illustration
tym·pa·ni·tes \,tim-pə-'nī-tēz\ n [ME, fr. LL, fr. Gk tympanitēs, fr. tympanon] (14c) : a distension of the abdomen caused by accumulation of gas in the intestinal tract or peritoneal cavity — **tym·pa·nit·ic** \-'ni-tik\ adj
tym·pa·num \'tim-pə-nəm\ n, pl **-na** \-nə\ also **-nums** [ML & L; ML, eardrum, fr. L, drum, architectural panel, fr. Gk tympanon drum, kettledrum; perh. akin to Gk typtein to beat] (1619) **1** a (1) : TYMPANIC MEMBRANE (2) : MIDDLE EAR **b** : a thin tense membrane covering an organ of hearing of an insect — see INSECT illustration **c** : a membranous resonator in a sound-producing organ **2** a : the recessed usu. triangular face of a pediment within the frame made by the upper and lower cornices **b** : the space within an arch and above a lintel or a subordinate arch

1 tympanum 2a

tym·pa·ny \-nē\ n, pl **-nies** [ML tympanias, fr. Gk, fr. tympanon] (1528) **1** : TYMPANITES **2** : BOMBAST, TURGIDITY
Tyn·dar·e·us \tin-'dar-ē-əs\ n [L, fr. Gk] : a king of Sparta and husband of Leda in Greek mythology
tyne var of TINE
typ·al \'tī-pəl\ adj (1853) **1** : serving as a type : TYPICAL **2** : of or relating to a type
¹**type** \'tīp\ n, often attrib [ME, fr. LL typus, fr. L & Gk; L typus image, fr. Gk typos blow, impression, model, fr. typtein to strike, beat; akin to Skt tupati he injures and prob. to L stupēre to be benumbed] (15c) **1** a : a person or thing (as in the Old Testament) believed to foreshadow another (as in the New Testament) **b** : one having qualities of a higher category : MODEL **c** : a lower taxonomic category selected as a standard of reference for a higher category; also : a specimen or series of specimens on which a taxonomic species or subspecies is actually based **2** : a distinctive mark or sign **3** a (1) : a rectangular block usu. of metal bearing a relief character from which an inked print can be made (2) : a collection of such blocks ⟨a font of ~⟩ (3) : alphanumeric characters for printing ⟨the ~ for this book has been photoset⟩ **b** : TYPEFACE ⟨italic ~⟩ **c** : printed letters **d** : matter set in type **4** a : qualities common to a number of individuals that distinguish them as an identifiable class: as (1) : the morphological, physiological, or ecological characters by which relationship between organisms may be recognized (2) : the form common to all instances of a linguistic element **b** : a typical and often superior specimen **c** : a member of an indicated class or variety of people ⟨the guests were mostly urban ~s —Lucy Cook⟩ **d** : a particular kind, class, or group ⟨oranges of the seedless ~⟩ ⟨leaders of the new ~ . . . did England yeoman's service —G. M. Trevelyan⟩ **e** : something distinguishable as a variety : SORT ⟨what ~ of food do you like?⟩
syn TYPE, KIND, SORT, NATURE, DESCRIPTION, CHARACTER mean a number of individuals thought of as a group because of a common quality or qualities. TYPE may suggest strong and clearly marked similarity throughout the items included so that each is typical of the group ⟨one of three basic body types⟩. KIND may suggest natural grouping ⟨a zoo seemingly having animals of every kind⟩. SORT often suggests some disparagement ⟨the sort of newspaper dealing in sensational stories⟩. NATURE may imply inherent, essential resemblance rather than obvious or superficial likenesses ⟨two problems of a similar nature⟩. DESCRIPTION implies a group marked by agreement in all details belonging to a type as described or defined ⟨not all acts of that description are actually illegal⟩. CHARACTER implies a group marked by distinctive likenesses peculiar to the type ⟨research on the subject so far has been of an elementary character⟩.
²**type** vb **typed; typ·ing** vt (1596) **1** : to represent beforehand as a type : PREFIGURE **2** a : to produce a copy of **b** : to represent in terms of typical characteristics : TYPIFY **3** : to produce (as a character or document) on a typewriter; also : KEYBOARD **4** : to identify as belonging to a type: as **a** : to determine the natural type of (as a blood sample) **b** : TYPECAST ~ vi : to write something on a typewriter or enter data into a computer by way of a keyboard — **type·able** \'tī-pə-bəl\ adj
type A adj (1970) : relating to, characteristic of, having, or being a personality that is marked by impatience, aggressiveness, and competitiveness and that is held to be associated with increased risk of cardiovascular disease ⟨type A behavior⟩
type·cast \'tīp-,kast\ vt **-cast; -cast·ing** (1927) **1** : to cast (an actor or actress) in a part calling for the same characteristics as those possessed by the performer **2** : to cast (an actor or actress) repeatedly in the same type of role **3** : STEREOTYPE ⟨~ as the grubby, unbeautiful place which is full of life —Miles Kington⟩
type·face \-,fās\ n (1887) **1** : the face of printing type **2** : all type of a single design
type·found·er \-,faůn-dər\ n (1797) : one engaged in the design and production of metal printing type for hand composition — **type·found·ing** \-diŋ\ n
type genus n (1840) : the genus of a taxonomic family or subfamily from which the name of the family or subfamily is formed
type I error \'tīp-'wən-\ n (1947) : rejection of the null hypothesis in statistical testing when it is true

type·script \'tīp-ˌskript\ n [*type* + manu*script*] (1893) : a typewritten manuscript; *esp* : one intended for use as printer's copy
type·set \-ˌset\ vt **-set; -set·ting** (1945) : to set in type : COMPOSE
type·set·ter \-ˌse-tər\ n (1883) : one that sets type
type·set·ting \-ˌse-tiŋ\ n (1846) : the process of setting material in type or into a form to be used in printing; *also* : the process of producing graphic matter (as through a computer system)
type species n (1840) : the species of a genus with which the generic name is permanently associated
type specimen n (ca. 1891) : a specimen or individual designated as type of a species or lesser group and serving as the final criterion of the characteristics of that group
type·style \'tīp-ˌstī(ə)l\ n (1954) : TYPEFACE
type II error \-'tü-\ n (1947) : acceptance of the null hypothesis in statistical testing when it is false
type·write \'tīp-ˌrīt\ vb **-wrote** \-ˌrōt\; **-writ·ten** \-ˌri-tᵊn\ [back-formation fr. *typewriter*] (1887) : TYPE 3 ~ vi : TYPE
type·writ·er \-ˌrī-tər\ n (1868) **1** : a machine for writing in characters similar to those produced by printer's type by means of keyboard=operated types striking a ribbon to transfer ink or carbon impressions onto the paper **2** : TYPIST
type·writ·ing \-ˌrī-tiŋ\ n (1867) **1** : the act or study of or skill in using a typewriter **2** : writing produced with a typewriter
typ·ey *also* **typy** \'tī-pē\ adj **typ·i·er; -est** [¹*type*] (1923) : characterized by strict conformance to type; *also* : exhibiting superior bodily conformation ⟨a ~ heifer⟩
typh·lo·sole \'ti-flə-ˌsōl\ n [Gk *typhlos* blind + *sōlēn* pipe, channel — more at DEAF] (1859) : a longitudinal fold of the intestinal wall that projects into the cavity esp. in bivalve mollusks, annelids, and star-fishes
Ty·pho·eus \tī-'fō-ˌyüs, -'fō-ē-əs\ n [L, fr. Gk *Typhōeus*] : TYPHON — **Ty·phoe·an** \-'fē-ən\ adj
¹ty·phoid \'tī-ˌfȯid, (ˌ)tī-'\ adj [NL *typhus*] (1800) **1** : of, relating to, or suggestive of typhus **2** [²*typhoid*] : of, relating to, or constituting typhoid
²typhoid n (1861) **1** : TYPHOID FEVER **2** : a disease of domestic animals resembling human typhus or typhoid
typhoid fever n (1845) : a communicable disease marked esp. by fever, diarrhea, prostration, headache, and intestinal inflammation and caused by a bacterium (*Salmonella typhi*)
Typhoid Mary n, pl **Typhoid Marys** [*Typhoid Mary*, nickname of Mary Mallon †1938 Irish cook in U.S. who was found to be a typhoid carrier] (1931) : one that is by force of circumstances a center from which something undesirable spreads
Ty·phon \'tī-ˌfän\ n [L, fr. Gk *Typhōn*] : a monster with a tremendous voice who according to classical mythology was father of Cerberus, the Chimera, and the Sphinx
ty·phoon \tī-'fün\ n [alter. (influenced by Chin — Guangdong — *daaih-fùng*, fr. *daaih* big + *fùng* wind) of earlier *touffon*, fr. Ar *ṭūfān* hurricane, fr. Gk *typhōn* violent storm] (1771) **1** : a tropical cyclone occurring in the region of the Philippines or the China sea **2** : WHIRL-WIND 2a ⟨a veritable ~ of interest and corporate investment —Norman Sklarewitz⟩
ty·phus \'tī-fəs\ n [NL, fr. Gk *typhos* fever; akin to Gk *typhein* to smoke — more at DEAF] (1785) : any of various bacterial diseases caused by rickettsias: as **a** : a severe human febrile disease that is caused by one (*Rickettsia prowazekii*) transmitted esp. by body lice and is marked by high fever, stupor alternating with delirium, intense headache, and a dark red rash **b** : MURINE TYPHUS **c** : TSUTSUGAMUSHI DISEASE
typ·ic \'ti-pik\ adj (1610) : TYPICAL 1
typ·i·cal \'ti-pi-kəl\ adj [LL *typicalis*, fr. *typicus*, fr. Gk *typikos*, fr. *typos* model — more at TYPE] (1612) **1** : constituting or having the nature of a type : SYMBOLIC **2 a** : combining or exhibiting the essential characteristics of a group ⟨~ suburban houses⟩ **b** : conforming to a type ⟨a specimen ~ of the species⟩ *syn* see REGULAR — **typ·i·cal·i·ty** \ˌti-pə-'ka-lə-tē\ n — **typ·i·cal·ness** \'ti-pi-kəl-nəs\ n
typ·i·cal·ly \'ti-pi-k(ə-)lē\ adv (1605) **1** : in a typical manner ⟨~ American⟩ **2** : on a typical occasion : in typical circumstances ⟨~, members of our staff receive little . . . recognition —Brendan Gill⟩
typ·i·fy \'ti-pə-ˌfī\ vt **-fied; -fy·ing** (1634) **1** : to represent in typical fashion : to constitute a typical mark or instance of ⟨realism . . . that *typified* his earlier work —*Current Biog.*⟩ **2** : to embody the essential or salient characteristics of : be the type of — **typ·i·fi·ca·tion** \ˌti-pə-fə-'kā-shən\ n
typ·ist \'tī-pist\ n (1885) : one who types or enters data into a computer esp. as a job
ty·po \'tī-(ˌ)pō\ n, pl **typos** [short for *typographical (error)*] (1892) : an error (as of spelling) in typed or typeset material
ty·po·graph \'tī-pə-ˌgraf\ vt (ca. 1933) : to produce (stamps) by letter-press
ty·pog·ra·pher \tī-'pä-grə-fər\ n (1643) : a person (as a compositor, printer, or designer) who specializes in the design, choice, and arrangement of type matter
ty·po·graph·ic \ˌtī-pə-'gra-fik\ *or* **ty·po·graph·i·cal** \-fi-kəl\ adj (1593) : of, relating to, or occurring or used in typography or typeset matter ⟨a ~ character⟩ ⟨a *typographical* error⟩ — **ty·po·graph·i·cal·ly** \-fi-k(ə-)lē\ adv
ty·pog·ra·phy \tī-'pä-grə-fē\ n [ML *typographia*, fr. Gk *typos* impression, cast + *-graphia* -graphy — more at TYPE] (1610) **1** : letterpress printing **2** : the style, arrangement, or appearance of typeset matter
ty·po·log·i·cal \ˌtī-pə-'lä-ji-kəl\ adj (1845) : of or relating to typology or types — **ty·po·log·i·cal·ly** \-ji-k(ə-)lē\ adv
ty·pol·o·gy \tī-'pä-lə-jē\ n, pl **-gies** (1845) **1** : a doctrine of theological types; *esp* : one holding that things in Christian belief are prefigured or symbolized by things in the Old Testament **2** : study of or analysis or classification based on types or categories — **ty·pol·o·gist** \-jist\ n
Tyr \'tir\ n [ON *Týr*; akin to OE *Tīw* Tiu — more at DEITY] : a god of war in Norse mythology
ty·ra·mine \'tī-rə-ˌmēn\ n [ISV *tyro*sine + *amine*] (1910) : a phenolic amine $C_8H_{11}NO$ found in various foods and beverages (as cheese and red wine) that has a sympathomimetic action and is derived from tyrosine
ty·ran·ni·cal \tə-'ra-ni-kəl, tī-\ *also* **ty·ran·nic** \-nik\ adj [L *tyrannicus*, fr. Gk *tyrannikos*, fr. *tyrannos* tyrant] (15c) : being or characteristic of a tyrant or tyranny : DESPOTIC ⟨~ rule⟩ ⟨a ~ ruler⟩ — **ty·ran·ni·cal·ly** \-ni-k(ə-)lē\ adv — **ty·ran·ni·cal·ness** \-kəl-nəs\ n
ty·ran·ni·cide \tə-'ra-nə-ˌsīd, tī-\ n [in sense 1, fr. F, fr. L *tyrannicidium*, fr. *tyrannus* + *-i-* + *-cidium* -cide (killing); in sense 2, fr. F, fr. L *tyrannicida*, fr. *tyrannus* + *-i-* + *-cida* -cide (killer)] (1650) **1** : the act of killing a tyrant **2** : the killer of a tyrant
tyr·an·nise *Brit var of* TYRANNIZE
tyr·an·nize \'tir-ə-ˌnīz\ vb **-nized; -niz·ing** vi (15c) : to exercise arbitrary oppressive power or severity ⟨some ways the living ~ over the dying —Thomas Powers⟩ ~ vt : to treat tyrannically : OPPRESS — **tyr·an·niz·er** n
ty·ran·no·saur \tə-'ra-nə-ˌsȯr, tī-\ n [NL *Tyrannosaurus*, genus name, fr. Gk *tyrannos* tyrant + *sauros* lizard] (1924) : a very large bipedal carnivorous dinosaur (*Tyrannosaurus rex*) with small forelegs that occurs in the Upper Cretaceous of No. America
ty·ran·no·sau·rus \tə-ˌra-nə-'sȯr-əs, (ˌ)tī-\ n [NL] (1905) : TYRANNOSAUR
tyr·an·nous \'tir-ə-nəs\ adj (15c) : marked by tyranny; *esp* : unjustly severe — **tyr·an·nous·ly** adv
tyr·an·ny \'tir-ə-nē\ n, pl **-nies** [ME *tyrannie*, fr. MF, fr. ML *tyrannia*, fr. L *tyrannus* tyrant] (14c) **1** : oppressive power ⟨every form of ~ over the mind of man —Thomas Jefferson⟩; *esp* : oppressive power exerted by government ⟨the ~ of a police state⟩ **2 a** : a government in which absolute power is vested in a single ruler; *esp* : one characteristic of an ancient Greek city-state **b** : the office, authority, and administration of a tyrant **3** : a rigorous condition imposed by some outside agency or force ⟨living under the ~ of the clock —Dixon Wecter⟩ **4** : a tyrannical act
ty·rant \'tī-rənt\ n [ME *tirant*, fr. OF *tyran, tyrant*, fr. L *tyrannus*, fr. Gk *tyrannos*] (14c) **1 a** : an absolute ruler unrestrained by law or constitution **b** : a usurper of sovereignty **2 a** : a ruler who exercises absolute power oppressively or brutally **b** : one resembling an oppressive ruler in the harsh use of authority or power
tyrant flycatcher n (ca. 1783) : any of various large American flycatchers (family Tyrannidae) that are usu. strictly insectivorous and have a flattened bill often hooked at the tip and usu. bristly at the gape
tyre *chiefly Brit var of* TIRE
Tyr·i·an purple \'tir-ē-ən-\ n [*Tyre*, maritime city of ancient Phoenicia] (ca. 1586) : a crimson or purple dye that is related to indigo, obtained by the ancient Greeks and Romans from gastropod mollusks, and now made synthetically
ty·ro \'tī-(ˌ)rō\ n, pl **tyros** often attrib [ML, fr. L *tiro* young soldier, tyro] (1611) : a beginner in learning : NOVICE *syn* see AMATEUR
ty·ro·ci·dine *also* **ty·ro·ci·din** \ˌtī-rə-'sī-dᵊn\ n [*tyro*thricin + *gramicidin*] (1940) : a basic polypeptide antibiotic produced by a soil bacillus (*Bacillus brevis*)
Ty·ro·le·an *also* **Ty·ro·li·an** \tī-'rō-lē-ən, tī-\ adj (1805) **1** : of or relating to the Tirol **2** *of a hat* : of a style originating in the Tirol and marked by soft often green felt, a narrow brim and pointed crown, and an ornamental feather
ty·ros·i·nase \tə-'rä-sə-ˌnās, tī-, -ˌnāz\ n (1896) : a copper-containing enzyme that promotes the oxidation of phenols (as tyrosine) and is widespread in plants and animals
ty·ro·sine \'tī-rə-ˌsēn\ n [ISV, irreg. fr. Gk *tyros* cheese — more at BUTTER] (1857) : a phenolic amino acid $C_9H_{11}NO_3$ that is a precursor of several important substances (as epinephrine and melanin)
ty·ro·thri·cin \ˌtī-rə-'thrī-sᵊn\ n [NL *Tyrothoric-, Tyrothrix*, genus name formerly applied to various bacteria including *Bacillus brevis*] (1940) : an antibiotic mixture that consists chiefly of tyrocidine and gramicidin, is usu. extracted from a soil bacillus (*Bacillus brevis*) as a gray to brown powder, and is used for local applications esp. for infection caused by gram-positive bacteria
tzaddik n, pl **tzaddikim** *var of* ZADDIK
tzar \'zär, '(t)sär\ *var of* CZAR
tzi·gane \(t)sē-'gän\ n [F, fr. Hung *cigány*] (1763) **1** : GYPSY 1 **2** : ROMANY 2
tzim·mes \'tsi-məs\ n [Yiddish *tsimes*, fr. MHG z, *zuo* at, too + *imbiz* light meal] (1892) : a sweetened combination of vegetables (as carrots and potatoes) or of meat and carrots often with dried fruits (as prunes) that is stewed or baked in a casserole
tzit·zis, tzi·tzit *var of* ZIZITH

\ə\ abut \ᵊ\ kitten, F table \ər\ further \a\ ash \ā\ ace \ä\ mop, mar \aú\ out \ch\ chin \e\ bet \ē\ easy \g\ go \i\ hit \ī\ ice \j\ job \ŋ\ sing \ō\ go \ȯ\ law \ȯi\ boy \th\ thin \t͟h\ the \ü\ loot \ú\ foot \y\ yet \zh\ vision \à, k̲, ⁿ, œ, œ̄, ᵫ, ᵫ̄, ᵞ\ *see* Guide to Pronunciation

U

u \'yü\ *n, pl* **u's** *or* **us** \'yüz\ *often cap, often attrib* (bef. 12c) **1 a** : the 21st letter of the English alphabet **b** : a graphic representation of this letter **c** : a speech counterpart of orthographic *u* **2** : a graphic device for reproducing the letter *u* **3** : one designated *u* esp. as the 21st in order or class **4** [abbr. for *unsatisfactory*] **a** : a grade rating a student's work as unsatisfactory **b** : one graded or rated with a U **5** : something shaped like the letter U

U \'yü\ *adj* [upper class] (1954) : characteristic of the upper classes

Uban·gi \yü-'baŋ-gē, ü-, -'baŋ-ē\ *n* [*Ubangi-Shari*, Africa] (1942) : a woman of the district of Kyabé village in Chad with lips pierced and distended to unusual dimensions with wooden disks — not used technically

ubi·qui·none \yü-'bi-kwə-ˌnōn, ˌyü-bə-kwi-'nōn\ *n* [blend of L *ubique* everywhere and E *quinone*; fr. its widespread occurrence in nature] (1958) : any of a group of lipid-soluble quinones that contain a long isoprenoid side chain and that function in the part of cellular respiration comprising oxidative phosphorylation as electron-carrying coenzymes in the transport of electrons from organic substrates to oxygen esp. along the chain of reactions leading from the Krebs cycle

ubiq·ui·tous \yü-'bi-kwə-təs\ *adj* (1837) : existing or being everywhere at the same time : constantly encountered : WIDESPREAD — **ubiq·ui·tous·ly** *adv* — **ubiq·ui·tous·ness** *n*

ubiq·ui·ty \-kwə-tē\ *n* [L *ubique* everywhere, fr. *ubi* where + *-que*, enclitic generalizing particle; akin to L *quis* who and to L *-que* and — more at WHO, SESQUI-] (1597) : presence everywhere or in many places esp. simultaneously : OMNIPRESENCE

U-boat \'yü-ˌbōt\ *n* [trans. of G *U-boot*, short for *Unterseeboot*, lit., undersea boat] (1916) : a German submarine

ud·der \'ə-dər\ *n* [ME, fr. OE *ūder*; akin to OHG *ūtar* udder, L *uber*, Gk *outhar*, Skt *ūdhar*] (bef. 12c) **1** : a large pendulous organ consisting of two or more mammary glands enclosed in a common envelope and each provided with a single nipple — see COW illustration **2** : MAMMARY GLAND

UFO \ˌyü-(ˌ)ef-'ō\ *n, pl* **UFO's** *or* **UFOs** \-'ōz\ [*unidentified flying object*] (1953) : an unidentified flying object; *esp* : FLYING SAUCER

ufol·o·gy \yü-'fä-lə-jē\ *n, often cap* UFO [UFO + *-logy*] (1959) : the study of unidentified flying objects — **ufo·log·i·cal** \ˌyü-fə-'lä-ji-kəl\ *adj, often cap* UFO — **ufol·o·gist** \yü-'fä-lə-jist\ *n, often cap* UFO

¹Uga·rit·ic \ˌyü-gə-'ri-tik, ˌü-gə-\ *n* (1936) : the Semitic language of ancient Ugarit closely related to Phoenician and Hebrew

²Ugaritic *adj* (1938) : of, relating to, or characteristic of the ancient city of Ugarit, its inhabitants, or Ugaritic

ugh *often read as* 'əg *or* 'ək *or* 'ə\ *interj* (1837) — used to indicate the sound of a cough or grunt or to express disgust or horror

Ug·li \'ə-glē\ *trademark* — used for a tangelo

ug·li·fy \'ə-gli-ˌfī\ *vt* **-fied; -fy·ing** (1576) : to make ugly — **ug·li·fi·ca·tion** \ˌə-gli-fə-'kā-shən\ *n*

ug·li·ness \'ə-glē-nəs\ *n* (14c) **1** : the quality or state of being ugly **2** : something that is ugly

¹ug·ly \'ə-glē\ *adj* **ug·li·er; -est** [ME, fr. ON *uggligr*, fr. *uggr* fear; akin to ON *ugga* to fear] (13c) **1** : FRIGHTFUL, DIRE **2 a** : offensive to the sight : HIDEOUS **b** : offensive or unpleasant to any sense **3** : morally offensive or objectionable ⟨corruption—the *ugliest* stain of all⟩ **4 a** : likely to cause inconvenience or discomfort ⟨the ~ truth⟩ **b** : SURLY, QUARRELSOME ⟨an ~ disposition⟩ ⟨the crowd got ~⟩ — **ug·li·ly** \-glə-lē\ *adv*

²ugly *adv* (14c) : in an ugly manner ⟨was acting ~⟩

Ugly American *n* [*The Ugly American* (1958), collection of stories by Eugene Burdick †1965 and William J. Lederer *b*1912 Am. authors] (1965) : an American in a foreign country whose behavior is offensive to the people of that country

ugly duckling *n* [*The Ugly Duckling*, story by Hans Christian Andersen] (1883) : one that appears very unpromising but often has great potential

Ugri·an \'yü-grē-ən, 'ü-\ *n* [ORuss *Ugre* Hungarians] (1841) : a member of a division of the Finno-Ugric peoples that includes the Hungarians and two peoples of western Siberia — **Ugrian** *adj*

Ugric \-grik\ *adj* (1854) : of, relating to, or characteristic of the languages of the Ugrians

ug·some \'əg-səm\ *adj* [ME, fr. *uggen* to fear, inspire fear, fr. ON *ugga* to fear] (15c) *archaic* : FRIGHTFUL, LOATHSOME

uh–huh \two m's *or* two n's *separated by the voiceless sound* h; 'ən-(ˌ)hən, (ˌ)ən-'\ *interj* (1899) — used to indicate affirmation, agreement, or gratification

uh·lan \'ü-ˌlän, ü-'; 'yü-lən, ü-\ *n* [G, fr. Pol *ulan* or Turk *oğlan* boy, servant] (1753) : any of a body of Prussian light cavalry orig. modeled on Tatar lancers

uh–oh \'ə-ˌō, *usu with strong glottal stops before the vowels*\ *interj* (1971) — used to indicate dismay or concern

uh–uh \two m's *or* two n's *preceded by glottal stops;* 'ən-ˌən\ *interj* (ca. 1924) — used to indicate negation

Ui·ghur *also* **Ui·gur** \'wē-ˌgùr\ *n* [Uighur *Uighur*] (1747) **1** : a member of a Turkic people powerful in Mongolia and eastern Turkestan between the 8th and 12th centuries A.D. who constitute a majority of the population of Chinese Turkestan **2** : the Turkic language of the Uighurs — **Uighur** *also* **Uigur** *adj*

uil·leann pipes \'i-lən-\ *n pl, often cap* [*uilleann* fr. Ir, gen. sing. of *uillinn* elbow, fr. OIr *uilen*; akin to OE *eln* ell — more at ELL] (1906) : an Irish bagpipe with air supplied by a bellows held under and worked by the elbow

uin·ta·ite *also* **uin·tah·ite** \yù-'in-tə-ˌīt\ *n* [*Uinta, Uintah*, mountains in Utah] (1888) : a black lustrous asphalt occurring esp. in Utah

Uit·land·er \'āt-ˌlan-dər, 'aùt-, -ˌlän-\ *n* [Afrik, fr. MD *utelander* foreigner, fr. *utelant* foreign territory, fr. *ute* out + *lant* land] (1892) : FOREIGNER; *esp* : a British resident in the former republics of the Transvaal and Orange Free State

ukase \yü-'kās, -'kāz, 'yü-ˌ; ü-'käz\ *n* [F & Russ; F, fr. Russ *ukaz*, fr. *ukazat'* to show, order; akin to OCS *u-* away, L *au-* away and- to OCS *kazati* to show] (1729) **1** : a proclamation by a Russian emperor or government having the force of law **2** : EDICT

uke \'yük\ *n* (1921) : UKULELE

uki·yo-e *also* **uki·yo-ye** \ˌü-ˌkē-ō-'yä, -'ā\ *n* [Jp *ukiyo-e* genre picture, fr. *ukiyo* world, life + *e* picture] (1879) : a Japanese art movement that flourished from the 17th to the 19th century and produced paintings and prints depicting the everyday life and interests of the common people; *also* : the paintings and prints themselves

Ukrai·ni·an \yü-'krā-nē-ən *also* -'krī-\ *n* (1823) **1** : a native or inhabitant of Ukraine **2** : the Slavic language of the Ukrainian people — **Ukrainian** *adj*

uku·le·le \ˌyü-kə-'lā-lē, ˌü-\ *n* [Hawaiian *'ukulele*, fr. *'uku* flea + *lele* jumping] (1896) : a small guitar of Portuguese origin popularized in Hawaii in the 1880s and strung typically with four strings

ukulele

-ular *adj suffix* [L *-ularis*, fr. *-ulus, -ula, -ulum -ule + -aris -ar*] : of, relating to, or resembling ⟨valv*ular*⟩

ul·cer \'əl-sər\ *n* [ME, fr. L *ulcer-, ulcus*; akin to Gk *helkos* wound] (14c) **1** : a break in skin or mucous membrane with loss of surface tissue, disintegration and necrosis of epithelial tissue, and often pus **2** : something that festers and corrupts like an open sore — **ulcer** *vb*

ul·cer·ate \'əl-sə-ˌrāt\ *vb* **-at·ed; -at·ing** *vi* (15c) : to become affected with or as if with an ulcer ~ *vt* : to affect with or as if with an ulcer

ul·cer·a·tion \ˌəl-sə-'rā-shən\ *n* (14c) **1** : the process of becoming ulcerated : the state of being ulcerated **2** : ULCER — **ul·cer·a·tive** \'əl-sə-ˌrā-tiv, 'əl-sə-rə-\ *adj*

ulcerative colitis *n* (ca. 1928) : a nonspecific inflammatory disease of the colon of unknown cause characterized by diarrhea with discharge of mucus and blood, cramping abdominal pain, and inflammation and edema of the mucous membrane with patches of ulceration

ul·cero·gen·ic \ˌəl-sə-rō-'je-nik\ *adj* (1950) : tending to produce or develop into ulcers or ulceration

ul·cer·ous \'əls-rəs, 'əl-sə-\ *adj* (1577) **1** : being or marked by an ulceration ⟨~ lesions⟩ **2** : affected with or as if with an ulcer : ULCERATED

-ule *n suffix* [F & L; F, fr. L *-ulus*, masc. dim. suffix, *-ula*, fem. dim. suffix, *-ulum*, neut. dim. suffix] : little one ⟨duct*ule*⟩

ule·ma *or* **ula·ma** \ˌü-lə-'mä\ *n* [Ar, Turk, & Per; Turk & Per *'ulemā*, fr. Ar *'ulamā*] (1688) **1** *pl in constr* : the body of mullahs **2** : MULLAH

-ulent *adj suffix* [L *-ulentus*] : that abounds in (a specified thing) ⟨flocculent⟩

ulex·ite \'yü-lək-ˌsīt\ *n* [George L. *Ulex* †1883 Ger. chemist] (1867) : a mineral consisting of a hydrous borate of sodium and calcium and usu. occurring in loosely packed white fibers that transmit light lengthwise with nearly undiminished intensity

ul·lage \'ə-lij\ *n* [ME *ulage*, fr. MF *eullage* act of filling a cask, fr. *eullier* to fill a cask, fr. OF *ouil* eye, bunghole, fr. L *oculus* eye — more at EYE] (15c) : the amount that a container (as a tank or cask) lacks of being full

ul·na \'əl-nə\ *n* [NL, fr. L, elbow — more at ELL] (1541) : the bone on the little-finger side of the human forearm; *also* : a corresponding part of the forelimb of vertebrates above fishes — **ul·nar** \-nər, -ˌnär\ *adj*

ul·ster \'əl-stər\ *n* [*Ulster*, Ireland] (1876) : a long loose overcoat of Irish origin made of heavy material (as frieze)

ul·te·ri·or \ˌəl-'tir-ē-ər\ *adj* [L, farther, further, compar. of (assumed) L *ulter* situated beyond, fr. *uls* beyond; akin to L *ollus, ille*, that one, OIr *indoll* beyond] (1646) **1 a** : FURTHER, FUTURE **b** : more distant : REMOTER **c** : situated on the farther side : THITHER **2** : going beyond what is openly said or shown and esp. what is proper ⟨~ motives⟩ — **ul·te·ri·or·ly** *adv*

ul·ti·ma \'əl-tə-mə\ *n* [L, fem. of *ultimus* last] (ca. 1864) : the last syllable of a word

ul·ti·ma·cy \'əl-tə-mə-sē\ *n, pl* **-cies** (1842) **1** : the quality or state of being ultimate **2** : ULTIMATE 1

ul·ti·ma ra·tio \ˌùl-tə-mə-'rä-tē-ˌō\ *n* [NL] (1780) : the final argument; *also* : the last resort (as force)

¹ul·ti·mate \'əl-tə-mət\ *adj* [ML *ultimatus* last, final, fr. LL, pp. of *ultimare* to come to an end, be last, fr. L *ultimus* farthest, last, final, superl. of (assumed) L *ulter* situated beyond] (1654) **1 a** : most remote in space or time : FARTHEST **b** : last in a progression or series ⟨their ~ destination was Paris⟩ **c** : EVENTUAL ⟨they hoped for ~ success⟩ **d** : the best or most extreme of its kind : UTMOST ⟨the ~ sacrifice⟩ **2** : arrived at as the last result ⟨the ~ question⟩ **3 a** : BASIC, FUNDAMENTAL ⟨the ~ nature of things —A. N. Whitehead⟩ **b** : ORIGINAL ⟨the ~ source⟩ **c** : incapable of further analysis, division, or separation **4** : MAXIMUM *syn* see LAST — **ul·ti·mate·ness** *n*

²ultimate *n* (1681) **1** : something ultimate; *esp* : FUNDAMENTAL **2** : ACME

³ul·ti·mate \-mət, -ˌmāt\ *vb* **-mat·ed; -mat·ing** (ca. 1834) : END

ul·ti·mate·ly \-mət-lē\ *adv* (1652) **1** : in the end : FINALLY, FUNDAMENTALLY **2** : EVENTUALLY

ul·ti·ma Thu·le \ˌəl-tə-mə-'thü-lē, -'thyü-\ *n* [L, farthest Thule] (1665) : THULE

ul·ti·ma·tum \ˌəl-tə-'mā-təm, -'mä-\ *n, pl* **-tums** *or* **-ta** \-tə\ [NL, fr. ML, neut. of *ultimatus* final] (1731) : a final proposition, condition, or demand; *esp* : one whose rejection will end negotiations and cause a resort to force or other direct action

ul·ti·mo \'əl-tə-ˌmō\ *adj* [L *ultimo mense* in the last month] (1616) : of or occurring in the month preceding the present

ul·ti·mo·gen·i·ture \ˌəl-tə-mō-'je-nə-ˌchùr, -ni-chər, -nə-ˌtyùr, -nə-ˌtùr\ *n* [L *ultimus* last + E *primogeniture*] (1882) : a system of inheritance by which the youngest child succeeds to the estate

¹ul·tra \'əl-trə\ *adj* [ultra-] (1818) : going beyond others or beyond due limit : EXTREME

²ultra *n* [ultra-] (1819) : one that is ultra : EXTREMIST

ultra- *prefix* [L, fr. ultra beyond, adv. & prep., fr. (assumed) L *ulter* situated beyond — more at ULTERIOR] **1** : beyond in space : on the other side : TRANS- ⟨*ultra*violet⟩ **2** : beyond the range or limits of

: transcending : SUPER- ⟨*ultra*microscopic⟩ **3** : beyond what is ordinary, proper, or moderate : excessively : extremely ⟨*ultra*modern⟩

ul·tra·care·ful	ul·tra·hip	ul·tra·ra·tio·nal
ul·tra·ca·su·al	ul·tra·hot	ul·tra·re·al·ism
ul·tra·cau·tious	ul·tra·hu·man	ul·tra·re·al·ist
ul·tra·chic	ul·tra·left	ul·tra·re·al·is·tic
ul·tra·civ·i·lized	ul·tra·left·ism	ul·tra·re·fined
ul·tra·clean	ul·tra·left·ist	ul·tra·re·li·able
ul·tra·cold	ul·tra·lib·er·al	ul·tra·re·spect·able
ul·tra·com·mer·cial	ul·tra·lib·er·al·ism	ul·tra·rev·o·lu·tion·ary
ul·tra·com·pact	ul·tra·light·weight	ul·tra·rich
ul·tra·com·pe·tent	ul·tra·low	ul·tra·right
ul·tra·con·ser·va·tism	ul·tra·mas·cu·line	ul·tra·right·ist
ul·tra·con·ser·va·tive	ul·tra·mil·i·tant	ul·tra·ro·man·tic
ul·tra·con·tem·po·rary	ul·tra·min·i·a·tur·ized	ul·tra·roy·al·ist
ul·tra·con·ve·nient	ul·tra·mod·ern	ul·tra·safe
ul·tra·cool	ul·tra·mod·ern·ist	ul·tra·se·cret
ul·tra·crit·i·cal	ul·tra·na·tion·al·ism	ul·tra·seg·re·ga·tion·ist
ul·tra·dem·o·crat·ic	ul·tra·na·tion·al·ist	ul·tra·sen·si·tive
ul·tra·dense	ul·tra·na·tion·al·is·tic	ul·tra·se·ri·ous
ul·tra·dis·tance	ul·tra·or·tho·dox	ul·tra·sharp
ul·tra·dis·tant	ul·tra·par·a·dox·i·cal	ul·tra·sim·ple
ul·tra·dry	ul·tra·pa·tri·ot·ic	ul·tra·slick
ul·tra·ef·fi·cient	ul·tra·phys·i·cal	ul·tra·slow
ul·tra·en·er·get·ic	ul·tra·pow·er·ful	ul·tra·small
ul·tra·ex·clu·sive	ul·tra·prac·ti·cal	ul·tra·smart
ul·tra·fa·mil·iar	ul·tra·pre·cise	ul·tra·smooth
ul·tra·fast	ul·tra·pre·ci·sion	ul·tra·soft
ul·tra·fas·tid·i·ous	ul·tra·pro·fes·sion·al	ul·tra·so·phis·ti·cat·ed
ul·tra·fem·i·nine	ul·tra·pro·gres·sive	ul·tra·thin
ul·tra·fine	ul·tra·pure	ul·tra·vac·u·um
ul·tra·glam·or·ous	ul·tra·qui·et	ul·tra·vi·o·lence
ul·tra·haz·ard·ous	ul·tra·rad·i·cal	ul·tra·vi·o·lent
ul·tra·heat	ul·tra·rap·id	ul·tra·vir·ile
ul·tra·heavy	ul·tra·rare	ul·tra·vi·ril·i·ty
ul·tra·high	ul·tra·rar·e·fied	ul·tra·wide

ul·tra·ba·sic \ˌəl-trə-'bā-sik\ *adj* [ISV] (1881) : extremely basic; *specif* : very low in silica and rich in iron and magnesium minerals — **ultrabasic** *n*

ul·tra·cen·trif·u·gal \-ˌsen-'tri-fyə-gəl, -fi-gəl\ *adj* (1930) : of, relating to, or obtained by means of an ultracentrifuge — **ul·tra·cen·trif·u·gal·ly** \-gə-lē\ *adv*

¹**ul·tra·cen·tri·fuge** \-'sen-trə-ˌfyüj\ *n* (1924) : a high-speed centrifuge able to sediment colloidal and other small particles and used esp. in determining sizes of such particles and molecular weights of large molecules

²**ultracentrifuge** *vt* (1930) : to subject to an ultracentrifuge — **ul·tra·cen·tri·fu·ga·tion** \-ˌsen-trə-fyü-'gā-shən\ *n*

ul·tra·fiche \'əl-trə-ˌfēsh\ *n* (1969) : a microfiche whose microimages are of printed matter reduced 90 or more times

ul·tra·fil·tra·tion \ˌəl-trə-fil-'trā-shən\ *n* (1908) : filtration through a medium (as a semipermeable capillary wall) which allows small molecules (as of water) to pass but holds back larger ones (as of protein) — **ul·tra·fil·trate** \-'fil-ˌtrāt\ *n*

ultrahigh frequency *n* (1932) : a radio frequency between superhigh frequency and very high frequency — see RADIO FREQUENCY table

ul·tra·ism \'əl-trə-ˌi-zəm\ *n* (1821) **1** : the principles of those who advocate extreme measures (as radicalism) **2** : an instance or example of radicalism — **ul·tra·ist** \-trə-ist\ *adj or n* — **ul·tra·is·tic** \ˌəl-trə-'is-tik\ *adj*

¹**ul·tra·light** \'əl-trə-ˌlīt\ *adj* (1974) : extremely light in mass or weight ⟨an ∼ alloy⟩ ⟨an ∼ pullover⟩

²**ultralight** *n* (1980) : a very light recreational aircraft typically for one person that is powered by a small gasoline engine

ul·tra·maf·ic \ˌəl-trə-'ma-fik\ *adj* (1933) : ULTRABASIC

ul·tra·mar·a·thon \-'mar-ə-ˌthän\ *n* (1977) : a footrace longer than a marathon — **ul·tra·mar·a·thon·er** \-ˌthä-nər\ *n*

¹**ul·tra·ma·rine** \-mə-'rēn\ *n* [ML *ultramarinus* coming from beyond the sea, fr. L *ultra-* + *mare* sea — more at MARINE] (1598) **1 a** (1) : a blue pigment prepared by powdering lapis lazuli (2) : a similar pigment prepared from kaolin, soda ash, sulfur, and charcoal **b** : any of several related pigments (2) : a vivid blue

²**ultramarine** *adj* (1652) : situated beyond the sea

ul·tra·mi·cro \ˌəl-trə-'mī-(ˌ)krō\ *adj* (1937) : being or dealing with something smaller than micro

ul·tra·mi·cro·scope \ˌəl-trə-'mī-krə-ˌskōp\ *n* [back-formation fr. *ultramicroscopic*] (1906) : an apparatus for making visible by scattered light particles too small to be perceived by an ordinary microscope

ul·tra·mi·cro·scop·ic \-ˌmī-krə-'skä-pik\ *also* **ul·tra·mi·cro·scop·i·cal** \-pi-kəl\ *adj* [ISV] (1870) **1** : too small to be seen with an ordinary microscope **2** : of or relating to an ultramicroscope — **ul·tra·mi·cro·scop·i·cal·ly** \-pi-k(ə-)lē\ *adv*

ul·tra·mi·cro·tome \-'mī-krə-ˌtōm\ *n* (1946) : a microtome for cutting extremely thin sections for electron microscopy — **ul·tra·mi·crot·o·my** \-mī-'krä-tə-mē\ *n*

ul·tra·min·i·a·ture \-'mi-nē-ə-ˌchúr, -'mi-ni-ˌchúr, -'min-yə-, -chər, -ˌtyúr, -ˌtúr\ *adj* (1942) : SUBMINIATURE

ul·tra·mon·tane \-'män-ˌtān, -ˌmän-'\ *adj* [ML *ultramontanus*, fr. L *ultra-* + *mont-, mons* mountain — more at MOUNT] (ca. 1618) **1** : of or relating to countries or peoples beyond the mountains (as the Alps) **2** : favoring greater or absolute supremacy of papal over national or diocesan authority in the Roman Catholic Church — **ultramontane** *n, often cap* — **ul·tra·mon·tan·ism** \-'män-tᵊn-ˌi-zəm\ *n*

ul·tra·short \-'shórt\ *adj* (1926) **1** : having a wavelength below 10 meters ⟨∼ radiation⟩ **2** : very short in duration ⟨an ∼ pulse of light⟩

ul·tra·son·ic \-'sä-nik\ *adj* (1923) **1** : having a frequency above the human ear's audibility limit of about 20,000 hertz — used of waves and vibrations **2** : utilizing, produced by, or relating to ultrasonic waves or vibrations ⟨∼ testing of metal⟩ — **ul·tra·son·i·cal·ly** \-ni-k(ə-)lē\ *adv*

ul·tra·son·ics \ˌəl-trə-'sä-niks\ *n pl* (1924) **1** : ultrasonic vibrations or compressional waves **2** *sing in constr* : the study of ultrasonic vibrations and their associated phenomena **3** : ultrasonic devices

ul·tra·so·nog·ra·phy \-sə-'nä-grə-fē, -sō-\ *n* [*ultrasonic* + *-o-* + *-graphy*] (1951) : ULTRASOUND 2 — **ul·tra·so·nog·ra·pher** \-fər\ *n* — **ul·tra·so·no·graph·ic** \-ˌsō-nə-'gra-fik, -ˌsä-\ *adj*

ul·tra·sound \'əl-trə-ˌsaúnd\ *n* (1923) **1** : vibrations of the same physical nature as sound but with frequencies above the range of human hearing **2** : the diagnostic or therapeutic use of ultrasound and esp. a technique involving the formation of a two-dimensional image used for the examination and measurement of internal body structures and the detection of bodily abnormalities — called also *sonography* **3** : a diagnostic examination using ultrasound

ul·tra·struc·ture \'əl-trə-ˌstrək-chər\ *n* (1939) : biological structure and esp. fine structure (as of a cell) not visible through an ordinary microscope — **ul·tra·struc·tur·al** \ˌəl-trə-'strək-chə-rəl, -'strək-shrəl\ *adj* — **ul·tra·struc·tur·al·ly** *adv*

ul·tra·vi·o·let \ˌəl-trə-'vī-(ə-)lət\ *adj* (1840) **1** : situated beyond the visible spectrum at its violet end — used of radiation having a wavelength shorter than wavelengths of visible light and longer than those of X rays **2** : relating to, producing, or employing ultraviolet radiation — **ultraviolet** *n*

ul·tra vi·res \ˌəl-trə-'vī-(ˌ)rēz\ *adv or adj* [NL, lit., beyond power] (1793) : beyond the scope or in excess of legal power or authority

ul·u·lant \'əl-yə-lənt\ *adj* (1868) : having a howling sound : WAILING ⟨dark wasteland . . . ∼ with bitter wind —Rudi Blesh⟩

ul·u·late \-ˌlāt\ *vi* **-lat·ed; -lat·ing** [L *ululatus*, pp. of *ululare*, of imit. origin] (1623) : HOWL, WAIL — **ul·u·la·tion** \ˌəl-yə-'lā-shən\ *n*

ul·va \'əl-və\ *n* [NL, genus name, fr. L *ulva*, fr. L, sedge] (1706) : SEA LETTUCE

Ulys·ses \yü-'li-(ˌ)sēz\ *n* [L *Ulysses, Ulixes*, fr. Gk *Oulixes, Olysseus, Odysseus*] : ODYSSEUS

um·bel \'əm-bəl\ *n* [NL *umbella*, fr. L, umbrella — more at UMBRELLA] (1597) : a racemose inflorescence typical of the carrot family in which the axis is very much contracted so that the pedicels appear to spring from the same point to form a flat or rounded flower cluster — see INFLORESCENCE illustration

um·bel·late \'əm-bə-ˌlāt, ˌəm-'be-lət\ *adj* (1760) **1** : bearing, consisting of, or arranged in umbels **2** : resembling an umbel in form

um·bel·lif·er \ˌəm-'be-lə-fər\ *n* [NL *Umbelliferae*, group name, fem. pl. of *umbellifer* bearing umbels] (1718) : a plant of the carrot family

um·bel·lif·er·ous \ˌəm-bə-'li-f(ə-)rəs\ *adj* (1662) : of or relating to the carrot family ⟨∼ flower heads⟩

¹**um·ber** \'əm-bər\ *n* [prob. fr. obs. E, shade, color, fr. ME *umbre* shade, shadow, fr. MF, fr. L *umbra* — more at UMBRAGE] (1568) **1 a** : a brown earth that is darker in color than ocher and sienna because of its content of manganese and iron oxides and is highly valued as a permanent pigment either in the raw or burnt state **2 a** : a moderate to dark yellowish brown **b** : a moderate brown

²**umber** *vt* **um·bered; um·ber·ing** \-b(ə-)riŋ\ (1610) : to darken with or as if with umber

³**umber** *adj* (1802) : of, relating to, or having the characteristics of umber; *specif* : of the color of umber

¹**um·bil·i·cal** \ˌəm-'bi-li-kəl, *Brit also* ˌəm-bə-'lī-kəl\ *adj* (1541) **1** : of, relating to, or used at the navel **2** : of or relating to the central region of the abdomen

²**umbilical** *n* (1774) : UMBILICAL CORD 2

umbilical cord *n* (1753) **1** : a cord arising from the navel that connects the fetus with the placenta; *also* : YOLK STALK **2** : a tethering or supply line (as for an astronaut outside a spacecraft or a diver underwater)

um·bil·i·cate \ˌəm-'bi-li-kət\ *or* **um·bil·i·cat·ed** \-lə-ˌkā-təd\ *adj* (1698) **1** : depressed like a navel **2** : having an umbilicus — **um·bil·i·ca·tion** \ˌəm-ˌbi-lə-'kā-shən\ *n*

um·bi·li·cus \ˌəm-'bi-li-kəs, ˌəm-bə-'lī-\ *n, pl* **um·bi·li·ci** \ˌəm-'bi-li-ˌkī, -ˌkē; ˌəm-bə-'lī-ˌkī, -ˌsī\ *or* **um·bi·li·cus·es** [L — more at NAVEL] (ca. 1615) **1 a** : NAVEL 1 **b** : any of several morphological depressions; *esp* : HILUM 1 **2** : a central point : CORE, HEART

um·bles \'əm-bəlz\ *n pl* [ME, alter. of *nombles*, fr. MF, pl. of *nomble* fillet of beef, pork loin, modif. of L *lumbulus*, dim. of *lumbus* loin — more at LOIN] (15c) : the edible viscera of an animal and esp. of a deer or hog

um·bo \'əm-(ˌ)bō\ *n, pl* **um·bo·nes** \ˌəm-'bō-(ˌ)nēz\ *or* **umbos** [L; akin to L *umbilicus* — more at NAVEL] (1721) **1** : the boss of a shield **2** : a rounded elevation: as **a** : an inward projection of the tympanic membrane of the ear **b** : one of the lateral prominences just above the hinge of a bivalve shell — **um·bo·nal** \'əm-bə-nᵊl, ˌəm-'bō-\ *adj* — **um·bo·nate** \'əm-bə-ˌnāt, ˌəm-'bō-nət\ *adj*

um·bra \'əm-brə\ *n, pl* **umbras** *or* **um·brae** \-(ˌ)brē, -ˌbrī\ [L] (1638) **1** : a shaded area **2 a** : a conical shadow excluding all light from a given source; *specif* : the conical part of the shadow of a celestial body excluding all light from the primary source **b** : the central dark part of a sunspot — **um·bral** \-brəl\ *adj*

um·brage \'əm-brij\ *n* [ME, fr. MF, fr. L *umbraticum*, neut. of *umbraticus* of shade, fr. *umbratus*, pp. of *umbrare* to shade, fr. *umbra* shade, shadow; akin to Lith *unksmė* shadow] (15c) **1** : SHADE, SHADOW **2** : shady branches : FOLIAGE **3 a** : an indistinct indication : vague suggestion : HINT **b** : a reason for doubt : SUSPICION **4** : a feeling of pique or resentment at some often fancied slight or insult ⟨took ∼ at the speaker's remarks⟩ *syn* see OFFENSE

um·bra·geous \ˌəm-'brā-jəs\ *adj* (1587) **1 a** : affording shade **b** : spotted with shadows **2** : inclined to take offense easily — **um·bra·geous·ly** *adv* — **um·bra·geous·ness** *n*

¹**um·brel·la** \ˌəm-'bre-lə, *esp Southern* 'əm-ˌ\ *n* [It *ombrella*, modif. of L *umbella*, dim. of *umbra*] (1611) **1** : a collapsible shade for protection against weather consisting of fabric stretched over hinged ribs radiating from a central pole; *esp* : a small one for carrying in the hand **2** : the bell-shaped or saucer-shaped largely gelatinous structure that

forms the chief part of the body of most jellyfishes **3** : something which provides protection: as **a** : defensive air cover (as over a battlefront) **b** : a heavy barrage **4** : something which covers or embraces a broad range of elements or factors ⟨decided to expand . . . by building new colleges under a federation ∼ —Diane Ravitch⟩

²**umbrella** *vt* **-laed; -la·ing** (ca. 1800) : to protect, cover, or provide with an umbrella

umbrella plant *n* (1874) : an African sedge (*Cyperus alternifolius*) that has large terminal whorls of slender leaves and is often grown as an ornamental

umbrella tree *n* (1738) **1** : a magnolia (*Magnolia tripetala*) of the eastern U.S. having large leaves clustered at the ends of the branches **2** : any of various trees or shrubs resembling an umbrella esp. in the arrangement of leaves or the shape of the crown

Um·bri·an \ˈəm-brē-ən\ *n* (1601) **1** : a native or inhabitant of Umbria **2** : the Italic language of ancient Umbria — see INDO-EUROPEAN LANGUAGES table — **Umbrian** *adj*

Um·bun·du \ˌəm-ˈbün-(ˌ)dü\ *n* (ca. 1895) : a Bantu language of central Angola

umi·ak \ˈü-mē-ˌak\ *n* [Inuit *umiaq*] (1769) : an open Eskimo boat made of a wooden frame covered with hide

umiak

¹**um·laut** \ˈüm-ˌlaút, ˈum-\ *n* [G, fr. *um-* around, transformation + *Laut* sound] (1852) **1 a** : the change of a vowel that is caused by partial assimilation to a succeeding sound or that occurs as a reflex of the former presence of a succeeding sound which has been lost or altered (as to mark pluralization in *goose, geese* or *mouse, mice*) **b** : a vowel resulting from such partial assimilation **2** : a diacritical mark ¨ placed over a vowel to indicate a more central or front articulation — compare DIAERESIS

²**umlaut** *vt* (1879) **1** : to produce by umlaut **2** : to write or print an umlaut over

¹**ump** \ˈəmp\ *n* (1912) : UMPIRE 2

²**ump** *vi* (1928) : to act as umpire

¹**um·pire** \ˈəm-ˌpīr\ *n* [ME *oumpere*, alter. (fr. misdivision of *a noumpere*) of *noumpere*, fr. MF *nomper* not equal, not paired, fr. *non-* + *per* equal, fr. L *par*] (15c) **1** : one having authority to decide finally a controversy or question between parties: as **a** : one appointed to decide between arbitrators who have disagreed **b** : an impartial third party chosen to arbitrate disputes arising under the terms of a labor agreement **2** : an official in a sport who rules on plays **3** : a military officer who evaluates maneuvers

²**umpire** *vb* **um·pired; um·pir·ing** *vt* (1609) : to supervise or decide as umpire ∼ *vi* : to act as umpire

ump·teen \ˈəm(p)-ˌtēn, -əm(p)-ˈ\ *adj* [blend of *umpty* (such and such) and *-teen* (as in *thirteen*)] (1918) : very many : indefinitely numerous — **ump·teenth** \-ˌtēn(t)th, -ˈtēn(t)th\ *adj*

¹**un-** \ˌən, ˈən *often* ˈən *before* ˈ-stressed syllable\ *prefix* [ME, fr. OE; akin to OHG *un-* un-, L *in-*, Gk *a-, an-*, OE *ne* not — more at NO] **1** : not : IN-, NON- — in adjectives formed from adjectives ⟨*un*ambitious⟩ ⟨*un*skilled⟩ or participles ⟨*un*dressed⟩, in nouns formed from nouns ⟨*una*vailability⟩, and rarely in verbs formed from verbs ⟨*un*be⟩; sometimes in words that have a meaning that merely negates that of the base word and are thereby distinguished from words that prefix *in-* or a variant of it (as *im-*) to the same base word and have a meaning positively opposite to that of the base word ⟨*un*artistic⟩ ⟨*un*moral⟩ **2** : opposite of : contrary to — in adjectives formed from adjectives ⟨*un*constitutional⟩ ⟨*un*graceful⟩ ⟨*un*mannered⟩ or participles ⟨*un*believing⟩ and in nouns formed from nouns ⟨*un*rest⟩

²**un-** *prefix* [ME, fr. OE *un-, on-*, alter. of *and-* against — more at ANTE] **1** : do the opposite of : reverse (a specified action) : DE- 1a, DIS- 1a — in verbs formed from verbs ⟨*un*bend⟩ ⟨*un*dress⟩ ⟨*un*fold⟩ **2 a** : deprive of : remove (a specified thing) from : remove — in verbs formed from nouns ⟨*un*frock⟩ ⟨*un*sex⟩ **b** : release from : free from — in verbs formed from nouns ⟨*un*hand⟩ **c** : remove from : extract from : bring out of — in verbs formed from nouns ⟨*un*bosom⟩ **d** : cause to cease to be — in verbs formed from nouns ⟨*un*man⟩ **3** : completely ⟨*un*loose⟩

un·abrad·ed	un·af·fec·tion·ate·ly	un·ar·gu·able
un·ab·sorbed	un·af·fil·i·at·ed	un·ar·gu·ably
un·ab·sor·bent	un·af·flu·ent	un·ar·mored
un·ac·a·dem·ic	un·af·ford·able	un·ar·ro·gant
un·ac·a·dem·i·cal·ly	un·afraid	un·ar·tis·tic
un·ac·cent·ed	un·ag·gres·sive	un·as·pi·rat·ed
un·ac·cept·ed	un·aid·ed	un·as·sailed
un·ac·cli·mat·ed	un·air-con·di·tioned	un·as·sem·bled
un·ac·cli·ma·tized	un·akin	un·as·signed
un·ac·com·mo·dat·ed	un·alien·at·ed	un·as·sim·i·la·ble
un·ac·com·mo·dat·ing	un·alike	un·as·sim·i·lat·ed
un·ac·cred·it·ed	un·al·le·vi·at·ed	un·as·so·ci·at·ed
un·ac·cul·tur·at·ed	un·al·lo·cat·ed	un·as·suaged
un·achieved	un·al·lur·ing	un·ath·let·ic
un·ac·knowl·edged	un·al·tered	un·at·tain·able
un·ac·quaint·ed	un·am·bi·tious	un·at·tend·ed
un·act·able	un·ame·na·ble	un·at·ten·u·at·ed
un·act·ed	un·amend·ed	un·at·test·ed
un·ac·tor·ish	un·ami·a·ble	un·at·trib·ut·able
un·adapt·able	un·am·or·tized	un·at·trib·ut·ed
un·adapt·ed	un·am·pli·fied	un·at·tuned
un·ad·dressed	un·amus·ing	un·au·dit·ed
un·ad·ju·di·cat·ed	un·an·a·lyz·able	un·au·then·tic
un·ad·just·ed	un·an·a·lyzed	un·au·tho·rized
un·ad·mired	un·an·no·tat·ed	un·au·to·mat·ed
un·ad·mit·ted	un·an·nounced	un·avail·abil·i·ty
un·adopt·able	un·apol·o·giz·ing	un·avail·able
un·adult	un·ap·par·ent	un·avowed
un·ad·ven·tur·ous	un·ap·peased	un·awak·ened
un·ad·ver·tised	un·ap·pre·ci·at·ed	un·award·ed
un·aes·thet·ic	un·ap·pre·cia·tive	un·awe·some
un·af·fect·ing	un·ap·pro·pri·at·ed	un·ban
un·af·fec·tion·ate	un·ap·proved	un·bap·tized

un·barbed	un·co·erced	un·de·filed
un·bar·ri·cad·ed	un·co·er·cive	un·de·fin·able
un·be·hold·en	un·co·er·cive·ly	un·de·fined
un·be·lig·er·ent	un·col·lect·ed	un·de·fo·li·at·ed
un·be·loved	un·col·lect·ible	un·de·formed
un·billed	un·col·ored	un·del·e·gat·ed
un·bit·ten	un·com·bat·ive	un·de·liv·er·able
un·bit·ter	un·combed	un·de·liv·ered
un·bleached	un·com·bined	un·de·lud·ed
un·blem·ished	un·come·ly	un·de·mand·ing
un·blend·ed	un·com·ic	un·de·nom·i·na·tion·al
un·blood·ed	un·com·mer·cial·ized	un·de·pend·able
un·book·ish	un·com·pas·sion·ate	un·de·scrib·able
un·bought	un·com·pel·ling	un·de·served
un·bowd·ler·ized	un·com·pen·sat·ed	un·de·serv·ing
un·brack·et·ed	un·com·pla·cent	un·des·ig·nat·ed
un·brake	un·com·plet·ed	un·de·sired
un·breach·able	un·com·pound·ed	un·de·tect·able
un·break·able	un·com·pre·hend·ed	un·de·tect·ed
un·bridge·able	un·com·pu·ter·ized	un·de·ter·min·able
un·bridged	un·con·cealed	un·de·ter·mined
un·briefed	un·con·fessed	un·de·terred
un·bright	un·con·fined	un·de·vel·oped
un·bril·liant	un·con·firmed	un·di·ag·nos·able
un·bruised	un·con·found·ed	un·di·ag·nosed
un·brushed	un·con·fuse	un·di·a·lec·ti·cal
un·bud·get·ed	un·con·ju·gat·ed	un·di·dac·tic
un·buf·fered	un·con·nect·ed	un·dif·fer·en·ti·at·ed
un·build·able	un·con·quered	un·di·gest·ed
un·bulky	un·con·se·crat·ed	un·di·gest·ible
un·bu·reau·crat·ic	un·con·strained	un·dig·ni·fied
un·bur·ied	un·con·strict·ed	un·di·lut·ed
un·burn·able	un·con·struc·tive	un·di·min·ished
un·burned	un·con·sumed	un·dimmed
un·burnt	un·con·sum·mat·ed	un·dis·charged
un·busi·ness·like	un·con·tain·able	un·dis·ci·plined
un·busy	un·con·tam·i·nat·ed	un·dis·closed
un·but·tered	un·con·tem·plat·ed	un·dis·cour·aged
un·cal·ci·fied	un·con·tem·po·rary	un·dis·cov·er·able
un·cal·cined	un·con·ten·tious	un·dis·cov·ered
un·cal·i·brat·ed	un·con·test·ed	un·dis·crim·i·nat·ing
un·called	un·con·tract·ed	un·dis·cussed
un·cal·loused	un·con·tra·dict·ed	un·dis·mayed
un·can·celed	un·con·trived	un·dis·pu·ta·ble
un·can·did	un·con·trolled	un·dis·put·ed
un·can·did·ly	un·con·tro·ver·sial	un·dis·solved
un·ca·non·i·cal	un·con·tro·ver·sial·ly	un·dis·tin·guished
un·cap	un·con·vert·ed	un·dis·tort·ed
un·cap·i·tal·ized	un·con·vinced	un·dis·tract·ed
un·cap·tioned	un·con·voyed	un·dis·trib·ut·ed
un·cap·tur·able	un·cooked	un·dis·turbed
un·cared-for	un·cooled	un·di·vid·ed
un·car·ing	un·co·op·er·a·tive	un·do·able
un·car·pet·ed	un·co·or·di·nat·ed	un·doc·ile
un·case	un·copy·right·able	un·doc·tored
un·cas·trat·ed	un·cor·rect·able	un·doc·tri·naire
un·cat·a·loged	un·cor·rect·ed	un·doc·u·ment·ed
un·catch·able	un·cor·re·lat·ed	un·do·mes·tic
un·catchy	un·cor·rob·o·rat·ed	un·do·mes·ti·cat·ed
un·cat·e·go·riz·able	un·cor·rupt	un·dot·ted
un·caught	un·count·able	un·doubt·able
un·cen·sored	un·cou·ra·geous	un·doubt·ing
un·cen·so·ri·ous	un·cov·e·nant·ed	un·drained
un·cen·sured	un·coy	un·dra·ma·tized
un·cer·ti·fied	un·cracked	un·drilled
un·chal·lenge·able	un·crate	un·dubbed
un·chal·lenged	un·cra·zy	un·dulled
un·chal·leng·ing	un·cre·a·tive	un·du·pli·cat·ed
un·changed	un·cre·den·tialed	un·dyed
un·chan·neled	un·cred·it·ed	un·dy·nam·ic
un·chap·er·oned	un·crip·pled	un·ea·ger
un·char·is·mat·ic	un·cropped	un·ear-marked
un·charm·ing	un·cross·able	un·eat·able
un·char·tered	un·crowd·ed	un·eat·en
un·chau·vin·is·tic	un·crush·able	un·ec·cen·tric
un·check·able	un·cuff	un·eco·log·i·cal
un·checked	un·cul·ti·va·ble	un·ed·i·fy·ing
un·chew·able	un·cul·ti·vat·ed	un·ed·u·ca·ble
un·chewed	un·cul·tured	un·ed·u·cat·ed
un·chic	un·cured	un·elab·o·rate
un·child·like	un·cu·ri·ous	un·elect·able
un·chlo·ri·nat·ed	un·cur·rent	un·elect·ed
un·cho·reo·graphed	un·cur·tained	un·elec·tri·fied
un·chris·tened	un·cus·tom·ar·i·ly	un·em·bar·rassed
un·chron·i·cled	un·cus·tom·ary	un·em·bel·lished
un·chro·no·log·i·cal	un·cute	un·em·bit·tered
un·church·ly	un·cyn·i·cal	un·em·phat·ic
un·cil·i·at·ed	un·cyn·i·cal·ly	un·em·phat·i·cal·ly
un·cin·e·mat·ic	un·dam·aged	un·em·pir·i·cal
un·clad	un·damped	un·en·chant·ed
un·claimed	un·dance·able	un·en·closed
un·clar·i·fied	un·dat·ed	un·en·cour·ag·ing
un·clas·si·fi·able	un·de·ca·dent	un·en·dear·ing
un·cleaned	un·de·cid·abil·i·ty	un·en·dur·able
un·clear	un·de·cid·able	un·en·dur·able·ness
un·cli·chéd	un·de·cid·ed	un·en·dur·ably
un·clip	un·de·ci·pher·able	un·en·force·able
un·cloy·ing	un·de·ci·phered	un·en·forced
un·co·alesce	un·de·clared	un·en·larged
un·coat·ed	un·de·com·posed	un·en·light·ened
un·coat·ing	un·dec·o·rat·ed	un·en·light·en·ing
un·cod·ed	un·ded·i·cat·ed	un·en·riched
un·cod·i·fied	un·de·feat·ed	un·en·ter·pris·ing
	un·de·fend·ed	un·en·thu·si·as·tic

un·en·thu·si·as·ti·cal·ly	un·hope·ful	un·ma·li·cious·ly	un·pre·pared·ness	un·re·strict·ed
un·en·vi·able	un·housed	un·man·age·able	un·pre·pos·sess·ing	un·re·touched
un·en·vi·ous	un·hu·mor·ous	un·man·age·ably	un·pressed	un·re·turn·able
un·erot·ic	un·hurt	un·man·aged	un·pres·sured	un·re·vealed
un·es·cap·able	un·hy·dro·lyzed	un·ma·nip·u·lat·ed	un·pres·sur·ized	un·re·view·able
un·es·tab·lished	un·hy·gien·ic	un·mapped	un·pret·ty	un·re·viewed
un·eth·i·cal	un·hy·phen·at·ed	un·marked	un·priv·i·leged	un·re·vised
un·eval·u·at·ed	un·hys·ter·i·cal	un·mar·ket·able	un·prob·lem·at·ic	un·rev·o·lu·tion·ary
un·ex·celled	un·hys·ter·i·cal·ly	un·marred	un·pro·cessed	un·re·ward·ed
un·ex·cit·able	un·iden·ti·fi·able	un·mas·cu·line	un·pro·duced	un·re·ward·ing
un·ex·cit·ed	un·iden·ti·fied	un·match·able	un·pro·duc·tive	un·rhe·tor·i·cal
un·ex·cit·ing	un·ideo·log·i·cal	un·matched	un·pro·fes·sion·al	un·rhymed
un·ex·cused	un·id·i·om·at·ic	un·meant	un·pro·gram·ma·ble	un·rhyth·mic
un·ex·ot·ic	un·ig·nor·able	un·mea·sur·able	un·pro·grammed	un·rid·able
un·ex·pend·ed	un·il·lu·mi·nat·ing	un·mea·sured	un·pro·gres·sive	un·ri·fled
un·ex·pired	un·imag·i·na·tive	un·mech·a·nized	un·prompt·ed	un·rip·ened
un·ex·plain·able	un·imag·i·na·tive·ly	un·med·i·cat·ed	un·pro·nounce·able	un·ro·man·tic
un·ex·plained	un·im·mu·nized	un·me·lo·di·ous	un·pro·pi·tious	un·ro·man·ti·cal·ly
un·ex·plod·ed	un·im·paired	un·me·lo·di·ous·ness	un·pros·per·ous	un·ro·man·ti·cized
un·ex·plored	un·im·pas·sioned	un·mem·o·ra·ble	un·pro·tect·ed	un·roofed
un·ex·posed	un·im·ped·ed	un·mem·o·ra·bly	un·prov·able	un·rushed
un·ex·pressed	un·im·por·tant	un·mer·it·ed	un·proved	un·safe
un·ex·pur·gat·ed	un·im·pos·ing	un·mer·ry	un·prov·en	un·sal·able
un·ex·traor·di·nary	un·im·pressed	un·met	un·pro·voked	un·sal·a·ried
un·faked	un·im·pres·sive	un·me·tab·o·lized	un·pruned	un·salt·ed
un·fa·mous	un·in·cor·po·rat·ed	un·mil·i·tary	un·pub·li·cized	un·sal·vage·able
un·fan·cy	un·in·dexed	un·milled	un·pub·lished	un·sanc·tioned
un·fas·tid·i·ous	un·in·dict·ed	un·mined	un·punc·tu·al	un·san·i·tary
un·fea·si·ble	un·in·dus·tri·al·ized	un·mix	un·punc·tu·al·i·ty	un·sat·is·fied
un·felt	un·in·fect·ed	un·mix·able	un·punc·tu·at·ed	un·scal·able
un·fem·i·nine	un·in·flat·ed	un·mixed	un·pun·ished	un·scarred
un·fenced	un·in·flect·ed	un·mod·ern·ized	un·quan·ti·fi·able	un·scent·ed
un·fer·ment·ed	un·in·flu·enced	un·mod·i·fied	un·quench·able	un·sched·uled
un·fer·tile	un·in·for·ma·tive	un·mod·ish	un·ques·tioned	un·schol·ar·ly
un·fer·til·ized	un·in·for·ma·tive·ly	un·mo·lest·ed	un·raised	un·screened
un·filled	un·in·formed	un·mon·i·tored	un·ranked	un·scrip·tur·al
un·fired	un·in·gra·ti·at·ing	un·mo·ti·vat·ed	un·rat·ed	un·sea·soned
un·flam·boy·ant	un·in·hab·it·able	un·mount·ed	un·rav·ished	un·sea·wor·thy
un·flashy	un·in·hab·it·ed	un·mov·able	un·reach·able	un·se·cured
un·fly·able	un·ini·ti·at·ed	un·moved	un·reached	un·seed·ed
un·fond	un·in·jured	un·mu·si·cal	un·read·able	un·seg·ment·ed
un·forced	un·in·oc·u·lat·ed	un·name·able	un·read·i·ness	un·self-con·scious
un·fore·see·able	un·in·spect·ed	un·named	un·ready	un·self-con·scious·ly
un·fore·seen	un·in·spired	un·need·ed	un·re·al·iz·able	un·self-con·scious·ness
un·for·est·ed	un·in·spir·ing	un·ne·go·tia·ble	un·re·al·ized	un·sell·able
un·for·giv·able	un·in·struct·ed	un·neu·rot·ic	un·re·cep·tive	un·sen·sa·tion·al
un·for·got·ten	un·in·struc·tive	un·news·wor·thy	un·re·claim·able	un·sen·si·tized
un·for·mu·lat·ed	un·in·su·lat·ed	un·no·tice·able	un·rec·og·niz·able	un·sent
un·forth·com·ing	un·in·sur·able	un·no·ticed	un·rec·og·niz·ably	un·sen·ti·men·tal
un·for·ti·fied	un·in·sured	un·nour·ish·ing	un·rec·og·nized	un·sep·a·rat·ed
un·fos·sil·if·er·ous	un·in·te·grat·ed	un·ob·jec·tion·able	un·rec·on·cil·able	un·se·ri·ous
un·framed	un·in·tel·lec·tu·al	un·ob·serv·able	un·rec·on·ciled	un·se·ri·ous·ness
un·free	un·in·tel·li·gent	un·ob·served	un·re·cord·ed	un·served
un·free·dom	un·in·tel·li·gent·ly	un·ob·struct·ed	un·re·cov·er·able	un·ser·vice·able
un·friv·o·lous	un·in·tel·li·gi·bil·i·ty	un·ob·tain·able	un·re·cov·ered	un·sex·u·al
un·ful·fill·able	un·in·tel·li·gi·ble	un·of·fi·cial	un·re·cy·cla·ble	un·sexy
un·ful·filled	un·in·tel·li·gi·ble·ness	un·of·fi·cial·ly	un·re·deem·able	un·shad·ed
un·fun·ny	un·in·tel·li·gi·bly	un·open·able	un·re·deemed	un·shak·able
un·fur·nished	un·in·tend·ed	un·opened	un·re·dressed	un·shak·ably
un·fused	un·in·ten·tion·al	un·op·posed	un·re·fined	un·shak·en
un·gal·lant	un·in·ten·tion·al·ly	un·or·dered	un·re·flec·tive	un·shape·ly
un·gal·lant·ly	un·in·ter·est·ing	un·orig·i·nal	un·re·formed	un·shared
un·gar·nished	un·in·ter·rupt·ed	un·or·na·ment·ed	un·re·frig·er·at·ed	un·sharp
un·ge·nial	un·in·ter·rupt·ed·ly	un·os·ten·ta·tious	un·reg·is·tered	un·shav·en
un·gen·teel	un·in·tim·i·dat·ed	un·os·ten·ta·tious·ly	un·reg·u·lat·ed	un·shelled
un·gen·tle	un·in·ven·tive	un·owned	un·re·hearsed	un·shock·able
un·gen·tle·man·ly	un·in·vit·ed	un·ox·y·gen·at·ed	un·re·in·forced	un·shorn
un·gen·tri·fied	un·in·vit·ing	un·paint·ed	un·re·lat·ed	un·showy
un·ger·mi·nat·ed	un·in·volved	un·par·a·sit·ized	un·re·laxed	un·signed
un·gift·ed	un·iron·i·cal·ly	un·par·don·able	un·re·li·abil·i·ty	un·sink·able
un·gim·micky	un·ir·ra·di·at·ed	un·pass·able	un·re·li·able	un·size
un·glam·or·ized	un·ir·ri·gat·ed	un·pas·teur·ized	un·re·lieved	un·slaked
un·glam·or·ous	un·is·sued	un·pas·to·ral	un·re·liev·ed·ly	un·smart
un·glazed	un·jad·ed	un·pat·ent·able	un·re·luc·tant	un·smil·ing
un·grace·ful	un·joint·ed	un·pa·tri·ot·ic	un·re·mark·able	un·smoothed
un·grace·ful·ly	un·jus·ti·fi·able	un·paved	un·re·mark·ably	un·soiled
un·grad·ed	un·jus·ti·fi·ably	un·pe·dan·tic	un·re·mem·bered	un·sol·dier·ly
un·grasp·able	un·jus·ti·fied	un·peeled	un·rem·i·nis·cent	un·so·lic·it·ed
un·ground	un·kept	un·per·ceived	un·re·mov·able	un·solv·able
un·grouped	un·knot	un·per·cep·tive	un·re·peat·able	un·solved
un·guess·able	un·knowl·edge·able	un·per·form·able	un·re·pen·tant	un·sort·ed
un·guid·ed	un·ko·sher	un·per·formed	un·re·pen·tant·ly	un·sound·ed
un·hack·neyed	un·la·beled	un·per·suad·ed	un·re·port·ed	un·sown
un·ham·pered	un·la·dy-like	un·per·sua·sive	un·rep·re·sen·ta·tive	un·spe·cial·ized
un·harmed	un·la·ment·ed	un·per·turbed	un·rep·re·sen·ta·tive·ness	un·spec·i·fi·able
un·har·ness	un·laun·dered	un·pic·tur·esque	un·rep·re·sent·ed	un·spe·cif·ic
un·har·vest·ed	un·learn·able	un·planned	un·re·pressed	un·spec·i·fied
un·hatched	un·leav·ened	un·plau·si·ble	un·re·sis·tant	un·spec·tac·u·lar
un·healed	un·lib·er·at·ed	un·play·able	un·re·solv·able	un·spent
un·health·ful	un·li·censed	un·pleased	un·re·solved	un·spir·i·tu·al
un·heat·ed	un·lik·able	un·pleas·ing	un·re·spect·able	un·split
un·hedged	un·lined	un·plowed	un·re·spon·sive	un·spoiled
un·heed·ed	un·lis·ten·able	un·po·et·ic	un·re·spon·sive·ly	un·spoilt
un·heed·ing	un·lit	un·po·liced	un·re·spon·sive·ness	un·spo·ken
un·help·ful	un·lit·er·ary	un·pol·ished	un·rest·ful	un·sprayed
un·help·ful·ly	un·liv·able	un·pol·lut·ed	un·re·stored	un·stained
un·her·ald·ed	un·lo·cal·ized	un·posed		un·stan·dard·ized
un·he·ro·ic	un·lov·able	un·prac·ti·cal		
un·hin·dered	un·loved	un·pre·dict·abil·i·ty		
un·hip	un·lov·ing	un·pre·dict·able		
un·his·tor·i·cal	un·lyr·i·cal	un·pre·dict·ably		
un·ho·mog·e·nized	un·ma·cho	un·prej·u·diced		
un·hon·ored	un·mag·ni·fied	un·pre·med·i·tat·ed		
	un·ma·li·cious	un·pre·pared		

				un·star·tling
				un·stat·ed
				un·stayed
				un·ster·ile
				un·ster·il·ized
				un·stint·ed
				un·stitch
				un·stop·per
				un·strained
				un·strat·i·fied
				un·stuffy
				un·styl·ish
				un·sub·dued
				un·sub·si·dized
				un·sub·stan·ti·at·ed
				un·sub·tle
				un·sub·tly
				un·suit·abil·i·ty
				un·suit·able
				un·suit·ably
				un·suit·ed
				un·sul·lied
				un·su·per·vised
				un·sup·port·able
				un·sup·port·ed
				un·sure
				un·sur·pass·able
				un·sur·passed
				un·sur·prised
				un·sus·cep·ti·ble
				un·sus·pect·ed
				un·sus·pect·ing
				un·sus·pi·cious
				un·sus·tain·able
				un·sweet·ened
				un·sym·pa·thet·ic
				un·sym·pa·thet·i·cal·ly
				un·syn·chro·nized
				un·sys·tem·at·ic
				un·sys·tem·at·i·cal·ly
				un·sys·tem·a·tized
				un·tact·ful
				un·tagged
				un·taint·ed
				un·tal·ent·ed
				un·tam·able
				un·tamed
				un·tanned
				un·tar·nished
				un·taxed
				un·teach·able
				un·tech·ni·cal
				un·tem·pered
				un·ten·ant·ed
				un·tend·ed
				un·ten·ured
				un·test·able
				un·test·ed
				un·the·o·ret·i·cal
				un·threat·en·ing
				un·thrifty
				un·till·able
				un·tilled
				un·to·geth·er
				un·trace·able
				un·tra·di·tion·al
				un·tra·di·tion·al·ly
				un·trained
				un·tram·meled
				un·trans·formed
				un·trans·lat·abil·i·ty
				un·trans·lat·able
				un·trans·lat·ed
				un·trav·eled
				un·tra·versed
				un·treat·ed
				un·trendy
				un·trimmed
				un·trust·ing
				un·trust·wor·thy
				un·tuck
				un·tuft·ed
				un·typ·i·cal
				un·typ·i·cal·ly
				un·un·der·stand·able
				un·us·able
				un·uti·lized
				un·vac·ci·nat·ed
				un·var·ied
				un·vary·ing
				un·ven·ti·lat·ed
				un·ver·bal·ized
				un·ver·i·fi·able
				un·versed
				un·vi·a·ble
				un·vis·it·ed
				un·want·ed

\ə\ abut \ʾ\ kitten, F table \ər\ further \a\ ash \ā\ ace \ä\ mop, mar
\aů\ out \ch\ chin \e\ bet \ē\ easy \g\ go \i\ hit \ī\ ice \j\ job
\ŋ\ sing \ō\ go \ȯ\ law \ȯi\ boy \th\ thin \t͟h\ the \ü\ loot \u̇\ foot
\y\ yet \zh\ vision \à, k̲, ⁿ, œ, œ̄, ʉ, ʉ̄, ʸ\ *see* Guide to Pronunciation

un·war·like
un·war·rant·ed
un·wa·ver·ing
un·wa·ver·ing·ly
un·waxed
un·weaned
un·wear·able
un·weath·ered

un·wed
un·weight·ed
un·wel·come
un·white
un·willed
un·win·na·ble
un·wom·an·ly
un·won

un·work·abil·i·ty
un·work·able
un·worked
un·wor·ried
un·wound·ed
un·wo·ven
un·young

un·abashed \ˌən-ə-'basht\ adj (1571) : not abashed : UNDISGUISED, UNAPOLOGETIC — **un·abash·ed·ly** \-'bash-əd-lē\ adv

un·abat·ed \ˌən-ə-'bā-təd\ adj (ca. 1611) : not abated : being at full strength or force — **un·abat·ed·ly** adv

un·able \ˌən-'ā-bəl\ adj (14c) : not able : INCAPABLE: as **a** : UNQUALIFIED, INCOMPETENT **b** : IMPOTENT, HELPLESS

un·abridged \ˌən-ə-'brijd\ adj (1599) **1** : not abridged : COMPLETE ⟨an ~ reprint of a novel⟩ **2** : being the most complete of its class : not based on one larger ⟨an ~ dictionary⟩

un·ac·cept·able \ˌən-ik-'sep-tə-bəl, -ak-\ adj (15c) : not acceptable : not pleasing or welcome — **un·ac·cept·abil·i·ty** \-ˌsep-tə-bi-lə-tē\ n — **un·ac·cept·ably** \-'sep-tə-blē\ adv

un·ac·com·pa·nied \ˌən-ə-'kəmp-nēd, -'kämp-; -'kəm-pə-, -'käm-\ adj (1545) : not accompanied; esp : being without instrumental accompaniment

un·ac·count·able \ˌən-ə-'kaün-tə-bəl\ adj (1643) **1** : not to be accounted for : INEXPLICABLE, STRANGE **2** : not to be called to account : not responsible — **un·ac·count·abil·i·ty** \-ˌkaün-tə-'bi-lə-tē\ n

un·ac·count·ably \-'kaün-tə-blē\ adv (15c) **1** : in an unaccountable manner ⟨looking ~ upset⟩ ⟨heat was ~ disappearing⟩ **2** : for reasons that are hard to understand ⟨~, he stayed right there⟩

un·ac·count·ed \-'kaün-təd\ adj (1689) : not accounted : UNEXPLAINED — often used with for

un·ac·cus·tomed \ˌən-ə-'kəs-təmd\ adj (1526) **1** : not customary : not usual or common **2** : not habituated — usu. used with to — **un·ac·cus·tomed·ly** \-təmd-lē\ adv

una cor·da \ˌü-nə-'kȯr-də, -ˌ(ˌ)dä\ adv or adj [It, lit., one string] (ca. 1849) : with soft pedal depressed — used as a direction in piano music

un·adorned \ˌən-ə-'dȯrnd\ adj (1634) : not adorned : lacking embellishment or decoration : PLAIN, SIMPLE

un·adul·ter·at·ed \ˌən-ə-'dəl-tə-ˌrā-təd\ adj (1719) **1** : not adulterated : PURE ⟨~ food⟩ **2** : COMPLETE, UNQUALIFIED ⟨an ~ fool⟩ — **un·adul·ter·at·ed·ly** adv

un·ad·vised \ˌən-əd-'vīzd\ adj (14c) **1** : done without due consideration : RASH ⟨~ and dangerous dealings with the terrorists⟩ **2** : not prudent : ILL-ADVISED ⟨done with ~ haste⟩ — **un·ad·vis·ed·ly** \-'vī-zəd-lē\ adv

un·af·fect·ed \ˌən-ə-'fek-təd\ adj (ca. 1586) **1** : not influenced or changed mentally, physically, or chemically **2** : free from affectation : GENUINE — **un·af·fect·ed·ly** adv — **un·af·fect·ed·ness** n

un·ag·ing or **un·age·ing** \ˌən-'ā-jiŋ\ adj (1860) : AGELESS

una·kite \'yü-nə-ˌkīt\ n [Unaka Mountains, Tenn. & N.C. + ¹-ite] (1874) : an altered igneous rock that is usu. opaque with green, black, pink, and white flecks and is usu. used as a gemstone

un·alien·able \ˌən-'āl-yə-nə-bəl, -'ā-lē-ə-\ adj (1611) : INALIENABLE

un·aligned \ˌən-ə-'līnd\ adj (ca. 1934) : NONALIGNED

un·al·loyed \ˌən-ə-'lȯid\ adj (1667) : not alloyed : UNMIXED, UNQUALIFIED, PURE ⟨~ metals⟩ ⟨~ happiness⟩

un·al·ter·able \ˌən-'ȯl-t(ə-)rə-bəl\ adj (1611) : not capable of being altered or changed ⟨an ~ resolve⟩ ⟨~ hatred⟩ — **un·al·ter·abil·i·ty** \ˌən-ˌȯl-t(ə)rə-'bi-lə-tē\ n — **un·al·ter·able·ness** \ˌən-'ȯl-t(ə)rə-bəl-nəs\ n — **un·al·ter·ably** \-blē\ adv

un·am·big·u·ous \ˌən-am-'bi-gyə-wəs\ adj (1751) : not ambiguous : CLEAR, PRECISE — **un·am·big·u·ous·ly** adv

un·am·biv·a·lent \-'bi-və-lənt\ adj (1945) : not ambivalent : CLEARCUT, DEFINITE — **un·am·biv·a·lent·ly** adv

un–Amer·i·can \ˌən-ə-'mer-ə-kən\ adj (1818) : not American : not characteristic of or consistent with American customs, principles, or traditions

un·an·chored \ˌən-'aŋ-kərd\ adj (1651) **1** : not anchored : not at anchor **2** : not having a firm basis or foundation

un·aneled \ˌən-ə-'nē(ə)ld\ adj [un- + aneled, pp. of anele to anoint, fr. ME, fr. an on + ¹elen to anoint, fr. ele oil, fr. OE, fr. L oleum — more at OIL] (1602) archaic : not having received extreme unction

un·anes·the·tized \ˌən-ə-'nes-thə-ˌtīzd\ adj (1950) : not having been subjected to an anesthetic

una·nim·i·ty \ˌyü-nə-'ni-mə-tē\ n (15c) : the quality or state of being unanimous

unan·i·mous \yu̇-'na-nə-məs\ adj [L unanimus, fr. unus one + animus mind — more at ONE, ANIMATE] (1624) **1** : being of one mind : AGREEING **2** : formed with or indicating unanimity : having the agreement and consent of all — **unan·i·mous·ly** adv

un·an·swer·able \ˌən-'an(t)s-rə-bəl, -'an(t)-sə-\ adj (1613) : not capable of being answered; also : IRREFUTABLE — **un·an·swer·abil·i·ty** \ˌən-ˌan(t)s-rə-'bi-lə-tē-, -ˌan(t)-sə-\ n — **un·an·swer·ably** \ˌən-'an(t)s-rə-blē, -'an(t)-sə-\ adv

un·an·swered \ˌən-'an(t)-sərd\ adj (14c) **1** : not answered ⟨~ letters⟩ **2** : scored in succession during a period in which an opponent fails to score ⟨scored 20 ~ points in the last quarter⟩

un·an·tic·i·pat·ed \ˌən-an-'ti-sə-ˌpā-təd\ adj (ca. 1779) : not anticipated : UNEXPECTED, UNFORESEEN — **un·an·tic·i·pat·ed·ly** adv

un·apol·o·get·ic \ˌən-ə-ˌpä-lə-'je-tik\ adj (1834) : not apologetic : offered, put forward, or being such without apology or qualification ⟨an ~ liberal⟩ — **un·apol·o·get·i·cal·ly** \-ti-k(ə-)lē\ adv

un·ap·peal·able \ˌən-ə-'pē-lə-bəl\ adj (1635) : not appealable : not subject to appeal

un·ap·peal·ing \-'pē-liŋ\ adj (ca. 1846) : not appealing : UNATTRACTIVE — **un·ap·peal·ing·ly** \-liŋ-lē\ adv

un·ap·peas·able \-'pē-zə-bəl\ adj (1561) : not to be appeased : IMPLACABLE — **un·ap·peas·ably** \-blē\ adv

un·ap·pe·tiz·ing \ˌən-'a-pə-ˌtī-ziŋ\ adj (1884) : not appetizing : INSIPID, UNATTRACTIVE — **un·ap·pe·tiz·ing·ly** \-ziŋ-lē\ adv

un·ap·pre·ci·a·tion \ˌən-ə-ˌprē-shē-'ā-shən\ n (1886) : failure to appreciate something

un·ap·proach·able \ˌən-ə-'prō-chə-bəl\ adj (1581) **1** : not approach-

able : physically inaccessible **2** : discouraging intimacies : RESERVED — **un·ap·proach·abil·i·ty** \-ˌprō-chə-'bi-lə-tē\ n — **un·ap·proach·ably** \-'prō-chə-blē\ adv

un·apt \ˌən-'apt\ adj (ca. 1513) **1** : INAPPROPRIATE, UNSUITABLE ⟨an ~ quote⟩ **2** : not accustomed and not likely ⟨a teacher ~ to tolerate carelessness⟩ **3** : DULL, BACKWARD ⟨~ scholars⟩ — **un·apt·ly** \-'ap(t)-lē\ adv — **un·apt·ness** \-nəs\ n

un·arm \ˌən-'ärm\ vt (1560) : DISARM

un·armed \-'ärmd\ adj (14c) **1** : not armed or armored **2** : having no hard and sharp projections (as spines, spurs, or claws)

un·ar·tic·u·lat·ed \ˌən-är-'ti-kyə-ˌlā-təd\ adj (ca. 1700) : not articulated; esp : not carefully reasoned or analyzed

una·ry \'yü-nə-rē\ adj [L unus one + E -ary] (1576) : having, consisting of, or acting on a single element, item, or component : MONADIC

un·ashamed \ˌən-ə-'shāmd\ adj (1600) : not ashamed : being without guilt, self-consciousness, or doubt — **un·asham·ed·ly** \-'shā-məd-lē\ adv

un·asked \ˌən-'as(k)t\ adj (13c) **1** : not being asked : UNINVITED **2** : not asked ⟨~ questions⟩ **3** : not asked for ⟨~ advice⟩

un·as·sail·able \ˌən-ə-'sā-lə-bəl\ adj (1596) : not assailable : not liable to doubt, attack, or question — **un·as·sail·abil·i·ty** \-ˌsā-lə-'bi-lə-tē\ n — **un·as·sail·able·ness** \-'sā-lə-bəl-nəs\ n — **un·as·sail·ably** \-blē\ adv

un·as·ser·tive \ˌən-ə-'sər-tiv\ adj (1861) : not assertive : MODEST, SHY — **un·as·ser·tive·ly** adv

un·as·sist·ed \ˌən-ə-'sis-təd\ adj (1614) **1** : not assisted : lacking help **2** : made or performed without an assist ⟨an ~ double play⟩

un·as·suag·able \ˌən-ə-'swā-jə-bəl\ adj (ca. 1611) : not capable of being assuaged

un·as·sum·ing \ˌən-ə-'sü-miŋ\ adj (1726) : not assuming : not arrogant or presuming : MODEST, RETIRING — **un·as·sum·ing·ness** n

un·at·tached \ˌən-ə-'tacht\ adj (1796) **1 a** : not assigned or committed (as to a particular task, organization, or person); esp : not married or engaged **b** : not seized as security for a legal judgment **2** : not joined or united ⟨~ buildings⟩

un·at·trac·tive \ˌən-ə-'trak-tiv\ adj (ca. 1775) : not attractive : PLAIN, DULL — **un·at·trac·tive·ly** adv — **un·at·trac·tive·ness** n

un·avail·ing \ˌən-ə-'vā-liŋ\ adj (1670) : not availing : FUTILE, USELESS — **un·avail·ing·ly** \-liŋ-lē\ adv — **un·avail·ing·ness** n

un·av·er·age \ˌən-'a-v(ə-)rij\ adj (1962) : not average : UNUSUAL, OUTSTANDING

un·avoid·able \ˌən-ə-'vȯi-də-bəl\ adj (1577) : not avoidable : INEVITABLE — **un·avoid·ably** \-blē\ adv

¹un·aware \ˌə-'war, -'wer\ adv (1592) : UNAWARES

²unaware adj (1704) : not aware : IGNORANT — **un·aware·ly** adv — **un·aware·ness** n

un·awares \-'warz, -'werz\ adv [un- + aware + -s, adv. suffix, fr. ME, fr. -s, gen. sing. ending of nouns — more at -s] (1535) **1** : without design, attention, preparation, or premeditation **2** : without warning : SUDDENLY, UNEXPECTEDLY

un·backed \ˌən-'bakt\ adj (1609) : lacking support or aid

¹un·bal·ance \ˌən-'ba-lən(t)s\ vt (1856) : to put out of balance; esp : to derange mentally

²unbalance n (1887) : lack of balance : IMBALANCE

un·bal·anced \-'lən(t)st\ adj (1650) : not balanced: as **a** : not in equilibrium **b** : mentally disordered or deranged **c** : not adjusted so as to make credits equal to debits ⟨an ~ account⟩

un·bal·last·ed \-'ba-lə-stəd\ adj (1657) : not furnished with or steadied by ballast : UNSTEADY

un·ban·dage \ˌən-'ban-dij\ vt (1840) : to remove a bandage from

un·bar \ˌən-'bär\ vt (14c) : to remove a bar from : UNBOLT, OPEN

un·bar·bered \-'bär-bərd\ adj (1845) : having long and esp. unkempt hair

un·barred \-'bärd\ adj (1603) **1** : not secured by a bar : UNLOCKED **2** : not marked with bars

un·bat·ed \-'bā-təd\ adj (1596) **1** : UNABATED **2** archaic : not blunted

un·be \-'bē\ vi (15c) archaic : to lack or cease to have being

un·bear·able \ˌən-'bar-ə-bəl, -'ber-\ adj (15c) : not bearable : UNENDURABLE — **un·bear·ably** \-blē\ adv

un·beat·able \-'bē-tə-bəl\ adj (1897) **1** : not capable of being defeated **2** : possessing unsurpassable qualities — **un·beat·ably** \-blē\ adv

un·beat·en \-'bē-t³n\ adj (13c) **1** : not pounded or beaten : not whipped **2** : not traversed : UNTROD **3** : not defeated

un·beau·ti·ful \-'byü-ti-fəl\ adj (15c) : not beautiful : UNATTRACTIVE — **un·beau·ti·ful·ly** \-f(ə-)lē\ adv

un·be·com·ing \ˌən-bi-'kə-miŋ\ adj (1598) : not becoming ⟨an ~ dress⟩; esp : not according with the standards appropriate to one's position or condition of life ⟨~ conduct⟩ **syn** see INDECOROUS — **un·be·com·ing·ly** \-miŋ-lē\ adv — **un·be·com·ing·ness** n

un·be·knownst \ˌən-bi-'nōn(t)st\ also **un·be·known** \-'nōn\ adj [¹un- + obs. E beknown known; unbeknownst, irreg. fr. unbeknown] (1636) : happening without one's knowledge : UNKNOWN — usu. used with to

un·be·lief \ˌən-bə-'lēf\ n (12c) : incredulity or skepticism esp. in matters of religious faith

un·be·liev·able \-'lē-və-bəl\ adj (1548) : too improbable for belief ⟨the plot is unreal and ~⟩; also : of such a superlative degree as to be hard to believe ⟨the destruction was ~⟩ ⟨made an ~ catch in center field⟩ — **un·be·liev·ably** \-blē\ adv

un·be·liev·er \-'lē-vər\ n (1526) **1** : one that does not believe : an incredulous person : DOUBTER, SKEPTIC **2** : one that does not believe in a particular religious faith

un·be·liev·ing \-'lē-viŋ\ adj (14c) : marked by unbelief : INCREDULOUS, SKEPTICAL — **un·be·liev·ing·ly** \-viŋ-lē\ adv

un·belt·ed \-'bel-təd\ adj (1814) : not furnished with a belt

un·bend \-'bend\ vb **-bent** \-'bent\; **-bend·ing** vt (13c) **1** : to free from flexure : make or allow to become straight ⟨~ a bow⟩ **2** : to cause (as the mind) to relax **3 a** : to unfasten (as a sail) from a spar or stay **b** : to cast loose (as a rope) : UNTIE ~ vi **1** : to relax one's severity, stiffness, or austerity **2** : to cease to be bent : become straight

un·bend·able \-'ben-də-bəl\ adj (ca. 1775) : SINGLE-MINDED, FIRM

un·bend·ing \-'ben-diŋ\ adj [¹un-] (ca. 1688) **1** : not bending : UNYIELDING, INFLEXIBLE ⟨an ~ will⟩ **2** : aloof or unsocial in manner : RESERVED

un·be·seem·ing \ˌən-bi-'sē-miŋ\ adj (1583) : not befitting : UNBECOMING

un·bi·ased \ˌən-'bī-əst\ adj (1647) 1 : free from bias; esp : free from all prejudice and favoritism : eminently fair 2 : having an expected value equal to a population parameter being estimated ⟨an ~ estimate of the population mean⟩ syn see FAIR — **un·bi·ased·ness** \-əs(t)-nəs\ n

un·bib·li·cal \ˌən-'bi-bli-kəl\ adj (1828) : contrary to or unsanctioned by the Bible

un·bid·den \ˌ'bi-dᵊn\ also **un·bid** \ˌ'bid\ adj [ME unbiden, unbeden, fr. OE unbeden, fr. un- + beden, pp. of biddan to entreat — more at BID] (bef. 12c) : not bidden : UNASKED, UNINVITED

un·bind \ˌ'bīnd\ vt **-bound** \ˌ'baúnd\; **-bind·ing** (bef. 12c) 1 : to remove a band from : free from fastenings : UNTIE, UNFASTEN 2 : to set free : RELEASE

un·bit·ted \ˌ'bi-təd\ adj [²bit] (ca. 1586) : UNBRIDLED, UNCONTROLLED

un·blenched \ˌ'blencht\ adj (1634) : not disconcerted : UNDAUNTED

un·blessed also **un·blest** \ˌən-'blest\ adj (14c) 1 : not blessed 2 : EVIL, ACCURSED

un·blind·ed \ˌ'blīn-dəd\ adj (ca. 1611) : not blinded; esp : free from illusion

un·blink·ing \ˌ'bliŋ-kiŋ\ adj (ca. 1909) 1 : not blinking 2 : not showing signs of emotion, doubt, or confusion — **un·blink·ing·ly** \-kiŋ-lē\ adv

un·block \ˌ'bläk\ vt (1611) : to free from being blocked

un·blush·ing \ˌ'blə-shiŋ\ adj (1595) 1 : not blushing 2 : SHAMELESS, UNABASHED — **un·blush·ing·ly** \-shiŋ-lē\ adv

un·bod·ied \ˌ'bä-dēd\ adj (1532) 1 : having no body : INCORPOREAL; also : freed from the body ⟨~ souls⟩ 2 : FORMLESS

un·bolt \ˌən-'bōlt\ vt (ca. 1598) : to open or unfasten by withdrawing a bolt

¹un·bolt·ed \ˌ'bōl-təd\ adj [²bolt] (ca. 1580) : not fastened by bolts

²unbolted adj [⁴bolt] (1598) : not sifted ⟨~ flour⟩

un·bon·net·ed \ˌən-'bä-nə-təd\ adj (1604) : BAREHEADED

un·born \ˌ'bórn\ adj (bef. 12c) 1 : not born : not brought into life 2 : still to appear : FUTURE 3 : existing without birth

un·bos·om \ˌ'bú-zəm\ also \ˌ'bü-\ vt (1588) 1 : to give expression to : DISCLOSE, REVEAL 2 : to disclose the thoughts or feelings of (oneself) ~ vi : to unbosom oneself

un·bound \ˌ'baúnd\ adj (bef. 12c) : not bound: as a (1) : not fastened (2) : not confined b : not having the leaves fastened together ⟨an ~ book⟩ c : not bound together with other issues ⟨~ periodicals⟩ d : not held in chemical or physical combination

un·bound·ed \ˌ'baún-dəd\ adj (1593) 1 : having no limit 2 : UNRESTRAINED, UNCONTROLLED — **un·bound·ed·ness** n

un·bowed \ˌən-'baúd\ adj (14c) 1 : not bowed down 2 : not subdued ⟨bloodied but ~⟩

un·box \ˌ'bäks\ vt (1611) : to remove from a box

un·brace \ˌ'brās\ vt (1593) 1 : to free or detach by or as if by untying or removing a brace or bond 2 : ENFEEBLE, WEAKEN

un·braid \ˌ'brād\ vt (ca. 1828) : to separate the strands of : UNRAVEL

un·branched \ˌ'brancht\ adj (1665) 1 : having no branches ⟨a straight ~ trunk⟩ 2 : not divided into branches ⟨a leaf with ~ veins⟩

un·brand·ed \ˌ'bran-dəd\ adj (1886) 1 : not marked with the owner's name or mark ⟨~ cattle⟩ 2 : not sold under a brand name

un·breath·able \ˌ'brē-thə-bəl\ adj (1846) : not fit for being breathed

un·bred \ˌ'bred\ adj (1662) 1 obs : ILL-BRED 2 : not taught : UNTRAINED 3 : not bred : never having been bred ⟨an ~ heifer⟩

un·bri·dle \ˌən-'brī-dᵊl\ vt (15c) : to free or loose from a bridle; broadly : to set loose : free from restraint

un·bri·dled \ˌ'brī-dᵊld\ adj (14c) 1 : UNRESTRAINED ⟨~ enthusiasm⟩ 2 : not confined by a bridle

un·broke \ˌ'brōk\ adj (14c) : UNBROKEN

un·bro·ken \ˌ'brō-kən\ adj (14c) : not broken: as a : not violated b : WHOLE, INTACT c : not subdued : UNTAMED; esp : not trained for service or use ⟨~ colts⟩ d : CONTINUOUS ⟨miles of ~ forest⟩ e : not plowed f : not disorganized ⟨advanced in ~ ranks⟩

un·buck·le \ˌ'bə-kəl\ vt (14c) : to loose the buckle of : UNFASTEN ~ vi 1 : to loosen buckles 2 : RELAX

un·budge·able \ˌ'bə-jə-bəl\ adj (1929) : not able to be budged or changed : INFLEXIBLE — **un·budge·ably** \-blē\ adv

un·budg·ing \ˌ'bə-jiŋ\ adj (ca. 1934) : not budging : resisting movement or change — **un·budg·ing·ly** \-jiŋ-lē\ adv

un·build \ˌən-'bild\ vb **-built** \ˌ'bilt\; **-build·ing** vt (1607) : to pull down : DEMOLISH, RAZE ~ vi : to destroy something

un·built \ˌ'bilt\ adj (15c) 1 : not built : not yet constructed 2 : not built on ⟨an ~ plot⟩

un·bun·dle \ˌ'bən-dᵊl\ vi (1969) : to give separate prices for equipment and supporting services ~ vt : to price separately

un·bur·den \ˌ'bər-dᵊn\ vt (1538) 1 : to free or relieve from a burden 2 : to relieve oneself of (as cares, fears, or worries) : cast off

un·bur·dened \ˌ'bər-dᵊnd\ adj (1548) : not burdened : having no weight or load

un·but·ton \ˌ'bə-tᵊn\ vt (14c) 1 : to loose the buttons of 2 : to open by or as if by loosing buttons ~ vi : to undo buttons

un·but·toned \ˌ'bə-tᵊnd\ adj (1583) 1 a : not buttoned b : not provided with buttons 2 : not under constraint : free and unrestricted in action and expression

un·cage \ˌən-'kāj\ vt (1620) : to release from or as if from a cage : free from restraint

un·cal·cu·lat·ed \ˌ'kal-kyə-ˌlā-təd\ adj (ca. 1828) : not planned or thought out beforehand : SPONTANEOUS

un·cal·cu·lat·ing \ˌ-ˌlā-tiŋ\ adj (ca. 1828) : not based on or marked by calculation

un·called–for \ˌən-'kóld(d)-ˌfór\ adj (ca. 1656) 1 : not called for or needed : UNNECESSARY 2 : being or offered without provocation or justification ⟨an ~ display of temper⟩ ⟨~ insults⟩

un·can·ny \ˌ'ka-nē\ adj (1843) 1 a : seeming to have a supernatural character or origin : EERIE, MYSTERIOUS b : being beyond what is normal or expected : suggesting superhuman or supernatural powers ⟨an ~ sense of direction⟩ 2 chiefly Scot : SEVERE, PUNISHING syn see WEIRD — **un·can·ni·ly** \ˌ'ka-nᵊl-ē\ adv — **un·can·ni·ness** \ˌ'ka-nē-nəs\ n

un·caused \ˌ'kózd\ adj (ca. 1628) : having no antecedent cause

un·ceas·ing \ˌ'sē-siŋ\ adj (14c) : never ceasing : CONTINUOUS, INCESSANT — **un·ceas·ing·ly** \-siŋ-lē\ adv

un·cel·e·brat·ed \ˌ'se-lə-ˌbrā-təd\ adj (1660) 1 : not formally honored or commemorated 2 : not famous : OBSCURE

un·cer·e·mo·ni·ous \ˌən-ˌser-ə-'mō-nē-əs\ adj (1598) 1 : not ceremonious : INFORMAL 2 : ABRUPT, RUDE ⟨an ~ dismissal⟩ — **un·cer·e·mo·ni·ous·ly** adv — **un·cer·e·mo·ni·ous·ness** n

un·cer·tain \ˌən-'sər-tᵊn\ adj (14c) 1 : INDEFINITE, INDETERMINATE ⟨the time of departure is ~⟩ 2 : not certain to occur : PROBLEMATICAL 3 : not reliable : UNTRUSTWORTHY 4 a : not known beyond doubt : DUBIOUS b : not having certain knowledge : DOUBTFUL c : not clearly identified or defined 5 : not constant : VARIABLE, FITFUL — **un·cer·tain·ly** adv — **un·cer·tain·ness** \-tᵊn-(n)əs\ n

un·cer·tain·ty \-tᵊn-tē\ n (14c) 1 : the quality or state of being uncertain : DOUBT 2 : something that is uncertain

syn UNCERTAINTY, DOUBT, DUBIETY, SKEPTICISM, SUSPICION, MISTRUST mean lack of sureness about someone or something. UNCERTAINTY may range from a falling short of certainty to an almost complete lack of conviction or knowledge esp. about an outcome or result ⟨assumed the role of manager without hesitation or uncertainty⟩. DOUBT suggests both uncertainty and inability to make a decision ⟨plagued by doubts as to what to do⟩. DUBIETY stresses a wavering between conclusions ⟨felt some dubiety about its practicality⟩. SKEPTICISM implies unwillingness to believe without conclusive evidence ⟨an economic forecast greeted with skepticism⟩. SUSPICION stresses lack of faith in the truth, reality, fairness, or reliability of something or someone ⟨regarded the stranger with suspicion⟩. MISTRUST implies a genuine doubt based upon suspicion ⟨had a great mistrust of doctors⟩.

uncertainty principle n (1929) : a principle in quantum mechanics: it is impossible to discern simultaneously and with high accuracy both the position and the momentum of a particle (as an electron) — called also Heisenberg uncertainty principle

un·chain \ˌən-'chān\ vt (1582) : to free by or as if by removing a chain : set loose

un·chancy \ˌ'chan(t)-sē\ adj (1533) 1 chiefly Scot : ILL-FATED 2 chiefly Scot : DANGEROUS

un·change·able \ˌ'chān-jə-bəl\ adj (14c) : not changing or to be changed : IMMUTABLE — **un·change·abil·i·ty** \ˌən-ˌchān-jə-bi-lə-tē\ n — **un·change·able·ness** \ˌən-'chān-jə-bəl-nəs\ n — **un·chan·ge·ably** \-blē\ adv

un·chang·ing \ˌ'chān-jiŋ\ adj (1593) : CONSTANT, INVARIABLE — **un·chang·ing·ly** \-jiŋ-lē\ adv — **un·chang·ing·ness** n

un·char·ac·ter·is·tic \ˌən-ˌkar-ik-tə-'ris-tik\ adj (1753) : not characteristic : not typical or distinctive — **un·char·ac·ter·is·ti·cal·ly** \-ti-k(ə-)lē\ adv

un·charge \ˌən-'chärj\ vt (1602) obs : ACQUIT

un·charged \ˌ'chärjd\ adj (1815) : not charged; specif : having no electric charge

un·char·i·ta·ble \ˌ'char-ə-tə-bəl\ adj (15c) : lacking in charity : severe in judging : HARSH — **un·char·i·ta·ble·ness** n — **un·char·i·ta·bly** \-blē\ adv

un·chart·ed \ˌ'chär-təd\ adj (ca. 1847) : not recorded or plotted on a map, chart, or plan; broadly : UNKNOWN ⟨~ territory⟩

un·chaste \ˌ'chāst\ adj (14c) : not chaste : lacking in chastity — **un·chaste·ly** adv — **un·chaste·ness** \ˌ'chās-(t)nəs\ n

un·chas·ti·ty \ˌ'chas-tə-tē\ n (14c) : the quality or state of being unchaste

un·chiv·al·rous \ˌ'shi-vəl-rəs\ adj (1846) : not chivalrous : lacking in chivalry — **un·chiv·al·rous·ly** adv

un·choke \ˌ'chōk\ vt (1588) : to clear of obstruction

un·chris·tian \ˌ'kris-chən, -'krish-\ adj (1555) 1 : not of the Christian faith 2 a : contrary to the Christian spirit or character b : UNCIVILIZED, BARBAROUS

un·church \ˌ'chərch\ vt (ca. 1620) 1 : to expel from a church : EXCOMMUNICATE 2 : to deprive of a church or of status as a church

un·churched \ˌ'chərcht\ adj (1681) : not belonging to or connected with a church

unci pl of UNCUS

¹un·cial \ˌ'ən(t)-shəl, -sē-əl\ adj [LL unciales (litterae) uncial (letters), fr. L, pl. of uncialis weighing an ounce, fr. uncia twelfth part, ounce — more at OUNCE] (1712) : written in the style or size of uncials — **un·cial·ly** adv

²uncial n (ca. 1775) 1 : a handwriting used esp. in Greek and Latin manuscripts of the 4th to the 8th centuries A.D. and made with somewhat rounded separated majuscules but having cursive forms for some letters 2 : an uncial letter 3 : a manuscript written in uncial

ROMAN UNCIAL

uncials

un·ci·form \ˌ'ən(t)-sə-ˌfórm\ adj [NL unciformis, fr. L uncus hook + -formis -form — more at ANGLE] (ca. 1734) : hook-shaped : UNCINATE

un·ci·na·ri·a·sis \ˌən-ˌsi-nə-'rī-ə-səs\ n [NL, fr. Uncinaria, genus that includes hookworms, fr. L uncinus hook] (1903) : ANCYLOSTOMIASIS

un·ci·nate \ˌ'ən(t)-sə-ˌnāt\ adj [L uncinatus, fr. uncinus hook, fr. uncus] (ca. 1760) : bent at the tip like a hook : HOOKED ⟨an ~ achene⟩

un·cir·cu·lat·ed \ˌən-'sər-kyə-ˌlā-təd\ adj (1917) : issued for use as money but kept out of circulation (as for preservation in a collection)

un·cir·cum·cised \ˌən-'sər-kəm-ˌsīzd\ adj (14c) 1 : not circumcised 2 : spiritually impure : HEATHEN — **un·cir·cum·ci·sion** \ˌən-ˌsər-kəm-'si-zhən\ n

un·civ·il \ˌən-'si-vəl\ adj (1553) 1 : not civilized : BARBAROUS 2 : lacking in courtesy : ILL-MANNERED, IMPOLITE 3 : not conducive to civic harmony and welfare — **un·civ·il·ly** \-və-lē\ adv

un·civ·i·lized \ˌ'si-və-ˌlīzd\ adj (1607) 1 : not civilized : BARBAROUS 2 : remote from settled areas : WILD

\ə\ abut \ᵊ\ kitten, F table \ər\ further \a\ ash \ā\ ace \ä\ mop, mar \aú\ out \ch\ chin \e\ bet \ē\ easy \g\ go \i\ hit \ī\ ice \j\ job \ŋ\ sing \ō\ go \ó\ law \ói\ boy \th\ thin \th\ the \ü\ loot \ú\ foot \y\ yet \zh\ vision \ä, k̲, ⁿ, œ, œ̄, ue, ūe, ᵞ\ see Guide to Pronunciation

un·clamp \-'klamp\ *vt* (1809) : to loosen the clamp of : to free from a clamp

un·clar·i·ty \-'klar-ə-tē\ *n, pl* **-ties** (1923) : lack of clarity : AMBIGUITY, OBSCURITY

un·clasp \-'klasp\ *vt* (1530) **1** : to open the clasp of **2** : to open or cause to be opened (as a clenched hand) ~ *vi* : to loosen a hold

un·clas·si·cal \-'kla-si-kəl\ *adj* (1725) : not classical; *esp* : unconcerned with the classics

un·clas·si·fied \-'kla-sə-ˌfīd\ *adj* (1865) **1** : not placed or belonging in a class **2** : not subject to a security classification

un·cle \'əŋ-kəl\ *n* [ME, fr. OF, fr. L *avunculus* mother's brother; akin to OE *ēam* uncle, W *ewythr* uncle, L *avus* grandfather] (14c) **1 a** : the brother of one's father or mother **b** : the husband of one's aunt **2** : one who helps, advises, or encourages **3** — used as a cry of surrender (was forced to cry ~) **4** *cap* : UNCLE SAM

un·clean \ˌən-'klēn\ *adj* (bef. 12c) **1** : morally or spiritually impure **2** : infected with a harmful supernatural contagion; *also* : prohibited by ritual law for use or contact **3** : DIRTY, FILTHY **4** : lacking in clarity and precision of conception or execution — **un·clean·ness** \-'klēn-nəs\ *n*

[1]un·clean·ly \-'klen-lē\ *adj* (bef. 12c) : morally or physically unclean — **un·clean·li·ness** *n*

[2]un·clean·ly \-'klēn-lē\ *adv* (bef. 12c) : in an unclean manner

un·clench \-'klench\ *vt* (1699) **1** : to open from a clenched position **2** : to release from a grip ~ *vi* : to become unclasped or relaxed

Un·cle Sam \ˌəŋ-kəl-'sam\ *n* [expansion of *U.S.*, abbr. of *United States*] (1813) **1** : the U.S. government **2** : the American nation or people

[1]Uncle Tom \-'täm\ *n* [*Uncle Tom*, pious and faithful black slave in *Uncle Tom's Cabin* (1851–52) by Harriet Beecher Stowe] (1922) **1** : a black who is overeager to win the approval of whites (as by obsequious behavior or uncritical acceptance of white values and goals) **2** : a member of a low-status group who is overly subservient to or cooperative with authority (the worst floor managers and supervisors by far are women . . . Some of them are regular *Uncle Toms* —Jane Fonda) — **Uncle Tom·ism** \-'tä-ˌmi-zəm\ *n*

[2]Uncle Tom *vi* **Uncle Tommed; Uncle Tom·ming** (1947) : to behave like an Uncle Tom

un·climb·able \ˌən-'klī-mə-bəl\ *adj* (1553) : not able to be climbed — **un·climb·able·ness** *n*

un·clinch \-'klinch\ *vt* (1598) : UNCLENCH

un·cloak \-'klōk\ *vt* (1598) **1** : to remove a cloak or cover from **2** : REVEAL, UNMASK ~ *vi* : to take off a cloak

un·clog \-'kläg\ *vt* (1607) : to free from a difficulty or obstruction

un·close \-'klōz\ *vt* (14c) **1** : OPEN **2** : DISCLOSE, REVEAL ~ *vi* : to become opened

un·closed \-'klōzd\ *adj* (15c) : not closed or settled : not concluded

un·clothe \-'klōth\ *vt* (14c) **1** : to strip of clothes **2** : DIVEST, UNCOVER

un·clothed \-'klōthd\ *adj* (15c) : not clothed

un·cloud·ed \-'klau̇-dəd\ *adj* (1594) : not covered by clouds : not darkened or obscured : CLEAR — **un·cloud·ed·ly** *adv*

un·club·ba·ble \ˌən-'klə-bə-bəl\ *adj* (ca. 1764) : UNSOCIABLE 1

un·clut·ter \-'klə-tər\ *vt* (1930) : to remove clutter from : make neat and orderly

un·clut·tered \-tərd\ *adj* (1925) : not cluttered

[1]un·co \'ən-(ˌ)kō, -kə\ *adj* [ME *unkow*, alter. of ME *uncouth*] (15c) **1** *chiefly Scot* **a** : STRANGE, UNKNOWN **b** : UNCANNY, WEIRD **2** *chiefly Scot* : EXTRAORDINARY

[2]unco *adv* (1724) : EXTREMELY, REMARKABLY, UNCOMMONLY

[3]unco *n, pl* **uncos** (1785) **1** *pl, chiefly Scot* : NEWS, TIDINGS **2** *chiefly Scot* : STRANGER

un·cock \ˌən-'käk\ *vt* (ca. 1775) : to remove the hammer of (a firearm) from a cocked position

un·cof·fin \-'kȯ-fən\ *vt* (1836) : to remove from or as if from a coffin

un·cof·fined \-'fȯnd\ *adj* (1648) : not placed in a coffin

un·coil \ˌən-'kȯi(ə)l\ *vt* (1713) : to release from a coiled state : UNWIND ~ *vi* : to become uncoiled

un·coiled \-'kȯi(ə)ld\ *adj* (1713) : not coiled

un·coined \-'kȯind\ *adj* (15c) **1** : not minted (~ metal) **2** : not fabricated : NATURAL

un·com·fort·able \ˌən-'kəm(p)(f)-tə(r)-bəl, -'kəm(p)-fə(r)-tə-bəl, -'kəm-fə(r)-bəl\ *adj* (1592) **1** : causing discomfort or annoyance (an ~ chair) (an ~ performance) **2** : feeling discomfort : UNEASY (was ~ with them) — **un·com·fort·ably** \-blē\ *adv*

un·com·mer·cial \ˌən-kə-'mər-shəl\ *adj* (1768) **1** : not engaged in or related to commerce **2** : not based on commercial principles **3** : not likely to result in financial success (an ~ book)

un·com·mit·ted \ˌən-kə-'mi-təd\ *adj* (1598) : not committed; *specif* : not pledged to a particular belief, allegiance, or program

un·com·mon \ˌən-'kä-mən\ *adj* (1611) **1** : not ordinarily encountered : UNUSUAL **2** : REMARKABLE, EXCEPTIONAL *syn* see INFREQUENT — **un·com·mon·ly** *adv* — **un·com·mon·ness** \-mən-nəs\ *n*

un·com·mu·ni·ca·ble \ˌən-kə-'myü-ni-kə-bəl\ *adj* (14c) : INCOMMUNICABLE

un·com·mu·ni·ca·tive \-'myü-nə-ˌkā-tiv, -ni-kə-tiv\ *adj* (1691) : not disposed to talk or impart information : RESERVED

un·com·pet·i·tive \-'pe-tə-tiv\ *adj* (1885) : not competitive : unable to compete — **un·com·pet·i·tive·ness** *n*

un·com·plain·ing \-'plā-niŋ\ *adj* (1744) : not complaining : PATIENT — **un·com·plain·ing·ly** \-niŋ-lē\ *adv*

un·com·pli·cat·ed \ˌən-'käm-plə-ˌkā-təd\ *adj* (ca. 1775) **1 a** : not complicated by something outside itself **b** : not involving medical complications (an ~ peptic ulcer) **2** : not complex : SIMPLE (~ machinery)

un·com·pli·men·ta·ry \ˌən-ˌkäm-plə-'men-tə-rē, -'men-trē\ *adj* (1842) : not complimentary : DEROGATORY

un·com·pre·hend·ing \-pri-'hen-diŋ\ *adj* (1838) : not comprehending : lacking understanding — **un·com·pre·hend·ing·ly** \-diŋ-lē\ *adv*

un·com·pro·mis·able \ˌən-'käm-prə-ˌmī-zə-bəl\ *adj* (1958) : not able to be compromised

un·com·pro·mis·ing \-ˌmī-ziŋ\ *adj* (ca. 1828) : not making or accepting a compromise : making no concessions : INFLEXIBLE, UNYIELDING — **un·com·pro·mis·ing·ly** \-ziŋ-lē\ *adv* — **un·com·pro·mis·ing·ness** \-nəs\ *n*

un·con·ceiv·able \ˌən-kən-'sē-və-bəl\ *adj* (ca. 1607) : INCONCEIVABLE

un·con·cern \ˌən-kən-'sərn\ *n* (1711) **1** : lack of care or interest : INDIFFERENCE **2** : freedom from excessive concern or anxiety

un·con·cerned \-'sərnd\ *adj* (ca. 1635) **1** : not involved : not having any part or interest **2** : not anxious or upset : free of worry *syn* see INDIFFERENT — **un·con·cerned·ly** \-'sər-nəd-lē, -'sərnd-lē\ *adv* — **un·con·cerned·ness** \-'sər-nəd-nəs, -'sərn(d)-nəs\ *n*

un·con·di·tion·al \ˌən-kən-'dish-nəl, -'di-shə-nᵊl\ *adj* (1666) **1** : not conditional or limited : ABSOLUTE, UNQUALIFIED (~ surrender) **2** : UNCONDITIONED **2** — **un·con·di·tion·al·ly** *adv*

un·con·di·tioned \-'di-shənd\ *adj* (ca. 1631) **1** : not subject to conditions or limitations **2 a** : not dependent on or subjected to conditioning or learning : NATURAL (~ responses) **b** : producing an unconditioned response (~ stimuli)

un·con·form·able \-'fȯr-mə-bəl\ *adj* (1594) **1** : not conforming **2** : exhibiting geological unconformity — **un·con·form·ably** \-blē\ *adv*

un·con·for·mi·ty \-'fȯr-mə-tē\ *n* (ca. 1600) **1** *archaic* : lack of conformity **2 a** : lack of continuity in deposition between rock strata in contact corresponding to a period of nondeposition, weathering, or erosion **b** : the surface of contact between unconformable strata

un·con·ge·nial \-'jē-nyəl, -nē-əl\ *adj* (ca. 1775) **1** : not sympathetic or compatible (~ roommates) **2 a** : not fitted : UNSUITABLE (a soil ~ to most crops) **b** : not to one's taste : DISAGREEABLE (an ~ task) — **un·con·ge·nial·i·ty** \-ˌjē-nē-'a-lə-tē, -ˌjēn-'ya-\ *n*

un·con·quer·able \ˌən-'käŋ-k(ə-)rə-bəl\ *adj* (1598) **1** : incapable of being conquered : INDOMITABLE (an ~ will) **2** : incapable of being surmounted (~ difficulties) — **un·con·quer·ably** \-blē\ *adv*

un·con·scio·na·ble \-'kän(t)-sh(ə-)nə-bəl\ *adj* (1570) **1** : not guided or controlled by conscience : UNSCRUPULOUS (an ~ villain) **2 a** : EXCESSIVE, UNREASONABLE (found an ~ number of defects in the car) **b** : shockingly unfair or unjust (~ sales practices) — **un·con·scio·na·bil·i·ty** \ˌən-ˌkän(t)-sh(ə-)nə-'bi-lə-tē\ *n* — **un·con·scio·na·ble·ness** \ən-'kän(t)-sh(ə-)nə-bəl-nəs\ *n* — **un·con·scio·na·bly** \-blē\ *adv*

[1]un·con·scious \ˌən-'kän(t)-shəs\ *adj* (1712) **1 a** : not knowing or perceiving : not aware **b** : free from self-awareness **2 a** : not possessing mind or consciousness (~ matter) **b** (1) : not marked by conscious thought, sensation, or feeling (~ motivation) (2) : of or relating to the unconscious **c** : having lost consciousness (was ~ for three days) **3** : not consciously held or deliberately planned or carried out (~ bias) — **un·con·scious·ly** *adv* — **un·con·scious·ness** *n*

[2]unconscious *n* (1912) : the part of the psychic apparatus that does not ordinarily enter the individual's awareness and that is manifested esp. by slips of the tongue or dissociated acts or in dreams

un·con·sid·ered \ˌən-kən-'si-dərd\ *adj* (1587) **1** : not considered or worth consideration **2** : not resulting from consideration

un·con·sol·i·dat·ed \-'sä-lə-ˌdā-təd\ *adj* (ca. 1775) **1** : loosely arranged (~ subsidiaries); *esp* : not stratified (~ soil)

un·con·sti·tu·tion·al \ˌən-ˌkän(t)-stə-'tü-shnəl, -'tyü-, -shə-nᵊl\ *adj* (1734) : not according or consistent with the constitution of a body politic (as a nation) — **un·con·sti·tu·tion·al·i·ty** \-ˌtü-shə-'na-lə-tē, -ˌtyü-\ *n* — **un·con·sti·tu·tion·al·ly** *adv*

un·con·straint \ˌən-kən-'strānt\ *n* (1711) : freedom from constraint : EASE

un·con·struct·ed \-'strək-təd\ *adj* (1970) *of clothing* : manufactured without added material for padding, stiffening, or shape retention

un·con·trol·la·ble \-'trō-lə-bəl\ *adj* (1593) **1** *archaic* : free from control by a superior power : ABSOLUTE **2** : incapable of being controlled : UNGOVERNABLE — **un·con·trol·la·bil·i·ty** \-ˌtrō-lə-'bi-lə-tē\ *n* — **un·con·trol·la·bly** \-'trō-lə-blē\ *adv*

un·con·ven·tion·al \-'vench-nəl, -'ven(t)-shə-nᵊl\ *adj* (1839) : not conventional : not bound by or in accordance with convention : being out of the ordinary — **un·con·ven·tion·al·i·ty** \-ˌven(t)-shə-'na-lə-tē\ *n* — **un·con·ven·tion·al·ly** *adv*

un·con·vinc·ing \-'vin(t)-siŋ\ *adj* (1653) : not convincing : IMPLAUSIBLE — **un·con·vinc·ing·ly** \-siŋ-lē\ *adv* — **un·con·vinc·ing·ness** *n*

un·cool \ˌən-'kül\ *adj* (1953) **1** : lacking in assurance **2** : failing to accord with the current styles (as of dress or behavior) of a particular group

un·cork \ˌən-'kȯrk\ *vt* (1727) **1** : to draw a cork from **2 a** : to release from a sealed or pent-up state (~ a surprise) **b** : to let go : RELEASE (~ a wild pitch)

un·corked \-'kȯrkt\ *adj* (1791) : not provided with a cork

un·cor·set·ed \-'kȯr-sə-təd\ *adj* (1856) **1** : not wearing a corset **2** : not controlled or inhibited (~ freedom)

un·count·ed \ˌən-'kau̇n-təd\ *adj* (15c) **1** : not counted **2** : INNUMERABLE

un·cou·ple \-'kə-pəl\ *vt* (14c) **1** : to release (dogs) from a couple **2** : DETACH, DISCONNECT (~ railroad cars) — **un·cou·pler** \-p(ə-)lər\ *n*

un·couth \-'küth\ *adj* [ME, fr. OE *uncūth*, fr. *un-* + *cūth* familiar, known; akin to OHG *kund* known, OE *can* know — more at CAN] (bef. 12c) **1** *archaic* : not known or not familiar to one : seldom experienced : UNCOMMON, RARE **b** *obs* : MYSTERIOUS, UNCANNY **2 a** : strange or clumsy in shape or appearance : OUTLANDISH **b** : lacking in polish and grace : RUGGED (~ verse) **c** : awkward and uncultivated in appearance, manner, or behavior — **un·couth·ly** *adv* — **un·couth·ness** *n*

un·cov·er \-'kə-vər\ *vt* (14c) **1** : to make known : bring to light : DISCLOSE, REVEAL **2** : to expose to view by removing some covering **3 a** : to take the cover from **b** : to remove the hat from **4** : to deprive of protection ~ *vi* **1** : to remove a cover or covering **2** : to take off the hat as a token of respect

un·cov·ered \-vərd\ *adj* (15c) : not covered: as **a** : not supplied with a covering **b** : not covered by insurance or included in a social insurance or welfare program **c** : not covered by collateral (an ~ note)

un·cre·at·ed \ˌən-krē-'ā-təd\ *adj* (ca. 1549) **1** : not existing by creation : ETERNAL, SELF-EXISTENT **2** : not created

un·crit·i·cal \ˌən-'kri-ti-kəl\ *adj* (1659) **1** : not critical : lacking in discrimination **2** : showing lack or improper use of critical standards or procedures — **un·crit·i·cal·ly** \-k(ə-)lē\ *adv*

un·cross \-'krȯs\ *vt* (1599) : to change from a crossed position

un·crown \-'krau̇n\ *vt* (14c) : to take the crown from : DEPOSE, DETHRONE

un·crum·ple \-'krəm-pəl\ *vt* (1611) : to restore to an original smooth condition

un·crys·tal·lized \-'kris-tə-,līzd\ *adj* (1759) : not crystallized; *also* : not finally or definitely formed

unc·tion \'əŋ(k)-shən\ *n* [ME *unctioun*, fr. L *unction-, unctio*, fr. *unguere* to anoint — more at OINTMENT] (14c) **1** : the act of anointing as a rite of consecration or healing **2** : something used for anointing : OINTMENT, UNGUENT **3 a** : religious or spiritual fervor or the expression of such fervor **b** : exaggerated, assumed, or superficial earnestness of language or manner : UNCTUOUSNESS

unc·tu·ous \'əŋ(k)-chə-wəs, -chəs, -shwəs\ *adj* [ME, fr. MF or ML; MF *unctueux*, fr. ML *unctuosus*, fr. L *unctus* act of anointing, fr. *unguere* to anoint] (14c) **1 a** : FATTY, OILY **b** : smooth and greasy in texture or appearance **2** : PLASTIC ⟨fine ~ clay⟩ **3** : full of unction; *esp* : revealing or marked by a smug, ingratiating, and false earnestness or spirituality — **unc·tu·ous·ly** *adv* — **unc·tu·ous·ness** *n*

un·curl \,ən-'kər(-ə)l\ *vi* (1588) : to become straightened out from a curled or coiled position ~ *vt* : to straighten the curls of : UNROLL

un·cus \'əŋ-kəs\ *n, pl* **un·ci** \'ən-,kī, -,kē; 'ən-,sī\ [NL, fr. L, hook — more at ANGLE] (1826) : a hooked anatomical part or process

un·cut \,ən-'kət\ *adj* (1548) **1** : not cut down or cut into **2** : not shaped by cutting ⟨an ~ diamond⟩ **3** *of a book* : not having the folds of the leaves slit **4** : not abridged, curtailed, or expurgated ⟨the ~ version of the film⟩ **5** : not diluted or adulterated ⟨~ vinegar⟩ ⟨~ heroin⟩

un·daunt·able \,ən-'dȯn-tə-bəl, -'dän-\ *adj* (1587) : incapable of being daunted : FEARLESS

un·daunt·ed \-təd\ *adj* (1587) : courageously resolute esp. in the face of danger or difficulty : not discouraged — **un·daunt·ed·ly** *adv*

un·dead \,ən-'ded\ *n, pl* **undead** (1897) **1** : VAMPIRE **2** : ZOMBIE 1b

un·de·bat·able \,ən-di-'bā-tə-bəl\ *adj* (1869) : not subject to debate : INDISPUTABLE — **un·de·bat·ably** \-blē\ *adv*

un·de·ceive \,ən-di-'sēv\ *vt* (1598) : to free from deception, illusion, or error

un·de·cil·lion \,ən-di-'sil-yən\ *n, often attrib* [L *undecim* eleven (fr. *unus* one + *decem* ten) + E *-illion* (as in *million*) — more at ONE, TEN] (1931) — see NUMBER table

un·dec·y·le·nic acid \,ən-,de-sə-'le-nik-, -'lē-\ *n* [*undecylene* (C₁₁H₂₂)] (1879) : an acid $C_{11}H_{20}O_2$ found in perspiration, obtained commercially from castor oil, and used in the treatment of fungal infections (as ringworm) of the skin

un·dem·o·crat·ic \,ən-,de-mə-'kra-tik\ *adj* (1839) : not democratic : not agreeing with democratic practice or ideals — **un·dem·o·crat·i·cal·ly** \-ti-k(ə-)lē\ *adv*

un·de·mon·stra·tive \,ən-di-'män(t)-strə-tiv\ *adj* (1846) : restrained in expression of feeling : RESERVED — **un·de·mon·stra·tive·ly** *adv* — **un·de·mon·stra·tive·ness** *n*

un·de·ni·able \,ən-di-'nī-ə-bəl\ *adj* (1547) **1** : plainly true : INCONTESTABLE **2** : unquestionably excellent or genuine ⟨an applicant with ~ references⟩ — **un·de·ni·able·ness** *n* — **un·de·ni·ably** \-blē\ *adv*

¹un·der \'ən-dər\ *adv* [ME, adv. & prep., fr. OE; akin to OHG *untar* under, L *inferus* situated beneath, lower, *infra* below, Skt *adha*] (bef. 12c) **1** : in or into a position below or beneath something **2** : below or short of some quantity, level, or limit ⟨$10 or ~⟩ — often used in combination ⟨*under*staffed⟩ **3** : in or into a condition of subjection, subordination, or unconsciousness **4** : down to defeat, ruin, or death **5** : so as to be covered

²under *prep* (bef. 12c) **1** : below or beneath so as to be overhung, surmounted, covered, protected, or concealed by ⟨~ sunny skies⟩ ⟨a soft heart ~ a stern exterior⟩ ⟨~ cover of darkness⟩ **2 a** : subject to the authority, control, guidance, or instruction of ⟨served ~ the general⟩ ⟨~ the terms of the contract⟩ **b** : receiving or undergoing the action or effect of ⟨~ pressure⟩ ⟨courage ~ fire⟩ ⟨~ the influence of alcohol⟩ ⟨the image of a point ~ a mapping⟩ **3** : within the group or designation of ⟨~ this heading⟩ **4** : less or lower than (as in size, amount, or rank); *esp* : falling short of a standard or required degree ⟨~ the legal age⟩ ⟨~ par⟩

³under *adj* (14c) **1 a** : lying or placed below, beneath, or on the ventral side — often used in combination ⟨*under*lip⟩ **b** : facing or protruding downward **2** : lower in rank or authority : SUBORDINATE **3** : lower than usual, proper, or desired in amount, quality, or degree ⟨an ~ dose of medicine⟩

un·der·achiev·er \,ən-dər-ə-'chē-vər\ *n* (1952) : a person and esp. a student who fails to attain a predicted level of achievement or does not do as well as expected — **un·der·achieve** \-ə-'chēv\ *vi* — **un·der·achieve·ment** \-mənt\ *n*

un·der·act \,ən-dər-'akt\ *vt* (ca. 1623) : to perform (a dramatic part) with restraint for effect : UNDERPLAY ~ *vi* : to perform feebly or with restraint

un·der·ac·tive \-'ak-tiv\ *adj* (1959) : characterized by an abnormally low level of activity ⟨an ~ thyroid gland⟩ — **un·der·ac·tiv·i·ty** \-ti-və-tē\ *n*

un·der·age \,ən-dər-'āj\ *adj* (1594) **1** : of less than mature or legal age **2** : done by or involving underage persons ⟨~ drinking⟩

un·der·ap·pre·ci·at·ed \,ən-dər-ə-'prē-shē-,ā-təd\ *adj* (1968) : not duly appreciated

¹un·der·arm \'ən-dər-,ärm\ *adj* (1816) **1** : UNDERHAND 4 **2** : placed under or on the underside of the arm ⟨~ seams⟩

²un·der·arm \,ən-dər-'ärm\ *adv* (ca. 1909) : UNDERHAND

³un·der·arm \'ən-dər-,ärm\ *n* (1923) **1** : ARMPIT 1 **2** : the part of a garment that covers the underside of the arm

un·der·bel·ly \'ən-dər-,be-lē\ *n* (1607) **1** : the underside of a body or mass **2** : a vulnerable area

un·der·bid \,ən-dər-'bid\ *vb* **-bid; -bid·ding** *vt* (ca. 1677) **1** : to bid less than (a competing bidder) **2** : to bid (a hand of cards) at less than the strength of the hand warrants ~ *vi* : to bid too low — **un·der·bid·der** *n*

un·der·body \'ən-dər-,bä-dē\ *n* (1879) : the lower part of something: as **a** : the lower part of an animal's body : UNDERPARTS **b** : the lower parts of the body of a vehicle

un·der·boss \'ən-dər-,bȯs\ *n* (1942) : a boss ranking next below the head of a branch of a crime syndicate

un·der·bred \,ən-dər-'bred\ *adj* (1650) : marked by lack of good breeding : ILL-BRED

un·der·brim \'ən-dər-,brim\ *n* (1886) : a facing on the underside of a hat brim

un·der·brush \'ən-dər-,brəsh\ *n* (1775) **1** : shrubs, bushes, or small trees growing beneath large trees in a wood or forest : BRUSH **2** : a tangled, obstructing, or impeding mass

un·der·bud·get·ed \,ən-dər-'bə-jə-təd\ *adj* (1965) : provided with an inadequate budget

un·der·cap·i·tal·ized \-'ka-pə-t²l-,īzd, -'kap-t²l-\ *adj* (1967) : having too little capital for efficient operation

un·der·card \'ən-dər-,kärd\ *n* (1948) : a program (as of boxing matches) supporting the featured match

un·der·car·riage \'ən-dər-,kar-ij\ *n* (ca. 1796) **1** : a supporting framework (as of an automobile) **2** *chiefly Brit* : the landing gear of an airplane

un·der·charge \,ən-dər-'chärj\ *vt* (1633) : to charge (as a person) too little — **undercharge** \'ən-dər-,\ *n*

un·der·class \,ən-dər-'klas\ *n* (1918) : the lowest social stratum usu. made up of disadvantaged minority groups

un·der·class·man \,ən-dər-'klas-mən\ *n* (1871) : a member of the freshman or sophomore class in a school or college

un·der·clothes \'ən-dər-,klō(th)z\ *n pl* (ca. 1859) : UNDERWEAR

un·der·cloth·ing \-,klō-thiŋ\ *n* (1835) : UNDERWEAR

un·der·coat \-,kōt\ *n* (1648) **1** : a coat or jacket worn under another **2** : a growth of short hair or fur partly concealed by the longer and usu. coarser guard hairs of a mammal **3 a** : a coat (as of paint) applied as a base for another coat **b** : UNDERCOATING **4** *dial* : PETTICOAT

un·der·coat·ing \-,kō-tiŋ\ *n* (1922) : a usu. asphalt-based waterproof coating applied to the underside of a vehicle

un·der·cool \,ən-dər-'kül\ *vt* (1902) : SUPERCOOL

un·der·count \-'kaunt\ *vt* (1951) : to count fewer than the actual number of — **undercount** *n*

un·der·cov·er \-'kə-vər\ *adj* (1920) : acting or executed in secret; *specif* : employed or engaged in spying or secret investigation ⟨an ~ agent⟩

un·der·croft \'ən-dər-,krȯft\ *n* [ME, fr. *under* + *crofte* crypt, fr. MD, fr. ML *crupta*, fr. L *crypta* — more at CRYPT] (14c) : a subterranean room; *esp* : a vaulted chamber under a church

un·der·cur·rent \-,kər-ənt, -,kə-rənt\ *n* (1683) **1** : a current below the upper currents or surface **2** : a hidden opinion, feeling, or tendency often contrary to the one publicly shown — **undercurrent** *adj*

¹un·der·cut \,ən-dər-'kət\ *vb* **-cut; -cut·ting** *vt* (1598) **1** : to cut away the underpart of ⟨~ a vein of ore⟩ **2** : to cut away material from the underside of (an object) so as to leave an overhanging portion in relief **3** : to offer to sell at lower prices than or to work for lower wages than (a competitor) **4** : to cut obliquely into (a tree) below the main cut and on the side toward which the tree will fall **5** : to strike (a ball) with a downward glancing blow so as to give a backspin or elevation to the shot **6** : to undermine or destroy the force, value, or effectiveness of ⟨inflation ~s consumer buying power⟩ ~ *vi* : to perform the action of cutting away beneath

²un·der·cut \'ən-dər-,kət\ *n* (1859) **1** *Brit* : TENDERLOIN 1 **2** : the action or result of cutting away from the underside or lower part of something **3** : a notch cut in the base of a tree before felling to determine the direction of falling and to prevent splitting

un·der·de·vel·oped \,ən-dər-di-'ve-ləpt\ *adj* (1892) **1** : not normally or adequately developed ⟨~ muscles⟩ ⟨an ~ film⟩ **2** : having a relatively low economic level of industrial production and standard of living (as from lack of capital) ⟨~ nations⟩ — **un·der·de·vel·op·ment** \-,lə-p-mənt\ *n*

un·der·dog \'ən-dər-,dȯg\ *n* (1887) **1** : a loser or predicted loser in a struggle or contest **2** : a victim of injustice or persecution

un·der·done \,ən-dər-'dən\ *adj* (1683) : not thoroughly cooked : RARE

un·der·draw·ers \'ən-dər-,drȯ(-ə)rz\ *n pl* (1894) : an article of underwear for the lower body

un·der·ed·u·cat·ed \,ən-dər-'e-jə-,kā-təd\ *adj* (1856) : poorly educated

un·der·em·pha·sis \,ən-dər-'em(p)-fə-səs\ *n* (1964) : less emphasis than is possible or desirable

un·der·em·pha·size \-,sīz\ *vt* (1967) : to fail to emphasize adequately

un·der·em·ployed \,ən-dər-im-'plȯid\ *adj* (1908) : having less than full-time, regular, or adequate employment

un·der·em·ploy·ment \-'plȯi-mənt\ *n* (1910) **1** : the condition in which people in a labor force are employed at less than full-time or regular jobs or at jobs inadequate with respect to their training or economic needs **2** : the condition of being underemployed

un·der·es·ti·mate \,ən-dər-'es-tə-,māt\ *vt* (1812) **1** : to estimate as being less than the actual size, quantity, or number **2** : to place too low a value on : UNDERRATE — **un·der·es·ti·mate** \-mət\ *n* — **un·der·es·ti·ma·tion** \-,es-tə-'mā-shən\ *n*

un·der·ex·pose \,ən-dər-ik-'spōz\ *vt* (1861) : to expose insufficiently; *esp* : to expose (as film) to insufficient radiation (as light) — **un·der·ex·po·sure** \-'spō-zhər\ *n*

un·der·feed \,ən-dər-'fēd\ *vt* **-fed** \-'fed\; **-feed·ing** (1659) : to feed with too little food

un·der·fi·nanced \-fə-'nan(t)st, -'fī-,, -fī-\ *adj* (1922) : inadequately financed

un·der·foot \-'fut\ *adv* (13c) **1** : under the foot esp. against the ground ⟨trampled the flowers ~⟩ **2** : below, at, or before one's feet ⟨warm sand ~⟩ **3** : in the way ⟨children always getting ~⟩

un·der·fund \-'fənd\ *vt* (1968) : to provide insufficient funds for

un·der·fur \'ən-dər-,fər\ *n* (1877) : an undercoat of fur esp. when thick and soft

un·der·gar·ment \-,gär-mənt\ *n* (1530) : a garment to be worn under another

un·der·gird \,ən-dər-'gərd\ *vt* (1526) **1** *archaic* : to make secure underneath ⟨took measures to ~ the ship —Acts 27:17 (RSV)⟩ **2** : to form the basis or foundation of : STRENGTHEN, SUPPORT ⟨facts and statistics subtly ~ his commentary —Susan Q. Stranahan⟩

un·der·glaze \'ən-dər-,glāz\ *adj* (1879) : applied or suitable for applying before the glaze is put on ⟨~ decorations⟩ ⟨~ colors⟩ — **underglaze** *n*

\ə\ abut \²\ kitten, F table \ər\ further \a\ ash \ā\ ace \ä\ mop, mar \au̇\ out \ch\ chin \e\ bet \ē\ easy \g\ go \i\ hit \ī\ ice \j\ job \ŋ\ sing \ō\ go \ȯ\ law \ȯi\ boy \th\ thin \t̲h̲\ the \ü\ loot \u̇\ foot \y\ yet \zh\ vision \ä, k̲, ⁿ, œ, œ̄, ᵫ, ūe, ᵞ\ *see* Guide to Pronunciation

un·der·go \ˌən-dər-ˈgō\ *vt* **-went** \-ˈwent\; **-gone** \-ˈgȯn *also* -ˈgän\; **-go·ing** \-ˈgō-iŋ, -ˈgȯ(-)iŋ\ (14c) **1 :** to submit to : ENDURE **2 :** to go through : EXPERIENCE **3** *obs* : UNDERTAKE **4** *obs* : to partake of
un·der·grad \ˈən-dər-ˌgrad\ *n* (1827) : UNDERGRADUATE
un·der·grad·u·ate \ˌən-dər-ˈgra-jə-wət, -ˌwāt; -ˈgraj-wət\ *n* (1630) : a student at a college or university who has not taken a first and esp. a bachelor's degree — **undergraduate** *adj*
¹un·der·ground \ˌən-dər-ˈgraund\ *adv* (1571) **1 :** beneath the surface of the earth **2 :** in or into hiding or secret operation
²underground \ˈən-dər-ˌ\ *n* (1594) **1 :** a subterranean space or channel **2 :** an underground city railway system **3 a :** a movement or group organized in strict secrecy among citizens esp. in an occupied country for maintaining communications, popular solidarity, and concerted resistive action pending liberation **b :** a clandestine conspiratorial organization set up for revolutionary or other disruptive purposes esp. against a civil order **c :** an unofficial, unsanctioned, or illegal but informal movement or group; *esp* : a usu. avant-garde group or movement that functions outside the establishment
³un·der·ground \ˈən-dər-ˌgraund\ *adj* (1610) **1 :** being, growing, operating, or situated below the surface of the ground **2 :** conducted by secret means **3 a :** existing outside the establishment ⟨an ~ literary reputation⟩ **b :** existing outside the purview of tax collectors or statisticians ⟨the ~ economy⟩ **4 a :** produced or published outside the establishment esp. by the avant-garde ⟨~ movies⟩ ⟨~ newspapers⟩ **b :** of or relating to the avant-garde underground ⟨an ~ moviemaker⟩ ⟨an ~ theater⟩
un·der·ground·er \ˈən-dər-ˌgraun-dər\ *n* (1882) : a member of the underground
Underground Railroad *n* (1842) : a system of cooperation among active antislavery people in the U.S. before 1863 by which fugitive slaves were secretly helped to reach the North or Canada — called also *Underground Railway*
un·der·growth \ˈən-dər-ˌgrōth\ *n* (1600) : low growth on the floor of a forest including seedlings and saplings, shrubs, and herbs
¹un·der·hand \ˈən-dər-ˌhand\ *adv* (1538) **1 a :** in a clandestine manner **b** *archaic* : in a quiet or unobtrusive manner **2 :** with the target seen below the hand holding the bow **3 :** with an underhand motion ⟨bowl ~⟩ ⟨pitch ~⟩
²underhand *adj* (1545) **1 :** aimed so that the target is seen below the hand holding the bow ⟨~ shooting at long range⟩ **2 :** UNDERHANDED **3 :** done so as to evade notice **4 :** made with the hand brought forward and up from below the shoulder level
¹un·der·hand·ed \ˌən-dər-ˈhan-dəd\ *adv* (ca. 1822) : UNDERHAND
²underhanded *adj* (1853) **1 :** marked by secrecy, chicanery, and deception : not honest and aboveboard *syn* see SECRET — **un·der·hand·ed·ly** *adv* — **un·der·hand·ed·ness** *n*
un·der·in·flat·ed \ˌən-dər-in-ˈflā-təd\ *adj* (1928) : not sufficiently inflated ⟨~ tires⟩ — **un·der·in·fla·tion** \-ˈflā-shən\ *n*
un·der·in·sured \-ˈshurd\ *adj* (1893) : not sufficiently insured
un·der·in·vest·ment \ˌən-dər-in-ˈves(t)-mənt\ *n* (1940) : an insufficient amount of investment
un·der·laid \ˌən-dər-ˈlād\ *adj* (bef. 12c) **1 :** laid or placed underneath **2 :** having something laid or lying underneath
¹un·der·lay \-ˈlā\ *vt* **-laid** \-ˈlād\; **-lay·ing** (bef. 12c) **1 :** to cover, line, or traverse the bottom of : give support to on the underside or below **2 :** to raise or support by something laid under
²un·der·lay \ˈən-dər-ˌlā\ *n* (1612) : something that is or is designed to be laid under
un·der·lay·ment \ˌən-dər-ˈlā-mənt\ *n* (1949) : UNDERLAY
un·der·let \ˌən-dər-ˈlet\ *vt* **-let**; **-let·ting** (1677) **1 :** to let below the real value **2 :** SUBLET
un·der·lie \-ˈlī\ *vt* **-lay** \-ˈlā\; **-lain** \-ˈlān\; **-ly·ing** \-ˈlī-iŋ\ (bef. 12c) **1** *archaic* : to be subject or amenable to **2 :** to lie or be situated under **3 :** to be at the basis of : form the foundation of : SUPPORT ⟨ideas *underlying* the revolution⟩ **4 :** to exist as a claim or security superior and prior to (another)
¹un·der·line \ˈən-dər-ˌlīn, ˌən-dər-ˈ\ *vt* (1721) **1 :** to mark (as a word) with a line underneath **2 :** to put emphasis on : STRESS **3 :** to show clearly or emphatically
²un·der·line \ˈən-dər-ˌlīn\ *n* (1886) **1 :** the outline of a quadruped's underbody; *also* : the ventral surface of a quadruped's body **2 :** a horizontal line placed underneath something
un·der·ling \ˈən-dər-liŋ\ *n* (12c) : one who is under the orders of another : SUBORDINATE, INFERIOR
un·der·lip \ˌən-dər-ˈlip\ *n* (1669) : the lower lip
un·der·ly·ing \ˌən-dər-ˈlī-iŋ\ *adj* (1611) **1 a :** lying beneath or below ⟨the ~ rock is shale⟩ **b :** BASIC, FUNDAMENTAL ⟨an investigation of the ~ issues⟩ **2 :** evident only on close inspection : IMPLICIT **3 :** anterior and prior in claim ⟨~ mortgage⟩ **4 :** of or being present in deep structure ⟨~ word order⟩
un·der·ly·ing·ly \-ˈlī-iŋ-lē\ *adv* (1973) : in deep structure
un·der·manned \ˌən-dər-ˈmand\ *adj* (ca. 1867) : inadequately staffed
un·der·mine \-ˈmīn\ *vt* (14c) **1 :** to excavate the earth beneath : form a mine under : SAP **2 :** to wash away supporting material from under **3 :** to subvert or weaken insidiously or secretly **4 :** to weaken or ruin by degrees *syn* see WEAKEN
un·der·most \ˈən-dər-ˌmōst\ *adj* (1555) : lowest in relative position — **undermost** *adv*
¹un·der·neath \ˌən-dər-ˈnēth\ *prep* [ME *undernethe*, prep. & adv., fr. OE *underneothan*, fr. *under* + *neothan* below — more at BENEATH] (bef. 12c) **1 a :** directly beneath ⟨write the date ~ the address⟩ **b :** close under esp. so as to be hidden ⟨treachery lying ~ a mask of friendliness⟩ ⟨a swimsuit ~ his slacks⟩ **2 :** under subjection to
²underneath *adv* (bef. 12c) **1 :** under or below an object or a surface : BENEATH **2 :** on the lower side — **underneath** *adj*
un·der·nour·ished \ˌən-dər-ˈnər-isht, -ˈnə-risht\ *adj* (1910) **1 :** supplied with less than the minimum amount of the foods essential for sound health and growth **2 :** poorly supplied with vital elements or qualities ⟨~ independent libraries⟩ — **un·der·nour·ish·ment** \-ˈnər-ish-mənt, -ˈnə-rish-\ *n*
un·der·nu·tri·tion \-nu̇-ˈtri-shən, -nyu̇-\ *n* (ca. 1889) : deficient bodily nutrition due to inadequate food intake or faulty assimilation

un·der·paint·ing \ˈən-dər-ˌpān-tiŋ\ *n* (1866) : preliminary painting; *esp* : such painting done on a canvas or panel and covered completely or partially by the final layers of paint
un·der·pants \ˈən-dər-ˌpan(t)s\ *n pl* (1925) : a usu. short undergarment for the lower trunk : DRAWERS
un·der·part \-ˌpärt\ *n* (1662) **1 :** a part lying on the lower side esp. of a bird or mammal **2 :** a subordinate or auxiliary part or role
un·der·pass \-ˌpas\ *n* (1903) : a crossing of a highway and another way (as a road or railroad) at different levels; *also* : the lower level of such a crossing
un·der·pay \ˌən-dər-ˈpā\ *vt* **-paid** \-ˈpād\; **-pay·ing** (1817) **:** to pay less than what is normal or required ⟨~ taxes⟩ — **un·der·pay·ment** *n*
un·der·pin \-ˈpin\ *vt* (1522) **1 :** SUPPORT, SUBSTANTIATE ⟨~ a thesis with evidence⟩ **2 :** to form part of, strengthen, or replace the foundation of ⟨~ a structure⟩ ⟨~ a sagging building⟩
un·der·pin·ning \ˈən-dər-ˌpi-niŋ\ *n* (1538) **1 :** the material and construction (as a foundation) used for support of a structure **2 :** something that serves as a foundation : BASIS, SUPPORT — often used in pl. ⟨the philosophical ~s of educational methods⟩ **3 :** UNDERWEAR — usu. used in pl. **4 :** a person's legs — usu. used in pl.
un·der·play \ˌən-dər-ˈplā\ *vi* (1896) **:** to play a role with subdued force ~ *vt* **1 :** to act or present (as a role or a scene) with restraint : PLAY DOWN **2 :** to play a card lower than (a held high card)
un·der·plot \ˈən-dər-ˌplät\ *n* (1668) : SUBPLOT 1
un·der·pop·u·lat·ed \ˌən-dər-ˈpä-pyə-ˌlā-təd\ *adj* (1884) : having a lower density of population than is normal or desirable
un·der·pow·ered \-ˈpau̇(-ə)rd\ *adj* (1905) **1 :** driven by an engine of insufficient power **2 :** having or supplied with insufficient power
un·der·pre·pared \-prə-ˈpard, -ˈperd\ *adj* (1964) : inadequately prepared
un·der·price \-ˈprīs\ *vt* (1756) **1 :** to price below what is normal or below the real value **2 :** to undercut (a competitor) in prices
un·der·priv·i·leged \-ˈpriv-lijd, -ˈpri-və-\ *adj* (1896) **1 :** deprived through social or economic condition of some of the fundamental rights of all members of a civilized society **2 :** of or relating to underprivileged people ⟨~ areas of the city⟩
un·der·pro·duc·tion \-prə-ˈdək-shən\ *n* (1887) : the production of less than enough to satisfy the demand or of less than the usual amount
un·der·proof \ˌən-dər-ˈprüf\ *adj* (1857) : containing less alcohol than proof spirit
un·der·pub·li·cized \-ˈpə-blə-ˌsīzd\ *adj* (1966) : insufficiently publicized
un·der·rate \ˌən-də(r)-ˈrāt\ *vt* (1650) : to rate too low : UNDERVALUE
un·der·re·act \-rē-ˈakt\ *vi* (1965) : to react with less than appropriate force or intensity
un·der·re·port \-ri-ˈpȯrt, -ˈpȯrt\ *vt* (1949) : to report to be less than is actually the case : UNDERSTATE ⟨~s his income⟩ ⟨the number of cases has been ~ed⟩
un·der·rep·re·sent·ed \-ˌre-pri-ˈzen-təd\ *adj* (1884) : inadequately represented — **un·der·rep·re·sen·ta·tion** \-ˌzen-ˈtā-shən, -zən-\ *n*
¹un·der·run \ˌən-də(r)-ˈrən\ *vt* **-ran** \-ˈran\; **-run**; **-run·ning** (1547) **1 :** to pass along under in order to examine (a cable) **2 :** to pass or extend under
²un·der·run \ˈən-də(r)-ˌrən\ *n* (1926) : the amount by which something produced (as a cut of lumber) falls below an estimate
un·der·sat·u·rat·ed \ˌən-dər-ˈsa-chə-ˌrā-təd\ *adj* (ca. 1828) : less than normally or adequately saturated
¹un·der·score \ˌən-dər-ˈskȯr, -ˈskȯr\ *vt* (1771) **1 :** to draw a line under : UNDERLINE **2 :** to make evident : EMPHASIZE, STRESS **3 :** to provide (action on film) with accompanying music
²underscore \ˈ \ *n* (1901) **1 :** a line drawn under a word or line esp. for emphasis or to indicate intent to italicize **2 :** music accompanying the action and dialogue of a film
¹un·der·sea \ˌən-dər-ˈsē\ *adj* (1613) **1 :** being or carried on under the sea or under the surface of the sea ⟨~ oil deposits⟩ ⟨~ fighting⟩ **2 :** designed for use under the surface of the sea ⟨an ~ fleet⟩
²undersea *or* **un·der·seas** \-ˈsēz\ *adv* (1684) : under the sea : beneath the surface of the sea ⟨photographs taken ~⟩
un·der·sec·re·tary \ˌən-dər-ˈse-krə-ˌter-ē, -ˈse-kə-\ *n* (1687) : a secretary immediately subordinate to a principal secretary ⟨~ of health⟩
un·der·sell \ˌən-dər-ˈsel\ *vt* **-sold** \-ˈsōld\; **-sell·ing** (1622) **1 :** to sell articles cheaper than ⟨~ a competitor⟩ ⟨we will not be *undersold*⟩ **2 :** to sell cheaper than ⟨imported cars that ~ domestic ones⟩
un·der·served \-ˈsərvd\ *adj* (1710) : provided with inadequate service
un·der·sexed \-ˈsekst\ *adj* (1931) : deficient in sexual desire
un·der·shirt \ˈən-dər-ˌshərt\ *n* (1648) : a collarless undergarment with or without sleeves — **un·der·shirt·ed** *adj*
un·der·shoot \ˌən-dər-ˈshüt\ *vt* **-shot** \-ˈshät\; **-shoot·ing** (ca. 1661) **1 :** to shoot short of or below (a target) **2 :** to fall short of (a runway) in landing an airplane
un·der·shorts \ˈən-dər-ˌshȯrts\ *n pl* (1949) : SHORT 4b
un·der·shot \ˈən-dər-ˌshät\ *adj* (1610) **1 :** moved by water passing beneath ⟨an ~ wheel⟩ **2 :** having the lower incisor teeth or lower jaw projecting beyond the upper when the mouth is closed
un·der·shrub \ˈən-dər-ˌshrəb, *esp Southern* -ˌsrəb\ *n* (1598) : SUBSHRUB
un·der·side \ˈən-dər-ˌsīd, ˌən-dər-ˈ\ *n* (1680) **1 :** the side or surface lying underneath **2 :** a side usu. hidden from sight; *specif* : the more unpleasant or reprehensible side ⟨the ~ of politics⟩
un·der·signed \ˌən-dər-ˈsīnd\ *n, pl* **undersigned** (1643) : one whose name is signed at the end of a document ⟨the ~ all agree⟩
un·der·sized \ˌən-dər-ˈsīzd\ *also* **un·der·size** \-ˈsīz\ *adj* (1706) : of a size less than is common, proper, normal, or average ⟨~ trout⟩
un·der·skirt \ˈən-dər-ˌskərt\ *n* (1861) : a skirt worn under an outer skirt; *esp* : PETTICOAT
un·der·slung \ˌən-dər-ˈsləŋ\ *adj* (1903) **1** *of a vehicle frame* : suspended below the axles **2 :** having a low center of gravity
un·der·spin \ˈən-dər-ˌspin\ *n* (1901) : BACKSPIN
un·der·staffed \ˌən-dər-ˈstaft\ *adj* (1891) : inadequately staffed — **un·der·staff·ing** \-ˈsta-fiŋ\ *n*
un·der·stand \ˌən-dər-ˈstand\ *vb* **-stood** \-ˈstu̇d\; **-stand·ing** [ME, fr. OE *understandan*, fr. *under* + *standan* to stand] *vt* (bef. 12c) **1 a :** to grasp the meaning of ⟨~ Russian⟩ **b :** to grasp the reasonableness of ⟨his behavior is hard to ~⟩ **c :** to have thorough or technical acquaintance with or expertness in the practice of ⟨~ finance⟩ **d :** to be thor-

oughly familiar with the character and propensities of ⟨~s children⟩ **2** : to accept as a fact or truth or regard as plausible without utter certainty ⟨we ~ that he is returning from abroad⟩ **3** : to interpret in one of a number of possible ways **4** : to supply in thought as though expressed ⟨"to be married" is commonly *understood* after the word *engaged*⟩ ~ *vi* **1** : to have understanding : have the power of comprehension **2** : to achieve a grasp of the nature, significance, or explanation of something **3** : to believe or infer something to be the case **4** : to show a sympathetic or tolerant attitude toward something — **un·der·stand·abil·i·ty** \-ˌstan-də-'bi-lə-tē\ *n* — **un·der·stand·able** \-'stan-də-bəl\ *adj*

syn UNDERSTAND, COMPREHEND, APPRECIATE mean to have a clear or complete idea of. UNDERSTAND and COMPREHEND are very often interchangeable. UNDERSTAND may, however, stress the fact of having attained a firm mental grasp of something ⟨orders that were fully *understood* and promptly obeyed⟩. COMPREHEND may stress the process of coming to grips with something intellectually ⟨I have trouble *comprehending* your reasons for doing this⟩. APPRECIATE implies a just evaluation or judgment of a thing's value or nature ⟨failed to *appreciate* the risks involved⟩.

un·der·stand·ably \ˌən-dər-'stan-də-blē\ *adv* (ca. 1921) : as can be easily understood : for understandable reasons ⟨is ~ nervous⟩
¹un·der·stand·ing \ˌən-dər-'stan-diŋ\ *n* (bef. 12c) **1** : a mental grasp : COMPREHENSION **2 a** : the power of comprehending; *esp* : the capacity to apprehend general relations of particulars **b** : the power to make experience intelligible by applying concepts and categories **3 a** : friendly or harmonious relationship **b** : an agreement of opinion or feeling : adjustment of differences **c** : a mutual agreement not formally entered into but in some degree binding on each side **4** : EXPLANATION, INTERPRETATION **5** : SYMPATHY 3a
²understanding *adj* (13c) **1** *archaic* : KNOWING, INTELLIGENT **2** : endowed with understanding : TOLERANT, SYMPATHETIC — **un·der·stand·ing·ly** \-'stan-diŋ-lē\ *adv*
un·der·state \ˌən-dər-'stāt\ *vt* (1824) **1** : to represent as less than is the case **2** : to state or present with restraint esp. for effect — **un·der·state·ment** \-mənt\ *n*
un·der·stat·ed \-'stā-təd\ *adj* (ca. 1909) : avoiding obvious emphasis or embellishment — **un·der·stat·ed·ly** *adv*
un·der·steer \'ən-dər-ˌstir\ *n* (1936) : the tendency of an automobile to turn less sharply than the driver intends — **un·der·steer** \ˌən-dər-\ *vi*
un·der·stood \ˌən-dər-'stůd\ *adj* (1605) **1** : fully apprehended **2** : agreed upon **3** : IMPLICIT
un·der·sto·ry \'ən-dər-ˌstōr-ē, -ˌstȯr-\ *n* (1902) **1** : an underlying layer of vegetation; *specif* : the vegetative layer and esp. the trees and shrubs between the forest canopy and the ground cover **2** : the plants that form the understory
un·der·strap·per \-ˌstra-pər\ *n* [³*under* + *strapper* one who harnesses horses] (ca. 1704) : a petty agent or subordinate : UNDERLING
un·der·strength \ˌən-dər-'streŋ(k)th\ *adj* (1925) : deficient in strength; *esp* : lacking sufficient or prescribed personnel
¹un·der·study \'ən-dər-ˌstə-dē, ˌən-dər-\ *vi* (1874) : to study another actor's part in order to substitute in an emergency ~ *vt* : to prepare (as a part) as understudy; *also* : to prepare as understudy to (as an actor)
²un·der·study \'ən-dər-ˌstə-dē\ *n* (1882) : one who is prepared to act another's part or take over another's duties
un·der·sup·ply \ˌən-dər-sə-'plī\ *n* (1848) : an inadequate supply or amount
¹un·der·sur·face \'ən-dər-ˌsər-fəs\ *n* (1733) : UNDERSIDE
²un·der·sur·face \ˌən-dər-'sər-fəs\ *adj* (ca. 1934) : existing or moving below the surface
un·der·take \ˌən-dər-'tāk\ *vb* **-took** \-'tůk\; **-tak·en** \-'tā-kən\; **-tak·ing** *vt* (14c) **1** : to take upon oneself : set about : ATTEMPT ⟨~ a task⟩ ⟨~ to learn to swim⟩ **2** : to put oneself under obligation to perform; *also* : to accept as a charge or responsibility ⟨the lawyer who *undertook* the case⟩ **3** : GUARANTEE, PROMISE ~ *vi, archaic* : to give surety or assume responsibility
un·der·tak·er \ˌən-dər-'tā-kər, 2 *is* 'ən-dər-\ *n* (1615) **1** : one that undertakes : one that takes the risk and management of business : ENTREPRENEUR **2** : one whose business is to prepare the dead for burial and to arrange and manage funerals **3** : an Englishman taking over forfeited lands in Ireland in the 16th and 17th centuries
un·der·tak·ing \ˌən-dər-ˌtā-kiŋ, ˌən-dər-'; 1b is 'ən-dər-, *only*\ *n* (15c) **1 a** : the act of one who undertakes or engages in a project or business **b** : the business of an undertaker **2** : something undertaken : ENTERPRISE **3** : PLEDGE, GUARANTEE
un·der·ten·ant \'ən-dər-ˌte-nənt\ *n* (1546) : one who holds lands or tenements by a sublease
under–the–counter *adj* [fr. the hiding of illicit wares under the counter of stores where they are sold] (1926) : surreptitious and usu. irregular or illicit ⟨~ liquor sales⟩
under–the–table *adj* (1948) : covert and usu. unlawful ⟨~ payoffs⟩
un·der·thrust \'ən-dər-ˌthrəst\ *vt* **-thrust; -thrust·ing** (1893) : to insert (a faulted rock mass) into position under a passive rock mass
un·der·tone \'ən-dər-ˌtōn\ *n* (1806) **1** : a low or subdued utterance or accompanying sound **2** : a quality (as of emotion) underlying the surface of an utterance or action **3** : a subdued color; *specif* : a color seen through and modifying another color
un·der·tow \-ˌtō\ *n* (1817) **1** : the current beneath the surface that sets seaward or along the beach when waves are breaking upon the shore **2** : an underlying current, force, or tendency that is in opposition to what is apparent
un·der·trick \-ˌtrik\ *n* (1903) : any of the tricks by which a declarer in bridge falls short of making the contract
un·der·used \ˌən-dər-'yüzd\ *adj* (1960) : not fully used
un·der·uti·lize \ˌən-dər-'yü-t²l-ˌīz\ *vt* (1951) : to utilize less than fully or below the potential use — **un·der·uti·li·za·tion** \'ən-dər-ˌyü-t²l-ə-'zā-shən\ *n*
un·der·val·u·a·tion \ˌən-dər-ˌval-yə-'wā-shən\ *n* (1653) **1** : the act of undervaluing **2** : a value below the real worth
un·der·val·ue \-'val-(ˌ)yü\ *vt* (1599) **1** : to value, rate, or estimate below the real worth ⟨~ stock⟩ **2** : to treat as having little value ⟨was *undervalued* as a poet⟩

un·der·wa·ter \ˌən-dər-'wȯ-tər, -'wä-\ *adj* (1627) **1** : lying, growing, worn, or operating below the surface of the water **2** : being below the waterline of a ship — **underwater** *adv*
un·der·way \ˌən-dər-'wā\ *adj* (1743) : occurring, performed, or used while traveling or in motion ⟨~ replenishment of fuel⟩
under way *adv* [prob. fr. D *onderweg*, fr. MD *onderwegen*, lit., under or among the ways] (1751) **1** : in motion : not at anchor or aground **2** : into motion from a standstill **3** : in progress : AFOOT ⟨preparations were *under way*⟩ ⟨the season got *under way* with a bang⟩
un·der·wear \'ən-dər-ˌwar, -ˌwer\ *n* (ca. 1879) : clothing or an article of clothing worn next to the skin and under other clothing
under weigh *adv* [by folk etymology] (1777) : UNDER WAY
¹un·der·weight \ˌən-dər-'wāt\ *n* (1596) : weight below normal, average, or requisite weight
²underweight *adj* (1890) : weighing less than the normal or requisite amount
un·der·whelm \-'hwelm, -'welm\ *vt* [*under* + overwhelm] (1949) : to fail to impress or stimulate
¹un·der·wing \'ən-dər-ˌwiŋ\ *n* (1535) **1** : one of the posterior wings of an insect **2** : any of various noctuid moths (esp. genus *Catocala*) that have the hind wings banded with contrasting colors (as red and black) — called also *underwing moth* **3** : the underside of a bird's wing
²underwing *adj* (1896) : placed or growing underneath the wing ⟨~ rockets⟩
un·der·wood \'ən-dər-ˌwůd\ *n* (14c) : UNDERGROWTH, UNDERBRUSH
un·der·wool \-ˌwůl\ *n* (1939) : short woolly underfur
un·der·world \-ˌwərld\ *n* (1608) **1** : the place of departed souls : HADES **2** *archaic* : EARTH **3** : the side of the earth opposite to one : ANTIPODES **4** : a social sphere below the level of ordinary life; *esp* : the world of organized crime
un·der·write \ˌən-də(r)-ˌrīt, ˌən-də(r)-'\ *vb* **-wrote** \-ˌrōt, -'rōt\; **-writ·ten** \-ˌri-t²n, -'ri-t²n\; **-writ·ing** \-ˌrī-tiŋ, -'rī-\ *vt* (15c) **1** : to write under or at the end of something else **2** : to set one's name to (an insurance policy) for the purpose of thereby becoming answerable for a designated loss or damage on consideration of receiving a premium percent : insure on life or property; *also* : to assume liability for (a sum or risk) as an insurer **3** : to subscribe to : agree to **4 a** : to agree to purchase (as security issue) usu. on a fixed date at a fixed price with a view to public distribution **b** : to guarantee financial support of ~ *vi* : to work as an underwriter
un·der·writ·er \'ən-də(r)-ˌrī-tər\ *n* (1622) **1** : one that underwrites : GUARANTOR **2 a** : one that underwrites a policy of insurance : INSURER **b** : one who selects risks to be solicited or rates the acceptability of risks solicited **3** : one that underwrites a security issue
un·de·scend·ed \ˌən-di-'sen-dəd\ *adj* (1701) : retained within the inguinal region rather than descending into the scrotum ⟨an ~ testis⟩
un·de·sign·ing \ˌən-di-'zī-niŋ\ *adj* (1697) : having no ulterior or fraudulent purpose : SINCERE
¹un·de·sir·able \-'zī-rə-bəl\ *adj* (1667) : not desirable : UNWANTED — **un·de·sir·abil·i·ty** \-ˌzī-rə-'bi-lə-tē\ *n* — **un·de·sir·able·ness** \-'zī-rə-bəl-nəs\ *n* — **un·de·sir·ably** \-blē\ *adv*
²undesirable *n* (1883) : one that is undesirable
un·de·vi·at·ing \ˌən-'dē-vē-ˌā-tiŋ\ *adj* (1732) : keeping a true course : UNSWERVING ⟨served their country with ~ loyalty and devotion⟩ — **un·de·vi·at·ing·ly** \-tiŋ-lē\ *adv*
un·dies \'ən-dēz\ *n pl* [by shortening & alter.] (1900) : UNDERWEAR; *esp* : women's underwear
un·dine \ˌən-'dēn, 'ən-,\ *n* [NL *undina*, fr. L *unda* wave — more at WATER] (1657) : an elemental being in the theory of Paracelsus inhabiting water : WATER NYMPH
un·dip·lo·mat·ic \ˌən-ˌdi-plə-'ma-tik\ *adj* (ca. 1828) : not diplomatic; *esp* : TACTLESS — **un·dip·lo·mat·i·cal·ly** \-ti-k(ə-)lē\ *adv*
un·di·rect·ed \ˌən-də-'rek-təd, -dī-\ *adj* (1596) : not directed : not planned or guided ⟨~ efforts⟩
un·dis·guised \ˌən-dis-'gīzd\ *adj* (ca. 1500) : not disguised or concealed : FRANK, OPEN — **un·dis·guis·ed·ly** \-'gī-zəd-lē\ *adv*
un·dis·so·ci·at·ed \ˌən-di-'sō-shē-ˌā-təd, -sē-\ *adj* (1899) : not electrolytically dissociated
un·do \ˌən-'dü, 'ən-\ *vb* **-did** \-'did\; **-done** \-'dən\; **-do·ing** \-'dü-iŋ\ *vt* (bef. 12c) **1** : to open or loose by releasing a fastening **2** : to make of no effect or as if not done : make null : REVERSE **3 a** : to ruin the worldly means, reputation, or hopes of **b** : to disturb the composure of : UPSET ⟨she's come *undone*⟩ **c** : SEDUCE 3 ~ *vi* : to come open or apart — **un·do·er** \-'dü-ər\ *n*
un·dock \'däk\ *vt* (1750) : to move away from a dock (as at sailing time) ~ *vt* : UNCOUPLE ⟨~ the shuttle from the space station⟩
un·dog·mat·ic \ˌən-dȯg-'ma-tik, -däg-\ *adj* (1857) : not dogmatic : not committed to dogma — **un·dog·mat·i·cal·ly** \-ti-k(ə-)lē\ *adv*
un·do·ing \ˌən-'dü-iŋ\ *n* (14c) **1** : an act of loosening : UNFASTENING **2** : RUIN; *also* : a cause of ruin ⟨greed was to prove his ~⟩ **3** : ANNULMENT, REVERSAL
un·done \ˌən-'dən\ *adj* (14c) : not done : not performed or finished
un·dou·ble \ˌən-'də-bəl\ *vb* (ca. 1611) : UNFOLD, UNCLENCH
un·dou·bled \-'də-bəld\ *adj* (1598) : not doubled
un·doubt·ed \-'daů-təd\ *adj* (15c) : not doubted : GENUINE, UNDISPUTED — **un·doubt·ed·ly** *adv*
un·dra·mat·ic \ˌən-drə-'ma-tik\ *adj* (1754) : lacking dramatic force or quality : UNSPECTACULAR — **un·dra·mat·i·cal·ly** \-ti-k(ə-)lē\ *adv*
un·drape \ˌən-'drāp\ *vt* (1869) : to strip of drapery : UNVEIL
un·draw \-'drȯ\ *vt* **-drew** \-'drü\; **-drawn** \-'drȯn\; **-draw·ing** (1677) : to draw aside (as a curtain) : OPEN
un·dreamed \-'drem(p)t, -'drēmd\ *also* **undreamt** \-'drem(p)t\ *adj* (1611) : not dreamed : not thought of : UNIMAGINED ⟨technical advances ~ of a few years ago⟩
¹un·dress \-'dres\ *vt* (1596) **1** : to remove the clothes or covering of : DIVEST, STRIP **2** : EXPOSE, REVEAL ~ *vi* : to take off one's clothes : DISROBE

\ə\ abut \²\ kitten, F table \ər\ further \a\ ash \ā\ ace \ä\ mop, mar \aů\ out \ch\ chin \e\ bet \ē\ easy \g\ go \i\ hit \ī\ ice \j\ job \ŋ\ sing \ō\ go \ȯ\ law \ȯi\ boy \th\ thin \t̷h\ the \ü\ loot \ů\ foot \y\ yet \zh\ vision \à, ḵ, ⁿ, œ, œ̄, ᵫ, ᵫ̄, ᵊ\ *see* Guide to Pronunciation

²**undress** n (1683) **1** : informal dress: as **a** : a loose robe or dressing gown **b** : ordinary dress — compare FULL DRESS **2** : the state of being undressed

un·dressed \,ən-'drest\ adj (1535) : not dressed: as **a** : partially, improperly, or informally clothed **b** : not fully processed or finished ⟨~ hides⟩ **c** : not cared for or tended ⟨an ~ wound⟩ ⟨~ fields⟩

un·drink·able \,ən-'driŋ-kə-bəl\ adj (1611) : unsuitable or unpleasant to drink

un·drunk \-'drəŋk\ adj (1637) : not swallowed

un·due \-'dü, -'dyü\ adj (14c) **1** : not due : not yet payable **2** : exceeding or violating propriety or fitness : EXCESSIVE

un·du·lant \'ən-jə-lənt, 'ən-dyə-, 'ən-də-\ adj (ca. 1830) **1** : rising and falling in waves **2** : having a wavy form, outline, or surface ⟨played her approach shot onto the ~ green⟩

undulant fever n (1896) : a persistent human brucellosis marked by remittent fever, pain and swelling in the joints, and great weakness and contracted by contact with infected domestic animals or consumption of their products

¹**un·du·late** \'ən-jə-lət, 'ən-dyə-, 'ən-də-, -,lāt\ or **un·du·lat·ed** \-,lā-təd\ adj [L undulatus, fr. (assumed) L undula, dim. of L unda wave — more at WATER] (1658) : having a wavy surface, edge, or markings ⟨the ~ margin of a leaf⟩

²**un·du·late** \-,lāt\ vb **-lat·ed; -lat·ing** [LL undula small wave, fr. (assumed) L] vi (1664) **1** : to form or move in waves : FLUCTUATE **2** : to rise and fall in volume, pitch, or cadence **3** : to present a wavy appearance ~ vt : to cause to move in a wavy, sinuous, or flowing manner **syn** see SWING

un·du·la·tion \,ən-jə-'lā-shən, ,ən-dyə-, ,ən-də-\ n (1646) **1 a** : a rising and falling in waves **b** : a wavelike motion to and fro in a fluid or elastic medium propagated continuously among its particles but with little or no permanent translation of the particles in the direction of the propagation : VIBRATION **2** : the pulsation caused by the vibrating together of two tones not quite in unison **3** : a wavy appearance, outline, or form : WAVINESS

un·du·la·to·ry \'ən-jə-lə-,tōr-ē, 'ən-dyə-, 'ən-də-,-,tór-\ adj (1728) : of or relating to undulation : moving in or resembling waves : UNDULATING

undulatory theory n (ca. 1828) : WAVE THEORY

un·du·ly \,ən-'dü-lē, -'dyü-\ adv (14c) : in an undue manner : EXCESSIVELY

un·du·ti·ful \-'dü-ti-fəl, -'dyü-\ adj (1582) : not dutiful — **un·du·ti·ful·ly** \-fə-lē\ adv — **un·du·ti·ful·ness** n

un·dy·ing \-'dī-iŋ\ adj (14c) : not dying : IMMORTAL, PERPETUAL

un·earned \-'ərnd\ adj (13c) **1** : not gained by labor, service, or skill ⟨~ income⟩ **2** : scored as a result of an error by the opposing team ⟨an ~ run⟩

unearned increment n (1871) : an increase in the value of property (as land) that is due to no labor or expenditure of the owner but to natural causes (as the increase of population) that create an increased demand for it

un·earth \,ən-'ərth\ vt (15c) **1** : to dig up out of or as if out of the earth : EXHUME ⟨~ a hidden treasure⟩ ⟨~ a forgotten photo album⟩ **2** : to make known or public : bring to light ⟨~ a plot⟩ **syn** see DISCOVER

un·earth·ly \-lē\ adj (1611) : not earthly: as **a** : not terrestrial ⟨~ radio sources⟩ **b** : PRETERNATURAL, SUPERNATURAL ⟨an ~ light⟩ **c** : WEIRD, EERIE ⟨~ howls⟩ **d** : not mundane : IDEAL ⟨~ love⟩ **e** : ABSURD 1, UNGODLY ⟨getting up at an ~ hour⟩ — **un·earth·li·ness** n

un·ease \,ən-'ēz\ n (14c) : mental or spiritual discomfort: as **a** : vague dissatisfaction : MISGIVING **b** : ANXIETY, DISQUIET **c** : lack of ease (as in social relations) : EMBARRASSMENT

un·eas·i·ly \-'ē-zə-lē\ adv (14c) : in an uneasy manner

¹**un·easy** \-'ē-zē\ adj (13c) **1** : causing physical or mental discomfort ⟨~ news of captures and killings —Marjory S. Douglas⟩ **2** : not easy : DIFFICULT **3** : marked by lack of ease : AWKWARD, EMBARRASSED ⟨gave an ~ laugh⟩ **4** : APPREHENSIVE, WORRIED **5** : RESTLESS, UNQUIET **6** : PRECARIOUS, UNSTABLE ⟨an ~ truce⟩ — **un·eas·i·ness** n

²**uneasy** adv (1596) : UNEASILY

un·eco·nom·ic \,ən-,e-kə-'nä-mik, -,ē-kə-\ or **un·eco·nom·i·cal** \-mi-kəl\ adj (1840) **1** : not economically practicable ⟨~ transportation routes⟩; also : COSTLY, WASTEFUL ⟨an ~ nuclear technology⟩

un·ed·it·ed \,ən-'e-də-təd\ adj (1829) : not edited: as **a** : left unrevised **b** : not yet edited ⟨~ books⟩ ⟨~ films⟩

un·emo·tion·al \,ən-i-'mō-shnəl, -shə-nəl\ adj (1876) : not emotional: as **a** : not easily aroused or excited : COLD **b** : involving a minimum of emotion : INTELLECTUAL — **un·emo·tion·al·ly** adv

un·em·ploy·able \,ən-im-'plói-ə-bəl\ adj (1887) : not acceptable for employment — **un·em·ploy·abil·i·ty** \-,plói-ə-'bi-lə-tē\ n — **unem·ployable** n

un·em·ployed \-'plóid\ adj (1600) : not employed: **a** : not being used **b** : not engaged in a gainful occupation : not invested — **unem·ployed** n

un·em·ploy·ment \-'plói-mənt\ n (1888) **1** : the state of being unemployed : involuntary idleness of workers; also : the rate of such unemployment **2** : UNEMPLOYMENT COMPENSATION

unemployment compensation n (1944) : compensation paid at regular intervals (as by a government agency) to an unemployed worker and esp. one who has been laid off — called also unemployment benefit

unemployment insurance n (1923) : social insurance against involuntary unemployment that provides unemployment compensation for a limited period to unemployed workers; also : UNEMPLOYMENT COMPENSATION

un·en·cum·bered \,ən-in-'kəm-bərd\ adj (1722) : free of encumbrance

un·end·ing \,ən-'en-diŋ\ adj (1661) : never ending : ENDLESS — **un·end·ing·ly** \-diŋ-lē\ adv

un·En·glish \,ən-'iŋ-glish also -'iŋ-lish\ adj (1633) **1** : not characteristically English **2** : not agreeing with standard or generally accepted usage of the English language

¹**un·equal** \,ən-'ē-kwəl\ adj (1565) **1 a** : not of the same measurement, quantity, or number as another **b** : not like or not the same as another in degree, worth, or status **2** : not uniform : VARIABLE, UNEVEN **3 a** : badly balanced or matched ⟨an ~ contest⟩ **b** : contracted between unequals ⟨~ marriages⟩ **c** archaic : not equable **4**

archaic : not equitable : UNJUST **5** : INADEQUATE, INSUFFICIENT ⟨~ to the task⟩ — **un·equal·ly** \-kwə-lē\ adv

²**unequal** n (1600) : one that is not equal to another

³**unequal** adv (1602) archaic : in an unequal manner ⟨~ match'd —Shak.⟩

un·equaled or **un·equalled** \-kwəld\ adj (1600) : not equaled : UNPARALLELED

un·equiv·o·ca·bly \,ən-i-'kwi-və-kə-blē\ adv [by alter.] (1917) nonstand : UNEQUIVOCALLY

un·equiv·o·cal \,ən-i-'kwi-və-kəl\ adj (1784) **1** : leaving no doubt : CLEAR, UNAMBIGUOUS **2** : UNQUESTIONABLE ⟨production of ~ masterpieces —Carole Cook⟩

un·equiv·o·cal·ly \-kə-lē, -klē\ adv (1794) : in an unequivocal manner

un·err·ing \,ən-'er-iŋ, ,ən-'ər-\ adj (1621) : committing no error : FAULTLESS, UNFAILING — **un·err·ing·ly** \-iŋ-lē\ adv

un·es·sen·tial \,ən-ə-'sen(t)-shəl\ adj (ca. 1656) **1** : not essential : DISPENSABLE, UNIMPORTANT **2** archaic : void of essence : INSUBSTANTIAL

un·Eu·ro·pe·an \,ən-,yur-ə-'pē-ən\ adj (1846) : not characteristically European

un·even \,ən-'ē-vən\ adj (bef. 12c) **1 a** archaic : UNEQUAL 1a **b** : ODD 3a **2 a** : not even : not level or smooth : RUGGED, RAGGED ⟨large ~ teeth⟩ ⟨~ handwriting⟩ **b** : varying from the straight or parallel **c** : not uniform : IRREGULAR **d** : varying in quality ⟨an ~ performance⟩ **3** : UNEQUAL 3a ⟨an ~ confrontation⟩ **syn** see ROUGH — **un·even·ly** adv — **un·even·ness** \-və(n)-nəs\ n

un·event·ful \,ən-i-'vent-fəl\ adj (1800) : marked by no noteworthy or untoward incidents : PLACID — **un·event·ful·ly** \-fə-lē\ adv — **un·event·ful·ness** \-fəl-nəs\ n

un·ex·am·pled \,ən-ig-'zam-pəld\ adj (1610) : having no example or parallel : UNPRECEDENTED

un·ex·cep·tion·able \,ən-ik-'sep-sh(ə-)nə-bəl\ adj [un- + obs. exception to take exception, object] (1664) : not open to objection or criticism : beyond reproach : UNIMPEACHABLE — **un·ex·cep·tion·able·ness** n — **un·ex·cep·tion·ably** \-blē\ adv

un·ex·cep·tion·al \-shnəl, -shə-nʰl\ adj (1806) : not out of the ordinary : COMMONPLACE

un·ex·er·cised \,ən-'ek-sər-,sīzd\ adj (14c) **1** : having terms that are not implemented ⟨~ options⟩ **2** : not subjected to exercise ⟨~ muscles⟩

un·ex·pect·ed \,ən-ik-'spek-təd\ adj (ca. 1586) : not expected : UNFORESEEN — **un·ex·pect·ed·ly** adv — **un·ex·pect·ed·ness** n

un·ex·ploit·ed \,ən-ik-'splói-təd\ adj (1888) : not exploited or developed : not taken advantage of

un·ex·pres·sive \,ən-ik-'spre-siv\ adj (1600) **1** obs : INEFFABLE **2** : not expressive : failing to convey the feeling or meaning intended

un·fad·ing \,ən-'fā-diŋ\ adj (1652) **1** : not losing color or freshness **2** : not losing value or effectiveness — **un·fad·ing·ly** \-diŋ-lē\ adv

un·fail·ing \-'fā-liŋ\ adj (14c) : not failing or liable to fail: **a** : CONSTANT, UNFLAGGING ⟨~ courtesy⟩ **b** : EVERLASTING, INEXHAUSTIBLE ⟨a subject of ~ interest⟩ **c** : INFALLIBLE, SURE ⟨an ~ test⟩ — **un·fail·ing·ly** \-liŋ-lē\ adv

un·fair \,ən-'far, -'fer\ adj (1700) **1** : marked by injustice, partiality, or deception : UNJUST **2** : not equitable in business dealings — **un·fair·ness** n

un·fair·ly \-lē\ adv (1713) : in an unfair manner

un·faith \,ən-'fāth, 'ən-,\ n (15c) : absence of faith : DISBELIEF

un·faith·ful \,ən-'fāth-fəl\ adj (15c) : not faithful: **a** : not adhering to vows, allegiance, or duty : DISLOYAL **b** : not faithful to marriage vows **c** : INACCURATE, UNTRUSTWORTHY — **un·faith·ful·ly** \-fə-lē\ adv — **un·faith·ful·ness** n

un·fall·en \,ən-'fó-lən\ adj (1653) : not morally fallen : INNOCENT 1a

un·fal·si·fi·able \,ən-'fól-sə-'fī-ə-bəl\ adj (ca. 1934) : not capable of being proved false ⟨~ hypotheses⟩

un·fal·ter·ing \,ən-'fól-t(ə-)riŋ\ adj (1727) : not wavering or weakening : FIRM — **un·fal·ter·ing·ly** \-t(ə-)riŋ-lē\ adv

un·fa·mil·iar \,ən-fə-'mil-yər\ adj (1594) : not familiar: **a** : not well-known : STRANGE ⟨an ~ place⟩ **b** : not well acquainted ⟨~ with the subject⟩ — **un·fa·mil·iar·i·ty** \-,mil-'yar-ə-tē, -,mi-lē-'yar-\ n — **un·fa·mil·iar·ly** \-'mil-yər-lē\ adv

un·fash·ion·able \-'fa-sh(ə-)nə-bəl\ adj (1648) **1** : not in keeping with the current fashion ⟨~ clothes⟩ **2** : not favored socially ⟨~ neighborhoods⟩ — **un·fash·ion·able·ness** \-bəl-nəs\ n — **un·fash·ion·ably** \-blē\ adv

un·fas·ten \-'fa-sʰn\ vt (15c) : to make loose: as **a** : UNPIN, UNBUCKLE **b** : UNDO ⟨~ a button⟩ **c** : DETACH ⟨~ a boat from its moorings⟩

un·fa·thered \,ən-'fä-thərd\ adj (1597) **1** : having no father : ILLEGITIMATE, BASTARD **2** : having no known origin ⟨~ slanders⟩

un·fath·om·able \-'fa-thə-mə-bəl\ adj (1640) : not capable of being fathomed: **a** : impossible to comprehend **b** : IMMEASURABLE

un·fa·vor·able \,ən-'fā-v(ə-)rə-bəl, -'fā-vər-bəl\ adj (1548) **1 a** : OPPOSED, CONTRARY **b** : expressing disapproval : NEGATIVE ⟨~ reviews⟩ **2** : not propitious : DISADVANTAGEOUS **3** : not pleasing — **un·fa·vor·able·ness** n — **un·fa·vor·ably** \-blē\ adv

un·fa·vor·ite \-'fā-v(ə-)rət, -'fā-vərt\ adj (ca. 1934) : not being a favorite; esp : being regarded with special disfavor or dislike

un·fazed \,ən-'fāzd\ adj (1945) : not fazed : UNDAUNTED

un·feel·ing \-'fē-liŋ\ adj (bef. 12c) **1** : devoid of feeling : INSENSATE ⟨an ~ corpse⟩ **2** : devoid of kindness or sympathy : HARDHEARTED, CRUEL ⟨an ~ wretch⟩ — **un·feel·ing·ly** \-liŋ-lē\ adv — **un·feel·ing·ness** n

un·feigned \-'fānd\ adj (14c) : not feigned or hypocritical : GENUINE **syn** see SINCERE — **un·feign·ed·ly** \-'fā-nəd-lē, -'fānd-lē\ adv

un·fet·ter \-'fe-tər\ vt (14c) **1** : to free from fetters ⟨~ a prisoner⟩ **2** : EMANCIPATE, LIBERATE ⟨~ the mind from prejudice⟩

un·fet·tered \-tərd\ adj (1601) : FREE, UNRESTRAINED

un·fil·ial \,ən-'fi-lē-əl, -'fil-yəl\ adj (1611) : not observing the obligations of a child to a parent : UNDUTIFUL — **un·fil·ial·ly** adv

un·fil·tered \,ən-'fil-tərd\ adj (ca. 1775) **1** : not filtered ⟨~ wine⟩; also : not modified, processed, or refined ⟨~ commercial publicity material —Paul Grimes⟩ **2** : lacking a filter ⟨an ~ cigarette⟩

un·find·able \-'fīn-də-bəl\ adj (1791) : not capable of being found

un·fin·ished \-'fi-nisht\ adj (1539) : not finished: **a** : not brought to an end or to the desired final state **b** : being in a rough state : UNPOL-

ISHED **c** : subjected to no other processes (as bleaching or dyeing) after coming from the loom

¹**un·fit** \-'fit\ *adj* (1545) : not fit: **a** : not adapted to a purpose : UNSUITABLE **b** : not qualified : INCAPABLE, INCOMPETENT **c** : physically or mentally unsound — **un·fit·ly** *adv* — **un·fit·ness** *n*

²**unfit** *vt* (1611) : to make unfit : DISABLE, DISQUALIFY

un·fit·ted \-ən-'fi-təd\ *adj* (1592) : not adapted : UNQUALIFIED

un·fit·ting \-'fi-tiŋ\ *adj* (1534) : not fitting : UNSUITABLE

un·fix \-'fiks\ *vt* (1597) **1** : to loosen from a fastening : DETACH, DISENGAGE **2** : to make unstable : UNSETTLE

un·flag·ging \-'fla-giŋ\ *adj* (1715) **1** : not flagging : TIRELESS **2** : UNRELENTING 2 — **un·flag·ging·ly** \-giŋ-lē\ *adv*

un·flap·pa·ble \-'fla-pə-bəl\ *adj* [¹*un-* + ¹*flap* (state of excitement) + *-able*] (1954) : marked by assurance and self-control — **un·flap·pa·bil·i·ty** \-,fla-pə-'bi-lə-tē\ *n* — **un·flap·pa·bly** \-'fla-pə-blē\ *adv*

un·flat·ter·ing \-'fla-tə-riŋ\ *adj* (1581) : not flattering; *esp* : UNFAVORABLE — **un·flat·ter·ing·ly** \-riŋ-lē\ *adv*

un·fledged \,ən-'flejd\ *adj* (1611) **1** : not feathered : not ready for flight **2** : not fully developed : IMMATURE ⟨an ∼ writer⟩

un·flinch·ing \-'flin-chiŋ\ *adj* (1728) : not flinching or shrinking : STEADFAST, UNCOMPROMISING — **un·flinch·ing·ly** \-chiŋ-lē\ *adv*

un·fo·cused *also* **un·fo·cussed** \-'fō-kəst\ *adj* (1886) **1** : not adjusted to a focus **2** : not concentrated on one point or objective ⟨∼ rage⟩

un·fold \-'fōld\ *vt* (bef. 12c) **1 a** : to open the folds of : spread or straighten out : EXPAND ⟨∼*ed* the map⟩ **b** : to remove (as a package) from the folds : UNWRAP **2** : to open to the view : REVEAL; *esp* : to make clear by gradual disclosure and often by recital ∼ *vi* **1 a** : to open from a folded state : open out : EXPAND **b** : BLOSSOM **2** : DEVELOP, EVOLVE ⟨as the story ∼*s*⟩ **3** : to open out gradually to the view or understanding : become known ⟨a panorama ∼*s* before their eyes⟩ — **un·fold·ment** \-'fōl(d)-mənt\ *n*

un·fold·ed *adj* (1683) : not folded

un·for·get·ta·ble \,ən-fər-'ge-tə-bəl\ *adj* (1806) : incapable of being forgotten : MEMORABLE — **un·for·get·ta·bly** \-'ge-tə-blē\ *adv*

un·for·giv·ing \,ən-fər-'gi-viŋ\ *adj* (1713) **1** : unwilling or unable to forgive **2** : having or making no allowance for error or weakness ⟨an ∼ environment where false moves can prove fatal —Jaclyn Fierman⟩ — **un·for·giv·ing·ness** *n*

un·formed \-'fȯrmd\ *adj* (14c) : not arranged in regular shape, order, or relations; *esp* : IMMATURE, UNDEVELOPED

¹**un·for·tu·nate** \-'fȯrch-nət, -'fȯr-chə-\ *adj* (15c) **1 a** : not favored by fortune : UNSUCCESSFUL, UNLUCKY ⟨an ∼ young man⟩ **b** : marked or accompanied by or resulting in misfortune ⟨an ∼ decision⟩ **2 a** : INFELICITOUS, UNSUITABLE ⟨an ∼ choice of words⟩ **b** : DEPLORABLE, REGRETTABLE ⟨an ∼ lack of taste⟩

²**unfortunate** *n* (1683) : an unfortunate person

un·for·tu·nate·ly \-lē\ *adv* (ca. 1548) **1** : in an unfortunate manner ⟨the marriage turned out ∼⟩ **2** : it is unfortunate ⟨∼ for him your letter has let the cat out of the bag —G. B. Shaw⟩

un·found·ed \,ən-'faùn-dəd\ *adj* (1648) : lacking a sound basis : GROUNDLESS, UNWARRANTED

un·freeze \-'frēz\ *vt* **-froze** \-'frōz\; **-fro·zen** \-'frō-z°n\; **-freez·ing** (1584) **1** : to cause to thaw **2** : to remove from a freeze

un·fre·quent·ed \,ən-frē-'kwen-təd, ;ən-'frē-kwən-\ *adj* (1588) : not often visited or traveled over

un·friend·ed \,ən-'fren-dəd\ *adj* (1513) : having no friends : not befriended

un·friend·li·ness \-'fren(d)-lē-nəs\ *n* (ca. 1684) : the quality or state of being unfriendly : HOSTILITY

un·friend·ly \-'fren(d)-lē\ *adj* (15c) : not friendly: as **a** : HOSTILE, UNSYMPATHETIC **b** : INHOSPITABLE, UNFAVORABLE

un·frock \-'fräk\ *vt* (1644) : DEFROCK

un·froz·en \-'frō-z°n\ *adj* (1596) : not frozen ⟨∼ ground⟩

un·fruit·ful \-'früt-fəl\ *adj* (14c) : not fruitful: as **a** : not producing offspring : BARREN **b** : yielding no valuable result : UNPROFITABLE ⟨an ∼ conference⟩ — **un·fruit·ful·ly** \-fə-lē\ *adv* — **un·fruit·ful·ness** *n*

un·fund·ed \-'fən-dəd\ *adj* (ca. 1770) **1** : not funded : FLOATING ⟨an ∼ debt⟩ **2** : not provided with funds ⟨∼ schools⟩

un·furl \-'fər-(ə)l\ *vt* (1641) : to release from a furled state ∼ *vi* : to open out from or as if from a furled state : UNFOLD

un·fussy \-'fə-sē\ *adj* (1825) : not fussy: as **a** : not particular : UNCONCERNED **b** : not cluttered with pretentious or nonessential matters : UNCOMPLICATED — **un·fuss·i·ly** \-'fə-sə-lē\ *adv*

un·gain·ly \,ən-'gān-lē\ *adj* (1611) **1 a** : lacking in smoothness or dexterity : CLUMSY **b** : hard to handle : UNWIELDY **2** : having an awkward appearance : UGLY — **un·gain·li·ness** *n*

un·gen·er·os·i·ty \,ən-,je-nə-'rä-sə-tē, -'räs-tē\ *n* (1757) : lack of generosity

un·gen·er·ous \,ən-'jen-rəs, -'je-nə-\ *adj* (1641) : not generous : a : PETTY, MEAN **b** : deficient in liberality : STINGY — **un·gen·er·ous·ly** *adv*

un·gird \-'gərd\ *vt* (bef. 12c) : to divest of a restraining band or girdle : UNBIND

un·girt \-'gərt\ *adj* (14c) **1** : having the belt or girdle off or loose **2** : lacking in discipline or compactness : LOOSE, SLACK

un·glue \-'glü\ *vt* (ca. 1548) : to separate by or as if by dissolving an adhesive

un·glued \-'glüd\ *adj* (1922) : UPSET, DISORDERED

un·god·li·ness \,ən-'gäd-lē-nəs *also* -'gȯd-\ *n* (1526) : the quality or state of being ungodly

un·god·ly \-lē\ *adj* (1526) **1 a** : denying or disobeying God : IMPIOUS, IRRELIGIOUS **b** : contrary to moral law : SINFUL, WICKED **2** : OUTRAGEOUS ⟨gets up at an ∼ hour⟩

un·got·ten \-'gä-t°n\ *or* **un·got** \-'gät\ *adj* (15c) **1** *obs* : not begotten **2** : not obtained

un·gov·ern·able \-'gə-vər-nə-bəl\ *adj* (1673) : not capable of being governed, guided, or restrained *syn* see UNRULY

un·gra·cious \-'grā-shəs\ *adj* (13c) **1** *archaic* : WICKED **2** : not courteous : RUDE **3** : not pleasing : DISAGREEABLE — **un·gra·cious·ly** *adv* — **un·gra·cious·ness** *n*

un·gram·mat·i·cal \,ən-grə-'ma-ti-kəl\ *adj* (1654) : not following rules of grammar — **un·gram·mat·i·cal·i·ty** \-,ma-tə-'ka-lə-tē\ *n*

un·grate·ful \,ən-'grāt-fəl\ *adj* (1533) **1** : showing no gratitude : making a poor return **2** : DISAGREEABLE; *also* : THANKLESS — **un·grate·ful·ly** \-fə-lē\ *adv* — **un·grate·ful·ness** *n*

un·grudg·ing \-'grə-jiŋ\ *adj* (ca. 1774) : being without envy or reluctance

un·gual \'əŋ-gwəl, 'ən-\ *adj* [L *unguis* nail, claw, hoof — more at NAIL] (1834) : of, relating to, or resembling a nail, claw, or hoof

un·guard \,ən-'gärd\ *vt* [back-formation fr. *unguarded*] (1745) : to leave unprotected

un·guard·ed \-'gär-dəd\ *adj* (ca. 1593) **1** : vulnerable to attack : UNPROTECTED **2** : free from guile or wariness : DIRECT, INCAUTIOUS — **un·guard·ed·ly** *adv* — **un·guard·ed·ness** *n*

un·guent \'əŋ-gwənt, 'ən-; 'ən-jənt\ *n* [ME, fr. L *unguentum* — more at OINTMENT] (15c) : a soothing or healing salve : OINTMENT

un·guis \'əŋ-gwəs, 'ən-\ *n*, *pl* **un·gues** \-,gwēz\ [L — more at NAIL] (ca. 1790) : a nail, claw, or hoof esp. on a digit of a vertebrate

¹**un·gu·late** \'əŋ-gyə-lət, 'ən-, -,lāt\ *adj* [LL *ungulatus*, fr. L *ungula* hoof, fr. *unguis* nail, hoof] (1839) **1** : having hoofs **2** : of or relating to the ungulates

²**ungulate** *n* [NL *Ungulata*, fr. LL, neut. pl. of *ungulatus*] (ca. 1842) : a hoofed typically herbivorous quadruped mammal (as a ruminant, swine, camel, hippopotamus, horse, tapir, rhinoceros, elephant, or hyrax) of a polyphyletic group formerly considered a major mammalian taxon (Ungulata)

un·hair \,ən-'har, -'her\ *vt* (14c) *archaic* : to deprive of hair

un·hal·low \-'ha-(,)lō\ *vt* (1535) *archaic* : to make profane

un·hal·lowed \-(,)lōd\ *adj* (bef. 12c) **1** : not blessed : UNCONSECRATED, UNHOLY **2 a** : unsanctioned by or showing lack of reverence for religion : IMPIOUS, PROFANE **b** : contrary to accepted standards : IMMORAL

un·hand \,ən-'hand\ *vt* (1602) : to remove the hand from : let go

un·hand·some \-'han(t)-səm\ *adj* (1530) : not handsome: as **a** : not beautiful : HOMELY **b** : UNBECOMING, UNSEEMLY **c** : lacking in courtesy or taste : RUDE — **un·hand·some·ly** *adv*

un·handy \-'han-dē\ *adj* (1664) **1** : hard to handle : INCONVENIENT **2** : lacking in skill or dexterity : AWKWARD — **un·hand·i·ly** \-də-lē\ *adv* — **un·hand·i·ness** \-dē-nəs\ *n*

un·hap·pi·ly \,ən-'ha-pə-lē\ *adv* (14c) **1** : UNFORTUNATELY **2** ⟨∼, medicine has not yet found a cure —Diana Trilling⟩ **2** : in an unhappy manner : without pleasure ⟨practiced law ∼ for a few years⟩

un·hap·py \-'ha-pē\ *adj* (14c) **1** : not fortunate : UNLUCKY **2** : not cheerful or glad : SAD, WRETCHED **3 a** : causing or subject to misfortune : INAUSPICIOUS **b** : INFELICITOUS, INAPPROPRIATE — **un·hap·pi·ness** *n*

un·healthy \-'hel-thē\ *adj* (1595) **1** : not conducive to health ⟨an ∼ climate⟩ **2** : not in good health : SICKLY, DISEASED **3 a** : DANGEROUS, RISKY **b** : BAD, INJURIOUS **c** : morally contaminated : CORRUPT, UNWHOLESOME ⟨an ∼ imagination⟩ — **un·health·i·ly** \-thə-lē\ *adv* — **un·health·i·ness** \-thē-nəs\ *n*

un·heard \-'hərd\ *adj* (14c) **1 a** : not perceived by the ear **b** : not given a hearing **2** *archaic* : UNHEARD-OF

un·heard–of \-,əv, -,äv\ *adj* (1592) : previously unknown; *esp* : UNPRECEDENTED

un·hes·i·tat·ing \-'he-zə-,tā-tiŋ\ *adj* (1753) : not hesitating : not checked or qualified — **un·hes·i·tat·ing·ly** \-tiŋ-lē\ *adv*

un·hinge \-'hinj\ *vt* (1616) **1** : to remove (as a door) from the hinges **2** : to make unstable : UNSETTLE, DISRUPT ⟨∼ the balance of world peace⟩ ⟨pressure that would ∼ a less experienced person⟩

un·hitch \-'hich\ *vt* (1706) : to free from or as if from being hitched

un·ho·ly \,ən-'hō-lē\ *adj* (bef. 12c) **1** : showing disregard for what is holy : WICKED **2** : SHOCKING, OUTRAGEOUS — **un·ho·li·ness** *n*

un·hood \-'hùd\ *vt* (1575) : to remove a hood or covering from

un·hook \-'hùk\ *vt* (1611) **1** : to remove from a hook **2** : to unfasten by disengaging a hook **3** : to free from a habit or dependency

un·hoped \-'hōpt\ *adj* (14c) *archaic* : not hoped for or expected

un·horse \-'hȯrs\ *vt* (14c) : to dislodge from or as if from a horse

un·hou·seled \-'haù-zəld\ *adj* (1532) *archaic* : not having received the Eucharist esp. shortly before death

un·hur·ried \-'hər-ēd, -'hə-rēd\ *adj* (ca. 1774) : not hurried : LEISURELY — **un·hur·ried·ly** *adv*

uni- *prefix* [ME, fr. MF, fr. L, fr. *unus* — more at ONE] : one : single ⟨*uni*cellular⟩

uni·al·gal \,yü-nē-'al-gəl\ *adj* (1914) : of, relating to, or derived from a single algal individual or cell ⟨a ∼ culture⟩

Uni·ate *or* **Uni·at** \'yü-nē-,at, 'ü-\ *n* [Ukrainian *uniat*, *uniyat* one in favor of the union of the Greek and Roman Catholic churches, fr. *uniya* union, fr. Pol *unija*, fr. LL *unio* — more at UNION] (1833) : a Christian of a church adhering to an Eastern rite and discipline but submitting to papal authority — **Uniate** *adj*

uni·ax·i·al \,yü-nē-'ak-sē-əl\ *adj* (ca. 1828) **1** : having only one axis **2** : of or relating to only one axis

uni·cam·er·al \,yü-ni-'kam-rəl, -'ka-mə-\ *adj* [*uni-* + LL *camera* room, chamber — more at CHAMBER] (1853) : having or consisting of a single legislative chamber — **uni·cam·er·al·ly** *adv*

uni·cel·lu·lar \,yü-ni-'sel-yə-lər\ *adj* (1858) : having or consisting of a single cell

uni·corn \'yü-nə-,kȯrn\ *n* [ME *unicorne*, fr. OF, fr. LL *unicornis*, fr. L, having one horn, fr. *uni-* + *cornu* horn — more at HORN] (13c) : a mythical animal generally depicted with the body and head of a horse, the hind legs of a stag, the tail of a lion, and a single horn in the middle of the forehead

unicorn plant *n* (1796) : DEVIL'S CLAW

uni·cy·cle \'yü-ni-,sī-kəl\ *n* [*uni-* + *-cycle* (as in *tricycle*)] (1869) : a vehicle that has a single wheel and is usu. propelled by pedals — **uni·cy·clist** \-,sī-k(ə-)list\ *n*

uni·di·men·sion·al \ˌyü-ni-də-'mench-nəl, -'men(t)-sh(ə-)nºl *also* -ˌdī-\ *adj* (1883) : ONE-DIMENSIONAL — **uni·di·men·sion·al·i·ty** \-ˌmen(t)-shə-'na-lə-tē\ *n*

uni·di·rec·tion·al \ˌyü-ni-də-'rek-shnəl, -dī-, -shə-nºl\ *adj* (1883) **1** : involving, functioning, moving, or responsive in a single direction **2** : not subject to change or reversal of direction — **uni·di·rec·tion·al·ly** *adv*

unidirectional current *n* (1883) : DIRECT CURRENT

uni·fi·ca·tion \ˌyü-nə-fə-'kā-shən\ *n* (1851) : the act, process, or result of unifying : the state of being unified

uni·fo·li·ate \-'fō-lē-ət\ *adj* [*uni-* + L *folium* leaf — more at BLADE] (1849) **1** : having only one leaf **2** : UNIFOLIOLATE

uni·fo·li·o·late \-'fō-lē-ə-ˌlāt\ *adj* [*uni-* + LL *foliolum* leaflet, dim. of L *folium* leaf] (ca. 1859) *of a leaf* : compound but having only a single leaflet and distinguishable from a simple leaf by the basal joint

¹uni·form \'yü-nə-ˌfórm\ *adj* [MF *uniforme*, fr. L *uniformis*, fr. *uni-* + *-formis* -form] (1538) **1** : consistent in conduct or opinion ⟨~ interpretation of laws⟩ **2** : having always the same form, manner, or degree : not varying or variable **3** : of the same form with others : conforming to one rule or mode : CONSONANT **4** : presenting an unvaried appearance of surface, pattern, or color ⟨~ red brick houses⟩ **5** : relating to or being convergence of a series whose terms are functions in such manner that the absolute value of the difference between the sum of the first *n* terms of the series and the sum of all terms can be made arbitrarily small for all values of the domain of the functions by choosing the *n*th term sufficiently far along in the series — **uni·form·ly** \'yü-nə-ˌfórm-lē, ˌyü-nə-'\ *adv* — **uni·form·ness** \'yü-nə-ˌfórm-nəs\ *n*

²uniform *vt* (ca. 1681) **1** : to bring into uniformity **2** : to clothe with a uniform

³uniform *n* (1748) : dress of a distinctive design or fashion worn by members of a particular group and serving as a means of identification; *broadly* : distinctive or characteristic clothing

Uniform (ca. 1956) — a communication code word for the letter *u*

uni·for·mi·tar·i·an \ˌyü-nə-ˌfór-mə-'ter-ē-ən\ *n* (1840) **1** : an adherent of the doctrine of uniformitarianism **2** : an advocate of uniformity — **uniformitarian** *adj*

uni·for·mi·tar·i·an·ism \-ē-ə-ˌni-zəm\ *n* (1865) : a geological doctrine that existing processes acting in the same manner as at present are sufficient to account for all geological changes — compare CATASTROPHISM

uni·for·mi·ty \ˌyü-nə-'fór-mə-tē\ *n, pl* **-ties** (15c) **1** : the quality or state of being uniform **2** : an instance of uniformity

uni·fy \'yü-nə-ˌfī\ *vt* **-fied; -fy·ing** [LL *unificare*, fr. L *uni-* + *-ficare* -fy] (1502) : to make into or a unit or a coherent whole : UNITE — **uni·fi·able** \-ˌfī-ə-bəl\ *adj* — **uni·fi·er** \-ˌfī(-ə)r\ *n*

uni·lat·er·al \ˌyü-ni-'la-tə-rəl, -'la-trəl\ *adj* (1802) **1 a** : done or undertaken by one person or party **b** : of, relating to, or affecting one side of a subject : ONE-SIDED **c** : constituting or relating to a contract or engagement by which an express obligation to do or forbear is imposed on only one party **2 a** : having parts arranged on one side ⟨a ~ raceme⟩ **b** : occurring on, performed on, or affecting one side of the body or one of its parts ⟨~ exophthalmos⟩ **3** : UNILINEAL **4** : having only one side — **uni·lat·er·al·ly** *adv*

uni·lin·e·al \-'li-nē-əl\ *adj* (1952) : tracing descent through either the maternal or paternal line only

uni·lin·e·ar \-'li-nē-ər\ *adj* (1851) : developing in or involving a series of stages usu. from the primitive to the more advanced ⟨a ~ cultural sequence⟩

uni·lin·gual \ˌyü-ni-'liŋ-gwəl, -gyə-wəl\ *adj* [*uni-* + L *lingua* tongue, language — more at TONGUE] (1866) : composed in or using one language only

un·il·lu·sioned \ˌən-i-'lü-zhənd\ *adj* (1926) : free from illusion

uni·loc·u·lar \ˌyü-ni-'lä-kyə-lər\ *adj* (1753) : containing a single cavity

un·imag·in·able \ˌən-ə-'maj-nə-bəl, -'ma-jə-\ *adj* (1611) : not imaginable or comprehensible — **un·imag·in·ably** \-blē\ *adv*

un·im·peach·able \ˌən-im-'pē-chə-bəl\ *adj* (1784) : not impeachable : not to be called in question : not liable to accusation : IRREPROACHABLE, BLAMELESS — **un·im·peach·ably** \-blē\ *adv*

¹un·im·proved \-'prüvd\ *adj* (1602) *obs* : not reproved or admonished

²unimproved (1665) : not improved: as **a** : not tilled, built on, or otherwise improved for use ⟨~ land⟩ **b** : not used or employed advantageously ⟨wasted time and ~ opportunities⟩ **c** : not selectively bred for better quality or productiveness

un·in·hib·it·ed \ˌən-in-'hi-bə-təd\ *adj* (1880) : free from inhibition; *also* : boisterously informal — **un·in·hib·it·ed·ly** *adv* — **un·in·hib·it·ed·ness** *n*

un·in·i·ti·ate \ˌən-ə-'ni-sh(ē-)ət\ *adj* (1801) : not initiated : INEXPERIENCED — **uninitiate** *n*

un·in·ter·est \ˌən-'in-trəst; -'in-tə-rəst, -tə-ˌrest, -tərst; -'in-ˌtrest\ *n* (1890) : lack of interest

uninterested *adj* (1661) : not interested : not having the mind or feelings engaged *usage* see DISINTERESTED

uni·nu·cle·ate \ˌyü-ni-'nü-klē-ət, -'nyü-\ *adj* (1885) : having a single nucleus ⟨a ~ yeast cell⟩

¹union \'yün-yən\ *n* [ME, fr. MF, fr. LL *union-, unio* oneness, union, fr. L *unus* one — more at ONE] (15c) **1 a** : an act or instance of uniting or joining two or more things into one: as **(1)** : the formation of a single political unit from two or more separate and independent units **(2)** : a uniting in marriage; *also* : SEXUAL INTERCOURSE **(3)** : the growing together of severed parts **b** : a unified condition : COMBINATION, JUNCTION ⟨a gracious ~ of excellence and strength⟩ **2** : something that is made one : something formed by a combining or coalition of parts or members: as **a** : a confederation of independent individuals (as nations or persons) for some common purpose **b (1)** : a political unit constituting an organic whole formed usu. from previously independent units (as England and Scotland in 1707) which have surrendered their principal powers to the government of the whole or to a newly created government (as the U.S. in 1789) **(2)** *cap* : the federal union of states during the period of the U.S. Civil War **c** *cap* : an organization on a college or university campus providing recreational, social, cultural, and sometimes dining facilities; *also* : the building housing such an organization **d** : the set of all elements belonging to one or more of a given collection of two or more sets — called also *join, sum* **e** : LABOR UNION **3 a** : a device emblematic of the union of two

or more sovereignties borne on a national flag typically in the upper inner corner or constituting the whole design of the flag **b** : the upper inner corner of a flag **4** : any of various devices for connecting parts (as of a machine); *esp* : a coupling for pipes or pipes and fittings

²union *adj* (1707) : of, relating to, dealing with, or constituting a union; *esp, cap* : of, relating to, or being the side favoring the Union in the U.S. Civil War ⟨*Union* troops⟩

union card *n* (1874) **1** : a card certifying personal membership in good standing in a labor union **2** : something that resembles a union card esp. in being necessary for employment or in providing evidence of in-group status

union church *n* (1847) : a local church uniting members of diverse denominational backgrounds in an interdenominational congregation

un·ion·i·sa·tion, union·ise Brit var of UNIONIZATION, UNIONIZE

union·ism \'yün-yə-ˌni-zəm\ *n* (1845) : the principle or policy of forming or adhering to a union: as **a** *cap* : adherence to the policy of a firm federal union between the states of the United States esp. during the Civil War period **b** : the principles, theory, advocacy, or system of trade unions

union·ist \-nist\ *n* (1799) : an advocate or supporter of union or unionism

union·i·za·tion \ˌyün-yə-nə-'zā-shən\ *n* (1896) **1** : the quality or state of being unionized **2** : the action of unionizing

union·ize \'yün-yə-ˌnīz\ *vb* **-ized; -iz·ing** *vt* (1890) : to organize into a labor union ~ *vi* : to form or join a labor union

unionized *adj* (1900) : characterized by the presence of labor unions ⟨~ states⟩

union jack *n* (1674) **1** : a jack consisting of the union of a national ensign **2** *cap U&J* : the state flag of the United Kingdom consisting of the union of the British national ensign

union shop *n* (1904) : an establishment in which the employer by agreement is free to hire nonmembers as well as members of the union but retains nonmembers on the payroll only on condition of their becoming members of the union within a specified time

union suit *n* (1892) : an undergarment with shirt and drawers in one piece

uni·pa·ren·tal \ˌyü-ni-pə-'ren-tºl\ *adj* (1900) : having or involving a single parent; *esp* : PARTHENOGENETIC — **uni·pa·ren·tal·ly** \-t-tºl-ē\ *adv*

unique \yu̇-'nēk\ *adj* [F, fr. L *unicus*, fr. *unus* one — more at ONE] (1602) **1** : being the only one : SOLE ⟨his ~ concern was his own comfort⟩ ⟨I can't walk away with a ~ copy. Suppose I lost it? —Kingsley Amis⟩ ⟨the ~ factorization of a number into prime factors⟩ **2 a** : being without a like or equal : UNEQUALED ⟨could stare at the flames, each one new, violent, ~ —Robert Coover⟩ **b** : distinctively characteristic : PECULIAR **1** ⟨this is not a condition ~ to California —Ronald Reagan⟩ **3** : UNUSUAL ⟨a very ~ ball-point pen⟩ ⟨we were fairly ~, the sixty of us, in that there wasn't one good mixer in the bunch —J. D. Salinger⟩ *syn* see STRANGE — **unique·ly** *adv* — **unique·ness** *n*

usage Many commentators have objected to the comparison or modification (as by *somewhat* or *very*) of *unique;* the statement that a thing is either unique or it is not has often been repeated by them. Objections are based chiefly on the assumption that *unique* has but a single absolute sense, an assumption contradicted by information readily available in a dictionary. *Unique* dates back to the 17th century but was little used until the end of the 18th when, according to the Oxford English Dictionary, it was reacquired from French. H. J. Todd entered it as a foreign word in his edition (1818) of Johnson's Dictionary, characterizing it as "affected and useless." Around the middle of the 19th century it ceased to be considered foreign and came into considerable popular use. With popular use came a broadening of application beyond the original two meanings (here numbered 1 and 2a). In modern use both comparison and modification are widespread and standard but are confined to the extended senses 2b and 3. When sense 1 or sense 2a is intended, *unique* is used without qualifying modifiers.

¹uni·sex \'yü-nə-ˌseks\ *n* (1966) : the state or condition of not being distinguishable (as by hair or clothing) as to sex

²unisex *adj* (1968) **1** : not distinguishable as male or female ⟨a ~ face⟩ **2** : suitable or designed for both males and females ⟨~ clothes⟩

uni·sex·u·al \ˌyü-nə-'sek-sh(ə-)wəl, -shəl\ *adj* (ca. 1802) **1** : of, relating to, or restricted to one sex: **a** : male or female but not hermaphroditic **b** : DICLINOUS ⟨a ~ flower⟩ **2** : UNISEX — **uni·sex·u·al·i·ty** \-ˌsek-shə-'wa-lə-tē\ *n*

uni·son \'yü-nə-sən, -nə-zən\ *n* [MF, fr. ML *unisonus* having the same sound, fr. L *uni-* + *sonus* sound — more at SOUND] (1575) **1 a** : identity in musical pitch; *specif* : the interval of a perfect prime **b** : the state of being so tuned or sounded **c** : the writing, playing, or singing of parts in a musical passage at the same pitch or in octaves **2** : a harmonious agreement or union : CONCORD — **unison** *adj* — **in unison 1** : in perfect agreement : so as to harmonize exactly **2** : at the same time : SIMULTANEOUSLY

unit \'yü-nət\ *n* [back-formation fr. *unity*] (1570) **1 a** : the first and least natural number : ONE **b** : a single quantity regarded as a whole in calculation **2** : a determinate quantity (as of length, time, heat, or value) adopted as a standard of measurement: as **a** : an amount of work used in education in calculating student credits **b** : an amount of a biologically active agent (as a drug or antigen) required to produce a specific result under strictly controlled conditions **3 a** : a single thing, person, or group that is a constituent of a whole **b** : a part of a military establishment that has a prescribed organization (as of personnel and materiel) **c** : a piece or complex of apparatus serving to perform one particular function **d** : a part of a school course focusing on a central theme **e** : a local congregation of Jehovah's Witnesses

²unit *adj* (1844) : being, relating to, or measuring one unit

unit·age \'yü-nə-tij\ *n* (1935) **1** : specifications of the amount constituting a unit **2** : arrangement in units

uni·tard \'yü-nə-ˌtärd\ *n* [*uni-* + *leotard*] (1961) : a close-fitting one-piece garment for the torso, legs, feet, and often the arms

uni·tar·i·an \ˌyü-nə-'ter-ē-ən\ *n* [NL *unitarius*, fr. L *unitas* unity] (1687) **1 a** *often cap* : one who believes that the deity exists only in

union suit

one person **b** *cap* : a member of a denomination that stresses individual freedom of belief, the free use of reason in religion, a united world community, and liberal social action **2** : an advocate of unity or a unitary system — **unitarian** *adj, often cap* — **uni·tar·i·an·ism** \-ē-ə-,ni-zəm\ *n, often cap*

uni·tary \'yü-nə-,ter-ē\ *adj* (1861) **1 a** : of or relating to a unit **b** : based on or characterized by unity or units **2** : having the character of a unit : UNDIVIDED, WHOLE — **uni·tar·i·ly** \,yü-nə-'ter-ə-lē\ *adv*

unit cell *n* (1915) : the simplest polyhedron that embodies all the structural characteristics of and by indefinite repetition makes up the lattice of a crystal

unit character *n* (1902) : a natural character inherited on an all-or-none basis; *esp* : one dependent on the presence or absence of a single gene

unit circle *n* (1955) : a circle having a radius of 1

¹**unite** \yü-'nīt\ *vb* **unit·ed; unit·ing** [ME, fr. L *unire*, fr. *unus* one — more at ONE] *vt* (15c) **1 a** : to put together to form a single unit **b** : to cause to adhere **c** : to link by a legal or moral bond **2** : to possess (as qualities) in combination ~ *vi* **1 a** : to become one or as if one **b** : to become combined by or as if by adhesion or mixture **2** : to act in concert *syn* see JOIN — **unit·er** *n*

²**unite** \'yü-nīt\ *n* [obs. *unite* united, fr. ME *unit*, fr. LL *unitus*, pp.] (1604) : an old British gold 20-shilling piece issued first by James I in 1604 for the newly united England and Scotland — called also *Jacobus*

unit·ed \yü-'nī-təd\ *adj* (1552) **1** : made one : COMBINED **2** : relating to or produced by joint action **3** : being in agreement : HARMONIOUS — **unit·ed·ly** *adv*

United Nations Day *n* (1947) : October 24 observed in commemoration of the founding of the United Nations

Unit·ed States \yü-'nī-təd-, *esp Southern* 'yü-,\ *n pl but sing or pl in constr* (1617) **1** : a federation of states esp. when forming a nation in a usu. specified territory ⟨advocating a *United States* of Europe⟩

uni·tive \'yü-nə-tiv, yü-'nī-\ *adj* (1526) : characterized by or tending to produce union

unit·ize \'yü-nə-,tīz\ *vt* **-ized; -iz·ing** (1860) **1** : to form or convert into a unit **2** : to divide into units ⟨the added cost of *unitizing* bulk products⟩ — **unit·i·za·tion** \,yü-nə-tə-'zā-shən\ *n*

unit membrane *n* [fr. its being the basic structural unit of the cell] (1959) : a 3-layered membrane that consists of an inner lipid layer surrounded by a protein layer on each side

unit rule *n* (1884) : a rule under which a delegation to a national political convention casts its entire vote as a unit as determined by a majority vote

uni·trust \'yü-ni-,trəst\ *n* (1970) : a trust from which the beneficiary receives annually a fixed percentage of the fair market value of its assets

units place *n* (1937) : the place just to the left of the decimal point in a number expressed in the Arabic system of writing numbers

unit train *n* (1964) : a railway train that transports a single commodity directly from producer to consumer

unit trust *n* (1936) **1** *Brit* : MUTUAL FUND **2** : an investment company whose portfolio consists of long-term bonds that are held to maturity

uni·ty \'yü-nə-tē\ *n, pl* **-ties** [ME *unite*, fr. MF *unité*, fr. L *unitat-, unitas*, fr. *unus* one — more at ONE] (14c) **1 a** : the quality or state of not being multiple : ONENESS **b** (1) : a definite amount taken as one or for which 1 is made to stand in calculation ⟨in a table of natural sines the radius of the circle is regarded as ~⟩ (2) : IDENTITY ELEMENT **2 a** : a condition of harmony : ACCORD **b** : continuity without deviation or change (as in purpose or action) **3 a** : the quality or state of being made one : UNIFICATION **b** : a combination or ordering of parts in a literary or artistic production that constitutes a whole or promotes an undivided total effect; *also* : the resulting singleness of effect or symmetry and consistency of style and character **4** : a totality of related parts : an entity that is a complex or systematic whole **5** : any of three principles of dramatic structure derived by French classicists from Aristotle's *Poetics* and requiring a play to have a single action represented as occurring in one place and within one day **6** *cap* : a 20th century American religious movement that emphasizes spiritual sources of health and prosperity

¹**uni·va·lent** \,yü-ni-'vā-lənt\ *adj* (1898) **1** : MONOVALENT 1 **2** : being a chromosomal univalent

²**univalent** *n* (1912) : a chromosome that lacks a synaptic mate

uni·valve \'yü-ni-,valv\ *n* (1668) **1** : a mollusk with a shell consisting of one valve; *esp* : GASTROPOD **2** : the shell of a univalve — **univalve** *adj*

uni·var·i·ate \,yü-ni-'ver-ē-ət, -'var-\ *adj* (1928) : characterized by or depending on only one random variable ⟨a ~ linear model⟩

¹**uni·ver·sal** \,yü-nə-'vər-səl\ *adj* [ME, fr. MF, fr. L *universalis*, fr. *universum* universe] (14c) **1** : including or covering all or a whole collectively or distributively without limit or exception **2 a** : present or occurring everywhere **b** : existent or operative everywhere or under all conditions ⟨~ cultural patterns⟩ **3 a** : embracing a major part or the greatest portion (as of mankind) ⟨a ~ state⟩ ⟨~ practices⟩ **b** : comprehensively broad and versatile ⟨a ~ genius⟩ **4 a** : affirming or denying something of all members of a class or of all values of a variable **b** : denoting every member of a class ⟨a ~ term⟩ **5** : adapted or adjustable to meet varied requirements (as of use, shape, or size) ⟨a ~ gear cutter⟩ — **uni·ver·sal·ly** \-s(ə-)lē\ *adv* — **uni·ver·sal·ness** \-səl-nəs\ *n*

²**universal** *n* (1553) **1** : one that is universal: as **a** : a universal proposition in logic **b** : a predicable of traditional logic **c** : a general concept or term or something in reality to which it corresponds : ESSENCE **2 a** : a behavior pattern or institution (as the family) existing in all cultures **b** : a culture trait characteristic of all normal adult members of a particular society

universal donor *n* (1922) : a person who belongs to ABO blood group O and can donate blood to any recipient

universal grammar *n* (1751) : the study of general principles believed to underlie the grammatical phenomena of all languages; *also* : such principles viewed as part of an innate human capacity for learning a language

uni·ver·sal·ism \,yü-nə-'vər-sə-,li-zəm\ *n* (1805) **1** *often cap* **a** : a theological doctrine that all human beings will eventually be saved **b** : the principles and practices of a liberal Christian denomination founded in the 18th century orig. to uphold belief in universal salvation

and now united with Unitarianism **2** : something that is universal in scope **3** : the state of being universal : UNIVERSALITY — **uni·ver·sal·ist** \-s(ə-)list\ *n or adj, often cap*

uni·ver·sal·is·tic \-,vər-sə-'lis-tik\ *adj* (1872) : of or relating to the whole : universal in scope or nature

uni·ver·sal·i·ty \-(,)vər-'sa-lə-tē\ *n* (14c) **1** : the quality or state of being universal **2** : universal comprehensiveness in range

uni·ver·sal·ize \-'vər-sə-,līz\ *vt* **-ized; -iz·ing** (1642) : to make universal : GENERALIZE — **uni·ver·sal·i·za·tion** \-,vər-sə-lə-'zā-shən\ *n*

universal joint *n* (1676) : a shaft coupling capable of transmitting rotation from one shaft to another not collinear with it — called also *universal coupling*

universal motor *n* (1925) : an electric motor that can be used on either an alternating or a direct current supply

Universal Product Code *n* (1974) : a combination of a bar code and numbers by which a scanner can identify a product and usu. assign a price

universal joint

universal recipient *n* (1922) : a person who belongs to ABO blood group AB and can receive blood from any donor

Universal time *n* (1882) : GREENWICH MEAN TIME

uni·verse \'yü-nə-,vərs\ *n* [L *universum*, fr. neut. of *universus* entire, whole, fr. *uni-* + *versus* turned toward, fr. pp. of *vertere* to turn — more at WORTH] (1589) **1** : the whole body of things and phenomena observed or postulated : COSMOS: as **a** : a systematic whole held to arise by and persist through the direct intervention of divine power **b** : the world of human experience **c** (1) : the entire celestial cosmos (2) : MILKY WAY GALAXY (3) : an aggregate of stars comparable to the Milky Way galaxy **2** : a distinct field or province of thought or reality that forms a closed system or self-inclusive and independent organization **3** : POPULATION 4 **4** : a set that contains all elements relevant to a particular discussion or problem **5** : a great number or quantity ⟨a large enough ~ of stocks . . . to choose from —G. B. Clairmont⟩

universe of discourse (1881) : an inclusive class of entities that is tacitly implied or explicitly delineated as the subject of a statement, discourse, or theory

uni·ver·si·ty \,yü-nə-'vər-sə-tē, -'vər-stē\ *n, pl* **-ties** [ME *universite*, MF *université*, fr. ML *universitat-, universitas*, fr. L *universus*] (14c) **1** : an institution of higher learning providing facilities for teaching and research and authorized to grant academic degrees; *specif* : one made up of an undergraduate division which confers bachelor's degrees and a graduate division which comprises a graduate school and professional schools each of which may confer master's degrees and doctorates **2** : the physical plant of a university

univ·o·cal \yü-'ni-və-kəl\ *adj* [LL *univocus*, fr. L *uni-* + *voc-, vox* voice — more at VOICE] (1599) : having one meaning only — **univ·o·cal·ly** \-k(ə-)lē\ *adv*

un·joined \,ən-'jóind\ *adj* (1538) : not joined

un·just \,ən-'jəst\ *adj* (14c) **1** : characterized by injustice : UNFAIR **2** *archaic* : DISHONEST, FAITHLESS — **un·just·ly** *adv* — **un·just·ness** \-'jəs(t)-nəs\ *n*

un·kempt \-'kem(p)t\ *adj* [*un-* + *kempt* combed, neat] (1579) **1** : deficient in order or neatness ⟨~ individuals⟩ ⟨~ hotel rooms⟩; *also* : ROUGH, UNPOLISHED ⟨~ prose⟩ **2** : not combed ⟨~ hair⟩

un·kenned \-'kend\ *adj* (14c) *chiefly dial* : UNKNOWN, STRANGE

un·ken·nel \-'ke-nᵊl\ *vt* (1575) **1 a** : to drive (as a fox) from a hiding place or den **b** : to free (dogs) from a kennel **2** : to bring out into the open : UNCOVER

un·kind \-'kīnd\ *adj* (13c) **1** : not pleasing or mild : INCLEMENT ⟨an ~ climate⟩ **2** : lacking in kindness or sympathy : HARSH, CRUEL — **un·kind·ness** \-'kīn(d)-nəs\ *n*

¹**un·kind·ly** \-'kīn(d)-lē\ *adj* (13c) : not kindly — **un·kind·li·ness** *n*

²**unkindly** *adv* (14c) : in an unkind manner ⟨dwells ~ long on his final decline —A. H. Johnston⟩

un·kink \,ən-'kiŋk\ *vt* (1891) : to free from kinks : STRAIGHTEN ~ *vi* : to become lax or loose : RELAX

un·knit \-'nit\ *vb* **-knit** *or* **-knit·ted; -knit·ting** (bef. 12c) : UNDO, UNRAVEL

un·know·able \,ən-'nō-ə-bəl\ *adj* (14c) : not knowable; *esp* : lying beyond the limits of human experience or understanding — **un·know·abil·i·ty** \-,nō-ə-'bi-lə-tē\ *n*

¹**un·know·ing** \-'nō-iŋ\ *adj* (14c) : not knowing — **un·know·ing·ly** \-iŋ-lē\ *adv*

²**unknowing** *n* (14c) : IGNORANCE

¹**un·known** \-'nōn\ *adj* (14c) : not known or not well-known; *also* : having an unknown value ⟨an ~ quantity⟩

²**unknown** *n* (1597) **1** : one that is not known or not well-known; *esp* : a person who is little known (as to the public) **2** : something that requires discovery, indentification, or clarification: as **a** : a symbol (as *x, y,* or *z*) in a mathematical equation representing an unknown quantity **b** : a specimen (as of bacteria or mixed chemicals) required to be identified as an exercise in appropriate laboratory techniques

Unknown Soldier *n* (1923) : an unidentified soldier whose body is selected to receive national honors as a representative of all of the same nation who died in a war and esp. in one of the world wars

un·lace \,ən-'lās\ *vt* (14c) **1** : to loose by undoing a lacing **2** *obs* : UNDO, DISGRACE

un·lade \-'lād\ *vb* **-lad·ed; -laded** *or* **-lad·en** \-'lā-dᵊn\ **-lad·ing** *vt* (14c) **1** : to take the load or cargo from **2** : DISCHARGE, UNLOAD ~ *vi* : to discharge cargo

un·lash \-'lash\ *vt* (1748) : to untie the lashing of

un·latch \-'lach\ *vt* (1642) : to open or loose by lifting the latch ~ *vi* : to become loosed or opened

---

\ə\ abut \ᵊ\ kitten, F table \ər\ further \a\ ash \ā\ ace \ä\ mop, mar
\aú\ out \ch\ chin \e\ bet \ē\ easy \g\ go \i\ hit \ī\ ice \j\ job
\ŋ\ sing \ō\ go \ò\ law \òi\ boy \th\ thin \th\ the \ü\ loot \ú\ foot
\y\ yet \zh\ vision \ä, k̲, ⁿ, œ, œ̄, ue, ue̅, ᵞ\ see Guide to Pronunciation

un·law·ful \,ən-'lȯ-fəl\ adj (14c) 1 : not lawful : ILLEGAL 2 : not morally right or conventional — **un·law·ful·ly** \-f(ə-)lē\ adv — **un·law·ful·ness** n

un·lay \-'lā\ vb -**laid** \-'lād\; **-lay·ing** vt (1726) : to untwist the strands of (as a rope) ~ vi : UNTWIST

un·lead·ed \-'le-dəd\ adj (ca. 1891) 1 : not having leads between the lines in printing 2 : not treated or mixed with lead or lead compounds ⟨~ fuels⟩

un·learn \-'lərn\ vt (15c) 1 : to put out of one's knowledge or memory 2 : to undo the effect of : discard the habit of

un·learned \-'lər-nəd for 1, 2, -'lərnd for 3\ adj (15c) 1 : possessing inadequate learning or education; esp : deficient in scholarly attainments 2 : characterized by or revealing ignorance 3 : not gained by study or training syn see IGNORANT

un·leash \-'lēsh\ vt (ca. 1671) : to free from or as if from a leash : let loose

¹**un·less** \ən-'les, 'ən-,\ conj [ME unlesse, alter. of onlesse, fr. on + lesse less] (1509) 1 : except on the condition that : under any other circumstance than 2 : without the accompanying circumstance or condition that : but that : BUT

²**unless** prep (ca. 1532) : except possibly : EXCEPT

un·let·tered \,ən-'le-tərd\ adj (14c) 1 a : lacking facility in reading and writing and ignorant of the knowledge to be gained from books b : ILLITERATE 2 : not marked with letters syn see IGNORANT

un·licked \-'likt\ adj (1593) 1 : lacking proper form or shape 2 archaic : not licked dry

¹**un·like** \-'līk\ adj (13c) : not like: as a : marked by lack of resemblance ⟨the two books are quite ~⟩ b : marked by inequality : UNEQUAL ⟨contributed ~ amounts⟩ — **un·like·ness** n

²**unlike** prep (1593) : not like: as a : different from b : not characteristic of c : in a different manner from

un·like·li·hood \,ən-'lī-klē-,hùd\ n (1548) 1 : IMPROBABILITY 2 : something unlikely

un·like·li·ness \-nəs\ n (1614) : IMPROBABILITY

un·like·ly \-'lī-klē\ adj (14c) 1 : not likely : IMPROBABLE 2 : likely to fail : UNPROMISING

un·lim·ber \,ən-'lim-bər\ vt (1802) 1 : to detach the limber from and so make ready ⟨~ a gun for action⟩ 2 : to prepare for operation or performance ⟨~ed his banjo and began to play⟩ ~ vi : to perform the task of preparing something for action

un·lim·it·ed \-'li-mə-təd\ adj (15c) 1 : lacking any controls : UNRESTRICTED 2 : BOUNDLESS, INFINITE 3 : not bounded by exceptions : UNDEFINED — **un·lim·it·ed·ly** adv

un·link \-'liŋk\ vt (1600) : to unfasten the links of : SEPARATE, DISCONNECT ~ vi : to become detached

un·linked \-'liŋ(k)t\ adj (1966) : not belonging to the same genetic linkage group ⟨~ genes⟩

un·list·ed \-'lis-təd\ adj (1644) 1 : not appearing on a list; esp : not appearing in a telephone book ⟨~ numbers⟩ 2 : being or involving a security not listed formally on an organized exchange : OVER-THE-COUNTER

un·live \-'liv\ vt (1614) : ANNUL, REVERSE

un·load \,ən-'lōd\ vt (1523) 1 a (1) : to take off : DELIVER (2) : to take the cargo from b : to give outlet to : pour forth ⟨~ed her bitter feelings⟩ 2 : to relieve of something burdensome, unwanted, or oppressive ⟨~ed the pack animals⟩ ⟨~ed himself to his friend⟩ 3 : to draw the charge from ⟨~ed the gun⟩ 4 : to sell or dispose of esp. in large quantities : DUMP 5 : to hit or propel with a great release of power ⟨~ed his ninth homer⟩ ~ vi 1 : to perform the act of unloading 2 : to release or deliver something esp. with power ⟨~ed on the ball⟩ — **un·load·er** n

un·lock \-'läk\ vt (15c) 1 : to unfasten the lock of 2 : OPEN, UNDO 3 : to free from restraints or restrictions ⟨the shock ~ed a flood of tears⟩ 4 : to furnish a key to : DISCLOSE ~ vi : to become unfastened or freed from restraints

un·looked-for \-'lùkt-,fȯr\ adj (1535) : not foreseen : UNEXPECTED

un·loose \,ən-'lüs\ vt (14c) 1 : to relax the strain of ⟨~ a grip⟩ 2 : to release from or as if from restraints : set free 3 : to loosen the ties of ⟨~ traditional social bonds⟩

un·loos·en \-'lü-sᵊn\ vt (15c) : UNLOOSE

un·love·ly \-'ləv-lē\ adj (14c) : not likable : DISAGREEABLE, UNPLEASANT — **un·love·li·ness** \-lē-nəs\ n

un·luck·i·ly \,ən-'lə-kə-lē\ adv (1530) : UNFORTUNATELY ⟨~, it has a nasty way of turning to rain —Ambrose Bierce⟩ ⟨his ascent being ~ a little out of the perpendicular —T. L. Peacock⟩

un·lucky \-'lə-kē\ adj (1530) 1 : marked by adversity or failure ⟨an ~ year⟩ 2 : likely to bring misfortune : INAUSPICIOUS 3 : having or meeting with bad luck ⟨~ people⟩ 4 : producing dissatisfaction : REGRETTABLE — **un·luck·i·ness** \-'lə-kē-nəs\ n

un·made \,ən-'mād\ adj (13c) : not made ⟨an ~ bed⟩

un·make \-'māk\ vt -**made** \-'mād\; -**mak·ing** (15c) 1 : to cause to disappear : DESTROY 2 : to deprive of rank or office : DEPOSE 3 : to deprive of essential characteristics : change the nature of

un·man \,ən-'man\ vt (ca. 1600) 1 : to deprive of manly vigor, fortitude, or spirit 2 : CASTRATE, EMASCULATE syn see UNNERVE

un·man·ly \-'man-lē\ adj (ca. 1547) : not manly: as a : being of weak character : COWARDLY b : EFFEMINATE — **un·man·li·ness** \-lē-nəs\ n

un·manned \-'mand\ adj (1544) 1 : not manned ⟨an ~ spaceflight⟩ 2 of a hawk : not trained

un·man·nered \-'ma-nərd\ adj (1594) 1 : marked by a lack of good manners : RUDE 2 : characterized by an absence of artificiality : UNAFFECTED — **un·man·nered·ly** adv

¹**un·man·ner·ly** \-'ma-nər-lē\ adv (14c) : in an unmannerly fashion

²**unmannerly** adj (14c) : not mannerly : DISCOURTEOUS — **un·man·ner·li·ness** \-lē-nəs\ n

un·mar·ried \-'mar-ēd\ adj (14c) : not married: a : not now or previously married b : being divorced or widowed — **unmarried** n

un·mask \,ən-'mask\ vt (1602) 1 : to remove a mask from 2 : to reveal the true nature of : EXPOSE ~ vi : to remove one's mask

un·mean·ing \-'mē-niŋ\ adj (1704) 1 : lacking intelligence : VAPID 2 : having no meaning : SENSELESS

un·me·di·at·ed \,ən-'mē-dē-,ā-təd\ adj (1648) : not mediated : not communicated or transformed by an intervening agency ⟨experience ~ by artifice⟩

un·meet \-'mēt\ adj (ca. 1529) : not meet : UNSUITABLE, IMPROPER

¹**un·men·tion·able** \-'men(t)-sh(ə-)nə-bəl\ adj (1837) : not fit or allowed to be mentioned or discussed : UNSPEAKABLE

²**unmentionable** n (1928) : one that is not to be mentioned or discussed: as a pl : ³PANT 1 b pl : UNDERWEAR

un·mer·ci·ful \-'mər-si-fəl\ adj (15c) 1 : not merciful : MERCILESS 2 : EXCESSIVE, EXTREME ⟨chatted for an ~ length of time⟩ — **un·mer·ci·ful·ly** \-f(ə-)lē\ adv

un·mind·ful \-'mīn(d)-fəl\ adj (14c) : not conscientiously aware, attentive, or heedful : INATTENTIVE, CARELESS

un·mis·tak·able \,ən-mə-'stā-kə-bəl\ adj (1666) : not capable of being mistaken or misunderstood : CLEAR — **un·mis·tak·ably** \-blē\ adv

un·mit·i·gat·ed \,ən-'mi-tə-,gā-təd\ adj (1599) 1 : not lessened : UNRELIEVED ⟨sufferings ~ by any hope of early relief⟩ 2 : being so definitely what is stated as to offer little chance of change or relief ⟨an ~ evil⟩ — **un·mit·i·gat·ed·ly** adv — **un·mit·i·gat·ed·ness** n

un·mold \,ən-'mōld\ vt (ca. 1900) : to remove from a mold

un·moor \-'mùr\ vt (15c) : to loosen from or as if from moorings ~ vi : to cast off moorings

un·mor·al \-'mȯr-əl, -'mär-\ adj (1841) 1 : having no moral perception or quality; also : not influenced or guided by moral considerations 2 : lying outside the bounds of morals or ethics : AMORAL — **un·mo·ral·i·ty** \,ən-mə-'ra-lə-tē, -mȯ-\ n

un·muf·fle \,ən-'mə-fəl\ vt (1611) : to free from something that muffles

un·muz·zle \-'mə-zəl\ vt (1601) : to free from or as if from a muzzle

un·my·elin·at·ed \-'mī-ə-lə-,nā-təd\ adj (1919) : lacking a myelin sheath

un·nail \,ən-'nā(ə)l\ vt (15c) : to unfasten by removing nails

un·nat·u·ral \,ən-'na-chə-rəl, -'nach-rəl\ adj (15c) 1 : not being in accordance with nature or consistent with a normal course of events 2 a : not being in accordance with normal human feelings or behavior : PERVERSE b : lacking ease and naturalness : CONTRIVED ⟨her manner was forced and ~⟩ c : inconsistent with what is reasonable or expected ⟨an ~ alliance⟩ syn see IRREGULAR — **un·nat·u·ral·ly** \-'na-chə-rə-lē, -'nach-rə-, -'na-chər-\ adv — **un·nat·u·ral·ness** \-'na-chə-rəl-nəs, -'nach-rəl-\ n

un·nec·es·sar·i·ly \,ən-,ne-sə-'ser-ə-lē\ adv (1594) : not by necessity : to an unnecessary degree

un·nec·es·sary \,ən-'ne-sə-,ser-ē\ adj (1548) : not necessary

un·nerve \-'nərv\ vt (1601) 1 : to deprive of courage, strength, or steadiness 2 : to cause to become nervous : UPSET — **un·nerv·ing·ly** \-'nər-viŋ-lē\ adv

syn UNNERVE, ENERVATE, UNMAN, EMASCULATE mean to deprive of strength or vigor and the capacity for effective action. UNNERVE implies marked often temporary loss of courage, self-control, or power to act ⟨unnerved by the near collision⟩. ENERVATE suggests a gradual physical or moral weakening (as through luxury or indolence) until one is too feeble to make an effort ⟨a nation's youth enervated by affluence and leisure⟩. UNMAN implies a loss of manly vigor, fortitude, or spirit ⟨a soldier unmanned by the terrors of battle⟩. EMASCULATE stresses a depriving of characteristic force by removing something essential ⟨an amendment that emasculates existing safeguards⟩.

un·nil·hex·i·um \,yü-n²l-'hek-sē-əm\ n [NL, fr. unnil- (fr. L unus one + nil nothing, zero) + Gk hex six + NL -ium — more at ONE, NIL, SIX] (1981) : the chemical element of atomic number 106 — see ELEMENT table

un·nil·pen·ti·um \-'pen-tē-əm\ n [NL, fr. unnil- + Gk pente five + NL -ium — more at FIVE] (1981) : the chemical element of atomic number 105 — see ELEMENT table

un·nil·qua·di·um \-'kwä-dē-əm\ n [NL, fr. unnil- + quadri- + -ium] (1979) : the chemical element of atomic number 104 — see ELEMENT table

un·num·bered \,ən-'nəm-bərd\ adj (14c) 1 : INNUMERABLE 2 : not having an identifying number ⟨~ pages⟩

un·ob·tru·sive \,ən-əb-'trü-siv, -ziv\ adj (1743) : not obtrusive : not blatant, arresting, or aggressive : INCONSPICUOUS — **un·ob·tru·sive·ly** adv — **un·ob·tru·sive·ness** n

un·oc·cu·pied \,ən-'ä-kyə-,pīd\ adj (14c) : not occupied: as a : not busy : UNEMPLOYED b : not lived in : EMPTY

un·or·ga·nized \-'ȯr-gə-,nīzd\ adj (ca. 1828) 1 : not organized: as a : not brought into a coherent or well-ordered whole b : not belonging to a labor union 2 : not having the characteristics of a living organism

un·or·tho·dox \-'ȯr-thə-,däks\ adj (1657) : not orthodox — **un·or·tho·dox·ly** adv

un·or·tho·doxy \-,däk-sē\ n (ca. 1704) 1 : the quality or state of being unorthodox 2 : something (as an opinion or doctrine) that is unorthodox

un·pack \,ən-'pak\ vt (15c) 1 a : to remove the contents of ⟨~ a trunk⟩ b : UNBURDEN, REVEAL ⟨must . . . ~ my heart with words —Shak.⟩ 2 : to remove or undo from packing or a container ⟨~ed his gear⟩ 3 : to analyze the nature of by examining in detail : EXPLICATE ⟨~ a concept⟩ ~ vi : to engage in unpacking a container — **un·pack·er** n

un·paged \-'pājd\ adj (1874) : having no page numbers

un·paid \-'pād\ adj (14c) 1 : not paid ⟨an ~ volunteer⟩ 2 : not paying a salary ⟨an ~ position⟩

un·paired \-'pard, -'perd\ adj (1648) 1 : not paired; esp : not matched or mated 2 : characterized by the absence of pairing ⟨electrons in the ~ state⟩

un·pal·at·able \-'pa-lə-tə-bəl\ adj (1682) 1 : not palatable : DISTASTEFUL 2 : UNPLEASANT, DISAGREEABLE — **un·pal·at·abil·i·ty** \,ən-,pa-lə-tə-'bi-lə-tē\ n

un·par·al·leled \,ən-'par-ə-,leld, -,ləld\ adj (1594) : having no parallel; esp : having no equal or match : unique in kind or quality

un·par·lia·men·ta·ry \,ən-,pär-lə-'men-tə-rē, -,pärl-yə-, -'men-trē\ adj (1626) : contrary to the practice of parliamentary bodies

un·peg \,ən-'peg\ vt (1602) 1 : to remove a peg from 2 : to unfasten by or as if by removing a peg

un·peo·ple \-'pē-pəl\ vt (ca. 1533) : DEPOPULATE

un·peo·pled \,ən-'pē-pəld\ adj (1586) : not filled with or occupied by people

un·per·fect \-'pər-fikt\ adj (14c) : IMPERFECT

un·per·son \'ən-'pər-s²n, -,pər-\ *n* (1949) : an individual who usu. for political or ideological reasons is removed completely from recognition or consideration

un·pick \,ən-'pik\ *vt* (ca. 1775) : to undo (as sewing) by taking out stitches

un·pile \-'pī(ə)l\ *vt* (1611) : to take or disentangle from a pile

un·pin \-'pin\ *vt* (14c) **1** : to remove a pin from **2** : to loosen, free, or unfasten by or as if by removing a pin

un·placed \,ən-'plāst\ *adj* (1512) **1** : not placed : not having a definite or assigned place ⟨taxonomically ~ organisms⟩ **2** : not finishing in one of the first three places in a horse race

un·pleas·ant \-'plez²nt\ *adj* (1538) : not pleasant : not amiable or agreeable : DISPLEASING ⟨~ odors⟩ — **un·pleas·ant·ly** *adv*

un·pleas·ant·ness *n* (1548) **1** : the quality or state of being unpleasant **2** : an unpleasant situation, experience, or event

un·plug \,ən-'pləg\ *vt* (ca. 1775) **1 a** : to take a plug out of **b** : to remove an obstruction from **2 a** : to remove (as an electric plug) from a socket or receptacle **b** : to disconnect from an electric circuit by removing a plug ⟨~ the refrigerator⟩

un·plumbed \-'pləmd\ *adj* (1623) **1** : not tested with a plumb line **2 a** : not measured with a plumb **b** : not thoroughly explored

un·po·lar·ized \-'pō-lə-,rīzd\ *adj* (ca. 1828) : not polarized; *specif* : having a random pattern of vibrations

un·po·lit·i·cal \,ən-pə-'li-ti-kəl\ *adj* (1643) : APOLITICAL 1

un·pop·u·lar \,ən-'pä-pyə-lər\ *adj* (1647) : not popular : viewed or received unfavorably by the public — **un·pop·u·lar·i·ty** \,ən-,pä-pyə-'lar-ə-tē\ *n*

un·prec·e·dent·ed \,ən-'pre-sə-,den-təd\ *adj* (1623) : having no precedent : NOVEL, UNEXAMPLED — **un·prec·e·dent·ed·ly** *adv*

un·preg·nant \,ən-'preg-nənt\ *adj* (1602) *obs* : INEPT 1

un·pre·tend·ing \,ən-pri-'ten-diŋ\ *adj* (1697) : UNPRETENTIOUS

un·pre·ten·tious \-'ten(t)-shəs\ *adj* (1859) : free from ostentation, elegance, or affectation : MODEST ⟨~ homes⟩ — **un·pre·ten·tious·ly** *adv* — **un·pre·ten·tious·ness** *n*

un·prin·ci·pled \,ən-'prin(t)-s(ə-)pəld, -sə-bəld\ *adj* (1644) : lacking moral principles : UNSCRUPULOUS — **un·prin·ci·pled·ness** *n*

un·print·able \-'prin-tə-bəl\ *adj* (1871) : unfit to be printed

un·pro·fessed \,ən-prə-'fest\ *adj* (15c) : not professed ⟨an ~ aim⟩

un·prof·it·able \,ən-'prä-fə-tə-bəl, -'präf-tə-bəl\ *adj* (14c) : not profitable : producing no gain, good, or result — **un·prof·it·able·ness** *n* — **un·prof·it·ably** \-blē\ *adv*

un·prom·is·ing \-'prä-mə-siŋ\ *adj* (1663) : appearing unlikely to prove worthwhile or result favorably — **un·prom·is·ing·ly** \-siŋ-lē\ *adv*

un·pro·nounced \,ən-prə-'naún(t)st\ *adj* (1611) : not pronounced; *esp* : MUTE

un·pub·lish·able \-'pə-bli-shə-bəl\ *adj* (1815) : UNPRINTABLE

un·qual·i·fied \,ən-'kwä-lə-,fīd\ *adj* (1556) **1** : not fit : not having requisite qualifications **2** : not modified or restricted by reservations : COMPLETE ⟨an ~ denial⟩ — **un·qual·i·fied·ly** \-,fī(-ə)d-lē\ *adv*

un·ques·tion·able \-'kwes-chə-nə-bəl, -'kwesh-\ *adj* (1631) : not questionable : INDISPUTABLE ⟨~ evidence⟩ — **un·ques·tion·ably** \-blē\ *adv*

un·ques·tion·ing \-'kwes-chə-niŋ, -'kwesh-\ *adj* (ca. 1828) : not questioning : not expressing or marked by doubt or hesitation ⟨~ obedience⟩ — **un·ques·tion·ing·ly** \-niŋ-lē\ *adv*

un·qui·et \-'kwī-ət\ *adj* (1523) **1** : not quiet : AGITATED, TURBULENT **2** : physically, emotionally, or mentally restless : UNEASY — **un·qui·et·ly** *adv* — **un·qui·et·ness** *n*

un·quote \'ən-,kwōt *also* -,kōt\ *n* (1915) — used orally to indicate the end of a direct quotation

un·rav·el \,ən-'ra-vəl\ *vt* (1603) **1 a** : to disengage or separate the threads of : DISENTANGLE **b** : to cause to come apart by or as if by separating the threads of **2** : to resolve the intricacy, complexity, or obscurity of : clear up ⟨~ a mystery⟩ ~ *vi* **1** : to become unraveled **2** : to fall apart

un·read \-'red\ *adj* (15c) **1** : not read : left unexamined **2** : lacking the experience or the benefits of reading ⟨~ in political science⟩

un·re·al \-'rē(-ə)l, -'ri(-ə)l\ *adj* (1605) : lacking in reality, substance, or genuineness : ARTIFICIAL, ILLUSORY; *also* : INCREDIBLE, FANTASTIC

un·re·al·is·tic \,ən-,rē-ə-'lis-tik\ *adj* (1865) : not realistic : inappropriate to reality or fact — **un·re·al·is·ti·cal·ly** \-ti-k(ə-)lē\ *adv*

un·re·al·i·ty \,ən-rē-'a-lə-tē\ *n* (1751) **1 a** : the quality or state of being unreal : lack of substance or validity **b** : something unreal, insubstantial, or visionary : FIGMENT **2** : ineptitude in dealing with reality

un·rea·son \,ən-'rē-z²n, 'ən-,\ *n* (1827) : the absence of reason or sanity : IRRATIONALITY, MADNESS

un·rea·son·able \-'rēz-nə-bəl, -'rē-z²n-ə-bəl\ *adj* (14c) **1 a** : not governed by or acting according to reason ⟨~ people⟩ **b** : not conformable to reason : ABSURD ⟨~ beliefs⟩ **2** : exceeding the bounds of reason or moderation ⟨working under ~ pressure⟩ — **un·rea·son·able·ness** \-nəs\ *n* — **un·rea·son·ably** \-blē\ *adv*

un·rea·soned \-'rē-z²nd\ *adj* (1790) : not founded on reason or reasoning

un·rea·son·ing \-'rēz-niŋ, -'rē-z²n-iŋ\ *adj* (1751) : not reasoning; *esp* : not moderated or controlled by reason ⟨~ fear⟩ — **un·rea·son·ing·ly** \-'rēz-niŋ-lē, -'rē-z²n-iŋ-lē\ *adv*

un·re·con·struct·ed \,ən-,rē-kən-'strək-təd\ *adj* (1867) : not reconciled to some political, economic, or social change ⟨an ~ rebel⟩; *also* : holding stubbornly to a particular belief, view, place, or style ⟨an ~ New Yorker⟩

un·reel \,ən-'rē(ə)l\ *vt* (1567) **1** : to unwind from a reel **2** : to perform successfully ⟨~ed a 66-yard pass play⟩ **3** : REEL OFF 2 ~ *vi* **1** : to become unwound **2** : to be presented ⟨the dress rehearsal ~ed flawlessly⟩

un·reeve \-'rēv\ *vt* **-rove** \-'rōv\ *or* **-reeved; -reev·ing** (1600) : to withdraw (a rope) from an opening (as a ship's block or thimble)

un·re·gen·er·ate \,ən-ri-'je-nə-rət, -'jen-rət\ *adj* (1589) **1** : not regenerate ⟨the ~ condition of humanity⟩ ⟨~ pagans⟩ **2 a** : not reformed : UNRECONSTRUCTED ⟨~ liberals⟩ ⟨~ Confederates⟩ **b** : OBSTINATE, STUBBORN ⟨struggling against ~ impulses⟩ ⟨his ~ competitiveness⟩ — **un·re·gen·er·ate·ly** *adv*

un·re·lent·ing \-'len-tiŋ\ *adj* (1588) **1** : not softening or yielding in determination : HARD, STERN ⟨an ~ leader⟩ **2** : not letting up or weakening in vigor or pace : CONSTANT ⟨the ~ struggle⟩ — **un·re·lent·ing·ly** \-tiŋ-lē\ *adv*

un·re·marked \-'märkt\ *adj* (ca. 1775) : not remarked : UNNOTICED

un·re·mit·ting \-'mi-tiŋ\ *adj* (1728) : not remitting : CONSTANT, INCESSANT — **un·re·mit·ting·ly** \-tiŋ-lē\ *adv*

un·re·quit·ed \,ən-ri-'kwī-təd\ *adj* (ca. 1542) : not requited : not reciprocated or returned in kind ⟨~ love⟩

un·re·serve \-'zərv\ *n* (1751) : absence of reserve : FRANKNESS

un·re·served \-'zərvd\ *adj* (1539) **1** : not limited or partial : ENTIRE, UNQUALIFIED ⟨~ enthusiasm⟩ **2** : not cautious or reticent : FRANK, OPEN **3** : not set aside for special use — **un·re·serv·ed·ly** \-'zər-vəd-lē\ *adv* — **un·re·served·ness** \-'zər-vəd-nəs, -'zərvd-nəs\ *n*

un·rest \,ən-'rest\ *n* (14c) : a disturbed or uneasy state : TURMOIL

un·re·strained \,ən-ri-'strānd\ *adj* (ca. 1600) **1** : not restrained : IMMODERATE, UNCONTROLLED ⟨~ proliferation of technology⟩ **2** : free of constraint : SPONTANEOUS ⟨felt happy and ~⟩ — **un·re·strain·ed·ly** \-'strā-nəd-lē\ *adv* — **un·re·strained·ness** \-'strā-nəd-nəs, -'strān(d)-nəs\ *n*

un·re·straint \-'strānt\ *n* (1804) : freedom from or lack of restraint

un·rid·dle \,ən-'ri-d²l\ *vt* (ca. 1586) : to find the explanation of : FIGURE OUT, SOLVE ⟨~ a puzzle⟩ ⟨no trouble *unriddling* three-part syllogisms —*New Yorker*⟩ *also* : to make understandable : EXPLAIN ⟨just trying to ~ the man —Helen Dudar⟩

un·rig \-'rig\ *vt* (ca. 1580) : to strip of rigging ⟨~ a ship⟩

un·righ·teous \-'rī-chəs\ *adj* (bef. 12c) **1** : not righteous : SINFUL, WICKED **2** : UNJUST, UNMERITED ⟨intolerable and ~ interference in their lives —W. W. Wagar⟩ — **un·righ·teous·ly** *adv* — **un·righ·teous·ness** *n*

un·ripe \-'rīp\ *adj* (13c) **1** : not ripe : IMMATURE **2** : not ready : UNPREPARED — **un·ripe·ness** *n*

un·ri·valed *or* **un·ri·valled** \,ən-'rī-vəld\ *adj* (1591) : having no rival : INCOMPARABLE, SUPREME

un·roll \-'rōl\ *vt* (15c) **1** : to unwind a roll of : open out : UNCOIL **2** : to spread out like a scroll for reading or inspection : UNFOLD, REVEAL ~ *vi* : to be unrolled : UNWIND

un·roof \-'rüf, -'rúf\ *vt* (1598) : to strip off the roof or covering of

¹un·round \,ən-'raúnd\ *vt* (1874) **1** : to pronounce (a sound) without lip rounding or with decreased lip rounding **2** : to spread (the lips) laterally ⟨necessary to ~ the lips in pronouncing \ē\⟩

²unround \-'raúnd\ *adj* (1958) : pronounced with the lips not rounded

un·ruf·fled \,ən-'rə-fəld\ *adj* (1659) **1** : poised and serene esp. in the face of setbacks or confusion **2** : not ruffled : SMOOTH ⟨~ water⟩ *syn* see COOL

un·ru·ly \-'rü-lē\ *adj* [ME *unreuly*, fr. *un-* + *reuly* disciplined, fr. *reule* rule] (15c) : not readily ruled, disciplined, or managed ⟨an ~ crowd⟩ ⟨a mane of ~ hair⟩ — **un·rul·i·ness** *n*

syn UNRULY, UNGOVERNABLE, INTRACTABLE, REFRACTORY, RECALCITRANT, WILLFUL, HEADSTRONG mean not submissive to government or control. UNRULY implies lack of discipline or incapacity for discipline and often connotes waywardness or turbulence of behavior ⟨*unruly* children⟩. UNGOVERNABLE implies either an escape from control or guidance or a state of being unsubdued and incapable of controlling oneself or being controlled by others ⟨*ungovernable* rage⟩. INTRACTABLE suggests stubborn resistance to guidance or control ⟨*intractable* opponents of the hazardous-waste dump⟩. REFRACTORY stresses resistance to attempts to manage or to mold ⟨special schools for *refractory* children⟩. RECALCITRANT suggests determined resistance to or defiance of authority ⟨acts of sabotage by a *recalcitrant* populace⟩. WILLFUL implies an obstinate determination to have one's own way ⟨a *willful* disregard for the rights of others⟩. HEADSTRONG suggests self-will impatient of restraint, advice, or suggestion ⟨a *headstrong* young calvary officer⟩.

un·sad·dle \,ən-'sa-d²l\ *vt* (14c) **1** : to take the saddle from **2** : to throw from the saddle ~ *vi* : to remove the saddle from a horse

un·said \-'sed\ *adj* (bef. 12c) : not said; *esp* : not spoken aloud

un·sat·is·fac·to·ry \-,sa-təs-'fak-t(ə-)rē\ *adj* (ca. 1650) : not satisfactory — **un·sat·is·fac·to·ri·ly** \-t(ə-)rə-lē\ *adv* — **un·sat·is·fac·to·ri·ness** \-t(ə-)rē-nəs\ *n*

un·sat·u·rate \-'sa-chə-rət, -'sach-rət\ *n* (1934) : an unsaturated chemical compound

un·sat·u·rat·ed \-'sa-chə-,rā-təd\ *adj* (1758) : not saturated: as **a** : capable of absorbing or dissolving more of something ⟨an ~ solution⟩ **b** : able to form products by chemical addition; *esp* : containing double or triple bonds between carbon atoms

un·saved \-'sāvd\ *adj* (1648) : not saved; *esp* : not absolved for eternal punishment : not regenerate

un·sa·vory \-'sā-və-rē, -'sāv-rē\ *adj* (13c) **1** : INSIPID, TASTELESS **2** : unpleasant to taste or smell **b** : DISAGREEABLE, DISTASTEFUL ⟨an ~ assignment⟩; *esp* : morally offensive

un·say \-'sā, Southern also -'se\ *vt* **-said** \-'sed\; **-say·ing** \-'sā-iŋ\ (15c) : to make as if not said : RECANT, RETRACT

un·say·able \-'sā-ə-bəl\ *adj* (1870) : not sayable : not easily expressed or related

un·scathed \-'skāthd\ *adj* (14c) : wholly unharmed : not injured

un·schooled \-'sküld\ *adj* (1589) **1** : not schooled : UNTAUGHT, UNTRAINED ⟨an ~ woodsman⟩ **2** : not artificial : NATURAL ⟨~ talent⟩

un·sci·en·tif·ic \,ən-,sī-ən-'ti-fik\ *adj* (ca. 1775) : not scientific: as **a** : not used in scientific work **b** : not being in accord with the principles and methods of science ⟨~ management of woodlands⟩ **c** : not showing scientific knowledge or familiarity with scientific methods — **un·sci·en·tif·i·cal·ly** \-fi-k(ə-)lē\ *adv*

un·scram·ble \,ən-'skram-bəl\ *vt* (ca. 1920) **1** : to separate (as a conglomeration or tangle) into original components : RESOLVE, CLARIFY **2** : to restore (scrambled communication) to intelligible form — **un·scram·bler** \-b(ə-)lər\ *n*

un·screw \-'skrü\ *vt* (1605) **1** : to draw the screws from **2** : to loosen or withdraw by turning ~ *vi* : to become or admit of being unscrewed

un·script·ed \-'skrip-təd\ *adj* (ca. 1950) : not following a prepared script

\ə\ abut \²\ kitten, F table \ər\ further \a\ ash \ā\ ace \ä\ mop, mar \aú\ out \ch\ chin \e\ bet \ē\ easy \g\ go \i\ hit \ī\ ice \j\ job \ŋ\ sing \ō\ go \ó\ law \ói\ boy \th\ thin \t͟h\ the \ü\ loot \ú\ foot \y\ yet \zh\ vision \á, k̲, ⁿ, œ, œ̄, ᵫ, ᵫ̄, ᵊ\ see Guide to Pronunciation

un·scru·pu·lous \-'skrü-pyə-ləs\ *adj* (1803) : not scrupulous : UN-PRINCIPLED — **un·scru·pu·lous·ly** *adv* — **un·scru·pu·lous·ness** *n*

un·seal \-'sē(ə)l\ *vt* (15c) : to break or remove the seal of : OPEN

un·sealed \-'sē(ə)ld\ *adj* (14c) : not sealed

un·seam \ˌən-'sēm\ *vt* (1592) : to open the seams of

un·search·able \-'sər-chə-bəl\ *adj* (14c) : not capable of being searched or explored : INSCRUTABLE — **un·search·ably** \-blē\ *adv*

un·sea·son·able \-'sēz-nə-bəl, -'sē-zᵊn-ə-\ *adj* (15c) **1** : occurring at other than the proper time : UNTIMELY **2** : not being in season **3 a** : not normal for the season of the year ⟨~ weather⟩ **b** : marked by unseasonable weather ⟨an ~ summer⟩ — **un·sea·son·able·ness** *n* — **un·sea·son·ably** \-blē\ *adv*

un·seat \-'sēt\ *vt* (1596) **1** : to dislodge from one's seat esp. on horse-back **2** : to remove from a place or position; *esp* : to remove from political office

¹un·seem·ly \-'sēm-lē\ *adj* (14c) : not seemly: as **a** : not according with established standards of good form or taste ⟨~ bickering⟩ **b** : not suitable for time or place : INAPPROPRIATE, UNSEASONABLE *syn* see INDECOROUS — **un·seem·li·ness** \-lē-nəs\ *n*

²unseemly *adv* (14c) : in an unseemly manner

un·seen \ˌən-'sēn\ *adj* (13c) **1** : not seen or perceived **2** : SIGHT 1 ⟨an ~ translation⟩

un·seg·re·gat·ed \-'se-gri-ˌgā-təd\ *adj* (1905) : not segregated; *esp* : free from racial segregation

un·se·lect·ed \ˌən-sə-'lek-təd\ *adj* (ca. 1891) : not selected : chosen at random

un·se·lec·tive \-'lek-tiv\ *adj* (ca. 1925) : not marked by selection : RANDOM, INDISCRIMINATE — **un·se·lec·tive·ly** \-lē\ *adv*

un·self·ish \ˌən-'sel-fish\ *adj* (1698) : not selfish : GENEROUS — **un·self·ish·ly** *adv* — **un·self·ish·ness** *n*

un·sell \-'sel\ *vt* **-sold** \-'sōld\; **-sell·ing** (ca. 1929) **1** : to dissuade from a belief in the truth, value, or desirability of something ⟨ads that ~ the public on energy consumption⟩ **2** : to discourage a belief in the truth, value, or desirability of ⟨I *unsold* the coat he wanted and sold him another⟩

un·set \-'set\ *adj* (14c) : not set: as **a** : not fixed in a setting : UN-MOUNTED ⟨~ diamonds⟩ **b** : not firmed or solidified ⟨~ concrete⟩

un·set·tle \ˌən-'set-ᵊl\ *vt* (1598) **1** : to loosen or move from a settled state or condition : make unstable : DISORDER **2** : to perturb or agi-tate mentally or emotionally : DISCOMPOSE ~ *vi* : to become unsettled

un·set·tled \-'se-tᵊld\ *adj* (1591) : not settled: as **a** (1) : not calm or tranquil : DISTURBED ⟨~ political conditions⟩ (2) : likely to vary widely esp. in the near future : VARIABLE ⟨~ weather⟩ (3) : not settled down ⟨~ dust⟩ **b** (1) : not decided or determined : DOUBTFUL ⟨an ~ state of mind⟩ (2) : not resolved or worked out : UNDECIDED ⟨an ~ question⟩ **c** : characterized by irregularity ⟨an ~ life⟩ **d** : not inhabited or pop-ulated ⟨~ land⟩ **e** : mentally unbalanced **f** (1) : not disposed of according to law ⟨an ~ estate⟩ (2) : not paid or discharged ⟨~ debts⟩ — **un·set·tled·ness** \-tᵊl(d)-nəs\ *n*

un·set·tling \ˌən-'set-liŋ, -'se-tᵊl-iŋ\ *adj* (1665) : having the effect of upsetting, disturbing, or discomposing ⟨~ images of the war⟩ — **un·set·tling·ly** \-lē\ *adv*

un·set·tle·ment \-'t²l-mənt\ *n* (1648) **1** : an act, process, or instance of unsettling **2** : the quality or state of being unsettled

un·sew \ˌən-'sō\ *vt* **-sewed; -sewn** \-'sōn\ *or* **-sewed; -sew·ing** (14c) : to undo the sewing of

un·sex \-'seks\ *vt* (1605) **1** : to deprive of sex or sexual power **2** : to deprive of the qualities typical of one's sex

un·shack·le \-'sha-kəl\ *vt* (1611) : to free from shackles

un·shaped \-'shāpt\ *adj* (1572) : not shaped: as **a** : not dressed or finished to final form ⟨an ~ timber⟩ **b** : imperfect in form or formula-tion ⟨~ ideas⟩

un·shap·en \-'shā-pən\ *adj* [ME, fr. ¹un- + *shapen*, pp. of *shapen* to shape] (14c) : UNSHAPED

un·sheathe \ˌən-'shēth\ *vt* (ca. 1542) : to draw from or as if from a sheath or scabbard

un·ship \-'ship\ *vt* (15c) **1** : to take out of a ship : DISCHARGE, UNLOAD **2** : to remove (as an oar or tiller) from position : DETACH ~ *vi* : to become or admit of being detached or removed

un·shod \ˌən-'shäd\ *adj* (bef. 12c) : not wearing or provided with shoes

¹un·sight \-'sīt\ *vt* (1615) : to prevent from seeing

²unsight *adj* (ca. 1622) : not sighted or examined

un·sight·ly \ˌən-'sīt-lē\ *adj* (15c) : not pleasing to the sight : not comely — **un·sight·li·ness** \-lē-nəs\ *n*

un·skilled \-'skild\ *adj* (1581) **1** : not skilled in a branch of work : lacking technical training ⟨an ~ worker⟩ **2** : not requiring skill ⟨~ jobs⟩ **3** : marked by lack of skill ⟨produced ~ poems⟩

un·skill·ful \-'skil-fəl\ *adj* (1565) : not skillful : lacking in skill or proficiency — **un·skill·ful·ly** \-fə-lē\ *adv* — **un·skill·ful·ness** *n*

un·slak·able \ˌən-'slā-kə-bəl\ *adj* (1820) : unable to be slaked : UN-QUENCHABLE ⟨an ~ thirst⟩ ⟨an ~ desire for excellence⟩

un·sling \-'sliŋ\ *vt* **-slung** \-'sləŋ\; **-sling·ing** \-'sliŋ-iŋ\ (1630) **1** : to take off the slings of esp. aboard ship : release from slings **2** : to re-move from being slung ⟨*unslung* the carbine⟩

un·snap \-'snap\ *vt* (1862) : to loosen or free by or as if by undoing a snap

un·snarl \-'snär(-ə)l\ *vt* (1555) : to disentangle a snarl in

un·so·cia·ble \ˌən-'sō-shə-bəl\ *adj* (1600) **1** : having or showing a disinclination for social activity : SOLITARY, RESERVED **2** : not condu-cive to sociability — **un·so·cia·bil·i·ty** \ˌən-ˌsō-shə-'bi-lə-tē\ *n* — **un·so·cia·ble·ness** \ˌən-'sō-shə-bəl-nəs\ *n* — **un·so·cia·bly** \-blē\ *adv*

un·so·cial \-'sō-shəl\ *adj* (1731) : lacking a taste or desire for society or close association; *also* : marked by or arising from such a lack ⟨an ~ disposition⟩ — **un·so·cial·ly** \-'sō-sh(ə-)lē\ *adv*

un·sold \-'sōld\ *adj* (14c) : not sold

un·so·phis·ti·cat·ed \ˌən-sə-'fis-tə-ˌkā-təd\ *adj* (1630) : not sophisti-cated: as **a** : not changed or corrupted : GENUINE **b** (1) : not world-ly-wise : lacking social or economic sophistication (2) : lacking com-plexity of structure : SIMPLE, STRAIGHTFORWARD ⟨an ~ analysis⟩ ⟨~ rhythms⟩ *syn* see NATURAL

un·so·phis·ti·ca·tion \-ˌfis-tə-'kā-shən\ *n* (1825) : lack of or freedom from sophistication

un·sought \ˌən-'sot\ *adj* (13c) : not searched for or sought out ⟨~ compliments⟩

un·sound \-'saúnd\ *adj* (14c) : not sound: as **a** : not healthy or whole **b** : not mentally normal : not wholly sane **c** : not firmly or made, placed, or fixed **d** : not valid or true : INVALID, SPECIOUS — **un·sound·ly** \-'saún(d)-lē\ *adv*

un·sound·ness \-'saún(d)-nəs\ *n* (1586) **1** : the quality or state of being unsound **2** : something (as a disease, injury, or defect) that causes one to be unsound

un·spar·ing \-'spar-iŋ, -'sper-\ *adj* (ca. 1586) **1** : not merciful or for-bearing : HARD, RUTHLESS **2** : not frugal : LIBERAL, PROFUSE — **un·spar·ing·ly** \-iŋ-lē\ *adv*

un·speak \-'spēk\ *vt* (1605) *obs* : UNSAY

un·speak·able \-'spē-kə-bəl\ *adj* (14c) **1** : incapable of being ex-pressed in words : UNUTTERABLE **b** : inexpressibly bad : HORRENDOUS **2** : that may not or cannot be spoken ⟨the bawdy thoughts that come into one's head — the words —L. P. Smith⟩ ⟨~ collections of con-sonants —Rosemary Jellis⟩ — **un·speak·ably** \-blē\ *adv*

un·sports·man·like \-'sports-mən-ˌlīk, -'sports-\ *adj* (1754) : not char-acteristic of or exhibiting good sportsmanship : not sportsmanlike

un·spot·ted \-'spä-təd\ *adj* (14c) : not spotted : free from spot or stain; *esp* : free from moral stain

un·sprung \-'sprəŋ\ *adj* (1600) : not sprung; *esp* : not equipped with springs

un·sta·ble \-'stā-bəl\ *adj* (13c) : not stable : not firm or fixed : not constant: as **a** : not steady in action or movement : IRREGULAR ⟨an ~ pulse⟩ **b** : wavering in purpose or intent : VACILLATING **c** : lacking steadiness : apt to move, sway, or fall ⟨an ~ tower⟩ **d** (1) : liable to change or alteration ⟨an ~ economy⟩ ⟨~ weather⟩ (2) : readily chang-ing (as by decomposing) in chemical composition or biological activity **e** : characterized by lack of emotional control *syn* see INCONSTANT — **un·sta·ble·ness** *n* — **un·sta·bly** \-b(ə-)lē\ *adv*

¹un·steady \ˌən-'ste-dē\ *vt* (1532) : to make unsteady

²unsteady *adj* (1598) : not steady: as **a** : not firm or solid : not fixed in position : UNSTABLE **b** : marked by change or fluctuation : CHANGE-ABLE **c** : not uniform or even : IRREGULAR — **un·stead·i·ly** \-'ste-dᵊl-ē\ *adv* — **un·stead·i·ness** \-'ste-dē-nəs\ *n*

un·step \ˌən-'step\ *vt* (1853) : to remove (a mast) from a step

un·stick \-'stik\ *vt* **-stuck** \-'stək\; **-stick·ing** (1706) : to release from a state of adhesion

un·stint·ing \-'stin-tiŋ\ *adj* (1845) : not restricting or holding back : giving or being given freely or generously ⟨an ~ volunteer⟩ ⟨~ praise⟩ — **un·stint·ing·ly** *adv*

un·stop \-'stäp\ *vt* (14c) **1** : to free from an obstruction : OPEN **2** : to remove a stopper from

un·stop·pa·ble \-'stä-pə-bəl\ *adj* (1836) : incapable of being stopped — **un·stop·pa·bly** \-blē\ *adv*

un·strap \-'strap\ *vt* (1828) : to remove or loose a strap from

un·stressed \ˌən-'strest\ *adj* (1883) **1** : not bearing a stress or accent ⟨~ syllables⟩ **2** : not subjected to stress ⟨~ wires⟩

un·string \-'striŋ\ *vt* **-strung** \-'strəŋ\; **-string·ing** \-'striŋ-iŋ\ (1611) **1** : to loosen or remove the strings of **2** : to remove from a string **3** : to make weak, disordered, or unstable ⟨was *unstrung* by the news⟩

un·struc·tured \-'strək-chərd\ *adj* (1936) : lacking structure or organi-zation: as **a** : not formally organized in a set or conventional pattern ⟨an ~ question⟩ ⟨feel insecure in an ~ situation⟩ **b** : not having a system or hierarchy typical of an organized society

un·stuck \ˌən-'stək\ *adj* (1934) : brought into a state of disarray, dis-composure, or incoherence ⟨the deal came ~⟩

un·stud·ied \-'stə-dēd\ *adj* (14c) : not studied: as **a** : not acquired by study **b** : not forced : not done or planned for effect

un·sub·stan·tial \ˌən-səb-'stan(t)-shəl\ *adj* (15c) : not substantial : lacking substance, firmness, or strength — **un·sub·stan·ti·al·i·ty** \-ˌstan(t)-shē-'a-lə-tē\ *n* — **un·sub·stan·tial·ly** \ˌən-səb-'stan(t)-sh(ə-)lē\ *adv*

un·suc·cess \ˌən-sək-'ses\ *n* (ca. 1586) : lack of success : FAILURE

un·suc·cess·ful \-fəl\ *adj* (1617) : not successful : not meeting with or producing success — **un·suc·cess·ful·ly** \-fə-lē\ *adv*

un·sung \ˌən-'səŋ\ *adj* (15c) **1** : not sung **2** : not celebrated or praised (as in song or verse) ⟨an ~ hero⟩

un·sur·pris·ing \ˌən-sə(r)-'prī-ziŋ\ *adj* (1671) : not surprising or unex-pected

un·sur·pris·ing·ly \-ziŋ-lē\ *adv* (1950) **1** : as is not surprising ⟨mat-ters complicate, ~ —Stanley Kauffmann⟩ **2** : in an unsurprising manner ⟨the story ended ~⟩

un·swathe \-'swäth, -'swoth, -'swäth\ *vt* (14c) : to free from something that swathes

un·swear \-'swar, -'swer\ *vb* **-swore** \-'swōr, -'swor\; **-sworn** \-'sworn, -'sworn\; **swear·ing** *vi* (1596) *archaic* : to unsay or retract something sworn ~ *vt, archaic* : to recant or recall (as an oath) esp. by a second oath

un·swerv·ing \-'swər-viŋ\ *adj* (1694) **1** : not swerving or turning aside **2** : STEADY, UNFALTERING ⟨~ loyalty⟩

un·sym·met·ri·cal \ˌən-sə-'me-tri-kəl\ *adj* (ca. 1755) : ASYMMETRIC — **un·sym·met·ri·cal·ly** \-k(ə-)lē\ *adv*

un·tan·gle \ˌən-'taŋ-gəl\ *vt* (1550) : to loose from tangles or entangle-ment : straighten out *syn* see EXTRICATE

un·tapped \-'tapt\ *adj* (ca. 1775) **1** : not subjected to tapping ⟨an ~ keg⟩ **2** : not drawn upon or utilized ⟨as yet ~ markets⟩

un·taught \-'tot\ *adj* (14c) **1** : not instructed or trained : IGNORANT **2** : NATURAL, SPONTANEOUS ⟨~ kindness⟩

un·teach \-'tēch\ *vt* **-taught** \-'tot\; **-teach·ing** (1532) **1** : to cause to unlearn something **2** : to teach the contrary of

un·ten·a·ble \-'te-nə-bəl\ *adj* (1647) **1** : not able to be defended **2** : not able to be occupied — **un·ten·a·bil·i·ty** \ˌən-ˌte-nə-'bi-lə-tē\ *n*

un·tent·ed \-'ten-təd\ *adj* [¹un- + obs. E *tented*, pp. of *tent* to probe] (1605) *archaic* : not probed or dressed ⟨the ~ woundings of a father's curse —Shak.⟩

un·teth·er \-'te-thər\ *vt* (ca. 1775) : to free from a tether

un·think \-'thiŋk\ *vt* **-thought** \-'thot\; **-think·ing** (ca. 1600) : to put out of mind

un·think·able \-'thiŋ-kə-bəl\ *adj* (15c) **1** : not capable of being grasped by the mind **2** : being contrary to what is reasonable, desir-able, or probable : being out of the question — **un·think·abil·i·ty** \ˌən-ˌthiŋ-kə-'bi-lə-tē\ *n* — **un·think·ably** \ˌən-'thiŋ-kə-blē\ *adv*

un·think·ing \ˌən-'thiŋ-kiŋ\ *adj* (1676) **1** : not taking thought : HEEDLESS, UNMINDFUL **2** : not indicating thought or reflection **3** : not having the power of thought — **un·think·ing·ly** \-kiŋ-lē\ *adv*
un·thought \-'thȯt\ *adj* (ca. 1548) : not anticipated : UNEXPECTED — often used with *of* ⟨an *unthought*-of development⟩
un·thread \ˌən-'thred\ *vt* (1595) **1** : to draw or take out a thread from **2** : to loosen the threads or connections of **3** : to make one's way through ⟨~ a maze⟩
un·throne \-'thrōn\ *vt* (1611) : to remove from or as if from a throne
un·ti·dy \ˌən-'tī-dē\ *adj* (14c) **1 a** : not neat : SLOVENLY **b** : not neat or orderly in habits or procedure ⟨an ~ mind⟩ **2 a** : not neatly organized or carried out ⟨an ~ manuscript⟩ **b** : conducive to a lack of neatness ⟨~ tasks like bathing the baby —*New Yorker*⟩ — **un·ti·di·ly** \-'tī-dᵊl-ē\ *adv* — **un·ti·di·ness** \-'tī-dē-nəs\ *n*
un·tie \-'tī\ *vb* **-tied; -ty·ing** *or* **-tie·ing** *vt* (bef. 12c) **1** : to free from something that ties, fastens, or restrains : UNBIND **2 a** : to disengage the knotted parts of **b** : DISENTANGLE, RESOLVE ⟨~ a traffic jam⟩ ~ *vi* : to become loosened or unbound
¹un·til \ən-'til, -'tel; 'ən-ₓ, -tᵊl\ *prep* [ME, fr. *un*- up to, until (akin to OE *oth* to, until, OHG *unt* up to, until, OE *ende* end) + *til, till* till] (13c) **1** *chiefly Scot* : TO **2** — used as a function word to indicate continuance (as of an action or condition) to a specified time ⟨stayed ~ morning⟩ **3** : BEFORE 2 ⟨not available ~ tomorrow⟩ ⟨we don't open ~ ten⟩
²until *conj* (14c) **1** : up to the time that : up to such time as ⟨play continued ~ it got dark⟩ ⟨never able to relax ~ he took up fishing⟩ ⟨ran ~ he was breathless⟩
¹un·time·ly \ˌən-'tīm-lē\ *adv* (13c) **1** : at an inopportune time : UNSEASONABLY **2** : before the due, natural, or proper time : PREMATURELY ⟨went ~ to the grave⟩
²untimely *adj* (1535) **1** : occurring or done before the due, natural, or proper time : too early : PREMATURE ⟨~ death⟩ **2** : INOPPORTUNE, UNSEASONABLE ⟨an ~ joke⟩ ⟨~ frost⟩ — **un·time·li·ness** *n*
un·time·ous \-'tī-məs\ *adj* (15c) *chiefly Scot* : UNTIMELY
un·tir·ing \-'tī-riŋ\ *adj* (1822) : not becoming tired : INDEFATIGABLE ⟨an ~ worker⟩ — **un·tir·ing·ly** *adv*
un·ti·tled \-'tī-tᵊld\ *adj* (1590) **1** *obs* : having no title or right to rule **2** : not named ⟨an ~ novel⟩ **3** : not called by a title ⟨~ nobility⟩
un·to \'ən-(ₓ)tü\ *prep* [ME, fr. *un*- up to, until + *to*] (14c) **1** : TO **2** — used as a function word to indicate reference or concern ⟨they became a world ~ themselves —Anne T. Fleming⟩
un·told \ˌən-'tōld\ *adj* (15c) **1** : too great or numerous to count : INCALCULABLE, VAST **2 a** : not told or related **b** : kept secret
un·touch·abil·i·ty \ˌən-ˌtə-chə-'bil-ə-tē\ *n* (1919) : the quality or state of being untouchable; *esp* : the state of being an untouchable
¹un·touch·able \ˌən-'tə-chə-bəl\ *adj* (1567) **1 a** : forbidden to the touch : not to be handled **b** : exempt from criticism or control **2** : lying beyond reach **3** : disagreeable or defiling to the touch
²untouchable *n* (1909) : one that is untouchable; *specif* : a member of a large formerly segregated hereditary group in India having in traditional Hindu belief the quality of defiling by contact with a member of a higher caste
un·touched \ˌən-'təcht\ *adj* (14c) **1** : not subjected to touching : not handled **2** : not described or dealt with **3** : not tasted **4** : being in the first or a primeval state or condition **4** : not influenced : UNAFFECTED
un·to·ward \ˌən-'tō(-ə)rd, -'tȯ(-ə)rd; ˌən-tə-'wȯrd\ *adj* (1526) **1** : difficult to guide, manage, or work with : UNRULY, INTRACTABLE **2 a** : marked by trouble or unhappiness : UNLUCKY **b** : not favorable : ADVERSE, UNPROPITIOUS ⟨~ side effects⟩ **3** : IMPROPER, INDECOROUS — **un·to·ward·ly** *adv* — **un·to·ward·ness** *n*
un·tread \ˌən-'tred\ *vt* (1592) *archaic* : to tread back : RETRACE
un·tried \-'trīd\ *adj* (1526) **1** : not tested or proved by experience or trial **2** : not tried in court
un·trod \-'träd\ *or* **un·trod·den** \-'trä-dᵊn\ *adj* (1593) : not trod : UNTRAVERSED
un·trou·bled \-'trə-bəld\ *adj* (15c) **1** : not given trouble : not made uneasy **2** : CALM, TRANQUIL
un·true \-'trü\ *adj* (bef. 12c) **1** : not faithful : DISLOYAL **2** : not according with a standard of correctness : not level or exact **3** : not according with the facts : FALSE — **un·tru·ly** \-'trü-lē\ *adv*
un·truss \-'trəs\ *vt* (1577) **1** *archaic* : UNTIE, UNFASTEN — used in the phrase *untruss one's points* **2** *archaic* : UNDRESS ~ *vi, archaic* : to unfasten or take off one's clothes and esp. one's breeches
un·truth \ˌən-'trüth, 'ən-ₓ\ *n* (bef. 12c) **1** *archaic* : DISLOYALTY **2** : lack of truthfulness : FALSITY **3** : something that is untrue : FALSEHOOD
un·truth·ful \-'trüth-fəl\ *adj* (ca. 1843) : not containing or telling the truth : FALSE, INACCURATE ⟨~ report⟩ *syn* see DISHONEST — **un·truth·ful·ly** \-fə-lē\ *adv* — **un·truth·ful·ness** *n*
un·tune \-'tün, -'tyün\ *vt* (1598) **1** : to put out of tune **2** : DISARRANGE, DISCOMPOSE
un·tu·tored \-'tü-tərd, -'tyü-\ *adj* (1593) **1 a** : having no formal learning or training **b** : NAIVE, UNSOPHISTICATED **2** : not produced or developed by instruction : NATIVE ⟨~ shrewdness⟩ *syn* see IGNORANT
un·twine \-'twīn\ *vt* (15c) **1** : to unwind the twisted or tangled parts of : DISENTANGLE **2** : to remove by unwinding ~ *vi* : to become disentangled or unwound
un·twist \ˌən-'twist\ *vt* (1538) : to separate the twisted parts of : UNTWINE ~ *vi* : to become untwined
un·twist·ed \-'twis-təd\ *adj* (1575) : not twisted
un·used \-'yüzd, *in the phrase "unused to" usu* -'yüs(t)\ *adj* (14c) **1** : not habituated : UNACCUSTOMED ⟨~ to crowds⟩ **2** : not used: as **a** : FRESH, NEW ⟨set an ~ canvas on the easel⟩ **b** : not put to use : IDLE ⟨~ land⟩ **c** : not consumed : ACCRUED ⟨~ sick leave⟩
un·usu·al \-'yü-zhə-wəl, -zhəl; -'yüzh-wəl\ *adj* (1582) : not usual : UNCOMMON, RARE — **un·usu·al·ly** *adv* — **un·usu·al·ness** *n*
un·ut·ter·able \ˌən-'ə-tə-rə-bəl\ *adj* (ca. 1586) : being beyond the powers of description : INEXPRESSIBLE — **un·ut·ter·ably** \-blē\ *adv*
un·val·ued \-'val-(ₓ)yüd, -yəd\ *adj* (1586) **1** *obs* : INVALUABLE **2** : not important or prized : DISREGARDED **b** : not appraised
un·var·nished \-'vär-nisht\ *adj* (1604) **1 a** : not adorned or glossed : PLAIN, STRAIGHTFORWARD ⟨told the ~ truth⟩ **b** : ARTLESS, FRANK ⟨the ~ candor of old people and children —Janet Flanner⟩ **2** : not coated with or as if with varnish : CRUDE, UNFINISHED

un·veil \ˌən-'vā(ə)l\ *vt* (1599) **1** : to remove a veil or covering from **2** : to make public : DIVULGE, REVEAL ~ *vi* : to throw off a veil or protective cloak
un·veiled \-'vā(ə)ld\ *adj* (1606) : not veiled : OPEN, REVEALED
un·vo·cal \ˌən-'vō-kəl\ *adj* (1773) **1** : not eloquent or outspoken : INARTICULATE **2** : not musical : DISCORDANT
un·voice \-'vȯis\ *vt* (1637) : DEVOICE
un·voiced \-'vȯist\ *adj* (1859) **1** : not verbally expressed **2** : VOICELESS 2
un·war·rant·able \-'wȯr-ən-tə-bəl, -'wär-\ *adj* (1612) : not justifiable : INEXCUSABLE — **un·war·rant·ably** \-blē\ *adv*
un·wary \ˌən-'war-ē, -'wer-\ *adj* (1579) : not alert : easily fooled or surprised : HEEDLESS, GULLIBLE — **un·war·i·ly** \-'war-ə-lē, -'wer-\ *adv* — **un·war·i·ness** \-'war-ē-nəs, -'wer-\ *n*
¹un·washed \-'wȯsht, -'wäsht\ *adj* (14c) **1** : not cleaned with or as if with soap and water **2** : IGNORANT, PLEBEIAN — **un·washed·ness** *n*
²unwashed *n* (1830) : an ignorant or underprivileged group : RABBLE — usu. used with *great* ⟨the great ~⟩
un·watch·able \ˌən-'wä-chə-bəl, -'wȯ-\ *adj* (1886) : not suitable or fit for watching : tending to discourage watching
un·wea·ried \-'wir-ēd\ *adj* (13c) : not tired or jaded : FRESH — **un·wea·ried·ly** *adv*
un·weave \-'wēv\ *vt* **-wove** \-'wōv\; **-wo·ven** \-'wō-vən\; **-weav·ing** (1542) : DISENTANGLE, UNRAVEL
un·weet·ing \-'wē-tiŋ\ *adj* (14c) *archaic* : UNWITTING — **un·weet·ing·ly** \-tiŋ-lē\ *adv, archaic*
un·weight \-'wāt\ *vt* (ca. 1939) : to reduce momentarily the force exerted by (as a ski) upon a surface by shifting the weight or position of one's body ~ *vi* : to unweight something by shifting the weight or position of one's body
un·well \ˌən-'wel\ *adj* (15c) **1** : being in poor health : AILING, SICK **2** : undergoing menstruation
un·whole·some \-'hōl-səm\ *adj* (13c) **1** : detrimental to physical, mental, or moral well-being : UNHEALTHY ⟨~ food⟩ ⟨~ pastimes⟩ **2 a** : CORRUPT, UNSOUND **b** : offensive to the senses : LOATHSOME — **un·whole·some·ly** *adv*
un·wieldy \-'wē(ə)l-dē\ *adj* (1530) : not easily managed, handled, or used (as because of bulk, weight, complexity, or awkwardness) : CUMBERSOME — **un·wield·i·ly** \-'wēl-də-lē\ *adv* — **un·wield·i·ness** \-dē-nəs\ *n*
un·will·ing \-'wi-liŋ\ *adj* (bef. 12c) : not willing: **a** : LOATH, RELUCTANT ⟨was ~ to learn⟩ **b** : done or given reluctantly ⟨~ approval⟩ **c** : offering opposition : OBSTINATE ⟨an ~ student⟩ — **un·will·ing·ly** \-liŋ-lē\ *adv* — **un·will·ing·ness** *n*
un·wind \-'wīnd\ *vb* **-wound** \-'waúnd\; **-wind·ing** *vt* (14c) **1 a** : to cause to uncoil : wind off : UNROLL **b** : to free from or as if from a binding or wrapping **c** : to release from tension : RELAX **2** *archaic* : to trace to the end ⟨~ing the labyrinth and bringing the hero out —Laurence Sterne⟩ ~ *vi* **1** : to become uncoiled or disentangled : UNFOLD **2** : to become released from tension
un·wis·dom \ˌən-'wiz-dəm\ *n* (bef. 12c) : lack of wisdom : FOOLISHNESS, FOLLY
un·wise \-'wīz\ *adj* (bef. 12c) : lacking wisdom or good sense : FOOLISH, IMPRUDENT — **un·wise·ly** *adv*
un·wish \-'wish\ *vt* (1594) *obs* : to wish away
un·wit·ting \-'wi-tiŋ\ *adj* (bef. 12c) **1** : not knowing : UNAWARE ⟨kept the truth from their ~ friends⟩ **2** : not intended : INADVERTENT ⟨an ~ mistake⟩ — **un·wit·ting·ly** \-tiŋ-lē\ *adv*
un·wont·ed \-'wȯn-təd, -'wȯn- also -'wən- or -'wän-\ *adj* (1553) **1** : being out of the ordinary : RARE, UNUSUAL **2** : not accustomed by experience — **un·wont·ed·ly** *adv* — **un·wont·ed·ness** *n*
un·world·ly \-'wər(-ə)l-dlē, -'wərl-lē\ *adj* (1707) **1** : not of this world : UNEARTHLY; *specif* : SPIRITUAL **2 a** : not wise in the ways of the world : NAIVE **b** : not swayed by mundane considerations — **un·world·li·ness** \-'wərl(d)-lē-nəs\ *n*
un·worn \-'wȯrn, -'wȯrn\ *adj* (ca. 1586) **1 a** : not impaired by use : not worn away **b** : not worn : NEW **2** : not jaded : FRESH, ORIGINAL
un·wor·thy \ˌən-'wər-thē\ *adj* (13c) **1 a** : lacking in excellence or value : POOR, WORTHLESS **b** : BASE, DISHONORABLE **2** : not meritorious : UNDESERVING ⟨~ of attention⟩ **3** : not deserved : UNMERITED ⟨~ treatment⟩ **4** : inappropriate to one's condition or station ⟨actions ~ of a gentleman⟩ — **un·wor·thi·ly** \-thə-lē\ *adv* — **un·wor·thi·ness** \-thē-nəs\ *n*
un·wrap \-'rap\ *vt* (14c) : to remove the wrapping from : DISCLOSE ⟨~ a package⟩ ⟨~ evidence in a criminal case⟩
un·wreathe \-'rēth\ *vt* (1591) : UNCOIL, UNTWIST
un·writ·ten \-'ri-tᵊn\ *adj* (14c) **1** : not expressed in writing : ORAL, TRADITIONAL **2** : containing no writing : BLANK
unwritten constitution *n* (1890) : a constitution not embodied in a single document but based chiefly on custom and precedent as expressed in statutes and judicial decisions
unwritten law *n* (1641) : law based chiefly on custom rather than legislative enactments
un·yield·ing \ˌən-'yē(ə)l-diŋ\ *adj* (1658) **1** : characterized by lack of softness or flexibility **2** : characterized by firmness or obduracy — **un·yield·ing·ly** \-diŋ-lē\ *adv*
un·yoke \-'yōk\ *vt* (14c) **1** : to free from a yoke or harness **2** : to take apart : DISJOIN ~ *vi* **1** *archaic* : to unharness a draft animal **2** *archaic* : to cease from work
un·zip \-'zip\ *vt* (1939) : to zip open ~ *vi* : to open by or as if by means of a zipper
¹up \'əp\ *adv* [partly fr. ME *up* upward, fr. OE *ūp*; partly fr. ME *uppe* on high, fr. OE; both akin to OHG *ūf* up and prob. to L *sub* under, Gk *hypo* under, *hyper* over — more at OVER] (bef. 12c) **1 a** (1) : in or into a higher position or level; *esp* : away from the center of the earth (2) : from beneath the ground or water to the surface (3) : from below the horizon (4) : UPSTREAM (5) : in or into an upright position

\ə\ abut \ᵊ\ kitten, F table \ər\ further \a\ ash \ā\ ace \ä\ mop, mar \aú\ out \ch\ chin \e\ bet \ē\ easy \g\ go \i\ hit \ī\ ice \j\ job \ŋ\ sing \ō\ go \ȯ\ law \ȯi\ boy \th\ thin \t̲h̲\ the \ü\ loot \ú\ foot \y\ yet \zh\ vision \á, k̲, ⁿ, œ, œ̄, ᵿ, ᵾ, ʸ\ *see* Guide to Pronunciation

⟨sit ~⟩; *esp* : out of bed   **b** : upward from the ground or surface ⟨pull ~ a daisy⟩   **c** : so as to expose a particular surface   **2** : with greater intensity ⟨speak ~⟩   **3** **a** : in or into a better or more advanced state   **b** : at an end ⟨your time is ~⟩   **c** : in or into a state of greater intensity or excitement   **d** : in a continual sequence : in continuance from a point or to a point ⟨from third grade ~⟩ ⟨at prices of $10 and ~⟩ ⟨~ until now⟩   **4** **a** (1) : into existence, evidence, prominence, or prevalence ⟨put ~ several new buildings⟩   (2) : into operation or practical form   **b** : into consideration or attention ⟨bring ~ for discussion⟩   **5** : into possession or custody   **6** **a** : ENTIRELY, COMPLETELY ⟨button ~ your coat⟩   **b** — used as an intensifier ⟨clean ~ the house⟩   **7** : in or into storage : BY ⟨lay ~ supplies⟩   **8** **a** : so as to arrive or approach   **b** : in a direction conventionally the opposite of down: (1) : to windward   (2) : NORTHWARD   (3) : to or at the top   (4) : to or at the rear of a theatrical stage   **9** : in or into parts   **10** : to a stop — usu. used with *draw, bring, fetch,* or *pull*   **11** : for each side ⟨the score is 15 ~⟩

²up *adj* (bef. 12c)   **1 a** : risen above the horizon ⟨the sun is ~⟩   **b** : STANDING   **c** : being out of bed   **d** : relatively high ⟨the river is ~⟩ ⟨was well ~ in her class⟩   **e** : being in a raised position : LIFTED ⟨windows are ~⟩   **f** : being in a state of completion : CONSTRUCTED, BUILT   **g** : having the face upward   **h** : mounted on a horse ⟨a new jockey ~⟩   **i** : grown above a surface ⟨the corn is ~⟩   **j** (1) : moving, inclining, or directed upward ⟨the ~ escalator⟩   (2) : bound in a direction regarded as up   **2 a** (1) : marked by agitation, excitement, or activity   (2) : positive or upbeat in mood or demeanor   **b** : being above a former or normal level (as of quantity or intensity) ⟨attendance is ~⟩ ⟨the wind is ~⟩   **c** : exerting enough power (as for operation) ⟨sail when steam is ~⟩   **d** : READY; *specif* : highly prepared ⟨~ is going on : taking place ⟨find out what is ~⟩   **3** : risen from a lower position ⟨men ~ from the ranks⟩   **b** : being at the same level or point ⟨did not feel ~ to par⟩   (1) : well informed : ABREAST ⟨~ on the news⟩   (2) : being on schedule ⟨~ on his homework⟩   **d** : being ahead of one's opponent   **4 a** : presented for or undergoing consideration ⟨contract ~ for negotiation⟩; *also* : charged before a court ⟨you're ~ next⟩   **b** : being the one whose turn it is ⟨you're ~ next⟩   **5** *of a quark* : having an electric charge of +²/₃, zero charm, and zero strangeness — compare ⁴DOWN 6 — **up against** : confronted with : face-to-face with ⟨the problem we are *up against*⟩ — **up to** **1** : capable of performing or dealing with ⟨feels *up to* her role⟩   **2** : engaged in ⟨what is he *up to*⟩   **3** : being the responsibility of ⟨it's *up to* me⟩

³up *prep* (1509)   **1 a** — used as a function word to indicate motion to or toward or situation at a higher point of ⟨went ~ the stairs⟩   **b** : up into or in the ⟨went ~ attic⟩   **2 a** : in a direction regarded as being toward or near the upper end or part of ⟨lives a few miles ~ the coast⟩ ⟨walked ~ the street⟩   **b** : toward or near a point closer to the source or beginning of ⟨sail ~ the river⟩   **3** : in the direction opposite to ⟨sailed ~ the wind⟩

⁴up *n* (1536)   **1** : one in a high or advantageous position   **2** : an upward slope   **3** : a period or state of prosperity or success   **4** : ³UPPER

⁵up *vb* **upped** \'əpt\ *or in vi 2* **up; upped; up-ping; ups** *or in vi 2* **up** *vi* (1643)   **1 a** : to rise from a lying or sitting position   **b** : to move upward : ASCEND   **2** — used with *and* and another verb to indicate that the action of the following verb was either surprisingly or abruptly initiated ⟨he ~ and married a showgirl⟩ ~ *vt* **1** : RAISE, LIFT   **2 a** : to advance to a higher level: (1) : INCREASE   (2) : PROMOTE 1a   **b** : RAISE 8d, e

up-and-com-ing \ˌəp-ən(d)-'kə-min, ˌəp-'m-\ *adj* (1926) : gaining prominence and likely to advance or succeed — **up-and-com-er** \-'kə-mər\ *n*

up-and-down \-'daùn\ *adj* (ca. 1755)   **1** : marked by alternate upward and downward movement, action, or surface   **2** : PERPENDICULAR

up and down *adv* (12c)   **1** : TO AND FRO ⟨paced *up and down*⟩   **2** : alternately upward and downward ⟨jump *up and down*⟩   **3** *archaic* : here and there esp. throughout an area   **4** : with regard to every particular : THOROUGHLY ⟨knew the territory *up and down*⟩ — **up and down** *prep*

up-and-up \'əp-ən-'əp\ *n* (1863) : an honest or respectable course — used in the phrase *on the up-and-up*

Upa·ni·shad \ü-'pä-ni-ˌshäd, yü-'pä-nə-ˌshad\ *n* [Skt *upaniṣad*] (1805) : one of a class of Vedic treatises dealing with broad philosophic problems — **Upa·ni·shad·ic** \(ˌ)ü-ˌpä-ni-'shä-dik, (ˌ)yü-ˌpä-nə-'sha-dik\ *adj*

upas \'yü-pəs\ *n* [Indonesian Malay *pohon upas* poison tree] (1783)   **1** : a tall tropical Asian tree (*Antiaris toxicaria*) of the mulberry family with a latex that contains poisonous glucosides used as an arrow poison; *also* : a poisonous concentrate of the juice or latex of a upas   **2** : a poisonous or harmful influence or institution

¹up-beat \'əp-ˌbēt\ *n* (1869)   **1** : an unaccented beat in a musical measure; *specif* : the last beat of the measure   **2** : an increase in activity or prosperity ⟨business that is on the ~⟩

²upbeat *adj* (1947) : CHEERFUL, OPTIMISTIC

up-bow \'əp-ˌbō\ *n* (ca. 1890) : a stroke in playing a bowed instrument in which the bow is moved across the strings from the tip to the heel

up-braid \ˌəp-'brād\ *vt* [ME *upbreyden*, fr. OE *ūpbregdan*, prob. fr. *ūp* up + *bregdan* to snatch, move suddenly — more at BRAID] (14c)   **1** : to criticize severely : find fault with   **2** : to reproach severely : scold vehemently   *syn* see SCOLD — **up-braid-er** *n*

up-bring-ing \'əp-ˌbrin-iŋ\ *n* (1520) : early training; *esp* : a particular way of bringing up a child ⟨had a strict ~⟩

up-build \ˌəp-'bild\ *vt* -**built** \-'bilt\; -**build-ing** (1513) : BUILD UP

up-cast \'əp-ˌkast\ *n* (1890) : something cast up

up-chuck \'əp-ˌchək\ *vb* (1936) : VOMIT

up close *adv or adj* (1851) : at close range

up-coast \'əp-ˌkōst\ *adv* (1909) : up the coast

up-com-ing \'əp-ˌkə-min\ *adj* (1944) : FORTHCOMING, APPROACHING

up-coun-try \'əp-ˌkən-trē\ *adj* (1835) : of, relating to, or characteristic of an inland, upland, or outlying region — **up-country** *n* — **up-country** \'əp-'\ *adv*

¹up-date \ˌəp-'dāt\ *vt* (1910) : to bring up to date

²up-date \'əp-ˌdāt\ *n* (1965)   **1** : an act or instance of updating   **2** : current information for updating something   **3** : an up-to-date version, account, or report

up-do \'əp-(ˌ)dü\ *n, pl* **updos** [*up*swept hair*do*] (1938) : an upswept hairdo

up-draft \'əp-ˌdraft, -ˌdráft\ *n* (ca. 1887) : an upward movement of gas (as air)

up-end \ˌəp-'end\ *vt* (1823)   **1** : to set or stand on end; *also* : OVERTURN   **2 a** : to affect to the point of being upset or flurried ⟨a . . . literary shocker, designed to ~ the credulous matrons —Wolcott Gibbs⟩   **b** : DEFEAT, BEAT ~ *vi* : to rise on an end

up-field \'əp-ˌfē(ə)ld\ *adv or adj* (ca. 1934) : in or into the part of the field toward which the offensive team is headed

up-front \ˌəp-'frənt, 'əp-ˌ\ *adj* (1945) : being or coming in or at the front: as   **a** (1) : being in a conspicuous or leading position   (2) : FRANK, FORTHRIGHT   **b** : playing in a front line (as in football)   **c** : paid or payable in advance

up front *adv* (1937)   **1** : in or at the front   **2** : in advance   **3** : in an up-front manner : FRANKLY

¹up-grade \'əp-ˌgrād\ *n* (1873)   **1** : an upward grade or slope   **2** : INCREASE, RISE   **3** : IMPROVEMENT 2b

²up-grade \'əp-ˌgrād, ˌəp-'\ *vt* (1901) : to raise or improve the grade of: as   **a** (1) : to improve (livestock) by use of purebred sires   **b** : to advance to a job requiring a higher level of skill esp. as part of a training program   **c** : to raise the quality of   **d** : to raise the classification and usu. the price of without improving the quality   **e** : to extend the usefulness of (as a device) — **up-grad-abil-i-ty** *or* **up-grade-abil-i-ty** \ˌəp-ˌgrā-də-'bi-lə-tē\ *n* — **up-grad-able** *or* **up-grade-able** \ˌəp-'grā-də-bəl\ *adj*

up-growth \'əp-ˌgrōth\ *n* (1844) : the process of growing upward : DEVELOPMENT; *also* : a product or result of this

up-heav-al \ˌəp-'hē-vəl, (ˌ)ə-'pē-\ *n* (1838)   **1** : the action or an instance of upheaving esp. of part of the earth's crust   **2** : extreme agitation or disorder : radical change; *also* : an instance of this

up-heave \ˌəp-'hēv, (ˌ)ə-'pē-\ *vt* (14c) : to heave up : LIFT ~ *vi* : to move upward esp. with power — **up-heav-er** *n*

¹up-hill \'əp-ˌhil\ *n* (1548) : rising ground : ASCENT

²up-hill \-'hil\ *adv* (1607)   **1** : upward on a hill or incline   **2** : against difficulties ⟨seemed to be talking ~ —Willa Cather⟩

³up-hill \-ˌhil\ *adj* (1613)   **1** : situated on elevated ground   **2 a** : going up : ASCENDING   **b** : being the higher one or part esp. of a set; *specif* : being nearer the top of an incline   **3** : DIFFICULT, LABORIOUS

up-hold \(ˌ)əp-'hōld\ *vt* -**held** \-'held\; -**hold-ing** (13c)   **1 a** : to give support to   **b** : to support against an opponent   **2 a** : to keep elevated   **b** : to lift up   *syn* see SUPPORT — **up-hold-er** *n*

up-hol-ster \(ˌ)əp-'hōl-stər, (ˌ)ə-'pōl-\ *vt* -**stered; -ster-ing** \-st(ə-)riŋ\ [back-formation fr. *upholstery*] (1864) : to furnish with or as if with upholstery — **up-hol-ster-er** \-stər-ər\ *n*

up-hol-stery \-st(ə-)rē\ *n, pl* -**ster-ies** [ME *upholdester* upholsterer, fr. *upholden* to uphold, fr. *up* + *holden* to hold] (1649) : materials (as fabric, padding, and springs) used to make a soft covering esp. for a seat

up-keep \'əp-ˌkēp\ *n* (1884)   **1** : the act of maintaining in good condition : the state of being maintained in good condition   **2** : the cost of maintaining in good condition

up-land \'əp-lənd, -ˌland\ *n* (1566)   **1** : high land esp. at some distance from the sea : PLATEAU   **2** : ground elevated above the lowlands along rivers or between hills — **upland** *adj* — **up-land-er** \-lən-dər, -ˌlan-\ *n*

upland cotton *n* (1819) : a widely cultivated American cotton plant (*Gossypium hirsutum*) having short- to medium-staple fibers

upland sandpiper *n* (ca. 1890) : a large No. American sandpiper (*Bartramia longicauda*) that frequents fields and prairies — called also *upland plover*

upland sandpiper

¹up-lift \(ˌ)əp-'lift\ *vt* (14c)   **1** : to lift up : ELEVATE; *esp* : to cause (a portion of the earth's surface) to rise above adjacent areas   **2** : to improve the spiritual, social, or intellectual condition of ~ *vi* : RISE — **up-lift-er** *n*

²up-lift \'əp-ˌlift\ *n* (ca. 1845)   **1** : an act, process, result, or cause of uplifting: as   **a** (1) : the uplifting of a part of the earth's surface   (2) : an uplifted mass of land   **b** : a bettering of a condition esp. spiritually, socially, or intellectually   **c** (1) : influences intended to uplift   (2) : a social movement to improve esp. morally or culturally   **2** : a brassiere designed to hold the breasts up

up-link \'əp-ˌliŋk\ *n* (1968)   **1** : a communications channel for transmissions to a spacecraft; *also* : the transmissions themselves   **2** : a facility on earth for transmitting to a spacecraft

up-load \ˌəp-'lōd, 'əp-ˌ\ *vt* (1983) : to transfer (information) from a microcomputer to a remote computer usu. with a modem

up-man-ship \'əp-mən-ˌship\ *n* (1959) : ONE-UPMANSHIP

up-mar-ket \'əp-ˌmär-kət\ *adj* (1972) : UPSCALE — **upmarket** *adv*

up-most \'əp-ˌmōst\ *adj* (1560) : UPPERMOST

¹up-on \ə-'pȯn, -'pän\ *prep* (13c) : ON

²up-on \ə-'pȯn, -'pän\ *adv* (14c)   **1** *obs* : on the surface : on it   **2** *obs* : THEREAFTER, THEREON

¹up-per \'ə-pər\ *adj* [ME, compar. of ²*up*] (14c)   **1 a** : higher in physical position, rank, or order   **b** : farther inland ⟨the ~ Mississippi⟩   **2** : constituting the branch of a bicameral legislature that is usu. smaller and more restricted in membership and possesses greater traditional prestige than the lower house   **3 a** : constituting a stratum relatively near the earth's surface   **b** *cap* : being a later epoch or series of the period or system named ⟨*Upper* Cretaceous⟩ ⟨*Upper* Paleolithic⟩   **4** : NORTHERN ⟨~ Manhattan⟩

²upper *n* (1789) : one that is upper: as   **a** : the parts of a shoe or boot above the sole   **b** : an upper tooth or denture   **c** : an upper berth — **on one's uppers** : in straitened circumstances : DESTITUTE

³upper *n* [*up* + ²-*er*] (ca. 1968)   **1** : a stimulant drug; *esp* : AMPHETAMINE   **2** : something that induces a state of good feeling or exhilaration

¹up-per-case \ˌə-pər-'kās\ *adj* [fr. the compositor's practice of keeping capital letters in the upper of a pair of type cases] (1738) : CAPITAL 1

²uppercase *n* (ca. 1916) : capital letters

³uppercase *vt* -**cased; -cas-ing** (1949) : to print or set in capital letters

upper case *n* (1683) : a type case containing capitals and usu. small capitals, fractions, symbols, and accents

upper-class *adj* (1837) : of, relating to, or characteristic of the upper class

upper class *n* (1839) : a social class occupying a position above the middle class and having the highest status in a society

up·per·class·man \ˌə-pər-ˈklas-mən\ *n* (1871) : a member of the junior or senior class in a school or college

upper crust *n* (1836) : the highest social class or group; *esp* : the highest circle of the upper class — **upper-crust** *adj*

up·per·cut \ˈə-pər-ˌkət\ *n* (1842) : a swinging blow (as in boxing) directed upward with a bent arm — **uppercut** *vb*

upper hand *n* (15c) : MASTERY, ADVANTAGE, CONTROL ⟨was determined not to let the opposition get the *upper hand*⟩

up·per·most \ˈə-pər-ˌmōst\ *adv* (15c) : in or into the highest or most prominent position — **uppermost** *adj*

up·per·part \-ˌpärt\ *n* (1526) : a part lying on the upper side (as of a bird)

upper respiratory *adj* (1950) : of, affecting, or being the part of the respiratory system that includes the nose, nasal passages, and nasopharynx ⟨*upper respiratory* tract⟩ ⟨*upper respiratory* infection⟩

up·pish \ˈə-pish\ *adj* (ca. 1734) : UPPITY — **up·pish·ly** *adv* — **up·pish·ness** *n*

up·pi·ty \ˈə-pə-tē\ *adj* [prob. fr. *up* + *-ity* (as in *persnickity*, var. of *persnickety*)] (1880) : putting on or marked by airs of superiority : ARROGANT, PRESUMPTUOUS ⟨~ technicians⟩ ⟨a small ~ country⟩ — **up·pi·ti·ness** *also* **up·pi·ty·ness** *n*

up·raise \ˌə-ˈrāz\ *vt* (14c) : to raise or lift up : ELEVATE

up·rate \ˈəp-ˌrāt\ *vt* (1965) : UPGRADE; *specif* : to improve the power output of (as an engine)

up·rear \-ˈrir\ *vt* (14c) **1** : to lift up : ERECT ~ *vi* : RISE

¹up·right \ˈəp-ˌrīt\ *adj* (bef. 12c) **1 a** : PERPENDICULAR, VERTICAL **b** : erect in carriage or posture **c** : having the main axis or a main part perpendicular ⟨~ freezer⟩ **2** : marked by strong moral rectitude — **up·right·ly** *adv* — **up·right·ness** *n*
syn UPRIGHT, HONEST, JUST, CONSCIENTIOUS, SCRUPULOUS, HONORABLE mean having or showing a strict regard for what is morally right. UPRIGHT implies a strict adherence to moral principles ⟨a stern and *upright* minister⟩. HONEST stresses adherence to such virtues as truthfulness, candor, fairness ⟨known for being *honest* in business dealings⟩. JUST stresses conscious choice and regular practice of what is right or equitable ⟨workers given *just* compensation⟩. CONSCIENTIOUS and SCRUPULOUS imply an active moral sense governing all one's actions and painstaking efforts to follow one's conscience ⟨*conscientious* in the completion of her assignments⟩ ⟨*scrupulous* in carrying out the terms of the will⟩. HONORABLE suggests a firm holding to codes of right behavior and the guidance of a high sense of honor and duty ⟨a difficult but *honorable* decision⟩.

²upright *adv* (1590) : vertically upward : in an upright position

³upright *n* (1683) **1** : the state of being upright : PERPENDICULAR ⟨a pillar out of ~⟩ **2** : something that stands upright; *esp* : a football goalpost — usu. used in pl. **3** : UPRIGHT PIANO

upright piano *n* (ca. 1890) : a piano with vertical frame and strings — compare GRAND PIANO

¹up·rise \ˌəp-ˈrīz\ *vi* **up·rose** \-ˈrōz\; **up·ris·en** \-ˈri-zᵊn\; **up·ris·ing** \-ˈrī-ziŋ\ (14c) **1 a** : to rise to a higher position **b** (1) : STAND UP (2) : to get out of bed **c** : to come into view esp. from below the horizon **2** : to rise up in sound — **up·ris·er** \ˌəp-ˈrī-zər, ˈəp-ˌ\ *n*

²up·rise \ˈəp-ˌrīz\ *n* (15c) **1** : an act or instance of uprising **2** : an upward slope

up·ris·ing \ˈəp-ˌrī-ziŋ\ *n* (13c) : an act or instance of rising up; *esp* : a usu. localized outbreak of popular violence in defiance usu. of an established government **syn** see REBELLION

up·riv·er \ˈəp-ˈri-vər\ *adv or adj* (1774) : toward or at a point nearer the source of a river

up·roar \ˈəp-ˌrōr, -ˌrȯr\ *n* [by folk etymology fr. D *oproer*, fr. MD, fr. *op* up (akin to OE *ūp*) + *roer* motion; akin to OE *hrēran* to stir] (1526) : a state of commotion, excitement, or violent disturbance

up·roar·i·ous \ˌəp-ˈrōr-ē-əs, -ˈrȯr-\ *adj* (1819) **1** : marked by uproar **2** : very noisy and full **3** : extremely funny ⟨an ~ comedy⟩ — **up·roar·i·ous·ly** *adv* — **up·roar·i·ous·ness** *n*

up·root \ˌ(ˌ)əp-ˈrüt, -ˈrů́t\ *vt* (ca. 1620) **1** : to remove as if by pulling up **2** : to pull up by the roots **3** : to displace from a country or traditional habitat **syn** see EXTERMINATE — **up·root·ed·ness** *n* — **up·root·er** *n*

up·rush \ˈəp-ˌrəsh\ *n* (1871) **1** : an upward rush (as of gas or liquid) **2** : a sudden increase

ups and downs *n pl* (1659) : alternating rise and fall esp. in fortune

up·scale \ˈəp-ˌskāl\ *adj* (1966) : relating to, being, or appealing to affluent consumers; *also* : of a superior quality — **upscale** *adv or vt*

¹up·set \(ˌ)əp-ˈset\ *vb* **-set**; **-set·ting** *vt* (1677) **1** : to thicken and shorten (as a heated bar of iron) by hammering on the end : SWAGE **2** : to force out of the usual upright, level, or proper position : OVERTURN **3 a** : to trouble mentally or emotionally : disturb the poise of **b** : to throw into disorder **c** : INVALIDATE **d** : to defeat unexpectedly **4** : to cause a physical disorder in; *specif* : to make somewhat ill ~ *vi* : to become overturned **syn** see DISCOMPOSE — **up·set·ter** *n*

²up·set \ˈəp-ˌset\ *n* (1804) **1** : an act of overturning : OVERTURN **2 a** (1) : an act of throwing into disorder : DERANGEMENT (2) : a state of disorder : CONFUSION **b** : an unexpected defeat **3 a** : a minor physical disorder ⟨a stomach ~⟩ **b** : an emotional disturbance ⟨went through a big ~ after his father's death⟩ **4 a** : a part of a rod (as the head on a bolt) that is upset **b** : the expansion of a bullet on striking

³up·set \(ˌ)əp-ˈset\ *adj* (1805) : emotionally disturbed or agitated ⟨was too ~ to speak to him⟩

upset price \ˈəp-ˌset-\ *n* (1814) : the minimum price set for property offered at auction or public sale

up·shift \ˈəp-ˌshift\ *vi* (1952) : to shift an automotive vehicle into a higher gear — **upshift** *n*

up·shot \ˈəp-ˌshät\ *n* (1604) : the final result : OUTCOME

¹up·side \ˈəp-ˌsīd\ *n* [²up + ¹side] (1927) **1** : an upward trend (as of prices) **2** : a positive aspect

²up·side \ˈəp-ˈsīd\ *prep* [perh. fr. ¹up + -side (as in *alongside*)] (1929) : up on or against the side of ⟨layin' in this death cell, writin' my time ~ the wall —Lonnie Johnson⟩ ⟨if they wish to knock a thug ~ the head, they do so —Robert MacKenzie⟩

up·side down \ˈəp-ˌsīd-ˈdau̇n\ *adv* [alter. of ME *up so doun*, fr. *up* + *so* + *doun* down] (15c) **1** : in such a way that the upper and the lower parts are reversed in position **2** : in or into great disorder — **upside-down** *adj*

upside-down cake *n* (1930) : a cake baked with its batter covering an arrangement of fruit (as pineapple) and served fruit side up

up·si·lon \ˈüp-sə-ˌlän, ˈyüp-, ˈəp-, -lən\ *n* [MGk *y psilon*, lit., simple *y*; fr. the desire to distinguish it from *oi*, which was pronounced the same in later Greek] (1621) **1** : the 20th letter of the Greek alphabet — see ALPHABET table **2** : any of a group of unstable electrically neutral elementary particles of the meson family that have a mass about 10 times that of a proton

up·spring \ˌəp-ˈspriŋ\ *vi* **-sprang** \-ˈspraŋ\ *or* **-sprung** \-ˈsprəŋ\; **-sprung**; **-spring·ing** \-ˈspriŋ-iŋ\ (bef. 12c) **1** : to spring up **2** : to come into being

¹up·stage \ˈəp-ˈstāj\ *adv* (1870) **1** : toward or at the rear of a theatrical stage **2** : away from a motion-picture or television camera

²upstage *adj* (1918) **1** [³upstage] : HAUGHTY **2** : of or relating to the rear of a stage

³up·stage \ˈəp-ˈstāj\ *vt* (1921) **1** : to draw attention away from **2** : to force (an actor) to face away from the audience by staying upstage **3** : to treat snobbishly

⁴up·stage \ˈəp-ˌstāj\ *n* (ca. 1931) : the part of a stage that is farthest from the audience or camera

¹up·stairs \ˈəp-ˈstarz, -ˈsterz\ *adv* (1596) **1** : up the stairs : on or to a higher floor **2** : to or at a high altitude or higher position ⟨kicked ~ to company management⟩ **3** : in the head : INTELLECTUALLY ⟨a little slow ~ —Tom Clancy⟩

²up·stairs \ˈəp-ˈ\ *adj* (1782) : situated above the stairs esp. on an upper floor ⟨an ~ bedroom⟩

³up·stairs \ˈəp-ˈ, ˈəp-ˌ\ *n pl but sing or pl in constr* (1842) : the part of a building above the ground floor

up·stand·ing \ˌəp-ˈstan-diŋ, ˈəp-ˌ\ *adj* (bef. 12c) **1** : ERECT, UPRIGHT **2** : marked by integrity — **up·stand·ing·ness** *n*

¹up·start \ˌəp-ˈstärt\ *vi* (14c) : to jump up (as to one's feet) suddenly

²up·start \ˈəp-ˌstärt\ *n* (1555) **1** : one that has risen suddenly (as from a low position to wealth or power) : PARVENU; *esp* : one that claims more personal importance than is warranted **2** : a start-up enterprise — **up·start** \ˈəp-ˈ\ *adj*

up·state \ˈəp-ˌstāt\ *n* (1901) : the chiefly northerly sections of a state; *also* : the chiefly rural part of a state when the major metropolitan area is in the south — **upstate** \-ˈstāt\ *adv or adj* — **up·stat·er** \-ˈstā-tər\ *n*

up·stream \ˈəp-ˈstrēm\ *adv or adj* (1681) **1** : in the direction opposite to the flow of a stream **2** : toward a portion of the production stream closer to basic extractive or manufacturing processes ⟨make most of its money ~, selling cheap crude . . . to refineries —John Quirt⟩

up·stroke \ˈəp-ˌstrōk\ *n* (1828) : a stroke (as of a pen) made in an upward direction

up·surge \ˈəp-ˌsərj\ *n* (1917) : a rapid or sudden rise

¹up·sweep \ˈəp-ˌswēp\ *vi* **-swept** \-ˌswept\; **-sweep·ing** (1791) : to sweep upward

²upsweep *n* (ca. 1891) **1** : an upward sweep **2** : an upswept hairdo

up·swept \ˈəp-ˌswept\ *adj* (1938) : swept upward; *esp* : brushed up to the top of the head ⟨~ hair⟩

up·swing \ˈəp-ˌswiŋ\ *n* (1924) **1** : an upward swing **2** : a marked increase or improvement — often used in the phrase *on the upswing*

up·take \ˈəp-ˌtāk\ *n* [Sc *uptake* to understand] (1816) **1** : UNDERSTANDING, COMPREHENSION ⟨quick on the ~⟩ **2** : a flue leading upward **3** : an act or instance of absorbing and incorporating esp. into a living organism

up–tem·po \ˈəp-ˌtem-(ˌ)pō\ *adj* (1948) : having a fast-moving tempo (as in jazz)

¹up–throw \ˈəp-ˌthrō\ *vt* **-threw** \-ˌthrü\; **-thrown** \-ˌthrōn\; **-throw·ing** (1600) : to throw or thrust upward

²upthrow *n* (1807) : an upward displacement (as of a rock stratum) : UPHEAVAL, UPTHRUST

¹up·thrust \ˈəp-ˌthrəst\ *vt* (1845) : to thrust up; *esp* : to elevate (a part of the earth's surface) in an upthrust ~ *vi* : to rise with an upward thrust

²upthrust *n* (1846) : an upward thrust; *specif* : an uplift of part of the earth's crust

up·tick \ˈəp-ˌtik\ *n* [²up + ³tick] (1955) : INCREASE, RISE

up·tight \ˈəp-ˈtīt, (ˌ)əp-\ *adj* (1934) **1 a** : being tense, nervous, or uneasy **b** : ANGRY, INDIGNANT **c** : rigidly conventional **2** : being in financial difficulties — **up·tight·ness** \(ˌ)əp-ˈtīt-nəs\ *n*

up·tilt \ˈəp-ˈtilt\ *vt* (1849) : to tilt upward

up·time \ˈəp-ˌtīm\ *n* (1958) : time during which a piece of equipment (as a computer) is functioning or able to function

up to *prep* (13c) **1** — used as a function word to indicate extension as far as a specified place ⟨sank *up* to his knees in the mud⟩ **2** — used as a function word to indicate a limit or boundary ⟨*up* to 50,000 copies a month⟩ ⟨worked *up* to the last minute⟩

up–to–date *adj* (1888) **1** : extending up to the present time : including the latest information ⟨~ maps⟩ **2** : abreast of the times : MODERN ⟨~ methods⟩ — **up–to–date·ly** *adv* — **up–to–date·ness** *n*

up–to–the–minute *adj* (1912) **1** : extending up to the immediate present : including the very latest information **2** : marked by complete up-to-dateness

¹up·town \ˈəp-ˈtau̇n\ *adj* (1838) **1** : of or relating to uptown **2** : UPSCALE, FASHIONABLE — **uptown** *adv*

²up·town \ˈəp-ˌtau̇n\ *n* (1844) : the upper part of a town or city; *esp* : the residential district

up·trend \ˈəp-ˌtrend\ *n* (1926) : an upturn esp. in business or economic activity

¹up·turn \ˈəp-ˌtərn, ˌəp-ˈ\ *vt* (1567) **1** : to turn up or over **2** : to direct upward ~ *vi* : to turn upward

²up·turn \ˈəp-ˌtərn\ *n* (1864) : an upward turn esp. toward better conditions or higher prices

---

\ə\ abut \ᵊ\ kitten, F table \ər\ further \a\ ash \ā\ ace \ä\ mop, mar \au̇\ out \ch\ chin \e\ bet \ē\ easy \g\ go \i\ hit \ī\ ice \j\ job \ŋ\ sing \ō\ go \ȯ\ law \ȯi\ boy \th\ thin \th\ the \ü\ loot \u̇\ foot \y\ yet \zh\ vision \à, k, ⁿ, œ, ɶ, ue, ūe, ᵌ\ *see* Guide to Pronunciation

¹up·ward \'əp-wərd\ *or* **up·wards** \-wərdz\ *adv* (bef. 12c) **1 a** : in a direction from lower to higher ⟨the kite rose ~⟩ **b** (1) : toward the source (as of a river) (2) : toward the interior (as of a region) **c** : in a higher position ⟨held out his hand, palm ~⟩ **d** : in the upper parts : toward the head : ABOVE ⟨from the waist ~⟩ **2** : toward a higher or better condition or level ⟨young lawyers moving ~⟩ **3 a** : to an indefinitely greater amount, figure, or rank ⟨from $5 ~⟩ **b** : toward a greater amount or higher number, degree, or rate ⟨attendance figures have risen ~⟩ **4** : toward or into later years ⟨from youth ~⟩
²upward *adj* (1607) **1** : directed toward or situated in a higher place or level : ASCENDING **2** : rising to a higher pitch — **up·ward·ly** *adv* — **up·ward·ness** *n*
upward mobility *n* (1949) : the capacity or facility for rising to a higher social or economic position — **upwardly mobile** *adj*
upwards of *also* **upward of** *adv* (1721) : more than : in excess of ⟨they cost *upwards of* $25⟩
up·well \,əp-'wel\ *vi* (1885) : to well up; *specif* : to move or flow upward
up·well·ing \-'we-liŋ\ *n* (1868) : the process or an instance of rising or appearing to rise to the surface and flowing outward; *esp* : the process of upward movement to the surface of marine often nutrient-rich lower waters esp. along some shores due to the offshore drift of surface water (as from the action of winds and the Coriolis force)
up·wind \'əp-'wind\ *adv or adj* (1838) : in the direction from which the wind is blowing
¹ur- *or* **uro-** *comb form* [NL, fr. Gk *our-, ouro-,* fr. *ouron* urine, fr. *ourein* to urinate — more at URINE] **1** : urine ⟨uric⟩ **2** : urinary tract ⟨urology⟩ **3** : urinary and ⟨urogenital⟩ **4** : urea ⟨uracil⟩
²ur- *or* **uro-** *comb form* [NL, fr. Gk *our-, ouro-,* fr. *oura* tail — more at ASS] : tail ⟨uropod⟩
³ur- \'ûr\ *prefix, often cap* [G, fr. OHG *ir-, ur-* thoroughly (perfective prefix) — more at ABIDE] **1** : original : primitive ⟨ur-form⟩ **2** : original version of ⟨urtext⟩ **3** : prototypical : ARCH- ⟨ur-anticommunist⟩
ura·cil \'yúr-ə-,sil, -səl\ *n* [ISV ¹ur- + *acetic* + -*il* (substance relating to)] (1890) : a pyrimidine base $C_4H_4N_2O_2$ that is one of the four bases coding genetic information in the polynucleotide chain of RNA — compare ADENINE, CYTOSINE, GUANINE, THYMINE
ura·e·us \yú-'rē-əs\ *n, pl* **urae·i** \-'rē-,ī\ [NL, fr. LGk *ouraios,* a kind of snake] (1832) : a representation of the sacred asp (*Naja haje*) appearing in ancient Egyptian art and esp. on the headdress of rulers and serving as a symbol of sovereignty
Ural–Al·ta·ic \,yûr-əl-al-'tā-ik\ *n* (1853) : a postulated language family comprising the Uralic and Altaic languages — **Ural–Altaic** *adj*
Ura·li·an \yú-'rā-lē-ən, -'ra-\ *adj* (1801) **1** : of or relating to the Ural mountains **2** : URALIC
¹Ural·ic \yù-'ra-lik\ *n* (1861) : a language family comprising the Finno-Ugric and Samoyed languages
²Uralic *adj* (1880) : of, relating to, or constituting the Finno-Ugric and Samoyed languages
Ura·nia \yù-'rā-nē-ə, -nyə\ *n* [L, fr. Gk *Ourania*] : the Greek Muse of astronomy
Ura·ni·an \yú-'rā-nē-ən, -nyən\ *adj* (1844) : of or relating to the planet Uranus
ura·ni·nite \yú-'rā-nə-,nīt\ *n* [G *Uranin* uraninite (fr. NL *uranium*) + E -*ite*] (1879) : a mineral that is basically a black octahedral or cubic oxide of uranium which contains thorium, lead, and rare earth elements and is the chief ore of uranium
ura·ni·um \yú-'rā-nē-əm\ *n, often attrib* [NL, fr. *Uranus*] (ca. 1797) : a silvery heavy radioactive polyvalent metallic element that is found esp. in pitchblende and uraninite and exists naturally as a mixture of three isotopes of mass number 234, 235, and 238 in the proportions of 0.006 percent, 0.71 percent, and 99.28 percent respectively — see ELEMENT table
uranium hexa·flu·o·ride \-,hek-sə-'flôr-,īd, -'flúr-\ *n* (1899) : a volatile compound UF_6 of uranium and fluorine that is used in one major process of enriching uranium in uranium 235
uranium 238 *n* (1942) : an isotope of uranium of mass number 238 that is the most abundant and stable uranium isotope, that is not fissionable but can be used to produce a fissionable isotope of plutonium, and that has a half-life of 4.51×10^9 years
uranium 235 *n* (1940) : a light isotope of uranium of mass number 235 that when bombarded with slow neutrons undergoes rapid fission into smaller atoms with the release of neutrons and energy and that is used in nuclear power plants and atomic bombs
ura·nog·ra·phy \,yûr-ə-'nä-grə-fē\ *n* [Gk *ouranographia* description of the heavens, fr. *ouranos* sky + *-graphia* -graphy] (1675) : the construction of celestial representations (as maps)
Ura·nus \'yûr-ə-nəs, yú-'rā-\ *n* [LL, fr. Gk *Ouranos*] **1** : the sky personified as a god and father of the Titans in Greek mythology **2** : the planet seventh in order from the sun — see PLANET table
ura·nyl \'yûr-ə-,nil, yú-'ra-n°l\ *n* [ISV, fr. NL *uranium* + ISV -*yl*] (1850) : a bivalent radical UO_2
urate \'yûr-,āt\ *n* [F, fr. *urique* uric, fr. E *uric*] (1800) : a salt of uric acid — **urat·ic** \yú-'ra-tik\ *adj*
ur·ban \'ər-bən\ *adj* [L *urbanus,* fr. *urbs* city] (1619) : of, relating to, characteristic of, or constituting a city
ur·bane \,ər-'bān\ *adj* [L *urbanus* urban, urbane] (ca. 1623) : notably polite or finished in manner : POLISHED *syn* see SUAVE — **ur·bane·ly** *adv*
ur·ban·i·sa·tion, ur·ban·ise *Brit var of* URBANIZATION, URBANIZE
ur·ban·ism \'ər-bə-,ni-zəm\ *n* (1889) **1** : the characteristic way of life of city dwellers **2 a** : the study of the physical needs of urban societies **b** : CITY PLANNING **3** : URBANIZATION
ur·ban·ist \'ər-bə-nist\ *n* (1930) : a specialist in city planning — **ur·ban·is·tic** \,ər-bə-'nis-tik\ *adj* — **ur·ban·is·ti·cal·ly** \-ti-k(ə-)lē\ *adv*
ur·ban·ite \'ər-bə-,nīt\ *n* (1897) : a person who lives in a city
ur·ban·i·ty \,ər-'ba-nə-tē\ *n, pl* **-ties** (1535) **1** : the quality or state of being urbane **2** *pl* : urbane acts or conduct
ur·ban·i·za·tion \,ər-bə-nə-'zā-shən\ *n* (1888) : the quality or state of being urbanized or the process of becoming urbanized

ur·ban·ize \'ər-bə-,nīz\ *vt* -**ized; -iz·ing** (1884) **1** : to cause to take on urban characteristics ⟨urbanized areas⟩ **2** : to impart an urban way of life to ⟨~ migrants from rural areas⟩
ur·ban·ol·o·gy \,ər-bə-'nä-lə-jē\ *n* (1961) : a study dealing with specialized problems of cities (as planning, education, sociology, and politics) — **ur·ban·ol·o·gist** \-jist\ *n*
urban renewal *n* (1954) : a construction program to replace or restore substandard buildings in an urban area
urban sprawl *n* (1958) : the spreading of urban developments (as houses and shopping centers) on undeveloped land near a city
ur·ce·o·late \,ər-'sē-ə-lət, ,ər-sē-ə-,lāt\ *adj* [NL *urceolatus,* fr. L *urceolus,* dim. of *urceus* pitcher] (1760) : shaped like an urn ⟨the ~ corolla of a blueberry⟩
ur·chin \'ər-chən\ *n* [ME, fr. MF *herichon, heriçon,* fr. (assumed) OF *eriz,* fr. L *ericius,* fr. *eris;* akin to Gk *chēr* hedgehog] (14c) **1** *archaic* : HEDGEHOG 1a **2** : a mischievous youngster : SCAMP **3** : SEA URCHIN
urd \'ûrd, 'ərd\ *n* [Hindi] (ca. 1934) : an annual Asian legume (*Vigna mungo* syn. *Phaseolus mungo*) widely grown in warm regions for its edible blackish seed, for green manure, or for forage; *also* : the seed
Ur·du \'ûr-(,)dü, 'ər-\ *n* [Hindi *urdū,* fr. Per *zabān-e-urdū-e-muallā* language of the Exalted Camp (the imperial bazaar in Delhi)] (1796) : an Indo-Aryan language that has the same colloquial basis as standard Hindi, is an official language of Pakistan, and is widely used by Muslims in urban areas of India
-ure *n suffix* [ME, fr. OF, fr. L -*ura*] **1** : act : process ⟨exposure⟩ **2** : office : function; *also* : body performing (such) a function ⟨legislature⟩
urea \yú-'rē-ə\ *n* [NL, fr. F *urée,* fr. *urine*] (1806) : a soluble weakly basic nitrogenous compound $CO(NH_2)_2$ that is the chief solid component of mammalian urine and an end product of protein decomposition, is synthesized from carbon dioxide and ammonia, and is used esp. in synthesis (as of resins and plastics) and in fertilizers and animal rations
urea–formaldehyde *n* (1928) : a thermosetting synthetic resin made by condensing urea with formaldehyde
ure·ase \'yúr-ē-,ās, -,āz\ *n* (1892) : an enzyme that catalyzes the hydrolysis of urea
ure·din·i·um \,yúr-ə-'di-nē-əm\ *n, pl* **-ia** \-nē-ə\ [NL, fr. L *uredin-, uredo* burning, blight, fr. *urere* to burn — more at EMBER] (1905) : a usu. reddish or black mass of hyphae and spores of a rust fungus forming pustules that rupture the host's cuticle — **ure·din·i·al** \-nē-əl\ *adj*
ure·do·spore \yú-'rē-də-,spōr, -,spôr\ *also* **ure·dio·spore** \-'rē-dē-ə-\ *or* **ure·din·io·spore** \yúr-ə-'di-nē-ə-\ *n* [NL *uredium uredinium* (fr. L *uredo*) + E -*o-* + *spore*] (1875) : one of the thin-walled spores that are produced by the uredinial hyphae of rust fungi and spread the fungus vegetatively
ure·ide \'yúr-ē-,īd\ *n* (1857) : a cyclic or acyclic acyl derivative of urea
ure·mia \yú-'rē-mē-ə\ *n* [NL] (ca. 1857) **1** : accumulation in the blood of constituents normally eliminated in the urine that produces a severe toxic condition and usu. occurs in severe kidney disease **2** : the toxic bodily condition associated with uremia ⟨the patient was in ~⟩ — **ure·mic** \-mik\ *adj*
ureo·tel·ic \yú-,rē-ə-'te-lik, ,yúr-ē-ō-\ *adj* [*urea* + -*o-* + *tel-* + -*ic;* fr. the fact that urea is the end product] (1924) : excreting nitrogen mostly in the form of urea ⟨~ mammals⟩ — **ureo·te·lism** \-'te-,li-zəm, ,yúr-ē-'ä-t°l-,i-zəm\ *n*
ure·ter \'yúr-ə-tər\ *n* [NL, fr. Gk *ourētēr,* fr. *ourein* to urinate — more at URINE] (1543) : a duct that carries away the urine from a kidney to the bladder or cloaca — **ure·ter·al** \yú-'rē-tə-rəl\ *or* **ure·ter·ic** \,yúr-ə-'ter-ik\ *adj*
ure·thane \'yúr-ə-,thān\ *or* **ure·than** \-,than\ *n* [F *uréthane,* fr. *ur-* ¹ur- + *éth-* eth- + -*ane*] (1838) **1 a** : a crystalline compound $C_3H_7NO_2$ that is the ethyl ester of carbamic acid and is used esp. as a solvent and medicinally as an antineoplastic agent **b** : an ester of carbamic acid other than the ethyl ester **2** : POLYURETHANE
ure·thra \yú-'rē-thrə\ *n, pl* -**thras** *or* -**thrae** \-(,)thrē\ [LL, fr. Gk *ourēthra,* fr. *ourein* to urinate] (1634) : the canal that in most mammals carries off the urine from the bladder and in the male serves also as a genital duct — **ure·thral** \-thrəl\ *adj*
ure·thri·tis \,yúr-i-'thrī-təs\ *n* [NL] (ca. 1823) : inflammation of the urethra
ure·thro·scope \yú-'rē-thrə-,skōp\ *n* [ISV] (1868) : an instrument for viewing the interior of the urethra
¹urge \'ərj\ *vb* **urged; urg·ing** [L *urgēre* to press, push, entreat — more at WREAK] *vt* (1560) **1** : to present, advocate, or demand earnestly or pressingly ⟨his conviction was upheld on a theory never *urged* at his ... trial —Leon Friedman⟩ **2** : to undertake the accomplishment of with energy, swiftness, or enthusiasm ⟨~ the attack⟩ **3 a** : SOLICIT, ENTREAT **b** : to serve as a motive or reason for **4** : to force or impel in an indicated direction or into motion or greater speed ⟨the dog *urged* the sheep toward the gate⟩ **5** : STIMULATE, PROVOKE ~ *vi* : to declare, advance, or press earnestly a statement, argument, charge, or claim — **urg·er** *n*
²urge *n* (ca. 1618) **1** : the act or process of urging : a force or impulse that urges; *esp* : a continuing impulse toward an activity or goal
ur·gen·cy \'ər-jən(t)-sē\ *n, pl* -**cies** (1540) **1** : the quality or state of being urgent : INSISTENCE **2** : a force or impulse that impels or constrains : URGE
ur·gent \'ər-jənt\ *adj* [ME, fr. MF, fr. L *urgent-, urgens,* prp. of *urgēre*] (15c) **1 a** : calling for immediate attention : PRESSING ⟨~ appeals⟩ **b** : conveying a sense of urgency **2** : urging insistently : IMPORTUNATE — **ur·gent·ly** *adv*
-urgy *n comb form* [NL -*urgia,* fr. Gk -*ourgos* working, fr. -*o-* + *ergon* work — more at WORK] : technique or art of dealing or working with (such) a product, matter, or tool ⟨metallurgy⟩
-uria *n comb form* [NL, fr. Gk -*ouria,* fr. *ouron* urine, fr. *ourein* to urinate — more at URINE] **1** : presence of (a specified substance) in urine ⟨albuminuria⟩ **2** : condition of having (such) urine ⟨polyuria⟩; *esp* : abnormal or diseased condition marked by the presence of (a specified substance) ⟨pyuria⟩
uri·al \'úr-ē-əl, -,äl\ *n* [Panjabi *huṛeāl*] (1860) : an upland wild sheep (*Ovis vignei*) of southern and central Asia which is reddish brown and the males of which have a beard from the neck to the chest
uric \'yúr-ik\ *adj* (1797) : of, relating to, or found in urine

uraeus

uric acid *n* (1800) : a white odorless and tasteless nearly insoluble acid $C_5H_4N_4O_3$ that is the chief nitrogenous waste present in the urine esp. of lower vertebrates (as birds and reptiles), is present in small quantity in human urine, and occurs pathologically in renal calculi and the tophi of gout

uri·co·su·ric \,yùr-i-kə-'shùr-ik, -'sùr-\ *adj* [irreg. fr. *uric*] (ca. 1947) : relating to or promoting the excretion of uric acid in the urine

uri·co·tel·ic \,yùr-i-kō-'te-lik\ *adj* [*uric* + *-o-* + *tel-* + *-ic;* fr. the fact that uric acid is the end product] (1924) : excreting nitrogen mostly in the form of uric acid ⟨birds are typical ~ animals⟩ — **uri·co·tel·ism** \-'te-,li-zəm, -'kä-t²l-,i-zəm\ *n*

uri·dine \'yùr-ə-,dēn\ *n* [ISV ¹*ur-* + *-idine*] (1911) : a pyrimidine nucleoside $C_9H_{12}N_2O_6$ that is composed of uracil attached to ribose, is derived by hydrolysis from nucleic acids, and in the form of phosphate derivatives plays an important role in carbohydrate metabolism

Uri·el \'yùr-ē-əl\ *n* [Heb *Ūrī'ēl*] : one of the four archangels named in Hebrew tradition

Urim and Thum·mim \,yùr-ə-mən(d)-'thə-məm, ,ùr-; ,ùr-ēm-ən(d)-'tù-mēm\ *n pl* [part trans. of Heb *ūrīm wĕthummīm*] (1537) : sacred lots used in early times by the Hebrews

urin- *or* **urino-** *comb form* [ME, fr. OF, fr. L, fr. *urina* urine] : ¹UR- ⟨*urino*genital⟩ ⟨*urinary*⟩

uri·nal \'yùr-ə-n²l, *Brit also* yù-'rī-n²l\ *n* [ME, fr. MF, fr. LL, fr. L *urina*] (13c) **1** : a vessel for receiving urine **2 a** : a building or enclosure with facilities for urinating **b** : a fixture used for urinating

uri·nal·y·sis \,yùr-ə-'na-lə-səs\ *n, pl* **-y·ses** [NL, irreg. fr. *urin-* + *analysis*] (1889) : chemical analysis of urine

uri·nary \'yùr-ə-,ner-ē\ *adj* (1578) **1** : relating to, occurring in, affecting, or constituting the organs concerned with the formation and discharge of urine ⟨~ system⟩ ⟨~ calculi⟩ **2** : of, relating to, or for urine **3** : excreted as or in urine

urinary bladder *n* (1728) : a membranous sac in many vertebrates that serves for the temporary retention of urine and discharges by the urethra

uri·nate \'yùr-ə-,nāt\ *vi* **-nat·ed; -nat·ing** (1599) : to discharge urine : MICTURATE — **uri·na·tion** \,yùr-ə-'nā-shən\ *n*

urine \'yùr-ən\ *n* [ME, fr. MF, fr. L *urina*, fr. *urinari* to dive; akin to Skt *vār* water and perh. to Skt *varṣati* it rains, Gk *ourein* to urinate] (14c) : waste material that is secreted by the kidney in vertebrates, is rich in end products of protein metabolism together with salts and pigments, and forms a clear amber and usu. slightly acid fluid in mammals but is semisolid in birds and reptiles — **urin·ous** \'yùr-ə-nəs\ *adj*

uri·no·gen·i·tal \,yùr-ə-nō-'je-nə-t²l\ *adj* (1836) : UROGENITAL

uri·nom·e·ter \,yùr-ə-'nä-mə-tər\ *n* [ISV] (1843) : a small hydrometer for determining the specific gravity of urine

urn \'ərn\ *n* [ME *urne*, fr. L *urna*] (14c) **1** : a vessel that is typically an ornamental vase on a pedestal and that is used for various purposes (as preserving the ashes of the dead after cremation) **2** : a closed vessel usu. with a spigot for serving a hot beverage ⟨a coffee ~⟩

uro- — see UR-

uro·ca·nic acid \,yùr-ə-'kä-nik-, -'ka-\ *n* [¹*ur-* + *canine* + *-ic;* fr. its being first obtained from the urine of a dog] (ca. 1903) : a crystalline acid $C_6H_6N_2O_2$ that is normally present in human skin

uro·chor·date \,yùr-ə-'kòr-dət, -,dāt\ *n* [NL *Urochordata*, former group name, fr. ²*ur-* + *chordatus* having a notochord, fr. *chorda* notochord, fr. L, string, cord — more at CORD] (1948) : TUNICATE — **urochordate** *adj*

uro·chrome \'yùr-ə-,krōm\ *n* (1864) : a yellow pigment to which the color of normal urine is principally due

uro·dele \'yùr-ə-,dēl\ *n* [F *urodèle*, ultim. fr. Gk *oura* tail + *dēlos* evident, showing — more at ASS] (1842) : any of an order (Caudata syn. Urodela) of amphibians (as newts) that have a tail throughout life — **urodele** *adj*

uro·gen·i·tal \,yùr-ō-'je-nə-t²l\ *adj* [ISV] (1848) : of, relating to, or being the organs or functions of excretion and reproduction

uro·ki·nase \,yùr-ō-'kī-,nās, -,nāz\ *n* (1952) : an enzyme that is produced by the kidney and found in urine, that activates plasminogen, and that is used therapeutically to dissolve blood clots (as in the heart)

uro·lith \'yùr-ə-,lith\ *n* [ISV] (ca. 1900) : a calculus in the urinary tract

uro·lith·i·a·sis \,yùr-ə-li-'thī-ə-səs\ *n* [NL] (ca. 1860) : a condition that is characterized by the formation or presence of calculi in the urinary tract

uro·log·ic \,yùr-ə-'lä-jik\ *also* **uro·log·i·cal** \-ji-kəl\ *adj* (1855) : of or relating to the urinary tract or to urology

urol·o·gist \yù-'rä-lə-jist\ *n* (1889) : a physician who specializes in the urinary or urogenital tract — **urol·o·gy** \-jē\ *n*

-uronic *adj suffix* [Gk *ouron* urine] : connected with urine — in names of certain aldehyde-acids derived from sugars or compounds of such acids ⟨hyaluronic⟩

uron·ic acid \yù-'rä-nik-\ *n* (1925) : any of a class of acidic compounds of the general formula HOOC(CHOH)ₙCHO that contain both carboxylic and aldehydic groups, are oxidation products of sugars, and occur combined in many polysaccharides and in urine

uro·pod \'yùr-ə-,päd\ *n* [ISV ²*ur-* + Gk *pod-, pous* foot — more at FOOT] (ca. 1890) : either of the flattened lateral appendages of the last abdominal segment of a crustacean; *broadly* : an abdominal appendage of a crustacean

uro·py·gi·al gland \,yùr-ə-'pī-jē-əl-\ *n* (1870) : a large gland that occurs in most birds, opens dorsally at the base of the tail feathers, and usu. secretes an oily fluid which the bird uses in preening its feathers — called also *oil gland*

uro·py·gi·um \,yùr-ə-'pī-jē-əm\ *n* [NL, fr. Gk *ouropygion*, fr. *ouro-* ²*ur-* + *pygē* rump] (1771) : the fleshy and bony prominence at the posterior extremity of a bird's body that supports the tail feathers

uro·style \'yùr-ə-,stīl\ *n* [ISV ²*ur-* + Gk *stylos* pillar — more at STEER] (1875) : a long unsegmented bone that represents a number of fused

---

vertebrae and forms the posterior part of the vertebral column of frogs and toads

Ur·sa Ma·jor \,ər-sə-'mā-jər\ *n* [L (gen. *Ursae Majoris*), lit., greater bear] : a constellation that is the most conspicuous of the northern constellations, is situated near the north pole of the heavens, and contains the stars forming the Big Dipper two of which are in a line indicating the direction of the North Star — called also *Great Bear*

Ursa Mi·nor \-'mi-nər\ *n* [L (gen. *Ursae Minoris*), lit., lesser bear] : a constellation that includes the north pole of the heavens and the stars which form the Little Dipper with the North Star at the tip of the handle — called also *Little Bear*

ur·sine \'ər-,sīn\ *adj* [L *ursinus*, fr. *ursus* bear — more at ARCTIC] (ca. 1550) **1** : of or relating to a bear or the bear family (Ursidae) **2** : suggesting or characteristic of a bear ⟨a lumbering ~ gait⟩

Ur·su·line \'ər-sə-lən, -,līn, -,lēn\ *n* [NL *Ursulina*, fr. *Ursula* St. Ursula, legendary Christian martyr] (1693) : a member of any of several Roman Catholic teaching orders of nuns; *esp* : a member of a teaching order founded by St. Angela Merici in Brescia, Italy, in 1535

ur·text \'ùr-,tekst\ *n* [G, fr. *ur-* ³*ur-* + *Text* text] (ca. 1932) : the original text (as of a musical score)

ur·ti·car·ia \,ər-tə-'kar-ē-ə, -'ker-\ *n* [NL, fr. L *urtica* nettle] (ca. 1771) : an allergic disorder marked by raised edematous patches of skin or mucous membrane and usu. intense itching and caused by contact with a specific precipitating factor (as a food, drug, or inhalant) either externally or internally — **ur·ti·car·i·al** \-ē-əl\ *adj*

ur·ti·cate \'ər-tə-,kāt\ *vi* **-cat·ed; -cat·ing** [ML *urticatus,* pp. of *urticare* to sting, fr. L *urtica*] (1843) : to produce wheals or itching; *esp* : to induce urticaria — **ur·ti·ca·tion** \,ər-tə-'kā-shən\ *n*

urus \'yùr-əs\ *n* [L, of Gmc origin; akin to OHG *ūro* aurochs — more at AUROCHS] (1601) : AUROCHS I

uru·shi·ol \yù-'rü-shē-,òl, ù-', -,ōl\ *n* [ISV, fr. Jp *urushi* lacquer + ISV ¹*-ol*] (1908) : a mixture of pyrocatechol derivatives with saturated or unsaturated side chains of 15 or 17 carbon atoms that is an oily toxic irritant principle present in poison ivy and some related plants (genus *Rhus*) and in oriental lacquers derived from such plants

us \'əs\ *pron* [ME, fr. OE *ūs;* akin to OHG *uns* us, L *nos*] *objective case of* WE

us·able *also* **use·able** \'yü-zə-bəl\ *adj* (14c) **1** : capable of being used **2** : convenient and practicable for use — **us·abil·i·ty** \,yü-zə-'bi-lə-tē\ *n* — **us·able·ness** \'yü-zə-bəl-nəs\ *n* — **us·ably** \-blē\ *adv*

us·age \'yü-sij, -zij\ *n* [ME, fr. MF, fr. *us* use] (14c) **1 a** : firmly established and generally accepted practice or procedure **b** : a uniform certain reasonable lawful practice existing in a particular locality or occupation and binding persons entering into transactions chiefly on the basis of presumed familiarity **c** : the way in which words and phrases are actually used (as in a particular form or sense) in a language community **2 a** : the action, amount, or mode of using ⟨a decrease in the ~ of electricity⟩ **b** : manner of treating ⟨suffered ill ~ at the hands of his captors⟩ **syn** see HABIT

us·ance \'yü-z²n(t)s\ *n* (14c) **1** : USAGE 1a **2** : USE, EMPLOYMENT **3** *a obs* : USURY **b** : INTEREST **4** : the time allowed by custom for payment of a bill of exchange in foreign commerce

¹use \'yüs\ *n* [ME us, fr. OF, fr. L *usus*, fr. *uti* to use] (13c) **1 a** : the act or practice of employing something : EMPLOYMENT, APPLICATION ⟨he made good ~ of his spare time⟩ **b** : the fact or state of being used ⟨a dish in daily ~⟩ **c** : a method or manner of employing or applying something ⟨gained practice in the ~ of the camera⟩ **2 a** (1) : habitual or customary usage (2) : an individual habit or group custom **b** : a liturgical form or observance; *esp* : a liturgy having modifications peculiar to a local church or religious order **3 a** : the privilege or benefit of using something ⟨gave him the ~ of her car⟩ **b** : the ability or power to use something (as a limb or faculty) **c** : the legal enjoyment of property that consists in its employment, occupation, exercise, or practice ⟨she had the ~ of the estate for life⟩ **4 a** : a particular service or end ⟨put learning to practical ~⟩ **b** : the quality of being suitable for employment ⟨saving things that might be of ~⟩ **c** : the occasion or need to employ ⟨took only what they had ~ for⟩ **5 a** : the benefit in law of one or more persons; *specif* : the benefit or profit of property established in one other than the legal possessor **b** : a legal arrangement by which such benefits and profits are so established **6** : a favorable attitude : LIKING ⟨had no ~ for modern art⟩

²use \'yüz\ *vb* **used** \'yüzd, *in the phrase "used to" usu* 'yüs(t)\; **us·ing** \'yü-ziŋ\ *vt* (14c) **1** *archaic* : ACCUSTOM, HABITUATE **2** : to put into action or service : avail oneself of : EMPLOY **3** : to consume or take (as liquor or drugs) regularly **4** : to carry out a purpose or action by means of : UTILIZE; *also* : MANIPULATE 2b ⟨used him only as a means up the corporate ladder⟩ **5** : to expend or consume by putting to use — often used with *up* **6** : to behave toward : act with regard to : TREAT ⟨*used* the prisoners cruelly⟩ **7** : STAND 1d ⟨the house could ~ a coat of paint⟩ ~ *vi* — used in the past with *to* to indicate a former fact or state ⟨claims winters *used* to be harder⟩ ⟨didn't ~ to smoke so much⟩

syn USE, EMPLOY, UTILIZE mean to put into service esp. to attain an end. USE implies availing oneself of something as a means or instrument to an end ⟨willing to *use* any means to achieve her ends⟩. EMPLOY suggests the use of a person or thing that is available but idle, inactive, or disengaged ⟨looking for better ways to *employ* their skills⟩. UTILIZE may suggest the discovery of a new, profitable, or practical use for something ⟨an old wooden bucket *utilized* as a planter⟩.

used \'yüzd, *in the phrase "used to" usu* 'yüs(t)\ *adj* (14c) **1** : employed in accomplishing something **2** : that has endured use; *specif* : SECOND-HAND ⟨a ~ car⟩ **3** : ACCUSTOMED, HABITUATED

use·ful \'yüs-fəl\ *adj* (1595) **1** : capable of being put to use; *esp* : serviceable for an end or purpose **2** : of a valuable or productive kind ⟨do something ~ with your life⟩ — **use·ful·ly** \-fə-lē\ *adv*

use·ful·ness *n* (1617) : the quality of having utility and esp. practical worth or applicability

urial

\ə\ abut \²\ kitten, F table \ər\ further \a\ ash \ā\ ace \ä\ mop, mar \aù\ out \ch\ chin \e\ bet \ē\ easy \g\ go \i\ hit \ī\ ice \j\ job \ŋ\ sing \ō\ go \ò\ law \òi\ boy \th\ thin \th\ the \ü\ loot \ù\ foot \y\ yet \zh\ vision \ä, k̟, ⁿ, œ, œ̄, ue, ūe, ᵞ\ see Guide to Pronunciation

use·less \'yü-sləs\ *adj* (1593) : having or being of no use: **a** : INEFFEC-
TUAL **b** : not able to give service or aid : INEPT — **use·less·ly** *adv* —
use·less·ness *n*
us·er \'yü-zər\ *n* (15c) : one that uses
user fee *n* (1967) : an excise tax often in the form of a license or supplemental charge levied to fund a public service — called also *user's fee*
us·er–friend·ly \,yü-zər-'fren(d)-lē\ *adj* (1977) : easy to learn, use,
understand, or deal with — **user–friendliness** *n*
use up *vt* (1833) : to exhaust of strength or useful properties ⟨land that
has been *used up*⟩
Ushak \ü-'shäk\ *var of* OUSHAK
¹ush·er \'ə-shər\ *n* [ME *ussher*, fr. MF *ussier*, fr. (assumed) VL *ustiarius*
doorkeeper, fr. L *ostium, ustium* door, mouth of a river — more at
OSTIUM] (14c) **1 a** : an officer or servant who has the care of the door
of a court, hall, or chamber **b** : an officer who walks before a person
of rank **c** : one who escorts persons to their seats (as in a theater) **2**
archaic : an assistant teacher
²usher *vb* **ush·ered; ush·er·ing** \'ə-sh(ə-)riŋ\ *vt* (1596) **1** : to conduct
to a place **2** : to precede as an usher, forerunner, or harbinger **3** : to
cause to enter : INTRODUCE ⟨a new theory ~*ed* into the world⟩ ~ *vi*
: to serve as an usher ⟨~ at a wedding⟩
ush·er·ette \,ə-shə-'ret\ *n* (1925) : a girl or woman who is an usher (as
in a theater)
usher in *vt* (ca. 1600) **1** : to serve to bring into being ⟨a discovery that
ushered in a period of prosperity⟩ **2** : to mark or observe the beginning of ⟨*ushered in* the new year with much merrymaking⟩ *syn* see
BEGIN
us·nea \'əs-nē-ə, 'əz-\ *n* [NL, fr. Ar *ushnah* moss] (ca. 1597) : any of a
genus (*Usnea*) of widely distributed lichens (as old-man's beard) that
have a grayish or yellow pendulous freely branched thallus
us·que·baugh \'əs-kwi-,bò, -,bä\ *n* [Ir *uisce beathadh*] (1581) *Irish &
Scot* : WHISKEY
¹usu·al \'yü-zhə-wəl, -zhəl; 'yüzh-wəl\ *adj* [ME, fr. LL *usualis*, fr. L
usus use] (14c) **1** : accordant with usage, custom, or habit : NORMAL
2 : commonly or ordinarily used ⟨followed his ~ route⟩ **3** : found in
ordinary practice or in the ordinary course of events : ORDINARY —
usu·al·ly \'yü-zhə-wə-lē, -zhə-lē; 'yüzh-wə-lē, 'yüzh-lē\ *adv* — **usu·al·
ness** \'yü-zhə-wəl-nəs, -zhəl-; 'yüzh-wəl-\ *n* — **as usual** : in the accustomed or habitual way ⟨*as usual* they were late⟩
  syn USUAL, CUSTOMARY, HABITUAL, WONTED, ACCUSTOMED mean familiar
through frequent or regular repetition. USUAL stresses the absence of
strangeness or unexpectedness ⟨my *usual* order for lunch⟩. CUSTOMARY
applies to what accords with the practices, conventions, or usages of
an individual or community ⟨the *customary* waiting period before the
application is approved⟩. HABITUAL suggests a practice settled or established by much repetition ⟨an *habitual* morning routine⟩. WONTED
stresses habituation but usu. applies to what is favored, sought, or
purposefully cultivated ⟨his *wonted* determination⟩. ACCUSTOMED is
less emphatic than WONTED or HABITUAL in suggesting fixed habit or
invariable custom ⟨accepted the compliment with her *accustomed*
modesty⟩.
²usual *n* (1589) : something usual
usu·fruct \'yü-zə-,frəkt, -sə-\ *n* [L *ususfructus*, fr. *usus et fructus* use
and enjoyment] (ca. 1630) **1** : the legal right of using and enjoying
the fruits or profits of something belonging to another **2** : the right to
use or enjoy something
¹usu·fruc·tu·ary \,yü-zə-'frək-chə-,wer-ē, -sə-\ *n* (ca. 1618) **1** : one
having the usufruct of property **2** : one having the use or enjoyment
of something
²usufructuary *adj* (1710) : of, relating to, or having the character of a
usufruct
usu·rer \'yü-zhər-ər, 'yüzh-rər\ *n* (14c) : one that lends money esp. at
an exorbitant rate
usu·ri·ous \yü-'zhùr-ē-əs, -'zùr-\ *adj* (1610) **1** : practicing usury **2**
: involving usury : of the character of usury — **usu·ri·ous·ly** *adv* —
usu·ri·ous·ness *n*
usurp \yü-'sərp *also* -'zərp\ *vb* [ME, fr. MF *usurper*, fr. L *usurpare* to
take possession of without legal claim, fr. *usu* (abl. of *usus* use) +
rapere to seize — more at RAPID] *vt* (14c) **1** : to seize and hold (as
office, place, or powers) in possession by force or without right ⟨~ a
throne⟩ **b** : to take or make use of without right ⟨~*ed* the rights to
her life story⟩ **2** : to take the place of by or as if by force : SUPPLANT
⟨must not let stock responses based on inherited prejudice ~ careful
judgment⟩ ~ *vi* : to seize or exercise authority or possession wrongfully — **usur·pa·tion** \,yü-sər-'pā-shən *also* ,yü-zər-\ *n* — **usurp·er**
\yü-'sərp-ər *also* -'zərp-\ *n*
usu·ry \'yü-zhə-rē, 'yüzh-rē\ *n, pl* **-ries** [ME, fr. ML *usuria*, alter. of L
usura, fr. *usus*, pp. of *uti* to use] (14c) **1** *archaic* : INTEREST **2** : the
lending of money with an interest charge for its use; *esp* : the lending of
money at exorbitant interest rates **3** : an unconscionable or exorbitant rate or amount of interest; *specif* : interest in excess of a legal rate
charged to a borrower for the use of money
ut \'ət, 'üt, 'üt\ *n* [ME, first note in the diatonic scale, fr. ML, fr. the
syllable sung to this note in a medieval hymn to St. John the Baptist]
(14c) : a syllable used for the first note in the diatonic scale in an early
solmization system and later replaced by *do*
Ute \'yüt\ *n, pl* **Ute** *or* **Utes** [short for earlier *Utah, Utaw*, fr. AmerSp
Yuta] (1776) **1** : a member of an American Indian people orig. ranging through Utah, Colorado, Arizona, and New Mexico **2** : the Uto-
Aztecan language of the Ute people
uten·sil \yù-'ten(t)-səl, 'yü-,\ *n* [ME, vessels for domestic use, fr. MF
utensile, fr. L *utensilia*, fr. neut. pl. of *utensilis* useful, fr. *uti* to use] (14c)
1 : an implement, instrument, or vessel used in a household and esp. a
kitchen **2** : a useful tool or implement *syn* see IMPLEMENT
uter·ine \'yü-tə-,rīn, -rən\ *adj* [ME, fr. LL *uterinus*, fr. L *uterus*] (15c)
1 : born of the same mother but by a different father **2** : of, relating
to, or affecting the uterus ⟨~ cancer⟩
uter·us \'yü-tə-rəs, 'yü-trəs\ *n, pl* **uteri** \'yü-tə-,rī\ *also* **uter·us·es** [L,
belly, womb; prob. akin to Gk *hoderos* belly, Skt *udara*] (1615) **1** : an
organ of the female mammal for containing and usu. for nourishing the
young during development previous to birth — called also *womb* **2** : a
structure in some lower animals analogous to the uterus in which eggs
or young develop
Uther \'ü-thər, 'yü-\ *n* : a legendary British king and father of Arthur

utile \'yü-t⁷l, 'yü-,tīl\ *adj* [MF, fr. L *utilis*] (15c) : USEFUL
uti·lise *Brit var of* UTILIZE
¹util·i·tar·i·an \(,)yü-,ti-lə-'ter-ē-ən\ *n* (ca. 1780) : an advocate or ad-
herent of utilitarianism
²utilitarian *adj* (1802) **1** : of or relating to or advocating utilitarianism **2** : marked by utilitarian views or practices **3 a** : of, relating
to, or aiming at utility **b** : exhibiting or preferring mere utility ⟨spare
~ furnishings⟩
util·i·tar·i·an·ism \-ē-ə-,ni-zəm\ *n* (1827) **1** : a doctrine that the useful is the good and that the determining consideration of right conduct
should be the usefulness of its consequences; *specif* : a theory that the
aim of action should be the largest possible balance of pleasure over
pain or the greatest happiness of the greatest number **2** : utilitarian
character, spirit, or quality
¹util·i·ty \yü-'ti-lə-tē\ *n, pl* **-ties** [ME *utilite*, fr. MF *utilité*, fr. L *utilitat,
utilitas*, fr. *utilis* useful, fr. *uti* to use] (14c) **1** : fitness for some purpose
or worth to some end **2** : something useful or designed for use **3 a**
: PUBLIC UTILITY **b** (1) : a service (as light, power, or water) provided
by a public utility (2) : equipment or a piece of equipment to provide
such service or a comparable service **4** : a program or routine designed to perform or facilitate esp. routine operations (as copying files
or editing text) on a computer
²utility *adj* (1851) **1** : capable of serving as a substitute in various
roles or positions ⟨a ~ infielder⟩ **2 a** : kept to provide a useful product or service rather than for show or as a pet ⟨~ livestock⟩ ⟨a ~ dog⟩
b : being of a usable but inferior grade ⟨~ beef⟩ **3** : serving primarily
for utility rather than beauty : UTILITARIAN **4** : designed or adapted
for general use ⟨a ~ knife⟩ **5** : of or relating to a utility ⟨a ~ com-
pany⟩
uti·lize \'yü-t⁷l-,īz\ *vt* **-lized; -liz·ing** [F *utiliser*, fr. *utile*] (1807) : to
make use of : turn to practical use or account ⟨I'm a great person for
utilizing waste power —Robert Frost⟩ *syn* see USE — **uti·liz·able**
\-,ī-zə-bəl\ *adj* — **uti·li·za·tion** \,yü-t⁷l-ə-'zā-shən\ *n* — **uti·liz·er**
\'yü-t⁷l-,ī-zər\ *n*
¹ut·most \'ət-,mōst, *also* Southern -məst\ *adj* [ME, alter. of *utmest*, fr.
OE *ūtmest*, superl. adj., fr. *ūt* out, adv. — more at OUT] (bef. 12c) **1**
: situated at the farthest or most distant point : EXTREME ⟨the ~ point
of the earth —John Hunt⟩ **2** : of the greatest or highest degree, quantity, number, or amount ⟨a matter of ~ concern⟩
²utmost *n* (bef. 12c) **1** : the most possible : the extreme limit : the
highest attainable point or degree ⟨the ~ in reliability⟩ **2** : the highest, greatest, or best of one's abilities, powers, and resources ⟨will do
our ~ to help⟩
Uto–Az·tec·an \,yü-tō-'az,-te-kən\ *n* [*Ute* + *-o-* + *Aztec*] (1891) : a
family of American Indian languages spoken by peoples from the U.S.
Great Basin south to Central America — **Uto–Aztecan** *adj*
uto·pia \yü-'tō-pē-ə\ *n* [*Utopia*, imaginary and ideal country in *Utopia*
(1516) by Sir Thomas More, fr. Gk *ou* not, no + *topos* place] (1610) **1**
: an imaginary and indefinitely remote place **2** *often cap* : a place of
ideal perfection esp. in laws, government, and social conditions **3** : an
impractical scheme for social improvement
¹uto·pi·an \-pē-ən\ *adj, often cap* (1551) **1** : of, relating to, or having
the characteristics of a utopia; *esp* : having impossibly ideal conditions
esp. of social organization **2** : proposing or advocating impractically
ideal social and political schemes ⟨~ idealists⟩ **3** : impossibly ideal
: VISIONARY ⟨recognised the ~ nature of his hopes —C. S. Kilby⟩ **4**
: believing in, advocating, or having the characteristics of utopian
socialism ⟨~ doctrines⟩ ⟨~ novels⟩
²utopian *n* (ca. 1873) **1** : one that believes in the perfectibility of human society **2** : one that proposes or advocates utopian schemes
uto·pi·an·ism \-pē-ə-,ni-zəm\ *n* (ca. 1661) **1** : a utopian idea or theory
2 *often cap* : the body of ideas, views, or aims of a utopian
utopian socialism *n* (ca. 1923) : socialism based on a belief that social
ownership of the means of production can be achieved by voluntary
and peaceful surrender of their holdings by propertied groups — **utopian socialist** *n*
uto·pism \'yü-tə-,pi-zəm, yù-'tō-\ *n* (1888) : UTOPIANISM 2 — **utopist**
\'yü-tō-pist\ *n* — **uto·pis·tic** \,yü-tə-'pis-tik, yù-,tō-\ *adj*
utri·cle \'yü-tri-kəl\ *n* [L *utriculus*, dim. of *uter* leather bag] (1731)
: any of various small pouches or saccate parts of an animal or plant
body: as **a** : the part of the membranous labyrinth of the inner ear
into which the semicircular canals open **b** : a small usu. indehiscent
one-seeded fruit with thin membranous pericarp — **utric·u·lar** \yü-
'tri-kyə-lər\ *adj*
utric·u·lus \yü-'tri-kyə-ləs\ *n* [L, small bag] (1847) : UTRICLE a
¹ut·ter \'ə-tər\ *adj* [ME, remote, fr. OE *ūtera* outer, compar. adj. fr. *ūt*
out, adv. — more at OUT] (15c) : carried to the utmost point or highest
degree : ABSOLUTE, TOTAL ⟨~ darkness⟩ ⟨~ strangers⟩ — **ut·ter·ly** *adv*
²utter *vb* [ME *uttren*, fr. *utter* outside, adv., fr. OE *ūtor*, compar. of *ūt*
out] *vt* (15c) **1** *obs* : to offer for sale **2 a** : to send forth as a sound
b : to give utterance to : PRONOUNCE, SPEAK **c** : to give public expression to : express in words **3** : to put (as currency) into circulation;
specif : to circulate (as a counterfeit note) as if legal or genuine ⟨~ false
tokens⟩ **4** : to put forth or out : DISCHARGE ~ *vi* : to make a statement or sound *syn* see EXPRESS — **ut·ter·able** \'ə-tə-rə-bəl\ *adj* —
ut·ter·er \'ə-tər-ər\ *n*
¹ut·ter·ance \'ə-tə-rən(t)s, 'ə-trən(t)s\ *n* [ME *uttraunce*, modif. of MF
outrance — more at OUTRANCE] (15c) *archaic* : the last extremity : BIT-
TER END
²ut·ter·ance \'ə-tə-rən(t)s *also* 'ə-trən(t)s\ *n* (15c) **1** : something uttered; *esp* : an oral or written statement : a stated or published expression **2** : vocal expression : SPEECH **3** : power, style, or manner of
speaking
¹ut·ter·most \'ə-tər-,mōst\ *adj* [ME, alter. of *uttermest*, fr. ¹*utter* +
-mest (as in *utmest* utmost)] (14c) **1** : OUTERMOST **2** : EXTREME, UT-
MOST
²uttermost *n* (14c) : UTMOST ⟨to the ~ of our capacity —H. S. Tru-
man⟩
U-turn \'yü-,tərn\ *n* (1930) **1** : a turn resembling the letter U; *esp* : a
180-degree turn made by a vehicle in a road **2** : something (as a reversal of policy) resembling a U-turn
U-val·ue \'yü-,val-(,)yü\ *n* [*unit*] (1949) : a measure of the heat transmission through a building part (as a wall or window) or a given thick-

ness of a material (as insulation) with lower numbers indicating better insulating properties — compare R-VALUE

uva·rov·ite \yü-'vär-ə-,vīt, ü-\ *n* [G *Uwarowit,* fr. Count Sergei S. *Uvarov* †1855 Russ. statesman] (1837) : an emerald green calcium‡ chromium garnet

uvea \'yü-vē-ə\ *n* [ML, fr. L *uva* grape] (1525) : the posterior pigmented layer of the iris; *also* : the iris and ciliary body together with the choroid coat — **uve·al** \-vē-əl\ *adj*

uve·itis \,yü-vē-'ī-təs\ *n* [NL] (ca. 1848) : inflammation of the uvea of the eye

uvu·la \'yü-vyə-lə\ *n, pl* **-las** *or* **-lae** \-,lē, -,lī\ [ME, fr. ML, dim. of L *uva* cluster of grapes, uvula; prob. akin to Gk *oa* service tree, OE *īw* yew — more at YEW] (14c) : the pendent fleshy lobe in the middle of the posterior border of the soft palate

uvu·lar \-lər\ *adj* (1843) **1** : of or relating to the uvula ⟨∼ glands⟩ **2** : produced with the aid of the uvula ⟨a ∼ sound⟩

ux·o·ri·al \,ək-'sōr-ē-əl, -'sôr-; ,əg-'zōr-, -'zôr-\ *adj* [L *uxorius*] (1800) : of, relating to, or characteristic of a wife

ux·or·i·cide \,ək-'sòr-ə-,sīd, -'sär-; ,əg-'zòr-, -'zär-\ *n* (1860) **1** [ML *uxoricidium,* fr. L *uxor* wife + *-i-* + *-cidium* -cide] : murder of a wife by her husband **2** [L *uxor* + E *-i-* + *-cide*] : a wife murderer

ux·o·ri·ous \,ək-'sōr-ē-əs, -'sòr-; ,əg-'zōr-, -'zôr-\ *adj* [L *uxorius* uxorious, uxorial, fr. *uxor* wife] (1598) : excessively fond of or submissive to a wife — **ux·o·ri·ous·ly** *adv* — **ux·o·ri·ous·ness** *n*

Uz·bek \'üz-,bek, 'əz-, üz-'\ *or* **Uz·beg** \-,beg, -'beg\ *n* (1616) **1** : a member of a Turkic people of Uzbekistan and adjacent regions of central Asia **2** : the Turkic language of the Uzbek people

---

v \'vē\ *n, pl* **v's** *or* **vs** \'vēz\ *often cap, often attrib* (15c) **1 a** : the 22d letter of the English alphabet **b** : a graphic representation of this letter **c** : a speech counterpart of orthographic *v* **2** : FIVE — see NUMBER table **3** : a graphic device for reproducing the letter *v* **4** : one designated *v* esp. as the 22d in order or class **5** : something shaped like the letter V

va·can·cy \'vā-kən(t)-sē\ *n, pl* **-cies** (1599) **1** *archaic* : an interval of leisure **2** : physical or mental inactivity or relaxation : IDLENESS **3 a** : a vacating of an office, post, or piece of property **b** : the time such office or property is vacant **4** : a vacant office, post, or tenancy **5** : empty space : VOID; *specif* : an unoccupied site for an atom or ion in a crystal **6** : the state of being vacant : VACUITY

va·cant \'vā-kənt\ *adj* [ME, fr. OF, fr. L *vacant-, vacans,* prp. of *vacare* to be empty, be free] (14c) **1** : not occupied by an incumbent, possessor, or officer ⟨a ∼ office⟩ ⟨∼ thrones⟩ **2** : being without content or occupant ⟨a ∼ seat in a bus⟩ ⟨a ∼ room⟩ **3** : free from activity or work : DISENGAGED ⟨∼ hours⟩ **4** : devoid of thought, reflection, or expression ⟨a ∼ smile⟩ **5** : not lived in ⟨∼ houses⟩ **6 a** : not put to use ⟨∼ land⟩ **b** : having no heir or claimant : ABANDONED ⟨a ∼ estate⟩ *syn* see EMPTY — **va·cant·ly** *adv* — **va·cant·ness** *n*

va·cate \'vā-,kāt, vā-'\ *vb* **va·cat·ed; va·cat·ing** [L *vacatus,* pp. of *vacare*] *vt* (1643) **1** : to make legally void : ANNUL **2 a** : to deprive of an incumbent or occupant **b** : to give up the incumbency or occupancy of ∼ *vi* : to vacate an office, post, or tenancy

¹va·ca·tion \vā-'kā-shən, və-\ *n, often attrib* [ME *vacacioun,* fr. MF *vacation,* fr. L *vacation-, vacatio* freedom, exemption, fr. *vacare*] (14c) **1** : a respite or a time of respite from something : INTERMISSION **2 a** : a scheduled period during which activity (as of a court or school) is suspended **b** : a period of exemption from work granted to an employee for rest and relaxation **3** : a period spent away from home or business in travel or recreation ⟨had a restful ∼ at the beach⟩ **4** : an act or an instance of vacating

²vacation *vi* **-tioned; -tion·ing** \-sh(ə-)niŋ\ (1896) : to take or spend a vacation — **va·ca·tion·er** \-sh(ə-)nər\ *n*

va·ca·tion·ist \-sh(ə-)nist\ *n* (1885) : a person taking a vacation

va·ca·tion·land \-shən-,land\ *n* (1927) : an area with recreational attractions and facilities for vacationists

vac·ci·nal \'vak-sə-n⁰l, vak-'sē-\ *adj* (ca. 1860) : of or relating to vaccine or vaccination

vac·ci·nate \'vak-sə-,nāt\ *vb* **-nat·ed; -nat·ing** *vt* (1803) **1** : to inoculate (a person) with cowpox virus in order to produce immunity to smallpox **2** : to administer a vaccine to usu. by injection ∼ *vi* : to perform or practice vaccination — **vac·ci·na·tor** \-,nā-tər\ *n*

vac·ci·na·tion \,vak-sə-'nā-shən\ *n* (1800) **1** : the act of vaccinating **2** : the scar left by vaccinating

vac·cine \vak-'sēn, 'vak-,\ *n* [L *vaccinus,* adj., of or from cows, fr. *vacca* cow; akin to Skt *vaśa* cow] (1803) **1** : matter or a preparation containing the virus of cowpox in a form used for vaccination **2** : a preparation of killed microorganisms, living attenuated organisms, or living fully virulent organisms that is administered to produce or artificially increase immunity to a particular disease — **vaccine** *adj*

vac·ci·nee \,vak-sə-'nē\ *n* (1889) : a vaccinated individual

vac·cin·ia \vak-'si-nē-ə\ *n* [NL, fr. *vaccinus*] (1803) **1** : COWPOX **2** : the virus that is the causative agent of cowpox — **vac·cin·i·al** \-nē-əl\ *adj*

vac·il·late \'va-sə-,lāt\ *vi* **-lat·ed; -lat·ing** [L *vacillatus,* pp. of *vacillare* to sway, waver — more at WINK] (1597) **1 a** : to sway through lack of equilibrium **b** : FLUCTUATE, OSCILLATE **2** : to waver in mind, will, or feeling : hesitate in choice of opinions or courses *syn* see HESITATE — **vac·il·lat·ing·ly** \-,lā-tiŋ-lē\ *adv* — **vac·il·la·tor** \-,lā-tər\ *n*

vac·il·la·tion \,va-sə-'lā-shən\ *n* (15c) **1** : an act or instance of vacillating **2** : inability to take a stand : IRRESOLUTION, INDECISION

va·cu·ity \va-'kyü-ə-tē, və-\ *n, pl* **-ties** [L *vacuitas,* fr. *vacuus* empty] (1541) **1** : an empty space **2** : the state, fact, or quality of being vacuous **3** : something (as an idea) that is vacuous or inane

vac·u·o·late \'va-kyü-(,)wō-,lāt\ *or* **vac·u·o·lat·ed** \-,lā-təd\ *adj* (1859) : containing one or more vacuoles ⟨highly *vacuolated* cells⟩

vac·u·o·la·tion \,va-kyü-(,)wō-'lā-shən\ *n* (1858) : the development or formation of vacuoles

vac·u·ole \'va-kyə-,wōl\ *n* [F, lit., small vacuum, fr. L *vacuum*] (1853)

1 : a small cavity or space in the tissues of an organism containing air or fluid **2** : a cavity or vesicle in the cytoplasm of a cell usu. containing fluid — see CELL illustration — **vac·u·o·lar** \,va-kyə-'wō-lər, -,lär\ *adj*

vac·u·ous \'va-kyə-wəs\ *adj* [L *vacuus*] (1655) **1** : emptied of or lacking content **2** : marked by lack of ideas or intelligence : STUPID, INANE ⟨a ∼ mind⟩ ⟨a ∼ expression⟩ **3** : devoid of serious occupation : IDLE *syn* see EMPTY — **vac·u·ous·ly** *adv* — **vac·u·ous·ness** *n*

¹vac·u·um \'va-(,)kyüm, -kyəm *also* -kyü-əm\ *n, pl* **vac·u·ums** *or* **vac·ua** \-kyə-wə\ [L, fr. neut. of *vacuus* empty, fr. *vacare* to be empty] (1550) **1** : emptiness of space **2 a** : a space absolutely devoid of matter **b** : a space partially exhausted (as to the highest degree possible) by artificial means (as an air pump) **c** : a degree of rarefaction below atmospheric pressure **3 a** : a state or condition resembling a vacuum : VOID ⟨the power ∼ in Indochina after the departure of the French —Norman Cousins⟩ **b** : a state of isolation from outside influences ⟨people who live in a ∼ . . . so that the world outside them is of no moment —W. S. Maugham⟩ **4** : a device creating or utilizing a partial vacuum; *esp* : VACUUM CLEANER

²vacuum *adj* (1825) **1** : of, containing, producing, or utilizing a partial vacuum ⟨separated by means of ∼ distillation⟩ **2** : of or relating to a vacuum device or system

³vacuum *vt* (1922) : to use a vacuum device (as a vacuum cleaner) on ∼ *vi* : to operate a vacuum device

vacuum bottle *n* (1910) : THERMOS

vacuum cleaner *n* (1903) : a household appliance for cleaning (as floors, carpets, or upholstery) by suction — called also *vacuum sweeper*

vacuum flask *n* (1917) : THERMOS

vacuum gauge *n* (ca. 1864) : a gauge indicating degree of rarefaction below atmospheric pressure

vacuum–packed *adj* (ca. 1926) : having much of the air removed before being hermetically sealed

vacuum pan *n* (1833) : a tank with a vacuum pump for rapid evaporation and condensation (as of sugar syrup) by boiling at a low temperature

vacuum pump *n* (ca. 1858) : a pump for exhausting gas from an enclosed space

vacuum tube *n* (1859) : an electron tube evacuated to a high degree of vacuum

va·de me·cum \,vā-dē-'mē-kəm, ,vä-dē-'mā-\ *n, pl* **vade mecums** [L, go with me] (1629) **1** : a book for ready reference : MANUAL **2** : something regularly carried about by a person

va·dose \'vā-,dōs\ *adj* [L *vadosus* shallow, fr. *vadum,* n., shallow, ford; akin to L *vadere* to go — more at WADE] (1894) : of, relating to, or being water or solutions in the earth's crust above the permanent groundwater level

vag- *or* **vago-** *comb form* [ISV, fr. NL *vagus*] : vagus nerve ⟨*vagal*⟩ ⟨*vagotomy*⟩

¹vag·a·bond \'va-gə-,bänd\ *adj* [ME, fr. MF, fr. LL *vagabundus,* fr. L *vagari* to wander] (15c) **1** : moving from place to place without a fixed home : WANDERING **2 a** : of, relating to, or characteristic of a wanderer **b** : leading an unsettled, irresponsible, or disreputable life — **vag·a·bond·ish** \-,bän-dish\ *adj*

²vagabond *n* (15c) : one leading a vagabond life; *esp* : TRAMP — **vag·a·bond·age** \-,bän-dij\ *n* — **vag·a·bond·ism** \-,bän-,di-zəm\ *n*

³vagabond *vi* (1586) : to wander in the manner of a vagabond : roam about

va·gal \'vā-gəl\ *adj* [ISV] (1854) : of, relating to, mediated by, or being the vagus nerve — **va·gal·ly** \-gə-lē\ *adv*

va·gar·i·ous \vā-'ger-ē-əs, və-, -'gar-\ *adj* (1798) : marked by vagaries : CAPRICIOUS, WHIMSICAL — **va·gar·i·ous·ly** *adv*

va·ga·ry \'vā-gə-rē\ *və-'ger-ē, -'gar-, vä-; also* 'va-gə-rē\ *n, pl* **-ries** [prob. fr. L *vagari* to wander, fr. *vagus* wandering] (1573) : an erratic, unpredictable, or extravagant manifestation, action, or notion *syn* see CAPRICE

vag·ile \'va-jəl, -,jīl\ *adj* [ISV, fr. L *vagus* wandering] (ca. 1890) : free to move about ⟨∼ organisms⟩ — **va·gil·i·ty** \və-'ji-lə-tē, va-\ *n*

\ə\ abut \ᵊ\ kitten, F table \ər\ further \a\ ash \ā\ ace \ä\ mop, mar \aú\ out \ch\ chin \e\ bet \ē\ easy \g\ go \i\ hit \ī\ ice \j\ job \ŋ\ sing \ō\ go \ò\ law \ói\ boy \th\ thin \t͟h\ the \ü\ loot \ú\ foot \y\ yet \zh\ vision \á, k̲, ⁿ, œ, œ̄, ᵫ, ᵫ̄, ʸ\ *see* Guide to Pronunciation

va·gi·na \və-'jī-nə\ *n, pl* **-nae** \-(,)nē\ *or* **-nas** [L, lit., sheath] (1682) **1** : a canal in a female mammal that leads from the uterus to the external orifice of the genital canal **2** : a canal that is similar in function or location to the vagina and occurs in various animals other than mammals

vag·i·nal \'va-jə-nᵊl\ *adj* (1726) **1** : of or relating to a theca **2** : of, relating to, or affecting the genital vagina — **vag·i·nal·ly** \-nᵊl-ē\ *adv*

vag·i·nis·mus \,va-jə-'niz-məs\ *n* [NL, fr. L *vagina*] (1866) : a painful spasmodic contraction of the vagina

vag·i·ni·tis \,va-jə-'nī-təs\ *n* [NL] (1846) : inflammation of the vagina or of a sheath (as a tendon sheath)

va·got·o·my \vā-'gä-tə-mē\ *n, pl* **-mies** [ISV] (ca. 1903) : surgical division of the vagus nerve

va·go·to·nia \,vā-gə-'tō-nē-ə\ *n* [NL] (ca. 1915) : excessive excitability of the vagus nerve resulting typically in vasomotor instability, constipation, and sweating — **va·go·ton·ic** \-'tä-nik\ *adj*

va·gran·cy \'vā-grən(t)-sē\ *n, pl* **-cies** (1641) **1** : VAGARY **2** : the state or action of being vagrant **3** : the offense of being a vagrant

¹va·grant \'vā-grənt\ *n* [ME *vagraunt*, prob. modif. of MF *waucrant, wacrant* wandering, fr. OF, fr. prp. of *waucrer, wacrer* to roll, wander, of Gmc origin; akin to OE *wealcan* to roll — more at WALK] (15c) **1 a** : one who has no established residence and wanders idly from place to place without lawful or visible means of support **b** : one (as a prostitute or drunkard) whose conduct constitutes statutory vagrancy **2** : WANDERER, ROVER

²vagrant *adj* (15c) **1** : wandering about from place to place usu. with no means of support **2 a** : having a fleeting, wayward, or inconstant quality **b** : having no fixed course : RANDOM — **va·grant·ly** *adv*

va·grom \'vā-grəm\ *adj* [by alter.] (1599) : VAGRANT

vague \'vāg\ *adj* **vagu·er; vagu·est** [MF, fr. L *vagus*, lit., wandering] (1548) **1 a** : not clearly expressed : stated in indefinite terms ⟨~ accusation⟩ **b** : not having a precise meaning ⟨~ term of abuse⟩ **2 a** : not clearly defined, grasped, or understood : INDISTINCT ⟨only a ~ notion of what's needed⟩; *also* : SLIGHT ⟨a ~ hint of a thickening waistline⟩ ⟨hasn't the *vaguest* idea⟩ **b** : not clearly felt or sensed : somewhat subconscious ⟨a ~ longing⟩ **3** : not thinking or expressing one's thoughts clearly or precisely ⟨~ about dates and places⟩ **4** : lacking expression : VACANT **5** : not sharply outlined : HAZY **syn** see OBSCURE — **vague·ly** *adv* — **vague·ness** *n*

va·gus nerve \'vā-gəs-\ *n* [NL *vagus nervus*, lit., wandering nerve] (1840) : either of the 10th pair of cranial nerves that arise from the medulla and supply chiefly the viscera esp. with autonomic sensory and motor fibers — called also *vagus*

vail \'vā(ə)l\ *vt* [ME *valen*, partly fr. MF *valer* (short for *avaler* to let fall) & partly short for ME *avalen* to let fall, fr. MF *avaler*, fr. OF, fr. *aval* downward, fr. *a* to (fr. L *ad*) + *val* valley — more at AT, VALE] (14c) : to lower often as a sign of respect or submission

vain \'vān\ *adj* [ME, fr. MF, fr. L *vanus* empty, vain — more at WANE] (14c) **1** : having no real value : IDLE, WORTHLESS **2** : marked by futility or ineffectualness : UNSUCCESSFUL, USELESS ⟨~ efforts to escape⟩ **3** *archaic* : FOOLISH, SILLY **4** : having or showing undue or excessive pride in one's appearance or achievements : CONCEITED **syn** see FUTILE — **vain·ly** *adv* — **vain·ness** \'vān-nəs\ *n* — **in vain** **1** : to no end : without success or result **2** : in an irreverent or blasphemous manner ⟨you shall not take the name of the Lord your God *in vain* —Deut 5:11 (RSV)⟩

syn VAIN, NUGATORY, OTIOSE, IDLE, EMPTY, HOLLOW mean being without worth or significance. VAIN implies either absolute or relative absence of value ⟨*vain* promises⟩. NUGATORY suggests triviality or insignificance ⟨a monarch with *nugatory* powers⟩. OTIOSE suggests that something serves no purpose and is either an encumbrance or a superfluity ⟨a film without a single *otiose* scene⟩. IDLE suggests being incapable of worthwhile use or effect ⟨*idle* speculations⟩. EMPTY and HOLLOW suggest a deceiving lack of real substance or soundness or genuineness ⟨an *empty* attempt at reconciliation⟩ ⟨a *hollow* victory⟩.

vain·glo·ri·ous \,vān-'glōr-ē-əs, -'glȯr-\ *adj* (15c) : marked by vainglory : BOASTFUL — **vain·glo·ri·ous·ly** *adv* — **vain·glo·ri·ous·ness** *n*

vain·glo·ry \'vān-,glōr-ē, -,glȯr-, ,vān-\ *n* (14c) **1** : excessive or ostentatious pride esp. in one's achievements **2** : vain display or show : VANITY

vair \'var, 'ver\ *n* [ME *veir*, fr. OF *vair*, fr. *vair*, adj., variegated, fr. L *varius* variegated, various] (14c) : the bluish gray and white fur of a squirrel prized for ornamental use in medieval times

Vaish·na·va \'vīsh-nə-və\ *n* [Skt *vaiṣnava* of Vishnu, fr. *Viṣṇu* Vishnu] (1815) : a member of a major Hindu sect devoted to the cult of Vishnu — **Vaishnava** *adj* — **Vaish·na·vism** \-,vi-zəm\ *n*

Vais·ya \'vīsh-yə, 'vī-shə\ *n* [Skt *vaiśya*, fr. *viś* settlement; akin to Gk *oikos* house — more at VICINITY] (1665) : a Hindu of an upper caste traditionally assigned to commercial and agricultural occupations

va·lance \'va-lən(t)s, 'vā-\ *n* [ME *vallance*, perh. fr. *Valence*, France] (15c) **1** : a drapery hanging along the edge of a bed, table, altar, canopy, or shelf **2** : a short drapery or wood or metal frame used as a decorative heading to conceal the top of curtains and fixtures — **va·lanced** \-lən(t)st\ *adj*

vale \'vā(ə)l\ *n* [ME, fr. MF, fr. OF *val*, fr. L *valles, vallis*; perh. akin to L *volvere* to roll — more at VOLUBLE] (14c) **1** : VALLEY, DALE **2** : WORLD ⟨this ~ of tears⟩

val·e·dic·tion \,va-lə-'dik-shən\ *n* [L *valedicere* to say farewell, fr. *vale* farewell + *dicere* to say — more at DICTION] (1614) **1** : an act of bidding farewell **2** : VALEDICTORY

val·e·dic·to·ri·an \-,dik-'tȯr-ē-ən, -'tȯr-\ *n* (1759) : the student usu. having the highest rank in a graduating class who delivers the valedictory address at the commencement exercises

¹val·e·dic·to·ry \-'dik-t(ə-)rē\ *adj* [L *valedicere*] (1651) : of or relating to a valediction : expressing or containing a farewell

²valedictory *n, pl* **-ries** (1779) : an address or statement of farewell or leave-taking

va·lence \'vā-lən(t)s\ *n* [LL *valentia* power, capacity, fr. L *valent-, valens*, prp. of *valēre* to be strong — more at WIELD] (1884) **1** : the degree of combining power of an element as shown by the number of atomic weights of a univalent element (as hydrogen) with which the atomic weight of the element will combine or for which it can be substituted or with which it can be compared **2 a** : relative capacity to unite, react, or interact (as with antigens or a biological substrate) **b**

: the degree of attractiveness an individual, activity, or object possesses as a behavioral goal

valence band *n* (1953) : the range of permissible energy values that are the highest energies an electron of an atom can have and still be associated with the atom and be used to form bonds — compare CONDUCTION BAND

valence electron *n* (1923) : a single electron or one of two or more electrons in the outer shell of an atom that is responsible for the chemical properties of the atom

Va·len·cia orange \və-'len-ch(ē-)ə, -len(t)-sē-ə\ *n* [*Valencia*, Spain] (1858) : a sweet orange of a juicy thin-skinned cultivar grown in the U.S. — called also *Valencia*

Va·len·ci·ennes \və-,len(t)-sē-'en(z), ,va-lən-sē-\ *n* [*Valenciennes*, France] (1717) : a fine bobbin lace

-valent *adj comb form* [ISV, fr. L *valent-, valens*] **1** : having a (specified) valence or valences ⟨bi*valent*⟩ ⟨multi*valent*⟩ **2** : having (so many) chromosomal strands or homologous chromosomes ⟨uni*valent*⟩

val·en·tine \'va-lən-,tīn\ *n* (15c) **1** : a sweetheart chosen or complimented on St. Valentine's Day **2** : a gift or greeting sent or given esp. to a sweetheart on St. Valentine's Day; *esp* : a greeting card sent on this day **b** : something (as a movie or piece of writing) expressing uncritical praise or affection : TRIBUTE

Valentine's Day *also* **Valentine Day** *n* (1668) : SAINT VALENTINE'S DAY

val·er·ate \'va-lə-,rāt\ *n* (1852) : a salt or ester of valeric acid

va·le·ri·an \və-'lir-ē-ən\ *n* [ME, fr. MF or ML; MF *valeriane*, fr. ML *valeriana*, prob. fr. fem. of *valerianus* of Valeria, fr. *Valeria*, Roman province formerly part of Pannonia] (14c) **1** : any of a genus (*Valeriana* of the family Valerianaceae, the valerian family) of perennial herbs many of which possess medicinal properties **2** : a drug consisting of the dried rootstock and roots of the garden heliotrope (*Valeriana officinalis*) formerly used as a carminative and sedative

va·le·ric acid \və-'lir-ik-, -'ler-\ *n* [*valerian*; fr. its occurrence in the root of valerian] (1857) : any of four isomeric fatty acids $C_5H_{10}O_2$ or a mixture of these; *esp* : a liquid acid of disagreeable odor obtained from valerian or made synthetically and used esp. in organic synthesis

¹va·let \'va-lət, 'va-(,)lā, va-'lā\ *n* [MF *vaslet, varlet, valet* young nobleman, page, domestic servant, fr. (assumed) ML *vassellittus*, dim. of ML *vassus* servant — more at VASSAL] (1567) **1 a** : a man's male servant who performs personal services (as taking care of clothing) **b** : an employee (as of a hotel or a public facility) who performs personal services for customers **2** : a device (as a rack or tray) for holding clothing or personal effects

²valet *vt* (1840) : to serve as a valet

valet de cham·bre \(,)va-lā-də-'shän̄br⟩\ *n, pl* **va·lets de chambre** *same*\ [F, lit., chamber valet] (1646) : VALET 1a

valet parking *n* (1960) : a service that provides parking of motor vehicles by an attendant

¹val·e·tu·di·nar·i·an \,va-lə-,tü-dᵊn-'er-ē-ən, -,tyü-\ *n* [L *valetudinarius* sickly, infirm, fr. *valetudin-, valetudo* state of health, sickness, fr. *valēre* to be strong, be well — more at WIELD] (1703) : a person of a weak or sickly constitution; *esp* : one whose chief concern is being or becoming a chronic invalid

²valetudinarian *adj* (1713) : of, relating to, or characteristic of a valetudinarian : SICKLY, WEAK

val·e·tu·di·nar·i·an·ism \-ē-ə-,ni-zəm\ *n* (1839) : the condition or state of mind of a valetudinarian

¹val·e·tu·di·nary \-'tü-dᵊn-,er-ē, -'tyü-\ *adj* [L *valetudinarius*] (1581) : VALETUDINARIAN

²valetudinary *n, pl* **-nar·ies** (1665) : VALETUDINARIAN

val·gus \'val-gəs\ *adj* [NL, fr. L, bowlegged] (1884) : of, relating to, or being a deformity in which an anatomical part is turned outward away from the midline of the body to an abnormal degree ⟨~ deformity of the ankle⟩ — **vargus** *n*

Val·hal·la \val-'ha-lə *also* väl-'hä-\ *n* [G & ON; G *Walhalla*, fr. ON *Valhǫll*, lit., hall of the slain, fr. *valr* the slain (akin to OE *wæl* slaughter, the slain) + *hǫll* hall; akin to OE *heall* hall] : the great hall in Norse mythology where the souls of heroes slain in battle are received

val·iance \'val-yən(t)s\ *n* (15c) : VALOR

val·ian·cy \-yən(t)-sē\ *n* (15c) : VALOR

¹val·iant \'val-yənt\ *adj* [ME *valiaunt*, fr. MF *vaillant*, fr. OF, fr. prp. of *valoir* to be of worth, fr. L *valēre* to be strong — more at WIELD] (14c) **1** : possessing or acting with bravery or boldness : COURAGEOUS ⟨~ soldiers⟩ **2** : marked by, exhibiting, or carried out with courage or determination : HEROIC ⟨~ feats⟩ — **val·iant·ly** *adv* — **val·iant·ness** *n*

²valiant *n* (1609) : a valiant person

val·id \'va-ləd\ *adj* [MF or ML; MF *valide*, fr. ML *validus*, fr. L, strong, fr. *valēre*] (1571) **1** : having legal efficacy or force; *esp* : executed with the proper legal authority and formalities ⟨a ~ contract⟩ **2 a** : well-grounded or justifiable : being at once relevant and meaningful ⟨a ~ theory⟩ **b** : logically correct ⟨a ~ argument⟩ ⟨a ~ inference⟩ **3** : appropriate to the end in view : EFFECTIVE ⟨every craft has its own ~ methods⟩ **4** *of a taxon* : conforming to accepted principles of sound biological classification — **va·lid·i·ty** \və-'li-də-tē, va-\ *n* — **val·id·ly** \'va-ləd-lē\ *adv*

syn VALID, SOUND, COGENT, CONVINCING, TELLING mean having such force as to compel serious attention and usu. acceptance. VALID implies being supported by objective truth or generally accepted authority ⟨a *valid* reason for being absent⟩ ⟨a *valid* marriage⟩. SOUND implies a basis of flawless reasoning or of solid grounds ⟨a *sound* proposal for reviving the economy⟩. COGENT may stress either weight of sound argument and evidence or lucidity of presentation ⟨the prosecutor's *cogent* summation won over the jury⟩. CONVINCING suggests a power to overcome doubt, opposition, or reluctance to accept ⟨a *convincing* argument for welfare reform⟩. TELLING stresses an immediate and crucial effect striking at the heart of a matter ⟨a *telling* example of bureaucratic waste⟩.

val·i·date \'va-lə-,dāt\ *vt* **-dat·ed; -dat·ing** (1648) **1 a** : to make legally valid **b** : to grant official sanction to by marking **c** : to confirm the validity of (an election); *also* : to declare (a person) elected **2** : to support or corroborate on a sound or authoritative basis ⟨experiments designed to ~ the hypothesis⟩ **syn** see CONFIRM

val·i·da·tion \ˌva-lə-'dā-shən\ n (ca. 1656) : an act, process, or instance of validating; esp : the determination of the degree of validity of a measuring device

va·line \'va-ˌlēn, 'vā-\ n [ISV, fr. valeric (acid)] (1907) : a crystalline essential amino acid $C_5H_{11}NO_2$ that is one of the building blocks of plant and animal proteins

va·lise \və-'lēs\ n [F, fr. It valigia] (1615) : SUITCASE

Val·ium \'va-lē-əm, 'val-yəm\ trademark — used for a preparation of diazepam

Val·ky·rie \val-'kir-ē also val-'kī-rē, 'val-kə-rē\ n [G & ON; G Walküre, fr. ON valkyrja, lit., chooser of the slain; akin to OE wælcyrige witch, ON valr the slain, OHG kiosan to choose — more at CHOOSE] : any of the maidens of Odin who choose the heroes to be slain in battle and conduct them to Valhalla

val·late \'va-ˌlāt\ adj [L vallatus, pp. of vallare to surround with a wall, fr. vallum wall, rampart — more at WALL] (1878) : having a raised edge surrounding a depression ⟨~ papillae of the tongue⟩

val·lec·u·la \va-'le-kyə-lə, və-\ n, pl -u·lae \-kyə-ˌlē, -ˌlī\ [NL, fr. LL, little valley, dim. of L valles valley — more at VALE] (1859) : an anatomical groove, channel, or depression; esp : one between the base of the tongue and the epiglottis — **val·lec·u·lar** \-lər\ adj

val·ley \'va-lē\ n, pl valleys [ME valey, fr. OF valee, fr. val valley — more at VALE] (14c) 1 a : an elongate depression of the earth's surface usu. between ranges of hills or mountains b : an area drained by a river and its tributaries 2 : a low point or condition 3 a : HOLLOW, DEPRESSION b : the place of meeting of two slopes of a roof that form on the plan a reentrant angle

valley fever n [fr. its prevalence in the San Joaquin valley of California] (1938) : COCCIDIOIDOMYCOSIS

Va·lois \'val-ˌwä, val-'\ adj [Philippe de Valois (Philip VI of France)] (ca. 1888) : of or relating to the French royal house that ruled from 1328 to 1589

va·lo·nia \və-'lō-nē-ə, -nyə\ n [It vallonia, fr. MGk balanidia, pl. of balanidion, dim. of Gk balanos acorn — more at GLAND] (1722) : dried acorn cups esp. from a Eurasian evergreen oak (Quercus macrolepis syn. Q. aegilops) used in tanning or dressing leather

val·or \'va-lər\ n [ME, fr. MF valour, fr. ML valor value, valor, fr. L valēre to be strong — more at WIELD] (15c) : strength of mind or spirit that enables a person to encounter danger with firmness : personal bravery

val·o·rize \'va-lə-ˌrīz\ vt -rized; -riz·ing [Pg valorizar, fr. valor value, price, fr. ML] (ca. 1906) : to enhance or try to enhance the price, value, or status of by organized and usu. governmental action (using subsidies to ~ coffee) — **val·o·ri·za·tion** \ˌva-lə-rə-'zā-shən\ n

val·or·ous \'va-lə-rəs\ adj (15c) : VALIANT — **val·or·ous·ly** adv

val·our \'va-lər\ chiefly Brit var of VALOR

val·po·li·cel·la \ˌväl-ˌpō-lə-'che-lə, -ˌväl-\ n, often cap [Valpolicella, district in northern Italy] (1903) : a dry red Italian table wine

Val·sal·va maneuver \val-'sal-və-\ n [Antonio Maria Valsalva †1723 Ital. anatomist] (1886) : the process of making a forceful attempt at expiration while holding the nostrils closed and keeping the mouth shut for the purpose of testing the patency of the eustachian tubes or of adjusting middle ear pressure — called also Valsalva

valse \väls\ n [F, fr. G Walzer — more at WALTZ] (1796) : WALTZ; specif : a concert waltz

¹valu·able \'val-yə-bəl, -yə-wə-bəl\ adj (1589) 1 a : having monetary value b : worth a good price 2 a : having desirable or esteemed characteristics or qualities (~ friendships) b : of great use or service (~ advice) — **valu·able·ness** n — **valu·ably** \-blē\ adv

²valuable n (ca. 1775) : a usu. personal possession (as jewelry) of relatively great monetary value — usu. used in pl

valuable consideration n (1638) : an equivalent or compensation having value that is given for something acquired or promised (as money or marriage) and that may consist either in a benefit accruing to one party or a loss falling upon the other

val·u·ate \'val-yə-ˌwāt\ vt -at·ed; -at·ing (1873) : to place a value on : APPRAISE

val·u·a·tion \ˌval-yə-'wā-shən\ n [MF, fr. valuer to value, fr. value] (1529) 1 : the act or process of valuing; specif : appraisal of property 2 : the estimated or determined market value of a thing 3 : judgment or appreciation of worth or character — **val·u·a·tion·al** \-shnəl, -shə-nᵊl\ adj — **val·u·a·tion·al·ly** adv

val·u·a·tor \'val-yə-ˌwā-tər\ n (1731) : one that valuates; specif : one that appraises

¹val·ue \'val-(ˌ)yü\ n [ME, fr. MF, fr. (assumed) VL valuta, fr. fem. of valutus, pp. of L valēre to be worth, be strong — more at WIELD] (14c) 1 : a fair return or equivalent in goods, services, or money for something exchanged 2 : the monetary worth of something : marketable price 3 : relative worth, utility, or importance (a good ~ at the price) (the ~ of base stealing in baseball) (had nothing of ~ to say) 4 a : a numerical quantity that is assigned or is determined by calculation or measurement (let x take on positive ~s) (a ~ for the age of the earth) b : precise signification (~ of a word) 5 : the relative duration of a musical note 6 a : relative lightness or darkness of a color : LUMINOSITY b : the relation of one part in a picture to another with respect to lightness and darkness 7 : something (as a principle or quality) intrinsically valuable or desirable (sought material ~s instead of human ~s —W. H. Jones) 8 : DENOMINATION 2 — **val·ue·less** \-(ˌ)yü-ləs, -yə-\ adj — **val·ue·less·ness** n

²value vt val·ued; val·u·ing (15c) 1 a : to estimate or assign the monetary worth of : APPRAISE (~ a necklace) b : to rate or scale in usefulness, importance, or general worth : EVALUATE 2 : to consider or rate highly : PRIZE, ESTEEM (~s your opinion) syn see ESTIMATE, APPRECIATE — **val·u·er** \-yə-wər\ n

value-added tax n (1935) : an incremental excise that is levied on the value added at each stage of the processing of a raw material or the production and distribution of a commodity and that typically has the impact of a sales tax on the ultimate consumer

val·ued \'val-(ˌ)yüd, -yəd\ adj (1595) : having a value or values esp. of a specified kind or number — often used in combination (real-valued)

val·ue–free \'val-(ˌ)yü-'frē\ adj (1948) : making or having no value judgments (~ distinctions) (~ economics)

value judgment n (1899) : a judgment assigning a value (as good or bad) to something

va·lu·ta \və-'lü-tə, -(ˌ)tä\ n [It, value, fr. (assumed) VL valuta] (1920) 1 : the agreed upon or exchange value of a currency 2 : FOREIGN EXCHANGE 2

val·vate \'val-ˌvāt\ adj (1829) : having valves or parts resembling a valve; esp : meeting at the edges without overlapping in the bud (as in the calyx of a mallow)

valve \'valv\ n [L valva; akin to L volvere to roll — more at VOLUBLE] (14c) 1 archaic : a leaf of a folding or double door 2 [NL valva, fr. L] : a structure esp. in a vein or lymphatic that closes temporarily a passage or orifice or permits movement of fluid in one direction only 3 a : any of numerous mechanical devices by which the flow of liquid, gas, or loose material in bulk may be started, stopped, or regulated by a movable part that opens, shuts, or partially obstructs one or more ports or passageways; also : the movable part of such a device b : a device in a brass instrument for quickly channeling air flow through an added length of tube in order to change the fundamental tone by some definite interval c chiefly Brit : ELECTRON TUBE 4 [NL valva, fr. L] : one of the distinct and usu. movably articulated pieces of which the shell of some shell-bearing animals (as lamellibranch mollusks, brachiopods, and barnacles) consists 5 [NL valva, fr. L] a : one of the segments or pieces into which a dehiscing capsule or legume separates b : the portion of various anthers (as of the barberry) resembling a lid c : one of the two encasing membranes of a diatom — **valved** \'valvd\ adj — **valve·less** \'valv-ləs\ adj

val·vu·la \'val-vyə-lə\ n, pl -lae \-ˌlē, -ˌlī\ [NL, dim. of L valva] (1615) : a small valve or fold

val·vu·lar \'val-vyə-lər\ adj (1797) 1 : resembling or functioning as a valve; also : opening by valves 2 : of, relating to, or affecting a valve esp. of the heart (~ heart disease)

val·vu·li·tis \ˌval-vyə-'lī-təs\ n [NL] (ca. 1891) : inflammation of a valve esp. of the heart

va·moose \və-'müs, va-\ vi va·moosed; va·moos·ing [Sp vamos let us go, suppletive 1st pl. imper. (fr. L vadere to go) of ir to go, fr. L ire — more at WADE, ISSUE] (1840) : to depart quickly

¹vamp \'vamp\ vb [²vamp] vt (1599) 1 a : to provide (a shoe) with a new vamp b : to piece (something old) with a new part : PATCH (~ up old sermons) 2 : INVENT, FABRICATE (~ up an excuse) ~ vi : to play a musical vamp — **vamp·er** n

²vamp n [ME vampe sock, fr. OF avantpié, fr. avant- fore- + pié foot, fr. L ped-, pes — more at VANGUARD, FOOT] (1654) 1 : the part of a shoe upper or boot upper covering esp. the forepart of the foot and sometimes also extending forward over the toe or backward to the back seam of the upper 2 [¹vamp] : a short introductory musical passage often repeated several times (as in vaudeville) before a solo or between verses

³vamp n [short for vampire] (ca. 1911) : a woman who uses her charm or wiles to seduce and exploit men — **vamp·ish** \'vam-pish\ adj

⁴vamp vt (ca. 1915) : to practice seductive wiles on

vam·pire \'vam-ˌpīr\ n [F, fr. G Vampir, fr. Serbo-Croatian vampir] (1734) 1 : the reanimated body of a dead person believed to come from the grave at night and suck the blood of persons asleep 2 a : one who lives by preying on others b : a woman who exploits and ruins her lover 3 : VAMPIRE BAT — **vam·pir·ish** \-ish\ adj

vampire bat n (1790) : any of several Central and So. American bats (Desmodus rotundus, Diaemus youngi, and Diphylla ecaudata of the subfamily Desmodontinae of the family Phyllostomidae) that feed on the blood of birds and mammals and esp. domestic animals and that are sometimes vectors of equine trypanosomiasis and of rabies; also : any of several other bats (as of the families Megadermatidae and Phyllostomidae) that do not feed on blood but are sometimes reputed to do so

vampire bat

vam·pir·ism \-ˌpīr-ˌi-zəm\ n (1794) 1 : belief in vampires 2 : the actions of a vampire

¹van \'van\ n [ME, fr. MF, fr. L vannus — more at WINNOW] (14c) 1 dial Eng : a winnowing device (as a fan) 2 : WING 1a

²van n [by shortening] (1610) : VANGUARD

³van n [short for caravan] (1829) 1 a : a usu. enclosed wagon or motortruck used for transportation of goods or animals; also : CARAVAN 2a b : a multipurpose enclosed motor vehicle having a boxlike shape, rear or side doors, and side panels often with windows c : a detachable passenger cabin transportable by aircraft or truck 2 chiefly Brit : an enclosed railroad freight or baggage car

⁴van vt vanned; van·ning (1840) : to transport by van

van·a·date \'va-nə-ˌdāt\ n [NL vanadium + E ¹-ate] (1835) : a salt derived from vanadium pentoxide and containing pentavalent vanadium

va·na·di·um \və-'nā-dē-əm\ n [NL, fr. ON Vanadis Freya] (1833) : a grayish malleable ductile metallic element found combined in minerals and used esp. to form alloys (as vanadium steel) — see ELEMENT table

vanadium pentoxide n (1885) : a yellowish red crystalline compound V_2O_5 used esp. in glass manufacture and as a catalyst

Van Al·len belt \van-'a-lən-\ n [James A. Van Allen] (1958) : a belt of intense radiation in the magnetosphere composed of energetic charged particles trapped by the earth's magnetic field; also : a similar belt surrounding another planet

va·nas·pa·ti \və-'nəs-pə-tē, -'näs-\ n [Skt, forest tree, soma plant, lit., lord of the forest, fr. vana forest + pati lord, master — more at POTENT] (1941) : a hydrogenated vegetable fat used as a butter substitute in India

van·dal \'van-dᵊl\ n [L Vandalii (pl.), of Gmc origin] (1555) 1 cap : a member of a Germanic people who lived in the area south of the Baltic

---

\ə\ abut \ᵊ\ kitten, F table \ər\ further \a\ ash \ā\ ace \ä\ mop, mar \au̇\ out \ch\ chin \e\ bet \ē\ easy \g\ go \i\ hit \ī\ ice \j\ job \ŋ\ sing \ō\ go \ȯ\ law \ȯi\ boy \th\ thin \t̲h̲\ the \ü\ loot \u̇\ foot \y\ yet \zh\ vision \á, k̲, ⁿ, œ, œ̄, ᵫ, ᵫ̄, ᵞ\ see Guide to Pronunciation between the Vistula and the Oder, overran Gaul, Spain, and northern Africa in the 4th and 5th centuries A.D., and in 455 sacked Rome **2** : one who willfully or ignorantly destroys, damages, or defaces property belonging to another or to the public — **vandal** *adj, often cap* — **Van·dal·ic** \,van-'da-lik\ *adj*

van·dal·ise *Brit var of* VANDALIZE

van·dal·ism \'van-d°l-,i-zəm\ *n* (1798) : willful or malicious destruction or defacement of public or private property

van·dal·is·tic \,van-d°l-'is-tik\ *adj* (1897) : of or relating to vandalism

van·dal·ize \'van-d°l-,iz\ *vt* **-ized; -iz·ing** (1845) : to subject to vandalism : DAMAGE — **van·dal·i·za·tion** \,van-d°l-ə-'zā-shən\ *n*

van·da orchid \'van-də-\ *n* [NL, fr. Hindi *vandā* mistletoe, fr. Skt, a parasitic plant] (1943) : any of a large genus (*Vanda*) of Indo-Malayan epiphytic orchids often grown for their loose racemes of showy flowers — called also *vanda*

Van de Graaff generator \'van-də-,graf-\ *n* [Robert J. *Van de Graaff* †1967 Am. physicist] (1937) : an apparatus for the production of electrical discharges at high voltage commonly consisting of an insulated hollow conducting sphere that accumulates in its interior the charge continuously conveyed from a source of direct current by an endless belt of flexible nonconducting material

van der Waals forces \'van-dər-,wölz-, 'vän-dər-,välz-\ *n pl* [Johannes D. *van der Waals* †1923 Du. physicist] (1926) : the relatively weak attractive forces that act on neutral atoms and molecules and that arise because of the electric polarization induced in each of the particles by the presence of other particles

Van·dyke \van-'dik, vən-\ *n* [Sir Anthony *Vandyke*] (1755) **1 a** : a wide collar with a deeply indented edge **b** : one of several V-shaped points forming a decorative edging **c** : a border of such points **2** : a trim pointed beard — **van·dyked** \-'dikt\ *adj*

Vandyke brown *n* [fr. its use by the painter Vandyke] (ca. 1850) : a natural brown-black pigment of organic matter obtained from bog earth or peat or lignite deposits; *also* : any of various synthetic brown pigments

vane \'vān\ *n* [ME (southern dial.), fr. OE *fana* banner; akin to OHG *fano* cloth, L *pannus* cloth, rag] (15c) **1 a** : a movable device attached to an elevated object (as a spire) for showing the direction of the wind **b** : one that is changeable or inconstant **2** : a thin flat or curved object that is rotated about an axis by a flow of fluid or that rotates to cause a fluid to flow or that redirects a flow of fluid (the ~*s* of a windmill) **3** : the web or flat expanded part of a feather — see FEATHER illustration **4** : a feather fastened to the shaft near the nock of an arrow — **vaned** \'vānd\ *adj*

van·guard \'van-,gärd *also* 'vaŋ-\ *n* [ME *vantgard*, fr. MF *avant-garde*, fr. OF, fr. *avant-* fore- (fr. *avant* before, fr. LL *abante*) + *garde* guard — more at ADVANCE] (15c) **1** : the troops moving at the head of an army **2** : the forefront of an action or movement — **van·guard·ism** \-,gär-,di-zəm\ *n* — **van·guard·ist** \-dist\ *n*

¹va·nil·la \və-'ni-lə, -'ne-\ *n* [NL, fr. Sp *vainilla* vanilla (plant and fruit), dim. of *vaina* sheath, fr. L *vagina* sheath, vagina] (1662) **1 a** : VANILLA BEAN **b** : a commercially important extract of the vanilla bean that is used esp. as a flavoring **2** : any of a genus (*Vanilla*) of tropical American climbing epiphytic orchids

²vanilla *adj* (1846) **1** : flavored with vanilla **2** : lacking distinction : PLAIN, ORDINARY

vanilla bean *n* (1874) : the long capsular fruit of a vanilla (esp. *Vanilla planifolia*) that is an important article of commerce

van·il·lin \'va-n°l-ən\ *n* (ca. 1868) : a crystalline phenolic aldehyde $C_8H_8O_3$ that is extracted from vanilla beans or prepared synthetically and is used esp. in flavoring and in perfumery

Va·nir \'vän-,ir\ *n pl* [ON] : a race of Norse gods who become united with the Aesir

van·ish \'va-nish\ *vb* [ME *vanisshen*, stem of *evanir*, fr. (assumed) VL *exvanire*, alter. of L *evanescere* to dissipate like vapor, vanish, fr. *e-* + *vanescere* to vanish, fr. *vanus* empty] *vi* (14c) **1 a** : to pass quickly from sight : DISAPPEAR **b** : to pass completely from existence **2** : to assume the value zero ~ *vt* : to cause to disappear — **van·ish·er** *n*

vanishing cream *n* (1916) : a cosmetic preparation that is less oily than cold cream and is used chiefly as a foundation for face powder

van·ish·ing·ly \'va-ni-shiŋ-lē\ *adv* (1870) : so as to be almost nonexistent or invisible (the difference is ~ small)

vanishing point *n* (1797) **1** : a point at which receding parallel lines seem to meet when represented in linear perspective **2** : a point at which something disappears or ceases to exist

van·i·ty \'va-nə-tē\ *n, pl* **-ties** [ME *vanite*, fr. OF *vanité*, fr. L *vanitat-, vanitas* quality of being empty or vain, fr. *vanus* empty, vain — more at WANE] (13c) **1** : something that is vain, empty, or valueless **2** : the quality or fact of being vain **3** : inflated pride in oneself or one's appearance : CONCEIT **4** : a fashionable trifle or knicknack **5 a** : ¹COMPACT a **b** : a small case or handbag for toilet articles used by women **6** : DRESSING TABLE

vanity fair *n, often cap* V&F [*Vanity-Fair*, a fair held in the frivolous town of Vanity in *Pilgrim's Progress* (1678) by John Bunyan] (1816) : a scene or place characterized by frivolity and ostentation

vanity plate *n* (1966) : a license plate bearing letters or numbers designated by the owner of the vehicle

vanity press *n* (1950) : a publishing house that publishes books at the author's expense — called also *vanity publisher*

van·ner \'va-nər\ *n* (1927) : a person who owns a usu. customized van

van·pool \'van-,pül\ *n* (1973) : an arrangement by which a group of people commute to work in a van — **van·pool·ing** *n*

van·quish \'vaŋ-kwish, 'van-\ *vt* [ME *venquissen*, fr. MF *venquis*, preterit of *veintre* to conquer, fr. L *vincere* — more at VICTOR] (14c) **1** : to overcome in battle : subdue completely **2** : to defeat in a conflict or contest **3** : to gain mastery over (an emotion, passion, or temptation) — *syn* see CONQUER — **van·quish·able** \-kwi-shə-bəl\ *adj* — **van·quish·er** *n*

van·tage \'van-tij\ *n* [ME, fr. AF, fr. MF *avantage* — more at ADVANTAGE] (14c) **1** *archaic* : BENEFIT, GAIN **2** : superiority in a contest **3** : a position giving a strategic advantage, commanding perspective, or comprehensive view : ADVANTAGE **4** — **to the vantage** *obs* : in addition

vantage point *n* (1865) : a position or standpoint from which something is viewed or considered; *esp* : POINT OF VIEW

van·ward \'van-wərd\ *adj* (1820) : located in the vanguard : ADVANCED — **vanward** *adv*

va·pid \'va-pəd, 'vā-\ *adj* [L *vapidus* flat-tasting; akin to L *vappa* vapid wine and perh. to L *vapor* steam] (ca. 1656) : lacking liveliness, tang, briskness, or force : FLAT, DULL (a gossipy, ~ woman, obsessed by her own elegance —R. F. Delderfield) (London was not all ~ dissipation —V. S. Pritchett) *syn* see INSIPID — **va·pid·ly** *adv* — **va·pid·ness** *n*

va·pid·i·ty \va-'pi-də-tē, vā-, və-\ *n, pl* **-ties** (ca. 1721) **1** : the quality or state of being vapid **2** : something vapid

¹va·por \'vā-pər\ *n* [ME *vapour*, fr. MF *vapeur*, fr. L *vapor* steam, vapor] (14c) **1** : diffused matter (as smoke or fog) suspended floating in the air and impairing its transparency **2 a** : a substance in the gaseous state as distinguished from the liquid or solid state **b** : a substance (as gasoline, alcohol, mercury, or benzoin) vaporized for industrial, therapeutic, or military uses; *also* : a mixture (as the explosive mixture in an internal combustion engine) of such a vapor with air **3 a** : something unsubstantial or transitory : PHANTASM **b** : a foolish or fanciful idea **4** *pl* **a** *archaic* : exhalations of bodily organs (as the stomach) held to affect the physical or mental condition **b** : a depressed or hysterical nervous condition

²vapor *vi* **va·pored; va·por·ing** \-p(ə-)riŋ\ (15c) **1 a** : to rise or pass off in vapor **b** : to emit vapor **2** : to indulge in bragging, blustering, or idle talk — **va·por·er** \-pər-ər\ *n*

vapor barrier *n* (ca. 1941) : a layer of material (as roofing paper or polyethylene film) used to retard or prevent the absorption of moisture into a construction (as a wall or floor)

va·po·ret·to \,vä-pə-'re-(,)tō\ *n, pl* **-ret·ti** \-'re-tē\ *also* **-ret·tos** [It, dim. of *vapore* steamboat, fr. F *vapeur*, fr. *bateau à vapeur* steamboat] (1926) : a motorboat serving as a canal bus in Venice, Italy

va·por·ing \'vā-p(ə-)riŋ\ *n* (ca. 1630) : the act or speech of one that vapors; *specif* : an idle, extravagant, or high-flown expression or speech — usu. used in pl.

va·por·ise *Brit var of* VAPORIZE

va·por·ish \'vā-p(ə-)rish\ *adj* (ca. 1644) **1** : resembling or suggestive of vapor **2** : given to fits of the vapors — **va·por·ish·ness** *n*

va·por·ize \'vā-pə-,riz\ *vb* **-ized; -iz·ing** *vt* (1803) **1** : to convert (as by the application of heat or by spraying) into vapor **2** : to cause to become dissipated ~ *vi* **1** : to become vaporized **2** : VAPOR 2 — **va·por·iz·able** \-,ri-zə-bəl\ *adj* — **va·por·i·za·tion** \,vā-pər-ə-'zā-shən\ *n*

va·por·iz·er \'vā-pə-,ri-zər\ *n* (ca. 1846) : one that vaporizes: as **a** : ATOMIZER **b** : a device for converting water or a medicated liquid into a vapor for inhalation

vapor lock *n* (1926) : partial or complete interruption of flow of a fluid (as fuel in an internal combustion engine) caused by the formation of bubbles of vapor in the feeding system

va·por·ous \'vā-p(ə-)rəs\ *adj* (1527) **1** : consisting or characteristic of vapor **2** : producing vapors : VOLATILE **3** : containing or obscured by vapors : MISTY **4 a** : ETHEREAL, UNSUBSTANTIAL **b** : consisting of or indulging in vaporings — **va·por·ous·ly** *adv* — **va·por·ous·ness** *n*

vapor pressure *n* (1875) : the pressure exerted by a vapor that is in equilibrium with its solid or liquid form — called also *vapor tension*

vapor trail *n* (1941) : CONTRAIL

va·por·ware \'vā-pər-,war, -,wer\ *n* (1984) : a new computer-related product that has been widely advertised but is not yet available

va·pory \'vā-p(ə-)rē\ *adj* (1598) : VAPOROUS, MISTY

va·pour *chiefly Brit var of* VAPOR

va·que·ro \vä-'ker-(,)ō\ *n, pl* **-ros** [Sp — more at BUCKAROO] (1826) : HERDSMAN, COWBOY

va·ra \'vär-ə\ *n* [AmerSp, fr. Sp, pole, fr. L, forked pole, fr. fem. of *varus* bent, bow-legged] (1831) : a Texas unit of length equal to 33.33 inches (84.66 centimeters)

vari- *or* **vario-** *comb form* [L *varius*] **1** : varied : diverse (*vari*colored) **2** : variation : variability (*vari*ometer)

var·ia \'ver-ē-ə, 'var-\ *n pl* [NL, fr. L, neut. pl. of *varius* various] (1926) : MISCELLANY; *esp* : a literary miscellany

¹var·i·able \'ver-ē-ə-bəl, 'var-\ *adj* [ME, fr. MF, fr. L *variabilis*, fr. *variare* to vary] (14c) **1 a** : able or apt to vary : subject to variation or changes (~ winds) (~ costs) **b** : FICKLE, INCONSTANT **2** : characterized by variations **3** : having the characteristics of a variable **4** : not true to type : ABERRANT — used of a biological group or character — **var·i·abil·i·ty** \,ver-ē-ə-'bi-lə-tē, ,var-\ *n* — **var·i·able·ness** \'ver-ē-ə-bəl-nəs, 'var-\ *n* — **var·i·ably** \-blē\ *adv*

²variable *n* (1816) **1 a** : a quantity that may assume any one of a set of values **b** : a symbol representing a variable **2** : something that is variable **3** : VARIABLE STAR

variable rate mortgage *n* (1975) : ADJUSTABLE RATE MORTGAGE

variable star *n* (1788) : a star whose brightness changes usu. in more or less regular periods

var·i·ance \'ver-ē-ən(t)s, 'var-\ *n* (14c) **1** : the fact, quality, or state of being variable or variant : DIFFERENCE, VARIATION (yearly ~ in crops) **2** : the fact or state of being in disagreement : DISSENSION, DISPUTE **3** : a disagreement between two parts of the same legal proceeding that must be consonant **4** : a license to do some act contrary to the usual rule (a zoning ~) **5** : the square of the standard deviation *syn* see DISCORD — **at variance** : not in harmony or agreement

¹var·i·ant \'ver-ē-ənt, 'var-\ *adj* (14c) **1** *obs* : VARIABLE **2** : manifesting variety, deviation, or disagreement : varying usu. slightly from the standard form (~ readings)

²variant *n* (1848) : one of two or more persons or things exhibiting usu. slight differences: as **a** : one that exhibits variation from a type or norm **b** : one of two or more different spellings (as *labor* and *labour*) or pronunciations (as of *economics* \ek-, ēk-\) of the same word **c** : one of two or more words (as *geographic* and *geographical*) or word elements (as *mon-* and *mono-*) of essentially the same meaning differing only in the presence or absence of an affix

var·i·ate \'ver-ē-,āt, 'var-, -ət\ *n* (1899) : RANDOM VARIABLE

var·i·a·tion \,ver-ē-'ā-shən, ,var-\ *n* (14c) **1 a** : the act or process of varying : the state or fact of being varied **b** : an instance of varying **c** : the extent to which or the range in which a thing varies **2** : DECLINATION 6 **3 a** : a change of algebraic sign between successive terms of a sequence **b** : a measure of the change in data, a variable, or a function **4** : the repetition of a musical theme with modifications in rhythm, tune, harmony, or key **5 a :** divergence in the characteristics of an organism from the species or population norm or average **b :** something (as an individual or group) that exhibits variation **6 a :** a solo dance in classic ballet **b :** a repetition in modern ballet of a movement sequence with changes — **var·i·a·tion·al** \-shnəl, -shə-nᵊl\ *adj* — **var·i·a·tion·al·ly** *adv*

var·i·cel·la \ˌvar-ə-'se-lə\ *n* [NL, irreg. dim. of *variola*] (ca. 1771) **:** CHICKEN POX

var·i·co·cele \'var-ə-kō-ˌsēl\ *n* [NL, fr. L *varic-, varix* + NL -o- + -*cele*] (1736) **:** a varicose enlargement of the veins of the spermatic cord

vari·col·ored \'ver-i-ˌkə-lərd, 'var-\ *adj* (1665) **:** having various colors **:** VARIEGATED ⟨the ∼ breeding plumage of a bird⟩; *also* **:** of various colors

var·i·cose \'var-ə-ˌkōs\ *also* **var·i·cosed** \-ˌkōst\ *adj* [L *varicosus* full of dilated veins, fr. *varic-, varix* dilated vein] (ca. 1730) **1 :** abnormally swollen or dilated ⟨∼ veins⟩ **2 :** affected with varicose veins ⟨∼ legs⟩

var·i·cos·i·ty \ˌvar-ə-'kä-sə-tē\ *n, pl* **-ties** (ca. 1842) **1 :** the quality or state of being abnormally or markedly swollen or dilated **2 :** VARIX

var·ied \'ver-ēd, 'var-\ *adj* (1588) **1 :** VARIOUS, DIVERSE **2 :** VARIEGATED 1 — **var·ied·ly** *adv*

var·ie·gate \'ver-ē-ə-ˌgāt, 'ver-i-ˌgāt, 'var-\ *vt* **-gat·ed; -gat·ing** [L *variegatus*, pp. of *variegare*, fr. *varius* various + -*egare* (akin to L *agere* to drive) — more at AGENT] (1653) **1 :** to diversify in external appearance esp. with different colors **:** DAPPLE **2 :** to enliven or give interest to by means of variety — **var·ie·ga·tor** \-ˌgā-tər\ *n*

var·ie·gat·ed \-ˌgā-təd\ *adj* (1661) **1 :** having discrete markings of different colors ⟨∼ leaves⟩ **2 :** VARIED 1

variegated cutworm *n* (1922) **:** a widespread noctuid moth (*Peridroma saucia*) whose larva is destructive to crops

var·ie·ga·tion \ˌver-ē-ə-'gā-shən, ˌver-i-'gā-, ˌvar-\ *n* (1646) **:** the act of variegating **:** the state of being variegated; *esp* **:** diversity of colors

var·i·er \'ver-ē-ər, 'var-\ *n* (1860) **:** one that varies

¹va·ri·e·tal \və-'rī-ə-tᵊl\ *adj* (1866) **1 :** of, relating to, or characterizing a variety ⟨∼ name⟩; *also* **:** being a variety in distinction from an individual or species **2 :** of, relating to, or producing a varietal

²varietal *n* (1950) **:** a wine bearing the name of the principal grape from which it is made

va·ri·e·ty \və-'rī-ə-tē\ *n, pl* **-ties** [MF or L; MF *varieté,* L *varietat-, varietas,* fr. *varius* various] (15c) **1 :** the quality or state of having different forms or types **:** MULTIFARIOUSNESS **2 :** a number or collection of different things esp. of a particular class **:** ASSORTMENT **3 a :** something differing from others of the same general kind **:** SORT **b :** any of various groups of plants or animals ranking below a species **:** SUBSPECIES **4 :** VARIETY SHOW

variety meat *n* (ca. 1946) **:** an edible part (as the liver or tongue) of a slaughter animal other than skeletal muscle

variety show *n* (1882) **:** a theatrical entertainment of successive separate performances (as of songs, dances, skits, acrobatic feats, and trained animal acts)

variety store *n* (ca. 1768) **:** a retail store that carries a wide variety of merchandise esp. of low unit value

vario- — see VARI-

va·ri·o·la \və-'rī-ə-lə, ˌver-ē-'ō-lə, ˌvar-\ *n* [NL, fr. ML, pustule, pox, fr. LL, pustule, prob. fr. *varius* various] (1543) **:** SMALLPOX

var·i·om·e·ter \ˌver-ē-'ä-mə-tər, ˌvar-\ *n* (ca. 1900) **1 :** an instrument for measuring magnetic declination **2 :** an aeronautical instrument for indicating rate of climb

¹var·i·o·rum \ˌver-ē-'ōr-əm, ˌvar-, -'ór-\ *n* [L *variorum* of various persons (gen. pl. masc. of *varius*), in the phrase *cum notis variorum* with the notes of various persons] (1728) **1 :** an edition or text with notes by different persons **2 :** an edition containing variant readings of the text

²variorum *adj* (1763) **:** relating to or being a variorum; *also* **:** VARIANT ⟨∼ readings⟩

¹var·i·ous \'ver-ē-əs, 'var-\ *adj* [L *varius*] (1552) **1** *archaic* **:** VARIABLE, INCONSTANT **2 :** VARICOLORED ⟨birds of ∼ plumage⟩ **3 a :** of differing kinds **:** MULTIFARIOUS **b :** dissimilar in nature or form **:** UNLIKE ⟨animals as ∼ as the jaguar and the sloth⟩ **4 :** having a number of different aspects or characteristics ⟨a ∼ place⟩ ⟨a ∼ talent⟩ **5 :** of an indefinite number greater than one ⟨stop at ∼ towns⟩ **6 :** INDIVIDUAL, SEPARATE ⟨rate increases granted in the ∼ states⟩ *syn* see DIFFERENT — **var·i·ous·ness** *n*

²various *pron, pl in constr* (1877) **:** an indefinite number of separate individuals greater than one ⟨conversations with people from ∼ of the schools —Patricia Linden⟩

var·i·ous·ly *adv* (1627) **1 :** in various ways **:** at various times ⟨was ∼ occupied teaching, farming, and clerking⟩ **2 :** by various designations ⟨known ∼ as principal, headmaster, and rector⟩

vari·sized \'ver-i-ˌsīzd, 'var-\ *adj* (1936) **:** of various sizes

va·ris·tor \va-'ris-tər, ve-\ *n* [*vari-* + *resistor*] (1937) **:** an electrical resistor whose resistance depends on the applied voltage

var·ix \'var-iks\ *n, pl* **var·i·ces** \'var-ə-ˌsēz\ [ME, fr. L *varic-, varix*] (14c) **:** an abnormally dilated and lengthened vein, artery, or lymph vessel; *esp* **:** a varicose vein

var·let \'vär-lət\ *n* [ME, fr. MF *vaslet, varlet* young nobleman, page — more at VALET] (15c) **1 a :** ATTENDANT, MENIAL **b :** a knight's page **2 :** a base unprincipled person **:** KNAVE

var·let·ry \-lə-trē\ *n* (1606) *archaic* **:** RABBLE

var·mint \'vär-mənt\ *n* [alter. of *vermin*] (1539) **1 :** an animal considered a pest; *specif* **:** one classed as vermin and unprotected by game law **2 :** a contemptible person **:** RASCAL; *broadly* **:** PERSON, FELLOW

¹var·nish \'vär-nish\ *n* [ME *vernisch,* fr. MF *vernis,* fr. OIt or ML; OIt *vernice,* fr. ML *veronic-, veronix* sandarac] (14c) **1 a :** a liquid preparation that when spread and allowed to dry on a surface forms a hard lustrous typically transparent coating **b :** the covering or glaze given by the application of varnish **c** (1) **:** something that suggests varnish by its gloss (2) **:** a coating (as of deposits in an internal combustion engine) comparable to varnish **2 :** ¹GLOSS **3** *chiefly Brit* **:** a liquid nail polish — **var·nishy** \-ni-shē\ *adj*

²varnish *vt* (14c) **1 :** to apply varnish to **2 :** to cover or conceal (as something unpleasant) with something that gives a fair appearance **:** ²GLOSS **3 :** ADORN, EMBELLISH — **var·nish·er** \'vär-ni-shər\ *n*

varnish tree *n* (1758) **:** any of various trees yielding a milky juice from which in some cases varnish or lacquer is prepared; *esp* **:** a Japanese sumac (*Rhus verniciflua*)

var·si·ty \'vär-sə-tē, -stē\ *n, pl* **-ties** [by shortening & alter. fr. *university*] (1646) **1** *Brit* **:** UNIVERSITY **2 a :** the principal squad representing a university, college, school, or club esp. in a sport **b :** REGULAR 1d

Var·so·vi·an \vär-'sō-vē-ən\ *n* [F *varsovien,* fr. *Varsovie* Warsaw] (1764) **:** a native or resident of Warsaw, Poland

Var·u·na \'vər-ə-nə\ *n* [Skt *Varuna*] **:** a chief Vedic god responsible for natural and moral order in the cosmos

var·us \'vər-əs, 'ver-\ *n* [NL, fr. L, bent, knock-kneed] (1800) **:** a deformed position of a bodily part characterized by bending or turning inward toward the midline of the body to an abnormal degree ⟨a moderate right metatarsus ∼ —*Jour. Amer. Med. Assoc.*⟩ — **varus** *adj*

varve \'värv\ *n* [Sw *varv* turn, layer; akin to ON *hvarf* ring, OE *hweorfan* to turn — more at WHARF] (1912) **:** a pair of layers of alternately finer and coarser silt or clay believed to comprise an annual cycle of deposition in a body of still water — **varved** \'värvd\ *adj*

vary \'ver-ē, 'var-\ *vb* **var·ied; vary·ing** [ME *varien,* fr. MF or L; MF *varier,* fr. L *variare,* fr. *varius* various] *vt* (14c) **1 a :** to make a partial change in **:** make different in some attribute or characteristic **b :** to make differences between items in **:** DIVERSIFY **2 :** to present under new aspects ⟨∼ the rhythm and harmonic treatment⟩ ∼ *vi* **1 :** to exhibit or undergo change ⟨the sky was constantly ∼ing⟩ **2 :** DEVIATE, DEPART **3 :** to take on successive values ⟨*y* varies inversely with *x*⟩ **4 :** to exhibit divergence in structural or physiological characters from the typical form *syn* see CHANGE — **vary·ing·ly** \-iŋ-lē\ *adv*

varying hare *n* (1781) **:** SNOWSHOE HARE

vas \'vas\ *n, pl* **va·sa** \'vā-zə\ [NL, fr. L, vessel] (1651) **:** an anatomical vessel **:** DUCT — **va·sal** \-zəl\ *adj*

vas- *or* **vaso-** *comb form* [NL, fr. L *vas*] **1 :** vessel: as **a :** blood vessel ⟨*vasomotor*⟩ **b :** vas deferens ⟨*vasectomy*⟩ **2 :** vascular and ⟨*vasovagal*⟩ **3 :** vasomotor ⟨*vasoactive*⟩

va·sa ef·fer·en·tia \'vā-zə-ˌe-fə-'ren(t)-shē-ə\ *n pl* [NL, lit., efferent vessels] (ca. 1860) **:** the 12 to 20 ductules that lead from the rete of the testis to the vas deferens and except near their commencement are greatly convoluted and form the compact head of the epididymis

vas·cu·lar \'vas-kyə-lər\ *adj* [NL *vascularis,* fr. L *vasculum* small vessel, dim. of *vas*] (1672) **1 :** of or relating to a channel for the conveyance of a body fluid (as blood of an animal or sap of a plant) or to a system of such channels; *also* **:** supplied with or made up of such channels and esp. blood vessels ⟨a ∼ tumor⟩ ⟨a ∼ system⟩ **2 :** marked by vigor and ardor **:** SPIRITED, PASSIONATE — **vas·cu·lar·i·ty** \ˌvas-kyə-'lar-ə-tē\ *n*

vascular bundle *n* (ca. 1884) **:** a strand of specialized vascular tissue of higher plants consisting mostly of xylem and phloem

vascular cylinder *n* (ca. 1889) **:** STELE

vas·cu·lar·i·za·tion \ˌvas-kyə-lə-rə-'zā-shən\ *n* (1818) **:** the process of becoming vascular; *also* **:** abnormal or excessive formation of blood vessels (as in the retina or on the cornea)

vascular plant *n* (1861) **:** a plant having a specialized conducting system that includes xylem and phloem **:** TRACHEOPHYTE

vascular ray *n* (1672) **:** a band of usu. parenchymatous cells partly in the xylem and partly in the phloem of a plant root or stem that conducts fluids radially and appears in a cross section like a spoke of a wheel

vascular tissue *n* (1815) **:** plant tissue concerned mainly with conduction; *esp* **:** the specialized tissue of higher plants consisting essentially of phloem and xylem

vas·cu·la·ture \'vas-kyə-lə-ˌchùr, -ˌtyùr, -ˌtùr\ *n* [L *vasculum* vessel + E -*ature* (as in *musculature*)] (ca. 1927) **:** the arrangement of blood vessels in an organ or part

vas·cu·li·tis \ˌvas-kyə-'lī-təs\ *n, pl* **-lit·i·des** \-'li-tə-ˌdēz\ [NL, fr. L *vasculum* vessel] (ca. 1900) **:** inflammation of a blood or lymph vessel

vas·cu·lum \'vas-kyə-ləm\ *n, pl* **-la** \-lə\ [NL, fr. L, small vessel] (1782) **:** a usu. metal and commonly cylindrical or flattened covered box used in collecting plants

vas def·er·ens \'vas-'de-fə-rənz, -ˌrenz\ *n, pl* **va·sa def·er·en·tia** \'vā-zə-ˌde-fə-'ren(t)-shē-ə\ [NL, lit., deferent vessel] (1578) **:** a spermatic duct esp. of a higher vertebrate that in the human male is a thickwalled tube about two feet (0.61 meters) long that begins at and is continuous with the tail of the epididymis and eventually joins the duct of the seminal vesicle to form the ejaculatory duct

vase \US *oftenest* 'vās; *Canad usu & US also* 'vāz; *Brit usu, Canad also, & US sometimes* 'väz\ *n* [F, fr. L *vas* vessel] (1563) **:** a usu. round vessel of greater depth than width used chiefly as an ornament or for holding flowers — **vase-like** \-ˌlīk\ *adj*

va·sec·to·mize \va-'sek-tə-ˌmīz, vā-'zek-\ *vt* **-mized; -miz·ing** (1900) **:** to perform a vasectomy on

va·sec·to·my \-tə-mē\ *n, pl* **-mies** [ISV] (1899) **:** surgical division or resection of all or part of the vas deferens usu. to induce sterility

Vas·e·line \'va-sə-ˌlēn, ˌva-sə-\ *trademark* — used for petroleum jelly

va·so·ac·tive \ˌvā-zō-'ak-tiv\ *adj* (ca. 1921) **:** affecting the blood vessels esp. in respect to the degree of their relaxation or contraction — **va·so·ac·tiv·i·ty** \-ˌak-'ti-və-tē\ *n*

va·so·con·stric·tion \-kən-'strik-shən\ *n* [ISV] (1899) **:** narrowing of the lumen of blood vessels esp. as a result of vasomotor action

va·so·con·stric·tive \-'strik-tiv\ *adj* (1890) **:** inducing vasoconstriction

va·so·con·stric·tor \-tər\ *n* (1877) **:** an agent (as a sympathetic nerve fiber or a drug) that induces or initiates vasoconstriction

va·so·di·la·tion \-dī-'lā-shən, -də-\ *or* **va·so·di·la·ta·tion** \-ˌdi-lə-'tā-shən, -ˌdī-lə-\ *n* [ISV] (1896) **:** widening of the lumen of blood vessels

va·so·di·la·tor \-dī-'lā-tər, -'dī-ˌlā-\ *n* (1881) **:** an agent (as a parasympathetic nerve fiber or a drug) that induces or initiates vasodilation

va·so·mo·tor \ˌvā-zə-'mō-tər\ *adj* [ISV] (1865) **:** of, relating to, or being nerves or centers controlling the size of blood vessels

---

\ə\ abut \ᵊ\ kitten, F table \ər\ further \a\ ash \ā\ ace \ä\ mop, mar
\aù\ out \ch\ chin \e\ bet \ē\ easy \g\ go \i\ hit \ī\ ice \j\ job
\ŋ\ sing \ō\ go \ò\ law \òi\ boy \th\ thin \t̲h̲\ the \ü\ loot \ù\ foot
\y\ yet \zh\ vision \ä, k̲, ⁿ, œ, œ̄, ᵫ, ᵫ̄, ᵊ\ see Guide to Pronunciation

va·so·pres·sin \\,vā-zō-'pre-s²n\\ *n* [fr. *Vasopressin*, a trademark] (1927) : a polypeptide hormone secreted by the posterior lobe of the pituitary gland that increases blood pressure and decreases urine flow — called also *antidiuretic hormone*

va·so·pres·sor \\-'pre-sər\\ *adj* (1928) : causing a rise in blood pressure by exerting a vasoconstrictor effect — **vasopressor** *n*

va·so·spasm \\'vā-zō-,spa-zəm\\ *n* [ISV] (ca. 1909) : sharp and often persistent contraction of a blood vessel reducing its caliber and blood flow — **va·so·spas·tic** \\,vā-zō-'spas-tik\\ *adj*

va·so·to·cin \\,vā-zə-'tō-s²n\\ *n* [*vaso-* + oxy*tocin*] (ca. 1963) : a polypeptide pituitary hormone of most vertebrates below mammals that is prob. the phylogenetic precursor of oxytocin and vasopressin

va·so·va·gal \\'vā-zō-'vā-gəl\\ *adj* (ca. 1923) : of, relating to, or involving both vascular and vagal factors

vas·sal \\'va-səl\\ *n* [ME, fr. MF, fr. ML *vassallus*, fr. *vassus* servant, vassal, of Celt origin; akin to W *gwas* young man, servant] (14c) **1** : a person under the protection of a feudal lord to whom he has vowed homage and fealty : a feudal tenant **2** : one in a subservient or subordinate position — **vassal** *adj*

vas·sal·age \\-sə-lij\\ *n* (1594) **1** : the state of being a vassal **2** : the homage, fealty, or services due from a vassal **3** : a position of subordination or submission (as to a political power)

¹vast \\'vast\\ *adj* [L *vastus*; akin to OHG *wuosti* empty, desolate, OIr *fás*] (1575) : very great in size, amount, degree, intensity, or esp. in extent or range **syn** see ENORMOUS — **vast·ly** *adv* — **vast·ness** \\'vas(t)-nəs\\ *n*

²vast *n* (1604) : a boundless space ⟨the ~ of heaven —John Milton⟩

vas·ti·tude \\'vas-tə-,tüd, -,tyüd\\ *n* [L *vastitudo*, fr. *vastus*] (1623) : IMMENSITY, VASTNESS

vasty \\'vas-tē\\ *adj* (1596) : VAST ⟨call spirits from the ~ deep —Shak.⟩

¹vat \\'vat\\ *n* [ME *fat*, *vat*, fr. OE *fæt*; akin to OHG *vaz* vessel, Lith *puodas* pot] (13c) **1** : a large vessel (as a cistern, tub, or barrel) esp. for holding liquors in an immature state or preparations for dyeing or tanning **2** : a liquor containing a dye converted into a soluble reduced colorless or weakly colored form that on textile material steeped in the liquor and exposed to the air is converted by oxidation to the original insoluble dye and precipitated in the fiber

²vat *vt* **vat·ted; vat·ting** (1784) : to put into or treat in a vat

vat dye *n* (ca. 1903) : a water-insoluble generally fast dye used in the form of a vat liquor — called also *vat color*

vat–dyed \\'vat-'dīd\\ *adj* (ca. 1947) : dyed with one or more vat dyes

vat·ic \\'va-tik\\ *adj* [L *vates* seer, prophet; akin to OE *wōth* poetry, OHG *wuot* madness, OIr *fáith* seer, poet] (1603) : PROPHETIC, ORACULAR

Vat·i·can \\'va-ti-kən\\ *n* [L *Vaticanus* Vatican Hill (in Rome)] (1555) **1** : the papal headquarters in Rome **2** : the papal government — **Vatican** *adj*

va·tic·i·nal \\və-'ti-sᵊn-ᵊl\\ *adj* [L *vaticinus*, fr. *vaticinari* to foretell, prophesy] (1586) : PROPHETIC

va·tic·i·nate \\-s²n-,āt\\ *vb* **-nat·ed; -nat·ing** [L *vaticinatus*, pp. of *vaticinari*, fr. *vates* + *-cinari* (akin to L *canere* to sing) — more at CHANT] (ca. 1623) : PROPHESY, PREDICT — **va·tic·i·na·tor** \\-,ā-tər\\ *n*

va·tic·i·na·tion \\-,ti-s²n-'ā-shən\\ *n* (1603) **1** : PREDICTION **2** : the act of prophesying

va·tu \\'vä-,tü\\ *n*, *pl* **vatu** [prob. alter. of *Vanuatu*] (1981) — see MONEY table

vaude·ville \\'vòd-wəl, 'väd-, 'vōd-, -,vil; 'vò-də-, 'vä-, 'vō-\\ *n* [F, fr. MF, popular satirical song, alter. of *vaudevire*, fr. *vau-de-Vire* valley of Vire, town in northwest France where such songs were composed] (1739) **1** : a light often comic theatrical piece frequently combining pantomime, dialogue, dancing, and song **2** : stage entertainment consisting of various acts (as performing animals, acrobats, comedians, dancers, or singers) — **vaude·vil·lian** \\,vòd-'vil-yən, ,väd-, ,vōd-; ,vò-də-, ,vä-, ,vō-\\ *n or adj*

Vau·dois \\vō-'dwä, 'vō-,\\ *n, pl* [MF, fr. ML *Valdenses*] (1560) : WALDENSES

¹vault \\'vòlt\\ *n* [ME *voute*, fr. MF, fr. (assumed) VL *volvita* turn, vault, fr. fem. of *volvitus*, alter. of L *volutus*, pp. of *volvere* to roll — more at VOLUBLE] (14c) **1 a** : an arched structure of masonry usu. forming a ceiling or roof **b** : something (as the sky) resembling a vault **c** : an arched or dome-shaped anatomical structure **2 a** : a space covered by an arched structure; *esp* : an underground passage or room **b** : an underground storage compartment **c** : a room or compartment for the safekeeping of valuables **3 a** : a burial chamber **b** : a prefabricated container usu. of metal or concrete into which a casket is placed at burial — **vaulty** \\'vòl-tē\\ *adj*

²vault *vt* (14c) : to form or cover with or as if with a vault : ARCH

³vault *vb* [MF *volter*, fr. OIt *voltare*, fr. (assumed) VL *volvitare* to turn, leap, freq. of L *volvere*] *vi* (1538) **1** : to bound vigorously; *esp* : to execute a leap using the hands or a pole **2** : to do or achieve something as if by a leap ⟨~ *vt* : to leap over; *esp* : to leap over by or as if by aid of the hands or a pole

⁴vault *n* (1576) : an act of vaulting : LEAP

vault·ed \\'vòl-təd\\ *adj* (1533) **1** : built in the form of a vault : ARCHED **2** : covered with a vault

vault·er \\-tər\\ *n* (ca. 1552) : one that vaults; *esp* : an athlete who competes in the pole vault

¹vault·ing \\-tiŋ\\ *n* (1512) : vaulted construction

²vaulting *adj* (1593) **1** : reaching or stretching for the heights ⟨~ ambition⟩ ⟨a ~ imagination⟩ **2** : designed for use in vaulting or in gymnastic exercises ⟨a ~ block⟩ — **vault·ing·ly** \\-tiŋ-lē\\ *adv*

vaulting horse *n* (ca. 1875) **1** : a gymnastics apparatus used in vaulting that consists of a padded rectangular or cylindrical form supported in a horizontal position above the floor **2** : an event in which vaults are made over a vaulting horse

¹vaunt \\'vònt, 'vänt\\ *vb* [ME, fr. MF *vanter*, fr. LL *vanitare*, freq. of (assumed) L *vanare*, fr. L *vanus* vain] *vi* (15c) : to make a vain display of one's own worth or attainments : BRAG ⟨~ *vt* : to call attention to pridefully and often boastfully ⟨people who ~ their ingenuity⟩ **syn** see BOAST — **vaunt·er** *n* — **vaunt·ing·ly** \\'vòn-tiŋ-lē, 'vän-\\ *adv*

²vaunt *n* (15c) **1** : a vainglorious display of what one is or has or has done **2** : a bragging assertive statement

vaunt–cou·ri·er \\,vònt-'kùr-ē-ər, ,vänt-, -'kər-ē-, -'kə-rē-\\ *n* [MF *avant-courrier*, lit., advance courier] (1560) *archaic* : FORERUNNER

vaunt·ed \\'vòn-təd, 'vän-\\ *adj* (1579) : highly or widely praised or boasted about ⟨his own much ~ ferocity —Calvin Tomkins⟩

vaunt·ful \\'vònt-fəl, 'vänt-\\ *adj* (1590) : VAINGLORIOUS, BOASTFUL

vaunty \\'vòn-tē, 'vän-\\ *adj* (1724) *Scot* : PROUD, BOASTFUL, VAIN

vav *var of* WAW

vav·a·sor *or* **vav·a·sour** \\'va-və-,sòr, -,sōr, -,sùr\\ *n* [ME *vavasour*, fr. MF *vavassor*, prob. fr. ML *vassus vassorum* vassal of vassals] (14c) : a feudal tenant ranking directly below a baron

va·ward \\'vaù-,òrd, -,wòrd\\ *n* [ME *vauntwarde*, *vaward*, fr. ONF *avant-warde*, fr. *avant* before (fr. LL *abante*) + *warde* guard, fr. *warder* to guard — more at ADVANCE, REWARD] (1597) *archaic* : the foremost part : FOREFRONT ⟨the ~ of our youth —Shak.⟩

VCR \\,vē-(,)sē-'är\\ *n* [*videocassette recorder*] (1971) : a videotape recorder that uses videocassettes

V–day \\'vē-,dā\\ *n* [*victory day*] (1941) : a day of victory

've \\v, əv\\ *vb* [by contr.] : HAVE ⟨we've been there⟩

Ve·adar \\'vā-ä-,där, 'vā-ə-\\ *n* [Heb *wĕ-Adhâr*, lit., and Adar (i.e., the second Adar)] (ca. 1864) : the intercalary month of the Jewish calendar following Adar in leap years — see MONTH table

¹veal \\'vē(ə)l\\ *n* [ME *veel*, fr. MF, fr. L *vitellus* small calf, dim. of *vitulus* calf — more at WETHER] (14c) **1** : the flesh of a young calf **2** : CALF; *esp* : VEALER

²veal *vt* (1847) : to kill and dress (a calf) for veal

veal·er \\'vē-lər\\ *n* (ca. 1895) : a calf grown for or suitable for veal

vealy \\'vē-lē\\ *adj* (1769) **1** : resembling or suggesting veal or a calf **2** : IMMATURE

¹vec·tor \\'vek-tər\\ *n* [NL, fr. L, carrier, fr. *vehere* to carry — more at WAY] (1846) **1 a** : a quantity that has magnitude and direction and that is commonly represented by a directed line segment whose length represents the magnitude and whose orientation in space represents the direction; *broadly* : an element of a vector space **b** : a course or compass direction esp. of an airplane **2 a** : an organism (as an insect) that transmits a pathogen **b** : POLLINATOR a **3** : a sequence of genetic material (as a transposon or the genome of a bacteriophage) used to introduce specific genes into the genome of an organism — **vec·to·ri·al** \\vek-'tōr-ē-əl, -'tòr-\\ *adj* — **vec·to·ri·al·ly** \\-ə-lē\\ *adv*

²vector *vt* **vec·tored; vec·tor·ing** \\-t(ə-)riŋ\\ (1941) **1** : to guide (as an airplane, its pilot, or a missile) in flight by means of a radioed vector **2** : to change the direction of (the thrust of a jet engine) for steering

vector product *n* (1878) : a vector *c* whose length is the product of the lengths of two vectors *a* and *b* and the sine of their included angle, whose direction is perpendicular to their plane, and whose direction is that in which a right-handed screw with axis *c* will move along *c* when *a* is rotated into *b* — called also *cross product*

vector space *n* (1937) : a set representing a generalization of a system of vectors and consisting of elements which comprise a commutative group under addition, each of which is left unchanged under multiplication by the multiplicative identity of a field, and for which multiplication by the multiplicative operation of the field is commutative, closed, distributive such that both $c(A + B) = cA + cB$ and $(c + d)A = cA + dA$, and associative such that $(cd)A = c(dA)$ where A, B are vectors and c, d are elements of the field

vector sum *n* (ca. 1890) : the sum of a number of vectors that for the sum of two vectors is geometrically represented by the diagonal of a parallelogram whose sides represent the two vectors being added

Ve·da \\'vā-də\\ *n* [Skt, lit., knowledge; akin to Gk *eidenai* to know — more at WIT] (1734) : any of four canonical collections of hymns, prayers, and liturgical formulas that comprise the earliest Hindu sacred writings

ve·da·lia \\vi-'dāl-yə\\ *n* [NL, genus name] (1889) : an Australian ladybug (*Rodolia cardinalis*) introduced to many countries to control scale insects

Ve·dan·ta \\vā-'dän-tə, və-, 'dan-\\ *n* [Skt *Vedānta*, lit., end of the Veda, fr. *Veda* + *anta* end; akin to OE *ende* end] (1788) : an orthodox system of Hindu philosophy developing esp. in a qualified monism the speculations of the Upanishads on ultimate reality and the liberation of the soul — **Ve·dan·tism** \\-'dän-,ti-zəm, -'dan-\\ *n* — **Ve·dan·tist** \\-'dän-tist, -'dan-\\ *n*

Ve·dan·tic \\-'dän-tik, -'dan-\\ *adj* (1882) **1** : of or relating to the Vedanta philosophy **2** : VEDIC

Ved·da *or* **Ved·dah** \\'ve-də\\ *n* [Sinhalese *vedda* hunter] (1681) : a member of an aboriginal people of Sri Lanka

Ved·doid \\'ve-,dòid\\ *n* (1928) : a member of an ancient race of southern Asia characterized by wavy to curly hair, chocolate-brown skin color, and slender body build — **Veddoid** *adj*

ve·dette \\vi-'det\\ *n* [F, fr. It *vedetta*, alter. of *veletta*, prob. fr. Sp *vela* watch, fr. *velar* to keep watch, fr. L *vigilare* to wake, watch, fr. *vigil* awake — more at VIGIL] (ca. 1702) : a mounted sentinel stationed in advance of pickets

Ve·dic \\'vā-dik\\ *adj* (1848) : of or relating to the Vedas, the language in which they are written, or Hindu history and culture between 1500 B.C. and 500 B.C.

vee \\'vē\\ *n* (ca. 1883) **1** : something shaped like the letter V **2** : the letter *v*

vee·jay \\'vē-,jā\\ *n* [*video jockey*] (1981) : an announcer of a program (as on television) that features music videos

vee·na *var of* VINA

veep \\'vēp\\ *n* [fr. *v. p.* (abbr. for *vice president*)] (1949) : VICE PRESIDENT

veal 1: *A* wholesale cuts: *1* leg, *2* loin, *3* flank, *4* rib, *5* breast, *6* shoulder, *7* shank; *B* retail cuts: *1* hind shank, *2* heel of round, *3* round, *4* rump roast, *5* sirloin steak, *6* loin chops, *7* kidney chops, *8* flank, *9* breast, *10* rib roast, *11* blade steak, *12* arm steak, *13* shoulder roast, *14* foreshank

¹**veer** \'vir\ vt [ME *veren*, of LG or D origin; akin to MD *vieren* to slacken, MLG *vīren*] (15c) : to let out (as a rope)

²**veer** vb [MF *virer*, fr. OF, to throw with a twisting motion, perh. modif. of L *vibrare* to wave, propel suddenly — more at VIBRATE] vi (1582) **1** of the wind : to shift in a clockwise direction — compare BACK **2** : to change direction or course **3** : to wear ship ~ vt : to direct to a different course; *specif* : WEAR 7 syn see SWERVE — **veer·ing·ly** \-iŋ-lē\ adv

³**veer** n (1611) : a change in course or direction ⟨a ~ to the right⟩

vee·ry \'vir-ē\ n, pl **veeries** [prob. imit.] (1838) : a thrush (*Catharus fuscescens*) common in the eastern U.S.

veg \'vej\ n, pl **veg** (1918) *chiefly Brit* : VEGETABLE

Ve·ga \'vē-gə, 'vā-\ n [NL, fr. Ar (*al-Nasr*) *al-Wāqi'*, lit., the falling (vulture)] : a star of the first magnitude that is the brightest in the constellation Lyra

veg·an \'vē-gən also 'vā- also 'vē-jən or -jan\ n [by contr. fr. *vegetarian*] (1944) : a strict vegetarian who consumes no animal food or dairy products; *also* : one who abstains from using animal products (as leather) — **veg·an·ism** \'vē-gə,ni-zəm, 'vā-gə-, 've-jə-\ n

¹**veg·e·ta·ble** \'vej-tə-bəl, 've-jə-\ adj [ME, fr. ML *vegetabilis* vegetative, fr. *vegetare* to grow, fr. L to animate, fr. *vegetus* lively, fr. *vegēre* to enliven — more at WAKE] (15c) **1 a** : of, relating to, constituting, or growing like plants **b** : consisting of plants : VEGETATIONAL **2** : made or obtained from plants or plant products **3** : resembling or suggesting a plant (as in inertness or passivity)

²**vegetable** n (1582) **1** : PLANT 1b **2** : a usu. herbaceous plant (as the cabbage, bean, or potato) grown for an edible part that is usu. eaten as part of a meal; *also* : such edible part **3** : a human being whose mental and physical functioning is severely impaired (as from accident or disease)

vegetable ivory n (1842) **1** : the hard white opaque endosperm of the ivory nut that takes a high polish and is used as a substitute for ivory **2** : IVORY NUT

vegetable marrow n (1816) : any of various smooth-skinned elongated summer squashes with creamy white to deep green skins

vegetable oil n (1797) : an oil of plant origin; *esp* : a fatty oil from seeds or fruits

vegetable oyster n (ca. 1818) : SALSIFY

vegetable pear n (1887) : CHAYOTE

vegetable wax n (1815) : a wax of plant origin secreted commonly in thin flakes by the walls of epidermal cells

veg·e·ta·bly \'vej-tə-blē, 've-jə-\ adv (1651) : in the manner of or like a vegetable

veg·e·tal \'ve-jə-t²l\ adj [ML *vegetare* to grow] (15c) **1** : VEGETABLE **2** : VEGETATIVE **3** : of or relating to the vegetal pole of an egg or to that part of an egg from which the endoderm normally develops ⟨~ blastomeres⟩

vegetal pole n (1896) : the point on the surface of an egg that is diametrically opposite to the animal pole and usu. marks the center of the protoplasm containing more yolk, dividing more slowly and into larger blastomeres than that about the animal pole, and giving rise to the hypoblast of the embryo

¹**veg·e·tar·i·an** \,ve-jə-'ter-ē-ən\ n [²*vegetable* + *-arian*] (1839) **1** : one who believes in or practices vegetarianism **2** : HERBIVORE

²**vegetarian** adj (1849) **1** : of or relating to vegetarians **2** : consisting wholly of vegetables, fruits, and sometimes eggs or dairy products ⟨a ~ diet⟩

veg·e·tar·i·an·ism \-ē-ə-,ni-zəm\ n (ca. 1851) : the theory or practice of living on a diet made up of vegetables, fruits, grains, nuts, and sometimes eggs or dairy products

veg·e·tate \'ve-jə-,tāt\ vb **-tat·ed; -tat·ing** [ML *vegetatus*, pp. of *vegetare* to grow] vi (1605) **1 a** : to grow in the manner of a plant; *also* : to grow exuberantly or with proliferation of fleshy or warty outgrowths **b** : to produce vegetation **2** : to lead a passive existence without exertion of body or mind ~ vt : to establish vegetation in or on

veg·e·ta·tion \,ve-jə-'tā-shən\ n (1564) **1** : the act or process of vegetating **2** : inert existence **3** : plant life or total plant cover (as of an area) **4** : an abnormal growth upon a body part — **veg·e·ta·tion·al** \-shnəl, -shə-n²l\ adj

veg·e·ta·tive \'ve-jə-,tā-tiv\ adj (14c) **1 a** (1) : growing or having the power of growing (2) : of, relating to, or engaged in nutritive and growth functions as contrasted with reproductive functions ⟨a ~ nucleus⟩ **b** : promoting plant growth ⟨the ~ properties of soil⟩ **c** : of, relating to, or involving propagation by nonsexual processes or methods **2** : relating to, composed of, or suggesting vegetation ⟨~ cover⟩ **3** : of or relating to the division of nature comprising the plant kingdom **4** : affecting, arising from, or relating to involuntary bodily functions **5** : VEGETABLE **3** — **veg·e·ta·tive·ly** adv — **veg·e·ta·tive·ness** n

ve·gete \və-'jēt\ adj [L *vegetus* — more at VEGETABLE] (1639) *archaic* : LIVELY, HEALTHY

veg·gie also **veg·ie** \'ve-jē\ n [by shortening & alter.] (1955) **1** : VEGETABLE **2** *slang* : VEGETARIAN

veg out \'vej-\ vi **vegged out; veg·ging out** [short for *vegetate*] (1980) : to spend time idly or passively

ve·he·mence \'vē-ə-mən(t)s\ n (15c) : the quality or state of being vehement : INTENSITY

ve·he·ment \-mənt\ adj [ME, fr. MF, fr. L *vehement-, vehemens, vement-, vemens*] (15c) : marked by forceful energy : POWERFUL ⟨a ~ wind⟩: as **a** : intensely emotional : IMPASSIONED, FERVID ⟨~ patriotism⟩ **b** (1) : deeply felt ⟨a ~ suspicion⟩ (2) : forcibly expressed ⟨~ denunciations⟩ **c** : bitterly antagonistic ⟨a ~ debate⟩ — **ve·he·ment·ly** adv

ve·hi·cle \'vē-ə-kəl also 'vē-,hi-kəl\ n [F *véhicule*, fr. L *vehiculum* carriage, conveyance, fr. *vehere* to carry — more at WAY] (1612) **1 a** : an inert medium (as a syrup) in which a medicinally active agent is administered **b** : any of various media acting usu. as solvents, carriers, or binders for active ingredients or pigments **2** : an agent of transmission : CARRIER **3** : a medium through which something is expressed, achieved, or displayed **4** : a means of carrying or transporting something : CONVEYANCE: as **a** : MOTOR VEHICLE **b** : a piece of mechanized equipment

ve·hic·u·lar \vē-'hi-kyə-lər\ adj (1616) **1 a** : of, relating to, or de-

signed for vehicles and esp. motor vehicles **b** : transported by vehicle **c** : caused by or resulting from the operation of a vehicle ⟨~ homicide⟩ **2** : serving as a vehicle

V–8 \'vē-'āt\ n (1942) : an internal combustion engine having two banks of four cylinders each with the banks at an angle to each other; *also* : an automobile having such an engine

¹**veil** \'vā(ə)l\ n [ME *veile*, fr. ONF, fr. L *vela*, pl. of *velum* sail, awning, curtain] (13c) **1 a** : a length of cloth worn by women as a covering for the head and shoulders and often esp. in Eastern countries for the face; *specif* : the outer covering of a nun's headdress **b** : a length of veiling or netting worn over the face or head or attached for protection or ornament to a hat or headdress **c** : any of various liturgical cloths; *esp* : a cloth used to cover the chalice **2** : the cloistered life of a nun **3** : a concealing curtain or cover of cloth **4** : something that hides or obscures like a veil **5** : a covering body part or membrane: as **a** : VELUM **b** : CAUL

²**veil** vt (14c) : to cover, provide, obscure, or conceal with or as if with a veil ~ vi : to put on or wear a veil

veiled \'vā(ə)ld\ adj (1593) **1 a** : having or wearing a veil or a concealing cover ⟨a ~ hat⟩ **b** : characterized by a softening tonal distortion **2** : obscured as if by a veil : DISGUISED ⟨~ threats⟩

veil·ing \'vā-liŋ\ n (14c) **1** : VEIL **2** : any of various light sheer fabrics

¹**vein** \'vān\ n [ME *veine*, fr. MF, fr. L *vena*] (14c) **1 a** : a narrow water channel in rock or earth or in ice **b** (1) : LODE 2, 3 (2) : a bed of useful mineral matter **2** : BLOOD VESSEL; *esp* : any of the tubular branching vessels that carry blood from the capillaries toward the heart **3 a** : any of the vascular bundles forming the framework of a leaf **b** : any of the thickened cuticular ribs that serve to stiffen the wings of an insect **4** : something suggesting veins (as in reticulation); *specif* : a wavy variegation (as in marble) **5 a** : a distinctive mode of expression : STYLE **b** : a pervasive element or quality : STRAIN **c** : a line of thought or action **6 a** : a special aptitude : TALENT **b** : a usu. transitory and casually attained mood **c** : top form : FETTLE — **vein·al** \'vā-n²l\ adj

²**vein** vt (1502) : to pattern with or as if with veins

veined \'vānd\ adj (ca. 1529) : patterned with or as if with veins : having venation : STREAKED ⟨a ~ leaf⟩ ⟨~ marble⟩ ⟨~ cheese⟩

vein·er \'vā-nər\ n (1895) : a small V gouge used in wood carving

vein·ing \'vā-niŋ\ n (1826) : a pattern of veins : VENATION

vein·let \'vān-lət\ n (1831) : a small vein

veiny \'vā-nē\ adj (1611) : full of veins : noticeably veined

ve·la·men \vi-'lā-mən\ n, pl **ve·lam·i·na** \-'la-mə-nə\ [NL, fr. L, covering, fr. *velare* to cover, fr. *velum* curtain] (1882) : the thick corky epidermis of aerial roots of an epiphytic orchid that absorbs water from the atmosphere

ve·lar \'vē-lər\ adj [NL *velaris*, fr. *velum*] (1876) **1** : formed with the back of the tongue touching or near the soft palate ⟨the ~ \k\ of \'kül\ *cool*⟩ **2** : of, forming, or relating to a velum and esp. the soft palate — **velar** n

ve·lar·i·um \vi-'lar-ē-əm, -'ler-\ n, pl **-ia** \-ē-ə\ [L, fr. *velum* curtain] (1834) : an awning over an ancient Roman theater or amphitheater

ve·lar·i·za·tion \,vē-lə-rə-'zā-shən\ n (1915) **1** : the quality or state of being velarized **2** : an act or instance of velarizing

ve·lar·ize \'vē-lə-,rīz\ vt **-ized; -iz·ing** (1915) : to modify (as the \l\ of \'pül\ *pool*) by a simultaneous velar articulation

Vel·cro \'vel-(,)krō\ *trademark* — used for a closure consisting of a piece of fabric of small hooks that sticks to a corresponding fabric of small loops

veld or **veldt** \'velt, 'felt\ n [Afrik *veld*, fr. D, field; akin to OE *feld* field] (1835) : a grassland esp. of southern Africa usu. with scattered shrubs or trees

ve·li·ger \'vē-lə-jər, 've-\ n [NL, fr. *velum* + *-ger* bearing, fr. *gerere* to bear] (1877) : a larval mollusk in the stage when it has developed the velum

vel·le·i·ty \ve-'lē-ə-tē, və-\ n, pl **-ties** [ML *velleitas*, fr. L *velle* to wish, will — more at WILL] (1618) **1** : the lowest degree of volition **2** : a slight wish or tendency : INCLINATION

¹**vel·lum** \'ve-ləm\ n [ME *velim*, fr. MF *veelin*, fr. *veelin*, adj., of a calf, fr. *veel* calf — more at VEAL] (15c) **1** : a fine-grained unsplit lambskin, kidskin, or calfskin prepared esp. for writing on or for binding books **2** : a strong cream-colored paper

²**vellum** adj (1565) **1** : of, resembling, or bound in vellum **2** : slightly rough ⟨paper with a ~ finish⟩

ve·lo·ce \vā-'lō-(,)chā\ adv or adj [It, fr. L *veloc-, velox*] (ca. 1823) : in a rapid manner — used as a direction in music

ve·lo·cim·e·ter \,vē-lō-'si-mə-tər, ,ve-\ n [*velocity* + *-meter*] (1842) : a device for measuring speed (as of fluid flow or sound)

ve·loc·i·pede \və-'lä-sə-,pēd\ n [F *vélocipède*, fr. L *veloc-, velox* + *ped-, pes* foot — more at FOOT] (1818) : a lightweight wheeled vehicle propelled by the rider: as **a** *archaic* : BICYCLE **b** : TRICYCLE **c** : a 3-wheeled railroad handcar

ve·loc·i·ty \və-'lä-sə-tē, -'läs-tē\ n, pl **-ties** [MF *velocité*, fr. L *velocitat-, velocitas*, fr. *veloc-, velox* quick; prob. akin to L *vegēre* to enliven — more at WAKE] (ca. 1550) **1 a** : quickness of motion : SPEED ⟨the ~ of sound⟩ **b** : rapidity of movement ⟨[my horse's] strong suit is grace & personal comeliness, rather than ~ —Mark Twain⟩ **c** : speed imparted to something ⟨the power pitcher relies on ~ —Tony Scherman⟩ **2** : the rate of change of position along a straight line with respect to time : the derivative of position with respect to time **3 a** : rate of occurrence or action : RAPIDITY ⟨the ~ of historical change —R. J. Lifton⟩ ⟨the narrative leaps from one frantic episode to another with impressive ~ —James Atlas⟩ **b** : rate of turnover ⟨the ~ of money⟩

ve·lo·drome \'vē-lə-,drōm, 've-,\ 'vē-\ n [F *vélodrome*, fr. *vélo* cycle (short for *vélocipède*) + *-drome*] (1895) : a track designed for cycling

ve·lour or **ve·lours** \və-'lur\ n, pl **velours** \-'lurz\ [F *velours* velvet, velour, fr. MF *velours, velour*, fr. OF *velous*, fr. OProv *velos*, fr. L *villosus* shaggy, fr. *villus* shaggy hair — more at VELVET] (ca. 1706) **1**

\ə\ abut \²\ kitten, F table \ər\ further \a\ ash \ā\ ace \ä\ mop, mar \aú\ out \ch\ chin \e\ bet \ē\ easy \g\ go \i\ hit \ī\ ice \j\ job \ŋ\ sing \ō\ go \o\ law \oi\ boy \th\ thin \th\ the \ü\ loot \ú\ foot \y\ yet \zh\ vision \ä, k̲, ⁿ, œ, œ̄, ue, ū̄, ᴿ\ *see* Guide to Pronunciation

: any of various fabrics with a pile or napped surface resembling velvet used in heavy weights for upholstery and curtains and in lighter weights for clothing; *also* : the article of clothing itself **2** : a fur felt (as of rabbit or nutria) finished with a long velvety nap and used esp. for hats

ve·lou·té \və-lü-'tā\ *n* [F, lit., velvetiness, fr. MF *velluté*, fr. OProv *velut* velvety, fr. (assumed) VL *villutus*] (1830) : a white sauce made of chicken, veal, or fish stock and cream and thickened with butter and flour

ve·lum \'vē-ləm\ *n, pl* **ve·la** \-lə\ [NL, fr. L, curtain] (1753) **1** : a membrane or membranous part resembling a veil or curtain: as **a** : SOFT PALATE **b** : an annular membrane projecting inward from the margin of the umbrella in some jellyfishes (as the hydromedusans) **2** : a swimming organ that is esp. well developed in the later larval stages of many marine gastropods

ve·lure \ve-'lur, vel-'yur, vel-yər\ *n* [modif. of MF *velour*] (1587) *obs* : VELVET; *also* : a fabric resembling velvet

¹vel·vet \'vel-vət\ *n* [ME *veluet, velvet*, fr. MF *velu* shaggy, fr. (assumed) VL *villutus*, fr. L *villus* shaggy hair; akin to L *vellus* fleece — more at WOOL] (14c) **1** : a clothing and upholstery fabric (as of silk, rayon, or wool) characterized by a short soft dense warp pile **2 a** : something suggesting velvet **b** : a characteristic (as softness or smoothness) of velvet **3** : the soft vascular skin that envelops and nourishes the developing antlers of deer **4 a** : the winnings of a player in a gambling game **b** : a profit or gain beyond ordinary expectation — **vel·vet·like** \-,līk\ *adj*

²velvet *adj* (14c) **1** : made of or covered with velvet; *also* : clad in velvet **2** : resembling or suggesting velvet : VELVETY ⟨a ~ voice⟩

velvet ant *n* (1748) : any of various solitary usu. brightly colored and hairy fossorial wasps (family Mutillidae) with the female wingless

velvet bean *n* (1898) : an annual legume (*Mucuna deeringiana* syn. *Stizolobium deeringianum*) grown esp. in the southern U.S. for green manure and grazing; *also* : its seed often used as stock feed

vel·ve·teen \,vel-və-'tēn\ *n* (1776) **1** : a clothing fabric usu. of cotton in twill or plain weaves made with a short close weft pile in imitation of velvet **2** *pl* : clothes made of velveteen

vel·vety \'vel-və-tē\ *adj* (1752) **1** : soft and smooth like velvet ⟨~ hair⟩ **2** : smooth to the taste : MILD ⟨a ~ wine⟩

ven- *or* **veni-** *or* **veno-** *comb form* [L *vena*] : vein ⟨*veni*puncture⟩ ⟨*ve*nography⟩

ve·na \'vē-nə\ *n, pl* **ve·nae** \-(,)nē\ [ME, fr. L] (14c) : VEIN

ve·na ca·va \vē-nə-'kā-və\ *n, pl* **ve·nae ca·vae** \-(,)nē-'kā-(,)vē\ [NL, lit., hollow vein] (1598) : any of the large veins by which in air-breathing vertebrates the blood is returned to the right atrium of the heart — **vena ca·val** \-vəl\ *adj*

ve·nal \'vē-n⁷l\ *adj* [L *venalis*, fr. *venum* (acc.) sale; akin to Gk *ōneisthai* to buy, Skt *vasna* price] (1652) **1** : capable of being bought or obtained for money or other valuable consideration : PURCHASABLE; *esp* : open to corrupt influence and esp. bribery : MERCENARY ⟨a ~ legislator⟩ **2** : originating in, characterized by, or associated with corrupt bribery ⟨a ~ arrangement with the police⟩ — **ve·nal·i·ty** \vi-'na-lə-tē\ *n* — **ve·nal·ly** \'vē-n⁷l-ē\ *adv*

ve·na·tion \vē-'nā-shən, vē-\ *n* [L *vena* vein] (1646) : an arrangement or system of veins (as in the tissue of a leaf or the wing of an insect)

vend \'vend\ *vb* [L *vendere* to sell, v.t., contr. for *venum dare* to give for sale] *vi* (1622) : to dispose of something by sale : SELL; *also* : to engage in selling ~ *vt* **1 a** : to sell esp. as a hawker or peddler **b** : to sell by means of vending machines **2** : to utter publicly

Ven·da \'ven-də\ *n* (1908) : a Bantu language spoken by a people of Northern Transvaal; *also* : a member of this people

vend·ee \ven-'dē\ *n* (1547) : one to whom a thing is sold : BUYER

ven·det·ta \ven-'de-tə\ *n* [It, lit., revenge, fr. L *vindicta* — more at VINDICTIVE] (1855) **1** : BLOOD FEUD **2** : an often prolonged series of retaliatory, vengeful, or hostile acts or exchange of such acts ⟨waged a personal ~ against those who opposed his nomination⟩

ven·deuse \vän-'də(r)z, vän-'düz\ *n* [F, fem. of *vendeur* salesman, fr. MF] (1913) : a saleswoman esp. in the fashion industry

vend·ible *or* **vend·able** \'ven-də-bəl\ *adj* (14c) : capable of being vended : SALABLE — **vend·ibil·i·ty** \,ven-də-'bi-lə-tē\ *n*

vending machine *n* (ca. 1895) : a coin-operated machine for selling merchandise

ven·dor \'ven-dər, *for 1 also* ven-'dȯr\ *also* **vend·er** \-dər\ *n* [MF *vendeur*, fr. *vendre* to sell, fr. L *vendere*] (1594) **1** : one that vends : SELLER **2** : VENDING MACHINE

ven·due \'ven-,dü, 'ven-,\ *also* ,'fen-,, ,dyü; ven-', vän-'\ *n* [obs. F, fr. MF, fr. *vendre*] (1668) : a public sale at auction

¹ve·neer \və-'nir\ *n* [G *Furnier*, fr. *furnieren* to veneer, fr. F *fournir* to furnish, equip — more at FURNISH] (1702) **1** : a thin sheet of a material: as **a** : a layer of wood of superior value or excellent grain to be glued to an inferior wood **b** : any of the thin layers bonded together to form plywood **2** : a protective or ornamental facing (as of brick or stone) **3** : a superficial or deceptively attractive appearance, display, or effect : FACADE, GLOSS

²veneer *vt* (1728) **1** : to overlay or plate (as a common wood) with a thin layer of finer wood for outer finish or decoration; *broadly* : to face with a material giving a superior surface **2** : to cover over with a veneer; *esp* : to conceal (as a defect of character) under a superficial and deceptive attractiveness — **ve·neer·er** *n*

ve·neer·ing *n* (ca. 1706) **1** : a veneered surface **2** : material used as veneer

ven·er·a·ble \'ve-nər(-ə)-bəl, 'ven-rə-bəl\ *adj* (15c) **1** : deserving to be venerated — used as a title for an Anglican archdeacon or for a Roman Catholic who has been accorded the lowest of three degrees of recognition for sanctity **2** : made sacred esp. by religious or historical association **3 a** : calling forth respect through age, character, and attainments; *broadly* : conveying an impression of aged goodness and benevolence **b** : impressive by reason of age ⟨under ~ pines⟩ **syn**

see OLD — **ven·er·a·bil·i·ty** \,ve-nə-rə-'bi-lə-tē, ,ven-rə-\ *n* — **ven·er·a·ble·ness** \'ve-nər(-ə)-bəl-nəs, 'ven-rə-\ *n* — **ven·er·a·bly** \-blē\ *adv*

ven·er·ate \'ve-nə-,rāt\ *vt* **-at·ed; -at·ing** [L *veneratus*, pp. of *venerari*, fr. *vener-, venus* love, charm — more at WIN] (ca. 1623) **1** : to regard with reverential respect or with admiring deference **2** : to honor (as an icon or a relic) with a ritual act of devotion **syn** see REVERE — **ven·er·a·tor** \-,rā-tər\ *n*

ven·er·a·tion \,ve-nə-'rā-shən\ *n* (15c) **1** : respect or awe inspired by the dignity, wisdom, dedication, or talent of a person **2** : the act of venerating **3** : the condition of one that is venerated

ve·ne·re·al \və-'nir-ē-əl\ *adj* [ME *venerealle*, fr. L *venereus*, fr. *vener-, venus* love, sexual desire] (15c) **1** : of or relating to sexual pleasure or indulgence **2 a** : resulting from or contracted during sexual intercourse ⟨~ infections⟩ **b** : of, relating to, or affected with venereal disease ⟨a high ~ rate⟩ **c** : involving the genital organs ⟨~ sarcoma⟩

venereal disease *n* (1658) : a contagious disease (as gonorrhea or syphilis) that is typically acquired in sexual intercourse — compare STD

¹ven·ery \'ve-nə-rē\ *n* [ME *venerie*, fr. MF, fr. *vener* to hunt, fr. L *venari* — more at VENISON] (14c) **1** : the art, act, or practice of hunting **2** : animals that are hunted : GAME

²venery *n* [ME *venerie*, fr. ML *veneria*, fr. L *vener-, venus* sexual desire] (15c) **1** : the pursuit of or indulgence in sexual pleasure **2** : SEXUAL INTERCOURSE

ve·ne·sec·tion \'ve-nə-,sek-shən, 'vē-\ *n* [NL *venae section-, venae sectio*, lit., cutting of a vein] (1661) : the operation of opening a vein for letting blood : PHLEBOTOMY

Ven·e·ti \'ve-nə-,ti\ *n pl* [L *Veneti*] (1881) **1** : an ancient people in Gaul conquered by Caesar in 56 B.C. **2** : an ancient people in northeastern Italy allied politically to the Romans

ve·ne·tian blind \və-'nē-shən-\ *n* [*Venetian* of Venice, Italy] (1770) : a blind (as for a window) having numerous horizontal slats that may be set simultaneously at any of several angles so as to vary the amount of light admitted

venetian glass *n, often cap V* (ca. 1845) : often colored glassware made at Murano near Venice of a soda-lime metal and typically elaborately decorated (as with gilt, enamel, or engraving)

Venetian red *n* (ca. 1753) : an earthy hematite used as a pigment; *also* : a synthetic iron oxide pigment

Ve·net·ic \və-'ne-tik\ *n* [L *veneticus* of the Veneti, fr. *Veneti*] (1902) : the language of the ancient Veneti of Italy — see INDO-EUROPEAN LANGUAGES table — **Venetic** *adj*

venge \'venj\ *vt* **venged; veng·ing** [ME, fr. MF *vengier*, fr. OF] (14c) *archaic* : AVENGE

ven·geance \'ven-jən(t)s\ *n* [ME, fr. OF, fr. *vengier* to avenge, fr. L *vindicare* to lay claim to, avenge — more at VINDICATE] (14c) : punishment inflicted in retaliation for an injury or offense : RETRIBUTION — **with a vengeance 1** : with great force or vehemence **2** : to an extreme or excessive degree

venge·ful \'venj-fəl\ *adj* [obs. E *venge* revenge] (1586) : REVENGEFUL: as **a** : seeking to avenge **b** : serving to gain vengeance — **venge·ful·ly** \-fə-lē\ *adv* — **venge·ful·ness** *n*

V–en·gine \'vē-\ *n* (ca. 1922) : an internal combustion engine whose cylinders are arranged in two banks forming an acute or right angle

veni- *or* **veno-** — see VEN-

ve·nial \'vē-nē-əl, -nyəl\ *adj* [ME, fr. MF, fr. LL *venialis*, fr. L *venia* favor, indulgence, pardon; akin to L *venus* love, charm — more at WIN] (14c) : of a kind that can be remitted : FORGIVABLE, PARDONABLE; *also* : meriting no particular censure or notice : EXCUSABLE ⟨~ faults⟩ — **ve·nial·ly** *adv* — **ve·nial·ness** *n*

venial sin *n* (14c) : a sin that is relatively slight or that is committed without full reflection or consent and so according to Thomist theology does not deprive the soul of sanctifying grace — compare MORTAL SIN

ve·ni·punc·ture \'vē-nə-,pəŋ(k)-chər, 've-\ *n* (ca. 1903) : surgical puncture of a vein esp. for the withdrawal of blood or for intravenous medication

ve·ni·re \və-'nī-rē\ *n* [*venire facias*] (1665) : an entire panel from which a jury is drawn

ve·ni·re fa·ci·as \-,nī-rē-'fā-shē-əs\ *n* [ME, fr. ML, you should cause to come] (15c) : a judicial writ directing the sheriff to summon a specified number of qualified persons to serve as jurors

ve·ni·re·man \və-'nī-rē-mən, -'nir-ē-\ *n* (1776) : a member of a venire

ven·i·son \'ve-nə-sən *also* -zən, *Brit usu* 'ven-zən\ *n, pl* **venisons** *also* **venison** [ME, fr. OF *veneison* hunting, game, fr. L *venation-, venatio*, fr. *venari* to hunt, pursue; akin to Skt *vanoti* he strives for — more at WIN] (14c) : the edible flesh of a game animal and esp. a deer

Ve·ni·te \və-'nī-tē, -'nē-,tā\ *n* [ME, fr. L, O come, fr. *venire* to come; fr. the opening word of Ps 95:1 — more at COME] (13c) : a liturgical chant composed of parts of Psalms 95 and 96

Venn diagram \'ven-\ *n* [John *Venn* †1923 Eng. logician] (1918) : a graph that employs closed curves and esp. circles to represent logical relations between and operations on sets and the terms of propositions by the inclusion, exclusion, or intersection of the circles

ve·nog·ra·phy \vi-'nä-grə-fē, vā-\ *n* [ISV] (1935) : roentgenography of a vein after injection of an opaque substance

¹ven·om \'ve-nəm\ *n* [ME *venim, venom*, fr. OF *venim*, fr. (assumed) VL *venimen*, alter. of L *venenum* magic charm, drug, poison; akin to L *venus* love, charm — more at WIN] (13c) **1** : poisonous matter normally secreted by some animals (as snakes, scorpions, or bees) and transmitted to prey or an enemy chiefly by biting or stinging; *broadly* : material that is poisonous **2** : ILL WILL, MALEVOLENCE

Venn diagram: *AB* represents the intersection of sets *A* and *B*

²venom *vt* (14c) : ENVENOM

ven·om·ous \'ve-nə-məs\ *adj* (14c) **1** : full of venom: as **a** : POISONOUS, ENVENOMED **b** : NOXIOUS, PERNICIOUS ⟨expose a ~ dope ring —Don Porter⟩ **c** : SPITEFUL, MALEVOLENT ⟨~ criticism⟩ **2** : having a venom-producing gland and able to inflict a poisoned wound ⟨~ snakes⟩ — **ven·om·ous·ly** *adv* — **ven·om·ous·ness** *n*

ve·nous \'vē-nəs\ *adj* [L *venosus*, fr. *vena* vein] (1626) **1** : of, relating

---

venation a: *1* parallel-veined, *2* net-veined, *3* dichotomously veined to, or full of veins ⟨a ~ rock⟩ ⟨a ~ system⟩ **2** *of blood* : having passed through the capillaries and given up oxygen for the tissues and become charged with carbon dioxide — **ve·nous·ly** *adv*

¹vent \'vent\ *vt* [ME, prob. fr. MF *esventer* to expose to the air, fr. *es*-ex- (fr. L *ex*-) + *vent* wind, fr. L *ventus* — more at WIND] (14c) **1** : to provide with a vent **2 a** : to serve as a vent for ⟨chimneys ~ smoke⟩ **b** : DISCHARGE, EXPEL **c** : to give often vigorous or emotional expression to **3** : to relieve by means of a vent **syn** see EXPRESS

²vent *n* (1508) **1** : an opportunity or means of escape, passage, or release : OUTLET ⟨finally gave ~ to his pent-up hostility⟩ **2 a** : an opening for the escape of a gas or liquid or for the relief of pressure: as **a** : the external opening of the rectum or cloaca : ANUS **b** : PIPE 3c, FUMAROLE **c** : an opening at the breech of a muzzle-loading gun through which fire is touched to the powder **d** *chiefly Scot* : CHIMNEY, FLUE — **vent·less** \-ləs\ *adj*

³vent *n* [ME *vente*, alter. of *fente*, fr. MF, slit, fissure, fr. *fendre* to split, fr. L *findere* — more at BITE] (15c) : a slit in a garment; *specif* : an opening in the lower part of a seam (as of a jacket or skirt) — **vent·less** *adj*

vent·age \'ven-tij\ *n* (1602) : a small hole (as a flute stop)

ven·tail \'ven-ˌtāl\ *n* [ME, fr. MF *ventaille*, fr. *vent* wind] (15c) : the lower movable front of a medieval helmet

ven·ter \'ven-tər\ *n* [AF, fr. L, belly, womb; perh. akin to OHG *wanast* paunch, L *vesica* bladder, Skt *vasti*] (1544) **1 a** : a wife or mother that is a source of offspring **2** : a protuberant and often hollow anatomical structure: as **a** : the undersurface of the abdomen of an arthropod **b** : the swollen basal portion of an archegonium in which an egg develops

ven·ti·fact \'ven-tə-ˌfakt\ *n* [L *ventus* + E art*ifact*] (1911) : a stone worn, polished, or faceted by windblown sand

ven·ti·late \'ven-tᵊl-ˌāt\ *vt* **-lat·ed; -lat·ing** [LL *ventilatus*, pp. of *ventilare*, fr. L, to fan, winnow, fr. *ventus* wind — more at WIND] (1527) **1 a** : to examine, discuss, or investigate freely and openly : EXPOSE ⟨*ventilating* family quarrels in public⟩ **b** : to make public : UTTER ⟨*ventilated* their objections at length⟩ **2** *archaic* : to free from chaff by winnowing **3 a** : to expose to air and esp. to a current of fresh air for purifying, curing, or refreshing ⟨~ stored grain⟩; *also* : OXYGENATE, AERATE ⟨~ blood in the lungs⟩ **b** : to subject the lungs to ventilation ⟨artificially ~ a patient in respiratory distress⟩ **4 a** *of a current of air* : to pass or circulate through so as to freshen **b** : to cause fresh air to circulate through (as a room or mine) **5** : to provide an opening in (a burning structure) to permit escape of smoke and heat

ven·ti·la·tion \ˌven-tᵊl-'ā-shən\ *n* (1519) **1** : the act or process of ventilating **2 a** : circulation of air ⟨a room with good ~⟩ **b** : the circulation and exchange of gases in the lungs or gills that is basic to respiration **3** : a system or means of providing fresh air

ven·ti·la·tor \'ven-tᵊl-ˌā-tər\ *n* (1743) : one that ventilates: as **a** : a contrivance for introducing fresh air or expelling foul or stagnant air **b** : RESPIRATOR 2

ven·ti·la·to·ry \'ven-tᵊl-ə-ˌtōr-ē, -ˌtór-\ *adj* (1850) : of, relating to, or provided with ventilation ⟨~ capacity of the lung⟩

ventr- *or* **ventro-** *comb form* [L *ventr-, venter* belly] : ventral and ⟨*ventro*lateral⟩

¹ven·tral \'ven-trəl\ *adj* [F, fr. L *ventralis*, fr. *ventr-, venter*] (1739) **1 a** : of or relating to the belly : ABDOMINAL **b** : being or located near or on the anterior or lower surface of an animal opposite the back **2** : being or located on the lower surface of a dorsiventral plant structure — **ven·tral·ly** \-trə-lē\ *adv*

²ventral *n* (1834) : a ventral part (as a scale or fin)

ventral root *n* (ca. 1923) : the one of the two roots of a spinal nerve that passes ventrally from the spinal cord and consists of motor fibers — compare DORSAL ROOT

ven·tri·cle \'ven-tri-kəl\ *n* [ME, fr. L *ventriculus*, fr. dim. of *ventr-, venter* belly] (14c) **a** : a cavity of a bodily part or organ: as **a** : a chamber of the heart which receives blood from a corresponding atrium and from which blood is forced into the arteries — see HEART illustration **b** : any of the system of communicating cavities in the brain that are continuous with the central canal of the spinal cord — see BRAIN illustration

ven·tri·cose \-ˌkōs\ *adj* [NL *ventricosus*, fr. L *ventr-, venter* + *-icosus* (as in *varicosus* varicose)] (1756) : markedly swollen, distended, or inflated esp. on one side ⟨~ corollas⟩

ven·tric·u·lar \ven-'tri-kyə-lər, vən-\ *adj* (1822) : of, relating to, or being a ventricle ⟨~ fibrillation⟩ ⟨~ pressure⟩ ⟨~ myocardium⟩

ven·tric·u·lus \ven-'tri-kyə-ləs, vən-\ *n, pl* **-li** \-ˌlī, -ˌlē\ [NL, fr. L, dim. of *venter*] (1693) : a digestive cavity: as **a** : STOMACH **b** : GIZZARD 1a **c** : the digestive part of an insect's stomach

ven·tril·o·quism \ven-'tri-lə-ˌkwi-zəm\ *n* [LL *ventriloquus* ventriloquist, fr. L *ventr-, venter* + *loqui* to speak; fr. the belief that the voice is produced from the ventriloquist's stomach] (ca. 1797) : the production of the voice in such a way that the sound seems to come from a source other than the vocal organs of the speaker — **ven·tri·lo·qui·al** \ˌven-trə-'lō-kwē-əl\ *adj* — **ven·tri·lo·qui·al·ly** \-ə-lē\ *adv*

ven·tril·o·quist \ven-'tri-lə-kwist\ *n* (ca. 1656) : one who uses or is skilled in ventriloquism; *esp* : one who provides entertainment by using ventriloquism to carry on an apparent conversation with a hand-manipulated dummy — **ven·tril·o·quis·tic** \(ˌ)ven-ˌtri-lə-'kwis-tik\ *adj*

ven·tril·o·quize \ven-'tri-lə-ˌkwīz\ *vb* **-quized; -quiz·ing** *vi* (1844) : to use ventriloquism ~ *vt* : to utter in the manner of a ventriloquist

ven·tril·o·quy \-kwē\ *n* (1584) : VENTRILOQUISM

ven·tro·lat·er·al \ˌven-trō-'la-tə-rəl, -'la-trəl\ *adj* (1835) : ventral and lateral

ven·tro·me·di·al \-'mē-dē-əl\ *adj* (1908) : ventral and medial

¹ven·ture \'ven(t)-shər\ *vb* **ven·tured; ven·tur·ing** \'ven(t)-sh(ə-)riŋ\ [ME *venteren*, by shortening & alter. fr. *aventuren*, fr. *aventure* adventure] *vt* (15c) **1** : to expose to hazard : RISK, GAMBLE ⟨*ventured* a buck or two on the race⟩ **2** : to undertake the risks and dangers of : BRAVE ⟨*ventured* the stormy sea⟩ **3** : to offer at the risk of rebuff, rejection, or censure ⟨~ an opinion⟩ ~ *vi* : to proceed esp. in the face of danger — **ven·tur·er** \'ven(t)-sh(ə-)rər\ *n*

²venture *n* (15c) **1** *obs* : DESTINY, FORTUNE, CHANCE **2 a** : an undertaking involving chance, risk, or danger; *esp* : a speculative business enterprise **b** : a venturesome act **3** : something (as money or prop-

erty) at hazard in a speculative venture — **at a venture** : at random ⟨a certain man drew a bow *at a venture*, and smote the king —1 Kings 22:34 (AV)⟩

venture capital *n* (1943) : capital (as retained corporate earnings or individual savings) invested or available for investment in the ownership element of new or fresh enterprise — called also *risk capital* — **venture capitalist** *n*

ven·ture·some \'ven(t)-shər-səm\ *adj* (1661) **1** : involving risk : HAZARDOUS ⟨a ~ journey⟩ **2** : inclined to court or incur risk or danger : DARING ⟨a ~ hunter⟩ **syn** see ADVENTUROUS — **ven·ture·some·ly** *adv* — **ven·ture·some·ness** *n*

ven·tu·ri \ven-'tur-ē\ *n* [G. B. *Venturi* †1822 Ital. physicist] (1887) : a short tube with a tapering constriction in the middle that causes an increase in the velocity of flow of a fluid and a corresponding decrease in fluid pressure and that is used esp. in measuring fluid flow or for creating a suction (as for driving aircraft instruments or drawing fuel into the flow stream of a carburetor)

ven·tur·ous \'ven(t)-sh(ə-)rəs\ *adj* (1565) : VENTURESOME — **ven·tur·ous·ly** *adv* — **ven·tur·ous·ness** *n*

ven·ue \'ven-ˌyü\ *n* [ME *venyw* action of coming, fr. MF *venue*, fr. *venir* to come, fr. L *venire* — more at COME] (1531) **1 a** : the place or county in which take place the alleged events from which a legal action arises **b** : the place from which a jury is drawn and in which trial is held ⟨requested a change of ~⟩ **c** : a statement showing that a case is brought to the proper court or authority **2** : LOCALE 1

ve·nule \'vēn-(ˌ)yü(ə)l, 'ven-\ *n* [L *venula*, dim. of *vena* vein] (ca. 1850) : a small vein; *esp* : any of the minute veins connecting the capillaries with the larger systemic veins

Ve·nus \'vē-nəs\ *n* [ME, fr. L *Vener-, Venus*] **1** : the Roman goddess of love and beauty — compare APHRODITE **2** : the planet second in order from the sun — see PLANET table

Ve·nus·berg \-ˌbərg\ *n* : a mountain in central Germany containing a cavern where in medieval legend Venus held court

Ve·nus-hair \-ˌhar, -ˌher\ *n* (1548) : a delicate maidenhair fern (*Adiantum capillus-veneris*) that grows chiefly on wet calcareous rocks

Ve·nu·sian \vi-'nü-zhən, -'nyü-\ *adj* (1874) : of or relating to the planet Venus

Ve·nus's-flow·er-bas·ket \'vē-nə-səz-, 'vē-nəs-\ *n* (1872) : any of several glass sponges (genus *Euplectella*) of the western Pacific and Indian oceans — called also *Venus flower basket*

Ve·nus's-fly·trap \-'flī-ˌtrap\ *n* (1770) : an insectivorous plant (*Dionaea muscipula*) of the sundew family of the Carolina coast with the leaf apex modified into an insect trap — called also *Venus flytrap*

ve·ra·cious \və-'rā-shəs\ *adj* [L *verac-, verax* — more at VERY] (1677) **1** : TRUTHFUL, HONEST **2** : marked by truth : ACCURATE — **ve·ra·cious·ly** *adv* — **ve·ra·cious·ness** *n*

ve·rac·i·ty \və-'ra-sə-tē\ *n, pl* **-ties** (ca. 1623) **1** : devotion to the truth : TRUTHFULNESS **2** : power of conveying or perceiving truth **3** : conformity with truth or fact : ACCURACY **4** : something true ⟨makes lies sound like *veracities*⟩

ve·ran·da *or* **ve·ran·dah** \və-'ran-də\ *n* [Hindi *varaṇḍā*] (1711) : a usu. roofed open gallery or portico attached to the exterior of a building

ve·ran·daed *also* **ve·ran·dahed** \-dəd\ *adj* (1818) : having a veranda

ve·rap·a·mil \və-'ra-pə-ˌmil\ *n* [ISV *valeric* (acid) + *-apam-* (prob. alter. of *amino* + *propyl*) + nitrile] (1967) : a calcium channel blocker $C_{27}H_{38}N_2O_4$ used esp. in the form of its hydrochloride

ve·rat·ri·dine \və-'ra-trə-ˌdēn\ *n* [*veratrine* + *-idine*] (1907) : a poisonous alkaloid $C_{36}H_{51}NO_{11}$ occurring esp. in sabadilla seed

ve·ra·trine \'ver-ə-ˌtrēn, -trən\ *n* [NL *veratrina*, fr. *Veratrum*, genus of herbs] (1822) : a poisonous irritant mixture of alkaloids from sabadilla seed that has been used as a counterirritant and insecticide

ve·ra·trum \və-'rā-trəm\ *n* [NL, genus name, fr. L, hellebore] (1577) : HELLEBORE 2

verb \'vərb\ *n* [ME *verbe*, fr. MF, fr. L *verbum* word, verb — more at WORD] (14c) : a word that characteristically is the grammatical center of a predicate and expresses an act, occurrence, or mode of being, that in various languages is inflected for agreement with the subject, for tense, for voice, for mood, or for aspect, and that typically has rather full descriptive meaning and characterizing quality but is sometimes nearly devoid of these esp. when used as an auxiliary or linking verb — **verb·less** \'vərb-ləs\ *adj*

¹ver·bal \'vər-bəl\ *adj* [MF or LL; MF, fr. LL *verbalis*, fr. L *verbum* word] (15c) **1 a** : of, relating to, or consisting of words ⟨~ instructions⟩ **b** : of, relating to, or involving words rather than meaning or substance ⟨a consistency that is merely ~ and scholastic —B. N. Cardozo⟩ **c** : consisting of or using words only and not involving action ⟨a ~ protest⟩ **2** : of, relating to, or formed from a verb ⟨a ~ adjective⟩ **3** : spoken rather than written ⟨a ~ contract⟩ **4** : VERBATIM, WORD-FOR-WORD ⟨a ~ translation⟩ **5** : of or relating to facility in the use and comprehension of words ⟨~ aptitude⟩ — **ver·bal·ly** \-b-lē\ *adv*

²verbal *n* (1530) : a word that combines characteristics of a verb with those of a noun or adjective — compare GERUND, INFINITIVE, PARTICIPLE

verbal auxiliary *n* (ca. 1958) : an auxiliary verb

ver·bal·ism \'vər-bə-ˌli-zəm\ *n* (1787) **1 a** : a verbal expression : TERM **b** : PHRASING, WORDING **2** : words used as if they were more important than the realities they represent ⟨the emancipation of science from ~ —G. A. L. Sarton⟩ **3 a** : a wordy expression of little meaning **b** : VERBOSITY

Venus's-flytrap

\ə\ abut \ᵊ\ kitten, F table \ər\ further \a\ ash \ā\ ace \ä\ mop, mar \au̇\ out \ch\ chin \e\ bet \ē\ easy \g\ go \i\ hit \ī\ ice \j\ job \ŋ\ sing \ō\ go \o̊\ law \o̊i\ boy \th\ thin \t̲h̲\ the \ü\ loot \u̇\ foot \y\ yet \zh\ vision \à, k̲, ⁿ, œ, œ̄, ᵫ, ᵫ̄, ᵊ\ *see* Guide to Pronunciation

ver·bal·ist \-list\ n (ca. 1609) **1** : one who stresses words above substance or reality **2** : a person who uses words skillfully — **ver·bal·is·tic** \ˌvər-bə-'lis-tik\ adj

ver·bal·ize \'vər-bə-ˌlīz\ vb **-ized; -iz·ing** vi (1609) **1** : to speak or write verbosely **2** : to express something in words ~ vt **1** : to convert into a verb **2** : to name or describe in words — **ver·bal·i·za·tion** \ˌvər-bə-lə-'zā-shən\ n — **ver·bal·iz·er** \'vər-bə-ˌlī-zər\ n

verbal noun n (ca. 1706) : a noun derived directly from a verb or verb stem and in some uses having the sense and constructions of a verb

¹ver·ba·tim \(ˌ)vər-'bā-təm\ adv [ME, fr. ML, fr. L verbum word] (15c) : in the exact words : word for word

²verbatim adj (1737) : being in or following the exact words : WORD-FOR-WORD

ver·be·na \(ˌ)vər-'bē-nə\ n [NL, genus of herbs or subshrubs, fr. L, leafy branch used ceremonially or medicinally — more at VERVAIN] (1562) : VERVAIN; esp : any of numerous garden plants of hybrid origin widely grown for their showy spikes of white, pink, red, or blue flowers which are borne in profusion over a long season

ver·biage \'vər-bē-ij also -bij\ n [F, fr. MF verbier to chatter, fr. verbe speech, fr. L verbum word] (ca. 1721) **1** : a profusion of words usu. of little or obscure content ⟨such a tangled maze of evasive ~ as a typical party platform —Marcia Davenport⟩ **2** : manner of expressing oneself in words : DICTION ⟨sportswriters guarded their ~ so jealously —Raymond Sokolov⟩

ver·bi·cide \'vər-bə-ˌsīd\ n [L verbum word + E -cide] (1858) **1** : deliberate distortion of the sense of a word (as in punning) **2** : one who distorts the sense of a word

ver·bid \'vər-bəd\ n (1914) : VERBAL

ver·big·er·a·tion \(ˌ)vər-ˌbi-jə-'rā-shən\ n [ISV, fr. L verbigerare to talk, chat, fr. verbum word + gerere to carry, wield — more at WORD] (1886) : continual repetition of stereotyped phrases (as in some forms of mental illness)

ver·bose \(ˌ)vər-'bōs\ adj [L verbosus, fr. verbum] (1672) **1** : containing more words than necessary : WORDY ⟨a ~ reply⟩; also : impaired by wordiness ⟨a ~ style⟩ **2** : given to wordiness ⟨a ~ orator⟩ syn see WORDY — **ver·bose·ly** adv — **ver·bose·ness** n — **ver·bos·i·ty** \-'bä-sə-tē\ n

ver·bo·ten \vər-'bōt-ən, fər-, ver-\ adj [G, fr. OHG farboten, pp. of farbioten to forbid (akin to OE forbēodan to forbid), fr. far-, fur-for- + biotan to offer — more at BID] (1912) : not allowed : FORBIDDEN; esp : prohibited by dictate

verb sap \'vərb-'sap\ (1841) : VERBUM SAP

ver·bum sap \ˌvər-bəm-'sap\ [short for NL verbum sapienti (sat est) a word to the wise (is sufficient)] (1818) : enough said — used to indicate that something left unsaid may or should be inferred

ver·dant \'vər-dᵊnt\ adj [modif. of MF verdoyant, fr. prp. of verdoyer to be green, fr. OF verdoier, fr. verd, vert green, fr. L viridis, fr. virēre to be green] (1581) **1 a** : green in tint or color ⟨~ grass⟩ **b** : green with growing plants ⟨~ fields⟩ **2** : unripe in experience or judgment : GREEN 9a, b — **ver·dan·cy** \-dᵊn(t)-sē\ n — **ver·dant·ly** \-dᵊnt-lē\ adv

verd an·tique or **verde an·tique** \ˌvərd-ˌan-'tēk\ n [It verde antico, lit., ancient green] (1745) : a green mottled or veined serpentine marble or calcareous serpentine much used for indoor decoration esp. by the ancient Romans

ver·der·er also **ver·der·or** \'vər-dər-ər\ n [AF, fr. OF verdier, fr. verd green] (ca. 1538) : a onetime English judicial officer in charge of the king's forest

ver·dict \'vər-(ˌ)dikt\ n [alter. of ME verdit, fr. AF, fr. OF ver true (fr. L verus) + dit saying, dictum, fr. L dictum — more at VERY] (1533) **1** : the finding or decision of a jury on the matter submitted to it in trial **2** : OPINION, JUDGMENT

ver·di·gris \'vər-də-ˌgrēs, -ˌgris, -ˌgris, -grəs also -ˌgrē\ n [ME vertegrez, fr. OF vert de Grice, lit., green of Greece] (14c) **1 a** : a green or greenish blue poisonous pigment resulting from the action of acetic acid on copper and consisting of one or more basic copper acetates **b** : normal copper acetate $Cu(C_2H_3O_2)_2 \cdot H_2O$ **2** : a green or bluish deposit esp. of copper carbonates formed on copper, brass, or bronze surfaces

ver·din \'vər-dᵊn\ n [F, a green songbird of Indochina, alter. of verdon, verdun bunting, yellowhammer, fr. vert green, fr. OF verd, vert] (1881) : a very small yellow-headed titmouse (Auriparus flaviceps) found from Texas to California and southward

ver·dure \'vər-jər also -dyər\ n [ME, fr. MF, fr. verd green] (14c) **1** : the greenness of growing vegetation; also : such vegetation itself **2** : a condition of health and vigor — **ver·dur·ous** \'vərj-rəs; 'vər-jə-rəs, -dyə-rəs\ adj

ver·dured \'vər-jərd also -dyərd\ adj (ca. 1718) : covered with verdure

¹verge \'vərj\ n [ME, fr. MF, fr. L virga rod, stripe] (15c) **1 a** (1) : a rod or staff carried as an emblem of authority or symbol of office (2) obs : a stick or wand held by a person being admitted to tenancy while he swears fealty **b** : the spindle of a watch balance; esp : a spindle with pallets in an old vertical escapement **c** : the male intromittent organ of any of various invertebrates **2 a** : something that borders, limits, or bounds: as (1) : an outer margin of an object or structural part (2) : the edge of roof covering (as tiling) projecting over the gable of a roof (3) Brit : a paved or planted strip of land at the edge of a road : SHOULDER **b** : BRINK, THRESHOLD ⟨a country on the ~ of destruction —Archibald MacLeish⟩

²verge vi **verged; verg·ing** (1787) **1** : to be contiguous **2** : to be on the verge or border

³verge vi **verged; verg·ing** [L vergere to bend, incline — more at WRENCH] (1610) **1 a** of the sun : to incline toward the horizon : SINK **b** : to move or extend in some direction or toward some condition **2** : to be in transition or change

verg·er \'vər-jər\ n (15c) **1** chiefly Brit : an attendant that carries a verge (as before a bishop or justice) **2** : a church official who keeps order during services or serves as an usher or a sacristan

ve·rid·i·cal \və-'ri-di-kəl\ adj [L veridicus, fr. verus true + dicere to say — more at VERY, DICTION] (1653) **1** : TRUTHFUL, VERACIOUS ⟨tried . . . to supply . . . a ~ background to the events and people portrayed —Laura Krey⟩ **2** : not illusory : GENUINE ⟨it is assumed that . . . perception is ~ —George Lakoff⟩ — **ve·rid·i·cal·i·ty** \-ˌri-də-'ka-lə-tē\ n — **ve·rid·i·cal·ly** \-'ri-di-k(ə-)lē\ adv

ver·i·fi·able \ˌver-ə-'fī-ə-bəl\ adj (1593) : capable of being verified — **ver·i·fi·abil·i·ty** \ˌver-ə-ˌfī-ə-'bi-lə-tē\ n — **ver·i·fi·able·ness** n

ver·i·fi·ca·tion \ˌver-ə-fə-'kā-shən\ n (1523) : the act or process of verifying : the state of being verified

ver·i·fy \'ver-ə-ˌfī\ vt **-fied; -fy·ing** [ME verifien, fr. MF verifier, fr. ML verificare, fr. L verus true] (14c) **1** : to confirm or substantiate in law by oath **2** : to establish the truth, accuracy, or reality of syn see CONFIRM — **ver·i·fi·er** \-ˌfī-(ə)r\ n

ver·i·ly \'ver-ə-lē\ adv [ME verraily, fr. verray very] (14c) **1** : in truth : CERTAINLY **2** : TRULY, CONFIDENTLY

veri·sim·i·lar \ˌver-ə-'si-mə-lər, -'sim-lər\ adj [L verisimilis] (1681) **1** : having the appearance of truth : PROBABLE **2** : depicting realism (as in art or literature) — **veri·sim·i·lar·ly** adv

veri·si·mil·i·tude \ˌver-ə-sə-'mi-lə-ˌtüd, -ˌtyüd\ n [L verisimilitudo, fr. verisimilis verisimilar, fr. veri similis like the truth] (1603) **1** : the quality or state of being verisimilar **2** : something that has verisimilitude — **veri·si·mil·i·tu·di·nous** \-ˌmi-lə-'tüd-nəs, -'tyüd-; -'tü-dᵊn-əs, -'tyü-\ adj

ve·rism \'vir-ˌi-zəm, 'ver-\ n [It verismo, fr. vero true, fr. L verus] (1892) : artistic use of contemporary everyday material in preference to the heroic or legendary esp. in grand opera — **ve·rist** \-ist\ n or adj — **ve·ris·tic** \vir-'is-tik, ver-\ adj

ve·ris·mo \vā-'rēz-(ˌ)mō\ n [It] (ca. 1908) : VERISM; also : REALISM 3

ver·i·ta·ble \'ver-ə-tə-bəl\ adj [ME, fr. MF, fr. verité] (15c) : being in fact the thing named and not false, unreal, or imaginary — often used to stress the aptness of a metaphor ⟨a ~ mountain of references⟩ — **ver·i·ta·ble·ness** n — **ver·i·ta·bly** \-blē\ adv

vé·ri·té \ˌver-ə-'tā\ n [cinema verité] (1966) : the art or technique of filming (as a motion picture) so as to convey candid realism

ver·i·ty \'ver-ə-tē\ n, pl **-ties** [ME verite, fr. MF verité, fr. L veritat-, veritas, fr. verus true] (14c) **1** : the quality or state of being true or real **2** : something (as a statement) that is true; esp : a fundamental and inevitably true value ⟨such eternal verities as honor, love, and patriotism⟩ **3** : the quality or state of being truthful or honest ⟨the king becoming graces, as justice, ~ —Shak.⟩

ver·juice \'vər-ˌjüs\ n [ME verjus, fr. MF, fr. vert jus, lit., green juice] (14c) **1** : the sour juice of crab apples or of unripe fruit (as grapes or apples); also : an acid liquor made from verjuice **2** : acidity of disposition or manner

ver·meil n [MF, fr. vermeil, adj. — more at VERMILION] (1590) **1** \'vər-məl, -ˌmāl\ : VERMILION **2** \ver-'mā\ : gilded silver — **vermeil** adj

vermi- comb form [NL, fr. LL, fr. L vermis — more at WORM] : worm ⟨vermiform⟩

ver·mi·cel·li \ˌvər-mə-'che-lē, -'se-\ n [It, pl. of vermicello, dim. of verme worm, fr. L vermis] (1669) : pasta made in long solid strings smaller in diameter than spaghetti

ver·mi·cide \'vər-mə-ˌsīd\ n (1849) : an agent that destroys worms

ver·mic·u·lar \(ˌ)vər-'mi-kyə-lər\ adj [NL vermicularis, fr. L vermiculus, dim. of vermis] (1672) **1 a** : resembling a worm in form or motion **b** : VERMICULATE **2** : of, relating to, or caused by worms

ver·mic·u·late \-lət\ or **ver·mic·u·lat·ed** \-lā-təd\ adj [L vermiculatus, fr. vermiculus] (1605) **1** : TORTUOUS, INVOLUTE **2** : full of worms : WORM-EATEN **3 a** : VERMIFORM **b** : marked with irregular fine lines or with wavy impressed lines ⟨a ~ nut⟩ — **ver·mic·u·la·tion** \-ˌmi-kyə-'lā-shən\ n

ver·mic·u·lite \(ˌ)vər-'mi-kyə-ˌlīt\ n [L vermiculus little worm] (1824) : any of various micaceous minerals that are hydrous silicates resulting usu. from expansion of the granules of mica at high temperatures to give a lightweight highly water-absorbent material

ver·mi·form \'vər-mə-ˌfȯrm\ adj [NL vermiformis, fr. vermi- + -formis -form] (ca. 1730) : resembling a worm in shape

vermiform appendix n (1778) : a narrow blind tube usu. about three to four inches (7.6 to 10.2 centimeters) long that extends from the cecum in the lower right-hand part of the abdomen

ver·mi·fuge \'vər-mə-ˌfyüj\ adj (1697) : serving to destroy or expel parasitic worms : ANTHELMINTIC — **vermifuge** n

ver·mil·ion also **ver·mil·lion** \vər-'mil-yən\ n [ME vermilioun, fr. OF vermeillon, fr. vermeil, adj., bright red, vermilion, fr. LL vermiculus kermes, fr. L, little worm] (13c) **1** : a bright red pigment consisting of mercuric sulfide; broadly : any of various red pigments **2** : a vivid reddish orange

ver·min \'vər-mən\ n, pl **vermin** [ME, fr. MF, fr. (assumed) VL verminum, fr. L verminare to be infested with maggots, have racking pains, fr. vermina racking pains] (14c) **1 a** : small common harmful or objectionable animals (as lice or fleas) that are difficult to control **b** : birds and mammals that prey on game **c** : animals that at a particular time and place compete (as for food) with humans or domestic animals **2** : an offensive person

ver·min·ous \'vər-mə-nəs\ adj (ca. 1616) **1** : consisting of or being vermin : NOXIOUS **2** : forming a breeding place for or infested by vermin : FILTHY ⟨~ garbage⟩ **3** : caused by vermin ⟨~ disease⟩

ver·mouth \vər-'müth\ n [F vermout, fr. G Wermut wormwood, fr. OHG wermuota — more at WORMWOOD] (1806) : a dry or sweet aperitif wine flavored with aromatic herbs and often used in mixed drinks

¹ver·nac·u·lar \və(r)-'na-kyə-lər\ adj [L vernaculus native, fr. verna slave born in the master's house, native] (1601) **1 a** : using a language or dialect native to a region or country rather than a literary, cultured, or foreign language **b** : of, relating to, or being a nonstandard language or dialect of a place, region, or country **c** : of, relating to, or being the normal spoken form of a language **2** : applied to a plant or animal in the common native speech as distinguished from the Latin nomenclature of scientific classification **3** : of, relating to, or characteristic of a period, place, or group; esp : of, relating to, or being the common building style of a period or place — **ver·nac·u·lar·ly** adv

²vernacular n (ca. 1706) **1** : a vernacular language, expression, or mode of expression **2** : the mode of expression of a group or class **3** : a vernacular name of a plant or animal

ver·nac·u·lar·ism \və(r)-'na-kyə-lə-ˌri-zəm\ n (ca. 1841) : a vernacular word or idiom

ver·nal \'vər-nᵊl\ adj [L vernalis, alter. of vernus, fr. ver spring; akin to Gk ear spring, Skt vasanta] (1534) **1** : of, relating to, or occurring in the spring ⟨~ equinox⟩ ⟨~ sunshine⟩ **2** : fresh or new like the spring; also : YOUTHFUL — **ver·nal·ly** \-nᵊl-ē\ adv

ver·nal·i·za·tion \ˌvər-nᵊl-ə-'zā-shən\ n (1933) : the act or process of hastening the flowering and fruiting of plants by treating seeds, bulbs, or seedlings so as to induce a shortening of the vegetative period — **ver·nal·ize** \'vər-nᵊl-,īz\ *vt*

ver·na·tion \(,)vər-'nā-shən\ *n* [NL *vernation-, vernatio,* fr. L *vernare* to behave as in spring, fr. *vernus* vernal] (1793) : the arrangement of foliage leaves within the bud

Ver·ner's law \'ver-nərz-\ *n* [Karl A. *Verner*] (1878) : a statement in historical linguistics: in medial or final position in voiced environments and when the immediately preceding vowel did not bear the principal accent in Proto-Indo-European, the Proto-Germanic voiceless fricatives *f, þ,* and χ derived from the Proto-Indo-European voiceless stops *p, t,* and *k* and the Proto-Germanic voiceless fricative *s* derived from Proto-Indo-European *s* became the voiced fricatives ƀ, ð, g, and *z* represented in various recorded Germanic languages by *b, d, g,* and *r*

ver·ni·cle *or* **ver·na·cle** \'vər-ni-kəl\ *n* [ME *vernicle,* fr. MF *veronique, vernicle,* fr. ML *veronica*] (14c) : ²VERONICA

¹**ver·ni·er** \'vər-nē-ər\ *n* [Pierre *Vernier*] (1766) **1** : a short scale made to slide along the divisions of a graduated instrument for indicating parts of divisions **2 a** : a small auxiliary device used with a main device to obtain fine adjustment **b** : any of two or more small supplementary rocket engines or gas nozzles on a missile or a rocket vehicle for making fine adjustments in the speed or course or controlling the attitude — called also *vernier engine*

²**vernier** *adj* (1788) : having or comprising a vernier

vernier caliper *n* (ca. 1876) : a measuring device that consists of a main scale with a fixed jaw and a sliding jaw with an attached vernier

ver·nis·sage \,ver-ni-'säzh\ *n* [F, day before an exhibition opens reserved for artists to varnish and put finishing touches to their paintings, lit., varnishing, fr. *vernis* varnish — more at VARNISH] (1912) : a private showing or preview of an art exhibition

¹**ve·ron·i·ca** \və-'rä-ni-kə\ *n* [NL, genus of herbs] (1527) : SPEEDWELL

²**veronica** *n* [ML, fr. *Veronica,* legendary saint of the 1st cent. A.D.] (ca. 1700) : an image of Christ's face said to have been impressed on the cloth that St. Veronica gave him to wipe his face with on the way to his crucifixion; *also* : a cloth resembling the legendary one of St. Veronica

³**veronica** *n* [Sp *verónica,* fr. St. *Veronica*] (1926) : a pass in bullfighting in which the cape is swung slowly away from the charging bull while the matador keeps his feet in the same position

Vé·ro·nique *also* **Ve·ro·nique** \,vā-rō-'nēk\ *adj* [F *Véronique* Veronica] (1907) : prepared or garnished with usu. white seedless grapes ⟨sole ~⟩

ver·ru·ca \və-'rü-kə\ *n, pl* **-cae** \-(,)kē, -,kī, -,sī\ [L, wart, hillock; akin to Lith *viršus* summit and prob. to OE *wearte* wart — more at WART] (1565) **1** : a wart or warty skin lesion **2** : a warty elevation on a plant or animal surface

verruca vul·ga·ris \-,vəl-'gar-əs, -'ger-\ *n* [NL, lit., common verruca] (1903) : WART 1a

ver·ru·cose \'ver-ə-,kōs\ *adj* (1686) : covered with warty elevations

ver·sal \'vər-səl, 'vär-\ *adj* [short for *universal*] (1592) *archaic* : ENTIRE, WHOLE ⟨as pale as any clout in the ~ world —Shak.⟩

ver·sant \'vər-sᵊnt\ *adj* [L *versant-, versans,* prp. of *versare, versari* to turn, occupy oneself, meditate] (1645) **1** *archaic* : EXPERIENCED, PRACTICED **2** : CONVERSANT

ver·sa·tile \'vər-sə-tᵊl, *esp Brit* -,tīl\ *adj* [F or L; F, fr. L *versatilis* turning easily, fr. *versare* to turn, freq. of *vertere*] (1605) **1** : changing or fluctuating readily : VARIABLE ⟨a ~ disposition⟩ **2** : embracing a variety of subjects, fields, or skills; *also* : turning with ease from one thing to another **3 a** (1) : capable of turning forward or backward : REVERSIBLE ⟨a ~ toe of a bird⟩ (2) : capable of moving laterally and up and down ⟨~ antennae⟩ **b** *of an anther* : having the filaments attached at or near the middle so as to swing freely **4** : having many uses or applications ⟨~ building material⟩ — **ver·sa·tile·ly** \-tᵊl-(l)ē, -,tīl-lē\ *adv* — **ver·sa·tile·ness** \-tᵊl-nəs, -,tīl-nəs\ *n*

ver·sa·til·i·ty \,vər-sə-'ti-lə-tē\ *n* (ca. 1755) : the quality or state of being versatile ⟨a writer of great ~⟩

vers de so·ci·é·té \,ver-də-,sō-sē-ə-'tā\ *n* [F, society verse] (1796) : witty and typically ironic light verse

¹**verse** \'vərs\ *n* [ME *vers,* fr. OF & OE; both fr. L *versus,* lit., turning, fr. *vertere* to turn — more at WORTH] (bef. 12c) **1** : a line of metrical writing **2 a** (1) : metrical language (2) : metrical writing distinguished from poetry esp. by its lower level of intensity (3) : POETRY 2 **b** : POEM **c** : a body of metrical writing (as of a period or country) **3** : STANZA **4** : one of the short divisions into which a chapter of the Bible is traditionally divided

²**verse** *vb* **versed; vers·ing** *vi* (bef. 12c) : to make verse : VERSIFY ~ *vt* **1** : to tell or celebrate in verse **2** : to turn into verse

³**verse** *vt* **versed; vers·ing** [back-formation fr. *versed,* fr. L *versatus,* pp. of *versari* to be active, be occupied (in), pass. of *versare* to turn] (1673) : to familiarize by close association, study, or experience ⟨well *versed* in the theater⟩

vers·et \'vər-sət, -,set; ,vər-'set\ *n* [ME, fr. OF, dim. of *vers* verse] (13c) : a short verse esp. from a sacred book (as the Koran)

ver·si·cle \'vər-si-kəl\ *n* [ME, fr. L *versiculus,* dim. of *versus* verse] (14c) **1** : a short verse or sentence (as from a psalm) said or sung by a leader in public worship and followed by a response from the people **2** : a little verse

ver·sic·u·lar \,vər-'si-kyə-lər\ *adj* [L *versiculus* little verse] (1812) : of or relating to verses or versicles

ver·si·fi·ca·tion \,vər-sə-fə-'kā-shən\ *n* (1603) **1** : the making of verses **2 a** : metrical structure : PROSODY **b** : a particular metrical structure or style **3** : a version in verse of something orig. in prose

ver·si·fi·er \'vər-sə-,fī(-ə)r\ *n* (14c) : one that versifies; *esp* : a writer of light or inferior verse

ver·si·fy \-,fī\ *vb* **-fied; -fy·ing** [ME *versifien,* fr. MF *versifier,* fr. L *versificare,* fr. *versus* verse, line] *vi* (14c) : to compose verses ~ *vt* **1** : to relate or describe in verse **2** : to turn into verse

ver·sion \'vər-zhən, -shən\ *n* [MF, fr. ML *version-, versio* act of turning, fr. L *vertere* to turn — more at WORTH] (1582) **1** : a translation from another language; *esp* : a translation of the Bible or a part of it **2** : an account or description from a particular point of view esp. as contrasted with another account **3** : an adaptation of a literary work ⟨the movie ~ of the novel⟩ **c** : an arrangement of a musical composition **3** : a form or variant of a type or original ⟨an experimental ~ of the plane⟩ **4 a** : a condition in which an organ and esp. the uterus is turned from its normal position **b** : manual turning of a fetus in the

uterus to aid delivery — **ver·sion·al** \'vərzh-nəl, 'vərsh-; 'vər-zhə-nᵊl, -shə-\ *adj*

vers li·bre \ver-'lēbrᵃ\ *n, pl* **vers li·bres** *same*\ [F] (1902) : FREE VERSE

vers–li·brist \-'lē-brist\ *n* [F *vers-libriste*] (1916) : a writer of free verse

ver·so \'vər-(,)sō\ *n, pl* **versos** [NL *verso (folio)* the page being turned] (1839) **1** : the side of a leaf (as of a manuscript) that is to be read second **2** : a left-hand page — compare RECTO

verst \'vərst\ *n* [F *verste* & G *Werst;* both fr. Russ *versta;* akin to L *vertere* to turn] (1555) : a Russian unit of distance equal to 0.6629 mile (1.067 kilometers)

ver·sus \'vər-səs, -səz\ *prep* [ML, towards, against, fr. L, adv., so as to face, fr. pp. of *vertere* to turn] (15c) **1** : AGAINST **2** : in contrast to or as the alternative of ⟨free trade ~ protection⟩

vert \'vərt\ *n* [ME *verte,* fr. MF *vert,* fr. *vert* green — more at VERDANT] (15c) **1 a** : green forest vegetation esp. when forming cover or providing food for deer **b** : the right or privilege (as in England) of cutting living wood or sometimes of pasturing animals in a forest **2** : the heraldic color green

ver·te·bra \'vər-tə-brə, -,brä\ *n, pl* **-brae** \-,brā, -,(,)brē, -brə\ *or* **-bras** [L, joint, vertebra, fr. *vertere* to turn] (1578) : one of the bony or cartilaginous segments composing the spinal column, consisting in some lower vertebrates of several distinct elements which never become united, and in higher vertebrates having a short more or less cylindrical body whose ends articulate by pads of elastic or cartilaginous tissue with those of adjacent vertebrae and a bony arch that encloses the spinal cord

ver·te·bral \(,)vər-'tē-brəl, 'vər-tə-\ *adj* (ca. 1681) **1** : of, relating to, or being vertebrae or the vertebral column : SPINAL **2** : composed of or having vertebrae

vertebral canal *n* (1831) : a canal that contains the spinal cord and is delimited by the arches on the dorsal side of the vertebrae — called also *spinal canal*

vertebral column *n* (1822) : SPINAL COLUMN

¹**ver·te·brate** \'vər-tə-brət, -,brāt\ *adj* [NL *vertebratus,* fr. L, jointed, fr. *vertebra*] (1826) **1** : having a spinal column **b** : of or relating to the vertebrates **2** : organized or constructed in orderly or developed form

²**vertebrate** *n* [NL *Vertebrata,* fr. neut. pl. of *vertebratus*] (1826) : any of a subphylum (Vertebrata) of chordates that possess a spinal column including the mammals, birds, reptiles, amphibians, and fishes

ver·tex \'vər-,teks\ *n, pl* **ver·ti·ces** \'vər-tə-,sēz\ *also* **ver·tex·es** [L *vertic-, vertex, vortic-, vortex* whirl, whirlpool, top of the head, summit, fr. *vertere* to turn] (1570) **1 a** : the point opposite to and farthest from the base in a figure **b** : a point (as of an angle, polygon, polyhedron, graph, or network) that terminates a line or curve or comprises the intersection of two or more lines or curves **c** : a point where an axis of an ellipse, parabola, or hyperbola intersects the curve itself **2** : the top of the head **3** : a principal or highest point : SUMMIT ⟨the ~ of the hill⟩

ver·ti·cal \'vər-ti-kəl\ *adj* [MF or LL; MF, fr. LL *verticalis,* fr. L *vertic-, vertex*] (1559) **1 a** : situated at the highest point : directly overhead or in the zenith **b** *of an aerial photograph* : taken with the camera pointing straight down or nearly so **2 a** : perpendicular to the plane of the horizon or to a primary axis : UPRIGHT **b** (1) : located at right angles to the plane of a supporting surface (2) : lying in the direction of an axis : LENGTHWISE **3 a** : relating to, involving, or integrating economic activity from basic production to point of sale ⟨~ monopoly⟩ **b** : of, relating to, or comprising persons of different status ⟨the ~ arrangement of society⟩ — **vertical** *n* — **ver·ti·cal·i·ty** \,vər-tə-'ka-lə-tē\ *n* — **ver·ti·cal·ly** \'vər-ti-k(ə-)lē\ *adv* — **ver·ti·cal·ness** \-kəl-nəs\ *n*

syn VERTICAL, PERPENDICULAR, PLUMB mean being at right angles to a base line. VERTICAL suggests a line or direction rising straight upward toward a zenith ⟨the side of the cliff is almost *vertical*⟩. PERPENDICULAR may stress the straightness of a line making a right angle with any other line, not necessarily a horizontal one ⟨the parallel bars are *perpendicular* to the support posts⟩. PLUMB stresses an exact verticality determined (as with a plumb line) by earth's gravity ⟨make sure that the wall is *plumb*⟩.

vertical angle *n* (1571) : either of two angles lying on opposite sides of two intersecting lines

vertical circle *n* (1559) : a great circle of the celestial sphere whose plane is perpendicular to that of the horizon

vertical file *n* (1906) : a collection of articles (as pamphlets and clippings) that is maintained (as in a library) to answer brief questions or to provide points of information not easily located

vertical union *n* (1933) : INDUSTRIAL UNION

ver·ti·cil \'vər-tə-,sil\ *n* [NL *verticillus,* dim. of L *vertex* whirl] (1793) : a circle of similar parts (as flowers around a stem or sensory hairs around an antennal joint) about the same point on the axis : WHORL

ver·ti·cil·late \,vər-tə-'si-lət\ *adj* (ca. 1793) : arranged in verticils

ver·ti·cil·li·um wilt \,vər-tə-'si-lē-əm-\ *n* [NL *Verticillium,* fr. *verticillus*] (1916) : a wilt disease of various plants that is caused by a soil=borne imperfect fungus (genus *Verticillium*)

ver·tig·i·nous \(,)vər-'ti-jə-nəs\ *adj* [L *vertiginosus,* fr. *vertigin-, vertigo*] (1608) **1 a** : characterized by or suffering from vertigo or dizziness **b** : inclined to frequent and often pointless change : INCONSTANT **2** : causing or tending to cause dizziness ⟨the ~ heights⟩ **3** : marked by turning : ROTARY ⟨the ~ motion of the earth⟩ — **ver·tig·i·nous·ly** *adv*

ver·ti·go \'vər-ti-,gō\ *n, pl* **-goes** *or* **-gos** [L *vertigin-, vertigo,* fr. *vertere* to turn] (1528) **1 a** : a disordered state in which the individual or the individual's surroundings seem to whirl dizzily **b** : a dizzy confused state of mind **2** : disordered vertiginous movement as a symptom of disease in lower animals; *also* : a disease (as gid) causing this

ver·tu \,vər-'tü, 'vər-\ *var of* VIRTU

ver·vain \'vər-,vān\ *n* [ME *verveine,* fr. MF, fr. L *verbena* leafy branch;

\ə\ abut \ᵊ\ kitten, F table \ər\ further \a\ ash \ā\ ace \ä\ mop, mar \aù\ out \ch\ chin \e\ bet \ē\ easy \g\ go \i\ hit \ī\ ice \j\ job \ŋ\ sing \ō\ go \ò\ law \òi\ boy \th\ thin \t̲h̲\ the \ü\ loot \ù\ foot \y\ yet \zh\ vision \á, k̲, ⁿ, œ, œ̄, ʊ, ūͤ, ᵞ\ see Guide to Pronunciation

akin to L *verber* rod, Lith *virbas,* and perh. to Gk *rhabdos* rod] (14c)
: any of a genus (*Verbena* of the family Verbenaceae, the vervain family) of chiefly American plants that have bracted spicate flowers, a regular corolla with a 5-lobed limb, and a fruit that separates into four nutlets

verve \'vərv\ *n* [F, fantasy, caprice, animation, fr. L *verba,* pl. of *verbum* word — more at WORD] (1697) **1** *archaic* : special ability or talent **2 a** : the spirit and enthusiasm animating artistic composition or performance : VIVACITY **b** : ENERGY, VITALITY

ver·vet monkey \'vər-vət-\ *n* [F *vervet*] (1893) : a monkey of any of several African races of a guenon (*Cercopithecus aethiops*) having the face, chin, hands, and feet black — called also *vervet*

vervet monkey

¹very \'ver-ē\ *adj* **veri·er; -est** [ME *verray, verry,* fr. OF *verai,* fr. (assumed) VL *veracus,* alter. of L *verac-, verax* truthful, fr. *verus* true; akin to OE *wǣr* true, OHG *wāra* trust, care, Gk *ēra* (acc.) favor] (13c) **1 a** : properly entitled to the name or designation : TRUE ⟨the fierce hatred of a ~ woman —J. M. Barrie⟩ **b** : ACTUAL, REAL ⟨the ~ blood and bone of our grammar —H. L. Smith †1972⟩ **c** : SIMPLE, PLAIN ⟨in ~ truth⟩ **2 a** : being exactly as stated ⟨the ~ heart of the city⟩ **b** : exactly suitable or necessary ⟨the ~ thing for the purpose⟩ **3 a** : ABSOLUTE, UTTER ⟨the *veriest* fool alive⟩ **b** : UNQUALIFIED, SHEER ⟨the ~ shame of it⟩ **4** — used as an intensive esp. to emphasize identity ⟨before my ~ eyes⟩ **5** : MERE, BARE ⟨the ~ thought terrified him⟩ **6** : being the same one : SELFSAME ⟨the ~ man I saw⟩ **7** : SPECIAL, PARTICULAR ⟨the ~ essence of truth is plainness and brightness —John Milton⟩ *syn* see SAME

²very *adv* (14c) **1** : in actual fact : TRULY ⟨the ~ best store in town⟩ ⟨told the ~ same story⟩ **2** : to a high degree : EXCEEDINGLY ⟨~ hot⟩ ⟨didn't hurt ~ much⟩

very hard *adj* (ca. 1943) *of cheese* : suitable chiefly for grating

very high frequency *n* (1920) : a radio frequency between ultrahigh frequency and high frequency — see RADIO FREQUENCY table

Ve·ry light \'ver-ē-, 'vir-ē-\ *n* [Edward W. *Very* †1910 Am naval officer] (1917) : a pyrotechnic signal in a system of signaling using white or colored balls of fire projected from a special pistol

very low–density lipoprotein *n* (1977) : VLDL

very low frequency *n* (1938) : a radio frequency between low frequency and voice frequency — see RADIO FREQUENCY table

Ve·ry pistol \'ver-ē-, 'vir-ē-\ *n* (1915) : a pistol for firing Very lights

Very Reverend \'ver-ē-\ (ca. 1828) — used as a title for various ecclesiastical officials (as cathedral deans and canons, rectors of Roman Catholic colleges and seminaries, and superiors of some religious houses)

ves·i·cal \'ve-si-kəl\ *adj* [L *vesica* bladder — more at VENTER] (1797) : of or relating to the urinary bladder ⟨~ burning⟩

ves·i·cant \-kənt\ *n* [L *vesica* bladder, blister] (1661) : an agent (as a drug or a chemical weapon) that induces blistering — **vesicant** *adj*

ves·i·cle \'ve-si-kəl\ *n* [MF *vesicule,* fr. L *vesicula* small bladder, blister, fr. dim. of *vesica*] (1578) **1 a** : a membranous and usu. fluid-filled pouch (as a cyst, vacuole, or cell) in a plant or animal **b** : a small abnormal elevation of the outer layer of skin enclosing a watery liquid : BLISTER **c** : a pocket of embryonic tissue that is the beginning of an organ **2** : a small cavity in a mineral or rock

ve·sic·u·lar \və-'si-kyə-lər, ve-\ *adj* [NL *vesicula* vesicle, fr. L, small bladder] (1715) **1** : containing, composed of, or characterized by vesicles ⟨~ lava⟩ **2** : having the form or structure of a vesicle **3** : of or relating to vesicles — **ve·sic·u·lar·i·ty** \-,si-kyə-'lar-ə-tē\ *n*

vesicular stomatitis *n* (ca. 1903) : an acute virus disease esp. of various domesticated animals (as horses and cows) that is marked by erosive blisters in and about the mouth and that much resembles foot-and-mouth disease

ve·sic·u·late \və-'si-kyə-,lāt, ve-\ *vb* **-lat·ed; -lat·ing** *vt* (1865) : to make vesicular ~ *vi* : to become vesicular — **ve·sic·u·la·tion** \-,si-kyə-'lā-shən\ *n*

¹ves·per \'ves-pər\ *n* [ME, fr. L, evening, evening star — more at WEST] (14c) **1** *cap, archaic* : EVENING STAR **2** : a vesper bell **3** *archaic* : EVENING, EVENTIDE

²vesper *adj* (1791) : of or relating to vespers or the evening

ves·per·al \'ves-p(ə-)rəl\ *adj* (ca. 1623) : VESPER ⟨a ~ breeze⟩

ves·pers \'ves-pərz\ *n pl but sing or pl in constr, often cap* [F *vespres,* fr. ML *vesperae,* fr. L, pl. of *vespera* evening; akin to L *vesper* evening star] (1611) **1** : the sixth of the canonical hours that is said or sung in the late afternoon **2** : a service of evening worship

ves·per·til·ian \,ves-pər-'ti-lē-ən, -'til-yən\ *adj* [L *vespertilio* bat, fr. *vesper*] (1874) : of, relating to, or resembling a bat ⟨flaunts ~ wing and cloven hoof —Robert Graves⟩

ves·per·tine \'ves-pər-,tīn\ *adj* [L *vespertinus,* fr. *vesper*] (1502) **1** : of, relating to, or occurring in the evening ⟨~ shadows⟩ **2** : active, flowering, or flourishing in the evening : CREPUSCULAR

ves·pid \'ves-pəd\ *n* [ultim. fr. L *vespa* wasp — more at WASP] (ca. 1900) : any of a cosmopolitan family (Vespidae) of chiefly social wasps that usu. live in colonies like bees — **vespid** *adj*

ves·pine \'ves-,pīn\ *adj* [L *vespa* wasp] (1843) : of, relating to, or resembling wasps and esp. vespid wasps

ves·sel \'ve-səl\ *n* [ME, fr. MF *vaissel,* fr. LL *vascellum,* dim. of L *vas* vase, vessel] (14c) **1 a** : a container (as a hogshead, bottle, kettle, cup, or bowl) for holding something **b** : a person into whom some quality (as grace) is infused ⟨a child of light, a true ~ of the Lord —H. J. Laski⟩ **2** : a watercraft bigger than a rowboat; *esp* : SHIP 1 **3 a** : a tube or canal (as an artery) in which a body fluid is contained and conveyed or circulated **b** : a conducting tube in the xylem of a vascular plant formed by the fusion and loss of end walls of a series of cells

¹vest \'vest\ *vb* [ME, fr. MF *vestir* to clothe, invest, fr. L *vestire* to clothe, fr. *vestis* clothing, garment — more at WEAR] *vt* (15c) **1 a** : to place or give into the possession or discretion of some person or authority; *esp* : to give to a person a legally fixed immediate right of present or future enjoyment of (as an estate) **b** : to grant or endow with a

particular authority, right, or property ⟨the retirement plan ~s the workers absolutely with the company's contribution after 10 years of continuous employment⟩ **2** : to clothe with or as if with a garment; *esp* : to robe in ecclesiastical vestments ~ *vi* **1** : to become legally vested **2** : to put on garments; *esp* : to put on ecclesiastical vestments

²vest *n* [F *veste,* fr. It. fr. L *vestis* garment] (1613) **1** *archaic* **a** : a loose outer garment : ROBE **b** : CLOTHING, GARB **2 a** : a man's sleeveless garment for the upper body usu. worn under a suit coat; *also* : a similar garment for women **b** : a protective usu. sleeveless garment (as a life preserver) that extends to the waist **c** : an insulated sleeveless waist-length garment often worn under or in place of a coat **3** *a chiefly Brit* : a man's sleeveless undershirt **b** : a knitted undershirt for women **4** : a plain or decorative piece used to fill in the front neckline of a woman's outer garment (as a waist, coat, or gown) — **vest·like** \-,līk\ *adj*

ves·ta \'ves-tə\ *n* [*L Vesta*] **1** *cap* : the Roman goddess of the hearth — compare HESTIA **2** : a short match with a shank of wax-coated threads; *also* : a short wooden match

¹ves·tal \'ves-t³l\ *adj* (15c) **1** : of or relating to the Roman goddess Vesta **2 a** : of or relating to a vestal virgin **b** : CHASTE

²vestal *n* (1549) : VESTAL VIRGIN

vestal virgin *n* (1600) **1** : a virgin consecrated to the Roman goddess Vesta and to the service of watching the sacred fire perpetually kept burning on her altar **2** : a chaste woman

vest·ed \'ves-təd\ *adj* (1766) **1** : fully and unconditionally guaranteed as a legal right, benefit, or privilege ⟨the ~ benefits of the pension plan⟩ **2** : having a vest (a ~ suit)

vested interest *n* (1818) **1 a** : an interest (as a title to an estate) carrying a legal right of present or future enjoyment **b** : a right vested in an employee under a pension plan **2** : a special concern or stake in maintaining or influencing a condition, arrangement, or action esp. for selfish ends **3** : one having a vested interest in something; *specif* : a group enjoying benefits from an existing economic or political privilege

vest·ee \ve-'stē\ *n* (1915) **1** : DICKEY; *esp* : one made to resemble a vest and worn under a coat **2** : VEST 4

ves·ti·ary \'ves-tē-,er-ē, 'vesh-chē-\ *n* [ME *vestiarie,* fr. MF, vestry — more at VESTRY] (15c) **1** : a room where clothing is kept **2** : CLOTHING, RAIMENT

ves·tib·u·lar \ve-'sti-byə-lər\ *adj* (ca. 1839) : of, relating to, or functioning as a vestibule

ves·ti·bule \'ves-tə-,byü(ə)l\ *n* [L *vestibulum*] (1728) **1** : any of various bodily cavities esp. when serving as or resembling an entrance to some other cavity or space: as **a** : the central cavity of the bony labyrinth of the ear or the parts of the membranous labyrinth that it contains **b** : the part of the left ventricle below the aortic orifice **c** : the space between the labia minora containing the orifice of the urethra **d** : the part of the mouth cavity outside the teeth and gums **2 a** : a passage, hall, or room between the outer door and the interior of a building : LOBBY **b** : an enclosed entrance at the end of a railway passenger car **3** : a course that offers access (as to something new) — **ves·ti·buled** \-,byü(ə)ld\ *adj*

vestibule school *n* (1918) : a school organized in an industrial plant to train new workers in specific skills

ves·tib·u·lo·co·chle·ar nerve \ve-,sti-byə-lō-'kō-klē-ər-, -'kä-\ *n* (1962) : AUDITORY NERVE

ves·tige \'ves-tij\ *n* [F, fr. L *vestigium* footstep, footprint, track, vestige] (1602) **1 a** (1) : a trace, mark, or visible sign left by something (as an ancient city or a condition or practice) vanished or lost (2) : the smallest quantity or trace **b** : FOOTPRINT 1 **2** : a bodily part or organ that is small and degenerate or imperfectly developed in comparison to one more fully developed in an earlier stage of the individual, in a past generation, or in closely related forms *syn* see TRACE — **ves·ti·gial** \ve-'sti-jē-əl, -jəl\ *adj* — **ves·ti·gial·ly** *adv*

vest·ing \'ves-tiŋ\ *n* (1944) : the conveying to an employee of the inalienable right to share in a pension fund esp. in the event of termination of employment prior to the normal retirement age; *also* : the right so conveyed

vest·ment \'ves(t)-mənt\ *n* [ME *vestement,* fr. MF, fr. L *vestimentum,* fr. *vestire* to clothe] (14c) **1 a** : an outer garment; *esp* : a robe of ceremony or office **b** *pl* : CLOTHING, GARB **2** : a covering resembling a garment **3** : one of the articles of the ceremonial attire and insignia worn by ecclesiastical officiants and assistants as indicative of their rank and appropriate to the rite being celebrated — **vest·men·tal** \ves(t)-'men-t³l\ *adj*

vest–pocket *adj* (1848) **1** : adapted to fit into the vest pocket ⟨a ~ edition of a book⟩ **2** : of very small size or scope

vest–pocket park *n* (1966) : a very small urban park

ves·try \'ves-trē\ *n, pl* **vestries** [ME *vestrie,* prob. modif. of MF *vestiarie,* fr. ML *vestiarium,* L *vestire*; fr. its use as a robing room for the clergy] (14c) **1 a** : SACRISTY **b** : a room used for church meetings and classes **2 a** : the business meeting of an English parish **b** : an elective body in an Episcopal parish composed of the rector and a group of elected parishioners administering the temporal affairs of the parish

ves·try·man \-trē-mən\ *n* (1614) : a member of a vestry

¹ves·ture \'ves-chər, 'vesh-\ *n* [ME, fr. MF, fr. *vestir* to clothe — more at VEST] (14c) **1 a** : a covering garment (as a robe or vestment) **b** : CLOTHING, APPAREL **2** : something that covers like a garment : CLOTHE

²vesture *vt* **ves·tured; ves·tur·ing** (1555) : to cover with vesture

ve·su·vi·an \və-'sü-vē-ən\ *n* [*Vesuvian*] (1853) : a match used esp. formerly for lighting cigars

Ve·su·vi·an \və-'sü-vē-ən\ *adj* (1673) **1** : of, relating to, or resembling the volcano Vesuvius **2** : marked by sudden outbursts ⟨has a ~ temper, but quickly controls himself —Sidney Shalett⟩

ve·su·vi·an·ite \-vē-ə-,nīt\ *n* (ca. 1888) : IDOCRASE

¹vet \'vet\ *n* (1862) : VETERINARIAN, VETERINARY

²vet *vt* **vet·ted; vet·ting** (1891) **1 a** : to provide veterinary care for (an animal) or medical care for (a person) **b** : to subject (a person or animal) to a physical examination or checkup **2** : to subject to expert appraisal or correction : EVALUATE

³vet *adj or n* (1848) : VETERAN

vetch \'vech\ *n* [ME *veeche,* fr. ONF *veche,* fr. L *vicia*; perh. akin to L *vincire* to bind] (14c) : any of a genus (*Vicia*) of herbaceous twining leguminous plants including some grown for fodder and green manure

vetch·ling \-liŋ\ n (1578) : any of various leguminous herbs (genus *Lathyrus* and esp. *L. pratensis*)

vet·er·an \'ve-tə-rən, 've-trən\ n [L *veteranus*, fr. *veteranus*, adj., old, of long experience, fr. *veter-, vetus* old — more at WETHER] (1509) **1 a** : an old soldier of long service **b** : a former member of the armed forces **2** : a person of long experience in some occupation or skill (as politics or the arts) — **veteran** *adj*

Veterans Day n (1952) : November 11 set aside in commemoration of the end of hostilities in 1918 and 1945 and observed as a legal holiday in the U.S. to honor the veterans of the armed forces

veterans' preference n (ca. 1941) : preferential treatment given qualified veterans of the U.S. armed forces under federal or state law; *specif* : special consideration (as by allowance of points) on a civil service examination

vet·er·i·nar·i·an \,ve-tə-rə-'ner-ē-ən, ,ve-trə-, ,ve-t°n-\ n (1646) : a person qualified and authorized to practice veterinary medicine

1vet·er·i·nary \'ve-tə-rə-,ner-ē, 've-trə-, 've-t°n-\ *adj* [L *veterinarius* of beasts of burden, fr. *veterinae* beasts of burden, fr. fem. pl. of *veterinus* of beasts of burden; akin to L *veter-, vetus* old] (1790) : of, relating to, or being the science and art of prevention, cure, or alleviation of disease and injury in animals and esp. domestic animals

2veterinary n, pl **-nar·ies** (1861) : VETERINARIAN

veterinary surgeon n (ca. 1802) *Brit* : VETERINARIAN

vet·i·ver \'ve-tə-vər\ n [F *vétiver*, fr. Tamil *vettivēr*] (ca. 1858) : an East Indian grass (*Vetiveria zizanioides*) cultivated in warm regions esp. for its fragrant roots which are used esp. in woven goods (as mats) and in perfumes; *also* : its root

1ve·to \'vē-(,)tō\ n, pl **vetoes** [L, I forbid, fr. *vetare* to forbid] (1629) **1** : an authoritative prohibition : INTERDICTION **2 a** : a power of one department or branch of a government to forbid or prohibit finally or provisionally the carrying out of projects attempted by another department; *esp* : a power vested in a chief executive to prevent permanently or temporarily the enactment of measures passed by a legislature **b** (1) : the exercise of such authority (2) : a message communicating the reasons of an executive and esp. the president of the U.S. for vetoing a proposed law

2veto vt (1706) : to refuse to admit or approve : PROHIBIT; *also* : to refuse assent to (a legislative bill) so as to prevent enactment or cause reconsideration — **ve·to·er** \-,tō(-ə)r\ n

ve·to-proof \-,prüf\ *adj* (1972) : having enough potential votes to be enacted over a veto or to override vetoes consistently ⟨a ~ bill⟩

vex \'veks\ vt **vexed** *also* **vext; vex·ing** [ME, fr. MF *vexer*, fr. L *vexare* to agitate, harry; prob. akin to L *vehere* to convey — more at WAY] (15c) **1 a** : to bring trouble, distress, or agitation to ⟨the restaurant is ~ed by slow service⟩ **b** : to bring physical distress to ⟨a headache ~ed him all morning⟩ **c** : to irritate or annoy by petty provocations : HARASS ⟨~ed by the children⟩ **d** : PUZZLE, BAFFLE ⟨a problem to ~ the keenest wit⟩ **2** : to shake or toss about **syn** see ANNOY

vex·a·tion \vek-'sā-shən\ n (15c) **1** : the act of harassing or vexing : TROUBLING **2** : the quality or state of being vexed : IRRITATION **3** : a cause of trouble : AFFLICTION

vex·a·tious \-shəs\ *adj* (1534) **1 a** : causing vexation : DISTRESSING **b** : intended to harass **2** : full of disorder or stress : TROUBLED — **vex·a·tious·ly** *adv* — **vex·a·tious·ness** n

vexed \'vekst\ *adj* (1657) : debated or discussed at length ⟨a ~ question⟩

vexed·ly \'vek-səd-lē, 'vekst-lē\ *adv* (1748) : with vexation

vex·il·lol·o·gy \,vek-sə-'lä-lə-jē\ n [L *vexillum*] (1959) : the study of flags — **vex·il·lo·log·ic** \(,)vek-,si-lə-'lä-jik\ *or* **vex·il·lo·log·i·cal** \-'lä-ji-kəl\ *adj* — **vex·il·lol·o·gist** \,vek-sə-'lä-lə-jist\ n

vex·il·lum \vek-'si-ləm\ n, pl **-la** \-lə\ [L; akin to L *velum* curtain, awning] (1726) **1** : a square flag of the ancient Roman cavalry **2** : the web or vane of a feather

via \'vī-ə, 'vē-ə\ *prep* [L, abl. of *via* way — more at WAY] (1779) **1** : by way of **2** : through the medium or agency of; *also* : by means of

vi·a·ble \'vī-ə-bəl\ *adj* [F, fr. MF, fr. *vie* life, fr. L *vita* — more at VITAL] (ca. 1832) **1** : capable of living; *esp* : capable of surviving outside the mother's womb without artificial support ⟨the normal human fetus is usually ~ by the end of the seventh month⟩ **2** : capable of growing or developing ⟨~ seeds⟩ ⟨~ eggs⟩ **3 a** : capable of working, functioning, or developing adequately ⟨~ alternatives⟩ **b** : capable of existence and development as an independent unit ⟨the colony is now a ~ state⟩ **c** (1) : having a reasonable chance of succeeding ⟨a ~ candidate⟩ (2) : financially sustainable ⟨a ~ enterprise⟩ — **vi·a·bil·i·ty** \,vī-ə-'bi-lə-tē\ n — **vi·a·bly** \'vī-ə-blē\ *adv*

via·duct \'vī-ə-,dəkt\ n [L *via* way, road + E aque*duct*] (1816) : a long elevated roadway usu. consisting of a series of short spans supported on arches, piers, or columns

vi·al \'vī(-ə)l\ n [ME *fiole, viole*, fr. MF *fiole*, fr. OProv *fiola*, fr. L *phiala* — more at PHIAL] (14c) : a small closed or closable vessel esp. for liquids

via me·dia \,vī-ə-'mē-dē-ə, ,vē-ə-'mā-dē-ə, -'me-\ n [L] (1834) : a middle way

vi·and \'vī-ənd\ n [ME, fr. MF *viande*, fr. ML *vivanda* food, alter. of L *vivenda*, neut. pl. of *vivendus*, gerundive of *vivere* to live — more at QUICK] (15c) **1** : an item of food; *esp* : a choice or tasty dish **2** *pl* : PROVISIONS, FOOD

vi·at·i·cum \vī-'a-ti-kəm, vē-\ n, pl **-cums** *or* **-ca** \-kə\ [L — more at VOYAGE] (1562) **1** : the Christian Eucharist given to a person in danger of death **2 a** : an allowance (as of transportation or supplies and money) for traveling expenses **b** : provisions for a journey

vibe \'vīb\ n (1967) : VIBRATION **4** ⟨seems to be in on every conversation, every deal, every ~ that is winging through the room —Albert Goldman⟩ — usu. used in pl. ⟨got bad ~s from him⟩

vibes \'vībz\ n pl (1940) : VIBRAPHONE — **vib·ist** \'vī-bist\ n

vi·bra·harp \'vī-brə-,härp\ n [fr. *Vibra-Harp*, a trademark] (1930) : VIBRAPHONE — **vi·bra·harp·ist** \-,här-pist\ n

vi·brance \'vī-brən(t)s\ n (1921) : VIBRANCY

vi·bran·cy \'vī-brən(t)-sē\ n (ca. 1890) : the quality or state of being vibrant

vi·brant \-brənt\ *adj* (1616) **1 a** (1) : oscillating or pulsating rapidly (2) : pulsating with life, vigor, or activity ⟨a ~ personality⟩ **b** (1) : readily set in vibration (2) : RESPONSIVE, SENSITIVE **2** : sounding as a result of vibration : RESONANT ⟨a ~ voice⟩ **3** : BRIGHT **4** ⟨a ~ orange⟩ — **vi·brant·ly** *adv*

vi·bra·phone \'vī-brə-,fōn\ n [L *vibrare* + ISV *-phone*] (1926) : a percussion instrument resembling the xylophone but having metal bars and motor-driven resonators for sustaining the tone and producing a vibrato — **vi·bra·phon·ist** \-,fō-nist\ n

vi·brate \'vī-,brāt, esp Brit vī-'\ vb **vi·brat·ed; vi·brat·ing** [L *vibratus*, pp. of *vibrare* to brandish, wave, rock — more at WIPE] vt (1616) **1** : to swing or move to and fro **2** : to emit with or as if with a vibratory motion **3** : to mark or measure by oscillation ⟨a pendulum *vibrating* seconds⟩ **4** : to set in vibration ~ vi **1 a** : to move to and fro or from side to side : OSCILLATE **b** : FLUCTUATE, VACILLATE ⟨~ between two choices⟩ **2** : to have an effect as or as if of vibration ⟨music, when soft voices die, ~s in the memory —P. B. Shelley⟩ **3** : to be in a state of vibration : QUIVER **4** : to respond sympathetically : THRILL ⟨~ to the opportunity⟩ **syn** see SWING

vi·bra·tile \'vī-brə-t°l, -,tīl\ *adj* (ca. 1826) **1** : characterized by vibration **2** : adapted to or used in vibratory motion ⟨the ~ organs of insects⟩

vi·bra·tion \vī-'brā-shən\ n (1655) **1 a** : a periodic motion of the particles of an elastic body or medium in alternately opposite directions from the position of equilibrium when that equilibrium has been disturbed (as when a stretched cord produces musical tones or particles of air transmit sounds to the ear) **b** : the action of vibrating : the state of being vibrated or in vibratory motion: as (1) : OSCILLATION (2) : a quivering or trembling motion : QUIVER **2** : an instance of vibration **3** : vacillation in opinion or action : WAVERING **4 a** : a characteristic emanation, aura, or spirit that infuses or vitalizes someone or something and that can be instinctively sensed or experienced — often used in pl. **b** : a distinctive usu. emotional atmosphere capable of being sensed — usu. used in pl. — **vi·bra·tion·al** \-shnəl, -shə-n°l\ *adj* — **vi·bra·tion·less** \-shən-ləs\ *adj*

vi·bra·to \vi-'brä-(,)tō, vī-\ n, pl **-tos** [It, fr. pp. of *vibrare* to vibrate, fr. L] (ca. 1876) : a slightly tremulous effect imparted to vocal or instrumental tone for added warmth and expressiveness by slight and rapid variations in pitch — **vi·bra·to·less** \-ləs\ *adj*

vi·bra·tor \'vī-,brā-tər\ n (1862) : one that vibrates or causes vibration: as **a** : a vibrating electrical apparatus used in massage or for sexual stimulation **b** : a vibrating device (as in an electric bell or buzzer)

vi·bra·to·ry \'vī-brə-,tōr-ē, -,tor-\ *adj* (1728) **1** : consisting in, capable of, or causing vibration or oscillation **2** : characterized by vibration

vib·rio \'vi-brē-,ō\ n, pl **-rios** [NL, *Vibrion-, Vibrio*, fr. L *vibrare* to wave] (ca. 1864) : any of a genus (*Vibrio*) of short rigid motile bacteria typically shaped like a comma or an S — **vib·ri·on·ic** \,vi-brē-'ä-nik\ *adj*

vib·ri·on \'vi-brē-,än\ n [NL *Vibrion-, Vibrio*] (1882) : VIBRIO; *also* : a motile bacterium

vib·ri·o·sis \,vi-brē-'ō-səs\ n, pl **-o·ses** \-,sēz\ [NL, fr. *Vibrio*] (1950) : abortion in sheep and cattle caused by a bacterium (*Campylobacter fetus* syn. *Vibrio fetus*) that invades the uterine and placental capillaries, interferes with fetal nutrition, and causes the death of the developing fetus

vi·bris·sa \vī-'bri-sə, və-\ n, pl **vi·bris·sae** \vī-'bri-(,)sē; və-'bri-(,)sē, -,sī\ [ML, fr. L *vibrare*] (ca. 1693) **1** : one of the stiff hairs that are located esp. about the nostrils or on other parts of the face in many mammals and that often serve as tactile organs **2** : one of the bristly feathers near the mouth of many and esp. insectivorous birds that may help to prevent the escape of insects

vi·bur·num \vī-'bər-nəm\ n [NL, fr. L, a viburnum] (ca. 1731) : any of a genus (*Viburnum*) of widely distributed shrubs or trees of the honeysuckle family with simple leaves and white or rarely pink cymose flowers

vic·ar \'vi-kər\ n [ME, fr. L *vicarius*, fr. *vicarius* vicarious] (14c) **1** : one serving as a substitute or agent; *specif* : an administrative deputy **2** : an ecclesiastical agent: as **a** : a Church of England incumbent receiving a stipend but not the tithes of a parish **b** : a member of the Episcopal clergy or laity who has charge of a mission or chapel **c** : a member of the clergy who exercises a broad pastoral responsibility as the representative of a prelate — **vic·ar·ship** \-,ship\ n

vic·ar·age \'vi-k(ə-)rij\ n (15c) **1** : the benefice of a vicar **2** : the house of a vicar **3** : VICARIATE 1

vicar apostolic n, pl **vicars apostolic** (1766) : a Roman Catholic titular bishop who administers a territory not organized as a diocese

vic·ar·ate \'vi-kə-rət, -,rāt\ n (1883) : VICARIATE

vicar–general n, pl **vicars–general** (15c) : an administrative deputy of a Roman Catholic or Anglican bishop or of the head of a religious order

vi·car·i·al \vī-'ker-ē-əl, və-, -'kar-\ *adj* [L *vicarius*] (1617) **1** : VICARIOUS 1 **2** : of or relating to a vicar

vi·car·i·ance \-ē-ən(t)s\ n (1957) : fragmentation of the environment (as by splitting of a tectonic plate) in contrast to dispersal as a factor in promoting biological evolution by division of large populations into isolated subpopulations — called also *vicariance biogeography*

vic·ar·i·ant \-ē-ənt\ *adj* [trans. of G *vikariirend*, prp. of *vikarieren* to act as a substitute, fr. *Vikar* representative, proxy, fr. MHG *vicar*, fr. L *vicarius* substitute] (1952) : of, relating to, or being the process of vicariance or organisms that evolved through this process ⟨the possible ~ origin of the Antillean arthropod fauna⟩ — **vicariant** n

vi·car·i·ate \-ē-ət\ n [ML *vicariatus*, fr. L *vicarius* vicar] (1610) **1** : the office, jurisdiction, or tenure of a vicar **2** : the office or district of a governmental administrative deputy

vi·car·i·ous \vī-'ker-ē-əs, və-, -'kar-\ *adj* [L *vicarius*, fr. *vicis* change,

\ə\ abut \ə\ kitten, F table \ər\ further \a\ ash \ā\ ace \ä\ mop, mar
\au̇\ out \ch\ chin \e\ bet \ē\ easy \g\ go \i\ hit \ī\ ice \j\ job
\ŋ\ sing \ō\ go \ȯ\ law \ȯi\ boy \th\ thin \tẖ\ the \ü\ loot \u̇\ foot
\y\ yet \zh\ vision \à, k̟, ⁿ, œ, œ̄, ue̮, ūe, ᵛ\ see Guide to Pronunciation

alternation, stead — more at WEEK] (1637)   **1 a :** serving instead of someone or something else   **b :** that has been delegated ⟨~ authority⟩   **2 :** performed or suffered by one person as a substitute for another or to the benefit or advantage of another : SUBSTITUTIONARY ⟨a ~ sacrifice⟩   **3 :** experienced or realized through imaginative or sympathetic participation in the experience of another   **4 :** occurring in an unexpected or abnormal part of the body instead of the usual one ⟨bleeding from the gums sometimes occurs in the absence of the normal discharge from the uterus in ~ menstruation⟩ — **vi·car·i·ous·ly** *adv* — **vi·car·i·ous·ness** *n*
Vicar of Christ (1570) : POPE 1
¹vice \'vīs\ *n* [ME, fr. OF, fr. L *vitium* fault, vice] (14c)   **1 a :** moral depravity or corruption : WICKEDNESS   **b :** a moral fault or failing   **c :** a habitual and usu. trivial defect or shortcoming : FOIBLE ⟨suffered from the ~ of curiosity⟩   **2 :** BLEMISH, DEFECT   **3 :** a physical imperfection, deformity, or taint   **4** *a often cap* **:** a character representing one of the vices in an English morality play   **b :** BUFFOON, JESTER   **5 :** an abnormal behavior pattern in a domestic animal detrimental to its health or usefulness   **6 :** sexual immorality; *esp* : PROSTITUTION   *syn* see FAULT, OFFENSE
²vice *chiefly Brit var of* VISE
³vice \'vīs *also* 'vī-sē\ *prep* [L, abl. of *vicis* change, alternation, stead — more at WEEK] (1770) : in the place of ⟨I will preside, ~ the absent chairman⟩; *also* : rather than
vice- \'vīs, vis\ *prefix* [ME *vis-, vice-*, fr. MF, fr. LL *vice-*, fr. L *vice*, abl. of *vicis*] : one that takes the place of ⟨*vice*-chancellor⟩
vice admiral *n* [MF *visamiral*, fr. *vis-* vice- + *amiral* admiral] (1520) : a commissioned officer in the navy or coast guard who ranks above a rear admiral and whose insignia is three stars
vice–chan·cel·lor \'vīs-'chan(t)-s(ə-)lər, ,vīs-\ *n* [ME *vichauncellor*, fr. MF *vischancelier*, fr. *vis-* + *chancelier* chancellor] (15c)   **1 :** an officer ranking next below a chancellor and serving as deputy to the chancellor   **2 :** chief administrative officer in a British university   **3 :** a judge appointed to act for or to assist a chancellor
vice–con·sul \-'kän(t)-səl\ *n* (1559) : a consular officer subordinate to a consul general or to a consul
vice·ge·ren·cy \-'jir-ən(t)-sē\ *n, pl* **-cies** (1596) : the office or jurisdiction of a vicegerent
vice·ge·rent \-'jir-ənt\ *n* [ML *vicegerent-, vicegerens*, fr. LL *vice-* + L *gerent-, gerens*, prp. of *gerere* to carry, carry on] (1536) : an administrative deputy of a king or magistrate
vi·cen·ni·al \vī-'sen-ē-əl\ *adj* [LL *vicennium* period of 20 years, fr. L *vicies* 20 times + *annus* year; akin to L *viginti* twenty — more at VIGESIMAL, ANNUAL] (ca. 1859) : occurring once every 20 years
vice presidency (1804) : the office of vice president
vice president *n* (1574)   **1 :** an officer next in rank to a president and usu. empowered to serve as president in that officer's absence or disability   **2 :** any of several officers serving as a president's deputies in charge of particular locations or functions — **vice presidential** *adj*
vice–re·gal \'vīs-'rē-gəl, ,vīs-\ *adj* (1836) : of or relating to a viceroy or viceroyalty — **vice·re·gal·ly** \-gə-lē\ *adv*
vice–re·gent \-'rē-jənt\ *n* (1556) : a regent's deputy
vice·reine \'vīs-,rān\ *n* [F, fr. *vice-* + *reine* queen, fr. L *regina*, fem. of *reg-, gerens, rex* king — more at ROYAL] (1823)   **1 :** the wife of a viceroy   **2 :** a woman who is a viceroy
vice·roy \'vīs-,ròi\ *n* [MF *vice-roi*, fr. *vice-* + *roi* king, fr. L *reg-, rex*] (1524)   **1 :** the governor of a country or province who rules as the representative of a king or sovereign   **2 :** a showy American nymphalid butterfly (*Limenitis archippus*) closely mimicking the monarch in coloration but smaller
vice·roy·al·ty \'vīs-,ròi(-ə)l-tē, ,vīs-'\ *n* (1703) : the office, jurisdiction, or term of service of a viceroy
vice·roy·ship \'vīs-,ròi-,ship\ *n* (1609) : VICEROYALTY
vice squad *n* (1905) : a police squad charged with enforcement of laws concerning gambling, pornography, prostitution, and the illegal use of liquor and narcotics
vice ver·sa \,vī-si-'vər-sə, 'vīs-'vər-\ *adv* [L] (1601) : with the order changed : with the relations reversed : CONVERSELY
vi·chys·soise \,vi-shē-'swäz, ,vē-\ *n* [F, fr. fem. of *vichyssois* of Vichy, fr. *Vichy*, France] (1939) : a soup made of pureed leeks or onions and potatoes, cream, and chicken stock and usu. served cold
Vi·chy water \'vi-shē-\ *n* (ca. 1858) : a natural sparkling mineral water from Vichy, France; *also* : an imitation of or substitute for this
vic·i·nage \'vi-s°n-ij, 'vis-nij\ *n* [ME *vesinage*, fr. MF, fr. *vesin* neighboring, fr. L *vicinus*] (14c) : a neighboring or surrounding district : VICINITY
vic·i·nal \'vi-s°n-əl, 'vis-nəl\ *adj* [L *vicinalis*, fr. *vicinus* neighbor, fr. *vicinus*, adj., neighboring] (ca. 1623)   **1 :** of or relating to a limited district : LOCAL   **2 :** of, relating to, or substituted in adjacent sites in a molecule ⟨a ~ disulfide group⟩
vi·cin·i·ty \və-'si-nə-tē\ *n, pl* **-ties** [MF *vicinité*, fr. L *vicinitat-, vicinitas*, fr. *vicinus* neighboring, fr. *vicus* row of houses, village; akin to Goth *weihs* village, OCS *vĭsĭ*, Gk *oikos, oikia* house] (1560)   **1 :** the quality or state of being near : PROXIMITY   **2 :** a surrounding area or district : NEIGHBORHOOD   **3 :** NEIGHBORHOOD 3b
vi·cious \'vi-shəs\ *adj* [ME, fr. MF *vicieus*, fr. L *vitiosus* full of faults, corrupt, fr. *vitium* vice] (14c)   **1 :** having the nature or quality of vice or immorality : DEPRAVED   **2 :** DEFECTIVE, FAULTY; *also* : INVALID   **3 :** IMPURE, NOXIOUS   **4** *a* **:** dangerously aggressive : SAVAGE ⟨a ~ dog⟩   **b :** marked by violence or ferocity : FIERCE ⟨a ~ fight⟩   **5 :** MALICIOUS, SPITEFUL ⟨~ gossip⟩   **6 :** worsened by internal causes that reciprocally augment each other ⟨a ~ wage-price spiral⟩ — **vi·cious·ly** *adv* — **vi·cious·ness** *n*
syn VICIOUS, VILLAINOUS, INIQUITOUS, NEFARIOUS, CORRUPT, DEGENERATE mean highly reprehensible or offensive in character, nature, or conduct. VICIOUS may directly oppose *virtuous* in implying moral depravity, or may connote malignancy, cruelty, or destructive violence ⟨a *vicious* gangster⟩. VILLAINOUS applies to any evil, depraved, or vile conduct or characteristic ⟨a *villainous* assault⟩. INIQUITOUS implies absence of all signs of justice or fairness ⟨an *iniquitous* system of taxation⟩. NEFARIOUS suggests flagrant breaching of time-honored laws and traditions of conduct ⟨the *nefarious* rackets of organized crime⟩. CORRUPT stresses a loss of moral integrity or probity causing betrayal of principle or sworn obligations ⟨city hall was rife with *corrupt* politi-

cians⟩. DEGENERATE suggests having sunk to an esp. vicious or enervated condition ⟨a *degenerate* regime propped up by foreign powers⟩.
vicious circle *n* (ca. 1792)   **1 :** a chain of events in which the response to one difficulty creates a new problem that aggravates the original difficulty   **2 :** an argument or definition that begs the question
vi·cis·si·tude \və-'si-sə-,tüd, vī-, -,tyüd\ *n* [MF, fr. L *vicissitudo*, fr. *vicissim* in turn, fr. *vicis* change, alternation — more at WEEK] (ca. 1576)   **1 a :** the quality or state of being changeable : MUTABILITY   **b :** natural change or mutation visible in nature or in human affairs   **2 a :** a favorable or unfavorable event or situation that occurs by chance : a fluctuation of state or condition ⟨the ~s of daily life⟩   **b :** a difficulty or hardship attendant on a way of life, a career, or a course of action and usu. beyond one's control   **c :** alternating change : SUCCESSION
vi·cis·si·tu·di·nous \və-,si-sə-'tüd-nəs, (,)vī-, -'tyüd-; -'tü-d°n-əs, -'tyü-\ *adj* [L *vicissitudin-, vicissitudo*] (ca. 1846) : marked by or filled with vicissitudes
vic·tim \'vik-təm\ *n* [ME *vyctym*, fr. L *victima*; perh. akin to OHG *wih* holy] (15c)   **1 :** a living being sacrificed to a deity or in the performance of a religious rite   **2 :** one that is acted on and usu. adversely affected by a force or agent ⟨the schools are ~s of the social system⟩: as **a** (1) **:** one that is injured, destroyed, or sacrificed under any of various conditions ⟨a ~ of cancer⟩ ⟨a ~ of the auto crash⟩ ⟨a murder ~⟩ (2) **:** one that is subjected to oppression, hardship, or mistreatment ⟨a frequent ~ of political attacks⟩   **b :** one that is tricked or duped ⟨a con man's ~⟩ — **vic·tim·hood** \-,hud\ *n*
vic·tim·ise *Brit var of* VICTIMIZE
vic·tim·ize \'vik-tə-,mīz\ *vt* **-ized; -iz·ing** (1830)   **1 :** to make a victim of   **2 :** to subject to deception or fraud : CHEAT — **vic·tim·i·za·tion** \,vik-tə-mə-'zā-shən\ *n* — **vic·tim·iz·er** \'vik-tə-,mī-zər\ *n*
vic·tim·less \'vik-təm-ləs\ *adj* (1965) : having no victim : not of a nature that may produce a complainant ⟨a ~ crime⟩
vic·tim·ol·o·gy \,vik-tə-'mä-lə-jē\ *n* (1958)   **1 :** the study of victims and victimization   **2 :** the claim that the problems of a person or group are the result of victimization — **vic·tim·ol·o·gist** \-jist\ *n*
vic·tor \'vik-tər\ *n* [ME, fr. L, fr. *vincere* to conquer, win; akin to OE *wigan* to fight, Lith *veikti* to be active] (14c) : one that defeats an enemy or opponent : WINNER — **victor** *adj*
Victor (1942) — a communications code word for the letter *v*
vic·to·ria \vik-'tōr-ē-ə, -'tòr-\ *n* [Queen *Victoria*] (ca. 1864) : a low four-wheeled pleasure carriage for two with a folding top and a raised seat in front for the driver

victoria

Victoria Cross *n* (1856) : a bronze Maltese cross awarded to members of the British armed services for acts of remarkable valor
Victoria Day *n* [Queen *Victoria*] (1901)   **1 :** formerly May 24 and now the Monday preceding May 25 observed in Canada as a legal holiday   **2 :** COMMONWEALTH DAY
¹Vic·to·ri·an \vik-'tōr-ē-ən, -'tòr-\ *adj* (1839)   **1 :** of, relating to, or characteristic of the reign of Queen Victoria of England or the art, letters, or tastes of her time   **2 :** typical of the moral standards, attitudes, or conduct of the age of Victoria esp. when considered stuffy or hypocritical
²Victorian *n* (1876)   **1 :** a person living during Queen Victoria's reign; *esp* : a representative figure of that time   **2 :** a typically large and ornate house built during Queen Victoria's reign
Vic·to·ri·ana \(,)vik-,tōr-ē-'a-nə, -,tòr-, -'ä-, -'ā-\ *n* [Queen *Victoria* + E *-ana*] (1940) : materials concerning or characteristic of the Victorian age; *also* : a collection of such materials
Vic·to·ri·an·ism \vik-'tōr-ē-ə-,ni-zəm, -'tòr-\ *n* (1905)   **1 :** a typical instance or product of Victorian expression, taste, or conduct   **2 :** the quality or state of being Victorian esp. in taste or conduct
vic·to·ri·ous \vik-'tōr-ē-əs, -'tòr-\ *adj* (14c)   **1 a :** having won a victory   **b :** of, relating to, or characteristic of victory   **2 :** evincing moral harmony or a sense of fulfillment : FULFILLED — **vic·to·ri·ous·ly** *adv* — **vic·to·ri·ous·ness** *n*
vic·to·ry \'vik-t(ə-)rē\ *n, pl* **-ries** [ME, fr. MF *victorie*, fr. L *victoria*, fr. *victor*] (14c)   **1 :** the overcoming of an enemy or antagonist   **2 :** achievement of mastery or success in a struggle or endeavor against odds or difficulties
Vic·tro·la \vik-'trō-lə\ *trademark* — used for a phonograph
¹vict·ual \'vi-t°l\ *n* [alter. of ME *vitaille*, fr. MF, fr. LL *victualia*, pl., provisions, victuals, fr. neut. pl. of *victualis* of nourishment, fr. L *victus* nourishment, way of living, fr. *vivere* to live — more at QUICK] (1523)   **1 :** food usable by people   **2** *pl* **:** supplies of food : PROVISIONS
²victual *vb* **-ualed** *or* **-ualled; -ual·ing** *or* **-ual·ling** *vt* (1558) **:** to supply with food ~ *vi*   **1 :** EAT   **2 :** to lay in provisions
vict·ual·ler *or* **vict·ual·er** \'vi-t°l-ər\ *n* (1568)   **1 :** the keeper of a restaurant or tavern   **2 :** one that provisions an army, a navy, or a ship with food   **3 :** an army or navy provision ship
vi·cu·ña *or* **vi·cu·na** \vi-'kün-yə, vī-; vī-'kü-nə, və-, -'kyü-\ *n* [Sp *vicuña*, fr. Quechua *wik'uña*] (1604)   **1 :** a wild ruminant (*Vicugna vicugna* syn. *Lama vicugna*) of the Andes from Peru to Argentina that is related to the llama and alpaca   **2 a :** the wool from the vicuña's fine lustrous undercoat   **b :** a fabric made of vicuña wool; *also* : a sheep's wool imitation of this
vi·de \'vī-dē, 'vē-,dā\ *vb imper* [L, fr. *videre* to see — more at WIT] (1565) : SEE — used to direct a reader to another item
vi·de·li·cet \və-'de-lə-,set, vī-; vi-'dā-li-,ket\ *adv* [ME, fr. L, fr. *videre* to see + *licet* it is permitted, fr. *licere* to be permitted] (15c) : that is to say : NAMELY
¹vid·eo \'vi-dē-,ō\ *n* [L *videre* to see + *-o* (as in *audio*)] (1937)   **1 :** TELEVISION; *also* : the visual portion of television   **2 :** VIDEOTAPE: as **a :** a recording of a motion picture or television program for playing through a television set   **b :** a videotaped performance of a song often featuring an interpretation of the lyrics through visual images
²video *adj* (1938)   **1 :** being, relating to, or used in the transmission or reception of the television image ⟨~ channel⟩ — compare AUDIO   **2 :** being, relating to, or involving images on a television screen or computer display ⟨~ terminal⟩

vid·eo·cas·sette \ˌvi-dē-ō-kə-ˈset, -ka-\ n (1970) 1 : a case containing videotape for use with a VCR 2 : a recording (as of a movie) on a videocassette

videocassette recorder n (1976) : VCR

vid·eo·con·fer·enc·ing \-ˈkän-f(ə-)rən(t)-siŋ, -fərn(t)-\ n (1977) : the holding of a conference among people at remote locations by means of transmitted audio and video signals — **vid·eo·con·fer·ence** \ˈkän-f(ə-)rən(t)s, -fərn(t)s\ n

vid·eo·disc or **vid·eo·disk** \ˈvi-dē-ō-ˌdisk\ n (1967) 1 : a disc similar in appearance and use to a phonograph record on which programs have been recorded for playback on a television set; also : OPTICAL DISK 2 : a recording (as of a movie) on a videodisc

video game n (1973) : an electronic game played by means of images on a video screen and often emphasizing fast action

vid·e·og·ra·phy \ˌvi-dē-ˈä-grə-fē\ n (1972) : the practice or art of recording images with a video camera — **vid·e·og·ra·pher** \-fər\ n

vid·eo·land \ˈ...ˌland\ n (1967) : television as a medium or industry

vid·eo·phile \ˈvi-dē-ə-ˌfīl\ n (1966) : a person fond of video; esp : one interested in video equipment or in producing videos

vid·eo·phone \ˈvi-dē-ə-ˌfōn\ n (ca. 1950) : a telephone equipped for transmission of video as well as audio signals so that users can see each other

¹vid·eo·tape \ˈvi-dē-ō-ˌtāp\ n (1953) : a recording of visual images and sound (as of a television production) made on magnetic tape; also : the magnetic tape used for such a recording

²videotape vt (1958) : to make a videotape of ⟨∼ a show⟩ ⟨∼ the president's speech⟩

videotape recorder n (1953) : a device for recording and playing back videotapes — called also video recorder

vid·eo·tex \-ˌteks\ also **vid·eo·text** \-ˌtekst\ n [²video + -tex (alter. of text)] (1978) : an electronic data retrieval system in which esp. textual information is transmitted via telephone or cable-television lines and displayed on a television set or video display terminal; esp : such a system that is interactive — compare TELETEXT

video vé·ri·té \-ˌver-ə-ˈtā\ n [cinema verité] (1969) : the filming or videotaping of a television program (as a documentary) so as to convey candid realism

vi·dette var of VEDETTE

vid·i·con \ˈvi-di-ˌkän\ n, often cap [²video + iconoscope] (1950) : a camera tube using the principle of photoconductivity

vi·du·ity \vi-ˈdü-ə-tē, -ˈdyü-\ n [ME (Sc) viduite, fr. MF viduite, fr. L viduitat-, viduitas, fr. vidua widow — more at WIDOW] (15c) : WIDOWHOOD

vie \ˈvī\ vb **vied; vy·ing** \ˈvī-iŋ\ [modif. of MF envier to invite, challenge, wager, fr. L invitare to invite; vi (1577) : to strive for superiority : CONTEND, COMPETE ∼ vt, archaic : WAGER, HAZARD; also : to exchange in rivalry : MATCH — **vi·er** \ˈvī(-ə)r\ n

Vi·en·na sausage \vē-ˈe-nə-\ n [Vienna, Austria] (ca. 1902) : a short slender frankfurter

Viet·cong \vē-ˈet-ˈkäŋ, vyet-, ˌvē-ət-, vēt-, -ˈkȯŋ\ n, pl **Vietcong** [Vietnamese Việt-cộng] (1957) : a guerrilla member of the Vietnamese communist movement

Viet·minh \-ˈmin\ n, pl **Vietminh** [Vietnamese Việt-Minh, short for Việt-Nam Độc-Lập Đồng-Minh League for the Independence of Vietnam] (1945) : an adherent of the Vietnamese communist movement from 1941 to 1951

Viet·nam·ese \vē-ˌet-nə-ˈmēz, ˌvyet-, ˌvē-ət-, ˌvēt-, -na-, -nä-, -ˈmēs\ n, pl **Vietnamese** (1947) 1 : a native or inhabitant of Vietnam 2 : the language of the largest group in Vietnam and the official language of the country — **Vietnamese** adj

¹view \ˈvyü\ n [ME vewe, fr. MF veue, vue, fr. OF, fr. fem. of veu, vu, pp. of veeir, voir to see, fr. L vidēre — more at WIT] (15c) 1 : the act of seeing or examining : INSPECTION; also : SURVEY ⟨a ∼ of English literature⟩ 2 a : a mode or manner of looking at or regarding something b : an opinion or judgment colored by the feeling or bias of its holder ⟨in my ∼ the conference has no chance of success⟩ 3 : SCENE, PROSPECT ⟨the lovely ∼ from the balcony⟩ 4 : extent or range of vision : SIGHT ⟨tried to keep the ship in ∼⟩ ⟨sat high in the bleachers to get a good ∼⟩ 5 : something that is looked toward or kept in sight : OBJECT ⟨studied hard with a ∼ to getting an A⟩ 6 : the foreseeable future ⟨no hope in ∼⟩ 7 : a pictorial representation syn see OPINION — **in view of** : in regard to : in consideration of — **on view** : open to public inspection : on exhibition

²view vt (1523) 1 : to look at attentively : SCRUTINIZE, OBSERVE ⟨∼ an exhibit⟩ ⟨∼ the landscape⟩ 2 a : SEE, WATCH ⟨∼ a film⟩ b : to look on in a particular light : REGARD ⟨doesn't ∼ himself as a rebel⟩ 3 : to survey or examine mentally : CONSIDER ⟨∼ all sides of a question⟩ — **view·able** \-ə-bəl\ adj

view·data \ˈvyü-ˌdā-tə also -ˌda-\ n (1975) : a videotex system usu. employing telephone lines

view·er \ˈvyü-ər\ n (15c) : one that views: as a : a person legally appointed to inspect and report on property b : an optical device used in viewing c : a person who watches television

view·er·ship \-ˌship\ n (1954) : a television audience esp. with respect to size or makeup

view·find·er \ˈvyü-ˌfīn-dər\ n (1889) : a device on a camera for showing the area of the subject to be included in the picture

view hal·loo \ˌvyü-hə-ˈlü\ interj (1761) — used in fox hunting on seeing a fox break cover

view·ing n (1535) : an act of seeing, watching, or taking a look; esp : an instance or the practice of watching television

view·less \ˈvyü-ləs\ adj (1603) 1 : not perceivable : INVISIBLE 2 : affording no view 3 : expressing no views or opinions — **view·less·ly** adv

view·point \-ˌpȯint\ n (1855) : POINT OF VIEW, STANDPOINT

viewy \ˈvyü-ē\ adj (1848) 1 : possessing visionary, impractical, or fantastic views 2 : spectacular or arresting in appearance : SHOWY

vig \ˈvig\ n (1968) : VIGORISH

vi·ga \ˈvē-gə\ n [Sp, beam, rafter] (1844) : one of the heavy rafters and esp. a log supporting the roof in American Indian and Spanish architecture of the Southwest

vi·ges·i·mal \vī-ˈje-sə-məl\ adj [L vicesimus, vigesimus twentieth; akin to L viginti twenty, Gk eikosi] (ca. 1656) : based on the number 20

vig·il \ˈvi-jəl\ n [ME vigile, fr. OF, fr. LL & L; LL vigilia watch on the eve of a feast, fr. L, wakefulness, watch, fr. vigil awake, watchful; akin to L vigēre to be vigorous, vegēre to enliven — more at WAKE] (13c) 1 a : a watch formerly kept on the night before a religious feast with prayer or other devotions b : the day before a religious feast observed as a day of spiritual preparation c : evening or nocturnal devotions or prayers — usu. used in pl. 2 : the act of keeping awake at times when sleep is customary; also : a period of wakefulness 3 : an act or period of watching or surveillance : WATCH

vig·i·lance \ˈvi-jə-lən(t)s\ n (1533) : the quality or state of being vigilant

vigilance committee n (1835) : a committee of vigilantes

vig·i·lant \ˈvi-jə-lənt\ adj [ME, fr. MF, fr. L vigilant-, vigilans, fr. prp. of vigilare to keep watch, stay awake, fr. vigil awake] (15c) : alertly watchful esp. to avoid danger syn see WATCHFUL — **vig·i·lant·ly** adv

vig·i·lan·te \ˌvi-jə-ˈlan-tē\ n [Sp, watchman, guard, fr. vigilante vigilant, fr. L vigilant-, vigilans] (1865) : a member of a volunteer committee organized to suppress and punish crime summarily (as when the processes of law appear inadequate); broadly : a self-appointed doer of justice — **vig·i·lan·tism** \-ˈlan-ˌti-zəm\ n

vigil light n (ca. 1931) : a candle lighted devotionally (as in a Roman Catholic church) before a shrine or image — called also vigil candle

vi·gin·til·lion \ˌvi-jin-ˈtil-yən\ n, often attrib [L viginti twenty + E -illion (as in million) — more at VIGESIMAL] (ca. 1903) — see NUMBER table

vi·gne·ron \ˌvēn-yə-ˈrōn\ n [ME, fr. MF, fr. OF vineron, fr. vine, vigne vine, vineyard] (15c) : WINEGROWER

¹vi·gnette \vin-ˈyet, vēn-\ n [F, fr. MF vignete, fr. dim. of vigne vine — more at VINE] (1751) 1 : a running ornament (as of vine leaves, tendrils, and grapes) put on or just before a title page or at the beginning or end of a chapter; also : a small decorative design or picture so placed 2 a : a picture (as an engraving or photograph) that shades off gradually into the surrounding paper b : the pictorial part of a postage stamp design as distinguished from the frame and lettering 3 a : a short descriptive literary sketch b : a brief incident or scene (as in a play or movie) — **vi·gnett·ist** \-ˈye-tist\ n

²vignette vt **vi·gnett·ed; vi·gnett·ing** (1853) 1 : to finish (as a photograph) in the manner of a vignette 2 : to describe briefly — **vi·gnett·er** n

vig·or \ˈvi-gər\ n [ME, fr. MF vigor, fr. L, fr. vigēre to be vigorous] (14c) 1 : active bodily or mental strength or force 2 : active healthy well-balanced growth esp. of plants 3 : intensity of action or effect : FORCE 4 : effective legal status

vig·o·rish \ˈvi-gə-rish\ n [perh. fr. Ukrainian vygrash or Russ vyigrysh winnings, profit] (1912) 1 : a charge taken (as by a bookie or a gambling house) on bets; also : the degree of such a charge ⟨a ∼ of five percent⟩ 2 : interest paid to a moneylender

vi·go·ro·so \ˌvi-gə-ˈrō-(ˌ)sō, ˌvē-, -(ˌ)zō\ adj or adv [It, lit., vigorous, fr. MF vigorous] (ca. 1724) : energetic in style — used as a direction in music

vig·or·ous \ˈvi-g(ə-)rəs\ adj [ME, fr. MF, fr. OF, fr. vigor] (14c) 1 : possessing vigor : full of physical or mental strength or active force : STRONG ⟨a ∼ youth⟩ ⟨a ∼ plant⟩ 2 : done with vigor : carried out forcefully and energetically ⟨∼ exercises⟩ — **vig·or·ous·ly** adv — **vig·or·ous·ness** n

syn VIGOROUS, ENERGETIC, STRENUOUS, LUSTY, NERVOUS mean having or showing great vitality and force. VIGOROUS further implies showing no signs of depletion or diminishing of freshness or robustness ⟨as vigorous as a youth half his age⟩. ENERGETIC suggests a capacity for intense activity ⟨an energetic campaigner⟩. STRENUOUS suggests a preference for coping with the arduous or the challenging ⟨the strenuous life on an oil rig⟩. LUSTY implies exuberant energy and capacity for enjoyment ⟨a lusty appetite for life⟩. NERVOUS suggests esp. the forcibleness and sustained effectiveness resulting from mental vigor ⟨full of nervous energy⟩.

vig·our \ˈvi-gər\ chiefly Brit var of VIGOR

Vi·king \ˈvī-kiŋ\ n [ON viking] (1807) 1 a : one of the pirate Norsemen plundering the coasts of Europe in the 8th to 10th centuries b not cap : SEA ROVER 2 : SCANDINAVIAN

vile \ˈvī(ə)l\ adj **vil·er** \ˈvī-lər\; **vil·est** \-ləst\ [ME, fr. OF vil, fr. L vilis] (14c) 1 a : morally despicable or abhorrent ⟨nothing is so ∼ as intellectual dishonesty⟩ b : physically repulsive : FOUL ⟨a ∼ slum⟩ 2 : of little worth or account : COMMON; also : MEAN 3 : tending to degrade ⟨∼ employments⟩ 4 : disgustingly or utterly bad : OBNOXIOUS, CONTEMPTIBLE ⟨∼ weather⟩ ⟨had a ∼ temper⟩ syn see BASE — **vile·ly** \ˈvī(ə)l-lē\ adv — **vile·ness** n

vil·i·fi·ca·tion \ˌvi-lə-fə-ˈkā-shən\ n (1630) 1 : the act of vilifying : ABUSE 2 : an instance of vilifying : a defamatory utterance

vil·i·fy \ˈvi-lə-ˌfī\ vt **-fied; -fy·ing** [ME vilifien, fr. ML vilificare, fr. L vilis cheap, vile] (15c) 1 : to lower in estimation or importance 2 : to utter slanderous and abusive statements against : DEFAME syn see MALIGN — **vil·i·fi·er** \-ˌfī(-ə)r\ n

vil·i·pend \ˈvi-lə-ˌpend\ vt [ME, fr. MF vilipender, fr. ML vilipendere, fr. L vilis + pendere to weigh, estimate] (15c) 1 : to hold or treat as of little worth or account : CONTEMN 2 : to express a low opinion of : DISPARAGE

vill \ˈvil\ n [AF, fr. OF ville village] (1596) 1 : a division of a hundred : TOWNSHIP 2 : VILLAGE

vil·la \ˈvi-lə\ n [It, fr. L; akin to L vicus village — more at VICINITY] (1611) 1 : a country estate 2 : the rural or suburban residence of a wealthy person 3 Brit : a detached or semidetached urban residence with yard and garden space

vil·la·dom \ˈvi-lə-dəm\ n (1880) Brit : the world constituted by villas and their occupants

vil·lage \ˈvi-lij\ n, often attrib [ME, fr. MF, fr. OF, fr. ville farm, village, fr. L villa] (14c) 1 a : a settlement usu. larger than a hamlet and smaller than a town b : an incorporated minor municipality 2 : the residents of a village 3 : something (as an aggregation of bur-

\ə\ abut \ᵊ\ kitten, F table \ər\ further \a\ ash \ā\ ace \ä\ mop, mar \au̇\ out \ch\ chin \e\ bet \ē\ easy \g\ go \i\ hit \ī\ ice \j\ job \ŋ\ sing \ō\ go \ȯ\ law \ȯi\ boy \th\ thin \t̶h̶\ the \ü\ loot \u̇\ foot \y\ yet \zh\ vision \a, ḵ, ⁿ, œ, œ̄, ᵫ, ᵻ, ᵿ\ see Guide to Pronunciation rows or nests) suggesting a village **4** : a territorial area having the status of a village esp. as a unit of local government

vil·lag·er \'vi-li-jər\ *n* (1570) : an inhabitant of a village

vil·lage·ry \'vi-lij-rē, -li-jə-\ *n* (1590) : VILLAGES

vil·lain \'vi-lən\ *n* [ME *vilain, vilein,* fr. MF, fr. ML *villanus,* fr. L *villa*] (14c) **1** : an uncouth person : BOOR **2** : VILLEIN **3** : a deliberate scoundrel or criminal **4** : a scoundrel in a story or play **5** : a person or thing blamed for a particular evil or difficulty ⟨automation as the ~ in job . . . displacement —M. H. Goldberg⟩

vil·lain·ess \-lə-nəs\ *n* (1586) : a woman who is a villain

vil·lain·ous \-lə-nəs\ *adj* (15c) **1 a** : befitting a villain (as in evil, depraved, or vile character) ⟨a ~ attack⟩ **b** : being or having the character of a villain : DEPRAVED ⟨the ~ foe⟩ **2** : highly objectionable : WRETCHED **syn** see VICIOUS — **vil·lain·ous·ly** *adv* — **vil·lain·ous·ness** *n*

vil·lainy \-lə-nē\ *n, pl* **-lain·ies** (13c) **1** : villainous conduct; *also* : a villainous act **2** : the quality or state of being villainous : DEPRAVITY

vil·la·nel·la \,vi-lə-'ne-lə\ *n, pl* **-nel·le** \-'ne-lē\ [It, fr. *villano* villein, peasant, fr. ML *villanus*] (1596) **1** : a 16th century Italian rustic part-song unaccompanied and in free form **2** : an instrumental piece in the style of a rustic dance

vil·la·nelle \,vi-lə-'nel\ *n* [F, fr. It *villanella*] (1877) : a chiefly French verse form running on two rhymes and consisting typically of five tercets and a quatrain in which the first and third lines of the opening tercet recur alternately at the end of the other tercets and together as the last two lines of the quatrain

vil·lat·ic \vi-'la-tik\ *adj* [L *villaticus,* fr. *villa*] (1671) : RURAL

-ville \,vil, *esp Southern* vil, *n suffix* [*-ville,* suffix occurring in names of towns, fr. F, fr. OF, fr. *ville* village] : place, category, or quality of a specified nature ⟨dulls*ville*⟩

vil·lein \'vi-lən, vi-'lān, vi-'lān\ *n* [ME *vilain, vilein* — more at VILLAIN] (14c) **1** : a free common villager or village peasant of any of the feudal classes lower in rank than the thane **2** : a free peasant of a feudal class lower than a sokeman and higher than a cotter **3** : an unfree peasant standing as the slave of a feudal lord but free in legal relations with respect to all others

vil·len·age \'vi-lə-nij\ *n* [ME *vilenage,* fr. MF, fr. OF, fr. *vilein, vilain*] (14c) **1** : tenure at the will of a feudal lord by villein services **2** : the status of a villein

vil·li·form \'vi-lə-,fórm\ *adj* [ISV] (1849) : having the form or appearance of villi

vil·los·i·ty \vi-'lä-sə-tē\ *n, pl* **-ties** (1777) **1** : the state of being villous **2** : a villous patch or area

vil·lous \'vi-ləs\ *adj* [ME, fr. L *villosus* hairy, shaggy, fr. *villus*] (14c) **1** : covered or furnished with villi **2** : having soft long hairs ⟨leaves ~ underneath⟩ — compare PUBESCENT

vil·lus \'vi-ləs\ *n, pl* **vil·li** \'vi-,lī, -(,)lē\ [NL, fr. L, tuft of shaggy hair — more at VELVET] (ca. 1704) : a small slender often vascular process: as **a** : one of the minute finger-shaped processes of the mucous membrane of the small intestine that serve in the absorption of nutriment **b** : one of the branching processes of the surface of the chorion of the developing embryo of most mammals that help to form the placenta

vim \'vim\ *n* [L, accus. of *vis* strength; akin to Gk *is* strength, Skt *vaya* meal, strength] (1843) : robust energy and enthusiasm

vi·na \'vē-nə\ *n* [Skt *vīṇā*] (1788) : a stringed instrument of India having usu. four strings on a long bamboo fingerboard with movable frets and a gourd resonator at each end

vina

vi·na·ceous \vī-'nā-shəs, vi-\ *adj* [L *vinaceus* of wine, fr. *vinum* wine — more at WINE] (1688) : of the color wine

vin·ai·grette \,vi-ni-'gret\ *n* [F, fr. *vinaigre* vinegar] (1699) **1** : a sauce made typically of oil and vinegar, onions, parsley, and herbs and used esp. on cold meats or fish — called also *vinaigrette dressing, vinaigrette sauce* **2** : a small ornamental box or bottle with perforated top used for holding an aromatic preparation (as smelling salts)

vi·nal \'vī-,nal\ *n* [poly*vinyl* alcohol] (ca. 1939) : a synthetic textile fiber that is a long-chain polymer consisting largely of vinyl alcohol units

vin·blas·tine \(,)vin-'blas-,tēn\ *n* [contr. of *vincaleukoblastine,* fr. *vinca* + *leukoblast* developing leukocyte, fr. *leuk-* + *-blast*] (1962) : an alkaloid $C_{46}H_{58}N_4O_9$ from Madagascar periwinkle used esp. in the form of its sulfate to treat human neoplastic diseases

vin·ca \'vin-kə\ *n* [NL, short for L *vincapervinca* periwinkle] (1578) : ¹PERIWINKLE

Vin·cen·tian \vin-'sen(t)-shən\ *n* (1854) **1** : a member of the Roman Catholic Congregation of the Mission founded by St. Vincent de Paul in Paris, France, in 1625 and devoted to missions and seminaries **2** : a native or inhabitant of the island of St. Vincent — **Vincentian** *adj*

Vin·cent's angina \'vin(t)-sən(t)s-, (,)van-'sän²-z-\ *n* [Jean Hyacinthe *Vincent* †1950 Fr. bacteriologist] (ca. 1903) : Vincent's infection in which the ulceration has spread to surrounding tissues (as of the pharynx and tonsils) — called also *trench mouth*

Vincent's infection *n* (ca. 1922) : a progressive painful disease of the mouth that is marked esp. by dirty gray ulceration of the mucous membranes, spontaneous hemorrhaging of the gums, and a foul odor to the breath and that is associated with the presence of large numbers of a bacillus (*Fusobacterium nucleatum* syn. *F. fusiforme*) and a spirochete (*Treponema vincentii* syn. *Borrelia vincentii*) in the lesions — called also *trench mouth*

vin·ci·ble \'vin(t)-sə-bəl\ *adj* [L *vincibilis,* fr. *vincere* to conquer — more at VICTOR] (1548) : capable of being overcome or subdued

vin·cris·tine \(,)vin-'kris-,tēn\ *n* [*vinca* + L *crista* crest + E ²*-ine* — more at CREST] (ca. 1962) : an alkaloid $C_{46}H_{56}N_4O_{10}$ from Madagascar

periwinkle used esp. in the form of its sulfate to treat some human neoplastic diseases (as leukemias)

vin·cu·lum \'vin-kyə-ləm\ *n, pl* **-lums** *or* **-la** \-lə\ [L, fr. *vincire* to bind] (1661) **1** : a unifying bond : LINK, TIE **2** : a straight horizontal mark placed over two or more members of a compound mathematical expression and equivalent to parentheses or brackets about them (as in $a-b-c=a-[b-c]$)

vin·da·loo \,vin-də-'lü\ *n* [prob. fr. Konkani *vindalu,* fr. Indo-Portuguese (Pg creole of India) *vinh d'alho,* lit., wine of garlic, fr. Pg *vinho de alho*] (1888) : a curried dish of Indian origin made with meat or shellfish, garlic, and wine or vinegar

vin·di·ca·ble \'vin-di-kə-bəl\ *adj* (1647) : capable of being vindicated

vin·di·cate \'vin-də-,kāt\ *vt* **-cat·ed; -cat·ing** [L *vindicatus,* pp. of *vindicare* to lay claim to, avenge, fr. *vindic-, vindex* claimant, avenger] (1570) **1 obs** : to set free : DELIVER **2** : AVENGE **3 a** : to free from allegation or blame **b** (1) : CONFIRM, SUBSTANTIATE (2) : to provide justification or defense for : JUSTIFY **c** : to protect from attack or encroachment : DEFEND **4** : to maintain a right to **syn** see EXCULPATE, MAINTAIN — **vin·di·ca·tor** \-,kā-tər\ *n*

vin·di·ca·tion \,vin-də-'kā-shən\ *n* (1613) : an act of vindicating : the state of being vindicated; *specif* : justification against denial or censure : DEFENSE

vin·dic·a·tive \vin-'di-kə-tiv\ *adj* (1521) **1 obs** : VINDICTIVE, VENGEFUL **2 archaic** : PUNITIVE

vin·di·ca·to·ry *adj* (1647) **1** \'vin-di-kə-,tör-ē, -,tör-\ : providing vindication : JUSTIFICATORY **2** \vin-'di-kə-\ : PUNITIVE, RETRIBUTIVE

vin·dic·tive \vin-'dik-tiv\ *adj* [L *vindicta* revenge, vindication, fr. *vindicare*] (1616) **1 a** : disposed to seek revenge : VENGEFUL **b** : intended for or involving revenge **2** : intended to cause anguish or hurt : SPITEFUL — **vin·dic·tive·ly** *adv* — **vin·dic·tive·ness** *n*

¹**vine** \'vīn\ *n* [ME, fr. MF, fr. OF *vigne,* fr. L *vinea* vine, vineyard, fr. fem. of *vineus* of wine, fr. *vinum* wine — more at WINE] (14c) **1** : GRAPE **2 a** : a plant whose stem requires support and which climbs by tendrils or twining or creeps along the ground; *also* : the stem of such a plant **b** : any of various sprawling herbaceous plants (as a tomato or potato) that lack specialized adaptations for climbing

²**vine** *vi* **vined; vin·ing** (1796) : to form or grow in the manner of a vine

vine·dress·er \'vīn-,dre-sər\ *n* (1560) : a person who cultivates and prunes grapevines

vin·e·gar \'vi-ni-gər\ *n* [ME *vinegre,* fr. MF *vinaigre,* fr. *vin* wine (fr. L *vinum*) + *aigre* keen, sour — more at EAGER] (14c) **1** : a sour liquid obtained by fermentation of dilute alcoholic liquids and used as a condiment or preservative **2** : ill humor : SOURNESS **3** : VIM

vin·e·gared \-gərd\ *adj* (1861) : flavored or marinated with vinegar

vinegar eel *n* (ca. 1839) : a minute nematode worm (*Turbatrix aceti*) often found in great numbers in vinegar or acid fermenting vegetable matter

vinegar fly *n* [fr. its breeding in pickles] (1901) : DROSOPHILA

vin·e·gar·ish \'vi-ni-g(ə-)rish\ *adj* (1648) : VINEGARY 2

vin·e·gary \'vi-ni-g(ə-)rē\ *adj* (ca. 1730) **1 a** : resembling vinegar : SOUR **b** : flavored with vinegar **2** : disagreeable, bitter, or irascible in character or manner

vin·ery \'vīn-rē, 'vi-nə-\ *n, pl* **-er·ies** (15c) : an area or building in which vines are grown

vine·yard \'vin-yərd\ *n* (14c) **1** : a planting of grapevines **2** : a sphere of activity : field of endeavor ⟨toilers in the ~ of diplomacy — Daniel Schorr⟩

vine·yard·ist \-yər-dist\ *n* (1848) : a person who owns or cultivates a vineyard

vingt-et-un \,van-,tā-'ən\ *n* [F, lit., twenty-one] (1772) : BLACKJACK 5

vi·ni·cul·ture \'vi-nə-,kəl-chər, 'vī-\ *n* [L *vinum* + ISV *-i-* + *culture*] (1871) : VITICULTURE

vi·nif·era \vī-'ni-f(ə-)rə\ *adj* [NL, fr. L *vinifer* wine-producing, fr. *vinum* wine] (1900) : of, relating to, being, or derived from a common European grape (*Vitis vinifera*) that is the chief source of Old World wine grapes and table grapes — **vinifera** *n*

vi·ni·fi·ca·tion \,vi-nə-fə-'kā-shən, ,vī-\ *n* [F, fr. *vin* wine + *-i-* + *-fication*] (1880) : the conversion of fruit juices (as grape juice) into wine by fermentation

vin·i·fy \'vi-nə-,fī, 'vī-\ *vt* **-fied; -fy·ing** [prob. back-formation fr. *vinification*] (1969) **1** : to make wine from (grapes often of a specified kind) **2** : to make (wine) from grapes

vi·no \'vē-(,)nō\ *n* [It & Sp, fr. L *vinum*] (ca. 1919) : WINE

vi·nos·i·ty \vī-'nä-sə-tē\ *n, pl* **-ties** (1658) : the characteristic body, flavor, and color of a wine

vi·nous \'vī-nəs\ *adj* [L *vinosus,* fr. *vinum* wine] (1664) **1** : of, relating to, or made with wine ⟨~ medications⟩ **2** : showing the effects of the use of wine **3** : VINACEOUS — **vi·nous·ly** *adv*

¹**vin·tage** \'vin-tij\ *n* [ME, alter. of *vendage,* fr. MF *vendenge,* fr. L *vindemia* grape-gathering, vintage, fr. *vinum* wine, grapes + *demere* to take off, fr. *de-* + *emere* to take — more at WINE, REDEEM] (15c) **1 a** (1) : a season's yield of grapes or wine from a vineyard (2) : WINE; *esp* : a usu. superior wine all or most of which comes from a single year **b** : a collection of contemporaneous and similar persons or things : CROP **2** : the act or time of harvesting grapes or making wine **3 a** : a period of origin or manufacture ⟨a piano of 1845 ~⟩ **b** : length of existence : AGE

²**vintage** *adj* (1601) **1** of *wine* : of, relating to, or produced in a particular vintage **2** : of old, recognized, and enduring interest, importance, or quality : CLASSIC **3 a** : dating from the past : OLD **b** : OUTMODED, OLD-FASHIONED **4** : of the best and most characteristic — used with a proper noun ⟨~ Shaw: a wise and winning comedy —*Time*⟩

vin·tag·er \'vin-ti-jər\ *n* (1589) : a person concerned with the production of grapes and wine

vintage year *n* (1933) **1** : a year of outstanding distinction or success **2** : a year in which a vintage wine is produced

vint·ner \'vint-nər\ *n* [ME *vineter,* fr. MF *vinetier,* fr. ML *vinetarius,* fr. L *vinetum* vineyard, fr. *vinum* wine] (15c) **1** : a wine merchant **2** : a person who makes wine

viny \'vī-nē\ *adj* **vin·i·er; -est** (1570) **1** : of, relating to, or resembling vines ⟨~ plants⟩ **2** : covered with or abounding in vines

vi·nyl \'vī-n²l\ *n* [ISV, fr. L *vinum* wine] (1863) **1** : a univalent group $CH_2=CH$ derived from ethylene by removal of one hydrogen atom **2**

: a polymer of a vinyl compound or a product (as a resin or a textile fiber) made from such a polymer — **vi·nyl·ic** \vī-'ni-lik\ *adj*
vinyl alcohol *n* (1873) : an unstable compound CH$_2$=CHOH isolated only in the form of its polymers or derivatives
vinyl chloride *n* (1872) : a flammable gaseous carcinogenic compound C$_2$H$_3$Cl that is used esp. to make vinyl resins
vi·nyl·i·dene \vī-'ni-lə-ˌdēn\ *n* [ISV *vinyl* + *-ide* + *-ene*] (1898) : a bivalent group CH$_2$=C derived from ethylene by removal of two hydrogen atoms from one carbon atom
vinyl resin *n* (1934) : any of various thermoplastic resinous materials that are essentially polymers of vinyl compounds
vi·ol \'vī(-ə)l, 'vī-(ˌ)ōl\ *n* [ME, fr. MF *viole* viol, viola, fr. OProv *viola* viol] (15c) : a bowed stringed instrument chiefly of the 16th and 17th centuries made in treble, alto, tenor, and bass sizes and distinguished from members of the violin family esp. in having a deep body, a flat back, sloping shoulders, usu. six strings, a fretted fingerboard, and a low-arched bridge
¹vi·o·la \vī-'ō-lə, vē-; 'vī-ə-\ *n* [ME, fr. L] (15c) : VIOLET 1a; *esp* : any of various garden hybrids with solitary white, yellow, or purple often variegated flowers resembling but smaller than typical pansies
²vi·o·la \vē-'ō-lə\ *n* [It & Sp, viol, viola, fr. OProv, viol] (ca. 1724) : a musical instrument of the violin family that is intermediate in size and compass between the violin and cello and is tuned a fifth below the violin — **vi·o·list** \-list\ *n*
vi·o·la·ble \'vī-ə-lə-bəl\ *adj* (1552) : capable of being or likely to be violated — **vi·o·la·bil·i·ty** \ˌvī-ə-lə-'bi-lə-tē\ *n* — **vi·o·la·ble·ness** \'vī-ə-lə-bəl-nəs\ *n* — **vi·o·la·bly** \-blē\ *adv*
vi·o·la·ceous \ˌvī-ə-'lā-shəs\ *adj* [L *violaceus*, fr. *viola* violet] (1657) : of the color violet
vi·o·la da gam·ba \vē-ˌō-lə-də-'gäm-bə, -'gam-\ *n, pl* **vi·o·las da gamba** \-ləz-də-\ *or* **vi·o·le da gamba** \-(ˌ)lā-\ [It, leg viol] (1597) : a bass member of the viol family having a range approximating the cello — **vi·o·list da gamba** \-lis(t)-də-\ *n*
viola d'a·mo·re \-də-'mȯr-ē, -mȯr-, -(ˌ)ā\ *n, pl* **violas d'amore** *or* **viole d'amore** [It, viol of love] (ca. 1700) : a tenor viol having usu. seven gut and seven wire strings
¹vi·o·late \'vī-ə-ˌlāt\ *vt* **-lat·ed; -lat·ing** [ME, fr. L *violatus*, pp. of *violare*, prob. fr. *violentus* violent] (15c) **1 :** BREAK, DISREGARD ⟨~ the law⟩ **2 :** to do harm to the person or esp. the chastity of; *specif* : RAPE **3 :** to fail to show proper respect for : PROFANE ⟨~ a shrine⟩ **4 :** INTERRUPT, DISTURB ⟨~ the peace of a spring evening —Nancy Larten⟩ — **vi·o·la·tive** \-ˌlā-tiv\ *adj* — **vi·o·la·tor** \-ˌlā-tər\ *n*
²vi·o·late \'vī-ə-lət\ *adj* (1503) *archaic* : subjected to violation
vi·o·la·tion \ˌvī-ə-'lā-shən\ *n* (15c) : the act of violating : the state of being violated: as **a :** INFRINGEMENT, TRANSGRESSION; *specif* : an infringement of the rules in sports that is less serious than a foul and usu. involves technicalities of play **b :** an act of irreverence or desecration : PROFANATION **c :** DISTURBANCE, INTERRUPTION **d :** RAPE, RAVISHMENT
vi·o·lence \'vī-ə-lən(t)s\ *n* (14c) **1 a :** exertion of physical force so as to injure or abuse (as in effecting illegal entry into a house) **b :** an instance of violent treatment or procedure **2 :** injury by or as if by distortion, infringement, or profanation : OUTRAGE ⟨a ~ : intense, turbulent, or furious and often destructive action or force ⟨the ~ of the storm⟩ **b :** vehement feeling or expression : FERVOR; *also* : an instance of such action or feeling **c :** a clashing or jarring quality : DISCORDANCE **4 :** undue alteration (as of wording or sense in editing a text)
vi·o·lent \-lənt\ *adj* [ME, fr. MF, fr. L *violentus*; akin to L *vis* strength — more at VIM] (14c) **1 :** marked by extreme force or sudden intense activity ⟨a ~ attack⟩ **2 a :** notably furious or vehement ⟨a ~ denunciation⟩ **b :** EXTREME, INTENSE ⟨~ pain⟩ ⟨~ colors⟩ **3 :** caused by force : not natural ⟨a ~ death⟩ **4 a :** emotionally agitated to the point of loss of self-control ⟨a mental patient becoming ~⟩ **b :** prone to commit acts of violence ⟨~ prison inmates⟩ — **vi·o·lent·ly** *adv*
violent storm *n* (ca. 1881) : STORM 1c(1) — see BEAUFORT SCALE table
vi·o·let \'vī-ə-lət\ *n* [ME, fr. MF *violete*, dim. of *viole* violet, fr. L *viola*] (14c) **1 a :** any of a genus (*Viola* of the family Violaceae, the violet family) of chiefly herbs with alternate stipulate leaves and showy flowers in spring and cleistogamous flowers in summer; *esp* : one with smaller usu. solid-colored flowers as distinguished from the true. larger-flowered violas and pansies **b :** any of several plants of genera other than that of the violet — compare DOGTOOTH VIOLET **2 :** any of a group of colors of reddish blue hue, low lightness, and medium saturation
vi·o·lin \ˌvī-ə-'lin\ *n* [It *violino*, dim. of *viola*] (1579) : a bowed stringed instrument having four strings tuned at intervals of a fifth and a usual range from G below middle C upward for more than 4$^1\!/_2$ octaves and having a shallow body, shoulders at right angles to the neck, a fingerboard without frets, and a curved bridge — **vi·o·lin·ist** \-ist\ *n* — **vi·o·lin·is·tic** \-ə-lə-'nis-tik\ *adj*
vi·o·lon·cel·lo \ˌvī-ə-lən-'che-(ˌ)lō, ˌvē-\ *n* [It, dim. of *violone*, aug. of *viola*] (ca. 1724) : CELLO — **vi·o·lon·cel·list** \-'che-list\ *n*
vio·my·cin \ˌvī-ə-'mī-sᵊn\ *n* [*violet* + *-mycin*; fr. the color of the soil organism] (1950) : a polypeptide antibiotic C$_{25}$H$_{43}$N$_{13}$O$_{10}$ that is produced by several soil actinomycetes (genus *Streptomyces*) and is administered in the form of its sulfate in the treatment of tuberculosis
VIP \ˌvē-ˌī-'pē\ *n, pl* **VIPs** \-'pēz\ [*very important person*] (1933) : a person of great influence or prestige; *esp* : a high official with special privileges
vi·per \'vī-pər\ *n* [MF *vipere*, fr. L *vipera*] (1526) **1 a :** a common Eurasian venomous snake (*Vipera berus*) that attains a length of two feet (0.6 meter), varies in color from red, brown, or gray with dark markings to black, and is usu. not fatal to humans; *broadly* : any of a family (Viperidae) of venomous snakes that includes Old World snakes (subfamily Viperinae) and the pit vipers **b :** a venomous or reputedly venomous snake **2 :** a vicious or treacherous person

violin: *1* bridge, *2* sound hole, *3* sound board, *4* fingerboard, *5* pegs, *6* scroll, *7* tailpiece, *g* G-string, *d* D-string, *a* A-string, *e* E-string

vi·per·ine \-pə-ˌrīn\ *adj* (ca. 1550) : of, relating to, or resembling a viper : VENOMOUS
vi·per·ish \-p(ə-)rish\ *adj* (1755) : spitefully vituperative : VENOMOUS
vi·per·ous \-p(ə-)rəs\ *adj* (1535) **1 :** VIPERINE **2 :** having the qualities attributed to a viper : MALIGNANT, VENOMOUS — **vi·per·ous·ly** *adv*
viper's bugloss *n* (1597) : a coarse Old World herb (*Echium vulgare*) of the borage family that is naturalized in No. America and has showy blue tubular flowers with exserted stamens — called also *blueweed*
vi·ra·go \və-'rä-(ˌ)gō, -'rā-; 'vir-ə-ˌgō\ *n, pl* **-goes** *or* **-gos** [ME, fr. L *viragin-, virago,* fr. *vir* man — more at VIRILE] (14c) **1 :** a loud overbearing woman : TERMAGANT **2 :** a woman of great stature, strength, and courage — **vi·rag·i·nous** \və-'ra-jə-nəs\ *adj*
vi·ral \'vī-rəl\ *adj* (1937) : of, relating to, or caused by a virus — **vi·ral·ly** \-rə-lē\ *adv*
vir·e·lay \'vir-ə-ˌlā\ *n* [ME, fr. MF *virelai*] (14c) : a chiefly French verse form consisting of stanzas of indeterminate length and number with alternating long and short lines and interlaced rhyme (as *abab bcbc cdcd dada*)
vi·re·mia \vī-'rē-mē-ə\ *n* [NL, fr. *virus* + *-emia*] (1946) : the presence of virus in the blood of a host — **vi·re·mic** \-mik\ *adj*
vir·eo \'vir-ē-ˌō\ *n, pl* **-e·os** [L, a small bird, fr. *virēre* to be green] (1834) : any of various small insectivorous American oscine birds (family Vireonidae and esp. genus *Vireo*) that are chiefly olivaceous and grayish in color
vires *pl of* VIS
vi·res·cence \və-'re-sᵊn(t)s, vī-\ *n* (ca. 1888) : the state or condition of becoming green; *esp* : such a condition due to the development of chloroplasts in plant organs (as petals) normally white or colored
vi·res·cent \-s'nt\ *adj* [L *virescent-, virescens,* prp. of *virescere* to become green, incho. of *virēre* to be green] (1826) **1 :** beginning to be green : GREENISH **2 :** developing or displaying virescence
vir·ga \'vər-gə\ *n* [NL, fr. L, branch, rod, streak in the sky suggesting rain] (1938) : wisps of precipitation evaporating before reaching the ground
¹vir·gate \'vər-gət\ *n* [ML *virgata*, fr. *virga,* a land measure, fr. L, rod] (1655) : an old English unit of land area equal to one quarter of a hide or one quarter of an acre
²virgate *adj* [NL *virgatus*, fr. L, made of twigs, fr. *virga*] (1821) : shaped like a rod or wand ⟨a ~ one-flowered branch⟩
¹vir·gin \'vər-jən\ *n* [ME, fr. OF *virgine,* fr. L *virgin-, virgo* young woman, virgin] (13c) **1 a :** an unmarried woman devoted to religion **b** *cap* : VIRGO **2 a :** an absolutely chaste young woman **b :** an unmarried girl or woman **3** *cap* : VIRGIN MARY **4 a :** a person who has not had sexual intercourse **b :** a person who is inexperienced in a usu. specified sphere of activity ⟨a ~ in politics⟩ **5 :** a female animal that has never copulated
²virgin *adj* (14c) **1 :** free of impurity or stain : UNSULLIED **2 :** CHASTE **3 :** characteristic of or befitting a virgin : MODEST **4 :** FRESH, UNSPOILED; *specif* : not altered by human activity ⟨a ~ forest⟩ **5 a** (1) : being used or worked for the first time (2) *of a metal* : produced directly from ore by primary smelting **b :** INITIAL, FIRST **6** *of a vegetable oil* : obtained from the first light pressing and without heating
¹vir·gin·al \'vər-jə-nᵊl, 'vərj-nəl\ *adj* (15c) **1 :** of, relating to, or characteristic of a virgin or virginity; *esp* : PURE, CHASTE **2 :** PRISTINE, UNSULLIED — **vir·gin·al·ly** *adv*
²virginal *n* [prob. fr. L *virginalis* of a virgin, fr. *virgin-, virgo*] (1530) : a small rectangular spinet having no legs and only one wire to a note and popular in the 16th and 17th centuries — often used in pl.; called also *pair of virginals* — **vir·gin·al·ist** \'vər-jə-nᵊl-ist, 'vərj-nə-list\ *n*
virgin birth *n* (1652) **1 :** birth from a virgin **2** *often cap V&B* : the theological doctrine that Jesus was miraculously begotten of God and born of a virgin mother
Vir·gin·ia bluebells \vər-'jin-yə-, -'ji-nē-ə-\ *n pl* [*Virginia,* state of the U.S.] (ca. 1922) : BLUEBELL 2b
Virginia creeper *n* (1704) : a common No. American tendril-climbing vine (*Parthenocissus quinquefolia*) of the grape family with palmately compound leaves and bluish black berries — called also *woodbine*
Virginia fence *n* (1671) : WORM FENCE — called also *Virginia rail fence*
Virginia ham *n* (1824) : a dry-cured, smoked, and aged ham esp. from a peanut-fed hog
Virginia pine *n* (1897) : a pine (*Pinus virginiana*) of the eastern U.S. that has short needles occurring in pairs — called also *Jersey pine*
Virginia rail *n* (1813) : an American long-billed rail (*Rallus limicola*) that has gray cheeks
Virginia reel *n* (1817) : an American dance in which two lines of couples face each other and all couples in turn participate in a series of figures
Virginia snakeroot *n* (1694) : a birthwort (*Aristolochia serpentaria*) of the eastern U.S. with oblong leaves cordate at the base and a solitary basal very irregular flower
vir·gin·i·ty \(ˌ)vər-'ji-nə-tē\ *n, pl* **-ties** (14c) **1 :** the quality or state of being virgin; *esp* : MAIDENHOOD **2 :** the unmarried life : CELIBACY, SPINSTERHOOD
Virgin Mary *n* : the mother of Jesus
virgin's bower *n* (1597) : any of several usu. small-flowered and climbing clematises (esp. *Clematis virginiana*)
virgin wool *n* (1915) : wool not used before in manufacture
Vir·go \'vər-(ˌ)gō, 'vir-\ *n* [L (gen. *Virginis*), lit., virgin] **1 :** a zodiacal constellation on the celestial equator that lies due south of the handle of the Big Dipper and is pictured as a woman holding a spike of grain **2 a :** the 6th sign of the zodiac in astrology — see ZODIAC table **b :** one born under the sign of Virgo — **Vir·go·an** *n*
vir·gule \'vər-(ˌ)gyü(ə)l\ *n* [F, fr. L *virgula* small stripe, obelus, fr. dim. of *virga* rod] (1837) : DIAGONAL 3
vi·ri·ci·dal \ˌvī-rə-'sī-dᵊl\ *adj* [NL *virus* + E *-i-* + *-cide*] (1924) : VIRUCIDAL — **vi·ri·cide** \'vī-rə-ˌsīd\ *n*
vir·id \'vir-əd\ *adj* [L *viridis* green] (1600) : vividly green : VERDANT

\ə\ abut \ᵊ\ kitten, F table \ər\ further \a\ ash \ā\ ace \ä\ mop, mar
\aù\ out \ch\ chin \e\ bet \ē\ easy \g\ go \i\ hit \ī\ ice \j\ job
\ŋ\ sing \ō\ go \ò\ law \òi\ boy \th\ thin \t̷h\ the \ü\ loot \ù\ foot
\y\ yet \zh\ vision \à, k̲, ⁿ, œ, œ̄, œ, ūe, ᵒ\ *see* Guide to Pronunciation

vir·i·des·cent \,vir-ə-'de-s³nt\ *adj* [L *viridis* green] (ca. 1847) : slightly green : GREENISH

vi·rid·i·an \və-'ri-dē-ən\ *n* [L *viridis*] (1882) : a chrome green that is a hydrated oxide of chromium

vi·rid·i·ty \və-'ri-də-tē\ *n* [ME *viridite*, fr. MF *viridité*, fr. L *viriditat-, viriditas*, fr. *viridis*] (15c) **1 a** : the quality or state of being green **b** : the color of grass or foliage **2** : naive innocence

vir·ile \'vir-əl, 'vir-,īl, *Brit also* 'vīr-,īl\ *adj* [MF or L; MF *viril*, fr. L *virilis*, fr. *vir* man, male; akin to OE & OHG *wer* man, Skt *vīra*] (15c) **1** : having the nature, properties, or qualities of an adult male; *specif* : capable of functioning as a male in copulation **2** : ENERGETIC, VIGOROUS **3 a** : characteristic of or associated with men : MASCULINE **b** : having traditionally masculine traits esp. to a marked degree **4** : MASTERFUL, FORCEFUL — **vir·ile·ly** *adv*

vir·il·ism \'vir-ə-,li-zəm\ *n* (1922) : the appearance of secondary male characteristics in the female

vi·ril·i·ty \və-'ri-lə-tē, *Brit also* vī-\ *n* (1586) : the quality or state of being virile: **a** : MANHOOD **b** : manly vigor : MASCULINITY

vi·ri·on \'vī-rē-,än, 'vir-ē-\ *n* [F, fr. *virien* viral (fr. *virus* virus) + *-on* ²*-on*] (1959) : a complete virus particle that consists of an RNA or DNA core with a protein coat sometimes with external envelopes and that is the extracellular infective form of a virus

virl \'vər(-ə)l\ *n* [ME *virole* — more at FERRULE] (15c) *Scot* : FERRULE 1

vi·roid \'vī-,roid\ *n* [NL *virus* + E -*oid*] (1971) : any of several causative agents of plant disease that consist solely of a single-stranded RNA of low molecular weight arranged in a closed loop or a linear chain

vi·rol·o·gy \vī-'rä-lə-jē\ *n* [NL *virus* + ISV -*logy*] (ca. 1935) : a branch of science that deals with viruses — **vi·ro·log·i·cal** \,vī-rə-'lä-ji-kəl\ *or* **vi·ro·log·ic** \-jik\ *adj* — **vi·ro·log·i·cal·ly** \-ji-k(ə-)lē\ *adv* — **vi·rol·o·gist** \vī-'rä-lə-jist\ *n*

vir·tu \,vər-'tü, vir-\ *n* [It *virtù*, lit., virtue, fr. L *virtut-, virtus*] (1722) **1** : a love of or taste for curios or objets d'art **2** : productions of art esp. of a curious or antique nature : OBJETS D'ART

vir·tu·al \'vər-chə-wəl, -chəl; 'vərch-wəl\ *adj* [ME, possessed of certain physical virtues, fr. ML *virtualis*, fr. L *virtus* strength, virtue] (1654) **1** : being such in essence or effect though not formally recognized or admitted ⟨a ~ dictator⟩ **2** : of, relating to, or using virtual memory **3** : of, relating to, or being a hypothetical particle whose existence is inferred from indirect evidence ⟨~ photons⟩ — compare REAL 3

virtual image *n* (1859) : an image (as seen in a plane mirror) formed of points from which divergent rays (as of light) seem to emanate without actually doing so

vir·tu·al·i·ty \,vər-chə-'wa-lə-tē\ *n, pl* -**ties** (1646) **1** : ESSENCE **2** : potential existence : POTENTIALITY

vir·tu·al·ly \'vər-chə-wə-lē, -chə-lē; 'vərch-wə-lē\ *adv* (15c) **1** : almost entirely : NEARLY **2** : for all practical purposes ⟨~ unknown⟩

virtual memory *n* (1959) : external memory (as magnetic disks) for a computer that can be used as if it were an extension of the computer's internal memory — called also *virtual storage*

virtual reality *n* (1989) : an artificial environment which is experienced through sensory stimuli (as sights and sounds) provided by a computer and in which one's actions partially determine what happens in the environment

vir·tue \'vər-(,)chü\ *n* [ME *virtu*, fr. OF, fr. L *virtut-, virtus* strength, manliness, virtue, fr. *vir* man — more at VIRILE] (13c) **1 a** : conformity to a standard of right : MORALITY **b** : a particular moral excellence **2** *pl* : an order of angels — see CELESTIAL HIERARCHY **3** : a beneficial quality or power of a thing **4** : manly strength or courage : VALOR **5** : a commendable quality or trait : MERIT **6** : a capacity to act : POTENCY **7** : chastity esp. in a woman — **vir·tue·less** \-(,)chü-ləs\ *adj* — **by virtue of** *or* **in virtue of** : through the force of : by authority of

vir·tu·o·sa \,vər-chü-'ō-sə, -zə\ *n* [It, fem. of *virtuoso*] (1668) : a girl or woman who is a virtuoso

vir·tu·os·i·ty \-'ä-sə-tē\ *n, pl* -**ties** (1673) **1** : a taste for or interest in virtu **2** : great technical skill (as in the practice of a fine art)

vir·tu·o·so \-'ō-(,)sō, -(,)zō\ *n, pl* -**sos** *or* -**si** \-(,)sē, -(,)zē\ [It, fr. *virtuoso*, adj., virtuous, skilled, fr. LL *virtuosus* virtuous, fr. L *virtus*] (1651) **1** : an experimenter or investigator esp. in the arts and sciences : SAVANT **2** : one skilled in or having a taste for the fine arts **3** : one who excels in the technique of an art; *esp* : a highly skilled musical performer (as on the violin) **4** : a person who has great skill at some endeavor ⟨a computer ~⟩ ⟨a ~ at public relations⟩ — **vir·tu·o·sic** \-'ō-sik, -zik\ *adj* — **virtuoso** *adj*

vir·tu·ous \'vər-chə-wəs, 'vərch-wəs\ *adj* (14c) **1** : POTENT, EFFICACIOUS **2 a** : having or exhibiting virtue **b** : morally excellent : RIGHTEOUS **3** : CHASTE *syn* see MORAL — **vir·tu·ous·ly** *adv* — **vir·tu·ous·ness** *n*

vi·ru·cid·al \,vī-rə-'sī-d³l\ *adj* [NL, *virus* + E -*cide*] (1925) : having the capacity to or tending to destroy or inactivate viruses ⟨~ agents⟩ ⟨~ activity⟩ — **vi·ru·cide** \'vī-rə-,sīd\ *n*

vir·u·lence \'vir-ə-lən(t)s, 'vir-yə-\ *n* (1663) : the quality or state of being virulent: as **a** : extreme bitterness or malignity of temper : RANCOR **b** : MALIGNANCY, VENOMOUSNESS ⟨ameliorate the ~ of a disease⟩ **c** : the relative capacity of a pathogen to overcome body defenses

vir·u·len·cy \-lən(t)-sē\ *n* (ca. 1617) : VIRULENCE

vir·u·lent \-lənt\ *adj* [ME, fr. L *virulentus*, fr. *virus* poison] (14c) **1 a** : marked by a rapid, severe, and malignant course ⟨a ~ infection⟩ **b** : able to overcome bodily defensive mechanisms ⟨a ~ pathogen⟩ **2** : extremely poisonous or venomous **3** : full of malice : MALIGNANT ⟨~ racists⟩ **4** : objectionably harsh or strong — **vir·u·lent·ly** *adv*

vir·u·lif·er·ous \,vir-ə-'li-f(ə-)rəs, ,vir-yə-\ *adj* [*virulence* + -*iferous*] (ca. 1899) : containing, producing, or conveying an agent of infection and esp. a virus ⟨~ insects⟩

vi·rus \'vī-rəs\ *n* [L, venom, poisonous emanation; akin to Gk *ios* poison, Skt *viṣa*; in senses 2 & 4, fr. NL, fr. L] (1599) **1** *archaic* : VENOM 1 **2 a** : the causative agent of an infectious disease **b** : any of a large group of submicroscopic infective agents that are regarded either as extremely simple microorganisms or as extremely complex molecules, that typically contain a protein coat surrounding an RNA or DNA core of genetic material but no semipermeable membrane, that are capable of growth and multiplication only in living cells, and that cause various important diseases in humans, lower animals, or plants;

also : FILTERABLE VIRUS **c** : a disease caused by a virus **3** : something that poisons the mind or soul ⟨the force of this ~ of prejudice —V. S. Waters⟩ **4** : a computer program usu. hidden within another seemingly innocuous program that produces copies of itself and inserts them into other programs and that usu. performs a malicious action (as destroying data)

vis \'vis\ *n, pl* **vi·res** \'vī-,rēz\ [L — more at VIM] (1601) : FORCE, POWER

¹vi·sa \'vē-zə *also* -sə\ *n* [F, fr. L, neut. pl. of *visus*, pp.] (1831) **1** : an endorsement made on a passport by the proper authorities denoting that it has been examined and that the bearer may proceed **2** : a signature of formal approval by a superior upon a document

²visa *vt* **vi·saed** \-zəd, -səd\; **vi·sa·ing** \-zə-iŋ, -sə-\ (ca. 1847) : to give a visa to (a passport)

vis·age \'vi-zij\ *n* [ME, fr. OF, fr. *vis* face, fr. L *visus* sight, fr. *vidēre* to see — more at WIT] (14c) **1** : the face, countenance, or appearance of a person or sometimes an animal **2** : ASPECT, APPEARANCE ⟨grimy ~ of a mining town⟩ — **vis·aged** \-zijd\ *adj*

¹vis-à-vis \'vēz-ə-'vē, ,vēs- *also* -ä-'vē\ *prep* [F, lit., face-to-face] (1755) **1** : face-to-face with **2** : in relation to **3** : as compared with

²vis-à-vis *n, pl* **vis-à-vis** \-ə-'vē(z), -ä-\ (ca. 1757) **1** : one that is face-to-face with another **2 a** : ESCORT, DATE **b** : COUNTERPART **3** : TÊTE-À-TÊTE 1

³vis-à-vis *adv* (1870) : in company : TOGETHER

Vi·sa·yan \və-'sī-ən\ *var of* BISAYAN

vis·ca·cha \vis-'kä-chə\ *n* [Sp *vizcacha*, fr. Quechua *wisk'acha*] (1604) : any of several So. American burrowing rodents (genera *Lagostomus* and *Lagidium*) closely related to the chinchilla

viscera *pl of* VISCUS

vis·cer·al \'vi-sə-rəl, 'vis-rəl\ *adj* (1575) **1** : felt in or as if in the viscera : DEEP ⟨~ conviction⟩ **2** : not intellectual : INSTINCTIVE, UNREASONING ⟨~ drives⟩ **3** : dealing with crude or elemental emotions : EARTHY ⟨a ~ novel⟩ **4** : of, relating to, or located on or among the viscera : SPLANCHNIC — **vis·cer·al·ly** \-rə-lē\ *adv*

vis·cid \'vi-səd\ *adj* [LL *viscidus*, fr. L *viscum* birdlime — more at VISCOUS] (1635) **1 a** : having an adhesive quality : STICKY **b** : having a glutinous consistency : VISCOUS **2** : covered with a sticky layer — **vis·cid·i·ty** \vi-'si-də-tē\ *n* — **vis·cid·ly** \'vi-səd-lē\ *adv*

vis·co·elas·tic \,vis-kō-ə-'las-tik\ *adj* [*viscous* + -*o-* + *elastic*] (1935) : having appreciable and conjoint viscous and elastic properties ⟨such ~ materials as asphalt⟩; *also* : constituting or relating to the state of viscoelastic materials ⟨~ data⟩ ⟨~ properties⟩ — **vis·co·elas·tic·i·ty** \-,las-'ti-sə-tē, -'tis-tē\ *n*

vis·com·e·ter \vis-'kä-mə-tər\ *n* [*viscosity* + -*meter*] (ca. 1883) : an instrument with which to measure viscosity — **vis·co·met·ric** \,vis-kə-'me-trik\ *adj* — **vis·com·e·try** \-mə-trē\ *n*

¹vis·cose \'vis-,kōs, -,kōz\ *n* [obs. *viscose*, adj., viscous] (1896) **1** : a viscous golden-brown solution made by treating cellulose with caustic alkali solution and carbon disulfide and used in making rayon and films of regenerated cellulose **2** : viscose rayon

²viscose *adj* (1900) : of, relating to, or made from viscose

vis·co·sim·e·ter \,vis-kə-'si-mə-tər\ *n* [ISV *viscosity* + -*meter*] (ca. 1868) : VISCOMETER — **vis·cosi·met·ric** \(,)vis-,kä-sə-'me-trik\ *adj*

vis·cos·i·ty \vis-'kä-sə-tē\ *n, pl* -**ties** [ME *viscosite*, fr. MF *viscosité*, fr. ML *viscositat-, viscositas*, fr. LL *viscosus* viscous] (15c) **1** : the quality or state of being viscous **2** : the property of resistance to flow in a fluid or semifluid **3** : the ratio of the tangential frictional force per unit area to the velocity gradient perpendicular to the direction of flow of a liquid — called also *coefficient of viscosity*

viscosity index *n* (1929) : an arbitrary number assigned as a measure of the constancy of the viscosity of a lubricating oil with change of temperature with higher numbers indicating viscosities that change little with temperature

vis·count \'vī-,kaunt\ *n* [ME *viscounte*, fr. MF *viscomte*, fr. ML *vicecomit-, vicecomes*, fr. LL *vice-* vice- + *comit-, comes* count — more at COUNT] (15c) : a member of the peerage in Great Britain ranking below an earl and above a baron — **vis·count·cy** \-,kaun(t)-sē\ *n* — **vis·county** \-,kaun-tē\ *n*

vis·count·ess \'vī-,kaun-təs\ *n* (15c) **1** : the wife or widow of a viscount **2** : a woman who holds the rank of viscount in her own right

vis·cous \'vis-kəs\ *adj* [ME *viscouse*, fr. LL *viscosus* full of birdlime, viscous, fr. L *viscum* mistletoe, birdlime; akin to OHG *wihsila* cherry, Gk *ixos* mistletoe] (14c) **1** : VISCID **2** : having or characterized by viscosity ⟨~ flow⟩ — **vis·cous·ly** *adv* — **vis·cous·ness** *n*

vis·cus \'vis-kəs\ *n, pl* **vis·cera** \'vi-sə-rə\ [L (pl. *viscera*)] (1651) **1** : an internal organ of the body; *esp* : one (as the heart, liver, or intestine) located in the great cavity of the trunk proper **2** *pl* : HEART 4

¹vise \'vīs\ *n* [MF *vis* screw, something winding, fr. L *vitis* vine — more at WITHY] (1500) **1** : any of various tools with two jaws for holding work that close usu. by a screw, lever, or cam **2** : something likened to a vise ⟨economic ~ of slow growth and rampant price increases —David Milne⟩ — **vise·like** \-,līk\ *adj*

²vise *vt* **vised**; **vis·ing** (1602) : to hold, force, or squeeze with or as if with a vise

³vi·sé \'vē-,zā, vē-'\ *vt* **vi·séd** *or* **vi·seed**; **vi·sé·ing** [F, pp. of *viser* to visa, fr. *visa*] (1810) : VISA

²visé *n* (1842) : VISA

vise 1

Vish·nu \'vish-(,)nü\ *n* [Skt *Viṣṇu*] (1638) : the preserver god of the Hindu sacred triad — compare BRAHMA, SIVA

vis·i·bil·i·ty \,vi-zə-'bi-lə-tē\ *n, pl* -**ties** (1581) **1** : the quality or state of being visible **2 a** : the degree of clearness of the atmosphere; *specif* : the greatest distance toward the horizon at which prominent objects can be identified with the naked eye **b** : capability of being readily noticed **c** : capability of affording an unobstructed view **d** : PUBLICITY 2d **3** : a measure of the ability of radiant energy to evoke visual sensation

vis·i·ble \'vi-zə-bəl\ *adj* [ME, fr. MF or L; MF, fr. L *visibilis*, fr. *visus*, pp. of *vidēre* to see] (14c) **1 a** : capable of being seen ⟨stars ~ to the naked eye⟩ **b** : situated in the region of the electromagnetic spectrum perceptible to human vision ⟨~ light⟩ — used of radiation having a wavelength between about 400 nanometers and 700 nanometers **2 a**

: exposed to view ⟨the ~ horizon⟩ **b** : CONSPICUOUS **3** : capable of being discovered or perceived : RECOGNIZABLE ⟨no ~ means of support⟩ **4** : ACCESSIBLE 4 **5** : devised to keep a particular part or item always in full view or readily seen or referred to ⟨a ~ index⟩ — **vis·i·ble·ness** n — **vis·i·bly** \-blē\ adv

visible speech n (1865) **1** : a set of phonetic symbols based on symbols for articulatory position **2** : speech reproduced spectrographically

Vis·i·goth \'vi-zə-,gäth\ n [LL Visigothi, pl.] (1611) : a member of the western division of the Goths — **Vis·i·goth·ic** \,vi-zə-'gä-thik\ adj

¹vi·sion \'vi-zhən\ n [ME, fr. OF, fr. L vision-, visio, fr. vidēre to see — more at WIT] (14c) **1 a** : something seen in a dream, trance, or ecstasy; esp : a supernatural appearance that conveys a revelation **b** : an object of imagination **c** : a manifestation to the senses of something immaterial ⟨look, not at ~s, but at realities —Edith Wharton⟩ **2 a** : the act or power of imagination **b** (1) : mode of seeing or conceiving (2) : unusual discernment or foresight ⟨a man of ~⟩ **c** : direct mystical awareness of the supernatural usu. in visible form **3 a** : the act or power of seeing : SIGHT **b** : the special sense by which the qualities of an object (as color, luminosity, shape and size) constituting its appearance are perceived and which is mediated by the eye **4 a** : something seen **b** : a lovely or charming sight — **vi·sion·al** \'vizh-nəl, 'vi-zhə-n³l\ adj — **vi·sion·al·ly** adv

²vision vt **vi·sioned; vi·sion·ing** \'vi-zhə-niŋ, 'vizh-niŋ\ (1795) : ENVISION

¹vi·sion·ary \'vi-zhə-,ner-ē\ adj (1648) **1 a** : of the nature of a vision : ILLUSORY **b** : incapable of being realized or achieved : UTOPIAN ⟨a ~ scheme⟩ **c** : existing only in imagination : UNREAL **2** : able or likely to see visions **b** : disposed to reverie or imagining : DREAMY **3** : of, relating to, or characterized by visions or the power of vision : having or marked by foresight and imagination ⟨a ~ leader⟩ ⟨a ~ invention⟩ **syn** see IMAGINARY — **vi·sion·ar·i·ness** \-ē-nəs\ n

²visionary n, pl **-ar·ies** (1702) **1** : one whose ideas or projects are impractical : DREAMER **2** : one who sees visions : SEER

vi·sioned \'vi-zhənd\ adj (1510) **1** : seen in a vision ⟨a ~ face⟩ **2** : produced by or experienced in a vision ⟨~ agony⟩ **3** : endowed with vision : INSPIRED

vi·sion·less \'vi-zhən-ləs\ adj (1820) **1** : SIGHTLESS, BLIND ⟨~ eyes⟩ **2** : lacking vision or inspiration ⟨a ~ leader⟩

¹vis·it \'vi-zət\ vb **vis·it·ed** \'vi-zə-təd, 'viz-təd\; **vis·it·ing** \'vi-zə-tiŋ, 'viz-tiŋ\ [ME, fr. OF visiter, fr. L visitare, freq. of visere to go to see, freq. of vidēre to see] vt (13c) **1 a** archaic : COMFORT — used of the Deity ⟨~ us with Thy salvation —Charles Wesley⟩ **b** (1) : AFFLICT ⟨~ed his people with distempers —Tobias Smollett⟩ (2) : INFLICT, IMPOSE ⟨~ed his wrath upon them⟩ **c** : AVENGE ⟨~ed the sins of the fathers upon the children⟩ **d** : to present itself to or come over momentarily ⟨was ~ed by a strange notion⟩ **2** : to go to see in order to comfort or help **3 a** : to pay a call on as an act of friendship or courtesy **b** : to reside with temporarily as a guest **c** : to go to see or stay at (a place) for a particular purpose (as business or sightseeing) **d** : to go or come officially to inspect or oversee ⟨a bishop ~ing his parishes⟩ ~ vi **1** : to make a visit; also : to make frequent or regular visits **2** : CHAT, CONVERSE

²visit n (1621) **1 a** : a short stay : CALL **b** : a brief residence as a guest **c** : an extended stay : SOJOURN **2** : a journey to and stay or short sojourn at a place **3** : an official or professional call or tour : VISITATION **4** : the act of a naval officer in boarding a merchant ship on the high seas in exercise of the right of search

vis·it·able \'vi-zə-tə-bəl, 'viz-tə-\ adj (1605) **1** : subject to or allowing visitation or inspection **2** : socially eligible to receive visits

vis·i·tant \'vi-zə-tənt, 'viz-tənt\ n (1599) **1** : VISITOR; esp : one thought to come from a spirit world **2** : a migratory bird that appears at intervals for a limited period — **visitant** adj

vis·i·ta·tion \,vi-zə-'tā-shən\ n (14c) **1** : an instance of visiting: as **a** : an official visit (as for inspection) **b** : ²WAKE 3 **c** : temporary custody of a child granted to a noncustodial parent ⟨~ rights⟩ **2 a** : a special dispensation of divine favor or wrath **b** : a severe trial : AFFLICTION **3** cap : the visit of the Virgin Mary to Elizabeth recounted in Luke and celebrated July 2 by a Christian feast

vis·i·ta·to·ri·al \,vi-zə-tə-'tōr-ē-əl, ,viz-tə-, -'tòr-\ adj (1688) : of or relating to visitation or to a judicial visitor or superintendent

visiting adj (1949) : invited to join or attend an institution (as a university) for a limited time ⟨a ~ professor⟩ ⟨a ~ fellow⟩

visiting card n (1782) : a small card presented when visiting that bears the name and sometimes the address of the visitor

visiting fireman n (1926) : a usu. important or influential visitor whom it is desirable or expedient to entertain impressively

visiting nurse n (ca. 1924) : a nurse employed by a hospital or social-service agency to perform public health services and esp. to visit sick persons in a community

vis·i·tor \'vi-zə-tər, 'viz-tər\ n (15c) : one that visits; esp : one that makes formal visits of inspection

vi·sive \'vi-ziv, 'vī-siv\ adj [ML visivus, fr. L visus, pp. of vidēre to see — more at WIT] (1543) archaic : of, relating to, or serving for vision

vi·sor \'vī-zər\ n [ME viser, fr. AF, fr. OF visiere, fr. vis face — more at VISAGE] (14c) **1** : the front piece of a helmet; esp : a movable upper piece **2 a** : a face mask **b** : DISGUISE **3 a** : a projecting front on a cap for shading the eyes **b** : a usu. movable flat sunshade attached at the top of an automobile windshield — **vi·sored** \-zərd\ adj — **vi·sor·less** \-zər-ləs\ adj

vis·ta \'vis-tə\ n [It, sight, fr. visto, visto, pp. of vedere to see, fr. L vidēre — more at WIT] (1644) **1** : a distant view through or along an avenue or opening : PROSPECT **2** : an extensive mental view (as over a stretch of time or a series of events)

vis·taed \'vis-təd\ adj (1835) **1** : affording or made to form a vista **2** : seen in or as if in a vista

¹vi·su·al \'vi-zhə-wəl, -zhəl; 'vizh-wəl\ adj [ME, fr. LL visualis, fr. L visus sight, fr. vidēre to see] (1603) **1** : of, relating to, or used in vision ⟨~ organs⟩ **2** : attained or maintained by sight ⟨~ impressions⟩ **3** : VISIBLE **4** : producing mental images : VIVID **5** : done or executed by sight only ⟨~ navigation⟩ **6** : of, relating to, or employing visual aids — **vi·su·al·ly** \'vi-zhə-wə-lē, -zhə-lē; 'vizh-wə-lē\ adv

²visual n (1938) : something (as a picture, chart, or film) that appeals to the sight and is variously used (as for illustration, demonstration, or promotion) — usu. used in pl.

visual acuity n (1889) : the relative ability of the visual organ to resolve detail that is usu. expressed as the reciprocal of the minimum angular separation in minutes of two lines just resolvable as separate and that forms in the average human eye an angle of one minute

visual aid n (1911) : an instructional device (as a chart, map, or model) that appeals chiefly to vision; esp : an educational motion picture or filmstrip

visual field n (1880) : the entire expanse of space visible at a given instant without moving the eyes — called also field of vision

vi·su·al·i·za·tion \,vi-zhə-wə-lə-'zā-shən, ,vi-zhə-lə-, ,vizh-wə-lə-\ n (1883) **1** : formation of mental visual images **2** : the act or process of interpreting in visual terms or of putting into visible form **3** : the process of making an internal organ visible by the introduction (as by swallowing, by an injection, or by an enema) of a radiopaque substance followed by roentgenography

vi·su·al·ize \'vi-zhə-wə-,līz, ¹vi-zhə-,līz, 'vizh-wə-,līz\ vb **-ized; -iz·ing** vt (1863) : to make visible: as **a** : to see or form a mental image of : ENVISAGE **b** : to make (an organ) visible by roentgenographic visualization ~ vi : to form a mental visual image

vi·su·al·iz·er \-,lī-zər\ n (1886) : one that visualizes; esp : a person whose mental imagery is prevailingly visual

visual literacy n (1971) : the ability to recognize and understand ideas conveyed through visible actions or images (as pictures)

visual purple n (1878) : a photosensitive red or purple pigment in the retinal rods of various vertebrates; esp : RHODOPSIN

vi·ta \'vē-tə, 'vī-tə\ n, pl **vi·tae** \'vē-,tī, -,tē\ [L, lit., life] (1939) **1** : a brief biographical sketch **2** : CURRICULUM VITAE

vi·tal \'vī-t³l\ adj [ME, fr. MF, fr. L vitalis of life, fr. vita life; akin to L vivere to live — more at QUICK] (14c) **1 a** : existing as a manifestation of life **b** : concerned with or necessary to the maintenance of life ⟨~ organs⟩ ⟨blood and other ~ fluids⟩ **2** : full of life and vigor : ANIMATED **3** : characteristic of life or living beings **4 a** : fundamentally concerned with or affecting life or living beings: as (1) : tending to renew or refresh the living : INVIGORATING (2) : destructive to life : MORTAL **b** : of the utmost importance **5** : recording data relating to lives **6** : of, relating to, or constituting the staining of living tissues **syn** see ESSENTIAL — **vi·tal·ly** \-t³l-ē\ adv

vital capacity n (1852) : the breathing capacity of the lungs expressed as the number of cubic inches or cubic centimeters of air that can be forcibly exhaled after a full inspiration

vi·tal·ism \'vī-t³l-,i-zəm\ n (1822) **1** : a doctrine that the functions of a living organism are due to a vital principle distinct from physicochemical forces **2** : a doctrine that the processes of life are not explicable by the laws of physics and chemistry alone and that life is in some part self-determining — **vi·tal·ist** \-t³l-ist\ n or adj — **vi·tal·is·tic** \,vī-t³l-'is-tik\ adj

vi·tal·i·ty \vī-'ta-lə-tē\ n, pl **-ties** (1592) **1 a** : the peculiarity distinguishing the living from the nonliving **b** : capacity to live and develop; also : physical or mental vigor esp. when highly developed **2 a** : power of enduring **b** : lively and animated character

vi·tal·ize \'vī-t³l-,īz\ vt **-ized; -iz·ing** (1678) : to endow with vitality : ANIMATE — **vi·tal·i·za·tion** \,vī-t³l-ə-'zā-shən\ n

vi·tals \'vī-t³lz\ n pl (ca. 1610) **1** : vital organs (as the heart, liver, lungs, and brain) **2** : essential parts

vital signs n pl (ca. 1919) : signs of life; specif : the pulse rate, respiratory rate, body temperature, and often blood pressure of a person

vital statistics n pl (1837) **1** : statistics relating to births, deaths, marriages, health, and disease **2** : facts (as physical dimensions or quantities) considered to be interesting or important; esp : a woman's bust, waist, and hip measurements

vi·ta·min \'vī-tə-mən, Brit usu 'vi-\ n [L vita life + ISV amine] (1912) : any of various organic substances that are essential in minute quantities to the nutrition of most animals and some plants, act esp. as coenzymes and precursors of coenzymes in the regulation of metabolic processes but do not provide energy or serve as building units, and are present in natural foodstuffs or sometimes produced within the body

vitamin A n (1920) : any of several fat-soluble vitamins (as retinol) found esp. in animal products (as egg yolk, milk, or fish-liver oils) or a mixture of them whose lack in the animal body causes epithelial tissues to become keratinous (as in the eye with resulting visual defects)

vitamin B n (1920) **1** : VITAMIN B COMPLEX **2** or **vitamin B₁** \-'bē-'wən\ : THIAMINE

vitamin B complex n (1928) : a group of water-soluble vitamins found esp. in yeast, seed germs, eggs, liver and flesh, and vegetables that have varied metabolic functions and include coenzymes and growth factors — called also B complex; compare BIOTIN, CHOLINE, NICOTINIC ACID, PANTOTHENIC ACID

vitamin B₆ \-'bē-'siks\ n (1934) : pyridoxine or a closely related compound found widely in combined form and considered essential to vertebrate nutrition

vitamin B₁₂ \-'bē-'twelv\ n (1948) **1** : a complex cobalt-containing compound $C_{63}H_{88}CoN_{14}O_{14}P$ that occurs esp. in liver, is essential to normal blood formation, neural function, and growth, and is used esp. in treating pernicious and related anemias and in animal feed as a growth factor — called also cyanocobalamin **2** : any of several compounds similar to vitamin B₁₂ in action but having different chemistry

vitamin B₂ \-'bē-'tü\ n (1928) : RIBOFLAVIN

vitamin C n (1920) : a water-soluble vitamin $C_6H_8O_6$ found in plants and esp. in fruits and leafy vegetables or made synthetically and used in the prevention and treatment of scurvy and as an antioxidant for foods — called also ascorbic acid

vitamin D n (1921) : any or all of several fat-soluble vitamins chemically related to steroids, essential for normal bone and tooth structure,

---

\a\ abut \³\ kitten, F table \ər\ further \a\ ash \ā\ ace \ä\ mop, mar
\aú\ out \ch\ chin \e\ bet \ē\ easy \g\ go \i\ hit \ī\ ice \j\ job
\ŋ\ sing \ō\ go \ò\ law \òi\ boy \th\ thin \th\ the \ü\ loot \ù\ foot
\y\ yet \zh\ vision \à, ᵏ, ⁿ, œ, œ, ue, ūe, ᵛ\ see Guide to Pronunciation

and found esp. in fish-liver oils, egg yolk, and milk or produced by activation (as by ultraviolet irradiation) of sterols: as **a** *or* **vitamin D₂**\-'dē-'tü\ : CALCIFEROL **b** *or* **vitamin D₃**\-'dē-'thrē\ : CHOLECALCIFEROL
vitamin E *n* (1925) : any of several fat-soluble vitamins that are chemically tocopherols, are essential in the nutrition of various vertebrates in which their absence is associated with infertility, degenerative changes in muscle, or vascular abnormalities, are found esp. in leaves and in seed germ oils, and are used chiefly in animal feeds and as antioxidants
vitamin G *n* (1929) : RIBOFLAVIN
vitamin H *n* (ca. 1935) : BIOTIN
vitamin K *n* [Dan *koagulation* coagulation] (1935) **1** : either of two naturally occurring fat-soluble vitamins C₃₁H₄₆O₂ and C₄₁H₅₆O₂ essential for the clotting of blood because of their role in the production of prothrombin — called also respectively *vitamin K₁, vitamin K₂* **2** : any of several synthetic compounds closely related chemically to natural vitamins K₁ and K₂ and of similar biological activity
vi·tel·line \vī-'te-lən, -,lēn, -,līn\ *adj* [ME, fr. MF *vitellin*, fr. ML *vitellinus*, fr. L *vitellus*] (15c) **1** : resembling the yolk of an egg esp. in yellow color **2** : of, relating to, or producing yolk
vitelline membrane *n* (1845) : a membrane that encloses the egg proper, corresponds to the plasmalemma of an ordinary cell, and in many animals forms the fertilization membrane by separating from the plasma membrane immediately after fertilization
vi·tel·lo·gen·e·sis \vī-,te-lō-'je-nə-səs, və-\ *n* [NL, fr. L *vitellus* + NL *-o- + genesis*] (1947) : yolk formation
vi·tel·lus \-'te-ləs\ *n* [L] (1728) : the egg cell proper including the yolk but excluding any albuminous or membranous envelopes; *also* : YOLK 1c
vi·ti·ate \'vi-shē-,āt\ *vt* **-at·ed; -at·ing** [L *vitiatus*, pp. of *vitiare*, fr. *vitium* fault, vice] (1534) **1** : to make faulty or defective : IMPAIR ⟨the comic impact is *vitiated* by obvious haste —William Styron⟩ **2** : to debase in moral or aesthetic status ⟨a mind *vitiated* by prejudice⟩ **3** : to make ineffective ⟨fraud ∼s a contract⟩ **syn** see DEBASE — **vi·ti·a·tion** \,vi-shē-'ā-shən\ *n* — **vi·ti·a·tor** \'vi-shē-,ā-tər\ *n*
vi·ti·cul·ture \'vi-tə-,kəl-chər, 'vī-\ *n* [L *vitis* vine + E *culture* — more at WITHY] (1872) : the cultivation or culture of grapes esp. for wine making — **vi·ti·cul·tur·al** \,vi-tə-'kəl-chə-rəl, ,vī-, -'kəlch-rəl\ *adj* — **vi·ti·cul·tur·al·ly** *adv* — **vi·ti·cul·tur·ist** \-rist\ *n*
vit·i·li·go \,vi-t²l-'ī-(,)gō, -'ē-\ *n* [NL, fr. L, tetter] (1842) : a skin disorder manifested by smooth white spots on various parts of the body
vit·rec·to·my \və-'trek-tə-mē\ *n, pl* **-mies** [*vitreous* humor + *-ectomy*] (1968) : surgical removal of all or part of the vitreous humor
¹**vit·re·ous** \'vi-trē-əs\ *adj* [L *vitreus*, fr. *vitrum* glass] (1646) **1** : of, relating to, derived from, or consisting of glass **2 a** : resembling glass (as in color, composition, brittleness, or luster) : GLASSY ⟨∼ rocks⟩ **b** : characterized by low porosity and usu. translucence due to the presence of a glassy phase ⟨∼ china⟩ **3** : of, relating to, or constituting the vitreous humor
²**vitreous** *n* (1869) : VITREOUS HUMOR
vitreous humor *n* (1663) : the clear colorless transparent jelly that fills the eyeball posterior to the lens — see EYE illustration
vitreous silica *n* (1925) : a chemically stable and refractory glass made from silica alone — compare QUARTZ GLASS
vit·ri·fy \'vi-trə-,fī\ *vb* **-fied; -fy·ing** [MF *vitrifier*, fr. L *vitrum* glass] *vt* (1594) : to convert into glass or a glassy substance by heat and fusion ∼ *vi* : to become vitrified — **vit·ri·fi·able** \,vi-trə-'fī-ə-bəl\ *adj* — **vit·ri·fi·ca·tion** \,vi-trə-fə-'kā-shən\ *n*
vi·trine \və-'trēn\ *n* [F, fr. *vitre* pane of glass, fr. OF, fr. L *vitrum*] (1880) : a glass showcase or cabinet esp. for displaying fine wares or specimens
vit·ri·ol \'vi-trē-əl\ *n* [ME, fr. MF, fr. ML *vitriolum*, alter. of LL *vitreolum*, neut. of *vitreolus* glassy, fr. L *vitreus* vitreous] (14c) **1 a** : a sulfate of any of various metals (as copper, iron, or zinc); *esp* : a glassy hydrate of such a sulfate **b** : OIL OF VITRIOL **2** : something felt to resemble vitriol esp. in caustic quality; *esp* : virulence of feeling or of speech — **vit·ri·ol·ic** \,vi-trē-'ä-lik\ *adj*
vit·ta \'vi-tə\ *n, pl* **vit·tae** \'vi-tē, 'vi-,tē, 'vi-,tī\ [NL, fr. L, fillet; akin to L *viēre* to plait — more at WIRE] (1819) **1** : STRIPE, STREAK **2** : one of the oil tubes in the fruits of plants of the carrot family
vit·tles \'vi-t²lz\ *n pl* (14c) : VICTUALS
vi·tu·per·ate \vī-'tü-pə-,rāt, və-, -'tyü-\ *vb* **-at·ed; -at·ing** [L *vituperatus*, pp. of *vituperare*, fr. *vitium* fault + *parare* to make, prepare — more at PARE] *vt* (1542) : to abuse or censure severely or abusively : BERATE ∼ *vi* : to use harsh condemnatory language **syn** see SCOLD — **vi·tu·per·a·tor** \-,rā-tər\ *n*
vi·tu·per·a·tion \(,)vī-,tü-pə-'rā-shən, və-, -,tyü-\ *n* (15c) **1** : sustained and bitter railing and condemnation : vituperative utterance **2** : an act or instance of vituperating **syn** see ABUSE
vi·tu·per·a·tive \vī-'tü-p(ə-)rə-tiv, -pə-,rā-\ *adj* (1727) : uttering or given to censure : containing or characterized by verbal abuse — **vi·tu·per·a·tive·ly** *adv*
vi·tu·per·a·to·ry \-p(ə-)rə-,tōr-ē, -,tòr-\ *adj* (1586) : VITUPERATIVE
vi·va \'vē-və, -,vä\ *interj* [It & Sp, long live, fr. 3d pers. sing. pres. subj. of *vivere* to live, fr. L — more at QUICK] (ca. 1700) — used to express goodwill or approval
¹**vi·va·ce** \vē-'vä-(,)chā, -chē\ *adv or adj* [It, vivacious, fr. L *vivac-, vivax*] (1683) : in a brisk spirited manner — used as a direction in music
²**vivace** *n* (ca. 1683) : a musical composition or movement in vivace tempo
vi·va·cious \və-'vā-shəs *also* vī-\ *adj* [L *vivac-, vivax*, lit., long-lived, fr. *vivere* to live] (1645) : lively in temper, conduct, or spirit : SPRIGHTLY **syn** see LIVELY — **vi·va·cious·ly** *adv* — **vi·va·cious·ness** *n*
vi·vac·i·ty \-'va-sə-tē\ *n* (15c) : the quality or state of being vivacious
vi·van·dière \,vē-,väⁿ-'dyer\ *n* [F, fem. of MF *vivandier*, fr. ML *vivanda* food — more at VIAND] (1848) : a female sutler
vi·var·i·um \vī-'var-ē-əm, -'ver-\ *n, pl* **-ia** \-ē-ə\ *or* **-iums** [L, park, preserve, fr. *vivus* alive — more at QUICK] (1853) : a terrarium used esp. for small animals
¹**vi·va vo·ce** \,vī-və-'vō-(,)sē *or* (*as if fr It*) ,vē-və-'vō-(,)chā\ *adv* [ML, with the living voice] (1563) : by word of mouth : ORALLY

²**viva voce** *adj* (1654) : expressed or conducted by word of mouth : ORAL
³**viva voce** *n* (1842) : an examination conducted viva voce — called also *viva*
vi·vax malaria \'vī-,vaks-\ *n* [NL *vivax*, specific epithet of *Plasmodium vivax*, parasite causing tertian] (ca. 1941) : malaria caused by a plasmodium (*Plasmodium vivax*) that induces paroxysms at 48-hour intervals
vi·ver·rid \vī-'ver-əd\ *n* [NL *Viverridae*, fr. *Viverra*, type genus, fr. L *viverra* ferret; akin to OE *ācweorna* squirrel, Lith *voverė*] (1902) : any of a family (*Viverridae*) of carnivorous mammals (as a civet, a genet, or a mongoose) that are rarely larger than a domestic cat but are long, slender, and like a weasel in build with short more or less retractile claws and rounded feet — **viverrid** *adj*
vi·vers \'vē-vərz, 'vī-\ *n pl* [MF *vivres*, pl. of *vivre* food, fr. *vivre* to live, fr. L *vivere*] (1536) *chiefly Scot* : VICTUALS, FOOD
Viv·i·an *or* **Viv·i·en** \'vi-vē-ən\ *n* : the mistress of Merlin in Arthurian legend — called also *Lady of the Lake*
viv·id \'vi-vəd\ *adj* [L *vividus*, fr. *vivere* to live — more at QUICK] (1638) **1** : having the appearance of vigorous life or freshness : LIVELY ⟨a ∼ sketch⟩ **2** *of a color* : very strong : very high in chroma **3** : producing a strong or clear impression on the senses : SHARP, INTENSE; *specif* : producing distinct mental images ⟨a ∼ description⟩ **4** : acting clearly and vigorously ⟨a ∼ imagination⟩ **syn** see GRAPHIC — **viv·id·ly** *adv* — **viv·id·ness** *n*
vi·vif·ic \vī-'vi-fik\ *adj* [L *vivificus*] (1551) : imparting spirit or vivacity
viv·i·fy \'vi-və-,fī\ *vt* **-fied; -fy·ing** [MF *vivifier*, fr. LL *vivificare*, fr. L *vivificus* enlivening, fr. *vivus* alive — more at QUICK] (1545) **1** : to endue with life or renewed life : ANIMATE ⟨rains that ∼ the barren hills⟩ **2** : to impart vitality or vividness to ⟨concentrating this union of quality and meaning in a way which *vivifies* both —John Dewey⟩ **syn** see QUICKEN — **viv·i·fi·ca·tion** \,vi-və-fə-'kā-shən\ *n* — **viv·i·fi·er** \'vi-və-,fī(-ə)r\ *n*
vi·vi·par·i·ty \,vī-və-'par-ət-ē, ,vi-\ *n* (1864) : the quality or state of being viviparous
vi·vip·a·rous \vī-'vi-p(ə)rəs, və-\ *adj* [L *viviparus*, fr. *vivus* alive + *-parus* -parous] (1646) **1** : producing living young instead of eggs from within the body in the manner of nearly all mammals, many reptiles, and a few fishes **2** : germinating while still attached to the parent plant ⟨the ∼ seed of the mangrove⟩ — **vi·vip·a·rous·ly** *adv*
viv·i·sect \'vi-və-,sekt\ *vb* [back-formation fr. *vivisection*] *vt* (1864) : to perform vivisection on : subject to vivisection ∼ *vi* : to practice vivisection — **viv·i·sec·tor** \-,sek-tər\ *n*
viv·i·sec·tion \,vi-və-'sek-shən, 'vi-və-,\ *n* [L *vivus* + E *section*] (1707) **1** : the cutting of or operation on a living animal usu. for physiological or pathological investigation; *broadly* : animal experimentation esp. if considered to cause distress to the subject **2** : minute or pitiless examination or criticism — **viv·i·sec·tion·al** \,vi-və-'sek-shnəl, -shə-n²l\ *adj* — **viv·i·sec·tion·ist** \-'sek-sh(ə-)nist\ *n*
vix·en \'vik-sən\ *n* [(assumed) ME (southern dial.) *vixen*, alter. of ME *fixen*, fr. OE *fyxe*, fem. of *fox*] (1590) **1** : a shrewish ill-tempered woman **2** : a female fox — **vix·en·ish** \-s(ə-)nish\ *adj*
viz·ard \'vi-zərd, -,zärd\ *n* [alter. of ME *viser* mask, visor] (ca. 1555) **1** : a mask for disguise or protection **2** : DISGUISE, GUISE
viz·ca·cha *var of* VISCACHA
vi·zier \və-'zir\ *n* [Turk *vezir*, fr. Ar *wazīr*] (1599) : a high executive officer of various Muslim countries and esp. of the Ottoman Empire — **vi·zier·ate** \-'zir-ət, -'zir-,āt\ *n* — **vi·zier·ial** \-'zir-ē-əl\ *adj* — **vi·zier·ship** \-'zir-,ship\ *n*
vi·zor *var of* VISOR
vizs·la \'vēz-lə, 'vēs-, 'vizh-\ *n* [Hung] (1945) : any of a breed of hunting dogs of Hungarian origin that resemble the weimaraner but have a rich deep red coat and brown eyes
VLDL \,vē-(,)el-(,)dē-'el\ *n* [*very low-density lipoprotein*] (1977) : a plasma lipoprotein that is produced primarily by the liver with lesser amounts contributed by the intestine, that contains relatively large amounts of triglycerides compared to protein, and that leaves a residue of cholesterol in the tissues during the process of conversion to LDL — compare HDL

vizsla

V neck *n* (1905) : a V-shaped neck of a garment; *also* : a garment (as a sweater) with a V-shaped neck — **V–necked** *adj*
vo·ca·ble \'vō-kə-bəl\ *n* [MF, fr. L *vocabulum*, fr. *vocare* to call, fr. *vox* voice — more at VOICE] (1530) : TERM; *specif* : a word composed of various sounds or letters without regard to its meaning
vo·cab·u·lar \vō-'ka-byə-lər, və-\ *adj* [back-formation fr. *vocabulary*] (1608) : of or relating to words or phraseology : VERBAL
vo·cab·u·lary \vō-'ka-byə-,ler-ē, və-\ *n, pl* **-lar·ies** [MF *vocabulaire*, prob. fr. ML *vocabularium*, fr. neut. of *vocabularius* verbal, fr. L *vocabulum*] (1532) **1** : a list or collection of words or of words and phrases usu. alphabetically arranged and explained or defined : LEXICON **2 a** : a sum or stock of words employed by a language, group, individual, or work or in a field of knowledge **b** : a list or collection of terms or codes available for use (as in an indexing system) **3** : a supply of expressive techniques or devices (as of an art form)
vocabulary entry *n* (ca. 1934) : a word (as the noun *book*), hyphenated or open compound (as the verb *book-match* or the noun *book review*), word element (as the affix *pro-*), abbreviation (as *agt*), verbalized symbol (as *Na*), or term (as *man in the street*) entered alphabetically in a dictionary for the purpose of definition or identification or expressly included as an inflected form (as the noun *mice* or the verb *saw*) or as a derived form (as the noun *godlessness* or the adverb *globally*) or related phrase (as *one for the book*) run on at its base word and usu. set in a type (as boldface) readily distinguishable from that of the lightface running text which defines, explains, or identifies the entry
¹**vo·cal** \'vō-kəl\ *adj* [ME, fr. L *vocalis*, fr. *voc-, vox* voice — more at VOICE] (14c) **1 a** : uttered by the voice : ORAL **b** : produced in the larynx : uttered with voice **2** : relating to, composed or arranged for, or sung by the human voice ⟨∼ music⟩ **3** : VOCALIC **4 a** : having or

exercising the power of producing voice, speech, or sound **b** : EX-PRESSIVE **c** : full of voices : RESOUNDING **d** : given to expressing one-self freely or insistently : OUTSPOKEN **e** : expressed in words **5** : of, relating to, or resembling the voice ⟨~ impairment⟩ — **vo·cal·i·ty** \vō-'ka-lə-tē\ *n* — **vo·cal·ly** \'vō-kə-lē\ *adv*

²**vocal** *n* (1582) **1** : a vocal sound **2** : a usu. accompanied musical composition for the human voice : SONG; *also* : a performance of such a composition

vocal cords *n pl* (1852) : either of two pairs of folds of mucous membranes that project into the cavity of the larynx and have free edges extending dorsoventrally toward the middle line

vocal folds *n pl* (1924) : the lower pair of vocal cords each of which when drawn taut, approximated to the contralateral member of the pair, and subjected to a flow of breath produces the voice

¹**vo·cal·ic** \vō-'ka-lik, və-\ *adj* [L *vocalis* vowel, fr. *vocalis* vocal] (1814) **1** : marked by or consisting of vowels **2 a** : being or functioning as a vowel **b** : of, relating to, or associated with a vowel — **vo·cal·i·cal·ly** \-li-k(ə-)lē\ *adv*

²**vocalic** *n* (1924) : a vowel sound or sequence in its function as the most sonorous part of a syllable

vo·cal·ise *Brit var of* VOCALIZE

vo·cal·ism \'vō-kə-,li-zəm\ *n* (ca. 1859) **1** : VOCALIZATION **2** : vocal art or technique : SINGING **3 a** : the vowel system of a language or dialect **b** : the pattern of vowels in a word or paradigm

vo·cal·ist \-kə-list\ *n* (1834) : ¹SINGER

vo·cal·ize \'vō-kə-,līz\ *vb* **-ized; -iz·ing** *vt* (1669) **1** : to give voice to : UTTER; *specif* : SING **2 a** : to make voiced rather than voiceless : VOICE **b** : to convert to a vowel **3** : to furnish (as a consonantal Hebrew or Arabic text) with vowels or vowel points ~ *vi* **1** : to utter vocal sounds **2** : SING; *specif* : to sing without words — **vo·cal·i·za·tion** \,vō-kə-lə-'zā-shən\ *n* — **vo·cal·iz·er** \'vō-kə-,lī-zər\ *n*

vo·ca·tion \vō-'kā-shən\ *n* [ME *vocacioun*, fr. L *vocation-*, *vocatio* summons, fr. *vocare* to call, fr. *vox* voice — more at VOICE] (15c) **1 a** : a summons or strong inclination to a particular state or course of action; *esp* : a divine call to the religious life **b** : an entry into the priesthood or a religious order **2 a** : the work in which a person is regularly employed : OCCUPATION **b** : the persons engaged in a particular occupation **3** : the special function of an individual or group

vo·ca·tion·al \-shnəl, -shə-n⁰l\ *adj* (1652) **1** : of, relating to, or concerned with a vocation **2** : of, relating to, or being in training in a skill or trade to be pursued as a career — **vo·ca·tion·al·ly** *adv*

vo·ca·tion·al·ism \-shnə-,li-zəm, -shə-n⁰l-,i-zəm\ *n* (1924) : emphasis on vocational training in education — **vo·ca·tion·al·ist** \-list, -ist\ *n*

¹**voc·a·tive** \'vä-kə-tiv\ *adj* [ME *vocatif*, fr. MF, fr. L *vocativus*, fr. *vocatus*, pp. of *vocare*] (15c) **1** : of, relating to, or being a grammatical case marking the one addressed (as Latin *Domine* in *miserere, Domine* "have mercy, O Lord") **2** *of a word or word group* : marking the one addressed (as *mother* in "mother, come here") — **voc·a·tive·ly** *adv*

²**vocative** *n* (ca. 1522) **1** : the vocative case of a language **2** : a form in the vocative case

vo·cif·er·ant \vō-'si-fə-rənt\ *adj* (1609) : CLAMOROUS, VOCIFEROUS

vo·cif·er·ate \-,rāt\ *vb* **-at·ed; -at·ing** [L *vociferatus*, pp. of *vociferari*, fr. *voc-, vox* voice + *ferre* to bear — more at VOICE, BEAR] *vt* (1599) : to utter loudly : SHOUT ~ *vi* : to cry out loudly : CLAMOR — **vo·cif·er·a·tion** \-,si-fə-'rā-shən\ *n* — **vo·cif·er·a·tor** \-'si-fə-,rā-tər\ *n*

vo·cif·er·ous \vō-'si-f(ə-)rəs\ *adj* (ca. 1611) : marked by or given to vehement insistent outcry — **vo·cif·er·ous·ly** *adv* — **vo·cif·er·ous·ness** *n*

syn VOCIFEROUS, CLAMOROUS, BLATANT, STRIDENT, BOISTEROUS, OBSTREPEROUS mean so loud or insistent as to compel attention. VOCIFEROUS implies a vehement shouting or calling out ⟨*vociferous* cries of protest and outrage⟩. CLAMOROUS may imply insistency as well as vociferousness in demanding or protesting ⟨*clamorous* demands for prison reforms⟩. BLATANT implies an offensive bellowing or insensitive loudness ⟨*blatant* rock music⟩ ⟨a *blatant* clamor for impeachment⟩. STRIDENT suggests harsh and discordant noise ⟨heard the *strident* cry of the crow⟩. BOISTEROUS suggests a noisiness and turbulence due to high spirits ⟨a *boisterous* crowd of party goers⟩. OBSTREPEROUS suggests unruly and aggressive noisiness and resistance to restraint ⟨the *obstreperous* demonstrators were removed from the hall⟩.

vo·cod·er \'vō-,kō-dər\ *n* [*voice coder*] (1939) : an electronic mechanism that reduces speech signals to slowly varying signals transmittable over communication systems of limited frequency bandwidth

vod·ka \'väd-kə\ *n* [Russ, fr. *voda* water; akin to OE *wæter* water] (ca. 1803) : a colorless liquor of neutral spirits distilled from a mash (as of rye or wheat)

vodka martini *n* (1948) : a martini made with vodka instead of gin

vo·dun *also* **vo·doun** \vō-'dün\ *n* [Haitian Creole] (1920) : VOODOO 1

vo·gie \'vō-gē\ *adj* [origin unknown] (1712) *Scot* : PROUD, VAIN

¹**vogue** \'vōg\ *n* [MF, action of rowing, course, fashion, fr. OIt *voga*, fr. *vogare* to row] (1571) **1** *archaic* : the leading place in popularity or acceptance **2 a** : popular acceptation or favor : POPULARITY **b** : a period of popularity **3** : one that is in fashion at a particular time **syn** see FASHION — **vogue** *adj*

²**vogue** *vi* **vogued; vogu·ing** *or* **vogue·ing** [fr. *Vogue*, a fashion magazine] (1989) : to strike poses in campy imitation of fashion models esp. as a kind of dance — **vogu·er** \'vō-gər\ *n*

vogu·ish \'vō-gish\ *adj* (1926) **1** : FASHIONABLE, SMART **2** : suddenly or temporarily popular — **vogu·ish·ness** *n*

¹**voice** \'vois\ *n* [ME, fr. OF *vois*, fr. L *voc-, vox;* akin to OHG *giwahanen* to mention, Gk *epos* word, speech, Skt *vāk* voice] (14c) **1 a** : sound produced by vertebrates by means of lungs, larynx, or syrinx; *esp* : sound so produced by human beings **b** (1) : musical sound produced by the vocal folds and resonated by the cavities of head and throat (2) : the power or ability to produce musical tones (3) : SINGER (4) : one of the melodic parts in a vocal or instrumental composition (5) : condition of the vocal organs with respect to production of musical tones (6) : the use of the voice (as in singing or acting) ⟨studying ~⟩ **c** : expiration of air with the vocal cords drawn close so as to vibrate audibly (as in uttering vowels and consonant sounds as \v\ or \z\) **d** : the faculty of utterance ⟨lost my ~⟩ **2** : a sound resembling or suggesting vocal utterance **3** : an instrument or medium of expression ⟨the party became the ~ of the workers⟩ **4 a** : wish, choice, or opinion openly or formally expressed ⟨the ~ of the people⟩

b : right of expression; *also* : influential power **5** : distinction of form or a system of inflections of a verb to indicate the relation of the subject of the verb to the action which the verb expresses ⟨active and passive ~s⟩ — **with one voice** : without dissent : UNANIMOUSLY

²**voice** *vt* **voiced; voic·ing** (15c) **1** : to express in words : UTTER ⟨~ a complaint⟩ **2** : to adjust for producing the proper musical sounds **3** : to pronounce (as a consonant) with voice **syn** see EXPRESS

voice box *n* (1912) : LARYNX

voiced \'voist\ *adj* (1593) **1** : having or furnished with a voice esp. of a specified kind — often used in combination ⟨soft-*voiced*⟩ **2** : uttered with vocal cord vibration ⟨a ~ consonant⟩

voice·ful \'vois-fəl\ *adj* (ca. 1611) : having a voice or vocal quality; *also* : having a loud voice or many voices — **voice·ful·ness** *n*

voice·less \-ləs\ *adj* (1535) **1** : having no voice : MUTE **2** : not voiced : SURD ⟨a ~ consonant⟩ — **voice·less·ly** *adv* — **voice·less·ness** *n*

voice mail *n* (1981) : an electronic communication system in which spoken messages are recorded or digitized for later playback to the intended recipient

voice-over \'vois-,ō-vər\ *n* (ca. 1947) **1 a** : the voice of an unseen narrator speaking (as in a motion picture or television commercial) **b** : the voice of a visible character (as in a motion picture) expressing unspoken thoughts **2** : a recording of a voice-over

voice part *n* (1776) : VOICE 1b(4)

voice·print \'vois-,print\ *n* [*voice* + *fingerprint*] (1962) : an individually distinctive pattern of certain voice characteristics that is spectrographically produced

voic·er \'vois-sər\ *n* (1879) : one that voices; *specif* : one that voices organ pipes

voice vote *n* (1924) : a parliamentary vote taken by calling for ayes and noes and estimating which response is stronger

¹**void** \'void\ *adj* [ME *voide*, fr. OF, fr. (assumed) VL *vocitus*, alter. of L *vocivus, vacivus* empty, fr. *vacare* to be empty] (14c) **1 a** : not occupied : VACANT ⟨a ~ bishopric⟩ **b** : not inhabited : DESERTED **2** : containing nothing ⟨~ space⟩ **3** : IDLE, LEISURE **4 a** : being without : DEVOID ⟨a nature ~ of all malice⟩ **b** : having no members or examples; *specif, of a suit* : having no cards represented in a particular hand **5** : VAIN, USELESS **6 a** : of no legal force or effect : NULL ⟨a ~ contract⟩ **b** : VOIDABLE **syn** see EMPTY — **void·ness** *n*

²**void** *n* (1616) **1 a** : OPENING, GAP **b** : empty space : EMPTINESS, VACUUM **2** : the quality or state of being without something : LACK, ABSENCE **3** : a feeling of want or hollowness **4** : absence of cards of a particular suit in a hand orig. dealt to a player

³**void** *vb* [ME, fr. MF *vuidier*, fr. (assumed) VL *vocitare*, fr. *vocitus*] *vt* (14c) **1 a** : to make empty or vacant : CLEAR **b** *archaic* : VACATE, LEAVE **2** : DISCHARGE, EMIT ⟨~ excrement⟩ **3** : NULLIFY, ANNUL ⟨~ a contract⟩ ~ *vi* : to eliminate solid or liquid waste from the body — **void·er** *n*

void·able \'voi-də-bəl\ *adj* (15c) : capable of being voided; *specif* : capable of being adjudged void — **void·able·ness** *n*

void·ance \'voi-d⁰n(t)s\ *n* (14c) **1** : the act of voiding **2** *of a benefice* : the state of being without an incumbent

void·ed \'voi-dəd\ *adj* (ca. 1539) : having the inner part cut away or left vacant with a narrow border left at the sides — used of a heraldic charge

voi·là *or* **voi·la** \vwä-'lä\ *interj* [F, lit., see there] (1739) — used to call attention, to express satisfaction or approval, or to suggest an appearance as if by magic

voile \'voi(ə)l\ *n* [F, veil, fr. L *vela*, neut. pl. of *velum*] (1889) : a fine soft sheer fabric used esp. for women's summer clothing or curtains

voir dire \'vwär-'dir, 'wär-\ *n* [AF, fr. OF, to speak the truth] (1676) : a preliminary examination to determine the competency of a witness or juror

vo·lant \'vō-lənt\ *adj* [MF, fr. L *volant-, volans*, prp. of *volare* to fly] (1572) **1** : having the wings extended as if in flight — used of a heraldic bird **2** : flying or capable of flying **3** : QUICK, NIMBLE

vo·lan·te \vō-'län-(,)tā\ *adj* [It, lit., flying, fr. L *volant-, volans*, prp.] (ca. 1854) : moving with light rapidity — used as a direction in music

Vo·la·pük \'vō-lə-,pük, 'vä-\ *n* [Volapük, world's speech, fr. *vola* of the world (gen. of *vol* world, modif. of E *world*) + *pük* speech, modif. of E *speak*] (1885) : an artificial international language based largely on English but with some root words from German, French, and Latin

vo·lar \'vō-lər, -,lär\ *adj* [L *vola* hollow in the palm of the hand or sole of the foot] (1814) : relating to the palm of the hand or the sole of the foot; *specif* : located on the same side as the palm of the hand ⟨the ~ part of the forearm⟩

¹**vol·a·tile** \'vä-lə-t⁰l, *esp Brit* -,til\ *adj* [F, fr. L *volatilis*, fr. *volare* to fly] (1605) **1** : readily vaporizable at a relatively low temperature **2** : flying or having the power to fly **3 a** : LIGHTHEARTED, LIVELY **b** : easily aroused ⟨~ suspicions⟩ **c** : tending to erupt into violence : EXPLOSIVE **4 a** : unable to hold the attention fixed because of an inherent lightness or fickleness of disposition **b** : characterized by or subject to rapid or unexpected change **5** : difficult to capture or hold permanently : EVANESCENT, TRANSITORY — **vol·a·tile·ness** *n* — **vol·a·til·i·ty** \,vä-lə-'ti-lə-tē\ *n*

²**volatile** *n* (1686) : a volatile substance

volatile oil *n* (1800) : an oil that vaporizes readily; *esp* : ESSENTIAL OIL

vol·a·til·ise *Brit var of* VOLATILIZE

vol·a·til·ize \'vä-lə-t⁰l-,īz, *Brit also* və-'la-\ *vb* **-ized; -iz·ing** *vt* (1657) : to make volatile; *esp* : to cause to pass off in vapor ~ *vi* : to pass off in vapor — **vol·a·til·iz·able** \-,ī-zə-bəl\ *adj* — **vol·a·til·i·za·tion** \,vä-lə-t⁰l-ə-'zā-shən, *Brit also* və-,la-\ *n*

vol-au-vent \,vō-lō-'väⁿ\ *n* [F, lit., flight in the wind] (1828) : a baked patty shell filled with meat, fowl, game, or seafood in sauce

¹**vol·ca·nic** \väl-'ka-nik, vōl- *also* -'kä-\ *adj* (1774) **1 a** : of, relating to, or produced by a volcano **b** : characterized by volcanoes ⟨a ~ range⟩ **c** : made of materials from volcanoes **2** : explosively violent : VOLATILE ⟨~ emotions⟩ — **vol·ca·ni·cal·ly** \-ni-k(ə-)lē\ *adv*

\ə\ abut \³\ kitten, F table \ər\ further \a\ ash \ā\ ace \ä\ mop, mar
\aú\ out \ch\ chin \e\ bet \ē\ easy \g\ go \i\ hit \ī\ ice \j\ job
\ŋ\ sing \ō\ go \ó\ law \oi\ boy \th\ thin \t̲h̲\ the \ü\ loot \ú\ foot
\y\ yet \zh\ vision \á, k̲, ⁿ, œ, œ̄, ᵫ, ᵫ̄, ᵊ\ *see* Guide to Pronunciation

²**vol·can·ic** n (1894) : a volcanic rock
volcanic glass n (ca. 1840) : natural glass produced by the cooling of molten lava too rapidly to permit crystallization
vol·ca·nic·i·ty \ˌväl-kə-'ni-sə-tē, ˌvȯl-\ n (1836) : VOLCANISM
vol·ca·nism \'väl-kə-ˌni-zəm, 'vȯl-\ n (ca. 1864) : volcanic action or activity
vol·ca·no \väl-'kā-(ˌ)nō, vȯl-\ n, pl **-noes** or **-nos** [It vulcano, fr. L Volcanus, Vulcanus Vulcan] (1613) **1** : a vent in the crust of the earth or another planet from which usu. molten or hot rock and steam issue; also : a hill or mountain composed wholly or in part of the ejected material **2** : something of explosively violent potential
vol·ca·no·log·i·cal \ˌväl-kə-nᵊl-'ä-ji-kəl, ˌvȯl-\ also **vol·ca·no·log·ic** \-jik\ adj (ca. 1891) : of, relating to, or involving volcanology or volcanic phenomena ⟨∼ processes that shape the planets⟩
vol·ca·nol·o·gy \ˌväl-kə-'nä-lə-jē, ˌvȯl-\ n (1886) : a branch of science that deals with volcanic phenomena — **vol·ca·nol·o·gist** \-jist\ n
¹**vole** \'vōl\ n [F, prob. fr. voler to fly — more at VOLLEY] (1679) : GRAND SLAM I
²**vole** n [earlier vole-mouse, fr. vole- (of Scand origin; akin to ON vǫllr field) + mouse; akin to OE weald forest — more at WOLD] (1805) : any of various small rodents (Microtus and related genera) that typically have a stout body, rather blunt nose, and short ears, inhabit both moist meadows and dry uplands and do much damage to crops, and are closely related to muskrats and lemmings
vo·li·tion \vō-'li-shən, və-\ n [F, fr. ML volition-, volitio, fr. L vol- (stem of velle to will, wish) + -ition-, -itio (as in L position-, positio position) — more at WILL] (1615) **1** : an act of making a choice or decision; also : a choice or decision made **2** : the power of choosing or determining : WILL — **vo·li·tion·al** \-'lish-nəl, -'li-shə-nᵊl\ adj
vol·i·tive \'vä-lə-tiv\ adj (1660) **1** : of or relating to the will **2** : expressing a wish or permission
volks·lied \'fȯks-ˌlēt, 'fōlks-\ n, pl **volks·lie·der** \-ˌlē-dər\ [G, fr. Volk people + Lied song] (ca. 1854) : a folk song
¹**vol·ley** \'vä-lē\ n, pl **volleys** [MF volee flight, fr. voler to fly, fr. L volare] (1573) **1 a** : a flight of missiles (as arrows) **b** : simultaneous discharge of a number of missile weapons **c** : one round per gun in a battery fired as soon as a gun is ready without regard to order **d** (1) : the flight of the ball (as in volleyball or tennis) or its course before striking the ground; also : a return of the ball before it touches the ground (2) : a kick of the ball in soccer before it rebounds (3) : the exchange of the shuttlecock in badminton following the serve **2 a** : a burst of many things or a large amount at once ⟨received a ∼ of angry letters⟩ ⟨a ∼ of praise⟩ **b** : a burst of simultaneous or immediately sequential nerve impulses passing to an end organ, synapse, or center
²**volley** vb **vol·leyed; vol·ley·ing** vt (1591) **1** : to discharge in or as if in a volley **2** : to propel (an object) while in the air and before touching the ground; esp : to hit (a tennis ball) on the volley ∼ vi **1** : to become discharged in or as if in a volley **2** : to make a volley; specif : to volley an object of play (as in tennis) — **vol·ley·er** n
vol·ley·ball \'vä-lē-ˌbȯl\ n (1896) : a game played by volleying an inflated ball over a net; also : the ball used in this game
vol·plane \'väl-ˌplān, 'vȯl-\ vi **vol·planed; vol·plan·ing** [F vol plané gliding flight] (1909) **1** : to glide in or as if in an airplane **2** : GLIDE 3
Vol·sci \'vȯl-ˌskē, 'väl-ˌsī\ n pl [L] (ca. 1909) : a people of ancient Italy dwelling between the Latins and Samnites
Vol·scian \'väl-shən, 'vȯl-skē-ən\ n, pl **Volscians** (1513) **1** : a member of the Volsci **2** : the Italic language of the Volsci — **Volscian** adj
¹**volt** \'vōlt, 'vȯlt\ n [F volte, fr. It volta turn, fr. voltare to turn, fr. (assumed) VL volvitare, freq. of L volvere to roll — more at VOLUBLE] (1688) **1** : a leaping movement in fencing to avoid a thrust **2 a** : a tread or gait in which a horse going sideways makes a turn around a center **b** : a circle traced by a horse in this movement
²**volt** \'vōlt\ n [Alessandro Volta] (1873) : the practical meter-kilogram-second unit of electrical potential difference and electromotive force equal to the difference of potential between two points in a conducting wire carrying a constant current of one ampere when the power dissipated between these two points is equal to one watt and equivalent to the potential difference across a resistance of one ohm when one ampere is flowing through it
volt·age \'vōl-tij\ n (1890) **1** : electric potential or potential difference expressed in volts **2** : intensity of feeling
voltage divider n (1922) : a resistor or series of resistors provided with taps at certain points and used to provide various potential differences from a single power source
vol·ta·ic \väl-'tā-ik, vōl-, vȯl-\ adj [Alessandro Volta] (1812) : of, relating to, or producing direct electric current by chemical action (as in a battery) : GALVANIC ⟨∼ cell⟩
volt-am·pere \'vōlt-'am-ˌpir also -ˌper\ n (1896) : a unit of electric measurement equal to the product of a volt and an ampere that for direct current constitutes a measure of power equivalent to a watt
volte–face \ˌvȯlt-'fäs, ˌvȯl-tə-\ n [F, fr. It voltafaccia, fr. voltare to turn + faccia face, fr. (assumed) VL facia — more at VOLT. FACE] (1819) : a reversal in policy : ABOUT-FACE
volt·me·ter \'vōlt-ˌmē-tər\ n [ISV] (1882) : an instrument (as a galvanometer) for measuring in volts the differences in potential between different points of an electrical circuit
vol·u·ble \'väl-yə-bəl\ adj [MF or L; MF, fr. L volubilis, fr. volvere to roll; akin to OE wealwian to roll, Gk eilyein to roll, wrap] (15c) **1** : easily rolling or turning : ROTATING **2** : characterized by ready or rapid speech : GLIB, FLUENT **syn** see TALKATIVE — **vol·u·bil·i·ty** \ˌväl-yə-'bi-lə-tē\ n — **vol·u·ble·ness** \'väl-yə-bəl-nəs\ n — **vol·u·bly** \-blē\ adv
¹**vol·ume** \'väl-yəm, -(ˌ)yüm\ n [ME, fr. MF, fr. L volumen roll, scroll, fr. volvere to roll] (14c) **1 a** : a series of printed sheets bound typically in book form : BOOK **b** : a series of issues of a periodical **c** : ALBUM 1c **2** : SCROLL 1a **3** : the amount of space occupied by a three-dimensional object as measured in cubic units (as quarts or liters) : cubic capacity — see METRIC SYSTEM table, WEIGHT table **4 a** (1) : AMOUNT; also : BULK, MASS (2) : a considerable quantity **b** : the amount of a substance occupying a particular volume **c** : mass or the representation of mass in art or architecture **5** : the degree of loudness or the intensity of a sound; also : LOUDNESS **syn** see BULK — **vol·umed** \-yəmd, -(ˌ)yümd\ adj

VOLUME FORMULAS

FIGURE	FORMULA	MEANING OF LETTERS
cube	$V = a^3$	a=length of one edge
rectangular solid	$V = lwh$	l=length of base; w=width of base; h=height
pyramid	$V = \dfrac{Ah}{3}$	A=area of base; h=height
cylinder	$V = \pi r^2 h$	π=3.1416; r=radius of the base; h=height
cone	$V = \dfrac{\pi r^2 h}{3}$	π=3.1416; r=radius of the base; h=height
sphere	$V = \dfrac{4\pi r^3}{3}$	π=3.1416; r=radius

²**volume** vb **vol·umed; vol·um·ing** vt (1815) : to send or give out in volume ∼ vi : to roll or rise in volume
³**volume** adj (ca. 1945) : involving large quantities ⟨offered ∼ discounts⟩
vol·u·me·ter \'väl-yù-ˌmē-tər\ n [ISV, blend of volume and -meter] (1829) : an instrument for measuring volumes (as of gases or liquids) directly or (as of solids) by displacement of a liquid
vol·u·met·ric \ˌväl-yù-'me-trik\ adj (1857) : of, relating to, or involving the measurement of volume — **vol·u·met·ri·cal·ly** \-tri-k(ə-)lē\ adv
vol·u·mi·nos·i·ty \və-ˌlü-mə-'nä-sə-tē\ n (1782) : the quality or state of being voluminous
vol·u·mi·nous \və-'lü-mə-nəs\ adj [LL voluminosus, fr. L volumin-, volumen] (1611) **1** : consisting of many folds, coils, or convolutions : WINDING **2 a** : having or marked by great volume or bulk : LARGE ⟨long ∼ tresses⟩; also : FULL ⟨a ∼ skirt⟩ **b** : NUMEROUS ⟨trying to keep track of ∼ slips of paper⟩ **3 a** : filling or capable of filling a large volume or several volumes ⟨a ∼ literature on the subject⟩ **b** : writing or speaking much or at great length — **vol·u·mi·nous·ly** adv — **vol·u·mi·nous·ness** n
vol·un·ta·rism \'vä-lən-tə-ˌri-zəm\ n (1838) **1** : the principle or system of doing something by or relying on voluntary action or volunteers **2** : a theory that conceives will to be the dominant factor in experience or in the world — **vol·un·ta·rist** \-rist\ n — **vol·un·ta·ris·tic** \ˌvä-lən-tə-'ris-tik\ adj
¹**vol·un·tary** \'vä-lən-ˌter-ē\ adj [ME, fr. L voluntarius, fr. voluntas will, fr. velle to will, wish — more at WILL] (14c) **1** : proceeding from the will or from one's own choice or consent **2** : unconstrained by interference : SELF-DETERMINING **3** : done by design or intention : INTENTIONAL ⟨∼ manslaughter⟩ **4** : of, relating to, subject to, or regulated by the will ⟨∼ behavior⟩ **5** : having power of free choice **6** : provided or supported by voluntary action ⟨a ∼ organization⟩ **7** : acting or done of one's own free will without valuable consideration or legal obligation — **vol·un·tar·i·ly** adv — **vol·un·tar·i·ness** n
syn VOLUNTARY, INTENTIONAL, DELIBERATE, WILLING mean done or brought about of one's own will. VOLUNTARY implies freedom and spontaneity of choice or action without external compulsion ⟨a voluntary confession⟩. INTENTIONAL stresses an awareness of an end to be achieved ⟨the intentional concealment of vital information⟩. DELIBERATE implies full consciousness of the nature of one's act and its consequences ⟨deliberate acts of sabotage⟩. WILLING implies a readiness and eagerness to accede to or anticipate the wishes of another ⟨willing obedience⟩.
²**voluntary** n, pl **-tar·ies** (1598) **1 a** : a prefatory often extemporized musical piece **b** : an improvisatory organ piece played before, during, or after a religious service **2** : one who participates voluntarily : VOLUNTEER
vol·un·tary·ism \'vä-lən-ˌter-ē-ˌi-zəm\ n (1835) : VOLUNTARISM — **vol·un·tary·ist** \-ē-ist\ n
voluntary muscle n (1788) : muscle (as most striated muscle) under voluntary control
¹**vol·un·teer** \ˌvä-lən-'tir\ n [obs. F voluntaire (now volontaire), fr. voluntaire, adj., voluntary, fr. L voluntarius] (ca. 1618) **1 a** : a person who voluntarily undertakes or expresses a willingness to undertake a service: as **a** : one who enters into military service voluntarily **b** (1) : one who renders a service or takes part in a transaction while having no legal concern or interest (2) : one who receives a conveyance or transfer of property without giving valuable consideration **2** : a volunteer plant **3** cap [Volunteers of America] : a member of a quasi-military religious and philanthropic organization founded in 1896 by Commander and Mrs. Ballington Booth
²**volunteer** adj (1649) **1** : being, consisting of, or engaged in by volunteers ⟨a ∼ army⟩ ⟨∼ activities to help the mentally handicapped⟩ **2** : growing spontaneously without direct human control or supervision esp. from seeds lost from a previous crop ⟨∼ corn plants⟩
³**volunteer** vi (1755) : to offer oneself as a volunteer ∼ vt : to offer or bestow voluntarily ⟨∼ one's services⟩
vol·un·teer·ism \ˌvä-lən-'tir-ˌi-zəm\ n (1844) **1** : VOLUNTARISM 1 **2** : the act or practice of doing volunteer work in community service
vo·lup·tu·ary \və-'ləp(t)-shə-ˌwer-ē\ n, pl **-ar·ies** (ca. 1610) : a person whose chief interests are luxury and the gratification of sensual appetites — **voluptuary** adj
vo·lup·tu·ous \-shə-wəs, -shəs\ adj [ME, fr. L voluptuosus, irreg. fr. voluptas pleasure, fr. volup pleasurable; akin to Gk elpesthai to hope, L velle to wish — more at WILL] (14c) **1 a** : full of delight or pleasure to the senses : conducive to or arising from sensuous or sensual gratification : LUXURIOUS ⟨a ∼ dance⟩ ⟨∼ ornamentation⟩ **b** : suggesting sensual pleasure by fullness and beauty of form ⟨∼ nudes⟩ **2** : given to or spent in enjoyments of luxury, pleasure, or sensual gratifications ⟨a long and ∼ holiday —Edmund Wilson⟩ **syn** see SENSUOUS — **vo·lup·tu·ous·ly** adv — **vo·lup·tu·ous·ness** n
vo·lute \və-'lüt\ n [L voluta, fr. fem. of volutus, pp. of volvere to roll — more at VOLUBLE] (ca. 1696) **1** : a spiral or scroll-shaped form **2** : a spiral scroll-shaped ornament forming the chief feature of the Ionic

capital **3 a :** any of various marine gastropod mollusks (family Volutidae) with a thick short-spired shell **b :** the shell of a volute — **volute** or **vo·lut·ed** \-'lü-təd\ adj

vo·lu·tin \'väl-yə-ˌtin, və-'lü-t²n\ n [G, fr. NL volutans, specific epithet of the bacterium *Spirillum volutans* in which it was first found] (1908) **:** a granular basophilic substance that is thought to be a nucleic acid compound and that is common in microorganisms

vol·va \'väl-və, 'vȯl-\ n [NL, fr. L volva, vulva integument — more at VULVA] (ca. 1753) **:** a membranous sac or cup about the base of the stipe in many gill fungi

vol·vox \-ˌväks\ n [NL, fr. L volvere to roll] (1798) **:** any of a genus (Volvox) of flagellated unicellular green algae that form spherical colonies

vol·vu·lus \'väl-vyə-ləs, 'vȯl-\ n [NL, fr. L volvere] (1679) **:** a twisting of the intestine upon itself that causes obstruction

vo·mer \'vō-mər\ n [NL, fr. L, plowshare] (ca. 1704) **:** a bone of the skull of most vertebrates that is situated below the ethmoid region and in the human skull forms part of the nasal septum — **vo·mer·ine** \'vō-mə-ˌrīn\ adj

volva

¹vom·it \'vä-mət\ n [ME, fr. MF, fr. L vomitus, fr. vomere to vomit; akin to ON vāma seasickness, Gk emein to vomit] (14c) **1 :** an act or instance of disgorging the contents of the stomach through the mouth; *also* **:** the disgorged matter **2 :** EMETIC

²vomit vi (15c) **1 :** to disgorge the stomach contents **2 :** to spew forth **:** BELCH, GUSH ~ vt **1 :** to disgorge (the contents of the stomach) through the mouth **2 :** to eject violently or abundantly **:** SPEW **3 :** to cause to vomit — **vom·it·er** n

vom·i·to·ry \'vä-mə-ˌtȯr-ē, -ˌtȯr-\ n, pl **-ries** [LL vomitorium, fr. L vomere; fr. its disgorging the spectators] (1730) **:** an entrance piercing the banks of seats of a theater, amphitheater, or stadium

vom·i·tus \'vä-mə-təs\ n [L] (ca. 1899) **:** material discharged by vomiting

V–1 \'vē-'wən\ n [G, abbr. for Vergeltungswaffe 1, lit., reprisal weapon 1] (1944) **:** BUZZ BOMB

¹voo·doo \'vü-(ˌ)dü\ n, pl **voodoos** [Louisiana Creole voudou, prob. fr. Ewe vódũ tutelary deity, demon] (1850) **1 :** a religion that is derived from African polytheism and ancestor worship and is practiced chiefly in Haiti **2 a :** a person who deals in spells and necromancy **b** (1) **:** a sorcerer's spell **:** HEX (2) **:** a hexed object **:** CHARM — **voodoo** adj

²voodoo vt (1880) **:** to bewitch by or as if by means of voodoo **:** HEX

voo·doo·ism \'vü-(ˌ)dü-ˌi-zəm\ n (1865) **1 :** VOODOO 1 **2 :** the practice of witchcraft — **voo·doo·ist** \-ist\ n — **voo·doo·is·tic** \ˌvü-(ˌ)dü-'is-tik\ adj

vo·ra·cious \vȯ-'rā-shəs, və-\ adj [L vorac-, vorax, fr. vorare to devour; akin to OE ācweorran to guzzle, L gurges whirlpool, Gk bibrōskein to devour] (1635) **1 :** having a huge appetite **:** RAVENOUS **2 :** excessively eager **:** INSATIABLE ⟨a ~ reader⟩ — **vo·ra·cious·ly** adv — **vo·ra·cious·ness** n

syn VORACIOUS, GLUTTONOUS, RAVENOUS, RAPACIOUS mean excessively greedy. VORACIOUS applies esp. to habitual gorging with food or drink ⟨teenagers are often *voracious* eaters⟩. GLUTTONOUS applies to one who delights in eating or acquiring things esp. beyond the point of necessity or satiety ⟨an admiral who was *gluttonous* for glory⟩. RAVENOUS implies excessive hunger and suggests violent or grasping methods of dealing with food or with whatever satisfies an appetite ⟨a nation with a *ravenous* lust for territorial expansion⟩. RAPACIOUS often suggests excessive and utterly selfish acquisitiveness or avarice ⟨*rapacious* developers indifferent to environmental concerns⟩.

vo·rac·i·ty \vȯ-'ra-sə-tē, və-\ n (1526) **:** the quality or state of being voracious

vor·la·ge \'fȯr-ˌlä-gə, 'fȯr-\ n [G, lit., forward position, fr. vor fore + Lage position] (1936) **:** the position of a skier leaning forward from the ankles usu. without lifting the heels from the skis

-vorous adj comb form [L -vorus, fr. vorare to devour] **:** eating **:** feeding on ⟨frugivorous⟩

vor·tex \'vȯr-ˌteks\ n, pl **vor·ti·ces** \'vȯr-tə-ˌsēz\ also **vor·tex·es** \'vȯr-ˌtek-səz\ [NL vortic-, vortex, fr. L vertex, vortex whirlpool — more at VERTEX] (1652) **1 a :** a mass of fluid (as a liquid) with a whirling or circular motion that tends to form a cavity or vacuum in the center of the circle and to draw toward this cavity or vacuum bodies subject to its action; *esp* **:** WHIRLPOOL, EDDY **b :** a region within a body of fluid in which the fluid elements have an angular velocity **2 :** something that resembles a whirlpool ⟨the hellish ~ of battle —*Time*⟩

vor·ti·cal \'vȯr-ti-kəl\ adj (1653) **:** of, relating to, or resembling a vortex **:** SWIRLING — **vor·ti·cal·ly** \-k(ə-)lē\ adv

vor·ti·cel·la \ˌvȯr-tə-'se-lə\ n, pl **-cel·lae** \-'se-(ˌ)lē\ or **-cellas** [NL, fr. L vortic-, vortex] (1787) **:** any of a genus (Vorticella) of stalked bell-shaped ciliates

vor·ti·cism \'vȯr-tə-ˌsi-zəm\ n [L vortic-, vortex] (1914) **:** an English abstract art movement from about 1912–15 embracing cubist and futurist concepts — **vor·ti·cist** \-sist\ n

vor·tic·i·ty \vȯr-'ti-sə-tē\ n (1888) **1 :** the state of a fluid in vortical motion; *broadly* **:** vortical motion **2 :** a measure of vortical motion; *esp* **:** a vector measure of local rotation in a fluid flow

vor·ti·cose \'vȯr-ti-ˌkōs\ adj (1783) archaic **:** VORTICAL

vo·ta·ress \'vō-tə-rəs\ n (1589) **:** a female votary

vo·ta·rist \-rist\ n (1603) **:** VOTARY

vo·ta·ry \'vō-tə-rē\ n, pl **-ries** [L votum vow] (1546) **1** archaic **:** a sworn adherent **2 a :** ENTHUSIAST, DEVOTEE **b :** a devoted adherent **3 a :** a devout or zealous worshiper **b :** a staunch believer or advocate

¹vote \'vōt\ n [ME (Sc), fr. L votum vow, wish — more at VOW] (15c) **1 a :** a usu. formal expression of opinion or will in response to a proposed decision; *esp* **:** one given as an indication of approval or disapproval of a proposal, motion, or candidate for office **b :** the total number of such expressions of opinion made known at a single time (as at an election) **c :** an expression of opinion or preference that resembles a vote **d :** BALLOT 1 **2 :** the collective opinion or verdict of a body of persons expressed by voting **3 :** the right to cast a vote; *specif* **:** the right of suffrage **:** FRANCHISE **4 a :** the act or process of voting ⟨brought the question to a ~⟩ **b :** a method of voting **5 :** a formal

expression of a wish, will, or choice voted by a meeting **6 a :** VOTER **b :** a group of voters with some common and identifying characteristics ⟨the labor ~⟩ **7** chiefly Brit **a :** a proposition to be voted on; *esp* **:** a legislative money item **b :** APPROPRIATION

²vote vb **vot·ed; vot·ing** vi (1552) **1 :** to express one's views in response to a poll; *esp* **:** to exercise a political franchise **2 :** to express an opinion ⟨consumers . . . ~ with their dollars —Lucia Mouat⟩ ~ vt **1 :** to choose, endorse, decide the disposition of, defeat, or authorize by vote **2 a :** to adjudge by general agreement **:** DECLARE **b :** to offer as a suggestion **:** PROPOSE ⟨I ~ we all go home⟩ **3 a :** to cause to vote in a given way **b :** to cause to be cast for or against a proposal **4 :** to vote in accordance with or in the interest of ⟨~ your conscience⟩ ⟨*voted* their pocketbooks⟩

vote·less \'vōt-ləs\ adj (1672) **:** having no vote; *esp* **:** denied the political franchise

vot·er \'vō-tər\ n (ca. 1578) **:** one that votes or has the legal right to vote

voting machine n (1900) **:** a mechanical device for recording and counting votes cast in an election

vo·tive \'vō-tiv\ adj [L votivus, fr. votum vow] (1597) **1 :** consisting of or expressing a vow, wish, or desire ⟨a ~ prayer⟩ **2 :** offered or performed in fulfillment of a vow or in gratitude or devotion — **vo·tive·ly** adv — **vo·tive·ness** n

votive candle n (1824) **1 :** a candle lit in devotion or gratitude **2 :** a small squat candle

votive mass n (1738) **:** a mass celebrated for a special intention (as for a wedding or funeral) in place of the mass of the day

vo·tress \'vō-trəs\ n [by alter.] (1590) archaic **:** VOTARESS

¹vouch \'vaúch\ vb [ME vochen, vouchen, fr. MF vocher, fr. L vocare to call, summon, fr. vox voice — more at VOICE] vt (14c) **1 :** to summon into court to warrant or defend a title **2** archaic **a :** ASSERT, AFFIRM **b :** ATTEST **3** archaic **:** to cite or refer to as authority or supporting evidence **4 a :** PROVE, SUBSTANTIATE **b :** to verify (a business transaction) by examining documentary evidence ~ vi **1 :** to give a guarantee **:** become surety **2 a :** to supply supporting evidence or testimony **b :** to give personal assurance *syn* see CERTIFY

²vouch n (1603) obs **:** ALLEGATION, DECLARATION

vouch·ee \vaú-'chē\ n (15c) **:** a person for whom another vouches

¹vouch·er \'vaú-chər\ n [MF vocher, voucher to vouch] (ca. 1523) **1 :** an act of vouching **2 a :** a piece of supporting evidence **:** PROOF **b :** a documentary record of a business transaction **c :** a written affidavit or authorization **:** CERTIFICATE **d :** a form or check indicating a credit against future purchases or expenditures

²voucher vt (1609) **1 :** to establish the authenticity of **2 :** to prepare a voucher for

³voucher n [¹vouch + ²-er] (1612) archaic **:** one that guarantees **:** SURETY

vouch·safe \vaúch-'sāf, 'vaúch-ˌ\ vt **vouch·safed; vouch·saf·ing** (1587) **1 a :** to grant or furnish often in a gracious or condescending manner **b :** to give by way of reply ⟨refused to ~ an explanation⟩ **2 :** to grant as a privilege or special favor *syn* see GRANT — **vouch·safe·ment** \vaúch-'sāf-mənt\ n

vous·soir \vü-'swär, 'vü-ˌ\ n [F, fr. (assumed) VL volsorium, fr. L volvere to roll — more at VOLUBLE] (1728) **:** one of the wedge-shaped pieces forming an arch or vault — see ARCH illustration

Vou·vray \vü-'vrā\ n [F, fr. Vouvray, village in France] (1885) **:** a semidry to semisweet white wine from the Loire Valley of France that is often produced as a sparkling wine

¹vow \'vaú\ n [ME vowe, fr. OF vou, fr. L votum, fr. vovēre to vow; akin to Gk euchesthai to pray, vow, Skt vāghat sacrificer] (14c) **:** a solemn promise or assertion; *specif* **:** one by which a person is bound to an act, service, or condition

²vow vt (14c) **1 :** to promise solemnly **:** SWEAR **2 :** to bind or consecrate by a vow ~ vi **1 :** to make a vow — **vow·er** \'vaú-(ə)r\ n

³vow vt [ME, short for avowen] (14c) **:** AVOW, DECLARE

vow·el \'vaú(-ə)l\ n [ME, fr. MF vouel, fr. L vocalis — more at VOCALIC] (14c) **1 :** one of a class of speech sounds in the articulation of which the oral part of the breath stream is not blocked and is not constricted enough to cause audible friction; *broadly* **:** the one most prominent sound in a syllable **2 :** a letter or other symbol representing a vowel — usu. used in English of a, e, i, o, u, and sometimes y

vow·el·ize \'vaú-(ə-)ˌlīz\ vt **-ized; -iz·ing** (1883) **:** to furnish with vowel points

vowel point n (1764) **:** a mark placed below or otherwise near a consonant in some languages (as Hebrew) and representing the vowel sound that precedes or follows the consonant sound

vowel rhyme n (1838) **:** ASSONANCE 2b

vox po·pu·li \ˌväks-'pä-pyü-ˌlī, -pyə-(ˌ)lē, -pə-(ˌ)lē\ n [L, voice of the people] (ca. 1550) **:** popular sentiment

¹voy·age \'vȯi-ij, 'vȯi-ij\ n [ME, fr. OF voiage, fr. LL viaticum, fr. L, traveling money, fr. neut. of viaticus of a journey, fr. via way — more at WAY] (14c) **1 :** an act or instance of traveling **:** JOURNEY **2 :** a course or period of traveling by other than land routes **3 :** an account of a journey esp. by sea

²voyage vb **voy·aged; voy·ag·ing** vi (15c) **:** to take a trip **:** TRAVEL ~ vt **:** SAIL, TRAVERSE — **voy·ag·er** n

voya·geur \ˌvȯi-ə-'zhər, ˌvwä-yä-\ n [CanF, fr. F, traveler, fr. voyager to travel, fr. voyage voyage, fr. OF voiage] (1793) **:** a man employed by a fur company to transport goods to and from remote stations esp. in the Canadian Northwest

voy·eur \vwä-'yər, vȯi-'ər\ n [F, lit., one who sees, fr. MF, fr. voir to see, fr. L vidēre — more at WIT] (1900) **1 :** one obtaining sexual gratification from seeing sex organs and sexual acts; *broadly* **:** one who habitually seeks sexual stimulation by visual means **2 :** a prying observer who is usu. seeking the sordid or the scandalous — **voy·eur·ism** \-ˌi-zəm\ n — **voy·eur·is·tic** \ˌvwä-(ˌ)yər-'is-tik, ˌvȯi-ər-\ adj — **voy·eur·is·ti·cal·ly** \-ti-k(ə-)lē\ adv

\ə\ abut \ˌ'\ kitten, F table \ər\ further \a\ ash \ā\ ace \ä\ mop, mar \aú\ out \ch\ chin \e\ bet \ē\ easy \g\ go \i\ hit \ī\ ice \j\ job \ŋ\ sing \ō\ go \ȯ\ law \ȯi\ boy \th\ thin \th\ the \ü\ loot \ú\ foot \y\ yet \zh\ vision \à, k̲, ⁿ, œ, œ̄, ʊœ, ⁱᴇ, ᵞ\ see Guide to Pronunciation

vroom \'vrüm, və-'rüm\ *vi* [imit. of the noise of an engine] (1965) : to operate a motor vehicle at high speed or so as to create a great deal of engine noise

V sign *n* (1942) : a sign made by raising the index and middle fingers in a V and used as a victory salute or a gesture of approval

V–2 \'vē-'tü\ *n* [G, abbr. for *Vergeltungswaffe 2*, lit., reprisal weapon 2] (1944) : a rocket-propelled bomb of German invention

vug \'vəg\ *n* [Corn dial. *vooga* underground chamber, fr. L *fovea* small pit] (1818) : a small unfilled cavity in a lode or in rock — **vug·gy** \'və-gē\ *adj*

Vul·can \'vəl-kən\ *n* [L *Volcanus, Vulcanus*] : the Roman god of fire and metalworking — compare HEPHAESTUS

vul·ca·ni·an \,vəl-'kā-nē-ən\ *adj* (1602) **1** *cap* : of or relating to Vulcan or to working in metals (as iron) **2** : of or relating to a volcanic eruption in which highly viscous or solid lava is blown into fragments and dust

vul·ca·nic·i·ty \,vəl-kə-'ni-sə-tē\ *n* (1873) : VOLCANISM

vul·ca·ni·sate, vul·ca·ni·sa·tion, vul·ca·nise *Brit var of* VULCANIZATE, VULCANIZATION, VULCANIZE

vul·ca·nism \'vəl-kə-,ni-zəm\ *n* (1877) : VOLCANISM

vul·ca·ni·zate \'vəl-kə-nə-,zāt, ,vəl-kə-'ni-\ *n* [back-formation fr. *vulcanization*] (1926) : a vulcanized product

vul·ca·ni·za·tion \,vəl-kə-nə-'zā-shən\ *n* (1846) : the process of treating crude or synthetic rubber or similar plastic material chemically to give it useful properties (as elasticity, strength, and stability)

vul·ca·nize \'vəl-kə-,nīz\ *vb* **-nized; -niz·ing** [ISV, fr. L *Vulcanus* Vulcan, fire] *vt* (1846) : to subject to vulcanization ~ *vi* : to undergo vulcanization — **vul·ca·niz·er** *n*

vulcanized fiber *n* [fr. *Vulcanized Fibre*, a trademark] (ca. 1884) : a tough substance made by treatment of cellulose and used for luggage and electrical insulation and in packaging

vul·ca·nol·o·gy \,vəl-kə-'nä-lə-jē\ *n* [ISV] (1858) : VOLCANOLOGY — **vul·ca·nol·o·gist** \-jist\ *n*

vul·gar \'vəl-gər\ *adj* [ME, fr. L *vulgaris* of the mob, vulgar, fr. *volgus, vulgus* mob, common people] (14c) **1 a** : generally used, applied, or accepted **b** : understood in or having the ordinary sense ⟨they reject the ~ conception of miracle —W. R. Inge⟩ **2** : VERNACULAR ⟨the ~ name of a plant⟩ **3 a** : of or relating to the common people : PLEBEIAN **b** : generally current : PUBLIC ⟨the ~ opinion of that time⟩ **c** : of the usual, typical, or ordinary kind **4 a** : lacking in cultivation, perception, or taste : COARSE **b** : morally crude, undeveloped, or unregenerate : GROSS **c** : ostentatious or excessive in expenditure or display : PRETENTIOUS **5 a** : offensive in language : EARTHY **b** : lewdly or profanely indecent *syn* see COMMON, COARSE — **vul·gar·ly** *adv*

vulgar era *n* (1716) : CHRISTIAN ERA

vul·gar·i·an \,vəl-'gar-ē-ən, -'ger-\ *n* (1804) : a vulgar person

vul·gar·ise *Brit var of* VULGARIZE

vul·gar·ism \'vəl-gə-,ri-zəm\ *n* (ca. 1676) **1** : VULGARITY **2 a** : a word or expression originated or used chiefly by illiterate persons **b** : a coarse word or phrase : OBSCENITY

vul·gar·i·ty \,vəl-'gar-ə-tē\ *n, pl* **-ties** (1579) **1** : something vulgar **2** : the quality or state of being vulgar

vul·gar·ize \'vəl-gə-,rīz\ *vt* **-ized; -iz·ing** (1709) **1** : to diffuse generally : POPULARIZE **2** : to make vulgar : COARSEN — **vul·gar·i·za·tion** \,vəl-gə-rə-'zā-shən\ *n* — **vul·gar·iz·er** \'vəl-gə-,rī-zər\ *n*

Vulgar Latin *n* (1818) : the nonclassical Latin of ancient Rome including the speech of plebeians and the informal speech of the educated established by comparative evidence as the chief source of the Romance languages

vul·gate \'vəl-,gāt, -gət\ *n* [ML *vulgata*, fr. LL *vulgata editio* edition in general circulation] (1728) **1** *cap* : a Latin version of the Bible authorized and used by the Roman Catholic Church **2** : a commonly accepted text or reading **3** : the speech of the common people and esp. of uneducated people

vul·gus \'vəl-gəs\ *n* [prob. alter. of obs. *vulgars* English sentences to be translated into Latin] (1856) : a short composition in Latin verse formerly common as an exercise in some English public schools

vul·ner·a·ble \'vəl-n(ə-)rə-bəl, 'vəl-nər-bəl\ *adj* [LL *vulnerabilis*, fr. L *vulnerare* to wound, fr. *vulner-, vulnus* wound; prob. akin to L *vellere* to pluck, Gk *oulē* wound] (1605) **1** : capable of being physically wounded **2** : open to attack or damage : ASSAILABLE **3** : liable to increased penalties but entitled to increased bonuses after winning a game in contract bridge — **vul·ner·a·bil·i·ty** \,vəl-n(ə-)rə-'bi-lə-tē\ *n* — **vul·ner·a·ble·ness** \'vəl-n(ə-)rə-bəl-nəs, 'vəl-nər-bəl-\ *n* — **vul·ner·a·bly** \-blē\ *adv*

¹vul·ner·ary \'vəl-nə-,rer-ē\ *adj* [L *vulnerarius*, fr. *vulner-, vulnus*] (1599) : used for or useful in healing wounds ⟨~ plants⟩

²vulnerary *n, pl* **-ar·ies** (1601) : a vulnerary remedy

vul·pine \'vəl-,pīn\ *adj* [L *vulpinus*, fr. *vulpes* fox; perh. akin to Gk *alōpēx* fox — more at ALOPECIA] (1628) **1** : of, relating to, or resembling a fox **2** : FOXY, CRAFTY

vul·ture \'vəl-chər\ *n* [ME, fr. L *vultur*] (14c) **1** : any of various large raptorial birds (families Accipitridae and Cathartidae) that are related to the hawks, eagles, and falcons but have weaker claws and the head usu. naked and that subsist chiefly or entirely on carrion **2** : a rapacious or predatory person — **vul·tur·ish** \-chə-rish\ *adj*

vul·tur·ine \-chə-,rīn\ *adj* (1647) **1** : of, relating to, or characteristic of vultures **2** : RAPACIOUS, PREDATORY ⟨~ legislators⟩

vul·tur·ous \'vəl-chə-rəs, 'vəlch-rəs\ *adj* (1623) : resembling a vulture esp. in rapacity or scavenging habits

vul·va \'vəl-və\ *n, pl* **vul·vae** \-,vē, -,vī\ [NL, fr. L *volva, vulva* womb, female genitals; akin to Skt *ulva* womb and perh. to L *volvere* to roll — more at VOLUBLE] (ca. 1577) : the external parts of the female genital organs — **vul·val** \'vəl-vəl\ *or* **vul·var** \-vər, -,vär\ *adj*

vul·vo·vag·i·ni·tis \,vəl-(,)vō-,va-jə-'nī-təs\ *n* [NL] (1897) : coincident inflammation of the vulva and vagina

vying *pres part of* VIE

---

w \'də-bəl-(,)yü, 'də-bə-; 'dəb-(,)yü, -yə; 'dəb-yē\ *n, pl* **w's** *or* **ws** \-(,)yüz, -yəz, -yēz\ *often cap, often attrib* (15c) **1 a** : the 23d letter of the English alphabet **b** : a graphic representation of this letter **c** : a speech counterpart of orthographic *w* **2** : a graphic device for reproducing the letter *w* **3** : one designated *w* esp. as the 23d in order or class **4** : something shaped like the letter W

W *n* (1960) : W PARTICLE

wab·ble \'wä-bəl\ *var of* WOBBLE

Wac \'wak\ *n* [Women's Army Corps] (1943) : a member of the Women's Army Corps

wacked–out *var of* WHACKED-OUT

wacko \'wa-(,)kō\ *adj* [by alter.] (1975) : WACKY — **wacko** *n*

wacky \'wa-kē\ *adj* **wack·i·er; -est** [perh. fr. E dial. *whacky* fool] (ca. 1935) : absurdly or amusingly eccentric or irrational : CRAZY — **wack·i·ly** \'wa-kə-lē\ *adv* — **wack·i·ness** \'wa-kē-nəs\ *n*

¹wad \'wäd\ *n* [ML *wadda*] (1573) **1** : a small mass, bundle, or tuft: as **a** : a soft mass esp. of a loose fibrous material variously used (as to stop an aperture, pad a garment, or hold grease around an axle) **b** (1) : a soft plug used to retain a powder charge or to avoid windage esp. in a muzzle-loading gun (2) : a felt or paper disk used to separate the components of a shotgun cartridge **c** : a small mass of a chewing substance ⟨a ~ of gum⟩ **2** : a considerable amount (as of money) **3 a** : a roll of paper money **b** : MONEY

²wad *vt* **wad·ded; wad·ding** (1579) **1 a** : to insert a wad into ⟨~ a gun⟩ **b** : to hold in by a wad ⟨~ a bullet in a gun⟩ **2** : to form into a wad or wadding; *esp* : to roll or crush into a tight wad **3** : to stuff or line with some soft substance — **wad·der** *n*

wad·ding \'wä-diŋ\ *n* (1627) **1** : wads or material for making wads **2** : a soft mass or sheet of short loose fibers used for stuffing or padding

¹wad·dle \'wä-d²l\ *vi* **wad·dled; wad·dling** \'wäd-liŋ, 'wä-d²l-iŋ\ [freq. of *wade*] (1592) **1** : to walk with short steps swinging the forepart of the body from side to side **2** : to move clumsily in a manner suggesting a waddle — **wad·dler** \'wäd-lər, 'wä-d²l-ər\ *n*

²waddle *n* (1691) : an awkward clumsy swaying gait

¹wad·dy \'wä-dē\ *n, pl* **waddies** [Dharuk (Australian aboriginal language of the Port Jackson area) *wadi* stick, wooden weapon] (ca. 1790) *Austral* : CLUB 1a

²waddy *vt* **wad·died; wad·dy·ing** (1833) *Austral* : to attack or beat with a waddy

³wad·dy *or* **wad·die** \'wä-dē\ *n, pl* **waddies** [origin unknown] (1897) *West* : COWBOY

¹wade \'wād\ *vb* **wad·ed; wad·ing** [ME, fr. OE *wadan*; akin to OHG *watan* to go, wade, L *vadere* to go] *vi* (13c) **1** : to step in or through a medium (as water) offering more resistance than air **2** : to move or proceed with difficulty or labor **3** : to set to work or attack with determination or vigor — used with *in* or *into* ⟨~ into a task⟩ ~ *vt* : to pass or cross by wading — **wad·able** *or* **wade·able** \'wā-də-bəl\ *adj*

²wade *n* (1665) : an act of wading ⟨a ~ in the brook⟩

Wade–Giles \'wād-'gīlz\ *n* [Thomas F. *Wade* †1895 Brit. diplomat & Herbert A. *Giles* †1935 Brit. sinologist] (1943) : a system for romanizing Chinese ideograms in which tones are indicated by superscript numbers and consonantal aspiration is indicated by an apostrophe — compare PINYIN

wad·er \'wā-dər\ *n* (1673) **1** : one that wades **2** : SHOREBIRD; *also* : WADING BIRD **3** *pl* : high waterproof boots or a one-piece waterproof garment usu. consisting of pants with attached boots that are used for wading (as when fishing)

wa·di \'wä-dē\ *n* [Ar *wādiy*] (1839) **1** : the bed or valley of a stream in regions of southwestern Asia and northern Africa that is usu. dry except during the rainy season and that often forms an oasis : GULLY, WASH **2** : a shallow usu. sharply defined depression in a desert region

wading bird *n* (ca. 1843) : any of an order (Ciconiiformes) of long-legged birds (as herons, bitterns, storks, and flamingos) that wade in water in search of food

wading pool *n* (1921) : a shallow pool of portable or permanent construction used by children for wading

waders

wad·mal or **wad·mol** or **wad·mel** \'wäd-məl\ n [ME wadmale, fr. ON vathmāl, lit., standard cloth, fr. vāth cloth, clothing + māl measure; akin to L metiri to measure — more at WEED, MEASURE] (14c) : a coarse rough woolen fabric formerly used in the British Isles and Scandinavia for protective coverings and warm clothing

wae·sucks \'wä-,səks\ interj [Sc wae woe (fr. ME wa) + sucks, alter. of E sakes — more at WOE] (ca. 1774) Scot — used to express pity

Waf \'waf\ n [Women in the Air Force] (1948) : a member of the women's component of the air force formed after World War II

¹wa·fer \'wā-fər\ n [ME, fr. ONF waufre, of Gmc origin; akin to MD wafel, wafer waffle] (14c) **1 a** : a thin crisp cake, candy, or cracker **b** : a round thin piece of unleavened bread used in the celebration of the Eucharist **2** : an adhesive disk of dried paste with added coloring matter used as a seal **3 a** : a thin disk or ring resembling a wafer and variously used (as for a valve or diaphragm) **b** : a thin slice of semiconductor (as silicon) used as a base for an electronic component or circuit

²wafer vt **wa·fered; wa·fer·ing** \-f(ə-)riŋ\ (1748) **1** : to seal, close, or fasten with a wafer **2** : to divide (as a silicon rod) into wafers

waff \'waf\ n [E dial. waff to wave] (1600) **1** chiefly Scot : a waving motion **2** chiefly Scot : PUFF, GUST

¹waf·fle \'wä-fəl, 'wo-\ n [D wafel, fr. MD wafel, wafer; akin to OE wefan to weave] (1744) : a crisp cake of batter baked in a waffle iron

²waffle vi **waf·fled; waf·fling** \-f(ə-)liŋ\ [freq. of obs. woff to yelp, of imit. origin] (1868) **1** : EQUIVOCATE, VACILLATE; also : YO-YO, FLIP-FLOP **2** : to talk or write foolishly : BLATHER ⟨can ~ . . . tiresomely off the point —Times Lit. Supp.⟩ — **waf·fler** \-f(ə-)lər\ n

³waffle n (ca. 1888) : empty or pretentious words : TRIPE

waffle iron n (1794) : a cooking utensil having two hinged metal parts that shut upon each other and impress surface projections on waffles that are being cooked

waf·fle·stomp·er \'wä-fəl-,stäm-pər, 'wo-, -,stom-\ n [fr. the pattern left by the soles] (1972) : a hiking boot with a lug sole

¹waft \'wäft, 'waft\ vb [assumed ME waughten to guard, convoy, fr. MD or MLG wachten to watch, guard; akin to OE wæccan to watch — more at WAKE] vi (ca. 1513) **1** : to move or go lightly on or as if on a buoyant medium ~ vt : to cause to move or go lightly by or as if by the impulse of wind or waves — **waft·er** n

²waft n (1607) **1** : something (as an odor) that is wafted : WHIFF **2** : a slight breeze : PUFF **3** : the act of waving **4** : a pennant or flag used to signal or to show wind direction

waft·age \'wäf-tij, 'waf-\ n (1558) : the act of wafting or state of being wafted; broadly : CONVEYANCE

waf·ture \'wäf(t)-shər, 'waf(t)-\ n (1601) : the act of waving or a wavelike motion

¹wag \'wag\ vb **wagged; wag·ging** [ME waggen; akin to MHG wacken to totter, OE wegan to move — more at WAY] vi (13c) **1** : to be in motion : STIR **2** : to move to and fro or up and down esp. with quick jerky motions **3** : to move in chatter or gossip ⟨scandal caused tongues to ~⟩ **4** archaic : DEPART **5** : WADDLE ~ vt **1** : to swing to and fro or up and down esp. with quick jerky motions : SWITCH; specif : to nod (the head) or shake (a finger) at (as in assent or mild reproof) **2** : to move (as the tongue) animatedly in conversation — **wag·ger** n

²wag n (1589) : an act of wagging : SHAKE

³wag n [prob. short for obs. E waghalter gallows bird, fr. E ¹wag + halter] (ca. 1553) **1** : WIT, JOKER **2** obs : a young man : CHAP

¹wage \'wāj\ n [ME, pledge, wage, fr. ONF, of Gmc origin; akin to Goth wadi pledge — more at WED] (14c) **1 a** : a payment usu. of money for labor or services usu. according to contract and on an hourly, daily, or piecework basis — often used in pl. **b** pl : the share of the national product attributable to labor as a factor in production **2** : RECOMPENSE, REWARD — usu. used in pl. but sing. or pl. in constr. ⟨the ~s of sin is death —Rom 6:23 (RSV)⟩ — **wage·less** \'wāj-ləs\ adj

²wage vb **waged; wag·ing** [ME, to pledge, give as security, fr. ONF wagier, fr. wage] vt (15c) : to engage in or carry on ⟨~ war⟩ ⟨~ a campaign⟩ ~ vi : to be in process of occurring ⟨the riot waged for several hours —Amer. Guide Series: Md.⟩

wage earner n (1885) : a person who works for wages or salary

¹wa·ger \'wā-jər\ n [ME, pledge, bet, fr. AF wageure, fr. ONF wagier to pledge] (14c) **1 a** : something (as a sum of money) risked on an uncertain event : STAKE **b** : something on which bets are laid : GAMBLE ⟨do a stunt as a ~⟩ **2** archaic : an act of giving a pledge to take and abide by the result of some action

²wager vb **wa·gered; wa·ger·ing** \'wāj-riŋ, 'wā-jə-\ vi (1602) : to make a bet ~ vt : to risk or venture on a final outcome; specif : to lay as a gamble : BET ⟨~ $5 on a horse⟩ — **wa·ger·er** \'wā-jər-ər\ n

wage scale n (1902) : a schedule of wage rates for related tasks; broadly : the general level of wages in an industry or region

wage slave n (1886) : a person dependent on wages or a salary for a livelihood

wage·work·er \'wāj-,wər-kər\ n (1876) : WAGE EARNER

wag·gery \'wa-gə-rē\ n, pl -ger·ies (1594) **1** : mischievous merriment : PLEASANTRY **2** : JEST; esp : PRACTICAL JOKE

wag·gish \'wa-gish\ adj (1589) **1** : resembling or characteristic of a wag ⟨a ~ friend⟩ ⟨a ~ prose style⟩ **2** : done or made in waggery or for sport : HUMOROUS ⟨~ spoofs of popular songs⟩ — **wag·gish·ly** adv — **wag·gish·ness** n

¹wag·gle \'wa-gəl\ vb **wag·gled; wag·gling** \-g(ə-)liŋ\ [freq. of ¹wag] vt (1594) : to move frequently one way and the other : WAG ~ vi : to reel, sway, or move from side to side : WAG — **wag·gly** \-g(ə-)lē\ adj

²waggle n (ca. 1866) **1** : an instance of waggling : a jerky motion back and forth or up and down **2** : a preliminary swinging of a golf club head back and forth over the ball before the swing

wag·gon chiefly Brit var of WAGON

¹Wag·ne·ri·an \väg-'nir-ē-ən, -'ner-\ adj [Richard Wagner] (1873) : of, relating to, characteristic of, or suggestive of Wagner or his music or theories

²Wagnerian n (1882) : an admirer of the musical theories and style of Wagner

Wag·ner·ite \'väg-nə-,rīt\ n (1855) : WAGNERIAN

¹wag·on \'wa-gən\ n [D wagen, fr. MD — more at WAIN] (15c) **1 a** : a usu. four-wheel vehicle for transporting bulky commodities and drawn orig. by animals **b** : a lighter typically horse-drawn vehicle for transporting goods or passengers **c** : PADDY WAGON **2** Brit : a railway

freight car **3** : a low four-wheel vehicle with an open rectangular body and a retroflex tongue for the play or use (as for carrying newspapers) of a child **4** : a small wheeled table used for the service of a dining room **5** : a delivery truck ⟨milk ~⟩ **6** : STATION WAGON — **off the wagon** : no longer abstaining from alcoholic beverages — **on the wagon** : abstaining from alcoholic beverages

²wagon vi (1606) : to travel or transport goods by wagon ~ vt : to transport (goods) by wagon

wag·on·er \'wa-gə-nər\ n (1544) **1** : a person who drives a wagon or transports goods by wagon **2** cap, obs : BOÖTES

wag·on·ette \,wa-gə-'net\ n (ca. 1858) : a light wagon with two facing seats along the sides behind a transverse front seat

wag·on–lit \vä-gōⁿ-'lē\ n, pl **wagons–lits** or **wagon–lits** \-gōⁿ-'lē(z)\ [F, fr. wagon railroad car + lit bed] (1884) : a railroad sleeping car

wagon master n (1645) : a person in charge of one or more wagons

wagon train n (1810) : a column of wagons (as of supplies for a group of settlers) traveling overland

wag·tail \'wag-,tāl\ n (1510) : any of various chiefly Old World oscine birds (family Motacillidae) related to the pipits and having a trim slender body and a very long tail that they habitually jerk up and down

Wah·habi also **Wa·habi** \wə-'hä-bē, wä-\ n [Ar wahhābiy, fr. Muhammad b. 'Abd al-Wahhāb (Abdul-Wahhab) †1787 Arab. religious reformer] (1807) : a member of a puritanical Muslim sect founded in Arabia in the 18th century by Muhammad ibn-Abdul Wahhab and revived by ibn-Saud in the 20th century — **Wah·hab·ism** \-'hä-,bizəm\ n — **Wah·hab·ite** \-,bīt\ adj or n

wa·hi·ne \wä-'hē-nē, -(,)nä\ n [Maori & Hawaiian, woman] (1773) **1** : a Polynesian woman **2** : a female surfer

¹wa·hoo \'wä-,hü, 'wo-\ n, pl **wahoos** [origin unknown] (1770) : WINGED ELM

²wahoo n, pl **wahoos** [Dakota wāhu, fr. wā- arrow + hu wood] (1857) : a shrubby No. American spindle tree (Euonymus atropurpureus) having purple capsules which in dehiscence expose the scarlet-ariled seeds — called also burning bush

³wahoo n, pl **wahoos** [origin unknown] (ca. 1900) : a large vigorous mackerel (Acanthocybium solandri) that is common in warm seas and esteemed as a food and sport fish

⁴wa·hoo \'wä-'hü\ interj (ca. 1924) chiefly West — used to express exuberance or enthusiasm or to attract attention

wah-wah pedal var of WA-WA PEDAL

¹waif \'wāf\ n [ME, fr. ONF, adj., lost, unclaimed, prob. of Scand origin; akin to ON veif something flapping, veifa to be in movement — more at WIPE] (14c) **1 a** : a piece of property found (as washed up by the sea) but unclaimed **b** pl : stolen goods thrown away by a thief in flight **2 a** : something found without an owner and esp. by chance **b** : a stray person or animal; esp : a homeless child — **waif·like** \-,līk\ adj

²waif n (1530) : WAFT 4

¹wail \'wā(ə)l\ vb [ME, of Scand origin; akin to ON væla, vála to wail; akin to ON vei woe — more at WOE] vi (14c) **1** : to express sorrow audibly : LAMENT **2** : to make a sound suggestive of a mournful cry **3** : to express dissatisfaction plaintively : COMPLAIN ~ vt, archaic : BEWAIL — **wail·er** \'wā-lər\ n

²wail n (15c) **1** : the act or practice of wailing : loud lamentation **2 a** : a usu. prolonged cry or sound expressing grief or pain **b** : a sound suggestive of wailing ⟨the ~ of an air-raid siren⟩ **c** : a querulous expression of grievance : COMPLAINT

wail·ful \'wā(ə)l-fəl\ adj (1544) **1** : uttering a sound suggestive of wailing **2** : expressing grief or pain : SORROWFUL, MOURNFUL — **wail·ful·ly** \-fə-lē\ adv

wailing wall n (1919) **1** cap : a surviving part of the wall which in ancient times formed a part of the enclosure of Herod's temple near the Holy of Holies and at which Jews traditionally gather for prayer and religious lament **2** : a source of comfort and consolation in misfortune

wain \'wān\ n [ME, wagon, chariot, fr. OE wægn; akin to MD wagen wagon, OE wegan to move — more at WAY] (bef. 12c) **1** : a usu. large and heavy vehicle for farm use **2** cap [short for Charles's Wain] : BIG DIPPER

¹wain·scot \'wān-skət, -,skōt, -,skät\ n [ME, fr. MD wagenschot, prob. fr. wagen wagon + schot shot, crossbar] (14c) **1** Brit : a fine grade of oak imported for woodwork **2 a** (1) : a usu. paneled wooden lining of an interior wall (2) : a lining of an interior wall irrespective of material **b** : the lower three or four feet (about one meter) of an interior wall when finished differently from the remainder of the wall

²wainscot vt **-scot·ed** or **-scot·ted; -scot·ing** or **-scot·ting** (ca. 1570) : to line with or as if with boards or paneling

wain·scot·ing or **wain·scot·ting** \-,skō-tiŋ, -,skä-, -skə-\ n (1580) **1** : WAINSCOT 2 **2** : material used to wainscot a surface

wain·wright \'wān-,rīt\ n (bef. 12c) : a maker and repairer of wagons

waist \'wāst\ n [ME wast; akin to OE wæstm growth, weaxan to grow — more at WAX] (14c) **1 a** : the narrowed part of the body between the thorax and hips **b** : the greatly constricted basal part of the abdomen of some insects (as wasps and flies) **2** : the part of something corresponding to or resembling the human waist: as **a** (1) : the part of a ship's deck between the poop and forecastle (2) : the middle part of a sailing ship between foremast and mainmast **b** : the middle section of the fuselage of an airplane **3** : a garment or the part of a garment covering the body from the neck to the waistline or just below: as **a** : BODICE 1 **b** : BLOUSE **4** : WAISTLINE 1b — **waist·ed** \'wā-stəd\ adj

waist·band \'wās(t)-,band\ n (1584) : a band (as of trousers or a skirt) fitting around the waist

waist·coat \'wes-kət, 'wās(t)-,kōt\ n (1519) **1** : an ornamental garment worn under a doublet **2** chiefly Brit : VEST 2a — **waist·coat·ed** \-,kō-təd\ adj

waist·line \'wāst-,līn\ n (1896) **1 a** : an arbitrary line encircling the narrowest part of the waist **b** : the part of a garment that covers the

\ə\ abut \ʲ\ kitten, F table \ər\ further \a\ ash \ā\ ace \ä\ mop, mar \aȯ\ out \ch\ chin \e\ bet \ē\ easy \g\ go \i\ hit \ī\ ice \j\ job \ŋ\ sing \ō\ go \ȯ\ law \ȯi\ boy \th\ thin \t͟h\ the \ü\ loot \u̇\ foot \y\ yet \zh\ vision \ä, k̲, ⁿ, œ, œ̄, ᵫ, ᵫ̄, ᵊ\ see Guide to Pronunciation waistline or may be above or below it as fashion dictates 2 : body circumference at the waist

¹wait \'wāt\ vb [ME, fr. ONF waitier to watch, of Gmc origin; akin to OHG wahta watch, OE wæccan to watch — more at WAKE] vt (14c) 1 : to stay in place in expectation of : AWAIT 2 : to delay serving (a meal) 3 : to serve as waiter for 〈~ tables〉 ~ vi 1 a : to remain stationary in readiness or expectation 〈~ for a train〉 b : to pause for another to catch up — usu. used with up 2 a : to look forward expectantly 〈just ~ing to see his rival lose〉 b : to hold back expectantly 〈~ing for a chance to strike〉 3 : to serve at meals — usu. used in such phrases as wait on tables or wait on table 4 a : to be ready and available 〈slippers ~ing by the bed〉 b : to remain temporarily neglected or unrealized — **wait on** also **wait upon** 1 a : to attend as a servant b : to supply the wants of : SERVE 2 : to make a formal call on 3 : to wait for — **wait up** : to delay going to bed : stay up

usage American dialectologists have evidence showing wait on (sense 3) to be more a Southern than a Northern form in speech. Handbook writers universally denigrate wait on and prescribe wait for in writing. Our evidence from printed sources does not show a regional preference; it does show that the handbooks' advice is not based on current usage 〈settlement of the big problems still waited on Russia —Time〉 〈I couldn't make out ... whether Harper was waiting on me for approval —E. B. White〉 〈the staggering bill that waited on them at the white commissary downtown —Maya Angelou〉. One reason for the continuing use of wait on may lie in its being able to suggest protracted or irritating waits better than wait for 〈for two days I've been waiting on weather —Charles A. Lindbergh〉 〈the boredom of black Africans sitting there, waiting on the whims of a colonial bureaucracy —Vincent Canby〉 〈doesn't care to sit around waiting on a House that's virtually paralyzed —Glenn A. Briere〉. Wait on is less common than wait for, but if it seems natural, there is no reason to avoid it.

²wait n [ME waite watchman, public musician, wait, fr. ONF, watchman, watch, of Gmc origin; akin to OHG wahta watch] (14c) 1 a : a hidden or concealed position — used chiefly in the expression lie in wait b : a state or attitude of watchfulness and expectancy 〈anchored in ~ for early morning fishing —Fred Zimmer〉 2 a : one of a band of public musicians in England employed to play for processions or public entertainments b (1) : one of a group who serenade for gratuities esp. at the Christmas season (2) : a piece of music by such a group 3 : an act or period of waiting 〈a long ~ in line〉

wait·er \'wā-tər\ n (15c) 1 : one that waits on another; esp : a person who waits tables (as in a restaurant) 2 : a tray on which something (as a tea service) is carried : SALVER

waiting game n (1890) : a strategy in which one or more participants withhold action temporarily in the hope of having a favorable opportunity for more effective action later

waiting list n (1897) : a list or roster of those waiting (as for election to a club or admission to an educational institution)

waiting room n (1683) : a room (as in a doctor's office) for the use of persons (as patients) who are waiting

wait out vt (1941) : to await an end to 〈wait the storm out〉

wait·per·son \'wāt-,pər-sᵊn\ n (1976) : a waiter or waitress

wait·ress \'wā-trəs\ n (1834) : a woman who waits tables (as in a restaurant) — **waitress** vi

waive \'wāv\ vt waived; waiv·ing [ME weiven, fr. ONF weyver, fr. waif lost, unclaimed — more at WAIF] (14c) 1 archaic : GIVE UP, FORSAKE 2 : to throw away (stolen goods) 3 archaic : to shunt aside (as a danger or duty) 〈evade 4 a : to relinquish voluntarily (as a legal right) 〈~ a jury trial〉 b : to refrain from pressing or enforcing (as a claim or rule) : FORGO 5 : to put off from immediate consideration : POSTPONE 6 : to dismiss with or as if with a wave of the hand 〈waived the problem aside〉 7 : to place (a ball player) on waivers; also : to release after placing on waivers syn see RELINQUISH

waiv·er \'wā-vər\ n [AF weyver, fr. ONF weyver to abandon, waive] (1628) 1 : the act of intentionally relinquishing or abandoning a known right, claim, or privilege; also : the legal instrument evidencing such an act 2 : the act of a club's waiving the right to claim a professional ball player who is being removed from another club's roster — often used in the phrase on waivers denoting the process by which a player to be removed from a roster is made available to other clubs 〈was placed on ~s before being released〉

Wa·kash·an \wȯ-'ka-shən, 'wȯ-,\ n (ca. 1895) : a family of American Indian languages spoken in coastal areas of British Columbia and northwest Washington

¹wake \'wāk\ vb woke \'wōk\ also waked \'wākt\; wo·ken \'wō-kən\ or waked also woke; wak·ing [partly fr. ME waken (past wook, pp. waken), fr. OE wacan to awake (past wōc, pp. wacen); partly fr. ME wakien (past & pp. waked), fr. OE wacian to be awake (past wacode, pp. wacod); akin to OE wæccan to watch, L vegēre to enliven] vi (bef. 12c) 1 a : to be or remain awake b archaic : to remain awake on watch esp. over a corpse c : to stay up late in revelry 2 : AWAKE — often used with up ~ vt 1 : to stand watch over (as a dead body); esp : to hold a wake over 2 a : to rouse from or as if from sleep : AWAKE — often used with up b : STIR, EXCITE 〈woke up latent possibilities —Norman Douglas〉 c : to arouse conscious interest in : ALERT — usu. used with to 〈woke the publishers to the fact that there was an enormous ... audience —Harrison Smith〉 — **wak·er** n

²wake n (13c) 1 : the state of being awake 2 a (1) : an annual English parish festival formerly held in commemoration of the church's patron saint 〈VIGIL 1a b : the festivities orig. connected with the wake of an English parish church — usu. used in pl. but sing. or pl. in constr. c Brit : an annual holiday or vacation — usu. used in pl. but sing. or pl. in constr. 3 : a watch held over the body of a dead person prior to burial and sometimes accompanied by festivity

³wake n [of Scand origin; akin to ON vǫk hole in ice] (ca. 1547) 1 : the track left by a moving body (as a ship) in a fluid (as water); broadly : a track or path left 2 : AFTERMATH 〈in the wake of 1 : close behind and in the same path of travel 〈in the wake of trappers and ... riflemen came ... settlers —Amer. Guide Series: Ind.〉 2 : as a result of : as a consequence of 〈power vacuums left in the wake of the second world war —A. M. Schlesinger b1917〉

wake·ful \'wāk-fəl\ adj (1549) : not sleeping or able to sleep : SLEEPLESS — **wake·ful·ly** \-fə-lē\ adv — **wake·ful·ness** n

wake·less \'wā-kləs\ adj (1824) : SOUND, UNBROKEN 〈~ sleep〉

wak·en \'wā-kən\ vb **wak·ened; wak·en·ing** \'wāk-niŋ, 'wā-kə-\ [ME waknen, fr. OE wæcnian; akin to ON vakna to awaken, OE wæccan to watch] vi (bef. 12c) : AWAKE — often used with up ~ vt : to rouse esp. out of sleep : WAKE

wak·en·er \'wāk-nər, 'wā-kə-\ n (1573) archaic : one that causes to waken

wake·rife \'wāk-,rīf\ adj [ME (Sc) walkryfe, fr. walk awake (fr. waken, walken to wake) + ryfe rife] (15c) Scot : WAKEFUL, ALERT

wake–rob·in \'wāk-,rä-bən\ n (ca. 1530) 1 : TRILLIUM 2 : JACK-IN-THE-PULPIT

wake–up \'wāk-,əp\ adj (1946) : serving to wake up 〈a ~ call〉 〈a ~ cup of coffee〉

wak·ing \'wā-kiŋ\ adj (1567) : passed in a conscious or alert state 〈every ~ hour〉

Wal·den·ses \wȯl-'den-(,)sēz, wäl-\ n pl [ME Waldensis, fr. ML Waldenses, Valdenses, fr. Peter Waldo (or Valdo)] (1537) : a Christian sect arising in southern France in the 12th century, adopting Calvinist doctrines in the 16th century, and later living chiefly in Piedmont — **Wal·den·sian** \-'den(t)-shən, -'den(t)-sē-ən\ adj or n

Wal·dorf salad \'wȯl-,dȯrf-\ n [Waldorf-Astoria Hotel, New York City] (1902) : a salad made typically of diced apples, celery, nuts, and mayonnaise

¹wale \'wā(ə)l\ n [ME, fr. OE walu; akin to ON vǫlr staff and perh. to ON valr round, L volvere to roll — more at VOLUBLE] (bef. 12c) 1 a : a streak or ridge made on the skin esp. by the stroke of a whip : WEAL b : a narrow raised surface : RIDGE 2 : any of a number of strakes usu. of extra thick and strong planks in the sides of a wooden ship — usu. used in pl. 3 a : one of a series of even ribs in a fabric b : the texture esp. of a fabric 4 : a horizontal constructional member (as of timber or steel) used for bracing vertical members

²wale vt waled; wal·ing (15c) : to mark (as the skin) with welts

³wale n [ME (Sc & northern dial.) wal, fr. ON val; akin to OHG wala choice, OE wyllan to wish — more at WILL] (14c) 1 dial Brit : CHOICE 2 dial Brit : the best part : PICK

⁴wale vb (14c) dial Brit : CHOOSE

wal·er \'wā-lər\ n, often cap [New So. Wales, Australia] (1849) : a horse from New So. Wales; esp : a rather large rugged saddle horse of mixed ancestry formerly exported in quantity from Australia to British India for military use

Wal·hal·la \väl-'hä-lə\ n [G] : VALHALLA

¹walk \'wȯk\ vb [partly fr. ME walken (past welk, pp. walken), fr. OE wealcan to roll, toss, journey about (past weolc, pp. wealcen) and partly fr. ME walkien (past walked, pp. walked), fr. OE wealcian to roll up, muffle up; akin to MD walken to knead, press, full] vi (bef. 12c) 1 a obs : ROAM, WANDER b of a spirit : to move about in visible form : APPEAR c of a ship : to make headway 2 a : to move along on foot : advance by steps b : to come or go easily or readily c : to go on foot for exercise or pleasure d : to go at a walk 3 a : to pursue a course of action or way of life : conduct oneself : BEHAVE 〈~ warily〉 b : to be or act in association : continue in union 〈the British and American peoples will ... ~ together side by side ... in peace —Sir Winston Churchill〉 c : WALK OUT 〈the workers didn't like the new contract so they ~ed〉 4 : to go to first base as a result of a base on balls 5 of an inanimate object a : to move in a manner that is suggestive of walking b : to stand with an appearance suggestive of strides 〈pylons ~ing across the valley〉 6 of an astronaut : to move about in space outside a spacecraft ~ vt 1 : to pass on foot or as if on foot through, along, over, or upon : TRAVERSE, PERAMBULATE 〈~ the streets〉 〈~ a tightrope〉 b : to perform or accomplish by going on foot 〈~ guard〉 2 a : to cause (an animal) to go at a walk : take for a walk 〈~ing a dog〉 b (1) : to cause to move by walking 〈~ed her bicycle up the hill〉 (2) : to haul (as an anchor) by walking round the capstan 3 : to follow on foot for the purpose of measuring, surveying, or inspecting 〈~ a boundary〉 4 a : to accompany on foot : walk with 〈~ed her home〉 b : to compel to walk (as by a command) c : to bring to a specified condition by walking 〈~ed us off our feet〉 5 : to move (an object) in a manner suggestive of walking 6 : to perform (a dance) at a walking pace 〈~ a quadrille〉 7 : to give a base on balls to — **walk away from** 1 : to outrun or get the better of without difficulty 2 : to survive (an accident) with little or no injury — **walk off with** 1 : to steal and take away b : to take over unexpectedly from someone else : STEAL 1d 〈walked off with the show〉 2 : to win or gain esp. by outdoing one's competitors without difficulty — **walk on** : to take advantage of : ABUSE — **walk over** : to treat contemptuously — **walk the plank** 1 : to walk under compulsion over the side of a ship into the sea 2 : to resign an office or position under compulsion — **walk through** 1 : to go through (as a theatrical role or familiar activity) perfunctorily (as in an early stage of rehearsal) 2 : to guide (a novice) through an unfamiliar or complex procedure step-by-step 3 : to deal with or carry out perfunctorily

²walk n (14c) 1 a : an act or instance of going on foot esp. for exercise or pleasure 〈go for a ~〉 b : SPACE WALK 2 : an accustomed place of walking : HAUNT 3 : a place designed for walking: a : a railed platform above the roof of a dwelling house b (1) : a path specially arranged or paved for walking (2) : SIDEWALK c : a public avenue for promenading : PROMENADE d : ROPEWALK 4 : a place or area of land in which animals feed and exercise with minimal restraint 5 : distance to be walked 〈a quarter mile ~ from here〉 6 Brit : a ceremonial procession 7 : manner of living : CONDUCT, BEHAVIOR 8 a : the gait of a biped in which the feet are lifted alternately with one foot not clear of the ground before the other touches b : the gait of a quadruped in which there are always at least two feet on the ground; specif : a four-beat gait of a horse in which the feet strike the ground in the sequence near hind, near fore, off hind, off fore c : a low rate of speed 〈the shortage of raw materials slowed production to a ~〉 9 : a route regularly traversed by a person in the performance of a particular activity (as patrolling, begging, or vending) 10 : characteristic manner of walking 〈his ~ is just like his father's〉 11 a : social or economic status 〈all ~s of life〉 b (1) : range or sphere of action : FIELD, PROVINCE (2) : VOCATION 12 : BASE ON BALLS

walk·about \'wȯ-kə-,baút\ n (1908) 1 : a short period of wandering bush life engaged in by an Australian aborigine as an occasional interruption of regular work 2 : a walking tour : walking trip

walk·a·thon \'wo̊-kə-ˌthän\ *n* [*walk* + *-athon*] (1932) : a walk covering a considerable distance organized esp. to raise money for a cause

walk-away \'wo̊-kə-ˌwā\ *n* (1888) : an easily won contest

walk·er \'wo̊-kər\ *n* (14c) **1** : one that walks: as **a** : a competitor in a walking race **b** : a peddler going on foot **c** : a temporary male escort of socially prominent women attending usu. public events **2** : something used in walking: as **a** : a framework designed to support a baby learning to walk or an infirm or handicapped person **b** : a walking shoe

walk·ie–talk·ie \ˌwo̊-kē-'to̊-kē, 'wo̊-kē-ˌ\ *n* (1939) : a compact easily transportable battery-operated radio transmitting and receiving set

¹walk-in \'wo̊k-ˌin\ *adj* (1926) **1** : large enough to be walked into ⟨a ~ closet⟩ **2** : arranged so as to be entered directly rather than through a lobby ⟨a ~ apartment⟩ **3 a** : being a person who walks in without an appointment ⟨a ~ blood donor⟩ **b** : of or relating to such persons ⟨~ clinic⟩

²walk-in \'wo̊k-ˌin\ *n* (1944) **1** : a walk-in refrigerator or cold storage room **2** : an easy election victory **3** : one who walks in without an appointment

¹walk·ing \'wo̊-kiŋ\ *n* (15c) **1** : the action of one that walks ⟨~ is good exercise⟩ **2** : the condition of a surface for one going on foot ⟨the ~ is slippery⟩

²walking *adj* (15c) **1 a** : able to walk : AMBULATORY ⟨the ~ wounded⟩ **b** : being the personification of a nonhuman quality or thing ⟨a ~ encyclopedia⟩ **2 a** : used for or in walking ⟨~ shoes⟩ **b** : characterized by or consisting of the action of walking ⟨a ~ tour⟩ **3** : that moves or appears to move in a manner suggestive of walking; *esp* : that swings or rocks back and forth ⟨~ beam⟩ **4** : guided or operated by a person on foot ⟨a ~ plow⟩

walking catfish *n* (1968) : an Asian freshwater catfish (*Clarias batrachus* of the family Clariidae) that is able to move about on land and has become established in Florida waters

walking delegate *n* (1889) : a labor union representative appointed to visit members and their places of employment, to secure enforcement of union rules and agreements, and at times to represent the union in dealing with employers

walking leaf *n* (1826) : any of a family (Phylliidae) of phasmid insects with wings and legs resembling leaves

walking papers *n pl* (1825) : DISMISSAL, DISCHARGE — called also *walking ticket*

walking pneumonia *n* (1964) : a usu. mild pneumonia caused by a mycoplasma (*Mycoplasma pneumoniae*) and characterized by malaise, cough, and often fever

walking stick *n* (1580) **1** : a stick used in walking **2** *usu* **walk·ing·stick** : STICK INSECT; *esp* : a phasmid insect (*Diapheromera femorata*) common in parts of the U.S.

Walk·man \'wo̊k-mən, -ˌman\ *trademark* — used for a small portable radio or cassette player listened to by means of headphones or earphones

walkingstick

walk–on \'wo̊k-ˌo̊n, -ˌän\ *n* (1902) **1** : a minor part (as in a dramatic production); *also* : an actor having such a part **2** : a college athlete who tries out for an athletic team without having been recruited or offered a scholarship

walk-out \'wo̊k-ˌau̇t\ *n* (1888) **1** : STRIKE 3a **2** : the action of leaving a meeting or organization as an expression of disapproval

walk out *vi* (1840) **1** : to leave suddenly often as an expression of disapproval **2** : to go on strike — **walk out on** : to leave in the lurch : ABANDON, DESERT

walk·over \'wo̊k-ˌō-vər\ *n* (1838) **1** : a one-sided contest : an easy or uncontested victory **2** : a horse race with only one starter

walk–through \'wo̊k-ˌthrü\ *n* (1940) **1** : a perfunctory performance of a play or acting part (as in an early stage of rehearsal) **2** : a television rehearsal without cameras

¹walk–up \'wo̊k-ˌəp\ *adj* (1919) **1** : located above the ground floor in a building with no elevator ⟨a ~ apartment⟩ **2** : consisting of several stories and having no elevator ⟨a ~ tenement⟩ **3** : designed to allow pedestrians to be served without entering a building ⟨the ~ window of a bank⟩

²walk–up *n* (1924) : a building or apartment house of several stories that has no elevator; *also* : an apartment or office in such a building

walk-way \'wo̊k-ˌwā\ *n* (1792) : a passage for walking : WALK

Wal·ky·rie \väl-'kir-ē *also* väl-'kī-rē *or* 'väl-kə-rē\ *n* [G *Walküre* & ON *valkyrja*] : VALKYRIE

¹wall \'wo̊l\ *n* [ME, fr. OE *weall*; akin to MHG *wall*; both fr. L *vallum* rampart, fr. *vallus* stake, palisade; perh. akin to ON *vo̧lr* staff — more at WALE] (bef. 12c) **1 a** : a high thick masonry structure forming a long rampart or an enclosure chiefly for defense — often used in pl. **b** : a masonry fence around a garden, park, or estate **c** : a structure that serves to hold back pressure (as of water or sliding earth) **2** : one of the sides of a room or building connecting floor and ceiling or foundation and roof **3** : the side of a footpath next to buildings **4** : an extreme or desperate position or a state of defeat, failure, or ruin — usu. used in the phrase *to the wall* **5** : a material layer enclosing space ⟨the ~ of a container⟩ ⟨heart ~s⟩ **6** : something resembling a wall (as in appearance, function, or effect); *esp* : something that acts as a barrier or defense ⟨a ~ of reserve⟩ ⟨tariff ~⟩ — **walled** \'wo̊ld\ *adj* — **wall·like** \'wo̊l-ˌlīk\ *adj* — **up the wall** *slang* : into a state of intense agitation, annoyance, or frustration ⟨the noise drove me *up the wall*⟩

²wall *vt* (13c) **1 a** : to provide, cover with, or surround with or as if with a wall ⟨~ in the garden⟩ **b** : to separate by or as if by a wall ⟨~ed off half the house⟩ **2 a** : IMMURE **b** : to close (an opening) with or as if with a wall

³wall *vb* [ME (Sc) *wawlen*, prob. fr. ME *wawil-* (in *wawil-eghed* wall-eyed)] *vi* (15c) *of the eyes* : to roll in a dramatic manner ~ *vt* : to roll (one's eyes) in a dramatic manner

wal·la·by \'wä-lə-bē\ *n, pl* **wallabies** *also* **wallaby** [Dharuk (Australian aboriginal language of the Port Jackson area) *walaba*] (ca. 1798) : any of various small or medium-sized kangaroos (esp. genus *Macropus*) — compare ROCK WALLABY

Wal·lace's line \'wä-lə-səz-\ *n* [Alfred Russel *Wallace*] (1868) : a hypothetical boundary that separates the highly distinctive floras and faunas of the Oriental and Australian biogeographic regions and passes between the islands of Bali and Lombok in Indonesia, between Borneo and Sulawesi, and between the Philippines and the Moluccas

wal·lah \'wä-lə, in combination usu ˌwä-lə\ *n* [Hindi -*vālā* one in charge, fr. Skt *pāla* protector, fr. *pālayati, pārayati* he guards; akin to Skt *piparti* he brings over, saves, OE *faran* to go — more at FARE] (1782) : a person who is associated with a particular work or who performs a specific duty or service — usu. used in combination ⟨the book ~ was an itinerant peddler —George Orwell⟩

wal·la·roo \ˌwä-lə-'rü\ *n, pl* **-roos** [Dharuk (Australian aboriginal language of the Port Jackson area) *walaru*] (1827) **1** : a large reddish gray kangaroo (*Macropus robustus*) — called also *euro* **2** : either of two kangaroos (*Macropus antelopinus* and *M. bernardus*) related to the wallaroo

wall·board \'wo̊l-ˌbo̊rd, -ˌbȯrd\ *n* (1906) : a structural boarding of any of various materials (as wood pulp, gypsum, or plastic) made in large rigid sheets and used esp. for sheathing interior walls and ceilings

wal·let \'wä-lət\ *n* [ME *walet*] (14c) **1** : a bag for carrying miscellaneous articles while traveling **2 a** : a folding pocketbook with compartments for personal papers and usu. unfolded paper money; *also* : BILLFOLD **b** : a container that resembles a money wallet: as (1) : a usu. flexible folding case fitted for carrying specific items (as tools or fishing flies) (2) : FOLDER 3

wall-eye \'wo̊-ˌlī\ *n* [back-formation fr. *walleyed*] (1523) **1 a** : an eye with a whitish or bluish white iris **b** : an eye with an opaque white cornea **2 a** : strabismus in which the eye turns outward away from the nose **b** : an eye affected with divergent strabismus **3** : a large vigorous No. American freshwater food and sport fish (*Stizostedion vitreum*) that has prominent eyes and is related to the perches but resembles the true pike — called also *walleyed pike*

wall-eyed \-'līd\ *adj* [by folk etymology fr. ME *wawil-eghed*, part trans. of ON *vagl-eygr* walleyed, fr. *vagl* beam (akin to Gk *ochleus* bar, OE *wegan* to move, carry) + *eygr* eyed — more at WAY] (15c) **1** : having walleyes or affected with walleye **2** : marked by a wild irrational staring of the eyes

walleye pollack *n* (1907) : POLLACK 2

wall-flow·er \'wo̊l-ˌflau̇(-ə)r\ *n* (1578) **1 a** : any of several Old World herbaceous or somewhat woody perennial plants (genus *Cheiranthus* of the mustard family; *esp* : a hardy erect herb (*C. cheiri*) widely cultivated for its showy fragrant flowers **b** : any of a related genus (*Erysimum*) of plants with showy flowers **2** : a person who from shyness or unpopularity remains on the sidelines of a social activity (as a dance)

Wal·loon \wä-'lün\ *n* [MF *Wallon*, adj. & n., of Gmc origin; prob. akin to OHG *Walah* Celt, Roman, OE *Wealh* Celt, Welshman — more at WELSH] (1567) **1** : a member of a people of southern and southeastern Belgium and adjacent parts of France **2** : a French dialect of the Walloons — **Walloon** *adj*

¹wal·lop \'wä-ləp\ *vb* [ME *walopen* to gallop, fr. ONF *waloper*] *vi* (1579) **1** : to boil noisily **2 a** : to move with reckless or disorganized haste : advance in a headlong rush **b** : WALLOW, FLOUNDER ~ *vt* **1 a** : to thrash soundly : LAMBASTE **b** : to beat by a wide margin : TROUNCE **2** : to hit with force : SOCK — **wal·lop·er** *n*

²wallop *n* [ME, gallop, fr. ONF *walop*, fr. *waloper* to gallop] (ca. 1823) **1 a** : a powerful blow : PUNCH **b** : something resembling a wallop esp. in suddenness of force ⟨c : the ability (as of a boxer) to hit hard⟩ **2 a** : emotional, sensory, or psychological force or influence : IMPACT ⟨a novel that packs a ~⟩ **b** : an exciting emotional response : THRILL **3** *Brit* : BEER

wal·lop·ing *adj* (ca. 1847) **1** : LARGE, WHOPPING **2** : exceptionally fine or impressive : SMASHING

¹wal·low \'wä-(ˌ)lō\ *vi* [ME *walwen*, fr. OE *wealwian* to roll — more at VOLUBLE] (bef. 12c) **1** : to roll oneself about in an indolent or ungainly manner **2** : to billow forth : SURGE **3** : to devote oneself entirely; *esp* : to take unrestrained pleasure : DELIGHT **4 a** : to become abundantly supplied : LUXURIATE ⟨a family that ~s in money⟩ **b** : to indulge oneself immoderately ⟨~ing in self-pity⟩ **5** : to become or remain helpless (allowed them to ~ in their ignorance⟩ — **wal·low·er** \'wä-lə-wər\ *n*

²wallow *n* (15c) **1** : an act or instance of wallowing **2 a** : a muddy area or one filled with dust used by animals for wallowing **b** : a depression formed by or as if by the wallowing of animals **3** : a state of degradation or degeneracy

wall painting *n* (1688) : FRESCO

¹wall-pa·per \'wo̊l-ˌpā-pər\ *n* (1827) : decorative paper for the walls of a room

²wallpaper *vt* (1924) : to provide the walls of (a room) with wallpaper ~ *vi* : to put wallpaper on a wall

wall plate *n* (14c) : PLATE 5

wall plug *n* (1888) : an electric receptacle in a wall

wall rock *n* (1876) : a rock through which a fault or vein runs

wall rocket *n* (1611) : any of several Old World herbs (genus *Diplotaxis*) of the mustard family; *esp* : a yellow-flowered European herb (*D. tenuifolia*) adventive in No. America

Wall Street \'wo̊l-\ *n* [*Wall Street*, New York City, site of the New York Stock Exchange] (1836) : the influential financial interests of the U.S. economy

Wall Street·er \-ˌstrē-tər\ *n* (1885) : a person who is involved in Wall Street

wall system *n* (1968) : a set of shelves often with cabinets or bureaus that can be variously arranged along a wall

wall–to–wall *adj* (1946) **1** : covering the entire floor ⟨~ carpeting⟩ **2 a** : covering or filling one entire space or time ⟨a party crammed with ~ bodies⟩ **b** : occurring or found everywhere : UBIQUITOUS

wal·ly \'wä-lē\ *adj* [prob. fr. ³*wale*] (ca. 1520) *Scot* : FINE, STURDY

\ə\ abut \ᵊ\ kitten, F table \ər\ further \a\ ash \ā\ ace \ä\ mop, mar \au̇\ out \ch\ chin \e\ bet \ē\ easy \g\ go \i\ hit \ī\ ice \j\ job \ŋ\ sing \ō\ go \o̊\ law \o̊i\ boy \th\ thin \th̶\ the \ü\ loot \u̇\ foot \y\ yet \zh\ vision \à, ḵ, ⁿ, œ, œ̄, ᵫ, ᵮ, ʸ\ *see* Guide to Pronunciation

wal·ly·drai·gle \'wä-lē-,drä-gəl, 'wä-lē-\ *n* [origin unknown] (1508) *chiefly Scot* : a feeble, imperfectly developed, or slovenly creature

wal·nut \'wȯl-(,)nət\ *n* [ME *walnot*, fr. OE *wealhhnutu*, lit., foreign nut, fr. *Wealh* Welshman, foreigner + *hnutu* nut — more at WELSH, NUT] (bef. 12c) **1 a** : a nut of any of a genus (*Juglans* of the family Juglandaceae, the walnut family) of trees; *esp* : the large edible nut of a Eurasian tree (*J. regia*) with a hard richly figured wood **b** : a tree that bears walnuts **c** : the wood of a walnut that is often used for cabinet-making and veneers **2** : a moderate reddish brown

Wal·pur·gis·nacht \väl-'pu̇r-gəs-,näkt\ *n* [G] (1822) : WALPURGIS NIGHT

Wal·pur·gis Night \väl-'pu̇r-gəs-\ *n* [part trans. of G *Walpurgisnacht*, fr. *Walpurgis* St. Walburga †A.D. 779 Eng. saint whose feast day falls on May Day + G *Nacht* night] (1823) **1** : the eve of May Day on which witches are held to ride to an appointed rendezvous **2** : something (as an event or situation) having a nightmarish quality

wal·rus \'wȯl-rəs, 'wäl-\ *n, pl* **walrus** *or* **wal·rus·es** [D, of Scand origin; akin to Dan & Norw *hvalros* walrus, ON *rosmhvalr*] (1728) : a large gregarious marine mammal (*Odobenus rosmarus* of the family Odobenidae) related to the seal that is found in Arctic seas, has long ivory tusks, a tough wrinkled hide, and stiff whiskers, and feeds mostly on bivalve mollusks

Wal·ter Mit·ty \,wȯl-tər-'mi-tē\ *n* [*Walter Mitty*, daydreaming hero of a story by James Thurber] (1949) : a commonplace unadventurous person who seeks escape from reality through daydreaming — **Walter Mit·ty·ish** \-ish\ *adj*

¹waltz \'wȯl(t)s\ *n* [G *Walzer*, fr. *walzen* to roll, dance, fr. OHG *walzan* to turn, roll — more at WELTER] (1781) **1** : a ballroom dance in ¾ time with strong accent on the first beat and a basic pattern of step-step-close **2** : music for a waltz or a concert composition in ¾ time

²waltz *vi* (ca. 1794) **1** : to dance a waltz **2** : to move or advance in a lively or conspicuous manner : FLOUNCE **3 a** : to advance easily and successfully : BREEZE — often used with *through* **b** : to approach boldly — used with *up* ⟨can't just ~ up and introduce ourselves⟩ ~ *vt* **1** : to dance a waltz with **2** : to grab and lead (as a person) unceremoniously : MARCH — **waltz·er** *n*

¹wam·ble \'wäm-bəl\ *vi* **wam·bled**; **wam·bling** \-b(ə-)liŋ\ [ME *wamlen*; akin to Dan *vamle* to become nauseated, L *vomere* to vomit — more at VOMIT] (14c) **1 a** : to feel nausea **b** *of a stomach* : RUMBLE 1 **2** : to move unsteadily or with a weaving or rolling motion

²wamble *n* (1552) **1** : a wambling esp. of the stomach **2** : a reeling or staggering gait or movement

wame \'wäm\ *n* [ME, alter. of *wamb* — more at WOMB] (15c) *chiefly Scot* : BELLY

Wam·pa·no·ag \,wäm-pə-'nō-(,)ag, ,wȯm-\ *n, pl* **Wampanoag** *or* **Wampanoags** [Narraganset, lit., easterners] (1676) : a member of an American Indian people of Rhode Island east of Narragansett Bay and neighboring parts of Massachusetts

wam·pum \'wäm-pəm\ *n* [short for *wampumpeag*] (1636) **1** : beads of polished shells strung in strands, belts, or sashes and used by No. American Indians as money, ceremonial pledges, and ornaments **2** : MONEY

wam·pum·peag \-,pēg\ *n* [Massachuset *wampompeag*, fr. *wampan* white + *api* string + *-ag*, pl. suffix] (1627) : WAMPUM

¹wan \'wän\ *adj* **wan·ner**; **wan·nest** [ME, fr. OE *wann* dark, livid] (14c) **1 a** : suggestive of poor health : SICKLY, PALLID **b** : lacking vitality : FEEBLE **2** : DIM, FAINT **3** : LANGUID ⟨a ~ smile⟩ — **wan·ly** *adv* — **wan·ness** \'wän-nəs\ *n*

²wan *vi* **wanned**; **wan·ning** (1582) : to grow or become pale or sickly

wand \'wänd\ *n* [ME, slender stick, fr. ON *vǫndr*; prob. akin to OE *windan* to wind, twist — more at WIND] (15c) **1** : a slender staff carried in a procession : VERGE **2** : a slender rod used by conjurers and magicians **3** : a slat 6 feet by 2 inches used as a target in archery; *also* : a narrow strip of paper pasted vertically on a target face **4** : any of various pipelike devices; *esp* : the rigid tube between the hose and the nozzle of a vacuum cleaner **5** : a handheld device used to enter information (as from a bar code) into a computer

wan·der \'wän-dər\ *vb* **wan·dered**; **wan·der·ing** \-d(ə-)riŋ\ [ME *wandren*, fr. OE *wandrian*; akin to MHG *wandern* to wander, OE *windan* to wind, twist] *vi* (bef. 12c) **1 a** : to move about without a fixed course, aim, or goal **b** : to go idly about : RAMBLE **2** : to follow a winding course : MEANDER **3 a** : to deviate (as from a course) : STRAY **b** : to go astray morally : ERR **c** : to lose normal mental contact : stray in thought ~ *vt* : to roam over — **wander** *n* — **wan·der·er** \-dər-ər\ *n*

syn WANDER, ROAM, RAMBLE, ROVE, TRAIPSE, MEANDER mean to go about from place to place usu. without a plan or definite purpose. WANDER implies an absence of or an indifference to a fixed course ⟨fond of *wandering* about the square just watching the people⟩. ROAM suggests wandering about freely and often far afield ⟨liked to *roam* through the woods⟩. RAMBLE stresses carelessness and indifference to one's course or objective ⟨the speaker *rambled* on without ever coming to the point⟩. ROVE suggests vigorous and sometimes purposeful roaming ⟨armed brigands *roved* over the countryside⟩. TRAIPSE implies a course that is erratic but may sometimes be purposeful ⟨*traipsed* all over town looking for the right dress⟩. MEANDER implies a winding or intricate course suggestive of aimless or listless wandering ⟨the river *meanders* for miles through rich farmland⟩.

¹wandering *adj* (bef. 12c) **1** : characterized by aimless, slow, or pointless movement: as **a** : that winds or meanders ⟨a ~ course⟩ **b** : not following a rational or sensible course : VAGRANT ⟨~ tribes⟩ **c** : NOMADIC ⟨~ tribes⟩ **d** *of a plant* : having long runners or tendrils

²wandering *n* (14c) **1** : a going about from place to place — often used in pl. **2** : movement away from the proper, normal, or usual course or place — often used in pl.

Wandering Jew *n* **1** : a Jew of medieval legend condemned by Christ to wander the earth till Christ's second coming **2** *not cap W* : any of several plants (genera *Zebrina* and *Tradescantia*) of the spiderwort family; *esp* : either of two trailing or creeping plants (*Z. pendula* and *T. fluminensis*) cultivated for their showy and often white-striped foliage

wan·der·lust \'wän-dər-,ləst\ *n* [G, fr. *wandern* to wander + *Lust* desire, pleasure] (1902) : strong longing for or impulse toward wandering

¹wane \'wän\ *vi* **waned**; **wan·ing** [ME, fr. OE *wanian*; akin to OHG

wanōn to wane, OE *wan* wanting, deficient, L *vanus* empty, vain] (bef. 12c) **1** : to decrease in size, extent, or degree : DWINDLE: as **a** : to diminish in phase or intensity — used chiefly of the moon **b** : to become less brilliant or powerful — DIM **c** : to flow out : EBB **2** : to fall gradually from power, prosperity, or influence *syn* see ABATE

²wane *n* (14c) **1** : the act or process of waning ⟨strength on the ~⟩ **b** : a period or time of waning; *specif* : the period from full phase of the moon to the new moon **2** [ME, defect, fr. OE *wana;* akin to OE *wan* deficient]: a defect in lumber characterized by bark or a lack of wood at a corner or edge

wan·gle \'waŋ-gəl\ *vb* **wan·gled**; **wan·gling** \-g(ə-)liŋ\ [perh. alter. of *waggle*] *vi* (ca. 1820) **1** : to extricate oneself (as from difficulty) : WIGGLE **2** : to resort to trickery or devious methods ~ *vt* **1** : SHAKE, WIGGLE **2** : to adjust or manipulate for personal or fraudulent ends **3** : to make or get by devious means : FINAGLE ⟨~ an invitation⟩ — **wan·gler** \-g(ə-)lər\ *n*

wan·i·gan *or* **wan·ni·gan** \'wä-ni-gən\ *n* [Ojibwa *wa·nikka·n* pit] (ca. 1848) : a shelter (as for sleeping, eating, or storage) often mounted on wheels or towed by tractor or mounted on a raft or boat

wan·ion \'wän-yən\ *n* [fr. the obs. phrase *in the waniand* unluckily, lit., in the waning (moon), fr. ME, fr. *waniand*, northern prp. of *wanien, wanen* to wane] (1549) *archaic* : PLAGUE, VENGEANCE — used in the phrase *with a wanion*

Wan·kel engine \'väŋ-kəl-, 'waŋ-\ *n* [Felix *Wankel* †1988 Ger. engineer] (1961) : an internal combustion rotary engine that has a rounded triangular rotor functioning as a piston and rotating in a space in the engine and that has only two major moving parts

wan·na·be \'wä-nə-,bē\ *n* [fr. the phrase *want to be*] (1981) : a person who wants or aspires to be someone or something else or who tries to look or act like someone else

¹want \'wȯnt *also* wänt & 'wənt\ *vb* [ME, fr. ON *vanta;* akin to OE *wan* deficient] *vi* (13c) **1** : to be needy or destitute **2** : to have or feel need ⟨never ~s for friends⟩ **3** : to be necessary or needed **4** : to desire to come, go, or be ⟨the cat ~s in⟩ ⟨~s out of the deal⟩ ~ *vt* **1** : to fail to possess esp. in customary or required amount : LACK ⟨the answer ~ed courtesy⟩ **2 a** : to have a strong desire for ⟨~ed a chance to rest⟩ **b** : to have an inclination to : LIKE ⟨say what you ~, he is efficient⟩ **3 a** : to have need of : REQUIRE ⟨the motor ~s a tune-up⟩ **b** : to suffer from the lack of ⟨thousands still ~ food and shelter⟩ **4** : OUGHT — used with the infinitive ⟨you ~ to be very careful what you say — Claudia Cassidy⟩ **5** : to wish or demand the presence of **6** : to hunt or seek in order to apprehend ⟨~ed for murder⟩ *syn* see DESIRE

²want *n* (14c) **1 a** : DEFICIENCY, LACK ⟨suffers from a ~ of good sense⟩ **b** : grave and extreme poverty that deprives one of the necessities of life **2** : something wanted : NEED, DESIRE **3** : personal defect : FAULT *syn* see POVERTY

want ad *n* (1897) : a newspaper advertisement stating that something (as an employee, employment, or a specified item) is wanted

¹want·ing *adj* (15c) **1** : not present or in evidence : ABSENT **2 a** : not being up to standards or expectations **b** : lacking in ability or capacity : DEFICIENT

²wanting *prep* (1693) **1** : LESS, MINUS ⟨a month ~ two days⟩ **2** : WITHOUT ⟨a book ~ a cover⟩

¹wan·ton \'wȯn-t°n, 'wän-\ *adj* [ME, fr. *wan-* deficient, wrong, mis- (fr. OE, fr. *wan* deficient) + *towen*, pp. of *teon* to draw, train, discipline, fr. OE *tēon* — more at TOW] (14c) **1 a** *archaic* : hard to control : UNDISCIPLINED, UNRULY **b** : playfully mean or cruel : MISCHIEVOUS **2 a** : LEWD, BAWDY **b** : causing sexual excitement : LUSTFUL, SENSUAL **3 a** : MERCILESS, INHUMANE ⟨~ cruelty⟩ **b** : having no just foundation or provocation : MALICIOUS ⟨a ~ attack⟩ **4** : being without check or limitation: as **a** : luxuriantly rank ⟨~ vegetation⟩ **b** : unduly lavish : EXTRAVAGANT — **wan·ton·ly** *adv* — **wan·ton·ness** \-t°n-nəs\ *n*

²wanton *n* (1526) **1** : a pampered person or animal : PET; *esp* : a spoiled child **2** : a frolicsome child or animal **3 a** : one given to self-indulgent flirtation or trifling — used esp. in the phrase *play the wanton* **b** : a lewd or lascivious person

³wanton *vi* (1582) : to be wanton or act wantonly ~ *vt* : to pass or waste wantonly or in wantonness — **wan·ton·er** *n*

wa·pen·take \'wa-pən-,tāk, 'wä-\ *n* [ME, fr. OE *wǣpentæc*, fr. ON *vápnatak* act of grasping weapons, fr. *vápn* weapon + *tak* act of grasping, fr. *taka* to take; prob. fr. the brandishing of weapons as an expression of approval when the chief of the wapentake entered upon his office — more at WEAPON, TAKE] (bef. 12c) : a subdivision of some English shires corresponding formerly to a hundred

wa·pi·ti \'wä-pə-tē\ *n, pl* **wapiti** *or* **wapitis** [Shawnee *wa'piti,* lit., white rump] (1806) : ELK 1b

wap·pen·schaw·ing \'wa-pən-,shȯ(-)iŋ, 'wä-\ *n* [ME (northern dial.) *wapynschawing*, fr. *wapen* weapon (fr. ON *vápn*) + *schawing*, gerund of *schawen* to show, fr. OE *scēawian* to look, look at — more at WEAPON, SHOW] (15c) : an inspection or muster of soldiers formerly held at various times in each district of Scotland

¹war \'wȯr\ *n, often attrib* [ME *werre*, fr. ONF, of Gmc origin; akin to OHG *werra* strife; akin to OHG *werran* to confuse] (12c) **1 a** (1): a state of usu. open and declared hostile conflict between states or nations (2) : a period of such armed conflict (3) : STATE OF WAR **b** : the art or science of warfare **c** (1) *obs* : weapons and equipment for war (2) *archaic* : soldiers armed and equipped for war **2 a** : a state of hostility, conflict, or antagonism **b** : a struggle or competition between opposing forces or for a particular end ⟨a class ~⟩ ⟨a ~ against disease⟩ **c** : VARIANCE, ODDS 3 — **war·less** \-ləs\ *adj*

²war *vi* **warred**; **war·ring** (13c) **1** : to be in active or vigorous conflict **2** : to engage in warfare

³war \'wär\ *adv or adj* [ME *werre*, fr. ON *verri,* adj., *verr,* adv.; akin to OE *wiersa* worse — more at WORSE] (13c) *chiefly Scot* : WORSE

⁴war \'wär\ *vt* **warred**; **war·ring** (15c) *Scot* : WORST, OVERCOME

war baby *n* (1901) : a person born or conceived during a war

¹war·ble \'wȯr-bəl\ *n* [ME *werble* tune, fr. ONF, of Gmc origin; akin to MHG *wirbel* whirl, tuning peg, OHG *wirbil* whirlwind — more at WHIRL] (14c) **1** : a melodious succession of low pleasing sounds **2** : a musical trill **3** : the action of warbling

²warble *vb* **war·bled**; **war·bling** \-b(ə-)liŋ\ *vi* (15c) **1** : to sing in a trilling manner or with many turns and variations **2** : to become sounded with trills, quavers, and rapid modulations in pitch **3** : SING ~ *vt* : to render with turns, runs, or rapid modulations : TRILL

³warble *n* [perh. of Scand origin; akin to obs. Sw *varbulde* boil, fr. *var* pus + *bulde* swelling] (ca. 1585) **1 a :** a swelling under the hide esp. of the back of cattle, horses, and wild mammals caused by the maggot of a botfly or warble fly **2 :** the maggot of a warble fly — **war·bled** \-bəld\ *adj*

warble fly *n* (1877) **:** any of various dipteran flies (family Oestridae) whose larvae live under the skin of various mammals and cause warbles

war·bler \ˈwȯr-blər\ *n* (1611) **1 :** one that warbles **:** SINGER, SONGSTER **2 a :** any of numerous small Old World oscine birds (family Sylviidae) many of which are noted songsters and are closely related to the thrushes **b :** any of numerous small brightly colored American oscine birds (family Parulidae) with a usu. weak and unmusical song — called also *wood warbler*

war·bon·net \ˈwȯr-ˌbä-nət\ *n* (1845) **:** an American Indian ceremonial headdress with a feathered extension down the back

war bride *n* (1916) **1 :** a woman who marries a serviceman ordered into active service in time of war **2 :** a woman who marries a serviceman esp. of a foreign nation met during a time of war

war chest *n* (1901) **:** a fund accumulated to finance a war; *broadly* **:** a fund earmarked for a specific purpose, action, or campaign

war club *n* (1776) **:** a club-shaped implement used as a weapon esp. by American Indians

war crime *n* (1906) **:** a crime (as genocide or maltreatment of prisoners) committed during or in connection with war — usu. used in pl. — **war criminal** *n*

war cry *n* (1748) **1 :** a cry used by a body of fighters in war **2 :** a slogan used esp. to rally people to a cause

¹ward \ˈwȯrd\ *n* [ME, fr. OE *weard;* akin to OHG *warta* act of watching, OE *warian* to beware of, guard, *wær* careful — more at WARY] (bef. 12c) **1 a :** the action or process of guarding **b :** a body of guards **2 :** the state of being under guard; *esp* **:** CUSTODY **3 a :** the inner court of a castle or fortress **b :** a division (as a cell or block) of a prison **c :** a division in a hospital; *esp* **:** a large room in a hospital where a number of patients often requiring similar treatment are accommodated **4 a :** a division of a city for representative, electoral, or administrative purposes **b :** a division of some English and Scottish counties corresponding to a hundred **c :** the Mormon local congregation having auxiliary organizations (as Sunday schools and relief societies) and one or more quorums of each office of the Aaronic priesthood **5 :** a projecting ridge of metal in a lock casing or keyhole permitting only the insertion of a key with a corresponding notch; *also* **:** a corresponding notch in a bit of a key **6 :** a person or thing under guard, protection, or surveillance: as **a :** a minor subject to wardship **b :** a person who by reason of incapacity (as minority or lunacy) is under the protection of a court either directly or through a guardian appointed by the court — called also *ward of court* **c :** a person or body of persons under the protection or tutelage of a government **7 :** a means of defense — **ward·ed** \ˈwȯr-dəd\ *adj*

²ward *vt* [ME, fr. OE *weardian;* akin to OHG *warten* to watch, ON *vartha* to guard, OE *weard* ward] (bef. 12c) **1 :** to keep watch over **:** GUARD **2 :** to turn aside (something threatening) **:** DEFLECT — usu. used with *off*

¹-ward *also* **-wards** *adj suffix* [-ward fr. ME, fr. OE *-weard;* akin to OHG *-wart, -wert* -ward, L *vertere* to turn; *-wards* fr. *-wards,* adv. suffix — more at WORTH] **1 :** that moves, tends, faces, or is directed toward ⟨river*ward*⟩ **2 :** that occurs or is situated in the direction of ⟨left*ward*⟩

²-ward *or* **-wards** *adv suffix* [-ward fr. ME, fr. OE *-weard,* fr. *-weard,* adj. suffix; *-wards* fr. ME, fr. OE *-weardes,* gen. sing. neut. of *-weard,* adj. suffix] **1 :** in a (specified) spatial or temporal direction ⟨up*ward*⟩ ⟨after*ward*⟩ **2 :** toward a (specified) point, position, or area ⟨earth*ward*⟩

war dance *n* (1711) **:** a dance performed (as by American Indians) in preparation for battle or in celebration of victory

ward·ed \ˈwȯr-dəd\ *adj* (1572) **:** provided with a ward ⟨a ~ lock⟩

war·den \ˈwȯr-d°n\ *n* [ME *wardein,* fr. ONF, fr. *warder* to guard, of Gmc origin; akin to OHG *warten* to watch] (13c) **1 :** one having care or charge of something **:** GUARDIAN, KEEPER **2 a :** REGENT **2 b :** the governor of a town, district, or fortress **c :** a member of the governing body of a guild **3 a :** an official charged with special supervisory duties or with the enforcement of specified laws or regulations ⟨game ~⟩⟨air raid ~⟩ **b :** an official in charge of the operation of a prison **c :** any of various British officials having designated administrative functions ⟨~ of the mint⟩ **4 a :** one of two ranking lay officers of an Episcopal parish **b :** any of various British college officials whose duties range from the administration of academic matters to the supervision of student discipline

war·den·ship \-ˌship\ *n* (15c) **:** the office, jurisdiction, or powers of a warden

¹ward·er \ˈwȯr-dər\ *n* [ME, fr. AF *wardere,* fr. *warde* act of guarding, of Gmc origin; akin to OHG *warta* act of watching] (15c) **1 :** WATCHMAN, PORTER **2** *Brit* **a :** WARDEN **b :** a prison guard

²war·der *n* [ME, staff, perh. fr. *warden* to ward] (ca. 1548) **:** a truncheon used by a king or commander in chief to signal orders

ward heeler *n* (1888) **:** a worker for a political boss in a ward or other local area

ward·ress \ˈwȯr-drəs\ *n* (1878) **:** a woman supervising female prisoners (as in a prison)

ward·robe \ˈwȯr-ˌdrōb\ *n* [ME *warderobe,* fr. ONF, fr. *warder* to guard + *robe* robe] (14c) **1 a :** a room or closet where clothes are kept **b :** CLOTHESPRESS **c :** a large trunk in which clothes may be hung upright **2 a :** a collection of wearing apparel (as of one person or for one activity) ⟨a summer ~⟩ **b :** a collection of stage costumes and accessories **3 :** the department of a royal or noble household entrusted with the care of wearing apparel, jewels, and personal articles

warbonnet

ward·room \ˈwȯr-ˌdrüm, -ˌdrum\ *n* (1758) **:** the space in a warship allotted for living quarters to the commissioned officers excepting the captain; *specif* **:** the mess assigned to these officers

ward·ship \ˈwȯrd-ˌship\ *n* (15c) **1 a :** care and protection of a ward **b :** the right to the custody of an infant heir of a feudal tenant and of the heir's property **2 :** the state of being under a guardian

¹ware \ˈwar, ˈwer\ *adj* [ME *war, ware* careful, aware, fr. OE *wær* — more at WARY] (bef. 12c) **1 :** AWARE, CONSCIOUS ⟨was ~ of black looks cast at me —Mary Webb⟩ **2** *archaic* **:** WARY, VIGILANT

²ware *vt* **wared;** **war·ing** [ME, fr. OE *warian;* akin to OHG bi*warōn* to protect, OE *wær* aware] (bef. 12c) **:** to beware of **:** AVOID — used chiefly as a command to hunting animals

³ware *n* [ME, fr. OE *waru;* akin to MHG *ware* ware and prob. to Skt *vasna* price — more at VENAL] (bef. 12c) **1 a :** manufactured articles, products of art or craft, or farm produce **:** GOODS — often used in combination ⟨tin*ware*⟩ **b :** an article of merchandise **2 :** articles (as pottery or dishes) of fired clay ⟨earthen*ware*⟩ **3 :** an intangible item (as a service or ability) that is a marketable commodity

⁴ware *vt* **wared;** **war·ing** [ME, fr. ON *verja* to clothe, invest, spend — more at WEAR] (14c) *Scot* **:** SPEND, EXPEND

¹ware·house \ˈwar-ˌhaüs, ˈwer-\ *n* (14c) **:** a structure or room for the storage of merchandise or commodities

²ware·house \-ˌhaüz, -ˌhaüs\ *vt* (1799) **1 :** to deposit, store, or stock in or as if in a warehouse **2 :** to confine or house (a person) in conditions suggestive of a warehouse

ware·house·man \-ˌhaüs-mən\ *n* (1635) **:** a person who manages or works in a warehouse

ware·hous·er \-ˌhaü-zər, -sər\ *n* (ca. 1927) **:** WAREHOUSEMAN

ware·room \ˈwar-ˌrüm, ˈwer-, -ˌrum\ *n* (1811) **:** a room in which goods are exhibited for sale

war·fare \ˈwȯr-ˌfar, -ˌfer\ *n* [ME, fr. *werre, warre* war + *fare* journey, passage — more at FARE] (15c) **1 :** military operations between enemies **:** HOSTILITIES, WAR; *also* **:** an activity undertaken by a political unit (as a nation) to weaken or destroy another ⟨economic ~⟩ **2 :** struggle between competing entities **:** CONFLICT

war·fa·rin \ˈwȯr-fə-rən\ *n* [Wisconsin Alumni Research Foundation (its patentee) + coum*arin*] (1950) **:** a crystalline anticoagulant compound $C_{19}H_{16}O_4$ used as a rodent poison and in medicine

war footing *n* (1847) **:** the condition of being prepared to undertake or maintain war

war–game *vt* (1942) **:** to plan or conduct in the manner of a war game ⟨war-gamed an invasion —Newsweek⟩ ~ *vi* **:** to conduct a war game

war game *n* (1828) **1 :** a simulated battle or campaign to test military concepts and usu. conducted in conferences by officers acting as the opposing staffs **2 :** a two-sided umpired training maneuver with actual elements of the armed forces participating

war hawk *n* (1798) **:** one who clamors for war; *esp* **:** an American jingo favoring war with Britain around 1812

war·head \ˈwȯr-ˌhed\ *n* (1898) **:** the section of a missile containing the explosive, chemical, or incendiary charge

war·horse \-ˌhȯrs\ *n* (1653) **1 :** a horse used in war **:** CHARGER **2 :** a person with long experience in a field; *esp* **:** a veteran soldier or public person (as a politician) **3 :** something (as a work of art or musical composition) that has become overly familiar or hackneyed due to much repetition in the standard repertoire

war·i·son \ˈwar-ə-sən\ *n* [prob. a misunderstanding by Sir Walter Scott in the *Lay of the Last Minstrel* (1805) of ME *waryson* reward, fr. ONF *warison* defense, possessions, fr. *warir* to protect, provide, of Gmc origin; akin to OHG *werien* to defend — more at WEIR] (1805) **:** a bugle call to attack

war·like \ˈwȯr-ˌlīk\ *adj* (15c) **1** *obs* **:** ready for war **:** equipped to fight **2 :** fit for, disposed to, or fond of war **:** BELLICOSE **3 :** of, relating to, or useful in war **4 :** befitting or characteristic of war or a soldier

war·lock \-ˌläk\ *n* [ME *warloghe,* fr. OE *wærloga* one that breaks faith, the Devil, fr. *wær* faith, troth + *-loga* (fr. *lēogan* to lie); akin to OE *wær* true — more at VERY, LIE] (14c) **1 :** a man practicing the black arts **:** SORCERER — compare WITCH **2 :** CONJURER

war·lord \-ˌlȯrd\ *n* (1856) **1 :** a supreme military leader **2 :** a military commander exercising civil power by force usu. in a limited area — **war·lord·ism** \-ˌlȯr-ˌdi-zəm\ *n*

¹warm \ˈwȯrm\ *adj* [ME, fr. OE *wearm;* akin to OHG *warm* warm and prob. to Lith *virti* to cook, boil] (bef. 12c) **1 a :** having or giving out heat to a moderate or adequate degree **b :** serving to maintain or preserve heat esp. to a satisfactory degree ⟨a ~ sweater⟩ **c :** feeling or causing sensations of heat brought about by strenuous exertion **2 :** comfortably established **:** SECURE **3 a :** marked by strong feeling **:** ARDENT **b :** marked by excitement, disagreement, or anger ⟨the argument grew ~⟩ **4 :** marked by or readily showing affection, gratitude, cordiality, or sympathy ⟨a ~ welcome⟩ ⟨~ regards⟩ **5 :** emphasizing or exploiting sexual imagery or incidents **6 :** accompanied or marked by extreme danger or duress **7 :** newly made **:** FRESH ⟨a ~ scent⟩ **8 :** having the color or tone of something that imparts heat; *specif* **:** of a hue in the range yellow through orange to red **9 :** near to a goal, object, or solution sought — **warm·ish** \ˈwȯr-mish\ *adj* — **warm·ness** \ˈwȯrm-nəs\ *n*

²warm *vt* (bef. 12c) **1 :** to make warm **2 a :** to infuse with a feeling of love, friendship, well-being, or pleasure **b :** to fill with anger, zeal, or passion **3 :** to reheat (cooked food) for eating — often used with *over* **4 :** to make ready for operation or performance by preliminary exercise or operation — often used with *up* ~ *vi* **1 :** to become warm **2 a :** to become ardent, interested, or receptive — usu. used with *to* or *toward* ⟨~ed to the idea⟩ **b :** to become filled with affection or love — used with *to* or *toward* **3 :** to experience feelings of pleasure **:** BASK **4 :** to become ready for operation or performance by preliminary activity — often used with *up*

³warm *adv* (bef. 12c) **:** WARMLY — usu. used in combination ⟨warm-clad⟩

\ə\ abut \ᵊ\ kitten, F table \ər\ further \a\ ash \ā\ ace \ä\ mop, mar \au\ out \ch\ chin \e\ bet \ē\ easy \g\ go \i\ hit \ī\ ice \j\ job \ŋ\ sing \ō\ go \o\ law \oi\ boy \th\ thin \t͟h\ the \ü\ loot \u\ foot \y\ yet \zh\ vision \á, k̲, ⁿ, œ, œ̄, ue, ūe, ᵊ\ see Guide to Pronunciation

warm—blood·ed \'wȯrm-'blə-dəd\ *adj* (1793) **1 :** having warm blood; *specif* : having a relatively high and constant body temperature relatively independent of the surroundings **2 :** fervent or ardent in spirit — **warm—blood·ed·ness** *n*

warmed—over \'wȯrmd-'ō-vər\ *adj* (1887) **1 :** not fresh or new : STALE ⟨~ ideas⟩ **2 :** heated again ⟨~ beans⟩

warm·er \'wȯr-mər\ *n* (ca. 1595) : one that warms; *esp* : a device for keeping something warm ⟨a hand ~⟩

warm front *n* (ca. 1921) : an advancing edge of a warm air mass

warm-heart·ed \'wȯrm-'här-təd\ *adj* (ca. 1520) : marked by ready affection, cordiality, generosity, or sympathy — **warm·heart·ed·ness** *n*

warming pan *n* (15c) : a long-handled covered pan filled with live coals that is used to warm a bed

warm·ly \'wȯrm-lē\ *adv* (1529) **1 :** in a manner characterized or accompanied by warmth of emotion **2 :** in a manner that causes or maintains warmth

war·mon·ger \'wȯr-ˌmən-gər, -ˌmän-\ *n* (1590) : one who urges or attempts to stir up war : JINGO — **war·mon·ger·ing** \-g(ə-)riŋ\ *n*

war·mouth \'wȯr-ˌmau̇th\ *n* [origin unknown] (ca. 1883) : a freshwater sunfish (*Lepomis gulosus*) chiefly of the eastern U.S. — called also *warmouth bass*

warm spot *n* (1951) : a lasting affection for a particular person or object

warmth \'wȯrm(p)th\ *n* (13c) **1 :** the quality or state of being warm in temperature **2 :** the quality or state of being warm in feeling ⟨a child needing human ~ and family life⟩ **3 :** a glowing effect produced by the use of warm colors

warm—up \'wȯrm-ˌəp\ *n* (1915) **1 :** the act or an instance of warming up; *also* : a preparatory activity or procedure **2 :** a suit for exercise or casual wear consisting of a jacket or sweatshirt and pants — often used in pl.; called also *warm-up suit*

warm up *vi* (1846) : to engage in exercise or practice esp. before entering a game or contest; *broadly* : to get ready

warn \'wȯrn\ *vb* [ME, fr. OE *warnian; akin* to OHG *warnōn* to take heed, OE *wær* careful, aware — more at WARY] *vt* (bef. 12c) **1 a :** to give notice to beforehand esp. of danger or evil **b :** to give admonishing advice to : COUNSEL **c :** to call to one's attention : INFORM **2 :** to order to go or stay away — often used with *off* ~ *vi* : to give a warning — **warn·er** *n*

¹warn·ing \'wȯr-niŋ\ *n* (bef. 12c) **1 :** the act of warning : the state of being warned ⟨he had ~ of his illness⟩ **2 :** something that warns or serves to warn; *esp* : a notice or bulletin that alerts the public that a tornado has been reported in the immediate vicinity or that the approach of a severe storm is imminent

²warning *adj* (ca. 1552) : serving as an alarm, signal, summons, or admonition ⟨~ bell⟩ ⟨~ shot⟩ — **warn·ing·ly** \'wȯr-niŋ-lē\ *adv*

warning coloration *n* (ca. 1928) : conspicuous coloration possessed by an animal (as an insect) otherwise effectively but not obviously defended that serves to warn off potential enemies

warning track *n* (1966) : a usu. dirt or cinder strip around the outside edge of a baseball outfield to warn a fielder when running to make a catch that the fence is near — called also *warning path*

war of nerves (1939) : a conflict characterized by psychological tactics (as bluff, threats, and intimidation) designed primarily to create confusion, indecision, or breakdown of morale

¹warp \'wȯrp\ *n* [ME, fr. OE *wearp*; akin to OHG *warf* warp, OE *weorpan* to throw, ON *verpa*] (bef. 12c) **1 a :** a series of yarns extended lengthwise in a loom and crossed by the weft **b :** FOUNDATION, BASE ⟨the ~ of the economic structure is agriculture —*Amer. Guide Series: N.C.*⟩ **2 :** a rope used for warping or mooring a ship or boat **3** [²*warp*] **a** : a twist or curve that has developed in something orig. flat or straight ⟨a ~ in a door panel⟩ **b :** a mental twist or aberration — **warp·age** \'wȯr-pij\ *n*

²warp *vt* (14c) **1 a :** to arrange (yarns) so as to form a warp **2 a :** to turn or twist out of or as if out of shape; *esp* : to twist or bend out of a plane **b :** to cause to judge, choose, or act wrongly or abnormally : PERVERT **c :** DISTORT 1 ⟨intellect and learning . . . ~ed by prejudices —Irving Wallace⟩ **d :** to deflect from a course **3 :** to move (as a ship) by hauling on a line attached to a fixed object ~ *vi* **1 :** to become warped **2 :** to move a ship by warping *syn* see DEFORM — **warp·er** *n*

war paint *n* (1826) **1 :** paint put on parts of the body (as the face) by American Indians as a sign of going to war **2 :** MAKEUP 3a

warp and woof *n* (1842) : FOUNDATION, BASE ⟨the vigorous Anglo-Saxon base had become the *warp and woof* of English speech —H. R. Warfel⟩

war party *n* (1755) **1 :** a group of American Indians on the warpath **2 :** a usu. jingoistic political party advocating or upholding a war

war·path \'wȯr-ˌpath, -ˌpàth\ *n* (1755) **1 :** the route taken by a party of American Indians going on a warlike expedition or to a war **2 :** a hostile course of action or frame of mind

warp beam *n* (ca. 1833) : a roll on which warp is wound for a loom

warp knit *n* (1946) : a knit fabric produced by machine with the yarns running in a lengthwise direction — compare WEFT KNIT — **warp·knit·ted** \-'ni-təd\ *adj* — **warp knitting** *n*

war·plane \'wȯr-ˌplān\ *n* (ca. 1911) : a military airplane; *specif* : one armed for combat

war power *n* (1766) : the power to make war; *specif* : an extraordinary power exercised usu. by the executive branch of a government in the prosecution of a war

¹war·rant \'wȯr-ənt, 'wär-\ *n* [ME, protector, warrant, fr. ONF *warant*, modif. of a Gmc noun represented by OHG *werēnto* guarantor, fr. prp. of *werēn* to warrant; akin to OHG *wāra* trust, care — more at VERY] (14c) **1 a :** SANCTION, AUTHORIZATION; *also* : evidence for or token of authorization (2) : GUARANTEE, SECURITY **b** (1) : GROUND, JUSTIFICATION (2) : CONFIRMATION, PROOF **2 a :** a commission or document giving authority to do something; *esp* : a writing that authorizes a person to pay or deliver to another and the other to receive money or other consideration **b :** a precept or writ issued by a competent magistrate authorizing an officer to make an arrest, a seizure, or a search or to do other acts incident to the administration of justice **c :** an official certificate of appointment issued to an officer of lower rank than a commissioned officer **d** (1) : a short-term obligation of a

governmental body (as a municipality) issued in anticipation of revenue (2) : an instrument issued by a corporation giving to the holder the right to purchase the capital stock of the corporation at a stated price either prior to a stipulated date or at any future time — **war·rant·less** \-ləs\ *adj*

²warrant *vt* [ME, fr. ONF *warantir*, fr. *warant*] (14c) **1 a :** to declare or maintain with certainty : be sure that ⟨I'll ~ he'll be here by noon⟩ **b :** to assure (a person) of the truth of what is said **2 a :** to guarantee to a person good title to and undisturbed possession of (as an estate) **b :** to provide a guarantee of the security of (as title to property sold) usu. by an express covenant in the deed of conveyance **c :** to guarantee to be as represented **d :** to guarantee (as goods sold) esp. in respect of the quality or quantity specified **3 :** to guarantee security or immunity to : SECURE ⟨I'll ~ him from drowning —Shak.⟩ **4 :** to give warrant or sanction to : AUTHORIZE ⟨the law ~s this procedure⟩ **5 a :** to give proof of the authenticity or truth of **b :** to give assurance of the nature of or for the undertaking of : GUARANTEE **6 :** to serve as or give adequate ground or reason for ⟨promising enough to ~ further consideration⟩

war·rant·able \'wȯr-ən-tə-bəl, 'wär-\ *adj* (1581) : capable of being warranted : JUSTIFIABLE — **war·rant·able·ness** *n* — **war·rant·ably** \-blē\ *adv*

war·ran·tee \ˌwȯr-ən-'tē, ˌwär-\ *n* (1706) : the person to whom a warranty is made

warrant officer *n* (1693) **1 :** an officer in the armed forces holding rank by virtue of a warrant and ranking above a noncommissioned officer and below a commissioned officer **2 :** a commissioned officer ranking below an ensign in the navy or coast guard and below a second lieutenant in the marine corps

war·ran·tor \ˌwȯr-ən-'tȯr, ˌwär-; 'wȯr-ən-tər, 'wär-\ *also* **war·rant·er** \'wȯr-ən-tər, 'wär-\ *n* (1583) : one that warrants or gives a warranty

war·ran·ty \'wȯr-ən-tē, 'wär-\ *n, pl* **-ties** [ME *warantie*, fr. ONF, fr. *warantir* to warrant] (14c) **1 a :** a real covenant binding the grantor of an estate and his heirs to warrant and defend the title **b :** a collateral undertaking that a fact regarding the subject of a contract is or will be as it is expressly or by implication declared or promised to be **2 :** something that authorizes, sanctions, supports, or justifies : WARRANT **3 :** a usu. written guarantee of the integrity of a product and of the maker's responsibility for the repair or replacement of defective parts

warranty deed *n* (1779) : a deed warranting that the grantor has a good title free and clear of all liens and encumbrances and will defend the grantee against all claims

war·ren \'wȯr-ən, 'wär-\ *n* [ME *warenne*, fr. ONF, prob. of Gmc origin; akin to OHG *werien* to defend, protect — more at WEIR] (15c) **1** *chiefly Brit* **a :** a place legally authorized for keeping small game (as hare or pheasant) **b :** the privilege of hunting game in such a warren **2 a** (1) : an area (as of uncultivated ground) where rabbits breed (2) : a structure where rabbits are kept or bred **b :** the rabbits of a warren **3 a :** a crowded tenement or district **b :** a maze of passageways or cubbies

war·ren·er \-ən-ər\ *n* (13c) **1 :** GAMEKEEPER **2 :** a person who maintains a rabbit warren

war·rior \'wȯr-yər, 'wȯr-ē-ər, 'wär-ē- *also* 'wär-yər\ *n, often attrib* [ME *werriour*, fr. ONF *werreier*, fr. *werreier* to make war, fr. *werre* war — more at WAR] (14c) : a man engaged or experienced in warfare; *broadly* : a person engaged in some struggle or conflict ⟨poverty ~s⟩

war room *n* (1914) **1 :** a room at a military headquarters where maps showing the current status of troops in battle are maintained **2 :** a room (as at a business headquarters) used for conferences and planning that is often specially equipped (as with computers, maps, or charts)

war·saw grouper \'wȯr-ˌsȯ-\ *n* [*warsaw* modif. of *warsaw guasa*] (1949) : any of several large groupers (esp. *Epinephelus nigritus*) — called also *warsaw*

war·ship \'wȯr-ˌship\ *n* (1533) : a naval vessel

war·sle *or* **wars·tle** \'wä(r)-səl\ *vb* [ME *werstelen, warstelen*, alter. of *wrestlen, wrastlen*] (14c) *Scot* : WRESTLE, STRUGGLE — **warsle** *n, Scot*

war story *n* (1981) : a story of a memorable personal experience typically involving an element of danger, hardship, or adventure ⟨politicians swapping *war stories* from past campaigns⟩

wart \'wȯrt\ *n* [ME, fr. OE *wearte*; akin to OHG *warza* wart, OCS *vrědŭ* injury] (bef. 12c) **1 a :** a horny projection on the skin usu. of the extremities that is caused by a virus — called also *verruca vulgaris* **b :** any of numerous similar skin lesions **2 :** an excrescence or protuberance resembling a true wart; *esp* : a glandular excrescence or hardened protuberance on a plant **3 a :** one that suggests a wart esp. in smallness, unpleasantness, or unattractiveness **b :** DEFECT, IMPERFECTION — often used in the phrase *warts and all* — **wart·ed** \'wȯr-təd\ *adj* — **wart·less** \'wȯrt-ləs\ *adj* — **warty** \'wȯr-tē\ *adj*

wart·hog \'wȯrt-ˌhȯg, -ˌhäg\ *n* (1840) : a wild African hog (*Phacochoerus aethiopicus*) which has large protruding tusks and the males of which have two pairs of rough warty excrescences on the face

warthog

war·time \'wȯr-ˌtīm\ *n, often attrib* (14c) : a period during which a war is in progress

warts—and—all *adj* (1930) : showing defects or imperfections frankly : not idealized ⟨a ~ biography⟩

war whoop *n* (1739) : a war cry esp. of American Indians

wary \'war-ē, 'wer-\ *adj* **war·i·er; -est** [¹*ware*, fr. ME *war, ware*, fr. OE *wær* careful, aware, wary; akin to OHG *giwar* aware, attentive, L *vereri* to fear, Gk *horan* to see] (15c) : marked by keen caution, cunning, and watchful prudence esp. in detecting and escaping danger *syn* see CAUTIOUS — **war·i·ly** \'war-ə-lē, 'wer-\ *adv* — **war·i·ness** \'war-ē-nəs, 'wer-\ *n*

war zone *n* (1914) **1 :** a zone in which belligerents are waging war **2 :** a designated area esp. on the high seas within which rights of neutrals are not respected by a belligerent nation in time of war

was [ME, fr. OE, 1st & 3d sing. past indic. of *wesan* to be; akin to ON *vera* to be, *var* was, Skt *vasati* he lives, dwells] *past 1st & 3d sing of* BE

wa·sa·bi \'wä-sə-bē\ *n* [Jp] (1903) **1 :** a condiment that is prepared from the thick pungent greenish root of an Asian herb (*Eutrema wasabi*) of the mustard family and is similar in flavor and use to horseradish; *also* : the root **2 :** the herb that yields wasabi

¹wash \'wȯsh, 'wäsh, *chiefly Midland also* 'wȯrsh *or* 'wärsh\ *vb* [ME, fr. OE *wascan*; akin to OHG *waskan* to wash and perh. to OE *wæter* water] *vt* (bef. 12c) **1 a :** to cleanse by or as if by the action of liquid (as water) **b :** to remove (as dirt) by rubbing or drenching with liquid **2 :** to cleanse (fur) by licking or by rubbing with a paw moistened with saliva **3 a :** to flush or moisten (a bodily part or injury) with a liquid **b** (1) : to wet thoroughly : DRENCH (2) : to overspread with light : SUFFUSE (3) : to pass a liquid (as water) over or through esp. so as to carry off material from the surface or interior **4 :** to flow along or dash or overflow against 〈waves ~*ing* the shore〉 **5 :** to move, carry, or deposit by or as if by the force of water in motion 〈houses ~*ed* away by the flood〉 **6 a :** to subject (as crushed ore) to the action of water to separate valuable material **b :** to separate (particles) from a substance (as ore) by agitation with or in water **c** (1) : to pass through a bath to carry off impurities or soluble components (2) : to pass (a gas or gaseous mixture) through or over a liquid to purify it esp. by removing soluble components **7 a :** to cover or daub lightly with or as if with an application of a thin liquid (as whitewash or varnish) **b :** to depict or paint by a broad sweep of thin color with a brush **8 :** to cause to swirl 〈~*ing* coffee around in his cup〉 **9 :** LAUNDER 3 〈how the mob ~*es* its money through corrupt bankers —Vincent Teresa〉 ~ *vi* **1 :** to wash oneself or a part of one's body **2 :** to become worn away by the action of water **3 :** to clean something by rubbing or dipping in water **4 a :** to become carried along on water : DRIFT 〈cakes of ice ~*ing* along〉 **b :** to pour, sweep, or flow in a stream or current 〈waves of pioneers ~*ing* westward —Green Peyton〉 **5 :** to serve as a cleansing agent 〈this soap ~*es* thoroughly〉 **6 a :** to undergo laundering 〈this dress doesn't ~ well〉 **b** (1) : to undergo testing successfully : WORK 4 〈an interesting theory, but it just won't ~〉 (2) : to gain acceptance : inspire belief 〈the story didn't ~ with me〉 — **wash one's hands of :** to disclaim interest in, responsibility for, or further connection with

²wash *n* (15c) **1 a :** a piece of ground washed by the sea or river **b** : BOG, MARSH **c** (1) : a shallow body of water (2) : a shallow creek **d** *West* : the dry bed of a stream — called also *dry wash* **2 a :** the act or process or an instance of washing or being washed **b :** articles to be washed, being washed, or having been washed **3 :** the surging action of waves **4 a :** worthless esp. liquid waste : REFUSE **b :** an insipid beverage **c :** vapid writing or speech **5 a :** a sweep or splash esp. of color made by or as if by a long stroke of a brush **b :** a thin coat of paint (as watercolor) **c :** a thin liquid used for coating a surface (as a wall) **6 :** LOTION **7 :** loose or eroded surface material of the earth (as rock debris) transported and deposited by running water **8 a :** BACKWASH 1 **b :** a disturbance in the air produced by the passage of an airfoil or propeller **9 :** a situation in which losses and gains or advantages and disadvantages balance each other

³wash *adj* (1634) **1 :** WASHABLE 〈~ fabric〉 **2 :** involving essentially simultaneous purchase and sale of the same security 〈spurious market activity resulting from ~ trading〉

wash·able \'wȯ-shə-bəl, 'wä-\ *adj* (1821) : capable of being washed without damage — **wash·abil·i·ty** \,wȯ-shə-'bi-lət-ē, ,wä-\ *n*

wash-and-wear *adj* (1956) : of, relating to, or constituting a fabric or garment that needs little or no ironing after washing

wash·a·te·ria *also* **wash·e·te·ria** \,wä-shə-'tir-ē-ə, ,wȯ-\ *n* [²*wash* + -*ateria* or -*eteria* (as in *cafeteria*)] (1937) *chiefly Southern* : a self-service laundry

wash·ba·sin \'wȯsh-,bā-sᵊn, 'wäsh-\ *n* (1812) : WASHBOWL

wash·board \'wȯsh-,bȯrd, 'wäsh-, -,bȯrd\ *n* (1742) **1 :** a broad thin plank along a gunwale or on the sill of a lower deck port to keep out the sea **2 :** BASEBOARD **3 a :** a corrugated rectangular surface that is used for scrubbing clothes or as a percussion instrument **b :** a road or pavement so worn by traffic as to be corrugated transversely

wash·bowl \-,bōl\ *n* (1816) : a large bowl for water that is used to wash one's hands and face

wash·cloth \-,klȯth\ *n* (ca. 1900) : a cloth that is used for washing one's face and body — called also *facecloth, washrag*

wash down *vt* (1600) **1 :** to move or carry downward by action of a liquid; *esp* : to facilitate the passage of (food) down the gullet with accompanying swallows of liquid 〈pizza *washed down* with beer〉 **2** : to wash the whole length or extent of 〈*washed down* and scrubbed the front porch〉

wash drawing *n* (1889) : watercolor painting in or chiefly in washes esp. in black, white, and gray tones only

washed-out \'wȯsht-'aut, 'wäsht-\ *adj* (1796) **1 :** faded in color **2** : depleted in vigor or animation : EXHAUSTED

washed-up \'wȯsht-'əp, 'wäsht-\ *adj* (1928) : no longer successful, skillful, popular, or needed

wash·er \'wȯ-shər, 'wä-\ *n* (13c) **1 :** a flat thin ring or a perforated plate used in joints or assemblies to ensure tightness, prevent leakage, or relieve friction **2 :** one that washes; *esp* : WASHING MACHINE

wash·er·man \-mən\ *n* (1715) : LAUNDRYMAN; *also* : a man operating any of various industrial washing machines

wash·er·wom·an \-,wu̇-mən\ *n* (1632) : a woman whose occupation is washing clothes : LAUNDRESS

wash·house \'wȯsh-,haus, 'wäsh-\ *n* (1577) : a building used or equipped for washing; *esp* : one for washing clothes

wash·ing \'wȯ-shiŋ, 'wä-\ *n* (13c) **1 :** the act or action of one that cleanses with water **2 :** material obtained by washing **3 :** articles washed or to be washed : WASH

washing machine *n* (ca. 1754) : a machine for washing; *esp* : one for washing clothes and household linen

washing soda *n* (1865) : a transparent crystalline hydrated sodium carbonate — called also *sal soda*

Wash·ing·ton pie \'wȯ-shiŋ-tən-, 'wä-, *chiefly Midland also* 'wȯr-shiŋ- *or* 'wär-shiŋ-\ *n* [George *Washington*] (1905) : cake layers put together with a jam or jelly filling

Washington's Birthday *n* [George *Washington*] (1829) **1 :** February 22 formerly observed as a legal holiday in most of the states of the U.S.

2 : the third Monday in February observed as a legal holiday in most of the states of the U.S. — called also *Presidents' Day*

wash-out \'wȯsh-,aut, 'wäsh-\ *n* (1873) **1 a :** the washing out or away of something and esp. of earth in a roadbed by a freshet **b :** a place where earth is washed away **2 :** one that fails to measure up : FAILURE: as **a :** one who fails in a course of training or study **b :** an unsuccessful enterprise or undertaking

wash out *vt* (1555) **1 :** to wash free of an extraneous substance (as dirt) **2 a :** to cause to fade by or as if by laundering **b :** to deplete the strength or vitality of **c :** to eliminate as useless or unsatisfactory : REJECT **3 a :** to destroy or make useless by the force or action of water 〈the storm *washed out* the bridge〉 **b :** RAIN OUT 〈the game was *washed out*〉 ~ *vi* **1 :** to become depleted of color or vitality : FADE **2** : to fail to meet requirements or measure up to a standard

wash·rag \'wȯsh-,rag, 'wäsh-\ *n* (1890) : WASHCLOTH

wash·room \-,rüm, -,ru̇m\ *n* (1806) : a room that is equipped with washing and toilet facilities : LAVATORY

wash·stand \-,stand\ *n* (1789) **1 :** a stand holding articles needed for washing one's face and hands **2 :** a washbowl permanently set in place and attached to water and drainpipes

wash·tub \-,təb\ *n* (1602) : a tub in which clothes are washed or soaked

wash·up \-,əp\ *n* (1884) : the act or process of washing clean

wash up *vt* (1751) **1 :** to get rid of by washing 〈*wash up* the spilled milk〉 **2 :** EXHAUST, FINISH ~ *vi* **1 :** to wash one's face and hands **2** *Brit* : to wash the dishes after a meal **3 :** to be deposited by or as if by a swell of waves 〈seaweed *washed up* on the shore〉

wash·wom·an \'wȯsh-,wu̇-mən, 'wäsh-\ *n* (1590) : WASHERWOMAN

washy \'wȯ-shē, 'wä-\ *adj* **wash·i·er; -est** (1615) **1 a :** WEAK, WATERY 〈~ tea〉 **b :** deficient in color : PALLID **c :** lacking in vigor, individuality, or definiteness **2 :** lacking in condition and in firmness of flesh

wasn't \'wə-zᵊnt, 'wä-, *dial also* 'wə-t³n(t)\ (ca. 1849) : was not

wasp \'wäsp, 'wȯsp\ *n* [ME *waspe*, fr. OE *wæps, wæsp*; akin to OHG *wafsa* wasp, L *vespa* wasp] (bef. 12c) **1 :** any of numerous social or solitary winged hymenopterous insects (esp. families Sphecidae and Vespidae) that usu. have a slender smooth body with the abdomen attached by a narrow stalk, well-developed wings, biting mouthparts, and in the females and workers an often formidable sting, and that are largely carnivorous and often provision their nests with caterpillars, insects, or spiders killed or paralyzed by stinging for their larvae to feed on — compare BEE **2 :** any of various hymenopterous insects (as a chalcid or ichneumon fly) other than wasps with larvae that are parasitic on other arthropods — **wasp·like** \-,līk\ *adj*

WASP *or* **Wasp** \'wäsp, 'wȯsp\ *n, often attrib* [white Anglo-Saxon Protestant] (1957) : an American of Northern European and esp. British ancestry and of Protestant background; *esp* : a member of the dominant and the most privileged class of people in the U.S. — sometimes used disparagingly — **Wasp·dom** \-dəm\ *n* — **Wasp·ish** \'wäs-pish, 'wȯs-\ *adj* — **Wasp·ish·ness** *n* — **Waspy** \-pē\ *adj*

wasp·ish \'wäs-pish, 'wȯs-\ *adj* (1566) **1 :** resembling a wasp in behavior; *esp* : SNAPPISH, PETULANT **2 :** resembling a wasp in form; *esp* : slightly built — **wasp·ish·ly** *adv* — **wasp·ish·ness** *n*

wasp waist *n* (1870) : a very slender waist — **wasp-waist·ed** \'wäsp-'wä-stəd, 'wȯsp-\ *adj*

¹was·sail \'wä-səl *also* wä-'sā(ə)l\ *n* [ME *wæs hæil*, fr. ON *ves heill* be well, fr. *ves* (imper. sing. of *vera* to be) + *heill* healthy — more at WAS, WHOLE] (13c) **1 :** an early English toast to someone's health **2 :** a hot drink that is made with wine, beer, or cider, spices, sugar, and usu. baked apples and is traditionally served in a large bowl esp. at Christmastime **3 :** riotous drinking : REVELRY

²wassail *vi* (14c) **1 :** to indulge in wassail : CAROUSE **2** *dial Eng* : to sing carols from house to house at Christmas ~ *vt* : to drink to the health or thriving of

was·sail bowl \'wä-səl-\ *n* (1606) **1 :** a bowl that is used for the serving of wassail **2 :** WASSAIL 2

was·sail·er \'wä-sə-lər *also* wä-'sā-lər\ *n* (1634) **1 :** one that carouses : REVELER **2** *archaic* : one who goes about singing carols

Was·ser·mann reaction \'wä-sər-mən-, 'vä-\ *n* [August von *Wassermann*] (1911) : the complement-fixing reaction that occurs in a positive complement-fixation test for syphilis using the serum of an infected individual

Wassermann test *n* (1909) : a test for the detection of syphilitic infection using the Wassermann reaction — called also *Wasserman*

wast \'wȯst, 'wäst\ *archaic past 2d sing of* BE

wast·age \'wā-stij\ *n* (1756) : loss, decrease, or destruction of something (as by use, decay, erosion, or leakage); *esp* : wasteful or avoidable loss of something valuable

¹waste \'wāst\ *n* [ME *waste, wast*; in sense 1, fr. ONF *wast*, fr. *wast, adj.*, desolate, waste, fr. L *vastus*; in other senses, fr. ME *wasten* to waste — more at VAST] (13c) **1 a :** a sparsely settled or barren region : DESERT **b :** uncultivated land **c :** a broad and empty expanse (as of water) **2 :** the act or an instance of wasting : the state of being wasted **3 a :** loss through breaking down of bodily tissue **b :** gradual loss or decrease by use, wear, or decay **4 a :** damaged, defective, or superfluous material produced by a manufacturing process: as (1) : material rejected during a textile manufacturing process and used usu. for wiping away dirt and oil 〈cotton ~〉 (2) : SCRAP (3) : an unwanted by-product of a manufacturing process, chemical laboratory, or nuclear reactor 〈toxic ~〉 〈hazardous ~〉 〈nuclear ~〉 **b :** refuse from places of human or animal habitation: as (1) : GARBAGE, RUBBISH (2) : EXCREMENT — often used in pl. (3) : SEWAGE **c :** material derived by mechanical and chemical weathering of the land and moved down sloping surfaces or carried by streams to the sea

²waste *vb* **wast·ed; wast·ing** [ME, fr. ONF *waster*, fr. L *vastare*, fr. *vastus* desolate, waste] *vt* (13c) **1 :** to damage or destroy gradually and progressively 〈reclaiming land *wasted* by strip-

\ə\ abut \ᵊ\ kitten, F table \ər\ further \a\ ash \ā\ ace \ä\ mop, mar
\au̇\ out \ch\ chin \e\ bet \ē\ easy \g\ go \i\ hit \ī\ ice \j\ job
\ŋ\ sing \ō\ go \ȯ\ law \ȯi\ boy \th\ thin \t͟h\ the \ü\ loot \u̇\ foot
\y\ yet \zh\ vision \à, k̲, ⁿ, œ, œ̄, ᴜᴇ, ᴜ̄ᴇ, ᵊ\ *see* Guide to Pronunciation

mining) **2 :** to cause to shrink in physical bulk or strength : EMACI-
ATE, ENFEEBLE **3 :** to wear away or diminish gradually : CONSUME **4 a**
: to spend or use carelessly : SQUANDER **b :** to allow to be used ineffi-
ciently or become dissipated **5 :** KILL; *also* **:** to injure severely ∼ *vi*
1 : to lose weight, strength, or vitality — often used with *away* **2 a**
: to become diminished in bulk or substance **b :** to become consumed
3 : to spend money or consume property extravagantly or improvidently *syn* see RAVAGE — **waste one's breath :** to accomplish
nothing by speaking

³**waste** *adj* [ME *waste, wast,* fr. ONF *wast*] (14c) **1 a** (1) **:** being wild
and uninhabited : DESOLATE (2) **:** ARID, EMPTY **b :** not cultivated
: not productive **2 :** being in a ruined or devastated condition **3**
[¹*waste*] **a :** discarded as worthless, defective, or of no use : REFUSE
⟨∼ material⟩ **b :** excreted from or stored in inert form in a living body
as a byproduct of vital activity ⟨∼ disposal in birds⟩ **4** [¹*waste*]**:** serving to conduct or hold refuse material; *specif* **:** carrying off superfluous
water **5 :** WASTED 4

waste·bas·ket \'wās(t)-,bas-kət\ *n* (1850) **:** a receptacle for refuse and
esp. for wastepaper — called also *wastepaper basket*

wast·ed *adj* (15c) **1 :** laid waste : RAVAGED **2 :** impaired in strength or
health : EMACIATED **3** *archaic* **:** gone by : ELAPSED ⟨the chronicle of ∼
time —Shak.⟩ **4 :** unprofitably used, made, or expended ⟨∼ effort⟩ **5**
slang **:** intoxicated from drugs or alcohol

waste·ful \'wāst-fəl\ *adj* (14c) **:** given to or marked by waste : LAVISH,
PRODIGAL — **waste·ful·ly** \-fə-lē\ *adv* — **waste·ful·ness** *n*

waste·land \'wāst-,land *also* -lənd\ *n* (14c) **1 :** barren or uncultivated
land ⟨a desert ∼⟩ **2 :** an ugly often devastated or barely inhabitable
place or area **3 :** something (as a way of life) that is spiritually and
emotionally arid and unsatisfying

waste·pa·per \'wās(t)-'pā-pər\ *n* (1585) **:** paper discarded as used,
superfluous, or not fit for use

waste pipe *n* (ca. 1512) **:** a pipe for carrying off waste fluid

wast·er \'wā-stər\ *n* (14c) **1 a** (1) **:** one that spends or consumes
extravagantly and without thought for the future (2) **:** a dissolute
person **b :** one that uses wastefully or causes or permits waste ⟨a procedure that is a ∼ of time⟩ **c :** one that lays waste : DESTROYER **2**
: an imperfect or inferior manufactured article or object

waste·wa·ter \'wāst-,wȯ-tər, -,wä-\ *n* (15c) **:** water that has been used
(as in a manufacturing process) : SEWAGE

wast·ing \'wā-stiŋ\ *adj* (13c) **1 :** laying waste : DEVASTATING **2 :** undergoing or causing decay or loss of strength ⟨∼ diseases such as tu-
berculosis⟩

wast·rel \'wās-trəl *also* 'wās-\ *n* [irreg. fr. ²*waste*] (ca. 1841) **1 :** VAGA-
BOND, WAIF **2 :** one who dissipates resources foolishly and self=
indulgently : PROFLIGATE

¹**watch** \'wäch, 'wȯch\ *vb* [ME *wacchen,* fr. OE *wæccan* — more at
WAKE] *vi* (bef. 12c) **1 a :** to keep vigil as a devotional exercise **b :** to
be awake during the night **2 a :** to be attentive or vigilant **b :** to
keep guard **3 a :** to keep someone or something under close observation **b :** to observe as a spectator ⟨the country ∼ed as stocks fell
sharply⟩ **4 :** to be expectant : WAIT ⟨∼ for the signal⟩ ∼ *vt* **1 :** to
keep under guard **2 a :** to observe closely in order to check on action
or change ⟨being ∼ed by the police⟩ **b :** to look at : OBSERVE ⟨sat and
∼ed the crowd⟩ **c :** to look on at ⟨∼ television⟩ ⟨∼ a ball game⟩ **3**
a : to take care of : TEND **b :** to be careful of ⟨∼es his diet⟩ **4 :** to be
on the alert for : BIDE ⟨∼ed her opportunity⟩ — **watch it :** look out
: be careful ⟨*watch it* when you handle the glassware⟩ — **watch one's
step :** to proceed with extreme care : act or talk warily — **watch
over :** to have charge of : SUPERINTEND

²**watch** *n* (bef. 12c) **1 a :** the act of keeping awake to guard, protect,
or attend **b** *obs* **:** the state of being wakeful **c :** a wake over a dead
body **d :** a state of alert and continuous attention **e :** close observation : SURVEILLANCE **f :** a notice or bulletin that alerts the public to
the possibility of severe weather conditions occurring in the near future
⟨winter storm ∼⟩ **2 a :** any of the definite divisions of the night
made by ancient peoples **b :** one of the indeterminate intervals marking the passage of night — usu. used in pl. ⟨the silent ∼es of the night⟩
3 a : LOOKOUT, WATCHMAN **b** *archaic* **:** the office or function of a sentinel or guard **4 a :** a body of soldiers or sentinels making up a guard
b : a watchman or body of watchmen formerly assigned to patrol the
streets of a town at night, announce the hours, and act as police **5 a**
(1) **:** a portion of time during which a part of a ship's company is on
duty (2) **:** the part of a ship's company required to be on duty during
a particular watch (3) **:** a sailor's assigned duty period **b :** a period
of duty : SHIFT **c :** a term as holder esp. of an overseeing or managerial
office ⟨the business grew on her ∼⟩ **6 :** a portable timepiece designed
to be worn (as on the wrist) or carried in the pocket — compare CLOCK

watch·able \'wä-chə-bəl, 'wȯ-\ *adj* (1954) **:** worth watching — **watch·
able** *n*

watch and ward *n* (14c) **1 :** continuous unbroken vigilance and
guard **2 :** service as a watchman or sentinel required from a feudal
tenant

watch·band \'wäch-,band, 'wȯch-\ *n* (1924) **:** the bracelet or strap of a
wristwatch

watch cap *n* (1886) **:** a knitted close-fitting usu. navy-blue cap worn
esp. by enlisted men in the U.S. navy in cold or stormy weather

watch·case \'wäch-,kās, 'wȯch-\ *n* (1671) **:** the outside metal covering
of a watch

¹**watch·dog** \-,dȯg\ *n* (1610) **1 :** a dog kept to guard property **2**
: one that guards against loss, waste, theft, or undesirable practices

²**watchdog** *vt* (1902) **:** to act as watchdog for

watch·er \'wä-chər, 'wȯ-\ *n* (1509) **:** one that watches: as **a :** one that
sits up or continues awake at night **b :** WATCHMAN **c** (1) **:** one that
keeps watch beside a dead person (2) **:** one that attends a sick person
at night **d :** a person who closely follows or observes someone or
something ⟨a Supreme Court ∼⟩ — often used in combination ⟨celebri-
ty-*watchers*⟩ **e :** a representative of a party or candidate who is stationed at the polls on an election day to watch the conduct of officials
and voters

watch fire *n* (1801) **:** a fire lighted as a signal or for the use of a guard

watch·ful \'wäch-fəl, 'wȯch-\ *adj* (1548) **1** *archaic* **a :** not able or
accustomed to sleep or rest : WAKEFUL **b :** causing sleeplessness **c**
: spent in wakefulness **2 :** carefully observant or attentive

: being on the watch — **watch·ful·ly** \-fə-lē\ *adv* — **watch·ful·ness**
n
    syn WATCHFUL, VIGILANT, WIDE-AWAKE, ALERT mean being on the look-
    out esp. for danger or opportunity. WATCHFUL is the least explicit term
    ⟨the *watchful* eye of the department supervisor⟩. VIGILANT suggests
    intense, unremitting, wary watchfulness ⟨eternally *vigilant* in the safe-
    guarding of democracy⟩. WIDE-AWAKE applies to watchfulness for op-
    portunities and developments more often than dangers ⟨*wide-awake*
    companies latched onto the new technology⟩. ALERT stresses readiness
    or promptness in meeting danger or in seizing opportunity ⟨*alert* trad-
    ers anticipated the stock market's slide⟩.

watch·mak·er \-,mā-kər\ *n* (1630) **:** one that makes or repairs watches
or clocks — **watch·mak·ing** \-,mā-kiŋ\ *n*

watch·man \-mən\ *n* (15c) **:** a person who keeps watch : GUARD

watch night *n* (1742) **:** a devotional service lasting until after midnight
esp. on New Year's Eve

watch out *vi* (1845) **:** to be vigilant or alert : be on the lookout ⟨you'd
better *watch out*⟩ ⟨*watch out* for the tree!⟩

watch pocket *n* (1831) **:** a small pocket just below the front waistband
of men's trousers

watch·tow·er \'wäch-,taur, 'wȯch-\ *n* (1544) **:** a tower for a lookout

watch·word \-,wərd\ *n* (15c) **1 :** a word or phrase used as a sign of
recognition among members of the same society, class, or group **2 a**
: a word or motto that embodies a principle or guide to action of an
individual or group : SLOGAN ⟨"safety" is our ∼⟩ **b :** a guiding principle ⟨change is the ∼ for both parties⟩

¹**wa·ter** \'wȯ-tər, 'wä-\ *n, often attrib* [ME, fr. OE *wæter;* akin to OHG
wazzar water, Gk *hydōr,* L *unda* wave] (bef. 12c) **1 a :** the liquid that
descends from the clouds as rain, forms streams, lakes, and seas, and is
a major constituent of all living matter and that when pure is an odorless, tasteless, very slightly compressible liquid oxide of hydrogen H_2O
which appears bluish in thick layers, freezes at 0° C and boils at 100° C,
has a maximum density at 4° C and a high specific heat, is feebly ionized to hydrogen and hydroxyl ions, and is a poor conductor of electricity and a good solvent **b :** a natural mineral water — usu. used in
pl. **2 :** a particular quantity or body of water: as **a** (1) *pl* **:** the water
occupying or flowing in a particular bed (2) *chiefly Brit* **:** LAKE, POND
b : a quantity or depth of water adequate for some purpose (as navigation) **c** *pl* (1) **:** a band of seawater abutting on the land of a particular sovereignty and under the control of that sovereignty (2) **:** the sea
of a particular part of the earth **d :** WATER SUPPLY ⟨threatened to turn
off the ∼⟩ **3 :** travel or transportation on water ⟨we went by ∼⟩ **4**
: the level of water at a particular state of the tide : TIDE **5 :** liquid
containing or resembling water: as **a** (1) **:** a pharmaceutical or cosmetic preparation made with water (2) **:** a watery solution of a gaseous or readily volatile substance — compare AMMONIA WATER **b** *archaic* **:** a distilled fluid (as an essence); *esp* **:** a distilled alcoholic liquor
c : a watery fluid (as tears, urine, or sap) formed or circulating in a
living body **d :** AMNIOTIC FLUID; *also* **:** BAG OF WATERS **6 a :** the degree of clarity and luster of a precious stone **b :** degree of excellence ⟨a
scholar of the first ∼⟩ **7 :** WATERCOLOR **8 a :** capital stock not representing assets of the issuing company and not backed by earning
power **b :** fictitious or exaggerated asset entries that give a stock an
unrealistic book value — **above water :** out of difficulty

²**water** *vt* (bef. 12c) **1 :** to moisten, sprinkle, or soak with water **2 :** to
supply with water for drink **3 :** to supply water to **4 :** to treat with
or as if with water; *specif* **:** to impart a lustrous appearance and wavy
pattern to (cloth) by calendering **5 a :** to dilute by the addition of
water — often used with *down* ⟨∼ down the punch⟩ **b :** to add to the
aggregate par value of (securities) without a corresponding addition to
the assets represented by the securities ∼ *vi* **1 :** to form or secrete
water or watery matter (as tears or saliva) **2 :** to get or take water: as
a : to take on a supply of water **b :** to drink water

water bag *n* (1638) **1 :** a bag for holding water; *esp* **:** one designed to
keep water cool for drinking by evaporation through a slightly porous
surface **2 :** the fetal membranes enclosing the amniotic fluid — used
esp. of domestic animals

water balance *n* (1911) **:** the ratio between the water assimilated into
the body and that lost from the body; *also* **:** the condition of the body
when this ratio approximates unity

water ballet *n* (1926) **:** a synchronized sequence of movements performed by a group of swimmers

water bear *n* (1852) **:** TARDIGRADE

Water Bearer *n* **:** AQUARIUS 1, 2a

water bed *n* (1844) **:** a bed whose mattress is a watertight bag filled
with water

water beetle *n* (ca. 1790) **:** any of numerous oval flattened aquatic
beetles (esp. family Dytiscidae) that swim by means of their fringed
hind legs which act together as oars

wa·ter·bird \'wȯ-tər-,bərd, 'wä-\ *n* (15c) **:** a swimming or wading bird
— compare WATERFOWL

water biscuit *n* (ca. 1790) **:** a cracker of flour and water and sometimes fat

water blister *n* (1895) **:** a blister with a clear watery content that is not
purulent or sanguineous

water bloom *n* (1903) **:** an accumulation of algae and esp. of blue=
green algae at or near the surface of a body of water

water boatman *n* (1815) **1 :** BACK SWIMMER **2 :** any of various
aquatic bugs (family Corixidae) with one pair of legs modified into
paddles

wa·ter·borne \'wȯ-tər-,bōrn, 'wä-, -,bȯrn\ *adj* (ca. 1559) **:** supported
or carried by water ⟨∼ commerce⟩ ⟨∼ infection⟩

water boy *n* (1859) **:** one who keeps a group (as of football players)
supplied with drinking water

wa·ter·buck \'wȯ-tər-,bək, 'wä-\ *n, pl* **waterbuck** *or* **waterbucks**
(1850) **:** an antelope (*Kobus ellipsiprymnus*) of sub-Saharan Africa that
commonly frequent streams or wet areas

water buffalo *n* (ca. 1890) **:** an often domesticated Asian buffalo
(*Bubalus bubalis* syn. *B. arnee*)

water bug *n* (1750) **:** any of various small arthropods and esp. insects
that frequent damp or wet places: as **a :** GERMAN COCKROACH **b :** WA-
TER BOATMAN **c :** any of various large aquatic bugs (family Belostomatidae) with the hind legs flattened and used for swimming

water cannon *n* (1964) : a large truck-mounted nozzle for directing a high-pressure stream of water (as at a crowd of rioters or demonstrators)

water chestnut *n* (1854) **1 :** any of a genus (*Trapa* and esp. *T. natans* of the family Trapaceae, the water-chestnut family) of Old World aquatic herbs sometimes grown as ornamentals; *also* : its edible nutlike spiny fruit **2 :** a whitish crunchy vegetable used esp. in Chinese cooking that is the peeled and often sliced tuber of a sedge (*Eleocharis dulcis* syn. *E. tuberosa*) native to Asia but widely cultivated elsewhere; *also* : the tuber or the sedge itself

water clock *n* (1601) : an instrument designed to measure time by the fall or flow of a quantity of water — called also *clepsydra*

water closet *n* (1755) **1 :** a compartment or room for defecation and excretion into a toilet bowl **2 :** a toilet bowl and its accessories

wa·ter·col·or \'wȯ-tər-ˌkə-lər, 'wä-\ *n* (1596) **1 :** a paint of which the liquid is a water dispersion of the binding material (as glue, casein, or gum) **2 :** the art or method of painting with watercolors **3 :** a picture or design executed in watercolors — **watercolor** *adj* — **wa·ter·col·or·ist** \-ˌkə-lə-rist\ *n*

wa·ter·cool·er \'wȯ-tər-ˌkü-lər, 'wä-\ *n* (1846) : a device for dispensing refrigerated drinking water

wa·ter·course \'wȯ-tər-ˌkȯrs, -ˌkȯrs\ *n* (1510) **1 :** a natural or artificial channel through which water flows **2 :** a stream of water (as a river, brook, or underground stream)

wa·ter·craft \-ˌkraft\ *n* (1566) **1 :** skill in aquatic activities (as managing boats) **2 a :** SHIP, BOAT **b :** craft for water transport

wa·ter·cress \-ˌkres\ *n* (14c) : any of several water-loving cresses; *esp* : a perennial European cress (*Nasturtium officinale*) naturalized in the U.S. and used esp. in salads or as a potherb

water cycle *n* (1928) : HYDROLOGIC CYCLE

water dog *n* (14c) **1 :** any of several large American salamanders; *esp* : any of a genus (*Necturus* of the family Proteidae) with external gills **2 :** a person (as a skilled sailor) who is quite at ease in or on water

water down *vt* (1850) : to reduce or temper the force or effectiveness of — **wa·tered–down** *adj*

wa·ter·er \'wȯ-tər-ər, 'wä-\ *n* (1549) : one that waters: as **a :** a person who obtains or supplies drinking water **b :** a device used for supplying water to livestock and poultry — called also *drinker*

wa·ter·fall \-ˌfȯl\ *n* (bef. 12c) **1 a :** a perpendicular or very steep descent of the water of a stream **b :** an artificial waterfall (as in a hotel lobby or a nightclub) **2 :** something resembling a waterfall

water flea *n* (ca. 1585) : any of various small active dark or brightly colored aquatic crustaceans (as a daphnia or cyclops)

¹wa·ter·flood \-ˌfləd\ *n* (1928) : the process of waterflooding an oil well

²waterflood *vi* (1928) : to pump water into the ground around an oil well nearing depletion in order to loosen and force out additional oil

wa·ter·fowl \'wȯ-tər-ˌfau̇l, 'wä-\ *n* (14c) **1 :** a bird that frequents water; *esp* : a swimming bird **2 waterfowl** *pl* : swimming game birds as distinguished from upland game birds and shorebirds

wa·ter·fowl·er \-ˌfau̇-lər\ *n* (1968) : a hunter of waterfowl — **wa·ter·fowl·ing** \-liŋ\ *n*

wa·ter·front \-ˌfrənt\ *n* (1766) : land, land with buildings, or a section of a town fronting or abutting on a body of water

water gap *n* (1756) : a pass in a mountain ridge through which a stream runs — compare WIND GAP

water garden *n* (1891) **1 :** a garden in which aquatic plants predominate **2 :** a garden built about a stream or pool as a central feature

water gas *n* (1851) : a poisonous flammable gaseous mixture that consists chiefly of carbon monoxide and hydrogen with small amounts of methane, carbon dioxide, and nitrogen, is usu. made by blowing air and then steam over red-hot coke or coal, and is used as a fuel or after carbureting as an illuminant

Wa·ter·gate \-ˌgāt\ *n* [*Watergate*, apartment and office complex in Washington, D.C.; fr. the scandal following the break-in at the Democratic National Committee headquarters there in 1972] (1973) : a scandal involving abuses of office, skulduggery, and a cover-up

water gate *n* (14c) **1 :** a gate (as of a building) giving access to a body of water **2 :** FLOODGATE

water gauge *n* (ca. 1706) : an instrument to measure or find the depth or quantity of water or to indicate the height of its surface esp. in a steam boiler

water glass *n* (1612) **1 :** a glass vessel (as a drinking glass) for holding water **2 :** an instrument consisting of an open box or tube with a glass bottom used for examining objects in or under water **3 :** a substance that consists usu. of the silicate of sodium, is found in commerce as a glassy mass, a stony powder, or dissolved in water as a viscous syrupy liquid, and is used esp. as a cement, a protective coating, and as a fireproofing agent

water gun *n* (1951) : WATER PISTOL

water hammer *n* (ca. 1890) : a concussion or sound of concussion of moving water against the sides of a containing pipe or vessel (as a steam boiler)

water haul *n* [fr. the figure of a fishing net that catches nothing but water] (1823) : a fruitless effort

water heater *n* (ca. 1876) : an apparatus for heating and usu. storing hot water (as for domestic use)

water hemlock *n* (1764) : a tall poisonous Eurasian perennial herb (*Cicuta virosa*) of the carrot family; *also* : any of several poisonous No. American plants (esp. *Cicuta maculata* and *C. douglasii*) of the same genus

water hen *n* (ca. 1529) : any of various birds (as a coot or gallinule) of the rail family

water hole *n* (ca. 1653) **1 :** a natural hole or hollow containing water **2 :** a hole in a surface of ice

water hyacinth *n* (ca. 1890) : a showy floating aquatic plant (*Eichhornia crassipes* of the family Pontederiaceae) of tropical America that often clogs waterways (as in the southern U.S.)

water ice *n* (1818) : a frozen dessert of water, sugar, and flavoring

watering can *n* (1692) : a vessel usu. with a spout used to sprinkle or pour water esp. on plants — called also *watering pot*

watering hole *n* (1955) : a place where people gather socially; *esp* : WATERING PLACE 3

watering place *n* (15c) **1 :** a place where water may be obtained; *esp*

: one where animals and esp. livestock come to drink **2 :** a health or recreational resort featuring mineral springs or bathing **3 :** a place (as a nightclub, bar, or lounge) where drink is available

wa·ter·ish \'wȯ-tər-ish, 'wä-\ *adj* (1542) : somewhat watery — **wa·ter·ish·ness** *n*

water jacket *n* (1869) : an outer casing which holds water or through which water circulates to cool the interior; *specif* : the enclosed space surrounding the cylinder block of an internal combustion engine and containing the cooling liquid

water jump *n* (1875) : an obstacle (as in a steeplechase) consisting of a pool, stream, or ditch of water

wa·ter·leaf \'wȯ-tər-ˌlēf, 'wä-\ *n, pl* **-leafs** \-ˌlēfs\ (1760) : any of a genus (*Hydrophyllum* of the family Hydrophyllaceae, the waterleaf family) of perennial No. American woodland herbs with lobed or pinnate toothed leaves and cymes of bell-shaped flowers

wa·ter·less \-ləs\ *adj* (bef. 12c) **1 :** lacking or destitute of water : DRY **2 :** not requiring water (as for cooling or cooking) — **wa·ter·less·ness** *n*

water level *n* (1563) **1 :** an instrument to show the level by means of the surface of water in a trough or in a U-shaped tube **2 :** the surface of still water: as **a :** the level assumed by the surface of a particular body or column of water **b :** the waterline of a vessel

water lily *n* (15c) : any of various aquatic plants (esp. genera *Nymphaea* and *Nuphar* of the family Nymphaeaceae, the water-lily family) with floating leaves and usu. showy flowers; *broadly* : an aquatic plant (as a water hyacinth) with showy flowers

wa·ter·line \'wȯ-tər-ˌlīn, 'wä-\ *n* (ca. 1625) : a line that marks the level of the surface of water on something: as **a** (1) : the point on the hull of a ship or boat to which the water rises (2) : a line marked on the outside of a ship that corresponds with the water's surface when the ship is afloat on an even keel under specified conditions of loading **b :** SHORELINE 1

wa·ter·log \-ˌlȯg, -ˌläg\ *vt* [back-formation fr. *waterlogged*] (1779) : to make waterlogged

wa·ter·logged \-ˌlȯgd, -ˌlägd\ *adj* [¹*water* + *log* to accumulate in the hold] (ca. 1776) **1 :** so filled or soaked with water as to be heavy or hard to manage (~ boats) **2 :** saturated with water (~ soil)

wa·ter·loo \ˌwȯ-tər-'lü, ˌwä-\ *n, pl* **-loos** [*Waterloo*, Belgium, scene of Napoleon's defeat in 1815] (1816) : a decisive or final defeat or setback

water main *n* (1803) : a pipe or conduit for conveying water

wa·ter·man \'wȯ-tər-mən, 'wä-\ *n* (15c) : one who works or lives on the water: as **a :** a man who makes his living from the water (as by fishing) **b :** a boatman who plies for hire usu. on inland waters or harbors

wa·ter·man·ship \-ˌship\ *n* (1882) : the business, skill, or art of a waterman: as **a :** technique or expertness in rowing **b :** technique or expertness in swimming

¹wa·ter·mark \'wȯ-tər-ˌmärk, 'wä-\ *n* (1678) **1 :** a mark indicating the height to which water has risen **2 :** a marking in paper resulting from differences in thickness usu. produced by pressure of a projecting design in the mold or on a processing roll and visible when the paper is held up to the light; *also* : the design of or the metal pattern producing the marking

²watermark *vt* (1866) **1 :** to mark (paper) with a watermark **2 :** to impress (a given design) as a watermark

wa·ter·mel·on \-ˌme-lən\ *n* (1615) **1 :** a large oblong or roundish fruit with a hard green or white rind often striped or variegated, a sweet watery pink, yellowish, or red pulp, and usu. many seeds **2 :** a widely grown African vine (*Citrullus lanatus* syn. *C. vulgaris*) of the gourd family that bears watermelons

water meter *n* (ca. 1858) : an instrument for recording the quantity of water passing through a particular outlet

water milfoil *n* (1578) : any of a genus (*Myriophyllum* of the family Haloragaceae) of aquatic plants with finely pinnate submersed leaves

water mill *n* (15c) : a mill whose machinery is moved by water

water moccasin *n* (1821) : a venomous semiaquatic pit viper (*Agkistrodon piscivorus*) chiefly of the southeastern U.S. that is closely related to the copperhead — called also *cottonmouth, cottonmouth moccasin* **2 :** an American water snake (genus *Nerodia*)

water moccasin 1

water mold *n* (1899) : an aquatic fungus (as of the genus *Saprolegnia*)

water nymph *n* (14c) : a nymph (as a naiad, Nereid, or Oceanid) associated with a body of water

water oak *n* (1687) : any of several American oaks (esp. *Quercus nigra*) that thrive in wet soils

water of crystallization (1791) : water of hydration present in many crystallized substances that is usu. essential for maintenance of a particular crystal structure

water of hydration (1889) : water that is chemically combined with a substance to form a hydrate and can be expelled (as by heating) without essentially altering the composition of the substance

water on the knee (ca. 1934) : an accumulation of inflammatory exudate in the knee joint often following an injury

water ouzel *n* (1622) : DIPPER 2

water parting *n* (1859) : DIVIDE 2a

water pepper *n* (ca. 1538) : an annual smartweed (*Polygonum hydropiper*) of moist soils with extremely acrid peppery juice

water pimpernel *n* (ca. 1760) : either of two small white-flowered herbs (*Samolus valerandi* of Eurasia and *S. floribundus* syn. *S. parviflorus* of America) of the primrose family that grow in wet places

water pipe *n* (15c) **1 :** a pipe for conveying water **2 :** a smoking device that consists of a bowl mounted on a vessel of water which is

\ə\ abut \ᵊ\ kitten, F table \ər\ further \a\ ash \ā\ ace \ä\ mop, mar
\au̇\ out \ch\ chin \e\ bet \ē\ easy \g\ go \i\ hit \ī\ ice \j\ job
\ŋ\ sing \ō\ go \ȯ\ law \ȯi\ boy \th\ thin \t̲h̲\ the \ü\ loot \u̇\ foot
\y\ yet \zh\ vision \ȧ, k̲, ⁿ, œ, ǣ, ᴜᴇ, ᵫ, ᵞ\ see Guide to Pronunciation

provided with a long tube and arranged so that smoke is drawn through the water where it is cooled and up the tube to the mouth

water pistol n (1905) : a toy pistol designed to squirt a jet of liquid — called also *water gun, squirt gun*

water plantain n (ca. 1538) : any of a genus (*Alisma* of the family Alismataceae, the water-plantain family) of marsh or aquatic herbs with acrid sap and scapose 3-petaled flowers

water polo n (1884) : a goal game similar to soccer that is played in water by teams of swimmers using a ball resembling a soccer ball

wa·ter·pow·er \'wȯ-tər-ˌpaü(-ə)r, 'wä-\ n (1817) **1** : the power of water employed to move machinery **2** : a fall of water suitable for being used to move machinery

water privilege n (1804) : the right to use water esp. as a source of mechanical power

¹wa·ter·proof \'wȯ-tər-ˌprüf, 'wä-\ adj (1736) : impervious to water; *esp* : covered or treated with a material (as a solution of rubber) to prevent permeation by water — **wa·ter·proof·ness** n

²waterproof n (1799) **1** : a waterproof fabric **2** *chiefly Brit* : RAINCOAT

³waterproof vt (1841) : to make waterproof — **wa·ter·proof·er** n

wa·ter·proof·ing \-ˌprü-fiŋ\ n (1845) **1 a** : the act or process of making something waterproof **b** : the condition of being made waterproof **2** : something (as a coating) capable of imparting waterproofness

water rat n (1552) **1** : a rodent that frequents water **2** : a waterfront loafer or petty thief

wa·ter·re·pel·lent \ˌwȯ-tə(r)-ri-'pe-lənt, ˌwä-\ adj (1896) : treated with a finish that is resistant but not impervious to penetration by water

wa·ter·re·sis·tant \-ri-'zis-tənt\ adj (1921) : WATER-REPELLENT

water right n (1793) : a right to the use of water (as for irrigation); *esp* : RIPARIAN RIGHT

water sapphire n (ca. 1741) : a deep blue cordierite sometimes used as a gem

wa·ter·scape \'wȯ-tər-ˌskāp, 'wä-\ n (ca. 1854) : a water or sea view : SEASCAPE 1

water scorpion n (1681) : any of numerous aquatic bugs (family Nepidae) with the end of the abdomen prolonged by a long breathing tube

wa·ter·shed \'wȯ-tər-ˌshed, 'wä-\ n (1803) **1 a** : DIVIDE 2a **b** : a region or area bounded peripherally by a divide and draining ultimately to a particular watercourse or body of water **2** : a crucial dividing point, line, or factor : TURNING POINT — **watershed** adj

water shield n (ca. 1818) : an aquatic plant (*Brasenia schreberi*) of the water-lily family having floating oval leaves with a gelatinous coating and small dull purple flowers; *also* : any of a related genus (*Cabomba*)

¹wa·ter·side \'wȯ-tər-ˌsīd, 'wä-\ n (14c) : the margin of a body of water : WATERFRONT

²waterside adj (1663) **1** : employed along the waterside ⟨~ workers⟩; *also* : of or relating to the workers along the waterside ⟨a ~ strike⟩ **2** : of, relating to, or located on the waterside ⟨a ~ café⟩

water ski n (1931) : a ski used in planing over water while being towed by a speedboat — **wa·ter·ski** vi

wa·ter·ski·er \-ˌskē-ər, 'wä-\ n (1931) : one that water-skis

wa·ter·ski·ing \-ˌskē-iŋ\ n (1931) : the sport of planing and jumping on water skis

water snake n (1601) : any of various snakes (esp. genus *Nerodia* formerly included in the genus *Natrix*) that frequent or inhabit fresh waters and feed largely on aquatic animals

wa·ter·soak \'wȯ-tər-ˌsōk, 'wä-\ vt (1791) : to soak in water

water spaniel n (1566) : a spaniel of either of two breeds: **a** : AMERICAN WATER SPANIEL **b** : IRISH WATER SPANIEL

water spot n (1939) : a physiological disorder of citrus fruits in the rainy season in which the epidermal air spaces of the rind become filled with liquid

wa·ter·spout \'wȯ-tər-ˌspaüt, 'wä-\ n (14c) **1** : a pipe, duct, or orifice from which water is spouted or through which it is carried **2** : a funnel-shaped or tubular column of rotating cloud-filled wind usu. extending from the underside of a cumulus or cumulonimbus cloud down to a cloud of spray torn up by the whirling winds from the surface of an ocean or lake

water sprite n (1798) : a sprite believed to inhabit or haunt water : WATER NYMPH

water sprout n (ca. 1892) : an extremely vigorous shoot from an adventitious or latent bud on a tree — compare SUCKER 2

water strider n (1849) : any of various long-legged bugs (family Gerridae) that move about on the surface of the water

water supply n (ca. 1882) : a source, means, or process of supplying water (as for a community) usu. including reservoirs, tunnels, and pipelines

water table n (15c) **1** : a stringcourse or similar member when projecting so as to throw off water **2** : the upper limit of the portion of the ground wholly saturated with water

water taxi n (1928) : a boat functioning (as within a harbor) as a taxi

wa·ter·thrush \'wȯ-tər-ˌthrəsh, 'wä-\ n (ca. 1813) : either of two No. American warblers (*Seiurus noveboracensis* and *S. motacilla*) found near freshwater (as a stream)

wa·ter·tight \ˌwȯ-tər-'tīt, ˌwä-\ adj (14c) **1** : of such tight construction or fit as to be impermeable to water except when under sufficient pressure to produce structural discontinuity **2** : leaving no possibility of misconstruction or evasion ⟨a ~ lease⟩ — **wa·ter·tight·ness** n

water tower n (ca. 1883) : a tower or standpipe serving as a reservoir to deliver water at a required head

water turkey n (1836) : a New World anhinga (*Anhinga anhinga*)

water vapor n (1880) : water in a vaporous form esp. when below boiling temperature and diffused (as in the atmosphere)

water–vascular system n (1870) : a system of canals in echinoderms containing a circulating watery fluid that is used for the movement of the tentacles and tube feet

water wagon n (1904) : a wagon or motortruck equipped with a tank or barrels for hauling water or for sprinkling — **on the water wagon** : abstaining from alcoholic beverages : on the wagon

water wave n (1882) : a method or style of setting hair by dampening with water and forming into waves — **wa·ter·waved** \'wȯ-tər-ˌwāvd, 'wä-\ adj

wa·ter·way \'wȯ-tər-ˌwā, 'wä-\ n (15c) **1** : a way or channel for water **2** : a navigable body of water

wa·ter·weed \-ˌwēd\ n (1842) : any of various aquatic plants (as a pondweed) with inconspicuous flowers — compare WATER LILY

wa·ter·wheel \-ˌhwēl, -ˌwēl\ n (15c) **1** : a wheel made to rotate by direct action of water **2** : a wheel for raising water

water wings n pl (1907) : a pneumatic device that buoys the body of a swimmer and is used esp. in learning to swim

water witch n (1817) : one that dowses for water — **water witch·ing** \-ˌwi-chiŋ\ n

water witch·er \-ˌwi-chər\ n (1917) : WATER WITCH

wa·ter·works \'wȯ-tər-ˌwərks, 'wä-\ n pl (ca. 1586) **1** : an ornamental fountain or cascade **2** : the system of reservoirs, channels, mains, and pumping and purifying equipment by which a water supply is obtained and distributed (as to a city) **3** : the shedding of tears : TEARS

wa·ter·worn \-ˌwȯrn, -ˌwȯrn\ adj (1815) : worn, smoothed, or polished by the action of water

wa·tery \'wȯ-tə-rē, 'wä-\ adj (bef. 12c) **1 a** : consisting of, filled with, or surrounded by water **b** : containing, sodden with, or yielding water or a thin liquid ⟨a ~ solution⟩ ⟨~ vesicles⟩ **2 a** : resembling water or watery matter esp. in thin fluidity, soggy texture, paleness, or lack of savor ⟨~ blood⟩ ⟨~ sunlight⟩ ⟨a ~ soup⟩ **b** : exhibiting weakness and vapidity : WISHY-WASHY ⟨a ~ writing style⟩ — **wa·ter·i·ly** \-tə-rə-lē\ adv — **wa·ter·i·ness** \-tə-rē-nəs\ n

wa·ter·zooi \'vä-tər-ˌzoi\ n [Flem, fr. *water* water + *zooi* quantity of cooked food] (1949) : a stew of fish or chicken and vegetables in a seasoned stock thickened with cream and egg yolks

Wat·son–Crick \ˌwät-sən-'krik\ adj (1964) : of or relating to the Watson-Crick model ⟨~ helix⟩ ⟨~ structure⟩ ⟨~ base pairs⟩

Watson–Crick model n [J. D. *Watson* & F. H. C. *Crick*] (1958) : a model of DNA structure in which the molecule is a cross-linked double-stranded helix, each strand is composed of alternating links of phosphate and deoxyribose, and the strands are cross-linked by pairs of purine and pyrimidine bases projecting inward from the deoxyribose sugars and joined by hydrogen bonds with adenine paired with thymine and with cytosine paired with guanine — compare DOUBLE HELIX

watt \'wät\ n [James *Watt* †1819] (1882) : the absolute meter-kilogram-second unit of power equal to the work done at the rate of one joule per second or to the power produced by a current of one ampere across a potential difference of one volt : ¹/₇₄₆ horsepower

watt·age \'wä-tij\ n (1903) : amount of power expressed in watts

Wat·teau \(ˌ)wä-'tō\ adj [Antoine *Watteau*] (1873) **1** *of women's dress* : having back pleats falling loosely from neckline to hem **2** *of a hat* : shallow-crowned and having a wide brim turned up at the back to hold flower trimmings

watt–hour \'wät-'aü(-ə)r\ n (1888) : a unit of work or energy equivalent to the power of one watt operating for one hour

¹wat·tle \'wä-t²l\ n [ME *wattel*, fr. OE *watel*; akin to OHG *wadal* bandage] (bef. 12c) **1 a** : a fabrication of poles interwoven with slender branches, withes, or reeds and used esp. formerly in building **b** : material for such construction **c** pl : poles laid on a roof to support thatch **2** : a fleshy dependent process usu. about the head or neck (as of a bird) **3** dial : ACACIA 2 — **wat·tled** \-t²ld\ adj

²wattle vt wat·tled; wat·tling \'wät-liŋ, 'wä-t²l-iŋ\ (14c) **1** : to form or build of or with wattle **2 a** : to form into wattle : interlace to form wattle **b** : to unite or make solid by interweaving light flexible material

wattle and daub n (1808) : a framework of woven rods and twigs covered and plastered with clay and used in building construction

wat·tle·bird \'wä-t²l-ˌbərd\ n (1819) : any of several Australasian honeyeaters (genus *Anthochaera*) having fleshy pendulous ear wattles

watt·me·ter \'wät-ˌmē-tər\ n [ISV] (1887) : an instrument for measuring electric power in watts

Wa·tu·si \wä-'tü-sē\ n, pl **Watusi** also **Watusis** (1899) : TUTSI

¹wave \'wāv\ vb **waved**; **wav·ing** [ME, fr. OE *wafian* to wave with the hands; akin to *wǣfan* to clothe and perh. to OE *wefan* to weave] vi (bef. 12c) **1** : to motion with the hands or with something held in them in signal or salute **2** : to float, play, or shake in an air current : move loosely to and fro : FLUTTER **3** *of water* : to move in waves : HEAVE **4** : to become moved or brandished to and fro **5** : to move before the wind with a wavelike motion ⟨field of *waving* grain⟩ **6** : to follow a curving line or take a wavy form : UNDULATE ~ vt **1** : to swing (something) back and forth or up and down **2** : to impart a curving or undulating shape to ⟨*waved* her hair⟩ **3 a** : to motion to (someone) to go in an indicated direction or to stop : FLAG, SIGNAL ⟨checked his name and *waved* him on⟩ ⟨*waved* down a passing car⟩ **b** : to gesture with (the hand or an object) in greeting or farewell or in homage **c** : to dismiss or put out of mind : DISREGARD — usu. used with *aside* or *off* **d** : to convey by waving ⟨*waved* farewell⟩ **4** : BRANDISH, FLOURISH ⟨*waved* a pistol menacingly⟩ **syn** see SWING

²wave n (1526) **1 a** : a moving ridge or swell on the surface of a liquid (as of the sea) **b** : open water **2 a** : a shape or outline having successive curves **b** : a waviness of the hair **c** : an undulating line or streak or a pattern formed by such lines **3** : something that swells and dies away: as **a** : a surge of sensation or emotion ⟨a ~ of anger swept over her⟩ **b** : a movement sweeping large numbers in a common direction ⟨~s of protest⟩ **c** : a peak or climax of activity ⟨a ~ of buying⟩ **4** : a sweep of hand or arm or of some object held in the hand used as a signal or greeting **5** : a rolling or undulatory movement or one of a series of such movements passing along a surface or through the air **6** : a movement like that of an ocean wave: as **a** : a surging movement of a group ⟨a big new ~ of women politicians⟩ **b** : one of a succession of influxes of people migrating into a region ⟨~ (1) : a moving group of animals of one kind (2) : a sudden rapid increase in a population⟩ **d** : a line of attacking or advancing troops or airplanes **e** : a display of people in a large crowd (as at a sports event) successively rising, lifting their arms overhead, and quickly sitting so as to form a swell moving through the crowd **7 a** : a disturbance or variation that transfers energy progressively from point to point in a medium and that may take the form of an elastic deformation or of a variation of pressure, electric or magnetic intensity, electric potential, or temperature **b** : one complete cycle of such a disturbance **8** : a marked change in temperature : a period of hot or cold weather **9** : an undulating or jagged line constituting a graphic representation of an action

— **wave·less** \'wāv-ləs\ *adj* — **wave·less·ly** *adv* — **wave·like** \-,līk\ *adj*

Wave \'wāv\ *n* [*W*omen *A*ccepted for *V*olunteer *E*mergency *S*ervice] (1942) : a woman serving in the navy

wave band *n* (1923) : a band of radio-wave frequencies

waved \'wāvd\ *adj* (1599) : having a wavelike form or outline: as **a** : having wavy lines of color ⟨WATERED ⟨~ cloth⟩ **b** : marked by undulations : CURVING ⟨the ~ cutting edge of a bread knife⟩

wave equation *n* (1926) : a partial differential equation of the second order whose solutions describe wave phenomena

wave·form \'wāv-,fȯrm\ *n* (1845) : a usu. graphic representation of the shape of a wave that indicates its characteristics (as frequency and amplitude) — called also *waveshape*

wave front *n* (ca. 1864) : a surface composed at any instant of all the points just reached by a vibrational disturbance in its propagation through a medium

wave·guide \'wāv-,gīd\ *n* (1932) : a device (as a duct, coaxial cable, or glass fiber) designed to confine and direct the propagation of electromagnetic waves (as light); *esp* : a metal tube for channeling ultrahigh-frequency waves

wave·length \-,leŋ(k)th\ *n* (1850) **1** : the distance in the line of advance of a wave from any one point to the next point of corresponding phase **2** : a particular course or line of thought esp. as related to mutual understanding ⟨two people on different ~s⟩

wave·let \-lət\ *n* (ca. 1810) : a little wave : RIPPLE

wave mechanics *n pl but sing or pl in constr* (1926) **1** : the mathematical description of atomic and subatomic particles in terms of their wave characteristics **2** : QUANTUM MECHANICS

wave number *n* (1873) : the number of waves per unit distance of radiant energy of a given wavelength : the reciprocal of the wavelength

wave of the future (1940) : an idea, product, or movement that is viewed as representing forces or a trend that will inevitably prevail

wave packet *n* (1928) : a pulse of radiant energy that is the resultant of a number of wave trains of differing wavelengths

¹**wa·ver** \'wā-vər\ *vi* **wa·vered; wa·ver·ing** \'wāv-riŋ, 'wā-və-riŋ\ [ME; akin to OE *wæfre* restless, *wafian* to wave with the hands — more at WAVE] (14c) **1** : to vacillate irresolutely between choices : fluctuate in opinion, allegiance, or direction **2 a** : to weave or sway unsteadily to and fro : REEL, TOTTER **b** : QUIVER, FLICKER ⟨~*ing* flames⟩ **c** : to hesitate as if about to give way : FALTER **3** : to give an unsteady sound : QUAVER *syn* see SWING, HESITATE — **wa·ver·er** \'wā-və-rər\ *n* — **wa·ver·ing·ly** \'wāv-riŋ-lē, 'wā-və-\ *adv*

²**waver** *n* (1519) : an act of wavering, quivering, or fluttering

³**wav·er** \'wā-vər\ *n* (1835) : one that waves

wa·very \'wāv-rē, 'wā-və-rē\ *adj* (1820) : that waves : WAVERING

wave·shape \'wāv-,shāp\ *n* (1907) : WAVEFORM

wave theory *n* (1833) : a theory in physics: light is transmitted from luminous bodies to the eye and other objects by an undulatory movement — called also *undulatory theory*

wave train *n* (1897) : a succession of similar waves at equal intervals

wavy \'wā-vē\ *adj* **wav·i·er; -est** (ca. 1586) **1** : rising or swelling in waves; *also* : abounding in waves ⟨~ hair⟩ **2** : moving with an undulating motion : FLUCTUATING; *also* : marked by wavering **3** : marked by undulation : ROLLING — **wav·i·ly** \'wā-və-lē\ *adv* — **wav·i·ness** \-vē-nəs\ *n*

waw \'väv, 'vȯv\ *n* [Heb *wāw*] (14c) : the 6th letter of the Hebrew alphabet — see ALPHABET table

wa–wa pedal \'wä-,wä-\ *n* [imit.] (1968) : an electronic device that is connected to an amplifier and operated by a foot pedal and that is used (as with an electric guitar) to produce a fluctuating muted effect

¹**wax** \'waks\ *n* [ME, fr. OE *weax*; akin to OHG *wahs* wax, Lith *vaškas*] (bef. 12c) **1** : a substance that is secreted by bees and is used by them for constructing the honeycomb, that is a dull yellow solid plastic when warm, and that is composed of a mixture of esters, cerotic acid, and hydrocarbons — called also *beeswax* **2** : any of various substances resembling beeswax: as **a** : any of numerous substances of plant or animal origin that differ from fats in being less greasy, harder, and more brittle and in containing principally compounds of high molecular weight (as fatty acids, alcohols, and saturated hydrocarbons) **b** : a solid substance (as ozokerite or paraffin wax) of mineral origin consisting usu. of hydrocarbons of high molecular weight **c** : a pliable or liquid composition used esp. in uniting surfaces, excluding air, making patterns or impressions, or producing a polished surface **3** : something likened to wax as soft, impressionable, or readily molded **4** : a waxy secretion; *esp* : CERUMEN **5** : a phonograph recording — **wax·like** \'waks-,līk\ *adj*

²**wax** *vt* (14c) **1** : to treat or rub with wax usu. for polishing or stiffening **2** : to record on phonograph records

³**wax** *vi* [ME, fr. OE *weaxan*; akin to OHG *wahsan* to increase, Gk *auxanein*, L *augēre* — more at EKE] (bef. 12c) **1 a** : to increase in size, numbers, strength, prosperity, or intensity **b** : to grow in volume or duration **c** : to grow toward full development **2** : to increase in phase or intensity — used chiefly of the moon, other satellites, and inferior planets **3** : to assume a (specified) characteristic, quality, or state : BECOME ⟨~ indignant⟩

⁴**wax** *n* (14c) : INCREASE, GROWTH — usu. used in the phrase *on the wax*

⁵**wax** *n* [perh. fr. ³*wax*] (1854) : a fit of temper : RAGE

wax bean *n* (1897) : a kidney bean with pods that turn creamy yellow to bright yellow when mature enough for use as snap beans

wax·bill \'waks-,bil\ *n* (1757) : any of numerous Old World oscine birds (family Estrildidae and esp. genus *Estrilda*) having white, pink, or reddish bills of a waxy appearance

waxed paper *n* (1853) : paper coated or treated with wax to make it resistant to water and grease and used esp. as a wrapping

wax·en \'wak-sən\ *adj* (bef. 12c) **1** : made of or covered with wax **2** : resembling wax: as **a** : easily molded : PLIABLE **b** : seeming to lack vitality or animation : PALLID **c** : lustrously smooth

wax·er \-sər\ *n* (ca. 1875) **1** : a device for applying wax **2** : one whose work is applying or polishing with wax

wax·ing *n* (15c) **1** : the act of applying wax (as in polishing) **2** : the process of removing body hair with a depilatory wax

wax light *n* (1599) : a wax candle : TAPER

wax moth *n* (1766) : a dull brownish or ashen pyralid moth (*Galleria mellonella*) with a larva that feeds on the comb wax of the honeybee

wax museum *n* (1953) : a place where wax effigies (as of historical persons) are exhibited

wax myrtle *n* (1806) : any of a genus (*Myrica* of the family Myricaceae, the wax-myrtle family) of trees or shrubs with aromatic foliage; *esp* : a shrub (*M. cerifera*) of the eastern U.S. having small hard berries with a thick coating of white wax used for candles

wax palm *n* (ca. 1828) : any of several palms that yield wax: as **a** : an Andean pinnate-leaved palm (*Ceroxylon alpinum* syn. *C. andicola*) whose stem yields a resinous wax used in candles **b** : CARNAUBA

wax paper *n* (ca. 1844) : WAXED PAPER

wax·wing \'waks-,wiŋ\ *n* (1817) : any of a genus (*Bombycilla*) of American and Eurasian chiefly brown to gray oscine birds (as a cedar waxwing) having a showy crest, red waxy material on the tips of the secondaries, and a yellow band on the tip of the tail

waxwing

wax·work \-,wərk\ *n* (1697) **1** : an effigy in wax usu. of a person **2** *pl but sing or pl in constr* : WAX MUSEUM

waxy \'wak-sē\ *adj* **wax·i·er; -est** (1552) **1** : made of, abounding in, or covered with wax : WAXEN ⟨a ~ surface⟩ ⟨~ berries⟩ **2** : resembling wax: as **a** : readily shaped or molded **b** : marked by smooth or lustrous whiteness ⟨a ~ complexion⟩ — **wax·i·ness** *n*

¹**way** \'wā\ *n* [ME, fr. OE *weg*; akin to OHG *weg* way, OE *wegan* to move, L *vehere* to carry, *via* way] (bef. 12c) **1 a** : a thoroughfare for travel or transportation from place to place **b** : an opening for passage ⟨this door is the only ~ out of the room⟩ **2** : the course traveled from one place to another : ROUTE **3 a** : a course (as a series of actions or sequence of events) leading in a direction or toward an objective ⟨led the ~ to eventual open heart operations —*Current Biog.*⟩ **b** (1) : a course of action ⟨took the easy ~ out⟩ (2) : opportunity, capability, or fact of doing as one pleases ⟨always manages to get her own ~⟩ **c** : a possible decision, action, or outcome : POSSIBILITY ⟨they were rude—no two ~s about it⟩ **4 a** : manner or method of doing or happening; *also* : method of accomplishing : MEANS **b** : FEATURE, RESPECT ⟨in no ~ resembles her mother⟩ **c** : a usu. specified degree of participation in an activity or enterprise ⟨active in real estate in a small ~⟩ **5 a** : characteristic, regular, or habitual manner or mode of being, behaving, or happening ⟨knows nothing of the ~s of women⟩ **b** : ability to get along well or perform well ⟨she has a ~ with kids⟩ ⟨a ~ with words⟩ **6** : the length of a course : DISTANCE ⟨has come a long ~ in her studies⟩ ⟨still have a ~ to go⟩ **7** : movement or progress along a course ⟨worked her ~ up the corporate ladder⟩ **8 a** : DIRECTION ⟨is coming this ~⟩ **b** : PARTICIPANT — usu. used in combination ⟨three-*way* discussion⟩ **9** : state of affairs : CONDITION, STATE ⟨that's the ~ things are⟩ **10** *a pl but sometimes sing in constr* : an inclined structure upon which a ship is built or supported in launching **b** *pl* : the guiding surfaces on the bed of a machine along which a table or carriage moves **11** : CATEGORY, KIND — usu. used in the phrase *in the way of* ⟨doesn't require much in the ~ of expensive equipment —*Forbes*⟩ **12** : motion or speed of a ship or boat through the water *syn* see METHOD — **all the way** : to the full or entire extent : as far as possible ⟨ran *all the way* home⟩ ⟨seated *all the way* in the back⟩ — **by the way** : by way of interjection or digression : INCIDENTALLY — **by way of 1** : for the purpose of **2** : by the route through : VIA — **in a way 1** : within limits : with reservations **2** : from one point of view — **in one's way** *also* **in the way 1** : in a position to be encountered by one : in or along one's course ⟨an opportunity had been put *in my way* —Ellen Glasgow⟩ **2** : in a position to hinder or obstruct — **on the way** *or* **on one's way** : moving along in one's course : in progress — **out of the way 1** : WRONG, IMPROPER ⟨didn't know I'd said anything *out of the way*⟩ **2 a** : in or to a secluded place **b** : UNUSUAL, REMARKABLE ⟨there's nothing *out of the way* about the plan⟩ **3** : DONE, COMPLETED ⟨got his homework *out of the way*⟩ — **the way 1** : in view of the manner in which ⟨you'd think she was rich, *the way* she spends money⟩ **2** : LIKE, AS ⟨we have cats *the way* other people have mice —James Thurber⟩

²**way** *adj* (1799) : of, connected with, or constituting an intermediate point on a route ⟨visited five major countries plus ~ points⟩

³**way** *adv* (1849) **1** : AWAY 7 ⟨is ~ ahead of the class⟩ **b** : by far : MUCH ⟨ate ~ too much⟩ **2** : all the way ⟨pull the switch ~ back⟩ — **from way back** : of long standing ⟨friends *from way back*⟩

way·bill \'wā-,bil\ *n* (1821) : a document prepared by the carrier of a shipment of goods that contains details of the shipment, route, and charges

way·far·er \'wā-,far-ər, -,fer-\ *n* [ME *weyfarere*, fr. *wey*, *way* way + *-farere* traveler, fr. *faren* to go — more at FARE] (15c) : a traveler esp. on foot — **way·far·ing** \-,far-iŋ, -,fer-\ *adj*

wayfaring tree *n* (1597) : a Eurasian shrub (*Viburnum lantana*) that has large ovate leaves and dense cymes of small white flowers and is common along waysides

way·go·ing \'wā-,gō-ən, -iŋ\ *n* (1633) *chiefly Scot* : the act of leaving : DEPARTURE

Way·land \'wā-lən(d)\ *n* [OE *Wēland*] : an heroic smith of Germanic legend

way·lay \'wā-,lā\ *vt* **-laid** \-,lād\; **-lay·ing** (1513) : to lie in wait for or attack from ambush

way·less \-ləs\ *adj* (12c) : having no road or path

Way of the Cross (1868) : STATIONS OF THE CROSS

way–out \'wā-'aȯt\ *adj* (1954) : FAR-OUT

ways \'wāz\ *n pl but sing in constr* [ME *wayes*, fr. gen. of ¹*way*] (1588) **1** : WAY 6 ⟨a long ~ from home⟩

-ways *adv suffix* [ME, fr. *ways*, gen. of *way*] : in (such) a way, course, direction, or manner ⟨side*ways*⟩

\ə\ abut \ᵊ\ kitten, F table \ər\ further \a\ ash \ā\ ace \ä\ mop, mar \aȯ\ out \ch\ chin \e\ bet \ē\ easy \g\ go \i\ hit \ī\ ice \j\ job \ŋ\ sing \ō\ go \ȯ\ law \ȯi\ boy \th\ thin \t͟h\ the \ü\ loot \ u̇\ foot \y\ yet \zh\ vision \ä, k̲, ⁿ, œ, œ̄, ᵫ, ᵫ̄, ᵊ\ *see* Guide to Pronunciation

ways and means *n pl* (15c) **1** : methods and resources for accomplishing something and esp. for defraying expenses **2** *often cap W&M* **a** : methods and resources for raising the necessary revenues for the expenses of a nation or state **b** : a legislative committee concerned with this function

way·side \'wā-ˌsīd\ *n* (15c) : the side of or land adjacent to a road or path — **wayside** *adj* — **by the wayside** : out of consideration : into a condition of neglect or disuse — usu. used with *fall*

way station *n* (1850) **1** : an intermediate station between principal stations on a line of travel (as a railroad) **2** : an intermediate stopping place

way·ward \'wā-wərd\ *adj* [ME, short for *awayward* turned away, fr. *away*, adv. + *-ward*] (14c) **1** : following one's own capricious, wanton, or depraved inclinations : UNGOVERNABLE **2** : following no clear principle or law : UNPREDICTABLE **3** : opposite to what is desired or expected ⟨~ fate⟩ *syn* see CONTRARY — **way·ward·ly** *adv* — **way·ward·ness** *n*

way·worn \-ˌwōrn, -ˌwȯrn\ *adj* (1788) : wearied by traveling

we \'wē\ *pron, pl in constr* [ME, fr. OE *wē*; akin to OHG *wir* we, Skt *vayam*] (bef. 12c) **1** : I and the rest of a group that includes me : you and I : you and I and another or others : I and another or others not including you — used as pronoun of the first person plural; compare I, OUR, OURS, US **2** : ¹I — used by sovereigns; used by writers to keep an impersonal character

weak \'wēk\ *adj* [ME *weike*, fr. ON *veikr*; akin to OE *wīcan* to yield, Gk *eikein* to give way, Skt *vijate* he speeds, flees] (14c) **1** : lacking strength: as **a** : deficient in physical vigor : FEEBLE, DEBILITATED **b** : not able to sustain or exert much weight, pressure, or strain **c** : not able to resist external force or withstand attack **2 a** : mentally or intellectually deficient **b** : not firmly decided : VACILLATING **c** : resulting from or indicating lack of judgment or discernment **d** : not able to withstand temptation or persuasion ⟨the spirit is willing but the flesh is ~⟩ **3** : not factually grounded or logically presented ⟨a ~ argument⟩ **4 a** : not able to function properly **b** (1) : lacking skill or proficiency ⟨tutoring for ~*er* students⟩ (2) : indicative of a lack of skill or aptitude ⟨history was my ~*est* subject⟩ **c** : wanting in vigor of expression or effect **5 a** : deficient in the usual or required ingredients : DILUTE ⟨~ coffee⟩ **b** : lacking normal intensity or potency ⟨~ strain of virus⟩ **6 a** : not having or exerting authority or political power ⟨~ government⟩ **b** : INEFFECTIVE, IMPOTENT **7** : of, relating to, or constituting a verb or verb conjugation that in English forms the past tense and past participle by adding the suffix *-ed* or *-d* or *-t* **8 a** : bearing the minimal degree of stress occurring in the language ⟨~ syllable⟩ **b** : having little or no stress and obscured vowel sound ⟨'*d* is the ~ form of *would*⟩ **9** : tending toward a lower price ⟨a ~ market⟩ **10** : ionizing only slightly in solution ⟨~ acids and bases⟩ — **weak·ly** *adv*

syn WEAK, FEEBLE, FRAIL, FRAGILE, INFIRM, DECREPIT mean not strong enough to endure strain, pressure, or strenuous effort. WEAK applies to deficiency or inferiority in strength or power of any sort ⟨students too *weak* to resist peer pressure⟩. FEEBLE suggests extreme weakness inviting pity or contempt ⟨a *feeble* attempt to get out of bed⟩. FRAIL implies delicacy and slightness of constitution or structure ⟨a *frail* teenager who was unable to enjoy contact sports⟩. FRAGILE suggests frailty and brittleness unable to resist rough usage ⟨a reclusive poet too *fragile* for the rigors of this world⟩. INFIRM suggests instability, unsoundness, and insecurity due to old age or crippling illness ⟨*infirm* residents requiring constant care⟩. DECREPIT implies being worn-out or broken-down from long use or old age ⟨the dowager's faithful, *decrepit* retainers⟩.

weak anthropic principle *n* (1985) : ANTHROPIC PRINCIPLE a

weak·en \'wē-kən\ *vb* **weak·ened**; **weak·en·ing** \'wēk-niŋ, 'wē-kə-\ *vt* (1530) **1** : to make weak : lessen the strength of **2** : to reduce in intensity or effectiveness ~ *vi* : to become weak — **weak·en·er** \'wēk-nər, 'wē-kə-\ *n*

syn WEAKEN, ENFEEBLE, DEBILITATE, UNDERMINE, SAP, CRIPPLE, DISABLE mean to lose or cause to lose strength or vigor. WEAKEN may imply loss of physical strength, health, soundness, or stability or of quality, intensity, or effective power ⟨a disease that *weakens* the body's defenses against infection⟩. ENFEEBLE implies an obvious and pitiable condition of weakness and helplessness ⟨*enfeebled* by starvation⟩. DEBILITATE suggests a less marked or more temporary impairment of strength or vitality ⟨the *debilitating* effects of surgery⟩. UNDERMINE and SAP suggest a weakening by something working surreptitiously and insidiously ⟨a poor diet *undermines* your health⟩ ⟨drugs had *sapped* his ability to think⟩. CRIPPLE implies causing a serious loss of functioning power through damaging or removing an essential part or element ⟨*crippled* by arthritis⟩. DISABLE suggests a usu. sudden crippling or enfeebling ⟨*disabled* soldiers received an immediate discharge⟩.

weak·fish \'wēk-ˌfish\ *n* [obs. D *weekvis*, fr. D *week* soft + *vis* fish; fr. its tender flesh] (1791) **1** : a common marine bony fish (*Cynoscion regalis* of the family Sciaenidae) that is a sport and food fish of the eastern coast of the U.S. — called also *sea trout* **2** : any of several fishes congeneric with the weakfish

weak force *n* (1971) : a fundamental physical force that governs interactions between hadrons and leptons (as in the emission and absorption of neutrinos) and is responsible for particle decay processes (as beta decay) in radioactivity, that is 10⁵ times weaker than the strong force, and that acts over distances smaller than those between nucleons in an atomic nucleus — called also *weak interaction, weak nuclear force*; compare ELECTROMAGNETISM 2a, GRAVITY 3a(2), STRONG FORCE

weak·heart·ed \-'här-təd\ *adj* (1549) : lacking courage : FAINTHEARTED

weak·ish \'wē-kish\ *adj* (1594) : somewhat weak ⟨~ tea⟩

weak–kneed \'wēk-'nēd\ *adj* (1863) : lacking willpower or resolution

weak·ling \'wē-kliŋ\ *n* (1548) : one that is weak in body, character, or mind — **weakling** *adj*

weak·ly \'wē-klē\ *adj* (1577) : FEEBLE, WEAK — **weak·li·ness** *n*

weak–mind·ed \'wēk-'mīn-dəd\ *adj* (1716) : having or indicating a weak mind: **a** : lacking in judgment or good sense : FOOLISH **b** : FEEBLEMINDED — **weak–mind·ed·ness** *n*

weak·ness \-nəs\ *n* (14c) **1** : the quality or state of being weak; *also* : an instance or period of being weak ⟨agreed in a moment of ~ to go along⟩ **2** : FAULT, DEFECT **3 a** : a special desire or fondness ⟨has a ~ for chocolates⟩ **b** : an object of special desire or fondness ⟨pizza is my ~⟩

weak side *n* (1940) **1** : the side of a football formation having the smaller number of players; *specif* : the side of a formation away from the tight end **2** : the side of a court or field (as in basketball or soccer) away from the ball — **weak·side** \'wēk-ˌsīd\ *adj*

weak sister *n* (1857) : a member of a group who needs aid; *also* : something that is weak and ineffective as compared with others in the group

¹**weal** \'wē(ə)l\ *n* [ME *wele*, fr. OE *wela*; akin to OE *wel* well] (bef. 12c) **1** : a sound, healthy, or prosperous state : WELL-BEING **2** *obs* : BODY POLITIC, COMMONWEAL

²**weal** *n* [alter. of *wale*] (ca. 1798) : WELT

weald \'wē(ə)ld\ *n* [the *Weald*, England, fr. ME *weeld*, fr. OE *weald* forest — more at WOLD] (bef. 12c) **1** : a heavily wooded area : FOREST ⟨the *Weald* of Kent⟩ **2** : a wild or uncultivated usu. upland region

wealth \'welth *also* 'weltth\ *n* [ME *welthe*, fr. *wele* weal] (13c) **1** *obs* : WEAL, WELFARE **2** : abundance of valuable material possessions or resources **3** : abundant supply : PROFUSION **4 a** : all property that has a money value or an exchangeable value **b** : all material objects that have economic utility; *esp* : the stock of useful goods having economic value in existence at any one time ⟨national ~⟩

wealthy \'wel-thē *also* 'welt-thē\ *adj* **wealth·i·er**; **-est** (15c) **1** : having wealth : extremely affluent **2** : characterized by abundance : AMPLE *syn* see RICH — **wealth·i·ly** \-thə-lē\ *adv* — **wealth·i·ness** \-thē-nəs\ *n*

wean \'wēn\ *vt* [ME *wenen*, fr. OE *wenian* to accustom, wean; akin to OE *wunian* to be used to — more at WONT] (bef. 12c) **1** : to accustom (as a child) to take food otherwise than by nursing **2** : to detach from a source of dependence ⟨being ~*ed* off the medication⟩ ⟨~ the bears from human food —*Sports Illus.*⟩; *also* : to free from a usu. unwholesome habit or interest ⟨~ him off his excessive drinking⟩ ⟨settling his soldiers on the land . . . , ~*ing* them from habits of violence —Geoffrey Carnall⟩ **3** : to accustom to something from an early age — used in the passive esp. with *on* ⟨students ~*ed* on the microcomputer⟩ ⟨I was ~*ed* on greasepaint —Helen Hayes⟩ ⟨the principles upon which he had been ~*ed* —J. A. Michener⟩

wean·er \'wē-nər\ *n* (1579) **1** : one that weans **2** : a young animal recently weaned from its mother

wean·ling \'wēn-liŋ\ *n* (1532) : a child or animal newly weaned — **wean·ling** *adj*

¹**weap·on** \'we-pən\ *n* [ME *wepen*, fr. OE *wǣpen*; akin to OHG *wāffan* weapon, ON *vāpn*] (bef. 12c) **1** : something (as a club, knife, or gun) used to injure, defeat, or destroy **2** : a means of contending against another

²**weapon** *vt* (bef. 12c) : ARM

weap·on·less \-ləs\ *adj* (bef. 12c) : lacking weapons : UNARMED

weap·on·ry \-rē\ *n* (1844) **1** : WEAPONS **2** : the science of designing and making weapons

¹**wear** \'war, 'wer\ *vb* **wore** \'wōr, 'wȯr\; **worn** \'wōrn, 'wȯrn\; **wear·ing** [ME *weren*, fr. OE *werian*; akin to ON *verja* to clothe, invest, spend, L *vestis* clothing, garment, Gk *hennynai* to clothe] *vt* (bef. 12c) **1** : to bear or have on the person ⟨wore a coat⟩ **2 a** : to use habitually for clothing, adornment, or assistance ⟨~*s* a toupee⟩ ⟨~ glasses⟩ **b** : to carry on the person ⟨~ a sword⟩ **3 a** : to hold the rank or dignity or position signified by (an ornament) ⟨~ the royal crown⟩ **b** : EXHIBIT, PRESENT ⟨wore a happy smile⟩ ⟨commend the book for ~*ing* its research so lightly —Brad Leithauser⟩ **c** : to show or fly (a flag or colors) on a ship **4 a** : to cause to deteriorate by use **b** : to impair or diminish by use or attrition : consume or waste gradually ⟨letters on the stone *worn* away by weathering⟩ **5** : to produce gradually by friction or attrition ⟨~ a hole in the rug⟩ **6** : to exhaust or lessen the strength of : WEARY, FATIGUE **7** : to cause (a ship) to go about with the stern presented to the wind **8** *Brit* : to accept or tolerate without complaint : put up with — usu. used in negative constructions ⟨your mates wouldn't ~ it —Colin MacInnes⟩ ~ *vi* **1 a** : to endure use : last under use or the passage of time ⟨material that will ~ for years⟩ **b** : to retain quality or vitality **2 a** : to diminish or decay through use ⟨the heels of his shoes began to ~⟩ **b** : to diminish or fail with the passage of time ⟨the effect of the drug *wore* off⟩ ⟨the day *wore* on⟩ **c** : to grow or become by attrition or use **3** *of a ship* : to change to an opposite tack by turning the stern to the wind — compare TACK — **wear·er** *n* — **wear on** : IRRITATE, FRAY — **wear the trousers** *or* **wear the pants** : to have the controlling authority in a household — **wear thin** **1** : to become weak or ready to give way ⟨my patience was *wearing thin*⟩ **2** : to become trite, unconvincing, or out-of-date ⟨an argument that quickly *wore thin*⟩

²**wear** *n* (15c) **1** : the act of wearing : the state of being worn : USE ⟨clothes for everyday ~⟩ **2 a** : clothing or an article of clothing usu. of a particular kind; *esp* : clothing worn for a special occasion or popular during a specific period **b** : FASHION, VOGUE **3** : wearing quality : durability under use **4** : the result of wearing or use : diminution or impairment due to use ⟨*wear*-resistant surface⟩

¹**wear·able** \'war-ə-bəl, 'wer-\ *adj* (1590) : capable of being worn : suitable to be worn — **wear·abil·i·ty** \ˌwar-ə-'bi-lə-tē, ˌwer-\ *n*

²**wearable** *n* (1711) : GARMENT — usu. used in pl.

wear and tear *n* (1666) : the loss, injury, or stress to which something is subjected by or in the course of use; *esp* : normal depreciation

wear down *vt* (1803) : to weary and overcome by persistent resistance or pressure

wea·ri·ful \'wir-ē-fəl\ *adj* (15c) **1** : causing weariness; *esp* : TEDIOUS **2** : full of weariness : WEARIED — **wea·ri·ful·ly** \-fə-lē\ *adv* — **wea·ri·ful·ness** *n*

wea·ri·less \'wir-ē-ləs\ *adj* (15c) : TIRELESS — **wea·ri·less·ly** *adv*

¹**wear·ing** \'war-iŋ, 'wer-\ *adj* (15c) : intended for wear ⟨~ apparel⟩

²**wearing** *adj* (1811) : subjecting to or inflicting wear; *esp* : causing fatigue ⟨a ~ journey⟩ — **wear·ing·ly** \-iŋ-lē\ *adv*

wea·ri·some \'wir-ē-səm\ *adj* (15c) : causing weariness : TIRESOME — **wea·ri·some·ly** *adv* — **wea·ri·some·ness** *n*

wear out *vt* (14c) **1** : TIRE, EXHAUST **2** : to make useless esp. by long or hard usage : ERASE, EFFACE **4** : to endure through : OUTLAST ⟨*wear out* a storm⟩ **5** : to consume (as time) tediously ⟨*wear out* idle days⟩ ~ *vi* : to become useless from long or excessive wear or use

¹**wea·ry** \'wir-ē\ *adj* **wea·ri·er**; **-est** [ME *wery*, fr. OE *wērig*; akin to

OHG *wuorag* intoxicated and perh. to Gk *aōros* sleep] (bef. 12c) **1** : exhausted in strength, endurance, vigor, or freshness **2** : expressing or characteristic of weariness **3** : having one's patience, tolerance, or pleasure exhausted — used with *of* **4** : WEARISOME — **wea·ri·ly** \'wir-ə-lē\ *adv* — **wea·ri·ness** \'wir-ē-nəs\ *n*
²**weary** *vb* **wea·ried; wea·ry·ing** *vi* (bef. 12c) : to become weary ∼ *vt* : to make weary *syn* see TIRE
wea·sand \'wē-z²nd, 'wi-z²n(d)\ *n* [ME *wesand,* fr. (assumed) OE *wāsend* gullet; akin to OE *wāsend* gullet, OHG *weisunt* windpipe] (bef. 12c): THROAT, GULLET; *also* : TRACHEA
¹**wea·sel** \'wē-zəl\ *n, pl* **weasels** [ME *wesele,* fr. OE *weosule;* akin to OHG *wisula* weasel] (bef. 12c) **1** *or pl* **weasel** : any of various small slender active carnivorous mammals (genus *Mustela* of the family Mustelidae, the weasel family) that are able to prey on animals (as rabbits) larger than themselves, are mostly reddish brown with white or yellowish underparts, and in northern forms turn white in winter **2** : a light self-propelled tracked vehicle built either for traveling over snow, ice, or sand or as an amphibious vehicle

weasel 1

²**weasel** *vi* **wea·seled; wea·sel·ing** \'wēz-liŋ, 'wē-zə-\ [*weasel word*] (1900) **1** : to use weasel words : EQUIVOCATE **2** : to escape from or evade a situation or obligation — often used with *out*
wea·sel·ly *also* **wea·sely** \'wēz-lē, 'wē-zə-\ *adj* (1838) : resembling or suggestive of a weasel
weasel word *n* [fr. the weasel's reputed habit of sucking the contents out of an egg while leaving the shell superficially intact] (1900) : a word used in order to evade or retreat from a direct or forthright statement or position
¹**weath·er** \'we-thər\ *n* [ME *weder,* fr. OE; akin to OHG *wetar* weather, OCS *vetrŭ* wind] (bef. 12c) **1** : the state of the atmosphere with respect to heat or cold, wetness or dryness, calm or storm, clearness or cloudiness **2** : state or vicissitude of life or fortune **3** : disagreeable atmospheric conditions: as **a** : RAIN, STORM **b** : cold air with dampness **4** : WEATHERING — **under the weather 1** : ILL **2** : DRUNK 1a
²**weather** *vb* **weath·ered; weath·er·ing** \'weth-riŋ, 'we-thə-\ *vt* (15c) **1** : to expose to the open air : subject to the action of the elements **2** : to bear up against and come safely through ⟨∼ a storm⟩ ⟨∼ a crisis⟩ ∼ *vi* : to undergo or endure the action of the elements
³**weather** *adj* (ca. 1625) : of or relating to the side facing the wind — compare LEE
weath·er·abil·i·ty \,weth-rə-'bi-lə-tē, ,we-thə-\ *n* (1947) : capability of withstanding the weathering process ⟨∼ of a plastic⟩
weath·er–beat·en \'we-thər-,bē-t²n\ *adj* (1530) **1** : toughened, tanned, or bronzed by the weather ⟨a ∼ face⟩ **2** : worn or damaged by exposure to weather
weath·er·board \-,bōrd, -,bȯrd\ *n* (ca. 1540) **1** : CLAPBOARD, SIDING **2** : the weather side of a ship — **weath·er·board·ed** *adj*
weath·er·board·ing \-,bōr-diŋ, -,bȯr-\ *n* (1632) : CLAPBOARDS, SIDING
weath·er–bound \-,baůnd\ *adj* (1590) : kept in port or at anchor or from travel or sport by bad weather
weather bureau *n* (1871) : a bureau engaged in the collection of weather reports as a basis for weather predictions, storm warnings, and the compiling of statistical records
weath·er–burned \'we-thər-,bərnd\ *adj* (1906) : browned by sun and wind
weath·er·cast \-,kast\ *n* [¹*weather* + ²*forecast*] (1866) : a weather forecast esp. on radio or television
weath·er·cast·er \-,kas-tər\ *n* (1607) : a weather forecaster esp. on radio or television
weath·er·cock \-,käk\ *n* (13c) **1** : a vane often in the figure of a cock mounted so as to turn freely with the wind and show its direction **2** : a person or thing that changes readily or often
weather deck *n* (1850) : a deck having no overhead protection from the weather
weath·ered \'we-thərd\ *adj* (1789) **1** : seasoned by exposure to the weather **2** : altered in color, texture, composition, or form by such exposure or by artificial means producing a similar effect ⟨∼ oak⟩
weather eye *n* (1839) **1** : an eye quick to observe coming changes in the weather **2** : constant and shrewd watchfulness and alertness
weath·er·glass \'we-thər-,glas\ *n* (1626) : a simple instrument for showing changes in atmospheric pressure by the changing level of liquid in a spout connected with a closed reservoir; *broadly* : BAROMETER
weathering *n* (1548) : the action of the elements in altering the color, texture, composition, or form of exposed objects; *specif* : the physical disintegration and chemical decomposition of earth materials at or near the earth's surface
weath·er·ize \'we-thə-,rīz\ *vt* **-ized; -iz·ing** (1943) : to make (as a house) better protected against winter weather (as by adding insulation) — **weath·er·i·za·tion** \,weth-rə-'za-shən, ,we-thə-\ *n*
weath·er·ly \'we-thər-lē\ *adj* (1729) : able to sail close to the wind with little leeway
weath·er·man \-,man\ *n* (1859) : one who reports and forecasts the weather : METEOROLOGIST
weather map *n* (1871) : a map or chart showing the principal meteorological elements at a given hour and over an extended region
weath·er·per·son \'we-thər-,pər-s²n\ *n* (1974) : a person who reports and forecasts the weather : METEOROLOGIST
weath·er·proof \'we-thər-,prüf\ *adj* (1620) : able to withstand exposure to weather without damage or loss of function — **weatherproof** *vt* — **weath·er·proof·ness** *n*
weather ship *n* (1946) : a ship that makes observations for use by meteorologists
weather station *n* (ca. 1895) : a station for taking, recording, and reporting meteorological observations
weather strip *n* (1846) : a strip of material to cover the joint of a door or window and the sill, casing, or threshold so as to exclude rain, snow, and cold air — called also *weather stripping* — **weath·er–strip** *vt*
weather vane *n* (ca. 1721) : VANE 1a

weath·er·wise \'we-thər-,wīz\ *adj* (14c) **1** : skillful in forecasting changes in the weather **2** : skillful in forecasting changes in opinion or feeling ⟨a ∼ politician⟩
weath·er·worn \-,wȯrn, -,wȯrn\ *adj* (1609) : worn by exposure to the weather
¹**weave** \'wēv\ *vb* **wove** \'wōv\ *or* **weaved; wo·ven** \'wō-vən\ *or* **weaved; weav·ing** [ME *weven,* fr. OE *wefan;* akin to OHG *weban* to weave, Gk *hyphainein* to weave, *hyphos* web] *vt* (bef. 12c) **1 a** : to form (cloth) by interlacing strands (as of yarn); *specif* : to make (cloth) on a loom by interlacing warp and filling threads **b** : to interlace (as threads) into cloth **c** : to make (as a basket) by intertwining **2** : SPIN 2 — used of spiders and insects **3** : to interlace esp. to form a texture, fabric, or design **4 a** : to produce by elaborately combining elements : CONTRIVE **b** : to unite in a coherent whole **c** : to introduce as an appropriate element : work in — usu. used with *in* or *into* **5** : to direct (as the body) in a winding or zigzag course esp. to avoid obstacles ∼ *vi* **1** : to work at weaving : make cloth **2** : to move in a devious, winding, or zigzag course esp. to avoid obstacles
²**weave** *n* (1581) **1** : something woven; *esp* : woven cloth **2** : any of the patterns or methods for interlacing the threads of woven fabrics
³**weave** *vi* **weaved; weav·ing** [ME *weven* to move to and fro, wave; akin to ON *veifa* to be in movement — more at WIPE] (1596) : to move waveringly from side to side : SWAY
weav·er \'wē-vər\ *n* (14c) **1** : one that weaves esp. as an occupation **2** : WEAVERBIRD
weav·er·bird \-,bərd\ *n* (1826) : any of numerous Old World passerine birds (family Ploceidae) that resemble finches and mostly construct elaborate nests of interlaced vegetation
weaver's knot *n* (1532) : SHEET BEND — called also *weaver's hitch*
¹**web** \'web\ *n* [ME, fr. OE; akin to ON *vefr* web, OE *wefan* to weave] (bef. 12c) **1** : a fabric on a loom or in process of being removed from a loom **2 a** : COBWEB, SPIDERWEB **b** : a network of silken thread spun esp. by the larvae of various insects (as a tent caterpillar) and usu. serving as a nest or shelter **3** : a tissue or membrane of an animal or plant; *esp* : that uniting fingers or toes either at their bases (as in humans) or for a greater part of their length (as in many waterbirds) **4 a** : a thin metal sheet, plate, or strip **b** : the plate connecting the upper and lower flanges of a girder or rail **c** : the arm of a crank **5** : something resembling a web: **a** : SNARE, ENTANGLEMENT ⟨a ∼ of intrigue⟩ ⟨ensnarled in a ∼ of folly —David A. Stockman⟩ **b** : an intricate pattern or structure suggestive of something woven : NETWORK ⟨a ∼ of little roads⟩ ⟨a complex ∼ of relationships⟩ **6** : the series of barbs implanted on each side of the shaft of a feather : VANE **7 a** : a continuous sheet of paper manufactured or undergoing manufacture on a paper machine **b** : a roll of paper for use in a rotary printing press **8** : the part of a ribbed vault between the ribs — **webbed** \'webd\ *adj* — **web·like** \'web-,līk\ *adj*
²**web** *vb* **webbed; web·bing** *vi* (1604) : to construct or form a web ∼ *vt* **1** : to cover with a web or network **2** : ENSNARE, ENTANGLE **3** : to provide with a web
web·bing \'we-biŋ\ *n* (1796) **1** : a strong narrow closely woven tape designed for bearing weight and used esp. for straps, harness, or upholstery **2** : TRAP 3c
web·by \'we-bē\ *adj* (1661) : of, relating to, or consisting of a web
we·ber \'we-bər, 'vā-bər\ *n* [Wilhelm E. *Weber* †1891 Ger. physicist] (1891) : the practical meter-kilogram-second unit of magnetic flux equal to that flux which in linking a circuit of one turn produces in it an electromotive force of one volt as the flux is reduced to zero at a uniform rate in one second : 10⁸ maxwells
web·fed \'web-,fed\ *adj* (1947) : of, relating to, or printed by a web press
web·foot *n* (1765) **1** \'web-'fůt\ : a foot having webbed toes **2** \-,fůt\ : an animal having web feet — **web–foot·ed** \-'fů-təd\ *adj*
web member *n* (ca. 1890) : one of the several members joining the top and bottom chords of a truss or lattice girder
web–off·set \'web-'ȯf-,set\ *n, often attrib* (1959) : offset printing by web press
web press *n* (1875) : a press that prints a continuous roll of paper
web spinner *n* (ca. 1907) : an insect that spins a web; *esp* : any of an order (Embioptera syn. Embiidina) of small slender insects with biting mouthparts that live in silken tunnels which they spin
web·ster \'web-stər\ *n* [ME, fr. OE *webbestre* female weaver, fr. *webbian* to weave; akin to OE *wefan* to weave] (12c) *archaic* : WEAVER 1
web·work \'web-,wərk\ *n* (1790) : WEB 5b ⟨a vast ∼ of real estate holdings⟩
web·worm \-,wərm\ *n* (1797) : any of various caterpillars that are more or less gregarious and spin large webs
wed \'wed\ *vb* **wed·ded** *also* **wed; wed·ding** [ME *wedden,* fr. OE *weddian;* akin to MHG *wetten* to pledge, OE *wedd* pledge, OHG *wetti,* Goth *wadi,* L *vad-, vas* bail, security] *vt* (bef. 12c) **1** : to take for wife or husband by a formal ceremony : MARRY **2** : to join in marriage **3** : to unite as if by the bond of marriage ∼ *vi* : to enter into matrimony — **wed·der** *n*
we'd \'wēd\ (1603) : we had : we would : we should
Wed·dell seal \wi-'del-, 'we-d²l-\ *n* [James *Weddell* †1834 Eng. navigator] (1914) : a vocal Antarctic hair seal (*Leptonychotes weddelli*) noted for its deep dives in search of food
wed·ding \'we-diŋ\ *n, often attrib* (bef. 12c) **1** : a marriage ceremony usu. with its accompanying festivities : NUPTIALS **2** : an act, process, or instance of joining in close association **3** : a wedding anniversary or its celebration — usu. used in combination ⟨a golden ∼⟩
wedding cake *n* (1648) **1** : a usu. elaborately decorated and tiered cake made for the celebration of a wedding **2** : something (as a large building) likened to a wedding cake esp. in elaborate ornamentation
wedding march *n* (1850) : a march of slow tempo and stately character composed or played to accompany the bridal procession

\ə\ abut \ᵊ\ kitten, F table \ər\ further \a\ ash \ā\ ace \ä\ mop, mar \aů\ out \ch\ chin \e\ bet \ē\ easy \g\ go \i\ hit \ī\ ice \j\ job \ŋ\ sing \ō\ go \ȯ\ law \ȯi\ boy \th\ thin \ṯẖ\ the \ü\ loot \ů\ foot \y\ yet \zh\ vision \à, ḵ, ⁿ, œ, œ̄, ʉe, ūe, ʸ\ *see* Guide to Pronunciation

wedding ring n (14c) : a ring often of plain gold or platinum given by the groom to the bride during the wedding service; *also* : a similar ring given by the bride to the groom in a double-ring service

we·del \'vā-dᵊl\ vi [G *Wedeln*] (ca. 1963) : to ski downhill by means of wedeln

we·deln \'vā-dᵊln\ n [G, fr. *wedeln*, lit., to fan, wag the tail, fr. *Wedel* fan, tail, fr. OHG *wadal*; akin to ON *veli* bird's tail] (ca. 1957) : a style of skiing in which a skier rhythmically swings the rear of the skis from side to side while following the fall line

¹wedge \'wej\ n [ME *wegge*, fr. OE *wecg*; akin to OHG *wecki* wedge, Lith *vagis*] (bef. 12c) **1** : a piece of a substance (as wood or iron) that tapers to a thin edge and is used for splitting wood and rocks, raising heavy bodies, or for tightening by being driven into something **2 a** : something (as a policy) causing a breach or separation **b** : something used to initiate an action or development **3** : something wedge-shaped: as **a** : an array of troops or tanks in the form of a wedge **b** : the wedge-shaped stroke in cuneiform characters **c** : a shoe having a heel extending from the back of the shoe to the front of the shank and a tread formed by an extension of the sole **d** : an iron golf club with a broad low-angled face for maximum loft

²wedge vb **wedged; wedg·ing** vt (15c) **1** : to fasten or tighten by driving in a wedge **2 a** : to force or press (something) into a narrow space : CRAM **b** : to force (one's way) into or through ⟨*wedged* his way into the crowd⟩ **3** : to separate or force apart with or as if with a wedge ～ vi : to become wedged

wedged \'wejd, 'we-jəd\ adj (1552) : shaped like a wedge

wedg·ie \'we-jē\ n (1939) **1** : a shoe having a wedge-shaped piece serving as the heel and joining the half sole to form a continuous flat undersurface **2** : the condition of having one's clothing wedged between the buttocks esp. from having one's pants or underpants yanked up from behind as a prank — often used with *get* or *give*

Wedg·wood \'wej-ˌwu̇d\ trademark — used for ceramic wares (as bone china or jasper)

wedgy \'we-jē\ adj (1799) : resembling a wedge in shape

wed·lock \'wed-ˌläk\ n [ME *wedlok*, fr. OE *wedlāc* marriage bond, fr. *wedd* pledge + *-lāc*, suffix denoting activity] (13c) : the state of being married : MARRIAGE, MATRIMONY — **out of wedlock** : with the natural parents not legally married to each other

Wednes·day \'wenz-dē, -(ˌ)dā; *Brit also* 'we-dᵊnz-\ n [ME, fr. OE *wōdnesdæg* (akin to ON *ōthinsdagr* Wednesday); akin to OE *Wōden* Odin and *dæg* day] (bef. 12c) : the fourth day of the week — **Wednes·days** \-dēz, -(ˌ)dāz\ adv

wee \'wē\ adj [ME *we*, fr. *we*, n., little bit, fr. OE *wǣge* weight; akin to OE *wegan* to move, weigh — more at WAY] (15c) **1** : very small : DIMINUTIVE **2** : very early ⟨～ hours of the morning⟩

¹weed \'wēd\ n [ME, fr. OE *wēod* weed, herb; akin to OS *wiod* weed] (bef. 12c) **1 a** (1) : a plant that is not valued where it is growing and is usu. of vigorous growth; *esp* : one that tends to overgrow or choke out more desirable plants (2) : a weedy growth of plants **b** : an aquatic plant; *esp* : SEAWEED **c** (1) : TOBACCO (2) : MARIJUANA **2 a** : an obnoxious growth, thing, or person **b** : something like a weed in detrimental quality; *esp* : an animal unfit to breed from

²weed vi (bef. 12c) : to remove weeds or something harmful ～ vt **1 a** : to clear of weeds ⟨～ a garden⟩ **b** (1) : to free from something hurtful or offensive (2) : to remove the less desirable portions of **2** : to get rid of (something harmful or superfluous) — often used with *out*

³weed n [ME *wede*, fr. OE *wǣd*, *gewǣde*; akin to ON *vāth* cloth, clothing and perh. to Lith *austi* to weave] (bef. 12c) **1** : GARMENT — often used in pl. **2 a** : dress worn as a sign of mourning (as by a widow) — usu. used in pl. **b** : a band of crape worn on a man's hat as a sign of mourning — usu. used in pl.

weed·er \'wē-dər\ n (15c) : one that weeds; *specif* : any of various devices for removing weeds from an area

weedy \'wē-dē\ adj **weed·i·er; -est** (15c) **1** : abounding with or consisting of weeds **2** : resembling a weed esp. in rank growth or ready propagation **3** : noticeably lean and scrawny : LANKY — **weed·i·ness** n

week \'wēk\ n [ME *weke*, fr. OE *wicu*, *wucu*; akin to OHG *wehha* week and perh. to L *vicis* change, alternation, OHG *wehsal* exchange] (bef. 12c) **1 a** : any of a series of 7-day cycles used in various calendars; *esp* : a 7-day cycle beginning on Sunday and ending on Saturday **b** (1) : a week beginning with a specified day or containing a specified holiday ⟨the ～ of the 18th⟩ ⟨Easter ～⟩ (2) : a week appointed for public recognition of some cause ⟨Fire Prevention *Week*⟩ **2 a** : any seven consecutive days **b** : a series of regular working, business, or school days during each 7-day period **3** : a time seven days before or after a specified day ⟨last Sunday ～⟩

week·day \'wēk-ˌdā\ n (15c) : a day of the week except Sunday or sometimes except Saturday and Sunday

week·days \-ˌdāz\ adv (1777) : on weekdays repeatedly : on any weekday ⟨takes a bus ～⟩

¹week·end \'wēk-ˌend\ n (1638) : the end of the week; *specif* : the period between the close of one working or business or school week and the beginning of the next

²weekend vi (1901) : to spend the weekend

³weekend adj (1935) : active in a specified role only on weekends or part-time ⟨a ～ father⟩ ⟨～ athletes⟩

weekend bag n (1921) : a suitcase of a size to carry clothing and personal articles for a weekend trip — called also *weekend case*

week·end·er \'wēk-ˌen-dər\ n (1880) **1** : one that vacations or visits for a weekend **2** : WEEKEND BAG

week·ends \'wēk-ˌen(d)z\ adv (1892) : on weekends repeatedly : on any weekend ⟨travels ～⟩

week·long \'wēk-ˌlȯn\ adj (1898) : lasting a week

¹week·ly \'wē-klē\ adv (15c) : every week : once a week : by the week

²weekly adj (15c) **1** : occurring, appearing, or done weekly **2** : reckoned by the week

³weekly n, pl **weeklies** (1833) : a weekly newspaper or periodical

week·night \'wēk-ˌnīt\ n (1859) : a weekday night

week·nights \-ˌnīts\ adv (1965) : on weeknights repeatedly : on any weeknight

ween \'wēn\ vt [ME *wenen*, fr. OE *wēnan*; akin to ON *væna* to hope and prob. to L *venus* love, charm — more at WIN] (bef. 12c) *archaic* : IMAGINE

wee·nie \'wē-nē\ n [alter. of *wienie*] (ca. 1906) **1** : FRANKFURTER **2** *slang* : PENIS **3** : NERD ⟨computer ～s⟩

wee·ny \'wē-nē\ *also* **ween·sy** \'wēn(t)-sē\ adj [alter. of *wee*] (ca. 1781) : exceptionally small : TINY

weep \'wēp\ vb **wept** \'wept\; **weep·ing** [ME *wepen*, fr. OE *wēpan*; akin to OHG *wuoffan* to weep, OCS *vabiti* to call to] vt (bef. 12c) **1** : to express deep sorrow for usu. by shedding tears : BEWAIL **2** : to pour forth (tears) from the eyes **3** : to exude (a fluid) slowly : OOZE ～ vi **1** : to express passion (as grief) by shedding tears **2 a** : to give off or leak fluid slowly : OOZE **b** *of a fluid* : to flow sluggishly or in drops **3** : to droop over : BEND

weep·er \'wē-pər\ n (14c) **1 a** : one that weeps **b** : a professional mourner **2** : a small statue of a figure in mourning on a funeral monument **3** : a badge of mourning worn esp. in the 18th and 19th centuries **4** *pl* : long and flowing side-whiskers **5** : TEARJERKER

weep hole n (1851) : a hole (as in a wall or foundation) that is designed to drain off accumulated water

weep·ie \'wē-pē\ n (1928) : TEARJERKER

weep·ing \'wē-piŋ\ adj (bef. 12c) **1** : TEARFUL **2** *archaic* : RAINY **3** : having slender pendent branches

weeping willow n (ca. 1731) : an Asian willow (*Salix babylonica*) introduced into No. America that has slender pendent branches

weepy \'wē-pē\ adj (1863) : inclined to weep : TEARFUL

weet \'wēt\ vb [ME *weten*, alter. of *witen* — more at WIT] (14c) *archaic* : KNOW

wee·vil \'wē-vəl\ n [ME *wevel*, fr. OE *wifel*; akin to OHG *wibil* beetle, OE *wefan* to weave] (bef. 12c) : any of a superfamily (Curculionoidea) of beetles which have the head prolonged into a more or less distinct snout and which include many that are injurious esp. as larvae to nuts, fruit, and grain or to living plants; *esp* : any of a family (Curculionidae) having a well-developed snout curved downward with the jaws at the tip and clubbed usu. elbowed antennae — **wee·vily** or **wee·vil·ly** \'wēv-lē, 'wē-və-lē\ adj

weevil

weft \'weft\ n [ME, fr. OE; akin to ON *veptr* weft, OE *wefan* to weave — more at WEAVE] (bef. 12c) **1 a** : a filling thread or yarn in weaving **b** : yarn used for the weft **2** : WEB, FABRIC; *also* : an article of woven fabric

weft knit n (1943) : a knit fabric produced in machine or hand knitting with the yarns running crosswise or in a circle — compare WARP KNIT — **weft-knit·ted** \-ˌni-təd\ adj — **weft knit·ing** n

wei·ge·la \wī-'jē-lə\ n [NL, fr. Christian E. *Weigel* †1831 Ger. physician] (1846) : any of a genus (*Weigela*) of showy shrubs of the honeysuckle family; *esp* : one (*W. florida*) of China widely grown for its usu. pink or red flowers

¹weigh \'wā\ vb [ME *weyen*, fr. OE *wegan* to move, carry, weigh — more at WAY] vt (bef. 12c) **1** : to ascertain the heaviness of by or as if by a balance **2** : OUTWEIGH **3** : COUNTERBALANCE **c** : to make heavy : WEIGHT — often used with *down* **3** : to consider carefully esp. by balancing opposing factors or aspects in order to reach a choice or conclusion : EVALUATE **4** : to heave up (an anchor) preparatory to sailing **5** : to measure or apportion (a definite quantity) on or as if on a scales ～ vi **1 a** : to have a certain heaviness : experience a specific force due to gravity **b** : to register a weight (as on a scales) — used with *in* or *out*; compare WEIGH IN **2** : to merit consideration as important : COUNT ⟨evidence will ～ heavily against him⟩ **3 a** : to press down with or as if with a heavy weight **b** : to have a saddening or disheartening effect **4** : to weigh anchor **syn** see CONSIDER — **weigh·able** \'wā-ə-bəl\ adj — **weigh·er** n

²weigh n [alter. of *way*] (1777) : WAY — used in the phrase *under weigh*

weigh down vt (14c) **1** : to cause to bend down : OVERBURDEN **2** : OPPRESS, DEPRESS

weigh–in \'wā-ˌin\ n (1939) : an act or instance of weighing in as a contestant esp. in sport

weigh in vi (1868) **1** : to have oneself or one's possessions (as baggage) weighed; *esp* : to have oneself weighed in connection with an athletic contest **2** : to enter as a participant

¹weight \'wāt\ n [ME *wight*, *weght*, fr. OE *wiht*; akin to ON *vætt* weight, OE *wegan* to weigh] (bef. 12c) **1 a** : the amount that a thing weighs **b** (1) : the standard or established amount that a thing should weigh (2) : one of the classes into which contestants in a sports event are divided according to body weight (3) : poundage required to be carried by a horse in a handicap race **2 a** : a quantity or thing weighing a fixed and usu. specified amount **b** : a heavy object (as a metal ball) thrown, put, or lifted as an athletic exercise or contest **3 a** : a unit of weight or mass — see METRIC SYSTEM table **b** : a piece of material (as metal) of known specified weight for use in weighing articles **c** : a system of related units of weight **4 a** : something heavy : LOAD **b** : a heavy object to hold or press something down or to counterbalance **5 a** : BURDEN, PRESSURE **b** : the quality or state of being ponderous **c** : CORPULENCE **6 a** : relative heaviness : MASS **b** : the force with which a body is attracted toward the earth or a celestial body by gravitation and which is equal to the product of the mass and the local gravitational acceleration **7 a** : the relative importance or authority accorded something **b** : measurable influence esp. on others **8** : overpowering force **9** : the quality (as lightness) that makes a fabric or garment suitable for a particular use or season — often used in combination ⟨summer-*weight*⟩ **10** : a numerical coefficient assigned to an item to express its relative importance in a frequency distribution **11** : the degree of thickness of the strokes of a type character **syn** see IMPORTANCE, INFLUENCE

²weight vt (1647) **1** : to oppress with a burden ⟨～ed down with cares⟩ **2 a** : to load or make heavy with or as if with a weight **b** : to increase in heaviness by adding an ingredient **3 a** : WEIGH 1 **b** : to feel the weight of : HEFT **4** : to assign a statistical weight to **5** : to cause to incline in a particular direction by manipulation ⟨the tax structure . . . which was ～ed so heavily in favor of the upper classes —A. S. Link⟩ **6** : to shift the burden of weight upon ⟨～ the inside ski⟩

weight·ed adj (ca. 1732) **1** : made heavy : LOADED ⟨～ silk⟩ **2 a** : having a statistical weight attached ⟨a ～ test score⟩ **b** : compiled or calculated from weighted data ⟨a ～ mean⟩ **3** : INCLINED 1

WEIGHTS AND MEASURES[1]

UNIT	ABBREVIATION OR SYMBOL	EQUIVALENTS IN OTHER UNITS OF SAME SYSTEM	METRIC EQUIVALENT
WEIGHT			
Avoirdupois[2]			
ton			
short ton		20 short hundredweight, 2000 pounds	0.907 metric ton
long ton		20 long hundredweight, 2240 pounds	1.016 metric tons
hundredweight	cwt		
short hundredweight		100 pounds, 0.05 short ton	45.359 kilograms
long hundredweight		112 pounds, 0.05 long ton	50.802 kilograms
pound	lb *or* lb avdp *also* #	16 ounces, 7000 grains	0.454 kilogram
ounce	oz *or* oz avdp	16 drams, 437.5 grains, 0.0625 pound	28.350 grams
dram	dr *or* dr avdp	27.344 grains, 0.0625 ounce	1.772 grams
grain	gr	0.037 dram, 0.002286 ounce	0.0648 gram
Troy			
pound	lb t	12 ounces, 240 pennyweight, 5760 grains	0.373 kilogram
ounce	oz t	20 pennyweight, 480 grains, 0.083 pound	31.103 grams
pennyweight	dwt *also* pwt	24 grains, 0.05 ounce	1.555 grams
grain	gr	0.042 pennyweight, 0.002083 ounce	0.0648 gram
Apothecaries'			
pound	lb ap	12 ounces, 5760 grains	0.373 kilogram
ounce	oz ap *or* ℥	8 drams, 480 grains, 0.083 pound	31.103 grams
dram	dr ap *or* ℨ	3 scruples, 60 grains	3.888 grams
scruple	s ap *or* ℈	20 grains, 0.333 dram	1.296 grams
grain	gr	0.05 scruple, 0.002083 ounce, 0.0166 dram	0.0648 gram
CAPACITY			
U.S. liquid measure			
gallon	gal	4 quarts (231 cubic inches)	3.785 liters
quart	qt	2 pints (57.75 cubic inches)	0.946 liter
pint	pt	4 gills (28.875 cubic inches)	473.176 milliliters
gill	gi	4 fluid ounces (7.219 cubic inches)	118.294 milliliters
fluid ounce	fl oz *or* f℥	8 fluid drams (1.805 cubic inches)	29.573 milliliters
fluid dram	fl dr *or* fℨ	60 minims (0.226 cubic inch)	3.697 milliliters
minim	min *or* ℳ	$1/_{60}$ fluid dram (0.003760 cubic inch)	0.061610 milliliter
U.S. dry measure			
bushel	bu	4 pecks (2150.42 cubic inches)	35.239 liters
peck	pk	8 quarts (537.605 cubic inches)	8.810 liters
quart	qt	2 pints (67.201 cubic inches)	1.101 liters
pint	pt	$1/_2$ quart (33.600 cubic inches)	0.551 liter
British imperial liquid and dry measure			
bushel	bu	4 pecks (2219.36 cubic inches)	36.369 liters
peck	pk	2 gallons (554.84 cubic inches)	9.092 liters
gallon	gal	4 quarts (277.420 cubic inches)	4.546 liters
quart	qt	2 pints (69.355 cubic inches)	1.136 liters
pint	pt	4 gills (34.678 cubic inches)	568.26 milliliters
gill	gi	5 fluid ounces (8.669 cubic inches)	142.066 milliliters
fluid ounce	fl oz *or* f℥	8 fluid drams (1.7339 cubic inches)	28.412 milliliters
fluid dram	fl dr *or* fℨ	60 minims (0.216734 cubic inch)	3.5516 milliliters
minim	min *or* ℳ	$1/_{60}$ fluid dram (0.003612 cubic inch)	0.059194 milliliter
LENGTH			
mile	mi	5280 feet, 1760 yards, 320 rods	1.609 kilometers
rod	rd	5.50 yards, 16.5 feet	5.029 meters
yard	yd	3 feet, 36 inches	0.9144 meter
foot	ft *or* '	12 inches, 0.333 yard	30.48 centimeters
inch	in *or* "	0.083 foot, 0.028 yard	2.54 centimeters
AREA			
square mile	sq mi *or* mi^2	640 acres, 102,400 square rods	2.590 square kilometers
acre		4840 square yards, 43,560 square feet	0.405 hectare, 4047 square meters
square rod	sq rd *or* rd^2	30.25 square yards, 0.00625 acre	25.293 square meters
square yard	sq yd *or* yd^2	1296 square inches, 9 square feet	0.836 square meter
square foot	sq ft *or* ft^2	144 square inches, 0.111 square yard	0.093 square meter
square inch	sq in *or* in^2	0.0069 square foot, 0.00077 square yard	6.452 square centimeters
VOLUME			
cubic yard	cu yd *or* yd^3	27 cubic feet, 46,656 cubic inches	0.765 cubic meter
cubic foot	cu ft *or* ft^3	1728 cubic inches, 0.0370 cubic yard	0.028 cubic meter
cubic inch	cu in *or* in^3	0.00058 cubic foot, 0.000021 cubic yard	16.387 cubic centimeters

[1] For U.S. equivalents of the metric units see Metric System table.
[2] The U.S. uses the avoirdupois units as the common system of measuring weight.

weight·less \'wāt-ləs\ *adj* (ca. 1547) : having little weight : lacking apparent gravitational pull — **weight·less·ly** *adv* — **weight·less·ness** *n*
weight lifter *n* (1897) : one that lifts barbells in competition or as an exercise — **weight lifting** *n*
weight man *n* (ca. 1949) : an athlete who competes in any of the field events in which a weight is thrown or put
weight room *n* (1973) : a room containing equipment for weight training
weight training *n* (1955) : a system of conditioning involving lifting weights esp. for strength and endurance
weighty \'wā-tē\ *adj* **weight·i·er; -est** (15c) **1 a** : of much importance or consequence : MOMENTOUS **b** : SOLEMN **2 a** : weighing a considerable amount **b** : heavy in proportion to its bulk ⟨~ metal⟩ **3** : POWERFUL, TELLING ⟨~ arguments⟩ *syn* see HEAVY — **weight·i·ly** \'wā-tᵊl-ē\ *adv* — **weight·i·ness** \'wā-tē-nəs\ *n*
wei·ma·ra·ner \,vī-mə-'rä-nər, ,wi-; 'vī-mə-,, 'wi-\ *n* [G, fr. *Weimar*, Germany] (1943) : any of a breed of large light gray usu. short-haired pointers of German origin
wei·ner *var of* WIENER
weir \'war, 'wer, 'wir\ *n* [ME *were*, fr. OE *wer*; akin to ON *ver* fishing place, OHG *werien, werren* to defend] (bef. 12c) **1** : a fence or enclosure set in a waterway for taking fish **2** : a dam in a stream or river to raise the water level or divert its flow
¹weird \'wird\ *n* [ME *wird, werd*, fr. OE *wyrd*; akin to ON *urthr* fate, OE *weorthan* to become — more at WORTH] (bef. 12c) **1** : FATE, DESTINY; *esp* : ill fortune **2** : SOOTHSAYER
²weird *adj* (15c) **1** : of, relating to, or caused by witchcraft or the supernatural : MAGICAL **2** : of strange or extraordinary character : ODD, FANTASTIC — **weird·ly** *adv* — **weird·ness** *n*
syn WEIRD, EERIE, UNCANNY mean mysteriously strange or fantastic. WEIRD may imply an unearthly or supernatural strangeness or it may stress queerness or oddness ⟨*weird* creatures from another world⟩. EERIE suggests an uneasy or fearful consciousness that mysterious and malign powers are at work ⟨an *eerie* calm preceded the bombing raid⟩. UNCANNY implies disquieting strangeness or mysteriousness ⟨an *uncanny* resemblance between total strangers⟩.

\ə\ abut \ᵊ\ kitten, F table \ər\ further \a\ ash \ā\ ace \ä\ mop, mar \aú\ out \ch\ chin \e\ bet \ē\ easy \g\ go \i\ hit \ī\ ice \j\ job \ŋ\ sing \ō\ go \ó\ law \ói\ boy \th\ thin \t͟h\ the \ü\ loot \ú\ foot \y\ yet \zh\ vision \á, k̠, ⁿ, œ, ᴀ̈, ᵫ, ᵫ, ᴀ̇\ *see* Guide to Pronunciation

weird·ie \'wir-dē\ or **weirdy** n, pl **weird·ies** (1894) : WEIRDO
weirdo \'wir-(,)dō\ n, pl **weird·os** (ca. 1955) : a person who is extraordinarily strange or eccentric
Weird Sisters n pl : FATES
wei·sen·hei·mer var of WISENHEIMER
weka \'we-kə\ n [Maori] (1845) : a flightless New Zealand rail (Gallirallus australis)
welch \'welch\ var of WELSH
Welch \'welch\ var of WELSH
¹wel·come \'wel-kəm\ vt **wel·comed; wel·com·ing** [ME, fr. OE welcumian, wylcumian, fr. wilcuma, n.] (bef. 12c) 1 : to greet hospitably and with courtesy or cordiality 2 : to accept with pleasure the occurrence or presence of ⟨~s danger⟩ — **wel·com·er** n
²welcome interj [ME, alter. of wilcume, fr. OE, fr. wilcuma desirable guest (akin to OHG willicomo desirable guest); akin to OE willa, will desire, cuman to come — more at WILL, COME] (12c) — used to express a greeting to a guest or newcomer upon arrival
³welcome adj (12c) 1 : received gladly into one's presence or companionship ⟨was always ~ in their home⟩ 2 : giving pleasure : received with gladness or delight esp. in response to a need ⟨a ~ relief⟩ 3 : willingly permitted or admitted ⟨he was ~ to come and go —W. M. Thackeray⟩ 4 — used in the phrase "You're welcome" as a reply to an expression of thanks — **wel·come·ly** adv — **wel·come·ness** n
⁴welcome n (1525) 1 : a greeting or reception usu. upon arrival 2 : the state of being welcome ⟨overstayed their ~⟩
welcome mat n (1946) : something likened to a mat placed before an entrance as a sign of welcome
¹weld \'weld\ vb [alter. of obs. E well to, weld, fr. ME wellen to boil, well, weld — more at WELL] vi (1599) : to become or be capable of being welded ~ vt 1 a : to unite (metallic parts) by heating and allowing the metals to flow together or by hammering or compressing with or without previous heating b : to unite (plastics) in a similar manner by heating c : to repair (as an article) by this method d : to produce or create as if by such a process 2 : to unite or reunite closely or intimately — **weld·able** \'wel-də-bəl\ adj
²weld n (1831) 1 : a welded joint 2 : union by welding : the state or condition of being welded
weld·er \'wel-dər\ n (ca. 1828) : one that welds: as a or **wel·dor** : one whose work is welding b : a machine used in welding
weld·ment \'wel(d)-mənt\ n (1941) : a unit formed by welding together an assembly of pieces
¹wel·fare \'wel-,far, -,fer\ n [ME, fr. the phrase wel faren to fare well] (14c) 1 : the state of doing well esp. in respect to good fortune, happiness, well-being, or prosperity 2 a : aid in the form of money or necessities for those in need b : an agency or program through which such aid is distributed
²welfare adj (1904) 1 : of, relating to, or concerned with welfare and esp. with improvement of the welfare of disadvantaged social groups ⟨~ legislation⟩ 2 : receiving public welfare benefits ⟨~ families⟩
welfare state n (1941) 1 : a social system based on the assumption by a political state of primary responsibility for the individual and social welfare of its citizens 2 : a nation or state characterized by the operation of the welfare state system
wel·far·ism \'wel-,far-,i-zəm, -,fer-\ n (1949) : the complex of policies, attitudes, and beliefs associated with the welfare state — **wel·far·ist** \-ist\ n or adj
wel·kin \'wel-kən\ n [ME, lit., cloud, fr. OE wolcen; akin to OHG wolkan cloud] (12c) 1 a : the vault of the sky : FIRMAMENT b : the celestial abode of God or the gods : HEAVEN 2 : the upper atmosphere
¹well \'wel\ n [ME welle, fr. OE welle; akin to OE weallan to bubble, boil, OHG wella wave, Lith vilnis] (bef. 12c) 1 a : an issue of water from the earth : a pool fed by a spring b : SOURCE, ORIGIN 2 a : a pit or hole sunk into the earth to reach a supply of water b : a shaft or hole sunk to obtain oil, brine, or gas 3 a : an enclosure in the middle of a ship's hold to protect from damage and facilitate the inspection of the pumps b : a compartment in the hold of a fishing boat in which fish are kept alive 4 : an open space extending vertically through floors of a structure 5 : a space having a construction or shape suggesting a well for water 6 a : something resembling a well in being damp, cool, deep, or dark b : a deep vertical hole c : a source from which something may be drawn as needed 7 : a pronounced minimum of a variable in physics ⟨a potential ~⟩
²well [ME, fr. OE wellan to cause to well; akin to OE weallan to bubble, boil] vi (bef. 12c) 1 : to rise to the surface and usu. flow forth ⟨tears ~ed from her eyes⟩ 2 : to rise like a flood of liquid ⟨longing ~ed up in his breast⟩ ~ vt : to emit in a copious free flow
³well adv **bet·ter** \'be-tər\; **best** \'best\ [ME wel, fr. OE; akin to OHG wela well, OE wyllan to wish — more at WILL] (bef. 12c) 1 a : in a good or proper manner : JUSTLY, RIGHTLY b : satisfactorily with respect to conduct or action ⟨did ~ in math⟩ 2 : in a kindly or friendly manner ⟨spoke ~ of your idea⟩ 3 a : with skill or aptitude : EXPERTLY ⟨paints ~⟩ b : SATISFACTORILY c : with good appearance or effect : ELEGANTLY ⟨carried himself ~⟩ 4 : with careful or close attention : ATTENTIVELY 5 : to a high degree ⟨~ deserved the honor⟩ ⟨a well-equipped kitchen⟩ — often used as an intensifier or qualifier ⟨there are . . . vacancies pretty ~ all the time —Listener⟩ 6 : FULLY, QUITE ⟨~ worth the price⟩ 7 a : in a way appropriate to the facts or circumstances : FITTINGLY, RIGHTLY b : in a prudent manner : SENSIBLY — used with do 8 : in accordance with the occasion or circumstances : with propriety or good reason ⟨cannot ~ refuse⟩ 9 a : as one could wish : FAVORABLY b : with material success : ADVANTAGEOUSLY ⟨married ~⟩ 10 a : EASILY, READILY ⟨could ~ afford a new car⟩ b : in all likelihood : INDEED ⟨it may ~ be true⟩ 11 : in a prosperous or affluent manner ⟨he lives ~⟩ 12 : to an extent approaching completeness : THOROUGHLY ⟨after being ~ dried with a sponge⟩ 13 : without doubt or question : CLEARLY ⟨~ knew the penalty⟩ 14 : in a familiar manner ⟨knew her ~⟩ 15 : to a large extent or degree : CONSIDERABLY, FAR ⟨~ over a million⟩ usage see GOOD — **as well** 1 : in addition : ALSO ⟨there were other features as well⟩ 2 : to the same extent or degree : as much ⟨open as well to the poor as to the rich⟩ 3 : with equivalent, comparable, or more favorable effect ⟨might just as well have stayed home⟩
⁴well interj (bef. 12c) 1 — used to indicate resumption of discourse or to introduce a remark 2 — used to express surprise or expostulation

⁵well adj (bef. 12c) 1 a : PROSPEROUS, WELL-OFF b : being in satisfactory condition or circumstances 2 : being in good standing or favor 3 : SATISFACTORY, PLEASING ⟨all's ~ that ends well⟩ 4 : ADVISABLE, DESIRABLE ⟨it might be ~ for you to leave⟩ 5 a : free or recovered from infirmity or disease : HEALTHY ⟨a ~ man⟩ b : completely cured or healed ⟨the wound is nearly ~⟩ 6 : pleasing or satisfactory in appearance 7 : being a cause for thankfulness : FORTUNATE ⟨it is ~ that this has happened⟩ syn see HEALTHY usage see GOOD
we'll \'wē(ə)l, wil\ (1578) : we will : we shall
well-ad·just·ed \,wel-ə-'jəs-təd\ adj (1692) : WELL-BALANCED 2
well-ad·vised \'wel-əd-'vīzd\ adj (14c) 1 : acting with wisdom, wise counsel, or proper deliberation : PRUDENT 2 : resulting from, based on, or showing careful deliberation or wise counsel ⟨~ plans⟩
well-ap·point·ed \'wel-ə-'pȯin-təd\ adj (1530) : having good and complete equipment : properly fitted out ⟨a ~ house⟩
well-la·way \,we-lə-'wä, 'we-lə-,\ interj [ME welaway, lit., woe! lo! woe!, alter. of wālāwā, fr. wā woe + lā lo + wā woe — more at WOE] (bef. 12c) archaic — used to express sorrow or lamentation
well-ba·lanced \'wel-'ba-lən(t)st\ adj (1629) 1 : nicely or evenly balanced, arranged, or regulated ⟨a ~ diet⟩ ⟨a ~ attack in football⟩ 2 : emotionally or psychologically untroubled
well-be·ing \'wel-'bē-iŋ\ n (ca. 1613) : the state of being happy, healthy, or prosperous : WELFARE
well-be·loved \,wel-bi-'ləvd\ adj (14c) 1 : sincerely and deeply loved ⟨my ~ wife⟩ 2 : sincerely respected — used in various ceremonial forms of address
well-born \'wel-'bȯrn\ adj (bef. 12c) : born of noble or wealthy lineage
well-bred \-'bred\ adj (1597) 1 : having or displaying good breeding : REFINED 2 : having a good pedigree ⟨~ swine⟩
well-con·di·tioned \,wel-kən-'di-shənd\ adj (15c) 1 : characterized by proper disposition, morals, or behavior 2 : having a good physical condition : SOUND
well deck n (1888) : a space on the weather deck of a ship lying at a lower level between a raised forecastle or poop and the bridge superstructure
well-de·fined \,wel-di-'find\ adj (1704) 1 : having clearly distinguishable limits, boundaries, or features ⟨a ~ scar⟩ 2 : clearly stated or described ⟨~ policies⟩
well-dis·posed \-dis-'pōzd\ adj (14c) : having a good disposition; esp : disposed to be friendly, favorable, or sympathetic
well-done \'wel-'dən\ adj (15c) 1 : rightly or properly performed 2 : cooked thoroughly
Wel·ler·ism \'we-lə-,ri-zəm\ n [Sam Weller, witty servant of Mr. Pickwick in the story Pickwick Papers (1836–37) by Charles Dickens] (1839) : an expression of comparison comprising a usu. well-known quotation followed by a facetious sequel (as "'every one to his own taste,' said the old woman as she kissed the cow")
well-fa·vored \'wel-'fā-vərd\ adj (15c) : GOOD-LOOKING, HANDSOME — **well-fa·vored·ness** n
well-fixed \-'fikst\ adj (1822) : having plenty of money or property
well-found \-'faŭnd\ adj (1793) : fully furnished : properly equipped ⟨a ~ ship⟩
well-found·ed \-'faŭn-dəd\ adj (14c) : based on excellent reasoning, information, judgment, or grounds
well-groomed \-'grümd, -'grŭmd\ adj (1886) 1 : well-dressed and scrupulously neat ⟨~ men⟩ 2 : made neat, tidy, and attractive down to the smallest details ⟨a ~ lawn⟩
well-ground·ed \-'graŭn-dəd\ adj (14c) 1 : having a firm foundation ⟨~ in Latin and Greek⟩ 2 : WELL-FOUNDED
well-han·dled \-'han-dᵊld\ adj (15c) 1 : managed or administered efficiently 2 : having been handled a great deal ⟨~ goods for sale⟩
well-head \'wel-,hed\ n (14c) 1 : the source of a spring or a stream 2 : principal source : FOUNTAINHEAD 3 : the top of a structure built over a well
wellhead price n (1953) : the price less transportation costs charged by the producer for petroleum or natural gas
well-heeled \-'hē(ə)ld\ adj (1897) : having plenty of money : WELL-FIXED
wel·lie or **wel·ly** \'we-lē\ n, pl **wellies** [by shortening & alter.] (1961) chiefly Brit : WELLINGTON — usu. used in pl.
well-in·formed \-in-'fȯrmd\ adj (15c) 1 : having extensive knowledge esp. of current topics and events 2 : thoroughly knowledgeable in a particular subject
Wel·ling·ton \'we-liŋ-tən\ n [Arthur Wellesley, 1st Duke of Wellington] (1817) : a boot having a loose top with the front usu. coming to or above the knee — usu. used in pl.
well-in·ten·tioned \,wel-in-'ten(t)-shənd\ adj (1598) : WELL-MEANING
well-knit \'wel-'nit\ adj (15c) : firmly knit ⟨a ~ group⟩; esp : firmly and strongly constructed, compacted, or framed ⟨a ~ drama⟩
well-known \-'nōn\ adj (15c) : fully or widely known
well-mean·ing \-'mē-niŋ\ adj (1532) 1 : having good intentions ⟨~ but misguided idealists⟩ 2 : based on good intentions ⟨~ advice⟩
well-meant \-'ment\ adj (15c) : WELL-MEANING 2
well-ness \'wel-nəs\ n (1654) : the quality or state of being in good health esp. as an actively sought goal ⟨~ clinics⟩ ⟨lifestyles that promote ~⟩
well-nigh \-'nī\ adv (12c) : ALMOST, NEARLY ⟨~ impossible⟩
well-off \-'ȯf\ adj (1733) 1 : being in good condition or favorable circumstances ⟨doesn't know when he's ~⟩ 2 : having no lack — usu. used with for 3 a : being in easy or affluent circumstances : WELL-TO-DO b : suggesting prosperity ⟨the house had a sleek ~ look⟩
well-oiled \-'ȯild\ adj (1847) : smoothly functioning ⟨a ~ political machine⟩
well-or·dered \-'ȯr-dərd\ adj (1589) 1 : having an orderly procedure or arrangement ⟨a ~ household⟩ 2 : partially ordered with every subset containing a first element and exactly one of the relationships "greater than", "less than", or "equal to" holding for any given pair of elements — **well-or·der·ing** \-'ȯrd-riŋ, -'ȯr-də-\ n
well-read \-'red\ adj (1596) : well informed or deeply versed through reading ⟨~ in history⟩
well-round·ed \-'raŭn-dəd\ adj (1875) : fully or broadly developed: as a : having a broad educational background ⟨schools that turn out ~ graduates⟩ b : COMPREHENSIVE ⟨a ~ program of activities⟩

well–set \-'set\ *adj* (14c)   **1** : well or firmly established ⟨~ in his own values —William Johnson⟩   **2** : strongly built ⟨a ~ athlete⟩

well–spo·ken \'wel-'spō-kən\ *adj* (15c)   **1** : speaking well, fitly, or courteously   **2** : spoken with propriety ⟨~ words⟩

well–spring \-,spriŋ\ *n* (bef. 12c) : a source of continual supply ⟨a ~ of information⟩

well–tak·en \-'tā-kən\ *adj* (1761) : WELL-GROUNDED, JUSTIFIABLE ⟨your point is ~⟩

well–thought–of \wel-'thȯt-,əv, -,äv\ *adj* (1579) : being of good repute

well–timed \'wel-'tīmd\ *adj* (ca. 1656) : happening at an opportune moment : TIMELY ⟨a ~ announcement⟩

well–to–do \,wel-tə-'dü\ *adj* (1825) : having more than adequate financial resources : PROSPEROUS ⟨a ~ family⟩

well–turned \'wel-'tərnd\ *adj* (1616)   **1** : symmetrically shaped or rounded : SHAPELY   **2** : concisely and appropriately expressed ⟨a ~ phrase⟩   **3** : expertly rounded or turned ⟨a ~ column⟩

well–wish·er \'wel-,wi-shər, -'wi-\ *n* (1590) : one that wishes well to another — **well–wish·ing** \-shiŋ\ *adj or n*

well–worn \-'wȯrn, -'wȯrn\ *adj* (1621)   **1 a** : made trite by overuse : HACKNEYED ⟨a ~ quotation⟩   **b** : having been much used or worn ⟨~ shoes⟩   **2** *archaic* : worn well or properly

welsh \'welsh, 'welch\ *vi* [prob. fr. *Welsh*, adj.] (1905)   **1** : to avoid payment — used with *on* ⟨~ed on his debts⟩   **2** : to break one's word : RENEGE ⟨~ed on their promises⟩ — **welsh·er** *n*

Welsh \'welsh *also* 'welch\ *n* [ME *Walsche, Welsse,* fr. *walisch, welisch,* adj., Welsh, fr. OE *wælisc, welisc* Celtic, Welsh, foreign, fr. OE *Wealh* Celt, Welshman, foreigner, of Celt origin; akin to the source of L *Volcae,* a Celtic people of southeastern Gaul] (bef. 12c)   **1** : the Celtic language of the Welsh people   **2** *pl in constr* : the natives or inhabitants of Wales   **3** : WELSH PONY — **Welsh** *adj*

Welsh black *n* (1919) : any of a breed of hardy medium-sized thick-haired horned black cattle of Welsh origin that are raised for meat and milk

Welsh cob *n* (1947) : any of a breed of medium-sized cobby horses that were developed by interbreeding Welsh mountain ponies with larger horses

Welsh corgi *n* (1926) : a short-legged long-backed dog with foxy head of either of two breeds of Welsh origin: **a** : CARDIGAN WELSH CORGI   **b** : PEMBROKE WELSH CORGI

Welsh·man \-mən\ *n* (13c) : a native or inhabitant of Wales

Welsh mountain pony *n* (1947) : any of a breed of small sturdy ponies native to the mountains of Wales that do not exceed 12.2 hands (124 centimeters) in height

Welsh pony *n* (1771) : a pony of any of several breeds of Welsh origin; *esp* : any of a breed of riding and light draft ponies measuring 12.2 to 13.2 hands (124 to 134 centimeters) in height

Welsh rabbit *n* (1725) : melted often seasoned cheese poured over toast or crackers

Welsh rare·bit \-'rar-bət, -'rer-\ *n* [by alter.] (1785) : WELSH RABBIT

Welsh springer spaniel *n* (ca. 1929) : any of a breed of red and white or orange and white small-eared springer spaniels of Welsh origin

Welsh corgi: *1* Pembroke, *2* Cardigan

Welsh terrier *n* (1885) : any of a breed of wiry-coated terriers resembling Airedales but smaller and developed in Wales for hunting

Welsh·wom·an \'welsh-,wu̇-mən *also* 'welch-\ *n* (15c) : a woman who is a native or inhabitant of Wales

¹welt \'welt\ *n* [ME *welte*] (15c)   **1** : a strip between a shoe sole and upper through which they are stitched or stapled together   **2** : a doubled edge, strip, insert, or seam (as on a garment) for ornament or reinforcement   **3 a** : a ridge or lump raised on the body usu. by a blow   **b** : a heavy blow

²welt *vt* (15c)   **1** : to furnish with a welt   **2 a** : to raise a welt on the body of   **b** : to hit hard

welt·an·schau·ung \'velt-,än-,shau̇-əŋ\ *n, pl* **weltanschauungs** \-əŋz\ *or* **welt·an·schau·ung·en** \-əŋ-ən\ *often cap* [G, fr. *Welt* world + *Anschauung* view] (1868) : a comprehensive conception or apprehension of the world esp. from a specific standpoint

¹wel·ter \'wel-tər\ *vi* **wel·tered; wel·ter·ing** \-t(ə-)riŋ\ [ME; akin to MD *welteren* to roll, OHG *walzan,* Lith *volioti,* L *volvere* — more at VOLUBLE] (14c)   **1 a** : WRITHE, TOSS; *also* : WALLOW   **b** : to rise and fall or toss about in or with waves   **2** : to become deeply sunk, soaked, or involved   **3** : to be in turmoil

²welter *n* (1596)   **1** : a state of wild disorder : TURMOIL   **2** : a chaotic mass or jumble ⟨a bewildering ~ of data⟩

³welter *n* (1900) : WELTERWEIGHT

wel·ter·weight \'wel-tər-,wāt\ *n* [*welter* (prob. fr. ¹*welt*) + *weight*] (ca. 1892) : a boxer in a weight division having a maximum limit of 147 pounds — compare LIGHTWEIGHT, MIDDLEWEIGHT

welt·schmerz \'velt-,shmerts\ *n, often cap* [G, fr. *Welt* world + *Schmerz* pain] (1875)   **1** : mental depression or apathy caused by comparison of the actual state of the world with an ideal state   **2** : a mood of sentimental sadness

¹wen \'wen\ *n* [ME *wenn,* fr. OE; akin to MLG *wene* wen] (bef. 12c) : an abnormal growth or a cyst protruding from a surface esp. of the skin

²wen *var of* WYNN

¹wench \'wench\ *n* [ME *wenche,* short for *wenchel* child, fr. OE *wencel;* akin to OHG *wankōn* to totter, waver and prob. to OHG *winchan* to stagger — more at WINK] (14c)   **1 a** : a young woman : GIRL   **b** : a female servant   **2** : a lewd woman : PROSTITUTE

²wench *vi* (1599) : to consort with lewd women; *esp* : to practice fornication — **wench·er** *n*

wend \'wend\ *vb* [ME, fr. OE *wendan;* akin to OHG *wenten* to turn, OE *windan* to twist — more at WIND] (bef. 12c)   ~ *vi* : to direct one's course : TRAVEL   ~ *vt* : to proceed on (one's way) : DIRECT

Wend \'wend\ *n* [G *Wende,* fr. OHG *Winida;* akin to OE *Winedas,* pl., Wends] (1786) : a member of a Slavic people of eastern Germany

¹Wend·ish \'wen-dish\ *adj* (1614) : of or relating to the Wends or their language

²Wendish *n* (1617) : the West Slavic language of the Wends

went [ME, past & pp. of *wenden* to wend] *past of* GO

wen·tle·trap \'wen-t²l-,trap\ *n* [D *wenteltrap* winding stair, fr. MD *wendeltrappe,* fr. *wendel* turning + *trappe* stairs] (1758) : any of a family (Epitoniidae) of marine snails with usu. white shells; *also* : one of the shells

wept *past and past part of* WEEP

were [ME *were* (suppletive sing. past subj. & 2d sing. past indic. of *been* to be), *weren* (suppletive past pl. of *been*), fr. OE *wǣre* (sing. past subj. & 2d sing. past indic. of *wesan* to be), *wǣron* (past pl. indic. of *wesan*), *wǣren* (past pl. subj. of *wesan*) — more at WAS] *past 2d sing, past pl, or past subjunctive of* BE

we're \'wir, 'wər, 'wē-ər\ (1608) : we are

weren't \(')wərnt, 'wər-ənt\ (1865) : were not

were·wolf \'wir-,wu̇lf, 'wer-, 'wər-\ *n, pl* **were·wolves** \-,wu̇lvz\ [ME, fr. OE *werwulf* (akin to OHG *werwolf* werewolf), fr. *wer* man + *wulf* wolf — more at VIRILE, WOLF] (bef. 12c) : a person transformed into a wolf or capable of assuming a wolf's form

wer·gild \'wər-,gild\ *or* **wer·geld** \-,geld\ *n* [ME *wergeld,* fr. OE, fr. *wer* man + *-geld,* alter. of *gield, geld* payment, tribute — more at GELD] (13c) : the value set in Anglo-Saxon and Germanic law upon human life in accordance with rank and paid as compensation to the kindred or lord of a slain person

wert \'wərt\ *archaic past 2d sing of* BE

wes·kit \'wes-kət\ *n* [alter. of *waistcoat*] (1856) : VEST 2a

Wes·ley·an·ism \'wes-lē-ə-,ni-zəm *also* 'wez-\ *n* (1774) : METHODISM 1; *specif* : the system of Arminian Methodism taught by John Wesley — **Wes·ley·an** \-lē-ən\ *adj or n*

¹west \'west\ *adv* [ME, fr. OE; akin to OHG *westar* to the west and prob. to L *vesper* evening, Gk *hesperos*] (bef. 12c) : to, toward, or in the west

²west *adj* (bef. 12c)   **1** : situated toward or at the west ⟨the ~ exit⟩   **2** : coming from the west ⟨a ~ wind⟩

³west *n* (12c)   **1 a** : the general direction of sunset : the direction to the left of one facing north   **b** : the compass point directly opposite to east   **2** *cap* **a** : regions or countries lying to the west of a specified or implied point of orientation   **b** : the noncommunist countries of Europe and America   **3** : the end of a church opposite the chancel   **4** *often cap* **a** : the one of four positions at 90-degree intervals that lies to the west or at the left of a diagram   **b** : a person (as a bridge player) occupying this position during a specified activity

west·bound \'wes(t)-,bau̇nd\ *adj* (1881) : traveling or heading west

west by north (1760) : a compass point that is one point north of due west : N78°45'W

west by south (1577) : a compass point that is one point south of due west : S78°45'W

west·er \'wes-tər\ *vi* **west·ered; west·er·ing** \-t(ə-)riŋ\ [ME *westren,* fr. ¹*west*] (14c) : to turn or move westward ⟨the half moon ~s low —A. E. Housman⟩

¹west·er·ly \'wes-tər-lē\ *adj or adv* [obs. *wester* western] (15c)   **1** : situated toward or belonging to the west ⟨the ~ end of the farm⟩   **2** : coming from the west ⟨a ~ breeze⟩

²westerly *n, pl* **-lies** (1876) : a wind from the west

¹west·ern \'wes-tərn\ *adj* [ME *westerne,* fr. OE; akin to OHG *westrōni* western, OE *west*] (bef. 12c)   **1 a** : coming from the west ⟨a ~ storm⟩   **b** : lying toward the west   **2** *cap* : of, relating to, or characteristic of a region conventionally designated West: as   **a** : steeped in or stemming from the Greco-Roman traditions   **b** : of or relating to the noncommunist countries of Europe and America   **c** : of or relating to the American West   **3** *cap* : of or relating to the Roman Catholic or Protestant segment of Christianity ⟨*Western* liturgies⟩ — **west·ern·most** \-,mōst\ *adj*

²western *n* (1612)   **1** : one that is produced in or characteristic of a western region and esp. the western U.S.   **2** *often cap* : a novel, story, motion picture, or broadcast dealing with life in the western U.S. esp. during the latter half of the 19th century

Western blot *n* [after *Southern blot*] (1983) : a blot that consists of a nitrocellulose sheet containing spots of protein for identification by a suitable molecular probe and is used esp. for the detection of antibodies — **Western blotting** *n*

West·ern·er \'wes-tə(r)-nər\ *n* (1599)   **1** : a native or inhabitant of the West; *esp* : a native or resident of the western part of the U.S.   **2** : one advocating the adoption of western European culture esp. in 19th century Russia

western hemisphere *n, often cap W&H* (1624) : the half of the earth comprising No. and So. America and surrounding waters

west·ern·i·sa·tion, west·ern·ise *Brit var of* WESTERNIZATION, WESTERNIZE

west·ern·i·za·tion \,wes-tər-nə-'zā-shən\ *n, often cap* (1904) : conversion to or adoption of western traditions or techniques

west·ern·ize \'wes-tər-,nīz\ *vb* **-ized; -iz·ing** *often cap, vt* (1837) : to imbue with qualities native to or associated with a western region and esp. the noncommunist countries of Europe and America   ~ *vi* : to become westernized

western omelet *n* (1951) : an omelet made usu. with diced ham, green pepper, and onion — called also *Denver omelet*

western red cedar *n* (1886) : RED CEDAR 2; *also* : its wood

western saddle *n, often cap W* (1897) : a deep-seated saddle with a high pommel and broad skirts and fenders used orig. by cattlemen — called also *stock saddle;* see SADDLE illustration

---

\ə\ abut   \ᵊ\ kitten, F table   \ər\ further   \a\ ash   \ā\ ace   \ä\ mop, mar
\au̇\ out   \ch\ chin   \e\ bet   \ē\ easy   \g\ go   \i\ hit   \ī\ ice   \j\ job
\ŋ\ sing   \ō\ go   \ȯ\ law   \ȯi\ boy   \th\ thin   \t̲h̲\ the   \ü\ loot   \u̇\ foot
\y\ yet   \zh\ vision   \ȧ, k̲, ⁿ, œ, œ̄, ᵫ, ᵬ, ᶾ\ see Guide to Pronunciation

western sandwich n (1926) : a sandwich filled with a western omelet — called also *Denver sandwich*

western swing n (1973) : swing music played typically on country music instruments (as guitar, fiddle, or steel guitar)

West Germanic n (1894) : a subdivision of the Germanic languages including English, Frisian, Dutch, and German — see INDO-EUROPEAN LANGUAGES table

West Highland white terrier n (ca. 1904) : any of a breed of small white long-coated terriers developed in Scotland — called also *West·ie* \'wes-tē\

west·ing \'wes-tiŋ\ n (1628) : westerly progress : a going westward

west–northwest n (15c) : a compass point that is two points north of due west : N67°30'W

West·pha·lian ham \wes(t)-'fāl-yən-, -'fā-lē-ən-\ n [*Westphalia*, Germany] (1664) : a ham of distinctive flavor produced by smoking with juniper brush

West Saxon n (14c) 1 : a member or a descendant of the Saxons who occupied England largely south of the Thames, west of the Downs, and east of Dartmoor 2 : a dialect of Old English used as the chief literary dialect in England before the Norman Conquest

west–southwest n (1555) : a compass point that is two points south of due west : S67°30'W

¹**west·ward** \'wes-twərd\ adv or adj (bef. 12c) : toward the west — **west·wards** \-twərdz\ adv

²**westward** n (1652) : westward direction or part ⟨sail to the ~⟩

¹**wet** \'wet\ adj **wet·ter**; **wet·test** [ME, partly fr. pp. of *weten* to wet & partly fr. OE *wǣt* wet; akin to ON *vātr* wet, OE *wǣter* water] (bef. 12c) 1 a : consisting of, containing, covered with, or soaked with liquid (as water) b *of natural gas* : containing appreciable quantities of readily condensable hydrocarbons 2 : RAINY 3 : still moist enough to smudge or smear ⟨~ paint⟩ 4 a : DRUNK 1a ⟨a ~ driver⟩ b : having or advocating a policy permitting the manufacture and sale of alcoholic beverages ⟨a ~ county⟩ ⟨a ~ candidate⟩ 5 : preserved in liquid 6 : employing or done by means of or in the presence of water or other liquid ⟨~ extraction of copper⟩ 7 : overly sentimental 8 *Brit* a : lacking strength of character : WEAK, SPINELESS ⟨thought him ~ and violence petrified him —William Golding⟩ b : belonging to the moderate or liberal wing of the Conservative party — **wet·ly** adv — **wet·ness** n — **all wet** : completely wrong : in error — **wet behind the ears** : IMMATURE, INEXPERIENCED

syn WET, DAMP, DANK, MOIST, HUMID mean covered or more or less soaked with liquid. WET usu. implies saturation but may suggest a covering of a surface with water or something (as paint) not yet dry ⟨slipped on the *wet* pavement⟩. DAMP implies a slight or moderate absorption and often connotes an unpleasant degree of moisture ⟨clothes will mildew if stored in a *damp* place⟩. DANK implies a more distinctly disagreeable or unwholesome dampness ⟨a prisoner in a cold, *dank* cell⟩. MOIST applies to what is slightly damp or not felt as dry ⟨treat the injury with *moist* heat⟩. HUMID applies to the presence of much water vapor in the air ⟨a hot, *humid* climate⟩.

²**wet** n (bef. 12c) 1 : WATER; *also* : MOISTURE, WETNESS 2 : rainy weather : RAIN 3 : an advocate of a policy permitting the sale of intoxicating liquors 4 *Brit* : one who is wet

³**wet** vb **wet** or **wet·ted**; **wet·ting** [ME, fr. OE *wǣtan*, fr. *wǣt*, adj.] vt (bef. 12c) 1 : to make wet 2 : to urinate in or on ~ vi 1 : to become wet 2 : URINATE — **wet one's whistle** : to take a drink esp. of liquor

wet·back \'wet-,bak\ n [fr. the practice of wading or swimming the Rio Grande where it forms the U.S.-Mexico border] (1929) : a Mexican who enters the U.S. illegally — sometimes taken to be offensive

wet bar n (1967) : a bar for mixing drinks (as in a home) that contains a sink with running water

wet blanket n (1857) : one that quenches or dampens enthusiasm or pleasure

wet down vt (1840) : to dampen by sprinkling with water

wet dream n (1851) : an erotic dream culminating in orgasm and in the male accompanied by seminal emission

weth·er \'we-thər\ n [ME, ram, fr. OE; akin to OHG *widar* ram, L *vitulus* calf, *vetus* old, Gk *etos* year] (bef. 12c) : a male sheep castrated before sexual maturity; *also* : a castrated male goat

wet·land \'wet-,land, -lənd\ n (1778) : land or areas (as tidal flats or swamps) containing much soil moisture — usu. used in pl.

wet–nurse vt (1784) 1 : to act as wet nurse to 2 : to give constant and often excessive care to

wet nurse n (1620) : a woman who cares for and suckles children not her own

wet suit n (1955) : a close-fitting suit made of material (as sponge rubber) that traps a thin layer of water against the body to retain body heat and that is worn (as by a skin diver) esp. in cold water

wet·ta·bil·i·ty \,we-tə-'bi-lə-tē\ n (1913) : the quality or state of being wettable : the degree to which something can be wet

wet·ta·ble \'we-tə-bəl\ adj (1885) : capable of being wetted

wet·ter \'we-tər\ n (1737) : one that wets; *also* : WETTING AGENT

wetting agent n (1927) : a substance that by becoming adsorbed prevents a surface from being repellent to a wetting liquid and is used esp. in mixing solids with liquids or spreading liquids on surfaces

wet·tish \'we-tish\ adj (1648) : somewhat wet : MOIST

wet wash n (1916) : laundry returned damp and not ironed

we've \'wēv\ (1742) : we have

¹**whack** \'hwak, 'wak\ vb [prob. imit. of the sound of a blow] vt (1719) 1 a : to strike with a smart or resounding blow b : to cut with or as if with a whack : CHOP 2 *chiefly Brit* : to get the better of : DEFEAT ~ vi : to strike a smart or resounding blow — **whack·er** n

²**whack** n (1736) 1 a : a smart or resounding blow; *also* : the sound of or as if of such a blow b : a critical attack 2 : PORTION, SHARE 3 : CONDITION, STATE 4 a : an opportunity or attempt to do something ⟨take a ~ at it⟩ b : a single action or occasion ⟨borrowed $50 all at one ~⟩ — **out of whack** 1 : out of proper order or shape ⟨threw his knee *out of whack*⟩ 2 : not in accord ⟨feeling *out of whack* with her contemporaries —S. E. Rubin⟩

whacked–out \'(h)wakt-,aút, ,(h)wakt-\ adj (1967) 1 : WORN-OUT, EXHAUSTED ⟨whacky ⟨a ~ parody⟩ 3 : STONED ⟨~ on drugs⟩

¹**whack·ing** \'hwa-kiŋ, 'wa-\ adj (1806) : very large : WHOPPING

²**whacking** adv (1853) : VERY ⟨a ~ good story⟩

whacko \'hwa-(,)kō, 'wa-\ *var of* WACKO

whack off vb (1969) : MASTURBATE — usu. considered vulgar

whack up vt (ca. 1893) : to divide into shares

whacky \'hwa-kē, 'wa-\ *var of* WACKY

¹**whale** \'hwā(ə)l, 'wā(ə)l\ n, pl **whales** *often attrib* [ME, fr. OE *hwæl*; akin to OHG *hwal* whale and perh. to L *squalus* sea fish] (bef. 12c) 1 *or pl* **whale** : CETACEAN; *esp* : one (as a sperm whale or killer whale) of larger size 2 : one that is impressive esp. in size ⟨a ~ of a difference⟩ ⟨a ~ of a good time⟩ — **whale·like** \-,līk\ adj

²**whale** vi **whaled**; **whal·ing** (1700) : to engage in whale fishing

³**whale** vt **whaled**; **whal·ing** [origin unknown] (ca. 1790) 1 : LASH, THRASH 2 : to strike or hit vigorously 3 : to defeat soundly

whale·back \'hwā(ə)l-,bak, 'wā(ə)l-\ n (1886) : something shaped like the back of a whale

whale·boat \-,bōt\ n (1682) 1 : a long narrow rowboat made with both ends sharp and raking, often steered with an oar, and formerly used by whalers for hunting whales 2 : a long narrow rowboat or motorboat resembling the original whaleboats and often carried by warships and merchant ships

whale·bone \-,bōn\ n (1601) 1 : BALEEN 2 : an article made of whalebone

whalebone whale n (1725) : BALEEN WHALE

whal·er \'hwā-lər, 'wā-\ n (1684) 1 : a person or ship engaged in whale fishing 2 : WHALEBOAT 2

whale shark n (ca. 1885) : a shark (*Rhincodon typus*) of warm waters that has small teeth, feeds chiefly on plankton strained by its gill rakers, may attain a length of up to 60 feet (18.3 meters), and is the largest known fish

whal·ing \'hwā-liŋ, 'wā-\ n (1688) : the occupation of catching and extracting commercial products from whales

¹**wham** \'hwam, 'wam\ n [imit.] (1739) 1 : a solid blow 2 : the loud sound of a hard impact

²**wham** or **wham·mo** \'hwa-(,)mō, 'wa-\ adv (1924) : with violent abruptness ⟨everything seemed to be going well, when ~ the deal fell through⟩

³**wham** vb **whammed**; **wham·ming** vt (1925) : to propel, strike, or beat so as to produce a loud impact ~ vi : to hit or explode with a loud impact

wham·my \'hwa-mē, 'wa-\ n, pl **whammies** [prob. fr. ¹*wham*] (1940) 1 a : a supernatural power bringing bad luck b : a magic curse or spell 2 : a potent force or attack; *specif* : a paralyzing or lethal blow

¹**whang** \'hwaŋ, 'waŋ\ n [alter. of ME *thong, thwang*] (1536) 1 *dial* a : THONG b : RAWHIDE 2 *Brit* : a large piece : CHUNK 3 : PENIS — often considered vulgar

²**whang** vt (1684) 1 *dial* : BEAT, THRASH 2 : to propel or strike with force ~ vi : to beat or work with force or violence

³**whang** n [imit.] (ca. 1824) : a loud sharp vibrant or resonant sound

⁴**whang** vi (1875) : to make a whang ~ vt : to strike with a whang

whan·gee \hwaŋ-'ē, waŋ-, -'gē\ n [prob. modif. of Chin (Beijing) *huáng* bamboo] (1790) 1 : any of several Chinese bamboos (genus *Phyllostachys*) 2 : a walking stick or riding crop of whangee

whap \'hwäp, 'wäp\ *var of* WHOP

wharf \'hwórf, 'wórf\ n, pl **wharves** \'hwórvz, 'wórvz\ *also* **wharfs** [ME, fr. OE *hwearf* embankment, wharf; akin to OE *hweorfan* to turn, OHG *hwerban*, Gk *karpos* wrist] (bef. 12c) 1 : a structure built along or at an angle from the shore of navigable waters so that ships may lie alongside to receive and discharge cargo and passengers 2 *obs* : the bank of a river or the shore of the sea

wharf·age \'hwór-fij, 'wór-\ n (15c) 1 a : the provision or the use of a wharf b : the handling or stowing of goods on a wharf 2 : the charge for the use of a wharf 3 : the wharf accommodations of a place : WHARVES

wharf·in·ger \-fən-jər\ n [irreg. fr. *wharfage*] (1552) : the operator or manager of a commercial wharf

wharf·mas·ter \'hwórf-,mas-tər, 'wórf-\ n (1618) : the manager of a wharf : WHARFINGER

¹**what** \'hwät, 'hwot, 'wät, 'wot\ pron [ME, fr. OE *hwæt*, neut. of *hwā* who — more at WHO] (bef. 12c) 1 a (1) — used as an interrogative expressing inquiry about the identity, nature, or value of an object or matter ⟨~ is this⟩ ⟨~ is wealth without friends⟩ ⟨~ does he earn⟩ ⟨~ hath God wrought⟩ (2) — often used to ask for repetition of an utterance or part of an utterance not properly heard or understood ⟨you said ~⟩ b (1) *archaic* : WHO 1 — used as an interrogative expressing inquiry about the identity of a person (2) — used as an interrogative expressing inquiry about the character, nature, occupation, position, or role of a person ⟨~ do you think I am, a fool⟩ ⟨~ is she, that all our swains commend her —Shak.⟩ c — used as an exclamation expressing surprise or excitement and frequently introducing a question ⟨~, no breakfast⟩ d — used in expressions directing attention to a statement that the speaker is about to make ⟨you know ~⟩ e — used at the end of a question to express inquiry about additional possibilities ⟨is it raining, or snowing, or ~⟩ f *chiefly Brit* — used at the end of an utterance as a form of tag question ⟨a clever play, ~⟩ 2 *chiefly dial* : ⁴THAT 1, WHICH 3, WHO 3 3 : that which : the one or ones that ⟨no income but ~ he gets from his writings⟩ — sometimes used in reference to a clause or phrase that is yet to come or is not yet complete ⟨gave also, ~ is more valuable, understanding⟩ 4 a : WHATEVER 1a ⟨say ~ you will⟩ b *obs* : WHOEVER — **what for** 1 : for what purpose or reason : WHY — usu. used with the other words of a question between *what* and *for* ⟨what did you do that *for*⟩ except when used alone 2 : harsh treatment esp. by blows or by a sharp reprimand ⟨gave him *what for* in violent Spanish —*New Yorker*⟩ — **what have you** : WHATNOT ⟨novels, plays, short stories, travelogues, and *what have you* —Haldeen Braddy⟩ — **what if** 1 : what will or would be the result if 2 : what does it matter if — **what of** 1 : what is the situation with respect to 2 : what importance can be assigned to — **what's what** : the true state of things ⟨knows *what's what* when it comes to fashion⟩ — **what though** : what does it matter if ⟨*what though* the rose have prickles, yet 'tis plucked —Shak.⟩

²**what** adv (bef. 12c) 1 *obs* : WHY 2 : in what respect : HOW ⟨~ does he care⟩ 3 — used to introduce prepositional phrases in parallel construction or a prepositional phrase that expresses cause and usu. has more than one object; used principally before phrases beginning with *with* ⟨~ with unemployment increasing⟩ ⟨~ with the war, ~ with the

sweat, ~ with the gallows, and ~ with poverty, I am custom-shrunk —Shak.⟩
³**what** *adj* (13c) **1 a** — used as an interrogative expressing inquiry about the identity, nature, or value of a person, object, or matter ⟨~ minerals do we export⟩ **b** : how remarkable or striking for good or bad qualities — used esp. in exclamatory utterances and dependent clauses ⟨~ mountains⟩ ⟨remember ~ fun we had⟩ ⟨~ a suggestion⟩ ⟨~ a charming girl⟩ **2 a** (1) : WHATEVER 1a (2) : ANY ⟨ornament of ~ description soever⟩ **b** : the . . . that : as much or as many . . . as ⟨rescued ~ survivors they found⟩
what all \'hwä-ˌdȯl, 'wä-, '(h)wə-\ *pron* (1702) : WHATNOT
what·cha·ma·call·it \'hwä-chə-mə-ˌkȯ-lət, 'wä-, '(h)wə-\ *n* [alter. of *what you may call it*] (1928) : THINGAMAJIG
¹**what·ev·er** \hwät-'e-vər, wät-, ˌ(ˌ)(h)wət-\ *pron* (14c) **1 a** : anything or everything that ⟨take ~ you want⟩ **b** : no matter what ⟨~ he says, they won't believe him⟩ **c** : WHATNOT ⟨buffalo or rhinoceros or ~ —Alan Moorehead⟩ **2** : WHAT 1a(1) — used to express astonishment or perplexity ⟨~ do you mean by that⟩
²**whatever** *adj* (14c) **1 a** : any . . . that : all . . . that ⟨buy peace . . . on ~ terms could be obtained —C. S. Forester⟩ **b** : no matter what ⟨money, in ~ hands, will confer power —Samuel Johnson⟩ **2** : of any kind at all — used after the substantive it modifies with *any* or with an expressed or implied negative ⟨in any order ~ —W. G. Moulton⟩ ⟨no food ~⟩
³**whatever** *adv* (1870) : in any case : whatever the case may be — sometimes used interjectionally to suggest the unimportance of a decision between alternatives
what–if \ˌhwät-'if, ˌwät-, ˌ(h)wət-\ *n* (1970) : a suppositional question
what·ness \'hwät-nəs, 'wät-, '(h)wət-\ *n* (1611) : QUIDDITY 1
¹**what·not** \'hwät-ˌnät, 'wät-, '(h)wət-\ *pron* [*what not?*] (1540) : any of various other things that might also be mentioned ⟨paper clips, pins, and ~⟩
²**whatnot** *n* (1602) **1** : a nondescript person or thing **2** : a light open set of shelves for bric-a-brac
what·sit \'hwät-sət, 'wät-, 'wət-\ *or* **what·sis** \-səs\ *also* **what–is–it** \-iz-ət\ *n* [*whatsit* & *whatsis* contr. of *what-is-it*] (ca. 1882) : THINGAMAJIG
what·so·ev·er \ˌhwät-sə-'we-vər, ˌwät-, ˌ(h)wət-\ *pron or adj* (13c) : WHATEVER
whaup \'hwȯp, 'wȯp\ *n, pl* **whaup** *also* **whaups** [imit.] (ca. 1512) *chiefly Scot* : a European curlew (*Numenius arquata*)
wheal \'hwē(ə)l, 'wē(ə)l\ *n* [alter. of ¹*wale*] (1808) : a suddenly formed elevation of the skin surface: as **a** : WELT **b** : a flat burning or itching eminence on the skin
wheat \'hwēt, 'wēt\ *n, often attrib* [ME *whete*, fr. OE *hwǣte*; akin to OHG *weizzi* wheat, *hwīz, wiz* white — more at WHITE] (bef. 12c) **1** : a cereal grain that yields a fine white flour, is the chief breadstuff of temperate climates, is used also in pastas (as macaroni or spaghetti), and is important in animal feeds **2** : any of various annual grasses (genus *Triticum* and esp. *T. aestivum* and *T. turgidum*) of wide climatic adaptability that are cultivated in most temperate areas for the wheat they yield **3** : a light yellow
wheat bread *n* (14c) : a bread made of a combination of white and whole wheat flours as distinguished from bread made entirely of white or whole wheat flour
wheat cake *n* (1772) : a pancake made of wheat flour
wheat·ear \'hwēt-ˌir, 'wēt-\ *n* [back-formation fr. earlier *wheatears* wheatear, prob. by folk etymology or euphemism fr. *white + arse*] (1591) : any of various small thrushes (genus *Oenanthe*) esp. a white-rumped one (*O. oenanthe*) of Eurasia and northern No. America
¹**wheat·en** \'hwē-t²n, 'wē-\ *adj* (bef. 12c) : of, relating to, or made of wheat
²**wheaten** *n* (ca. 1931) : a pale yellowish to ruddy fawn color characteristic of the coat of some dogs
wheat germ *n* (1897) : the embryo of the wheat kernel separated in milling and used esp. as a source of vitamins and protein
wheat rust *n* (1884) : a destructive disease of wheat caused by rust fungi; *also* : a fungus (as *Puccinia graminis*) causing a wheat rust
Wheat·stone bridge \'hwēt-ˌstōn-, 'wēt-, *chiefly Brit* -stən-\ *n* [Sir Charles *Wheatstone*] (1872) : a bridge for measuring electrical resistances that consists of a conductor joining two branches of a circuit
whee \'hwē, 'wē\ *interj* (1898) — used to express delight or exuberance
whee·dle \'hwē-d²l, 'wē-d²l\ *vb* **whee·dled**; **whee·dling** \'(h)wēd-liŋ, '(h)wē-d²l-iŋ\ [origin unknown] *vt* (ca. 1661) **1** : to influence or entice by soft words or flattery **2** : to gain or get by wheedling ⟨~ one's way into favor⟩ ~ *vi* : to use soft words or flattery
¹**wheel** \'hwē(ə)l, 'wē(ə)l\ *n, often attrib* [ME, fr. OE *hwēogol, hwēol*; akin to ON *hvēl* wheel, Gk *kyklos* circle, wheel, Skt *cakra*, L *colere* to cultivate, inhabit, Skt *carati* he moves, wanders] (bef. 12c) **1** : a circular frame of hard material that may be solid, partly solid, or spoked and that is capable of turning on an axle **2** : a contrivance or apparatus having as its principal part a wheel: as **a** : a chiefly medieval instrument of torture designed for mutilating a victim (as by stretching or disjointing) **b** : BICYCLE **c** : any of many revolving disks or drums used as gambling paraphernalia **d** : POTTER'S WHEEL **e** : STEERING WHEEL **3 a** : an imaginary turning wheel symbolizing the inconstancy of fortune **b** : a recurring course, development, or action : CYCLE **4** : something resembling a wheel in shape or motion: as **a** : a round flat cheese **b** : a firework that rotates while burning **c** : a propeller on a boat **5 a** : a curving or circular movement **b** : a rotation or turn usu. about an axis or center; *specif* : a turning movement of troops or ships in line in which the units preserve alignment and relative positions as they change direction **6 a** : a moving or essential part of something compared to a machine ⟨the ~s of government⟩ **b** : a directing or controlling force **c** : a person of importance esp. in an organization ⟨a big ~⟩ **7** : the refrain or burden of a song **8 a** : a circuit of theaters or places of entertainment **b** : a sports league **9** *pl, slang* : a wheeled vehicle; *esp* : AUTOMOBILE — **wheel·less** \'hwē(ə)l-ləs, 'wē(ə)l-\ *adj*

wheel 1: *1* hub, *2* spoke, *3* felly, *4* tire

²**wheel** *vi* (13c) **1** : to turn on or as if on an axis : REVOLVE **2** : to change direction as if revolving on a pivot ⟨the battalion would have ~ed to the flank —Walter Bernstein⟩ ⟨her mind will ~ around to the other extreme —Liam O'Flaherty⟩ **3** : to move or extend in a circle or curve ⟨birds in ~ing flight⟩ ⟨valleys where young cotton ~ed slowly in fanlike rows —William Faulkner⟩ **4** : to drive or go on or as if on wheels or in a wheeled vehicle ~ *vt* **1** : to cause to turn on or as if on an axis : ROTATE **2** : to convey or move on or as if on wheels or in a wheeled vehicle; *esp* : to drive (a vehicle) at high speed **3** : to cause to change direction as if revolving on a pivot **4** : to make or perform in a circle or curve — **wheel and deal** : to make deals or do business esp. shrewdly or briskly
wheel and axle *n* (ca. 1773) : a mechanical device consisting of a grooved wheel turned by a cord or chain with a rigidly attached axle (as for winding up a weight) together with the supporting standards
wheel animal *n* (1788) : ROTIFER
wheel animalcule *n* (1834) : ROTIFER
¹**wheel·bar·row** \'hwē(ə)l-ˌbar-(ˌ)ō, 'wē(ə)l-\ *n* (14c) : a small usu. single-wheeled vehicle that is used for carrying small loads and is fitted with handles at the rear by which it can be pushed and guided
²**wheelbarrow** *vt* (1721) : to convey in a wheelbarrow
wheel·base \'hwē(ə)l-ˌbās, 'wē(ə)l-\ *n* (1886) : the distance in inches between the front and rear axles of an automotive vehicle
wheel bug *n* (1815) : a large No. American bug (*Arilus cristatus*) that has a high serrated crest on its prothorax and preys on other insects
wheel·chair \'hwē(ə)l-ˌcher, 'wē(ə)l-, -ˌchar\ *n* (ca. 1700) : a chair mounted on wheels esp. for the use of disabled persons
wheeled \'hwē(ə)ld, 'wē(ə)ld\ *adj* (1606) **1** : equipped with wheels ⟨~ vehicles⟩ **2** : moving or functioning by means of wheels ⟨~ traffic⟩
wheel·er \'hwē-lər, 'wē-\ *n* (1683) **1** : one that wheels **2** : a draft animal (as a horse) pulling in the position nearest the front wheels of a wagon **3** : something (as a vehicle or ship) that has wheels — used esp. in combination ⟨side-*wheeler*⟩
wheeler and dealer *n, pl* **wheelers and dealers** (1966) : WHEELER-DEALER
wheel·er–deal·er \ˌhwē-lər-'dē-lər, ˌwē-\ *n* (1954) : a shrewd operator esp. in business or politics
wheel·horse \'hwē(ə)l-ˌhȯrs, 'wē(ə)l-\ *n* (1708) **1** : a horse (as in a tandem) in a position nearest the wheels **2** : a steady and effective worker esp. in a political body
wheel·house \-ˌhau̇s\ *n* (1835) : PILOTHOUSE
wheel·ie \'hwē-lē, 'wē-\ *n* (ca. 1965) : a maneuver in which a wheeled vehicle (as a bicycle) is momentarily balanced on its rear wheel or wheels
wheel·ing \'hwē-liŋ, 'wē-\ *n* (15c) **1** : the act or process of one that wheels **2** : the condition of a road relative to passage on wheels
wheel lock *n* (1670) : a gun's lock for a muzzle-loading firearm in which sparks are struck from a flint or a piece of iron pyrites by a revolving wheel
wheel·man \'hwē(ə)l-mən, 'wē(ə)l-\ *n* (1865) **1 a** : HELMSMAN **b** : the driver of an automobile **2** : CYCLIST
wheels·man \'hwē(ə)lz-mən, 'wē(ə)lz-\ *n* (1866) : one who steers with a wheel; *esp* : HELMSMAN
wheel–thrown \'hwēl-ˌthrōn, 'wēl-\ *adj* (1975) : made on a potter's wheel ⟨~ pottery⟩
wheel·work \'hwē(ə)l-ˌwərk, 'wē(ə)l-\ *n* (1670) : wheels in gear and their connections in a machine or mechanism
wheel·wright \-ˌrīt\ *n* (13c) : a maker and repairer of wheels and wheeled vehicles
¹**wheen** \'hwēn, 'wēn\ *adj* [ME (Sc) *quheyne*, fr. OE *hwǣne, hwēne*, adv., somewhat, fr. instr. of *hwōn* little, few] (14c) *dial Brit* : FEW 2
²**wheen** *n* (1680) *dial Brit* : a considerable number or amount
¹**wheeze** \'hwēz, 'wēz\ *vi* **wheezed**; **wheez·ing** [ME *whesen*, prob. fr. Scand origin; akin to ON *hvæsa* to hiss; akin to OE *hwǣst* action of blowing, Skt *śvasiti* he blows, snorts] (15c) **1** : to breathe with difficulty. with a whistling sound **2** : to make a sound resembling that of wheezing
²**wheeze** *n* (1834) **1** : a sound of wheezing **2 a** : an often repeated and widely known joke used esp. by entertainers **b** : a trite saying or proverb
wheezy \'hwē-zē, 'wē-\ *adj* **wheez·i·er**; **-est** (1818) **1** : inclined to wheeze **2** : having a wheezing sound — **wheez·i·ly** \-zə-lē\ *adv* — **wheez·i·ness** \-zē-nəs\ *n*
¹**whelk** \'hwelk, 'welk, 'wilk\ *n* [ME *welke*, fr. OE *weoloc*; akin to MD *willoc* whelk and perh. to L *volvere* to turn — more at VOLUBLE] (bef. 12c) : any of numerous large marine snails (as of the genus *Buccinum*); *esp* : one (*B. undatum*) much used as food in Europe
²**whelk** \'hwelk, 'welk\ *n* [ME *whelke*, fr. OE *hwylca*, fr. *hwelian* to suppurate] (bef. 12c) : PAPULE, PUSTULE
whelm \'hwelm, 'welm\ *vb* [ME] *vt* (14c) **1** : to turn (as a dish or vessel) upside down usu. to cover something : cover or engulf completely with usu. disastrous effect **2** : to overcome in thought or feeling : OVERWHELM ~ *vi* : to pass or go over something so as to bury or submerge it
¹**whelp** \'hwelp, 'welp\ *n* [ME, fr. OE *hwelp*; akin to OHG *hwelf* whelp] (bef. 12c) **1** : any of the young of various carnivorous mammals and esp. of the dog **2** : a young boy or girl
²**whelp** *vt* (13c) : to give birth to — used of various carnivores and esp. the dog ~ *vi* : to bring forth young
¹**when** \'hwen, 'wen, (h)wən\ *adv* [ME, fr. OE *hwanne, hwenne*; akin to OHG *hwanne* when, OE *hwā* who — more at WHO] (bef. 12c) **1** : at what time ⟨~ will you return⟩ **2 a** : at or during which time **b** : and then **3** : at a former and usu. less prosperous time ⟨brag fondly of having known him — —Vance Packard⟩
²**when** *conj* [ME, fr. OE *hwanne, hwenne*, fr. *hwanne, hwenne*, adv.] (bef. 12c) **1 a** : at or during the time that : WHILE ⟨went fishing ~ he was a boy⟩ **b** : just at the moment that ⟨stop writing ~ the bell rings⟩ **c**

\ə\ abut \²\ kitten, F table \ər\ further \a\ ash \ā\ ace \ä\ mop, mar
\au̇\ out \ch\ chin \e\ bet \ē\ easy \g\ go \i\ hit \ī\ ice \j\ job
\ŋ\ sing \ō\ go \ȯ\ law \ȯi\ boy \th\ thin \th\ the \ü\ loot \u̇\ foot
\y\ yet \zh\ vision \à, k̲, ⁿ, œ, œ̄, ᵫ, ᵫ̄, �究\ see Guide to Pronunciation

: at any or every time that ⟨∼ he listens to music, he falls asleep⟩ 2 : in the event that : IF ⟨a contestant is disqualified ∼ he disobeys the rules⟩ 3 a : considering that ⟨why use water at all ∼ you can drown in it —Stuart Chase⟩ b : in spite of the fact that : ALTHOUGH ⟨quit politics ∼ I might have had a great career in it⟩ 4 : the time or occasion at or in which ⟨tomorrow is ∼ we must decide⟩ ⟨humor is ∼ you laugh —Earl Rovit⟩
³when \'hwen, 'wen\ *pron* (14c) : what or which time ⟨life-long homes for those . . . who have lived here since ∼ —Kim Waller⟩
⁴when *n* (1616) : the time in which something is done or comes about ⟨troubled his head very little about the hows and ∼s of life —Laurence Sterne⟩
when·as \hwe-'naz, we-, (h)wə-\ *conj* [ME (Sc) *when as,* fr. ME *when + as*] (15c) *archaic* : WHEN
¹whence \'hwen(t)s, 'wen(t)s\ *adv* [ME *whennes,* fr. *whenne* whence (fr. OE *hwanon*) + *-s,* adv. suffix, fr. *-s,* gen. sing. ending; akin to OHG *hwanān* whence, OE *hwā* who] (13c) 1 : from what place, source, or cause ⟨then ∼ comes this paradox —*Changing Times*⟩ — **from whence** : from what place, source, or cause ⟨no one could tell me *from whence* the gold had come —Graham Greene⟩
²whence *conj* (14c) 1 : from what place, source, or cause ⟨inquired ∼ the water came —Maria Edgeworth⟩ 2 a : from or out of which place, source, or cause ⟨the lawless society ∼ the ballads sprang —DeLancey Ferguson⟩ b : by reason of which fact : WHEREFORE ⟨nothing broke — ∼ I infer that my bones are not yet chalky —O. W. Holmes †1935⟩
whence·so·ev·er \'hwen(t)s-sə-,we-vər, 'wen(t)s-\ *conj* (1511) : from whatever place or source
¹when·ev·er \hwe-'ne-vər, we-, (h)wə-\ *conj* (14c) : at any or every time that
²whenever *adv* (1667) : at whatever time
¹when·so·ev·er \'hwen(t)s-sə-,we-vər, 'wen(t)s-\ *conj* (14c) : WHENEVER
²whensoever *adv* (1526) *obs* : at any time whatever
¹where \'hwer, 'hwar, 'wer, 'war, (,)(h)wər\ *adv* [ME, fr. OE *hwǣr;* akin to OHG *hwār* where, OE *hwā* who — more at WHO] (bef. 12c) 1 a : at, in, or to what place ⟨∼ is the house⟩ ⟨∼ are we going⟩ b : at, in, or to what situation, position, direction, circumstances, or respect ⟨∼ does this plan lead⟩ ⟨∼ am I wrong⟩ 2 *archaic* : HERE, THERE ⟨lo, ∼ it comes again —Shak.⟩
²where *conj* (13c) 1 a : at, in, or to what place ⟨knows ∼ the house is⟩ b : at, in, or to what situation, position, direction, circumstances, or respect ⟨shows ∼ the plan leads⟩ c : the place or point at, in, or to which ⟨couldn't see from ∼ he was sitting⟩ ⟨kept that horse and gentled him to ∼ I finally rode him —William Faulkner⟩ 2 : WHEREVER ⟨goes ∼ she likes⟩ 3 a : at, in, or to which place ⟨the town ∼ she lives⟩ b : at or in which ⟨has reached the size ∼ traffic is a problem⟩ ⟨two fireplaces ∼ you can bake bread in the ovens —Randall Jarrell⟩ 4 a : at, in, or to the place at, in, or to which ⟨stay ∼ you are⟩ ⟨send him away ∼ he'll forget⟩ b : in a case, situation, or respect in which ⟨outstanding ∼ endurance is called for⟩ 5 : THAT ⟨I've read ∼ they do it that way in some Middle Eastern countries —Andy Rooney⟩
³where \'hwer, 'hwar, 'wer, 'war\ *n* (15c) 1 : PLACE, LOCATION ⟨the ∼ and the how of the accident⟩ 2 : what place, source, or cause ⟨I know ∼ that comes from⟩ — **where it's at** 1 a : a place of central interest or activity b : something (as a topic or field of interest) of primary concern or importance ⟨education is *where it's at*⟩ 2 : the true nature of things — **where one is at** : one's true position, state, or nature
¹where·abouts \-ə-,baůts\ *also* **where·about** \-,baůt\ *adv* [ME *wher aboutes* (fr. *wher aboute + -s,* adv. suffix) & *wher aboute,* fr. *where, wher* where + *about, aboute* about — more at WHENCE] (14c) : about where : near what place ⟨∼ is the house⟩
²whereabouts *also* **whereabout** *conj* (14c) 1 *obs* : on what business or errand 2 : near what place : WHERE ⟨know ∼ he lives⟩
³whereabouts *n pl but sing or pl in constr, also* **whereabout** (1605) : the place or general locality where a person or thing is ⟨their present ∼ are a secret⟩
¹where·as \hwer-'az, hwar-, wer-, war-, (,)(h)wər-\ *conj* [ME *where as,* fr. *where + as*] (14c) 1 a : while on the contrary ⟨∼ ALTHOUGH 2 : in view of the fact that : SINCE — used esp. to introduce a preamble
²whereas *n* (1795) 1 : an introductory statement of a formal document : PREAMBLE 2 : a conditional or qualifying statement
where·at \-'at\ *conj* (15c) 1 : at or toward which 2 : in consequence of which : WHEREUPON
¹where·by \-'bī\ *conj* (13c) : by, through, or in accordance with which
²whereby *adv* (14c) *obs* : by what : HOW
¹where·fore \'hwer-,fōr, 'hwar-, 'wer-, 'war-, -,fòr\ *adv* [ME *wherfor, wherfore,* fr. *where, wher + for, fore* for] (13c) 1 : for what reason or purpose : WHY 2 : THEREFORE
²wherefore *n* (1590) : an answer or statement giving an explanation : REASON ⟨wants to know the whys and ∼s⟩
where·from \-,frəm, -,främ\ *conj* (15c) : from which
¹where·in \hwer-'in, hwar-, wer-, war-, (,)(h)wər-\ *adv* (13c) : in what : in what particular or respect ⟨∼ was I wrong⟩
²wherein *conj* (15c) 1 a : in which : WHERE ⟨the city ∼ he lives⟩ b : during which 2 : in what way : HOW ⟨showed me ∼ I was wrong⟩
where·in·to \-'in-(,)tü, -in-'tü\ *conj* (1539) : into which
¹where·of \-'əv, -'äv\ *conj* (13c) 1 *archaic* : with or by which 2 : of what ⟨knows ∼ she speaks⟩ 3 a : of which ⟨books ∼ the best are lost⟩ b : of whom
²whereof *adv* (15c) *archaic* : of what ⟨∼ are you made —Shak.⟩
¹where·on \-'ȯn, -'än\ *conj* (13c) 1 *archaic* : on what ⟨tell me ∼ the likelihood depends —Shak.⟩ 2 : on which ⟨the base ∼ it rests⟩
²whereon *adv* (15c) *archaic* : on what ⟨∼ do you look —Shak.⟩
where·so·ev·er \'hwer-sə-,we-vər, 'hwar-, 'wer-, 'war-\ *conj* (13c) : WHEREVER
where·through \'hwer-,thrü, 'hwar-, 'wer-, 'war-\ *conj* (13c) : through which
¹where·to \-,tü\ *adv* (13c) : to what place, purpose, or end ⟨∼ tends all this —Shak.⟩
²whereto *conj* (14c) : to which
where·un·to \'hwer-ən-(,)tü, hwar-, wer-, war-, (,)(h)wər-\ *adv or conj* (15c) : WHERETO
where·up·on \'hwer-ə-,pȯn, 'hwar-, 'wer-, 'war-, -,pän\ *conj* (14c) 1 : on which 2 : closely following and in consequence of which

¹wher·ev·er \hwer-'e-vər, hwar-, wer-, war-, (,)(h)wər-\ *adv* (13c) 1 : where in the world ⟨∼ did you get that tie⟩ 2 : anywhere at all ⟨explore northward or ∼ —Bernard De Voto⟩
²wherever *conj* (14c) 1 : at, in, or to any or all places that ⟨thrives ∼ he goes⟩ 2 : in any circumstance in which ⟨∼ it is possible, we try to help⟩
¹where·with \'hwer-,with, 'hwar-, 'wer-, 'war-, -,with\ *pron* (13c) *archaic* : that with or by which — used with an infinitive ⟨so shall I have ∼ to answer him —Ps 119:42 (AV)⟩
²wherewith *adv* (13c) *obs* : with what ⟨∼ shall it be salted —Mt 5:13 (AV)⟩
³wherewith *conj* (14c) : with or by means of which ⟨metal tools ∼ to break ground —Russell Lord⟩
¹where·with·al \'hwer-wi-,thȯl, 'hwar-, 'wer-, 'war-, -,thȯl\ *conj* [*where + ²withal*] (1534) : WHEREWITH
²wherewithal *pron* (1583) : WHEREWITH
³wherewithal *n* (1659) : MEANS, RESOURCES; *specif* : MONEY ⟨didn't have the ∼ for an expensive dinner⟩
wher·ry \'hwer-ē, 'wer-\ *n, pl* **wherries** [ME *whery*] (15c) 1 : any of various light boats: as a : a long light rowboat made sharp at both ends and used to transport passengers on rivers and about harbors b : a racing scull for one person 2 : a large light barge, lighter, or fishing boat varying in type in different parts of Great Britain
¹whet \'hwet, 'wet\ *vt* **whet·ted; whet·ting** [ME *whetten,* fr. OE *hwettan;* akin to OHG *wezzen* to whet, *waz* sharp] (bef. 12c) 1 : to sharpen by rubbing on or with something (as a stone) ⟨∼ a knife⟩ 2 : to make keen or more acute : EXCITE, STIMULATE ⟨∼ the appetite⟩ — **whet·ter** *n*
²whet *n* (ca. 1628) 1 *dial* a : a spell of work done with a scythe between the time it is sharpened and the time it needs to be sharpened again b : TIME, WHILE 2 : something that sharpens or makes keen: a : GOAD, INCITEMENT b : APPETIZER; *also* : a drink of liquor
¹wheth·er \'hwe-thər, 'we-, (,)(h)wə-\ *pron* [ME, fr. OE *hwæther, hwether;* akin to OHG *hwedar* which of two, L *uter,* Gk *poteros,* OE *hwā* who — more at WHO] (bef. 12c) 1 *archaic* : which one of the two 2 *archaic* : whichever one of two
²whether *conj* (bef. 12c) — used as a function word usu. with correlative *or* or with *or whether* to indicate (1) until the early 19th century a direct question involving alternatives; (2) an indirect question involving stated or implied alternatives ⟨decide ∼ he should agree or raise objections⟩ ⟨wondered ∼ to stay⟩; (3) alternative conditions or possibilities ⟨see me no more, ∼ he be dead or no —Shak.⟩ ⟨seated him next to her ∼ by accident or design⟩ — **whether or no** *or* **whether or not** : in any case
whet·stone \'hwet-,stōn, 'wet-\ *n* (bef. 12c) : a stone for whetting edge tools
whew \often read as 'hwü, 'wü, 'hyü; *the interj is a whistle concluded with a voiceless* ü\ *n* [imit.] (1513) : a whistling sound or a sound like a half-formed whistle uttered as an exclamation ⟨gave a long ∼ when he realized the size of the job⟩ — used interjectionally chiefly to express amazement, discomfort, or relief
whey \'hwā, 'wā\ *n* [ME, fr. OE *hwæg;* akin to MD *wey* whey] (bef. 12c) : the watery part of milk that is separated from the coagulable part or curd esp. in the process of making cheese and that is rich in lactose, minerals, and vitamins and contains lactalbumin and traces of fat — **whey·like** \-,līk\ *adj*
whey·face \'hwā-,fās, 'wā-\ *n* (1605) : a person having a pale face (as from fear) — **whey–faced** \-,fāst\ *adj*
¹which \'hwich, 'wich\ *adj* [ME, of what kind, which, fr. OE *hwilc;* akin to OHG *wilih* of what kind, which, OE *hwā* who, *gelīk* like — more at WHO, LIKE] (bef. 12c) 1 : being what one or ones out of a group — used as an interrogative ⟨∼ tie should I wear⟩ ⟨kept a record of ∼ employees took their vacations in July⟩ 2 : WHICHEVER ⟨it will not fit, turn it ∼ way you like⟩ 3 — used as a function word to introduce a nonrestrictive relative clause and to modify a noun in that clause and to refer together with that noun to a word or word group in a preceding clause or to an entire preceding clause or sentence or longer unit of discourse ⟨in German, ∼ language might . . . have been the medium of transmission —Thomas Pyles⟩ ⟨that this city is a rebellious city . . . : for ∼ cause was this city destroyed —Ezra 4:15 (AV)⟩
²which *pron* (bef. 12c) 1 : what one or ones out of a group — used as an interrogative ⟨∼ of those houses do you live in⟩ ⟨∼ of you want tea and ∼ want lemonade⟩ ⟨he is swimming or canoeing, I don't know ∼⟩ 2 : WHICHEVER ⟨take ∼ you like⟩ 3 — used as a function word to introduce a relative clause; used in any grammatical relation except that of a possessive; used esp. in reference to animals, inanimate objects, groups, or ideas ⟨the bonds ∼ represent the debt —G. B. Robinson⟩ ⟨the Samnite tribes, ∼ settled south and southeast of Rome —Ernst Pulgram⟩; used freely in reference to persons as recently as the 17th century ⟨our Father ∼ art in heaven —Mt 6:9 (AV)⟩, and still occas. so used but usu. with some implication of emphasis on the function or role of the person rather than on the person as such ⟨chiefly they wanted husbands, ∼ they got easily —Lynn White⟩; used by speakers on all educational levels and by many reputable writers, though disapproved by some grammarians, in reference to an idea expressed by a word or group of words that is not necessarily a noun or noun phrase ⟨he resigned that post, after ∼ he engaged in ranching —*Current Biog.*⟩ *usage* see ⁴THAT
¹which·ev·er \hwich-'e-vər, wich-\ *adj* (14c) : being whatever one or ones out of a group : no matter which ⟨its soothing . . . effect will be the same ∼ way you take it —*Punch*⟩
²whichever *pron* (15c) : whatever one or ones out of a group ⟨take two of the four elective subjects, ∼ you prefer⟩
which·so·ev·er \,hwich-sə-'we-vər, ,wich-\ *pron or adj* (15c) *archaic* : WHICHEVER
whick·er \'hwi-kər, 'wi-\ *vi* **whick·ered; whick·er·ing** \-k(ə-)riŋ\ [imit.] (1753) 1 : NEIGH, WHINNY — **whicker** *n*
whid \'hwid, 'wid\ *vi* **whid·ded; whid·ding** [Sc *whid* silent rapid motion] (1728) *Scot* : to move nimbly and silently
¹whiff \'hwif, 'wif\ *n* [origin unknown] (1591) 1 a : a quick puff or slight gust esp. of air, odor, gas, smoke, or spray b : an inhalation of odor, gas, or smoke c : a slight puffing or whistling sound 2 : a slight trace or indication 3 : STRIKEOUT
²whiff *vi* (1591) 1 : to move with or as if with a puff of air 2 : to emit whiffs : PUFF 3 : to inhale an odor 4 : STRIKE OUT 3 ∼ *vt* 1 a : to

carry or convey by or as if by a whiff : BLOW　**b** : to expel or puff out in a whiff : EXHALE　**c** : SMOKE 3　**2** : FAN 8

whif·fet \'hwi-fət, 'wi-\ *n* [prob. alter. of *whippet*] (1839) : a small, young, or unimportant person

whif·fle \'hwi-fəl, 'wi-\ *vb* **whif·fled; whif·fling** \-f(ə-)liŋ\ [prob. freq. of *whiff*] *vi* (1568)　**1**　**a** *of the wind* : to blow unsteadily or in gusts　**b** : VACILLATE　**2** : to emit or produce a light whistling or puffing sound　**~** *vt* : to blow, disperse, emit, or expel with or as if with a whiff

¹**whif·fler** \'hwi-flər, 'wi-\ *n* [alter. of earlier *wifler*, fr. obs. *wifle* battle=ax] (1539) *Brit* : one that clears the way for a procession

²**whif·fler** \'hwi-f(ə-)lər, 'wi-\ *n* [*whiffle*] (1607)　**1** : a person who frequently changes opinions or course　**2** : a person who uses shifts and evasions in argument

whif·fle·tree \'hwi-fəl-(ˌ)trē, 'wi-\ *n* [alter. of *whippletree*] (ca. 1806) : the pivoted swinging bar to which the traces of a harness are fastened and by which a vehicle or implement is drawn

1 whiffletree

Whig \'hwig, 'wig\ *n* [short for *Whiggamore*, member of a Scottish group that marched to Edinburgh in 1648 to oppose the court party] (ca. 1680)　**1** : a member or supporter of a major British political group of the late 17th through early 19th centuries seeking to limit the royal authority and increase parliamentary power — compare TORY　**2** : an American favoring independence from Great Britain during the American Revolution　**3** : a member or supporter of an American political party formed about 1834 in opposition to the Jacksonian Democrats, associated chiefly with manufacturing, commercial, and financial interests, and succeeded about 1854 by the Republican party — **Whig** *adj* — **Whig·gism** \'hwi-gi-zəm\ *n*

Whig·gery \'hwi-gə-rē, 'wi-\ *n* (1714) : the principles or practices of Whigs

Whig·gish \'hwi-gish, 'wi-\ *adj* (1684)　**1** : characteristic of Whigs or Whiggery　**2** : of, relating to, or characterized by a view which holds that history follows a path of inevitable progression and improvement and which judges the past in light of the present

whig·ma·lee·rie \ˌhwig-mə-'lir-ē, ˌwig-\ *n* [origin unknown] (1730)　**1** *chiefly Scot* : WHIM　**2** *chiefly Scot* : an odd or fanciful contrivance : GIMCRACK

¹**while** \'hwi(ə)l, 'wi(ə)l\ *n* [ME, fr. OE *hwil;* akin to OHG *hwila* time, L *quies* rest, quiet] (bef. 12c)　**1** : a period of time esp. when short and marked by the occurrence of an action or a condition : TIME ⟨stay here for a ~⟩　**2** : the time and effort used (as in the performance of an action) : TROUBLE ⟨worth your ~⟩

²**while** *conj* (12c)　**1**　**a** : during the time that ⟨take a nap ~ I'm out⟩　**b** : as long as ⟨~ there's life there's hope⟩　**2**　**a** : when on the other hand : WHEREAS ⟨easy for an expert, ~ it is dangerous for a novice⟩　**b** : in spite of the fact that : ALTHOUGH ⟨~ respected, he is not liked⟩　**3** : similarly and at the same time that ⟨~ the book will be welcomed by scholars, it will make an immediate appeal to the general reader —*Brit. Book News*⟩

³**while** *prep* (15c) *dial Brit* : UNTIL

⁴**while** *vt* **whiled; whil·ing** (1635) : to cause to pass esp. without boredom or in a pleasant manner — usu. used with *away* ⟨~ away the time⟩

¹**whiles** \'hwi(ə)lz, 'wi(ə)lz\ *conj* [ME, fr. *while* + *-s*, adv. suffix — more at WHENCE] (13c) *archaic* : WHILE

²**whiles** *adv* (15c) *chiefly Scot* : SOMETIMES

¹**whi·lom** \'hwi-ləm, 'wi-\ *adv* [ME, lit., at times, fr. OE *hwilum*, dat. pl. of *hwil* time, while] (13c) *archaic* : FORMERLY

²**whilom** *adj* (1837) : FORMER

whilst \'hwi(ə)lst, 'wi(ə)lst\ *conj* [ME *whilest*, alter. of *whiles*] (14c) *chiefly Brit* : WHILE

whim \'hwim, 'wim\ *n* [short for *whim-wham*] (1697)　**1** : a capricious or eccentric and often sudden idea or turn of the mind : FANCY　**2** : a large capstan that is made with one or more radiating arms to which a horse may be yoked and that is used in mines for raising ore or water　*syn* see CAPRICE

whim·brel \'hwim-brəl, 'wim-\ *n* [origin unknown] (ca. 1531) : a small curlew (*Numenius phaeopus*) chiefly of the northern regions of No. America and Eurasia; *broadly* : any small curlew

¹**whim·per** \'hwim-pər, 'wim-\ *vi* **whim·pered; whim·per·ing** \-p(ə-)riŋ\ [imit.] (1513)　**1** : to make a low whining plaintive or broken sound　**2** : to complain or protest with or as if with a whimper

²**whimper** *n* (ca. 1700)　**1** : a whimpering cry or sound　**2** : a petulant complaint or protest

whim·si·cal \'hwim-zi-kəl, 'wim-\ *adj* [*whimsy*] (1653)　**1** : full of, actuated by, or exhibiting whims　**2**　**a** : resulting from or characterized by whim or caprice; *esp* : lightly fanciful　**b** : subject to erratic behavior or unpredictable change — **whim·si·cal·i·ty** \ˌhwim-zə-'ka-lə-tē, ˌwim-\ *n* — **whim·si·cal·ly** \'hwim-zi-k(ə-)lē, 'wim-\ *adv* — **whim·si·cal·ness** \-kəl-nəs\ *n*

whim·sy *also* **whim·sey** \'hwim-zē, 'wim-\ *n, pl* **whimsies** *also* **whimseys** [irreg. fr. *whim-wham*] (1605)　**1** : WHIM, CAPRICE　**2** : the quality or state of being whimsical or fanciful ⟨the designer's new line showed a touch of ~⟩　**3** : a fanciful or fantastic device, object, or creation esp. in writing or art

whim–wham \'hwim-ˌhwam, 'wim-ˌwam\ *n* [origin unknown] (1500)　**1** : a whimsical object or device esp. of ornament or dress　**2** : FANCY, WHIM　**3** *pl* : JITTERS

whin \'hwin, 'win\ *n* [ME *whynne*, of Scand origin; akin to Norw *kvein* bent grass] (15c) : GORSE

whin·chat \'hwin-ˌchat, 'win-\ *n* [*whin*] (1678) : a small brown and buff European singing bird (*Saxicola rubetra*) of grassy meadows

¹**whine** \'hwīn, 'wīn\ *vb* **whined; whin·ing** [ME, fr. OE *hwīnan* to whiz; akin to ON *hvīna* to whiz] *vi* (13c)　**1 a** : to utter a high-pitched plaintive or distressed cry　**b** : to make a sound similar to such a cry ⟨the wind *whined* in the chimney⟩　**2** : to complain with or as if with a whine　**3** : to move or proceed with the sound of a whine ⟨the bullet *whined* ... across the ice —Berton Roueché⟩　**~** *vt* : to utter or express with or as if with a whine — **whin·er** *n* — **whin·ing·ly** \'hwī-niŋ-lē, 'wī-\ *adv*

²**whine** *n* (1633)　**1**　**a** : a prolonged high-pitched cry usu. expressive of distress or pain　**b** : a sound resembling such a cry　**2** : a complaint uttered with or as if with a whine — **whiny** *or* **whin·ey** \'hwī-nē, 'wī-\ *adj*

whin·ding \'win-ˌdiŋ, 'hwin-\ *n* [by alter.] (ca. 1945) : WINGDING

whinge \'hwinj, 'winj\ *vi* **whinged; whing·ing** *or* **whinge·ing** [fr. (assumed) ME, fr. OE *hwinsian;* akin to OHG *winsōn* to moan] (12c) *Brit* : to complain fretfully : WHINE

¹**whin·ny** \'hwi-nē, 'wi-\ *vb* **whin·nied; whin·ny·ing** [prob. imit.] *vi* (1530) : to neigh esp. in a low or gentle way　**~** *vt* : to utter with or as if with a whinny

²**whinny** *n, pl* **whinnies** (ca. 1823)　**1** : the neigh of a horse esp. when low or gentle　**2** : a sound resembling a neigh

whin·stone \'hwin-ˌstōn, 'win-\ *n* [*whin*, a hard rock] (1513) : basaltic rock : TRAP; *also* : any of various other dark resistant rocks (as chert)

¹**whip** \'hwip, 'wip\ *vb* **whipped; whip·ping** [ME *wippen, whippen;* akin to MD *wippen* to move up and down, sway, OE *wīpian* to wipe] *vt* (14c)　**1** : to take, pull, snatch, jerk, or otherwise move very quickly and forcefully ⟨*whipped* out his gun —Green Peyton⟩　**2**　**a** (1) : to strike with a slender lithe implement (as a lash or rod) esp. as a punishment　(2) : SPANK　**b** : to drive or urge on by or as if by using a whip　**c** : to strike as a lash does ⟨rain *whipped* the pavement⟩　**3**　**a** : to bind or wrap (as a rope or fishing rod) with cord for protection and strength　**b** : to wind or wrap around something　**4** : to belabor with stinging words : ABUSE　**5** : to seam or hem with shallow overcasting stitches　**6** : to overcome decisively : DEFEAT　**7** : to stir up : INCITE — usu. used with *up* ⟨trying to ~ up a new emotion —Ellen Glasgow⟩　**8** : to produce in a hurry — usu. used with *up* ⟨a sketch ... an artist might ~ up —*N.Y. Times*⟩　**9** : to fish (water) with rod, line, and artificial lure　**10** : to beat (as eggs or cream) into a froth with a utensil (as a whisk or fork)　**11** : to gather together or hold together for united action in the manner of a party whip　**~** *vi*　**1** : to proceed nimbly or quickly ⟨*whipping* through the supper dishes —C. B. Davis⟩　**2** : to thrash about flexibly in the manner of a whiplash ⟨a flag ... *whipping* out from its staff —H. A. Calahan⟩ — **whip·per** *n* — **whip into shape** : to bring forcefully to a desired state or condition

²**whip** *n* (14c)　**1** : an instrument consisting usu. of a handle and lash forming a flexible rod that is used for whipping　**2** : a stroke or cut with or as if with a whip　**3**　**a** : a dessert made by whipping a portion of the ingredients ⟨prune ~⟩　**b** : a kitchen utensil made of braided or coiled wire or perforated metal with a handle and used in whipping　**4** : one that handles a whip: as　**a** : a driver of horses : COACHMAN　**b** : WHIPPER-IN 1　**5**　**a** : a member of a legislative body appointed by a political party to enforce party discipline and to secure the attendance of party members at important sessions　**b** *often cap* : a notice of forthcoming business sent weekly to each member of a political party in the British House of Commons　**6** : a whipping or thrashing motion　**7** : the quality of resembling a whip esp. in being flexible　**8** : a flexible vertical rod radio antenna — called also *whip antenna* — **whip·like** \'hwip-ˌlīk, 'wip-\ *adj*

whip·cord \'hwip-ˌkórd, 'wip-\ *n* [fr. its use in making whips] (14c)　**1** : a thin tough cord made of braided or twisted hemp or catgut　**2** : a cloth that is made of hard-twisted yarns and has fine diagonal cords or ribs

whip hand *n* (1680)　**1** : positive control : ADVANTAGE　**2** : the hand holding the whip in driving

whip in *vt* (1742)　**1** : to collect or keep together (members of a political party) for legislative action　**2** : to keep (hounds in a pack) from scattering by use of a whip

whip·lash \'hwip-ˌlash, 'wip-\ *n* (ca. 1580)　**1** : the lash of a whip　**2** : something resembling a blow from a whip ⟨the ~ of fear —R. S. Banay⟩　**3** : WHIPLASH INJURY

whiplash injury *n* (ca. 1953) : injury resulting from a sudden sharp whipping movement of the neck and head (as of a person in a vehicle that is struck head-on or from the rear by another vehicle)

whip·per–in \ˌhwi-pər-'in, ˌwi-\ *n, pl* **whip·pers–in** \-pərz-\ (1739)　**1** : a huntsman's assistant who whips in the hounds　**2** : WHIP 5a

whip·per·snap·per \'hwi-pər-ˌsna-pər, 'wi-\ *n* [alter. of *snippersnapper*] (1700) : a diminutive, insignificant, or presumptuous person

whip·pet \'hwi-pət, 'wi-\ *n* [prob. fr. ¹*whip*] (1610) : any of a breed of small swift slender dogs that are widely used for racing

whip·ping *n* (1540)　**1** : the act of one that whips: as　**a** : a severe beating or chastisement　**b** : a stitching made with small overcasting stitches　**2** : material used to whip or bind

whipping boy *n* (1647)　**1** : a boy formerly educated with a prince and punished in his stead　**2** : SCAPEGOAT 2

whipping cream *n* (1921) : a cream suitable for whipping that by law contains not less than 30 percent butterfat

whipping post *n* (1600) : a post to which offenders are tied to be legally whipped

whip·ple·tree \'hwi-pəl-(ˌ)trē, 'wi-\ *n* [perh. irreg. fr. *whip + tree*] (1733) : WHIFFLETREE

whip·poor·will \'hwi-pər-ˌwil, ˌhwi-pər-', 'wi-, ˌwi-\ *n* [imit.] (1709) : a nocturnal nightjar (*Caprimulgus vociferus*) of eastern No. America with a loud repeated call suggestive of its name

whip·py \'hwi-pē, 'wi-\ *adj* **whip·pi·er; -est** (1867)　**1** : unusually resilient : SPRINGY ⟨a ~ fishing rod⟩　**2** : of, relating to, or resembling a whip

whip–round \'hwip-ˌraúnd, 'wip-\ *n* (1887) *chiefly Brit* : a collection of money made usu. for a benevolent purpose ⟨had a ~ to help the couple pay for a Paris honeymoon —*The People*⟩

whippoorwill

\ə\ abut　\ᵊ\ kitten, F table　\ər\ further　\a\ ash　\ā\ ace　\ä\ mop, mar
\aú\ out　\ch\ chin　\e\ bet　\ē\ easy　\g\ go　\i\ hit　\ī\ ice　\j\ job
\ŋ\ sing　\ō\ go　\ó\ law　\ói\ boy　\th\ thin　\t͟h\ the　\ü\ loot　\ú\ foot
\y\ yet　\zh\ vision　\à, k̲, ⁿ, œ, œ̄, ᵫ, ūe, ᵞ\ see Guide to Pronunciation

¹whip·saw \'hwip-,sȯ, 'wip-\ *n* [²*whip*] (1538) : a narrow pit saw averaging from 5 to 7½ feet (1.5 to 2.3 meters) in length
²whipsaw *vt* (1842) **1** : to saw with a whipsaw **2** : to beset or victimize in two opposite ways at once, by a two-phase operation, or by the collusive action of two opponents ⟨wage earners were ~ed by inflation and high taxes⟩
whip-sawed \-,sȯd\ *adj* (1892) : subjected to a double market loss through trying inopportunely to recoup a loss by a subsequent short sale of the same security
whip scorpion *n* (ca. 1890) : any of an order (Uropygi) of arachnids somewhat resembling true scorpions but having a long slender caudal process and no sting
whip stall *n* (1924) : a stall during a vertical climb in which the nose of the airplane whips violently forward and then downward
¹whip·stitch \'hwip-,stich, 'wip-\ *vt* (1592) : WHIP 5
²whipstitch *n* (1640) : a shallow overcasting stitch
whip·stock \-,stäk\ *n* (ca. 1530) : the handle of a whip
whip·worm \-,wǝrm\ *n* (1875) : a parasitic nematode worm (genus *Trichuris*) with a body that is thickened posteriorly and that is very long and slender anteriorly; *esp* : one (*T. trichiura*) of the human intestine
¹whir *also* **whirr** \'hwǝr, 'wǝr\ *vb* **whirred; whir·ring** [ME (Sc) *quir-ren*, prob. of Scand origin; akin to Dan *hvirre* to whirl, whir] *vi* (15c) : to fly, revolve, or move rapidly with a whir ~ *vt* : to move or carry rapidly with a whir
²whir *also* **whirr** *n* (1677) : a continuous fluttering or vibratory sound made by something in rapid motion
¹whirl \'hwǝr(-ǝ)l, 'wǝr(-ǝ)l\ *vb* [ME, prob. of Scand origin; akin to ON *hvirfla* to whirl; akin to OHG *wirbil* whirlwind, OE *hweorfan* to turn — more at WHARF] *vi* (14c) **1** : to move in a circle or similar curve esp. with force or speed **2 a** : to turn on or around an axis like a wheel : ROTATE **b** : to turn abruptly around or aside : WHEEL **3** : to pass, move, or go quickly ⟨~ed down the hallway⟩ **4** : to become giddy or dizzy : REEL ⟨my head is ~ing⟩ ~ *vt* **1** : to drive, impel, or convey with or as if with a rotary motion **2 a** : to cause to turn usu. rapidly on or around an axis : ROTATE **b** : to cause to turn abruptly around or aside **3** *obs* : to throw or hurl violently with a revolving motion — **whirl·er** \'hwǝr-lǝr, 'wǝr-\ *n*
²whirl *n* (15c) **1 a** : a rapid rotating or circling movement **b** : something undergoing such a movement **2 a** : a busy or fast-paced succession of events : BUSTLE ⟨a ~ of activity⟩ ⟨the social ~⟩ **b** : a confused or disturbed mental state : TURMOIL ⟨a ~ of febrile excitement — Emily Skeel⟩ **3** : an experimental or brief attempt : TRY ⟨gave it a ~⟩
whirl·i·gig \'hwǝr-li-,gig, 'wǝr-\ *n* [ME *whirlegigg*, fr. *whirlen* to whirl + *gigg* top — more at GIG] (15c) **1** : a child's toy having a whirling motion **2** : MERRY-GO-ROUND **3 a** : one that continuously whirls, moves, or changes **b** : a whirling or circling course (as of events)
whirligig beetle *n* (1855) : any of a family (Gyrinidae) of beetles with two pairs of eyes and clubbed antennae that live mostly on the surface of water where they swim swiftly about in circles
whirl·pool \'hwǝr(-ǝ)l-,pül, 'wǝr(-ǝ)l-\ *n* (1529) **1 a** : a confused tumult and bustle : WHIRL **b** : a magnetic or impelling force by which something may be ⟨refusing to be drawn into this ~ of intrigue —A. D. White⟩ **2 a** : water moving rapidly in a circle so as to produce a depression in the center into which floating objects may be drawn : EDDY, VORTEX **b** : WHIRLPOOL BATH
whirlpool bath *n* (ca. 1916) : a therapeutic bath in which all or part of the body is exposed to forceful whirling currents of hot water
¹whirl·wind \-,wind\ *n* (14c) **1** : a small rotating windstorm of limited extent **2 a** : a confused rush : WHIRL **b** : a violent or destructive force or agency
²whirlwind *adj* (1614) : resembling a whirlwind esp. in speed or force ⟨a ~ campaign⟩ ⟨a ~ romance⟩
¹whirly \'hwǝr-lē, 'wǝr-\ *adj* (15c) : marked by or exhibiting a whirling motion
²whirly *n*, *pl* **whirl·ies** (1914) : a small whirlwind
whirly·bird \-,bǝrd\ *n* (1951) : HELICOPTER
whir·ry \'hwǝr-ē, 'wǝr-, '(h)wǝ-rē\ *vb* **whir·ried; whir·ry·ing** [perh. blend of *whir* and *hurry*] *vt* (1582) *Scot* : to convey quickly ~ *vi*, *Scot* : HURRY
¹whish \'hwish, 'wish\ *vb* [imit.] *vt* (1518) : to urge on or cause to move with a whish ~ *vi* **1** : to make a sibilant sound **2** : to move with a whish esp. at high speed ⟨an elevator . . . ~es down to the lower level —Natalie Cooper⟩
²whish *n* (ca. 1802) : a rushing sound : SWISH
whisht \'hwisht, 'wisht\ *vi* [ME; imit.] (15c) *chiefly Irish* : HUSH — often used interjectionally to enjoin silence
¹whisk \'hwisk, 'wisk\ *n* [ME *wisk*, prob. of Scand origin; akin to ON *visk* wisp; akin to OE *wiscian* to plait] (14c) **1** : a quick light brushing or whipping motion **2 a** : a usu. wire kitchen utensil used for beating food by hand **b** : a flexible bunch (as of twigs, feathers, or straw) attached to a handle for use as a brush
²whisk *vt* (15c) **1** : to move nimbly and quickly ~ *vt* **1** : to move or convey briskly ⟨~ed the children off to bed⟩ **2** : to mix or fluff up by or as if by beating with a whisk ⟨~ egg whites⟩ **3** : to brush or wipe off lightly
whisk broom *n* (1857) : a small broom with a short handle used esp. as a clothes brush
whis·ker \'hwis-kǝr, 'wis-\ *n* [sing. of *whiskers* mustache, fr. ²*whisk*] (ca. 1600) **1 a** : a hair of the beard **b** *pl* (1) *archaic* : MUSTACHE (2) : the part of the beard growing on the sides of the face or on the chin **c** : HAIRBREADTH ⟨lost the race by a ~⟩ **2** : one of the long projecting hairs or bristles growing near the mouth of an animal (as a cat or bird) **3** : an outrigger extending on each side of the bowsprit to spread the jib and flying jib guys — usu. used in pl. **4 a** : a shred or filament resembling a whisker **b** : a thin hairlike crystal (as of sapphire or copper) of exceptional mechanical strength used esp. to reinforce composite structural material — **whis·kered** \-kǝrd\ *adj* — **whis·kery** \-k(ǝ-)rē\ *adj*
whis·key *or* **whis·ky** \'hwis-kē, 'wis-\ *n*, *pl* **whiskeys** *or* **whiskies** [Ir *uisce beathadh* & ScGael *uisge beatha*, lit., water of life] (1715) **1** : a liquor distilled from the fermented mash of grain (as rye, corn, or barley) **2** : a drink of whiskey
Whiskey (ca. 1952) — a communication code word for the letter *w*

whiskey sour *n* (ca. 1889) : a cocktail usu. consisting of whiskey, sugar, and lemon juice shaken with ice
¹whis·per \'hwis-pǝr, 'wis-\ *vb* **whis·pered; whis·per·ing** \-p(ǝ-)riŋ\ [ME, fr. OE *hwisperian*; akin to OHG *hwispalōn* to whisper, ON *hvīsla* — more at WHISTLE] *vi* (bef. 12c) **1** : to speak softly with little or no vibration of the vocal cords esp. to avoid being overheard **2** : to make a sibilant sound that resembles whispering ~ *vt* **1** : to address in a whisper **2** : to utter or communicate in or as if in a whisper
²whisper *n* (1595) **1** : something communicated by or as if by whispering; *esp* : RUMOR ⟨~s of scandal⟩ **2** : an act or instance of whispering; *esp* : speech without vibration of the vocal cords **b** : a sibilant sound that resembles whispered speech **3** : HINT, TRACE
whis·per·er \-pǝr-ǝr\ *n* (1547) : one that whispers; *specif* : RUMORMONGER
¹whispering *n* (bef. 12c) **1 a** : whispered speech **b** : GOSSIP, RUMOR **2** : a sibilant sound : WHISPER
²whispering *adj* (1547) **1** : making a sibilant sound **2** : spreading confidential and esp. derogatory reports ⟨~ tongues can poison truth —S. T. Coleridge⟩ — **whis·per·ing·ly** \-p(ǝ-)riŋ-lē\ *adv*
whispering campaign *n* (1920) : the systematic dissemination by word of mouth of derogatory rumors or charges esp. against a candidate for public office
whis·pery \'hwis-p(ǝ-)rē, 'wis-\ *adj* (1834) **1** : resembling a whisper **2** : full of whispers
¹whist \'hwist, 'wist, 'wist\ *vi* [ME; imit.] (14c) *dial Brit* : to be silent : HUSH — often used interjectionally to enjoin silence
²whist *adj* (15c) : QUIET, SILENT
³whist *n* [alter. of earlier *whisk*, prob. fr. ²*whisk*; fr. whisking up the tricks] (1663) : a card game for four players in two partnerships that is played with a pack of 52 cards and that scores one point for each trick in excess of six
whis·tle \'hwi-sǝl, 'wi-\ *n*, *often attrib* [ME, fr. OE *hwistle*; akin to ON *hvīsla* to whisper] (bef. 12c) **1 a** : a small wind instrument in which sound is produced by the forcible passage of breath through a slit in a short tube ⟨police ~⟩ **b** : a device through which air or steam is forced into a cavity or against a thin edge to produce a loud sound ⟨a factory ~⟩ **2 a** : a shrill clear sound produced by forcing breath out or air in through the puckered lips **b** : the sound produced by a whistle **c** : a signal given by or as if by whistling **3** : a sound that resembles a whistle; *esp* : a shrill clear note of or as if of a bird
²whistle *vb* **whis·tled; whis·tling** \-s(ǝ-)liŋ\ *vi* (bef. 12c) **1 a** : to utter a shrill sound by blowing or drawing air through the puckered lips **b** : to utter a shrill note or call resembling a whistle **c** : to make a shrill clear sound esp. by rapid movement ⟨the wind *whistled*⟩ **d** : to blow or sound a whistle **2 a** : to give a signal or issue an order or summons by or as if by whistling **b** : to make a demand without result ⟨did a sloppy job so he can ~ for his money⟩ ~ *vt* **1 a** : to send, bring, signal, or call by or as if by whistling **b** : to charge (as a basketball or hockey player) with an infraction **2** : to produce, utter, or express by whistling ⟨~ a tune⟩ — **whis·tle·able** \-sǝ-lǝ-bǝl\ *adj* —
whistle in the dark : to keep up one's courage by or as if by whistling
whis·tle–blow·er \-,blō(-ǝ)r\ *n* (1970) : one who reveals something covert or who informs against another ⟨pledges to protect ~s who fear reprisals —*Wall Street Jour.*⟩ — **whis·tle–blow·ing** \-,blō-iŋ\ *n*
whis·tler \'hwi-s(ǝ-)lǝr, 'wi-\ *n* (bef. 12c) : one that whistles: as **a** : any of various birds; *esp* : any of numerous Australian and Polynesian oscine birds (esp. genus *Pachycephala*) that are related to the shrikes and have a whistling call **b** : a large mountain marmot (*Marmota caligata*) of northwestern No. America **c** : a broken-winded horse **d** : a very-low-frequency radio signal that is generated by lightning discharge, travels along the earth's magnetic-field lines, and produces a sound resembling a whistle of descending pitch in radio receivers
¹whis·tle–stop \'hwi-sǝl-,stäp, 'wi-\ *n*, *often attrib* (ca. 1925) **1** : a small station at which trains stop only on signal : FLAG STOP **b** : a small community **2** : a brief personal appearance esp. by a political candidate usu. on the rear platform of a train during the course of a tour
²whistle–stop *vi* (1952) : to make a tour esp. in a political campaign with many brief personal appearances in small communities
whistling *n* (14c) : the act or sound of one that whistles : WHISTLE
whistling swan *n* (1785) : a native No. American swan (*Cygnus columbianus* syn. *Olor columbianus*) that calls with a soft musical note, breeds in the Arctic tundra, and winters in shallow fresh or salt water esp. along the eastern and western coasts of the U.S.
whit \'hwit, 'wit\ *n* [ME, prob. alter. of *wiht*, *wight* creature, thing — more at WIGHT] (15c) : the smallest part or particle imaginable : BIT ⟨what some people will do for a ~ of publicity —Patrick Quinn⟩
¹white \'hwit, 'wit\ *adj* **whit·er; whit·est** [ME, fr. OE *hwit*; akin to OHG *hwiz* white and prob. to OCS *světŭ* light, Skt *śveta* white, bright] (bef. 12c) **1 a** : free from color **b** : of the color of new snow or milk; *specif* : of the color white **c** : light or pallid in color ⟨~ hair⟩ ⟨lips ~ with fear⟩ **d** : lustrous pale gray : SILVERY; *also* : made of silver **2 a** : being a member of a group or race characterized by reduced pigmentation and usu. specif. distinguished from persons belonging to groups marked by black, brown, yellow, or red skin coloration **b** : of, relating to, characteristic of, or consisting of white people **c** : marked by upright fairness **3** : free from spot or blemish: as **a** (1) : free from moral impurity : INNOCENT (2) : marked by the wearing of white by the woman as a symbol of purity ⟨a ~ wedding⟩ **b** : unmarked by writing or printing **c** : not intended to cause harm ⟨a ~ lie⟩ ⟨~ magic⟩ **d** : FAVORABLE, FORTUNATE ⟨one of the ~ days of his life —Sir Walter Scott⟩ **4 a** : wearing or habited in white **b** : marked by the presence of snow : SNOWY ⟨a ~ Christmas⟩ **5 a** : heated to the point of whiteness **b** : notably ardent : PASSIONATE ⟨~ fury⟩ **6 a** : conservative or reactionary in political outlook and action **b** : instigated or carried out by reactionary forces as a counterrevolutionary measure ⟨a ~ terror⟩ **7** : of, relating to, or constituting a musical tone quality characterized by a controlled pure sound, a lack of warmth and color, and a lack of resonance **8** : consisting of a wide range of frequencies — used of light, sound, and electromagnetic radiation — **whit·ish** \'hwi-tish, 'wi-\ *adj*
²white *n* (bef. 12c) **1** : the achromatic object color of greatest lightness

characteristically perceived to belong to objects that reflect diffusely nearly all incident energy throughout the visible spectrum **2 a** : a white or light-colored part of something: as **(1)** : a mass of albuminous material surrounding the yolk of an egg **(2)** : the white part of the ball of the eye **(3)** : the light-colored pieces in a two-handed board game; *also* : the player by whom these are played **(4)** : the area of a page unmarked by writing, printing, or illustration **b (1)** *archaic* : a white target **(2)** : the fifth or outermost circle of an archery target; *also* : a shot that hits it **3** : one that is or approaches white in color: as **a** : white clothing — often used in pl. **b** : WHITE WINE **c** : a white mammal (as a horse or a hog) **d (1)** : a white-colored product (as flour, pins, or sugar) — usu. used in pl. **(2)** : any of numerous butterflies (subfamily Pierinae of the family Pieridae) that usu. have the ground color of the wings white and are related to the sulphur butterflies **4** *pl* : LEUKORRHEA **5** : a person belonging to a light-skinned race **6** *often cap* : a member of a conservative or reactionary political group

³**white** *vt* **whit·ed; whit·ing** [ME, fr. *white,* adj.] (bef. 12c) *archaic* : WHITEN

white amur \-ä-'mùr\ *n* [*amur* fr. *Amur* River] (1968) : GRASS CARP

white ant *n* (1684) : TERMITE

white ash *n* (1683) : an American ash (*Fraxinus americana*) having compound leaves with a pale green or silvery white underside; *also* : its hard brownish wood

white·bait \'hwīt-,bāt, 'wīt-\ *n* (1758) **1** : the young of any of several European herrings and esp. of the common herring (*Clupea harengus*) or of the sprat (*C. sprattus*) **2** : any of various small fishes likened to the European whitebait and used as food

white bass *n* (1813) : a No. American freshwater bony fish (*Morone chrysops* of the family Percichthyidae) that is used for food

white bean *n* (1969) : a dried white kidney bean seed; *also* : a plant that is a source of white beans

white·beard \'hwīt-,bird, 'wīt-\ *n* (15c) : an old man : GRAYBEARD

white birch *n* (1789) **1** : PAPER BIRCH; *also* : GRAY BIRCH **2** : either of two European birches (*Betula pubescens* and *B. pendula*) with white or ash-colored bark that are often planted as ornamentals in the U.S.

white blood cell *n* (1885) : any of the blood cells that are colorless, lack hemoglobin, contain a nucleus, and include the lymphocytes, monocytes, neutrophils, eosinophils, and basophils — called also *white blood corpuscle*

white book *n* (15c) : an official report of government affairs bound in white

white–bread \'hwīt-'bred, 'wīt-\ *adj* (1979) : being, typical of, or having qualities (as blandness) associated with the white middle class

white·cap \'hwīt-,kap, 'wīt-\ *n* (1773) : a wave crest breaking into white foam — usu. used in pl.

white cedar *n* (1674) **1** : a strong-scented evergreen swamp tree (*Chamaecyparis thyoides*) of the cypress family that occurs along the eastern coast of the U.S. and that has smaller leaves than an arborvitae and globose cones with peltate scales; *also* : its wood **2** : NORTHERN WHITE CEDAR

white cell *n* (1861) : WHITE BLOOD CELL

white chip *n* (1897) **1** : a white-colored poker chip usu. of minimum value **2** : a thing or quantity of little worth — compare BLUE CHIP

white chocolate *n* (1923) : a confection of cocoa butter, sugar, milk solids, lecithin, and flavorings

white clover *n* (bef. 12c) : a Eurasian clover (*Trifolium repens*) with round heads of white flowers that is widely used in lawn and pasture grass-seed mixtures and is an important source of nectar for bees — called also *white Dutch clover*

white–col·lar \'hwīt-'kä-lər, 'wīt-\ *adj* (1920) : of, relating to, or constituting the class of salaried employees whose duties do not call for the wearing of work clothes or protective clothing — compare BLUE-COLLAR

white crappie *n* (ca. 1926) : a silvery No. American sunfish (*Pomoxis annularis*) with 5 or 6 protruding spines on the dorsal fins that is used as a panfish and often for stocking small ponds

white–crowned sparrow \'hwīt-'kraünd-, 'wīt-\ *n* (1839) : a migratory sparrow (*Zonotrichia leucophrys*) that breeds in northern and western No. America and has a grayish breast, pink bill, and head striped with black and white

whit·ed \'hwī-təd, 'wī-\ *adj* (14c) **1** : covered with white or whiting and esp. with whitewash **2** : made white : WHITENED

whited sepulcher *n* [fr. the simile in Mt 23:27 (AV)] (1582) : a person inwardly corrupt or wicked but outwardly or professedly virtuous or holy : HYPOCRITE

white dwarf *n, pl* **white dwarfs** (1924) : a small whitish star of low intrinsic brightness usu. with a mass approximately equal to that of the sun but with a density many times larger

white elephant *n* (15c) **1** : an Indian elephant of a pale color that is sometimes venerated in India, Sri Lanka, Thailand, and Myanmar **2 a** : a property requiring much care and expense and yielding little profit **b** : an object no longer of value to its owner but of value to others **c** : something of little or no value

white–face \'hwīt-,fās, 'wīt-\ *n* (1709) **1** : a white-faced animal; *specif* : HEREFORD **2** : dead-white facial makeup ⟨a clown in ~⟩

white–faced \-'fāst\ *adj* (1595) **1** : having a wan pale face **2** : having the face white in whole or in part — used esp. of an animal otherwise dark in color

white feather *n* [fr. the superstition that a white feather in the plumage of a gamecock is a mark of a poor fighter] (ca. 1785) : a mark or symbol of cowardice — used chiefly in the phrase *show the white feather*

white·fish \'hwīt-,fish, 'wīt-\ *n* (15c) **1 a** : any of various freshwater salmonid food fishes (esp. of genera *Coregonus* and *Prosopium*) **b** : any of various fishes resembling the true whitefishes **c** *Brit* : any of various market fishes with white flesh that is not oily **2** : the flesh of a whitefish esp. as an article of food

white flag *n* (1600) **1** : a flag of plain white used as a flag of truce or as a token of surrender **2** : a token of weakness or yielding

white flight *n* (1967) : the departure of white families usu. from urban neighborhoods undergoing racial integration or from cities implementing school desegregation

white·fly \'hwīt-,flī, 'wīt-\ *n* (ca. 1889) : any of numerous small homopterous insects (family Aleyrodidae) that are injurious plant pests

white–foot·ed mouse \'hwīt-,fù-təd-, 'wīt-\ *n* (1869) : any of various largely nocturnal mice (genus *Peromyscus*) of No. and Central America typically having whitish feet and underparts; *esp* : a common woodland mouse (*P. leucopus*) of No. America

white-footed mouse

white friar *n, often cap W&F* [fr. his white habit] (15c) : CARMELITE

white–fringed beetle \'hwīt-,frinj(d)-, 'wīt-\ *n* (1939) : any of a genus (*Graphognathus*) of So. American flightless beetles of which one (*G. leucoloma*) has been accidentally introduced into the southeastern U.S. where it is a pest on cultivated plants

white gas *n* (1926) : unleaded gasoline — called also *white gasoline*

white gold *n* (1666) : a pale alloy of gold esp. with nickel or palladium that resembles platinum in appearance

white goods *n pl* (ca. 1871) **1 a** : white fabrics esp. of cotton or linen **b** : articles (as sheets, towels, or curtains) orig. or typically made of white cloth **2** : major household appliances (as stoves and refrigerators) that are typically finished in white enamel

white grub *n* (ca. 1817) : a grub that is a destructive pest of grass roots and is the larva of various beetles and esp. june bugs

White·hall \'hwīt-,hól, 'wīt-\ *n* [*Whitehall,* thoroughfare of London in which are located the chief offices of British government] (1827) : the British government

white·head \-,hed\ *n* (ca. 1931) : MILIUM

white–head·ed \-'he-dəd\ *adj* (1525) **1** : having the hair, fur, or plumage of the head white or very light **2** : specially favored : FORTUNATE — used esp. in the phrase *white-headed boy*

white heat *n* (ca. 1710) **1** : a temperature for copper and iron from 1500° to 1600° C) which is higher than red heat and at which a body becomes brightly incandescent **2** : a state of intense mental or physical strain, emotion, or activity

white hole *n* (1971) : a hypothetical extremely dense celestial object that radiates enormous amounts of energy and matter — compare BLACK HOLE 1

white hope *n* (1911) **1** : a white contender for a boxing championship held by a black; *also* : one who is felt to represent white **2** : one from whom much is expected; *esp* : a person undertaking a difficult task

white–hot \'hwīt-'hät, 'wīt-\ *adj* (1820) **1** : being at or radiating white heat **2** : ardently zealous : FERVID

White House \-,haùs\ *n* [the *White House,* mansion in Washington, D.C., assigned to the use of the president of the U.S.] (1811) **1** : the executive department of the U.S. government **2** : a residence of the president of the U.S.

white hunter *n* (1945) : a white man serving as guide and professional hunter to an African safari

white knight *n* (1951) **1** : one that comes to the rescue of another; *esp* : a corporation invited to buy out a second corporation in order to prevent an undesired takeover by a third **2** : one that champions a cause

white–knuck·le \'hwīt-'nə-kəl, 'wīt-\ *also* **white–knuck·led** \-kəld\ *adj* (1974) : showing or causing tense nervousness ⟨a ~ ride on a roller coaster⟩

white lead *n* (15c) : any of several white lead-containing pigments; *esp* : a heavy poisonous basic carbonate of lead of variable composition that is marketed as a powder or as a paste in linseed oil, has good hiding power, and is used chiefly in exterior paints

white lightning *n* (1915) : MOONSHINE 3

white line *n* (15c) : a band or edge of something white; *esp* : a stripe painted on a road and used to guide traffic

white list \-,list\ *n* (1900) : a list of approved or favored items — compare BLACKLIST — **white–list·ed** \-,lis-təd\ *adj*

white–liv·ered \-'li-vərd\ *adj* [fr. the former belief that the choleric temperament depends on the body's producing large quantities of yellow bile] (1549) : PUSILLANIMOUS, LILY-LIVERED

white·ly \'hwīt-lē, 'wīt-\ *adv* (14c) : with an effect of whiteness : so as to show or appear white

white man's burden *n* ["The White Man's Burden" (1899), poem by Rudyard Kipling] (1911) : the alleged duty of the white peoples to manage the affairs of the less developed nonwhite peoples

white matter *n* (ca. 1847) : neural tissue that consists largely of myelinated nerve fibers, has a whitish color, and underlies the gray matter of the brain and spinal cord or is gathered into nerves

white metal *n* (1613) **1** : any of several light-colored alloys used esp. as a base for plated silverware and ornaments and novelties **2** : any of several lead-base or tin-base alloys (as babbitt) used esp. for bearings, fusible plugs, and type metal

whit·en \'hwī-t°n, 'wī-\ *vb* **whit·ened; whit·en·ing** \'hwīt-niŋ, 'wīt-, -°n-iŋ\ *vt* (14c) : to make white or whiter ⟨snow ~ed the hills⟩ ~ *vi* : to become white or whiter

whit·en·er \'hwīt-nər, 'wīt-; 'hwī-t°n-ər, 'wī-\ *n* (1611) : one that whitens; *specif* : an agent (as a bleach) used to impart whiteness to something

white·ness \'hwīt-nəs, 'wīt-\ *n* (bef. 12c) **1** : the quality or state of being white: as **a** : white color **b** : PALLOR, PALENESS **c** : freedom from stain : CLEANNESS **2** : white substance

whitening *n* (1601) **1** : the act or process of making or becoming white **2** : something that is used to make white : WHITING

white noise *n* (1943) : a heterogeneous mixture of sound waves extending over a wide frequency range

---

\ə\ abut \³\ kitten, F table \ər\ further \a\ ash \ā\ ace \ä\ mop, mar \aù\ out \ch\ chin \e\ bet \ē\ easy \g\ go \i\ hit \ī\ ice \j\ job \ŋ\ sing \ō\ go \ò\ law \òi\ boy \th\ thin \t͟h\ the \ü\ loot \ù\ foot \y\ yet \zh\ vision \à, k̲, ⁿ, œ, œ̄, ue, ūe, ᵫ, ʸ\ see Guide to Pronunciation

white oak n (1634) : any of various oaks (esp. *Quercus alba* of eastern No. America) with acorns that mature in one year and leaf veins that never extend beyond the margin of the leaf; *also* : its hard strong durable wood

white oil n (ca. 1900) : any of various colorless odorless tasteless mineral oils used esp. in medicine and in pharmaceutical and cosmetic preparations

white-out \'hwīt-ˌaut, 'wīt-\ n [*white* + *blackout*] (1942) : a surface weather condition in a snow-covered area (as a polar region) in which no object casts a shadow, the horizon cannot be seen, and only dark objects are discernible; *also* : a blizzard that severely reduces visibility

white pages n pl (1952) : the section of a telephone directory that lists individuals and businesses alphabetically

white oak: leaves and acorns

white paper n (1899) **1** : a government report on any subject; *esp* : a British publication that is usu. less extensive than a blue book **2** : a detailed or authoritative report

white pepper n (14c) : a pungent condiment that consists of the fruit of an East Indian plant (*Piper nigrum*) ground after the black husk has been removed

white perch n (1775) **1** : a silvery anadromous bass (*Morone americana*) chiefly of the coast and coastal streams of the eastern U.S. **2** : FRESHWATER DRUM **3** : WHITE CRAPPIE

white pine n (1682) **1 a** : a tall-growing pine (*Pinus strobus*) of eastern No. America with long needles in clusters of five — called also *eastern white pine* **b** : any of several trees that resemble the white pine esp. in having leaves in bundles of five **2** : the wood of a white pine and esp. of the eastern white pine

white–pine blister rust n (1911) : a destructive disease of white pine caused by a rust fungus (*Cronartium ribicola*) that passes part of its complex life cycle on currant or gooseberry bushes; *also* : this fungus

white potato n (ca. 1890) : POTATO 2b

white rice n (1923) : rice from which the hull and bran have been removed by milling

white room n (1961) : CLEAN ROOM

White Russian n (1850) **1** : BELORUSSIAN **2** : a cocktail made of vodka, coffee liqueur, and cream or milk

white rust n (ca. 1848) : any of various plant diseases caused by a fungus (genus *Albugo* of the order Peronosporales) and characterized by the presence of masses of white spores that escape through ruptures of the host tissue; *also* : a fungus causing a white rust

white sale n (1914) : a sale of white goods

white sauce n (1723) : a sauce consisting essentially of a roux with milk, cream, or stock and seasoning

white sea bass n (1884) : a large croaker (*Atractoscion nobilis*) of the Pacific coast that is an important sport and food fish

white shark n (1674) : GREAT WHITE SHARK

white slave n (1882) : a woman or girl held unwillingly for purposes of commercial prostitution

white slav·er \-'slā-vər\ n (1912) : one engaged in white-slave traffic

white slavery n (1857) : enforced prostitution

white·smith \'hwīt-ˌsmith, 'wīt-\ n (14c) **1** : TINSMITH **2** : a worker in iron who finishes or polishes the work

white space n (1849) : the areas of a page without print or pictures

white spruce n (1770) **1** : any of several spruces; *esp* : a widely distributed spruce (*Picea glauca*) of coniferous forests of Canada and the northern U.S. that has short stiff blue-green needles and slender cones **2** : the wood of a white spruce; *esp* : the light pale tough straight-grained wood of the common white spruce (*Picea glauca*) used esp. for construction and as a source of paper pulp

white sucker n (ca. 1902) : a common and widespread edible sucker (*Catostomus commersoni*) of the U.S. and Canada

white supremacist n (1945) : an advocate of or believer in white supremacy

white supremacy n (1867) : a doctrine based on a belief in the inherent superiority of the white race over the black race and the correlative necessity for the subordination of blacks to whites in all relationships

white·tail \'hwīt-ˌtāl, 'wīt-\ n (1872) : WHITE-TAILED DEER

white–tailed deer \-ˈtāld-\ n (1849) : a No. American deer (*Odocoileus virginianus*) with a rather long tail white on the undersurface and the males of which have forward-arching antlers

white·throat \'hwīt-ˌthrōt, 'wīt-\ n (1676) : any of several birds with white on the throat: as **a** : an Old World warbler (*Sylvia communis*) with rusty upper parts and largely pale buff underparts **b** : WHITE-THROATED SPARROW

white–throat·ed sparrow \-ˌthrō-təd-\ n (1811) : a common brown sparrow (*Zonotrichia albicollis*) chiefly of eastern No. America with a black-and-white striped crown and a white patch on the throat

white–tie adj (1936) : characterized by or requiring the wearing of formal evening clothes consisting of white tie and tailcoat for men and a formal gown for women ⟨a ~ dinner⟩ — compare BLACK-TIE

white trash n sing but pl in constr (1831) : POOR WHITE — usu. used disparagingly

white-wall \'hwīt-ˌwol, 'wīt-\ n (1953) : an automobile tire having a white band on the sidewall

white walnut n (1743) **1** : BUTTERNUT 1 **2** : the light-colored wood of a butternut

¹white·wash \'hwīt-ˌwosh, 'wīt-, -ˌwäsh\ vt (1591) **1** : to whiten with whitewash **2 a** : to gloss over or cover up (as vices or crimes) **b** : to exonerate by means of a perfunctory investigation or through biased presentation of data **3** : to hold (an opponent) scoreless in a game or contest — **white·wash·er** n

²whitewash n (1689) **1** : a liquid composition for whitening a surface: as **a** : a preparation for whitening the skin **b** : a composition (as of lime and water or whiting, size, and water) for whitening structural surfaces **2** : an act or instance of glossing over or of exonerating **3** : a defeat in a contest in which the loser fails to score

white·wash·ing n (1663) : an act or instance of applying whitewash; *also* : WHITEWASH 3

white water n (1586) : frothy water (as in breakers, rapids, or falls) — **white–water** adj

white way n [the *Great White Way*, nickname for the theatrical section of Broadway, New York City] (1909) : a brilliantly lighted street or avenue esp. in a city's business or theater district

white whale n (ca. 1834) : a cetacean (*Delphinapterus leucas*) that is about 10 feet (3.0 meters) long and white when adult — called also *beluga*

white wine n (14c) : a wine ranging in color from faintly yellow to amber that is produced from the juice alone of dark- or light-colored grapes

white·wing \'hwīt-ˌwiŋ, 'wīt-\ n (1898) : a person and esp. a street sweeper wearing a white uniform

white·wood \-ˌwud\ n (1663) **1** : any of various trees with pale or white wood: as **a** : TULIP TREE 1 **b** : an Australian tree (*Atalaya hemiglauca*) of the soapberry family **2** : the wood of a whitewood; *esp* : TULIPWOOD 1

whit·ey \'hwī-tē, 'wī-\ n, often cap (1828) : the white man : white society — usu. used disparagingly

white zinfandel n (1976) : a blush wine made from zinfandel grapes

¹whith·er \'hwi-thər, 'wi-\ adv [ME, fr. OE *hwider*; akin to L *quis* who and to OE *hider* hither — more at WHO, HITHER] (bef. 12c) **1** : to what place ⟨~ will they go⟩ **2** : to what situation, position, degree, or end ⟨~ will this abuse drive him⟩

²whither conj (bef. 12c) **1 a** : to what place ⟨knew ~ to go —Daniel Defoe⟩ **b** : to what situation, position, degree, or end **2 a** : to the place at, in, or to which **b** : to which place **3** : to whatever place

whith·er·so·ev·er \ˌhwi-thər-sə-'we-vər, ˌwi-\ conj (14c) : to whatever place ⟨will go ~ you lead⟩

whith·er·ward \'hwi-thər-wərd, 'wi-\ adv (13c) archaic : toward what or which place

¹whit·ing \'hwī-tiŋ, 'wī-\ n [ME, fr. MD *witinc*, fr. *wit* white; akin to OE *hwīt* white] (15c) : any of various marine food fishes: as **a** : a common European fish (*Merlangus merlangus*) of the cod family **b** : SILVER HAKE

²whiting n [ME, fr. gerund of *whiten* to white] (15c) : calcium carbonate ground into fine powder, washed, and used esp. as a pigment and extender, in putty, and in rubber compounding and paper coating

whit·low \'hwit-(ˌ)lō, 'wit-\ n [ME *whitflawe, whitflowe, whitlowe*] (14c) : a deep usu. suppurative inflammation of the finger or toe esp. near the end or around the nail — called also *felon*

Whit·mon·day \'hwit-ˌmən-dē, 'wit-, -'mən-\ n [*Whitsunday* + *Monday*] (1557) : the day after Whitsunday observed as a legal holiday in England, Wales, and Ireland

Whit·sun \'hwit-sən, 'wit-\ adj [ME *Whitson*, fr. *Whitsunday*] (14c) : of, relating to, or observed on Whitsunday or at Whitsuntide

Whit·sun·day \-'sən-dē, -sən-ˌdā\ n [ME *Whitsonday*, fr. OE *hwīta sunnandæg*, lit., white Sunday; prob. fr. the custom of wearing white robes by those newly baptized at this season] (12c) : PENTECOST 2

Whit·sun·tide \-sən-ˌtīd\ n (13c) : the week beginning with Whitsunday and esp. the first three days of this week

¹whit·tle \'hwi-t³l, 'wi-\ n [ME *whittel*, alter. of *thwitel*, fr. *thwiten* to whittle, fr. OE *thwītan*; akin to ON *thveita* to hew] (15c) archaic : a large knife

²whittle vb whit·tled; whit·tling \'hwit-liŋ, 'wit-; 'hwi-t³l-iŋ, 'wi-\ vt (1552) **1 a** : to pare or cut off chips from the surface of (wood) with a knife **b** : to shape or form by so paring or cutting **2** : to reduce, remove, or destroy gradually as if by cutting off bits with a knife : PARE ⟨~ down expenses⟩ ~ vi **1** : to cut or shape something (as wood) by or as if by paring with a knife **2** : to wear oneself or another out with fretting — **whit·tler** \'hwit-lər, 'wit-; 'hwi-t³l-ər, 'wi-\ n

whit·tling n (1854) **1** : the act or art of whittling **2** : a piece cut away in whittling

whit·tret \'hwi-trət, 'wi-\ n [ME *whitrat*, fr. *white, whit* white + *rat* rat] (15c) chiefly Scot : WEASEL

whity or **whit·ey** \'hwī-tē, 'wī-\ adj (1593) : somewhat white : WHITISH — usu. used in combination

¹whiz or **whizz** \'hwiz, 'wiz\ vb whizzed; whiz·zing [imit.] vi (1547) **1** : to hum, whir, or hiss like a speeding object (as an arrow or ball) passing through air **2** : to fly or move swiftly esp. with a whiz ~ vt : to cause to whiz, rotate, or spin rapidly

²whiz or **whizz** n, pl **whiz·zes** (1620) **1** : a hissing, buzzing, or whirring sound **2** : a movement or passage of something accompanied by a whizzing sound

³whiz n, pl **whiz·zes** [prob. by shortening & alter.] (1914) : WIZARD 3 ⟨a ~ at math⟩

whiz·bang also **whizz·bang** \'hwiz-ˌbaŋ, 'wiz-, -ˈbaŋ\ n (1915) : one that is conspicuous for noise, speed, excellence, or startling effect — **whiz–bang** adj

whiz kid also **whizz kid** n [³whiz] (ca. 1942) : a person who is unusually intelligent, clever, or successful esp. at an early age

whiz·zer \'hwi-zər, 'wi-\ n (1881) : one that whizzes; *esp* : a centrifugal machine for drying something (as grain, sugar, or nitrated cotton)

who \'hü, ü\ pron [ME, fr. OE *hwā*; akin to OHG *hwer*, interrog. pron., who, L *quis*, Gk *tis*, L *qui*, rel. pron., who] (bef. 12c) **1** : what or which person or persons — used as an interrogative ⟨~ was elected?⟩ ⟨find out ~ they are⟩; used by speakers on all educational levels and by many reputable writers, though disapproved by some grammarians, as the object of a verb or a following preposition ⟨~ did I see but a Spanish lady —Padraic Colum⟩ ⟨do not know ~ the message is from —G. K. Chesterton⟩ **2** : the person or persons that : WHOEVER **3** — used as a function word to introduce a relative clause; used esp. in reference to persons ⟨my father, ~ was a lawyer⟩ but also in reference to groups ⟨a generation ~ had known nothing but war —R. B. West⟩ or to animals ⟨dogs ~ . . . fawn all over tramps —Nigel Balchin⟩ or to inanimate objects esp. with the implication that the reference is really to a person ⟨earlier sources ~ maintain a Davidic ancestry —F. M. Cross⟩; used by speakers on all educational levels and by many reputable writers, though disapproved by some grammarians, as the object of a verb or a following preposition ⟨a character ~ we are meant to pity —*Times Lit. Supp.*⟩ *usage* see WHOM, THAT — **who·so** archaic : as one that : as if someone — **as who should say** archaic : so to speak — **who is who** or **who's who** or **who was who** : the identity of or the noteworthy facts about each of a number of persons

whoa \'wō, 'hō, 'hwō\ *vb imper* [ME *whoo, who*] (15c) — a command (as to a draft animal) to stand still

who'd \'hüd\ (1640) : who had : who would

who·dun·it *also* **who·dun·nit** \hü-'də-nət\ *n* [alter. of *who done it?*] (1930) : a detective story or mystery story

who·ev·er \hü-'e-vər\ *pron* (13c) : whatever person : no matter who — used in any grammatical relation except that of a possessive ⟨sells to ~ has the money to buy⟩

¹whole \'hōl\ *adj* [ME *hool* healthy, unhurt, entire, fr. OE *hāl;* akin to OHG *heil* healthy, unhurt, ON *heill,* OCS *cělŭ*] (bef. 12c) **1 a** (1) : free of wound or injury : UNHURT (2) : recovered from a wound or injury : RESTORED (3) : being healed ⟨~ of an ancient evil, I sleep sound —A. E. Housman⟩ **b** : free of defect or impairment : INTACT **c** : physically sound and healthy : free of disease or deformity **d** : mentally or emotionally sound **2** : having all its proper parts or components : COMPLETE, UNMODIFIED ⟨~ milk⟩ ⟨a ~ egg⟩ **3 a** : constituting the total sum or undiminished entirety : ENTIRE ⟨owns the ~ island⟩ **b** : each or all of the ⟨took part in the ~ series of athletic events⟩ **4 a** : constituting an undivided unit : UNBROKEN, UNCUT ⟨a ~ roast suckling pig⟩ **b** : directed to one end : CONCENTRATED ⟨promised to give it his ~ attention⟩ **5 a** : seemingly complete or total ⟨the ~ idea is to help, not hinder⟩ **b** : very great in quantity, extent, or scope ⟨feels a ~ lot better now⟩ **6** : constituting the entirety of a person's nature or development ⟨educate the ~ student⟩ **7** : having the same father and mother ⟨~ brother⟩ *syn* see PERFECT — **whole·ness** *n*

syn WHOLE, ENTIRE, TOTAL, ALL mean including everything or everyone without exception. WHOLE implies that nothing has been omitted, ignored, abated, or taken away ⟨read the *whole* book⟩. ENTIRE may suggest a state of completeness or perfection to which nothing can be added ⟨the *entire* population was wiped out⟩. TOTAL implies that everything has been counted, weighed, measured, or considered ⟨the *total* number of people present⟩. ALL may equal WHOLE, ENTIRE, or TOTAL ⟨*all* proceeds go to charity⟩.

²whole *n* (14c) **1** : a complete amount or sum : a number, aggregate, or totality lacking no part, member, or element **2** : something constituting a complex unity : a coherent system or organization of parts fitting or working together as one — **in whole** : to the full or entire extent : WHOLLY — usu. used in the phrase *in whole or in part* — **on the whole 1** : in view of all the circumstances or conditions : all things considered **2** : in general : in most instances : TYPICALLY

³whole *adv* (14c) **1** : WHOLLY, ENTIRELY ⟨a ~ new age group —Henry Chauncey⟩ **2** : as a complete entity

whole cloth *n* (1840) : pure fabrication — usu. used in the phrase *out of whole cloth*

whole gale *n* (ca. 1805) : wind having a speed of 55 to 63 miles (88 to 101 kilometers) per hour — see BEAUFORT SCALE table

whole·heart·ed \'hōl-'här-təd\ *adj* (1840) **1** : completely and sincerely devoted, determined, or enthusiastic ⟨a ~ student of social problems⟩ **2** : marked by complete earnest commitment : free from all reserve or hesitation ⟨gave the proposal ~ approval⟩ *syn* see SINCERE — **whole·heart·ed·ly** *adv*

whole·hog *adj* (1829) : committed without reservation : THOROUGHGOING ⟨a ~ patriot⟩

¹whole hog *n* (1829) : the whole way or farthest limit — usu. used adverbially in the phrase *go the whole hog*

²whole hog *adv* (1844) : to the fullest extent : without reservation : COMPLETELY ⟨accepting *whole hog* the standards . . . of the majority —R. B. Kaplan⟩

whole-life \'hōl-'līf\ *adj* (1845) : of, relating to, or being life insurance with a fixed premium for the life of the policyholder and a cash value that can be redeemed on sale of the policy or can be the basis of low-interest loans

whole note *n* (1597) : a musical note equal in time value to four quarter notes or two half notes — see NOTE illustration

whole number *n* (1557) : any of the set of nonnegative integers; *also* : INTEGER

whole rest *n* (ca. 1890) : a musical rest corresponding in time value to a whole note — see REST illustration

¹whole·sale \'hōl-,sāl\ *n* (15c) : the sale of commodities in quantity usu. for resale (as by a retail merchant)

²wholesale *adj* (1642) **1** : performed or existing on a large scale esp. without discrimination ⟨~ slaughter⟩ **2** : of, relating to, or engaged in the sale of commodities in quantity for resale ⟨a ~ grocer⟩

³wholesale *adv* (1759) : in a wholesale manner

⁴wholesale *vb* **whole·saled; whole·sal·ing** *vt* (1800) : to sell (something) in quantity usu. for resale ~ *vi* : to sell in quantity usu. for resale

whole·sal·er \'hōl-,sā-lər\ *n* (1857) : a merchant middleman who sells chiefly to retailers, other merchants, or industrial, institutional, and commercial users mainly for resale or business use

whole·some \'hōl-səm\ *adj* (13c) **1** : promoting health or well-being of mind or spirit **2** : promoting health of body **3 a** : sound in body, mind, or morals **b** : having the simple health or vigor of normal domesticity **4 a** : based on well-grounded fear : PRUDENT ⟨a ~ respect for the law⟩ **b** : SAFE ⟨it wouldn't be ~ for you to go down there —Mark Twain⟩ *syn* see HEALTHFUL, HEALTHY — **whole·some·ly** *adv* — **whole·some·ness** *n*

whole–souled \'hōl-'sōld\ *adj* (1834) : moved by ardent enthusiasm or single-minded devotion : WHOLEHEARTED

whole step *n* (ca. 1899) : a musical interval (as C–D or G–A) comprising two half steps — called also *whole tone*

whole wheat *adj* (1880) : made of ground entire wheat kernels

who·lis·tic \hō-'lis-tik\ *var of* HOLISTIC

whol·ly \'hō(l)-lē\ *adv* [ME *hoolly,* fr. *hool* whole] (14c) **1** : to the full or entire extent : COMPLETELY ⟨a ~ owned subsidiary⟩ **2** : to the exclusion of other things : SOLELY ⟨a book dealing ~ with herbs⟩

whom \'hüm, üm\ *pron, objective case of* WHO [ME, fr. OE *hwām,* dat. of *hwā* who] (bef. 12c) — used as an interrogative or relative; used as object of a verb or a preceding preposition ⟨to know for ~ the bell tolls —John Donne⟩ or less frequently as the object of a following preposition ⟨the man ~ you wrote to⟩ though now often considered stilted esp. as an interrogative and esp. in oral use; occas. used as predicate nominative with a copulative verb or as subject of a verb esp. in the vicinity of a preposition or a verb of which it might mistakenly be considered the object ⟨~ say ye that I am —Mt 16:15 (AV)⟩ ⟨people . . . ~ you never thought would sympathize —Shea Murphy⟩

usage Observers of the language have been predicting the demise of *whom* from about 1870 down to the present day ⟨one of the pronoun cases is visibly disappearing—the objective case *whom* —R. G. White (1870)⟩ ⟨*whom* is dying out in England, where "Whom did you see?" sounds affected —Anthony Burgess (1980)⟩. Our evidence shows that no one—English or not—should expect *whom* to disappear momentarily; it shows every indication of persisting quite a while yet. Actual usage of *who* and *whom*—accurately described at the entries in this dictionary—does not appear to be markedly different from that usage of Shakespeare's time. But the 18th century grammarians, propounding rules and analogies, rejecting other rules and analogies, and usu. justifying both with appeals to Latin or Greek, have intervened between us and Shakespeare. It seems clear that the grammarians' rules have had little effect on the traditional uses. One thing they have accomplished is to encourage hypercorrect uses of *whom* ⟨*whom* shall I say is calling?⟩. Another is that they have made some people unsure of themselves ⟨said he was asked to step down, although it is not known exactly *who* or *whom* asked him —*Redding (Conn.) Pilot*⟩.

whom·ev·er \hü-'me-vər\ *pron, objective case of* WHOEVER

¹whomp \'hwämp, 'hwómp, 'wämp, 'wómp\ *n* [imit.] (1926) : a loud slap, crash, or crunch

²whomp *vi* (1942) : to strike with a sharp noise or thump ~ *vt* **1** : to hit or slap sharply **2** : to defeat decisively : TROUNCE **3** : to create or put together esp. hastily — usu. used with *up*

whomp up *vt* (1949) : to stir up : AROUSE

whom·so \'hüm-(,)sō\ *pron, objective case of* WHOSO

whom·so·ev·er \,hüm-sə-'we-vər\ *pron, objective case of* WHOSOEVER

¹whoop \'hüp, 'hup, 'hwüp, 'hwup, 'wüp, 'wup\ *vb* [ME *whopen,* fr. MF *houpper,* of imit. origin] *vi* (14c) **1** : to utter a whoop in expression of eagerness, enthusiasm, or enjoyment : SHOUT **2** : to utter the cry of an owl : HOOT **3** : to make the characteristic whoop of whooping cough **4 a** : to go or pass with a loud noise **b** : to be rushed through by acclamation or with noisy support ⟨the bill ~ed through both houses⟩ ~ *vt* **1 a** : to utter or express with a whoop **b** : to urge, drive, or cheer on with a whoop **2** : to agitate in behalf of **3** : RAISE, BOOST ⟨~ up the price⟩ — **whoop it up 1** : to celebrate riotously : CAROUSE **2** : to stir up enthusiasm

²whoop *n* (1593) **1 a** : a loud yell expressive of eagerness, exuberance, or jubilation — often used interjectionally **b** : a shout of hunters or of men in battle or pursuit **2** : the cry of an owl : HOOT **3** : the crowing intake of breath following a paroxysm in whooping cough **4** : a minimum amount or degree : the least bit ⟨not worth a ~⟩

whoop–de–do *or* **whoop–de–doo** \,h(w)üp-dē-'dü, ,h(w)up-, -tē-\ *n* [prob. irreg. fr. ²*whoop*] (1929) **1** : noisy and exuberant or attention-getting activity (as at a social affair or in a political campaign) **2** : a lively social affair **3** : agitated public discussion or debate

¹whoop·ee \'(h)wü-(,)pē, '(h)wü-; (h)wü-'pē, (h)wü-\ *interj* [irreg. fr. ²*whoop*] (1845) — used to express exuberance

²whoop·ee \'(h)wü-(,)pē, '(h)wü-\ *n* (1924) **1** : boisterous convivial fun : MERRYMAKING — usu. used with *make* **2** : sexual play — usu. used with *make*

whoopee cushion *n* (1953) : a cushion that makes a sound like the breaking of wind when sat upon

whoop·er \'h(w)ü-pər, 'h(w)ü-\ *n* (1660) : one that whoops; *specif* : WHOOPING CRANE

whooper swan *n* (1880) : a chiefly Eurasian swan (*Cygnus cygnus*) with a yellow and black bill — compare TRUMPETER SWAN

whooping cough *n* (ca. 1670) : an infectious disease esp. of children caused by a bacterium (*Bordetella pertussis*) and marked by a convulsive spasmodic cough sometimes followed by a crowing intake of breath — called also *pertussis*

whooping crane *n* (ca. 1730) : a large white nearly extinct No. American crane (*Grus americana*) noted for its loud trumpeting call

whoop·la \'h(w)üp-,lä, 'h(w)up-\ *n* [alter. of *hoopla*] (1931) **1** : HOOPLA **2** : boisterous merry-making

whooping crane

whoops \'(w)ú(ə)ps\ *var of* OOPS

¹whoosh \'hwüsh, 'wüsh, '(h)wush\ *n* [imit.] (1880) : a swift or explosive rush; *also* : the sound created by such a rush — often used interjectionally

²whoosh *vi* (1909) : to rush past or move explosively ⟨cars ~ing along the expressway⟩ ~ *vt* : to move (a person or thing) with or as if with a whoosh

¹whop \'hwäp, 'wäp\ *vt* **whopped; whop·ping** [ME *whappen,* alter. of *wappen* to throw violently] (15c) **1** : to pull or whip out **2 a** : BEAT, STRIKE **b** : to defeat totally

²whop *n* (15c) : a heavy blow : THUMP

whop·per \'hwä-pər, 'wä-\ *n* [¹*whop*] (ca. 1785) **1** : something unusually large or otherwise extreme of its kind **2** : an extravagant or monstrous lie

whop·ping \'hwä-piŋ, 'wä-\ *adj* (ca. 1625) : extremely large; *also* : EXTRAORDINARY, INCREDIBLE

¹whore \'hōr, 'hòr, 'hùr\ *n* [ME *hore,* fr. OE *hōre;* akin to ON *hōra* whore, *hōrr* adulterer, L *carus* dear — more at CHARITY] (bef. 12c) **1** : a woman who engages in sexual acts for money : PROSTITUTE; *also* : a promiscuous or immoral woman **2** : a male who engages in sexual acts for money **3** : a venal or unscrupulous person

²whore *vb* **whored; whor·ing** *vi* (1583) **1** : to have unlawful sexual intercourse as or with a whore **2** : to pursue a faithless, unworthy, or idolatrous desire ~ *vt, obs* : to corrupt by lewd intercourse : DEBAUCH

\ə\ abut \ᵊ\ kitten, F table \ər\ further \a\ ash \ā\ ace \ä\ mop, mar \aú\ out \ch\ chin \e\ bet \ē\ easy \g\ go \i\ hit \ī\ ice \j\ job \ŋ\ sing \ō\ go \ò\ law \òi\ boy \th\ thin \t͟h\ the \ü\ loot \ú\ foot \y\ yet \zh\ vision \à, k̲, ⁿ, œ, œ̄, ᵫ, ū̇, ᵞ\ *see* Guide to Pronunciation

whore·dom \'hȯr-dəm, 'hȯr-, 'hu̇r-\ n [ME *hordom* sexual immorality, idolatrous practices, fr. ON *hōrdōmr* adultery, fr. *hōrr*] (12c) **1** : the practice of whoring : PROSTITUTION **2** : faithless, unworthy, or idolatrous practices or pursuits

whore·house \'hȯr-ˌhau̇s, 'hȯr-, 'hu̇r-\ n (14c) : a building in which prostitutes are available : BORDELLO

whore·mas·ter \-ˌmas-tər\ n (14c) : a man consorting with whores or given to lechery

whore·mon·ger \-ˌməŋ-gər, -ˌmäŋ-\ n (1526) : WHOREMASTER

whore·son \'hȯr-sᵊn, 'hȯr-, 'hu̇r-\ n, *often attrib* (14c) **1** : BASTARD **2** : a coarse fellow — used as a generalized term of abuse

Whorf·ian hypothesis \'wȯr-fē-ən-, 'hwȯr-\ n [Benjamin Lee *Whorf* †1941 Am. anthropologist] (1954) : a theory in linguistics: one's language determines one's conception of the world

whor·ish \'hȯr-ish, 'hȯr-, 'hu̇r-\ adj (1535) : of or befitting a whore

whorl \'hwȯr(-ə)l, 'wȯr(-ə)l, '(h)wər(-ə)l\ n [ME *wharle, whorle*, prob. alter. of *whirle*, fr. *whirlen* to whirl] (15c) **1** : a drum-shaped section on the lower part of a spindle in spinning or weaving machinery serving as a pulley for the tape drive that rotates the spindle **2** : an arrangement of similar anatomical parts (as leaves) in a circle around a point on an axis **3** : something that whirls, coils, or spirals or whose form suggests such movement : SWIRL ⟨~s of snow⟩ **4** : one of the turns of a univalve shell **5** : a fingerprint in which the central papillary ridges turn through at least one complete circle

whorled \'hwȯr(-ə)ld, 'wȯr(-ə)ld, '(h)wər(-ə)ld\ adj (ca. 1776) : having or arranged in whorls ⟨leaves ~ at the nodes of the stem⟩

whor·tle·ber·ry \'hwȯr-tᵊl-ˌber-ē, 'wər-\ n [alter. of earlier *hurtleberry*, fr. ME *hurtilberye*, irreg. fr. OE *horte* whortleberry + ME *berye* berry] (1578) **1** : a European blueberry (*Vaccinium myrtillus*); *also* : its glaucous blackish edible berry **2** : BLUEBERRY

¹whose \'hüz, üz\ adj [ME *whos*, gen. of *who, what*] (bef. 12c) : of or relating to whom or which esp. as possessor or possessors ⟨~ gorgeous vesture heaps the ground —Robert Browning⟩; agent or agents ⟨the law courts, ~ decisions were important —F. L. Mott⟩, or object or objects of an action ⟨the first poem ~ publication he ever sanctioned —J. W. Krutch⟩

²whose pron, *sing or pl in constr* (13c) : that which belongs to whom — used without a following noun as a pronoun equivalent in meaning to the adjective *whose* ⟨tell me ~ it was —Shak.⟩

whose·so·ev·er \ˌhüz-sə-'we-vər\ adj (1611) : of or relating to whomsoever ⟨~ sins ye remit —Jn 20:23 (AV)⟩

who·so \'hü-(ˌ)sō\ pron (12c) : WHOEVER

who·so·ev·er \ˌhü-sə-'we-vər\ pron (13c) : WHOEVER

who's who \ˌhüz-'hü\ n, *often cap both Ws* (1917) **1** : a compilation of brief biographical sketches of prominent persons in a particular field ⟨a *who's who* of sports figures⟩ **2** : the leaders of a group : ELITE; *also* : a listing of such figures

whump \'hwəmp, 'wəmp\ vi [imit.] (1897) : BANG, THUMP — **whump** n

¹why \'hwī, 'wī\ adv [ME, fr. OE *hwȳ*, instr. case of *hwæt* what — more at WHAT] (bef. 12c) : for what cause, reason, or purpose ⟨~ did you do it?⟩

²why conj (bef. 12c) **1** : the cause, reason, or purpose for which ⟨know ~ you did it⟩ ⟨that is ~ you did it⟩ **2** : for which : on account of which ⟨know the reason ~ you did it⟩

³why n, pl **whys** (14c) **1** : REASON, CAUSE ⟨wants to know the ~s and wherefores⟩ **2** : a baffling problem : ENIGMA

⁴why interj (1519) — used to express mild surprise, hesitation, approval, disapproval, or impatience ⟨~, here's what I was looking for⟩

whyd·ah \'hwi-də, 'wi-\ n [alter. of *widow (bird)*] (1783) : any of various mostly black and white African weaverbirds (genera *Euplectes* and *Vidua*) often kept as cage birds and distinguished in the male by long drooping tail feathers during the breeding season

¹wick \'wik\ n [ME *weke, wicke*, fr. OE *wēoce*; akin to OHG *wiohha* wick, MIr *figid* he weaves] (bef. 12c) : a bundle of fibers or a loosely twisted, braided, or woven cord, tape, or tube usu. of soft spun cotton threads that by capillary attraction draws up to be burned a steady supply of the oil in lamps or the melted tallow or wax in candles

²wick vt (1949) : to carry (as moisture) by capillary action — often used with *away* ⟨a fabric that ~s away perspiration⟩

¹wick·ed \'wi-kəd\ adj [ME, alter. of *wicke* wicked] (13c) **1** : morally very bad : EVIL **2 a** : FIERCE, VICIOUS ⟨a ~ dog⟩ **b** : disposed to or marked by mischief : ROGUISH ⟨does ~ impersonations⟩ **3 a** : disgustingly unpleasant : VILE ⟨a ~ odor⟩ **b** : causing or likely to cause harm, distress, or trouble ⟨a ~ storm⟩ **4** : going beyond reasonable or predictable limits : of exceptional quality or degree ⟨throws a ~ fastball⟩ — **wick·ed·ly** adv

²wicked adv (1980) : VERY, EXTREMELY ⟨~ fast⟩

wick·ed·ness n (14c) **1** : the quality or state of being wicked **2** : something wicked

wick·er \'wi-kər\ n [ME *wiker*, of Scand origin; akin to Sw dial. *vikker* willow, ON *veikr* weak — more at WEAK] (14c) **1** : a small pliant twig or branch : OSIER, WITHE **2 a** : WICKERWORK **b** : something made of wicker — **wicker** adj

wick·er·work \-ˌwərk\ n (1719) : work consisting of interlaced osiers, twigs, or rods ⟨a cage of ~⟩

wick·et \'wi-kət\ n [ME *wiket*, fr. ONF, of Gmc origin; akin to ON *vik* corner, *vīkja* to move, turn] (13c) **1** : a small gate or door; *esp* : one forming part of or placed near a larger gate or door **2** : an opening like a window; *esp* : a grilled or grated window through which business is transacted **3 a** : either of the two sets of three stumps topped by two crosspieces and set 66 feet apart at which the ball is bowled in cricket **b** : an area 10 feet wide bounded by these wickets **c** : one innings of a batsman; *specif* : one that is not completed or never begun ⟨win by three ~s⟩ **4** : an arch or hoop in croquet

wick·ing \'wi-kiŋ\ n (1847) : material for wicks

wick·i·up \'wi-kē-ˌəp\ n [Fox (Algonquian language of the Fox, Sauk, and Kickapoo Indians) *wī́kiyapi* house] (1852) : a hut used by the nomadic Indians of the arid regions of the western and southwestern U.S. with a usu.

wickiup

oval base and a rough frame covered with reed mats, grass, or brushwood; *also* : a rude temporary shelter or hut

wid·der·shins \'wi-dər-shənz\ adv [MLG *weddersinnes*, fr. MHG *widersinnes*, fr. *widersinnen* to go against, fr. *wider* back against (fr. OHG *widar*) + *sinnen* to travel, go; akin to OHG *sendan* to send — more at WITH, SEND] (1513) : in a left-handed, wrong, or contrary direction : COUNTERCLOCKWISE — compare DEASIL

wid·dy \'wi-dē\ n, pl **widdies** [ME *withy*] (15c) **1** *Scot & dial Eng* : a rope of osiers **2** *Scot & dial Eng* : a hangman's noose

¹wide \'wīd\ adj **wid·er; wid·est** [ME, fr. OE *wīd*; akin to OHG *wīt* wide] (bef. 12c) **1 a** : having great extent : VAST ⟨a ~ area⟩ **b** : extending over a vast area : EXTENSIVE ⟨a ~ reputation⟩ **c** : extending throughout a specified area or scope — usu. used in combination ⟨nationwide⟩ ⟨industry-wide⟩ **d** : COMPREHENSIVE, INCLUSIVE ⟨a ~ assortment⟩ **2 a** : having a specified extension from side to side ⟨3 feet ~⟩ **b** : having much extent between the sides : BROAD ⟨a ~ doorway⟩ **c** : fully opened ⟨wide-eyed⟩ **d** : LAX **4 3 a** : extending or fluctuating considerably between limits ⟨a ~ variation⟩ **b** : straying or deviating from something specified — used with *of* ⟨the accusation was ~ of the truth⟩ **4** *of an animal ration* : relatively rich in carbohydrate as compared with protein *syn* see BROAD — **wide·ness** n

²wide adv **wid·er; wid·est** (bef. 12c) **1 a** : over a great distance or extent : WIDELY ⟨searched far and ~⟩ **b** : over a specified distance, area, or extent — usu. used in combination ⟨expanded the business country= wide⟩ **2 a** : so as to leave much space or distance between ~ b : so as to pass at or clear by a considerable distance ⟨ran ~ around left end⟩ **3** : to the fullest extent : COMPLETELY, FULLY ⟨~ open⟩

wide–an·gle \'wid-ˌaŋ-gəl\ adj (1878) **1** : having or covering an angle of view wider than the ordinary — used esp. of lenses of shorter than normal focal length **2** : having, involving the use of, or relating to a wide-angle lens ⟨a ~ shot⟩

wide–awake \ˌwid-ə-'wāk\ n (1837) **1** : a soft felt hat with a low crown and a wide brim **2** : SOOTY TERN

wide–awake adj (1818) **1** : fully awake **2** : alertly watchful esp. for advantages or opportunities *syn* see WATCHFUL

wide·band \'wid-ˌband\ adj (1935) : BROADBAND

wide–body \'wid-ˌbä-dē\ n (1968) : a large jet aircraft

wide–eyed \'wid-'īd\ adj (1853) **1** : having the eyes wide open esp. with wonder or astonishment **2** : having or marked by unsophisticated or uncritical acceptance or admiration : NAIVE ⟨~ innocence⟩

wide·ly adv (1579) **1** : over or through a wide area ⟨has traveled ~⟩ **2** : to a great extent ⟨departed ~ from the previous edition⟩ **3** : by or among a large well-dispersed group of people ⟨a ~ known political figure⟩ **4** : over a broad range ⟨persons with ~ fluctuating incomes —*Current Biog.*⟩

wide–mouthed \'wid-'mau̇thd, -'mau̇tht\ adj (1593) **1** : having one's mouth opened wide (as in awe) **2** : having a wide mouth ⟨~ jars⟩

wid·en \'wī-dᵊn\ vb **wid·ened; wid·en·ing** \'wid-niŋ, 'wi-dᵊn-iŋ\ vt (1650) : to increase the width, scope, or extent of ~ vi : to become wide or wider — **wid·en·er** \'wid-nər, 'wi-dᵊn-ər\ n

wide–open \'wid-'ō-pən, -ˌō-\ adj (1852) : having virtually no limits or restrictions ⟨a ~ town⟩

wide·out \'wid-ˌau̇t\ n (1979) : WIDE RECEIVER

wide–rang·ing \'wid-ˌrān-jiŋ\ adj (1816) : extensive in scope : COMPREHENSIVE ⟨~ interests⟩

wide receiver n (1968) : a football receiver who normally lines up several yards to the side of the offensive formation

wide–screen adj (1931) : of or relating to a projected picture whose aspect ratio is substantially greater than 1.33:1

wide·spread \'wid-'spred\ adj (1705) **1** : widely diffused or prevalent ⟨~ public interest⟩ **2** : widely extended or spread out ⟨low, ~ hood and fenders —*Time*⟩ ⟨a ~ erosion surface —C. B. Hitchcock⟩

wide–spread·ing \-ˌspre-diŋ\ adj (1591) : stretching or extending over a wide space or area ⟨~ thatch roofs —*Nat'l Geographic*⟩

wid·get \'wi-jət\ n [alter. of *gadget*] (1926) **1** : GADGET **2** : an unnamed article manufactured for purposes of hypothetical example

wid·ish \'wi-dish\ adj (1845) : somewhat wide

¹wid·ow \'wi-(ˌ)dō\ n [ME *widewe*, fr. OE *wuduwe*; akin to OHG *wituwa* widow, L *vidua*, Skt *vidhavā*, L *-videre* to separate] (bef. 12c) **1 a** : a woman who has lost her husband by death and usu. has not remarried **b** : GRASS WIDOW **2 c** : a woman whose husband leaves her alone frequently or for long periods to engage in a usu. specified activity ⟨a golf ~⟩ **2** : an extra hand or part of a hand of cards dealt face down and usu. placed at the disposal of the highest bidder **3** : a single usu. short last line (as of a paragraph) separated from its related text and appearing at the top of a printed page or column

²widow vt (14c) **1** : to cause to become a widow or widower **2** *obs* : to survive as the widow of **3** : to deprive of something greatly valued or needed

wid·ow·er \'wi-də-wər\ n [ME *widewer*, alter. of *wedow* widow, widower, fr. OE *wuduwa* widower; akin to OE *wuduwe* widow] (14c) : a man who has lost his wife by death and usu. has not remarried

wid·ow·er·hood \-ˌhu̇d\ n (1796) **1** : the fact or state of being a widower **2** : the period during which a man remains a widower

wid·ow·hood \'wi-dō-ˌhu̇d, -də-\ n (bef. 12c) **1** : the fact or state of being a widow **2** : the period during which a woman remains a widow **3** : WIDOWERHOOD

widow's cruse n [fr. the widow's cruse of oil that miraculously supplies Elijah during a famine (I Kings 17:8–16)] (1816) : an inexhaustible supply

widow's peak n (1849) : a point formed by the hairline in front

widow's walk n (1937) : a railed observation platform atop a usu. coastal house

width \'width, 'witth\ n [¹*wide*] (1627) **1** : the horizontal measurement taken at right angles to the length : BREADTH **2** : largeness of extent or scope **3** : a measured and cut piece of material ⟨a ~ of calico⟩

wield \'wē(ə)ld\ vt [ME *welden* to control, fr. OE *wieldan*; akin to OHG *waltan* to rule, L *valēre* to be strong, be worth] (bef. 12c) **1** *chiefly dial* : to deal successfully with : MANAGE **2** : to handle (as a tool) esp. effectively ⟨~ a broom⟩ **3 a** : to exert one's authority by means of ⟨~ influence⟩ **b** : have at one's command or disposal ⟨did not ~ appropriate credentials —G. W. Bonham⟩ — **wield·er** n

wieldy \'wē(ə)l-dē\ adj (14c) : capable of being wielded easily

wie·ner \'wē-nər, 'wē-nē also 'wi-nē\ n [short for wienerwurst] (1900) : FRANKFURTER

Wie·ner schnit·zel \'vē-nər-,shnit-səl, 'wē-nər-,snit-\ n [G, lit., Vienna cutlet] (1862) : a thin breaded veal cutlet

wie·ner·wurst \'wē-nə(r)-,wərst also -,wúrst sometimes -,wúsht or -,wùst; also with v for w\ n [G, fr. Wiener of Vienna + Wurst sausage] (1889) **1** : VIENNA SAUSAGE **2** : FRANKFURTER

wie·nie \'wē-nē also 'wi-nē\ n [by shortening & alter. fr. wienerwurst] (1897) : FRANKFURTER

wife \'wīf\ n, pl **wives** \'wīvz\ [ME wif, fr. OE wif; akin to OHG wīb wife] (bef. 12c) **1** a dial : WOMAN **b** : a woman acting in a specified capacity — used in combination ⟨fishwife⟩ **2** : a female partner in a marriage — used with out — **wife·hood** \'wīf-,húd, 'wī-,fúd\ n — **wife·less** \'wī-fləs\ adj

¹wife·like \'wī-,flīk\ adv (1598) : in a wifely manner

²wifelike adj (1613) : WIFELY

wife·ly \-flē\ adj (bef. 12c) : of, relating to, or befitting a wife — **wife·li·ness** \-flē-nəs\ n

Wif·fle \'wi-fl\ trademark — used for a hollow plastic ball with cut-outs in one hemisphere

wif·ty \'wif-tē\ adj [origin unknown] (1979) : DITSY

¹wig \'wig\ n [short for periwig] (1675) **1** a : a manufactured covering of natural or synthetic hair for the head **b** : TOUPEE 2 **2** : an act of wigging : REBUKE

²wig vb **wigged; wig·ging** vt (1829) : to scold severely : REBUKE ~ vi, slang : to lose one's composure or reason : FLIP — usu. used with out

wig·an \'wi-gən\ n [Wigan, England] (ca. 1875) : a stiff plain-weave cotton fabric used for interlining

wi·geon or **wid·geon** \'wi-jən\ n, pl **wigeon** or **wigeons** or **widgeon** or **widgeons** [origin unknown] (1513) : any of several freshwater ducks (genus Anas): as **a** : an Old World duck (Anas penelope) with a large white patch on each wing and in the male with a red brown head and a buff crown **b** : BALDPATE 2

wigged \'wigd\ adj (1777) : wearing a wig esp. of a specified kind ⟨the mute, blond-wigged . . . member of the team —Current Biog.⟩

wigged–out \'wigd-'aút\ adj (1970) slang : having lost touch with reality : CRAZY

¹wig·gle \'wi-gəl\ vb **wig·gled; wig·gling** \-g(ə-)liŋ\ [ME wiglen, fr. or akin to MD or MLG wiggelen to totter; akin to OE wegan to move — more at WAY] vi (14c) **1** : to move to and fro with quick jerky or shaking motions : JIGGLE **2** : to proceed with or as if with twisting and turning movements : WRIGGLE ~ vt : to cause to wiggle

²wiggle n (1816) **1** : the act of wiggling **2** : shellfish or fish in cream sauce with peas — **wig·gly** \'wi-g(ə-)lē\ adj

wig·gler \'wi-g(ə-)lər\ n (1859) **1** : a larva or pupa of the mosquito — called also wriggler **2** : one that wiggles

¹wight \'wīt\ n [ME, creature, thing, fr. OE wiht; akin to OHG wiht creature, thing, OCS vešti thing] (bef. 12c) : a living being : CREATURE; esp : a human being

²wight adj [ME, of Scand origin; akin to ON vīgr skilled in fighting (neut. vīgt); akin to OE wīgan to fight — more at VICTOR] (13c) archaic : VALIANT, STALWART

wig·let \'wi-glət\ n (1831) : a small wig used esp. to enhance a hairstyle

¹wig·wag \'wig-,wag\ vb [E dial. wig to move + E wag] vt (1892) **1** : to signal by wigwagging **2** : to cause to wigwag ~ vi **1** : to send a signal by or as if by a flag or light waved according to a code **2** : to make a signal (as by waving the hand or arm)

²wigwag n (1886) : the art or practice of wigwagging

wig·wam \'wig-,wäm\ n [Eastern Abenaki wikəwam house] (1628) : a hut of the American Indians of the Great Lakes region and eastward having typically an arched framework of poles overlaid with bark, rush mats, or hides; also : a rough hut

wil·co \'wil-(,)kō\ interj [will comply] (ca. 1938) — used esp. in radio and signaling to indicate that a message received will be complied with

¹wild \'wī(ə)ld\ adj [ME wilde, fr. OE wilde; akin to OHG wildi wild, W gwyllt] (bef. 12c) **1** a : living in a state of nature and not ordinarily tame or domesticated ⟨~ duck⟩ **b** (1) : growing or produced without human aid or care ⟨~ honey⟩ (2) : related to or resembling a corresponding cultivated or domesticated organism **c** : of or relating to wild organisms ⟨the ~ state⟩ **2** a : not inhabited or cultivated ⟨~ land⟩ **b** : not amenable to human habitation or cultivation; also : DESOLATE **3** a (1) : not subject to restraint or regulation : UNCONTROLLED; also : UNRULY (2) : emotionally overcome ⟨~ with grief⟩; also : passionately eager or enthusiastic ⟨was ~ to own a toy train —J. C. Furnas⟩ **b** : marked by turbulent agitation : STORMY ⟨a ~ night⟩ **c** : going beyond normal or conventional bounds : FANTASTIC ⟨~ ideas⟩; also : SENSATIONAL **d** : indicative of strong passion, desire, or emotion ⟨a ~ gleam of delight in his eyes —Irish Digest⟩ **4** : UNCIVILIZED, BARBARIC **5** : characteristic of, appropriate to, or expressive of wilderness, wildlife, or a simple or uncivilized society **6** a : deviating from the intended or expected course ⟨~ spelling —C. W. Cunnington⟩ ⟨the throw was ~⟩; also : tending to throw inaccurately **b** : having no basis in known or surmised fact ⟨a ~ guess⟩ **7** of a playing card : able to represent any card designated by the holder — **wild·ish** \'wīl-dish\ adj — **wild·ness** \-nəs\ n

²wild adv (1549) : in a wild manner: as **a** : without regulation or control **b** : off an intended or expected course

³wild n (1596) **1** : a sparsely inhabited or uncultivated region or tract : WILDERNESS **2** : a wild, free, or natural state or existence

wild bergamot n (1843) : a fragrant No. American herbaceous mint (Monarda fistulosa) having a terminal capitate cluster of rather large pink or purple flowers

wild boar n (13c) : an Old World wild hog (Sus scrofa) from which most domestic swine have been derived

wild card n [wild card, playing card with arbitrarily determined value] (1972) **1** : one picked to fill a leftover playoff or tournament berth after regularly qualifying competitors have all been determined **2** : an unknown or unpredictable factor

wild carrot n (ca. 1538) : QUEEN ANNE'S LACE

¹wild·cat \'wī(ə)ld-,kat\ n, pl **wildcats** (14c) **1** a : a cat (Felis silvestris) of Eurasia and Africa that resembles but is heavier in build than the domestic tabby cat and is usu. held to be among the ancestors of the domestic cat **b** or pl **wildcat** : any of various small or medium-sized cats (as the lynx or ocelot) **c** : a feral domestic cat **2** : a savage

quick-tempered person **3** a : wildcat money **b** : a wildcat oil or gas well **c** : a wildcat strike

²wildcat adj (1838) **1** a (1) : financially irresponsible or unreliable ⟨~ banks⟩ (2) : issued by a financially irresponsible banking establishment ⟨~ currency⟩ **b** : operating, produced, or carried on outside the bounds of standard or legitimate business practices ⟨~ insurance schemes —H. H. Reichard⟩ **c** : of, relating to, or being an oil or gas well drilled in territory not known to be productive **d** : initiated by a group of workers without formal union approval or in violation of a contract ⟨a ~ strike⟩ ⟨~ work stoppages⟩ **2** a of a cartridge : having a bullet of standard caliber but using an expanded case or a case designed for a bullet of greater caliber necked down for the smaller bullet **b** of a firearm : using wildcat cartridges

³wildcat vi **wild·cat·ted; wild·cat·ting** (1883) : to prospect and drill an experimental oil or gas well or sink a mine shaft in territory not known to be productive

wild·cat·ter \-,ka-tər\ n (1883) **1** : one that drills wells in the hope of finding oil in territory not known to be an oil field **2** : one that promotes unsafe and unreliable enterprises; esp : one that sells stocks in such enterprises **3** : one that designs, builds, or fires wildcat cartridges and firearms **4** : a worker who goes out on a wildcat strike

wild celery n (1874) : TAPE GRASS

wil·de·beest \'wil-də-,bēst\ n, pl **wildebeests** also **wildebeest** [Afrik wildebees, fr. wilde wild + bees ox] (1824) : GNU

wil·der \'wil-dər\ vb [prob. irreg. fr. wilderness] vt (1613) **1** archaic : to lead astray **2** archaic : BEWILDER, PERPLEX ~ vi, archaic : to move at random : WANDER — **wil·der·ment** \-dər-mənt\ n, archaic

wil·der·ness \'wil-dər-nəs\ n [ME, fr. wildern wild, fr. OE wilddēoren of wild beasts] (13c) **1** a (1) : a tract or region uncultivated and uninhabited by human beings (2) : an area essentially undisturbed by human activity together with its naturally developed life community **b** : an empty or pathless area or region ⟨in remote ~es of space groups of nebulae are found —G. W. Gray †1960⟩ **c** : a part of a garden devoted to wild growth **2** obs : wild or uncultivated state **3** a : a confusing multitude or mass : an indefinitely great number or quantity ⟨I would not have given it for a ~ of monkeys —Shak.⟩ **b** : a bewildering situation ⟨those moral ~es of civilized life —Norman Mailer⟩

wilderness area n, often cap W&A (1928) : an often large tract of public land maintained essentially in its natural state and protected against introduction of intrusive artifacts (as roads and buildings)

wild–eyed \'wi(ə)ld-'īd\ adj (1817) **1** : having a wild expression in the eyes **2** : consisting of or favoring extreme or visionary ideas ⟨~ schemes⟩

wild·fire \-,fīr\ n (12c) **1** : a sweeping and destructive conflagration esp. in a wilderness or a rural area **2** : GREEK FIRE **3** : a phosphorescent glow (as ignis fatuus or fox fire) **4** : a destructive leaf-spot disease of tobacco caused by several strains of a bacterium (Pseudomonas syringae) — **like wildfire** : very rapidly

wild·flow·er \-,flaú(-ə)r\ n (1797) : the flower of a wild or uncultivated plant or the plant bearing it

wild·fowl \-,faúl\ n (bef. 12c) : a game bird; esp : a game waterfowl (as a wild duck or goose) — **wild·fowl·er** \-,faú-lər\ n — **wild·fowl·ing** \-liŋ\ n

wild geranium n (1840) : a common geranium (Geranium maculatum) of eastern No. America with deeply parted leaves and flowers of rosy purple; also : any of several related geraniums

wild ginger n (1804) : a No. American perennial herb (Asarum canadense) of the birthwort family with a pungent creeping rhizome

wild–goose chase n (1592) : a complicated or lengthy and usu. fruitless pursuit or search

wild hyacinth n (1847) : any of several plants with flowers suggestive of hyacinths: as **a** : a camas (Camassia scilloides) of the central U.S. and southern Ontario with white racemose flowers **b** : BLUEBELL 2a **c** : any of several western No. American plants (genus Brodiaea) of the lily family with grasslike basal leaves and variously colored flowers

wild indigo n (1744) : BAPTISIA; esp : a tumbleweed (Baptisia tinctoria) with bright yellow flowers and trifoliolate leaves

¹wild·ing \'wīl-diŋ\ n [¹wild + ²-ing] (ca. 1525) **1** : a plant growing uncultivated in the wild either as a native or an escape; esp : a wild apple or crab apple **b** : the fruit of a wilding **2** : a wild animal

²wilding adj (1697) : not domesticated or cultivated : WILD

wild·land \'wī(ə)l(d)-,land\ n (1813) : land that is uncultivated or unfit for cultivation

wild·life \-,līf\ n, often attrib (1879) : living things and esp. mammals, birds, and fishes that are neither human nor domesticated

wild·ling \-liŋ\ n (1840) : WILDING

wild·ly \'wī(ə)l(d)-lē\ adv (14c) **1** : in a wild manner ⟨was talking ~⟩ **2** : EXTREMELY 2 ⟨~ popular⟩

wild marjoram n (1550) : OREGANO 1

wild mustard n (1597) : CHARLOCK

wild oat n (15c) **1** : any of several wild grasses (genus Avena); esp : a European annual weed (A. fatua) common in meadows and pastures **2** pl : offenses and indiscretions ascribed to youthful exuberance — usu. used in the phrase sow one's wild oats

wild pansy n (ca. 1900) : JOHNNY-JUMP-UP

wild pink n (1814) : an American catchfly (Silene caroliniana) of the eastern U.S. with pink or whitish flowers

wild pitch n (1867) : a baseball pitch not hit by the batter that cannot be caught or controlled by the catcher with ordinary effort and that enables a base runner to advance — compare PASSED BALL

wild rice n (1748) : a tall aquatic No. American perennial grass (Zizania aquatica) that yields an edible grain; also : the grain

wild rye n (ca. 1500) : any of several grasses (genus Elymus)

wild sarsaparilla n (1814) : a common No. American perennial herb (Aralia nudicaulis) of the ginseng family with long-stalked basal compound leaves, umbels of greenish flowers, and an aromatic root used as a substitute of true sarsaparilla

---

\ə\ abut \ᵊ\ kitten, F table \ər\ further \a\ ash \ā\ ace \ä\ mop, mar
\aú\ out \ch\ chin \e\ bet \ē\ easy \g\ go \i\ hit \ī\ ice \j\ job
\ŋ\ sing \ō\ go \ò\ law \òi\ boy \th\ thin \ṯẖ\ the \ü\ loot \ù\ foot
\y\ yet \zh\ vision \á, k̄, ⁿ, œ, œ̄, ᵫ, ᵬ, ᶌ\ see Guide to Pronunciation

wild type n (1914) : a phenotype, genotype, or gene that predominates in a natural population of organisms or strain of organisms in contrast to that of natural or laboratory mutant forms; *also* : an organism or strain displaying the wild type — **wild–type** *adj*

Wild West n (1849) : the western U.S. in its frontier period characterized by roughness and lawlessness — **Wild West** *adj*

wild·wood \'wī(ə)l(d)-,wu̇d\ n (12c) : a wood unaltered or unfrequented by humans

¹**wile** \'wī(ə)l\ n [ME *wil*, prob. fr. Scand origin; akin to ON *vēl* deceit, artifice] (12c) **1 a** : a trick or stratagem intended to ensnare or deceive; *also* : a beguiling or playful trick **2** : skill in outwitting : TRICKERY, GUILE *syn* see TRICK

²**wile** *vt* **wiled; wil·ing** (14c) **1** : to lure by or as if by a magic spell : ENTICE **2** [by alter.]: WHILE

¹**will** \wəl, (ə)l, ²l, 'wil\ *vb, past* **would** \wəd, (ə)d, 'wu̇d\; *pres sing & pl* **will** [ME (1st & 3d sing. pres. indic.), fr. OE *wille* (infin. *wyllan*); akin to OHG *wili* (3d sing. pres. indic.) wills, L *velle* to wish, will] *vt* (bef. 12c) : DESIRE, WISH ⟨call it what you ~⟩ ~ *verbal auxiliary* **1** — used to express desire, choice, willingness, consent, or in negative constructions refusal ⟨no one *would* take the job⟩ ⟨if we ~ all do our best⟩ ⟨~ you please stop that racket⟩ **2** — used to express frequent, customary, or habitual action or natural tendency or disposition ⟨~ get angry over nothing⟩ ⟨~ work one day and loaf the next⟩ **3** — used to express futurity ⟨tomorrow morning I ~ wake up in this first-class hotel suite —Tennessee Williams⟩ **4** — used to express capability or sufficiency ⟨the back seat ~ hold three passengers⟩ **5** — used to express probability and often equivalent to the simple verb ⟨that ~ be the milkman⟩ **6 a** — used to express determination, insistence, persistence, or willfulness ⟨I have made up my mind to go and go I ~⟩ **b** — used to express inevitability ⟨accidents ~ happen⟩ **7** — used to express a command, exhortation, or injunction ⟨you ~ do as I say, at once⟩ ~ *vi* : to have a wish or desire ⟨whether we ~ or no⟩ *usage* see SHALL — **if you will** : if you wish to call it that ⟨a kind of preoccupation, or obsession *if you will* —Louis Auchincloss⟩

²**will** \'wil\ n [ME, fr. OE *willa* will, desire; akin to OE *wille*] (bef. 12c) **1** : DESIRE, WISH: as **a** : DISPOSITION, INCLINATION ⟨where there's a ~ there's a way⟩ **b** : APPETITE, PASSION **c** : CHOICE, DETERMINATION **2 a** : something desired; *esp* : a choice or determination of one having authority or power **b** (1) *archaic* : REQUEST, COMMAND (2) [fr. the phrase *our will is* which introduces it]: the part of a summons expressing a royal command **3** : the act, process, or experience of willing : VOLITION **4 a** : mental powers manifested as wishing, choosing, desiring, or intending **b** : a disposition to act according to principles or ends **c** : the collective desire of a group ⟨the ~ of the people⟩ **5** : the power of control over one's own actions or emotions ⟨a man of iron ~⟩ **6** : a legal declaration of a person's wishes regarding the disposal of his or her property or estate after death; *esp* : a written instrument legally executed by which a person makes disposition of his or her estate to take effect after death — **at will** : as one wishes : as or when it pleases or suits oneself

³**will** \'wil\ *vt* (bef. 12c) **1 a** : to order or direct by a will **b** : to dispose of by or as if by a will : BEQUEATH **2 a** : to determine by an act of choice **b** : DECREE, ORDAIN ⟨Providence ~s it⟩ **c** : INTEND, PURPOSE **d** : to cause or change by an act of will; *also* : to try to do so ~ *vi* **1** : to exercise the will **2** : CHOOSE

willed \'wild\ *adj* (14c) **1** : having a will esp. of a specified kind — usu. used in combination ⟨strong-*willed*⟩ **2** : DELIBERATE

wil·lem·ite \'wi-lə-,mīt\ n [G *Willemit*, fr. *Willem* (William) I †1843 king of the Netherlands] (ca. 1841) : a mineral consisting of a silicate of zinc, occurring in hexagonal prisms and in massive or granular forms, and varying in color

wil·let \'wi-lət\ *n, pl* **willet** [imit.] (1791) : a large American shorebird (*Catoptrophorus semipalmatus*) that resembles the greater yellowlegs but has a thicker bill and gray legs and that displays a black and white wing pattern when in flight

will·ful *or* **wil·ful** \'wil-fəl\ *adj* (13c) **1** : obstinately and often perversely self-willed **2** : done deliberately : INTENTIONAL *syn* see UNRULY — **will·ful·ly** \-fə-lē\ *adv* — **will·ful·ness** n

Wil·liam Tell \,wil-yəm-'tel\ n : an heroic archer in Swiss legend who complies with an order to shoot an apple off his son's head

wil·lies \'wi-lēz\ *n pl* [origin unknown] (ca. 1896) : a fit of nervousness : JITTERS — used with *the*

will·ing \'wi-liŋ\ *adj* (14c) **1** : inclined or favorably disposed in mind : READY **2** : prompt to act or respond **3** : done, borne, or accepted by choice or without reluctance **4** : of or relating to the will or power of choosing : VOLITIONAL *syn* see VOLUNTARY — **will·ing·ly** \-liŋ-lē\ *adv* — **will·ing·ness** n

wil·li·waw \'wi-li-,wȯ\ n [origin unknown] (1842) **1 a** : a sudden violent gust of cold land air common along mountainous coasts of high latitudes **b** : a sudden violent wind **2** : a violent commotion

will·less \'wil-ləs\ *adj* (1747) **1** : involving no exercise of the will : INVOLUNTARY ⟨~ obedience⟩ **2** : not exercising the will ⟨~ slaves⟩

will-o'-the-wisp \,wil-ə-thə-'wisp\ n [*Will* (nickname for *William*) + *of* + *the* + *wisp*] (1661) **1** : IGNIS FATUUS 1 **2** : a delusive or elusive goal — **will-o'-the-wisp** *adj*

wil·low \'wi-(,)lō\ n [ME *wilghe, wilowe*, fr. OE *welig*; akin to MHG *wilge* willow] (bef. 12c) **1** : any of a genus (*Salix* of the family Salicaceae, the willow family) of trees and shrubs bearing catkins of apetalous flowers and including forms of value for wood, osiers, or tanbark and a few ornamentals **2** : an object made of willow wood; *esp* : a cricket bat — **wil·low·like** \-lō-,līk\ *adj*

willow herb n (1578) : any of a genus (*Epilobium*) of herbs of the evening-primrose family; *esp* : FIREWEED b

wil·low·ware \'wi-lō-,war, 'wi-lō-, -,wer\ n (ca. 1885) : dinnerware that is usu. blue-and-white and that is decorated with a story-telling design featuring a large willow tree by a little bridge

wil·lowy \'wi-lə-wē\ *adj* (1766) **1** : abounding with willows **2** : resembling a willow: **a** : PLIANT **b** : gracefully tall and slender

will-pow·er \'wil-,pau̇(-ə)r\ n (1874) : energetic determination

will to power (1907) **1** : the drive of the superman in the philosophy of Nietzsche to perfect and transcend the self through the possession and exercise of creative power **2** : a conscious or unconscious desire to exercise authority over others

wil·ly–nil·ly \,wi-lē-'ni-lē\ *adv or adj* [alter. of *will I nill I* or *will ye nill ye* or *will he nill he*] (1608) **1** : by compulsion : without choice **2** : in a haphazard or spontaneous manner

Wilms' tumor \'vilm-zz-, 'vilmz-\ n [Max *Wilms* †1918 Ger. surgeon] (ca. 1910) : a malignant tumor of the kidney that primarily affects children and is made up of embryonic elements

Wil·son's disease \'wil-sənz-\ n [Samuel A. K. *Wilson* †1937 Eng. neurologist] (ca. 1915) : a hereditary disease that is determined by an autosomal recessive gene and is marked esp. by cirrhotic changes in the liver and severe mental disorder due to a ceruloplasmin deficiency and resulting inability to metabolize copper

¹**wilt** \'wilt, 'wilt\ *archaic pres 2d sing of* WILL

²**wilt** \'wilt\ *vb* [alter. of earlier *welk*, fr. ME *welken*, prob. fr. MD; akin to OHG *erwelken* to wilt] *vi* (ca. 1691) **1 a** : to lose turgor from lack of water ⟨the plants ~ed in the heat⟩ **b** : to become limp **2** : to grow weak or faint : LANGUISH ~ *vt* : to cause to wilt

³**wilt** \'wilt\ n (1855) **1** : an act or instance of wilting : the state of being wilted **2 a** : a disorder (as a fungus disease) of plants marked by loss of turgidity in soft tissues with subsequent drooping and often shriveling — called also *wilt disease* **b** : a destructive virus disease of various caterpillars marked by visceral liquefaction and shriveling of the body

Wil·ton \'wil-t²n\ n [*Wilton*, borough in England] (1774) : a carpet woven with loops like the Brussels carpet but having a velvet cut pile and being generally of better materials

wily \'wī-lē\ *adj* **wil·i·er; -est** (14c) : full of wiles : CRAFTY *syn* see SLY — **wil·i·ly** \-lə-lē\ *adv* — **wil·i·ness** \-lē-nəs\ n

¹**wim·ble** \'wim-bəl\ n [ME, fr. AF, fr. MD *wimmel* auger; akin to MLG *wimmel* auger] (13c) : any of various instruments for boring holes

²**wimble** *vt* **wim·bled; wim·bling** \-b(ə-)liŋ\ (15c) *archaic* : to bore with or as if with a wimble

wimp \'wimp\ n [origin unknown] (1920) : a weak, cowardly, or ineffectual person — **wimp·i·ness** \'wim-pē-nəs\ n — **wimp·ish** \'wim-pish\ *adj* — **wimp·ish·ness** \-nəs\ n — **wimpy** \'wim-pē\ *adj*

¹**wim·ple** \'wim-pəl\ n [ME *wimpel*, fr. OE; perh. akin to OE *wīpian* to wipe] (bef. 12c) **1** : a cloth covering worn over the head and around the neck and chin esp. by women in the late medieval period and by some nuns **2** *Scot* **a** : a crafty turn : TWIST **b** : CURVE, BEND

²**wimple** *vb* **wim·pled; wim·pling** \-p(ə-)liŋ\ *vt* (13c) **1** : to cover with or as if with a wimple : VEIL **2** : to cause to ripple ~ *vi* **1** *archaic* : to fall or lie in folds **2** *chiefly Scot* : to follow a winding course : MEANDER **3** : RIPPLE

wimp out *vi* (1982) : to behave like a wimp : chicken out; *esp* : to choose the easiest course of action

wimple 1

¹**win** \'win\ *vb* **won** \'wən\; **win·ning** [ME *winnen*, fr. OE *winnan* to struggle; akin to OHG *winnan* to struggle and prob. to L *venus* sexual desire, charm, Skt *vanas* desire, *vanoti* he strives for] *vt* (bef. 12c) **1 a** : to get possession of by effort or fortune **b** : to obtain by work : EARN ⟨striving to ~ a living from the sterile soil⟩ **2 a** : to gain in or as if in battle or contest **3 a** : to be the victor in ⟨*won* the war⟩ **3 a** : to make friendly or favorable to oneself or to one's cause — often used with *over* ⟨*won* him over with persuasive arguments⟩ **b** : to induce to accept oneself in marriage **4 a** : to obtain (as ore, coal, or clay) by mining **b** : to prepare (as a vein or bed) for regular mining **c** : to recover (as metal) from ore **5** : to reach by expenditure of effort ~ *vi* **1** : to gain the victory in a contest : SUCCEED **2** : to succeed in arriving at a place or a state — **win·less** \'win-ləs\ *adj* — **win·na·ble** \'wi-nə-bəl\ *adj*

²**win** n (1862) : VICTORY; *esp* : first place at the finish (as of a horse race)

wince \'win(t)s\ *vi* **winced; winc·ing** [ME *wincen* to kick impatiently, fr. (assumed) ONF *wincier* to turn aside, of Gmc origin; akin to OHG *wankōn* to totter — more at WENCH] (ca. 1748) : to shrink back involuntarily (as from pain) : FLINCH *syn* see RECOIL — **wince** n

¹**winch** \'winch\ n [ME *winche* roller, reel, fr. OE *wince*; akin to OE *wincian* to wink] (bef. 12c) **1** : any of various machines or instruments for hauling or pulling; *esp* : a powerful machine with one or more drums on which to coil a rope, cable, or chain for hauling or hoisting : WINDLASS **2** : a crank with a handle for giving motion to a machine (as a grindstone)

²**winch** *vt* (1529) : to hoist or haul with or as if with a winch — **winch·er** n

Win·ches·ter \'win-,ches-tər\ *adj* [fr. the code name used by the original developer] (1973) : relating to or being computer disk technology that permits high-density storage by sealing the rigid metal disks within the disk drive mechanism as protection against dust

¹**wind** \'wind, *archaic or poetic* 'wīnd\ *n, often attrib* (bef. 12c) **1 a** : a natural movement of air of any velocity; *esp* : the earth's air or the gas surrounding a planet in natural motion horizontally **b** : an artificially produced movement of air **c** : SOLAR WIND, STELLAR WIND **2 a** : a destructive force or influence : a force or agency that carries along or influences : TENDENCY, TREND ⟨withstood the ~s of popular opinion —Felix Frankfurter⟩ **3 a** : BREATH 4a **b** : BREATH 2a **c** : the pit of the stomach : SOLAR PLEXUS **4** : gas generated in the stomach or the intestines **5 a** : compressed air or gas **b** *archaic* : AIR **6** : something that is insubstantial: as **a** : mere talk : idle words **b** : NOTHING, NOTHINGNESS **c** : vain self-satisfaction **7 a** : air carrying a scent (as of a hunter or game) **b** : slight information esp. about something secret : INTIMATION ⟨got ~ of the plan⟩ **8 a** : musical wind instruments esp. as distinguished from strings and percussion **b** *pl* : players of wind instruments **9 a** : a direction from which the wind may blow : a point of the compass; *esp* : one of the cardinal points **b** : the direction from which the wind is blowing — **wind·less** \-ləs\ *adj* — **wind·less·ly** *adv* — **before the wind** : in the same direction as the main force of the wind — **close to the wind** : as nearly as possible against the main force of the wind — **have the wind**

of **1** : to be to windward of **2** : to be on the scent of **3** : to have a superior position to — **in the wind** : about to happen : ASTIR, AFOOT ⟨change is *in the wind*⟩ — **near the wind** **1** : close to the wind **2** : close to a point of danger : near the permissible limit — **off the wind** : away from the direction from which the wind is blowing — **on the wind** : toward the direction from which the wind is blowing — **to the wind** *or* **to the winds** : ASIDE, AWAY ⟨threw caution *to the wind*⟩ — **under the wind** **1** : to leeward **2** : in a place protected from the wind : under the lee

²**wind** \'wind\ *vt* (15c) **1** : to detect or follow by scent **2** : to expose to the air or wind : dry by exposing to air **3** : to make short of breath **4** : to regulate the wind supply of (an organ pipe) **5** : to rest (as a horse) in order to allow the breath to be recovered ~ *vi* **1** : to scent game **2** *dial* : to pause for breath

³**wind** \'wind, 'wind\ *vb* **wound** \'wünd\ *also* **wind·ed**; **'win-** *or* **wound** \'waünd\; **wind·ing** ['wind] *vt* (1586) **1** : to cause (as a horn) to sound by blowing : BLOW **2** : to sound (as a call or note) on a horn ⟨*wound* a rousing call —R. L. Stevenson⟩ ~ *vi* : to produce a sound on a horn

⁴**wind** \'wind\ *vb* **wound** \'waünd\ *also* **wind·ed**; **wind·ing** [ME, fr. OE *windan* to twist, move with speed or force, brandish; akin to OHG *wintan* to wind, Umbrian oha*vendu* let him turn aside] *vt* (bef. 12c) **1 a** *obs* : WEAVE **b** : ENTANGLE, INVOLVE **c** : to introduce sinuously or stealthily : INSINUATE **2 a** : to encircle or cover with something pliable : bind with loops or layers **b** : to turn completely or repeatedly about an object : COIL, TWINE **c** (1) : to hoist or haul by means of a rope or chain and a windlass (2) : to move (a ship) by hauling on a capstan **d** (1) : to tighten the spring of ⟨~ a clock⟩ (2) *obs* : to make tighter : TIGHTEN, TUNE (3) : CRANK **e** : to raise to a high level (as of excitement or tension) — usu. used with *up* **3 a** : to cause to move in a curving line or path **b** *archaic* : to turn the course of; *esp* : to lead (a person) as one wishes **c** (1) : to cause (as a ship) to change direction : TURN (2) : to turn (a ship) end for end **d** : to traverse on a curving course ⟨the river ~s the valley⟩ **e** : to effect by or as if by curving ~ *vi* **1** : BEND, WARP **2 a** : to have a curving course or shape : extend in curves **b** : to proceed as if by winding **3** : to move so as to encircle something **4** : to turn when lying at anchor

⁵**wind** \'wind\ *n* (14c) **1** : a mechanism (as a winch) for winding **2** : an act of winding : the state of being wound **3** : COIL, TURN **4** : a particular method of winding

wind·age \'win-dij\ *n* ['wind] (ca. 1710) **1 a** : the space between the projectile of a smoothbore gun and the surface of the bore **b** : the difference between the diameter of the bore of a muzzle-loading rifled cannon and that of the projectile cylinder **2 a** : the amount of sight deflection necessary to compensate for wind displacement in aiming a gun **b** (1) : the influence of the wind in deflecting the course of a projectile (2) : the amount of deflection due to the wind **3** : the surface exposed (as by a ship) to the wind

wind·bag \'win(d)-,bag\ *n* (1827) : an exhaustively talkative person

wind–bell \-,bel\ *n* (1901) **1** : WIND CHIME — usu. used in pl. **2** : a bell that is light enough to be moved and sounded by the wind

wind·blast \-,blast\ *n* (1942) : the destructive effect of air friction on a pilot ejected from a high-speed airplane

wind·blown \-,blōn\ *adj* (1600) : blown by the wind; *esp* : having a permanent set or character of growth determined by the prevailing winds ⟨~ trees⟩

wind–borne \-,bórn, -,bòrn\ *adj* (1842) : carried by the wind ⟨~ pollen⟩ ⟨~ soil deposits⟩

wind·break \-,brāk\ *n* (1861) : a growth of trees or shrubs serving to break the force of wind; *broadly* : a shelter (as a fence) from the wind

wind·break·er \-,brā-kər\ *n* [fr. a trademark] (1918) : an outer jacket made of wind-resistant material

wind–bro·ken \-,brō-kən\ *adj* (1603) *of a horse* : affected with pulmonary emphysema or heaves

wind–burn \-,bərn\ *n* (1925) : irritation of the skin caused by wind — **wind·burned** \-,bərnd\ *adj*

Wind·cheat·er \'win(d)-,chē-tər\ *trademark* — used for a windbreaker

wind–chill \'win(d)-,chil\ *n* (1939) : a still-air temperature that would have the same cooling effect on exposed human skin as a given combination of temperature and wind speed — called also *chill factor, windchill factor, windchill index*

wind chime *n* (1927) : a cluster of small often sculptured pieces (as of metal or glass) suspended so as to chime when blown by the wind — usu. used in pl.

wind down *vi* (1952) **1** : to draw gradually toward an end **2** : RELAX, UNWIND ~ *vt* : to cause a gradual lessening of usu. with the intention of bringing to an end

wind·er \'wīn-dər\ *n* [⁴*wind*] (1552) : one that winds: as **a** : a worker or machine that winds thread and yarn **b** : a key for winding a mechanism (as a clock) **c** : a step that is wider at one end than at the other (as in a spiral staircase)

wind·fall \'win(d)-,fól\ *n* (15c) **1** : something (as a tree or fruit) blown down by the wind **2** : an unexpected, unearned, or sudden gain or advantage

wind farm *n* (1980) : an area of land with a cluster of wind turbines for driving electrical generators

wind·flow·er \-,flaü(-ə)r\ *n* (1551) : ANEMONE 1

wind·gall \-,gól\ *n* (ca. 1534) : a soft tumor or synovial swelling on a horse's leg in the region of the fetlock joint

wind gap *n* (1769) : a notch in the crest of a mountain ridge : a pass not occupied by a stream — compare WATER GAP

wind harp *n* (1813) : AEOLIAN HARP

wind·hov·er \'wind-,hə-vər, -,hä-\ *n* (1674) *Brit* : KESTREL

¹**wind·ing** \'wīn-diŋ\ *n* (bef. 12c) **1** : material (as wire) wound or coiled about an object (as an armature); *also* : a single turn of the wound material **2 a** : the act of one that winds **b** : the manner of winding something **3** : a curved or sinuous course, line, or progress

²**winding** *adj* (1530) **1** : marked by winding: as **a** : having a curved or spiral course or form ⟨a ~ stairway⟩ **b** : having a course that winds ⟨a ~ road⟩

wind·ing–sheet \'wīn-diŋ-,shēt\ *n* (15c) : a sheet in which a corpse is wrapped

wind·ing–up \,wīn-diŋ-'əp\ *n* (ca. 1858) *Brit* : the process of liquidating the assets of a partnership or corporation in order to pay creditors and make distributions to partners or shareholders upon dissolution

wind instrument *n* (1582) : a musical instrument (as a trumpet, clarinet, or organ) sounded by wind; *esp* : one sounded by the player's breath

wind·jam·mer \'win(d)-,ja-mər\ *n* (1880) : a sailing ship; *also* : one of its crew — **wind·jam·ming** \-,miŋ\ *n*

¹**wind·lass** \'win(d)-ləs\ *n* [ME *wyndlas*, alter. of *wyndas*, fr. ON *vindāss*, fr. *vinda* to wind (akin to OHG *wintan* to wind) + *āss* pole; akin to Goth *ans* beam] (15c) : any of various machines for hoisting or hauling: as **a** : a horizontal barrel supported on vertical posts and turned by a crank so that the hoisting rope is wound around the barrel **b** : a steam or electric winch with horizontal or vertical shaft and two drums used to raise a ship's anchor

²**windlass** *vt* (1834) : to hoist or haul with a windlass

win·dle·straw \'win-dᵊl-,stró, 'wi-nᵊl-\ *n* [(assumed) ME, fr. OE *windelstrēaw*, fr. *windel* basket (fr. *windan* to wind) + *strēaw* straw] (bef. 12c) *Brit* : a dry thin stalk of grass

¹**wind·mill** \'win(d)-,mil\ *n* (14c) **1 a** : a mill or machine operated by the wind usu. acting on oblique vanes or sails that radiate from a horizontal shaft; *esp* : a wind-driven water pump or electric generator **b** : the wind-driven wheel of a windmill **2** : something that resembles or suggests a windmill **b** : a calisthenic exercise that involves alternately lowering each outstretched hand to touch the toes of the opposite foot **3** [fr. the episode in *Don Quixote* by Cervantes in which the hero attacks windmills under the illusion that they are giants] : an imaginary wrong, evil, or opponent — usu. used in the phrase *to tilt at windmills*

²**windmill** *vt* (1914) : to cause to move like a windmill ~ *vi* : to move like a windmill; *esp* : to spin from the force of wind

win·dow \'win-(,)dō\ *n*, *often attrib* [ME *windowe*, fr. ON *vindauga*, fr. *vindr* wind (akin to OE *wind*) + *auga* eye; akin to OE *ēage* eye — more at EYE] (13c) **1 a** : an opening esp. in the wall of a building for admission of light and air that is usu. closed by casements or sashes containing transparent material (as glass) and capable of being opened and shut **b** : WINDOWPANE **c** : a space behind a window of a retail store containing displayed merchandise **d** : an opening in a partition or wall through which business is conducted ⟨a bank teller's ~⟩ **2 a** : a means of entrance or access; *esp* : a means of obtaining information ⟨a ~ on history⟩ **3** : an opening (as a shutter, slot, or valve) that resembles or suggests a window **4** : the transparent panel or opening of a window envelope **5** : the framework (as a shutter or sash with its fittings) that closes a window opening **6** : CHAFF 4 **7** : a range of wavelengths in the electromagnetic spectrum to which a planet's atmosphere is transparent **8 a** : an interval of time within which a rocket or spacecraft must be launched to accomplish a particular mission **b** : an interval of time during which certain conditions or an opportunity exists ⟨a ~ of vulnerability⟩ **9** : an area into which a portion of the earth's sensible atmosphere through which a spacecraft must pass for successful reentry **10** : any of the areas into which a computer display may be divided and on which distinctly different types of information are displayed — **win·dow·less** \-dō-ləs, -də-\ *adj* — **out the window** : out of existence, use, or consideration

window box *n* (ca. 1885) : a box designed to hold soil for growing plants at a windowsill

window dressing *n* (1895) **1** : the display of merchandise in a retail store window **2 a** : the act or an instance of making something appear deceptively attractive or favorable **b** : something used to create a deceptively favorable or attractive impression — **win·dow–dress** \'win-dō-,dres\ *vt* — **window dresser** *n*

win·dowed \'win-(,)dōd, -dəd\ *adj* (15c) : having windows esp. of a specified kind — often used in combination

window envelope *n* (1914) : an envelope having an opening through which the address on the enclosure is visible

win·dow·pane \'win-dō-,pān, -də-\ *n* (1819) **1** : a pane in a window **2** : TATTERSALL

window seat *n* (1745) **1** : a seat built into a window recess **2** : a seat next to a window (as in a bus or airplane)

window shade *n* (1810) : a shade or curtain for a window

win·dow–shop \'win-dō-,shäp, -də-\ *vi* (1922) : to look at the displays in retail store windows without going inside the stores to make purchases — **win·dow–shop·per** *n*

win·dow·sill \-,sil\ *n* (1703) : the horizontal member at the bottom of a window opening

wind·pipe \'win(d)-,pīp\ *n* (1530) : TRACHEA 1

wind–pol·li·nat·ed \-'pä-lə-,nā-təd\ *adj* (1884) : pollinated by wind–borne pollen

wind·proof \-'prüf\ *adj* (1616) : impervious to wind ⟨a ~ jacket⟩

wind rose \'wind-,rōz\ *n* [G *Windrose* compass card] (1846) : a diagram showing for a given place the relative frequency or frequency and strength of winds from different directions

¹**wind·row** \'win(d)-,rō\ *n* (ca. 1534) **1 a** : a row of hay raked up to dry before being baled or stored **b** : a similar row of cut vegetation (as grain) for drying **2** : a row heaped up by or as if by the wind **3 a** : a long low ridge of road-making material scraped to the side of a road **b** : BANK, RIDGE, HEAP

²**windrow** *vt* (1729) : to form (as hay) into a windrow

wind–screen \'win(d)-,skrēn\ *n* (1858) **1** : a screen that protects against the wind **2** *chiefly Brit* : WINDSHIELD

wind shake *n* (1545) : a split in timber attributed to high winds

wind shear *n* (1941) : a radical shift in wind speed and direction that occurs over a very short distance

wind·shield \'win(d)-,shēld\ *n* (1902) : a transparent screen (as of glass) in front of the occupants of a vehicle

wind sock *n* (1928) : a truncated cloth cone open at both ends and mounted in an elevated position to indicate the direction of the wind

---

\ə\ abut \ᵊ\ kitten, F table \ər\ further \a\ ash \ā\ ace \ä\ mop, mar \aü\ out \ch\ chin \e\ bet \ē\ easy \g\ go \i\ hit \ī\ ice \j\ job \ŋ\ sing \ō\ go \ó\ law \ói\ boy \th\ thin \t͟h\ the \ü\ loot \ù\ foot \y\ yet \zh\ vision \á, k̲, ⁿ, œ, œ̄, ᵫ, ᵫ̄, ᵋ\ see Guide to Pronunciation

Wind·sor chair \'win-zər-\ *n* [*Windsor*, England] (1740) : a wooden chair with spindle back, raking legs, and usu. a saddle seat — called also *Windsor*

Windsor knot *n* [prob. after Edward, Duke of *Windsor*] (1947) : a symmetrical necktie knot that is wider than the usual four-in-hand knot

Windsor tie *n* (1895) : a broad necktie usu. tied in a loose bow

wind sprint *n* (1948) : a sprint performed as a training exercise to develop breathing capacity esp. during exertion

wind·storm \'win(d)-,storm\ *n* (14c) : a storm marked by high wind with little or no precipitation

Wind·surf·er \-,sər-fər\ *trademark* — used for a sail-board

wind·surf·ing \-,sər-fiŋ\ *n* (1969) : the sport or activity of riding a sailboard — **wind·surf** \-,sərf\ *vi*

wind·swept \'win(d)-,swept\ *adj* (1812) : swept by or as if by wind

wind tee *n* (1932) : a large weather vane shaped like a horizontal letter T on or near a landing field

wind·throw \'win(d)-,thrō\ *n* (1916) : the uprooting and overthrowing of trees by the wind

wind tunnel *n* (1911) : a tunnellike passage through which air is blown at a known velocity to investigate air flow around an object (as an airplane part or model) placed in the passage

wind turbine *n* (1909) : a wind-driven turbine for generating electricity

¹wind·up \'wīn-,dəp\ *n* (1665)　**1 a** : the act of bringing to an end　**b** : a concluding act or part : FINISH　**2 a** : a series of regular and distinctive motions (as swinging the arms) made by a pitcher preparatory to releasing a pitch　**b** : an exaggerated backswing (as in tennis)

²wind·up *adj* (1784) : operated by a spring mechanism wound by hand

wind up *vt* (1583)　**1** : to bring to a conclusion : END　**2 a** : to put in order for the purpose of bringing to an end ⟨*winds up* the meeting⟩　**b** *Brit* : to effectuate a winding up ～ *vi*　**1 a** : to come to a conclusion　**b** : to arrive in a place, situation, or condition at the end or as a result of a course of action ⟨*wound up* as millionaires⟩　**2** : to make a pitching windup

¹wind·ward \'win-(d)wərd\ *n* (1549) : the side or direction from which the wind is blowing — **to windward** : into or in an advantageous position

²windward *adj* (1627) : being in or facing the direction from which the wind is blowing — compare LEEWARD

wind·way \'win(d)-,wā\ *n* (ca. 1875) : a passage for air (as in an organ pipe)

windy \'win-dē\ *adj* **wind·i·er; -est** (bef. 12c)　**1 a** (1) : WINDSWEPT (2) : marked by strong wind or by more wind than usual　**b** : VIOLENT, STORMY　**2** : FLATULENT 1 ⟨a ～ bellyache⟩　**3 a** : VERBOSE, BOMBASTIC　**b** : lacking substance : EMPTY — **wind·i·ly** \-də-lē\ *adv* — **wind·i·ness** \-dē-nəs\ *n*

¹wine \'wīn\ *n, often attrib* [ME *win*, fr. OE *wīn* wine; both fr. L *vinum* wine, prob. of non-IE origin; akin to the source of Gk *oinos* wine] (bef. 12c)　**1 a** : the fermented juice of fresh grapes used as a beverage　**b** : wine or a substitute used in Christian communion services　**2** : the usu. fermented juice of a plant product (as a fruit) used as a beverage　**3** : something that invigorates or intoxicates　**4** : a dark red

²wine *vb* **wined; win·ing** *vi* (1829) : to drink wine ～ *vt* : to give wine to ⟨*wined* and dined his friends⟩

wine cellar *n* (14c) : a room for storing wines; *also* : a stock of wines

wine cooler *n* (1815)　**1** : a vessel or container in which wine is cooled　**2** : a usu. carbonated beverage that contains a mixture of wine and fruit juice

wine·glass \'wīn-,glas\ *n* (1709) : a stemware drinking glass for wine

wine·grow·er \-,grō(-ə)r\ *n* (1844) : a person who cultivates a vineyard and makes wine

wine·press \-,pres\ *n* (1526) : a vat in which juice is expressed from grapes by treading or by means of a plunger

win·ery \'wī-nə-rē, 'wīn-rē\ *n, pl* **-er·ies** (1882) : a wine-making establishment

wine·shop \'wīn-,shäp\ *n* (1848) : a tavern that specializes in serving wine

wine·skin \-,skin\ *n* (1821) : a bag that is made from the skin of an animal (such as a goat) and that is used for holding wine

wine taster *n* (1632)　**1** : one who tastes and evaluates wine esp. professionally　**2** : a small shallow vessel used to sample wine

win·ey *var of* WINY

¹wing \'wiŋ\ *n, often attrib* [ME *winge*, of Scand origin; akin to Dan & Sw *vinge* wing; akin to Skt *vāti* it blows — more at WIND] (13c)　**1 a** : one of the movable feathered or membranous paired appendages by means of which a bird, bat, or insect is able to fly; *also* : such an appendage even though rudimentary if possessed by an animal belonging to a group characterized by the power of flight　**b** : any of various anatomical structures esp. of a flying fish or flying lemur providing means of limited flight　**2** : an appendage or part resembling a wing in appearance, position, or function: as　**a** : ALA　**c** : a turned-back or extended edge on an article of clothing　**d** : a sidepiece at the top of an armchair　**e** (1) : a foliaceous, membranous, or woody expansion of a plant esp. along a stem or on a samara or capsule (2) : either of the two lateral petals of a papilionaceous flower　**f** : a vane of a windmill or arrow　**g** : SAIL　**h** : an airfoil that develops a major part of the lift which supports a heavier-than-air aircraft　**i** *chiefly Brit* : FENDER　**d**　**3** : a means of flight or rapid progress　**4** : the act or manner of flying : FLIGHT　**5** : a side or outlying region or district　**6** : a part or feature usu. projecting from and subordinate to the main or central part ⟨the servants' ～ of

wing 1a: *1* coverts, *2* primaries, *3* secondaries

the mansion⟩　**7 a** : one of the pieces of scenery at the side of a stage　**b** *pl* : the area at the side of the stage out of sight　**8 a** : a left or right section of an army or fleet : FLANK　**b** : one of the offensive positions or players on either side of a center position in certain team sports; *also* : FLANKER　**9 a** : either of two opposing groups within an organization or society : FACTION　**b** : a section of an organized body (as a legislative chamber) representing a group or faction holding distinct opinions or policies — compare LEFT WING, RIGHT WING　**10 a** : a unit of the U.S. Air Force higher than a group and lower than a division　**b** : two or more squadrons of naval airplanes　**11** : a dance step marked by a quick outward and inward rolling glide of one foot　**12** *pl* : insignia consisting of an outspread pair of stylized bird's wings which are awarded on completion of prescribed training to a qualified pilot, aircrew member, or military balloon pilot — **wingy** \'wiŋ-ē\ *adj* — **in the wings**　**1** : out of sight in the stage wings　**2** : close at hand in the background : readily available ⟨had a plan waiting *in the wings*⟩ — **on the wing**　**1** : in flight　**2** : in motion — **under one's wing** : under one's protection : in one's care

²wing *vt* (1591)　**1 a** : to fit with wings　**b** : to enable to fly or move swiftly　**2 a** : to traverse with or as if with wings　**b** : to effect or achieve by flying　**3** : to let fly : DISPATCH ⟨would start to ～ punches —A. J. Liebling⟩　**4 a** : to wound in the wing : disable the wing of ⟨～ed the duck⟩　**b** : to wound (as with a bullet) without killing ⟨～ed by a sniper⟩　**5** : to do or perform without preparation or guidelines : IMPROVISE ⟨～*ing* it⟩ ～ *vi* : to go with or as if with wings : FLY

wing and wing *adv* (1781) : with sails extended on both sides

wing·back \'wiŋ-,bak\ *n* (1933) : an offensive back in football who lines up outside the tight end; *also* : the position of such a player

wing bar *n* (1855) : a line of contrasting color across the middle of a bird's wing made by markings on the wing coverts

wing case *n* (1661) : ELYTRON

wing chair *n* (1904) : an upholstered armchair with high solid back and sides that provide a rest for the head and protection from drafts

wing commander *n* (1914) : a commissioned officer in the British air force who ranks with a lieutenant colonel in the army

wing covert *n* (1815) : one of the feathers covering the bases of the wing quills

wing·ding \'wiŋ-,diŋ\ *n* [origin unknown] (1944) : a wild, lively, or lavish party

winged \'wiŋd *also except for* 1a(2) 'wiŋ-əd\ *adj* (14c)　**1 a** (1) : having wings ⟨～ seeds⟩ (2) : having wings of a specified kind — used in combination ⟨strong-*winged*⟩　**b** : using wings in flight　**2 a** : soaring with or as if with wings : ELEVATED　**b** : SWIFT, RAPID

winged bean \'wiŋd-\ *n* (1910) : an Asian twining legume (*Psophocarpus tetragonolobus*) cultivated in warm regions for its edible high-protein 4-winged pods; *also* : its pod

winged elm *n* (1820) : an elm (*Ulmus alata*) of the U.S. having twigs and young branches with prominent corky projections

wing·er \'wiŋ-ər\ *n* (1896) : a player (as in soccer or ice hockey) in a wing position

wing-foot·ed \'wiŋ-'fú-təd\ *adj* (1591)　**1** : having winged feet　**2** : SWIFT

wing·less \'wiŋ-ləs\ *adj* (1591) : having no wings or very rudimentary wings — **wing·less·ness** *n*

wing·let \'wiŋ-lət\ *n* (1816) : a small wing; *also* : a small nearly vertical airfoil at an airplane's wingtip that reduces drag by inhibiting turbulence

wing·like \-,līk\ *adj* (ca. 1804) : resembling a wing in form or lateral position

wing·man \-mən\ *n* (1942) : a pilot who flies behind and outside the leader of a flying formation

wing nut *n* (ca. 1900) : a nut with wings that provide a grip for the thumb and finger

wing·over \'wiŋ-,ō-vər\ *n* (1927) : a flight maneuver in which a plane is put into a climbing turn until nearly stalled after which the nose is allowed to fall while the turn is continued until normal flight is attained in a direction opposite to that in which the maneuver was entered

wing shooting *n* (1881) : the act or practice of shooting at game birds in flight or at flying targets

wing·span \'wiŋ-,span\ *n* (ca. 1917) : the distance from the tip of one of a pair of wings to that of the other; *also* : SPAN 2c

wing·spread \-,spred\ *n* (1897) : the spread of the wings : WINGSPAN; *specif* : the extreme measurement between the tips or outer margins of the wings (as of a bird or insect)

wing tip *n* (ca. 1908)　**1** : a toe cap having a point that extends back toward the throat of the shoe and curving sides that extend toward the shank　**2** : a shoe having a wing tip　**3 a** : the edge or outer margin of a bird's wing　**b** *usu* **wingtip** : the outer end of an airplane wing

¹wink \'wiŋk\ *vb* [ME, fr. OE *wincian*; akin to OHG *winchan* to stagger, wink and perh. to L *vacillare* to sway, Skt *vañcati* he goes crookedly] *vi* (bef. 12c)　**1** : to shut one eye briefly as a signal or in teasing　**2** : to close and open the eyelids quickly　**3** : to avoid seeing or noting something — usu. used with *at*　**4** : to gleam or flash intermittently : TWINKLE　**5 a** : to come to an end — usu. used with *out*　**b** : to stop shining — usu. used with *out*　**6** : to signal a message with a light ～ *vt*　**1** : to cause to open and shut　**2** : to affect or influence by or as if by blinking the eyes

²wink *n* (14c)　**1** : a brief period of sleep : NAP　**2 a** : a hint or sign given by winking　**b** : an act of winking　**3** : the time of a wink : INSTANT ⟨quick as a ～⟩　**4** : a flicker of the eyelids : BLINK

wink·er \'wiŋ-kər\ *n* (1549)　**1** : one that winks　**2** : a horse's blinder

¹win·kle \'wiŋ-kəl\ *n* [by shortening] (1585) : ²PERIWINKLE

²winkle *vi* **win·kled; win·kling** \-k(ə-)liŋ\ [freq. of *wink*] (1791) : TWINKLE

³winkle *vt* **win·kled; win·kling** \-k(ə-)liŋ\ [¹*winkle*; fr. the process of extracting a winkle from its shell] (1918) *chiefly Brit* : to displace, extract, or evict from a position — usu. used with *out*

win·ner \'wi-nər\ *n* (14c) : one that wins: as　**a** : one that is successful esp. through praiseworthy ability and hard work　**b** : a victor esp. in games and sports　**c** : one that wins admiration　**d** : a shot in a court game that is not returned and that scores for the player making it

winner's circle *n* (1951) : an enclosure near a racetrack where the winning horse and jockey are brought for photographs and awards

Win·nie \'wi-nē\ n [winner + -ie] (ca. 1944) : an award presented annually by a professional organization for notable achievement in fashion design

¹**win·ning** \'wi-niŋ\ n (14c) 1 : the act of one that wins : VICTORY 2 : something won: as a : a captured territory : CONQUEST b : money won by success in a game or competition — usu. used in pl.

²**winning** adj (15c) 1 a : of or relating to winning : that wins ⟨the ~ ticket⟩ b : successful esp. in competition ⟨a ~ team⟩ 2 : tending to please or delight ⟨a ~ smile⟩ — **win·ning·ly** \-niŋ-lē\ adv

win·nock \'wi-nək\ n [ME (Sc) windok, windowe] (15c) Scot : WINDOW

¹**win·now** \'wi-(,)nō\ vb [ME winewen, fr. OE windwian to fan, winnow; akin to OHG wintōn to fan, L vannus winnowing fan, ventus wind — more at WIND] vt (bef. 12c) 1 a (1) : to remove (as chaff) by a current of air (2) : to get rid of (something undesirable or unwanted) : REMOVE — often used with out ⟨~ out certain inaccuracies —Stanley Walker⟩ b (1) : SEPARATE, SIFT ⟨an old hand at ~ing what is true and significant —Oscar Lewis⟩ (2) : SELECT 2 a : to treat (as grain) by exposure to a current of air so that waste matter is eliminated b : to free of unwanted or inferior elements : PARE 3 : to blow on : FAN ⟨the wind ~ing his thin white hair —Time⟩ ~ vi 1 : to separate chaff from grain by fanning 2 : to separate desirable and undesirable elements — **win·now·er** \'wi-nō-wər\ n

²**winnow** n (1580) 1 a : a device for winnowing 2 a : the action of winnowing b : a motion resembling that of winnowing

wino \'wī-(,)nō\ n, pl **win·os** (ca. 1915) : one who is chronically addicted to drinking wine

win·some \'wi(n)t-səm\ adj [ME winsum, fr. OE wynsum, fr. wynn joy; akin to OHG wunna joy, L venus desire — more at WIN] (bef. 12c) 1 : generally pleasing and engaging often because of a childlike charm and innocence 2 : CHEERFUL, GAY — **win·some·ly** adv — **win·some·ness** n

¹**win·ter** \'win-tər\ n [ME, fr. OE; akin to OHG wintar winter and perh. to Lith vanduo water, OE wæter — more at WATER] (bef. 12c) 1 : the season between autumn and spring comprising in the northern hemisphere usu. the months of December, January, and February or as reckoned astronomically extending from the December solstice to the March equinox 2 : the colder half of the year 3 : YEAR ⟨happened many ~s ago⟩ 4 : a period of inactivity or decay

²**winter** vb **win·tered; win·ter·ing** \'win-t(ə-)riŋ\ vi (14c) 1 : to pass the winter 2 : to feed or find food during the winter — used with on ~ vt : to keep, feed, or manage during the winter

³**winter** adj (15c) 1 : of, relating to, or suitable for winter ⟨a ~ vacation⟩ ⟨~ clothes⟩ 2 : sown in the autumn and harvested in the following spring or summer ⟨~ wheat⟩ ⟨~ rye⟩ — compare SUMMER

winter aconite n (1794) : a small European perennial herb (Eranthis hyemalis) of the buttercup family grown for its bright yellow flowers which often bloom through the snow

win·ter·ber·ry \'win-tər-,ber-ē\ n (1759) 1 : an eastern No. American shrub (Ilex verticillata) of the holly family with clusters of axillary flowers, usu. bright red berries, and deciduous leaves that turn black in the fall — called also black alder 2 : a shrub (Ilex laevigata) of the holly family similar to the winterberry but of more restricted range

winter crookneck n (ca. 1909) : any of several crooknecks that are winter squashes of the pumpkin group noted for their keeping qualities

win·ter·er \'win-tər-ər\ n (1783) : one that winters; specif : a winter resident or visitor

winter flounder n (1814) : a rusty brown flounder (Pseudopleuronectes americanus of the family Pleuronectidae) of the northwestern Atlantic important as a market fish esp. in winter

win·ter·green \'win-tər-,grēn\ n (1548) 1 : any of a genus (Pyrola of the family Pyrolaceae, the wintergreen family) of evergreen perennial herbs (as the shinleafs) that have basal leaves and racemose flowers 2 a : any of a genus (Gaultheria) of evergreen plants of the heath family; esp : a low creeping evergreen shrub (G. procumbens) of No. America with white flowers and spicy red berries — compare CHECKERBERRY b (1) : an essential oil from this plant (2) : the flavor of this oil ⟨~ lozenges⟩

win·ter·ize \'win-tə-,rīz\ vt **-ized; -iz·ing** (1934) : to make ready for winter or winter use and esp. resistant or proof against winter weather ⟨~ a car⟩ — **win·ter·i·za·tion** \,win-tə-rə-'zā-shən\ n

win·ter·kill \'win-tər-,kil\ vt (ca. 1800) : to kill (as a plant) by exposure to winter conditions ~ vi : to die as a result of exposure to winter conditions — **winterkill** n

win·ter·ly \'win-tər-lē\ adj (1559) : of, relating to, or occurring in winter : WINTRY

winter melon n (ca. 1900) 1 : any of several muskmelons (as a casaba or honeydew melon) that are fruits of a cultivated vine (Cucumis melo indorus) 2 : a large white-fleshed melon that is the fruit of an Asian vine (Benincasa hispida) and is used esp. in Chinese cooking

winter quarters n pl but sing or pl in constr (1641) : a winter residence or station (as of a military unit or a circus)

winter savory n (1597) : a perennial European mint (Satureja montana) with leaves used for seasoning — compare SUMMER SAVORY

winter squash n (1775) : any of various hard-shelled squashes that belong to cultivars derived from several species (esp. Cucurbita maxima, C. moschata, and C. pepo) and that can be stored for several months

win·ter·tide \'win-tər-,tīd\ n (bef. 12c) : WINTERTIME

win·ter·time \-,tīm\ n (14c) : the season of winter

win through vi (1644) : to survive difficulties and reach a desired or satisfactory end

win·tle \'wi-n²l, 'win-t²l\ vi **win·tled; win·tling** \'win(t)-liŋ; 'wi-n²l-iŋ, 'win-t²l-\ [perh. fr. Flem windtelen to reel] (1786) 1 Scot : STAGGER, REEL 2 Scot : WRIGGLE

win·try \'win-trē\ also **win·tery** \'win-t(ə-)rē\ adj **win·tri·er; -est** [OE wintrig, fr. winter] (bef. 12c) 1 : of, relating to, or characteristic of winter 2 a : weathered by or as if by winter : AGED, HOARY b : CHEERLESS, CHILLING ⟨a ~ greeting⟩ — **win·tri·ness** \'win-trē-nəs\ n

winy \'wī-nē\ adj **win·i·er; -est** (14c) 1 : having the taste or qualities of wine : VINOUS 2 of the air : crisply fresh : EXHILARATING

¹**winze** \'winz\ n [alter. of earlier winds, prob. fr. pl. of ⁵wind] (1757) : a steeply inclined passageway in a mine

²**winze** n [Flem or D wensch wish] (1785) Scot : CURSE

¹**wipe** \'wīp\ vb **wiped; wip·ing** [ME wipen, fr. OE wīpian; akin to OHG wīfan to wind around, L vibrare to brandish, and prob. to ON veipa to be in movement, Skt vepate it trembles] vt (bef. 12c) 1 a : to rub with or as if with something soft for cleaning b : to clean or dry by rubbing c : to draw, pass, or move for or as if for rubbing or cleaning 2 a : to remove by or as if by rubbing b : to expunge completely ⟨~ from memory the gruesome scenes —Amer. Guide Series: Del.⟩ 3 : to spread by or as if by wiping ~ vi : to make a motion of or as if of wiping something — **wipe one's boots on** : to treat with indignity — **wipe the floor with** or **wipe the ground with** : to defeat decisively

²**wipe** n (1550) 1 a : BLOW, STRIKE b : JEER, GIBE 2 a : an act or instance of wiping b : a transition from one scene or picture to another (as in movies or television) made by a line moving across the screen 3 : something (as a towel) used for wiping

wiped out adj (1965) slang : INTOXICATED, HIGH

wipe·out \'wīp-,aut\ n (1921) 1 : the act or an instance of wiping out : complete or utter destruction 2 : a fall or crash caused usu. by losing control

wipe out vt (1535) : to destroy completely : ANNIHILATE ~ vi : to fall or crash usu. as a result of losing control

wip·er \'wī-pər\ n (1552) 1 : one that wipes 2 a : something (as a towel or sponge) used for wiping b : a moving contact for making connections with the terminals of an electrical device (as a rheostat) c : a usu. motor-driven arm with a flexible blade for wiping a window (as the windshield of an automobile or airplane)

¹**wire** \'wīr\ n, often attrib [ME, fr. OE wīr; akin to OHG wiara fine gold work, L viēre to plait, and prob. to Gk iris rainbow] (bef. 12c) 1 a : metal in the form of a usu. very flexible thread or slender rod b : a thread or rod of such material 2 a : WIREWORK b : the meshwork of parallel or woven wire on which the wet web of paper forms 3 : something (as a thin plant stem) that is wirelike 4 a : a system of wires used to operate the puppets in a puppet show b : hidden influences controlling the action of a person or organization 5 a : a line of wire for conducting electrical current — compare CORD 3b b : a telephone or telegraph wire or system; esp : WIRE SERVICE c : TELEGRAM, CABLEGRAM 6 : fencing or a fence of usu. barbed wire 7 : the finish line of a race 8 : WIREHAIR — **wire·like** \-,līk\ adj — **under the wire** 1 : at the finish line 2 : at the last moment

²**wire** vb **wired; wir·ing** vt (15c) 1 : to provide with wire : use wire on for a specific purpose 2 : to send or send word to by telegraph 3 : to connect by or as if by a wire ~ vi : to send a telegraphic message — **wir·er** \'wīr-ər\ n

wire cloth n (1798) : a fabric of woven metallic wire (as for strainers)

wired \'wīrd\ adj (15c) 1 : reinforced by wire (as for strength) 2 : furnished with wires (as for electric connections) 3 : bound with wire ⟨a ~ container⟩ 4 : having a wirework netting or fence 5 : feverishly excited

wire·draw \'wīr-,drò\ vt (1598) 1 : to draw or stretch forcibly : ELONGATE 2 : to draw or spin out to great length, tenuity, or overrefinement : ATTENUATE — **wire·draw·er** \-,drò(-ə)r\ n

wire·drawn \-,dròn\ adj (1603) : excessively minute and subtle ⟨curious speculations, ~ comparisons, obsolete erudition —Virginia Woolf⟩

wire fox terrier n (1929) : a wirehaired fox terrier

wire fraud n (1976) : fraud committed using a means of electronic communication (as a telephone)

wire gauge n (1833) 1 : a gauge esp. for measuring the diameter of wire or the thickness of sheet metal 2 : any of various systems consisting of a series of standard sizes used in describing the diameter of wire or the thickness of sheet metal

wire gauze n (1816) : a gauzelike wire cloth

wire grass n (1751) : any of various grasses or rushes having wiry culms or leaves: as a : a European slender-stemmed meadow grass (Poa compressa) widely naturalized in the U.S. and Canada b : any of several coarse grasses (genus Aristida) with 3-awned lemma that grow extensively in open dry, sandy, or sterile areas esp. of the southeastern and south-central U.S.

wire·hair \'wīr-,har, -,her\ n (1884) : a wirehaired dog or cat

wire·haired \-'hard, -'herd\ adj (1801) : having a stiff wiry outer coat of hair — used esp. of a dog or cat; compare ROUGH, SMOOTH

wirehaired pointing griffon n (1929) : any of a breed of dogs of Dutch origin that both hunt and retrieve and have a long head and a harsh wiry often chestnut or white and chestnut colored coat

wirehaired terrier n (ca. 1885) : WIRE FOX TERRIER

¹**wire·less** \'wīr-ləs\ adj (1894) 1 : having no wire or wires 2 chiefly Brit : of or relating to radiotelegraphy, radiotelephony, or radio

²**wireless** n (1903) 1 : WIRELESS TELEGRAPHY 2 : two-way wireless transmission of sound using radio waves 3 chiefly Brit : RADIO

wireless telegraphy n (1898) : telegraphy carried on by radio waves and without connecting wires — called also wireless telegraph

wireless telephone n (1894) : RADIOTELEPHONE

wire·man \'wīr-mən\ n (ca. 1548) 1 : a maker of or worker with wire; esp : LINEMAN 1 2 : WIRETAPPER

wire netting n (1801) : a wire cloth coarser than wire gauze

wire·pho·to \'wīr-'fō-(,)tō\ n [fr. Wirephoto, a trademark] (1935) : a photograph transmitted by electrical signals over telephone wires

wire·pull·er \-,pu̇-lər\ n (1832) : one who uses secret or underhanded means to influence the acts of a person or organization — **wire·pull·ing** \-,pu̇-liŋ\ n

wire recorder n (1943) : a magnetic recorder using a thin wire as the recording medium — **wire·re·cord·ing** n

wire rope n (1841) : a rope formed wholly or chiefly of wires

wire service n (1944) : a news agency that sends out syndicated news copy to subscribers by wire or by satellite transmission

¹**wire·tap** \'wīr-,tap\ vi (1904) : to tap a telephone or telegraph wire in order to get information ~ vt : to tap the telephone or

²**wiretap** n (1948) 1 : the act or an instance of wiretapping 2 : an electrical connection for wiretapping

---

\ə\ abut \ᵊ\ kitten, F table \ər\ further \a\ ash \ā\ ace \ä\ mop, mar
\au̇\ out \ch\ chin \e\ bet \ē\ easy \g\ go \i\ hit \ī\ ice \j\ job
\ŋ\ sing \ō\ go \ȯ\ law \ȯi\ boy \th\ thin \th̲\ the \ü\ loot \u̇\ foot
\y\ yet \zh\ vision \à, ḵ, ⁿ, œ, œ̄, ue, ūe, �956\ see Guide to Pronunciation

wire·tap·per \-,tap-ər\ *n* (1893) : one that taps telephone or telegraph wires

wire·work \-,wərk\ *n* (1587) **1** : a work of wires; *esp* : meshwork, netting, or grillwork of wire ⟨plan the ~ for new circuitry⟩ **2** : walking on wires esp. by acrobats

wire·worm \-,wərm\ *n* (1790) : any of the slender hard-coated larvae of various click beetles that include some destructive esp. to plant roots

wir·ing \'wir-iŋ\ *n* (1809) **1** : the act of providing or using wire **2** : a system of wires; *esp* : an arrangement of wires used for electric distribution

wir·ra \'wir-ə\ *interj* [oh wirra, fr. Ir *a Mhuire*, lit., Mary!] (1829) *Irish* — usu. used to express lament, grief, or concern

wiry \'wir-ē\ *adj* **wir·i·er** \'wi-rē-ər\; **-est** (1588) **1 a** *archaic* : made of wire **b** : resembling wire esp. in form and flexibility **c** *of sound* : produced by or suggestive of the vibration of wire ⟨the violinist . . . often let his tone go nasal and ~ —D. J. Henahan⟩ **2** : being lean, supple, and vigorous : SINEWY — **wir·i·ly** \'wi-rə-lē\ *adv* — **wir·i·ness** \-rē-nəs\ *n*

wis \'wis\ *vb* [by misdivision fr. *iwis* (understood as *I wis*, with *wis* taken to be an archaic pres. indic. of [1]*wit*)] (1508) *archaic* : KNOW

wis·dom \'wiz-dəm\ *n* [ME, fr. OE *wīsdōm*, fr. *wīs* wise] (bef. 12c) **1 a** : accumulated philosophic or scientific learning : KNOWLEDGE **b** : ability to discern inner qualities and relationships : INSIGHT **c** : good sense : JUDGMENT **d** : generally accepted belief ⟨challenges what has become accepted ~ among many historians —Robert Darnton⟩ **2 a** : a wise attitude or course of action **3** : the teachings of the ancient wise men *syn* see SENSE

Wisdom *n* : a didactic book included in the Roman Catholic canon of the Old Testament and corresponding to the Wisdom of Solomon in the Protestant Apocrypha — see BIBLE table

Wisdom of Sol·o·mon \-'sä-lə-mən\ : a didactic book included in the Protestant Apocrypha — see BIBLE table

wisdom tooth *n* [fr. being cut usu. in the late teens] (1848) : the third molar that is the last tooth to erupt on each side of the upper and lower jaws in humans

[1]**wise** \'wiz\ *n* [ME, fr. OE *wīse*; akin to OHG *wīsa* manner, Gk *eidos* form, *idein* to see — more at WIT] (bef. 12c) : MANNER, WAY ⟨in any ~⟩

[2]**wise** *adj* **wis·er**; **wis·est** [ME *wis*, fr. OE *wīs*; akin to OHG *wīs* wise, OE *witan* to know — more at WIT] (bef. 12c) **1 a** : characterized by wisdom : marked by deep understanding, keen discernment, and a capacity for sound judgment **b** : exercising sound judgment : PRUDENT **2 a** : evidencing or hinting at the possession of inside information : KNOWING **b** : possessing inside information **c** : CRAFTY, SHREWD **3** *archaic* : skilled in magic or divination **4** : INSOLENT, SMART-ALECKY, FRESH — **wise·ly** *adv* — **wise·ness** *n*

syn WISE, SAGE, SAPIENT, JUDICIOUS, PRUDENT, SENSIBLE, SANE mean having or showing sound judgment. WISE suggests great understanding of people and of situations and unusual discernment and judgment in dealing with them ⟨wise beyond his tender years⟩. SAGE suggests wide experience, great learning, and wisdom ⟨the *sage* advice of my father⟩. SAPIENT suggests great sagacity and discernment ⟨the *sapient* musings of an old philosopher⟩. JUDICIOUS stresses a capacity for reaching wise decisions or just conclusions ⟨*judicious* parents using kindness and discipline in equal measure⟩. PRUDENT suggests exercise of the restraint of sound practical wisdom and discretion ⟨a *prudent* decision to wait out the storm⟩. SENSIBLE applies to action guided and restrained by good sense and rationality ⟨a *sensible* woman who was not fooled by flattery⟩. SANE stresses mental soundness, rationality, and levelheadedness ⟨remained *sane* even in times of crises⟩.

[3]**wise** *vb* **wised**; **wis·ing** *vt* (1905) : to give instruction or information to : TEACH — usu. used with *up* ~ *vi* : to become informed or knowledgeable : LEARN — used with *up*

[4]**wise** *vt* **wised**; **wis·ing** [ME, fr. OE *wīsian*; akin to ON *vīsa* to show the way, OE *wīs* wise] (bef. 12c) **1** *chiefly Scot* **a** : DIRECT, GUIDE **b** : ADVISE, PERSUADE **2** *chiefly Scot* : to divert or impel in a given direction : SEND

-wise *adv comb form* [ME, fr. OE *-wīsan*, fr. *wīse* manner] **1 a** : in the manner of ⟨crab*wise*⟩ ⟨fan*wise*⟩ **b** : in the position or direction of ⟨slant*wise*⟩ ⟨clock*wise*⟩ **2** : with regard to : in respect of ⟨dollar*wise*⟩

wise·acre \'wi-,zā-kər\ *n* [MD *wijssegger* soothsayer, modif. of OHG *wizzago*; akin to OE *wītega* soothsayer, *witan* to know] (1595) : one who pretends to knowledge or cleverness; *esp* : SMART ALECK

wise-ass \'wiz-,as\ *n* (1971) : SMART ALECK

[1]**wise-crack** \'wiz-,krak\ *n* (1924) : a clever or sarcastic remark

[2]**wisecrack** *vi* (1924) : to make a wisecrack — **wise·crack·er** *n*

wised–up \'wizd-'əp\ *adj* (1926) : KNOWING 1

wise guy \'wiz-,gi\ *n* (1896) : SMART ALECK

wise man *n* (bef. 12c) **1** : a man of unusual learning, judgment, or insight : SAGE **2** : a man versed in esoteric lore (as of magic or astrology); *esp* : MAGUS 1b

wi·sen·hei·mer \'wi-z°n-,hi-mər\ *n* [²wise + -enheimer (as in family names such as *Guggenheimer, Oppenheimer*)] (1904) : SMART ALECK

wi·sent \'vē-,zent\ *n* [G, fr. OHG *wisant* — more at BISON] (1866) : a European bison (*Bison bonasus*) sometimes considered conspecific with the No. American buffalo (*B. bison*) — called also *aurochs*

wise-wom·an \'wiz-,wu̇-mən\ *n* (14c) : a woman versed in charms, conjuring, or fortune-telling

[1]**wish** \'wish\ *vb* [ME *wisshen*, fr. OE *wȳscan*; akin to OHG *wunsken* to wish, Skt *vāñchati* he wishes, *vanoti* he strives for — more at WIN] *vt* (bef. 12c) **1** : to have a desire for (as something unattainable) ⟨~ed he could live his life over⟩ **2** : to give expression to as a wish : BID ⟨~ them good night⟩ **3 a** : to give form to (a wish) **b** : to express a wish for **c** : to request in the form of a wish : ORDER **d** : to desire (a person or thing) to be as specified ⟨cannot ~ our problems away⟩ **4** : to confer (something unwanted) on someone : FOIST ~ *vi* **1** : to have a desire : WANT **2** : to make a wish *syn* see DESIRE — **wish·er** *n*

[2]**wish** *n* (14c) **1 a** : an act or instance of wishing or desire : WANT **b** : an object of desire : GOAL **2 a** : an expressed will or desire : MANDATE **b** : a request or command couched as a wish **3** : an invocation of good or evil fortune on someone

wisha \'wi-shə\ *interj* [Ir *mhuise*] (1826) *chiefly Irish* — used as an intensive or to express surprise

wish·bone \'wish-,bōn\ *n* [fr. the superstition that when two persons pull it apart the one getting the longer fragment will have a wish

granted] (1853) **1** : a forked bone in front of the breastbone in a bird consisting chiefly of the two clavicles fused at their median or lower end **2** : a variation of the T formation in which the halfbacks line up farther from the line of scrimmage than the fullback does

wish·ful \'wish-fəl\ *adj* (1593) **1 a** : expressive of a wish : HOPEFUL **b** : having a wish : DESIROUS **2** : according with wishes rather than reality — **wish·ful·ly** \-fə-lē\ *adv* — **wish·ful·ness** *n*

wish fulfillment *n* (1908) : the gratification of a desire esp. symbolically (as in dreams, daydreams, or neurotic symptoms)

wishful thinking *n* (1932) : the attribution of reality to what one wishes to be true or the tenuous justification of what one wants to believe

wish·ing *adj* (ca. 1530) **1** *archaic* : WISHFUL **2** : regarded as having the power to grant wishes ⟨threw a coin in the ~ well⟩

wish list *n* (1972) : a list of desired but often realistically unobtainable items

wish–wash \'wish-,wȯsh, -,wäsh\ *n* [redupl. of ²*wash*] (1786) **1** : a weak drink **2** : insipid talk or writing

wishy–washy \'wi-shē-,wȯ-shē, -,wä-\ *adj* [redupl. of *washy*] (ca. 1693) **1** : lacking in character or determination : WEAK — **wishy–wash·i·ness** *n*

[1]**wisp** \'wisp\ *n* [ME] (14c) **1** : a small handful (as of hay or straw) **2 a** : a thin strip or fragment **b** : a thready streak ⟨a ~ of smoke⟩ **c** : something frail, slight, or fleeting ⟨a ~ of a girl⟩ ⟨a ~ of a smile⟩ **3** *archaic* : WILL-O'-THE-WISP — **wisp·i·ly** \'wis-pə-lē\ *adv* — **wisp·i·ness** \'wis-pē-nəs\ *n* — **wispy** \'wis-pē\ *adj*

[2]**wisp** *vt* (1753) **1** : to roll into a wisp **2** : to make wisps of ⟨a cigarette ~ing smoke at the corner of his mouth —Raymond Chandler⟩ ~ *vi* : to emerge or drift in wisps ⟨her hair began to ~ into her eyes —Mary Manning⟩

wisp·ish \'wis-pish\ *adj* (1896) : resembling a wisp : INSUBSTANTIAL

wist \'wist\ *vt* [alter. of *wis*] (1508) *archaic* : KNOW

wis·te·ria \wis-'tir-ē-ə\ *or* **wis·tar·ia** \-'tir-ē-ə *also* -'ter-\ *n* [NL *Wisteria*, fr. Caspar *Wistar* †1818 Am. physician] (1842) : any of a genus (*Wisteria*) of chiefly Asian mostly woody leguminous vines that have pinnately compound leaves and long racemes of showy blue, white, purple, or rose papilionaceous flowers and that include several grown as ornamentals

wist·ful \'wist-fəl\ *adj* [blend of *wishful* and obs. E *wistly* intently] (1714) **1** : full of yearning or desire tinged with melancholy; *also* : inspiring such yearning ⟨a ~ memoir⟩ **2** : musingly sad : PENSIVE — **wist·ful·ly** \-fə-lē\ *adv* — **wist·ful·ness** *n*

wisteria

[1]**wit** \'wit\ *vb* **wit·ting**; *pres 1st & 3d sing* **wot** \'wät\ [ME *witen* (1st & 3d sing. pres. *wot*, past *wiste*), fr. OE *witan* (1st & 3d sing. pres. *wāt*, past *wisse, wiste*); akin to OHG *wizzan* to know, L *vidēre* to see, Gk *eidenai* to know, *idein* to see] (bef. 12c) **1** *archaic* : KNOW **2** *archaic* : to come to know : LEARN

[2]**wit** *n* [ME, fr. OE; akin to OHG *wizzi* knowledge, OE *witan* to know] (bef. 12c) **1 a** : MIND, MEMORY **b** : reasoning power : INTELLIGENCE **2 a** : SENSE 2a — usu. used in pl. ⟨alone and warming his five ~s, the white owl in the belfry sits —Alfred Tennyson⟩ **b** (1) : mental soundness : SANITY — usu. used in pl. (2) : mental capability and resourcefulness : INGENUITY **3 a** : astuteness of perception or judgment : ACUMEN **b** : the ability to relate seemingly disparate things so as to illuminate or amuse **c** (1) : a talent for banter or persiflage (2) : a witty utterance or exchange **d** : clever or apt humor **4 a** : a person of superior intellect : THINKER **b** : an imaginatively perceptive and articulate individual esp. skilled in banter or persiflage — **at one's wit's end** *or* **at one's wits' end** : at a loss for a means of solving a problem

syn WIT, HUMOR, IRONY, SARCASM, SATIRE, REPARTEE mean a mode of expression intended to arouse amusement. WIT suggests the power to evoke laughter by remarks showing verbal felicity or ingenuity and swift perception esp. of the incongruous ⟨a playful *wit*⟩. HUMOR implies an ability to perceive the ludicrous, the comical, and the absurd in human life and to express these usu. without bitterness ⟨a sense of *humor*⟩. IRONY applies to a manner of expression in which the intended meaning is the opposite of what is seemingly expressed ⟨the *irony* of the title⟩. SARCASM applies to expression frequently in the form of irony that is intended to cut or wound ⟨given to heartless *sarcasm*⟩. SATIRE applies to writing that exposes or ridicules conduct, doctrines, or institutions either by direct criticism or more often through irony, parody, or caricature ⟨a *satire* on the Congress⟩. REPARTEE implies the power of answering quickly, pointedly, or wittily ⟨a dinner guest noted for *repartee*⟩.

wi·tan \'wi-,tän\ *n pl* [OE, pl. of *wita* sage, adviser; akin to OHG *wizzo* sage, OE *witan* to know] (1807) : members of the witenagemot

[1]**witch** \'wich\ *n* [ME *wicche*, fr. OE *wicca*, masc., wizard & *wicce*, fem., witch; akin to MHG *wicken* to bewitch, OE *wigle* divination, and perh. to OHG *wīh* holy — more at VICTIM] (bef. 12c) **1** : one that is credited with usu. malignant supernatural powers; *esp* : a woman practicing usu. black witchcraft often with the aid of a devil or familiar : SORCERESS — compare WARLOCK **2** : an ugly old woman : HAG **3** : a charming or alluring girl or woman — **witch·like** \'wich-,līk\ *adj* — **witchy** \'wi-chē\ *adj*

[2]**witch** *vt* (14c) **1** : to affect injuriously with witchcraft **2** *archaic* : to influence or beguile with allure or charm ~ *vi* : DOWSE

witch·craft \'wich-,kraft\ *n* (bef. 12c) **1 a** : the use of sorcery or magic **b** : communication with the devil or with a familiar **2** : an irresistible influence or fascination

witch doctor *n* (1718) : a professional worker of magic usu. in a primitive society who often works to cure sickness

witch·ery \'wi-chə-rē, 'wich-rē\ *n, pl* **-er·ies** (1546) **1 a** : the practice of witchcraft : SORCERY **b** : an act of witchcraft **2** : an irresistible fascination

witches' brew *n* (1929) : a potent or fearsome mixture ⟨a *witches' brew* of untamed sex and brutality —Harrison Smith⟩

witch·es'–broom \'wi-chəz-ˌbrüm, -ˌbrům\ *n* (1881) : an abnormal tufted growth of small branches on a tree or shrub caused esp. by fungi or viruses

witches' Sabbath *n* (ca. 1676) : a midnight assembly of witches, devils, and sorcerers for the celebration of rites and orgies

witch-grass \'wich-ˌgras\ *n* [prob. alter. of *quitch (grass)*] (1790) 1 : QUACK GRASS 2 [¹*witch*]: a No. American grass (*Panicum capillare*) with slender brushy panicles that is often a weed on cultivated land

witch ha·zel \'wich-ˌhā-zəl\ *n* [*witch*, a tree with pliant branches, fr. ME *wyche*, fr. OE *wice*; prob. akin to OE *wīcan* to yield — more at WEAK] (1542) 1 : any of a genus (*Hamamelis* of the family Hamamelidaceae, the witch-hazel family) of shrubs or small trees with slender-petaled yellow flowers borne in late fall or early spring; *esp* : one (*H. virginiana*) of eastern No. America that blooms in the fall 2 : an alcoholic solution of a distillate of the bark of a witch hazel (*H. virginiana*) used as a soothing and mildly astringent lotion

witch–hunt \'wich-ˌhənt\ *n* (1885) 1 : a searching out for persecution of persons accused of witchcraft 2 : the searching out and deliberate harassment of those (as political opponents) with unpopular views — **witch–hunt·er** *n* — **witch–hunt·ing** *n or adj*

witch of Agne·si \-än-'yā-zē\ *n* [Maria Gaetana *Agnesi* †1799 Ital. mathematician; *witch*, trans. of It *versiera* cubic curve (influenced by It *versiera* female demon)] (1875) : a plane cubic curve that is symmetric about the y-axis and approaches the x-axis as an asymptote that is constructed by drawing lines from the origin intersecting an upright circle tangent to the x-axis at the origin and taking the locus of points of intersection of pairs of lines parallel to the x-axis and y-axis each pair of which consists of a line parallel to the x-axis through the point where a line through the origin intersects the circle and a line parallel to the y-axis through the point where the same line through the origin intersects the line parallel to the x-axis through the point of intersection of the circle and the y-axis and that has the equation $x^2y = 4a^2(2a - y)$ — called also *witch*

witch·weed \'wich-ˌwēd\ *n* (1904) : any of a genus (*Striga*) of yellow-flowered Old World plants of the snapdragon family that are damaging root parasites of grasses (as sorghum and maize) and that include one (*S. lutea*) which is an introduced pest in parts of the southeastern U.S.

¹wite \'wīt\ *vt* **wit·ed; wit·ing** [ME, fr. OE *wītan*; akin to OHG *wīzan* to blame, OE *wītan* to know] (bef. 12c) *chiefly Scot* : BLAME

²wite *n* (13c) *chiefly Scot* : BLAME, RESPONSIBILITY

wi·te·na·ge·mot *or* **wi·te·na·ge·mote** \'wi-t⁸n-ə-gə-ˌmōt, -yə-ˌmōt\ *n* [OE *witena gemōt*, fr. *witena* (gen. pl. of *wita* sage, adviser) + *gemōt* gemot] (bef. 12c) : an Anglo-Saxon council made up of a varying number of nobles, prelates, and influential officials and convened from time to time to advise the king on administrative and judicial matters

with \'with, 'with, wəth, wəth\ *prep* [ME, against, from, with, fr. OE; akin to OE *wither* against, OHG *widar* against, back, Skt *vi* apart] (bef. 12c) 1 a : in opposition to : AGAINST ⟨had a fight ~ his brother⟩ b : so as to be separated or detached from ⟨broke ~ her family⟩ 2 a — used as a function word to indicate a participant in an action, transaction, or arrangement ⟨works ~ his father⟩ ⟨a talk ~ a friend⟩ ⟨got into an accident ~ the car⟩ b — used as a function word to indicate the object of attention, behavior, or feeling ⟨get tough ~ him⟩ ⟨angry ~ her⟩ c : in respect to : so far as concerns ⟨on friendly terms ~ all nations⟩ d — used to indicate the object of an adverbial expression of imperative force ⟨off ~ his head⟩ e : OVER, ON ⟨no longer has any influence ~ them⟩ f : in the performance, operation, or use of ⟨the trouble ~ this machine⟩ 3 a — used as a function word to indicate the object of a statement of comparison or equality ⟨a dress identical ~ her hostess's⟩ b — used as a function word to express agreement or sympathy ⟨must conclude, ~ you, that the painting is a forgery⟩ c : on the side of : FOR ⟨if he's for lower taxes, I'm ~ him⟩ d : as well as ⟨can pitch ~ the best of them⟩ 4 a — used as a function word to indicate combination, accompaniment, presence, or addition ⟨heat milk ~ honey⟩ ⟨went there ~ her⟩ ⟨his money, ~ his wife's, comes to a million⟩ b : inclusive of ⟨costs $5 ~ the tax⟩ 5 a : in the judgment or estimation of ⟨stood well ~ her classmates⟩ b : in or according to the experience or practice of ⟨~ many of us, our ideas seem to fall by the wayside —W. J. Reilly⟩ 6 a — used as a function word to indicate the means, cause, agent, or instrumentality ⟨hit him ~ a rock⟩ ⟨pale ~ anger⟩ ⟨threatened ~ tuberculosis⟩ ⟨he amused the crowd ~ his antics⟩ b *archaic* : by the direct act of 7 a — used as a function word to indicate manner of action ⟨ran ~ effort⟩ ⟨acknowledge your contribution ~ thanks⟩ b — used as a function word to indicate an attendant fact or circumstance ⟨stood there ~ his hat on⟩ c — used as a function word to indicate a result attendant on a specified action ⟨got off ~ a light sentence⟩ 8 a (1) : in possession of ⟨came ~ good news⟩ (2) : in the possession or care of ⟨left the money ~ her mother⟩ b : characterized or distinguished by ⟨a person ~ a sharp nose⟩ 9 a — used as a function word to indicate a close association in time ⟨~ the outbreak of war they went home⟩ ⟨mellows ~ time⟩ b : in proportion to ⟨the pressure varies ~ the depth⟩ 10 a : in spite of : NOTWITHSTANDING ⟨a really tip-top man, ~ all his wrongheadedness —H. J. Laski⟩ b : except for ⟨finds that, ~ one group of omissions and one important addition, they reflect that curriculum —Gilbert Highet⟩ 11 : in the direction of ⟨~ the wind⟩ ⟨~ the grain⟩

¹with·al \wi-'thȯl, -'thȯl\ *adv* [ME, fr. *with* + *all*, *al* all] (13c) 1 : together with this : BESIDES ⟨a supporter of all constructive work and ... an excellent businessman —A. W. Long⟩ 2 *archaic* : THEREWITH 1 3 : on the other hand : NEVERTHELESS

²withal *prep* (14c) *archaic* : WITH — used postpositively with a relative or interrogative pronoun as object

with·draw \with-'drȯ, with-\ *vb* **-drew** \-'drü\; **-drawn** \-'drȯn\; **-draw·ing** \-'drȯ(-)iŋ\ [ME, fr. *with* from + *drawen* to draw] *vt* (13c) 1 a : to take back or away : REMOVE ⟨pressure upon educational administrators to ~ academic credit —J. W. Scott⟩ b : to remove from use or cultivation c : to remove (money) from a place of deposit d : to turn away (as the eyes) from an object of attention ⟨withdrew their gaze⟩ e : to draw (as a curtain) back or aside 2 a : to remove from consideration or set outside a group ⟨withdrew his name from the list of nominees⟩ ⟨withdrew their child from the school⟩ b (1) : TAKE BACK,

RETRACT (2) : to recall or remove (a motion) under parliamentary procedure ~ *vi* 1 a : to move back or away : RETIRE b : to draw back from a battlefield : RETREAT 2 a : to remove oneself from participation b : to become socially or emotionally detached ⟨had *withdrawn* farther and farther into herself —Ethel Wilson⟩ 3 : to recall a motion under parliamentary procedure — **with·draw·able** \-'drȯ-ə-bəl\ *adj*

with·draw·al \-'drȯ(-ə)l\ *n* (1749) 1 a : the act of taking back or away something that has been granted or possessed b : removal from a place of deposit or investment c (1) : the discontinuance of administration or use of a drug (2) : a period following the discontinuance of an addicting drug that is marked by often painful physical and psychological symptoms ⟨a heroin addict going through ~⟩ 2 a : retreat or retirement esp. into a more secluded or less exposed place or position b : an operation by which a military force disengages from the enemy c (1) : social or emotional detachment (2) : a pathological retreat from objective reality (as in some schizophrenic states) 3 : RETRACTION, REVOCATION ⟨threatened us with ~ of consent⟩ 4 a : the act of drawing someone or something back from or out of a place or position b : COITUS INTERRUPTUS

withdrawing room *n* (1591) : a room to retire to (as from a dining room); *esp* : DRAWING ROOM

with·drawn \with-'drȯn, with-\ *adj* (1615) 1 : removed from immediate contact or easy approach : ISOLATED 2 : socially detached and unresponsive : exhibiting withdrawal : INTROVERTED — **with·drawn·ness** \-'drȯn-nəs\ *n*

withe \'with, 'with, 'with\ *n* [ME, fr. OE *withthe*; akin to OE *wīthig* withy] (bef. 12c) : a slender flexible branch or twig; *esp* : one used as a band or line

¹with·er \'wi-thər\ *vb* **with·ered; with·er·ing** \'with-riŋ, 'wi-thə-\ [ME *widren*; prob. akin to ME *weder* weather] *vi* (14c) 1 : to become dry and sapless; *esp* : to shrivel from or as if from loss of bodily moisture 2 : to lose vitality, force, or freshness ~ *vt* 1 : to cause to wither 2 : to make speechless or incapable of action : STUN ⟨~ed him with a look —Dorothy Sayers⟩

²wither *n* (1607) *chiefly Brit* : WITHERS

withering *adj* (1579) : acting or serving to cut down or destroy : DEVASTATING ⟨a ~ fire from the enemy⟩ — **with·er·ing·ly** \'with-riŋ-lē, 'wi-thə-\ *adv*

with·er·ite \'wi-thə-ˌrīt\ *n* [G *Witherit*, irreg. fr. William *Withering* †1799 Eng. physician] (1794) : a mineral consisting of a carbonate of barium in the form of white or gray twin crystals or columnar or granular masses

withe rod *n* (1846) : a No. American viburnum (*Viburnum cassinoides*) with tough slender shoots

with·ers \'wi-thərz\ *n pl* [prob. fr. obs. E *wither*- against, fr. ME, fr. OE, fr. *wither* against; fr. the withers being the parts which resist the pull in drawing a load — more at WITH] (1580) 1 : the ridge between the shoulder bones of a horse — see HORSE illustration 2 : a part corresponding to the withers in a quadruped other than a horse

with·er·shins \'wi-thər-shənz\ *var of* WIDDERSHINS

with·hold \with-'hōld, with-\ *vb* **-held** \-'held\; **-hold·ing** [ME, *with* from + *holden* to hold — more at WITH] *vt* (13c) 1 : to hold back from action : CHECK 2 *archaic* : to keep in custody 3 : to refrain from granting, giving, or allowing ⟨~ permission⟩ 4 : to deduct (withholding tax) from income ~ *vi* : FORBEAR, REFRAIN *syn* see KEEP — **with·hold·er** *n*

withholding tax *n* (1940) : a deduction (as from wages, fees, or dividends) levied at a source of income as advance payment on income tax

¹with·in \wi-'thin, -'thin\ *adv* [ME *withinne*, fr. OE *withinnan*, fr. *with* + *innan* inwardly, within, fr. *in*] (bef. 12c) 1 : in or into the interior : INSIDE 2 : in one's inner thought, disposition, or character : INWARDLY ⟨search ~ for a creative impulse —Kingman Brewster, Jr.⟩

²within *prep* (12c) 1 — used as a function word to indicate enclosure or containment 2 — used as a function word to indicate situation or circumstance in the limits or compass of: as a : before the end of ⟨gone ~ a week⟩ b (1) : not beyond the quantity, degree, or limitations of ⟨live ~ your income⟩ (2) : in or into the scope or sphere of ⟨~ the jurisdiction of the state⟩ (3) : in or into the range of ⟨~ reach⟩ ⟨~ sight⟩ (4) — used as a function word to indicate a specified difference or margin ⟨came ~ two points of a perfect mark⟩ ⟨~ a mile of the town⟩ 3 : to the inside of : INTO

³within *n* (15c) : an inner place or area ⟨revolt from ~⟩

⁴within *adj* (1748) : being inside : ENCLOSED ⟨the ~ indictment⟩

with·in·doors \wi-ˌthin-'dȯrz, -ˌthin-, -'dȯrz\ *adv* (1581) : INDOORS

with–it \'wi-thət\ *adj* (1959) : socially or culturally up-to-date ⟨the intelligent, disaffected, ~ young —Eliot Fremont-Smith⟩

¹with·out \wi-'thaủt, -'thaủt\ *prep* [ME *withoute*, fr. OE *withūtan*, fr. *with* + *ūtan* outside, fr. *ūt* out — more at OUT] (bef. 12c) 1 : OUTSIDE 2 — used as a function word to indicate the absence or lack of something or someone ⟨fight ~ fear⟩ ⟨left ~ him⟩ ⟨looks ~ seeing⟩

²without *adv* (bef. 12c) 1 : on the outside : EXTERNALLY 2 : with something lacking or absent ⟨has learned to do ~⟩

³without *conj* (14c) *chiefly dial* : UNLESS ⟨you don't know about me ~ you have read a book —Mark Twain⟩

⁴without *n* (15c) : an outer place or area ⟨came from ~⟩

with·out·doors \wi-ˌthaủt-'dȯrz, -ˌthaủt-\ *adv* (1617) : OUTDOORS

with·stand \with-'stand, with-\ *vt* **-stood** \-'stủd\; **-stand·ing** [ME, fr. OE *withstandan*, fr. *with* against + *standan* to stand] (bef. 12c) 1 a : to stand up against : oppose with firm determination; *esp* : to resist successfully b : to be proof against : resist the effect of ⟨~ the impact of a landing —*Current Biog.*⟩ 2 *archaic* : to stop or obstruct the course of *syn* see OPPOSE

¹withy \'wi-thē\ *n, pl* **with·ies** [ME, fr. OE *wīthig*; akin to OHG *wīda* willow, L *vitis* vine, *viēre* to plait — more at WIRE] (bef. 12c) 1 : WILLOW; *esp* : OSIER 1 2 : a flexible slender twig or branch (as of osier) : WITHE

\ə\ abut \ᵊ\ kitten, F table \ər\ further \a\ ash \ā\ ace \ä\ mop, mar \aủ\ out \ch\ chin \e\ bet \ē\ easy \g\ go \i\ hit \ī\ ice \j\ job \ŋ\ sing \ō\ go \ȯ\ law \ȯi\ boy \th\ thin \t̲h̲\ the \ü\ loot \ủ\ foot \y\ yet \zh\ vision \á, k̲, ⁿ, œ, œ̄, ᵫ, ᵫ̄, ᵊ\ *see* Guide to Pronunciation

²**withy** \'wi-thē, 'wi-thē, 'wī-thē\ *adj* [*withe*] (1598) : flexibly tough
wit·less \'wit-ləs\ *adj* (bef. 12c) **1** : destitute of wit or understanding : FOOLISH **2** : mentally deranged : CRAZY ⟨drive one ~ with anxiety — William Styron⟩ — **wit·less·ly** *adv* — **wit·less·ness** *n*
wit·ling \-liŋ\ *n* (1693) **1** : a would-be wit **2** : a person of little wit
wit·loof \'wit-,lōf, -,lüf\ *n* [D dial. *witloof* chicory, fr. D *wit* white + *loof* foliage] (1885) : CHICORY 1; *also* : ENDIVE 2
¹**wit·ness** \'wit-nəs\ *n* [ME *witnesse*, fr. OE *witnes* knowledge, testimony, witness, fr. ²*wit*] (bef. 12c) **1** : attestation of a fact or event : TESTIMONY **2** : one that gives evidence; *specif* : one who testifies in a cause or before a judicial tribunal **3** : one asked to be present at a transaction so as to be able to testify to its having taken place **4** : one who has personal knowledge of something **5 a** : something serving as evidence or proof : SIGN **b** : public affirmation by word or example of usu. religious faith or conviction ⟨the heroic ~ to divine life —*Pilot*⟩ **6** *cap* : a member of the Jehovah's Witnesses
²**witness** *vt* (14c) **1** : to testify to : ATTEST **2** : to act as legal witness of **3** : to furnish proof of : BETOKEN **4** : to have personal or direct cognizance of — see for oneself ⟨*~ed* the historic event⟩ **b** : to take note of ⟨our grammar — ~ our verb system—is a marvel of flexibility, variety, and exactitude —Charlton Laird⟩ **5** : to constitute the scene or time of ⟨structures . . . which this striking Dorset hilltop once *~ed* —*Times Lit. Supp.*⟩ ~ *vi* **1** : to bear witness : TESTIFY **2** : to bear witness to one's religious convictions ⟨opportunity to ~ for Christ — Billy Graham⟩ *syn* see CERTIFY
wit·ness–box \-,bäks\ *n* (1806) *chiefly Brit* : an enclosure in which a witness sits or stands while testifying in court
witness stand *n* (1853) : a stand or an enclosure from which a witness gives evidence in a court
wit·ted \'wi-təd\ *adj* (14c) : having wit or understanding — usu. used in combination ⟨dull-*witted*⟩ ⟨quick-*witted*⟩
wit·ti·cism \'wi-tə-,si-zəm\ *n* [*witty* + *-cism* (as in *criticism*)] (1651) : a cleverly witty and often biting or ironic remark
¹**wit·ting** \'wi-t°n, -tiŋ\ *n* (14c) **1** *dial* : knowledge or awareness of something : COGNIZANCE **2** *chiefly dial* : information obtained or communicated : NEWS
²**wit·ting** \-tiŋ\ *adj* (ca. 1520) **1** : cognizant or aware of something : CONSCIOUS **2** : done deliberately : INTENTIONAL — **wit·ting·ly** \-tiŋ-lē\ *adv*
wit·tol \'wi-t°l\ *n* [ME *wetewold*, fr. *weten, witen* to know + *cokewold* cuckold — more at WIT] (15c) **1** *archaic* : a man who knows of his wife's infidelity and puts up with it **2** *archaic* : a witless person
wit·ty \'wi-tē\ *adj* **wit·ti·er; -est** (bef. 12c) **1** *archaic* : having good intellectual capacity : INTELLIGENT **2** : amusingly or ingeniously clever in conception or execution ⟨the costumes are sumptuous and ~ — Virgil Thomson⟩ ⟨the musical background is ~ —Wolcott Gibbs⟩ **3** : marked by or full of wit : smartly facetious or jocular **4** : quick or ready to see or express illuminating or amusing relationships or insights — **wit·ti·ly** \'wi-t°l-ē\ *adv* — **wit·ti·ness** \'wi-tē-nəs\ *n*
syn WITTY, HUMOROUS, FACETIOUS, JOCULAR, JOCOSE mean provoking or intended to provoke laughter. WITTY suggests cleverness and quickness of mind ⟨a *witty* remark⟩. HUMOROUS applies broadly to anything that evokes usu. genial laughter and may contrast with *witty* in suggesting whimsicality or eccentricity ⟨*humorous* anecdotes⟩. FACETIOUS stresses a desire to produce laughter and may be derogatory in implying dubious or ill-timed attempts at wit or humor ⟨*facetious* comments⟩. JOCULAR implies a usu. habitual fondness for jesting and joking ⟨a *jocular* fellow⟩. JOCOSE is somewhat less derogatory than FACETIOUS in suggesting habitual waggishness or playfulness ⟨*jocose* proposals⟩.
wive \'wiv\ *vb* **wived; wiv·ing** [ME, fr. OE *wīfian*, fr. *wīf* woman, wife] *vi* (bef. 12c) : to marry a woman ~ *vt* **1** : to marry to a woman **2** : to take for a wife
wives *pl of* WIFE
wiz \'wiz\ *n* (1902) : WIZARD 3
¹**wiz·ard** \'wi-zərd\ *n* [ME *wysard*, fr. *wis, wys* wise] (15c) **1** *archaic* : a wise man : SAGE **2** : one skilled in magic : SORCERER **3** : a very clever or skillful person
²**wizard** *adj* (1579) **1** *archaic* : having magical influence or power **2** *archaic* : of or relating to wizardry : ENCHANTED **3** *chiefly Brit* : worthy of the highest praise : EXCELLENT
wiz·ard·ly \'wi-zərd-lē\ *adj* (1588) **1** : having characteristics of a wizard **2** : marvelous in construction or operation ⟨uses ~ circuitry to distort images —*Time*⟩
wiz·ard·ry \'wi-zə(r)-drē\ *n, pl* **-ries** (1583) **1** : the art or practices of a wizard : SORCERY **2 a** : a seemingly magical transforming power or influence ⟨electronic ~⟩ **b** : great skill or cleverness in an activity
¹**wiz·en** \'wi-z°n *also* 'wē-\ *vb* **wiz·ened; wiz·en·ing** \'wiz-niŋ *also* 'wēz-; 'wi-z°n-iŋ *also* 'wē-\ [ME *wisenen*, fr. OE *wisnian*; akin to OHG *wesanēn* to wither, Lith *vysti*] *vi* (bef. 12c) : to become dry, shrunken, and wrinkled often as a result of aging or of failing vitality ~ *vt* : to cause to wizen
²**wizen** *adj* [alter. of *wizened*] (1786) : that is wizened
woad \'wōd\ *n* [ME *wod*, fr. OE *wād*; akin to OHG *weit* woad, L *vitrum*] (bef. 12c) : a European herb (*Isatis tinctoria*) of the mustard family formerly grown for the blue dyestuff yielded by its leaves; *also* : this dyestuff
¹**wob·ble** \'wä-bəl\ *vb* **wob·bled; wob·bling** \-b(ə-)liŋ\ [prob. fr. LG *wabbeln*; akin to OE *wǣfre* restless — more at WAVER] *vi* (1657) **1 a** : to move or proceed with an irregular rocking or staggering motion or unsteadily and clumsily from side to side **b** : TREMBLE, QUAVER **2** : WAVER, VACILLATE ~ *vt* : to cause to wobble — **wob·bler** \-b(ə-)lər\ *n* — **wob·bli·ness** \'wä-blē-nəs\ *n* — **wob·bly** \'wä-b(ə-)lē\ *adj*
²**wobble** *n* (1699) **1 a** : a hobbling or rocking unequal motion (as of a wheel unevenly mounted) **b** : an uncertainly directed movement **2** : an intermittent variation (as in volume of sound)
Wob·bly \'wä-blē\ *n, pl* **Wobblies** [origin unknown] (1914) : a member of the Industrial Workers of the World
Wo·den \'wō-d°n\ *n* [OE *Wōden*] : ODIN
wodge \'wäj\ *n* [prob. alter. of *wedge*] (1860) *chiefly Brit* : a bulky mass or chunk : LUMP, WAD
¹**woe** \'wō\ *interj* [ME *wa, wo*, fr. OE *wā*; akin to ON *vei*, interj., woe, L *vae*] (bef. 12c) — used to express grief, regret, or distress

²**woe** *n* (13c) **1** : a condition of deep suffering from misfortune, affliction, or grief **2** : ruinous trouble : CALAMITY, AFFLICTION ⟨economic ~s⟩ *syn* see SORROW
woe·be·gone \'wō-bi-,gȯn *also* -,gän\ *adj* [ME *wo begon*, fr. *wo*, n. + *begon*, pp. of *begon* to go about, beset, fr. OE *begān*, fr. *be-* + *gān* to go — more at GO] (14c) **1** : strongly affected with woe : WOEFUL **2 a** : exhibiting great woe, sorrow, or misery ⟨a ~ expression⟩ **b** : being in a sorry state ⟨~ tattered clothes⟩ — **woe·be·gone·ness** *n*
woe·ful *also* **wo·ful** \'wō-fəl\ *adj* (14c) **1** : full of woe : GRIEVOUS ⟨~ prophecies⟩ **2** : involving or bringing woe **3** : lamentably bad or serious : DEPLORABLE ⟨~ ignorance⟩ — **woe·ful·ly** \-f(ə-)lē\ *adv* — **woe·ful·ness** \-fəl-nəs\ *n*
wog \'wäg, 'wȯg\ *n* [perh. short for *golliwog*] (ca. 1929) *chiefly Brit* : a dark-skinned foreigner; *esp* : one from the Middle East or Far East — usu. used disparagingly
wok \'wäk\ *n* [Chin (Guangdong) *wohk*] (1952) : a bowl-shaped cooking utensil used esp. in stir-frying
woke *past and past part of* WAKE
woken *past part of* WAKE
wold \'wōld\ *n* [ME *wald, wold*, fr. OE *weald, wald* forest; akin to OHG *wald* forest, ON *vollr* field] (bef. 12c) **1** : a usu. upland area of open country **2** *cap* : a hilly or rolling region — used in names of various English geographical areas ⟨Yorkshire Wolds⟩
¹**wolf** \'wùlf\ *n, pl* **wolves** \'wùlvz\ *often attrib* [ME, fr. OE *wulf*; akin to OHG *wolf* wolf, L *lupus*, Gk *lykos*] (bef. 12c) **1** *pl also* **wolf a** : any of various large predatory canids (genus *Canis*) that live and hunt in packs and resemble the related dogs; *esp* : GRAY WOLF — compare COYOTE, JACKAL **b** : the fur of a wolf **2 a** (1) : a fierce, rapacious, or destructive person (2) : a man forward, direct, and zealous in amatory attentions to women **b** : dire poverty : STARVATION ⟨keep the ~ from the door⟩ **c** : the maggot of a warble fly **3** [G; fr. the howling sound] **a** (1) : dissonance in some chords on organs, pianos, or other instruments with fixed tones tuned by unequal temperament (2) : an instance of such dissonance **b** : a harshness due to faulty vibration in various tones in a bowed instrument — **wolf-like** \'wùlf-,līk\ *adj* — **wolf in sheep's clothing** : one who cloaks a hostile intention with a friendly manner
²**wolf** *vt* (1862) : to eat greedily : DEVOUR
wolf·ber·ry \'wùlf-,ber-ē\ *n* (ca. 1834) : a white-berried No. American shrub (*Symphoricarpos occidentalis*) of the honeysuckle family
wolf dog *n* (1652) **1** : any of various large dogs formerly kept for hunting wolves **2** : the offspring of a wolf and a domestic dog
wolf·er \'wùl-fər\ *n* (1872) : a hunter of wolves
wolff·ian body \'wùl-fē-ən-\ *n, often cap* W [Kaspar Friedrich *Wolff*] (ca. 1844) : MESONEPHROS
Wolffian duct *n* (1879) : the duct of the mesonephros that persists in the female chiefly as part of a vestigial organ and in the male as the duct system leaving the testis and including the epididymis, vas deferens, and ejaculatory duct
wolf·fish \'wùlf-,fish\ *n* (1569) : any of several large marine blennies (genus *Anarhichas* of the family Anarhicadidae) having strong canine teeth in the front of the jaws and molar teeth on the sides and that feed chiefly on shellfish, starfish, and sea urchins
wolf·hound \'wùlf-,haùnd\ *n* (1786) : any of several large dogs used esp. formerly in hunting large animals (as wolves)
wolf·ish \'wùl-fish\ *adj* (1563) **1** : of or relating to wolves **2 a** : suggestive of a wolf ⟨~ mongrel dogs —Hoffman Birney⟩ ⟨a ~ and withdrawn youth —Marshall Frady⟩ **b** : befitting or characteristic of a wolf ⟨a ~ appetite⟩ — **wolf·ish·ly** *adv* — **wolf·ish·ness** *n*
wolf pack *n* (1941) : a group of submarines that make a coordinated attack on shipping
wol·fram \'wùl-frəm\ *n* [G] (1757) **1** : WOLFRAMITE **2** : TUNGSTEN
wol·fram·ite \'wùl-frə-,mīt\ *n* [G *Wolframit*, fr. *Wolfram*] (ca. 1868) : a mineral that consists of a tungstate of iron and manganese usu. of a brownish or grayish black color and slightly metallic luster, occurs in monoclinic crystals and in granular or columnar masses, and is used as a source of tungsten
wolfs·bane \'wùlfs-,bān\ *n* (1548) : MONKSHOOD; *esp* : a highly variable yellow-flowered poisonous European herb (*Aconitum vulparia*)
wolf spider *n* (1608) : any of various active wandering ground spiders (family Lycosidae)
wolf whistle *n* (1946) : a distinctive whistle sounded by a boy or man to express sexual admiration for a girl or woman in his vicinity
wol·las·ton·ite \'wù-lə-stə-,nīt, 'wä-\ *n* [William H. *Wollaston*] (1823) : a triclinic mineral consisting of a native calcium silicate occurring usu. in cleavable masses
Wo·lof \'wō-,lȯf\ *n* (1823) : a Niger-Congo language of Senegambia
wol·ver·ine \,wùl-və-'rēn\ *n, pl* **wolverines** [prob. irreg. fr. *wolv-* (as in *wolves*)] (1574) **1** *pl also* **wolverine a** : a carnivorous usu. solitary mammal (*Gulo gulo*) of the weasel family of northern forests and associated tundra that is blackish with a light brown band on each side of the body and is noted esp. for its strength **b** : the fur of the wolverine **2** *cap* : a native or resident of Michigan — used as a nickname
wom·an \'wù-mən, *esp Southern* 'wö- *or* 'wə-\ *n, pl* **wom·en** \'wi-mən\ [ME, fr. OE *wīfman*, fr. *wīf* woman, wife + *man* human being, man] (bef. 12c) **1 a** : an adult female person **b** : a woman belonging to a particular category (as by birth, residence, membership, or occupation) — usu. used in combination ⟨council*woman*⟩ **2** : WOMANKIND **3** : distinctively feminine nature : WOMANLINESS **4** : a female servant or personal attendant **5** *chiefly dial* : WIFE **b** : MISTRESS **c** : GIRLFRIEND **2** — **woman** *adj* — **wom·an·less** \-ləs\ *adj*
wom·an·hood \-,hùd\ *n* (14c) **1 a** : the state of being a woman **b** : the distinguishing character or qualities of a woman or of womankind **2** : WOMEN, WOMENKIND
wom·an·ise *Brit var of* WOMANIZE
wom·an·ish \'wù-mə-nish\ *adj* (14c) **1** : characteristic of or suitable for a woman **2** : unsuitable to a man or to a strong character of either sex : EFFEMINATE ⟨~ fears⟩ — **wom·an·ish·ly** *adv* — **wom·an·ish·ness** *n*
wom·an·ize \'wù-mə-,nīz\ *vb* **-ized; -iz·ing** *vt* (1593) : to make effeminate ~ *vi* : to pursue multiple casual relationships with women — **wom·an·iz·er** *n*
wom·an·kind \'wù-mən-,kīnd\ *n sing but sing or pl in constr* (14c) : WOMENKIND

¹**wom·an·like** \-,līk\ *adj* (15c) : WOMANLY
²**womanlike** *adv* (15c) : in the manner of a woman
wom·an·ly \-lē\ *adj* (13c) **1** : having qualities generally associated with a woman **2** : appropriate in character to a woman — **wom·an·li·ness** *n*
woman of letters (1818) **1** : a woman who is a scholar **2** : a woman who is an author
woman of the street (1928) : PROSTITUTE
wom·an·pow·er \'wu̇-mən-,paú(-ə)r\ *n* (1938) : women available and prepared for work (as in industry or a particular line of endeavor)
woman's rights *n pl* (1840) **1** : legal, political, and social rights for women equal to those of men **2** : FEMINISM 2
woman suffrage *n* (1867) : possession and exercise of suffrage by women
womb \'wüm\ *n* [ME *wamb, womb,* fr. OE; akin to OHG *wamba* belly] (bef. 12c) **1** : UTERUS **2 a** : a cavity or space that resembles a womb in containing and enveloping **b** : a place where something is generated — **wombed** \'wümd\ *adj*
wom·bat \'wäm-,bat\ *n* [Dharuk (Australian aboriginal language of the Port Jackson area) *wambat*] (1798) : any of several stocky Australian marsupials (genera *Vombatus* and *Lasiorhinus* of the family Vombatidae) resembling small bears
wom·en·folk \'wi-mən-,fōk\ *also* **wom·en·folks** \-,fōks\ *n pl* (1833) : WOMEN
wom·en·kind \-,kīnd\ *n* (14c) : female human beings : women esp. as distinguished from men

wombat

women's rights *n pl* (1632) : WOMAN'S RIGHTS
women's room *n* (ca. 1937) : LADIES' ROOM
wom·mera \'wä-mə-rə\ *var of* WOOMERA
¹**won** \'wən, 'wōn\ *vi* wonned; won·ning [ME, fr. OE *wunian* — more at WONT] (bef. 12c) *archaic* : DWELL 2a, ABIDE 2
²**won** \'wən\ *past and past part of* WIN
³**won** \'wōn\ *n, pl* **won** [Korean *wŏn*] (ca. 1917) — see MONEY table
¹**won·der** \'wən-dər\ *n* [ME, fr. OE *wundor;* akin to OHG *wuntar* wonder] (bef. 12c) **1 a** : a cause of astonishment or admiration : MARVEL ⟨it's a ~ you weren't killed⟩ **b** : MIRACLE **2** : the quality of exciting amazed admiration **3 a** : rapt attention or astonishment at something awesomely mysterious or new to one's experience **b** : a feeling of doubt or uncertainty
²**wonder** *vb* **won·dered; won·der·ing** \-d(ə-)riŋ\ *vi* (bef. 12c) **1 a** : to be in a state of wonder **b** : to feel surprise **2** : to feel curiosity or doubt ~ *vt* : to be curious or in doubt about — **won·der·er** \-dər-ər\ *n*
³**wonder** *adj* (12c) : WONDROUS, WONDERFUL; *as* **a** : exciting amazement or admiration **b** : effective or efficient far beyond anything previously known or anticipated
wonder drug *n* (1939) : MIRACLE DRUG
won·der·ful \'wən-dər-fəl\ *adj* (bef. 12c) **1** : exciting wonder : MARVELOUS, ASTONISHING ⟨a sight ~ to behold⟩ **2** : unusually good : ADMIRABLE — **won·der·ful·ly** \-f(ə-)lē\ *adv* — **won·der·ful·ness** \-fəl-nəs\ *n*
won·der·land \'wən-dər-,land, -lənd\ *n* (1790) **1** : an imaginary place of delicate beauty or magical charm **2** : a place that excites admiration or wonder
won·der·ment \-mənt\ *n* (1535) **1** : ASTONISHMENT, SURPRISE **2** : a cause or occasion for wonder **3** : curiosity about something
won·der·work \-də(r)-,wərk\ *n* (bef. 12c) : a marvelous act, work, or accomplishment
won·der–work·er \-,wər-kər\ *n* (1599) : one that performs wonders
won·der–work·ing \-,wər-kiŋ\ *n* : producing wonders
won·drous \'wən-drəs\ *adj* [ME, alter. of *wonders,* fr. gen. of ¹*wonder*] (15c) : that is to be marveled at : EXTRAORDINARY — **wondrous** *adv, archaic* — **won·drous·ly** *adv* — **won·drous·ness** *n*
wonk \'wäŋk, 'wȯŋk\ *n* [origin unknown] (1954) : NERD
won·ky \'wäŋ-kē\ *adj* [prob. alter. of E dial. *wankle,* fr. ME *wankel,* fr. OE *wancol;* akin to OHG *wankōn* to totter — more at WENCH] (1919) **1** *Brit* : UNSTEADY, SHAKY **2** *Brit* : AWRY, WRONG
¹**wont** \'wȯnt, 'wōnt *also* 'wänt, 'wänt\ *adj* [ME *woned, wont,* pp. pp. of *wonen* to dwell, be used to, fr. OE *wunian;* akin to OHG *wonēn* to dwell, be used to, Skt *vanoti* he strives for — more at WIN] (bef. 12c) **1** : ACCUSTOMED, USED ⟨got up early as he is ~ to do⟩ **2** : INCLINED, APT ⟨revealing as letters are ~ to be —Gladys M. Wrigley⟩
²**wont** *vb* wont; wont *or* wont·ed; wont·ing *vt* (15c) : ACCUSTOM, HABITUATE ~ *vi* : to have the habit of doing something
³**wont** *n* (1530) : habitual way of doing something : USE *syn* See HABIT
won't \'wōnt; *NewEng, upstate NY, nPa* ,wȯnt, 'wənt; *greater NYC* 'wünt; *eSC* 'wünt, 'wu̇nt\ (1652) : will not
wont·ed \'wȯn-təd, 'wōn- *also* 'wən- *or* 'wän-\ *adj* (15c) : usual or ordinary esp. by reason of established habit ⟨spoke with his ~ slowness⟩ *syn* See USUAL — **wont·ed·ly** *adv* — **wont·ed·ness** *n*
won·ton \'wän-,tän\ *n* [Chin (Guangdong) *wàhn-tān*] (1934) : filled pockets of noodle dough served boiled in soup or fried
woo \'wü\ *vb* [ME *wowen,* fr. OE *wōgian*] *vt* (bef. 12c) **1** : to sue for the affection of and usu. marriage with : COURT **2** : to solicit or entreat esp. with importunity **3** : to seek to gain or bring about ~ *vi* : to court a woman — **woo·er** *n*
¹**wood** \'wu̇d\ *adj* [ME, fr. OE *wōd* insane; akin to OHG *wuot* madness — more at VATIC] (12c) *archaic* : violently mad
²**wood** \'wu̇d\ *n* [ME *wode,* fr. OE *widu, wudu;* akin to OHG *witu* wood, OIr *fid* tree] (bef. 12c) **1 a** : a dense growth of trees usu. greater in extent than a grove and smaller than a forest — often used in pl. but sing. or pl. in constr. **b** : WOODLAND **2 a** : the hard fibrous substance consisting basically of xylem that makes up the greater part of the stems, branches, and roots of trees or shrubs beneath the bark and is found to a limited extent in herbaceous plants **b** : wood suitable or prepared for some use (as burning or building) **3 a** : something made of wood **b** : a golf club having a thick wooden head; *also* : a golf club having a similar head made of metal — **out of the woods** : clear of danger or difficulty

³**wood** \'wu̇d\ *adj* (1538) **1** : WOODEN **2** : suitable for cutting or working with wood ⟨a ~ saw⟩ **3** *or* **woods** \'wu̇dz\ : living, growing, or existing in woods ⟨*woods* trails⟩
⁴**wood** \'wu̇d\ *vi* (1630) : to gather or take on wood ~ *vt* : to cover with a growth of trees or plant with trees
wood alcohol *n* (1861) : METHANOL
wood anemone *n* (1657) : any of several anemones; *esp* : one (*Anemone quinquefolia*) of No. America with solitary often pink-tinged flowers
wood bet·o·ny \-'be-t³n-ē\ *n* [ME *betone,* fr. OF *betoine,* fr. L *vettonica, betonica,* fr. *Vettones,* an ancient people inhabiting the Iberian peninsula] (1657) : a lousewort (*Pedicularis canadensis*) of eastern No. America with yellow or reddish flowers in bracted spikes
wood·bine \'wu̇d-,bīn\ *n* [ME *wodebinde,* fr. OE *wudubinde,* fr. *wudu* wood + *bindan* to tie, bind; fr. its winding around trees] (bef. 12c) **1** : any of several honeysuckles; *esp* : a Eurasian twining shrub (*Lonicera periclymenum*) **2** : VIRGINIA CREEPER
wood·block \-,bläk\ *n* (1837) : WOODCUT — **wood–block** *adj*
wood–bor·ing \-,bōr-iŋ, -,bȯr-\ *adj* (1815) : excavating galleries in wood in feeding or in constructing a nest — used chiefly of an insect
wood carving *n* (1847) : the art of fashioning or ornamenting objects of wood by cutting with a sharp handheld implement; *also* : an object of wood so fashioned or ornamented — **wood–carv·er** \-,kär-vər\ *n*
wood·chat shrike \'wu̇d-,chat-\ *n* (1781) : a European shrike (*Lanius senator*) — called also *woodchat*
wood·chop·per \-,chä-pər\ *n* (1779) : one engaged esp. in chopping down trees
wood·chuck \-,chək\ *n* [by folk etymology fr. a word of Algonquian origin; akin to Narraganset *ockqutchaun* woodchuck] (1674) : a grizzled thickset marmot (*Marmota monax*) chiefly of Alaska, Canada, and the northeastern U.S. — called also *groundhog*
wood·cock \'wu̇d-,käk\ *n, pl* **woodcocks** (bef. 12c) **1** *or pl* **woodcock** : a widespread Old World woodland bird (*Scolopax rusticola*) that is related to the sandpipers and snipes; *also* : a smaller related game bird (*Scolopax minor* syn. *Philohela minor*) of eastern No. America **2** [fr. the ease with which the woodcock is snared]: *archaic* : SIMPLETON
wood·craft \-,kraft\ *n* (14c) **1** : skill and practice in anything relating to the woods and esp. in maintaining oneself and making one's way in the woods **2** : skill in shaping or constructing articles from wood
wood·cut \-,kət\ *n* (1594) **1** : a relief printing surface consisting of a wooden block cut with a usu. pictorial design cut with the grain **2** : a print from a woodcut
wood·cut·ter \-,kə-tər\ *n* (1761) : one that cuts wood
wood·cut·ting \-,kə-tiŋ\ *n* (1683) **1** : the action or occupation of cutting wood or timber **2** : the producing of woodcuts
wood duck *n* (1777) : a showy American duck (*Aix sponsa*) which nests in tree cavities and the males of which have a large crest and iridescent plumage varied with green, purple, black, white, and chestnut

wood duck

wood ear *n* (1917) : TREE EAR
wood·ed \'wu̇-dəd\ *adj* (1605) : covered with growing trees
wood·en \'wu̇-d³n\ *adj* (1538) **1** : made or consisting of wood **2** : lacking ease or flexibility : awkwardly stiff — **wood·en·ly** *adv* — **wood·en·ness** \-d³n-(n)əs\ *n*
wood engraving *n* (1816) **1** : a relief printing surface consisting of a wooden block with a usu. pictorial design cut in the end grain **2** : a print from a wood engraving
wood·en·head \'wu̇-d³n-,hed\ *n* (1831) : BLOCKHEAD
wood·en·head·ed \,wu̇-d³n-'he-dəd\ *adj* (ca. 1854) : DENSE, STUPID
wooden Indian *n* (1879) : a wooden image of a standing American Indian brave used esp. formerly as a sign for a cigar store
wood·en·ware \'wu̇-d³n-,war, -,wer\ *n* (1647) : articles made of wood for domestic use
wood fiber *n* (1875) : any of various fibers in or associated with xylem
¹**wood·land** \'wu̇d-lənd, -,land\ *n* (bef. 12c) : land covered with woody vegetation : TIMBERLAND, FOREST — **wood·land·er** \-lən-dər, -,lan-\ *n*
²**woodland** *adj* (14c) **1** : growing, living, or existing in woodland **2** : of, relating to, or being woodland
wood·lore \'wu̇d-,lōr, -,lȯr\ *n* (1918) : knowledge of the woods
wood·lot \-,lät\ *n* (1643) : a restricted area of woodland usu. privately maintained as a source of fuel, posts, and lumber
wood louse *n* (1611) : a terrestrial isopod crustacean (suborder Oniscoidea) with a flattened elliptical body often capable of being rolled into a ball — called also *pill bug, sow bug*
wood·man \'wu̇d-mən\ *n* (15c) **1** : WOODSMAN **2** *cap* [Modern *Woodmen* of America & *Woodmen* of the World]: a member of either of two independent benevolent and fraternal societies
wood·note \-,nōt\ *n* [fr. its likeness to the call of a bird in the woods] (1632) : verbal expression that is natural and artless
wood nymph *n* (1577) : a nymph living in woods — called also *dryad*
wood·peck·er \'wu̇d-,pe-kər\ *n* (ca. 1530) : any of numerous birds (family Picidae) with zygodactyl feet, stiff spiny tail feathers used in climbing or resting on tree trunks, a usu. extensile tongue, a very hard bill used to drill the bark or wood of trees for insect food or to excavate nesting cavities, and generally showy parti-colored plumage
wood·pile \-,pīl\ *n* (ca. 1552) : a pile of wood (as firewood) — **in the woodpile** : doing or responsible for covert mischief
wood pulp *n* (1866) : pulp from wood used in making cellulose derivatives (as paper or rayon)
wood pussy *n* (ca. 1899) : SKUNK

\ə\ abut \ᵊ\ kitten, F table \ər\ further \a\ ash \ā\ ace \ä\ mop, mar \aú\ out \ch\ chin \e\ bet \ē\ easy \g\ go \i\ hit \ī\ ice \j\ job \ŋ\ sing \ō\ go \ȯ\ law \ȯi\ boy \th\ thin \t̲h̲\ the \ü\ loot \ü\ foot \y\ yet \zh\ vision \á, k̲, ⁿ, œ, œ̄, ᵫ, ūe, ᵞ\ *see* Guide to Pronunciation

wood rat n (1763) : any of numerous cricetid rodents (esp. genus *Neotoma*) of No. and Central America with soft fur, well-furred tails, and large ears

wood ray n (1925) : XYLEM RAY

wood·ruff \'wu̇d-(ˌ)rəf\ n [ME *woderove*, fr. OE *wudurofe*, fr. *wudu* wood + -*rofe* (of unknown origin)] (bef. 12c) **1** : any of a genus (*Asperula*) of Old World herbs of the madder family **2** : a small Eurasian and No. African sweet-scented herb (*Galium odoratum* syn. *Asperula odorata*) used in perfumery and for flavoring wine

¹wood·shed \-ˌshed\ n (1844) **1** : a shed for storing wood and esp. firewood **2** : a place, means, or session for administering discipline

²woodshed vi -**shed·ded; -shed·ding** [prob. fr. the former use of woodsheds for private practicing] (1936) : PRACTICE; esp : to practice on a musical instrument

wood shot n (1927) **1** : a golf shot played with a wood **2** : a stroke in a racket game in which the ball or shuttlecock is hit with the frame of the racket rather than the strings

woods·man \'wu̇dz-mən\ n (1688) : a person who frequents or works in the woods; esp : one skilled in woodcraft

wood sorrel n (1525) : any of a genus (*Oxalis* of the family Oxalidaceae, the wood-sorrel family) of herbs with acid sap, compound leaves, and regular flowers; esp : either of two stemless herbs (*O. montana* of No. America and *O. acetosella* of Eurasia) with trifoliolate leaves

wood spirit n (1842) : METHANOL

wood stork n (1884) : a white stork (*Mycteria americana*) with black wing flight feathers and tail that frequents wooded swamps from the southeastern U.S. to Argentina — called also *wood ibis*

wood-stove \'wu̇d-ˌstōv\ n (1847) : a stove that uses wood for fuel

wood sugar n (ca. 1900) : XYLOSE

woodsy \'wu̇d-zē\ adj (1860) : characteristic or suggestive of woods

wood tar n (1857) : tar obtained by the destructive distillation of wood either as a deposit from pyroligneous acid or as a residue from the distillation of the acid or of wood turpentine

wood tick n (1668) : any of several ixodid ticks: as **a** : a widely distributed tick (*Dermacentor andersonii*) of western No. America that is a vector of Rocky Mountain spotted fever **b** : AMERICAN DOG TICK

wood turning n (ca. 1876) : the art or process of fashioning wooden pieces or blocks into various forms and shapes by means of a lathe

wood turpentine n (ca. 1909) : TURPENTINE 2b

wood warbler n (1817) : WARBLER 2b

wood·wind \'wu̇d-ˌwind\ n (1876) **1** : any of a group of wind instruments (as a clarinet, flute, oboe, or saxophone) that are characterized by a cylindrical or conical tube of wood or metal usu. ending in a slightly flared bell, that produce tones by the vibration of one or two reeds in the mouthpiece or by the passing of air over a mouth hole, and that usu. have finger holes or keys by which the player may produce all the tones within an instrument's range **2** pl : the woodwind section of a band or orchestra

wood·work \-ˌwərk\ n (1650) **1** : work made of wood; esp : interior fittings (as moldings or stairways) of wood **2** : a place or state of concealment, seclusion, or anonymity ⟨witnesses came out of the ~ when a reward was offered⟩

¹wood·work·ing \-ˌwər-kiŋ\ adj (1872) : used for woodworking

²woodworking n (1875) : the act, process, or occupation of working wood into a useful or desired form — **wood·work·er** \-kər\ n

wood·worm \'wu̇d-ˌwərm\ n (1725) : an insect larva (as of a furniture beetle) that bores esp. in dead wood; *also* : an infestation of woodworms

¹woody \'wu̇d-ē\ adj **wood·i·er; -est** (14c) **1** : abounding or overgrown with woods **2** a : of or containing wood or wood fibers : LIGNEOUS ⟨~ tissues⟩ **b** : having woody parts : rich in xylem and associated structures ⟨~ plants⟩ **3** : characteristic or suggestive of wood ⟨wine with a ~ flavor⟩ — **wood·i·ness** n

²woody or **wood·ie** \'wu̇d-ē\ n, pl **woodies** [alter. of ³*wood*] (1961) : a wood-paneled station wagon

¹woof \'wu̇f, 'wu̇f\ n [alter. of ME *oof*, fr. OE *ōwef*, fr. *ō-* (fr. *on*) + *wefan* to weave — more at WEAVE] (bef. 12c) **1** a : WEFT 1a **b** : woven fabric; *also* : the texture of such a fabric **2** : a basic or essential element or material

²woof \'wu̇f\ vi [imit.] (1804) **1** : to make the low gruff sound typically produced by a dog **2** : to express oneself in a usu. stylized boastful, aggressive, or exaggeratedly deceitful manner

³woof \'wu̇f\ n (1839) **1** : a low gruff sound typically produced by a dog **2** : a low note emitted by sound reproducing equipment

woof·er \'wu̇f-ər\ n (1935) : a loudspeaker usu. larger than a tweeter, responsive only to the lower acoustic frequencies, and used for reproducing sounds of low pitch — compare TWEETER

wool \'wu̇l\ n, often attrib [ME *wolle*, fr. OE *wull*; akin to OHG *wolla* wool, L *vellus* fleece, *lana* wool] (bef. 12c) **1** : the soft wavy or curly hypertrophied undercoat of various hairy mammals and esp. the sheep made up of a matrix of keratin fibers and covered with minute scales **2** : a product of wool; esp : a woven fabric or garment of such fabric **3** a : a dense felted pubescence esp. on a plant : TOMENTUM **b** : a filamentous mass — usu. used in combination; compare MINERAL WOOL, STEEL WOOL

wooled also **woolled** \'wu̇ld\ adj (ca. 1859) : having wool esp. of a specified kind — used in combination ⟨long-*wooled*⟩

¹wool·en or **wool·len** \'wu̇-lən\ adj (bef. 12c) **1** : made of wool **2** : of or relating to the manufacture or sale of woolen products ⟨~ mills⟩ ⟨the ~ industry⟩

²woolen or **woollen** n (14c) **1** : a fabric made of wool and esp. of woolen yarns having a hairy or napped face (as for use in clothing or blankets) — compare WORSTED **2** : garments of woolen fabric — usu. used in pl.

wool fat n (1875) : wool grease esp. after refining : LANOLIN

wool-gath·er \'wu̇l-ˌga-thər, -ˌge-thər\ vi (1850) : to indulge in woolgathering — **wool-gath·er·er** \-thər-ər\ n

wool-gath·er·ing \-ˌga-th(ə-)riŋ, -ˌge-th(ə-)riŋ\ n (1553) : indulgence in idle daydreaming

wool grease n (1875) : a fatty slightly sticky wax coating the surface of the fibers of sheep's wool — compare WOOL FAT

¹wool·ly also **wooly** \'wu̇-lē\ adj **wool·li·er; -est** (1578) **1** a : of, relating to, or bearing wool **b** : resembling wool **2** a : lacking in

clearness or sharpness of outline ⟨a ~ TV picture⟩ **b** : marked by mental confusion ⟨~ thinking⟩ **3** : marked by boisterous roughness or lack of order or restraint ⟨where the West is still ~ —Paul Schubert⟩ — used esp. in the phrase *wild and woolly* — **wool·li·ly** \-lə-lē\ adv — **wool·li·ness** n

²wool·ly also **wool·ie** or **wooly** \'wu̇-lē\ n, pl **wool·lies** also **wool·ies** (ca. 1865) **1** : a garment made from wool; esp : underclothing of knitted wool — usu. used in pl. **2** *West & Austral* : SHEEP

woolly aphid n (1842) : any of several plant lice (esp. genus *Eriosoma*) covered with a dense coat of white filaments — called also *woolly aphis*

woolly bear n (ca. 1841) : any of various rather large very hairy moth caterpillars; esp : one of a tiger moth

wool·ly-head·ed \ˌwu̇-lē-'he-dəd\ adj (1650) **1** : having hair suggesting wool **2** : marked by vague or confused perception or thinking

woolly mammoth n (1933) : a heavy-coated mammoth (*Mammuthus primigenius*) of the colder parts of the northern hemisphere

wool·pack \'wu̇l-ˌpak\ n (14c) **1** : a wrapper of strong fabric into which fleeces are packed for shipment **2** : the complete package of wool and wrapper

wool·sack \-ˌsak\ n (14c) **1** *archaic* : WOOLPACK 2 **2** : a cushion that is the official seat of the Lord Chancellor or his deputy in presiding over the House of Lords

wool·shed \-ˌshed\ n (1850) : a building or range of buildings (as on an Australian sheep station) in which sheep are sheared and wool is prepared for market

wool·skin \-ˌskin\ n (15c) : a sheepskin having the wool still on it

wool·sort·er's disease \'wu̇l-ˌsȯr-tərz-\ n (1880) : pulmonary anthrax resulting esp. from inhalation of bacterial spores (*Bacillus anthracis*) from contaminated wool or hair

wool stapler n (1709) : a dealer in wool

woom·era \'wu̇-mə-rə\ n [Dharvk (Australian aboriginal language of the Port Jackson area) *wumera*] (1817) : a wooden rod with a hooked end used by Australian aborigines for throwing a spear

woops \'(w)u̇(ə)ps\ *var of* OOPS

woo·zy \'wü-zē, 'wu̇-\ adj **woo·zi·er; -est** [origin unknown] (1897) **1** : mentally unclear or hazy ⟨seems a little ~, not quite knowing what to say —J. A. Lukacs⟩ **2** : affected with dizziness, mild nausea, or weakness — **woo·zi·ly** adv — **woo·zi·ness** n

wop \'wäp\ n, often cap [It dial. *guappo* swaggerer, tough, fr. Sp *guapo*, prob. fr. MF dial. *vape, wape* weak, insipid, fr. L *vappa* wine gone flat] (1908) : ITALIAN — usu. used disparagingly

Worces·ter \'wu̇s-tər\ n (1802) : low-fired porcelain containing a frit and steatite produced at Worcester, England, from about 1751 — called also *Worcester china, Worcester porcelain*

Worces·ter·shire sauce \'wu̇s-tə(r)-ˌshir-, -shər-, also -ˌshir-\ n [*Worcestershire*, England, where it was orig. made] (1843) : a pungent sauce whose ingredients include soy, vinegar, and garlic

¹word \'wərd\ n [ME, fr. OE; akin to OHG *wort* word, L *verbum*, Gk *eirein* to say, speak, Hitt *weriya-* to call, name] (bef. 12c) **1** a : something that is said **b** pl (1) : TALK, DISCOURSE ⟨putting one's feelings into ~s⟩ (2) : the text of a vocal musical composition **c** : a brief remark or conversation ⟨would like to have a ~ with you⟩ **2** a (1) : a speech sound or series of speech sounds that symbolizes and communicates a meaning without being divisible into smaller units capable of independent use (2) : the entire set of linguistic forms produced by combining a single base with various inflectional elements without change in the part of speech elements **b** (1) : a written or printed character or combination of characters representing a spoken word ⟨the number of ~s to a line⟩ — sometimes used with the first letter of a real or pretended taboo word prefixed often as a humorous euphemism ⟨we were not afraid to use the d ~ and talk about death —Erma Bombeck⟩ ⟨the first man to utter the f ~ on British TV —*Time*⟩ (2) : any segment of written or printed discourse ordinarily appearing between spaces or between a space and a punctuation mark **c** : a number of bytes processed as a unit and conveying a quantum of information in communication and computer work **3** : ORDER, COMMAND ⟨don't move till I give the ~⟩ **4** often cap **a** : LOGOS **b** : GOSPEL 1a **c** : the expressed or manifested mind and will of God **5** a : NEWS, INFORMATION ⟨sent ~ that he would be late⟩ **b** : RUMOR **6** : the act of speaking or of making verbal communication **7** : SAYING, PROVERB **8** : PROMISE, DECLARATION ⟨kept her ~⟩ **9** : a quarrelsome utterance or conversation — usu. used in pl. ⟨they had ~s and parted⟩ **10** : a verbal signal : PASSWORD — **good word 1** : a favorable statement ⟨put in a *good word* for me⟩ **2** : good news ⟨what's the *good word*⟩ — **in a word** : in short — **in so many words 1** : in exactly those terms ⟨implied that such actions were criminal but did not say so *in so many words*⟩ **2** : in plain forthright language ⟨*in so many words*, she wasn't fit to be seen — Jean Stafford⟩ — **of few words** : not inclined to say more than is necessary : LACONIC — **of one's word** : that can be relied on to keep a promise — used only after *man* or *woman* — **upon my word** : with my assurance : INDEED, ASSUREDLY ⟨*upon my word*, I've never heard of such a thing⟩

²word vi (13c) *archaic* : SPEAK ~ vt : to express in words : PHRASE

word·age \'wər-dij\ n (1829) **1** a : WORDS **b** : VERBIAGE 1 **2** : the number or quantity of words **3** : WORDING

word–association test n (1946) : a test of personality and mental function in which the subject is required to respond to each of a series of words with the first one that comes to mind or with one of a specified class of words

word·book \'wərd-ˌbu̇k\ n (1598) : VOCABULARY, DICTIONARY

word class n (1914) : a linguistic form class whose members are words; esp : PART OF SPEECH

word–for–word adj (1611) : being in the exact words : VERBATIM

word for word adv (14c) : in the exact words : VERBATIM

word–hoard \'wərd-ˌhōrd, -ˌhȯrd\ n [trans. of OE *wordhord*] (ca. 1869) : a supply of words : VOCABULARY

word·ing \'wər-diŋ\ n (1649) : the act or manner of expressing in words : PHRASEOLOGY

word·less \'wərd-ləs\ adj (15c) **1** : not expressed in or accompanied by words **2** : SILENT, SPEECHLESS — **word·less·ly** adv — **word·less·ness** n

word·mon·ger \-ˌməŋ-gər, -ˌmäŋ-\ n (1590) : a writer who uses words for show or without particular regard for meaning

word-mon·ger·ing \-g(ə-)riŋ\ *n* (1879) : the use of empty or bombastic words

word-of-mouth \ˌwərd-ə(v)-ˈmaùth\ *adj* (1802) : orally communicated; *also* : generated from or reliant on oral publicity ⟨~ customers⟩ ⟨a ~ business⟩

word of mouth (1553) : oral communication; *esp* : oral often inadvertent publicity

word order *n* (1892) : the order or arrangement of words in a phrase, clause, or sentence

word·play \ˈwərd-ˌplā\ *n* (1855) : verbal wit

word processing *n* (1970) : the production of typewritten documents (as business letters) with automated and usu. computerized typing and text-editing equipment — **word process** *vb*

word processor *n* (1970) : a keyboard-operated terminal usu. with a video display and a magnetic storage device for use in word processing; *also* : software (as for a computer system) to perform word processing

word·smith \ˈwərd-ˌsmith\ *n* (1896) : a person who works with words; *esp* : a skillful writer — **word·smith·ery** \-ˌsmi-thə-rē\ *n*

word square *n* (ca. 1879) : a series of words of equal length arranged in a square pattern to read the same horizontally and vertically

word stress *n* (ca. 1914) : the manner in which stresses are distributed on the syllables of a word — called also *word accent*

wordy \ˈwər-dē\ *adj* **word·i·er; -est** (12c) **1** : using or containing many and usu. too many words **2** : of or relating to words : VERBAL — **word·i·ly** \ˈwər-dᵊl-ē\ *adv* — **word·i·ness** \ˈwər-dē-nəs\ *n*

syn WORDY, VERBOSE, PROLIX, DIFFUSE mean using more words than necessary to express thought. WORDY may also imply loquaciousness or garrulity ⟨a *wordy* speech⟩. VERBOSE suggests a resulting dullness, obscurity, or lack of incisiveness or precision ⟨the *verbose* position papers⟩. PROLIX suggests unreasonable and tedious dwelling on details ⟨habitually transformed brief anecdotes into *prolix* sagas⟩. DIFFUSE stresses lack of compactness and pointedness of style ⟨*diffuse* memoirs that are so many shaggy-dog stories⟩.

wore *past of* WEAR

¹work \ˈwərk\ *n* [ME *werk, work,* fr. OE *werc, weorc;* akin to OHG *werc,* Gk *ergon,* Av *varəzəm* activity] (bef. 12c) **1** : activity in which one exerts strength or faculties to do or perform something: **a** : sustained physical or mental effort to overcome obstacles and achieve an objective or result **b** : the labor, task, or duty that is one's accustomed means of livelihood **c** : a specific task, duty, function, or assignment often being a part or phase of some larger activity **2 a** : energy expended by natural phenomena **b** : the result of such energy ⟨sand dunes are the ~ of sea and wind⟩ **c** : the transference of energy that is produced by the motion of the point of application of a force and is measured by multiplying the force and the displacement of its point of application in the line of action **3 a** : something that results from a particular manner or method of working, operating, or devising ⟨careful police ~⟩ ⟨clever camera ~⟩ **b** : something that results from the use or fashioning of a particular material ⟨porcelain ~⟩ **4 a** : a fortified structure (as a fort, earthen barricade, or trench) **b** *pl* : structures in engineering (as docks, bridges, or embankments) or mining (as shafts or tunnels) **5** *pl but sing or pl in constr* : a place where industrial labor is carried on : PLANT, FACTORY **6** *pl* : the working or moving parts of a mechanism ⟨~s of a clock⟩ **7 a** : something produced or accomplished by effort, exertion, or exercise of skill ⟨this book is the ~ of many hands⟩ **b** : something produced by the exercise of creative talent or expenditure of creative effort : artistic production **8** *pl* : performance of moral or religious acts ⟨salvation by ~s⟩ **9 a** : effective operation : EFFECT, RESULT ⟨wait for time to do its healing ~⟩ **b** : manner of working : WORKMANSHIP, EXECUTION **10** : the material or piece of material that is operated upon at any stage in the process of manufacture **11** *pl* **a** : everything possessed, available, or belonging ⟨the whole ~s, rod, reel, tackle box, went overboard⟩ ⟨ordered pizza with the ~s⟩ **b** : subjection to drastic treatment : all possible abuse — usu. used with *get* ⟨get the ~s⟩ or *give* ⟨gave them the ~s⟩ — **at work 1** : engaged in working : BUSY; *esp* : engaged in one's regular occupation **2** : having effect : OPERATING, FUNCTIONING — **in the works** : in process of preparation, development, or completion — **in work 1** : in process of being done **2** *of a horse* : in training — **out of work** : without regular employment : JOBLESS

syn WORK, LABOR, TRAVAIL, TOIL, DRUDGERY, GRIND mean activity involving effort or exertion. WORK may imply activity of body, of mind, of a machine, or of a natural force ⟨too tired to do any *work*⟩. LABOR applies to physical or intellectual work involving great and often strenuous exertion ⟨farmers demanding fair compensation for their *labor*⟩. TRAVAIL is bookish for labor involving pain or suffering ⟨years of *travail* were lost when the house burned⟩. TOIL implies prolonged and fatiguing labor ⟨his lot would be years of back-breaking *toil*⟩. DRUDGERY suggests dull and irksome labor ⟨an editorial job with a good deal of *drudgery*⟩. GRIND implies labor exhausting to mind or body ⟨the *grind* of the assembly line⟩.

syn WORK, EMPLOYMENT, OCCUPATION, CALLING, PURSUIT, MÉTIER, BUSINESS mean a specific sustained activity engaged in esp. in earning one's living. WORK may apply to any purposeful activity whether remunerative or not ⟨her *work* as a hospital volunteer⟩. EMPLOYMENT implies work for which one has been engaged and is being paid by an employer ⟨your *employment* with this firm is hereby terminated⟩. OCCUPATION implies work in which one engages regularly esp. as a result of training ⟨his *occupation* as a trained auto mechanic⟩. CALLING applies to an occupation viewed as a vocation or profession ⟨the ministry seemed my true *calling*⟩. PURSUIT suggests a trade, profession, or avocation followed with zeal or steady interest ⟨her family considered medicine the only proper *pursuit*⟩. MÉTIER implies a calling or pursuit for which one believes oneself to be esp. fitted ⟨acting was my one and only *métier*⟩. BUSINESS suggests activity in commerce or the management of money and affairs ⟨the *business* of managing a hotel⟩.

²work *adj* (14c) **1** : used for work ⟨~ elephant⟩ **2** : suitable or styled for wear while working ⟨~ clothes⟩ **3** : involving or engaged in work ⟨~ gang⟩ ⟨~ hours⟩

³work *vb* **worked** \ˈwərkt\ *or* **wrought** \ˈròt\; **work·ing** [ME *werken, worken,* fr. OE *wyrcan;* akin to OE *weorc*] *vt* (bef. 12c) **1** : to bring to pass : EFFECT ⟨~ miracles⟩ **2 a** : to fashion or create a useful or desired product by expending labor or exertion on : FORGE, SHAPE ⟨~ flint into tools⟩ **b** : to make or decorate with needlework; *esp* : EM-

BROIDER **3 a** : to prepare for use by stirring or kneading **b** : to bring into a desired form by a gradual process of cutting, hammering, scraping, pressing, or stretching ⟨~ cold steel⟩ **4** : to set or keep in motion, operation, or activity : cause to operate or produce ⟨a pump ~ed by hand⟩ ⟨~ farmland⟩ **5** : to solve (a problem) by reasoning or calculation — often used with *out* **6 a** : to cause to toil or labor ⟨~ed their horses nearly to death⟩ **b** : to make use of : EXPLOIT **c** : to control or guide the operation of ⟨switches are ~ed from a central tower⟩ **7 a** : to carry on an operation or perform a job through, at, in, or along ⟨the salespeople ~ed both sides of the street⟩ ⟨a sportscaster hired to ~ the game⟩ **b** : to greet and talk with in a friendly way in order to ingratiate oneself or achieve a purpose ⟨politicians ~ing the crowd⟩ ⟨~ed the room⟩ **8** : to pay for or achieve with labor or service ⟨~ed my way through college⟩ ⟨~ed my way up in the company⟩ **9 a** : to get (oneself or an object) into or out of a condition or position by gradual stages **b** : CONTRIVE, ARRANGE ⟨we can ~ it so that you can take your vacation⟩ **10 a** : to practice trickery or cajolery on for some end ⟨~ed the management for a free ticket⟩ **b** : EXCITE, PROVOKE ⟨~ed myself into a rage⟩ ~ *vi* **1 a** : to exert oneself physically or mentally esp. in sustained effort for a purpose or under compulsion or necessity **b** : to perform or carry through a task requiring sustained effort or continuous repeated operations ⟨~ed all day over a hot stove⟩ **c** : to perform work or fulfill duties regularly for wages or salary **2** : to function or operate according to plan or design ⟨hinges ~ better with oil⟩ **3** : to exert an influence or tendency **4** : to produce a desired effect or result : SUCCEED **5 a** : to make way slowly and with difficulty : move or progress laboriously ⟨~ed up to the presidency⟩ **b** : to sail to windward **6** : to permit of being worked : react in a specified way to being worked ⟨this wood ~s easily⟩ **7 a** : to be in agitation or restless motion **b** : FERMENT 1 **c** : to move slightly in relation to another part **d** : to get into a specified condition by slow or imperceptible movements ⟨the knot ~ed loose⟩ — **work on 1** : AFFECT ⟨worked on my sympathies⟩ **2** : to strive to influence or persuade — **work upon** : to have effect upon : operate on : INFLUENCE

work·able \ˈwər-kə-bəl\ *adj* (1545) **1** : capable of being worked **2** : PRACTICABLE, FEASIBLE ⟨a ~ system⟩ — **work·abil·i·ty** \ˌwər-kə-ˈbi-lə-tē\ *n* — **work·able·ness** \ˈwər-kə-bəl-nəs\ *n*

work·a·day \ˈwər-kə-ˌdā\ *adj* [alter. of earlier *workyday,* fr. obs. *workyday,* n. workday] (1554) **1** : of, relating to, or suited for working days **2** : ORDINARY, PROSAIC

work·a·hol·ic \ˌwər-kə-ˈhò-lik, -ˈhä-\ *n* [*work* + *-aholic,* alter. of *-oholic* (as in *alcoholic*)] (1968) : a compulsive worker — **workaholic** *adj* — **work·a·hol·ism** \ˈwər-kə-ˌhò-ˌli-zəm, -ˌhä-\ *n*

work·bag \ˈwərk-ˌbag\ *n* (1775) : a bag for implements or materials for work; *esp* : a bag for needlework

work·bas·ket \-ˌbas-kət\ *n* (1743) : a basket for needlework

work·bench \-ˌbench\ *n* (1781) : a bench on which work esp. of mechanics, machinists, and carpenters is performed

work·boat \-ˌbōt\ *n* (1937) : a boat used for work purposes (as commercial fishing and ferrying supplies) rather than for sport or for passenger or naval service

work·book \-ˌbùk\ *n* (1910) **1** : a worker's manual **2** : a book outlining a course of study **3** : a record of work done **4** : a student's book of problems to be solved directly on the pages

work·box \-ˌbäks\ *n* (1605) : a box for work instruments and materials

work camp *n* (1933) : a camp for workers: as **a** : PRISON CAMP 1 **b** : a short-term group project in which individuals from one or more religious organizations volunteer their labor

work·day \ˈwərk-ˌdā\ *n* (15c) **1** : a day on which work is performed as distinguished from a day off **2** : the period of time in a day during which work is performed — **workday** *adj*

worked \ˈwərkt\ *adj* (1740) : that has been subjected to some process of development, treatment, or manufacture ⟨a newly ~ field⟩

worked up *adj* (1903) : emotionally aroused : EXCITED

work·er \ˈwər-kər\ *n* (14c) **1 a** : one that works esp. at manual or industrial labor or with a particular material — often used in combination **b** : a member of the working class : any of the sexually underdeveloped and usu. sterile members of a colony of social ants, bees, wasps, or termites that perform most of the labor and protective duties of the colony

worker–priest *n* (1949) : a French Roman Catholic priest who for missionary purposes spends part of each weekday as a worker in a secular job

workers' compensation *n* (1948) : a system of insurance that reimburses an employer for damages that must be paid to an employee for injury occurring in the course of employment

work ethic *n* (1951) : a belief in work as a moral good

work·fare \ˈwərk-ˌfar, -ˌfer\ *n* [*work* + *welfare*] (1968) : a welfare program in which recipients are required to perform usu. public-service work

work farm *n* (1953) : a farm on which persons guilty of minor law violations are confined

work·folk \ˈwərk-ˌfōk\ *or* **work·folks** \-ˌfōks\ *n pl* (15c) : working people; *esp* : farm workers

work·force \ˈwərk-ˌfōrs, -ˌfòrs\ *n* (1943) **1** : the workers engaged in a specific activity or enterprise ⟨the factory's ~⟩ **2** : the number of workers potentially assignable for any purpose ⟨the nation's ~⟩

work·horse \ˈwərk-ˌhòrs\ *n* (1543) **1** : a horse used chiefly for labor as distinguished from driving, riding, or racing **2 a** (1) : a person who performs most of the work of a group task (2) : a hardworking person **b** : a markedly useful or durable vehicle, craft, or machine **c** : HORSE 7

work·house \-ˌhaùs\ *n* (1652) **1** *Brit* : POORHOUSE **2** : a house of correction for persons guilty of minor law violations

work in *vt* (1675) **1** : to insert or cause to penetrate by repeated or continued effort **2** : to interpose or insinuate gradually or unobtrusively ⟨worked in a few topical jokes⟩

\ə\ abut \ᵊ\ kitten, F table \ər\ further \a\ ash \ā\ ace \ä\ mop, mar
\aù\ out \ch\ chin \e\ bet \ē\ easy \g\ go \i\ hit \ī\ ice \j\ job
\ŋ\ sing \ō\ go \ò\ law \òi\ boy \th\ thin \t͟h\ the \ü\ loot \ù\ foot
\y\ yet \zh\ vision \ä, k̲, ⁿ, œ, œ̄, ᵫ, ᵫ̄, ʸ\ *see* Guide to Pronunciation

¹**work·ing** n (14c) **1** : the manner of functioning or operating : OPERA-TION — usu. used in pl. **2** : an excavation or group of excavations made in mining, quarrying, or tunneling — usu. used in pl.

²**working** adj (1613) **1** : engaged in work ⟨a ~ journalist⟩ **2** : adequate to permit work to be done ⟨a ~ majority⟩ **3** : assumed or adopted to permit or facilitate further work or activity ⟨~ draft⟩ **4** : spent at work ⟨~ life⟩ **5** : being in use or operation ⟨a ~ farm⟩

working asset n (ca. 1914) : an asset other than a capital asset

working capital n (ca. 1901) : capital actively turned over in or available for use in the course of business activity: **a** : the excess of current assets over current liabilities **b** : all capital of a business except that invested in capital assets

working–class adj (1839) : of, relating to, deriving from, or suitable to the class of wage earners ⟨~ virtues⟩ ⟨~ family⟩

working class n (1789) : the class of people who work for wages usu. at manual labor

working day n (15c) : WORKDAY

working dog n (1891) : a dog fitted by size, breeding, or training for useful work (as draft or herding) esp. as distinguished from one fitted primarily for pet, show, or sporting use

working fluid n (1903) : a fluid working substance

work·ing·man \'wər-kiŋ-,man\ n (1638) : one who works for wages usu. at manual labor

working papers n pl (1928) : official documents legalizing the employment of a minor

working substance n (1897) : a usu. fluid substance that through changes of temperature, volume, and pressure is the means of carrying out thermodynamic processes or cycles (as in a heat engine)

work·ing·wom·an \'wər-kiŋ-,wu̇-mən\ n (1853) : WORKWOMAN

work·less \'wərk-kləs\ adj (15c) : being without work : UNEMPLOYED — **work·less·ness** n

work·load \'wərk-,lōd\ n (1943) **1** : the amount of work or of working time expected or assigned **2** : the amount of work performed or capable of being performed (as by a mechanical device) usu. within a specific period

work·man \'wərk-mən\ n (bef. 12c) **1** : WORKINGMAN **2** : ARTISAN

work·man·like \-,līk\ adj (1739) : characterized by the skill and efficiency typical of a good workman

work·man·ly \-lē\ adj (1545) : WORKMANLIKE

work·man·ship \-,ship\ n (1523) **1** : something effected, made, or produced : WORK **2** : the art or skill of a workman : CRAFTSMANSHIP; also : the quality imparted to a thing in the process of making ⟨a vase of exquisite ~⟩

work·mate \'wərk-,māt\ n (1851) chiefly Brit : a fellow worker

workmen's compensation insurance n (ca. 1917) : WORKERS' COMPENSATION

work of art (1834) **1** : a product of one of the fine arts; esp : a painting or sculpture of high artistic quality **2** : something giving high aesthetic satisfaction to the viewer or listener

work off vt (1678) : to dispose of or get rid of by work or activity

work·out \'wərk-,au̇t\ n (ca. 1894) **1** : a practice or exercise to test or improve one's fitness for athletic competition, ability, or performance **2** : a test of one's ability, capacity, stamina, or suitability

work out vt (1534) **1 a** : to bring about by labor and exertion ⟨work out your own salvation —Phil 2:12 (AV)⟩ **b** : to solve (as a problem) by a process of reasoning or calculation ⟨~ the answer⟩ **c** : to devise, arrange, or achieve by resolving difficulties ⟨after many years of wrangling, worked out a definite agreement —A. A. Butkus⟩ **d** : DEVELOP ⟨the final situation is not worked out with psychological profundity —Leslie Rees⟩ **2** : to discharge (as a debt) by labor **3** : to exhaust (as a mine) by working ~ vi **1 a** : to prove effective, practicable, or suitable ⟨how this will actually work out I don't know —Milton Kotler⟩ **b** : to amount to a total or calculated figure — used with at or to **2** : to engage in a workout ⟨works out in gymnasiums . . . to keep in shape —Current Biog.⟩

work over vt (1874) **1** : to do over : REWORK ⟨saved the play by working the first act over⟩ **2** : to subject to thorough examination, study, or treatment ⟨shelf stock worked over by shoppers⟩ **3** : to beat up or manhandle with thoroughness ⟨the gang worked me over⟩

work·peo·ple \'wərk-,pē-pəl\ n pl (1708) chiefly Brit : WORKERS, EMPLOYEES

work·piece \-,pēs\ n (1926) : a piece of work in process of manufacture

work·place \-,plās\ n (ca. 1828) : a place (as a shop or factory) where work is done

work print n (1937) : a completely edited motion-picture print used as a guide in cutting the original negative from which the final production prints will be made

work·room \'wərk-,rüm, -,ru̇m\ n (1828) : a room used for work

work·shop \-,shäp\ n (1562) **1** : a small establishment where manufacturing or handicrafts are carried on **2** : WORKROOM **3** : a usu. brief intensive educational program for a relatively small group of people that focuses esp. on techniques and skills in a particular field

work song n (1911) : a song sung in rhythm with work

work·sta·tion \-,stā-shən\ n (1931) **1** : an area with equipment for the performance of a specialized task usu. by a single individual **2 a** : an intelligent terminal or personal computer usu. connected to a computer network **b** : a powerful microcomputer used esp. for scientific or engineering work

work stoppage n (1945) : concerted cessation of work by a group of employees usu. more spontaneous and less serious than a strike

work–study program n (1946) : a program planned to give high school or college students work experience

work·ta·ble \'wərk-,tā-bəl\ n (1790) : a table for holding working materials and implements; esp : a small table with drawers and other conveniences for needlework

work–to–rule n (1950) : the practice of working to the strictest interpretation of the rules as a job action

work·up \'wərk-,əp\ n (1939) : an intensive diagnostic study

work–up \'wərk-,əp\ n (1903) : an unintended mark on a printed sheet caused by the rising of spacing material

work up vt (15c) **1** : to stir up : ROUSE **2** : to produce by mental or physical work ⟨worked up a comedy act⟩ ⟨worked up a sweat in the gymnasium⟩ ~ vi : to rise gradually in intensity or emotional tone

work·week \'wərk-,wēk\ n (1921) : the hours or days of work in a calendar week ⟨40-hour ~⟩ ⟨a 5-day ~⟩ ⟨a shortened ~⟩

work·wom·an \-,wu̇-mən\ n (ca. 1530) : a woman who works

¹**world** \'wər(-ə)ld\ n [ME, fr. OE woruld human existence, this world, age (akin to OHG weralt age, world); akin to OE wer man, eald old — more at VIRILE, OLD] (bef. 12c) **1 a** : the earthly state of human existence **b** : life after death — used with a qualifier ⟨the next ~⟩ **2** : the earth with its inhabitants and all things upon it **3** : individual course of life : CAREER **4** : the inhabitants of the earth : the human race **5 a** : the concerns of the earth and its affairs as distinguished from heaven and the life to come **b** : secular affairs **6** : the system of created things : UNIVERSE **7 a** : a division or generation of the inhabitants of the earth distinguished by living together at the same place or at the same time ⟨the medieval ~⟩ **b** : a distinctive class of persons or their sphere of interest ⟨the academic ~⟩ ⟨the sports ~⟩ **8** : human society ⟨withdraw from the ~⟩ **9** : a part or section of the earth that is a separate independent unit **10** : the sphere or scene of one's life and action ⟨living in your own little ~⟩ **11** : an indefinite multitude or a great quantity or distance ⟨makes a ~ of difference⟩ ⟨a ~ away⟩ **12** : the whole body of living persons : PUBLIC ⟨announced their discovery to the ~⟩ **13** : KINGDOM 5 ⟨the animal ~⟩ **14** : a celestial body (as a planet) — **for all the world** : in every way : EXACTLY ⟨copies which look for all the world like the original⟩ — **in the world** : among innumerable possibilities : EVER — used as an intensive ⟨what in the world is it⟩ — **out of this world** : of extraordinary excellence : SUPERB

²**world** adj (13c) **1** : of or relating to the world ⟨a ~ championship⟩ **2 a** : extending or found throughout the world : WORLDWIDE ⟨brought about ~ peace⟩ **b** : involving or applying to part of or the whole world ⟨a ~ tour⟩ ⟨a ~ state⟩

world–beat·er \'wər(d)-,bē-tər\ n (ca. 1888) : one that excels all others of its kind : CHAMPION

world–class adj (1950) : being of the highest caliber in the world ⟨a ~ polo player⟩

world federalism n (1950) **1** : federalism on a worldwide basis **2** cap W&F **a** : the principles and policies of the World Federalists **b** : the body or movement composed of World Federalists

world federalist n (1951) **1** : an adherent or advocate of world federalism **2** cap W&F : a member of a movement arising after World War II advocating the formation of a federal union of the nations of the world with limited but positive governmental powers

world·ling \'wər(-ə)ld-liŋ, 'wərl-liŋ\ n (1549) : a person engrossed in the concerns of this present world

world·ly \'wər(-ə)ld-lē, 'wərl-lē\ adj (bef. 12c) **1** : of, relating to, or devoted to this world and its pursuits rather than to religion or spiritual affairs **2** : WORLDLY-WISE **syn** see EARTHLY — **world·li·ness** n

world·ly–mind·ed \,wər(d)-lē-'mīn-dəd\ adj (1601) : devoted to or engrossed in worldly interests — **world·ly–mind·ed·ness** n

world·ly–wise \'wər(d)-lē-,wiz\ adj (15c) : possessing a practical and often shrewd understanding of human affairs **syn** see SOPHISTICATED

world power n (1860) : a political unit (as a nation or state) powerful enough to affect the entire world by its influence or actions

world premiere n (1925) : the first regular performance (as of a theatrical production) anywhere in the world

World Series n [fr. World Series, annual championship of U.S. major-league baseball] (1951) : a contest or event that is the most important or prestigious of its kind ⟨the World Series of the equestrian world⟩

world's fair n (1850) : an international exposition featuring exhibits and participants from all over the world

world–shak·ing \'wərl(d)-,shā-kiŋ\ adj (1598) : EARTHSHAKING

world soul n (1848) : an animating spirit or creative principle related to the world as the soul is to the individual being

world·view \-,vyü\ n (1858) : WELTANSCHAUUNG

world war n (1909) : a war engaged in by all or most of the principal nations of the world; esp, cap both Ws : either of two such wars of the first half of the 20th century

world–wea·ry \'wərl(d)-,wir-ē\ adj (1768) : feeling or showing fatigue from or boredom with the life of the world and esp. material pleasures — **world–wea·ri·ness** n

¹**world–wide** \-'wīd\ adj (1632) : extended throughout or involving the entire world

²**worldwide** adv (1892) : throughout the world

¹**worm** \'wərm\ n, often attrib [ME, fr. OE wyrm serpent, worm; akin to OHG wurm serpent, worm, L vermis worm] (bef. 12c) **1 a** : EARTHWORM; broadly : an annelid worm **b** : any of numerous relatively small elongated usu. naked and soft-bodied animals: as (1) : an insect larva; esp : one that is a destructive grub, caterpillar, or maggot (2) : SHIPWORM (3) : BLINDWORM **2 a** : a human being who is an object of contempt, loathing, or pity : WRETCH **b** : something that torments or devours from within **3** archaic : SNAKE, SERPENT **4** : HELMINTHIASIS — usu. used in pl. **5** : something (as a mechanical device) spiral or vermiculate in form or appearance: as **a** : the thread of a screw **b** : a short revolving screw whose threads gear with the teeth of a worm wheel or a rack **c** : a spiral condensing tube used in distilling **d** : ARCHIMEDES' SCREW; also : a conveyor working on the principle of such a screw **6** : a usu. small self-contained computer program that invades computers on a network and usu. performs a malicious action — **worm·like** \-,līk\ adj

²**worm** vi (1610) : to move or proceed sinuously or insidiously ~ vt **1 a** : to proceed or make (one's way) insidiously or deviously ⟨~ their way into positions of power —Bill Franzen⟩ **b** : to insinuate or introduce (oneself) by devious or subtle means **c** : to cause to move or proceed in or as if in the manner of a worm **2** : to wind rope or yarn spirally round and between the strands of (a cable or rope) before serving **3** : to obtain or extract by artful or insidious questioning or by pleading, asking, or persuading — usu. used with out of **4** : to treat (an animal) with a drug to destroy or expel parasitic worms

worm–eat·en \'wərm-,ē-t²n\ adj (14c) **1 a** : eaten or burrowed by worms ⟨~ timber⟩ **b** : PITTED **2** : WORN-OUT, ANTIQUATED

worm·er \'wər-mər\ n (ca. 1934) : a drug used in veterinary medicine to worm an animal

worm fence n (1652) : a zigzag fence consisting of interlocking rails supported by crossed poles — called also snake fence, Virginia fence

worm gear *n* (ca. 1876) **1** : WORM WHEEL **2** : a gear of a worm and a worm wheel working together

worm·hole \'wǝrm-,hōl\ *n* (1593) **1** : a hole or passage burrowed by a worm **2** : a hypothetical structure of space-time envisioned as a long thin tunnel connecting points that are separated in space and time

worm·seed \-,sēd\ *n* (15c) : any of various plants whose seeds possess anthelmintic properties: as **a** : any of several artemisias **b** : a goosefoot (*Chenopodium ambrosioides*)

worm's-eye \'wǝrm-,zī\ *adj* (1908) : seen from ground level or from the lowest levels of a hierarchy ⟨the bird's-eye view of the executive and the ~ view of the employee —*Current Biog.*⟩

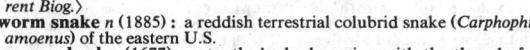

worm fence

worm snake *n* (1885) : a reddish terrestrial colubrid snake (*Carphophis amoenus*) of the eastern U.S.

worm wheel *n* (1677) : a toothed wheel gearing with the thread of a worm

worm·wood \'wǝrm-,wùd\ *n* [ME *wormwode*, alter. of *wermode*, fr. OE *wermōd*; akin to OHG *wermuota* wormwood] (15c) **1** : ARTEMISIA; *esp* : a European plant (*Artemisia absinthium*) that has silvery silky-haired leaves and drooping yellow nearly globular flower heads and yields a bitter dark green oil used in absinthe **2** : something bitter or grievous : BITTERNESS

wormy \'wǝr-mē\ *adj* **worm·i·er; -est** (15c) **1** : containing, abounding in, or infested with or as if with worms ⟨~ flour⟩ ⟨a ~ dog⟩; *also* : damaged by worms : WORM-EATEN ⟨~ timbers⟩ **2** : resembling or suggestive of a worm

worn *past part of* WEAR

worn-out \'wōrn-'aùt, 'wòrn-\ *adj* (1589) : exhausted or used up by or as if by wear

wor·ri·ment \'wǝr-ē-mǝnt, 'wǝ-rē-\ *n* (1833) : an act or instance of worrying; *also* : TROUBLE, WORRY

wor·ri·some \-sǝm\ *adj* (1845) **1** : causing distress or worry **2** : inclined to worry or fret — **wor·ri·some·ly** *adv* — **wor·ri·some·ness** *n*

¹wor·ry \'wǝr-ē, 'wǝ-rē\ *vb* **wor·ried; wor·ry·ing** [ME *worien*, fr. OE *wyrgan*; akin to OHG *wurgen* to strangle, Lith *veržti* to constrict] *vt* (bef. 12c) **1** *dial Brit* : CHOKE, STRANGLE **2 a** : to harass by tearing, biting, or snapping esp. at the throat **b** : to shake or pull at with the teeth ⟨a terrier ~*ing* a rat⟩ **c** : to touch or disturb something repeatedly **d** : to change the position of or adjust by repeated pushing or hauling **3 a** : to assail with rough or aggressive attack or treatment : TORMENT **b** : to subject to persistent or nagging attention or effort **4** : to afflict with mental distress or agitation : make anxious ~ *vi* **1** *dial Brit* : STRANGLE, CHOKE **2** : to move, proceed, or progress by unceasing or difficult effort : STRUGGLE **3** : to feel or experience concern or anxiety : FRET — **wor·ried·ly** \-(r)ēd-lē, -(r)ǝd-\ *adv* — **wor·ri·er** \-(r)ē-ǝr\ *n*

syn WORRY, ANNOY, HARASS, HARRY, PLAGUE, PESTER, TEASE mean to disturb or irritate by persistent acts. WORRY implies an incessant goading or attacking that drives one to desperation ⟨pursued a policy of *worrying* the enemy⟩. ANNOY implies disturbing one's composure or peace of mind by intrusion, interference, or petty attacks ⟨you're doing that just to *annoy* me⟩. HARASS implies petty persecutions or burdensome demands that exhaust one's nervous or mental power ⟨*harassed* on all sides by creditors⟩. HARRY may imply heavy oppression or maltreatment ⟨the strikers had been *harried* by thugs⟩. PLAGUE implies a painful and persistent affliction ⟨*plagued* all her life by poverty⟩. PESTER stresses the repetition of petty attacks ⟨constantly *pestered* with trivial complaints⟩. TEASE suggests an attempt to break down one's resistance or rouse to wrath ⟨children *teased* the dog⟩.

²worry *n, pl* **worries** (1804) **1 a** : mental distress or agitation resulting from concern usu. for something impending or anticipated : ANXIETY **b** : an instance or occurrence of such distress or agitation **2** : a cause of worry : TROUBLE, DIFFICULTY **syn** see CARE

worry beads *n pl* (1956) : a string of beads that can be fingered to keep one's hands occupied

wor·ry·wart \'wǝr-ē-,wòrt, 'wǝ-rē-\ *n* (1936) : one who is inclined to worry unduly

¹worse \'wǝrs\ *adj, comparative of* BAD *or of* ILL [ME *werse, worse,* fr. OE *wiersa, wyrsa*; akin to OHG *wirsiro* worse] (bef. 12c) **1** : of more inferior quality, value, or condition **2 a** : more unfavorable, difficult, unpleasant, or painful **b** : more faulty, unsuitable, or incorrect **c** : less skillful or efficient **3** : bad, evil, or corrupt in a greater degree : more reprehensible **4** : being in poorer health **3** : SICKER

²worse *n* (bef. 12c) : one that is worse ⟨thought he was an atheist and ~ —Van Wyck Brooks⟩

³worse *adv, comparative of* BAD *or of* ILL (bef. 12c) **1** : in a worse manner : to a worse extent or degree **2** : what is worse

wors·en \'wǝrs-²n\ *vb* **wors·ened; wors·en·ing** \'wǝrs-niŋ, 'wǝr-s²n-iŋ\ *vt* (13c) : to make worse ~ *vi* : to become worse

wors·er \'wǝr-sǝr\ *adj or adv* (15c) *archaic* : WORSE ⟨I cannot hate thee ~ than I do —Shak.⟩

¹wor·ship \'wǝr-shǝp\ *n* [ME *worshipe* worthiness, respect, reverence paid to a divine being, fr. OE *weorthscipe* worthiness, respect, fr. *weorth* worthy, worth + *-scipe* -ship] (bef. 12c) **1** *chiefly Brit* : a person of importance — used as a title for various officials (as magistrates and some mayors) **2** : reverence offered a divine being or supernatural power; *also* : an act of expressing such reverence **3** : a form of religious practice with its creed and ritual **4** : extravagant respect or admiration for or devotion to an object of esteem ⟨~ of the dollar⟩

²worship *vb* **-shiped** *or* **-shipped; -ship·ing** *or* **-ship·ping** *vt* (13c) **1** : to honor or reverence as a divine being or supernatural power **2** : to regard with great or extravagant respect, honor, or devotion ~ *vi* : to perform or take part in worship or an act of worship **syn** see REVERE — **wor·ship·er** *or* **wor·ship·per** *n*

wor·ship·ful \'wǝr-shǝp-fǝl\ *adj* (14c) **1 a** *archaic* : NOTABLE, DISTINGUISHED **b** *chiefly Brit* — used as a title for various persons or groups of rank or distinction **2** : giving or expressing worship or veneration — **wor·ship·ful·ly** \-fǝ-lē\ *adv* — **wor·ship·ful·ness** *n*

wor·ship·less \-shǝ-plǝs\ *adj* (1765) : lacking worship or worshipers

¹worst \'wǝrst\ *adj, superlative of* BAD *or of* ILL [ME *werste, worste,* fr. OE *wierresta, wyrsta,* superl. of the root of OE *wiersa* worse] (bef. 12c) **1** : most corrupt, bad, evil, or ill **2 a** : most unfavorable, difficult, unpleasant, or painful **b** : most unsuitable, faulty, unattractive, or ill-conceived **c** : least skillful or efficient **3** : most wanting in quality, value, or condition — **the worst way** : very much ⟨such men . . . need indoctrination *the worst way* —J. G. Cozzens⟩ — often used with *in* ⟨wanted a new bicycle in *the worst way*⟩

²worst *adv, superlative of* ILL *or* ILLY *or of* BAD *or* BADLY (bef. 12c) **1** : to the extreme degree of badness or inferiority **2** : to the greatest or highest degree ⟨groups who need the subsidies ~ lose out —T. W. Arnold⟩

³worst *n, pl* **worst** (14c) : one that is worst — **at worst** : under the worst circumstances

⁴worst *vt* (1636) : to get the better of : DEFEAT

worst-case *adj* (1964) : involving, projecting, or providing for the worst possible circumstances or outcome of a given situation

wor·sted \'wùs-tǝd, 'wǝr-stǝd\ *n* [ME, fr. *Worsted* (now *Worstead*), England] (13c) : a smooth compact yarn from long wool fibers used esp. for firm napless fabrics, carpeting, or knitting; *also* : a fabric made from worsted yarns — **worsted** *adj*

¹wort \'wǝrt, 'wòrt\ *n* [ME, fr. OE *wyrt* root, herb, plant — more at ROOT] (bef. 12c) : PLANT; *esp* : an herbaceous plant — usu. used in combination ⟨louse*wort*⟩

²wort *n* [ME, fr. OE *wyrt*; akin to MHG *würze* brewer's wort, OE *wyrt* root, herb] (bef. 12c) : a liquid formed by soaking mash in hot water and then fermented to make beer

¹worth \'wǝrth\ *vi* [ME, fr. OE *weorthan*; akin to OHG *werdan* to become, L *vertere* to turn, Lith *versti* to overturn, Skt *vartate* he turns] (bef. 12c) *archaic* : BECOME — usu. used in the phrase *woe worth*

²worth *adj* [ME, fr. OE *weorth* worthy, of (a specified) value; akin to OHG *werd* worthy, worth] (bef. 12c) **1** *archaic* : having monetary or material value **2** : ESTIMABLE — **for all one is worth** : to the fullest extent of one's value or ability

³worth *n* (bef. 12c) **1 a** : monetary value ⟨farmhouse and lands of little ~⟩ **b** : the equivalent of a specified amount or figure ⟨a dollar's ~ of gas⟩ **2** : the value of something measured by its qualities or by the esteem in which it is held ⟨a literary heritage of great ~⟩ **3 a** : moral or personal value ⟨trying to teach human ~⟩ **b** : MERIT, EXCELLENCE ⟨a field in which we have proved our ~⟩ **4** : WEALTH, RICHES

⁴worth *prep* (13c) **1 a** : equal in value to **b** : having assets or income equal to **2** : deserving of ⟨well ~ the effort⟩ — **worth one's salt** : of substantial or significant value or merit

worth·ful \'wǝrth-fǝl\ *adj* (bef. 12c) **1** : full of merit ⟨a good and ~ person⟩ **2** : having value ⟨the ~ aspects of their culture⟩

worth·less \'wǝrth-lǝs\ *adj* (1588) **1 a** : lacking worth : VALUELESS ⟨~ currency⟩ **b** : USELESS ⟨~ to continue searching⟩ **2** : CONTEMPTIBLE, DESPICABLE — **worth·less·ly** *adv* — **worth·less·ness** *n*

worth·while \-'hwī(ǝ)l, -'wī(ǝ)l\ *adj* (1903) **1** : being worth the time or effort spent **2** : WORTHY 1 — **worth·while·ness** *n*

¹wor·thy \'wǝr-thē\ *adj* **wor·thi·er; -est** (13c) **1 a** : having worth or value : ESTIMABLE ⟨a ~ cause⟩ **b** : HONORABLE, MERITORIOUS ⟨~ candidates⟩ **2** : having sufficient worth or importance ⟨~ to be remembered⟩ — **wor·thi·ly** \'wǝr-thǝ-lē\ *adv* — **wor·thi·ness** \-thē-nǝs\ *n*

²worthy *n, pl* **worthies** (14c) : a worthy or prominent person

-wor·thy \,wǝr-thē\ *adj comb form* **1** : fit or safe for ⟨a sea*worthy* vessel⟩ **2** : of sufficient worth for ⟨a news*worthy* event⟩

¹wot *pres 1st & 3d sing of* WIT

²wot \'wät\ *vb* **wot·ted; wot·ting** [ME, alter. of *witen* — more at WIT] (14c) *chiefly Brit* : KNOW — often used with *of*

would \wǝd, ǝd, d, 'wùd\ *past of* WILL [ME *wolde,* fr. OE; akin to OHG *wolta* wished, desired] (bef. 12c) **1 a** *archaic* : WISHED, DESIRED **b** *archaic* : wish for : WANT **c** (1) : strongly desire : WISH ⟨I ~ I were young again⟩ — often used without a subject and with *that* in a past or conditional construction ⟨~ that I had heeded your advice⟩ (2) — used in auxiliary function with *rather* or *sooner* to express preference ⟨he ~ sooner die than face them⟩ **2 a** — used in auxiliary function to express wish, desire, or intent ⟨those who ~ forbid gambling⟩ **b** — used in auxiliary function to express willingness or preference ⟨as ye ~ that men should do to you —Lk 6:31 (AV)⟩ **c** — used in auxiliary function to express plan or intention ⟨said we ~ come⟩ **3** — used in auxiliary function to express custom or habitual action ⟨we ~ meet often for lunch⟩ **4** — used in auxiliary function to express consent or choice ⟨~ put it off if he could⟩ **5 a** — used in auxiliary function in the conclusion of a conditional sentence to express a contingency or possibility ⟨if he were coming, he ~ be here now⟩ **b** — used in auxiliary function in a noun clause ⟨as one completing a statement of desire, request, or advice⟩ ⟨we wish that he ~ go⟩ **6** — used in auxiliary function to express probability or presumption in past or present time ⟨~ have won if I had not tripped⟩ **7** : COULD ⟨the barrel ~ hold 20 gallons⟩ **8** — used in auxiliary function to express a request with which voluntary compliance is expected ⟨~ you please help us⟩ **9** — used in auxiliary function to express doubt or uncertainty ⟨the explanation . . . ~ seem satisfactory⟩ **10** : SHOULD ⟨knew I ~ enjoy the trip⟩ ⟨~ be glad to know the answer⟩

would-be \'wùd-'bē\ *adj* (1647) : desiring, professing, or having the potential to be

would·est \'wù-dǝst\ *archaic past 2d sing of* WILL

wouldn't \'wù-d²nt, -d²n, *dial also* 'wù-t²n(t) *or* ,wùnt\ (ca. 1828) : would not

wouldst \wǝdst, 'wùdst, wǝtst\ *archaic past 2d sing of* WILL

¹wound \'wünd, *archaic or dial* 'waùnd\ *n* [ME, fr. OE *wund;* akin to OHG *wunta* wound] (bef. 12c) **1 a** : an injury to the body (as from violence, accident, or surgery) that involves laceration or breaking of a membrane (as the skin) and usu. damage to underlying tissues **b** : a cut or breach in a plant due to external violence **2** : a mental or emo-

\ǝ\ abut \²\ kitten, F table \ǝr\ further \a\ ash \ā\ ace \ä\ mop, mar
\aù\ out \ch\ chin \e\ bet \ē\ easy \g\ go \i\ hit \ī\ ice \j\ job
\ŋ\ sing \ō\ go \ò\ law \òi\ boy \th\ thin \th\ the \ü\ loot \ù\ foot
\y\ yet \zh\ vision \á, k̲, ⁿ, œ, œ̄, ᵫ, ᵬ̄, ᵗ\ see Guide to Pronunciation

tional hurt or blow **3** : something resembling a wound in appearance or effect; *esp* : a rift in or blow to a political body or social group
²**wound** *vt* (bef. 12c) : to cause a wound to or in ~ *vi* : to inflict a wound
³**wound** \'waủnd\ *past and past part of* WIND
¹**wound-ed** \'wün-dəd\ *n pl* (bef. 12c) : wounded persons
²**wounded** *adj* (14c) : injured, hurt by, or suffering from a wound
wound-less \'wün(d)-ləs\ *adj* (1579) **1** : free from wounds : UN-WOUNDED **2** *obs* : INVULNERABLE ⟨the ~ air —Shak.⟩
wove *past of* WEAVE
¹**woven** *past part of* WEAVE
²**wo-ven** \'wō-vən\ *n* (1930) : a woven fabric
wove paper \'wōv-\ *n* [*wove* (archaic pp. of *weave*)] (1815) : paper made with a revolving roller covered with wires so woven as to produce no fine lines running across the grain — compare LAID PAPER
¹**wow** \'waủ\ *interj* (1513) — used to express strong feeling (as pleasure or surprise)
²**wow** *n* (1920) : a striking success : HIT
³**wow** *vt* (1924) : to excite to enthusiastic admiration or approval
⁴**wow** *n* [imit.] (1932) : a distortion in reproduced sound consisting of a slow rise and fall of pitch caused by speed variation in the reproducing system
wow-ser \'waủ-zər\ *n* [origin unknown] (1899) *chiefly Austral* : an obtrusively puritanical person
W particle *n* [*weak*] (1963) : either of two particles about 80 times heavier than a proton that along with the Z particle are transmitters of the weak force and that can have a positive or negative charge
¹**wrack** \'rak\ *n* [ME *wrak*, fr. MD or MLG; akin to OE *wræc* something driven by the sea] (14c) **1 a** : a wrecked ship **b** : WRECKAGE **c** : WRECK **d** *dial* : the violent destruction of a structure, machine, or vehicle **2 a** : marine vegetation; *esp* : KELP **b** : dried seaweeds
²**wrack** *n* [ME, fr. OE *wræc* misery, punishment, something driven by the sea; akin to OE *wrecan* to drive, punish — more at WREAK] (15c) **1** : RUIN, DESTRUCTION **2** : a remnant of something destroyed
³**wrack** *vt* (1562) : to utterly ruin : WRECK
⁴**wrack** *vb* [by alter.] (ca. 1555) : ⁴RACK
⁵**wrack** *n* (1591) : ³RACK 2
⁶**wrack** *n* (1796) : ¹RACK
wrack-ful \'rak-fəl\ *adj* (1558) : DESTRUCTIVE
wraith \'rāth\ *n, pl* **wraiths** \'rāths *also* 'rāthz\ [origin unknown] (1513) **1 a** : the exact likeness of a living person seen usu. just before death as an apparition **b** : GHOST, SPECTER **2** : an insubstantial form or semblance : SHADOW **3** : a barely visible gaseous or vaporous column — **wraith-like** \-ˌlīk\ *adj*
¹**wran-gle** \'raŋ-gəl\ *vb* **wran-gled; wran-gling** \-g(ə-)liŋ\ [ME; akin to OHG *ringan* to struggle — more at WRING] (14c) **1** : to dispute angrily or peevishly : BICKER **2** : to engage in argument or controversy ~ *vt* **1** : to obtain by persistent arguing or maneuvering : WANGLE **2** [back-formation fr. *wrangler*] : to herd and care for (livestock and esp. horses) on the range
²**wrangle** *n* (1547) **1** : an angry, noisy, or prolonged dispute or quarrel **2** : the action or process of wrangling
wran-gler \-g(ə-)lər\ *n* (ca. 1515) **1** : a bickering disputant **2** [short for *horse-wrangler*, prob. part trans. of MexSp *caballerango* groom] : a ranch hand who takes care of the saddle horses; *broadly* : COWBOY
¹**wrap** \'rap\ *vb* **wrapped; wrap-ping** [ME *wrappen*] *vt* (14c) **1 a** : to cover esp. by winding or folding **b** : to envelop and secure for transportation or storage : BUNDLE **c** : ENFOLD, EMBRACE **d** : to coil, fold, draw, or twine (as string or cloth) around something **2 a** : SUR-ROUND, ENVELOP **b** : to suffuse or surround with an aura or state ⟨the affair was *wrapped* in scandal⟩ **c** : to involve completely : ENGROSS — usu. used with *up* **3** : to conceal or obscure as if by enveloping **4** : to enclose as if with a protective covering **5** : to finish filming or video-taping ⟨~ a movie⟩ ~ *vi* **1** : to wind, coil, or twine so as to encircle or cover something **2** : to put on clothing : DRESS — usu. used with *up* **3** : to be subject to covering, enclosing, or packaging — usu. used with *up* **4** : to come to completion in filming or videotaping
²**wrap** *n* (15c) **1 a** (1) : WRAPPER, WRAPPING (2) : material used for wrapping ⟨plastic ~⟩ **b** : an article of clothing that may be wrapped round a person; *esp* : an outer garment (as a coat or shawl) **c** : BLAN-KET **2** : a single turn or convolution of something wound round an object **3** *pl* **a** : RESTRAINT **b** : a shroud of secrecy ⟨a plan kept under ~s⟩ **4** : the completion of a schedule or session for filming or video-taping
³**wrap** *adj* (1948) : WRAPAROUND 1
¹**wrap-around** \'rap-ə-ˌraủnd\ *n* (1924) **1** : a garment (as a dress) made with a full-length opening and adjusted to the figure by wrapping around **2** : an object that encircles or esp. curves and laps over another
²**wraparound** *adj* (1926) **1** : made to be wrapped around something and esp. the body ⟨a ~ skirt⟩ **2 a** : shaped to follow a contour; *esp* : made to curve from the front around to the side ⟨~ sunglasses⟩ ⟨~ terraces⟩ **b** : extending laterally to the outermost limits of the field of vision ⟨a ~ movie screen⟩
wrap-per \'ra-pər\ *n* (15c) **1** : that in which something is wrapped: as **a** : a tobacco leaf used for the outside covering esp. of cigars **b** (1) : JACKET 3c(1) (2) : the paper cover of a book not bound in boards **c** : a paper wrapped around a newspaper or magazine in the mail **2** : one that wraps **3** : an article of clothing worn wrapped around the body
wrap-ping \'ra-piŋ\ *n* (14c) : something used to wrap an object : WRAPPER
wrap–up \'rap-ˌəp\ *n* (1951) **1** : a summarizing report **2** : a conclud-ing part : FINALE
wrap up *vt* (ca. 1568) **1** : SUMMARIZE, SUM UP **2 a** : to bring to a usu. successful conclusion **b** : CINCH, SEW UP ⟨has the nomination *wrapped up*⟩
wrasse \'ras\ *n, pl* **wrasses** *also* **wrasse** [Corn *gwragh, wragh* hag, wrasse] (ca. 1672) : any of a large family (Labridae) of elongate com-pressed usu. brilliantly colored marine bony fishes that usu. bury them-selves in sand at night and include important food fishes as well as a number of popular aquarium fishes
¹**wrath** \'rath, *chiefly Brit* 'roth\ *n* [ME, fr. OE *wrǣththo*, fr. *wrāth* wroth — more at WROTH] (bef. 12c) **1** : strong vengeful anger or in-

dignation **2** : retributory punishment for an offense or a crime : di-vine chastisement *syn* see ANGER
²**wrath** *adj* [alter. of *wroth*] (1535) *archaic* : WRATHFUL
wrath-ful \-fəl\ *adj* (14c) **1** : filled with wrath : IRATE **2** : arising from, marked by, or indicative of wrath — **wrath-ful-ly** \-fə-lē\ *adv* — **wrath-ful-ness** *n*
wrathy \'ra-thē, *chiefly Brit* 'rò-\ *adj* (1828) : WRATHFUL
wreak \'rēk *also* 'rek\ *vt* [ME *wreken*, fr. OE *wrecan* to drive, punish, avenge; akin to OHG *rehhan* to avenge and perh. to L *urgēre* to drive on, urge] (bef. 12c) **1 a** *archaic* : AVENGE **b** : to cause the infliction of (vengeance or punishment) **2** : to give free play or course to (ma-levolent feeling) **3** : BRING ABOUT, CAUSE ⟨~ havoc⟩
wreath \'rēth\ *n, pl* **wreaths** \'rēthz, 'rēths\ [ME *wrethe*, fr. OE *writha*; akin to OE *writhan* to twist — more at WRITHE] (bef. 12c) : something intertwined into a circular shape; *esp* : GARLAND, CHAPLET
wreathe \'rēth\ *vb* **wreathed; wreath-ing** [*wreath*] (1530) **1 a** : to shape into a wreath **b** : INTERWEAVE **c** : to cause to coil about something **2** : to twist or contort so as to show folds or creases **3** : to encircle or adorn with or as if with a wreath ~ *vi* **1** : to twist in coils : WRITHE **2 a** : to take on the shape of a wreath **b** : to move or extend in circles or spirals
wreathy \'rē-thē, -thē\ *adj* (1644) **1** : having the form of a wreath **2** : constituting a wreath
¹**wreck** \'rek\ *n* [ME *wrek*, fr. AF, of Scand origin; akin to ON *rek* wreck; akin to OE *wrecan* to drive] (13c) **1** : something cast up on the land by the sea esp. after a shipwreck **2 a** : SHIPWRECK **b** : the ac-tion of wrecking or fact or state of being wrecked : DESTRUCTION **3 a** : a hulk or the ruins of a wrecked ship **b** : the broken remains of something wrecked or otherwise ruined **c** : something disabled or in a state of ruin or dilapidation; *also* : a person or animal of broken consti-tution, health, or spirits
²**wreck** *vt* (15c) **1** : to cast ashore **2** : to reduce to a ruinous state by or as if by violence : SHIPWRECK **c** : to ruin, damage, or imperil by a wreck **d** : to involve in disaster or ruin **3** : BRING ABOUT, WREAK ⟨~ havoc⟩ ~ *vi* **1** : to become wrecked **2** : to rob, salvage, or repair wreckage or a wreck
wreck-age \'re-kij\ *n* (1837) **1** : the act of wrecking : the state of being wrecked **2 a** : something that has been wrecked **b** : broken and disordered parts or material from something wrecked
wreck-er \'re-kər\ *n* (1802) **1 a** : one that searches for or works on the wrecks of ships (as for rescue or for plunder) **b** : TOW TRUCK **2** : one that wrecks; *esp* : one whose work is the demolition of buildings
wrecker's ball *n* (1967) : a heavy iron or steel ball swung or dropped by a derrick to demolish old buildings — called also *wrecking ball*
wrecking bar *n* (1924) : a small crowbar with a claw for pulling nails at one end and a slight bend for prying at the other end
wren \'ren\ *n* [ME *wrenne*, fr. OE *wrenna*; akin to OHG *rentilo* wren] (bef. 12c) **1** : any of a family (Troglodytidae) of nu-merous small more or less brown oscine singing birds; *esp* : a very small widely distributed bird (*Troglodytes troglodytes*) that has a short erect tail and is noted for its song **2** : any of various small singing birds resembling the true wrens in size and habits

wren 1

¹**wrench** \'rench\ *vb* [ME, fr. OE *wrencan*; akin to OHG *renken* to twist and perh. to L *vergere* to bend, incline] *vi* (bef. 12c) **1** : to move with a violent twist; *also* : to undergo twisting **2** : to pull or strain at something with violent twisting ~ *vt* **1** : to twist violently **2** : to injure or dis-able by a violent twisting or straining **3** : CHANGE; *esp* : DISTORT, PERVERT **4 a** : to pull or tighten by violent twisting or with violence **b** : to snatch forcibly : WREST **5** : to cause to suffer mental anguish : RACK — **wrench-ing-ly** \'ren-chiŋ-lē\ *adv*
²**wrench** *n* (1530) **1 a** : a violent twisting or a pull with or as if with twisting **b** : a sharp twist or sudden jerk straining muscles or liga-ments; *also* : the resultant injury (as of a joint) **c** : a distorting or perverting alteration **d** : acute emotional distress : sudden violent mental change **2** : a hand or power tool for holding, twisting, or turn-ing an object (as a bolt or nut) **3** : MONKEY WRENCH 2
¹**wrest** \'rest\ *vt* [ME *wrasten, wresten*, fr. OE *wrǣstan*; akin to ON *reista* to bend and prob. to OE *wrigian* to turn — more at WRY] (bef. 12c) **1** : to pull, force, or move by violent wringing or twisting move-ments **2** : to gain with difficulty by or as if by force, violence, or de-termined labor
²**wrest** *n* (14c) **1** : the action of wresting : WRENCH **2** *archaic* : a key or wrench used for turning pins in a stringed instrument (as a harp or piano)
¹**wres-tle** \'re-səl, 'ra-\ *vb* **wres-tled; wres-tling** \'res-liŋ, 'ras-; 're-sᵊl-iŋ, 'ra-\ [ME *wrastlen, wrestlen*, fr. OE *wrǣstlian*, freq. of *wrǣstan*] *vi* (bef. 12c) **1** : to contend by grappling with and striving to trip or throw an opponent down or off balance **2** : to combat an opposing tendency or force ⟨*wrestling* with his conscience⟩ **3** : to engage in deep thought, consideration, or debate **4** : to engage in or as if in a violent or determined struggle ⟨*wrestling* with cumbersome luggage⟩ ~ *vt* **1 a** : to engage in (a match, bout, or fall) in wrestling **b** : to wrestle with ⟨~ an alligator⟩ **2** : to move, maneuver, or force with difficulty — **wres-tler** \'res-lər, 'ras-; 're-sᵊl-ər, 'ra-\ *n*
²**wrestle** *n* (1593) : the action or an instance of wrestling : STRUGGLE; *esp* : a wrestling bout
wres-tling \'res-liŋ, 'ras-; 're-sᵊl-iŋ, 'ra-\ *n* (bef. 12c) : a sport or contest in which two opposing individuals struggle hand to hand with each attempting to subdue or unbalance the other
wretch \'rech\ *n* [ME *wrecche*, fr. OE *wrecca* outcast, exile; akin to OHG *hrechjo* fugitive, OE *wrecan* to drive, drive out — more at WREAK] (bef. 12c) **1** : a miserable person : one who is profoundly unhappy or in great misfortune **2** : a base, despicable, or vile person
wretch-ed \'re-chəd\ *adj* [ME, irreg. fr. *wretch*] (12c) **1** : deeply af-flicted, dejected, or distressed in body or mind **2** : extremely or de-plorably bad or distressing ⟨was in ~ health⟩ ⟨a ~ accident⟩ **3 a** : being or appearing mean, miserable, or contemptible ⟨dressed in ~

old clothes⟩ **b** : very poor in quality or ability : INFERIOR ⟨~ workmanship⟩ — **wretch·ed·ly** *adv* — **wretch·ed·ness** *n*

¹**wrig·gle** \'ri-gəl\ *vb* **wrig·gled; wrig·gling** \-g(ə-)liŋ\ [ME, fr. akin to MLG *wriggeln* to wriggle; akin to OE *wrigian* to turn — more at WRY] *vi* (15c) **1** : to move the body or a bodily part to and fro with short writhing motions like a worm : SQUIRM **2** : to move or advance by twisting and turning **3** : to extricate or insinuate oneself or reach a goal as if by wriggling ~ *vt* **1** : to cause to move in short quick contortions **2** : to introduce, insinuate, or bring into a state or place by or as if by wriggling — **wrig·gly** \-g(ə-)lē\ *adj*

²**wriggle** *n* (1709) **1** : a short or quick writhing motion or contortion **2** : a formation or marking of sinuous design

wrig·gler \'ri-g(ə-)lər\ *n* (1631) : one that wriggles; *esp* : WIGGLER 1

wright \'rīt\ *n* [ME, fr. OE *wyrhta, wryhta* worker, maker; akin to OE *weorc* work — more at WORK] (bef. 12c) : a worker skilled in the manufacture esp. of wooden objects — usu. used in combination ⟨ship*wright*⟩ ⟨wheel*wright*⟩

wring \'riŋ\ *vb* **wrung** \'rəŋ\; **wring·ing** \'riŋ-iŋ\ [ME, fr. OE *wringan;* akin to OHG *ringan* to struggle, Lith *rengtis* to bend down, OE *wyrgan* to strangle — more at WORRY] *vt* (bef. 12c) **1** : to squeeze or twist esp. so as to make dry or to extract moisture or liquid ⟨~ a towel dry⟩ **2** : to extract or obtain by or as if by twisting and compressing ⟨~ water from a towel⟩ ⟨~ a confession from the suspect⟩ **3** a : to twist so as to strain or sprain into a distorted shape ⟨I could ~ your neck⟩ **b** : to twist together (clasped hands) as a sign of anguish **4** : to affect painfully as if by wringing : TORMENT ⟨a tragedy that ~s the heart⟩ ~ *vi* : SQUIRM, WRITHE — **wring** *n*

wring·er \'riŋ-ər\ *n* (14c) : one that wrings: as **a** : a machine or device for pressing out liquid or moisture ⟨a clothes ~⟩ **b** : something that causes pain, hardship, or exertion

¹**wrin·kle** \'riŋ-kəl\ *n* [ME, back-formation fr. *wrinkled* twisted, winding, prob. fr. OE *gewrinclod,* pp. of *gewrinclian* to wind, fr. *ge-,* perfective prefix + *-wrinclian* (akin to *wrencan* to wrench) — more at CO-] (15c) **1** : a small ridge or furrow esp. when formed on a surface by the shrinking or contraction of a smooth substance : CREASE; *specif* : one in the skin esp. when due to age, worry, or fatigue **2** a : METHOD, TECHNIQUE **b** : a change in a customary procedure or method ⟨: something new or different : INNOVATION **3** : IMPERFECTION, IRREGULARITY — **wrin·kly** \-k(ə-)lē\ *adj*

²**wrinkle** *vb* **wrin·kled; wrin·kling** \-k(ə-)liŋ\ *vi* (1523) : to become marked with or contracted into wrinkles ~ *vt* : to contract into wrinkles : PUCKER

wrist \'rist\ *n* [ME, fr. OE; akin to MHG *rist* wrist, ankle, OE *wrǣstan* to twist — more at WREST] (bef. 12c) **1** : the joint or the region of the joint between the human hand and the arm or a corresponding part on a lower animal **2** : the part of a garment or glove covering the wrist

wrist·band \'ris(t)-,band\ *n* (1571) **1** : the part of a sleeve covering the wrist **2** : a band encircling the wrist

wrist·let \'ris(t)-lət\ *n* (ca. 1847) **1** : a band encircling the wrist; *esp* : a close-fitting knitted band attached to the top of a glove or the end of a sleeve

wrist·lock \'rist-,läk\ *n* (1921) : a wrestling hold in which one contestant is thrown or made helpless by a twisting grip on the wrist

wrist pin *n* (ca. 1875) : a stud or pin that forms a journal (as in a crosshead) for a connecting rod

wrist shot *n* (ca. 1899) : a quick usu. short-range shot in ice hockey made while the puck is against the blade of the stick by snapping the blade quickly forward

wrist·watch \'rist-,wäch\ *n* (1896) : a small watch that is attached to a bracelet or strap and is worn around the wrist

wrist wrestling *n* (1968) : a form of arm wrestling in which opponents interlock thumbs instead of gripping hands

wristy \'ris-tē\ *adj* **wrist·i·er; -est** (1867) : involving or using a lot of wrist movement (as in stroking a ball)

writ \'rit\ *n* [ME, fr. OE; akin to OE *wrītan* to write] (bef. 12c) **1** : something written : WRITING ⟨Sacred *Writ*⟩ **2** a : a formal written document; *specif* : a legal instrument in epistolary form issued under seal in the name of the English monarch **b** : an order or mandatory process in writing issued in the name of the sovereign or of a court or judicial officer commanding the person to whom it is directed to perform or refrain from performing an act specified therein ⟨~ of detinue⟩ ⟨~ of entry⟩ ⟨~ of execution⟩ **c** : the power and authority of the issuer of such a written order — usu. used with *run* ⟨outside the United States where . . . our ~ does not run —Dean Acheson⟩

writ·able \'rī-tə-bəl\ *adj* (1782) : capable of being put in writing

write \'rīt\ *vb* **wrote** \'rōt\; **writ·ten** \'ri-t³n\ *also* **writ** \'rit\ *or dial* **wrote; writ·ing** \'rī-tiŋ\ [ME, fr. OE *wrītan* to scratch, draw, inscribe; akin to OHG *rizan* to tear and perh. to Gk *rhīnē* file, rasp] *vt* (bef. 12c) **1** a : to form (as characters or symbols) on a surface with an instrument (as a pen) **b** : to form (as words) by inscribing the characters or symbols of on a surface **c** : to spell in writing ⟨words *written* alike but pronounced differently⟩ **d** : to cover, fill, or fill in by writing ⟨*wrote* ten pages⟩ ⟨~ a check⟩ **2** : to set down in writing: as **a** : DRAW UP, DRAFT ⟨~ a will⟩ **b** (1) : to be the author of : COMPOSE ⟨~s poems and essays⟩ (2) : to compose in musical form ⟨~ a string quartet⟩ **c** : to express in literary form ⟨if I could ~ the beauty of your eyes —Shak.⟩ **d** : to communicate by letter ⟨~s that they are coming⟩ **e** : to use or exhibit (a specific script, language, or literary form or style) in writing ⟨~ Braille⟩ ⟨~s French with ease⟩ **f** : to write contracts or orders for; *esp* : UNDERWRITE ⟨~ life insurance⟩ **3** : to make a permanent impression of **4** : to communicate with in writing ⟨we'll ~ you when we get there⟩ **5** : ORDAIN, FATE ⟨so be it, it is *written* —D. C. Peattie⟩ **6** : to make evident or obvious ⟨guilt *written* on his face⟩ **7** : to force, effect, introduce, or remove by writing ⟨~ oneself into fame and fortune —Charles Lee⟩ **8** : to take part in or bring about (something worth recording⟩ **9** a : to introduce (information) into the storage device or medium of a computer **b** : to transfer (information) from the main memory of a computer to a storage or output device **10** : SELL ⟨a stock option⟩ ~ *vi* **1** a : to make significant characters or inscriptions; *also* : to permit or be adapted to writing **b** : to form or produce written letters, words, or sentences **2** : to compose, communicate by, or send a letter **3** a : to produce a written work **b** : to compose music — **write one's own ticket** : to select a course of action or position entirely according to one's wishes — **writ large**

: on a larger scale or in a more prominent manner ⟨the problems of modern totalitarianism are only our own problems *writ large* —Times Lit. Supp.⟩ — **writ small** : on a smaller scale

write—down \'rīt-,daún\ *n* (1932) : a deliberate reduction in the book value of an asset (as to reflect the effect of obsolescence)

write down *vt* (1588) **1** : to record in written form **2** a : to depreciate, disparage, or injure by writing **b** : to reduce in status, rank, or value; *esp* : to reduce the book value of ~ *vi* : to write so as to appeal to a lower level of taste, comprehension, or intelligence

write—in \'rīt-,in\ *n* (1932) **1** : a vote cast by writing in the name of a candidate **2** : a candidate whose name is written in

write in *vt* (14c) **1** : to insert in a document or text **2** a : to insert (a name not listed on a ballot or voting machine) in an appropriate space **b** : to cast (a vote) in this manner

write—off \'rīt-,óf\ *n* (1905) **1** : an elimination of an item from the books of account **2** : a reduction in book value of an item (as by way of depreciation)

write off *vt* (1682) **1** a : to reduce the estimated or book value of : DEPRECIATE **b** : to take off the books : CANCEL ⟨*write off* a bad debt⟩ **2** : to regard or concede to be lost ⟨most were content to *write off* 1979 and look optimistically ahead —*Money*⟩; *also* : DISMISS ⟨was *written off* as an expatriate highbrow —Brendan Gill⟩

write out *vt* (1548) : to write esp. in a full and complete form

writ·er \'rī-tər\ *n* (bef. 12c) : one that writes: as **a** : AUTHOR **b** : one who writes stock options

writ·er·ly \'rī-tər-lē\ *adj* (1957) : of, relating to, or typical of a writer

writer's block *n* (1950) : a psychological inhibition preventing a writer from proceeding with a piece

writer's cramp *n* (1853) : a painful spasmodic cramp of muscles of the hand or fingers brought on by excessive writing

write—up \'rīt-,əp\ *n* (1885) **1** : a written account; *esp* : a flattering article **2** : a deliberate increase in the book value of an asset (as to reflect the effect of inflation)

write up *vt* (15c) **1** : to make a write-up of **2** : to report (a person) esp. for some violation of law or rules

writhe \'rīth\ *vb* **writhed; writh·ing** [ME, fr. OE *writhan;* akin to ON *rītha* to twist] *vt* (bef. 12c) **1** a : to twist into coils or folds **b** : to twist so as to distort : WRENCH **c** : to twist (the body or a bodily part) in pain **2** : INTERTWINE ~ *vi* **1** : to move or proceed with twists and turns **2** : to twist from or as if from pain or struggling **3** : to suffer keenly — **writhe** *n*

writh·en \'ri-thən\ *adj* [ME, fr. OE, fr. pp. of *writhan*] (bef. 12c) : being twisted or contorted ⟨~ trees⟩ ⟨a ~ smile⟩

writ·ing \'rī-tiŋ\ *n* (13c) **1** : the act or process of one who writes: as **a** : the act or art of forming visible letters or characters; *specif* : HANDWRITING 1 **b** : the act or practice of literary or musical composition **2** : something written: as **a** : letters or characters that serve as visible signs of ideas, words, or symbols **b** : a letter, note, or notice used to communicate or record **c** : a written composition **d** : INSCRIPTION **3** : a style or form of composition **4** : the occupation of a writer; *esp* : the profession of authorship — **writing on the wall** : HANDWRITING ON THE WALL

writing desk *n* (1611) : a desk that often has a sloping top for writing on; *also* : a portable case that contains writing materials and has a surface for writing

writing paper *n* (1548) : paper that is usu. finished with a smooth surface and sized and that can be written on with ink

Writ·ings \'rī-tiŋz\ *n pl* [trans. of LHeb *kĕthūbhīm*] (14c) : HAGIOGRAPHA

writ of assistance (1706) **1** : a writ issued to a law officer (as a sheriff or marshal) for the enforcement of a court order or decree; *esp* : one used to enforce an order for the possession of lands **2** : a writ used esp. in colonial America authorizing a law officer to search in unspecified locations for unspecified illegal goods

writ of certiorari (ca. 1532) : CERTIORARI

writ of error (15c) : a common law writ directing an inferior court to remit the record of a legal action to the reviewing court in order that an error of law may be corrected if it exists

writ of extent (ca. 1861) : a writ formerly used to recover debts of record to the British crown and under which the lands, goods, and person of the debtor might all be seized to secure payment

writ of habeas corpus (1771) : HABEAS CORPUS

writ of mandamus (ca. 1861) : MANDAMUS

writ of prohibition (ca. 1876) : a writ issued by a superior court to prevent an inferior court from acting beyond its jurisdiction

writ of right *n* (15c) **1** : a common law writ for restoring to its owner property held by another **2** : a writ granted as a matter of right

writ of summons (1660) : a writ issued on behalf of the British monarch summoning a lord spiritual or a lord temporal to attend parliament

¹**wrong** \'róŋ\ *n* [ME, fr. OE, fr. (assumed) *wrang,* adj., wrong] (bef. 12c) **1** : an injurious, unfair, or unjust act : action or conduct inflicting harm without due provocation or just cause **b** : a violation or invasion of the legal rights of another; *esp* : TORT **2** : something wrong, immoral, or unethical; *esp* : principles, practices, or conduct contrary to justice, goodness, equity, or law **3** : the state, position, or fact of being or doing wrong: as **a** : the state of being mistaken or incorrect **b** : the state of being guilty **syn** see INJUSTICE

²**wrong** *adj* **wrong·er** \'róŋ-ər\; **wrong·est** \'róŋ-əst\ [ME, fr. (assumed) OE *wrang,* of Scand origin; akin to ON *rangr* awry, wrong; akin to OE *wringan* to wring] (13c) **1** : not according to the moral standard : SINFUL, IMMORAL ⟨thought that war was ~⟩ **2** : not right or proper according to a code, standard, or convention : IMPROPER ⟨it was ~ not to thank your host⟩ **3** : not according to truth or facts : INCORRECT ⟨gave a ~ date⟩ **4** : not satisfactory (as in condition, results, health, or temper⟩ **5** : not in accordance with one's needs, intent, or expectations ⟨took the ~ bus⟩ **6** : of, relating to, or consti-

\ə\ abut \ᵊ\ kitten, F table \ər\ further \a\ ash \ā\ ace \ä\ mop, mar \aú\ out \ch\ chin \e\ bet \ē\ easy \g\ go \i\ hit \ī\ ice \j\ job \ŋ\ sing \ō\ go \ò\ law \òi\ boy \th\ thin \<u>th</u>\ the \ü\ loot \ù\ foot \y\ yet \zh\ vision \ä, ᵏ, ⁿ, œ, œ̄, ᵫ, ū̄, ᵊ\ *see* Guide to Pronunciation tuting the side of something that is usu. held to be opposite to the principal one, that is the one naturally or by design turned down, inward, or away, or that is the least finished or polished — **wrong·ly** \'rȯŋ-lē\ *adv* — **wrong·ness** *n* — **wrong side of the tracks** : a run-down or unfashionable neighborhood

³**wrong** *adv* (13c) **1** : without accuracy : INCORRECTLY ⟨guessed ~⟩ **2** : without regard for what is proper or just **3** : in a wrong direction **4 a** : in an unsuccessful or unfortunate way **b** : out of working order or condition **5** : in a false light ⟨don't get me ~⟩

⁴**wrong** *vt* **wronged; wrong·ing** \'rȯŋ-iŋ\ (14c) **1 a** : to do wrong to : INJURE, HARM **b** : to treat disrespectfully or dishonorably : VIOLATE **2** : DEFRAUD — usu. used with *of* **3** : DISCREDIT, MALIGN — **wrong·er** \'rȯŋ-ər\ *n*

syn WRONG, OPPRESS, PERSECUTE, AGGRIEVE mean to injure unjustly or outrageously. WRONG implies inflicting injury either unmerited or out of proportion to what one deserves ⟨a penal system that had *wronged* him⟩. OPPRESS suggests inhumane imposing of burdens one cannot endure or exacting more than one can perform ⟨a people *oppressed* by a warmongering tyrant⟩. PERSECUTE implies a relentless and unremitting subjection to annoyance or suffering ⟨a child *persecuted* by constant criticism⟩. AGGRIEVE implies suffering caused by an infringement or denial of rights ⟨a legal aid society representing *aggrieved* minority groups⟩.

wrong·do·er \'rȯŋ-ˌdü-ər\ *n* (15c) : one that does wrong; *esp* : one who transgresses moral laws
wrong·do·ing \-ˌdü-iŋ\ *n* (14c) **1** : evil or improper behavior or action **2** : an instance of doing wrong
wronged *adj* (ca. 1547) : being injured unjustly : suffering a wrong
wrong·ful \'rȯŋ-fəl\ *adj* (14c) **1** : WRONG, UNJUST **2 a** : having no legal sanction : UNLAWFUL **b** : ILLEGITIMATE — **wrong·ful·ly** \-fə-lē\ *adv* — **wrong·ful·ness** *n*
wrong·head·ed \'rȯŋ-'he-dəd\ *adj* (1732) : stubborn in adherence to wrong opinion or principles ⟨a ~ policy⟩ — **wrong·head·ed·ly** *adv* — **wrong·head·ed·ness** *n*
wrote *past and dial past part of* WRITE
wroth \'rȯth *also* 'rōth\ *adj* [ME, fr. OE *wrāth;* akin to OHG *reid* twisted, OE *writhan* to writhe] (bef. 12c) : intensely angry : highly incensed : WRATHFUL
¹**wrought** \'rȯt\ *past and past part of* WORK
²**wrought** *adj* [ME, fr. pp. of *worken* to work] (14c) **1** : worked into shape by artistry or effort ⟨carefully ~ essays⟩ **2** : elaborately embellished : ORNAMENTED **3** : processed for use : MANUFACTURED ⟨~ silk⟩ **4** : beaten into shape by tools : HAMMERED — used of metals **5** : deeply stirred : EXCITED — often used with *up* ⟨gets easily ~ up over nothing⟩
wrought iron *n* (1678) : a commercial form of iron that is tough, malleable, and relatively soft, contains less than 0.3 percent and usu. less than 0.1 percent carbon, and carries 1 or 2 percent of slag mechanically mixed with it
wrung *past and past part of* WRING
¹**wry** \'rī\ *vb* **wried; wry·ing** [ME *wrien,* fr. OE *wrigian* to turn; akin to MHG *rigel* kerchief wound around the head, Gk *rhiknos* shriveled, Av

urvisyeiti he turns] *vi* (14c) : TWIST, WRITHE ~ *vt* : to pull out of or as if out of proper shape : make awry
²**wry** *adj* **wry·er** \'rī-(-ə)r\; **wry·est** \'rī-əst\ (1523) **1** : having a bent or twisted shape or condition ⟨a ~ smile⟩; *esp* : turned abnormally to one side ⟨a ~ neck⟩ **2** : WRONGHEADED **3** : cleverly and often ironically or grimly humorous — **wry·ly** \'rī-lē\ *adv* — **wry·ness** *n*
wry·neck \'rī-ˌnek\ *n* (1585) **1** : either of two Old World woodpeckers (*Jynx torquilla* or *J. ruficollis*) that differ from the typical woodpeckers in having soft tail feathers and a peculiar manner of writhing the neck **2** : TORTICOLLIS
Wu \'wü\ *n* [Chin (Beijing) *Wú,* historical kingdom coextensive with the dialect area] (1908) : a group of Chinese dialects spoken principally in Jiangsu and Zhejiang provinces
wud \'wüd\ *adj* [alter. of ¹*wood*] (1772) *chiefly Scot* : INSANE, MAD
wul·fen·ite \'wu̇l-fə-ˌnīt\ *n* [G *Wulfenit,* fr. F. X. von *Wulfen* †1805 Austrian mineralogist] (1849) : a tetragonal mineral that is a complex oxide of lead and molybdenum and occurs esp. in bright orange-yellow tabular crystals
wun·der·kind \'vu̇n-dər-ˌkint\ *n, pl* **wun·der·kin·der** \-ˌkin-dər\ [G, fr. *Wunder* wonder + *Kind* child] (1891) : a child prodigy; *also* : one who succeeds in a competitive or highly difficult field or profession at an early age
wurst \'wərst *also* 'wu̇rst *sometimes* 'wu̇sht *or* 'wu̇st; *also with* v *for* w\ *n* [G, fr. OHG] (1855) : SAUSAGE
wurzel *n* [short for *mangel-wurzel*] (ca. 1888) : MANGEL
wuss \'wu̇s\ *also* **wus·sy** \'wu̇-sē\ *n, pl* **wuss·es** *also* **wus·sies** [origin unknown] (1983) : WIMP — **wussy** *adj*
wuth·er \'wə-thər\ *vi* [alter. of *whither* to rush, bluster, hurl] (ca. 1825) *dial Eng* : to blow with a dull roaring sound
Wy·an·dot \'wī-ən-ˌdät *also* 'win-\ *n* (1749) : a member of an American Indian group formed in the 17th century by Hurons and other Indians fleeing the Iroquois
wy·an·dotte \-ˌdät\ *n* [prob. fr. *Wyandotte* Wyandot] (1884) : any of a U.S. breed of medium-sized domestic fowls raised for meat and eggs
Wyc·liff·ite \'wi-klə-ˌfīt\ *n* [John *Wycliffe*] (1580) : LOLLARD — **Wyc·liffite** *adj*
wye \'wī\ *n* (1857) **1** : a Y-shaped part or object **2** : the letter *y*
wy·lie·coat \'wi-lē-ˌkōt, 'wi-\ *n* [ME (Sc) *wyle cot*] (15c) **1** *chiefly Scot* : a warm undergarment **2** *chiefly Scot* : PETTICOAT
wynd \'wīnd\ *n* [ME (Sc) *wynde,* prob. fr. *wynden* to wind, proceed, go, fr. OE *windan* to twist — more at WIND] (15c) *chiefly Scot* : a very narrow street
wynn *or* **wyn** \'win\ *n* [OE *wynn,* lit., joy — more at WINSOME] (bef. 12c) : a runic letter used in Old English and Middle English to represent the consonant \w\
WYS·I·WYG \'wi-zē-ˌwig, -zə-\ *adj* [*what you see is what you get*] (1982) : of, relating to, or being a display generated by word-processing or desktop-publishing software that exactly reflects the appearance of the printed document
wy·vern \'wī-vərn\ *n* [alter. of ME *wyvere* viper, fr. ONF *wivre,* modif. of L *vipera*] (1610) : a mythical animal usu. represented as a 2-legged winged creature resembling a dragon

¹**x** \'eks\ *n, pl* **x's** *or* **xs** \'ek-səz\ *often cap, often attrib* (bef. 12c) **1 a** : the 24th letter of the English alphabet **b** : a graphic representation of this letter **c** : a speech counterpart of orthographic *x* **2** : TEN — see NUMBER table **3** : a graphic device for reproducing the letter *x* **4** : one designated *x* esp. as the 24th in order or class, or the first in an order or class that includes x, y, and sometimes z **5** : an unknown quantity **6** : something shaped like or marked with the letter X
²**x** *vt* **x—ed** *also* **x'd** *or* **xed** \'ekst\; **x—ing** *or* **x'ing** \'ek-siŋ\ (ca. 1849) **1** : to mark with an *x* **2** : to cancel or obliterate with a series of *x*'s — usu. used with *out*
X \'eks\ *adj* (1950) *of a motion picture* : of such a nature that admission is denied to persons under a specified age (as 17) — used before the adoption of *NC-17*
Xan·a·du \'za-nə-ˌdü, -ˌdyü\ *n* [*Xanadu,* locality in *Kubla Khan* (1798), poem by Samuel T. Coleridge] (1919) : an idyllic, exotic, or luxurious place
xanth- *or* **xantho-** *comb form* [NL, fr. Gk, fr. *xanthos*] : yellow ⟨*xanthene*⟩
xan·than gum \'zan-thən-\ *n* [*xanth-* (fr. NL *Xanthomonas,* genus name) + ³*-an*] (1964) : a polysaccharide that is produced by fermentation of carbohydrates by a gram-negative bacterium (*Xanthomonas campestris* of the family Pseudomonadaceae) and is a thickening and suspending agent used esp. in pharmaceuticals and prepared foods — called also *xanthan*
xan·thate \'zan-ˌthāt\ *n* (1831) : a salt or ester of any of various thio acids and esp. $C_3H_6OS_2$
xan·thene \-ˌthēn\ *n* (1898) **1** : a white crystalline heterocyclic compound $C_{13}H_{10}O$; *also* : an isomer of this that is the parent of the colored forms of the xanthene dyes **2** : any of various derivatives of xanthene
xanthene dye *n* (1930) : any of various brilliant fluorescent yellow to pink to bluish red dyes that are characterized by the presence of the xanthene nucleus

xan·thine \'zan-ˌthēn\ *n* [ISV] (1857) : a feebly basic compound $C_5H_4N_4O_2$ that occurs esp. in animal or plant tissue, is derived from guanine and hypoxanthine, and yields uric acid on oxidation; *also* : any of various derivatives of this
Xan·thip·pe \zan-'thi-pē, -'ti-\ *or* **Xan·tip·pe** \-'ti-pē\ *n* [Gk *Xanthippē,* shrewish wife of Socrates] (1691) : an ill-tempered woman
xan·thone \'zan-ˌthōn\ *n* [ISV] (ca. 1894) : a ketone $C_{13}H_8O_2$ that is the parent of several natural yellow pigments
xan·tho·phyll \'zan(t)-thə-ˌfil\ *n* [F *xanthophylle,* fr. *xanth-* + *-phylle* -phyll] (1838) : any of several neutral yellow to orange carotenoid pigments that are oxygen derivatives of carotenes; *esp* : LUTEIN
Xa·ve·ri·an Brother \zā-'vir-ē-ən-, za-\ *n* [*Xaverian* of St. Francis Xavier] (1882) : a member of a Roman Catholic congregation of lay brothers founded by Theodore J. Ryken in Bruges, Belgium, in 1839 and dedicated to education
x–ax·is \'eks-ˌak-səs\ *n* (1886) **1** : the axis in a plane Cartesian coordinate system parallel to which abscissas are measured **2** : one of the three axes in a three-dimensional rectangular coordinate system
X band *n* (ca. 1946) : a segment of the superhigh-frequency radio spectrum that lies between 5.2 GHz and 10.9 GHz and is used esp. for radars and for spacecraft communication
X chromosome *n* (1911) : a sex chromosome that usu. occurs paired in each female cell and single in each male cell in species in which the male typically has two unlike sex chromosomes — compare Y CHROMOSOME
x–co·or·di·nate \ˌeks-kō-'ȯrd-nət; -'ȯr-d°n-ət, -də-ˌnāt\ *n* (1927) : a coordinate whose value is determined by measuring parallel to an x-axis; *specif* : ABSCISSA
xe·bec \'zē-ˌbek, zi-\ *n* [modif. of F *chebec,* fr. Ar *shabbāk*] (1756) : a usu. 3-masted Mediterranean sailing ship with long overhanging bow and stern
xen- *or* **xeno-** *comb form* [LL, fr. Gk, fr. *xenos* stranger, guest, host] **1** : guest

xebec

: foreigner ⟨*xenophobia*⟩ **2** : strange : foreign ⟨*xenolith*⟩
xe·nia \'zē-nē-ə, -nyə\ *n* [NL, fr. Gk, hospitality, fr. *xenos* host] (1899)
: the effect of genes introduced by pollen esp. on endosperm and embryo development
xe·no·bi·ot·ic \,zē-nō-bī-'ä-tik, ,zē-, -bē-\ *n* (1965) : a chemical compound (as a drug, pesticide, or carcinogen) that is foreign to a living organism — **xenobiotic** *adj*
xe·no·di·ag·no·sis \-,dī-ig-'nō-səs\ *n* [NL] (ca. 1929) : the detection of a parasite (as of humans) by feeding a suitable intermediate host (as an insect) on supposedly infected material (as blood) and later examining the host for the parasite — **xe·no·di·ag·nos·tic** \-'näs-tik\ *adj*
xe·no·ge·ne·ic \-jə-'nē-ik\ *adj* [*xen-* + *-geneic* (as in *isogeneic*)] (1961) : derived from, originating in, or being a member of another species
xe·no·graft \'ze-nə-,graft, 'zē-\ *n* (1961) : HETEROGRAFT
xe·no·lith \'ze-nᵊl-,ith, 'zē-\ *n* (1894) : a fragment of a rock included in another rock — **xe·no·lith·ic** \,ze-nᵊl-'i-thik, ,zē-\ *adj*
xe·non \'zē-,nän, 'ze-\ *n* [Gk, neut. of *xenos* strange] (1898) : a heavy, colorless, and relatively inert gaseous element that occurs in air as about one part in 20 million by volume and is used esp. in thyratrons and specialized flashtubes — see ELEMENT table
xe·no·phile \'ze-nə-,fīl, 'zē-\ *n* [ISV] (1948) : one attracted to foreign things (as styles or people)
xe·no·phobe \'ze-nə-,fōb, 'zē-\ *n* [ISV] (1922) : one unduly fearful of what is foreign and esp. of people of foreign origin — **xe·no·pho·bic** \,ze-nə-'fō-bik, ,zē-\ *adj* — **xe·no·pho·bi·cal·ly** \-bi-k(ə-)lē\ *adv*
xe·no·pho·bia \,ze-nə-'fō-bē-ə, ,zē-\ *n* [NL] (1903) : fear and hatred of strangers or foreigners or of anything that is strange or foreign
xe·no·tro·pic \-'trä-pik, -trō-\ *adj* (1973) : replicating or reproducing only in cells other than those of the host species ⟨~ viruses⟩
xer- or **xero-** *comb form* [LL, fr. Gk *xēr-, xēro-,* fr. *xēros*] : dry ⟨*xeric*⟩ ⟨*xerophyte*⟩
xe·ric \'zir-ik, 'zer-\ *adj* (1926) : characterized by, relating to, or requiring only a small amount of moisture ⟨a ~ habitat⟩ ⟨a ~ plant⟩ — compare HYDRIC, MESIC
Xeri·scape \'zir-ə-,skāp, 'zer-\ *trademark* — used for a water-conserving method of landscaping in arid or semiarid climates
xe·ro·der·ma pig·men·to·sum \,zir-ə-'dər-mə-,pig-mən-'tō-səm, -,men-\ *n* [NL, lit., pigmented dryness of the skin] (1884) : a genetic condition inherited as a recessive autosomal trait that is caused by a defect in mechanisms that repair DNA mutations (as those caused by ultraviolet light) and is characterized by the development of pigment abnormalities and multiple skin cancers in body areas exposed to the sun
xe·rog·ra·phy \zə-'rä-grə-fē\ *n* [ISV] (1948) : a process for copying graphic matter by the action of light on an electrically charged photoconductive insulating surface in which the latent image is developed with a resinous powder **2** : XERORADIOGRAPHY — **xe·ro·graph·ic** \,zir-ə-'gra-fik\ *adj* — **xe·ro·graph·i·cal·ly** \-fi-k(ə-)lē\ *adv*
xe·roph·i·lous \zə-'rä-fə-ləs\ *or* **xe·ro·phile** \'zir-ə-,fīl\ *adj* (1863) : thriving in or tolerant or characteristic of a xeric environment — **xe·roph·i·ly** \zə-'rä-fə-lē\ *n*
xe·roph·thal·mia \,zir-,äf-'thal-mē-ə, -,äp-'thal-\ *n* [LL, fr. Gk *xēroph-thalmia,* fr. *xēr-* *xer-* + *ophthalmia* ophthalmia] (ca. 1656) : a dry thickened lusterless condition of the eyeball resulting esp. from a severe systemic deficiency of vitamin A — **xe·roph·thal·mic** \-mik\ *adj*
xe·ro·phyte \'zir-ə-,fīt\ *n* (1897) : a plant structurally adapted for life and growth with a limited water supply esp. by means of mechanisms that limit transpiration or that provide for the storage of water — **xe·ro·phyt·ic** \,zir-ə-'fi-tik\ *adj* — **xe·ro·phyt·ism** \'zir-ə-,fī,ti-zəm\ *n*
xe·ro·ra·di·og·ra·phy \,zir-ō-,rā-dē-'ä-grə-fē\ *n* (1949) : radiography used esp. in mammographic screening for breast cancer that produces an image using X rays in a manner similar to the way an image is produced by light in xerography
xe·ro·ther·mic \,zir-ə-'thər-mik\ *adj* (1904) **1** : characterized by heat and dryness **2** : adapted to or thriving in a hot dry environment
xe·rox \'zir-,äks, 'zē-,räks\ *vt* [fr. *Xerox*] (1965) **1** : to copy on a Xerox copier **2** : to make (a copy) on a Xerox copier
Xe·rox \'zir-,äks, 'zē-,räks\ *trademark* — used for a xerographic copier
x–height \'eks-,hīt, -,hītth\ *n* (ca. 1945) : the height of a lowercase x used to represent the height of the main body of a lowercase letter
Xho·sa \'kō-sə, 'hō-, 'kō-* or with* ȯ *for* ō\ *n* (1801) **1** : a member of a Bantu-speaking people of Eastern Cape province **2** : a Bantu language of the Xhosas
xi \'zī, 'ksī\ *n, pl* **xis** [Gk *xei*] (1823) : the 14th letter of the Greek alphabet — see ALPHABET table
x–in·ter·cept \'eks-'in-tər-,sept\ *n* (ca. 1939) : the x-coordinate of a point where a line, curve, or surface intersects the x-axis
xi·phi·ster·num \,zī-fə-'stər-nəm, ,zi-\ *n, pl* **-na** \-nə\ [NL, fr. Gk *xiphos* sword + NL *sternum*] (ca. 1860) : XIPHOID PROCESS
xi·phoid \'zī-,fȯid, 'zi-\ *n* [NL *xiphoides,* fr. Gk *xiphoeidēs,* fr. *xiphos*] (ca. 1860) : XIPHOID PROCESS — **xiphoid** *adj*
xiphoid process *n* (1873) : the segment of the human sternum that is the third and closest to the feet

x–ir·ra·di·a·tion \,eks-i-,rā-dē-'ā-shən\ *n, often cap* (1927) : X-RADIATION 1
Xmas \'kris-məs *also* 'eks-məs\ *n* [*X* (symbol for *Christ,* fr. the Gk letter chi (X), initial of *Christos* Christ) + *-mas* (in *Christmas*)] (1551) : CHRISTMAS
x–ra·di·a·tion \,eks-,rā-dē-'ā-shən\ *n, often cap* (1896) **1** : exposure to X rays **2** : radiation composed of X rays
X–rated \'eks-'rā-təd\ *adj* (1970) **1** : having a rating of X; *broadly* : relating to or characterized by explicit sexual material or activity ⟨an ~ book⟩ **2** : OBSCENE, VULGAR ⟨an ~ gesture⟩
Xray \'eks-,rā\ (1943) — a communications code word for the letter x
x–ray \'eks-,rā\ *vt, often cap* (1899) : to examine, treat, or photograph with X rays
X ray \'eks-,rā\ *n* (1896) **1** : any of the electromagnetic radiations of the same nature as visible radiation but having an extremely short wavelength of less than 100 angstroms that is produced by bombarding a metallic target with fast electrons in vacuum or by transition of atoms to lower energy states and that has the properties of ionizing a gas upon passage through it, of penetrating various thicknesses of all solids, of producing secondary radiations by impinging on material bodies, of acting on photographic films and plates as light does, and of causing fluorescent screens to emit light **2** : a photograph obtained by use of X rays — **X–ray** *adj*
X–ray astronomy *n* (1963) : astronomy dealing with investigations of celestial bodies by means of the X rays they emit
X–ray diffraction *n* (1924) : a scattering of X rays by the atoms of a crystal that produces an interference effect so that the diffraction pattern gives information on the structure of the crystal or the identity of a crystalline substance
X–ray star *n* (1964) : a luminous celestial object emitting a major portion of its radiation in the form of X rays — called also *X-ray source*
X–ray therapy *n* (1926) : medical treatment (as of cancer) by controlled application of X rays
X–ray tube *n* (1896) : a vacuum tube in which a concentrated stream of electrons strikes a metal target and produces X rays
x–sec·tion \'krȯs-'sek-shən, -,sek-\ *n* [*x,* rebus for *cross*] (1962) : CROSS SECTION — **x–sec·tion·al** \-shnəl, -shə-nᵊl\ *adj*
xu \'sü\ *n, pl* **xu** [Vietnamese, fr. F *sou* sou] (1948) **1** : a coin formerly minted by South Vietnam equivalent to the cent **2** — see *dong* at MONEY table
xyl- or **xylo-** *comb form* [L, fr. Gk, fr. *xylon*] **1** : wood ⟨*xylophone*⟩ **2** : xylene ⟨*xylidine*⟩
xy·lan \'zī-,lan\ *n* [ISV] (ca. 1894) : a yellow gummy pentosan that yields xylose on hydrolysis and is abundantly present in plant cell walls and woody tissue
xy·lem \'zī-ləm, -,lem\ *n* [G, fr. Gk *xylon*] (1873) : a complex tissue in the vascular system of higher plants that consists of vessels, tracheids, or both usu. together with wood fibers and parenchyma cells, functions chiefly in conduction of water and dissolved minerals but also in support and food storage, and typically constitutes the woody element (as of a plant stem) — compare PHLOEM
xylem ray *n* (1875) : a vascular ray or portion of a vascular ray located in xylem — called also *wood ray;* compare PHLOEM RAY
xy·lene \'zī-,lēn\ *n* [ISV] (1851) : any of three toxic flammable oily isomeric aromatic hydrocarbons C_8H_{10} that are di-methyl homologues of benzene and are usu. obtained from petroleum or natural gas distillates; *also* : a mixture of xylenes and ethyl benzene used chiefly as a solvent
xy·li·dine \'zī-lə-,dēn\ *n* [ISV] (1850) : any or a mixture of six toxic liquid or low-melting crystalline isomeric amino derivatives $C_8H_{11}N$ of the xylenes used chiefly as intermediates for azo dyes and in organic synthesis
xy·li·tol \'zī-lə-,tȯl, -,tōl\ *n* (1891) : a crystalline alcohol $C_5H_{12}O_5$ that is a derivative of xylose, is obtained esp. from birch bark, and is used as a sweetener
xy·log·ra·phy \zī-'lä-grə-fē\ *n* [F *xylographie,* fr. *xyl-* + *-graphie* -graphy] (1816) : the art of making engravings on wood esp. for printing — **xy·lo·graph** \'zī-lə-,graf\ *n* — **xy·log·ra·pher** \zī-'lä-grə-fər\ *n* — **xy·lo·graph·ic** \,zī-lə-'gra-fik\ *also* **xy·lo·graph·i·cal** \-fi-kəl\ *adj*
xy·lol \'zī-,lȯl, -,lōl\ *n* [ISV] (1851) : XYLENE
xy·loph·a·gous \zī-'lä-fə-gəs\ *adj* [Gk *xylophagos,* fr. *xyl-* + *-phagos* -phagous] (1739) : feeding on or in wood
xy·lo·phone \'zī-lə-,fōn *also* 'zi-\ *n* (1866) : a percussion instrument consisting of a series of wooden bars graduated in length to produce the musical scale, supported on belts of straw or felt, and sounded by striking with two small wooden hammers — **xy·lo·phon·ist** \-,fō-nist\ *n*
xy·lose \'zī-,lōs, -,lōz\ *n* [ISV] (ca. 1894) : a crystalline aldose sugar $C_5H_{10}O_5$ that is not fermentable with ordinary yeasts and occurs esp. as a constituent of xylans from which it is obtained by hydrolysis

---

\ə\ abut \ᵊ\ kitten, F table \ər\ further \a\ ash \ā\ ace \ä\ mop, mar
\au̇\ out \ch\ chin \e\ bet \ē\ easy \g\ go \i\ hit \ī\ ice \j\ job
\ŋ\ sing \ō\ go \ȯ\ law \ȯi\ boy \th\ thin \t͟h\ the \ü\ loot \u̇\ foot
\y\ yet \zh\ vision \á, k̲, ⁿ, œ, œ̄, ue, ūe, ʸ\ *see* Guide to Pronunciation

Y \'wī\ *n, pl* **y's** *or* **ys** \'wīz\ *often cap, often attrib* (bef. 12c) **1 a** : the 25th letter of the English alphabet **b** : a graphic representation of this letter **c** : a speech counterpart of orthographic *y* **2** : a graphic device for reproducing the letter *y* **3** : one designated *y* esp. as the 25th in order or class or the second in order or class when x is made the first **4** : something shaped like the letter Y

Y \'wī\ *n* (ca. 1915) : YMCA, YWCA

¹-y *also* **-ey** \ē\ *in some dialects, esp Brit, Southern, & NewEng, often* i *but not shown at individual entries\ adj suffix* [ME, fr. OE *-ig;* akin to OHG *-ig -y,* L *-icus,* Gk *-ikos,* Skt *-ika*] **1 a** : characterized by : full of ⟨blossom*y*⟩ ⟨dirt*y*⟩ ⟨mudd*y*⟩ ⟨clay*y*⟩ **b** : having the character of : composed of ⟨ic*y*⟩ ⟨wax*y*⟩ **c** : like : like that of ⟨home*y*⟩ ⟨wintr*y*⟩ — often with a disparaging connotation ⟨stag*y*⟩ **2 a** : tending or inclined to ⟨sleep*y*⟩ ⟨chatt*y*⟩ **b** : giving occasion for (specified) action ⟨tear*y*⟩ **c** : performing (specified) action ⟨curl*y*⟩

²-y \same\ *n suffix, pl* **-ies** [ME *-ie,* fr. OF, fr. L *-ia,* fr. Gk *-ia, -eia*] **1** : state : condition : quality ⟨beggar*y*⟩ **2** : activity, place of business, or goods dealt with ⟨chandler*y*⟩ ⟨laundr*y*⟩ **3** : whole body or group ⟨soldier*y*⟩

³-y *n suffix, pl* **-ies** [ME *-ie,* fr. AF, fr. L *-ium*] : instance of a (specified) action ⟨entreat*y*⟩ ⟨inquir*y*⟩

⁴-y — see -IE

yab·ber \'ya-bər\ *n* [prob. modif. of Wuywurung (Australian aboriginal language of the Melbourne area) *yaba* speak] (1855) *Austral* : TALK, JABBER ⟨all ∼ and chatter ceased around the campfires —Francis Birtles⟩ — **yabber** *vi*

¹yacht \'yät\ *n* [obs. D *jaght,* fr. MLG *jacht,* short for *jachtschiff,* lit., hunting ship] (1557) : any of various recreational watercraft: as **a** : a sailboat used for racing **b** : a large usu. motor-driven craft used for pleasure cruising

²yacht *vi* (1836) : to race or cruise in a yacht

yacht club *n* (1834) : a club organized to promote and regulate yachting and boating

yacht·ing *n* (1836) : the action, fact, or pastime of racing or cruising in a yacht

yachts·man \'yäts-mən\ *n* (1862) : a person who owns or sails a yacht

YAG \'yag\ *n* [*y*ttrium *a*luminum *g*arnet] (1964) : a synthetic yttrium aluminum garnet of marked hardness and high refractive index that is used esp. as a gemstone and in laser technology

ya·gi \'yä-gē, 'ya-\ *n* [Hidetsugu *Yagi* b1886 Jp. engineer] (1943) : a highly directional and selective shortwave antenna consisting of a horizontal conductor of one or two dipoles connected with the receiver or transmitter and of a set of nearly equal insulated dipoles parallel to and on a level with the horizontal conductor

ya·hoo \'yä-(,)hü, 'yä-\ *n, pl* **yahoos** (1726) **1** *cap* : a member of a race of brutes in Swift's *Gulliver's Travels* who have the form and all the vices of humans **2** : a boorish, crass, or stupid person — **ya·hoo·ism** \-,i-zəm\ *n*

Yah·weh \'yä-(,)wā, -(,)vä\ *also* **Yah·veh** \-(,)vä\ *n* [Heb *Yahweh*] (1869) : GOD 1a — used esp. by the Hebrews; compare TETRAGRAMMATON

Yah·wism \-,wi-zəm, -,vi-\ *n* (1867) : the worship of Yahweh among the ancient Hebrews

Yah·wis·tic \yä-'wis-tik, -'vis-\ *adj* (1874) **1** : characterized by the use of *Yahweh* as the name of God **2** : of or relating to Yahwism

¹yak \'yak\ *n, pl* **yaks** *also* **yak** [Tibetan *gyagk*] (1795) : a large long-haired wild or domesticated ox (*Bos grunniens* syn. *B. mutus*) of Tibet and adjacent elevated parts of central Asia

²yak \'yak, 'yak\ *n* [imit.] (1948) **1** *slang* : LAUGH **2** *slang* : JOKE, GAG

³yak *also* **yack** *vi* **yakked** *also* **yacked;** **yak·king** *also* **yack·ing** [prob. imit.] (1949) : to talk persistently : CHATTER

⁴yak *also* **yack** \'yak\ *n* (1950) : persistent or voluble talk

Yak·i·ma \'ya-kə-,mó\ *n, pl* **Yakima** *or* **Yakimas** (1838) **1** : a member of a group of Shahaptian peoples of the lower Yakima River valley, south central Washington **2** : the language of the Yakima people

ya·ki·to·ri \,yä-ki-'tór-ē\ *n* [Jp, grilled chicken, fr. *yaki* broil, roast + *tori* bird] (1962) : bite-sized marinated pieces of beef, seafood, or chicken on skewers

y'all \'yôl\ *var of* YOU-ALL

yam \'yam\ *n* [earlier *iname,* fr. Pg *inhame* & Sp *ñame,* of African origin; akin to Fulani *nyami* to eat] (1657) **1** : the edible starchy tuberous root of various plants (genus *Dioscorea* of the family Dioscoreaceae) used as a staple food in tropical areas; *also* : a plant producing yams **2** : a moist-fleshed and usu. orange-fleshed sweet potato

ya·men \'yä-mən\ *n* [Chin (Beijing) *yámen*] (1747) : the headquarters or residence of a Chinese government official or department

yam·mer \'ya-mər\ *vi* **yam·mered; yam·mer·ing** \'ya-mə-riŋ, 'yam-riŋ\ [ME *yameren,* alter. of *yomeren* to murmur, be sad, fr. OE *gēomrian;* akin to OHG *jāmaron* to be sad] (15c) **1 a** : to utter repeated cries of distress or sorrow **b** : WHIMPER **2** : to utter persistent complaints : WHINE **3** : to talk persistently or volubly and often loudly ⟨caused the purists to ∼ for censorship —D. W. Maurer⟩ — **yammer** *n*

yang \'yäŋ, 'yaŋ\ *n* [Chin (Beijing) *yáng*] (1671) : the masculine active principle in nature that in Chinese cosmology is exhibited in light, heat, or dryness and that combines with yin to produce all that comes to be

¹yank \'yaŋk\ *n* [origin unknown] (ca. 1864) : a strong sudden pull : JERK

²yank *vi* (1822) : to pull on something with a quick vigorous movement ∼ *vt* **1** : to pull or extract with a quick vigorous movement **2** : to

remove in or as if in an abrupt manner ⟨∼ed the story from the evening edition⟩

Yank \'yaŋk\ *n* (1778) : YANKEE

¹Yan·kee \'yaŋ-kē\ *n* [origin unknown] (1758) **1 a** : a native or inhabitant of New England **b** : a native or inhabitant of the northern U.S. **2** : a native or inhabitant of the U.S. — **Yan·kee·dom** \-kē-dəm\ *n* — **Yan·kee·ism** \-kē-,i-zəm\ *n*

²Yankee (1952) — a communications code word for the letter *y*

Yan·kee–Doo·dle \,yaŋ-kē-'dü-d³l\ *n* [*Yankee Doodle,* popular song during the American Revolution] (1770) : YANKEE

yan·qui \'yäŋ-kē\ *n, often cap* [Sp, fr. E *¹Yankee*] (1928) : a citizen of the U.S. as distinguished from a Latin American

yan·tra \'yən-trə, 'yan-, 'yän-\ *n* [Skt] (1877) : a geometrical diagram used like an icon usu. in meditation

¹yap \'yap\ *vi* **yapped; yap·ping** [imit.] (1668) **1** : to bark snappishly : YELP **2** : to talk in a shrill insistent way : CHATTER — **yap·per** *n*

²yap *n* (1826) **1 a** : a quick sharp bark : YELP **b** : shrill insistent talk : CHATTER **2** : an unsophisticated, ignorant, or uncouth person : BUMPKIN **3** *slang* : MOUTH

Ya·qui \'yä-kē\ *n* (1861) **1** : a member of an American Indian people of Sonora, Mexico **2** : the Uto-Aztecan language of the Yaqui people

Yar·bor·ough \'yär-,bər-ə, -,bə-rə, -b(ə-)rə\ *n* [Charles Anderson Worsley, 2d Earl of *Yarborough* †1897 Eng. nobleman said to have bet a thousand to one against the dealing of such a hand] (1900) : a hand in bridge or whist containing no ace and no card higher than a nine

¹yard \'yärd\ *n* [ME, fr. OE *geard* enclosure, yard; akin to OHG *gart* enclosure, L *hortus* garden] (bef. 12c) **1 a** : a small usu. walled and often paved area open to the sky and adjacent to a building : COURT **b** : the grounds of a building or group of buildings **2** : the grounds immediately surrounding a house that are usu. covered with grass **3 a** : an enclosure for livestock (as poultry) **b** (1) : an area with its buildings and facilities set aside for a particular business or activity (2) : an assembly or storage area **c** : a system of tracks for storage and maintenance of cars and making up trains **4** : a locality in a forest where deer herd in winter

²yard *adj* (15c) **1** : of, relating to, or employed in the yard surrounding a building ⟨∼ light⟩ **2** : of, relating to, or employed in a railroad yard ⟨a ∼ engine⟩

³yard *vt* (1758) **1** : to drive into or confine in a restricted area : HERD, PEN **2** : to deliver to or store in a yard ∼ *vi* : to congregate in or as if in a yard

⁴yard *n* [ME *yarde,* fr. OE *gierd* twig, measure, yard; akin to OHG *gart* stick, L *hasta* spear] (bef. 12c) **1** : any of various units of measure: as **a** : a unit of length equal in the U.S. to 0.9144 meter — see WEIGHT table **b** : a unit of volume equal to a cubic yard **2 a** : a great length or quantity ⟨remembered ∼s of facts and figures⟩ **b** *slang* : one hundred dollars **3** : a long spar tapered toward the ends to support and spread the head of a square sail, lateen, or lugsail **4** : a slender horn= shaped glass about three feet tall; *also* : the amount it contains ⟨a ∼ of ale⟩ — **the whole nine yards** : all of a related set of circumstances, conditions, or details ⟨who could learn the most about making records, about electronics and engineering, *the whole nine yards* —Stephen Stills⟩ — sometimes used adverbially with *go* to indicate an all-out effort

¹yard·age \'yär-dij\ *n* [*¹yard*] (1867) **1** : the use of a livestock enclosure for animals in transit provided by a railroad at a station **2** : a charge made by a railroad for the use of a livestock enclosure

²yardage *n* [*⁴yard*] (1900) **1 a** : an aggregate number of yards **b** : the length, extent, or volume of something as measured in yards **2** : YARD GOODS

yard·arm \'yärd-,ärm\ *n* (1553) : either end of the yard of a square-rigged ship

yard·bird \-,bərd\ *n* [*¹yard*] (ca. 1941) **1** : a soldier assigned to a menial task or restricted to a limited area as a disciplinary measure **2** : an untrained or inept enlisted man

yard goods *n pl* (1905) : fabrics sold by the yard : PIECE GOODS

yard grass *n* [*¹yard*] (1822) : a coarse annual grass (*Eleusine indica*) with digitate spikes that is widely distributed as a weed — called also *goosegrass*

yard line *n* (1949) : any of a series of marked or imaginary lines one yard apart on a football field that are parallel to the goal lines and that indicate the distance to the nearest goal line

yard–long bean \'yärd-'lóŋ-\ *n* (1926) : the edible 1- to 3-foot (0.3- to 0.9- meter) long thin stringless fruit of a plant of a subspecies (*Vigna unguiculata sesquipedalis*) of the cowpea; *also* : the plant

yard·man \'yärd-mən, -,man\ *n* (ca. 1825) **1** : a person employed to do outdoor work (as mowing lawns) **2** : a person who works in the yard of a commercial establishment; *esp* : one who supervises the handling of building materials in a lumberyard **3** : a railroad hand employed in yard service

yard·mas·ter \-,mas-tər\ *n* (1864) : the person in charge of operations in a railroad yard

yard sale *n* (1972) : GARAGE SALE

yard·stick \'yärd-,stik\ *n* (1816) **1 a** : a graduated measuring stick three feet (0.9144 meter) long **b** : a standard basis of calculation **2** : a standard for making a critical judgment : CRITERION **syn** see STANDARD

yare \'yar, 'yer, 'yär\ *adj* [ME, fr. OE *gearu;* akin to OHG *garo* ready] (bef. 12c) **1** *archaic* : set for action : READY **2** *or* **yar** \'yär\ **a** : characterized by speed and agility : NIMBLE, LIVELY **b** : HANDY 1c, MANEUVERABLE — **yare** *adv, archaic* — **yare·ly** *adv, archaic*

yar·mul·ke *also* **yar·mel·ke** \'yä-mə-kə, 'yär-mə(l)-kə\ *n* [Yiddish *yarmlke,* fr. Pol *jarmułka* & Ukrainian *yarmulka* skullcap, of Turkic origin; akin to Turk *yağmurluk* rainwear] (1903) : a skullcap worn esp. by Orthodox and Conservative Jewish males in the synagogue and the home

¹yarn \'yärn\ *n* [ME, fr. OE *gearn;* akin to OHG *garn* yarn, Gk *chordē* string, L *hernia* rupture, Skt *hira* band] (bef. 12c) **1 a** : a continuous often plied strand composed of either natural or man-made fibers or filaments and used in weaving and knitting to form cloth **b** : a similar strand of another material (as metal, glass, or plastic) **2** : a narrative of adventures; *esp* : a tall tale

²yarn *vi* (1812) : to tell a yarn — **yarn·er** *n*

yarn–dye \'yärn-,dī\ *vt* (1885) : to dye before weaving or knitting

yar·row \'yar-(,)ō\ n [ME *yarowe,* fr. OE *gearwe;* akin to OHG *garwa* yarrow] (bef. 12c) : a widely naturalized strong-scented Eurasian composite herb (*Achillea millefolium*) with finely dissected leaves and small usu. white corymbose flowers; *also* : any of several congeneric plants
yash·mak *also* **yas·mak** \'yash-,mak, 'yas-\ n [Turk *yaşmak*] (1844) : a veil worn by Muslim women that is wrapped around the upper and lower parts of the face so that only the eyes remain exposed to public view
yat·a·ghan \'ya-tə-,gan, 'ya-ti-gən\ n [Turk *yatağan*] (1819) : a long knife or short saber that lacks a guard for the hand at the juncture of blade and hilt and that usu. has a double curve to the edge and a nearly straight back

yataghan

yauld \'yól(d)\ adj [origin unknown] (1786) *chiefly Scot* : VIGOROUS, ENERGETIC
yau·pon \'yü-,pän *also* 'yō-, 'yó-\ n [Catawba *yápa,* fr. *ya-* tree + *pa* leaf] (1709) : a holly (*Ilex vomitoria*) of the southeastern U.S. that has smooth elliptical leaves with emetic and purgative properties
yau·tia \'yaù-tē-ə\ n [AmerSp *yautia,* fr. Taino] (1899) : any of several aroid plants (genus *Xanthosoma* and esp. *X. sagittifolium*) chiefly of tropical America with starchy edible shaggy brown tubers that are cooked and eaten like yams or potatoes; *esp* : one of these tubers
¹**yaw** \'yó\ n [origin unknown] (1546) **1** : the action of yawing; *esp* : a side to side movement **2** : the extent of the movement in yawing
²**yaw** vi (1586) **1 a** *of a ship* : to deviate erratically from a course (as when struck by a heavy sea); *esp* : to move from side to side **b** *of an airplane, spacecraft, or projectile* : to turn by angular motion about the vertical axis **2** : ALTERNATE ⟨restlessly ~ing between apparent extremes —Martin Kasindorf⟩
yawl \'yól\ n [LG *jolle*] (1670) **1** : a ship's small boat : JOLLY BOAT **2** : a fore-and-aft rigged sailboat carrying a mainsail and one or more jibs with a mizzenmast far aft
¹**yawn** \'yón, 'yän\ vb [ME *yenen, yanen,* fr. OE *ginian;* akin to OHG *ginēn* to yawn, L *hiare,* Gk *chainein*] vi (bef. 12c) **1** : to open wide : GAPE **2** : to open the mouth wide usu. as an involuntary reaction to fatigue or boredom ~ vt **1** : to utter with a yawn **2** : to accomplish with or impel by yawns ⟨his grandchildren ~ed him to bed —L. L. King⟩
²**yawn** n (1602) **1** : GAP, CAVITY **2** : a deep usu. involuntary intake of breath through the wide open mouth often as an involuntary reaction to fatigue or boredom; *also* : a reaction resembling a yawn ⟨a . . . success at the box office but drew only ~s from critics —*Current Biog.*⟩ **3** : ⁵BORE
yawn·er n (1687) **1** : one that yawns **2** : something that causes boredom ⟨the show was a real ~⟩
yawn·ing adj (bef. 12c) **1** : wide open : CAVERNOUS ⟨a ~ hole⟩ ⟨a dreadful, ~ gap of . . . weeks —*Times Educational Supp.*⟩ **2** : showing fatigue or boredom by yawns ⟨a ~ audience⟩ — **yawn·ing·ly** \'yó-niŋ-lē\ adv
¹**yawp** *or* **yaup** \'yóp\ vi [ME *yolpen*] (14c) **1** : to make a raucous noise : SQUAWK **2** : CLAMOR, COMPLAIN — **yawp·er** n
²**yawp** *also* **yaup** n (1824) **1** : a raucous noise : SQUAWK **2** : something suggestive of a raucous noise; *specif* : rough vigorous language
yawp·ing n (1876) : a strident utterance
yaws \'yóz\ n pl but sing or pl in constr [prob. fr. an English-based creole of the Caribbean] (1679) : an infectious contagious tropical disease caused by a spirochete (*Treponema pertenue*) closely resembling the causative agent of syphilis and marked by ulcerating lesions with later bone involvement — called also *frambesia*
y–ax·is \'wī-,ak-səs\ n (1875) **1** : the axis of a plane Cartesian coordinate system parallel to which ordinates are measured **2** : one of the three axes in a three-dimensional rectangular coordinate system
Y chromosome n (1911) : a sex chromosome that is characteristic of male cells in species in which the male typically has two unlike sex chromosomes — compare X CHROMOSOME
yclept *or* **ycleped** [ME, fr. OE *geclipod,* pp. of *clipian* to cry out, name] *past part of* CLEPE
y–co·or·di·nate \,wī-kō-'órd-nət, -'ór-d³n-ət, -də-,nāt\ n (1927) : a coordinate whose value is determined by measuring parallel to a y-axis; *specif* : ORDINATE
¹**ye** \'yē\ pron [ME, fr. OE *gē;* akin to OHG *ir* you — more at YOU] (bef. 12c) : YOU 1 — used orig. only as a plural pronoun of the second person in the subjective case and now used esp. in ecclesiastical or literary language and in various English dialects
²**ye** \yē, yə; *orig same as* ¹THE\ *definite article* [alter. of ME *þe* the, fr. OE *þē;* fr. the use of the letter *y* by printers and scribes of late ME to represent *þ* (*th*) of earlier manuscripts] (1551) *archaic* : THE ⟨*Ye* Olde Gifte Shoppe⟩
¹**yea** \'yā\ adv [ME *ye,* *ya,* fr. OE *gēa;* akin to OHG *jā*] (bef. 12c) **1** : YES — used in oral voting **2** : more than this : not only so but — used as a function word to introduce a more explicit or emphatic phrase ⟨yet the impression, ~ the evidence, is inescapable —J. G. Harrison⟩
²**yea** n (13c) **1** : AFFIRMATION, ASSENT **2 a** : an affirmative vote **b** : a person casting a yea vote
yeah \'ye-ə, 'yeù, 'ya-ə\ adv [by alter.] (1902) : YES
yean \'yēn, ēn\ vi [ME *yenen,* fr. (assumed) OE *geēanian,* fr. OE *ge-,* perfective prefix + *ēanian* to yean; akin to L *agnus* lamb, Gk *amnos*] (1548) : to bring forth young — used of a sheep or goat
yean·ling \-liŋ, -lən\ n (1637) : LAMB, KID 1a
year \'yir\ n [ME *yere,* fr. OE *gēar;* akin to OHG *jār* year, Gk *hōros* year, *hōra* season, hour] (bef. 12c) **1 a** : the period of about 365¼ solar days required for one revolution of the earth around the sun **b** : the time required for the apparent sun to return to an arbitrary fixed or moving reference point in the sky **c** : the time in which a planet completes a revolution about the sun ⟨a ~ of Jupiter⟩ **2 a** : a cycle in the Gregorian calendar of 365 or 366 days divided into 12 months

beginning with January and ending with December **b** : a period of time equal to one year of the Gregorian calendar but beginning at a different time **3** : a calendar year specified usu. by a number ⟨died in the ~ 1900⟩ **4** pl : a time or era having a special significance ⟨their glory ~s⟩ **5 a** : 12 months that constitute a measure of age or duration ⟨her 21st ~⟩ — often used in combination ⟨a *year*-old child⟩ **b** pl : AGE ⟨an adult in ~s but a child in understanding⟩; *also* : the final stage of the normal life span **6** : a period of time (as the usu. nine-month period in which a school is in session) other than a calendar year
year–book \-,bùk\ n (1710) **1** : a book published yearly as a report or summary of statistics or facts : ANNUAL **2** : a school publication that is compiled usu. by a graduating class and that serves as a record of the year's activities
¹**year–end** \'yir-'end\ n (1872) : the end of usu. the fiscal year
²**year–end** adj (1899) : made, occurring, or existing at the year-end ⟨a ~ report⟩
year·ling \'yir-liŋ, 'yər-lən\ n (15c) : one that is a year old: as **a** : an animal one year old or in the second year of its age **b** : a racehorse between January 1st of the year after the year in which it was foaled and the next January 1st — **yearling** adj
year-long \'yir-'lóŋ\ adj (1813) : lasting through a year
¹**year·ly** \'yir-lē\ adj (bef. 12c) **1** : reckoned by the year **2** : occurring, appearing, made, done, or acted upon every year or once a year : ANNUAL
²**yearly** adv (bef. 12c) : every year : ANNUALLY
Yearly Meeting n (1688) : an organization uniting several Quarterly Meetings of the Society of Friends
yearn \'yərn\ vi [ME *yernen,* fr. OE *giernan;* akin to OHG *gerōn* to desire, L *hortari* to urge, encourage, Gk *chairein* to rejoice] (bef. 12c) **1** : to long persistently, wistfully, or sadly **2** : to feel tenderness or compassion *syn* see LONG — **yearn·er** n — **yearn·ing·ly** \'yər-niŋ-lē\ adv
yearn·ing n (bef. 12c) : a tender or urgent longing
year of grace (14c) : a calendar year of the Christian era ⟨the *year of grace* 1993⟩
year–round \'yir-'raùnd\ adj (1924) : occurring, effective, employed, staying, or operating for the full year : not seasonal ⟨a ~ resort⟩ — **year–round** adv — in the year round
yea–say·er \'yā-,sā-ər, -,se(-ə)r\ n (1920) **1** : one whose attitude is that of confident affirmation **2** : YES-MAN
¹**yeast** \'yēst, *esp Southern & Midland* 'ēst\ n [ME *yest,* fr. OE *gist;* akin to OHG *jesen, gesen* to ferment, Gk *zein* to boil] (bef. 12c) **1 a** : a yellowish surface froth or sediment that occurs esp. in saccharine liquids (as fruit juices) in which it promotes alcoholic fermentation, consists largely of cells of a fungus (family Saccharomycetaceae), and is used esp. in the making of alcoholic liquors and as a leaven in baking **b** : a commercial product containing yeast plants in a moist or dry medium **c** (1) : a minute fungus (esp. *Saccharomyces cerevisiae*) that is present and functionally active in yeast, usu. has little or no mycelium, and reproduces by budding (2) : any of various similar fungi (esp. orders Endomycetales and Moniliales) **2** archaic : the foam or spume of waves **3** : something that causes ferment or activity ⟨were all seething with the ~ of revolt —J. F. Dobie⟩
²**yeast** n (1819) : FERMENT, FROTH
yeasty \'yē-stē, 'ē-stē\ adj **yeast·i·er; -est** (1598) **1** : of, relating to, or resembling yeast **2 a** : IMMATURE, UNSETTLED **b** : marked by change **c** : full of vitality **d** : FRIVOLOUS 1a, 2 — **yeast·i·ness** \-stē-nəs\ n
yech *or* **yecch** \'yək, 'yək, 'yek, 'yek\ *interj* (1969) — used to express rejection or disgust
yegg \'yeg, 'yāg\ n [origin unknown] (1903) : SAFECRACKER; *also* : ROBBER
¹**yell** \'yel\ vb [ME, fr. OE *giellan;* akin to OHG *gellan* to yell, OE *galan* to sing] vi (bef. 12c) **1** : to utter a loud cry, scream, or shout **2** : to give a cheer usu. in unison ~ vt : to utter or declare with or as if with a yell : SHOUT — **yell·er** n
²**yell** n (14c) **1** : SCREAM, SHOUT **2** : a usu. rhythmic cheer used esp. in schools or colleges to encourage athletic teams
¹**yel·low** \'ye-(,)lō, *dial* 'ye-lər *or* 'ya-\ adj [ME *yelwe, yelow,* fr. OE *geolu;* akin to OHG *gelo* yellow, L *helvus* light bay, Gk *chlōros* greenish yellow, Skt *hari* yellowish] (bef. 12c) **1 a** : of the color yellow **b** : become yellowish through age, disease, or discoloration : SALLOW **c** : having a yellow or light brown complexion or skin **2 a** : featuring sensational or scandalous items or ordinary news sensationally distorted ⟨~ journalism⟩ **b** : MEAN, COWARDLY — **yel·low·ish** \'ye-lə-wish\ adj
²**yellow** n (bef. 12c) **1** : something yellow or marked by a yellow color: as **a** : a person having yellow or light brown skin **b** : the yolk of an egg **2 a** : a color whose hue resembles that of ripe lemons or sunflowers or is that of the portion of the spectrum lying between green and orange **b** : a pigment or dye that colors yellow **3** pl : JAUNDICE **4** pl but sing in constr : any of several plant diseases caused esp. by mycoplasma-like organisms and marked by yellowing of the foliage and stunting
³**yellow** vt (1598) : to make yellow : give a yellow tinge or color to ⟨~ed by time⟩ ~ vi : to become or turn yellow
yellow bile n (1881) : a humor believed in medieval physiology to be secreted by the liver and to cause irascibility
yellow birch n (1787) : a No. American birch (*Betula alleghaniensis* syn. *B. lutea*) with thin lustrous gray or yellow bark forming plates with ragged edges in older trees; *also* : its strong hard dark brown to reddish brown wood
yel·low–dog \,ye-lō-'dóg, -lə-'dóg\ adj (1880) **1** : MEAN, CONTEMPTIBLE **2** : of or relating to opposition to trade unionism or a labor union
yellow–dog contract n (1920) : an employment contract in which a worker disavows membership in and agrees not to join a labor union in order to get a job

\ə\ abut \³\ kitten, F table \ər\ further \a\ ash \ā\ ace \ä\ mop, mar \aù\ out \ch\ chin \e\ bet \ē\ easy \g\ go \i\ hit \ī\ ice \j\ job \ŋ\ sing \ō\ go \ò\ law \òi\ boy \th\ thin \th\ the \ü\ loot \ù\ foot \y\ yet \zh\ vision \à, k̲, ⁿ, œ, œ̄, ʉe, ʉ̄e, ᵘ\ see Guide to Pronunciation

yellow dwarf *n* (1928) : any of several virus diseases esp. of cereal grasses (as oats and barley) characterized by yellowing and stunting

yellow fever *n* (1739) : an acute destructive infectious disease of warm regions marked by sudden onset, prostration, fever, albuminuria, jaundice, and often hemorrhage and caused by a virus transmitted by the yellow-fever mosquito

yellow–fever mosquito *n* (1905) : a small dark-colored mosquito (*Aedes aegypti*) that is the usual vector of yellow fever

yel·low·fin tuna \'ye-lō-,fin-, 'ye-lə-\ *n* (1922) : a rather small and nearly cosmopolitan tuna (*Thunnus albacares*) with yellowish fins — called also *yellowfin*

yellow–green alga *n* (1930) : any of a class (Xanthophyceae of the division Chrysophyta) of algae with the chlorophyll masked by brown or yellow pigment

yel·low·ham·mer \'ye-lō-,ha-mər, 'ye-lə-\ *n* [alter. of earlier *yelambre*, fr. (assumed) ME *yelwambre*, fr. ME *yelwe* yellow + (assumed) ME *ambre* yellowhammer, fr. OE *amore*; akin to OHG *amaro* yellowhammer, *amari* emmer] (1556) 1 : a common Palearctic finch (*Emberiza citrinella*) having the male largely bright yellow — called also *yellow bunting*   2 : YELLOW-SHAFTED FLICKER

yellow jack *n* (1836) 1 : YELLOW FEVER   2 : a yellowish carangid marine food fish (*Caranx bartholomaei*) found from Massachusetts to Brazil

yellow jacket *n* (1796) 1 : any of various small yellow-marked vespid wasps (esp. genus *Vespula*) that commonly nest in the ground and can sting repeatedly and painfully   2 *slang* : pentobarbital esp. in a yellow capsule

yellow jessamine *n* (1709) : a twining evergreen shrub (*Gelsemium sempervirens* of the family Loganiaceae) with fragrant yellow flowers — called also *yellow jasmine*

yel·low·legs \'ye-lō-,legz, 'ye-lə-, -,lāgz\ *n pl but sing or pl in constr* (1772) : either of two American shorebirds with yellow legs: a : GREATER YELLOWLEGS   b : LESSER YELLOWLEGS

yellow ocher *n* (15c) 1 : a mixture of limonite usu. with clay and silica used as a pigment   2 : a moderate orange yellow

yellow pages *n pl, often cap Y&P* (1952) : the section of a telephone book that lists business and professional firms alphabetically by category and that includes classified advertising; *also* : a listing of products or services that is independently published

yellow perch *n* (1805) : a common No. American freshwater bony fish (*Perca flavescens*) of the perch family that is yellowish with dark green bands and is an excellent food and sport fish

yellow peril *n, often cap Y&P* (1898) 1 : a danger to Western civilization held to arise from expansion of the power and influence of eastern Asian peoples   2 : a threat to Western living standards from the influx of eastern Asian laborers willing to work for very low wages

yellow pine *n* (1709) 1 : any of several No. American pines (as a Ponderosa pine or longleaf pine) with yellowish wood   2 : the wood of a yellow pine

yellow poplar *n* (1774) 1 : TULIP TREE 1   2 : TULIPWOOD 1

yellow rain *n* (1979) : a yellow substance reported to occur as a mist or as spots on rocks and vegetation in Southeast Asia and variously held to be a chemical warfare agent used in the Vietnam War or a natural substance similar if not identical to pollen or the feces of bees

yel·low–shaft·ed flicker \'ye-lō-,shaf-təd-, 'ye-lə-\ *n* (1888) : a flicker of eastern No. America that is golden yellow on the underside of the tail and wings, has a red mark on the nape, and in the male has a black streak on each cheek

yellow spot *n* (1869) : MACULA LUTEA

yel·low·tail \'ye-lō-,tāl, 'ye-lə-\ *n, pl* **yellowtail** *or* **yellowtails** (1709) : any of various fishes having a yellow or yellowish tail: as a : any of several carangid fishes (genus *Seriola*); *esp* : a sport fish (*S. lalandei*) of the California coast and southward that reaches a length of about three feet (one meter)   b : SILVER PERCH a   c : a common snapper (*Ocyurus chrysurus*) that is a sport and food fish of the tropical western Atlantic and West Indies and is olive above and broadly striped with yellow along the sides and on the tail — called also *yellowtail snapper*

yel·low·throat \-,thrōt\ *n* (1702) : any of several largely olive American warblers (genus *Geothlypis*); *esp* : one (*G. trichas*) with yellow breast and throat and a whitish belly

yel·low·ware \-,war, -,wer\ *n* (1785) : pottery made from buff clay and covered with a yellowish transparent glaze

yel·low·wood \-,wud\ *n* (1666) 1 : any of various trees having yellowish wood or yielding a yellow extract; *esp* : a leguminous tree (*Cladrastis lutea*) of the southern U.S. having showy white fragrant flowers and yielding a yellow dye   2 : the wood of a yellowwood tree

¹yelp \'yelp\ *n* [²*yelp*] (1501) : a sharp shrill bark or cry (as of a dog); *also* : SQUEAL

²yelp *vb* [ME, to boast, cry out, fr. OE *gielpan* to boast, exult; akin to OHG *gelph* outcry] *vi* (1553) : to utter a sharp quick shrill cry ⟨dogs ~⟩ ~ *vt* : to utter a yelp

yelp·er \'yel-pər\ *n* (1673) 1 : one that yelps; esp : a yelping dog   2 : an instrument used by hunters to produce a call or whistle imitating the yelp of the wild turkey hen

¹yen \'yen\ *n, pl* **yen** [Jp *en*] (1875) — see MONEY table

²yen *n* [obs. E argot *yen-yen* craving for opium, fr. Chin (Guangdong) *yin-yáhn*, fr. *yin* opium + *yáhn* craving] (1906) : a strong desire or propensity : LONGING; *also* : URGE

³yen *vi* **yenned; yen·ning** (1919) : to have an intense desire : LONG, YEARN

yen–shee \'yen-'shē\ *n* [Chin (Guangdong) *yin-sí*, fr. *yin* opium + *sí* excrement, filth] (1882) : the residue formed in the bowl of an opium pipe by smoking

yen·ta \'yen-tə\ *n* [Yiddish *yente*, fr. the name *Yente*] (1923) : one that meddles; *also* : BLABBERMOUTH, GOSSIP

yeo·man \'yō-mən\ *n* [ME *yoman*] (14c) 1 a : an attendant or officer in a royal or noble household   b : a person attending or assisting another : RETAINER   c : YEOMAN OF THE GUARD   d : a naval petty officer who performs clerical duties   2 a : a person who owns and cultivates a small farm; *specif* : one belonging to a class of English freeholders below the gentry   b : a person of the social rank of yeoman   3 : one that performs great and loyal service ⟨did a ~'s job in seeing the program through⟩

¹yeo·man·ly \-lē\ *adv* (14c) *archaic* : in a manner befitting a yeoman : BRAVELY

²yeomanly *adj* (1576) 1 : of, relating to, or having the rank of a yeoman   2 : becoming or suitable to a yeoman : STURDY, LOYAL

yeoman of the guard *n* (ca. 1520) : a member of a military corps attached to the British royal household that serves as ceremonial attendants of the sovereign and as warders of the Tower of London

yeo·man·ry \'yō-mən-rē\ *n* (14c) 1 : the body of yeomen; *specif* : the body of small landed proprietors of the middle class   2 : a British volunteer cavalry force created from yeomen in 1761 as a home defense force and reorganized in 1907 as part of the territorial force

yep \'yep, *or with glottal stop instead of p*\ *adv* [by alter.] (1891) : YES

-yer — see -ER

yer·ba ma·té \,yer-bə-'mä-,tā, ,yer-\ *n* [AmerSp *yerba mate*, fr. *yerba* herb + *mate* maté] (1839) : MATÉ

¹yerk \'yərk\ *vt* [ME, to bind tightly] (ca. 1520) 1 *dial* : to beat vigorously : THRASH   2 *dial* : to attack or excite vigorously : GOAD

²yerk *n* (1581) 1 *Scot* : a lashing out : KICK   2 *dial* : JERK 1

¹yes \'yes\ *adv* [ME, fr. OE *gēse*] (bef. 12c) 1 — used as a function word to express assent or agreement ⟨are you ready? *Yes,* I am⟩   2 — used as a function word usu. to introduce correction or contradiction of a negative assertion or direction ⟨don't say that! *Yes,* I will⟩   3 — used as a function word to introduce a more emphatic or explicit phrase   4 — used as a function word to indicate uncertainty or polite interest or attentiveness

²yes *n* (1712) : an affirmative reply : YEA

ye·shi·va *also* **ye·shi·vah** \yə-'shē-və\ *n, pl* **yeshivas** *or* **ye·shi·vot** \-,shē-'vōt, -'vōth\ [LHeb *yĕshibhāh*] (1851) 1 : a school for talmudic study   2 : an Orthodox Jewish rabbinical seminary   3 : a Jewish day school providing secular and religious instruction

yes–man \'yes-,man\ *n* (1913) : a person who agrees with everything that is said; *esp* : one who endorses or supports without criticism every opinion or proposal of an associate or superior

yes·ter \'yes-tər\ *adj* (1577) *archaic* : of or relating to yesterday

¹yes·ter·day \'yes-tər-dē, -(,)dā\ *adv* [ME *yesterday*, fr. OE *giestran dæg*, fr. *giestran* yesterday + *dæg* day; akin to OHG *gestaron* yesterday, L *heri*, Gk *chthes*] (bef. 12c) 1 : on the day last past : on the day preceding today   2 : at a time not long past : only a short time ago ⟨I wasn't born ~⟩ — **yesterday** *adj*

²yesterday *n* (bef. 12c) 1 : the day last past : the day next before the present   2 : recent time : time not long past   3 : past time — usu. used in pl.

¹yes·ter·night \'yes-tər-,nīt\ *adv* [ME, fr. OE *gystran niht*, fr. *giestran* yesterday + *niht* night] (bef. 12c) *archaic* : on the night last past

²yesternight *n* (1513) : the night last past

yes·ter·year \'yes-tər-,yir\ *n* [*yesterday* + *year*] (1870) 1 : last year   2 : time gone by; *esp* : the recent past — **yesteryear** *adv*

yes·treen \ye-'strēn\ *n* [ME (Sc) *yistrevin*, fr. *yisterday* + *evin* evening, alter. of ME *even*] (1785) *chiefly Scot* : last evening or night — **yestreen** *adv*

¹yet \'yet\ *adv* [ME, fr. OE *giet*; akin to OFris *ieta* yet] (bef. 12c) 1 a : in addition : BESIDES ⟨gives ~ another reason⟩   b : EVEN 2c ⟨a ~ higher speed⟩   c : on top of everything else : no less ⟨had wells going dry. Between two large lakes, ~ —J. H. Buzard⟩   2 a (1) : up to now : so far ⟨hasn't done much ~⟩ — often used to imply the negative of a following infinitive ⟨have ~ to win a game⟩   (2) : at this or that time : so soon as now ⟨not time to go ~⟩   b : continuously up to the present or a specified time : STILL ⟨is ~ a new country⟩   c : at a future time : EVENTUALLY ⟨may ~ see the light⟩   3 : NEVERTHELESS, HOWEVER — as yet : up to the present or a specified time — **yet again** : one more time ⟨arrived late *yet again*⟩

²yet *conj* (13c) : but nevertheless : BUT

ye·ti \'ye-tē, 'yā-\ *n* [Tibetan] (1937) : ABOMINABLE SNOWMAN

yeuk \'yük\ *vi* [ME (northern) *yukyn*, fr. OE *giccan* — more at ITCH] (15c) *chiefly Scot* : ITCH

yew \'yü\ *n* [ME *ew*, fr. OE *īw*; akin to OHG *īwa* yew, MIr *eó*] (bef. 12c) 1 a : any of a genus (*Taxus* of the family Taxaceae, the yew family) of evergreen trees and shrubs with stiff linear leaves and fruit with a fleshy aril: as   (1) : a long-lived Eurasian tree or shrub (*T. baccata*) — called also *English yew*   (2) : a low straggling bush (*T. canadensis*) of the eastern U.S. and Canada   b : the wood of a yew; *esp* : the heavy fine-grained wood of English yew   2 *archaic* : an archery bow made of yew

Ygerne \ē-'gern\ *n* : IGRAINE

Ygg·dra·sil \'ig-drə-,sil\ *n* [ON] : a huge ash tree in Norse mythology that overspreads the world and binds earth, hell, and heaven together

yew 1a

YHWH \'yä-(,)wä, -(,)vä\ *n* : YAHWEH — compare TETRAGRAMMATON

Yid \'yid\ *n* [Yiddish, fr. MHG *Jüde*, fr. OHG *Judeo*, fr. L *Judaeus* — more at JEW] (ca. 1874) : JEW — usu. taken to be offensive

Yid·dish \'yi-dish\ *n* [Yiddish *yidish*, short for *yidish daytsh*, lit., Jewish German, fr. MHG *jüdisch diutsch*, fr. *jüdisch* Jewish (fr. *Jude* Jew) + *diutsch* German] (1886) : a High German language written in Hebrew characters that is spoken by Jews and descendants of Jews of central and eastern European origin — **Yiddish** *adj*

Yid·dish·ism \'yi-di-,shi-zəm\ *n* (1904) 1 : a usage, word, phrase, or idiom peculiar to Yiddish   2 : a movement characterized by advocacy of the Yiddish language and culture — **Yid·dish·ist** \-shist\ *n or adj*

¹yield \'yē(ə)ld\ *vb* [ME, fr. OE *gieldan*; akin to OHG *geltan* to pay] *vt* (bef. 12c) 1 *archaic* : RECOMPENSE, REWARD   2 : to give or render as fitting, rightfully owed, or required   3 : to give up possession of on claim or demand: as   a : to give up (as one's breath) and so die   b : to surrender or relinquish to the physical control of another : hand over possession of   c : to surrender or submit (oneself) to another   d : to give (oneself) up to an inclination, temptation, or habit   e : to relinquish one's possession of (as a position of advantage or point of superiority) ⟨~ precedence⟩   4 a : to bear or bring forth as a natural product esp. as a result of cultivation ⟨the tree always ~s good fruit⟩   b : to produce or furnish as return ⟨this soil should ~ good crops⟩   c   (1)

: to produce as return from an expenditure or investment : furnish as profit or interest ⟨a bond that ~s 12 percent⟩ (2) : to produce as revenue : BRING IN ⟨the tax is expected to ~ millions⟩ 5 : to give up (as a hit or run) in baseball ⟨~ed two runs in the third inning⟩ ~ vi 1 : to be fruitful or productive : BEAR, PRODUCE 2 : to give up and cease resistance or contention : SUBMIT, SUCCUMB 3 : to give way to pressure or influence : submit to urging, persuasion, or entreaty 4 : to give way under physical force (as bending, stretching, or breaking) 5 a : to give place or precedence : acknowledge the superiority of someone else b : to be inferior ⟨our dictionary ~s to none⟩ c : to give way to or become succeeded by someone or something else 6 : to relinquish the floor of a legislative assembly

syn YIELD, SUBMIT, CAPITULATE, SUCCUMB, RELENT, DEFER mean to give way to someone or something that one can no longer resist. YIELD may apply to any sort or degree of giving way before force, argument, persuasion, or entreaty ⟨yields too easily in any argument⟩. SUBMIT suggests full surrendering after resistance or conflict to the will or control of another ⟨a repentant sinner vowing to submit to the will of God⟩. CAPITULATE stresses the fact of ending all resistance and may imply either a coming to terms (as with an adversary) or hopelessness in the face of an irresistible opposing force ⟨officials capitulated to the protesters' demands⟩. SUCCUMB implies weakness and helplessness to the one that gives way or an overwhelming power to the opposing force ⟨a stage actor succumbing to the lure of Hollywood⟩. RELENT implies a yielding through pity or mercy by one who holds the upper hand ⟨finally relented and let the children stay up late⟩. DEFER implies a voluntary yielding or submitting out of respect or reverence for or deference and affection toward another ⟨I defer to your superior expertise in these matters⟩. syn see in addition RELINQUISH

²yield n (15c) 1 : something yielded : PRODUCT; esp : the amount or quantity produced or returned ⟨~ of wheat per acre⟩ 2 : the capacity of yielding produce

yield·er \'yēl-dər\ n (1590) : one that yields: as a : a person who surrenders, concedes, or gives in b : something that yields produce or products

yield·ing \-diŋ\ adj (1533) 1 : PRODUCTIVE ⟨a high-yielding wheat⟩ 2 : lacking rigidity or stiffness : FLEXIBLE 3 : disposed to submit or comply

yikes \'yīks\ interj [prob. alter. of yoicks] (1957) — used to express fear or astonishment

yin \'yin\ n [Chin (Beijing) yīn] (1671) : the feminine passive principle in nature that in Chinese cosmology is exhibited in darkness, cold, or wetness and that combines with yang to produce all that comes to be

Yin·glish \'yin-glish, -lish\ n [blend of Yiddish and English] (1951) : English marked by numerous borrowings from Yiddish

y–in·ter·cept \'wī-'in-tər-,sept\ n (ca. 1939) : the y-coordinate of a point where a line, curve, or surface intersects the y-axis

yip \'yip\ vi yipped; yip·ping [imit.] (1907) 1 : to bark sharply, quickly, and often continuously 2 : to utter a short sharp cry — yip n

yip·pee \'yi-pē\ interj (1914) — used to express exuberant delight or triumph

yip·pie \'yi-pē\ n [Youth International Party + -ie (as in hippie)] (1968) : a person belonging to or identified with a politically active group of hippies

yips \'yips\ n pl [origin unknown] (1962) : a state of nervous tension affecting an athlete (as a golfer) in the performance of a crucial action ⟨had a bad case of the ~ on short putts⟩

-yl \'əl, ²l, (,)il, ,ēl, chiefly Brit ,il\ n comb form [Gk hylē matter, material, lit., wood] : chemical and usu. univalent group ⟨ethyl⟩

ylang–ylang \,ē-,läŋ-'ē-,läŋ\ n [Tag] (1876) 1 : a tree (Cananga odorata syn. Canangium odoratum) of the custard-apple family of the Malay Archipelago, the Philippines, and adjacent areas that has very fragrant greenish yellow flowers 2 : a perfume distilled from the flowers of the ylang-ylang tree

YMCA \,wī-,em-(,)sē-'ā\ n [Young Men's Christian Association] (1881) : an international organization that promotes the spiritual, intellectual, social, and physical welfare orig. of young men

YMHA \,wī-,em-,ā-'chā\ n [Young Men's Hebrew Association] (1918) : an organization that promotes the religious, intellectual, social, and physical welfare of Jewish young men

Ymir \'ē-,mir\ n [ON] : a giant from whose body the gods create the world in Norse mythology

yo \'yō\ interj [ME yo, io, interj.] (15c) — used esp. to call attention, to indicate attentiveness, or to express affirmation

yob \'yäb\ n [backward spelling for boy] (1908) Brit : YOBBO

yob·bo \'yä-bō\ n, pl yobbos or yobboes [yob + ¹-o] (1922) 1 Brit : LOUT, YOKEL 2 Brit : HOODLUM

yock \'yäk\ var of ²YAK

yod \'yōd, 'yud\ n [Heb yōdh] (1735) : the 10th letter of the Hebrew alphabet — see ALPHABET table

¹yo·del \'yō-dᵊl\ vb -deled or -delled; -del·ing or -del·ling \'yōd-liŋ, 'yō-dᵊl-iŋ\ [G jodeln] vi (1838) : to sing by suddenly changing from a natural voice to a falsetto and back; also : to shout or call in a similar manner ~ vt : to sing (a tune) by yodeling — yo·del·er \'yōd-lər, 'yō-dᵊl-ər\ n

²yodel n (1849) : a song or refrain sung by yodeling; also : a yodeled shout or cry

yo·ga \'yō-gə\ n [Skt, lit., yoking, fr. yunakti he yokes; akin to L jungere to join — more at YOKE] (1820) 1 cap : a Hindu theistic philosophy teaching the suppression of all activity of body, mind, and will in order that the self may realize its distinction from them and attain liberation 2 : a system of exercises for attaining bodily or mental control and well-being — yo·gic \-gik\ adj, often cap

yogh \'yōk, 'yōg, 'yóḥ\ n [ME] (14c) : the letter ȝ used esp. in Middle English chiefly to represent voiced and voiceless velar and palatal fricatives

yo·gi \'yō-gē\ also yo·gin \-gən, -,gin\ n [Skt yogin, fr. yoga] (1619) 1 : a person who practices yoga 2 cap : an adherent of Yoga philosophy 3 : a markedly reflective or mystical person

yo·gurt also yo·ghurt \'yō-gərt\ n [Turk yoğurt] (1625) : a fermented slightly acid often flavored semisolid food made of whole or skimmed cow's milk and milk solids to which cultures of two bacteria (Lactobacillus bulgaricus and Streptococcus thermophilus) have been added

yo·him·bine \yō-'him-,bēn, -bən\ n [ISV, fr. yohimbé, a tropical Afri-

can tree (Corynanthe yohimbe) from which it is obtained] (1898) : an alkaloid $C_{21}H_{26}N_2O_3$ that is a weak blocker of alpha-adrenergic receptors and has been used as an aphrodisiac

yoicks \'yóiks\ interj (1774) — used as a cry of encouragement to fox-hounds

¹yoke \'yōk\ n, pl yokes [ME yok, fr. OE geoc; akin to OHG joh yoke, L jugum, Gk zygon, Skt yuga, L jungere to join] (bef. 12c) 1 a : a wooden bar or frame by which two draft animals (as oxen) are joined at the heads or necks for working together b : an arched device formerly laid on the neck of a defeated person c : a frame fitted to a person's shoulders to carry a load in two equal portions d : a bar by which the end of the tongue of a wagon or carriage is suspended from the collars of the harness e (1) : a crosspiece on the head of a boat's rudder (2) : the control device for an airplane's ailerons that is mounted on a column which also serves to operate the elevator f : a frame from which a bell is hung g : a clamp or similar piece that embraces two parts to hold or unite them in position 2 pl usu yoke : two animals yoked or worked together 3 a (1) : an oppressive agency (2) : SERVITUDE, BONDAGE b : TIE, LINK; esp : MARRIAGE 4 : a fitted or shaped piece at the top of a skirt or at the shoulder of various garments

²yoke vb yoked; yok·ing vt (bef. 12c) 1 a (1) : to put a yoke on (2) : to join in or with a yoke b : to attach a draft animal to; also : to attach (a draft animal) to something 2 : to join as if by a yoke 3 : to put to work ~ vi : to become joined or linked

yoke·fel·low \'yōk-,fe-(,)lō\ n (1526) : a close companion : MATE

yo·kel \'yō-kəl\ n [perh. fr. E dial. yokel green woodpecker, of imit. origin] (ca. 1812) : a naive or gullible inhabitant of a rural area or small town

yolk \'yōk, 'yelk (in cultivated speech, esp Southern), also 'yōlk, 'yólk, 'yälk, 'yəlk\ also yoke \'yōk\ n [ME yolke, fr. OE geoloca, fr. geolu yellow — more at YELLOW] (bef. 12c) 1 a : the yellow spheroidal mass of stored food that forms the inner portion of the egg of a bird or reptile and is surrounded by the white — see EGG illustration b archaic : the whole contents of an ovum consisting of a protoplasmic formative portion and an inert nutritive portion c : material stored in an ovum that supplies food to the developing embryo and consists chiefly of proteins, lecithin, and cholesterol 2 [akin to MD ieke yolk (of wool), OE ēowu ewe]: oily material in unprocessed sheep wool consisting of wool fat, suint, and debris — yolked adj — yolky adj

yolk sac n (1861) : a membranous sac that is attached to an embryo and encloses food yolk, that is continuous in most forms through the yolk stalk with the intestinal cavity of the embryo, that being abundantly supplied with blood vessels is throughout embryonic life and in some forms later the chief organ of nutrition, and that in placental mammals is nearly vestigial and functions chiefly prior to the elaboration of the placenta

yolk stalk n (1900) : the narrow tubular stalk connecting the yolk sac with the embryo

Yom Kip·pur \,yōm-ki-'púr, ,yóm-, ,yäm-; -'ki-pər, -(,)púr\ n [Heb yōm kippūr, lit., day of atonement] (1854) : a Jewish holiday observed with fasting and prayer on the 10th day of Tishri in accordance with the rites described in Leviticus 16 — called also Day of Atonement

¹yon \'yän\ adj [ME, fr. OE geon; akin to OHG iener, adj., that, Gk enē day after tomorrow] (bef. 12c) : YONDER

²yon pron (14c) dial : that or those yonder

³yon adv (15c) 1 : YONDER 2 : THITHER ⟨ran hither and ~⟩

¹yond \'yänd\ adv [ME, fr. OE geond; akin to OE geon] (bef. 12c) archaic : YONDER

²yond adj (13c) dial : YONDER

¹yon·der \'yän-dər\ adv [ME, fr. yond + -er (as in hither)] (14c) : at or in that indicated more or less distant place usu. within sight

²yonder adj (14c) 1 : farther removed : more distant 2 : being at a distance within view or at a place or in a direction known or indicated

³yonder pron (14c) : something that is or is in an indicated more or less distant place

yo·ni \'yō-nē\ n [Skt, vulva] (1799) : a stylized representation of the female genitalia symbolizing the feminine principle in Hindu cosmology — compare LINGAM — yo·nic \'yō-nik\ adj

yoo–hoo \'yü-(,)hü\ interj (ca. 1924) — used to attract attention or as a call to persons

yore \'yōr, 'yór\ n [ME, fr. yore, adv., long ago, fr. OE gēara, fr. gēar year — more at YEAR] (14c) : time past and esp. long past — usu. used in the phrase of yore

York·ie \'yór-kē\ n [by shortening & alter.] (1946) : YORKSHIRE TERRIER

York·ist \'yór-kist\ adj [Edward, Duke of York (Edward IV of England)] (1823) : of or relating to the English royal house that ruled from 1461 to 1485 — Yorkist n

York rite \'yórk-\ n [York, England] (ca. 1878) 1 : a ceremonial observed by one of the Masonic systems 2 : a system or organization that observes the York rite and confers in the U.S. 13 degrees of which the last three are in commanderies of Knights Templar — compare SCOTTISH RITE

York·shire \'yórk-,shir, -shər\ n (1902) : a white swine of any of several breeds or strains originated in Yorkshire, England

Yorkshire pudding n (1747) : batter consisting of eggs, flour, and milk that is baked in meat drippings

Yorkshire terrier n (1872) : any of a breed of compact toy terriers with long straight silky hair mostly bluish gray but tan on the head and chest

Yor·u·ba \'yór-ə-bə\ n, pl Yoruba or Yorubas (1841) : a Niger-Congo language of southwestern Nigeria and parts of Benin and Togo; also : a member of any of the Yoruba-speaking peoples of this region — Yo·ru·ban \'yór-ə-bən\ n or adj

you \'yü, yə also yē\ pron [ME, fr. OE ēow, dat. & accus. of gē you; akin to OHG iu, dat. of ir you, Skt yūyam you] (bef. 12c) 1 : the one or

---

\ə\ abut \ᵊ\ kitten, F table \ər\ further \a\ ash \ā\ ace \ä\ mop, mar \aú\ out \ch\ chin \e\ bet \ē\ easy \g\ go \i\ hit \ī\ ice \j\ job \ŋ\ sing \ō\ go \ó\ law \ói\ boy \th\ thin \th̲\ the \ü\ loot \ú\ foot \y\ yet \zh\ vision \a̱, k̲, ⁿ, œ, œ̄, ᵫ, ᵫ̄, ᵊ\ see Guide to Pronunciation ones being addressed — used as the pronoun of the second person singular or plural in any grammatical relation except that of a possessive ⟨~ may sit in that chair⟩ ⟨~ are my friends⟩ ⟨can I pour ~ a cup of tea⟩; used formerly only as a plural pronoun of the second person in the dative or accusative case as direct or indirect object of a verb or as object of a preposition; compare THEE, THOU, YE, YOUR, YOURS 2 : ONE 2a

you–all \yü-'ol, 'yü-,; 'yol\ *pron* (1824) *chiefly Southern* : YOU — usu. used in addressing two or more persons or sometimes one person as representing also another or others

you'd \'yüd, 'yud, yəd\ (1602) : you had : you would

you'll \'yü(ə)l, 'yul, yəl\ (1592) : you will : you shall

¹young \'yəŋ\ *adj* **youn·ger** \'yəŋ-gər\; **youn·gest** \'yəŋ-gəst\ [ME *yong*, fr. OE *geong*; akin to OHG *jung* young, L *juvenis*] (bef. 12c) **1 a** : being in the first or an early stage of life, growth, or development **b** : JUNIOR 1a **c** : of an early, tender, or desirable age for use as food or drink ⟨fresh ~ lamb⟩ ⟨a ~ wine⟩ **2** : having little experience **3 a** : recently come into being : NEW **b** : YOUTHFUL **5 4** : of, relating to, or having the characteristics of youth or a young person **5** *cap* : representing a new or rejuvenated esp. political group or movement — **young·ish** \'yəŋ-ish\ *adj* — **young·ness** \'yəŋ-nəs\ *n*

²young *n, pl* **young** (bef. 12c) **1** *pl* **a** : young persons : YOUTH **b** : immature offspring esp. of lower animals **2** : a single recently born or hatched animal — **with young** : PREGNANT — used of a female animal

young·ber·ry \'yəŋ-,ber-ē\ *n* [B. M. *Young fl* 1900 Am. fruit grower] (1927) : the large sweet reddish black fruit of a cultivar of a hybrid bramble closely related to the boysenberry and loganberry and grown in the western and southern U.S.; *also* : a bramble bearing youngberries

youn·ger \'yəŋ-gər\ *n* (bef. 12c) : an inferior in age : JUNIOR — usu. used with a possessive pronoun ⟨is several years his ~⟩

youn·gest \'yəŋ-gəst\ *n, pl* **youngest** (13c) : one that is the least old; *esp* : the youngest child or member of a family

young·ling \'yəŋ-liŋ\ *n* (bef. 12c) : one that is young; *esp* : a young person or animal — **youngling** *adj*

young·ster \'yəŋ(k)-stər\ *n* (1589) **1 a** : a young person : YOUTH **b** : CHILD **2** : a young mammal, bird, or plant esp. of a domesticated or cultivated breed or type

Young Turk *n* [*Young Turks*, a 20th cent. revolutionary party in Turkey] (1908) : an insurgent or a member of an insurgent group esp. in a political party : RADICAL; *broadly* : one advocating changes within a usu. established group

youn·ker \'yəŋ-kər\ *n* [D *jonker* young nobleman] (1513) **1** : a young man **2** : CHILD, YOUNGSTER

your \yər, 'yur, 'yor, 'yor\ *adj* [ME, fr. OE *ēower*; akin to OE *ēow* you — more at YOU] (bef. 12c) **1** : of or relating to you or yourself or yourselves esp. as possessor or possessors ⟨~ bodies⟩, agent or agents ⟨~ contributions⟩, or object or objects of an action ⟨~ discharge⟩ **2** : of or relating to one or oneself ⟨when you face the north, east is at ~ right⟩ **3** — used with little or no meaning almost as an equivalent to the definite article *the* ⟨a trait . . . that sets him apart from ~ average professor —James Breckenridge⟩

you're \yər, 'yur, 'yor, 'yor, yü-ər\ (1593) : you are

yours \'yurz, 'yorz, 'yorz\ *pron, sing or pl in constr* [ME fr. *your* + *-s* -'s] (1526) : that which belongs to you — used without a following noun as a pronoun equivalent in meaning to the adjective *your*, often used esp. with an adverbial modifier in the complimentary close of a letter ⟨~ truly⟩ — **yours truly** : I, ME, MYSELF ⟨I can take care of *yours truly*⟩

your·self \yər-'self, *Southern also* -'sef\ *pron* (14c) **1 a** : that identical one that is you — used reflexively ⟨you might hurt ~⟩, for emphasis ⟨carry them ~⟩, or in absolute constructions **b** : your normal, healthy, or sane condition **2** : ONESELF

your·selves \-'selvz, *Southern also* -'sevz\ *pron pl* (1523) **1** : those identical ones that are you — used reflexively ⟨get ~ a treat⟩, for emphasis, or in absolute constructions **2** : your normal, healthy, or sane condition

youth \'yüth\ *n, pl* **youths** \'yüthz, 'yüths\ *often attrib* [ME *youthe*, fr. OE *geoguth*; akin to OE *geong* young — more at YOUNG] (bef. 12c) **1 a** : the time of life when one is young; *esp* : the period between childhood and maturity **b** : the early period of existence, growth, or development **2 a** : a young person; *esp* : a young male between adolescence and maturity **b** : young persons or creatures — usu. pl. in constr. **3** : the quality or state of being youthful : YOUTHFULNESS

youth·ful \'yüth-fəl\ *adj* (1590) **1** : of, relating to, or characteristic of youth **2** : being young and not yet mature **3** : marked by or possessing youth **4** : having the vitality or freshness of youth : VIGOROUS **5** : having accomplished or undergone little erosion — **youth·ful·ly** \-fə-lē\ *adv* — **youth·ful·ness** *n*

youth hostel *n* (1929) : HOSTEL 2b

youth·quake *n* \-,kwāk\ *n* [*youth* + earth*quake*] (1966) : the impact of the values, tastes, and mores of youth on the established norms of society

you've \'yüv, yəv\ (1691) : you have

¹yowl \'yaù(ə)l\ *vb* [ME] *vi* (13c) **1** : to utter a loud long cry of grief, pain, or distress : WAIL **2** : to complain or protest with or as if with yowls ~ *vt* : to express with yowling

²yowl *n* (15c) : a loud long mournful wail or howl (as of a cat)

¹yo–yo \'yō-(,)yō\ *n, pl* **yo-yos** [perh. fr. a language of the Philippines] (1915) **1** : a thick grooved double disk with a string attached to its center which is made to fall and rise to the hand by unwinding and rewinding on the string **2** : one that resembles a yo-yo esp. in moving up and down unexpectedly or repeatedly **3** : a stupid or foolish person

²yo–yo *adj* (1932) : shifting back and forth or up and down uncertainly or unexpectedly

³yo–yo *vi* **yo-yoed; yo-yo·ing** (1967) : to move from one position to another repeatedly : FLUCTUATE

yt·ter·bi·um \i-'tər-bē-əm\ *n* [NL, fr. *Ytterby*, town in southern Sweden] (1879) : a metallic element of the rare-earth group that resembles yttrium and occurs with it and related elements in several minerals — see ELEMENT table

yt·tri·um \'i-trē-əm\ *n* [NL, fr. *yttria* yttrium oxide (Y₂O₃), irreg. fr. *Ytterby*, town in southern Sweden] (1822) : a metallic element usu. included among the rare-earth metals which it resembles chemically and with which it usu. occurs in minerals — see ELEMENT table

yu·an \'yü-ən, yü-'än\ *n, pl* **yuan** [Chin (Beijing) *yuán*] (1914) **1** — see MONEY table **2** : the dollar of the Republic of China (Taiwan)

yu·ca \'yü-kə\ *n* [NL *jucca*, fr. Taino *yuca*] (1555) : CASSAVA

Yu·ca·tec \'yü-kə-,tek\ *n* [Sp *yucateco*] (1843) **1** : a member of an American Indian people of the Yucatán peninsula, Mexico **2** : the Mayan language of the Yucatecs — **Yu·ca·tec·an** \,yü-kə-'te-kən\ *adj or n*

yuc·ca \'yə-kə\ *n* [NL, fr. Sp *yuca*, of unknown origin] (1664) **1** : any of a genus (*Yucca*) of sometimes arborescent plants of the agave family that occur in warm regions chiefly of western No. America and have long often rigid fibrous-margined leaves on a woody base and bear a large panicle of white blossoms **2** : CASSAVA

yucca

¹yuck \'yək\ *var of* ²YAK

²yuck *also* **yuk** *interj* (1966) — used to express rejection or disgust ⟨spending hours over some dish and getting, "~, I hate that" —Anne Dowie⟩

yucky \'yə-kē\ *adj* [²yuck] (1970) : OFFENSIVE, DISTASTEFUL

yu·ga \'yù-gə, 'yü-\ *n* [Skt, yoke, age — more at YOKE] (1784) : one of the four ages of a Hindu world cycle

yuk \'yək\ *var of* ²YAK

yule \'yü(ə)l\ *n, often cap* [ME *yol*, fr. OE *gēol*; akin to ON *jōl*, a pagan midwinter festival] (bef. 12c) : the feast of the nativity of Jesus Christ : CHRISTMAS

Yule log *n* (1725) : a large log formerly put on the hearth on Christmas Eve as the foundation of the fire

yule·tide \'yü(ə)l-,tīd\ *n, often cap* (15c) : CHRISTMASTIDE

Yu·man \'yü-mən\ *n* (1891) : an American Indian language family of southwestern U.S. and northern Mexico — **Yuman** *adj*

yum·my \'yə-mē\ *adj* **yum·mi·er; -est** [*yum-yum*] (1899) : highly attractive or pleasing; *esp* : DELICIOUS, DELECTABLE

yum–yum \'yəm-'yəm\ *interj* (1878) — used to express pleasurable satisfaction esp. in the taste of food

¹yup \'yəp\ *var of* YEP

²yup *n* (1983) : YUPPIE

Yu·pik \'yü-pik\ *n, pl* **Yupiks** *or* **Yupik** [Central Alaskan Yupik *yúppik*, lit., authentic person] (1951) **1** : the language of the Eskimo people of southwestern Alaska **2** : a member of the Yupik-speaking people

yup·pie \'yə-pē\ *n, often cap* [prob. fr. *young urban professional* + *-ie*] (1983) : a young college-educated adult who is employed in a well-paying profession and who lives and works in or near a large city

yurt \'yùrt\ *n* [Russ dial. *yurta*, of Turkic origin; akin to Turk *yurt* home] (1784) : a circular domed tent of skins or felt stretched over a collapsible lattice framework and used by pastoral peoples of inner Asia; *also* : a structure that resembles a yurt usu. in size and design

YWCA \,wī-,də-bəl-yü-(,)sē-'ā, -,də-bə-yü-\ *n* [Young Women's Christian Association] (1887) : an international organization that promotes the spiritual, intellectual, social, and physical welfare orig. of young women

YWHA \-, āch-'ā\ *n* [Young Women's Hebrew Association] (1918) : an organization that promotes the religious, intellectual, social, and physical welfare of Jewish young women

z \'zē, *Canad, Brit, & Austral* 'zed, *chiefly dial* 'izərd\ *n, pl* **z's** *or* **zs** *often cap, often attrib* (bef. 12c) **1 a** : the 26th and last letter of the English alphabet **b** : a graphic representation of this letter **c** : a speech counterpart of orthographic *z* **2** : a graphic device for reproducing the letter *z* **3** : one designated *z* esp. as the 26th in order or class or the third in order or class when *x* is made the first **4** : something shaped like the letter Z **5** : WINK 1 — usu. used in pl. ⟨catch some *z's* before dinner⟩

Z *n* (1967) : Z PARTICLE

za·ba·glio·ne \ˌzä-bəl-'yō-nē\ *n* [It] (1899) : a whipped dessert consisting of a mixture of egg yolks, sugar, and usu. Marsala wine that is often served on fruit

Zach·a·ri·as \ˌza-kə-'rī-əs\ *n* [LL, fr. Gk, fr. Heb *Zĕkharyāh*] : ZECHARIAH

zad·dik \'tsä-dik\ *n, pl* **zad·dik·im** \tsä-'di-kəm\ [Yiddish *tsadek*, fr. Heb *saddiq* just, righteous] (1873) **1** : a righteous and saintly person by Jewish religious standards **2** : the spiritual leader of a modern Hasidic community

zaf·tig \'zäf-tig, 'zòf-\ *adj* [Yiddish *zaftik* juicy, succulent, fr. *zaft* juice, sap, fr. MHG *saf, saft*, fr. OHG *saf* — more at SAP] (ca. 1936) *of a woman* : having a full rounded figure : pleasingly plump

¹zag \'zag\ *n* [*zigzag*] (1793) **1 a** : one of the sharp turns, angles, or alterations in a zigzag course **b** : one of the short straight lines or sections of a zigzag course at an angle to a zig **2** : ZIG 2

²zag *vi* **zagged; zag·ging** (1900) : to execute a zag — usu. contrasted with *zig*

zaire \'zīr, zä-'ir\ *n, pl* **zaires** *or* **zaire** [F *zaïre*, fr. *Zaïre*, former country in central Africa] (1967) — see MONEY table

za·mia \'zā-mē-ə\ *n* [NL, fr. L *zamiae nuces*, false MS reading for *azaniae nuces* pine nuts] (1819) : any of a genus (*Zamia* of the family Zamiaceae) of American cycads with a short thick woody base, a crown of palmlike leaves, and oblong cones

za·min·dar *or* **ze·min·dar** \'za-mən-ˌdär, 'ze-; zə-ˌmēn-'där\ *n* [Hindi *zamīndār*, fr. Per, fr. *zamīn* land + *-dār* holder] (1683) **1** : a collector of the land revenue of a district for the government during the period of Mogul rule in India **2** : a feudal landlord in British India paying the government a fixed revenue

za·min·dari *or* **ze·min·dary** \ˌza-mən-'där-ē, ˌze-; zə-ˌmēn-\ *n, pl* **-dar·is** *or* **-dar·ies** [Hindi *zamīndārī*, fr. Per, fr. *zamīndār*] (1757) **1** : the system of landholding and revenue collection by zamindars **2** : the land held or administered by a zamindar

zan·der \'zan-dər, 'tsän-\ *n, pl* **zander** *or* **zanders** [G] (1854) : a pike perch (*Stizostedion lucioperca*) of central Europe related to the walleye

¹za·ny \'zā-nē\ *n, pl* **zanies** [It *zanni*, a traditional masked clown, fr. It dial. *Zanni*, nickname for It *Giovanni* John] (1588) **1** : a subordinate clown or acrobat in old comedies who mimics ludicrously the tricks of the principal : MERRY-ANDREW **2** : a slavish follower : TOADY **3 a** : one who acts the buffoon to amuse others **b** : NUT, KOOK

²zany *adj* **za·ni·er; -est** (1616) **1** : being or having the characteristics of a zany **2** : fantastically or absurdly ludicrous — **za·ni·ly** \'zā-nə-lē, 'zā-n³l-ē\ *adv* — **za·ni·ness** \'zā-nē-nəs\ *n*

¹zap \'zap\ *interj* [imit.] (1929) **1** — used to express a sound made by or as if by a gun **2** — used to indicate a sudden or instantaneous occurrence

²zap *vb* **zapped; zap·ping** *vt* (1942) **1 a** : to get rid of, destroy, or kill esp. with or as if with sudden force **b** : to hit with or as if with a sudden concentrated application of force or energy **c** : to irradiate esp. with microwaves **2 a** : to propel suddenly or speedily **b** : to transport instantaneously **3** : to avoid watching (as a television commercial) by changing channels esp. with a remote control or by fast forwarding a videotape **~** *vi* **1** : to move with speed or force **2** : to change television channels using a remote control

³zap *n* (1963) : a pungent or zestful quality : ZIP; *also* : a sudden forceful blow

za·pa·te·ado \ˌzä-pə-tä-'ä-(ˌ)dō, ˌsä-pə-tä-'aù\ *n* [Sp, fr. *zapatear* to strike or tap with the shoe, fr. *zapato* shoe] (1845) : a Latin-American dance marked by rhythmic stamping or tapping of the feet

za·pa·teo \ˌzä-pə-'tä-(ˌ)ō, ˌsä-\ *n* [Sp, fr. *zapatear*] (1922) : ZAPATEADO

Za·po·tec \ˌzä-pə-'tek, ˌsä-\ *n* (1797) : a member of an American Indian people of Oaxaca state, Mexico

zap·per \'za-pər\ *n* (1969) : one that zaps: as **a** : an electronic device designed to attract and kill insects **b** : a person who habitually changes channels (as to avoid commercials) **c** : a remote control device used for zapping

zap·py \'za-pē\ *adj* (1969) : ZIPPY

za·re·ba *or* **za·ri·ba** \zə-'rē-bə\ *n* [Ar *zarībah* enclosure] (1849) : an improvised stockade constructed in parts of Africa esp. of thorny bushes

zar·zue·la \ˌzär-zə-'wā-lə, ˌzär-'zwä-\ *n* [Sp, prob. fr. *La Zarzuela*, royal residence near Madrid where it was first performed] (1888) : a usu. comic Spanish operetta

z–ax·is \'zē-ˌak-səs; *Canad, Brit, & Austral* 'zed-\ *n* (ca. 1949) : one of the axes in a three-dimensional rectangular coordinate system

za·yin \'zä-yən, 'zī(-ə)n\ *n* [Heb] (1823) : the 7th letter of the Hebrew alphabet — see ALPHABET table

z–co·or·di·nate \ˌzē-kō-'òrd-nət, -'òr-d³n-ət, -də-ˌnät; *Canad, Brit, & Austral* ˌzed-\ *n* (ca. 1956) : a coordinate whose value is determined by measuring parallel to a z-axis

zeal \'zē(ə)l\ *n* [ME *zele*, fr. LL *zelus*, fr. Gk *zēlos*] (15c) : eagerness and ardent interest in pursuit of something : FERVOR **syn** see PASSION

zeal·ot \'ze-lət\ *n* [LL *zelotes*, fr. Gk *zēlōtēs*, fr. *zēlos*] (1537) **1** *cap* : a member of a fanatical sect arising in Judea during the first century A.D. and militantly opposing the Roman domination of Palestine **2** : a zealous person; *esp* : a fanatical partisan

zeal·ot·ry \'ze-lə-trē\ *n, pl* **-ries** (1656) : excess of zeal : fanatical devotion

zeal·ous \'ze-ləs\ *adj* (1535) : filled with or characterized by zeal ⟨**~** missionaries⟩ — **zeal·ous·ly** *adv* — **zeal·ous·ness** *n*

ze·a·tin \'zē-ə-tən\ *n* [NL *Zea*, genus of grasses including Indian corn + *kinetin* — more at ZEIN] (1963) : a cytokinin first isolated from the endosperm of Indian corn

ze·bra \'zē-brə, *Canad & Brit also* 'ze-\ *n, pl* **zebras** [Pg *zebra, zebro* wild ass, perh. fr. L *equiferus*, kind of wild horse, fr. *equus* horse + *ferus* wild — more at EQUINE, FIERCE] (1600) **1** *pl also* **zebra** : any of several fleet African mammals (*Equus burchelli, E. grevyi,* and *E. zebra*) related to the horse but distinctively and conspicuously patterned in stripes of black or dark brown and white or buff **2** [fr. the shirts patterned in black and white stripes worn by football referees] : REFEREE 2 **3** : ZEBRA CROSSING — **ze·brine** \-ˌbrīn\ *adj or n*

ze·bra crossing \'ze-brə-, 'zē-\ *n* (1950) *Brit* : a crosswalk marked by a series of broad white stripes to indicate a crossing point at which pedestrians have the right of way

zebra finch *n* (1889) : a small largely gray-and-white Australian waxbill (*Poephila guttata*) that has black bars on the tail coverts and is often kept as a cage bird

zebra fish *n* (1771) : any of various barred fishes; *esp* : a very small blue-and-silver-striped Indian danio (*Brachydanio rerio* syn. *Danio rerio*) often kept in the tropical aquarium

zebra mussel *n* (1883) : a freshwater Eurasian lamellibranch mollusk (*Dreissena polymorpha*) that was accidentally introduced into the Great Lakes and is spreading to surrounding waterways where it colonizes and clogs water intake pipes and competes with native fish for food

ze·bra·wood \'zē-brə-ˌwùd, 'ze-\ *n* (1783) **1** : any of several trees or shrubs having mottled or striped wood: as **a** : any of various leguminous African timber trees (genus *Brachystegia*) **b** : a tall So. American timber tree (*Astronium fraxinifolium*) of the cashew family **2** : the wood of a zebrawood

ze·bu \'zē-(ˌ)bü, -(ˌ)byü\ *n* [F *zébu*] (1774) : any of various breeds of domestic oxen developed in India that are often considered conspecific with the common ox (*Bos taurus*) or sometimes as a separate species (*B. indicus*) and are characterized by a large fleshy hump over the shoulders, a dewlap, pendulous ears, and marked resistance to the injurious effects of heat and insect attack

Zeb·u·lun \'ze-byə-lən\ *n* [Heb *Zĕbhūlūn*] : a son of Jacob and the traditional eponymous ancestor of one of the tribes of Israel

zec·chi·no \ze-'kē-(ˌ)nō, tse-\ *n, pl* **-ni** \-(ˌ)nē\ *or* **-nos** [It — more at SEQUIN] (1617) : SEQUIN 1

Zech·a·ri·ah \ˌze-kə-'rī-ə\ *n* [Heb *Zĕkharyāh*] **1** : a Hebrew prophet of the 6th century B.C. **2** : a prophetic book of canonical Jewish and Christian Scripture — see BIBLE table

ze·chin \'ze-kən, ze-'kēn\ *n* [It *zecchino*] (1575) : SEQUIN 1

zed \'zed\ *n* [ME, fr. MF *zede*, fr. LL *zeta* zeta, fr. Gk *zēta*] (15c) *chiefly Brit* : the letter z

zee \'zē\ *n* (1677) : the letter z

ze·in \'zē-ən\ *n* [NL *Zea*, genus of grasses including Indian corn, fr. Gk *zeai*, pl., wheat; akin to Skt *yava* barley] (1822) : a protein from Indian corn that lacks lysine and tryptophan and is used esp. in making textile fibers, plastics, printing inks, coatings, and adhesives and sizes

zeit·ge·ber \'tsīt-ˌgä-bər, 'zīt-\ *n* [G, fr. *Zeit* time + *Geber* giver] (1964) : an environmental agent or event (as the occurrence of light or dark) that provides the stimulus setting or resetting a biological clock of an organism

zeit·geist \'tsīt-ˌgīst, 'zīt-\ *n, often cap* [G, fr. *Zeit* + *Geist* spirit] (1884) : the general intellectual, moral, and cultural climate of an era

zel·ko·va \'zel-kə-və, zel-'kō-və\ *n* [NL, fr. Russ *zel'kova, zel'kva,* fr. Georgian *dzelkva*] (ca. 1890) : a tall widely spreading Japanese tree (*Zelkova serrata*) of the elm family that is often used as an ornamental and shade tree in place of the American elm because of its resistance to Dutch elm disease

zemst·vo \'zem(p)st-(ˌ)vō, -və\ *n, pl* **zemstvos** [Russ; akin to Russ *zemlya* earth, land, L *humus* — more at HUMBLE] (1865) : one of the district and provincial assemblies established in Russia in 1864

Zen \'zen\ *n* [Jp, religious meditation] (1727) : a Japanese sect of Mahayana Buddhism that aims at enlightenment by direct intuition through meditation

ze·na·na \zə-'nä-nə\ *n* [Hindi *zanāna,* fr. Per, fr. *zan* woman] (1760) : HAREM 1a

Zend–Aves·ta \ˌzend-ə-'ves-tə\ *n* [F, fr. MPer *Avastāk va Zand* Avesta and commentary] (1630) : AVESTA

ze·ner diode \'zē-nər-, 'ze-\ *n, often cap* Z [Clarence M. *Zener* b1905 Am. physicist] (1957) : a silicon semiconductor device used esp. as a voltage regulator

ze·nith \'zē-nəth, *Canad & Brit usu* 'ze-nəth, -nith\ *n* [ME *senith,* fr. MF *cenith,* fr. ML, fr. OSp *zenit,* modif. of Ar *samt (ar-ra's)* way (over one's head)] (14c) **1** : the point of the celestial sphere that is directly opposite the nadir and vertically above the observer **2** : the highest point reached in the heavens by a celestial body **3** : culminating point : ACME ⟨at the **~** of his powers —John Buchan⟩

ze·nith·al \-nə-thəl\ *adj* (1860) **1** : of, relating to, or located at or near the zenith **2** : showing correct directions from the center ⟨a **~** map⟩

ze·o·lite \'zē-ə-ˌlīt\ *n* [Sw *zeolit,* fr. Gk *zein* to boil + *-o-* + Sw *-lit* -lite, fr. F *-lite* — more at YEAST] (1777) : any of various hydrous silicates that are analogous in composition to the feldspars, occur as secondary minerals in cavities of lavas, and can act as ion-exchangers; *also* : any of various natural or synthesized silicates of similar structure used esp. in water softening and as adsorbents and catalysts — **ze·o·lit·ic** \ˌzē-ə-'li-tik\ *adj*

Zeph·a·ni·ah \ˌze-fə-'nī-ə\ *n* [Heb *Sĕphanyāh*] **1** : a Hebrew prophet of the 7th century B.C. **2** : an apocalyptic book of canonical Jewish and Christian Scripture — see BIBLE table

zeph·yr \'ze-fər\ *n* [ME *Zephirus,* west wind (personified), fr. L *Zephyrus,* god of the west wind & *zephyrus* west wind, zephyr, fr. Gk *Zephyros & zephyros*] (1611) **1 a** : a breeze from the west **b** : a gentle breeze **2** : any of various lightweight fabrics and articles of clothing

Zeph·y·rus \'ze-fə-rəs\ *n* [L] : the Greek god of the west wind

---

\ə\ abut \ᵊ\ kitten, F table \ər\ further \a\ ash \ā\ ace \ä\ mop, mar
\aù\ out \ch\ chin \e\ bet \ē\ easy \g\ go \i\ hit \ī\ ice \j\ job
\ŋ\ sing \ō\ go \ò\ law \òi\ boy \th\ thin \t͟h\ the \ü\ loot \ù\ foot
\y\ yet \zh\ vision \ä, k̲, ⁿ, œ, œ̄, ue, ūe, ᵜ\ see Guide to Pronunciation

zep·pe·lin \'ze-p(ə-)lən\ *n* [Count Ferdinand von *Zeppelin*] (1900) : a rigid airship consisting of a cylindrical trussed and covered frame supported by internal gas cells; *broadly* : AIRSHIP

zeppelin

zerk \'zərk\ *n* [Oscar U. *Zerk* †1968 Am. (Austrian-born) inventor] (1926) : a grease fitting

¹ze·ro \'zē-(,)rō, 'zir-(,)ō\ *n, pl* **zeros** *also* **zeroes** [F or It; F *zéro*, fr. It *zero*, fr. ML *zephirum*, fr. Ar *sifr*] (1604) **1 a** : the arithmetical symbol 0 or Ø denoting the absence of all magnitude or quantity **b** : ADDITIVE IDENTITY; *specif* : the number between the set of all negative numbers and the set of all positive numbers **c** : a value of an independent variable that makes a function equal to zero ⟨+2 and −2 are ∼*s* of $f(x)=x^2-4$⟩ **2** — see NUMBER table **3 a** (1) : the point of departure in reckoning; *specif* : the point from which the graduation of a scale (as of a thermometer) begins (2) : the temperature represented by the zero mark on a thermometer **b** : the setting or adjustment of the sights of a firearm that causes it to shoot to point of aim at a desired range **4** : an insignificant person or thing : NONENTITY **5 a** : a state of total absence or neutrality **b** : the lowest point : NADIR **6** : something arbitrarily or conveniently designated zero

²zero *adj* (1810) **1 a** : of, relating to, or being a zero **b** : having no magnitude or quantity : not any ⟨∼ growth⟩ **c** (1) : having no phonetic manifestation ⟨the ∼ modification in the past tense of *cut*⟩ (2) : having no modified inflectional form ⟨a ∼ plural⟩ **2 a** *of a cloud ceiling* : limiting vision to 50 feet (15 meters) or less **b** *of horizontal visibility* : limited to 165 feet (50.3 meters) or less

³zero *vt* (1913) **1** : to determine or adjust the zero of (as a rifle) **2 a** : to concentrate firepower on the exact range of — usu. used with *in* **b** : to bring to bear on the exact range of a target — usu. used with *in* ∼ *vi* **1** : to adjust fire on a specific target — usu. used with *in* **2** : to close in on or focus attention on an objective — usu. used with *in*

zero–based *or* **zero–base** *adj* (1970) : having each item justified on the basis of cost or need ⟨∼ budgeting⟩

zero coupon *adj* (1979) : of, relating to, or being an investment security that is sold at a deep discount, is redeemable at face value on maturity, and that pays no periodic interest ⟨zero coupon municipal bonds⟩

zero gravity *n* (1951) : the state or condition of lacking apparent gravitational pull : WEIGHTLESSNESS

zero hour *n* [fr. its being marked by the count of zero in a countdown] (1917) **1 a** : the hour at which a planned military operation is scheduled to start **b** : the time at which a usu. significant or notable event is scheduled to take place **2** : a time when a vital decision or decisive change must be made

zero–sum *adj* (1944) : of, relating to, or being a situation (as a game or relationship) in which a gain for one side entails a corresponding loss for the other side

ze·roth \'zē-(,)rōth, 'zir-(,)ōth\ *adj* (1896) : being numbered zero in a series; *also* : ZERO 1 ⟨the ∼ power of a number⟩

zero tillage *n* (1963) : NO-TILLAGE

zero vector *n* (ca. 1901) : a vector which is of zero length and all of whose components are zero

zero–zero *adj* (ca. 1939) **1** : characterized by or being atmospheric conditions that reduce ceiling and visibility to zero **2** : limited to zero by atmospheric conditions

zest \'zest\ *n* [obs. F (now *zeste*), orange or lemon peel (used as flavoring)] (ca. 1674) **1** : a piece of the peel or of the thin outer skin of an orange or lemon used as flavoring **2** : an enjoyably exciting quality : PIQUANCY **b** : keen enjoyment : RELISH, GUSTO — **zest·ful** \-fəl\ *adj* — **zest·ful·ly** \-fə-lē\ *adv* — **zest·ful·ness** *n* — **zest·less** \-ləs\ *adj*

zest·er \'zes-tər\ *n* (1973) : a small utensil for peeling zest

zesty \'zes-tē\ *adj* **zest·i·er; -est** (1930) : having or characterized by zest

ze·ta \'zā-tə, 'zē-\ *n* [Gk *zēta*] (1823) : the 6th letter of the Greek alphabet — see ALPHABET table

zeug·ma \'züg-mə\ *n* [L, fr. Gk, lit., joining, fr. *zeugnynai* to join; akin to L *jungere* to join — more at YOKE] (1523) : the use of a word to modify or govern two or more words usu. in such a manner that it applies to each in a different sense or makes sense with only one (as in "opened the door and her heart to the homeless boy")

Zeus \'züs\ *n* [Gk] : the king of the gods and husband of Hera in Greek mythology — compare JUPITER

zib·e·line *or* **zib·el·line** \'zi-bə-,lēn, -,līn\ *n* [MF, sable, fr. OIt *zibellino*, of Slav origin; akin to Russ *sobol'* sable] (1892) : a soft lustrous wool fabric with mohair, alpaca, or camel's hair

zi·do·vu·dine \zi-'dō-vyü-,dēn\ *n* [by shortening & alter. fr. *azidothymidine*] (1987) : AZIDOTHYMIDINE

¹zig \'zig\ *n* [*zigzag*] (1840) **1 a** : one of the sharp turns, angles, or alterations in a zigzag course **b** : one of the short straight lines or sections of a zigzag course at an angle to a zag **2 a** : a sharp alteration or change of direction (as in a process or policy) ⟨the quick ∼*s* and zags of his international maneuverings —*N.Y. Times*⟩

²zig *vi* **zigged; zig·ging** (1940) : to execute a zig — usu. contrasted with *zag*

zig·gu·rat \'zi-gə-,rat\ *n* [Akkadian *ziqqurratu*] (1877) : an ancient Mesopotamian temple tower consisting of a lofty pyramidal structure built in successive stages with outside staircases and a shrine at the top

¹zig·zag \'zig-,zag\ *n* [F] (1712) : one of a series of short sharp turns, angles, or alterations in a course; *also* : something having the form or character of such a series ⟨a blouse with green ∼*s*⟩ ⟨endured the ∼*s* of policy —Richard Bernstein⟩

²zigzag *adv* (ca. 1730) : in or by a zigzag path or course

ziggurat

³zigzag *adj* (1750) : having short sharp turns or angles ⟨a ∼ trail⟩

⁴zigzag *vb* **zig·zagged; zig·zag·ging** *vt* (1777) : to form into a zigzag or move along a zigzag course ∼ *vi* : to lie in, proceed along, or consist of a zigzag course

zilch \'zilch\ *adj or n* [origin unknown] (ca. 1966) : ZERO, NOTHING

zil·lion \'zil-yən\ *n* [*z* + *-illion* (as in *million*)] (1934) : an indeterminately large number ⟨∼*s* of mosquitoes⟩ — **zil·lionth** \-yən(t)th\ *adj*

zil·lion·aire \,zil-yə-'nar, -'ner\ *n* [*zillion* + *-aire* (as in *millionaire*)] (1946) : an immeasurably wealthy person

zin \'zin\ *n, often cap* (1980) : ZINFANDEL

¹zinc \'ziŋk\ *n, often attrib* [G *Zink*] (1651) : a bluish white crystalline metallic element of low to intermediate hardness that is ductile when pure but in the commercial form is brittle at ordinary temperatures and becomes ductile on slight heating, occurs abundantly in minerals, is an essential micronutrient for both plants and animals, and is used esp. as a protective coating for iron and steel — see ELEMENT table

²zinc *vt* **zinced** *or* **zincked** \'ziŋ(k)t\; **zinc·ing** *or* **zinck·ing** \'ziŋ-kiŋ\ (1841) : to treat or coat with zinc : GALVANIZE

zinc blende *n* (1842) : SPHALERITE

zinc chloride *n* (1851) : a poisonous caustic deliquescent salt $ZnCl_2$ used esp. as a wood preservative, drying agent, and catalyst

zinc·ite \'ziŋ-,kīt\ *n* [G *Zinkit*, fr. *Zink*] (1854) : a brittle deep-red to orange-yellow hexagonal mineral that consists essentially of zinc oxide and occurs in massive or granular form

zinc oxide *n* (1849) : an infusible white solid ZnO used esp. as a pigment, in compounding rubber, and in pharmaceutical and cosmetic preparations

zinc oxide ointment *n* (1936) : an ointment that contains about 20 percent of zinc oxide and is used in treating skin disorders

zinc sulfate *n* (1851) : a crystalline salt $ZnSO_4$ used esp. in making a white paint pigment, in printing and dyeing, in sprays and fertilizers, and in medicine as an astringent, emetic, and weak antiseptic

zinc sulfide *n* (1851) : a fluorescent white to yellowish compound ZnS used esp. as a white pigment and a phosphor

zinc white *n* (1847) : a white pigment that consists of zinc oxide

zin·eb \'zi-,neb\ *n* [*zinc* + *ethylene* + *bis*-] (1950) : a zinc-containing agricultural fungicide $C_4H_6N_2S_4Zn$ used on fruits and vegetables

zin·fan·del \'zin-fən-,del\ *n* [origin unknown] (1896) : a dry red table wine made from a small black grape that is grown chiefly in California; *also* : the grape

¹zing \'ziŋ\ *n* [imit.] (1911) **1** : a shrill humming noise **2 a** : an enjoyably exciting or stimulating quality : ZEST ⟨really put some ∼ into this industry —Erwin Fine⟩ **b** : a sharply piquant flavor ⟨barbecue sauce with ∼⟩

²zing *vi* (1920) **1** : to make or move with a humming sound **2** : ZIP, SPEED ∼ *vt* **1** : to hit suddenly : ZAP **2** : to criticize in a pointed or witty manner

zing·er \'ziŋ-ər\ *n* (1955) **1** : something causing or meant to cause interest, surprise, or shock **2** : a pointed witty remark or retort

zingy \'ziŋ-ē\ *adj* **zing·i·er; -est** ['*zing*] (1945) **1** : enjoyably exciting ⟨a ∼ musical⟩ **2** : strikingly attractive or appealing ⟨wore a ∼ new outfit⟩ **3** : sharply piquant ⟨a ∼ salad⟩

zin·nia \'zi-nē-ə, 'zēn-ē-, 'zin-yə, 'zēn-\ *n* [NL, fr. Johann G. *Zinn* †1759 Ger. botanist] (1767) : any of a small genus (*Zinnia*) of tropical American composite herbs and low shrubs with showy flower heads and long-lasting ray flowers

Zi·on \'zī-ən\ *n* [ME *Sion*, fr. OE, citadel in Palestine which was the nucleus of Jerusalem, fr. LL, fr. Gk *Seiōn*, fr. Heb *Siyōn*] (14c) **1 a** : the Jewish people : ISRAEL **b** : the Jewish homeland that is symbolic of Judaism or of Jewish national aspiration **2** : HEAVEN **3** : UTOPIA

Zi·on·ism \'zī-ə-,ni-zəm\ *n* (1896) : an international movement orig. for the establishment of a Jewish national or religious community in Palestine and later for the support of modern Israel — **Zi·on·ist** \-nist\ *adj or n* — **Zi·on·is·tic** \,zī-ə-'nis-tik\ *adj*

¹zip \'zip\ *vb* **zipped; zip·ping** [imit. of the sound of a speeding object] *vi* (1852) **1** : to move, act, or function with speed and vigor **2** : to travel with a sharp hissing or humming sound ∼ *vt* **1** : to impart speed or force to **2** : to add zest, interest, or life to — often used with *up* **3** : to transport or propel with speed

²zip *n* (1875) **1** : a sudden sharp hissing or sibilant sound **2** : ENERGY, VIM — **zip·less** \-ləs\ *adj*

³zip *n* [origin unknown] (ca. 1900) : NOTHING, ZERO ⟨the final score was 27 to ∼⟩

⁴zip *n* (1920) *chiefly Brit* : ZIPPER

⁵zip *vb* **zipped; zip·ping** [back-formation fr. *zipper*] *vt* (1932) **1 a** : to close or open with or as if with a zipper **b** : to enclose or wrap by fastening a zipper **2** : to cause (a zipper) to open or shut ∼ *vi* : to become open, closed, or attached by means of a zipper

⁶zip *n, often cap* Z&I&P (1965) : ZIP CODE

zip–code *vt* (1964) : to furnish with a zip code

zip code *n, often cap* Z&I&P [*zone improvement plan*] (1963) : a number that identifies each postal delivery area in the U.S.

zip fastener *n* (1927) *chiefly Brit* : ZIPPER

zip gun *n* (1950) : a crudely homemade single-shot pistol

¹zip·per \'zi-pər\ *n* [fr. *Zipper*, a trademark] (1925) : a fastener consisting of two rows of metal or plastic teeth on strips of tape and a sliding piece that closes an opening by drawing the teeth together

²zipper *vt* (1930) : ⁵ZIP

zip·pered \-pərd\ *adj* (1939) : equipped with a zipper

zip·py \'zi-pē\ *adj* **zip·pi·er; -est** (1904) : full of zip : BRISK, SNAPPY

zi·ram \'zī-,ram\ *n* [*zinc* + *dithiocarbamate*] (1949) : an organic zinc salt $C_6H_{12}N_2S_4Zn$ used esp. as an agricultural fungicide

zir·con \'zər-,kän, -kən\ *n* [G, modif. of F *jargon* jargoon, zircon, fr. It *giargone*] (1794) : a tetragonal mineral consisting of a silicate of zirconium and occurring usu. in brown or grayish square prisms of adamantine luster or sometimes in transparent forms which are used as gems

zir·co·nia \,zər-'kō-nē-ə\ *n* [NL, fr. ISV *zircon*] (1797) : a white crystalline compound ZrO_2 used esp. in refractories, in thermal and electric insulation, in abrasives, and in enamels and glazes — called also *zirconium oxide*

zir·co·ni·um \,zər-'kō-nē-əm\ *n* [NL, fr. ISV *zircon*] (1808) : a steel‑gray strong ductile metallic element with a high melting point that occurs widely in combined form (as in zircon), is highly resistant to corrosion, and is used esp. in alloys and in refractories and ceramics — see ELEMENT table

zit \'zit\ *n* [origin unknown] (ca. 1966) *slang* : PIMPLE 1

zith·er \'zi-thər, -thər\ *n* [G, fr. L *cithara* cithara — more at CITHER] (1850) : a stringed instrument having usu. 30 to 40 strings over a shallow horizontal soundboard and played with pick and fingers — **zith·er·ist** \-thə-rist, -thə-\ *n*

zi·ti \'zē-tē\ *n, pl* **ziti** [It., pl. of *zito*, alter. of *zita* piece of tubular pasta, prob. short for *maccheroni di zita*, lit., bride's macaroni] (ca. 1845) : medium-sized tubular pasta

zi·zith \'tsit-səs, tsēt-'sēt\ *n pl* [Heb *ṣiṣith*] (1675) : the fringes or tassels worn on traditional or ceremonial garments by Jewish males as reminders of the commandments of Deut 22:12 and Num 15:37–41

Z line *n* (1916) : any of the dark thin lines across a striated muscle fiber that mark the boundaries between adjacent sarcomeres

zlo·ty \'zlȯ-tē\ *n, pl* **zlo·tys** \-tēz\ *or* **zloty** [Pol *złoty*] (1915) — see MONEY table

zo- *or* **zoo-** *comb form* [Gk *zōi-*, *zōio-*, fr. *zōion*; akin to Gk *zōē* life — more at QUICK] **1** : animal : animal kingdom or kind ⟨*zooid*⟩ ⟨*zoology*⟩ **2** [Gk *zō-* alive, fr. *zōos*; akin to Gk *zōē*] : motile ⟨*zoospore*⟩

-zoa \'zō-ə\ *n pl comb form* [NL, fr. Gk *zōia*, pl. of *zōion*] : animals — in taxa ⟨Metazoa⟩ ⟨Protozoa⟩

zo·an·thar·i·an \,zō-ən-'ther-ē-ən, -'thar-\ *n* [ultim. fr. *zo-* + Gk *anthos* flower — more at ANTHOLOGY] (1887) : any of a subclass (Zoantharia) of anthozoans having a hexameral arrangement of tentacles or septa or both and including most of the recent corals and sea anemones — **zoantharian** *adj*

zo·di·ac \'zō-dē-,ak\ *n* [ME, fr. MF *zodiaque*, fr. L *zodiacus*, fr. Gk *zōidiakos*, fr. *zōidiakos*, adj., of carved figures, of the zodiac, fr. *zōidion* carved figure, sign of the zodiac, fr. dim. of *zōion* living being, figure; akin to Gk *zōē* life] (14c) **1 a** : an imaginary band in the heavens centered on the ecliptic that encompasses the apparent paths of all the planets except Pluto and is divided into 12 constellations or signs each taken for astrological purposes to extend 30 degrees of longitude **b** : a figure representing the signs of the zodiac and their symbols **2** : a cyclic course ⟨a ~ of feasts and fasts —R. W. Emerson⟩ — **zo·di·a·cal** \zō-'dī-ə-kəl, zə-\ *adj*

SIGNS OF THE ZODIAC

NUMBER	NAME	SYMBOL	SUN ENTERS
1	Aries the Ram	♈	March 21
2	Taurus the Bull	♉	April 20
3	Gemini the Twins	♊	May 21
4	Cancer the Crab	♋	June 22
5	Leo the Lion	♌	July 23
6	Virgo the Virgin	♍	August 23
7	Libra the Balance	♎	September 23
8	Scorpio the Scorpion	♏	October 24
9	Sagittarius the Archer	♐	November 22
10	Capricorn the Goat	♑	December 22
11	Aquarius the Water Bearer	♒	January 20
12	Pisces the Fishes	♓	February 19

zodiacal light *n* (1734) : a diffuse glow seen in the west after twilight and in the east before dawn

zo·ea \zō-'ē-ə\ *n, pl* **zo·eae** \-'ē-,ē\ *or* **zo·eas** \-'ē-əz\ [NL, fr. Gk *zōē* life] (ca. 1890) : a free-swimming planktonic larval form of many decapod crustaceans and esp. crabs that has a relatively large cephalothorax, conspicuous eyes, and fringed antennae and mouthparts

zof·tig \'zȯf-tig\ *var of* ZAFTIG

¹-zoic *adj comb form* [Gk *zōikos* of animals, fr. *zōion* animal — more at ZO-] : having a (specified) animal mode of existence ⟨holozoic⟩

²-zoic *adj comb form* [Gk *zōē* life] : of, relating to, or being a (specified) geological era ⟨Archeozoic⟩ ⟨Mesozoic⟩

zois·ite \'zȯi-,sīt\ *n* [G *Zoisit*, fr. Baron Sigismund *Zois* von Edelstein †1819 Slovenian nobleman] (1805) : an orthorhombic mineral that consists of a basic silicate of calcium and aluminum and is related to epidote

zom·bie *also* **zom·bi** \'zäm-bē\ *n* [prob. fr. Kongo *nzambi* god] (ca. 1871) **1** *usu* **zombi** : the supernatural power that according to voodoo belief may enter into and reanimate a dead body **b** : a willless and speechless human in the West Indies capable only of automatic movement who is held to have died and been supernaturally reanimated **2 a** : a person held to resemble the so-called walking dead; *esp* : AUTOMATON **b** : a person markedly strange in appearance or behavior **3** : a mixed drink made of several kinds of rum, liqueur, and fruit juice — **zom·bie·like** \-bē-,līk\ *adj*

zom·bi·fy \'zäm-bə-,fī\ *vt* **-fied; -fy·ing** (1946) : to turn (a human being) into a zombie — **zom·bi·fi·ca·tion** \,zäm-bə-fə-'kā-shən\ *n*

zom·bi·ism \-bē-,i-zəm\ *n* (1932) : the beliefs and practices of the cult of the zombi

zon·al \'zō-n⁼l\ *adj* (1873) **1** : of, relating to, affecting, or having the form of a zone ⟨a ~ boundary⟩ **2** : of, relating to, or being a soil or a major soil group marked by well-developed characteristics that are determined primarily by the action of climate and organisms esp. vegetation — compare AZONAL, INTRAZONAL — **zon·al·ly** \-n⁼l-ē\ *adv*

zo·na pel·lu·ci·da \,zō-nə-pə-'lü-sə-də, -pel-'yü-\ *n, pl* **zo·nae pel·lu·ci·dae** \-(,)nē . . . -(,)dē, -,dī\ [NL, transparent zone] (1841) : the transparent more or less elastic outer layer or envelope of a mammalian ovum often traversed by numerous radiating striae

zo·na·tion \zō-'nā-shən\ *n* (1902) **1** : structure or arrangement in zones **2** : distribution of kinds of organisms in biogeographic zones

¹zone \'zōn\ *n* [ME, fr. L *zona* belt, zone, fr. Gk *zōnē*; akin to Lith *juosti* to gird] (15c) **1 a** : any of five great divisions of the earth's surface with respect to latitude and temperature — compare FRIGID ZONE, TEMPERATE ZONE, TORRID ZONE **b** : a portion of the surface of a sphere included between two parallel planes **2** *archaic* : GIRDLE, BELT **3 a** : an encircling anatomical structure **b** (1) : a subdivision of a biogeographic region that supports a similar fauna and flora throughout its extent (2) : such a zone dominated by a particular life form **c** : a distinctive belt, layer, or series of layers of earth materials (as rock) **4**

: a region or area set off as distinct from surrounding or adjoining parts **5** : one of the sections of an area or territory created for a particular purpose: as **a** : a zoned section of a city **b** : any of the eight concentric bands of territory centered on a given postal shipment point designated as a distance bracket for U.S. parcel post to which mail is charged at a single rate **c** : a distance within which the same fare is charged by a common carrier **d** : an area on a field of play **e** : a stretch of roadway or a space in which certain traffic regulations are in force

²zone *vt* **zoned; zon·ing** (1795) **1** : to surround with a zone : ENCIRCLE **2** : to arrange in or mark off into zones; *specif* : to partition (a city, borough, or township) by ordinance into sections reserved for different purposes (as residence or business) — **zon·er** *n*

³zone *adj* (1795) **1** : ZONAL 1 **2** : of, relating to, or being a system of defense (as in basketball or football) in which each player guards an assigned area rather than a specified opponent

zone out (1984) : to become oblivious to one's surroundings esp. in order to relax

zone refining *n* (1952) : a technique for the purification of a crystalline material and esp. a metal in which a molten region travels through the material to be refined, picks up impurities at its advancing edge, and then allows the purified part to recrystallize at its opposite edge — called also *zone melting* — **zone–refined** *adj*

Zon·ian \'zō-nē-ən, -nyən\ *n* (1910) : a U.S. citizen who lives in the Panama Canal Zone

zonk \'zäŋk, 'zȯŋk\ *vb* [prob. imit.] *vt* (1950) : STUN, STUPEFY; *also* : STRIKE, ZAP — often used with *out* ~ *vi* : to pass out from or as if from alcohol or a drug — often used with *out*

zonked \'zäŋkt, 'zȯŋ(k)t\ *adj* (ca. 1959) : stupefied by or as if by alcohol or a drug

zonked–out \-'aȯt\ *adj* (1967) : ZONKED

Zon·ti·an \'zän-tē-ən\ *n* [*Zonta International*, a service club] (1934) : a member of a service club made up of executive women each of whom is a sole representative of one business or profession in a community

zoo \'zü\ *n, pl* **zoos** [short for *zoological garden*] (ca. 1847) **1 a** : ZOOLOGICAL GARDEN **b** : a collection of living animals usu. for public display **2** : a place, situation, or group marked by crowding, confusion, or unrestrained behavior ⟨the convention was a ~⟩

zoo- — see ZO-

zo·oe·ci·um *or* **zo·e·ci·um** \zō-'ē-shē-əm\ *n, pl* **-cia** [NL, fr. *zo-* + Gk *oikia* house — more at VICINITY] (1880) : a sac or chamber secreted and lived in by a bryozoan zooid

zoo·gen·ic \,zō-ə-'je-nik\ *adj* [ISV] (ca. 1864) : caused by or associated with animals or their activities ⟨~ humus⟩

zoo·ge·og·ra·phy \,zō-ə-jē-'ä-grə-fē\ *n* [ISV] (1868) : a branch of biogeography concerned with the geographical distribution of animals and esp. with the determination of the areas characterized by special groups of animals and the study of the causes and significance of such groups — **zoo·ge·og·ra·pher** \-fər\ *n* — **zoo·geo·graph·ic** \-,jē-ə-'gra-fik\ *or* **zoo·geo·graph·i·cal** \-fi-kəl\ *adj* — **zoo·geo·graph·i·cal·ly** \-fi-k(ə-)lē\ *adv*

zo·oid \'zō-,ȯid\ *n* (1851) : one of the asexually produced individuals of a compound organism (as a bryozoan, hydroid, or coral colony)

zoo·keep·er \'zü-,kē-pər\ *n* (1924) : one who maintains or cares for animals in a zoo

zooks \'zúks\ *interj* [short for *gadzooks*] (1634) *archaic* — used as a mild oath

zo·ol·a·try \zō-'ä-lə-trē, zə-'wä-\ *n* [NL *zoolatria*, fr. *zo-* + LL *-latria* -latry] (1817) : animal worship

zoo·log·i·cal \,zō-ə-'lä-ji-kəl\ *also* **zoo·log·ic** \-jik\ *adj* (1807) **1** : of, relating to, or occupied with zoology **2** : of, relating to, or affecting lower animals often as distinguished from humans — **zoo·log·i·cal·ly** \-ji-k(ə-)lē\ *adv*

zoological garden *n* (1829) : a garden or park where wild animals are kept for exhibition

zo·ol·o·gy \zō-'ä-lə-jē, zə-'wä-\ *n* [NL *zoologia*, fr. *zo-* + *-logia* -logy] (1669) **1** : a branch of biology concerned with the classification and the properties and vital phenomena of animals **2 a** : animal life (as of a region) : FAUNA **b** : the properties and vital phenomena exhibited by an animal, animal type, or group — **zo·ol·o·gist** \-jist\ *n*

¹zoom \'züm\ *vb* [imit.] *vi* (1886) **1 a** : to move with a loud low hum or buzz **b** : to go speedily : ZIP **2** *of an airplane* : to climb for a short time at an angle greater than that which can be maintained in steady flight so that the machine is carried upward at the expense of stored kinetic energy **3** : to focus a camera or microscope on an object using a zoom lens so that the object's apparent distance from the observer changes — often used with *in* or *out* **4** : to increase sharply ⟨retail sales ~ed⟩ ~ *vt* : to cause to zoom

²zoom *n* (1918) **1 a** : an act or process of zooming; *esp* : a sharp upward movement **b** : an image created by zooming **2** : a zooming sound **3** : ZOOM LENS

zoom lens *n* (1936) : a lens (as of a camera or projector) in which the image size can be varied continuously while the image remains in focus

zoo·mor·phic \,zō-ə-'mȯr-fik\ *adj* [ISV] (1872) **1** : having the form of an animal **2** : of, relating to, or being a deity conceived of in animal form or with animal attributes — **zoo·morph** \'zō-ə-,mȯrf\ *n*

-zoon *n comb form, pl* **-zoa** [NL, fr. Gk *zōion*] : animal : zooid ⟨spermatozoon⟩

zoo·no·sis \zō-'ä-nə-səs, ,zō-ə-'nō-səs\ *n, pl* **-no·ses** \-,sēz\ [NL, fr. *zo-* + Gk *nosos* disease] (1876) : a disease communicable from animals to humans under natural conditions — **zoo·not·ic** \,zō-ə-'nä-tik\ *adj*

zoo·phil·ic \,zō-ə-'fi-lik\ *or* **zo·oph·i·lous** \zō-'ä-fə-ləs, zə-'wä-\ *adj* (1886) : having an attraction to or preference for animals; *esp, of an insect* : preferring animals to humans as a source of food

zoo·phyte \'zō-ə-,fīt\ *n* [Gk *zōophyton*, fr. *zōi-*, *zō-* zo- + *phyton* plant — more at PHYT-] (1621) : an invertebrate animal (as a coral or sponge) more or less resembling a plant in appearance or mode of growth

\ə\ abut \ᵊ\ kitten, F table \ər\ further \a\ ash \ā\ ace \ä\ mop, mar \aú\ out \ch\ chin \e\ bet \ē\ easy \g\ go \i\ hit \ī\ ice \j\ job \ŋ\ sing \ō\ go \ȯ\ law \ȯi\ boy \th\ thin \th\ the \ü\ loot \ú\ foot \y\ yet \zh\ vision \ȧ, ḵ, ⁿ, œ, œ̄, ᵫ, ᵫ̄, ᵑ\ see Guide to Pronunciation

zoo·plank·ter \'zō-ə-ˌplaŋ(k)-tər\ *n* [*zo-* + *plankter*] (1943) : a planktonic animal

zoo·plank·ton \ˌzō-ə-'plaŋ(k)-tən, -ˌtän\ *n* (1901) : plankton composed of animals — **zoo·plank·ton·ic** \-ˌplaŋ(k)-'tä-nik\ *adj*

zoo·spo·ran·gi·um \ˌzō-ə-spə-'ran-jē-əm\ *n* [NL] (1874) : a spore case or sporangium bearing zoospores

zoo·spore \'zō-ə-ˌspōr, -ˌspȯr\ *n* [ISV] (1846) : an independently motile spore; *esp* : a motile usu. naked and flagellated asexual spore esp. of an alga or lower fungus — **zoo·spor·ic** \ˌzō-ə-'spōr-ik, -'spȯr-\ *adj*

zo·os·ter·ol \zō-'äs-tə-ˌrȯl, -ˌrōl\ *n* (1926) : a sterol (as cholesterol) of animal origin — compare PHYTOSTEROL

zoo·tech·ni·cal \ˌzō-ə-'tek-ni-kəl\ *adj* (1926) : of or relating to the technology of animal husbandry — **zoo·tech·nics** \-'tek-niks\ *n pl but sing or pl in constr*

zoot suit \'züt-\ *n* [coined by Harold C. Fox *b*1910 Am. clothier and bandleader] (1942) : a suit of extreme cut typically consisting of a thigh-length jacket with wide padded shoulders and peg pants with narrow cuffs — **zoot–suit·er** \-ˌsü-tər\ *n*

zooty \'zü-tē\ *adj* (1946) : typical of a zoot-suiter : flashy in manner or style ⟨a ~ haircut⟩

zo·o·xan·thel·la \ˌzō-ə-zan-'the-lə\ *n, pl* **-lae** \-(ˌ)lē\ [NL, fr. *zo-* + *xanth-* + *-ella* (dim. suffix)] (ca. 1891) : any of various symbiotic dinoflagellates that live within the cells of other organisms (as reef-building coral polyps)

zo·ri \'zōr-ē, 'zȯr-\ *n, pl* **zori** *also* **zoris** [Jp *zōri*] (1823) : a flat thonged sandal usu. made of straw, cloth, leather, or rubber

Zorn's lemma \'zȯrnz-, 'tsȯrnz-\ *n* [Max August *Zorn* †1993 Ger. mathematician] (ca. 1950) : a lemma in set theory: if a set S is partially ordered and if each subset for which every pair of elements is related by exactly one of the relationships "less than," "equal to," or "greater than" has an upper bound in S, then S contains at least one element for which there is no greater element in S — compare AXIOM OF CHOICE

Zo·ro·as·tri·an·ism \ˌzōr-ə-'was-trē-ə-ˌni-zəm\ *n* (1854) : a Persian religion founded in the 6th century B.C. by the prophet Zoroaster, promulgated in the Avesta, and characterized by worship of a supreme god Ahura Mazda who requires good deeds for help in his cosmic struggle against the evil spirit Ahriman — **Zo·ro·as·tri·an** \-trē-ən\ *adj or n*

zoster *n* [L, fr. Gk *zōstēr* girdle; akin to Gk *zōnē* zone] (ca. 1706) : HERPES ZOSTER

Zou·ave \zü-'äv\ *n* [F, fr. Berber *Zwāwa*, Berber tribe] (1830) **1** : a member of a French infantry unit orig. composed of Algerians wearing a brilliant uniform and conducting a quick spirited drill **2** : a member of a military unit adopting the dress and drill of the Zouaves

zounds \'zaùn(d)z, 'zünd)z, 'zwaùn(d)z, 'zwün(d)z\ *interj* [euphemism for *God's wounds*] (ca. 1600) — used as a mild oath

zow·ie \'zaù-ē\ *interj* [imit. of the sound of a speeding vehicle] (1902) — used to express astonishment or admiration esp. in response to something sudden or speedy

zoy·sia \'zói-shə, -zhə, -sē-ə, -zē-ə\ *n* [NL, alter. of *Zoisia*, fr. Karl von *Zois* †1800 Ger. botanist] (1924) : any of a genus (*Zoysia*) of creeping perennial grasses of southeastern Asia and New Zealand having fine wiry leaves and including some suitable for lawn grasses esp. in warm regions

Z particle *n* (1979) : a neutral elementary particle about 90 times heavier than a proton that along with the W particle is a transmitter of the weak force — called also Z^0 or Z^0 *particle*

zuc·chet·to \zü-'ke-(ˌ)tō, tsü-\ *n, pl* **-tos** [It, dim. of *zucca* gourd, head] (1853) : a small round skullcap worn by Roman Catholic ecclesiastics in colors that vary according to the rank of the wearer

zuc·chi·ni \zü-'kē-nē\ *n, pl* **-ni** *or* **-nis** [It, pl. of *zucchino*, dim. of *zucca* gourd] (1929) : a summer squash of bushy growth with smooth cylindrical usu. dark green fruits; *also* : its fruit

¹Zu·lu \'zü-(ˌ)lü\ *n, pl* **Zulu** *or* **Zulus** (1824) **1** : a member of a Bantu-speaking people of Natal **2** : the Bantu language of the Zulus — **Zulu** *adj*

²Zulu (1952) — a communications code word for the letter *z*

Zu·ni \'zü-nē\ *also* **Zu·ñi** \'zün-yē\ *n, pl* **Zuni** *or* **Zunis** *also* **Zuñi** *or* **Zuñis** [AmerSp *Zuñí*] (1834) **1** : a member of an American Indian people of western New Mexico **2** : the language of the Zuni people

zup·pa in·gle·se \ˌtsü-pə-iŋ-'glā-(ˌ)zā, ˌzü-, -in-, -(ˌ)sä\ *n, often cap I* [It, lit., English soup] (1941) : a dessert consisting of sponge cake and custard or pudding that is flavored with rum, covered with cream, and garnished with fruit

zwie·back \'swē-ˌbak, 'swī-, 'zwē-, 'zwī-, -ˌbäk\ *n* [G, lit., twice baked, fr. *zwie-* twice (fr. OHG *zwi-*) + *backen* to bake, fr. OHG *bahhan* — more at TWI-, BAKE] (1894) : a usu. sweetened bread enriched with eggs that is baked and then sliced and toasted until dry and crisp

Zwing·li·an \'zwiŋ-glē-ən, 'swiŋ-, -lē-; 'tsfiŋ-lē-\ *adj* (1532) : of or relating to Ulrich Zwingli or his teachings and esp. his doctrine that Christ's presence in the Eucharist is not corporeal but symbolic — **Zwinglian** *n* — **Zwing·li·an·ism** \-ə-ˌni-zəm\ *n*

zwit·ter·ion \'tsvi-tər-ˌī-ˌän *also* 'zwi-\ *n* [G, fr. *Zwitter* hybrid (fr. OHG *zwitaran*, fr. *zwi-*) + *Ion* ion — more at TWI-] (1906) : a dipolar ion — **zwit·ter·ion·ic** \ˌzwi-tər-ī-'ä-nik, ˌswi-\ *adj*

zy·de·co \'zī-də-ˌkō\ *n, often attrib* [perh. modif. of F *les haricots* beans, fr. the Cajun dance tune *Les Haricots Sont Pas Salés*] (1960) : popular music of southern Louisiana that combines tunes of French origin with elements of Caribbean music and the blues and that features guitar, washboard, and accordion

zyg- *or* **zygo-** *comb form* [NL, fr. Gk, fr. *zygon* — more at YOKE] **1** : yoke ⟨zygomorphic⟩ **2** : pair ⟨zygodactyl⟩ **3** : union ⟨zygospore⟩

zyg·apoph·y·sis \ˌzī-gə-'pä-fə-səs\ *n, pl* **-y·ses** \-ˌsēz\ [NL] (1854) : any of the articular processes of the neural arch of a vertebra of which there are usu. two anterior and two posterior

zy·go·dac·tyl \ˌzī-gə-'dak-t⁹l\ *adj* [ISV *zyg-* + Gk *daktylos* toe] (1831) : having the toes arranged two in front and two behind — used of a bird

zy·go·dac·ty·lous \-tə-ləs\ *adj* (ca. 1828) : ZYGODACTYL

zy·go·ma \zī-'gō-mə\ *n, pl* **-ma·ta** \-mə-tə\ *also* **-mas** [NL *zygomat-, zygoma*, fr. Gk *zygōma*, fr. *zygoun* to join, fr. *zygon* yoke] (ca. 1684) **1 a** : ZYGOMATIC ARCH **b** : a slender bony process of the zygomatic arch **2** : ZYGOMATIC BONE

zy·go·mat·ic \ˌzī-gə-'ma-tik\ *adj* (1709) : of, relating to, constituting, or situated in the region of the zygoma and esp. the zygomatic arch

zygomatic arch *n* (1825) : the arch of bone that extends along the front or side of the skull beneath the orbit

zygomatic bone *n* (1709) : a bone of the side of the face below the eye that in mammals forms part of the zygomatic arch and part of the orbit — called also *cheekbone*

zygomatic process *n* (1741) : any of several bony processes that enter into or strengthen the zygomatic arch

zy·go·mor·phic \ˌzī-gə-'mȯr-fik\ *adj* (1875) : having one or more similar parts unequal in size or form so that the whole structure is capable of division into essentially symmetrical halves by only one longitudinal plane passing through the axis ⟨the flower of the pea is ~⟩ — **zy·go·mor·phy** \'zī-gə-ˌmȯr-fē\ *n*

zy·gos·i·ty \zī-'gä-sə-tē\ *n* [prob. fr. *-zygous*] (1946) : the makeup or characteristics of a particular zygote

zy·go·spore \'zī-gə-ˌspōr, -ˌspȯr\ *n* [ISV] (1864) : a thick-walled spore of some algae and fungi that is formed by union of two similar sexual cells, usu. serves as a resting spore, and produces the sporophytic phase of the plant — compare OOSPORE

zy·gote \'zī-ˌgōt\ *n* [Gk *zygōtos* yoked, fr. *zygoun* to join — more at ZYGOMA] (ca. 1887) : a cell formed by the union of two gametes; *broadly* : the developing individual produced from such a cell — **zy·got·ic** \zī-'gä-tik\ *adj*

zy·go·tene \'zī-gə-ˌtēn\ *n* [ISV] (1911) : the stage of meiotic prophase which immediately follows the leptotene and during which synapsis of homologous chromosomes occurs — **zygotene** *adj*

-zygous *adj comb form* [Gk *-zygos* yoked, fr. *zygon* yoke — more at YOKE] : having (such) a zygotic constitution ⟨heterozygous⟩

zym- *or* **zymo-** *comb form* [ISV, fr. Gk, leaven, fr. *zymē* — more at JUICE] **1** : yeast ⟨zymosan⟩ **2** : enzyme ⟨zymogen⟩

zy·mase \'zī-ˌmās, -ˌmäz\ *n* [ISV] (1875) : an enzyme or enzyme complex of yeast that promotes fermentation of sugar

-zyme *n comb form* [Gk *zymē* leaven] : enzyme ⟨lysozyme⟩

zy·mo·gen \'zī-mə-jən\ *n* [ISV] (1877) : an inactive protein precursor of an enzyme secreted by living cells and activated by catalysis (as by a kinase or an acid) — called also *proenzyme*

zy·mo·gram \'zī-mə-ˌgram\ *n* (1957) : an electrophoretic strip (as of starch gel) or a representation of it exhibiting the pattern of separated enzymes and esp. isoenzymes after electrophoresis

zy·mo·san \'zī-mə-ˌsan\ *n* [*zym-* + *-osan* (as in *hexosan*)] (1943) : an insoluble largely polysaccharide fraction of yeast cell walls

Abbreviations

AND SYMBOLS FOR CHEMICAL ELEMENTS

The following list of abbreviations is not intended to be all-inclusive; it does, however, contain many of those most commonly used. Symbols for chemical elements are also included. Most of these abbreviations have been normalized to one form. In practice, however, there is considerable variation in the use of periods and in capitalization (as *mph, m.p.h., Mph,* and *MPH*), and stylings other than those given in this dictionary are often acceptable. For a small number of abbreviations about which the question of punctuation is raised very frequently, a note is added at the entry.

For a list of abbreviations regularly used in this dictionary, see the section Abbreviations in This Work in the front matter. Many of these are also in general use, but as a rule an abbreviation is entered either in that list or this one, not both.

For a list of special signs and symbols not readily alphabetizable, see the section Signs and Symbols in the back matter.

a absent, acceleration, acre, adult, alto, anode, answer, ante, anterior, are, area, atto-, author
Å ace, adenine, ampere, argon
Å angstrom unit
aa ana
AA administrative assistant, Alcoholics Anonymous, antiaircraft, associate in arts, author's alterations
AAA Agricultural Adjustment Administration, American Automobile Association
AAAL American Academy of Arts and Letters
AAAS American Association for the Advancement of Science
AAFP American Academy of Family Physicians
AAMC American Association of Medical Colleges
A and M agricultural and mechanical, ancient and modern
A and R artists and repertory
AAR against all risks
AARP American Association of Retired Persons
AAS associate in applied science
AASCU American Association of State Colleges and Universities
AAU Amateur Athletic Union
AAUP American Association of University Professors
AAUW American Association of University Women
ab about
AB able-bodied seaman, airborne, airman basic, Alberta, [NL *artium baccalaureus*] bachelor of arts
ABA Amateur Boxing Association, American Bankers Association, American Bar Association, American Booksellers Association
abbr abbreviation
ABC American Bowling Congress, American Broadcasting Companies, Australian Broadcasting Corporation
ABCD accelerated business collection and delivery
abd *or* **abdom** abdomen, abdominal
abl ablative
abn airborne
abp archbishop
abr abridged, abridgment
abs absolute, abstract
ABS American Bible Society, antilock braking system
abstr abstract
ac account, acre
Ac actinium, altocumulus
AC air-conditioning, alternating

current, [ML *ante Christum*] before Christ; [L *ante cibum*] before meals; area code, athletic club
acad academic, academy
acc accusative
accel accelerando
acct account, accountant
accus accusative
ACE American Council on Education
ack acknowledge, acknowledgment
ACLU American Civil Liberties Union
ACP African, Caribbean and Pacific (states), American College of Physicians
acpt acceptance
ACS American Chemical Society, American College of Surgeons
act active, actor, actual
ACT Action for Children's Television, American College Test, Association of Classroom Teachers, Australian Capital Territory
actg acting
ACV actual cash value, air cushion vehicle
AD active duty, after date, anno Domini — often printed in small capitals and often punctuated; assembly district, assistant director, athletic director
A/D analog/digital
ADA American Dental Association, Americans for Democratic Action, average daily attendance
ADC aide-de-camp, Aid to Dependent Children, Air Defense Command, assistant division commander
ADD American Dialect Dictionary, attention deficit disorder
addn addition
addnl additional
ADF automatic direction finder
ad int ad interim
ADIZ air defense identification zone
adj adjective, adjunct, adjustment, adjutant
ad loc [L *ad locum*] to or at the place
adm administration, administrative
ADM admiral
admin administration, administrative
adv adverb, [L *adversus*] against; advertisement, advertising, advisory
ad val ad valorem
advt advertisement
AEC Atomic Energy Commission

AEF American Expeditionary Force
aeq [L *aequalis*] equal
aero aeronautical, aeronautics
aet *or* **aetat** [L *aetatis*] of age, aged
af affix
AF air force, audio frequency
AFB air force base
AFC American Football Conference, automatic frequency control
A/1C airman first class
AFDC Aid to Families with Dependent Children
aff affirmative
afft affidavit
AFL American Football League
AFL–CIO American Federation of Labor and Congress of Industrial Organizations
AFP alpha-fetoprotein
Afr Africa, African
aft afternoon
AFT American Federation of Teachers, automatic fine tuning
AFTRA American Federation of Television and Radio Artists
Ag [L *argentum*] silver
AG adjutant general, attorney general
AGC advanced graduate certificate
agcy agency
agl above ground level
agr *or* **agric** agricultural, agriculture
agt agent
AH ampere-hour, anno hegirae, arts and humanities
AHL American Hockey League
AI ad interim, airborne intercept, air interception, artificial insemination, artificial intelligence
AIA American Institute of Architects
AID Agency for International Development, artificial insemination by donor
AIM American Indian Movement
AK Alaska
aka also known as
AKC American Kennel Club
Al aluminum
AL Alabama, American League, American Legion
Ala Alabama
ALA American Library Association
Alb Albania, Albanian
alc alcohol
ALCS American League Championship Series
ald alderman
alg algebra
alk alkaline

alky alkalinity
ALS amyotrophic lateral sclerosis, autographed letter signed
alt alternate, altitude, alto
Alta Alberta
alum aluminum
alw allowance
Am America, American, americium
AM airmail, Air Medal, [L *anno mundi*] in the year of the world — often printed in small capitals; ante meridiem — often not cap and often punctuated; [NL *artium magister*] master of arts
AMA American Medical Association
amb ambassador
amdt amendment
AmE American English
Amer America, American
AmerInd American Indian
AMG allied military government
Amn airman
amp hr ampere-hour
AMSLAN American Sign Language
amt amount
AMU atomic mass unit
AMVETS American Veterans (of World War II)
an annum
AN airman (Navy)
ANA American Nurses Association
anal analogy, analysis, analytic
anat anatomical, anatomy
anc ancient
ANC African National Congress
Angl Anglican
anhyd anhydrous
ann annals, annual
anon anonymous, anonymously
ANOVA analysis of variance
ans answer
ANSI American National Standards Institute
ant antenna, antonym
Ant Antarctica, Antrim
anthrop anthropological, anthropology
antiq antiquarian, antiquary
AO account of, and others
aor aorist
ap apostle, apothecaries'
AP additional premium, adjective phrase, airplane, American plan, antipersonnel, arithmetic progression, armor-piercing, Associated Press, author's proof
APB all points bulletin
APC armored personnel carrier
API air position indicator
APO army post office

Apoc Apocalypse, Apocrypha, apocryphal
app apparatus, appendix, appliance
appl applied
appro approval
approx approximate, approximately
appt appoint, appointed, appointment
apptd appointed
Apr April
APR annual percentage rate
apt apartment, aptitude
aq aqua, aqueous
ar arrival, arrive
Ar Arabic, argon
AR accounts receivable, acknowledgment of receipt, all rail, all risks, annual return, Arkansas, army regulation, autonomous republic
Arab Arabian, Arabic
ARC AIDS-related complex, American Red Cross
arch archaic, archery, architect, architectural, architecture
Arch Archbishop
archeol archeology
arg argent, argument
Arg Argentina
arith arithmetic, arithmetical
Ariz Arizona
Ark Arkansas
Arm Armagh, Armenian
ARM adjustable rate mortgage
ARP air-raid precautions
arr arranged, arrival, arrive
ARRT American Registry of Radiologic Technologists
art article, artificial, artillery
arty artillery
ARV American Revised Version
ARVN Army of the Republic of Vietnam (South Vietnam)
As altostratus, arsenic
AS after sight, airspeed, American Samoa, Anglo-Saxon, antisubmarine, associate in science
ASAP as soon as possible
asb asbestos
ASCAP American Society of Composers, Authors and Publishers
ASE American Stock Exchange
ASEAN Association of Southeast Asian Nations
asgd assigned
asgmt assignment
ASI airspeed indicator
ASL American Sign Language
ASPCA American Society for the Prevention of Cruelty to Animals
ASR airport surveillance radar, air-sea rescue
assn association
assoc associate, associated, association
ASSR Autonomous Soviet Socialist Republic
asst assistant, assorted
asstd assented, assorted
assy assembly
Assyr Assyrian
AST Alaska standard time
ASTM American Society for Testing and Materials
ASTP army specialized training program
astrol astrologer, astrology
astron astronomer, astronomy
ASV American Standard Version
ASW antisubmarine warfare
at airtight, atmosphere, atomic
At astatine
AT air temperature, ampere-turn, automatic transmission
ATC air traffic control
Atl Atlantic
atm atmosphere, atmospheric
ATM automated teller machine, automatic teller machine
at no atomic number
att attached, attention, attorney
attn attention
attrib attributive, attributively
atty attorney
atty gen attorney general
ATV all-terrain vehicle
at wt atomic weight
Au [L *aurum*] gold; author
AU angstrom unit, astronomical unit

AUC [L *ab urbe condita*] from the year of the founding of the city (of Rome)
aud audit, auditor
aug augmentative
Aug August
Aus Austria, Austrian
AUS Army of the United States
Austral Australia
auth authentic, author, authorized
auto automatic
aux auxiliary verb
av avenue, average, avoirdupois
AV ad valorem, audiovisual, Authorized Version
AVC automatic volume control
avdp avoirdupois
ave avenue
avg average
avn aviation
AW actual weight, aircraft warning, articles of war, automatic weapon
AWACS airborne warning and control system
ax axiom, axis
AYC American Youth Congress
AYD American Youth for Democracy
AYH American Youth Hostels
az azimuth, azure
AZ Arizona
b bachelor, bacillus, back, bag, bale, bass, basso, bat, Baumé, before, Bible, billion, bishop, black, blue, bolivar, book, born, bottom, brick, brightness, British, bulb, butut
B boron
Ba barium
BA bachelor of arts, batting average, Buenos Aires
BAA bachelor of applied arts
BAAE bachelor of aeronautical and astronautical engineering
bac [ML *baccalaureus*] bachelor
bact bacterial, bacteriology, bacterium
BAE bachelor of aeronautical engineering, bachelor of agricultural engineering, bachelor of architectural engineering, bachelor of art education, bachelor of arts in education
BAEd bachelor of arts in education
BAeE bachelor of aeronautical engineering
BAEE bachelor of arts in elementary education
BAg bachelor of agriculture
bal balance
BAM bachelor of applied mathematics, bachelor of arts in music
B and B bed-and-breakfast
B and E breaking and entering
b and w black and white
Bap *or* **Bapt** Baptist
bar barometer, barometric, barrel
Bar Baruch
BAr bachelor of architecture
BAR Browning automatic rifle
Bart baronet
BAS bachelor of applied science, bachelor of arts and sciences
BAT bachelor of arts in teaching
Bav Bavaria, Bavarian
BB bachelor of business, ball bearing, base on balls, blue book, B'nai B'rith
BBA bachelor of business administration
BBB Better Business Bureau
BBC British Broadcasting Corporation
BBE bachelor of business education
bbl barrel, barrels
BBQ barbecue
BC before Christ — often printed in small capitals and often punctuated; British Columbia
BCD bad conduct discharge
BCE bachelor of chemical engineering, bachelor of civil engineering, before the Christian Era — often punctuated; before the Common Era — often punctuated
bcf billion cubic feet
BCh bachelor of chemistry
BChE bachelor of chemical engineering

BCL bachelor of canon law, bachelor of civil law
bcn beacon
BCS bachelor of chemical science, bachelor of commercial science
bd barrels per day, board, bound, boundary, bundle
BD bachelor of divinity, bank draft, bills discounted, bomb disposal, brought down
BDA bachelor of dramatic art
bd ft board foot
bdl *or* **bdle** bundle
bdrm bedroom
Be beryllium
BE bachelor of education, bachelor of engineering, bill of exchange, Black English
Bé Baumé
BEC Bureau of Employees' Compensation
BEd bachelor of education
Beds Bedfordshire
BEE bachelor of electrical engineering
bef before
BEF British Expeditionary Force
beg begin, beginning
Belg Belgian, Belgium
BEM bachelor of engineering of mines, British Empire Medal
BEngr bachelor of engineering
BEngS bachelor of engineering science
Berks Berkshire
bet between
BeV billion electron volts
BEV Black English vernacular
bf boldface
BF bachelor of forestry, board foot, brought forward
BFA bachelor of fine arts
bg background, bag, beige, being
BG *or* **B Gen** brigadier general
BH bill of health, Brinell hardness
bhd bulkhead
BHL bachelor of Hebrew letters, bachelor of Hebrew literature
BHN Brinell hardness number
bhp bishop
Bi bismuth
BIA bachelor of industrial administration, Bureau of Indian Affairs
bib Bible, biblical
bibliog bibliography
bid [L *bis in die*] twice a day
BID bachelor of industrial design
BIE bachelor of industrial engineering
bil billion
biog biographer, biographical, biography
biol biologic, biological, biologist, biology
BJ bachelor of journalism
bk bank, book, break, brook
Bk berkelium
bkg banking, bookkeeping, breakage
bkgd background
bks barracks
bkt basket, bracket
bl bale, barrel, black, block, blue
BL bachelor of law, bachelor of letters, baseline, bats left, bill of lading, breadth-length
bld blond, blood
bldg building
bldr builder
BLEVE boiling liquid expanding vapor explosion
BLitt *or* **BLit** [ML *baccalaureus litterarum*] bachelor of letters, bachelor of literature
blk black, block, bulk
BLM Bureau of Land Management
BLS bachelor of liberal studies, bachelor of library science, Bureau of Labor Statistics
blvd boulevard
bm beam
BM bachelor of medicine, bachelor of music, basal metabolism, bill of material, board measure, bowel movement, bronze medal
BME bachelor of mechanical engineering, bachelor of mining engineering, bachelor of music education
BMOC big man on campus
BMR basal metabolic rate
BMS bachelor of marine science

BMT bachelor of medical technology
BMX bicycle motocross
bn baron, battalion, beacon, been
BN bachelor of nursing, bank note, Bureau of Narcotics
BNDD Bureau of Narcotics and Dangerous Drugs
BNS bachelor of naval sciences
BO back order, best offer, body odor, box office, branch office, buyer's option
BOD biochemical oxygen demand, biological oxygen demand
BOQ bachelor officers' quarters
bor borough
bot botanical, botanist, botany, bottle, bottom, bought
botan botanical
bp baptized, base pair, birthplace, bishop
BP batting practice, beautiful people, before the present, bills payable, blood pressure, blueprint, boiling point
bpd barrels per day
BPE bachelor of petroleum engineering, bachelor of physical education
BPh bachelor of philosophy
BPharm bachelor of pharmacy
bpi bits per inch, bytes per inch
bpl birthplace
BPOE Benevolent and Protective Order of Elks
bps bits per second
BPW Board of Public Works, Business and Professional Women's Clubs
br branch, brass, brown
Br Britain, British, bromine
BR bats right, bedroom, bills receivable
Braz Brazil, Brazilian
BRE bachelor of religious education, business reply envelope
Breck Brecknockshire
brig brigade, brigadier
Brig Gen brigadier general
Brit Britain, British
brl barrel
bros brothers
BS bachelor of science, balance sheet, bill of sale, British standard, bullshit — sometimes considered vulgar
BSA bachelor of science in agriculture, Boy Scouts of America
BSAA bachelor of science in applied arts
BSAE bachelor of science in aeronautical engineering, bachelor of science in agricultural engineering, bachelor of science in architectural engineering
BSAg bachelor of science in agriculture
BSArch bachelor of science in architecture
BSB bachelor of science in business
BSc bachelor of science
BSCE bachelor of science in chemical engineering
BSCh bachelor of science in chemistry
BSEc *or* **BSEcon** bachelor of science in economics
BSEd *or* **BSE** bachelor of science in education
BSEE bachelor of science in electrical engineering, bachelor of science in elementary education
BSFor bachelor of science in forestry
BSFS bachelor of science in foreign service
BSI British Standards Institution
bskt basket
BSL bachelor of sacred literature, bachelor of science in languages, bachelor of science in law, bachelor of science in linguistics
BSME bachelor of science in mechanical engineering
bsmt basement
BSN bachelor of science in nursing
BSW bachelor of social work
Bt baronet
btry battery
Btu British thermal unit
bu bureau, bushel
Bucks Buckinghamshire

buff buffalo
Bulg Bulgaria, Bulgarian
bull bulletin
bur bureau
bus business
BV Blessed Virgin
bvt brevet
BW bacteriological warfare, biological warfare, black and white
BWI British West Indies
bx box
BX base exchange
by billion years
BYO bring your own
BYOB bring your own beer, bring your own booze, bring your own bottle
byp bypass
c calm, calorie, Canadian, canceled, candle, carat, case, castle, catcher, Catholic, cedi, cent, centavo, center, centi-, centime, centimeter, centum, century, chairman, chapter, circa, circuit, circumference, clockwise, cloudy, cocaine, codex, coefficient, college, colon, color, colt, [L *congius*] gallon; congress, conservative, contralto, copyright, cost, cubic, cup, curie
C capacitance, carbon, Celsius, centigrade, Coulomb, cytosine
ca circa
Ca calcium
CA California, Central America, certified acupuncturist, chartered accountant, chief accountant, chronological age, commercial agent, controller of accounts, current account
CAB Civil Aeronautics Board
CAD computer-aided design
CAF cost and freight
CAFE corporate average fuel economy
CAGS Certificate of Advanced Graduate Study
CAI computer-aided instruction, computer-assisted instruction
cal calendar, caliber, calorie, small calorie
Cal California, large calorie
calc calculate, calculated
Calif California
cam camera
CAM computer-aided manufacturing
Cambs Cambridgeshire
can canceled, cancellation, cannon, canto
Can or **Canad** Canada, Canadian
canc canceled
C and F cost and freight
C and W country and western
Cant Canticle of Canticles, Cantonese
cap capacity, capital, capitalize, capitalized
CAP Civil Air Patrol
caps capitals, capsule
Capt captain
Car Carlow
CAR civil air regulations
card cardinal
CARE Cooperative for American Relief to Everywhere
CAS certificate of advanced study
cat catalog, catalyst
CAT clear-air turbulence, college ability test, computerized axial tomography
cath cathedral, cathode
CATV community antenna television
caus causative
cav cavalry, cavity
CAVU ceiling and visibility unlimited
Cb columbium, cumulonimbus
CBC Canadian Broadcasting Corporation
CBD cash before delivery, central business district
CBE commander of the Order of the British Empire, companion of the Order of the British Empire
CBI computer-based instruction, Cumulative Book Index
CBO Congressional Budget Office
CBS Columbia Broadcasting System
CBW chemical and biological warfare

cc cubic centimeter
Cc cirrocumulus
CC carbon copy, chief clerk, common carrier, community college, country club
CCC Civilian Conservation Corps
CCD Confraternity of Christian Doctrine
CCF Chinese communist forces
cckw counterclockwise
CCTV closed-circuit television
CCU cardiac care unit, coronary care unit, critical care unit
ccw counterclockwise
cd candela, candle, cord
Cd cadmium
CD carried down, certificate of deposit, civil defense, [F *corps diplomatique*] diplomatic corps
CDC Centers for Disease Control
CDD certificate of disability for discharge
cdg commanding
Cdn Canadian
CDP certificate in data processing
CDR commander
CDT central daylight time
Ce cerium
CE chemical engineer, civil engineer, Christian Era — often punctuated; Common Era — often punctuated; Corps of Engineers
CEA College English Association, Council of Economic Advisors
CED Committee for Economic Development
cem cement
CEMF counter electromotive force
cent centigrade, central, centum, century
Cent Central
CENTO Central Treaty Organization
CERN [*Conseil Européen pour la Recherche Nucléaire*] European Organization for Nuclear Research
cert certificate, certification, certified, certify
CETA Comprehensive Employment and Training Act
CEU continuing education credit
cf calf, [L *confer*, imper. of *conferre* to compare] compare
Cf californium
CF carried forward, centrifugal force, cost and freight, cystic fibrosis
CFC chlorofluorocarbon
CFI certified flight instructor, chief flying instructor; cost, freight, and insurance
CFL Canadian Football League
cfm cubic feet per minute
CFO chief financial officer
CFP Certified Financial Planner
cfs cubic feet per second
cg centigram
CG center of gravity, coast guard, commanding general
cgs centimeter-gram-second
CGT [F *Confédération Générale du Travail*] General Confederation of Labor
ch chain, champion, chaplain, chapter, chief, child, children, church
CH clearinghouse, courthouse, customhouse
chan channel
chap chapter
CHD coronary heart disease
chem chemical, chemist, chemistry
Ches Cheshire
chg change, charge
Chin Chinese
chm chairman, checkmate
Chmn chairman
chron chronicle, chronological, chronology
Chron Chronicles
Ci cirrus, curie
CI cast iron, certificate of insurance, Channel Islands, cost and insurance
CIA Central Intelligence Agency, certified internal auditor
cía [Sp *compañía*] company
CIAA Central Intercollegiate Athletic Association
CIC counterintelligence corps

CID Criminal Investigation Department, cubic inch displacement
cie [F *compagnie*] company
CIF central information file; cost, insurance, and freight
C in C commander in chief
CIP Cataloging in Publication
cir circle, circuit, circular, circumference
circ circular
cit citation, cited, citizen
civ civil, civilian, civilization
CIWS close-in weapons system
CJ chief justice
ck cask, check
cl centiliter, claiming, class, clause, close, closet, cloth
Cl chlorine
CL carload, center line, civil law, common law
cld called, cleared
CLEP College Level Examination Program
clin clinical
clk clerk
clo clothing
clr clear, clearance
CLU chartered life underwriter
cm centimeter, cumulative
Cm curium
CM center matched, circular mil, common meter, [Commonwealth of the Northern Mariana Islands] Northern Mariana Islands, Congregation of the Mission
CMA certified medical assistant
cmd command
cmdg commanding
cmdr commander
CMG Companion of the Order of St. Michael and St. George
cml commercial
CMSgt chief master sergeant
CMV cytomegalovirus
CN credit note
CNC computer numerical control
CNO chief of naval operations
CNS central nervous system
co company, county
Co cobalt
CO cash order, Colorado, commanding officer, conscientious objector
c/o care of
cod codex
COD carrier onboard delivery, cash on delivery, collect on delivery
coeff or **coef** coefficient
C of C Chamber of Commerce
C of S chief of staff
cog cognate
col colonial, colony, color, colored, column, counsel
col or **coll** collateral, collect, collected, collection, college, collegiate
Col colonel, Colorado, Colossians
COL colonel, cost of living
COLA cost-of-living allowance
collat collateral
colloq colloquial
Colo Colorado
colog cologarithm
com comedy, comic, comma
COM computer output microfilm, computer output microfilmer
comb combination, combined, combining, combustion
comd command
comdg commanding
comdr commander
comdt commandant
COMECON Council for Mutual Economic Assistance
coml commercial
comm command, commandant, commander, commanding, commentary, commerce, commercial, commission, commissioned, commissioner, committee, common, commoner, commonwealth, commune, communication, communist, community
commo commodore
comp comparative, compare, compensation, compiled, compiler, composition, compositor, compound, comprehensive, comptroller
compd compound
comr commissioner

con [L *conjunx*] consort; consolidated, consul, continued
conc concentrate, concentrated, concentration, concrete
concn concentration
cond condition, conductivity
conf conference, confidential
Confed Confederate
cong congress, congressional
conj conjunction, conjunctive
Conn Connecticut
cons consecrated, conservative, consigned, consignment, consol, consolidated, consonant, constable, constitution, construction, consul, consulting
consol consolidated
const constant, constitution, constitutional, construction
constr construction
cont containing, contents, continent, continental, continued, control
contd continued
contg containing
contr contract, contraction, contralto, contrary, control, controller
contrib contribution, contributor
conv convention, conventional, convertible, convocation
COO chief operating officer
cop copper, copulative, copy, copyright
cor corner, coroner, corpus, corresponding
Cor Corinthians
CORE Congress of Racial Equality
Corn Cornish, Cornwall
corp corporal, corporation
corr correct, corrected, correction, correspondence, correspondent, corresponding, corrupt, corruption
cos companies, consul, consulship, cosine, counties
COS cash on shipment, chief of staff
cosec cosecant
cot cotangent
cp compare, coupon
CP candlepower, Cape Province, center of pressure, cerebral palsy, charter party, chemically pure, command post, communist party, Congregation of the Passion, custom of port
CPA certified public accountant
CPB Corporation for Public Broadcasting
CPCU chartered property casualty underwriter
cpd compound
CPFF cost plus fixed fee
cpi characters per inch
CPI consumer price index
cpl complete, compline
Cpl corporal
CPM cost per thousand
CPO chief petty officer
CPOM master chief petty officer
CPOS senior chief petty officer
CPR cardiopulmonary resuscitation
CPS cards per second, certified professional secretary, characters per second, Civilian Public Service, cycles per second
CPSC Consumer Product Safety Commission
CPT captain
cpu central processing unit
CQ call to quarters, charge of quarters, commercial quality
cr center, circular, commander, cream, creased, credit, creditor, creek, crescendo, cruzeiro
Cr chromium
CR carrier's risk, cathode ray, class rate, conditioned reflex, conditioned response, consciousness-raising, Costa Rica, current rate
CRC Civil Rights Commission
cresc crescendo
crim criminal
crim con criminal conversation
criminol criminologist, criminology
crit critical, criticism, criticized
CRNA certified registered nurse anesthetist
CRT carrier route

cryst crystalline, crystallized
cs case, cases, census, consciousness, consul
Cs cesium, cirrostratus
CS capital stock, cesarean section, chief of staff, Christian Science practitioner, civil service, conditioned stimulus, county seat
CSA Confederate States of America
csc cosecant
CSC Civil Service Commission
CSF cerebrospinal fluid
CSM command sergeant major
CST central standard time
ct carat, cent, count, county, court
CT central time, certificated teacher, certified teacher, code telegram, computed tomography, computerized tomography, Connecticut
CTC centralized traffic control
ctf certificate
ctn carton, cotangent
c to c center to center
ctr center, counter
cu cubic, cumulative
Cu cumulus, [L *cuprum*] copper
CU close-up
cum cumulative
Cumb Cumbria
cur currency, current
cv *or* **cvt** convertible
CV cardiovascular, chief value, curriculum vitae
CVA Columbia Valley Authority
cw clockwise
CW chemical warfare, chief warrant officer, continuous wave
CWO cash with order, chief warrant officer
cwt hundredweight
CY calendar year
cyl cylinder
CYO Catholic Youth Organization
cytol cytological, cytology
CZ Canal Zone
d date, daughter, day, dead, deceased, deci-, degree, [L *denarius, denarii*] penny, pence; depart, departure, diameter, differential, dimensional, distance, dorsal, drive, driving
D Democrat, derivative, deuterium, Dutch
da deka-
DA days after acceptance, delayed action, deposit account, Dictionary of Americanisms, district attorney, doctor of arts, documents against acceptance, documents for acceptance, don't answer
DAB Dictionary of American Biography
DAE Dictionary of American English
dag dekagram
DAH Dictionary of American History
dal dekaliter
dam dekameter
Dan Daniel, Danish
D & C dilation and curettage
DAR Daughters of the American Revolution
DARE Dictionary of American Regional English
DARPA Defense Advanced Research Projects Agency
dat dative
DAT differential aptitude test, digital audiotape
dau daughter
DAV Disabled American Veterans
db debenture
dB decibel
DB daybook
d/b/a doing business as
DBA doctor of business administration
DBE Dame Commander of the Order of the British Empire
DBH diameter at breast height
dbl *or* **dble** double
DBMS data base management system
DBS direct broadcast satellite
DC [It *da capo*] from the beginning; decimal classification, direct current, District of Columbia,

doctor of chiropractic, double crochet
DChE doctor of chemical engineering
DCL doctor of canon law, doctor of civil law
dd dated, delivered
DD days after date, demand draft, dishonorable discharge, doctor of divinity, due date
DDC Dewey Decimal Classification
DDD direct distance dialing
DDS doctor of dental science, doctor of dental surgery
DE defensive end, Delaware, doctor of engineering
DEA Drug Enforcement Administration
deb debenture
dec deceased, declaration, declared, declination, decorated, decorative, decrease, decrescendo
Dec December
decd deceased
def defendant, defense, deferred, defined, definite, definition
deg degree
del delegate, delegation, delete
Del Delaware
dely delivery
dem demonstrative, demurrage
Dem Democrat, Democratic
Den Denmark
dent dental, dentist, dentistry
dep depart, department, departure, deponent, deposed, deposit, depot, deputy
depr depreciation, depression
dept department
der *or* **deriv** derivation, derivative
Derbys Derbyshire
derm dermatologist, dermatology
det detached, detachment, detail, determine
detd determined
detn detention, determination
Deut Deuteronomy
dev deviation
Devon Devonshire
DEW distant early warning
DF damage free, direction finder, direction finding
DFA doctor of fine arts
DFC Distinguished Flying Cross
dft defendant, draft
dg decigram
DG [LL *Dei gratia*] by the grace of God; director general
DH designated hitter, doctor of humanities
DHL doctor of Hebrew letters, doctor of Hebrew literature
DI drill instructor
dia diameter
diag diagonal, diagram
dial dialect, dialectical
diam diameter
dict dictionary
dif *or* **diff** difference
dig digest
dil dilute
dim dimension, diminished, diminuendo, diminutive
dimin diminuendo
din dinar
DIN [G *Deutsche Industrie Normen*] German Industrial Standards
dip diploma
dir direction, director
dis discharge, discount, distance
disc discount
disp dispensary
diss dissertation
dist distance, district
distn distillation
distr distribute, distribution
div divided, dividend, division, divorced
DJ district judge, doctor of jurisprudence, dust jacket
DJIA Dow-Jones Industrial Average
dk dark, deck, dock
dl deciliter
DL disabled list
DLitt *or* **DLit** [NL *doctor litterarum*] doctor of letters, doctor of literature
DLO dead letter office, dispatch loading office
DLS doctor of library science
dm decimeter

DM deutsche mark
DMA doctor of musical arts
DMD [NL *dentariae medicinae doctor*] doctor of dental medicine
DMin doctor of ministry
DML doctor of modern languages
DMZ demilitarized zone
dn down
DNB Dictionary of National Biography
DNF did not finish
DNR do not resuscitate
do ditto
DO defense order, doctor of osteopathy
DOA dead on arrival
DOB date of birth
doc document
DOD Department of Defense
DOE Department of Energy
dol dollar
dom domestic, dominant, dominion
Don Donegal
Dors Dorset
DOS disk operating system
DOT Department of Transportation
doz dozen
DP data processing, degree of polymerization, dew point, doctor of podiatry, double play
DPE doctor of physical education
DPh doctor of philosophy
DPH department of public health, doctor of public health
DPM doctor of podiatric medicine
dpt department, deponent
DPT diphtheria, pertussis, tetanus
DQ disqualification, disqualify
dr debtor, drachma, dram, drive, drum
Dr doctor
DR dead reckoning, dining room
dram dramatic, dramatist
DS [It *dal segno*] from the sign; days after sight, detached service, document signed
DSc doctor of science
DSC Distinguished Service Cross, doctor of surgical chiropody
DSM Distinguished Service Medal
DSO Distinguished Service Order
DSP [L *decessit sine prole*] died without issue
DST daylight saving time, doctor of sacred theology
DSW doctor of social welfare, doctor of social work
DT daylight time, doctor of theology, double time
DTh doctor of theology
DTP desktop publishing; diphtheria, tetanus, pertussis
Du Dutch
Dub Dublin
DUI driving under the influence
Dumf Gal Dumfries and Galloway
dup duplex, duplicate
Dur Durham
DV [L *Deo volente*] God willing; Douay Version
DVM doctor of veterinary medicine
DW deadweight, delayed weather, distilled water, dust wrapper
DWI driving while intoxicated, Dutch West Indies
dwt deadweight ton, pennyweight
DX distance
dy delivery, deputy, duty
Dy dysprosium
dynam dynamics
dz dozen
e earth, east, easterly, eastern, edge, eldest, ell, empty, end, energy, erg, error, excellent
E electromotive force, energy, English, exponent
ea each
E and OE errors and omissions excepted
EB eastbound
EBC Educational Broadcasting Corporation
EBV Epstein-Barr virus
EC European Community
eccl ecclesiastic, ecclesiastical
Eccles Ecclesiastes

Ecclus Ecclesiasticus
ECG electrocardiogram
ECM electronic countermeasure, European Common Market
ecol ecological, ecology
econ economics, economist, economy
ECT electroconvulsive therapy
Ecua Ecuador
ed edited, edition, editor, education
EDB ethylene dibromide
EdD doctor of education
EDD English Dialect Dictionary
EDP electronic data processing
EdS specialist in education
EDT eastern daylight time
educ education, educational
EE electrical engineer
EEC European Economic Community
EEG electroencephalogram, electroencephalograph
EENT eye, ear, nose, and throat
EEO equal employment opportunity
eff efficiency
EFT *or* **EFTS** electronic funds transfer (system)
e.g. [L *exempli gratia*] for example
Eg Egypt, Egyptian
EGF epidermal growth factor
EHF extremely high frequency
EHP effective horsepower, electric horsepower
EHV extra high voltage
EKG [G *Elektrokardiogramm*] electrocardiogram, electrocardiograph
el elevation
elec electric, electrical, electricity
elem elementary
elev elevation
ELF extremely low frequency
Eliz Elizabethan
EM electromagnetic, electron microscope, electron microscopy, end matched, engineer of mines, enlisted man
emer emeritus
EMG electromyogram, electromyograph, electromyography
emp emperor, empress
EMP electromagnetic pulse
emu electromagnetic unit
enc *or* **encl** enclosure
ency *or* **encyc** encyclopedia
ENE east-northeast
eng engine, engineer, engineering
Eng England, English
engr engineer, engraved, engraver, engraving
enl enlarged, enlisted
ENS ensign
ENT ear, nose, and throat
entom *or* **entomol** entomological, entomology
env envelope
EO executive order
EOE equal opportunity employer
EOM end of month
EP estimated position, European plan, extended play
EPA Environmental Protection Agency
Eph *or* **Ephes** Ephesians
Episc Episcopal
eq equal, equation
equip equipment
equiv equivalency, equivalent
Er erbium
ER earned run, emergency room
ERA earned run average, Equal Rights Amendment
ERISA Employee Retirement Income Security Act
Es einsteinium
ESB electrical stimulation of the brain
Esd Esdras
ESE east-southeast
Esk Eskimo
ESL English as a second language
ESOP employee stock ownership plan
esp especially
Esq *or* **Esqr** esquire
est established, estimate, estimated
EST eastern standard time
Esth Esther
Et ethyl
ET eastern time
ETA estimated time of arrival

et al [L *et alii* (masc.), *et aliae* (fem.), or *et alia* (neut.)] and others
etc et cetera
ETD estimated time of departure
ETO European theater of operations
et seq [L *et sequens*] and the following one; [L *et sequentes* (masc. & fem. pl.), or *et sequentia* (neut. pl.)] and the following ones
et ux [L *et uxor*] and wife
ETV educational television
Eu europium
Eur Europe, European
eV electron volt
EVA extravehicular activity
eval evaluation
evap evaporate
evg evening
EW enlisted woman
ex example, exchange, executive, express, extra
Ex Exodus
exc excellent, except
exch exchange, exchanged
excl exclude, excluded, excluding
exec executive
exhbn exhibition
Exod Exodus
exor executor
exp expense, experience, experiment, experimental, exponent, export, express
expt experiment
exptl experimental
expwy expressway
exrx executrix
ext extension, exterior, external, externally, extra, extract
Ez or **Ezr** Ezra
Ezech Ezechiel
Ezek Ezekiel
f failure, false, family, faraday, feast, female, feminine, femto-, fermi, fine, finish, fluid, fluidness, focal length, [following] and the following one; force, forte, fragile, frequency, from, full
F Fahrenheit, farad, fluorine, French, Friday
FA field artillery, fielding average, football association
FAA Federal Aviation Administration, free of all average
fac facsimile, faculty
FADM fleet admiral
Fah or **Fahr** Fahrenheit
fam familiar, family
F and A fore and aft
FAO Food and Agriculture Organization of the United Nations
FAQ fair average quality
far farthing
FAS firsts and seconds, free alongside (ship)
fasc fascicle
fath fathom
FB foreign body, freight bill
FBI Federal Bureau of Investigation
FC fire control, fire controlman, follow copy, food control, footcandle
FCA Farm Credit Administration
FCC Federal Communications Commission
fcp foolscap
fcy fancy
FD fire department, free dock
FDA Food and Drug Administration
FDIC Federal Deposit Insurance Corporation
Fe [L *ferrum*] iron
Feb February
fec [L *fecit*] he made it
fed federal, federation
fedn federation
fem female, feminine
FEMA Federal Emergency Management Agency
FEPA Fair Employment Practices Act
FEPC Fair Employment Practices Commission
FERA Federal Emergency Relief Administration
Ferm Fermanagh
FET Federal excise tax, field-effect transistor
ff folios, [following] and the following ones; fortissimo

FHA Federal Housing Administration
FICA Federal Insurance Contributions Act
fict fiction, fictitious
fi fa fieri facias
FIFO first in, first out
fig figurative, figuratively, figure
fin finance, financial, finish
FIO free in and out
fl flanker, floor, florin, [L *floruit*] flourished; fluid
FL Florida, focal length, foreign language
Fla Florida
fl dr fluid dram
Flem Flemish
Flint or **Flints** Flintshire
FLIR forward-looking infrared
fl oz fluid ounce
FLSA Fair Labor Standards Act
fm fathom
Fm fermium
FM field manual
FMCS Federal Mediation and Conciliation Service
fn footnote
fo or **fol** folio
FO field officer, field order, finance officer, flight officer, foreign office, forward observer
FOB free on board
FOC free of charge
FOE Fraternal Order of Eagles
FOIA Freedom of Information Act
for foreign, forestry
FOR free on rail
forz forzando
FOS free on steamer
FOT free on truck
4WD four-wheel drive
fow first open water
fp freezing point
FPA Foreign Press Association, free of particular average
FPC fish protein concentrate
fpm feet per minute
FPO fleet post office
fps feet per second, foot-pound-second, frames per second
fr father, franc, friar, from
Fr France, francium, French, Friday
FRB Federal Reserve Board
freq frequency, frequent, frequentative, frequently
FRG Federal Republic of Germany
Fri Friday
FRM fixed rate mortgage
front frontispiece
FRS Federal Reserve System
frt freight
frwy freeway
fs femtosecond
FS filmstrip, Foreign Service
FSH follicle-stimulating hormone
FSLIC Federal Savings and Loan Insurance Corporation
FSO Foreign Service Officer
ft feet, foot, fort
FT Fourier transform, free throw, full time
FTC Federal Trade Commission
FTE full-time equivalent
fth fathom
ft lb foot-pound
fund fundamental
fur furlong
fut future
FV [L *folio verso* the page being turned] on the back of the page
fwd foreword, forward
FWD front-wheel drive
FX foreign exchange
FY fiscal year
FYI for your information
g acceleration of gravity, game, gauge, gelding, gender, good, gram, grand, gravity
G German, giga-, guanine, Gulf
ga gauge
Ga gallium, Georgia
GA Gamblers Anonymous, general agent, general assembly, general average, general of the army, Georgia
GAAP generally accepted accounting principles
gal gallery, gallon
Gal Galatians
galv galvanized
GAO General Accounting Office

gar garage
GAR Grand Army of the Republic
GATT General Agreement on Tariffs and Trade
gaz gazette
GB Great Britain
GBF Great Books Foundation
GC gas chromatograph, gas chromatography
GCA ground-controlled approach
GCB Knight Grand Cross of the Bath
GCD greatest common divisor
GCF greatest common factor
GCT Greenwich civil time
gd good
Gd gadolinium
GDR German Democratic Republic
Ge germanium
GE gilt edges
GED General Educational Development (tests), general equivalency diploma
GEM ground-effect machine
gen general, genitive, genus
Gen Genesis
Gen AF general of the air force
genl general
geog geographic, geographical, geography
geol geologic, geological, geology
geom geometric, geometrical, geometry
ger gerund
Ger German, Germany
GeV giga-electron-volt
GHQ general headquarters
GHz gigahertz
gi gill
GI galvanized iron, gastrointestinal, general issue, government issue
Gib or **Gibr** Gibraltar
GIGO garbage in, garbage out
GIT Group Inclusive Tour
Gk Greek
Glos Gloucestershire
gm gram
GM general manager, grand master, guided missile
GMT Greenwich mean time
GMW gram-molecular weight
gn guinea
GNI gross national income
GNP gross national product
GO general order
GOP Grand Old Party (Republican)
Goth Gothic
gov government, governor
govt government
gp group
GP general practice, general practitioner, geometric progression
GPA grade point average
GPD gallons per day
GPH gallons per hour
GPM gallons per minute
GPO general post office, Government Printing Office
GPS gallons per second
GQ general quarters
gr grade, grain, gram, gravity, gross
Gr Greece, Greek
grad graduate, graduated
gram grammar, grammatical
Gramp Grampian
GRAS generally recognized as safe
GRE Graduate Record Examination
gro gross
GRP glass-reinforced plastic
GRU [Russ *Glavnoe razvedyvatel'noe upravlenic*] Chief Intelligence Directorate
gr wt gross weight
GS general staff, giant slalom, government service, ground speed
GSA General Services Administration, Girl Scouts of America
GSC general staff corps
GSL Guaranteed Student Loan
GSO general staff officer
GSR galvanic skin response
GST Greenwich sidereal time
GSUSA Girl Scouts of the United States of America
gt gilt top, great
GT gross ton
Gt Brit Great Britain

gtd guaranteed
Gtr Man Greater Manchester
gtt [L *gutta*, pl. *guttae*] drop
GU genitourinary, Guam
GUT grand unified theory, grand unification theory
GWRBI game winning run batted in
Gwyn Gwynedd
gyn or **gynecol** gynecology
Gy Sgt gunnery sergeant
h half, harbor, hard, hardness, hecto-, height, high, hit, horse, hour, humidity, hundred, Hungary, husband
H Hamiltonian, henry, heroin, hydrogen
ha hectare
HA hour angle
Hab Habakkuk
hab corp habeas corpus
Hag Haggai
Hants Hampshire
Hb hemoglobin
HBM Her Britannic Majesty, His Britannic Majesty
HC Holy Communion, House of Commons, hydrocarbon
HCF highest common factor
HCG human chorionic gonadotropin
HCL high cost of living
hd head
HD heavy-duty
hdbk handbook
hdkf handkerchief
HDTV high-definition television
hdwe hardware
He helium
HE Her Excellency, high explosive, His Eminence, His Excellency
Heb Hebrew, Hebrews
her heraldry
Heref/Worcs Hereford and Worcester
Herts Hertfordshire
HEW Department of Health, Education, and Welfare
hex hexagon, hexagonal
hf half
Hf hafnium
HF height finding, high frequency, home forces
hg hectogram, heliogram, hemoglobin
Hg [NL *hydrargyrum*, lit., water silver] mercury
HGH human growth hormone
hgt height
hgwy highway
HH Her Highness, His Highness, His Holiness
HHD [NL *humanitatum doctor*] doctor of humanities
HHS Department of Health and Human Services
HI Hawaii, high intensity, humidity index
hist historian, historical, history
Hitt Hittite
HJ [L *hic jacet*] here lies
HJR House joint resolution
hl hectoliter
HL House of Lords
hld hold
hlqn harlequin
HLS [L *hoc loco situs*] laid in this place; holograph letter signed
hlt halt
hm hectometer
HM Her Majesty, Her Majesty's, His Majesty, His Majesty's
HMAS Her Majesty's Australian ship, His Majesty's Australian ship
HMBS Her Majesty's British ship, His Majesty's British ship
HMC Her Majesty's Customs, His Majesty's Customs
HMCS Her Majesty's Canadian ship, His Majesty's Canadian ship
HMS Her Majesty's ship, His Majesty's ship
HN head nurse
Ho holmium
hom homiletics, homily
hon honor, honorable, honorary
Hon or **Hond** Honduras
HOPE Health Opportunity for People Everywhere
hor horizontal
hort horticultural, horticulture

Hos Hosea
hosp hospital
HOV high-occupancy vehicle
hp horsepower
HP half pay, high pressure, hire purchase
HPA high-power amplifier
HPF highest possible frequency, high power field
HPV human-powered vehicle
HQ headquarters
hr here, hour
HR home run, House of Representatives
H Res House resolution
HRH Her Royal Highness, His Royal Highness
hrzn horizon
HS high school
HSL high-speed launch
HST Hawaiian standard time, hypersonic transport
ht height
HT half time, halftone, hardtop, Hawaii time, high-tension, high tide, [L *hoc tempore*] at this time; [L *hoc titulo*] under this title
HUAC House Un-American Activities Committee
HUD Department of Housing and Urban Development
Humber Humberside
Hung Hungarian, Hungary
hv have
HV high velocity, high voltage
HVAC heating, ventilating, and air-conditioning
hvy heavy
hw how
HW high water, highway, hot water
HWM high-water mark
hwy highway
hyd hydraulics, hydrostatics
hyp hypothesis, hypothetical
Hz hertz
i industrial, initial, intelligence, intensity, intransitive, island, isle
I electric current, Indian, interstate, iodine, Israeli
Ia *or* **IA** Iowa
IAA indoleacetic acid
IAAF International Amateur Athletic Federation
IABA International Amateur Boxing Association
IAEA International Atomic Energy Agency
IALC instrument approach and landing chart
IAM International Association of Machinists and Aerospace Workers
IAP international airport
IAS indicated airspeed
IATA International Air Transport Association
IAU International Association of Universities, International Astronomical Union
ib *or* **ibid** ibidem
IB in bond, incendiary bomb
IBRD International Bank for Reconstruction and Development
ICA International Cooperative Alliance
ICAO International Civil Aviation Organization
ICC International Chamber of Commerce, Interstate Commerce Commission
Ice Iceland
ICE internal combustion engine, International Cultural Exchange
Icel Icelandic
ICF intermediate care facility
ICFTU International Confederation of Free Trade Unions
ICJ International Court of Justice
ICRC International Committee of the Red Cross
ICU intensive care unit
id idem
ID Idaho, identification, independent distributor, industrial design, inner diameter, inside dimensions, intelligence department, internal diameter
IDA International Development Association
IDP international driving permit
i.e. [L *id est*] that is
IE industrial engineer

IEEE The Institute of Electrical and Electronics Engineers
IF intermediate frequency
IFC International Finance Corporation
IFF identification, friend or foe
IFO identified flying object
IFR instrument flight rules
Ig immunoglobulin
IG inspector general
IGY International Geophysical Year
ihp indicated horsepower
IIE Institute of Industrial Engineers
IL Illinois
ILA International Longshoremen's Association
ILGWU International Ladies' Garment Workers' Union
ill illustrated, illustration, illustrator
Ill Illinois
illust *or* **illus** illustrated, illustration
ILO International Labor Organization
ILS instrument landing system
IL–2 interleukin-2
IM individual medley, intramural
IMCO Inter-Governmental Maritime Consultative Organization
IMF International Monetary Fund
imit imitative
immed immediate, immediately
immun immunity, immunization
immunol immunology
imp imperative, imperfect, imperial, import, imported
IMP international match point
imperf imperfect, imperforate
in inch, inlet
In indium
IN Indiana
inc incomplete, incorporated, increase
incl include, included, including, inclusive
incog incognito
incr increase, increased
ind independent, index, industrial, industry
Ind Indian, Indiana
IND investigational new drug
IndE industrial engineer
indef indefinite
indic indicative
indiv individual
indn indication
Indon Indonesia, Indonesian
indus industrial, industry
inf infantry, infinitive
INF intermediate range nuclear forces
infl influenced
INH [*iso-nicotinic acid hydrazide*] isoniazid
inorg inorganic
INP International News Photo
inq inquire
INRI [L *Iesus Nazarenus Rex Iudaeorum*] Jesus of Nazareth, King of the Jews
ins inches, insurance
INS Immigration and Naturalization Service, inertial navigation system
insol insoluble
insp inspector
inst instant, institute, institution, institutional
instr instructor, instrument, instrumental
insur insurance
int intelligence, intercept, interest, interim, interior, interjection, interleaved, intermediate, internal, international, interpreter, intersection, interval, interview, intransitive
intel intelligence
interj interjection
Interpol International Criminal Police Organization
interrog interrogative
intl *or* **intnl** international
intrans intransitive
in trans [L *in transitu*] in transit
introd introduction
inv inventor, invoice
I/O input/output
IOC International Olympic Committee

IOM Isle of Man
Ion Ionic
IOOF Independent Order of Odd Fellows
IORM Improved Order of Red Men
IOW Isle of Wight
IP initial point, innings pitched, intermediate pressure
IPA individual practice association
ipm inches per minute
ips inches per second
IPTS International Practical Temperature Scale
iq [L *idem quod*] the same as
Ir iridium, Irish
IR information retrieval, infrared, inland revenue, intelligence ratio, internal revenue
IRA Irish Republican Army
IRBM intermediate range ballistic missile
Ire Ireland
irid iridescent
irred irredeemable
irreg irregular
IRS Internal Revenue Service
is island, isle
Isa *or* **Is** Isaiah
ISBN International Standard Book Number
ISC interstate commerce
isl island
ISO International Organization for Standardization
isoln isolation
Isr Israel, Israeli
ISSN International Standard Serial Number
isth isthmus
ISV International Scientific Vocabulary
It Italian, Italy
ital italic, italicized
Ital Italian
ITO International Trade Organization
ITU International Telecommunication Union, International Typographical Union
ITV instructional television
IU international unit
IV intravenous, intravenously
IVF in vitro fertilization
IW inside width, isotopic weight
IWW Industrial Workers of the World
j jack, journal, judge, justice
J joule, jump shot
JA joint account, judge advocate
JAG judge advocate general
Jam Jamaica
Jan January
Jas James
Jav Javanese
JBS John Birch Society
JC junior college
JCAHO Joint Commission on Accreditation of Healthcare Organizations
JCB [NL *juris canonici baccalaureus*] bachelor of canon law
JCD [NL *juris canonici doctor*] doctor of canon law
JCL [NL *juris canonici licentiatus*] licentiate in canon law
JCS joint chiefs of staff
jct junction
JD [NL *juris doctor*] doctor of jurisprudence, doctor of law; [NL *jurum doctor*] doctor of laws; justice department, juvenile delinquent
Jer Jeremiah, Jeremias
jg junior grade
JIT job instruction training, just in time
Jn *or* **Jno** John
JND just noticeable difference
jnr *Brit* junior
Jo Joel
Jon Jonah, Jonas
Josh Joshua
jour journal, journeyman
JP jet propulsion, justice of the peace
Jpn Japan, Japanese
Jr junior
JSD [NL *juris scientiae doctor*] doctor of science of law
jt *or* **jnt** joint
Jud Judith
Judg Judges

Jul July
jun junior
Jun June
junc junction
juv juvenile
JV junior varsity
k karat, kindergarten, king, kitchen, knit, knot, koruna, kosher — often enclosed in a circle; kyat
K [NL *kalium*] potassium; Kelvin, kilometer
ka [G *Kathode*] cathode
Kan *or* **Kans** Kansas
kb kilobar, kilobase
KB kilobyte
kbar kilobar
kc kilocycle
KC Kansas City, King's Counsel, Knights of Columbus
kcal kilocalorie, kilogram calorie
KCB knight commander of the Order of the Bath
kc/s kilocycles per second
KD kiln-dried, knockdown, knocked down
Ker Kerry
keV kilo-electron volt
kg keg, kilogram, king
kG kilogauss
KG knight of the Order of the Garter
KGB [Russ *Komitet gosudarstvennoi bezopasnosti*] (Soviet) State Security Committee
kgps kilograms per second
kHz kilohertz
KIA killed in action
Kild Kildare
Kilk Kilkenny
kit kitchen
kJ kilojoule
KJV King James Version
KKK Ku Klux Klan
kl kiloliter
km kilometer
kmh *or* **kmph** kilometers per hour
kmps kilometers per second
kn knot
K of C Knights of Columbus
Kor Korea, Korean
kPa kilopascal
kpc kiloparsec
kph kilometers per hour
Kr krypton
KS Kansas, Kaposi's sarcoma
kt karat, knight, knot
KT kiloton
kV kilovolt
kW kilowatt
kWh kilowatt-hour
Ky *or* **KY** Kentucky
l lady, lake, lambert, land, large, late, left, [L *libra*] pound; line, liquid, lira, lire, liter, little, low
L Lagrangian, Latin, long
La lanthanum, Louisiana
LA law agent, legislative assistant, Los Angeles, Louisiana
Lab Labrador
lam laminated
Lam Lamentations
Lancs Lancashire
lang language
lat latitude
Lat Latin, Latvia
LAT local apparent time
lav lavatory
lb [L *libra*] pound
LB Labrador
LBO leveraged buyout
lc lowercase
LC landing craft, left center, letter of credit, Library of Congress
LCD least common denominator, lowest common denominator
LCDR lieutenant commander
LCL less-than-carload lot
LCM least common multiple, lowest common multiple, [NL *legis comparativae magister*] master of comparative law
LCpl lance corporal
LCS League Championship Series
LCT local civil time
ld load, lord
LD learning disabled, learning disability; lethal dose — often used with a numerical subscript to indicate the percent of a test group of organisms the dose is expected to kill $\langle LD_{50}\rangle$; line of departure
LDC less developed country

ldg landing, loading
LDH lactate dehydrogenase, lactic dehydrogenase
ldr leader
LDS Latter-day Saints
LE leading edge
lea leather
Leb Lebanese, Lebanon
lect lecture, lecturer
leg legal, legato, legislative, legislature
legis legislation, legislative, legislature
Leics Leicestershire
Leit Leitrim
LEM lunar excursion module
LEP limited English proficiency, limited English proficient
Lev or **Levit** Leviticus
lf lightface
LF ledger folio, low frequency
lg large, long
LH left hand, lower half, luteinizing hormone
LHD [NL *litterarum humaniorum doctor*] doctor of humane letters, doctor of humanities
li link
Li lithium
LI Long Island
lib liberal, librarian, library
lic license
lieut lieutenant
LIFO last in, first out
Lim Limerick
lin lineal, linear
Lincs Lincolnshire
ling linguistics
liq liquid, liquor
lit liter, literal, literally, literary, literature
lith lithographic, lithography
Litt B or **Lit B** [ML *litterarum baccalaureus*] bachelor of letters, bachelor of literature
Litt D or **Lit D** [ML *litterarum doctor*] doctor of letters, doctor of literature
Lk Luke
ll lines
LL lending library, limited liability, lower left
LLB [NL *legum baccalaureus*] bachelor of laws
LLD [NL *legum doctor*] doctor of laws
LLM [NL *legum magister*] master of laws
lm lumen
LM Legion of Merit, long meter, lunar module
LMG light machine gun
LMT local mean time
ln lane, natural logarithm
lndg landing
LNG liquefied natural gas
LOA length overall
loc cit [L *loco citato*] in the place cited
log logic
Lond London, Londonderry
long longitude
Long Longford
loq [L *loquitur*] he speaks, she speaks
LOS line of scrimmage, line of sight
Loth Lothian
Lou Louth
LP low pressure
LPG liquefied petroleum gas
LPGA Ladies Professional Golf Association
Lr lawrencium
LR living room, log run, lower right
LRT light-rail transit
LRV light-rail vehicle
LS left side, letter signed, library science, [L *locus sigilli*] place of the seal; long shot
LSAT Law School Admission Test
LSI large-scale integrated circuit, large-scale integration
LSM letter-sorting machine
LSS lifesaving service, lifesaving station, life-support system
LST landing ship, tank; local sidereal time
lt light
Lt lieutenant
LT long ton, low-tension

LTC lieutenant colonel, long term care
Lt Col lieutenant colonel
Lt Comdr lieutenant commander
ltd limited
LTG or **Lt Gen** lieutenant general
lt gov lieutenant governor
LTh licentiate in theology
LTJG lieutenant, junior grade
LTL less than truckload
ltr letter, lighter
LTS launch telemetry station, launch tracking system
Lu lutetium
lub lubricant, lubricating
Luth Lutheran
lv leave
LVT landing vehicle, tracked
LW low water
LWM low-water mark
LWV League of Women Voters
lx lux
LZ landing zone
m male, manual, married, martyr, masculine, mass, meridian, [L *meridies*] noon; meter, middle, mile, [L *mille*] thousand; milli-, minute, molal, molality, molar, molarity, mole, month, moon, morning, muscle
m- meta-
M Mach, March, May, medium, mega-, million, monsieur
mA milliampere
MA [ML *magister artium*] master of arts; Massachusetts, mental age, Middle Ages
MAA master of applied arts
Mac Machabees
Mac or **Macc** Maccabees
MAC military airlift command
mach machine, machining, machinist
MAD mutual assured destruction
MAE or **MA Ed** master of arts in education
mag magnesium, magnetism, magneto, magnitude
Maj major
Maj Gen major general
Mal Malachi
MALS master of arts in liberal studies, master of arts in library science
man manual
Man Manitoba
M&A mergers and acquisitions
manuf manufacture, manufacturing
MAO monoamine oxidase
MAP modified American plan
mar maritime
Mar March
MARC machine readable cataloging
MARV maneuverable reentry vehicle
masc masculine
MASH mobile army surgical hospital
Mass Massachusetts
MAT master of arts in teaching, Miller analogy test
math mathematical, mathematician
matric matriculated, matriculation
Matt Matthew
MATV master antenna television
max maximum
mb millibar
MB bachelor of medicine, Manitoba, megabyte, municipal borough
MBA master of business administration
mbd million barrels per day
MBD minimal brain dysfunction
MBE member of the Order of the British Empire
MBO management by objective
MBS Mutual Broadcasting System
mc megacycle, millicurie
MC member of Congress
MCAT Medical College Admission Test
MCC mission control center
mcf thousand cubic feet
mcg microgram
MCL Marine Corps League, master of civil law, master of comparative law

MCP male chauvinist pig
MCPO master chief petty officer
Md Maryland, mendelevium
MD [NL *medicinae doctor*] doctor of medicine; [It *mano destra*] right hand; Maryland, medical department, months after date, muscular dystrophy
MDC more developed country
MDiv master of divinity
mdnt midnight
mdse merchandise
MDT mountain daylight time
Me Maine, methyl
ME Maine, managing editor, mechanical engineer, medical examiner
Mea Meath
meas measure
mech mechanical, mechanics
med medicine, medieval, medium
Med Mediterranean
MEd master of education
meg megohm
MEGO my eyes glaze over
MEK methyl ethyl ketone
mem member, memoir, memorial
MEng master of English
MEP member of the European Parliament
mer meridian
Mersey Merseyside
met meteorological, meteorology, metropolitan
metal or **metall** metallurgical, metallurgy
metaph metaphysics
METO Middle East Treaty Organization
MeV million electron volts
Mex Mexican, Mexico
mf mezzo forte
mF millifarad
MF medium frequency, microfiche
MFA master of fine arts
mfd manufactured
mfg manufacturing
MFH master of foxhounds
MFN most favored nation
mfr manufacture, manufacturer
mg milligram
Mg magnesium
MG machine gun, major general, military government
mgal milligal
MGB [Russ *Ministerstvo gosudarstvennoĭ bezopasnosti*] Ministry of State Security
mgd million gallons per day
mgr manager, monseigneur, monsignor
mgt or **mgmt** management
MGy Sgt master gunnery sergeant
MH medal of honor, mental health, mobile home
MHA master of hospital administration
MHC major histocompatibility complex
MHD magnetohydrodynamic, magnetohydrodynamics
mhg mahogany
MHW mean high water
MHz megahertz
mi mile, mileage, mill
MI Michigan, military intelligence
Mic Micah
MIC methyl isocyanate
Mich Michigan
MICR magnetic ink character recognition
mid middle
Middx Middlesex
Mid Glam Mid Glamorgan
midn midshipman
mil military, million
min minim, minimum, mining, minister, minor, minute
Minn Minnesota
MIO minimum identifiable odor
MIPS or **mips** million instructions per second
misc miscellaneous
Miss Mississippi
mixt mixture
mk mark, markka
Mk Mark
mks meter-kilogram-second
mkt market
mktg marketing
ml milliliter
mL millilambert

MLA Member of the Legislative Assembly
MLD median lethal dose, minimum lethal dose
MLF multilateral force
Mlle [F] mademoiselle
Mlles [F] mesdemoiselles
MLS master of library science
MLW mean low water
mm millimeter
MM [F] messieurs; mutatis mutandis
Mme [F] madame
Mmes [F] mesdames
mmf magnetomotive force
MMPI Minnesota Multiphasic Personality Inventory
Mn manganese
MN magnetic north, Minnesota
MNC multinational company, multinational corporation
mo month
Mo Missouri, molybdenum, Monday
MO mail order, medical officer, Missouri, modus operandi, money order
mod moderate, modern, modification, modified, modulo, modulus
modif modification
mol mole, molecular, molecule
MOL manned orbiting laboratory
mol wt molecular weight
MOM middle of month
mon monastery, monetary
Mon Monaghan, Monday
Mont Montana
mor morocco
MOR middle of the road
morph morphology
mos months
MOS metal-oxide semiconductor, military occupational specialty
MOSFET metal-oxide-semiconductor field-effect transistor
MP melting point, member of parliament, metropolitan police, milepost, military police, military policeman
MPA master of public administration
MPAA Motion Picture Association of America
mpg miles per gallon
mph miles per hour
MPH master of public health
MPhil master of philosophy
MPM meters per minute
MPS meters per second
MPV multi-purpose vehicle
MPX multiplex
mR milliroentgen
MR map reference, mentally retarded
MRE meals ready to eat
MRI magnetic resonance imaging
mRNA messenger RNA
ms millisecond
MS [It *mano sinistra*] left hand; manuscript, master of science, military science, Mississippi, motor ship, multiple sclerosis
MSc master of science
msec millisecond
msg message
MSG master sergeant, monosodium glutamate
msgr monseigneur, monsignor
MSgt master sergeant
MSH melanocyte-stimulating hormone
MSL mean sea level
MSN master of science in nursing
MSS manuscripts
MST mountain standard time
MSW master of social welfare, master of social work
mt mount, mountain
Mt Matthew
MT machine translation, metric ton, Montana, mountain time
mtg meeting, mortgage
mtge mortgage
mth month
mtn mountain
MTO Mediterranean theater of operations
mun or **munic** municipal
mus museum, music, musical, musician
mV millivolt
MV main verb, mean variation, motor vessel

MVD [Russ *Ministerstvo vnutrennikh del*] Ministry of Internal Affairs

MVP most valuable player

mW milliwatt

MW megawatt

MWe megawatts electric

mxd mixed

my million years

myc *or* **mycol** mycology

Myr million years

n name, nano-, navy, net, neuter, *usu ital* neutron, noon, normal, north, northern, note, noun, number

N newton, nitrogen

Na [NL *natrium*] sodium

NA national association, no account, North America, not applicable, not available

NAACP National Association for the Advancement of Colored People

NAB New American Bible

NAD no appreciable disease

Nah Nahum

NAIA National Association of Intercollegiate Athletes

NAS National Academy of Sciences, naval air station

NASA National Aeronautics and Space Administration

NASCAR National Association for Stock Car Auto Racing

NASD National Association of Securities Dealers

NASL North American Soccer League

NASW National Association of Social Workers

nat national, native, natural

natl national

NATO North Atlantic Treaty Organization

naut nautical

nav naval, navigable, navigation

Nb niobium

NB New Brunswick, northbound, nota bene

NBA National Basketball Association, National Boxing Association

NBC National Broadcasting Company

NBS National Bureau of Standards

NC no charge, no credit, North Carolina, nurse corps

NCAA National Collegiate Athletic Association

NCE New Catholic Edition

NCV no commercial value

nd no date

Nd neodymium

ND doctor of naturopathy, North Dakota

N Dak North Dakota

NDE near-death experience

NDP New Democratic Party (Canad)

Ne neon

NE Nebraska, New England, no effects, northeast

NEA National Education Association, National Endowment for the Arts

Neb *or* **Nebr** Nebraska

NEB New English Bible

NED New English Dictionary

neg negative, negotiable

Neh Nehemiah

NEH National Endowment for the Humanities

NEI not elsewhere included

nem con [NL *nemine contradicente*] no one contradicting

nem diss [NL *nemine dissentiente*] no one dissenting

NEP New Economic Policy

NES not elsewhere specified

Neth Netherlands

neurol neurological, neurology

neut neuter

Nev Nevada

New Eng New England

NF Newfoundland, no funds

NFC National Football Conference

NFL National Football League

Nfld Newfoundland

NFP natural family planning

NFS not for sale

ng nanogram

NG national guard, no good

NGF nerve growth factor

NGO nongovernmental organization

NGU nongonococcal urethritis

NH never hinged, New Hampshire

NHL National Hockey League

Ni nickel

NIC newly industrialized country, newly industrializing country

NIH National Institutes of Health, not invented here

NIMBY not in my backyard

NIT National Invitational Tournament

NIU network interface unit

NJ New Jersey

NKVD [Russ *Narodnyi komissariat vnutrennikh del*] People's Commissariat of Internal Affairs

NL National League, new line, night letter, [L *non licet*] it is not permitted; north latitude

NLCS National League Championship Series

NLF National Liberation Front

NLRB National Labor Relations Board

NLT night letter

nm nanometer

NM nautical mile, New Mexico, no mark, not marked

N Mex New Mexico

NMHA National Mental Health Association

NMI no middle initial

NMR nuclear magnetic resonance

NNE north-northeast

NNW north-northwest

no north, northern, [L *numero*, abl. of *numerus*] number

No nobelium

NOAA National Oceanic and Atmospheric Administration

NOIBN not otherwise indexed by name

nom nominative

non obst *or* **non obs** non obstante

non seq non sequitur

NOP not otherwise provided for

Nor Norway, Norwegian

NORAD North American Air Defense Command

Norf Norfolk

norm normal

Northants Northamptonshire

Norw Norway, Norwegian

nos numbers

NOS not otherwise specified

Notts Nottinghamshire

nov novelist

Nov November

NOW National Organization for Women

NO$_x$ nitrogen oxide

np no pagination, no place (of publication)

Np neptunium

NP neuropsychiatric, neuropsychiatry, no protest, notary public, noun phrase

NPF not provided for

NPN nonprotein nitrogen

NPR National Public Radio

NPS National Park Service

nr near

NR not rated

NRA National Recovery Administration, National Rifle Association

NRC National Research Council, Nuclear Regulatory Commission

ns *also* **nsec** nanosecond

Ns nimbostratus

NS new series, new style, not specified, not sufficient, Nova Scotia

NSA National Security Agency

NSC National Security Council

NSF National Science Foundation, not sufficient funds

NSW New South Wales

NT New Territories, New Testament, Northern Territory, Northwest Territories

Nthmb Northumberland

NTP normal temperature and pressure

NTSB National Transportation Safety Board

nt wt *or* **n wt** net weight

NU name unknown

num numeral

Num *or* **Numb** Numbers

numis numismatic, numismatical, numismatics

NV Nevada, nonvoting

NW northwest

NWT Northwest Territories

NY New York

NYC New York City

NYSE New York Stock Exchange

NZ New Zealand

o ocean, ohm, old, order, oriental, over

O Ohio, oxygen, [NL *octarius*] pint

o- ortho-

o/a on or about

OAS Organization of American States

OASDHI Old Age, Survivors, Disability, and Health Insurance

OAU Organization of African Unity

ob [L *obiit*] he died, she died; observation

Ob *or* **Obad** Obadiah

OB obstetric, obstetrician, obstetrics

OBE officer of the Order of the British Empire, out-of-body experience

OB–GYN obstetrician gynecologist, obstetrics gynecology

obj object, objective

obl oblique, oblong

obstet obstetrical, obstetrics

obv obverse

oc ocean

OC off center, officer candidate, on center, on course, over-the-counter

occas occasionally

oceanog oceanography

OCR optical character reader, optical character recognition

OCS officer candidate school

oct octavo

Oct October

OD doctor of optometry, [L *oculus dexter*] right eye; officer of the day, olive drab, on demand, outside diameter, outside dimension, overdraft, overdrawn

Oe oersted

OECD Organization for Economic Cooperation and Development

OED Oxford English Dictionary

OEO Office of Economic Opportunity

OER officer efficiency report

OES Order of the Eastern Star

OF outfield

off office, officer, official

offic official

OG officer of the guard, original gum

OH Ohio

OHMS on Her Majesty's service, on His Majesty's service

OIT Office of International Trade

OJ orange juice

OJT on-the-job training

OK Oklahoma, outer keel

Okla Oklahoma

OM order of merit

OMB Office of Management and Budget

ON *or* **Ont** Ontario

OOD officer of the deck

op operation, operative, operator, opportunity, opus

OP observation post, out of print

op cit [L *opere citato*] in the work cited

OPEC Organization of Petroleum Exporting Countries

opp opposite

opt optical, optician, optics, option, optional

OR operating room, operational research, operations research, Oregon, owner's risk, own recognizance

orch orchestra

ord order, ordnance

Ore *or* **Oreg** Oregon

org organic, organization, organized

orig original, originally, originator

Ork Orkney

ornith ornithology

ORV off-road vehicle

Os osmium

OS [L *oculus sinister*] left eye; old series, old style, ordinary seaman, out of stock

OSHA Occupational Safety and Health Administration

OSS Office of Strategic Services

OT occupational therapy, Old Testament, overtime

OTA Office of Technology Assessment

OTB offtrack betting

OTC over-the-counter

OTR occupational therapist, registered

OTS officers' training school

OW one-way

Oxfam Oxford Committee for Famine Relief

Oxon [ML *Oxonia*] Oxford; Oxfordshire, [ML *Oxoniensis*] of Oxford

oz [obs. It *onza* (now *oncia*)] ounce, ounces

p page, pages, parental generation, part, participle, past, pater, pawn, pence, penny, per, peseta, peso, petite, piano, pico-, pint, pipe, pitch, pole, port, power, pro, proton, purl

P phosphorus, pressure, [F *poids*] weight

p- para-

Pa pascal, Pennsylvania, protactinium

PA particular average, passenger agent, Pennsylvania, per annum, personal appearance, personal assistant, power amplifier, power of attorney, press agent, private account, professional association, public address, purchasing agent

Pac Pacific

PAC political action committee

paleon paleontology

pam pamphlet

Pan Panama

p and h postage and handling

P&I principal and interest

P&L profit and loss

par paragraph, parallel, parish

para paragraph

part participial, participle, particular

PAS para-aminosalicylic acid

pass passenger, passive

pat patent

PAT point after touchdown

path *or* **pathol** pathological, pathology

PAYE *Brit* pay as you earn

payt payment

pb paperback

Pb [L *plumbum*] lead

PB personal best, power brakes

PB&J peanut butter and jelly

PBS Public Broadcasting Service

pc parsec

PC Peace Corps, percent, percentage, politically correct, postcard, [L *post cibum*] after meals; printed circuit, professional corporation

PCP pneumocystis carinii pneumonia, primary care physician

PCR polymerase chain reaction

pct percent, percentage

pd paid

Pd palladium

PD per diem, police department, postal district, potential difference, program director, public domain

PDA predicted drift angle, public display of affection

PDD past due date

PDT Pacific daylight time

PE physical education, printer's error, probable error, professional engineer

P/E price/earnings

PEI Prince Edward Island

pen peninsula

PEN International Association of Poets, Playwrights, Editors, Essayists and Novelists

Penn *or* **Penna** Pennsylvania

per period, person

perf perfect, perforated, performance

perh perhaps

perm permanent

perp perpendicular, perpetrator

pers person, personal, personnel

Pers Persia, Persian

pert pertaining
pet petroleum
Pet Peter
PET positron-emission tomography
pf personal foul, pfennig, picofarad, preferred
PF power factor, pianoforte, [It *più forte*] louder
PFC *or* **Pfc** private first class
pfd preferred
PFD personal flotation device
pg page, picogram
Pg Portugal, Portuguese
PG paying guest, postgraduate, prostaglandin
PGA Professional Golfers' Association
ph phase
PH pinch hit, public health, Purple Heart
phar pharmacopoeia, pharmacy
pharm pharmaceutical, pharmacist, pharmacy
PhB [NL *philosophiae baccalaureus*] bachelor of philosophy
PhD [NL *philosophiae doctor*] doctor of philosophy
phil *or* **philol** philological, philology
Phil Philippians
philos philosopher, philosophy
phon phonetics
photog photographic, photography
phr phrase
phys physical, physics
physiol physiologist, physiology
PI Philippine Islands, private investigator, programmed instruction
PID pelvic inflammatory disease
PIK payment in kind
PIN personal identification number
PINS persons in need of supervision
pinx [L *pinxit*] he painted it, she painted it
PIRG Public Interest Research Group
pizz pizzicato
pk park, peak, peck, pike
PK preacher's kid
pkg package
pkt packet, pocket
PKU phenylketonuria
pkwy parkway
pl place, plate, plural
PL partial loss, private line, Public Law
plat plateau, platoon
PLC *Brit* public limited company
plf plaintiff
PLO Palestine Liberation Organization
pls please
PLSS portable life-support system
pm phase modulation, premium
Pm promethium
PM paymaster, permanent magnet, police magistrate, postmaster, post meridiem — often not cap and often punctuated; postmortem, prime minister, provost marshal
pmk postmark
PMS premenstrual syndrome
pmt payment
PN promissory note
pnxt [L *pinxit*] he painted it, she painted it
Po polonium
PO [L *per os*] by mouth, orally; petty officer, postal order, post office, purchase order
POB post office box
POC port of call
POD pay on delivery, post office department
POE port of embarkation, port of entry
Pol Poland, Polish
polit political, politician
poly polytechnic
pon pontoon
pop population
POP point of purchase
por portrait
POR pay on return, price on request
port portable, portrait
Port Portugal, Portuguese

pos position, positive
POS point of sale
poss possessive
pot potential, potentiometer
POV point of view
pp pages, [L *per procurationem*] by proxy; pianissimo
PP parcel post, past participle, postpaid, prepaid
ppa per power of attorney
ppb parts per billion
ppd postpaid, prepaid
PPI plan position indicator
ppm parts per million
PPS [NL *post postscriptum*] an additional postscript
ppt parts per thousand, parts per trillion, precipitate
pptn precipitation
PQ Province of Quebec
pr pair, price, printed
Pr praseodymium, propyl
PR payroll, proportional representation, public relations, Puerto Rico
PRC People's Republic of China
prec preceding
pred predicate
pref preface, preference, preferred, prefix
prem premium
prep preparatory, preposition
prepd prepared
prepg preparing
prepn preparation
pres present, president
Presb Presbyterian
prev previous, previously
prf proof
prim primary, primitive
prin principal, principle
priv private, privately, privative
PRN [L *pro re nata*] for the emergency, as needed
PRO public relations officer
prob probable, probably, probate, problem
proc proceedings
prod product, production
prof professional, professor
prog program
proj project, projector
prom promontory
pron pronoun, pronounced, pronunciation
prop property, proposition, proprietor
pros prosody
Prot Protestant
prov province, provincial, provisional
Prov Proverbs
prox proximo
ps picosecond
Ps *or* **Psa** Psalms
PS [NL *postscriptum*] postscript; power steering, power supply, public school
PSA public service announcement
psec picosecond
pseud pseudonym, pseudonymous
psf pounds per square foot
PSG platoon sergeant
psi pounds per square inch
psig pounds per square inch gauge
PST Pacific standard time
psych psychology
psychol psychologist, psychology
pt part, payment, pint, point, port
Pt platinum
PT Pacific time, part-time, physical therapy, physical training
pta peseta
PTA Parent-Teacher Association
pte *Brit* private
ptg printing
PTO Parent-Teacher Organization, please turn over, power takeoff
PTSD post-traumatic stress disorder
PTV public television
Pty *Brit* proprietary
Pu plutonium
PU pickup
pub public, publication, publicity, published, publisher, publishing
publ publication, published, publisher
PUD pickup and delivery
pulv [L *pulvis*] powder
PUSH People United to Serve Humanity
PV photovoltaic, polyvinyl

PVA polyvinyl acetate
PVC polyvinyl chloride
PVO private voluntary organization
pvt private
PVT pressure, volume, temperature
PW prisoner of war
PWA person with AIDS
pwr power
PWR pressurized water reactor
pwt pennyweight
PX please exchange, post exchange
PYO pick your own
q quart, quartile, quarto, queen, query, question, quetzal, quire
QA quality assurance
QB quarterback, queen's bench
QC quality control, queen's counsel
qd [L *quaque die*] daily
QED quantum electrodynamics, [L *quod erat demonstrandum*] which was to be demonstrated
QEF [L *quod erat faciendum*] which was to be done
QEI [L *quod erat inveniendum*] which was to be found out
QF quick-firing
qid [L *quater in die*] four times a day
Qld Queensland
qm [L *quoque matutino*] every morning
QM quartermaster
QMC quartermaster corps
QMG quartermaster general
qp *or* **q pl** [L *quantum placet*] as much as you please
qq questions
qq v [L *quae vide*] which (*pl*) see
qr quarter, quire
qs [L *quantum sufficit*] as much as suffices
qt quantity, quart
qtd quartered
qto quarto
qty quantity
qu *or* **ques** question
quad quadrant
qual qualitative, quality
quant quantitative
quar quarterly
Que Quebec
quot quotation
qv [L *quod vide*] which see
qy query
r rabbi, radius, rain, range, Rankine, rare, real, Reaumur, recto, red, repeat, rerun, resistance, right, river, roentgen, rook, rough, run
R radial, radical — used esp. of a univalent hydrocarbon radical; recipe; registered trademark — often enclosed in a circle; regular, Republican
ra range
Ra radium
RA regular army, right ascension, Royal Academician, Royal Academy
RAAF Royal Australian Air Force
rad radical, radian, radiator, radio, radius, radix
RADM rear admiral
RAF Royal Air Force
R & B rhythm and blues
R and R rest and recreation, rest and recuperation
rap rappel
Rb rubidium
RBC red blood cells, red blood count
RBE relative biological effectiveness
RC Red Cross, resistance-capacitance, Roman Catholic
RCAF Royal Canadian Air Force
RCMP Royal Canadian Mounted Police
RCN Royal Canadian Navy
rct recruit
rd road, rod, round
RD registered dietitian, rural delivery
RDA recommended daily allowance, recommended dietary allowance
RDF radio direction finder, radio direction finding, Rapid Deployment Force, refuse-derived fuel

Re rhenium
REA Rural Electrification Administration
reas reasonable
rec receipt, record, recording, recreation
recd received
recip reciprocal, reciprocity
rec sec recording secretary
rect receipt, rectangle, rectangular, rectified
red reduce, reduction
ref reference, referred, refining, reformed, refunding
refl reflex, reflexive
refr refraction
refrig refrigerating, refrigeration
reg region, register, registered, registration, regular
regd registered
regt regiment
REIT real estate investment trust
rel relating, relative, released, religion, religious
relig religion
rep repair, repeat, report, reporter, representative, republic
Rep Republican
repl replace, replacement
rept report
req request, require, required, requisition
reqd required
res research, reservation, reserve, reservoir, residence, resident, resolution
RES reticuloendothelial system
resp respective, respectively
ret retain, retired, return
retd retained, retired, returned
rev revenue, reverse, review, reviewed, revised, revision, revolution
Rev Revelation, reverend
Revd *Brit* reverend
rf refunding
RF radio frequency
RFD rural free delivery
RFP request for proposal
Rh rhodium
RH relative humidity, right hand
rhet rhetoric
RHIP rank has its privileges
RI refractive index, Rhode Island
RIA radioimmunoassay
RICO Racketeer Influenced and Corrupt Organizations (Act)
RIF reduction in force
RIO radar intercept officer
RIP [L *requiescat in pace*] may he rest in peace, may she rest in peace; [L *requiescant in pace*] may they rest in peace
rit ritardando
riv river
RJ road junction
rm ream, room
rms root-mean-square
Rn radon
RN Royal Navy
rnd round
RNZAF Royal New Zealand Air Force
ROC Republic of China (Taiwan)
ROG receipt of goods
ROI return on investment
ROK Republic of Korea (South Korea)
Rom Roman, Romance, Romania, Romanian, Romans
ROP record of production, run-of-paper
ROR release on own recognizance
rot rotating, rotation
ROTC Reserve Officers' Training Corps
RP Received Pronunciation, relief pitcher, reply paid, reprint, reprinting, Republic of the Philippines
RPh registered pharmacist
rpm revolutions per minute
rps revolutions per second
rpt repeat, report
RQ respiratory quotient
RR railroad, rural route
RRT registered record technician
RS Received Standard, recording secretary, revised statutes, right side, Royal Society
RSA Republic of South Africa
RSFSR [Russ *Rossiiskaya Sovetskaya Federativnaya Sotsialisti-*

cheskaya Respublika] Russian Soviet Federated Socialist Republic
RSV Revised Standard Version
RSVP [F *répondez s'il vous plaît*] please reply
RSWC right side up with care
rt right, route
RT radiologic technologist, radiotelephone, respiratory therapy, room temperature, round-trip
rte route
rtw ready-to-wear
Ru ruthenium
Rum Rumania, Rumanian
Russ Russia, Russian
RV Revised Version
RW radiological warfare, right worshiful, right worthy
rwy *or* **ry** railway
s sabbath, saint, schilling, scruple, second, secondary, section, senate, series, shilling, [L *signa*] label; siemens, signor, sine, singular, small, smooth, snow, society, son, sou, south, southern, subject, symmetrical
S satisfactory, short, standard deviation of a sample, sulfur, svedberg
Sa Saturday
SA Salvation Army, seaman apprentice, sex appeal, [L *sine anno* without year] without date; South Africa, South America, South Australia, subject to approval
sac sacrifice
SAC special agent in charge, Strategic Air Command
SAD seasonal affective disorder
SAE self-addressed envelope, Society of Automotive Engineers, stamped addressed envelope
SAG Screen Actors Guild
sal salary
SALT Strategic Arms Limitation Talks
Sam *or* **Saml** Samuel
san sanatorium
S&H shipping and handling
S and M sadism and masochism, sadist and masochist
sanit sanitary, sanitation
SAR search and rescue
SASE self-addressed stamped envelope
Sask Saskatchewan
sat saturate, saturated, saturation
Sat Saturday
satd saturated
S Aust South Australia
sb substantive
Sb [L *stibium*] antimony
SB [NL *scientiae baccalaureus*] bachelor of science; simultaneous broadcast, southbound
SBA Small Business Administration
SBN Standard Book Number
sc scale, scene, science, scilicet, screw, [L *sculpsit*] he carved it, she carved it, he engraved it, she engraved it
Sc scandium, Scots, stratocumulus
SC small capitals, South Carolina, supercalendered, supreme court
Scand Scandinavia, Scandinavian
SCAT School and College Ability Test, supersonic commercial air transport
ScD doctor of science
sch school
sci science, scientific
SCID severe combined immune deficiency, severe combined immunodeficiency
scil scilicet
SCLC Southern Christian Leadership Conference
Scot Scotland, Scottish
SCPO senior chief petty officer
script scripture
sct scout
sctd scattered
sd said, sewed
SD sea-damaged, sine die, South Dakota, special delivery, stage direction, standard deviation
S Dak South Dakota
SDI Strategic Defense Initiative
SDRs special drawing rights
SDS Students for a Democratic Society

Se selenium
SE self-explanatory, southeast, Standard English, stock exchange, straight edge
SEAL sea, air, land (team)
SEATO Southeast Asia Treaty Organization
sec secant, second, secondary, secretary, section, [L *secundum*] according to; security
SEC Securities and Exchange Commission
sect section, sectional
secy secretary
sed sediment, sedimentation
sel select, selected, selection
sem semicolon, seminar, seminary
Sem Semitic
sen senate, senator, senior
sep separate, separated
Sep September
SEP simplified employee pension
sepd separated
sepg separating
sepn separation
Sept September
seq [L *sequens, sequentes, sequentia*] the following
seqq [L *sequentia*] the following ones
ser serial, series, service
Serb Serbian
serg *or* **sergt** sergeant
serv service
SES socioeconomic status
sess session
sf *or* **sfz** sforzando
SF sacrifice fly, science fiction, sinking fund, square feet, square foot
SFC sergeant first class
SG senior grade, sergeant, solicitor general, *often not cap* specific gravity; surgeon general
sgd signed
Sgt sergeant
Sgt Maj sergeant major
sh share
Shak Shakespeare
shd should
Shet Shetland
SHF superhigh frequency
shipt shipment
shp shaft horsepower
shpt shipment
sht sheet
shtg shortage
Si silicon
SI [F *Système International d'Unités*] International System of Units
SIDS sudden infant death syndrome
sig signal, signature, signor
Sig [L *signa*] label
SIG special interest group
sigill [L *sigillum*] seal
sin sine
sing singular
SIS Secret Intelligence Service (Brit)
SJ Society of Jesus
SK Saskatchewan
sl slightly, slip, slow
SL salvage loss, sea level, south latitude
SLAN [L *sine loco, anno, (vel) nomine*] without place, year, or name
SLBM submarine-launched ballistic missile
sld sailed, sealed, sold
SLE systemic lupus erythematosus
Slo Sligo
SLR single-lens reflex
sm small
Sm samarium
SM [NL *scientiae magister*] master of science; sergeant major, service mark, soldier's medal, stage manager, station master
S–M *or* **S/M** sadomasochism, sadomasochist
SMA sergeant major of the army
SMaj sergeant major
SMSA Standard Metropolitan Statistical Area
SMSgt senior master sergeant
SMV slow-moving vehicle
Sn [LL *stannum*] tin
SN seaman
SNCC Student Nonviolent Coordinating Committee

SNF skilled nursing facility
SNG substitute natural gas, synthetic natural gas
Snr *Brit* senior
so south, southern
SO seller's option, strikeout
soc social, society, sociology
sociol sociologist, sociology
sol solicitor, soluble, solution
soln solution
Som Somersetshire
SOP standard operating procedure, standing operating procedure
soph sophomore
SO_x sulfur oxide
sp special, species, specific, specimen, spelling, spirit
Sp Spain, Spanish
SP self-propelled, shore patrol, shore patrolman, shore police, [L *sine prole*] without issue; single pole, specialist
Span Spanish
SPCA Society for the Prevention of Cruelty to Animals
SPCC Society for the Prevention of Cruelty to Children
spd speed
spec special, specialist, specifically, specification
specif specific, specifically
SPF sun protection factor
sp gr specific gravity
sp ht specific heat
SPOT satellite positioning and tracking
spp *pl* species
SPQR [L *senatus populusque Romanus*] the senate and the people of Rome; small profits, quick returns
sps [L *sine prole superstite*] without surviving issue
sq squadron, square
Sr senior, senor, señor, sister, strontium
SR seaman recruit, sedimentation rate, shipping receipt
Sra senora, señora
SRO standing room only
Srta senorita, señorita
ss scilicet — used in legal documents, [L *semis*] one half
SS saints, same size, Social Security, steamship, sworn statement
SSA Social Security Administration
SSE south-southeast
SSG *or* **SSgt** staff sergeant
SSI supplemental security income
SSM staff sergeant major
SSN Social Security number
ssp subspecies
SSPE subacute sclerosing panencephalitis
SSR Soviet Socialist Republic
SSS Selective Service System
SSW south-southwest
st stanza, state, stitch, stone, street
St saint, stratus
ST short ton, single throw, standard time
sta station, stationary
Staffs Staffordshire
START strategic arms limitation talks
stat [L *statim*] immediately; statute
STB [NL *sacrae theologiae baccalaureus*] bachelor of sacred theology; [NL *scientiae theologicae baccalaureus*] bachelor of theology
stbd starboard
std standard
STD [NL *sacrae theologiae doctor*] doctor of sacred theology
Ste [F *sainte*] saint (female)
ster *or* **stg** sterling
stge storage
stk stock
STL [NL *sacrae theologiae licentiatus*] licentiate of sacred theology
STM [NL *sacrae theologiae magister*] master of sacred theology
STOL short takeoff and landing
stor storage
STP standard temperature and pressure
str steamer, strophe
stud student
STV subscription television

Su Sunday
sub subaltern, subscription, subtract, suburb
subj subject, subjunctive
suff sufficient, suffix
Suff Suffolk
Sun Sunday
sup superior, supplement, supplementary, supply, supra
supp *or* **suppl** supplement, supplementary
supr supreme
supt superintendent
supvr supervisor
sur surface
surg surgeon, surgery, surgical
surv survey, surveying, surveyor
Suss Sussex
sv sailing vessel, saves, [L *sub verbo* or *sub voce*] under the word
svc *or* **svce** service
svgs savings
sw switch
Sw Sweden
SW seawater, shipper's weight, shortwave, southwest
SWAK sealed with a kiss
SWAT Special Weapons and Tactics
Swed Sweden
SWG standard wire gauge
Switz Switzerland
syl *or* **syll** syllable
sym symbol, symmetrical
syn synonym, synonymous, synonymy
syst system
t metric ton, tablespoon, target, teaspoon, technical, temperature, [L *tempore*] in the time of; tense, tension, tertiary, time, ton, township, transitive, troy, true
T tera-, tesla, thymine, toddler, tritium, T-shirt
Ta tantalum
TA teaching assistant, transactional analysis
TAC Tactical Air Command
TAG the adjutant general
tan tangent
TAT thematic apperception test
taxon taxonomic, taxonomy
Tay Tayside
tb tablespoon, tablespoonful
Tb terbium
TB thoroughbred, trial balance, tubercle bacillus
TBA *often not cap* to be announced
TBD to be determined
tbs *or* **tbsp** tablespoon, tablespoonful
TBS talk between ships
tc tierce
Tc technetium
TC teachers college, terra-cotta, till countermanded
TCE trichloroethylene
tchr teacher
TD tank destroyer, touchdown, Treasury Department
TDD telecommunications device for the deaf
TDN total digestible nutrients
TDY temporary duty
Te tellurium
tec technical, technician
tech technical, technically, technician, technological, technology
technol technological, technology
TEFL teaching English as a foreign language
tel telegram, telegraph, telephone
teleg telegraphy
temp temperance, template, temporal, temporary, [L *tempore*] in the time of
Tenn Tennessee
ter terrace, territory
terr territory
TESL teaching English as a second language
TESOL Teachers of English to Speakers of Other Languages
Test Testament
Tex Texas
TF task force, territorial force
tfr transfer
TFR total fertility rate
TG transformational grammar, type genus
TGIF thank God it's Friday
tgt target

TGV [F *train à grande vitesse*] high-speed train
Th thorium, Thursday
TH true heading
Thai Thailand
ThD [NL *theologiae doctor*] doctor of theology
theat theater, theatrical
theol theological, theology
therm thermometer
Thess Thessalonians
ThM [NL *theologiae magister*] master of theology
Thurs *or* **Thu** Thursday
Ti titanium
TIA transient ischemic attack
tid [L *ter in die*] three times a day
Tim Timothy
TIN taxpayer identification number
tinc tincture
Tip Tipperary
tit title
Tit Titus
tk tank, truck
tkt ticket
Tl thallium
TL total loss, truckload
TLC tender loving care, thin-layer chromatography
TLO total loss only
tlr tailor, trailer
Tm thulium
TM trademark, transcendental meditation
TMJ temporomandibular joint
TMO telegraph money order
tn ton, town, train
TN Tennessee, true north
TNF tumor necrosis factor
tng training
tnpk turnpike
TO table of organization, telegraph office, traditional orthography, turn over
Tob Tobit
TOEFL Test of English as a Foreign Language
tol tolerance
tonn tonnage
topo topographic, topographical
topog topography
tot total
TOT time on target
tp title page, township
TP triple play
TPA tissue plasminogen activator
tpk *or* **tpke** turnpike
tps townships, troops
tr translated, translation, translator, transpose, troop, trustee
trag tragedy, tragic
trans transaction, transitive, translated, translation, translator, transmission, transportation, transverse
transf transfer, transferred
transl translated, translation
transp transportation
trav travel, traveler, travels
treas treasurer, treasury
trib tributary
trit triturate
trop tropic, tropical
ts tensile strength
TSgt technical sergeant
TSH thyroid-stimulating hormone
tsp teaspoon, teaspoonful
TSS toxic shock syndrome
TT telegraphic transfer, teletypewriter, Trust Territories
TTY teletypewriter
Tu Tuesday
TU trade union, transmission unit
TUC Trades Union Congress
Tues *or* **Tue** Tuesday
Turk Turkey, Turkish
TV terminal velocity, transvestite
TVA Tennessee Valley Authority
2WD two-wheel drive
twp township
TWX teletypewriter exchange
TX Texas
Tyr Tyrone
u uncle, unit, unsymmetrical, upper
U [*Union of Orthodox Hebrew Congregations*] kosher certification — often enclosed in a circle;

university, unsatisfactory, uracil, uranium
UAE United Arab Emirates
UAR United Arab Republic
UAW United Automobile Workers
UC undercharge, uppercase
ugt urgent
UHF ultrahigh frequency
UI unemployment insurance
UK United Kingdom
ult ultimate, ultimo
UMWA United Mine Workers of America
UN United Nations
unan unanimous
Unc uncirculated
UNCF United Negro College Fund
UNESCO United Nations Educational, Scientific, and Cultural Organization
Unh unnilhexium
uni uniform
UNICEF [*United Nations International Children's Emergency Fund,* its former name] United Nations Children's Fund
univ universal, university
unp unpaged
Unp unnilpentium
Unq unnilquadium
UNRWA United Nations Relief and Works Agency
uns unsymmetrical
UP underproof, Upper Peninsula (of Michigan)
UPC Universal Product Code
UPI United Press International
urol urological, urology
US [L *ubi supra*] where above mentioned; United States, [L *ut supra*] as above
USA United States Army, United States of America
USAF United States Air Force
USCG United States Coast Guard
USDA United States Department of Agriculture
USES United States Employment Service
USG United States government
USGA United States Golf Association
USGS United States Geological Survey
USIA United States Information Agency
USMC United States Marine Corps
USN United States Navy
USNR United States Naval Reserve
USNS United States Naval Ship
USO United Service Organizations
USP United States Pharmacopeia
USPS United States Postal Service
USS United States ship
USSR Union of Soviet Socialist Republics
USTA United States Tennis Association
usu usual, usually
UT Universal time, Utah
UTC Coordinated Universal Time
ut dict [L *ut dictum*] as directed
util utility
UV ultraviolet
UW underwriter
ux [L *uxor*] wife
UXB unexploded bomb
v vector, velocity, verb, verse, verso, versus, very, vice, victory, vide, voice, voltage, volume, vowel
V vanadium, volt
Va Virginia
VA Veterans Administration, vicar apostolic, vice admiral, Virginia, visual aid, volt-ampere
vac vacuum
VADM vice admiral
vag vagrancy
val value, valued
var variable, variant, variation, variety, various
VAR visual-aural range, volt-ampere reactive

VAT value-added tax
vb verb, verbal
VC veterinary corps, vice-chancellor, vice-consul, Victoria Cross, Vietcong
VD vapor density, various dates, venereal disease
VDRL venereal disease research laboratory
VDT video display terminal
VDU visual display unit
veg vegetable
vel vellum, velocity
Ven venerable
ver verse
vert vertebrate, vertical
VF very fair, very fine, video frequency, visual field, voice frequency
VFD volunteer fire department
VFR visual flight rules
VFW Veterans of Foreign Wars
VG very good, vicar-general
VHF very high frequency
vi verb intransitive, [L *vide infra*] see below
VI Virgin Islands, viscosity index, volume indicator
vic vicinity
Vic Victoria
vil village
VIN vehicle identification number
vis visibility, visible, visual
VISTA Volunteers in Service to America
viz videlicet
VJ veejay
VLF very low frequency
VMD [NL *veterinariae medicinae doctor*] doctor of veterinary medicine
VNA Visiting Nurse Association
VOA Voice of America
voc vocational, vocative
vocab vocabulary
vol volcano, volume, volunteer
VOM volt-ohmmeter
VOR very-high-frequency omnidirectional radio range
vou voucher
VP variable pitch, various places, verb phrase, vice president
VRM variable rate mortgage
vs verse, versus
VS veterinary surgeon, [L *vide supra*] see above
vss verses, versions
V/STOL vertical or short takeoff and landing
vt verb transitive
Vt Vermont
VT vacuum tube, variable time, Vermont, voice tube
VTOL vertical takeoff and landing
VTR videotape recorder
VU volume unit
Vulg Vulgate
vv verses, vice versa
w warden, water, week, weight, Welsh, west, western, white, wicket, wide, width, wife, with, withdrawal, work
W energy, [G *Wolfram*] tungsten; watt
WA Washington, Western Australia
war warrant
Warks Warwickshire
Wash Washington
Wat Waterford
WATS Wide-Area Telecommunications Service
W Aust Western Australia
Wb weber
WB water ballast, waybill, weather bureau, westbound, wheelbase
WBC white blood cells
WBF wood-burning fireplace
WC water closet, without charge
WCTU Women's Christian Temperance Union
wd wood, word, would
WD War Department
We *or* **Wed** Wednesday
Westm Westmeath, Westmorland
Wex Wexford
wf wrong font
WFTU World Federation of Trade Unions

wh which, white
WH watt-hour, withholding
WHA World Hockey Association
whf wharf
WHO World Health Organization
whr watt-hour
whs *or* **whse** warehouse
whsle wholesale
wi when issued
WI West Indies, Wisconsin, wrought iron
WIA wounded in action
Wick Wicklow
wid widow, widower
Wilts Wiltshire
Wis *or* **Wisc** Wisconsin
Wisd Wisdom
wk week, work
wkly weekly
WL waterline, wavelength
wm wattmeter
wmk watermark
WNW west-northwest
WO warrant officer
w/o without
WOC without compensation
WP weather permitting, wettable powder, white phosphorus, without prejudice, word processing, word processor
WPA Works Progress Administration
wpc watts per candle, watts per channel
WPI Wholesale Price Index
WPM words per minute
wpn weapon
WR warehouse receipt, world record
WRAC Women's Royal Army Corps
WRAF Women's Royal Air Force
WRNS Women's Royal Naval Service
wrnt warrant
WRVS Women's Royal Voluntary Service
WSW west-southwest
wt weight
WT watertight, wireless telegraphy
wtd wanted
WV *or* **W Va** West Virginia
WVS Women's Voluntary Services
WW warehouse warrant, with warrants, world war
w/w wall-to-wall
WY *or* **Wyo** Wyoming
x cross, ex, experimental, extra
X–C cross-country
XD *or* **x div** ex dividend
Xe xenon
XL extra large, extra long
Xn Christian
Xnty Christianity
XO executive officer
XS extra small
XW ex warrants
y yard, year, yeoman
Y yttrium
YA young adult
Yb ytterbium
YB yearbook
YBP years before present
yd yard
yeo *or* **yeom** yeomanry
YO year old
YOB year of birth
Yorks Yorkshire
yr year, younger, your
yrbk yearbook
YT Yukon Territory
Yug Yugoslavia
z zero, zone
Z *or* **ZD** zenith distance
Zach Zacharias
Zech Zechariah
Zeph Zephaniah
ZI zone of interior
Zn [azimuth + *north*] azimuth; zinc
zool zoological, zoology
ZPG zero population growth
Zr zirconium

Foreign Words and Phrases

ab·eunt stu·di·a in mo·res \'ä-be-ˌünt-'stü-dē-ˌä-ˌin-'mō-ˌrās\ [L] : practices zealously pursued pass into habits

à bien·tôt \à-byaⁿ-'tō\ [F] : so long

ab in·cu·na·bu·lis \ˌäb-ˌiŋ-kü-'nä-bü-ˌlēs\ [L] : from the cradle : from infancy

à bon chat, bon rat \à-bōⁿ-'shà bōⁿ-'rà\ [F] : to a good cat, a good rat : retaliation in kind

à bouche ou·verte \à-bü-shü-vert\ [F] : with open mouth : eagerly : uncritically

ab ovo us·que ad ma·la \ˌäb-'ō-vō-ˌùs-kwe-ˌäd-'mä-lä\ [L] : from egg to apples : from soup to nuts : from beginning to end

à bras ou·verts \à-brà-zü-ver\ [F] : with open arms : cordially

ab·sit in·vi·dia \'äb-ˌsit-in-'wi-dē-ˌä\ [L] : let there be no envy or ill will

ab uno dis·ce om·nes \äb-'ü-nō-ˌdis-ke-'óm-ˌnäs\ [L] : from one learn to know all

ab ur·be con·di·ta \äb-'ùr-be-'kón-di-ˌtä\ [L] : from the founding of the city (Rome, founded 753 B.C.) — used by the Romans in reckoning dates

ab·usus non tol·lit usum \'ä-ˌbü-sùs-ˌnōn-ˌtò-lit-'ü-sùm\ [L] : abuse does not take away use, i.e., is not an argument against proper use

à compte \à-'kōⁿt\ [F] : on account

à coup sûr \à-kü-sūēr\ [F] : with sure stroke : surely

acte gra·tuit \àk-tə-grà-twʸē\ [F] : gratuitous impulsive act

ad ar·bi·tri·um \ˌad-är-'bi-trē-ùm\ [L] : at will : arbitrarily

ad as·tra per as·pe·ra \äd-'as-trə-ˌpər-'as-pə-rə\ [L] : to the stars by hard ways — motto of Kansas

ad ex·tre·mum \äd-ik-'strē-məm\ [L] : to the extreme : at last

ad ka·len·das Grae·cas \ˌäd-kä-'len-däs-'grī-ˌkäs\ [L] : at the Greek calends : never (since the Greeks had no calends)

ad ma·jo·rem Dei glo·ri·am \äd-mä-'yōr-ˌem-'de-ˌē-'glōr-ē-ˌäm, -'yór-, -'glór-\ [L] : to the greater glory of God — motto of the Society of Jesus

ad pa·tres \äd-'pä-ˌträs\ [L] : (gathered) to his fathers : deceased

ad re·fe·ren·dum \ˌäd-ˌre-fe-'ren-dùm\ [L] : for reference : for further consideration by one having the authority to make a final decision

à droite \à-drwàt\ [F] : to or on the right hand

ad un·guem \äd-'ùŋ-ˌgwem\ [L] : to the fingernail : to a nicety : exactly (from the use of the fingernail to test the smoothness of marble)

ad utrum·que pa·ra·tus \ˌäd-ù-'trùm-kwe-pä-'rä-tùs\ [L] : prepared for either (event)

ad vi·vum \äd-'wē-ˌwùm\ [L] : to the life

ae·gri som·nia \ˌī-grē-'sóm-nē-ˌä\ [L] : a sick man's dreams

ae·quam ser·va·re men·tem \'ī-ˌkwäm-ser-ˌwä-rä-'men-ˌtem\ [L] : to preserve a calm mind

ae·quo ani·mo \ˌī-kwō-'ä-ni-ˌmō\ [L] : with even mind : calmly

ae·re per·en·ni·us \ˌī-rä-pe-'re-nē-ùs\ [L] : more lasting than bronze

à gauche \à-gōsh\ [F] : to or on the left hand

age quod agis \'ä-ge-ˌkwòd-'ä-ˌgis\ [L] : do what you are doing : to the business at hand

à grands frais \à-grän-fre\ [F] : at great expense

à huis clos \à-wʸē-klō\ [F] : with closed doors

aide—toi, le ciel t'ai·dera \ed-twá lə-'syel-te-drà\ [F] : help yourself (and) heaven will help you

aî·né \e-nä\ [F] : elder : senior (masc.)

aî·née \e-nä\ [F] : elder : senior (fem.)

à l'aban·don \à-là-bäⁿ-dōⁿ\ [F] : carelessly : in disorder

à la belle étoile \à-là-bel-ä-twàl\ [F] : under the beautiful star : in the open air at night

à la bonne heure \à-là-bò-nœr\ [F] : at a good time : well and good : all right

à la fran·çaise \à-là-fräⁿ-sez\ [F] : in the French manner

à l'amé·ri·caine \à-là-mä-rē-ken\ [F] : in the American manner : of the American kind

à l'an·glaise \à-läⁿ-glez\ [F] : in the English manner

à la page \à-là-päzh\ [F] : at the page : up-to-the-minute

à la russe \à-là-rūēs\ [F] : in the Russian manner

alea jac·ta est \'ä-lē-ˌä,-yàk-tä-'est\ [L] : the die is cast

à l'im·pro·viste \à-laⁿ-prò-vēst\ [F] : unexpectedly

ali·quan·do bo·nus dor·mi·tat Ho·me·rus \ä-li-ˌkwän-dō-'bò-nùs-dòr-ˌmē-ˌtät-hō-'mer-ùs\ [L] : sometimes (even) good Homer nods

alis vo·lat pro·pri·is \'ä-ˌlēs-'wò-ˌlät-'prō-prē-ˌēs\ [L] : she flies with her own wings — motto of Oregon

al·ki \'al-ˌkī, -kē\ [Chinook Jargon] : by and by — motto of Washington

alo·ha oe \ä-ˌlō-hä-'ói, -'ō-ē\ [Hawaiian] : love to you : greetings : farewell

al·ter Chris·tus \ˌäl-ter-'kris-tùs\ [L] : another Christ

al·ter idem \ˌól-tər-'ī-ˌdem, ˌäl-ter-'ē-\ [L] : second self

a max·i·mis ad mi·ni·ma \ä-'mäk-si-ˌmēs-ˌäd-'mi-ni-ˌmä\ [L] : from the greatest to the least

à mer·veille \à-mer-vey\ [F] : marvelously

ami·cus hu·ma·ni ge·ne·ris \ä-'mē-kùs-hü-ˌmä-nē-'ge-ne-ris\ [L] : friend of the human race

ami·cus us·que ad aras \-ˌùs-kwe-ˌäd-'är-ˌäs\ [L] : a friend as far as to the altars, i.e., except in what is contrary to one's religion; *also* : a friend to the last extremity

ami de cour \à-ˌmē-də-'kùr\ [F] : court friend : insincere friend

amor pa·tri·ae \ˌä-ˌmòr-'pä-trē-ˌī\ [L] : love of one's country

amor vin·cit om·nia \'ä-ˌmòr-ˌwiŋ-kit-'óm-nē-ä\ [L] : love conquers all things

an·cienne no·blesse \äⁿ-syen-nò-bles\ [F] : old-time nobility : the French nobility before the Revolution of 1789

an·guis in her·ba \ˌäŋ-gwis-in-'her-ˌbä\ [L] : snake in the grass

ani·mal bi·pes im·plu·me \'ä-ni-ˌmäl-ˌbī-ˌpäs-im-'plü-me\ [L] : two= legged animal without feathers (i.e., the human race)

ani·mis opi·bus·que pa·ra·ti \'ä-ni-ˌmēs-ˌó-pi-'bùs-kwe-pä-'rä-tē\ [L] : prepared in mind and resources — one of the mottoes of South Carolina

an·no ae·ta·tis su·ae \'ä-nō-ī-ˌtä-tis-'sü-ˌī\ [L] : in the (specified) year of his (or her) age

an·no mun·di \ˌä-nō-'mùn-dē\ [L] : in the year of the world — used in reckoning dates from the supposed period of the creation of the world, esp. as fixed by James Ussher at 4004 B.C. or by the Jews at 3761 B.C.

an·no ur·bis con·di·tae \ˌä-nō-ˌùr-bis-'kòn-di-ˌtī\ [L] : in the year of the founded city (Rome, founded 753 B.C.)

an·nu·it coep·tis \'ä-nü-ˌit-'kóip-ˌtēs\ [L] : He (God) has approved our beginnings — motto on the reverse of the Great Seal of the United States

à peu près \à-pœ̄-pre\ [F] : nearly : approximately

à pied \à-pyä\ [F] : on foot

après moi le dé·luge \à-pre-mwá-lə-dā-lūēzh\ *or* **après nous le dé·luge** \à-pre-nü-\ [F] : after me the deluge — attributed to Louis XV

à pro·pos de bottes \à-prə-pō-də-bót\ [F] : apropos of boots — used to change the subject

à pro·pos de rien \-ryaⁿ\ [F] : apropos of nothing

aqua et ig·ni in·ter·dic·tus \ˌä-kwä-et-'ig-nē-ˌin-ter-'dik-tùs\ [L] : forbidden to be furnished with water and fire : outlawed

Ar·ca·des am·bo \'är-kä-ˌdes-'äm-bō\ [L] : both Arcadians : two persons of like occupations or tastes; *also* : two rascals

ar·gu·men·tum ad ba·cu·lum \ˌär-gù-'men-tùm-ˌäd-'bä-kù-lùm\ [L] : argument of the staff : appeal to force

ar·rec·tis au·ri·bus \ä-'rek-ˌtēs-'aù-ri-ˌbùs\ [L] : with ears pricked up : attentively

ar·ri·ve·der·ci \ˌär-ē-vä-'der-chē\ [It] : till we meet again : farewell

ars est ce·la·re ar·tem \ˌärs-ˌest-kä-ˌlär-ä-'är-ˌtem\ [L] : it is (true) art to conceal art

ars lon·ga, vi·ta bre·vis \ˌärs-'lóŋ-ˌgä, wē-ˌtä-'bre-wis\ [L] : art is long, life is short

a ter·go \ä-'ter-(ˌ)gō\ [L] : from behind

à tort et à tra·vers \à-ˌtòr-ä-à-trà-ver\ [F] : wrong and crosswise : at random : without rhyme or reason

au bout de son la·tin \ō-büd-sōⁿ-là-taⁿ, -bü-də-\ [F] : at the end of one's Latin : at the end of one's mental resources

au con·traire \ō-kōⁿ-trer\ [F] : on the contrary

au·de·mus ju·ra nos·tra de·fen·de·re \aù-'dä-mùs-ˌyùr-ä-'nò-strä-dā-'fen-de-rä\ [L] : we dare defend our rights — motto of Alabama

au·den·tes for·tu·na ju·vat \aù-'den-ˌtäs-fòr-ˌtü-nä-'yù-ˌwät\ [L] : fortune favors the bold

au·di al·te·ram par·tem \'aù-ˌdē-ˌäl-te-ˌräm-'pär-ˌtem\ [L] : hear the other side

au fait \ō-fet, -fe\ [F] : to the point : fully competent : fully informed : socially correct

au fond \ō-fōⁿ\ [F] : at bottom : fundamentally

au grand sé·rieux \ō-grän-sä-ryœ̄\ [F] : in all seriousness

au mieux \ō-myœ̄\ [F] : on the best terms : on intimate terms

au pays des aveugles les borgnes sont rois \ō-pä-ē-dä-zà-vœgl²-lä-bórnʸ-ə-sōⁿ-rwà, -rwä\ [F] : in the country of the blind the one-eyed men are kings

au·rea me·di·o·cri·tas \'aù-rē-ä-ˌme-dē-'ó-kri-ˌtäs\ [L] : the golden mean

au reste \ō-rest\ [F] : for the rest : besides

au sé·rieux \ō-sä-ryœ̄\ [F] : seriously

au·spi·ci·um me·li·o·ris ae·vi \aù-ˌspi-kē-ˌùm-ˌme-lē-ˌōr-is-'ī-ˌwē\ [L] : an omen of a better age — motto of the Order of St. Michael and St. George

aus·si·tôt dit, aus·si·tôt fait \ō-sē-tō-dē ō-sē-tō-fe\ [F] : no sooner said than done

aut Cae·sar aut ni·hil \aut-'kī-sär-,aut-'ni-,hil\ [L] : either a Caesar or nothing
aut Caesar aut nul·lus \-'nú-lús\ [L] : either a Caesar or a nobody
au·tres temps, au·tres mœurs \ō-tr∂-täⁿ ō-tr∂-mœrs\ [F] : other times, other customs
aut vin·ce·re aut mo·ri \aut-'wiŋ-ke-rä-,aut-'mó-,rē\ [L] : either to conquer or to die
aux armes \ō-zárm\ [F] : to arms
avant la lettre \ä-väⁿ-lä-letr[∂]\ [F] : before the letter : before a (specified) name existed
avant–pro·pos \ä-väⁿ-pró-pō\ [F] : preface
ave at·que va·le \'ä-,wä-,ät-kwe-'wä-,lä\ [L] : hail and farewell
à vo·tre san·té \ä-vót-säⁿ-tä, -vó-tr∂-\ [F] : to your health — used as a toast
beaux yeux \bō-zyœ\ [F] : beautiful eyes : beauty of face
bel·la fi·gu·ra \'bel-l∂-fē-'gü-rä\ [It] : fine appearance or impression
belle laide \bel-led\ [F] : beautiful ugly woman : woman who is attractive though not conventionally beautiful
bel·lum om·ni·um con·tra om·nes \'be-lùm-'óm-nē-ùm-,kón-trä-'óm-,näs\ [L] : war of all against all
bien en·ten·du \byaⁿ-näⁿ-täⁿ-dū̄ē\ [F] : well understood : of course
bien–pen·sant \byaⁿ-päⁿ-säⁿ\ [F] : right-minded : one who holds orthodox views
bien·sé·ance \byaⁿ-sā-äⁿs\ [F] : propriety
bien vu \byaⁿ-vū̄ē\ [F] : well regarded
bis dat qui ci·to dat \'bis-,dät-kwē-'ki-tō-,dät\ [L] : he gives twice who gives promptly
bon ap·pé·tit \bó-nä-pä-tē\ [F] : good appetite : enjoy your meal
bon gré, mal gré \'bōⁿ,grä-'mál,grä\ [F] : whether with good grace or bad : willy-nilly
bo·nis avi·bus \,bó-,nēs-'ä-wi-,bùs\ [L] : under good auspices
bon·jour \bōⁿ-zhür\ [F] : good day : good morning
bonne foi \bón-fwä\ [F] : good faith
bon·soir \bōⁿ-swär\ [F] : good evening
bru·tum ful·men \brü-tùm-'fùl-men\ [L] : insensible thunderbolt : a futile threat or display of force
ca·dit quae·stio \,kä-dit-'kwī-stē-,ō\ [L] : the question drops : the argument collapses
ca·pable de tout \ká-pábl[∂]-d∂-tü\ [F] : capable of anything : unpredictable
carte d'iden·ti·té \kárt-dē-däⁿ-tē-tä\ [F] : identity card
cau·sa si·ne qua non \'kaù-,sä-,si-nä-kwä-'nōn\ [L] : an indispensable cause or condition
ça va sans dire \sä-vä-säⁿ-dēr\ [F] : it goes without saying
ca·ve·at lec·tor \'kä-vē-,ät-'lek-,tòr, 'ka-\ [L] : let the reader beware
ca·ve ca·nem \,kä-wä-'kä-,nem\ [L] : beware the dog
ce·dant ar·ma to·gae \'kä-,dänt-,är-m∂-'tō-,gi\ [L] : let arms yield to the toga : let military power give way to civil power — motto of Wyoming
ce n'est que le pre·mier pas qui coûte \snek-l∂-pr∂-myā-pä-kē-küt\ [F] : it is only the first step that costs
c'est–à–dire \se-tá-dēr\ [F] : that is to say : namely
c'est au·tre chose \se-tōt-shóz, -tō-tr∂-\ [F] : that's a different thing
c'est la guerre \se-lá-ger\ [F] : that's war : it cannot be helped
c'est la vie \se-lá-vē\ [F] : that's life : that's how things happen
c'est plus qu'un crime, c'est une faute \se-plūē-kœⁿ-krēm se-tūēn-fōt\ [F] : it is worse than a crime, it is a blunder
ce·te·ra de·sunt \,kä-te-,rä-'dā-,sùnt\ [L] : the rest is missing
cha·cun à son goût \shá-kœⁿ-ná-sōⁿ-gü\ [F] : everyone to his taste
châ·teau en Es·pagne \shä-tō-äⁿ-nes-pán^y\ [F] : castle in Spain : a visionary project
cher·chez la femme \sher-shä-lá-fám\ [F] : look for the woman
che sa·rà, sa·rà \,kä-sä-,rä-sä-'rä\ [It] : what will be, will be
che·val de ba·taille \sh∂-vál-d∂-bä-tä^y\ [F] : war-horse : argument constantly relied on : favorite subject
ci–gît \sē-zhē\ [F] : here lies — used preceding a name on a tombstone
co·gi·to, er·go sum \'kō-gi-,tō-,er-gō-'sùm\ [L] : I think, therefore I exist
co·mé·die hu·maine \kó-mä-dē-ūē-men\ [F] : human comedy : the whole variety of human life
comédie lar·moy·ante \-lár-mwá-yäⁿt\ [F] : tearful comedy : sentimental comedy
comme ci, comme ça \kòm-sē-kóm-sá\ [F] : so-so
com·pa·gnon de voy·age \kōⁿ-pá-n^yōⁿ-d∂-vwá-yázh\ [F] : traveling companion
compte ren·du \kōⁿt-räⁿ-dūē\ [F] : report (as of proceedings in an investigation)
con·cor·dia dis·cors \kón-'kòr-dē-ä-'dis-,kòrs\ [L] : discordant harmony
con·fes·sio fi·dei \kón-'fe-sē-ō-'fi-dē-,ē\ [L] : confession of faith
con·temp·tus mun·di \kón-'tem(p)-tùs-'mùn-dē\ [L] : contempt for the world
cor·rup·tio op·ti·mi pes·si·ma \kò-'rúp-tē-,ō-'äp-ti-,mē-'pe-si-,mä\ [L] : the corruption of the best is the worst of all
coup de maî·tre \küd-metr[∂], kü-d∂-\ [F] : masterstroke
coup d'es·sai \kü-dä-se\ [F] : experiment : trial
coûte que coûte \küt-k∂-küt\ [F] : cost what it may
cre·do quia ab·sur·dum est \,krä-dō-'kwē-ä-äp-,sùr-dùm-'est\ [L] : I believe it because it is absurd
cre·do ut in·tel·li·gam \,krä-dō-,ùt-in-'te-lē-,gäm\ [L] : I believe so that I may understand
cres·cit eun·do \,kres-kit-'eùn-dō\ [L] : it grows as it goes — motto of New Mexico
crise de conscience \krēz-d∂-kōⁿ-syäⁿs\ [F] : crisis of conscience : agonizing period of moral uncertainty
crise de nerfs *or* **crise des nerfs** \krēz-d∂-ner\ [F] : crisis of nerves : nervous collapse : hysterical fit
crux cri·ti·co·rum \'krúks-,kri-ti-'kòr-ùm\ [L] : crux of critics
cuj·us re·gio, ej·us re·li·gio \,kü-yùs-'re-gē-,ō ,e-yùs-re-'li-gē-,ō\ [L] : whose region, his or her religion : subjects are to accept the religion of their ruler
cum gra·no sa·lis \kúm-,grä-nō-'sä-lis\ [L] : with a grain of salt
cur·sus ho·no·rum \'kùr-sùs-hò-'nō-rùm\ [L] : course of honors : succession of offices of increasing importance

cus·tos mo·rum \,kùs-tōs-'mōr-ùm\ [L] : guardian of manners or morals : censor
d'ac·cord \dá-kór\ [F] : in accord : agreed
dame d'hon·neur \dám-dò-nœr\ [F] : lady-in-waiting
dam·nant quod non in·tel·li·gunt \'däm-,nänt-,kwòd-,nōn-in-'te-li-,gùnt\ [L] : they condemn what they do not understand
de bonne grâce \d∂-bón-gräs\ [F] : with good grace : willingly
de gus·ti·bus non est dis·pu·tan·dum \dā-'gùs-t∂-,bùs-,nōn-,est-,dis-pù-'tän-,dùm\ [L] : there is no disputing about tastes
Dei gra·tia \,de-ē-'grä-tē-,ä\ [L] : by the grace of God
de in·te·gro \dā-'in-te-,grō\ [L] : anew : afresh
de l'au·dace, en·core de l'au·dace, et tou·jours de l'au·dace \d∂-lō-'däs äⁿ-'kòr-d∂-lō-däs ā-tü-'zhür-d∂-lō-däs\ [F] : audacity, more audacity, and ever more audacity
de·len·da est Car·tha·go \dā-'len-dä-,est-kär-'tä-gō\ [L] : Carthage must be destroyed
de·li·ne·a·vit \dā-,lē-nä-'ä-wit\ [L] : he (or she) drew it
de mal en pis \d∂-má-läⁿ-pē\ [F] : from bad to worse
de mi·ni·mis non cu·rat lex \dā-'mi-ni-,mēs-,nōn-,kü-,rät-'leks\ [L] : the law takes no account of trifles
de mor·tu·is nil ni·si bo·num \dā-'mòr-tù-,ēs-,nēl-,ni-sē-'bó-,nùm\ [L] : of the dead (say) nothing but good
de nos jours \d∂-nō-zhür\ [F] : of our time : contemporary — used postpositively esp. after a proper name
Deo fa·ven·te \,dā-ō-fä-'ven-tä\ [L] : with God's favor
Deo gra·ti·as \,dā-ō-'grä-tē-,äs\ [L] : thanks (be) to God
de pro·fun·dis \,dā-prō-'fùn-dēs, -'f∂n-\ [L] : out of the depths
der Geist der stets ver·neint \d∂r-'gist-d∂r-,shtäts-fer-'nīnt\ [G] : the spirit that ever denies — applied originally to Mephistopheles
de·si·pe·re in lo·co \dā-'si-pe-rä-in-'lō-kō\ [L] : to indulge in trifling at the proper time
De·us ab·scon·di·tus \,dā-ùs-,äp-'skòn-di-,tùs\ [L] : hidden God : God unknowable by the human mind
De·us vult \dā-ùs-'wùlt\ [L] : God wills it — rallying cry of the First Crusade
di·es fau·stus \,dē-,äs-'faù-stùs\ [L] : lucky day
dies in·fau·stus \-'in-,faù-stùs\ [L] : unlucky day
dies irae \-'ē-,rī, -,rä\ [L] : day of wrath — used of the Judgment Day
Dieu et mon droit \dyœ-ā-móⁿ-drwä\ [F] : God and my right — motto on the British royal arms
Dieu vous garde \dyœ-vü-gárd\ [F] : God keep you
di·ri·go \'dē-ri-,gō\ [L] : I direct — motto of Maine
dis ali·ter vi·sum \,dēs-ä-li-,ter-'wē-,sùm\ [L] : the Gods decreed otherwise
dis·cor·dia con·cors \dis-'kòr-dē-ä-'kòn-,kòrs\ [L] : harmonious discord : harmony or unity gained by combining disparate or conflicting elements
di·tat De·us \,dē-,tät-'dā-,ùs\ [L] : God enriches — motto of Arizona
di·vi·de et im·pe·ra \'dē-wi-,de-,et-'im-p∂-,rä\ [L] : divide and rule
do·cen·do dis·ci·mus \dō-,ken-dō-'dis-ki-,mùs\ [L] : we learn by teaching
dol·ce stil nuo·vo \'dòl-chä-stēl-'nwó-vō\ [It] : sweet new style
Do·mi·ne, di·ri·ge nos \'dò-mi-,ne-'dē-ri-,ge-'nōs\ [L] : Lord, direct us — motto of the City of London
Do·mi·nus vo·bis·cum \dó-mi-,nùs-wō-'bēs-,kùm\ [L] : the Lord be with you
dul·ce et de·co·rum est pro pa·tria mo·ri \,dùl-,ke-et-de-'kòr-ùm-,est-prō-,pä-trē-,ä-'mó-,rē\ [L] : it is sweet and seemly to die for one's country
dum spi·ro, spe·ro \dùm-'spē-rō-'spä-rō\ [L] : while I breathe, I hope — one of the mottoes of South Carolina
dum vi·vi·mus vi·va·mus \dùm-'wē-wē-,mùs-wē-'wä-mùs\ [L] : while we live, let us live
d'un cer·tain âge \dœⁿ-ser-te-näzh\ [F] : of a certain age : no longer young
dux fe·mi·na fac·ti \,dùks-,fä-mi-nä-'fäk-,tē\ [L] : a woman was leader of the exploit
ec·ce sig·num \,e-ke-'sig-,nùm\ [L] : behold the sign : look at the proof
e con·tra·rio \,ā-kón-'trär-ē-,ō\ [L] : on the contrary
écra·sez l'in·fâme \ā-krä-zä-laⁿ-fám\ [F] : crush the infamous thing
eheu fu·ga·ces la·bun·tur an·ni \,ā-,heù-fú-'gä-,käs-lä-'bùn-,túr-'ä-,nē\ [L] : alas! the fleeting years glide on
ein' fes·te Burg ist un·ser Gott \īn-,fes-t∂-'bùrk-ist-,ún-z∂r-'gót\ [G] : a mighty fortress is our God
em·bar·ras de ri·chesses *or* **embarras de ri·chesse** \äⁿ-bá-räd-rē-shes, -rä-d∂-\ [F] : embarrassing surplus of riches : confusing abundance
em·bar·ras de choix \äⁿ-,bá-rä-d∂-shwä\ *or* **embarras du choix** \-dūē-shwä\ [F] : embarrassing variety of choice
en ami \äⁿ-ná-mē\ [F] : as a friend
en ef·fet \äⁿ-nä-fe\ [F] : in fact : indeed
en fa·mille \äⁿ-fá-mēy\ [F] : in or with one's family : at home : informally
en·fant ché·ri \äⁿ-fäⁿ-shä-rē\ [F] : loved or pampered child : one that is highly favored
en·fant gâ·té \äⁿ-fäⁿ-gä-tä\ [F] : spoiled child
en·fants per·dus \äⁿ-fäⁿ-per-dūē\ [F] : lost children : soldiers sent to a dangerous post
en·fin \äⁿ-faⁿ\ [F] : in conclusion : in a word
en gar·çon \äⁿ-gär-sōⁿ\ [F] : as or like a bachelor
en garde \äⁿ-gárd\ [F] : on guard
en pan·tou·fles \äⁿ-päⁿ-tüfl[∂]\ [F] : in slippers : at ease : informally
en plein air \äⁿ-ple-ner\ [F] : in the open air
en plein jour \äⁿ-pläⁿ-zhür\ [F] : in broad day
en poste \äⁿ-pòst\ [F] : in a diplomatic post
en règle \äⁿ-regl[∂]\ [F] : in order : in due form

\∂\ abut \[∂]\ kitten, F table \∂r\ further \a\ ash \ā\ ace \ä\ mop, mar \aù\ out \ch\ chin \e\ bet \ē\ easy \g\ go \i\ hit \ī\ ice \j\ job \ŋ\ sing \ō\ go \ò\ law \òi\ boy \th\ thin \t͟h\ the \ü\ loot \ù\ foot \y\ yet \zh\ vision \á, k̲, ⁿ, œ, œ̄, ue, ūē, ^y\ *see* Guide to Pronunciation

en re·tard \äⁿr-(ə-)tár\ [F] : behind time : late

en re·traite \äⁿr-(ə-)tret\ [F] : in retreat : in retirement

en re·vanche \äⁿr-(ə-)väⁿsh\ [F] : in return : in compensation

en se·condes noces \äⁿs-gōⁿd-nós, äⁿ-sə-\ [F] : in a second marriage

en·se pe·tit pla·ci·dam sub li·ber·ta·te qui·e·tem \en-se-,pe-tit-'plä-ki-,däm-sùb-,lē-ber-,tä-te-kwē-'ä-,tem\ [L] : with the sword she seeks calm repose under liberty : by the sword we seek peace, but peace only under liberty — motto of Massachusetts

eo ip·so \ā-ō-'ip-(,)sō\ [L] : by that itself : by that fact alone

épa·ter le bour·geois \ā-pä-tä-lə-bür-zhwä\ *or* **épater les bourgeois** \-lā-bür-\ [F] : to shock the middle classes

e plu·ri·bus unum \,ē-,plür-ə-bəs-'(y)ü-nəm, ,ä-,plùr-i-bùs-'ü-nùm\ [L] : one out of many — used on the Great Seal of the U.S. and on several U.S. coins

ep·pur si muo·ve \āp-,pür-sē-'mwò-vā\ [It] : and yet it does move — attributed to Galileo after recanting his assertion of the earth's motion

Erin go bragh \er-ən-gə-'brò, -gō-'brä\ [Ir *go brách* or *go bráth*, lit., till doomsday] : Ireland forever

er·ra·re hu·ma·num est \e-'rär-ä-hü-,mä-núm-'est\ [L] : to err is human

es·prit de l'es·ca·lier \es-prēd-les-kà-lyä\ *or* **es·prit d'es·ca·lier** \-prē-des-\ [F] : wit of the staircase : repartee thought of only too late, on the way home

es·se quam vi·de·ri \'e-sā-,kwäm-wi-'dā-rē\ [L] : to be rather than to seem — motto of North Carolina

est mo·dus in re·bus \est-'mò-,dùs-in-'rā-,bùs\ [L] : there is a proper measure in things, i.e., the golden mean should always be observed

es·to per·pe·tua \'es-,tō-per-'pe-tü-,ä\ [L] : may she endure forever — motto of Idaho

et hoc ge·nus om·ne \et-,hōk-,ge-nùs-'òm-ne\ *or* **et id genus omne** \et-,id-\ [L] : and everything of this kind

et in Ar·ca·dia ego \,et-in-är-,kä-dē-ä-'e-gō\ [L] : I too (lived) in Arcadia

et sic de si·mi·li·bus \et-,sēk-dā-si-'mi-li-,bùs\ [L] : and so of like things

et tu Bru·te \et-'tü-'brü-te\ [L] : thou too, Brutus — exclamation attributed to Julius Caesar on seeing his friend Brutus among his assassins

eu·re·ka \yù-'rē-kä\ [Gk] : I have found it — motto of California

Ewig—Weib·li·che \,ā-vik-'vīp-li-kə\ [G] : eternal feminine

ex·al·té \eg-zál-tā\ [F] : emotionally excited or elated : fanatic

ex ani·mo \eks-'ä-ni-,mō\ [L] : from the heart : sincerely

ex·cel·si·or \ik-'sel-sē-ər, eks-'kel-sē-,ór\ [L] : still higher — motto of New York

ex·cep·tio pro·bat re·gu·lam de re·bus non ex·cep·tis \eks-'kep-tē-,ō-,prō-bät-'rā-gù-,läm-dā-'rä-,bùs-,nōn-eks-'kep-,tēs\ [L] : an exception establishes the rule as to things not excepted

ex·cep·tis ex·ci·pi·en·dis \eks-'kep-,tēs-eks-,ki-pē-'en-,dēs\ [L] : with the proper or necessary exceptions

ex·i·tus ac·ta pro·bat \'ek-si-,tùs-,äk-tä-'prò-,bät\ [L] : the outcome justifies the deed

ex li·bris \eks-'lē-bris\ [L] : from the books of — used on bookplates

ex me·ro mo·tu \,eks-,mer-ō-'mō-tü\ [L] : out of mere impulse : of one's own accord

ex ne·ces·si·ta·te rei \,eks-ne-,ke-si-'tä-te-'rā(-,ē)\ [L] : from the necessity of the case

ex ni·hi·lo ni·hil fit \eks-'ni-hi-,lō-,ni-,hil-'fit\ [L] : from nothing nothing is produced

ex pe·de Her·cu·lem \eks-,pe-de-'her-kù-,lem\ [L] : from the foot (we may judge of the size of) Hercules : from a part we may judge of the whole

ex·per·to cre·de \eks-,per-tō-'krä-de\ *or* **experto cre·di·te** \-'krä-di-,te\ [L] : believe one who has had experience : trust me

ex un·gue le·o·nem \eks-'ùŋ-gwe-le-'ō-,nem\ [L] : from the claw (we may judge of) the lion : from a part we may judge of the whole

ex vi ter·mi·ni \eks-,wē-'ter-mə-,nē\ [L] : from the force of the term

fa·ci·le prin·ceps \,fä-ki-le-'prin-,keps\ [L] : easily first

fa·ci·lis de·scen·sus Aver·no \'fä-ki-,lis-dā-,skän-,sùs-ä-'wer-nō\ *or* **facilis descensus Aver·ni** \-(,)nē\ [L] : the descent to Avernus is easy : the road to evil is easy

fa·çon de par·ler \fà-sōⁿ-də-pár-lā\ [F] : manner of speaking : figurative or conventional expression

faire suivre \fer-swⁱⁿēvr\ [F] : have forwarded : please forward

fas est et ab ho·ste do·ce·ri \fäs-'est-et-äb-'hò-ste-dó-'kä-(,)rē\ [L] : it is right to learn even from an enemy

Fa·ta vi·am in·ve·ni·ent \,fä-tä-'wē-,äm-in-'we-nē-,ent\ [L] : the Fates will find a way

fat·ti mas·chii, pa·ro·le fe·mi·ne \,fät-tē-'mäs-,kē pä-,rò-lä-'fä-mē-,nä\ [It] : deeds are males, words are females : deeds are more effective than words — motto of Maryland, where it is generally interpreted as meaning "manly deeds, womanly words"

faux bon·homme \fō-bô-nòm\ [F] : pretended good fellow

faux—naïf \fō-nä-ēf\ [F] : spuriously or affectedly childlike : artfully simple

fe·lix cul·pa \'fā-liks-'kùl-pä\ [L] : fortunate fault — used esp. of original sin in relation to the consequent coming of Christ

femme de cham·bre \fäm-də-shäⁿbr\ [F] : chambermaid : lady's maid

fes·ti·na len·te \fe-,stē-nä-'len-,tä\ [L] : make haste slowly

feux d'ar·ti·fice \fœ-dár-tē-fēs\ [F] : fireworks : display of wit

fi·at ex·pe·ri·men·tum in cor·po·re vi·li \'fē-,ät-ek-,sper-ē-'men-,tùm-in-,kór-pó-re-'wē-lē\ [L] : let experiment be made on a worthless body

fi·at jus·ti·tia, ru·at cae·lum \,fē-,ät-yùs-'ti-tē-ä ,rú-,ät-'kī-,lùm\ [L] : let justice be done though the heavens fall

fi·at lux \,fē-,ät-'lùks\ [L] : let there be light

Fi·dei De·fen·sor \,fi-de-ē-dā-'fän-,sór\ [L] : Defender of the Faith — a title of the sovereigns of England

fille de cham·bre \fēy-də-shäⁿbr\ [F] : lady's maid

fille d'hon·neur \fēy-dò-nœr\ [F] : maid of honor

fils \fēs\ [F] : son — used orig. after French and now also after other family names to distinguish a son from his father

fi·nem re·spi·ce \,fē-,nem-'rā-spi-,ke\ [L] : consider the end

fi·nis co·ro·nat opus \,fē-nis-kó-,rō-,nät-'ō-,pùs\ [L] : the end crowns the work

flo·re·at \'flō-re-,ät\ [L] : may (he, she, or it) flourish — usu. followed by a name

fluc·tu·at nec mer·gi·tur \'flùk-tù-,ät-,nek-'mer-gi-,tùr\ [L] : it is tossed by the waves but does not sink — motto of Paris

fo·lie de gran·deur *or* **fo·lie des gran·deurs** \fó-lē-də-grä-dœr\ [F] : delusion of greatness : megalomania

force de frappe \fórs-də-fráp\ [F] : military striking force esp. with nuclear weapons

fors·an et haec olim me·mi·nis·se ju·va·bit \,fòr-,sän-,et-'hīk-,ō-lim-,me-mi-'ni-se-yù-'wä-bit\ [L] : perhaps this too will be a pleasure to look back on one day

for·tes for·tu·na ju·vat \'fór-,täs-fór-,tü-nä-'yù-,wät\ [L] : fortune favors the brave

fron·ti nul·la fi·des \'fròn-,tē-,nù-lä-'fi-,dās\ [L] : no reliance can be placed on appearance

fu·it Ili·um \'fù-it-'i-lē-ùm\ [L] : Troy has been (i.e., is no more)

fu·ror lo·quen·di \,fùr-,ór-lō-'kwen-(,)dē\ [L] : rage for speaking

furor po·e·ti·cus \-pó-'ä-ti-kùs\ [L] : poetic frenzy

furor scri·ben·di \-skrē-'ben-(,)dē\ [L] : rage for writing

Gal·gen·hu·mor \'gäl-gən-hü-,mōr\ [G] : gallows humor

Gal·li·ce \'gä-li-,ke\ [L] : in French : after the French manner

gar·çon d'hon·neur \gär-sōⁿ-dò-nœr\ [F] : bridegroom's attendant

garde du corps \gärd-dü-kór\ [F] : bodyguard

gar·dez la foi \gár-,dā-lä-fwä\ [F] : keep faith

gau·de·a·mus igi·tur \,gaú-dē-'ä-,mùs-'i-gi-,tùr\ [L] : let us then be merry

gens d'é·glise \zhäⁿ-dā-glēz\ [F] : church people : clergy

gens de guerre \zhäⁿ-də-ger\ [F] : military people : soldiery

gens du monde \zhäⁿ-dǖ-mōⁿd\ [F] : people of the world : fashionable people

gno·thi se·au·ton \'gnō-thē-,se-aú-'tòn\ [Gk] : know thyself

goût de ter·roir \gü-də-te-rwár\ [F] : taste of the earth

grande école \grä-dā-kól\ [F] : great school : French institution of higher education for postbaccalaureate professional or technological training

grand monde \grä-mōⁿd\ [F] : great world : high society

gros·so mo·do \'gròs-(,)sō-'mō-(,)dō\ [It] : roughly

guerre à ou·trance \ger-à-ü-träⁿs\ [F] : war to the uttermost

gu·ten Tag \,gü-tən-'täk\ [G] : good day

has·ta la vis·ta \,äs-tə-lä-'vēs-tə\ [Sp] : good-bye

haute vul·ga·ri·sa·tion \ōt-,vül-gä-rē-zä-syōⁿ\ [F] : high popularization : effective presentation of a difficult subject to a general audience

haut goût \ō-gü\ [F] : high flavor : slight taint of decay

hic et nunc \'hēk-et-'nùŋk\ [L] : here and now

hic et ubi·que \,hēk-et-ù-'bē-kwe\ [L] : here and everywhere

hic ja·cet \hik-'jä-sət, hēk-'yä-ket\ [L] : here lies — used preceding a name on a tombstone

hinc il·lae la·cri·mae \,hiŋk-,i-,lī-'lä-kri-,mī\ [L] : hence those tears

hoc age \hōk-'ä-ge\ [L] : do this : apply yourself to what you are about

hoc opus, hic la·bor est \hōk-'ò-,pùs,-hēk-'lä-,bòr-'est\ [L] : this is the hard work, this is the toil

homme d'af·faires \òm-dä-fer\ [F] : man of business : business agent

homme d'es·prit \-des-prē\ [F] : man of wit

homme moyen sen·suel \òm-mwä-yaⁿ-säⁿ-swⁿel\ [F] : the average nonintellectual man

ho·mo sum: hu·ma·ni nil a me ali·e·num pu·to \'hò-mō-,sùm hü-,mä-nē-'nēl-ä-,mä-,ä-lē-'ä-nùm-'pú-tō\ [L] : I am a human being : I regard nothing of human concern as foreign to my interests

ho·ni soit qui mal y pense \ò-nē-swä-kē-mál-ē-päⁿs\ [F] : shamed be he who thinks evil of it — motto of the Order of the Garter

hon·nête homme \ò-net-òm\ [F] : honest man : respectable and honorable citizen of the middle class

hors com·merce \òr-kó-mers\ [F] : outside the trade : not offered through regular commercial means

hu·ma·num est er·ra·re \hü-,mä-nùm-,est-e-'rär-ä\ [L] : to err is human

ich dien \ik-'dēn\ [G] : I serve — motto of the Prince of Wales

ici on parle fran·çais \ē-sē-ōⁿ-pärl-fräⁿ-se, -pár-lə-\ [F] : French is spoken here

idées re·çues \ē-dār-(ə-)sⁿē\ [F] : received ideas : conventional opinions

id est \id-'est\ [L] : that is

ig·no·ran·tia ju·ris ne·mi·nem ex·cu·sat \,ig-nó-,rän-tē-ä-'yùr-is-'nä-mi-,nem-eks-'kü-,sät\ [L] : ignorance of the law excuses no one

ig·no·tum per ig·no·ti·us \ig-,nō-tùm,-per-ig-'nō-tē-,ùs\ [L] : (explaining) the unknown by means of the more unknown

il faut cul·ti·ver no·tre jar·din \ēl-fō-kⁿēl-tē-vä-nòt-zhár-daⁿ, -nò-trə-zhár-\ [F] : we must cultivate our garden : we must tend to our own affairs

ils ne pas·se·ront pas \ēl-nə-pás-rōⁿ-pä, -pá-sə-rōⁿ-\ [F] : they shall not get past

in ae·ter·num \,in-ī-'ter-,nùm\ [L] : forever

in du·bio \in-'dü-bē-,ō\ [L] : in doubt : undetermined

in fu·tu·ro \,in-fú-'tùr-ō\ [L] : in the future

in hoc sig·no vin·ces \in-hōk-'sig-nō-'wiŋ-,käs\ [L] : by this sign (the Cross) you will conquer

in li·mi·ne \in-'lē-mi-,ne\ [L] : on the threshold : at the beginning

In·nig·keit \'i-ni(k)-,kīt\ [G] : poignant intimacy of feeling — used esp. of music

in om·nia pa·ra·tus \in-'òm-nē-ä-pä-'rä-,tùs\ [L] : ready for all things

in par·ti·bus in·fi·de·li·um \in-'pär-ti-,bùs-,in-fi-'dä-lē-,ùm\ [L] : in the regions of the infidels — used of a titular bishop having no diocesan jurisdiction, usu. in non-Christian countries

in prae·sen·ti \,in-prī-'sen-,tē\ [L] : at the present time

in sae·cu·la sae·cu·lo·rum \in-'sī-kù-,lä-,sī-kù-'lòr-,ùm, -'sä-kù-,lä-,sä-\ [L] : for ages of ages : forever and ever

in·shal·lah \,in-shä-'lä\ [Ar] : if Allah wills : God willing

in sta·tu quo an·te bel·lum \in-'stä-,tü-kwō-,än-te-'be-lùm\ [L] : in the same state as before the war

in·te·ger vi·tae sce·le·ris·que pu·rus \ˌin-te-ˌger-'wē-ˌtī-ˌske-le-'ris-kwe-'pü-rùs\ [L] : upright of life and free from wickedness

in·ter nos \ˌin-ter-'nōs\ [L] : between ourselves

in·tra mu·ros \ˌin-trä-'mü-ˌrōs\ [L] : within the walls

in usum Del·phi·ni \in-'ü-sùm-del-'fē-nē\ [L] : for the use of the Dauphin : expurgated

in utrum·que pa·ra·tus \ˌin-ü-'trüm-kwe-pä-'rä-ˌtùs\ [L] : prepared for either (event)

in·ve·nit \in-'wā-nit\ [L] : he or she devised it

in vi·no ve·ri·tas \in-wē-nō-'wä-ri-ˌtäs\ [L] : there is truth in wine

in·vi·ta Mi·ner·va \in-'wē-tä-mi-'ner-ˌwä\ [L] : Minerva being unwilling : without natural talent or inspiration

ip·sis·si·ma ver·ba \ip-ˌsi-si-ˌmä-'wer-ˌbä\ [L] : the very words

ira fu·ror bre·vis est \ˌē-rä-'für-ˌòr-'bre-wis-ˌest\ [L] : anger is a brief madness

j'ac·cuse \zhá-kūēz\ [F] : I accuse : bitter denunciation

jac·ta alea est \'yäk-ˌtä-ˌä-lē-ä-'est\ [L] : the die is cast

j'adoube \zhá-düb\ [F] : I adjust — used in chess when touching a piece without intending to move it

ja·nu·is clau·sis \ˌyä-nü-ˌēs-'klaú-ˌsēs\ [L] : behind closed doors

je main·tien·drai \zhə-maⁿ-tyaⁿ-drā\ [F] : I will maintain — motto of the Netherlands

jeu de mots \zhœd-mō, zhœ-də-\ [F] : play on words : pun

Jo·an·nes est no·men eius \yō-'ä-näs-est-ˌnō-men-'ä-yùs\ [L] : John is his name — motto of Puerto Rico

jo·lie laide \zhò-lē-led\ [F] : good-looking ugly woman : woman who is attractive though not conventionally pretty

jour·nal in·time \zhür-nál-aⁿ-tēm\ [F] : intimate journal : private diary

jus di·vi·num \ˌyüs-di-'wē-ˌnùm\ [L] : divine law

jus·ti·tia om·ni·bus \yüs-ˌti-tē-ˌä-'òm-ni-ˌbùs\ [L] : justice for all — motto of the District of Columbia

j'y suis, j'y reste \zhē-swē-zhē-rest\ [F] : here I am, here I remain

Kin·der, Kir·che, Küche \'kin-dər 'kir-kə 'kǔe-kə\ [G] : children, church, kitchen

kte·ma es aei \(kə-)'tä-ˌmä-es-ä-'ä\ [Gk] : a possession for ever — applied to a work of art or literature of enduring significance

la belle dame sans mer·ci \lä-bel-dám-säⁿ-mer-sē\ [F] : the beautiful lady without mercy

la·bo·ra·re est ora·re \'lä-bō-ˌrär-ä-ˌest-'ō-ˌrär-ä\ [L] : to work is to pray

la·bor om·nia vin·cit \'lä-ˌbòr-ˌòm-nē-ˌä-'wiⁿ-kit\ [L] : labor conquers all things — motto of Oklahoma

la·cri·mae re·rum \ˌlä-kri-ˌmi-'rä-ˌrùm\ [L] : tears for things : pity for misfortune; also : tears in things : tragedy of life

lais·sez–al·ler or **lais·ser–al·ler** \le-sä-ä-lä\ [F] : letting go : lack of restraint

lap·sus ca·la·mi \ˌläp-sùs-'kä-lä-ˌmē, ˌlap-səs-'ka-lə-ˌmī\ [L] : slip of the pen

lap·sus lin·guae \ˌlap-səs-'liⁿ-ˌgwī, ˌläp-ˌsùs-\ [L] : slip of the tongue

la reine le veut \lä-ren-lə-vœ\ [F] : the queen wills it

la·scia·te ogni spe·ran·za, voi ch'en·tra·te \läsh-'shä-tä-ō-nʸē-spä-'rän-tsä-ˌvō-ē-kän-'trä-tä\ [It] : abandon all hope, ye who enter

lau·da·tor tem·po·ris ac·ti \laú-'dä-ˌtòr-ˌtem-pó-ris-'äk-ˌtē\ [L] : one who praises past times

laus Deo \laús-'dä-ō\ [L] : praise (be) to God

Le·bens·welt \'lā-bəns-ˌvelt\ [G] : life world : world of lived experience

le cœur a ses rai·sons que la rai·son ne con·naît point \lə-kœr-ä-sä-re-zōⁿ-la-re-zōⁿn-kò-ne-pwaⁿ, -zōⁿ-nə-\ [F] : the heart has its reasons that reason knows nothing of

le roi est mort, vive le roi \lə-rwä-e-mór vēv-lə-rwä\ [F] : the king is dead, long live the king

le roi le veut \lə-rwä-lə-vœ\ [F] : the king wills it

le roi s'avi·se·ra \lə-rwä-sä-vēz-rá\ [F] : the king will consider

le style, c'est l'homme \lə-stēl-se-lòm\ [F] : the style is the man

l'état, c'est moi \lā-tä-se-mwá\ [F] : the state, it is I

l'étoile du nord \lā-twál-dūē-nór\ [F] : the star of the north — motto of Minnesota

Lie·der·kranz \'lē-dər-ˌkränts\ [G] : wreath of songs : German singing society

lit·tera scrip·ta ma·net \ˌli-te-ˌrä-ˌskrip-tä-'mä-net\ [L] : the written letter abides

lo·cus in quo \ˌlò-kùs-in-'kwò\ [L] : place in which

l'union fait la force \lūē-nyōⁿ-fe-lä-fórs\ [F] : union makes strength — motto of Belgium

lu·sus na·tu·rae \ˌlü-sùs-nä-'tùr-ē, -'tùr-ˌī\ [L] : freak of nature

ma foi \mä-fwä\ [F] : my faith! : indeed

mag·na est ve·ri·tas et prae·va·le·bit \ˌmäg-nä-ˌest-'wä-ri-ˌtäs-et-ˌprī-wä-'lä-bit\ [L] : truth is mighty and will prevail

mag·ni no·mi·nis um·bra \ˌmäg-nē-ˌnō-mi-nis-'ùm-brä\ [L] : the shadow of a great name

ma·ha·lo \'mä-hä-lō\ [Hawaiian] : thank you

mai·son de san·té \mä-zōⁿd-säⁿ-tā, -zōⁿ-də-\ [F] : private hospital : asylum

ma·lade ima·gi·naire \má-lád-ē-má-zhē-ner\ [F] : imaginary invalid : hypochondriac

ma·lis avi·bus \ˌmä-ˌlēs-'ä-wi-ˌbùs\ [L] : under evil auspices

mal vu \mál-vūē\ [F] : badly regarded : disapproval of

ma·no a ma·no \ˌmä-nō-ä-'mä-nō\ [Sp] : hand to hand : in direct competition or confrontation

man spricht Deutsch \män-shpri̇kt-'dòich\ [G] : German spoken

ma·riage de con·ve·nance \má-ryázh-də-kōⁿv-näns\ [F] : marriage of convenience

ma·ri com·plai·sant \má-rē-kōⁿ-ple-zäⁿ\ [F] : complaisant husband : cuckold who accepts his wife's infidelity

mau·vaise honte \mò-vez-ōⁿt\ [F] : bad shame : bashfulness

mau·vais quart d'heure \mò-ve-kár-dœr\ [F] : bad quarter hour : an uncomfortable though brief experience

me·den agan \ˌ(ˌ)mä-ˌden-'ä-ˌgän\ [Gk] : nothing in excess

me·dio tu·tis·si·mus ibis \'me-dē-ō-tü-ˌti-si-mùs-'ē-bis\ [L] : you will go most safely by the middle course

me ju·di·ce \mā-'yü-di-ke\ [L] : I being judge : in my judgment

mens sa·na in cor·po·re sa·no \mäns-'sä-nä-in-ˌkòr-pó-re-'sä-nō\ [L] : a sound mind in a sound body

met·teur en scène \me-tœr-äⁿ-sen\ [F] : one who puts on the stage : director of a play or film

me·um et tu·um \ˌmē-əm-ˌet-'tü-əm, ˌme-ùm-ˌet-'tü-ùm\ [L] : mine and thine : distinction of private property

mi·ra·bi·le vi·su \mi-ˌrä-bi-lä-'wē-sü\ [L] : wonderful to behold

mi·ra·bi·lia \ˌmir-ə-'bi-lē-ˌä\ [L] : wonders : miracles

mœurs \mœr(s)\ [F] : mores : attitudes, customs, and manners of a society

mo·le ru·it sua \'mō-le-'rú-it-ˌsú-ä\ [L] : it collapses from its own bigness

monde \mōⁿd\ [F] : world : fashionable world : society

mon·ta·ni sem·per li·be·ri \mōⁿ-'tä-nē-ˌsem-per-'lē-be-ˌrē\ [L] : mountaineers are always free — motto of West Virginia

mo·nu·men·tum ae·re per·en·ni·us \ˌmó-nù-'men-tùm-ˌī-re-pe-'re-nē-ùs\ [L] : a monument more lasting than bronze — used of an immortal work of art or literature

mo·re suo \ˌmòr-ä-'sü-ō\ [L] : in his (or her) own manner

mo·ri·tu·ri te sa·lu·ta·mus \ˌmòr-i-'tùr-ē-ˌtā-ˌsä-lü-'tä-mùs\ or **morituri te sa·lu·tant** \-'sä-lù-ˌtänt\ [L] : we (or those) who are about to die salute thee

mul·tum in par·vo \ˌmùl-tùm-in-'pär-vō, -'pär-wō\ [L] : much in little

mu·sée ima·gi·naire \mü-zä-ē-má-zhē-ner\ [F] : imaginary museum

mu·ta·to no·mi·ne de te fa·bu·la nar·ra·tur \mü-ˌtä-tō-'nō-mi-ne-ˌdä-ˌtä-'fä-bù-lä-nä-'rä-ˌtùr\ [L] : with the name changed the story applies to you

my·ster·i·um tre·men·dum \mi-'ster-ē-ˌùm-tre-'men-dùm\ [L] : overwhelming mystery

na·tu·ram ex·pel·las fur·ca, ta·men us·que re·cur·ret \nä-'tü-ˌräm-ek-ˌspe-läs-'für-ˌkä, ˌtä-men-'ús-kwe-re-'kùr-et\ [L] : you may drive nature out with a pitchfork, but she will keep coming back

na·tu·ra non fa·cit sal·tum \nä-'tü-rä-ˌnōn-ˌfä-kit-'säl-ˌtùm\ [L] : nature makes no leap

ne ce·de ma·lis \nä-ˌkä-de-'mä-ˌlēs\ [L] : yield not to misfortunes

ne·mo me im·pu·ne la·ces·sit \'nä-mō-'mä-im-ˌpü-nä-lä-'ke-sit\ [L] : no one attacks me with impunity — motto of Scotland and of the Order of the Thistle

ne quid ni·mis \ˌnä-ˌkwid-'ni-mis\ [L] : not anything in excess

n'est–ce pas? \nes-pä\ [F] : isn't it so?

nicht wahr? \nikt-'vär\ [G] : not true? : isn't it so?

nil ad·mi·ra·ri \'nēl-ˌäd-mi-'rär-ē\ [L] : to be excited by nothing : equanimity

nil de·spe·ran·dum \'nēl-ˌdä-spä-'rän-dùm\ [L] : never despair

nil si·ne nu·mi·ne \'nēl-si-nä-'nü-mi-ne\ [L] : nothing without the divine will — motto of Colorado

n'im·porte \naⁿ-pòrt\ [F] : it's no matter

no·lens vo·lens \ˌnō-ˌlenz-'vō-ˌlenz\ [L] : unwilling (or) willing : willy-nilly

non om·nia pos·su·mus om·nes \nōn-'òm-nē-ˌä-ˌpó-sù-mùs-'òm-ˌnäs\ [L] : we can't all (do) all things

non om·nis mo·ri·ar \nōn-'òm-nis-'mòr-ē-ˌär\ [L] : I shall not wholly die

non sans droict \nōⁿ-säⁿ-drwä\ [OF] : not without right — motto on Shakespeare's coat of arms

non sum qua·lis eram \nōn-ˌsùm-ˌkwä-lis-'er-ˌäm\ [L] : I am not what I used to be

nos·ce te ip·sum \ˌnōs-ke-ˌtä-'ip-ˌsùm\ [L] : know thyself

nos·tal·gie de la boue \nòs-tál-zhēd-lä-bü, -zhē-də-\ [F] : yearning for the mud : attraction to what is unworthy, crude, or degrading

nous avons chan·gé tout ce·la \nü-zá-vōⁿ-shäⁿ-zhä-tü-sə-lá\ [F] : we have changed all that

nous ver·rons ce que nous ver·rons \nü-ve-rōⁿs-kə-nü-ve-rōⁿ, -rōⁿ-sə-kə-\ [F] : we shall see what we shall see

no·vus ho·mo \ˌnò-wùs-'hò-mō\ [L] : new man : man newly ennobled : upstart

novus or·do se·clo·rum \-'òr-ˌdō-sä-'klòr-ùm\ [L] : a new cycle of the ages — motto on the reverse of the Great Seal of the United States

nu·gae \'nü-ˌgī\ [L] : trifles

nuit blanche \nwēⁿ-blä̈sh\ [F] : white night : a sleepless night

nyet \'nyet\ [Russ] : no

O al·ti·tu·do \'ō-ˌäl-ti-'tü-ˌdō\ [L] : O (the) height : feeling of spiritual exaltation

ob·iit \'ò-bē-ˌit\ [L] : he or she died

ob·scu·rum per ob·scu·ri·us \òb-'skyúr-ùm-ˌper-òb-'skyúr-ē-ùs\ [L] : (explaining) the obscure by means of the more obscure

ode·rint dum me·tu·ant \'ō-de-ˌrint-ˌdùm-me-tù-ˌänt\ [L] : let them hate, so long as they fear

odi et amo \'ō-ˌdē-et-'ä-(ˌ)mō\ [L] : I hate and I love

omer·tà \ò-'mer-tä\ [It] : submission : code chiefly among members of the criminal underworld that enjoins private vengeance and the refusal to give information to outsiders (as the police)

om·ne ig·no·tum pro mag·ni·fi·co \ˌòm-ne-ig-'nō-ˌtùm-prō-mäg-'ni-fi-ˌkō\ [L] : everything unknown (is taken) as grand : the unknown tends to be exaggerated in importance or difficulty

om·nia mu·tan·tur, nos et mu·ta·mur in il·lis \ˌòm-nē-ä-mü-'tän-ˌtùr ˌnōs-ˌet-mü-ˌtä-mùr-in-'i-ˌlēs\ [L] : all things are changing, and we are changing within them

om·nia vin·cit amor \'òm-nē-ä-'wiⁿ-kit-'ä-ˌmòr\ [L] : love conquers all

onus pro·ban·di \ˌō-nùs-prō-'ban-ˌdī, -dē\ [L] : burden of proof

ora pro no·bis \ˌō-rä-prō-'nò-ˌbēs\ [L] : pray for us

ore ro·tun·do \ˌòr-ē-rō-'tùn-dō\ [L] : with round mouth : eloquently

oro y pla·ta \ˌò-rō-ē-'plä-tə\ [Sp] : gold and silver — motto of Montana

o tem·po·ra! o mo·res! \ō-'tem-pó-rä-ō-'mò-ˌräs\ [L] : oh the times! oh the manners!

\ə\ abut \ᵊ\ kitten, F table \ər\ further \a\ ash \ā\ ace \ä\ mop, mar
\aú\ out \ch\ chin \e\ bet \ē\ easy \g\ go \i\ hit \ī\ ice \j\ job
\ŋ\ sing \ō\ go \ò\ law \òi\ boy \th\ thin \t͟h\ the \ü\ loot \ù\ foot
\y\ yet \zh\ vision \á, k̲, ⁿ, œ, œ̄, œ, ūē, ʸ\ see Guide to Pronunciation

oti·um cum dig·ni·ta·te \'ō-tē-,ùm-kùm-,dig-ni-'tä-te\ [L] : leisure with dignity

où sont les neiges d'an·tan? \ü-sōⁿ-lā-nezh-däⁿ-täⁿ\ [F] : where are the snows of yesteryear?

outre—mer \ütr'-mer\ [F] : overseas : distant lands

pal·li·da Mors \,pa-li-dä-'mórz\ [L] : pale Death

pa·nem et cir·cen·ses \'pä-,nem-et-kir-'kän-,säs\ [L] : bread and circuses : provision of the means of life and recreation by government to appease discontent

pan·ta rhei \,pän-,tä-'rā, ,pan-tə-'rā\ [Gk] : all things are in flux

par avance \pär-ä-väⁿs\ [F] : in advance : by anticipation

par avion \pär-ä-vyōⁿ\ [F] : by airplane — used on airmail

par ex·em·ple \pär-āg-zäⁿpl'\ [F] : for example

pars pro to·to \'pärs-(,)prō-'tō-(,)tō\ [L] : part (taken) for the whole

par·tu·ri·unt mon·tes, nas·ce·tur ri·di·cu·lus mus \pär-'tùr-ē-,ùnt-'mòn-,tās näs-'kā-,tùr-ri-,di-kù-lùs-'müs\ [L] : the mountains are in labor, and a ridiculous mouse will be brought forth

pa·ter pa·tri·ae \,pä-,ter-'pä-trē-,i\ [L] : father of his country

pau·cis ver·bis \,paù-,kēs-'wer-,bēs\ [L] : in a few words

pax vo·bis·cum \,päks-vō-'bēs-,kùm\ [L] : peace (be) with you

peine forte et dure \pen-fòr-tā-dǖr\ [F] : strong and hard punishment : torture

per an·gus·ta ad au·gus·ta \per-'än-,gùs-tä-äd-'aù-,gùs-tä, per-'äŋ-\ [L] : through difficulties to honors

père \per\ [F] : father — used orig. after French and now also after other family names to distinguish a father from his son

per·eant qui an·te nos nos·tra dix·e·runt \'per-e-,änt-kwē-,än-te-'nōs-'nōs-trä-dēk-'sä-,rùnt\ [L] : may they perish who have expressed our bright ideas before us

per·eunt et im·pu·tan·tur \'per-e-,ùnt-et-,im-pù-'tän-,tùr\ [L] : they (the hours) pass away and are reckoned on (our) account

per·fide Al·bion \per-fēd-äl-byōⁿ\ [F] : perfidious Albion (England)

peu à peu \pœ-ä-pœ\ [F] : little by little

peu de chose \pœd-shōz, pœ-də-\ [F] : a trifle

pièce d'oc·ca·sion \pyes-dò-kä-zyōⁿ\ [F] : piece for a special occasion

pièce jus·ti·fi·ca·tive \pyes-zhūes-tē-fē-kä-tēv\ [F] : justificatory paper : document serving as evidence

pièce mon·tée \pyes-mōⁿ-tä\ [F] : set piece : food that has been decoratively shaped or arranged

pinx·it \'pink-sit\ [L] : he or she painted it

place aux dames \pläs-ō-dám\ [F] : (make) room for the ladies

ple·no ju·re \,plä-nō-'yùr-e\ [L] : with full right

plus ça change, plus c'est la même chose \plūe-sä-shäⁿzh plūe-se-lä-mem-shōz\ [F] : the more that changes, the more it's the same thing — often shortened to *plus ça change*

plus roy·a·liste que le roi \plūe-rwä-yä-lēst-kəl-rwä\ [F] : more royalist than the king

po·cas pa·la·bras \,pō-käs-pä-'lä-vräs\ [Sp] : few words

po·eta nas·ci·tur, non fit \pò-,ä-tä-'näs-ki-,tùr nōn-'fit\ [L] : a poet is born, not made

point de re·père \pwaⁿ-də-ra-per\ [F] : point of reference

pol·li·ce ver·so \,pò-li-ke-'wer-sō\ [L] : with thumb turned : with a gesture or expression of condemnation

post hoc, er·go prop·ter hoc \'pòst-,hōk ,er-gō-'pròp-ter-,hōk\ [L] : after this, therefore on account of it (a fallacy of argument)

post ob·itum \pòst-'ò-bi-,tùm\ [L] : after death

pour ac·quit \pür-ä-kē\ [F] : received payment

pour le mé·rite \pür-lə-mä-rēt\ [F] : for merit

pour rire \pür-rēr\ [F] : for laughing : not to be taken seriously

pri·mum no·no·ce·re \,prē-mùm-,nōn-nó-'kā-rä\ [L] : the first thing (is) to do no harm

pro aris et fo·cis \,prō-,ä-,rēs-et-'fò-,kēs\ [L] : for altars and firesides

pro bo·no pu·bli·co \,prō-,bò-nō-'pü-bli-,kō\ [L] : for the public good

pro hac vi·ce \,prō-,häk-'wi-ke\ [L] : for this occasion

pro pa·tria \,prō-'pä-trē-,ä\ [L] : for one's country

pro re·ge, le·ge, et gre·ge \,prō-'rā-,ge-'lä-,ge-et-'gre-,ge\ [L] : for the king, the law, and the people

pro re na·ta \,prō-,rā-'nä-tä\ [L] : for an occasion that has arisen : as needed — used in medical prescriptions

quand même \kä-mem\ [F] : even so : all the same

quan·tum mu·ta·tus ab il·lo \,kwän-tùm-mü-'tä-tùs-äb-'i-lō\ [L] : how changed from what he once was

quan·tum suf·fi·cit \,kwän-təm-'sə-fə-,kit\ [L] : as much as suffices : a sufficient quantity — used chiefly in medical prescriptions

¿quién sa·be? \kyän-'sä-vä\ [Sp] : who knows?

qui fa·cit per ali·um fa·cit per se \kwē-,fä-kit-,per-'ä-lē-,ùm-,fä-kit-,per-'sā\ [L] : he who does (something) through another does it through himself

quis cus·to·di·et ip·sos cus·to·des? \,kwis-kùs-'tō-dē-,et-,ip-,sōs-kùs-'tō-,dās\ [L] : who will keep the keepers themselves?

qui s'ex·cuse s'ac·cuse \kē-'sek-,skūēz-'sä-,kūēz\ [F] : he who excuses himself accuses himself

quis se·pa·ra·bit? \,kwis-,sä-pə-'rä-bit\ [L] : who shall separate (us)? — motto of the Order of St. Patrick

qui trans·tu·lit sus·ti·net \kwē-'träns-tù-,lit-'sùs-ti-,net\ [L] : He who transplanted sustains (us) — motto of Connecticut

qui va là? \kē-vä-lä\ [F] : who goes there?

quo·ad hoc \,kwò-,äd-'hōk\ [L] : as far as this : to this extent

quod erat de·mon·stran·dum \,kwòd-'er-,ät-,de-mən-'stran-dəm, -,dä-,mōn-'strän-,dùm\ [L] : which was to be proved

quod erat fa·ci·en·dum \-,fä-kē-'en-,dùm\ [L] : which was to be done

quod sem·per, quod ubi·que, quod ab om·ni·bus \kwòd-'sem-,per kwòd-'ü-bi,kwä kwòd-äb-'òm-ni-,bùs, -,kwòd-ù-'bē-(,)kwä-\ [L] : what (has been held) always, everywhere, by everybody

quod vi·de \kwòd-'wi-,de\ [L] : which see

quo·rum pars mag·na fui \'kwōr-ùm,pärs-,mäg-nä-'fù-ē\ [L] : in which I played a great part

quos de·us vult per·de·re pri·us de·men·tat \kwōs-'dā-ùs-,wùlt-'per-de-,rä,pri-ùs-dā-'men-,tät\ [L] : those whom a god wishes to destroy he first drives mad

quot ho·mi·nes, tot sen·ten·ti·ae \kwòt-'hò-mi-,nās-,tòt-sen-'ten-tē-,ī\ [L] : there are as many opinions as there are men

quo va·dis? \kwō-'wä-dis, -'vä-dəs\ [L] : whither are you going?

rai·son d'état \re-zōⁿ-dä-tä\ [F] : reason of state

re·cu·ler pour mieux sau·ter \rə-kūe-lä-pür-myœ-sō-tā\ [F] : to draw back in order to make a better jump

reg·nat po·pu·lus \,reg-,nät-'pò-pù-,lùs\ [L] : the people rule — motto of Arkansas

re in·fec·ta \,rā-in-'fek-,tä\ [L] : the business being unfinished : without accomplishing one's purpose

re·li·gio lo·ci \re-'li-gē-,ō-'lò-,ke\ [L] : religious sanctity of a place

rem acu te·ti·gis·ti \rem-'ä-,kü-,te-ti-'gis-tē\ [L] : you have touched the point with a needle : you have hit the nail on the head

ré·pon·dez s'il vous plaît \rā-pōⁿ-dā-sēl-vü-ple\ [F] : reply, if you please

re·qui·es·cat in pa·ce \,re-kwē-'es-,kät-in-'pä-,ke, ,rä-kwē-'es-,kät-in-'pä-,chä\ [L] : may he or she rest in peace — used on tombstones

re·spi·ce fi·nem \,rā-spi-,ke-'fē-,nem\ [L] : look to the end : consider the outcome

re·sur·gam \re-'sùr-,gäm\ [L] : I shall rise again

re·te·nue \rət-nūe\ [F] : self-restraint : reserve

re·ve·nons à nos mou·tons \rəv-nōⁿ-ä-nō-mü-tōⁿ\ [F] : let us return to our sheep : let us get back to the subject

ruse de guerre \rūez-də-ger\ [F] : war stratagem

rus in ur·be \,rüs-in-'ùr-,be\ [L] : the business being unfinished : country in the city

sae·va in·dig·na·tio \,sī-wä-,in-dig-'nä-tē-ō\ [L] : fierce indignation

sal At·ti·cum \,sal-'a-ti-kəm\ [L] : Attic salt : wit

salle à man·ger \,säl-ä-mäⁿ-zhä\ [F] : dining room

sa·lon des re·fu·sés \sä-lōⁿ-dār-(ə-)fūe-zā\ [F] : salon of the refused : exhibition of art that has been rejected by an official body

sal·to mor·ta·le \,säl-tō-mór-'tä-lä\ [It] : deadly jump : full somersault : dangerous or crucial undertaking

sa·lus po·pu·li su·pre·ma lex es·to \,sä-,lüs-'pò-pù-,lē-sù-,prä-mä-,leks-'es-tō\ [L] : let the welfare of the people be the supreme law — motto of Missouri

sanc·ta sim·pli·ci·tas \,säŋk-tä-sim-'pli-ki-,täs\ [L] : holy simplicity — often used ironically in reference to another's naïveté

sans doute \säⁿ-düt\ [F] : without doubt

sans gêne \säⁿ-zhen\ [F] : without embarrassment or constraint

sans peur et sans re·proche \säⁿ-pœr-ä-säⁿ-rə-'pròsh\ [F] : without fear and without reproach

sans sou·ci \säⁿ-sü-sē\ [F] : without worry

sa·yo·na·ra \,sī-ə-'när-ə, ,sä-yə-\ [Jp] : good-bye

scène à faire \sen-ä-fer\ [F] : obligatory scene

sculp·sit \'skəlp-sət, 'skùlp-sit\ [L] : he or she carved it

scu·to bo·nae vo·lun·ta·tis tu·ae co·ro·nas·ti nos \'skü-,tō-'bò-,nī-,vō-lùn-,tä-tis-'tù-,ī-'kòr-ò-,näs-tē-'nōs\ [L] : Thou hast crowned us with the shield of Thy good will — a motto on the Great Seal of Maryland

se·cun·dum ar·tem \se-,kùn-dùm-'är-,tem\ [L] : according to the art : according to the accepted practice of a profession or trade

secundum na·tu·ram \-,nä-'tü-,räm\ [L] : according to nature : naturally

se de·fen·den·do \'sā-,dā-,fen-'den-dō\ [L] : in self-defense

se ha·bla es·pa·ñol \sā-,äv-lä-,äs-pä-'nyòl\ [Sp] : Spanish spoken

sem·per ea·dem \,sem-,per-'e-ä-,dem\ [L] : always the same (fem.) — motto of Queen Elizabeth I

sem·per fi·de·lis \,sem-pər-fə-'dä-ləs\ [L] : always faithful — motto of the U.S. Marine Corps

sem·per idem \,sem-,per-'ē-,dem\ [L] : always the same (masc.)

sem·per pa·ra·tus \,sem-pər-pə-'rä-təs\ [L] : always prepared — motto of the U.S. Coast Guard

se non è ve·ro, è ben tro·va·to \sā-,nōn-e-'vā-rō-e-,ben-trō-'vä-tō\ [It] : even if it is not true, it is well conceived

sic itur ad as·tra \sēk-,i-,tùr-,äd-'äs-trə\ [L] : thus one goes to the stars : such is the way to immortality

sic sem·per ty·ran·nis \,sik-,sem-pər-tə-'ra-nəs\ [L] : thus ever to tyrants — motto of Virginia

sic trans·it glo·ria mun·di \sēk-'trän-sit-,glòr-ē-ä-'mùn-dē\ [L] : so passes away the glory of the world

sic·ut pa·tri·bus sit De·us no·bis \,sē-,kùt-'pä-tri-,bùs-sit-,dā-ùs-'nō-,bēs\ [L] : as to our fathers may God be to us — motto of Boston

si jeu·nesse sa·vait, si vieil·lesse pou·vait! \sē-'zhœ-nes-'sä-ve sē-'vye-yes-'pü-ve\ [F] : if youth only knew, if age only could!

si·lent le·ges in·ter ar·ma \,si-,lent-'lā-,gäs-,in-ter-'är-mä\ [L] : the laws are silent in the midst of arms

s'il vous plaît \sēl-vü-ple\ [F] : if you please

si·mi·lia si·mi·li·bus cu·ran·tur \si-'mi-lē-ä-si-'mi-li-bùs-kü-'rän-,tùr\ [L] : like is cured by like

si·mi·lis si·mi·li gau·det \'si-mi-lis-'si-mi-lē-'gaù-,det\ [L] : like takes pleasure in like

si mo·nu·men·tum re·qui·ris, cir·cum·spi·ce \sē-,mò-nú-,men-tùm-re-'kwē-ris kir-'kùm-spi-ke\ [L] : if you seek his monument, look around — epitaph of Sir Christopher Wren in St. Paul's, London, of which he was architect

sim·pliste \saⁿ-plēst\ [F] : simplistic : overly simple or naive

si quae·ris pen·in·su·lam amoe·nam, cir·cum·spi·ce \sē-'kwī-ris-pā-'nin-sə-,läm-ä-'mòi-,näm kir-'kùm-spi-ke\ [L] : if you seek a beautiful peninsula, look around — motto of Michigan

sis·te vi·a·tor \,sis-te-wē-'ä-,tór\ [L] : stop, traveler — used on Roman roadside tombs

si vis pa·cem, pa·ra bel·lum \sē-'wēs-'pä-,kem 'pä-rä-'be-,lùm\ [L] : if you wish peace, prepare for war

sol·vi·tur am·bu·lan·do \'sòl-wi-,tùr-,äm-bù-'län-dō\ [L] : it is solved by walking : the problem is solved by a practical experiment

splen·di·de men·dax \,splen-di-,dä-'men-,däks\ [L] : nobly untruthful

spo·lia opi·ma \,spò-lē-ä-ō-'pē-mä\ [L] : rich spoils : the arms taken by the victorious from the vanquished general

Sta·bat Ma·ter \,stä-bät-'mä-ter\ [L] : the mother was standing — title of a Latin hymn

sta·tus in quo \,stä-tùs-,in-'kwō\ [L] : state in which : the existing state

sta·tus quo an·te bel·lum \'stä-tùs-kwō-,än-te-'be-lùm\ [L] : the state existing before the war

Stim·mung \shti-mùŋ\ [G] : tone : mood : atmosphere

sua·vi·ter in mo·do, for·ti·ter in re \'swä-wi-,ter-in-'mò-dō 'fòr-ti-,ter-in-'rä\ [L] : gently in manner, strongly in deed sub ver·bo \sŭb-'wer-bō, ˌsəb-'vər-bō\ or sub vo·ce \sŭb-'wō-ke, ˌsəb-'vō-sē\ [L] : under the word — introducing a cross-reference in a dictionary or index

sunt la·cri·mae re·rum \sŭnt-ˌlä-kri-ˌmī-'rä-rům\ [L] : there are tears for things : tears attend trials

suo ju·re \ˌsů-ō-'yůr-e\ [L] : in his (or her) own right

suo lo·co \-'lō-kō\ [L] : in its proper place

suo Mar·te \-'mär-te\ [L] : by one's own exertions

sur place \sůēr-plás\ [F] : in place : on the spot

su·um cui·que \ˌsů-ům-'kwi-kwe\ [L] : to each his own

tant mieux \tän-'myœ̄\ [F] : so much the better

tant pis \-pē\ [F] : so much the worse : too bad

tem·po·ra mu·tan·tur, nos et mu·ta·mur in il·lis \ˌtem-pô-rä-mü-'tän-ˌtůr ˌnōs-et-mü-ˌtä-můr-in-'i-ˌlēs\ [L] : the times are changing, and we are changing with them

tem·pus edax re·rum \'tem-půs-ˌe-ˌdäks-'rä-rům\ [L] : time, that devours all things

tem·pus fu·git \ˌtem-pəs-'fyü-jət, ˌtem-půs-'fü-git\ [L] : time flies

ti·meo Da·na·os et do·na fe·ren·tes \ˌti-mē-ˌō-'dä-nä-ˌōs-et-ˌdō-nä-fe-'ren-ˌtäs\ [L] : I fear the Greeks even when they bring gifts

to·ti·dem ver·bis \ˌtō-ti-ˌdem-'wer-bēs\ [L] : in so many words

to·tis vi·ri·bus \ˌtō-ˌtēs-'wē-ri-ˌbůs\ [L] : with all one's might

to·to cae·lo \ˌtō-tō-'kī-lō\ or toto coe·lo \-'kói-lō\ [L] : by the whole extent of the heavens : diametrically

tou·jours per·drix \tü-zhür-per-drē\ [F] : always partridge : too much of a good thing

tour d'ho·ri·zon \tür-dó-rē-zōⁿ\ [F] : circuit of the horizon : general survey

tous frais faits \tü-fre-fe\ [F] : all expenses defrayed

tout à fait \tü-tá-fe\ [F] : altogether : quite

tout au con·traire \tü-tō-kōⁿ-trer\ [F] : quite the contrary

tout à vous \tü-tá-vü\ [F] : wholly yours : at your service

tout bien ou rien \tü-'byaⁿ-nü-'ryaⁿ\ [F] : everything well (done) or nothing (attempted)

tout com·pren·dre c'est tout par·don·ner \'tü-kōⁿ-prän-drə se-'tü-pár-dó-nä\ [F] : to understand all is to forgive all

tout court \tü-kür\ [F] : quite short : and nothing more : simply : just; also : brusquely

tout de même \tüt-mem\ [F] : all the same : nevertheless

tout de suite \tüt-swēt\ [F] : immediately; also : all at once : consecutively

tout en·sem·ble \tü-tän-sänbl\ [F] : all together : general effect

tout est per·du fors l'hon·neur \tü-te-per-dūē-fór-lò-nœr\ or tout est perdu hors l'honneur \-dūē-ór-\ [F] : all is lost save honor

tout le monde \tü-lə-mōnd\ [F] : all the world : everybody

tra·hi·son des clercs \trá-ē-zōⁿ-dä-klerk\ [F] : treason of the intellectuals

tranche de vie \tränsh-də-'vē\ [F] : slice of life

tria junc·ta in uno \ˌtri-ä-'yůnk-tä-in-'ü-nō\ [L] : three joined in one — motto of the Order of the Bath

trist·esse \trē-stes\ [F] : melancholy

tru·di·tur di·es die \'trü-di-ˌtůr-'di-ˌäs-'di-ˌä\ [L] : day is pushed forth by day : one day hurries on another

tu·e·bor \tü-'ā-ˌbór\ [L] : I will defend — a motto on the Great Seal of Michigan

ua mau ke ea o ka ai·na i ka po·no \ˌů-ä-'mä-ů-kä-'ä-ä-ō-kä-'ä-ē-nä-ˌē-kä-'pō-nō\ [Hawaiian] : the life of the land is perpetuated in righteousness — motto of Hawaii

über al·les \ˌūē-ber-'ä-les\ [G] : above everything else

ue·ber·mensch \'ūē-bər-ˌmench\ [G] : superman

ul·ti·ma ra·tio re·gum \'ůl-ti-mä-ˌrä-tē-ō-'rä-gům\ [L] : the final argument of kings, i.e., war

und so wei·ter \ůnt-zō-'vī-tər\ [G] : and so on

uno ani·mo \ˌü-nō-'ä-ni-ˌmō\ [L] : with one mind : unanimously

ur·bi et or·bi \ˌůr-bē-ˌet-'ór-bē\ [L] : to the city (Rome) and the world : to everyone

uti·le dul·ci \ˌü-ti-le-'důl-ˌkē\ [L] : the useful with the agreeable

ut in·fra \ůt-'in-frä\ [L] : as below

ut su·pra \ůt-'sü-prä\ [L] : as above

va·de re·tro me, Sa·ta·na \ˌwä-de-'rä-trō-ˌmä-'sä-tä-ˌnä\ [L] : get thee behind me, Satan

va et vient \vá-ä-vyäⁿ\ [F] : coming and going : active movement : traffic

vae vic·tis \wī-'wik-ˌtēs\ [L] : woe to the vanquished

va·ria lec·tio \ˌwär-ē-ä-'lek-tē-ˌō\ pl va·ri·ae lec·ti·o·nes \'wär-ē-ˌī-ˌlek-tē-'ō-ˌnäs\ [L] : variant reading

va·ri·um et mu·ta·bi·le sem·per fe·mi·na \ˌwär-ē-ům-ˌet-ˌmü-'tä-bi-le-ˌsem-ˌper-'fä-mi-nä\ [L] : woman is ever a fickle and changeable thing

ve·di Na·po·li e poi mo·ri \ˌvä-dē-'nä-pō-lē-ä-ˌpó-ē-'mó-rē\ [It] : see Naples and then die

ve·ni, vi·di, vi·ci \ˌvä-nē-ˌwē-dē-'wē-kē, ˌvä-nē-ˌvē-dē-'vē-chē\ [L] : I came, I saw, I conquered

ven·tre à terre \väⁿ-trá-ter\ [F] : belly to the ground : at very great speed

ver·ba·tim ac lit·te·ra·tim \wer-'bä-tim-ˌäk-ˌli-te-'rä-tim\ [L] : word for word and letter for letter

ver·bum sat sa·pi·en·ti est \ˌwer-bům-'sät-ˌsä-pē-'en-tē-ˌest\ [L] : a word to the wise is sufficient

vieux jeu \vyœ̄-zhœ̄\ [F] : old game : old hat

vin·cit om·nia ve·ri·tas \ˌwiŋ-kit-'óm-nē-ä-'wä-ri-ˌtäs\ [L] : truth conquers all things

vin·cu·lum ma·tri·mo·nii \ˌwiŋ-ků-lům-ˌmä-tri-'mō-nē-ˌē\ [L] : bond of marriage

vin du pays \vaⁿ-dūē-pä-ē\ or vin de pays \vaⁿ-də-\ [F] : wine of the locality

vir·gi·ni·bus pu·e·ris·que \wir-'gi-ni-bůs-ˌpů-e-'rēs-kwe\ [L] : for girls and boys

vir·go in·tac·ta \'vir-ˌgō-in-'täk-tä\ [L] : untouched virgin

vir·tu·te et ar·mis \wir-'tü-te-ˌet-'är-mēs\ [L] : by valor and arms — motto of Mississippi

vis me·di·ca·trix na·tu·rae \'wēs-ˌme-di-'kä-triks-nä-'tü-ˌrī\ [L] : the healing power of nature

vi·ta nuo·va \ˌvē-tä-'nwó-vä\ [It] : new life

vive la dif·fé·rence \vēv-lä-dē-fä-räⁿs, vē-və-\ [F] : long live the difference (between the sexes)

vive la reine \vēv-lá-ren\ [F] : long live the queen

vive le roi \vēv-lə-rwä\ [F] : long live the king

vix·e·re for·tes an·te Aga·mem·no·na \wik-ˌsä-re-'fór-ˌtäs-ˌän-te-ˌä-gä-'mem-nó-ˌnä\ [L] : brave men lived before Agamemnon

vogue la ga·lère \vòg-lä-gá-ler\ [F] : let the galley be kept rowing : keep on, whatever may happen

voi·là tout \vwä-lä-tü\ [F] : that's all

vo·lup·té \vò-lūēp-tä\ [F] : pleasure : sensuality

vou·lu \vü-lūē\ [F] : willed : contrived or forced

vox et prae·te·rea ni·hil \'wōks-et-prī-'ter-e-ä-'ni-ˌhil\ [L] : voice and nothing more

vox po·pu·li vox Dei \wōks-'pó-pů-ˌlē-ˌwōks-'dä-ē\ [L] : the voice of the people is the voice of God

Wan·der·jahr \'vän-dər-ˌyär\ [G] : year of wandering

Welt·bild \'velt-ˌbilt\ [G] : conception of the world

Wert·frei·heit \'vert-ˌfrī-ˌhīt\ [G] : freedom from value judgments : ethical neutrality

wie geht's? \vē-'gäts\ [G] : how goes it?

Wis·sen·schaft \'vi-sən-ˌshäft\ [G] : learning : science

wun·der·bar \'vůn-dər-ˌbär\ [G] : wonderful

\ə\ abut \ˀ\ kitten, F table \ər\ further \a\ ash \ā\ ace \ä\ mop, mar \aů\ out \ch\ chin \e\ bet \ē\ easy \g\ go \i\ hit \ī\ ice \j\ job \ŋ\ sing \ō\ go \ò\ law \òi\ boy \th\ thin \t̲h̲\ the \ü\ loot \ů\ foot \y\ yet \zh\ vision \á, k̲, ⁿ, œ, œ̄, ů, ūē, ʸ\ see Guide to Pronunciation

Biographical Names

This section contains the names of many notable persons both living and dead. Persons are generally entered under the name or title by which they are most commonly known. Entries typically consist of last name, personal names, birth and death dates, nationality, and occupation or status. Also included, when appropriate, are pseudonyms, original names, epithets, alternate names, reign names, and titles. The pronunciation and end-of-line division of elements in boldface are usually shown. The pronunciation and end-of-line division of names or titles in italics or roman are given only occasionally. Transliterations of names from alphabets other than the roman have been made as exact and consistent as possible. For most Chinese names, the traditional Wade-Giles system has been used. The Pinyin system has been used only for Chinese still living or recently deceased.

A number of names contain connectives like *d'*, *de*, *di*, *van*, and *von*. With some exceptions, chiefly American or British, names are not alphabetized under these connectives but rather under the principal element of the surname. If the surname of a person is usually construed as containing this connective, the entry appears at the principal element and the connective appears immediately after, separated by a comma:

Gogh, van . . . Vincent

If the full name contains a connective which is not usually construed as an inseparable part of the surname, then the connective follows the personal name.

Bee·tho·ven . . . Ludwig van

Birth and death dates about which there is little or no doubt are entered without qualification. Doubtful dates are followed by a question mark, and approximate dates are preceded by *ca* (circa). In some instances only the years of principal activity are given, preceded by the abbreviation *fl* (flourished). The dates of a reign or other term of office are enclosed in parentheses.

At the end of many entries are derivative adjectives with such endings as *-ian*, *-ic*, or *-esque*. While it is possible to form these derivatives from any name, only the more common are shown:

Dan·te . . .— Dan·te·an . . . or Dan·tes·can . . . or Dan·tesque . . . adj

Of necessity many abbreviations have been used. For a key see the section Abbreviations in This Work in the front matter.

Ab·bey \'a-bē\ Edwin Austin 1852–1911 Am. painter & illustrator
Ab·bott \'a-bət\ Berenice 1898–1991 Am. photographer
Abbott Sir John Joseph Caldwell 1821–1893 Canad. polit.; prime min. (1891–92)
Abbott Lyman 1835–1922 Am. clergyman & author
Ab·del·ka·der \,ab-,del-'kä-dər\ *or* **Abd al–Qā·dir** \,ab-dəl-\ 1808–1883 Arab leader in Algeria
'Ab·dor·rah·mān Khān \,ab-,dòr-rə-'män-'kän\ *ca* 1844–1901 emir of Afghanistan (1880–1901)
Ab·dül·a·ziz \,ab-,dü-lə-'zēz\ 1830–1876 Ottoman sultan (1861–76)
Ab·dül·ha·mīd II \,ab-,dül-hä-'mēd\ 1842–1918 Ottoman sultan (1876–1909)
Abd·ul·lah \,ab-də-'lä\ 1882–1951 *'Abd Allāh ibn al-Husayn* emir of Transjordan (1921–46); king of Jordan (1946–51)
Ab·dül·me·cid I \,ab-,dül-mə-'jēd\ 1823–1861 Ottoman sultan (1839–61)
Abel \'ā-bəl\ Sir Frederick Augustus 1827–1902 Eng. chem.
Abe·lard \'a-bə-,Järd\ Peter *F* Pierre **Alé·lard** *or* **Abai·lard** \,a-bā-'lär\ 1079–?1144 *husband of Héloïse* Fr. philos. & theol.
Ab·er·crom·bie *or* **Ab·er·crom·by** \'a-bər-,kräm-bē, -,krəm-\ James 1706–1781 Brit. gen. in America
Abercromby Sir Ralph 1734–1801 Brit. gen.
Ab·er·nathy \'a-bər-,na-thē\ Ralph David 1926–1990 Am. clergyman & civil rights leader
Ab·ing·ton \'a-biŋ-tən\ Fanny 1737–1815 née *Frances Barton* Eng. actress
Abruz·zi Duke of the — SEE LUIGI AMEDEO
Abū al–Qā·sim *or* **Abul Ka·sim** \ə-,bül-'kä-səm\ *L* **Al·bu·ca·sis** \,al-byü-'kä-səs\ *ca* 936–*ca* 1013 Span. Arab physician & medical writer
Abū Bakr \ə-,bü-'ba-kər\ *ca* 573–634 1st caliph of Mecca
Ach·e·son \'a-chə-sən\ Dean Gooderham 1893–1971 Am. statesman

Ac·ton \'ak-tən\ 1st Baron 1834–1902 *John Emerich Edward Dal·berg= Acton* \,dal-,bərg-\ Eng. hist.
Ad·am \'a-dəm\ Robert 1728–1792 & his bro. James 1730–1794 Scot. architects & furniture designers
Ad·ams \'a-dəmz\ Ansel Easton 1902–1984 Am. photographer
Adams Charles Francis 1807–1886 *son of J.Q.* Am. author & diplomat
Adams Franklin Pierce 1881–1960 *known as F.P.A.* Am. journalist
Adams Henry Brooks 1838–1918 *son of C.F.* Am. hist.
Adams James Truslow 1878–1949 Am. hist.
Adams John 1735–1826 Am. diplomat; 2d pres. of the U.S. (1797–1801)
Adams John Quin·cy \'kwin-zē, 'kwin(t)-sē\ 1767–1848 *son of John* 6th pres. of the U.S. (1825–29)
Adams Maude 1872–1953 orig. *Maude Kiskadden* Am. actress
Adams Samuel 1722–1803 Am. Revolutionary patriot
Adams Samuel Hopkins 1871–1958 Am. author
Ad·dams \'a-dəmz\ Jane 1860–1935 Am. social worker
Ad·di·son \'a-də-sən\ Joseph 1672–1719 Eng. essayist & poet — **Ad·di·so·nian** \,a-də-'sō-nē-ən, -nyən\ *adj*
Ade \'ād\ George 1866–1944 Am. humorist & playwright
Ade·nau·er \'a-d'n-,aů(-ə)r, 'ä-\ Konrad 1876–1967 chancellor of West Germany (1949–63)
Ad·ler \'äd-lər, 'ad-\ Alfred 1870–1937 Austrian psychiatrist
Ad·ler \'ad-lər\ Cyrus 1863–1940 Am. educ. & scholar
Ad·ler \'ad-lər\ Felix 1851–1933 Am. educ. & reformer
Ad·ler \'ad-lər\ Mortimer Jerome 1902– Am. philos.
Adri·an \'ā-drē-ən\ name of 6 popes: esp. **IV** (*Nicholas Break·spear* \'brāk-,spi(ə)r\) 1100?–1159 the only Eng. pope (1154–59)
Adrian Rom. emp. — SEE HADRIAN
Adrian Edgar Douglas 1889–1977 1st Baron of *Cambridge* Eng. physiol.
Æ — see George William RUSSELL

Æl·fric \'al-frik\ ca 955–ca 1010 Eng. abbot & writer
Aeneas Silvius or Sylvius — see PIUS II
Aes·chi·nes \'es-kə-‚nēz, 'ēs-\ 389–314 B.C. Athenian orator
Aes·chy·lus \'es-kə-ləs, 'ēs-\ 525–456 B.C. Greek dram. — Aes·chy·le·an \‚es-kə-'lē-ən, ‚ēs-\ adj
Ae·sop \'ē-‚säp, -səp\ Greek fabulist; prob. legendary
Aeth·el·berht \'a-thəl-‚berkt\ or Eth·el·bert \'e-thəl-‚bert, -thəl-, -‚bərt\ or Aed·il·berct \'a-d°l-‚berkt\ d 616 king of Kent (560–616)
Aeth·el·red \'a-thəl-‚red\ or Eth·el·red II \'e-thəl-\ 968?–1016 the Unready king of England (978–1016)
Afon·so \ə-'fōⁿ(n)-sü\ name of 6 kings of Portugal: esp. I Hen·ri·ques \ānᵊ-'rē-kish\ 1109?–1185 (1st king of Portugal; 1139–85); V 1432–1481 (reigned 1438–81)
Aga Khan III \‚ä-gə-'kän, ‚a-\ 1877–1957 Aga Sultan Sir Mohammed Shah imam of a branch of Shiism (1885–1957)
Aga Khan IV 1936–   grandson of prec., Shah Karim imam of a branch of Shiism (1957–   )
Ag·as·siz \'a-gə-(‚)sē\ Alexander 1835–1910 son of J.L.R. Am. zool.
Agassiz (Jean) Louis (Rodolphe) 1807–1873 Am. (Swiss-born) naturalist
Agath·o·cles \ə-'ga-thə-‚klēz\ 361–289 B.C. tyrant of Syracuse
Agee \'ā-(‚)jē\ James 1909–1955 Am. author
Ages·i·la·us II \ə-‚je-sə-'lā-əs\ ca 444–360 B.C. king of Sparta (399–360)
Ag·nes \'ag-nəs\ Saint d A.D. 304 virgin martyr
Ag·new \'ag-‚nü, -‚nyü\ Spi·ro \'spir-(‚)ō\ Theodore 1918–   Am. polit.; vice pres. of the U.S. (1969–73)
Ag·non \'ag-‚nän\ Shmuel Yosef 1888–1970 Israeli (Austrian-born) author
Agric·o·la \ə-'gri-kə-lə\ Gnaeus Julius A.D. 40–93 Rom. gen.
Agrip·pa \ə-'gri-pə\ Marcus Vipsanius 63?–12 B.C. Rom. statesman
Ag·rip·pi·na \‚a-grə-'pī-nə, -'pē-\ the elder ca 14 B.C.–A.D. 33 dau. of Agrippa, wife of Germanicus Caesar, mother of Caligula
Agrippina the younger A.D. 15?–59 dau. of prec. & mother of Emp. Nero
Agui·nal·do \‚ä-gē-'näl-(‚)dō\ Emilio 1869–1964 Filipino leader
Ah·med III \ä-'met, -'med\ 1673–1736 Ottoman sultan (1703–30)
Ai·ken \'ā-kən\ Conrad Potter 1889–1973 Am. writer
Ai·ley \'ā-lē\ Alvin 1931–1989 Am. dancer & choreographer
Ains·worth \'ānz-(‚)wərth\ (William) Harrison 1805–1882 Eng. nov.
Ai·shah \'ä-ē-shə\ 611–678 favorite wife of Muhammad
Ak·bar \'ak-bər, -‚bär\ 1542–1605 Mughal emp. of India (1556–1605)
à Kempis — see THOMAS À KEMPIS
Aken·side \'ā-kən-‚sīd\ Mark 1721–1770 Eng. poet & physician
Akhe·na·ton \‚äk-'nä-t°n, ‚ä-kə-\ also Ikh·na·ton \ik-'nä-t°n\ king of Egypt (1379–1362 B.C.)
Aki·ba ben Jo·seph \ä-'ki-vä-ben-'jō-zəf\ A.D. 40–135 Jewish sage & martyr in Palestine
Aki·hi·to \‚ä-kē-'hē-(‚)tō\ 1933–   emp. of Japan (1989–   )
'Alam·gīr \'ä-ləm-‚gir\ Muhī-ud-Dīn Muhammad 1618–1707 Au·rang·zeb \‚aü-rən-'zeb, ó-, -'zēb\ Mughal emp. of India
Alanbrooke Viscount — see Sir Alan Francis BROOKE
Alar·cón, de \‚ä-‚lär-'kōn, -'kón\ Pedro Antonio 1833–1891 Span. writer & statesman
Al·a·ric \'a-lə-rik\ ca 370–410 Visigoth king; conqueror of Rome
Alaric II d 507 Visigoth king; issued legal code
Al·bee \'ól-(‚)bē, 'al-\ Edward Franklin 1928–   Am. dram.
Albemarle Duke of — see George MONCK
Al·bé·niz \äl-'bā-(‚)nēs, -(‚)nēth\ Isaac 1860–1909 Span. pianist & composer
Al·bers \'al-bərz, 'äl-bərs\ Josef 1888–1976 Am. (Ger.-born) painter
Albert I \'al-bərt\ 1875–1934 king of Belgium (1909–34)
Albert Carl Bert 1908–   Am. polit.
Albert of Saxe–Coburg–Gotha 1819–1861 prince consort of Queen Victoria of Great Britain (1840–61)
Al·ber·tus Mag·nus \al-'bər-təs-'mag-nəs\ Saint ca 1200–1280 Albert Count von Boll·städt \'ból-‚shtet\ Ger. philos. & theol.
Al·boin \'al-‚bóin, -bə-wən\ d 572 Lombard king (ca 565–572)
Albucasis — see ABŪ AL-QĀSIM
Al·bu·quer·que, de \'al-bə-‚kər-kē, ‚al-bə-'\ Afonso 1453–1515 Port. viceroy & conqueror in India
Al·cae·us \al-'sē-əs\ ca 620–ca 580 B.C. Greek poet
Al·ci·bi·a·des \‚al-sə-'bī-ə-‚dēz\ ca 450–404 B.C. Athenian gen. & polit.
Al·cott \'ól-kət, 'al-, -‚kät\ Amos Bronson 1799–1888 Am. teacher & philos.
Alcott Louisa May 1832–1888 dau. of A.B. Am. author
Al·cuin \'al-kwən\ ca 732–804 Anglo-Saxon theol. & scholar
Al·da \'äl-də, 'ól-, 'al-\ Frances 1883–1952 orig. Frances Davis N.Z.-born soprano
Al·den \'ól-dən\ John 1599?–1687 Mayflower pilgrim
Al·der \'äl-dər\ Kurt 1902–1958 Ger. chem.
Al·drich \'ól-drich\ Thomas Bailey 1836–1907 Am. author
Al·drin \'ól-drən\ Edwin Eugene Jr. 1930–   Am. astronaut
Alei·chem Sha·lom \‚shó-ləm-ə-'lā-kəm, ‚shō-\ 1859–1916 pseud. of Sholem Ra·bin·o·witz \rə-'bi-nə-‚wits\ Am. (Russ.-born) humorist
Aleix·an·dre \‚ä-lek-'sän-dre\ Vicente 1898–1984 Span. poet
Ale·mán \‚ä-lā-'män\ Mateo 1547–ca 1614 Span. nov.
Alemán Val·dés \väl-'des\ Miguel 1902–1983 Mex. lawyer; pres. of Mexico (1946–52)
Alem·bert, d' \‚da-ləm-'bar, -'ber\ Jean Le Rond 1717–1783 Fr. math. & philos.
Al·ex·an·der \‚a-lig-'zan-dər, ‚e-\ name of 8 popes: esp. VI (Rodrigo Borgia) 1431–1503 (pope 1492–1503)
Alexander III of Macedon 356–323 B.C. the Great king (336–323)
Alexander Russ Alek·sandr \‚ä-lik-'sän-dər\ name of 3 emps. of Russia: I 1777–1825 (reigned 1801–25); II 1818–1881 (reigned 1855–81); III 1845–1894 (reigned 1881–94)
Alexander Serb Alek·san·dar Obre·no·vić \‚ä-lik-'sän-dər-ó-'bre-nə-‚vich\ 1876–1903 king of Serbia (1889–1903)
Alexander Harold Rupert Leofric George 1891–1969 1st Earl Alexander of Tunis Brit. field marshal; gov.-gen. of Canada (1946–52)
Alexander I 1888–1934 king of Yugoslavia (1929–34)
Alexander Nev·sky \'nev-skē, 'nef-\ ca 1220–1263 Russ. saint & mil. hero
Alexander Se·ve·rus \sə-'vir-əs\ A.D. 208–235 Rom. emp. (222–235)

Alex·is I Mi·khay·lo·vich \ə-‚lek-səs-mi-'kī-lə-‚vich\ 1629–1676 father of Peter the Great czar of Russia (1645–76)
Alexis Pe·tro·vich \pe-'trō-vich\ 1690–1718 son of Peter the Great czarevitch of Russia
Alex·i·us I Com·ne·nus \ə-'lek-sē-əs-‚käm-'nē-nəs\ 1048–1118 Byzantine emp. (1081–1118)
Al·fie·ri \‚al-fē-'er-ē\ Conte Vittorio 1749–1803 Ital. tragic poet
Al·fon·so XIII \al-'fän(t)-(‚)sō, -'fän-(‚)zō\ 1886–1941 king of Spain (1886–1931)
Al·fred or Æl·fred \'al-frəd, -fərd\ 849–899 the Great king of Wessex (871–899)
Alf·vén \(‚)al(f)-'vän, -'ven\ Hannes Olof Gösta 1908–1995 Swed. astrophysicist
Al·ger \'al-jər\ Horatio 1832–1899 Am. author
Al·gren \'ól-grən\ Nelson 1909–1981 Am. author
'Alī \ä-'lē, 'ä-lē\ Ar 'Alī ibn Abī Ṭā·lib \‚i-bən-‚ä-bē-'tä-lib\ ca 600–661 cousin & son-in-law of Muhammad 4th orthodox caliph (656–661)
Ali Pa·şa \'pä-shə, 'pa-; pə-'shä\ 1741–1822 the Lion of Janina Turk. pasha
Ali \ä-'lē\ Muhammad 1942–   orig. Cassius Marcellus Clay Am. boxer
Al·lais \ä-lā\ Maurice 1911–   Fr. econ.
Al·len \'a-lən\ Ethan 1738–1789 Am. Revolutionary soldier
Allen William 1532–1594 Eng. cardinal
Al·len·by \'a-lən-bē\ Edmund Henry Hynman 1861–1936 1st Viscount Allenby of Megiddo and Felixstowe Brit. field marshal
Allen·de Gos·sens \ä-‚yen-dā-'gó-‚sen(t)s\ Salvador 1908–1973 Chilean Marxist; pres. of Chile (1970–73)
Al·leyne \'a-lən, -‚lēn, -‚län\ Edward 1566–1626 Eng. actor
All·ston \'ól-stən\ Washington 1779–1843 Am. painter
Al·ma–Tad·e·ma \‚al-mə-'ta-də-mə\ Sir Lawrence 1836–1912 Eng. (Du.-born) painter
Alt·man \'ólt-mən\ Sidney 1939–   Am. (Canad.-born) biophysicist
Alva Duke of — see ÁLVAREZ DE TOLEDO
Al·va·ra·do, de \‚äl-vä-'rä-thō\ Pedro ca 1485–1541 Span. conquistador
Ál·va·rez \'al-və-‚rez\ Luis Walter 1911–1988 Am. physicist
Ál·va·rez de To·le·do \‚äl-vä-‚räth-thä-tō-'lā-thō\ Fernando 1507–1582 3d Duke of Alba \'äl-bə\ or Al·va \'al-və\ Span. gen.
Alvarez Quin·te·ro \kēn-'tä-rō\ Serafín 1871–1938 & his bro. Joaquín 1873–1944 Span. dram.
Ama·ti \ä-'mä-tē, ə-\ family of Ital. violin makers of Cremona: esp. Nicolò 1596–1684
Am·brose \'am-‚brōz\ Saint 339–397 bishop of Milan — Am·bro·sian \am-'brō-zhən, -zē-ən\ adj
Amen·ho·tep \‚ä-mən-'hō-‚tep, ‚a-\ or Am·e·no·phis \‚a-mə-'nō-fəs\ name of 4 kings of Egypt: esp. III (1417–1379 B.C.); IV — see AKHENATON
Amerigo Vespucci — see VESPUCCI
Am·herst \'a-(‚)mərst\ Jeffrey 1717–1797 Baron Amherst Brit. gen.; gov.-gen. of Brit. No. America (1760–63)
Amis \'ä-məs\ Kingsley 1922–   Eng. author
Am·père \äⁿ-'per\ André-Marie 1775–1836 Fr. physicist
Amund·sen \'ä-mən-sən\ Roald 1872–1928 Norw. polar explorer
Anac·re·on \ə-'na-krē-ən\ ca 582–ca 485 B.C. Greek poet
An·ax·ag·o·ras \‚a-‚nak-'sa-gə-rəs\ ca 500–ca 428 B.C. Greek philos. — An·ax·ag·o·re·an \-‚sa-gə-'rē-ən\ adj
Anax·i·man·der \ə-'nak-sə-‚man-dər\ ca 610–ca 547 B.C. Greek philos. & astron. — Anax·i·man·dri·an \ə-‚nak-sə-'man-drē-ən\ adj
An·ders \'än-dərs, -dərz\ Władysław 1892–1970 Pol. gen.
An·der·sen \'an-dər-sən\ Hans Christian 1805–1875 Dan. writer
An·der·son \'an-dər-sən\ Carl David 1905–1991 Am. physicist
Anderson John 1882–1958 1st Viscount Wa·ver·ley \'wä-vər-lē\ Brit. polit.
Anderson Dame Judith 1898–1992 orig. Frances Margaret Anderson Austral. actress
Anderson Marian 1897–1993 Am. contralto
Anderson Maxwell 1888–1959 Am. dram.
Anderson Philip Warren 1923–   Am. physicist
Anderson Sherwood 1876–1941 Am. writer
An·drás·sy \'ón-‚drä-shē\ Gyula, count; father 1823–1890 & son 1860–1929 Hung. statesmen
An·dré \'an-drē, 'än-(‚)drā\ John 1750–1780 Brit. spy
An·drea del Sar·to \än-'drā-ə-‚del-'sär-(‚)tō\ 1486–1530 Andrea d'Agnolo Florentine painter
An·dre·ot·ti \‚än-drā-'ä-(‚)tē\ Giulio 1919–   prime min. of Italy (1972–73; 1976–79; 1989–92)
An·drews \'an-‚drüz\ Roy Chapman 1884–1960 Am. naturalist
An·dre·yev \än-'drā-yəf\ Leonid Nikolayevich 1871–1919 Russ. author
An·drić \'än-drich\ Ivo 1892–1975 Serbo-Croatian author
An·dro·pov \an-'drä-‚pöf\ Yuri Vladimirovich 1914–1984 Russ. polit.; pres. U.S.S.R. (1982–84); 1st secy. of communist party (1982–84)
An·dros \'an-‚dräs, -drəs\ Sir Edmund 1637–1714 Brit. colonial gov. in America
An·fin·sen \'an-fən-sən\ Christian Boehmer 1916–1995 Am. chem.
An·ge·la Me·ri·ci \'an-jə-lə-mə-'rē-chē\ Saint 1474?–1540 Ital. religious & founder of Ursuline order
An·ge·li·co \an-'je-li-‚kō\ Fra ca 1400–1455 orig. Guido di Pietro Florentine painter
An·gell \'än-jəl\ Sir Norman 1872–1967 orig. Ralph Norman Angell Lane Eng. author & lecturer
Ång·ström \'aŋ-strəm, 'óŋ-\ Anders Jonas 1814–1874 Swed. physicist
An·na Iva·nov·na \'a-nə-ē-'vä-nəv-nə\ 1693–1740 empress of Russia (1730–40)

\ə\ abut \ᵊ\ kitten, F table \ər\ further \a\ ash \ā\ ace \ä\ mop, mar
\aú\ out \ch\ chin \e\ bet \ē\ easy \g\ go \i\ hit \ī\ ice \j\ job
\ŋ\ sing \ō\ go \ó\ law \ói\ boy \th\ thin \t͟h\ the \ü\ loot \ú\ foot
\y\ yet \zh\ vision \á, k̲, ⁿ, œ, œ̄, ɶ, ᵜ, ᶣ\ see Guide to Pronunciation

Anne \'an\ 1665–1714 *dau. of James II* queen of Great Britain (1702–14)

Anne of Austria 1601–1666 *consort of Louis XIII of France* regent (1643–51) for her son Louis XIV

Anne of Cleves \'klēvz\ 1515–1557 *4th wife of Henry VIII of England*

Annunzio, D' Gabriele — see D'ANNUNZIO

Anouilh \a-'nü-ē\ Jean 1910–1987 Fr. dram.

An·selm \'an-,selm\ Saint 1033/34–1109 archbishop of Canterbury (1093–1109)

An·tall \'ȯn-,tȯl\ József 1932–1993 prime min. of Hungary (1990–93)

An·tho·ny \'an(t)-thə-nē, *chiefly Brit* 'an-tə-\ Saint *ca* 250–355 Egypt. monk

Anthony Mark — see Marcus ANTONIUS

Anthony Susan Brownell 1820–1906 Am. suffragist

Anthony *or* **An·to·ny** \'an-tə-nē\ **of Padua** Saint 1195–1231 Franciscan monk

An·tig·o·nus I \an-'ti-gə-nəs\ 382–301 B.C. *Antigonus Cyclops* gen. of Alexander the Great & king of Macedonia (306–301)

An·ti·o·chus \an-'tī-ə-kəs\ name of 13 Seleucid kings of Syria: esp. **III** *the Great* 242–187 B.C. (reigned 223–187); **IV** *Epiph·a·nes* \i-'pi-fə-,nēz\ *ca* 215–164 B.C. (reigned 175–164)

An·tip·a·ter \an-'ti-pə-tər\ *ca* 397–*ca* 319 B.C. Macedonian gen.

An·tis·the·nes \an-'tis-thə-,nēz\ *ca* 445–*ca* 365 B.C. Athenian philos.

An·to·ne·scu \,an-tə-'nes-(,)kü\ Ion \'yȯn\ 1882–1946 Romanian gen.; dictator (1940–44)

An·to·ni·nus \,an-tə-'nī-nəs\ Marcus Au·re·lius \ȯ-'rēl-yəs, -'rē-lē-əs\ A.D. 121–180 *nephew, son-in-law, and adopted son of Antoninus Pius* Rom. emp. (161–180) & Stoic philos.

Antoninus Pi·us \-'pī-əs\ A.D. 86–161 Rom. emp. (138–161)

An·to·ni·us \an-'tō-nē-əs\ Marcus *E* Mark *or* Marc An·to·ny \'an-tə-nē\ *or* An·tho·ny \'an(t)-thə-nē, *chiefly Brit* 'an-tə-\ *ca* 82–30 B.C. Rom. orator, triumvir, & gen.

Apel·les \ə-'pe-lēz\ 4th cent. B.C. Greek painter

Apol·li·naire \ä-,pä-lə-'nar, -'ner\ Guillaume 1880–1918 orig. *Wilhelm Apollinaris de Kos·tro·wit·zki* \,kȯs-trə-'vēt-skē\ Fr. poet

Ap·ol·lo·ni·us \,a-pə-'lō-nē-əs\ **of Rhodes** 3d cent. B.C. Greek poet — **Ap·ol·lo·nian** \-nē-ən, -nyən\ *adj*

Appius Claudius — see CLAUDIUS

Appleseed Johnny — see John CHAPMAN

Ap·ple·ton \'a-pəl-tən\ Sir Edward 1892–1965 Eng. physicist

Aprak·sin *or* **Aprax·in** \ə-'prak-sən\ Fyodor Matveyevich 1661–1728 Russ. admiral

Ap·u·le·ius \,a-pə-'lā-əs\ Lucius *ca* A.D. 124–after 170? Rom. philos. & rhetorician

Aquinas Saint Thomas — see THOMAS AQUINAS

Aqui·no \ə-'kē-nō\ Corazon 1933–   pres. of Philippines (1986–92)

'Ar·a·fāt \är-ə-'fät, 'ar-ə-,fat\ Yāsir 1929–   *Raḥmān 'Abd Arra'üf Al-Qudwah* Palestinian polit. leader

Ar·am \'ar-əm, 'er-\ Eugene 1704–1759 Eng. philologist & murderer

Ara·nha \ə-'ran-yə\ Oswaldo 1894–1960 Braz. lawyer & polit.

Ar·ber \'är-bər\ Werner 1929–   Swiss microbiologist

Arblay, d' Madame — see Fanny BURNEY

Ar·buth·not \är-'bəth-nət, 'är-bəth-,nät\ John 1667–1735 Scot. physician & author

Ar·cher \'är-chər\ William 1856–1924 Scot. critic & dram.

Ar·chi·me·des \,är-kə-'mē-dēz\ *ca* 287–212 B.C. Greek math. & inventor — **Ar·chi·me·de·an** \-'mē-dē-ən, -mi-'dē-\ *adj*

Ar·chi·pen·ko \,är-kə-'peŋ-(,)kō\ Aleksandr Porfiryevich 1887–1964 Am. (Ukrainian-born) sculptor

Are·ti·no \,ar-ə-'tē-(,)nō\ Pietro 1492–1556 Ital. satirist

Ar·gall \'är-,gȯl, -gəl\ Sir Samuel *ca* 1572–*ca* 1626 Eng. mariner

Argyll 9th Duke of — see John D.S. CAMPBELL

Ar·i·as Sán·chez \'är-ē-,äs-'sän-chez\ Oscar 1941–   pres. of Costa Rica (1986–90)

Ari·os·to \,är-ē-'ȯ-(,)stō\ Ludovico 1474–1533 Ital. poet

Ar·is·tar·chus \,ar-ə-'stär-kəs\ *ca* 217–145 B.C. Greek grammarian

Aristarchus of Samos *fl ca* 270 B.C. Greek astron.

Ar·is·tide \,ar-i-'stēd, ä-rē-stēd\ Jean-Bertrand 1953–   pres. of Haiti (1991; 1994–   )

Ar·is·ti·des *or* **Ar·is·tei·des** \,ar-ə-'stī-dēz\ *ca* 530–*ca* 468 B.C. *the Just* Athenian statesman

Ar·is·tip·pus \,ar-ə-'sti-pəs\ *ca* 435–366 B.C. Greek philos.

Ar·is·toph·a·nes \,ar-ə-'stä-fə-,nēz\ *ca* 450–*ca* 388 B.C. Athenian dram. — **Ar·is·to·phan·ic** \,ar-ə-stə-'fa-nik\ *adj*

Aristophanes of Byzantium *ca* 257–180 B.C. Greek scholar

Ar·is·tot·le \'ar-ə-,stä-t°l\ 384–322 B.C. Greek philos.

Ari·us \'ar-ē-əs, 'er-\ *ca* A.D. 250–336 Greek theol.

Ark·wright \'ärk-,rīt\ Sir Richard 1732–1792 Eng. inventor

Ar·len \'är-lən\ Michael 1895–1956 orig. *Dik·ran* \'di-krän\ *Kou·youm·djian* \kü-'yüm-jē-ən\ Brit. (Bulg.-born) nov.

Ar·min·i·us \är-'mi-nē-əs\ *or* **Ar·min** \är-'mēn\ 18 B.C.?–A.D. 19 sometimes *Her·mann* \'her-,män\ Ger. hero

Arminius Jacobus 1560–1609 Jacob *Har·men·sen* \'här-mən-sən\ *or* *Her·mansz* \'her-,män(t)s\ Du. theol.

Ar·mour \'är-mər\ Philip Danforth 1832–1901 Am. industrialist

Armstrong Louis 1901–1971 *Satch·mo* \'sach-,mō\ Am. jazz musician

Armstrong Neil Alden 1930–   Am. astronaut

Armstrong William George 1810–1900 Baron *Armstrong of Cragside* Eng. inventor & industrialist

Arm·strong–Jones \'ärm-,strȯŋ-'jȯnz\ Antony Charles Robert 1930–   Earl of *Snowdon* Eng. photographer

Arne \'ärn\ Thomas Augustine 1710–1778 Eng. composer

Ar·nold \'är-n°ld\ Benedict 1741–1801 Am. Revolutionary gen. & traitor

Arnold Henry Harley 1886–1950 *Hap Arnold* Am. gen.

Arnold Matthew 1822–1888 *son of Thomas* Eng. poet & critic — **Arnold·ian** \är-'nȯl-dē-ən\ *adj*

Arnold Thomas 1795–1842 Eng. educ.

Ar·nold·son \'är-nəld-sən\ Klas Pontus 1844–1916 Swed. pacifist

Arou·et \är-we\ François-Marie — see VOLTAIRE

Arp \'ärp\ Jean (or Hans) 1887–1966 Fr. artist & poet

Ar·pád \'är-,päd\ *d* 907 Hung. national hero

Ar·rau \ə-'raü\ Claudio 1903–1991 Am. (Chilean-born) pianist

Ar·rhe·ni·us \ə-'rē-nē-əs, -'rä-\ Svante August 1859–1927 Swed. physicist & chem.

Ar·row \'ar-(,)ō\ Kenneth Joseph 1921–   Am. econ.

Ar·son·val, d' \'där-s°n-,väl\ Jacques Arsène 1851–1940 Fr. biophysicist

Ar·ta·xer·xes \,är-tə(g)-'zərk-,sēz\ name of 3 Pers. kings: **I** *d.* 425 B.C. (reigned 465–25); **II** *d* 359/58 B.C. (reigned 404–359/58); **III** *d* 338 B.C. (reigned 359/58–338)

Ar·te·vel·de, van \vän-'är-tə-,vel-də\ Jacob *ca* 1295–1345 & his son Philip 1340–1382 Flem. leaders

Ar·thur \'är-thər\ Chester Alan 1829–1886 21st pres. of the U.S. (1881–85)

As·bury \'az-,ber-ē, -b(ə-)rē\ Francis 1745–1816 Methodist bishop

Asch \'ash\ Sho·lem \'shȯ-ləm, 'shō-\ *or* Sha·lom \shə-'lōm\ *or* Sho·lom \'shȯ-ləm, 'shō-\ 1880–1957 Am. (Pol.-born) Yiddish writer

As·cham \'as-kəm\ Roger 1515–1568 Eng. scholar & author

Ash·croft \'ash-,krȯft\ Dame Peggy 1907–1991 Brit. actress

Ashton Winifred — see Clemence DANE

Ashur·ba·ni·pal *also* **As·sur·ba·ni·pal** *or* **Asur·ba·ni·pal** \,ä-sər-'bä-nə-,päl, ,ä-shər-\ king of Assyria (668–627 B.C.)

Aśo·ka *or* **Aço·ka** \ə-'shō-kə, -'sō-\ *d* 238 *or* 232 B.C. king of Magadha, India (*ca* 265–238 *or ca* 273–232 B.C.)

As·pa·sia \as-'pā-zh(ē-)ə\ 470?–410 B.C. *consort of Pericles*

As·quith \'as-,kwith, -kwəth\ Herbert Henry 1852–1928 1st Earl of *Oxford and Asquith* Brit. statesman

Assad, al- \al-'ä-,säd\ Hafiz 1928–   pres. of Syria (1971–   )

As·ser \'ä-sər\ Tobias Michael Carel 1838–1913 Du. jurist

Astaire \ə-'star, -'ster\ Fred 1899–1987 Am. dancer & actor

As·ton \'as-tən\ Francis William 1877–1945 Eng. physicist

As·tor \'as-tər\ John Jacob 1763–1848 Am. (Ger.-born) fur trader & capitalist

Astor Nancy Witcher 1879–1964 Viscountess *Astor* 1st woman member of Brit. Parliament (1919–45)

As·tu·ri·as \ə-'stür-ē-əs, -'styùr-\ Miguel Angel 1899–1974 Guatemalan author

Ata·huall·pa *or* **Ata·hual·pa** \,ä-tə-'wäl-pə\ *ca* 1502–1533 last Incan king of Peru

Ath·a·na·si·us \,a-thə-'nä-zh(ē-)əs, -sh(ē-)əs\ Saint *ca* 293–373 Greek (Egyptian-born) church father

Ath·el·stan \'a-thəl-,stan\ *d* 939 Anglo-Saxon ruler

Ath·er·ton \'a-thər-t°n\ Gertrude Franklin 1857–1948 née *Horn* Am. nov.

'At·tār \'a-tər, -,tär\ Farīd od-Dīn Mohammad ebn Ebrāhīm *ca* 1142–*ca* 1220 Pers. mystical poet

At·ti·la \'a-t°l-ə, ə-'ti-lə\ 406?–453 *the Scourge of God* king of the Huns

Att·lee \'at-lē\ Clement Richard 1883–1967 1st Earl *Attlee* Eng. polit.

At·tucks \'a-təks\ Crispus 1723?–1770 Am. patriot

At·wood \'at-,wüd\ Margaret Eleanor 1939–   Canad. author

Au·ber \ō-'ber\ Daniel-François-Esprit 1782–1871 Fr. composer

Au·brey \'ō-brē\ John 1626–1697 Eng. antiquarian

Au·chin·closs \'ȯ-kən-,kläs\ Louis Stanton 1917–   Am. writer

Au·den \'ȯ-d°n\ Wystan Hugh 1907–1973 Am. (Eng.-born) poet — **Au·den·esque** \,ȯ-d°n-'esk\ *adj*

Au·du·bon \'ȯ-də-bən, -,bän\ John James 1785–1851 Am. (Haitian-born) artist & ornithologist

Au·er·bach \'aú-(ə)r-,bäk, -,bäk\ Berthold 1812–1882 Ger. nov.

Au·gier \ō-'zhä, -'zhyä; ,ō-zhē-'ā\ Émile 1820–1889 Fr. poet & dram.

Au·gus·tine \'ȯ-gə-,stēn; ȯ-'gəs-tən, ə-\ Saint 354–430 church father; bishop of Hippo (396–430)

Augustine *also* **Aus·tin** \'ȯs-tən, 'äs-\ Saint *d* 604 *Apostle of the English* 1st archbishop of Canterbury (601–04)

Au·gus·tus \ȯ-'gəs-təs, ə-\ 63 B.C.–A.D. 14 orig. *Gaius Oc·ta·vi·us* \äk-'tā-vē-əs\ then *Gaius Julius Caesar* 1st Rom. emp. (27 B.C.–A.D. 14)

Aung San Suu Kyi \'ȯŋ-'sän-'sü-'chē\ 1945–   Burmese human rights activist

Aurangzeb — see 'ĀLAMGĪR

Au·re·lian \ȯ-'rēl-yən\ *ca* A.D. 215–275 *Lucius Domitius Aurelianus* Rom. emp. (270–275)

Au·riol \,ȯr-ē-'ȯl, -'ōl\ Vincent 1884–1966 Fr. polit.; 1st pres. of 4th Republic (1947–54)

Au·ro·bin·do \,ȯr-ə-'bin-dō\ Sri 1872–1950 orig. *Sri Aurobindo Ghose* \'gōs\ Indian seer, poet, & nationalist

Aus·ten \'ȯs-tən, 'äs-\ Jane 1775–1817 Eng. nov.

Aus·tin \'ȯs-tən, 'äs-\ Alfred 1835–1913 Eng. poet; poet laureate (1896–1913)

Austin John 1790–1859 Eng. jurist

Austin John Langshaw 1911–1960 Eng. philos.

Austin Mary 1868–1934 née *Hunter* Am. nov.

Austin Stephen Fuller 1793–1836 Am. colonizer in Texas

Avebury 1st Baron — see LUBBOCK

Avenzoar — see IBN ZUHR

Aver·ro·ës *or* **Aver·rho·ës** \ə-'ver-ə-,wēz, ,a-və-'rō-(,)ēz\ 1126–1198 *also Ibn-Rushd* Span.-Arab philos. & physician

Avery \'ā-və-rē, -vrē\ Milton Clark 1885–1965 Am. artist

Avi·cen·na \,a-və-'se-nə\ 980–1037 *also Ibn Sīnā* Islamic (Pers.-born) philos. & scientist

Avi·la Ca·ma·cho \'ä-vē-lə-kə-'mä-(,)chō\ Manuel 1897–1955 Mex. soldier & polit.; pres. of Mexico (1940–46)

Avo·ga·dro \,a-və-'gä-(,)drō, ,ä-\ Amedeo 1776–1856 Conte *di Quaregna e Ceretto* Ital. chem. & physicist

Avon Earl of — see Anthony EDEN

Ax·el·rod \'ak-səl-,räd\ Julius 1912–   Am. biochem.

Ay·de·lotte \'ā-d°l-,ät\ Frank 1880–1956 Am. educ.

Ayer \'ar, 'er\ Sir Alfred Jules 1910–1989 Eng. philos.

Ayl·win Azó·car \'äl-win-ä-'sō-kär\ Patricio 1918–   pres. of Chile (1990–94)

Aza·ña y Di·az \ə-'thän-yə-ē-'thē-äth\ Manuel 1880–1940 Span. polit.; pres. of Spain (1936–39)

Ba'al Shem Tov — see ISRAEL BEN ELIEZER

Bab·bitt \'ba-bət\ Bruce Edward 1938–   U.S. secy. of interior (1993–   )

Babbitt Irving 1865–1933 Am. scholar

Ba·beuf \bä-'bəf, bá-bœf\ François-Noël 1760–1797 Fr. agitator

Bab·ing·ton \'ba-biŋ-tən\ Anthony 1561–1586 Eng. conspirator against Queen Elizabeth I

Bab·son \'bab-sən\ Roger Ward 1875–1967 Am. statistician

Bā·bur \'bä-bər\ 1483–1530 *Zahīr-ud-Dīn Muhammad* founder of Mogul dynasty of India; emp. (1526–30)

Ba·bu·ren \bä-'bū̇-rən, -'bir-ən\ Dirck van *ca* 1590–1624 Du. painter

Bach \'bäk, 'bäk\ Carl Philipp Emanuel 1714–1788 *son of J.S.* Ger. composer

Bach Johann Christian 1735–1782 *son of J.S.* Ger. organist & composer

Bach Johann Sebastian 1685–1750 Ger. organist & composer

Bach Wilhelm Friedemann 1710–1784 *son of J.S.* Ger. organist & composer

Ba·con \'bā-kən\ Francis 1561–1626 1st Baron *Ver·u·lam* \'ver-(y)ə-ləm\ Viscount *St. Al·bans* \sȯnt-'ȯl-bənz, sȯnt-\ Eng. philos.

Bacon Francis 1909–1992 Brit. (Irish-born) painter

Bacon Nathaniel 1647–1676 Am. colonial leader

Bacon Roger *ca* 1220–1292 Eng. philos. and scientist

Ba·den–Pow·ell \'bā-dᵊn-'pō-əl\ Robert Stephenson Smyth 1857–1941 1st Baron of *Gilwell* founder of Boy Scout movement

Ba·do·glio \bə-'dōl-(ˌ)yō\ Pietro 1871–1956 Ital. gen.; prime min. (1943–44)

Bae·yer, von \'bā-ər\ Adolf 1835–1917 Ger. chem.

Baf·fin \'ba-fən\ William *ca* 1584–1622 Eng. navigator

Bage·hot \'baj-ət\ Walter 1826–1877 Eng. econ. & journalist

Ba·gra·tion \bä-grä-tē-'ȯn, -ˌgrät-sē-; ˌbä-grə-'tyȯn\ Prince Pyotr Ivanovich 1765–1812 Russ. gen.

Ba·hā' Al·lāh *or* Ba·ha·ul·lah \bä-'hä-ü-'lä\ Mīrzā Ḥoseyn Alī Nūrī 1817–1892 Pers. founder of the Bahā'ī faith

Bai·ley \'bā-lē\ Liberty Hyde 1858–1954 Am. botanist

Bailey Nathan *or* Nathaniel *d* 1742 Eng. lexicographer

Bailey Pearl Mae 1918–1990 Am. singer

Bail·lie \'bā-lē\ Joanna 1762–1851 Scot. dram. & poet

Bain \'bān\ Alexander 1818–1903 Scot. psychol.

Baird \'bard, 'berd\ John Logie 1888–1946 *father of television* Scot. inventor

Bairns·fa·ther \'barnz-ˌfä-thər, 'bernz-\ Bruce 1888–1959 Eng. cartoonist

Ba·jer \'bī(-ə)r\ Fredrik 1837–1922 Dan. statesman & writer

Ba·ker \'bā-kər\ James Addison 1930–   U.S. secy. of treasury (1985–88); secy. of state (1989–92)

Baker Newton Diehl 1871–1937 Am. statesman

Baker Ray Stannard 1870–1946 pseud. *David Gray·son* \'grās-ᵊn\ Am. author

Baker Sir Samuel White 1821–1893 Eng. explorer in Africa

Bakst \'bäkst\ Léon 1866–1924 orig. *Lev Samoylovich Rosenberg* Russ. painter

Ba·ku·nin \bə-'kün-yən, bä-, -'kü-nən\ Mikhail Aleksandrovich 1814–1876 Russ. anarchist

Bal·an·chine \ˌba-lən-'shēn, 'ba-lən-ˌ\ George 1904–1983 *Georgy Melitonovich Balanchivadze* Am. (Russ.-born) choreographer

Bal·bo \'bäl-(ˌ)bō\ Italo 1896–1940 Ital. aviator & polit.

Bal·boa \bal-'bō-ə\ Vasco Núñez de 1475–1519 Span. explorer & conquistador

Balch \'bȯlch\ Emily Greene 1867–1961 Am. econ. & sociol.

Bald·win I \'bȯl-dwən\ 1058?–1118 *bro. of Godfrey of Bouillon* king of Jerusalem (1100–18)

Baldwin James 1924–1987 Am. writer

Baldwin James Mark 1861–1934 Am. psychol.

Baldwin Stanley 1867–1947 1st Earl *Baldwin of Bewd·ley* \'byüd-lē\ Eng. statesman

Balfe \'balf\ Michael William 1808–1870 Irish composer & singer

Bal·four \'bal-fər, -ˌfōr, -ˌfȯr\ Arthur James 1848–1930 1st Earl of *Balfour*; Brit. philos. & statesman

Ba·liol *or* Bal·liol \'bāl-yəl\ John de 1249–1315 king of Scotland (1292–96)

Ball \'bȯl\ John *d* 1381 Eng. priest & social agitator

Bal·lan·tyne \'ba-lən-ˌtīn\ James 1772–1833 Scot. printer

Bal·ti·more \'bȯl-tə-ˌmȯr, -ˌmȯr, -mər\ David 1938–   Am. microbiologist

Baltimore Baron — see George CALVERT

Bal·zac \'bȯl-ˌzak, 'bal-, *F* bál-zák\ Honoré de 1799–1850 Fr. nov. — Bal·za·cian \bȯl-'zā-shən, bal-, -'za-kē-ən\ *adj*

Ban·croft \'ban-ˌkrȯft, 'baŋ-\ George 1800–1891 Am. hist.

Bancroft Richard 1544–1610 Eng. prelate; archbishop of Canterbury (1604–10)

Ban·del·lo \ban-'de-(ˌ)lō, bän-\ Matteo 1485–1561 Ital. writer

Bangs \'baŋz\ John Kendrick 1862–1922 Am. humorist

Banks \'baŋ(k)s\ Sir Joseph 1743–1820 Eng. naturalist

Ban·ting \'ban-tiŋ\ Sir Frederick Grant 1891–1941 Canad. physician

Ba·ra·nov \bə-'rä-nəf\ Aleksandr Andreyevich 1747–1819 Russ. fur trader; first gov. of Russ. America

Bá·rány \'bär-ˌän-yə\ Robert 1876–1936 Austrian physician

Barbarossa — see FREDERICK I

Bar·ba·ros·sa \ˌbär-bə-'rä-sə, -'rȯ-\ *d* 1546 *Khayr ad-Dīn* Barbary pirate

Bar·ber \'bär-bər\ Samuel 1910–1981 Am. composer

Bar·bie \'bär-bē\ Klaus 1913–1991 Ger. Nazi leader

Bar·busse \bär-bües; *F* bär-'büs, -'byüs\ Henri 1873–1935 Fr. author

Bar·clay de Tol·ly \ˌbär-'klī-də-'tȯ-lē, -'klä-\ Prince Mikhail 1761–1818 Russ. field marshal

Bar·deen \bär-'dēn\ John 1908–1991 Am. physicist

Ba·rents \'bär-ən(t)s, 'bär-\ Willem *ca* 1550–1597 Du. navigator

Bar·ing \'bar-iŋ, 'ber-\ Alexander 1774–1848 1st Baron *Ash·bur·ton* \'ash-ˌbər-tᵊn\ Brit. financier & diplomat

Baring Evelyn 1841–1917 1st Earl of *Cro·mer* \'krō-mər\ Brit. diplomat

Bark·la \'bär-klə\ Charles Glover 1877–1944 Eng. physicist

Bark·ley \'bär-klē\ Al·ben \'al-bən\ William 1877–1956 Am. lawyer & polit.; vice pres. of U.S. (1949–53)

Bar·low \'bär-ˌlō\ Joel 1754–1812 Am. poet & diplomat

Bar·nard \'bär-nərd, -ˌnärd\ Christiaan Neethling 1922–   So. African surgeon

Bar·nard \'bär-nərd\ George Grey 1863–1938 Am. sculptor

Barnevelt Jan van Olden — see OLDENBARNEVELT

Bar·num \'bär-nəm\ Phineas Taylor 1810–1891 Am. showman — Bar·num·esque \ˌbär-nə-'mesk\ *adj*

Ba·ro·ja \bä-'rō-(ˌ)hä\ Pío 1872–1956 Span. writer

Barozzi Giacomo — see VIGNOLA

Bar·rès \ba-'res\ Auguste-Maurice 1862–1923 Fr. nov. & polit.

Bar·rie \'bar-ē\ Sir James Matthew 1860–1937 Scot. nov. & dram.

Bar·ros \'bär-üsh\ João de *ca* 1496–1570 Port. hist.

Bar·row \'bar-(ˌ)ō\ Isaac 1630–1677 Eng. math. & theol.

Bar·ry \'bar-ē\ Jeanne Bécu 1743–1793 *Comtesse du Barry* mistress of Louis XV of France

Bar·ry \'bar-ē\ Philip 1896–1949 Am. dram.

Bar·ry·more \'bar-i-ˌmōr, -ˌmȯr\ family of Am. actors: Maurice 1847–1905 orig. *Herbert Blythe*; his wife Georgiana Emma 1854–1893 *dau. of John Drew*; their children Lionel 1878–1954, Ethel 1879–1959, & John Blythe 1882–1942

Bart \'bär\ *or* Barth \'bärt\ Jean 1650–1702 Fr. naval hero

Barth \'bärth\ John Simmons 1930–   Am. author

Barth \'bärt, 'bärth\ Karl 1886–1968 Swiss theol. — Barth·ian \'bär-tē-ən, -thē-\ *adj*

Bar·thol·di \ˌbär-'täl-dē, -'tȯl-, -'thäl-, -'thȯl-\ Frédéric-Auguste 1834–1904 Fr. sculptor

Bar·thol·o·mew \bär-'thä-lə-ˌmyü\ 1940–   archbishop of Constantinople and ecumenical patriarch (1991–   )

Bart·lett \'bärt-lət\ John 1820–1905 Am. publisher & editor

Bar·tók \'bär-ˌtäk, -ˌtȯk\ Béla 1881–1945 Hung. composer

Bar·to·lom·meo \ˌbär-ˌtō-lə-'mā-(ˌ)ō\ Fra 1472–1517 *Baccio della Porta* Florentine painter

Bar·ton \'bär-tᵊn\ Clara 1821–1912 in full *Clarissa Harlow Barton* founder of Am. Red Cross Society

Barton Sir Derek Harold Richard 1918–   Brit. chem.

Bar·tram \'bär-trəm\ John 1699–1777 Am. botanist

Bartram William 1739–1823 *son of John* Am. naturalist

Ba·ruch \bə-'rük\ Bernard Man·nes \'ma-nəs\ 1870–1965 Am. businessman & statesman

Ba·rysh·ni·kov \bə-'rish-nə-ˌkȯf\ Mikhail 1948–   Am. (Latvian-born) ballet dancer

Bashō — see MATSUO

Ba·sie \'bā-sē\ William 1904–1984 *Count* Am. bandleader & composer

Bas·il \'bä-zəl, 'ba-, -səl\ *or* Ba·sil·i·us \bə-'si-lē-əs, -'zi-\ Saint *ca* 329–379 *the Great* church father; bishop of Caesarea

Bas·ker·ville \'bas-kər-ˌvil\ John 1706–1775 Eng. typographer

Ba·sov \'bä-ˌsȯf, -ˌsȯv\ Nikolay Gennadiyevich 1922–   Russ. physicist

Bates \'bāts\ Katharine Lee 1859–1929 Am. poet & educ.

Ba·tis·ta y Zal·di·var \bə-'tēs-tə-ə̄-zäl-'dē-ˌvär\ Fulgencio 1901–1973 Cuban soldier; pres. of Cuba (1940–44; 1952–59)

Bat·tā·ni, al- \ˌal-bə-'tä-nē\ *ca* 858–929 *Al·ba·te·gni* \ˌal-bə-'tän-yē\ *or* *Al·ba·te·ni·us* \-'tē-nē-əs\ Arab astron.

Bau·de·laire \bōd-'lar, -'ler\ Charles-Pierre 1821–1867 Fr. poet — Bau·de·lair·ean *also* Bau·de·lair·ian \-ē-ən\ *adj*

Bau·douin \bō-'dwan\ 1930–1993 king of Belgium (1951–93)

Baum \'bäm\ Lyman Frank 1856–1919 Am. journalist & writer

Baum \'baụm\ Vicki 1888–1960 Am. (Austrian-born) nov.

Bau·mé \bō-'mā\ Antoine 1728–1804 Fr. chem.

Bax·ter \'bak-stər\ Richard 1615–1691 Eng. Puritan scholar & writer

Ba·yard \'bī-ərd, 'bā-ərd, *F* bà-yár\ Pierre Terrail *ca* 1473–1524 *Seigneur de Bayard* Fr. mil. hero

Bayle \'bā(ə)l, 'bel\ Pierre 1647–1706 Fr. philos. & critic

Beaconsfield Earl of — see Benjamin DISRAELI

Bea·dle \'bē-dᵊl\ George Wells 1903–1989 Am. biol.

Beard \'bird\ Charles Austin 1874–1948 & his wife Mary née *Ritter* 1876–1958 Am. historians

Beard Daniel Carter 1850–1941 Am. painter, illustrator, & organizer of Boy Scouts in U.S.

Beards·ley \'birdz-lē\ Aubrey Vincent 1872–1898 Eng. illustrator — Beards·ley·esque \ˌbirdz-lē-'yesk\ *adj*

Be·a·trix \'bē-ə-ˌtriks\ 1938–   queen of the Netherlands (1980–   )

Beat·tie \'bē-tē\ James 1735–1803 Scot. poet

Beau·fort \'bō-fərt\ Sir Francis 1774–1857 Brit. admiral

Beaufort Henry *ca* 1374–1447 Eng. cardinal & statesman

Beau·har·nais, de \ˌbō-ˌär-'nā\ Fr. family including: Vicomte Alexandre 1760–1794 gen.; his wife Joséphine 1763–1814 later the *1st wife of Napoleon I*; their son Eugène 1781–1824 prince of Eich·stätt \'ik-ˌshtet\; their daughter Hortense \ȯr-täⁿs\ 1783–1837 *wife of Louis Bonaparte & mother of Napoleon III*

Beau·mar·chais \ˌbō-ˌmär-'shā\ Pierre-Augustin Caron de 1732–1799 Fr. dram. & businessman

Beau·mont \'bō-ˌmänt, -mənt\ Francis 1584–1616 Eng. dram.

Beau·mont \-ˌmänt\ William 1785–1853 Am. surgeon

Beau·re·gard \'bōr-ə-ˌgärd, 'bȯr-\ Pierre Gustave Toutant 1818–1893 Am. Confed. gen.

Beau·voir, de \də-bō-'vwär\ Simone 1908–1986 Fr. author

Bea·ver·brook \'bē-vər-ˌbru̇k\ 1st Baron 1879–1964 *William Maxwell Aitken* Brit. (Canad.-born) newspaper publisher

Be·bel \'bā-bəl\ August 1840–1913 Ger. Social Democrat leader & writer

Beck·er \'be-kər\ Gary Stanley 1930–   Am. econ.

Beck·et \'be-kət\ Saint Thomas *ca* 1118–1170 *Thomas à Becket* archbishop of Canterbury (1162–70)

Beck·ett \'be-kət\ Samuel 1906–1989 Irish author in France — Beck·ett·ian \be-'ke-tē-ən\ *adj*

Beck·ford \'bek-fərd\ William 1760–1844 Eng. author

Bec·que·rel \be-'krel, ˌbe-kə-'rel\ family of Fr. physicists including: Antoine-César 1788–1878; his son Alexandre-Edmond 1820–1891; the latter's son Antoine-Henri 1852–1908

Bed·does \'be-(ˌ)dōz\ Thomas Lovell 1803–1849 Eng. writer

\ə\ abut \ᵊ\ kitten, F table \ər\ further \a\ ash \ā\ ace \ä\ mop, mar \aú\ out \ch\ chin \e\ bet \ē\ easy \g\ go \i\ hit \ī\ ice \j\ job \ŋ\ sing \ō\ go \ȯ\ law \ȯi\ boy \th\ thin \t͟h\ the \ü\ loot \ú\ foot \y\ yet \zh\ vision \à, k̟, ⁿ, œ, œ̄, ᵫ, ū̆, ᵫ̄, ᫬\ *see* Guide to Pronunciation

Bede \'bēd\ or Bae·da or Be·da \'bē-də\ Saint ca 672–735 the Venerable Bede Anglo-Saxon scholar, hist., & theol.
Bedford Duke of — see JOHN OF LANCASTER
Bed·norz \'bed-ˌnȯrts\ Johannes Georg 1950–   Ger. physicist
Bee·be \'bē-bē\ Charles William 1877–1962 Am. naturalist & explorer
Bee·cham \'bē-chəm\ Sir Thomas 1879–1961 Eng. conductor
Bee·cher \'bē-chər\ Henry Ward 1813–1887 Am. clergyman
Beecher Lyman 1775–1863 father of H.W. & of Harriet Beecher Stowe Am. Presbyterian clergyman
Beer·bohm \'bir-ˌbōm, -bəm\ Sir Max 1872–1956 Eng. critic & caricaturist
Beer·naert \'ber-ˌnärt\ Auguste Marie François 1829–1912 Belg. statesman
Bee·tho·ven \'bā-ˌtō-vən\ Ludwig van 1770–1827 Ger. composer —
Bee·tho·ve·nian \ˌbā-tō-'vē-nyən\ adj
Be·gin \'bā-gin\ Me·na·chem \mə-'nä-kəm\ 1913–1992 prime min. of Israel (1977–83)
Be·han \'bē-ən\ Brendan Francis 1923–1964 Irish dram.
Beh·ring \'ber-iŋ\ Emil von 1854–1917 Ger. bacteriol.
Behr·man \'ber-mən\ Samuel Nathaniel 1893–1973 Am. dram.
Bé·ké·sy \'bā-kə-shē\ Georg von 1899–1972 Am. (Hung.-born) physicist
Be·las·co \bə-'las-(ˌ)kō\ David 1853–1931 Am. dram. & producer
Bel·i·sar·i·us \ˌbel-ə-'sar-ē-əs, -'ser-\ ca 505–565 Byzantine gen.
Bell \'bel\ Alexander Graham 1847–1922 Am. (Scot.-born) inventor
Bel·la·my \'bel-ə-mē\ Edward 1850–1898 Am. author
Bel·lay, du \ˌdü-bə-'lā, ˌdyü-\ Joachim ca 1522–1560 Fr. poet
Bel·li·ni \bə-'lē-nē\ family of Venetian painters including: Jacopo ca 1400–ca 1470 and his sons Gentile ca 1429–1507 and Giovanni ca 1430–1516
Bellini Vincenzo 1801–1835 Ital. composer
Bel·loc \'be-ˌläk, -lək\ (Joseph-Pierre) Hilaire 1870–1953 Eng. author
Bel·low \'be-(ˌ)lō\ Saul 1915–   Am. (Canad.-born) writer
Bel·lows \'be-(ˌ)lōz\ George Wesley 1882–1925 Am. painter & lithographer
Be·na·cer·raf \be-'na-sə-ˌräf\ Baruj 1920–   Am. (Venezuelan-born) pathologist
Be·na·ven·te y Mar·ti·nez \ˌbe-nə-'ven-tē-ˌē-mär-'tē-nəs\ Jacinto 1866–1954 Span. dram.
Bench·ley \'bench-lē\ Robert Charles 1889–1945 Am. humorist
Ben·e·dict \'be-nə-ˌdikt\ name of 15 popes: esp. **XIV** (Prospero Lambertini) 1675–1758 (pope 1740–58); **XV** (Giacomo della Chiesa) 1854–1922 (pope 1914–22)
Benedict of Nur·sia \'nər-sh(ē-)ə\ Saint ca 480–ca 547 Ital. founder of Benedictine order
Benedict Ruth 1887–1948 née Fulton Am. anthropol.
Be·neš \'be-ˌnesh\ Edvard 1884–1948 Czech statesman; pres. (1935–38; 1940–48)
Be·nét \bə-'nā\ Stephen Vincent 1898–1943 bro. of W.R. Am. poet
Benét William Rose 1886–1950 Am. poet, nov., & editor
Ben–Gu·rion \ˌben-gùr-'yōn, ben-'gùr-ē-ən\ David 1886–1973 Israeli (Pol.-born) statesman; prime min. of Israel (1949–53; 1955–63)
Ben·ja·min \'ben-jə-mən\ Judah Philip 1811–1884 Am. Confed. statesman & lawyer
Ben·nett \'be-nət\ (Enoch) Arnold 1867–1931 Eng. nov.
Bennett James Gordon 1795–1872 Am. (Scot.-born) journalist
Bennett Richard Bedford 1870–1947 Viscount Bennett Canad. prime min. (1930–35)
Be·noît de Sainte–Maure \ben-'wä-də-(ˌ)saⁿ(n)t-'mȯr\ 12th cent. Fr. trouvère
Ben·son \'ben(t)-sən\ Edward White 1829–1896 Brit. prelate; archbishop of Canterbury (1882–96)
Ben·tham \'ben(t)-thəm\ Jeremy 1748–1832 Eng. jurist & philos.
Ben·tinck \'ben-ti(ŋ)k\ Lord William Cavendish 1774–1839 son of W.H.C. 1st gov.-gen. of India (1833)
Bentinck William Henry Cavendish 1738–1809 3d Duke of Portland Brit. prime min. (1783; 1807–09)
Bent·ley \'bent-lē\ Richard 1662–1742 Eng. clergyman, scholar, & critic
Ben·ton \'ben-tᵊn\ Thomas Hart 1782–1858 Old Bullion Am. polit.
Benton Thomas Hart 1889–1975 Am. painter
Bent·sen \'ben(t)-sən\ Lloyd Millard, Jr. 1921–   U.S. secy. of treasury (1993–   )
Bé·ran·ger \bā-räⁿ-zhā\ Pierre-Jean de 1780–1857 Fr. poet
Ber·dya·yev \bərd-'yä-yəf, bər-jä-\ Nikolay Aleksandrovich 1874–1948 Russ. philos.
Ber·en·son \'ber-ən-sən\ Bernard 1865–1959 Am. (Lith.-born) art critic
Berg \'berg\ Alban 1885–1935 Austrian composer
Berg \'bərg\ Paul 1926–   Am. chem.
Bergerac, de Cyrano — see CYRANO DE BERGERAC
Ber·gi·us \'ber-gē-əs\ Friedrich 1884–1949 Ger. chem.
Berg·man \'bərg-mən, Sw 'ber-è-mán\ Ingmar 1918–   Swed. film & theater director
Berg·son \'berg-sən, berk-sōⁿ\ Henri-Louis 1859–1941 Fr. philos. —
Berg·son·ian \berg-'sō-nē-ən, berk-\ adj
Berg·ström \berg-strəm, 'bär-ē-strüm\ K. Sune D. 1916–   Swed. biochem.
Be·ria or Be·ri·ya \'ber-iŋ, 'bir-\ Lavrenty Pavlovich 1899–1953 Russ. polit.
Be·ring \'ber-iŋ, 'bir-\ Vitus Jonassen 1681–1741 Dan. navigator
Berke·ley \'bär-klē, 'bər-\ George 1685–1753 Irish bishop & philos.
Berke·ley \'bər-klē\ Sir William 1606–1677 colonial gov. of Virginia
Ber·lich·ing·en \'ber-li-ˌkiŋ-ən\ Götz or Gottfried von 1480–1562 Ger. knight
Ber·lin \(ˌ)bər-'lin\ Irving 1888–1989 Am. (Russ.-born) composer
Ber·li·ner \'bər-lə-nər\ Emile 1851–1929 Am. (Ger.-born) inventor
Ber·li·oz \'ber-lē-ˌōz\ Hector 1803–1869 in full Louis-Hector Berlioz Fr. composer — Ber·li·oz·ian \ˌber-lē-'ō-zē-ən\ adj
Ber·na·dette of Lourdes \ˌbər-nə-'det\ Saint 1844–1879 Marie Bernarde Sou·bi·rous \ˌsü-bē-'rü\ Fr. religious
Bernadotte Jean Baptiste Jules — see CHARLES XIV JOHN
Ber·nard \ber-'när\ Claude 1813–1878 Fr. physiol.

Ber·nard of Clair·vaux \bər-'närd-əv-ˌklar-'vō, ber-'när-, -ˌkler-\ Saint 1090–1153 Fr. ecclesiastic — Ber·nar·dine \'bər-nə(r)-ˌdēn\ adj
Ber·nar·din de Saint–Pierre \ˌber-nər-'daⁿ-də-ˌsänt-pē-'er\ Jacques-Henri 1737–1814 Fr. author
Berners Baron — see TYRWHITT-WILSON
Bern·hardt \'bərn-ˌhärt, ber-'när\ Sarah 1844–1923 orig. Henriette-Rosine Ber·nard \ber-när\ Fr. actress
Ber·ni·ni \ber-'nē-nē\ Gian or Giovanni Lorenzo 1598–1680 Ital. sculptor, architect, & painter
Bern·stein \'bərn-ˌstīn also -ˌstēn\ Leonard 1918–1990 Am. conductor & composer
Bern·storff \'bern-ˌshtȯrf\ Johann-Heinrich 1862–1939 Graf von Bernstorff Ger. diplomat
Ber·ry·man \'ber-ē-mən\ John 1914–1972 Am. poet
Ber·thier \ber-'tyä\ Louis-Alexandre 1753–1815 Prince de Neuchâtel; Prince de Wagram Fr. soldier; marshal of France
Ber·til·lon \ˌber-tē-'yōⁿ\ Alphonse 1853–1914 Fr. criminol.
Ber·ton \'bər-tᵊn\ Pierre 1920–   Canad. writer
Ber·ze·li·us \(ˌ)bər-'zē-lē-əs, ber-'zä-\ Baron Jöns Jakob 1779–1848 Swed. chem.
Bes·ant \'be-sᵊnt, -zᵊnt\ Annie 1847–1933 née Wood Eng. theosophist
Bes·se·mer \'be-sə-mər\ Sir Henry 1813–1898 Eng. engineer
Best \'best\ Charles Herbert 1899–1978 Canad. (Am.-born) physiol.
Be·tan·court \ˌbe-ˌtän-'kúr(t), -tän-\ Rómulo 1908–1981 Venezuelan pres. (1959–64)
Be·the \'bā-tə\ Hans Albrecht 1906–   Am. (Ger.-born) physicist
Beth·mann–Holl·weg \'bet-mən-'hōl-ˌväg, -ˌmän-\ Theobald Theodor Friedrich Alfred von 1856–1921 Ger. statesman; chancellor (1909–17)
Be·thune \bə-'thün, -'thyün\ Mary 1875–1955 née McLeod Am. educ.
Bet·je·man \'be-chə-mən\ Sir John 1906–1984 Brit. author; poet laureate (1972–84)
Bet·tel·heim \'be-təl-ˌhīm\ Bruno 1903–1990 Am. (Austrian-born) psychol.
Bet·ter·ton \'be-tər-tᵊn\ Thomas ca 1635–1710 Eng. actor
Bev·er·idge \'be-və-rij, 'bev-rij\ Albert Jeremiah 1862–1927 Am. polit. & hist.
Beveridge William Henry 1879–1963 1st Baron Beveridge of Tug·gal \'tə-gəl\ Eng. econ.
Bev·in \'be-vən\ Ernest 1881–1951 Brit. labor leader & polit.
Beyle Marie-Henri — see STENDHAL
Bhu·mi·bol Adul·ya·dej \'pü-mē-ˌpōn-ä-'dùn-lə-ˌdät —sic\ 1927–   king of Thailand (1946–   )
Bhut·to \'bü-tō\ Benazir 1953–   prime min. of Pakistan (1988–90; 1993–   )
Bi·dault \bē-'dō\ Georges 1899–1983 Fr. statesman
Bid·dle \'bi-dᵊl\ John 1615–1662 founder of Eng. Unitarianism
Biddle Nicholas 1786–1844 Am. financier
Bien·ville \'bē-en-ˌvil, -vəl; byä-'vēl\ Jean-Baptiste Le Moyne, sieur de 1680–1768 Fr. colonial gov. of Louisiana
Bierce \'birs\ Ambrose Gwinnett 1842–?1914 Am. author
Bier·stadt \'bir-ˌstat\ Albert 1830–1902 Am. (Ger.-born) painter
Bing·ham \'biŋ-əm\ George Caleb 1811–1879 Am. painter
Bin·nig \'bi-nik\ Gerd 1947–   Ger. physicist
Bi·on \'bī-ˌän, -ən\ fl 100 B.C. Greek bucolic poet
Birk·beck \'bər(k)-ˌbek\ George 1776–1841 Eng. physician
Bir·ken·head \'bər-kən-ˌhed\ 1st Earl of 1872–1930 Frederick Edwin Smith Eng. jurist & statesman
Bi·ron \'bē-ˌrōn\ Ernst Johann 1690–1772 orig. Büh·ren \'bǖ-rən\ Duke of Kurland Ger. polit. in Russia
Bish·op \'bi-shəp\ Elizabeth 1911–1979 Am. poet
Bishop John Michael 1936–   Am. microbiologist
Bis·marck \'biz-ˌmärk\ Prince Otto Eduard Leopold von 1815–1898 in full Bismarck-Schön·hau·sen \-shōn-'haú-zᵊn\ 1st chancellor of Ger. Empire (1871–90) — Bis·marck·ian \biz-'mär-kē-ən\ adj
Bi·zet \bē-'zā\ Alexandre-César-Léopold 1838–1875 called Georges Fr. composer
Bjørn·son \'byȯrn-sən\ Bjørnstjerne Martinius 1832–1910 Norw. poet, dram., & nov.
Black \'blak\ Hugo LaFayette 1886–1971 Am. jurist & polit.
Black Sir James Whyte 1924–   Brit. pharmacologist
Black·ett \'bla-kət\ Patrick Maynard Stuart 1897–1974 Brit. physicist
Black Hawk \'blak-ˌhȯk\ 1767–1838 Ma-ka-ta-i-me-she-kia-kiak Sauk Indian chief
Black·more \'blak-ˌmȯr, -ˌmȯr\ Richard Doddridge 1825–1900 Eng. nov.
Black·mun \'blak-mən\ Harry Andrew 1908–   Am. jurist
Black·stone \'blak-ˌstōn, chiefly Brit -stən\ Sir William 1723–1780 Eng. jurist
Black·well \'blak-ˌwel, -wəl\ Elizabeth 1821–1910 Am. physician
Black·wood \'blak-ˌwùd\ William 1776–1834 Scot. publisher
Blaine \'blän\ James Gillespie 1830–1893 Am. statesman
Blake \'blāk\ Eugene Carson 1906–1985 Am. clergyman
Blake Robert 1599–1657 Eng. admiral
Blake William 1757–1827 Eng. artist, poet, & mystic — Blak·ean \'blā-kē-ən\ adj
Blanc \'blaŋk\ Melvin Jerome 1908–1989 Mel Am. actor
Blas·co Ibá·ñez \'bläs-(ˌ)kō-ē-'bän-(ˌ)yäs\ Vicente 1867–1928 Span. nov.
Bla·vat·sky \blə-'vat-skē, -'vät-\ Helena Petrovna 1831–1891 née Hahn Russ. traveler & theosophist
Blé·riot \'bler-ē-ˌō\ Louis 1872–1936 Fr. engineer & pioneer aviator
Bligh \'blī\ William 1754–1817 Eng. naval officer
Bloch \'bläk, 'blȯk, 'blȯ́k\ Ernest 1880–1959 Am. (Swiss-born) composer
Bloch \'bläk\ Felix 1905–1983 Am. physicist
Bloch \'bläk, 'blȯk, 'blȯ́k\ Konrad Emil 1912–   Am. (Ger.-born) biochem.
Block \'bläk\ Herbert Lawrence 1909–   Her·block \'hər-ˌbläk\ Am. editorial cartoonist
Bloem·ber·gen \'blüm-ˌbər-gən\ Nicolaas 1920–   Am. (Du.-born) physicist
Bloom·er \'blü-mər\ Amelia 1818–1894 née Jenks Am. reformer
Bloom·field \'blüm-ˌfēld\ Leonard 1887–1949 Am. linguist —
Bloom·field·ian \ˌblüm-'fēl-dē-ən\ adj

Blü·cher \'blü-kər, 'blʉ-kər\ Gebhard Leberecht von 1742–1819 prince of *Wahlstatt* Pruss. field marshal
Blum \'blüm\ Léon 1872–1950 Fr. polit.; provisional pres. (1946–47)
Blum·berg \'bləm-,bərg, 'blüm-\ Baruch Samuel 1925–   Am. virologist
Bluntsch·li \'blünch-lē\ Johann Kaspar 1808–1881 Swiss legal scholar
Boabdil — see MUḤAMMAD XI
Boadicea — see BOUDICCA
Bo·as \'bō-,az\ Franz 1858–1942 Am. (Ger.-born) anthropol. & ethnol.
— Bo·as·ian \bō-'a-zē-ən, -zh(ē-)ən\ *adj*
Bo·ba·di·lla \,bō-bə-'dē-yə\ Francisco de *d* 1502 Span. viceroy of Indies
Boc·cac·cio \bō-'kä-ch(ē-,)ō\ Giovanni 1313–1375 Ital. author
Boc·che·ri·ni \,bä-kə-'rē-nē\ Luigi 1743–1805 Ital. composer
Bod·ley \'bäd-lē\ Sir Thomas 1545–1613 Eng. diplomat & founder of Bodleian library
Bo·do·ni \bə-'dō-nē\ Giambattista 1740–1813 Ital. printer & type designer
Bo·e·thi·us \bō-'ē-thē-əs\ Anicius Manlius Severinus *ca* 480–524 Rom. philos.
Boh·len \'bō-lən\ Charles Eustis 1904–1974 Am. diplomat
Böh·me \'bə(r)m-ə, 'bœ-mə\ Ja·kob \'yä-,köp\ 1575–1624 Ger. mystic
Bohr \'bōr, 'bȯr\ Aage Niels 1922–   *son of Niels* Dan. physicist
Bohr Niels Henrik David 1885–1962 Dan. physicist
Bo·iar·do \bȯi-'är-(,)dō, bō-'yär-\ Matteo Maria 1441?–1494 Ital. poet
Boi·leau–Des·pré·aux \'bwä-lō-,dä-prē-'ō\ Nicolas 1636–1711 Fr. critic & poet
Boj·er \'bȯi-ər\ Johan \yō-'hän\ 1872–1959 Norw. writer
Bok \'bäk\ Edward William 1863–1930 Am. (Du.-born) editor
Bo·leyn \bu·'lin, -'lēn; 'bu·lən\ Anne 1507?–1536 *2d wife of Henry VIII of England & mother of Queen Elizabeth I*
Bol·ger \'bäl-jər, 'bȯl-\ James Brendan 1935–   prime min. of New Zealand (1990–   )
Bo·ling·broke \'bä-liŋ,brùk, 'bu-, US also 'bō-liŋ-, -,brōk\ 1st Viscount 1678–1751 *Henry St. John* \'sin-jən, US also (,)sänt-'jän, sənt-\ Eng. statesman
Bo·lí·var Si·món \sē-,mōn-bə-'lē-,vär; ,sī-mən-'bä-lə-,vär, -vər\ 1783–1830 So. Am. liberator
Böll \'bəl, 'bœl\ Heinrich Theodor 1917–1985 Ger. writer
Bo·na·parte \'bō-nə-,pärt\ *It* **Buo·na·par·te** \,bwȯ-nə-'pär-tē\ Corsican family including Na·po·léon I \nə-'pōl-yən, -'pō-lē-ən\ (*q. v.*) & his bros.: Joseph 1768–1844 king of Naples & Spain; Lucien 1775–1840 prince of Ca·ni·no \kə-'nē-(,)nō\; Louis 1778–1846 *father of Napoléon III* king of Holland; Jérôme 1784–1860 king of Westphalia
Bonar Law — see LAW
Bon·a·ven·tu·ra \,bä-nə-,ven-'túr-ə, -'tyúr-\ *or* **Bon·a·ven·ture** \,bä-nə-'ven-chər, 'bä-nə-,\ Saint *ca* 1217–1274 *the Seraphic Doctor* Ital. philos.
Bone \'bōn\ Sir Muirhead 1876–1953 Scot. etcher & painter
Bon·heur \bä-'nər\ Rosa 1822–1899 *Marie-Rosalie* Fr. painter
Bon·i·face \'bä-nə-fəs, -,fäs\ Saint *ca* 675–754 *Wynfrid* or *Wynfrith* Eng. missionary in Germany
Boniface name of 9 popes: esp. **VIII** (*Benedict Caetani*) *ca* 1235(or 1240)–1303 (pope 1294–1303)
Bon·nard \bȯ-'när\ Pierre 1867–1947 Fr. painter
Bon·ner *or* **Bon·er** \'bä-nər\ Edmund *ca* 1500–1569 Eng. prelate
Bon·net \bȯ-'nā\ Georges-Étienne 1889–1973 Fr. polit. & diplomat
Bon·ney \'bä-nē\ William orig. *Henry* 1859–1881 *Billy the Kid* Am. outlaw
Bon·temps \bän-'täm\ Arna Wendell 1902–1973 Am. writer
Boone \'bün\ Daniel 1734–1820 Am. pioneer
Booth \'büth, *chiefly Brit* 'büth\ family of Am. actors: Junius Brutus 1796–1852 *b* in England & his sons Edwin Thomas 1833–1893 & John Wilkes 1838–1865 assassin of Lincoln
Booth William 1829–1912 Eng. founder of Salvation Army *father of:* William Bramwell 1856–1929 Salvation Army gen.; Ballington 1857–1940 founder of Volunteers of America; Evangeline Cory 1865–1950 Salvation Army gen.
Boothe Clare — see Clare Boothe LUCE
Bo·rah \'bōr-ə, 'bȯr-\ William Edgar 1865–1940 Am. polit.
Bor·den \'bȯr-dᵊn\ Sir Robert (Laird) 1854–1937 Canad. lawyer & statesman; prime min. (1911–20)
Bor·det \bȯr-'dā\ Jules 1870–1961 Belg. bacteriol.
Bor·ges \'bȯr-,hās\ Jorge Luis 1899–1986 Argentine author
Bor·gia \'bȯr-(,)jä, -jə, -zhə\ Cesare 1475(or 1476)–1507 *son of Rodrigo* Ital. cardinal & mil. leader
Borgia Lucrezia 1480–1519 *dau. of Rodrigo* duchess of Ferrara
Borgia Rodrigo — see Pope ALEXANDER VI
Bor·glum \'bȯr-gləm\ (John) Gut·zon \'gət-sən\ (de la Mothe) 1867–1941 Am. sculptor
Bo·ris III \'bȯr-əs, 'bȯr-, 'bär-\ 1894–1943 czar of Bulgaria (1918–43)
Bor·laug \'bȯr-,lȯg\ Norman Ernest 1914–   Am. agronomist
Born \'bȯrn\ Max 1882–1970 Ger. physicist
Bo·ro·din \,bȯr-ə-'dēn, ,bär-\ Aleksandr Porfiryevich 1833–1887 Russ. composer & chem.
Bor·row \'bär-(,)ō\ George Henry 1803–1881 Eng. author
Bosch \'bäsh, 'bȯsh\ Carl 1874–1940 Ger. industrial chem.
Bosch \'bäsh, 'bȯsh, *D* 'bȯs\ Hieronymus *ca* 1450–*ca* 1516 Du. painter
Bo·sco \'bäs-kō\ Saint Giovanni Melchior 1815–1888 *Don Bosco* Ital. religious & founder of Society of St. Francis de Sales
Bose \'bōs, 'bȯs, 'bȯsh\ Sir Ja·ga·dis \,jə-gə-'dēs\ Chan·dra \'chən-drə\ 1858–1937 Indian physicist & plant physiol.
Bos·suet \bȯ-'swā\ Jacques-Bénigne 1627–1704 Fr. bishop
Bos·well \'bäz-,wel, -wəl\ James 1740–1795 Scot. biographer & diarist
Bo·tha \'bō-tə, 'bù(ə)-\ Louis 1862–1919 Boer gen.; 1st prime min. of Transvaal (1907) & of Union of So. Africa (1910–19)
Botha Pieter Willem 1916–   prime min. of Republic of So. Africa (1978–89)
Bo·the \'bō-tə\ Walther Wilhelm Georg Franz 1891–1957 Ger. physicist
Bot·ti·cel·li \,bä-tə-'che-lē\ Sandro 1445–1510 *Alessandro di Mariano Filipepi* Ital. painter
Bou·cher \bü-'shā\ François 1703–1770 Fr. painter

Bou·ci·cault \'bü-si-,kō\ *or* **Bour·ci·cault** \'búr-\ Dion 1820(or 1822)–1890 *Dionysius Lardner Boursiquot* Am. (Irish-born) actor & dram.
Bou·dic·ca \bü-'di-kə\ *also* **Bo·a·di·cea** \,bō-ə-də-'sē-ə\ *d* A.D. 60 ancient Brit. queen
Bou·gain·ville \'bü-gən-,vil, bü-gaⁿ-vēl\ Louis-Antoine de 1729–1811 Fr. navigator
Bou·lan·ger \bü-län-zhā\ Georges-Ernest-Jean-Marie 1837–1891 Fr. gen.
Boulanger Nadia-Juliette 1887–1979 Fr. music teacher & conductor
Bou·lez \bü-'lez\ Pierre 1925–   Fr. composer & conductor
Bour·bon \'búr-bən, búr-'bōⁿ\ Charles de 1490–1527 Duc *de Bourbon* Fr. gen.; constable of France
Bour·geois \búrzh-'wä, 'búrzh-,\ Léon-Victor-Auguste 1851–1925 Fr. statesman
Bour·get \búr-'zhā\ Paul-Charles-Joseph 1852–1935 Fr. author
Bour·gui·ba \búr-'gē-bə\ Habib ibn Ali 1903–   Tunisian pres. (1957–87)
Bou·tros–Gha·li \,bü-trōs-'gä-lē\ Boutros 1922–   Egypt. U.N. official; secy.-gen. (1992–   )
Bo·vet \bō-'vä\ Daniele 1907–1992 Ital. (Swiss-born) pharmacologist
Bow·ditch \'baú-,dich\ Nathaniel 1773–1838 Am. math. & astron.
Bow·ell \'bō-əl\ Sir Mackenzie 1823–1917 Canad. polit.; prime min. of Canada (1894–96)
Bow·en \'bō-ən\ Elizabeth 1899–1973 Irish author
Bow·ie \'bü-ē, 'bō-\ James 1796–1836 hero of Texas revolution
Bowles \'bōlz\ Chester 1901–1986 Am. econ. & diplomat
Boy·den \'bȯi-dᵊn\ Seth 1788–1870 Am. inventor
Boyd Orr \'bȯid-'ȯr, -'ȯr\ John 1880–1971 Baron *Boyd-Orr of Brechin Mearns* Scot. agriculturist
Boyle \'bȯi(ə)l\ Kay 1902–1992 Am. author
Boyle Robert 1627–1691 Brit. physicist & chem.
Brad·bury \'brad-,ber-ē, -b(ə-)rē\ Ray Douglas 1920–   Am. writer
Brad·dock \'bra-dək\ Edward 1695–1755 Brit. gen. in America
Brad·ford \'brad-fərd\ Gamaliel 1863–1932 Am. biographer
Bradford William 1590–1657 Pilgrim father; 2d gov. of Plymouth colony
Bradford William 1663–1752 Am. printer
Brad·ley \'brad-lē\ Francis Herbert 1846–1924 Eng. philos. — **Brad·le·ian** *also* **Brad·ley·an** \'brad-lē-ən, brad-'\ *adj*
Bradley Henry 1845–1923 Eng. philologist & lexicographer
Bradley Omar Nelson 1893–1981 Am. gen.
Brad·street \'brad-,strēt\ Anne *ca* 1612–1672 née *Dudley; wife of Simon* Am. poet
Bradstreet Simon 1603–1697 colonial gov. of Massachusetts
Bra·dy \'brā-dē\ Mathew B. 1823?–1896 Am. photographer
Bragg \'brag\ Braxton 1817–1876 Am. Confed. gen.
Bragg Sir (William) Lawrence 1890–1971 *son of W.H.* Eng. physicist
Bragg Sir William Henry 1862–1942 Eng. physicist
Brahe \'brä; 'brä-hē, -hə\ Ty·cho \'tē-(,)kō, 'tī-\ 1546–1601 Dan. astron.
Brahms \'brämz\ Johannes 1833–1897 Ger. composer & pianist — **Brahms·ian** \'bräm-zē-ən\ *adj*
Braille \'brä(ə)l, 'brī\ Louis 1809–1852 Fr. blind teacher of the blind
Bra·man·te \brə-'män-tē, -,(,)tä\ Donato 1444–1514 orig. *Donato d'Agnolo* or *d'Angelo* Ital. architect
Bran·cu·si \bran-'kü-sē\ Constantin 1876–1957 Fr. (Romanian-born) sculptor
Bran·deis \'bran-,dīs, -,dīz\ Louis Dembitz 1856–1941 Am. jurist
Bran·des \'brän-dəs\ Georg Morris 1842–1927 Dan. lit. critic
Brandt \'bränt, 'brant\ Wil·ly \'vi-lē, 'wi-\ 1913–1992 orig. *Herbert Ernst Karl Frahm* W. Ger. polit.; chancellor of West Germany (1969–74)
Brant \'brant\ Joseph 1742–1807 *Thayendanegea* Mohawk Indian chief
Bran·ting \'bran-tiŋ\ Karl Hjal·mar \'yäl-,mär\ 1860–1925 Swed. statesman & socialist leader
Braque \'brak, 'bräk\ Georges 1882–1963 Fr. painter
Brat·tain \'bra-tᵊn\ Walter Houser 1902–1987 Am. physicist
Brau·chitsch \'braú-kich, -kich\ Heinrich Alfred Hermann Walther von 1881–1948 Ger. gen.
Braun \'braún\ Karl Ferdinand 1850–1918 Ger. physicist
Braun Wernher von 1912–1977 Am. (Ger.-born) engineer
Breas·ted \'bres-təd\ James Henry 1865–1935 Am. orientalist
Brecht \'brekt, 'brekt\ Bertolt 1898–1956 Ger. dram. — **Brecht·ian** \'brek-tē-ən, 'brek-\ *adj*
Breck·in·ridge \'bre-kən-,(,)rij\ John Cabell 1821–1875 Am. polit.; vice pres. of the U.S. (1857–61)
Bren·nan \'bre-nən\ William Joseph, Jr. 1906–   Am. jurist
Bre·ton \brə-'tōⁿ\ André 1896–1966 Fr. surrealist poet
Brew·ster \'brü-stər\ William 1567–1644 Pilgrim father
Brey·er \'brī-ər\ Stephen Gerald 1938–   Am. jurist
Brezh·nev \'brezh-,nef\ Leonid Ilyich 1906–1982 Russ. polit.; pres. of U.S.S.R. (1960–64, 1977–82); 1st secy. of Communist party (1964–82)
Bri·an \'brī-ən, 'brēn\ *also* **Brian Bo·ru** \bə-'rü\ 941–1014 king of Ireland (1002–14)
Bri·and \brē-äⁿ\ Aristide 1862–1932 Fr. statesman
Brid·ger \'bri-jər\ James 1804–1881 Am. pioneer & scout
Brid·ges \'bri-jəz\ Robert Seymour 1844–1930 Eng. poet; poet laureate (1913–30)
Bridg·man \'brij-mən\ Percy Williams 1882–1961 Am. physicist
Bright \'brīt\ John 1811–1889 Eng. orator & statesman
Brig·it \'bri-jət, 'brē-yit\ *also* **Brid·get** \'bri-jət\ *or* **Brig·id** \'bri-jəd, 'brē-yid\ *or* **Brighid** \'brēd\ Saint *d ca* 524–528 *Bride of Kildare* or *Bride of Ireland* a patron saint of Ireland
Bril·lat–Sa·va·rin \brē-'yä-,sa-və-'raⁿ, -'sa-və-rən\ Anthelme 1755–1826 Fr. gastronome

\ə\ abut \ᵊ\ kitten, F table \ər\ further \a\ ash \ā\ ace \ä\ mop, mar \aú\ out \ch\ chin \e\ bet \ē\ easy \g\ go \i\ hit \ī\ ice \j\ job \ŋ\ sing \ō\ go \ȯ\ law \ȯi\ boy \th\ thin \t͟h\ the \ü\ loot \ú\ foot \y\ yet \zh\ vision \à, k̲, ⁿ, œ, œ̄, ʉ, ᵾ, ᵊ\ *see* Guide to Pronunciation

Brit·ten \'bri-tᵊn\ (Edward) Benjamin 1913–1976 Baron *Britten of Aldeburgh* Eng. composer
Brock·house \'bräk-ˌhaůs\ Bertram Neville 1918–   Canad. physicist
Brod·sky \'bräd-skē\ Joseph 1940–   Am. (Russ.-born) poet & essayist
Bro·gan \'brō-gən\ Sir Denis William 1900–1974 Brit. hist.
Broglie \bròi\ Louis-Victor-Pierre-Raymond de 1892–1987 Fr. physicist
Bron·të \'brän-tē, -(ˌ)tä\ a family of Eng. writers: Charlotte 1816–1855 & her sisters Emily 1818–1848 & Anne 1820–1849
Brooke \'brůk\ Sir Alan Francis 1883–1963 1st Viscount *Al·an·brooke* \'a-lən-ˌbrůk\ Brit. field marshal
Brooke Edward William 1919–   Am. polit.
Brooke Rupert 1887–1915 Eng. poet
Brooks \'brůks\ Gwendolyn Elizabeth 1917–   Am. poet
Brooks Phillips 1835–1893 Am. bishop
Brooks Van Wyck \van-'wīk, vən-\ 1886–1963 Am. essayist & critic
Brow·der \'braů-dər\ Earl 1891–1973 Am. Communist polit.
Brown \'braůn\ Charles Brockden 1771–1810 Am. nov.
Brown Ford Mad·ox \'ma-dəks\ 1821–1893 Eng. painter
Brown Herbert Charles 1912–   Am. (Eng.-born) chem.
Brown Jesse 1944–   U.S. secy. of veteran affairs (1993–   )
Brown John 1800–1859 *Old Brown of Osa·wat·o·mie* \ˌō-sə-'wä-tə-mē\ Am. abolitionist
Brown Michael Stuart 1941–   Am. biochemist
Brown Ronald Harmon 1941–   U.S. secy. of commerce (1993–   )
Browne \'braůn\ Charles Farrar 1834–1867 pseud. *Ar·te·mus* \'är-tə-məs\ *Ward* Am. humorist
Browne Sir Thomas 1605–1682 Eng. physician & author
Brow·ning \'braů-niŋ\ Elizabeth Barrett 1806–1861 *wife of Robert* Eng. poet
Browning Robert 1812–1889 Eng. poet
Broz Josip — see TITO
Bruce \'brüs\ Sir David 1855–1931 Brit. physician & bacteriol.
Bruce Robert — see ROBERT I the Bruce
Bruce Stanley Melbourne 1883–1967 1st Viscount *Bruce of Melbourne* Austral. statesman; prime min. (1923–29)
Bruck·ner \'brůk-nər\ Anton 1824–1896 Austrian composer — **Bruck·ner·ian** \ˌbrůk-'ner-ē-ən\ *adj*
Brue·ghel or **Breu·ghel** \'brü-gəl, 'brói-, *Dutch* 'brȫ-kəl\ family of Flem. painters including: Pieter *ca* 1525(or 1530)–1569 & his sons Pieter 1564–1638 & Jan 1568–1625
Brum·mell \'brə-məl\ George Bryan 1778–1840 *Beau Brummell* Eng. dandy
Bru·nel·le·schi \ˌbrü-nᵊl-'es-kē\ or **Bru·nel·le·sco** \-(ˌ)kō\ Filippo 1377–1446 Ital. architect
Bru·ne·tière \ˌbrü-nə-'tyer, ˌbrüē-\ Vincent de Paul-Marie-Ferdinand 1849–1906 Fr. critic
Brü·ning \'brü-niŋ, 'brüē-\ Heinrich 1885–1970 chancellor of Germany (1930–32)
Bru·no \'brü-(ˌ)nō\ Giordano 1548–1600 Ital. philos.
Bru·tus \'brü-təs\ Marcus Junius 85–42 B.C. Rom. polit. & conspirator
Bry·an \'brī-ən\ William Jennings 1860–1925 Am. lawyer & polit.
Bry·ant \'brī-ənt\ William Cullen 1794–1878 Am. poet & editor
Bu·ber \'bü-bər\ Martin 1878–1965 Israeli (Austrian-born) philos.
Buch·an \'bə-kən, -ˌkən\ Sir John 1875–1940 1st Baron *Tweeds·muir* \'twēdz-ˌmyůr\ Scot. author; gov.-gen. of Canada (1935–40)
Bu·chan·an \byü-'ka-nən, bə-\ James 1791–1868 Am. polit. & diplomat; 15th pres. of the U.S. (1857–61)
Buchanan James McGill 1919–   Am. econ.
Buch·man \'bůk-mən, 'bək-\ Frank Nathan Daniel 1878–1961 Am. evangelist
Buch·ner \'bůk-nər, 'bük-\ Eduard 1860–1917 Ger. chem.
Buck \'bək\ Pearl 1892–1973 née *Sy·den·strick·er* \'sī-dᵊn-ˌstri-kər\ Am. nov.
Buckingham 1st & 2d Dukes of — see VILLIERS
Buck·ley \'bə-klē\ William Frank 1925–   Am. editor & writer
Buck·ner \'bək-nər\ Simon Bolivar 1823–1914 Am. Confed. gen. & polit.
Buckner Simon Bolivar 1886–1945 *son of prec.* Am. gen.
Buddha — see SIDDHĀRTHA GAUTAMA
Bu·den·ny \bü-'dyó-nē, bü-'de-\ Semyon Mikhaylovich 1883–1973 Russ. gen.
Buffalo Bill — see William Frederick CODY
Buf·fon \bə-'fōⁿ, byü-, büē-\ Comte Georges-Louis Leclerc de 1707–1788 Fr. naturalist
Buis·son \bwē-'sōⁿ\ Ferdinand-Édouard 1841–1932 Fr. educ.
Bu·kha·rin \bü-'kär-ən\ Nikolay Ivanovich 1888–1938 Russ. Communist leader & editor
Bul·finch \'bůl-ˌfinch\ Charles 1763–1844 Am. architect
Bul·ga·nin \bůl-'ga-nən\ Nikolay Aleksandrovich 1895–1975 Russ. polit. & marshal
Bull \'bůl\ Ole \'ō-lə\ Bornemann 1810–1880 Norw. violinist
Bul·litt \'bů-lət\ William Christian 1891–1967 Am. diplomat
Bü·low \'byü-(ˌ)lō, 'büē-\ Bernhard Heinrich Martin Karl 1849–1929 Prince *von Bülow* Ger. diplomat & statesman; chancellor of Germany (1900–09)
Bult·mann \'bůlt-ˌmän\ Rudolf Karl 1884–1976 Ger. theol. — **Bultmann·ian** \bůlt-'mä-nē-ən\ *adj*
Bul·wer \'bůl-wər\ William Henry Lytton Earle 1801–1872 *bro. of 1st Baron Lytton* Brit. diplomat
Bulwer–Lytton — see LYTTON
Bunche \'bənch\ Ralph Johnson 1904–1971 Am. diplomat
Bu·nin \'bün-yən, -ˌyēn; 'bü-nən, -ˌnēn\ Ivan Alekseyevich 1870–1953 Russ. poet & nov.
Bun·ker \'bəŋ-kər\ Ellsworth 1894–1984 Am. diplomat
Bun·sen \'bůn-zən, 'bən(t)-sən\ Robert Wilhelm 1811–1899 Ger. chem.
Bun·yan \'bən-yən\ John 1628–1688 Eng. preacher & author
Buonaparte Ital. spelling of BONAPARTE
Bur·bage \'bər-bij\ Richard *ca* 1567–1619 Eng. actor
Bur·bank \'bər-ˌbaŋk\ Luther 1849–1926 Am. horticulturist
Burch·field \'bərch-ˌfēld\ Charles Ephraim 1893–1967 Am. painter

Bur·ger \'bər-gər\ Warren Earl 1907–1995 Am. jurist; chief justice U.S. Supreme Court (1969–86)
Bür·ger \'bůr-gər, 'bir-, 'büēr-\ Gottfried August 1747–1794 Ger. poet
Bur·gess \'bər-jəs\ Anthony 1917–1993 Brit. writer
Burgess (Frank) Gelett 1866–1951 Am. humorist & illustrator
Burgess Thornton Waldo 1874–1965 Am. writer
Burghley or **Burleigh** 1st Baron — see William CECIL
Bur·goyne \(ˌ)bər-'góin, 'bər-\ John 1722–1792 Brit. gen. in America
Burk \'bərk\ Martha Jane 1852?–1903 née *Can·nary* \'ka-nə-rē\ pseud. *Calamity Jane* Am. frontier figure
Burke \'bərk\ Edmund 1729–1797 Brit. statesman & orator — **Burk·ean** or **Burk·ian** \'bər-kē-ən\ *adj*
Bur·lin·game \'bər-lən-ˌgäm\ Anson 1820–1870 Am. diplomat
Burne–Jones \'bərn-'jōnz\ Sir Edward Co·ley \'kō-lē\ 1833–1898 orig. surname *Jones* Eng. painter & designer
Bur·net \(ˌ)bər-'net, 'bər-nət\ Sir (Frank) Macfarlane 1899–1985 Austral. physician
Bur·nett \(ˌ)bər-'net, 'bər-nət\ Frances Eliza 1849–1924 née *Hodg·son* \'häj-sən\ Am. (Eng.-born) writer
Bur·ney \'bər-nē\ Fanny 1752–1840 orig. *Frances; Madame d'Ar·blay* \'där-ˌblä\ Eng. nov. & diarist
Burns \'bərnz\ Robert 1759–1796 Scot. poet — **Burns·ian** \'bərn-zē-ən\ *adj*
Burn·side \'bərn-ˌsīd\ Ambrose Everett 1824–1881 Am. gen.
Burr \'bər\ Aaron 1756–1836 3d vice pres. of the U.S. (1801–05)
Bur·roughs \'bər-(ˌ)ōz, 'bə-(ˌ)rōz\ Edgar Rice 1875–1950 Am. writer
Burroughs John 1837–1921 Am. naturalist
Burroughs William Seward 1914–   Am. writer
Bur·ton \'bər-tᵊn\ Harold Hitz 1888–1964 Am. jurist
Burton Richard 1925–1984 Brit. actor
Burton Sir Richard Francis 1821–1890 Brit. explorer & orientalist
Burton Robert 1577–1640 Eng. clergyman & author
Bush \'bůsh\ George Herbert Walker 1924–   Am. polit.; 41st pres. of the U.S. (1989–93)
Bush Van·ne·var \və-'nē-vər\ 1890–1974 Am. electrical engineer
Bu·so·ni \byü-'zō-nē, bü-\ Ferruccio Benvenuto 1866–1924 Ital. composer & pianist
Bu·sta·man·te y Sir·vén \bü-stä-'män-(ˌ)tā-ē-sir-'ven\ Antonio Sánchez \'sän-(ˌ)chez\ 1865–1951 Cuban jurist
Bu·te·nandt \'bü-tᵊn-ˌänt\ Adolph Friedrich Johann 1903–1995 Ger. chem.
But·ler \'bət-lər\ Benjamin Franklin 1818–1893 Am. gen. & polit.
Butler Joseph 1692–1752 Eng. theol.
Butler Nicholas Murray 1862–1947 Am. educ.
Butler Samuel 1612–1680 Eng. satirical poet
Butler Samuel 1835–1902 Eng. nov. & satirist
Bux·te·hu·de \ˌbůk-stə-'hü-də\ Dietrich 1637–1707 Dan. organist & composer
Byng \'biŋ\ George 1663–1733 1st Viscount *Torrington* Brit. admiral
Byng Julian Hedworth George 1862–1935 1st Viscount *Byng of Vimy* Brit. gen.; gov.-gen. of Canada (1921–26)
Byrd \'bərd\ Richard Evelyn 1888–1957 Am. admiral & polar explorer
Byrnes \'bərnz\ James Francis 1879–1972 Am. polit. & jurist
By·ron \'bī-rən\ Lord 1788–1824 in full *George Gordon Byron*, 6th Baron *Byron* Eng. poet — **By·ron·ic** \bī-'rä-nik\ *adj*
Ca·be·za de Va·ca \kə-'bā-zə-də-'vä-kə\ Álvar Núñez *ca* 1490–*ca* 1560 Span. explorer
Ca·ble \'kā-bəl\ George Washington 1844–1925 Am. nov.
Cab·ot \'ka-bət\ John *ca* 1450–*ca* 1499 It. *Giovanni Ca·bo·to* \kä-'bō-(ˌ)tō\ Venetian navigator & explorer for England
Cabot Sebastian 1476?–1557 *son of John* Eng. navigator & explorer
Ca·bral \kə-'bräl\ Pedro Alvares 1467(or 1468)–1520 Port. navigator
Ca·bril·ho \kə-'brē-(ˌ)yō, -'(ˌ)lō\ João Rodrigues *d* 1543 Sp. *Juan Rodríguez Cabrillo* Span. (Port.-born) explorer in Mexico & California
Ca·bri·ni \kə-'brē-nē\ Saint Frances Xavier 1850–1917 *Mother Cabrini* 1st Am. citizen canonized (1946)
Cade \'kād\ John *d* 1450 *Jack Cade* Eng. rebel
Cad·il·lac \'ka-dᵊl-ˌak, *F* kä-dē-yák\ Antoine de la Mothe, sieur de 1658–1730 Fr. founder of Detroit
Caed·mon \'kad-mən\ *fl* 658–680 Anglo-Saxon poet
Cae·sar \'sē-zər\ Gaius Julius 100–44 B.C. Rom. gen., statesman, & writer
Cage \'kāj\ John Milton 1912–1992 Am. composer
Ca·glio·stro \kal-'yó-(ˌ)strō, käl-\ Count Alessandro di 1743–1795 orig. *Giuseppe Bal·sa·mo* \'bäl-sə-ˌmō\ Ital. adventurer
Caine \'kän\ Sir (Thomas Henry) Hall 1853–1931 Eng. nov.
Calamity Jane — see Martha Jane BURK
Cal·der \'kól-dər\ Alexander 1898–1976 Am. sculptor
Cal·de·ra Rod·rí·guez \käl-'thä-rä-róth-'rē-gäs\ Rafael 1916–   pres. of Venezuela (1969–74; 1993–   )
Cal·de·rón de la Bar·ca \ˌkäl-də-'rōn-dā-lə-'bär-kə\ Pedro 1600–1681 Span. dram. & poet
Cal·de·rón Sol \ˌkäl-dä-'rōn-'sòl\ Armando 1949–   pres. of El Salvador (1994–   )
Cald·well \'kól-ˌdwel, -dwəl, 'käl-\ Erskine 1903–1987 Am. nov.
Caldwell (Janet) Taylor 1900–1985 Am. (Eng.-born) author
Cal·houn \kal-'hün\ John Caldwell 1782–1850 Am. polit.; vice pres. of the U.S. (1825–32)
Ca·lig·u·la \kə-'li-gyə-lə\ A.D. 12–41 *Gaius Caesar* Rom. emp. (37–41)
Cal·la·ghan \'ka-lə-hən, -ˌhan\ (Leonard) James 1912–   Brit. prime min. (1976–79)
Callaghan Morley Edward 1903–1990 Canad. author
Cal·las \'ka-ləs, 'kä-\ Maria 1923–1977 orig. *Maria Anna Sofia Cecilia Kalogeropoulos* Am. soprano
Cal·les \'kä-ˌyäs\ Plutarco Elías 1877–1945 Mex. gen.; pres. of Mexico (1924–28)
Cal·lim·a·chus \kə-'li-mə-kəs\ 5th cent. B.C. Greek sculptor
Callimachus *ca* 305–*ca* 240 B.C. Greek scholar & Alexandrian librarian
Cal·lis·the·nes \kə-'lis-thə-ˌnēz\ *ca* 360–328 B.C. Greek philos. & hist.
Cal·lis·tra·tus \kə-'lis-trə-təs\ *d* 355 B.C. Athenian orator & polit.
Cal·vert \'kal-vərt\ George 1580?–1632 1st Baron *Baltimore* Eng. proprietor in America
Calvert Leonard 1606–1647 *son of George* gov. of Maryland province (1634–47)

Cal·vin \'kal-vən\ John 1509–1564 orig. *Jean Chau·vin* \shō-vaⁿ\ or *Caul·vin* \kōl-vaⁿ\ Fr. theol. & reformer

Calvin Melvin 1911–   Am. chem.

Camacho Manuel Ávila — see ÁVILA CAMACHO

Cam·ba·cé·rès \,käⁿ-,ba-sə-'res, -,bä-\ Jean-Jacques-Régis de 1753–1824 Duc de *Parme* Fr. jurist; counselor of Napoléon I

Cambridge 1st Baron of — see Edgar Douglas ADRIAN

Cam·by·ses II \kam-'bī-(,)sēz\ *d* 522 B.C. *son of Cyrus II the Great* king of Persia (529–22)

Cam·den \'kam-dən\ William 1551–1623 Eng. antiquarian & hist.

Cam·er·on of Loch·iel \'ka-mə-rən-əv-lä-'kē(ə)l, 'kam-rən-, -‿kē(ə)l\ 1629–1719 Sir *Ewen Cameron* Scot. chieftain

Cameron of Lochiel 1695?–1748 *Donald Cameron; the gentle Lochiel* Scot. chieftain

Ca·mões \kə-'mōiⁿsh\ *E* **Ca·mo·ëns** \kə-'mō-ənz, 'ka-mə-wənz\ Luiz Vaz de 1524(or 1525)–1580 Port. poet

Camp \'kamp\ Walter Chauncey 1859–1925 Am. football coach

Camp·bell \'kam-bəl, 'ka-məl\ Alexander 1788–1866 Am. (Irish-born) founder of Disciples of Christ

Campbell Colin 1792–1863 orig. surname *Mac·li·ver* \mə-'klē-vər\; Baron *Clyde* Brit. field marshal

Campbell John 1705–1782 4th Earl of *Lou·doun* \'lau̇-d^ən\ Brit. gen. in America

Campbell John Douglas Sutherland 1845–1914 9th Duke of *Argyll* gov.-gen. of Canada (1878–83)

Campbell Joseph 1904–1987 Am. mythologist & folklorist

Campbell Kim 1947–   orig. *Avril Phaedra Campbell* prime min. of Canada (1993)

Campbell Thomas 1777–1844 Brit. poet

Camp·bell–Ban·ner·man \-'ba-nər-mən\ Sir Henry 1836–1908 Brit. statesman; prime min. (1905–08)

Cam·pi \'käm-(,)pē\ Ital. family of painters in Cremona including: Galeazzo 1477–1536 & his three sons Giulio 1502–1572, Antonio 1536–*ca* 1591, & Vincenzo 1536–1591

Cam·pi·on \'kam-pē-ən\ Thomas 1567–1620 Eng. poet & composer

Ca·mus \kà-mūē\ Albert 1913–1960 Fr. nov., essayist, & dram.

Ca·na·let·to \,ka-n^əl-'e-(,)tō\ 1697–1768 orig. *Giovanni Antonio Canal* Ital. painter

Can·by \'kan-bē\ Henry Sei·del \'sī-d^əl\ 1878–1961 Am. editor & author

Can·dolle \kän-dȯl\ Augustin Pyrame de 1778–1841 Swiss botanist

Can·dra·gup·ta \,kən-drə-'gu̇p-tə\ *or* **Chan·dra·gup·ta** \,chən-\ *d ca* 297 B.C. Indian emp. (*ca* 321–*ca* 297 B.C.)

Candra Gup·ta II \'kən-drə-'gu̇p-tə\ *also* **Chan·dra Gup·ta II** \'chən-\ Indian ruler of Gupta dynasty (*ca* 380–*ca* 415)

Ca·net·ti \kə-'ne-tē\ Elias 1905–1994 Brit. (Bulg.-born) author writing in German

Canfield Dorothy — see Dorothy Canfield FISHER

Can·ning \'ka-niŋ\ Charles John 1812–1862 Earl *Canning* Brit. gov.‑gen. of India (1856–58); 1st viceroy of India (1858–62)

Canning George 1770–1827 *father of C.J.* Brit. statesman; prime min. (1827)

Canning Stratford 1786–1880 1st Viscount *Stratford de Red·cliffe* \'red-,klif\ Brit. diplomat

Can·non \'ka-nən\ Joseph Gurney 1836–1926 *Uncle Joe* Am. polit.

Ca·no·va \kə-'nō-və\ Antonio 1757–1822 Ital. sculptor

Ca·nute \kə-'nüt, -'nyüt\ *d* 1035 *the Great* king of England (1016–35); of Denmark (1018–35); of Norway (1028–35)

Ca·pek \'chä-,pek\ Ka·rel \'kär-əl\ 1890–1938 Czech nov. & dram.

Capet Hugh — see HUGH CAPET

Ca·pone \kə-'pōn\ Alphonse 1899–1947 *Scarface* Am. gangster

Ca·pote \kə-'pō-tē\ Truman 1924–1984 Am. writer

Cap·ra \'ka-prə\ Frank 1897–1991 Am. film director & producer —
Cap·ra·esque \,ka-prə-'esk\ *adj*

Car·a·cal·la \,kar-ə-'ka-lə\ A.D. 188–217 *Marcus Aurelius Antoninus* orig. *Bassi·a·nus* \,ba-sē-'ä-nəs\ Rom. emp. (211–217)

Ca·rat·a·cus \kə-'ra-ti-kəs\ *also* **Ca·rac·ta·cus** \-'rak-ti-\ *W* **Ca·ra·doc** \-'ra-,dȯg\ 1st cent. A.D. Brit. chieftain

Ca·ra·vag·gio \,kar-ə-'vä-j(ē,)ō, -'vä-zhō\ Michelangelo da 1573–1610 *Michelangelo Merisi* Ital. painter — **Ca·ra·vag·gesque** \,kär-ə-,vä-'jesk\ *adj*

Car·ber·ry \'kär-,ber-ē, -bə-rē\ John Joseph 1904–   Am. cardinal

Cár·de·nas \'kär-d^ən-,äs, kär-thä-,näs\ Lázaro 1895–1970 Mex. gen. & polit.; pres. of Mexico (1934–40)

Car·do·so \kár-'dō-(,)zü\ Fernando Henrique 1931–   pres. of Brazil (1995–)

Car·do·zo \kär-'dō-(,)zō\ Benjamin Nathan 1870–1938 Am. jurist

Car·duc·ci \kär-'dü-(,)chē\ Giosuè 1835–1907 Ital. poet

Ca·rew \kə-'rü; 'kar-ē; 'ker-ē\ Thomas 1595?–?1640 Eng. poet

Car·ey \'kar-ē, 'ker\ George Leonard 1935–   archbishop of Canterbury (1991–)

Carl XVI Gus·taf \'kärl-,gəs-,täv, -'gu̇s-, -,täf\ 1946–   king of Sweden (1973–)

Carle·ton \'kär(-ə)l-tən\ Sir Guy 1724–1808 1st Baron *Dorchester* Brit. gen. & administrator in America

Car·los \'kär-ləs, -,lōs\ Don 1788–1855 infante & pretender to Span. throne

Carlos de Aus·tria \-thä-'au̇-strē-ə\ Don 1545–1568 *son of Philip II of Spain* prince of Asturias & heir to Span. throne

Car·lo·ta \kär-'lō-tə, -'lä-\ 1840–1927 *Marie-Charlotte-Amélie-Augustine-Victoire-Clémentine-Léopoldine* empress of Mexico (1864–67)

Car·lyle \kär-'lī(ə)l, 'kär-,\ Thomas 1795–1881 Scot. essayist & hist. — **Car·lyl·ean** *or* **Car·lyl·ian** \kär-'lī-,lē-ən\ *adj*

Car·mo·na \kär-'mō-nə\ António Óscar de Fragoso 1869–1951 Port. gen.; pres. of Portugal (1928–51)

Car·nap \'kär-,nap\ Rudolf 1891–1970 Am. (Ger.-born) philos.

Car·ne·gie \kär-'ne-gē, 'kär-nə-gē\ Andrew 1835–1919 Am. (Scot.-born) industrialist & philanthropist

Car·not \kär-'nō\ Lazare-Nicolas-Marguerite 1753–1823 Fr. statesman & gen.

Carnot Marie-François-Sadi 1837–1894 pres. of France (1887–94)

Car·ol II \'kar-əl\ 1893–1953 king of Romania (1930–40)

Car·pac·cio \kär-'pä-ch(ē,)ō\ Vittore *ca* 1460–1525(or 1526) Ital. painter

Car·ran·za \kə-'ran-zə, -'rän-\ Venustiano 1859–1920 pres. of Mexico (1915–20)

Car·rel \kə-'rel, 'kar-əl\ Alexis 1873–1944 Fr. surgeon & biol.

Car·rère \kə-'rer\ John Merven 1858–1911 Am. architect

Car·roll \'kar-əl\ Charles 1737–1832 *Carroll of Carrollton* Am. patriot

Carroll Lewis — see Charles Lutwidge DODGSON — **Car·roll·ian** \ka-'rō-lē-ən\ *adj*

Car·son \'kär-s^ən\ Christopher 1809–1868 *Kit* \'kit\ *Carson* Am. scout

Carson Rachel Louise 1907–1964 Am. scientist & writer

Carte, D'Oy·ly \,dȯi-lē-'kärt\ Richard 1844–1901 Eng. opera impresario

Car·ter \'kär-tər\ Elliott Cook 1908–   Am. composer

Carter Howard 1873–1939 Eng. archaeol.

Carter Jimmy 1924–   *James Earl Carter, Jr.* Am. polit.; 39th pres. of the U.S. (1977–81)

Car·ter·et \,kär-tə-'ret, 'kär-tə-,\ John 1690–1763 Earl *Gran·ville* \'gran-,vil\ Eng. statesman

Car·tier \kär-'tyā, kär-tē-,ā\ George Étienne 1814–1873 Canad. polit.

Cartier Jacques 1491–1557 Fr. navigator & explorer

Cart·wright \'kärt-,rīt\ Edmund 1743–1823 Eng. inventor

Ca·ru·so \kə-'rü-(,)sō, -(,)zō\ En·ri·co \en-'rē-(,)kō\ 1873–1921 orig. *Errico* Ital. tenor

Car·ver \'kär-vər\ George Washington *ca* 1864–1943 Am. botanist

Carver John 1576–1621 Eng. *Mayflower* pilgrim; 1st gov. of Plymouth colony

Cary \'kar-ē, 'ker-ē\ (Arthur) Joyce (Lunel) 1888–1957 Brit. nov.

Cary Henry Francis 1772–1844 Eng. clergyman & translator

Ca·sals \kə-'sälz, -'zälz\ Pablo 1876–1973 Catalan *Pau* Span.-born cellist, conductor, & composer

Ca·sa·no·va \,ka-zə-'nō-və, ,ka-sə-\ Giovanni Giacomo 1725–1798 *Chevalier de Seingalt* Ital. adventurer

Ca·sau·bon \kə-'sȯ-bən, ,ka-zō-'bōⁿ\ Isaac 1559–1614 Fr. theol. & scholar

Case·ment \'kās-mənt\ Sir Roger David 1864–1916 Irish rebel

Ca·si·mir–Pé·rier \'kä-zə-,mir-'per-ē-,ā\ Jean-Paul-Pierre 1847–1907 Fr. statesman; pres. of France (1894–95)

Cas·lon \'kaz-lən\ William 1692–1766 Eng. typefounder

Cass \'kas\ Lewis 1782–1866 Am. statesman

Cas·satt \kə-'sat\ Mary Stevenson 1845–1926 Am. painter in France

Cas·sin \ka-'saⁿ, kä-\ René-Samuel 1887–1976 Fr. statesman

Cas·si·o·do·rus \,ka-sē-ə-'dȯr-əs, -'dȯr-\ Flavius Magnus Aurelius *ca* 490–*ca* 585 Rom. statesman & author

Cas·sius Lon·gi·nus \'ka-sh(ē-)əs-,län-'jī-nəs, -s(ē-)əs-\ Gaius *d* 42 B.C. Rom. gen. & conspirator

Cas·te·lar y Ri·poll \,kas-tə-'lär-ē-rē-'pȯl'\ Emilio 1832–1899 Span. statesman & writer

Ca·stel·ve·tro \,kä-,stel-'ve-(,)trō\ Lodovico *ca* 1505–1571 Ital. critic & philologist

Ca·sti·glio·ne \,käs-tēl-'yō-(,)nā\ Baldassare 1478–1529 Ital. writer

Cas·ti·lho \kash-'tēl-(,)yü, kas-\ Antônio Feliciano de 1800–1875 Port. poet

Castlereagh Viscount — see Robert STEWART

Cas·tro \'kas-(,)trō, 'käs-\ Cipriano 1858–1924 Venezuelan gen.; pres. of Venezuela (1902–08)

Cas·tro \'käs-(,)trō\ Inés \ē-'nəs\ de 1320?–1355 Span. noblewoman

Castro (Ruz) \'rüs\ Fi·del \fē-'del\ 1926–   Cuban leader (1959–)

Cates·by \'käts-bē\ Mark 1679?–1749 Eng. naturalist

Catesby Robert 1573–1605 Eng. rebel

Cath·er \'ka-thər\ Willa Sibert 1873–1947 Am. nov.

Cath·er·ine \'ka-th(ə-)rən\ name of 1st, 5th, & 6th wives of Henry VIII of England: Catherine of Aragon 1485–1536; Catherine Howard 1520?–1542; Catherine Parr \'pär\ 1512–1548

Catherine I 1684–1727 *wife of Peter the Great* empress of Russia (1725–27)

Catherine II 1729–1796 *the Great* empress of Russia (1762–96)

Catherine of Bra·gan·za \brə-'gan-zə\ 1638–1705 *queen of Charles II of England*

Cath·er·ine de Mé·di·cis \,kä-mə-dē-'sēs, -'me-də-(,)chē *also* kà-'trēn-\ *It* **Ca·te·ri·na de' Me·di·ci** \,kä-tä-'rē-nä-dā-'me-dē-(,)chē\ 1519–1589 *queen of Henry II of France*

Cat·i·line \'ka-t^əl-,īn\ *ca* 108–62 B.C. *Lucius Sergius Cat·i·li·na* \,ka-t^əl-'i-nə, -'ē-nə\ Rom. polit. & conspirator

Cat·lin \kat-lən\ George 1796–1872 Am. artist

Ca·to \'kā-(,)tō\ Marcus Porcius 234–149 B.C. *the Elder; the Censor* Rom. statesman

Cato Marcus Porcius 95–46 B.C. *the Younger; great-grandson of prec.* Rom. statesman

Catt \'kat\ Carrie Chapman 1859–1947 née *Lane* Am. suffragist

Cat·tell \kə-'tel\ James McKeen 1860–1944 Am. psychol. & editor

Cat·ton \'ka-t^ən\ (Charles) Bruce 1899–1978 Am. journalist & hist.

Ca·tul·lus \kə-'tə-ləs\ Gaius Valerius *ca* 84–*ca* 54 B.C. Rom. poet

Cau·lain·court \,kō-,laⁿ-'kür\ Marquis Armand-Augustin-Louis de 1773–1827 Fr. gen. & diplomat

Ca·vell \'ka-vəl, kə-'vel\ Edith Louisa 1865–1915 Eng. nurse

Cav·en·dish \'ka-vən-(,)dish\ Henry 1731–1810 Eng. scientist

Cavendish Spencer Compton 1833–1908 8th Duke of *Devonshire* Eng. statesman

Cavendish Sir William 1505?–1557 Eng. statesman

Cavendish William 1640–1707 1st Duke of *Devonshire* Eng. statesman

Ca·vour \kə-'vu̇r, kä-\ Con·te \'kōn-(,)tā\ Camillo Benso di 1810–1861 Ital. statesman

Ca·xi·as \kə-'shē-əs\ Du·que \'dü-kə\ de 1803–1880 *Luiz Alves de Lima e Silva* Braz. gen. & statesman

Cax·ton \'kak-stən\ William *ca* 1422–1491 1st Eng. printer

Ceau·şes·cu \chau̇-'shes-(,)kü\ Nicolae 1918–1989 pres. of Romania (1974–1989)

Cech \'chek\ Thomas Robert 1947–   Am. biochem.

\ə\ abut \^ə\ kitten, F table \ər\ further \a\ ash \ā\ ace \ä\ mop, mar \au̇\ out \ch\ chin \e\ bet \ē\ easy \g\ go \i\ hit \ī\ ice \j\ job \ŋ\ sing \ō\ go \ȯ\ law \ȯi\ boy \th\ thin \ṯh\ the \ü\ loot \u̇\ foot \y\ yet \zh\ vision \à, k̲, ⁿ, œ, œ̄, ue, ūe, ^y\ *see* Guide to Pronunciation

Cec·il \'se-səl, 'si-\ (Edgar Algernon) Robert 1864–1958 1st Viscount *Cecil of Chel·wood* \'chel-ˌwud\ Eng. statesman
Cecil Lord (Edward Christian) David 1902–1986 Eng. biographer
Cecil Robert 1563–1612 1st Earl of *Salisbury* & 1st Viscount *Cranborne* \'kran-ˌbȯrn\ Eng. statesman
Cecil Robert Arthur Talbot Gas·coyne- \'gas-ˌkȯin\ 1830–1903 3d Marquis of *Salis·bury* \'sȯlz-b(ə-)rē, 'sälz-\ Eng. statesman
Cecil William 1520–1598 1st Baron *Burgh·ley* or *Bur·leigh* \'bər-lē\ Eng. statesman
Ce·la \'sā-lə\ Camilo José 1916–   Span. writer
Cel·li·ni \chə-'lē-nē\ Ben·ve·nu·to \ˌben-və-'nü-(ˌ)tō\ 1500–1571 Ital. goldsmith & sculptor
Cel·sius \'sel-sē-əs, -shəs\ Anders 1701–1744 Swed. astron.
Cen·ci \'chen-(ˌ)chē\ Be·a·tri·ce \ˌbä-ä-'trē-(ˌ)chä\ 1577–1599 Ital. woman executed for parricide
Cer·van·tes \sər-'van-ˌtēz, -'vän-ˌtäs\ Miguel de 1547–1616 full surname *Cervantes Saa·ve·dra* \ˌsä-(ə-)'vä-drə\ Span. writer
Cé·zanne \sā-'zan\ Paul 1839–1906 Fr. painter — **Cé·zann·esque** \(ˌ)sā-ˌza-'nesk\ *adj*
Cha·bri·er \ˌshä-brē-'ā, ˌsha-\ (Alexis-) Emmanuel 1841–1894 Fr. composer
Chad·wick \'chad-(ˌ)wik\ Sir James 1891–1974 Eng. physicist
Cha·gall \shə-'gäl, -'gal\ Marc 1887–1985 Russ. painter in France
Chag·a·tai \ˌcha-gə-'tī\ *or* **Jag·a·tai** \ˌja-\ *d* 1241 *2d son of Genghis Khan* Mongol ruler
Chain \'chān\ Ernst Boris 1906–1979 Brit. (Ger.-born) biochem.
Cha·lia·pin \shəl-'yä-(ˌ)pēn, -pən\ Fyodor Ivanovich 1873–1938 Russ. basso
Chal·mers \'chal-mərz, 'chä-mərz\ Alexander 1759–1834 Scot. biographer & editor
Cham·ber·lain \'chăm-bər-lən\ Joseph 1836–1914 & his sons Sir (Joseph) Austen 1863–1937 & (Arthur) Neville 1869–1940 Brit. statesmen
Chamberlain Owen 1920–   Am. physicist
Cham·ber·lin \'chăm-bər-lən\ Thomas Chrow·der \'kraü-dər\ 1843–1928 Am. geologist
Cham·bers \'chăm-bərz\ Robert 1802–1871 Scot. publisher & editor
Cham·bord \shäm-'bȯr\ Comte de 1820–1883 *Henri-Charles-Ferdinand=Marie Dieudonné d'Artois* Duc de Bordeaux Bourbon claimant to Fr. throne
Cha·mor·ro \chä-'mȯr-rō\ Violeta Barrios de 1929–   pres. of Nicaragua (1990–   )
Cham·plain \ˌsham-'plān, shän-plänⁿ\ Samuel de *ca* 1567–1635 Fr. navigator, explorer, & founder of Quebec
Cham·pol·lion \shäⁿ-pȯl-yōⁿ\ Jean-François 1790–1832 Fr. Egyptologist
Cham·pol·lion–Fi·geac \-fē-zhák\ Jacques-Joseph 1778–1867 *bro. of prec.* Fr. archaeol.
Chan·dra·gup·ta — see CANDRAGUPTA
Chandra Gupta II — see CANDRA GUPTA II
Chan·dra·se·khar \ˌchən-drə-'shä-kär\ Subrahmanyan 1910–   Am. (Indian-born) physicist
Cha·nel \shə-'nel, sha-\ Gabrielle 1883–1971 *Co·co* \'kō-(ˌ)kō\ Chanel Fr. fashion designer & perfumer
Chang Hsüeh-liang \'jäŋ-shü-'ä-lē-'äŋ\ *son of Chang Tso-lin* 1898–   Chin. gen.
Chang Tso-lin \-'(t)sō-'lin\ 1873–1928 Chin. gen.
Chan·ning \'cha-niŋ\ William Ellery 1780–1842 Am. clergyman
Chao K'uang-yin \'jaü-'kwäŋ-'yin\ 927–976 *T'ai Tsu* \'tīd-'zü\ Chin. emp. (960–976) & founder of Sung dynasty
Chap·lin \'cha-plən\ Sir Charles Spencer 1889–1977 Brit. actor & producer — **Chap·lin·esque** \ˌcha-plə-'nesk\ *adj*
Chap·man \'chap-mən\ Frank Mich·ler \'mi-klər\ 1864–1945 Am. ornithologist
Chapman George 1559?–1634 Eng. dram. & translator
Chapman John 1774–1845 *Johnny Ap·ple·seed* \'ap-əl-ˌsēd\ Am. pioneer
Char·cot \shär-'kō, 'shär-\ Jean-Mar·tin \'zhäⁿ-mär-'taⁿ\ 1825–1893 Fr. neurologist
Char·din \shär-'daⁿ\ Jean-Baptiste-Siméon 1699–1779 Fr. painter
Char·le·magne \'shär-lə-ˌmän\ 742–814 *Charles the Great* or *Charles I* Frankish king (768–814) & emp. of the West (800–814)
Charles I \'chär(-ə)lz\ 1600–1649 *Charles Stuart* king of Great Britain (1625–49)
Charles II 1630–1685 *son of Charles I* king of Great Britain (1660–85)
Charles 1948–   *son of Elizabeth II* prince of Wales
Charles 1771–1847 archduke of Austria
Charles I 1887–1922 *Charles Francis Joseph; nephew of Francis Ferdinand* emp. of Austria & (as *Charles IV*) king of Hungary (1916–18)
Charles I *or* **II** 823–877 *the Bald* king of France as *Charles I* (840–877); Holy Rom. emp. as *Charles II* (875–877)
Charles IV 1294–1328 *the Fair* king of France (1322–28)
Charles V 1337–1380 *the Wise* king of France (1364–80)
Charles VI 1368–1422 *the Mad* or *the Beloved* king of France (1380–1422)
Charles VII 1403–1461 king of France (1422–61)
Charles IX 1550–1574 king of France (1560–74)
Charles X 1757–1836 king of France (1824–30)
Charles V 1500–1558 Holy Rom. emp. (1519–56); king of Spain as *Charles I* (1516–56)
Charles XII 1682–1718 king of Sweden (1697–1718)
Charles Prince 1903–1983 *bro. of King Leopold* regent of Belgium (1944–50)
Charles XIV John 1763–1844 orig. *Jean-Baptiste-Jules Ber·na·dotte* \ber-nà-dȯt\ king of Sweden & Norway (1818–44)
Charles Edward 1720–1788 *the Young Pretender; (Bonnie) Prince Charlie* Brit. prince
Charles Mar·tel \-mär-'tel\ *ca* 688–741 *grandfather of Charlemagne* Frankish ruler (719–741)
Charlotte Empress of Mexico — see CARLOTA
Char·pak \shär-pák\ Georges 1924–   Fr. (Pol.-born) physicist
Chase \'chās\ Mary Ellen 1887–1973 Am educ. & author
Chase Sal·mon \'sa-mən, 'sal-\ Portland 1808–1873 Am. statesman; chief justice U.S. Supreme Court (1864–73)

Cha·teau·bri·and \(ˌ)sha-ˌtō-brē-'äⁿ\ Vi·comte \vē-kōⁿt\ François= Auguste-René de 1768–1848 Fr. author
Chatham 1st Earl of — see William PITT
Chatrian Alexandre — see ERCKMANN-CHATRIAN
Chat·ter·jee \'chä-tər-jē\ Ban·kim \'bȯŋ-kim\ Chan·dra \'chən-(ˌ)drə\ 1838–1894 Indian nov.
Chat·ter·ton \'cha-tər-tⁿn\ Thomas 1752–1770 Eng. poet
Chau·cer \'chȯ-sər\ Geoffrey *ca* 1342–1400 Eng. poet — **Chau·ce·ri·an** \chȯ-'sir-ē-ən\ *adj*
Chau·temps \shō-täⁿ\ Camille 1885–1963 Fr. lawyer & polit.; premier (1930; 1933–34; 1937–38)
Chavannes, de — see PUVIS DE CHAVANNES
Chá·vez \'chä-vəs, -ˌvez\ Carlos 1899–1978 Mex. conductor & composer
Chee·ver \'chē-vər\ John 1912–1982 Am. writer
Che·khov *also* **Che·kov** \'che-ˌkȯf, -ˌkȯv\ Anton Pavlovich 1860–1904 Russ. dram. & writer — **Che·kho·vi·an** \che-'kō-vē-ən\ *adj*
Ché·nier \shän-'yā\ André-Marie de 1762–1794 Fr. poet
Chen·nault \shə-'nȯlt\ Claire Lee 1890–1958 Am. gen.
Cheops — see KHUFU
Che·ren·kov \chə-'reŋ-kəf\ Pavel Alekseyevich 1904–1990 Russ. physicist
Cher·nen·ko \cher-'nyeŋ-kō\ Konstantin Ustinovich 1911–1985 Soviet polit.; pres. U.S.S.R. (1984–85); 1st secy. of Communist party (1984–85)
Cher·ny·shev·sky \ˌcher-ni-'shef-skē, -'shev\ Nikolay Gavrilovich 1829–1889 Russ. revolutionary & author
Che·ru·bi·ni \ˌker-ə-'bē-nē, ˌkä-rü-\ (Maria) Lu·i·gi \lü-'ē-(ˌ)jē\ Carlo Zenobio Salvatore 1760–1842 Ital. composer
Ches·ter·field \'ches-tər-ˌfēld\ 4th Earl of 1694–1773 *Philip Dormer Stan·hope* \'sta-nəp\ Eng. statesman & author
Ches·ter·ton \'ches-tər-tⁿn\ Gilbert Keith 1874–1936 Eng. journalist & author — **Ches·ter·to·nian** \ˌches-tər-'tō-nē-ən, -nyən\ *adj*
Che·va·lier \shə-'val-(ˌ)yā\ Mau·rice \mȯ-'rēs\ 1888–1972 Fr. entertainer
Chiang Kai–shek \jē-'äŋ-'kī-'shek, 'chaŋ-\ 1887–1975 pinyin *Jiang Jie·shi* \jē-'äŋ-jē-'ä-'shē\ Chin. gen. & polit.; pres. of China (1948–49; Taiwan, 1950–75)
Chi·ca·go \shə-'kä-(ˌ)gō, -'kȯ-, -gə\ Judy 1939–   orig. surname *Cohen* Am. artist
Ch'ien–lung \chē-'en-'lùŋ\ 1711–1799 Chin. emp. (1736–96)
Chi·ka·ma·tsu \ˌchē-kä-'mät-(ˌ)sü\ Monzaemon 1653–1724 *the Shakespeare of Japan* Jp. dram.
Child \'chī(ə)ld\ Francis James 1825–1896 Am. philologist & ballad editor
Childe \'chī(ə)ld\ Vere Gordon 1892–1957 Brit. anthropol. & archaeol.
Chil·ders \'chil-dərz\ Erskine Hamilton 1905–1974 Irish (Eng.-born) polit.; pres. of Ireland (1973–74)
Ch'in Shih Huang Ti \'chin-'shir-'hwäŋ-'dē\ *ca* 259–210 B.C. prename *Cheng* \'jeŋ\ Chin. emp. (221–210 B.C.)
Chip·pen·dale \'chi-pən-ˌdāl\ Thomas 1718–1779 Eng. cabinetmaker
Chi·rac \shē-räk\ Jacques-René 1932–   prime min. of France (1974–76; 1986–88); pres. (1995–)
Chi·ri·co, De \'kir-i-ˌkō, 'kē-ri-\ Gior·gio \'jȯr-(ˌ)jō\ 1888–1978 Ital. painter
Choate \'chōt\ Joseph Hodges 1832–1917 Am. lawyer & diplomat
Choate Rufus 1799–1859 Am. jurist
Choi·seul \shwä-'zəl, -'zər(-ə)l, -'zœl\ Étienne-François de 1719–1785 Duc *de Choiseul* Fr. statesman
Chom·sky \'chäm(p)-skē\ (Avram) Noam 1928–   Am. linguist — **Chom·sky·an** *also* **Chom·ski·an** \-skē-ən\ *adj*
Cho·pin \'shō-ˌpan, -ˌpaⁿ\ Frédéric François 1810–1849 Pol. pianist & composer
Chou En–lai \'jō-'en-'lī\ 1898–1976 pinyin *Zhou Enlai* Chin. Communist polit.
Chré·tien \krā-tyaⁿ\ (Joseph Jacques) Jean 1934–   prime min. of Canada (1993–)
Chré·tien de Troyes \krā-tyaⁿ-də-trwä\ *fl* 1170 Fr. trouvère
Christ Jesus — see JESUS
Chris·tian X \'kris-chən, 'krish-\ 1870–1947 king of Denmark (1912–47)
Chris·tie \'kris-tē\ Dame Agatha 1890–1976 née *Miller* Eng. writer
Chris·ti·na \kris-'tē-nə\ 1626–1689 *dau. of Gustav II Adolphus* queen of Sweden (1632–54)
Christine de Pi·san \krēs-tēn-də-pē-zäⁿ\ 1364–*ca* 1430 Fr. poet
Chris·to·phe \krē-stȯf\ Henri 1767–1820 king of Haiti (1811–20)
Chris·to·pher \'kris-tə-fər\ Warren Minor 1925–   U.S. secy. of state (1993–)
Chris·ty \'kris-tē\ Howard Chandler 1873–1952 Am. artist
Chry·sos·tom \'kri-səs-təm, kri-'säs-təm\ Saint John *ca* 347–407 church father & patriarch of Constantinople
Chu Hsi \'jü-'shē\ 1130–1200 Chin. philos.
Chun Doo–Hwan \'jùn-'dō-'hwän\ 1931–   pres. of So. Korea (1980–88)
Church \'chərch\ Frederic Edwin 1826–1900 Am. painter
Chur·chill \'chər-ˌchil, 'chərch-ˌhil\ John 1650–1722 1st Duke of *Marlbor·ough* \'märl-ˌbər-ə, 'mȯl-, -ˌbə-rə, -b(ə-)rə\ Eng. gen.
Churchill Randolph Henry Spencer 1849–1895 Lord *Randolph Churchill* Brit. statesman
Churchill Sir Winston Leonard Spencer 1874–1965 *son of Lord Randolph* Brit. statesman; prime min. (1940–45; 1951–55) — **Chur·chill·ian** \ˌchər-'chi-lē-ən, 'chərch-'hi-\ *adj*
Chu Teh \'jü-'də\ 1886–1976 Chin. gen.
Cia·no \'chä-(ˌ)nō\ Galeazzo 1903–1944 Conte *di Cortellazzo* Ital. statesman
Ciar·di \'chär-dē\ John 1916–1986 Am. poet
Cib·ber \'si-bər\ Col·ley \'kä-lē\ 1671–1757 Eng. dram. & actor; poet laureate (1730–57)
Cic·ero \'si-sə-ˌrō\ Marcus Tullius 106–43 B.C. Rom. statesman, orator, & author — **Cic·ero·nian** \ˌsi-sə-'rō-nyən, -nē-ən\ *adj*
Cid, El \'sid\ *ca* 1043–1099 *Rodrigo Dí·az de Vi·var* \'dē-äs-də-vē-'vär, -äz-\ Span. soldier & hero
Çil·ler \chi-'lesh\ Tan·su \tän-'sü\ 1946–   prime min. of Turkey (1993–)

Ci·ma·bue \,chē-mə-'bü-(,)ā\ Giovanni ca 1251-1302 orig. *Bencivieni di Pepo* Florentine painter

Ci·mon \'sī-mən, -,män\ ca 570-ca 451 B.C. Athenian gen. & statesman

Cin·cin·na·tus \,sin(t)-sə-'na-təs, -'nä-\ Lucius Quinctius b ca 519 B.C. Rom. gen. & statesman

Cis·ner·os \sis-'ner-(,)ōs\ Henry Gabriel 1947-   U.S. secy. of housing & urban development (1993-   )

Clare \'klar, 'kler\ John 1793-1864 Eng. poet

Clare of Assisi Saint 1194-1253 Ital. religious

Clarendon Earl of — see Edward HYDE

Clark \'klärk\ Champ \'champ\ 1850-1921 *James Beau-champ* \'bē-chəm\ *Clark* Am. polit.

Clark George Rogers 1752-1818 Am. soldier & frontiersman

Clark Joe 1939-   *Charles Joseph* Canad. polit.; prime min. (1979-80)

Clark Kenneth Bancroft 1914-   Am. psychol.

Clark Kenneth Mackenzie 1903-1983 Baron *Clark of Saltwood* Brit. art hist.

Clark Mark Wayne 1896-1984 Am. gen.

Clark Tom Campbell 1899-1977 Am. jurist

Clark William 1770-1838 *bro. of G.R.* Am. explorer

Clarke \'klärk\ Charles Cow·den \'kaü-dᵊn\ 1787-1877 & his wife Mary Victoria Cowden-Clarke 1809-1898 Eng. Shakespearean scholars

Claude \'klōd\ Albert 1898-1983 Belg. physiol. in U.S.

Claude Lor·rain \klōd-lȯ-raⁿ\ 1600-1682 pseud. of *Claude Gel·lée* \zhə-lā\ Fr. painter

Clau·di·us \'klȯ-dē-əs\ Rom. gens including: Ap·pi·us \'a-pē-əs\ Claudius Cras·sus \'kra-səs\ consul (471 & 451 B.C.) & decemvir (451-450 B.C.); Appius Claudius Cae·cus \'sē-kəs\ censor (312-307 B.C.), consul (307 & 296 B.C.), & dictator

Claudius I 10 B.C.-A.D. 54 *Tiberius Claudius Drusus Ne·ro* \'nē-(,)rō, 'nir-(,)ō\ *Germanicus* Rom. emp. (41-54)

Claudius II A.D. 214-270 *Marcus Aurelius Claudius Gothicus* Rom. emp. (268-270)

Clau·se·witz \'klaü-zə-,vits\ Carl von 1780-1831 Pruss. gen. & military strategist — Clau·se·witz·ian \,klaü-zə-'vit-sē-ən\ *adj*

Clay \'klā\ Henry 1777-1852 Am. statesman & orator

Clay Lucius Du Bi·gnon \dü-'bin-yən\ 1897-1978 Am. gen.

Cle·an·thes \klē-'an-,thēz\ 331(or 330)-232(or 231) B.C. Greek Stoic philos.

Cle·ar·chus \klē-'är-kəs\ 5th cent. B.C. Greek soldier; gov. of Byzantium

Cleis·the·nes \'klīs-thə-,nēz\ or Clis·the·nes \'klis-\ ca 570-after 508 B.C. Athenian statesman

Cle·men·ceau \,kle-mən-'sō, klā-mäⁿ-sō\ Georges 1841-1929 Fr. statesman

Clem·ens \'kle-mənz\ Samuel Langhorne 1835-1910 pseud. *Mark Twain* \'twān\ Am. writer

Clem·ent \'kle-mənt\ name of 14 popes: esp. VII (*Giulio de'Me·di·ci* \'me-də-(,)chē\) 1478-1534 (pope 1523-34)

Cle·men·ti \'klə-'men-tē\ Muzio 1752-1832 Ital. pianist & composer in England

Clement of Alexandria Saint ca 150-between 211 and 215 *Titus Flavius Cle·mens* \'kle-,menz\ Greek Christian theol. & church father

Cle·om·e·nes \klē-'ä-mə-,nēz\ name of 3 kings of Sparta: esp. III (reigned 235-222 B.C.)

Cle·o·pa·tra \klē-ə-'pa-trə, -'pä-\ 69-30 B.C. queen of Egypt (51-30)

Cleve·land \'klēv-lənd\ (Stephen) Grover 1837-1908 22d & 24th pres. of the U.S. (1885-89; 1893-97)

Cli·burn \'klī-bərn\ Van 1934-   *Harvey Lavan Cliburn* Am. pianist

Clin·ton \'klin-tᵊn\ De Witt 1769-1828 Am. statesman

Clinton George 1739-1812 vice pres. of the U.S. (1805-12)

Clinton Sir Henry 1738-1795 Eng. gen. in America

Clinton William Jefferson 1946-   Am. polit.; 42d pres. of the U.S. (1993-   )

Clive \'klīv\ Robert 1725-1774 Baron *Clive of Plassey* Brit. gen. & founder of the empire of Brit. India

Cloots \'klōts\ Baron de 1755-1794 *Jean-Baptiste du Val-de-Grâce*; known as An·a·char·sis \,a-nə-'kär-səs\ *Cloots* Pruss.-Fr. revolutionary

Clough \'kləf\ Arthur Hugh 1819-1861 Eng. poet

Clo·vis I \'klō-vəs\ G *Chlod·wig* \'klȯt-(,)vik\ ca 466-511 king of the Salian Franks (481-511)

Clyde Baron — see Colin CAMPBELL

Cnut see 'nüt, -'nyüt\ *var of* CANUTE

Coase \'kōz\ Ronald Harry 1910-   Am. (Brit.-born) econ.

Coates \'kōts\ Joseph Gordon 1878-1943 N. Z. statesman

Cobb \'käb\ Tyrus Raymond 1886-1961 *Ty* Am. baseball player

Cob·bett \'kä-bət\ William 1763-1835 pseud. *Peter Porcupine* Eng. polit. writer

Cob·den \'käb-dən\ Richard 1804-1865 Eng. statesman & econ.

Cobham Lord — see Sir John OLDCASTLE

Co·chise \kō-'chēs\ 1812?-1874 Chiricahua Apache Indian chief

Cock·croft \'kä(k)-,krȯft\ Sir John Douglas 1897-1967 Brit. physicist

Coc·teau \kȯk-'tō, kȯk-\ Jean 1889-1963 Fr. author & artist

Co·dy \'kō-dē\ William Frederick 1846-1917 *Buffalo Bill* Am. scout & showman

Coen \'kün\ Jan Pieterszoon 1587-1629 Du. colonial gov. & founder of Du. East Indian empire

Coeur de Lion — see RICHARD I of England

Cof·fin \'kȯ-fən, 'kä-\ Robert Peter Tristram 1892-1955 Am. author

Cog·gan \'kä-gən\ Frederick Donald 1909-   archbishop of Canterbury (1974-80)

Co·han \'kō-,han\ George Michael 1878-1942 Am. actor, dram., & producer

Co·hen \'kō-ən\ Stanley 1922-   Am. biochem.

Cohn \'kōn\ Ferdinand Julius 1828-1898 Ger. botanist

Coke \'kük, 'kōk\ Sir Edward 1552-1634 *Lord Coke* Eng. jurist

Col·bert \kȯl-'ber, 'kōl-,\ Jean-Baptiste 1619-1683 Fr. statesman & financier

Cole \'kōl\ Thomas 1801-1848 Am. (Eng.-born) painter

Cole·pep·er or Cul·pep·er \'kəl-,pe-pər\ Thomas 1635-1689 2d Baron *Colepeper* Eng. colonial administrator; gov. of Virginia

Cole·ridge \'kōl-rij, 'kō-lə-rij\ Samuel Taylor 1772-1834 Eng. poet — Cole·ridg·ean also Cole·ridg·ian \,kōl-'ri-jē-ən, ,kō-lə-\ *adj*

Col·et \'kä-lət\ John 1466(or 1467)-1519 Eng. theol. & scholar

Co·lette \kȯ-'let\ Sidonie-Gabrielle 1873-1954 Fr. author

Col·fax \'kōl-,faks\ Schuy·ler \'skī-lər\ 1823-1885 vice pres. of the U.S. (1869-73)

Co·li·gny \,kȯ-,lēn-'yē, kə-'lēn-yē\ Gaspard II de 1519-1572 *Seigneur de Châtillon* Fr. admiral & Huguenot leader

Col·lier \'käl-yər, 'kä-lē-ər\ Jeremy 1650-1726 Eng. clergyman

Collier John Payne 1789-1883 Eng. editor

Collier Peter Fen·e·lon \'fe-nᵊl-ən\ 1849-1909 Am. publisher

Col·lins \'kä-lənz\ Michael 1890-1922 Irish revolutionary

Collins Michael 1930-   Am. astronaut

Collins William 1721-1759 Eng. poet

Collins (William) Wilkie 1824-1889 Eng. nov.

Col·lor de Mel·lo \kō-'lȯr-də-'me-lü\ Fernando Affonso 1949-   pres. of Brazil (1990-92)

Col·man \'kōl-mən\ George 1732-1794 Eng. dram.

Col·um \'kä-ləm\ Pad·raic \'pȯth-rig\ 1881-1972 Am. (Irish-born) writer

Co·lum·ba \kə-'ləm-bə\ *Ir* Col·um \'kə-ləm\ or Col·um·cille \'kə-ləm-,kil\ Saint ca 521-597 Irish missionary in Scotland

Co·lum·bus \kə-'ləm-bəs\ Christopher *It* Christoforo Co·lom·bo \kə-'lōm-(,)bō\ *Sp* Cristóbal Co·lón \kə-'lōn\ 1451-1506 Genoese navigator & explorer for Spain

Co·me·ni·us \kə-'mē-nē-əs\ John Amos *Czech* Jan Ámos Ko·men·ský \'kȯ-mən-skē\ 1592-1670 Czech theol. & educ.

Com·ma·ger \'kä-mi-jər\ Henry Steele 1902-   Am. hist.

Com·mo·dus \'kä-mə-dəs\ Lucius Aelius Aurelius A.D. 161-192 Rom. emp. (180-192)

Com·mo·ner \'kä-mə-nər\ Barry 1917-   Am. biol. & educ.

Com·mynes or Co·mines or Com·mines \kȯ-'mēn\ Philippe de ca 1447-1511 Fr. polit. & chronicler

Comp·ton \'käm(p)-tən\ Arthur Holly 1892-1962 Am. physicist

Compton Karl Taylor 1887-1954 *bro. of A.H.* Am. physicist

Com·stock \'käm-,stäk also 'kəm-\ Anthony 1844-1915 Am. reformer

Comte \'kōⁿ(n)t\ Auguste 1798-1857 in full *Isidore-Auguste-Marie-François-Xavier* Fr. math. & philos.

Conan Doyle — see DOYLE

Co·nant \'kō-nənt\ James Bryant 1893-1978 Am. chem. & educ.

Con·dé \kōⁿ-dā\ Prince de 1621-1686 *Louis II de Bour·bon* \'bur-bən, bur-'bōⁿ\; Duc *d'En·ghien* \däⁿ-gaⁿ\ Fr. gen.

Con·don \'kän-dən\ Edward Uhler 1902-1974 Am. physicist

Con·dor·cet \kōⁿ-dȯr-sā\ Marquis de 1743-1794 *Marie-Jean-Antoine-Nicholas de Ca·ri·tat* \,kä-rē-'tä\ Fr. philos. & polit.

Con·fu·cius \kən-'fyü-shəs\ *Chin* K'ung-Fu-tzu \'kuŋ-'fü-'dzü\ or K'ung-tzu \,kuŋ-'dzü\ 551-479 B.C. Chin. philos.

Con·greve \'kän-,grēv, 'käŋ-\ William 1670-1729 Eng. dram.

Con·ing·ham \'kə-niŋ-,ham, *chiefly Brit* -niŋ-əm\ Sir Arthur 1895-1948 Brit. air marshal

Con·rad \'kän-,rad\ Joseph 1857-1924 orig. *Józef Teodor Konrad Korzeniow·ski* \,kȯ-zhən-'yȯf-skē, -'yȯv-\ Brit. (Ukrainian-born of Pol. parents) nov. — Con·rad·ian \,kän-'ra-dē-ən\ *adj*

Con·sta·ble \'kən(t)-stə-bəl, 'kän(t)-\ John 1776-1837 Eng. painter

Con·stant de Re·becque \kōⁿ-'stäⁿ-də-rə-'bek\ Benjamin 1767-1830 Fr. writer & polit.

Con·stan·tine \'kän(t)-stən-,tēn, -,tīn\ name of 2 kings of Greece: I 1868-1923 (reigned 1913-17; 1920-22); II 1940-   (reigned 1964-73; deposed)

Constantine I d 337 *the Great* Rom. emp. (306-337) — Con·stan·tin·ian \,kän(t)s-tən-'ti-nē-ən\ *adj*

Con·ta·ri·ni \,kän-tə-'rē-nē\ Venetian family including esp. Gasparo 1483-1542 cardinal & diplomat

Con·ti \'kōn-tē, 'kän-\ Niccolò de' ca 1395-1469 Venetian traveler

Cook \'kük\ James 1728-1779 Eng. navigator & explorer

Cooke \'kük\ (Alfred) Al·is·tair \'a-lə-stər\ 1908-   Am. (Brit.-born) essayist & journalist

Cooke Terence James 1921-1983 Am. cardinal

Coo·lidge \'kü-lij\ (John) Calvin 1872-1933 30th pres. of the U.S. (1923-29)

Cooper Anthony Ashley — see SHAFTESBURY

Coo·per \'kü-pər, 'kù-\ James Fen·i·more \'fen-ə-,mōr, -,mȯr\ 1789-1851 Am. nov.

Cooper Leon N. 1930-   Am. physicist

Cooper Peter 1791-1883 Am. manufacturer & philanthropist

Co·per·ni·cus \kō-'pər-ni-kəs\ Nicolaus *Pol* Mikołaj Ko·per·nik \kȯ-'per-nēk\ or Niklas Kop·per·nigk \'kä-pər-,nik\ 1473-1543 Pol. astron.

Cop·land \'kō-plənd\ Aaron 1900-1990 Am. composer

Cop·ley \'kä-plē\ John Sin·gle·ton \'siŋ-gəl-tən\ 1738-1815 Am. portrait painter

Co·que·lin \,kȯk-'laⁿ, ,kȯ-kə-\ Benoît-Constant 1841-1909 Fr. actor

Cor·bu·sier, Le \lə-kȯr-bües-'yā\ 1887-1965 orig. *Charles-Edouard Jean-ne-ret* \zhän-'ne-ret\ Fr. (Swiss-born) architect, painter, & sculptor

Cor·day \kȯr-'dā, 'kȯr-\ Charlotte 1768-1793 *Marie-Anne-Charlotte Corday d'Ar·mont* \där-'mōⁿ\ Fr. patriot

Co·rel·li \kə-'re-lē\ Arcangelo 1653-1713 Ital. violinist & composer

Co·rey \'kȯr-ē, 'kȯr-\ Elias James 1928-   Am. chem.

Co·ri \'kȯr-ē, 'kȯr-\ Carl Ferdinand 1896-1984 & his wife Ger·ty \'ger-tē\ Theresa 1896-1957 née *Rad·nitz* \'räd-,nits\ Am. (Czech-born) biochemists

Cor·mack \'kȯr-mək\ Allan MacLeod 1924-   Am. (So. African-born) physicist

Cor·neille \kȯr-'nā\ Pierre 1606-1684 Fr. dram.

Cor·ne·lia \kȯr-'nēl-yə, -'nē-lē-ə\ 2d cent. B.C. *Mother of the Gracchi* Rom. matron

Cornelia d 67? B.C. *wife of Julius Caesar*

\ə\ abut \ᵊ\ kitten, F table \ər\ further \a\ ash \ā\ ace \ä\ mop, mar \aü\ out \ch\ chin \e\ bet \ē\ easy \g\ go \i\ hit \ī\ ice \j\ job \ŋ\ sing \ō\ go \ȯ\ law \ȯi\ boy \th\ thin \th\ the \ü\ loot \ù\ foot \y\ yet \zh\ vision \à, k̲, ⁿ, œ, œ̄, ue, ūe, ᵞ\ see Guide to Pronunciation

Cor·ne·lius \kȯr-'nāl-yəs, -'nā-lē-əs\ Pe·ter \'pā-tər\ von 1783–1867 Ger. painter

Cor·nell \kȯr-'nel\ Ezra 1807–1874 Am. financier & philanthropist

Cornell Katharine 1893–1974 Am. actress

Corn·forth \'kȯrn-farth, -,fȯrth, -,fȯrth\ John Warcup 1917– Brit. (Austral.-born) chem.

Corn·wal·lis \kȯrn-'wä-ləs\ 1st Marquis 1738–1805 Charles Cornwallis Brit. gen. & statesman

Co·ro·na·do \,kȯr-ə-'nä-(,)dō, ,kär-\ Francisco Vásquez de ca 1510–1554 Span. explorer & conquistador

Co·rot \kȯ-'rō, kō-\ Jean-Baptiste-Camille 1796–1875 Fr. painter

Cor·reg·gio \kə-'re-j(ē-,)ō\ 1494–1534 Antonio Allegri da Correggio Ital. painter

Cor·ri·gan \'kȯr-i-gən\ Mairead 1944– Irish peace worker

Cor·tés \kȯr-'tez, ,kȯr-,\ Hernán or Hernando 1485–1547 Span. conquistador

Cos·grave \'käz-,grāv\ Liam 1920– prime min. of Ireland (1973–77)

Cosgrave William Thomas 1880–1965 father of Liam Irish statesman

Cos·ta Ca·bral \,kȯsh-tə-kə-'bräl, ,kȯs-\ António Bernardo da 1803–1889 Conde de Thomar Port. statesman

Cos·tel·lo \'käs-tə-,lō\ John Aloysius 1891–1976 prime min. of Ireland (1948–51; 1954–57)

Cot·ton \'kä-tᵊn\ Charles 1630–1687 Eng. author & translator

Cotton John 1585–1652 Am. (Eng.-born) Puritan clergyman

Co·ty \kȯ-'tē, kō-\ René-Jules-Gustave 1882–1962 Fr. lawyer; 2d pres. of 4th Republic (1954–59)

Cou·lomb \kü-lōⁿ; 'kü-,läm, -,lōm, kü-'\ Charles-Augustin de 1736–1806 Fr. physicist

Cou·pe·rin \,kü-'pər, ,kü-pə-\ François 1668–1733 Fr. composer

Cou·pe·rus \kü-'pā-rəs, -'per-əs\ Louis Marie Anne 1863–1923 Du. nov.

Cour·bet \kur-'bä\ Gustave 1819–1877 Fr. painter

Cour·nand \kur-'näⁿ\ André Frédéric 1895–1988 Am. (Fr.-born) physiol.

Cou·sin \kü-zaⁿ\ Victor 1792–1867 Fr. philos.

Cous·ins \'kə-zᵊnz\ Norman 1912–1990 Am. editor & essayist

Cous·teau \kü-'stō\ Jacques-Yves 1910– Fr. marine explorer

Co·var·ru·bias \,kō-və-'rü-bē-əs\ Miguel 1904–1957 Mex. artist

Cov·er·dale \'kə-vər-,dāl\ Miles 1488?–1569 Eng. Bible translator

Cow·ard \'kau̇(-ə)rd\ Sir Noël Peirce 1899–1973 Eng. actor & dram.

Cow·ell \'kau̇-(ə)l\ Henry Dixon 1887–1965 Am. composer

Cow·en \'kau̇-ən, 'kō-\ Sir Zelman 1919– gov.-gen. of Australia (1977–82)

Cowl \'kau̇(ə)l\ Jane 1883–1950 orig. Cowles Am. actress

Cow·ley \'kau̇-lē\ Abraham 1618–1667 Eng. poet

Cowley Malcolm 1898–1989 Am. lit. critic

Cow·per \'kü-pər, 'kü-, 'kau̇-\ William 1731–1800 Eng. poet

Cox·ey \'käk-sē\ Jacob Sechler 1854–1951 Am. polit. reformer

Coz·zens \'kə-zᵊnz\ James Gould 1903–1978 Am. author

Crabbe \'krab\ George 1754–1832 Eng. poet

Craig·av·on \krä-'ga-vən\ 1st Viscount 1871–1940 James Craig Brit. statesman; 1st prime min. of Northern Ireland (1921–40)

Crai·gie \'krä-gē\ Sir William Alexander 1867–1957 Brit. philologist & lexicographer

Cram \'kram\ Donald James 1919– Am. chem.

Cram Ralph Adams 1863–1942 Am. architect & author

Cra·nach \'krä-,näk\ Lucas 1472–1553 Ger. painter & engraver

Cranborne Viscount — see Robert CECIL

Crane \'krän\ (Harold) Hart 1899–1932 Am. poet

Crane Stephen 1871–1900 Am. writer

Crane Walter 1845–1915 Eng. artist

Cran·mer \'kran-mər\ Thomas 1489–1556 Eng. reformer; archbishop of Canterbury (1533–56)

Cras·sus \'kra-səs\ Marcus Licinius 115?–53 B.C. Di·ves \'dī-(,)vēz\ Rom. polit.

Crazy Horse \'krä-zē-,hȯrs\ 1842–1877 Ta-sunko-witko or Tashunca= Uitco Sioux Indian chief

Cré·bil·lon \,krā-bē-'yōⁿ\ 1674–1762 pseud. of Prosper Jolyot Fr. dram.

Cre·mer \'krē-mər\ Sir William Randal 1838–1908 Eng. pacifist

Cres·ton \'kres-tən\ Paul 1906–1985 orig. Giuseppe Guttoveggio Am. composer

Crève·coeur \krev-'kər, krēv-, -'kur\ Michel-Guillaume-Jean de 1735–1813 pseud. J. Hector St. John Am. (Fr.-born) essayist

Crich·ton \'kri-tᵊn\ James 1560–1582 the Admirable Crichton Scot. man of letters

Crick \'krik\ Francis Harry Compton 1916– Brit. biophysicist

Crile \'krī(ə)l\ George Washington 1864–1943 Am. surgeon

Cripps \'krips\ Sir (Richard) Stafford 1889–1952 Brit. statesman

Cri·spi \'kris-pē, 'krēs\ Francesco 1819–1901 Ital. statesman; premier (1887–91; 1893–96)

Cris·ti·ani \,kris-tē-'ä-nē\ Alfredo 1947– pres. of El Salvador (1989–94)

Cro·ce \'krō-(,)chā\ Benedetto 1866–1952 Ital. philos. & statesman

Crock·ett \'krä-kət\ David 1786–1836 Davy Am. frontiersman & polit.

Croe·sus \'krē-səs\ d ca 546 B.C. king of Lydia (ca 560–546)

Cro·ker \'krō-kər\ John Wilson 1780–1857 Brit. essayist & editor

Cromer 1st Earl of — see Evelyn BARING

Cromp·ton \'kräm(p)-tən\ Samuel 1753–1827 Eng. inventor

Crom·well \'kräm-,wel, 'kram-, -wəl\ Oliver 1599–1658 Eng. gen. & statesman; lord protector of England (1653–58) — Crom·well·ian \kräm-'we-lē-ən, ,krəm-\ adj

Cromwell Richard 1626–1712 son of Oliver lord protector (1658–59)

Cromwell Thomas 1485?–1540 Earl of Essex Eng. statesman

Cro·nin \'krō-nən\ Archibald Joseph 1896–1981 Eng. physician & nov.

Cronin James Watson 1931– Am. physicist

Cron·jé \krōn-'yä\ Piet Arnoldus ca 1835–1911 Boer leader & gen.

Crookes \'kruks\ Sir William 1832–1919 Eng. physicist & chem.

Cross \'krȯs\ Wilbur Lucius 1862–1948 Am. educ. & polit.

Crouse \'kraus\ Russel 1893–1966 Am. journalist & dram.

Cru·den \'krü-dᵊn\ Alexander 1701–1770 Scot. compiler of a biblical concordance

Cruik·shank \'kruk-,shaŋk\ George 1792–1878 Eng. caricaturist & illustrator

Cruz \'krüs\ Juana Inés de la 1651–1695 orig. Juana Inés de Asbaje Mex. religious & poet

Cud·worth \'kəd-(,)wərth\ Ralph 1617–1688 Eng. philos.

Cul·pep·er \'kəl-,pe-pər\ var of COLEPEPER

Cum·mings \'kə-miŋz\ Edward Estlin 1894–1962 known as e. e. cummings Am. poet

Cu·nha \'kün-yə\ Tris·tão da \,tris-tən-də-'kü-nə, trēsh-,tauⁿ-də-'kün-yə, trēs-\ 1460–1540 Port. navigator & explorer

Cun·ning·ham \'kə-niŋ-,ham, chiefly Brit -niŋ-əm\ Allan 1784–1842 Scot. author

Cunningham Merce 1919?– Am. choreographer

Cu·rie \kyü-'rē, 'kyur-(,)ē\ Eve 1904– dau. of Marie & Pierre Am. (Fr.-born) author

Curie Marie 1867–1934 née Maria Skło·dow·ska \skłə-'dȯf-skə, -'dȯv-\ Fr. (Pol.-born) chem.

Curie Pierre 1859–1906 husband of Marie Fr. chem.

Curie Joliot — see JOLIOT-CURIE

Cur·ley \'kər-lē\ James Michael 1874–1958 Am. polit.

Cur·ri·er \'kər-ē-ər, 'kə-rē-\ Nathaniel 1813–1888 Am. lithographer

Cur·ry \'kər-ē, 'kə-rē\ John Steuart 1897–1946 Am. painter

Cur·tin \'kər-tᵊn\ John 1885–1945 Austral. polit.; prime min. (1941–45)

Cur·tis \'kər-təs\ Charles 1860–1936 vice pres. of the U.S. (1929–33)

Curtis Cyrus Hermann Kotzschmar 1850–1933 Am. publisher

Curtis George Ticknor 1812–1894 Am. lawyer & writer

Curtis George William 1824–1892 Am. author & editor

Cur·tiss \'kər-təs\ Glenn Hammond 1878–1930 Am. aviator & inventor

Cur·ti·us \'kurt-sē-əs\ Ernst 1814–1896 Ger. hist. & archaeol.

Cur·wen \'kər-wən\ John 1816–1880 Eng. music teacher

Cur·zon \'kər-zᵊn\ George Nathaniel 1859–1925 1st Baron & 1st Marquis Curzon of Ked·le·ston \'ke-dᵊl-stən\ Eng. statesman; viceroy of India (1899–1905)

Cush·ing \'ku-shiŋ\ Caleb 1800–1879 Am. lawyer & diplomat

Cushing Harvey 1869–1939 Am. surgeon

Cushing Richard James 1895–1970 Am. cardinal

Cush·man \'kush-mən\ Charlotte Saunders 1816–1876 Am. actress

Cus·ter \'kəs-tər\ George Armstrong 1839–1876 Am. gen.

Cuth·bert \'kəth-bərt\ Saint 635?–687 Eng. monk

Cu·vier \'kü-vē-,ā, 'kyü-, kū̄-vyä\ Baron Georges 1769–1832 orig. Jean-Léopold-Nicolas-Frédéric Cuvier Fr. naturalist

Cuyp or Cuijp \'kīp\ Aelbert Jacobsz 1620–1691 Du. painter

Cyn·e·wulf \'ki-nə-,wulf\ or Cyn·wulf \'kin-,wulf\ 9th cent. Anglo= Saxon poet

Cyp·ri·an \'si-prē-ən\ Saint d 258 Thascius Caecilius Cyprianus Christian martyr; bishop of Carthage (ca 248–258)

Cy·ran·kie·wicz \,(t)sir-ən-'kyä-vich\ Józef 1911–1989 Pol. polit.; prime min. (1947–52; 1954–70)

Cy·ra·no de Ber·ge·rac \'sir-ə-,nō-də-'ber-zhə-,rak\ Savinien de 1619–1655 Fr. poet & soldier

Cyr·il \'sir-əl\ Saint ca 827–869 Constantine apostle to the Slavs

Cy·rus II \'sī-rəs\ ca 585–ca 529 B.C. the Great or the Elder king of Persia (ca 550–529)

Cyrus 424?–401 B.C. the Younger Persian prince & satrap

Czer·ny \'cher-nē, 'chər-\ Carl 1791–1857 Austrian pianist & composer

D' \d-\, De \də-, di-; in Dutch names dē-\, Du \dü, dyü-, də-\, etc. for many names beginning with these elements see the specific family names

Da·guerre \də-'ger\ Louis-Jacques-Mandé 1789–1851 Fr. painter & inventor

Daim·ler \'dīm-lər\ Gottlieb Wilhelm 1834–1900 Ger. automotive manuf.

Da·kin \'dā-kən\ Henry Drysdale 1880–1952 Eng. chem.

Da·la·dier \də-'lä-dē-,ā, ,da-lə-'dyä\ Edouard 1884–1970 Fr. statesman

Da·lai La·ma \'dä-,lī-'lä-mə\ 1935– Tenzin Gyatso Tibetan religious & political leader

D' Al·bert \'dal-bərt\ Eugen Francis Charles 1864–1932 Scot. pianist & composer

Dalcroze Émile Jaques — see Émile JAQUES-DALCROZE

Dale \'dā(ə)l\ Sir Henry Hallett 1875–1968 Eng. physiol.

Dale Sir Thomas d 1619 Eng. colonial administrator in Virginia

Da·lén \də-'län\ Nils Gustaf 1869–1937 Swed. inventor

Da·ley \'dā-lē\ Richard Joseph 1902–1976 Am. polit.

Dal·housie Earl & Marquis of — see RAMSAY

Da·lí \'dä-lē, by himself dä-'lē\ Salvador 1904–1989 Span. surrealistic painter — Da·li·esque \,dä-lē-'esk\ adj

Dal·las \'da-ləs, -lis\ George Mifflin 1792–1864 vice pres. of the U.S. (1845–49)

Dal·rym·ple \dal-'rim-pəl, 'dal-,\ Sir James 1619–1695 1st Viscount Stair \'ster\ Scot. jurist

Dalrymple Sir John 1673–1747 2d Earl of Stair Brit. gen. & diplomat

Dal·ton \'dȯl-tᵊn\ Baron 1887–1962 Hugh Dalton Brit. polit.

Dalton John 1766–1844 Eng. chem. & physicist

Da·ly \'dā-lē\ (John) Augustin 1838–1899 Am. dram. & theater manager

Dam \'dam, 'däm\ (Carl Peter) Henrik 1895–1976 Dan. biochem.

Da·mien \'dä-mē-ən, ,da-mē-'aⁿ\ Father 1840–1889 orig. Joseph de Veuster Belg. R.C. missionary in Hawaiian islands

Dam·pi·er \'dam-pē-ər\ William 1652–1715 Eng. buccaneer & navigator

Dam·rosch \'dam-,räsh\ Walter Johannes 1862–1950 Am. (Ger.-born) musician & conductor

Da·na \'dä-nə\ Charles Anderson 1819–1897 Am. newspaper editor

Dana James Dwight 1813–1895 Am. geologist

Dana Richard Henry 1815–1882 Am. lawyer & author

Dane \'dän\ Clemence 1888–1965 pseud. of Winifred Ash·ton \'ash-tən\ Eng. nov.

Dan·iel \'dan-yəl\ Samuel 1562?–1619 Eng. poet

Dan·iels \'dan-yəlz\ Josephus 1862–1948 Am. journalist & statesman

Da·ni·lo·va \də-'nē-lə-və\ Aleksandra 1903?– Am. (Russ.-born) choreographer & dancer

D'An·nun·zio \dä-'nün(t)-sē-,ō\ Gabriele 1863–1938 Ital. author & soldier

Dan·te \\'dän-(,)tā, 'dan-, -(,)tē\\ 1265–1321 *Dante* or *Durante Ali·ghie·ri* \\,a-lə-'gyer-ē\\ Ital. poet — **Dan·te·an** \\'dan-tē-ən, 'dän-\\ or **Dan·tes·can** \\dan-'tes-kən, dän-\\ or **Dan·tesque** \\-'tesk\\ *adj*

Dan·ton \\dän-tōⁿ\\ Georges-Jacques 1759–1794 Fr. revolutionary

Dare \\'dar, 'der\\ Virginia 1587–? 1st child born in America of Eng. parents

Da·ri·us \\də-'rī-əs\\ name of 3 kings of Persia: esp. **I** 550–486 B.C. (reigned 522–486) *Darius Hys·tas·pes* \\his-'tas-pəs\\; *the Great*

Dar·lan \\där-'läⁿ\\ Jean-Louis-Xavier-François 1881–1942 Fr. admiral

Darn·ley \\'därn-lē\\ Lord 1545–1567 *Henry Stewart* or *Stuart; husband of Mary, Queen of Scots*

Dar·row \\'dar-(,)ō\\ Clarence Seward 1857–1938 Am. lawyer & author

Dar·win \\'där-wən\\ Charles Robert 1809–1882 Eng. naturalist

Darwin Erasmus 1731–1802 *grandfather of C. R.* Eng. physiol. & poet

Dau·bi·gny \\,dō-bēn-'yē, dō-'bē-nyē\\ Charles-François 1817–1878 Fr. painter

Dau·det \\dō-'dā\\ Alphonse 1840–1897 Fr. nov.

Daudet Léon 1867–1942 *son of Alphonse* Fr. journalist & writer

Dau·mier \\dō-myā, 'dō-mē-,ā\\ Honoré 1808–1879 Fr. caricaturist & painter

Daus·set \\dō-se, -sā\\ Jean-Baptiste-Gabriel 1916–   Fr. physician

Dav·e·nant or **D'Av·e·nant** \\'dav-nənt, 'da-və-\\ Sir William 1606–1668 Eng. poet & dram.; poet laureate (1638–68)

Dav·en·port \\'da-vən-,pört, 'da-v^əm-, -,pórt\\ John 1597–1670 Am. (Eng.-born) clergyman & founder of New Haven colony

Da·vid I \\'dä-vəd\\ *ca* 1082–1153 king of Scotland (1124–53)

Da·vid \\'dä-vət\\ Gerard *ca* 1460–1523 Du. painter

Da·vid \\dä-'vēd\\ Jacques-Louis 1748–1825 Fr. painter

Da·vid d'An·gers \\däⁿ-'zhä\\ Pierre-Jean 1788–1856 Fr. sculptor

Da·vid·son \\'dä-vəd-sən\\ Jo 1883–1952 Am. sculptor

Davidson Randall Thomas 1848–1930 archbishop of Canterbury (1903–28)

Da·vies \\'dä-vēz\\ Arthur Bowen 1862–1928 Am. painter

Davies (William) Robertson 1913–   Canad. author

Dá·vi·la Pa·di·lla \\'dä-vi-lə-pä-'dē-yə\\ Agustín 1562–1604 Mex. monk & hist.

Da·vis \\'dä-vəs\\ Bet·te \\'be-tē\\ 1908–1989 orig. *Ruth Elizabeth Davis* Am. actress

Davis Dwight Filley 1879–1945 Am. statesman

Davis Elmer Holmes 1890–1958 Am. radio broadcaster & news commentator

Davis Harold Le·noir \\lə-'nór, -'nòr\\ 1896–1960 Am. writer

Davis Jefferson 1808–1889 Am. statesman; pres. of Confed. states (1861–65)

Davis Miles 1926–1991 Am. jazz composer & musician

Da·vis·son \\'dä-və-sən\\ Clinton Joseph 1881–1958 Am. physicist

Da·vout \\dä-'vü\\ Louis-Nicolas 1770–1823 Duc *d'Au·er·städt* \\'daú(-ə)r-,stet\\ & Prince *d'Eck·mühl* \\'dek-,myül\\ marshal of France

Da·vy \\'dä-vē\\ Sir Humphry 1778–1829 Eng. chem.

Dawes \\'dòz\\ Charles Gates 1865–1951 Am. lawyer & financier; vice pres. of U.S. (1925–29)

Daw·son \\'dò-s^ən\\ Sir John William 1820–1899 Canad. geologist

Day \\'dā\\ Clarence Shepard, Jr. 1874–1935 Am. author

Day Thomas 1748–1789 Eng. author

Day William Rufus 1849–1923 Am. statesman & jurist

Da·yan \\dī-'än\\ Moshe 1915–1981 Israeli soldier & polit.

Day–Le·wis \\'dä-'lü-əs\\ Cecil 1904–1972 pseud. *Nicholas Blake* Brit. writer; poet laureate (1968–72)

De·ák \\dā-,äk\\ Fe·renc \\'fer-,en(t)s\\ 1803–1876 Hung. statesman

Dean \\'dēn\\ Sir Patrick 1909–1994 Brit. diplomat

Deane \\dēn\\ Silas 1737–1789 Am. lawyer & diplomat

De·bierne \\də-'byern\\ André-Louis 1874–1949 Fr. chem.

De·breu \\də-'brœ\\ Gerard 1921–   Am. (Fr.-born) econ.

Debs \\'debz\\ Eugene Victor 1855–1926 Am. socialist

De·bus·sy \\,de-byü-'sē, ,dä-; də-'byü-sē\\ (Achille-) Claude 1862–1918 Fr. composer — **De·bus·sy·an** \\de-byü-'sē-ən, ,dä-; də-'byü-sē-ən\\ *adj*

De·bye \\də-'bī\\ Peter Joseph William 1884–1966 Am. (Du.-born) physicist

De·ca·tur \\di-'kā-tər\\ Stephen 1779–1820 Am. naval officer

De·cazes \\də-käz\\ Duc Élie 1780–1860 Fr. statesman

De·cius \\'dē-sh(ē-)əs\\ Gaius Messius Quintus Trajanus *ca* 201–251 Rom. emp. (249–51)

Dee·ping \\'dē-piŋ\\ (George) Warwick 1877–1950 Eng. nov.

Deere \\'dir\\ John 1804–1886 Am. inventor

Def·fand, du \\dä-fäⁿ\\ Marquise 1697–1780 née *Marie de Vichy-Chamrond* \\də-vē-shē-shä-rōⁿ\\ Fr. woman of letters

De·foe \\di-'fō\\ Daniel 1660–1731 Eng. journalist & nov.

De For·est \\di-'fòr-əst, -'fär-\\ Lee 1873–1961 Am. inventor

De·gas \\də-gä\\ (Hilaire-Germain-) Edgar 1834–1917 Fr. artist

de Gaulle Charles — see GAULLE

De Gennes \\də-zhen\\ Pierre-Gilles 1932–   Fr. physicist

Deh·melt \\'dā-məlt\\ Hans Georg 1922–   Am. (Ger.-born) physicist

Dei·sen·hof·er \\'dī-zən-,hō-fər\\ Johann 1943–   Ger. biochem.

Dek·ker \\'de-kər\\ Thomas 1572?–?1632 Eng. dram.

de Klerk \\də-'klərk, -'klerk\\ Frederik Willem 1936–   pres. of Republic of So. Africa (1989–94); vice pres. (1994–   )

de Koo·ning \\də-'kö-niŋ\\ Willem 1904–   Am. (Du.-born) painter

de Kruif \\də-'krif\\ Paul Henry 1890–1971 Am. bacteriol. & author

De·la·croix \\,de-lə-'k(r)wä\\ (Ferdinand-Victor-) Eugène 1798–1863 Fr. painter

de la Mare \\,de-lə-'mar, -'mer\\ Walter John 1873–1956 Eng. poet & nov.

De·land \\də-'land\\ Margaret 1857–1945 née *Margaretta Wade Campbell* Am. nov.

De La Rey \\,de-lə-'rī, -'rā\\ Jacobus Hercules 1847–1914 Boer gen. & statesman

De·la·roche \\,de-lə-'rōsh, -'rósh\\ (Hippolyte-) Paul 1797–1859 Fr. painter

De·la·vigne \\,de-lə-'vēn^y, -'vēn-yə\\ Jean-François-Casimir 1793–1843 Fr. poet & dram.

De La Warr \\'de-lə-,war, -,wer\\ Baron 1577–1618 *Thomas West; Lord Delaware* Eng. colonial administrator in America

Del·brück \\'del-,bruek, -,brük\\ Max 1906–1981 Am. (Ger.-born) biol.

De·led·da \\dā-'le-də, də-\\ Grazia 1875–1936 Ital. author

De·libes \\də-'lēb\\ (Clément-Philibert-) Léo 1836–1891 Fr. composer

De·lius \\'dē-lē-əs, 'dēl-yəs\\ Frederick 1862–1934 Eng. composer

Del·la Rob·bia \\,de-lə-'rä-bē-ə, -'rō\\ Luca 1399(or 1400)–1482 orig. *Luca di Simone di Marco* Florentine sculptor

De Long \\də-'lòŋ\\ George Washington 1844–1881 Am. naval officer & explorer

De·lorme or **de l'Orme** \\de-'lòrm\\ Philibert 1515?–1570 Fr. architect

de Mille \\də-'mil\\ Agnes George 1905–1993 Am. dancer & choreographer

De·Mille \\də-'mil\\ Cec·il \\'se-səl\\ Blount \\'blənt\\ 1881–1959 Am. film director & producer

De·moc·ri·tus \\di-'mä-krə-təs\\ *ca* 460–*ca* 370 B.C. *the Laughing Philosopher* Greek philos.

De Mor·gan \\di-'mòr-gən\\ William Frend 1839–1917 Eng. artist & nov.

De·mos·the·nes \\di-'mäs-thə-,nēz\\ 384–322 B.C. Athenian orator & statesman — **De·mos·then·ic** \\di-,mäs-'the-nik, ,dē-, -'thē-\\ *adj*

Demp·sey \\'dem(p)-sē\\ William Harrison 1895–1983 *Jack* Am. boxer

Deng Xiaoping — see TENG HSIAO-P'ING

De·ni·ker \\,dā-nē-'ker\\ Joseph 1852–1918 Fr. anthropol.

De·nis or **De·nys** \\'de-nəs, də-nē\\ Saint *d* 258? 1st bishop of Paris & patron saint of France

Dent \\'dent\\ Joseph Mal·a·by \\'ma-lə-bē\\ 1849–1926 Eng. publisher

De·pew \\di-'pyü\\ Chauncey Mitchell 1834–1928 Am. lawyer & polit.

De Quin·cey \\di-'kwin(t)-sē, -'kwin-zē\\ Thomas 1785–1859 Eng. author

De·rain \\də-raⁿ\\ André 1880–1954 Fr. painter

Der·ri·da \\de-rē-dä\\ Jacques 1930–   Fr. philos. & critic — **Der·ri·de·an** *also* **Der·ri·di·an** \\,de-ri-'dē-ən\\ *adj*

Der·win·ski \\dər-'win-skē\\ Edward Joseph 1926–   U.S. secy. of veterans affairs (1989–93)

Der·zha·vin \\der-'zhä-vən\\ Gavrila Romanovich 1743–1816 Russ. poet

De·sai \\de-'sī\\ Morarji Ranchhodji 1896–1995 prime min. of India (1977–79)

De·saix de Vey·goux \\də-'sä-də-(,)vā-'gü\\ Louis-Charles-Antoine 1768–1800 Fr. gen.

De·sargues \\dā-'zärg\\ Gérard or Girard 1591–1661 Fr. math.

Des·cartes \\dā-'kärt\\ René 1596–1650 L. *Renatus Cartesius* Fr. math. & philos.

Des·cha·nel \\,dā-shə-'nel\\ Paul-Eugène-Louis 1855–1922 Fr. statesman; pres. of France (1920)

De Se·ver·sky \\də-sə-'ver-skē\\ Alexander Procofieff 1894–1974 Am. (Russ.-born) aeronautical engineer

Des·mou·lins \\dā-mü-laⁿ\\ Camille 1760–1794 *Lucie-Simplice-Camille-Benoît Desmoulins* Fr. revolutionary

de Soto Hernando — see SOTO, DE

Des Prez Josquin — see JOSQUIN DES PREZ

Des·saix \\dā-'sä\\ Comte Joseph-Marie 1764–1834 Fr. gen.

Des·sa·lines \\,dā-sə-'lēn, ,de-\\ Jean-Jacques 1758?–1806 emp. as *Jacques I* \\zhäk\\ of Haiti (1804–06)

De·taille \\də-'tī\\ (Jean-Baptiste-) Édouard 1848–1912 Fr. painter

De·us Ra·mos \\'dā-əsh-'ra-(,)müsh\\ João \\'zhwaúⁿ\\ de 1830–1896 Port. poet

De Va·le·ra \\,de-və-'ler-ə, -'lir-ə\\ Ea·mon \\'ā-mən\\ 1882–1975 Irish polit.; prime min. of Ireland (1937–48; 1951–54; 1957–59); pres. of Ireland (1959–73)

De Vere \\də-'vir\\ Aubrey Thomas 1814–1902 Irish poet

Dev·er·eux \\'de-və-,rüks, -,rü\\ Robert 1566–1601 2d Earl of *Essex* Eng. soldier & courtier

Devonshire dukes of — see CAVENDISH

De Vo·to \\di-'vō-(,)tō\\ Bernard Augustine 1897–1955 Am. author

De Vries Hugo — see VRIES, DE

Dew·ar \\'dü-ər, 'dyü-\\ Sir James 1842–1923 Scot. chem. & physicist

De Wet Christiaan Rudolph — see WET, DE

Dew·ey \\'dü-ē, 'dyü-\\ George 1837–1917 Am. admiral

Dewey John 1859–1952 Am. philos. & educ. — **Dew·ey·an** \\-ən\\ *adj*

Dewey Melvil 1851–1931 Am. librarian

Dewey Thomas Edmund 1902–1971 Am. lawyer & polit.

De Witt Johan — see WITT, DE

De Witte Emanuel — see WITTE, DE

Dia·ghi·lev \\dē-'ä-gə-,lef\\ Sergey Pavlovich 1872–1929 Russ. ballet producer & art critic

Di·as \\'dē-,äsh\\ Bartholomeu *ca* 1450–1500 Port. navigator

Di·az \\'dē-,äts\\ Armando 1861–1928 Duca *della Vittoria* Ital. gen.; marshal of Italy

Dí·az \\'dē-,äs, -,äz\\ Porfirio 1830–1915 *José de la Cruz Porfirio* Mex. gen.; pres. of Mexico (1877–80; 1884–1911)

Díaz de Vivar — see CID

Dí·az Or·daz \\'dē-əs-òr-'däz\\ Gustavo 1911–1979 pres. of Mexico (1964–70)

Dick \\'dik\\ George Frederick 1881–1967 & Gladys Henry 1881–1963 Am. physicians

Dick·ens \\'di-kənz\\ Charles John Huffam 1812–1870 pseud. *Boz* \\'bäz, 'bòz\\ Eng. nov. — **Dick·en·si·an** \\di-'ken-zē-ən, -sē-\\ *adj*

Dick·in·son \\'di-kən-sən\\ Emily Elizabeth 1830–1886 Am. poet

Dickinson John 1732–1808 Am. statesman

Di·de·rot \\'dē-drō, 'dē-də-,rō\\ Denis 1713–1784 Fr. encyclopedist

Die·fen·ba·ker \\'dē-fən-,bā-kər\\ John George 1895–1979 prime min. of Canada (1957–63)

Diels \\'dē(ə)lz, 'dē(ə)ls\\ Otto Paul Hermann 1876–1954 Ger. chem.

Die·sel \\'dē-zəl, -səl\\ Rudolf 1858–1913 Ger. mechanical engineer

Die·trich \\'dē-trik, -trik\\ Marlene 1901?–1992 Am. (Ger.-born) actress & singer

Diez \\'dēts\\ Friedrich Christian 1794–1876 Ger. philologist

---

\\ə\\ abut \\^ə\\ kitten, F table \\ər\\ further \\a\\ ash \\ā\\ ace \\ä\\ mop, mar \\aú\\ out \\ch\\ chin \\e\\ bet \\ē\\ easy \\g\\ go \\i\\ hit \\ī\\ ice \\j\\ job \\ŋ\\ sing \\ō\\ go \\ò\\ law \\òi\\ boy \\th\\ thin \\t̷h\\ the \\ü\\ loot \\ú\\ foot \\y\\ yet \\zh\\ vision \\à, k̲, ⁿ, œ, œ̄, ue, uē, ^y\\ see Guide to Pronunciation

Dig·by \'dig-bē\ Sir Ken·elm \'ke-ˌnelm\ 1603–1665 Eng. naval commander, diplomat, & author

Dill \'dil\ Sir John Greer 1881–1944 Brit. gen.

Dil·lon \'di-lən\ John 1851–1927 Irish nationalist polit.

Di·Mag·gio \də-'mä-zhē-(ˌ)ō, -'ma-jē-(ˌ)ō, -'ma-jō\ Joseph Paul 1914– Am. baseball player

Di·mi·tri·os I \the-'mē-trē-òs; də-'mē-trē-əs\ 1914–1991 archbishop of Constantinople and ecumenical patriarch (1972–91)

Di·ne·sen \'dē-nə-sən, 'di-\ Isak \'ē-ˌsäk\ 1885–1962 pseud. of *Karen Christence Dinesen*, Baroness *Blixen-Finecke* Dan. author

Din·wid·die \din-'wi-dē\ Robert 1693–1770 Eng. colonial administrator in America

Di·o·cle·tian \ˌdī-ə-'klē-shən\ 245(or 248)–313(or 316) *Gaius Aurelius Valerius Diocletianus* Rom. emp. (284–305)

Di·og·e·nes \dī-'ä-jə-ˌnēz\ *d ca* 320 B.C. Greek Cynic philos.

Di·o·ny·sius \ˌdī-ə-'ni-shē-əs, -sē-əs, -shəs; -'nī-sē-əs\ *ca* 430–367 B.C. *the Elder* Greek tyrant of Syracuse (405–367)

Dionysius *the Younger* tyrant of Syracuse (367–356; 354–343 B.C.)

Dionysius Ex·ig·u·us \eg-'zi-gyə-wəs\ *ca* 500–*ca* 560 Christian monk

Dionysius of Alexandria Saint *ca* 200–*ca* 265 theol. & bishop of Alexandria (247)

Dionysius of Hal·i·car·nas·sus \ˌha-lə-(ˌ)kär-'na-səs\ *fl ca* 20 B.C. Greek scholar

Di·rac \di-'rak\ Paul Adrien Maurice 1902–1984 Eng. physicist

Dirk·sen \'dərk-sən\ Everett McKinley 1896–1969 Am. polit.

Dis·ney \'diz-nē\ Walter Elias 1901–1966 Am. film producer

Dis·rae·li \diz-'rā-lē\ Benjamin 1804–1881 1st Earl of *Bea·cons·field* \'bē-kənz-ˌfēld\ Brit. polit. & author; prime min. (1868; 1874–80)

Dit·mars \'dit-ˌmärz\ Raymond Lee 1876–1942 Am. naturalist

Dix \'diks\ Dorothea Lynde 1802–1887 Am. social reformer

Dix Dorothy — see Elizabeth Meriwether GILMER

Dix·on \'dik-sən\ Jeremiah *d* 1777 Eng. surveyor in America

Dmow·ski \də-'móf-skē, -'móv-\ Roman 1864–1939 Pol. statesman

Dö·be·rei·ner \'də(r)-bə-ˌrī-nər, -ˌrē-\ Johann Wolfgang 1780–1849 Ger. chem.

Do·bie \'dō-bē\ James Frank 1888–1964 Am. folklorist

Do·brée \'dō-ˌbrā\ Bon·a·my \'bä-nə-mē\ 1891–1974 Eng. scholar

Dob·son \'däb-sən\ (Henry) Austin 1840–1921 Eng. poet & essayist

Dodge \'däj\ Mary Elizabeth 1831–1905 née *Mapes* \'māps\ Am. author

Dodg·son \'däd-sən, 'däj-\ Charles Lut·widge \'lət-wij\ 1832–1898 pseud. *Lewis Car·roll* \'kar-əl\ Eng. math. & author

Dods·ley \'dädz-lē\ Robert 1703–1764 Eng. author & bookseller

Doi·sy \'dòi-zē\ Edward Adelbert 1893–1986 Am. biochem.

Dole \'dōl\ Robert Joseph 1923– Am. polit.

Dole Sanford Ballard 1844–1926 Am. jurist; pres. (1894–1900) & gov. (1900–03) of Hawaii

Doll·fuss \'dòl-ˌfüs\ Engelbert 1892–1934 Austrian statesman

Do·magk \'dō-ˌmäk\ Gerhard 1895–1964 Ger. bacteriol.

Do·me·ni·chi·no \(ˌ)dō-ˌmā-nə-'kē-(ˌ)nō\ 1581–1641 *Domenico Zampieri* \ˌtsäm-pē-'er-ē, ˌzäm-\ Ital. painter

Do·min·go \dō-'miŋ-gō\ Placido 1941– Span. tenor

Dom·i·nic \'dä-mə-(ˌ)nik\ Saint *ca* 1170–1221 *Domingo de Guz·mán* \güz-'män, güs-\ Span.-born founder of the Dominican order of friars

Do·mi·tian \də-'mi-shən\ A.D. 51–96 *Titus Flavius Domitianus* Rom. emp. (81–96)

Don·a·tel·lo \ˌdä-nə-'te-(ˌ)lō\ 1386?–1466 *Donato de Betto di Bardi* Florentine sculptor

Dong·en \'dòŋ-ən\ Kees van 1877–1968 orig. *Cornelis Theodorus Maria Dongen* Fr. (Du.-born) painter

Dö·nitz \'də(r)-nəts, 'dō-\ Karl 1891–1980 Ger. admiral

Don·i·zet·ti \ˌdä-nə(d)-'ze-tē, ˌdō-\ Gaetano 1797–1848 Ital. composer — **Don·i·zet·ti·an** \-'ze-tē-ən\ *adj*

Donne \'dən *also* 'dän\ John 1572–1631 Eng. poet & clergyman — **Donn·ean** *or* **Donn·ian** \'də-nē-ən, 'dä-\ *adj*

Don·o·van \'dä-nə-vən, 'də-\ William Joseph 1883–1959 *Wild Bill* Am. lawyer & gen.

Doo·lit·tle \'dü-ˌli-tᵊl\ James Harold 1896–1993 Am. aviator & gen.

Dopp·ler \'dä-plər\ Christian Johann 1803–1853 Austrian physicist

Do·ra·ti \də-'rä-tē\ An·tal \'än-ˌtäl\ 1906–1988 Am. (Hung.-born) conductor

Do·ré \dò-'rā, do-\ (Paul-) Gustave 1832–1883 Fr. illustrator & painter

Dor·ge·les \ˌdòr-zhə-'les\ Roland 1886–1973 Fr. nov.

Dor·nier \'dòrn-ˌyā\ Claudius 1884–1969 Ger. airplane builder

Dorr \'dòr\ Thomas Wilson 1805–1854 Am. lawyer & polit.

Dorset 1st Earl of — see Thomas SACKVILLE

Dos Pas·sos \däs-'pa-səs\ John Roderigo 1896–1970 Am. writer

Dos·to·yev·sky \ˌdäs-tə-'yef-skē, -'yev-\ Fyodor Mikhaylovich 1821–1881 Russ. nov. — **Dos·to·yev·ski·an** *or* **Dos·to·ev·ski·an** \-skē-ən\ *adj*

Dou *or* **Douw** \'daù\ Gerrit *or* Gerard 1613–1675 Du. painter

Dou·ble·day \'də-bəl-ˌdā\ Abner 1819–1893 Am. soldier & reputed inventor of baseball

Dough·ty \'daù-tē\ Charles Montagu 1843–1926 Eng. poet & traveler

Doug·las \'də-gləs\ John Shol·to \'shòl-(ˌ)tō\ 1844–1900 8th Marquis & Earl of *Queens·ber·ry* \'kwēnz-ˌber-ē, -b(ə-)rē\ Scot. boxing patron

Douglas Stephen Arnold 1813–1861 Am. polit.

Douglas William Orville 1898–1980 Am. jurist

Douglas–Home — see HOME

Douglas of Kir·tle·side \'kər-tᵊl-ˌsīd\ 1st Baron 1893–1969 *William Sholto Douglas* Brit. air marshal

Doug·lass \'də-gləs\ Frederick 1817–1895 orig. *Frederick Augustus Washington Bailey* Am. abolitionist

Dou·mer \dü-'mer\ Paul 1857–1932 pres. of France (1931–32)

Dou·mergue \dü-'merg\ Gaston 1863–1937 Fr. statesman; pres. of France (1924–31)

Dow·den \'daù-dᵊn\ Edward 1843–1913 Irish lit. critic

Dow·ie \'daù-ē\ John Alexander 1847–1907 Am. (Scot.-born) religious leader

Dow·son \'daù-sᵊn\ Ernest Christopher 1867–1900 Eng. lyric poet

Dox·ia·dis \ˌdòk-sē-'ä-thēs\ Konstantinos Apostolos 1913–1975 Greek architect

Doyle \'dòi(ə)l\ Sir Arthur Co·nan \'kō-nən\ 1859–1930 Brit. physician, nov., & detective-story writer

D'Oyly Carte — see CARTE

Drach·mann \'dräk-mən\ Holger Henrik Herholdt 1846–1908 Dan. author

Dra·co \'drā-(ˌ)kō\ late 7th cent. B.C. Athenian lawgiver

Drake \'drāk\ Sir Francis 1540(or 1543)–1596 Eng. navigator & buccaneer

Dra·per \'drā-pər\ Henry 1837–1882 Am. astron.

Dray·ton \'drā-tᵊn\ Michael 1563–1631 Eng. poet

Drei·ser \'drī-sər, -zər\ Theodore 1871–1945 Am. editor & nov. — **Drei·ser·ian** \ˌdrī-'ser-ē-ən, -'zər-\ *adj*

Drew \'drü\ John 1827–1862 Am. (Irish-born) actor

Drew John 1853–1927 *son of prec.* Am. actor

Drey·fus \'drī-fəs, 'drā-; dre-fü͞es\ Alfred 1859–1935 Fr. army officer

Driesch \'drēsh\ Hans Adolf Eduard 1867–1941 Ger. biol. & philos.

Drink·wa·ter \'driŋk-ˌwò-tər, -ˌwä-\ John 1882–1937 Eng. writer

Drou·et \drü-'e, -'ā\ Jean-Baptiste 1765–1844 Comte *d'Er·lon* \der-'lōⁿ\ Fr. gen.; marshal of France

Drum·mond \'drə-mənd\ Henry 1851–1897 Scot. clergyman & writer

Drummond William Henry 1854–1907 Canad. (Irish-born) poet

Drummond of Haw·thorn·den \'hò-ˌthórn-dən\ William 1585–1649 Scot. poet

Dru·sus \'drü-səs\ 38–9 B.C. *Ne·ro* \'nē-(ˌ)rō, 'nir-(ˌ)ō\ *Claudius Drusus Ger·man·i·cus* \(ˌ)jer-'ma-ni-kəs\ Rom. gen.

Dry·den \'drī-dᵊn\ John 1631–1700 Eng. poet & dram.; poet laureate (1668–88) — **Dry·de·ni·an** \ˌdrī-'dē-nē-ən, -'de-\ *adj*

Du Barry Comtesse — see Jeanne BARRY

Du·bois \dü-'bwä, dyü-; dü͞e-bwä\ Paul 1829–1905 Fr. sculptor

Dubois (François-Clément-) Théodore 1837–1924 Fr. composer

DuBois \dü-'bòis, dyü-\ William Edward Burghardt 1868–1963 Am. educ. & writer

Du·buf·fet \ˌdü-bə-'fā, ˌdyü-; dü͞e-bü͞e-fe\ Jean 1901–1985 Fr. artist

Du Cange \dü-'käⁿzh, dyü-\ Sieur Charles Du Fresne 1610–1688 Fr. scholar & glossarist

Du Chail·lu \də-'shal-(ˌ)yü, -'shī-(ˌ)ü\ Paul Belloni 1831–1903 Am. (Fr.-born) explorer in Africa

Du·champ \dü-'shäⁿ, dyü-\ Marcel 1887–1968 Fr. painter — **Du·champ·ian** \-'shäm-pē-ən\ *adj*

Du·com·mun \ˌdü-kə-'mœⁿ, ˌdyü-\ Élie 1833–1906 Swiss journalist

Dudevant Aurore — see George SAND

Dud·ley \'dəd-lē\ Robert 1532(or 1533)–1588 1st Earl of *Leicester* Eng. courtier

Dudley Thomas 1576–1653 colonial administrator in Massachusetts Bay Colony

Duf·fer·in and Ava \ˌdə-fə-rin-ən-(ə)-'ä-və\ 1st Marquis of 1826–1902 *Frederick Temple Hamilton-Temple-Blackwood* Brit. diplomat

Duff–Gor·don \ˌdəf-'gòr-dᵊn\ Lady Lucie 1821–1869 Eng. author

Duf·fy \'də-fē\ Sir Charles Gavan 1816–1903 Irish nationalist & Austral. polit.

Du·fy \dü-'fē, dyü-\ Raoul 1877–1953 Fr. painter

Du Gard Roger Martin — see MARTIN DU GARD

Du Guesclin Bertrand — see GUESCLIN

Du·ha·mel \ˌdü-ä-'mel, ˌdyü-; dü͞e-á-mel\ Georges 1884–1966 Fr. writer

Du·ka·kis \dü-'kä-kis\ Michael Stanley 1933– Am. polit.

Duke \dük, 'dyük\ Benjamin Newton 1855–1929 & his bro. James Buchanan 1856–1925 Am. tobacco industrialists

Dul·bec·co \(ˌ)dəl-'be-(ˌ)kō\ Renato 1914– Am. (Ital.-born) virologist

Dul·les \'də-ləs\ John Foster 1888–1959 Am. diplomat; secy. of state (1953–59)

Du·mas \dü-'mä, dyü-; 'd(y)ü-ˌ\ Alexandre 1802–1870 *Dumas père* \'per\ Fr. nov. & dram.

Dumas Alexandre 1824–1895 *Dumas fils* \'fēs\ Fr. nov. & dram.

du Mau·rier \dü-'mòr-ē-ˌā, dyü-\ Dame Daphne 1907–1989 Brit. writer

du Maurier George Louis Palmella Busson 1834–1896 *grandfather of prec.* Brit. artist & nov.

Du·mou·riez \dü-'mür-ē-ˌā, dyü-\ Charles-François du Périer 1739–1823 Fr. gen.

Du·nant \dü-'näⁿ, dyü-\ Jean-Henri 1828–1910 Swiss philanthropist & founder of the Red Cross

Dun·bar \'dən-ˌbär\ Paul Laurence 1872–1906 Am. poet

Dunbar \'dən-ˌbär, -'bär\ William 1460?–?1530 Scot. poet

Dun·can \'dəŋ-kən\ Isadora 1877–1927 Am. dancer

Dun·das \dən-'das\ Henry 1742–1811 1st Viscount *Melville* & Baron *Dun·ira* \də-'nir-ə\ Brit. statesman

Dun·lop \dən-'läp, 'dən-ˌ\ John Boyd 1840–1921 Scot. inventor

Dunne \'dən\ Finley Peter 1867–1936 Am. humorist

Du·nois \dün-'wä, dyün-\ Comte de 1403–1468 *Jean d'Orléans; the bastard of Orléans* Fr. gen.

Dun·sa·ny \ˌdən-'sä-nē\ 18th Baron 1878–1957 *Edward John Moreton Drax Plunkett* Irish poet & dram.

Duns Sco·tus \'dənz-'skō-təs\ John 1266?–1308 Scot. scholastic theol.

Dun·stan \'dən(t)-stən\ Saint 924–988 archbishop of Canterbury (959–988)

Du·pleix \dü-'pleks, dyü-\ Marquis Joseph-François 1697–1763 Fr. colonial administrator in India

Duplessis–Mornay — see Philippe de MORNAY

Du Pont \dü-'pänt, dyü-; 'd(y)ü-ˌ\ Éleuthère Irénée 1771–1834 *son of P.S. Du Pont de Nemours* Am. (Fr.-born) industrialist

Du Pont de Ne·mours \-də-nə-'mur\ Pierre-Samuel 1739–1817 Fr. econ. & statesman

Du·quesne \dü-'kän, dyü-\ Marquis Abraham 1610–1688 Fr. naval officer

Du·rant \du-'rant\ William James 1885–1981 Am. educ. & writer

Dü·rer \'dür-ər, 'dyür-; 'dü͞er-\ Albrecht 1471–1528 Ger. painter & engraver — **Dü·rer·esque** \ˌdur-ər-'esk, ˌdyür-, ˌdü͞er-\ *adj*

D'Ur·fey \'dər-fē\ Thomas 1653–1723 Eng. songwriter & dram.

Durk·heim \'dur-ˌkem\ Émile 1858–1917 Fr. sociol. — **Durk·heim·ian** \-'ke-mē-ən\ *adj*

Du·roc \dü-'räk, dyü-\ Géraud-Christophe-Michel 1772–1813 Duc de *Fri·oul* \frē-ül\ Fr. gen. under Napoleon

Dur·rell \'dər-əl, 'də-rəl\ Lawrence 1912–1990 Eng. nov. & poet

Dür·ren·matt \'du͞er-ən-ˌmät, 'dur-\ Friedrich 1921–1990 Swiss author

Du·ruy \,dùr-'wē, dūē-rwʸē\ Victor 1811–1894 Fr. hist.
Du·se \'dü-(,)zā\ Eleonora 1858–1924 Ital. actress
Du·tra \'dü-trə\ Eurico Gaspar 1885–1974 Braz. gen.; pres. of Brazil (1946–51)
Du·va·lier \dù-'val-(,)yā, dyù-\ François 1907–1971 *Papa Doc* pres. of Haiti (1957–71)
Du·ve \'dü-və\ Christian René Marie Joseph 1917– Belg. (Eng.=born) physiol.
Du Vi·gneaud \dù-'vēn-(,)yō, dyù-\ Vincent 1901–1978 Am. biochem.
Dvo·řák \(də-)'vȯr-,zhäk\ Antonín 1841–1904 Bohemian composer
Dwig·gins \'dwi-gənz\ William Addison 1880–1956 Am. type designer
Dwight \'dwīt\ Timothy 1752–1817 Am. clergyman; pres. Yale U. (1795–1817)
Dwight Timothy 1828–1916 *grandson of prec.* Am. clergyman; pres. Yale U. (1886–99)
Dwyfor Earl of — see LLOYD GEORGE
Dyce \'dīs\ Alexander 1798–1869 Scot. editor
Dy·er \'dī(-ə)r\ John 1699–1757 Brit. poet
Dyer Mary *d* 1660 Am. Quaker martyr
Eads \'ēdz\ James Buchanan 1820–1887 Am. engineer & inventor
Ea·kins \'ā-kənz\ Thomas 1844–1916 Am. artist
Ear·hart \'er-,härt, 'ir-\ Amelia 1897–1937 Am. aviator
Ear·ly \'ər-lē\ Ju·bal \'jü-bəl\ Anderson 1816–1894 Am. Confed. gen.
Earp \'ȯrp\ Wyatt 1848–1929 Am. lawman
East·man \'ēst-mən\ George 1854–1932 Am. inventor & industrialist
Eastman Max Forrester 1883–1969 Am. editor & writer
Ea·ton \'ē-t²n\ Theophilus 1590–1658 Eng. colonial administrator in America; gov. of New Haven colony (1638–58)
Ebert \'ā-bərt\ Friedrich 1871–1925 pres. of Germany (1919–25)
Ec·cles \'e-kəlz\ Sir John Carew 1903– Brit. physiol.
Eccles Marriner Stoddard 1890–1977 Am. banker & econ.
Eche·ga·ray y Ei·za·guir·re \,ā-chə-gə-'rī-,ē-,ā-thə-'gwir-(,)ā, -sə-'gwir-\ José 1832–1916 Span. dram.
Eche·ver·ría Ál·va·rez \,ā-chə-və-'rē-ə-'al-və-,rez, ,e-chə-\ Luis 1922– pres. of Mexico (1970–76)
Eck \'ek\ Johann 1486–1543 orig. *Maier* Ger. R.C. theol.
Ecke·hart \'e-kə-,härt\ *or* Eck·art *or* Eck·hart \'ek-,härt, 'e-,kärt\ Johannes 1260?–?1327 *Meister Eckehart* Ger. mystic
Eck·er·mann \'e-kər-,män, -mən\ Johann Peter 1792–1854 Ger. writer
Ed·ding·ton \'e-diŋ-tən\ Sir Arthur Stanley 1882–1944 Eng. astron.
Ed·dy \'e-dē\ Mary Morse 1821–1910 née *Baker* Am. founder of the Christian Science Church
Ed·el·man \'e-d²l-mən\ Gerald Maurice 1929– Am. biochem.
Eden \'ē-d²n\ (Robert) Anthony 1897–1977 Earl of *Avon* \'ā-vən\ Eng. statesman; prime min. (1955–57)
Edge·worth \'ej-(,)wərth\ Maria 1767–1849 Brit. nov.
Edinburgh Duke of — see PHILIP
Ed·i·son \'e-də-sən\ Thomas Alva 1847–1931 Am. inventor
Ed·mund *or* Ead·mund II \'ed-mənd\ *ca* 993–1016 *Ironside* king of the English (1016)
Ed·ward \'ed-wərd\ name of 8 post-Norman Eng. (Brit.) kings: **I** 1239–1307 (reigned 1272–1307); **II** 1284–1327 (reigned 1307–27); **III** 1312–1377 (reigned 1327–77); **IV** 1442–1483 (reigned 1461–70; 1471–83); **V** 1470–1483 (reigned 1483); **VI** 1537–1553 (reigned 1547–53) *son of Henry VIII & Jane Seymour;* **VII** 1841–1910 (reigned 1901–10) *Albert Edward, son of Victoria;* **VIII** 1894–1972 (reigned 1936; abdicated) Duke of *Windsor, son of George V*
Edward 1330–1376 *the Black Prince; son of Edward III* prince of Wales
Edward *or* Ead·ward \'ed-\ 1003?–1066 *the Confessor* king of the English (1042–66)
Ed·wards \'ed-wərdz\ Jonathan 1703–1758 Am. theol. — Ed·ward·ean \ed-'wär-dē-ən, -'wȯr-\ *adj*
Ed·win *or* Ead·wine \'ed-wən\ 585?–633 king of Northumbria (616–633)
Egas Mo·niz \'ā-gäs-mȯ-'nēz\ António Caetano de Abreu Freire 1874–1955 Port. neurologist & polit.
Eg·bert \'eg-bərt\ *d* 839 king of the West Saxons (802–839) & 1st king of the English (828–839)
Eg·gle·ston \'e-gəl-stən\ Edward 1837–1902 Am. writer
Eggleston George Cary 1839–1911 *bro. of Edward* Am. writer
Eg·mond \'eg-,mänt\ *or* Eg·mont Lamoraal 1522–1568 Graaf *van Egmond* Flem. gen. & statesman
Eh·ren·burg \'er-ən-,bùrg, -,bùrk\ Ilya Grigoryevich 1891–1967 Russ. writer
Ehr·lich \'er-lik\ Paul 1854–1915 Ger. bacteriol.
Ehr·lich \'ȯr-lik\ Paul Ralph 1932– Am. biol.
Eif·fel \'ī-fəl, e-fel\ Alexandre-Gustave 1832–1923 Fr. engineer
Ei·gen \'ī-gən\ Manfred 1927– Ger. chem.
Eijk·man \'īk-,män, 'āk-\ Christiaan 1858–1930 Du. pathologist
Ein·stein \'īn-,stīn\ Albert 1879–1955 Am. (Ger.-born) physicist — Ein·stein·ian \īn-'stī-nē-ən\ *adj*
Eint·ho·ven \'īnt-,hō-vən, 'änt-\ Willem 1860–1927 Du. physiol.
Ei·sen·how·er \'ī-z²n-,haú(-ə)r\ Dwight David 1890–1969 Am. gen.; 34th pres. of the U.S. (1953–61)
Ei·sen·stein \'ī-z²n-,stīn\ Sergey Mikhaylovich 1898–1948 Soviet (Russ.-born) film director
El·a·gab·a·lus \,e-lə-'ga-bə-ləs\ *Gk* He·li·o·gab·a·lus \,hē-lē-ō-'ga-bə-ləs\ 204–222 Rom. emp. (218–222)
El·ders \'el-dərz\ (Minnie) Joycelyn 1933– U.S. surgeon general (1993–94)
El·don \'el-dən\ 1st Earl of 1751–1838 *John Scott* Eng. jurist
El·ea·nor \'e-lə-nər, -,nȯr\ of Aquitaine 1122?–1204 *queen of Louis VII of France (divorced 1152) & of Henry II of England*
Eleanor of Castile 1246–1290 *queen of Edward I of England*
Eleanor of Provence 1223–1291 *queen of Henry III of England*
El·gar \'el-,gär, -gər\ Sir Edward 1857–1934 Eng. composer
El·i·on \'e-lē-ən\ Gertrude Belle 1918– Am. biochem.
El·iot \'e-lē-ət, 'el-yət\ Charles William 1834–1926 Am. educ.; pres. Harvard U. (1869–1909)
Eliot George 1819–1880 pseud. *of Mary Ann (or Marian) Evans* Eng. nov.
Eliot Sir John 1592–1632 Eng. statesman
Eliot John 1604–1690 *apostle to the Indians* Am. clergyman

Eliot Thomas Stearns 1888–1965 Brit. (Am.-born) poet & critic — El·i·ot·ian \,e-lē-'ō-tē-ən, -'ō-sh(ē-)ən\ *adj* — El·i·ot·ic \,e-lē-'ä-tik\ *adj*
Eliz·a·beth \i-'li-zə-bəth\ name of 2 Eng. (Brit.) queens: **I** 1533–1603 *dau. of Henry VIII & Anne Boleyn* (reigned 1558–1603); **II** 1926– *Elizabeth Alexandra Mary; dau. of George VI* (reigned 1952–)
Elizabeth *also* Elizabeth Stu·art \-'stü-ərt, -'styü-; 'stú(-ə)rt, 'styü(-ə)rt\ 1596–1662 *queen of Frederick V of Bohemia*
Elizabeth 1900– *Elizabeth Angela Marguerite Bowes-Ly·on* \'bōz-'lī-ən\; *queen of George VI of Great Britain*
Elizabeth 1843–1916 pseud. *Car·men Syl·va* \'kär-mən-'sil-və\ *queen of Romania & writer*
Elizabeth Pe·trov·na \pə-'trȯv-nə\ 1709–1762 empress of Russia (1741–62)
Ellenborough 1st Baron — see LAW
El·ling·ton \'e-liŋ-tən\ Edward Kennedy 1899–1974 *Duke Ellington* Am. bandleader & composer
El·liott \'e-lē-ət, 'el-yət\ Maxine 1868–1940 pseud. *of Jessie Dermot* Am. actress
El·lis \'e-ləs\ Alexander John 1814–1890 orig. surname *Sharpe* Eng. philologist
Ellis (Henry) Have·lock \'hav-,läk, -lək\ 1859–1939 Eng. psychol. & writer
Ell·son \'e-lə-sən\ Ralph Waldo 1914–1994 Am. writer
Ells·worth \'elz-(,)wərth\ Lincoln 1880–1951 Am. explorer
Ellsworth Oliver 1745–1807 Am. jurist; chief justice U.S. Supreme Court (1796–1800)
El·man \'el-mən\ Mi·scha \'mē-shə\ 1891–1967 Am. (Russ.-born) violinist
El·phin·stone \'el-fən-,stȯn, *chiefly Brit* -stən\ Mount·stu·art \maúnt-'st(y)ü-ərt\ 1779–1859 Brit. statesman in India
Elphinstone William 1431–1514 Scot. bishop & statesman
El·yot \'e-lē-ət, 'el-yət\ Sir Thomas 1490?–1546 Eng. scholar & diplomat
El·y·tis \'e-lē-(,)tēs\ Odysseus 1911– Greek poet
El·ze·vir *or* El·ze·vier \'el-zə-,vir\ family of Du. printers including esp. Lodewijk *or* Louis 1546?–1617, his son Bonaventura 1583–1652, & his grandson Abraham 1592–1652
Em·er·son \'e-mər-sən\ Ralph Waldo 1803–1882 Am. essayist & poet — Em·er·so·nian \,e-mər-'sō-nē-ən, -nyən\ *adj*
Em·met \'e-mət\ Robert 1778–1803 Irish nationalist & rebel
Em·ped·o·cles \em-'pe-də-,klēz\ *ca* 490–430 B.C. Greek philos. & statesman
Endara (Galimany) \en-'där-ə-,gä-lē-'mä-nē\ Guillermo 1936– pres. of Panama (1989–94)
En·de·cott *or* En·di·cott \'en-di-kət, -də-,kät\ John 1588–1665 colonial gov. of Massachusetts
En·ders \'en-dərz\ John Franklin 1897–1985 Am. bacteriol.
Enes·cu \ə-'nes-(,)kü\ Gheorghe *or* George *Fr* Enes·co \-(,)kō\ Georges 1881–1955 Romanian composer
Eng·els \'eŋ-gəlz, -əlz, *G* 'eŋ-əls\ Friedrich 1820–1895 Ger. socialist
En·ver Pa·şa \'en-,ver-'pä-shə, -'pa-shə, -pə-'shä\ 1881–1922 Turk. soldier & polit.
Epam·i·non·das \i-,pa-mə-'nän-dəs\ *ca* 410–362 B.C. Theban gen. & statesman
Ep·ic·te·tus \,e-pik-'tē-təs\ *ca* A.D. 55–*ca* 135 Greek Stoic philos. in Rome — Ep·ic·te·tian \-'tē-shən\ *adj*
Ep·i·cu·rus \,e-pi-'kyùr-əs\ 341–270 B.C. Greek philos.
Ep·stein \'ep-,stīn\ Sir Jacob 1880–1959 Brit. (Am.-born) sculptor
Eras·mus \i-'raz-məs\ Desiderius 1466?–1536 Du. scholar — Eras·mi·an \-,mē-ən\ *adj*
Er·a·tos·the·nes \,er-ə-'täs-thə-,nēz\ *ca* 276–*ca* 194 B.C. Greek astron.
Erck·mann—Cha·tri·an \'erk-,män-,shä-trē-'äⁿ, -,sha-\ joint pseud. of Émile Erckmann 1822–1899 & Alexandre Chatrian 1826–1890 Fr. authors
Er·hard \'er-,härt\ Ludwig 1897–1977 chancellor of West Germany (1963–66)
Er·ics·son \'er-ik-sən\ John 1803–1889 Am. (Swed.-born) engineer & inventor
Erig·e·na \i-'ri-jə-nə\ John Sco·tus \'skō-təs\ *ca* 810–*ca* 877 Scot. (Irish-born) philos. & theol.
Er·ik \'er-ik\ *the Red* 10th cent. Norw. navigator & explorer
Eriksson Leif — see LEIF ERIKSSON
Er·lan·der \er-'län-dər\ Tage Frithiof 1901–1985 Swed. polit.
Er·lang·er \'ər-,laŋ-ər\ Joseph 1874–1965 Am. physiol.
Er·len·mey·er \'ər-lən-,mī(-ə)r, 'er-\ Richard August Carl Emil 1825–1909 Ger. chem.
Ernst \'ern(t)st, 'ərn(t)st\ Max 1891–1976 Ger. painter
Ernst Richard Robert 1933– Swiss chem.
Er·skine \'ər-skən\ John 1879–1951 Am. educ. & writer
Erskine of Car·nock \'kär-nək\ John 1695–1768 Scot. jurist
Er·vine \'ər-vən\ St. John \,sänt-'jän, sənt-; 'sin-jən\ Greer 1883–1971 Irish dram. & nov.
Erz·ber·ger \'erts-,ber-gər\ Matthias 1875–1921 Ger. statesman
Es·a·ki \e-'sä-kē\ Leo 1925– Jp. physicist
Esch·er \'e-shər, 'es-kər\ Maurits Cornelis 1898–1972 Du. graphic artist
Esh·kol \esh-'kȯl\ Levi 1895–1969 prime min. of Israel (1963–69)
Es·par·te·ro \,es-pər-'ter-(,)ō\ Baldomero 1793–1879 Conde *de Luchana* Span. gen. & statesman
Es·py \'es-pē\ Mike 1953– U.S. secy. of agriculture (1993–94)
Es·qui·vel \,ä-skē-'vel\ Adolfo Pérez 1931– Argentine sculptor and dissident
Es·sen \'e-s²n\ Count Hans Henrik von 1755–1824 Swed. field marshal & statesman
Essex 2d Earl of — see DEVEREUX
Es·taing, d' \des-taⁿ\ Comte Jean-Baptiste-Charles-Henri-Hector 1729–1794 Fr. admiral

---

\ə\ abut \ᵊ\ kitten, F table \ər\ further \a\ ash \ā\ ace \ä\ mop, mar \aú\ out \ch\ chin \e\ bet \ē\ easy \g\ go \i\ hit \ī\ ice \j\ job \ŋ\ sing \ō\ go \ȯ\ law \ȯi\ boy \th\ thin \t͟h\ the \ü\ loot \ú\ foot \y\ yet \zh\ vision \à, k̲, ⁿ, œ, œ̄, ᵫ, ᵫ, ʸ\ *see* Guide to Pronunciation

Este \'es-(,)tā\ Ital. princely family beginning with *Alberto Az-zo II* \'äd-(,)zō\ 996–1097 & ending with *Er-co-le III* \'er-kə-,lā\ *Rinaldo* 1727–1803

Es-ter-ha-zy \'es-tər-,hä-zē\ Marie-Charles-Ferdinand-Walsin 1847–1923 Fr. army officer

Es-tienne \ā-'tyen\ *or* Étienne Fr. family of printers & booksellers including esp.: Henri I *ca* 1470–1520; his son Robert 1503–1559; & Robert's son Henri II 1528–1598

Es-tra-da Pal-ma \ā-'strä-thə-'päl-mə\ Tomás 1835–1908 1st pres. of Cuba (1902–06)

Ethelbert — see AETHELBERHT

Ethelred — see AETHELRED

Eth-er-ege \'e-th(ə-)rij\ Sir George 1635?–1692 Eng. dram.

Euck-en \'ói-kən\ Rudolf Christoph 1846–1926 Ger. philos.

Eu-clid \'yü-kləd\ *fl ca* 300 B.C. Greek geometer

Eu-gene \yü-'jēn, 'yü-,\ *F* œ-zhen\ 1663–1736 *François-Eugène de Sav-oie-Carignan* prince of Savoy & Austrian gen.

Eu-gé-nie \'yü-jə-,nē; yü-'jä-nē, -'jē-; *F* œ-zhä-nē\ 1826–1920 *Eugénia Maria de Montijo de Guzmán; wife of Napoleon III* empress of the French (1853–71)

Eu-ler \'ói-lər\ Leonhard 1707–1783 Swiss math. & physicist

Eu-ler–Chel-pin \'ói-lər-'kel-pən\ Hans Karl August Simon von 1873–1964 Swed. (Ger.-born) chem.

Eu-rip-i-des \yü-'ri-pə-,dēz\ *ca* 484–406 B.C. Greek dram. — Eu-rip-i-de-an \-,ri-pə-'dē-ən\ *adj*

Eus-den \'yüz-dən\ Laurence 1688–1730 Eng. poet; poet laureate (1718–30)

Eu-se-bi-us of Caesarea \yü-'sē-bē-əs\ *ca* 260–*ca* 339 theol. & church hist.

Eu-sta-chio \eú-'stä-kē-,ō\ Bartolomeo 1520–1574 L. *Eu-sta-chius* \yü-'stä-kē-əs, -'stä-sh(ē-)əs\ Ital. anatomist

Ev-ans \'e-vənz\ Sir Arthur John 1851–1941 Eng. archaeol.

Evans Herbert McLean 1882–1971 Am. anatomist & embryologist

Evans Maurice 1901–1989 Am. (Eng.-born) actor

Evans Rudolph 1878–1960 Am. sculptor

Evans Walker 1903–1975 Am. photographer

Ev-arts \'e-vərts\ William Maxwell 1818–1901 Am. lawyer & states-man

Ev-att \'e-vət\ Herbert Vere 1894–1965 Austral. jurist & statesman

Eve-lyn \'ēv-lən, 'ev-\ John 1620–1706 Eng. diarist

Ev-er-ett \'ev-rət, 'ev-ə-\ Edward 1794–1865 Am. clergyman, orator, & statesman

Ewald \'ī-,väl\ Johannes 1743–1781 Dan. poet & dram.

Ew-ell \'yü-əl\ Richard Stoddert 1817–1872 Am. Confed. gen.

Eyck, van \van-'īk\ Hubert *or* Huybrecht *ca* 1370–1426 & his bro. Jan before 1395–1441 Flem. painters

Eze-kiel \i-'zēk-yəl\ Moses Jacob 1844–1917 Am. sculptor

Fa-bio-la \,fa-bē-'ō-lə, fə-'byō-\ 1928–   queen of King Baudouin I of Belgium

Fa-bi-us \'fā-bē-əs\ *d* 203 B.C. *Quintus Fabius Maximus Verrucosus Cunc-ta-tor* \,kənk-'tā-tər\ Rom. gen. against Hannibal

Fa-bre \fäbr⁰\ Jean-Henri 1823–1915 Fr. entomologist

Fad-den \'fa-d⁰n\ Sir Arthur William 1895–1973 Austral. statesman

Fad-i-man \'fa-də-mən\ Clifton 1904–   Am. writer & editor

Fahd \'fäd\ 1923–   *Fahd ibn 'Abd al-'Aziz as-Sa'ūd* king of Saudi Arabia (1982–   )

Fah-ren-heit \'far-ən-,hīt, 'fär-\ Daniel Gabriel 1686–1736 Ger. physi-cist

Fair-banks \'far-,baŋ(k)s, 'fer-\ Charles Warren 1852–1918 Am. law-yer & polit.; vice pres. of U.S. (1905–09)

Fairbanks Douglas Elton 1883–1939 Am. actor

Fair-child \'far-,chīld, 'fer-\ David Grandison 1869–1954 Am. botanist

Fair-fax \'far-,faks, 'fer-\ Baron Thomas 1612–1671 Eng. gen.

Fairfax Baron Thomas 1692–1782 proprietor in Virginia

Fai-sal \'fī-səl, 'fā-\ *ca* 1906–1975 king of Saudi Arabia (1964–75)

Fai-sal I *Ar* Fay-sal \'fī-səl, 'fā-\ 1885–1933 king of Syria (1920), of Iraq (1921–1933)

Faisal II *Ar* Fay-sal 1935–1958 king of Iraq (1939–58)

Fa-lier \fəl-'yer\ *or* Fa-lie-ro \-(,)ō\ Marino 1274–1355 doge of Venice (1354–55)

Fal-ken-hau-sen \'fäl-kən-,haú-z⁰n, 'fal-\ Ludwig 1844–1936 Freiherr *von Falkenhausen* Ger. gen.

Fal-ken-hayn \'fäl-kən-,hīn, 'fal-\ Erich von 1861–1922 Ger. gen.

Falkner William — see FAULKNER

Fal-la \'fä-yə, 'fäl-\ Manuel de 1876–1946 Span. composer

Fal-lières \fal-'yer\ Clément-Armand 1841–1931 Fr. statesman; pres. of France (1906–13)

Fan-euil \'fan-yəl, 'fan-ⁿl, 'fan-yə-wəl\ Peter 1700–1743 Am. merchant

Far-a-day \'far-ə-,dā, -dē\ Michael 1791–1867 Eng. chem. & physicist

Fa-ri-na \fə-'rē-nə\ Salvatore 1846–1918 Ital. nov.

Far-ley \'fär-lē\ James Aloysius 1888–1976 Am. polit.

Far-man \'fär-,mäⁿ, 'fär-mən\ Henri 1874–1958 & his bro. Maurice 1877–1964 Fr. pioneer aviators and airplane manufacturers

Far-mer \'fär-mər\ Fannie Merritt 1857–1915 Am. cookery expert

Farmer James Leonard 1920–   Am. civil rights leader

Far-ne-se \fär-'nä-zē, -sē\ Alessandro 1545–1592 Duke of *Parma* Ital. gen. in Span. service

Fa-rouk I \fə-'rük\ *Ar* Fā-rūq al–Aw-wal \fär-'ük-al-'a-wal\ 1920–1965 king of Egypt (1936–52; abdicated)

Far-quhar \'fär-kər, -kwər\ George 1678–1707 Brit. dram.

Far-ra-gut \'far-ə-gət\ David Glasgow 1801–1870 Am. admiral

Far-rar \'far-ər\ Frederic William 1831–1903 Eng. clergyman & translator

Far-rar \fə-'rär\ Geraldine 1882–1967 Am. soprano

Far-rell \'far-əl\ James Thomas 1904–1979 Am. nov.

Fa-ruk *var of* FAROUK

Fāt-i-mah \fa-tə-mə\ *ca* 606–633 *az-Zahrā* ('Shining One') dau. of Muhammad

Faulk-ner \'fók-nər\ William Cuthbert 1897–1962 orig. *Falkner* Am. nov. — Faulk-ner-ian \,fók-'nir-ē-ən, -'ner-\ *adj*

Faure \'fōr\ François-Félix 1841–1899 Fr. statesman; pres. of France (1895–99)

Fau-ré \fō-'rä\ Gabriel-Urbain 1845–1924 Fr. composer

Faus-ta \'fó-stə, 'faú-\ 289–326 *Flavia Maximiana Fausta; wife of Con-stantine the Great* Rom. empress

Fawkes \'fóks\ Guy 1570–1606 Eng. conspirator

Fech-ner \'fek-nər, 'fek-\ Gustav Theodor 1801–1887 Ger. physicist & psychol.

Feif-fer \'fī-fər\ Jules 1929–   Am. cartoonist and writer

Fei-ning-er \'fī-niŋ-ər\ Lyonel Charles Adrian 1871–1956 Am. painter

Feke \'fēk\ Robert *ca* 1705–*ca* 1750 Am. painter

Fel-li-ni \fə-'lē-nē\ Federico 1920–1993 Ital. film director — Fel-li-ni-esque \fə-,lē-nē-'esk\ *adj*

Fell-tham \'fel-thəm\ Owen 1602?–1668 Eng. writer

Fé-ne-lon \,fā-n⁰l-'ō⁰, fen-'lō⁰\ François de Salignac de La Mothe-1651–1715 Fr. prelate & writer

Feng Yü–hsiang \'fəŋ-'yü-shē-'äŋ\ 1882–1948 Chin. gen.

Fer-ber \'fər-bər\ Edna 1887–1968 Am. writer

Fer-di-nand I \'fər-d⁰n-,and\ 1503–1564 Holy Rom. emp. (1558–64)

Ferdinand II 1578–1637 king of Bohemia (1617–19; 1620–27) & of Hungary (1618–25); Holy Rom. emp. (1619–37)

Ferdinand III 1608–1657 king of Hungary (1625–47); Holy Rom. emp. (1637–57)

Ferdinand I 1861–1948 king of Bulgaria (1908–18)

Ferdinand I 1016(or 1018)–1065 *the Great* king of Castile (1035–65); of León (1037–65)

Ferdinand II of Aragon *or* V of Castile 1452–1516 *the Catholic; hus-band of Isabella I* king of Castile (1474–1504); of Aragon (1479–1516); of Naples (1504–16); founder of the Span. monarchy

Ferdinand VII 1784–1833 king of Spain (1808; 1814–33)

Fer-mat \fer-'mä\ Pierre de 1601–1665 Fr. math.

Fer-mi \'fer-(,)mē\ Enrico 1901–1954 Am. (Ital.-born) physicist

Fer-nán-dez \fər-'nan-,dez\ Juan *ca* 1536–*ca* 1604 Span. navigator

Fernández de Cór-do-ba \-,thä-'kör-də-bə, -və\ Gon-za-lo \gón-'zä-lō\ 1453–1515 *El Gran Capitán* Span. soldier & statesman

Fer-re-ro \fə-'rer-(,)ō\ Guglielmo 1871–1943 Ital. hist. & author

Fes-sen-den \'fe-s⁰n-dən\ William Pitt 1806–1869 Am. polit.; secy. of the treasury (1864–65)

Fes-tus \'fes-təs\ Porcius *d ca* A.D. 62 Rom. procurator of Judea (58 or 60–62)

Feucht-wang-er \'fóikt-,väŋ-ər, 'fóikt-\ Li-on \'lē-,ón\ 1884–1958 Ger. nov. & dram.

Feuil-let \,fə-'yā\ Octave 1821–1890 Fr. nov. & dram.

Feyn-man \'fīn-mən\ Richard Phillips 1918–1988 Am. physicist

Fi-bi-ger \'fē-bē-gər\ Johannes Andreas Grib 1867–1928 Dan. pathol-ogist

Fich-te \'fik-tə, 'fik-\ Johann Gottlieb 1762–1814 Ger. philos. — Fich-te-an \-tē-ən\ *adj*

Fied-ler \'fēd-lər\ Arthur 1894–1979 Am. conductor

Field \'fē(ə)ld\ Cyrus West 1819–1892 Am. financier

Field Eugene 1850–1895 Am. poet & journalist

Field Marshall 1834–1906 Am. merchant

Field-ing \'fē(ə)l-diŋ\ Henry 1707–1754 Eng. nov.

Fields \'fē(ə)ldz\ W.C. 1880–1946 orig. *William Claude Dukenfield* Am. actor

Figl \'fē-gəl\ Leopold 1902–1965 Austrian polit.

Fi-guei-re-do \,fē-ge-'rä-(,)dü\ João Baptista de Oliveira 1918–   pres. of Brazil (1979–85)

Fi-gue-roa \,fē-gə-'rō-ə\ Francisco de *ca* 1536–*ca* 1620 Span. poet

Fill-more \'fil-,mōr, -,mór\ Millard 1800–1874 13th pres. of the U.S. (1850–53)

Fin-lay \fin-'lī\ Carlos Juan 1833–1915 Cuban physician & biol.

Finn-bo-ga-dot-tir \'fin-,bō-gə-,dó-tər\ Vigdis 1930–   pres. of Ice-land (1980–   )

Fin-sen \'fin(t)-sən\ Niels Ryberg 1860–1904 Dan. physician

Fir-bank \'fər-,baŋk\ (Arthur Annesley) Ronald 1886–1926 Eng. au-thor — Fir-bank-ian \,fər-'baŋ-kē-ən\ *adj*

Fir-daw-si *or* Fer-dow-si \,fər-'daú-sē, -'dó-\ *or* Fir-du-si \-'dü-\ *or* Fir-dou-si \-'daú-, -'dó-\ *ca* 935–*ca* 1020(or 1026) orig. *Abū ol-Qāsem Mansūr* Pers. poet

Fire-stone \'fīr-,stōn\ Harvey Samuel 1868–1938 Am. industrialist

Fi-scher \'fi-shər\ Edmond Henri 1920–   Am. (Chin.-born of Fr. parents) biochem.

Fischer Emil 1852–1919 Ger. chem.

Fischer Ernst Otto 1918–   Ger. chem.

Fischer Hans 1881–1945 Ger. chem.

Fi-scher–Dies-kau \'fi-shər-'dēs-,kaú\ Dietrich 1925–   Ger. bari-tone

Fish \'fish\ Hamilton 1808–1893 Am. statesman

Fish-bein \'fish-,bīn\ Morris 1889–1976 Am. physician & editor

Fish-er \'fi-shər\ Dorothy 1879–1958 *Dorothea Frances* née *Can-field* \'kan-,fēld\ Am. nov.

Fisher Irving 1867–1947 Am. econ.

Fisher John Arbuthnot 1841–1920 1st Baron *Fisher of Kil-ver-stone* \'kil-vər-stən\ Brit. admiral

Fisher Mary Frances Kennedy 1908–1992 Am. writer

Fiske \'fisk\ John 1842–1901 orig. *Edmund Fisk Green* Am. philos. & hist.

Fitch \'fich\ (William) Clyde 1865–1909 Am. dram.

Fitch John 1743–1798 Am. inventor

Fitch Val Logsdon 1923–   Am. physicist

Fitz-ger-ald \'fits-'jer-əld\ Ella 1918–   Am. singer

Fitzgerald Francis Scott Key 1896–1940 Am. writer

FitzGerald Edward 1809–1883 Eng. poet & translator

FitzGerald Garret 1926–   prime min. of Ireland (1981–87)

Fitz-her-bert \'fits-'hər-bərt\ Maria Anne 1756–1837 née *Smythe; wife of George IV of England*

Flagg \'flag\ James Montgomery 1877–1960 Am. illustrator

Flag-stad \'flag-,stad, *Norw* 'fläg-,stä\ Kir-sten \'kish-tən, 'kir-stən\ 1895–1962 Norw. soprano

Fla-min-i-us \flə-'mi-nē-əs\ Gaius *d* 217 B.C. Rom. gen. & statesman

Flam-ma-rion \flə-,mar-ē-'ō⁰\ (Nicolas-) Camille 1842–1925 Fr. astron. & writer

Flan-a-gan \'fla-ni-gən\ Edward Joseph 1886–1948 Am. (Irish-born) R. C. priest & founder of Boys Town

Flan-din \'flä⁰-da⁰\ Pierre-Étienne 1889–1958 Fr. polit.; premier (1934–35)

Flau·bert \flō-'ber\ Gustave 1821–1880 Fr. nov. — **Flau·ber·tian** \-'bər-shən, -'ber-tē-ən\ *adj*
Flax·man \'flaks-mən\ John 1755–1826 Eng. sculptor
Fleet·wood \'flēt-ˌwůd\ Charles *d* 1692 Eng. gen.
Flem·ing \'fle-miŋ\ Sir Alexander 1881–1955 Brit. bacteriol.
Fleming Ian Lancaster 1908–1964 Brit. writer
Fleming Sir John Ambrose 1849–1945 Eng. electrical engineer
Fletch·er \'fle-chər\ John 1579–1625 Eng. dram.
Fleu·ry \flər-'ē\ André-Hercule de 1653–1743 Fr. cardinal & statesman
Fleury Claude 1640–1723 Fr. ecclesiastical hist.
Flint \'flint\ Austin: father 1812–1886 & son 1836–1915 Am. physicians
Flo·res \'flōr-ˌās, 'flȯr-\ Juan José 1800–1864 Ecuadorian soldier; pres. of Ecuador (1830–35; 1839–45)
Flo·rey \'flōr-ē, 'flȯr-\ Sir Howard Walter 1898–1968 Brit. pathologist
Flo·rio \'flōr-ē-ˌō, 'flȯr-\ John *ca* 1553–*ca* 1625 Eng. lexicographer & translator
Flo·ry \'flōr-ē, 'flȯr-\ Paul John 1910–85 Am. chem.
Flo·tow \'flō-(ˌ)tō\ Friedrich 1812–1883 Freiherr *von Flotow* Ger. composer
Foch \'fȯsh, 'fȧsh\ Ferdinand 1851–1929 Fr. gen.; marshal of France
Fo·gel \'fō-gəl\ Robert William 1926– Am. econ.
Fo·kine \'fō-ˌkēn, fȯ-'\ Michel 1880–1942 Am (Russ.-born) choreographer
Fok·ker \'fä-kər, 'fȯ-\ Anthony Herman Gerard 1890–1939 Am. (Du.-born) aircraft designer & builder
Fol·ger \'fōl-jər\ Henry Clay 1857–1930 Am. bibliophile
Fon·tanne \fän-'tan, 'fän-\ Lynn 1887?–1983 *wife of Alfred Lunt* Am. (Eng.-born) actress
Fon·teyn \fän-'tān, 'fän-\ Dame Margot 1919–1991 orig. *Margot Hook·ham* \'hů-kəm\ Eng. ballerina
Foote \'fůt\ Andrew Hull 1806–1863 Am. admiral
Foote Samuel 1720–1777 Eng. actor & playwright
Foote Shelby 1916– Am. hist. & nov.
Forbes–Rob·ert·son \ˌfȯrbz-'rä-bərt-sən\ Sir Johnston 1853–1937 Eng. actor
Ford \'fōrd, 'fȯrd\ Ford Mad·ox \'ma-dəks\ 1873–1939 orig. *Huef·fer* \'hü-fər; 'hwe-fər, 'we-\ Eng. author
Ford Gerald Rudolph 1913– Am. polit.; 38th pres. of the U.S. (1974–77)
Ford Henry 1863–1947 Am. automobile manuf.
Ford John 1586–?1639 Eng. dram.
For·es·ter \'fȯr-əs-tər, 'fär-\ Cecil Scott 1899–1966 Brit. writer
For·rest \'fȯr-əst, 'fär-\ Edwin 1806–1872 Am. actor
Forrest Nathan Bedford 1821–1877 Am. Confed. gen.
For·res·tal \'fȯr-əs-tᵊl, 'fär-, -ˌtȯl\ James Vincent 1892–1949 Am. banker; 1st secy. of defense (1947–49)
Forss·mann \'fȯrs-ˌmän\ Werner Theodor Otto 1904–1979 Ger. surgeon
For·ster \'fȯr-stər\ Edward Morgan 1879–1970 Brit. nov. — **For·ste·ri·an** \fȯr-'stir-ē-ən\ *adj*
For·syth \'fȯr-ˌsīth, fər-\ John 1780–1841 Am. statesman
For·tas \'fȯr-təs\ Abe 1910–1982 Am. jurist
Fos·dick \'fäz-(ˌ)dik\ Harry Emerson 1878–1969 Am. clergyman
Fos·sey \'fȯ-sē, 'fä-\ Dian 1932–1985 Am. ethologist
Fos·ter \'fȯs-tər, 'fäs-\ Stephen Collins 1826–1864 Am. songwriter
Foster William Zebulon 1881–1961 Am. Communist
Fou·cault \fü-'kō\ Jean-Bernard-Léon 1819–1868 Fr. physicist
Fou·qué \fü-'kā\ Friedrich Heinrich Karl de la Motte \mȯt\ 1777–1843 Freiherr *Fouqué* Ger. author
Fou·quet *or* **Fouc·quet** \fü-'kā\ Nicolas 1615–1680 Fr. govt. official
Fou·quier–Tin·ville \fü-kyā-taⁿ-'vēl\ Antoine-Quentin 1746–1795 Fr. polit.
Four·dri·nier \ˌfōr-drə-'nir, ˌfȯr-; fůr-'dri-nē-ər, fōr-, fȯr-\ Henry 1766–1854 & his bro. Sealy *d* 1847 Eng. papermakers & inventors
Fou·ri·er \'fůr-ē-ˌā\ (François-Marie-) Charles 1772–1837 Fr. sociol. & reformer
Fow·ler \'faů-lər\ Henry Watson 1858–1933 Eng. lexicographer
Fowler William Alfred 1911–1995 Am. physicist
Fox \'fäks\ Charles James 1749–1806 Eng. statesman & orator
Fox George 1624–1691 Eng. preacher & founder of Society of Friends
Fox Henry 1705–1774 1st Baron *Hol·land* \'hä-lənd\ Brit. statesman
Foxe \'fäks\ John 1516–1587 Eng. martyrologist
Foxe *or* **Fox** Richard *ca* 1448–1528 Eng. prelate & statesman
Fra·go·nard \ˌfra-gə-'när\ Jean-Honoré 1732–1806 Fr. artist
France \'fran(t)s, fräⁿs\ Anatole 1844–1924 pseud. of *Jacques-Anatole François Thibault* Fr. nov. & satirist
Francesca Piero della — see PIERO DELLA FRANCESCA
Francesca da Rimini — see POLENTA
Fran·cis I \'fran(t)-səs\ 1494–1547 king of France (1515–47)
Francis II 1768–1835 last Holy Rom. emp. (1792–1806); emp. of Austria (as *Francis I*) 1804–35
Francis Fer·di·nand \'fər-də-ˌnand, 'fer-dē-ˌnänt\ 1863–1914 archduke of Austria
Francis Jo·seph I \'jō-səf, 'yō-sef\ 1830–1916 emp. of Austria (1848–1916)
Francis of Assisi Saint 1181(or 1182)–1226 in full *Francesco di Pietro di Bernardone* Ital. friar; founder of Franciscan order
Francis of Sales \'sä(ə)lz\ Saint 1567–1622 Fr. R. C. bishop of Geneva
Franck \'fräŋk\ César Auguste 1822–1890 Fr. (Belg.-born) organist & composer
Franck James 1882–1964 Am. (Ger.-born) physicist
Francke \'fräŋ-kə\ Kuno 1855–1930 Am. (Ger.-born) hist. & educ.
Fran·co \'fräŋ-(ˌ)kō, 'fraŋ-\ Francisco 1892–1975 *Francisco Paulino Hermenegildo Teódulo Franco Bahamonde* Span. gen. & head of Span. state (1936–75)
Frank \'fraŋk, 'fräŋk\ Anne 1929–1945 Ger.-born diarist during the Holocaust
Frank Ilya Mikhaylovich 1908–1990 Russ. physicist
Frank·en·thal·er \'fraŋ-kən-ˌtä-lər, -ˌthä-\ Helen 1928– Am. artist
Frank·furt·er \'fraŋk-fə(r)-tər, -fər-\ Felix 1882–1965 Am. (Austrian-born) jurist

Frank·lin \'fraŋ-klən\ Benjamin 1706–1790 Am. statesman & philos.
Franklin Sir John 1786–1847 Eng. arctic explorer
Franklin Rosalind Elsie 1920–1958 Eng. biophysicist
Franks \'fraŋks\ Oliver Shewell 1905–1992 Baron *Franks of Heading·ton* Eng. philos. & diplomat
Fra·ser \'frā-zər, -zhər\ James Earle 1876–1953 Am. sculptor
Fraser (John) Malcolm 1930– prime min. of Australia (1975–83)
Fraser Peter 1884–1950 N.Z. statesman; prime min. (1940–49)
Fraun·ho·fer \'fraůn-ˌhō-fər\ Joseph von 1787–1826 Bavarian optician & physicist
Fra·zer \'frā-zər, -zhər\ Sir James George 1854–1941 Scot. anthropol.
Fré·chette \frā-'shet\ Louis-Honoré 1839–1908 Canad. poet
Fred·er·ick I \'fre-d(ə-)rik\ *ca* 1123–1190 *Frederick Bar·ba·ros·sa* \ˌbär-bə-'rä-sə, -'rȯ-\ Holy Rom. emp. (1152–90)
Frederick II 1194–1250 Holy Rom. emp. (1215–50); king of Sicily (1198–1250)
Frederick I 1657–1713 king of Prussia (1701–13)
Frederick II 1712–1786 *the Great* king of Prussia (1740–86)
Frederick IX 1899–1972 king of Denmark (1947–72)
Frederick William 1620–1688 *the Great Elector* elector of Brandenburg (1640–88)
Frederick William name of 4 kings of Prussia: **I** 1688–1740 (reigned 1713–40); **II** 1744–1797 (reigned 1786–97); **III** 1770–1840 (reigned 1797–1840); **IV** 1795–1861 (reigned 1840–61)
Free·man \'frē-mən\ Douglas Sou·thall \'saů-ˌthȯl, -ˌthȯl\ 1886–1953 Am. editor & hist.
Freeman Mary Eleanor 1852–1930 née *Wilkins* Am. writer
Fre·ge \'frā-gə\ (Friedrich Ludwig) Gottlob 1848–1925 Ger. math. & philos.
Frei Ru·íz-Ta·gle \'frā-rü-'ēs-'tä-glä\ Eduardo 1941– pres. of Chile (1994–)
Fre·ling·huy·sen \'frē-liŋ-ˌhī-zᵊn\ Frederick Theodore 1817–1885 Am. statesman
Fré·mont \'frē-ˌmänt\ John Charles 1813–1890 Am. gen. & explorer
French \'french\ Daniel Chester 1850–1931 Am. sculptor
Fre·neau \fri-'nō\ Philip Morin 1752–1832 Am. poet
Fres·co·bal·di \ˌfres-kə-'bäl-dē, -'bȯl-\ Girolamo 1583–1643 Ital. composer
Fres·nel \frā-'nel\ Augustin-Jean 1788–1827 Fr. physicist
Freud \'frȯid\ Sigmund 1856–1939 Austrian neurologist
Frey·berg \'frī-ˌbərg\ 1st Baron 1889–1963 *Bernard Cyril Freyberg* N.Z. gen.
Frey·tag \'frī-ˌtäk, -ˌtäg\ Gustav 1816–1895 Ger. author
Frick \'frik\ Henry Clay 1849–1919 Am. industrialist
Fried \'frēt, 'frēd\ Alfred Hermann 1864–1921 Austrian pacifist
Fried·man \'frēd-mən\ Jerome Isaac 1930– Am. physicist
Friedman Milton 1912– Am. econ.
Frie·drich \'frē-drik\ Caspar David 1774–1840 Ger. painter
Frisch \'frish\ Karl von 1886–1982 Austrian zool.
Frisch Ragnar 1895–1973 Norw. econ.
Fro·bi·sher \'frō-bi-shər\ Sir Martin 1535?–1594 Eng. navigator
Froe·bel *or* **Frö·bel** \'frā-bəl, 'frē-, 'frœ-\ Friedrich Wilhelm August 1782–1852 Ger. educ.
Froh·man \'frō-mən\ Charles 1860–1915 Am. theater manager
Frois·sart \'frȯi-ˌsärt, frwä-'sär\ Jean 1333?–*ca* 1405 Fr. chronicler
Fromm \'frōm, 'främ\ Erich 1900–1980 Am. (Ger.-born) psychoanalyst
Fron·di·zi \frän-'dē-zē, -sē\ Arturo 1908–1995 Argentine pres. (1958–62)
Fron·te·nac et Pal·lu·au \frōⁿ-tə-näk-ā-pá-lwʸō\ Comte de 1622–1698 *Louis de Buade* \'bwᵛäd\ Fr. gen. & colonial administrator in America
Frost \'frȯst\ Robert Lee 1874–1963 Am. poet — **Frost·ian** \'frȯs-tē-ən, -chən\ *adj*
Froude \'früd\ James Anthony 1818–1894 Eng. hist.
Fry \'frī\ Christopher 1907– Eng. dram.
Frye \'frī\ (Herman) Northrop 1912–1991 Canad. lit. critic
Fu·'ad I \fü-'äd\ 1868–1936 sultan (1917–22) & king (1922–36) of Egypt
Fu·en·tes \fü-'en-ˌtäs\ Carlos 1928– Mex. author
Fuer·tes \'fyůr-(ˌ)tēz\ Louis Agassiz 1874–1927 Am. illustrator
Fu·gard \fü-'gärd\ Athol 1932– So. African playwright
Fu·ji·mo·ri \ˌfü-jē-'mō-rē\ Alberto 1938– pres. of Peru (1990–)
Fu·kui \'fü-kü-ē, fü-'kü-ē\ Kenichi 1918– Jp. chem.
Ful·bright \'fůl-ˌbrīt\ (James) William 1905–1995 Am. polit.
Full·er \'fů-lər\ Melville Weston 1833–1910 Am. jurist; chief justice U.S. Supreme Court (1888–1910)
Fuller (Richard) Buckminster 1895–1983 Am. engineer
Fuller (Sarah) Margaret 1810–1850 Marchioness *Os·so·li* \'ȯ-sə-(ˌ)lē\ Am. critic & reformer
Fuller Thomas 1608–1661 Eng. divine & author
Ful·ton \'fůl-tᵊn\ Robert 1765–1815 Am. engineer & inventor
Funk \'fůŋk, 'fäŋk\ Casimir 1884–1967 Am. (Pol.-born) biochem.
Funk \'fäŋk\ Isaac Kauffman 1839–1912 Am. editor & publisher
Fun·ston \'fən(t)-stən\ Frederick 1865–1917 Am. gen.
Fur·ness \'fər-nəs, -ˌnes\ Horace Howard: father 1833–1912 & son 1865–1930 Am. Shakespeare scholars
Fur·ni·vall \'fər-nə-vəl\ Frederick James 1825–1910 Eng. philologist
Furt·wäng·ler \'fůrt-ˌveŋ-lər\ (Gustav Heinrich Ernst Martin) Wilhelm 1886–1954 Ger. conductor
Ga·ble \'gā-bəl\ (William) Clark 1901–1960 Am. actor
Ga·bo \'gä-(ˌ)bō\ Naum 1890–1977 orig. *Naum Pevs·ner* \'pevz-nər\ Am. (Russ.-born) sculptor
Gabor \'gä-(ˌ)bȯr, gə-'bȯr\ Dennis 1900–1979 Brit. (Hung.-born) physicist
Ga·bo·riau \gə-'bȯr-ē-ˌō\ Émile 1832(or 1833 or 1835)–*ca* 1873 Fr. writer

---

\ə\ abut \ᵊ\ kitten, F table \ər\ further \a\ ash \ā\ ace \ä\ mop, mar \aů\ out \ch\ chin \e\ bet \ē\ easy \g\ go \i\ hit \ī\ ice \j\ job \ŋ\ sing \ō\ go \ȯ\ law \ȯi\ boy \th\ thin \th\ the \ü\ loot \ů\ foot \y\ yet \zh\ vision \à, k̲, ⁿ, œ, œ̄, ue, ᵫ, ʸ\ see Guide to Pronunciation

1412 Biographical Names

Ga·bri·eli \,gä-brē-'e-lē\ Giovanni *ca* 1556–1612 Ital. composer
Gad·ha·fi \gə-'dä-fē, kə-, -'da-\ Mu'ammar Muḥammad al- 1942– Libyan leader (1969–   )
Gads·den \'gadz-dən\ James 1788–1858 Am. army officer & diplomat
Ga·ga·rin \gə-'gär-ən\ Yu·ry \'yùr-ē\ Alekseyevich 1934–1968 Russ. astronaut
Gage \'gāj\ Thomas 1721–1787 Brit. gen. & colonial gov. in America
Gail·lard \gil-'yärd\ David DuBose \dü-'bōz, dyü-\ 1859–1913 Am. army officer & engineer
Gaines \'gānz\ Edmund Pendleton 1777–1849 Am. gen.
Gains·bor·ough \'gānz-,bər-ə, -,bə-rə, -b(ə-)rə\ Thomas 1727–1788 Eng. painter
Gait·skell \'gāt-skəl\ Hugh Todd Naylor 1906–1963 Eng. polit.
Ga·ius \'gā-əs, 'gī-əs\ *fl* A.D. 130–180 Rom. jurist
Gaj·du·sek \'gī-də-,shek\ D(aniel) Carleton 1923–   Am. virologist
Gal·ba \'gal-bə, 'gól-\ Servius Sulpicius 3 B.C.–A.D. 69 Rom. emp. (68–69)
Gal·braith \'gal-,brāth\ John Kenneth 1908–   Am. (Canad.-born) econ. — Gal·braith·ian \gal-'brā-thē-ən, -'brāth-yən\ *adj*
Gale \'gā(ə)l\ Zona 1874–1938 Am. nov.
Ga·len \'gā-lən\ A.D. 129–*ca* 199 Greek physician & writer — Ga·len·ic \gə-'le-nik\ *or* Ga·len·i·cal \-ni-kəl\ *adj*
Ga·le·ri·us \gə-'lir-ē-əs\ *d* 311 *Gaius Galerius Valerius Maximianus* Rom. emp. (305–311)
Ga·li·leo \,ga-lə-'lē-(,)ō, -'lā-\ 1564–1642 in full *Galileo Galilei* Ital. astron. & physicist
Gal·land \gä-'läⁿ\ Antoine 1646–1715 Fr. orientalist & translator
Gal·la·tin \'ga-lə-t⁰n\ (Abraham Alfonse) Albert 1761–1849 Am. (Swiss-born) financier & statesman
Gal·lau·det \,ga-lə-'det\ Thomas Hopkins 1787–1851 Am. teacher of the hearing- and speech-impaired
Ga·lle·gos Frei·re \gä-'yā-(,)gōs-'frā-(,)rā\ Rómulo 1884–1969 Venezuelan nov.; pres. of Venezuela (1948)
Gal·li–Cur·ci \,ga-li-'kùr-chē, ,gä-, -'kər-\ Amelita 1889–1963 née *Galli* Am. (Ital.-born) soprano
Gal·lie·ni \,gal-yā-'nē, gal-'yā-nē\ Joseph-Simon 1849–1916 Fr. gen. & colonial administrator
Gal·lie·nus \,ga-lē-'ē-nəs, -'ā-nəs\ Publius Licinius Valerianus Egnatius *d* 268 Rom. emp. (253–268)
Gal·lup \'ga-ləp\ George Horace 1901–1984 Am. statistician
Ga·lois \gal-'wä\ Évariste 1811–1832 Fr. math.
Gals·wor·thy \'gólz-,wər-thē\ John 1867–1933 Eng. nov. & dram.
Galt \'gólt\ John 1779–1839 Scot. nov.
Gal·ton \'gól-t⁰n\ Sir Francis 1822–1911 Eng. scientist — Gal·to·nian \gól-'tō-nē-ən, -nyən\ *adj*
Gal·va·ni \gal-'vä-nē, gäl-\ Luigi 1737–1798 Ital. physician & physicist
Gál·vez \'gäl-,ves\ José 1729–1787 Marqués *de la Sonora* Span. jurist & colonial administrator
Ga·ma, da \dä-'gä-mə, -'gä-\ Vas·co \'vas-kō, 'väs-\ *ca* 1460–1524 Port. navigator & explorer
Ga·mar·ra \gə-'mär-ə\ Augustín 1785–1841 Peruvian gen.; pres. of Peru (1829–33; 1839–41)
Gam·bet·ta \gam-'be-tə, ,gän-bə-'tä\ Léon-Michel 1838–1882 Fr. lawyer & statesman
Ga·me·lin \,gam-'la⁰, ,ga-mə-\ Maurice-Gustave 1872–1958 Fr. gen.
Gan·dhi \'gän-dē, 'gan-\ In·dira \in-'dir-ə, 'in-də-rə\ Nehru 1917–1984 *dau. of Jawaharlal Nehru* prime min. of India (1966–77; 1980–84)
Gandhi Mohandas Karamchand 1869–1948 *Ma·hat·ma* \mə-'hät-mə, -'hat-\ Indian nationalist leader — Gan·dhi·an \-ən\ *adj*
Gandhi Ra·jiv \rä-'jēv\ Ratna 1944–1991 *son of Indira* prime min. of India (1984–89)
Gar·a·mond \'gar-ə-,mänd, ,gar-ə-'mō⁰\ *or* Gar·a·mont \-'mänt, -'mō⁰\ Claude *ca* 1480–1561 Fr. typefounder
Ga·rand \gə-'rand, 'gar-ənd\ John Cantius 1888–1974 Am. (Canad.-born) inventor
Gar·bo \'gär-(,)bō\ Greta 1905–1990 orig. *Greta Lovisa Gustafsson* Am. (Swed.-born) actress — Gar·bo·esque \,gär-bō-'wesk\ *adj*
Gar·cía Gu·tiér·rez \gär-'sē-ə-gü-'tyer-əs\ Antonio 1813–1884 Span. dram.
García Íñi·guez \-'ēn-yi-,gäs\ Calixto 1839–1898 Cuban revolutionary
García Lor·ca \-'lór-kə\ Federico 1898–1936 Span. poet & dram.
García Már·quez \-'mär-,käs\ Gabriel 1928–   Colombian author
García Mo·re·no \-mə-'rä-(,)nō\ Gabriel 1821–1875 Ecuadorian journalist; pres. of Ecuador (1861–65; 1869–75)
Gar·ci·la·so de la Ve·ga \,gär-si-'lä-sō-,dä-lə-'vä-gə\ 1539–1616 *El Inca* Peruvian hist.
Gar·den \'gär-d⁰n\ Mary 1874–1967 Am. (Scot.-born) soprano
Gar·di·ner \'gärd-nər, 'gär-d⁰n-ər\ Samuel Rawson 1829–1902 Eng. hist.
Gardiner Stephen *ca* 1482–1555 Eng. prelate & statesman
Gard·ner \'gärd-nər\ Erle Stanley 1889–1970 Am. writer
Gar·field \'gär-,fēld\ James Abram 1831–1881 20th pres. of the U.S. (1881)
Gar·i·bal·di \,gar-ə-'ból-dē\ Giuseppe 1807–1882 Ital. patriot — Gar·i·bal·di·an \-dē-ən\ *adj*
Gar·land \'gär-lənd\ (Hannibal) Hamlin 1860–1940 Am. nov.
Gar·ner \'gär-nər\ John Nance 1868–1967 Am. polit.; vice pres. of the U.S. (1933–41)
Gar·nett \'gär-nət\ Constance 1862–1946 née *Black* Eng. translator
Gar·rick \'gar-ik\ David 1717–1779 Eng. actor
Gar·ri·son \'gar-ə-sən\ William Lloyd 1805–1879 Am. abolitionist
Gar·shin \'gär-shən\ Vsevolod Mikhaylovich 1855–1888 Russ. writer
Gar·vey \'gär-vē\ Marcus Moziah 1887–1940 Jamaican black leader
Gary \'gar-ē, 'ger-ē\ Elbert Henry 1846–1927 Am. industrialist
Gas·coigne \'gas-,kóin\ George *ca* 1525–1577 Eng. poet
Gas·kell \'gas-kəl\ Elizabeth Cleghorn 1810–1865 née *Stevenson* Eng. nov.
Gas·ser \'ga-sər\ Herbert Spencer 1888–1963 Am. physiol.
Gates \'gāts\ Horatio *ca* 1728–1806 Am. gen. in Revolution
Gau·guin \gō-ga⁰\ (Eugène-Henri-) Paul 1848–1903 Fr. painter — Gau·guin·esque \(,)gō-,ga-'nesk\ *adj*
Gaulle \di-'gól, -'gōl\ Charles-André-Marie-Joseph 1890–1970 Fr. gen. & polit.; pres. of Fifth Republic (1958–69)
Gauss \'gaús\ Carl Friedrich 1777–1855 Ger. math. & astron.

Gautama Buddha — see SIDDHĀRTHA GAUTAMA
Gau·tier \gō-tyā\ Théophile 1811–1872 Fr. author
Gay \'gā\ John 1685–1732 Eng. poet & dram.
Gay–Lus·sac \'gā-lə-'sak\ Joseph-Louis 1778–1850 Fr. chem. & physicist
Geber — see JĀBIR IBN ḤAYYĀN
Ged·des \'ge-dēz\ Norman Bel 1893–1958 Am. designer
Gei·kie \'gē-kē\ Sir Archibald 1835–1924 Scot. geologist
Gei·sel \'gī-zəl\ Theodor Seuss 1904–1991 pseud. *Dr. Seuss* \'süs\ Am. writer & illustrator
Gellée Claude — see CLAUDE LORRAIN
Gell–Mann \'gel-,män\ Murray 1929–   Am. physicist
Ge·net \zhə-'nā\ Edmond-Charles-Édouard 1763–1834 Fr. diplomat in U.S.
Genet Jean 1910–1986 Fr. dram. & nov.
Gen·ghis Khan \,jen-gəs-'kän, ,gen-\ *ca* 1162–1227 Mongol conqueror
Gen·ser·ic \'gen(t)-sə-rik, 'jen(t)-\ *or* Gai·se·ric \'gī-zə-(,)rik, -sə-\ *d* 477 king of the Vandals (428–477)
Gen·ti·le da Fa·bri·a·no \jen-'tē-lē-də-,fä-brē-'ä-(,)nō\ *ca* 1370–1427 orig. *Niccolo di Giovanni di Massio* Ital. painter
Gen·ti·les·chi \,jen-t⁰l-'es-kē\ Orazio Lomi *ca* 1562–*ca* 1647 & his dau. Artemisia *ca* 1597–after 1651 Ital. painters
Geof·frey of Monmouth \'jef-rē-əv-'män-məth\ *ca* 1100–1154 Brit. ecclesiastic & chronicler
George \'jórj\ Saint 3d cent. Christian martyr & patron saint of England
George name of 6 kings of Great Britain: I 1660–1727 (reigned 1714–27); II 1683–1760 (reigned 1727–60); III 1738–1820 (reigned 1760–1820); IV 1762–1830 (reigned 1820–30); V 1865–1936 (reigned 1910–36); VI 1895–1952 (reigned 1936–52)
George name of 2 kings of Greece: I 1845–1913 (reigned 1863–1913); II 1890–1947 (reigned 1922–23; 1935–47)
George David Lloyd — see David LLOYD GEORGE
George Henry 1839–1897 Am. econ.
Ge·rard \jə-'rärd, 'jer-,ärd\ Charles 1618?–1694 1st Baron *Gerard of Bran·don* \'bran-dən\; Viscount *Brandon* Eng. royalist commander
Gé·rard \zhā-'rär\ Comte Étienne-Maurice 1773–1852 Fr. Napoleonic gen.; marshal of France
Ger·hard·sen \'ger-,här-s⁰n\ Einar Henry 1897–1987 Norw. polit.
Gé·ri·cault \,zhā-ri-'kō\ (Jean-Louis-André-) Théodore 1791–1824 Fr. painter
Ger·man·i·cus Cae·sar \jər-,ma-ni-kə(s)-'sē-zər\ 15 B.C.–A.D. 19 Rom. gen.
Gé·rôme \zhā-'rōm\ Jean-Léon 1824–1904 Fr. painter
Ge·ron·i·mo \jə-'rä-nə-,mō\ 1829–1909 *Goyathlay* Chiricahua Apache leader
Ger·ry \'ger-ē\ Elbridge 1744–1814 Am. polit.; vice pres. of the U.S. (1813–14)
Gersh·win \'gər-shwən\ George 1898–1937 orig. *Jacob Gershvin* Am. composer
Ge·sell \gə-'zel\ Arnold Lucius 1880–1961 Am. psychol. & pediatrician
Ges·ner \'ges-nər\ Conrad 1516–1565 Swiss naturalist
Get·ty \'ge-tē\ Jean Paul 1892–1976 Am. business executive
Gha·zā·lī, al- \,al-gə-'za-lē\ 1058–1111 *Abu Ḥāmid Muḥammad ibn Muḥammad at-Tūsi al-Ghazālī* Islamic jurist, theol., & mystic
Ghi·ber·ti \gē-'ber-tē\ Lorenzo *ca* 1378–1455 Florentine goldsmith, painter, & sculptor
Ghir·lan·da·jo *or* Ghir·lan·da·io \,gir-lən-'dä-(,)yō\ Domenico 1449–1494 orig. *Domenico di Tommaso Bigordi* Florentine painter
Ghose Sri Aurobindo — see AUROBINDO
Gia·co·met·ti \,jä-kə-'me-tē\ Alberto 1901–1966 Swiss artist
Giae·ver \'yā-vər\ Ivar 1929–   Am. (Norw.-born) physicist
Gi·auque \jē-'ók\ William Francis 1895–1982 Am. chem.
Gib·bon \'gi-bən\ Edward 1737–1794 Eng. hist. — Gib·bon·ian \gi-'bō-nē-ən\ *adj*
Gib·bons \'gi-bənz\ James 1834–1921 Am. cardinal
Gibbons Orlando 1538–1625 Eng. organist & composer
Gibbs \'gibz\ James 1682–1754 Brit. architect
Gibbs Josiah Willard 1839–1903 Am. math. & physicist
Gib·ran *or* Jib·ran \jə-'brän\ Kahlil 1883–1931 *Jubrān Khalīl Jubrān* Lebanese nov., poet, & artist in U.S.
Gib·son \'gib-sən\ Charles Dana 1867–1944 Am. illustrator
Gibson William 1914–   Am. dram.
Gide \'zhēd\ André 1869–1951 Fr. nov., critic, & essayist
Giel·gud \'gil-,gùd, 'gēl-\ Sir (Arthur) John 1904–   Eng. actor
Gie·rek \'gyer-ək\ Edward 1913–   1st secy. of Polish Communist party (1970–80)
Gie·se·king \'gē-zə-kiŋ\ Walter Wilhelm 1895–1956 Ger. (Fr.-born) pianist
Gil·bert \'gil-bərt\ Cass 1859–1934 Am. architect
Gilbert Sir Humphrey *ca* 1539–1583 Eng. navigator
Gilbert Walter 1932–   Am. biochem.
Gilbert William 1540–1603 Eng. physician & physicist
Gilbert Sir William Schwenck 1836–1911 Eng. librettist & poet — Gilbert·ian \gi-'bər-tē-ən\ *adj*
Gil·les·pie \gə-'les-pē\ John Birks 1917–1993 *Dizzy* Am. jazz musician
Gil·lette \jə-'let\ King Camp 1855–1932 Am. inventor & manuf.
Gillette William Hooker 1855–1937 Am. actor
Gil·man \'gil-mən\ Alfred Goodman 1941–   Am. pharmacologist
Gilman Daniel Coit \'kóit\ 1831–1908 Am. educ.; pres. Johns Hopkins U. (1875–1901)
Gil·mer \'gil-mər\ Elizabeth 1870–1951 née *Mer·i·weth·er* \'mer-ə-,wethər\ pseud. *Dorothy Dix* \'diks\ Am. journalist
Gil·pin \'gil-pən\ Charles Sidney 1878–1930 Am. actor
Gi·na·ste·ra \,hē-nə-'ster-ə\ Alberto Evaristo 1916–1983 Argentine composer
Gin·grich \'giŋ-(,)grich, -(,)rich\ Newton Leroy 1943–   Am. polit.
Gins·berg \'ginz-,bərg\ Allen 1926–   Am. poet
Gins·burg \'ginz-,bərg\ Ruth Bader 1933–   Am. jurist
Gior·gio·ne \(,)jór-'jō-nē\ *ca.* 1477–1511 *Giorgione da Castelfranco* Venetian painter
Giot·to \'jō(t)-(,)tō, jē-'ä-(,)tō\ 1266/67(or 1276)–1337 *Giotto di Bondone* Florentine painter, architect, & sculptor

Gi·rard \zhē-'rär\ Jean-Baptiste 1765–1850 Swiss Franciscan & educ.
Gi·rard \jə-'rärd\ Stephen 1750–1831 Am. (Fr.-born) financier
Gi·raud \zhē-'rō\ Henri-Honoré 1879–1949 Fr. gen.
Gi·rau·doux \ˌzhē-rō-'dü\ (Hyppolyte-) Jean 1882–1944 Fr. writer
Gir·tin \'gər-t²n\ Thomas 1775–1802 Eng. painter
Gis·card d'Es·taing \zhis-kär-des-taⁿ, -ˌkär-des-'taŋ\ Valéry 1926– pres. of France (1974–81)
Gis·sing \'gis-iŋ\ George Robert 1857–1903 Eng. nov.
Giu·lio Ro·ma·no \ˌjül-yō-rə-'mä-(ˌ)nō\ ca 1499–1546 Giulio di Pietro di Filippo de' Gianuzzi Ital. painter & architect
Gjel·le·rup \'ge-lə-ˌrúp\ Karl 1857–1919 Dan. writer
Glad·stone \'glad-ˌstōn, chiefly Brit -stən\ William Ewart 1809–1898 Brit. statesman; prime min. (1868–74; 1880–85; 1886; 1892–94) — **Glad·ston·ian** \ˌglad-'stō-nē-ən\ adj
Gla·ser \'glä-zər\ Donald Arthur 1926–   Am. physicist
Glas·gow \'glas-(ˌ)kō, -(ˌ)gō; 'glaz-(ˌ)gō\ Ellen Anderson Gholson 1873–1945 Am. nov.
Glash·ow \'gla-(ˌ)shō\ Sheldon Lee 1932–   Am. physicist
Glas·pell \'glas-ˌpel\ Susan 1882–1948 Am. nov. & dram.
Glass \'glas\ Carter 1858–1946 Am. statesman
Glass Philip 1937–   Am. composer
Gla·zu·nov \glen-'daú\ Aleksandr Konstantinovich 1865–1936 Russ. composer
Glen·dow·er \glen-'daú(-ə)r\ Owen ca 1359–ca 1416 Welsh rebel
Glenn \'glen\ John Herschel 1921–   Am. astronaut & polit.
Glick·man \'glik-mən\ Daniel Robert 1941–   U.S. secy. of agriculture (1995–)
Glin·ka \'gliŋ-kə\ Mikhail Ivanovich 1804–1857 Russ. composer
Gloucester Duke of — see HUMPHREY
Glov·er \'glə-vər\ John 1732–1797 Am. gen. in Revolution
Glover Sarah Ann 1785–1867 Eng. music teacher
Gluck \'glük\ Alma 1884–1938 née (Reba) Fiersohn Am. (Romanian-born) soprano
Gluck Christoph Willibald 1714–1787 Ger. composer
Go·bat \gō-'bä\ Charles Albert 1834–1914 Swiss statesman
God·dard \'gä-dərd\ Robert Hutchings 1882–1945 Am. physicist
God·frey of Bouillon \ˌgäd-frē\ F Gode·froy de Bouillon \gōt-frwä\ ca 1060–1100 Fr. crusader
Go·dol·phin \gə-'däl-fən\ Sidney 1645–1712 1st Earl of Godolphin Eng. statesman
Go·doy \gō-'dói\ Manuel de 1767–1851 Span. statesman
Go·du·nov \'gō-d²n-ˌóf, 'gó-, 'gä-\ Boris Fyodorovich ca 1551–1605 czar of Russia (1598–1605)
God·win \'gäd-wən\ or **God·wine** \'gäd-(ˌ)wi-nə\ d 1053 earl of Wessex
Godwin William 1756–1836 Eng. philos. & nov. — **God·win·ian** \ˌgäd-'wi-nē-ən\ adj
Godwin-Aus·ten \-'ós-tən, -'äs-\ Henry Haversham 1834–1923 Eng. explorer & geologist
Goeb·bels \'gə(r)-bəlz, 'gœ-bəls\ (Paul) Joseph 1897–1945 Ger. Nazi propagandist
Goe·ring var of GÖRING
Goes \'güs\ Hugo van der ca 1440–1482 Du. painter
Goe·thals \'gō-thəlz\ George Washington 1858–1928 Am. gen. & engineer
Goe·the \'gə(r)-tə, 'gœ-tə\ Johann Wolfgang von 1749–1832 Ger. poet & dram. — **Goe·the·an** \-tē-ən\ adj
Gogh, van \van-'gō, -'gäk, -'kók, Brit also -'gəf\ Vincent Willem 1853–1890 Du. painter
Go·gol \'gó-gəl, 'gō-ˌgól\ Nikolay Vasilyevich 1809–1852 Russ. writer — **Go·gol·ian** \gō-'gōl-yən, gō-'gól-\ adj
Gold·berg \'gōl(d)-ˌbərg\ Arthur Joseph 1908–1990 Am. lawyer and jurist; U.S. ambassador to U.N. (1965–68)
Gol·den·wei·ser \'gōl-dən-ˌwī-zər\ Alexander Alexandrovich 1880–1940 Am. (Russ.-born) anthropol. & sociol.
Gold·ing \'gōl-diŋ\ William Gerald 1911–1993 Eng. author
Gol·do·ni \gäl-'dō-nē, gōl-\ Carlo 1707–1793 Ital. dram.
Gold·smith \'gōl(d)-ˌsmith\ Oliver 1730–1774 Brit. author
Gold·stein \'gōl(d)-ˌstīn\ Joseph Leonard 1940–   Am. medical geneticist
Gold·wa·ter \'gōld-ˌwó-tər, -ˌwä-\ Barry Morris 1909–   Am. polit.
Gold·wyn \'gōl-dwən\ Samuel 1879?–1974 orig. Schmuel Gelbfisz Am. (Pol.-born) motion-picture producer
Gol·gi \'gōl-(ˌ)jē\ Camillo 1843(or 1844)–1926 Ital. physician
Gol·lancz \gə-'lan(t)s\ Sir Hermann 1852–1930 Eng. Semitic scholar
Gó·mez \'gō-ˌmez\ Juan Vicente 1864–1935 Venezuelan gen. & polit.; dictator (1908–35)
Gom·pers \'gäm-pərz\ Samuel 1850–1924 Am. (Brit.-born) labor leader
Go·muł·ka \gō-'múl-kə, -'məl-\ Władysław 1905–1982 Pol. polit.
Gon·çal·ves Di·as \gən-'säl-vəs-'dē-əs\ Antônio 1823–1864 Braz. poet
Gon·cha·ro·va \gən-'chär-ə-və\ Nathalie 1883–1962 Russ. artist
Gon·court \gō⁽ⁿ⁾-'kúr\ Edmond-Louis-Antoine Huot de 1822–1896 & his bro. Jules-Alfred Huot de 1830–1870 Fr. nov. & collaborators
Gon·do·mar \ˌgän-də-'mär\ Conde de 1567–1626 Diego Sarmiento de Acuña Span. diplomat
Gon·za·ga \gən-'zä-gə, gän-, -'za-\ Saint Aloysius 1568–1591 Ital. Jesuit
Gon·zá·lez \gən-'zä-ləs\ Manuel 1833–1893 Mex. gen.; pres. of Mexico (1880–84)
Gon·za·lo de Cór·do·ba — see FERNÁNDEZ DE CÓRDOBA
Goo·dall \'gú-(ˌ)dòl, -(ˌ)däl\ Jane 1934–   Brit. ethologist
Good·hue \'gúd-(ˌ)hyü, -(ˌ)yü\ Bertram Grosvenor 1869–1924 Am. architect
Good·man \'gúd-mən\ Benjamin David 1909–1986 Benny Goodman Am. musician and bandleader
Good·rich \'gúd-(ˌ)rich\ Samuel Griswold 1793–1860 pseud. Peter Parley \'pär-lē\ Am. writer
Good·year \'gúd-ˌyir\ Charles 1800–1860 Am. inventor
Gor·ba·chev \ˌgór-bə-'chóf, -'chef; 'gór-bə-ˌ\ Mikhail Sergeyevich 1931–   Soviet polit.; 1st secy. of communist party (1985–91); pres. of U.S.S.R. (1990–91)

Gor·cha·kov \ˌgór-chə-'kóf, -'kóv\ Prince Aleksandr Mikhaylovich 1798–1883 Russ. statesman & diplomat
Gor·di·mer \'gór-də-mər\ Nadine 1923–   So. African writer
Gor·din \'gór-d²n\ Jacob 1853–1909 Am. (Russ.-born) Yiddish dram.
Gor·don \'gór-d²n\ Charles George 1833–1885 Chinese Gordon, Gordon Pasha Brit. soldier
Gordon Charles William 1860–1937 pseud. Ralph Connor Canad. clergyman & nov.
Gordon Lord George 1751–1793 Eng. polit. agitator
Gore \'gór, 'gór\ Albert, Jr. 1948–   Am. polit.; vice pres. of the U.S. (1993–)
Go·re·my·kin \ˌgór-ə-'mē-kən\ Ivan Logginovich 1839–1917 Russ. statesman; prime min. (1906; 1914–16)
Gor·gas \'gór-gəs\ William Crawford 1854–1920 Am. army surgeon & sanitation expert
Gö·ring \'gər-iŋ, 'ger-, 'gōer-\ Hermann 1893–1946 Ger. Nazi polit.
Gor·ky \'gór-kē\ Maksim 1868–1936 pseud. of Aleksey Maksimovich Pesh·kov \'pesh-ˌkóf, -ˌkóv\ Russ. writer
Gor·ky \'gór-kē\ Arshile 1905–1948 Am. (Armenian-born) artist
Gort Viscount — see VEREKER
Gosse \'gäs\ Sir Edmund William 1849–1928 Eng. poet & critic
Gott·schalk \'gä-chók, 'gät-ˌshók\ Louis Moreau 1829–1869 Am. composer
Gou·dy \'gaú-dē\ Frederic William 1865–1947 Am. type designer
Gough \'gäf\ Hugh 1779–1869 1st Viscount Gough Eng. field marshal
Gould \'güld\ Jay 1836–1892 orig. Jason Gould Am. financier
Gou·nod \gü-'nō; 'gü-ˌnō\ Charles-François 1818–1893 Fr. composer
Gour·mont \gúr-'mō⁽ⁿ⁾\ Remy de 1858–1915 Fr. writer
Gove \'gōv\ Philip Babcock 1902–1972 Am. lexicographer
Gow·er \'gaú(-ə)r, 'gō(-ə)r, 'gó(-ə)r\ John 1330?–1408 Eng. poet
Go·ya y Lu·cien·tes \'gói-ə-,ē-,lü-sē-'en-,täs\ Francisco José de 1746–1828 Span. painter — **Go·ya·esque** \ˌgói-ə-'esk\ or **Go·yesque** \gói-'yesk\ adj
Goy·en or **Goij·en, van** \van-'gói-ən, 'kói-\ Jan Josephszoon 1596–1656 Du. painter
Grac·chus \'gra-kəs\ Gaius Sempronius 153–121 B.C. & his bro. Tiberius Sempronius 163–133 B.C. the Grac·chi \'gra-ˌkī\ Rom. statesmen
Gra·ham \'grä-əm, 'gra-əm\ John 1648–1689 Graham of Claverhouse; Bonny Dundee; 1st Viscount of Dundee Scot. Jacobite
Graham Martha 1893–1991 Am. choreographer & dancer
Graham Thomas 1805–1869 Scot. chem.
Graham William Franklin 1918–   Billy Graham Am. evangelist
Gra·hame \'grä-əm, 'gra(-ə)m\ Kenneth 1859–1932 Brit. writer
Gramme \'gram\ Zénobe Théophile 1826–1901 Belg. engineer
Gra·na·dos \grə-'nä-(ˌ)dōs, -(ˌ)thōs\ Enrique 1867–1916 Span. composer
Gran·di \'grän-(ˌ)dē\ Dino 1895–1988 Conte di Mordano Ital. Fascist polit.
Gra·nit \grä-'nēt\ Ragnar Arthur 1900–1991 Swed. (Finn.-born) physiol.
Grant \'grant\ Ulysses 1822–1885 orig. Hiram Ulysses Grant Am. gen.; 18th pres. of the U.S. (1869–77)
Gran·ville–Bar·ker \'gran-ˌvil-'bär-kər\ Harley Granville 1877–1946 Eng. actor, manager, & dram.
Grass \'gräs\ Günter Wilhelm 1927–   Ger. writer
Grasse \'gras, 'gräs\ François-Joseph-Paul 1722–1788 Comte de Grasse & Marquis de Grasse-Tilly \-tē-'yē\ Fr. naval officer
Gra·tian \'grä-sh(ē-)ən\ L Flavius Gratianus 359–383 Rom. emp. (367–383)
Grat·tan \'gra-t²n\ Henry 1746–1820 Irish orator & statesman
Grau San Mar·tín \ˌgraú-ˌsan-(ˌ)mär-'tēn, -ˌsän\ Ramón 1887–1969 Cuban physician & polit.; pres. of Cuba (1944–48)
Graves \'grävz\ Robert Ranke 1895–1985 Brit. author
Gray \'grä\ Asa 1810–1888 Am. botanist
Gray Thomas 1716–1771 Eng. poet
Grayson David — see Ray Stannard BAKER
Gra·zia·ni \ˌgrät-sē-'ä-nē\ Rodolfo 1882–1955 Marchese di Neghelli Ital. marshal & colonial administrator
Gre·co, El \el-'gre-(ˌ)kō also -'grä-\ 1541–1614 Doménikos Theotokópoulos Span. (Cretan-born) painter
Gree·ley \'grē-lē\ Horace 1811–1872 Am. journalist & polit.
Gree·ly \'grē-lē\ Adolphus Washington 1844–1935 Am. gen. & arctic explorer
Green \'grēn\ John Richard 1837–1883 Eng. hist.
Green Julien 1900–   Fr. nov.
Green William 1873–1952 Am. labor leader
Gree·na·way \'grē-nə-ˌwä\ Catherine 1846–1901 Kate Eng. artist
Greene \'grēn\ Graham 1904–1991 Brit. nov.
Greene Nathanael 1742–1786 Am. gen. in Revolution
Greene Robert 1558?–1592 Eng. poet & dram.
Gree·nough \'grē-ˌnō\ Horatio 1805–1852 Am. sculptor
Greg·o·ry \'gre-g(ə-)rē\ Saint 240–332 the Illuminator apostle & founder of the Armenian Church
Gregory name of 16 popes: esp. **I** Saint ca 540–604 the Great (pope 590–604); **VII** Saint orig. Hil·de·brand \'hil-də-ˌbrand\ ca 1020–1085 (pope 1073–85); **XIII** orig. Ugo Buon·com·pa·gni \'ü-gō-bwón-kōm-ˌpän-yē\ 1502–1585 (pope 1572–85)
Gregory Isabella Augusta 1852–1932 Lady Gregory née Persse Irish dram.
Gregory of Nys·sa \'ni-sə\ Saint ca 335–ca 394 Eastern church father
Gregory of Tours Saint 538–594 Frankish ecclesiastic & hist.
Gren·fell \'gren-ˌfel, -fəl\ Sir Wilfred Thomason 1865–1940 Eng. medical missionary
Gren·ville \'gren-vil, -vəl\ George 1712–1770 Eng. statesman
Grenville or **Greyn·ville** \'grän-\ Sir Richard 1542–1591 Brit. naval commander
Gresh·am \'gre-shəm\ Sir Thomas 1519–1579 Eng. financier

\ə\ abut \²\ kitten, F table \ər\ further \a\ ash \ā\ ace \ä\ mop, mar \aú\ out \ch\ chin \e\ bet \ē\ easy \g\ go \i\ hit \ī\ ice \j\ job \ŋ\ sing \ō\ go \ó\ law \ói\ boy \th\ thin \th̸\ the \ü\ loot \ú\ foot \y\ yet \zh\ vision \à, ḵ, ⁿ, œ, œ̄, ue, ūe, ᵞ\ see Guide to Pronunciation

Greuze \'grə(r)z, 'grœz\ Jean-Baptiste 1725–1805 Fr. painter
Gré·vy \grā-'vē\ (François-Paul-) Jules 1807–1891 Fr. lawyer; 3d pres. of the Republic (1879–87)
Grey \'grā\ 2d Earl 1764–1845 *Charles Grey* Eng. statesman; prime min. (1830–34)
Grey Edward 1862–1933 Viscount *Grey of Fal·lo·don* \'fa-lə-d°n\ Eng. polit.
Grey Lady Jane 1537–1554 titular queen of England for 9 days
Grey Zane 1875–1939 Am. nov.
Grieg \'grēg\ Edvard Hagerup 1843–1907 Norw. composer
Grieve Christopher Murray — see Hugh MACDIARMID
Grif·fin \'gri-fən\ Walter Burley 1876–1937 Am. architect
Grif·fith \'gri-fəth\ Arthur 1872–1922 Irish journalist & nationalist
Griffith David Lewelyn Wark 1875–1948 Am. motion-picture producer & director
Gri·gnard \grēn-'yär\ (François-Auguste-) Victor 1871–1935 Fr. chem.
Grill·par·zer \'gril-,pärt-sər\ Franz 1791–1872 Austrian dram. & poet
Grimm \'grim\ Jacob 1785–1863 & his bro. Wilhelm 1786–1859 Ger. philologists & folklorists
Gris \'grēs\ Juan 1887–1927 *José Victoriano González* Span. painter in France
Gro·fé \'grō-,fā\ Fer·de \'fər-dē\ 1892–1972 Am. conductor & composer
Gro·lier de Ser·vières \,grōl-'yā-də-,ser-vē-'er, 'grōl-yər-\ Jean 1479–1565 Vicomte *d'Aguisy* Fr. bibliophile
Gro·my·ko \grə-'mē-(,)kō, grō-\ Andrey Andreyevich 1909–1989 Russ. econ. & diplomat; pres. of U.S.S.R. (1985–88)
Groo·te \'grō-tə\ Gerhard 1340–1384 *Ge·rar·dus Mag·nus* \jə-,rär-dəs-'mag-nəs\ Du. religious reformer
Gro·pi·us \'grō-pē-əs\ Walter 1883–1969 Am. (Ger.-born) architect
Grop·per \'grä-pər\ William 1897–1977 Am. artist
Gros·ve·nor \'grōv-nər, 'grō-və-\ Gilbert Hovey 1875–1966 Am. geographer and editor
Grosz \'grōs\ George 1893–1959 Am. (Ger.-born) painter
Grote \'grōt\ George 1794–1871 Eng. hist.
Gro·tius \'grō-sh(ē-)əs\ Hugo 1583–1645 *Huigh de Groot* \də-'grōt\ Du. jurist & statesman
Grou·chy \grü-'shē\ Emmanuel 1766–1847 Marquis *de Grouchy* Fr. gen.
Grove \'grōv\ Sir George 1820–1900 Eng. musicologist
Groves \'grōvz\ Leslie Richard 1896–1970 Am. gen.
Grü·ne·wald \'grü-nə-,wōld, 'grüē-nə-,vält\ Matthias *ca* 1455–1528 Ger. painter
Gryph·i·us \gri-fē-əs\ Andreas 1616–1664 *G Greif* \'grīf\ Ger. poet & dram.
Guar·ne·ri \gwär-'ner-ē\ *L* **Guar·ne·ri·us** \gwär-'nir-ē-əs, -'ner-\ family of Ital. violin makers: esp. Giuseppe Antonio 1687–1745
Gu·de·ri·an \gü-'der-ē-ən\ Heinz Wilhelm 1888–1954 Ger. gen.
Gue·dal·la \gwi-'da-lə\ Philip 1889–1944 Eng. writer
Gue·rin \'ger-ən\ Jules 1866–1946 Am. painter
Gues·clin \ges-'klan\ Bertrand du *ca* 1320–1380 Fr. soldier
Guesde \ged\ Jules 1845–1922 *Mathieu Basile* Fr. socialist
Guest \'gest\ Edgar Albert 1881–1959 Am. journalist & poet
Gue·va·ra \ge-'vär-ə, gā-\ Ernesto 1928–1967 *Che* Latin-Am. (Argentine-born) revolutionary leader
Gui·do of Arezzo \'gwē-(,)dō\ *or* **Guido Are·ti·nus** \,ar-ə-'tē-nəs\ *ca* 991–1050 Benedictine monk & music reformer
Guil·laume \gē-'yōm\ Charles Edouard 1861–1938 Fr. physicist
Guille·min \gē(-ə)-'ma°\ Roger Charles Louis 1924– Am. (Fr.-born) physiol.
Guiscard Robert — see ROBERT GUISCARD
Guise \'gēz *also* 'gwēz\ 2d Duc de 1519–1563 *François de Lorraine* Fr. soldier & polit.
Guise 3d Duc de 1550–1588 *Henri I de Lorraine* Fr. soldier & polit.
Gui·te·ras \gē-'ter-əs\ Juan 1852–1925 Cuban physician
Gui·zot \gē-'zō\ François-Pierre-Guillaume 1787–1874 Fr. hist. & statesman
Gull·strand \'gəl-,strand\ Allvar 1862–1930 Swed. ophthalmologist
Gun·nars·son \'gə-nər-sən\ Gunnar 1889–1975 Icelandic writer
Gun·ter \'gən-tər\ Edmund 1581–1626 Eng. math.
Gus·tav \'güs-,täv\ *or* **Gus·ta·vus** \(,)gə-'stä-vəs, -'stä-\ name of 6 kings of Sweden, the first 4 of the Vasa dynasty: **I** (*Gustav Eriksson*) 1496?–1560 (reigned 1523–60); **II** (*Gustav Adolph*)1594–1632 (reigned 1611–32); **III** 1746–1792 (reigned 1771–92); **IV** (*Gustav Adolph*) 1778–1837 (reigned 1792–1809); **V** 1858–1950 (reigned 1907–50); **VI** (*Gustav Adolph*)1882–1973 (reigned 1950–73)
Gu·ten·berg \'gü-t°n-,bərg\ Johannes *ca* 1390–1468 Ger. inventor of printing from movable type
Guth·rie \'gə-thrē\ Woodrow Wilson 1912–1967 *Woody* Am. folk-singer
Gutz·kow \'güts-(,)kō\ Karl Ferdinand 1811–1878 Ger. journalist, nov., & dram.
Guz·mán Blan·co \güs-,män-'bläŋ-(,)kō\ Antonio 1829–1899 Venezuelan soldier & statesman; dictator of Venezuela (1870–89)
Gwin·nett \gwi-'net\ Button *ca* 1735–1777 Am. Revolutionary leader
Gwyn *or* **Gwynn** *or* **Gwynne** \'gwin\ Eleanor 1650–1687 *Nell* Eng. actress *mistress of Charles II*
Haa·kon VII \'hō-kən, -,kän\ 1872–1957 king of Norway (1905–57)
Haa·vel·mo \'hō-vəl-,mō\ Trygve 1911– Norw. econ.
Ha·ber \'hä-bər\ Fritz 1868–1934 Ger. chem.
Há·cha \'hä-(,)kä\ Emil 1872–1945 Czech jurist & statesman
Had·field \'had-,fēld\ Sir Robert Abbott 1858–1940 Eng. metallurgist
Had·ley \'had-lē\ Henry Kimball 1871–1937 Am. composer
Had·ow \'ha-(,)dō\ Sir (William) Henry 1859–1937 Eng. educ. & musicologist
Ha·dri·an \'hā-drē-ən\ *var of* ADRIAN
Hadrian A.D. 76–138 Rom. emp. (117–138)
Haeck·el \'he-kəl\ Ernst Heinrich 1834–1919 Ger. biol. & philos.
Hā·fez \hä-'fez\ 1325(or 1326)–1389(or 1390) *Moḥammad Shams od-Din Ḥāfez* Pers. poet
Hag·gard \'ha-gərd\ Sir (Henry) Rider 1856–1925 Eng. nov.
Hahn \'hän\ Otto 1879–1968 Ger. physical chem.

Hah·ne·mann \'hä-nə-mən\ (Christian Friedrich) Samuel 1755–1843 Ger. physician
Haider Ali — see HYDER ALI
Haig \'hāg\ 1st Earl 1861–1928 *Douglas Haig* Brit. field marshal
Hai·le Se·las·sie \'hī-lē-sə-'la-sē, -'lä-\ 1892–1975 Ras *Tafari* emp. of Ethiopia (1930–36; 1941–74)
Hak·luyt \'hak-,lüt\ Richard *ca* 1552–1616 Eng. geographer & hist.
Hal·dane \'hōl-,dān, -dən\ John Burdon Sanderson 1892–1964 *son of J.S.* Brit. biol.
Haldane John Scott 1860–1936 Brit. physiol.
Haldane Richard Burdon 1856–1928 Viscount *Haldane of Cloan* \'klōn\; *bro. of J.S.* Brit. lawyer, philos., & statesman
Hal·der \'häl-dər\ Franz 1884–1972 Ger. gen.
Hale \'hā(ə)l\ Edward Everett 1822–1909 Am. Unitarian clergyman & writer
Hale George Ellery 1868–1938 Am. astron.
Hale Sir Matthew 1609–1676 Eng. jurist
Hale Nathan 1755–1776 Am. Revolutionary hero
Ha·lé·vy \,(h)a-lā-'vē, ,(h)ä-\ (Jacques-François-) Fromental (-Elie) 1799–1862 pseud. of *Élie Lé·vy* \lä-'ve\ Fr. composer
Halévy Ludovic 1834–1908 *nephew of prec.* Fr. dram. & nov.
Hal·i·fax \'ha-lə-,faks\ Earl of 1881–1959 *Edward Frederick Lindley Wood* Eng. statesman & diplomat
Hall \'hōl\ Charles Francis 1821–1871 Am. arctic explorer
Hall Charles Martin 1863–1914 Am. chem. & manuf.
Hall Granville Stanley 1844–1924 Am. psychol. & educ.
Hall James Norman 1887–1951 Am. nov.
Hal·lam \'ha-ləm\ Henry 1777–1859 Eng. hist.
Hal·leck \'ha-lək, -lik\ Fitz-Greene 1790–1867 Am. poet
Halleck Henry Wager 1815–1872 Am. gen.
Hal·ley \'ha-lē *also* 'hā-lē\ Edmond *or* Edmund 1656–1742 Eng. astron.
Hals \'hälz, 'häls\ Frans *ca* 1581–1666 Du. painter
Hal·sey \'hōl-sē, -zē\ William Frederick 1882–1959 Am. admiral
Hal·sted \'hōl-stəd, -,sted\ William Stewart 1852–1922 Am. surgeon
Ham·bro \'häm-,brō\ Carl Joachim 1885–1964 Norw. statesman
Ha·mil·car Bar·ca \hə-'mil-,kär-'bär-kə, 'ha-məl-\ *or* **Bar·cas** \'bär-kəs\ 270?–229(or 228) B.C. *father of Hannibal* Carthaginian gen.
Ham·il·ton \'ha-məl-tən, -t°n\ Alexander 1755–1804 Am. statesman
Hamilton Edith 1867–1963 Am. classicist
Hamilton Lady Emma 1765–1815 née *Amy Lyon* mistress of Lord Nelson
Ham·lin \'ham-lən\ Hannibal 1809–1891 Am. polit.; vice pres. of the U.S. (1861–65)
Ham·mar·skjöld \'ha-mər-,shəld, 'häm-, -,shüld, -,sheld\ Dag \'däg\ Hjalmar Agne Carl 1905–1961 Swed. U.N. official; secy.-gen. (1953–61)
Ham·mer·stein \'ha-mər-,stīn, -,stēn\ Oscar 1846–1919 Am. (Ger.= born) theater impresario
Hammerstein Oscar 1895–1960 *grandson of prec.* Am. lyricist & librettist
Ham·mett \'ha-met\ (Samuel) Dashiell 1894–1961 Am. writer
Ham·mond \'ha-mənd\ John Hays 1855–1936 Am. mining engineer
Hammond John Hays 1888–1965 *son of prec.* Am. electrical engineer & inventor
Hammond Laurens 1895–1973 Am. inventor
Ham·mu·ra·bi \,ha-mu-'rä-bē\ *or* **Ham·mu·ra·pi** \-'rä-pē\ *d* 1750 B.C. king of Babylon (1792–50)
Hamp·den \'ham(p)-dən\ John 1594–1643 Eng. statesman
Hampden Walter 1879–1955 stage name of *W. H. Dougherty* Am. actor
Hamp·ton \'ham(p)-tən\ Wade 1751?–1835 Am. gen.
Hampton Wade 1818–1902 *grandson of prec.* Am. polit. & Confed. gen.
Ham·sun \'häm-sən\ Knut 1859–1952 pseud. of *Knut Pedersen* Norw. writer
Han·cock \'han-,käk\ John 1737–1793 Am. statesman in Revolution
Hancock Winfield Scott 1824–1886 Am. gen. & polit.
Hand \'hand\ (Billings) Learned 1872–1961 Am. jurist
Han·del \'han-d°l\ George Frideric 1685–1759 Brit. (Ger.-born) composer — **Han·de·li·an** \han-'dē-lē-ən\ *adj*
Han·dy \'han-dē\ William Christopher 1873–1958 Am. blues musician
Han·na \'ha-nə\ Marcus Alonzo 1837–1904 *Mark* Am. businessman & polit.
Han·nay \'ha-,nā, 'ha-nē\ James Owen 1865–1950 Irish clergyman & nov.
Han·ni·bal \'ha-nə-bəl\ 247–183 B.C. *son of Hamilcar Barca* Carthaginian gen.
Han·no \'ha-(,)nō\ 3d cent. B.C. *the Great* Carthaginian statesman
Ha·no·taux \,a-nə-'tō, ,ä-\ (Albert-Auguste-) Gabriel 1853–1944 Fr. hist. & statesman
Han·sard \'han-,särd, 'han(t)-sərd\ Luke 1752–1828 Eng. printer
Han·son \'han(t)-sən\ Howard 1896–1981 Am. composer
Hans·son \'han(t)-sən\ Per Albin 1885–1946 Swed. statesman
Han Wu Ti \'hän-'wü-'dē\ 156–87 B.C. orig. *Liu Ch'e* often called *Wu Ti* Chin. emp. (140–87)
Han Yü \'hän-'yü\ 768–824 *Han Wen-kung* Chin. poet, essayist, & philos.
Har·bach \'här-,bäk\ Otto Abels 1873–1963 Am. dram. & librettist
Har·de·ca·nute *or* **Har·di·ca·nute** \,här-di-kə-'nüt, -'nyüt\ *ca* 1019–1042 king of Denmark (1028–42) and of England (1040–42)
Har·den \'här-d°n\ Sir Arthur 1865–1940 Eng. chem.
Harden Maximilian 1861–1927 orig. *Felix Ernst Witkowski* Ger. writer
Har·den·berg \'här-d°n-,bərg, -,berk\ Prince Karl August von 1750–1822 Pruss. statesman
Har·ding \'här-diŋ\ Warren Gamaliel 1865–1923 29th pres. of the U.S. (1921–23)
Har·dy \'här-dē\ Thomas 1840–1928 Eng. nov. & poet — **Har·dy·esque** \,här-dē-'esk\ *adj*
Har·greaves \'här-,grēvz\ James *d* 1778 Eng. inventor
Har·ing·ton *or* **Har·ring·ton** \'har-iŋ-tən\ Sir John 1561–1612 Eng. writer & translator
Ha·rī·rī, al- \,al-hə-'rir-ē\ 1054–1122 Arab scholar & poet

Har·lan \'här-lən\ John Marshall 1833–1911 & his grandson 1899–1971 Am. jurists
Har·ley \'här-lē\ Robert 1661–1724 1st Earl of *Oxford* Eng. statesman
Harms·worth \'härmz-(,)wərth\ Alfred Charles William 1865–1922 Viscount *North·cliffe* \'north-,klif\ Eng. publisher & polit.
Harmsworth Harold Sidney 1868–1940 1st Viscount *Roth·er·mere* \'rä-thər-mir\ *bro. of A.C.W.* Eng. publisher & polit.
Har·old \'har-əld\ name of 2 kings of the English: **I** *d* 1040 *Harold Hare·foot* \'har-,fut, 'her-\ (reigned 1035–40); **II** *ca* 1022–1066 (reigned 1066)
Harold name of 3 kings of Norway: esp. **III** *Hard·raa·de* \'hor-,rö-də\ 1015–1066 (reigned 1045–66)
Har·ri·man \'har-ə-mən\ William Aver·ell \'av-rəl, 'ā-və-\ 1891–1986 Am. businessman, diplomat, & polit.
Har·ris \'har-əs\ Barbara Clementine 1930– Am. bishop
Harris Frank 1856–1931 Am. (Irish-born) writer
Harris Joel Chandler 1848–1908 Am. writer
Harris Roy 1898–1979 Am. composer
Harris William Torrey 1835–1909 Am. philos. & educ.
Har·ri·son \'har-ə-sən\ Benjamin 1833–1901 *grandson of W. H. Harrison* 23d pres. of the U.S. (1889–93)
Harrison Frederic 1831–1923 Eng. writer & philos.
Harrison Sir Rex 1908–1990 *orig. Reginald Carey Harrison* Brit. actor
Harrison William Henry 1773–1841 9th pres. of the U.S. (1841)
Har·san·yi \här-'shä-nē\ John Charles 1920– Am. (Hung.-born) econ.
Hart \'härt\ Albert Bushnell 1854–1943 Am. hist. & editor
Hart Basil Henry Liddell — see LIDDELL HART
Hart Lorenz 1895–1943 Am. lyricist
Hart Moss 1904–1961 Am. librettist & dram.
Hart Sir Robert 1835–1911 Brit. diplomat
Hart William Surrey 1872–1946 Am. actor
Harte \'härt\ Francis Bret 1836–1902 *Bret Harte* Am. writer
Hart·line \'härt-,līn\ Haldan Keffer 1903–1983 Am. biophysicist
Har·tung \'här-,tung\ Hans 1904–1989 Fr. (Ger.-born) painter
Hä·rün ar–Ra·shid \hə-'rün-är-rə-'shēd\ 763(or 766)–809 *Hārūn ar-Rashīd ibn Muhammad al-Mahdi ibn al-Manṣūr al-'Abbāsī* caliph of Baghdad (786–809)
Har·vard \'här-vərd\ John 1607–1638 Am. clergyman & benefactor
Har·vey \'här-vē\ George Brinton McClellan 1864–1928 Am. journalist & diplomat
Harvey Sir John Martin 1863–1944 Eng. actor & producer
Harvey William 1578–1657 Eng. physician & anatomist
Has·dru·bal \'haz-,drü-bəl, haz-'\ *d* 207 B.C. *bro. of Hannibal* Carthaginian gen.
Has·sam \'ha-səm\ (Frederick) Childe 1859–1935 Am. artist
Has·sel \'hä-səl\ Odd 1897–1981 Norw. chem.
Hass·ler \'häs-lər\ Hans Leo 1564–1612 Ger. composer
Has·tings \'häs-tinz\ 1st Marquess of 1754–1826 *Francis Raw·don= Hastings* \'rö-d°n-\ Brit. gen. & colonial administrator
Hastings Warren 1732–1818 Eng. statesman & administrator in India
Haugh·ey \'hö-hē\ Charles James 1925– prime min. of Ireland (1979–81; 1982; 1987–92)
Haupt·man \'haupt-mən\ Herbert Aaron 1917– Am. biophysicist
Haupt·mann \'haupt-,män\ Gerhart 1862–1946 Ger. writer
Haus·ho·fer \'haus-,hō-fər\ Karl Ernst 1869–1946 Ger. gen. & geographer
Hauss·mann \ōs-'män, 'haus-mən\ Baron Georges-Eugène 1809–1891 Fr. administrator
Ha·vel \'hä-vel, -vəl\ Vá·clav \'vät-,släf\ 1936– Czech writer & polit.; pres. of Czechoslovakia (1989–92); pres. of Czech Republic (1993–)
Have·lock \'hav-,läk, -lək\ Sir Henry 1795–1857 Brit. gen.
Hawke \'hök\ 1st Baron 1705–1781 *Edward Hawke* Eng. admiral
Hawke Robert James Lee 1929– prime min. of Australia (1983–91)
Haw·king \'hö-kin\ Stephen William 1942– Brit. physicist
Haw·kins \'hö-kənz\ Sir Anthony Hope 1863–1933 pseud. *Anthony Hope* Eng. nov. & dram.
Hawkins *or* **Haw·kyns** Sir John 1532–1595 Eng. admiral
Haw·orth \'hau-ərth\ Sir (Walter) Norman 1883–1950 Eng. chem.
Haw·thorne \'hö-,thörn\ Nathaniel 1804–1864 Am. author
Hay \'hā\ John Milton 1838–1905 Am. statesman
Hay·den \'hā-d°n\ Carl Trumbull 1877–1972 Am. polit.
Haydn \'hī-d°n\ (Franz) Joseph 1732–1809 Austrian composer
Hay·ek \'hī-ak\ Friedrich August von 1899–1992 Brit. (Austrian= born) econ.
Hayes \'hāz\ Helen 1900–1993 *Helen Hayes Brown* Am. actress
Hayes Isaac Israel 1832–1881 Am. arctic explorer
Hayes Roland 1887–1977 Am. tenor
Hayes Rutherford Birchard 1822–1893 19th pres. of the U.S. (1877–81)
Haynes \'hānz\ Elwood 1857–1925 Am. inventor
Hays \'hāz\ Will Harrison 1879–1954 Am. lawyer & polit.
Ha·zard \ä-'zär\ Paul-Gustave-Marie-Camille 1878–1944 Fr. lit. hist.
Haz·litt \'haz-lət, 'häz-\ William 1778–1830 Eng. essayist
Hea·ly \'hē-lē\ Timothy Michael 1855–1931 Irish statesman
Hearn \'hərn\ Laf·ca·dio \laf-'kä-dē-,ō\ 1850–1904 Jp. *Yakumo Koizumi* Am. (Greek-born) writer in Japan
Hearst \'hərst\ William Randolph 1863–1951 Am. newspaper publisher
Heath \'hēth\ Edward 1916– Brit. prime min. (1970–74)
Heav·i·side \'he-vē-,sīd\ Oliver 1850–1925 Eng. physicist
Heb·bel \'he-bəl\ (Christian) Friedrich 1813–1863 Ger. dram.
He·ber \'hē-bər\ Reginald 1783–1826 Eng. prelate & hymn writer
Hé·bert \ā-'ber\ Jacques-René 1757–1794 Fr. radical journalist
He·din \'hā-dēn\ Sven Anders 1865–1952 Swed. explorer
Heem \'hām\ Jan Davidsz de 1606–1683(or 1684) Du. painter
He·gel \'hā-gəl\ Georg Wilhelm Friedrich 1770–1831 Ger. philos. —
Hei·deg·ger \'hī-,de-gər, 'hī-di-gər\ Martin 1889–1976 Ger. philos. — **Hei·deg·ger·ian** \,hī-di-'gar-ē-ən, -'ger-\ *adj*
Hei·den·stam \'hā-d°n-,stam, -,stäm\ (Carl Gustaf) Verner von 1859–1940 Swed. writer

Hei·fetz \'hī-fəts\ Ja·scha \'yä-shə\ 1901–1987 Am. (Russ.-born) violinist
Hei·ne \'hī-nə *also* -nē\ Heinrich 1797–1856 Ger. poet & critic
Hei·sen·berg \'hī-z°n-bərg, -,berk\ Werner Karl 1901–1976 Ger. physicist
Heliogabalus — see ELAGABALUS
Hel·ler \'he-lər\ Joseph 1923– Am. nov.
Hell·man \'hel-mən\ Lillian 1905–1984 Am. dram.
Helm·holtz \'helm-,hōlts\ Hermann Ludwig Ferdinand von 1821–1894 Ger. physicist, anatomist, & physiol.
Hé·lo·ïse \'ā-lə-,wēz, 'e-lə-\ *ca* 1098–1164 *wife of Abelard* Fr. abbess
Hel·vé·tius \hel-'vā-sh(ē-)əs, -'vē-; ,(h)el-,vās-'yüs, -'yūes\ Claude= Adrien 1715–1771 Fr. philos.
He·mans \'he-mənz, 'hē-\ Felicia Dorothea 1793–1835 née *Browne* Eng. poet
Hem·inge *or* **Hem·minge** \'he-min\ John *ca* 1556–1630 Eng. actor
Hem·ing·way \'he-min-,wā\ Ernest Miller 1899–1961 Am. writer & journalist — **Hem·ing·way·esque** \,he-min-,wā-'esk\ *adj*
Hench \'hench\ Philip Showalter 1896–1965 Am. physician
Hen·der·son \'hen-dər-sən\ Arthur 1863–1935 Brit. labor leader & statesman
Henderson Sir Nev·ile \'ne-vəl\ Meyrick 1882–1942 Brit. diplomat
Hen·dricks \'hen-driks\ Thomas Andrews 1819–1885 Am. polit.; vice pres. of the U.S. (1885)
Hen·gist *or* **Hen·gest** \'hen-gəst, -,gist\ & *his bro.* **Hor·sa** \'hör-sə\ 5th cent. Jute invaders of Britain
Hen·ley \'hen-lē\ William Ernest 1849–1903 Eng. editor & author
Hen·ne·pin \'he-nə-pən, ,e-nə-'pa°\ Louis 1626–after 1701 Belg. friar & explorer in America
Hen·ri \'hen-rē\ Robert 1865–1929 Am. painter
Hen·ry \'hen-rē\ name of 8 kings of England: **I** 1068–1135 (reigned 1100–35); **II** 1133–1189 (reigned 1154–89); **III** 1207–1272 (reigned 1216–72); **IV** 1366–1413 (reigned 1399–1413); **V** 1387–1422 (reigned 1413–22); **VI** 1421–1471 (reigned 1422–61 & 1470–71); **VII** 1457–1509 (reigned 1485–1509); **VIII** 1491–1547 (reigned 1509–47)
Henry name of 4 kings of France: **I** *ca* 1008–1060 (reigned 1031–60); **II** 1519–1559 (reigned 1547–59); **III** 1551–1589 (reigned 1574–89); **IV** (Henry III of Navarre) 1553–1610 (reigned 1589–1610)
Henry 1394–1460 *the Navigator* Port. prince
Henry Joseph 1797–1878 Am. physicist
Henry O. — see William Sydney PORTER
Henry Patrick 1736–1799 Am. statesman & orator
Hens·lowe \'henz-(,)lö\ Philip *ca* 1550–1616 Eng. theater manager
Hep·burn \'hep-(,)bərn\ Katharine 1907– Am. actress
Hep·ple·white \'he-pəl-,hwīt, -,wīt\ George *d* 1786 Eng. cabinetmaker and designer
Hep·worth \'hep-(,)wərth\ Dame Barbara 1903–1975 Brit. sculptor
Her·a·clei·tus *or* **Her·a·cli·tus** \,her-ə-'klī-təs\ *ca* 540–*ca* 480 B.C. Greek philos. — **Her·a·cli·te·an** \-'klī-tē-ən, -klī-'tē-\ *adj*
He·ra·cli·us \,her-ə-'klī-əs, hi-'ra-klē-\ *ca* 575–641 Byzantine emp. (610–641)
Her·bart \'her-,bärt\ Johann Friedrich 1776–1841 Ger. philos. & educ.
Her·bert \'hər-bərt\ George 1593–1633 Eng. divine & poet
Herbert Victor 1859–1924 Am. (Irish-born) composer & conductor
Herbert William 1580–1630 3d Earl of *Pembroke* Eng. statesman & poet
Herblock — see Herbert Lawrence BLOCK
Her·der \'her-dər\ Johann Gottfried von 1744–1803 Ger. philos.
He·re·dia \ā-rā-'dyä, (h)ä-'rä-dē-ə\ José María de 1842–1905 Fr. (Cuban-born) poet
Her·ford \'hər-ford\ Oliver 1863–1935 Eng. writer & illustrator
He·ring \'her-in, 'hä-rin\ Ewald 1834–1918 Ger. physiol. & psychol.
Her·ki·mer \'hər-kə-mər\ Nicholas 1728–1777 Am. gen.
Her·man \'hər-mən\ Woodrow Charles 1913–1987 *Woody Herman* Am. musician & bandleader
Hern·don \'hərn-dən\ William Henry 1818–1891 Am. lawyer
He·ro \'hē-(,)rō, 'hir-(,)ō\ *or* **He·ron** \'hē-,rän\ 1st cent. A.D. Greek scientist
Her·od \'her-əd\ 73–4 B.C. *the Great* Rom. king of Judea (37–4)
Herod An·ti·pas \'an-tə-pəs, -,pas\ 21 B.C.–A.D. 39 *son of prec.* Rom. tetrarch of Galilee (4 B.C.–A.D. 39)
He·rod·o·tus \hi-'rä-də-təs\ *ca* 484–between 430 and 420 B.C. Greek hist. — **He·rod·o·te·an** \-,rä-də-'tē-ən\ *adj*
Her·re·ra \(h)ə-'rer-ə\ Francisco de 1576–*ca* 1656 *el Viejo* Span. painter
Her·rick \'her-ik\ Robert 1591–1674 Eng. poet
Her·riot \,er-ē-'ō\ Édouard 1872–1957 Fr. statesman
Hersch·bach \'hərsh-,bäk\ Dudley Robert 1932– Am. chem.
Her·schel \'hər-shəl\ Sir John Frederick William 1792–1871 & his father Sir William 1738–1822 Eng. astronomers
Her·sey \'hər-sē\ John Richard 1914–1993 Am. nov.
Her·shey \'hər-shē\ Alfred Day 1908– Am. geneticist
Her·ter \'hər-tər\ Christian Archibald 1895–1966 Am. diplomat; secy. of state (1959–61)
Hertz \'herts, 'härts\ Gustav Ludwig 1887–1975 Ger. physicist
Hertz Heinrich Rudolf 1857–1894 Ger. physicist
Hert·zog \'hert-,sök\ James Barry Munnik 1866–1942 So. African gen.
Herz·berg \'herts-,bərg\ Gerhard 1904– Canad. (Ger.-born) physicist
Herzl \'hert-s°l\ Theodor 1860–1904 Austrian (Hung.-born) Zionist
He·si·od \'hē-sē-əd, 'he-\ *fl ca* 800 B.C. Greek poet
Hess \'hes\ Dame Myra 1890–1965 Eng. pianist
Hess (Walther Richard) Rudolf 1894–1987 Ger. Nazi polit.
Hess Victor Franz 1883–1964 Austrian physicist
Hess Walter Rudolf 1881–1973 Swiss physiol.
Hes·se \'hes\ Hermann 1877–1962 Ger. author
He·ve·sy \'he-və-shē, -,ve-shē\ Georg Karl 1885–1966 Hung. chem.

\ə\ abut \°\ kitten, F table \ər\ further \a\ ash \ā\ ace \ä\ mop, mar \au\ out \ch\ chin \e\ bet \ē\ easy \g\ go \i\ hit \ī\ ice \j\ job \n\ sing \ō\ go \o\ law \oi\ boy \th\ thin \th\ the \ü\ loot \u\ foot \y\ yet \zh\ vision \à, k̲, °, œ, œ̄, ue, ūe, ʸ\ see Guide to Pronunciation

Hew·ish \'hyü-ish\ Antony 1924–   Brit. astron.
Hey·drich \'hī-drik, -drik\ Reinhard 1904–1942 *the Hangman* Ger. Nazi administrator
Hey·er·dahl \'hā-ər-‚däl\ Thor 1914–   Norw. explorer & writer
Hey·mans \ā-'män(t)s, -'man(t)s\ Corneille-Jean-François 1892–1968 Belg. physiol.
Hey·rov·ský \'hā-‚róf-skē, -‚róv-\ Jaroslav 1890–1967 Czech chem.
Hey·se \'hī-zə\ Paul Johann Ludwig von 1830–1914 Ger. writer
Hey·ward \'hā-wərd\ (Edwin) Du·Bose \dü-'bōz, dyü-\ 1885–1940 Am. author
Hey·wood \'hā-‚wùd\ John 1497?–?1580 Eng. author
Heywood Thomas 1574?–1641 Eng. dram.
Hick·ok \'hi-‚käk\ James Butler 1837–1876 *Wild Bill* Am. scout & U.S. marshal
Hicks \'hiks\ Edward 1780–1849 Am. painter
Hicks Sir John Richard 1904–1989 Brit. econ.
Hi·ero I \'hī-ə-‚rō\ *or* **Hi·er·on** \-‚rän\ *d* 467(or 466) B.C. tyrant of Syracuse (478–467 or 466)
Hieronymus Saint Eusebius — see JEROME
Hig·gin·son \'hi-gən-sən\ Thomas Wentworth Storrow 1823–1911 Am. clergyman & writer
Hil·bert \'hil-bərt\ David 1862–1943 Ger. math.
Hildebrand — see Pope GREGORY VII
Hill \'hil\ Ambrose Powell 1825–1865 Am. Confed. gen.
Hill Archibald Vivian 1886–1977 Eng. physiol.
Hill James Jerome 1838–1916 Am. financier
Hill Sir Rowland 1795–1879 Eng. postal reformer
Hil·la·ry \'hi-lə-rē\ Sir Edmund Percival 1919–   N.Z. mountaineer & explorer
Hil·lel \'hi-ləl, -‚lel\ 1st cent. B.C.–1st cent. A.D. Jewish teacher
Hil·liard \'hil-yərd\ Nicholas 1547–1619 Eng. painter
Hill·man \'hil-mən\ Sidney 1887–1946 Am. labor leader
Hil·ton \'hil-t³n\ Conrad Nicholson 1887–1979 Am. hotelier
Hilton James 1900–1954 Eng. nov.
Himm·ler \'him-lər\ Heinrich 1900–1945 Ger. Nazi polit.
Hin·de·mith \'hin-də-‚mit, -‚mith, -mət, -məth\ Paul 1895–1963 Am. (Ger.-born) composer
Hin·den·burg \'hin-dən-‚bərg, -‚bùrg\ Paul von 1847–1934 *Paul Ludwig Hans Anton von Beneckendorff und von Hindenburg* Ger. field marshal; pres. of Germany (1925–34)
Hin·shel·wood \'hin(t)-shəl-‚wùd\ Sir Cyril Norman 1897–1967 Brit. chem.
Hip·par·chus \hi-'pär-kəs\ *d* 514 B.C. tyrant of Athens (527–514)
Hipparchus *or* **Hip·par·chos** \hi-'pär-kəs\ *fl* 146–127 B.C. Greek astron.
Hip·pi·as \'hi-pē-əs\ *d* 490 B.C. *bro. of Hipparchus* ruled Athens with his brother
Hip·poc·ra·tes \hi-'pä-krə-‚tēz\ *ca* 460–*ca* 377 B.C. *father of medicine* Greek physician
Hi·ro·hi·to \‚hir-ō-'hē-(‚)tō\ 1901–1989 emp. of Japan (1926–89)
Hi·ro·shi·ge \‚hir-ə-'shē-‚gā\ Ando 1797–1858 Jp. painter
Hitch·cock \'hich-‚käk\ Sir Alfred Joseph 1899–1980 Brit. film director — **Hitch·cock·ian** \hich-'kä-kē-ən\ *adj*
Hitchcock Edward 1793–1864 Am. geologist
Hitch·ings \'hi-chiŋz\ George Herbert 1905–   Am. biochem.
Hit·ler \'hit-lər\ Adolf 1889–1945 Ger. chancellor & führer — **Hit·ler·ian** \hit-'lir-ē-ən, -'ler-\ *adj*
Hit·ti \'hi-tē\ Philip Khuri 1886–1978 Am. (Lebanese-born) orientalist
Hit·torf \'hi-‚tórf\ Johann Wilhelm 1824–1914 Ger. physicist
Hoare \'hòr, 'hór\ Sir Samuel John Gurney 1880–1959 Viscount *Templewood* Eng. statesman
Ho·bart \'hō-‚bärt, -bərt\ Garret Augustus 1844–1899 Am. polit.; vice pres. of the U.S. (1897–99)
Hob·be·ma \'hä-bə-mə\ Mein·dert *or* Meyn·dert \'mīn-‚dert\ 1638–1709 Du. painter
Hobbes \'häbz\ Thomas 1588–1679 Eng. philos.
Hoc·cleve \'häk-‚lēv\ *or* **Oc·cleve** \'äk-\ Thomas 1368(or 1369)–*ca* 1450 Eng. poet
Ho Chi Minh \'hō-'chē-'min, -'shē-\ 1890–1969 orig. *Nguyen That Thanh* pres. of No. Vietnam (1945–69)
Hock·ing \'hä-kiŋ\ William Ernest 1873–1966 Am. philos.
Hodg·kin \'häj-kin\ Sir Alan Lloyd 1914–   Brit. physiol.
Hodgkin Dorothy May Crowfoot 1910–1994 Brit. physicist
Hoe \'hō\ Richard March 1812–1886 *son of Robert* Am. inventor
Hoe Robert 1784–1833 Am. (Eng.-born) printing-press manuf.
Ho·fer \'hō-fər\ Andreas 1767–1810 Tyrolese patriot
Hof·fa \'hä-fə\ James Riddle 1913–?1975 Am. labor leader
Hoff·man \'häf-mən, 'hòf-\ Mal·vi·na \mal-'vē-nə\ 1887–1966 Am. sculptor
Hoff·mann \'häf-mən, 'hòf-, -‚män\ August Heinrich 1798–1874 Ger. poet, philologist, & hist.
Hoffmann Ernst Theodor Wilhelm 1776–1822 known as *Ernst Theodor Amadeus Hoffmann* Ger. composer, writer, & illustrator
Hoffmann Roald 1937–   Am. (Pol.-born) chem.
Hof·mann \'häf-mən, 'hòf-, -‚män\ August Wilhelm von 1818–1892 Ger. chem.
Hofmann Hans 1880–1966 Am. (Ger.-born) painter
Hofmann Josef Casimir 1876–1957 Pol. pianist
Hof·manns·thal \'häf-mənz-‚täl, 'hòf-\ Hugo von 1874–1929 Austrian poet & dram.
Hof·stadt·er \'hòf-‚sta-tər\ Robert 1915–1990 Am. physicist
Ho·garth \'hō-‚gärth\ William 1697–1764 Eng. painter & engraver — **Ho·garth·ian** \hō-'gär-thē-ən\ *adj*
Hog·ben \'hòg-bən, 'häg-\ Lancelot Thomas 1895–1975 Eng. scientist
Hogg \'hòg, 'häg\ James 1770–1835 *the Ettrick Shepherd* Scot. poet
Ho·hen·zol·lern \‚hō-ənt-'sò-lərn\ Michael — see MICHAEL
Ho·ku·sai \'hō-kù-‚sī, ‚hō-kù-'\ Katsushika 1760–1849 Jp. artist
Hol·bein \'hōl-‚bīn, 'hòl-\ Hans 1465?–1524 *the Elder* & Hans 1497?–1543 *the Younger* Ger. painters
Hol·berg \'hōl-‚berg\ Baron 1684–1754 *Ludwig Holberg* Dan. (Norw.-born) author
Hol·i·day \'hä-lə-‚dā\ Eleanora 1915–1959 *Billie* Am. jazz singer
Hol·in·shed \'hä-lən-‚shed\ *or* **Hol·lings·head** \-liŋz-‚hed\ Raphael *d* *ca* 1580 Eng. chronicler

Hol·land \'hä-lənd\ John Philip 1840–1914 Am. (Irish-born) inventor
Holland Sir Sidney George 1893–1961 prime min. of New Zealand (1945–57)
Hol·ley \'hä-lē\ Robert William 1922–1993 Am. biochem.
Holman–Hunt William — see Holman HUNT
Holmes \'hōmz, 'hòlmz\ Oliver Wendell 1809–1894 Am. physician & author
Holmes Oliver Wendell 1841–1935 *son of prec.* Am. jurist
Holst \'hōlst\ Gustav Theodore 1874–1934 Eng. composer
Holt \'hōlt\ Harold Edward 1908–1967 Austral. polit.; prime min. (1966–67)
Holt Luther Emmett 1855–1924 Am. pediatrician
Hol·yoake \'hōl-‚yōk, 'hō-lē-‚ōk\ Sir Keith Jacka 1904–1983 prime min. of New Zealand (1960–72)
Home \'hyüm, 'hòm\ Sir Alec Douglas- 1903–   Brit. prime min. (1963–64)
Home William Douglas- 1912–1992 Brit. dram.
Ho·mer \'hō-mər\ 9th–8th? cent. B.C. Greek epic poet
Homer Winslow 1836–1910 Am. artist
Ho·neck·er \'hō-nə-kər\ Erich 1912–1994 gen. secy. of East German Communist party (1971–89)
Ho·neg·ger \‚ò-nā-'ger, '(h)ä-ni-gər\ Arthur 1892–1955 Fr. composer
Ho·no·ri·us \hə-'nòr-ē-əs, -'nòr-\ Flavius 384–423 Rom. emp. of the West (395–423)
Hont·horst \'hònt-‚hòrst\ Gerrit van 1590–1656 Du. painter
Hooch *or* **Hoogh** \'hōk\ Pieter de 1629–after 1684 Du. painter
Hood \'hùd\ John Bell 1831–1879 Am. Confed. gen.
Hood Samuel 1724–1816 1st Viscount *Hood* Brit. admiral
Hood Thomas 1799–1845 Eng. poet
Hooke \'hùk\ Robert 1635–1703 Eng. scientist
Hook·er \'hù-kər\ Joseph 1814–1879 Am. gen.
Hooker Sir Joseph Dalton 1817–1911 Eng. botanist
Hooker Richard 1554–1600 Eng. theol.
Hooker Thomas 1586?–1647 Eng. Puritan clergyman & founder of Connecticut
Hoo·ton \'hü-t³n\ Earnest Albert 1887–1954 Am. anthropol.
Hoo·ver \'hü-vər\ Herbert Clark 1874–1964 31st pres. of the U.S. (1929–33)
Hoover John Edgar 1895–1972 Am. criminologist; F.B.I. director (1924–72)
Hope \'hōp\ Anthony — see Sir Anthony Hope HAWKINS
Hope Victor Alexander John 1887–1951 8th Earl of *Hope·toun* \'hòp-tən\ & 2d Marquis of *Lin·lith·gow* \lin-'lith-(‚)gō\ Brit. soldier; viceroy of India (1936–43)
Hop·kins \'häp-kənz\ Sir Frederick Gow·land \'gaù-lənd\ 1861–1947 Eng. biochem.
Hopkins Gerard Manley 1844–1889 Eng. poet
Hopkins Harry Lloyd 1890–1946 Am. polit. & administrator
Hopkins Johns \'jänz\ 1795–1873 Am. financier
Hopkins Mark 1802–1887 Am. educ.
Hop·kin·son \'häp-kən-sən\ Francis 1737–1791 Am. lawyer & satirist
Hop·pe \'hä-pē\ William Frederick 1887–1959 Am. billiard player
Hop·per \'hä-pər\ Edward 1882–1967 Am. artist
Hopper Grace 1906–1992 Am. admiral, math., & computer scientist
Hopper (William) DeWolf 1858–1935 Am. actor
Hop·wood \'häp-‚wùd\ (James) Avery 1882–1928 Am. dram.
Hor·ace \'hòr-əs, 'här-\ 65–8 B.C. *Quintus Horatius Flaccus* Rom. poet & satirist — **Ho·ra·tian** \hə-'rā-shən\ *adj*
Hore–Be·li·sha \'hòr-bə-'lē-shə, 'hòr-\ Leslie 1893–1957 Eng. polit.
Hor·na·day \'hòr-nə-‚dā\ William Temple 1854–1937 Am. zool.
Hor·ney \'hòr-‚nī\ Karen 1885–1952 née *Danielsen* Am. (Ger.-born) psychoanalyst & author
Ho·ro·witz \'hòr-ə-‚wits, 'här-\ Vladimir 1903–1989 Am. (Russ.-born) pianist
Horsa — see HENGIST
Hortense de Beauharnais — see BEAUHARNAIS
Hor·thy de Nagy·bán·ya \'hòr-tē-dä-'näj-‚bán-yə\ Miklós 1868–1957 Hung. admiral; regent of Hungary (1920–44)
Hou·di·ni \hü-'dē-nē\ Harry 1874–1926 orig. *Erik Weisz* Am. (Hung.-born) magician
Hou·don \'hü-‚dän, ü-dōⁿ\ Jean-Antoine 1741–1828 Fr. sculptor
Houns·field \'haùnz-‚fē(ə)ld\ Godfrey Newbold 1919–   Brit. engineer & inventor
House \'haùs\ Edward Mandell 1858–1938 *Colonel House* Am. diplomat
Hous·man \'haùs-mən\ Alfred Edward 1859–1936 Eng. classical scholar & poet
Housman Laurence 1865–1959 *bro. of prec.* Eng. writer & illustrator
Hous·say \ü-'sī\ Bernardo Alberto 1887–1971 Argentine physiol.
Hous·ton \'hyü-stən, 'yü-\ Samuel 1793–1863 Am. gen.; pres. of the Republic of Texas (1836–38; 1841–44)
How·ard \'haù(-ə)rd\ Catherine — see CATHERINE
Howard Henry 1517?–1547 Earl of *Surrey* Eng. soldier & poet
Howard Oliver Otis 1830–1909 Am. gen. & educ.
Howard Sidney Coe 1891–1939 Am. dram.
Howe \'haù\ Ed 1853–1937 *Edgar Watson* Am. journalist
Howe Elias 1819–1867 Am. inventor
Howe Julia 1819–1910 née *Ward* Am. suffragist & reformer
Howe Richard 1726–1799 *Earl Howe* Eng. admiral
Howe William 1729–1814 5th Viscount *Howe*; *bro. of prec.* Eng. gen. in America
How·ells \'haù-əlz\ William Dean 1837–1920 Am. author
Hr·dlič·ka \'hərd-lich-‚kä\ Aleš \'ä-‚lesh\ 1869–1943 Am. (Bohemian-born) anthropol.
Hsüan–t'ung \shü-'än-'túŋ\ — see PU-I
Hua Kuo-feng \'hwä-'gwō-'fəŋ\ 1920–   pinyin *Hua Guo·feng* Chin. premier (1976–80)
Huás·car \'wäs-‚kär\ *d* 1532 Inca prince
Hub·bard \'hə-bərd\ Elbert Green 1856–1915 Am. writer
Hub·ble \'hə-bəl\ Edwin Powell 1889–1953 Am. astron.
Hu·bel \'hyü-bəl, 'yü-\ David Hunter 1926–   Am. (Canad.-born) neurobiologist
Hu·ber \'hü-bər, 'hyü-\ Robert 1937–   Ger. biochem.
Hud·son \'həd-sən\ Henry *d* 1611 Eng. navigator & explorer

Hudson Manley Ottmer 1886–1960 Am. jurist
Hudson William Henry 1841–1922 Eng. naturalist & writer
Huer·ta \'wer-tə, ü-'er-\ Victoriano 1854–1916 Mex. gen.; provisional pres. of Mexico (1913–14)
Hug·gins \'hə-gənz\ Charles Brenton 1901–   Am. (Canad.-born) physician
Huggins Sir William 1824–1910 Eng. astron.
Hugh Ca·pet \'hyü-'kā-pət, -'ka-, -ka-'pā\ ca 938–996 king of France (987–996)
Hughes \'hyüz also 'yüz\ Charles Evans 1862–1948 Am. jurist; chief justice U.S. Supreme Court (1930–41)
Hughes Howard Robard 1905–1976 Am. businessman
Hughes (James) Langston 1902–1967 Am. writer
Hughes Ted 1930–   Brit. poet; poet laureate (1984–)
Hughes Thomas 1822–1896 Eng. jurist, reformer, & writer
Hughes William Morris 1864–1952 Austral. statesman
Hu·go \'hyü-(,)gō, 'yü-\ Victor-Marie 1802–1885 Fr. poet, nov., & dram. — **Hu·go·esque** \,hyü-(,)gō-'esk, ,yü-\ adj
Hui·zin·ga \'hi-zin-gə\ Johan 1872–1945 Du. hist.
Hü·le·gü \'hü-'lā-(,)gü\ ca 1217–ca 1265 grandson of Genghis Khan Mongol ruler
Hull \'həl\ Cordell 1871–1955 Am. statesman; secy. of state (1933–44)
Hull Isaac 1773–1843 Am. naval officer
Hull William 1753–1825 Am. gen.
Hulse \'həls\ Russell Alan 1950–   Am. physicist
Hu·mā·yun \hü-'mä-,yün\ 1508–1556 Mogul emp. of India (1530–56)
Hum·boldt \'hüm-,bōlt, 'hùm-\ (Friedrich Wilhelm Karl Heinrich) Alexander von 1769–1859 Ger. naturalist, traveler, & statesman
Humboldt (Karl) Wilhelm von 1767–1835 bro. of prec. Ger. philologist & diplomat
Hume \'hyüm also 'yüm\ David 1711–1776 Scot. philos. & hist. — **Hum·ean** or **Hum·ian** \'(h)yü-mē-ən\ adj
Hum·per·dinck \'hùm-pər-,dink, 'həm-\ Engelbert 1854–1921 Ger. composer
Hum·phrey \'həm(p)-frē\ 1391–1447 son of Henry IV Duke of Gloucester (the Good Duke) & Earl of Pembroke Eng. statesman & book collector
Humphrey Hubert Horatio 1911–1978 Am. polit.; vice pres. of the U.S. (1965–69)
Hun·e·ker \'hə-ni-kər\ James Gibbons 1860–1921 Am. critic
Hung·wu \'hùn-'wü\ 1328–1398 Chu Yüan-chang \'jü-yü-'än-'jän\ Chin. emp. (1368–98); founder of Ming dynasty
Hunt \'hənt\ (James Henry) Leigh 1784–1859 Eng. writer
Hunt (William) Hol·man \'hōl-mən\ 1827–1910 Eng. painter
Hun·ter \'hən-tər\ John 1728–1793 Brit. anatomist & surgeon
Hun·ting·ton \'hən-tiŋ-tən\ Collis Potter 1821–1900 Am. railroad builder
Huntington Ellsworth 1876–1947 Am. geographer & explorer
Huntington Henry Edwards 1850–1927 Am. bibliophile
Huntington Samuel 1731–1796 Am. Revolutionary polit.
Hun·tzi·ger \,(h)ənt-sē-'zher\ Charles-Léon-Clément 1880–1941 Fr. gen.
Hu·nya·di \'hùn-,yä-dē, -,yò-\ Já·nos \'yä-(,)nōsh\ 1407?–1456 Hung. soldier & hero
Hur·ley \'hər-lē\ Patrick Jay 1883–1963 Am. lawyer & diplomat
Hurst \'hərst\ Sir Cecil James Barrington 1870–1963 Eng. jurist
Hurst Fannie 1889–1968 Am. writer
Hus \'həs, 'hùs\ Jan 1372(or 1373)–1415 Bohemian religious reformer
Hu·sák \'hü-(,)säk, 'hyü-\ Gustav 1913–1991 pres. of Czechoslovakia (1975–87)
Hu·sayn ibn 'Alī \hü-'sän-,i-bən-ä-'lē\ ca 1854–1931 1st king of the Hejaz (1916–24)
Hu Shih \'hü-'shir\ 1891–1962 Chin. philos.
Hus·sein I \hü-'sän\ 1935–   king of Jordan (1952–)
Hussein Saddam al-Tikriti 1937–   pres. of Iraq (1979–)
Hus·serl \'hù-sə-rəl\ Edmund 1859–1938 Ger. philos. — **Hus·serl·ian** \hù-'sər-lē-ən\ adj
Hus·ton \'hyü-stən, 'yü-\ John 1906–1987 Am. motion-picture director, writer, & actor
Hu·szár \'hù-,sär\ Károly 1882–1941 Hung. journalist & polit.
Hutch·ins \'hə-chənz\ Robert Maynard 1899–1977 Am. educ.
Hutch·in·son \'hə-chə(n)-sən\ Anne 1591–1643 née Marbury Am. (Eng.-born) religious dissident
Hutchinson Thomas 1711–1780 Am. colonial administrator
Hut·ten \'hù-t³n\ Ulrich von 1488–1523 Ger. humanist & supporter of Luther
Hux·ley \'həks-lē\ Al·dous \'òl-dəs\ Leonard 1894–1963 bro. of J.S. Eng. nov. & critic — **Hux·lei·an** \,həks-'lē-ən, 'həks-lē-\ or **Hux·ley·an** \'həks-lē-ən\ adj
Huxley Andrew Fielding 1917–   Brit. physiol. & educ.
Huxley Sir Julian Sorell 1887–1975 grandson of T.H. Eng. biol.
Huxley Thomas Henry 1825–1895 Eng. biol.
Huy·gens \'hī-gənz, 'hòi-\ Christian 1629–1695 Du. math., physicist, & astron.
Huys·mans \wē-'smä³s\ Camille 1871–1968 Belg. polit.
Huysmans Joris-Karl 1848–1907 orig. Georges-Charles Fr. nov.
Hy·att \'hī-ət\ Alpheus 1838–1902 Am. naturalist
Hyde \'hīd\ Douglas 1860–1949 pseud. An Craoibhín Aoibhinn Irish author; pres. of Republic of Ireland (1938–45)
Hyde Edward 1609–1674 1st Earl of Clar·en·don \'klar-ən-dən, 'kler\ Eng. statesman & hist.
Hy·der Ali or **Hai·dar Ali** \'hī-dər-ä-'lē\ 1722–1782 Indian ruler & soldier
Hy·mans \'hī-,män(t)s, ē-mä³s\ Paul 1865–1941 Belg. statesman
Hy·pse·lan·tes \,ēp-sə-'län-dēs\ var of YPSILANTIS
Ibáñez Vicente Blasco— see BLASCO IBÁÑEZ
Iber·ville \'ē-bər-,vil, -,vēl; 'ī-bər,vil\ Sieur d' 1661–1706 Pierre Le Moyne \'mwä³\ Fr.-Canad. explorer & founder of Louisiana
Ibn—Khal·dūn \,i-bən-,kal-'dün, -,kal-\ 1332–1406 Arab hist.
Ibn—Rushd \,i-bən-'rùsht\ — see AVERROËS
Ibn Sa·'ūd \,i-bən-sä-'üd, -'saùd\ ca 1880–1953 king of Saudi Arabia (1932–53)
Ibn Zuhr \,i-bən-'zúr\ L **Av·en·zo·ar** \,a-vən-'zō-ər, -zō-'är\ or **Abu-me·ron** \,a-byù-'mer-,än\ ca 1090–1162 Muslim physician

Ibrā·hīm Pa·sha \i-,brä-'him-'pä-shə, -'pa-shə, -pə-'shä\ 1789–1848 Egypt. gen. & viceroy
Ib·sen \'ib-sən, 'ip-\ Henrik 1828–1906 Norw. poet & dram. — **Ib·se·ni·an** \ib-'sē-nē-ən, ip-, -'se-nē-\ or **Ib·sen·esque** \,ib-sə-'nesk, ,ip-\ adj
Ick·es \'i-kəs\ Harold LeClair 1874–1952 Am. polit.
Ic·ti·nus \ik-'tī-nəs\ 5th cent. B.C. Greek architect
Ig·na·tius \ig-'nā-sh(ē-)əs\ Saint d ca A.D. 110 Theophorus bishop of Antioch & church father
Ignatius of Loyola Saint 1491–1556 orig. Iñigo de Oñaz y Loyola Span. religious & founder of Society of Jesus — **Ig·na·tian** \-sh(ē-)ən\ adj
Ike·da \ē-'kä-də, -'ke-\ Hayato 1899–1965 Jp. polit.; prime min. (1960–64)
Ikhnaton — see AKHENATON
Il·ies·cu \i-lē-'es-(,)kü, il-'yes-\ Ion 1930–   pres. of Romania (1989–)
Im·mel·mann \'i-məl-,män, -mən\ Max 1890–1916 Ger. aviator
In·dy, d' \'dan-dē; dan-'dē, dan-\ (Paul-Marie-Théodore-) Vincent 1851–1931 Fr. composer
Inés de Castro — see CASTRO
Inge \'inj\ William 1913–1973 Am. playwright
Inge \'iŋ\ William Ralph 1860–1954 Eng. prelate & author
In·ger·soll \'iŋ-gər-,sòl, -səl\ Robert Green 1833–1899 Am. orator
In·gres \'a³(ŋ)gr³\ Jean-Auguste-Dominique 1780–1867 Fr. painter
In·ness \'i-nəs\ George: father 1825–1894 & son 1854–1926 Am. painters
In·no·cent \'i-nə-sənt\ name of 13 popes: esp. **II** d 1143 (pope 1130–43); **III** 1160(or 1161)–1216 (pope 1198–1216); **IV** d 1254 (pope 1243–54); **XI** 1611–1689 (pope 1676–89)
İnö·nü \,i-nə-'nü, -'nyü\ İs·met \is-'met\ 1884–1973 Turk. statesman; pres. of Turkey (1938–50); premier (1961–65)
In·sull \'in(t)-səl\ Samuel 1859–1938 Am. (Eng.-born) financier
Io·nes·co \,ē-ə-'nes-(,)kō\ Eugène 1909–1994 Fr. (Rom.-born) dram.
Ipa·tieff \i-'pä-tē-,ef, -'pä-chəf\ Vladimir Nikolayevich 1867–1952 Am. (Russ.-born) chem.
Ire·dell \'ir-,del\ James 1751–1799 Am. jurist
Ire·ton \'ir-t³n\ Henry 1611–1651 Eng. soldier & polit.
Iri·go·yen \,ir-i-'gō-,yen\ Hi·pó·li·to \ē-'pò-lē-,tō\ 1852–1933 pres. of Argentina (1916–22; 1928–30)
Iron·side \'ī-(ə)rn-,sīd\ William Edmund 1880–1959 1st Baron Ironside Brit. field marshal
Ir·ving \'ər-vin\ Sir Henry 1838–1905 orig. John Henry Brodribb Eng. actor
Irving Washington 1783–1859 Am. essayist, nov., & hist.
Ir·win \'ər-wən\ William Henry 1873–1948 Will Irwin Am. journalist
Isaacs \'ī-ziks, -zəks\ Sir Isaac Alfred 1855–1948 Austral. jurist & statesman; gov.-gen. of Australia (1931–36)
Isaacs Rufus Daniel — see Marquis of READING
Is·a·bel·la I \,i-zə-'be-lə\ 1451–1504 wife of Ferdinand V of Castile queen of Castile (1474–1504) & of Aragon (1479–1504)
Ish·er·wood \'i-shər-,wùd\ Christopher William Bradshaw 1904–1986 Am. (Brit.-born) writer
Ishii \'ē-shē-,ē, 'i-\ Viscount Kikujiro 1866–1945 Jp. diplomat
Is·i·dore of Seville \'i-zə-,dòr, -,dòr\ Saint ca 560–636 L. Isidorus Hispalensis Span. prelate & scholar
Iskander Bey — see SKANDERBEG
Is·mā·'īl Pa·sha \is-'mä-,ēl-'pä-shə, -'pa-shə, -pə-'shä\ 1830–1895 viceroy of Egypt (1863–79)
Isoc·ra·tes \ī-'sä-krə-,tēz\ 436–338 B.C. Athenian orator
Is·ra·el ben Eli·ezer \'iz-rē-əl-,ben-,e-lē-'ā-zər\ ca 1700–1760 Ba'al Shem Tov \'bä(-ə)l-'shem-'tòv\ Pol.-Jewish religious leader
Ito \'ē-(,)tō\ Prince Hirobumi 1841–1909 Jp. statesman
Itur·bi \i-'tùr-bē\ José 1895–1980 Span.-born pianist & conductor
Itur·bi·de \,ē-,tùr-'bē-(,)thä\ Agustín de 1783–1824 Mex. soldier; emp. of Mexico (1822–23)
Ivan III \ē-'vän, 'i-vən\ Va·si·lye·vich \və-'sil-yə-,vich\ 1440–1505 the Great grand prince of Russia (1462–1505)
Ivan IV Vasilyevich 1530–1584 the Terrible ruler of Russia (1533–84)
Ives \'īvz\ Charles Edward 1874–1954 Am. composer — **Ives·ian** \'īv-zē-ən\ adj
Ives James Merritt 1824–1895 Am. lithographer
Iyeyasu or **Ieyasu** — see TOKUGAWA
Jā·bir ibn Hay·yān \'ja-,bir-,i-bən-hī-'yan\ Abū Mūsā ca 721–ca 851 L. Ge·ber \'ja-,bir, 'ga-, 'ge-\ Arab alchemist & mystic
Jack·son \'jak-sən\ Andrew 1767–1845 Am. gen.; 7th pres. of the U.S. (1829–37) — **Jack·son·ian** \jak-'sō-nē-ən\ adj
Jackson Helen Maria Hunt 1830–1885 née Fiske Am. nov.
Jackson Jesse Louis 1941–   Am. clergyman & polit. activist
Jackson Mahalia 1911–1972 Am. gospel singer
Jackson Robert Hough·wout \'haù-ət\ 1892–1954 Am. jurist
Jackson Thomas Jonathan 1824–1863 Stone·wall \'stòn-,wòl\ Jackson Am. Confed. gen.
Ja·cob \zhä-kòb\ François 1920–   Fr. geneticist
Ja·co·po del·la Quer·cia \yä-'kō-(,)pō-,dä-lə-'kwer-chä\ ca 1374–1438 Ital. sculptor
Jac·quard \zhə-'kär, 'ja-,kärd\ Joseph-Marie 1752–1834 Fr. inventor
Jacques I — see Jean-Jacques DESSALINES
Jag·a·tai — see CHAGATAI
Ja·hān·gīr \jə-'hän-,gir\ 1569–1627 emp. of India (1605–27)
Ja·lāl ad–Dīn ar–Rū·mī \jə-'lä-lə-'dē-när-'rü-mē\ ca 1207–1273 Pers. poet
James \'jāmz\ name of 6 kings of Scotland & 2 kings of Great Britain: esp. **VI** 1566–1625 of Scotland (reigned 1567–1603) or **I** of Great Britain (reigned 1603–25); **II** 1633–1701 (reigned 1685–88)
James Henry 1811–1882 Am. philos.

\ə\ abut \ᵊ\ kitten, F table \ər\ further \a\ ash \ā\ ace \ä\ mop, mar \aù\ out \ch\ chin \e\ bet \ē\ easy \g\ go \i\ hit \ī\ ice \j\ job \ŋ\ sing \ō\ go \ò\ law \òi\ boy \th\ thin \th\ the \ü\ loot \ù\ foot \y\ yet \zh\ vision \à, k̲, ⁿ, œ, œ̄, ṳe, ᵫ, ᵊ\ see Guide to Pronunciation

James Henry 1843–1916 *son of prec.* Brit. (Am.-born) writer — **James·ian** \'jām-zē-ən\ *adj*
James Jesse Woodson 1847–1882 Am. outlaw
James Phyllis Dorothy 1920– Brit. writer
James William 1842–1910 *bro. of Henry* Am. psychol. & philos. — **James·ian** \'jām-zē-ən\ *adj*
James Edward 1688–1766 *James Francis Edward Stuart; the Old Pretender* Eng. prince
Jame·son \'jām-sən, 'je-mə-sən\ Sir Leander Starr 1853–1917 *Doctor Jameson* Scot. physician & administrator in So. Africa
Jā·mī \'jä-mē\ 1414–1492 Pers. poet & mystic
Ja·ná·cek \'yä-nə-,chek\ Leoš 1854–1928 Czech composer
Jan·sen \'jan(t)-sən, 'yän(t)-\ Cor·ne·lis \kȯr-'nä-ləs\ 1585–1638 L. *Cornelius Jansenius* Du. R.C. theol.
Jaques–Dal·croze \'zhäk-,dal-'krōz, 'zhak-\ Émile 1865–1950 Swiss composer & creator of eurythmics
Ja·rīr \jə-'rir\ *ca* 650–*ca* 729 Arab poet
Jar·rell \jə-'rel, ja-\ Randall 1914–1965 Am. writer
Ja·ru·zel·ski \,yär-ü-'zel-skē\ Woj·ciech \'vȯi-,chek\ Witold 1923– gen.; 1st secy. of the communist party in Poland (1981–89)
Jas·pers \'yäs-pərs\ Karl Theodor 1883–1969 Ger. philos.
Jauregg Julius Wagner von — *see* WAGNER VON JAUREGG
Jau·rès \zhō-res\ Jean-Joseph-Marie-Auguste 1859–1914 Fr. socialist
Jay \'jä\ John 1745–1829 Am. jurist & statesman; 1st chief justice U.S. Supreme Court (1789–95)
Jeanne d'Arc — *see* JOAN OF ARC
Jeans \'jēnz\ Sir James Hopwood 1877–1946 Eng. physicist, astron., & author
Jebb \'jeb\ Sir Richard Claverhouse 1841–1905 Scot. scholar
Jef·fers \'je-fərz\ (John) Robinson 1887–1962 Am. poet
Jef·fer·son \'je-fər-sən\ Thomas 1743–1826 3d pres. of the U.S. (1801–09) — **Jef·fer·so·nian** \,je-fər-'sō-nē-ən, -nyən\ *adj*
Jef·frey \'je-frē\ Lord Francis 1773–1850 Scot. critic & jurist
Jef·freys \'je-frēz\ George 1645–1689 1st Baron *Jeffreys of Wem* Eng. jurist
Jel·li·coe \'je-li-,kō\ 1st Earl 1859–1935 *John Rushworth Jellicoe* Brit. admiral
Jen·ner \'je-nər\ Edward 1749–1823 Eng. physician — **Jen·ne·ri·an** \je-'nir-ē-ən\ *adj*
Jenner Sir William 1815–1898 Eng. physician
Jen·sen \'yen-zən\ (Johannes) Hans Daniel 1907–1973 Ger. physicist
Jen·sen \'yen(t)-sən, 'jen(t)-\ Johannes Vilhelm 1873–1950 Dan. poet & nov.
Jen·son \'jen-sən, zhäⁿ-sōⁿ\ Nicolas *ca* 1420–1480 Fr. printer & engraver in Venice
Jerne \'yer-ne\ Niels Kai 1911–1994 Dan. (Eng.-born) immunologist
Je·rome \jə-'rōm *also* 'jer-əm\ Saint *ca* 347–419(or 420) L. *Eusebius Hi·eron·y·mus* \,hī-ə-'rä-nə-məs, hi-\ church father
Jer·vis \'jär-vəs, 'jär-\ John 1735–1823 Earl of *St. Vincent* Brit. admiral
Jes·per·sen \'yes-pər-sən\ (Jens) Otto Harry 1860–1943 Dan. philologist
Je·sus \'jē-zəs, -zəz\ *or* **Jesus Christ** \'krīst\ *or* **Christ Jesus** *ca* 6 B.C.–*ca* A.D. 30 *Jesus of Nazareth; the Son of Mary* source of the Christian religion & Savior in the Christian faith
Jev·ons \'je-vənz\ William Stanley 1835–1882 Eng. econ.
Jew·ett \'jü-ət\ Sarah Orne 1849–1909 Am. writer
Ji·ang Ze·min \jē-'äŋ-zə-'min\ 1926– gen. secy. of Chin. communist party (1989–); pres. of China (1993–)
Ji·mé·nez \hē-'mä-nəs\ Juan Ramón 1881–1958 Span. poet
Jiménez de Cis·ne·ros \-,dä-sis-'ner-əs\ Francisco 1436–1517 Span. prelate & statesman
Jin·nah \'ji-(,)nä, 'ji-nə\ Mohammed Ali 1876–1948 Indian polit.; 1st gov.-gen. of dominion of Pakistan (1947–48)
Jo·achim \yō-'ä-kim, -,kim; 'yō-ə-,kim, -,kim\ Joseph 1831–1907 Hung. violinist
Joan of Arc \,jōn-əv-'ärk\ *F* **Jeanne d'Arc** \zhän-dárk\ Saint *ca* 1412–1431 *the Maid of Orleans* Fr. national heroine
Jodl \'yō-d°l\ Alfred 1890–1946 Ger. gen.
Jof·fre \zhȯfr°\ Joseph-Jacques-Césaire 1852–1931 Fr. field marshal; marshal of France
John \'jän\ name of 21 popes: esp. **XXIII** (*Angelo Giuseppe Roncalli*) 1881–1963 (pope 1958–63)
John 1167–1216 *John Lack·land* \'lak-,land\ king of England (1199–1216)
John I 1357–1433 *the Great* king of Portugal (1385–1433)
John Augustus Edwin 1878–1961 Brit. painter & etcher
John of Austria 1547–1578 *Don John* Span. gen.
John of Gaunt \'gȯnt, 'gänt\ 1340–1399 Duke of *Lancaster; son of Edward III of England*
John of Lancaster 1389–1435 Duke of *Bedford; son of Henry IV of England*
John of Leiden *ca* 1509–1536 Du. Anabaptist
John of Salisbury 1115(or 1120)–1180 Eng. ecclesiastic
John of the Cross 1542–1591 *Juan de Yepes y Alvarez* Span. mystic & poet
John Paul \'pȯl\ name of 2 popes: esp. **II** (*Karol Wojtyla*) 1920– (pope 1978–)
John III So·bies·ki \sō-'byes-kē, ,sō-bē-'es-\ 1629–1696 king of Poland (1674–96)
John·son \'jän(t)-sən\ Andrew 1808–1875 17th pres. of the U.S. (1865–69) — **John·so·nian** \jän-'sō-nē-ən, -nyən\ *adj*
Johnson (Jonathan) Eastman 1824–1906 Am. painter
John·son \'yün-sȯn\ Eyvind 1900–1976 Swed. author
John·son \'jän(t)-sən\ James Weldon 1871–1938 Am. author
Johnson Lyndon Baines 1908–1973 Am. polit.; 36th pres. of the U.S. (1963–69) — **John·so·nian** \jän-'sō-nē-ən, -nyən\ *adj*
Johnson Philip Cortelyou 1906– Am. architect
Johnson Richard Mentor 1780–1850 vice pres. of the U.S. (1837–41)
Johnson Samuel 1709–1784 *Dr. Johnson* Eng. lexicographer & author — **John·so·nian** \jän-'sō-nē-ən, -nyən\ *adj*
Johnson Sir William 1715–1774 Brit. administrator in America
John·ston \'jän(t)-stən, -sən\ Albert Sidney 1803–1862 Am. Confed. gen.
Johnston Joseph Eggleston 1807–1891 Am. Confed. gen.

Join·ville \zhwaⁿ-'vē(ə)l\ Jean de *ca* 1224–1317 Fr. chronicler
Jó·kai \'yō-,kȯi\ Mór 1825–1904 Hung. nov. & dram.
Jo·liot–Cu·rie \zhȯl-,yō-kyù-'rē, -'kyùr-(,)ē\ (Jean-) Frédéric 1900–1958 orig. *Joliot* Fr. physicist
Joliot–Curie Irène 1897–1956 formerly *Irène Curie-Joliot, dau. of Marie & Pierre Curie & wife of prec.* Fr. physicist
Jol·liet *or* **Jo·liet** \zhȯl-'yä\ Louis 1645–1700 Fr. explorer
Jo·mi·ni \zhō-mə-'nē\ Henri de 1779–1869 Swiss-born soldier & mil. strategist
Jones \'jōnz\ Anson 1798–1858 pres. of the Republic of Texas (1844–46)
Jones Daniel 1881–1967 Eng. phonetician
Jones Howard Mumford 1892–1980 Am. educ. & critic
Jones In·i·go \'i-ni-,gō\ 1573–1652 Eng. architect
Jones John Paul 1747–1792 orig. in full *John Paul* Am. (Scot.-born) naval officer
Jones Thomas Hudson 1892–1969 Am. sculptor
Jon·son \'jän(t)-sən\ Benjamin 1572–1637 *Ben Jonson* Eng. dram. — **Jon·so·nian** \jän-'sō-nē-ən, -nyən\ *adj*
Jop·lin \'jä-plən\ Scott 1868–1917 Am. pianist & composer
Jor·daens \'yȯr-dän(t)s\ Jacob 1593–1678 Flem. painter
Jor·dan \'jȯr-d°n\ David Starr 1851–1931 Am. biol. & educ.
Jo·seph \'jō-zəf *also* -səf\ *ca* 1840–1904 *In-mut-too-yah-lat-lat* Nez Percé Indian chief
Joseph II 1741–1790 Holy Rom. emp. (1765–90)
Jo·se·phine \'jō-zə-,fēn\ Empress — *see* BEAUHARNAIS
Jo·seph·son \'jō-zəf-sən *also* -səf-\ Brian David 1940– Brit. physicist
Jo·se·phus \jō-'sē-fəs\ Flavius *ca* A.D. 37–*ca* 100 Jewish hist.
Jos·quin des Prez \zhȯ-'skaⁿ-de-'prā\ *or* **Des·prez** \de-'prā\ *ca* 1440–1521 Fr. composer
Jou·bert \zhü-'ber\ Joseph 1754–1824 Fr. essayist & moralist
Joubert \'zhü-'ber, yō-\ Petrus Jacobus 1834–1900 known as *Piet Joubert* Boer gen. & statesman
Jou·haux \zhü-ō\ Léon 1879–1954 Fr. trade-union leader
Joule \'jül\ James Prescott 1818–1889 Eng. physicist
Jour·dan \zhùr-'dän\ Comte Jean-Baptiste 1762–1833 Fr. soldier; marshal of France
Jo·vi·an \'jō-vē-ən\ *ca* 331–364 *Flavius Jovianus* Rom. emp. (363–364)
Jow·ett \'jaù-ət, 'jō-\ Benjamin 1817–1893 Eng. Greek scholar
Joyce \'jȯis\ James Augustine 1882–1941 Irish writer — **Joyc·ean** \'jȯi-sē-ən\ *adj*
Juan Car·los \'(h)wän-'kär-,lōs\ 1938– king of Spain (1975–)
Juan Manuel Don — *see* MANUEL
Juá·rez \'hwär-əs, 'wär-\ Benito Pablo 1806–1872 Mex. lawyer; pres. of Mexico (1861–65; 1867–72)
Judas Maccabaeus — *see* MACCABEES
Ju·gur·tha \jù-'gər-thə\ *or* **Iu·gur·tha** \yù-\ *ca* 160–104 B.C. king of Numidia (118–105 B.C.)
Ju·lian \'jül-yən\ *ca* 331–363 *Flavius Claudius Julianus, the Apostate* Rom. emp. (361–363)
Ju·li·ana \,jü-lē-'a-nə\ 1909– *dau. of Wilhelmina* queen of the Netherlands (1948–80)
Jung \'yùŋ\ Carl Gustav 1875–1961 Swiss psychol.
Ju·nius \'jü-nyəs, -nē-əs\ Franciscus 1589–1677 Eng. (Ger.-born) philologist
Jun·kers \'yùŋ-kərz, -kərs\ Hugo 1859–1935 Ger. airplane designer & builder
Ju·not \zhüē-'nō\ Andoche 1771–1813 Duc *d'Abran·tès* \,da-,bräⁿ-'tes\ Fr. gen.
Jus·se·rand \zhüēs-räⁿ, zhüē-sə-\ Jean-(Adrien-Antoine-) Jules 1855–1932 Fr. scholar & diplomat
Jus·tin \'jəs-tən\ Saint *ca* 100–*ca* 165 *Justin (the) Martyr* church father
Jus·tin·i·an I \jə-'sti-nē-ən\ 483–565 *the Great* Byzantine emp. (527–565)
Ju·ve·nal \'jü-və-n°l\ A.D. 55 to 60–*ca* 127 *Decimus Junius Juvenalis* Rom. poet & satirist — **Ju·ve·na·lian** \,jü-və-'nāl-yən\ *adj*
Ká·dár \'kä-,dár\ János 1912–1989 1st secy. of Hung. communist party (1956–88)
Kaf·ka \'käf-kə, 'kaf-\ Franz 1883–1924 Czech-born author writing in German
Ka·ga·wa \kä-'gä-wə\ Toyohiko 1888–1960 Jp. social reformer
Kai·fu \'ki-(,)fü\ Toshiki 1931– prime min. of Japan (1989–91)
Kai·ser \'kī-zər\ Henry John 1882–1967 Am. industrialist
Kalb \'kälp, 'kalb\ Johann 1721–1780 Baron *de Kalb* \di-'kalb\ Ger. gen. in Am. Revolution
Kā·li·dā·sa \,kä-li-'dä-sə\ 5th cent. A.D. Indian dram. & poet
Ka·li·nin \kə-'lē-nyən, -nyən\ Mikhail Ivanovich 1875–1946 Russ. polit.; formal head of Soviet state (1919–46)
Ka·me·ha·me·ha I \kə-,mä-ə-'mä-(,)hä\ 1758?–1819 *the Great* king of Hawaii (1795–1819)
Ka·me·nev \'käm-yə-,nef, 'kam-; 'kä-mə-, 'ka-\ Lev Borisovich 1883–1936 Russ. Communist leader
Ka·mer·lingh On·nes \,kä-mər-liŋ-'ȯn-əs\ Heike 1853–1926 Du. physicist
Kan·din·sky \kan-'din(t)-skē\ Wassily 1866–1944 Russ. painter
Kane \'kān\ Elisha Kent 1820–1857 Am. arctic explorer
K'ang-hsi \'käŋ-'shē\ 1654–1722 Chin. emp. (1661–1722)
Kant \'kant, 'känt\ Immanuel 1724–1804 Ger. philos.
Kan·to·ro·vich \,kän-tə-'rȯ-vich\ Leonid Vitalyevich 1912–1986 Russ. econ.
Ka·pit·sa \'kä-pyit-sə\ Pyotr Leonidovich 1894–1984 Russ. physicist
Kar·a·george \,kar-ə-'jȯrj\ 1762–1817 orig. *George Petrovič Karageorge* Serbian nationalist & founder of Kar·a·geor·ge·vić \-'jȯr-jə-,vich\ dynasty
Ka·ra·jan \'kär-ə-,yän\ Herbert von 1908–1989 Austrian conductor
Ka·ra·man·lis \,kär-ə-,män-'lēs, -'män-\ Konstantinos 1907– prime min. (1974–80) & pres. (1980–85; 1990–) of Greece
Karle \'kärl\ Jerome 1918– Am. physical chem.
Karl·feldt \'kär(ə)l-,felt\ Erik Axel 1864–1931 Swed. poet
Ká·ro·lyi \'kar-əl-yē, 'kär-\ Count Mihály 1875–1955 Hung. polit.
Kar·rer \'kär-ər\ Paul 1889–1971 Swiss chem.
Kar·sa·vi·na \kär-'sä-və-nə, -'sä-\ Tamara 1885–1978 Russ. dancer
Kast·ler \käst-ler\ Alfred 1902–1984 Fr. physicist

Kastrioti George — see SKANDERBEG
Katz \'kats\ Sir Bernhard 1911–   Brit. (Ger.-born) biophysicist
Kauf·man \'kȯf-mən\ George Simon 1889–1961 Am. dram.
Kau·nitz \'kau̇-nəts\ Wenzel Anton von 1711–1794 Prince *von Kaunitz-Rietberg* Austrian statesman
Kaut·sky \'kau̇t-skē\ Karl Johann 1854–1938 Ger. socialist writer
Ka·wa·ba·ta \ˌkä-wə-'bä-tə, kə-'wä-bə-ˌtä\ Yasunari 1899–1972 Jp. writer
Kaye–Smith \'kā-'smith\ Sheila 1887–1956 Eng. nov.
Ka·zan·tza·kis \ˌkä-zᵊn-'tsä-kēs, -'chä-\ Nikos 1885–1957 Greek poet, nov., & translator
Kean \'kēn\ Edmund 1789–1833 Eng. actor
Kear·ny \'kär-nē\ Philip 1814–1862 Am. gen.
Keat·ing \'kē-tiŋ\ Paul John 1944–   prime min. of Australia (1991–   )
Keats \'kēts\ John 1795–1821 Eng. poet — **Keats·ian** \'kēt-sē-ən\ adj
Ke·ble \'kē-bəl\ John 1792–1866 Eng. clergyman & poet
Ke·fau·ver \'kē-ˌfȯ-vər\ (Carey) Estes 1903–1963 Am. polit.
Kei·tel \'kī-t'l\ Wilhelm 1882–1946 Ger. field marshal
Kek·ko·nen \'ke-kə-nən, -ˌnen\ Urho Kaleva 1900–1986 pres. of Finland (1956–81)
Kel·ler \'ke-lər\ Helen Adams 1880–1968 Am. deaf & blind lecturer
Kel·logg \'ke-ˌlȯg, -ˌläg\ Frank Billings 1856–1937 Am. statesman
Kel·vin \'kel-vən\ 1st Baron 1824–1907 *William Thomson* Brit. math. & physicist
Ke·mal Ata·türk \kə-'mal-'a-tə-ˌtȯrk, -'ä-\ 1881–1938 orig. *Mus·ta·fa Ke·mal* \mü-stä-'fä-kä-'mäl\ Turk. gen.; pres. of Turkey (1923–38)
Kem·ble \'kem-bəl\ Frances Anne 1809–1893 *Fanny* Eng. actress
Kemble John Philip 1757–1823 Eng. actor
Kempis Thomas à — see THOMAS À KEMPIS
Ken or **Kenn** \'ken\ Thomas 1637–1711 Eng. prelate & hymn writer
Ken·dall \'ken-d'l\ Edward Calvin 1886–1972 Am. biochem.
Kendall Henry Way 1926–   Am. physicist
Ken·drew \'ken-(ˌ)drü\ Sir John Cowdery 1917–   Brit. chem.
Ken·nan \'ke-nən\ George Frost 1904–   Am. hist. & diplomat
Ken·ne·dy \'ke-nə-dē\ Anthony M. 1936–   Am. jurist
Kennedy John Fitzgerald 1917–1963 Am. polit.; 35th pres. of the U.S. (1961–63) — **Ken·ne·dy·esque** \ˌke-nə-dē-'esk\ adj
Kennedy Joseph Patrick 1888–1969 *father of J. F. & R. F.* Am. businessman & diplomat
Kennedy Robert Francis 1925–1968 Am. polit.; atty. gen. (1961–64)
Ken·nel·ly \'ke-nᵊl-ē\ Arthur Edwin 1861–1939 Am. engineer
Ken·ny \'ke-nē\ Elizabeth 1880–1952 *Sister Kenny* Austral. nurse & physiotherapist
Kent \'kent\ James 1763–1847 Am. jurist
Kent Rockwell 1882–1971 Am. painter & illustrator
Ken·yon \'ken-yən\ John Samuel 1874–1959 Am. phonetician
Kep·ler \'ke-plər\ Johannes 1571–1630 Ger. astron. — **Kep·ler·ian** \ke-'plir-ē-ən, -'pler-\ adj
Kep·pel \'ke-pəl\ 1st Viscount 1725–1786 *Augustus Keppel* Brit. admiral
Ker \'ker, 'kər, 'kär\ William Paton 1855–1923 Brit. scholar
Ke·ren·sky \'ker-ən-skē, kə-'ren-\ Aleksandr Fyodorovich 1881–1970 Russ. revolutionary
Kern \'kərn\ Jerome David 1885–1945 Am. composer
Ker·ou·ac \'ker-ə-ˌwak\ Jack 1922–1969 *Jean-Louis* Am. writer
Kes·sel·ring \'ke-səl-riŋ\ Albert 1885–1960 Ger. field marshal
Ket·ter·ing \'ke-tə-riŋ\ Charles Franklin 1876–1958 Am. electrical engineer & inventor
Key \'kē\ Francis Scott 1779–1843 Am. lawyer & author of "The Star-Spangled Banner"
Keynes \'kānz\ John Maynard 1883–1946 1st Baron *Keynes of Tilton* Eng. econ.
Key·ser·ling \'kī-zər-liŋ\ Hermann Alexander 1880–1946 Graf *Keyserling* Ger. philos. & writer
Kha·cha·tu·ri·an \ˌkä-chə-'tùr-ē-ən, ˌka-\ Aram Ilich 1903–1978 Soviet (Armenian-born) composer
Kha·da·fy — see GADHAFI
Khā·lid \'ka-lid, 'kä-\ in full *Khālid ibn 'Abd al-'Azīz ibn 'Abd ar-Raḥmān al-Sa'ūd* 1913–1982 king of Saudi Arabia (1975–82)
Kha·me·nei \ˌkä-'mä-nä\ Hojatolislam Sayyed Ali 1939–   religious leader of Iran (1989–   )
Khayyám Omar — see OMAR KHAYYÁM
Khe·ra·skov \ᵊ-'räs-kəf\ Mikhail Matveyevich 1733–1807 Russ. poet
Kho·mei·ni \kō-'mä-nē, kō-, hō-\ Ayatollah Ruholla Mussaui 1900–1989 religious leader of Iran (1979–89)
Kho·ra·na \kō-'rä-nə\ Har Gobind 1922–   Am. (Indian-born) biochem.
Khru·shchev \'krüsh-'chȯf, -'chȯv; 'krüsh-ˌ; krü-'shȯf, -'shȯv; 'krü-ˌ; also with e for ȯ\ Ni·ki·ta \nə-'kē-tə\ Sergeyevich 1894–1971 Soviet polit.; premier of the Soviet Union (1958–64) — **Khru·shchev·ian** \krüsh-'chȯ-vē-ən, -'chō- also -'che-; krü-'shȯ-, -'shō- also -'she-\ adj — **Khru·shchev·ite** \krüsh-'chȯ-ˌvīt, -'che-ˌvit, 'krüsh-ˌ; krü-'shȯ-, -'she-, 'krü-ˌ\ adj
Khu·fu \'kü-(ˌ)fü\ Gk Che·ops \'kē-ˌäps\ 26th cent. B.C. king of Egypt & pyramid builder
Khwā·riz·mī, al– \al-'kwär-əz-mē, -'kwär-\ ca 780–ca 850 *Muḥammad ibn Mūsā al-Khwārizmī* Islamic (Persian-born) math. & astron.
Kidd \'kid\ William ca 1645–1701 *Captain Kidd* Scot. pirate
Kie·ran \'kir-ən\ John Francis 1892–1981 Am. journalist
Kier·ke·gaard \'kir-kə-ˌgär(d), -ˌgȯr\ Søren Aabye 1813–1855 Dan. philos. & theol. — **Kier·ke·gaard·ian** \ˌkir-kə-'gär-dē-ən, -'gȯr-\ adj
Kie·sing·er \'kē-ziŋ-ər\ Kurt Georg 1904–1988 chancellor of West Germany (1966–69)
Kil·lian \'ki-lē-ən, 'kil-yən\ James Rhyne 1904–1988 Am. educ.
Kil·mer \'kil-mər\ (Alfred) Joyce 1886–1918 Am. poet
Kim Il Sung \'kim-'il-'səŋ, -'sùŋ\ 1912–1994 No. Korean communist leader (1948–94) and pres. (1972–94)
Kim·mel \'ki-məl\ Husband Edward 1882–1968 Am. admiral
Kim Young Sam \'kim-'yəŋ-'säm, -'sam\ 1927–   pres. of So. Korea (1993–   )
Kin·di, al– \al-'kin-dē\ d ca 870 Arab philos.
King \'kiŋ\ Ernest Joseph 1878–1956 Am. admiral
King Martin Luther, Jr. 1929–1968 Am. clergyman & civil rights leader

King Rufus 1755–1827 Am. polit. & diplomat
King William Lyon Mackenzie 1874–1950 Canad. statesman; prime min. (1921–26; 1926–30; 1935–48)
King William Rufus de Vane 1786–1853 Am. polit.; vice pres. of the U.S. (1853)
Kings·ley \'kiŋz-lē\ Charles 1819–1875 Eng. clergyman & nov.
Kin·kaid \kin-'kād\ Thomas Cassin 1888–1972 Am. admiral
Kin·sey \'kin-zē\ Alfred Charles 1894–1956 Am. sexologist
Kip·ling \'kip-liŋ\ (Joseph) Rud·yard \'rəd-yərd, 'rə-jərd\ 1865–1936 Eng. author — **Kip·ling·esque** \ˌkip-liŋ-'esk\ adj
Kir·by–Smith \ˌkər-bē-'smith\ Edmund 1824–1893 orig. surname *Smith* Am. Confed. gen.
Kirch·hoff \'kir-ˌkȯf\ Gustav Robert 1824–1887 Ger. physicist
Kirch·ner \'kirk-nər, 'kirk-\ Ernst Ludwig 1880–1938 Ger. painter
Ki·rov \'kē-ˌrȯf, -ˌrȯv\ Sergey Mironovich 1886–1934 Soviet polit.
Kir·wan \'kər-wən\ Richard 1733–1812 Irish chem.
Kis·sin·ger \'ki-sᵊn-jər\ Henry Alfred 1923–   Am. (Ger.-born) scholar & govt. official; secy. of state (1973–77)
Kitch·e·ner \'kich-nər, 'ki-chə-\ Horatio Herbert 1850–1916 1st Earl *Kitchener of Khartoum and of Broome* Brit. field marshal
Kit·tredge \'ki-trij\ George Lyman 1860–1941 Am. educ.
Klee \'klā\ Paul 1879–1940 Swiss painter
Klein \'klīn\ Lawrence Robert 1920–   Am. econ.
Kleist \'klīst\ (Bernd) Heinrich Wilhelm von 1777–1811 Ger. dram.
Kleist (Paul Ludwig) Ewald von 1881–1954 Ger. field marshal
Klem·per·er \'klem-pər-ər\ Otto 1885–1973 Ger. conductor
Kles·til \'kles-ˌtil\ Thomas 1932–   pres. of Austria (1992–   )
Klitz·ing \'klit-siŋ\ Klaus von 1943–   Ger. physicist
Klop·stock \'kläp-ˌstäk, 'klȯp-ˌshtȯk\ Friedrich Gottlieb 1724–1803 Ger. poet
Klug \'klüg\ Aaron 1926–   So. African (Lith.-born) molecular biol.
Knel·ler \'ne-lər, 'kne-\ Sir Godfrey 1646(or 1649)–1723 orig. *Gottfried Kniller* Eng. (Ger.-born) painter
Knox \'näks\ Henry 1750–1806 Am. gen. in Revolution
Knox John ca 1514–1572 Scot. religious reformer
Knox Philander Chase 1853–1921 Am. statesman
Knud·sen \'nüd-sən, 'knüd-\ William Signius 1879–1948 Am. (Dan.-born) industrialist & administrator
Knut \'knüt, 'knyüt\ var of CANUTE
Koch \'kȯk, 'kȯḵ, or with ō or ä for ȯ\ Robert 1843–1910 Ger. bacteriol.
Ko·cher \'kȯ-kər, -kər\ Emil Theodor 1841–1917 Swiss surgeon
Kock \'kȯk\ Charles-Paul de 1793–1871 Fr. nov. & dram.
Ko·dály \'kō-ˌdī\ Zol·tán \'zȯl-ˌtän\ 1882–1967 Hung. composer
Koest·ler \'kes(t)-lər\ Arthur 1905–1983 Brit. (Hung.-born) writer
Kohl \'kōl\ Helmut 1930–   chancellor of West Germany (1982–90)
Koh·ler \'kō-lər\ Foy David 1908–1990 Am. diplomat
Köhler \'kœ-lər\ Georges J. F. 1946–   Ger. immunologist
Koi·so \'kȯi-(ˌ)sō, 'kō-ē-(ˌ)sō\ Kuniaki 1880–1950 Jp. gen.
Kokh·ba \'kȯk-bä\ Bar d A.D. 135 orig. *Sim·e·on bar Ko·zi·ba* \'si-mē-ən-bär-'kō-zē-ˌbä\ Jewish leader in Palestine
Ko·kosch·ka \kə-'kȯsh-kə\ Oskar 1886–1980 Brit. (Austrian-born) painter
Kol·chak \kȯl-'chäk\ Aleksandr Vasilyevich 1873–1920 Russ. admiral & counterrevolutionary
Kol·lon·tay \ˌkä-lən-'tī\ Aleksandra Mikhaylovna 1872–1952 Russ. diplomat
Koll·witz \'kȯl-ˌwits, 'kȯl-ˌvits\ Käthe 1867–1945 Ger. artist
Kol·mo·go·rov \kəl-mə-'gȯ-rəf\ Andrey Nikolayevich 1903–1987 Soviet math.
Kol·tsov \kȯl-'tsȯf, -'tsȯv\ Aleksey Vasilyevich 1808–1842 Russ. poet
Ko·mu·ra \kō-'mùr-ä, 'kō-mə-ˌrä\ Marquis Jutarō 1855–1911 Jp. diplomat
Kon·di·lis \kȯn-'dē-ləs, -lēs\ Géorgios 1879–1936 Greek gen. & polit.
Ko·nev \'kȯn-yef, -ˌyev, -yəf\ Ivan Stepanovich 1897–1973 Soviet gen.
Ko·noe \'kȯ-nō-ˌe\ Prince Fumimaro 1891–1945 Jp. statesman
Koo \'kü\ Vi Kyuin Wel·ling·ton \'we-liŋ-tən\ 1888–1985 orig. *Ku Wei-chün* Chin. statesman & diplomat
Koop·mans \'küp-mənz, 'kōp-ˌmänz\ Tjalling Charles 1910–1985 Am. (Du.-born) econ.
Kopernik or **Koppernigk** — see COPERNICUS
Korn·berg \'kȯrn-ˌbərg\ Arthur 1918–   Am. biochem.
Korn·gold \'kȯrn-ˌgōld, -ˌgȯlt\ Erich Wolfgang 1897–1957 Am. (Austrian-born) composer, conductor, & pianist
Kor·ni·lov \kȯr-'nē-ləf\ Lavr Georgiyevich 1870–1918 Russ. gen. & counterrevolutionary
Ko·ro·len·ko \ˌkȯr-ə-'leŋ-(ˌ)kō, ˌkär-\ Vladimir Galaktionovich 1853–1921 Russ. nov.
Kor·zyb·ski \kȯr-'zhip-skē, kȯr-'zib-\ Alfred Habdank Skarbek 1879–1950 Am. (Pol.-born) scientist & writer
Koś·ciusz·ko \ˌkȯsh-'chùsh-(ˌ)kō, ˌkä-sē-'əs-ˌkō\ Tadeusz Andrzej Bonawentura 1746–1817 Pol. patriot & soldier in Am. Revolution
Kos·sel \'kȯ-səl\ Albrecht 1853–1927 Ger. biochem.
Kos·suth \'kä-ˌsüth, kä-'; 'kȯ-ˌshùt\ La·jos \'lȯi-ˌōsh\ 1802–1894 Hung. patriot & statesman
Ko·sy·gin \kə-'sē-gən\ Aleksey Nikolayevich 1904–1980 Soviet polit.; premier of Soviet Union (1964–80)
Kot·ze·bue \'kät-sə-ˌbü, 'kȯt-\ August Friedrich Ferdinand von 1761–1819 Ger. dram.
Kous·se·vitz·ky \ˌkü-sə-'vit-skē\ Serge \'sərj, 'serzh\ 1874–1951 *Sergey Aleksandrovich Kusevitsky* Am. (Russ.-born) conductor
Krafft–Ebing \ˌkräft-'ā-biŋ, 'kraft-\ Richard 1840–1902 Freiherr *von Krafft-Ebing* Ger. neurologist
Krebs \'krebz\ Edwin Gerhard 1918–   Am. biochem.
Krebs Sir Hans Adolf 1900–1981 Brit. (Ger.-born) biochem.

\ə\ abut \'ᵊ\ kitten, F table \ər\ further \a\ ash \ā\ ace \ä\ mop, mar
\aù\ out \ch\ chin \e\ bet \ē\ easy \g\ go \i\ hit \ī\ ice \j\ job
\ŋ\ sing \ō\ go \ȯ\ law \ȯi\ boy \th\ thin \th̲\ the \ü\ loot \ù\ foot
\y\ yet \zh\ vision \á, k̲, ⁿ, œ, œ̄, ᵫ, ᵬ, ᷓ\ see Guide to Pronunciation

Kreis·ky \'krī-skē\ Bruno 1911–1990 chancellor of Austria (1970–83)
Kreis·ler \'krīs-lər\ Fritz 1875–1962 Am. (Austrian-born) violinist
Krogh \'króg\ (Schack) August Steenberg 1874–1949 Dan. physiol.
Kro·pot·kin \krə-'pät-kən\ Pyotr Alekseyevich 1842–1921 Russ. geographer & revolutionary
Kru·ger \'krü-gər *Afrik* 'krǖ-ər\ Paul 1825–1904 *Stephanus Johannes Paulus* So. African statesman
Krupp \'krúp, 'krəp\ family of Ger. munition makers: including Friedrich 1787–1826; his son Alfred 1812–1887; Alfred's son Friedrich Alfred 1854–1902; Friedrich Alfred's daughter Bertha 1886–1957; & Bertha's son Alfried 1907–1967
Krup·ska·ya \'krúp-skə-yə\ Nadezhda Konstantinovna 1869–1939 *wife of Lenin* Russ. revolutionary
Krutch \'krüch\ Joseph Wood 1893–1970 Am. author & critic
Ku·bi·tschek de Oli·vei·ra \'kü-bə-,chek-ä-ō-lē-'vä-rə\ Juscelino 1902–1976 pres. of Brazil (1956–61)
Ku·blai Khan \'kü-,blə-'kän, -,blī-\ 1215–1294 founder of Mongol dynasty in China
Ku·brick \'kü-brik, 'kyü-\ Stanley 1928–   Am. film director, writer, & producer
Kuhn \'kün\ Richard 1900–1967 Austrian chem.
Kuhn Thomas Samuel 1922–   Am. philos. & scientist — **Kuhn·ian** \'kü-nē-ən\ *adj*
Kun \'kün\ Béla 1885–1937 Hung. Communist
Kung \'gün\ Prince 1833–1898 Manchu statesman
K'ung \'kún\ H. H. 1881–1967 orig. *K'ung Hsiang-hsi* Chin. statesman
Ku·ro·pat·kin \,kúr-ə-'pat-kən, -'pät-\ Aleksey Nikolayevich 1848–1921 Russ. gen.
Ku·ro·sa·wa \,kúr-ə-'saú-ə\ Akira 1910–   Jp. filmmaker
Kusch \'kúsh\ Polykarp 1911–1993 Am. (Ger.-born) physicist
Ku·tu·zov \kə-'tü-,zóf, -,zóv\ Mikhail Illarionovich 1745–1813 Prince of *Smolensk* Russ. field marshal
Kuz·nets \kəz-(,)nets\ Simon 1901–1985 Am. (Ukrainian-born) econ.
Kyd *or* **Kid** \'kid\ Thomas 1558–1594 Eng. dram.
Kynewulf *var of* CYNEWULF
La Bru·yère \,lä-brü-'yer, -brē-'er\ Jean de 1645–1696 Fr. moralist
La·chaise \lə-'shäz\ Gaston 1882–1935 Am. (Fr.-born) sculptor
La Farge \lə-'färzh, -'färj\ John 1835–1910 Am. artist
La Farge Oliver Hazard Perry 1901–1963 Am. writer & anthropol.
La·fa·yette \,lä-fē-'et, ,la-\ Marquis de 1757–1834 *Marie-Joseph-Paul=Yves-Roch-Gilbert du Motier* Fr. gen. & statesman
Laf·fite *or* **La·fitte** \lə-'fēt, la-\ Jean *ca* 1780–*ca* 1826 Fr. pirate in America
La Fol·lette \lə-'fä-lət\ Robert Marion 1855–1925 Am. polit.
La·fon·taine \,lä-fōⁿ-'ten\ Henri 1854–1943 Belg. lawyer & statesman
La Fon·taine \,lä-,fōⁿ-'ten\ Jean 1621–1695 Fr. poet
La·ger·kvist \'lä-gər-,kvist, -,kwist\ Pär Fabian 1891–1974 Swed. dram., poet, & nov.
La·ger·löf \'lä-gər-,lə(r)v\ Selma Ottiliana Lovisa 1858–1940 Swed. nov. & poet
La·grange \lə-'gränj, -'gräⁿzh\ Joseph-Louis 1736–1813 Comte *de Lagrange* Fr. math.
La Guar·dia \lə-'gwär-dē-ə\ Fi·o·rel·lo \,fē-ə-'re-(,)lō\ Henry 1882–1947 Am. polit.
Laing \'laŋ\ Ronald David 1927–1989 Brit. psychiatrist — **Laing·ian** \-ē-ən\ *adj*
Lake \'lāk\ Simon 1866–1945 Am. naval architect
La·marck \lə-'märk\ Jean-Baptiste de Monet de 1744–1829 Chevalier *de Lamarck* Fr. naturalist
La·mar·tine \,lä-,mär-'tēn, ,la-mər-\ Alphonse-Marie-Louis de Prat de 1790–1869 Fr. poet
Lamas Carlos Saavedra — *see* Carlos SAAVEDRA LAMAS
Lamb \'lam\ Charles 1775–1834 Eng. essayist & critic
Lamb William 1779–1848 2d Viscount *Melbourne* Eng. statesman
Lamb Willis Eugene 1913–   Am. physicist
Lam·bert \'lam-bərt\ John 1619–1683 Eng. gen.
Lam·masch \'lä-,mäsh\ Heinrich 1853–1920 Austrian jurist
La Motte-Fouqué — *see* FOUQUÉ
L'Amour \lä-'mór, -'mür\ Louis Dearborn 1908–1988 Am. writer
Land \'land\ Edwin Herbert 1909–1991 Am. inventor & industrialist
Lan·dau \län-'daú\ Lev Davidovich 1908–1968 Russ. physicist
Lan·dis \'lan-dəs\ Ken·e·saw \'ke-nə-,só\ Mountain 1866–1944 Am. jurist & baseball commissioner
Lan·don \'lan-dən\ Alfred Mossman 1887–1987 Am. polit.
Lan·dor \'lan-,dór\ Walter Savage 1775–1864 Eng. author
Lan·dow·ska \lan-'dóf-skə, -'dóv-\ Wanda Louise 1879–1959 Pol. pianist
Land·seer \'lan(d)-,sir\ Sir Edwin Henry 1802–1873 Eng. painter
Land·stei·ner \'lan(d)-,stī-nər, 'länt-,shtī-\ Karl 1868–1943 Am. (Austrian-born) pathologist
Lane \'lān\ Edward William 1801–1876 Eng. orientalist
Lan·franc \'lan-,fraŋk\ 1005?–1089 Ital.-born prelate in England
Lang \'laŋ\ Andrew 1844–1912 Scot. scholar & author
Lang Cosmo Gordon 1864–1945 Brit. prelate; archbishop of Canterbury (1928–42)
Lange \'läŋ-ə\ Christian Louis 1869–1938 Norw. pacifist & hist.
Lange \'lóⁿ-ē\ David Russell 1942–   prime min. of New Zealand (1984–89)
Lang·er \'laŋ-ər\ Susanne Knauth 1895–1985 Am. philos. & educ.
Lang·land \'laŋ-lənd\ William *ca* 1330–*ca* 1400 Eng. poet
Lang·ley \'laŋ-lē\ Samuel Pierpont 1834–1906 Am. astron. & airplane pioneer
Lang·muir \'laŋ-,myúr\ Irving 1881–1957 Am. chem.
Lang·ton \'laŋ(k)-tən\ Stephen *d* 1228 Eng. prelate
Lang·try \'laŋ(k)-trē\ Lillie 1853–1929 née (*Emilie Charlotte*) *Le Breton; the Jersey Lily* Brit. actress
La·nier \lə-'nir\ Sidney 1842–1881 Am. poet
Lan·kes·ter \'laŋ-kəs-tər; 'lan-,kes-, 'laŋ-\ Sir Edwin Ray 1847–1929 Eng. zool.
Lannes \'län, 'lan\ Jean 1769–1809 Duc *de Montebello* Fr. soldier
Lan·sing \'lan(t)-siŋ\ Robert 1864–1928 Am. lawyer & statesman
Lao—tzu \'laúd-'zə\ orig. *Li Erh* \'lē-'er\ 6th cent. B.C. Chin. philos.
La Pé·rouse \,lä-pā-'rüz, -pə\ Comte de 1741–1788 *Jean-François de Galoup* Fr. navigator & explorer

La·place \lə-'pläs\ Pierre-Simon 1749–1827 Marquis *de Laplace* Fr. astron. & math.
Lard·ner \'lärd-nər\ Ring 1885–1933 in full *Ringgold Wilmer Lardner* Am. writer
La·re·do Brú \lə-'rä-dō-'brü\ Federico 1875–1946 Cuban soldier; pres. of Cuba (1936–40)
La Roche·fou·cauld \lä-,rōsh-,fü-'kō, -,rōsh-\ François 1613–1680 Duc *de La Rochefoucauld* Fr. writer & moralist
La·rousse \lä-'rüs\ Pierre-Athanase 1817–1875 Fr. grammarian & lexicographer
Lar·tet \lär-'tä\ Édouard-Armand-Isidore-Hippolyte 1801–1871 Fr. archaeol.
La Salle \lə-'sal\ Sieur de 1643–1687 *René-Robert Cavelier* Fr. explorer in America
Las Ca·sas \läs-'kä-səs\ Bartolomé de 1474–1566 Span. Dominican missionary & hist.
Las·ki \'las-kē\ Harold Joseph 1893–1950 Eng. polit. scientist
Las·salle \lə-'sal, -'säl\ Ferdinand 1825–1864 Ger. socialist
Lat·i·mer \'la-tə-mər\ Hugh *ca* 1485–1555 Eng. religious reformer
La Tour \lə-'túr\ Georges de 1593–1652 Fr. painter
La Tour Maurice-Quentin de 1704–1788 Fr. painter
La·trobe \lə-'trōb\ Benjamin Henry 1764–1820 Am. (Eng.-born) architect & engineer
Lat·ti·more \'la-tə-,mōr, -,mór\ Owen 1900–1989 Am. orientalist
Lattimore Richmond 1906–1984 Am. poet & translator
Lau·bach \'laú-,bäk\ Frank Charles 1884–1970 Am. educator & missionary
Laud \'lód\ William 1573–1645 Eng. prelate; archbishop of Canterbury (1633–45) — **Laud·ian** \'ló-dē-ən\ *adj*
Lau·der \'ló-dər\ Sir Harry Maclennan 1870–1950 Scot. singer
Laue \'laú-ə\ Max von 1879–1960 Ger. physicist
Laugh·ton \'ló-tᵉn\ Charles 1899–1962 Am. (Eng.-born) actor
Lau·rence \'lór-ən(t)s, 'lär-\ (Jean) Margaret 1926–1987 née *Wemyss* Can. author
Lau·ren·cin \ló-rä°-sa°\ Marie 1885–1956 Fr. painter
Lau·ri·er \'lór-ē-,ā, 'lär-\ Sir Wilfrid 1841–1919 Canad. statesman
Lautrec — *see* TOULOUSE-LAUTREC
La·val \lə-'val, -'väl\ Pierre 1883–1945 Fr. polit.
La Val·lière \lä-val-'yer\ Duchesse de 1644–1710 *Françoise-Louise de La Baume Le Blanc* mistress of Louis XIV of France
La·ve·ran \,la-və-'rä°\ Charles-Louis-Alphonse 1845–1922 Fr. physiol. & bacteriol.
La Vé·ren·drye \lä-,ver-ən-'drē, -'ver-ən-,drī\ Sieur de 1685–1749 *Pierre Gaultier de Varennes* Canad. explorer in America
La·very \'lä-və-rē, 'la-\ Sir John 1856–1941 Brit. painter
La·voi·sier \ləv-'wä-zē-,ā\ Antoine-Laurent 1743–1794 Fr. chem.
Law \'ló\ (Andrew) Bon·ar \'bä-nər\ 1858–1923 Brit. (Canad.-born) statesman
Law Edward 1750–1818 1st Baron *El·len·bor·ough* \'e-lən-,bər-ə, -,bə-rə, -brə\ Eng. jurist
Law John 1671–1729 Scot. financier & speculator
Law William 1686–1761 Eng. writer
Lawes \'lóz\ Henry 1596–1662 Eng. composer
Lawes Lewis Edward 1883–1947 Am. penologist
Law·rence \'lór-ən(t)s, 'lär-\ David 1888–1973 Am. journalist
Lawrence David Herbert 1885–1930 Eng. nov. — **Law·ren·cian** \lō-'ren(t)-sē-ən\ *or* **Law·ren·tian** *or* **Lau·ren·tian** \-sh(ē-)ən\ *adj*
Lawrence Ernest Orlando 1901–1958 Am. physicist
Lawrence Gertrude 1898–1952 orig. *Gertrud Alexandra Dagmar Lawrence Klasen* Eng. actress
Lawrence James 1781–1813 Am. naval officer
Lawrence Sir Thomas 1769–1830 Eng. painter
Lawrence Thomas Edward 1888–1935 *Lawrence of Arabia* later surname *Shaw* Brit. archaeol., soldier, & writer
Lax·ness \'läks-,nes\ Halldór Kiljan 1902–   Icelandic writer
Lay·a·mon \'lī-ə-mən, 'lä-\ *fl* 1200 Eng. poet
Lay·ard \'lā-,ärd, -ərd\ Sir Austen Henry 1817–1894 Eng. archaeol. & diplomat
Lea·cock \'lē-,käk\ Stephen Butler 1869–1944 Canad. econ. & humorist
Leadbelly — *see* Huddie LEDBETTER
Lea·hy \'lā-(,)hē\ William Daniel 1875–1959 Am. admiral
Lea·key \'lē-kē\ Louis Seymour Bazett 1903–1972 Brit. paleontologist
Leakey Mary Douglas 1913–   *wife of prec.* Brit. paleontologist
Lean \'lēn\ Sir David 1908–1991 Brit. film director
Lear \'lir\ Edward 1812–1888 Eng. painter & nonsense poet
Lea·vis \'lē-vəs\ Frank Raymond 1895–1978 Eng. critic — **Lea·vis·ian** \lē-'vi-zh(ē-)ən\ *adj* — **Lea·vis·ite** \'lē-və-,sīt\ *adj*
Le·brun \lə-'brə°(n), -'brœ°\ Albert 1871–1950 Fr. statesman; pres. of France (1932–40)
Lebrun Mme. Vigée- — *see* VIGÉE-LEBRUN
Le Brun *or* **Le·brun** \lə-'brə°(n), -'brœ°\ Charles 1619–1690 Fr. painter
Le Car·ré \lə-kä-'rā\ John 1931–   pseud. of *David Corn·well* \'kórn-,wel\ Eng. nov.
Lecky \'le-kē\ William Edward Hartpole 1838–1903 Irish hist.
Le·conte de Lisle \lə-,kōⁿ(n)t-də-'lē(ə)l\ Charles-Marie 1818–1894 orig. *Leconte* Fr. poet
Le Corbusier — *see* CORBUSIER
Led·bet·ter \'led-,be-tər\ Huddie 1888–1949 *Lead·bel·ly* \'led-,be-lē\ Am. blues singer
Le·der·berg \'lā-dər-,bərg\ Joshua 1925–   Am. geneticist
Led·er·man \'lä-dər-mən\ Leon Max 1922–   Am. physicist
Le Duc Tho \'läd-'ək-'tō\ 1911–1990 Vietnamese diplomat
Lee \'lē\ Ann 1736–1784 Am. (Eng.-born) Shaker
Lee Charles 1731–1782 Am. (Eng.-born) gen.
Lee Fitzhugh 1835–1905 *nephew of R. E. Lee* Am. gen.
Lee Francis Lightfoot 1734–1797 Am. statesman in Revolution
Lee Henry 1756–1818 *Light-Horse Harry* Am. soldier
Lee Richard Henry 1732–1794 Am. statesman in Revolution
Lee Robert Edward 1807–1870 Am. Confed. gen.
Lee Sir Sidney 1859–1926 Eng. editor & scholar
Lee Yuan Tseh 1936–   Am. (Taiwanese-born) chem.
Lee Tsung-Dao \'lē-'dzúŋ-'daú\ 1926–   Chin. physicist

Leeu·wen·hoek \'lā-vən-ˌhúk\ Antonie van 1632–1723 Du. naturalist
Le·feb·vre \lə-'fevrᵊ\ François-Joseph 1755–1820 Duc de Dantzig Fr. gen.; marshal of France
Le Gal·lienne \lə-'gal-yən\ Eva 1899–1991 Am. (Eng.-born) actress
Le Gallienne Richard 1866–1947 Eng. writer
Le·gen·dre \lə-'zhäⁿdrᵊ\ Adrien-Marie 1752–1833 Fr. math.
Lé·ger \lā-'zhā\ Alexis Saint-Léger 1887–1975 pseud. St. John Perse \saⁿ-ˌjóⁿ-'pers\ Fr. diplomat & poet
Léger Fernand 1881–1955 Fr. painter
Le·guía y Sal·ce·do \lə-'gē-ə-ˌē-säl-'sä-(ˌ)dō, -(ˌ)thō\ Augusto Bernardino 1863–1932 Peruvian banker; pres. of Peru (1908–12; 1919–30)
Le·hár \'lā-ˌhär\ Franz 1870–1948 Hung. composer
Leh·man \'lē-mən\ Herbert Henry 1878–1963 Am. banker & polit.
Leh·mann \'lā-ˌmän\ Lot·te \'ló-tə\ 1888–1976 Ger. soprano
Lehn \'lān\ Jean-Marie 1939–   Fr. chem.
Leib·niz \'līb-nəts, G 'līp-nits\ Gottfried Wilhelm 1646–1716 Ger. philos. & math. — Leib·niz·ian \līb-'nit-sē-ən, līp-\ adj
Lei·bo·vitz \'lē-bō-ˌvits\ Annie 1949–   Am. photographer
Leicester 1st Earl of — see Robert DUDLEY; see also de MONTFORT
Leif Er·iks·son \ˌlāv-'er-ik-sən, ˌlēf-\ or Er·ics·son \same\ fl 1000 son of Erik the Red Norw. explorer
Leigh·ton \'lā-tᵊn\ Frederick 1830–1896 Baron Leighton of Stretton Eng. painter
Leins·dorf \'līnz-ˌdórf, 'līn(t)s-\ Erich 1912–1993 Am. (Austrian-born) conductor
Le·jeune \lə-'jün\ John Archer 1867–1942 Am. marine-corps gen.
Le·land \'lē-lənd\ John 1506?–1552 Eng. antiquarian
Leloir \lā-'lwär\ Luis Federico 1906–1987 Argentine biochem.
Le·ly \'lē-lē\ Sir Peter 1618–1680 orig. Pieter Van der Faes Brit. (Westphalian-born) painter
Le·maî·tre \lə-'metrᵊ\ (François-Élie) Jules 1853–1914 Fr. writer
Le Moyne Pierre — see IBERVILLE
Le·nard \'lā-ˌnärt\ Philipp 1862–1947 Ger. physicist
Len·clos \län-'klō\ Anne de 1620–1705 Ninon de Lenclos Fr. courtesan
L'En·fant \läⁿ-ˌfänt, län-'fäⁿ\ Pierre-Charles 1754–1825 Am. (Fr.⸗born) architect & engineer
Le·nin \'le-nən\ 1870–1924 orig. Vladimir Ilyich Ul·ya·nov \úl-'yä-nəf, -ˌnóf, -ˌnóv\ Russ. Communist leader
Leo \'lē-(ˌ)ō\ name of 13 popes: esp. I Saint d 461 (pope 440–61); III Saint d 816 (pope 795–816); XIII 1810–1903 (pope 1878–1903)
Leon·ard \'le-nərd\ William Ellery 1876–1944 Am. educ. & poet
Le·o·nar·do da Vin·ci \ˌlē-ə-'när-(ˌ)dō-də-'vin-chē, ˌlā-, -'vēn-\ 1452–1519 It. painter, sculptor, architect, & engineer — Le·o·nar·desque \ˌlē-ə-ˌnär-'desk, ˌlā-\ adj
Le·on·ca·val·lo \lā-ˌōn-kə-'vä-(ˌ)lō\ Ruggiero 1858–1919 Ital. composer & librettist
Le·on·i·das \lē-'ä-nə-dəs\ d 480 B.C. Greek hero; king of Sparta (490?–480)
Le·ont·ief \lē-'ónt-yəf, lyē-\ Wassily 1906–   Am. (Russ.-born) econ.
Le·o·par·di \ˌlā-ə-'pär-dē\ Giacomo 1798–1837 Ital. poet
Leopold I \'lē-ə-ˌpōld\ 1640–1705 king of Hungary (1655–1705) & Holy Rom. emp. (1658–1705)
Leopold II 1747–1792 Holy Rom. emp. (1790–92)
Leopold I 1790–1865 king of Belgium (1831–65)
Leopold II 1835–1909 king of Belgium (1865–1909)
Leopold III 1901–1983 king of Belgium (1934–51)
Lep·i·dus \'le-pə-dəs\ Marcus Aemilius d 13(or 12) B.C. Rom. triumvir
Ler·mon·tov \'ler-mən-ˌtóf, -ˌtóv\ Mikhail Yuryevich 1814–1841 Russ. poet & nov.
Ler·ner \'lər-nər\ Alan Jay 1918–1986 Am. dram. & librettist
Le·sage \lə-'säzh\ Alain-René 1668–1747 Fr. nov. & dram.
Le·sche·tiz·ky \ˌle-shə-'tit-skē\ Theodor 1830–1915 Pol. pianist & composer
Les·seps \'lā-ˌseps, 'le-səps\ Ferdinand-Marie de 1805–1894 Vicomte de Lesseps Fr. diplomat & promoter of Suez Canal
Les·sing \'le-siŋ\ Gotthold Ephraim 1729–1781 Ger. critic & dram.
L'Es·trange \lā-'stränj\ Sir Roger 1616–1704 Eng. journalist & translator
Leu·tze \'lóit-sə\ Emanuel 1816–1868 Am. (Ger.-born) painter
Le·ver \'lē-vər\ Charles James 1806–1872 Brit. nov.
Le·vi–Mon·tal·ci·ni \ˌlā-vē-ˌmōn-täl-'chē-nē\ Rita 1909–   Am. (Ital.-born) neurologist
Lé·vi–Strauss \ˌlā-vē-'straús, ˌle-vē-\ Claude 1908–   Fr. (Belg.⸗ born) social anthropol. — Lé·vi–Strauss·i·an \-'straú-sē-ən\ adj
Lew·es \'lü-əs\ George Henry 1817–1878 Eng. philos. & critic
Lew·is \'lü-əs\ Sir (William) Arthur 1915–1991 Brit. econ.
Lewis Cecil Day — see DAY-LEWIS
Lewis Clive Staples 1898–1963 Eng. nov. & essayist
Lewis Isaac Newton 1858–1931 Am. army officer & inventor
Lewis John Llewellyn 1880–1969 Am. labor leader
Lewis Matthew Gregory 1775–1818 Monk Lewis Eng. author
Lewis Meriwether 1774–1809 Am. explorer
Lewis (Harry) Sinclair 1885–1951 Am. nov.
Lewis (Percy) Wyndham 1882–1957 Brit. painter & author
Ley \'lī\ Robert 1890–1945 Ger. Nazi leader
Lib·by \'li-bē\ Willard Frank 1908–1980 Am. chem.
Lich·ten·stein \'lik-tən-ˌstīn, -ˌstēn\ Roy 1923–   Am. artist
Li·cin·i·us \lə-'si-nē-əs\ d 325 Valerius Licinianus Licinius Rom. emp. (308–324)
Lid·dell Hart \'li-dᵊl-'härt\ Sir Basil Henry 1895–1970 Eng. mil. scientist
Lie \'lē\ Jonas 1833–1908 Norw. nov. & dram.
Lie Trygve Halvdan 1896–1968 Norw. lawyer; secy.-gen. of U.N. (1946–52)
Lie·big \'lē-big\ Justus von 1803–1873 Freiherr von Liebig Ger. chem.
Lieb·knecht \'lēp-ˌknekt, -ˌnekt\ Karl 1871–1919 Ger. socialist leader
Li·far \'lē-ˌfär, lē-'\ Serge 1905–1986 Fr. (Russ.-born) choreographer & dancer
Li Hung–chang \'lē-'húŋ-'jäŋ\ 1823–1901 Chin. statesman
Lil·ien·thal \'lil-yən-ˌtäl, -ˌthól\ Otto 1848–1896 Ger. aeronautical engineer

Li·li·u·o·ka·la·ni \li-ˌlē-ə-(ˌ)wō-kə-'lä-nē\ 1838–1917 Lydia Paki Liliuokalani; Liliu Kamakaeha queen of the Hawaiian Islands (1891–93)
Lil·lo \'li-(ˌ)lō\ George 1693–1739 Eng. dram.
Li·món \li-'mōn\ José Arcadio 1908–1972 Am. (Mex.-born) dancer & choreographer
Lin·a·cre \'li-ni-kər\ Thomas ca 1460–1524 Eng. humanist & physician
Lin·coln \'liŋ-kən\ Abraham 1809–1865 16th pres. of the U.S. (1861–65) — Lin·coln·esque \ˌliŋ-kə-'nesk\ or Lin·coln·ian \liŋ-'kō-nē-ən\ adj
Lincoln Benjamin 1733–1810 Am. gen. in Revolution
Lind \'lind\ Jenny 1820–1887 orig. Johanna Maria; the Swedish Nightingale Swed. soprano
Lind·bergh \'lin(d)-ˌbərg\ Anne Spencer 1906–   née Morrow; wife of C. A. Am. author
Lindbergh Charles Augustus 1902–1974 Am. aviator
Lind·ley \'lin(d)-lē\ John 1799–1865 Eng. botanist — Lind·ley·an \-ən-\ adj
Lind·say \'lin-zē\ Howard 1889–1968 Am. dram. & actor
Lindsay (Nicholas) Va·chel \'vā-chəl, 'va-\ 1879–1931 Am. poet
Link·la·ter \'liŋk-ˌlā-tər, -lə-tər\ Eric 1899–1974 Brit. writer
Linlithgow Marquis of — see HOPE
Lin·nae·us \lə-'nē-əs, -'nā-\ Carolus 1707–1778 Sw. Carl von Lin·né \lə-'nā\ Swed. botanist
Lin Yü–t'ang \'lin-'yü-'täŋ\ 1895–1976 Chin. author & philologist
Li·o·tard \ˌlē-ō-'tär\ Jean-Étienne 1702–1789 Swiss painter
Lip·chitz \'lip-shits\ Jacques 1891–1973 Am. (Latvian-born) sculptor
Li Peng \'lē-'pəŋ, -'peŋ\ 1928–   Chin. Communist leader (1987–   )
Lip·mann \'lip-mən\ Fritz Albert 1899–1986 Am. (Ger.-born) biochem.
Li Po \'lē-'bō, -'pō\ 701–762 Chin. poet
Lip·pi \'li-pē\ Fra Filippo ca 1406–1469 Florentine painter
Lippi Filippo or Filippino ca 1457–1504 son of prec. Florentine painter
Lipp·mann \'lēp-'män, -'man\ Gabriel 1845–1921 Fr. physicist
Lipp·mann \'lip-mən\ Walter 1889–1974 Am. journalist & author
Lips·comb \'lips-kəm\ William Nunn, Jr. 1919–   Am. chem.
Lip·ton \'lip-tən\ Sir Thomas Johnstone 1850–1931 Eng. merchant & yachtsman
Li Shih–min — see T'ANG T'AI TSUNG
Lisle, de — see LECONTE DE LISLE, ROUGET DE LISLE
Lis·ter \'lis-tər\ Joseph 1827–1912 1st Baron Lister of Lyme Regis Eng. surgeon
Liszt \'list\ Franz 1811–1886 Hung. pianist & composer — Liszt·ian \'lis-tē-ən\ adj
Lit·tle·ton or Lyt·tel·ton \'li-tᵊl-tən\ or Lut·tel·ton \'lə-\ Sir Thomas 1422–1481 Eng. jurist
Lit·tré \li-'trā\ Maximilien-Paul-Émile 1801–1881 Fr. lexicographer
Lit·vi·nov \lit-'vē-ˌnóf, -ˌnóv, -nəf\ Maksim Maksimovich 1876–1951 Soviet diplomat
Liu Shao–ch'i \lē-'ü-'shaú-'chē\ 1898–1974 Chin. Communist polit.
Liv·ing·ston \'li-viŋ-stən\ Robert R. 1746–1813 Am. statesman
Liv·ing·stone \'li-viŋ-stən\ David 1813–1873 Scot. missionary & explorer in Africa
Livy \'li-vē\ 59 B.C.–A.D. 17 Titus Livius Rom. hist.
Lloyd George \'lóid-'jórj\ David 1863–1945 1st Earl of Dwy·for \'dü-ē-ˌvòr\ Brit. statesman; prime min. (1916–22)
Llull \'lyül\ Ramon ca 1235–1316 Raymond Lul·ly \'lú-lē\ Catalan mystic & poet
Lo·ba·chev·sky \ˌlō-bə-'chef-skē, ˌlä-, -'chev-\ Nikolay Ivanovich 1792–1856 Russ. math.
Lo·ben·gu·la \lō-bən-'gü-lə, -'gyü-\ ca 1836–1894 Zulu king of the Matabele
Locke \'läk\ John 1632–1704 Eng. philos. — Lock·ean also Locke·ian \'lä-kē-ən\ adj
Lock·hart \'lä-kərt, -ˌkärt; 'läk-ˌhärt\ John Gibson 1794–1854 Scot. nov. & biographer
Lock·yer \'lä-kyər\ Sir Joseph Norman 1836–1920 Eng. astron.
Lodge \'läj\ Henry Cabot 1850–1924 Am. statesman & author
Lodge Henry Cabot 1902–1985 grandson of prec. Am. polit. & diplomat
Lodge Sir Oliver Joseph 1851–1940 Eng. physicist
Lodge Thomas 1558–1625 Eng. poet & dram.
Loeb \'lōb\ Jacques 1859–1924 Am. (Ger.-born) physiol.
Loewe \'lō\ Frederick 1901–1988 Am. (Austrian-born) composer
Loewi \'lō-ē\ Otto 1873–1961 Am. (Ger.-born) pharmacologist
Löff·ler \'le-flər\ Friedrich August Johannes 1852–1915 Ger. bacteriol.
Lo·max \'lō-ˌmaks\ John Avery 1867–1948 and his son Alan 1915–   Am. folklorists
Lombard Peter — see PETER LOMBARD
Lom·bro·so \lòm-'brō-(ˌ)sō\ Ce·sa·re \'chā-zä-ˌrā\ 1836–1909 Ital. physician & psychiatrist
Lon·don \'lən-dən\ John Griffith 1876–1916 Jack Am. writer
Long \'lóŋ\ Crawford Williamson 1815–1878 Am. surgeon
Long Hu·ey \'hyü-ē\ Pierce 1893–1935 Am. polit.
Long Stephen Harriman 1784–1864 Am. army officer & explorer
Long·fel·low \'lóŋ-ˌfe-(ˌ)lō\ Henry Wads·worth \'wädz-(ˌ)wərth\ 1807–1882 Am. poet
Lon·gi·nus \län-'jī-nəs\ 1st cent. A.D. Greek critic
Long·street \'lóŋ-ˌstrēt\ James 1821–1904 Am. Confed. gen.
Lönn·rot \'lœn-ˌrüt\ Elias 1802–1884 Finn. folklorist
Lons·dale \'länz-ˌdāl\ Frederick 1881–1954 Brit. dram.
Ló·pez \'lō-ˌpez\ Carlos Antonio 1790–1862 pres. of Paraguay (1844–62)
López Francisco Solano 1827–1870 son of prec. pres. of Paraguay (1862–70)
López Ma·te·os \-mə-'tā-əs, -(ˌ)ōs\ Adolfo 1910–1969 pres. of Mexico (1958–64)

\ə\ abut \ᵊ\ kitten, F table \ər\ further \a\ ash \ā\ ace \ä\ mop, mar \aú\ out \ch\ chin \e\ bet \ē\ easy \g\ go \i\ hit \ī\ ice \j\ job \ŋ\ sing \ō\ go \ò\ law \òi\ boy \th\ thin \th\ the \ü\ loot \ú\ foot \y\ yet \zh\ vision \á, k̲, ⁿ, œ, œ̄, ᵫ, ᵬ, ᵊ\ see Guide to Pronunciation

López Por·til·lo \-pòr-'tē-yō\ José 1920– pres. of Mexico (1976–82)

Lorca Federico García — see Federico GARCÍA LORCA

Lo·rentz \'lòr-,en(t)s, 'lòr-\ Hendrik Antoon 1853–1928 Du. physicist

Lo·renz \'lòr-,en(t)s, 'lòr-\ Konrad 1903–1989 Ger. (Austrian-born) ethologist

Lorrain Claude — see CLAUDE LORRAIN

Lo·thair I \lō-'tar, -'ter, -'thar, -'ther, 'lō-,\ 795–855 Holy Rom. emp. (840–855)

Lothair II (or III) 1075–1137 king of Germany & Holy Rom. emp. (1125–37)

Lo·ti \lō-'tē, lò-\ Pierre 1850–1923 pseud. of Louis-Marie-Julien Viaud Fr. naval officer & nov.

Lou·bet \lü-'bā\ Émile-François 1838–1929 Fr. statesman; pres. of France (1899–1906)

Loudoun 4th Earl of — see John CAMPBELL

Lou·is \'lü-ē, lü-'ē\ name of 18 kings of France: esp. **I** 778–840 (reigned 814–840); **V** (le Fainéant) 967–987 (reigned—last Carolingian—986–987); **IX** (Saint) 1214–1270 (reigned 1226–70); **XI** 1423–1483 (reigned 1461–83); **XII** 1462–1515 (reigned 1498–1515); **XIII** 1601–1643 (reigned 1610–43); **XIV** 1638–1715 (reigned 1643–1715); **XV** 1710–1774 (reigned 1715–74); **XVI** 1754–1793 (reigned 1774–92; guillotined); **XVII** 1785–1795 (nominally reigned 1793–95); **XVIII** 1755–1824 (reigned 1814–15; 1815–24)

Louis IV 1283?–1347 Duke of Bavaria king of Germany & Holy Rom. emp. (1314–47)

Louis II de Bourbon — see CONDÉ

Louis-Napoléon — see NAPOLÉON III

Louis Phi·lippe \-fi-'lēp\ 1773–1850 the Citizen King king of the French (1830–48)

L'Ouverture — see Pierre Dominique TOUSSAINT LOUVERTURE

Louÿs \lü-'ē\ Pierre 1870–1925 Fr. writer

Love·lace \'ləv-,lās\ Richard 1618–1657 Eng. poet

Lov·ell \'lə-vəl\ Sir (Alfred Charles) Bernard 1913–   Brit. astron.

Lov·er \'lə-vər\ Samuel 1797–1868 Irish nov.

Low \'lō\ Sir David Alexander Cecil 1891–1963 Brit. cartoonist

Low·ell \'lō-əl\ Amy 1874–1925 Am. poet & critic

Lowell James Russell 1819–1891 Am. poet, essayist, & dram.

Lowell Percival 1855–1916 bro. of Amy Am. astron.

Lowell Robert Traill Spence 1917–1977 Am. poet

Lowes \'lōz\ John Livingston 1867–1945 Am. educ.

Lowndes \'laün(d)z\ William Thomas 1798–1843 Eng. bibliographer

Low·ry \'laú-(ə)r-ē\ (Clarence) Malcolm 1909–1957 Brit. writer

Loyola Saint Ignatius — see IGNATIUS OF LOYOLA

Lub·bock \'lə-bək\ Sir John 1834–1913 1st Baron Ave·bury \'āv-b(ə-)rē, 'ā-\ son of Sir J. W. Eng. financier & author

Lubbock Sir John William 1803–1865 Eng. astron. & math.

Luc·an \'lü-kən\ A.D. 39–65 Marcus Annaeus Lucanus Rom. poet

Luce \'lüs\ Clare 1903–1987 née Boothe \'büth\ wife of H. R. Am. dram., polit., & diplomat

Luce Henry Robinson 1898–1967 Am. editor & publisher

Lu·cre·tius \lü-'krē-sh(ē-)əs\ ca 96–ca 55 B.C. Titus Lucretius Carus Rom. poet & philos. — **Lu·cre·tian** \-shən\ adj

Lu·cul·lus \lü-'kə-ləs\ Lucius Licinius ca 117–58(or 56) B.C. Rom. gen. & epicure

Lu·den·dorff \'lü-d°n-,dòrf\ Erich Friedrich Wilhelm 1865–1937 Ger. gen.

Lu Hsün \'lü-'shün\ 1881–1936 pseud. of Chou Shu-Jen Chin. writer

Lu·i·gi Ame·deo \lə-'wē-jē-,ä-mə-'dā-(,)ō\ 1873–1933 Duca D'Abruz·zi \dä-'brüt-tsē\ & Prince of Savoy-Aosta Ital. explorer & naval officer

Lu·jan \'lü-hən\ Manuel, Jr. 1928–   U.S. secy. of interior (1989–93)

Lul·ly \lü-'lē\ Jean-Baptiste 1632–1687 Fr. (Ital.-born) composer

Lully Raymond — see Ramon LLULL

Lunt \'lənt\ Alfred 1893–1977 husband of Lynn Fontanne Am. actor

Lu·ria \'lùr-ē-ə\ Salvador Edward 1912–1991 Am. (Ital.-born) microbiologist

Lu·ther \'lü-thər\ Martin 1483–1546 Ger. Reformation leader

Lu·thu·li \lù-'tü-lē, -'thü-\ Albert John 1898–1967 So. African reformer

Lux·em·burg \'lək-səm-,bərg, 'lùk-səm-,bùrk\ Rosa 1870–1919 Ger. socialist leader

Lwoff \'lwòf\ André-Michael 1902–1995 Fr. microbiologist

Lyau·tey \lē-,ō-'tā\ Louis-Hubert-Gonzalve 1854–1934 Fr. soldier & colonial administrator

Ly·cur·gus \lī-'kər-gəs\ 9th cent. B.C. Spartan lawgiver

Lyd·gate \'lid-,gāt, -gət\ John ca 1370–ca 1450 Eng. poet

Ly·ell \'lī-əl\ Sir Charles 1797–1875 Brit. geologist

Lyly \'li-lē\ John 1554?–1606 Eng. author

Lynd \'lind\ Robert Staugh·ton \'stò-t°n\ 1892–1970 & his wife Helen née Merrell 1896–1982 Am. sociologists

Ly·nen \'lü-nən\ Feodor Felix Konrad 1911–1979 Ger. biochem.

Ly·on \'lī-ən\ Mary 1797–1849 Am. educ.

Ly·ons \'lī-ənz\ Joseph Aloysius 1879–1939 Austral. statesman; prime min. (1931–39)

Ly·san·der \lī-'san-dər\ d 395 B.C. Spartan commander

Ly·sen·ko \lī-'sen-(,)kō\ Trofim Denisovich 1898–1976 Soviet biol.

Lys·i·as \'li-sē-əs\ ca 445–after 380 B.C. Athenian orator

Ly·sim·a·chus \lī-'si-mə-kəs\ ca 355–ca 281 B.C. Macedonian gen. under Alexander the Great; king of Thrace (306)

Ly·sip·pus \lī-'si-pəs\ 4th cent. B.C. Greek sculptor

Lyt·ton \'li-t°n\ 1st Baron 1803–1873 Edward George Earle Bul·wer= Lytton \'bùl-wər-\; bro. of Sir Henry Bulwer Eng. author

Lytton 1st Earl of 1831–1891 (Edward) Robert Bulwer-Lytton; pseud. Owen Meredith; son of prec. Brit. statesman & poet

Mac·Ar·thur \mə-'kär-thər\ Arthur 1845–1912 Am. gen.

MacArthur Charles 1895–1956 Am. dram.

MacArthur Douglas 1880–1964 son of Arthur Am. gen.

Ma·cau·lay \mə-'kò-lē\ Dame Rose 1881–1958 Eng. nov.

Macaulay Thomas Babington 1800–1859 1st Baron Macaulay Eng. hist., author, & statesman

Mac·beth \mək-'beth\ d 1057 king of Scotland (1040–57)

Mac·Bride \mək-'brīd\ Seán 1904–1988 Irish statesman

Mac·ca·bees \'ma-kə-,bēz\ Judas or Judah d 161 B.C. surname Mac·ca·ba·eus \,ma-kə-'bē-əs\ Jewish patriot

Mac·Diar·mid \mək-'dər-məd, -mət\ Hugh 1892–1978 pseud. of Christopher Murray Grieve \'grēv\ Scot. poet

Mac·don·ald \mək-'dä-n°ld\ George 1824–1905 Scot. nov. & poet

Macdonald Sir John Alexander 1815–1891 Canad. statesman; 1st prime min. of Dominion of Canada (1867–73; 1878–91)

Mac·Don·ald \mək-'dä-n°ld\ (James) Ramsay 1866–1937 Brit. statesman

Mac·don·ough \mək-'dä-nə, -'də-\ Thomas 1783–1825 Am. naval officer

Mac·Dow·ell \mək-'daù(-ə)l\ Edward Alexander 1860–1908 Am. composer

Mach \'mäk, 'mäk\ Ernst 1838–1916 Austrian physicist & philos.

Ma·cha·do y Mo·ra·les \mä-'chä-dō-,ē-mə-'rä-ləs\ Gerardo 1871–1939 pres. of Cuba (1925–33)

Ma·chi·a·vel·li \,ma-kē-ə-'ve-lē\ Niccolò 1469–1527 Ital. polit. philos.

Mac·Kaye \mə-'kī\ Percy 1875–1956 Am. poet & dram.

Mack·en·sen \'mäk-kən-zən\ August von 1849–1945 Ger. field marshal

Mac·ken·zie \mə-'ken-zē\ Alexander 1822–1892 Canad. (Scot.-born) statesman; prime min. (1873–78)

Mackenzie Sir Alexander Campbell 1847–1935 Brit. composer & conductor

Mackenzie Sir Compton 1883–1972 Eng. nov.

Mackenzie William Lyon 1795–1861 Canad. (Scot.-born) insurgent leader

Mac·kin·der \mə-'kin-dər\ Sir Halford John 1861–1947 Eng. geographer

Maclaren Ian — see John WATSON

Mac·Leish \mə-'klēsh\ Archibald 1892–1982 Am. poet & administrator

Mac·Len·nan \mə-'kle-nən\ (John) Hugh 1907–1990 Canad. nov.

Mac·leod \mə-'klaùd\ John James Rickard 1876–1935 Scot. physiol.

Mac·Ma·hon \,mäk-,mä-'ō°; mək-'ma(-ə)n, -'män\ Marie-Edme= Patrice-Maurice 1808–1893 Comte de Mac-Mahon; duc de Magenta marshal (1859) & pres. (1873–79) of France

Mac·mil·lan \mək-'mi-lən\ (Maurice) Harold 1894–1986 Brit. prime min. (1957–63)

Mac·Mil·lan \mək-'mi-lən\ Donald Baxter 1874–1970 Am. explorer

Mac·Neice \mək-'nēs\ Louis 1907–1963 Irish poet

Mac·pher·son \mək-'fər-s°n\ James 1736–1796 Scot. writer

Mac·rea·dy \mə-'krē-dē\ William Charles 1793–1873 Eng. actor

Ma·da·ria·ga y Ro·jo \,mä-də-rē-'ä-gə-(,)ē-'rō-(,)hō\ Salvador de 1886–1978 Span. writer & diplomat

Ma·de·ro \mə-'der-(,)ō\ Francisco Indalecio 1873–1913 pres. of Mexico (1911–13)

Mad·i·gan \'ma-də-gən\ Edward R. 1936–1994 U.S. secy. of agriculture (1991–93)

Mad·i·son \'ma-də-sən\ Dolley 1768–1849 née (Dorothea) Payne; wife of James Am. socialite

Madison James 1751–1836 4th pres. of the U.S. (1809–17) — **Mad·i·so·nian** \,ma-də-'sō-nē-ən, -nyən\ adj

Mae·ce·nas \mi-'sē-nəs\ Gaius ca 70–8 B.C. Rom. statesman & patron of literature

Maes \'mäs\ Nicolaes 1634–1693 also called Nicolas Maas Du. painter

Mae·ter·linck \'mä-tər-,liŋk also 'me-, 'ma-\ Maurice-Polydore-Marie= Bernard 1862–1949 Belg. poet, dram., & essayist — **Mae·ter·linck·ian** \,mä-tər-'liŋ-kē-ən, ,me-, ,ma-\ adj

Ma·gel·lan \mə-'je-lən, chiefly Brit -'ge-\ Ferdinand ca 1480–1521 Pg. Fernão de Magalhães Port. navigator & explorer

Ma·gi·not \,ma-zhə-'nō, ,ma-jə-\ André 1877–1932 Fr. polit.

Ma·gritte \mə-'grēt\ René-François-Ghislain 1898–1967 Belg. painter

Mag·say·say \mäg-'sī-,sī, -,sī-'sī\ Ramon 1907–1957 pres. of Philippines (1953–57)

Mah·fouz \'mäk-füz\ Naguib 1911–   Egypt. writer

Mah·ler \'mä-lər\ Gustav 1860–1911 Austrian composer — **Mah·ler·ian** \mä-'lir-ē-ən, -'ler-\ adj

Mah·mud II \mä-'müd\ 1785–1839 Ottoman sultan (1808–39)

Mai·ler \'mā-lər\ Norman 1923–   Am. author

Mail·lol \mä-'yòl, -'yōl\ Aristide 1861–1944 Fr. sculptor

Mai·mon·i·des \mī-'mä-nə-,dēz\ Moses 1135–1204 Heb. Moses ben Maimon Jewish philos., jurist, & physician

Maine \'mān\ Sir Henry James Sumner 1822–1888 Eng. jurist

Main·te·non \,ma°(n)-t°n-'ō°, ma°(n)t-°n-'nō°\ Marquise de 1635–1719 Françoise d'Aubigné; consort of Louis XIV

Mait·land \'māt-lənd\ Frederic William 1850–1906 Eng. hist.

Ma·jor \'mā-jər\ John 1943–   Brit. prime min. (1990–   )

Mal·a·mud \'ma-lə-(,)məd\ Bernard 1914–1986 Am. writer

Ma·lan \mə-'lan, -'län\ Daniel François 1874–1959 So. African editor; prime min. (1948–54)

Mal·colm X \'mal-kəm-'eks\ 1925–1965 orig. Malcolm Little Am. civil rights leader

Male·branche \,mal-'brä°sh, ,mäl-; ,ma-lə-, ,mä-\ Nicolas de 1638–1715 Fr. philos.

Ma·len·kov \,ma-lən-'kòf, -,kóv, -'leŋ-kəf; ,ma-lən-'kòf, -'kóv\ Georgy Maksimilianovich 1902–1988 Soviet polit.

Mal·herbe \ma-'lerb, mä-\ François de 1555–1628 Fr. poet

Ma·li·nov·sky \,ma-lə-'nòf-skē, mä-, -'nòv-\ Rodion Yakovlevich 1898–1967 Soviet gen.

Ma·li·now·ski \,ma-lə-'nòf-skē, mä-, -'nòv-\ Bronislaw Kasper 1884–1942 Am. (Pol.-born) anthropol.

Mal·lar·mé \,ma-,lär-'mā\ Stéphane 1842–1898 Fr. poet

Ma·lone \mə-'lōn\ Edmond 1741–1812 Irish scholar

Mal·o·ry \'ma-lə-rē, 'mal-rē\ Sir Thomas fl 1470 Eng. author

Mal·pi·ghi \mal-'pē-gē, -'pi-\ Marcello 1628–1694 Ital. anatomist — **Mal·pi·gh·i·an** \-°n\ adj

Mal·raux \mal-'rō\ André 1901–1976 Fr. writer & art historian

Mal·thus \'mal-thəs\ Thomas Robert 1766–1834 Eng. econ.

Mam·et \'ma-mət\ David Alan 1947–   Am. dram.

Man·del \mä°(n)-'del\ Georges 1885–1944 orig. Louis-Georges Roth·schild Fr. polit.

Man·dela \man-'de-lə\ Nelson Rolihlahla 1918–   So. African black political leader; pres. of So. Africa (1994–   )

Man·del·brot \'man-dəl-,brōt\ Benoit 1924–   Am. (Pol.-born) math. & scientist

Man·de·ville \\'man-də-ˌvil\\ Bernard de 1670–1733 Brit. (Du.-born) satirist & philos.
Mandeville Sir John *fl* 1356 pseud. of an unidentified travel writer
Ma·net \\ma-'nā, mä-\\ Édouard 1832–1883 Fr. painter
Ma·nil·i·us \\mə-'ni-lē-əs\\ Gaius 1st cent. B.C. Rom. polit.
Mann \\'man\\ Horace 1796–1859 Am. educ.
Mann \\'män, 'man\\ Thomas 1875–1955 Am. (Ger.-born) author
Man·ner·heim \\'mä-nər-ˌhām, 'ma-, -ˌhim\\ Baron Carl Gustaf Emil von 1867–1951 Finn. gen. & statesman
Man·ning \\'ma-niŋ\\ Henry Edward 1808–1892 Eng. cardinal
Mans·field \\'mans-ˌfēld, 'manz-\\ Katherine 1888–1923 pseud. of *Kathleen Mansfield Beau·champ* \\'bē-chəm\\ Brit. (N.Z.-born) writer
Man·son \\'man(t)-sən\\ Sir Patrick 1844–1922 Brit. parasitologist
Man·stein \\'män-shtīn\\ Fritz Erich von 1887–1973 orig. surname *von Lewinski* Ger. field marshal
Man·sūr, al- \\ˌal-ˌman-'sùr\\ 709(to 714)–775 in full *Abū Ja'far al-Manṣūr* or *al-Manṣūr al-'Abbāsī* Arab caliph (754–775) & founder of Baghdad
Man·te·gna \\män-'tän-yə\\ Andrea 1431–1506 Ital. painter & engraver
Man·uel \\'man-'wel\\ Don Juan 1282–1349 Span. nobleman & writer
Man·zo·ni \\män(d)-'zō-nē\\ Alessandro Francesco Tommaso Antonio 1785–1873 Ital. nov. & poet
Mao Tse–tung \\'maú-(')(d)zə-'dùŋ, -(')tsə-\\ 1893–1976 pinyin *Mao Ze-dong* Chin. Communist; leader of People's Republic of China (1949–76)
Map \\'map\\ Walter *ca* 1140–*ca* 1209 Eng. writer
Ma·rat \\mə-'rä\\ Jean-Paul 1743–1793 Fr. (Swiss-born) revolutionary
Mar·cel·lus \\mär-'se-ləs\\ Marcus Claudius 268?–208 B.C. Rom. gen.
March 1st Earl of — see Roger de MORTIMER
Mar·co·ni \\mär-'kō-nē\\ Guglielmo 1874–1937 Ital. physicist & inventor
Marco Polo — see POLO
Mar·cos \\'mär-(ˌ)kōs\\ Ferdinand Edralin 1917–1989 pres. of the Philippines (1965–86)
Mar·cus \\'mär-kəs\\ Rudolph Arthur 1923– Am. (Canad.-born) chem.
Marcus Aurelius — see Marcus Aurelius ANTONINUS
Mar·cu·se \\mär-'kü-zə\\ Herbert 1898–1979 Am. (Ger.-born) social & polit. philos.
Mar·ga·ret \\'mär-g(ə-)rət\\ **of Angoulême** 1492–1549 *queen of Henry of Navarre* & writer
Margaret of Anjou 1430–1482 *queen of Henry VI of England*
Margaret of Valois or **Margaret of France** 1553–1615 *queen consort of Henry of Navarre*
Margaret Rose \\'rōz\\ 1930– *princess of Great Britain*
Mar·gre·the II \\mär-'grā-tə\\ 1940– queen of Denmark (1972–)
Ma·ria The·re·sa \\mə-'rē-ə-tə-'rā-sə, -'rā-zə\\ 1717–1780 *wife of Holy Rom. Emp. Francis I* archduchess of Austria & queen of Hungary & Bohemia
Ma·rie \\mə-'rē\\ 1875–1938 queen of Romania (1914–27); queen dowager (1927–38)
Marie An·toi·nette \\ˌan-twə-'net, -tə-\\ 1755–1793 *dau. of Maria Theresa* & *wife of Louis XVI of France*
Ma·rie–Lou·ise \\mə-'rē-lə-'wēz, -'lwēz\\ 1791–1847 *dau. of Francis II of Austria* & *2d wife of Napoléon I*
Ma·rie de Mé·di·cis \\mə-'rē-də-'me-də-(ˌ)chē, -ˌmā-də-'sē(s)\\ 1573–1642 *2d wife of Henry IV of France* regent for Louis XIII
Mar·in \\'mar-ən\\ John Cheri 1870–1953 Am. painter
Ma·ri·net·ti \\ˌmar-ə-'ne-tē, ˌmär-\\ (Emilio) Filippo Tommaso 1876–1944 Ital. poet
Ma·ri·ni \\mə-'rē-nē\\ or **Ma·ri·no** \\-(ˌ)nō\\ Giambattista 1569–1625 Ital. poet
Mar·i·on \\'mer-ē-ən, 'mar-ē-\\ Francis 1732?–1795 *the Swamp Fox* Am. gen. in Revolution
Ma·ri·otte \\már-yòt\\ Edme *ca* 1620–1684 Fr. physicist
Ma·ri·tain \\ˌmar-ə-'tan⁵\\ Jacques 1882–1973 Fr. philos. & diplomat
Ma·ri·us \\'mer-ē-əs, 'mar-\\ Gaius *ca* 157–86 B.C. Rom. gen.
Ma·ri·vaux \\ˌmar-ə-'vō\\ Pierre Carlet de Chamblain de 1688–1763 Fr. dram. & nov.
Mark Antony or **Anthony** — see Marcus ANTONIUS
Mark·ham \\'mär-kəm\\ Beryl 1902–1986 Brit. aviator
Markham Edwin 1852–1940 orig. *Charles Edward Anson Markham* Am. poet
Mar·ko·va \\mär-'kō-və\\ Dame Ali·cia \\ə-'lē-sē-ə\\ 1910– orig. *Lilian Alicia Marks* Eng. dancer
Mar·ko·witz \\'mär-kə-ˌwits\\ Harry M. 1927– Am. econ.
Marlborough 1st Duke of — see John CHURCHILL
Mar·lowe \\'mär-ˌlō\\ Christopher 1564–1593 Eng. dram. — **Mar·lo·vi·an** \\mär-'lō-vē-ən, -vyən\\ *adj*
Marlowe Julia 1866–1950 orig. *Sarah Frances Frost* Am. (Eng.-born) actress
Mar·mont \\mär-'mō⁵\\ Auguste-Frédéric-Louis Viesse de 1774–1852 Duc *de Raguse* Fr. gen.; marshal of France
Mar·mon·tel \\ˌmär-(ˌ)mō⁵-'tel\\ Jean-François 1723–1799 Fr. author
Ma·rot \\ma-'rō\\ Clément 1496?–1544 Fr. poet
Mar·quand \\mär-'kwänd\\ John Phillips 1893–1960 Am. nov.
Mar·quette \\mär-'ket\\ Jacques 1637–1675 *Père* \\ˌpir, ˌper\\ *Marquette* Fr.-born Jesuit missionary & explorer in America
Mar·quis \\'mär-kwəs\\ Donald Robert Perry 1878–1937 Am. humorist
Mar·ry·at \\'mar-ē-ət\\ Frederick 1792–1848 Eng. naval commander & nov.
Marsh \\'märsh\\ Dame (Edith) Ngaio \\'nī-(ˌ)ō\\ 1899–1982 N.Z. writer
Mar·shall \\'mär-shəl\\ Alfred 1842–1924 Eng. econ.
Marshall George Catlett 1880–1959 Am. gen. & statesman
Marshall John 1755–1835 Am. jurist; chief justice U.S. Supreme Court (1801–35)
Marshall Thomas Riley 1854–1925 vice pres. of the U.S. (1913–21)
Marshall Thurgood 1908–1993 Am. jurist
Mar·sil·i·us \\mär-'si-lē-əs\\ **of Padua** *ca* 1280–*ca* 1343 Ital. scholar
Mar·ston \\'mär-stən\\ John 1576–1634 Eng. dram.
Martel Charles — see CHARLES MARTEL
Mar·tens \\'mär-t⁵nz\\ Fyodor Fyodorovich 1845–1909 Russ. jurist
Martens Wilfried 1936– prime min. of Belgium (1979–92)

Mar·tial \\'mär-shəl\\ *ca* A.D. 40–*ca* 103 *Marcus Valerius Martialis* Rom. epigrammatist
Mar·tin \\'mär-t⁵n, mär-ta⁵\\ Saint *ca* 316–397 *Martin of Tours* patron saint of France
Mar·tin \\'mär-t⁵n\\ Archer John Porter 1910– Brit. chem.
Martin Glenn Luther 1886–1955 Am. airplane manuf.
Martin Homer Dodge 1836–1897 Am. painter
Martin Joseph William 1884–1968 Am. publisher & polit.
Martin Lynn Morley 1939– U.S. secy. of labor (1991–93)
Mar·tin du Gard \\mär-ta⁵-dē-gár\\ Roger 1881–1958 Fr. author
Mar·ti·neau \\'mär-t⁵n-ˌō\\ Harriet 1802–1876 Eng. nov. & econ.
Martineau James 1805–1900 *bro. of Harriet* Eng. theol. & philos.
Mar·ti·ni \\mär-'tē-nē\\ Simone *ca* 1284–1344 Ital. painter
Mar·tin·son \\'mär-tēn-(ˌ)sòn\\ Harry Edmund 1904–1978 Swed. author
Mar·vell \\'mär-vəl\\ Andrew 1621–1678 Eng. poet & satirist
Marx \\'märks\\ Karl Heinrich 1818–1883 Ger. polit. philos. & socialist
Mary I \\'mer-ē, 'mar-ē, 'mä-rē\\ 1516–1558 *Mary Tudor; Bloody Mary* queen of England (1553–58)
Mary II 1662–1694 joint Brit. sovereign with William III
Mary Stuart 1542–1587 *Mary, Queen of Scots* queen of Scotland (1542–67)
Ma·sac·cio \\mə-'zä-ch(ē-ˌ)ō\\ 1401–1428 orig. *Tommaso di Giovanni di Simone Guidi* Ital. painter
Ma·sa·ryk \\'mä-sə-(ˌ)rik, 'ma-\\ Jan \\'yän, 'yan\\ Gar·rigue \\gə-'rēg\\ 1886–1948 *son of T. G.* Czech diplomat & polit.
Masaryk To·máš \\'tó-ˌmäsh, 'tä-məs\\ Garrigue 1850–1937 Czech philos. & statesman; 1st pres. of Czechoslovakia (1918–35)
Ma·sca·gni \\mä-'skän-yē, ma-\\ Pietro 1863–1945 Ital. composer
Mase·field \\'mäs-ˌfēld\\ John 1878–1967 Eng. author; poet laureate (1930–67)
Mas·i·nis·sa or **Mas·si·nis·sa** \\ˌmas-ə-'ni-sə\\ *ca* 240–148 B.C. king of Numidia
Ma·son \\'mä-s⁵n\\ Charles 1728–1786 Eng. astron. & surveyor
Mason George 1725–1792 Am. statesman in Revolution
Mas·soit \\ma-sə-'sòit\\ *d* 1661 Wampanoag Indian chief
Mas·sé·na \\ˌma-sä-'nä, mə-'sä-nə\\ André 1758–1817 Duc *de Rivoli*; Prince *d'Ess·ling* \\des-le⁵\\ Fr. gen.
Mas·se·net \\ˌma-s⁵n-'ā, ma-'snä\\ Jules-Émile-Frédéric 1842–1912 Fr. composer
Mas·sey \\'ma-sē\\ William Ferguson 1856–1925 N.Z. statesman
Mas·sine \\ma-'sēn\\ Léonide 1896–1979 orig. *Leonid Fedorovich Miassin* Am. (Russ.-born) dancer & choreographer
Mas·sing·er \\'ma-s⁵n-jər\\ Philip 1583–1640 Eng. dram.
Mas·son \\'ma-s⁵n\\ David 1822–1907 Scot. editor & author
Mas·sys \\'mä-ˌsis\\ or **Mat·sys** \\'mät-sis\\ or **Mes·sys** \\'me-sis\\ or **Met·sys** \\'met-sis\\ Quentin *ca* 1466–1530 Flem. painter
Mas·ters \\'mas-tərz\\ Edgar Lee 1869–1950 Am. author
Math·er \\'ma-thər, -thər\\ Cotton 1663–1728 Am. clergyman & author
Mather Increase 1639–1723 *father of Cotton* Am. clergyman & author; pres. Harvard College (1685–1701)
Ma·tisse \\ma-'tēs, mə-\\ Henri-Émile-Benoît 1869–1954 Fr. painter
Ma·tsuo \\mät-'sü-ō, 'mät-sü-ō\\ Bashō \\'bä-ˌshō\\ 1644–1694 pseud. of *Matsuo Munefusa* Jp. haiku poet
Ma·tsu·o·ka \\ˌmat-sə-'wō-kə, ˌmät-, -(ˌ)kä\\ Yōsuke 1880–1946 Jp. statesman
Mat·te·ot·ti \\ˌma-tē-'ō-tē, ˌmä-, -'ò-\\ Giacomo 1885–1924 Ital. socialist
Mat·thews \\'ma-(ˌ)thyüz\\ (James) Brander 1852–1929 Am. educ. & author
Maugham \\'mòm\\ (William) Somerset 1874–1965 Eng. nov. & dram.
Mau·nou·ry \\ˌmō-nə-'rē\\ Michel-Joseph 1847–1923 Fr. gen.
Mau·pas·sant \\ˌmō-pə-'sä⁵\\ (Henri-René-Albert-) Guy de 1850–1893 Fr. writer
Mau·riac \\mòr-'yäk, ˌmòr-ē-'äk\\ François 1885–1970 Fr. author
Mau·rice \\'mòr-əs, 'mär-; mò-'rēs\\ *G* **Mo·ritz** \\'mōr-əts, 'mòr-\\ 1521–1553 elector of Saxony (1547–53) & gen.
Maurice of Nassau 1567–1625 Prince of *Orange* Du. gen. & statesman
Mau·rois \\mòr-'wä\\ André 1885–1967 pseud. of *Émile-Salomon-Wilhelm Her·zog* \\er-zóg\\ Fr. writer
Mau·ry \\'mòr-ē, 'mär-\\ Matthew Fontaine 1806–1873 Am. naval officer & oceanographer
Mau·ser \\maú-zər\\ Peter Paul 1838–1914 & his bro. Wilhelm 1834–1882 Ger. inventors
Maw·son \\'mó-s⁵n\\ Sir Douglas 1882–1958 Austral. explorer & geologist
Max·im \\'mak-səm\\ Sir Hiram Stevens 1840–1916 Brit. (Am.-born) inventor
Maxim Hudson 1853–1927 *bro. of Sir Hiram* Am. inventor
Max·i·mil·ian \\ˌmak-sə-'mil-yən\\ 1832–1867 *bro. of Francis Joseph I of Austria* emp. of Mexico (1864–67)
Maximilian I 1459–1519 Holy Rom. emp. (1493–1519)
Maximilian II 1527–1576 Holy Rom. emp. (1564–76)
Max·well \\'maks-ˌwel, -wəl\\ James Clerk \\'klärk\\ 1831–1879 Scot. physicist — **Max·wel·li·an** \\maks-'we-lē-ən\\ *adj*
May \\'mā\\ Sir Thomas Erskine 1815–1886 1st Baron *Farn·bor·ough* \\'färn-ˌbər-ə, -ˌbə-rə, -b(ə-)rə\\ Eng. jurist
Ma·ya·kov·ski \\ˌmä-yə-'kóf-skē, -'kòv-\\ Vladimir Vladimirovich 1893–1930 Russ. poet
May·er \\'mī(-ə)r\\ Maria Goeppert 1906–1972 Am. (Ger.-born) physicist
Mayo \\'mā-(ˌ)ō\\ Charles Horace 1865–1939 & his bro. William James 1861–1939 Am. surgeons
Ma·za·rin \\ˌma-zə-'ra⁵\\ Jules 1602–1661 Fr. cardinal & statesman
Ma·zo·wie·cki \\ˌmä-zō-'vyet-skē\\ Tadeusz 1927– prime min. of Poland (1989–91)
Maz·zi·ni \\mät-'sē-nē, mäd-'zē-\\ Giuseppe 1805–1872 Ital. patriot

---

\ə\ abut \ᵊ\ kitten, F table \ər\ further \a\ ash \ā\ ace \ä\ mop, mar
\aú\ out \ch\ chin \e\ bet \ē\ easy \g\ go \i\ hit \ī\ ice \j\ job
\ŋ\ sing \ō\ go \ò\ law \òi\ boy \th\ thin \t̶h̶\ the \ü\ loot \ú\ foot
\y\ yet \zh\ vision \á, k̠, ⁿ, œ, œ̄, ɶ, ūē, ʳ\ see Guide to Pronunciation

Mc·Adoo \'ma-kə-,dü\ William Gibbs 1863–1941 Am. administrator

M'·Car·thy \mə-'kär-thē also -tē\ Justin 1830–1912 Irish writer & polit.

Mc·Car·thy \mə-'kär-thē also -tē\ Eugene Joseph 1916–   Am. polit.

McCarthy Joseph Raymond 1908–1957 Am. polit.

McCarthy Mary Therese 1912–1989 Am. writer

Mc·Clel·lan \mə-'kle-lən\ George Brinton 1826–1885 Am. gen. & polit.

Mc·Clin·tock \mə-'klin-tək\ Barbara 1902–1992 Am. botanist

Mc·Clos·key \mə-'kläs-kē\ John 1810–1885 1st Am. cardinal

Mc·Cloy \mə-'klȯi\ John Jay 1895–1989 Am. banker & govt. official

Mc·Clure \mə-'klu̇r\ Samuel Sidney 1857–1949 Am. (Irish-born) editor & publisher

Mc·Cor·mack \mə-'kȯr-mək, -mik\ John 1884–1945 Am. (Irish-born) tenor

McCormack John William 1891–1980 Am. polit.

Mc·Cor·mick \mə-'kȯr-mik\ Cyrus Hall 1809–1884 Am. inventor

McCormick Robert Rutherford 1880–1955 Am. newspaper publisher

Mc·Cul·lers \mə-'kə-lərz\ Carson 1917–1967 née Smith Am. writer

Mc·Dow·ell \mək-'dau̇(-ə)l\ Ephraim 1771–1830 Am. surgeon

McDowell Irvin 1818–1885 Am. gen.

Mc·Gill \mə-'gil\ James 1744–1813 Canad. (Scot.-born) businessman & philanthropist

Mc·Gov·ern \mə-'gə-vərn\ George Stanley 1922–   Am. polit.

Mc·Guf·fey \mə-'gə-fē\ William Holmes 1800–1873 Am. educ.

Mc·Ken·na \mə-'ke-nə\ Siobhan \shə-'vȯn\ 1923?–1986 Irish actress

Mc·Kim \mə-'kim\ Charles Follen 1847–1909 Am. architect

Mc·Kin·ley \mə-'kin-lē\ William 1843–1901 25th pres. of the U.S. (1897–1901)

Mc·Lu·han \mə-'klü-ən\ (Herbert) Marshall 1911–1980 Canad. educ.

Mc·Ma·hon \mək-'mä(-ə)n\ Sir William 1908–1988 prime min. of Australia (1971–72)

Mc·Mil·lan \mək-'mi-lən\ Edwin Mattison 1907–1991 Am. chem.

Mc·Na·mara \,mak-nə-'mar-ə, 'mak-nə-,mar-ə\ Robert Strange 1916–   U.S. secy. of defense (1961–68)

Mc·Naugh·ton \mək-'nȯ-t³n\ Andrew George Latta 1887–1966 Canad. gen. & diplomat

Mead \'mēd\ Margaret 1901–1978 Am. anthropol.

Meade \'mēd\ George Gordon 1815–1872 Am. gen.

Meade James Edward 1907–   Brit. econ.

Mea·ny \'mē-nē\ George 1894–1980 Am. labor leader

Med·a·war \'me-də-wər\ Peter Brian 1915–1987 Eng. anatomist

Me·dei·ros \mə-'der-əs, -(,)ōs\ Humberto 1915–1983 Am. (Port.-born) cardinal

Me·di·ci, de' \'me-də-(,)chē\ Catherine — see CATHERINE DE MÉDICIS

Medici, de' Cosimo 1389–1464 the Elder Florentine financier & ruler

Medici, de' Cosimo I 1519–1574 the Great; Duke of Florence; Grand Duke of Tuscany

Medici, de' Giulio — see CLEMENT VII

Medici, de' Lorenzo 1449–1492 the Magnificent Florentine statesman, ruler, & patron

Me·di·na–Si·do·nia \mə-'dē-nə-sə-'dōn-yə\ Duque de d 1619 Alonso Pérez de Guzmán Span. admiral

Meer van Delft, van der — see Jan VERMEER

Meigh·en \'mē-ən\ Arthur 1874–1960 Canad. statesman; prime min. (1920–21; 1926)

Me·ir \me-'ir\ Golda 1898–1978 orig. Goldie Mabovitch, later Goldie Myerson prime min. of Israel (1969–74)

Meis·so·nier \,mä-s³n-'yā\ Jean-Louis-Ernest 1815–1891 Fr. painter

Meit·ner \'mīt-nər\ Li·se \'lē-zə\ 1878–1968 Ger. physicist

Me·lanch·thon \mə-'laŋ(k)-thən, -tən\ Philipp 1497–1560 orig. surname Schwartzerd Ger. scholar & religious reformer

Mel·ba \'mel-bə\ Dame Nellie 1861–1931 orig. Helen Porter Mitchell Austral. soprano

Mel·chers \'mel-chərz\ (Julius) Gari 1860–1932 Am. painter

Mel·chi·or \'mel-kē-,ȯr\ Lau·ritz \'lau̇-rəts\ Lebrecht Hommel 1890–1973 Am. (Dan.-born) tenor

Mel·lon \'me-lən\ Andrew William 1855–1937 Am. financier

Mel·ville \'mel-,vil\ Herman 1819–1891 Am. author

Mem·ling \'mem-liŋ\ or Mem·linc \-liŋk\ Hans ca 1430–1494 Flem. painter

Me·nan·der \mə-'nan-dər\ 342–292 B.C. Greek dram.

Men·chú \'men-,chü\ Rigoberta 1959–   Guatemalan human rights activist

Mencius — see MENG-TZU

Menck·en \'meŋ-kən, 'men-\ Henry Louis 1880–1956 Am. editor — Menck·e·nian \,meŋ-'kē-nē-ən, men-\ adj

Men·del \'men-d³l\ Gregor Johann 1822–1884 Austrian botanist — Men·del·ian \men-'dē-lē-ən, -'dē-\ adj

Men·de·le·yev \,men-də-'lā-əf\ Dmitry Ivanovich 1834–1907 Russ. chem.

Men·dels·sohn \'men-d³l-sən\ Moses 1729–1786 Ger. philos.

Mendelssohn–Bar·thol·dy \-bär-'tȯl-dē, -'thȯl-\ (Jakob Ludwig) Felix 1809–1847 grandson of prec. Ger. composer, pianist, & conductor — Men·dels·sohn·ian \,men-d³l-'sō-nē-ən, -nyən\ adj

Mendès–France \ma³-des-frä³s\ Pierre 1907–1982 Fr. statesman

Men·do·za \men-'dō-zə\ Antonio de ca 1490–1552 Span. colonial gov.

Men·e·lik II \'me-n³l-(,)ik\ 1844–1913 emp. of Ethiopia (1889–1913)

Men·em \'me-,nem, -nəm\ Carlos Saúl 1930–   pres. of Argentina (1989–   )

Me·nén·dez de Av·i·lés \mə-'nen-dəs-dā-,ä-və-'lās\ Pedro 1519–1574 Span. navigator & explorer

Me·nes \'mē-(,)nēz\ fl ca 3100 B.C. king of Egypt

Mengs \'meŋ(k)s\ Anton Raphael 1728–1779 Ger. painter

Meng–tzu \'məŋ-'dzü\ ca 371–ca 289 B.C. orig. Meng K'o L. Men·cius \'men-ch(ē)-əs\ Chin. philos.

Men·ning·er \'me-niŋ-ər\ Karl Augustus 1893–1990 Am. psychiatrist

Men·no Si·mons \'me-nō-'sē-mōns, -'sī-\ 1469–1561 Dutch religious reformer

Me·not·ti \mə-'nä-tē, -'nȯ-\ Gian Carlo 1911–   Am. (Ital.-born) composer

Me·nu·hin \'men-yə-wən\ Ye·hu·di \yə-'hü-dē\ 1916–   Am. violinist

Men·zies \'men-(,)zēz\ Sir Robert Gordon 1894–1978 Austral. statesman; prime min. (1939–41; 1949–66)

Mer·ca·tor \(,)mər-'kā-tər\ Gerardus 1512–1594 Gerhard Kremer Flem. cartographer

Mer·cier \mer-'syā, 'mer-sē-,ā\ Désiré-Joseph 1851–1926 Belg. cardinal & philos.

Mer·e·dith \'mer-ə-dəth\ George 1828–1909 Eng. nov. & poet

Meredith Owen — see E. R. Bulwer-LYTTON

Mer·gen·tha·ler \'mər-gən-,thä-lər, 'mer-gən-,tä-\ Ottmar 1854–1899 Am. (Ger.-born) inventor

Mé·ri·mée \'mer-ə-,mā, ,mä-rə-'\ Prosper 1803–1870 Fr. writer

Mer·ri·field \'mer-i-,fēld\ Robert Bruce 1921–   Am. biochem.

Mer·ton \'mər-t³n\ Thomas 1915–1968 Am. religious & author

Mes·mer \'mez-mər, 'mes-\ Franz or Friedrich Anton 1734–1815 Ger. physician

Mes·sa·la (or Mes·sal·la) Cor·vi·nus \mə-'sä-lə-,kȯr-'vī-nəs\ Marcus Valerius ca 64 B.C.–A.D. 8 Rom. gen. & statesman

Mes·sa·li·na \,me-sə-'lī-nə, -'lē-\ Valeria ca A.D. 22–48 3d wife of Emp. Claudius

Mes·ser·schmitt \'me-sər-,shmit\ Willy 1898–1978 Ger. aircraft designer & manuf.

Mes·sier \mäs-yā, 'me-sē-,ā\ Charles 1730–1817 Fr. astron.

Meš·tro·vić \'mesh-trə-,vich, 'mes-\ Ivan 1883–1962 Am. (Yugoslavian-born) sculptor

Me·tax·as \me-'täk-'säs\ Ioannis 1871–1941 Greek gen. & dictator

Metch·ni·koff \'mech-nə-,kȯf\ Elie 1845–1916 orig. Ilya Ilich Mech·ni·kov \'myäch-nyi-,kȯf\ Fr. (Russ.-born) zool. & bacteriol.

Met·ter·nich \'me-tər-(,)nik, -,nik\ Klemens Wenzel Nepomuk Lothar 1773–1859 Fürst von Metternich Austrian statesman — Met·ter·nich·ian \,me-tər-'ni-kē-ən, -kē-ən\ adj

Mey·er \'mī(-ə)r\ Annie 1867–1951 née Nathan Am. educ. & writer

Mey·er·beer \'mī-ər-,bir, -,ber\ Giacomo 1791–1864 orig. Jakob Liebmann Beer Ger. composer

Mey·er·hof \'mī-ər-,hȯf\ Otto 1884–1951 Ger. biochem.

Mi·chael \'mī-kəl\ Romanian Mi·hai \mē-'hī\ 1921–   Michael Hohenzollern king of Romania (1927–30; 1940–47)

Mich·el \'mī-kəl\ Hartmut 1948–   Ger. biochem.

Mi·chel·an·ge·lo \,mī-kə-'lan-jə-,lō, ,mi-, ,me-kə-'län-\ 1475–1564 Michelangelo di Lodovico Buonarroti Simoni Ital. sculptor, painter, architect, & poet — Mi·chel·an·ge·lesque \-,lan-jə-'lesk\ adj

Mi·che·let \,mēsh-'lā, ,mē-shə-\ Jules 1798–1874 Fr. hist.

Mi·chel·son \'mī-kəl-sən\ Albert Abraham 1852–1931 Am. (Ger.-born) physicist

Mich·e·ner \'mich-nər\ (Daniel) Roland 1900–   Canad. polit.; gov.-gen. (1967–74)

Mich·e·ner \'mich-nər, 'mi-chə-\ James Albert 1907–   Am. author

Mi·chu·rin \myi-'chür-yin\ Ivan Vladimirovich 1855–1935 Soviet horticulturist

Mic·kie·wicz \mits-'kyä-vich\ Adam 1798–1855 Pol. poet

Mid·dle·ton \'mi-d³l-tən\ Thomas 1570?–1627 Eng. dram.

Mies van der Ro·he \,mēs-,van-dər-'rō(-ə), ,mis-\ Ludwig 1886–1969 Am. (Ger.-born) architect — Mies·ian \'mē-sē-ən, 'mē-shən\ adj

Miff·lin \'mif-lən\ Thomas 1744–1800 Am. gen. in Revolution

Mi·haj·lo·vić \mi-'hi-lə-,vich\ Dragoljub 1893–1946 Draža \'drä-zhə\ Yugoslav gen.

Mi·ki \'mē-kē\ Tak·eo \'tä-kā-ō\ 1907–1988 prime min. of Japan (1974–76)

Mi·ko·yan \,mē-kō-'yän\ Ana·stas \,ä-nə-'stäs\ Ivanovich 1895–1978 Soviet polit.; head of Presidium (1964–65)

Miles \'mī(ə)lz\ Nelson Appleton 1839–1925 Am. gen.

Mi·lhaud \mē-'yō\ Darius 1892–1974 Fr. composer

Mill \'mil\ James 1773–1836 Scot. philos., hist., & econ.

Mill John Stuart 1806–1873 son of James Eng. philos. & econ.

Mil·lais \'mi-,lā, mi-'lā\ Sir John Everett 1829–1896 Eng. painter

Mil·lay \mi-'lā\ Edna St. Vincent 1892–1950 Am. poet

Mil·ler \'mi-lər\ Arthur 1915–   Am. dram. & nov.

Miller Henry 1891–1980 Am. writer

Miller Joa·quin \wä-'kēn, wȯ-\ 1837–1913 pseud. of Cincinnatus Hiner Miller Am. poet

Miller Merton Howard 1923–   Am. econ.

Miller Perry Gilbert Eddy 1905–1963 Am. lit. critic & scholar

Miller William 1782–1849 Am. religious leader

Mil·le·rand \mēl-rä³, mē-lə-\ Alexandre 1859–1943 Fr. statesman; pres. of France (1920–24)

Mil·les \'mi-ləs\ Carl 1875–1955 Swed. sculptor

Mil·let \mē-'yā, mi-'lā\ Jean-François 1814–1875 Fr. painter

Mil·li·kan \'mi-li-kən\ Robert Andrews 1868–1953 Am. physicist

Mil·man \'mil-mən\ Henry Hart 1791–1868 Eng. poet & hist.

Milne \'mil(n)\ Alan Alexander 1882–1956 Eng. poet & dram.

Mi·losz \'mē-lȯsh\ Czeslaw 1911–   Pol. writer

Mil·stein \'mil-,stīn, -,stēn\ César 1927–   Brit. (Argentine-born) immunologist

Mil·ti·a·des \mil-'tī-ə-,dēz\ ca 554–?489 B.C. the Younger Athenian gen.

Mil·ton \'mil-t³n\ John 1608–1674 Eng. poet — Mil·to·nian \mil-'tō-nē-ən, -nyən\ or Mil·ton·ic \-'tä-nik\ adj

Mil·yu·kov \,mil-yə-'kȯf, -'kȯv\ Pavel Nikolayevich 1859–1943 Russ. polit. & hist.

Mi·not \'mī-nət\ George Richards 1885–1950 Am. physician

Min·ton \'min-t³n\ Sherman 1890–1965 Am. jurist

Min·u·it \'min-yə-wət\ or Min·ne·wit \'mi-nə-,wit\ Peter 1580–1638 Du. colonial administrator in America

Mi·ra·beau \'mir-ə-,bō\ Comte de 1749–1791 Honoré-Gabriel Riqueti Fr. orator & revolutionary

Mi·ró \mē-'rō\ Joan \zhü-'än\ 1893–1983 Span. painter

Mi·shi·ma \'mē-shi-,mä, mə-'shē-mə\ Yukio 1925–1970 Jp. writer

Mis·tral \mi-'sträl, -'sträl\ Frédéric 1830–1914 Provençal poet

Mistral \mi-'sträl, -'sträl\ Gabriela 1889–1957 orig. Lucila Godoy Alcayaga Chilean poet & educ.

Mitch·ell \'mi-chəl\ John 1870–1919 Am. labor leader

Mitchell Margaret Munnerlyn 1900–1949 Am. nov.

Mitchell Maria 1818–1889 Am. astron.

Mitchell Peter Dennis 1920–   Brit. chem.

Mitchell William 1879–1936 Billy Am. gen.

Mit·ford \'mit-fərd\ Mary Russell 1787–1855 Eng. nov. & dram.

Mitford William 1744–1827 Eng. hist.
Mith·ra·da·tes VI Eu·pa·tor \\,mi-thrə-'dā-tēz-'yü-,pā-tər\\ *d* 63 B.C. *the Great* king of Pontus (120–63)
Mi·tro·pou·los \\mə-'trä-pə-ləs\\ Di·mi·tri \\də-'mē-trē\\ 1896–1960 Am. (Greek-born) conductor
Mit·ter·rand \\,mē-ter-'än\\ François-Maurice 1916–   pres. of France (1981–   )
Mi·ya·za·wa \\,mē-ə-'zä-wə\\ Kiichi 1919–   prime min. of Japan (1991–93)
Mo·bu·tu Se·se Se·ko \\mə-'bü-(,)tü-'sä-sä-'sä-(,)kō\\ 1930–   orig. *Joseph-Désiré Mobutu* pres. of Zaire (1965–   )
Mo·di·glia·ni \\,mō-dēl-'yä-nē, -d⁹l-\\ Amedeo 1884–1920 Ital. painter
Modigliani Franco 1918–   Am. (Ital.-born) econ.
Mo·djes·ka \\mə-'jes-kə\\ Helena 1840–1909 Am. (Pol.-born) actress
Mo·ham·mad Re·za Pah·la·vi \\mō-'ha-məd-ri-'zä-'pə-lə-(,)vē, -'hä-\\ 1919–1980 shah of Iran (1941–79)
Mo·ham·med *var of* MUHAMMAD
Mois·san \\mwä-'säⁿ\\ Henri 1852–1907 Fr. chem.
Mo·ley \\'mō-lē\\ Raymond Charles 1886–1975 Am. journalist
Mo·lière \\mōl-'yer, 'mōl,-\\ 1622–1673 orig. *Jean-Baptiste Poquelin* Fr. actor & dram.
Molina Tirso de — see TIRSO DE MOLINA
Mol·nár \\'mōl-,när, 'mól-\\ Fe·renc \\'fer-ən(t)s\\ 1878–1952 Hung. author
Mo·lo·tov \\'mä-lə-,tóf, 'mò-, 'mō-, -,tóv\\ Vyacheslav Mikhaylovich 1890–1986 orig. surname *Skryabin* Soviet statesman
Molt·ke \\'mōlt-kə\\ Helmuth Karl Bernhard 1800–1891 Graf *von Moltke* Pruss. field marshal
Momm·sen \\'mōm-zən\\ Theodor 1817–1903 Ger. scholar & hist.
Monck *or* **Monk** \\'məŋk\\ George 1608–1670 1st Duke of *Al·be·marle* \\'al-bə-,märl\\ Eng. gen.
Mon·dale \\'män-,dāl\\ Walter Frederick 1928–   Am. polit.; vice pres. of the U.S. (1977–81)
Mon·dri·an \\'món-drē-,än\\ Piet 1872–1944 *Pieter Cornelis Mondriaan* Du. painter
Mo·net \\mō-'nä\\ Claude 1840–1926 Fr. painter
Mo·ne·ta \\mō-'nā-tə\\ Ernesto Teodoro 1833–1918 Ital. journalist & pacifist
Mo·niz Antonio Egas — see EGAS MONIZ
Monk \\'məŋk\\ Thelonious Sphere 1920–1982 Am. jazz musician
Mon·mouth \\'mən-məth, 'män-\\ Duke of 1649–1685 *James Scott, son of Charles II of England* Eng. rebel & claimant to the throne
Mon·net \\mō-'ne\\ Jean-Omer-Marie-Gabriel 1888–1979 Fr. econ. & diplomat
Mo·nod \\mó-nô\\ Jacques-Lucien 1910–1976 Fr. biochem.
Mon·roe \\mən-'rō\\ James 1758–1831 5th pres. of U.S. (1817–25)
Mon·ta·gna \\mən-'tän-yə\\ Bartolommeo *ca* 1450–1523 Ital. painter
Mon·ta·gu \\'män-tə-,gyü, 'mən-\\ Lady Mary Wortley 1689–1762 Eng. letter writer & poet
Mon·taigne \\män-'tän, mō⁻-ten^y\\ Michel Eyquem de 1533–1592 Fr. essayist
Mon·ta·le \\mōn-'tä-(,)lä\\ Eugenio 1896–1981 Ital. poet
Mont·calm de Saint-Véran \\mänt-'kälm-də-,sa⁻-vä-'rä⁻, -'käm-\\ Marquis de 1712–1759 *Louis-Joseph de Montcalm-Grozon* Fr. field marshal
Mon·tes·pan \\,mōⁿ-tes-pä⁻, 'mänt-es-,span\\ Marquise de 1641–1707 née (*Françoise-Athénaïs*) *Rochechouart de Mortemart* mistress of Louis XIV
Mon·tes·quieu \\,män-təs-'kyü, -'kyə(r), -'kyœ\\ Baron *de La Brède et de* 1689–1755 *Charles-Louis de Secondat* Fr. lawyer & polit. philos.
Mon·tes·so·ri \\,män-tə-'sōr-ē, -'sór-\\ Maria 1870–1952 Ital. physician & educ.
Mon·teux \\mōⁿ-'tə(r), -'tœ\\ Pierre 1875–1964 Am. (Fr.-born) conductor
Mon·te·ver·di *or* **Mon·te·ver·de** \\,män-tə-'ver-dē, -'vər-\\ Claudio 1567–1643 Ital. composer
Mon·te·zu·ma II \\,män-tə-'zü-mə\\ *or* **Moc·te·zu·ma** \\,mäk-tə-\\ 1466–1520 last Aztec emp. of Mexico (1502–20)
Mont·fort \\'mänt-fərt, mōⁿ-'fōr\\ Simon de 1165?–1218 *Simon IV de Montfort l'Amaury* Fr. soldier
Mont·fort \\'mänt-fərt\\ Simon de *ca* 1208–1265 Earl of *Leicester* Eng. soldier & statesman
Mont·gol·fier \\mänt-'gäl-fē-ər, -fē-,ā\\ Joseph-Michel 1740–1810 & his bro. Jacques-Étienne 1745–1799 Fr. inventors & balloonists
Mont·gom·ery \\(,)mən(t)-'gəm-rē, män(t)-, -'gäm-; -'gə-mə-, -'gä-\\ Bernard Law 1887–1976 1st Viscount *Montgomery of Alamein* Brit. field marshal
Montgomery Lucy Maud 1874–1942 Canad. nov.
Mont·mo·ren·cy \\,mänt-mə-'ren(t)-sē\\ Anne 1493–1567 1st duc *de Montmorency* Fr. soldier; constable (1537)
Mon·trose \\män-'trōz\\ 1st Marquess of 1612–1650 *James Graham* Scot. Royalist
Moo·dy \\'mü-dē\\ Dwight Lyman 1837–1899 Am. evangelist
Moody William Vaughn 1869–1910 Am. poet & dram.
Moore \\'mōr, 'mòr, 'mùr\\ George 1852–1933 Irish author
Moore George Edward 1873–1958 Eng. philos.
Moore Henry 1898–1986 Brit. sculptor
Moore John Bassett 1860–1947 Am. jurist
Moore Marianne Craig 1887–1972 Am. poet
Moore Stanford 1913–1982 Am. biochem.
Moore Thomas 1779–1852 Irish poet
Mo·ra·via \\mō-'rä-vē-ə\\ Alberto 1907–1990 pseud. of *Alberto Pincherle* Ital. writer
More \\'mōr, 'mòr\\ Hannah 1745–1833 Eng. religious writer
More Henry 1614–1687 Eng. philos.
More Paul Elmer 1864–1937 Am. essayist & critic
More Sir Thomas 1478–1535 *Saint* Eng. statesman & author
Mo·reau \\mó-rō\\ (Jean-) Victor-Marie 1763–1813 Fr. gen.
Mor·gan \\'mór-gən\\ Daniel 1736–1802 Am. gen. in Revolution
Morgan Sir Henry 1635–1688 Eng. buccaneer
Morgan John Hunt 1825–1864 Am. Confed. cavalry officer
Morgan John Pier·pont \\'pir-,pänt\\ 1837–1913 Am. financier
Morgan John Pierpont 1867–1943 *son of J. P.* Am. financier
Morgan Thomas Hunt 1866–1945 Am. geneticist
Morgan William Wilson 1906–1994 Am. astron.

Mor·gen·thau \\'mór-gən-,thó\\ Henry 1891–1967 U.S. secy. of the treasury (1934–45)
Mor·i·son \\'mór-ə-sən, 'mär-\\ Samuel Eliot 1887–1976 Am. hist.
Morison Stanley 1889–1968 Eng. type designer
Mo·ri·sot \\mó-rē-zō\\ Berthe 1841–1895 Fr. painter
Mor·ley \\'mór-lē\\ Christopher Darlington 1890–1957 Am. writer
Morley John 1838–1923 Viscount *Morley* Eng. statesman & writer
Mor·nay \\mór-nā\\ Philippe de 1549–1623 Seigneur *du Plessis-Marly; usu. called Du·ples·sis-Mor·nay* \\dɯ-plä-sä-mór-ne\\ Fr. Huguenot
Mor·ris \\'mór-əs, 'mär-\\ Gou·ver·neur \\,gə-və(r)-'nir\\ 1752–1816 Am. statesman & diplomat
Morris Robert 1734–1806 Am. financier & statesman
Morris William 1834–1896 Eng. poet, artist, & socialist
Mor·ri·son \\'mór-ə-sən, 'mär-\\ Herbert Stanley 1888–1965 Baron *Morrison of Lambeth* Eng. polit.
Morrison Robert 1782–1834 Scot. missionary
Morrison Toni 1931–   orig. *Chloe Anthony Wofford* Am. novelist
Morse \\'mórs\\ Samuel Finley Breese 1791–1872 Am. artist & inventor
Mor·ti·mer \\'mór-tə-mər\\ Roger de 1287–1330 1st Earl of *March & 8th Baron of Wigmore* Welsh rebel
Mor·ton \\'mór-t⁹n\\ Levi Parsons 1824–1920 Am. banker & polit.; vice pres. of the U.S. (1889–93)
Morton William Thomas Green 1819–1868 Am. dentist
Mos·by \\'mōz-bē\\ John Singleton 1833–1916 Am. Confed. cavalry officer
Moś·cic·ki \\mósh-'chēt-skē, -'chit-\\ Ignacy 1867–1946 Pol. chem.; pres. of Poland (1926–39)
Mo·ses \\'mō-zəz *also* -zəs\\ Anna Mary née *Robertson* 1860–1961 *Grandma Moses* Am. painter
Mos·ley \\'mōz-lē\\ Sir Oswald Er·nald \\'ər-n⁹ld\\ 1896–1980 Eng. polit.
Möss·bau·er \\'mœs-,baů-(ə)r, 'mes-\\ Rudolf Ludwig 1929–   Ger. physicist
Moth·er·well \\'mə-thər-,wel, -wəl\\ Robert 1915–1991 Am. artist
Mo Ti — see MO-TZU
Mot·ley \\'mät-lē\\ John Lothrop 1814–1877 Am. hist.
Mo·ton \\'mō-t⁹n\\ Robert Russa 1867–1940 Am. educ.
Mott \\'mät\\ John Raleigh 1865–1955 Am. religious leader
Mott Lucretia 1793–1880 née *Coffin* Am. social reformer
Mott Sir Nevill Francis 1905–   Brit. physicist
Mot·tel·son \\'mō-t⁹l-sən, -(,)sòn\\ Ben Roy 1926–   Dan. (Am.≠born) physicist
Mot·teux \\mä-'tə(r), 'mä-,\\ Peter Anthony 1660–1718 Brit. (Fr.-born) dram. & translator
Mo–tzu \\'mōd-'zə\\ 470?–?391 B.C. orig. *Mo Ti* \\'mō-'dē\\ L. *Mi·cius* \\'mē-sh(ē-)əs\\ Chin. philos.
Moul·ton \\'mōl-t⁹n\\ Forest Ray 1872–1952 Am. astron.
Moul·trie \\'mül-trē, 'mōl-\\ William 1730–1805 Am. gen. in Revolution
Mount·bat·ten \\maůnt-'ba-t⁹n\\ Louis 1900–1979 1st Earl *Mountbatten of Burma* Brit. admiral; 1st gov.-gen. of India (1947–48); chief of defense staff (1959–65)
Mountbatten Philip, Duke of Edinburgh — see Prince PHILIP
Mow·at \\'mō-ət\\ Farley McGill 1921–   Canad. writer
Mo·zart \\'mōt-,särt\\ Wolfgang Amadeus 1756–1791 Austrian composer — **Mo·zart·ean** *or* **Mo·zart·ian** \\mōt-'sär-tē-ən\\ *adj*
Mu·bar·ak \\mü-'bär-ək\\ Muhammad Hosni 1929–   pres. of Egypt (1981–   )
Muench \\'minch\\ Aloisius Joseph 1889–1962 Am. cardinal
Mu·ga·be \\mü-'gä-bē\\ Robert Gabriel 1924–   prime min. of Zimbabwe (1980–87); executive pres. (1987–   )
Mug·ge·ridge \\'mə-gə-,rij\\ Malcolm Thomas 1903–1990 Brit. writer & social critic
Mu·ham·mad \\mō-'ha-məd, -'hä- *also* mü-\\ *ca* 570–632 *Abū al-Qāsim Muhammad ibn ʿAbd Allāh ibn ʿAbd al-Muṭṭalib ibn Hāshim* Arab prophet & founder of Islam
Mu·ham·mad \\mō-'ha-məd, mü-\\ Elijah 1897–1975 orig. *E. Poole* Am. religious leader
Muhammad XI \\mō-'ha-məd, -'hä- *also* mü-\\ *d* 1527 *Abū ʿAbd Allāh Muhammad* Sp. *Bo·ab·dil* \\bō-äv-'dēl\\ last sultan of Granada
Müh·len·berg \\'myü-lən-,bərg\\ Henry Melchior 1711–1787 Am. (Ger.-born) Lutheran clergyman
Muir \\'myůr\\ John 1838–1914 Am. (Scot.-born) naturalist
Mul·ler \\'mə-lər\\ Hermann Joseph 1890–1967 Am. geneticist
Mül·ler \\'myü-lər, 'mi-, 'mə-\\ (Friedrich) Max 1823–1900 Brit. (Ger.≠born) philologist
Müller Johann 1436–1476 *Regiomontanus* Ger. astron.
Müller Karl Alexander 1927–   Swiss physicist
Müller Paul Hermann 1899–1965 Swiss chem.
Mul·li·ken \\'mə-li-kən\\ Robert Sanderson 1896–1986 Am. chem. & physicist
Mul·lis \\'mə-lis\\ Kary Banks 1944–   Am. biochem.
Mul·ro·ney \\məl-'rü-nē\\ (Martin) Brian 1939–   Canad. polit.; prime min. (1984–93)
Mum·ford \\'məm(p)-fərd\\ Lewis 1895–1990 Am. philos.
Munch \\'műnch, 'műnch\\ Charles 1891–1968 Fr.-born conductor
Munch \\'műŋk\\ Edvard 1863–1944 Norw. painter
Münch·hau·sen \\'műnk-,haů-z⁹n\\ Karl Friedrich Hieronymus von 1720–1797 Baron *Mun·chau·sen* \\'mən-,chaů-z⁹n, 'mün-\\ Ger. hunter, soldier, & raconteur
Mu·ñoz Ma·rín \\(,)mün-'yōs-mə-'rēn, -'yōz-\\ Luis 1898–1980 Puerto Rican polit.
Mun·ro \\(,)mən-'rō\\ Alice 1931–   née *Laidlaw* Canad. writer
Munro Hecto Hugh 1870–1916 pseud. *Saki* Scot. writer
Mün·ster·berg \\'mün(t)-stər-,bərg, 'myün(t)-, 'mən(t)-\\ Hugo 1863–1916 Am. (Ger.-born) psychol.
Mu·ra·sa·ki \\,műr-ə-'sä-kē, ,myůr-\\ Shikibu 978?–?1026 Jp. court lady & nov.

\\ə\\ abut \\⁹\\ kitten, F table \\ər\\ further \\a\\ ash \\ā\\ ace \\ä\\ mop, mar
\\aů\\ out \\ch\\ chin \\e\\ bet \\ē\\ easy \\g\\ go \\i\\ hit \\ī\\ ice \\j\\ job
\\ŋ\\ sing \\ō\\ go \\ò\\ law \\òi\\ boy \\th\\ thin \\t͟h\\ the \\ü\\ loot \\ů\\ foot
\\y\\ yet \\zh\\ vision \\á, k̲, ⁿ, œ, œ̄, ɯ, ūe, ᵞ\\ see Guide to Pronunciation

Mu·rat \myủ-'rä, mü̅ē-\ Joachim 1767–1815 Fr. gen.; marshal of France; king of Naples (1808–15)

Mu·ra·ya·ma \ˌmủ-rä-'yä-mä\ Tomiichi 1924–   prime min. of Japan (1994–)

Mur·doch \'mər-dək, -ˌdäk\ Dame (Jean) Iris 1919–   Brit. (Irish-born) writer

Mu·ril·lo \myủ-'ri-(ˌ)lō; mủ-'rē-(ˌ)ō, myủ-\ Bartolomé Esteban 1617–1682 Span. painter

Mur·phy \'mər-fē\ Frank 1890–1949 Am. jurist

Murphy William Parry 1892–1987 Am. physician

Mur·ray \'mər-ē, 'mə-rē\ (George) Gilbert Aimé 1866–1957 Brit. classical scholar

Murray Sir James Augustus Henry 1837–1915 Brit. lexicographer

Murray Joseph Edward 1919–   Am. surgeon

Murray Lindley 1745–1826 Am. grammarian

Murray Philip 1886–1952 Am. labor leader

Mur·row \'mər-(ˌ)ō, 'mə-(ˌ)rō\ Edward Roscoe 1908–1965 Am. journalist

Mus·set \myü-'sä\ (Louis-Charles-) Alfred de 1810–1857 Fr. poet

Mus·so·li·ni \ˌmü-sə-'lē-nē, ˌmü-\ Be·ni·to \bə-'nē-(ˌ)tō\ 1883–1945 *Il Du·ce* \ēl-'dü-(ˌ)chā\ Ital. Fascist premier (1922–43)

Mus·sorg·sky \mü-'sȯrg-skē, -'zȯrg-\ Mo·dest \mō-'dest\ Petrovich 1839–1881 Russ. composer

Mustafa Kemal — see KEMAL ATATÜRK

Mu·tsu·hi·to \ˌmüt-sə-'hē-(ˌ)tō\ 1852–1912 *Mei·ji* \'mā-(ˌ)jē\ emp. of Japan (1867–1912)

Mu·zo·re·wa \ˌmü-zə-'rä-wə\ Abel Tendekayi 1925–   prime min. of Zimbabwe Rhodesia (1979–80)

Myr·dal \'mᵘer-ˌdäl, 'mər-, 'mir-\ Alva 1902–1986 Swed. sociologist & diplomat

Myrdal (Karl) Gunnar 1898–1987 Swed. econ.

My·ron \'mī-rən\ *fl ca* 480–440 B.C. Greek sculptor

Na·bo·kov \nə-'bȯ-kəf\ Vladimir Vladimirovich 1899–1977 Am. (Russ.-born) nov. & poet — **Na·bo·ko·vi·an** \ˌnä-bə-'kȯ-vē-ən\ *adj*

Na·der \'nä-dər\ Ralph 1934–   Am. consumer advocate

Nai·du \'nī-(ˌ)dü\ Sarojini 1879–1949 Indian poet & reformer

Na·ka·so·ne \ˌnä-kə-'sō-nē\ Yasuhiro 1918–   prime min. of Japan (1982–87)

Na·mier \'na-ˌmir\ Sir Lewis Bernstein 1888–1960 Brit. hist.

Nā·nak \'nä-nək\ 1469–1539 founder of the Sikh faith in India

Nan·sen \'nän(t)-sən, 'nan(t)-\ Frid·tjof \'fri-ˌchȯf\ 1861–1930 Norw. arctic explorer, zool., & statesman

Na·pier \'nä-pē-ər, -ˌpir; nə-'pir\ Sir Charles James 1782–1853 Brit. gen.

Napier *or* **Ne·per** \'nä-pər\ John 1550–1617 Laird of *Mer·chis·ton* \'mər-kə-stən\ Scot. math.

Napier Robert Cornelis 1810–1890 1st Baron *Napier of Mag·da·la* \'mag-də-lə\ Brit. field marshal

Na·po·léon I \nə-'pōl-yən, -'pō-lē-ən\ *or* **Napoléon Bo·na·parte** \'bō-nə-ˌpärt\ 1769–1821 emp. of the French (1804–15) — **Na·po·le·on·ic** \nə-ˌpō-lē-'ä-nik\ *adj*

Napoléon II 1811–1832 Duc *de Reichstadt; son of Napoléon I & Marie Louise*

Napoléon III 1808–1873 *Louis-Napoléon; son of Louis Bonaparte & nephew of Napoléon I* emp. of the French (1852–71)

Nar·vá·ez \när-'vä-ˌās\ Pánfilo de *ca* 1480–1528 Span. soldier

Nash \'nash\ John F. 1928–   Am. econ.

Nash Ogden 1902–1971 Am. poet

Nash *or* **Nashe** \'nash\ Thomas 1567–1601 Eng. satirist & dram.

Nash Walter 1882–1968 prime min. of New Zealand (1957–60)

Na·smyth \'nä-ˌsmith, 'näz-məth\ Alexander 1758–1840 Scot. painter

Nas·ser \'nä-sər, 'na-\ Ga·mal \gə-'mäl\ Ab·del \'äb-dᵊl\ 1918–1970 Egypt. polit.; pres. of Egypt (1956–70)

Nast \'nast\ Thomas 1840–1902 Am. (Ger.-born) cartoonist

Na·than \'nä-thən\ George Jean 1882–1958 Am. editor & drama critic

Na·thans \'nä-thənz\ Daniel 1928–   Am. microbiologist

Na·tion \'nä-shən\ Car·ry \'kar-ē\ Amelia 1846–1911 *née Moore* Am. temperance agitator

Nat·ta \'nät-(ˌ)tä\ Giulio 1903–1979 Ital. chem.

Neb·u·cha·drez·zar II \ˌne-byə-kə-'dre-zər, -bə-\ *or* **Neb·u·chad·nez·zar** \-kəd-'ne-\ *ca* 630–562 B.C. Chaldean king of Babylon (605–562)

Nec·ker \nä-'ker, 'ne-kər\ Jacques 1732–1804 *father of Mme. de Staël* Fr. (Swiss-born) financier & statesman

Né·el \nä-el\ Louis-Eugène-Félix 1904–   Fr. physicist

Neh·er \'nä-(ə)r\ Erwin 1944–   Ger. biochem.

Neh·ru \'ner-(ˌ)ü, 'nä-(ˌ)rü\ Ja·wa·har·lal \jə-'wä-hər-ˌläl\ 1889–1964 *son of Motilal* Indian nationalist; prime min. (1947–64)

Nehru Pan·dit \'pən-dət\ Mo·ti·lal \'mō-tᵊl-ˌäl\ 1861–1931 Indian nationalist

Neil·son \'nē(ə)l-sən\ William Allan 1869–1946 Am. (Scot.-born) educ.; pres. Smith College (1917–39)

Nel·son \'nel-sən\ Horatio 1758–1805 Viscount *Nelson* Brit. admiral

Nem·e·rov \'ne-mə-ˌrȯf, -ˌrȯv\ Howard 1920–1991 Am. writer; poet laureate (1988–90)

Ne·pos \'nē-ˌpäs, 'ne-\ Cornelius *ca* 100–*ca* 25 B.C. Rom. hist.

Ne·ri \'ner-ē, 'nä-rē\ Saint Philip 1515–1595 It. *Filippo Neri* Ital. founder (1564) of "Fathers of the Oratory"

Nernst \'nern(t)st\ Walther Hermann 1864–1941 Ger. physicist & chem.

Ne·ro \'nē-(ˌ)rō, 'nir-(ˌ)ō\ A.D. 37–68 *Nero Claudius Caesar Drusus Germanicus* orig. *Lucius Domitius Ahenobarbus* Rom. emp. 54–68 — **Ne·ro·ni·an** \ni-'rō-nē-ən\ *or* **Ne·ron·ic** \-'rä-nik\ *adj*

Ne·ru·da \nā-'rü-də, -(ˌ)thä\ Pablo 1904–1973 *Neftalí Ricardo Reyes Basoalto* Chilean poet & diplomat

Ner·va \'nər-və\ Marcus Cocceius *ca* A.D. 30–98 Rom. emp. (96–98)

Ner·vi \'ner-vē\ Pier Luigi 1891–1979 Ital. engineer & architect

Nes·to·ri·us \ne-'stȯr-ē-əs, -'stȯr-\ *d ca* 451 patriarch of Constantinople (428–431)

Neu·rath \'nȯi-ˌrät\ Konstantin 1873–1956 Freiherr *von Neurath* Ger. diplomat

Nev·el·son \'ne-vəl-sən\ Louise 1900–1988 Am. (Russ.-born) sculptor

Neville Richard — see Earl of WARWICK

Nev·in \'ne-vən\ Ethelbert Woodbridge 1862–1901 Am. composer

Nev·ins \'ne-vənz\ Allan 1890–1971 Am. hist.

New·bolt \'nü-ˌbōlt, 'nyü-\ Sir Henry John 1862–1938 Eng. author

New·comb \'nü-kəm, 'nyü-\ Simon 1835–1909 Am. (Canad.-born) astron.

New·man \'nü-mən, 'nyü-\ John Henry 1801–1890 Eng. cardinal & writer

New·ton \'nü-tᵊn, 'nyü-\ Sir Isaac 1642–1727 Eng. math. & physicist — **New·to·ni·an** \nü-'tō-nē-ən, nyü-, -nyən\ *adj*

Ney \'nā\ Michel 1769–1815 Duc *d'Elchingen; Prince de la Moskova* Fr. soldier; marshal of France

Nich·o·las \'ni-k(ə-)ləs\ Saint 4th cent. Christian prelate

Nicholas name of 2 czars of Russia: **I** 1796–1855 (reigned 1825–55); **II** 1868–1918 (reigned 1894–1917)

Nicholas *Russ* **Ni·ko·lay Ni·ko·lay·e·vich** \'nyē-kə-ˌlī-,nyē-kə-'lī(-ə)-ˌyyich\ 1856–1929 Russ. grand duke & army officer

Nicholas of Cu·sa \-'kyü-sə, -zə\ 1401–1464 Ger. cardinal, math., & philos.

Nich·ol·son \'ni-kəl-sən\ Ben 1894–1982 Brit. painter

Ni·ci·as \'ni-shē-əs, -sē-\ *d* 413 B.C. Athenian gen. & statesman

Nic·o·lay \'ni-kə-ˌlā\ John George 1832–1901 Am. biographer

Nic·o·let \ˌni-kə-'lā, -'let\ Jean 1598–1642 Fr. explorer in No. America

Ni·colle \nē-kȯl\ Charles-Jean-Henri 1866–1936 Fr. physician & bacteriol.

Nic·ol·son \'ni-kəl-sən\ Sir Harold George 1886–1968 Eng. biographer & diplomat

Nie·buhr \'nē-ˌbủr, -bər\ Barthold Georg 1776–1831 Ger. hist., statesman, & philologist

Niebuhr Rein·hold \'rīn-ˌhōld\ 1892–1971 Am. theol. — **Nie·buhr·ian** \nē-'bủr-ē-ən\ *adj*

Niel·sen \'nē(ə)l-sən\ Carl August 1865–1931 Dan. composer

Niem·ce·wicz \nyemt-'sä-vich\ Julian Ursyn 1758–1841 Pol. patriot & writer

Nie·mey·er \'nē-ˌmī(-ə)r\ Oscar 1907–   in full *Oscar Niemeyer Soares Filho* Braz. architect

Nie·möl·ler \'nē-ˌmə(r)l-ər, -ˌmȯel-\ (Friedrich Gustav Emil) Martin 1892–1984 Ger. Protestant theol.

Nietz·sche \'nē-chə, -chē\ Friedrich Wilhelm 1844–1900 Ger. philos. — **Nietz·sche·an** \-chē-ən\ *adj*

Night·in·gale \'nī-tᵊn-ˌgāl, -tiŋ-\ Florence 1820–1910 Eng. nurse & philanthropist

Ni·jin·ska \nə-'zhin-skə, -'jin-\ Bro·ni·sła·wa \ˌbrä-nə-'slä-və\ 1891–1972 *sister of following* Russ. (Pol.-born) dancer & choreographer

Ni·jin·sky \nə-'zhin-skē, -'jin-\ Vas·lav \'vät-släf\ Fomich 1890–1950 Russ. dancer

Nils·son \'nil-sən\ Birgit 1918–   Swed. soprano

Nim·itz \'ni-məts\ Chester William 1885–1966 Am. admiral

Nin \'nēn\ Anaïs 1903–1977 Am. (Fr.-born) author

Ni·ren·berg \'nir-ən-ˌbərg\ Marshall Warren 1927–   Am. geneticist

Nit·ti \'ni-tē, 'nē-\ Francesco Saverio 1868–1953 Ital. econ. & polit.

Nix·on \'nik-sən\ Richard Milhous 1913–1994 Am. polit.; 37th pres. of the U.S. (1969–74) — **Nix·on·esque** \ˌnik-sə-'nesk\ *or* **Nix·o·ni·an** \nik-'sō-nē-ən, -nyən\ *adj*

Nkru·mah \en-'krü-mə, eŋ-\ Kwa·me \'kwä-mē\ 1909–1972 prime min. (1952–60) & 1st pres. (1960–66) of Ghana

No·bel \nō-'bel\ Alfred Bernhard 1833–1896 Swed. manuf., inventor, & philanthropist

No·bi·le \'nȯ-bə-ˌlā\ Umberto 1885–1978 Ital. arctic explorer & aeronautical engineer

No·el–Ba·ker \ˌnō-əl-'bā-kər\ Philip John 1889–1982 Brit. polit.

No·gu·chi \nō-'gü-chē\ Hideyo 1876–1928 Am. (Jp.-born) bacteriol.

Noguchi Isamu 1904–1988 Am. sculptor

Nor·dau \'nȯr-ˌdaú\ Max Simon 1849–1923 orig. *Süd·feld* \'zü̅et-ˌfelt\ Ger. (Hung.-born) physician, author, & Zionist

Nor·den·skiöld \'nủr-dᵊn-ˌshȯld, -ˌshủld, -ˌshēld\ Baron (Nils) Adolf Erik 1832–1901 Swed. arctic explorer

Nor·ris \'nȯr-əs, 'när-\ Benjamin Franklin 1870–1902 *Frank; bro. of C. G.* Am. nov.

Norris Charles Gilman 1881–1945 Am. nov.

Norris George William 1861–1944 Am. statesman

Nor·rish \'nȯr-ish\ Ronald George Wreyford 1897–1978 Brit. chem.

North \'nȯrth\ Christopher — see John WILSON

North Douglass Cecil 1920–   Am. econ.

North Frederick 1732–1792 *Lord North* Eng. statesman; prime min. (1770–82)

North Sir Thomas 1535–?1603 Eng. translator

Northcliffe Viscount — see Alfred C. W. HARMSWORTH

Nor·throp \'nȯr-thrəp\ John Howard 1891–1987 Am. biochem.

Nor·ton \'nȯr-tᵊn\ Charles Eliot 1827–1908 Am. author & educ.

Norton Thomas 1532–1584 Eng. lawyer & poet

Nos·tra·da·mus \ˌnäs-trə-'dä-məs, ˌnōs-, -'dä-\ 1503–1566 *Michel de Notredame* or *Nostredame* Fr. physician & astrologer

No·vel·lo \nō-'ve-(ˌ)lō\ Antonia Coello 1944–   U.S. surgeon general (1990–93)

Noyes \'nȯiz\ Alfred 1880–1958 Eng. poet

Nu·re·yev \nủ-'rä-yəf\ Rudolf Hametovich 1938–1993 Russ.-born ballet dancer

Nut·ting \'nə-tiŋ\ Wallace 1861–1941 Am. antiquarian

Nye \'nī\ Edgar Wilson 1850–1896 *Bill Nye* Am. humorist

Oates \'ōts\ Joyce Carol 1938–   Am. writer

Oates Titus 1649–1705 Brit. fabricator of the Popish Plot

O'·Boyle \ō-'bȯi(ə)l\ Patrick Aloysius 1896–1987 Am. cardinal

Obrenović Alexander I — see ALEXANDER

O'·Ca·sey \ō-'kā-sē\ Sean \'shȯn\ 1880–1964 orig. *John Casey* Irish dram.

Occleve — see Thomas HOCCLEVE

Ochoa \ō-'chō-ə\ Severo 1905–1993 Am. (Span.-born) biochem.

Ochs \'äks\ Adolph Simon 1858–1935 Am. newspaper publisher

Ock·ham *or* **Oc·cam** \'ä-kəm\ William of *ca* 1285–?1349 Eng. philos. — **Ock·ham·is·tic** *or* **Oc·cam·is·tic** \ˌä-kə-'mis-tik\ *adj*

O'·Con·nell \ō-'kä-nᵊl\ Daniel 1775–1847 Irish nationalist

O'Connell William Henry 1859–1944 Am. cardinal

O'·Con·nor \ō-'kä-nər\ (Mary) Flannery 1925–1964 Am. writer

O'Connor Frank 1903–1966 pseud. of *Michael John O'Donovan* Irish author

O'Connor Sandra Day 1930–   Am. jurist
O'Connor Thomas Power 1848–1929 *Tay Pay* \'tā-'pā\ Irish journalist
Octavius — see AUGUSTUS
Odets \ō-'dets\ Clifford 1906–1963 Am. dram.
Odo·a·cer \'ō-də-,wā-sər, 'ä-\ *also* Odo·va·car *or* Odo·va·kar \-vä-kər\ 433–493 1st barbarian ruler of Italy (476–493)
Oe \'ō-ē\ Kenzaburo 1935–   Jp. writer
Oeh·len·schlä·ger \'ə(r)-lən-,shlä-gər, 'œl-\ Adam Gottlob 1779–1850 Dan. poet & dram.
O'·Fao·láin \ō-fə-'lōn\ Seán \'shón\ 1900–1991 Irish author
Of·fen·bach \'ò-fən-,bäk, -,bäk\ Jacques 1819–1880 Fr. composer
O'·Fla·her·ty \ō-'fla-(h)ər-tē\ Li·am \'lē-əm\ 1896–1984 Irish nov.
Og·den \'ò(g)-dən, 'äg-\ Charles Kay 1889–1957 Brit. psychol.
Ogle·thorpe \'ō-gəl-,thórp\ James Edward 1696–1785 Eng. philanthropist, gen., & founder of Georgia
Ogö·dei \'ō-gə-,dā\ *also* Oga·dai \-,dī\ *or* Og·dai \'ò-,dī\ *or* Uge·dei \'ü-gə-,dā\ 1185–1241 Mongol Khan (1229–41)
O'·Hara \ō-'har-ə\ John Henry 1905–1970 Am. author
O'·Hig·gins \ō-'hi-gənz, ō-'ē-gən(t)s\ Bernardo 1778–1842 *Liberator of Chile* Chilean soldier & statesman
Ohira \ō-'hir-ə\ Masayoshi 1910–1980 prime min. of Japan (1978–80)
Oh·lin \'ō-lin\ Bertil Gotthard 1899–1979 Swed. econ.
Ohm \'ōm\ Georg Simon 1787–1854 Ger. physicist
Ois·trakh \'óis-trək\ David Fyodorovich 1908–1974 Russ. violinist
O'·Keeffe \ō-'kēf\ Georgia 1887–1986 Am. painter
O'·Kel·ly \ō-'ke-lē\ Seán \'shón\ Thomas 1883–1966 Irish journalist; pres. of Republic of Ireland (1945–59)
O'·Kelly Seu·mas \'shā-məs\ 1881–1918 Irish writer
Olaf \'ō-ləf, -,läf, -,laf; 'ü-läf\ name of 5 kings of Norway: esp. **Olaf I** Trygg·va·son \'trig-və-sən\ *ca* 964–1000 (reigned 995–1000); **Olaf II** Har·alds·son \'har-əld(z)-sən\ *Saint Olaf* 995?–1030 (reigned 1016–28); **Olaf V** 1903–1991 (reigned 1957–91)
Olah \'ō-la\ George Andrew 1927–   Am. (Hung.-born) chem.
Old·cas·tle \'ōl(d)-,ka-səl\ Sir John 1377?–1417 Baron *Cob·ham* \-'kä-bəm\ Eng. Lollard leader
Ol·den·bar·ne·velt \,ōl-dən-'bär-nə-vəlt\ Johan van 1547–1619 Du. statesman
O'·Lea·ry \ō-'lir-ē\ Hazel Reid 1937–   U.S. secy. of energy (1993–)
Oliv·i·er \ō-'li-vē-,ā\ Laurence Kerr 1907–1989 Baron *Olivier of Brighton* Eng. actor
Olm·sted \'ōm-,sted, 'äm-, -stəd\ Frederick Law 1822–1903 Am. landscape architect
Omar Khay·yám \,ō-,mär-,kī-'yäm, ,ō-mər-, -'yam\ 1048?–1122 Pers. poet & astron.
O'·Neill \ō-'nē(ə)l\ Eugene Gladstone 1888–1953 Am. dram.
On·ions \'ən-yənz\ Charles Talbut 1873–1965 Eng. lexicographer
On·sa·ger \'ón-,sä-gər\ Lars 1903–1976 Am. (Norw.-born) chem.
Op·pen·heim \'ä-pən-,hīm\ Edward Phillips 1866–1946 Eng. nov.
Op·pen·hei·mer \'ä-pən-,hī-mər\ (Julius) Robert 1904–1967 Am. physicist
Or·ca·gna \or-'kän-yə\ Andrea *ca* 1308–*ca* 1368 *Andrea di Cione* Florentine painter, sculptor, & architect
Or·czy \'órt-sē\ Baroness Em·mus·ka \'e-məsh-kə\ 1865–1947 Eng. (Hung.-born) nov. & dram.
Orff \'órf\ Carl 1895–1982 Ger. composer
Or·i·gen \'ór-ə-jən, 'är-\ 185?–?254 Greek (Egypt.-born) Christian writer, teacher, & mystic
Or·lan·do \ór-'lan-(,)dō, -'län-\ Vittorio Emanuele 1860–1952 Ital. statesman
Or·man·dy \'ór-mən-dē\ Eugene 1899–1985 Am. (Hung.-born) conductor
Oroz·co \ō-'ró-(,)skō\ José Clemente 1883–1949 Mex. painter
Ør·sted \'ə(r)-stəd, 'œr-\ Hans Christian 1777–1851 Dan. physicist & chem.
Or·te·ga y Gas·set \ór-'tä-gə-,ē-gä-'set\ José 1883–1955 Span. philos., writer, & statesman
Or·well \'ór-,wel, -wəl, -wəl\ George 1903–1950 pseud. of *Eric Blair* Eng. author — **Or·well·ian** \ór-'we-lē-ən\ *adj*
Os·born \'äz-bərn, -,bórn\ Henry Fairfield 1857–1935 Am. paleontologist
Os·borne \'äz-bərn, -,bórn, -,börn\ John James 1929–1994 Brit. dram.
Osborne Thomas Mott 1859–1926 Am. penologist
Os·car II \'äs-kər\ 1829–1907 king of Sweden (1872–1907) & of Norway (1872–1905)
Osce·o·la \,ä-sē-'ō-lə, ,ō-\ *ca* 1800–1838 Seminole Indian chief
Os·ler \'ōs-lər, 'óz-\ Sir William 1849–1919 Canad. physician
Os·man I \ōs-'män\ 1258–*ca* 1326 founder of the Ottoman Empire
Os·me·ña \óz-'män-yə, ōs-\ Sergio 1878–1961 pres. of Philippine Commonwealth (1944–46)
Os·si·etz·ky \,ä-sē-'et-skē\ Carl von 1889–1938 Ger. writer & pacifist
Ossoli Marchioness — see Margaret FULLER
Ost·wald \'óst-,wóld, -,vóld\ Friedrich Wilhelm 1853–1932 Ger. physical chem. & philos.
Otis \'ō-təs\ Elwell Stephen 1838–1909 Am. gen.
Otis Harrison Gray 1837–1917 Am. gen. & journalist
Otis James 1725–1783 Am. statesman in Revolution
Ot·ter·bein \'ä-tər-,bīn\ Philip William 1726–1813 Am. (Ger.-born) clergyman
Ot·to I \'ä-(,)tō\ 912–973 *the Great* Holy Rom. emp. (936–973)
Ot·way \'ät-,wā\ Thomas 1652–1685 Eng. dram.
Ouida — see Marie Louise de la RAMÉE
Ov·id \'ä-vəd\ 43 B.C.–?A.D. 17 *Publius Ovidius Naso* Rom. poet — **Ovid·ian** \ä-'vi-dē-ən\ *adj*
Ow·en \'ō-ən\ Robert 1771–1858 Welsh social reformer
Owen Wilfred 1893–1918 Brit. poet
Ox·en·stier·na \'ük-sen-,sher-nä\ Count Axel Gustafsson 1583–1654 Swed. statesman
Oxford Earl of — see Robert HARLEY
Paa·si·ki·vi \'pä-sə-,kē-vē\ Ju·ho \'yü-(,)hò\ Kusti 1870–1956 Finn. businessman; pres. of Finland (1946–56)
Pa·de·rew·ski \,pa-də-'ref-skē, -'rev-\ Ignacy \ēn-'yäs\ Jan \'yän\ 1860–1941 Pol. pianist, composer, & statesman
Pa·ga·ni·ni \,pa-gə-'nē-nē, ,pä-\ Niccolò 1782–1840 Ital. violinist

Page \'pāj\ Thomas Nelson 1853–1922 Am. nov. & diplomat
Page Walter Hines 1855–1918 Am. journalist & diplomat
Pag·et \'pa-jət\ Sir James 1814–1899 Eng. surgeon & pathologist
Pahlavi — see REZA SHAH PAHLAVI & MOHAMMAD REZA PAHLAVI
Paine \'pān\ Albert Bigelow 1861–1937 Am. author
Paine Thomas 1737–1809 Am. (Eng.-born) polit. philos. & author
Pain·le·vé \'pan-lə-vä\ Paul 1863–1933 Fr. math. & statesman
Pa·la·de \pə-'lä-dē\ George Emil 1912–   Am. (Romanian-born) biol.
Pa·le·stri·na \,pa-lə-'strē-nə\ Giovanni Pierluigi da *ca* 1525–1594 Ital. composer
Pa·ley \'pā-lē\ William 1743–1805 Eng. theol. & philos.
Pal·grave \'pal-,grāv, 'pòl-\ Francis Turner 1824–1897 Eng. writer
Pal·la·dio \pə-'lä-dē-,ō\ Andrea 1508–1580 Ital. architect
Palma Tomás Estrada — see ESTRADA PALMA
Palm·er \'pä-mər, 'päl-mər\ Alice Elvira 1855–1902 née *Freeman; wife of G. H.* Am. educ.
Palmer Daniel David 1845–1913 Am. chiropractor
Palmer George Herbert 1842–1933 Am. scholar & educ.
Palm·er·ston \'pä-mər-stən, 'päl-\ 3d Viscount 1784–1865 *Henry John Temple* Eng. statesman; prime min. (1855–58; 1859–65) — **Palm·er·sto·nian** \,pä-mər-'stō-nē-ən, ,päl-, -nyən\ *adj*
Palm·gren \'päm-grən, 'pälm-\ Selim 1878–1951 Finn. pianist & composer
Pä·ni·ni \'pä-nə-(,)nē, 'pän-yə-; pä-'nē-nē\ *fl ca* 400 B.C. Indian grammarian of Sanskrit
Pank·hurst \'paŋk-,hərst\ Emmeline 1858–1928 née *Goulden* Eng. suffragist
Pan·ni·ni *or* Pa·ni·ni \pä-'nē-(,)nē\ Giovanni Paolo 1691–1765 Ital. painter
Pa·nof·sky \pä-'nóf-skē\ Erwin 1892–1968 Am. (Ger.-born) art historian
Pa·o·li \'paù-lē, 'pä-ō-(,)lē\ Pasquale 1725–1807 Corsican patriot
Pa·pan·dre·ou \,pä-pän-'drä-ü\ Andreas Georgios 1919–   prime min. of Greece (1981–89; 1993–)
Pa·pen \'pä-pən\ Franz von 1879–1969 Ger. diplomat
Pap·pen·heim \'pä-pən-,hīm, 'pa-\ Gottfried Heinrich 1594–1632 Graf *zu Pappenheim* Ger. gen.
Par·a·cel·sus \,par-ə-'sel-səs\ 1493–1541 pseud. of *Philippus Aureolus Theophrastus Bombast von Hohenheim* Swiss-born alchemist & physician
Pa·re·to \pə-'rā-(,)tō\ Vilfredo 1848–1923 Ital. econ. & sociol.
Par·is \pä-'rēs, pə-\ (Bruno-Paulin-) Gaston 1839–1903 Fr. philologist
Par·is \'par-əs\ Matthew *d* 1259 Eng. monk & hist.
Park Chung Hee \'pärk-'chəŋ-'hē\ 1917–1979 So. Korean leader (1961–79) & pres. (1963–79)
Park \'pärk\ Mungo 1771–1806 Scot. explorer
Par·ker \'pär-kər\ Dorothy 1893–1967 née *Rothschild* Am. writer
Parker Sir Gilbert 1862–1932 Canad. author
Parker Matthew 1504–1575 Eng. theol.
Parker Theodore 1810–1860 Am. Unitarian clergyman
Parkes \'pärks\ Sir Henry 1815–1896 Austral. statesman
Park·man \'pärk-mən\ Francis 1823–1893 Am. hist.
Parks \'pärks\ Rosa Lee 1913–   Am. civil rights activist
Parley Peter — see Samuel Griswold GOODRICH
Par·men·i·des \pär-'me-nə-,dēz\ *b ca* 515 B.C. Greek philos.
Par·mi·gia·ni·no \,pär-mi-jä-'nē-(,)nō\ *or* Par·mi·gia·no \-mə-'jä-(,)nō\ 1503–1540 *Girolamo Francesco Maria Mazzuoli or Mazzola* Ital. painter
Par·nell \pär-'nel\ Charles Stewart 1846–1891 Irish nationalist
Parr Catherine — see CATHERINE
Par·ring·ton \'par-iŋ-tən\ Vernon Louis 1871–1929 Am. lit. hist.
Par·rish \'par-ish\ Maxfield Frederick 1870–1966 Am. painter
Par·ry \'par-ē\ Sir William Edward 1790–1855 Eng. explorer
Par·sons \'pär-s²nz\ Talcott 1902–1979 Am. sociol.
Parsons William 1800–1867 3d Earl of *Rosse* Irish astron.
Pas·cal \pa-'skal, päs-kä´l\ Blaise 1623–1662 Fr. math. & philos. — **Pas·cal·ian** \pa-'skä-lē-ən\ *adj*
Pa·šić \'pä-(,)shich\ Nicola \'nē-kō-lä\ 1845–1926 Serbian & Yugoslav statesman
Pass·field \'pas-,feld\ 1st Baron — see WEBB
Pas·sy \'pa-sē, pä-\ Frédéric 1822–1912 Fr. econ. & statesman
Passy Paul-Edouard 1859–1940 *son of prec.* Fr. phonetician
Pas·ter·nak \'pas-tər-,nak\ Boris Leonidovich 1890–1960 Soviet (Russ.-born) poet, nov., & translator
Pas·teur \pas-'tər\ Louis 1822–1895 Fr. chem. & microbiologist — **Pas·teur·ian** \-ē-ən\ *adj*
Pa·ter \'pä-tər\ Walter Horatio 1839–1894 Eng. essayist & critic
Pat·more \'pat-,mōr, -,mór\ Coventry Kersey Dighton 1823–1896 Eng. poet
Pa·ton \'pä-t³n\ Alan Stewart 1903–1988 So. African writer
Patrick \'pa-trik\ Saint 5th cent. A.D. apostle & patron saint of Ireland
Pat·ti \'pä-tē, 'pä-\ Adelina 1843–1919 Am. (Span.-born) soprano
Pat·ti·son \'pa-tə-sən\ Mark 1813–1884 Eng. scholar & author
Pat·ton \pa-t³n\ George Smith 1885–1945 Am. gen.
Paul \'pòl\ name of 6 popes: esp. **III** 1468–1549 (pope 1534–49); **V** 1552–1621 (pope 1605–21); **VI** (*Giovanni Battista Montini*) 1897–1978 (pope 1963–78)
Paul I 1754–1801 emp. of Russia (1796–1801)
Paul I 1901–1964 king of Greece (1947–64)
Paul Jean — see RICHTER
Paul \'paùl\ Wolfgang 1913–1993 Ger. physicist
Paul–Bon·cour \'pòl-(,)bōⁿ-'kúr\ Joseph 1873–1972 Fr. lawyer & statesman
Paul·ding \'pòl-diŋ\ James Kirke 1778–1860 Am. author
Pau·li \'paù-lē\ Wolfgang 1900–1958 Am. (Austrian-born) physicist
Pau·ling \'pò-liŋ\ Li·nus \'lī-nəs\ Carl 1901–1994 Am. chem.

\ə\ abut \'\ kitten, F table \ər\ further \a\ ash \ā\ ace \ä\ mop, mar
\aù\ out \ch\ chin \e\ bet \ē\ easy \g\ go \i\ hit \ī\ ice \j\ job
\ŋ\ sing \ō\ go \ó\ law \ói\ boy \th\ thin \th\ the \ü\ loot \ù\ foot
\y\ yet \zh\ vision \à, k̟, ⁿ, œ, œ̄, ü, ǖ, ᵊ\ see Guide to Pronunciation

Pau·lus \'paù-ləs\ Friedrich 1890–1957 Ger. field marshal
Pau·lus \'pò-ləs\ Julius 2d–3d cent. A.D. Rom. jurist
Pau·sa·ni·as \pò-'sä-nē-əs\ fl A.D. 143–176 Greek traveler & geographer
Pav·lov \'päv-,lòf, 'pav-, -,lòv\ Ivan Petrovich 1849–1936 Russ. physiol. — Pav·lov·ian \pav-'lò-vē-ən, -'lò-; -'lò-fē-\ adj
Pav·lo·va \'pav-lə-və, pav-'lò-\ Anna 1882–1931 Russ. ballerina
Paz \'päs, 'päz\ Octavio 1914–   Mex. author
Pea·body \'pē-,bä-dē, -bə-dē\ Endicott 1857–1944 Am. educ.
Peabody George 1795–1869 Am. merchant & philanthropist
Pea·cock \'pē-,käk\ Thomas Love 1785–1866 Eng. nov. & poet
Peale \'pē(ə)l\ Charles Willson 1741–1827 & his bro. James 1749–1831 & Charles's son Rembrandt 1778–1860 Am. painters
Pear·son \'pir-s°n\ Karl 1857–1936 Eng. math.
Pearson Lester Bowles 1897–1972 prime min. of Canada (1963–68)
Pea·ry \'pir-ē\ Robert Edwin 1856–1920 Am. polar explorer
Pe·der·sen \'pē-dər-sən\ Charles John 1904–1989 Am. (Korean-born) chem.
Pe·dro \'pā-drō, -drü\ Dom; name of 2 emps. of Brazil: I 1798–1834 (reigned as emp. 1822–31; as king of Portugal 1826); II 1825–1891 (reigned 1831–1889)
Peel \'pē(ə)l\ Sir Robert 1788–1850 Eng. statesman
Peele \'pē(ə)l\ George 1556–1596 Eng. dram. & poet
Pei \'pā\ Ieoh Ming 1917–   Am. (Chin.-born) architect
Peirce \'pərs, 'pirs\ Charles Sanders 1839–1914 Am. physicist, math., & logician — Peirc·ean \'pər-sē-ən, 'pir-\ adj
Pei·sis·tra·tus or Pi·sis·tra·tus \pi-'sis-trə-təs, pə-\ d 527 B.C. Athenian tyrant
Pe·la·gius \pə-'lā-j(ē-)əs\ ca 354–after 418 Brit. monk & theol.
Pe·lop·i·das \pə-'läp-ə-dəs\ d 364 B.C. Theban gen.
Pe·ña \'pe-nyə, 'pā-\ Federico Fabian 1947–   U.S. secy. of transportation (1993–)
Pen·de·rec·ki \,pen-də-'ret-skē\ Krzysztof 1933–   Pol. composer
Penn \'pen\ Sir William 1621–1670 Eng. admiral
Penn William 1644–1718 son of prec. Eng. Quaker & founder of Pennsylvania
Pen·nell \'pe-n°l, pə-'nel\ Joseph 1857–1926 Am. etcher
Pen·rose \'pen-,rōz, pen-'rōz\ Roger 1931–   Brit. math. & physicist
Pen·zi·as \'pent-sē-əs\ Arno Allan 1933–   Am. (Ger.-born) physicist
Pép·in III \'pe-pən\ 714?–768 the Short king of the Franks (751–768)
Pepys \'pēps\ Samuel 1633–1703 Eng. diarist — Pepys·ian \'pēp-sē-ən\ adj
Per·cy \'pər-sē\ Sir Henry 1364–1403 Hotspur Eng. soldier
Percy Thomas 1729–1811 Eng. antiquarian & poet
Percy Walker 1916–1990 Am. writer
Per·el·man \'per-əl-mən (his own pron.), 'pər(-ə)l-\ Sidney Joseph 1904–1979 Am. writer
Per·es \'per-(,)ez\ Shimon 1923–   Israeli foreign minister (1986–88; 1992–)
Pé·rez Gal·dós \'per-əs-(,)gäl-'dōs\ Benito 1843–1920 Span. writer
Pérez Ro·drí·guez \-,ròth-'rē-gäs\ Carlos Andrés 1922–   pres. of Venezuela (1974–79; 1989–93)
Per·go·le·si \,pər-gə-'lā-zē, ,per-gə-'lā-sē\ Giovanni Battista 1710–1736 Ital. composer
Per·i·cles \'per-ə-,klēz\ ca 495–429 B.C. Athenian statesman — Per·i·cle·an \,per-ə-'klē-ən\ adj
Per·kins \'pər-kənz\ Frances 1882–1965 Am. public official
Pe·rón \pā-'rōn, pə-\ Juan Domingo 1895–1974 Argentine polit.; pres. of Argentina (1946–55; 1973–74)
Per·rault \pə-'rō, pe-\ Charles 1628–1703 Fr. writer
Per·rin \pe-'ra°(n), pə-\ Jean-Baptiste 1870–1942 Fr. physicist
Per·ry \'per-ē\ Bliss 1860–1954 Am. educ. & critic
Perry Matthew Calbraith 1794–1858 Am. commodore
Perry Oliver Hazard 1785–1819 bro. of prec. Am. naval officer
Perry Ralph Barton 1876–1957 Am. philos. & educ.
Perry William James 1927–   U.S. secy. of defense (1994–)
Perse St. John — see Aléxis Saint-Léger LÉGER
Per·shing \'pər-shiŋ, -zhiŋ\ John Joseph 1860–1948 Am. gen.
Per·sius \'pər-shəs, 'pər-sē-əs\ A.D. 34–62 Aulus Persius Flaccus Rom. satirist
Pe·ru·gi·no \,per-ə-'jē-(,)nō\ ca 1450–1523 Pietro di Cristoforo Vannucci Ital. painter
Per·utz \pə-'rüts\ Max Ferdinand 1914–   Brit. (Austrian-born) chem.
Pe·ruz·zi \pə-'rüt-sē, pä-\ Baldassare 1481–1536 Ital. architect & painter
Pes·ta·loz·zi \,pes-tə-'lät-sē\ Johann Heinrich 1746–1827 Swiss educ.
Pé·tain \pā-ta°\ Philippe 1856–1951 Fr. gen.; marshal of France; premier of Vichy France (1940–44)
Pe·ter I \'pē-tər\ 1672–1725 the Great czar of Russia (1682–1725)
Peter I 1844–1921 king of Serbia (1903–21)
Peter II 1923–1970 king of Yugoslavia (1934–45)
Peter Cla·ver \'kläv-ər\ Saint 1581–1654 Span. Jesuit missionary
Peter Lom·bard \'läm-,bärd\ ca 1095–1160 L. Petrus Lombardus Ital. theol.
Peter the Hermit ca 1050–1115 Fr. preacher of the 1st Crusade
Pe·ters \'pā-tərz, -tərs\ Carl 1856–1918 Ger. explorer
Pe·tő·fi \'pe-tə-fē\ Sán·dor \'shän-,dòr\ 1823–1849 Hung. poet
Pe·trarch \'pē-,trärk, 'pe-\ 1304–1374 It. Francesco Petrarca Ital. poet — Pe·trarch·an \pē-'trär-kən, pe-\ adj
Pe·trie \'pē-trē\ Sir (William Matthew) Flin·ders \'flin-dərz\ 1853–1942 Eng. Egyptologist
Pe·tro·ni·us \pə-'trō-nē-əs\ d A.D. 66 in full prob. Titus Petronius Niger Rom. satirist — Pe·tro·ni·an \-nē-ən\ adj
Pet·ty \'pe-tē\ Sir William 1623–1687 Eng. polit. econ.
Pevs·ner \'pevz-nər\ Antoine 1886–1962 bro. of Naum Gabo Fr. (Russ.-born) sculptor & painter
Pevsner Sir Nikolaus 1902–1983 Brit. (Ger.-born) art hist.
Phae·drus \'fē-drəs\ 5th cent. B.C. Greek philos.
Phaedrus ca 15 B.C.–ca A.D. 50 Rom. fabulist
Phid·i·as \'fi-dē-əs\ fl ca 490–430 B.C. Greek sculptor
Phil·ip \'fi-ləp\ 1639?–1676 Met·a·com·et \,me-tə-'kä-mət\ Wampanoag Indian chief

Philip name of 6 kings of France: esp. II or Philip Augustus 1165–1223 (reigned 1179–1223); IV (the Fair) 1268–1314 (reigned 1285–1314); VI 1293–1350 (reigned 1328–50)
Philip name of 5 kings of Spain: esp. II 1527–1598 (reigned 1556–98); V 1683–1746 (reigned 1700–24, 1724–46)
Philip II 382–336 B.C. king of Macedon (359–336)
Philip III 1396–1467 the Good Duke of Burgundy (1419–67)
Philip Prince 1921–   consort of Queen Elizabeth II of Great Britain 3d Duke of Edinburgh
Phil·ips \'fi-ləps\ Ambrose 1674–1749 Nam·by-Pam·by \,nam-bē-'pam-bē\ Eng. poet & dram.
Phil·lips \'fi-ləps\ Wendell 1811–1884 Am. orator & reformer
Phill·potts \'fil-,päts\ Eden 1862–1960 Eng. nov. & dram.
Phi·lo Ju·dae·us \'fī-(,)lō-jü-'dē-əs, -'dā-\ ca 13 B.C.–A.D. 45 to 50 Jewish philos. of Alexandria
Pho·ci·on \'fō-sē-,än\ ca 402–318 B.C. Athenian gen. & statesman
Phyfe \'fīf\ Duncan 1768–1854 Am. (Scot.-born) cabinetmaker
Pia·get \pyä-'zhā\ Jean 1896–1980 Swiss psychol. — Pia·get·ian \,pē-ə-'je-tē-ən, pyä-'zhā-ən\ adj
Pi·card \pē-'kär, pi-'kärd\ Jean 1620–1682 Fr. astron.
Pi·cas·so \pi-'kä-(,)sō, -'ka-\ Pablo 1881–1973 Span. painter & sculptor in France
Pic·card \pi-'kär, -'kärd\ Auguste 1884–1962 Swiss physicist
Piccard Jacques-Ernest-Jean 1922–   son of Auguste Swiss (Belg.-born) oceanographer
Pick·er·ing \'pi-k(ə-)riŋ\ Edward Charles 1846–1919 & his bro. William Henry 1858–1938 Am. astron.
Pick·ett \'pi-kət\ George Edward 1825–1875 Am. Confed. gen.
Pi·co del·la Mi·ran·do·la \'pē-(,)kō-,de-lə-mə-'ran-də-lə, -'rän-\ Conte Giovanni 1463–1494 Ital. humanist
Pierce \'pirs\ Franklin 1804–1869 14th pres. of the U.S. (1853–57)
Pie·ro del·la Fran·ces·ca \'pyer-ō-,de-lə-fran-'ches-kə, -frän-\ or de'·Fran·ces·chi \-dā-fran-'ches-kē, -frän-\ ca 1420–1492 Ital. painter
Pike \'pīk\ Zebulon Montgomery 1779–1813 Am. gen. & explorer
Pi·late \'pī-lət\ Pon·tius \'pän-chəs, 'pən-chəs\ d after A.D. 36 Rom. procurator of Judea (26–ca 36)
Pił·sud·ski \pil-'süt-skē, -'züt-\ Józef Klemens 1867–1935 Pol. gen. & statesman
Pin·chot \'pin-,shō\ Gifford 1865–1946 Am. conservationist & polit.
Pinck·ney \'piŋk-nē\ Charles Cotesworth 1746–1825 Am. statesman
Pin·dar \'pin-dər, -,där\ ca 522–ca 438 B.C. Greek poet
Pi·ne·ro \pə-'nir-(,)ō, -'ner-\ Sir Arthur Wing 1855–1934 Eng. dram.
Pin·ker·ton \'piŋ-kər-t°n\ Allan 1819–1884 Am. (Scot.-born) detective
Pi·no·chet Ugar·te \,pē-nō-'chet-ü-'gär-tä\ Augusto 1915–   Chilean gen.; pres. of Chile (1974–90)
Pin·ter \'pin-tər\ Harold 1930–   Eng. dram. — Pin·ter·esque \,pin-tə-'resk\ adj
Pin·tu·ric·chio \,pin-tə-'rē-kē-,ō\ ca 1454–1513 Bernardino di Betto di Biago Ital. painter
Pin·zón \pin-'zōn\ Martín Alonso ca 1441–1493 & his bro. Vicente Yáñez ca 1460–ca 1523 Span. navigators & explorers
Pioz·zi \pē-'òt-sē\ Hester Lynch 1741–1821 Mrs. Thrale \'thrā(ə)l\ Eng. writer
Pi·ran·del·lo \,pir-ən-'de-(,)lō\ Luigi 1867–1936 Ital. author — Pi·ran·del·li·an \-'de-lē-ən\ adj
Pi·ra·ne·si \,pir-ə-'nä-zē\ Giambattista 1720–1778 Ital. architect, painter, & engraver
Pire \'pir\ Dominique Georges 1910–1969 Belg. humanitarian
Pi·sa·no \pi-'sä-(,)nō, -'zä-\ Giovanni ca 1250–after 1314 & his father Nicola ca 1220–1278(or 1284) Ital. sculptors
Pisistratus — see PEISISTRATUS
Pis·sar·ro \pə-'sär-(,)ō\ Camille 1830–1903 Fr. painter
Pis·ton \'pis-tən\ Walter Hamor 1894–1976 Am. composer
Pit·man \'pit-mən\ Sir Isaac 1813–1897 Eng. phonographer
Pitt \'pit\ William 1708–1778 Earl of Chatham; the Elder Pitt Eng. statesman
Pitt William 1759–1806 the Younger Pitt; son of prec. Eng. statesman
Pitt–Riv·ers \'pit-'ri-vərz\ Augustus Henry 1827–1900 Eng. archaeol.
Pi·us \'pī-əs\ name of 12 popes: esp. II (Enea Silvio Piccolomini or Aeneas Sil·vi·us \i-'nē-əs-'sil-vē-əs\ or Syl·vi·us \'sil-vē-əs\) 1405–1464 (pope 1458–64); VII 1742–1823 (pope 1800–23); IX 1792–1878 (pope 1846–78); X 1835–1914 (pope 1903–14); XI (Ambrogio Damiano Achille Ratti) 1857–1939 (pope 1922–39); XII (Eugenio Pacelli) 1876–1958 (pope 1939–58)
Pi·zar·ro \pə-'zär-(,)ō\ Francisco ca 1475–1541 Span. conquistador
Planck \'pläŋk\ Max Karl Ernst Ludwig 1858–1947 Ger. physicist
Plan·tin \plä-ta°\ Christophe ca 1520–1589 Fr. printer
Plath \'plath\ Sylvia 1932–1963 Am. poet
Pla·to \'plā-(,)tō\ ca 428–348(or 347) B.C. Greek philos.
Plau·tus \'plò-təs\ Titus Maccius ca 254–184 B.C. Rom. dram. — Plau·tine \'plò-,tīn\ adj
Ple·kha·nov \plə-'kä-,nòf, pli-'kä-\ Georgy Valentinovich 1857–1918 Russ. Marxist philos.
Ple·ven \plā-'ven\ René 1901–1993 Fr. polit.
Pliny \'pli-nē\ A.D. 23–79 Gaius Plinius Secundus; the Elder Rom. scholar
Pliny A.D. 61(or 62)–ca 113 Gaius Plinius Caecilius Secundus; the Younger; nephew of prec. Rom. author
Plo·ti·nus \plō-'tī-nəs\ A.D. 205–270 Rom. (Egypt.-born) philos. — Plo·tin·i·an \-'ti-nē-ən\ adj
Plu·tarch \'plü-,tärk\ ca A.D. 46–after 119 Greek biographer & moralist — Plu·tarch·an \plü-'tär-kən\ or Plu·tarch·ian \-kē-ən\ adj
Po·ca·hon·tas \,pō-kə-'hän-təs\ ca 1595–1617 dau. of Powhatan Am. Indian
Pod·gor·ny \päd-'gòr-nē\ Nikolay Viktorovich 1903–1983 Soviet polit.; head of Presidium (1965–77)
Poe \'pō\ Edgar Allan 1809–1849 Am. poet & short-story writer
Poin·ca·ré \,pwa°-,kä-'rā\ Jules-Henri 1854–1912 Fr. math.
Poincaré Raymond 1860–1934 cousin of J. H. Fr. statesman; pres. of France (1913–20)
Po·lan·yi \pō-'län-yē\ John Charles 1929–   Canad. (Ger.-born) chem.

Pole \'pōl, 'pül\ Reginald 1500–1558 Eng. cardinal; archbishop of Canterbury (1556–58)
Po·len·ta \pō-'len-tə\ Francesca da d 1283(or 1284) Fran·ces·ca da Ri·mi·ni \,fran-'ches-kə-dä-'ri-mə-(,)nē, ,frän-, -'rē-\ Ital. noblewoman famous for tragic adulterous love affair
Po·li·tian \pə-'li-shən\ 1454–1494 Angelo Poliziano or Angelo Ambrogini Ital. classical scholar & poet
Polk \'pōk\ James Knox 1795–1849 11th pres. of the U.S. (1845–49)
Pol·lio \'pä-lē-,ō\ Gaius Asinius 76 B.C.–A.D. 4 Rom. soldier, orator, & polit.
Pol·lock \'pä-lək\ Sir Frederick 1845–1937 Eng. jurist
Pollock (Paul) Jackson 1912–1956 Am. painter
Po·lo \'pō-(,)lō\ Mar·co \'mär-(,)kō\ 1254–1324 Venetian traveler
Po·lyb·i·us \pə-'li-bē-əs\ ca 200–ca 118 B.C. Greek hist.
Pol·y·carp \'pä-li-,kärp\ Saint 2d cent. Christian martyr & Apostolic Father; bishop of Smyrna
Pol·y·cli·tus or Pol·y·clei·tus \,pä-li-'klī-təs\ 5th cent. B.C. Greek sculptor & architect
Po·lyc·ra·tes \pə-'li-krə-,tēz\ d ca 522 B.C. tyrant of Samos
Pol·y·do·rus \,pä-li-'dōr-əs, -'dȯr-\ 1st cent. B.C. Rhodian sculptor
Pol·yg·no·tus \,pä-lig-'nō-təs\ ca 500–ca 440 B.C. Greek painter
Pom·pa·dour \'päm-pə-,dōr, -,dȯr, -,dur\ Madame de 1721–1764 Jeanne-Antoinette Poisson; mistress of Louis XV
Pom·pey \'päm-pē\ 106–48 B.C. Gnaeus Pompeius Magnus; the Great Rom. gen. & statesman
Pom·pi·dou \'päm-pi-,dü\ Georges-Jean-Raymond 1911–1974 Fr. polit.; premier (1962–68) & pres. (1969–74) of France
Ponce de Le·ón \'pän(t)-sə-,dā-lē-'ōn, ,pänts-də-, -'lē-ən\ Juan 1460–1521 Span. explorer
Pon·chi·el·li \,pȯn-kē-'e-lē\ Amilcare 1834–1886 Ital. composer
Pons \'pänz, 'pōⁿs\ Lily 1904–1976 Am. (Fr.-born) soprano
Pon·selle \pän-'sel\ Rosa Melba 1897–1981 Am. soprano
Pon·ti·ac \'pän-tē-,ak\ ca 1720–1769 Ottawa Indian chief
Pon·top·pi·dan \pän-'tä-pə-,dan\ Henrik 1857–1943 Dan. nov.
Pon·tor·mo \pōn-'tȯr-(,)mō\ Jacopo da 1494–1557 orig. J. Carrucci Ital. painter
Pope \'pōp\ Alexander 1688–1744 Eng. poet — Pop·ian also Pop·ean \'pō-pē-ən\ adj
Pope John 1822–1892 Am. gen.
Por·son \'pȯr-sᵊn\ Richard 1759–1808 Eng. scholar
Por·tal \'pȯr-tᵊl, 'pȯr-\ Charles Frederick Algernon 1893–1971 1st Viscount Portal of Hungerford Brit. air marshal
Por·ter \'pōr-tər, 'pȯr-\ Cole Albert 1891–1964 Am. composer & lyricist
Porter David 1780–1843 & his son David Dixon 1813–1891 Am. naval officers
Porter Eliot Furness 1901–1990 Am. photographer
Porter Gene 1868–1924 née Stratton Am. nov.
Porter Sir George 1920– Brit. chem.
Porter Katherine Anne 1890–1980 Am. writer
Porter Noah 1811–1892 Am. philos. & lexicographer
Porter Rodney Robert 1917–1985 Brit. biochem.
Porter William Sydney 1862–1910 pseud. O. Hen·ry \(')ō-'hen-rē\ Am. short-story writer
Portland Duke of — see BENTINCK
Post \'pōst\ Emily 1872–1960 née Price Am. columnist & writer
Po·tem·kin \pə-'tyȯm(p)-kən, pō-'tem(p)-\ Grigory Aleksandrovich 1739–1791 Russ. field marshal & statesman
Pot·ter \'pä-tər\ Beatrix 1866–1943 Brit. writer & illustrator
Potter Paul or Paulus 1625–1654 Du. painter
Pou·lenc \'pü-,laŋk\ Fran·cis \fräⁿ-sēs\ 1899–1963 Fr. composer
Pound \'paund\ Ezra Loomis 1885–1972 Am. poet — Pound·ian \'paun-dē-ən\ adj
Pound Roscoe 1870–1964 Am. jurist
Pound·mak·er \'paund-,mä-kər\ 1826–1886 Canad. Cree chief
Pous·sin \pü-saⁿ\ Nicolas 1594–1665 Fr. painter
Pow·ell \'pau̇(-ə)l\ Adam Clayton 1908–1972 Am. clergyman & polit.
Pow·ell \'pō-əl, 'pau̇(-ə)l\ Anthony 1905– Eng. writer
Powell Cecil Frank 1903–1969 Brit. physicist
Powell (also Colin Luther 1937– Am. gen.
Powell John Wesley 1834–1902 Am. geologist & explorer
Powell Lewis Franklin 1907– Am. jurist
Pow·ell \'pō-əl, 'pau̇(-ə)l\ Michael Latham 1905–1990 Brit. film director, writer, & producer
Pow·ers \'pau̇(-ə)rz\ Hiram 1805–1873 Am. sculptor
Pow·ha·tan \,pau̇-ə-'tan, pau̇-'ha-tᵊn\ 1550?–1618 Wa-hun-sen-a-cawh or Wahunsonacock; father of Pocahontas Am. Indian chief
Pow·ys \'pō-əs\ John Cow·per \'kü-pər\ 1872–1963 & his bros. Theodore Francis 1875–1953 & Llewelyn 1884–1939 Eng. authors
Pra·do Ugar·te·che \'prä-(,)dō-,ü-gär-'tä-chē\ Manuel 1889–1967 Peruvian banker; pres. of Peru (1939–45; 1956–62)
Pra·ja·dhi·pok \prə-'chä-ti-,päk\ 1893–1941 king of Siam (1925–35)
Pratt \'prat\ Edwin John 1883–1964 Canad. poet
Prax·it·e·les \prak-'si-tᵊl-,ēz\ fl 370–330 B.C. Athenian sculptor — Prax·it·e·le·an \(,)prak-,si-tᵊl-'ē-ən\ adj
Pre·ble \'pre-bəl\ Edward 1761–1807 Am. naval officer
Pregl \'prā-gəl\ Fritz 1869–1930 Austrian chem.
Pre·log \'pre-,lȯg\ Vladimir 1906– Swiss (Bosnian-born) chem.
Pres·cott \'pres-kət also -,kät\ William Hickling 1796–1859 Am. hist.
Pre·to·ri·us \pri-'tȯr-ē-əs, -'tȯr-\ Andries Wilhelmus Jacobus 1798–1853 & his son Marthinus Wessels 1819–1901 So. African Du. colonizers & soldiers
Pré·vost d'Ex·iles \prä-'vō-,deg-'zē(ə)l\ Antoine-François 1697–1763 Fr. abbé & writer
Price \'prīs\ (Mary) Le·on·tyne \lē-'än-,tēn; 'lē-ən-,, 'lä-\ 1927– Am. soprano
Pride \'prīd\ Thomas d 1658 Eng. parliamentary commander
Priest·ley \'prēst-lē\ John Boynton 1894–1984 Eng. author
Priestley Joseph 1733–1804 Eng. clergyman & chem.
Pri·go·gine \prə-'gō-zhən, -(,)gō-'zhēn\ Ilya 1917– Belg. (Russ.-born) chem.
Pri·mo de Ri·ve·ra y Or·ba·ne·ja \'prē-(,)mō-thä-ri-'ver-ə-,ē-,ȯr-bə-'nä-(,)hä\ Miguel 1870–1930 Marqués de Estella Span. gen. & polit.
Primrose Archibald Philip — see ROSEBERY

Prior \'prī(-ə)r\ Matthew 1664–1721 Eng. poet
Pri·scian \'pri-shən, 'pri-shē-ən\ fl A.D. 500 Priscianus Caesariensis Latin grammarian at Constantinople
Pro·clus \'prō-kləs, 'prä-\ 410?–485 Greek philos.
Pro·co·pi·us \prə-'kō-pē-əs\ 6th cent. Byzantine hist.
Pro·kho·rov \,prȯ-kə-'rȯf\ Aleksandr Mikhaylovich 1916– Russ. physicist
Pro·kof·iev \prə-'kȯf-yəf, -,yef, -,yev\ Sergey Sergeevich 1891–1953 Russ. composer — Pro·kof·iev·ian \-,kȯf-'ye-vē-ən\ adj
Pro·per·tius \prō-'pər-sh(ē-)əs\ Sextus ca 50–ca 15 B.C. Rom. poet
Pro·tag·o·ras \prō-'ta-gə-rəs\ ca 485–410 B.C. Greek philos. — Pro·tag·o·re·an \-,ta-gə-'rē-ən\ adj
Proud·hon \prü-dōⁿ\ Pierre-Joseph 1809–1865 Fr. journalist
Proust \'prüst\ Marcel 1871–1922 Fr. nov. — Proust·ian \'prü-stē-ən\ adj
Prynne \'prin\ William 1600–1669 Eng. Puritan pamphleteer
Przhe·val·sky \,pər-zhə-'väl-skē, ,pshə-'väl-\ Nikolay Mikhaylovich 1839–1888 Russ. explorer
Ptol·e·my \'tä-lə-mē\ name of 15 kings of Egypt 323–30 B.C.
Ptolemy 2d cent. A.D. Claudius Ptolemaeus Alexandrian astron.
Puc·ci·ni \pü-'chē-nē\ Giacomo 1858–1924 Ital. composer — Puc·ci·ni·an \-nē-ən\ adj
P'u–i \'pü-'ē, -'yē\ Henry 1906–1967 Hsüan-T'ung Chin. emp. (1908–12); last of Manchu dynasty; puppet emp. of Manchukuo (1934–45)
Pu·las·ki \pə-'las-kē, pyü-\ Kazimierz 1747–1779 Pol. soldier in Am. Revolution
Pu·lit·zer \'pu̇-lət-sər (family's pron.), 'pyü-\ Joseph 1847–1911 Am. (Hung.-born) journalist
Pull·man \'pu̇l-mən\ George Mortimer 1831–1897 Am. inventor
Pu·pin \'pyü-,pēn, pü-\ Michael Idvorsky 1858–1935 Am. (Hung.-born) physicist & inventor
Pur·cell \(,)pər-'sel\ Edward Mills 1912– Am. physicist
Pur·cell \'pər-səl, (,)pər-'sel\ Henry ca 1659–1695 Eng. composer
Pur·chas \'pər-chəs\ Samuel ca 1577–1626 Eng. compiler of travel books
Pur·ky·ně or Pur·kin·je \'pu̇r-kən-,yā\ Jan Evangelista 1787–1869 Bohemian physiol.
Pu·sey \'pyü-zē\ Edward Bouverie 1800–1882 Eng. theol.
Push·kin \'pu̇sh-kən\ Aleksandr Sergeyevich 1799–1837 Russ. poet — Push·kin·ian \'pu̇sh-'ki-nē-ən\ adj
Put·nam \'pət-nəm\ Israel 1718–1790 Am. gen. in Revolution
Putnam Rufus 1738–1824 cousin of prec. Am. gen. in Revolution
Pu·vis de Cha·vannes \pü-,vē-də-shä-'vàn, -vēs-; pyü-,vē(s)-də-shä-'vàn\ Pierre-Cécile 1824–1898 Fr. painter & muralist
Pye \'pī\ Henry James 1745–1813 Eng. poet laureate (1790–1813)
Pyle \'pī(ə)l\ Ernest Taylor 1900–1945 Ernie Am. journalist
Pym \'pim\ John 1584–1643 Eng. statesman
Pyn·chon \'pin-chən\ Thomas 1937– Am. writer — Pyn·chon·esque \,pin-chə-'nesk\ adj
Pyr·rhus \'pir-əs\ 319–272 B.C. king of Epirus (306–302; 297–272 B.C.)
Py·thag·o·ras \pə-'tha-gə-rəs, pī-\ ca 580–ca 500 B.C. Greek philos. & math.
Qad·da·fi — see GADHAFI
Qua·dros \'kwä-,drōs\ Jânio da Silva 1917–1992 pres. of Brazil (1960–61)
Quarles \'kwȯr(-ə)lz, 'kwär(-ə)lz\ Francis 1592–1644 Eng. poet
Qua·si·mo·do \,kwä-'zē-mə-,dō\ Salvatore \,säl-vä-'tō-(,)rä\ 1901–1968 Ital. poet & critic
Quayle \'kwā(ə)l\ James Danforth 1947– Dan Am. polit.; vice pres. of the U.S. (1989–93)
Queensberry Marquis of — see DOUGLAS
Quercia, della Jacopo — see JACOPO DELLA QUERCIA
Ques·nay \kā-'nā\ François 1694–1774 Fr. physician & econ.
Que·zon y Mo·li·na \'kā-,sȯn-,ē-mə-'lē-nə\ Manuel Luis 1878–1944 pres. of the Philippine Commonwealth (1935–44)
Quid·de \'kvi-də, 'kwi-\ Ludwig 1858–1941 Ger. hist. & pacifist
Quil·ler–Couch \'kwi-lər-'küch\ Sir Arthur Thomas 1863–1944 pseud. Q Eng. author
Quin·cy \'kwin-zē, 'kwin(t)-sē\ Josiah 1744–1775 Am. lawyer
Quine \'kwīn\ Willard Van Orman 1908– Am. philos.
Quintero Serafín & Joaquín — see ALVAREZ QUINTERO
Quin·til·ian \kwin-'til-yən\ ca A.D. 35–ca 100 Marcus Fabius Quintilianus Rom. rhetorician
Qui·ri·no \ki-'rē-(,)nō\ Elpidio 1890–1956 pres. of the Philippine Republic (1948–53)
Quoirez Françoise — see Françoise SAGAN
Ra·be·lais \'ra-bə-,lā, ,ra-bə-'lā\ François ca 1483–1553 Fr. humorist & satirist
Ra·bi \'rä-bē\ Isidor Isaac 1898–1988 Am. (Austrian-born) physicist
Ra·bin \,rä-'bēn\ Yitzhak 1922– prime min. of Israel (1974–77; 92–)
Rabinowitz Solomon — see Shalom ALEICHEM
Rach·ma·ni·noff \räk-'mä-nə-,nȯf\ Sergey Vasilyevich 1873–1943 Russ. composer, pianist, & conductor
Ra·cine \rə-'sēn, ra-\ Jean 1639–1699 Fr. dram. — Ra·cin·ian \rə-'si-nē-ən, ra-\ adj
Rack·ham \'ra-kəm\ Arthur 1867–1939 Brit. illustrator
Rad·cliffe \'rad-,klif\ Ann 1764–1823 née Ward Eng. nov.
Ra·detz·ky \rə-'det-skē\ Joseph 1766–1858 Graf Radetzky von Radetz Austrian field marshal
Rae \'rā\ John 1813–1893 Scot. explorer
Rae·burn \'rā-(,)bərn\ Sir Henry 1756–1823 Scot. painter
Rae·der \'rā-dər\ Erich 1876–1960 Ger. admiral
Rae·mae·kers \'rä-,mä-kərz, -kərs\ Louis 1869–1956 Du. cartoonist
Raf·san·ja·ni \,räf-sän-'jä-nē\ Ali Akbar Hashemi 1934– pres. of Iran (1989–)

\ə\ abut \ᵊ\ kitten, F table \ər\ further \a\ ash \ā\ ace \ä\ mop, mar \au̇\ out \ch\ chin \e\ bet \ē\ easy \g\ go \i\ hit \ī\ ice \j\ job \ŋ\ sing \ō\ go \ȯ\ law \ȯi\ boy \th\ thin \th̲\ the \ü\ loot \u̇\ foot \y\ yet \zh\ vision \à, k̲, ⁿ, œ, œ̄, ᵫ, ūe, ʸ\ see Guide to Pronunciation

Rag·lan \'ra-glən\ 1st Baron 1788–1855 *FitzRoy James Henry Somerset* Brit. field marshal

Rai·mon·di \rī-'män-dē, -'mōn-\ Marcantonio *ca* 1480–*ca* 1534 Ital. engraver

Rai·nier III \rə-'nir, ra-, rā-\ 1923–   prince of Monaco (1949–)

Rain·wa·ter \'rān-,wȯ-tər, -,wä-\ L(eo) James 1917–1986 Am. physicist

Ra·ja·go·pa·la·cha·ri \,rä-jə-(,)gō-,pä-lə-'chär-ē\ Chakravarti 1879–1972 Indian polit.; gov.-gen. of India (1948–50)

Ra·leigh *or* **Ra·legh** \'rȯ-lē, 'rä- *also* 'ra-\ Sir Walter 1554–1618 Eng. courtier, navigator, & hist.

Ra·ma·krish·na \,rä-mə-'krish-nə\ 1836–1886 Hindu religious

Ra·man \'rä-mən\ Sir Chan·dra·se·kha·ra \,chən-drə-'shä-kə-rə\ Venkata 1888–1970 Indian physicist

Ra·meau \ra-'mō\ Jean-Philippe 1683–1764 Fr. composer

Ra·mée \rə-'mā\ Marie Louise de la 1839–1908 pseud. *Oui·da* \'wē-də\ Eng. nov.

Ra·món y Ca·jal \rə-'mōn-(,)ē-kə-'häl\ Santiago 1852–1934 Span. histologist

Ra·mos \'rä-(,)mōs\ Fidel V. 1928–   pres. of the Philippines (1992–)

Ram·say \'ram-zē\ Allan 1686–1758 Scot. poet

Ramsay James Andrew Broun 1812–1860 10th Earl & 1st Marquis of *Dal·hou·sie* \dal-'haù-zē\ Brit. colonial administrator

Ramsay Sir William 1852–1916 Brit. chem.

Ram·ses \'ram-,sēz\ *or* **Ram·e·ses** \'ra-mə-,sēz\ name of 11 kings of Egypt: esp. **II** (reigned 1304–1237 B.C.); **III** (reigned 1198–1166 B.C.)

Ram·sey \'ram-zē\ (Arthur) Michael 1904–1988 archbishop of Canterbury (1961–74)

Ramsey Norman Foster 1915–   Am. physicist

Rand \'rand\ Ayn \'īn\ 1905–1982 Am. (Russ.-born) writer

Ran·dolph \'ran-,dälf\ Asa Philip 1889–1979 Am. labor leader

Randolph Edmund Jennings 1753–1813 Am. statesman

Randolph John 1773–1833 *John Randolph of Roanoke* Am. statesman

Ran·jit Singh \'rən-jət-'siŋ\ 1780–1839 *Lion of the Punjab* founder of Sikh kingdom

Ran·ke \'räŋ-kə\ Leopold von 1795–1886 Ger. hist.

Ran·som \'ran(t)-səm\ John Crowe 1888–1974 Am. educ. & poet

Rao \raù, 'rä-ō\ Pamulaparti Venkata Narasimha 1921–   prime min. of India (1991–)

Ra·pha·el \'ra-fē-əl, 'rä-, 'rä-\ 1483–1520 It. *Raffaello Sanzio* Ital. painter — **Ra·pha·el·esque** \,ra-fē-ə-'lesk, ,rä-, ,rä-\ *adj*

Rask \'rask, 'räsk\ Rasmus Kristian 1787–1832 Dan. philologist & orientalist

Ras·mus·sen \'ras-mə-sən, 'räs-,mù-s³n\ Knud Johan Victor 1879–1933 Dan. explorer & ethnologist

Ras·pu·tin \ra-'spyü-t³n, -'spü-, -'spü-\ Grigory Yefimovich 1872–1916 Russ. mystic

Rausch·en·berg \'raù-shən-,berg\ Robert 1925–   Am. artist

Ra·vel \rə-'vel, ra-\ Mau·rice \mȯ-'rēs\ Joseph 1875–1937 Fr. composer — **Ra·vel·ian** \rə-'vel-yən, ra-, -lē-ən\ *adj*

Raw·lin·son \'rȯ-lən-sən\ Sir Henry Cres·wicke \'kre-zik\ 1810–1895 Eng. orientalist

Ray \'rā\ John 1627–1705 Eng. naturalist

Ray Satyajit 1921–1992 Indian film director, writer, & producer

Ray·burn \'rā-(,)bərn\ Samuel Taliaferro 1882–1961 Am. polit.

Ray·leigh \'rā-lē\ Lord 1842–1919 *John William Strutt* Eng. math. & physicist

Read \'rēd\ George 1733–1798 Am. statesman in Revolution

Read Sir Herbert 1893–1968 Eng. writer

Reade \'rēd\ Charles 1814–1884 Eng. nov. & dram.

Read·ing \'re-diŋ\ 1st Marquis of 1860–1935 *Rufus Daniel Isaacs* Brit. statesman; viceroy of India (1921–26)

Rea·gan \'rā-gən\ Ronald Wilson 1911–   Am. actor & polit.; 40th pres. of the U.S. (1981–89) — **Rea·gan·esque** \,rā-gə-'nesk\ *adj*

Ré·au·mur \,rā-ō-'myùr, -'mūēr\ René-Antoine Ferchault de 1683–1757 Fr. naturalist & physicist

Ré·ca·mi·er \rā-'ka-mē-ā, rā-,kä-myā\ Jeanne-Françoise-Julie Adélaïde 1777–1849 Fr. society wit

Red Cloud \'red-,klaùd\ 1822–1909 Sioux Indian chief

Red·mond \'red-mənd\ John Edward 1856–1918 Irish polit.

Re·don \rə-'dōⁿ\ Odilon 1840–1916 Fr. artist

Reed \'rēd\ John 1887–1920 Am. journalist, poet, & communist

Reed Stanley Forman 1884–1980 Am. jurist

Reed Thomas Brackett 1839–1902 Am. polit.

Reed Walter 1851–1902 Am. army surgeon

Reg·u·lus \'re-gyə-ləs\ Marcus Atilius *d ca* 250 B.C. Rom. gen.

Rehn·quist \'ren-,kwist, 'reŋ-kwəst\ William Hubbs 1924–   Am. jurist; chief justice U.S. Supreme Court (1986–)

Reich \'rīsh, 'rīk\ Robert Bernard 1946–   U.S. secy. of labor (1993–)

Reich \'rīk\ Wilhelm 1897–1957 Austrian psychol. — **Reich·ian** \'rī-kē-ən\ *adj*

Reich·stein \'rīk-,shtīn, -,stīn\ Tadeus 1897–   Swiss (Pol.-born) chem.

Reid \'rēd\ Thomas 1710–1796 Scot. philos.

Reid Whitelaw 1837–1912 Am. journalist & diplomat

Rei·ner \'rī-nər\ Fritz 1888–1963 Am. (Hung.-born) conductor

Rein·hardt \'rīn-,härt\ Max 1873–1943 orig. surname *Goldmann* Austrian theater director

Re·marque \rə-'märk\ Erich Maria 1898–1970 Am. (Ger.-born) nov.

Rem·brandt \'rem-,brant *also* -,bränt\ 1606–1669 in full *Rembrandt Harmensz* \,rem-,bran-'tesk, -,brän-\ *adj* *van Rijn* (*or Ryn*) Du. painter — **Rem·brandt·esque** \,rem-,bran-'tesk, -,brän-\ *adj*

Rem·ing·ton \'re-miŋ-tən\ Frederic 1861–1909 Am. artist

Rem·sen \'rem(p)-sən, 'rem-zən\ Ira 1846–1927 Am. chem.

Re·nan \rə-'näⁿ(n)\ Joseph Ernest 1823–1892 Fr. philologist & hist.

Re·nault \rə-'nō\ Louis 1843–1918 Fr. jurist & pacifist

Re·ni \'rā-nē\ Guido 1575–1642 Ital. painter

Ren·ner \'re-nər\ Karl 1870–1950 pres. of Austria (1945–50)

Re·no \'rē-(,)nō\ Janet 1938–   U.S. atty. gen. (1993–)

Re·noir \'ren-,wär, rən-'\ Jean 1894–1979 *son of P.-A.* Fr. film director & writer

Renoir Pierre-Auguste 1841–1919 Fr. painter

Ren·wick \'ren-(,)wik\ James 1818–1895 Am. architect

Rep·plier \'re-,plir, -plē-ər\ Agnes 1855–1950 Am. essayist

Re·spi·ghi \rə-'spē-gē, re-\ Ottorino 1879–1936 Ital. composer

Res·ton \'res-tən\ James Barrett 1909–   Am. journalist

Retz \'rets, *Fr* re(s)\ Cardinal de 1613–1679 *Jean-François-Paul de Gondi* Fr. ecclesiastic & polit.

Reuch·lin \'rȯi-klən; -,klēn, rȯi-'\ Johannes 1455–1522 *Cap·nio* \'kap-nē-,ō\ Ger. humanist

Reu·ter \'rȯi-tər\ Baron Paul Julius von 1816–1899 orig. *Israel Beer Josaphat* Brit. (Ger.-born) journalist

Reu·ther \'rü-thər\ Walter Philip 1907–1970 Am. labor leader

Re·vere \ri-'vir\ Paul 1735–1818 Am. patriot & silversmith

Rex·roth \'reks-,rȯth\ Kenneth 1905–1982 Am. writer

Rey·mont \'rā-,mänt\ *or* **Rej·ment** \'rā-,ment\ Wła·dy·sław \vlä-'di-,släf\ Sta·ni·sław \stä-'nē-,släf\ 1867–1925 Pol. nov.

Rey·naud \rā-'nō\ Paul 1878–1966 premier of France (1940)

Reyn·olds \'re-n³l(d)z\ Sir Joshua 1723–1792 Eng. painter

Re·za Shah Pah·la·vi \ri-'zä-'shä-'pa-lə-(,)vē, -'shȯ-\ 1878–1944 *father of Mohammad Reza Pahlavi* shah of Iran (1925–41)

Rhee \'rē\ Syng·man \'siŋ-mən, 'sig-\ 1875–1965 So. Korean polit.; pres. of So. Korea (1948–60)

Rhodes \'rōdz\ Cecil John 1853–1902 Brit. administrator & financier in So. Africa

Rhond·da \'rän-də, -thə\ 1st Viscount 1856–1918 *David Alfred Thomas* Brit. industrialist & administrator

Rib·ben·trop \'ri-bən-,träp, -,trȯp\ Joachim von 1893–1946 Ger. diplomat

Ri·be·ra \rē-'ber-ə\ José (*or* Jusepe) de 1591–1652 *Lo Spa·gno·let·to* \,lō-,spän-yə-'le-(,)tō\ Span. painter & etcher in Naples

Ri·car·do \ri-'kär-(,)dō\ David 1772–1823 Eng. econ.

Rice \'rīs\ Elmer Leopold 1892–1967 orig. *Elmer Reizenstein* Am. dram.

Rich·ard \'ri-chərd\ name of 3 kings of England: **I** (*Coeur de Li·on* \,kər-də-'lī-ən, -'lē-; -lē-'ōⁿ\) 1157–1199 (reigned 1189–99); **II** 1367–1400 (reigned 1377–99); **III** 1452–1485 (reigned 1483–85)

Rich·ards \'ri-chərdz\ Ann 1933–   orig. *Dorothy Ann Willis* Am. polit.

Richards Dickinson Woodruff 1895–1973 Am. physician

Richards Theodore William 1868–1928 Am. chem.

Rich·ard·son \'ri-chərd-sən\ Henry Handel 1870–1946 pseud. of *Ethel Florence Lindesay Richardson* Austral. nov.

Richardson Henry Hobson 1838–1886 Am. architect

Richardson Sir Owen Willans 1879–1959 Eng. physicist

Richardson Sir Ralph David 1902–1983 Brit. actor

Richardson Samuel 1689–1761 Eng. nov.

Ri·che·lieu \'ri-shə-,lü, -shəl-,yü; rē-shə-lyœ\ Duc de 1585–1642 *Armand-Jean du Plessis* Fr. cardinal & statesman

Ri·chet \rē-'shā\ Charles Robert 1850–1935 Fr. physiol.

Rich·ter \'rik-tər\ Burton 1931–   Am. physicist

Richter Charles Francis 1900–1985 Am. seismologist

Richter \'rik-tər, 'rik\ Jean Paul Friedrich 1763–1825 pseud. *Jean Paul* \'zhäⁿ-'paùl\ Ger. writer

Ric·i·mer \'ri-sə-mər\ Flavius *d* 472 Rom. gen.

Rick·en·back·er \'ri-kən-,ba-kər\ Edward Vernon 1890–1973 Am. aviator

Rick·o·ver \'ri-,kō-vər\ Hyman George 1900–1986 Am. admiral

Rid·ley \'rid-lē\ Nicholas *ca* 1503–1555 Eng. reformer & martyr

Ri·el \rē-'el\ Louis 1844–1885 Canad. insurgent

Rie·mann \'rē-,män\ Georg Friedrich Bernhard 1826–1866 Ger. math. — **Rie·mann·ian** \rē-'mä-nē-ən\ *adj*

Rien·zo \'ryent-sō\ Cola di 1313–1354 prename *Niccolò* Ital. leader

Ries·man \'rēs-mən\ David 1909–   Am. social scientist

Riis \'rēs\ Jacob August 1849–1914 Am. (Dan.-born) social reformer

Ri·ley \'rī-lē\ James Whit·comb \'hwit-kəm, 'wit-\ 1849–1916 Am. poet

Riley Richard Wilson 1933–   U.S. secy. of education (1993–)

Ril·ke \'ril-kə, -kē\ Rai·ner \'rī-nər\ Maria 1875–1926 Ger. poet

Rim·baud \ra(m)-'bō, 'ram-,\ (Jean-Nicholas-)Arthur 1854–1891 Fr. poet

Rimini Francesca da — see POLENTA

Rim·sky–Kor·sa·kov \,rim(p)-skē-'kȯr-sə-,kȯf, -,kȯv, -,kȯr-sə-\ Nikolay Andreyevich 1844–1908 Russ. composer

Rine·hart \'rīn-,härt\ Mary 1876–1958 née *Roberts* Am. writer

Rí·os \'rē-,ōs\ Juan Antonio 1888–1946 pres. of Chile (1942–46)

Rip·ley \'ri-plē\ George 1802–1880 Am. lit. critic & socialist

Ri·ve·ra \ri-'ver-ə\ Diego 1886–1957 Mex. painter

Riv·ers \'ri-vərz\ Larry 1923–   Am. artist

Ri·zal \ri-'zäl, -'säl\ José Protasio 1861–1896 Filipino patriot

Riza Shah Pahlavi *var of* REZA SHAH PAHLAVI

Riz·zio \'rit-sē-,ō\ *or* **Ric·cio** \'ri-chē-,ō\ David *ca* 1533–1566 Ital. musician & favorite of Mary, Queen of Scots

Robbe–Gril·let \,rȯb-bə-grē-'yä\ Alain 1922–   Fr. writer

Robbia, della Luca — see DELLA ROBBIA

Rob·bins \'rä-bənz\ Frederick Chapman 1916–   Am. physician

Robbins Jerome 1918–   Am. dancer & choreographer

Robert I \'rä-bərt\ *d* 1035 *the Devil* Duke of Normandy (1027–35) *father of William the Conqueror*

Robert I 1274–1329 *the Bruce* \'brüs\ king of Scotland (1306–1329)

Robert Guis·card \-gē-'skär\ *ca* 1015–1085 *Robert de Hauteville* Norman mil. leader

Rob·erts \'rä-bərts\ Sir Charles George Douglas 1860–1943 Canad. poet

Roberts Frederick Sleigh 1832–1914 1st Earl *Roberts* Brit. field marshal

Roberts Kenneth 1885–1957 Am. nov.

Roberts Owen Josephus 1875–1955 Am. jurist

Roberts Richard John 1943–   Am. (Brit.-born) biol.

Rob·ert·son \'rä-bərt-sən\ William 1721–1793 Scot. hist.

Robe·son \'rōb-sən\ Paul Bustill 1898–1976 Am. actor & singer

Robes·pierre \'rōbz-,pir, -,pyer; ,rō-,bes-'pyer\ Maximilien-François-Marie-Isidore de 1758–1794 Fr. revolutionary

Rob·in·son \'rä-bən-sən\ Edwin Arlington 1869–1935 Am. poet

Robinson George Frederick Samuel 1827–1909 1st Marquis & 2d Earl of *Ripon* Brit. statesman

Robinson James Harvey 1863–1936 Am. hist.
Robinson Sir Robert 1886–1975 Eng. chem.
Ro·cham·beau \,rō-,sham-'bō\ Comte de 1725–1807 *Jean-Baptiste Donatien de Vimeur* Fr. field marshal
Rocke·fel·ler \'rä-ki-,fe-lər\ John Davison father 1839–1937 & son 1874–1960 Am. oil magnates & philanthropists
Rockefeller Nelson Aldrich 1908–1979 *grandson & son of prec.* Am. polit.; vice pres. of the U.S. (1974–77)
Rock·ing·ham \'rä-kiŋ-əm, *US also* -kiŋ-,ham\ 2d Marquis of 1730–1782 *Charles Watson-Wentworth* Eng. statesman
Rock·ne \'räk-nē\ Knute \'nüt\ Kenneth 1888–1931 Am. (Norw.-born) football coach
Rock·well \'räk-,wel, -wəl\ Norman 1894–1978 Am. illustrator
Rod·bell \'räd-(,)bel\ Martin 1925– Am. biochem.
Ro·de \'rō-thə\ Hel·ge \'hel-gə\ 1870–1937 Dan. poet
Rod·gers \'rä-jərz\ Richard 1902–1979 Am. composer
Ro·din \'rō-daⁿ(n)\ (François-)Auguste(-René) 1840–1917 Fr. sculptor — Ro·din·esque \,rō,da-'nesk\ *adj*
Rod·ney \'räd-nē\ George Bryd·ges \'bri-jəz\ 1718–1792 1st Baron *Rodney* Eng. admiral
Ro·dri·guez Pe·dot·ti \,rōth-'rē-gäs-pā-'dòt-tē\ Andrés 1923– pres. of Paraguay (1989–93)
Roeb·ling \'rō-bliŋ\ John Augustus 1806–1869 Am. (Ger.-born) civil engineer
Roentgen — see RÖNTGEN
Roe·rich \'rer-ik, 'rer-\ Nikolay Konstantinovich 1874–1947 Russ. painter
Roeth·ke \'ret-kē, 'reth-\ Theodore 1908–1963 Am. poet
Rog·ers \'rä-jərz\ Bruce 1870–1957 Am. printer & book designer
Rogers Carl Ranson 1902–1987 Am. psychol.
Rogers Henry Hut·tle·ston \'hə-tᵊl-stən\ 1840–1909 Am. financier
Rogers Robert 1731–1795 Am. frontiersman
Rogers William Penn Adair 1879–1935 *Will* Am. actor & humorist
Ro·get \rō-'zhā, 'rō-,\ Peter Mark 1779–1869 Eng. physician & scholar
Rohr·er \'ròr-ər\ Heinrich 1933– Swiss physicist
Roh Tae Woo \'rō-'tā-'ü, 'nò-, -'wü\ 1932– pres. of So. Korea (1988–93)
Ro·kos·sov·sky \,rä-kə-'sòf-skē, -'sòv-\ Konstantin Konstantinovich 1896–1968 marshal of Soviet Union
Rolfe \'rälf\ John 1585–1622 Eng. colonist
Rol·land \rō-'läⁿ, rò-\ Romain 1866–1944 Fr. author
Röl·vaag \'rōl-,väg\ Ole \'ō-lə\ Ed·vart \'ed-,värt\ 1876–1931 Am. (Norw.-born) educ. & nov.
Ro·mains \rō-'maⁿ\ Jules 1885–1972 pseud. of *Louis-Henri-Jean Farigoule* Fr. author
Romano Giulio — see GIULIO ROMANO
Ro·ma·nov *or* Ro·ma·noff \rō-'mä-nəf, 'rō-mə-,näf\ Michael 1596–1645 1st czar (1613–45) of Russ. Romanov dynasty (1613–1917)
Rom·berg \'räm-,bərg\ Sigmund 1887–1951 Am. (Hung.-born) composer
Rom·mel \'rä-məl\ Erwin Johannes Eugen 1891–1944 Ger. field marshal
Rom·ney \'räm-nē, 'rəm-\ George 1734–1802 Eng. painter
Ron·sard \rōⁿ-'sär\ Pierre de 1524–1585 Fr. poet
Rönt·gen *or* Roent·gen \'rent-gən, 'rənt-, -jən\ \'ren-chən, 'rən-\ Wilhelm Conrad 1845–1923 Ger. physicist
Roo·se·velt \'rō-zə-,velt (*Roosevelts' usual pron.*), -,velt *also* \'rü-\ (Anna) Eleanor 1884–1962 née *Roosevelt, wife of F.D.* Am. humanitarian & writer
Roosevelt Franklin Del·a·no \'de-lə-,nō\ 1882–1945 32d pres. of the U.S. (1933–45) — Roo·se·velt·ian \,rō-zə-'vel-tē-ən, -vel-tē-ən, -sh(ē-)ən\ *adj*
Roosevelt Theodore 1858–1919 26th pres. of the U.S. (1901–09)
Root \'rüt, 'rüt\ Elihu 1845–1937 Am. lawyer & statesman
Ro·sa \'rō-zə\ Salvator 1615–1673 Ital. painter & poet
Rose·bery \'rōz-,ber-ē, -b(ə)rē\ 5th Earl of 1847–1929 *Archibald Philip Prim·rose* \'prim-,rōz\ Eng. statesman
Rose·crans \'rō-zə-,kranz, 'rōz-,kran(t)s\ William Starke 1819–1898 Am. gen.
Ro·sen·berg \'rō-zᵊn-,bərg, -,berg\ Alfred 1893–1946 Ger. Nazi & writer
Ro·sen·wald \'rō-zᵊn-,wóld\ Julius 1862–1932 Am. merchant & philanthropist
Ross \'ròs\ Betsy 1752–1836 née *Griscom* reputed maker of 1st Am. flag
Ross Sir James Clark 1800–1862 Scot. explorer
Ross Sir John 1777–1856 *uncle of prec.* Scot. explorer
Ross Sir Ronald 1857–1932 Brit. physician
Rosse Earl of — see William PARSONS
Ros·set·ti \rō-'ze-tē, -'se-\ Christina Georgina 1830–1894 *sister of D.G.* Eng. poet
Rossetti Dante Gabriel 1828–1882 Eng. painter & poet
Ros·si \'rò-sē\ Bruno 1905–1993 Am. (Ital.-born) physicist
Ros·si·ni \rō-'sē-nē, rə-\ Gio·ac·chi·no \,jō-ə-'kē-(,)nō\ Antonio 1792–1868 Ital. composer — Ros·si·ni·an \-'sē-nē-ən\ *adj*
Ros·tand \rò-stäⁿ, 'räs-,tand\ Edmond 1868–1918 Fr. poet & dram.
Ro·ta \'rō-(,)tä\ Nino 1911–1979 Ital. composer
Roth \'ròth\ Philip 1933– Am. writer
Roth·ko \'räth-(,)kō\ Mark 1903–1970 Am. (Russ.-born) painter
Roth·schild \'ròth(s)-,chīld, 'rós-, G 'rōt-,shilt\ Mayer Amschel 1744–1812 Ger. financier
Rothschild Nathan Mayer 1777–1836 *son of prec.* financier in London
Rou·ault \rü-'ō\ Georges 1871–1958 Fr. painter
Rou·get de Lisle \(,)rü-'zhā-də-'lē(ə)l\ Claude-Joseph 1760–1836 Fr. army officer & composer
Rous \'raùs\ Francis Peyton 1879–1970 Am. pathologist
Rous·seau \rü-'sō, 'rü-,\ Henri-Julien-Félix 1844–1910 *le Douanier* Fr. painter
Rousseau Jean-Jacques 1712–1778 Fr. (Swiss-born) philos. & writer — Rous·seau·esque \,rü-sō-'esk, ,rü-\ *or* Rous·seau·ian \-'sō-ē-ən\ *adj*
Rousseau (Pierre-Étienne-) Théodore 1812–1867 Fr. painter
Rowe \'rō\ Nicholas 1674–1718 Eng. poet & dram.; poet laureate (1715–18)
Row·land·son \'rō-lən(d)-sən\ Thomas 1756–1827 Eng. caricaturist
Row·ley \'rō-lē, 'raù-\ William 1585?–?1642 Eng. actor & dram.

Ro·xas y Acu·ña \'rò-,häs-,ē-ə-'kün-yə\ Manuel 1892–1948 Philippine statesman; pres. of the Philippine Republic (1946–48)
Royce \'ròis\ Josiah 1855–1916 Am. philos.
Rub·bia \'rü-bē-ə\ Carlo 1934– Ital. physicist
Ru·bens \'rü-bənz\ Peter Paul 1577–1640 Flem. painter — Ru·ben·si·an \'rü-'ben-zē-ən\ *adj*
Ru·bin \'rü-bən\ Robert Edward 1938– U.S. secy. of treasury (1995–)
Ru·bin·stein \'rü-bən-,stīn\ An·ton \än-'tòn\ 1829–1894 Russ. pianist & composer
Rubinstein Arthur 1887–1982 Am. (Pol.-born) pianist
Rud·olf \'rü-,dälf\ 1858–1889 archduke & crown prince of Austria
Rudolf I 1218–1291 Holy Rom. emp. (1273–91); 1st of the Hapsburgs
Ruis·dael *or* Ruys·dael \'rīz-,däl, 'rīs-\ Jacob van 1628(or 1629)–1682 & his uncle Salomon van *ca* 1602–1670 Du. painters
Rumford Count — see Benjamin THOMPSON
Run·cie \'rən(t)-sē\ Robert Alexander Kennedy 1921– archbishop of Canterbury (1980–91)
Rund·stedt \'rùn(t)-,shtet\ Karl Rudolf Gerd von 1875–1953 Ger. field marshal
Ru·ne·berg \'rü-nə-,bərg, -,ber-ē\ Johan Ludvig 1804–1877 Finn. poet
Run·yon \'rən-yən\ (Alfred) Da·mon \'dā-mən\ 1884–1946 Am. author — Run·yon·esque \,rən-yə-'nesk\ *adj*
Ru·pert \'rü-pərt\ Prince 1619–1682 Count *Palatine of Rhine* & Duke of *Bavaria* Eng. (Ger.-born) Royalist gen. & admiral
Rush \'rəsh\ Benjamin 1745–1813 Am. physician & patriot
Rush Richard 1780–1859 *son of prec.* Am. diplomat & statesman
Rush·die \'rəsh-(,)dē, 'rúsh-\ (Ahmed) Salman 1947– Brit. (Indian-born) writer
Rusk \'rəsk\ (David) Dean 1909–1994 U.S. secy. of state (1961–69)
Rus·ka \'rüs-kə\ Ernst August Friedrich 1906–1988 Ger. physicist
Rus·kin \'rəs-kən\ John 1819–1900 Eng. essayist, critic, & reformer — Rus·kin·ian \,rəs-'ki-nē-ən\ *adj*
Rus·sell \'rə-səl\ Bertrand Arthur William 1872–1970 3d Earl *Russell* Eng. math. & philos.
Russell Charles Taze 1852–1916 Am. religious leader
Russell George William 1867–1935 pseud. Æ \'ä-'ē\ Irish author
Russell John 1792–1878 1st Earl *Russell of Kingston Russell* Brit. statesman
Russell Lillian 1861–1922 *Helen Louise Leonard* Am. singer & actress
Rus·tin \'rəs-tən\ Bayard 1910–1987 Am. civil rights leader
Ruth \'rüth\ George Herman 1895–1948 *Babe Ruth* or *the Babe* Am. baseball player — Ruth·ian \'rü-thē-ən\ *adj*
Ruth·er·ford \'rə-thə(r)-fərd, -thə(r)-\ Ernest 1871–1937 1st Baron *Rutherford of Nelson* Brit. physicist
Rutherford Joseph Franklin 1869–1942 Am. leader of Jehovah's Witnesses
Rut·ledge \'rət-lij\ John 1739–1800 Am. statesman & jurist; chief justice U.S. Supreme Court (1795)
Rutledge Wiley Blount \'blənt\ 1894–1949 Am. jurist
Ru·žič·ka \'rü-,zhich-kə, -,zich-, -,zhits-\ Leopold 1887–1976 Swiss (Croatian-born) chem.
Ry·der \'rī-dər\ Albert Pinkham 1847–1917 Am. painter
Rydz–Smig·ly \'rits-'shmē-glē\ Edward 1886–1941 Pol. gen.
Ryle \'rī(ə)l\ Sir Martin 1918–1984 Brit. astron.
Saa·ri·nen \'sär-ə-nən\ Ee·ro \er-(,)ō\ 1910–1961 Am. architect
Saarinen (Gottlieb) Eliel 1873–1950 *father of prec.* Finn. architect
Saa·ve·dra La·mas \sä-'vä-drə-'lä-məs, -'vä-thrə-\ Carlos 1878–1959 Argentine lawyer & diplomat
Sa·ba·tier \,sa-bə-'tyā\ Paul 1854–1941 Fr. chem.
Sa·ba·ti·ni \,sa-bə-'tē-nē, sä-\ Rafael 1875–1950 Eng. (Ital.-born) author
Sa·bin \'sā-bin\ Albert Bruce 1906–1993 Am. physician
Sac·a·ga·wea *also* Sac·a·ja·wea \,sa-kə-jə-'wē-ə\ 1786?–1812 Am. Indian guide
Sac·co \'sa-(,)kō\ Nicola 1891–1927 & Van·zet·ti \van-'ze-tē\ Bartolomeo 1888–1927 Am. (Ital.-born) anarchists
Sachs \'zäks, 'saks\ Hans 1494–1576 Ger. poet & Meistersinger
Sachs \'saks, 'zäks\ Nelly 1891–1970 Swed. (Ger.-born) dram. & poet
Sack·ville \'sak-,vil\ Thomas 1536–1608 1st Earl of *Dorset* Eng. poet & diplomat
Sackville–West \-'west\ Victoria Mary 1892–1962 *Vita* Eng. writer
Sā·dāt \sə-'dat, -'dät\ Anwar el- 1918–1981 pres. of Egypt (1970–81)
Sade, de \də-'säd\ Comte Donatien-Alphonse-François 1740–1814 *Marquis de Sade* Fr. writer of erotica
Sa·gan \sä-'gäⁿ\ Françoise 1935– pseud. of *Françoise Quoi·rez* \kwä-rā\ Fr. writer
Sage \'sāj\ Russell 1816–1906 Am. financier
St. Den·is \sänt-'de-nəs, sənt-\ Ruth 1878–1968 Am. dancer & choreographer
Sainte–Beuve \saⁿt-bœv; sänt-'bə(r)v, sənt-\ Charles-Augustin 1804–1869 Fr. critic & author
Saint–Gau·dens \sänt-'gò-d'nz, sənt-\ Augustus 1848–1907 Am. (Irish-born) sculptor
St. John Henry — see BOLINGBROKE
Saint–Just \saⁿ-zhüest; sänt-'jəst, sənt-\ Louis-Antoine-Léon de 1767–1794 Fr. revolutionary
St. Lau·rent \saⁿ-lò-räⁿ\ Louis Stephen 1882–1973 Canad. polit.; prime min. (1948–57)
Saint–Pierre — see BERNARDIN DE SAINT-PIERRE
Saint–Saëns \saⁿ-säⁿs\ (Charles-) Camille 1835–1921 Fr. composer
Saints·bury \'sänts-,ber-ē, -b(ə-)rē\ George Edward Bateman 1845–1933 Eng. critic
Saint–Si·mon \saⁿ-sē-mōⁿ\ Claude-Henri de Rouvroy 1760–1825 Comte *de Saint-Simon* Fr. philos. & social scientist
Saint–Simon Louis de Rouvroy 1675–1755 Duc *de Saint-Simon* Fr. soldier, statesman, & writer

---

\ə\ abut \ᵊ\ kitten, F table \ər\ further \a\ ash \ā\ ace \ä\ mop, mar
\aù\ out \ch\ chin \e\ bet \ē\ easy \g\ go \i\ hit \ī\ ice \j\ job
\ŋ\ sing \ō\ go \ò\ law \òi\ boy \th\ thin \t̲h̲\ the \ü\ loot \ù\ foot
\y\ yet \zh\ vision \à, k̲, ⁿ, œ, œ̄, ɷ, ūe, ᵞ\ *see* Guide to Pronunciation

Sai·on·ji \sī-'än-jē, -'òn-\ Prince Kimmochi 1849–1940 Jp. statesman
Sa·kha·rov \'sä-kə-,róf, -kə-, -,ròv\ Andrey Dmitriyevich 1921–1989 Russ. physicist
Sa·ki \'sä-kē\ — see H. H. MUNRO
Sak·mann \'zäk-,män, 'säk-\ Bert 1942– Ger. biochem.
Sal·a·din \'sa-lə-,dēn, -dən; ,sa-lə-'dēn\ 1137(or 1138)–1193 *Salāḥ Ad-dīn Yūsuf Ibn Ayyūb* Syrian commander & vizier in Egypt
Sa·lam \sä-'läm\ Abdus 1926– Pakistani physicist
Sa·la·zar \sä-lə-'zär, ,sä-\ Antonio de Oliveira 1889–1970 Port. dictator (1932–68)
Sa·li·nas de Gor·ta·ri \sä-'lē-näs-thä-gòr-'tä-rē\ Carlos 1948– pres. of Mexico (1988–94)
Sal·in·ger \'sa-lən-jər\ Jerome David 1919– Am. nov.
Salisbury 1st Earl of & 3d Marquis of — see CECIL
Salk \'sò(l)k\ Jonas Edward 1914–1995 Am. physician
Sal·lust \'sa-ləst\ *ca* 86–35(or 34) B.C. *Gaius Sallustius Crispus* Rom. hist. & polit. — **Sal·lus·ti·an** \sə-'ləs-tē-ən, sa-\ *adj*
Sal·o·mon \'sa-lə-mən\ Haym 1740–1785 Am. (Pol.-born) merchant
Sam·per Pi·za·no \'säm-per-pē-'sä-nō\ Ernesto 1950– pres. of Colombia (1994–)
Sam·u·el·son \'sam-yə-(wə)l-sən\ Paul Anthony 1915– Am. econ.
Sam·u·els·son \'sam-yə-(wə)l-sən\ Bengt I. 1934– Swed. biochem.
Sánchez de Bustamante y Sirvén Antonio — see BUSTAMANTE Y SIRVÉN
Sand \'sand, 'sän(d)d, säⁿ\ George 1804–1876 pseud. of *Amandine Aurore-Lucie* (or *-Lucile*) *Du·de·vant* \düed-vän, düe-də-\ née *Dupin* Fr. writer
Sand·burg \'san(d)-,bərg\ Carl 1878–1967 Am. author
San·gal·lo \sän-'gä-(,)lō, säŋ-\ Giuliano da 1445?–1516 Florentine architect & sculptor
Sang·er \'saŋ-ər\ Frederick 1918– Brit. chem.
Sanger Margaret 1883–1966 née *Higgins* Am. birth-control leader
San Mar·tín \,san-(,)mär-'tēn, ,sän-\ José de 1778–1850 So. Am. soldier & statesman
San·ta An·na \,san-tə-'a-nə, ,sän-tə-'ä-nə\ Antonio López de 1794–1876 Mex. gen., revolutionary, & pres.
San·tan·der \,san-tən-'der, ,san-,tan-\ Francisco de Paula 1792–1840 Colombian gen. & polit.
San·ta·ya·na \,san-tə-'yä-nə, ,san-tē-'ä-, ,sän-\ George 1863–1952 Am. (Span.-born) poet & philos.
San·tos–Du·mont \,san-təs-dü-'mänt, -dyü-; säⁿ-tōs-düe-'mōⁿ\ Alberto 1873–1932 Fr. (Braz.-born) aviation pioneer
Sa·pir \sə-'pir\ Edward 1884–1939 Am. (Pomeranian-born) anthropol. & linguist
Sap·pho *also* **Psap·pho** \'sa-(,)fō\ *fl ca* 610–*ca* 580 B.C. Greek poet
Sar·da·na·pa·lus *or* **Sar·da·na·pal·lus** \,sär-dⁿn-'a-p(ə-)ləs, -dⁿn-ə-'pä-ləs\ king of Assyria; sometimes identified with Ashurbanipal (reigned 668–627 B.C.)
Sar·dou \sär-'dü\ Victorien 1831–1908 Fr. dram.
Sar·gent \'sär-jənt\ John Sing·er \'siŋ-ər\ 1856–1925 Am. painter
Sar·gon II \'sär-,gän, -gən\ king of Assyria (722–705 B.C.)
Sa·roy·an \sə-'ròi-ən\ William 1908–1981 Am. writer
Sar·tre \'särtrʳ\ Jean-Paul 1905–1980 Fr. philos., dram., & nov. — **Sar·tre·an** *or* **Sar·tri·an** \'sär-trē-ən\ *adj*
Sas·soon \sa-'sün, sə-\ Siegfried Lorraine 1886–1967 Eng. writer
Sa·tie \sa-'tē, sä-\ Erik-Alfred-Leslie 1866–1925 Fr. composer
Sa·ud \sä-'üd\ 1902–1969 king of Saudi Arabia (1953–64)
Saus·sure \sō-süer\ Ferdinand de 1857–1913 Swiss linguist — **Saus·sur·ean** *also* **Saus·sur·ian** \sō-'sür-ē-ən, sō-\ *adj*
Sav·age \'sa-vij\ Michael Joseph 1872–1940 prime min. of New Zealand (1935–40)
Savage Richard 1697?–1743 Eng. poet
Sa·vo·na·ro·la \,sa-və-nə-'rō-lə, sə-,vä-nə-'rō-\ Gi·ro·la·mo \ji-'rò-lə-,mō\ 1452–1498 Ital. reformer
Saxe \'saks\ Hermann-Maurice 1696–1750 Comte *de Saxe* Fr. gen.
Saxo Gram·mat·i·cus \,sak-(,)sō-gra-'ma-ti-kəs\ *ca* 1150–after 1216 Dan. hist.
Say·ers \'sä-ərz, 'serz\ Dorothy Leigh 1893–1957 Eng. writer
Sca·lia \skə-'lē-ə\ Antonin 1936– Am. jurist
Scal·i·ger \'ska-lə-jər\ Joseph Justus 1540–1609 Fr. scholar
Scaliger Julius Caesar 1484–1558 *father of prec.* Ital. physician
Scanderbeg — see SKANDERBEG
Scar·lat·ti \skär-'lä-tē\ (Pietro) Alessandro Gaspare 1660–1725 & his son (Giuseppe) Domenico 1685–1757 Ital. composers
Scar·ron \ska-'rōⁿ\ Paul 1610–1660 Fr. author
Schacht \'shäkt, 'shäkt\ (Horace Greeley) Hjal·mar \'yäl-,mär\ 1877–1970 Ger. financier
Schal·ly \'sha-lē\ Andrew Victor 1926– Am. (Pol.-born) physiol.
Scharn·horst \'shärn-,hòrst\ Gerhard Johann David von 1755–1813 Pruss. gen.
Schar·wen·ka \shär-'veŋ-kə\ (Ludwig) Philipp 1847–1917 & his bro. (Franz) Xaver 1850–1924 Ger. pianists & composers
Schaw·low \'shò-(,)lō\ Arthur Leonard 1921– Am. physicist
Schei·de·mann \'shī-də-,män\ Philipp 1865–1939 Ger. polit.
Schel·ling \'she-liŋ\ Friedrich Wilhelm Joseph von 1775–1854 Ger. philos. — **Schel·ling·ian** \she-'liŋ-ē-ən\ *adj*
Schia·pa·rel·li \skē-,ä-pə-'re-lē, ,ska-\ Giovanni Virginio 1835–1910 Ital. astron.
Schick \'shik\ Bé·la \'bā-lə\ 1877–1967 Am. (Hung.-born) pediatrician
Schil·ler \'shi-lər\ (Johann Christoph) Friedrich von 1759–1805 Ger. poet & dram.
Schin·dler \'shind-lər\ Oskar 1908–1974 Ger. humanitarian
Schi·rach \'shē-,räk, -,räk\ Baldur von 1907–1974 Ger. Nazi polit.
Schle·gel \'shlā-gəl\ August Wilhelm von 1767–1845 Ger. author
Schlegel Friedrich von 1772–1829 *bro. of prec.* Ger. philos. & writer
Schlei·cher \'shlī-kər, -,kər\ Kurt von 1882–1934 Ger. soldier & polit.
Schlei·er·ma·cher \'shlī-ər-,mä-kər, -,kər\ Friedrich Ernst Daniel 1768–1834 Ger. theol. & philos.
Schle·sing·er \'shlā-ziŋ-ər, 'shle-siŋ-jər\ Arthur Meier father 1888–1965 & son 1917– Am. historians
Schley \'shlī, 'slī\ Winfield Scott 1839–1909 Am. admiral
Schlie·mann \'shlē-,män\ Heinrich 1822–1890 Ger. archaeol.
Schmidt \'shmit\ Helmut 1918– chancellor of West Germany (1974–82)

Schna·bel \'shnä-bəl\ Ar·tur \'är-,túr\ 1882–1951 Austrian pianist & composer
Schnitz·ler \'shnits-lər\ Arthur 1862–1931 Austrian dram. & nov.
Schoen·berg \'shə(r)n-,bərg, 'shœn-,berk\ Arnold Franz Walter 1874–1951 Am. (Austrian-born) composer — **Schoen·berg·ian** \-,bər-gē-ən\ *adj*
Scho·field \'skō-,fēld\ John McAllister 1831–1906 Am. gen.
Scho·pen·hau·er \'shō-pən-,haù(-ə)r\ Arthur 1788–1860 Ger. philos. — **Scho·pen·hau·er·ian** \,shō-pən-'haù-(ə-)rē-ən\ *adj*
Schrief·fer \'shrē-fər\ John Robert 1931– Am. physicist
Schrö·ding·er \'shrœ-diŋ-ər, shrä-\ Erwin 1887–1961 Austrian physicist
Schu·bert \'shü-bərt, -,bert\ Franz Peter 1797–1828 Austrian composer — **Schu·bert·ian** \shü-'bər-tē-ən, -'ber-\ *adj*
Schultz \'shúlts\ Theodore 1902– Am. econ.
Schulz \'shúlts\ Charles Monroe 1922– Am. cartoonist
Schu·man \'shü-,män, -mən\ Robert 1886–1963 Fr. statesman
Schu·man \'shü-mən\ William Howard 1910–1992 Am. composer
Schu·mann \'shü-,män, -mən\ Robert 1810–1856 Ger. composer
Schu·mann–Heink \'shü-mən-'hiŋk\ Ernestine 1861–1936 née *Roessler* Am. (Austrian-born) contralto
Schur·man \'shúr-mən, 'shər-\ Jacob Gould 1854–1942 Am. philos. & diplomat
Schurz \'shúrts, 'shərts\ Carl 1829–1906 Am. (Ger.-born) lawyer, gen., & polit.
Schusch·nigg \'shùsh-(,)nik, -(,)nig\ Kurt von 1897–1977 Austrian statesman
Schuy·ler \'skī-lər\ Philip John 1733–1804 Am. gen. & statesman
Schwartz \'shwòrts\ Melvin 1932– Am. physicist
Schwarz·kopf \'shwòrts-,kòpf, 'swòrts-\ H. Norman 1934– Am. gen.
Schwarz·kopf \shvärts-,kòpf\ (Olga Maria) Elisabeth Friederike 1915– Ger. (Pol.-born) soprano
Schweit·zer \'shwīt-sər, 'shvīt-, 'swīt-\ Albert 1875–1965 Fr. theol., philos., missionary physician, & music scholar
Schwing·er \'shwiŋ-ər\ Julian Seymour 1918– Am. physicist
Scip·io \'si-pē-,ō, 'ski-\ **Ae·mil·ia·nus Af·ri·ca·nus** \-,a-frə-'ka-nəs, -'kä-, -'kä-\ **Numantinus** Publius Cornelius 185(or 184)–129 B.C. *Scipio the Younger* Rom. gen.
Scipio Africanus Publius Cornelius 236–184(or 183) B.C. *Scipio the Elder* Rom. gen.
Scopes \'skōps\ John Thomas 1900–1970 Am. teacher
Scott \'skät\ Dred \'dred\ 1795?–1858 Am. slave
Scott Sir George Gilbert 1811–1878 Eng. architect
Scott Robert Falcon 1868–1912 Eng. polar explorer
Scott Sir Walter 1771–1832 Scot. poet & nov.
Scott Winfield 1786–1866 Am. gen.
Scotus Duns — see DUNS SCOTUS
Scotus John — see ERIGENA
Scria·bin *or* **Skrya·bin** \skrē-'ä-bən\ Aleksandr Nikolayevich 1872–1915 Russ. composer
Scribe \skrēb\ Augustin-Eugène 1791–1861 Fr. dram.
Scu·dé·ry \,skü-dò-'rē, sküe-dä-rē\ Madeleine de 1607–1701 *Sa·pho* \sà-fō\ Fr. poet, nov., & hostess of literary salon
Sea·borg \'sē-,bòrg\ Glenn Theodore 1912– Am. chem.
Sears \'sirz\ Richard Warren 1863–1914 Am. merchant
See \'sē\ Thomas Jefferson Jackson 1866–1962 Am. astron. & math.
Seeckt \zäkt\ Hans von 1866–1936 Ger. army officer
See·ger \'sē-gər\ Peter 1919– *Pete* Am. folksinger
Se·fe·ri·a·des \se-'fer-ē-əs\ Giorgos Stylianou 1900–1971 pseud. *George Se·fer·is* \se-'fer-ēs\ Greek diplomat & poet
Se·go·via \sā-'gō-vyə, -vē-ə\ Andrés 1893?–1987 Span. guitarist & composer
Se·grè \sə-'grā, sä-\ Emilio Gino 1905–1989 Am. (Ital.-born) physicist
Sei·fert \'zi-fərt\ Jaroslav 1901–1986 Czech poet
Se·ja·nus \si-'jä-nəs\ Lucius Aelius *d* A.D. 31 Rom. conspirator
Sel·den \'sel-dən\ George Baldwin 1846–1922 Am. lawyer & inventor
Selden John 1584–1654 Eng. jurist & antiquarian
Se·leu·cus I Ni·ca·tor \sə-,lü-kəs-'nī-,kä-tər\ 358(to 354)–281 B.C. Macedonian gen. & founder of Seleucid dynasty
Sel·kirk \'sel-,kərk\ Alexander 1676–1721 Scot. marooned sailor
Sel·ten \'zel-t'n\ Reinhard 1930– Ger. econom.
Se·me·nov \sə-'myò-nəf\ Nikolay Nikolayevich 1896–1986 Soviet chem.
Semmes \'semz\ Raphael 1809–1877 Am. Confed. admiral
Sen·e·ca \'se-ni-kə\ Lucius Annaeus 4 B.C.?–A.D. 65 Rom. statesman, dram., & philos. — **Sen·e·can** \-kən\ *adj*
Sen·ghor \seŋ-'gòr, säⁿ-'gòr\ Léopold Sédar 1906– pres. of Senegal (1960–80)
Sen·nach·er·ib \sə-'na-kə-rəb\ *d* 681 B.C. king of Assyria (704–681)
Se·quoya *or* **Se·quoy·ah** *or* **Se·quoia** \si-'kwòi-ə\ *ca* 1760–1843 *George Guess* Cherokee Indian scholar
Ser·kin \'sər-kən\ Rudolf 1903–1991 Am. (Bohemian-born) pianist
Ser·ra \'ser-ə\ Ju·ní·pe·ro \hü-'nē-pə-,rō\ 1713–1784 orig. *Miguel José* Span. missionary in Mexico & California
Ser·to·ri·us \(,)sər-'tòr-ē-əs, -'tòr-\ Quintus *ca*123–72 B.C. Rom. gen. & statesman
Ser·ve·tus \(,)sər-'vē-təs\ Michael 1511?–1553 Span. *Miguel Serveto* Span. theol. & physician
Ser·vice \'sər-vəs\ Robert William 1874–1958 Canad. writer
Ses·sions \'se-shənz\ Roger Huntington 1896–1985 Am. composer
Se·ton \'sē-t'n\ Saint Elizabeth Ann née *Bayley* 1774–1821 *Mother Seton* Am. religious leader
Seton Ernest Thompson 1860–1946 orig. surname *Thompson* Am. (Eng.-born) writer & illustrator
Seu·rat \sə-'rä\ Georges 1859–1891 Fr. painter
Seuss — see Theodor Seuss GEISEL
Se·ve·rus \sə-'vir-əs\ Lucius Septimius A.D. 146–211 Rom. emp. (193–211)
Sé·vi·gné \,sä-(,)vēn-'yä, sä-'vēn-(,)yä\ Marquise de 1626–1696 née (*Marie*) *de Rabutin-Chantal* Fr. letter writer
Sew·ard \'sü-ərd, 'sù(-ə)rd\ William Henry 1801–1872 Am. statesman; secy. of state (1861–69)
Sew·ell \'sü-əl\ Anna 1820–1878 Brit. writer

Sey·mour \'sē-ˌmȯr, -ˌmȯr\ Jane 1509?–1537 *3d wife of Henry VIII of England & mother of Edward VI*
Seyss–In·quart \'zīs-ˌiŋk-ˌvärt\ Ar·tur \'är-ˌtur\ 1892–1946 Austrian Nazi polit.
Shack·le·ton \'sha-kəl-tən\ Sir Ernest Henry 1874–1922 Brit. polar explorer
Shad·well \'shad-ˌwel, -wəl\ Thomas 1642?–1692 Eng. dram.; poet laureate (1688–92)
Shaf·ter \'shaf-tər\ William Rufus 1835–1906 Am. gen.
Shaftes·bury \'shaf(t)s-ˌber-ē, -b(ə-)rē\ 1st Earl of 1621–1683 *Anthony Ashley Coo·per* \'kü-pər, 'kü-\ Eng. statesman
Shāh Jā·han \'shä-jə-'hän\ 1592–1666 Mogul emp. of India (1628–57 or 58)
Shahn \'shän\ Ben 1898–1969 Am. (Lithuanian-born) painter
Shake·speare \'shāk-ˌspir\ William 1564–1616 Eng. dram. & poet
Sha·la·la \shə-'lä-lə, -'lä-\ Donna Edna 1941–   U.S. secy. of health & human services (1993–)
Sha·mir \shə-'mēr\ Yitzhak 1914–   orig. surname *Yizernitzky* prime min. of Israel (1983–92)
Sha·piro \shə-'pir-(ˌ)ō\ Karl Jay 1913–   Am. poet & critic
Sha·rif \shä-'rēf\ Nawaz 1949–   prime min. of Pakistan (1990–93)
Sharp \'shärp\ Phillip Allen 1944–   Am. biol.
Sharpe \'shärp\ William Forsyth 1934–   Am. econ.
Shas·tri \'shäs-trē\ Lal \'läl\ Bahadur 1904–1966 prime min. of India (1964–66)
Shaw \'shȯ\ George Bernard 1856–1950 Brit. (Irish-born) author
Shaw Thomas Edward — see T. E. LAWRENCE
Shawn \'shȯn\ Ted 1891–1972 Am. dancer & choreographer
Shays \'shāz\ Daniel 1747?–1825 Am. soldier & insurrectionist
Shee·ler \'shē-lər\ Charles 1883–1965 Am. painter & photographer
Shel·don \'shel-dən\ William Herbert 1898–1977 Am. psychologist & physical anthropologist
Shel·ley \'she-lē\ Mary Woll·stone·craft \'wu̇l-stən-ˌkraft\ 1797–1851 née *Godwin; wife of P. B. Eng. nov.*
Shelley Percy Bysshe \'bish\ 1792–1822 Eng. poet — **Shel·ley·an** \'she-lē-ən\ *or* **Shel·ley·esque** \ˌshe-lē-'esk\ *adj*
Shen·stone \'shen-ˌstōn, 'shen(t)-stən\ William 1714–1763 Eng. poet
Shep·ard \'she-pərd\ Alan Bartlett 1923–   Am. astronaut
Sher·a·ton \'sher-ə-t²n\ Thomas 1751–1806 Eng. furniture designer
Sher·i·dan \'sher-ə-d²n\ Philip Henry 1831–1888 Am. gen.
Sheridan Richard Brins·ley \'brinz-lē\ 1751–1816 Irish dram. & orator
Sher·man \'shər-mən\ James Schoolcraft 1855–1912 vice pres. of the U.S. (1909–12)
Sherman John 1823–1900 *bro. of W. T.* Am. statesman
Sherman Roger 1721–1793 Am. jurist & statesman
Sherman William Tecumseh 1820–1891 Am. gen. — **Sher·man·esque** \ˌshər-mə-'nesk\ *adj*
Sher·riff \'sher-əf\ Robert Cedric 1896–1975 Eng. writer
Sher·ring·ton \'sher-iŋ-tən\ Sir Charles Scott 1857–1952 Eng. physiol.
Sher·wood \'shər-ˌwu̇d *also* 'sher-\ Robert Emmet 1896–1955 Am. dram.
Shev·ard·nad·ze \ˌshe-vər(d)-'näd-zə\ Eduard Amvrosiyevich 1928– Soviet foreign minister (1985–90; 1991); pres. of Georgia (1992–)
Shev·chen·ko *or* **Šev·čen·ko** \shef-'cheŋ-(ˌ)kō\ Taras Hryhorovych 1814–1861 Ukrainian poet
Shi·de·ha·ra \ˌshē-də-'här-ə\ Kijūrō Baron 1872–1951 Jp. statesman
Shi·ge·mit·su \ˌshē-gə-'mit-(ˌ)sü, ˌshi-\ Mamoru 1887–1957 Jp. diplomat
Shih Huang–ti — see CH'IN SHIH HUANG TI
Shi·rer \'shir-ər\ William Lawrence 1904–1993 Am. author
Shir·ley \'shər-lē\ James 1596–1666 Eng. dram.
Shock·ley \'shä-klē\ William Bradford 1910–1989 Am. physicist
Sho·lo·khov \'shȯ-lə-ˌkȯf, -ˌkȯv\ Mikhail Aleksandrovich 1905–1984 Soviet (Russ.-born) nov.
Sho·sta·ko·vich \ˌshäs-tə-'kō-vich, ˌshȯs-, -'kȯ-\ Dmi·try \də-'mē-trē\ Dmitriyevich 1906–1975 Soviet (Russ.-born) composer
Shull \'shəl\ Clifford Glenwood 1915–   Am. physicist
Shultz \'shu̇lts\ George Pratt 1920–   U.S. secy. of labor (1969–70); secy. of the treasury (1972–73); secy. of state (1982–89)
Shute \'shüt\ Nev·il \'ne-vəl\ 1899–1960 pseud. of *Nevil Shute Norway* Eng. aeronautical engineer & writer
Shver·nik \'shver-nik\ Nikolay Mikhaylovich 1888–1970 Soviet polit.; chairman of the Presidium (1946–54)
Si·be·lius \sə-'bāl-yəs, -'bā-lē-əs\ Jean \'zhän, 'yän\ 1865–1957 Finn. composer
Sick·les \'si-kəlz\ Daniel Edgar 1825–1914 Am. gen. & polit.
Sid·dhār·tha Gau·ta·ma \si-'där-tə-'gau̇-tə-mə, -'gō-\ *ca* 563–*ca* 483 B.C. *The Bud·dha* \'bü-də, 'bu̇-\ Indian philos. & founder of Buddhism
Sid·dons \'si-d²nz\ Sarah 1755–1831 née *Kemble* Eng. actress
Sid·ney \'sid-nē\ Sir Philip 1554–1586 Eng. poet, statesman, & soldier
Sieg·bahn \'sēg-ˌbän\ Kai Manne 1918–   Swed. physicist
Siegbahn Karl Manne Georg 1886–1978 Swed. physicist *father of prec.*
Sie·mens \'sē-mənz\ Sir William 1823–1883 Brit. (Ger.-born) inventor
Sien·kie·wicz \shen-'kyä-vich\ Henryk 1846–1916 pseud. *Litwas* Pol. nov.
Sie·yès \sē-ā-'yes\ Emmanuel-Joseph 1748–1836 Fr. revolutionary
Sig·is·mund \'si-gəs-mənd\ 1368–1437 Holy Rom. emp. (1433–37)
Sigs·bee \'sigz-bē\ Charles Dwight 1845–1923 Am. admiral
Si·gurds·son \'si-gərd-sən, -gərth-\ Jón \'yōn\ 1811–1879 Icelandic statesman & author
Si·kor·ski \sə-'kȯr-skē\ Władysław 1881–1943 Pol. gen. & statesman
Si·kor·sky \sə-'kȯr-skē\ Igor Ivan 1889–1972 Am. (Russ.-born) aeronautical engineer
Sil·lan·pää \'sil-lən-ˌpä\ Frans Eemil 1888–1964 Finn. nov.
Si·lo·ne \si-'lō-nē\ Ignazio 1900–1978 pseud. of *Secondo Tranquilli* Ital. author
Si·me·non \ˌsē-mə-'nōⁿ\ Georges-Joseph-Christian 1903–1989 Fr. (Belg.-born) author
Sim·e·on Sty·li·tes \'si-mē-ən-stə-'lī-tēz, -ˌstī-\ Saint *ca* 390–459 Syrian ascetic & pillar dweller
Si·mon \sē-mōⁿ\ Claude 1913–   Fr. writer
Si·mon \'sī-mən\ 1st Viscount 1873–1954 *John Allsebrook Simon* Brit. jurist & statesman

Simon Herbert Alexander 1916–   Am. econ.
Simon Neil 1927–   Am. dram.
Si·mon·i·des \sī-'mä-nə-ˌdēz\ of Ceos *ca* 556–*ca* 468? B.C. Greek poet
Sims \'simz\ William Sow·den \'sau̇-d²n\ 1858–1936 Am. admiral
Sin·clair \sin-'kler, siŋ-\ Upton Beall \'bel\ 1878–1968 Am. writer & polit.
Sing·er \'siŋ-ər\ Isaac Ba·shev·is \bə-'she-vəs\ 1904–1991 Am. (Pol.⁼born) author
Singer Isaac Merrit 1811–1875 Am. inventor
Singh \'siŋ, 'siⁿ-hə\ Vishwanath Pratap 1931–   prime min. of India (1989–90)
Si·quei·ros \si-'kā-(ˌ)rōs\ David Alfaro 1896–1974 Mex. painter
Si·rāj–ud–Daw·lah \sə-ˌräj-ə-'daù-lə\ *ca* 1732–1757 nawab of Bengal (1756–57)
Sis·ley \'siz-lē, sēs-le\ Alfred 1839–1899 Fr. (Eng.-born) painter
Sis·mon·di \sis-mōn-dē, sēs-mōⁿ-dē\ Jean-Charles-Léonard Simonde de 1773–1842 Swiss hist. & econ.
Sit·ter \'si-tər\ Willem de 1872–1934 Du. astron.
Sit·ting Bull \ˌsi-tiŋ-'bu̇l\ *ca* 1831–1890 Sioux leader
Sit·well \'sit-ˌwel, -wəl\ Sir George Reres·by \'rirz-bē\ 1860–1943 & his 3 children: Dame Edith 1887–1964; Sir Osbert 1892–1969; & Sa·chev·er·ell \sə-'she-və-rəl\ 1897–1988 Eng. authors
Skan·der·beg *or* **Scan·der·beg** \'skan-dər-ˌbeg\ 1405–1468 orig. *George Kas·tri·o·ti* \ˌkäs-trē-'ō-(ˌ)tē\ Turk. *Is·kan·der Bey* \i-skän-'der-'bä\ Albanian hero
Skeat \'skēt\ Walter William 1835–1912 Eng. philologist
Skel·ton \'skel-t²n\ John *ca* 1460–1529 Eng. poet — **Skel·ton·ic** \skel-'tä-nik\ *adj*
Skin·ner \'ski-nər\ Burrhus Frederic 1904–1990 Am. psychol. — **Skin·ner·ian** \ski-'nir-ē-ən, -'ner-\ *adj*
Skinner Cornelia Otis 1901–1979 *dau. of Otis* Am. actress
Skinner Otis 1858–1942 Am. actor
Sko·da \'skō-də, 'shkȯ-(ˌ)dä\ Emil von 1839–1900 Czech engineer & industrialist
Sla·ter \'slā-tər\ Samuel 1768–1835 Am. (Eng.-born) industrialist
Sli·dell \slī-'del, *by collateral descendants* 'sli-d²l\ John 1793–1871 Am. Confed. diplomat
Sloan \'slōn\ John French 1871–1951 Am. painter
Slo·cum \'slō-kəm\ Henry Warner 1827–1894 Am. gen.
Slo·nim·sky \slō-'nim(p)-skē\ Nicolas 1894–   Am. (Russ.-born) composer & musicologist
Sme·ta·na \'sme-t²n-ə\ Be·dřich \'be-dər-ˌzhik\ 1824–1884 Czech composer
Śmigły–Rydz Edward — see RYDZ–ŚMIGŁY
Smith \'smith\ Adam 1723–1790 Scot. econ.
Smith Alfred Emanuel 1873–1944 Am. polit.
Smith Bessie 1894(or 1898)–1937 Am. blues singer
Smith David 1906–1965 Am. sculptor
Smith Edmund Kirby — see KIRBY–SMITH
Smith Hamilton Othanel 1931–   Am. microbiologist
Smith John *ca* 1580–1631 Eng. explorer & colonist
Smith Joseph 1805–1844 Am. founder of Mormon Church
Smith Michael 1932–   Canad. (Brit-born) biochem.
Smith Sydney 1771–1845 Eng. essayist
Smith Walter Be·dell \bə-'del\ 1895–1961 Am. gen. & diplomat
Smith William 1769–1839 Eng. geologist
Smith–Dor·ri·en \'smith-'dȯr-ē-ən, -'där-\ Sir Horace Lockwood 1858–1930 Brit. gen.
Smith·son \'smith-sən\ James 1765–1829 Brit. chem. & mineralogist & benefactor of the Smithsonian Inst.
Smol·lett \'smä-lət\ Tobias George 1721–1771 Brit. author
Smuts \'sməts, 'smœts\ Jan \'yän\ Christiaan 1870–1950 So. African field marshal; prime min. (1919–24; 1939–48)
Smyth \'smith\ Henry DeWolf 1898–1986 Am. physicist
Snell \snel\ George 1903–   Am. research geneticist
Snor·ri Stur·lu·son \'snȯr-ē-'stər-lə-sən, ˌsnär-\ 1179–1241 Icelandic statesman & hist.
Snow \'snō\ Charles Percy 1905–1980 Baron *Snow* Eng. nov. & physicist
Snow·den \'snō-d²n\ Philip 1864–1937 1st Viscount *Snowden of Ickorn·shaw* \i-ˌkȯrn-ˌshȯ\ Eng. polit.
Snow·don \'snō-d²n\ Earl of — see ARMSTRONG–JONES
Sny·ders \'snī-dərs\ Frans 1579–1657 Flem. painter
Soar·es \'swär-ish\ Mário 1924–   prime min. of Portugal (1976–78; 1983–85) & pres. (1986–)
Sobieski John — see JOHN III SOBIESKI
So·ci·nus \sō-'sī-nəs\ Faustus 1539–1604 *Fausto Soz·zi·ni or So·ci·ni or Sozi·ni* \sōt-'sē-nē\ Ital. theol.
Soc·ra·tes \'sä-krə-ˌtēz\ *ca* 470–399 B.C. Greek philos.
Sod·dy \'sä-dē\ Frederick 1877–1956 Eng. chem.
Sö·der·blom \'sə(r)-dər-ˌblüm, 'sœ-\ Nathan 1866–1931 Swed. theol.
So·do·ma \sō-'dō-mə\ Il 1477–1549 *Giovanni Antonio Bazzi* Ital. painter
So·lon \'sō-lən, -ˌlän\ *ca* 630–*ca* 560 B.C. Athenian lawgiver
So·low \'sō-lō\ Robert Merton 1924–   Am. econ.
Sol·zhe·ni·tsyn \ˌsōl-zhə-'nēt-sən, ˌsōl-\ Aleksandr Isayevich 1918– Russ. nov.
Som·er·ville \'sə-mər-ˌvil\ Sir James Fownes 1882–1949 Brit. admiral
Son·tag \'sän-ˌtag\ Susan 1933–   Am. writer
Soong Ai–ling \'su̇ŋ-'ī-'liŋ\ 1888–1973 *wife of H. H. K'ung*
Soong Ch'ing–ling \-'chiŋ-'liŋ\ 1892–1981 *wife of Sun Yat-sen*
Soong Mei–ling \-'mā-'liŋ\ 1897–   *wife of Chiang Kai-shek*
Soong Tzu–wen *or* **Tse–ven** *or* **Tsŭ–wên** \-'tsü-'wən\ 1894–1971 *T. V. Soong; bro. of prec.* Chin. financier & statesman
Soph·o·cles \'sä-fə-ˌklēz\ *ca* 496–406 B.C. Greek dram. — **Soph·o·cle·an** \ˌsä-fə-'klē-ən\ *adj*
Sor·del·lo \sȯr-'de-(ˌ)lō\ *ca* 1200–before 1269 Ital. troubadour

---

\ə\ abut \'ə\ kitten, F table \ər\ further \a\ ash \ā\ ace \ä\ mop, mar \au̇\ out \ch\ chin \e\ bet \ē\ easy \g\ go \i\ hit \ī\ ice \j\ job \ŋ\ sing \ō\ go \ȯ\ law \ȯi\ boy \th\ thin \t͟h\ the \ü\ loot \u̇\ foot \y\ yet \zh\ vision \ä, k̲, ⁿ, œ, œ̄, ue, ue̅, ᵞ\ see Guide to Pronunciation

1434 Biographical Names

So·rol·la y Bas·ti·da \sə-'rôl-yə-ē-bä-'stē-də, -'rôi-ə-, -'stē-thə\ Joaquín 1863–1923 Span. painter
So·to, de \thä-'sôt-(,)ō, di-\ Hernando 1496(or 1499 or 1500)–1542 Span. explorer
Soult \sült\ Nicolas-Jean de Dieu 1769–1851 Duc de Dal·ma·tie \dàl-má-sē\ Fr. soldier; marshal of France
Sou·sa \'sü-zə, 'sü-sə\ John Philip 1854–1932 the March King Am. bandmaster & composer
Sou·ter \'sü-tər\ David 1939–   Am. jurist
South \'saùth\ Robert 1634–1716 Eng. clergyman
Sou·they \'saù-thē, 'sə-thē\ Robert 1774–1843 Eng. author; poet laureate (1813–43)
Sou·tine \sü-'tēn\ Chaim 1893–1943 Fr. (Lith.-born) painter
So·yin·ka \shô-'yiŋ-ka\ Wo·le \'wô-lā\ 1934–   Nigerian dram. & poet
Spaak \'späk\ Paul-Henri Charles 1899–1972 Belg. lawyer & polit.; premier (1938–39; 1947–50); secy.-gen. of NATO (1957–61)
Spaatz \'späts\ Carl 1891–1974 Am. gen.
Spal·ding \'spôl-diŋ\ Albert 1888–1953 Am. violinist & composer
Spark \'spärk\ Muriel Sarah 1918–   née Camberg Brit. writer
Sparks \'spärks\ Jar·ed \'jar-əd, 'jer-\ 1789–1866 Am. hist.
Spar·ta·cus \'spär-tə-kəs\ d 71 B.C. Rom. slave & insurrectionist
Spell·man \'spel-mən\ Francis Joseph 1889–1967 Am. cardinal
Spe·mann \'shpā-,män\ Hans 1869–1941 Ger. embryologist
Spen·cer \'spen(t)-sər\ Herbert 1820–1903 Eng. philos.
Spen·der \'spen-dər\ Stephen Harold 1909–1995 Eng. poet & critic
Speng·ler \'shpeŋ-lər, 'speŋ-\ Oswald 1880–1936 Ger. philos.
Spen·ser \'spen(t)-sər\ Edmund 1552–1599 Eng. poet — Spen·se·ri·an \spen-'sir-ē-ən\ adj
Sper·ry \'sper-ē\ Elmer Ambrose 1860–1930 Am. inventor
Sperry Roger Wolcott 1913–1994 Am. psychobiologist
Spiel·berg \'spē(ə)l-,bərg\ Steven 1947–   Am. motion-picture director, writer, & producer — Spiel·berg·ian \,spēl-'bər-gē-ən\ adj
Spi·no·za \spi-'nō-zə\ Benedict de 1632–1677 Hebrew prename Baruch Du. philos.
Spit·te·ler \'shpi-t⁹l-ər, 'spi-; 'shpit-lər, 'spit-\ Carl 1845–1924 pseud. Felix Tan·dem \'tän-,dem\ Swiss writer
Spock \'späk\ Benjamin McLane 1903–   Am. physician
Spode \'spōd\ Josiah 1754–1827 Eng. potter
Spru·ance \'sprü-ən(t)s\ Raymond Ames 1886–1969 Am. admiral
Spy·ri \'shpir-ē, 'spir-\ Johanna 1827–1901 née Heusser Swiss author
Staël, de \də-'stäl, -stàl\ Mme. Anne-Louise-Germaine 1766–1817 née Necker Baronne de Staël-Holstein Fr. writer & hostess of literary salon
Ståhl·berg \'stól-,bərg, -,ber-ē\ Kaarlo Ju·ho \'yü-(,)hò\ 1865–1952 Finn. statesman
Stair Viscount & Earl of — see DALRYMPLE
Sta·lin \'stä-lən, 'sta-, -,lēn\ Joseph 1879–1953 Iosif Vissarionovich Dzhu·gash·vi·li \,jü-gəsh-'vē-lē\ Soviet leader
Stan·dish \'stan-dish\ Myles or Miles 1584?–1656 Am. colonist
Stan·is·lav·sky \,sta-ni-'släf-skē\ Konstantin 1863–1938 pseud. of Konstantin Sergeyevich Alekseyev Russ. actor, director, & producer
Stan·is·ław I \'sta-nə-,slòv, -,släv\ Lesz·czyń·ski \lesh-'chin-skē\ 1677–1766 king of Poland (1704–09; 1733–35)
Stan·ley \'stan-lē\ Edward George Geoffrey Smith 1799–1869 Earl of Derby Brit. statesman
Stanley Sir Henry Morton 1841–1904 orig. John Rowlands Brit. explorer
Stanley Wendell Meredith 1904–1971 Am. biochem.
Stan·ton \'stan-t⁹n\ Edwin McMasters 1814–1869 Am. lawyer & secy. of war (1862–68)
Stanton Elizabeth 1815–1902 née Cady Am. suffragist
Star·hem·berg \'stär-əm-,bərg, 'shtär-əm-,berk\ Ernst Rüdiger 1899–1956 Fürst von Starhemberg Austrian polit.
Stark \'stärk\ Harold Raynsford 1880–1972 Am. admiral
Stark \'shtärk, 'stärk\ Johannes 1874–1957 Ger. physicist
Stark \'stärk\ John 1728–1822 Am. gen. in Revolution
Sta·tius \'stä-sh(ē-)əs\ Publius Papinius ca A.D. 45–96 Rom. poet
Stau·ding·er \'shtaù-diŋ-ər, 'staù-\ Hermann 1881–1965 Ger. chem.
Steele \'stē(ə)l\ Sir Richard 1672–1729 Brit. essayist & dram.
Steen \'stān\ Jan 1626–1679 Du. painter
Ste·fans·son \'ste-fən-sən\ Vil·hjal·mur \'vil-,yaùl-mər\ 1879–1962 Am. (Canad.-born) explorer
Stef·fens \'ste-fənz\ (Joseph) Lincoln 1866–1936 Am. journalist
Stei·chen \'stī-kən\ Edward Jean 1879–1973 Am. photographer
Stein \'stīn\ Gertrude 1874–1946 Am. writer
Stein William Howard 1911–1980 Am. biochem.
Stein \'shtīn, 'stīn\ (Heinrich Friedrich) Karl 1757–1831 Freiherr vom und zum Stein Pruss. statesman
Stein·beck \'stīn-,bek\ John Ernst 1902–1968 Am. nov.
Stein·berg·er \'stīn-,bər-gər\ Jack 1921–   Am. (Ger.-born) physicist
Stei·nem \'stī-nəm\ Gloria 1934–   Am. feminist writer & editor
Stein·metz \'shtīn-,mets, 'stīn-\ Charles Proteus 1865–1923 Am. (Ger.-born) electrical engineer
Sten·dhal \sten-'däl, stan-, F stan-dàl\ 1783–1842 pseud. of Marie-Henri Beyle \'bel\ Fr. writer — Sten·dhal·ian \-'dä-lē-ən\ adj
Ste·phen \'stē-vən\ ca 1097–1154 king of England (1135–54)
Stephen Sir Leslie 1832–1904 Eng. philos., critic, & biographer
Ste·phens \'stē-vənz\ Alexander Hamilton 1812–1883 Am. polit.; vice pres. of the Confed. states
Stephens James 1882–1950 Irish poet & nov.
Ste·phen·son \'stē-vən-sən\ George 1781–1848 Eng. inventor & founder of railroads
Stephenson Robert 1803–1859 son of George Eng. engineer
Stern \'stərn\ Isaac 1920–   Am. (Russ.-born) violinist
Stern Otto 1888–1969 Am. (Ger.-born) physicist
Stern·berg \'stərn-,bərg\ George Miller 1838–1915 Am. physician & bacteriol.
Sterne \'stərn\ Laurence 1713–1768 Brit. nov.
Stet·tin·i·us \stə-'ti-nē-əs, ste-\ Edward Reilly 1900–1949 Am. financier & statesman
Steu·ben \'stü-bən, 'styü-\ Baron Friedrich Wilhelm Ludolf Gerhard Augustin von 1730–1794 Pruss.-born gen. in Am. Revolution
Ste·vens \'stē-vənz\ John 1749–1838 Am. inventor

Stevens John Paul 1920–   Am. jurist
Stevens Thaddeus 1792–1868 Am. polit.
Stevens Wallace 1879–1955 Am. poet
Ste·ven·son \'stē-vən-sən\ Ad·lai \'ad-lē, -(,)lā\ Ewing 1835–1914 Am. polit.; vice pres. of U.S. (1893–97)
Stevenson Adlai Ewing 1900–1965 grandson of prec. Am. polit.
Stevenson Robert Louis Balfour 1850–1894 Scot. author
Stew·art \'stü-ərt, 'styü-; 'st(y)ù(-ə)rt\ Du·gald \'dü-gəld\ 1753–1828 Scot. philos.
Stewart Potter 1915–1985 Am. jurist
Stewart Robert 1769–1822 Viscount Cas·tle·reagh \'ka-səl-,rā\ Eng. statesman
Steyn \'stīn\ Marthinus Theunis 1857–1916 So. African statesman
Stieg·litz \'stē-gləts, -,glits\ Alfred 1864–1946 Am. photographer
Stig·ler \'sti-glər\ George J. 1911–1991 Am. econ.
Stil·i·cho \'sti-li-,kō\ Flavius ca 365–408 Rom. gen. & statesman
Still \'stil\ Andrew Taylor 1828–1917 Am. founder of osteopathy
Stil·well \'stil-,wel, -wəl\ Joseph Warren 1883–1946 Am. gen.
Stim·son \'stim(p)-sən\ Henry Lewis 1867–1950 Am. statesman
Stin·nes \'shti-nəs, 'sti-\ Hugo 1870–1924 Ger. industrialist
Stir·ling \'stər-liŋ\ James Frazer 1926–1992 Brit. architect
Stock·hau·sen \'shtòk-,haù-zən, 'stäk-\ Karlheinz 1928–   Ger. composer & theorist
Stock·mar \'stäk-,mär\ Christian Friedrich 1787–1863 Baron von Stockmar Anglo-Belg. statesman
Stock·ton \'stäk-tən\ Francis Richard 1834–1902 Frank R. Stockton Am. writer
Stod·dard \'stä-dərd\ Richard Henry 1825–1903 Am. poet & critic
Sto·ker \'stō-kər\ Bram 1847–1912 Brit. writer
Stokes \'stōks\ Sir Frederick Wilfrid Scott 1860–1927 Eng. engineer & inventor
Sto·kow·ski \stə-'kòf-skē, -'kòv- also -'kaù-\ Leopold Antoni Stanislaw Boleslawowicz 1882–1977 Am. (Eng.-born) conductor
Stone \'stōn\ Harlan Fiske 1872–1946 Am. jurist; chief justice U.S. Supreme Court (1941–46)
Stone Irving 1903–1989 orig. surname Tennenbaum Am. writer
Stone Lucy 1818–1893 Am. suffragist
Stone Sir (John) Richard Nicholas 1913–1991 Eng. econ.
Stoph \'shtòf, 'stòf\ Willi 1914–   prime min. of East Germany (1976–89)
Sto·ry \'stōr-ē, 'stòr-ē\ Joseph 1779–1845 Am. jurist
Story William Wetmore 1819–1895 son of prec. Am. sculptor
Stow \'stō\ John 1525–1605 Eng. hist. & antiquarian
Stowe \'stō\ Harriet Elizabeth 1811–1896 née Beecher Am. author
Stra·bo \'strā-(,)bō\ 64(or 63) B.C.–after A.D. 23 Greek geographer
Stra·chey \'strā-chē\ (Evelyn) John St. Loe 1901–1963 Eng. socialist
Strachey (Giles) Lytton 1880–1932 Eng. biographer
Stra·di·va·ri \,stra-də-'vär-ē, -'var-, -'ver-\ Antonio 1644–1737 L. Antonius Strad·i·var·i·us \,stra-də-'var-ē-əs, -'ver-\ Ital. violin maker
Straf·ford \'stra-fərd\ 1st Earl of 1593–1641 Thomas Wentworth Eng. statesman
Stratford de Redcliffe Viscount — see Stratford CANNING
Strath·co·na \strath-'kō-nə\ and Mount Royal 1st Baron 1820–1914 Donald Alexander Smith Canad. (Scot.-born) railroad builder & polit.
Straus \'shtraùs, 'straùs\ Oscar 1870–1954 Fr. (Austrian-born) composer
Strauss \'shtraùs, 'straùs\ David Friedrich 1808–1874 Ger. theol. & philos.
Strauss Johann father 1804–1849 & his sons Johann Baptist 1825–1899 & Josef 1827–1870 Austrian composers
Strauss Ri·chard \'ri-,kärt, -,kärt\ 1864–1949 Ger. composer — Strauss·ian \'strau-sē-ən, 'shtraù-\ adj
Stra·vin·sky \strə-'vin(t)-skē\ Igor \'ē-,gór\ Fyodorovich 1882–1971 Am. (Russ.-born) composer — Stra·vin·sky·an or Stra·vin·ski·an \-skē-ən\ adj
Strei·cher \'shtrī-kər, 'strī-, -kər\ Julius 1885–1946 Ger. Nazi administrator
Stre·se·mann \'shtrā-zə-,män, 'strā-\ Gustav 1878–1929 Ger. polit.
Strij·dom \'strī-dəm, 'strā-\ Johannes Gerhardus 1893–1958 prime min. of So. Africa (1954–58)
Strind·berg \'strin(d)-,bərg, Sw 'strind-,ber-ē\ August 1849–1912 Swed. dram. & nov. — Strind·berg·ian \strin(d)-'bər-gē-ən\ adj
Stroess·ner \'stres-nər\ Alfredo 1912–   pres. of Paraguay (1954–89)
Stru·en·see \'shtrü-ən-,zā, 'strü-\ Johann Friedrich 1737–1772 Graf Struensee Dan. (Ger.-born) physician & polit.
Stu·art \'stü-ərt, 'styü-; 'st(y)ù(-ə)rt\ — see CHARLES I & MARY STUART
Stuart Charles the Young Pretender — see CHARLES EDWARD
Stuart Gilbert Charles 1755–1828 Am. painter
Stuart James Ewell Brown 1833–1864 Jeb Stuart Am. Confed. gen.
Stuart James Francis Edward the Old Pretender — see JAMES EDWARD
Stubbs \'stəbz\ George 1724–1806 Eng. painter
Stubbs William 1825–1901 Eng. hist. & prelate
Stülp·na·gel \'shtülp-,nä-gəl, 'stülp-, 'shtuelp-\ Karl Heinrich von 1886–1944 Ger. gen.
Sturluson — see SNORRI STURLUSON
Stur·sa \'shtùr-sə\ Jan \'yän\ 1880–1925 Czech sculptor
Stuy·ve·sant \'stī-və-sənt\ Peter ca 1610–1672 Du. colonial administrator in America
Sty·ron \'stī-rən\ William 1925–   Am. writer
Sua·rez Gon·zá·lez \'swär-əz-gən-'zä-ləs\ Adolfo 1932–   prime min. of Spain (1976–81)
Su·choc·ka \sü-'kòt-,skä\ Hanna 1946–   prime min. of Poland (1992–93)
Suck·ling \'sə-kliŋ\ Sir John 1609–1642 Eng. Cavalier poet
Su·cre \'sü-(,)krā\ Antonio José de 1795–1830 So. Am. liberator
Sue \'sü, süē\ Eugène 1804–1857 orig. Marie-Joseph Sue Fr. nov.
Sue·to·ni·us \swē-'tō-nē-əs, ,sü-ə-'tō-\ ca A.D. 69–after 122 Gaius Suetonius Tranquillus Rom. biographer & hist.
Su·gi·ya·ma \,sü-gē-'yä-mə\ Hajime 1880–1945 Jp. field marshal
Su·har·to \sə-'här-(,)tò, sù-\ 1921–   pres. of Indonesia (1967–   )
Su·kar·no \sü-'kär-(,)nō\ 1901–1970 pres. of Indonesian Republic (1945–1967)

Sü·ley·man *or* So·li·man *or* Su·lei·man I \'sü-lā-ˌmän, -li-\ 1494(or 1495)–1566 *the Magnificent* Ottoman sultan (1520–66)
Sul·la \'sə-lə\ 138–78 B.C. *Lucius Cornelius Sulla Felix* Rom. gen. & polit.
Sul·li·van \'sə-lə-vən\ Sir Arthur Seymour 1842–1900 Eng. composer
Sullivan John 1740–1795 Am. gen. in Revolution
Sullivan John Lawrence 1858–1918 Am. boxer
Sullivan John Lawrence 1899–1982 Am. lawyer & administrator
Sullivan Louis Henri 1856–1924 Am. architect
Sul·ly \'sə-lē, (ˌ)sə-'lē, süel-lē\ Duc de 1560–1641 *Maximilien de Béthune* Baron *de Ros·ny* \də-rō-'nē\ Fr. statesman
Sul·ly \'sə-lē\ Thomas 1783–1872 Am. (Eng.-born) painter
Sul·ly Prud·homme \süel-lē-prüе-dəm\ 1839–1907 pseud. of *René= François-Armand Prudhomme* Fr. poet & critic
Sum·ner \'səm-nər\ Charles 1811–1874 Am. statesman & orator
Sumner James Batcheller 1887–1955 Am. biochem.
Sumner William Graham 1840–1910 Am. sociol. & educ.
Sun·day \'sən-dē\ William Ashley 1862–1935 *Billy* Am. evangelist
Sun Yat–sen \'sün-'yät-'sen\ 1866–1925 orig. *Sun Wen* or *Sun Chung= shan* Chin. statesman
Surrey Earl of — see Henry HOWARD
Sur·tees \'sər-(ˌ)tēz\ Robert Smith 1803–1864 Eng. nov. & editor
Suth·er·land \'sə-thər-lənd\ Earl Wilbur, Jr. 1915–1974 Am. physiol.
Sutherland Dame Joan 1926– Austral. soprano
Sut·ter \'sə-tər, 'sü-\ John Augustus 1803–1880 orig. *Johann August Suter* Am. (Ger.-born) pioneer
Sutt·ner \'zút-nər, 'süt-\ Bertha 1843–1914 née *Kinsky* Baroness *von Suttner* Austrian writer & pacifist
Su·vo·rov \sü-'vór-əf, -'vär-\ Aleksandr Vasilyevich 1729–1800 Russ. field marshal
Sved·berg \'sved-ˌbərg, Sw -ˌber-ē\ The *or* Theodor 1884–1971 Swed. chem.
Sver·drup \'sver-drəp\ Otto Neumann 1855–1930 Norw. explorer
Sver·rir \'sver-ər\ *ca* 1149–1202 *Sverrir Si·gurds·son* \'si-gərd-sən\ king of Norway (1184–1202)
Swe·den·borg \'swē-dᵊn-ˌbórg\ Emanuel 1688–1772 orig. *Svedberg* Swed. philos. & religious writer
Swee·linck \'swä-liŋk\ Jan Pieterszoon 1562–1621 Du. organist & composer
Sweet \'swēt\ Henry 1845–1912 Eng. phonetician
Swift \'swift\ Gustavus Franklin 1839–1903 Am. meat packer
Swift Jonathan 1667–1745 Eng. satirist — **Swift·ian** \-tē-ən\ *adj*
Swin·burne \'swin-(ˌ)bərn\ Algernon Charles 1837–1909 Eng. poet — **Swin·burn·ian** \swin-'bər-nē-ən\ *adj*
Swin·ner·ton \'swi-nər-tᵊn\ Frank Arthur 1884–1982 Eng. nov. & critic
Sylva Carmen — see ELIZABETH Queen of Romania
Sy·ming·ton \'sī-miŋ-tən\ (William) Stuart 1901–1988 Am. industrialist & polit.
Sy·monds \'si-mən(d)z, 'sī-\ John Addington 1840–1893 Eng. scholar
Symons \'si-mənz, 'sī-\ Arthur William 1865–1945 Brit. poet & critic
Synge \'siŋ\ John Millington 1871–1909 Irish poet & dram.
Synge Richard Laurence Millington 1914– Brit. biochem.
Szell \'sel, 'zel\ George 1897–1970 Am. (Hung.-born) conductor
Szent–Györ·gyi \sänt-'jórj, -'jör-jē\ Albert von Nagyrapolt 1893–1986 Am. (Hung.-born) chem.
Szi·lard \'zi-ˌlärd, zə-'lärd\ Leo 1898–1964 Am. (Hung.-born) physicist
Szold \'zōld\ Henrietta 1860–1945 Am. Zionist & founder of Hadassah
Tac·i·tus \'ta-sə-təs\ Cornelius *ca* A.D. 56–*ca* 120 Rom. hist. — **Tac·i·te·an** \ˌta-sə-'tē-ən\ *adj*
Taft \'taft\ Lo·ra·do \lə-'rä-(ˌ)dō\ 1860–1936 Am. sculptor
Taft Robert Alphonso 1889–1953 *son of W. H.* Am. polit.
Taft William Howard 1857–1930 27th pres. of the U.S. (1909–13); chief justice U.S. Supreme Court (1921–30)
Ta·gore \tə-'gór, -'gór\ Ra·bin·dra·nath \rə-'bin-drə-ˌnät\ 1861–1941 Indian poet
Taine \'tān, 'ten\ Hippolyte-Adolphe 1828–1893 Fr. philos. & critic
Tait \'tāt\ Archibald Campbell 1811–1882 archbishop of Canterbury (1869–82)
T'ai–tsu — see CHAO K'UANG-YIN
Ta·ke·shi·ta \ˌtä-'kä-shə-ˌtä\ Noboru 1924– prime min. of Japan (1987–89)
Tall·chief \'tól-ˌchēf\ Maria 1925– Am. dancer
Tal·ley·rand–Pé·ri·gord \'ta-lē-ˌran(d)-ˌper-ə-'gór, F tȧl-räⁿ-\ Charles-Maurice de 1754–1838 Prince *de Bénévent* Fr. statesman
Ta·ma·yo \tə-'mī-(ˌ)ō\ Rufino 1899–1991 Mex. painter
Tamerlane *or* Tamburlaine — see TIMUR
Tamm \'täm, 'tam\ Igor Yevgenyevich 1895–1971 Soviet physicist
Tan·cred \'taŋ-krəd\ 1078?–1112 Norman leader in 1st Crusade
Tan·dy \'tan-dē\ Jessica 1909–1994 Am. (Brit.-born) actress
Ta·ney \'tó-nē\ Roger Brooke 1777–1864 Am. jurist; chief justice U.S. Supreme Court (1836–64)
Tan·ge \'tän-gä\ Kenzo 1913– Jp. architect
T'ang T'ai Tsung \'täŋ-'tī-'dzüŋ\ 600–649 orig. *Li Shih-min* \'le-'shir-ˌmin\ Chin. emp.
Tan·guy \täⁿ-'gē\ Yves 1900–1955 Am. (Fr.-born) artist
Tar·bell \'tär-bəl\ Ida Minerva 1857–1944 Am. author
Tar·dieu \tär-'dyə(r), -'dyœ\ André-Pierre-Gabriel-Amédée 1876–1945 Fr. statesman
Tar·king·ton \'tär-kiŋ-tən\ (Newton) Booth 1869–1946 Am. nov.
Tas·man \'taz-mən\ Abel Janszoon 1603?–?1659 Du. navigator & explorer
Tas·so \'ta-(ˌ)sō, 'tä-\ Tor·qua·to \tòr-'kwä-(ˌ)tō\ 1544–1595 Ital. poet
Tate \'tāt\ (John Orley) Allen 1899–1979 Am. poet & critic
Tate Nahum 1652–1715 Brit. dram.; poet laureate (1692–1715)
Ta·tum \'tā-təm\ Edward Lawrie 1909–1975 Am. biochem.
Taube \'taúb\ Henry 1915– Am. (Canad.-born) chem.
Taw·ney \'tó-nē\ Richard Henry 1880–1962 Eng. economic hist.
Tay·lor \'tā-lər\ (James) Bay·ard \'bī-ərd, 'bā-\ 1825–1878 Am. writer
Taylor (Joseph) Deems 1885–1966 Am. composer & music critic
Taylor Edward 1645?–1729 Am. clergyman & poet
Taylor Jeremy 1613–1667 Eng. prelate & author
Taylor Joseph Hooton 1941– Am. physicist

Taylor Maxwell Davenport 1901–1987 Am. gen.
Taylor Richard Edward 1929– Canad. physicist
Taylor Tom 1817–1880 Eng. dram.
Taylor Zachary 1784–1850 12th pres. of the U.S. (1849–50)
Tchai·kov·sky \chī-'kóf-skē, chə-, -'kóv-\ Pyotr Ilich 1840–1893 Russ. composer — **Tchai·kov·sky·an** *or* **Tchai·kov·ski·an** \-skē-ən\ *adj*
Teas·dale \'tēz-ˌdāl\ Sara 1884–1933 Am. poet
Te·cum·seh \tə-'kəm(p)-sə, -sē\ *or* Te·cum·tha \-'kəm(p)-thə\ *or* Ti·kam·the \-'kəm(p)-thə, -'käm(p)-\ 1768–1813 Shawnee Indian chief
Ted·der \'te-dər\ 1st Baron 1890–1967 *Arthur William Tedder* Brit. air marshal
Teil·hard de Char·din \tā-yȧr-də-shär-daⁿ\ Pierre 1881–1955 Fr. philos. & paleontologist
Tek·a·kwitha \ˌte-kə-'kwi-thə\ *or* Teg·a·kwitha \ˌte-gə-\ *or* Teg·a·kouita \ˌte-gə-'kwi-tə\ Ka·teri \'kä-tə-rē\ 1656–1680 *Lily of the Mohawks* Am. Indian religious
Te·le·mann \'tā-lə-ˌmän, 'tē-\ Georg Philipp 1681–1767 Ger. composer
Tel·ler \'te-lər\ Edward 1908– Am. (Hung.-born) physicist
Téllez Gabriel — see TIRSO DE MOLINA
Tem·in \'te-mən\ Howard Martin 1934–1994 Am. oncologist
Tem·ple \'tem-pəl\ Frederick 1821–1902 archbishop of Canterbury (1896–1902)
Temple Shirley 1928– Am. actress & polit.
Temple Sir William 1628–1699 Brit. statesman
Temple William 1881–1944 *son of Frederick* archbishop of Canterbury (1942–44)
Templewood Viscount — see HOARE
Teng Hsiao–p'ing *or* Deng Xiao·ping \'dəŋ-'shaú-'piŋ\ 1904– Chin. Communist leader (1977–)
Te·niers \tə-'nirs, tä-'nyä\ David *the Elder* 1582–1649 & *the Younger* 1610–1690 Flem. painters
Ten·niel \'ten-yəl\ Sir John 1820–1914 Eng. cartoonist & illustrator
Ten·ny·son \'te-nə-sən\ Alfred 1809–1892 1st Baron *Tennyson* known as *Alfred, Lord Tennyson* Eng. poet; poet laureate (1850–92) — **Ten·ny·so·nian** \ˌte-nə-'sō-nē-ən, -nyən\ *adj*
Ter·borch *or* Ter Borch \tər-'bórk, -'bórk\ Gerard 1617–1681 Du. painter
Ter·brug·ghen \tər-'brü-gən\ Hendrik 1588–1629 Du. painter
Ter·ence \'ter-ən(t)s\ 186(or 185)–?159 B.C. *Publius Terentius Afer* Rom. dram.
Te·re·sa \tə-'rā-zə, -'rē-sə\ Mother 1910– *Agnes Gonxha Bojaxhiu* Albanian religious in India
Teresa of Avila Saint 1515–1582 Span. Carmelite & mystic
Te·resh·ko·va \ˌter-əsh-'kò-və, -'kō-\ Valentina Vladimirovna 1937– Soviet (Russ.-born) cosmonaut
Ter·hune \(ˌ)tər-'hyün\ Albert Payson 1872–1942 Am. author
Ter·ry \'ter-ē\ (Alice) Ellen 1847–1928 Eng. actress
Ter·tul·lian \(ˌ)tər-'təl-yən\ *ca* A.D. 155(or 160)–after 220 *Quintus Septimius Florens Tertullianus* church father
Tes·la \'tes-lə\ Nikola 1856–1943 Am. (Croatian-born) electrical engineer & inventor
Tet·zel *or* Te·zel \'tet-səl\ Johann *ca* 1465–1519 Ger. Dominican monk
Thack·er·ay \'tha-k(ə-)rē\ William Makepeace 1811–1863 Eng. author — **Thack·er·ay·an** \-k(ə-)rē-ən\ *adj*
Tha·les \'thā-(ˌ)lēz\ *of* Miletus 625?–?547 B.C. Greek philos. — **Tha·le·sian** \thā-'lē-zhən\ *adj*
Thant \'thant, 'thänt\ U \'ü\ 1909–1974 Burmese U.N. official; secy.= gen. (1961–71)
Thatch·er \'tha-chər\ Margaret Hilda 1925– née *Roberts* Brit. prime min. (1979–90)
Thayer \'thar, 'ther, 'thä-ər\ Sylvanus 1785–1872 *father of West Point* Am. army officer & educ.
Thei·ler \'tī-lər\ Max 1899–1972 Am. (So. African-born) microbiologist
The·mis·to·cles \thə-'mis-tə-ˌklēz\ *ca* 524–*ca* 460 B.C. Athenian gen. & statesman
The·oc·ri·tus \thē-'ä-krə-təs\ *ca* 310–250 B.C. Greek poet
The·od·o·ric \thē-'ä-də-rik\ 454?–526 *the Great* king of the Ostrogoths (493–526)
The·o·do·sius I \ˌthē-ə-'dō-sh(ē-)əs\ 347–395 *the Great* Rom. gen. & emp. (379–395)
The·o·phras·tus \ˌthē-ə-'fras-təs\ *ca* 372–*ca* 287 B.C. Greek philos. & naturalist
The·o·rell \ˌtä-ə-'rel\ Axel Hugo Theodor 1903–1982 Swed. biochem.
Theresa Saint — see TERESA OF AVILA
Thes·pis \'thes-pəs\ 6th cent. B.C. Greek poet
Thiers \tē-'er\ Louis-Adolphe 1797–1877 Fr. statesman & hist.
Tho·mas \tò-'mä\ (Charles-Louis=)Ambroise 1811–1896 Fr. composer
Thom·as \'tä-məs\ Augustus 1857–1934 Am. dram.
Thomas Clarence 1948– Am. jurist
Thomas Dyl·an \'di-lən\ Marlais 1914–1953 Welsh poet
Thomas Edward Donnall 1920– Am. physician
Thomas Lowell Jackson 1892–1981 Am. traveler, journalist, & author
Thomas Norman Mat·toon \ma-'tün, mə-\ 1884–1968 Am. socialist polit.
Thomas Seth 1785–1859 Am. clock manuf.
Thomas (Christian Friedrich) Theodore 1835–1905 Am. (Ger.-born) conductor
Thomas à Becket — see BECKET
Thomas à Kem·pis \ə-'kem-pəs, (ˌ)ä-'kem-\ 1379(or 1380)–1471 orig. *Thomas Hemerken* Du. ecclesiastic & writer
Thomas Aqui·nas \ə-'kwī-nəs\ Saint 1224(or 1225)–1274 It. *Tommaso d'Aquino* Ital. religious & philos.
Thomas of Er·cel·doune \'ər-səl-ˌdün\ *fl* 1220–1297 *Thomas the Rhymer* and *Thomas Learmont* Scot. seer & poet

---

\ə\ abut \'ᵊ\ kitten, F table \ər\ further \a\ ash \ā\ ace \ä\ mop, mar
\aú\ out \ch\ chin \e\ bet \ē\ easy \g\ go \i\ hit \ī\ ice \j\ job
\ŋ\ sing \ō\ go \ó\ law \ói\ boy \th\ thin \t̲h̲\ the \ü\ loot \ú\ foot
\y\ yet \zh\ vision \á, k̲, ⁿ, œ, œ̄, ɶ, ᵫ, �\ see Guide to Pronunciation

Thomp·son \'täm(p)-sən\ Benjamin 1753–1814 Count *Rum·ford* \'rəm(p)-fərd\ Brit. (Am.-born) physicist & statesman
Thompson Dorothy 1894–1961 Am. journalist
Thompson Francis 1859–1907 Eng. poet
Thompson Sir John Sparrow David 1844–1894 Canad. statesman; prime min. (1892–94)
Thom·son \'täm(p)-sən\ Sir George Pag·et \'pa-jət\ 1892–1975 *son of Sir Joseph John* Eng. physicist
Thomson James 1700–1748 Scot. poet
Thomson James 1834–1882 *B. V.* or *Bysshe Vanolis* Scot. poet
Thomson John Arthur 1861–1933 Scot. biol.
Thomson Sir Joseph John 1856–1940 Eng. physicist
Thomson Virgil Garnett 1896–1989 Am. composer & critic
Thomson William — see Baron KELVIN
Tho·reau \thə-'rō, thó-; 'thôr-(,)ō, 'thər-(,)ō\ Henry David 1817–1862 orig. *David Henry Thoreau* Am. writer — Tho·reau·vi·an \thə-'rō-vē-ən, thó-\ *adj*
Tho·rez \tō-'rez\ Maurice 1900–1964 Fr. polit.
Thorn·dike \'thôrn-,dīk\ Edward Lee 1874–1949 Am. psychol.
Thorndike Lynn 1882–1965 Am. historian
Thorndike Dame (Agnes) Sybil 1882–1976 Brit. actress
Thorn·ton \'thôrn-t°n\ William 1759–1828 Am. architect
Thorpe \'thôrp\ James Francis 1866–1953 *Jim* Am. athlete
Thor·vald·sen or Thor·wald·sen \'tór-,wòl-sən, 'thôr-; 'tùr-,väl-sən\ Ber·tel \'ber-t°l\ 1768(or 1770)–1844 Dan. sculptor
Thras·y·bu·lus \,thra-sə-'byü-ləs\ *d* 388 B.C. Athenian gen.
Thu·cyd·i·des \thü-'si-də-,dēz, thyü-\ *d ca* 401 B.C. Greek hist. — Thu·cyd·i·de·an \(,)thü-,si-də-'dē-ən, (,)thyü-\ *adj*
Thur·ber \'thər-bər\ James Grover 1894–1961 Am. writer — Thur·ber·esque \,thər-bə-'resk\ *adj*
Thut·mo·se \thüt-'mō-sə\ name of 4 kings of Egypt: esp. III *d* 1450 B.C. (reigned 1504–1450 B.C.)
Thys·sen \'ti-s°n\ Fritz 1873–1951 Ger. industrialist
Tib·bett \'ti-bət\ Lawrence Mervil 1896–1960 Am. baritone
Ti·be·ri·us \tī-'bir-ē-əs\ 42 B.C.–A.D. 37 *Tiberius Claudius Nero Caesar Augustus* Rom. emp. (14–37)
Ti·bul·lus \tə-'bə-ləs\ Albius *ca* 55–*ca* 19 B.C. Rom. poet
Tieck \'tēk\ (Johann) Ludwig 1773–1853 Ger. author
Tie·po·lo \tē-'ä-pə-,lō, -'e-\ Giovanni Battista 1696–1770 Ital. painter
Tif·fa·ny \'ti-fə-nē\ Charles Lewis 1812–1902 Am. jeweler
Tiffany Louis Comfort 1848–1933 *son of C.L.* Am. painter & stained= glass artist
Tig·lath–pi·le·ser III \'ti-,glath-(,)pī-'lē-zər-, -pə-\ *d* 727 B.C. king of Assyria (745–727)
Til·den \'til-dən\ Samuel Jones 1814–1886 Am. polit.
Til·dy \'til-dē\ Zol·tán \'zol-,tän\ 1889–1961 Hung. polit.
Til·lich \'ti-lik, -lik\ Paul Johannes 1886–1965 Am. (Ger.-born) theol.
Till·ot·son \'ti-lət-sən\ John 1630–1694 Eng. prelate
Til·ly \'ti-lē\ Graf von 1559–1632 *Johann Tser·claes* \tsər-'kläs\ Bavarian gen.
Ti·mo·shen·ko \,ti-mə-'shen-(,)kō\ Semyon \səm-'yón\ Konstantinovich 1895–1970 Soviet marshal
Tim·ur \'ti-(,)mùr\ or Timur Lenk \-'leŋk\ 1336–1405 E. *Tam·er·lane* \'ta-mər-,län\ or *Tam·bur·laine* \'tam-bər-,län\ Turkic conqueror
Tin·ber·gen \'tin-,bər-gə(n)\ Jan 1903–1994 Du. econ.
Tinbergen Nikolaas 1907–1988 *bro. of Jan* Du. ethologist
Ting \'tiŋ\ Samuel Chao Chung 1936–   Am. physicist
Ting·ley \'tiŋ-lē\ Katherine Augusta 1847–1929 née *Westcott* Am. theosophist
Tin·to·ret·to \,tin-tə-'re-(,)tō\ *ca* 1518–1594 *Jacopo Robusti* Ital. painter
Ti·pu or Tip·pu Sul·tan \,ti-(,)pü-'sùl-,tän\ 1749(or 1753)–1799 sultan of Mysore (1782–99)
Tir·pitz \'tir-pəts, 'tər-\ Alfred von 1849–1930 Ger. admiral
Tir·so de Mo·li·na \'tir-(,)sō-,dā-mə-'lē-nə\ *ca* 1584–1648 pseud. of *Gabriel Tel·lez* \'tā(l)-yäth\ Span. dram.
Ti·se·li·us \tə-'sā-lē-əs, -'zä-\ Arne Wilhelm Kaurin 1902–1971 Swed. biochem.
Ti·so \'tē-(,)sō\ Josef or Joseph 1887–1947 Slovak priest & polit.
Titch·e·ner \'ti-chə-nər\ Edward Bradford 1867–1927 Am. psychol.
Ti·tian \'ti-shən\ *ca* 1488–1576 *Tiziano Vecellio* Ital. painter — Ti·tian·esque \,ti-shə-'nesk\ *adj*
Ti·to \'tē-(,)tō\ 1892–1980 orig. *Josip Broz* \'bròz, 'brōz\ usu. called *Marshal Tito* leader of Yugoslavia (1943–80)
Ti·tus \'tī-təs\ A.D. 39–81 *Titus Flavius Vespasianus* Rom. emp. (79–81)
To·bin \'tō-bən\ James 1918–   Am. econ.
Tocque·ville \'tōk-,vil, 'tòk-, 'täk-, -,vēl, -vəl\ Alexis-Charles-Henri Clérel de 1805–1859 Fr. statesman & author
Todd \'täd\ Sir Alexander Robertus 1907–   Brit. chem.
Todt \'tōt\ Fritz 1891–1942 Ger. military engineer
To·gliat·ti \tōl-'yä-tē\ Pal·mi·ro \päl-'mē-(,)rō\ 1893–1964 Ital. polit.
Tō·gō \'tō-(,)gō\ Marquis Heihachirō 1848–1934 Jp. admiral
Tō·jō \'tō-(,)jō\ Hideki 1884–1948 Jp. gen. & polit.
To·ku·ga·wa \,tō-kù-'gä-wə\ Ieyasu 1543–1616 orig. *Matsudaira Take·chiyo* Jp. shogun (1603–05); founder of last Jp. shogunate (1603–1867)
Tol·kien \'tól-,kēn\ John Ronald Reuel 1892–1973 Eng. author — Tol·kien·esque \,tól-(,)kē-'nesk\ *adj*
Tol·ler \'tō-lər, 'tä-\ Ernst 1893–1939 Ger. dram. & polit.
Tol·stoy \tòl-'stòi, tōl-', täl-', 'tòl-,, 'tōl-,, 'täl-,\ Count Lev Nikolayevich 1828–1910 Russ. nov., philos., & mystic — Tol·stoy·an also Tol·stoi·an \-ən\ *adj*
Tom·baugh \'täm-,bò\ Clyde William 1906–   Am. astron.
Tom·ma·si·ni \,tä-mə-'zē-nē\ Vincenzo 1878–1950 Ital. composer
To·mo·na·ga \,tō-mə-'nä-gə, -mō-\ Shin'ichirō 1906–1979 Jp. physicist
Tomp·kins \'tämp-)kənz\ Daniel D. 1774–1825 Am. polit.; vice pres. of the U.S. (1817–25)
Tone \'tōn\ (Theobald) Wolfe 1763–1798 Irish revolutionary
To·ne·ga·wa \,tō-nə-'gä-wə\ Susumu 1939–   Am. (Jp.-born) biol.
Tooke \'tùk\ (John) Horne 1736–1812 Eng. polit. radical & philologist
Toombs \'tümz\ Robert Augustus 1810–1885 Am. polit.
Tor·que·ma·da \,tór-kə-'mä-də, -thə\ Tomás de 1420–1498 Span. grand inquisitor
Tor·ri·cel·li \,tór-ə-'che-lē, ,tär-\ Evangelista 1608–1647 Ital. math. & physicist

Tos·ca·ni·ni \,täs-kə-'nē-nē, ,tòs-\ Ar·tu·ro \är-'tùr-(,)ō\ 1867–1957 Ital. conductor
Tou·louse–Lau·trec (–Mon·fa) \tù-,lüz-lō-'trek(-mō°-'fä)\ Henri= Marie-Raymond de 1864–1901 Fr. painter
Tour·neur \'tər-nər\ Cyril *ca* 1575–1626 Eng. dram.
Tous·saint–Lou·ver·ture \'tü-,san-'lü-vər-,tür, -,tyùr\ *ca* 1743–1803 orig. *François-Dominique Toussaint* Haitian gen. & liberator
Townes \'taùnz\ Charles Hard 1915–   Am. physicist
Toyn·bee \'tóin-bē\ Arnold Joseph 1889–1975 Eng. hist.
Tra·jan \'trā-jən\ A.D. 53–117 orig. *Marcus Ulpius Traiánus* usu. called *Germanicus* Rom. emp. (98–117)
Trau·bel \'traù-bəl\ Helen 1903–1972 Am. soprano
Tree \'trē\ Sir Herbert Draper Beerbohm 1853–1917 Eng. actor= manager
Treitsch·ke \'trīch-kə\ Heinrich von 1834–1896 Ger. hist.
Tre·vel·yan \tri-'vel-yən, -'vil-\ George Macaulay 1876–1962 Eng. hist.
Trevelyan Sir George Otto 1838–1928 *father of prec.* Eng. polit., biographer, & hist.
Trol·lope \'trä-ləp\ Anthony 1815–1882 Eng. nov. — Trol·lo·pi·an \trä-'lō-pē-ən\ *adj*
Tromp \'trómp, 'trämp\ Maarten Harpertszoon 1598–1653 Du. admiral
Trots·ky \'trät-skē also 'tròt-\ Leon 1879–1940 orig. *Lev Davidovich Bronstein* Russ. Communist leader
Tru·deau \trü-(,)dō\ Pierre Elliott 1919–   Canad. polit.; prime min. (1968–79; 1980–84)
Tru·ji·llo Mo·li·na \trü-'hē-(,)yō-mə-'lē-nə\ Rafael Leónidas 1891–1961 Dominican gen. & polit.; pres. of Dominican Republic (1930–38; 1942–52)
Tru·man \'trü-mən\ Harry S. 1884–1972 33d pres. of the U.S. (1945–53)
Trum·bull \'trəm-bəl\ John 1756–1843 Am. painter
Trumbull Jonathan 1710–1785 *father of prec.* Am. statesman
Truth \'trüth\ Sojourner *ca* 1797–1883 Am. evangelist & reformer
Ts'ao Chan \'tsaù-'jän\ 1715?–1763 *Ts'ao Hsüeh-ch'in* Chin. nov.
Tschaikovsky *var of* TCHAIKOVSKY
Tu Fu \'tü-'fü\ 712–770 Chin. poet
Tub·man \'təb-mən\ Harriet *ca* 1820–1913 Am. abolitionist
Tubman William Vacanarat Shadrach 1895–1971 Liberian lawyer; pres. of Liberia (1944–71)
Tuch·man \'tùk-mən\ Barbara 1912–1989 Am. hist.
Tu·dor \'tü-dər, 'tyü-\ Antony 1908 (or 1909)–1987 Am. (Brit.-born) ballet dancer & choreographer
Tul·sī·dās \,tùl-sē-'däs\ 1543?–1623 Hindu poet
Tup·per \'tə-pər\ Sir Charles 1821–1915 Canad. polit.; prime min. (1896)
Tu·renne \tü-'ren\ Vicomte de 1611–1675 *Henri de La Tour d'Auvergne* marshal of France
Tur·ge·nev \tùr-'gän-yəf, -'gen-\ Ivan Sergeyevich 1818–1883 Russ. nov.
Tur·got \tür-'gō\ Anne-Robert-Jacques 1727–1781 Baron *de l'Aulne* \'lōn\ Fr. statesman & econ.
Tur·ner \'tər-nər\ Frederick Jackson 1861–1932 Am. hist.
Turner Joseph Mallord William 1775–1851 Eng. painter
Turner Nat 1800–1831 Am. slave insurrectionist
Tut·ankh·a·men \,tü-,taŋ-'kä-mən, -,tän-\ or Tut·ankh·a·ten \-'kä-t°n\ *ca*1370–1352 B.C. king of Egypt (1361–1352 B.C.)
Tutu \'tü-,tü\ Desmond Mpilo 1931–   So. African clergyman & polit. activist
Twacht·man \'twäkt-mən\ John Henry 1853–1902 Am. painter
Twain Mark — see CLEMENS
Tweed \'twēd\ William Marcy 1823–1878 *Boss Tweed* Am. polit.
Tweedsmuir — see BUCHAN
Ty·ler \'tī-lər\ Anne 1941–   Am. writer
Tyler John 1790–1862 10th pres. of the U.S. (1841–45)
Tyler Wat \'wät\ or Walter *d* 1381 Eng. leader of Peasants' Revolt (1381)
Tyn·dale or Tin·dal or Tin·dale \'tin-d°l\ William *ca*1494–1536 Eng. reformer & translator
Tyn·dall \'tin-d°l\ John 1820–1893 Brit. physicist
Tyr·whitt–Wil·son \'tir-ət-'wil-sən\ Gerald Hugh 1883–1950 14th Baron *Ber·ners* \'bər-nərz\ Eng. composer & painter
Tz'u–hsi \'tsü-'shē\ 1835–1908 Chin. empress dowager
Uc·cel·lo \ü-'che-(,)lō\ Paolo 1397–1475 orig. *Paolo di Dono* Florentine painter
Udall \'yü-,dòl, 'yü-d°l\ Nicholas 1505–1556 Eng. schoolmaster & dram.
Ugar·te \ü-'gär-tē\ Manuel 1874–1951 Argentine writer
Uh·land \'ü-,länt\ Johann Ludwig 1787–1862 Ger. poet & hist.
Ul·bricht \'ùl-(,)brikt, -(,)brikt\ Walter 1893–1973 East German polit.
Ul·fi·las \'ùl-fə-ləs, 'ul-, -ləs, -,las\ or Goth. Wul·fi·la \'wùl-fə-lə\ *ca* 311–*ca* 382 Gothic missionary
Ul·pi·an \'əl-pē-ən\ *d* A.D. 228 *Domitius Ulpianus* Rom. jurist
Um·ber·to \(,)əm-'ber-(,)tō\ name of 2 kings of Italy: I 1844–1900 Duke of *Savoy* (reigned 1878–1900); II 1904–1983 Prince of *Piedmont*; Count of *Sarre* (reigned 1946)
Una·mu·no y Ju·go \,ü-nə-'mü-(,)nō-ē-'hü-(,)gō\ Miguel de 1864–1936 Span. philos. & writer
Un·cas \'əŋ-kəs\ 1588?–?1683 Pequot Indian chief
Und·set \'ün-,set\ Sigrid \'si-grē, -grəd\ 1882–1949 Norw. nov.
Uno \'ü-(,)nō\ Sousuke 1922–   prime min. of Japan (1989)
Un·ter·mey·er \'ən-tər-,mī(-ə)r\ Louis 1885–1977 Am. poet
Up·dike \'əp-,dīk\ John Hoyer 1932–   Am. writer
Up·john \'əp-,jän\ Richard 1802–1878 Am. (Eng.-born) architect
Up·ton \'əp-tən\ Emory 1839–1881 Am. gen. & author
Ur·ban \'ər-bən\ name of 8 popes: esp. II (*Odo* \'ō-(,)dō\ *of Lagery*) *ca* 1035–1099 (pope 1088–99)
Urey \'yùr-ē\ Harold Clayton 1893–1981 Am. chem.
Ur·quhart \'ər-kərt, -,kärt\ or Ur·chard \,ər-chərd\ Sir Thomas 1611–1660 Scot. author & translator
Ussh·er \'ə-shər\ James 1581–1656 Irish prelate
Utril·lo \yü-'tri-(,)lō; ,yü-trē-'ō, ,üe-\ Maurice 1883–1955 Fr. painter

Val·de·mar \'väl-də-,mär, 'val-\ or Wal·de·mar \'wòl-\ name of 4 kings of Denmark: esp. I 1131–1182 (reigned 1157–82)

Valdes Peter — see WALDO

Val·di·via \val-'dē-vē-ə\ Pedro de ca 1498–1553 Span. conquistador

Va·lens \'vä-lənz, -,lenz\ 328?–378 Rom. emp. of the East (364–378)

Val·en·tin·ian \,va-lən-'ti-nē-ən, -'tin-yən\ L Val·en·tin·i·a·nus \'va-lən-,ti-nē-'ä-nəs\ name of 3 Rom. emperors: I 321–375 (reigned 364–375); II 371–392 (reigned 375–392); III 419–455 (reigned 425–455))

Valera Eamon de — see DE VALERA

Va·le·ra y Al·ca·lá Ga·lia·no \və-'ler-ə-,ē-,al-kə-'lä-,ga-lē-'ä-(,)nō, -,äl-kə-, -,gä-\ Juan 1824–1905 Span. writer & statesman

Va·le·ri·an \və-'lir-ē-ən\ d A.D. 260 Publius Licinius Valerianus Rom. emp. (253–260)

Va·lé·ry \,va-lə-'rē, 'va-lə-rē\ (Ambroise-) Paul-Toussaint-Jules 1871–1945 Fr. poet & philos.

Val·le·jo \və-'lā-(,)ō, -'yä-(,)(h)ō\ Mariano Guadalupe 1808–1890 Am. soldier & pioneer

Van Al·len \van-'a-lən\ James Alfred 1914– Am. physicist

Van·brugh \'van-brə, van-'brü\ Sir John 1664–1726 Eng. dram. & architect

Van Bu·ren \van-'byùr-ən, vən-\ Martin 1782–1862 8th pres. of the U.S. (1837–41)

Van·cou·ver \van-'kü-vər\ George 1757–1798 Eng. navigator & explorer

Van·de·grift \'van-də-,grift\ Alexander Archer 1887–1973 Am. marine-corps gen.

Van·den·berg \'van-dən-,bərg\ Arthur Hendrick 1884–1951 Am. journalist & polit.

Van·der·bilt \'van-dər-,bilt\ Cornelius 1794–1877 Am. industrialist

van der Meer \van-dər-'mer\ Simon 1925– Du. physicist

Van Dine — see Willard Huntington WRIGHT

van Dongen Kees — see DONGEN

Van Do·ren \van-'dōr-ən, vən-, -'dòr-\ Carl Clinton 1885–1950 & his bro. Mark 1894–1972 Am. writers & editors

Van Dyck or Van·dyke \van-'dīk, vən-\ Sir Anthony 1599–1641 Flem. painter

Vane \'vän\ Sir Henry 1613–1662 the Younger Eng. statesman

Vane John R. 1927– Eng. pharmacologist

Van Eyck — see EYCK, VAN

van Gogh Vincent Willem — see GOGH, VAN

Van·ier \'van-yā\ Georges-Philéas 1888–1967 Canad. polit.; gov.-gen. (1959–67)

Van Rens·se·laer \,van-,ren(t)-sə-'lir, -,ren-'slir, vən-; -'ren(t)-s(ə-)lər\ Stephen 1764–1839 Am. gen. & polit.

van't Hoff \vänt-'hòf, vant-\ Jacobus Hen·dri·cus \hen-'drē-kəs\ 1852–1911 Du. physical chem.

Van Vleck \van-'vlek\ John Hasbrouck 1899–1980 Am. physicist

Vanzetti Bartolomeo — see Nicola SACCO

Va·rèse \və-'räz, -'rez\ Edgard 1883–1965 orig. Edgar Victor Achille Charles Varèse Am. (Fr.-born) composer

Var·gas \'vär-gəs\ Getúlio Dornelles 1883–1954 Braz. lawyer; pres. of Brazil (1930–45; 1951–54)

Var·mus \'vär-məs\ Harold Elliot 1939– Am. microbiologist

Var·ro \'var-(,)ō\ Marcus Terentius 116–27 B.C. Rom. scholar

Va·sa·ri \və-'zär-ē\ Giorgio 1511–1574 Ital. artist & art hist.

Vasco da Gama — see GAMA

Va·tu·tin \vo-'tü-tin\ Nikolay Fyodorovich 1900–1944 Soviet gen.

Vau·ban \vō-'bän\ Sébastien Le Prestre de 1633–1707 Fr. mil. engineer; marshal of France

Vaughan \'vòn, 'vän\ Henry 1621?–1695 Brit. poet

Vaughan Sarah Lois 1924–1990 Am. singer

Vaughan Wil·liams \-'wil-yəmz\ Ralph 1872–1958 Eng. composer

Veb·len \'ve-blən\ Thor·stein \'thòr-,stīn\ Bunde 1857–1929 Am. sociol. & econ. — Veb·le·ni·an \ve-'blē-nē-ən\ adj

Ve·ga \'vā-gə\ Lo·pe \'lō-(,)pā\ de 1562–1635 Lope Félix de Vega Carpio Span. dram.

Ve·láz·quez \və-'läs-kəs, -'läs-, -kwiz, -(,)käs\ Diego Rodríguez de Silva 1599–1660 Span. painter

Ven·dôme \vä n(n)-'dōm\ Duc de 1654–1712 Louis-Joseph Fr. soldier

Ve·ni·zé·los \,ve-nə-'zä-ləs, -'ze-ləs\ Eleuthérios 1864–1936 Greek statesman

Ver·di \'ver-dē\ Giuseppe Fortunio Francesco 1813–1901 Ital. composer — Ver·di·an \-ən\ adj

Ve·re·ker \'ver-ə-kər\ John Standish Surtees Prendergast 1886–1946 6th Viscount Gort \'gòrt\ Brit. soldier

Ve·re·shcha·gin \,ver-əsh-'chä-gən, ,ver-ə-'shä-\ Vasily Vasilyevich 1842–1904 Russ. painter

Vergil — see VIRGIL

Ver·laine \ver-'län, -'len\ Paul 1844–1896 Fr. poet

Ver·meer \vər-'mer, -'mir\ Jan 1632–1675 also called Jan van der Meer van Delft \vän-dər-'mer-van-'delft, -'mir-\ Du. painter

Verne \'vərn, 'vern\ Jules \'jülz, 'zhüēl\ 1828–1905 Fr. writer

Ver·ner \'vər-nər\ Karl Adolph 1846–1896 Dan. philologist

Ver·nier \vern-'yā, 'vər-nē-ər\ Pierre ca 1580–1637 Fr. math.

Ver·non \'vər-nən\ Edward 1684–1757 Eng. admiral

Ve·ro·ne·se \,ver-ə-'nä-sē, -zē\ Paolo 1528–1588 orig. Paolo Caliari Ital. painter

Ver·ra·za·no or Ver·raz·za·no \,ver-ə-'zä-(,)nō, -ət-'sä-\ Giovanni da 1485?–?1528 Florentine navigator & explorer

Ver·roc·chio \və-'rò-kē-,ō\ Andrea del 1435–1488 orig. Andrea di Michele Cione Florentine sculptor & painter

Verulam — see Francis BACON

Ve·rus \'vir-əs\ Lucius Aurelius A.D. 130–169 orig. Lucius Ceionius Commodus Rom. emp. (161–169)

Ver·woerd \fər-'vùrt, -\ Hendrik Frensch 1901–1966 So. African polit.; prime min. (1958–66)

Ve·sa·li·us \və-'sā-lē-əs, -'zā-\ Andreas 1514–1564 Belg. anatomist

Ve·sey \'vē-zē\ Denmark ca 1767–1822 Am. slave insurrectionist

Ves·pa·sian \ve-'spā-zh(ē-)ən\ A.D. 9–79 Titus Flavius Sabinus Vespasianus Rom. emp. (69–79)

Ves·puc·ci \ve-'spü-chē, -'spyü-\ Ame·ri·go \ə-'mer-i-,gō, It ,ä-mə-'rē-(,)gō\ 1454–1512 L. Amer·i·cus Ves·pu·cius \ə-'mer-ə-kəs,ves-'pyüsh(ē-)əs\ Ital. navigator & explorer

Vi·co \'vē-kō\ Giambattista 1668–1744 Ital. philos.

Vic·tor Em·man·u·el I \'vik-tər-i-'man-yə-wəl\ 1759–1824 king of Sardinia (1802–21)

Victor Emmanuel II 1820–1878 king of Sardinia-Piedmont (1849–61) & 1st king of Italy (1861–78)

Victor Emmanuel III 1869–1947 king of Italy (1900–46)

Vic·to·ria \vik-'tōr-ē-ə, -'tòr-\ 1819–1901 Alexandrina Victoria queen of Great Britain (1837–1901)

Victoria Tomás Luis de ca 1548–1611 Span. composer

Vi·da \'vē-də\ Marco Girolamo ca1490–1566 Ital. poet

Vi·gée—Le·brun \vē-'zhä-lə-'brœ n(n), -'brœ n\ Marie-Louise-Élisabeth 1755–1842 Fr. painter

Vi·gno·la \vēn-'yō-lə\ Giacomo da 1507–1573 Giacomo Ba·roz·zi \bä-'ròt-sē\ Ital. architect

Vi·gny \vēn-'yē\ Alfred-Victor de 1797–1863 Fr. author

Vil·la \'vē-yə\ Francisco usu. called Pan·cho \'pän-(,)chō, 'pan-\ 1878–1923 orig. Doroteo Arango Mex. bandit & revolutionary

Vil·la—Lo·bos \,vē-lə-'lō-(,)bōsh, -(,)bōs, -bəs\ Heitor \'ā-,tòr\ 1887–1959 Braz. composer

Vil·lard \və-'lär(d)\ Oswald Garrison 1872–1949 Am. journalist

Vil·lars \vi-'lär\ Claude-Louis-Hector 1653–1734 Duc de Villars Fr. soldier; marshal of France

Ville·neuve \,vēl-'nə(r)v, -'nœv\ Pierre-Charles-Jean-Baptiste-Silvestre de 1763–1806 Fr. admiral

Vil·liers \'vil-yərz, 'vi-lərz\ George 1592–1628 1st Duke of Buck·ing·ham \'bə-kiŋ-əm, US also -kiŋ-,ham\ Eng. courtier & polit.

Villiers George 1628–1687 2d Duke of Buckingham, son of prec. Eng. courtier & dram.

Vil·lon \vē-'yō n also -'lō\ François 1431–after 1463 orig. François de Montcorbier or Des Loges Fr. poet

Vil·lon \vē-'lō n, -'yō n\ Jacques 1875–1963 orig. Gaston Duchamp; bro. of Marcel Duchamp Fr. painter

Vin·cent de Paul \'vin(t)-sənt-də-'pòl\ Saint 1581–1660 Fr. religious

Vinci, da Leonardo — see LEONARDO DA VINCI

Vi·no·gra·doff \,vi-nə-'gra-,dòf\ Sir Paul Gavrilovitch 1854–1925 Brit. (Russ.-born) jurist & hist.

Vin·son \'vin(t)-sən\ Frederick Moore 1890–1953 Am. jurist; chief justice U.S. Supreme Court (1946–53)

Viol·let—le—Duc \vē-ə-'lā-lə-'dük, -'dyük; vyò-le-lə-dūēk\ Eugène Emmanuel 1814–1879 Fr. architect

Vir·chow \'fir-(,)kō, 'vir-\ Rudolf 1821–1902 Ger. pathologist

Vir·gil also Ver·gil \'vər-jəl\ 70–19 B.C. Publius Vergilius Maro Rom. poet — Vir·gil·ian also Ver·gil·ian \(,)vər-'ji-lē-ən\ adj

Vir·ta·nen \'vir-tə-,nen\ Art·tu·ri \'är-tə-rē\ Ilmari 1895–1973 Finn. biochem.

Vi·tru·vi·us \və-'trü-vē-əs\ fl 1st cent. B.C. Marcus Vitruvius Pollio Rom. architect & engineer

Vi·val·di \vi-'väl-dē, -'vòl-\ Antonio Lucio 1678–1741 Ital. composer

Vla·di·mir I \'vla-də-,mir, vlə-'dē-,mir\ Saint ca 956–1015 grand prince of Kiev (980–1015)

Vla·minck \vlə-'maŋk\ Maurice de 1876–1958 Fr. painter

Vo·gler \'fō-glər\ Georg Joseph 1749–1814 Abt \äpt, apt\ or Abbé Vogler Ger. composer & writer

Vol·stead \'väl-,sted, 'vòl-, 'vōl-, -stəd\ Andrew John 1860–1947 Am. legislator

Vol·ta \'vōl-tə, 'väl-, 'vòl-\ Conte Alessandro Giuseppe Antonio Anastasio 1745–1827 Ital. physicist

Vol·taire \vōl-'tar, väl-, vòl-, -'ter\ 1694–1778 orig. François-Marie Arouet Fr. writer — Vol·tair·ean or Vol·tair·ian \-'tar-ē-ən, -'ter-\ adj

Von Braun Wernher — see BRAUN

Von Eu·ler \fòn-'òi-lər\ Ulf Svante 1905–1983 Swed. physiol.

Von·ne·gut \'vä-ni-gət\ Kurt 1922– Am. writer

Vo·ro·shi·lov \'för-stər\ \,vòr-ə-'shē-,lòf, -,vär-, -,lòv\ Kliment Yefremovich 1881–1969 Soviet marshal; chairman of the Presidium (1953–60)

Vor·ster \'för-stər\ Balthazar Johannes 1915–1983 prime min. of Republic of So. Africa (1966–78)

Voz·ne·sen·sky \,väz-nə-'sen(t)-skē\ Andrey 1933– Soviet (Russ.-born) poet

Vries, de \də-'vrēs\ Hugo Marie 1848–1935 Du. botanist & geneticist

Vuil·lard \vwē-'yär\ (Jean-)Édouard 1868–1940 Fr. painter

Vy·shin·sky \və-'shin(t)-skē\ Andrey Yanuaryevich 1883–1954 Soviet lawyer, polit., & diplomat

Waals, van der \'van-dər-,wòlz\ Johannes Diderik 1837–1923 Du. physicist

Wace \'wās, 'wäs\ ca1100–after 1174 Anglo-Norman poet

Wag·ner \'väg-nər\ (Wilhelm) Ri·chard \'ri-,kärt, -,kärt\ 1813–1883 Ger. composer

Wagner von Jau·regg or Wagner—Jau·regg \-'yaù-,rek\ Julius 1857–1940 Austrian neurologist & psychiatrist

Wain·wright \'wān-,rīt\ Jonathan Mayhew 1883–1953 Am. gen.

Wainwright Richard father 1817–1862 & his son 1849–1926 Am. naval officers

Waite \'wāt\ Morrison Remick 1816–1888 Am. jurist; chief justice U.S. Supreme Court (1874–88)

Waks·man \'wäks-mən, 'waks-\ Sel·man \'sel-mən\ Abraham 1888–1973 Am. (Ukrainian-born) microbiologist

Wal·cott \'wäl-(,)kät\ Derek Alton 1930– West Indian poet & playwright

Wald \'wòld\ George 1906– Am. biol.

Wald Lillian D. 1867–1940 Am. social worker

Waldemar — see VALDEMAR

Wal·der·see \'väl-dər-,zā, 'wòl-\ Alfred von 1832–1904 Ger. soldier

Wald·heim \'vält-,hīm\ Kurt 1918– Austrian U.N. official; secy.-gen. (1972–82); pres. of Austria (1986–92)

Wal·do \'wòl-(,)dō, 'wäl-\ or Val·des \'val-(,)dās, 'väl-\ Peter d before 1218 Fr. religious leader

\ə\ abut \'ə\ kitten, F table \ər\ further \a\ ash \ā\ ace \ä\ mop, mar \aù\ out \ch\ chin \e\ bet \ē\ easy \g\ go \i\ hit \ī\ ice \j\ job \ŋ\ sing \ō\ go \ò\ law \òi\ boy \th\ thin \th\ the \ü\ loot \ù\ foot \y\ yet \zh\ vision \á, k̲, n, œ, œ̄, ue, ūe, ᵻ\ see Guide to Pronunciation

Wa·łe·sa \vä-'len(t)-sə, wä-; wä-'wen-sə\ Lech \'lek, 'lek\ 1943–
Pol. polit.; pres. of Poland (1990–   )
Walk·er \'wȯ-kər\ Alice Malsenior 1944–   Am. writer
Walker Francis Am·a·sa \'a-mə-sə\ 1840–1897 Am. econ.
Walker William 1824–1860 Am. filibuster
Wal·lace \'wä-ləs\ Alfred Russel 1823–1913 Eng. naturalist
Wallace George Corley 1919–   Am. polit.
Wallace Henry Agard \'ā-,gärd\ 1888–1965 Am. agriculturist, editor,
& polit.; vice pres. of the U.S. (1941–45)
Wallace Lewis 1827–1905 *Lew* Am. lawyer, gen., & nov.
Wallace Sir William *ca* 1270–1305 Scot. patriot
Wal·lach \'wä-läk, 'väl-\ Otto 1847–1931 Ger. chem.
Wal·len·berg \'wä-lən-,bərg, *Sw* -,ber-ē\ Raoul 1912–1947? Swed.
diplomat & hero of the Holocaust
Wal·len·stein \'vä-lən-,shtīn, 'wä-lən-,stīn\ Albrecht Eusebius Wenzel
von 1583–1634 Duke of *Friedland and Mecklenburg;* Prince of *Sagan*
Austrian gen.
Wal·ler \'wä-lər\ Edmund 1606–1687 Eng. poet
Waller Thomas Wright 1904–1943 *Fats* Am. pianist & composer
Wal·pole \'wȯl-,pōl, 'wäl-\ Horace 1717–1797 orig. *Horatio* 4th Earl of
Or·ford \'ȯr-fərd\ Eng. author
Walpole Sir Hugh Seymour 1884–1941 Eng. nov.
Walpole Sir Robert 1676–1745 1st Earl of *Orford; father of Horace*
Eng. statesman — **Wal·pol·ian** \wȯl-'pō-lē-ən, wäl-\ *adj*
Wal·ter \'väl-tər, 'wȯl-\ Bruno 1876–1962 orig. *Bruno Schle·sing·er*
\'shlā-ziŋ-ər\ Am. (Ger.-born) conductor
Wal·ther von der Vo·gel·wei·de \'väl-tər-,fȯn-dər-'fō-gəl-,vī-də\
*ca*1170–*ca*1230 Ger. minnesinger
Wal·ton \'wȯl-t°n\ Ernest Thomas Sinton 1903–1995 Irish physicist
Walton Izaak \'ī-zik, -zək\ 1593–1683 Eng. writer
Walton Sir William Turner 1902–1983 Eng. composer
Wan·a·ma·ker \'wä-nə-,mā-kər\ John 1838–1922 Am. merchant
Wang Ching–wei \'wäŋ-'jiŋ-'wä\ 1883–1944 Chin. polit.
War·beck \'wȯr-,bek\ Perkin 1474–1499 Flem. imposter & pretender
to the English throne
War·burg \'wȯr-,bərg, 'vär-,bu̇rk\ Otto Heinrich 1883–1970 Ger. bio-
chem.
Ward \'wȯrd\ Aaron Montgomery 1843–1913 Am. merchant
Ward Ar·te·mas \'är-tə-məs\ 1727–1800 Am. gen. in Revolution
Ward Artemus — see Charles Farrar BROWNE
Ward Barbara 1914–1981 Baroness *Jackson of Lodsworth* Eng. econ.
Ward Sir George 1856–1930 N.Z. statesman
Ward Mary Augusta 1851–1920 *Mrs. Humphry Ward* née *Arnold* Eng.
nov.
War·hol \'wȯr-,hȯl, -,hōl\ Andy 1927?–1987 Am. artist & filmmaker
— **War·hol·ian** \(,)wȯr-'hō-lē-ən, -'hȯ-\ *adj*
War·ner \'wȯr-nər\ Charles Dudley 1829–1900 Am. editor & essayist
War·ren \'wȯr-ən, 'wär-\ Earl 1891–1974 Am. jurist; chief justice U.S.
Supreme Court (1953–69)
Warren Gou·ver·neur \,gə-və(r)-'nir\ Kemble 1830–1882 Am. gen.
Warren Joseph 1741–1775 Am. physician & gen. in Revolution
Warren Robert Penn 1905–1989 Am. author & educ.; poet laureate
(1986–87)
War·ton \'wȯr-t°n\ Thomas 1728–1790 Eng. lit. hist. & critic; poet
laureate (1785–90)
War·wick \'wär-ik, *US also* 'wȯr-ik, 'wȯr-(,)wik\ Earl of 1428–1471
Richard Nev·ille \'ne-vəl\; *the Kingmaker* Eng. soldier & statesman
Wash·ing·ton \'wȯ-shiŋ-tən, *chiefly Midland also* 'wȯr- *or* 'wär-\
Book·er \'bu̇-kər\ Tal·ia·ferro \'tä-lə-vər\ 1856–1915 Am. educ.
Washington George 1732–1799 Am. gen.; 1st pres. of the U.S.
(1789–97) — **Wash·ing·to·nian** \,wȯ-shiŋ-'tō-nē-ən, ,wä-, ,wȯr-,
,wär-, -nyən\ *adj*
Was·mo·sy \wäs-'mō-sē\ Juan Carlos 1939–   pres. of Paraguay
(1993–   )
Was·ser·mann \'wä-sər-mən, 'vä-\ August von 1866–1925 Ger. bac-
teriol.
Was·ser·stein \'wä-sər-,stīn\ Wendy 1950–   Am. dram.
Wa·ters \'wȯ-tərz, 'wä-\ Ethel 1896–1977 Am. actress & singer
Wat·son \'wät-sən\ James Dewey 1928–   Am. geneticist
Watson John 1850–1907 pseud. *Ian Mac·lar·en* \mə-'klar-ən\ Scot.
clergyman & author
Watson John Broadus 1878–1958 Am. psychol.
Watson Sir (John) William 1858–1935 Eng. poet
Watson–Watt \-'wät\ Sir Robert Alexander 1892–1973 Scot. physi-
cist
Watt \'wät\ James 1736–1819 Scot. inventor
Wat·teau \wä-'tō, vä-\ (Jean-) Antoine 1684–1721 Fr. painter
Wat·ter·son \'wä-tər-sən, 'wȯ-\ Henry 1840–1921 Am. journalist &
polit.
Watts \'wäts\ George Frederic 1817–1904 Eng. painter & sculptor
Watts Isaac 1674–1748 Eng. theol. & hymn writer
Watts–Dun·ton \-'dən-t°n\ Walter Theodore 1832–1914 Eng. critic &
poet
Waugh \'wȯ\ Evelyn Arthur St. John 1903–1966 Eng. writer
Wa·vell \'wä-vəl\ 1st Earl 1883–1950 *Archibald Percival Wavell* Brit.
field marshal; viceroy of India (1943–47)
Wayne \'wān\ Anthony 1745–1796 *Mad Anthony* Am. gen. in Revolu-
tion
Webb \'web\ Beatrice 1858–1943 née *Potter; wife of S.J.* Eng. socialist
Webb Sidney James 1859–1947 1st Baron *Passfield* Eng. socialist
We·ber \'vā-bər\ Ernst Heinrich 1795–1878 Ger. physiol.
Weber Carl Maria von 1786–1826 Ger. composer & conductor
Weber Max 1864–1920 Ger. sociol. & econ. — **We·be·ri·an** \vā-'bir-ē-
ən\ *adj*
We·ber \'we-bər\ Max 1881–1961 Am. (Russ.-born) painter
We·bern \'vā-bərn\ Anton von 1883–1945 Austrian composer
Web·ster \'web-stər\ Daniel 1782–1852 Am. statesman & orator
Webster John *ca*1580–*ca*1625 Eng. dram.
Webster Noah 1758–1843 Am. lexicographer & author
Wedg·wood \'wej-,wu̇d\ Josiah 1730–1795 Eng. potter
Weems \'wēmz\ Mason Locke 1759–1825 *Parson Weems* Am. clergy-
man & biographer
We·ge·ner \'vā-gə-nər\ Alfred Lothar 1880–1930 Ger. geophysicist &
meteorologist

Weill \'wī(ə)l, 'vī(ə)l\ Kurt \'ku̇rt\ 1900–1950 Am. (Ger.-born) com-
poser
Wein·berg \'wīn-,bərg\ Steven 1933–   Am. physicist
Wein·ber·ger \'wīn-,bər-gər\ Caspar Willard 1917–   U.S. secy. of
defense (1981–87)
Weir \'wir\ Robert Walter 1803–1889 Am. painter
Weis·mann \'vis-,män, 'wīs-mən\ August Friedrich Leopold
1834–1914 Ger. biol.
Weiz·mann \'vits-mən, 'wīts-\ Chaim \'kīm, 'hīm\ Azriel 1874–1952
Israeli (Russ.-born) chem.; 1st pres. of Israel (1949–52)
Welch \'welch, 'welsh\ William Henry 1850–1934 Am. pathologist
Wel·ler \'we-lər\ Thomas Huckle 1915–   Am. virologist
Welles \'welz\ (George) Or·son \'ȯr-s°n\ 1915–1985 Am. film & the-
ater director, writer, producer, & actor
Welles Gideon 1802–1878 Am. polit. & writer
Welles Sumner 1892–1961 Am. diplomat
Welles·ley \'welz-lē\ 1st Marquis of 1760–1842 *Richard Colley Welles-
ley* Brit. statesman; gov.-gen. of India (1797–1805)
Wel·ling·ton \'we-liŋ-tən\ 1st Duke of 1769–1852 *Arthur Wellesley; the
Iron Duke* Brit. gen. & statesman
Wells \'welz\ Herbert George 1866–1946 Eng. nov. & hist. — **Wells-
ian** \'wel-zē-ən\ *adj*
Wel·ty \'wel-tē\ Eudora 1909–   Am. writer
Wen·ces·las \'wen(t)-sə-,sləs, -sləs\ *G* **Wen·zel** \'ven(t)-səl\
1361–1419 king of Germany & Holy Rom. emp. (1378–1400) & (as
Wenceslas IV) king of Bohemia (1378–1419)
Wen·dell \'wen-d°l\ Barrett 1855–1921 Am. scholar
Went·worth \'went-(,)wərth\ William Charles 1793–1872 Austral.
statesman
Wer·fel \'ver-fəl\ Franz 1890–1945 Ger. author
Wer·ner \'ver-nər\ Alfred 1866–1919 Swiss chem.
Wes·ley \'wes-lē, 'wez-\ Charles 1707–1788 *bro. of John* Eng. Method-
ist preacher & hymn writer
Wesley John 1703–1791 Eng. theol., evangelist, & founder of Method-
ism
West \'west\ Benjamin 1738–1820 Am. painter
West Nathanael 1903–1940 orig. *Nathan Wallenstein Weinstein* Am.
nov.
West Dame Rebecca 1892–1983 pseud. of *Cicily Isabel Andrews* née
Fairfield Eng. critic & nov.
West Thomas — SEE DE LA WARR
Wes·ter·marck \'wes-tər-,märk\ Edward Alexander 1862–1939 Finn.
philos. & anthropol.
Wes·ting·house \'wes-tiŋ-,hau̇s\ George 1846–1914 Am. inventor
Wet, de \də-'vet\ Christiaan Rudolf 1854–1922 Boer soldier & polit.
Wey·den \'vī-d°n, 'vā-\ Rogier van der 1399?–1464 Flem. painter
Wey·gand \vā-gäⁿ\ Maxime 1867–1965 Fr. gen.
Whar·ton \'hwȯr-t°n, 'wȯr-\ Edith Newbold 1862–1937 née *Jones* Am.
nov.
Whate·ly \'hwāt-lē, 'wāt-\ Richard 1787–1863 Eng. theol. & logician
Wheat·ley \'hwēt-lē, 'wēt-\ Phillis 1753?–1784 Am. (African-born)
poet
Wheat·stone \'hwēt-,stōn, 'wēt-, *chiefly Brit* -stən\ Sir Charles
1802–1875 Eng. physicist & inventor
Whee·ler \'hwē-lər, 'wē-\ Joseph 1836–1906 Am. gen.
Wheeler William Almon 1819–1887 Am. polit.; vice pres. of the U.S.
(1877–81)
Whee·lock \'hwē-,läk, 'wē-\ Eleazar 1711–1779 Am. clergyman &
educ.
Whip·ple \'hwi-pəl, 'wi-\ George Hoyt 1878–1976 Am. pathologist
Whis·tler \'hwis-lər, 'wis-\ James Abbott McNeill 1834–1903 Am.
painter & etcher — **Whis·tler·ian** \hwis-'lir-ē-ən, wis-\ *adj*
White \'hwīt, 'wīt\ Andrew Dickson 1832–1918 Am. educ. & diplomat
White Byron Raymond 1917–   Am. jurist & polit.
White Edward Douglass 1845–1921 Am. jurist; chief justice U.S. Su-
preme Court (1910–21)
White Elwyn Brooks 1899–1985 Am. journalist & writer
White Gilbert 1720–1793 Eng. clergyman & naturalist
White Patrick Victor Martindale 1912–1990 Austral. writer
White Stanford 1853–1906 Am. architect
White Stewart Edward 1873–1946 Am. writer
White Theodore Harold 1915–1986 Am. writer
White William Allen 1868–1944 Am. journalist & writer
White·field \'hwit-,fēld, 'hwīt-, 'wit-, 'wīt-\ George 1714–1770 Eng.
Methodist revivalist
White·head \'hwit-,hed, 'wīt-\ Alfred North 1861–1947 Eng. math &
philos.
Whitehead William 1715–1785 Eng. dram.; poet laureate (1757–85)
Whit·man \'hwit-mən, 'wit-\ Marcus 1802–1847 & his wife Narcissa
1808–1847 née *Prentiss* Am. missionaries & pioneers
Whitman Walt \'wȯlt\ 1819–1892 orig. *Walter* Am. poet — **Whit-
man·esque** \,hwit-mə-'nesk, ,wit-\ *or* **Whit·man·ni·an** \hwit-'mā-nē-
ən, wit-\ *adj*
Whit·ney \'hwit-nē, 'wit-\ Eli 1765–1825 Am. inventor
Whitney Josiah Dwight 1819–1896 Am. geologist
Whitney William Dwight 1827–1894 *bro. of J.D.* Am. philologist
Whit·ta·ker \'hwi-ti-kər, 'wit-\ Charles Evans 1901–1973 Am. jurist
Whit·ti·er \'hwi-tē-ər, 'wit-\ John Greenleaf 1807–1892 Am. poet
Wic·lif *or* **Wick·liffe** *var of* WYCLIFFE
Wi·dor \vē-'dȯr\ Charles-Marie 1844–1937 Fr. organist & composer
Wie·land \'vē-,länt\ Christoph Martin 1733–1813 Ger. author
Wieland Heinrich 1877–1957 Ger. chem.
Wien \'vēn\ Wilhelm 1864–1928 Ger. physicist
Wie·ner \'wē-nər\ Norbert 1894–1964 Am. math.
Wie·sel \vē-'zel, wē-\ El·ie \'e-lē\ 1928–   Am. (Rom.-born) writer
Wie·sel \'vē-səl\ Torsten N. 1924–   Swed. neurobiologist
Wig·gin \'wi-gən\ Kate Douglas 1856–1923 Am. writer & educ.
Wig·ner \'wig-nər\ Eugene Paul 1902–1995 Am. (Hung.-born) physi-
cist
Wil·ber·force \'wil-bər-,fȯrs, -,fȯrs\ William 1759–1833 Eng. philan-
thropist & abolitionist
Wil·bur \'wil-bər\ Richard Purdy 1921–   Am. poet & translator;
poet laureate (1987–88)

Wilde \'wī(ə)ld\ Oscar Fingal O'Flahertie Wills 1854–1900 Irish writer — Wil·de·an \'wĭl-dē-ən\ adj
Wil·der \'wĭl-dər\ Thornton Niven 1897–1975 Am. author
Wi·ley \'wī-lē\ Harvey Washington 1844–1930 Am. chem. & reformer
Wil·hel·mi·na \,wil-(,)hel-'mē-nə, ,wi-lə-'mē-\ 1880–1962 queen of the Netherlands (1890–1948)
Wilkes \'wilks\ Charles 1798–1877 Am. naval officer & explorer
Wilkes John 1725–1797 Eng. polit.
Wil·kins \'wil-kənz\ Sir George Hubert 1888–1958 Austral. explorer
Wilkins Mary Eleanor — see Mary E. FREEMAN
Wilkins Maurice Hugh Frederick 1916–   Brit. biophysicist
Wilkins Roy 1901–1981 Am. civil rights leader
Wil·kin·son \'wil-kən-sən\ Ellen Cicely 1891–1947 Eng. polit.
Wilkinson Sir Geoffrey 1921–   Brit. chem.
Wilkinson James 1757–1825 Am. gen. & adventurer
Wil·lard \'wi-lərd\ Emma 1787–1870 née Hart Am. educ.
Willard Frances Elizabeth Caroline 1839–1898 Am. educ. & reformer
Will·cocks \'wil-,käks\ Sir William 1852–1932 Brit. engineer
Wil·liam \'wil-yəm\ name of 4 kings of England: I (the Conqueror) ca1028–1087 (reigned 1066–87); II (Ru·fus \'rü-fəs\) ca1056–1100 (reigned 1087–1100); III 1650–1702 (reigned 1689–1702—see MARY); IV 1765–1837 (reigned 1830–37)
William I 1533–1584 the Silent prince of Orange & founder of the Du. Republic
William I 1797–1888 Wilhelm Friedrich Ludwig king of Prussia (1861–88) Ger. emp. (1871–88)
William II 1859–1941 Friedrich Wilhelm Viktor Albert Ger. emp. & king of Prussia (1888–1918)
William 1882–1951 Friedrich Wilhelm Victor August Ernst crown prince of Germany (1888–1918)
William of Malmes·bury \'mämz-,ber-ē, 'mälmz-, -b(ə-)rē\ ca 1090–ca 1143 Eng. hist.
Wil·liams \'wil-yəmz\ Elizabeth 1943–   Betty Irish peace worker
Williams Ralph Vaughan — see VAUGHAN WILLIAMS
Williams Roger 1603?–1683 Am. (Eng.-born) clergyman & founder of Rhode Island colony
Williams Tennessee 1911–1983 orig. Thomas Lanier Williams Am. dram.
Williams William Carlos 1883–1963 Am. writer
Will·kie \'wil-kē\ Wendell Lewis 1892–1944 Am. polit.
Wil·loch \'vi-lək\ Kå·re \'kòr-ə\ Isaachsen 1928–   prime min. of Norway (1981–86)
Will·stät·ter \'vil-,shte-tər, 'wil-,ste-\ Richard 1872–1942 Ger. chem.
Wil·son \'wil-sən\ Charles Thomson Rees 1869–1959 Scot. physicist
Wilson Edmund 1895–1972 Am. writer
Wilson Sir (James) Harold 1916–1995 Brit. prime min. (1964–70; 1974–76)
Wilson Henry 1812–1875 orig. Jeremiah Jones Colbath Am. polit.; vice pres. of the U.S. (1873–75)
Wilson John 1785–1854 pseud. Christopher North Scot. author
Wilson Kenneth G. 1936–   Am. physicist
Wilson Robert Woodrow 1936–   Am. physicist
Wilson (Thomas) Wood·row \'wù-,drō\ 1856–1924 28th pres. of the U.S. (1913–21) — Wil·so·ni·an \wil-'sō-nē-ən\ adj
Winck·el·mann \'viŋ-kəl-,män, 'wiŋ-kəl-mən\ Johann Joachim 1717–1768 Ger. archaeol. & art hist.
Win·daus \'vin-,daùs\ Adolf Otto Reinhold 1876–1959 Ger. chem.
Win·disch·grätz \,vin-dish-'grets\ Alfred Candidus Ferdinand 1787–1862 Fürst zu Windischgrätz Austrian field marshal
Windsor Duke of — see EDWARD VIII
Win·gate \'win-,gāt, -gət\ Orde \'òrd\ Charles 1903–1944 Brit. gen.
Wingate Sir (Francis) Reginald 1861–1953 Brit. gen.
Wins·low \'winz-,lō\ Edward 1595–1655 gov. of Plymouth colony
Win·sor \'win-zər\ Justin 1831–1897 Am. librarian & hist.
Win·throp \'win(t)-thrəp\ John 1588–1649 1st gov. of Massachusetts Bay colony
Winthrop John 1606–1676 son of prec. gov. of Connecticut colony
Winthrop John 1638–1707 son of prec. gov. of Connecticut colony
Wise \'wīz\ Stephen Samuel 1874–1949 Am. (Hung.-born) rabbi
Wise Thomas James 1859–1937 Eng. bibliophile & forger
Wise·man \'wīz-mən\ Nicholas Patrick Stephen 1802–1865 Eng. cardinal & author
Wiss·ler \'wis-lər\ Clark 1870–1947 Am. anthropol.
Wis·ter \'wis-tər\ Owen 1860–1938 Am. nov.
With·er \'wi-thər\ George 1588–1667 Eng. poet & pamphleteer
Witt, de \də-'vit\ Johan 1625–1672 Du. statesman
Wit·te \'vi-tə\ Sergey Yulyevich 1849–1915 Russ. statesman
Wit·te, de \də-'vi-tə\ Emanuel 1617–1692 Du. painter
Wit·te·kind \'vi-tə-,kint\ or Wi·du·kind \'vē-də-\ d ca 807 Saxon warrior
Witt·gen·stein \'vit-gən-,shtīn, -,stīn\ Ludwig Josef Johan 1889–1951 Brit. (Austrian-born) philos. — Witt·gen·stein·ian \,vit-gən-'shtī-nē-ən, -'stī-\ adj
Wit·tig \'vi-tik\ Georg 1897–1987 Ger. chem.
Wode·house \'wùd-,haùs\ Sir Pel·ham \'pe-ləm\ Grenville 1881–1975 Am. (Eng.-born) author
Wof·fing·ton \'wä-fiŋ-tən\ Margaret ca1714–1760 Peg Irish actress
Wol·cott \'wùl-kət\ Oliver 1726–1797 son of Roger Am. polit.
Wolcott Oliver 1760–1833 son of prec. Am. polit.
Wolcott Roger 1679–1767 Am. colonial administrator
Wolf \'vòlf\ Friedrich August 1759–1824 Ger. philologist
Wolf Hugo Philipp Jakob 1860–1903 Austrian composer
Wolfe \'wùlf\ Charles 1791–1823 Irish poet
Wolfe James 1727–1759 Brit. gen.
Wolfe Thomas Clayton 1900–1938 Am. nov.
Wolff \'vòlf\ Caspar Friedrich 1734–1794 Ger. anatomist
Wolff or Wolf \vòlf\ Christian 1679–1754 Freiherr von Wolff Ger. philos. & math.
Wol·fram von Esch·en·bach \'wùl-frəm-vän-'e-shən-,bäk, 'vòl-,främ-, -,bäk\ ca1170–ca1220 Ger. poet & minnesinger
Wol·las·ton \'wù-lə-stən\ William Hyde 1766–1828 Eng. chem. & physicist
Woll·stone·craft \'wùl-stən-,kraft\ Mary 1759–1797 wife of William Godwin & mother of M.W. Shelley Eng. feminist & writer

Wolse·ley \'wùlz-lē\ 1st Viscount 1833–1913 Garnet Joseph Wolseley Brit. field marshal
Wol·sey \'wùl-zē\ Thomas ca1475–1530 Eng. cardinal & statesman
Wood \'wùd\ Grant 1892–1942 Am. painter
Wood Leonard 1860–1927 Am. physician & gen.
Wood·ward \'wùd-wərd\ Robert Burns 1917–1979 Am. chem.
Woolf \'wùlf\ (Adeline) Virginia 1882–1941 née Stephen Eng. author
Wooll·cott \'wùl-kət\ Alexander 1887–1943 Am. writer
Wool·ley \'wù-lē\ Sir Charles Leonard 1880–1960 Eng. archaeol.
Wool·worth \'wùl-(,)wərth\ Frank Winfield 1852–1919 Am. merchant
Worces·ter \'wùs-tər\ Joseph Emerson 1784–1865 Am. lexicographer
Worde \'wòrd\ Wynkyn de d 1534? Eng. (Alsatian-born) printer
Words·worth \'wərdz-(,)wərth\ William 1770–1850 Eng. poet; poet laureate (1843–50) — Words·worth·ian \,wərdz-'wər-thē-ən, -thē-\ adj
Wot·ton \'wù-tᵊn, 'wä-\ Sir Henry 1568–1639 Eng. diplomat & poet
Wran·gel \'raŋ-gəl\ Baron Pyotr Nikolayevich 1878–1928 Russ. gen.
Wren \'ren\ Sir Christopher 1632–1723 Eng. architect
Wright \'rīt\ Frank Lloyd 1867–1959 Am. architect
Wright Joseph 1734–1797 Wright of Derby Eng. painter
Wright Louis Booker 1899–1984 Am. educ. & librarian
Wright Or·ville \'òr-vəl\ 1871–1948 & his bro. Wilbur 1867–1912 Am. pioneers in aviation
Wright Richard 1908–1960 Am. author
Wright Willard Huntington 1888–1939 pseud. S. S. Van Dine \van-'dīn, vən-\ Am. writer
Wundt \'vùnt\ Wilhelm 1832–1920 Ger. physiol. & psychol.
Wu-ti — see HAN WU TI
Wy·att or Wy·at \'wī-ət\ Sir Thomas 1503–1543 Eng. poet & diplomat
Wych·er·ley \'wi-chər-lē\ William 1640–1716 Eng. dram.
Wyc·liffe \'wi-,klif, -kləf\ John ca1330–1384 Eng. religious reformer & theol. — Wyc·liff·ian \wi-'kli-fē-ən\ adj
Wy·eth \'wī-əth\ Andrew Newell 1917–   Am. painter
Wyeth Newell Convers 1882–1945 father of A. N. Am. painter
Wyld \'wī(ə)ld\ Henry Cecil Kennedy 1870–1945 Eng. lexicographer
Wy·lie \'wī-lē\ Elinor Morton 1885–1928 Mrs. William Rose Benét, née Hoyt Am. poet & nov.
Wylie Philip Gordon 1902–1971 Am. writer
Wynd·ham \'win-dəm\ George 1863–1913 Eng. polit. & writer
Xan·thip·pe \zan-'thi-pē, -'ti-\ 5th cent. B.C. wife of Socrates
Xa·vi·er \'zāv-yər, 'zā-vē-ər, ig-'zā-\ Saint Francis 1506–1552 Span. Francisco Ja·vier \-'vyer\ Span. Jesuit missionary
Xe·noc·ra·tes \zi-'nä-krə-,tēz\ 396–314 B.C. Greek philos.
Xe·noph·a·nes \zi-'nä-fə-,nēz\ ca 560–ca 478 B.C. Greek philos.
Xen·o·phon \'ze-nə-fən\ ca 431–ca 352 B.C. Greek hist.
Xer·xes I \'zərk-,sēz\ ca 519–465 B.C. the Great king of Persia (486–465)
Yale \'yā(ə)l\ Elihu 1649–1721 Eng. (Am.-born) colonial administrator
Yal·ow \'ya-(,)lō\ Rosalyn Sussman 1921–   Am. med. physicist
Ya·ma·ga·ta \,yä-mə-'gä-tə\ Prince Aritomo 1838–1922 Jp. gen. & statesman
Ya·ma·mo·to \,yä-mə-'mō-(,)tō\ Isoroku 1884–1943 Jp. admiral
Ya·ma·shi·ta \,yä-'mä-shi-,tä\ Tomoyuki 1885–1946 Jp. gen.
Yang Chen Ning \'yäŋ-'jən-'niŋ\ 1922–   Chin. physicist
Yeats \'yāts\ William Butler 1865–1939 Irish poet & dram. — Yeats·ian \'yāt-sē-ən\ adj
Yelt·sin \'yelt-sən, 'yel-sin\ Boris Nikolayevich 1931–   pres. of Russian Federation (1990–   )
Yen Hsi–shan \'yen-'shē-'shän\ 1883–1960 Chin. gen.
Yer·kes \'yər-kēz\ Charles Ty·son \'tī-sᵊn\ 1837–1905 Am. financier
Yev·tu·shen·ko \,yef-tə-'sheŋ-(,)kō\ Yevgeny Aleksandrovich 1933–   Soviet (Russ.-born) writer
Yo·nai \'yō-,nī\ Mitsumasa 1880–1948 Jp. admiral & statesman
York \'yòrk\ Alvin Cullum 1887–1964 Am. soldier
Yo·shi·hi·to \,yō-shi-'hē-(,)tō\ 1879–1926 emp. of Japan (1912–26)
You·mans \'yü-mənz\ Vincent 1898–1946 Am. composer
Young \'yəŋ\ Andrew Jackson, Jr. 1932–   U.S. ambassador to U.N. (1977–79)
Young Brig·ham \'bri-gəm\ 1801–1877 Am. Mormon leader
Young Edward 1683–1765 Eng. poet
Young Francis Brett 1884–1954 Eng. nov.
Young Owen D. 1874–1962 Am. lawyer
Young Whitney Moore 1921–1971 Am. civil rights leader
Young·hus·band \'yəŋ-,həz-bənd\ Sir Francis Edward 1863–1942 Brit. explorer & author
Your·ce·nar \,yür-sə-'när\ Marguerite 1903–1987 orig. surname de Crayencour Fr. author
Yp·si·lan·tis \,ip-sə-'lan-tē\ Alexandros 1792–1828 & his bro. Demetrios 1793–1832 Greek revolutionaries
Yüan Shih–k'ai \yü-'än-'shir-'kī, -'sh(ē\ 1859–1916 Chin. soldier & statesman; pres. of China (1913–16)
Yu·ka·wa \yü-'kä-wə\ Hideki 1907–1981 Jp. physicist
Yung–lo \'yùn-'lō\ 1360–1424 orig. Chu Ti; often called Ch'eng Tsu Chin. emp. (1402–24)
Zagh·lūl \zag-'lül\ Sa'd \'säd\ 1857–1927 Sa'd Zaghlūl Pasha ibn Ibrāhīm Egypt. statesman
Za·ha·roff \zə-'här-əf, -,òf\ Sir Basil 1849–1936 orig. Basileios Zacharias Fr. (Russ.-born) banker & armament contractor
Za·ï·mis \zä-'ē-məs, -mēs\ Alexandros 1855–1936 Greek statesman
Zan·gwill \'zaŋ-,gwil, -,wil\ Israel 1864–1926 Eng. dram. & nov.
Ze·dil·lo Pon·ce de Le·ón \sä-'thē-(,)yō-'pòn-sä-(,)thä-lā-'ón\ Ernesto 1951–   pres. of Mexico (1994–   )
Zee·man \'zā-,män, -mən\ Pieter 1865–1943 Du. physicist
Zeng·er \'zeŋ-gər, -ər\ John Peter 1697–1746 Am. (Ger.-born) journalist & printer

\ə\ abut \ᵊ\ kitten, F table \ər\ further \a\ ash \ā\ ace \ä\ mop, mar
\aù\ out \ch\ chin \e\ bet \ē\ easy \g\ go \i\ hit \ī\ ice \j\ job
\ŋ\ sing \ō\ go \ò\ law \òi\ boy \th\ thin \t͟h\ the \ü\ loot \ù\ foot
\y\ yet \zh\ vision \à, k̲, ⁿ, œ, œ̄, ᵫ, ᵬ, ᵊ\ see Guide to Pronunciation

Ze·no of Citium \'zē-(,)nō-əv-'si-sh(ē-)-əm\ *ca* 335–*ca* 263 B.C. Greek philos. & founder of Stoic school

Zeno of Elea \'ē-lē-ə\ *ca* 495–*ca* 430 B.C. Greek philos.

Ze·no·bia \zə-'nō-bē-ə\ *d* after A.D. 274 queen of Palmyra (267 or 268–272)

Zep·pe·lin \,tse-pə-'lēn, 'ze-p(ə-)lən\ Ferdinand Adolf August Heinrich 1838–1917 Graf *von Zeppelin* Ger. gen. & aeronaut

Zer·ni·ke \'zer-ni-kə, 'zər-\ Frits 1888–1966 Du. physicist

Zeux·is \'zük-səs\ 5th cent. B.C. Greek painter

Zhao Zi·yang *or* **Chao Tzu–yang** \'jaü-(d)zə-'yäŋ\ 1919–   Chin. Communist leader (1987–89)

Zhda·nov \zhə-'dä-nəf, 'shtä-\ Andrey Aleksandrovich 1896–1948 Soviet polit.

Zhu·kov \'zhü-,kóf, -,kóv\ Georgy Konstantinovich 1896–1974 Soviet marshal

Zieg·feld \'zig-,feld, 'zēg- *also* -,fēld, -fəld\ Florenz 1869–1932 Am. theatrical producer

Zieg·ler \'tsē-glər\ Karl 1898–1973 Ger. chem.

Zim·mer·mann \'zi-mər-mən, 'tsi-mər-,män\ Arthur 1864–1940 Ger. statesman

Zi·nov·yev *or* **Zi·nov·iev** \zyi-'nóf-yəf\ Grigory Yevseyevich 1883–1936 orig. *Ovsel Gershon Aronov Radomyslsky* Soviet revolutionary

Zins·ser \'zin(t)-sər\ Hans 1878–1940 Am. bacteriol.

Zin·zen·dorf \'zin-zən-,dórf, 'tsin-sən-\ Nikolaus Ludwig 1700–1760 Graf *von Zinzendorf* religious reformer

Žiž·ka \'zhish-kə\ Count Jan *ca*1376–1424 Bohemian gen. & Hussite leader

Zog I \'zōg\ 1895–1961 prename *Ahmed Bey Zogu* king of the Albanians (1928–39)

Zo·la \'zō-lə, 'zō-,lä, zō-'lä\ Émile 1840–1902 Fr. nov. — **Zo·la·esque** \,zō-lə-'esk, -lä-\ *adj*

Zorn \'sórn, 'zórn\ Anders Leonhard 1860–1920 Swed. painter, etcher, & sculptor

Zo·ro·as·ter \'zór-ə-,was-tər, 'zór-\ *Old Iranian* **Zar·a·thu·shtra** \,zar-ə-'thüsh-trə, -'thəsh-, -'thüs-, -'thəs-\ *ca* 628–*ca* 551 B.C. founder of Zoroastrianism

Zor·ri·lla y Mo·ral \zə-'rē-yə-,ē-mə-'räl\ José 1817–1893 Span. poet & dram.

Zsig·mon·dy \'zhig-,món-dē\ Richard 1865–1929 Ger. chem.

Zu·lo·a·ga \,zü-lə-'wä-gə\ Ignacio 1870–1945 Span. painter

Zur·ba·rán \,zür-bə-'rän\ Francisco de 1598–1664 Span. painter

Zweig \'zwīg, 'swīg, 'tsvīk\ Arnold 1887–1968 Ger. author

Zweig Stefan 1881–1942 Austrian writer

Zwing·li \'zwiŋ-glē, 'swiŋ-, -lē; 'tsfiŋ-lē\ Huldrych 1484–1531 Swiss Reformation leader

Geographical Names

This section gives basic information about the countries of the world and their most important regions, cities, and physical features. The information includes spelling, end-of-line division, and pronunciation of the name, nature of the feature, its location, and for the more important entries statistical data. Cities in the United States having 19,000 or more inhabitants at the 1990 census and incorporated places in Canada having 21,500 or more inhabitants at the 1991 census have been included.

This section complements the A–Z vocabulary by entering many derivative forms:

Ab·ys·sin·ia . . . — Ab·ys·sin·ian . . . *adj or n*

Cos·ta Ri·ca . . . — Cos·ta Ri·can . . . *adj or n*

Mo·na·co . . . — Mo·na·can . . . *adj or n* — Mon·e·gasque . . . *adj or n*

The abbreviations used are listed in the section Abbreviations in This Work or in the back-matter section Abbreviations and Symbols for Chemical Elements. The letters N, E, S, and W when not followed by a period indicate direction and are not part of a place-name; thus N Vietnam indicates northern Vietnam and not North Vietnam. The symbol ✳ denotes a capital. Areas, altitudes, and lengths are given first in conventional units with metric equivalents in parentheses.

The Pinyin transliteration of place-names for the People's Republic of China is the first spelling shown; the Wade-Giles transliteration is second. Where no variant is given, the two spellings are identical.

Aa·chen \'ä-kən\ *or F* **Aix–la–Cha·pelle** \ˌäks-ˌlä-shə-'pel, ˌeks-\ city W Germany near Belgian & Dutch borders *pop* 243,947

Aai·ún, El \ˌe-lī-'üin\ *or* **Ai·un** \ī-'ün\ town NW Africa ✳ of Western Sahara

Aaland — see AHVENANMAA

Aalborg — see ÅLBORG

Aalst \'älst\ *or* **Alost** \ä-'lòst\ commune *cen* Belgium WNW of Brussels *pop* 76,382

Aa·rau \'är-ˌaù\ commune N Switzerland ✳ of Aargau canton *pop* 15,836

Aa·re \'är-ə\ *or* **Aar** \'är\ river 175 *mi* (280 *km*), *cen* & N Switzerland flowing E & NE into the Rhine

Aar·gau \'är-ˌgaù\ *or F* **Ar·go·vie** \ˌär-gə-'vē\ canton N Switzerland ✳ Aarau *area* 542 *sq mi* (1409 *sq km*), *pop* 489,567

Aarhus — see ÅRHUS

Ab·a·co \'a-bə-ˌkō\ two islands of the Bahamas (**Great Abaco** & **Lit·tle Abaco**) N of New Providence Is. *area* 776 *sq mi* (2018 *sq km*)

Aba·dan \ˌä-bə-'dän, ˌa-bə-'dan\ 1 island W Iran in delta of Shatt-al-Arab 2 city & port on Abadan Is.

Ab·bai \ä-'bī\ the upper course of the Blue Nile

Ab·be·ville \ab-'vēl, 'a-bi-ˌvil\ commune N France on the Somme NW of Amiens *pop* 25,252

Ab·er·dare \ˌa-bər-'dar, -'der\ town S Wales in Mid Glamorgan *pop* 36,621

Ab·er·deen 1 \'a-bər-ˌdēn\ city NE S.Dak. *pop* 24,927 2 \ˌa-bər-'dēn\ *or* **Ab·er·deen·shire** \-ˌshir, -shər\ former county NE Scotland ✳ Aberdeen 3 city & port NE Scotland ✳ of Grampian *pop* 190,200 — **Ab·er·do·ni·an** \ˌa-bər-'dō-nē-ən\ *adj or n*

Ab·er·yst·wyth \ˌa-bə-'ris-ˌtwith, -'rəs-\ borough W Wales in Dyfed on Cardigan Bay *pop* 8666

Ab–i–Diz — see DEZ

Ab·i·djan \ˌa-bi-'jän\ city & port ✳ of Ivory Coast *pop* 685,828

Abila — see MUSA (Jebel)

Ab·i·lene \'a-bə-ˌlēn\ city NW *cen* Tex. *pop* 106,654

Ab·i·tibi, Lake \ˌa-bə-'ti-bē\ 1 lake Canada on E boundary of Ont. *area* 356 *sq mi* (926 *sq km*) 2 river 230 *mi* (368 *km*) Canada flowing N into Moose River

Ab·khaz Republic \ab-'käz\ *or* **Ab·kha·zia** \ab-'kä-zh(ē-)ə, -'kä-zē-ə\ *or* **Ab·kha·zian Republic** \-'kä-zh(ē-)ən, -'kä-zē-ən\ autonomous republic NW Republic of Georgia on Black Sea ✳ Sukhumi *area* 3358 *sq mi* (8731 *sq km*), *pop* 499,000 — **Ab·khas** \-'käs\ *n* — **Ab·kha·sian** *or* **Ab·kha·zian** \-'kä-zh(ē-)ən, -'kä-zē-ən\ *adj or n*

Abo·mey \ˌa-bə-'mā, ə-'bō-mē\ city S Benin *pop* 54,418

Abruz·zi \ä-'brüt-sē, ə-\ region *cen* Italy bordering on the Adriatic & including highest of the Apennines ✳ L'Aquila *pop* 1,266,448; with Molise (to S), formerly comprised **Abruzzi e Mo·li·se** \ˌä-'mò-li-ˌzā\ region

Ab·sa·ro·ka Range \ab-'sär-ə-kə, -'sòr-kē, -'zór-\ mountain range S Mont. & NW Wyo. E of Yellowstone National Park — see FRANCS PEAK

Ab·se·con Inlet \ab-'sē-kən\ inlet SE N.J. bet. barrier islands N of Atlantic City

Abu Dha·bi \ˌä-bü-'thä-bē, -'dä-\ 1 sheikhdom, member of United Arab Emirates 2 town, its ✳ & ✳ of United Arab Emirates *pop* 347,000

Abu·ja \ä-'bü-jä\ city *cen* Nigeria, its ✳ since 1991

Ab·u·kir \ˌa-(ˌ)bü-'kir, ä-\ 1 bay N Egypt bet. Alexandria & Rosetta mouth of the Nile 2 village on this bay — see CANOPUS

Abu Sim·bel \ˌä-ˌbü-'sim-bəl\ *or* **Ip·sam·bul** \ˌip-səm-'bül\ locality S Egypt on left bank of the Nile SW of Aswân; site of two rock temples which were moved 1964–66 to higher ground when area was flooded after completion of Aswan High Dam

Aby·dos \ə-'bī-dəs\ 1 ancient town Asia Minor on the Hellespont 2 ancient town S Egypt on left bank of the Nile S of Thebes

Abyla — see MUSA (Jebel)

Ab·ys·sin·ia \ˌa-bə-'si-nē-ə, -'sin-yə\ — see ETHIOPIA — **Ab·ys·sin·ian** \-nē-ən, -yən\ *adj or n*

Aca·dia \ə-'kā-dē-ə\ *or F* **Aca·die** \ä-kà-dē\ NOVA SCOTIA — an early name

Acadia National Park section of coast of Maine including chiefly mountainous areas on Mount Desert Is. & Isle au Haut

Aca·pul·co \ˌä-kə-'pül-(ˌ)kō, ˌa-\ *or* **Acapulco de Juá·rez** \də-'wär-əs\ city & port S Mexico in Guerrero on the Pacific *pop* 309,254

Ac·ar·na·nia \ˌa-kər-'nä-nē-ə, -'nä-nyə\ *or NGk* **Akar·na·nia** \ˌä-ˌkär-nə-'nē-ə\ region W Greece on Ionian Sea — **Ac·ar·na·nian** \ˌa-kər-'nä-nē-ən, -'nä-nyən\ *adj or n*

Ac·cad \'a-ˌkad, 'ä-ˌkäd\ — see AKKAD — **Ac·ca·di·an** \ə-'kä-dē-ən, -'kä-\ *adj or n*

Ac·cra \ə-'krä\ city & port ✳ of Ghana on Gulf of Guinea *pop* 867,459

Ac·cring·ton \'a-kriŋ-tən\ town NW England in SE Lancashire N of Manchester *pop* 35,891

Achaea \ə-'kē-ə\ *or* **Acha·ia** \ə-'kī-ə, -'kā-\ region S Greece in N Peloponnisos bordering on Gulfs of Corinth & Patras — **Achae·an** \ə-'kē-ən\ *or* **Acha·ian** \ə-'kī-ən, -'kā-\ *adj or n*

Ach·e·lo·us *or NGk* **Akhe·ló·os** *or* **Ach·e·lo·os** \ˌa-kə-'lō-əs\ river 100 *mi* (160 *km*) W Greece flowing S to Ionian Sea

Ach·ill \'a-kəl\ island 15 *mi* (24 *km*) long NW Ireland in County Mayo

Achray, Loch \ə-'krā\ lake *cen* Scotland in SW Tayside

\ə\ abut \ˀ\ kitten, F table \ər\ further \a\ ash \ā\ ace \ä\ mop, mar
\aù\ out \ch\ chin \e\ bet \ē\ easy \g\ go \i\ hit \ī\ ice \j\ job
\ŋ\ sing \ō\ go \ò\ law \òi\ boy \th\ thin \t̲h̲\ the \ü\ loot \ù\ foot
\y\ yet \zh\ vision \à, k̲, ⁿ, œ, œ̄, ᵫ, ᵫ̄, ˀ\ see Guide to Pronunciation

Acon·ca·gua \‚a-kən-'kä-gwə, ‚ä-, -kən-\ mountain 22,834 *ft* (6960 *m*) W Argentina WNW of Mendoza near Chilean border; highest in Andes & western hemisphere

Açores — see AZORES

Acragas — see AGRIGENTO

Acre \'ä-krə, -(‚)krä\ state W Brazil bordering on Peru & Bolivia ✳ Rio Branco *area* 57,153 *sq mi* (148,598 *sq km*), *pop* 306,893

Acre \'ä-kər, 'ä-krə, 'ä-krə\ *or Heb* **Ak·ko** *or* **Ac·cho** \ä-'kō\ *or anc* **Ptol·e·ma·is** \‚tä-lə-'mä-əs\ city & port NW Israel N of Mt. Carmel *pop* 33,900

Ac·te *or* **Ak·te** \'ak-tē\ peninsula NE Greece, the most easterly of the three peninsulas of Chalcidice — see ATHOS

Ac·ti·um \'ak-shē-əm, 'ak-tē-\ promontory & ancient town W Greece in NW Acarnania

Adak \ä-ˌdak\ island SW Alaska in Andreanof group

Adalia — see ANTALYA

Ad·ams, Mount \'a-dəmz\ **1** mountain 5798 *ft* (1767 *m*) N N.H. in White Mountains N of Mt. Washington **2** mountain 12,307 *ft* (3751 *m*) SW Wash. in Cascade Range SSE of Mt. Rainier

Ad·am's Bridge \'a-dəmz\ chain of shoals 30 *mi* (48 *km*) long bet. Sri Lanka & SE India

Adam's Peak *or Sinhalese* **Sa·ma·na·la** \'sə-mə-nə-lə\ mountain 7360 *ft* (2243 *m*) S *cen* Sri Lanka

Ada·na \'ä-də-nə, -ˌnä, ä-'dä-nə\ *or* **Sey·han** \sā-'hän\ city S Turkey on Seyhan River *pop* 568,513

Ada·pa·za·ri \ˌä-də-ˌpä-zə-'rē\ city NW Turkey E of Istanbul *pop* 152,171

Ad·dis Aba·ba \ˌa-dəs-'a-bə-bə\ city *cen* Ethiopia, its ✳ *pop* 1,408,068

Ad·di·son \'a-də-sən\ village NE Ill. W of Chicago *pop* 32,058

Ad·e·laide \'a-d²l-ˌād\ city Australia ✳ of S. Australia *metropolitan area pop* 917,000

Aden \'ä-d²n, 'ā-\ **1** former Brit. protectorate S Arabia comprising coast area bet. Yemen on W & Oman on E; became part of People's Democratic Republic of Yemen 1967 *area* 112,000 *sq mi* (291,200 *sq km*) **2** former Brit. colony on coast of & surrounded by Aden protectorate comprising Aden & Little Aden peninsulas, a small area of hinterland, & Perim Is.; became part of People's Democratic Republic of Yemen 1967 *area* 75 *sq mi* (195 *sq km*) **3** city & port S Yemen; formerly ✳ of People's Democratic Republic of Yemen & before that ✳ of Aden colony & protectorate *pop* 240,370

Aden, Gulf of arm of Indian Ocean bet. Aden & Somalia

Adi·ge \'ä-də-ˌjä\ river 220 *mi* (354 *km*) N Italy flowing SE into the Adriatic

Ad·i·ron·dack Mountains \ˌa-də-'rän-ˌdak\ mountains NE N.Y.

Ad·mi·ral·ty Inlet \'ad-m(ə-)rəl-tē\ branch of Puget Sound NW Washington

Admiralty Island island 100 *mi* (161 *km*) long SE Alaska in N Alexander Archipelago

Admiralty Islands islands W Pacific N of New Guinea in Bismarck Archipelago *area* 800 *sq mi* (2080 *sq km*), *pop* 30,160

Adour \ə-'dúr\ river 200 *mi* (322 *km*) SW France flowing from the Pyrenees NW & W into Bay of Biscay

Adri·an \'ä-drē-ən\ city SE Mich. SW of Detroit *pop* 22,097

Adrianople — see EDIRNE

Adri·at·ic Sea \ˌä-drē-'a-tik, ˌa-\ arm of the Mediterranean bet. Italy & Balkan Peninsula

Ad·vent Bay \'ad-ˌvent, -vənt\ inlet of Arctic Ocean West Spitsbergen on W coast

Ad·wa \'äd-(ˌ)wä\ city N Ethiopia S of Asmara *pop* 26,782

Ady·gea *or* **Ady·ge·ya** \ˌä-də-'gä-ə\ republic S Russia in Europe ✳ Maikop *area* 1505 *sq mi* (3913 *sq km*), *pop* 400,000

Adzhar Republic \ə-'jär\ autonomous republic SW Republic of Georgia on Black Sea ✳ Batum *area* 1080 *sq mi* (2808 *sq km*), *pop* 339,000 — **Adzhar** *n* — **Adzhar·i·an** \ə-'jär-ē-ən\ *adj or n*

Aegates — see EGADI

Ae·ge·an Islands \i-'jē-ən\ islands Aegean Sea including the Cyclades & the Northern & Southern Sporades

Aegean Sea arm of the Mediterranean bet. Asia Minor & Greece

Ae·gi·na \i-'jī-nə\ *or NGk* **Ai·gi·na** \'e-yē-ˌnä\ island & ancient state SE Greece in Saronic Gulf — **Ae·gi·ne·tan** \ˌē-jə-'nē-t²n\ *adj or n*

Ae·gos·pot·a·mi \ˌē-gə-'spä-tə-ˌmī\ *or* **Ae·gos·pot·a·mos** \-məs\ river & town of ancient Thrace in the Chersonese

Aemilia — see EMILIA-ROMAGNA

Ae·o·lis \'ē-ə-ləs\ *or* **Ae·o·lia** \ē-'ō-lē-ə, -'ōl-yə\ ancient country of NW Asia Minor

Ae·to·lia \ē-'tō-lē-ə, -'tōl-yə\ region W *cen* Greece N of Gulf of Patras & E of Acarnania — **Ae·to·lian** \-lē-ən, -yən\ *adj or n*

Afars and the Issas, French Territory of the — see DJIBOUTI

Af·ghan·i·stan \af-'ga-nə-ˌstan, -ˌstän\ country W Asia E of Iran; a republic ✳ Kabul *area* 250,000 *sq mi* (650,000 *sq km*), *pop* 13,051,358

Afog·nak \ə-'fóg-ˌnak, -'fäg-\ island S Alaska N of Kodiak Is.

Af·ri·ca \'a-fri-kə *also* 'ä-\ continent of the eastern hemisphere S of the Mediterranean & adjoining Asia on NE *area* 11,596,000 *sq mi* (30,149,600 *sq km*)

Afyon·ka·ra·hi·sar \ä-'fyōn-ˌkär-ə-hi-'sär\ *or* **Afyon** \ä-'fyōn\ city W *cen* Turkey *pop* 73,832

Aga·dir \ˌä-gə-'dir, ˌa-\ city & port SW Morocco *pop* 110,479

Aga·na \ə-'gä-nyə\ town ✳ of Guam on W coast *pop* 881

Agar·ta·la \ˌa-gər-tə-'lä\ city E India ✳ of Tripura *pop* 131,513

Ag·ate Fossil Beds National Monument \'a-gət\ reservation W Nebr.

Ag·a·wam \'a-gə-ˌwäm\ town SW Mass. *pop* 27,323

Age·nais \ä-zhə-'nä\ *or* **Age·nois** \ä-zhən-'wä\ ancient region SW France S of Périgord ✳ Agen

Aghrim — see AUGHRIM

Agincourt — see AZINCOURT

Ag·no \'äg-(ˌ)nō\ river 128 *mi* (206 *km*) Philippines in NW Luzon

Agou·ra Hills \ə-'gúr-ə\ city SW Calif. W of Los Angeles *pop* 20,390

Agra \'ä-grə\ **1** region N India roughly equivalent to present Uttar Pradesh excluding Oudh region **2** city N India in W Uttar Pradesh SSE of Delhi *pop* 770,352

Agri Dagi — see ARARAT

Agri·gen·to \ˌä-gri-'jen-(ˌ)tō, ˌa-\ *or formerly* **Gir·gen·ti** \jər-'jen-tē\ *or anc* **Ag·ri·gen·tum** \ˌa-grə-'jen-təm\ *or* **Ac·ra·gas** \'a-krə-gəs\ commune Italy in SW Sicily near coast *pop* 56,372

Agua·di·lla \ˌä-gwə-'thē-yə\ city NW Puerto Rico *pop* 59,335

Aguas·ca·lien·tes \ˌä-gwə-ˌskäl-'yen-ˌtäs\ **1** state *cen* Mexico *area* 2499 *sq mi* (6497 *sq km*), *pop* 503,410 **2** city, its ✳ *pop* 222,105

Agul·has, Cape \ə-'gə-ləs\ headland Republic of S. Africa in S Western Cape province; southernmost point of Africa, at 34°50'S, 20°E

Ahag·gar Mountains \ə-'hä-gər, ä-hə-'gär\ *or* **Hog·gar Mountains** \'hä-gər, hə-'gär\ mountains S Algeria in W *cen* Sahara; highest Tahat 9573 *ft* (2918 *m*)

Ah·mad·abad *or* **Ah·med·abad** \'ä-mə-də-ˌbäd, -ˌbad\ city W India N of Bombay in Gujarat *pop* 1,550,779

Ah·ven·an·maa \'ä-və-ˌnän-ˌmä, 'ä-fə-\ *or Sw* **Åland** *or* **Aa·land** \'ō-ˌländ\ **1** archipelago SW Finland in Baltic Sea ✳ Mariehamn **2** island, chief of this group

Ah·waz \ä-'wäz\ city SW Iran on the Karun *pop* 579,826

Ai·ken \'ä-kən\ city W S.C. SW of Columbia *pop* 19,872

Ail·sa Craig \'āl-zə-ˌkrāg\ small rocky island Scotland S of Arran at mouth of Firth of Clyde

Ain \aⁿ\ river 118 *mi* (190 *km*) E France rising in Jura Mountains & flowing SSW into the Rhône

Aintab — see GAZIANTEP

Air·drie \'ar-drē, 'er-\ burgh S *cen* Scotland in Strathclyde E of Glasgow *pop* 45,643

Aire \'ar, 'er\ river 70 *mi* (113 *km*) N England in W Yorkshire flowing to the Ouse; its valley is **Aire·dale** \-ˌdāl\

Aisne \'ān\ river *ab* 175 *mi* (282 *km*) N France flowing NW & W from Argonne Forest into the Oise near Compiègne

Aiun — see AAIÚN, EL

Aix–en–Pro·vence \ˌäks-äⁿ-prō-'väⁿs, ˌeks-\ *or* **Aix** \'äks, 'eks\ city SE France N of Marseilles *pop* 91,665

Aix–la–Chapelle — see AACHEN

Aix–les–Bains \ˌäks-lā-'baⁿ, ˌeks-\ commune E France N of Chambéry *pop* 21,884

Ajac·cio \ä-'yä-(ˌ)chō, ä-zhäk-syō\ city & port France in Corsica *pop* 47,065

Ajan·ta \ə-'jən-tə\ village W *cen* India in N *cen* Maharashtra in Ajanta Range NNE of Aurangabad; caves

Ajax \'ä-ˌjaks\ town Canada in SE Ont. *pop* 57,350

Aj·man \äj-'man\ sheikhdom, member of United Arab Emirates

Aj·mer \ˌəj-'mir, -'mer\ **1** *or* **Ajmer–Mer·wa·ra** \-ˌmer-'wär-ə\ former state NW India, now part of Rajasthan *area* 2425 *sq mi* (6305 *sq km*) **2** city, its ✳, SW of Delhi *pop* 374,350

Akaba — see AQABA

Akarnania — see ACARNANIA

Akheloós — see ACHELOUS

Ak·hi·sar \ˌäk-hi-'sär, ˌä-ki-\ *or anc* **Thy·a·ti·ra** \ˌthī-ə-'tī-rə\ city W Turkey in Asia NE of Izmir *pop* 46,167

Aki·ta \ä-'kē-tə, 'ä-ki-ˌtä\ city & port Japan in N Honshu on Sea of Japan *pop* 302,359

Ak·kad *or* **Ac·cad** \'a-ˌkad, 'ä-ˌkäd\ **1** the N division of ancient Babylonia **2** *or* **Aga·de** \ə-'gä-də\ ancient city, its ✳

Akkerman — see BELGOROD-DNESTROVSKIY

Akko — see ACRE

Ak·ron \'a-krən\ city NE Ohio SE of Cleveland *pop* 223,019

Ak·sum *or* **Ax·um** \'äk-ˌsüm\ town N Ethiopia ✳ of an ancient kingdom (the Axumite Empire)

Akte — see ACTE

Akyab — see SITTWE

Al·a·bama \ˌa-lə-'ba-mə\ **1** river 315 *mi* (507 *km*) S Ala. flowing SW into Tensaw & Mobile rivers — see TALLAPOOSA **2** state SE U.S. ✳ Montgomery *area* 51,609 *sq mi* (134,183 *sq km*), *pop* 4,040,587 — **Al·a·bam·i·an** \-'ba-mē-ən\ *or* **Al·a·bam·an** \-'ba-mən\ *adj or n*

Ala·go·as \ˌa-lə-'gō-əs\ state NE Brazil ✳ Maceió *area* 11,031 *sq mi* (28,681 *sq km*), *pop* 2,011,875

Alai \'ä-ˌlī\ mountain range SW Kyrgyzstan; highest peak 19,554 *ft* (5960 *m*)

Al·a·me·da \ˌa-lə-'mē-də\ city & port W Calif. on island in San Francisco Bay near Oakland *pop* 76,459

Ala·mein *or* **El Alamein** \ˌel-ˌa-lə-'mān\ village NW Egypt on the Mediterranean N of NE corner of Qattara Depression

Al·a·mo·gor·do \ˌa-lə-mə-'gór-(ˌ)dō\ city S N.Mex. *pop* 27,596

Ala·se·hir \ˌa-lə-shə-'hir, ˌä-\ *or anc* **Philadelphia** city W Turkey 75 *mi* (121 *km*) E of Izmir *pop* 23,243

Alas·ka \ə-'las-kə\ state (territory 1912–59) of the U.S. NW N. America ✳ Juneau *area* 586,412 *sq mi* (1,524,671 *sq km*), *pop* 550,043 — **Alas·kan** \-kən\ *adj or n*

Alaska, Gulf of inlet of the Pacific off S Alaska between Alaska Peninsula on W & Alexander Archipelago on E

Alaska Peninsula peninsula SW Alaska SW of Cook Inlet

Alaska Range mountain range S Alaska extending from Alaska Peninsula to Yukon boundary — see MCKINLEY (Mount)

Ala Tau \ˌa-lə-'taú, ˌä-\ several ranges of the Tian Shan mountain system E Kazakhstan & Kyrgyzstan around & NE of Issyk Kul

Ala·va \'ä-lə-və\ province N Spain S of Vizcaya; one of the Basque Provinces ✳ Vitoria *area* 1175 *sq mi* (3055 *sq km*), *pop* 286,499

Al·a·va, Cape \'a-lə-və\ cape NW Wash. S of Cape Flattery; westernmost point of conterminous U.S., at 124°44'W

Al·ba·ce·te \ˌal-bə-'sä-tē\ **1** province SE Spain N of Murcia province *area* 5737 *sq mi* (14,916 *sq km*), *pop* 317,498 **2** commune, its ✳ *pop* 116,484

Al·ban Hills \'ól-bən, 'al-\ *or anc* **Al·ba·nus Mons** \ˌäl-ˌbä-nəs-'món(t)s\ mountain group Italy SE of Rome

Al·ba·nia \al-'bä-nē-ə, -nyə *also* ól-\ **1** ancient country Europe in E Caucasus region on W side of Caspian Sea **2** country S Europe in Balkan Peninsula on the Adriatic; a republic ✳ Tiranë *area* 10,630 *sq mi* (27,638 *sq km*), *pop* 3,841,000

Al·ba·no, Lake \al-'bä-(ˌ)nō, äl-\ *or anc* **La·cus Al·ba·nus** \ˌlä-kəs-äl-'bä-nəs\ lake Italy SE of Rome

Al·ba·ny \'ól-bə-nē\ **1** city SW Ga. *pop* 78,122 **2** city ✳ of N.Y., on Hudson River *pop* 101,082 **3** city NW Oreg. S of Salem *pop* 29,462 **4**

\'al-\ river 610 *mi* (982 *km*) Canada in N Ont. flowing E into James Bay — **Al·ba·ni·an** \òl-'bā-nē-ən\ *adj or n*
Al Basrah — see BASRA
Al·be·marle Island \'al-bə-,märl\ — see ISABELA ISLAND
Albemarle Sound inlet of Atlantic Ocean NE N.C.
Al·bert, Lake \'al-bərt\ lake 100 *mi* (161 *km*) long E Africa bet. Uganda & Zaire in course of the Victoria Nile
Al·ber·ta \al-'bər-tə\ province W Canada ✽ Edmonton *area* 248,800 *sq mi* (646,880 *sq km*), *pop* 2,545,553 — **Al·ber·tan** \-'bər-t°n\ *adj or n*
Albert Nile — see NILE
Albertville — see KALEMIE
Al·bi \al-'bē\ commune S France NE of Toulouse *pop* 43,942
Al Biqa — see BEKAA
Al·borg *or* **Aal·borg** \'òl-,bòrg\ city & port Denmark in NE Jutland *pop* 154,547
Al·bu·quer·que \'al-bə-,kər-kē\ city *cen* N.Mex. *pop* 384,736 — **Al·bu·quer·que·an** \-kē-ən\ *n*
Al·ca·mo \'äl-kə-,mò\ commune Italy in NW Sicily *pop* 43,231
Al·ca·traz \'al-kə-,traz\ island Calif. in San Francisco Bay
Al·coy \'al-'kòi\ commune E Spain N of Alicante *pop* 61,371
Al·da·bra \'al-də-brə\ island (atoll) NW Indian Ocean N of Madagascar, chief of Aldabra group belonging to Seychelles
Al·dan \äl-'dän\ river 1500 *mi* (2414 *km*) E Russia in Asia, in SE Yakut Republic flowing into the Lena
Al·der·ney \'òl-dər-nē\ island in English Channel, northernmost of the Channel Islands ✽ St. Anne *area* 3 *sq mi* (7.8 *sq km*), *pop* 2086
Al·der·shot \'òl-dər-,shät\ borough S England in NE Hampshire *pop* 32,654
Aleksandrovsk — see ZAPOROZH 'YE
Aleksandrovsk Grushevski — see SHAKHTY
Alen·çon \,ä-,län-'sòⁿ, a-lä-'sòⁿ\ city NW France N of Le Mans *pop* 32,917
Alep·po \ə-'le-(,)pò\ *or anc* **Be·roea** *or* **Be·rea** \bə-'rē-ə\ city N Syria *pop* 639,000 — **Alep·pine** \ə-'le-pən, -,pīn, -,pēn\ *adj or n*
Ales·san·dria \,a-lə-'san-drē-ə\ commune NW Italy *pop* 93,866
Aleu·tian Islands \ə-'lü-shən\ islands SW Alaska extending in an arc 1200 *mi* (1931 *km*) SW & W from Alaska Peninsula — see ANDREANOF ISLANDS, FOX ISLANDS, NEAR ISLANDS, RAT ISLANDS
Aleutian Range mountain range SW Alaska, the SW extension of Alaska Range, running along NW shore of Cook Inlet to SW tip of Alaska Peninsula with mountains of the Aleutian chain forming its SW extension — see SHISHALDIN
Al·ex·an·der Archipelago \,a-lig-'zan-dər, ,e-\ archipelago of *ab* 1100 islands SE Alaska — see ADMIRALTY ISLAND, BARANOF, CHICHAGOF, KUPREANOF, PRINCE OF WALES ISLAND, REVILLAGIGEDO ISLAND
Alexander I Island island Antarctica W of base of Antarctic Peninsula
Alexandretta — see ISKENDERUN
Al·ex·an·dria \,a-lig-'zan-drē-ə, -,e-\ **1** city *cen* La. *pop* 49,188 **2** city N Va. on the Potomac S of Washington, D.C. *pop* 111,183 **3** city & port N Egypt bet. Lake Mareotis & the Mediterranean *pop* 2,317,705 — **Al·ex·an·dri·an** \-drē-ən\ *adj or n*
Al·föld \'òl-,fə(r)ld, -,fœld\ the central plain of Hungary
Al·gar·ve \äl-'gär-və, al-\ medieval Moorish kingdom now a province of Portugal on S coast
Al·ge·ci·ras \,al-jə-'sir-əs\ city & port SW Spain W of Gibraltar on Bay of Algeciras *pop* 81,662
Al·ge·ria \al-'jir-ē-ə\ country NW Africa bordering on the Mediterranean ✽ Algiers *area* 918,497 *sq mi* (2,390,315 *sq km*), *pop* 16,948,000 — **Al·ge·ri·an** \-ē-ən\ *adj or n*
Al·giers \al-'jirz\ **1** former Barbary state N Africa now Algeria **2** city & port ✽ of Algeria on **Bay of Algiers** (inlet of Mediterranean) *pop* 1,365,400 — **Al·ge·rine** \,al-jə-'rēn\ *adj or n*
Al·goa Bay \al-'gō-ə\ inlet of Indian Ocean S Republic of S. Africa on SE coast of Eastern Cape province
Al Hamad — see HAMAD, AL
Al·ham·bra \al-'ham-brə, *for 2 also* ä-'lam-brə\ **1** city SW Calif. E of Los Angeles *pop* 82,106 **2** hill in Granada, Spain; site of remains of the palace of the Moorish kings
Al Hijāz — see HEJAZ
Al·i·ba·tes Flint Quarries National Monument \,a-lə-'bä-tēz\ archaeological site N Tex. NE of Amarillo
Ali·can·te \,a-lə-'kan-tē, ,ä-lə-'kän-tē\ **1** province E Spain on the Mediterranean S of Valencia province *area* 2185 *sq mi* (5681 *sq km*), *pop* 1,217,729 **2** city & port, its ✽ *pop* 245,963
Al·ice \'a-ləs\ city S Tex. W of Corpus Christi *pop* 19,788
Ali·garh \,a-li-'gär\ city N India in NW Uttar Pradesh N of Agra *pop* (including old town of **Ko·il** \'kō-əl\) 319,981
Al Ittihad — see MADINAT ASH SHA'B
Al Jazirah — see GEZIRA, EL
Alk·maar \'alk-,mär\ commune NW Netherlands *pop* 80,992
Al Ku·frah \al-'kü-frə\ *or* **Ku·fra** \'kü-frə\ group of five oases SE Libya
Al–Kut — see KUT
Al·lah·abad \'a-lə-hə-,bad, -,bäd\ city N India in S Uttar Pradesh on the Ganges W of Banaras *pop* 642,420
Al·le·ghe·ny \,a-lə-'gā-nē *also* -'ge-\ river 325 *mi* (523 *km*) W Pa. & SW N.Y. uniting with the Monongahela at Pittsburgh to form the Ohio — **Al·le·ghe·ni·an** \-'gā-nē-ən, -'ge-\ *adj*
Allegheny Mountains mountains of Appalachian system E U.S. in Pa., Md., Va., & W.Va.
Al·len Park \'a-lən\ city SE Mich. WSW of Detroit *pop* 31,092
Allenstein — see OLSZTYN
Al·len·town \'a-lən-,taún\ city E Pa. on the Lehigh *pop* 105,090
Al·lep·pey \ə-'le-pē\ city & port S India in Kerala *pop* 169,934
Al·li·ance \ə-'lī-ən(t)s\ city NE Ohio NE of Canton *pop* 23,376
Al·lier \al-'yā\ river *ab* 250 *mi* (402 *km*) S *cen* France flowing to the Loire
Al·ma \'al-mə\ **1** river 50 *mi* (80 *km*) in SW Crimea **2** city Canada in E Que. on the Saguenay *pop* 25,910
Al·ma–Ata \,al-mə-ə-'tä, ,äl-\ *or formerly* **Ver·nyi** \'vern-yē\ city SE Kazakhstan, its ✽ *pop* 1,128,000
Al·ma·dén \,al-mə-'dän, ,äl-\ town S *cen* Spain in Sierra Morena
Al·me·lo \'äl-mə-,lō\ commune E Netherlands *pop* 63,079

Al·me·ría \,al-mə-'rē-ə\ **1** province S Spain SE of Granada province *area* 3360 *sq mi* (8736 *sq km*), *pop* 389,922 **2** city & port, its ✽ *pop* 140,745
Al Minyā — see MINYĀ, AL
Alor \'a-,lòr, 'ä-\ island Indonesia in Lesser Sunda Is. N of Timor; with **Pan·tar** \'pan-,tär\, forms **Alor Islands** group
Alor Se·tar \sə-'tär\ city Malaysia in NW Peninsular Malaysia ✽ of Kedah *pop* 66,179
Alost — see AALST
Al·phe·us \al-'fē-əs\ *or NGk* **Al·fiós** \äl-'fyòs\ river *ab* 75 *mi* (121 *km*) S Greece in W Peloponnisos flowing NW into Ionian Sea
Alps \'alps\ mountain system *cen* Europe extending from Mediterranean coast at border bet. France & Italy into Slovenia, Croatia, Bosnia and Herzegovina, Montenegro, & W Serbia — see MONT BLANC
Al·sace \al-'sas, -'säs, 'al-,\ *or G* **El·sass** \'el-,zäs\ *or anc* **Al·sa·tia** \al-'sā-sh(ē-)ə\ region & former province NE France bet. Rhine River & Vosges Mountains — **Al·sa·tian** \al-'sā-shən\ *adj or n*
Alsace–Lor·raine \-lə-'rän, -lò-\ region NE France including Alsace & part of Lorraine
Al·sek \'al-,sek\ river 260 *mi* (418 *km*) NW Canada & SE Alaska flowing S into the Pacific
Al·ta California \'al-tə\ former Spanish & Mexican province (1772–1848) comprising the present state of Calif. — a name used to differentiate it from Baja California
Al·tai \,al-'tī\ **1** mountain system *cen* Asia bet. Mongolia (republic) & Xinjiang Uygur region of W China & bet. Kazakhstan & Russia in Asia — see TABUN BOGDO **2** territory SW Russia in Asia ✽ Barnaul *area* 71,885 *sq mi* (186,901 *sq km*)
Al·ta·ma·ha \'òl-tə-mə-,hò\ river 137 *mi* (220 *km*) SE Ga. formed by junction of the Ocmulgee & the Oconee & flowing SE into **Altamaha Sound** (estuary)
Al·ta·mi·ra \,al-tə-'mir-ə\ caverns N Spain WSW of Santander
Al·ta·monte Springs \'al-tə-,mänt\ city *cen* Fla. *pop* 34,879
Alt·dorf \'alt-,dòrf, 'ält-\ *or* **Al·torf** \'al-,tòrf, 'äl-\ town *cen* Switzerland ✽ of Uri canton *pop* 8249
Al·ten·burg \'äl-t°n-,bùrg\ city E *cen* Germany E of Weimar *pop* 55,468
Al·to Adi·ge \,äl-(,)tō-'ä-di-jä\ *or* **Upper Adige** *or* **South Tirol** district N Italy in S Tirol in N Trentino-Alto Adige region
Al·ton \'òl-t°n\ city SW Ill. on the Mississippi *pop* 32,905
Al·too·na \al-'tü-nə\ city S *cen* Pa. *pop* 51,881
Alto Paraná — see PARANÁ
Al·trinc·ham \'òl-trin-əm\ borough NW England in Greater Manchester SSW of Manchester *pop* 39,641
Al·tus \'al-təs\ city SW Okla. *pop* 21,910
Al·tyn Tagh \,al-tin-'täg\ *or* **Al·tun Shan** \,al-tən-'shän\ mountain range W China in S Xinjiang Uygur; highest peak 20,213 *ft* (6161 *m*)
Al·vin \'al-vən\ city SE Tex. S of Houston *pop.* 19,220
Ama·do·ra \,a-mə-'dòr-ə, -ä-\ city W Portugal *pop* 95,518
Ama·ga·sa·ki \,a-mə-gə-'sä-kē\ city Japan in W *cen* Honshu on Osaka Bay *pop* 498,998
Amal·fi \ə-'mäl-fē\ commune & port S Italy in Campania on Gulf of Salerno — **Amal·fi·an** \-fē-ən\ *adj or n*
Ama·mi \ə-'mä-mē\ island group W Pacific in *cen* Ryukyus *area* 498 *sq mi* (1295 *sq km*)
Ama·pá \,a-mə-'pä\ territory N Brazil NW of Amazon delta ✽ Macapá *area* 55,489 *sq mi* (144,271 *sq km*), *pop* 180,078
'Ama·ra \ə-'mär-ə\ city SE Iraq on the Tigris
Am·a·ril·lo \,a-mə-'ri-(,)lō, -lə\ city NW Tex. *pop* 157,615 — **Am·a·ril·lo·an** \-'ri-lō-ən\ *n*
Am·a·zon \'a-mə-,zän, -zən\ river *ab* 3900 *mi* (6276 *km*) N S. America flowing from Peruvian Andes into the Atlantic in N Brazil — see UCAYALI, SOLIMÕES
Ama·zo·nas \,a-mə-'zō-nəs\ state NW Brazil ✽ Manaus *area* 595,474 *sq mi* (1,548,232 *sq km*), *pop* 1,449,135
Ama·zo·nia \,a-mə-'zō-nē-ə\ region N S. America, the basin of the Amazon
Am·ba·to \äm-'bä-(,)tō\ city *cen* Ecuador S of Quito *pop* 75,300
Am·bon \'am-,bän\ *or* **Am·boi·na** \am-'bòi-nə\ **1** island E Indonesia in the Moluccas S of Ceram *area* 314 *sq mi* (816 *sq km*) **2** city & port on Ambon Is. *pop* 276,955
Am·bra·cian Gulf \am-'brā-shən\ *or* **Gulf of Ar·ta** \'är-tə\ *or NGk* **Am·vra·ki·kós Kól·pos** \am-'vrä-kē-,kòs-'kòl-,pòs\ inlet of Ionian Sea 25 *mi* (40 *km*) long W Greece in S Epirus
Am·brose \'am-,bròz\ dredged channel SE N.Y. at entrance to N.Y. harbor N of Sandy Hook; 40 *ft* (12 *m*) deep, 2000 *ft* (606 *m*) wide
Am·chit·ka \am-'chit-kə\ island SW Alaska at E end of Rat group
Amer·i·ca \ə-'mer-ə-kə\ **1** either continent (N. America or S. America) of the western hemisphere **2** *or* **Amer·i·cas** \-kəz\ the lands of the western hemisphere including N., Central, & S. America & the W. Indies **3** UNITED STATES OF AMERICA
American Samoa *or* **Eastern Samoa** island group of E Samoa SW *cen* Pacific ✽ Pago Pago (on Tutuila Is.) *area* 76 *sq mi* (198 *sq km*), *pop* 32,297
Amers·foort \'ä-mərz-,fòrt, -mərs-, -,fòrt\ commune *cen* Netherlands NE of Utrecht *pop* 87,471
Ames \'āmz\ city *cen* Iowa N of Des Moines *pop* 47,198
Am·ga \äm-'gä\ river 800 *mi* (1280 *km*) E *cen* Russia in Asia, flowing NE to the Aldan
Am·hara \am-'har-ə, -'här-ə\ former kingdom (now a province) NW Ethiopia ✽ Gondar
Am·herst \'a-(,)mərst, *chiefly by outsiders* 'am-,hərst\ town W *cen* Mass. N of Springfield *pop* 35,228
Amiens \'am-yaⁿ\ city N France on the Somme *pop* 129,453
Amin·di·vi \,ə-mən-'dē-vē\ island group India in the N Laccadives
Am·i·rante \'a-mə-,rant\ islands W Indian Ocean SW of Seychelles; a dependency of Seychelles

---

\ə\ abut \'ə\ kitten, F table \ər\ further \a\ ash \ā\ ace \ä\ mop, mar \aú\ out \ch\ chin \e\ bet \ē\ easy \g\ go \i\ hit \ī\ ice \j\ job \ŋ\ sing \ō\ go \ò\ law \òi\ boy \th\ thin \t̲h̲\ the \ü\ loot \ú\ foot \y\ yet \zh\ vision \ä, k̲, ⁿ, œ, œ̄, ᵫ, ᵬ, ʸ\ see Guide to Pronunciation

Am·man \ä-'män, -'man\ *or anc* Philadelphia *or bib* Rab·bah \'ra-bə\ *or* Rab·bath \'ra-bəth\ city * of Jordan, NE of Dead Sea *pop* 711,850

Am·mon \'a-mən\ ancient country NW Arabia E of Gilead * Rabbah

Ammonium — see SIWA

Amne Machin — see A'NYÊMAQÊN

Amor·gos \ə-'mȯr-gäs\ *or NGk* Amor·gós \ä-(.)mȯr-'gȯs\ island Greece in the Aegean in SE Cyclades SE of Naxos *area* 52 *sq mi* (135 *sq km*)

Amoy — see XIAMEN

Am·ra·va·ti \,əm-'rä-və-tē, äm-\ *or* Am·rao·ti \-'rau̇-tē\ city *cen* India in NE Maharashtra, chief city of Berar region *pop* 261,387

Am·rit·sar \,əm-'rit-sər\ city N India in NW Punjab *pop* 589,229

Am·ster·dam \'am(p)-stər-,dam, *for 2 also* 'äm(p)-stər-'däm\ 1 city E N.Y. on the Mohawk *pop* 20,714 2 city & port, official * of Netherlands *pop* 688,100 — Am·ster·dam·mer \-,da-mər, -,dä-\ *n*

Amu Dar·ya \,ä-mü-'där-yə\ *or* Ox·us \'äk-səs\ river over 1400 *mi* (2253 *km*), *cen* & W Asia flowing from Pamir plateau into Aral Sea

Amund·sen Gulf \'ä-mən-sən, 'a-\ arm of Beaufort Sea N Canada

Amundsen Sea arm of the S Pacific W Antarctica off Marie Byrd Land

Amur \ä-'mu̇r\ river 1780 *mi* (2865 *km*) E Asia formed by junction of the Shilka & the Argun, flowing into the Pacific at N end of Tatar Strait, & forming part of boundary bet. China & Russia

Ana·dyr *or* Ana·dir \,ä-nə-'dir, ,a-\ river 450 *mi* (724 *km*) E Russia in Asia flowing S & E to Gulf of Anadyr

Anadyr, Gulf of inlet of N Bering Sea E Russia in Asia S of Chukotski Peninsula

An·a·heim \'a-nə-,hīm\ city SW Calif. E of Long Beach *pop* 266,406

Aná·huac \ə-'nä-,wäk\ the central plateau of Mexico

An·a·to·lia \,a-nə-'tō-lē-ə, -'tōl-yə\ the part of Turkey comprising the peninsula of Asia Minor

An·cas·ter \'aŋ,kas-tər, 'an-\ town Canada in SE Ont. W of Hamilton *pop* 21,988

An–ch'ing — see ANQING

An·chor·age \'aŋ-k(ə-)rij\ city S *cen* Alaska at head of Cook Inlet *pop* 226,338

An·co·hu·ma \,aŋ-kə-'hü-mə, -'hyü-\ mountain peak 20,873 *ft* (6362 *m*) W Bolivia; highest in the Illampu massif

An·co·na \aŋ-'kō-nə, an-\ city & port *cen* Italy * of the Marches on the Adriatic *pop* 103,454

An·da·lu·sia \,an-də-'lü-zh(ē-)ə\ *or Sp* An·da·lu·cía \,än-də-(,)lü-'sē-ə\ region S Spain including Sierra Nevada & valley of the Guadalquivir — An·da·lu·sian \,an-də-'lü-zhən\ *adj or n*

An·da·man and Nic·o·bar \,an-də-mən...ni-kə-,bar, -,man-\ union territory India comprising Andaman & Nicobar groups * Port Blair *area* 3143 *sq mi* (8172 *sq km*), *pop* 188,254

Andaman Islands islands India in Bay of Bengal S of Myanmar & N of Nicobar Islands *area* 2508 *sq mi* (6521 *sq km*) — An·da·man·ese \,an-də-mə-'nēz, -'nēs\ *adj or n*

Andaman Sea sea SE Asia, the E section of Bay of Bengal

An·der·lecht \'än-dər-,lekt\ commune *cen* Belgium, *pop* 87,884

An·der·matt \'än-dər-,mät\ commune *cen* Switzerland S of Altdorf

An·der·son \'an-dər-sən\ 1 city *cen* Ind. *pop* 59,459 2 city NW S.C. *pop* 26,184 3 river 430 *mi* (692 *km*) Canada in Northwest Territories flowing W & N into Beaufort Sea

An·des \'an-(,)dēz\ mountain system of S. America extending along W coast from Panama to Tierra del Fuego — see ACONCAGUA — An·de·an \'an-(,)dē-ən, an-'\ *adj* — An·dine \'an-,dēn, -'\ *adj*

An·dhra Pra·desh \,än-drə-prə-'däsh, -'desh\ state SE India N of Tamil Nadu state bordering on Bay of Bengal * Hyderabad *area* 105,677 *sq mi* (274,760 *sq km*), *pop* 53,403,619

An·di·zhan *or* An·di·jon \,an-di-'zhan, ,än-di-'zhän\ city Uzbekistan ESE of Tashkent *pop* 188,000

An·dor·ra \an-'dȯr-ə, -'där-ə\ country SW Europe in E Pyrenees bet. France & Spain; a republic * Andorra la Vella *area* 179 *sq mi* (465 *sq km*), *pop* 40,000 — An·dor·ran \-ən\ *adj or n*

An·do·ver \'an-,dō-vər, -də-\ town NE Mass. *pop* 29,151

An·dre·a·nof Islands \,an-drē-'a-nȯf, -,nȯf\ islands SW Alaska in *cen* Aleutian chain — see ADAK, ATKA

An·dria \'än-drē-ə\ commune SE Italy in Apulia *pop* 89,762

Andropov — see RYBINSK

An·dros 1 \'an-drəs\ island, largest of the Bahamas *area* 1600 *sq mi* (4160 *sq km*) 2 \'an-drəs, -,dräs; 'än-thrȯs\ island 25 *mi* (40 *km*) long Greece in N Cyclades

An·dros·cog·gin \,an-drə-'skä-gən\ river 157 *mi* (253 *km*) NE N.H. & SW Maine flowing into the Kennebec

Ane·to, Pi·co de \'pē-(,)kō-,dā-ə-'nä-(,)tō\ *or F* Pic de Né·thou \,pēk-də-(,)nä-'tü\ mountain 11,168 *ft* (3404 *m*) NE Spain; highest in the Pyrenees

An·ga·ra \,äŋ-gə-'rä\ river 1100 *mi* (1770 *km*) Russia, flowing from Lake Baikal into the Yenisei — see TUNGUSKA

An·garsk \an-'gärsk\ city S Russia in Asia on the Angara NW of Irkutsk *pop* 224,000

An·gel Falls \'än-jəl\ waterfall 3212 *ft* (979 *m*) SE Venezuela on Auyán-tepuí mountain in a headstream of the Caroní

An·gers \ä-'zhā\ city W France ENE of Nantes *pop* 136,603

Ang·kor \'aŋ-,kȯr\ ruins of ancient city NW Cambodia N of Tonle Sap; * of the Khmers

An·gle·sey *or* An·gle·sea \'aŋ-gəl-sē\ 1 *or anc* Mo·na \'mō-nə\ island NW Wales 2 former county comprising Anglesey Is. & Holyhead Is. * Llangefni

Anglia 1 — see ENGLAND 2 — see EAST ANGLIA — An·gli·an \'aŋ-glē-ən\ *adj or n*

Anglo–Egyptian Sudan — see SUDAN

An·go·la \aŋ-'gō-lə, an-\ *or formerly* Portuguese West Africa country SW Africa S of mouth of the Congo; until 1975 a dependency of Portugal * Luanda *area* 481,351 *sq mi* (1,251,513 *sq km*), *pop* 6,761,000 — An·go·lan \-lən\ *adj or n*

An·gou·lême \,äⁿ-gü-'läm, -'lem\ city W France *pop* 46,293

An·gou·mois \,äⁿ-güm-'wä\ region & former duchy & province W France S of Poitou * Angoulême

An·guil·la \aŋ-'gwi-lə, an-\ island Brit. West Indies NW of St. Kitts *area* 34 *sq mi* (88 *sq km*) — An·guil·lan \-'gwi-lən\ *adj or n*

An·gus \'aŋ-gəs\ *or earlier* For·far \'fȯr-fər\ *or* For·far·shire \-,shir-, -shər\ former county E Scotland * Forfar

An·halt \'än-,hält\ former state *cen* Germany * Dessau

An·hui *or* An·hwei \'än-'hwā, -'wā\ province E China W of Jiangsu * Hefei *area* 54,015 *sq mi* (140,439 *sq km*), *pop* 49,665,724

An·i·ak·chak Crater \,a-nē-'ak-,chak\ active volcano 4420 *ft* (1347 *m*) SW Alaska on Alaska Peninsula in Aniakchak National Monument; crater 6 *mi* (10 *km*) in diameter

A–ni–ma–ch'ing — see A'NYÊMAQÊN

An·jou \'an-,jü, äⁿ-zhü\ 1 region & former province NW France in Loire valley * Angers 2 town Canada in S Que. *pop* 37,210

An·ka·ra \'aŋ-kə-rə, 'äŋ-\ *or formerly* An·go·ra \aŋ-'gȯr-ə, an-, -'gȯr-\ *or anc* An·cy·ra \an-'sī-rə\ city * of Turkey in N *cen* Anatolia *pop* 2,203,729

Ann, Cape \'an\ peninsula NE Mass.

An·na·ba \ə-'nä-bə\ *or formerly* Bône \'bōn\ commune & port NE Algeria NE of Constantine *pop* 255,900

An Nafūd — see NAFŪD, AN

An Na·jaf \an-'na-,jaf\ city S *cen* Iraq W of the Euphrates *pop* 134,027

An·nam \a-'nam, ə-; 'a-,nam\ region & former kingdom E Indochina in *cen* Vietnam * Hue *area* 57,000 *sq mi* (148,200 *sq km*)

An·nap·o·lis \ə-'nap-(ə-)ləs\ city & port * of Md. *pop* 33,187

Annapolis Basin inlet of Bay of Fundy Canada in W N.S.

An·na·pur·na \,a-nə-'pu̇r-nə, -'pər-\ massif N Nepal in the Himalayas; highest peak 26,334 *ft* (8027 *m*)

Ann Ar·bor \(,)an-'är-bər\ city SE Mich. W of Detroit *pop* 109,592

An·ne·cy \,a-nə-'sē\ city E France ENE of Lyons *pop* 53,058

An Nhon \'än-'nȯn\ *or formerly* Binh Dinh \'bin-'din\ city *cen* Vietnam in S Annam

An·nis·ton \'a-nə-stən\ city NE Ala. *pop* 26,623

An·qing *or* An–ch'ing \'än-'chiŋ\ *or* An·king \'än-'kiŋ\ *or formerly* Hwai·ning \'hwī-'niŋ\ city E China in Anhui on the Chang *pop* 105,300

An·shan \'än-'shän\ city NE China in E *cen* Liaoning SSW of Shenyang *pop* 833,000

An·ta·kya \,an-tə-'kyä\ *or* An·ta·ki·yah \-'kē-yə\ *or anc* An·ti·och \'an-tē-,äk\ city S Turkey on the Orontes *pop* 91,551

An·tal·ya \an-'täl-yə\ *or formerly* Ada·lia \ä-d°l-ē-'yä\ city & port SW Turkey on Gulf of Antalya *pop* 176,446

An·ta·nan·a·ri·vo \,än-tə-,na-nə-'rē-(,)vō\ *or Malagasy* Ta·nan·a·ri·vo \tə-,na-nə-'rē-(,)vō\ *or formerly* Ta·nan·a·rive \tə-'na-nə-,rēv\ city * of Madagascar *pop* 339,233

Ant·arc·tic \ant-'ärk-tik, -'är-tik\ region including Antarctica, Antarctic Ocean, Antarctic Peninsula, and the Antarctic Ocean

Ant·arc·ti·ca \ant-'ärk-ti-kə, -'är-ti-kə\ *or* Antarctic Continent body of land around the S. Pole; a plateau covered by a great ice cap & mountain peaks *area ab* 5,500,000 *sq mi* (14,300,000 *sq km*), divided into West Antarctica (including Antarctic Peninsula) & East Antarctica by Transantarctic Mountains

Antarctic Archipelago *or* Palm·er Archipelago \,pä-mər, ,päl-mər\ islands W of N end of Antarctic Peninsula in Falkland Islands Dependencies

Antarctic Ocean ocean surrounding Antarctica including the southern regions of the S. Atlantic, S. Pacific, & Indian oceans esp. S of *ab* 60°S

Antarctic Peninsula *or formerly* Palmer Peninsula *or* Gra·ham Land \'grä-əm, 'gra(-ə)m\ peninsula 1200 *mi* (1931 *km*) long W Antarctica S end of S. America

An·tibes \ä-'tēb\ city & port SE France SW of Nice *pop* 44,226

Antibes, Cap d' — see CAP D'ANTIBES

An·ti·cos·ti Island \,an-tə-'kȯ-stē\ island E Canada in E Que. at mouth of the St. Lawrence *area* 3043 *sq mi* (7912 *sq km*)

An·tie·tam Creek \an-'tē-təm\ creek S Pa. & N Md. flowing S into the Potomac N of Harpers Ferry, W.Va.

An·ti·gua \an-'tē-gə, -gwə\ 1 island Brit. West Indies in the Leewards *area* 108 *sq mi* (281 *sq km*); with Barbuda an independent nation (Antigua and Barbuda) since 1981 (*pop* 77,000) — see WEST INDIES ASSOCIATED STATES 2 *or* Antigua Guatemala city S *cen* Guatemala; former * of Guatemala *pop* 27,014 — An·ti·guan \an-'tē-gən, -gwən\ *adj or n*

An·ti–Leb·a·non \,an-ti-'le-bə-nən, -,nän\ mountain range SW Asia E of Bekaa Valley on Syria-Lebanon border — see HERMON (Mount)

An·til·les \an-'ti-lēz\ the W. Indies excluding the Bahamas — see GREATER ANTILLES, LESSER ANTILLES — An·til·le·an \an-'ti-lē-ən\ *adj*

An·ti·och \'an-tē-,äk\ 1 city W Calif. NE of Oakland *pop* 62,195 2 — see ANTAKYA 3 ancient city Asia Minor in Pisidia, at certain periods within boundaries of Phrygia; ruins in W *cen* Turkey — An·ti·o·chene \an-'tī-ə-,kēn, ,an-tē-(,)ä-'kēn\ *adj or n* — An·ti·och·i·an \,an-tē-'ō-kē-ən, -'ä-\ *adj or n*

An·ti·sa·na \an-ti-'sä-nə\ volcano 18,714 *ft* (5704 *m*) N *cen* Ecuador

An·to·fa·gas·ta \,an-tə-fə-'gäs-tə\ city & port N Chile N of Santiago *pop* 125,081

An·trim \'an-trəm\ 1 traditional county NE Northern Ireland 2 district E Northern Ireland, established 1974 *area* 217 *sq mi* (564 *sq km*), *pop* 44,384

Antung — see DANDONG

Ant·werp \'ant-,wərp, 'an-,twərp\ *or F* An·vers \äⁿ-'ver(s)\ *or Flem* Ant·wer·pen \'änt-,ver-pə(n)\ 1 province N Belgium *area* 1104 *sq mi* (2870 *sq km*), *pop* 1,605,167 2 city & port, its *, on the Scheldt *pop* 467,518

Anu·ra·dha·pu·ra \,ə-nə-,rä-də-'pu̇r-ə\ town N *cen* Sri Lanka; an ancient * of Ceylon *pop* 37,000

An·yang \'än-'yäŋ\ 1 city E China in N Henan 2 city NW S. Korea *pop* 361,577

A'·nyê·ma·qên \,an-yē-mə-'jin\ *or* Am·ne Ma·chin \,am-nē-mə-'jin\ *or* A–ni–ma–ch'ing \'ä-'nē-'mä-'chiŋ\ range of the Kunlun Mountains W China in E *cen* Qinghai; highest peak *ab* 25,000 *ft* (7620 *m*)

An·zio \'an-zē-,ō, 'än-\ city & port Italy SSE of Rome *pop* 33,523

Ao·mo·ri \'au̇-mə-(,)rē\ city & port N Japan in NE Honshu on Mutsu Bay *pop* 287,813

Aorangi — see COOK (Mount)

Aos·ta \ä-'ȯ-stə\ 1 commune NW Italy in Piedmont at junction of Great & Little Saint Bernard passes *pop* 36,339 2 — see VALLE D'AOSTA

Ap·a·lach·i·co·la \ˌa-pə-ˌla-chi-ˈkō-lə\ river 90 *mi* (145 *km*) NW Fla. flowing from Lake Seminole S into **Apalachicola Bay** (inlet of Gulf of Mexico)

Apa·po·ris \ˌä-pə-ˈpōr-(ˌ)ēs, -ˈpȯr-\ river *ab* 500 *mi* (805 *km*) S Colombia flowing SE into the Japurá on Colombia-Brazil boundary

Apel·doorn \ˈa-pəl-ˌdȯrn, -ˌdȯrn\ commune E *cen* Netherlands N of Arnhem *pop* 143,276

Ap·en·nines \ˈa-pə-ˌnīnz\ mountain chain Italy extending the length of the peninsula — see CORNO (Monte) — **Ap·en·nine** \-ˌnīn\ *adj*

Apia \ə-ˈpē-ə\ town & port Samoa * of Western Samoa on Upolu Is.

Apo, Mount \ˈä-(ˌ)pō\ volcano 9689 *ft* (2953 *m*) S Philippines in SE Mindanao; highest peak in the Philippines

Ap·pa·la·chia \ˌa-pə-ˈlā-chə, -ˈla-chə, -ˈlā-shə\ region E U.S. comprising Appalachian Mountains from S *cen* N.Y. to *cen* Ala.

Ap·pa·la·chian Mountains \ˌa-pə-ˈlā-ch(ē-)ən, -sh(ē-)ən; -ˈla-ch(ē-)ən\ mountain system E N. America extending from SE Que., Nfld., & N.B. SW to N Ala.; highest peak Mt. Mitchell 6684 *ft* (2037 *m*)

Ap·pen·zell \ˈa-pən-ˌzel, ˈä-pən(t)-ˌsel\ former canton NE Switzerland, now divided into two cantons (formerly half cantons): **Appenzell Inner Rhodes** \ˌrōdz\ *or G* **Appenzell Inner Rho·den** \ˈi-nə(r)-ˈrō-d°n\ (* Appenzell *area* 61 *sq mi or* 159 *sq km, pop* 13,656) & **Appenzell Outer Rhodes** *or G* **Appenzell Aus·ser Rhoden** \ˈau̇-sə(r)\ (* Herisau *area* 101 *sq mi or* 263 *sq km, pop* 51,167)

Ap·pi·an Way \ˈa-pē-ən\ ancient paved highway extending from Rome to Brundisium (in Apulia)

Ap·ple·ton \ˈa-pəl-tən\ city E Wis. *pop* 65,695

Apple Valley 1 town SE Calif. N of San Bernardino *pop* 46,079 2 city SE Minn. *pop* 34,598

Apra Harbor \ˈä-prə\ seaport Guam on W coast

Ap·she·ron \ˌäp-shə-ˈrȯn\ peninsula E Azerbaijan projecting into the Caspian Sea

Apu·lia \ə-ˈpyül-yə, -ˈpyü-lē-ə\ *or It* **Pu·glia** \ˈpül-yä\ *or* **Le Pu·glie** \lä-ˈpül-yä\ region SE Italy on the Adriatic & Gulf of Taranto * Bari *pop* 4,069,359 — **Apu·lian** \ə-ˈpyül-yən, -ˈpyü-lē-ən\ *adj or n*

Apu·re \ə-ˈpür-(ˌ)ā\ river 420 *mi* (676 *km*) W Venezuela flowing E into the Orinoco

Apu·ri·mac \ˌä-pə-ˈrē-ˌmäk\ river 550 *mi* (885 *km*) S & *cen* Peru flowing N to unite with the Urubamba forming the Ucayali

'Aqa·ba *or* **Aka·ba** \ˈä-kə-bə\ *or anc* **Elath** \ˈē-ˌlath\ town & port SW Jordan on border of Israel at head of NE arm (**Gulf of 'Aqaba**) of Red Sea

Aquid·neck Island \ə-ˈkwid-ˌnek\ *or* **Rhode Island** island SE R.I. in Narragansett Bay; site of city of Newport

Aq·ui·taine \ˈa-kwə-ˌtān\ old region of SW France comprising area later known as Guienne * Toulouse

Aq·ui·ta·nia \ˌa-kwə-ˈtā-nyə, -nē-ə\ a Roman division of SW Gaul under Caesar consisting of country bet. Pyrenees & Garonne River & under Augustus expanded to Loire & Allier rivers — **Aq·ui·ta·nian** \-nyən, -nē-ən\ *adj or n*

Ara·ba, Wa·di el \ˌwä-dē-el,ˌel-ˈar-ə-bə\ *or* **Ar·a·bah** \ˈar-ə-bə\ valley extending S from Dead Sea to Gulf of 'Aqaba

Ara·bia \ə-ˈrā-bē-ə\ peninsula SW Asia *ab* 1400 *mi* (2253 *km*) long & 1250 *mi* (2012 *km*) wide including Saudi Arabia, Yemen, & Persian Gulf States; in early times divided into **Arabia Pe·traea** \pə-ˈtrē-ə\, "Rocky Arabia", the NW part; **Arabia De·ser·ta** \di-ˈzər-tə\, "Desert Arabia", the N part; & **Arabia Fe·lix** \ˈfē-liks\, "Fertile Arabia", the main part but by some geographers restricted to Yemen

Arabian Desert desert E Egypt bet. the Nile & the Red Sea

Arabian Sea sea, NW section of the Indian Ocean bet. India & Arabia

Ar·a·by \ˈar-ə-bē\ ARABIA

Ara·ca·ju \ˌar-ə-kə-ˈzhü\ city & port NE Brazil * of Sergipe *pop* 293,285

Arad \ä-ˈräd\ city W Romania on the Mures *pop* 191,428

Ara·fu·ra Sea \ˌar-ə-ˈfür-ə\ sea bet. N Australia & W New Guinea

Ar·a·gon \ˈar-ə-ˌgän, -gən\ region NE Spain bordering on France; once an independent kingdom * Zaragoza — **Ar·a·go·nese** \ˌar-ə-gə-ˈnēz, -ˈnēs\ *adj or n*

Ara·gua·ia *or* **Ara·gua·ya** \ˌar-ə-ˈgwī-ə\ river *ab* 1100 *mi* (1770 *km*), *cen* Brazil flowing N into the Tocantins

Arak \ä-ˈräk, ə-ˈrak\ city W Iran SW of Tehran *pop* 265,349

Ara·kan \ˌar-ə-ˈkän, -ˈkan\ coast region SW Myanmar on Bay of Bengal; chief town Sittwe

Araks \ə-ˈräks\ *or* **Aras** \ə-ˈräs\ *or anc* **Arax·es** \ə-ˈrak-(ˌ)sēz\ river 635 *mi* (1022 *km*) W Asia rising in mountains of Turkish Armenia & flowing E to join the Kura in E Azerbaijan

Ar·al Sea \ˈar-əl\ *or formerly* **Lake Aral** brackish lake bet. Kazakhstan & Kyrgyzstan *area* 26,000 *sq mi* (67,600 *sq km*)

Ar·am \ˈar-əm, ˈer-\ ancient Syria — its Hebrew name

Ar·an Islands \ˈar-ən\ islands W Ireland off coast of Galway; largest island Inishmore

Aran·sas Bay \ə-ˈran(t)-səs\ inlet of Gulf of Mexico S Tex. NE of Corpus Christi Bay bet. mainland & St. Joseph Is.

Aransas Pass channel S Tex. bet. Mustang & St. Joseph islands leading to Corpus Christi & Aransas bays

Ar·a·rat \ˈar-ə-ˌrat\ *or* **Ag·ri Da·gi** \ˌä-(g)rē-dä-ˈ(g)ē\ mountain 16,946 *ft* (5165 *m*) E Turkey near border of Iran

Ara·val·li Range \ə-ˈrä-və-(ˌ)lē\ mountain range NW India E of Thar Desert; highest peak Mt. Abu 5650 *ft* (1722 *m*)

Ar·bil *or* **Ir·bil** *or* **Er·bil** \ər-ˈbēl\ *or anc* **Ar·be·la** \är-ˈbē-lə\ city N Iraq E of Mosul *pop* 460,758

Ar·bon \är-ˈbōn\ commune NE Switzerland *pop* 11,333

Ar·buck·le Mountains \ˈär-ˌbə-kəl\ hilly region S *cen* Okla.

Ar·ca·dia \är-ˈkā-dē-ə\ 1 city SW Calif. ENE of Los Angeles *pop* 48,290 2 mountainous region S Greece in *cen* Peloponnisos

Archangel, Gulf of — see DVINA GULF

Arch·es National Park \ˈär-chəz\ reservation E Utah including wind-eroded natural arch formations

Ar·cos de la Fron·te·ra \ˈär-kōs-ˌde-lə-ˌfrän-ˈter-ə\ commune SW Spain NE of Cádiz *pop* 16,217

Ar·cot \är-ˈkät\ city SE India in N Tamil Nadu WSW of Madras; once * of the nawabs of Carnatic *pop* 30,230

Arc·tic \ˈärk-tik, ˈär-tik\ the Arctic Ocean and lands in it and adjacent to it

Arctic Archipelago archipelago N & E Northwest Territories, Canada in Arctic Ocean

Arctic Ocean ocean N of the Arctic Circle

Arctic Red river 310 *mi* (499 *km*) Canada in W Northwest Territories, flowing N into the Mackenzie

Ar·cueil \är-ˈkœi\ commune N France S of Paris *pop* 20,303

Ar·da·bil *or* **Ar·de·bil** \ˌär-də-ˈbē(ə)l\ city NW Iran in E Azerbaijan region *pop* 281,973

Ar·den \ˈär-d°n\ district *cen* England in SW Warwickshire W of Stratford-upon-Avon; site of former **Forest of Arden**

Ar·dennes \är-ˈden\ wooded plateau region in NE France, W Luxembourg, & SE Belgium E of the Meuse

Ard·more \ˈärd-ˌmōr, -ˌmȯr\ city S Okla. *pop* 23,079

Ards \ˈärdz\ district E Northern Ireland, established 1974 *area* 143 *sq mi* (372 *sq km*), *pop* 57,626

Are·ci·bo \ˌar-ə-ˈsē-(ˌ)bō\ city & port N Puerto Rico *pop* 93,385

Are·na, Point \ə-ˈrē-nə\ promontory N Calif. in the Pacific *ab* midway bet. Cape Mendocino & San Francisco Bay

Are·qui·pa \ˌar-ə-ˈkē-pə\ city S Peru at foot of El Misti *pop* 108,023

Arez·zo \ə-ˈret-(ˌ)sō, ä-\ commune *cen* Italy in Tuscany *pop* 91,527

Ar·gen·tan \ˌär-zhən-ˈtän\ commune NW France in Normandy NNW of Alençon *pop* 16,063

Ar·gen·teuil \ˌär-zhən-ˈtəi\ commune N France on the Seine NNW of Paris *pop* 101,542

Ar·gen·ti·na \ˌär-jən-ˈtē-nə\ *or the* **Ar·gen·tine** \ˈär-jən-ˌtīn, -ˌtēn\ country S S. America bet. the Andes & the Atlantic S of the Pilcomayo; a federal republic * Buenos Aires *area* 1,079,965 *sq mi* (2,807,909 *sq km*), *pop* 27,947,446 — **Argentine** *adj or n* — **Ar·gen·tin·ean** *or* **Ar·gen·tin·i·an** \ˌär-jən-ˈti-nē-ən\ *adj or n*

Ar·gi·nu·sae \ˌär-jə-ˈnü-(ˌ)sē, -ˈnyü-\ group of small islands in the Aegean SE of Lésvos

Ar·go·lis \ˈär-gə-ləs\ district & ancient country S Greece in E Peloponnisos comprising a plain around Argos & area between Gulf of Argolis & Saronic Gulf — **Ar·gol·ic** \är-ˈgä-lik\ *adj*

Argolis, Gulf of *or* **Gulf of Nau·plia** \-ˈnȯ-plē-ə\ inlet of the Aegean S Greece on E coast of Peloponnisos

Ar·gonne \är-ˈgän, -ˈgȯn\ wooded plateau NE France S of the Ardennes near Belgian border bet. the Meuse & the Aisne

Ar·gos \ˈär-ˌgȯs, -gəs\ town Greece in E Peloponnisos on Argive plain at head of Gulf of Argolis; once a Greek city-state

Argovie — see AARGAU

Ar·guel·lo, Point \är-ˈgwe-(ˌ)lō\ cape SW Calif. WNW of Santa Barbara

Ar·gun \är-ˈgün\ river 450 *mi* (724 *km*) NE Asia forming boundary bet. Inner Mongolia (China) & Russia & uniting with the Shilka to form the Amur

Ar·gyll \är-ˈgī(ə)l, ˌär-ˌgīl\ *or* **Ar·gyll·shire** \-ˌshir, -shər\ former county W Scotland * Lochgilphead

Ar·hus *or* **Aar·hus** \ˈȯr-ˌhüs\ city & port Denmark in E Jutland on the Kattegat *pop* 259,493

Aria \ˈär-ē-ə, ə-ˈrī-ə\ 1 an E province of ancient Persian Empire; district now in NW Afghanistan & E Iran 2 — see HERAT

Ari·ca \ə-ˈrē-kə\ city & port N Chile *pop* 63,160 — see TACNA

Ar·i·ma·thea *or* **Ar·i·ma·thaea** \ˌar-ə-mə-ˈthē-ə\ town in ancient Palestine; location not certainly identified

Ariminum — see RIMINI

Ari·pua·nã \ˌar-ə-pwə-ˈnäⁿ\ river 600 *mi* (966 *km*) W *cen* Brazil rising in Mato Grosso state & flowing N into the Madeira

Arius — see HARI RUD

Ar·i·zo·na \ˌar-ə-ˈzō-nə\ state SW U.S. * Phoenix *area* 113,909 *sq mi* (296,163 *sq km*), *pop* 3,665,228 — **Ar·i·zo·nan** \-nən\ *or* **Ar·i·zo·nian** \-nē-ən, -nyən\ *adj or n*

Ar·kan·sas \ˈär-kən-ˌsȯ; *1 is also* är-ˈkan-zəs\ 1 river 1450 *mi* (2334 *km*) SW *cen* U.S. rising in *cen* Colo. & flowing E & SE through S Kans., NE Okla., & Ark. into the Mississippi 2 state S *cen* U.S. * Little Rock *area* 53,104 *sq mi* (138,070 *sq km*), *pop* 2,350,725 — **Ar·kan·san** \är-ˈkan-zən\ *adj or n*

Ar·khan·gel'sk \är-ˈkan-gelsk\ *or* **Arch·an·gel** \ˈär-ˌkän-jəl\ city & port Russia in Europe on the Northern Dvina *pop* 385,000

Arl·berg \ˈär(-ə)l-ˌbərg, -ˌberg\ Alpine valley, pass, & tunnel W Austria in the Tirol

Arles \ˈär(-ə)l\ 1 medieval kingdom E & SE France; also called Kingdom of Burgundy 2 *or anc* **Ar·e·las** \ˈar-ə-ˌlas\ *or* **Ar·e·la·te** \ˌar-ə-ˈlā-tē\ city SE France on the Rhône *pop* 37,337 — **Ar·le·sian** \är-ˈlē-zhən\ *n*

Ar·ling·ton \ˈär-liŋ-tən\ 1 town E Mass. NW of Boston *pop* 44,630 2 city N Tex. E of Fort Worth *pop* 261,721 3 unincorporated population center N Va. *pop* 170,936

Arlington Heights village NE Ill. NW of Chicago *pop* 75,460

Ar·lon \är-ˈlōⁿ\ commune SE Belgium * of Luxembourg province *pop* 23,422

Ar·magh \är-ˈmä, ˈär-\ 1 traditional county SE Northern Ireland 2 district S Northern Ireland, established 1974 *area* 260 *sq mi* (676 *sq km*), *pop* 47,618 3 town *cen* Armagh district, Northern Ireland *pop* 12,700

Ar·ma·gnac \ˌär-mən-ˈyak\ district SW France in old province of Gascony; chief town Auch

Ar·me·nia \är-ˈmē-nē-ə, -nyə\ 1 *or bib* **Min·ni** \ˈmi-ˌnī\ former kingdom W Asia in mountainous region SE of Black Sea & SW of Caspian Sea; area now divided bet. Armenia, Turkey, & Iran 2 independent country SE Europe; a constituent republic (**Armenian Republic**) of the U.S.S.R. 1936–91 * Yerevan *area* 11,580 *sq mi* (30,108 *sq km*), *pop* 3,283,000 — see LESSER ARMENIA

Ar·men·tières \ˌär-mən-ˈtyer, -ˈtirz\ commune N France W of Lille *pop* 23,850

Ar·mor·i·ca \är-ˈmȯr-ə-kə, -ˈmär-\ 1 *or* **Ar·e·mor·i·ca** \ˌar-ə-\ ancient region NW France bet. the Seine & the Loire 2 BRITTANY

\ə\ abut \°\ kitten, F table \ər\ further \a\ ash \ā\ ace \ä\ mop, mar
\au̇\ out \ch\ chin \e\ bet \ē\ easy \g\ go \i\ hit \ī\ ice \j\ job
\ŋ\ sing \ō\ go \ȯ\ law \ȯi\ boy \th\ thin \th\ the \ü\ loot \u̇\ foot
\y\ yet \zh\ vision \ä, k̟, ⁿ, œ, œ̄, ue, ūe, ᵊ\ *see* Guide to Pronunciation

Arn·hem \\'ärn-ˌhem, 'är-nəm\\ commune E Netherlands ✳ of Gelderland *pop* 128,641

Arn·hem Land \\'är-nəm\\ region N Australia on N coast of Northern Territory

Ar·no \\'är-(ˌ)nō\\ *or anc* **Ar·nus** \\-nəs\\ river 140 *mi* (225 *km*) *cen* Italy flowing W from the Apennines through Florence into Ligurian Sea

Aroos·took \\ə-'rüs-tək, -'rüs-\\ river 140 *mi* (225 *km*) N Maine flowing NE across N.B. border & into St. John River

Ar·ran \\'ar-ən\\ island SW Scotland in Firth of Clyde *area* 165 *sq mi* (429 *sq km*)

Ar·ras \\ə-'räs, 'ar-əs\\ city N France SSW of Lille *pop* 45,804

Arsanias — see MURAT

Arta, Gulf of — see AMBRACIAN GULF

Ar·tois \\är-'twä\\ former province N France bet. Flanders & Picardy ✳ Arras

Aru·ba \\ə-'rü-bə\\ internally self-governing Dutch island off NW Venezuela; chief town Oranjestad *area* 69 *sq mi* (179 *sq km*), *pop* 60,312

Aru Islands *or* **Aroe Islands** *or* **Ar·roe Islands** \\'är-(ˌ)ü\\ islands E Indonesia S of W New Guinea *area* 3305 *sq mi* (8593 *sq km*), *pop* 29,604

Arun·a·chal Pra·desh \\ˌär-ə-ˌnä-chəl-prə-'däsh, -'desh\\ *or formerly* **North East Frontier Agency** state NE India N of Assam ✳ Itanagar *area* 31,439 *sq mi* (81,741 *sq km*), *pop* 628,050

Aru·wi·mi \\ˌär-ə-'wē-mē, ˌar-\\ river 800 *mi* (1287 *km*) N Zaire flowing SW & W into Congo River

Ar·va·da \\är-'va-də\\ city N of Denver *pop* 89,235

Ar·wad \\är-'wad, -'wäd\\ *or* **Ru·ad** \\rü-'ad\\ *or bib* **Ar·vad** \\'är-,vad\\ island Syria off coast of S Latakia

Asa·hi·ka·wa \\ˌä-sə-hē-'kä-wə\\ *or* **Asa·hi·ga·wa** \\-'gä-wə\\ city Japan in *cen* Hokkaido *pop* 359,069

Asa·ma \\ə-'sä-mə\\ *or* **Asa·ma·ya·ma** \\ə-ˌsä-mə-'yä-mə\\ volcano 8340 *ft* (2542 *m*) Japan in *cen* Honshu

Asan·sol \\'ä-s'n-ˌsōl\\ city NE India in W. Bengal *pop* 365,371

As·cen·sion \\ə-'sen(t)-shən\\ island in S Atlantic belonging to Brit. colony of St. Helena *area* 34 *sq mi* (88 *sq km*), *pop* 849

As·co·li Pi·ce·no \\ˌäs-kə-(ˌ)lē-pi-'chā-(ˌ)nō\\ *or anc* **As·cu·lum Pi·ce·num** \\ˌas-kyə-ləm-(ˌ)pi-'sē-nəm\\ commune *cen* Italy in the Marches NE of Rome *pop* 52,667

Ascoli Sa·tria·no \\ˌsä-trē-'ä-(ˌ)nō\\ *or anc* **As·cu·lum Ap·u·lum** \\ˌas-kyə-ləm-'a-pyə-ləm\\ *or* **Aus·cu·lum Apulum** \\ˌós-\\ commune SE Italy in Apulia S of Foggia

As·cot \\'as-kət\\ village S England in Berkshire SW of London

As·cut·ney, Mount \\'as-kət-nē\\ mountain 3144 *ft* (958 *m*) SE Vt.

Ashan·ti \\ə-'shan-tē, -'shän-\\ *or* **Asan·te** \\-'sän-tē\\ region *cen* Ghana; formerly a native kingdom & later a Brit. colony ✳ Kumasi *area* 24,379 *sq mi* (63,385 *sq km*), *pop* 1,996,821

Ash·bur·ton \\'ash-ˌbər-t'n\\ river 500 *mi* (805 *km*) Australia in NW Western Australia flowing NW into Indian Ocean

Ash·dod \\'ash-ˌdäd\\ city & port Israel W of Jerusalem *pop* 40,500

Ashe·ville \\'ash-ˌvil, -vəl\\ city W N.C. *pop* 61,607

Ash·ke·lon \\'ash-kə-ˌlän\\ *or* **As·ca·lon** \\'as-\\ ancient city & port SW Palestine, site in Israel WSW of Jerusalem

Ashkh·a·bad \\'ash-kə-ˌbad, -ˌbäd\\ *or* **Ash·ga·bat** \\'äsh-gə-ˌbät\\ *or formerly* **Pol·to·ratsk** \\ˌpäl-tə-'rätsk\\ city ✳ of Turkmenistan *pop* 398,000

Ash·land \\'ash-lənd\\ **1** city NE Ky. on the Ohio *pop* 23,622 **2** city N *cen* Ohio *pop* 20,079

Ash·ley \\'ash-lē\\ river 40 *mi* (64 *km*) S S.C. flowing SE into Charleston harbor

Ash·ta·bu·la \\ˌash-tə-'byü-lə\\ city NE Ohio on Lake Erie *pop* 21,633

Asia \\'ā-zhə, -shə\\ continent of the eastern hemisphere N of equator forming a single landmass with Europe (the conventional dividing line bet. Asia & Europe being the Ural Mountains & main range of the Caucasus Mountains); has numerous large offshore islands including Cyprus, Sri Lanka, Malay Archipelago, Taiwan, the Japanese chain, & Sakhalin *area* 16,988,000 *sq mi* (44,168,800 *sq km*)

Asia Mi·nor \\'mī-nər\\ peninsula forming W extremity of Asia bet. Black Sea on N, Mediterranean Sea on S, & Aegean Sea on W — see ANATOLIA

Asir \\a-'sir\\ province S Saudi Arabia on Red Sea SE of Hejaz ✳ As Sabya *area* 13,857 *sq mi* (36,028 *sq km*)

As·ma·ra \\az-'mär-ə, -'mar-ə\\ city ✳ of Eritrea *pop* 474,241

As·nières \\an-'yer, än-\\ commune N France NW of Paris

Aso \\'ä-(ˌ)sō\\ *or* **Aso·san** \\ˌä-sō-'sän\\ volcanic mountain Japan in *cen* Kyushu; has five volcanic cones grouped around crater 15 *mi* (24 *km*) long with walls 2000 *ft* (610 *m*) high

Aso·lo \\'ä-zə-ˌlō\\ commune NE Italy NW of Treviso

Asphaltites, Lacus — see DEAD SEA

As·sam \\ə-'sam, a-; 'a-ˌsam\\ state NE India on edge of Himalayas ✳ Dispur *area* 30,318 *sq mi* (78,827 *sq km*), *pop* 19,902,226

As·sen \\'ä-s'n\\ commune NE Netherlands ✳ of Drenthe

As·sin·i·boine \\ə-'si-nə-ˌbóin\\ river 450 *mi* (724 *km*) Canada rising in SE Sask. & flowing S & E across S Man. into Red River

Assiniboine, Mount mountain 11,870 *ft* (3618 *m*) Canada in SW Alta. on B.C. border

As·si·si \\ə-'si-sē, -'sē-, -zē\\ commune *cen* Italy ESE of Perugia *pop* 24,669

As·syr·ia \\ə-'sir-ē-ə\\ *or bib* **As·sur** \\ä-'sùr, 'ä-,\\ *or* **Ashur** \\'ä-,shùr\\ ancient empire W Asia extending along middle Tigris & over foothills to the E; early ✳ Calah, later ✳ Nineveh

Astacus — see IZMIT

Asti \\'äs-tē\\ commune NW Italy W of Alessandria *pop* 74,649

As·tra·khan \\'as-trə-ˌkan, -kən\\ city Russia in Europe, on the Volga at head of its delta *pop* 461,000

As·tu·ri·as \\ə-'stür-ē-əs, a-, -'styùr-\\ **1** region & old kingdom NW Spain on Bay of Biscay **2** OVIEDO (province) — **As·tu·ri·an** \\-ē-ən\\ *adj or n*

Asun·ción \\ä-ˌsün(t)-sē-'ōn, (ˌ)ä-\\ city ✳ of Paraguay on Paraguay River at confluence with the Pilcomayo *pop* 455,517

As·wân \\a-'swän, ä-\\ *or anc* **Sy·e·ne** \\sī-'ē-nē\\ city S Egypt on right bank of the Nile near site of dam built 1898–1902 & of **Aswân High Dam** (completed 1970 to form **Lake Nas·ser** \\'nä-sər, 'na-\\ *pop* 144,654

As·yût \\äs-'yüt\\ city *cen* Egypt on left bank of the Nile *pop* 213,751

Ata·ca·ma \\ˌa-tə-'kä-mə, ˌä-\\ — see PUNA DE ATACAMA

Atacama Desert desert N Chile bet. Copiapó & Peru border

Atas·ca·de·ro \\ə-ˌtas-kə-'der-(ˌ)ō\\ city W Calif. *pop* 23,138

At·ba·ra \\'at-bə-rə\\ river *ab* 500 *mi* (805 *km*) NE Africa rising in N Ethiopia & flowing through E Sudan into the Nile

Atchaf·a·laya \\(ə-)ˌcha-fə-'lī-ə\\ river 225 *mi* (362 *km*) S La. flowing S into **Atchafalaya Bay** (inlet of Gulf of Mexico)

Ath·a·bas·ca *or* **Ath·a·bas·ka** \\ˌa-thə-'bas-kə, ˌä-\\ river 765 *mi* (1231 *km*) Canada in Alta. flowing NE & N into Lake Athabasca

Athabasca, Lake lake Canada on Alta.-Sask. boundary *area* 3058 *sq mi* (7951 *sq km*)

Ath·ens \\'a-thənz\\ **1** city NE Ga. *pop* 45,734 **2** city SE Ohio *pop* 21,265 **3** *or NGk* **Athí·nai** \\ä-'thē-(ˌ)nē\\ *or anc* **Athe·nae** \\ə-'thē-(ˌ)nē\\ city ✳ of Greece near Saronic Gulf *pop* 748,110 — **Athe·nian** \\ə-'thē-nē-ən, -nyən\\ *adj or n*

Athos \\'a-ˌthös, 'ä-\\ mountain NE Greece at E end of Acte Peninsula; site of a number of monasteries comprising **Mount Athos** (autonomous area)

Ati·tlán \\ˌä-tē-'tlän\\ lake 24 *mi* (39 *km*) long SW Guatemala at 4700 *ft* (1432 *m*) altitude occupying a crater 1000 *ft* (305 *m*) deep N of **Atitlán Volcano**

At·ka \\'at-kə, 'ät-\\ island SW Alaska in Andreanof group

At·lan·ta \\ət-'lan-tə, at-\\ city NW *cen* Ga., its ✳ *pop* 394,017 — **At·lan·tan** \\-'lan-t'n\\ *adj or n*

At·lan·tic City \\ət-'lan-tik, at-\\ city SE N.J. on Atlantic coast *pop* 37,986

Atlantic Ocean ocean separating N. & S. America from Europe & Africa *area* 41,105,000 *sq mi* (106,873,000 *sq km*); often divided into **North Atlantic Ocean** & **South Atlantic Ocean**

Atlantic Provinces the Canadian provinces of Nfld., N.B., N.S., & P.E.I. — see MARITIME PROVINCES

At·las Mountains \\'at-ləs\\ mountains NW Africa extending from SW Morocco to NE Tunisia; its highest peaks are in the **Grand,** or **High, Atlas** in SW *cen* Morocco — see TOUBKAL (Jebel)

Atrek \\ə-'trek\\ *or* **Atrak** \\-'trak\\ river 300 *mi* (483 *km*) NE Iran flowing into the Caspian Sea on Turkmenistan border

Atropatene — see AZERBAIJAN

At·ta·wa·pis·kat \\ˌa-tə-wə-'pis-kət\\ river 465 *mi* (748 *km*) Canada in N Ont. flowing E into James Bay

At·ti·ca \\'a-ti-kə\\ region E Greece, chief city Athens; a state of ancient Greece

At·tle·boro \\'a-t'l-ˌbər-ə, -ˌbə-rə\\ city SE Mass. *pop* 38,383

At·tu \\'a-(ˌ)tü\\ island SW Alaska, most westerly of the Aleutians, in Near group — see WRANGELL (Cape)

At·wa·ter \\'at-ˌwò-tər, -ˌwä-\\ city *cen* Calif. *pop* 22,282

Aube \\'ōb\\ river 125 *mi* (201 *km*) N *cen* France flowing into the Seine

Au·ber·vil·liers \\ˌō-bər-vēl-'yä\\ commune N France *pop* 72,859

Au·burn \\'ò-bərn\\ **1** city E Ala. *pop* 33,830 **2** city SW Maine *pop* 24,309 **3** city *cen* N.Y. *pop* 31,258 **4** city W Wash. *pop* 33,102

Auck·land \\'ò-klənd\\ city & port N New Zealand on North Is. *pop* 144,963 — **Auck·land·er** \\-klən-dər\\ *n*

Audenarde — see OUDENAARDE

Au·ghra·bies Falls \\ò-'grä-bēz\\ *or* **King George's Falls** waterfall 480 *ft* (146 *m*) Republic of S. Africa in Orange River in Northern Cape province

Au·ghrim *or* **Aghrim** \\'ò-grəm, -krəm\\ town W Ireland in E Galway

Augs·burg \\'ógz-ˌbərg, 'aùgz-ˌbürg\\ city S Germany in Bavaria on the Lech *pop* 248,346

Au·gus·ta \\ò-'gəs-tə, ə-\\ **1** city E Ga. on Savannah River *pop* 44,639 **2** city ✳ of Maine on the Kennebec *pop* 21,325

Au·lis \\'ò-ləs\\ harbor E Greece in Boeotia on Evripos Strait

Au·nis \\ō-'nēs\\ former province W France on Gironde Estuary & Bay of Biscay ✳ La Rochelle

Au·rang·a·bad \\aù-'rəŋ-gə-ˌbäd, -'rəŋ-ə-, -ˌbad\\ city W India in *cen* Maharashtra ENE of Bombay *pop* 316,244

Au·rès \\ó-'res\\ massif *ab* 7600 *ft* (2316 *m*) NE Algeria in Saharan Atlas

Au·ri·gnac \\ˌó-rēn-'yak\\ village SW France SW of Toulouse

Au·ril·lac \\ˌó-rē-'yak\\ city S *cen* France *pop* 29,458

Au·ro·ra \\ə-'rōr-ə, ó-, -'ròr-\\ **1** city *cen* Colo. E of Denver *pop* 222,103 **2** city NE Ill. *pop* 99,581 **3** town Canada in SE Ont. *pop* 29,454

Au·sa·ble \\ò-'sä-bəl\\ river 20 *mi* (32 *km*) NE N.Y. flowing E into Lake Champlain through **Ausable Chasm** gorge

Auschwitz — see OŚWIĘCIM

Austerlitz — see SLAVKOV

Aus·tin \\'òs-tən, 'äs-\\ **1** city S Minn. *pop* 21,907 **2** city ✳ of Tex. on the Colorado *pop* 465,622

Austral Islands — see TUBUAI ISLANDS

Aus·tral·asia \\ˌós-trə-'lā-zhə, ˌäs-, -'lā-shə\\ Australia, Tasmania, New Zealand, & Melanesia — **Aus·tral·asian** \\-zhən, -shən\\ *adj or n*

Aus·tra·lia \\ò-'strāl-yə, ä-, ə-\\ **1** continent of the E hemisphere SE of Asia & S of the equator *area* 2,948,366 *sq mi* (7,665,751 *sq km*) **2** *or* **Commonwealth of Australia** dominion of the Commonwealth of Nations including the continent of Australia & island of Tasmania ✳ Canberra *area* 2,967,909 *sq mi* (7,716,563 *sq km*), *pop* 14,574,488

Australian Alps mountain range SE Australia in E Victoria & SE New S. Wales forming S end of Great Dividing Range

Australian Capital Territory *or formerly* **Federal Capital Territory** district SE Australia including two areas, one around Canberra & the other on Jervis Bay, surrounded by New S. Wales *area* 939 *sq mi* (2441 *sq km*), *pop* 221,609

Aus·tra·sia *or* **Os·tra·sia** \\ò-'strä-zhə, ä-, -shə\\ the E dominions of the Merovingian Franks extending from the Meuse to Böhmerwald — **Aus·tra·sian** \\-zhən, -shən\\ *adj or n*

Aus·tria \\'òs-trē-ə, 'äs-\\ *or G* **Os·ter·reich** \\' œ-stə(r)-ˌrīk\\ country *cen* Europe in & N of E Alps with the Danube crossing it in N; a republic ✳ Vienna *area* 32,375 *sq mi* (84,175 *sq km*), *pop* 7,812,100 — **Aus·tri·an** \\-ən\\ *adj or n*

Austria–Hun·ga·ry \\-'həŋ-gə-rē\\ dual monarchy 1867–1918 *cen* Europe including Bohemia, Moravia, Bukovina, Transylvania, Galicia, and what is now Austria, Hungary, Slovenia, Croatia, & NE Italy — **Aus·tro–Hun·gar·i·an** \\ˌós-(ˌ)trō-ˌhəŋ-'gar-ē-ən, ˌäs-, -'ger-\\ *adj or n*

Aus·tro·ne·sia \\ˌós-trə-'nē-zhə, -shə\\ **1** the islands of the S Pacific **2** area extending from Madagascar through the Malay Peninsula & Archipelago to Hawaii & Easter Is.

Au·teuil \ō-'tœ̄i, -'tə(r)\ district in W Paris, France

Au·vergne \ō-'vernʸ, -'vərn\ region & former province S *cen* France ✱ Clermont (now Clermont-Ferrand)

Auvergne Mountains mountains S *cen* France; highest in the Massif Central — see SANCY (Puy de)

Aux Cayes — see CAYES

Aux Sources, Mont \,mōⁿ-,tō-'sùrs\ mountain 10,822 *ft* (3298 *m*) N Lesotho in Drakensberg Mountains on South Africa border

Au·yán—te·pui \aú-,yän-tə-'pwĕ\ *or* Devil Mountain plateau *ab* 20 *mi* (32 *km*) long SE Venezuela E of the Caroní — see ANGEL FALLS

Au·yuit·tuq National Park \aú-'yü-ə-,tək\ reservation NE Canada in E Baffin Is.

Av·a·lon \'a-və-,län\ peninsula Canada in SE Newfoundland

Avalon, Isle of — see ISLE OF AVALON

Ave·bury \'āv-b(ə-)rē, *US also* -,ber-ē\ village S England in Wiltshire E of Bristol; has megalithic remains

Ave·lla·ne·da \,ä-və-zhə-'nä-də\ city E Argentina, E suburb of Buenos Aires, on Río de la Plata *pop* 330,654

Avenches \ä-'vänsh\ *or anc* Aven·ti·cum \ə-'ven-ti-kəm\ town W Switzerland in Vaud canton ✱ of ancient Helvetia

Av·en·tine \'a-vən-,tīn, -,tēn\ hill in Rome, Italy, one of seven (including also the Caelian, Capitoline, Esquiline, Palatine, Quirinal, & Viminal) on which the ancient city was built

Aver·nus, Lake \ə-'vər-nəs\ *or It* Lago d'Aver·no \,lä-gō-dä-'ver-(,)nō\ lake S Italy in crater of extinct volcano W of Naples

Avi·gnon \,a-(,)vēn-'yōⁿ\ city SE France *pop* 73,482

Avi·la \'ä-vi-lä\ 1 province *cen* Spain *area* 3042 *sq mi* (7909 *sq km*), *pop* 165,427 2 city, its ✱, WNW of Madrid *pop* 36,745

Avlona — see VLORË

Avon \'ā-vən, 'a-, *US also* 'ā-,vän\ 1 river 96 *mi* (154 *km*) *cen* England rising in Northamptonshire & flowing WSW past Stratford-upon-Avon into Severn River at Tewkesbury 2 river 65 *mi* (105 *km*) S England rising near Devizes in Wiltshire & flowing S into English Channel 3 river 62 *mi* (100 *km*) SW England rising in Gloucestershire & flowing S & W through city of Bristol into Bristol Channel at Avonmouth 4 \'a-vən\ — see SWAN 5 \'ā-vən, 'a-, *US also* 'ā-,vän\ county SW England ✱ Bristol *area* 520 *sq mi* (1352 *sq km*), *pop* 925,700

Avranches \av-'ränsh\ town NW France in SW Normandy

Awa·ji \ə-'wä-jē\ island Japan S of Honshu & NE of Shikoku

Awash \'ä-,wäsh\ river 500 *mi* (805 *km*) E Ethiopia flowing NE

Ax·el Hei·berg \'ak-səl-'hī-,bərg\ island N Canada in the Sverdrup Islands W of Ellesmere Is. *area* 15,779 *sq mi* (41,025 *sq km*)

Axum — see AKSUM — Ax·um·ite \'ak-sə-mīt\ *adj or n*

Aya·cu·cho \,ī-ə-'kü-(,)chō\ town S Peru SE of Lima

Ay·dın \ī-'din\ city SW Turkey SE of Izmir *pop* 71,576

Ayers Rock \'arz, 'erz\ outcrop *cen* Australia in SW Northern Territory; 1143 *ft* (348 *m*) high

Ayles·bury \'ā(ə)lz-b(ə-)rē, *US also* -,ber-ē\ borough SE *cen* England ✱ of Buckinghamshire *pop* 41,288

Ayl·mer \'ā(ə)l-mər\ town Canada in SW Que. *pop* 32,244

Ayr \'är, 'er\ 1 *or* Ayr·shire \-,shir, -shər\ former county SW Scotland 2 burgh & port SW Scotland in Strathclyde *pop* 49,481

Ayut·tha·ya \ä-'yü-tə-yə\ city S Thailand N of Bangkok

Azer·bai·jan \,a-zər-,bī-'jän, ,ä-\ independent country SE Europe bordering on Caspian Sea; a constituent republic of the U.S.S.R. 1936–91 ✱ Baku 33,200 *sq mi* (86,320 *sq km*), *pop* 7,029,000

Azerbaijan *or anc* At·ro·pa·te·ne \,a-trō-pə-'tē-nē\ *or* Me·dia Atro·pa·te·ne \me-dē-ə\ region NW Iran; chief city Tabriz

Azin·court \á-zaⁿ-'kür\ *or earlier* Agin·court \á-jən-,kört, -,kórt; 'a-zhən-,kùr\ village N France WNW of Arras

Azores \'ā-,zōrz, -,zórz\ *or Pg* Aço·res \ə-'sór-esh\ islands N Atlantic belonging to Portugal & lying *ab* 800 *mi* (1287 *km*) off coast of Portugal; chief town Ponta Delgada *area* 888 *sq mi* (2309 *sq km*), *pop* 336,100 — Azor·e·an *or* Azor·i·an \ā-'zōr-ē-ən, -'zór-, ə-\ *adj or n*

Azov, Sea of \'a-,zóf, 'ā-,-,zäv\ gulf of the Black Sea E of Crimea connected with the Black Sea by the Kerch Strait *area* 14,520 *sq mi* (37,752 *sq km*)

Az·tec Ruins National Monument \'az-,tek\ reservation NW N.Mex. NE of Farmington; site of a prehistoric pueblo

Azu·sa \ə-'zü-sə\ city SW Calif. ENE of Los Angeles *pop* 41,333

Az Zaqāzīq — see ZAGAZIG

Baal·bek \'bä-əl-,bek, 'bäl-,bek\ town E Lebanon N of Damascus on site of ancient city of He·li·op·o·lis \,hē-lē-'ä-p(ə-)ləs\

Ba·bar Islands \'bä-,bär\ islands Indonesia ENE of Timor

Bab el Man·deb \'bab-əl-'man-dəb\ strait between SW Arabia & Africa connecting Red Sea & Gulf of Aden

Ba·bel·thu·ap \,bä-bəl-'tü-,äp\ island W Pacific, chief island in Belau *area* 143 *sq mi* (372 *sq km*)

Ba·bian \'bä-bē-'än\ *or* Pa–Pien \'pä-pē-'en\ *or* Black \'blak\ river 500 *mi* (800 *km*) SE Asia rising in *cen* Yunnan, China & flowing SE to Red River

Babruysk — see BOBRUYSK

Ba·bu·yan \,bä-bü-'yän\ chief island of the Babuyan group

Babuyan Islands islands of N Philippines N of Luzon *area* 225 *sq mi* (585 *sq km*)

Bab·y·lon \'ba-bə-lən, -,län\ ancient city ✱ of Babylonia; its site *ab* 50 *mi* (80 *km*) S of Baghdad near the Euphrates

Bab·y·lo·nia \,ba-bə-'lō-nyə, -nē-ə\ ancient country in valley of the lower Euphrates & the Tigris ✱ Babylon

Ba·cau \bə-'kaú\ city E *cen* Romania *pop* 193,269

Back \'bak\ river 605 *mi* (974 *km*) Canada in Northwest Territories flowing ENE into Arctic Ocean

Ba·co·lod \bä-'kō-,lód\ city Philippines on Negros Is. *pop* 262,415

Bactra — see BALKH

Bac·tria \'bak-trē-ə\ ancient country SW Asia between Hindu Kush & Oxus River ✱ Bactra — see BALKH — Bac·tri·an \'bak-trē-ən\ *adj or n*

Ba·da·joz \,bä-thə-'hōs, ,bä-də-'hōz\ 1 province SW Spain in valley of the Guadiana *area* 8451 *sq mi* (21,973 *sq km*), *pop* 572,798 2 city, its ✱ *pop* 111,456

Ba·da·lo·na \,bä-thə-'lō-nə, ,bä-dᵊl-'ō-nə\ city & port NE Spain on the Mediterranean NE of Barcelona *pop* 229,780

Bad Ems — see EMS

Ba·den \'bä-dᵊn\ 1 region SW Germany bordering on Switzerland & France; formerly a grand duchy (1805–1918), a state of the Weimar

---

Republic (1918–33), an administrative division of the Third Reich (1933–49), & a state of the Bonn Republic (1949–51) ✱ Karlsruhe — see BADEN-WÜRTTEMBERG 2 BADEN-BADEN

Ba·den—Ba·den \,bä-dᵊn-'bä-dᵊn\ city & spa SW Germany in Baden≈ Württemberg SSW of Karlsruhe *pop* 49,142

Ba·den—Würt·tem·berg \,bä-dᵊn-'wər-təm-,bərg, -'wùr-; -'vuer-təm-,berk\ state SW Germany W of Bavaria; formed 1951 from former Baden, Württemberg-Baden, & Württemberg-Hohenzollern states ✱ Stuttgart *area* 13,800 *sq mi* (35,880 *sq km*), *pop* 9,258,947

Bad Godesberg — see GODESBERG

Bad Hom·burg \,bät-'hóm-,bùrk, -'häm-,bərg\ city SW *cen* Germany N of Frankfurt am Main *pop* 41,847

Badlands National Park reservation SW S.Dak. E of Black Hills comprising an area of badlands topography

Bad Mergentheim — see MERGENTHEIM

Baer·um \'bar-əm\ city SE Norway, a suburb of Oslo *pop* 89,221

Baf·fin Bay \'ba-fən\ inlet of the Atlantic bet. W Greenland & E Baffin Is.

Baffin Island island NE Canada N of Hudson Strait; largest in Arctic Archipelago *area* 183,810 *sq mi* (477,906 *sq km*)

Ba·fing \bə-'faŋ, bä-'fēŋ\ river 350 *mi* (560 *km*) W Africa in W Mali & Guinea; the upper course of the Senegal

Bagh·dad \'bag-,dad, ,bag-'dad\ city ✱ of Iraq on the middle Tigris *pop* 1,490,759 — Bagh·dadi \bag-'da-dē\ *n*

Ba·guio \,bä-gē-'ō\ city, summer ✱ of the Philippines, in NW *cen* Luzon *pop* 119,009

Ba·ha·ma Islands \bə-'hä-mə, *by outsiders also* -'hā-\ islands in the Atlantic SE of Fla.; an independent member of the Commonwealth of Nations since 1973 ✱ Nassau *area* 4404 *sq mi* (11,450 *sq km*), *pop* 223,455 — see TURKS AND CAICOS — Ba·ha·mi·an \bə-'hä-mē-ən, -'hā-\ *adj or n*

Ba·ha·wal·pur \bə-'hä-wəl-,pùr\ region Pakistan in SW Punjab in Thar Desert; until 1947 a princely state of India

Ba·hia \bə-'hē-ə, bä-'ē-ə\ 1 *or formerly* Ba·ía \bä-'ē-ə\ state E Brazil ✱ Salvador *area* 215,329 *sq mi* (559,855 *sq km*), *pop* 9,597,393 2 — see SALVADOR — Ba·hi·an \-ən\ *adj or n*

Ba·hía Blan·ca \bə-,hē-ə-'blaŋ-kə, bä-,ē-ə-'bläŋ-\ city & port E Argentina SW of Buenos Aires *pop* 182,158

Bahnasa, El — see OXYRHYNCHUS

Bah·rain *or* Bah·rein \bä-'rän\ 1 islands in Persian Gulf off coast of Arabia; an independent sultanate ✱ Manama (on Bahrain Is.) *area* 213 *sq mi* (554 *sq km*), *pop* 358,857 2 island, largest of the group, 27 *mi* (43 *km*) long — Bah·raini *or* Bah·reini \-'rä-nē\ *adj or n*

Bahr el Gha·zal \,bär-el-gə-'zal\ river *ab* 500 *mi* (800 *km*) SW Sudan flowing E to unite with the Bahr el Jebel forming the White Nile

Ba·ia—Ma·re \,bä-yə-'mär-ə\ city NW Romania *pop* 150,456

Baie—Co·meau \,bä-'kō-(,)mō, ,bä-kō-'mō\ town Canada in SE Que. *pop* 26,012

Bai·kal, Lake *or* Lake Bay·kal \bī-'käl, -'kal\ lake Russia in Asia; 5712 *ft* (1731 *m*) deep, *ab* 375 *mi* (600 *km*) long

Baile Atha Cliath — see DUBLIN

Ba·ja California \'bä-(,)hä\ peninsula 760 *mi* (1216 *km*) long NW Mexico bet. the Pacific & Gulf of California; divided into the states of Baja California (to the N ✱ Mexicali *area* 27,653 *sq mi* or 71,898 *sq km*, *pop* 1,225,436) & Baja California Sur \'sùr\ to the S ✱ La Paz *area* 27,976 *sq mi* or 72,738 *sq km*, *pop* 221,389)

Bakan — see SHIMONOSEKI

Ba·ker Island \'bā-kər\ atoll *cen* Pacific near the equator at 176°31′W; belongs to U.S.

Baker, Mount mountain 10,778 *ft* (3266 *m*) NW Wash. in Cascade Range

Baker Lake — see DUBAWNT

Ba·kers·field \'bā-kərz-,fēld\ city S *cen* Calif. on the Kern *pop* 174,820

Bakh·ta·ran \,bäk-tə-'rän\ *or formerly* Ker·man·shah \,ker-,män-'shä\ city W Iran *pop* 560,514

Ba·ku \bä-'kü\ city, ✱ of Azerbaijan *pop* 1,150,000

Bakwanga — see MBUJI-MAYI

Ba·la·kla·va *or* Ba·la·cla·va \,ba-lə-'klä-və, -'kla-; ,bä-lə-'klä-və\ village in Crimea SE of Sevastopol

Bal·a·ton \'ba-lə-,tän, 'bö-lə-,tōn\ *or G* Plat·ten·see \'plä-tᵊn-,zä\ lake W Hungary; largest in *cen* Europe *area* 266 *sq mi* (692 *sq km*)

Bal·boa Heights \(,)bal-'bō-ə\ town Panama at Pacific entrance to Panama Canal adjacent to Panama (city); former administrative center of Canal Zone

Bald·win \'bȯl-dwən\ borough SW Pa. S of Pittsburgh *pop* 21,923

Baldwin Park city SW Calif. E of Los Angeles *pop* 69,330

Bâle — see BASEL

Bal·e·ar·es \,ba-lē-'är-ēz, ,bä-lē-'är-əs\ 1 BALEARIC ISLANDS 2 province E Spain comprising the Balearic Islands ✱ Palma *area* 1936 *sq mi* (5034 *sq km*)

Bal·e·ar·ic Islands \,ba-lē-'ar-ik\ islands E Spain in the W Mediterranean — see BALEARES, IBIZA, MAJORCA, MINORCA

Ba·li \'bä-lē, 'ba-\ island Indonesia off E Java *area* 2147 *sq mi* (5582 *sq km*), *pop* 2,247,000 — Ba·li·nese \,bä-li-'nēz, ,ba-, -'nēs\ *adj or n*

Ba·lı·ke·sir \,bä-lē-ke-'sir\ city NW Turkey in Asia *pop* 124,122

Ba·lik·pa·pan \,bä-lik-'pä-,pän\ city & port Indonesia on SE Borneo on inlet of Makassar Strait *pop* 344,405

Bal·kan Mountains \'bȯl-kən\ mountain range *cen* Bulgaria extending from Yugoslavia border to Black Sea; highest point Botev Peak 7746 *ft* (2324 *m*)

Balkan Peninsula peninsula SE Europe bet. Adriatic & Ionian seas on W & Aegean & Black seas on E — Balkan *adj* — Bal·kan·ic \bȯl-'ka-nik\ *adj*

Bal·kans \'bȯl-kənz\ *or* Balkan States the countries occupying the Balkan Peninsula; Slovenia, Croatia, Bosnia and Herzegovina, Macedonia, Yugoslavia, Romania, Bulgaria, Albania, Greece, & Turkey in Europe

---

\ə\ abut \ᵊ\ kitten, F table \ər\ further \a\ ash \ā\ ace \ä\ mop, mar \aú\ out \ch\ chin \e\ bet \ē\ easy \g\ go \i\ hit \ī\ ice \j\ job \ŋ\ sing \ō\ go \ó\ law \ói\ boy \th\ thin \t̲h\ the \ü\ loot \ù\ foot \y\ yet \zh\ vision \å, ḵ, ⁿ, œ, œ̄, ɶ, ūe, ᵜ\ *see* Guide to Pronunciation

Bal·kar·ia \bȯl-'kär-ē-ə, bal-, -'ker-\ mountain region S Russia in Europe, in S Kabardino-Balkar Republic

Balkh \'bälk\ **1** district N Afghanistan corresponding closely to ancient Bactria **2** or anc **Bac·tra** \'bak-trə\ town N Afghanistan ✱ of ancient Bactria

Bal·khash \bal-'kash, bäl-'käsh\ lake 440 mi (704 km) long SE Kazakhstan area 6700 sq mi (17,420 sq km)

Bal·la·rat \'ba-lə-ˌrat\ city SE Australia in cen Victoria pop 63,802

Bal·ly·me·na \ˌba-lē-'mē-nə\ district NE Northern Ireland, established 1974 area 246 sq mi (640 sq km), pop 54,426

Bal·ly·mon·ey \ˌba-lē-'mə-nē\ district Northern Ireland, established 1974 area 162 sq mi (421 sq km), pop 22,873

Bal·sas \'bȯl-ˌsäs, 'bäl-, -säs\ river 426 mi (682 km) con Mexico flowing from Tlaxcala to the Pacific on border bet. Michoacán & Guerrero

Bal·tic Sea \'bȯl-tik\ arm of the Atlantic N Europe enclosed by Denmark & Scandinavia area ab 160,000 sq mi (256,000 sq km)

Bal·ti·more \'bȯl-tə-ˌmȯr, -ˌmȯr, -mər; 'bȯlt-mər; by residents usu 'bȯltē-ˌmȯr or 'bȯl-mər\ city & port N cen Md. on the Patapsco estuary near Chesapeake Bay pop 736,014 — **Bal·ti·mor·e·an** \ˌbȯl-tə-'mȯr-ē-ən, -'mȯr-\ n

Bal·ti·stan \ˌbȯl-tə-'stan, -'stän\ region Ladakh district N Kashmir; under Pakistani control

Ba·lu·chi·stan \bə-ˌlü-chə-'stan, -'stän; bə-'lü-chə-ˌ\ **1** arid region S Asia bordering on Arabian Sea in SW Pakistan & SE Iran S & SW of Afghanistan **2** province SW Pakistan ✱ Quetta pop 4,305,000

Ba·ma·ko \ˌbä-mə-'kō\ city ✱ of Mali on Niger River pop 435,313

Bam·ba·ri \bäm-bə-rē\ town S cen Central African Republic

Bam·berg \'bam-ˌbərg, 'bäm-ˌberk\ city S cen Germany in N Bavaria NNW of Nuremberg pop 71,928

Ba·na·hao \bə-'nä-ˌhau\ extinct volcano 7141 ft (2142 m) Philippines on S Luzon SE of Manila

Banana River \bə-'na-nə\ lagoon E Fla. bet. Canaveral Peninsula & Merritt Is.

Ba·na·ras or **Be·na·res** \bə-'när-əs, -ēz\ or **Va·ra·na·si** \və-'rä-nə-(ˌ)sē\ city N India in SE Uttar Pradesh pop 793,542

Ba·nat \bə-'nät, 'bä-ˌnät\ region SE con Europe in Danube basin bet. the Tisza & the Mures & the Transylvanian Alps; once entirely in Hungary, divided 1919 bet. Yugoslavia & Romania

Ban·bridge \ban-'brij\ district SE Northern Ireland, established 1974 area 171 sq mi (445 sq km), pop 29,885

Ban·da Islands \'bän-də, 'bän-\ islands Indonesia in Moluccas S of Ceram area 16 sq mi (42 sq km)

Banda Sea sea E Malay Archipelago SE of Sulawesi, S of the Moluccas, W of Aru Islands, & NE of Timor

Ban·da Ori·en·tal \'bän-də-ˌȯr-ē-ˌen-'täl, -ˌȯr-\ URUGUAY — a former name, used with reference to its position on E shore of Río de la Plata

Bandar — see MACHILIPATNAM

Ban·dar Ab·bas \ˌbən-dər-ə-'bäs\ city S Iran on Strait of Hormuz pop 201,642

Ban·dar Kho·mei·ni \ˌbən-dər-ˌkō-mā-'nē, -kō-'mā-nē\ town & port SW Iran at head of Persian Gulf ENE of Abadan pop 49,355

Ban·dar Lam·pung \ˌbən-dər-'läm-pùŋ\ city & port Indonesia in S Sumatra pop 636,706

Ban·dar Se·ri Be·ga·wan \ˌbən-dər-ˌser-ē-bə-'gä-wən\ or formerly Brunei town, ✱ of Brunei pop 49,902

Ban·de·lier National Monument \ˌban-də-'lir\ reservation N cen N.Mex. W of Santa Fe containing cliff-dweller ruins

Ban·dung or D **Ban·doeng** \'bän-ˌdùŋ\ city Indonesia in W Java SE of Djakarta pop 2,057,442

Banff \'bam(p)f\ or **Banff·shire** \-ˌshir, -shər\ former county NE Scotland ✱ Banff

Banff National Park reservation W Canada in SW Alta. on E slope of Rocky Mountains

Ban·ga·lore \'baŋ-gə-ˌlȯr, -ˌlȯr\ city S India W of Madras ✱ of Karnataka pop 2,913,537

Bang·ka or **Ban·ka** \'baŋ-kə\ island Indonesia off SE Sumatra; chief town Pangkalpinang area 4609 sq mi (11,983 sq km), pop 251,639

Bang·kok \'baŋ-ˌkäk, baŋ-'\ or Thai **Krung Thep** \'krùŋ-'tep\ city & port ✱ of Thailand on the Chao Phraya ab 20 mi (32 km) above its mouth pop 2,132,000

Ban·gla·desh \ˌbäŋ-glə-'desh, ˌbaŋ-, ˌbəŋ-, -'däsh\ country S Asia E of India on Bay of Bengal; a republic in the Commonwealth of Nations since 1971 ✱ Dacca area 55,126 sq mi (143,328 sq km), pop 87,052,024 — see EAST PAKISTAN — **Ban·gla·deshi** \-'de-shē, -'dä-\ adj or n

Ban·gor \'baŋ-ˌgȯr & 'ban-ˌgȯr (these usual for 1), 'baŋ-gər\ **1** city E cen Maine on the Penobscot pop 33,181 **2** municipal borough SE Northern Ireland in North Down district pop 46,585 **3** borough & city NW Wales in Gwynedd pop 12,174

Ban·gui \bäŋ-gē, bäŋ-'gē\ city ✱ of Central African Republic, on the Ubangi pop 300,723

Bang·we·u·lu, Lake \ˌbaŋ-wē-'ü-(ˌ)lü\ lake ab 50 mi (80 km) long N Zambia in swamp region; its area fluctuates seasonally; drains into the Luapula, a headstream of Congo River

Ban·jar·ma·sin \ˌban-jər-'mä-sᵊn, ˌbän-\ city Indonesia in S Borneo pop 481,371

Ban·jul \'bän-ˌjül\ or formerly **Bath·urst** \'ba-(ˌ)thərst\ city & port ✱ of Gambia on island of St. Mary in Gambia River pop 44,188

Banks Island \'baŋks\ island N Canada at W end of Canadian Arctic archipelago area 23,230 sq mi (60,398 sq km)

Banks Islands islands SW Pacific N of Vanuatu pop 5521

Ban·nock·burn \'ba-nək-ˌbərn, ˌba-nək-'\ town cen Scotland in Central region SSE of Stirling

Ban·tam \'ban-təm\ village Indonesia in NW corner of Java; once ✱ of Sultanate of Bantam

Ban·try Bay \'ban-trē\ bay SW Ireland in SW County Cork

Bao·ding or **Pao·ting** \'bau̇-diŋ\ or formerly **Tsing·yuan** \'chiŋ-yü-'än\ city NE China SW of Beijing pop 250,000

Bao·ji or **Pao·chi** \'bau̇-'jē\ city N cen China in SW Shaanxi on the Wei W of Xi'an pop 180,000

Bao·tou or **Pao·t'ou** \'bau̇-'tō\ city N China in SW Inner Mongolia on the Huang pop 1,400,000

Ba·paume \bä-'pōm, ba-\ town N France S of Arras pop 3683

Ba·ra·cal·do \ˌbar-ə-'käl-(ˌ)dō, ˌbär-\ commune N Spain W of Bilbao pop 118,615

Ba·ra·coa \ˌbar-ə-'kō-ə, ˌbär-\ city & port E Cuba on N coast near E tip of island pop 76,873

Ba·ra·na·gar \bə-'rä-nə-gər\ city E India in W. Bengal N of Calcutta pop 136,842

Ba·ra·nof \'bar-ə-ˌnȯf, bə-'rä-nəf\ island SE Alaska in Alexander Archipelago S of Chichagof Is. area ab 1600 sq mi (4160 sq km)

Bar·a·tar·ia Bay \ˌbar-ə-'tar-ē-ə, -'ter-\ lagoon SE La. on coast NW of delta of Mississippi River

Bar·ba·dos \bär-'bā-(ˌ)dōs, -dəs, -(ˌ)dōz, -(ˌ)däs\ island Brit. West Indies in Lesser Antilles E of the Windward group; a dominion of the Commonwealth of Nations since 1966 ✱ Bridgetown area 166 sq mi (432 sq km), pop 249,000 — **Bar·ba·di·an** \-'bā-dē-ən\ adj or n

Bar·ba·ry \'bär-b(ə-)rē\ region N Africa on **Barbary Coast** extending from Egyptian border to the Atlantic & including the former **Barbary States** (Morocco, Algiers, Tunis, & Tripoli) — a chiefly former name

Bar·bers Point \'bär-bərz\ or **Ka·la·e·loa Point** \kə-ˌlä-ā-(ˌ)'lō-ə\ cape Hawaii at SW corner of Oahu W of Pearl Harbor

Bar·ber·ton \'bär-bər-tᵊn\ city NE Ohio SW of Akron pop 27,623

Bar·bi·zon \ˌbär-bə-'zōⁿ, 'bär-bə-ˌzän\ village N France SSE of Paris

Bar·bu·da \bär-'bü-də\ island Brit. West Indies in the Leewards. area 62 sq mi (161 sq km) — see ANTIGUA 1

Bar·ca or **Bar·ka** \'bär-kə\ town Libya in NW Cyrenaica

Bar·ce·lo·na \ˌbär-sə-'lō-nə\ **1** province N Spain in Catalonia on the Mediterranean area 2968 sq mi (7717 sq km), pop 4,949,892 **2** city & port, its ✱ pop 1,752,627 **3** city NE Venezuela near coast pop 221,792 — **Bar·ce·lo·nan** \-'lō-nən\ n — **Bar·ce·lo·nese** \-lō-'nēz, -'nēs, -'lō-,\ adj or n

Bar·dia \'bär-dē-ə\ town & port Libya in NE Cyrenaica

Ba·reil·ly or **Ba·re·li** \bə-'rä-lē\ **1** city N India in NW cen Uttar Pradesh ESE of Delhi pop 437,801 **2** — see ROHILKHAND

Ba·rents Sea \'bar-ənts, 'bär-\ sea comprising the part of the Arctic Ocean bet. Spitsbergen & Novaya Zemlya

Ba·ri \'bär-ē\ or anc **Bar·i·um** \'bar-ē-əm, 'ber-\ commune & port SE Italy ✱ of Apulia on the Adriatic pop 355,352

Ba·ri·lo·che \ˌbär-ə-'lō-chē\ or **San Car·los de Bariloche** \san-'kär-ləs-də-, -(ˌ)lōs-\ city SW Argentina on Lake Nahuel Huapí pop 15,995

Ba·ri·nas \bä-'rē-nəs\ city W cen Venezuela pop 153,630

Bar·i·sal \'bar-ə-ˌsȯl\ city S Bangladesh in Ganges delta pop 98,127

Bar·king and Dag·en·ham \'bär-kiŋ-ən(d)-'da-g²n-ᵊm\ borough of E Greater London, England pop 150,900

Bar·let·ta \bär-'le-tə\ commune & port SE Italy in Apulia on the Adriatic pop 88,074

Bar·na·ul \ˌbär-nə-'ül\ city Russia in Asia on the Ob ✱ of Altai territory pop 533,000

Bar·ne·gat Bay \'bär-ni-ˌgat, -gət\ inlet of the Atlantic E N.J.

Barnes \'bärnz\ former municipal borough SE England, now part of Richmond

Bar·net \'bär-nət\ borough of N Greater London, England pop 296,300

Barns·ley \'bärnz-lē\ borough N England in S. Yorkshire pop 73,646

Barn·sta·ble \'bärn-stə-bəl\ town SE Mass. pop 40,949

Ba·ro·da \bə-'rō-də\ **1** former state W India near head of Gulf of Cambay ✱ Baroda area 8176 sq mi (21,258 sq km) **2** city W India in SE Gujarat SE of Ahmadabad pop 744,043

Ba·rot·se·land \bə-'rät-sē-ˌland\ region W Zambia; formerly a protectorate

Bar·qui·si·me·to \ˌbär-kə-sə-'mä-(ˌ)tō\ city NW Venezuela pop 625,450

Bar·ran·quil·la \ˌbär-ən-'kē-yə, ˌbär-\ city & port N Colombia on the Magdalena pop 703,488

Barren Grounds treeless plains N Canada W of Hudson Bay

Bar·rie \'bar-ē\ city Canada SE Ont. pop 62,728

Bar·row, Point \'bar-(ˌ)ō\ most northerly point of Alaska & of the U.S., at ab 71°25′N, 156°30′W

Bar·row–in–Fur·ness \ˌbar-ō-in-'fər-nəs\ borough NW England in S Cumbria pop 73,900

Bar·stow \'bär-ˌstō\ city S Calif. NNE of San Bernardino pop 21,472

Bar·tles·ville \'bär-t²lz-ˌvil\ city NE Okla. pop 34,256

Bart·lett \'bär-lət\ **1** village N Ill. W of Chicago pop 19,373 **2** city SW Tenn. pop 26,989

Ba·rú \bä-'rü\ or formerly **Chi·ri·quí** \chir-i-'kē\ volcano 11,400 ft (3475 m) Panama near Costa Rican border

Ba·ru·ta \bə-'rü-tə\ city N Venezuela, a S suburb of Caracas pop 182,941

Ba·sel \'bä-zəl\ or F **Bâle** or older **Basle** \'bäl\ **1** former canton NW Switzerland, now divided into two half cantons: **Ba·sel–Land** \ˌbäzəl-ˌlänt\ (✱ Liestal area 165 sq mi or 429 sq km, pop 229,787) & **Ba·sel–Stadt** \-ˌshtät\ (✱ Basel area 14 sq mi or 36 sq km, pop 192,271) **2** city NW Switzerland ✱ of Basel-Stadt pop 171,465

Ba·shan \'bä-shən\ region in ancient Palestine E & NE of Sea of Galilee

Ba·shi Channel \'bä-shē\ strait between Philippines & Taiwan

Bash·kir Republic \ˌbash-'kir, ˌbäsh-\ autonomous republic E Russia in Europe, in S Ural Mountains ✱ Ufa area 54,233 sq mi (141,006 sq km), pop 3,819,000

Ba·si·lan \bä-'sē-ˌlän\ **1** island Philippines SW of Mindanao area 495 sq mi (1287 sq km) **2** city comprising Basilan Is. and several small nearby islands

Bas·il·don \'ba-zəl-dən\ town SE England in Essex pop 152,301

Ba·si·li·ca·ta \bə-ˌzi-lə-'kä-tə, -ˌsi-\ or formerly **Lu·ca·nia** \lü-'kā-nyə, 'kä-\ region S Italy on Gulf of Taranto ✱ Potenza pop 623,175

Basin Ranges — see GREAT BASIN

Basque Provinces \'bask\ autonomous region N Spain on Bay of Biscay including provinces of Álava, Guipúzcoa, & Vizcaya

Bas·ra \'bäs-rə, 'bəs-, 'bas-, 'bäz-, 'baz-, 'bäz-\ or **Al Bas·rah** \al-'\ city & port S Iraq on Shatt-al-Arab pop 310,950

Bass Strait \'bas\ strait separating Tasmania & continent of Australia

Bas·sein \bə-'sān\ city S Myanmar W of Yangon pop 126,045

Basse·terre \bas-'ter, bäs-\ town & port Brit. West Indies ✱ of St. Kitts Is. & of St. Kitts-Nevis state pop 14,725

Basse–Terre \bas-'ter, bäs-\ **1** island French West Indies constituting the W part of Guadeloupe area 364 sq mi (946 sq km) **2** town & port ✱ of Guadeloupe pop 13,796

Bas·tia \'bas-tē-ə, 'bäs-\ city & port France on NE coast of Corsica pop 45,387

Bas·togne \ba-'stōn, -'stȯ-nyə\ town SE Belgium in the Ardennes pop 12,187

Basutoland — see LESOTHO

Ba·ta \'bä-tə\ city ✱ of Mbini, Equatorial Guinea *pop* 30,474

Ba·taan \bə-'tan, -'tän\ peninsula Philippines in W Luzon on W side of Manila Bay

Ba·ta·via \bə-'tā-vē-ə\ — see DJAKARTA — **Ba·ta·vi·an** \-vē-ən\ *adj or n*

Batavian Republic the Netherlands under the French (1795–1806)

Bath \'bath, 'báth\ city SW England in Avon *pop* 79,965

Bath·urst \'ba-(,)thərst\ — see BANJUL

Bathurst Island island N Canada in Parry group *area* 6041 *sq mi* (15,707 *sq km*)

Bat·on Rouge \,ba-t°n-'rüzh\ city ✱ of La. on Mississippi River *pop* 219,531

Bat·ter·sea \'ba-tər-sē\ former metropolitan borough SW London, England, on S bank of the Thames, now part of Wandsworth

Bat·tle Creek \,ba-t°l-'krēk\ city S Mich. *pop* 53,540

Ba·tu·mi \bä-'tü-mē\ city & port SW Republic of Georgia on Black Sea ✱ of Adzhar Republic *pop* 82,000

Baut·zen \'baút-sən\ city E Germany on the Spree ENE of Dresden *pop* 48,866

Ba·var·ia \bə-'ver-ē-ə, -'var-\ *or G* **Bay·ern** \'bī-ərn\ state SE Germany bordering on Austria & the Czech Republic ✱ Munich *area* 27,232 *sq mi* (70,803 *sq km*), *pop* 10,928,151

Ba·ya·món \,bī-ə-'mōn\ city NE *cen* Puerto Rico *pop* 220,262

Bay City city E Mich. near head of Saginaw Bay *pop* 38,936

Ba·yeux \bī-'yü, bä-; bä-'yə(r); bâ-yœ\ town NW France WNW of Caen

Baykal, Lake — see BAIKAL (Lake)

Bay·onne \bā-'ōn\ city & port NE N.J. *pop* 61,444

Ba·yonne \bä-'ōn, bā-'yōn\ city SW France on the Adour near Bay of Biscay *pop* 41,281

Bay·reuth \bī-'ròit, 'bī-,\ city Germany in Bavaria NE of Nuremberg *pop* 70,633

Bay·town \'bā-,taún\ city SE Tex. on Galveston Bay *pop* 63,850

Beachy Head \'bē-chē\ headland SE England on coast of E. Sussex

Bear \'bar, 'ber\ **1** river 75 *mi* (121 *km*) N Calif. flowing SW to Feather River **2** river 350 *mi* (563 *km*) N Utah, SW Wyo., & SE Idaho flowing to Great Salt Lake

Beard·more \'bird-,mōr, -,mòr\ glacier Antarctica descending to Ross Ice Shelf at *ab* 170°E

Bear Mountain mountain 1314 *ft* (401 *m*) SE N.Y. on the Hudson

Bé·arn \bā-'arn\ region & former province SW France in Pyrenees SW of Gascony ✱ Pau

Be·as *or* **Bi·as** \'bē-,äs\ river 300 *mi* (483 *km*) N India in the Punjab

Beau·fort Sea \'bō-fərt\ sea comprising the part of the Arctic Ocean NE of Alaska & NW of Canada

Beau·mar·is \bō-'mar-əs\ borough NW Wales in Gwynedd on E Anglesey Is. on **Beaumaris Bay** *pop* 2088

Beau·mont \'bō-,mänt, bō-'\ city & port SE Tex. on the Neches *pop* 114,323

Beaune \'bōn\ commune E France SSW of Dijon *pop* 16,386

Beau·port \bō-'pòr, 'bō-(,)pòrt\ city Canada in S Que. *pop* 69,158

Beau·so·leil \bō-sò-'lā\ commune SE France N of Monaco

Beau·vais \bō-'vā\ commune N France NNW of Paris *pop* 53,493

Bea·ver \'bē-vər\ **1** river 280 *mi* (451 *km*) NW Okla. forming upper course of the N. Canadian **2** river 305 *mi* (491 *km*) Canada in Alta. & Sask. flowing E into the Churchill

Bea·ver·creek \'bē-vər-,krēk\ city SW Ohio E of Dayton *pop* 33,626

Bea·ver·head Mountains \'bē-vər-,hed\ mountains on Idaho-Mont. boundary; SE part of Bitterroot Range of the Rockies — see GARFIELD MOUNTAIN

Bea·ver·ton \'bē-vər-t°n\ city NW Oreg. W of Portland *pop* 53,310

Bé·char \bā-'shär\ *or formerly* **Co·lomb–Béchar** \kə-,lōⁿ(m)-\ commune NW Algeria SSE of Oran *pop* 72,800

Bech·u·a·na·land \,bech-'wä-nə-,land, ,be-chə-\ **1** region S Africa N of Orange River & including Kalahari Desert & Okanvango Swamps **2** — see BOTSWANA **3** *or* **British Bechuanaland** former Brit. colony in the region S of the Molopo; became part of Union of South Africa 1895 — **Bech·u·a·na** \,bech-'wä-nə, ,be-chə-\ *adj or n*

Beck·en·ham \'be-kə-nəm, -kə-,nam\ former urban district SE England in Kent, now part of Bromley

Bed·ford \'bed-fərd\ **1** city N Tex. *pop* 43,762 **2** borough SE *cen* England ✱ of Bedfordshire *pop* 74,245

Bed·ford·shire \'bed-fərd-,shir, -shər\ *or* **Bed·ford** \'bed-fərd\ county SE *cen* England *area* 477 *sq mi* (1240 *sq km*), *pop* 509,200

Bedloe's Island — see LIBERTY ISLAND

Bę·dzin \'ben-jēn\ commune S Poland in Silesia *pop* 76,846

Beer·she·ba \bir-'shē-bə, ber-, bər-\ city S Israel in N Negeb, in Bible times marking extreme S limit of Palestine *pop* 101,000

Behistun — see BISITUN

Bei·da \'bā-də\ town NE Libya in Cyrenaica NE of Benghazi

Bei·jing \'bā-'jiŋ\ *or* **Pe·king** \'pē-'kiŋ, 'pā-\ *or formerly* **Pei·ping** \'pā-'piŋ, 'bā-\ municipality NE China, its ✱ *pop* 9,230,687

Bei·ra \'bā-rə\ town & port SE Mozambique; chief port for *cen* Mozambique & landlocked Zimbabwe & Malawi *pop* 130,398

Bei·rut \bā-'rüt\ *or anc* **Be·ry·tus** \bə-'rī-təs\ city & port ✱ of Lebanon — **Bei·ruti** \-'rü-tē\ *n*

Be·jaïa \bā-'zhī-ə\ *or formerly* **Bou·gie** \bü-'zhē\ city & port NE Algeria *pop* 89,500

Be·kaa \bi-'kä\ *or* **Al Bi·qa** \,al-bi-'kä\ *or anc* **Coe·le–Syr·ia** \,sē-lē-'sir-ē-ə\ valley Lebanon bet. Lebanon & Anti-Lebanon mountain ranges

Be·la·rus \,bē-lə-'rüs, ,bye-lə-\ *or* **Bye·la·rus** \,bē-,e-lə-, ,bye-lə-\ independent country N *cen* Europe; a constituent republic (**Belorussia** *or* **Byelorussia**) of the U.S.S.R. 1919–91 ✱ Minsk *area* 88,044 *sq mi* (228,914 *sq km*), *pop* 10,200,000

Be·lau \bə-'laú\ *or* **Pa·lau** \pə-'laú\ island group W Pacific comprising a trust territory in association with U.S.; usu. considered part of the Carolines

Be·la·wan \bə-'lä-,wän\ town & port Indonesia in NE Sumatra

Be·la·ya \'be-lə-yə\ river 700 *mi* (1126 *km*) Russia in Europe rising in the S Urals & flowing S, W, & NW to the Kama

Be·lém \bə-'lem\ *or* **Pa·rá** \pə-'rä\ city N Brazil ✱ of Pará state on Pará River *pop* 1,200,000

Bel·fast \'bel-,fast, bel-'\ **1** district E Northern Ireland, established 1974 *area* 54 *sq mi* (140 *sq km*), *pop* 295,223 **2** city & port ✱ of Northern Ireland at head of **Belfast Lough** (inlet) *pop* 295,223

Bel·fort \bel-'fòr, bä-'fòr\ commune E France commanding **Belfort Gap** (wide pass bet. Vosges & Jura Mountains) *pop* 54,469

Belgian Congo *or earlier* **Congo Free State** former Belgian colony W *cen* Africa — see ZAIRE

Belgian East Africa — see RUANDA-URUNDI

Bel·gium \'bel-jəm\ *or F* **Bel·gique** \bel-zhēk\ *or Flem* **Bel·gië** \'bel-kē-ə\ country W Europe bordering on North Sea; a constitutional monarchy ✱ Brussels *area* 11,774 *sq mi* (30,612 *sq km*), *pop* 9,978,681

Bel·go·rod–Dnes·trov·skiy \'bel-gə-,räd-(,)nes-'tróf-skē, -'stróv-, 'byel-gə-rat-\ *or* **Byel·go·rod–Dnes·trov·ski** \'byel-\ *or formerly* **Turk** & **Russ Ak·ker·man** \,ä-kər-'män\ city SW Ukraine on the Dniester estuary *pop* 29,000

Bel·grade \'bel-,grād, -,gräd, -,grad, bel-'\ *or* **Beo·grad** \'beú-,gräd\ city ✱ of Yugoslavia & of Serbia *pop* 727,945

Bel·gra·via \bel-'grā-vē-ə\ district of W *cen* London, England, in Kensington and Chelsea borough S of Hyde Park

Be·li·tung \bə-'lē-tən\ *or* **Bil·li·ton** \-,tän\ island Indonesia bet. Sumatra & Borneo *area* 1866 *sq mi* (4852 *sq km*), *pop* 102,375

Be·lize \bə-'lēz\ **1** *or formerly* **British Honduras** country Central America bordering on the Caribbean; an independent member of the Commonwealth of Nations ✱ Belmopan *area* 8866 *sq mi* (23,052 *sq km*), *pop* 184,340 **2** *or* **Belize City** seaport Belize; former ✱ of British Honduras *pop* 43,621 — **Be·liz·ean** \-'lē-zē-ən\ *adj or n*

Bell \'bel\ city SW Calif. SE of Los Angeles *pop* 34,365

Bel·la Coo·la \,be-lə-'kü-lə\ river *ab* 60 *mi* (96 *km*) Canada in B.C. flowing W to Burke Channel E of Queen Charlotte Sound

Bel·leau \be-'lō, 'be-,\ village N France NW of Château-Thierry & N of **Belleau Wood** (*F* **Bois de Bel·leau** \,bwä-də-be-'lō\)

Belle Fourche \,bel-'füsh\ river *ab* 290 *mi* (467 *km*) NE Wyo. & W S.Dak. flowing NE & E into Cheyenne River

Belle Isle, Strait of \be-'lī(ə)l\ channel bet. N tip of Newfoundland (island) & SE Labrador

Belle·ville \'bel-,vil\ **1** city SW Ill. *pop* 42,785 **2** town NE N.J. N of Newark *pop* 34,213 **3** city Canada in SE Ont. *pop* 37,243

Belle·vue \'bel-,vyü\ **1** city E Nebr. S of Omaha *pop* 30,982 **2** city W Wash. E of Seattle *pop* 86,874

Bell·flow·er \'bel-,flaú(-ə)r\ city SW Calif. E of Los Angeles *pop* 61,815

Bell Gardens city SW Calif. E of Los Angeles *pop* 42,355

Bel·ling·ham \'be-liŋ-,ham\ city & port NW Wash. on **Bellingham Bay** (inlet at N end of Puget Sound) *pop* 52,179

Bel·lings·hau·sen Sea \'be-liŋz-,haú-z°n\ sea comprising a large bay of the S Pacific W of base of Antarctic Peninsula

Bel·lin·zo·na \,be-lən-'zō-nə\ commune S Switzerland E of Locarno ✱ of Ticino *pop* 17,142

Bell·wood \'bel-,wúd\ village NE Ill. W of Chicago *pop* 20,241

Bel·mont \'bel-,mänt\ **1** city W Calif. SE of San Francisco *pop* 24,127 **2** town E Mass. W of Boston *pop* 24,720

Bel·mo·pan \,bel-mō-'pan\ city ✱ of Belize *pop* 5256

Be·lo Ho·ri·zon·te \'bā-lō-,hòr-ə-'zän-tē, 'be-, -,här-\ city E Brazil ✱ of Minas Gerais *pop* 2,300,000

Be·loit \bə-'lòit\ city S Wis. on Ill. border *pop* 35,573

Be·lo·rus·sia \,be-lō-'rə-shə, ,bye-lō-\ *or* **Bye·lo·rus·sia** \,bē-,e-lō-, ,bye-lō-\ constituent republic of the U.S.S.R. bordering on Poland, Lithuania, & Latvia; became independent 1991 — see BELARUS

Beloye More — see WHITE SEA

Bel·sen \'bel-zən, -son\ *or* **Ber·gen–Belsen** \,ber-gən-, ,bər-\ locality N Germany on Lüneburg Heath NW of Celle; site of Nazi concentration camp during World War II

Be·lu·kha \bə-'lü-kə\ mountain 15,157 *ft* (4620 *m*) Russia in Asia; highest in Altai mountain range

Benares — see BANARAS

Ben·brook \'ben-,brúk\ village N Tex. SW of Fort Worth *pop* 19,564

Bend \'bend\ city *cen* Oreg. on the Deschutes *pop* 20,469

Ben·di·go \'ben-di-,gō\ city SE Australia in N Victoria NNW of Melbourne *pop* 53,944

Be·ne·lux \'be-n°l-,əks\ economic union comprising Belgium, the Netherlands, & Luxembourg; formed 1947

Be·ne·ven·to \,be-nə-'ven-(,)tō\ commune S Italy in Campania NE of Naples *pop* 64,842

Ben·gal \ben-'gòl, beŋ-, -'gäl\ region E India (subcontinent) including delta of the Ganges & the Brahmaputra; formerly a presidency & (1937–47) a province of Brit. India; divided 1947 bet. Pakistan & India (republic) — see EAST BENGAL, EAST PAKISTAN, WEST BENGAL — **Ben·gal·ese** \,ben-gə-'lēz, ,beŋ-, -'lēs\ *adj or n*

Bengal, Bay of arm of the Indian Ocean between India & Sri Lanka on the W & Myanmar & Malay Peninsula on the E

Beng·bu \'bəŋ-'bü\ *or* **Peng·pu** \'pəŋ-'pü\ *or* **Pang·fou** \'bəŋ-'fü\ city E China in N Anhui *pop* 253,000

Ben·gha·zi \ben-'gä-zē, beŋ-, -'ga-\ *or anc* **Ber·e·ni·ce** \,ber-ə-'nī-sē\ city & port NE Libya, a former ✱ of Libya *pop* 267,700

Ben·guela \ben-'gwä-lə\ city & port W Angola *pop* 40,996

Be·ni \'bā-nē\ river 1000 *mi* (1609 *km*) *cen* & N Bolivia flowing N to unite with Mamoré River forming Madeira River

Be·ni·cia \bə-'nē-shə\ city *cen* Calif. NNE of Oakland *pop* 24,437

Be·nin \bə-'nin, -'nēn; 'be-\ **1** river *ab* 100 *mi* (161 *km*) S Nigeria W of the Niger flowing into mouth of Benin **2** former kingdom W Africa on lower Niger River; incorporated in Nigeria after 1897 **3** *or formerly* **Da·ho·mey** \də-'hō-mē\ country W Africa on Gulf of Guinea; a republic, formerly a territory of French West Africa ✱ Porto-Novo *area* 44,743 *sq mi* (116,347 *sq km*), *pop* 3,338,240 **4** *or* **Benin City** city SW Nigeria in W delta of Niger River *pop* 161,700 — **Be·ni·nese** \bə-,ni-'nēz, -,nē-, -'nēs; ,be-ni-'nēz, -'nēs\ *adj or n*

Benin, Bight of the N section of Gulf of Guinea W Africa SW of Nigeria

---

\ə\ abut \'ᵊ\ kitten, F table \ər\ further \a\ ash \ā\ ace \ä\ mop, mar \aú\ out \ch\ chin \e\ bet \ē\ easy \g\ go \i\ hit \ī\ ice \j\ job \ŋ\ sing \ō\ go \ò\ law \òi\ boy \th\ thin \t͟h\ the \ü\ loot \ú\ foot \y\ yet \zh\ vision \á, k̶, ⁿ, œ, œ̄, ᵫ, ᵫ̄, �验\ see Guide to Pronunciation

Be·ni Su·ef \,be-nē-sù-'āf\ city N *cen* Egypt *pop* 117,910

Ben Lomond — see LOMOND (Ben)

Ben Nev·is \ben-'ne-vəs\ mountain 4406 *ft* (1343 *m*) W Scotland in Grampian Hills; highest in Great Britain

Be·no·ni \bə-'nō-nē\ city NE Republic of S. Africa in Pretoria–Witwatersrand-Vereeniging on the Witwatersrand E of Johannesburg *pop* 151,294

Be·nue \'bān-(,)wā\ river 870 *mi* (1400 *km*) W Africa flowing W into Niger River

Ben·xi \'bən-'shē\ *or* **Pen·ki** \-'jē\ *or* **Pen–hsi** \-'shē\ city NE China in E *cen* Liaoning *pop* 449,000

Be·rar \bā-'rär, bə-\ region W *cen* India; in Central Provinces & Berar 1903–47, in Madhya Pradesh 1947–56, in Bombay 1956–60, in Maharashtra since 1960; chief city Amravati

Ber·be·ra \'bər-b(ə-)rə\ town & port N Somalia *pop* 12,219

Be·rea \bə-'rē-ə\ **1** city NE Ohio SW of Cleveland *pop* 19,051 **2** — see VÉROIA

Be·re·zi·na \bə-'rā-z°n-ə, -'re-\ river 350 *mi* (563 *km*) Belarus flowing SE into the Dnieper

Bergama — see PERGAMUM

Ber·ga·mo \'ber-gə-,mō, 'bər-\ commune N Italy in Lombardy NE of Milan *pop* 117,584

Ber·gen **1** \'bər-gən, 'ber-\ city & port SW Norway *pop* 211,826 **2** — see MONS

Ber·gen·field \'bər-gən-,fēld\ borough NE N.J. *pop* 24,458

Be·ring Sea \'bir-iŋ, 'ber-\ arm of the N Pacific bet. Alaska & NE Siberia & bet. the Aleutians & Bering Strait *area* 878,000 *sq mi* (2,282,800 *sq km*)

Bering Strait strait *ab* 56 *mi* (90 *km*) wide separating Asia (Russia) from N. America (Alaska)

Berke·ley \'bər-klē\ city W Calif. on San Francisco Bay N of Oakland *pop* 102,724

Berk·shire \'bərk-,shir, -shər\ **1** hills W Mass. W of Connecticut River — see GREYLOCK (Mount) **2** *Brit usu* 'bärk-\ county S England in Thames River basin ✳ Reading *area* 485 *sq mi* (1261 *sq km*), *pop* 688,100

Ber·lin \(,)bər-'lin, *G* ber-'lēn\ city ✳ of (reunified) Germany on Spree River, before 1945 ✳ of Germany & of Prussia, divided under postwar occupation bet. E. & W. Germany, E. Berlin being made ✳ of E. Germany (1949) & W. Berlin a state (not formally incorporated) of W. Germany — **Ber·lin·er** \(,)bər-'li-nər\ *n*

Ber·me·jo \ber-'mā-(,)hō, ber-\ river 1000 *mi* (1609 *km*) N Argentina rising on Bolivian frontier & flowing SE into Paraguay River

Ber·mond·sey \'bər-mən(d)-zē\ former metropolitan borough E *cen* London, England, now part of Southwark

Ber·mu·da \(,)bər-'myü-də\ islands W Atlantic ESE of Cape Hatteras; a self-governing Brit. colony ✳ Hamilton *area* 21 *sq mi* (55 *sq km*), *pop* 67,761 — **Ber·mu·di·an** \-dē-ən\ *or* **Ber·mu·dan** \-d°n\ *adj or n*

Bermuda Triangle triangular area N. Atlantic Ocean bet. Bermuda, Fla., & Puerto Rico; site of numerous reported disappearances of planes & ships

Bern \'bərn, 'bern\ **1** canton NW & W *cen* Switzerland *area* 2658 *sq mi* (6911 *sq km*), *pop* 942,721 **2** city, its ✳ & ✳ of Switzerland on the Aare *pop* 135,825 — **Ber·nese** \(,)bər-'nēz, -'nēs\ *adj or n*

Bern·burg \'bərn-,borg, 'bern-,bùrk\ city *cen* Germany W of Dessau *pop* 44,428

Ber·ner Al·pen \,ber-nər-'äl-pən\ *or* **Ber·nese Ober·land** \(,)bər-'nēz-'ō-bər-,länt, -'nēs-\ *or* **Bernese Alps** *or* **Oberland** section of the Alps S Switzerland in Bern & Valais cantons bet. Thuner See & Brienz on the N & the valley of the upper Rhône on the S

Ber·ni·cia \(,)bər-'ni-sh(ē-)ə\ Anglian kingdom of 6th century A.D. located bet. Tyne & Forth rivers ✳ Bamborough

Ber·ni·na \(,)bər-'nē-nə\ the S extension of Rhaetian Alps on border bet. Italy & Switzerland; highest peak **Piz Bernina** \,pēts-\ (highest in the Rhaetian Alps) 13,200 *ft* (4023 *m*)

Beroea **1** — see ALEPPO **2** — see VÉROIA

Ber·ry *or* **Ber·ri** \be-'rē\ former province *cen* France ✳ Bourges

Ber·thoud Pass \'bər-thəd\ mountain pass 11,315 *ft* (3449 *m*) N Colo. in Front range WNW of Denver

Ber·wick \'ber-ik\ *or* **Ber·wick·shire** \-,shir, -shər\ former county SE Scotland ✳ Duns

Ber·wyn \'bər-wən\ city NE Ill. W of Chicago *pop* 45,426

Berytus — see BEIRUT

Be·san·con \bə-'zan(t)-sən, bə-zän-'sōⁿ\ city E France E of Dijon *pop* 119,803

Bes·kids \'bes-,kidz, be-'skēdz\ mountain ranges *cen* Europe in W Carpathians; include **West Beskids** (in Poland, Slovakia, & the Czech Republic) & **East Beskids** (in Poland & NE Slovakia)

Bes·sa·ra·bia \,be-sə-'rā-bē-ə\ region SE Europe bet. the Dniester & Prut rivers; now mostly in Moldova — **Bes·sa·ra·bi·an** \-bē-ən\ *adj or n*

Bes·se·mer \'be-sə-mər\ city N *cen* Ala. *pop* 33,497

Beth·a·ny \'be-thə-nē\ **1** city *cen* Okla. *pop* 20,075 **2** village Palestine E of Jerusalem on Mount of Olives *pop* 3560

Beth·el \'be-thəl, 'be-'thel\ ruined town Palestine in W Jordan N of Jerusalem

Bethel Park \'be-thəl\ borough SW Pa. *pop* 33,823

Be·thes·da \bə-'thez-də\ population center Md., a N suburb of Washington, D.C. *pop* 62,936

Beth·le·hem \'beth-li-,hem, -lē-həm, -lē-əm\ **1** city E Pa. on the Lehigh *pop* 71,428 **2** city Palestine in Judea SW of Jerusalem *pop* 16,313

Beth·nal Green \'beth-nəl\ former metropolitan borough E London, England, now part of Tower Hamlets

Beth·sa·i·da \beth-'sā-i-də\ ruined town Palestine on NE side of Sea of Galilee E of the Jordan; its site in SE Syria

Be·tio \'bā-chē-,ō, -shē-\ \'bāt-sē-\ islet & village W Pacific in N Kiribati at S end of Tarawa

Bet·ten·dorf \'be-t°n-,dorf\ city E Iowa E of Davenport *pop* 28,132

Beuthen — see BYTOM

Bev·er·ley \'be-vər-lē\ town N England in Humberside *pop* 16,433

Bev·er·ly \'be-vər-lē\ city NE Mass. *pop* 38,195

Beverly Hills city SW Calif. within city of Los Angeles *pop* 31,971

Bex·ley \'bek-slē\ borough of E Greater London, England *pop* 216,900

Bey·o·glu \,bā-ə-'(g)lü\ *or formerly* **Pera** \'per-ə\ section of Istanbul, Turkey, comprising area N of the Golden Horn

Bé·ziers \bāz-'yā\ city S France SW of Montpellier *pop* 79,213

Bezwada — see VIJAYAWADA

Bha·gal·pur \'bä-gəl-,pùr\ city E India on the Ganges in E Bihar *pop* 221,276

Bhak·ra Dam \'bä-krə\ hydroelectric & irrigation dam 680 *ft* (207 *m*) high N India in Punjab NW of Bilaspur in gorge of the Sutlej

Bha·mo \bə-'mō, -'mō\ city N Myanmar on the upper Irrawaddy *pop* 13,767

Bhat·pa·ra \bät-'pär-ə\ city E India in W. Bengal *pop* 204,750

Bhav·na·gar *or* **Bhau·na·gar** \baù-'nə-gər\ city & port W India in S Gujarat on Gulf of Cambay *pop* 308,194

Bho·pal \bō-'päl\ **1** former state N *cen* India in & N of Vindhya Mountains ✳ Bhopal; now part of Madhya Pradesh **2** city N *cen* India NW of Nagpur ✳ of Madhya Pradesh *pop* 672,329

Bhu·ba·nesh·war *or* **Bhu·va·nesh·war** \,bù-və-'näsh-wər\ city E India S of Cuttack ✳ of Orissa *pop* 219,419

Bhu·tan \bü-'tän, -'tan\ country Asia in Himalayas on NE border of India; a protectorate of India ✳ Thimbu *area* 18,000 *sq mi* (46,800 *sq km*), *pop* 1,333,000 — **Bhu·ta·nese** \,bü-t°n-'ēz, -'ēs\ *adj or n*

Bi·a·fra \bē-'ä-frə, bī-, -'a-\ name adopted by the SE part of Nigeria during its secession 1967–70 — **Bi·a·fran** \-frən\ *adj or n*

Biafra, Bight of *or* **Bight of Bon·ny** \'bä-nē\ the E section of Gulf of Guinea, W Africa

Bi·ak \bē-'yäk\ island off W New Guinea; largest of the Schoutens

Bia·ły·stok \bē-'ä-li-,stók\ city NE Poland *pop* 268,085

Biar·ritz \,bē-ə-'rits, 'bē-ə-,\ commune SW France on Bay of Biscay *pop* 27,453

Bias — see BEAS

Bid·de·ford \'bi-də-fərd\ city SW Maine SW of Portland *pop* 20,710

Biel \'bē(ə)l\ *or F* **Bienne** \bē-'en\ commune NW Switzerland in Bern canton NE of **Lake of Biel** (10 *mi* or 17 *km* long) *pop* 52,038

Bie·le·feld \'bē-lə-,felt\ city W *cen* Germany E of Münster *pop* 312,708

Biel·sko—Bia·ła \bē-,el-skó-bē-'ä-lə, ,byel-skó-'byä-, -wə\ city S Poland *pop* 179,879

Big Bend **1** area W Tex. in large bend of the Rio Grande; partly included in **Big Bend National Park** **2** section of Columbia River E *cen* Wash.

Big Black river 330 *mi* (531 *km*) W *cen* Miss. flowing to Mississippi River

Big Diomede — see DIOMEDE ISLANDS

Big·horn \'big-,horn\ river 336 *mi* (541 *km*) N Wyo. & SE Mont. flowing N into Yellowstone River — see WIND

Bighorn Mountains mountains N Wyo. extending S from Mont. border E of Bighorn River — see CLOUD PEAK

Big Sandy river 22 *mi* (35 *km*) bet. W.Va. & Ky. flowing N into Ohio River

Big Sioux \'sü\ river 300 *mi* (483 *km*) S.Dak. & Iowa flowing S to Missouri River & forming Iowa-S.Dak. boundary

Big Spring city W Tex. NE of Odessa *pop* 23,093

Big Stone lake *ab* 30 *mi* (48 *km*) long bet. W Minn. & NE S.Dak. — see MINNESOTA 1

Big Sur \'sər\ region W Calif. centering on Big Sur River & extending *ab* 80 *mi* (129 *km*) along coast SE of Point Sur

Big Thicket wilderness area E Tex. NE of Houston *area ab* 450 *sq mi* (1170 *sq km*)

Bi·har \bi-'här\ **1** state NE India bordering on Nepal; winter ✳ Patna, summer ✳ Ranchi *area* 67,164 *sq mi* (174,626 *sq km*), *pop* 59,823,154 **2** city *cen* Bihar state SE of Patna *pop* 151,308

Bijanagar — see VIJAYANAGAR

Bi·ka·ner \,bi-kə-'ner, ,bē-, -'nir\ city NW India in N Rajasthan in Thar Desert *pop* 280,366

Bi·ki·ni \bə-'kē-nē\ island (atoll) W Pacific in Marshall Islands — **Bi·ki·ni·an** \-nē-ən\ *n*

Bi·las·pur \bi-'läs-,pùr\ city E *cen* India in SE Madhya Pradesh SE of Jabalpur *pop* 186,885

Bil·bao \bil-'bä-,ō, -'baù, -'bä-(,)ō\ city N Spain ✳ of Vizcaya *pop* 433,115

Bil·ler·i·ca \(,)bil-'ri-kə\ town NE Mass. *pop* 37,609

Bil·lings \'bi-liŋz\ city S *cen* Mont. *pop* 81,151

Billiton — see BELITUNG

Bi·lo·xi \bə-'lək-sē, -'läk-\ city & port SE Miss. *pop* 46,319

Bim·i·ni \'bi-mə-nē\ two islands of the Bahamas NW of Andros

Bing·en \'biŋ-ən\ city W Germany *pop* 23,528

Bing·ham·ton \'biŋ-əm-tən\ city S *cen* N.Y. *pop* 53,008

Binh Dinh — see AN NHON

Bío–Bío \,bē-ō-'bē-(,)ō\ river 238 *mi* (383 *km*) S *cen* Chile flowing into the Pacific at Concepción

Bi·o·ko \bē-'ō-(,)kō\ *or formerly* **Fer·nan·do Po** *or* **Fernando Póo** \fər-'nan-(,)dō-'pō\ *or 1973–79* **Ma·ci·as Ngue·ma Bi·yo·go** \mä-'sē-əs-əŋ-'gwä-mə-bi-'yō-(,)gō\ island Equatorial Guinea in Bight of Biafra *area* 778 *sq mi* (2023 *sq km*)

Bir·ken·head \'bər-kən-,hed, ,bər-kən-'\ borough NW England in Merseyside on the Mersey estuary opposite Liverpool *pop* 123,907

Bir·ming·ham \'bər-miŋ-,ham, *Brit usu* -miŋ-əm\ **1** city N *cen* Ala. *pop* 265,968 **2** city SE Mich. N of Detroit *pop* 19,997 **3** city & borough W *cen* England in West Midlands *pop* 920,389

Bi·ro·bi·dzhan \,bir-ō-bi-'jän, -'jan\ city Russia in Asia ✳ of Yevreyskaya autonomous oblast *pop* 69,000

Bisayas — see VISAYAN

Biscay *or* **Biscaya** — see VIZCAYA — **Bis·cay·an** \bis-'kī-ən, -'kā-\ *adj or n*

Bis·cay, Bay of \'bis-,kā, -kē\ inlet of the Atlantic bet. W coast of France & N coast of Spain

Bis·cayne Bay \bis-'kān, 'bis-,\ inlet of the Atlantic SE Fla.; S part forms **Biscayne National Park**

Bish·kek \bish-'kek\ *or 1926–91* **Frun·ze** \'frün-zə\ city on Chu River ✳ of Kyrgyzstan *pop* 616,000

Bi·sho \'bē-(,)shō\ town S Republic of South Africa; formerly ✳ of Ciskei

Bi·si·tun \,bē-sə-'tün\ *or* **Be·his·tun** \,bā-his-\ *or* **Bi·so·tun** \,bē-sə-\ ruined town W Iran E of Kermanshah

Bis·kra \'bis-krə, -(,)krä\ city NE Algeria at an oasis on S edge of Atlas Mountains *pop* 90,500

Bis·marck \'biz-,märk\ city ✳ of N.Dak. on Missouri River *pop* 49,256

Bismarck Archipelago archipelago W Pacific N of E end of New Guinea *area* 22,290 *sq mi* (57,954 *sq km*)

Bismarck Range mountain range North-East New Guinea NW of Owen Stanley Range; highest point Mt. Wilhelm 14,107 *ft* (4300 *m*)

Bismarck Sea sea comprising the part of the W Pacific enclosed by the islands of the Bismarck Archipelago

Bis·sau \bi-'saú(ⁿ)\ city & port ✳ of Guinea-Bissau *pop* 105,273

Bi·thyn·ia \bə-'thi-nē-ə\ ancient country NW Asia Minor bordering on the Sea of Marmara & Black Sea — **Bi·thyn·i·an** \-nē-ən\ *adj or n*

Bi·to·la \'bē-t°l-,yä\ *or* **Bi·tolj** \'bē-,tõl(-yə), -,tõi\ *or* **Mon·a·stir** \,mä-nə-'stir\ city S Macedonia *pop* 64,467

Bitter Lakes two lakes (Great Bitter Lake & Little Bitter Lake) in NE Egypt N of Suez; connected & traversed by the Suez Canal

Bit·ter·root Range \'bi-tə(r)-,rüt, -,rüt\ range of the Rocky Mountains on Idaho-Mont. boundary — see BEAVERHEAD MOUNTAINS, GARFIELD MOUNTAIN

Bi·wa \'bē-(,)wä\ lake 40 *mi* (64 *km*) long Japan on W *cen* Honshu

Biysk \'bēsk\ city Russia in Asia, in E Altai territory *pop* 212,000

Bi·zerte \bə-'zər-tē, bi-'zert\ *or* **Bi·zer·ta** \bə-'zər-tə\ city & port N Tunisia on **Lake Bizerte** (a deep lagoon) *pop* 62,856

Black — see BABIAN

Black·burn \'blak-(,)bərn\ borough NW England in Lancashire *pop* 88,236

Blackburn, Mount mountain 16,390 *ft* (4996 *m*) S Alaska; highest in the Wrangell Mountains

Black Canyon 1 canyon of Colorado River bet. Ariz. & Nev. S of Hoover Dam 2 canyon of the Gunnison SW *cen* Colo. partly in **Black Canyon of the Gunnison National Monument**

Black Forest *or G* **Schwarz·wald** \'shvärts-,vält\ forested mountain region SW Germany along the upper Rhine bet. the Neckar River & Swiss border

Black Hills mountains W S.Dak. & NE Wyo. — see HARNEY PEAK

Black Mountains mountains W N.C., a range of the Blue Ridge Mountains — see MITCHELL (Mount)

Black·pool \'blak-,pül\ borough NW England in Lancashire on Irish Sea *pop* 147,854

Blacks·burg \'blaks-,bərg\ city W Va. W of Roanoke *pop* 34,590

Black Sea *or anc* **Pon·tus Eux·i·nus** \'pän-təs-,yük-'sī-nəs\ *or* **Pon·tus** sea bet. Europe & Asia connected with Aegean Sea through the Bosporus, Sea of Marmara, & Dardanelles *area* 168,500 *sq mi* (438,100 *sq km*)

Black Volta — see VOLTA

Black Warrior river 178 *mi* (286 *km*) *cen* Ala. flowing into the Tombigbee

Bla·go·vesh·chensk \,blä-gə-'ve-shən(t)sk, -'vesh-chən(t)sk\ city Russia in Asia on the Amur *pop* 172,000

Blaine \'blān\ city E Minn. N of St. Paul *pop* 38,975

Blain·ville \'blān-,vil, blenⁿ-'vēl\ town Canada in S Que. *pop* 22,679

Blanc, Cape \'blank, 'blänⁿ\ 1 cape N Tunisia; northernmost point of Africa, at 37°14'N 2 promontory NW Africa on the Atlantic in Mauritania at SW tip of Río de Oro

Blanc, Mont — see MONT BLANC

Blan·ca Peak \'blaŋ-kə, 'bläŋ-\ mountain 14,317 *ft* (4364 *m*) S Colo.; highest in Sangre de Cristo Mountains

Blan·co, Cape \'blaŋ-(,)kō\ cape SW Oreg.

Blan·tyre \'blan-,tīr\ city S Malawi *pop* 222,153

Blar·ney \'blär-nē\ town SW Ireland in *cen* County Cork *pop* 1952

Blen·heim \'ble-nəm\ *or G* **Blind·heim** \'blint-,hīm\ village S Germany in Bavaria NNW of Augsburg *pop* 1619

Bli·da \'blē-də\ city N Algeria SW of Algiers *pop* 160,900

Block Island \'bläk\ island R.I. in the Atlantic at E entrance to Long Island Sound

Bloem·fon·tein \'blüm-fən-,tān, -,fän-\ city *cen* Republic of South Africa, judicial ✳ of the Republic *pop* 149,836

Blois \'blwä\ city N *cen* France SW of Orléans *pop* 49,134

Bloom·field \'blüm-,fēld\ 1 town N *cen* Conn. NW of Hartford *pop* 18,608 2 town NE N.J. *pop* 45,061

Bloo·ming·ton \'blü-miŋ-tən\ 1 city *cen* Ill. *pop* 51,972 2 city SW *cen* Ind. *pop* 60,633 3 village SE Minn. *pop* 86,335

Blooms·bury \'blümz-b(ə-)rē, US also -,ber-ē\ district of N *cen* London, England, in borough of Camden

Blue Grotto sea cave Italy on N shore of Capri

Blue Island city NE Ill. S of Chicago *pop* 21,203

Blue Mountains 1 mountains NE Oreg. & SE Wash.; highest Rock Creek Butte 9105 *ft* (2775 *m*) 2 mountains SE Australia in Great Dividing Range in E New S. Wales; highest 4460 *ft* (1359 *m*) 3 mountains E Jamaica; highest Blue Mountain Peak 7402 *ft* (2256 *m*)

Blue Nile river 850 *mi* (1368 *km*) Ethiopia & Sudan flowing from Lake Tana NNW into the Nile at Khartoum — see ABBAI

Blue Ridge the E range of the Appalachians E U.S. extending from South Mountain, S Pa. into N Ga. — see MITCHELL (Mount)

Blue Springs city W Mo. SE of Independence *pop* 40,153

Bluff \'bləf\ town S New Zealand; port for Invercargill *pop* 2720

Blythe·ville \'blī-vəl, 'blĭth-,vil\ city NE Ark. *pop* 22,906

Bo·bo–Diou·las·so \'bō-(,)bō-dyü-'la-(,)sō\ town W Burkina Faso *pop* 290,000

Bo·bruysk *or* **Ba·bruysk** \bə-'brü-isk\ city *cen* Belarus on the Berezina *pop* 138,000

Bo·ca Ra·ton \,bō-kə-rə-'tōn\ city SE Fla. N of Fort Lauderdale *pop* 61,492

Bo·chum \'bō-kəm\ city W Germany in Ruhr valley *pop* 400,757

Bodensee — see CONSTANCE (Lake)

Bod·min \'bäd-min\ borough SW England, a ✳ of Cornwall and Isles of Scilly *pop* 12,148

Boe·o·tia \bē-'ō-sh(ē-)ə\ *or NGk* **Voi·o·tía** \vē-ō-'tē-ə\ district E *cen* Greece NW of Attica — **Boe·o·tian** \bē-'ō-shən\ *adj or n*

Bo·go·tá \,bō-gə-'tä, -'tó, 'bō-gə-,\ city ✳ of Colombia on plateau in the Andes *pop* 2,293,919

Bo Hai *or* **Po Hai** \'bō-'hī\ *or* **Gulf of Chih·li** \'chē-'lē, 'jir-\ arm of Yellow Sea NE China bounded on NE by Liaodong Peninsula & on SE by Shandong Peninsula

Bo·he·mia \bō-'hē-mē-ə\ *or* **Če·chy** \'che-kē, -ˌkē\ region W Czech Republic once a kingdom, later a province ✳ Prague

Böh·mer·wald \'bə(r)-mər-,vält, 'bōē-\ *or* **Bohemian Forest** forested mountain region Czech Republic & Germany along boundary bet. E Bavaria & SW Bohemia

Bo·hol \bō-'hōl\ island S *cen* Philippines, one of the Visayan Islands, N of Mindanao *area* 1492 *sq mi* (3879 *sq km*)

Bois de Belleau — see BELLEAU

Bois de Bou·logne \,bwä-də-bü-'lōn, -'lô-nyə, -'lóin\ park France W of Paris

Boi·se \'bói-sē, -zē\ city ✳ of Idaho on Boise River (60 *mi or* 96 *km* long) *pop* 125,738

Bo·ja·dor, Cape \'bä-jə-,dór\ headland NW Africa in the Atlantic on W coast of Western Sahara

Bokhara — see BUKHARA

Boks·burg \'bäks-,bərg\ city NE Republic of South Africa in Pretoria–Witwatersrand–Vereeniging E of Johannesburg *pop* 108,850

Bo·lan Pass \bō-'län\ mountain pass 5900 *ft* (1798 *m*) Pakistan in N Baluchistan

Bolbitine — see ROSETTA

Bo·ling·brook \'bō-liŋ-,brúk\ city NE Ill. SW of Chicago *pop* 40,843

Bo·lí·var, Cer·ro \'ser-(,)ō-bə-'lē-,vär\ *or formerly* **La Pa·ri·da** \,lä-pə-'rē-də\ iron mountain 2018 *ft* (615 *m*) E Venezuela S of Ciudad Bolívar

Bo·lí·var, Pi·co \'pē-(,)kō-bə-'lē-,vär\ mountain 16,427 *ft* (5007 *m*) W Venezuela in Cordillera Mérida; highest in Venezuela

Bo·liv·ia \bə-'li-vē-ə\ country W *cen* S. America; a republic; administrative ✳ La Paz, constitutional ✳ Sucre *area* 424,200 *sq mi* (1,102,920 *sq km*), *pop* 6,547,000 — **Bo·liv·i·an** \-vē-ən\ *adj or n*

Bo·lo·gna \bə-'lō-nyə\ *or anc* **Bo·no·nia** \bə-'nō-nē-ə\ commune N Italy ✳ of Emilia-Romagna at foot of the Apennines *pop* 417,410 — **Bo·lo·gnan** \bə-'lō-nyən\ *or* **Bo·lo·gnese** \,bō-lə-'nēz, -'nēs, -'nyēz, -'nyēs\ *adj or n*

Bol·se·na, Lake \bōl-'sā-nə\ lake *cen* Italy in NW Latium

Bol·ton \'bōl-t°n\ borough NW England in NW Greater Manchester *pop* 147,099

Bol·za·no \bōlt-'sä-(,)nō, bōl-'zä-\ 1 former province N Italy in S Tirol, now part of Trentino-Alto Adige region 2 commune in Trentino-Alto Adige region *pop* 100,707

Bo·ma \'bō-mə\ city & port W Congo on Congo River *pop* 79,230

Bom·bay \bäm-'bā\ 1 former state W India ✳ Bombay; divided 1960 into Gujarat & Maharashtra states; once a presidency & (1937–47) a province of Brit. India 2 city & port W India ✳ of Maharashtra & of former Bombay state *pop* 8,227,332

Bombay Island island W India on which city of Bombay is situated *area* 24 *sq mi* (62 *sq km*)

Bo·mu \'bō-(,)mü\ *or* **Mbo·mou** \əm-'bō-(,)mü\ river 500 *mi* (805 *km*) W *cen* Africa forming boundary bet. Zaire & Central African Republic & uniting with the Uele to form the Ubangi

Bon, Cape \'bōⁿ\ *or* **Ras el Tib** \,räs-,el-'tib\ headland NE Tunisia on **Cape Bon Peninsula**

Bo·na, Mount \'bō-nə\ mountain 16,420 *ft* (5005 *m*) S Alaska at W end of Wrangell Mountains

Bon·aire \bə-'nar, -'ner\ island Netherlands Antilles E of Curaçao *area* 95 *sq mi* (247 *sq km*), *pop* 11,058

Bon·di \'bän-,dī\ town SE Australia, SE suburb of Sydney, S of entrance to Port Jackson on **Bondi Beach**

Bône — see ANNABA

Bo·nin Islands \'bō-nən\ *or* **Oga·sa·wa·ra Islands** \(,)ō-,gä-sə-'wär-ə\ islands W Pacific *ab* 600 *mi* (966 *km*) SSE of Tokyo; belong to Japan; administered by U.S. 1945–68 *area* 40 *sq mi* (104 *sq km*), *pop* 1507

Bonn \'bän, 'bón\ city W Germany on the Rhine SSE of Cologne ✳ of Federal Republic of Germany (sometimes called **Bonn Republic**) before reunification *pop* 288,148

Bon·ne·ville Salt Flats \'bä-nə-,vil\ *or* **Bonneville Flats** broad level area of Great Salt Lake Desert E of Wendover, Utah

Bonny, Bight of — see BIAFRA, BIGHT OF

Booker T. Washington National Monument historic site W *cen* Va. SE of Roanoke

Boo·thia, Gulf of \'bü-thē-ə\ gulf N Canada bet. Baffin Is. & Melville Peninsula on E & Boothia Peninsula on W

Boothia Peninsula peninsula N Canada W of Baffin Is.; its N tip (at *ab* 72°N, 94°W) is the northernmost point on N. American mainland

Boo·tle \'bü-t°l\ borough NW England in W Merseyside *pop* 62,463

Bo·phu·tha·tswa·na \,bō-(,)pü-tät-'swä-nə\ former group of noncontiguous black enclaves in the Republic of South Africa ✳ Mmabatho; granted independence 1977; abolished 1994

Bo·ra Bo·ra \,bōr-ə-'bōr-ə, ,bór-ə-'bór-ə\ island S Pacific in Leeward group of the Society Islands NW of Tahiti *area ab* 15 *sq mi* (38 *sq km*)

Bo·rah Peak \'bōr-ə, 'bór-\ mountain 12,662 *ft* (3859 *m*) E *cen* Idaho in Lost River Range; highest point in state

Bo·rås \bü-'rós\ city SW Sweden E of Göteborg *pop* 101,231

Bor·deaux \bór-'dō\ city & port SW France on the Garonne *pop* 220,830 — **Bor·de·lais** \,bór-d°l-'ā\ *n*

Bor·ders \'bór-dərz\ region S Scotland, established 1975 ✳ Newtown St. Boswells *area* 1804 *sq mi* (4690 *sq km*), *pop* 99,248

Bor·di·ghe·ra \,bór-di-'ger-ə\ commune & port NW Italy in Liguria

Borgne, Lake \'bórn\ inlet of the Mississippi Sound E of New Orleans, La.

Bor·neo \'bór-nē-,ō\ island Malay Archipelago SW of Philippines *area* 290,012 *sq mi* (754,031 *sq km*) — see BRUNEI, KALIMANTAN, SABAH, SARAWAK — **Bor·ne·an** \-nē-ən\ *adj or n*

Born·holm \'bórn-,hōlm, -,hōm\ island Denmark in Baltic Sea ✳ Rönne *area* 228 *sq mi* (593 *sq km*), *pop* 46,105

Bos·nia \'bäz-nē-ə, 'bóz-\ region S Europe in the Balkans; with Herzegovina forms independent state of **Bosnia and Her·ze·go·vi·na** \,hert-sə-gō-'vē-nə, ,hərt-, -'gō-və-nə\, a federated republic of Yugosla-

\ə\ abut \ᵊ\ kitten, F table \ər\ further \a\ ash \ā\ ace \ä\ mop, mar \aú\ out \ch\ chin \e\ bet \ē\ easy \g\ go \i\ hit \ī\ ice \j\ job \ŋ\ sing \ō\ go \ó\ law \ói\ boy \th\ thin \t͟h\ the \ü\ loot \ú\ foot \y\ yet \zh\ vision \à, k̲, ⁿ, œ, œ̄, ᴜ, ᵫ, ᵞ\ *see* Guide to Pronunciation via 1946–92 ✱ Sarajevo *area* 19,904 *sq mi* (51,750 *sq km*), *pop* 4,021,000 — **Bos·ni·an** \-nē-ən\ *adj or n*

Bos·po·rus \'bäs-p(ə-)rəs\ *or* **Bos·pho·rus** \-f(ə-)rəs\ strait *ab* 18 *mi* (29 *km*) long bet. Turkey in Europe & Turkey in Asia connecting Sea of Marmara & Black Sea — **Bos·po·ran** \-pə-rən\ *adj*

Bos·sier City \'bō-zhər\ city NW La. *pop* 52,721

Bos·ton \'bòs-tən\ 1 city & port ✱ of Mass. on Massachusetts Bay *pop* 535,721 2 borough & port E England in SE Lincolnshire in Parts of Holland *pop* 26,425 — **Bos·to·nian** \bò-'stō-nē-ən, -nyən\ *adj or n*

Boston Mountains mountains NW Ark. & E Okla. in Ozark Plateau

Bo·ta·fo·go Bay \,bō-tə-'fō-(,)gō\ inlet of Guanabara Bay in Rio de Janeiro, Brazil

Bot·a·ny Bay \'bä-t°n-ē, 'bät-nē\ inlet of the S Pacific SE Australia in New South Wales on S border of city of Sydney

Both·nia, Gulf of \'bäth-nē-ə\ arm of Baltic Sea bet. Sweden & Finland

Bo·tswa·na \bät-'swä-nə\ country S Africa N of the Molopo; an independent republic since 1966, formerly Brit. protectorate of **Bechuanaland** ✱ Gaborone *area ab* 222,000 *sq mi* (577,200 *sq km*), *pop* 936,600

Bot·trop \'bä-,träp\ city W Germany N of Essen *pop* 114,571

Bou·cher·ville \'bü-shər-,vil, ,bü-shā-'vēl\ town Canada in S Que. NE of Montreal *pop* 33,796

Bou·gain·ville \'bü-gən-,vil, 'bō-, 'bù-\ island S Pacific, largest of the Solomons; chief town Kieta *area* 3880 *sq mi* (10,088 *sq km*)

Bougie — see BEJAÏA

Bouil·lon \bü-'yōⁿ\ town SE Belgium in the Ardennes *pop* 5468

Boul·der \'bōl-dər\ city N cen Colo. *pop* 83,312

Boulder Dam — see HOOVER DAM

Bou·logne \bü-'lōn, -'lò-nyə, -'lòin\ *or* **Bou·logne–sur–Mer** \-,sùr-'mer\ city & port N France on English Channel *pop* 48,309

Boulogne–Bil·lan·court \,bē-,yäⁿ-'kùr\ commune N France SW of Paris on the Seine *pop* 103,527

Boundary Peak mountain 13,140 *ft* (4005 *m*) SW Nev. in White Mountains; highest in state

Bountiful city N Utah N of Salt Lake City *pop* 36,659

Bour·bon·nais \,bùr-bə-'nā\ former province *cen* France W of Burgundy

Bourges \'bùrzh\ commune *cen* France SSE of Orléans *pop* 75,200

Bourgogne — see BURGUNDY

Bourne·mouth \'bòrn-məth, 'bòrn-, 'bùrn-\ town S England in Dorset on English Channel *pop* 144,803

Bou·vet \bü-'vā\ island S Atlantic SSW of Cape of Good Hope at *ab* 54°S, 5°E; belongs to Norway

Bow \'bō\ river 315 *mi* (507 *km*) Canada in SW Alta. rising in Banff National Park

Bow·ie \'bü-ē\ town NE Md. NE of Washington, D.C. *pop* 37,589

Bowling Green 1 city S Ky. *pop* 40,641 2 city NW Ohio S of Toledo *pop* 28,176

Boyne \'bòin\ river 70 *mi* (113 *km*) E Ireland in Leinster flowing to Irish Sea S of Drogheda

Boyn·ton Beach \'bòin-t°n\ city SE Fla. *pop* 46,194

Bo·yo·ma Falls \bòi-'ō-mə\ *or formerly* **Stanley Falls** series of seven cataracts NE Zaire in the Lualaba near head of Congo River with total fall of *ab* 200 *ft* (61 *m*) in 60 *mi* (96 *km*)

Boz·caa·da \,bòz-jä-'dä\ *or anc* **Ten·e·dos** \'te-nə-,däs\ island Turkey in NE Aegean Sea S of the Dardanelles

Boze·man \'bōz-mən\ city SW Mont. *pop* 22,660

Bra·bant \brä-bənt; brə-'bant, -'bänt\ 1 old duchy of W Europe including region now forming N. Brabant province of the Netherlands & Brabant & Antwerp provinces of Belgium 2 province *cen* Belgium ✱ Brussels *pop* 2,245,890

Bra·den·ton \'brā-d°n-tən\ city & port W Fla. N of Sarasota *pop* 43,779

Brad·ford \'brad-fərd\ city N England in W. Yorkshire *pop* 280,691

Bra·ga \'brä-gə\ commune NW Portugal NNE of Porto *pop* 63,033

Bra·gan·ça \brə-'gan(t)-sə\ commune NE Portugal near Spanish border *pop* 34,803

Brah·ma·pu·tra \,brä-mə-'pü-trə\ river 1680 *mi* (2704 *km*) S Asia flowing from the Himalayas in Tibet to the Ganges delta in E India (subcontinent) — see JAMUNA, TSANGPO

Bra·i·la \brə-'ē-lə\ city E Romania on the Danube *pop* 242,595

Brain·tree \'brān-(,)trē\ town E Mass. S of Boston *pop* 33,836

Brak·pan \'brak-,pan\ city NE Republic of S. Africa in Pretoria-Witwatersrand-Vereeniging on the Witwatersrand S of Johannesburg *pop* 85,044

Bramp·ton \'bramp-tən\ city Canada in SE Ont. *pop* 234,445

Bran·co \'braŋ-(,)kō, -(,)kü\ river 350 *mi* (563 *km*) N Brazil flowing S into Negro River

Bran·den·burg \'bran-dən-,bərg, 'brän-dən-,bùrk\ 1 region & former province NE *cen* Germany 2 city E Germany *pop* 94,071

Bran·don \'bran-dən\ city Canada in SW Man. *pop* 38,567

Bran·dy·wine \'bran-dē-,wīn\ creek *ab* 20 *mi* (32 *km*) SE Pa. & N Del. flowing SE to Wilmington, Del.

Bran·ford \'bran-fərd\ town S Conn. E of New Haven *pop* 27,603

Brant·ford \'brant-fərd\ city Canada in SE Ont. *pop* 81,997

Bras d'Or Lake \brä-'dòr\ tidal lake *ab* 50 *mi* (80 *km*) long Canada in N.S. on Cape Breton Is.

Bra·sí·lia \brə-'zil-yə\ city ✱ of Brazil in Federal District *metropolitan area pop* 1,803,478

Bra·sov \brä-'shòv\ *or formerly* **Sta·lin** \'stä-lən, 'sta-, -,lēn\ *or* **Ora·sul Stalin** \,ò-,rä-shü, -shül-\ city *cen* Romania in foothills of Transylvanian Alps *pop* 352,640

Bra·ti·sla·va \,brä-tə-'slä-və, ,brä-\ *or G* **Press·burg** \'pres-,bərg, -,bùrk\ *or Hung* **Po·zsony** \'pō-,zhō-nyə\ city SW Slovakia, its ✱, on the Danube *pop* 440,421

Bratsk \'brätsk\ city Russia in Asia, NNE of Irkutsk near site of **Bratsk Dam** (in the Angara) *pop* 214,000

Braunschweig — see BRUNSWICK

Bravo, Rio — see RIO GRANDE

Bray \'brā\ urban district & port E Ireland *pop* 24,686

Bra·zil *or Pg* **Bra·sil** \brə-'zil\ country E S. America; a federal republic ✱ Brasília *area* 3,286,169 *sq mi* (8,544,039 *sq km*), *pop* 150,051,784 — **Bra·zil·ian** \brə-'zil-yən\ *adj or n*

Braz·os \'bra-zəs\ river *ab* 950 *mi* (1529 *km*), *cen* Tex. flowing SE into Gulf of Mexico

Braz·za·ville \'bra-zə-,vil, 'brä-zə-,vēl\ city & port ✱ of Congo on W bank of Malebo Pool in Congo River *pop* 302,460

Brea \'brā-ə\ city SW Calif. SE of Los Angeles *pop* 32,873

Brec·on \'bre-kən\ *or* **Breck·nock** \'brek-,näk, -,nək\ 1 *or* **Brec·on·shire** *or* **Breck·nock·shire** \-,shir, -shər\ former county SE Wales ✱ Brecon 2 borough SE Wales in Powys *pop* 7422

Brecon Beacons two mountain peaks SE Wales in S Powys

Bre·da \'brā-də\ commune S Netherlands in N. Brabant province *pop* 118,813

Bre·genz \'brā-,gents\ commune W Austria on Lake Constance ✱ of Vorarlberg *pop* 24,683

Bre·men \'bre-mən, 'brā-\ 1 former duchy N Germany bet. the lower Weser & the lower Elbe 2 state NW Germany *area* 156 *sq mi* (406 *sq km*), *pop* 693,846 3 city & port, its ✱, on the Weser *pop* 555,118

Bre·mer·ha·ven \'bre-mər-,hä-vən, ,brä-mər-'hä-fən\ city & port NW Germany in Bremen state at mouth of the Weser; includes former city of Wesermünde *pop* 138,728

Brem·er·ton \'bre-mər-tən, -t°n\ city & port W Wash. on Puget Sound *pop* 38,142

Bren·ner Pass \'bre-nər\ mountain pass 4495 *ft* (1370 *m*) in the Alps bet. Austria & Italy

Brent \'brent\ *or formerly* **Brent·ford and Chis·wick** \'brent-fərd-°n-'chi-zik\ borough of W Greater London, England *pop* 254,400

Bren·ta \'bren-tə\ river 100 *mi* (161 *km*) N Italy flowing SE into the Adriatic S of Chioggia

Bre·scia \'bre-shə, 'brā-ə\ *or anc* **Brix·ia** \'brik-sē-ə\ commune N Italy in E Lombardy ENE of Milan *pop* 196,935

Breslau — see WROCŁAW

Brest \'brest\ 1 commune & port NW France in Brittany *pop* 163,940 2 *or formerly* **Brest Li·tovsk** \lə-'tòfsk\ city SW Belarus on Bug River *pop* 177,000

Bre·ton, Cape \,kāp-'bre-t°n, kə-'bre-, -'bri-\ headland Canada, easternmost point of Cape Breton Is. & of N.S., at 59°48′W

Briansk — see BRYANSK

Bridge·port \'brij-,pòrt, -,pòrt\ city SW Conn. on Long Island Sound *pop* 141,686

Bridge·town \'brij-,taùn\ city & port Brit. West Indies ✱ of Barbados *pop* 8868

Bridge·wa·ter \'brij-,wò-tər, -,wä-\ city SE Mass. S of Brockton *pop* 21,249

Brie \brē\ district & medieval county NE France E of Paris; chief town Meaux

Bri·enne \brē-'en\ 1 former county NE France in Champagne NNE of Troyes 2 town, its ✱

Bri·enz \brē-'ents\ town Switzerland in SE Bern canton at NE end of **Lake of Brienz** (9 *mi* or 14 *km* long, in course of the Aare)

Brigh·ton \'brī-t°n\ borough S England in E. Sussex on English Channel *pop* 146,134

Brin·di·si \'brin-də-(,)zē, 'brēn-\ *or anc* **Brun·di·si·um** \,brən-'di-zē-əm, -zhē-\ city & port SE Italy in Apulia *pop* 92,815

Bris·bane \'briz-bən, -,bān\ city & port E Australia ✱ of Queensland on Brisbane River (215 *mi* or 344 *km*) near its mouth *pop* 1,037,815

Bris·tol \'bris-t°l\ 1 city W *cen* Conn. WSW of Hartford *pop* 60,640 2 town E R.I. SE of Providence *pop* 21,625 3 city NE Tenn. *pop* 23,421 4 city & port SW England in Avon on Avon River near Severn estuary *pop* 387,977 — **Bris·to·li·an** \bri-'stō-lē-ən, -'stòl-yən\ *n*

Bristol Bay arm of Bering Sea SW Alaska W of Alaska Peninsula

Bristol Channel channel bet. S Wales & SW England

Brit·ain \'bri-t°n\ 1 *or L* **Bri·tan·nia** \brə-'ta-nyə, -nē-ə\ the island of Great Britain 2 UNITED KINGDOM 3 COMMONWEALTH OF NATIONS

British America 1 *or* **British North America** CANADA 2 all Brit. possessions in & adjacent to N. & S. America

British Bechuanaland — see BECHUANALAND

British Cameroons former Brit. trust territory W equatorial Africa comprising two areas in the Cameroons bet. Nigeria & Cameroon ✱ Buea; divided 1961 bet. Nigeria (N section) & Cameroon (S section)

British Columbia province W Canada on Pacific coast ✱ Victoria *area* 359,279 *sq mi* (934,125 *sq km*), *pop* 3,282,061 — **British Co·lum·bi·an** \kə-'ləm-bē-ən\ *n or adj*

British Commonwealth COMMONWEALTH OF NATIONS — a former name

British East Africa 1 KENYA — a former name 2 the former Brit. dependencies in E Africa: Kenya, Uganda, Zanzibar, & Tanganyika

British Empire Great Britain & the Brit. dominions & dependencies — a former usage

British Guiana — see GUYANA

British Honduras — see BELIZE

British India the part of India formerly under direct Brit. administration — see INDIAN STATES

British Indian Ocean Territory Brit. colony in Indian Ocean comprising Chagos Archipelago & formerly Aldabra, Farquhar, & Desroches islands (returned to Seychelles 1976) *area* 23 *sq mi* (60 *sq km*)

British Isles island group W Europe comprising Great Britain, Ireland, & adjacent islands

British Malaya former dependencies of Great Britain on Malay Peninsula & in Malay Archipelago including Malaya (federation), Singapore, N. Borneo, Sarawak, & Brunei

British Solomon Islands former Brit. protectorate comprising the Solomons (except Bougainville, Buka, & adjacent small islands) & the Santa Cruz Islands ✱ Honiara (on Guadalcanal)

British Somaliland former Brit. protectorate E Africa bordering on Gulf of Aden ✱ Hargeisa; since 1960 part of Somalia

British Virgin Islands the E part of the Virgin Islands group; a Brit. possession ✱ Road Town (on Tortola Is.) *area* 58 *sq mi* (151 *sq km*), *pop* 14,746

British West Indies islands of the West Indies including Jamaica, the Bahamas, Caymans, Brit. Virgin Islands, Brit. Leeward & Windward Islands, Trinidad, & Tobago

Brit·ta·ny \'bri-t°n-ē\ *or F* **Bre·tagne** \brə-tán\ᵞ\ region & former province NW France SW of Normandy

Br·no \'bər-(,)nō\ *or G* **Brünn** \bruen, 'brün\ city E Czech Republic, chief city of Moravia *pop* 391,093

Broad \'bröd\ **1** river 220 *mi* (354 *km*) N.C. & S.C. — see SALUDA **2** river 70 *mi* (113 *km*) S S.C. flowing into the Atlantic

Broads \'brödz\ low-lying district E England in Norfolk (the **Norfolk Broads**) & Suffolk (the **Suffolk Broads**)

Brock·en \'bräk-kən\ mountain 3747 *ft* (1142 *m*) *cen* Germany near former E. Germany–W. Germany border; highest in Harz Mountains

Brock·ton \'bräk-tən\ city SE Mass. *pop* 92,788

Brock·ville \'bräk-,vil\ city Canada in SE Ont. *pop* 21,582

Bro·ken Ar·row \'brō-kən-'ar-ō\ city NE Okla. SE of Tulsa *pop* 58,043

Broken Hill **1** city SE Australia in W New South Wales *pop* 26,913 **2** — see KABWE

Bromberg — see BYDGOSZCZ

Brom·ley \'bräm-lē\ borough of SE Greater London, England *pop* 299,500

Bronx \'bränks\ *or* **The Bronx** borough of New York City on the mainland NE of Manhattan Is. *pop* 1,203,789

Brook·field \'brúk-,fēld\ city SE Wis. W of Milwaukee *pop* 35,184

Brook·line \'brúk-,līn\ town E Mass. W of Boston *pop* 54,718

Brook·lyn \'brúk-klən\ borough of New York City at SW end of Long Is. *pop* 2,300,664 — **Brook·lyn·ite** \-klə-,nīt\ *n*

Brooklyn Center village SE Minn. NW of Minneapolis *pop* 28,887

Brooklyn Park village E Minn. NW of Minneapolis *pop* 56,381

Brook Park \'brúk\ city NE Ohio *pop* 22,865

Brooks Range \'brúks\ mountain range N Alaska extending from Kotzebue Sound to Canadian border; highest peak Mt. Michelson 9239 *ft* (2816 *m*)

Broom·field \'brüm-,fēld, 'brùm-\ city N *cen* Colo. NNW of Denver *pop* 24,638

Bros·sard \brō-'sär(d)\ town Canada in S Que. *pop* 64,793

Browns·ville \'braùnz-,vil, -vəl\ city & port S Tex. *pop* 98,962

Bruce \'brüs\ peninsula SE Ontario, Canada, projecting bet. Lake Huron & Georgian Bay

Bruges \'brüzh, brüĒzh\ *or Flem* **Brug·ge** \'brœ-kə, 'brü-gə\ commune NW Belgium ✳ of W. Flanders *pop* 117,063

Bru·nei \brü-'nī, 'brü-,nī\ **1** independent sultanate & former Brit. protectorate NW Borneo ✳ Bandar Seri Begawan *area* 2226 *sq mi* (5788 *sq km*), *pop* 260,863 **2** — see BANDAR SERI BEGAWAN — **Bru·nei·an** \brü-'nī-ən\ *adj or n*

Bruns·wick \'brənz-(,)wik\ **1** town SW Maine *pop* 20,906 **2** city NE Ohio SSW of Cleveland *pop* 28,230 **3** *or G* **Braun·schweig** \'braùn-shvīk\ former state *cen* Germany ✳ Brunswick **4** *or G* **Braunschweig** city N *cen* Germany W of Berlin *pop* 261,141

Brus·sels \'brə-səlz\ *or F* **Bru·xelles** \brüĒ(k)-sel\ *or Flem* **Brus·sel** \'brüĒ-səl\ city ✳ of Belgium & of Brabant *pop* 136,424 — **Brus·xel·lois** \brüĒ-sel-wä *also* brüēk-\ *adj or n*

Bruttium — see CALABRIA

Bry·an \'brī-ən\ city E *cen* Tex. *pop* 55,002

Bryansk *or* **Briansk** \brē-'än(t)sk\ city Russia in Europe SW of Moscow *pop* 394,000

Bryce Canyon National Park \'brīs\ reservation S Utah NE of Zion National Park

Bu·bas·tis \byü-'bas-təs\ ancient city N Egypt near modern Zagazig

Bu·ca·ra·man·ga \,bü-kä-rə-'mäŋ-gə\ city N Colombia NNE of Bogotá *pop* 291,661

Bu·cha·rest \'bü-kə-,rest, 'byü-\ *or Romanian* **Bu·cu·res·ti** \,bü-kə-'resht, -'resh-tē\ city ✳ of Romania *pop* 2,036,894

Bu·chen·wald \'bü-kən-,wôld, -,vält\ village *cen* Germany NW of Weimar; site of Nazi concentration camp

Buck·ing·ham·shire \'bə-kiŋ-əm-,shir, -shər, *US also* -kiŋ-,ham-\ *or* **Buckingham** *or* **Bucks** \'bəks\ county SE *cen* England ✳ Aylesbury *area* 727 *sq mi* (1890 *sq km*), *pop* 571,600

Buck Island Reef National Monument \'bək\ reservation St. Croix, Virgin Islands; contains marine gardens

Bu·da·pest \'bü-də-,pest *also* 'bú-, 'byü-, -,pesht\ city ✳ of Hungary on the Danube *pop* 2,013,900

Buddh Ga·ya \,búd-gə-'yä\ village NE India in *cen* Bihar

Budweis — see CESKE BUDEJOVICE

Bue·na Park \'bwā-nə\ city Calif. W of Anaheim *pop* 68,784

Bue·na·ven·tu·ra \,bwe-nə-,ven-'túr-ə, ,bwā-, -'tyúr-\ city & port W Colombia on the Pacific *pop* 115,770

Bue·nos Ai·res \,bwā-nəs-'ar-ēz, *Sp* bwā-nōs-'ī-räs\ city & port ✳ of Argentina on Río de la Plata *pop* 2,908,001

Buenos Aires, Lake lake 80 *mi* (129 *km*) long S Argentina & S Chile

Buf·fa·lo \'bə-fə-,lō\ city & port W N.Y. on Lake Erie & the Niagara *pop* 328,123 — **Buf·fa·lo·ni·an** \,bə-fə-'lō-nē-ən\ *n*

Buffalo Grove city NE Ill. *pop* 36,427

Bug \'büg\ **1** river 450 *mi* (724 *km*) *cen* Poland rising in W Ukraine, & flowing into the Vistula **2** river 500 *mi* (805 *km*) SW Ukraine flowing SE to the Dnieper estuary

Bu·gan·da \bü-'gan-də, byü-\ region & former native kingdom E Africa in SE Uganda ✳ Kampala

Bu·jum·bu·ra \,bü-jəm-'bur-ə\ *or formerly* **Usum·bu·ra** \,ü-səm-\ city ✳ of Burundi on Lake Tanganyika *pop* 376,000

Bu·ka \'bü-kə\ island W Pacific in the Solomons N of Bougainville *pop* 33,770

Bu·ka·vu \bü-'kä-(,)vü\ *or formerly* **Cos·ter·mans·ville** \'käs-tər-mənz-,vil\ city E Zaire at S end of Lake Kivu *pop* 152,193

Bu·kha·ra \bü-'kär-ə, -'kar-, -'här-, -'har-\ *or* **Bo·kha·ra** \bō-\ **1** former emirate W Asia around city of Bukhara **2** city W Uzbekistan E of the Amu Darya *pop* 139,000 — **Bu·kha·ran** *or* **Bo·kha·ran** \-ən\ *adj or n*

Bu·ko·vi·na *or* **Bu·co·vi·na** \,bü-kə-'vē-nə\ region E *cen* Europe in foothills of E Carpathians; now in NE Romania & W Ukraine

Bu·la·wayo *or* **Bu·lu·wayo** \,bü-lə-'wä-(,)ō, -'wī-\ city SW Zimbabwe, chief town of Matabeleland *pop* 495,317

Bul·gar·ia \,bəl-'gar-ē-ə, búl-, -'ger-\ country SE Europe on Black Sea; a republic ✳ Sofia *area* 42,858 *sq mi* (111,431 *sq km*), *pop* 8,942,976

Bull Run \'bùl-'rən\ stream 20 *mi* (32 *km*) N Va. W of Washington, D.C., flowing into Occquan Creek (small tributary of the Potomac)

Bun·del·khand \'bùn-d''l-,kənd\ region N *cen* India containing headwaters of the Jumna; now chiefly in N Madhya Pradesh

Bundesrepublik Deutschland — see GERMANY

Bun·ker Hill \'bəŋ-kər\ height in Charlestown section of Boston, Mass.

Bur·bank \'bər-,baŋk\ **1** city SW Calif. *pop* 93,643 **2** city NE Ill. *pop* 27,600

Bur·gas \bùr-'gäs\ city & port SE Bulgaria *pop* 144,449

Bur·gen·land \'bər-gən-,land, 'búr-gən-,länt\ province E Austria SE of Vienna on Hungarian border ✳ Eisenstadt

Bur·gos \'bùr-,gōs\ **1** province N Spain *area* 5480 *sq mi* (14,248 *sq km*), *pop* 327,926 **2** city, its ✳ & once ✳ of Old Castile *pop* 152,545

Bur·gun·dy \'bər-gən-dē\ *or F* **Bour·gogne** \bùr-gôn'\ **1** region & with varying limits former kingdom, duchy, & province E France S of Champagne **2** former county France E of Burgundy province; later called **Franche–Com·té** \frän̄sh-kōⁿ-tä\— **Bur·gun·di·an** \(,)bər-'gən-dē-ən\ *adj or n*

Bur·ki·na Fa·so \bùr-'kē-nə-'fä-sō, bər-\ *or formerly* **Upper Vol·ta** \'vōl-tə, 'vôl-, 'väl-\ republic W Africa; until 1958 a French territory ✳ Ouagadougou *area* 121,892 *sq mi* (316,919 *sq km*), *pop* 7,967,019

Bur·lin·game \'bər-liŋ-,gäm\ city W Calif. *pop* 26,801

Bur·ling·ton \'bər-liŋ-tən\ **1** city SE Iowa *pop* 27,208 **2** town NE Mass. *pop* 23,302 **3** city N *cen* N.C. *pop* 39,498 **4** city NW Vt. *pop* 39,127 **5** city Canada in SE Ont. N of Hamilton *pop* 129,575

Burma — see MYANMAR

Bur·na·by \'bər-nə-bē\ municipality Canada in SW B.C. *pop* 158,858

Burn·ley \'bərn-lē\ borough NW England in SE Lancashire *pop* 69,864

Burns·ville \'bərnz-,vil\ village SE Minn. S of Minneapolis *pop* 51,288

Bur·rard Inlet \bə-'rärd\ inlet of Strait of Georgia W Canada in B.C.; city of Vancouver is situated on it

Bur·sa \bùr-'sä, 'bər-sə\ *or formerly* **Bru·sa** \brü-'sä, 'brü-sə\ city NW Turkey in Asia near Sea of Marmara *pop* 466,178

Bur·ton \'bər-t²n\ city SE Mich. SE of Flint *pop* 27,617

Bu·run·di \bù-'rün-dē, -'rùn-\ *or formerly* **Urun·di** \ù-'rün-\ country E *cen* Africa; a republic ✳ Bujumbura *area* 10,744 *sq mi* (27,934 *sq km*), *pop* 3,992,130 — see RUANDA-URUNDI — **Bu·run·di·an** \-dē-ən\ *adj or n*

Bury \'ber-ē\ borough NW England in Greater Manchester NNW of Manchester *pop* 67,529

Bur·yat Republic \bùr-'yät, ,bùr-ē-'ät\ autonomous republic S Russia in Asia adjacent to Mongolia & E of Lake Baikal ✳ Ulan-Ude *area* 127,020 *sq mi* (330,252 *sq km*), *pop* 812,000 — **Buryat** *n*

Bury Saint Ed·munds \,ber-ē-sänt-'ed-mən(d)z, -sənt-\ borough SE England in Suffolk *pop* 28,914

Bu·shire \bü-'shir\ city & port SW Iran *pop* 120,787

Butaritari — see MAKIN

Bute \'byüt\ **1** island SW Scotland W of Firth of Clyde **2** *or* **Buteshire** \-,shir, -shər\ former county SW Scotland comprising several islands in the Firth of Clyde ✳ Rothesay (on Bute)

Butte \'byüt\ city SW Mont. in plateau of Rockies *pop* 33,336

Bu·tung \'bü-,tùŋ\ island Indonesia off SE Sulawesi *area ab* 2000 *sq mi* (5200 *sq km*), *pop* 253,262

Bu·zau \bə-'zō, -'zəù\ city E Romania *pop* 145,423

Buz·zards Bay \'bə-zərdz\ inlet of the Atlantic SE Mass. W of Cape Cod

Byd·goszcz \'bid-,gósh(ch)\ *or G* **Brom·berg** \'bräm-,bərg, 'brōm-,berk\ city NW *cen* Poland NE of Poznan *pop* 380,385

Byelarus — see BELARUS

Byelgorod–Dnestrovski — see BELGOROD-DNESTROVSKIY

Byelorussia — see BELORUSSIA — **Byelorussian** *adj or n*

By·tom \'bē-,tóm, 'bi-\ *or G* **Beu·then** \'bói-t²n\ city SW Poland in Silesia *pop* 229,851

Byzantium — see ISTANBUL

Ca·ba·na·tuan \,kä-bə-nə-'twän\ city Philippines in S *cen* Luzon *pop* 138,298

Ca·bi·mas \kə-'bē-məs\ city NW Venezuela on NE coast of Lake Maracaibo *pop* 165,755

Ca·bin·da \kə-'bin-də\ territory W equatorial Africa on the Atlantic bet. Congo & Zaire; belongs to Angola ✳ Cabinda *area* 3000 *sq mi* (7800 *sq km*), *pop* 58,547

Cab·ot Strait \'ka-bət\ strait *ab* 70 *mi* (113 *km*) wide E Canada bet. SW Newfoundland & Cape Breton Is. connecting Gulf of Saint Lawrence with the Atlantic

Ca·bril·lo National Monument \kə-'brē-(,)yō\ historic site SW Calif. on San Diego Bay

Ca·ca·hua·mil·pa \,kä-kə-wə-'mil-pə\ caverns S Mexico in Guerrero NNE of Taxco

Cá·ce·res \'kä-sə-,räs\ **1** province W Spain in N Estremadura *area* 7667 *sq mi* (19,934 *sq km*), *pop* 380,020 **2** city, its ✳ *pop* 67,392

Cache la Pou·dre \,kash-lə-'pü-dər\ river 125 *mi* (201 *km*) N Colo. flowing into the S. Platte

Cad·do Lake \'ka-(,)dō\ lake 20 *mi* (32 *km*) long NW La. & NE Tex. draining to Red River

Cá·diz \kə-'diz; 'kä-dəz, 'kä-, 'ka-; *Sp* 'kä-(,)thēs\ **1** province SW Spain in Andalusia *area* 2834 *sq mi* (7368 *sq km*), *pop* 992,296 **2** *or anc* **Ga·dir** \'gä-dər\ *or* **Ga·des** \'gä-(,)dēz\ city & port, its ✳, on Bay of Cádiz NW of Gibraltar *pop* 156,711

Cadiz, Gulf of arm of the Atlantic SW Spain

Cae·li·an \'sē-lē-ən\ hill in Rome, Italy, one of seven on which the ancient city was built — see AVENTINE

Caen \kän̄\ city NW France in Normandy *pop* 116,987

Caerdydd — see CARDIFF

Caer·nar·von *or* **Caer·nar·fon** \kär-'när-vən, kə(r)-\ **1** *or* **Caer·nar·von·shire** \-,shir, -shər\ former county NW Wales **2** borough NW Wales ✳ of Gwynedd *pop* 9506

Cae·sa·rea \,sē-zə-'rē-ə; ,se-sə-, ,se-zə-\ **1** ancient seaport Palestine S of Haifa **2** *or* **Caesarea Mazaca** — see KAYSERI

Caesarea Phi·lip·pi \'fi-lə-,pī, fə-'li-,pī\ ancient city N Palestine SW of Mt. Hermon; site at modern village of Baniyas \,ba-nē-'yas\ in SW Syria

Caesena — see CESENA

\ə\ abut \'ə\ kitten, F table \ər\ further \a\ ash \ā\ ace \ä\ mop, mar \aù\ out \ch\ chin \e\ bet \ē\ easy \g\ go \i\ hit \ī\ ice \j\ job \ŋ\ sing \ō\ go \ò\ law \òi\ boy \th\ thin \t̲h̲\ the \ü\ loot \ù\ foot \y\ yet \zh\ vision \à, k̲, ⁿ, œ, œ̄, ᵫ, ᵫ̄, ᵊ\ *see* Guide to Pronunciation

Ca·ga·yan \ˌkä-gə-'yän\ *or* **Rio Gran·de de Cagayan** \ˌrē-ō-'grändē-dä-\ river 220 *mi* (354 *km*) Philippines in NE Luzon flowing N

Ca·glia·ri \'käl-yə-(ˌ)rē\ commune & port Italy ✱ of Sardinia *pop* 219,095

Ca·guas \'kä-(ˌ)gwäs\ city E *cen* Puerto Rico *pop* 133,447

Ca·ho·kia Mounds \kə-'hō-kē-ə\ group of prehistoric Indian mounds Ill. ENE of E. St. Louis

Ca·hors \kä-'(h)òr\ city SW France N of Toulouse *pop* 19,288

Caicos — *see* TURKS AND CAICOS

Cairn·gorm \'karn-ˌgòrm, 'kern-\ mountain 4084 *ft* (1245 *m*) in Cairngorm Mountains on boundary bet. Highlands and Grampian regions

Cairngorm Mountains mountain range of the Grampians NE *cen* Scotland; highest point Ben Macdhui 4296 *ft* (1309 *m*)

Cairns \'karnz, 'kernz\ city & port NE Australia in NE Queensland *pop* 54,862

Cai·ro \'kī-(ˌ)rō\ city N Egypt, its ✱ *pop* 5,074,016 — **Cai·rene** \kī-'rēn\ *adj or n*

Caith·ness \'käth-nis, ˌkäth-'nes\ *or* **Caith·ness–shire** \-nish-ˌshir, -shər; -'nesh-\ former county N Scotland ✱ Wick

Ca·ja·mar·ca \ˌkä-hə-'mär-kə\ city NW Peru *pop* 77,182

Ca·jon Pass \kə-'hōn\ pass 4301 *ft* (1303 *m*) S Calif. NW of San Bernardino bet. San Bernardino Mountains & San Gabriel Mountains

Cal·a·bar \ˌka-lə-ˌbär\ city & port SE Nigeria *pop* 122,800

Ca·la·bria \kə-'lä-brē-ə, -'lä-\ **1** district of ancient Italy comprising area forming heel of the Italian Peninsula; now the S part of Apulia **2** *or It* **Le Ca·la·brie** \ˌlä-kə-'lä-brē-ˌā\ *or anc* **Brut·ti·um** \'brü-tē-əm, 'brə-\ region S Italy occupying toe of the Italian Peninsula ✱ Catanzaro *area* 5823 *sq mi* (15,140 *sq km*), *pop* 2,152,539 — **Ca·la·bri·an** \kə-'lä-brē-ən, -'lä-\ *adj or n*

Ca·lah \'kā-lə\ *or* **Kal·hu** \'kal-(ˌ)hü\ ancient city ✱ of Assyria on the Tigris 20 *mi* (32 *km*) SE of modern Mosul, Iraq; site now called **Nimrud** \nim-'rüd\

Ca·lais \ka-'lā, 'ka-(ˌ)lā\ city & port N France on Strait of Dover *pop* 73,009

Calais, Pas de — *see* DOVER (Strait of)

Ca·la·mian \ˌka-lə-mē-'än\ islands W Philippines NE of Palawan Is.

Cal·ca·sieu \'kal-kə-ˌshü\ river 200 *mi* (322 *km*) SW La. flowing through **Calcasieu Lake** (*ab* 15 *mi or* 24 *km* long) & **Calcasieu Pass** (channel 5 *mi or* 8 *km* long) into Gulf of Mexico

Cal·cut·ta \kal-'kə-tə\ city & port E India on the Hooghly ✱ of W. Bengal *pop* 9,165,650 — **Cal·cut·tan** \-'kə-tᵊn\ *n*

Cal·e·don \'ka-lə-dən\ town Canada in SE Ont. *pop* 34,965

Cal·e·do·nia \ˌka-lə-'dō-nyə, -nē-ə\ — *see* SCOTLAND — **Cal·e·do·nian** \-nyən, -nē-ən\ *adj or n*

Caledonian Canal ship canal N Scotland connecting Loch Linnhe & Moray Firth & uniting Lochs Ness, Oich, Lochy, & Eil

Cal·ga·ry \'kal-gə-rē\ city Canada in SW Alta. *pop* 710,677 — **Cal·gar·i·an** \kal-'gar-ē-ən, -'ger-\ *n*

Ca·li \'kä-lē\ city W Colombia on the Cauca *pop* 820,809

Cal·i·cut \'ka-li-(ˌ)kət\ *or* **Ko·zhi·kode** \'kō-zhə-ˌkōd\ city & port SW India on Malabar coast in Kerala *pop* 546,060

Cal·i·for·nia \ˌka-lə-'fòr-nyə\ state SW U.S. ✱ Sacramento *area* 158,693 *sq mi* (412,602 *sq km*), *pop* 29,760,020 — **Cal·i·for·nian** \-nyən\ *adj or n* — **Cal·i·for·nio** \-nyō\ *n*

California, Gulf of arm of the Pacific NW Mexico bet. Baja California & states of Sonora & Sinaloa

Ca·llao \kə-'yä-(ˌ)ō, -'yaù\ city & port W Peru on Callao Bay W of Lima *pop* 260,581

Ca·loo·sa·hatch·ee \kə-ˌlü-sə-'ha-chē\ river 75 *mi* (121 *km*) S Fla. flowing W into Gulf of Mexico

Calpe — *see* GIBRALTAR (Rock of)

Cal·ta·nis·set·ta \ˌkäl-tə-ni-'se-tə, ˌkal-\ commune Italy in *cen* Sicily *pop* 62,588

Cal·u·met \'kal-yə-ˌmet, -mət\ industrial region NW Ind. & NE Ill. SE of & adjacent to Chicago; includes chiefly cities of E. Chicago, Gary, & Hammond, Ind., & Calumet City & Lansing, Ill.

Calumet City city NE Ill. S of Chicago *pop* 37,840

Cal·va·dos Reef \ˌkal-və-'dòs\ *or F* **Ro·chers du Calvados** \rō-ˌshädə-\ long reef of rocks NW France in English Channel at mouth of the Orne

Cal·va·ry \'kal-v(ə-)rē\ *or Heb* **Gol·go·tha** \'gäl-gə-thə, gäl-'gä-thə\ place outside ancient Jerusalem where Jesus was crucified

Cal·y·don \'ka-lə-ˌdän, -dᵊn\ ancient city *cen* Greece in S Aetolia near Gulf of Patras — **Cal·y·do·nian** \ˌka-lə-'dō-nyən, -nē-ən\ *adj or n*

Cam \'kam\ river 40 *mi* (64 *km*) E *cen* England in Cambridgeshire flowing into the Ouse

Ca·ma·güey \ˌka-mə-'gwā\ city E *cen* Cuba *pop* 261,831

Ca·margue \kə-'märg\ *or* **La Camargue** \ˌlä-\ marshy island S France in delta of the Rhône

Cam·a·ril·lo \ˌka-mə-'rē-(ˌ)ō\ city SW Calif. W of Los Angeles *pop* 52,303

Cam·bay \kam-'bā\ city W India in Gujarat W of Baroda *pop* 51,291

Cambay, Gulf of inlet of Arabian Sea in W India N of Bombay

Cam·ber·well \'kam-bər-ˌwel, -wəl\ **1** city SE Australia in S Victoria E of Melbourne *pop* 85,883 **2** former metropolitan borough S London, England, now part of Southwark

Cam·bo·dia \kam-'bō-dē-ə\ *or* **Kam·pu·chea** \ˌkam-pù-'chē-ə\ *or 1970–75* **Khmer Republic** \kə-'mer\ country SE Asia bordering on Gulf of Siam ✱ Phnom Penh *area* 69,866 *sq mi* (181,652 *sq km*), *pop* 7,492,000

Cam·brai *or formerly* **Cam·bray** \kam-'brā, käⁿ-\ city N France on the Scheldt *pop* 38,706

Cam·bria \'kam-brē-ə\ — *see* WALES

Cam·bri·an \'kam-brē-ə\ mountains *cen* Wales

Cam·bridge \'kām-brij\ **1** city E Mass. W of Boston *pop* 95,802 **2** city Canada in SE Ont. *pop* 92,772; includes former cities of Galt & Preston **3** *or ML* **Can·ta·brig·ia** \ˌkan-tə-'bri-j(ē-)ə\ city & borough E England ✱ of Cambridgeshire *pop* 90,440

Cam·bridge·shire \'kām-brij-ˌshir, -shər\ *or* **Cambridge** *or formerly* **Cambridgeshire and Isle of Ely** \'ē-lē\ county E England ✱ Cambridge *area* 1316 *sq mi* (3422 *sq km*), *pop* 540,300

Cam·den \'kam-dən\ **1** city & port SW N.J. on Delaware River opposite Philadelphia, Pa. *pop* 87,492 **2** borough of N Greater London, England *pop* 183,800

Cam·er·oon \ˌka-mə-'rün\ **1** *or* **Fa·ko** \'fä-(ˌ)kō\ massif 13,350 *ft* (4069 *m*) Cameroon (republic) NW of Buea **2** *or* **Cam·er·oun** \-'rün\ country W equatorial Africa in Cameroons region; a republic, formerly a trust territory under France ✱ Yaoundé *area* 183,080 *sq mi* (476,008 *sq km*), *pop* 10,446,000 — **Cam·er·oo·nian** \-'rü-nē-ən, -nyən\ *adj or n*

Cam·er·oons \ˌka-mə-'rünz\ region W Africa bordering on NE Gulf of Guinea formerly comprising Brit. & French Cameroons but now divided bet. Nigeria & Cameroon — **Cam·er·oo·nian** \-'rü-nē-ən, -nyən\ *adj or n*

Ca·mi·guin \ˌka-mə-'gēn\ **1** island N Philippines N of Luzon; site of Camiguin Volcano 2602 *ft* (793 *m*) **2** island S Philippines off N coast of Mindanao — *see* HIBOKHIBOK

Ca·mo·tes Sea \kə-'mō-ˌtäs\ sea S *cen* Philippines W of Leyte

Cam·pa·gna di Ro·ma \kam-ˌpä-nyə-dē-'rō-mə, -'pa-\ *or* **Roman Campagna** region *cen* Italy around Rome

Cam·pa·nia \kam-'pā-nyə, -nē-ə\ region S Italy bordering on Tyrrhenian Sea ✱ Naples *area* 5214 *sq mi* (13,556 *sq km*), *pop* 5,808,705 — **Cam·pa·nian** \-nyən, -nē-ən\ *adj or n*

Camp·bell \'kam-bel, 'ka-məl\ city W Calif. SW of San José *pop* 36,048

Cam·pe·che \kam-'pē-chē, käm-'pā-chä\ **1** state SE Mexico in W Yucatán Peninsula *area* 19,670 *sq mi* (51,142 *sq km*), *pop* 372,277 **2** city & port, its ✱, on Bay of Campeche *pop* 59,627

Campeche, Bay of the SW section of Gulf of Mexico

Cam·pi·na Gran·de \ˌkam-ˌpē-nə-'gran-də, -dē\ city E Brazil in E Paraíba *pop* 247,964

Cam·pi·nas \kam-'pē-nəs\ city SE Brazil in E São Paulo state *pop* 664,356

Cam·po·bel·lo \ˌkam-pə-'be-(ˌ)lō\ island Canada in SW N.B.

Cam·po·for·mi·do \ˌkam-(ˌ)pō-'fòr-mə-ˌdō\ *or formerly* **Cam·po For·mio** \-mē-ō\ village NE Italy SW of Udine

Cam·po Gran·de \ˌkam-(ˌ)pü-'gran-də, -dē\ city SW Brazil ✱ of Mato Grosso do Sul *pop* 291,807

Cam·pos \'kam-pəs\ city SE Brazil in Rio de Janeiro state on the Paraíba *pop* 349,036

Cam Ranh Bay \'kam-'ran\ inlet of S. China Sea SE Vietnam *ab* 180 *mi* (290 *km*) NE of Ho Chi Minh City

Ca·na \'kā-nə\ village in Galilee NE of Nazareth; now in Israel

Ca·naan \'kā-nən\ ancient region corresponding vaguely to later Palestine

Can·a·da \'ka-nə-də\ country N N. America including Newfoundland & Arctic islands N of mainland; a dominion of the Commonwealth of Nations ✱ Ottawa *area* 3,851,809 *sq mi* (10,014,703 *sq km*), *pop* 27,296,859

Ca·na·di·an \kə-'nā-dē-ən\ *or, above its junction with the N. Canadian,* **South Canadian** river 906 *mi* (1458 *km*) S *cen* U.S. flowing E from NE N. Mex. to Arkansas River in E Okla.

Canadian Shield *or* **Lau·ren·tian Shield** \lò-'ren(t)-shən\ plateau region E Canada & NE U.S. extending from Mackenzie River basin E to Davis Strait & S to S Que., NE Minn., N Wis., NW Mich., & NE N.Y. including the Adirondacks

Canal Zone *or* **Panama Canal Zone** strip of territory Panama; ceased to exist as a formal political entity Oct. 1, 1979, but remains under U.S. control through 1999 for administration of the Panama Canal

Can·an·dai·gua \ˌka-nən-'dā-gwə\ lake 15 *mi* (24 *km*) long W *cen* N.Y.; one of the Finger Lakes

Ca·nary Islands \kə-'ner-ē\ islands in the Atlantic off NW Africa belonging to Spain *area* 2897 *sq mi* (7298 *sq km*), *pop* 1,367,646 — *see* LAS PALMAS, SANTA CRUZ DE TENERIFE — **Ca·nar·i·an** \kə-'ner-ē-ən\ *adj or n*

Ca·nav·er·al, Cape \kə-'nav-rəl, -'na-və-\ *or 1963–1973 officially* **Cape Ken·ne·dy** \'ke-nə-dē\ cape E shore of Canaveral Peninsula; site of Air Force Missile Test Center & John F. Kennedy Space Center

Canaveral Peninsula peninsula E Fla. enclosing Indian River (lagoon)

Can·ber·ra \'kan-b(ə-)rə, -ˌber-ə\ city ✱ of Australia in Australian Capital Territory W of Sydney *pop* 196,538

Can·cún \kan-'kün\ resort SE Mexico on island off NE coast of Yucatán Peninsula

Can·dia \'kan-dē-ə\ **1** CRETE **2** — *see* IRÁKLION

Candia, Sea of — *see* CRETE (Sea of)

Ca·nea \kə-'nē-ə\ *or NGk* **Kha·niá** \kä-'nyä\ *or anc* **Cy·do·nia** \sī-'dōnē-ə, -nyə\ city & port Greece ✱ of Crete *pop* 50,077

Can·i·a·pis·kau \ˌka-nē-ə-'pis-(ˌ)kō\ river 575 *mi* (925 *km*) Canada in N Que. flowing N to unite with the Larch forming the Koksoak

Can·nae \'ka-(ˌ)nē\ ancient town SE Italy in Apulia WSW of modern Barletta

Can·na·nore \'ka-nə-ˌnōr, -ˌnòr\ **1** *or* **Ka·na·nur** \kə-nə-'nùr\ city SW India in Kerala NNW of Calicut *pop* 157,777 **2** — *see* LACCADIVE ISLANDS

Cannes \'kan\ commune & port SE France SW of Nice *pop* 70,226

Ca·no·pus \kə-'nō-pəs\ ancient city N Egypt E of Alexandria at modern Abukir — **Ca·no·pic** \kə-'nō-pik, -'nä-\ *adj*

Can·so, Cape \'kan(t)-(ˌ)sō\ cape Canada on NE N.S. mainland

Canso, Strait of narrow channel Canada separating Cape Breton Is. from N.S. mainland

Can·ta·bri·an Mountains \kan-'tā-brē-ən\ mountains N & NW Spain running E–W near coast of Bay of Biscay — *see* CERREDO

Cantabrigia — *see* CAMBRIDGE

Can·ter·bury \'kan-tə(r)-ˌber-ē, -b(ə-)rē\ **1** city SE Australia in E New South Wales, SW suburb of Sydney **2** city & county borough SE England in Kent *pop* 34,404 — **Can·ter·bu·ri·an** \ˌkan-tə(r)-'byùr-ēən\ *adj*

Can·ti·gny \käⁿ-ˌtē-'nyē\ village N France S of Amiens

Can·ton \'kan-tᵊn\ **1** city NE Ohio SSE of Akron *pop* 84,161 **2** — *see* GUANGZHOU

Canyon de Chelly National Monument \də-'shā\ reservation NE Ariz. containing cliff-dweller ruins

Can·yon·lands National Park \'kan-yən-ˌlan(d)z\ reservation SE Utah surrounding junction of Colorado & Green rivers

Cap d'An·tibes \ˌkap-dän-'tēb\ cape SE France SW of Antibes

Cap-de-la-Ma·de·leine \ˌkap-də-lä-ˌma-d'l-'än, -'en\ city Canada in S Que. on St. Lawrence River ENE of Trois-Rivières *pop* 33,716

Cape Breton — *see* BRETON (Cape)

Cape Bret·on Highlands National Park \kāp-'bret-t⁾n, kə-'bre-, -'bri-\ reservation Canada in NE N.S. near N end of Cape Breton Is.

Cape Breton Island island Canada in NE N.S. *area* 3970 *sq mi* (10,322 *sq km*)

Cape Cod — see COD (Cape)

Cape Cod Bay the S end of Massachusetts Bay W of Cape Cod

Cape Cor·al \'kȯr-əl, 'kär-\ city SW Fla. *pop* 74,991

Cape Fear \'fir\ **1** river 202 *mi* (325 *km*) *cen* & SE N.C. flowing SE into the Atlantic **2** — see FEAR (Cape)

Cape Gi·rar·deau \jə-'rär-(,)dō, jə-'rä-də\ city SE Mo. on Mississippi River *pop* 34,438

Cape Kru·sen·stern National Monument \'krü-zən-,stərn\ reservation NW Alaska on Chukchi Sea

Cape of Good Hope **1** — see GOOD HOPE (Cape of) **2** *or* **Cape Province** *or* **Kaap·land** \'käp-,länt\ *or earlier* **Cape Colony** former province S Republic of South Africa ✻ Cape Town *area* 278,465 *sq mi* (724,009 *sq km*)

Ca·per·na·um \kə-'pər-nē-əm\ city of ancient Palestine on NW shore of Sea of Galilee

Cape Sable — see SABLE (Cape)

Cape Sa·ble Island \'sā-bəl\ island 7 *mi* (11 *km*) long Canada off S coast of N.S.

Cape Town \'kāp-,taùn\ city & port, legislative ✻ of Republic of South Africa ✻ of Cape of Good Hope, on Table Bay *pop* 790,880 — **Cape·to·ni·an** \kāp-'tō-nē-ən\ *n*

Cape Verde — see VERDE (Cape)

Cape Verde \'vərd\ country E Atlantic comprising the Cape Verde Islands; until 1975 belonged to Portugal ✻ Praia *area* 1557 *sq mi* (4048 *sq km*), *pop* 303,000 — **Cape Verd·ean** \'vər-dē-ən\ *adj or n*

Cape Verde Islands islands in the Atlantic off W Africa

Cape York Peninsula \'yȯrk\ peninsula NE Australia in N Queensland having at its N tip **Cape York** (on Torres Strait)

Cap Hai·tien \kạ-pạ-'hā-shən\ *or* **F Cap–Ha·i·tien** \kà-pà-ē-syaⁿ, -ē-tyaⁿ\ city & port N Haiti *pop* 74,761

Cap·i·to·line \'ka-pə-t⁾l-,īn, *Brit often* kə-'pi-t⁾l-\ hill in Rome, Italy, one of seven on which the ancient city was built — see AVENTINE

Capitol Reef National Park reservation S *cen* Utah containing archaeological remains, petrified forests, & unusual erosion forms

Capodistria — see KOPER

Caporetto — see KOBARID

Cap·pa·do·cia \,ka-pə-'dō-sh(ē-)ə\ ancient district E Asia Minor chiefly in valley of the upper Kizil Irmak in modern Turkey ✻ Caesarea Mazaca — **Cap·pa·do·cian** \-sh(ē-)ən\ *adj or n*

Ca·pri \kä-'prē, kə-; 'kä-(,)prē, 'ka-\ *or anc* **Cap·re·ae** \'ka-prē-ē\ island Italy S Bay of Naples *area* 5 *sq mi* (13 *sq km*) — **Ca·pri·ote** \'ka-prē-,ōt, 'kä-, -prē-ət\ *n*

Capsa — see GAFSA

Cap·ua \'ka-pyə-wə\ commune S Italy on the Volturno N of Naples NW of site of ancient city of Capua

Cap·u·lin, Mount \'ka-pyə-lən, -pə-\ cinder cone 8215 *ft* (2504 *m*) NE N. Mex.; main feature of **Capulin Mountain National Monument**

Ca·ra·cas \kə-'rä-kəs, -'ra-\ city ✻ of Venezuela near Caribbean coast *pop* 1,822,465

Car·bon·dale \'kär-bən-,dāl\ city SW Ill. *pop* 27,033

Car·cas·sonne \,kär-kə-'sȯn, -'sön\ city S France *pop* 38,887

Car·che·mish \'kär-kə-,mish, kär-'kē-mish\ ruined city S Turkey on the Euphrates at Syrian border N of modern Jerablus, Syria

Cár·de·nas \'kär-d⁾n-,äs\ city & port N Cuba E of Matanzas *pop* 73,521

Car·diff \'kär-dəf\ *or W* **Caer–dydd** \kīr-'dēth\ borough & port ✻ of Wales & of S. Glamorgan *pop* 260,574

Car·di·gan \'kär-di-gən\ *or* **Car·di·gan·shire** \-,shir, -shər\ former county W Wales ✻ Aberystwyth

Cardigan Bay inlet of St. George's Channel on W coast of Wales

Ca·ren·tan \,kar-ən-'täⁿ\ town NW France at base of Cotentin Peninsula

Car·ia \'kar-ē-ə, 'ker-\ ancient region SW Asia Minor bordering on Aegean Sea ✻ Halicarnassus — **Car·i·an** \-ē-ən\ *adj or n*

Ca·rib·be·an Sea \,kar-ə-'bē-ən, kə-'ri-bē-\ arm of the Atlantic bounded on N & E by West Indies, on S by S. America, & on W by Central America

Car·ib·bees \'kar-ə-,bēz\ LESSER ANTILLES

Car·i·boo \'kar-ə-,bü\ mountains W Canada in E *cen* B.C. W of the Rocky Mountains; highest point *ab* 11,750 *ft* (3581 *m*)

Ca·rin·thia \kə-'rin(t)-thē-ə\ region *cen* Europe in E Alps; once a duchy, Austrian crown land 1849–1918, divided bet. Austria & Yugoslavia 1918 — **Ca·rin·thi·an** \-thē-ən\ *adj or n*

Car·lisle \kär-'lī(ə)l, kər-, 'kär-\ city & borough NW England ✻ of Cumbria *pop* 70,930

Car·low \'kär-,lō\ **1** county SE Ireland in Leinster *area* 346 *sq mi* (900 *sq km*), *pop* 40,946 **2** urban district, its ✻ *pop* 11,509

Carls·bad \'kär(-ə)lz-,bad\ **1** caverns SE N. Mex. in **Carlsbad Caverns National Park** **2** city SW Calif. NNW of San Diego *pop* 63,126 **3** city SE N. Mex. on the Pecos *pop* 24,952

Carmana, Carmania — see KERMAN

Car·mar·then \kär-'mär-thən, kə(r)-\ **1** *or* **Car·mar·then·shire** \-,shir, -shər\ former county S Wales ✻ Carmarthen **2** borough & port S Wales ✻ of Dyfed *pop* 12,302

Car·mel **1** \kär-'mel\ city W Calif. S of Monterey Bay *pop* 4239 **2** \'kär-məl\ city *cen* Ind. N of Indianapolis *pop* 25,380

Car·mel, Mount \'kär-məl\ mountain ridge NW Israel; highest point 1791 *ft* (546 *m*)

Car·men de Pat·a·go·nes \'kär-mən-dä-,pa-tə-'gō-nəs\ town Argentina on the Negro River opposite Viedma *pop* 13,981

Car·nat·ic \kär-'na-tik\ region SE India bet. Eastern Ghats & Coromandel coast now in Andhra Pradesh & Karnataka

Car·nic Alps \'kär-nik\ mountain range E Alps bet. Austria & Italy

Car·nio·la \,kär-nē-'ō-lə, kär-'nyō-\ region S & W Slovenia NE of Istrian Peninsula — **Car·nio·lan** \-lən\ *adj*

Car·o·li·na \,kar-ə-'lī-nə\ English colony 1663–1729 on E coast of N. America divided 1729 into N.C. & S.C. (the **Car·o·li·nas** \-nəz\) — **Car·o·lin·i·an** \,kar-ə-'li-nē-ən, -nyən\ *n*

Ca·ro·li·na \,kär-ə-'lē-nə\ city NE *cen* Puerto Rico *pop* 177,806

Car·o·line Islands \'kar-ə-,līn, -lən\ islands W Pacific Ocean comprising Belau & the Federated States of Micronesia; formerly part of Trust Territory of the Pacific Islands

Car·ol Stream \'kar-əl\ village NE Ill. W of Chicago *pop* 31,716

Ca·ro·ní \,kär-ə-'nē\ river 373 *mi* (600 *km*) E Venezuela flowing N into the Orinoco

Car·pa·thi·an Mountains \kär-'pā-thē-ən\ mountain system E *cen* Europe along boundary bet. Slovakia & Poland & in N & *cen* Romania — see GERLACHOVKA, TATRY, TRANSYLVANIAN ALPS

Carpathian Ruthenia — see RUTHENIA

Car·pen·tar·ia, Gulf of \,kär-pən-'ter-ē-ə, -'tar-\ inlet of Arafura Sea on N coast of Australia

Car·pen·ters·ville \'kär-pən-tərz-,vil\ village NE Ill. NW of Chicago *pop* 23,049

Car·qui·nez Strait \kär-'kē-nəs\ strait 8 *mi* (13 *km*) long Calif. joining San Pablo & Suisun bays

Car·ran·tuo·hill \,kar-ən-'tü-əl\ mountain 3414 *ft* (1041 *m*) SW Ireland in County Kerry; highest in Macgillicuddy's Reeks & in Ireland

Car·ra·ra \kə-'rär-ə\ commune N Italy ESE of La Spezia *pop* 68,528

Car·rhae \'kar-(,)ē\ ancient city N Mesopotamia SSE of modern Urfa

Car·rick·fer·gus \,kar-ik-'fər-gəs\ district E Northern Ireland, established 1974 *area* 34 *sq mi* (88 *sq km*), *pop* 28,458

Car·rick on Shan·non \'kar-ik-òn-'sha-nən, -än-\ town N *cen* Ireland ✻ of County Leitrim *pop* 1621

Car·roll·ton \'kar-əl-tən, -t⁾n\ city N Tex. *pop* 82,169

Car·shal·ton \kär-'shȯl-t⁾n, kər-\ former urban district S England in Surrey, now part of Sutton

Carso — see KARST

Car·son \'kär-s⁾n\ **1** river 125 *mi* (201 *km*) W Nev. flowing NE into Carson Lake **2** city SW Calif. SE of Los Angeles *pop* 83,995

Carson City city ✻ of Nev. E of Lake Tahoe *pop* 40,443

Carson Sink intermittent lake W Nev. S of Humboldt Lake

Carstensz, Mount — see DJAJA (Mount)

Car·ta·ge·na \,kär-tə-'gä-nə, -'hä-, -'jē-\ **1** city & port NW Colombia *pop* 292,512 **2** city & port SE Spain on the Mediterranean *pop* 167,936

Car·ta·go \kär-'tä-(,)gō\ city *cen* Costa Rica *pop* 21,753

Car·ter·et \,kär-tə-'ret\ borough NE N.J. S of Elizabeth *pop* 19,025

Car·thage \'kär-thij\ *or anc* **Car·tha·go** \kär-'tä-(,)gō, -'thä-\ ancient city & state N Africa on coast NE of modern Tunis — **Car·tha·gin·ian** \,kär-thə-'ji-nyən, -nē-ən\ *adj or n*

Cary \'kar-ē, 'ker-ē\ city E *cen* N.C. *pop* 43,858

Ca·sa·blan·ca \,ka-sə-'blaŋ-kə, ,käs-ə-'bläŋ-, -zə-\ *or Ar* **Dar el Bei·da** \,där-,el-bā-'dä\ city & port N Morocco on the Atlantic *pop* 2,139,204

Casa Gran·de Ruins National Monument \,ka-sə-'gran-dē\ reservation S Ariz. SE of Phoenix; prehistoric ruins

Cas·cade Range \(,)kas-'kād\ mountain range W U.S., N continuation of the Sierra Nevada extending N from Lassen Peak across Oreg. & Wash. — see COAST MOUNTAINS, COAST RANGES, RAINIER (Mount)

Cas·co Bay \'kas-(,)kō\ inlet of the Atlantic S Maine

Ca·ser·ta \kə-'zer-tə, -'zər-\ commune S Italy *pop* 67,769

Cash·el \'ka-shəl\ urban district S Ireland in *cen* Tipperary at base of **Rock of Cashel** (hill with ruins of cathedral & castle)

Cashmere — see KASHMIR

Ca·si·quia·re \,kä-si-'kyär-ē\ river 125 *mi* (201 *km*) S Venezuela connecting the upper course of Negro River with Orinoco River

Cas·per \'kas-pər\ city *cen* Wyo. on N. Platte River *pop* 46,742

Cas·pi·an Gates \'kas-pē-ən\ pass on W shore of Caspian Sea near Derbent

Caspian Sea sea (salt lake) bet. Europe & Asia; *ab* 85 *ft* (30 *m*) below sea level *area* 169,381 *sq mi* (440,391 *sq km*)

Cas·si·no \kä-'sē-(,)nō\ commune *cen* Italy ESE of Frosinone; site of Monte Cassino monastery *pop* 34,565

Cas·tel Gan·dol·fo \(,)kä-,stel-gän-'dȯl-(,)fō\ commune *cen* Italy on Lake Albano SE of Rome

Cas·te·llón *or* **Castellón de la Pla·na** \,kas-tə(l)-'yȯn-,de-lə-'plä-nə\ **1** province E Spain *area* 2495 *sq mi* (6487 *sq km*), *pop* 430,171 **2** city & port, its ✻, on the Mediterranean NE of Valencia *pop* 124,487

Castellorizo *or* **Castelrosso** — see KASTELLORIZON

Cas·tile \ka-'stē(ə)l\ *or Sp* **Cas·ti·lla** \kä-'stē-lᵊ, -'stē-yä\ region & ancient kingdom *cen* & N Spain divided by the Sierra de Guadarrama into regions & old provinces of **Old Castile** *or Sp* **Castilla la Vie·ja** \lä-'vyä-hä\ (to the N, ✻ Burgos) & **New Castile** *or Sp* **Castilla la Nue·va** \lä-'nwä-vä\ (to the S, ✻ Toledo)

Cas·ti·llo de San Mar·cos National Monument \ka-'stē-yō-də-san-'mär-(,)kōs\ historic site NE Fla.; contains a Spanish fort

Cas·tle·bar \,ka-stəl-'bär\ urban district NW Ireland ✻ of Mayo *pop* 6349

Castle Clin·ton National Monument \'klin-t⁾n\ historic site Manhattan Is. SE N.Y.; contains a fort

Cas·tle·reagh \'ka-səl-(,)rā\ district E Northern Ireland, established 1974 *area* 33 *sq mi* (86 *sq km*), *pop* 60,757

Castres \'kästr⁾\ city S France E of Toulouse *pop* 41,037

Cas·tries \'kas-,trēz, -,trēs\ city & port ✻ of St. Lucia *administrative area pop* 56,147

Ca·strop–Raux·el *or* **Ka·strop–Rauxel** \,käs-,tròp-'raùk-səl\ city W Germany SSW of Münster *pop* 78,877

Ça·tal·ca \,chä-t⁾l-'jä\ city Turkey in Europe W of Istanbul

Cat·a·li·na \,ka-t⁾l-'ē-nə\ *or* **San·ta Catalina** \'san-tə\ island SW Calif. in Channel Islands *area* 70 *sq mi* (182 *sq km*)

Cat·a·lo·nia \,ka-t⁾l-'ō-nyə, -nē-ə\ *or Sp* **Ca·ta·lu·ña** \,kä-t⁾l-'ü-nyə\ autonomous region NE Spain bordering on France & the Mediterranean; chief city Barcelona *area* 12,431 *sq mi* (32,321 *sq km*) — **Cat·a·lo·nian** \-'ō-nyən, -nē-ən\ *adj or n*

Ca·ta·mar·ca \,kä-tə-'mär-kə\ city NW Argentina *pop* 64,410

Ca·ta·nia \kə-'tä-nyə, -'tä-\ *or anc* **Cat·a·na** \'ka-tə-nə\ commune Italy in E Sicily on E coast on Gulf of Catania *pop* 366,226

\ə\ abut \ᵊ\ kitten, F table \ər\ further \a\ ash \ā\ ace \ä\ mop, mar \aù\ out \ch\ chin \e\ bet \ē\ easy \g\ go \i\ hit \ī\ ice \j\ job \ŋ\ sing \ō\ go \ȯ\ law \ȯi\ boy \th\ thin \th\ the \ü\ loot \ù\ foot \y\ yet \zh\ vision \à, k̭, ⁿ, œ, œ̄, ᵫ, ᵫ̄, ᵊ\ *see* Guide to Pronunciation

Ca·tan·za·ro \ˌkä-ˌtän(d)-'zär-(ˌ)ō\ city S Italy ✱ of Calabria *pop* 103,521

Ca·taw·ba \kə-'tȯ-bə\ river 250 *mi* (402 *km*) flowing S from W N.C. into S.C. — see WATEREE

Ca·thay \ka-'thā\ CHINA — an old name

Cathedral City city SW Calif. *pop* 30,085

Catherine, Mount — see KATHERINA (Gebel)

Ca·toc·tin Mountain \kə-'täk-tən\ mountain ridge NW Md. & N Va. in Blue Ridge Mountains

Cats·kill Mountains \'kat-ˌskil\ mountains SE N.Y. in the Appalachian system W of Hudson River — see SLIDE MOUNTAIN

Cattaro — see KOTOR

Cau·ca \'kaů-kə\ river 600 *mi* (966 *km*) W Colombia flowing N into the Magdalena

Cau·ca·sus \'kȯ-kə-səs\ *or* **Cau·ca·sia** \kȯ-'kā-zhə, -shə\ region SE Europe bet. the Black & Caspian seas; divided by Caucasus Mountains into **Cis·cau·ca·sia** \ˌsis-\ (to the N) & **Trans·cau·ca·sia** \ˌtran(t)s-\ (to the S)

Caucasus Indicus — see HINDU KUSH

Caucacus Mountains mountain system SE Europe in Russia, Georgia, Azerbaijan, and Armenia

Cau·dine Forks \'kȯ-ˌdīn, -ˌdēn\ two mountain passes S Italy in the Apennines bet. Benevento & Capua

Caul·field \'kȯl-ˌfēld\ city SE Australia in S Victoria SE of Melbourne; part of Greater Melbourne *pop* 69,922

Causses \'kōs\ limestone region S cen France on S border of Massif Central

Cau·ve·ry \'kȯ-və-rē\ *or* **Ka·ve·ri** \'kä-və-rē\ river 475 *mi* (764 *km*) S India flowing E & entering Bay of Bengal in a wide delta

Cauvery Falls waterfall 300 *ft* (91 *m*) India in the Cauvery on Karnataka-Tamil Nadu boundary

Cav·an \'ka-vən\ **1** county NE Ireland (republic) in Ulster *area* 730 *sq mi* (1898 *sq km*), *pop* 52,756 **2** urban district, its ✱ *pop* 3381

Ca·vi·te \kə-'vē-tē\ city Philippines in Luzon on **Cavite Peninsula** in Manila Bay SW of Manila *pop* 87,666

Ca·xi·as \kə-'shē-əs\ **1** town NE Brazil in Maranhão WNW of Teresina *pop* 125,771 **2** — see DUQUE DE CAXIAS **3** *or* **Caxias do Sul** \də-'sül\ city S Brazil in Rio Grande do Sul *pop* 220,725

Cay·enne \kī-'en, kā-\ city & port ✱ of French Guiana on island in Cayenne River near the coast *pop* 38,135

Cayes \'kī\ *or* **Aux Cayes** \ō-'kī\ city & port SW Haiti *pop* 105,383

Ca·yey \kä-'yā\ city SE cen Puerto Rico *pop* 46,553

Cay·man Islands \(ˌ)kā-'man, *attributively* 'kā-mən\ islands W. Indies NW of Jamaica; a Brit. colony ✱ George Town (on **Grand Cayman**, chief island) *area* 93 *sq mi* (242 *sq km*), *pop* 25,355 — **Cay·man·i·an** \kā-'ma-nē-ən\ *adj or n*

Ca·yu·ga \ˌsā-ə-'rä\ lake 40 *mi* (64 *km*) long W cen N.Y.; one of the Finger Lakes

Ce·a·rá \ˌsā-ə-'rä\ state NE Brazil bordering on the Atlantic ✱ Fortaleza *area* 57,371 *sq mi* (149,165 *sq km*), *pop* 5,380,432

Ce·bu \sā-'bü\ **1** island E cen Philippines, one of the Visayans *area* 1707 *sq mi* (4438 *sq km*) *pop* 2,091,602 **2** city on E Cebu Is. *pop* 490,281

Cechy — see BOHEMIA

Ce·dar \'sē-dər\ river 329 *mi* (529 *km*) SE Minn. & E Iowa flowing SE into the Iowa

Cedar Breaks National Monument reservation SW Utah NE of Zion National Park containing unusual erosion forms

Cedar Falls city NE Iowa NW of Waterloo *pop* 34,298

Cedar Hill town NE Tex. SW of Dallas *pop* 19,976

Cedar Rapids city E Iowa on the Cedar *pop* 108,751

Ce·le·bes \'se-lə-ˌbēz, sə-'lē-bēz\ — see SULAWESI

Celebes Sea arm of W Pacific enclosed on N by Mindanao & the Sulu Archipelago, on S by Sulawesi, & on W by Borneo — **Cel·e·be·sian** \ˌse-lə-'bē-zhən\ *adj*

Celestial Empire the former Chinese Empire

Cel·le \'(t)se-lə\ city N cen Germany NE of Hannover *pop* 72,820

Celt·ic Sea \'kel-tik, 'sel-\ inlet of the Atlantic in British Isles SE of Ireland, SW of Wales, & W of Cornwall

Ce·nis, Mont \ˌmōⁿ-sə-'nē\ **1** mountain pass 6831 *ft* (2082 *m*) bet. France & Italy over Mont Cenis massif (11,792 *ft or* 3573 *m*) in Graian Alps **2** *or* **Fré·jus** \frā-'zhüs, -'zhūes\ tunnel 8.5 *mi* (13.6 *km*) long piercing the Fréjus massif SW of Mont Cenis

Cen·ter·ville \'sen-tər-ˌvil, -vəl\ city SW Ohio *pop* 21,082

Central region cen Scotland, established 1975 ✱ Stirling *area* 972 *sq mi* (2527 *sq km*), *pop* 373,078

Central African Republic *or* 1976–79 **Central African Empire** *or earlier* **Ubangi–Shari** republic N cen Africa ✱ Bangui *area* 240,376 *sq mi* (624,978 *sq km*), *pop* 2,740,000

Central America **1** the narrow S portion of N. America connecting with S. America & extending from the Isthmus of Tehuantepec to the Isthmus of Panama **2** the republics of Guatemala, El Salvador, Honduras, Nicaragua, & Costa Rica & often also Panama & Belize

Central Europe the countries of cen Europe — usu. considered as including the countries extending from Baltic Sea on the N to Alps on the S and from Russia, Lithuania, Belarus, & Ukraine on the E to North Sea & France on the W

Central India former group of 89 Indian states N cen India ✱ Indore; area now chiefly in W & N Madhya Pradesh

Central Karroo — see KARROO

Central Provinces and Be·rar \bā-'rär, bə-\ former province of India reorganized 1950 & renamed Madhya Pradesh

Central Valley valley cen Calif. comprising the valleys of the Sacramento & San Joaquin rivers

Ceos — see KEOS

Ceph·a·lo·nia \ˌse-fə-'lō-nyə, -nē-ə\ *or NGk* **Ke·fal·li·nía** \ˌke-fə-lə-'nē-ə\ island W Greece in the Ionians *area* 277 *sq mi* (720 *sq km*)

Ce·ram *or* **Se·ram** \'sā-ˌräm\ island E Indonesia in cen Moluccas *area* 6621 *sq mi* (17,215 *sq km*), *pop* 96,797

Ce·res \'sir-(ˌ)ēz\ city cen Calif. SE of Modesto *pop* 26,314

Cerigo — see KÍTHIRA

Cernauti — see CHERNOVTSY

Cer·re·do \sə-'rä-(ˌ)dō\ *or* **Tor·re de Cerredo** \'tȯr-ē-də-, 'tȯr-ā-\ mountain 8787 *ft* (2678 *m*) N Spain SW of Santander; highest in the Cantabrians

Cer·ri·tos \sə-'rē-təs\ city SW Calif. NE of Long Beach *pop* 53,240

Cerro Bolívar — see BOLÍVAR (Cerro)

Cer·ro de Pas·co \ˌser-ō-də-'pas-(ˌ)kō\ **1** mountain 15,100 *ft* (4602 *m*) cen Peru NE of Lima **2** city near the mountain *pop* 71,558

Cerro de Pun·ta \də-'pün-tə\ mountain 4390 *ft* (1338 *m*), cen Puerto Rico in Cordillera Central; highest on the island

Cerro Gor·do \'gȯr-(ˌ)dō\ mountain pass E Mexico bet. Veracruz & Jalapa

Cervin, Mont — see MATTERHORN

Ce·se·na \chā-'zā-nə\ *or anc* **Cae·se·na** \sə-'zē-nə\ commune N Italy in Emilia-Romagna SE of Forlì *pop* 89,606

Ces·ke Bu·de·jo·vi·ce \'ches-kə-'bü-də-ˌyȯ-vət-sə\ *or G* **Bud·weis** \'bůt-ˌvīs\ city Czech Republic in S Bohemia *pop* 98,761

Ce·ti·nje \'(t)se-t*ⁿ*-ˌyä\ town S Yugoslavia SE of Kotor near coast; formerly ✱ of Montenegro *pop* 12,089

Cette — see SÈTE

Ceu·ta \'sā-ˌü-tə, 'seů-(ˌ)tä\ city & port N Morocco opposite Gibraltar; a Spanish presidio *pop* 67,187

Cé·vennes \sā-'ven\ mountain range S France W of the Rhône at E edge of Massif Central — see MÉZENC

Cey·lon \si-'län, sā-\ *or* **Lan·ka** \'läŋ-kə, 'laŋ-\ **1** *or Ar* **Ser·en·dib** \'ser-ən-ˌdib, -ˌdip\ *or L & Gk* **Ta·prob·a·ne** \tə-'prä-bə-(ˌ)nē\ island 270 *mi* (434 *km*) long & 140 *mi* (225 *km*) wide in Indian Ocean off S India **2** — see SRI LANKA — **Cey·lon·ese** \ˌsā-lə-'nēz, ˌsē-, ˌse-, -'nēs\ *adj or n*

Cha·co \'chä-(ˌ)kō\ *or* **Gran Chaco** \'grän\ region S cen S. America drained by the Paraguay & its chief W tributaries the Pilcomayo & Bermejo; divided bet. Argentina, Bolivia, & Paraguay

Chad *or F* **Tchad** \'chad\ country N cen Africa ✱ N'Djamena; a republic; until 1959 a territory of French Equatorial Africa *area* 495,752 *sq mi* (1,288,955 *sq km*), *pop* 4,681,000 — **Chad·ian** \'cha-dē-ən\ *adj or n*

Chad, Lake shallow lake N cen Africa at junction of boundaries of Chad, Niger, & Nigeria

Chae·ro·nea \ˌker-ə-'nē-ə, ˌkir-\ *or* **Chae·ro·neia** \-'nī-ə\ ancient city E cen Greece in N Boeotia SE of Mt. Parnassus

Cha·gos Archipelago \'chä-gəs\ archipelago cen Indian Ocean S of Maldives; comprises Brit. Indian Ocean Territory — see DIEGO GARCIA

Cha·gres \'chä-grəs, 'cha-\ river Panama flowing through Gatun Lake to the Caribbean

Cha·gua·ra·mas \ˌchä-gwə-'rä-məs\ district NW Trinidad W of Port of Spain on **Chaguaramas Bay** (inlet of Gulf of Paria)

Cha·har \'chä-'här\ former province NE China in E Inner Mongolia ✱ Kalgan

Chalcedon — see KADIKOY

Chal·cid·i·ce \kal-'si-də-(ˌ)sē\ *or NGk* **Khal·ki·di·kí** \ˌkäl-kē-thē-'kē\ peninsula NE Greece in E Macedonia projecting SE into N Aegean Sea; terminates in three peninsulas: Kassandra (ancient Pallene), Sithonia, & Acte — see ACTE

Chalcis — see KHALKÍS — **Chal·cid·i·an** \kal-'si-dē-ən\ *adj or n*

Chal·dea *or* **Chal·daea** \kal-'dē-ə\ ancient region SW Asia on Euphrates River & Persian Gulf

Cha·leur Bay \shə-'lůr, -'lȯr\ inlet of Gulf of St. Lawrence SE Canada bet. N N.B. & Gaspé Peninsula, Que.

Cha·lon \sha-'lōⁿ\ *or* **Chalon–sur–Saône** \-ˌsůr-'sōn\ city E cen France N of Mâcon *pop* 55,495

Châ·lons \shä-'lōⁿ\ *or* **Châlons–sur–Marne** \-ˌsůr-'märn\ commune NE France on the Marne *pop* 50,870

Cham·bal \'chəm-bal\ river 650 *mi* (1046 *km*) cen India flowing from Vindhya Mountains E into the Jumna

Cham·bé·ry \ˌshän-bā-'rē\ city E France E of Lyons *pop* 52,286

Cham·bord \shäⁿ-'bȯr\ village N cen France NE of Blois *pop* 166

Cha·mi·zal \ˌsha-mə-'zäl, ˌchä-mi-'säl\ tract of land 630 *acres* (252 *hectares*) on N bank of the Rio Grande formerly in El Paso, Tex.; ceded to Mexico 1963 — see CORDOVA ISLAND

Cha·mo·nix \ˌsha-mə-'nē\ **1** valley SE France NW of Mont Blanc **2** *or* **Chamonix–Mont–Blanc** \-(ˌ)mōⁿ-'bläⁿ\ town SE France in Chamonix valley *pop* 5907

Cham·pagne \sham-'pān\ region & former province NE France W of Lorraine & N of Burgundy ✱ Troyes

Cham·paign \sham-'pān\ city E cen Ill. *pop* 63,502

Cham·pi·gny–sur–Marne \ˌshäⁿ-(ˌ)pē-'nyē-ˌsůr-'märn\ commune N France, SSE suburb of Paris *pop* 80,189

Cham·plain, Lake \sham-'plān\ lake 125 *mi* (201 *km*) long bet. N.Y. & Vt. extending N into Que. *area* 600 *sq mi* (1500 *sq km*)

Chan–chiang — see ZHENJIANG

Chan·der·na·gore \ˌchən-dər-nə-'gȯr, -'gȯr\ *or* **Chan·dan·na·gar** \ˌchən-də-'nə-gər\ *or* **Chan·dar·na·gar** \ˌdər-'nə-gər\ city E India in W. Bengal N of Calcutta; before 1950 part of French India *pop* 421,256

Chan·di·garh \'chən-dē-gər\ city N India N of Delhi; a union territory administered by the national government; ✱ of Punjabi Suba & of Haryana; founded 1953, *pop* 450,061

Chan·dler \'chan(d)-lər\ city SW cen Ariz. *pop* 90,533

Chan·dra·pur \ˌchən-drə-'půr\ *or formerly* **Chan·da** \'chən-də\ town cen India in E Maharashtra *pop* 115,352; ✱ of anc. Gond dynasty

Chang \'chäŋ\ *or* **Yang·tze** \'yaŋ-ˌsē, 'yaŋ(k)t-'sē\ river 3100 *mi* (4989 *km*) cen China flowing from Kunlun Mountains in SW Qinghai E into E. China Sea

Changan — see XI'AN

Ch'ang–chia–k'ou — see ZHANGJIAKOU

Chang–chou — see ZHANGZHOU

Chang·chun \'chäŋ-'chůn\ city NE China ✱ of Jilin *pop* 975,000

Chang·de *or* **Chang·te** \'chäŋ-'də\ city SE cen China in N Hunan on the Yuan *pop* 120,000

Chang·hua \'chäŋ-'hwä, -'wä\ city China in W Taiwan *pop* 58,227

Chang·sha \'chäŋ-'shä\ city SE cen China ✱ of Hunan on the Xiang *pop* 975,000

Chang·zhou *or* **Ch'ang–chou** \'chäŋ-'jō\ *or* **Chang–chow** *same or* 'chaŋ-'chaů\ *or formerly* **Wu–tsin** \'wüd-'zin\ city E China in S Jiangsu *pop* 300,000

Channel Islands **1** *or* **Santa Barbara Islands** Calif. in the Pacific off SW coast — see CATALINA, SAN CLEMENTE ISLAND, SANTA CRUZ, SANTA ROSA ISLAND **2** islands in English Channel; a possession of Brit. Crown *area* 75 *sq mi* (195 *sq km*), *pop* 129,000 — see ALDERNEY, GUERNSEY, JERSEY, SARK

Channel Islands National Park reserve SW Calif. in Channel Islands including areas on Anacapa Islands (E of Santa Cruz Is.) & Santa Barbara Is. (W of Santa Catalina Is.)

Chan·til·ly \shär-tē-'yē, shan-'ti-lē\ town N France NNE of Paris

Ch'ao–an \'chaù-'än\ *or* **Chao·chow** \'chaù-'jō\ city E China in NE Guangdong on Han River *pop* 101,000

Chao Phra·ya \chaù-'prī-ə, prä-'yä\ *or* **Me Nam** \mä-'näm\ river 160 *mi* (257 *km*) W *cen* Thailand formed by confluence of Nan & Ping rivers & flowing S into Gulf of Siam

Cha·pa·la \chə-'pä-lə\ lake 50 *mi* (80 *km*) long W *cen* Mexico in Jalisco & Michoacán SE of Guadalajara

Chapel Hill town N N.C. SW of Durham *pop* 38,719

Cha·rente \shə-'ränt\ river 225 *mi* (362 *km*) W France flowing W into Bay of Biscay

Cha·ri *or* **Sha·ri** \'shär-ē\ river 1400 *mi* (2253 *km*) N *cen* Africa in Chad flowing NW into Lake Chad

Char·i·ton \'shar-ə-t°n\ river 280 *mi* (451 *km*) S Iowa & N Mo. flowing S into the Missouri

Charle·roi \'shär-lə-ˌròi, -lər-ˌwä\ city SW Belgium in Hainaut *pop* 206,214

Charles \'chär(-ə)lz\ river 47 *mi* (76 *km*) Mass. flowing into Boston harbor

Charles, Cape cape E Va. N of entrance to Chesapeake Bay

Charles·bourg \shärl-'bùr, 'chär(-ə)lz-ˌbòrg\ city Canada in SE Que. NE of Quebec city *pop* 70,788

Charles·ton \'chär(-ə)l-stən\ **1** city E *cen* Ill. *pop* 20,398 **2** city & port SE S.C. *pop* 80,414 **3** city * W. Va. on the Kanawha *pop* 57,287 — **Charles·to·nian** \chär(-ə)l-'stō-nē-ən, -nyən\ *n*

Charleston Peak mountain 11,919 *ft* (3633 *m*) SE Nev. WNW of Las Vegas

Charles·town \'chär(-ə)lz-ˌtaùn\ section of Boston, Mass., on Boston harbor between mouths of Charles & Mystic rivers

Char·lotte \'shär-lət\ city S N.C. near S.C. border *pop* 395,934

Charlotte Ama·lie \ə-'mäl-yə, 'a-mə-lē\ *or formerly* **Saint Thomas** city & port * of Virgin Islands of the U.S., on St. Thomas Is. *pop* 12,331

Charlotte Harbor inlet of Gulf of Mexico SW Fla.

Char·lottes·ville \'shär-ləts-ˌvil, -vəl\ city *cen* Va. *pop* 40,341

Char·lotte·town \'shär-lət-ˌtaùn\ city & port Canada * of P.E.I. on Northumberland Strait *pop* 15,396

Chartres \'shärt, 'shärtrª\ city N *cen* France SW of Paris *pop* 38,574

Châ·teau·guay \'sha-tə-ˌgä\ town Canada in S Que. SW of Montreal *pop* 39,833

Châ·teau·roux \ˌshä-tō-'rü, sha-\ commune France S of Orléans *pop* 53,166

Châ·teau–Thier·ry \ˌsha-ˌtō-tye-'rē, ˌshä-\ town N France on the Marne SW of Reims *pop* 13,379

Chat·ham \'cha-təm\ **1** — see SAN CRISTÓBAL **2** city Canada in SE Ont. E of Lake Saint Clair *pop* 43,557 **3** borough SE England in Kent *pop* 61,909

Chatham Islands islands S Pacific belonging to New Zealand & comprising two islands (Chatham & Pitt) *area* 372 *sq mi* (967 *sq km*)

Chatham Strait strait SE Alaska bet. Admiralty Is. & Kuiu Is. on E & Baranof Is. & Chichagof Is. on W

Chat·ta·hoo·chee \ˌcha-tə-'hü-chē\ river 410 *mi* (660 *km*) SE U.S. rising in N Ga., flowing SW & S along Ala.-Ga. boundary into Lake Seminole

Chat·ta·noo·ga \ˌcha-tə-'nü-gə, ˌcha-t°n-'ü-\ city SE Tenn. on Tennessee River *pop* 152,466

Chau·tau·qua \shə-'tò-kwə\ lake 18 *mi* (29 *km*) long SW N.Y.

Che·bok·sa·ry \ˌche-ˌbäk-'sär-ē\ city Russia in Europe * of Chuvash Republic WNW of Kazan *pop* 308,000

Che·cheno–In·gush Republic \chə-ˌche-nō-in-'güsh\ autonomous republic SE Russia in Europe on N slopes of Caucasus Mountains *area* 6064 *sq mi* (15,766 *sq km*), *pop* 1,065,000

Che·du·ba \chə-'dü-bə\ island W Myanmar *area* 220 *sq mi* (572 *sq km*), *pop* 2635

Chefoo — see YANTAI

Che·ju \'chē-jü\ *or* **Quel·part** \'kwel-ˌpärt\ island S. Korea in N E. China Sea *area* 710 *sq mi* (1846 *sq km*)

Chekiang — see ZHEJIANG

Che·lan, Lake \shə-'lan\ lake *ab* 55 *mi* (88 *km*) long N *cen* Wash.

Chelms·ford **1** \'chemz-fərd *also* 'chelmz-\ town NE Mass. S of Lowell *pop* 32,383 **2** \'chelmz-, 'chemz-\ borough SE England * of Essex *pop* 58,159

Chel·sea \'chel-sē\ **1** city E Mass. NE of Boston *pop* 28,710 **2** former metropolitan borough SW London, England, on N bank of Thames River, now part of Kensington and Chelsea

Chel·ten·ham \'chelt-nəm, 'chel-t°n-əm, U.S. also -t°n-ˌham\ borough SW *cen* England in Gloucestershire *pop* 73,229

Che·lya·binsk \chel-'yä-bən(t)sk\ city W Russia in Asia S of Sverdlovsk *pop* 1,030,000

Che·lyu·skin, Cape \chel-'yü-skən\ headland Russia in Asia on Taimyr Peninsula; northernmost point of Asian mainland, at 77°35'N, 105°E

Chem·nitz \'kem-ˌnits, -nəts\ *or* 1953–90 **Karl–Marx–Stadt** \ˌkärl-'märk-ˌshtät, -ˌstät\ city E Germany SE of Leipzig *pop* 317,696

Chemulpo — see INCHON

Che·nab \chə-'näb\ river 590 *mi* (950 *km*) NW India (subcontinent) in Kashmir & the Punjab flowing SW to unite with the Sutlej forming the Panjnad

Chen–chiang — see ZHENJIANG

Cheng–chou — see ZHENGZHOU

Cheng·de *or* **Ch'eng–te** *or* **Cheng·teh** \'chəŋ-'də\ city NE China in NE Hebei NE of Beijing *pop* 120,000

Cheng·du *or* **Ch'eng–tu** \'chəŋ-'dü\ city SW *cen* China * of Szechwan on Min River *pop* 1,107,000

Chenstokhov — see CZESTOCHOWA

Cher \'sher\ river 220 *mi* (354 *km*), *cen* France flowing into the Loire

Cher·bourg \'sher-ˌbùr(g), sher-'bùr\ city & port NW France on Cotentin Peninsula on English Channel *pop* 31,333

Che·rem·kho·vo \chə-'rem-kə-və, ˌcher-əm-'kò-və\ city Russia in Asia NW of Irkutsk *pop* 77,000

Cheribon — see TJIREBON

Cher·kessk \chər-'kesk\ city S Russia in Europe in N Caucasus region SE of Stavropol * of Karachay-Cherkess Autonomous Region *pop* 91,000

Cher·ni·gov \cher-'nē-gəf\ city N Ukraine *pop* 238,000

Cher·no·byl \chər-'nō-bəl, (ˌ)cher-\ site N Ukraine of town abandoned after 1986 nuclear accident

Cher·nov·tsy \cher-'nòft-sē\ *or Romanian* **Cer·na·u·ti** \ˌcher-nə-'üts, -'üt-sē\ city W Ukraine on the Prut near Romania border *pop* 187,000

Cher·o·kee Outlet *or* **Cherokee Strip** \'cher-ə-(ˌ)kē\ strip of land N Okla. along S border of Kans. E of 100°W opened to settlement 1893; 50 *mi* (80 *km*) wide, *ab* 220 *mi* (354 *km*) long

Cher·so·nese \'kər-sə-ˌnēz, -ˌnēs\ *or anc* **Cher·so·ne·sus** \ˌkər-sə-'nē-səs\ any of several peninsulas: as (1) Jutland (the **Cim·bri·an Chersonese** \'sim-brē-ən\ *or* **Cim·bric Chersonese** \-brik\); (2) the Malay Peninsula (the **Golden Chersonese**); (3) the Crimea (the **Tau·ric Chersonese** \'tòr-ik\); (4) the Gallipoli Peninsula (the **Thra·cian Chersonese** \'thrä-shən\)

Cher·well \'chär-wəl\ river 30 *mi* (48 *km*) *cen* England in Northamptonshire & Oxfordshire flowing into the Thames at Oxford

Ches·a·peake \'che-sə-ˌpēk, 'ches-ˌpēk\ city SE Va. S of Norfolk *pop* 151,976

Chesapeake Bay inlet of the Atlantic 200 *mi* (322 *km*) long in Va. & Md.

Chesh·ire \'che-shər, -ˌshir\ **1** town S Conn. SW of Meriden *pop* 25,684 **2** *or* **Ches·ter** \'ches-tər\ county NW England * Chester *area* 899 *sq mi* (2337 *sq km*), *pop* 928,300

Ches·ter \'ches-tər\ **1** city SE Pa. *pop* 41,856 **2** city NW England * of Cheshire on Dee River *pop* 58,436

Ches·ter·field \'ches-tər-ˌfēld\ **1** city E Mo. W of St. Louis *pop* 37,991 **2** borough N *cen* England in Derbyshire S of Sheffield *pop* 70,546

Chesterfield Inlet inlet *ab* 250 *mi* (402 *km*) long N Canada on NW coast of Hudson Bay

Che·tu·mal \ˌchä-tü-'mäl\ city SE Mexico * of Quintana Roo

Chev·i·ot \'chē-vē-ət, 'che-\ peak 2676 *ft* (816 *m*) highest in the Cheviot Hills

Cheviot Hills hills extending NE to SW along English-Scottish border

Chey·enne \shī-'an, -'en\ **1** river 290 *mi* (467 *km*) S. Dak. flowing NE into Missouri River **2** city * of Wyo. *pop* 50,008

Chia–i \jē-'ä-ē\ city W *cen* Taiwan *pop* 200,000

Chia–mu–ssu — see JIAMUSI

Chiang Mai \jē-'äŋ-'mī\ *or* **Chieng·mai** \jē-'eŋ-'mī\ city NW Thailand on the Ping *pop* 89,272

Chi·a·pas \chē-'ä-pəs\ state SE Mexico bordering on the Pacific * Tuxtla Gutiérrez *area* 28,729 *sq mi* (74,695 *sq km*), *pop* 2,096,812

Chi·ba \'chē-bə\ city E Japan in Honshu on Tokyo Bay E of Tokyo *pop* 829,467

Chi·ca·go \shə-'kä-(ˌ)gō, -'kò-, -gə\ **1** river Chicago, Ill., having two branches (N. Branch & S. Branch) & orig. flowing E into Lake Michigan but now flowing S through S. Branch & Chicago Sanitary & Ship Canal into Des Plaines River **2** city & port NE Ill. on Lake Michigan *pop* 2,783,726 — **Chi·ca·go·an** \-'kä-gō-ən, -'kò-\ *n*

Chicago Heights city NE Ill. S of Chicago *pop* 33,072

Chich·a·gof \'chi-chə-ˌgòf, -ˌgäf\ island SE Alaska in Alexander Archipelago N of Baranof Is. *area* 2062 *sq mi* (5460 *sq km*)

Chi·chén It·zá \chē-ˌchen-ēt-'sä, -'ēt-sə\ village SE Mexico in Yucatán ESE of Mérida at site of ruins of important Mayan city

Chich·es·ter \'chi-chəs-tər\ city & borough S England ENE of Portsmouth * of W. Sussex *pop* 24,189

Ch'i–ch'i–ha–erh — see QIQIHAR

Chick·a·hom·i·ny \ˌchi-kə-'hä-mə-nē\ river 90 *mi* (145 *km*) E Va. flowing SE into James River

Chi·cla·yo \chə-'klī-(ˌ)ō\ city NW Peru near coast *pop* 207,269

Chi·co \'chē-(ˌ)kō\ city W Calif. N of Sacramento *pop* 40,079

Chic·o·pee \'chi-kə-(ˌ)pē\ city SW Mass. *pop* 56,632

Chi·cou·ti·mi \shə-'kü-tə-mē\ **1** river 100 *mi* (161 *km*) Canada in S Que. flowing N into the Saguenay **2** city Canada in S *cen* Que. on the Saguenay *pop* 62,670

Chihli — see HEBEI

Chihli, Gulf of — see BO HAI

Chi·hua·hua \chə-'wä-(ˌ)wä, shə-, -wə\ **1** state N Mexico bordering on the U.S. *area* 94,822 *sq mi* (246,537 *sq km*), *pop* 1,933,856 **2** city, its * *pop* 363,850

Chi·le \'chi-lē, 'chē-(ˌ)lä\ country S S. America bet. the Andes & the Pacific; a republic * Santiago *area* 286,396 *sq mi* (744,630 *sq km*), *pop* 11,275,440 — **Chil·ean** \'chi-lē-ən, chə-'lā-ən\ *adj or n*

Chil·koot \'chil-ˌküt\ pass 3502 *ft* (1067 *m*) bet. SE Alaska & SW Yukon Territory, Canada, in N Coast Mountains

Chil·li·cothe \ˌchi-lə-'kä-thē, -'kò-\ city S Ohio *pop* 21,923

Chil·li·wack \'chi-lə-ˌwak\ municipality Canada in S B.C. *pop* 49,531

Chil·oé \ˌchi-lō-'ā\ island S *cen* Chile *area* 4700 *sq mi* (12,220 *sq km*), *pop* 65,161

Chil·pan·cin·go \ˌchil-pən-'siŋ-(ˌ)gō\ city S Mexico * of Guerrero *pop* 36,193

Chil·tern Hills \'chil-tərn\ hills S *cen* England in Oxfordshire, Buckinghamshire, Hertfordshire, & Bedfordshire

Chim·bo·ra·zo \ˌchim-bə-'rä-(ˌ)zō\ mountain 20,561 *ft* (6267 *m*) W *cen* Ecuador

Chim·kent *or* **Shym·kent** \chim-'kent, shim-\ city S Kazakhstan N of Tashkent *pop* 322,000

Chi·na, People's Republic of \'chī-nə\ country E Asia; a republic, * Beijing; *area* 3,691,502 *sq mi* (9,597,905 *sq km*), *pop* 1,031,882,511

China, Republic of — see TAIWAN

\ə\ abut \ªˌ\ kitten, F table \ər\ further \a\ ash \ā\ ace \ä\ mop, mar
\aù\ out \ch\ chin \e\ bet \ē\ easy \g\ go \i\ hit \ī\ ice \j\ job
\ŋ\ sing \ō\ go \ò\ law \òi\ boy \th\ thin \th̲\ the \ü\ loot \ù\ foot
\y\ yet \zh\ vision \à, k̲, ⁿ, œ, œ̄, ᵫ, ᵫ̄, ʸ\ see Guide to Pronunciation

Chinan — see JINAN
China Sea the E. & S. China seas
Chin-chou, Chinchow — see JINZHOU
Chin-co-teague Bay \‚shin-kə-'tēg\ bay Md. & Va. on Atlantic coast
Chin-dwin \'chin-'dwin\ river 550 mi (885 km) NW Myanmar flowing S into the Irrawaddy
Chinese Turkestan region W China in W & cen Xinjiang Uygur
Ch'ing Hai — see QINGHAI
Chin Hills \'chin\ hills W Myanmar; highest Mt. Victoria 10,016 ft (3053 m)
Ch'in–huang-tao, Chin-wang-tao — see QINHUANGDAO
Chinkiang — see ZHENJIANG
Chinnampo — see NAMPO
Chinnereth, Sea of — see GALILEE (Sea of)
Chi-no \'chē-(‚)nō\ city SW Calif. E of Los Angeles pop 59,682
Chiog-gia \kē-'ô-jə\ commune & port NE Italy on island in Lagoon of Venice pop 53,581
Chi-os \'kī-‚äs\ or NGk Khí-os \'kē-‚òs\ island E Greece in the Aegean off W coast of Turkey area 355 sq mi (923 sq km) pop 52,691 — **Chi-an** \'kī-ən\ adj or n
Chip-pe-wa \'chi-pə-‚wò, -‚wä, -‚wä, -wə\ river 183 mi (294 km) NW Wis. flowing S into Mississippi River
Chir-i-ca-hua National Monument \‚chir-ə-'kä-wə, locally also 'chir-ə-‚kaù\ reservation SE Ariz. containing curious natural rock formations
Chiriquí — see BARÚ
Chis-holm Trail \'chi-zəm\ pioneer cattle trail bet. San Antonio (Tex.) & Abilene (in E cen Kans.), used esp. 1866–85
Chi-şi-nău \‚kē-shə-'naù\ or **Ki-shi-nev** \‚ki-shi-'nyòf; 'ki-shə-‚nef, -‚nev\ city cen Moldova, its ✱ pop 665,000
Chis-le-hurst and Sid-cup \'chi-zəl-‚hərst-ən(d)-'sid-kəp\ former urban district SE England in Kent, now partly in Bexley, partly in Bromley
Chi-ta \chi-'tä\ city Russia in Asia E of Lake Baikal pop 303,000
Chi-tral \chi-'träl\ **1** river 300 mi (483 km) N Pakistan & Afghanistan flowing SW into Kabul River **2** district N North-West Frontier Province Pakistan ✱ Chitral
Chit-ta-gong \'chi-tə-‚gäŋ, -‚gòŋ\ city & port SE Bangladesh on Bay of Bengal pop 889,760
Chi-tun-gwi-za \‚chē-tùŋ-'gwē-zə\ city NE cen Zimbabwe, SSE of Harare pop 172,000
Ch'iung-chou — see QIONGZHOU
Chiu-si \'kyü-sē\ or anc **Clu-si-um** \'klü-zhē-əm, -zē-\ town cen Italy in Tuscany SE of Siena
Chkalov — see ORENBURG
Choaspes — see KARKHEH
Choi-seul \shwä-'zə(r)l, -'zœl\ island W Pacific in the Solomons SE of Bougainville Is. area 1500 sq mi (3900 sq km); nearly surrounded by barrier reef
Choi-sy \shwä-'zē\ or **Choi-sy–le–Roi** \shwä-‚zē-lər-'wä\ commune N France on the Seine SSE of Paris pop 38,629
Cho-lon \shə-'lōn, chə-'lən\ former city S Vietnam, now part of Ho Chi Minh City
Cho-lu-la \chə-'lü-lə\ town SE cen Mexico in Puebla state
Cho-mo Lha-ri \‚chō-mō-'lär-ē\ mountain 23,997 ft (7314 m) in the Himalayas bet. Tibet & NW Bhutan; sacred to Buddhists
Chomolungma — see EVEREST (Mount)
Chong-jin \'chòŋ-‚jin\ city & port NE N. Korea on Sea of Japan pop 265,000
Chong-ju \'chòŋ-‚jü\ city W cen S. Korea N of Taejon pop 350,256
Chong-qing or **Ch'ung–ch'ing** \'chùŋ-'chiŋ\ or **Chung-king** \'chùŋ-'kiŋ\ city SE Sichuan on the Chang; ✱ of China 1937–43 pop 3,500,000
Chon-ju \'jən-‚jü\ city SW S. Korea SW of Taejon pop 426,473
Cho Oyu \‚chō-ō-'yü\ mountain 26,749 ft (8153 m) Nepal & Tibet in the Himalayas; 6th highest in the world
Cho-ras-mia \kə-'raz-mē-ə\ province of ancient Persia on Oxus River extending W to Caspian Sea; equivalent to Khwarazm — see KHIVA
Cho-rzow \'kò-‚zhúf, 'hò-, -‚zhüv\ city SW Poland in Silesia pop 132,674
Chosen — see KOREA
Cho-ta Nag-pur \‚chō-tə-'näg-‚pùr\ plateau region E India N of Mahanadi basin in N Orissa & S Bihar
Chou–shan — see ZHOUSHAN
Cho-wan \chə-'wän\ river 50 mi (80 km) NE N.C. flowing into Albemarle Sound
Christ-church \'krīs(t)-‚chərch\ city New Zealand on E coast of South Is. pop 164,680 — see LYTTELTON
Christiania — see OSLO
Chris-tians-haab \'kris-chənz-‚hòb, 'krish-\ town W Greenland on Disko Bay SE of Godhavn
Chris-tian-sted \'kris-chən-‚sted, 'krish-\ town Virgin Islands of the U.S. on N coast of St. Croix Is. pop 2555
Christ-mas Island \'kris-məs\ **1** island E Indian ocean 225 mi (360 km) S of W end of Java; administered by Australia area 64 sq mi (166 sq km), pop 2871 **2** — see KIRITIMATI
Chu \'chü\ or ZHU **2** river 600 mi (966 km) SE Kazakhstan flowing E into Issyk Kul
Ch'üan–chou, Chuanchow — see QUANZHOU
Chubb Crater — see NEW QUEBEC CRATER
Chu-but \chə-'büt, -'vüt\ river 500 mi (805 km) S Argentina flowing E across Patagonia into the Atlantic
Chu–chou, Chuchow — see ZHUZHOU
Chudskoe — see PEIPUS
Chu-gach Mountains \'chü-‚gach also -‚gash\ mountains S Alaska extending along coast from Cook Inlet to St. Elias Range; highest Mt. Marcus Baker 13,176 ft (4016 m)
Chuk-chi Sea or **Chuck-chee Sea** \'chək-chē, 'chúk-\ sea of the Arctic Ocean N of Bering Strait
Chu-kot-skiy Peninsula \chə-'kät-skē\ peninsula NE Russia in Asia, bet. Bering & Chukchi seas
Chu-la Vis-ta \‚chü-lə-'vis-tə\ city SW Calif. S of San Diego pop 135,163
Chu-lym or **Chu-lim** \chə-'lim\ river 700 mi (1126 km) Russia in Asia flowing W into the Ob

Ch'ung–ch'ing, Chungking — see CHONGQING
Chur \'kúr\ or F **Coire** \'kwär\ commune E Switzerland ✱ of Graubünden canton pop 31,078
Chur-chill \'chər-‚chil\ **1** river ab 1000 mi (1609 km) Canada flowing E across N Sask. & N Man. into Hudson Bay **2** or formerly **Hamilton** river 208 mi (335 km) Canada in Nfld. in S cen Labrador flowing E to Lake Melville
Churchill Falls or formerly **Grand Falls** waterfall 245 ft (75 m) high Canada in W Labrador in Churchill River
Chu-vash Republic \chü-'väsh\ autonomous republic E cen Russia in Europe S of the Volga ✱ Cheboksary area 6909 sq mi (17,963 sq km), pop 1,224,000
Chu-zen-ji \chü-'zen-jē\ lake Japan in cen Honshu W of Nikko
Cí-bo-la \'sē-bə-lə, 'si-\ historical region in present N N. Mex. including seven pueblos the **Seven Cities of Cibola**) believed by early Spanish explorers to contain vast treasures
Cic-ero \'si-sə-‚rō\ town NE Ill. W of Chicago pop 67,436
Cien-fue-gos \sē-en-'fwā-(‚)gōs\ city & port W cen Cuba on S coast on **Cienfuegos Bay** pop 114,650
Cie-szyn \'che-shən\ or G **Te-schen** \'te-shən\ region cen Europe in Silesia; once an Austrian duchy; divided 1920 bet. Poland & Czechoslovakia (now the Czech Republic)
Ci-li-cia \sə-'li-sh(ē-)ə\ ancient country SE Asia Minor extending along Mediterranean coast S of Taurus Mountains — see LESSER ARMENIA — **Ci-li-cian** \-'li-shən\ adj or n
Cilician Gates mountain pass S Turkey in Taurus Mountains
Cim-ar-ron \'si-mə-‚rän, -‚rōn, -rən\ river 600 mi (966 km) flowing E from NE N. Mex. through SW Kans. into Arkansas River in NE Okla.
Cimbrian Chersonese, Cimbric Chersonese — see CHERSONESE
Cim-me-ri-an Bosporus \sə-'mir-ē-ən\ KERCH STRAIT
Cin-cin-nati \‚sin(t)-sə-'na-tē, -'na-tə\ city SW Ohio on Ohio River pop 364,040 — **Cin-cin-nat-i-an** \-'na-tē-ən\ n
Cinque Ports \'siŋk\ group of seaport towns SE England on coast of Kent & Sussex, orig. five (Dover, Sandwich, Romney, Hastings, & Hythe) to which were later added Winchelsea, Rye, & other minor places, granted special privileges (abolished in 19th century) in return for services in coast defense
Cintra — see SINTRA
Circars — see NORTHERN CIRCARS
Cir-cas-sia \(‚)sər-'ka-sh(ē-)ə\ region S Russia in Europe on Black Sea N of W end of Caucasus Mountains
Cirenaica — see CYRENAICA
Cis-al-pine Gaul \(‚)sis-'al-‚pīn\ the part of Gaul lying S & E of the Alps
Ciscaucasia — see CAUCASUS
Cis-kei \'sis-‚kī\ former black enclave in the Republic of South Africa ✱ Bisho; granted independence 1981; abolished 1994 — **Cis-kei-an** \(‚)sis-'kī-ən\ adj or n
Ci-thae-ron \sə-'thē-‚rän\ or NGk **Ki-thai-rón** \‚kē-the-'ròn\ or formerly **El-a-tea** \‚e-lə-'tē-ə\ mountain 4623 ft (1409 m) Greece on NW border of ancient Attica
Ci-tlal-te-petl \sēt-‚läl-'tä‚pe-t?l\ or **Ori-za-ba** \‚ò-rē-'zä-bə, ‚òr-, -'sä-\ inactive volcano 18,700 ft (5700 m) SE Mexico on Puebla-Veracruz boundary; highest mountain in Mexico & 3d highest in N. America
Citrus Heights urban center N cen Calif. NE of Sacramento pop 107,439
Città del Vaticano — see VATICAN CITY
Ci-u-dad Bo-lí-var \‚sē-ü-‚thäth-bə-'lē-‚vär, -ü-'dad-\ city & port E cen Venezuela on the Orinoco pop 103,663
Ciudad Gua-ya-na \‚gwə-'yä-nə\ city E Venezuela near junction of the Caroní & the Orinoco pop 453,047
Ciudad Juá-rez or **Juárez** \'wär-əs, 'wär-\ city Mexico in Chihuahua on Rio Grande opposite El Paso, Tex. pop 424,135
Ciudad Re-al \rā-'äl\ **1** province S cen Spain area 7620 sq mi (19,812 sq km), pop 438,621 **2** commune, its ✱, S of Toledo pop 48,115
Ciudad Trujillo — see SANTO DOMINGO
Ciudad Vic-to-ria \vik-'tōr-ē-ə, -'tòr-\ city E cen Mexico ✱ of Tamaulipas pop 94,304
Ci-vi-ta-vec-chia \‚chē-vē-tä-'ve-(‚)kyä\ commune & port cen Italy in Latium on Tyrrhenian sea WNW of Rome pop 51,094
Clack-man-nan \klak-'ma-nən\ or **Clack-man-nan-shire** \-‚shir, -shər\ **1** former county cen Scotland bordering on the Forth **2** town, its ✱
Clac-ton \'klak-tən\ or **Clacton–on–Sea** town SE England in Essex on North Sea pop 43,571
Clare \'klar, 'kler\ county W Ireland in Munster ✱ Ennis area 1231 sq mi (3201 sq km), pop 90,826
Clare-mont \-‚mänt\ city SW Calif. E of Los Angeles pop 32,503
Clark Fork \'klärk\ river 300 mi (483 km) W Mont. & N Idaho flowing NW into Pend Oreille Lake
Clarks-dale \'klärks-‚dāl\ city NW Miss. pop 19,717
Clarks-ville \'klärks-‚vil, -vəl\ **1** town S Ind. pop 19,833 **2** city N Tenn. NW of Nashville pop 75,494
Clear-field \'klir-‚fēld\ city N Utah S of Ogden pop 21,435
Clear-wa-ter \'klir-‚wò-tər, -‚wä-\ city W Fla. NW of St. Petersburg on Gulf of Mexico pop 98,784
Clearwater Mountains mountains N cen Idaho; highest ab 8000 ft (2438 m)
Cle-burne \'klē-bərn\ city NE cen Tex. pop 22,205
Clee Hills \'klē\ hills W England in S Salop
Cler-mont–Fer-rand \‚kler-‚mōⁿ-fə-'räⁿ\ city S cen France in Allier valley on edge of Auvergne Mountains pop 153,379
Cleve-land \'klēv-lənd\ **1** city & port NE Ohio on Lake Erie pop 505,616 **2** city SE Tenn. ENE of Chattanooga pop 30,354 **3** county N England N of N. Yorkshire ✱ Middlesbrough area 226 sq mi (588 sq km), pop 568,400; includes the **Cleveland Hills** — **Cleve-land-er** \-lən-dər\ n
Cleveland, Mount mountain 10,448 ft (3184 m) N Mont., highest in Glacier National Park
Cleveland Heights city NE Ohio E of Cleveland pop 54,052
Cli-chy \klē-'shē\ commune N France NW of Paris pop 47,731
Cliff-side Park \'klif-‚sīd\ borough NE N.J. pop 20,393
Clif-ton \'klif-tən\ city NE N.J. N of Newark pop 71,742

Clinch \'klinch\ river 200 *mi* (322 *km*) SW Va. & E Tenn. flowing SW into Tennessee River

Cling·mans Dome \'kliŋ-mənz\ mountain 6642 *ft* (2024 *m*) on N.C.≈Tenn. boundary; highest in Great Smoky Mountains

Clin·ton \'klin-tᵊn\ **1** city E Iowa on Mississippi River *pop* 29,201 **2** town SW *cen* Miss. *pop* 21,847

Clon·mel \klän-'mel\ municipal borough S Ireland ✷ of County Tipperary *pop* 11,759

Cloud Peak mountain 13,165 *ft* (4013 *m*) N Wyo.; highest in Bighorn Mountains

Clo·vis \'klō-vəs\ **1** city *cen* Calif. NE of Fresno *pop* 50,323 **2** city E N. Mex. *pop* 30,954

Cluj–Na·po·ca \'klüzh-'nä-pō-kə\ city NW *cen* Romania in Transylvania *pop* 317,914

Clu·ny \'klü-nē, klü-'\ town E *cen* France NNW of Lyons *pop* 4335

Clusium — see CHIUSI

Clu·tha \'klü-thə\ river 210 *mi* (338 *km*) New Zealand in SE South Is. flowing SE into the Pacific

Clwyd \'klü-id\ county NE Wales ✷ Mold *area* 937 *sq mi* (2436 *sq km*), *pop* 392,200

Clyde \'klīd\ river 106 *mi* (171 *km*) SW Scotland flowing NW into **Firth of Clyde** (estuary)

Clyde·bank \'klīd-,baŋk\ burgh W *cen* Scotland in Strathclyde on Clyde River *pop* 51,656

Clydes·dale \'klīdz-,dāl\ valley of the upper Clyde River in Scotland

Cni·dus \'nī-dəs\ ancient town SW Asia Minor in Caria

Cnossus — see KNOSSOS

Coa·chel·la Valley \kō-'che-lə\ valley SE Calif. bet. Salton Sea & San Bernardino Mountains

Coa·hui·la \,kō-ə-'wē-lə, kwä-'wē-\ state N Mexico bordering on the U.S. ✷ Saltillo *area* 58,062 *sq mi* (150,961 *sq km*), *pop* 1,558,401

Coast Mountains mountains Canada in W B.C.; N continuation of Cascade Range

Coast Ranges mountain ranges W N. America extending along Pacific coast W of Sierra Nevada & Cascade Range & N through Vancouver Is., B.C., to Kenai Peninsula & Kodiak Is., Alaska — see LOGAN (Mount)

Coat·bridge \'kōt-(,)brij\ burgh S *cen* Scotland in Strathclyde *pop* 50,866

Coats Land \'kōts\ section of Antarctica SE of Weddell Sea

Cobh \'kōv\ *or formerly* **Queens·town** \'kwēnz-,taun\ urban district & port SW Ireland on island in Cork harbor *pop* 6369

Coblenz — see KOBLENZ

Co·burg **1** \'kō-,bərg\ city SE Australia in S Victoria, N suburb of Melbourne *pop* 55,035 **2** \'kō-,bərg, -,burk\ city *cen* Germany in N Bavaria NW of Bayreuth *pop* 45,633

Co·cha·bam·ba \,kō-chə-'bäm-bə\ city W *cen* Bolivia *pop* 204,684

Co·chin \'kō-chən\ region SW India in Kerala on Malabar Coast — see TRAVANCORE

Cochin China region S Vietnam bordering on S. China Sea & Gulf of Siam *area* 29,974 *sq mi* (77,932 *sq km*)

Co·chi·nos, Ba·hia de \bä-'ē-ə-,thä-kō-'chē-nōs\ *or* **Bay of Pigs** bay W Cuba on S coast

Co·co \'kō-(,)kō\ *or* **Se·go·via** \sä-'gō-vyə, sə-, -vē-ə\ river 450 *mi* (724 *km*) N Nicaragua flowing NE into the Caribbean & forming part of Honduras-Nicaragua boundary

Co·co·ni·no Plateau \,kō-kə-'nē-(,)nō, -'nē-nə\ plateau NW Ariz. S of Grand Canyon

Coconut Creek city SE Fla. NNW of Fort Lauderdale *pop* 27,485

Co·cos Islands \'kō-kəs\ *or* **Kee·ling Islands** \'kē-liŋ\ islands E Indian Ocean belonging to Australia *area* 1 *sq mi* (2.6 *sq km*), *pop* 555

Cod, Cape \'käd\ peninsula 65 *mi* (105 *km*) long SE Mass. — **Cape Cod·der** \'kä-dər\ *n*

Coele–Syria — see BEKAA

Coeur d'Alene \,kȯr-dᵊl-'ān\ city N Idaho *pop* 24,563

Coeur d'Alene Lake lake *ab* 25 *mi* (40 *km*) long N Idaho E of Spokane, Wash.; drained by Spokane River

Co·glians, Mon·te \,mȯn-tē-kōl-'yän(t)s\ mountain 9121 *ft* (2780 *m*) on Austria-Italy border; highest in the Carnic Alps

Coim·ba·tore \,kȯim-bə-'tȯr, -'tȯr\ city S India in W Tamil Nadu on S slope of Nilgiri Hills *pop* 917,155

Co·im·bra \kō-'im-brə, kü-\ city W *cen* Portugal *pop* 74,616

Coire — see CHUR

Col·ches·ter \'kōl-,ches-tər, -chəs-\ borough SE England in Essex *pop* 81,945

Col·chis \'käl-kəs\ ancient country bordering on Black Sea S of Caucasus Mountains; area now constitutes W part of Republic of Georgia — **Col·chi·an** \'käl-kē-ən\ *adj or n*

Cole·raine \kōl-'rān, 'kōl-,\ district N Northern Ireland, established 1974 *area* 187 *sq mi* (486 *sq km*), *pop* 46,272

Co·li·ma \kə-'lē-mə\ **1** volcano SW Mexico in S Jalisco **2** state SW Mexico bordering on the Pacific *area* 2009 *sq mi* (5223 *sq km*), *pop* 339,202 **3** city, its ✷, SSW of Guadalajara *pop* 70,219

College Park **1** city NW Ga. S of Atlanta *pop* 20,457 **2** city SW Md. NE of Washington, D.C. *pop* 21,927

College Station city E *cen* Tex. SE of Bryan *pop* 52,456

Col·lins·ville \'kä-lənz-,vil\ city SW Ill. NE of E. St. Louis *pop* 22,446

Col·mar *or* **Kol·mar** \'kōl-,mär, kōl-'\ commune NE France at E edge of Vosges Mountains *pop* 58,585

Co·logne \kə-'lōn\ *or* G **Köln** \'kœln\ city W Germany in N. Rhine≈Westphalia on the Rhine *pop* 976,694

Colomb–Béchar — see BÉCHAR

Co·lombes \kə-'lōm(m)b\ commune N France, NW suburb of Paris *pop* 83,241

Co·lom·bia \kə-'ləm-bē-ə\ country N S. America bordering on Caribbean Sea & Pacific Ocean ✷ Bogotá *area* 439,825 *sq mi* (1,143,545 *sq km*), *pop* 27,867,326 — **Co·lom·bi·an** \-bē-ən\ *adj or n*

Co·lom·bo \kə-'ləm-(,)bō\ city & port ✷ of Sri Lanka *pop* 612,000

Co·lón \kə-'lōn\ city & port N Panama on the Caribbean at entrance to Panama Canal *pop* 54,469

Colón, Archipiélago de — see GALÁPAGOS ISLANDS

Col·o·phon \'kä-lə-fən, -,fän\ ancient city W Asia Minor in Lydia

Col·o·ra·do \,kä-lə-'ra-(,)dō, -'rä-\ **1** river 1450 *mi* (2334 *km*) SW U.S. & NW Mexico rising in N Colo. & flowing SW into Gulf of California **2** river 840 *mi* (1352 *km*) S Tex. flowing SE into Gulf of Mexico **3** state W U.S. ✷ Denver *area* 104,247 *sq mi* (271,042 *sq km*), *pop* 3,294,394 **4** river 530 *mi* (853 *km*) *cen* Argentina flowing SE to the Atlantic — **Col·o·ra·dan** \-'ra-dᵊn, -'rä-\ *adj or n* — **Col·o·ra·do·an** \-'ra-dō-ən, -'rä-\ *adj or n*

Colorado Desert desert SE Calif. W of Colorado River

Colorado National Monument reservation W Colo. W of Grand Junction containing many unusual erosion formations

Colorado Plateau plateau SW U.S. W of Rocky Mountains in Colorado River basin in N Ariz., S & E Utah, W Colo., & NW N. Mex

Colorado Springs city *cen* Colo. E of Pikes Peak *pop* 281,140

Co·los·sae \kə-'lä-(,)sē\ ancient city SW *cen* Asia Minor in SW Phrygia — **Co·los·sian** \kə-'lä-shən\ *adj or n*

Col·ton \'kōl-tᵊn\ city SW Calif. S of San Bernardino *pop* 40,213

Co·lum·bia \kə-'ləm-bē-ə\ **1** river 1270 *mi* (2044 *km*) SW Canada & NW U.S. rising in SE B.C. & flowing S & W into the Pacific **2** city *cen* Mo. *pop* 69,101 **3** city ✷ of S.C. *pop* 98,052 **4** city *cen* Tenn. *pop* 28,583 — **Co·lum·bi·an** \-bē-ən\ *adj or n*

Columbia, Cape cape N Canada on Ellesmere Is.; northernmost point of Canada, at 83°07'N

Columbia, District of — see DISTRICT OF COLUMBIA

Columbia Plateau plateau E Wash., E Oreg., & SW Idaho in Columbia River basin

Co·lum·bus \kə-'ləm-bəs\ **1** city W Ga. on the Chattahoochee *pop* 178,681 **2** city S *cen* Ind. *pop* 31,802 **3** city E Miss. *pop* 23,799 **4** city E Nebr. *pop* 19,480 **5** city *cen* Ohio, its ✷ *pop* 632,910

Col·ville \'kōl-,vil, 'käl-\ river 320 *mi* (515 *km*) N Alaska flowing NE into Beaufort Sea

Col·wyn Bay \'käl-wən\ borough N Wales in Clwyd *pop* 26,278

Co·mil·la \kə-'mi-lə\ city E Bangladesh SE of Dacca *pop* 86,446

Commander — see KOMANDORSKIE ISLANDS

Common Market — see EUROPEAN ECONOMIC COMMUNITY

Commonwealth of Independent States association of the former constituent republics of the U.S.S.R. except for Lithuania, Latvia, & Estonia; formed 1991

Commonwealth of Nations *or* **Commonwealth** political organization consisting of nations loyal to the British monarch

Communism Peak *or* Russ **Pik Kom·mu·niz·ma** \'pēk-kə-mü-'nēz-mə\ mountain 24,590 *ft* (7495 *m*) NE Tajikistan in the Pamirs; highest in Tajikistan & the former U.S.S.R.

Co·mo \'kō-(,)mō\ commune N Italy in Lombardy at SW end of **Lake Como** (37 *mi or* 59 *km* long) *pop* 89,602

Co·mo·do·ro Ri·va·da·via \,kä-mə-'dȯr-(,)ō-,rē-və-'dä-vē-ə, -'dȯr-\ city & port S Argentina *pop* 96,865

Com·o·rin, Cape \'kä-mə-rən; kə-'mȯr-ən, -'mȯr-, -'mär-\ cape S India in Tamil Nadu; southernmost point of India, at 8°5'N

Com·o·ro Islands \'kä-mə-,rō\ country off SE Africa bet. Mozambique & Madagascar; formerly a French possession; a republic (except for Mayotte Is., which remains French) since 1975 ✷ Moroni *area* 790 *sq mi* (2054 *sq km*), *pop* 519,527

Com·piègne \kōm-'pyän\ town N France on the Oise *pop* 37,009

Compostela SANTIAGO DE COMPOSTELA

Comp·ton \'käm(p)-tən\ city SW Calif. SSE of Los Angeles *pop* 90,454

Com·stock Lode \'käm-,stäk\ gold & silver lode at Virginia City, Nev.

Con·a·kry *or* **Kon·a·kry** \'kä-nə-krē\ city & port ✷ of Guinea on the Atlantic *pop* 581,000

Co·nan·i·cut Island \kə-'na-ni-kət\ island R.I. in Narragansett Bay W of Aquidneck Is.

Con·cep·ción \,kän-,sep-sē-'ōn, -'sep-shən\ city S *cen* Chile *pop* 267,891

Con·chos \'kän-(,)chōs\ river 300 *mi* (483 *km*) N Mexico flowing NE into Rio Grande

Con·cord **1** \'kän-,kȯrd, 'käŋ-\ city W Calif. NE of Oakland *pop* 111,348 **2** \'käŋ-kərd\ town E Mass. NW of Boston *pop* 17,076 **3** \'käŋ-kərd\ city ✷ of N.H. on the Merrimack *pop* 36,006 **4** \'kän-,kȯrd, 'käŋ-\ city S *cen* N.C. *pop* 27,347

Co·ney Island \'kō-nē\ resort section of New York City in S Brooklyn; formerly an island

Con·ga·ree \'käŋ-gə-,rē\ river 60 *mi* (96 *km*) *cen* S.C. flowing SE to unite with the Wateree forming the Santee

Congaree Swamp National Monument reservation *cen* S.C. S of Columbia

Con·go \'käŋ-(,)gō\ **1** *or* **Zaire** river *ab* 3000 *mi* (4828 *km*) *cen* Africa flowing N, W, & SW into the Atlantic — see LUALABA **2** — see ZAIRE **3** *or formerly* **Middle Congo** country W *cen* Africa W of the lower Congo ✷ Brazzaville *area* 132,046 *sq mi* (343,320 *sq km*), *pop* 1,853,828 — see FRENCH EQUATORIAL AFRICA — **Con·go·lese** \,käŋ-gə-'lēz, -'lēs\ *adj or n*

Congo Free State — see BELGIAN CONGO

Con·nacht \'kä-,nȯt\ *or formerly* **Con·naught** province W Ireland *area* 6611 *sq mi* (17,189 *sq km*), *pop* 422,909

Con·nect·i·cut \kə-'ne-ti-kət\ **1** river 407 *mi* (655 *km*) NE U.S. rising in N N.H. & flowing S into Long Island Sound **2** state NE U.S. ✷ Hartford *area* 5009 *sq mi* (13,023 *sq km*), *pop* 3,287,116

Con·ne·ma·ra \,kä-nə-'mär-ə\ district Ireland in W Galway

Con·roe \'kän-(,)rō\ city E Tex. *pop* 27,610

Con·stance \'kän(t)-stən(t)s\ *or* G **Kon·stanz** \'kȯn-,stänts\ commune S Germany on **Lake Constance** *pop* 68,305

Constance, Lake *or* G **Bo·den·see** \'bō-dᵊn-,zā\ lake 46 *mi* (74 *km*) long W Europe on border bet. Germany, Austria, & Switzerland

Con·stan·ta \kän-'stän(t)-sə\ city & port SE Romania on Black Sea

Con·stan·tine \'kän(t)-stən-,tēn\ city NE Algeria *pop* 335,100

Constantinople — see ISTANBUL — **Con·stan·ti·no·pol·i·tan** \,kän-,stan-tᵊn-ō-'pä-lə-tᵊn\ *adj*

Continental Divide *or* **Great Divide** the watershed of N. America comprising the line of highest points of land separating the waters flowing W from those flowing N or E, coinciding with various ranges of the Rockies, and extending SSE from NW Canada to NW S. America

---

\ə\ abut \ᵊ\ kitten, F table \ər\ further \a\ ash \ā\ ace \ä\ mop, mar \au\ out \ch\ chin \e\ bet \ē\ easy \g\ go \i\ hit \ī\ ice \j\ job \ŋ\ sing \ō\ go \ȯ\ law \ȯi\ boy \th\ thin \t͟h\ the \ü\ loot \u̇\ foot \y\ yet \zh\ vision \à, k̲, ⁿ, œ, œ̄, ue, ūe, ᵊ\ *see* Guide to Pronunciation

Con·way \'kän-ˌwā\ city cen Ark. N of Little Rock pop 26,481

Cooch Be·har \ˌküch-bə-'här\ former state NE India W of Assam; since 1947 attached to West Bengal

Cook, Mount or **Ao·rangi** \aú-'räŋ-ē\ mountain 12,349 ft (3764 m) New Zealand in W cen South Is.; highest peak in Southern Alps & New Zealand

Cooke·ville \'kúk-ˌvil, -vəl\ city N cen Tenn. pop 21,744

Cook Inlet \'kúk\ inlet of the Pacific S Alaska W of Kenai Peninsula

Cook Islands islands S Pacific SW of Society Islands; self-governing territory of New Zealand ✱ Avarua (on Rarotonga Is.) area 89 sq mi (231 sq km), pop 17,614

Cooks·town \'kúks-ˌtaún\ district cen Northern Ireland, established 1974 area 241 sq mi (627 sq km), pop 26,624

Cook Strait strait New Zealand bet. North Is. & South Is.

Coon Rapids \'kün\ city E Minn. N of St. Paul pop 52,978

Coo·per City \'kü-pər\ city SE Fla. WNW of Hollywood pop 20,791

Coorg or **Kurg** \'kúrg\ former state S India ✱ Mercara; merged with Mysore state (now Karnataka) 1956

Coo·sa \'kü-sə\ river 286 mi (460 km) NW Ga. & N Ala. flowing SW to join Tallapoosa River forming Alabama River

Coos Bay \'küs\ inlet of the Pacific SW Oreg.

Co·pán \kō-'pän\ ruins of Mayan city W Honduras

Co·pen·ha·gen \ˌkō-pən-'hā-gən, -'hä-; 'kō-pən-ˌ\ or Dan **Kø·ben·havn** \ˌkœ-bən-'haún\ city & port ✱ of Denmark on E Sjælland Is. & N Amager Is. pop 467,850 — **Co·pen·ha·gen·er** \ˌkō-pən-'hā-gə-nər, -'hä-; 'kō-pən-ˌ\ n

Co·pia·pó \ˌkō-pē-ə-'pō\ **1** volcano 19,948 ft (6080 m) N cen Chile **2** city W of the volcano

Cop·per·as Cove \'kä-p(ə-)rəs\ city cen Tex. pop 24,079

Cop·per·mine \'kä-pər-ˌmīn\ river 525 mi (845 km) N Canada in Northwest Territories flowing NW into Arctic Ocean

Coquilhatville — see MBANDAKA

Co·quit·lam \kō-'kwit-ləm\ municipality Canada in SW B.C. E & NE of Burnaby pop 84,021

Coral Gables city SE Fla. SW of Miami pop 40,091

Coral Sea arm of the SW Pacific bounded on W by Queensland, Australia, on N by the Solomons, & on E by Vanuatu & New Caledonia

Coral Springs city SE Fla. pop 79,443

Cor·co·va·do \ˌkor-kə-'vä-(ˌ)dō\ mountain 2310 ft (704 m) SE Brazil on S side of city of Rio de Janeiro

Cor·di·lle·ra Cen·tral \ˌkor-d'l-'yer-ə-ˌsen-'träl, ˌkor-də-'ler-, ˌkor-dē-'yer-\ **1** range of the Andes in Colombia **2** range of the Andes in Peru E of the Marañón **3** chief range of the Dominican Republic **4** range Philippines in N Luzon — see PULOG (Mount) **5** range S cen Puerto Rico — see CERRO DE PUNTA

Cordillera Mé·ri·da \'mer-ə-də\ or **Sier·ra Ne·va·da de Mérida** \sē-ˌer-ə-nə-'vä-də-də-, -'va-\ mountain range W Venezuela — see BOLÍVAR (Pico)

Cór·do·ba \'kor-də-bə, -və\ **1** province S Spain area 5299 sq mi (13,777 sq km) pop 684,974 **2** or **Cor·do·va** \'kor-də-və\ city, its ✱, on the Guadalquivir pop 279,386 **3** city N cen Argentina pop 586,015 — **Cor·do·ban** \-bən\ adj or n

Cor·do·va Island \'kor-də-və\ tract on the Rio Grande 382 acres (153 hectares) adjoining Chamizal, formerly belonging to Mexico; 191 acres (76 hectares) ceded to U.S. in 1963

Cor·fu \'kor-fü; 'kor-(ˌ)fü, -(ˌ)fyü\ or NGk **Kér·ki·ra** or **Kér·ky·ra** \'ker-ki-rə\ or anc **Cor·cy·ra** \kor-'sī-rə\ **1** island NW Greece, one of the Ionian Islands area 227 sq mi (590 sq km) pop 105,043 **2** city & port on E Corfu pop 36,875 — **Cor·fi·ote** \'kor-fē-ˌōt, -ət\ n

Cor·inth \'kor-ən(t)th, 'kär-\ or NGk **Kó·rin·thos** \'kor-ən-ˌthos\ or **Co·rin·thia** \kə-'rin(t)-thē-ə\ region of ancient Greece occupying most of Isthmus of Corinth & part of NE Peloponnisos

Corinth, Gulf of or **Gulf of Le·pan·to** \li-'pan-(ˌ)tō, 'le-pən-ˌtō\ inlet of Ionian Sea cen Greece W of **Isthmus of Corinth** (neck of land 20 mi or 32 km long connecting Peloponnisos with rest of Greece)

Cork \'kork\ **1** county SW Ireland in Munster area 2881 sq mi (7491 sq km), pop 409,814 **2** city & county borough & port, its ✱, at head of Cork harbor pop 127,024

Corn \'korn\ two small islands Nicaragua in the Caribbean

Cor·ner Brook \'kor-nər-ˌbrúk\ city Canada on W Nfld. on Gulf of Saint Lawrence pop 22,410

Corneto — see TARQUINIA

Cor·no, Mon·te \ˌmän-tē-'kor-(ˌ)nō\ mountain 9560 ft (2897 m) cen Italy NE of Rome; highest in the Apennines

Corn·wall \'korn-ˌwol, -wəl\ **1** city Canada in SE Ont. pop 47,137 **2** or since 1974 **Cornwall and Isles of Scil·ly** \'si-lē\ county SW England ✱ Bodmin & ✱ Truro area 1375 sq mi (3575 sq km), pop 426,500

Co·ro \'kor-(ˌ)ō, 'kor-\ city NW Venezuela near coast pop 68,701

Cor·o·man·del \ˌkor-ə-'man-d'l, ˌkär-\ coast region SE India on Bay of Bengal S of the Krishna

Co·ro·na \kə-'rō-nə\ city SW Calif. E of Los Angeles pop 76,095

Cor·o·na·do \ˌkor-ə-'nä-(ˌ)dō, ˌkär-\ city SW Calif. on San Diego Bay opposite San Diego pop 26,540

Cor·pus Chris·ti \ˌkor-pəs-'kris-tē\ city & port S Tex. on **Corpus Christi Bay** (inlet of Gulf of Mexico) at mouth of the Nueces pop 257,453

Cor·reg·i·dor \kə-'re-gə-ˌdor\ island N Philippines at entrance to Manila Bay area ab 2 sq mi (5 sq km)

Cor·rien·tes \ˌkor-ē-'en-ˌtās, ˌkär-\ city NE Argentina pop 179,590

Cor·si·ca \'kor-si-kə\ or F **Corse** \'kors\ island France in the Mediterranean N of Sardinia area 3367 sq mi (8754 sq km), pop 289,842 — **Cor·si·can** \'kor-si-kən\ adj or n

Cor·si·cana \ˌkor-sə-'ka-nə\ city NE cen Tex. pop 22,911

Cor·ti·na or **Cortina d'Am·pez·zo** \ˌkor-'tē-nə-ˌdäm-'pet-(ˌ)sō\ resort village N Italy in the Dolomites N of Belluno

Cort·land \'kort-lənd\ city S cen N.Y. pop 19,801

Cor·to·na \kor-'tō-nə\ commune cen Italy NW of Perugia pop 22,627

Coruña, La; Corunna — see LA CORUÑA

Cor·val·lis \kor-'va-ləs\ city W Oreg. SW of Salem pop 44,757

Cos — see KOS

Co·sen·za \kō-'zen(t)-sə\ commune S Italy in Calabria pop 105,349

Cos·ta Bra·va \ˌkäs-tə-'brä-və, ˌkos-, ˌkos-\ coast region NE Spain in Catalonia on the Mediterranean extending NE from Barcelona

Costa del Sol \-del-'sōl, -'sol\ coast region S Spain on the Mediterranean extending E from Gibraltar

Costa Me·sa \'mā-sə\ city SW Calif. SE of Long Beach on Pacific coast pop 96,357

Costa Ri·ca \'rē-kə\ country Central America bet. Nicaragua & Panama; a republic ✱ San José area 19,238 sq mi (50,019 sq km), pop 2,435,000 — **Cos·ta Ri·can** \-kən\ adj or n

Costermansville — see BUKAVU

Côte d'A·zur \ˌkōt-də-'zúr, -dä-'zūr\ coast region SE France on the Mediterranean; part of the Riviera

Côte d'Ivoire — see IVORY COAST

Côte d'Or \ˌkōt-'dor\ range of hills E France SW of Dijon

Co·ten·tin Peninsula \ˌkō-ˌtäⁿ-'taⁿ\ peninsula NW France projecting into English Channel W of mouth of the Seine

Côte–Saint–Luc \ˌkōt-saⁿ-'lük, -sänt-, -sənt-\ city Canada in S Que. W of Montreal pop 28,700

Co·to·nou \ˌkō-tə-'nü\ city & port S Benin, former ✱ of Dahomey pop 449,000

Co·to·paxi \ˌkō-tə-'pak-sē, -'päk-\ volcano 19,347 ft (5897 m) N cen Ecuador

Cots·wold \'kät-ˌswōld, -swäld\ hills SW cen England in Gloucestershire; highest point Cleeve Cloud 1031 ft (314 m)

Cottage Grove city E Minn. pop 22,935

Cott·bus or **Kott·bus** \'kät-bəs, -ˌbús\ city E Germany on Spree River SE of Berlin pop 114,840

Cot·ti·an Alps \'kä-tē-ən\ range of W Alps France & Italy — see VISO

Couls·don and Pur·ley \'kōlz-dən-ən(d)-'pər-lē\ former urban district S England in Surrey, now part of Croydon

Coun·cil Bluffs \'kaún(t)-səl-'bləfs\ city SW Iowa on Missouri River pop 54,315

Cou·ran·tyne or **Co·ren·tyne** \'kor-ən-ˌtīn, 'kor-\ or D **Co·ran·tijn** \-ˌtīn\ river 300 mi (483 km) N S. America flowing N into the Atlantic & forming boundary bet. Guyana & Suriname

Cour·be·voie \ˌkúr-bə-'vwä\ commune N France on the Seine NW of Paris pop 54,391

Courland — see KURLAND

Courland Lagoon — see KURISCHES HAFF

Cour·ma·yeur \ˌkúr-mə-'yər\ resort village NW Italy in Valle d'Aosta SE of Mont Blanc

Courtrai — see KORTRIJK

Cov·en·try **1** \'kə-vən-trē\ town W R.I. pop 31,083 **2** \'kä-, 'kə-\ city & borough cen England in W. Midlands pop 312,605

Co·vi·na \kō-'vē-nə\ city SW Calif. E of Los Angeles pop 43,207

Cov·ing·ton \'kə-viŋ-tən\ city N Ky. pop 43,264

Cowes \'kaúz\ town S England on Isle of Wight pop 19,663

Cow·litz \'kaú-ləts\ river 150 mi (241 km) SW Wash. flowing into Columbia River

Co·zu·mel \ˌkō-zə-'mel\ island SE Mexico off Quintana Roo

Cracow — see KRAKÓW

Craig·av·on \krā-'ga-vən\ district cen Northern Ireland, established 1974 area 147 sq mi (382 sq km), pop 71,202

Cra·io·va \krä-'yō-və\ city S Romania pop 300,030

Cran·ston \'kran(t)-stən\ city E R.I. S of Providence pop 76,060

Cra·ter Lake \'krā-tər\ lake 1932 ft (589 m) deep SW Oreg. in Cascade Range at altitude of 6164 ft (1879 m); main feature of **Crater Lake National Park**

Craters of the Moon National Monument reservation SE cen Idaho including lava flows & other volcanic formations

Cré·cy \krā-'sē, 'kre-sē\ or **Cré·cy–en–Pon·thieu** \krā-sē-ˌäⁿ-pōⁿ-'tyə(r), -'tyœ\ commune N France NW of Amiens

Cre·mo·na \kri-'mō-nə\ commune N Italy in Lombardy on the Po ESE of Milan pop 75,547 — **Crem·o·nese** \ˌkre-mə-'nēz, -'nēs\ adj

Crete \'krēt\ or NGk **Krí·ti** \'krē-tē\ island Greece in the E Mediterranean ✱ Canea area 3199 sq mi (8317 sq km), pop 536,980 — **Cre·tan** \'krē-t'n\ adj or n

Crete, Sea of or **Sea of Can·dia** \'kan-dē-ə\ the S section of Aegean Sea bet. Crete & the Cyclades

Crewe \'krü\ borough NW England in Cheshire pop 47,759

Cri·mea \krī-'mē-ə, krə-\ or Russ **Krim** \'krim\ peninsula SE Europe, extending into Black Sea SW of Sea of Azov — **Cri·me·an** \krī-'mē-ən, krə-\ adj

Cris·to·bal or Sp **Cris·tó·bal** \kri-'stō-bəl\ town N Panama adjoining Colón at Caribbean entrance to Panama Canal

Cro·a·tan \ˌkrō-ə-'tan\ or **Cro·a·to·an** \-'tō-ən\ island of uncertain identity, prob. Ocracoke Is., off coast of N.C. bet. Pamlico Sound & the Atlantic thought to be place to which Raleigh's Roanoke Is. colony moved 1587

Cro·a·tia \krō-'ā-sh(ē-)ə\ independent country SE Europe; a constituent republic of Yugoslavia 1946–91 comprising Croatia, Slavonia, & most of Istria & the Dalmatian coast ✱ Zagreb area 21,726 sq mi (56,488 sq km), pop 4,396,397

Crocodile — see LIMPOPO

Cros·by \'kroz-bē\ or **Great Crosby** borough NW England in Merseyside on Irish Sea NNW of Liverpool pop 53,660

Cross \'kros\ river 300 mi (483 km) W Africa in W Cameroon & SE Nigeria flowing W & S into Gulf of Guinea

Cro·to·ne \krō-'tō-nē\ or anc **Cro·to·na** \-nə\ or **Cro·ton** \'krō-ˌtän, 'krō-t'n\ commune S Italy in Calabria on Gulf of Taranto pop 61,688

Croy·don \'kroi-d'n\ borough of S Greater London, England pop 322,000

Cro·zet Islands \krō-'zā\ islands S Indian Ocean WNW of Kerguelen; a French dependency

Crys·tal \'kris-t'l\ city SE Minn. N of Minneapolis pop 23,788

Crystal Lake city N Ill. pop 24,512

Cte·si·phon \'te-sə-ˌfän, 'tē-\ ancient city cen Iraq on the Tigris opposite Seleucia ✱ of Parthia & of later Sassanid empire

Cuan·za \'kwän-zə\ river 500 mi (805 km) SW Africa in cen Angola flowing NW into the Atlantic

Cu·ba \'kyü-bə\ **1** island in the W. Indies N of Caribbean Sea area 41,634 sq mi (108,248 sq km) **2** country largely coextensive with island; a republic ✱ Havana area 46,736 sq mi (121,514 sq km), pop 9,706,369 — **Cu·ban** \-bən\ adj or n

Cubango — see OKAVANGO

Cú·cu·ta \'kü-kə-tə, -ˌtä\ city N Colombia near Venezuela border *pop* 219,772

Cud·a·hy \'kə-də-(ˌ)hē\ city SW Calif. NW of Downey *pop* 22,817

Cuen·ca \'kwen-kə\ **1** city S Ecuador *pop* 104,470 **2** province E *cen* Spain *area* 6636 *sq mi* (17,254 *sq km*), *pop* 188,958 **3** commune, its *, ESE of Madrid *pop* 39,403

Cuer·na·va·ca \ˌkwer-nə-'vä-kə, -'va-\ city S *cen* Mexico S of Mexico City. * of Morelos *pop* 239,814

Cu·lia·cán \ˌkül-yə-'kän\ **1** river 175 *mi* (282 *km*) NW Mexico flowing SW into the Pacific at mouth of Gulf of California **2** city NW Mexico on the Culiacán * of Sinaloa *pop* 228,001

Cul·lo·den Moor \kə-'lä-dᵊn, -'lō-\ moorland N Scotland in N Highland region E of Inverness

Cul·ver City \'kəl-vər\ city SW Calif. *pop* 38,793

Cu·mae \'kyü-(ˌ)mē\ ancient town S Italy on Tyrrhenian coast W of modern Naples — Cu·mae·an \kyü-'mē-ən\ *adj*

Cu·ma·ná \ˌkü-mə-'nä\ city & port NE Venezuela on the Caribbean NE of Barcelona *pop* 212,432

Cum·ber·land \'kəm-bər-lənd\ **1** river 687 *mi* (1106 *km*) S Ky. & N Tenn. flowing W into Ohio River **2** city NW Md. on the Potomac *pop* 23,706 **3** town NE R.I. *pop* 29,038 **4** former county NW England * Carlisle — see CUMBRIA **5** settlement Canada in SE Ont. on Ottawa River NE of Ottawa *pop* 40,697

Cumberland Caverns caverns *cen* Tenn. SE of McMinnville

Cumberland Falls falls SE Ky. in upper course of Cumberland River

Cumberland Gap mountain pass 1304 *ft* (397 *m*) NE Tenn. through a ridge of the Cumberlands SE of Middlesboro, Ky.

Cumberland Plateau *or* Cumberland Mountains mountain region E U.S., part of the S Appalachian Mountains W of Tennessee River extending from S W.Va. to NE Ala.

Cumbre, La — see USPALLATA

Cum·bria \'kəm-brē-ə\ **1** — see STRATHCLYDE **2** county NW England including former counties of Cumberland & Westmorland * Carlisle *area* 2659 *sq mi* (6913 *sq km*), *pop* 476,700 — Cum·bri·an \'kəm-brē-ən\ *adj or n*

Cumbrian Mountains mountains NW England chiefly in Cumbria & Lancashire — see SCAFELL PIKE

Cu·naxa \kyü-'nak-sə\ town in ancient Babylonia NW of Babylon

Cu·ne·ne *or* Ku·ne·ne \kü-'nä-nə\ river 700 *mi* (1126 *km*) SW Africa in SW Angola flowing S & W into the Atlantic

Cu·par \'kü-pər\ burgh E Scotland * of Fife *pop* 6642

Cu·per·ti·no \ˌkü-pər-'tē-(ˌ)nō\ city W Calif. W of San José *pop* 40,263

Cu·ra·çao \'kür-ə-ˌsō, 'kyür-, -ˌsaú; ˌk(y)ùr-ə-', -'sä-(ˌ)ō\ island Netherlands Antilles in the S Caribbean; chief town Willemstad *area* 210 *sq mi* (546 *sq km*), *pop* 144,952

Cu·ri·ti·ba \ˌkür-ə-'tē-bə\ city S Brazil * of Paraná *pop* 1,400,000

Cush *or* Kush \'kəsh, 'kùsh\ ancient country NE Africa in Nile valley S of Egypt — Cush·ite \'kə-ˌshīt, 'kù-\ *adj or n* — Cush·it·ic \ˌkə-'shi-tik, kù-\ *adj*

Cus·ter Battlefield National Monument \'kəs-tər\ site SE Mont. on the Little Bighorn of battle 1876

Cutch — see KUTCH

Cut·tack \'kə-tək\ city E India in Orissa *pop* 326,463

Cux·ha·ven \'küks-ˌhä-fən\ city & port NW Germany on North Sea at mouth of the Elbe *pop* 58,666

Cuy·a·ho·ga \ˌkī-(ə-)'hò-gə, kə-'hò-, -'hä-, -'hō-\ river 100 *mi* (161 *km*) NE Ohio flowing into Lake Erie at Cleveland

Cuyahoga Falls city NE Ohio N of Akron *pop* 48,950

Cu·yu·ni \kü-'yü-nē\ river 300 *mi* (483 *km*) N S. America rising in E Venezuela & flowing E into the Essequibo in N Guyana

Cuz·co *or* Cus·co \'küs-(ˌ)kō\ city S Peru *pop* 88,104

Cwm·bran \kúm-'brän\ urban district SE Wales * of Gwent

Cyc·la·des \'si-klə-ˌdēz\ *or* NGk Ki·klá·dhes \kē-'klä-(ˌ)thes\ islands Greece in the S Aegean *area* 996 *sq mi* (2590 *sq km*) *pop* 95,083 — Cyc·lad·ic \si-'kla-dik, sī-\ *adj*

Cydonia — see CANEA — Cy·do·nian \sī-'dō-nē-ən, -nyən\ *adj or n*

Cymru — see WALES

Cy·press \'sī-prəs\ city SW Calif. SE of Los Angeles *pop* 42,655

Cy·prus \'sī-prəs\ **1** island E Mediterranean S of Turkey **2** country coextensive with the island; a republic of the Commonwealth of Nations * Nicosia *area* 3572 *sq mi* (9287 *sq km*), *pop* 698,800 — Cyp·ri·ot \'si-prē-ət, -ˌät\ *or* Cyp·ri·ote \-ˌōt, -ət\ *adj or n*

Cy·re·na·ica \ˌsir-ə-'nā-ə-kə, ˌsī-rə-\ *or It* Ci·re·na·ica *same or* ˌchē-rā-'nä-ē-(ˌ)kä\ **1** *or* Cy·re·ne \sī-'rē-(ˌ)nē\ ancient coastal region N Africa dominated by city of Cyrene **2** region E Libya, formerly a province — Cy·re·na·ic \ˌsir-ə-'nā-ik, ˌsī-rə-\ *adj or n* — Cy·re·na·ican \-'nä-ə-kən\ *adj or n*

Cy·re·ne \sī-'rē-(ˌ)nē\ ancient city N Africa on the Mediterranean in NE Libya — Cy·re·ni·an \sī-'nē-ən\ *adj or n*

Cyz·i·cus \'si-zi-kəs\ **1** — see KAPIDAGI **2** ancient city in Mysia on isthmus leading to Kapidagi Peninsula

Czech·o·slo·va·kia \ˌche-kə-slō-'vä-kē-ə, -slə-, -'va-\ country 1918–92 *cen* Europe; a republic * Prague *area* 49,373 *sq mi* (128,370 *sq km*), *pop* 15,283,095; divided Jan. 1, 1993 into separate countries of Czech Republic & Slovakia — Czech·o·slo·vak \-'slō-ˌväk, -ˌvak\ *adj or n* — Czech·o·slo·ki·an \-slō-'vä-kē-ən, -slə-, -'va-\ *adj or n*

Czech Republic country *cen* Europe; a constituent republic of Czechoslovakia 1918–92 * Prague *area* 30,448 *sq mi* (78,860 *sq km*), *pop* 10,291,927

Cze·sto·cho·wa \ˌchen(t)-stə-'kō-və\ *or Russ* Chen·sto·khov \ˌchen(t)-stə-'kóf, -'kóv\ city S Poland on the Warta *pop* 257,497

Da — see DA YUNHE

Da·bro·wa Gor·ni·cza \dòm-'brò-və-gùr-'nē-chə\ city S Poland *pop* 135,960

Dac·ca *or* Dha·ka \'da-kə, 'dä-\ city * of Bangladesh *pop* 1,679,572

Da·chau \'dä-ˌkaủ, -ˌkaủ\ city S Germany in S Bavaria *pop* 33,950; site of Nazi concentration camp

Da·cia \'dā-sh(ē-)ə\ ancient country & Roman province SE Europe roughly equivalent to Romania & Bessarabia — Da·cian \-shən\ *adj or n*

Da·dra and Na·gar Ha·ve·li \də-'drä . . . ˌnə-gər-ə-'ve-lē\ union territory India bordering on Gujarat and Maharashtra *area* 189 *sq mi* (491 *sq km*), *pop* 103,677

Dag·en·ham \'da-gə-nəm, 'dag-nəm\ former municipal borough SE England in Essex, now part of Barking and Dagenham

Da·ge·stan \ˌda-gə-'stan, ˌdä-gə-'stän\ autonomous republic SE Russia in Europe, on W shore of the Caspian * Makhachkala *area* 13,124 *sq mi* (34,122 *sq km*), *pop* 1,429,000

Dahomey — see BENIN — Da·ho·man \də-'hō-mən\ *adj or n* — Da·ho·me·an \-mē-ən\ *or* Da·ho·mey·an \-mē-ən\ *adj or n*

Dairen — see LÜDA

Da·kar \'da-ˌkär, də-'kär\ city & port * of Senegal *pop* 798,792

Dakh·la \'dä-klə\ *or formerly* Vi·lla Cis·ne·ros \ˌvē-yə-sis-'ner-əs\ town & port NW Africa in Western Sahara * of Río de Oro

Da·ko·ta \də-'kō-tə\ territory (1861–89) NW U.S. divided 1889 into states of N.D. & S.D. (the Da·ko·tas \-təz\) — Da·ko·tan \-'kō-tᵊn\ *adj or n*

Dal·e·car·lia \ˌda-lə-'kär-lē-ə\ region W *cen* Sweden — Dal·e·car·li·an \-lē-ən\ *adj*

Dal·las \'da-ləs, -lis\ city NE Tex. on Trinity River *pop* 1,006,877 — Dal·las·ite \'da-lə-ˌsīt\ *n*

Dal·ma·tia \dal-'mā-sh(ē-)ə\ region W Balkan Peninsula on the Adriatic — Dal·ma·tian \-shən\ *adj or n*

Dal·ton \'dòl-tᵊn\ city NW Ga. *pop* 21,761

Da·ly City \'dā-lē\ city W Calif. S of San Francisco *pop* 92,311

Da·man \də-'män, -'man\ *or* Da·mão \də-'maúⁿ\ district W India on Gulf of Cambay; a constituent part of the union territory of Daman and Diu *area* 148 *sq mi* (385 *sq km*) — see GOA, PORTUGUESE INDIA

Da·man·hûr \ˌda-mən-'hùr\ city N Egypt E of Alexandria *pop* 170,633

Da·mas·cus \də-'mas-kəs\ city SW Syria, its * *pop* 1,251,028

Dam·a·vand \'dä-mə-ˌvand\ *or* Dem·a·vend \'de-mə-ˌvend\ mountain 18,934 *ft* (5771 *m*) N Iran; highest in Elburz Mountains

Dam·i·et·ta \ˌda-mē-'e-tə\ city & port N Egypt *pop* 93,488

Dam·mam \də-'mäm\ town & port Saudi Arabia on Persian Gulf

Da·mo·dar \'dä-mə-ˌdär\ river 350 *mi* (563 *km*) NE India in *cen* Bihar & W. Bengal flowing ESE into the Hooghly

Dan \'dan\ **1** river 180 *mi* (290 *km*) S Va. & N N.C. flowing E into Roanoke River **2** ancient village at N extremity of Palestine

Da Nang \(ˌ)dä-'näŋ, -'naŋ\ *or formerly* Tou·rane \tü-'rän\ city & port *cen* Vietnam in Annam

Dan·bury \'dan-ˌber-ē, -b(ə-)rē\ city SW Conn. *pop* 65,585

Dan·dong \'dän-'dùŋ\ *or* An·tung \'än-'dùŋ\ *or* Tan–tung \'dän-'dùŋ\ city & port NE China in SE Liaoning at mouth of the Yalu *pop* 420,000

Danger Islands — see PUKAPUKA

Danish West Indies the W islands of the Virgin Islands group that were until 1917 a Danish possession & now constitute the Virgin Islands of the U.S.

Danmark — see DENMARK

Dan·ube \'dan-(ˌ)yüb\ *or G* Do·nau \'dō-ˌnaú\ *or anc* Da·nu·bi·us \də-'nü-bē-əs, da-, -'nyü-\ *or* Is·ter \'is-tər\ river 1771 *mi* (2850 *km*) *cen* & SE Europe flowing SE from SW Germany into Black Sea — Da·nu·bi·an \də-'nyü-bē-ən\ *adj*

Dan·vers \'dan-vərz\ town NE Mass. N of Lynn *pop* 24,174

Dan·ville \'dan-ˌvil\ city E Ill. *pop* 33,828 **2** \-ˌvil, -vəl\ city S Va. on Dan River *pop* 53,056

Dan·zig \'dan(t)-sig, 'dän(t)-\ **1** — see GDANSK **2** territory surrounding & including Gdansk that (1920–39) constituted a free city under the League of Nations

Danzig, Gulf of — see GDANSK, GULF OF

Dar·da·nelles \ˌdär-dᵊn-'elz\ *or* Hel·les·pont \'he-lə-ˌspänt\ *or anc* Hel·les·pon·tus \ˌhe-lə-'spän-təs\ strait NW Turkey connecting Sea of Marmara with the Aegean

Dar el Beida — see CASABLANCA

Dar es Sa·laam \ˌdär-ˌe(s)-sə-'läm\ city & port * of Tanzania & of Tanganyika on Indian Ocean *pop* 757,346

Dar·fur \där-'fùr\ region W Sudan; chief city El Fasher

Dar·i·en \ˌder-ē-'en, der-, där-\ Spanish colonial settlement Central America W of Gulf of Darien

Darien, Gulf of inlet of the Caribbean bet. E Panama & NW Colombia

Darien, Isthmus of — see PANAMA (Isthmus of)

Dar·jee·ling *or* Dar·ji·ling \där-'jē-liŋ\ city NE India in W. Bengal on Sikkim border *pop* 42,873

Dar·ling \'där-liŋ\ river 1160 *mi* (1867 *km*) SE Australia in Queensland & New South Wales flowing SW into Murray River

Darling Range mountain range SW Western Australia extending *ab* 250 *mi* (400 *km*) N–S along coast; highest point Mt. Cooke 1910 *ft* (582 *m*)

Dar·ling·ton \'där-liŋ-tən\ borough N England in Durham *pop* 85,396

Darm·stadt \'därm-ˌstat, -ˌshtät, -ˌstät\ city *cen* Germany in Hesse SSW of Frankfurt am Main *pop* 138,201

Dart·moor \'därt-ˌmủr, -ˌmōr, -ˌmór\ tableland SW England in S Devon *area* 215 *sq mi* (559 *sq km*)

Dart·mouth \'därt-məth\ **1** town SE Mass. W of New Bedford *pop* 27,244 **2** city Canada in S N.S. on Halifax harbor opposite Halifax *pop* 67,798 **3** borough & port SW England in S Devon on Dart River *pop* 6298

Dar·win \'där-wən\ city & port N Australia * of Northern Territory on Port Darwin (inlet of Timor Sea) *pop* 72,937

Dar·yal Gorge *or* Dar·ial Gorge \där-'yal\ mountain pass SE Russia in Europe through Caucasus Mountains

Da·tong \'dä-'tùŋ\ *or* Ta·tung \'dä-'tùŋ\ city NE China in N Shanxi *pop* 243,000

Dau·gav·pils \'daù-gəf-ˌpilz\ *or Russ* Dvinsk \də-'vin(t)sk\ city E Latvia on Dvina River *pop* 116,000

Dau·phi·né \ˌdō-fi-'nā\ region & former province SE France N of Provence * Grenoble

Da·vao \'dä-ˌvaù, dä-'vaù\ city Philippines on Davao Gulf *pop* 610,375

Davao Gulf gulf of the Pacific, Philippines in SE Mindanao

\ə\ abut \ᵊ\ kitten, F table \ər\ further \a\ ash \ā\ ace \ä\ mop, mar \aú\ out \ch\ chin \e\ bet \ē\ easy \g\ go \i\ hit \ī\ ice \j\ job \ŋ\ sing \ō\ go \ò\ law \òi\ boy \th\ thin \t̲h̲\ the \ü\ loot \ù\ foot \y\ yet \zh\ vision \à, k̲, ⁿ, œ, œ̄, ue, ūe, ᵞ\ *see* Guide to Pronunciation

Dav·en·port \'da-vən-ˌpōrt, 'da-vᵊm-, -ˌpȯrt\ city E Iowa on Mississippi River *pop* 95,333
Da·vid \dä-'vēd\ town W Panama *pop* 65,635
Da·vie \'dā-vē\ city SE Fla. *pop* 47,217
Da·vis \'dā-vəs\ city W Calif. W of Sacramento *pop* 46,209
Davis Mountains mountains W Tex. N of the Big Bend of the Rio Grande
Davis Strait strait connecting Baffin Bay with the Atlantic
Daw·son \'dȯ-sᵊn\ city N Canada in Yukon *pop* 972
Dax \'daks\ commune SW France in the Landes on the Adour NE of Biarritz *pop* 18,019
Day·ton \'dā-tᵊn\ city SW Ohio on Miami River *pop* 182,044
Day·to·na Beach \dā-'tō-nə, də-\ city NE Fla. *pop* 61,921
Da Yun·he \'dä-'yùn-'hə\ *or* **Grand Canal** canal *ab* 1000 *mi* (1609 *km*) long E China from Hengshui to Tianjin
Dead Sea *or bib* **Salt Sea** *or* L **La·cus As·phal·ti·tes** \'lā-kəs-ˌas-ˌfȯl-'tī-tēz\ salt lake *ab* 50 *mi* (80 *km*) long on boundary bet. Israel & Jordan *area* 370 *sq mi* (962 *sq km*), surface 1286 *ft* (392 *m*) below sea level
Dean, Forest of \'dēn\ forested district SW England in W Gloucester bet. Severn & Wye rivers; an ancient royal forest
Dear·born \'dir-ˌbȯrn, -bərn\ city SE Mich. *pop* 89,286
Dearborn Heights city SE Mich. W of Detroit *pop* 60,838
Death Valley arid valley E Calif. & S Nev. containing lowest point in the U.S. at 280 *ft* (85 *m*) below sea level; most of area included in **Death Valley National Monument**
Deau·ville \'dō-ˌvil, dō-'vē(ə)l\ town NW France on Bay of the Seine SSW of Le Havre *pop* 5655
De·bre·cen \'de-brət-ˌsen\ city E Hungary *pop* 222,300
De·cap·o·lis \di-'ka-pə-ləs\ confederation of 10 ancient cities N Palestine in region chiefly SE of Sea of Galilee
De·ca·tur \di-'kā-tər\ 1 city N Ala. *pop* 48,761 2 city *cen* Ill. *pop* 83,885
Dec·can \'de-kən, -ˌkan\ plateau region S *cen* India lying bet. Eastern Ghats & Western Ghats
Ded·ham \'de-dəm\ town E Mass. SW of Boston *pop* 23,782
Dee \'dē\ 1 river 90 *mi* (145 *km*) NE Scotland flowing E into North Sea 2 river 50 *mi* (80 *km*) S Scotland flowing S into Solway Firth 3 river 70 *mi* (113 *km*) N Wales & W England flowing E & N into Irish Sea
Deep South region SE U.S. — usu. considered as including Ala., Ga., La., Miss., N.C., S.C., and all or part of the adjacent states of Fla., Va., Tenn., Ark., & Tex.
Deer·field Beach \'dir-ˌfēld\ city SE Fla. N of Fort Lauderdale *pop* 46,325
Deer Park city SE Tex. *pop* 27,652
De·hi·wa·la–Mount La·vin·ia \ˌdā-hē-'wä-lə . . . lə-'vi-nē-ə\ town W Sri Lanka on coast S of Colombo *pop* 193,000
Deh·ra Dun \ˌder-ə-'dün\ city N India in NW Uttar Pradesh *pop* 293,628
De Kalb \di-'kalb\ city N Ill. *pop* 34,925
Del·a·goa Bay \ˌde-lə-'gō-ə\ inlet of Indian Ocean S Mozambique
De·la·no \də-'lā-(ˌ)nō\ city S Calif. NNW of Bakersfield *pop* 22,762
Del·a·ware \'de-lə-ˌwar, -ˌwer, -wər\ 1 river 296 *mi* (476 *km*) E U.S. flowing S from S N.Y. into Delaware Bay 2 state E U.S. ✻ Dover *area* 2057 *sq mi* (5348 *sq km*), *pop* 666,168 3 city *cen* Ohio NNW of Columbus *pop* 20,030 — **Del·a·war·ean** \ˌde-lə-'war-ē-ən, -'wer-\ *n*
Delaware Bay inlet of the Atlantic bet. SW N.J. & E Del.
Del City \'del\ city *cen* Okla. E of Oklahoma City *pop* 23,928
De·lé·mont \də-lā-'mōⁿ\ commune NW Switzerland ✻ of Jura canton *pop* 11,467
Delft \'delft\ commune SW Netherlands *pop* 86,287
Del·ga·do, Cape \del-'gä-(ˌ)dō\ cape NE Mozambique
Del·hi \'de-lē\ 1 union territory N India W of Uttar Pradesh ✻ Delhi *area* 578 *sq mi* (1503 *sq km*) 2 city, its ✻ *pop* 5,713,581 — see NEW DELHI
Dells of the Wisconsin *or* **Wisconsin Dells** \'delz\ gorge of Wisconsin River S *cen* Wis. N of Baraboo
Del·mar·va Peninsula \del-'mär-və\ peninsula E U.S. bet. Chesapeake & Delaware bays comprising Del. & parts of Md. & Va. — see EASTERN SHORE
Del·men·horst \'del-mən-ˌhȯrst\ city NW Germany in Lower Saxony WSW of Bremen *pop* 72,370
De·los \'dē-ˌläs\ *or NGk* **Dhí·los** \'thē-ˌlȯs\ island Greece in cen Cyclades *area* 2 *sq mi* (5.2 *sq km*) — **De·lian** \'dē-lē-ən, 'dēl-yən\ *adj or n*
Del·phi \'del-ˌfī\ ancient town *cen* Greece in Phocis on S slope of Mt. Parnassus near present village of **Dhel·foí** \thel-'fē\
Del·ray Beach \'del-ˌrā\ city SE Fla. S of Palm Beach *pop* 47,181
Del Río \del-'rē-(ˌ)ō\ city S Tex. on Rio Grande *pop* 30,705
Del·ta \'del-tə\ municipality Canada in SW B.C. *pop* 88,978
Delta, The region NW Miss. bet. Mississippi & Yazoo rivers
Demavend — see DAMAVAND
Dem·e·ra·ra \ˌde-mə-'rär-ə, -'rar-, -'rer-\ river 200 *mi* (322 *km*) Guyana flowing N into the Atlantic
Denali, Denali National Park — see MCKINLEY (Mount)
Den·bigh \'den-bē\ *or* **Den·bigh·shire** \-ˌshir, -shər\ former county N Wales ✻ Ruthin
Den·der·mon·de \ˌden-dər-'män-də\ *or* **Ter·monde** \ter-'mōⁿ(n)d\ commune NW *cen* Belgium *pop* 42,499
Den Hel·der \den-'hel-dər\ commune W Netherlands in N. Holland on an outlet from Wadden Zee to North Sea *pop* 63,647
Den·i·son \'de-nə-sən\ city NE Tex. on Red River *pop* 21,505
De·niz·li \ˌde-naz-'lē\ city SW Turkey SE of Izmir *pop* 134,673
Den·mark \'den-ˌmärk\ *or* **Dan Dan·mark** \'dän-ˌmärk\ country N Europe occupying most of Jutland Peninsula & adjacent islands in Baltic & North seas; a kingdom ✻ Copenhagen *area* 16,576 *sq mi* (43,098 *sq km*), *pop* 5,129,778
Denmark Strait strait 130 *mi* (209 *km*) wide bet. SE Greenland & Iceland connecting Arctic Ocean with the Atlantic
Dent Blanche \ˌdäⁿ-'bläⁿsh\ mountain 14,295 *ft* (4357 *m*) S Switzerland in Pennine Alps
Dent du Mi·di \ˌdäⁿ-də-mi-'dē\ mountain 10,686 *ft* (3257 *m*) SW Switzerland in W Alps
Den·ton \'den-tᵊn\ city N Tex. NW of Dallas *pop* 66,270

D'En·tre·cas·teaux Islands \ˌdän-trə-'kas-(ˌ)tō\ islands SW Pacific N of E tip of New Guinea belonging to Papua New Guinea *area* 1200 *sq mi* (3120 *sq km*) *pop* 38,894
Den·ver \'den-vər\ city NE *cen* Colo., its ✻ *pop* 467,610 — **Den·ver·ite** \-və-ˌrīt\ *n*
Dept·ford \'det-fərd\ former metropolitan borough SE London, England, now part of Lewisham
Der·be \'dər-(ˌ)bē\ ancient town S Asia Minor in S Lycaonia on border of Cilicia; exact site unknown
Der·bent *or* **Der·bend** \dər-'bent\ city S Russia in Europe in Dagestan on Caspian Sea *pop* 61,000
Der·by \'där-bē, *chiefly U.S.* 'dər-\ borough N *cen* England in Derbyshire *pop* 215,736
Der·by·shire \'där-bē-ˌshir, -shər; *US also* 'dər-\ *or* **Derby** county N *cen* England ✻ Matlock *area* 1016 *sq mi* (2642 *sq km*), *pop* 910,200
Der·na \'der-nə\ city & port NE Libya *pop* 36,900
Der·ry \'der-ē\ 1 city SE N.H. SE of Manchester *pop* 29,603 2 *or* **Lon·don·der·ry** \ˌlən-dən-'der-ē; 'lən-dən-ˌder-ē, -d(ə-)rē\ district NW Northern Ireland, established 1974 *area* 148 *sq mi* (385 *sq km*), *pop* 83,384 3 *or* **Londonderry** county borough & port, NW Derry district *pop* 62,697
Der·went \'dər-wənt\ river 130 *mi* (209 *km*) Australia in Tasmania flowing SE into Tasman Sea
Derwent Water lake NW England in Lake District in Cumbria
Desaguadero — see SALADO
Des·chutes \dā-'shüt\ river 250 *mi* (402 *km*) *cen* & N Oreg. E of Cascade Range flowing N into Columbia River
Des·er·et \ˌde-zə-'ret\ provisional state of the U.S. S of 42d parallel & W of the Rockies organized 1849 by Mormons
Des Moines \di-'mȯin\ 1 river 327 *mi* (526 *km*) Iowa flowing SE into Mississippi River 2 city ✻ of Iowa on Des Moines River *pop* 193,187
Des·na \də-'snä\ river 550 *mi* (885 *km*) SW Russia in Europe & N Ukraine flowing S into the Dnieper
De So·to \di-'sō-(ˌ)tō\ city NE Tex. S of Dallas *pop* 30,544
Des Plaines \des-'plānz\ 1 river 150 *mi* (241 *km*) NE Ill. flowing S to unite with Kankakee River forming Illinois River 2 city NE Ill. NW of Chicago *pop* 53,223
Des·roches \dā-'rȯsh\ island NW Indian Ocean NNE of Madagascar belonging to Seychelles
Des·sau \'de-ˌsaù\ city *cen* Germany NE of Halle *pop* 102,957
De·troit \di-'trȯit\ 1 river 31 *mi* (50 *km*) Ont. & SE Mich. connecting Lake Erie & Lake Saint Clair 2 city SE Mich. on Detroit River *pop* 1,027,974 — **De·troit·er** \-'trȯi-tər\ *n*
Detskoe Selo — see PUSHKIN
Deur·ne \'dər-nə, 'dȯrn\ commune N Belgium, E suburb of Antwerp
Deutsche Demokratische Republik — see GERMANY
Deutschland — see GERMANY
De·ven·ter \'dā-vən-tər\ commune E Netherlands *pop* 64,453
Devil Mountain — see AUYÁN-TEPUÍ
Devil's Island *or F* **Île du Dia·ble** \ēl-dᵫ-dyäbl'\ island French Guiana in the Safety Islands group; former penal colony
Devils Post·pile \'pōst-ˌpīl\ lava formation E *cen* Calif. SE of Yosemite National Park; feature of **Devils Postpile National Monument**
Devils Tower *or* **Ma·to Tepee** \'ma-(ˌ)tō\ columnar rock formation NE Wyo. rising 865 *ft* (264 *m*) in **Devils Tower National Monument**
Dev·on \'de-vən\ *or* **Dev·on·shire** \'de-vən-ˌshir, -shər\ county SW England ✻ Exeter *area* 2591 *sq mi* (6737 *sq km*), *pop* 959,700
Devon Island island Northwest Territories, Canada in E Parry Islands N of Baffin Is. *area* 20,861 *sq mi* (54,239 *sq km*)
Dews·bury \'düz-ˌber-ē, 'dyüz-, -b(ə-)rē\ borough N England in W. Yorkshire S of Leeds *pop* 48,339
Dez \'dez\ *or* **Ab–I–Diz** \ˌä-bi-'dēz\ river 250 *mi* (402 *km*) W Iran flowing S to the Karun
Dezh·ne·va, Cape \dezh-nē-'ȯ-və, 'desh-\ *or* **Cape Dezh·nev** \-nē-'ȯf, -'ȯv\ *or* **East Cape** cape NE Russia in Asia at E end of Chukotskiy Peninsula
Dhah·ran \dä-'rän, thäh-'ran\ town SE Saudi Arabia on Persian Gulf near Bahrain Islands *pop* 12,500
Dhaka — see DACCA
Dhau·la·gi·ri \ˌdaù-lə-'gir-ē\ mountain 26,810 *ft* (8172 *m*) W *cen* Nepal in the Himalayas
Di·a·blo, Mount \dē-'ä-(ˌ)blō, dī-'a-\ mountain 3849 *ft* (1173 *m*) *cen* Calif. at N end of **Diablo Range**
Di·a·man·ti·na \ˌdē-ə-ˌman-'tē-nə\ river 470 *mi* (756 *km*) E *cen* Australia in SW Queensland flowing SW into the Warburton 2 \ˌdē-ə-\ city E Brazil in *cen* Minas Gerais *pop* 36,018
Di·a·mond \'dī-(ə-)mənd\ *or* **Kum·gang** \'kùm-ˌgäŋ\ mountains SE N. Korea; highest 5374 *ft* (1638 *m*)
Diamond Bar city S Calif. E of Los Angeles *pop* 53,672
Diamond Head promontory Hawaii on Oahu Is. in SE Honolulu
Die·go Gar·cia \dē-ˌā-gō-ˌgär-'sē-ə\ island in Indian Ocean, chief island of Chagos Archipelago
Dié·go–Suá·rez \dē-ˌā-gō-'swär-es\ city & port Madagascar near N tip of island *pop* 40,443
Dien Bien Phu \'dyen-ˌbyen-'fü\ village NW Vietnam
Di·eppe \dē-'ep\ city & port N France N of Rouen *pop* 25,607
Di·jon \dē-'zhōⁿ\ city E France *pop* 149,899
Diks·mui·de \'dēk-ˌsmī-də\ *or* **Dix·mude** \dēk-smᵫd\ town W Belgium in W. Flanders N of Ieper *pop* 15,273
Di·li \'dē-lē\ city & port N Timor, formerly ✻ of Portuguese Timor
Di·mi·trov·grad \də-'mē-trəf-ˌgrad, -ˌgräd\ city S Bulgaria on the Maritsa ESE of Plovdiv *pop* 45,596
Dimitrovo — see PERNIK
Di·nar·ic Alps \də-'nar-ik\ range of E Alps W Slovenia, W Croatia, Bosnia and Herzegovina, & Montenegro; highest point Djeravica (SW of Pec) 8714 *ft* (2656 *m*)
Din·gle Bay \'diŋ-gəl\ inlet of the Atlantic SW Ireland
Ding·wall \'diŋ-ˌwȯl\ burgh N Scotland NW of Inverness *pop* 4815
Dinosaur National Monument reservation NW Colo. & NE Utah at junction of Green & Yampa rivers; rich fossil deposits
Di·o·mede Islands \'dī-ə-ˌmēd\ islands in Bering Strait comprising **Big Diomede** (Russia) & **Little Diomede** (U.S.)
Diospolis — see THEBES

Di·re·dawa \,dir-ə-'daủ-ə\ city E Ethiopia *pop* 91,629
Dis·ko \'dis-(,)kō\ island W Greenland in Davis Strait
Dismal Swamp *or* **Great Dismal Swamp** swamp SE Va. & NE N.C. between Chesapeake Bay & Albemarle Sound *ab* 40 *mi* (64 *km*) long, 10 *mi* (16 *km*) wide
District of Co·lum·bia \kə-'ləm-bē-ə\ federal district E U.S. coextensive with city of Washington *area* 67 *sq mi* (174 *sq km*), *pop* 606,900
Dis·tri·to Fe·de·ral \di-'strē-tō,-fe-thə-'räl\ 1 district E Argentina largely comprising ✳ city of Buenos Aires *area* 74 *sq mi* (192 *sq km*) 2 — see FEDERAL DISTRICT 1 3 *or* **Federal District** district *cen* Mexico including ✳ city of Mexico City *area* 573 *sq mi* (1490 *sq km*) 4 *or* **Federal District** district N Venezuela including ✳ city of Caracas *area* 745 *sq mi* (1937 *sq km*)
Diu \'dē-(,)ü\ district W India at S end of Kathiawar Peninsula; a constituent part of the union territory of Daman and Diu *area* 20 *sq mi* (52 *sq km*) — see GOA, PORTUGUESE INDIA
Di·yar·ba·kir \di-,yär-bä-'kir\ *or* **Di·ar·bekr** \-'be-kər\ city SE Turkey on the Tigris *pop* 233,289
Dja·ja, Mount \'jä-yə\ *or formerly* **Mount Car·stensz** \'kär-stənz\ mountain 16,503 *ft* (5030 *m*) Indonesia in W. Irian in Sudirman Range; highest in New Guinea
Dja·ja·pu·ra \,jä-yə-'pủr-ə\ *or formerly* **Hol·lan·dia** \hä-'lan-dē-ə\ *or* **Ko·ta·ba·ru** \,kō-tə-'bär-(,)ü\ *or* **Su·kar·na·pu·ra** \sü-,kär-nə-'pủr-ə\ city & port Indonesia ✳ of W. Irian
Dja·kar·ta *or* **Ja·kar·ta** \jə-'kär-tə\ *or formerly* **Ba·ta·via** \bə-'tä-vē-ə\ city & port ✳ of Indonesia in NW Java *pop* 6,503,449
Djambi — see TELANAIPURA
Djawa — see JAVA
Djer·ba *or* **Jer·ba** \'jər-bə, 'jer-\ island SE Tunisia in the Mediterranean at entrance to Gulf of Gabes *area* 16 *sq mi* (42 *sq km*), *pop* 70,217
Dji·bou·ti \jə-'bü-tē\ 1 *or formerly* **French Territory of the Afars and the Is·sas** \'ä-,fär(z) . . . ē-'sä(z)\ *or earlier* **French Somaliland** country E Africa on Gulf of Aden; a republic *area* 8880 *sq mi* (23,088 *sq km*), *pop* 510,000 2 *or* **Ji·bu·ti** city, its ✳ *pop* 300,000
Djokjakarta — see YOGYAKARTA
Dne·pro·dzer·zhinsk \,ne-(,)prō-dər-'zhin(t)sk\ city E *cen* Ukraine on the Dnieper W of Dnepropetrovsk *pop* 227,000
Dne·pro·pe·trovsk \,ne-(,)prō-pə-'trỏfsk\ *or formerly* **Eka·te·ri·no·slav** \i-,ka-tə-'rē-nə-,släf, -,släv\ city E Ukraine *pop* 863,000
Dnie·per \'nē-pər\ river 1400 *mi* (2253 *km*) Ukraine, E Belarus, & W Russia in Europe rising in S Valdai Hills & flowing S into Black Sea
Dnies·ter \'nēs-tər\ river 850 *mi* (1368 *km*) W Ukraine & E Moldova rising on N slope of Carpathian Mountains near Polish border & flowing SE into Black Sea
Do·be·rai \'dō-bə,rī\ *or* **Vo·gel·kop** \'vō-gəl-,käp\ peninsula Indonesia in NW W. Irian
Do·bru·ja *or* **Do·bru·dja** \'dỏ-brə-,jä, -jə\ region S Europe in Romania & Bulgaria on Black Sea S of the Danube
Do·de·ca·nese \dō-'de-kə-,nēz, -,nēs; ,dō-di-kə-'\ islands Greece in the SE Aegean comprising the Southern Sporades S of Icaria & Samos; belonged to Italy 1923–47 *area* 486 *sq mi* (1264 *sq km*) *pop* 162,439 — see RHODES — **Do·de·ca·ne·sian** \(,)dō-,de-kə-'nē-zhən, ,dō-di-kə-, -shən\ *adj or n*
Dodge City \'däj\ city S Kans. on Arkansas River *pop* 21,129
Do·do·ma \dō-'dō-(,)mä\ town NE *cen* Tanzania, since 1974 designated as the future national ✳
Dog·ger Bank \'dỏ-gər, 'dä-\ submerged sandbank *ab* 150 *mi* (241 *km*) long in North Sea E of N England
Do·ha \'dō-(,)hä\ city & port ✳ of Qatar on Persian Gulf *pop* 217,294
Dol·gel·lau \dỏl-'ge-,(h)lī\ *or* **Dol·gel·ley** \-'ge-(h)lē\ town W Wales in Gwynedd, formerly ✳ of Merionethshire
Dol·lard—des—Or·meaux \dỏ-'lär-,dā-,zỏr-'mō\ town Canada in S Que. NW of Montreal *pop* 46,922
Do·lo·mites \'dō-lə-,mīts, 'dä-\ *or* **Dolomite Alps** range of E Alps NE Italy bet. Adige & Piave rivers — see MARMOLADA
Dol·ton \'dōl-t*ə*n\ village NE Ill. S of Chicago *pop* 23,930
Dôme, Puy de \,pwē-də-'dōm\ mountain 4806 *ft* (1465 *m*) S *cen* France in Auvergne Mountains
Dom·i·ni·ca \,dä-mə-'nē-kə, ÷də-'mi-nə-kə\ island Brit. West Indies in the Lesser Antilles; a republic of the Commonwealth of Nations since 1978 ✳ Roseau *area* 305 *sq mi* (793 *sq km*), *pop* 74,089
Do·min·i·can Republic \də-'mi-ni-kən\ *or formerly* **San·to Do·min·go** \,san-tə-də-'miŋ-(,)gō\ *or* **San Domingo** \,san-də-\ country W. Indies on E Hispaniola; a republic ✳ Santo Domingo *area* 18,700 *sq mi* (48,620 *sq km*), *pop* 5,647,977 — **Dominican** *adj or n*
Don \'dän\ river 1200 *mi* (1931 *km*) Russia in Europe flowing SE & then SW into Sea of Azov
Donau — see DANUBE
Don·cas·ter \'däŋ-kəs-tər\ borough N England in S. Yorkshire *pop* 81,610
Don·e·gal \,dä-ni-'gỏl, ,də-\ county NW Ireland (republic) in Ulster ✳ Lifford *area* 1865 *sq mi* (4849 *sq km*), *pop* 127,994
Donegal Bay inlet of the Atlantic NW Ireland
Do·nets \də-'nets\ river 670 *mi* (1078 *km*) SE Ukraine & SW Russia in Europe flowing SE into Don River
Donets Basin *or* **Don·bass** *or* **Don·bas** \,dən-'bas\ region E Ukraine SW of the Donets
Do·netsk \də-'netsk\ *or formerly* **Sta·li·no** \'stä-li-,nō, 'sta-\ *or* **Sta·lin** \'stä-lən, 'sta-, -,lēn\ *or* **Yu·zov·ka** \'yü-zəf-kə\ city E Ukraine in Donets Basin *pop* 879,000
Don·ner Pass \'dä-nər\ mountain pass 7135 *ft* (2175 *m*) E Calif. in Sierra Nevada
Don·ny·brook \'dä-nē-,brủk\ city E Ireland in Leinster, SE suburb of Dublin
Doornik — see TOURNAI
Door Peninsula \'dỏr, 'dỏr\ peninsula E Wis. bet. Green Bay & Lake Michigan
Dor·ches·ter \'dỏr-chəs-tər, -,ches-\ borough S England ✳ of Dorset *pop* 14,049
Dor·dogne \dỏr-'dōn, -'dỏ-nyə\ river 300 *mi* (483 *km*) SW France flowing SW & W to unite with the Garonne forming the Gironde Estuary
Dor·drecht \'dỏr-,drekt\ *or* **Dordt** *or* **Dort** \'dỏrt\ commune SW Netherlands in S. Holland on the Meuse *pop* 107,947

Dore, Monts \mōⁿ-'dỏr, -'dỏr\ mountain group S *cen* France in Auvergne Mountains — see SANCY (Puy de)
Do·ris \'dỏr-əs, 'dỏr-, 'där-\ 1 ancient country *cen* Greece bet. Mounts Oeta & Parnassus 2 ancient district SW Asia Minor on coast of Caria
Dor·noch \'dỏr-nək, -nək\ royal burgh N Scotland in Highland region N of Inverness
Dorpat — see TARTU
Dor·set \'dỏr-sət\ *or* **Dor·set·shire** \-,shir, -shər\ county S England ✳ Dorchester *area* 973 *sq mi* (2530 *sq km*), *pop* 596,600
Dort·mund \'dỏrt-,mủnt, -mənd\ city W Germany in the Ruhr *pop* 608,297
Do·than \'dō-thən\ city SE Ala. *pop* 53,589
Dou·ai \dü-'ā\ city N France S of Lille *pop* 43,954
Dou·a·la *or* **Du·a·la** \dü-'ä-lə\ city & port SW Cameroon on Bight of Biafra *pop* 458,426
Doug·las \'də-gləs\ borough ✳ of Isle of Man *pop* 20,385
Dou·ro \'dỏr-(,)ü, 'dỏr-\ *or* **Sp Due·ro** \'dwer-(,)ō\ river 485 *mi* (781 *km*) N Spain & N Portugal flowing W into the Atlantic
Do·ver \'dō-vər\ 1 city *cen* Del., its ✳ *pop* 27,630 2 city SE N.H. *pop* 25,042 3 borough SE England in Kent on Strait of Dover *pop* 32,843
Dover, Strait of *or* **F Pas de Ca·lais** \päd-kä-le, pä-də-\ channel bet. SE England & N France, easternmost section of English Channel; 20 *mi* (32 *km*) wide at narrowest point
Down \'daủn\ 1 district SE Northern Ireland, established 1974 *area* 250 *sq mi* (650 *sq km*), *pop* 52,869 2 traditional county SE Northern Ireland
Dow·ners Grove \'daủ-nərz\ village NE Ill. *pop* 46,858
Dow·ney \'daủ-nē\ city SW Calif. SE of Los Angeles *pop* 91,444
Down·pat·rick \daủn-'pa-trik\ town SE Northern Ireland in Down district *pop* 8245
Downs \'daủnz\ 1 two ranges of hills SE England — see NORTH DOWNS, SOUTH DOWNS 2 roadstead in English Channel along E coast of Kent protected by the Goodwin Sands
Down Under Australia or New Zealand
Dra·chen·fels \'drä-kən-,fels\ hill 1053 *ft* (321 *m*) W Germany in the Siebengebirge on the Rhine S of Bonn
Dra·cut \'drä-kət\ town NE Mass. N of Lowell *pop* 25,594
Dra·kens·berg Mountains \'drä-kənz-,bərg\ *or* **Quath·lam·ba** \kwät-'läm-bə\ mountains E Republic of S. Africa & in Lesotho; highest Thabana Ntlenyana 11,425 *ft* (3482 *m*)
Drake Passage \'dräk\ strait S of S. America bet. Cape Horn & S. Shetlands
Dram·men \'drä-mən\ city & port SE Norway *pop* 51,978
Dran·cy \drän-'sē\ commune N France, NE of Paris *pop* 64,258
Dra·va *or* **Dra·ve** \'drä-və\ river 450 *mi* (724 *km*) S Austria, NE Slovenia, & N tip of Croatia flowing SE into the Danube
Dren·the *or* **Dren·te** \'dren-tə\ province NE Netherlands ✳ Assen *area* 1030 *sq mi* (2678 *sq km*), *pop* 424,694
Dres·den \'drez-dən\ city E Germany in Saxony *pop* 516,604
Dri·na \'drē-nə\ river 160 *mi* (257 *km*) flowing N along the border bet. Bosnia & Serbia into the Sava
Dro·ghe·da \'drỏi-ə-də, 'drỏ-i-də\ municipal borough E Ireland in County Louth on the Boyne *pop* 24,086
Drug — see DURG
Drum·mond·ville \'drə-mən(d)-,vil\ town Canada in S Que. NE of Montreal *pop* 35,462
Dry Tor·tu·gas \tỏr-'tü-gəz\ island group S Fla. W of Key West; site of Fort Jef·fer·son National Monument \'je-fər-sən\
Duar·te \dü-'är-tē, dü-'är-\ city SW Calif. *pop* 20,688
Du·bai \(,)dü-'bī\ 1 sheikhdom, member of United Arab Emirates 2 city, its ✳ *pop* 265,702
Du·bawnt \dü-'bỏnt\ river 580 *mi* (933 *km*) N Canada flowing NE through Dubawnt Lake to Ba·ker Lake \'bā-kər\ (W expansion of Chesterfield Inlet)
Dubawnt Lake lake N Canada in SE Northwest Territories E of Great Slave Lake *area* 1654 *sq mi* (4300 *sq km*)
Dub·lin \'də-blən\ *or for* 2 *and* 3 *IrGael* **Bai·le Atha Cli·ath** \blä-'klē-ə\ 1 city W Calif. ESE of Oakland *pop* 23,229 2 county E Ireland in Leinster *area* 356 *sq mi* (926 *sq km*), *pop* 1,024,429 3 city & county borough & port ✳ of Ireland (republic) & of County Dublin at mouth of the Liffey on Dublin Bay (inlet of Irish Sea) *pop* 477,675 — **Dub·lin·er** \'də-blə-nər\ *n*
Du·brov·nik \'dü-,brỏv-nik, dủ-'brỏv-nik\ city & port S Croatia *pop* 31,213
Du·buque \də-'byük\ city E Iowa on Mississippi River *pop* 57,546
Dud·ley \'dəd-lē\ borough W *cen* England in W. Midlands WNW of Birmingham *pop* 187,228
Duis·burg \'dü-əs-,bərg, 'düz-,, 'dyüz-,, *G* 'dứes-,bủrk\ *or formerly* **Duis·burg—Ham·born** \-,häm-'bỏrn\ city W Germany at junction of Rhine & Ruhr rivers *pop* 558,089
Du·luth \də-'lüth\ city & port NE Minn. at W end of Lake Superior *pop* 85,493 — **Du·luth·ian** \-'lü-thē-ən\ *adj or n*
Dul·wich \'də-lij, -lich\ a SE district of London, England
Dum·bar·ton \,dəm-'bär-t*ə*n\ 1 burgh W *cen* Scotland in Strathclyde *pop* 23,204 2 *or* **Dum·bar·ton·shire** \-,shir, -shər\ — see DUNBARTON
Dum·fries \,dəm-'frēs, -'frēz\ 1 *or* **Dum·fries·shire** \-'frēsh-,shir, -shər\ former county S Scotland ✳ Dumfries 2 burgh S Scotland ✳ of Dumfries and Galloway *pop* 32,084
Dumfries and Gal·lo·way \'ga-lə-,wā\ region S Scotland, established 1975 ✳ Dumfries *area* 2460 *sq mi* (6396 *sq km*), *pop* 145,078
Dun·bar·ton \,dən-'bär-t*ə*n\ *or* **Dun·bar·ton·shire** \-,shir, -shər\ former county *cen* Scotland ✳ Dumbarton
Dun·can \'dəŋ-kən\ city S Okla. ✳ *pop* 21,732
Dun·can·ville \'dəŋ-kən-,vil, -vəl\ city NE Tex. *pop* 35,748
Dun·dalk \,dən-'dỏ(l)k\ urban district & port NE Ireland (republic) on Dundalk Bay ✳ of County Louth *pop* 26,669
Dun·das \,dən-dəs\ town Canada in SE Ont. *pop* 21,868

\ə\ abut \ᵊ\ kitten, F table \ər\ further \a\ ash \ā\ ace \ä\ mop, mar \aủ\ out \ch\ chin \e\ bet \ē\ easy \g\ go \i\ hit \ī\ ice \j\ job \ŋ\ sing \ō\ go \ỏ\ law \ỏi\ boy \th\ thin \th\ the \ü\ loot \ủ\ foot \y\ yet \zh\ vision \ä, k̠, ⁿ, œ, œ̄, ừ, ứ, ʸ\ see Guide to Pronunciation

Dun·dee \ˌdən-ˈdē\ city & port E Scotland ✻ of Tayside on Firth of Tay *pop* 174,746
Dun·e·din \ˌdə-ˈnē-dᵊn\ **1** city W Fla. N of Clearwater *pop* 34,012 **2** — see EDINBURGH **3** city New Zealand on SE coast of South Is. at head of Otago Harbor *pop* 77,176
Dun·ferm·line \ˌdən-ˈfərm-lən\ royal burgh E Scotland in Fife *pop* 52,057
Dun·gan·non \ˌdən-ˈga-nən\ district S Northern Ireland, established 1974 *area* 301 *sq mi* (*783 sq km*), *pop* 41,073
Dun·kerque or **Dun·kirk** \ˈdən-ˌkərk, ˌdən-ˈ\ city & port N France on Strait of Dover *pop* 78,171
Dun Laoghai·re \ˌdən-ˈler-ə\ or formerly **Kings·town** \ˈkinz-ˌtaùn\ borough & port E Ireland in Leinster on Dublin Bay *pop* 54,715
Dun·net Head \ˈdə-nət\ headland N Scotland on N coast W of John o'Groat's; northernmost point of mainland, at 58°50′N
Duns \ˈdənz\ burgh SE Scotland in Borders region *pop* 2249
Du·que de Ca·xi·as \ˌdü-kə-də-kə-ˈshē-əs\ city SE Brazil in Rio de Janeiro state N of city of Rio de Janeiro *pop* 575,533
Du·ran·go \dù-ˈraŋ-(ˌ)gō, dyù-\ **1** state NW cen Mexico *area* 42,272 *sq mi* (*109,907 sq km*), *pop* 1,160,196 **2** city, its ✻ *pop* 182,633
Dur·ban \ˈdər-bən\ city & port E Republic of South Africa in E Natal on Natal Bay *pop* 736,852
Durg \ˈdùrg\ or formerly **Drug** \ˈdrüg\ city E cen India in SE Madhya Pradesh E of Nagpur *pop* 64,132
Dur·ham \ˈdər-əm, ˈdə-rəm, ˈdùr-əm\ **1** city NE cen N.C. NW of Raleigh *pop* 136,611 **2** county N England bordering on North Sea *area* 911 *sq mi* (*2369 sq km*), *pop* 606,400 **3** city, its ✻, S of Newcastle *pop* 26,422
Dur·res \ˈdùr-əs\ or It **Du·raz·zo** \dù-ˈrät-(ˌ)sō\ or anc **Ep·i·dam·nus** \ˌe-pə-ˈdam-nəs\ or **Dyr·ra·chi·um** \də-ˈrā-kē-əm\ city & port Albania on Adriatic Sea W of Tiranë *pop* 65,900
Du·shan·be \dü-ˈsham-bə, dyü-, -ˈshäm-\ or formerly **Sta·lin·a·bad** \ˌstä-li-nə-ˈbäd, ˌsta-li-nə-ˈbad\ city ✻ of Tajikistan *pop* 595,000
Düs·sel·dorf \ˈdü-səl-ˌdorf, ˈdyü-, ˈdùe-\ city W Germany on the Rhine N of Cologne ✻ of N. Rhine-Westphalia *pop* 590,479
Dutch Borneo — see KALIMANTAN
Dutch Guiana — see SURINAME
Dutch New Guinea — see WEST IRIAN
Dvi·na \də-ˌvē-ˈnä\ **1** river 630 *mi* (*1014 km*) Latvia, W Belarus, & W Russia in Europe rising in Valdai Hills & flowing W into Gulf of Riga **2** — see NORTHERN DVINA
Dvina Gulf or **Dvina Bay** or formerly **Gulf of Arch·an·gel** \ˈär-ˌkān-jəl\ arm of White Sea N Russia in Europe
Dvinsk — see DAUGAVPILS
Dyf·ed \ˈdə-ved, -vəd\ county SW Wales ✻ Carmarthen *area* 2226 *sq mi* (*5788 sq km*), *pop* 332,300
Dzaudzhikau — see VLADIKAVKAZ
Dzer·zhinsk \dər-ˈzhin(t)sk\ city cen Russia in Europe on Oka River W of Gorki *pop* 285,000
Dzungaria or **Dzungarian Basin** — see JUNGGAR
E¹ — see LHOTSE
Ea·gan \ˈē-gən\ city SE Minn. *pop* 47,409
Ea·gle Lake \ˈē-gəl\ lake 13 *mi* (*21 km*) long N Calif. ENE of Lassen Peak
Eagle Pass city SW Tex. on Rio Grande *pop* 20,651
Ea·ling \ˈē-liŋ\ borough of W Greater London, England *pop* 284,000
East An·glia \ˈaŋ-glē-ə\ region E England including Norfolk & Suffolk; one of kingdoms in Anglo-Saxon heptarchy *pop* 1,224,400 — **East An·gli·an** \-ən\ adj or n
East Antarctica — see ANTARCTICA
East Bengal the part of Bengal now in Bangladesh
East Beskids — see BESKIDS
East·bourne \ˈēs(t)-ˌbórn, -ˌbórn\ borough S England in E. Sussex on English Channel *pop* 77,608
East Cape — see DEZHNEVA (Cape)
East Chicago city NW Ind. SE of Chicago, Ill. *pop* 33,892
East China Sea sea W Pacific bet. China (on W), S. Korea (on N), Japan & Ryukyu Islands (on E), & Taiwan (on S)
East Cleveland city NE Ohio NE of Cleveland *pop* 33,096
East Detroit city SE Mich. NE of Detroit *pop* 35,283
Eas·ter Island \ˈē-stər\ or **Ra·pa Nui** \ˌrä-pə-ˈnü-ē\ or Sp **Is·la de Pas·cua** \ˌēz-lä-də-ˈpäs-kwə\ island Chile in SE Pacific 2000 *mi* (*3200 km*) W of coast *area* 50 *sq mi* (*130 sq km*) — **Easter Islander** n
Eastern Cape province SE Republic of South Africa *area* 65,875 *sq mi* (*170,616 sq km*), *pop* 6,665,400
Eastern Ghats \ˈgäts, ˈgóts, ˈgəts\ chain of mountains SE India extending SW & S from near delta of the Mahanadi in Orissa to W Tamil Nadu; highest point Mt. Dodabetta (in Nilgiri Hills) 8640 *ft* (*2633 m*) — see WESTERN GHATS
Eastern Rumelia region S Bulgaria including Rhodope Mountains & the Maritsa valley
Eastern Samoa — see AMERICAN SAMOA
Eastern Shore region E Md. & E Va. E of Chesapeake Bay; sometimes considered as including Del. — see DELMARVA PENINSULA
Eastern Thrace — see THRACE
Eastern Transvaal province NE Republic of South Africa *area* 31,590 *sq mi* (*81,818 sq km*), *pop* 2,838,500
East Flanders province NW cen Belgium ✻ Ghent *area* 1147 *sq mi* (*2982 sq km*), *pop* 1,335,793
East Frisian — see FRISIAN ISLANDS
East Germany the German Democratic Republic — see GERMANY
East Ham \ˈēst-ˈham\ former county borough SE England in Essex, now part of Newham
East Hartford town cen Conn. *pop* 50,452
East Ha·ven \ˈēst-ˌhā-vən\ town S Conn. SE of New Haven *pop* 26,144
East Indies **1** or **East India** southeastern Asia including India, Indochina, & Malay Archipelago — a chiefly former name **2** the Malay Archipelago — **East Indian** adj or n
East·lake \ˈēst-ˌlāk\ city NE Ohio NE of Cleveland *pop* 21,161
East Lansing city S Mich. *pop* 50,677
East London city & port S Republic of South Africa in SE Cape of Good Hope on Indian Ocean *pop* 119,727
East Los Angeles urban center SW Calif. *pop* 126,379

East Lo·thi·an \ˈlō-thē-ən\ or **Had·ding·ton** \ˈha-diŋ-tən\ or **Had·ding·ton·shire** \-ˌshir, -shər\ former county SE Scotland ✻ Haddington — see LOTHIAN
East·main \ˈēst-ˌmān\ river 375 *mi* (*604 km*) Canada in W Que.
East Malaysia the parts of Malaysia on the island of Borneo, comprising Sabah and Sarawak
East Moline city NW Ill. on Mississippi River *pop* 20,147
Eas·ton \ˈēs-tən\ **1** city SE Mass. SW of Brockton *pop* 19,807 **2** city E Pa. NE of Allentown *pop* 26,276
East Orange city NE N.J. NW of Newark *pop* 73,552
East Pakistan the former E division of Pakistan comprising the E portion of Bengal — see BANGLADESH
East Palo Alto city W Calif. *pop* 23,451
East Peoria city N cen Ill. *pop* 21,378
East Point \ˈēst-ˌpóint\ city NW cen Ga. SW of Atlanta *pop* 34,402
East Providence city E R.I. *pop* 50,380
East Prussia region N Europe bordering on the Baltic E of Pomerania; formerly a province of Prussia, for a time (1919–39) separated from rest of Prussia by Polish Corridor; divided 1945 bet. Poland & U.S.S.R. (Russia & Lithuania)
East Punjab — see PUNJAB
East Ridge \ˈēst-ˌrij\ town SE Tenn. SE of Chattanooga *pop* 21,101
East Riding — see YORK
East River strait SE N.Y. connecting Upper New York Bay with Long Island Sound & separating Manhattan Is. from Long Is.
East Saint Louis city SW Ill. *pop* 40,944
East Siberian Sea sea, arm of Arctic Ocean N of Yakut Republic, E Russia in Asia extending from New Siberian Islands to Wrangel Is.
East Strouds·burg \ˈstraùdz-ˌbərg\ borough E Pa. *pop* 8781
East Suffolk — see SUFFOLK
East Sus·sex \ˈsə-siks, US also -ˌseks\ county SE England ✻ Lewes *area* 693 *sq mi* (*1802 sq km*), *pop* 666,700
East York borough Canada in SE Ont. near Toronto *pop* 102,696
Eau Claire \ō-ˈklar, -ˈkler\ city W Wis. *pop* 56,856
Eb·bw Vale \ˈe-bü-ˈväl\ town SE Wales in W Gwent *pop* 24,422
Eboracum — see YORK
Ebro \ˈā-(ˌ)brō\ river 480 *mi* (*772 km*) NE Spain flowing from Cantabrian Mountains ESE into the Mediterranean
Ecbatana — see HAMADAN
Ec·ua·dor \ˈe-kwə-ˌdór\ country W S. America bordering on the Pacific; a republic ✻ Quito *area* 104,510 *sq mi* (*271,726 sq km*), *pop* 6,521,710 — **Ec·ua·dor·an** \ˌe-kwə-ˈdór-ən, -ˈdór-\ adj or n — **Ec·ua·dor·ean** or **Ec·ua·dor·ian** \-ē-ən\ adj or n
Edam \ˈē-dəm, -ˌdam, D ā-ˈdäm\ commune NW Netherlands on the IJsselmeer NNE of Amsterdam *pop* 23,853
Ede **1** \ˈā-də\ commune E Netherlands NW of Arnhem *pop* 85,892 **2** \ˈā-ˌdā\ city SW Nigeria NE of Ibadan *pop* 216,400
Eden Prairie \ˈē-dᵊn\ village SE cen Minn., a suburb of Minneapolis *pop* 39,311
Edes·sa \i-ˈde-sə\ **1** or **Vo·de·na** \ˌvó-the-ˈnä\ city N Greece in W Macedonia; ancient ✻ of Macedonian kings *pop* 15,980 **2** — see URFA
Edi·na \i-ˈdī-nə\ village SE Minn. SW of Minneapolis *pop* 46,070
Ed·in·boro \ˈe-dᵊn-ˌbar-ə, -ˌbə-rə\ borough NW corner of Pa. *pop* 7736
Ed·in·burg \ˈe-dᵊn-ˌbərg\ city S Tex. NW of Brownsville *pop* 29,885
Ed·in·burgh \ˈe-dᵊn-ˌbar-ə, -ˌbə-rə, -b(ə-)rə\ **1** or ScGael **Dun·e·din** \ˌdə-ˈnē-dᵊn\ city ✻ of Scotland & of Lothian region on Firth of Forth *pop* 419,187 **2** or **Ed·in·burgh·shire** \-ˌshir, -shər\ — see MIDLOTHIAN
Edir·ne \ā-ˈdir-nə\ or formerly **Adri·a·no·ple** \ˌā-drē-ə-ˈnō-pəl\ city Turkey in Europe on the Maritsa *pop* 71,927
Ed·is·to \ˈe-də-ˌstō\ river 150 *mi* (*241 km*) S S.C. flowing SE into the Atlantic
Edith Ca·vell, Mount \ˈē-dəth-ˈka-vəl, -kə-ˈvel\ mountain 11,033 *ft* (*3363 m*) Canada in SW Alta. in Jasper National Park
Ed·mond \ˈed-mənd\ city cen Okla. N of Oklahoma City *pop* 52,315
Ed·monds \ˈed-mən(d)z\ city W Wash. N of Seattle *pop* 30,744
Ed·mon·ton \ˈed-mən-tən\ **1** city Canada ✻ of Alta. on the N. Saskatchewan *pop* 616,741 **2** former municipal borough SE England in Middlesex, now part of Enfield — **Ed·mon·to·ni·an** \ˌed-mən-ˈtō-nē-ən, -nyən\ n
Edo — see TOKYO
Edom \ˈē-dəm\ or **Id·u·maea** or **Id·u·mea** \ˌi-jə-ˈmē-ə\ ancient country SW Asia S of Judea & the Dead Sea
Ed·ward, Lake \ˈed-wərd\ lake E Africa SW of Lake Albert on boundary bet. NE Zaire & SW Uganda *area* 830 *sq mi* (*2158 sq km*)
Ed·wards \ˈed-wərdz\ plateau 2000–5000 *ft* (*610–1524 m*) SW Tex.
Efa·te \ā-ˈfä-ˌtā\ or F **Va·té** \vä-ˈtā\ island SW Pacific in cen Vanuatu; chief town Port-Vila (✻ of Vanuatu) *area* 200 *sq mi* (*520 sq km*), *pop* 30,422
Effigy Mounds National Monument site NE Iowa on Mississippi River NW of Dubuque including prehistoric mounds
Ega·di Islands \ˈe-gə-dē\ or anc **Ae·ga·tes Islands** \ē-ˈgā-tēz\ islands Italy off W coast of Sicily *area* 15 *sq mi* (*6 sq km*)
Eger \ˈā-gər\ or Czech **Ohře** \ˈór-zhə\ river 193 *mi* (*311 km*) E Germany & NW Czech Republic flowing NE into the Elbe
Eg·mont, Mount \ˈeg-ˌmänt\ or **Ta·ra·na·ki** \ˌtar-ə-ˈna-kē, ˌtär-\ mountain 8260 *ft* (*2518 m*) New Zealand in SW cen North Is.
Egypt \ˈē-jəpt\ or Ar **Miṣr** \ˈmisrᵊ\ country NE Africa bordering on Mediterranean & Red seas ✻ Cairo *area* 386,198 *sq mi* (*1,004,115 sq km*), *pop* 36,626,204 — see UNITED ARAB REPUBLIC
Ei·fel \ˈī-fəl\ plateau region W Germany NW of the Moselle & NE of Luxembourg
Ei·ger \ˈī-gər\ mountain 13,025 *ft* (*3970 m*) W cen Switzerland NE of the Jungfrau
Eind·ho·ven \ˈint-ˌhō-və(n), ˈänt-\ commune S Netherlands in N. Brabant *pop* 194,641
Eire — see IRELAND
Ei·se·nach \ˈī-zᵊn-ˌäk, -ˌäk\ city cen Germany in Thuringia W of Erfurt *pop* 50,754
Ekaterinodar — see KRASNODAR
Ekaterinoslav — see DNEPROPETROVSK
El Aiún — see AAIÚN, EL
El Alamein — see ALAMEIN

Elam \'ē-ləm\ *or* **Su·si·ana** \ˌsü-zē-'a-nə, -'ä-, -'ä-\ ancient kingdom SW Asia at head of Persian Gulf E of Babylonia ✱ Susa — **Elam·ite** \'ē-lə-ˌmīt\ *adj or n*

Elatea — see CITHAERON

Elath \'ē-ˌlath\ **1** — see 'AQABA **2** *or* **Ei·lat** \ā-'lät\ town & port S Israel at head of Gulf of 'Aqaba

Ela·zig \ˌe-lə-'zə, -'zē(g)\ city E *cen* Turkey in valley of the upper Murat *pop* 142,787

El·ba \'el-bə\ island Italy in the Mediterranean bet. Corsica & mainland; chief town Portoferraio *area* 86 *sq mi* (224 *km*)

El Bahnasa — see OXYRHYNCHUS

El·be \'el-bə, 'elb\ *or Czech* **La·be** \'lä-be\ river 720 *mi* (1159 *km*) N Czech Republic & NE Germany flowing NW into North Sea

El·bert, Mount \'el-bərt\ mountain 14,431 *ft* (4398 *m*) *cen* Colo. in Sawatch Range; highest in Colo. & Rocky Mountains

El·blag \'el-ˌblónk\ *or G* **El·bing** \'el-biŋ\ city & port N Poland near the Frisches Haff *pop* 125,154

El'·brus *or* **El·brus** \el-'brüz, -'brüs\ mountain 18,481 *ft* (5633 *m*) S Russia in Europe in Kabardino-Balkar Republic; highest in the Caucasus & in Europe

El·burz Mountains \el-'bùrz\ mountains N Iran parallel with S shore of Caspian Sea — see DAMAVAND

El Ca·jon \ˌel-kə-'hōn\ city SW Calif. E of San Diego *pop* 88,693

El Cen·tro \el-'sen-(ˌ)trō\ city S Calif. in Imperial Valley *pop* 31,384

El Cer·ri·to \ˌel-sə-'rē-(ˌ)tō\ city W Calif. on San Francisco Bay N of Berkeley *pop* 22,869

El·che \'el-(ˌ)chā\ city SE Spain SW of Alicante *pop* 164,779

El Do·ra·do \ˌel-də-'rä-(ˌ)dō, -'rä-də\ city S Ark. *pop* 23,146

Electric Peak mountain 11,155 *ft* (3400 *m*) S Mont. in Yellowstone National Park; highest in Gallatin Range

El·e·phan·ta \ˌe-lə-'fan-tə\ *or* **Gha·ra·pu·ri** \ˌgär-ə-'pùr-ē\ island W India in Bombay harbor

El·e·phan·ti·ne \ˌe-lə-ˌfan-'tī-nē, -fən-, -'tē-\ island S Egypt in the Nile opposite Aswān *pop* 1814

Eleu·sis \i-'lü-səs\ ancient deme W Attica NW of Athens; ruins at modern town of **Elev·sís** \ˌe-lef-'sēs\ in E Greece — **El·eu·sin·i·an** \ˌe-lyü-'si-nē-ən\ *n*

Eleu·thera \i-'lü-thə-rə\ island Bahamas E of New Providence Is. *area* 164 *sq mi* (426 *sq km*)

El Fai·yûm \ˌel-fā-'yüm, -(ˌ)fī-\ city N Egypt SSW of Cairo *pop* 166,910

El Fa·sher \el-'fa-shər\ city W Sudan in Darfur

El Fer·rol \el-fə-'ról\ *or* **El Ferrol del Cau·di·llo** \ˌdel-kaù-'thē-(ˌ)yō, -'thēl-(ˌ)yō\ city & port NW Spain on the Atlantic *pop* 87,736

El Gezira — see GEZIRA, EL

El·gin **1** \'el-jən\ city NE Ill. *pop* 77,010 **2** \'el-gən\ *or* **El·gin·shire** \-ˌshir, -shər\ — see MORAY **3** \'el-gən\ royal burgh NE Scotland in Moray district of Grampian region *pop* 18,905

El·gon, Mount \'el-ˌgän\ extinct volcano 14,178 *ft* (4321 *m*) E Africa on boundary bet. Uganda & Kenya NE of Lake Victoria

El Hasa — see HASA

Elis \'ē-ləs\ *or NGk* **Ilía** \ē-'lē-ä\ region S Greece in NW Peloponnisos S of Achaea bordering on Ionian Sea

Elisabethville — see LUBUMBASHI

Elisavetgrad — see KIROVOGRAD

Elisavetpol — see GYANDZHA

Eliz·a·beth \i-'li-zə-bəth\ **1** short river SE Va. flowing bet. cities of Norfolk & Portsmouth into Hampton Roads **2** city & port NE N.J. SW of Newark on Newark Bay *pop* 110,002

Elizabeth Islands islands SE Mass. bet. Buzzards Bay & Vineyard Sound

Elk Grove Village village NE Ill. NW of Chicago *pop* 33,429

Elk·hart \'el-kärt\ city N Ind. E of S. Bend *pop* 43,627

Elk Island National Park reservation Canada in E *cen* Alta.

Ellás — see GREECE

Elles·mere Island \'elz-ˌmir\ island Canada in Northwest Territories W of NW Greenland — see COLUMBIA (Cape)

Ellice — see TUVALU

El·lis Island \'e-ləs\ island SE N.Y. in Upper New York Bay; served as immigrant station 1892–1954

El·lo·ra \e-'lòr-ə, -'lór-\ *or* **Elu·ra** \-'lúr-ə\ village W India in *cen* Maharashtra NW of Aurangabad; caves

Ells·worth Land \'elz-(ˌ)wərth\ region W Antarctica on Bellingshausen Sea

El Maghreb al Aqsa — see MAGHREB

El Mansûra — see MANSÚRA

Elm·hurst \'elm-ˌhərst\ city NE Ill. W of Chicago *pop* 42,029

El Minya — see MINYĀ, AL

El·mi·ra \el-'mī-rə\ city S N.Y. *pop* 33,724

El Misti — see MISTI

El Mon·te \el-'män-tē\ city SW Calif. E of Los Angeles *pop* 106,209

El Mor·ro National Monument \el-'mär-(ˌ)ō, -'mór-\ reservation W N.Mex. SE of Gallup; rock carvings, pueblo

Elm·wood Park \'elm-ˌwùd\ village NE Ill. *pop* 23,206

El Obeid \el-ō-'bād\ city W Sudan in Kordofan *pop* 66,270

El Paso \el-'pa-(ˌ)sō\ city Tex. at W tip on Rio Grande *pop* 515,342 — **El Paso·an** \-pa-sō-ən\ *n*

El Sal·va·dor \el-'sal-və-ˌdòr, ˌsal-və-'\ country Central America bordering on the Pacific; a republic ✱ San Salvador *area* 8236 *sq mi* (21,414 *sq km*) *pop* 4,813,000 — **El Sal·va·dor·an** \-ˌsal-və-'dór-ən\ *n or adj*

Elsass — see ALSACE

Elsene — see IXELLES

El Uqsor — see LUXOR

Elu·ru \e-'lúr-(ˌ)ü\ *or formerly* **El·lore** \e-'lōr, -'lór\ city SE India in E Andhra Pradesh *pop* 168,148

Ely \'ē-lē\ town E England in N *cen* Cambridgeshire

Ely, Isle of district & former administrative county (✱ Ely) E England in Cambridgeshire — see CAMBRIDGESHIRE

Elyr·ia \i-'lir-ē-ə\ city NE Ohio SW of Cleveland *pop* 56,746

Em·bar·ras *or* **Em·bar·rass** \'am-ˌbró\ river 150 *mi* (241 *km*) E Ill. flowing SE into the Wabash

Em·den \'em-dən\ city & port NW Germany at mouth of Ems River *pop* 51,186

Emesa — see HOMS

Emi·lia \ā-'mēl-yə\ **1** district N Italy comprising the W part of Emilia=Romagna region **2** — see EMILIA-ROMAGNA

Emi·lia–Ro·ma·gna \ā-ˌmēl-yə-rō-'mä-nyə\ *or formerly* **Emilia** *or anc* **Ae·mil·ia** \ē-'mil-yə\ region N Italy bounded by the Po, the Adriatic, & the Apennines ✱ Bologna *area* 8546 *sq mi* (22,220 *sq km*), *pop* 3,921,597

Em·me \'e-mə\ river 45 *mi* (72 *km*) *cen* Switzerland in E Bern canton

Em·men \'e-mən\ commune NE Netherlands *pop* 90,816

Em·men·tal *or* **Em·men·thal** \'e-mən-ˌtäl\ valley of the upper Emme River

Em·po·ria \em-'pōr-ē-ə, -'pòr-\ city E *cen* Kans. *pop* 25,512

Empty Quarter RUB' AL KHALI

Ems \'emz, 'em(p)s\ **1** river 200 *mi* (322 *km*) NW Germany flowing N into North Sea **2** *or* **Bad Ems** \ˌbät-\ town W Germany SE of Koblenz *pop* 10,358

Enchanted Mesa sandstone butte W N.Mex. NE of Acoma

En·ci·ni·tas \ˌen(t)-sə-'nē-təs\ city S Calif. on coast N of San Diego *pop* 55,386

En·der·bury \'en-dər-ˌber-ē\ island (atoll) *cen* Pacific in the Phoenix Islands chain of Kiribati

En·di·cott Mountains \'en-di-kət, -də-ˌkät\ mountains N Alaska, the central range of Brooks Range

En·field \'en-ˌfēld\ **1** town N Conn. *pop* 45,532 **2** borough of N Greater London, England *pop* 261,100

En·ga·dine \'eŋ-gə-ˌdēn, 'eŋ-gə-ˌ\ valley of upper Inn River 60 *mi* (96 *km*) long E Switzerland in Graubünden

En·gland \'iŋ-glənd, 'iŋ-lənd\ **1** *or LL* **An·glia** \'aŋ-glē-ə\ country S Great Britain; a division of the United Kingdom of Great Britain and Northern Ireland ✱ London *area* 50,331 *sq mi* (130,861 *sq km*), *pop* 46,220,955 **2** England & Wales **3** UNITED KINGDOM

En·gle·wood \'eŋ-gəl-ˌwùd\ **1** city N *cen* Colo. S of Denver *pop* 29,387 **2** city NE N.J. on the Hudson *pop* 24,850

English Channel *or F* **La Manche** \lä-'mänsh\ strait bet. S England & N France connecting North Sea & Atlantic Ocean

Enid \'ē-nəd\ city N Okla. *pop* 45,309

Eni·we·tok \ˌe-ni-'wē-ˌtäk\ island (atoll) W Pacific in the NW Marshalls

En·na \'e-nə\ commune Italy in *cen* Sicily *pop* 29,350

En·nis \'e-nəs\ urban district W Ireland ✱ of County Clare *pop* 5917

En·nis·kil·len \ˌe-nəs-'ski-lən\ *or* **In·nis·kil·ling** \ˌi-nə-'ski-liŋ\ municipal borough SW Northern Ireland in *cen* Fermanagh district

Enns \'enz, 'en(t)s\ river 160 *mi* (257 *km*) C Austria flowing E & N from Styria into the Danube

En·sche·de \'en(t)-skə-ˌdā, -skə-\ commune E Netherlands in Overijssel near German frontier *pop* 144,897

En·se·na·da \ˌen(t)-sə-'nä-də\ city & port NW Mexico in Baja California on the Pacific SE of Tijuana *pop* 113,320

En·teb·be \en-'te-bə, -bē\ town S Uganda on N shore of Lake Victoria; former ✱ of Uganda *pop* 21,096

En·ter·prise \'en-tə(r)-ˌprīz\ city SE Ala. *pop* 20,123

Eph·e·sus \'e-fə-səs\ ancient city W Asia Minor in Ionia near Aegean coast; its site SSE of Izmir — **Ephe·sian** \i-'fē-zhən\ *adj or n*

Ephra·im \'ē-frē-əm\ **1** *or* **Mount Ephraim** hilly region *cen* Palestine in N Jordan E of Jordan River **2** — see ISRAEL

Epidamnus — see DURRES

Ep·i·dau·rus \ˌe-pə-'dòr-əs\ ancient town S Greece in Argolis on Saronic Gulf

Épi·nal \ˌā-pi-'nál\ commune NE France on the Moselle *pop* 39,000

Epi·rus *or* **Epei·rus** \i-'pī-rəs\ *or NGk* **Ípi·ros** \'ē-pē-ˌròs\ region NW Greece bordering on Ionian Sea — **Epi·rote** \i-'pī-ˌrōt, -rət\ *n*

Ep·ping Forest \'e-piŋ\ forested region SE England in Essex NE of London & S of town of Epping

Ep·som and Ew·ell \'ep-səm-ən(d)-'yü-əl\ borough SE England in Surrey SW of London *pop* 69,230

Equatorial Guinea country W Africa on Bight of Biafra comprising former Spanish Guinea; an independent republic since 1968 ✱ Malabo *area* 10,831 *sq mi* (28,161 *sq km*), *pop* 300,000 — see SPANISH GUINEA

Erbil — see ARBIL

Er·ci·yas Da·gi \er-jē-ˌyäs-dä-'ē, -dä-'gē\ mountain 12,848 *ft* (3916 *m*) *cen* Turkey; highest in Asia Minor

Er·e·bus, Mount \'er-ə-bəs\ volcano 12,450 *ft* (3795 *m*) E Antarctica on Ross Is. in SW Ross Sea

Ere·gli \er-ā-'lē, -'glē\ **1** city S Turkey SSE of Ankara *pop* 38,362 **2** town & port NW Turkey in Asia on Black Sea *pop* 18,978

Er·furt \'er-fərt, -ˌfùrt\ city *cen* Germany WSW of Leipzig *pop* 212,035

Erie \'ir-ē\ city & port NW Pa. on Lake Erie *pop* 108,718

Erie, Lake lake E *cen* N. America on boundary bet. the U.S. & Canada; one of the Great Lakes *area* 9940 *sq mi* (25,844 *sq km*)

Erie Canal canal 363 *mi* (584 *km*) long N N.Y. from Hudson River at Albany to Lake Erie at Buffalo; built 1817–25; superseded by **New York State Barge Canal** (*ab* 525 *mi* or 840 *km* long)

Eriha — see JERICHO

Er·in \'er-ən\ IRELAND — a poetic name

Er·i·trea \ˌer-ə-'trē-ə, -'trā-\ country NE Africa bordering on Red Sea ✱ Asmara; incorporated (1962) into Ethiopia; voted (1993) in favor of independence *area* 46,000 *sq mi* (119,600 *sq km*) — **Er·i·tre·an** \-ən\ *adj or n*

Er·lang·en \'er-ˌläŋ-ən\ city S Germany in Bavaria NNW of Nuremberg *pop* 101,845

Er·moú·po·lis *or* **Her·moú·po·lis** \er-'mü-pə-ləs, -pō-ˌlēs\ *or* **Sy·ros** \'si-ˌräs, 'sē-, -ˌròs\ town & port Greece on Síros; chief town of the Cyclades *pop* 12,987

Er Rif \ər-'rif\ *or* **Rif** \'rif\ mountain range N Morocco on the Mediterranean

Erz·ge·bir·ge \'erts-gə-ˌbir-gə\ mountain range Germany & NW Czech Republic on boundary bet. Saxony & Bohemia; highest Klinovec (in Czech Republic) 4081 *ft* (1244 *m*)

\ə\ abut \ᵊ\ kitten, F table \ər\ further \a\ ash \ā\ ace \ä\ mop, mar \aù\ out \ch\ chin \e\ bet \ē\ easy \g\ go \i\ hit \ī\ ice \j\ job \ŋ\ sing \ō\ go \ò\ law \òi\ boy \th\ thin \th̲\ the \ü\ loot \ù\ foot \y\ yet \zh\ vision \ä, k̲, ⁿ, œ, œ̄, ᵾ, ᵫ, ᵿ, ᵊ\ see Guide to Pronunciation

Er·zin·can \\,er-zin-'jän\ city E cen Turkey on the Euphrates pop 73,335

Er·zu·rum \\,er-zə-'rüm, ,ər-; ,erz-'rüm, ,ərz-\ city NE Turkey in mountains of W Turkish Armenia pop 190,121

Es·bjerg \\'es-,byer(g)\ city & port SW Denmark in SW Jutland Peninsula on North Sea pop 81,480

Escaut — see SCHELDT

Es·con·di·do \\,es-kən-'dē-(,)dō\ city SW Calif. N of San Diego pop 108,635

Es·dra·e·lon, Plain of \\,ez-drə-'ē-lən\ or **Plain of Jez·re·el** \\'jez-rē-,el, -,rē(ə)l\ plain N Israel NE of Mt. Carmel in valley of the upper Qishon

Es·fa·hān \\,es-fə-'hän, -'han\ or **Is·fa·han** \\,is-\ or **Is·pa·han** \\,is-pə-\ city W cen Iran; former ✳ of Persia pop 986,753

Esher \\'ē-shər\ town S England in Surrey pop 61,446

Es·kils·tu·na \\'es-kəl-,stü-nə\ city SE Sweden pop 89,460

Es·ki·se·hir \\,es-ki-shə-'hir\ or **Es·ki·shehr** \\-'sher\ city W cen Turkey on tributary of the Sakarya pop 309,335

España — see SPAIN

Española — see HISPANIOLA

Es·pí·ri·to San·to \\ə-'spir-ə-,tü-'san-(,)tü\ state E Brazil bordering on the Atlantic ✳ Vitória area 16,543 sq mi (43,012 sq km), pop 2,063,679

Es·pí·ri·tu San·to \\ə-'spir-ə-,tü-'san-(,)tü\ island SW Pacific in NW Vanuatu largest in the group area 1875 sq mi (4875 sq km), pop 22,663

Es·poo \\'es-(,)pō\ town S Finland W of Helsinki pop 169,851

Es·qui·line \\'es-kwə-,līn, -lən\ hill in Rome, Italy, one of seven on which the ancient city was built — see AVENTINE

Es·sa·oui·ra \\,e-sə-'wir-ə\ or **Mog·a·dor** \\'mä-gə-,dór\ city & port W Morocco on the Atlantic W of Marrakech pop 30,061

Es·sen \\'e-s³n\ city W Germany in the Ruhr pop 647,643

Es·se·qui·bo \\,e-sə-'kē-(,)bō\ river 600 mi (966 km) Guyana flowing N into the Atlantic through a wide estuary

Es·sex \\'e-siks\ county SE England bordering on North Sea & N shore of Thames River; one of kingdoms in Anglo-Saxon heptarchy ✳ Chelmsford area 1419 sq mi (3689 sq km), pop 1,480,100

Ess·ling·en \\'es-liŋ-ən\ city SW Germany on the Neckar pop 90,835

Es·te·rel \\,es-tə-'rel\ forested mountain region SE France on coast bet. Fréjus & Cannes; highest point 2020 ft (616 m)

Es·tes Park \\'es-tēz\ valley N Colo. in Front Range of the Rocky Mountains at E border of Rocky Mountain National Park

Es·to·nia \\e-'stō-nē-ə, -nyə\ or **Es·tho·nia** \\e-'stō-, es-'thō-\ country N Europe bordering on Baltic Sea; one of the Baltic Provinces of Russia 1721–1917, an independent republic 1918–40, a constituent republic **(Estonian Republic)** of the U.S.S.R 1940–91 ✳ Tallinn area 18,361 sq mi (47,739 sq km), pop 1,573,000

Es·to·ril \\,ēsh-tə-'ril\ resort town Portugal on coast W of Lisbon pop 15,740

Es·tre·ma·du·ra \\,es-trə-mə-'dur-ə\ **1** region & old province W cen Portugal ✳ Lisbon **2** or **Ex·tre·ma·du·ra** \\,ek-strə-\ region & old province W Spain bordering on Portugal; area included in present Cáceres & Badajoz provinces

Ethi·o·pia \\,ē-thē-'ō-pē-ə\ **1** ancient country NE Africa bordering on Red Sea and extending from S Egypt to N (present-day) Ethiopia **2** or **Ab·ys·sin·ia** \\,a-bə-'sin-yə, -'si-nē-ə\ country E Africa; formerly an empire, since 1975 a republic ✳ Addis Ababa area 471,776 sq mi (1,226,618 sq mi) pop 32,775,000

Et·na, Mount \\'et-nə\ volcano 10,902 ft (3323 m) Italy in NE Sicily

Eto·bi·coke \\e-'tō-bi-,kō—sic\ city Canada in SE Ont. pop 309,993

Eton \\'ē-t³n\ town SE cen England in Berkshire

Etru·ria \\i-'trür-ē-ə\ ancient country cen Italy coextensive with modern Tuscany & part of Umbria; home of the Etruscans

Et·trick Forest \\'e-trik\ region, formerly a forest & hunting ground, in SE Scotland in Borders region

Euboea — see ÉVVOIA — **Eu·boe·an** \\yü-'bē-ən\ adj or n

Eu·clid \\'yü-kləd\ city NE Ohio NE of Cleveland pop 54,875

Eu·ga·ne·an Hills \\yü-'gā-nē-ən, ,yü-gə-'nē-\ hills NE Italy in SW Veneto bet. Padua & the Adige

Eu·gene \\yü-'jēn\ city W Oreg. on the Willamette pop 112,669

Eu·less \\'yü-ləs\ city NE Tex. NE of Fort Worth pop 38,149

Eu·pen \\'ói-pən; ,ə(r)-'pen, œ-\ commune E Belgium E of Liège; formerly in Germany, transferred (with Malmédy) to Belgium 1919 pop 17,161

Eu·phra·tes \\yü-'frā-(,)tēz\ river 1700 mi (2736 km) SW Asia flowing from E Turkey SW & SE to unite with the Tigris forming the Shatt-al-Arab — see KARA SU — **Eu·phra·te·an** \\-'frä-tē-ən\ adj

Eur·asia \\yü-'rā-zhə, -shə\ name given to Asia & Europe as one continent

Eure \\'ər\ river 140 mi (225 km) NW France flowing N into the Seine

Eu·re·ka \\yü-'rē-kə\ city & port NW Calif. pop 27,025

Eu·rope \\'yúr-əp\ **1** continent of the E hemisphere bet. Asia & the Atlantic area ab 3,800,000 sq mi (9,880,000 sq km) **2** the European continent exclusive of the British Isles

European Economic Community or **Common Market** economic organization subsumed within the European Union

European Union or formerly **European Communities** or **European Community** economic, scientific, and political organization consisting of Belgium, France, Italy, Luxembourg, Netherlands, Germany, Denmark, Greece, Ireland, United Kingdom, Spain, & Portugal

Ev·ans, Mount \\'e-vənz\ mountain 14,264 ft (4348 m) N cen Colo. in Front Range WSW of Denver

Ev·ans·ton \\'e-vən(t)-stən\ city NE Ill. N of Chicago pop 73,233

Ev·ans·ville \\'e-vənz-,vil\ city SW Ind. on Ohio River pop 126,272

Ev·er·est, Mount \\'ev-rəst, 'e-və-\ or Tibetan **Cho·mo·lung·ma** \\,chō-mə-'lúŋ-mə\ mountain 29,028 ft (8848 m) S Asia on border bet. Nepal & Tibet in the Himalayas; highest in the world

Ev·er·ett \\'ev-rət, 'e-və-\ **1** city E Mass. N of Boston pop 35,701 **2** city NW cen Wash. on Puget Sound N of Seattle pop 69,961

Ev·er·glades \\'e-vər-,glādz\ swamp region S Fla. S of Lake Okeechobee; now partly drained; SW part forms **Everglades National Park**

Evergreen Park village NE Ill. S of Chicago pop 20,874

Eve·sham \\'ēv-shəm\ borough W cen England in Hereford and Worcester S of Birmingham in **Vale of Evesham** pop 15,271

Évian or **Évian-les-Bains** \\ā-vyäⁿ-le-baⁿ\ commune E France on Lake Geneva; health resort pop 5765

Évo·ra \\'e-və-rə\ city S cen Portugal pop 50,545

Évreux \\āv-'rœ, -'rə(r)\ commune N France WNW of Paris pop 46,181

Ev·ri·pos \\'ev-ri-,pós\ or **Eu·ri·pus** \\yü-'rī-pəs\ or NGk **Ev·rí·pou Porth·mós** \\ev-'rē-pü-(,)pórth-'mós\ narrow strait E Greece bet. Évvoia & mainland

Évros — see MARITSA

Ev·voia \\'ev-(,)yä\ or **Eu·boea** \\yü-'bē-ə\ island 90 mi (145 km) long E Greece in the Aegean NE of Attica & Boeotia ✳ Chalcis area 1457 sq mi (3788 sq km)

Ex·e·ter \\'ek-sə-tər\ city SW England ✳ of Devon pop 95,621

Ex·moor \\'eks-,múr, -,mór, -,mór\ moorland SW England in Somerset & Devonshire area 32 sq mi (83 sq km)

Extremadura — see ESTREMADURA

Ex·u·ma \\ik-'sü-mə, ig-'zü-\ islands in cen Bahamas S of **Exuma Sound** (SE of New Providence Is.); chief island **Great Exuma**

Eyre, Lake intermittent lake cen Australia in NE S. Australia

Eyre Peninsula \\'ar, 'er\ peninsula Australia in S S. Australia W of Spencer Gulf

Eyzies, Les — see LES EYZIES

Fa·en·za \\fä-'en-zə, -'en(t)-sə\ commune N Italy pop 54,118

Faer·oe Islands or **Far·oe Islands** \\'far-(,)ō, 'fer-\ islands Denmark in the NE Atlantic NW of the Shetlands ✳ Thorshavn area 540 sq mi (1404 sq km), pop 47,653

Fa·ial \\fə-'yäl, fi-'äl\ island cen Azores area 64 sq mi (166 sq km)

Fair·banks \\'far-,baŋks, 'fer-\ city E cen Alaska pop 30,843

Fair·born \\'far-,bórn, 'fer-\ city SW cen Ohio pop 31,300

Fair·fax \\'far-,faks, 'fer-\ city NE Va. pop 19,622

Fair·field \\'far-,fēld, 'fer-\ **1** city W Calif. NE of Berkeley pop 77,211 **2** city SW Conn. SW of Bridgeport pop 53,418 **3** city SW Ohio pop 39,729

Fair Lawn borough NE N.J. NE of Paterson pop 30,548

Fair·mont \\'far-,mänt, 'fer-\ city N W.Va. pop 20,210

Fair·weath·er, Mount \\'far-,we-thər, 'fer-\ mountain 15,300 ft (4663 m) on boundary bet. Alaska & B.C.; highest in **Fairweather Range** of the Coast Ranges

Fai·sa·la·bad \\,fī-,sä-lə-'bäd, -,sa-lə-'bad\ or formerly **Lyall·pur** \\lē-,äl-'púr\ city NE Pakistan W of Lahore pop 1,092,000

Faiyûm, El — see EL FAIYÛM

Faiz·a·bad \\'fī-zə-,bad, -,bäd\ **1** city NE Afghanistan pop 70,871 **2** or **Fyz·a·bad** \\'fī-\ city N India in Uttar Pradesh pop 141,714

Fa·ka·ra·va \\,fä-kə-'rä-və\ island (atoll) S Pacific, principal island of the Tuamotu Archipelago pop 651

Fako — see CAMEROON

Fa·laise \\fə-'lāz\ town NW France SSE of Caen pop 8133

Fal·kirk \\'fól-(,)kərk\ royal burgh cen Scotland in Central region ENE of Glasgow pop 36,875

Falk·land Islands \\'fó-klənd, 'fól-\ or Sp **Is·las Mal·vi·nas** \\,ēz-läz-mäl-'vē-näs\ islands SW Atlantic E of S end of Argentina; a Brit. crown colony ✳ Stanley area 4618 sq mi (12,007 sq km)

Falkland Islands Dependencies islands & territories in the S Atlantic & in Antarctica administered by the British from Falkland Islands, including S. Orkney, S. Sandwich, & S. Shetland Islands, S. Georgia Is., Antarctic Peninsula, & Antarctic Archipelago

Fall River \\'fól\ city & port SE Mass. pop 92,703

Fal·mouth \\'fal-məth\ town SE Mass. on Cape Cod pop 27,960

False Bay \\'fóls\ inlet Republic of South Africa in SW Western Cape province E of Cape of Good Hope

Fal·ster \\'fäl-stər, 'fól-\ island Denmark in Baltic Sea S of Sjælland pop 42,841

Fa·ma·gus·ta \\,fä-mə-'güs-tə, ,fa-\ city & port E Cyprus on **Famagusta Bay** (inlet of the Mediterranean) pop 42,500

Fanning — see TABUAERAN

Far·al·lon Islands \\'far-ə-,län\ islands in the Pacific W cen Calif. W of San Francisco

Far East the countries of E Asia & the Malay Archipelago — usu. considered as comprising the Asian countries bordering on the Pacific but sometimes as including also India, Sri Lanka, Bangladesh, Tibet, & Myanmar — **Far Eastern** adj

Fare·well, Cape \\'far-,wel, 'fer-\ cape Greenland at S tip

Far·go \\'fär-(,)gō\ city E N.Dak. on Red River pop 74,111

Farm·ers Branch \\'fär-mərz\ city NE Tex. pop 24,250

Far·ming·ton \\'fär-miŋ-tən\ **1** town N Conn. W of Hartford pop 20,608 **2** city NW N.Mex. pop 33,997

Farmington Hills city SE Mich. pop 74,652

Far·quhar Islands \\'fär-kwər, -kər\ island group NW Indian Ocean NE of Madagascar belonging to Seychelles

Far·rukh·a·bad \\fə-'rü-kə-,bad, -,bäd\ city N India in Uttar Pradesh on the Ganges WNW of Lucknow pop 160,927

Fársala — see PHARSALUS

Fashoda — see KODOK

Fá·ti·ma \\'fa-tə-mə, 'fä-\ village cen Portugal NNE of Lisbon

Fatshan — see FOSHAN

Fay·ette·ville \\'fā-ət-,vil, -vəl; 2 is also 'fed-vəl\ **1** city NW Ark. pop 42,099 **2** city SE cen N.C. on Cape Fear River pop 75,695

Fear, Cape \\'fir\ cape SE N.C. at mouth of Cape Fear River

Feath·er \\'fe-thər\ river 100 mi (161 km) N cen Calif. flowing S into Sacramento River

Federal Capital Territory — see AUSTRALIAN CAPITAL TERRITORY

Federal District 1 or Pg **Dis·tri·to Fe·de·ral** \\dish-'trē-tü-,fe-thə-'räl\ district E cen Brazil including ✳ city of Brasília area 2260 sq mi (5876 sq km) **2** — see DISTRITO FEDERAL 3 **3** — see DISTRITO FEDERAL 4

Federated Malay States former Brit. protectorate (1895–1945) comprising the Malay states of Negri Sembilan, Pahang, Perak, & Selangor ✳ Kuala Lumpur

Federated Shan States — see SHAN STATE

Fen \\'fen, 'fən\ river 300 mi (483 km) N China in cen Shanxi flowing SSE into the Huang

Fengtien 1 — see LIAONING **2** — see SHENYANG

Fer·ga·na or **Fer·gha·na** \\fər-'gä-nə\ valley W cen Asia in the Tian Shan in Kyrgyzstan, Tajikistan, & Uzbekistan SE of Tashkent

Fer·gu·son \\'fär-gə-sən\ city E Mo. N of St. Louis pop 22,286

Fer·man·agh \\fər-'ma-nə\ **1** district SW Northern Ireland, established 1974 area 724 sq mi (1882 sq km), pop 51,008 **2** traditional county W Northern Ireland

Fer·nan·do de No·ro·nha \fər-'nan-(,)dō-də-nə-'rō-nyə\ island Brazil in the Atlantic NE of city of Natal *area* 7 *sq mi* (18 *sq km*)
Fernando Po *or* **Fernando Póo** — see BIOKO
Fern·dale \'fərn-,dāl\ city SE Mich. N of Detroit *pop* 25,084
Fer·ra·ra \fə-'rär-ə\ commune N Italy in Emilia-Romagna NE of Bologna near the Po *pop* 141,404
Ferro — see HIERRO
Ferrol, El — see EL FERROL
Ferryville — see MENZEL-BOURGUIBA
Fertile Crescent semicircle of fertile land stretching from SE coast of Mediterranean around Syrian Desert N of Arabia to Persian Gulf
Fez \'fez\ *or* **Fès** \'fes\ city N cen Morocco *pop* 448,823
Fez·zan \fe-'zan\ region SW Libya, chiefly desert
Fich·tel·ge·bir·ge \'fik-t°l-gə-,bir-gə\ mountains Germany in NE Bavaria; highest Schneeberg 3448 *ft* (1051 *m*)
Fie·so·le \fe-'ä-zə-lē, -,lā\ *or anc* **Fae·su·lae** \'fē-zə-,lē\ commune *cen* Italy in Tuscany NE of Florence
Fife \'fīf\ *or* **Fife·shire** \-,shir, -shər\ region, formerly a county E Scotland bet. Firths of Tay & Forth ✱ Cupar *area* 504 *sq mi* (1310 *sq km*), *pop* 326,480
Fi·ji \'fē-(,)jē\ islands SW Pacific E of Vanuatu constituting (with Rotuma Is.) an independent dominion of the Commonwealth of Nations ✱ Suva (on Viti Levu) *area* 7083 *sq mi* (18,416 *sq km*), *pop* 715,735 — **Fi·ji·an** \'fē-(,)jē-ən, fi-\ *adj or n*
Filch·ner Ice Shelf \'filk-nər\ area of shelf ice Antarctica in Weddell Sea
Filipinas, República de — see PHILIPPINES
Finch·ley \'finch-lē\ former municipal borough SE England in Middlesex, now part of Barnet
Find·lay \'fin(d)-lē\ city NW Ohio *pop* 35,703
Fin·gal's Cave \'fiŋ-gəlz\ sea cave W Scotland on Staffa Is.
Fin·ger Lakes \'fiŋ-gər\ group of long narrow lakes W cen N.Y. comprising Cayuga, Seneca, Keuka, Canandaigua, Skaneateles, Owasco, & several smaller lakes
Fin·is·terre, Cape \,fi-nə-'ster, -'ster-ē\ cape NW Spain on coast of La Coruña province; westernmost point of Spanish mainland, at 9°18'W
Fin·land \'fin-lənd\ *or* **Finn Suo·mi** \'swò-mē\ country N Europe bordering on Gulf of Bothnia & Gulf of Finland; a rep. ✱ Helsinki *area* 130,165 *sq mi* (338,429 *sq km*), *pop* 4,974,383 — **Fin·land·er** n
Finland, Gulf of arm of Baltic Sea bet. Finland & Estonia
Fin·lay \'fin-lē\ river 250 *mi* (402 *km*) Canada in N cen B.C. flowing SE to unite with **Pars·nip** \'pär-snəp\ River (145 *mi or* 232 *km*) forming Peace River
Fins·bury \'finz-,ber-ē, -b(ə-)rē\ former metropolitan borough E cen London, England, now part of Islington
Fin·ster·aar·horn \,fin(t)-stər-'är-,hórn\ mountain 14,022 *ft* (4274 *m*) S Switzerland; highest of the Berner Alpen
Fiord·land \fē-'órd-,land, 'fē-,; 'fyórd-\ mountain region S New Zealand in SW South Is.
Fitch·burg \'fich-,bərg\ city N cen Mass. *pop* 41,194·
Fiume — see RIJEKA
Fiu·mi·ci·no \,fyü-mə-'chē-(,)nō\ town cen Italy on Tyrrhenian Sea SW of Rome & WNW of Ostia
Flag·staff \'flag-,staf\ city N cen Ariz. *pop* 45,857
Flam·bor·ough \'flam-,bər-ə, -,bə-rə, -b(ə-)rə\ town Canada in SE Ont. near Hamilton *pop* 29,616
Flamborough Head promontory NE England on Humberside coast
Flan·ders \'flan-dərz\ *or F* **Flan·dre** \fläⁿdⁿ\ *or* **Flem Vlaan·de·ren** \'vlän-də-rə(n)\ 1 medieval country along coast of what is now Belgium and adjacent parts of France & Netherlands ✱ Lille 2 semiautonomous region W Belgium — see EAST FLANDERS, WEST FLANDERS
Flat·head \'flat-,hed\ river 250 *mi* (402 *km*) SE B.C. & NW Mont. flowing S through **Flathead Lake** (reservoir in Mont.) into Clark Fork
Flat·tery, Cape \'fla-tə-rē\ cape NW Wash. at entrance to Strait of Juan de Fuca
Flens·burg \'flenz-,bərg, 'flen(t)s-,bùrk\ city & port N Germany on inlet of the Baltic near Danish border *pop* 87,862
Fletsch·horn \'flech-,hórn\ *or* **Ross·bo·den·horn** \'rós-'bō-d°n-,hórn\ mountain 13,127 *ft* (4001 *m*) S Switzerland in Pennine Alps S of Simplon Pass
Flevo·land \'fle-vō-,land\ province cen Netherlands ✱ Lelystad *area* 548 *sq mi* (1420 *sq km*)
Flin·ders \'flin-dərz\ river 500 *mi* (805 *km*) Australia in cen Queensland flowing NW into Gulf of Carpentaria
Flinders Ranges mountain ranges Australia in E S. Australia E of Lake Torrens
Flint \'flint\ 1 river 265 *mi* (426 *km*) W Ga. flowing S & SW into Lake Seminole 2 city SE cen Mich. NNW of Detroit *pop* 140,761 3 *or* **Flint·shire** \-,shir, -shər\ former county NE Wales ✱ Mold
Flod·den \'flä-d°n\ hill N England in N Northumberland near Scottish border
Flor·ence \'flór-ən(t)s, 'flär-\ 1 city NW Ala. on Tennessee River *pop* 36,426 2 city E S.C. *pop* 29,813 3 *or It* **Fi·ren·ze** \fē-'rent-sā\ commune cen Italy on the Arno ✱ of Tuscany *pop* 413,069 — **Flor·en·tine** \'flór-ən-,tēn, 'flär-, -,tīn\ n
Flo·res \'flór-əs, 'flór-\ 1 island NW Azores *area* 57 *sq mi* (148 *sq km*) 2 island Indonesia in Lesser Sunda Islands *area* 5509 *sq mi* (14,323 *sq km*), *pop* 6556
Flo·ri·a·nó·po·lis \,flór-ē-ə-'nä-pə-ləs, ,flór-\ city S Brazil ✱ of Santa Catarina state on island off coast *pop* 187,800
Flor·i·da \'flór-ə-də, 'flär-\ state SE U.S. ✱ Tallahassee *area* 58,560 *sq mi* (152,256 *sq km*), *pop* 12,937,926 — **Flo·rid·i·an** \flə-'ri-dē-ən\ *adj or n* — **Flor·i·dan** \'flór-ə-d°n, 'flär-\ *adj or n*
Florida, Straits of channel bet. Florida Keys (on NW) & Cuba & Bahamas (on S & E) connecting Gulf of Mexico with the Atlantic
Flor·i·da Island \'flór-ə-də, 'flär-; flə-'rē-də\ island W Pacific in SE Solomons N of Guadalcanal
Florida Keys chain of islands S Florida extending SW from S tip of the peninsula
Flo·ris·sant \'flór-ə-sənt, 'flór-\ city E Mo. NNW of St. Louis *pop* 51,206
Florissant Fossil Beds National Monument reservation cen Colo.

Flush·ing \'flə-shiŋ\ 1 section of New York City on Long Is. in Queens 2 — see VLISSINGEN
Fly \'flī\ river 650 *mi* (1046 *km*) S New Guinea flowing SE into Gulf of Papua
Fog·gia \'fò-jə, -(,)jä\ commune SE Italy in Apulia *pop* 159,199
Foggy Bottom section of Washington, D.C., near the Potomac where the State Department building is located
Foix \'fwä\ region & former province S France in the Pyrenees SE of Gascony
Folke·stone \'fōk-stən, US also -,stōn\ borough SE England in Kent on Strait of Dover *pop* 43,742
Fol·som \'fōl-səm\ city Calif. NE of Sacramento *pop* 29,802
Fond du Lac \'fän-d°l-,ak, 'fän-jə-,lak\ city E Wis. on Lake Winnebago *pop* 37,757
Fon·se·ca, Gulf of \fän-'sä-kə\ *or* **Fonseca Bay** inlet of the Pacific in Central America in El Salvador, Honduras, & Nicaragua
Fon·taine·bleau \'fän-t°n-,blō\ commune N France *pop* 16,436
Fon·tana \fän-'ta-nə\ city SW Calif. E of Los Angeles *pop* 87,535
Foochow — see FUZHOU
For·a·ker, Mount \'fór-i-kər, 'fär-\ mountain 17,400 *ft* (5304 *m*) S Alaska in Alaska Range SW of Mt. McKinley
For·far \'fór-fər\ 1 *or* **For·far·shire** \-,shir, -shər\ — see ANGUS 2 royal burgh E Scotland in Tayside *pop* 12,742
Fo·ril·lon National Park \,fór-ē(l)-'yōⁿ\ reservation E Canada in Gaspé Peninsula
For·lì \fór-'lē\ commune N Italy in Emilia-Romagna SE of Bologna *pop* 109,986
Formosa — see TAIWAN — **For·mo·san** \fór-'mō-s°n, fər-, -'z°n\ *adj or n*
For·mo·sa Strait \fór-'mō-sə, fər-, -zə\ strait between Taiwan & China mainland connecting E. China & S. China seas
For·ta·le·za \,fór-t°l-'ā-zə\ city & port NE Brazil on the Atlantic ✱ of Ceará *pop* 1,700,000
Fort Col·lins \'kä-lənz\ city N Colo. *pop* 87,758
Fort–de–France \,fór-də-'fräⁿs\ city French West Indies ✱ of Martinique on W coast *pop* 93,598
Fort Dodge \'däj\ city NW cen Iowa *pop* 25,894
Fort Erie \'ir-ē\ town Canada in SE Ont. on Niagara River *pop* 26,006
Fort Fred·e·ri·ca National Monument \,fre-də-'rē-kə, fre-'drē-\ reservation SE Ga. on W shore of St. Simons Is. containing site of fort built by Oglethorpe 1736
Fort George \'jórj\ river 480 *mi* (772 *km*) Canada in cen Que. flowing W into James Bay
Forth \'fórth, 'fòrth\ river 114 *mi* (183 *km*) S cen Scotland flowing E into **Firth of Forth** (estuary 48 *mi or* 77 *km* long, inlet of North Sea)
Fort Jefferson National Monument — see DRY TORTUGAS
Fort Knox \'näks\ military reservation N cen Ky. SSW of Louisville; location of U.S. Gold Bullion Depository
Fort–Lamy — see N'DJAMENA
Fort Lau·der·dale \'lò-dər-,dāl\ city SE Fla. on the Atlantic *pop* 149,377
Fort Lee \'lē\ borough NE N.J. on the Hudson *pop* 31,997
Fort Ma·tan·zas National Monument \mə-'tan-zəs\ reservation SSE of St. Augustine, Fla., containing fort built ab 1736 by the Spanish
Fort Mc·Hen·ry National Monument \mə-'ken-rē\ site in Baltimore, Md., of a fort bombarded 1814 by the British
Fort Mc·Mur·ray \mək-'mər-ē\ city Canada in NE Alta. *pop* 34,706
Fort My·ers \'mī(-ə)rz\ city SW Fla. *pop* 45,206
Fort Nel·son \'nel-sən\ river 260 *mi* (418 *km*) Canada in NE B.C. flowing NW into the Liard
Fort Peck Reservoir \'pek\ reservoir ab 130 *mi* (209 *km*) long NE Mont. formed in Missouri River by **Fort Peck Dam**
Fort Pierce \'pirs\ city E Fla. on the Atlantic *pop* 36,830
Fort Pu·las·ki National Monument \pə-'las-kē, pyü-\ reservation E Ga. comprising island in mouth of Savannah River, site of a fort built 1829–47 to replace Revolutionary Fort Greene
Fort Smith \'smith\ city NW Ark. on Arkansas River *pop* 72,798
Fort Stan·wix National Monument \'stan-(,)wiks\ historic site E cen N.Y. in Rome
Fort Sum·ter National Monument \'səm(p)-tər\ reservation S.C. at entrance to Charleston harbor containing site of Fort Sumter
Fort Union National Monument reservation NE N.Mex. ENE of Santa Fe containing site of military post 1851–91
Fort Wal·ton Beach \'wól-t°n\ city NW Fla. E of Pensacola *pop* 21,471
Fort Wayne \'wān\ city NE Ind. *pop* 173,072
Fort William — see THUNDER BAY
Fort Worth \'wərth\ city N Tex. W of Dallas *pop* 447,619
Fos \'fòs\ port S France on Gulf of Fos in Rhône delta *pop* 2693
Fo·shan \'fō-'shän\ *or* **Fat·shan** \'fät-'shän\ city SE China in cen Guangdong SW of Guangzhou *pop* 120,000
Fossil Butte National Monument reservation SW Wyo. containing aquatic fossils
Fos·ter City \'fòs-tər, 'fäs-\ city W Calif. SSE of San Francisco *pop* 28,176
Fountain Valley city SW Calif. SE of Los Angeles *pop* 53,691
Four Forest Cantons the cantons of Uri, Schwyz, Unterwalden, & Lucerne in cen Switzerland surrounding Vierwaldstätter See
Fou·ta Djal·lon *or* **Fu·ta Jal·lon** \,fü-tə-jə-'lōn\ mountain region W Guinea; highest point ab 4200 *ft* (1280 *m*)
Fox \'fäks\ 1 river 220 *mi* (354 *km*) SE Wis. & NE Ill. flowing S into Illinois River 2 river 176 *mi* (282 *km*) E Wis. flowing NE & N through Lake Winnebago into Green Bay
Foxe Basin \'fäks\ inlet of the Atlantic N Canada in E Northwest Territories W of Baffin Is.; connected with Hudson Bay by **Foxe Channel**

\ə\ abut \ᵊ\ kitten, F table \ər\ further \a\ ash \ā\ ace \ä\ mop, mar
\aù\ out \ch\ chin \e\ bet \ē\ easy \g\ go \i\ hit \ī\ ice \j\ job
\ŋ\ sing \ō\ go \ò\ law \òi\ boy \th\ thin \t̲h̲\ the \ü\ loot \ù\ foot
\y\ yet \zh\ vision \à, k̲, ⁿ, œ, œ̄, ᵫ, ᵫ̄, �\ see Guide to Pronunciation

Fox Islands islands SW Alaska in E Aleutians — see UMNAK, UN-ALASKA, UNIMAK

Foyle \'foi(ə)l\ river *ab* 20 *mi* (32 *km*) N Ireland flowing NE past city of Derry to **Lough Foyle** (inlet of the Atlantic 18 *mi* or 29 *km* long)

Fra·ming·ham \'frā-miŋ-,ham\ town E Mass. WSW of Boston *pop* 64,989

France \'fran(t)s\ country W Europe bet. English Channel & the Mediterranean; a republic * Paris *area* 212,659 *sq mi* (552,913 *sq km*), *pop* 52,655,802

Franche–Com·té \fränsh-kōⁿ-tā\ region & former county & province E France E of the Saône — see BURGUNDY

Fran·cis Case, Lake \'fran(t)-səs-'kās\ reservoir *ab* 100 *mi* (161 *km*) long S S.Dak. formed in Missouri River by **Fort Ran·dall Dam** \'ran-dᵊl\

Fran·co·nia \fraŋ-'kō-nē-ə, -nyə\ former duchy in Austrasia, now included chiefly in Baden-Wurtemburg, Bavaria, & Hesse states, Germany — **Fran·co·ni·an** \-nē-ən, -nyən\ *adj or n*

Francs Peak *or* **Franks Peak** \'fraŋks\ mountain 13,140 *ft* (4005 *m*) NW Wyo; highest in Absaroka Range

Frank·fort \'fraŋk-fərt\ city * of Ky., on Kentucky River E of Louisville *pop* 25,968

Frank·furt \'fraŋk-fərt, 'fräŋk-,fûrt\ **1** *or in full* **Frankfurt am Main** \(,)äm-'mīn\ city W Germany on Main River *pop* 629,375 **2** *or in full* **Frankfurt an der Oder** \-,än-dər-'ō-dər\ city E Germany on Oder River *pop* 70,817

Frank·lin \'fraŋ-klən\ **1** town E *cen* Mass. SW of Boston *pop* 22,095 **2** town *cen* Tenn. S of Nashville *pop* 20,098 **3** city SE Wis., a SSW suburb of Milwaukee *pop* 21,855 **4** former district Canada in N Northwest Territories including Arctic islands & Boothia & Melville peninsulas

Franklin D. Roosevelt Lake reservoir 151 *mi* (243 *km*) long NE Wash. formed in Columbia River by Grand Coulee Dam

Franz Jo·sef Land \,frants-'jō-zəf-,land, -səf-; ,fränts-'yō-zəf-,länt\ archipelago Russia in Arctic Ocean N of Novaya Zemlya

Fras·ca·ti \fra-'skä-tē, frä-\ commune *cen* Italy in Latium SE of Rome

Fra·ser \'frā-zər, -zhər\ river 850 *mi* (1368 *km*) Canada in S *cen* B.C. flowing into Strait of Georgia

Frau·en·feld \'fraú(-ə)n-,felt\ commune NE Switzerland * of Thurgau canton *pop* 19,538

Fred·er·ick \'fre-drik, 'fre-də-rik\ city N Md. *pop* 40,148

Fred·er·icks·burg \'fre-driks-,bərg, 'fre-də-riks-\ city NE Va. SW of Alexandria *pop* 19,027

Fred·er·ic·ton \'fre-drik-tən, 'fre-də-rik-\ city Canada * of N.B. on St. John River *pop* 46,466

Fred·er·iks·berg \'fre-driks-,bərg, 'fre-də-riks-\ city Denmark on Sjælland Is., W suburb of Copenhagen *pop* 85,327

Free·port \'frē-,pōrt, -,pȯrt\ **1** city N Ill. W of Rockford *pop* 25,840 **2** village SE N.Y. on Long Is. *pop* 39,894 **3** city NW Bahamas on *cen* Grand Bahama Is. *pop* 22,301

Free·town \'frē-,taun\ city & port * of Sierra Leone on the Atlantic *pop* 178,600

Frei·burg \'frī-,bu̇rg, -,bərg, -,bûrk\ *or* **Freiburg im Breis·gau** \im-'brīs-,gau̇\ city SW Germany at N foot of Black Forest *pop* 175,106

Fréjus — see CENIS (Mont) 2

Fré·jus, Mas·sif du \ma-,sēf-dü-frā-'zhüs, -'zhüⁱs\ mountain on border bet. France & Italy at SW end of Graian Alps

Fre·man·tle \'frē-,man-tᵊl\ city Australia in SW Western Australia at mouth of Swan River; port for Perth *pop* 22,484

Fre·mont \'frē-,mänt\ **1** city W Calif. SE of Oakland *pop* 173,339 **2** city E Nebr. *pop* 23,680

French Broad \'brȯd\ river 210 *mi* (338 *km*) flowing from W N.C. to E Tenn.

French Community *or* **F Com·mu·nau·té fran·çaise** \kȯ-mü-nō-tā-frä⁻-sez\ former federation comprising metropolitan France, its overseas departments & territories, & the former French territories in Africa that on becoming republics chose to maintain their ties with France

French Equatorial Africa *or* **French Congo** former country W *cen* Africa N of Congo River comprising a federation of Chad, Gabon, Middle Congo, & Ubangi-Shari territories * Brazzaville

French Guiana country N S. America; an overseas department of France * Cayenne *area* 34,740 *sq mi* (90,324 *sq km*), *pop* 73,022

French Guinea — see GUINEA

French India former French possessions in India including Chandernagore (ceded to India 1950) & Pondicherry, Karikal, Yanaon, & Mahé (ceded to India 1954) * Pondicherry

French Indochina — see INDOCHINA

French Morocco — see MOROCCO

French Polynesia *or formerly* **French Oceania** islands in S Pacific belonging to France & including Society, Marquesas, Tuamotu, Gambier, & Tubuai groups * Papeete (on Tahiti) *pop* 188,814

French Somaliland — see DJIBOUTI

French Sudan — see MALI

French Territory of the Afars and the Issas — see DJIBOUTI

French Togo — see TOGOLAND

French Union former federation (1946–58) comprising metropolitan France & its overseas departments, territories, & associated states — see FRENCH COMMUNITY

French West Africa former federation of French dependencies W Africa consisting of Dahomey, French Guinea, French Sudan, Ivory Coast, Mauritania, Niger, Senegal, & Upper Volta

French West Indies islands of the W. Indies belonging to France & including Guadeloupe, Martinique, Désirade, Les Saintes, Marie Galante, St. Barthélemy, & part of St. Martin

Fres·no \'frez-(,)nō\ city S *cen* Calif. SE of San Francisco *pop* 354,202

Fria, Cape \'frē-ə\ cape NW Namibia on the Atlantic

Fri·bourg \frē-'bu̇r\ **1** canton W *cen* Switzerland *area* 647 *sq mi* (1682 *sq km*), *pop* 203,878 **2** commune, its *, SW of Bern *pop* 34,089

Frid·ley \'frid-lē\ city SE Minn. N of St. Paul *pop* 28,335

Friends·wood \'fren(d)z-,wud\ city SE Tex. SE of Houston *pop* 22,814

Fries·land \'frēs-,land, 'frēz-, -lənd; 'frēs-länt\ **1** old region N Europe bordering on North Sea **2** province N Netherlands * Leeuwarden *area* 1431 *sq mi* (3721 *sq km*), *pop* 595,131

Frio, Cape \'frē-(,)ō\ cape SE Brazil E of Rio de Janeiro

Fri·sches Haff \'fri-shəs-,häf\ lagoon N Poland & W Russia in Europe; inlet of Gulf of Gdansk

Fri·sian Islands \'fri-zhən, 'frē-\ islands NW Europe in North Sea including **West Frisian Islands** (off N Netherlands), **East Frisian Islands** (off NW Germany), & **North Frisian Islands** (off NW Germany & Denmark, including Helgoland & Sylt)

Fri·u·li \frē-'ü-lē\ district N Italy in Friuli-Venezia Giulia on Slovenia border — **Fri·u·li·an** \frē-'ü-lē-ən\ *adj or n*

Friuli–Ve·ne·zia Giu·lia \-,və-,net-sē-ə-'jül-yə\ region N Italy E of Veneto * Trieste *area* 6223 *sq mi* (16,180 *sq km*), *pop* 1,202,877

Fro·bi·sher Bay \,frō-bi-shər-\ inlet of the Atlantic N Canada in E Northwest Territories on SE coast of Baffin Is.

Front Range \'frənt\ range of the Rockies extending from *cen* Colo. N into SE Wyo. — see GRAYS PEAK

Frost·belt \'frȯst-,belt\ the N & NE states of the U.S.

Fro·ward, Cape \'frō-(w)ərd\ headland S Chile N of Strait of Magellan; southernmost point of mainland of S. America at *ab* 53°54'S

Frunze — see BISHKEK

Fu–chou — see FUZHOU

Fu·jai·ra \fü-'jī-rə\ sheikhdom, member of United Arab Emirates

Fu·ji \'fü-jē\ *or* **Fu·ji·ya·ma** \,fü-jē-'yä-mə\ *or* **Fu·ji·san** \-'sän\ mountain 12,388 *ft* (3776 *m*) Japan in S *cen* Honshu; highest in Japan

Fu·jian \'fü-jän, -jē-'än\ *or* **Fu·kien** \'fü-'kyen, -kē-'en\ province SE China bordering on Formosa Strait * Fuzhou *area* 47,529 *sq mi* (123,575 *sq km*), *pop* 25,931,106

Fu·ji·sa·wa \,fü-jē-'sä-wə\ city Japan on Honshu *pop* 350,335

Fu·ku·o·ka \,fü-kü-'ō-kə\ city & port Japan on N Kyushu on inlet of Tsushima Strait *pop* 1,237,107

Fu·ku·ya·ma \,fü-kü-'yä-mə\ city Japan on SW Honshu *pop* 365,615

Ful·da \'fu̇l-də\ city *cen* Germany *pop* 57,035

Ful·ham \'fu̇-ləm\ former metropolitan borough SW London, England, now part of Hammersmith

Ful·ler·ton \'fu̇-lər-tᵊn, -tən\ city SW Calif. NE of Long Beach *pop* 114,144

Fu·na·ba·shi \,fü-nə-'bä-shē\ city Japan on Honshu, a suburb of Tokyo *pop* 533,273

Fu·na·fu·ti \,fü-nə-'fü-tē\ island (atoll) S Pacific in *cen* Tuvalu Islands; contains * of the group *pop* 1328

Fun·chal \fün-'shäl, fən-\ city & port Portugal * of Madeira Islands *pop* 119,022

Fun·dy, Bay of \'fən-dē\ inlet of the Atlantic SE Canada bet. N.B. & N.S.

Fundy National Park reservation SE Canada in N.B. on upper Bay of Fundy

Fur·neaux \'fər-(,)nō\ islands Australia off NE Tasmania

Fur·ness \'fər-nəs\ district N England comprising peninsula in Irish Sea in SW Cumbria

Fürth \'fu̇rt, 'fûrt\ city S *cen* Germany NW of Nuremberg *pop* 99,088

Fu·shun \'fü-'shùn\ city NE China in NE Liaoning E of Shenyang *pop* 1,019,000

Futa Jallon — see FOUTA DJALLON

Fu·tu·na \fə-'tü-nə\ **1** island SW Pacific in Futuna Islands **2** island SW Pacific in SE Vanuatu

Futuna Islands *or* **Hoorn Islands** \'hȯrn, 'hȯrn\ islands SW Pacific NE of Fiji; formerly a French protectorate, since 1959 part of Wallis & Futuna Islands territory *pop* 2689

Fu·xin *or* **Fu·sin** \'fü-'shin\ city NE China in *cen* Liaoning

Fu·zhou \'fü-'jō\ *or* **Foo·chow** *or* **Fu–chou** \'fü-'jō, -chau̇\ *or formerly* **Min·how** \'min-'hō\ city & port SE China * of Fujian on Min River *pop* 623,000

Fyn \'fin\ island Denmark in the Baltic bet. Sjælland & Jutland; chief city Odense *area* 1149 *sq mi* (2987 *sq km*), *pop* 458,111

Fyzabad — see FAIZABAD

Ga·bès \'gä-bəs, -,bes\ city & port SE Tunisia on **Gulf of Gabès** *or anc* **Syr·tis Minor** \'sər-təs\ (arm of the Mediterranean) *pop* 40,585

Ga·bon \ga-'bōⁿ\ **1** *or* **Ga·boon** *or* **Ga·bun** \gə-'bün, ga-\ river NW Gabon flowing into the Atlantic through long wide estuary **2** country W Africa on the Atlantic; formerly a territory of French Equatorial Africa, since 1958 a republic * Libreville *area* 103,089 *sq mi* (268,031 *sq km*), *pop* 1,206,000 — **Gab·o·nese** \,ga-bə-'nēz, -'nēs\ *adj or n*

Ga·bo·rone \,gä-bə-'rō-(,)nä, ,kä-\ *or formerly* **Ga·be·ro·nes** \-'rō-nəs\ town SE Botswana, its *, * *pop* 59,000

Gad·a·ra \'ga-də-rə\ ancient town Palestine SE of Sea of Galilee — **Gad·a·rene** \'ga-də-,rēn, ,ga-də-'\ *adj or n*

Gades *or* **Gadir** — see CÁDIZ — **Gad·i·tan** \'ga-də-tən\ *adj or n*

Gads·den \'gadz-dən\ city NE Ala. on the Coosa *pop* 42,523

Gadsden Purchase tract of land S of Gila River in present Ariz. & N.Mex. purchased 1853 by the U.S. from Mexico *area* 29,640 *sq mi* (77,064 *sq km*)

Ga·e·ta \gä-'ā-tə\ city & port *cen* Italy in Latium on **Gulf of Gaeta** (inlet of Tyrrhenian Sea N of Bay of Naples) *pop* 24,038

Gaf·sa \'gaf-sə\ *or anc* **Cap·sa** \'kap-sə\ oasis W *cen* Tunisia

Ga·han·na \gə-'ha-nə\ city *cen* Ohio NE of Columbus *pop* 27,791

Gaines·ville \'gānz-,vil, -vəl\ city N *cen* Fla. *pop* 84,770

Gaird·ner, Lake \'gard-nər, 'gerd-\ salt lake Australia in S. Australia W of Lake Torrens *area* 1840 *sq mi* (4784 *sq km*)

Gai·thers·burg \'gā-thərz-,bərg\ town W Md. NW of Washington, D.C. *pop* 39,542

Ga·lá·pa·gos Islands \gə-'lä-pə-gəs, -'lä-, -,gōs\ *or* **Ar·chi·pié·la·go de Co·lón** \,är-chē-'pye-lə-gō-thä-kə-'lōn\ island group Ecuador in the Pacific W of mainland * on San Cristóbal Is. *area* 3029 *sq mi* (7875 *sq km*), *pop* 4037 — see ISABELA

Gal·a·ta \'ga-lə-tə\ port & commercial section of Istanbul, Turkey

Ga·la·ti \gə-'läts, -'lät-sē\ city E Romania on the Danube *pop* 307,376

Ga·la·tia \gə-'lā-sh(ē-)ə\ ancient country & Roman province *cen* Asia Minor in region centered on modern Ankara, Turkey — **Ga·la·tian** \-shən\ *adj or n*

Gald·hö·pig·gen \'gäl-,hə(r)-,pi-gən\ mountain 8100 *ft* (2469 *m*) S *cen* Norway in Jotunheim Mountains

Gales·burg \'gā(ə)lz-,bərg\ city NW Ill. WNW of Peoria *pop* 33,530

Ga·li·cia \gə-'li-sh(ē-)ə\ **1** region E *cen* Europe including N slopes of the Carpathians & valleys of the upper Vistula, Dniester, Bug, & Seret rivers; former Austrian crown land; belonged to Poland bet. the two world wars; now divided bet. Poland & Ukraine **2** region & ancient kingdom NW Spain bordering on the Atlantic — **Ga·li·cian** \-'li-shən\ *adj or n*

Gal·i·lee \'ga-lə-,lē\ hill region N Israel N of Plain of Esdraelon — **Gal·i·le·an** \,ga-lə-'lē-ən\ *adj or n*

Galilee, Sea of *or bib* **Lake of Gen·nes·a·ret** \gə-'ne-sə-,ret, -rət\ *or* **Sea of Ti·be·ri·as** \tī-'bir-ē-əs\ *or* **Sea of Chin·ne·reth** \'ki-nə-,reth\ *or Heb* **Yam Kin·ne·ret** \'yäm-'ki-nə-,ret\ lake 14 *mi* (22 *km*) long & 8 *mi* (13 *km*) wide N Israel on Syrian border traversed by Jordan River; 686 *ft* (209 *m*) below sea level

Gal·la·tin \'ga-lə-t'n\ river 125 *mi* (201 *km*) SW Mont. — see THREE FORKS

Gallatin Range mountain range S Mont. — see ELECTRIC PEAK

Ga·lli·nas, Point \gə-'ye-nəs\ cape N Colombia; northernmost point of S. America, at 12°15′ N

Gal·lip·o·li \gə-'li-pə-lē\ *or* **Ge·li·bo·lu** \,ge-lə-bə-'lü\ peninsula Turkey in Europe bet. the Dardanelles & Saros Gulf — see CHERSONESE

Gal·lo·way \'ga-lə-,wā\ former district SW Scotland comprising area formerly in counties of Wigtown & Kirkcudbright — see DUMFRIES AND GALLOWAY — **Gal·we·gian** \gal-'wē-j(ē-)ən\ *adj or n*

Gal·lup \'ga-ləp\ city NW N.Mex. near Indian reservations *pop* 19,154

Galt \'gōlt\ former city, Ont., Canada — see CAMBRIDGE

Gal·ves·ton \'gal-vəs-tən\ city SE Tex. on **Galveston Island** (30 *mi* or 48 *km* long) at entrance to **Galveston Bay** (inlet of Gulf of Mexico) *pop* 59,070 — **Gal·ves·to·nian** \,gal-və-'stō-nē-ən, -nyən\ *n*

Gal·way \'gōl-,wā\ **1** county W Ireland in Connacht bordering on the Atlantic *area* 2293 *sq mi* (5962 *sq km*), *pop* 180,304 **2** municipal borough & port, its ✻, on **Galway Bay** (inlet of Atlantic) *pop* 50,842

Gam·bia \'gam-bē-ə\ **1** river 460 *mi* (740 *km*) W Africa flowing from Fouta Djallon in W Guinea W through Senegal into the Atlantic in Gambia **2** *or* **The Gambia** country W Africa; a republic in the Commonwealth of Nations ✻ Banjul *area* 3977 *sq mi* (10,340 *sq km*), *pop* 687,817 — **Gam·bi·an** \-bē-ən\ *adj or n*

Gam·bier Islands \'gam-,bir\ islands S Pacific SE of Tuamotu Archipelago belonging to France *pop* 620 — see MANGAREVA

Gan *or* **Kan** \'gän\ river 350 *mi* (563 *km*) SE China in Jiangxi flowing N through Poyang Lake into the Chang

Gana — see GHANA

Gand — see GHENT

Gan·dhi·na·gar \'gən-də-,nə-gər\ town W India ✻ of Gujarat

Gan·ges \'gan-jēz\ river 1550 *mi* (2494 *km*) N India flowing from the Himalayas SE & E to unite with the Brahmaputra & empty into Bay of Bengal through the vast **Ganges Delta** — see HOOGHLY — **Gan·get·ic** \gan-'je-tik\ *adj*

Gangetic Plain low-lying plains region India & Bangladesh formed by Ganges River & its tributaries

Gang·tok \'gaŋ-,täk, 'gəŋ-\ town NE India ✻ of Sikkim *pop* 12,000

Gan·nett Peak \'ga-nət\ mountain 13,785 *ft* (4202 *m*) cen Wyo.; highest in Wind River Range & in the state

Gan·su *or* **Kan·su** \'gän-'sü\ province N cen China ✻ Lanzhou *area* 137,104 *sq mi* (356,470 *sq km*), *pop* 19,569,261

Gar \'gär\ *or* **Ka·erh** \'kä-'er\ town China in W Tibet

Gar·da, Lake \'gär-də\ lake 35 *mi* (56 *km*) long N Italy bet. Lombardy & Veneto draining through the Mincio into the Po

Gar·de·na \gär-'dē-nə\ city SW Calif. S of Los Angeles *pop* 49,847

Garden City **1** city W Kans. on Arkansas River *pop* 24,097 **2** city SE Mich. SW of Detroit *pop* 31,846 **3** village SE N.Y. on Long Is. *pop* 21,686

Garden Grove city SW Calif. SW of Los Angeles *pop* 143,050

Gard·ner \'gärd-nər\ city N cen Mass. *pop* 20,125

Gar·field \'gär-,fēld\ city NE N.J. N of Newark *pop* 26,727

Garfield Heights city NE Ohio SSE of Cleveland *pop* 31,739

Garfield Mountain mountain 10,961 *ft* (3341 *m*) SW Mont. near Idaho border; highest in Beaverhead & Bitterroot ranges

Ga·ri·glia·no \,gär-ēl-'yä-(,)nō\ river 100 *mi* (161 *km*) cen Italy in Latium flowing SE & SW into Gulf of Gaeta

Gar·land \'gär-lənd\ city NE Tex. NNE of Dallas *pop* 180,650

Gar·misch–Par·ten·kir·chen \'gär-mish-'pär-t'n,kir-kən\ city S Germany in Bavaria SW of Munich in foothills of the Alps *pop* 27,828

Ga·ronne \gə-'rän, -'rōn\ river 355 *mi* (571 *km*) SW France flowing NW to unite with the Dordogne forming Gironde estuary

Gar·ri·son Dam \'gar-ə-sən\ dam 210 *ft* (64 *m*) high in Missouri River W cen N. Dak. — see SAKAKAWEA (Lake)

Gary \'gar-ē, 'ger-\ city NW Ind. on Lake Michigan *pop* 116,646

Gas·co·nade \,gas-kə-'näd\ river 250 *mi* (402 *km*) S cen Mo. flowing NE into Missouri River

Gas·co·ny \'gas-kə-nē\ *or F* **Gas·cogne** \gȧ-skôn'\ region & former province SW France ✻ Auch

Ga·sher·brum \'gə-shər-,brüm, -,brùm\ mountain 26,470 *ft* (8068 *m*) N Kashmir in Karakoram Range SE of K2

Gas·pé Peninsula \ga-'spā, 'ga-,\ peninsula Canada in SE Que. bet. mouth of St. Lawrence River & Chaleur Bay — **Gas·pe·sian** \ga-'spē-zhən\ *adj*

Gas·ti·neau Channel \'gas-tə-,nō\ channel SE Alaska bet. Douglas Is. & mainland; Juneau is situated on it

Gas·to·nia \ga-'stō-nē-ə, -nyə\ city SW N.C. W of Charlotte *pop* 54,732

Gates·head \'gāts-,hed\ borough N England in Tyne and Wear county on the Tyne opposite Newcastle *pop* 181,367

Gates of the Arctic National Park wilderness area N cen Alaska in Brooks Range N of the Arctic Circle

Gath \'gath\ city of ancient Philistia ENE of Gaza

Gat·i·neau \,ga-t'n-'ō\ **1** river 240 *mi* (386 *km*) Canada in SW Que. flowing S into Ottawa River at Hull **2** town Canada in SW Que. *pop* 92,284

Ga·tun Lake \gə-'tün\ lake cen Panama formed by the **Gatun Dam** in the Chagres; formerly in Canal Zone

Gaul \'gōl\ *or L* **Gal·lia** \'ga-lē-ə\ ancient country W Europe comprising chiefly the region occupied by modern France & Belgium & at one time including also the Po valley in N Italy — see CISALPINE GAUL, TRANSALPINE GAUL

Ga·var·nie \,ga-vər-'nē\ waterfall 1385 *ft* (422 *m*) SW France S of Lourdes in the **Cirque de Gavarnie** \,sirk-də-\ (natural amphitheater at head of Gave de Pau) — see PAU

Gave de Pau — see PAU

Gav·ins Point Dam \'ga-vənz\ dam SE S.Dak. & NE Nebr. in Missouri River — see LEWIS AND CLARK LAKE

Gäv·le \'yev-lə\ city & port E Sweden on Gulf of Bothnia NNW of Stockholm *pop* 88,081

Ga·ya \gə-'yä\ city NE India in cen Bihar *pop* 246,778

Ga·za *or Ar* **Ghaz·ze** \'gä-zə\ city S Palestine near the Mediterranean; with surrounding coastal district (**Gaza Strip**, adjoining Sinai Peninsula), administered 1949–67 by Egypt, since 1967 by Israel *pop* 118,300 — **Ga·zan** \-zən\ *n*

Ga·zi·an·tep \,gä-zē-(,)än-'tep\ *or formerly* **Ain·tab** \īn-'tab\ city S Turkey N of Aleppo, Syria *pop* 371,000

Gdansk \gə-'dän(t)sk, -'dan(t)sk\ *or G* **Dan·zig** \'dan(t)-sig, 'dän(t)-\ city & port N Poland on Gulf of Gdansk *pop* 464,649

Gdansk, Gulf of *or* **Gulf of Danzig** inlet of S Baltic Sea in N Poland & W Russia

Gdyn·ia \gə-'di-nē-ə\ city & port N Poland on Gulf of Gdansk NNW of Gdansk *pop* 250,936

Gebel Katherina — see KATHERINA (Gebel)

Gebel Musa — see MUSA (Gebel)

Ge·diz \gə-'dēz\ *or* **Sa·ra·bat** \,sär-ə-'bät\ river 200 *mi* (322 *km*) W Turkey in Asia flowing W into Gulf of Izmir

Gee·long \jə-'lóŋ\ city & port SE Australia in S Victoria on Port Phillip Bay SW of Melbourne *metropolitan area pop* 125,833

Geelvink Bay — see SARERA BAY

Ge·jiu \gə-jē-'ü\ *or* **Ko–chiu** \'gō-jē-'ü\ city S China in SE Yunnan S of Kunming *pop* 180,000

Gel·der·land \'gel-dər-,land, 'kel-dər-,länt\ province E Netherlands bordering on IJsselmeer ✻ Arnhem *area* 1965 *sq mi* (5109 *sq km*), *pop* 1,727,500

Gelibolu — see GALLIPOLI

Gel·sen·kir·chen \,gel-zən-'kir-kən\ city W Germany in the Ruhr W of Dortmund *pop* 304,386

General San Martín — see SAN MARTÍN

Gen·e·see \,je-nə-'sē\ river 144 *mi* (232 *km*) W N.Y. flowing N into Lake Ontario

Ge·ne·va \jə-'nē-və\ *or F* **Ge·nève** \zhə-'nev\ *or G* **Genf** \'genf\ **1** canton SW Switzerland *area* 107 *sq mi* (278 *sq km*), *pop* 377,108 **2** city, its ✻, at SW tip of Lake of Geneva on the Rhône *pop* 167,934 — **Gen·e·vese** \,je-nə-'vēz, -'vēs\ *adj or n*

Geneva, Lake of *or* **Lake Le·man** \'lē-mən, 'le-; lə-'man\ lake 45 *mi* (72 *km*) long on border bet. SW Switzerland & E France; traversed by the Rhône

Gennesaret, Lake of — see GALILEE (Sea of)

Gen·oa \'je-nō-ə\ *or It* **Ge·no·va** \'je-nō-(,)vä\ *or anc* **Gen·ua** \'jen-yə-wə\ commune & port NW Italy ✻ of Liguria at foot of the Apennines & at head of **Gulf of Genoa** (arm of Ligurian Sea) *pop* 706,754 — **Gen·o·ese** \,je-nō-'ēz, -'ēs\ *adj or n* — **Gen·o·vese** \-nə-'vēz, -'vēs\ *adj or n*

Gen·tof·te \'gen-,təf-tə\ city Denmark on Sjælland Is., N suburb of Copenhagen *pop* 65,032

George \'jórj\ river 345 *mi* (555 *km*) Canada in NE Que. flowing N into Ungava Bay

George, Lake **1** lake 14 *mi* (22 *km*) long NE Fla. in course of St. Johns River WNW of Daytona Beach **2** lake 33 *mi* (53 *km*) long E N.Y. S of Lake Champlain

George·es Bank \'jór-jəz\ submerged sandbank E of Mass.

George·town \'jórj-,taún\ **1** section of Washington, D.C., in W part of the city **2** city & port ✻ of Guyana on the Atlantic *pop* 162,000

George Town \'jórj-,taún\ **1** town ✻ of Cayman Islands on Grand Cayman Is. **2** *or* **Pi·nang** \pi-'naŋ\ *or* **Pe·nang** \pə-\ city & port Malaysia ✻ of Penang on Penang Is. *pop* 234,930

George Washington Birthplace National Monument historic site E Va.

George Washington Carver National Monument historic site SW Mo. SE of Joplin

Geor·gia \'jór-jə\ **1** state SE U.S. ✻ Atlanta *area* 58,876 *sq mi* (153,078 *sq km*), *pop* 6,478,216 **2** *or* **Republic of Georgia** independent country SE Europe bordering on Black Sea; an ancient & medieval kingdom & later (1936–91) a constituent republic of the U.S.S.R. ✻ Tbilisi *area* 26,875 *sq mi* (69,875 *sq km*), *pop* 5,449,000

Georgia, Strait of channel 150 *mi* (241 *km*) long NW Wash. & SW B.C. bet. S Vancouver Is. & mainland NW of Puget Sound

Georgian Bay inlet of Lake Huron, Canada, in SE Ont.

Georgian Bay Islands National Park reservation SE Canada including Flowerpot Is. SE of Manitoulin Is. & a group of small islands N of Midland, Ont.

Geor·gi·na \jór-'jē-nə\ town Canada in SE Ont. *pop* 29,746

Ge·ra \'ger-ə\ city E Germany ESE of Erfurt *pop* 126,069

Ger·la·chov·ka \'ger-lə-,kóf-kə, -,kóv-\ *or* **Ger·la·chov·sky** \-skē\ mountain 8711 *ft* (2655 *m*) N Slovakia in Tatry mountains; highest in Carpathians

German East Africa former country E Africa comprising Tanganyika & Ruanda-Urundi (now Rwanda & Burundi); a German protectorate 1885–1920

Ger·ma·nia \(,)jər-'mā-nē-ə, -nyə\ **1** region of ancient Europe E of the Rhine & N of the Danube **2** region of Roman Empire just W of the Rhine in what is now NE France & part of Belgium & the Netherlands

German Southwest Africa — see NAMIBIA

Ger·man·town \'jər-mən-,taún\ **1** city SW Tenn. *pop* 32,893 **2** a NW section of Philadelphia, Pa.

Ger·ma·ny \'jər-mə-nē, 'jərm-nē\ *or G* **Deutsch·land** \'dóich-,länt\ country cen Europe bordering on North & Baltic seas, divided 1949–90 into two republics: **Federal Republic of Germany** *or* **Bun·des·re·pu·blik Deutschland** \,bùn-dəs-,rā-pü-'blēk\ to the W (✻ Bonn, *area* 96,000 *sq mi* or 249,600 *sq km*) & **German Democratic Republic** *or* **Deutsche De·mo·krat·ische Re·pu·blik** \'dói-chə-,dā-mō-'krä-ti-shə-,rā-pü-'blēk\ to the E (✻ East Berlin *area* 41,804 *sq mi* or 108,690 *sq km*); ✻ Berlin *pop* 76,281,635

\ə\ abut \ᵊ\ kitten, F table \ər\ further \a\ ash \ā\ ace \ä\ mop, mar
\aú\ out \ch\ chin \e\ bet \ē\ easy \g\ go \i\ hit \ī\ ice \j\ job
\ŋ\ sing \ō\ go \ó\ law \ói\ boy \th\ thin \th\ the \ü\ loot \ù\ foot
\y\ yet \zh\ vision \á, k̲, ⁿ, œ, œ̄, ue, ūe, ᵊ\ see Guide to Pronunciation

Ger·mis·ton \'jər-məs-tən\ city NE Republic of South Africa in Pretoria-Witwatersrand-Vereeniging E of Johannesburg *pop* 221,972

Ge·ro·na \hā-'rō-nə, jə-\ **1** province NE Spain in NE Catalonia *area* 2264 *sq mi* (5886 *sq km*), *pop* 466,992 **2** commune, its ✱ *pop* 116,477

Ge·zi·ra, El \el-jə-'zir-ə\ *or* **Al Ja·zi·rah** \,al-jə-'zir-ə\ district E *cen* Sudan bet. the Blue Nile & the White Nile

Gha·da·mes *or* **Gha·da·mis** \gə-'dä-məs, -'dä-\ oasis & town NW Libya in Tripolitania near Algerian border *pop* 6172

Gha·gha·ra \'gä-gə-,rä\ *or* **Ghagh·ra** \'gä-grə, -,grä\ river 570 *mi* (1207 *km*) S *cen* Asia flowing S from SW Tibet through Nepal into the Ganges in N India

Gha·na \'gä-nə, 'ga-\ **1** *or* **Ga·na** ancient empire W Africa in what is now W Mali; flourished 4th–13th centuries **2** *or formerly* **Gold Coast** country W Africa bordering on Gulf of Guinea; a republic within the Commonwealth of Nations; formerly (as Gold Coast) a Brit. territory comprising Gold Coast colony, Ashanti, Northern Territories, & Togoland trust territory ✱ Accra *area* 91,843 *sq mi* (238,792 *sq km*), *pop* 12,296,081 — **Gha·na·ian** \gä-'nä-ən, ga-, -'nī-ən\ *adj or n* — **Gha·nian** \'gä-nē-ən, 'ga-, -nyən\ *adj or n* — **Gha·nese** \gä-'nēz, ga-, -'nēs\ *adj*

Gharapuri — see ELEPHANTA

Ghar·da·ïa \gär-'dī-ə\ commune N *cen* Algeria *pop* 70,500

Ghats — see EASTERN GHATS, WESTERN GHATS

Ghazal, Bahr el — see BAHR EL GHAZAL

Ghaz·ni \'gäz-nē\ city E *cen* Afghanistan; once ✱ of a Muslim kingdom extending from the Tigris to the Ganges *pop* 30,425

Ghazze — see GAZA

Ghent \'gent\ *or Flem* **Gent** \'kent\ *or F* **Gand** \gän\ city NW *cen* Belgium ✱ of E. Flanders *pop* 230,246

Giant's Causeway formation of prismatic basaltic columns Northern Ireland on N coast of Moyle

Gib·e·on \'gi-bē-ən\ city of ancient Palestine NW of Jerusalem — **Gib·e·on·ite** \-ə-,nīt\ *n*

Gi·bral·tar \jə-'brȯl-tər\ town & port on Rock of Gibraltar; a Brit. colony *area* 2.5 *sq mi* (6.5 *sq km*), *pop* 29,760 — **Gi·bral·tar·i·an** \jə-,brȯl-'ter-ē-ən, jī-,brȯl-, -'tar-\ *n*

Gibraltar, Rock of *or an* **Cal·pe** \'kal-(,)pē\ headland on S coast of Spain at E end of Strait of Gibraltar; highest point 1396 *ft* (426 *m*) — see PILLARS OF HERCULES

Gibraltar, Strait of passage bet. Spain & Africa connecting the Atlantic & Mediterranean *ab* 8 *mi* (12.8 *km*) wide at narrowest point

Gies·sen \'gē-s°n\ city W *cen* Germany N of Frankfurt am Main *pop* 76,374

Gi·fu \'gē-(,)fü\ city Japan in *cen* Honshu *pop* 410,318

Gi·jón \hē-'hōn\ city & port NW Spain in Oviedo province on Bay of Biscay *pop* 256,433

Gi·la \'hē-lə\ river 630 *mi* (1014 *km*) N.Mex. & Ariz. flowing W into Colorado River

Gila Cliff Dwellings National Monument reservation SW N.Mex. including cliff-dweller ruins

Gil·bert \'gil-bərt\ town SW *cen* Ariz. SE of Mesa *pop* 29,188

Gilbert and El·lice \'e-ləs\ island group W Pacific; until 1976 a Brit. colony; now divided into the independent countries of Kiribati and Tuvalu

Gilbert Islands islands Kiribati in *cen* Pacific — **Gil·bert·ese** \,gil-bər-'tēz, -'tēs\ *n or adj*

Gil·boa, Mount \gil-'bō-ə\ mountain 1631 *ft* (497 *m*) N Palestine W of Jordan River & S of Valley of Jezreel

Gil·e·ad \'gi-lē-əd\ mountainous region of Palestine E of Jordan River; now in Jordan — **Gil·e·ad·ite** \-lē-ə-,dīt\ *n*

Gil·git \'gil-gət\ **1** district NW Kashmir **2** town NW Kashmir on Gilgit River (tributary of the Indus) *pop* 4671

Gil·ling·ham \'ji-liŋ-əm\ borough SE England in Kent *pop* 93,741

Gil·roy \'gil-,rȯi\ city W Calif. SE of San Jose *pop* 31,487

Gin·za \'gin-zə\ shopping street & entertainment district in downtown Tokyo, Japan

Gi·re·sun \,gir-ə-'sün\ *or* **Ke·ra·sun** \,ker-ə-\ city & port NE Turkey on Black Sea W of Trabzon *pop* 46,068

Girgenti — see AGRIGENTO

Gi·ronde \jə-'ränd, zhə-\ estuary 45 *mi* (72 *km*) W France formed by junction of the Garonne & the Dordogne & flowing NW into Bay of Biscay

Gis·borne \'giz-bərn, -,bȯrn\ borough & port New Zealand on E North Is. *pop* 29,986

Gi·za \'gē-zə\ city N Egypt on W bank of the Nile near Cairo *pop* 1,230,446

Gju·he·zes, Cape \jü-'hə-,zəs\ *or formerly* **Cape Lin·guet·ta** \liŋ-'gwe-tə\ *or* **Cape Glos·sa** \glä-sə, 'glȯ-\ cape SW Albania projecting into Strait of Otranto

Gla·cier Bay \'glā-shər *also* -zhər\ inlet SE Alaska at S end of St. Elias Range in Glacier Bay National Park

Glacier National Park 1 — see WATERTON-GLACIER INTERNATIONAL PEACE PARK **2** reservation W Canada in SE B.C. in Selkirk Mountains W of Yoho National Park

Glad·beck \'glät-,bek, 'glad-\ city W Germany in the Ruhr *pop* 79,747

Glades \'glādz\ EVERGLADES

Glad·sak·se \'glath-,sak-sə\ city Denmark; a suburb of Copenhagen *pop* 61,198

Glad·stone \'glad-,stōn\ city W Mo. N of Kansas City *pop* 26,243

Gla·mor·gan \glə-'mȯr-gən\ *or* **Gla·mor·gan·shire** \-,shir, -shər\ former county SE Wales ✱ Cardiff — see MID GLAMORGAN, SOUTH GLAMORGAN, WEST GLAMORGAN

Gla·rus \'glär-əs\ *or F* **Gla·ris** \gla-'rēs\ **1** canton E *cen* Switzerland *area* 267 *sq mi* (694 *sq km*), *pop* 37,686 **2** commune, its ✱ *pop* 5623

Glas·gow \'glas-(,)kō, 'glas-(,)gō, 'glaz-(,)gō\ city & port S *cen* Scotland on the Clyde ✱ of Strathclyde *pop* 762,288 — **Glas·we·gian** \glas-'wē-jən, glaz-\ *n or adj*

Glas·ton·bury 1 \'glas-tən-,ber-ē\ town *cen* Conn. SE of Hartford *pop* 27,901 **2** \'glas-tən-b(ə-)rē, 'gläs-\ borough SW England in Somerset *pop* 6773

Glen Canyon Dam \'glen\ dam N Ariz. in Glen Canyon of Colorado River forming **Lake Pow·ell** \'paủ(-ə)l\ (chiefly in SE Utah)

Glen·coe \glen-'kō\ valley W Scotland SW of Loch Leven

Glen Cove \'glen-'kōv\ city SE N.Y. on NW Long Is. *pop* 24,149

Glen·dale \'glen-,dāl\ **1** city *cen* Ariz. NW of Phoenix *pop* 148,134 **2** city SW Calif. just N of Los Angeles *pop* 180,038

Glendale Heights city NE Ill. *pop* 27,973

Glen·do·ra \glen-'dȯr-ə, -'dȯr-\ city SW Calif. *pop* 47,828

Glen El·lyn \glen-'e-lən\ village NE Ill. W of Chicago *pop* 24,944

Glen More \glen-'mȯr, -'mȯr\ valley *ab* 50 *mi* (80 *km*) long N Scotland running SW to NE & connecting Loche Linnhe & Moray Firth — see CALEDONIAN CANAL

Glen·view \'glen-,vyü\ village NE Ill. NNW of Chicago *pop* 37,093

Glit·ter·tind \'gli-tər-,tin\ mountain 8110 *ft* (2472 *m*) S *cen* Norway in Jotunheim Mountains; highest in Scandinavia

Gli·wi·ce \gli-'vēt-sə\ *or G* **Glei·witz** \'glī-(,)vits\ city SW Poland in Silesia W of Katowice *pop* 222,084

Glom·ma \'glȯ-,mä, 'glä-mə\ river 185 *mi* (298 *km*) E Norway flowing S into the Skagerrak

Glouces·ter \'gläs-tər, 'glȯs-\ **1** city NE Mass. on Cape Ann *pop* 28,716 **2** city Canada in SE Ont. near Ottawa *pop* 101,677 **3** borough SW *cen* England ✱ of Gloucestershire

Glouces·ter·shire \'gläs-tər-,shir, -shər, -'glȯs-\ *or* **Glouces·ter** \'gläs-tər, 'glȯs-\ county SW *cen* England *area* 1020 *sq mi* (2652 *sq km*), *pop* 503,800

Gnossus — see KNOSSOS

Goa *or Pg* **Gôa** \'gō-ə\ state W India on Malabar Coast; before 1962 belonged to Portugal; with Daman & Diu constituted a union territory 1962–1987; ✱ Panaji *area* 1301 *sq mi* (3383 *sq km*), *pop* 626,978 — see PORTUGUESE INDIA — **Go·an** \'gō-ən\ *adj or n* — **Goa·nese** \,gō-ə-'nēz, -'nēs\ *adj or n*

Go·bi \'gō-(,)bē\ desert E *cen* Asia in Mongolia & China *area ab* 500,000 *sq mi* (1,300,000 *sq km*)

Go·da·va·ri \gə-'dä-və-rē\ river 900 *mi* (1448 *km*) *cen* India flowing SE across the Deccan into Bay of Bengal

Go·des·berg \'gō-dəs-,bərg, -,berk\ *or* **Bad Godesberg** \,bät-\ commune W Germany on the Rhine S of Bonn *pop* 73,512

Godt·haab \'gȯt-,hȯb, 'gät-\ town ✱ of Greenland on SW coast

Godwin Austen — see K2

Go·ge·bic \gō-'gē-bik\ iron range N Wis. & NW Mich.

Goi·â·nia *or formerly* **Goy·a·nia** \gȯi-'a-nē-ə\ city SE *cen* Brazil ✱ of Goiás *pop* 717,948

Goi·ás *or* **Goi·az** *or* **Goy·az** \gȯi-'äs\ state SE *cen* Brazil ✱ Goiânia *area* 244,330 *sq mi* (635,258 *sq km*), *pop* 3,967,907

Gök·çe·ada \,gœk-jä-ə-'dä\ *or formerly* **Im·roz** \im-'róz\ island Turkey in NE Aegean *area* 110 *sq mi* (286 *sq km*)

Go·lan Heights \'gō-,län, -lən\ hilly region NE of Sea of Galilee; annexed by Israel 1981

Gol·con·da \gäl-'kän-də\ ruined city *cen* India in W Andhra Pradesh W of Hyderabad ✱ (1512–1687) of Golconda kingdom

Gold Coast 1 region W Africa on N shore of Gulf of Guinea bet. the Ivory Coast (on W) & the Slave Coast (on E) **2** — see GHANA **3** former Brit. colony in S Gold Coast region ✱ Accra; now part of Ghana

Golden Chersonese — see CHERSONESE

Golden Gate strait 2 *mi* (3.2 *km*) wide W Calif. connecting San Francisco Bay with Pacific Ocean

Golden Horn inlet of the Bosporus, Turkey; harbor of Istanbul

Golden Valley village E Minn. W of Minneapolis *pop* 20,971

Golds·boro \'gōl(d)z-,bər-ə, -,bə-rə\ city E *cen* N.C. *pop* 40,709

Golgotha — see CALVARY

Go·mel \'gō-məl, 'gó-\ *or* **Ho·myel'** \kō-'myel\ city SE Belarus *pop* 383,000

Go·mor·rah \gə-'mȯr-ə, -'mär-\ city of ancient Palestine in the plain of Jordan River

Go·nâve, Gulf of \gō-'näv\ arm of Caribbean Sea on W coast of Haiti

Gon·dar \'gän-dər, -,där\ city NW Ethiopia N of Lake Tana ✱ of Amhara & former ✱ of Ethiopia *pop* 85,941

Gond·wa·na·land \gän-'dwä-nə-,land\ *or* **Gond·wa·na** \-'dwä-nə\ hypothetical land area believed to have once connected the Indian subcontinent & the landmasses of the southern hemisphere

Gong·ga \'gäŋ-gə\ *or* **Min·ya Kon·ka** \,mi-nyə-'käŋ-kə\ mountain 24,900 *ft* (7590 *m*) W China in SW *cen* Szechwan; highest in China

Good Hope, Cape of \,gủd-'hōp\ cape S Republic of South Africa in SW Western Cape province W of False Bay, at 34°21′ S — see CAPE OF GOOD HOPE

Good·win Sands \'gủd-dwən\ shoals SE England in Strait of Dover off E coast of Kent — see DOWNS

Goose Creek city SE S.C. *pop* 24,692

Go·rakh·pur \'gȯr-ək-,púr, 'gȯr-\ city NE India in E Uttar Pradesh N of Banaras *pop* 306,399

Go·ri·zia \gə-'rēt-sē-ə\ commune NE Italy in Venetia

Gorkiy *or* **Gorky** — see NIZHNI NOVGOROD

Gör·litz \'gȯr-,lits, -ləts\ city E Germany on Neisse River *pop* 81,003

Gor·lov·ka \gȯr-'lȯf-kə, -'lȯv-\ city E Ukraine in the Donets Basin N of Donetsk *pop* 335,000

Gor·no–Al·tai \'gȯr-(,)nō-,al-'tī\ *or formerly* **Oi·rot** \'ȯi-rət\ autonomous region S Russia in Asia in SE Altai Territory in Altai Mountains ✱ Gorno-Altaisk (formerly Oirot-Tura) *area* 35,800 *sq mi* (93,080 *sq km*), *pop* 168,000

Gor·no–Ba·dakh·shan \'gȯr-(,)nō-,bä-,däk-'shän\ autonomous region SE Tajikistan in the Pamirs ✱ Khorog *area* 25,784 *sq mi* (67,038 *sq km*), *pop* 98,000

Gor·zow–Wiel·ko·pol·ski \'gȯ-zhüf-,vyel-kə-'pȯl-skē\ city W Poland *pop* 123,350

Go·shen \'gō-shən\ **1** city N Ind. *pop* 23,797 **2** district of ancient Egypt E of the Nile delta

Gos·port \'gäs-,pȯrt, -,pȯrt\ borough S England in Hampshire on Portsmouth harbor *pop* 77,276

Gö·te·borg \,yə(r)-tə-'bȯr-ē\ *or* **Goth·en·burg** \'gä-thən-,bərg\ city & port SW Sweden on the Kattegat *pop* 431,840

Go·tha \'gō-tə, 'gō-thə\ city *cen* Germany W of Erfurt *pop* 57,847

Goth·am \'gä-thəm\ NEW YORK CITY — an informal name — **Goth·am·ite** \-thə-,mīt\ *n*

Got·land \'gät-,land, -lənd\ island Sweden in the Baltic off SE coast; chief town Visby *area* 1167 *sq mi* (3034 *sq km*), *pop* 54,093

Göt·ting·en \'gə(r)-tiŋ-ən, 'ge-tiŋ-\ city *cen* Germany SSW of Brunswick *pop* 129,656

Gou·da \'gaủ-də, 'gü-, 'kaủ-\ commune SW Netherlands *pop* 59,179

Gow·er \'gaü(-ə)r\ peninsula S Wales W of Swansea

Gra·ham Land \'grā-əm, 'gra(-ə)m\ 1 — see ANTARCTIC PENINSULA 2 the N section of the Antarctic Peninsula

Gra·hams·town \'grā-əmz-,taün, 'gra(-ə)mz-\ city S Republic of South Africa in Eastern Cape province ENE of Port Elizabeth *pop* 41,302

Gra·ian Alps \'grā-ən, 'grī-\ section of W Alps S of Mont Blanc on border bet. France & Italy — see GRAN PARADISO

Grain coast \'grān\ region W Africa in Liberia on Gulf of Guinea

Gram·pi·an \'gram-pē-ən\ region NE *cen* Scotland, established 1975 ✳ Aberdeen *area* 3360 *sq mi* (8736 *sq km*), *pop* 470,596

Grampian Hills hills *cen* Scotland bet. the Lowlands & the Highlands — see BEN NEVIS

Gra·na·da \grə-'nä-də\ 1 city SW Nicaragua on NW shore of Lake Nicaragua *pop* 56,232 2 medieval Moorish kingdom S Spain 3 province S Spain in Andalusia bordering on the Mediterranean *area* 4928 *sq mi* (12,813 *sq km*), *pop* 724,299 4 city, ✳ of Granada province, Spain, in the Sierra Nevada *pop* 246,642

Gran·by \'gran-bē\ town Canada in S Que. *pop* 42,804

Gran Chaco — see CHACO

Grand 1 river 260 *mi* (418 *km*) SW Mich. flowing N & W into Lake Michigan 2 river 300 *mi* (483 *km*) NW Mo. flowing SE into Missouri River 3 river 140 *mi* (225 *km*) W Mo. flowing SE into Lake of the Ozarks 4 river 200 *mi* (322 *km*) N S.Dak. flowing E into Missouri River 5 the Colorado River from its source to junction with Green River in SE Utah — a former name 6 — see NEOSHO

Grand Atlas — see ATLAS

Grand Bahama island Bahamas, NW island of group *area* 430 *sq mi* (1118 *sq km*)

Grand Bank *or* Grand Banks shoals in W Atlantic SE of Newfoundland

Grand Canal — see DA YUNHE

Grand Canary *or Sp* Gran Ca·na·ria \,grän-kə-'när-yä\ island Spain in the Canaries; chief city Las Palmas *area* 523 *sq mi* (1360 *sq km*)

Grand Canyon gorge of the Colorado NW Ariz. extending from mouth of the Little Colorado W to the Grand Wash Cliffs; over 1 *mi* (1.6 *km*) deep; area largely comprised in **Grand Canyon National Park**— see MARBLE CANYON

Grand Canyon of the Snake — see HELLS CANYON

Grand Cayman — see CAYMAN

Grand Cou·lee \'kü-lē\ valley E Wash. extending SSW from S wall of canyon of Columbia River where it turns W in forming the Big Bend

Grand Coulee Dam dam NE *cen* Wash. in Columbia River — see FRANKLIN D. ROOSEVELT LAKE

Grande Prai·rie \'gran(d)-'prer-ē, -'prä-rē\ city Canada in W Alta. *pop* 28,271

Grande, Rio 1 \,rē-ō-'grand, -'gran-dē *also* ,rī-ō-'grand\ river U.S. & Mexico — see RIO GRANDE 2 \,rē-ō-'gran-də, -dē\ river 680 *mi* (1094 *km*) E Brazil in Minas Gerais flowing W to unite with Paranaíba River forming Paraná River

Grande–Terre \grän-'ter\ island French West Indies constituting the E portion of Guadeloupe *area* 220 *sq mi* (572 *sq km*)

Grand Falls — see CHURCHILL FALLS

Grand Forks city E N.Dak. on Red River *pop* 49,425

Grand Island city SE *cen* Nebr. near Platte River *pop* 39,386

Grand Junction city W Colo. on Colorado River *pop* 29,034

Grand Lac — see TONLE SAP

Grand Ma·nan Island \mə-'nan\ island 20 *mi* (32 *km*) long Canada in N.B. at entrance to Bay of Fundy

Grand Mesa mountain *ab* 10,000 *ft* (3048 *m*) W Colo. near junction of Colorado & Gunnison rivers; summit *area ab* 53 *sq mi* (138 *sq km*)

Grand Portage National Monument historic site NE Minn. on Lake Superior

Grand Prairie city NE *cen* Tex. W of Dallas *pop* 99,616

Grand Rapids city SW Mich. on Grand River *pop* 189,126

Grand Te·ton \'tē-,tän, 'tē-t°n\ mountain 13,766 *ft* (4196 *m*) W Wyo. in Grand Teton National Park; highest in Teton Range

Grand Teton National Park reservation NW Wyo. including Jackson Lake & main part of Teton Range

Grand Trav·erse Bay \'tra-vərs\ inlet of Lake Michigan in Mich. on NW coast of Lower Michigan

Grand Turk — see TURKS AND CAICOS

Grand·view \'gran(d)-,vyü\ city W Mo. *pop* 24,967

Grange·mouth \'gränj-məth, -,maüth\ burgh & port *cen* Scotland in Central region on Firth of Forth *pop* 21,666

Granicus — see KOCABAS

Granite City city SW Ill. on Mississippi River *pop* 32,862

Granite Peak mountain 12,799 *ft* (3901 *m*) S Mont. NE of Yellowstone National Park in Beartooth Range (spur of Absaroka Range); highest point in state

Gran Pa·ra·di·so \,gran-,par-ə-'dē-(,)zō\ mountain 13,323 *ft* (4061 *m*) NW Italy in NW Piedmont; highest in Graian Alps

Grape·vine \'grāp-,vin\ city N Tex. NE of Fort Worth *pop* 29,202

Gras·mere \'gras-,mir\ lake 1 *mi* (1.6 *km*) long NW England in Cumbria in Lake District

Grasse \'gras, 'gräs\ commune SE France W of Nice *pop* 24,260

Grass·lands National Park \'gras-,lan(d)z, -,lən(d)z\ reservation Canada in SW Sask.

Grau·bün·den \graü-'bün-dən, -'buen-\ *or F* Gri·sons \grē-zō°\ canton E Switzerland ✳ Chur *area* 2744 *sq mi* (7134 *sq km*), *pop* 177,096

Graudenz — see GRUDZIADZ

Gravenhage, 's — see HAGUE (The)

Graves·end \,grävz-'end\ borough SE England in Kent on Thames estuary *pop* 52,963

Grays Harbor \'grāz\ inlet of the Pacific W Wash.

Grays Peak mountain 14,270 *ft* (4349 *m*) *cen* Colo., highest in Front Range

Graz \'gräts\ city S Austria ✳ of Styria on the Mur *pop* 232,155

Great Abaco — see ABACO

Great Australian Bight wide bay on S coast of Australia; part of Indian Ocean

Great Barrier Reef coral reef 1250 *mi* (2012 *km*) long Australia in Coral Sea off NE coast of Queensland; in part comprises a marine park

Great Basin region W U.S. bet. Sierra Nevada & Wasatch Range including most of Nev. & parts of Calif., Idaho, Utah, Wyo. & Oreg. &

having no drainage to ocean; contains many isolated mountain ranges (the **Basin Ranges**)

Great Basin National Park reservation E Nev. including Wheeler Peak & Lehman Caves

Great Bear Lake lake Canada in W Northwest Territories *area* 12,000 *sq mi* (31,200 *sq km*)

Great Brit·ain \'brit-t°n\ *or* Britain 1 island W Europe comprising England, Scotland, & Wales *area* 88,745 *sq mi* (230,737 *sq km*), *pop* 54,397,000 2 UNITED KINGDOM

Great Crosby — see CROSBY

Great Dismal — see DISMAL

Great Divide — see CONTINENTAL DIVIDE

Great Dividing Range mountain system E Australia extending from Cape York Peninsula to S Victoria &, interrupted by Bass Strait, into Tasmania — see KOSCIUSKO (Mount)

Greater Antilles group of islands in the West Indies including Cuba, Hispaniola, Jamaica, & Puerto Rico

Greater London metropolitan area SE England comprising London (city) & 32 surrounding boroughs *area* 620 *sq mi* (1612 *sq km*), *pop* 6,851,400

Greater Manchester metropolitan area NW England comprising Manchester and nearby boroughs *area* 498 *sq mi* (1295 *sq km*), *pop* 2,624,400

Greater Sunda Islands — see SUNDA ISLANDS

Greater Walachia — see MUNTENIA

Great Exuma — see EXUMA

Great Falls 1 *or* Great Falls of the Potomac waterfall 35 *ft* (11 *m*) in the Potomac N of Washington 2 city W *cen* Mont. on Missouri River WSW of the Great Falls of the Missouri (waterfall, now in modified form) *pop* 55,097

Great Inagua — see INAGUA

Great Indian Desert — see THAR DESERT

Great Kabylia — see KABYLIA

Great Karroo — see KARROO

Great Lakes 1 chain of five lakes (Superior, Michigan, Huron, Erie, & Ontario) *cen* N. America in the U.S. & Canada draining through St. Lawrence River into the Atlantic 2 group of lakes E *cen* Africa including Lakes Rudolf, Albert, Victoria, Tanganyika, & Malawi

Great Namaqualand — see NAMAQUALAND

Great Ouse — see OUSE

Great Plains elevated plains region W *cen* U.S. & W Canada E of Rocky Mountains & chiefly W of 100th meridian extending from NE B.C. & NW Alta. SE & S to include the Llano Estacado of N.Mex. & Tex.

Great Rift Valley depression SW Asia & E Africa extending with several breaks from valley of Jordan River S to *cen* Mozambique

Great Saint Ber·nard \,sänt-bər-'närd\ mountain pass 8111 *ft* (2472 *m*) through Pennine Alps bet. Switzerland & Italy

Great Salt Lake lake *ab* 70 *mi* (113 *km*) long N Utah having strongly saline waters & no outlet

Great Salt Lake Desert flat barren region NW Utah

Great Sand Dunes National Monument reservation S Colo. on W slope of Sangre de Cristo Mountains

Great Slave Lake \'slāv\ lake NW Canada in S Northwest Territories receiving Slave River on S & draining into Mackenzie River on W *area* 11,170 *sq mi* (29,042 *sq km*)

Great Smoky Mountains mountains on N.C.-Tenn. boundary partly in Great Smoky Mountains National Park— see CLINGMANS DOME

Great Yarmouth — see YARMOUTH

Greece \'grēs\ *or Gk* Hel·las \'he-ləs\ *or NGk* El·lás \e-'läs\ country S Europe at S end of Balkan Peninsula; a republic ✳ Athens *area* 50,147 *sq mi* (130,382 *sq km*), *pop* 10,264,156

Gree·ley \'grē-lē\ city N Colo. *pop* 60,536

Green \'grēn\ river 730 *mi* (1175 *km*) W U.S. flowing from Wind River Range in W Wyo. S into Colorado River in SE Utah

Green Bay 1 inlet of W Lake Michigan 120 *mi* (193 *km*) long in NW Mich. & NE Wis. 2 city NE Wis. on Green Bay *pop* 96,466

Green·belt \'grēn-,belt\ city *cen* Md. *pop* 21,096

Green·field \'grēn-,fēld\ city SE Wis. near Milwaukee *pop* 33,403

Green·land \'grēn-land, -,land\ *or* Ka·laa·llit Nu·naat \kä-'lät-,lēt-nü-'nät\ island in N Atlantic off NE N. America belonging to Denmark ✳ Godthaab *area* 839,800 *sq mi* (2,183,480 *sq km*), *pop* 55,171 — Green·land·er \-lən-dər, -,lan-\ n

Greenland Sea arm of Arctic Ocean bet. Greenland & Spitsbergen

Green Mountains mountains E N. America in Appalachian system extending from S Que. S through Vt. into W Mass. — see MANSFIELD (Mount)

Gree·nock \'grē-nək\ burgh & port SW Scotland in Strathclyde on Firth of Clyde *pop* 57,324

Greens·boro \'grēnz-,bər-ə, -,bə-rə\ city N *cen* N.C. *pop* 183,521

Green·ville \'grēn-,vil, -vəl\ 1 city W Miss. on Mississippi River *pop* 45,226 2 city E N.C. *pop* 44,972 3 city N.C. 4 city NE Tex. NE of Dallas on the Sabine *pop* 23,071

Green·wich \'gre-nich, 'grēn-,wich, 'grin-,wich\ town SW Conn. on Long Island Sound *pop* 58,441 2 \'gri-nij, 'gre-, -nich\ borough of E Greater London, England *pop* 214,900

Green·wich Village \'gre-nich\ section of New York City in Manhattan on lower W side

Green·wood \'grēn-,wüd\ 1 city *cen* Ind. *pop* 26,265 2 city W S.C. *pop* 20,807

Gre·na·da \grə-'nā-də\ island Brit. West Indies in S Windward Islands; with S Grenadines, independent member of the Commonwealth of Nations since 1974 ✳ St. George's *area* 133 *sq mi* (346 *sq km*), *pop* 98,000 — Gre·na·dan \-'nä-d°n\ *adj or n* — Gre·na·di·an \-'nä-dē-ən\ *adj or n*

\ə\ abut \°\ kitten, F table \ər\ further \a\ ash \ā\ ace \ä\ mop, mar
\aü\ out \ch\ chin \e\ bet \ē\ easy \g\ go \i\ hit \ī\ ice \j\ job
\ŋ\ sing \ō\ go \ȯ\ law \ȯi\ boy \th\ thin \t̲h̲\ the \ü\ loot \ u̇\ foot
\y\ yet \zh\ vision \ā, k̲, n, œ, œ̄, ue, uē, ʸ\ see Guide to Pronunciation

Gren·a·dines \,gre-nə-'dēnz, 'gre-nə-,\ islands Brit. West Indies in cen Windward Islands bet. Grenada & St. Vincent; divided administratively bet. Grenada & St. Vincent and the Grenadines

Gre·no·ble \grə-'nō-bəl, -'nóbl'\ city SE France on the Isère pop 165,431

Gresh·am \'gre-shəm\ city NW Oreg. E of Portland pop 68,235

Grey·lock, Mount \'grā-,läk\ mountain 3491 ft (1064 m) NW Mass.; highest in Berkshire Hills & in state

Grif·fin \'gri-fən\ city W cen Ga. pop 21,347

Grims·by \'grimz-bē\ borough E England in Humberside near mouth of the Humber pop 92,147

Grin·del·wald \'grin-d'l-,vält, -,wold\ valley & village cen Switzerland in Bern canton in the Berner Alpen E of Interlaken

Gri·qua·land West \'gri-kwə-,land\ district NW Republic of South Africa in N Cape of Good Hope N of Orange River; chief town Kimberley

Gris–Nez, Cape \grē-'nā\ headland N France projecting into Strait of Dover

Grisons — see GRAUBÜNDEN

Grod·no \'gräd-(,)nō, 'gród-\ city W Belarus on the Neman pop 195,000

Gro·ning·en \'grō-niŋ-ən, 'krō-niŋ-ə(n)\ **1** province NE Netherlands area 866 sq mi (2252 sq km), pop 560,614 **2** city, its * pop 166,951

Gros Morne National Park \grō-'mórn\ reservation Canada in Newfoundland (island)

Gross·glock·ner \'grōs-,gläk-nər\ mountain 12,457 ft (3797 m) SW Austria, highest in the Hohe Tauern & in Austria

Gros Ventre \'grō-,vänt\ river 100 mi (161 km) W Wyo. flowing W into Snake River

Grot·on \'grä-t²n\ town SE Conn. E of New London pop 45,144

Grove City \'grōv\ city cen Ohio pop 19,661

Groz·ny or **Groz·nyy** \'gróz-nē, 'gräz-\ city S Russia in Europe, N of Caucasus Mountains pop 375,000

Gru·dziadz \'grü-,jō⁽ⁿ⁾(t)s\ or G **Grau·denz** \'grau-,dents\ city N Poland on the Vistula NE of Bydgoszcz pop 100,861

Gua·da·la·ja·ra \,gwä-d'l-ə-'här-ə\ **1** city W cen Mexico * of Jalisco pop 2,343,034 **2** province E cen Spain in NE New Castile area 4676 sq mi (12,158 sq km), pop 125,834 **3** commune, * of Guadalajara province, Spain pop 64,334

Gua·dal·ca·nal \,gwä-d'l-kə-'nal, ,gwä-də-kə-\ island W Pacific in the SE Solomons area 2500 sq mi (6500 sq km), pop 23,922 — see HONIARA

Gua·dal·qui·vir \,gwä-d'l-ki-'vir, -'kwi-vər\ river 374 mi (602 km) S Spain flowing W & SW into Gulf of Cádiz

Gua·da·lupe \'gwä-d'l-,üp\ river 300 mi (483 km) SE Tex. flowing SE into San Antonio River

Gua·da·lupe Hi·dal·go \'gwä-d'l-,üp-hi-'dal-(,)gō, ,gwä-d'l-'ü-pē-, -ē-'thäl-(,)gō\ **1** former city cen Mexico N of Mexico City now part of city of Gustavo A. Madero **2** GUSTAVO A. MADERO

Guadalupe Mountains mountains S N.Mex. & W Tex., the S extension of Sacramento Mountains; highest point **Guadalupe Peak**, 8751 ft (2667 m) in **Guadalupe Mountains National Park** (in Tex.)

Gua·de·loupe \'gwä-d'l-,üp, ,gwä-d'l-'\ two islands, Basse-Terre (or Guadeloupe proper) & Grande-Terre, in French West Indies in cen Leeward Islands; an overseas department of France * Basse-Terre (on Basse-Terre Is.) area 583 sq mi (1516 sq km), pop 327,002 — **Gua·de·lou·pe·an** \,gwä-d'l-'ü-pē-ən\ n

Gua·di·a·na \,gwä-dē-'ä-nə, -'a-nə\ river 515 mi (829 km) Spain & Portugal flowing W & S into Gulf of Cádiz

Guairá Falls — see SETE QUEDAS

Guam \'gwäm\ island W Pacific in S Marianas belonging to U.S. * Agana area 212 sq mi (551 sq km), pop 133,152 — **Gua·ma·ni·an** \gwä-'mä-nē-ən\ adj or n

Gua·na·ba·coa \,gwä-nə-bə-'kō-ə\ city W Cuba E of Havana pop 89,741

Gua·na·ba·ra Bay \,gwä-nə-'bar-ə, -'bär-ə\ inlet of Atlantic Ocean SE Brazil

Gua·na·jua·to \,gwä-nə-'hwä-(,)tō, -'wä-\ **1** state cen Mexico area 11,804 sq mi (30,690 sq km), pop 3,044,402 **2** city, its * pop 65,258

Guang·dong \'gwäŋ-'dúŋ\ or **Kwang·tung** \'gwäŋ-'dúŋ, 'kwäŋ-, -'túŋ\ province SE China bordering on S. China Sea & Gulf of Tonkin * Guangzhou area 76,344 sq mi (198,494 sq km), pop (with Hainan) 59,299,220

Guang·xi Zhuang·zu \'gwäŋ-'shē-jə-'wäŋ-'zü\ or **Kwang·si Chuang** \'gwäŋ-'sē-chə-'wäŋ\ region & former province S China W of Guangdong * Nanning area 85,096 sq mi (221,250 sq km)

Guang·zhou or **Kuang–chou** \'gwäŋ-'jō\ or **Can·ton** \'kan-,tän, kan-'\ city & port SE China * of Guangdong on Zhu River pop 1,840,000

Guan·tá·na·mo \gwän-'tä-nə-,mō\ city SE Cuba NW of **Guantánamo Bay** (inlet of the Caribbean; site of U.S. naval station) pop 204,268

Gua·po·ré \,gwä-pə-'rā\ **1** or **Ité·nez** \ē-'tā-nəs\ river 950 mi (1529 km) W Brazil & NE Bolivia flowing NW to the Mamoré **2** — see RONDÔNIA

Guar·da·fui, Cape \,g(w)är-də-'fwē, -'fü-ē\ cape NE Somalia at entrance to Gulf of Aden

Guá·ri·co \'gwär-i-,kō\ river 225 mi (362 km) W Venezuela flowing SW & S into the Orinoco

Gua·te·ma·la \,gwä-tə-'mä-lə\ **1** country Central America S of Mexico bordering on the Pacific & the Caribbean; a republic area 42,042 sq mi (109,309 sq km), pop 8,681,100 **2** or **Guatemala City** city, its * pop 749,784 — **Gua·te·ma·lan** \-'mä-lən\ adj or n

Gua·via·re \,gwä-'vyär-ē\ river 650 mi (1046 km) Colombia flowing E into the Orinoco

Gua·ya·ma \gwə-'yä-mə\ town SE Puerto Rico pop 41,588

Gua·ya·quil \,gwī-ə-'kē(ə)l, -'kil\ city & port W Ecuador on Guayas River 40 mi (64 km) from **Gulf of Guayaquil** (inlet of the Pacific) pop 823,219

Gua·yas \'gwī-əs\ river ab 100 mi (161 km) W Ecuador forming delta in Gulf of Guayaquil

Guay·mas \'gwī-məs\ city & port NW Mexico in Sonora on Gulf of California pop 57,492

Guay·na·bo \gwī-'nä-(,)bō\ city NE cen Puerto Rico pop 92,886

Guelph \'gwelf\ city Canada in SE Ont. pop 87,976

Guern·sey \'gərn-zē\ island English Channel in the Channel Islands * St. Peter Port area 25 sq mi (65 sq km), pop 46,182

Guer·re·ro \gə-'rer-(,)ō\ state S Mexico bordering on the Pacific * Chilpancingo area 24,885 sq mi (64,701 sq km), pop 2,174,162

Gui \'gwē\ or **Kuei** \'gwā\ river 200 mi (322 km) SE China in E Guangxi Zhuangzu flowing S into the Xi

Gui·a·na \gē-'a-nə, -'ä-nə; gi-'a-nə\ region N S. America bordering on the Atlantic & bounded on W & S by Orinoco, Negro, & Amazon rivers; includes Guyana, French Guiana, Suriname, & adjoining parts of Brazil & Venezuela — **Gui·a·nan** \-nən\ adj or n — **Gui·a·nese** \,gī-ə-'nēz, ,gē-ə-, -'nēs\ adj or n

Gui·enne or **Guy·enne** \gwē-'yen\ region & former province SW France bordering on Bay of Biscay * Bordeaux — see AQUITAINE

Guil·ford \'gil-fərd\ city S Conn. on Long Island Sound pop 19,848

Gui·lin \'gwē-'lin\ or **Kuei–lin** or **Kwei·lin** \'gwä-'lin\ city S China in NE Guangxi Zhuangzu on the Gui pop 170,000

Guin·ea \'gi-nē\ or F **Gui·née** \gē-nā\ **1** region W Africa bordering on the Atlantic from Gambia (on N) to Angola (on S) **2** or formerly **French Guinea** republic W Africa bordering on the Atlantic; formerly a territory of French West Africa * Conakry area 108,455 sq mi (281,983 sq km), pop 7,300,000 — **Guin·ean** \'gi-nē-ən\ adj or n

Guinea, Gulf of arm of the Atlantic W cen Africa; includes Bights of Benin & Biafra

Guin·ea–Bis·sau \,gi-nē-bi-'sau⁽ⁿ⁾\ or formerly **Portuguese Guinea** republic W Africa S of Senegal; until 1974 a Portuguese colony * Bissau area 13,948 sq mi (36,265 sq km), pop 767,739

Gui·púz·coa \gē-'püs-kō-ə\ province N Spain; one of the Basque Provinces * San Sebastian area 728 sq mi (1893 sq km), pop 733,042

Gui·yang \'gwē-'yäŋ\ or **Kuei–yang** or **Kwei·yang** \'gwä-'yäŋ\ city S China * of Guizhou pop 530,000

Gui·zhou \'gwē-'jō\ or **Kwei·chow** \'gwä-'jō, 'kwä-\ province S China S of Szechwan * Guiyang area 67,181 sq mi (174,671 sq km), pop 28,552,997

Gu·ja·rat or **Gu·je·rat** \,gü-jə-'rät, ,gú-\ **1** region W India where Gujarati is spoken **2** state W India N & E of Gulf of Cambay * Gandhinagar area 72,226 sq mi (187,788 sq km), pop 33,960,905

Guj·ran·wala \,güj-rən-'wä-lə, ,gúj-\ city NE Pakistan N of Lahore pop 785,000

Gulf·port \'gəlf-,pōrt, -,pòrt\ city & port SE Miss. pop 40,775

Gulf Stream warm current in N Atlantic flowing from Gulf of Mexico NE along U.S. coast to Nantucket & thence eastward

Gulja — see YINING

Gum·ti \'gùm(p)-tē\ river 500 mi (805 km) N India flowing SE into the Ganges

Gun·ni·son \'gə-nə-sən\ river 150 mi (241 km) W cen Colo. flowing W & NW into Colorado River — see BLACK CANYON

Gun·tur \gún-'túr\ city E India in cen Andhra Pradesh W of Machilipatnam pop 367,219

Gus·ta·vo A Ma·de·ro \gù-'stä-(,)vō-'ä-mə-'der-(,)ō\ city cen Mexico in Distrito Federal N of Mexico City pop 1,182,895

Guy·ana \gī-'a-nə\ or formerly **British Guiana** country N S. America on Atlantic coast; a republic within the Commonwealth of Nations since 1970 * Georgetown area 83,000 sq mi (215,800 sq km), pop 758,619 — **Guy·anese** \,gī-ə-'nēz, -'nēs\ adj or n

Gwa·dar or **Gwa·dur** \'gwä-dər\ town & port SW Pakistan on Arabian Sea; until 1958 belonged to Sultan of Oman pop 17,000

Gwa·li·or \'gwä-lē-,ór\ **1** former state N cen India * Lashkar; part of Madhya Pradesh since 1956 **2** city N cen India in NW Madhya Pradesh SSE of Agra pop (including adjacent city of **Lash·kar** \'ləsh-kər\) 559,776

Gwent \'gwent\ county SE Wales * Cwmbran area 531 sq mi (1381 sq km), pop 440,100

Gwyn·edd \'gwi-neth\ county NW Wales * Caernarvon area 1493 sq mi (3882 sq km), pop 234,100

Gyan·dzha \'gyän-jə\ or 1919–91 **Ki·ro·va·bad** \ki-'rō-və-,bad, -,bäd\ or earlier **Eli·sa·vet·pol** \i-,li-zə-'vet-,pól\ city W Azerbaijan pop 232,000

Gyor \'jər\ city NW Hungary WNW of Budapest pop 134,200

Haar·lem \'här-ləm\ city W Netherlands * of N. Holland pop 154,423

Haar·lem·mer·meer \,här-lə-mər-'mer\ commune W Netherlands pop 82,250

Habana — see HAVANA

Ha·chi·o·ji \,hä-chē-'ō-jē\ city Japan on Honshu pop 466,373

Hack·en·sack \'ha-kən-,sak\ city NE N.J. pop 37,049

Hack·ney \'hak-nē\ borough of N Greater London, England pop 187,000

Had·ding·ton \'ha-diŋ-tən\ **1** or **Had·ding·ton·shire** \-shir, -shər\ — see EAST LOTHIAN **2** royal burgh Scotland in Lothian pop 8117

Ha·dhra·maut or **Ha·dra·maut** \,hä-drə-'maùt\ region S Arabia bordering on Arabian Sea E of Aden, Yemen; chief city Mukalla area 58,500 sq mi (152,100 sq km)

Hadrumetum — see SOUSSE

Hae·ju \'hī-(,)jü\ city SW N. Korea on inlet of Yellow Sea pop 140,000

Ha–erh–pin — see HARBIN

Ha·gen \'hä-gən\ or **Hagen in West·fa·len** \-in-,vest-'fä-lən\ city W Germany ENE of Düsseldorf pop 218,927

Hague, The \,thə-'hāg\ or D 's **Gra·ven·ha·ge** \'skrä-vən-,hä-kə\ city SW Netherlands in S. Holland near coast of North Sea; de facto * of the Netherlands pop 449,700

Haidarabad — see HYDERABAD

Hai·fa \'hī-fə\ city & port NW Israel at foot of Mt. Carmel pop 227,800

Hai·kou \'hī-'kō\ city & port SE China * of Hainan pop 402,000

Hai·nan \'hī-'nän\ **1** island SE China in S. China Sea; a province * Haikou area 13,000 sq mi (33,800 sq km) **2** — see QIONGZHOU

Hai·naut \ā-'nō, hā-\ **1** medieval county in Low Countries SE of Flanders in modern SW Belgium & N France **2** province SW Belgium * Mons area 1436 sq mi (3734 sq km), pop 1,278,791

Hai·phong \'hī-'fòŋ, -'fäŋ\ city & port N Vietnam in Tonkin in delta of Red River pop 812,000

Hai·ti or formerly **Hay·ti** \'hā-tē also hä-'ē-tē\ **1** — see HISPANIOLA **2** country W. Indies on W Hispaniola; a republic * Port-au-Prince area 10,714 sq mi (27,856 sq km), pop 5,053,792

Ha·ka·pe·hi \,hä-kə-'pā-(,)hē\ town Nuku Hiva Is. * of the Marquesas

Ha·ko·da·te \,hä-kə-'dä-tē\ city & port Japan in SW Hokkaido on Tsugaru Strait pop 307,251

Hal·ber·stadt \'häl-bər-,shtät, -,stät\ city cen Germany SE of Brunswick pop 47,713

Ha·le·a·ka·la Crater \,hä-lē-,ä-kə-'lä\ crater of dormant volcano 10,023 ft (3055 m) Hawaii on E Maui; 2720 ft (829 m) deep, 20 mi (32 km) in circumference; in Haleakala National Park

Hal·i·car·nas·sus \,ha-lə-kär-'na-səs\ ancient city SW Asia Minor in SW Caria on Aegean Sea

Hal·i·fax \'ha-lə-,faks\ 1 city & port Canada ✽ of N.S. pop 114,455 2 borough N England in W. Yorkshire pop 87,488 — Hal·i·go·ni·an \,ha-lə-'gō-nē-ən\ n

Hal·lan·dale \'ha-lən-,dāl\ city SE Fla. S of Fort Lauderdale pop 30,996

Hal·le \'hä-lə\ city E cen Germany on the Saale NW of Leipzig pop 232,396

Hall·statt \'hôl-,stat, 'häl-,shtät, -,stät\ village W cen Austria on shore of Hall·stät·ter Lake \'hôl-,ste-tər; 'häl-,shte-, -,ste-\

Hal·ma·hera \,hal-mə-'her-ə, ,häl-\ island E Indonesia in Moluccas; lies on the equator & is largest in group area 6928 sq mi (18,013 sq km), pop 54,000

Halm·stad \'hälm-,stä(d)\ city & port SW Sweden pop 79,362

Hälsingborg — see HELSINGBORG

Hal·tom City \'hôl-təm\ village N Tex. NE of Fort Worth pop 32,856

Hal·ton Hills \'hôl-tᵊn\ town Canada in S Ont. pop 36,816

Halys — see KIZIL IRMAK

Ha·ma \'ha-,mä\ or bib Ha·math \'hä-,math\ city W Syria on the Orontes pop 176,640

Ha·mad, Al \,al-hə-'mad\ the SW portion of Syrian Desert

Ha·ma·dan \,ha-mə-'dan, -'dän\ or anc Ec·bat·a·na \ek-'ba-tᵊn-ə\ city W Iran WSW of Tehran pop 272,499

Ha·ma·ma·tsu \,hä-mə-'mät-(,)sü\ city Japan in S Honshu SE of Nagoya near Pacific coast pop 534,624

Ham·burg \'ham-,bərg; 'häm-,bùrg, -,bùrk\ city & port N Germany on the Elbe 90 mi (145 km) from its mouth; a state of the Federal Republic of Germany 1948–90 & of reunified Germany since then area 288 sq mi (749 sq km), pop 1,645,095 — Ham·burg·er \-,bər-gər, -,bùr-\ n

Ham·den \'ham-dən\ town S Conn. N of New Haven pop 52,434

Ha·meln \'hä-məln\ city N cen Germany in Lower Saxony SW of Hannover pop 58,390

Ham·hung \'häm-,hùn\ city E cen N. Korea near coast pop 420,000

Ham·il·ton \'ha-məl-tən, -tᵊn\ 1 city SW Ohio N of Cincinnati pop 61,368 2 town & port ✽ of Bermuda pop 1617 3 — see CHURCHILL 4 city & port Canada in SE Ont. on Lake Ontario pop 318,499 5 borough New Zealand on cen North Is. pop 91,109

Hamilton, Mount mountain 4261 ft (1299 m) W Calif. E of San Jose

Hamilton Inlet inlet of the Atlantic 150 mi (241 km) long (with Lake Melville) Canada in SE Labrador

Hamm \'häm, 'ham\ city W Germany on Lippe River pop 171,869

Ham·mer·fest \'ha-mər-,fest, 'hä-\ town & port N Norway on island in Arctic Ocean; northernmost town in Europe, at 70°38′N

Ham·mer·smith \'ha-mər-,smith\ borough of SW Greater London, England pop 153,800

Ham·mond \'ha-mənd\ city NW Ind. SE of Chicago pop 84,236

Hamp·shire \'ham(p)-,shir, -shər\ or Hants \'hants\ county S England on English Channel ✽ Winchester area 1457 sq mi (3788 sq km), pop 1,479,500

Hamp·stead \'ham(p)-stəd, -,sted\ former metropolitan borough NW London, England, now part of Camden

Hamp·ton \'ham(p)-tən\ city & port SE Va. E Newport News on Hampton Roads pop 133,793

Hampton Roads channel SE Va. through which James & Elizabeth rivers flow into Chesapeake Bay

Han \'hän\ 1 river 900 mi (1448 km) E cen China in Shaanxi & Hubei flowing SE into the Chang 2 river 220 mi (354 km) N cen S. Korea flowing W & NW into Yellow Sea

Han·ford \'han-fərd\ city S cen Calif. SE of Fresno pop 30,897

Hang·zhou \'häŋ-'jō\ or Hang·chou \-'jō\ or Hang·chow \'haŋ-'chaů, 'häŋ-'jō\ city E China ✽ of Zhejiang at head of Hangzhou Bay (inlet of E. China Sea) pop 784,000

Han·ko \'haŋ-,kō\ or Sw Hangö \'häŋ-,ə(r)\ town & port SW Finland on Hanko (Hangö) Peninsula in the Baltic SE of Turku

Han·kow \'haŋ-'kaů, -'kō; 'hän-'kō\ former city E cen China — see WUHAN

Han·ni·bal \'ha-nə-bəl\ city NE Mo. on Mississippi River pop 18,004

Han·no·ver or Han·o·ver \'ha-,nō-vər, -nə-vər, G hä-'nō-vər, -'nō-fər\ city N cen Germany WNW of Brunswick pop 534,451

Ha·noi \ha-'nói, hə-, hä-\ city ✽ of Vietnam in Tonkin on Red River; formerly ✽ of French Indochina & of N. Vietnam pop 414,600

Han·o·ver Park \'ha-,nō-vər, -nə-vər\ city NE Ill. pop 32,895

Han·yang \'hän-'yäŋ\ former city E cen China — see WUHAN

Ha·rap·pa \hə-'ra-pə\ locality W Pakistan in Indus valley NE of Multan; center of a prehistoric civilization

Ha·rar \'här-ər\ city E Ethiopia E of Addis Ababa pop 70,289

Ha·ra·re \hə-'rä-(,)rä\ or formerly Salisbury city ✽ of Zimbabwe pop 658,364

Har·bin \'här-bən, här-'bin\ or Ha—erh—pin \'hä-'er-'bin\ or formerly Pin·kiang \'bin-jē-'äŋ\ city NE China ✽ of Heilongjiang on Songhua River pop 2,624,000

Har·in·gey \'har-iŋ-,gä\ borough of N Greater London, England pop 208,600

Ha·ri Rud \,har-ē-'rüd\ or anc Ari·us \'ar-ē-əs, 'er-; ə-'rī-əs\ river 700 mi (1126 km) NW Afghanistan, NE Iran, & S Turkmenistan flowing SW & N into Kara Kum Desert

Har·lem \'här-ləm\ 1 river channel SE N.Y. NE of Manhattan Is.; with Spuyten Duyvil Creek, connects Hudson & East rivers 2 section of New York City in NE Manhattan bordering on Harlem & East rivers 3 HAARLEM — Har·lem·ite \-lə-,mīt\ n

Har·lin·gen 1 \'här-lən-jən\ city S Tex. NNW of Brownsville pop 48,735 2 \-liŋ-ən\ town & port N Netherlands in Friesland

Har·ney Lake \'här-nē\ intermittent salt lake SE Oreg. in Harney Basin (depression, area 2500 sq mi or 6500 sq km)

Harney Peak mountain 7242 ft (2207 m) SW S.Dak.; highest in Black Hills & in state

Harris — see LEWIS WITH HARRIS

Har·ris·burg \'har-əs-,bərg\ city ✽ of Pa. pop 52,376

Har·ri·son \'har-ə-sən\ village SE N.Y. on Long Island Sound pop 23,308

Har·ri·son·burg \'har-ə-sən-,bərg\ city N Va. pop 30,707

Har·ro·gate \'har-ə-gət, -,gät\ borough N England in N. Yorkshire N of Leeds pop 66,475

Har·row \'har-,ō\ borough of NW Greater London, England pop 199,200

Hart·ford \'härt-fərd\ city N cen Conn., its ✽ pop 139,739 — Hartford·ite \-fər-,dīt\ n

Hart·le·pool \'härt-lē-,pül\ borough N England in Cleveland on North Sea pop 94,359

Har·vard, Mount \'här-vərd\ mountain 14,420 ft (4395 m) cen Colo. in Sawatch Mountains SE of Mt. Elbert

Har·vey \'här-vē\ city NE Ill. S of Chicago pop 29,771

Har·wich \'har-ij, -ich\ borough SE England in Essex on North Sea pop 15,076

Ha·ry·a·na or Ha·ri·a·na \,hə-rē-'ä-nə\ state NW India in E Punjab formed 1966 from southern part of former state of Punjab ✽ Chandigarh area 17,010 sq mi (44,226 sq km), pop 12,850,902

Harz \'härts\ mountains cen Germany bet. the Elbe & the Leine — see BROCKEN

Ha·sa \'ha-sə\ or El Ha·sa \el-'ha-sə\ region NE Saudi Arabia in E Nejd bordering on Persian Gulf

Has·selt \'hä-səlt\ commune NE Belgium ✽ of Limburg pop 66,611

Has·tings \'hās-tiŋz\ 1 city S Nebr. pop 22,837 2 borough SE England in E. Sussex on Strait of Dover pop 74,803

Ha·tay \hä-'tī\ district S Turkey E of Gulf of Iskenderun

Hat·ter·as Island \'ha-tə-rəs, 'ha-trəs\ island N.C. bet. Pamlico Sound & Atlantic Ocean; a long barrier island

Hatteras, Cape cape N.C. on SE Hatteras Is.

Hat·ties·burg \'ha-tēz-,bərg\ city SE Miss. pop 41,882

Hau·ra·ki Gulf \haů-'ra-kē, -'rä-\ inlet of the S Pacific N New Zealand on N coast of North Is.

Haute—Vol·ta \ōt-vòl-tä\ UPPER VOLTA — French name

Ha·vana or Ha·bana \hə-'va-nə\ or Sp La Ha·ba·na \lä-(ä-)'vä-nə\ city & port ✽ of Cuba on Gulf of Mexico pop 990,000 — Ha·van·an \hə-'va-nən\ adj or n

Hav·ant and Wa·ter·loo \'ha-vən-t²n-,wò-tər-'lü, -,wä-; -'wò-tər-,, -'wä-\ town S England in Hampshire NE of Portsmouth pop 116,649

Ha·vel \'hä-fəl\ river 225 mi (362 km) NE Germany flowing SW through Berlin into the Elbe

Have·lock \'hav-,läk, -lək\ city SE N.C. pop 20,268

Hav·er·ford·west \'ha-vər-fərd-'west, ,här-fərd-\ borough & port SW Wales in Dyfed pop 9936

Ha·ver·hill \'hāv-rəl, 'hā-və-rəl\ city NE Mass. pop 51,418

Ha·ver·ing \'häv-riŋ, 'hä-və-riŋ\ borough of NE Greater London, England pop 241,800

Ha·ví·rov \'hä-və-,róf, -vər-,zhóf\ city E Czech Republic pop 92,142

Havre — see LE HAVRE

Ha·waii \hə-'wä-yē, -'wä-,ē also -'vä- or -'wò-; sometimes -yə\ 1 or Ha·wai·ian Islands \-yən\ or formerly Sand·wich Islands \'san(d)-,wich\ group of islands cen Pacific belonging to U.S. 2 island SE Hawaii, largest of the group; chief city Hilo area 4021 sq mi (10,455 sq km) 3 state of the U.S. comprising Hawaiian Islands except Midway Islands; annexed 1898, a territory 1900–59 ✽ Honolulu area 6450 sq mi (16,770 sq km), pop 1,108,229

Hawaii Volcanoes National Park reservation Hawaii including Mauna Loa & Kilauea volcanoes on Hawaii (island)

Hawke Bay \'hòk\ inlet of the S Pacific N New Zealand on SE coast of North Is.

Haw·thorne \'hò-,thórn\ 1 city SW Calif. SW of Los Angeles pop 71,349 2 borough NE N.J. N of Paterson pop 17,084

Hay \'hā\ river 530 mi (853 km) Canada in N Alta. & SW Mackenzie district flowing NE into Great Slave Lake

Hayes \'hāz\ 1 river 300 mi (483 km) Canada in E Man. flowing NE into Hudson Bay 2 or Hayes and Har·ling·ton \'här-liŋ-tən\ former urban district SE England in Middlesex, now part of Hillingdon

Hayti — see HAITI

Hay·ward \'hā-wərd\ city W Calif. SE of Oakland pop 111,498

Ha·zle·ton \'hā-zəl-tən\ city E Pa. S of Wilkes-Barre pop 24,730

Heard \'hərd\ island S Indian Ocean SE of Kerguelen, at 53°10′S, 74°10′E; claimed by Australia

He·bei \'hə-'bä\ or Ho·peh or Ho·pei \'hō-'bä\ or formerly Chih-li \'chē-'lē, 'jir-'lē\ province NE China ✽ Shijiazhuang area 84,865 sq mi (220,649 sq km), pop 53,005,875

Heb·ri·des \'he-brə-,dēz\ islands W Scotland in the Atlantic divided by Little Minch into Inner Hebrides (near the mainland) & Outer Hebrides (to NW) area 2900 sq mi (7540 sq km), pop 60,000 — see LEWIS WITH HARRIS, WESTERN ISLES — Heb·ri·de·an \,he-brə-'dē-ən\ adj or n

He·bron \'hē-brən\ or anc Kir·jath—ar·ba \,kər-yəth-'är-bə, ,kir-\ city cen Palestine SSW of Jerusalem in modern Jordan pop 38,348

Hec·ate Strait \'he-kət\ strait Canada in W B.C., inlet of the Pacific bet. Queen Charlotte Islands & the coast

Heer·len \'her-lən\ commune SE Netherlands in Limburg NE of Maastricht pop 92,158

He·fei or Ho·fei \'hə-'fā\ or formerly Lu·chow \'lü-'jō\ city E China ✽ of Anhui W of Nanjing pop 360,000

Hei·del·berg \'hī-d²l-,bərg, -,berg, -,berk\ city SW Germany on the Neckar SE of Mannheim pop 133,227

Heil·bronn \'hī(ə)l-,brän, hīl-'brón\ city SW Germany on the Neckar N of Stuttgart pop 111,938

Hei·long·jiang or Hei·lung·kiang \'hä-'lùŋ-jē-'äŋ\ province NE China in N Manchuria bordering on the Amur ✽ Harbin area 178,996 sq mi (465,390 sq km), pop 32,665,546

\ə\ abut \ᵊ\ kitten, F table \ər\ further \a\ ash \ā\ ace \ä\ mop, mar
\aů\ out \ch\ chin \e\ bet \ē\ easy \g\ go \i\ hit \ī\ ice \j\ job
\ŋ\ sing \ō\ go \ò\ law \òi\ boy \th\ thin \t̲h̲\ the \ü\ loot \ů\ foot
\y\ yet \zh\ vision \à, k̲, ⁿ, œ, œ̄, Ꭓ, ᵫ, ʸ\ see Guide to Pronunciation

He·jaz \he-'jaz, hi-\ *or* **Al Ḥi·jāz** \,al-hi-'jaz\ region W Saudi Arabia on Red Sea; a viceroyalty ✱ Mecca *area* 150,000 *sq mi* (390,000 *sq km*), *pop* 1,400,000

Hek·la \'he-klə\ volcano 4892 *ft* (1491 *m*) SW Iceland

Hel·e·na \'he-lə-nə\ city W *cen* Mont., its ✱ *pop* 24,569

Hel·go·land \'hel-gō-,land, -,länt\ *or* **Hel·i·go·land** \'he-lə-gō-\ island NW Germany in North Sea, in N. Frisian Islands

Hel·i·con \'he-lə-,kän, -li-kən\ mountain 5735 *ft* (1748 *m*) E *cen* Greece in SW Boeotia near Gulf of Corinth

He·li·op·o·lis \,hē-lē-'ä-pə-ləs\ **1** — see BAALBEK **2** ancient ruined city N Egypt S of modern Cairo **3** ancient ruined city NE of modern Cairo

Hellas — see GREECE

Hel·les, Cape \he-(,)lēz\ headland Turkey in Europe at S tip of Gallipoli Peninsula

Hellespont, Hellespontus — see DARDANELLES

Hell Gate a narrow part of East River in New York City bet. Long Is. & Manhattan Is.

Hells Canyon \'helz\ *or* **Grand Canyon of the Snake** canyon of Snake River on Idaho-Oreg. border

Hel·mand \'hel-mənd\ river 650 *mi* (1046 *km*) SW Afghanistan flowing SW & W into a morass on Iran border

Hel·mond \'hel-,mònt\ commune S Netherlands *pop* 59,345

Helm·stedt \'helm-,shtet, -,stet\ city *cen* Germany E of Brunswick near former E. Germany–W. Germany border *pop* 26,718

Hel·sing·borg *or* **Häl·sing·borg** \'hel-siŋ-,bòrg, hel-siŋ-'bòr-ē\ city & port SW Sweden on Øresund opposite Helsingør, Denmark *pop* 108,359

Hel·sing·ör \,hel-siŋ-'ər\ city & port Denmark on N Sjælland Is. *pop* 56,754

Hel·sin·ki \'hel-,siŋ-kē, hel-'\ *or Sw* **Hel·sing·fors** \'hel-siŋ-,fòrz\ city & port ✱ of Finland on Gulf of Finland *pop* 490,629

Hel·vel·lyn \hel-'ve-lən\ mountain 3118 *ft* (950 *m*) NW England in Cumbria SW of Ullswater

Helvetia — see SWITZERLAND — **Hel·ve·tian** \hel-'vē-shən\ *adj or n*

Hem·et \'he-mət\ city SE Calif. SE of San Bernardino *pop* 36,094

Hemp·stead \'hem(p)-,sted, -stəd\ village SE N.Y. on Long Is. *pop* 49,453

He·nan \'hə-'nän\ *or* **Ho·nan** \'hō-'nän\ province E *cen* China ✱ Zhengzhou *area* 64,479 *sq mi* (167,645 *sq km*), *pop* 74,422,739

Hen·der·son \'hen-dər-sən\ **1** city NW Ky. *pop* 25,945 **2** city S Nev. *pop* 64,942

Hen·der·son·ville \'hen-dər-sən-,vil, -vəl\ city N Tenn. NE of Nashville *pop* 32,188

Hen·don \'hen-dən\ former urban district SE England in Middlesex, now part of Barnet

Heng·e·lo \'heŋ-ə-,lō\ commune E Netherlands in Overijssel *pop* 76,535

Heng·yang \'həŋ-'yäŋ\ city SE *cen* China in SE Hunan on the Xiang *pop* 240,000

Hen·ley \'hen-lē\ *or* **Henley on Thames** borough SE *cen* England in Oxfordshire W of London *pop* 31,744

Hen·lo·pen, Cape \hen-'lō-pən\ headland SE Del. at entrance to Delaware Bay

Hen·ry, Cape \'hen-rē\ headland SE Va. S of entrance to Chesapeake Bay

He·rat \he-'rät, hə-\ *or anc* **Aria** \'ar-ē-ə, 'er-; ə-'rī-ə\ city NW Afghanistan on the Hari Rud *pop* 163,960

Her·cu·la·ne·um \,hər-kyə-'lā-nē-əm\ ancient city S Italy in Campania on Tyrrhenian Sea; destroyed A.D. 79 by eruption of Mt. Vesuvius

Her·e·ford \'hə-fərd, *US also* 'hər-fərd\ **1** *or* **Her·e·ford·shire** \-,shir, -shər\ former county W England on Welsh border **2** borough W England in Hereford and Worcester *pop* 47,652

Hereford and Worces·ter \'wüs-tər\ county W England ✱ Worcester *area* 1516 *sq mi* (3942 *sq km*), *pop* 634,700

Her·ford \'her-fórt\ city W *cen* Germany in N. Rhine-Westphalia NE of Bielefeld *pop* 62,881

He·ri·sau \'her-ə-,zaú\ commune NE Switzerland ✱ of Appenzell Outer Rhodes canton *pop* 14,600

Her·mon, Mount \'hər-mən\ mountain 9232 *ft* (2814 *m*) on border bet. Syria & Lebanon; highest in Anti-Lebanon Mountains

Her·mo·si·llo \,er-mə-'sē-(,)yō\ city NW Mexico ✱ of Sonora on Sonora River *pop* 232,691

Hermoúpolis — see ERMOÚPOLIS

Her·ne \'her-nə\ city W Germany in the Ruhr *pop* 182,542

Her·ning \'her-niŋ, 'har-niŋ\ city Denmark in cen Jutland *pop* 56,376

Her·ten \'her-t^n\ city W Germany in N. Rhine-Westphalia N of Essen *pop* 69,247

Hert·ford \'här-fərd, 'härt-, *US also* 'hart-\ borough SE England ✱ of Hertfordshire *pop* 21,412

Hert·ford·shire \'här-fərd-,shir, 'härt-, -shər, *US also* 'hart-\ *or* **Hertford** \'här-fərd *also* 'härt-, *US also* 'hart-\ county SE England *area* 654 *sq mi* (1699 *sq km*), *pop* 964,800

Her·to·gen·bosch, 's — see 'S HERTOGENBOSCH

Her·ze·go·vi·na \,hert-sə-gō-'vē-nə, ,hart-, -'gō-və-nə\ *or Serb* **Her·ce·go·vi·na** \,kert-sə-gō-vē-nə\ region S Europe S of Bosnia & NW of Montenegro; part of Bosnia and Herzegovina — **Her·ze·go·vi·nian** \,hert-sə-gō-'vē-nē-ən, ,hart-, -nyən\ *n*

Hes·pe·ria \he-'sper-ē-ə\ city SE Calif. N of San Bernardino *pop* 50,418

Hesse \'hes, 'he-sē\ *or G* **Hes·sen** \'he-s^n\ **1** region W *cen* Germany N of Baden-Württemberg divided into **Hesse–Darmstadt** (in the S) & **Hesse–Cas·sel** \-'ka-səl, -'kä-\ (in the N), the latter being united with Prussia in 1866 as part of the province of **Hesse–Nassau** along with the duchy of Nassau & the city of Frankfurt am Main **2** state of the Weimar Republic, equivalent to Hesse-Darmstadt **3** state of Germany & formerly of W. Germany including larger part of Hesse–Darmstadt & part of Hesse-Nassau ✱ Wiesbaden *area* 8148 *sq mi* (21,185 *sq km*), *pop* 5,601,031

Hes·ton and Isle·worth \'hes-tən-ən(d)-'ī-zəl-(,)wərth, 'he-s^n-\ former municipal borough SE England in Middlesex, now part of Hounslow

Hi·a·le·ah \,hī-ə-'lē-ə\ city SE Fla. N of Miami *pop* 188,004

Hibernia — see IRELAND

Hi·bok·hi·bok \,hē-,bòk-'hē-,bòk\ volcano 5620 *ft* (1713 *m*) S Philippines on Camiguin Is.

Hick·o·ry \'hi-k(ə-)rē\ city W *cen* N.C. *pop* 28,301

Hi·dal·go \hi-'dal-(,)gō, ē-'thäl-(,)gō\ state *cen* Mexico ✱ Pachuca *area* 8057 *sq mi* (20,948 *sq km*), *pop* 1,516,511

Hierosolyma — see JERUSALEM

Hier·ro \'yer-(,)ō\ *or formerly* **Fer·ro** \'fer-(,)ō\ island Spain, westernmost of the Canary Islands *area* 107 *sq mi* (278 *sq km*)

Hi·ga·shi·ōsa·ka \hē-,gä-shē-ō-'sä-kə\ city Japan in S Honshu; suburb of Osaka *pop* 518,251

High Atlas — see ATLAS

High·land \'hī-lənd\ **1** city SE Calif. E of San Bernardino *pop* 34,439 **2** town NW Ind. S of Hammond *pop* 23,696 **3** region N Scotland, established 1975 ✱ Inverness *area* 9813 *sq mi* (25,514 *sq km*), *pop* 200,030

Highland Park 1 city NE Ill. N of Chicago *pop* 30,575 **2** city SE Mich. within city of Detroit *pop* 20,121

High·lands \'hī-lən(d)z\ the chiefly mountainous N part of Scotland N of a line connecting Firth of Clyde & Firth of Tay

Highlands of Navesink — see NAVESINK (Highlands of)

Highlands of the Hudson hilly region SE N.Y. on both sides of Hudson River; includes Storm King (W of the Hudson) 1340 *ft* (408 *m*)

High Plains the Great Plains esp. from Nebr. southward

High Point \'hī-,pòint\ city N *cen* N.C. SW of Greensboro *pop* 69,496

High Sierra the Sierra Nevada (in Calif.)

High Wyc·ombe \'wi-kəm\ borough SE *cen* England in Buckinghamshire WNW of London *pop* 60,516

Hii·u·maa \'hē-ə-,mä\ island Estonia in Baltic Sea N of Sarema Is. *area* 371 *sq mi* (965 *sq km*)

Hijāz, Al — see HEJAZ

Hil·des·heim \'hil-dəs-,hīm\ city N *cen* Germany SSE of Hannover *pop* 102,619

Hil·ling·don \'hi-liŋ-dən\ borough of W Greater London, England *pop* 232,800

Hills·boro \'hilz-,bər-ə, -,bə-rə, -brə\ city NW Oreg. W of Portland *pop* 37,520

Hi·lo \'hē-(,)lō\ city & port Hawaii in E Hawaii (island) *pop* 37,808

Hil·ton Head Island \'hil-t^n-'hed\ island comprising a town off S.C. coast *pop* 23,694

Hil·ver·sum \'hil-vər-səm\ city *cen* Netherlands in N. Holland SE of Amsterdam *pop* 89,510

Hi·ma·chal Pra·desh \hi-'mä-chəl-prə-'desh, -'däsh\ state NW India NW of Uttar Pradesh ✱ Simla *area* 21,629 *sq mi* (56,235 *sq km*), *pop* 4,237,569

Hi·ma·la·ya \,hi-mə-'lā-ə; hə-'mäl-yə, -'mä-lē-ə\ mountains S Asia on border bet. India & Tibet & in Kashmir, Nepal, & Bhutan — see EVEREST (Mount) — **Hi·ma·la·yan** \,hi-mə-'lā-ən; hə-'mäl-yən, -'mä-lē-ən\ *adj*

Hi·me·ji \hi-'me-jē\ city Japan in W Honshu *pop* 454,360

Hindenburg — see ZABRZE

Hin·du Kush \'hin-(,)dü-'kush, -'kəsh\ *or anc* **Cau·ca·sus In·di·cus** \'kò-kə-səs-'in-di-kəs\ mountain range *cen* Asia SW of the Pamirs on border of Kashmir & in Afghanistan

Hin·du·stan *or* **Hin·do·stan** \,hin-(,)dü-'stan, -də-, -'stän\ **1** region N India N of the Deccan including the plain drained by the Indus, the Ganges, & the Brahmaputra **2** the subcontinent of India **3** the Republic of India

Hines·ville \'hīnz-,vil, -vəl\ town SE Ga. *pop* 21,603

Hing·ham \'hiŋ-əm\ town E Mass. SE of Boston *pop* 19,821

Hip·po \'hi-(,)pō\ *or* **Hippo Re·gi·us** \-'rē-jəs, -jē-əs\ ancient city N Africa S of modern Bône, Algeria; chief town of Numidia

Hi·ra·ka·ta \,hir-ə-'kä-tə\ city Japan on Honshu *pop* 390,790

Hi·ro·shi·ma \,hir-ə-'shē-mə, hə-'rō-shə-mə\ city & port Japan in SW Honshu on Inland Sea *pop* 1,085,677

His·pa·nia \hi-'spä-nē-ə, -'spā-nyə, -'spa-\ IBERIAN PENINSULA

His·pan·io·la \,his-pə-'nyō-lə\ *or Sp* **Es·pa·ño·la** \,es-,pä-'nyō-lə\ *or formerly* **Hai·ti** \'hā-tē\ *or* **San·to Do·min·go** \,san-tə-də-'miŋ-(,)gō\ *or* **San Domingo** \,san-də-\ island West Indies in the Greater Antilles; divided bet. Haiti (on W) & Dominican Republic (on E) *area* 29,979 *sq mi* (77,945 *sq km*)

His·sar·lik \,hi-sər-'lik\ site of ancient Troy NW Turkey in Asia 4 *mi* (6.4 *km*) S of mouth of the Dardanelles

Hi·was·see \hī-'wä-sē\ river 150 *mi* (241 *km*) E U.S. flowing from NE Ga. WNW through W N.C. into Tennessee River in Tenn.

Ho·bart 1 \'hō-bərt\ city NW Ind. *pop* 21,822 **2** \-,bärt\ city & port Australia ✱ of Tasmania *pop* 127,106

Hobbs \'häbz\ city SE corner of N.Mex. *pop* 29,115

Ho·bo·ken \'hō-,bō-kən\ city NE N.J. N of Jersey City *pop* 33,397

Ho Chi Minh City \,hō-(,)chē-,min, -(,)shē-\ *or formerly* **Sai·gon** \sī-'gän, 'sī-,\ city & port S Vietnam; formerly (as Saigon) ✱ of S. Vietnam

Ho·dei·da \hō-'dā-də\ city & port W Yemen *pop* 40,000

Hof \'hōf, 'hòf\ city Germany in Bavaria on the Saale near former E. Germany–W. Germany border *pop* 53,180

Hofei — see HEFEI

Hoff·man Estates \'häf-mən, 'hòf-\ village NE Ill. *pop* 46,561

Ho·fuf \hù-'füf, hō-\ city NE Saudi Arabia in E Nejd; chief town of Hasa region *pop* 85,000

Hoggar — see AHAGGAR

Ho·hen·zol·lern \'hō-ən-,zä-lərn\ region SW Germany, formerly a province of Prussia — see WÜRTTEMBERG

Ho·he Tau·ern \,hō-ə-'taú-(ə)rn\ range of the E Alps W Austria bet. Carinthia & Tirol — see GROSSGLOCKNER

Hoh·hot \'hō-'hōt\ *or* **Hu·he·hot** \'hü-(,)hä-'hōt\ *or* **Hu–ho–hao–t'e** \'hü-'hō-'haú-'tə\ city N China ✱ of Inner Mongolia *pop* 320,000

Ho·ho·kam Pi·ma National Monument \hō-'hō-kəm-'pē-mə\ reservation SE of Phoenix, Ariz.; not open to the public

Hok·kai·do \hä-'kī-(,)dō\ *or formerly* **Ye·zo** \'ye-(,)zō\ island N Japan N of Honshu *area* 30,077 *sq mi* (78,200 *sq km*), *pop* 5,643,715

Hol·guín \(h)òl-'gēn\ city E Cuba in plateau region *pop* 239,641

Hol·land \'hä-lənd\ **1** city W Mich. on Lake Michigan *pop* 30,745 **2** medieval county of Holy Roman Empire bordering on North Sea, now forming N. & S. Holland provinces of the Netherlands **3** — see NETHERLANDS — **Hol·land·er** \-lən-dər\ *n*

Holland, Parts of district & former administrative county E England in SE Lincolnshire ✱ Boston *area* 420 *sq mi* (1092 *sq km*)

Hollandia — see DJAJAPURA

Hol·lis·ter \'hä-lə-stər\ city W Calif. E of Monterey Bay *pop* 19,212

Hol·ly·wood \'hä-lē-,wůd\ **1** section of Los Angeles, Calif. NW of the downtown district **2** city SE Fla. N of Miami *pop* 121,697

Hol·stein \'hōl-,stīn, -,stēn\ region N Germany S of Jutland Peninsula adjoining Schleswig; once a duchy of Denmark, became a part of Prussia 1866 — see SCHLESWIG-HOLSTEIN

Hol·ston \'hōl-stən\ river 140 *mi* (225 *km*) E Tenn. flowing SW to unite with French Broad River forming the Tennessee River

Holy Cross, Mount of the mountain 14,005 *ft* (4269 *m*) NW *cen* Colo. in Sawatch Range

Holy·head \'hä-lē-,hed\ urban area & port NW Wales in Gwynedd on Holy Is.

Ho·ly Island \'hō-lē\ **1** or **Lin·dis·farne** \'lin-dəs-,färn\ island N England off NE coast of Northumberland; connected to mainland at low tide *pop* 190 **2** or **Holy·head** \'hä-lē-,hed\ island NW Wales in St. George's Channel off W coast of Anglesey

Holy Land a name for Palestine first used in Zech. 2:12

Holy Loch inlet of Firth of Clyde W Scotland on NW shore of the firth opposite mouth of the Clyde

Hol·yoke \'hōl-,yōk\ city SW Mass. N of Springfield *pop* 43,704

Holy Roman Empire realm of *cen* Europe in medieval & modern periods; of varying extent, but with Germany as chief component

Home·stead \'hōm-,sted\ city SE Fla. SW of Miami *pop* 26,866

Homestead National Monument site SE Nebr. (W of Beatrice) of first homestead entered under General Homestead Act of 1862

Home·wood \'hōm-,wůd\ **1** city *cen* Ala. *pop* 22,922 **2** village NE Ill. S of Chicago *pop* 19,278

Homs \'hómz, 'húms\ **1** *or formerly* **Leb·da** \'leb-də\ town & port Libya ESE of Tripoli **2** *or anc* **Em·e·sa** \'e-mə-sə\ city W Syria on the Orontes *pop* 354,508

Homyel' — see GOMEL

Honan — see HENAN

Hon·du·ras \hän-'dúr-əs, -'dyúr-\ country Central America bordering on the Caribbean & the Pacific; a republic ✱ Tegucigalpa *area* 59,160 *sq mi* (153,816 *sq km*), *pop* 4,604,800 — **Hon·du·ran** \-ən\ *adj or n* — **Hon·du·ra·ne·an** *or* **Hon·du·ra·ni·an** \,hän-dú-'rä-nē-ən, -dyú-\ *adj or n*

Honduras, Gulf of inlet of the Caribbean bet. S Belize, E Guatemala, & N Honduras

Hon·fleur \ōⁿ-'flər\ town & port N France on Seine estuary *pop* 8995

Hong — see RED

Hong Kong \'häŋ-,käŋ, -'käŋ; 'hóŋ-,kòŋ, -'kòŋ\ **1**.Brit. crown colony on SE coast of China E of mouth of Zhu River including Hong Kong Is., Kowloon Peninsula & adjacent area (New Territories) on mainland, & nearby islands ✱ Victoria *area* 391 *sq mi* (1017 *sq km*), *pop* 4,986,560 **2** — see VICTORIA — **Hong Kong·er** *n*

Hong·shui *or* **Hung·shui** \'hůŋ-'shwä\ river 800 *mi* (1287 *km*) S China flowing from E Yunnan E to unite with the Yu in E Guangxi Zhuangzu forming the Xun

Hong·ze *or* **Hung·tse** \'hůŋ-'(d)zə\ lake 65 *mi* (105 *km*) long E China in W Jiangsu; traversed by the Huang

Ho·ni·a·ra \,hō-nē-'är-ə\ town W Pacific ✱ of Solomon Islands on Guadalcanal Is. *pop* 14,942

Ho·no·lu·lu \,hä-nᵊl-'ü-(,)lü, ,hō-nᵊl-\ city & port ✱ of Hawaii on Oahu *pop* 365,272 — **Ho·no·lu·lan** \-'ü-lən\ *n*

Hon·shu \'hän-(,)shü\ *or* **Hon·do** \-(,)dō\ island Japan, chief island of the group *area* 88,000 *sq mi* (228,800 *sq km*), *pop* 100,254,208

Hood, Mount \'hůd\ mountain 11,245 *ft* (3427 *m*) NW Oreg. in Cascade Range; highest point in state

Hood Canal inlet of Puget Sound 80 *mi* (129 *km*) long W Wash. along E shore of Olympic Peninsula

Hoo·ghly \'hü-glē\ river 120 *mi* (193 *km*) E India flowing S into Bay of Bengal; most westerly channel of the Ganges in its delta

Hook of Holland \'hůk\ headland SW Netherlands in S. Holland on coast SW of The Hague

Hoorn Islands — see FUTUNA ISLANDS

Hoo·sac Mountains \'hü-sək\ mountain range NW Mass. & SW Vt., a southern extension of Green Mountains

Hoo·ver \'hü-vər\ city *cen* Ala. *pop* 39,788

Hoover Dam *or* **Boul·der Dam** \'bōl-dər\ dam 726 *ft* (221 *m*) high in Colorado River bet. Nev. & Ariz. — see MEAD (Lake)

Ho·pat·cong, Lake \hə-'pat-,kän, -,käŋ\ lake 8 *mi* (13 *km*) long N N.J.

Hopeh *or* **Hopei** — see HEBEI

Hope·well \'hōp-,wel, -wəl\ city SE Va. *pop* 23,101

Hop·kins·ville \'häp-kənz-,vil\ city SW Ky. *pop* 29,809

Ho·reb, Mount \'hór-,eb, 'hór-\ *or* **Mount Si·nai** \'sī-,nī *also* -nē-,ī\ mountain where according to the Bible the Law was given to Moses; thought to be in the Gebel Musa on Sinai peninsula

Hor·muz *or* **Or·muz** \'(h)ór-,məz, (h)ór-'müz\ **1** ancient town S Iran on **Strait of Hormuz** (strait connecting Persian Gulf & Gulf of Oman) **2** island SE Iran in Strait of Hormuz

Horn \'hórn\ *or* **North Cape** cape NW Iceland

Horn, Cape headland S Chile on **Horn Island** in Tierra del Fuego; southernmost point of S. America, at 55°59′S

Horn·church \'hórn-,chərch\ former urban district SE England in Essex, now part of Havering

Horn of Africa the easternmost projection of Africa; variously used of Somalia, SE or all of Ethiopia & sometimes Djibouti; its E tip is Cape Guardafui

Hor·sens \'hór-sᵊnz, -s²n(t)s\ city & port Denmark *pop* 54,940

Hos·pi·ta·let \,(h)äs-,pi-tᵊl-'et\ city NE Spain in Barcelona province, SW suburb of Barcelona *pop* 295,074

Ho·tan \'hō-'tän\ *or* **Ho·t'ien** \'hō-tē-'en\ *or* **Kho·tan** \'kō-'tän\ town & oasis W China in SW Xinjiang Uygur on S edge of the Taklimakan

Hot Springs city W *cen* Ark. adjoining **Hot Springs National Park** (reservation containing hot mineral springs) *pop* 32,462

Hou·ma \'hō-mə, 'hü-\ city SE La. *pop* 30,495

Houns·low \'haůnz-(,)lō\ borough of SW Greater London, England *pop* 204,300

Hou·sa·ton·ic \,hü-sə-'tä-nik, ,hü-zə-\ river 148 *mi* (238 *km*) W Mass. & W Conn. flowing from Berkshire Hills S into Long Island Sound

Hous·ton \'hyü-stən, 'yü-\ city & port SE Tex. connected with Galveston Bay by ship canal *pop* 1,630,553 — **Hous·to·nian** \hyü-'stō-nē-ən, yü-, -nyən\ *n* — **Hous·ton·ite** \'hyü-stə-,nit, 'yü-\ *n*

Hove \'hōv\ borough S England in E. Sussex *pop* 66,612

Ho·ven·weep National Monument \'hō-vən-,wēp\ site SE Utah & SW Colo. of prehistoric pueblos & cliff dwellings

How·rah \'haů-rə\ city E India in W. Bengal on the Hooghly opposite Calcutta *pop* 599,740

Hra·dec Kra·lo·ve \'(h)rä-,dets-'krä-lə-,vä\ *or G* **Kö·nig·grätz** \'kā-nig-,gräts, Ger 'kœ-nik-,grets\ city N *cen* Czech Republic *pop* 101,159

Hsi — see XI

Hsia—men — see XIAMEN

Hsiang — see XIANG

Hsiang–t'an — see XIANGTAN

Hsin·chu \'shin-'chü\ city & port China in NW Taiwan on coast SW of Taipei *pop* 125,814

Hsin–hsiang — see XINXIANG

Hsi—ning — see XINING

Hsinkao — see YÜ SHAN

Hsüan—hua — see XUANHUA

Huai \hü-'ī, 'hwī\ river 600 *mi* (966 *km*) E China flowing from S Henan E into Hongze Lake

Huai·nan \hü-'ī-'nän, 'hwī-\ city E China in N *cen* Anhui SW of Bengbu *pop* 685,000

Hua·lla·ga \wä-'yä-gə, kwä-\ river 700 *mi* (1126 *km*) N *cen* Peru flowing N into the Marañón

Huam·bo \'wäm-(,)bō, 'hwäm-\ *or formerly* **No·va Lis·boa** \'nō-və-,lēzh-'bō-ə\ city Angola in W *cen* highlands *pop* 49,823

Huang *or* **Hwang** \'hwäŋ\ *or* **Yellow** river 3000 *mi* (4828 *km*) N China flowing from Kunlun Mountains in Qinghai E into Bo Hai

Huang·pu *or* **Whang·poo** \'hwäŋ-'pü\ river 70 *mi* (113 *km*) E China flowing E & N past Shanghai into the Chang

Huas·ca·rán \,wäs-kə-'rän\ mountain 22,205 *ft* (6768 *m*) W Peru; highest in the country

Hu·bei \'hü-'bā\ *or* **Hu·peh** \'hü-'be\ *or* **Hu·pei** \'hü-'bā, -'pā\ province E *cen* China ✱ Wuhan *area* 72,394 *sq mi* (188,224 *sq km*), *pop* 47,804,150

Hu·ber Heights \'hyü-bər, 'yü-\ city W Ohio *pop* 38,696

Hu·bli–Dhar·war \,hüb-lē-,där-'wär\ city SW India in W Karnataka *pop* 648,298

Hud·ders·field \'hə-dərz-,fēld\ borough N England in W. Yorkshire NE of Manchester *pop* 123,888

Hud·son \'həd-sən\ river 306 *mi* (492 *km*) E N.Y. flowing from Adirondack Mountains S into New York Bay — **Hud·so·ni·an** \,həd-'sō-nē-ən\ *adj*

Hudson Bay inlet of the Atlantic in N Canada; an inland sea 850 *mi* (1368 *km*) long

Hudson Strait strait 450 *mi* (724 *km*) long NE Canada bet. S Baffin Is. & N Que. connecting Hudson Bay with the Atlantic

Hue *or* **F Hué** \'hwä, 'wä, hü-'ā, hyü-'ā\ city & port *cen* Vietnam in Annam; formerly ✱ of Annam *pop* 209,043

Huel·va \'wel-və, 'hwel-\ **1** province SW Spain in Andalusia on Gulf of Cádiz *area* 3913 *sq mi* (10,174 *sq km*), *pop* 392,954 **2** city, its ✱ *pop* 127,822

Hues·ca \'wes-kə, 'hwes-\ **1** province NE Spain in Aragon *area* 5848 *sq mi* (15,205 *sq km*), *pop* 199,211 **2** commune, its ✱ *pop* 41,593

Huhehot — see HOHHOT

Hui·la \'wē-(,)lä, 'hwē-\ volcano 18,865 *ft* (5750 *m*) SW *cen* Colombia

Hull \'həl\ **1** town Canada in SW Que. on Ottawa River opposite Ottawa, Ont. *pop* 60,707 **2** *or in full* **Kings·ton upon Hull** \'kiŋ(k)-stən\ city & borough & port N England in Humberside *pop* 285,472

Hu·ma·cao \,ü-mə-'kaů\ town E Puerto Rico *pop* 55,203

Hum·ber \'həm-bər\ estuary 40 *mi* (64 *km*) E England formed by Ouse & Trent rivers & flowing E & SE into North Sea

Hum·ber·side \'həm-bər-,sīd\ county E England; area formerly in Yorkshire; ✱ Kingston upon Hull *area* 1356 *sq mi* (3526 *sq km*), *pop* 852,400

Hum·boldt \'həm-,bōlt\ river 290 *mi* (467 *km*) N Nev. flowing W & SW into Rye Patch reservoir & formerly into Humboldt Lake

Humboldt Bay bay NW Calif. on which Eureka is situated

Humboldt Glacier glacier NW Greenland

Humboldt Lake *or* **Humboldt Sink** intermittent lake W Nev. formerly receiving Humboldt River; has no outlet

Hum·phreys Peak \'həm(p)-frēz\ mountain peak 12,633 *ft* (3851 *m*) N *cen* Ariz. — see SAN FRANCISCO PEAKS

Hu·nan \'hü-'nän\ province SE *cen* China ✱ Changsha *area* 81,274 *sq mi* (211,312 *sq km*), *pop* 54,008,851

Hun·ga·ry \'həŋ-g(ə-)rē\ *or Hung* **Ma·gyar·or·szag** \,mä-,jär-'ór-,säg\ country *cen* Europe; formerly a kingdom, since 1946 a republic ✱ Budapest *area* 35,912 *sq mi* (93,371 *sq km*), *pop* 10,709,463

Hung·nam \'hůŋ-,näm\ city & port *cen* N. Korea on Sea of Japan *pop* 143,600

Hungshui — see HONGSHUI

Hungtse — see HONGZE

Hun·ter \'hən-tər\ river 287 *mi* (462 *km*) SE Australia in E New South Wales flowing E into the Pacific

Hun·ting·don \'hən-tiŋ-dən\ **1** *or* **Hun·ting·don·shire** \-,shir, -shər\ *or* **Huntingdon and Pe·ter·bor·ough** \'pē-tər-,bər-ə, -,bə-rə, -b(ə-)rə\ *or* **Hunts** \'hənts\ former county E *cen* England ✱ Huntingdon and Godmanchester; since 1974 part of Cambridgeshire **2** *or* **Huntingdon and God·man·ches·ter** \'gäd-mən-,ches-tər\ borough E *cen* England in Cambridgeshire *pop* 17,467

Hun·ting·ton \'hən-tiŋ-tən\ city W W.Va. on Ohio River *pop* 54,844

Huntington Beach city SW Calif. SE of Los Angeles *pop* 181,519

Huntington Park city SW Calif. S of Los Angeles *pop* 56,065

\ə\ abut \ᵊ\ kitten, F table \ər\ further \a\ ash \ā\ ace \ä\ mop, mar \aů\ out \ch\ chin \e\ bet \ē\ easy \g\ go \i\ hit \ī\ ice \j\ job \ŋ\ sing \ō\ go \ó\ law \ói\ boy \th\ thin \t̲h̲\ the \ü\ loot \ů\ foot \y\ yet \zh\ vision \à, k̲, ⁿ, œ, œ̄, ŭe, ūe, ᵞ\ *see* Guide to Pronunciation

Hunts·ville \'hənts-,vil, -vəl\ **1** city N Ala. *pop* 159,789 **2** city E Tex. N of Houston *pop* 27,925
Hu·on Gulf \'hyü-,än\ inlet of Solomon Sea on SE coast of North-East New Guinea S of Huon Peninsula
Hu·ron, Lake \'hyur-ən, 'hyür-,än, *or without* h\ lake E *cen* N. America bet. the U.S. & Canada; one of the Great Lakes *area* 23,010 *sq mi* (59,826 *sq km*)
Hurst \'hərst\ city NE Tex. NE of Fort Worth *pop* 33,574
Hutch·in·son \'hə-chə(n)-sən\ city *cen* Kans. *pop* 39,308
Hutt \'hət\ urban area New Zealand on S North Is. *pop* 122,000
Huy \'wē, 'hwē\ commune E Belgium SW of Liège *pop* 18,197
Huy·ton with Ro·by \'hī-t'n-with-'rō-bē, -with-\ town NW England in Lancashire E of Liverpool *pop* 57,671
Hwaining — see ANQING
Hy·bla \'hī-blə\ ancient town in Sicily on S slope of Mt. Etna
Hydaspes — see JHELUM
Hy·der·a·bad \'hī-d(ə-)rə-,bad, -,bäd\ **1** former state S *cen* India in the Deccan ✱ Hyderabad **2** *or* **Hai·dar·a·bad** city S *cen* India ✱ of Andhra Pradesh *pop* 2,528,198 **3** city S Pakistan in Sind on the Indus *pop* 795,000
Hy·dra \'hī-drə\ *or NGk* **Ídhra** \'ēth-rä\ island Greece in S Aegean Sea off E coast of Peloponnisos *area* 20 *sq mi* (52 *sq km*), *pop* 2794 —
Hy·dri·ot \'hī-drē-ət, -drē-,ät\ *or* **Hy·dri·ote** \-,ōt, -ət\ *n*
Hydraotes — see RAVI
Hy·ères \ē-'er, 'yer\ commune SE France on Côte d'Azur E of Toulon *pop* 29,366
Hyères Islands *or F* **Îles d'Hyères** \,ēl-dē-'er, ēl-'dyer\ islands in the Mediterranean off SE coast of France
Hy·met·tus \hī-'me-təs\ mountain ridge 3370 *ft* (1027 *m*) *cen* Greece E & SE of Athens — **Hy·met·ti·an** \-'me-tē-ən\ *adj*
Hyr·ca·nia \(,)hər-'kā-nē-ə\ province of ancient Persia on SE coast of Caspian NE of Media & NW of Parthia — **Hyr·ca·ni·an** \-nē-ən\ *adj*
Ia·si \'yäsh, 'yä-shē\ *or* **Jas·sy** \'yä-sē\ city NE Romania *pop* 330,195
Iba·dan \i-'bä-d'n, -'ba-\ city SW Nigeria NNE of Lagos *pop* 1,009,000
Ibe·ria \ī-'bir-ē-ə\ **1** ancient Spain **2** IBERIAN PENINSULA **3** ancient region of the Caucasus W of Colchis in modern Georgia
Ibe·ri·an Peninsula \-ē-ən\ peninsula SW Europe bet. the Mediterranean & the Atlantic occupied by Spain & Portugal
Ibi·cuí \,ē-bi-'kwē\ river 400 *mi* (644 *km*) S Brazil in Rio Grande do Sul flowing W into Uruguay River
Ibi·za *or* **Ivi·za** \ē-'vē-thə, -'bē-, -sə, -zə\ island Spain in the Balearics SW of Majorca *area* 230 *sq mi* (598 *sq km*)
Içá — see PUTUMAYO
Icar·ia \ī-'ker-ē-ə, i-, -'kar-\ *or NGk* **Ika·ria** \,ē-kə-'rē-ə\ island Greece in Southern Sporades WSW of Samos *area* 99 *sq mi* (257 *sq km*) — **Icar·i·an** \ī-'ker-ē-ən, i-, -'kar-\ *adj or n*
Ice·land \'īs-lənd, 'īs-,land\ *or Dan* **Is·land** \'ēs-,län\ *or Icelandic* **Ís·land** \'ēs-,länt\ island bet. the Arctic & the Atlantic SE of Greenland; a republic formerly (1380–1918) belonging to Denmark, later (1918–44) an independent kingdom in personal union with Denmark ✱ Reykjavik *area* 39,709 *sq mi* (103,243 *sq km*), *pop* 255,855 — **Ice·land·er** \'īs-,lan-dər, 'īs-lən-\ *n*
I–ch'ang — see YICHANG
Ichi·ka·wa \i-'chē-,kä-wə\ city Japan in SE Honshu E of Tokyo *pop* 436,597
Iconium — see KONYA
Ida — see KAZ DAGI
Ida·ho \'ī-də-,hō\ state NW U.S. ✱ Boise *area* 83,557 *sq mi* (217,248 *sq km*), *pop* 1,006,749 — **Ida·ho·an** \,ī-də-'hō-ən\ *adj or n*
Idaho Falls city SE Idaho on Snake River *pop* 43,929
Id·fu \'id-(,)füi\ city S Egypt on the Nile *pop* 34,858
Idhi \'ē-thē\ *or* **Ida** \'ī-də\ mountain 8058 *ft* (2456 *m*) Greece in *cen* Crete; highest on island
Idumaea *or* **Idumea** — see EDOM — **Id·u·mae·an** *or* **Id·u·me·an** \,i-jə-'mē-ən\ *adj or n*
Ie·per \'yä-pər\ *or F* **Ypres** \'ēpr'\ commune NW Belgium in W. Flanders *pop* 35,235
Ife \'ē-(,)fe\ city SW Nigeria NE of Ibadan *pop* 209,100
If·ni \'if-nē\ former territory SW Morocco; administered by Spain 1934–69 ✱ Sidi Ifni
Igua·çú \,ē-gwə-'sü\ river 380 *mi* (612 *km*) S Brazil in Paraná state flowing W into Alto Paraná River; contains **Iguaçú Falls** (waterfall over 2 *mi* or 3.2 *km* wide composed of numerous cataracts averaging 200 *ft* or 61 *m* in height)
IJs·sel \'ī-səl\ river 70 *mi* (113 *km*) E Netherlands flowing out of the Rhine N into IJsselmeer
IJs·sel·meer \,ī-səl-'mer\ *or* **Lake IJs·sel** \'ī-səl\ freshwater lake N Netherlands separated from North Sea by a dike & bordered by reclaimed lands; part of former Zuider Zee (inlet of North Sea)
Île–de–France \,ēl-də-'fräⁿs\ region & former province N *cen* France bounded on N by Picardy, on E by Champagne, on S by Orléanais, & on W by Normandy ✱ Paris
Ile des Pins \,ēl-dā-'paⁿ\ *or* **Isle of Pines** \'pīnz\ island SW Pacific in New Caledonia territory SE of New Caledonia Is. *area* 58 *sq mi* (151 *sq km*)
Île du Diable — see DEVIL'S ISLAND
Îles de la Société — see SOCIETY ISLANDS
Îles du Vent — see WINDWARD ISLANDS
Îles sous le Vent — see LEEWARD ISLANDS
Il·ford \'il-fərd\ former municipal borough SE England in Essex, now part of Redbridge
Il·fra·combe \'il-frə-,küm\ town SW England in Devon on Bristol Channel *pop* 10,133
Ili \'ē-lē\ river 800 *mi* (1287 *km*) *cen* Asia flowing from W Xinjiang Uygur, China, W & NW into Lake Balkhash in Kazakhstan
Ilía — see ELIS
Il·i·am·na \,i-lē-'am-nə\ volcano 10,016 *ft* (3053 *m*) NE of Iliamna Lake
Iliamna Lake lake 80 *mi* (129 *km*) long SW Alaska NE of Bristol Bay
Ilion *or* **Ilium** — see TROY — **Il·i·an** \'i-lē-ən\ *adj or n*
Illam·pu \ē-'yäm-(,)pü\ *or* **So·ra·ta** \sə-'rä-tə\ massif in the Andes W Bolivia E of Lake Titicaca — see ANCOHUMA **2** peak 20,873 *ft* (6325 *m*) in the Illampu massif

Illi·ma·ni \,ē-yə-'mä-nē\ mountain 21,201 *ft* (6462 *m*) Bolivia E of La Paz
Il·li·nois \,i-lə-'noi *also* -'noiz\ **1** river 273 *mi* (439 *km*) Ill. flowing SW into Mississippi River **2** state *cen* U.S. ✱ Springfield *area* 56,400 *sq mi* (146,640 *sq km*), *pop* 11,430,602 — **Il·li·nois·an** \,i-lə-'noi-ən *also* -'noi-z'n\ *adj or n*
Il·lyr·ia \i-'lir-ē-ə\ ancient region S Europe in Balkan Peninsula bordering on the Adriatic — **Il·lyr·ic** \-'lir-ik\ *adj*
Il·lyr·i·cum \i-'lir-i-kəm\ province of Roman Empire in Illyria
Il·men \'il-mən\ lake W Russia in Europe S of Lake Ladoga
Ilo·ilo \,ē-lō-'ē-(,)lō\ city Philippines on Panay Is. *pop* 244,827
Im·pe·ria \im-'pir-ē-ə, -'per-\ commune & port NW Italy in Liguria SW of Genoa *pop* 41,111
Im·pe·ri·al Beach \im-'pir-ē-əl\ city SW Calif. S of San Diego *pop* 26,512
Imperial Valley valley U.S. & Mexico in SE Calif. & NE Baja California in Colorado Desert; most of area below sea level
Imp·hal \'imp-,həl\ city NE India ✱ of Manipur *pop* 155,639
Imroz — see GÖKÇEADA
Ina·gua \i-'nä-gwə\ two islands in the SE Bahamas: **Great Inagua** (50 *mi or* 80 *km* long) & **Little Inagua** (8 *mi or* 13 *km* long)
In·chon \'in-,chän\ *or* **Che·mul·po** \,chə-'mül-(,)pō\ city & port NW S. Korea W of Seoul *pop* 1,386,911
In·de·pen·dence \,in-də-'pen-dən(t)s\ city W Mo. E of Kansas City *pop* 112,301
In·dia \'in-dē-ə\ **1** peninsula region (often called a subcontinent) S Asia S of the Himalayas bet. Bay of Bengal & Arabian Sea occupied by India, Pakistan & Bangladesh & formerly often considered as also including Burma (but not Ceylon) **2** those parts of India until 1947 under Brit. rule or protection together with Baluchistan & the Andaman & Nicobar islands &, prior to 1937, Burma **3** country comprising major portion of peninsula; a republic within the Commonwealth of Nations; until 1947 a part of the Brit. Empire ✱ New Delhi *area* 1,265,093 *sq mi* (3,289,242 *sq km*), *pop* 685,184,692
In·di·ana \,in-dē-'a-nə\ state E *cen* U.S. ✱ Indianapolis *area* 36,291 *sq mi* (94,357 *sq km*), *pop* 5,544,159 — **In·di·an·an** \-'a-nən\ *adj or n* — **In·di·an·i·an** \-'a-nē-ən\ *adj or n*
Indiana Harbor harbor district in E. Chicago, Ind., on Lake Michigan
In·di·a·nap·o·lis \,in-dē-ə-'na-p(ə-)ləs\ city *cen* Ind., its ✱ *pop* 731,327
Indian Ocean \'in-dē-ən\ ocean E of Africa, S of Asia, W of Australia & Tasmania, & N of Antarctica *area* 28,925,000 *sq mi* (75,205,000 *sq km*)
Indian River lagoon 165 *mi* (266 *km*) long E Fla. bet. mainland & coastal islands
Indian States *or* **Native States** former semi-independent states of the Indian Empire ruled by native princes subject to varying degrees of Brit. authority — see BRITISH INDIA
Indian Territory former territory S U.S. in present state of Okla.
In·dies \'in-(,)dēz\ **1** EAST INDIES **2** WEST INDIES
In·di·gir·ka \,in-də-'gir-kə\ river 850 *mi* (1368 *km*) E *cen* Russia in Asia in NE Yakut Republic flowing N into E. Siberian Sea
In·dio \'in-dē-,ō\ city SE Calif. SE of San Bernardino *pop* 36,793
In·do·chi·na \,in-(,)dō-'chī-nə\ **1** peninsula SE Asia; includes Myanmar, Cambodia, Laos, Malay Peninsula, Thailand, & Vietnam **2** *or* **French Indochina** former country SE Asia comprising Annam, Cochin China, & Tonkin (all now a part of Vietnam), Cambodia, & Laos ✱ Hanoi
In·do·ne·sia \,in-də-'nē-zhə, -shə\ **1** country SE Asia in Malay Archipelago comprising Sumatra, Java, S & E Borneo, Sulawesi, Timor, W New Guinea, the Moluccas, & many adjacent smaller islands; formerly (as **Netherlands East Indies**) an overseas territory of the Netherlands ✱ Djakarta *area* 575,450 *sq mi* (1,496,170 *sq km*), *pop* 147,490,298 **2** MALAY ARCHIPELAGO
In·dore \in-'dōr, -'dor\ **1** former state *cen* India in Narmada valley ✱ Indore; area now in Madhya Pradesh **2** city NW *cen* India in W Madhya Pradesh *pop* 827,071
In·dus \'in-dəs\ river 1800 *mi* (2897 *km*) S Asia flowing from Tibet NW & SSW through Pakistan into Arabian Sea
In·gle·wood \'iŋ-gəl-,wùd\ city SW Calif. SW of Los Angeles *pop* 109,602
In·gol·stadt \'iŋ-gəl-,shtät, -,stät\ city S Germany in *cen* Bavaria *pop* 90,490
Ink·ster \'iŋk-stər\ village SE Mich. W of Detroit *pop* 30,772
In·land Empire \'in-,land, -lənd\ region NW U.S. bet. Cascade Range & Rocky Mountains in E Wash., N Idaho, NW Mont., & NE Oreg.
Inland Sea inlet of the Pacific 240 *mi* (386 *km*) long SW Japan bet. Honshu on E & N, Kyushu on W, & Shikoku on S
Inn \'in\ river 320 *mi* (515 *km*) flowing from SE Switzerland NE through Austria into the Danube in SE Germany — see ENGADINE
Inner Hebrides — see HEBRIDES
Inner Mon·go·lia \-män-'gōl-yə, män-, -'gō-lē-ə\ *or* **Nei Mong·gol** \'nā-'män-,gōl, -'män-\ region N China in SE Mongolia & W Manchuria ✱ Hohhot *area* 454,633 *sq mi* (1,182,046 *sq km*), *pop* 19,274,279
In·nis·fil \'i-nəs-,fil, -fəl\ town Canada in SE Ont. *pop* 21,667
Inniskilling — see ENNISKILLEN
Inns·bruck \'inz-,brùk, 'in(t)s-\ city W Austria *pop* 114,996
Inside Passage *or* **Inland Passage** protected shipping route from Puget Sound, Wash., to Skagway, Alaska, following channels bet. mainland & coastal islands
In·ter·la·ken \'in-tər-,lä-kən\ commune W *cen* Switzerland in Bern canton on the Aare bet. Thuner See & Lake of Brienz
International Zone — see MOROCCO
In·ver·car·gill \,in-vər-'kär-gəl\ borough New Zealand on S coast of South Is. *pop* 49,446 — see BLUFF
In·ver Grove Heights \'in-vər\ city SE Minn. *pop* 22,477
In·ver·ness \,in-vər-'nes\ **1** *or* **In·ver·ness–shire** \-'nesh-,shir, -shər\ former county NW Scotland **2** burgh NW Scotland ✱ of Highland region *pop* 39,736
Io·an·ni·na \yō-'ä-nē-(,)nä\ city NW Greece in N Epirus *pop* 56,496
Io·na \ī-'ō-nə\ island Scotland in S Inner Hebrides off SW tip of Mull Is. *area* 6 *sq mi* (16 *sq km*), *pop* 120
Io·nia \ī-'ō-nē-ə\ ancient region W Asia Minor bordering on the Aegean W of Lydia & Caria — **Io·ni·an** \-nē-ən\ *adj or n*

Io·ni·an Islands \ī-'ō-nē-ən\ islands W Greece in Ionian Sea *pop* 191,003

Ionian Sea arm of the Mediterranean Sea bet. SE Italy & W Greece

Io·wa \'ī-ə-wə\ **1** river 291 *mi* (468 *km*) Iowa flowing SE into Mississippi River **2** state cen U.S. ✱ Des Moines *area* 56,290 *sq mi* (146,354 *sq km*), *pop* 2,776,755 — **Io·wan** \-wən\ *adj or n*

Iowa City city E Iowa *pop* 59,738

J–pin — see YIBIN

Ipiros — see EPIRUS

Ipoh \'ē-(,)pō\ city Malaysia (federation) in Perak *pop* 125,766

Ipsambul — see ABU SIMBEL

Ips·wich \'ip-(,)swich\ **1** city E Australia in SE Queensland *pop* 68,297 **2** borough SE England ✱ of Suffolk *pop* 120,447

Iqa·lu·it \ē-'ka-lü-ət\ town Canada, on Baffin Is., Northwest Territories *pop* 3552

Iqui·que \i-'kē-kē, -(,)kä\ city & port N Chile on the Pacific *pop* 65,288

Iqui·tos \i-'kē-(,)tōs\ city NE Peru on the Amazon *pop* 203,568

Irák·li·on \i-'ra-klē-ən, ē-'rä-klē-,ón\ *or* **Can·dia** \'kan-dē-ə\ city & port Greece on N coast of Crete *pop* 117,167

Iran \i-'rän, -'ran; i-'ran\ *or esp formerly* **Per·sia** \'pər-zhə, *esp Brit* -shə\ country SW Asia bordering in N on Caspian Sea & in S on Persian Gulf & Gulf of Oman; an Islamic republic since 1979, formerly an empire ✱ Tehran *area* 628,000 *sq mi* (1,632,800 *sq km*), *pop* 33,591,875 — **Irani** \i-'rä-nē, -'ra-\ *adj or n*

Iraq \i-'räk, -'rak\ country SW Asia in Mesopotamia; a republic since 1958, formerly a kingdom ✱ Baghdad *area* 171,555 *sq mi* (446,043 *sq km*), *pop* 12,000,497 — **Iraqi** \i-'rä-kē, -'ra-\ *adj or n*

Irbil — see ARBIL

Ire·land \'īr-lənd\ **1** *or L* **Hi·ber·nia** \hī-'bər-nē-ə\ island W Europe in the Atlantic, one of the British Isles *area* 32,375 *sq mi* (84,175 *sq km*); divided bet. Ireland (republic) & Northern Ireland **2** *or* **Éi·re** \'ar-ə, 'ar-ē, 'er-, 'ār-, 'ir-\ country occupying major portion of the island; a republic since 1949; a division of the United Kingdom of Great Britain and Ireland 1801–1921 & (as **Irish Free State**) a dominion of the Commonwealth of Nations 1922–37 ✱ Dublin *area* 26,602 *sq mi* (69,165 *sq km*), *pop* 3,523,401 **3** — see NORTHERN IRELAND

Irian Jaya — see WEST IRIAN

Irish Sea arm of the Atlantic bet. Great Britain & Ireland

Ir·kutsk \ir-'kütsk, ,ər-\ city S Russia in Asia on the Angara near Lake Baikal *pop* 550,000

Iron Gate \'ī(-ə)rn\ gorge 2 *mi* (3.2 *km*) long of the Danube where it cuts around Transylvanian Alps on border bet. Romania & Yugoslavia

Ir·ra·wad·dy \,ir-ə-'wä-dē\ river 1350 *mi* (2173 *km*) Myanmar flowing S into Bay of Bengal through several mouths

Ir·tysh \ir-'tish, ,ər-\ river 2200 *mi* (3541 *km*) cen Asia flowing from Altai mountains in China, NW & N through Kazakhstan & into the Ob in W Russia in Asia

Irún \ē-'rün\ commune N Spain in Guipúzcoa *pop* 45,060

Ir·vine \'ər-,vīn\ city SW Calif. SE of Santa Ana *pop* 110,330

Ir·ving \'ər-viŋ\ city NE Tex. W of Dallas *pop* 155,037

Is·a·bela Island \,i-zə-'be-lə\ *or* **Al·be·marle Island** \'al-bə-,märl\ island Ecuador; largest of the Galápagos *area* 1650 *sq mi* (4290 *sq km*), *pop* 336

Isar \'ē-,zär\ river 219 *mi* (352 *km*) W Europe flowing from Tirol, Austria, through Bavaria, Germany, into the Danube

Isau·ria \i-'sór-ē-ə\ ancient district in E Pisidia S Asia Minor on N slope of W Taurus Mountains — **Isau·ri·an** \-ē-ən\ *adj or n*

Is·chia \'is-kē-ə\ island Italy in Tyrrhenian Sea WSW of Naples *area* 18 *sq mi* (47 *sq km*)

Ise Bay \'ē-,sā\ inlet of the Pacific S Japan on S coast of Honshu

Iseo, Lake \ē-'(,)ō\ lake 14 *mi* (22 *km*) long N Italy in Lombardy

Isère \ē-'zer\ river 150 *mi* (241 *km*) SE France flowing from Graian Alps WSW into the Rhône

Iser·lohn \,ē-zər-'lōn, 'ē-zər-,\ city W Germany *pop* 93,823

Isfahan — see ESFAHAN

Ishim \i-'shim\ river 1330 *mi* (2140 *km*) flowing from N Kazakhstan N into the Irtysh in W Russia in Asia

Isis \'ī-səs\ the Thames River, England, at & upstream from Oxford

Is·ken·de·run \(,)is-,ken-də-'rün\ *or* **Is·ken·de·ron** \-'rän\ *or formerly* **Al·ex·an·dret·ta** \,a-lig-(,)zan-'dre-tə, ,e-\ city & port S Turkey on Gulf of Iskenderun (inlet of the Mediterranean) *pop* 69,382

Is·lam·a·bad \is-'lä-mə-,bäd, iz-, -'la-mə-,bad\ city ✱ of Pakistan in NE Pakistan NE of Rawalpindi *pop* 250,000

Island *or* **Islande** — see ICELAND

Is·lay \'ī-(,)lā, -lə\ island Scotland in S Inner Hebrides *area* 234 *sq mi* (608 *sq km*), *pop* 3855

Isle au Haut \,ī-lə-'hō(t), ,ē-lə-'hō\ island Maine at entrance to Penobscot Bay — see ACADIA NATIONAL PARK

Isle of Av·a·lon \'a-və-,län\ district, orig. an island, SW England in Somerset including Glastonbury

Isle of Ely — see ELY (Isle of)

Isle of Man — see MAN (Isle of)

Isle of Pines — see YOUTH (Isle of)

Isle of Wight — see WIGHT (Isle of)

Isle Roy·ale \'ī(ə)l-'rói(-ə)l\ island Mich. in NW Lake Superior in **Isle Royale National Park**

Is·ling·ton \'iz-liŋ-tən\ borough of N Greater London, England *pop* 167,400

Is·ma·i·lia \,iz-mā-ə-'lē-ə, ,is-\ city NE Egypt on the Suez Canal *pop* 145,930

Isole Eolie — see LIPARI ISLANDS

Ison·zo \ē-'zōn(t)-(,)sō\ *or* **So·ča** \'sò-chə\ river 75 *mi* (121 *km*) W Slovenia & NE Italy flowing S into Gulf of Trieste

Ispahan — see ESFAHAN

Is·par·ta \,is-(,)pär-'tä\ city SW Turkey N of Antalya *pop* 91,544

Is·ra·el \'iz-rē-əl, -(,)rā- *also* 'is- *or* 'iz-rəl\ **1** ancient kingdom Palestine comprising the lands occupied by the Hebrew people; established *ab* 1025 B.C.; divided *ab* 933 B.C. into a S kingdom (Judah) & a N kingdom (Israel) **2** *or* **Northern Kingdom** *or* **Ephra·im** \'ē-frē-əm\ the N portion of the Hebrew kingdom after the division **3** country in SW Asia; a republic established 1948 ✱ Jerusalem *area* 7993 *sq mi* (20,782 *sq km*), *pop* 4,037,620 — see PALESTINE

Is·sus \'i-səs\ ancient town S Asia Minor N of modern Iskenderun

Is·syk Kul *or* **Ys·yk–Köl** \,i-sik-'kəl, -'kœl\ lake 115 *mi* (185 *km*) long in NE Kyrgyzstan *area* 2250 *sq mi* (5850 *sq km*)

Is·tan·bul \,is-tən-'bül, -,tan-, -,tän-, -'bùl, 'is-tən-,, *or with m for* n\ *or formerly* **Con·stan·ti·no·ple** \,kän-,stan-t⁰n-'ō-pəl\ *or anc* **By·zan·ti·um** \bə-'zan-tē-əm, -'zan-sh(ē-)əm\ city NW Turkey on the Bosporus & Sea of Marmara; former ✱ of Turkey & of Ottoman Empire *pop* 2,853,539

Ister — see DANUBE

Is·tria \'is-trē-ə\ *or* **Is·tri·an Peninsula** \-trē-ən\ peninsula in Croatia & Slovenia projecting into the N Adriatic — **Istrian** *adj or n*

Itai·pu \ē-'ti-pü\ dam in Paraná River bet. Brazil & Paraguay

Italian East Africa former territory E Africa comprising Eritrea, Ethiopia, & Italian Somaliland

Italian Somaliland former Italian colony E Africa bordering on Indian Ocean ✱ Mogadishu; since 1960 part of Somalia

It·a·ly \'i-t⁰l-ē\ *or* **It** Ita·lia \ē-'täl-yə\ *or L* Ita·lia \ə-'tal-yə, i-\ **1** peninsula 760 *mi* (1223 *km*) S Europe projecting into the Mediterranean bet. Adriatic & Tyrrhenian seas **2** country comprising the peninsula of Italy, Sicily, Sardinia, & numerous other islands; a republic since 1946, formerly a kingdom ✱ Rome *area* 119,764 *sq mi* (311,336 *sq km*), *pop* 57,576,429

Ita·na·gar \,ē-tə-'nə-gər\ town NE India ✱ of Arunachal Pradesh

Itas·ca, Lake \i-'tas-kə\ lake NW cen Minn.; generally considered as source of Mississippi River

Iténez — see GUAPORÉ

Ith·a·ca \'i-thi-kə\ **1** city S cen N.Y. on Cayuga Lake *pop* 29,541 **2** *or NGk* Itha·ki \ē-'thä-kē\ island W Greece in the Ionian Islands NE of Cephalonia *area* 36 *sq mi* (94 *sq km*) — **Ith·a·can** \'i-thi-kən\ *adj or n*

Itsu·ku·shi·ma \it-,sü-kə-'shē-mə\ *or* **Mi·ya·ji·ma** \,mē-ə-'jē-mə\ island *ab* 5 *mi* (8 *km*) long Japan in Inland Sea SW of Hiroshima

It·u·raea *or* **It·u·rea** \,i-tyù-'rē-ə\ ancient country NE Palestine S of Damascus — **It·u·rae·an** *or* **It·u·re·an** \-'rē-ən\ *adj or n*

Iva·no–Fran·kovsk \i-'vä-nō-frän-'kófsk\ *or formerly* **Sta·ni·slav** \,sta-nə-'släf, -'släv\ city SW Ukraine *pop* 134,000

Iva·no·vo \i-'vä-nə-və\ *or formerly* **Ivanovo Voz·ne·sensk** \,väz-nə-'sen(t)sk\ city cen Russia in Europe WNW of Nizhni Novgorod *pop* 419,000

Iviza — see IBIZA

Ivory Coast *or* **Côte d'Ivoire** \,kōt-dē-'vwär\ **1** region W Africa bordering on the Atlantic W of the Gold Coast **2** country W Africa including the Ivory Coast & its hinterland; a republic; formerly a territory of French West Africa ✱ Abidjan *area* 127,520 *sq mi* (331,552 *sq km*), *pop* 9,300,000 — **Ivor·i·an** \(,)ī-'vōr-ē-ən, -'vòr-\ *adj or n* —

Ivory Coast·er \'kō-stər\ *n*

Iwo \'ē-(,)wō\ city SW Nigeria NE of Ibadan *pop* 255,100

Iwo Ji·ma \,ē-(,)wō-'jē-mə\ island Japan in W Pacific in the Volcano Islands *area* 8 *sq mi* (21 *sq km*)

Ix·elles \ēk-'sel\ *or* **Flem El·se·ne** \'el-sə-nə\ commune cen Belgium in Brabant; suburb of Brussels *pop* 72,610

Ix·tac·ci·huatl *or* **Iz·tac·ci·huatl** \,ēs-(,)täk-'sē-,wä-t⁰l\ *or* **Ix·ta·ci·huatl** \-(,)tä-'sē-\ extinct volcano 17,343 *ft* (5286 *m*) S Mexico N of Popocatepetl

Iza·bal, Lake \,ē-zə-'bäl, -sə-\ lake 25 *mi* (40 *km*) long E Guatemala

Izal·co \i-'zal-(,)kō, ē-'säl-\ volcano 7828 *ft* (2386 *m*) W El Salvador

Izhevsk \'ē-,zhefsk\ *or* 1985–1987 **Usti·nov** \'üs-ti-,nóf, -,nóv\ city E Russia in Europe ✱ of Udmurt Republic *pop* 422,000

Iz·ma·il *or Romanian* **Is·ma·il** \,iz-mä-'ē(ə)l, ,is-\ city SW Ukraine on the Danube delta *pop* 63,000

Iz·mir \iz-'mir\ *or formerly* **Smyr·na** \'smər-nə\ city & port W Turkey in Asia on an inlet of the Aegean *pop* 753,749

Iz·mit *or* **Iz·mid** \iz-'mit\ *or anc* **As·ta·cus** \'as-tə-kəs\ *or* **Nic·o·me·dia** \,ni-kə-'mē-dē-ə\ city & port NW Turkey in Asia on **Gulf of Iz·mit** (E arm of Sea of Marmara) *pop* 191,340

Iz·nik \iz-'nik\ lake 14 *mi* (22 *km*) long NW Turkey in Asia

Jabal Katrinah — see KATHERINA (Gebel)

Ja·bal·pur \,jə-bəl-,pùr\ city cen India in cen Madhya Pradesh *pop* 757,726

Jack·son \'jak-sən\ **1** city S Mich. *pop* 37,446 **2** city ✱ of Miss. on Pearl River *pop* 196,637 **3** city W Tenn. *pop* 48,949

Jackson Hole valley NW Wyo. E of Teton Range & partly in Grand Teton National Park; contains **Jackson Lake** (reservoir)

Jack·son·ville \'jak-sən-,vil\ **1** city cen Ark. NE of Little Rock *pop* 29,101 **2** city NE Fla. near mouth of St. Johns River *pop* 635,230 **3** city W cen Ill. *pop* 19,324 **4** city E N.C. *pop* 30,013

Jadotville — see LIKASI

Ja·én \hä-'ān\ **1** province S Spain in N Andalusia *area* 5203 *sq mi* (13,528 *sq km*), *pop* 611,655 **2** commune, its ✱ *pop* 86,001

Jaf·fa \'ja-fə, 'ya-, 'yä-\ *or* **Jop·pa** \'jä-pə\ *or* **Ya·fo** \yä-'fō\ former city W Israel, since 1950 a S section of Tel Aviv

Jaff·na \'jäf-nə\ city N Sri Lanka on Jaffna Peninsula *pop* 128,000

Jaffna Peninsula peninsula N extremity of Sri Lanka extending into Palk Strait

Jain·tia Hills \'jin-tē-ə\ hills E India in N cen Assam E of Khasi Hills

Jai·pur \'jī-,pùr\ **1** former state NW India; now part of Rajasthan **2** city, its ✱, now ✱ of Rajasthan *pop* 1,004,669

Jakarta — see DJAKARTA

Ja·la·pa \hə-'lä-pə\ city E Mexico ✱ of Veracruz *pop* 151,419

Ja·lis·co \hə-'lis-(,)kō\ state W cen Mexico ✱ Guadalajara *area* 31,149 *sq mi* (80,987 *sq km*), *pop* 4,293,549

Jal·u·it \'ja-lə-wət, 'jal-yə-wət\ island (atoll) W Pacific, in Ralik chain of the Marshalls

Ja·mai·ca \jə-'mā-kə\ island West Indies in the Greater Antilles; a dominion of the Commonwealth of Nations since 1962; formerly a Brit. colony ✱ Kingston *area* 4411 *sq mi* (11,469 *sq km*), *pop* 2,095,878 — **Ja·mai·can** \-kən\ *adj or n*

Jamaica Bay inlet of Atlantic Ocean SE N.Y. in SW Long Is.

Jambi — see TELANAIPURA

\ə\ abut \'ə\ kitten, F table \ər\ further \a\ ash \ā\ ace \ä\ mop, mar \aù\ out \ch\ chin \e\ bet \ē\ easy \g\ go \i\ hit \ī\ ice \j\ job \ŋ\ sing \ō\ go \ò\ law \òi\ boy \th\ thin \t̲h̲\ the \ü\ loot \ù\ foot \y\ yet \zh\ vision \à, k̲, ⁿ, œ, œ̄, ᵫ, ūe, ᵫ̄, ᵞ\ *see* Guide to Pronunciation

James \'jāmz\ **1** river 710 *mi* (1143 *km*) N.Dak. & S.Dak. flowing S to Missouri River **2** river 340 *mi* (547 *km*) Va. flowing E into Chesapeake Bay at Hampton Roads

James Bay the S extension of Hudson Bay 280 *mi* (448 *km*) long & 150 *mi* (240 *km*) wide Canada bet. NE Ont. & W Que.

James·town \'jāmz-ˌtaún\ **1** city SW N.Y. *pop* 34,681 **2** ruined village E Va. SW of Williamsburg on James River; first permanent English settlement in America (1607)

Jam·mu \'jə-(ˌ)mü\ **1** district N India (subcontinent) S of Kashmir in valley of the upper Chenab **2** city S of Srinagar, winter * of Jammu & Kashmir *pop* 135,522

Jammu and Kash·mir \'kash-ˌmir, 'kazh-, kash-', kazh-'\ *or* **Kashmir** state N India including Kashmir region & Jammu (to the S); claimed also by Pakistan; summer * Srinagar, winter * Jammu *area* 92,780 *sq mi* (241,228 *sq km*), *pop* 5,981,600

Jam·na·gar \jäm-'nə-gər\ city W India in W Gujarat on Gulf of Kutch *pop* 317,037

Ja·mu·na \'jə-mə-nə\ the lower Brahmaputra

Janes·ville \'jānz-ˌvil\ city S Wis. SE of Madison *pop* 52,133

Ja·nic·u·lum \jə-'ni-kyə-ləm\ hill in Rome, Italy, on right bank of the Tiber opposite the seven hills on which the ancient city was built — see AVENTINE

Jan Ma·yen Island \yän-'mī-ən\ island in Arctic Ocean E of Greenland & NNE of Iceland belonging to Norway *area* 147 *sq mi* (382 *sq km*)

Ja·pan \jə-'pan, ja-\ *or Jp* **Nip·pon** \ni-'pän\ *or* **Ni·hon** \'nē-'hón\ country E Asia comprising Honshu, Hokkaido, Kyushu, Shikoku, & other islands in the W Pacific; a constitutional monarchy * Tokyo *area* 146,690 *sq mi* (381,394 *sq km*), *pop* 123,611,541

Japan, Sea of arm of the N Pacific W of Japan

Ja·pu·rá \ˌzhä-pu̇-'rä\ river 1750 *mi* (2816 *km*) S Colombia & NW Brazil flowing SE into the Amazon

Jar·vis \'jär-vəs\ island *cen* Pacific in the Line Islands; claimed by the U.S.

Jasper National Park \'jas-pər\ reservation W Canada in W Alta. on E slopes of the Rockies NW of Banff National Park

Jassy — see IASI

Ja·strze·bie–Zdroj \yäsh-'che-byəz-'dròi\ city S Poland *pop* 102,661

Ja·va \'jä-və, 'ja-\ *or Indonesian* **Dja·wa** \'jä-və\ island Indonesia SE of Sumatra; chief city Djakarta *area* 51,007 *sq mi* (132,618 *sq km*), *pop* 78,201,001

Java Head cape Indonesia at W end of Java on Sunda Strait

Ja·va·ri \ˌzhä-və-'rē\ *or Sp* **Ya·va·rí** \ˌyä-və-'rē\ *or formerly* **Ya·ca·ra·na** \ˌyä-kə-'rä-nə\ river 650 *mi* (1046 *km*) Peru & Brazil flowing NE on the boundary & into the Amazon

Java Sea arm of the Pacific bounded on S by Java, on W by Sumatra, on N by Borneo, & on E by Sulawesi

Jaxartes — see SYR DARYA

Jazirah, Al — see GEZIRA, EL

Jebel, Bahr el — see BAHR EL GHAZAL

Je·bel ed Druz \ˌje-bəl-ed-'drüz\ *or* **Jebel Druz** region S Syria E of Sea of Galilee on border of Jordan

Jebel Musa — see MUSA (Jebel)

Jebel Toubkal — see TOUBKAL (Jebel)

Je·bus \'jē-bəs\ a Biblical name for Jerusalem

Jed·burgh \'jed-b(ə-)rə\ royal burgh SE Scotland in Borders region

Jef·fer·son \'je-fər-sən\ river 250 *mi* (402 *km*) SW Mont. — see THREE FORKS

Jefferson, Mount mountain 10,495 *ft* (3199 *m*) NW Oreg. in Cascades

Jefferson City city * of Mo. on Missouri River *pop* 35,481

Jef·fer·son·town \'je-fər-sən-ˌtaún\ city N Ky. E of Louisville *pop* 23,221

Jef·fer·son·ville \'je-fər-sən-ˌvil\ city S Ind. *pop* 21,841

Je·hol \jə-'hōl, 'rō-'hō\ former province NE China * Chengteh; divided 1955 among Hopeh, Liaoning, & Inner Mongolia

Je·mappes \zhə-'map\ commune SW Belgium W of Mons

Je·na \'yā-nə, -(ˌ)nä\ city E cen Germany E of Erfurt *pop* 104,282

Je·qui·ti·nho·nha \zhə-ˌkē-tə-'nyō-nyə, -'nō-nyə\ river 500 *mi* (805 *km*) E Brazil flowing NE into the Atlantic

Jerba — see DJERBA

Je·rez \hə-'räs\ *or* **Je·rez de la Fron·te·ra** \hə-'rez-de-lə-ˌfrän-'ter-ə\ *or formerly* **Xe·res** \'sher-ēz\ city SW Spain SE of Cádiz *pop* 175,653

Jer·i·cho \'jer-i-ˌkō\ **1** *or Ar* **Eri·ha** \ə-'rē-ə\ town W Jordan 5 *mi* (8 *km*) NW of Dead Sea **2** ancient Palestinian city near site of modern Jericho

Jer·sey \'jər-zē\ **1** island English Channel in the Channel Islands * St. Helier *area* 45 *sq mi* (117 *sq km*) **2** NEW JERSEY — **Jer·sey·an** \-ən\ *n* — **Jer·sey·ite** \-ˌīt\ *n*

Jersey City city * of N.J. *pop* 228,537

Je·ru·sa·lem \jə-'rü-s(ə-)ləm, -'rüz-ləm, -'rü-zə-\ *or anc* **Hi·ero·sol·y·ma** \ˌhī-(ə-)rō-'sä-lə-mə\ city *cen* Palestine NW of Dead Sea; divided 1948–67 bet. Jordan (old city) & Israel (new city) * of Israel since 1950 & formerly * of ancient kingdoms of Israel & Judah; old city under Israeli control since 1967 *pop* 376,000 — **Je·ru·sa·lem·ite** \-ˌmīt\ *n*

Jer·vis Bay \'jär-vəs\ inlet of the Pacific SE Australia on SE coast of New South Wales on which is situated district (*area* 28 *sq mi* or 73 *sq km*) that is part of Australian Capital Territory

Jesselton — see KOTA KINABALU

Jewel Cave National Monument limestone cave SW S.Dak.

Jewish — see YEVREYSKAYA

Jez·re·el \'jez-rē-ˌel, -ˌrē(ə)l\ ancient town *cen* Palestine in Samaria NW of Mt. Gilboa in Valley of Jezreel; now in N Israel

Jezreel, Plain of the Plain of Esdraelon

Jezreel, Valley of the E end of the Plain of Esdraelon

Jhan·si \'jän(t)-sē\ city N India in S Uttar Pradesh *pop* 281,332

Jhe·lum \'jā-ləm\ *or anc* **Hy·das·pes** \hī-'das-(ˌ)pēz\ river 450 *mi* (724 *km*) NW India (subcontinent) flowing from Kashmir S & SW into the Chenab

Jia·mu·si \jē-'ä-'mü-ˌsē\ *or* **Chia–mu–ssu** \jē-'ä-'mü-'sü\ *or* **Kia·mu·sze** \jē-'ä-'mü-sə\ city NE China in E Heilongjiang *pop* 300,000

Jiang·su *or* **Kiang·su** \jē-'äŋ-'sü\ province E China bordering on Yellow Sea * Nanjing *area* 41,699 *sq mi* (108,417 *sq km*), *pop* 60,521,114

Jiang·xi *or* **Kiang·si** \jē-'äŋ-shē\ province SE China * Nanchang *area* 63,629 *sq mi* (165,435 *sq km*), *pop* 33,184,827

Jiao·zhou *or* **Kiao·chow** \jē-'aú-'jō\ inlet of Yellow Sea E China in E Shandong *area* 200 *sq mi* (520 *sq km*)

Jibuti — see DJIBOUTI

Jid·da \'ji-də\ *or* **Jed·da** \'je-də\ city W Saudi Arabia in Hejaz on Red Sea; port for Mecca *pop* 561,104

Jih–k'a–tse — see XIGAZE

Ji·lin \jē-'lin\ *or* **Ki·rin** \'kē-'rin\ **1** province NE China in E Manchuria * Changchun *area* 72,201 *sq mi* (187,723 *sq km*), *pop* 22,560,053 **2** *or formerly* **Yung·ki** \'yúŋ-'jē\ city NE China in E *cen* Jilin *pop* 583,000

Ji·nan *or* **Chi·nan** *or* **Tsi·nan** \jē-'nän\ city E China * of Shandong *pop* 1,500,000

Jin·ja \'jin-jə\ city & port SE Uganda on Lake Victoria *pop* 228,520

Jin·zhou *or* **Chin·chow** *or* **Chin–chou** \'jin-'jō\ city NE China in SW Liaoning *pop* 400,000

João Pes·soa \ˌzhwaú(m)-pə-'sō-ə\ *or formerly* **Pa·ra·í·ba** \ˌpar-ə-'ē-bə\ city NE Brazil * of Paraíba *pop* 330,176

Jodh·pur \'jäd-pər, -'pur\ **1** *or* **Mar·war** \'mär-ˌwär\ former state NW India bordering on Thar Desert & Rann of Kutch; since 1949 part of Rajasthan state **2** city, its * *pop* 493,609

Jod·rell Bank \'jä-drəl\ locality W England in NE Cheshire near Macclesfield

Jogjakarta — see YOGYAKARTA

Jo·han·nes·burg \jō-'ha-nəs-ˌbərg, -'hä-\ city NE Republic of South Africa in Pretoria-Witwatersrand-Vereeniging *pop* 654,232

John Day \'jän-'dā\ river 281 *mi* (452 *km*) N Oreg. flowing W & N into Columbia River

John Day Fossil Beds National Monument reservation N *cen* Oreg.

John o' Groat's \ˌjän-ō-'grōts\ *or* **John o' Groat's House** locality N Scotland; popularly considered the northernmost point of mainland of Scotland & Great Britain — see DUNNET HEAD

John·son City \'jän(t)-sən\ city NE Tenn. S of Va. border *pop* 49,381

John·ston \'jän(t)-stən\ **1** island (atoll) *cen* Pacific SW of Honolulu, Hawaii; belongs to the U.S. **2** town N R.I. SW of Providence *pop* 26,542

Johns·town \'jänz-ˌtaún\ city SW *cen* Pa. *pop* 28,134

Jo·hore \jə-'hōr, -'hór\ state Malaysia in Peninsular Malaysia at S end of Malay Peninsula * Johore Bahru *area* 7321 *sq mi* (19,035 *sq km*), *pop* 1,601,504

Johore Bah·ru \'bär-(ˌ)ü\ city S Malaysia (federation) * of Johore on an inlet opposite Singapore Is. *pop* 135,936

Join·vi·le *or formerly* **Join·vil·le** \zhóin-'vē-lē\ city S Brazil NNW of Florianópolis *pop* 235,612

Jo·li·et \ˌjō-lē-'et, *chiefly by outsiders* jä-\ city NE Ill. *pop* 76,836

Jo·lo \hō-'lō\ island S Philippines, chief island of Sulu Archipelago *area* 345 *sq mi* (897 *sq km*)

Jones·boro \'jōnz-ˌbər-ə, -ˌbə-rə\ city NE Ark. *pop* 46,535

Jön·kö·ping \'yə(r)n-ˌshə(r)-piŋ\ city S Sweden at S end of Vättern Lake *pop* 110,860

Jon·quière \ˌzhōn-kē-'er\ town Canada in S *cen* Que. *pop* 57,933

Jop·lin \'jä-plən\ city SW Mo. *pop* 40,961

Joppa — see JAFFA

Jor·dan \'jór-dᵊn\ **1** river 45 *mi* (72 *km*) *cen* Utah flowing from Utah Lake N into Great Salt Lake **2** river 200 *mi* (322 *km*) NE Palestine flowing from Anti-Lebanon Mountains S through Sea of Galilee into Dead Sea **3** *or formerly* **Trans·jor·dan** \(ˌ)tran(t)s-, (ˌ)tranz-\ country SW Asia in NW Arabia * Amman *area* 37,737 *sq mi* (98,116 *sq km*), *pop* 2,152,273 — **Jor·da·ni·an** \jór-'dä-nē-ən\ *adj or n*

Josh·ua Tree National Monument \'jä-sh(ə-)wə\ reservation S Calif. N of Salton Sea containing unusual desert flora

Jo·tun·heim \'yō-t°n-ˌhäm\ *or Norw* **Jo·tun·hei·men** \-ˌhä-mən\ mountains S *cen* Norway — see GLITTERTIND

Juana Dí·az \ˌwä-nə-'dē-ˌäs, ˌhwä-\ town S Puerto Rico *pop* 45,198

Juan de Fu·ca, Strait of \ˌwän-də-'fyü-kə, ˌhwän-\ strait 100 *mi* (161 *km*) long bet. Vancouver Is., B.C., & Olympic Peninsula, Wash.

Juan Fer·nán·dez \ˌwän-fər-'nan-dəs, ˌhwän-\ group of three islands SE Pacific W of Chile; belongs to Chile *area* 70 *sq mi* (182 *sq km*)

Juan–les–Pins \ˌwän-lā-'paⁿ\ town SE France on Cap d'Antibes

Juárez — see CIUDAD JUÁREZ

Ju·ba \'jü-bə\ river 1000 *mi* (1609 *km*) E Africa flowing from S Ethiopia S through Somalia into Indian Ocean

Ju·by, Cape \'jü-bē, 'yü-\ cape NW Africa on NW coast of Western Sahara

Jú·car \'hü-ˌkär\ river 300 *mi* (483 *km*) E Spain flowing S & E into the Mediterranean S of Valencia

Ju·daea *or* **Ju·dea** \jü-'dē-ə, -'dā-\ ancient region Palestine constituting the S division (Judah) of the country under Persian, Greek, & Roman rule; bounded on N by Samaria, on E by Jordan River & Dead Sea, on SW by Sinai Peninsula, & on W by the Mediterranean — **Ju·dae·an** *or* **Ju·de·an** \-ən\ *adj or n*

Ju·dah \'jü-də\ ancient kingdom S Palestine * Jerusalem — see ISRAEL

Jugoslavia — see YUGOSLAVIA — **Ju·go·slav** \ˌyü-gō-'släv, -'släv\ *or* **Ju·go·sla·vi·an** \-'slä-vē-ən\ *adj or n*

Juiz de Fo·ra \ˌzhwēzh-də-'fór-ə, -'fór-\ city E Brazil in S Minas Gerais *pop* 307,820

Ju·juy \hü-'hwē\ city NW Argentina N of Tucumán *pop* 44,188

Ju·lian Alps \'jül-yən\ section of E Alps W Slovenia N of Istrian Peninsula; highest peak Triglav 9393 *ft* (2863 *m*)

Julian Venetia — see VENEZIA GIULIA

Jul·lun·dur \'jə-lən-dər\ city NW India in Punjab *pop* 405,700

Jum·na \'jəm-nə\ river 860 *mi* (1384 *km*) N India in Uttar Pradesh flowing from the Himalayas S & SE into the Ganges

Junction City city NE *cen* Kans. *pop* 20,604

Ju·neau \'jü-(ˌ)nō, jü-'\ city & port * of Alaska in SE coastal strip *pop* 26,751

Jung·frau \'yún-ˌfraú\ mountain 13,642 *ft* (4158 *m*) SW *cen* Switzerland in Berner Alpen bet. Bern & Valais cantons

Jung·gar *or* **Zhun·gar·ia** *or* **Dzun·gar·ian Basin** \ˌ(d)zən-'gar-ē-ən, (d)zúŋ-, -'ger-\ *or* **Dzun·gar·ia** \-ē-ə\ region W China in N Xinjiang Uygur N of the Tian Shan

Ju·ni·ata \ˌjü-nē-'a-tə\ river 150 *mi* (241 *km*) S *cen* Pa. flowing E into the Susquehanna

Ju·nín \hü-'nēn\ 1 city E Argentina W of Buenos Aires *pop* 62,080 2 town *cen* Peru at S end of **Lake Junín** (25 *mi or* 40 *km* long)
Ju·pi·ter \'jü-pə-tər\ town SE Fla. *pop* 24,986
Jupiter Island island SE Fla. in the Atlantic
Ju·ra \'jür-ə\ 1 canton W Switzerland *pop* 65,376 2 mountains France & Switzerland extending 200 *mi* (322 *km*) along the boundary; highest Crête de la Neige (in France) 5652 *ft* (1723 *m*) 3 island 24 *mi* (39 *km*) long W Scotland in the Inner Hebrides S of Mull
Juramento — see SALADO
Ju·ruá \,zhür-(ə-)'wä\ river 1200 *mi* (1931 *km*) NW *cen* S. America flowing from E *cen* Peru NE into the Solimões in NW Brazil
Ju·rue·na \,zhür-(ə-)'wä-nə\ river 600 *mi* (966 *km*) W *cen* Brazil flowing N to unite with the São Manuel forming the Tapajoz
Jut·land \'jət-lənd\ *or Dan* Jyl·land \'yüœ-,lán, 'yœ-\ 1 peninsula N Europe projecting into North Sea & comprising mainland of Denmark & N portion of Schleswig-Holstein, Germany 2 the mainland of Denmark
Kaapland — see CAPE OF GOOD HOPE
Kab·a·le·ga Falls \,kä-bə-'lē-gə, -'lä-\ *or formerly* Mur·chi·son Falls \'mər-chə-sən\ waterfall 120 *ft* (36 *m*) W Uganda in the Victoria Nile
Kab·ar·di·no–Bal·kar Republic \,ka-bər-dē-(,)nō-'bȯl-,kär, -'bal-\ *or* Kab·ar·din–Balkar Republic \,ka-bər-'dēn-\ autonomous republic S Russia in Europe on N slopes of the Caucasus ✻ Nalchik *area* 4600 *sq mi* (11,960 *sq km*), *pop* 539,000 — Kab·ar·din·ian \,ka-bər-'dē-nē-ən\ *adj or n*
Kabia — see SELAJAR
Ka·bul \'kä-bəl, kə-'bül\ 1 river 360 *mi* (579 *km*) Afghanistan & N Pakistan flowing E into the Indus 2 city ✻ of Afghanistan on Kabul River *pop* 913,164 — Ka·buli \'kä-bə-(,)lē, kə-'bü-lē\ *adj or n*
Kab·we \'kä-(,)bwä\ *or formerly* Bro·ken Hill \'brō-kən\ city *cen* Zambia *pop* 143,635
Ka·by·lia \kə-'bi-lē-ə, -'bi-\ mountainous region N Algeria on coast E of Algiers; comprises two areas: **Great Kabylia** (to W) & **Little Kabylia** (to E)
Ka·desh–bar·nea \,kä-(,)desh-'bär-nē-ə, -bär-'nē-ə\ ancient town S Palestine SW of Dead Sea; exact location uncertain
Ka·di·koy \,kä-di-'kȯi\ *or anc* Chal·ce·don \'kal-sə-,dän, kal-'sē-d²n\ former city Asia on the Bosporus; now a district of Istanbul
Kadiyevka — see STAKHANOV
Kaerh — see GAR
Kae·song \'kā-,sȯŋ\ city SW N. Korea SE of Pyongyang *pop* 140,000
Kaf·fe·klub·ben \'kä-fə-,klü-bən, -,klə-\ island in Arctic Ocean off N coast of Greenland; northernmost point of land in the world, at 83°40′N
Kaf·frar·ia \kə-'frar-ē-ə, ka-, -'frer-\ region Republic of South Africa in Eastern Cape province S of Natal & bordering on Indian Ocean
Kafiristan — see NURISTAN
Ka·fue \kə-'fü-ē\ river 500 *mi* (805 *km*) Zambia flowing into the Zambezi
Ka·ge·ra \kə-'ger-ə\ river 430 *mi* (692 *km*) Burundi, Rwanda, & NW Tanganyika flowing N & E into Lake Victoria on Uganda border
Ka·go·shi·ma \,kä-gə-'shē-mə, kä-'gō-shə-\ city & port S Japan in S Kyushu on Kagoshima Bay (inlet of the Pacific) *pop* 536,685
Ka·hoo·la·we \,kä-hō-ə-'lä-(,)vä, -(,)wä\ island Hawaii SW of Maui *area* 45 *sq mi* (117 *sq km*)
Kai·bab Plateau \'kī-,bab\ plateau N Ariz. & SW Utah N of Grand Canyon
Kai·e·teur Falls \,kī-ə-'túr, ,kī-'chúr\ waterfall 741 *ft* (226 *m*) high & 350 *ft* (107 *m*) wide *cen* Guyana
Kai·feng \'kī-'fəŋ\ city E *cen* China in NE Henan *pop* 318,000
Kai·lua \kī-'lü-ə\ city Hawaii in NE Oahu *pop* 36,818
Kair·ouan \ker-'wän\ city NE Tunisia *pop* 54,546
Kai·sers·lau·tern \,kī-zərz-'laú-tərn\ city SW Germany W of Ludwigshafen *pop* 98,745
Ka·ki·na·da \,kä-kə-'nä-də\ city & port E India in NE Andhra Pradesh on Bay of Bengal *pop* 226,642
Kalaallit Nunaat — see GREENLAND
Ka Lae \kä-'lä-ā\ *or* South Cape headland Hawaii, southernmost point of Hawaii (island)
Kalaeloa Point — see BARBERS POINT
Kal·a·ha·ri Desert \,ka-lə-'här-ē\ desert region S Africa N of Orange River & S E of Natal in Botswana & NW Republic of South Africa
Kal·a·ma·zoo \,ka-lə-mə-'zü\ city SW Mich. *pop* 80,277
Ka·lat *or* Khe·lat \kə-'lät\ region NW Pakistan including S & *cen* Baluchistan; a former princely state ✻ Kalat
Ka·le·mie \kə-'lä-mē\ *or formerly* Al·bert·ville \,al-,ber-'vē(ə)l, 'al-bərt-,vil\ city & port E Zaire on Lake Tanganyika *pop* 27,500
Kalgan — see ZHANGJIAKOU
Kal·goor·lie \kal-'gúr-lē\ town Australia in S *cen* W. Australia
Kalhu — see CALAH
Ka·li·man·tan \,ka-lə-'man-,tan, ,kä-lə-'män-,tän\ 1 an Indonesian name for Borneo 2 the S & E part of Borneo belonging to Indonesia; formerly (as **Dutch Borneo**) part of Netherlands India
Ka·li·nin \kə-'lē-nən, -,nyēn\ *or* Tver \tə-'ver\ city W *cen* Russia in Europe on the Volga *pop* 412,000
Ka·li·nin·grad \kə-'lē-nən-,grad, -nyən-, -,gräd\ *or G* Kö·nigs·berg \'kä-nigz-,bərg, *Ger* 'kœ-niks-,berk\ city & port W Russia in Europe near the Frisches Haff; formerly ✻ of E. Prussia *pop* 355,000
Ka·lisz \'kä-lish\ commune *cen* Poland W of Lodz *pop* 106,087
Kal·mar \'käl-,mär, 'kal-\ city & port SE Sweden *pop* 52,846
Kal·myk Republic \(,)kal-'mik\ autonomous republic S Russia in Europe on NW shore of Caspian Sea W of the Volga ✻ Elista *area* 29,417 *sq mi* (76,484 *sq km*), *pop* 268,000
Ka·lu·ga \kə-'lü-gə\ city W *cen* Russia in Europe on Oka River WNW of Tula *pop* 265,000
Ka·ma \'kä-mə\ river 1200 *mi* (1931 *km*) E Russia in Europe flowing SW into the Volga S of Kazan
Ka·ma·ku·ra \,kä-'mä-kə-,rä, ,kä-mə-'kúr-ə\ city Japan in SE Honshu on Sagami Sea S of Yokohama *pop* 174,299
Kam·chat·ka \kam-'chat-kə, -'chät-\ peninsula 750 *mi* (1207 *km*) long E Russia in Asia bet. Sea of Okhotsk & Bering Sea
Ka·met \'kə-,mät\ mountain 25,447 *ft* (7756 *m*) N India in Uttar Pradesh in the NW Himalayas
Kam·loops \'kam-,lüps\ city Canada in S B.C. *pop* 67,057

Kam·pa·la \käm-'pä-lə, kam-\ city ✻ of Uganda N of Lake Victoria *pop* 458,423
Kampuchea — see CAMBODIA — Kam·pu·che·an \,kam-pú-'chē-ən\ *adj*
Kan — see GAN
Ka·nan·ga \kə-'näŋ-gə\ *or formerly* Lu·lua·bourg \lü-'lü-ə-,bür(g)\ city S *cen* Zaire *pop* 285,470
Kananur — see CANNANORE
Ka·na·ta \kə-'nä-tə\ city Canada in SE Ont. *pop* 37,344
Ka·na·wha \kə-'nȯ-(w)ə\ river 97 *mi* (156 *km*) W W.Va. flowing NW into Ohio River
Ka·na·za·wa \kə-'nä-zə-wə, ,kä-nə-'zä-wə\ city & port Japan in W *cen* Honshu near Sea of Japan *pop* 442,872
Kan·chen·jun·ga \,kän-chən-'jəŋ-gə, -'jüŋ-\ mountain 28,208 *ft* (8598 *m*) Nepal & Sikkim in the Himalayas; 3d highest in world
Kan·chi·pu·ram \kän-'chē-pə-rəm\ city SE India in N Tamil Nadu SW of Madras *pop* 145,329
Kan·da·har \'kan-də-,här\ city SE Afghanistan *pop* 130,212
Kand·la \'kənd-lə\ port W India in Gujarat on Gulf of Kutch
Kan·dy \'kan-dē\ city W *cen* Sri Lanka ENE of Colombo *pop* 103,000 — Kan·dy·an \-dē-ən\ *adj*
Kane Basin \'kän\ section of the passage bet. NW Greenland & Ellesmere Is. N of Baffin Bay
Ka·ne·o·he Bay \,kä-nē-'ō-ē, -'ō-(,)hä\ inlet Hawaii on E Oahu
Kan·ka·kee \,kaŋ-kə-'kē\ 1 river Ind. & Ill. flowing SW & W to unite with Des Plaines River forming Illinois River 2 city NE Ill. on Kankakee River *pop* 27,575
Kan·nap·o·lis \kə-'na-p(ə-)ləs\ town S *cen* N.C. *pop* 29,696
Ka·no \'kä-(,)nō\ city N *cen* Nigeria *pop* 475,000
Kan·pur \'kän-,púr\ city N India in S Uttar Pradesh on the Ganges *pop* 1,688,242
Kan·sas \'kan-zəs\ 1 *or* Kaw \'kȯ\ river 169 *mi* (272 *km*) E Kans. flowing E into Missouri River — see SMOKY HILL 2 state *cen* U.S. ✻ Topeka *area* 82,264 *sq mi* (213,886 *sq km*), *pop* 2,477,574 — Kan·san \'kan-zən\ *adj or n*
Kansas City 1 city NE Kans. adjacent to Kansas City, Mo. *pop* 149,767 2 city W Mo. on Missouri River *pop* 435,146
Kansu — see GANSU
Kan·ton Island \'kan-t²n\ island (atoll) *cen* Pacific in Phoenix Islands
Kan·to Plain \'kän-(,)tō\ region Japan in E *cen* Honshu; Tokyo is situated on it
Kao·hsiung \'kaú-shē-'úŋ, 'gaú-\ city & port SW Taiwan *pop* 1,227,454
Ka·pi·da·gi \,kä-pē-dä-'(g)ē\ *or anc* Cyz·i·cus \'si-zi-kəs\ peninsula NW Turkey in Asia projecting into Sea of Marmara
Ka·ra·chay–Cher·kess \,kär-ə-'chī-ə-,'chər-'kes\ *or* Ka·ra·cha·ye·vo–Cherkess \,kär-ə-'chī-ə-,võ\ autonomous region SE Russia in Europe in N Caucasus *area* 5442 *sq mi* (14,149 *sq km*) ✻ Cherkessk
Ka·ra·chi \kə-'rä-chē\ city & port S Pakistan ✻ of Sind *pop* 5,103,000
Karafuto — see SAKHALIN
Ka·ra·gan·da \,kar-ə-gən-'dä\ *or* Qa·ra·ghan·dy \,kar-ə-gən-'dē\ city *cen* Kazakhstan *pop* 572,000
Ka·raj \kə-'räj\ city N Iran NW of Tehran *pop* 275,100
Ka·ra–Kal·pak Republic \,kar-ə-,kal-'pak\ autonomous republic NW Uzbekistan SE of Aral Sea ✻ Nukus *area* 61,600 *sq mi* (160,160 *sq km*), *pop* 829,000
Kar·a·ko·ram Pass \,kar-ə-'kȯr-əm, -'kȯr-\ mountain pass 18,290 *ft* (5575 *m*) NE Kashmir through Karakoram Range
Karakoram Range mountain system S *cen* Asia in N Kashmir & NW Tibet on Xinjiang Uygur border; westernmost system of the Himalaya complex, connecting the Himalayas with the Pamirs — see K2
Kar·a·ko·rum \,kar-ə-'kȯr-əm\ ruined city Mongolia on the upper Orkhon ✻ of Mongol Empire
Ka·ra Kum \,kar-ə-'küm, ,kär-\ desert Turkmenistan S of Aral Sea bet. the Caspian Sea & the Amu Darya *area* 110,000 *sq mi* (286,000 *sq km*)
Kara Sea arm of Arctic Ocean off coast of Russia E of Novaya Zemlya
Ka·ra Su \,kar-ə-'sü, ,kär-\ the Euphrates above its junction with the Murat in E *cen* Turkey
Kar·ba·lā' \,kär-bə-lä, 'kär-bə-lə\ city *cen* Iraq SSW of Baghdad *pop* 83,301
Ka·re·lia \kə-'rē-lē-ə, -'rēl-yə\ region NE Europe bet. Gulf of Finland & White Sea in Finland & Russia in Europe
Ka·re·lian Isthmus \kə-'rē-lē-ən, -'rēl-yən\ isthmus Russia in Europe in Karelia bet. Gulf of Finland & Lake Ladoga
Karelian Republic autonomous republic NW Russia in Europe in Karelia region; formerly (1940–56), as the Ka·re·lo–Finn·ish Republic \kə-'rē-(,)lō-'fi-nish\ constituent republic of the U.S.S.R. ✻ Petrozadovsk *area* 68,900 *sq mi* (179,140 *sq km*), *pop* 738,000
Ka·ri·ba \kə-'rē-bə\ lake 165 *mi* (266 *km*) long SE Zambia & N Zimbabwe formed in the Zambezi by **Kariba Dam**
Ka·ri·kal \,kar-i-'käl\ 1 territory of former French India S of Pondicherry; incorporated 1954 in India *area* 52 *sq mi* (135 *sq km*) 2 city & port, its ✻, on Bay of Bengal *pop* 22,252
Kar·kheh \kär-'kä\ *or anc* Cho·as·pes \kō-'as-(,)pēz\ river 340 *mi* (547 *km*) flowing from W Iran S & W into marshlands E of the Tigris in SE Iraq
Karl–Marx–Stadt — see CHEMNITZ
Karls·kro·na \kär(-ə)lz-'krü-nə\ city & port SE Sweden on Baltic Sea *pop* 60,141
Karls·ru·he \'kär(-ə)lz-,rü-ə\ city SW Germany in Baden-Württemberg on the Rhine *pop* 271,892 — Karls·ru·her \-,rü-ər\ *n*
Karl·stad \'kär(-ə)l-,stä(d)\ city SW Sweden *pop* 76,120
Kar·nak \'kär-,nak\ town S Egypt on the Nile N of Luxor on N part of site of ancient Thebes
Kar·na·ta·ka \kər-'nä-tə-kə\ *or formerly* My·sore \mī-'sōr, -'sȯr\ state SW India ✻ Bangalore *area* 74,326 *sq mi* (193,248 *sq km*), *pop* 37,034,451

\ə\ abut \ᵊ\ kitten, F table \ər\ further \a\ ash \ā\ ace \ä\ mop, mar
\aú\ out \ch\ chin \e\ bet \ē\ easy \g\ go \i\ hit \ī\ ice \j\ job
\ŋ\ sing \ō\ go \ȯ\ law \ȯi\ boy \th\ thin \th̷\ the \ü\ loot \ú\ foot
\y\ yet \zh\ vision \á, k̲, ⁿ, œ, œ̄, ue, ue̅, ᵞ\ see Guide to Pronunciation

Kár·pa·thos \'kär-pə-ˌthós\ island Greece in the S Dodecanese *area* 118 *sq mi* (307 *sq km*), *pop* 8129

Kar·roo *or* **Ka·roo** \kə-'rü\ plateau region W Republic of South Africa W of Drakensberg Mountains divided into **Little Karroo** *or* **South·ern Karroo** (in *cen* Western Cape province); **Great Karroo** *or* **Cen·tral Karroo** (in Western Cape & Eastern Cape provinces); and **Northern Karroo** *or* **Upper Karroo** (in Northern Cape, Orange Free State, & North West provinces)

Kars \'kärz, 'kärs\ city NE Turkey *pop* 58,651

Karst \'kärst\ *or* **Kras** \'kräs\ *or* *It* **Car·so** \'kär-(,)sō\ limestone plateau NE of Istrian Peninsula in E Italy, W Slovenia, & W Croatia

Ka·run \kä-'rün\ river 450 *mi* (724 *km*) W Iran flowing into Shatt-al-Arab

Ka·sai \kə-'sī\ **1** river 1200 *mi* (1931 *km*) N Angola & W Zaire flowing N & W into Congo River **2** region S *cen* Zaire

Kashi \'kä-shē, 'kä-\ *or* **Kash·gar** \'kash-,gär, 'käsh-\ city W China in SW Xinjiang Uygur *pop* 100,000

Ka·shi·wa \'kä-shē-(,)wä\ city Japan on Honshu *pop* 305,060

Kash·mir \'kash-,mir, 'kazh-, kash-', kazh-'\ **1** *or formerly* **Cash·mere** mountainous region N India (subcontinent) W of Tibet & SW of Xinjiang Uygur; includes valley (**Vale of Kashmir**) watered by the Jhelum **2** — see JAMMU AND KASHMIR

Kas·kas·kia \ka-'skas-kē-ə\ river 300 *mi* (483 *km*) SW Ill. flowing SW into Mississippi River

Kas·sa·la \'kä-sə-lə\ city NE Sudan *pop* 99,000

Kas·sel \'ka-səl, 'kä-\ city *cen* Germany WNW of Erfurt *pop* 195,912

Kas·ser·ine Pass \'ka-sə-,rēn\ mountain pass *cen* Tunisia

Ka·stel·lór·i·zon \,kä-stə-'lōr-ə-,zón\ *or* **Ca·stel·lo·ri·zo** \,käs-tə-'lōr-ə-,zō\ *or* *It* **Cas·tel·ros·so** \,käs-,tel-'rō-(,)sō\ island Greece in the E Dodecanese off SW coast of Turkey *area* 4 *sq mi* (10 *sq km*)

Kás·tron \'käs-,trón\ town Greece on Lemnos

Kastrop-Rauxel — see CASTROP-RAUXEL

Ka·tah·din, Mount \kə-'tä-d³n\ mountain 5268 *ft* (1606 *m*) N *cen* Maine; highest point in state

Katanga — see SHABA

Ka·te·ri·nē \,kä-tə-'rē-nē\ town N Greece *pop* 46,304

Kath·er·i·na, Ge·bel \,je-bəl-,kä-thə-'rē-nə\ *or* **Ja·bal Kat·ri·nah** \jä-bəl-kä-'trē-nə\ mountain 8652 *ft* (2637 *m*) NE Egypt on Sinai Peninsula; highest in the Gebel Musa

Ka·thi·a·war \,kä-tē-ə-'wär\ peninsula W India in Gujarat bet. Gulf of Kutch & Gulf of Cambay

Kath·man·du *or* **Kat·man·du** \,kat-,man-'dü, ,kät-,män-\ city ✴ of Nepal *pop* 235,211

Kat·mai, Mount \'kat-,mī\ volcano 6715 *ft* (2047 *m*) S Alaska in Aleutian Range at NE end of Alaska Peninsula

Katmai National Park reservation S Alaska including Mt. Katmai & Valley of Ten Thousand Smokes

Ka·to·wi·ce \,kä-tə-'vēt-sə\ city S Poland in Silesia *pop* 367,041

Kat·rine, Loch \'kat-rən\ lake 9 *mi* (14 *km*) long *cen* Scotland in Central region E of Loch Lomond

Ka·tsi·na \'kät-si-nə\ city N Nigeria ✴ of old kingdom of Katsina *pop* 145,500

Kat·te·gat \'ka-ti-,gat\ arm of North Sea bet. Sweden & Jutland Peninsula of Denmark

Kau·ai \'kaú-,ī\ island Hawaii WNW of Oahu *area* 551 *sq mi* (1433 *sq km*)

Kau·nas \'kaú-nəs, -,näs\ *or* *Russ* **Kov·no** \'kòv-(,)nō, -nə\ city *cen* Lithuania on the Neman; a former (1918–40) ✴ of Lithuania *pop* 370,000

Ka·vál·la \kə-'va·lə, -'vä-\ city & port NE Greece in Macedonia *pop* 58,576

Kaveri — see CAUVERY

Kaw — see KANSAS

Ka·wa·goe \kə-'wä-,gói\ city Japan on SE *cen* Honshu *pop* 304,860

Ka·wa·gu·chi \,kä-wə-'gü-chē, kä-'wä-gü-(,)chē\ city Japan in E Honshu N of Tokyo *pop* 438,667

Ka·war·tha Lakes \kə-'wòr-thə\ group of lakes Canada in SE Ont. E of Lake Simcoe; traversed by Trent Canal system

Ka·wa·sa·ki \,kä-wə-'sä-kē\ city Japan in E Honshu on Tokyo Bay, S suburb of Tokyo *pop* 1,173,606

Kay·se·ri \,kī-zə-'rē\ *or anc* **Cae·sa·rea** \,sē-zə-'rē-ə, ,se-zə-, ,se-sə-\ *or* **Maz·a·ca** \'ma-zə-kə\ *or* **Caesarea Mazaca** city *cen* Turkey in Asia at foot of Erciyas Dagi; chief city of ancient Cappadocia *pop* 273,362

Ka·zakh·stan \,ka-(,)zak-'stan; ,kä-(,)zäk-'stän *also* kə-\ independent country NW *cen* Asia extending from Caspian Sea to Altai mountain range; a constituent republic of the U.S.S.R. 1936–91 ✴ Alma-Ata *area* 1,047,930 *sq mi* (2,724,618 *sq km*), *pop* 14,684,000

Ka·zan \kə-'zan\ **1** river 455 *mi* (732 *km*) Canada flowing through a series of lakes into Baker Lake **2** \-'zan, -'zän, -'zä-nyə\ city E *cen* Russia in Europe ✴ of Tatar Republic *pop* 993,000

Kazan Retto — see VOLCANO

Kaz·bek \käz-'bek\ mountain 16,558 *ft* (5047 *m*) bet. Georgia & Russia in Europe in *cen* Caucasus Mountains

Kaz Da·gi \,käz-dä-'(g)ē\ *or* **Ida** \'ī-də\ mountain 5797 *ft* (1767 *m*) NW Turkey in Asia SE of ancient Troy

Kazvin — see QAZVIN

Ke·a·la·ke·kua Bay \kā-,ä-lə-lə-kə-'kü-ə\ inlet of the Pacific Hawaii in W Hawaii (island) on Kona coast W of Mauna Loa

Kear·ney \'kär-nē\ city S *cen* Nebr. on Platte River *pop* 24,396

Kear·ny \'kär-nē\ town NE N.J. N of Newark *pop* 34,874

Kecs·ke·met \'kech-kə-,mēt\ city *cen* Hungary *pop* 108,000

Ked·ah \'ke-də\ state Malaysia in N Peninsular Malaysia bordering on Strait of Malacca ✴ Alor Star *area* 3660 *sq mi* (9516 *sq km*), *pop* 1,102,200

Keeling — see COCOS

Kee·lung \'kē-'lúŋ\ city & port N Taiwan *pop* 347,828

Keene \'kēn\ city SW N.H. *pop* 22,430

Kee·wa·tin \kē-'wā-t³n\ former district Canada in E Northwest Territories N of Man. & Ont. & including the islands in Hudson Bay

Kefallinía — see CEPHALONIA

Kef·la·vík \'kye-blə-,vēk, 'ke-flə-\ town SW Iceland WSW of Reykjavík *pop* 7520

Keigh·ley \'kēth-lē—*sic*\ borough N England in W. Yorkshire, NW of Leeds *pop* 57,451

Kei·zer \'kī-zər\ city NW Oreg. N of Salem *pop* 21,884

Kej·im·ku·jik National Park \,ke-jə-mə-'kü-jik, ,kej-mə-\ reservation Canada in SW N.S.

Ke·lan·tan \kə-'lan-,tan\ state Malaysia in N Peninsular Malaysia on S. China Sea ✴ Kota Bharu *area* 5746 *sq mi* (14,940 *sq km*), *pop* 877,575

Ke·low·na \kə-'lō-nə\ city Canada in S B.C. *pop* 75,950

Keltsy — see KIELCE

Ke·me·ro·vo \'ke-mə-rə-və, -,rō-və, -rə-,vō\ city Russia in Asia in Kuznetsk Basin on Tom River *pop* 471,000

Ke·nai Peninsula \'kē-,nī\ peninsula S Alaska E of Cook Inlet; site of **Kenai Fjords National Park** (ice field)

Ken·dal \'ken-d³l\ borough NW England in Cumbria *pop* 23,411

Ken·il·worth \'ke-n³l-,wərth\ town *cen* England in Warwickshire *pop* 19,315

Ke·ni·tra \kə-'nē-trə\ *or formerly* **Port Lyau·tey** \,pòr-lē-,ō-'tā, -'ō-,\ city N Morocco NE of Rabat *pop* 139,206

Ken·ne·bec \'ke-ni-,bek, ,ke-ni-'\ river 164 *mi* (264 *km*) S Maine flowing S from Moosehead Lake into the Atlantic

Kennedy, Cape — see CANAVERAL (Cape)

Ken·ne·dy, Mount \'ke-nə-dē\ mountain 13,905 *ft* (4238 *m*) NW Canada in Yukon Territory in St. Elias Range near Alaska border

Ken·ner \'ke-nər\ city SE La. W of New Orleans *pop* 72,033

Ken·ne·saw Mountain \'ke-nə-,sò\ mountain 1809 *ft* (551 *m*) NW Ga. NW of Atlanta

Ken·ne·wick \'ke-nə-,wik\ city SE Wash. *pop* 42,155

Ke·no·sha \kə-'nō-shə\ city SE Wis. S of Racine *pop* 80,352

Ken·sing·ton and Chel·sea \,ken-ziŋ-tən-ən(d)-'chel-sē, ,ken(t)-siŋ-\ royal borough W Greater London, England *pop* 146,900; includes former boroughs of Kensington & Chelsea

Kent \'kent\ **1** city NE Ohio SE of Cleveland *pop* 28,835 **2** city W Wash. S of Seattle *pop* 37,960 **3** county SE England bordering on Strait of Dover; one of kingdoms in Anglo-Saxon heptarchy ✴ Maidstone *area* 1441 *sq mi* (3747 *sq km*), *pop* 1,482,900 — **Kent·ish** \'ken-tish\ *adj*

Kent Island island Md. in Chesapeake Bay 15 *mi* (25 *km*) long; largest island in the bay

Ken·tucky \kən-'tə-kē\ **1** river 259 *mi* (417 *km*) N *cen* Ky. flowing NW into Ohio river **2** state E *cen* U.S. ✴ Frankfort *area* 40,395 *sq mi* (105,027 *sq km*), *pop* 3,685,296 — **Ken·tuck·i·an** \-kē-ən\ *adj or n*

Kent·wood \'kent-,wúd\ city SW Mich. *pop* 37,826

Ke·nya \'ke-nyə, 'kē-\ **1** extinct volcano 17,058 *ft* (5199 *m*) *cen* Kenya near equator **2** republic E Africa S of Ethiopia bordering on Indian Ocean; member of the Commonwealth of Nations, formerly Brit. crown colony & protectorate ✴ Nairobi *area* 224,960 *sq mi* (584,896 *sq km*), *pop* 15,327,061 — **Ke·nyan** \-nyən\ *adj or n*

Ke·os \'kē-,äs, 'kä-,òs\ *or* **Kea** \'kē-ə, 'kä-ə\ *or anc* **Ce·os** \'kē-,äs\ island Greece in NW Cyclades; chief town Kea *area* 67 *sq mi* (174 *sq km*)

Ker·a·la \'ker-ə-lə\ state S India bordering on Arabian Sea ✴ Trivandrum *area* 15,035 *sq mi* (39,091 *sq km*), *pop* 25,403,217

Kerasun — see GIRESUN

Kerch \'kerch\ **1** peninsula projecting E from the Crimea **2** city & port in the Crimea on Kerch Strait *pop* 149,000

Kerch Strait strait bet. Kerch & Taman peninsulas connecting Sea of Azov & Black Sea

Ker·gue·len \'kər-gə-lən, ,ker-gə-'len\ island in the Kerguelen Archipelago

Kerguelen Archipelago archipelago S Indian Ocean belonging to France *area* 7000 *sq mi* (18,200 *sq km*)

Ke·rin·tji \kə-'rin-chē\ volcano 12,484 *ft* (3805 *m*) Indonesia in W *cen* Sumatra; highest on the island

Kérkira *or* **Kérkyra** — see CORFU

Kerk·ra·de \'kerk-,rä-də\ commune SE Netherlands *pop* 53,353

Ker·mad·ec Islands \(,)kər-'ma-dək\ islands SW Pacific NE of New Zealand; belong to New Zealand *area* 13 *sq mi* (34 *sq km*), *pop* 9

Ker·man \kər-'män, ker-\ **1** *or anc* **Car·ma·nia** \kär-'mā-nē-ə, -nyə\ region SE Iran bordering on Gulf of Oman & Persian Gulf S of ancient Parthia **2** *or anc* **Car·ma·na** \'kär-'mä-nə, -'ma-, -'mä-\ city SE *cen* Iran in NW Kerman region *pop* 257,284

Kermanshah — see BAKHTARAN

Kern \'kərn\ river 150 *mi* (241 *km*) S *cen* Calif. flowing SW into Buena Vista reservoir

Ker·ry \'ker-ē\ county SW Ireland in Munster ✴ Tralee *area* 1815 *sq mi* (4719 *sq km*), *pop* 121,719

Ke·ru·len \'ker-ə-lən\ river 650 *mi* (1046 *km*) E Mongolia flowing S & E into the Argun in Manchuria

Kes·te·ven, Parts of \ke-'stē-vən, 'kes-ti-vən\ district & former administrative county E England in SW Lincolnshire ✴ Sleaford *area* 724 *sq mi* (1882 *sq km*)

Kes·wick \'ke-zik\ town NW England in Cumbria in Lake District

Ket·ter·ing \'ke-tə-riŋ\ city SW Ohio S of Dayton *pop* 60,569

Keu·ka Lake \'kyü-kə, kā-'yü-\ lake 18 *mi* (29 *km*) long W *cen* N.Y.; one of the Finger Lakes

Kew \'kyü\ **1** city SE Australia in S Victoria, NE suburb of Melbourne *pop* 28,870 **2** parish S England in Surrey, now in the Greater London borough of Richmond upon Thames

Ke·wee·naw Peninsula \'kē-wə-,nò\ peninsula NW Mich. projecting from Upper Peninsula into Lake Superior W of **Keweenaw Bay**

Key Lar·go \'lär-(,)gō\ island S Fla. in the Florida Keys

Key West \'west\ city SW Fla. on Key West (island) at W end of Florida Keys *pop* 24,832 — **Key West·er** \'wes-tər\ *n*

Kha·ba·rovsk \kə-'bär-əfsk\ **1** territory E Russia in Asia bordering on Sea of Okhotsk *area* 965,400 *sq mi* (2,510,040 *sq km*), *pop* 1,346,000 **2** city, its ✴, on the Amur *pop* 437,000

Kha·kass \kə-'kas\ autonomous region S Russia in Asia in SW Krasnoyarsk Territory N of the Sayan Mountains ✴ Abakan *area* 24,000 *sq mi* (62,400 *sq km*), *pop* 446,000

Khalkidikí — see CHALCIDICE

Khal·kís \käl-'kēs, käl-\ *or* **Chal·cis** \'kal-səs, -kəs\ city *cen* Greece ✴ of Evvoia on Evripos Strait *pop* 51,482

Khaniá — see CANEA

Khan·ka \'kaŋ-kə\ lake E Asia bet. Maritime Territory, Russia & Heilongjiang, China *area* 1700 *sq mi* (4420 *sq km*)

Khan Ten·gri \ˌkän-ˈteŋ-grē\ mountain 22,949 ft (6995 m) on border bet. Kyrgyzstan & Xinjiang Uygur (China) in Tian Shan

Kha·rag·pur \ˈkär-əg-ˌpùr, ˈkər-\ city E India in SW W. Bengal WSW of Calcutta pop 234,931

Khar·kov \ˈkär-ˌkóf, ˈkär-, -ˌkòv\ city NE Ukraine, its ✳ 1921–34, on edge of Donets Basin pop 1,444,000

Khar·toum or **Khar·tum** \kär-ˈtüm\ city ✳ of Sudan at junction of White Nile & Blue Nile rivers pop 1,089,339

Khartoum North city cen Sudan pop 151,000

Kha·si Hills \ˈkä-sē\ hills E India in NW cen Assam

Kha·tan·ga \kə-ˈtäŋ-gə, -ˈtaŋ-\ river 800 mi (1287 km) N Russia in Asia, in NE Krasnoyarsk Territory flowing N into Laptev Sea

Khelat — see KALAT

Kher·son \ker-ˈsòn\ city & port S Ukraine on the Dnieper near its mouth pop 319,000

Khí·os \ˈkē-ˌòs, ˈkē-\ 1 — see CHIOS 2 city & port Greece on E coast of Chios Is. pop 21,261

Khirbat Qumran — see QUMRAN

Khi·va \ˈkē-və\ 1 or **Kho·rezm** \kə-ˈre-zəm\ oasis Uzbekistan on the lower Amu Darya 2 or **Khwa·razm** \kwə-ˈra-zəm, kwä-\ former khanate cen Asia including Khiva oasis 3 city in the oasis, ✳ of the khanate pop 24,139

Khmer Republic — see CAMBODIA

Khor·a·san \ˌkòr-ə-ˈsän, ˌkór-\ or **Khu·ra·san** \ˌkùr-ə-ˈsän, ˌkùr-\ region NE Iran; chief city Meshed

Khor·ra·ma·bad \kò-ˈra-mə-ˌbäd, -ˌbad\ city W Iran pop 208,592

Khor·ram·shahr \ˌkòr-əm-ˈshä(-ˌhə)r, ˌkòr-\ city & port W Iran in Khuzistan on Shatt-al-Arab NNW of Abadan

Khotan — see HOTAN

Khu·zi·stan \ˌkü-zi-ˈstän, -ˈstan\ region SW Iran bordering on Persian Gulf; chief city Khorramshahr

Khy·ber Pass \ˈkī-bər\ mountain pass 33 mi (53 km) long on border bet. Afghanistan & Pakistan in Safed Koh range WNW of Peshawar

Kiamusze — see JIAMUSI

Kiangsi — see JIANGXI

Kiangsu — see JIANGSU

Kiaochow — see JIAOZHOU

Ki·bo \ˈkē-(ˌ)bō\ mountain peak 19,340 ft (5895 m) Tanzania in NE Tanganyika; highest peak of Kilimanjaro & highest point in Africa

Kid·der·min·ster \ˈki-dər-ˌmin(t)-stər\ borough W cen England in Hereford and Worcester SW of Birmingham pop 51,261

Kid·ron \ˈki-drən, ˈkī-\ valley cen Palestine bet. Jerusalem & Mount of Olives; source of stream (Kidron) flowing E to Dead Sea

Kiel \ˈkē(ə)l\ 1 city & port N Germany ✳ of Schleswig-Holstein on SE coast of Jutland Peninsula pop 250,062 2 ship canal 61 mi (98 km) N Germany across base of Jutland Peninsula connecting Baltic Sea & North Sea

Kiel·ce \kē-ˈelt-(ˌ)sä, ˈkyelt-\ or Russ **Kelt·sy** \ˈkelt-sē\ city S Poland S of Warsaw pop 212,901

Ki·ev or **Ki·yev** \ˈkē-ˌef, -ˌev, -əf\ city ✳ of Ukraine on the Dnieper pop 2,587,000 — **Ki·ev·an** \ˈkē-ˌe-fən, -vən\ adj or n

Ki·ga·li \ki-ˈgä-lē\ city cen Rwanda, its ✳ pop 117,749

Kikládhes — see CYCLADES

Ki·lau·ea \ˌkē-ˌlaü-ˈā-ə\ volcanic crater 2 mi (3.2 km) wide Hawaii on Hawaii (island) in Hawaii Volcanoes National Park on E slope of Mauna Loa

Kil·dare \kil-ˈdar, -ˈder\ county E Ireland in Leinster ✳ Naas area 654 sq mi (1700 sq km), pop 122,516

Kil·i·man·ja·ro \ˌki-lə-mən-ˈjär-(ˌ)ō, -ˈjar-\ mountain Tanzania on NE mainland near Kenya border — see KIBO

Kil·ken·ny \kil-ˈke-nē\ 1 county SE Ireland in Leinster area 796 sq mi (2070 sq km), pop 73,613 2 municipal borough, its ✳ pop 8969

Kil·lar·ney, Lakes of \ki-ˈlär-nē\ three lakes SW Ireland in County Kerry

Kill Dev·il \ˈkil-ˌde-vəl\ hill E N.C. near village of **Kit·ty Hawk** \ˈki-tē-ˌhòk\ on sand barrier opposite Albemarle Sound

Kil·leen \ki-ˈlēn\ city cen Tex. N of Austin pop 63,535

Kil·lie·cran·kie \ˌki-lē-ˈkraŋ-kē\ mountain pass cen Scotland in Tayside in the SE Grampians NW of Pitlochry

Kill Van Kull \ˌkil-(ˌ)van-ˈkəl, -vən-\ channel bet. N.J. & Staten Is., N.Y., connecting Newark Bay & Upper New York Bay

Kil·mar·nock \kil-ˈmär-nək\ burgh SW Scotland in Strathclyde pop 52,080

Kim·ber·ley \ˈkim-bər-lē\ city Republic of South Africa in N Cape of Good Hope WNW of Bloemfontein pop 105,258

Kim·ber·leys \-lēz\ plateau region N Western Australia N of 19°30′S lat.

Kin·a·ba·lu or **Kin·a·bu·lu** \ˌki-nə-bə-ˈlü\ mountain 13,455 ft (4101 m) N cen N. Borneo; highest in Borneo Is.

Kin·car·dine \kin-ˈkär-dᵊn\ or **Kin·car·dine·shire** \-ˌshir, -shər\ or **The Mearns** \ˈmərnz, ˈmernz\ former county E Scotland ✳ Stonehaven

Ki·nesh·ma \ˈkē-nish-mə\ city cen Russia in Europe NE of Moscow pop 94,000

King George's Falls — see AUGHRABIES FALLS

King·man \ˈkiŋ-mən\ reef cen Pacific at N end of Line Islands

King's — see OFFALY

Kings Canyon National Park \ˈkiŋz\ reservation SE cen Calif. in the Sierra Nevada N of Sequoia National Park

King's Lynn \ˈkiŋz-ˈlin\ or **Lynn** or **Lynn Re·gis** \ˈrē-jəs\ borough E England in Norfolk near The Wash pop 33,340

Kings Mountain ridge N.C. & S.C. SW of Gastonia, N.C.

Kings Peak mountain 13,528 ft (4123 m) NE Utah in Uinta Mountains; highest point in state

Kings·port \ˈkiŋz-ˌpōrt, -ˌpòrt\ city NE Tenn. on the Holston pop 36,365

Kings·ton \ˈkiŋ(k)-stən\ 1 city SE N.Y. on the Hudson pop 23,095 2 city Canada in SE Ont. on Lake Ontario near head of St. Lawrence River; ✳ of Canada 1841–44 pop 56,597 3 or in full **Kingston upon** (or on) **Thames** royal borough of SW Greater London, England ✳ of Surrey pop 135,000 4 city & port ✳ of Jamaica on **Kingston Harbor** (inlet of the Caribbean) pop 117,400

Kingston upon Hull — see HULL

Kings·town \ˈkiŋz-ˌtaün\ 1 town & port ✳ of St. Vincent and the Grenadines on St. Vincent Is. at head of Kingstown Bay 2 — see DUN LAOGHAIRE

Kings·ville \ˈkiŋz-ˌvil, -vəl\ city S Tex. pop 25,276

Kinneret, Yam — see GALILEE (Sea of)

Kin·ross \kin-ˈròs\ or **Kin·ross-shire** \-ˈròsh-ˌshir, -shər\ former county E cen Scotland ✳ Kinross

Kin·sha·sa \kin-ˈshä-sə\ or formerly **Lé·o·pold·ville** \ˈlē-ə-ˌpōld-ˌvil, ˈlā-\ city ✳ of Zaire on Congo River at outlet of Malebo Pool pop 2,242,297

Kin·ston \ˈkin(t)-stən\ city E N.C. pop 25,295

Kin·tyre \kin-ˈtīr\ peninsula 40 mi (64 km) long SW Scotland bet. the Atlantic & Firth of Clyde; terminates in **Mull of Kintyre** \ˈməl\ (cape in N. channel)

Kioga — see KYOGA

Kirghiz Republic or **Kirgiz Republic** or **Kirghizia** — see KYRGYZSTAN

Ki·ri·bati \ˈkir-ə-ˌbas—sic\ island nation W Pacific SSE of the Marshalls comprising Ocean Island and the Gilbert, Line, & Phoenix groups ✳ Tarawa area 102 sq mi (265 sq km), pop 63,848

Ki·rik·ka·le \ˌkə-ˈri-kə-ˌlä\ city cen Turkey E of Ankara

Kirin — see JILIN

Ki·riti·mati \kə-ˈris-məs—sic\ or formerly **Christ·mas** \ˈkris-məs\ island (atoll) in the Line Islands; largest atoll in the Pacific area 234 sq mi (608 sq km), pop 674

Kirjath–arba — see HEBRON

Kirk·cal·dy \(ˌ)kər-ˈkò-dē, -ˈkòl-, -ˈkä-\ royal burgh & port E Scotland in Fife on Firth of Forth N of Edinburgh pop 46,314

Kirk·cud·bright \(ˌ)kər-ˈkü-brē\ or **Kirk·cud·bright·shire** \-ˌshir, -shər\ former county S Scotland ✳ Kirkcudbright (pop 2574)

Kirk·land \ˈkərk-lənd\ city W Wash. NE of Seattle pop 40,052

Kirk·pat·rick, Mount \ˌkərk-ˈpa-trik\ mountain 14,856 ft (4528 m) E Antarctica in Queen Alexandra Range S of Ross Sea

Kir·kuk \kir-ˈkük\ city NE Iraq SE of Mosul pop 175,303

Kirk·wall \ˈkərk-ˌwòl\ burgh & port N Scotland ✳ of Orkney, on Mainland Is. pop 5947

Kirk·wood \ˈkərk-ˌwùd\ city E Mo. W of St. Louis pop 27,291

Ki·rov \ˈkē-ˌròf, -ˌròv, -rəf\ or formerly **Vyat·ka** \vē-ˈat-kə, -ˈät-\ city E cen Russia in Europe pop 390,000

Kirovabad — see GYANDZHA

Ki·ro·vo·grad \ki-ˈrō-və-ˌgrad, -ˌgräd\ or formerly **Zi·nov·ievsk** \zə-ˈnòv-ˌyefsk\ or **Eli·sa·vet·grad** \i-ˌli-zə-ˈvet-ˌgrad, -ˌgräd\ city S cen Ukraine pop 237,000

Ki·ru·na \ˈkē-rə-ˌnä\ city N Sweden in Lapland pop 29,705

Ki·san·ga·ni \ˌkē-sən-ˈgä-nē\ or formerly **Stan·ley·ville** \ˈstan-lē-ˌvil\ city NE Zaire on Congo River pop 291,888

Kish \ˈkish\ ancient city of Sumer & Akkad E of site of Babylon

Kishinev — see CHIŞINĂU

Kis·ka \ˈkis-kə\ island SW Alaska; largest & westernmost of Rat Islands of the Aleutians

Kis·ma·yu \ˌkis-ˈmī-(ˌ)ü\ city & port S Somalia pop 30,115

Kis·sim·mee \ki-ˈsi-mē\ 1 river 150 mi (241 km) S cen Fla. flowing SSE from Tohopekaliga Lake through **Lake Kissimmee** (12 mi or 19 km long) into Lake Okeechobee 2 city Fla. on Tohopekaliga Lake pop 30,050

Kistna — see KRISHNA

Ki·su·mu \ki-ˈsü-(ˌ)mü\ city W Kenya on Lake Victoria pop 152,643

Ki·ta·kyu·shu \ˌkē-tä-kē-ˈü-(ˌ)shü\ city & port Japan in N Kyushu formed 1963 by amalgamation of former cities of Kokura, Moji, Tobata, Wakamatsu, & Yahata pop 1,026,467

Kitch·e·ner \ˈkich-nər, ˈki-chə-\ city Canada in SE Ont. pop 168,282

Kithairón — see CITHAERON

Ki·thi·ra \ˈkē-thē-(ˌ)rä\ or It **Ce·ri·go** \ˈcher-i-ˌgō\ island W Greece, southernmost of Ionian Islands ✳ Kíthira area 110 sq mi (286 sq km)

Kit·i·mat \ˈki-tə-ˌmat\ river ab 50 mi (80 km) W Canada in NW B.C. flowing to Douglas Channel (inlet of the Pacific)

Kit·ta·tin·ny Mountain \ˌki-tə-ˈti-nē\ ridge E U.S. in the Appalachians extending from SE N.Y. through NW N.J. into E Pa.

Kit·tery Point \ˈki-tə-rē\ cape Maine at S tip

Kitt Peak \ˈkit\ mountain 6875 ft (2096 m) S Ariz. SW of Tucson

Kitty Hawk — see KILL DEVIL

Kitz·bü·hel \ˈkits-ˌbyü(-)əl, -ˌbū̇(-ə)l\ resort town W Austria in the Tirol

Ki·vu, Lake \ˈkē-(ˌ)vü\ lake 60 mi (96 km) long & 30 mi (48 km) wide E Zaire in Great Rift Valley N of Lake Tanganyika area 1025 sq mi (2665 sq km)

Ki·zil Ir·mak \kə-ˌzil-ir-ˈmäk\ or anc **Ha·lys** \ˈhā-ləs\ river 600 mi (966 km) N cen Turkey flowing W & NE into Black Sea

Kjö·len Mountains \ˈchə(r)-lən\ mountains on border bet. NE Norway & NW Sweden; highest Kebnekaise (in Sweden) 6965 ft (2123 m)

Kla·gen·furt \ˈklä-gən-ˌfürt\ city S Austria ✳ of Carinthia WSW of Graz pop 89,502

Klai·pe·da \ˈklī-pə-də\ or **Me·mel** \ˈmä-məl\ city & port W Lithuania on the Baltic pop 176,000

Klam·ath \ˈkla-məth\ river 250 mi (402 km) S Oreg. & NW Calif. flowing from Upper Klamath Lake SW into the Pacific

Klamath Mountains mountains S Oreg. & NW Calif. in the Coast Ranges; highest Mt. Eddy (in Calif.) 9038 ft (2755 m)

Kle·ve \ˈklā-və\ city W Germany WSW of Münster pop 44,026

Klon·dike \ˈklän-ˌdīk\ 1 river 90 mi (145 km) Canada in cen Yukon Territory flowing W into the Yukon 2 the Klondike River valley

Klu·ane National Park \klü-ˈö-nē, -ˈä-\ reservation Canada in SW Yukon Territory

Kly·az·ma \klē-ˈaz-mə\ river 425 mi (684 km) cen Russia in Europe flowing E to join the Oka W of Nizhni Novgorod

Knok·ke–Heist \kə-ˈnä-kə-ˌhīst, -ˈhäst\ town NW Belgium NNE of Bruges pop 31,787

\ə\ abut \ᵊ\ kitten, F table \ər\ further \a\ ash \ā\ ace \ä\ mop, mar \aü\ out \ch\ chin \e\ bet \ē\ easy \g\ go \i\ hit \ī\ ice \j\ job \ŋ\ sing \ō\ go \ò\ law \òi\ boy \th\ thin \t͟h\ the \ü\ loot \ù\ foot \y\ yet \zh\ vision \à, k̲, ⁿ, œ, œ̄, ᵫ, ᵫ̄, ꞓ\ see Guide to Pronunciation

Knos·sos or **Cnos·sus** \(kə-)'nä-səs\ or **Gnos·sus** \(g̱ə-)'nä-səs\ ruined city ✻ of ancient Crete near N coast SE of modern Candia

Knox·ville \'näks-ˌvil, -vəl\ city E Tenn. on Tennessee River *pop* 165,121

Knud Ras·mus·sen Land \'(k)nüd-'ras-mə-sən, -'räs-ˌmü-s²n\ region N & NW Greenland NE of Baffin Bay

Ko·ba·rid \'kō-bə-ˌred\ or It **Ca·po·ret·to** \ˌkä-pə-'re-(ˌ)tō, ˌkä-\ village W Slovenia on the Isonzo NE of Udine, Italy

Ko·be \'kō-bē, -ˌbä\ city & port Japan in S Honshu on Osaka Bay *pop* 1,477,423

Kö·ben·havn — see COPENHAGEN

Ko·blenz or **Co·blenz** \'kō-ˌblents\ city W Germany SSE of Cologne at confluence of the Rhine & the Moselle *pop* 113,676

Ko·buk Valley National Park \'kō-'bùk\ reservation W Alaska N of the arctic circle along **Kobuk River**

Ko·ca \'kō-'jä\ river 75 *mi* (121 *km*) S Turkey flowing SW & S into the Mediterranean

Ko·ca·bas \ˌkō-jə-'bäsh\ or *anc* **Gra·ni·cus** \grə-'nī-kəs\ river *ab* 30 *mi* (48 *km*) NW Turkey in Asia flowing NE to Sea of Marmara

Ko·chi \'kō-chē\ city & port Japan in S Shikoku *pop* 317,090

Ko·chiu — see GEJIU

Ko·di·ak \'kō-dē-ˌak\ island S Alaska in Gulf of Alaska E of Alaska Peninsula *area* 3465 *sq mi* (9009 *sq km*)

Ko·dok \'kō-ˌdäk\ or *formerly* **Fa·sho·da** \fə-'shō-də\ town SE Sudan on White Nile River

Ko·ha·la Mountains \kō-'hä-lə\ mountains Hawaii in N Hawaii (island); highest *ab* 5500 *ft* (1676 *m*)

Ko·hi·ma \'kō-hē-mə, 'kō-hē-\ town NE India ✻ of Nagaland

Koil — see ALIGARH

Ko·kand \kō-'kand\ or **Qŭ·qon** \kü-'kòn\ 1 region & former khanate E Uzbekistan 2 city in Kokand region SE of Tashkent *pop* 153,000

Ko·ko·mo \'kō-kə-ˌmō\ city N cen Ind. *pop* 44,962

Koko Nor — see QINGHAI

Kok·so·ak \'käk-sō-ˌak\ river 85 *mi* (136 *km*) Canada N Que. formed by confluence of the Caniapiskau and the Larch and flowing into Ungave Bay

Ko·la Peninsula \'kō-lə\ peninsula 250 *mi* (402 *km*) long & 150 *mi* (241 *km*) wide NW Russia in Europe bet. Barents & White seas

Ko·lar Gold Fields \kō-'lär\ city S India in SE Karnataka *pop* 144,406

Kold·ing \'kə-liŋ\ city & port Denmark *pop* 57,128

Kol·ha·pur \'kō-lə-ˌpùr\ city W India in SW Maharashtra SSE of Bombay *pop* 351,073

Kolmar — see COLMAR

Köln — see COLOGNE

Ko·ly·ma or **Ko·li·ma** \kə-'lē-mə\ river 1110 *mi* (1786 *km*) NE Russia in Asia flowing from Kolyma Mountains NE into E. Siberian Sea

Kolyma Mountains or **Kolima Mountains** mountain range Russia in Asia in NE Khabarovsk Territory parallel to coast of Penzhinskaya Bay

Ko·man·dor·skie Islands \ˌkä-mən-'dòr-skē\ or **Com·mand·er Islands** \kə-'man-dər\ islands E Russia in Asia in Bering Sea E of Kamchatka Peninsula *area* 850 *sq mi* (2210 *sq km*)

Ko·ma·ti \kə-'mä-tē\ river 500 *mi* (805 *km*) S Africa flowing from N Drakensberg Mountains in NE Republic of South Africa E & N into Delagoa Bay in S Mozambique

Ko·mi Republic \'kō-mē\ autonomous republic NE Russia in Europe W of N Ural Mountains ✻ Syktyvkar *area* 145,221 *sq mi* (377,575 *sq km*), *pop* 965,000

Kommunizma, Pik — see COMMUNISM PEAK

Ko·mo·do \kə-'mō-(ˌ)dō\ island Indonesia in the Lesser Sundas E of Sumbawa Is. & W of Flores Is. *area* 185 *sq mi* (481 *sq km*)

Kom·so·molsk \ˌkäm-sə-'mòlsk\ city E Russia in Asia in S Khabarovsk Territory on the Amur

Ko·na \'kō-nə\ coast region Hawaii in W Hawaii (island)

Konakry — see CONAKRY

Königgrätz — see HRADEC KRALOVE

Königsberg — see KALININGRAD

Kö·niz \'kä-nəts, 'kə(r)-, 'kœ̄-\ commune W cen Switzerland SW of Bern *pop* 35,670

Kon·kan \'kän-kən\ region W India in W Maharashtra bordering on Arabian Sea & extending from Bombay S to Goa

Konstanz — see CONSTANCE

Kon·ya \kō-'nyä\ or *anc* **Ico·ni·um** \i-'kō-nē-əm\ city SW cen Turkey on edge of *cen* plateau *pop* 325,850

Ko·o·lau \'kō-nə\ mountains Hawaii in E Oahu

Koo·te·nai or (*in Canada*) **Koo·te·nay** \'kü-t²n-ˌä, -t²n-ē\ river 407 *mi* (655 *km*) SW Canada & NW U.S. in B.C., Mont., & Idaho flowing through **Kootenay Lake** (65 *mi* or 104 *km* long, in B.C.) into Columbia River

Kootenay National Park reservation Canada in SE B.C. including section of the upper Kootenay River

Ko·per \'kō-ˌper\ or **Ko·par** \-ˌpär\ or It **Ca·po·dis·tria** \ˌkä-pō-'dēs-trē-ə, ˌkä-pə-'dēs-\ town & port SW Slovenia at N end of Istrian Peninsula SSW of Trieste *pop* 16,683

Ko·peysk or **Ko·peisk** \'kō-ˌpäsk\ city SW Russia in Asia SE of Chelyabinsk *pop* 146,000

Kor·do·fan \ˌkòr-də-'fan\ region cen Sudan W & N of White Nile River; chief city El Obeid

Ko·rea \kə-'rē-ə, *esp South* (ˌ)kō-\ 1 peninsula 600 *mi* (966 *km*) long & 135 *mi* (217 *km*) wide E Asia bet. Yellow Sea & Sea of Japan 2 *or Jp* **Cho·sen** \'chō-'sen\ country coextensive with the peninsula; once a kingdom & (1910–1945) a Japanese dependency ✻ Seoul; divided 1948 at 38th parallel into republics of **North Korea** (✻ Pyongyang *area* 47,839 *sq mi or* 124,381 *sq km, pop* 18,747,000) & **South Korea** (✻ Seoul *area* 37,427 *sq mi or* 97,310 *sq km, pop* 40,448,486)

Korea Bay arm of Yellow Sea bet. Liaodong Peninsula & N. Korea

Korea Strait strait 120 *mi* (193 *km*) wide bet. S. Korea & SW Japan connecting Sea of Japan & Yellow Sea

Kórinthos — see CORINTH

Kort·rijk \'kòrt-ˌrīk\ or **Cour·trai** \kùr-'trä\ commune NW Belgium in W. Flanders on the Lys NNE of Lille *pop* 76,141

Kos or **Cos** \'käs, 'kòs\ 1 island Greece in the Dodecanese *area* 111 *sq mi* (289 *sq km*) 2 chief town on the island

Kos·ci·us·ko, Mount \ˌkä-zē-'əs-(ˌ)kō, ˌkä-sē-\ mountain 7316 *ft* (2230 *m*) SE Australia in SE New South Wales; highest in Great Dividing Range & in Australia

Ko·shi·ga·ya \kō-'shē-gä-yə; ˌkō-shi-'gä-yə, -'gī-ə\ city Japan on Honshu *pop* 285,280

Ko·si·ce \'kō-shət-ˌsä\ city E Slovakia *pop* 235,623

Ko·so·vo \'kō-sə-ˌvō, 'kä-\ autonomous region S Yugoslavia

Ko·stro·ma \ˌkäs-trə-'mä\ city cen Russia in Europe on the Volga *pop* 255,000

Ko·sza·lin \kō-'shä-ˌlēn\ city NW Poland *pop* 107,580

Kotabaru — see DJAJAPURA

Ko·ta Bha·ru \ˌkō-tə-'bär-(ˌ)ü\ city Malaysia in N Peninsular Malaysia ✻ of Kelantan *pop* 281,161

Ko·ta Kin·a·ba·lu \'kō-tə-ˌki-nə-bə-'lü\ or *formerly* **Jes·sel·ton** \'je-səl-tən\ city & port Malaysia ✻ of Sabah *pop* 112,758

Ko·tor \'kō-ˌtòr\ or It **Cat·ta·ro** \'kä-tə-ˌrō\ town & port SW Yugoslavia in Montenegro on an inlet of the Adriatic

Kottbus — see COTTBUS

Kot·te \'kō-(ˌ)tä\ town W Sri Lanka, a suburb ESE of Colombo *pop* 108,000

Kot·ze·bue Sound \'kät-si-ˌbyü\ arm of Chuckchee Sea NW Alaska NE of Bering Strait

Kou·chi·bou·guac National Park \kü-ˌshē-bü-'gwäk\ reservation SE Canada in E N.B.

Kou·dou·gou \kü-'dü-(ˌ)gü\ town cen Burkina Faso *pop* 106,000

Kovno — see KAUNAS

Kow·loon \'kaù-'lün\ 1 peninsula SE China in Hong Kong colony opposite Hong Kong Is. 2 city on Kowloon Peninsula

Koy·u·kuk \'kī-ə-ˌkək\ river 425 *mi* (684 *km*) N cen Alaska flowing from Brooks Range SW into Yukon River

Kozhikode — see CALICUT

Kra, Isthmus of \'krä\ isthmus S Thailand in N cen Malay Peninsula; 40 *mi* (64 *km*) wide at narrowest part

Krak·a·tau or **Krak·a·tao** \ˌkra-kə-'taù\ or **Krak·a·toa** \-'tō-ə\ island & volcano Indonesia bet. Sumatra & Java

Kra·ków or **Cra·cow** \'krä-ˌkaù, 'kra-, 'krä-, -(ˌ)kō, Pol 'krä-ˌküf\ city S Poland on the Vistula *pop* 748,356

Kras — see KARST

Kras·no·dar \'kras-nə-ˌdär\ 1 territory S Russia in Europe in N Caucasus region *area* 32,800 *sq mi* (85,280 *sq km*), *pop* 4,511,000 2 *or formerly* **Eka·te·ri·no·dar** \i-ˌkä-tə-'rē-nə-ˌdär\ city, its ✻, on the Kuban *pop* 560,000

Kras·no·yarsk \ˌkras-nə-'yärsk\ 1 territory W cen Russia in Asia extending along valley of the Yenisey from Arctic Ocean to Sayan Mountains *area* 928,000 *sq mi* (2,412,800 *sq km*), *pop* 2,962,000 2 city, its ✻, on the upper Yenisey *pop* 796,000

Kre·feld \'krä-ˌfelt\ or *formerly* **Krefeld–Uer·ding·en** \-'ür-diŋ-ən, -'uer-\ city W Germany on the Rhine WSW of Essen *pop* 223,969

Krim — see CRIMEA

Krish·na \'krish-nə\ or *formerly* **Kist·na** \'kist-nə\ river 800 *mi* (1287 *km*) S India flowing from Western Ghats E into Bay of Bengal

Kristiania — see OSLO

Kris·tian·sand \'kris-chən-ˌsan(d), 'krish-\ city & port SW Norway on the Skagerrak SW of Oslo *pop* 64,888

Kris·tian·sund \-ˌsün(d)\ city & port W Norway *pop* 17,936

Kríti — see CRETE

Kri·voy Rog \ˌkri-ˌvòi-'rōg, -'ròk\ or **Kryv·yy Rih** \kri-'vē-ˈrik\ city SE cen Ukraine NE of Odessa *pop* 650,000

Kron·shtadt \'krän-'shtät\ city W Russia in Europe on island in E Gulf of Finland W of St. Petersburg *pop* 45,000

Kru·ger National Park \'krü-gər\ game reserve NE Republic of South Africa in E parts of Northern Transvaal & Eastern Transvaal provinces on Mozambique border

Kru·gers·dorp \'krü-gərz-ˌdòrp, 'krǖ-ərz-\ city NE Republic of South Africa in Pretoria-Witwatersrand-Vereeniging W of Johannesburg *pop* 92,725

Krung Thep — see BANGKOK

K2 \ˌkä-'tü\ or **God·win Aus·ten** \ˌgä-dwən-'ós-tən, -'äs-\ mountain 28,250 *ft* (8611 *m*) N Kashmir in Karakoram Range; 2d highest in the world

Kua·la Lum·pur \ˌkwä-lə-'lùm-ˌpùr, -'ləm-, ˌlù-'\ city ✻ of Malaysia in Peninsular Malaysia *pop* 937,875

Kuang–chou — see GUANGZHOU

Ku·ban \kü-'ban\ river 512 *mi* (824 *km*) S Russia in Europe flowing from the Caucasus N & W into Sea of Azov

Ku·ching \'kü-chiŋ\ city & port Malaysia ✻ of Sarawak *pop* 231,490

Ku·dus \'kü-ˌdüs\ city Indonesia in cen Java NE of Semarang

Kuei — see GUI

Kuei–lin — see GUILIN

Kuei–yang — see GUIYANG

Kufra — see AL KUFRAH

Ku·iu Island \'kü-(ˌ)yü\ island SE Alaska in cen Alexander Archipelago

Ku·la Gulf \'kü-lə\ body of water 17 *mi* (27 *km*) long in the Solomons bet. New Georgia & adjacent islands

Kuldja — see YINING

Kum \'küm\ river 247 *mi* (398 *km*) cen S. Korea flowing into Yellow Sea

Ku·ma·mo·to \ˌkü-mə-'mō-(ˌ)tō\ city Japan in W Kyushu *pop* 579,305

Ku·ma·si \kü-'mä-sē, -'ma-\ city S cen Ghana in Ashanti *pop* 376,346

Kumgang — see DIAMOND

Kunene — see CUNENE

Kun·lun \'kün-'lün\ mountains W China extending from the Pamirs & Karakoram Range E along N edge of Tibetan plateau to SE Qinghai — see MUZTAG

Kun·ming \'kün-'miŋ\ or *formerly* **Yun·nan** \yü-'nän\ or **Yun·nan·fu** \-'fü\ city S China ✻ of Yunnan *pop* 900,000

Kun·san \'kün-ˌsän\ city & port W S. Korea on Yellow Sea at mouth of the Kum *pop* 185,649

Kuo·pio \'kwò-pē-ˌò\ city S cen Finland *pop* 80,002

Ku·pre·a·nof \ˌkü-prē-'a-ˌnòf\ island SE Alaska in E Alexander Archipelago

Ku·ra \kə-'rä, 'kür-ə\ river 825 *mi* (1328 *km*) W Asia in Transcaucasia flowing from NE Turkey ESE through Georgia & Azerbaijan into Caspian Sea

Ku·ra·shi·ki \kü-'rä-shē-kē, ˌkur-ə-'shē-kē\ city Japan on Honshu *pop* 414,692

Kur·di·stan \ˌkur-də-'stan, ˌkər-, -'stän; 'kər-də-,\ region SW Asia chiefly in E Turkey, NW Iran, & N Iraq

Ku·re Island \'kur-ē, 'kyur-; 'kü-(ˌ)rä\ *or* **Ocean Island** island *cen* Pacific in Hawaii, westernmost of the Leewards

Kurg — see COORG

Kur·gan \kur-'gan, -'gän\ city SW Russia in Asia E of Chelyabinsk *pop* 310,000

Ku·ria Mu·ria Islands \ˌkur-ē-ə-'mur-ē-ə, ˌkyur-, -'myur-\ islands in Arabian Sea off SW Oman belonging to Oman *area* 28 *sq mi* (73 *sq km*), *pop* 85

Ku·ril Islands *or* **Ku·rile Islands** \'kyur-ˌēl, 'kur-; kyù-'rē(ə)l, ku-\ islands Russia in the Pacific bet. S Kamchatka & NE Hokkaido, Japan; belonged 1875–1945 to Japan *area* 3960 *sq mi* (10,296 *sq km*)

Kur·isch·es Haff \ˌkur-i-shəs-'häf\ *or* **Cour·land Lagoon** \'kur-lənd\ *or* **Kur·skiy Za·liv** \ˌkur-skyē-'zä-lif\ inlet of the Baltic on border bet. Lithuania & Russia *area* 625 *sq mi* (1625 *sq km*)

Kur·land *or* **Cour·land** \'kur-lənd\ region W Latvia bordering on the Baltic & Gulf of Riga

Kur·nool \kər-'nül\ city S India in W Andhra Pradesh SSW of Hyderabad *pop* 206,661

Kursk \'kursk\ city SW Russia in Europe on the Seym *pop* 375,000

Ku·saie \kü-'sï-ˌä\ island E Carolines, part of Federated States of Micronesia

Kush — see CUSH

Kus·ko·kwim \'kəs-kə-ˌkwim\ river 550 *mi* (885 *km*) SW Alaska flowing SW into Kuskokwim Bay (inlet of Bering Sea)

Kut \'küt\ *or* **Al–kut** \al-\ *or* **Kut–al–Ima·ra** \ˌal-ē-'mär-ə\ city SE *cen* Iraq on the Tigris SE of Baghdad *pop* 42,116

Ku·tah·ya \kü-'tä-yə\ city W *cen* Turkey *pop* 101,087

Kutch *or* **Cutch** \'kəch\ former principality & state W India N of Gulf of Kutch **☀** Bhuj; now part of Gujarat

Kutch, Gulf of inlet of Arabian Sea W India N of Kathiawar

Kutch, Rann of \'rən\ salt marsh in S Pakistan & W India stretching in an arc from the mouths of the Indus to the head of Gulf of Kutch

Ku·wait \ku-'wät\ **1** country SW Asia in Arabia at head of Persian Gulf; a sheikhdom, before 1961 under Brit. protection *area* 6178 *sq mi* (16,063 *sq km*), *pop* 1,355,827 **2** city & port, its **☀** *pop* 181,774 — **Ku·waiti** \-'wä-tē\ *adj or n*

Kuybyshev — see SAMARA

Kuz·netsk \kuz-'netsk\ city SE *cen* Russia in Europe

Kuznetsk Basin *or* **Kuz·bass** *or* **Kuz·bas** \'kuz-,bas\ basin of the Tom R. Russia in Asia extending from Novokuznetsk to Tomsk

Kwa·ja·lein \'kwä-jə-lən, -,län\ island (atoll) 78 *mi* (126 *km*) long W Pacific in Ralik chain of the Marshalls; encloses lagoon (*area* 650 *sq mi or* 1690 *sq km*)

Kwan·do \'kwän-(ˌ)dō\ river 600 *mi* (966 *km*) S Africa flowing from *cen* Angola SE & E into the Zambezi just above Victoria Falls

Kwang·cho·wan \'gwän-'jō-'wän, 'kwän-\ former territory SE China in Kwangtung on Leizhou Peninsula; leased 1898–1946 to France **☀** Fort Bayard *area* 325 *sq mi* (845 *sq km*)

Kwang·ju \'gwän-(ˌ)jü, 'kwän-\ city SW S. Korea *pop* 905,896

Kwangsi Chuang — see GUANGXI ZHUANGZU

Kwangtung — see GUANGDONG

Kwan·tung \'gwän-'duŋ, 'kwän-, -'tuŋ\ former territory NE China in S Manchuria at tip of Liaodong Peninsula; leased to Russia 1898–1905, to Japan 1905–45, & to Russia again 1945–55; included cities of Port Arthur & Dairen

Kwa·Zu·lu \kwä-'zü-(ˌ)lü\ former group of noncontiguous black enclaves in E Republic of South Africa; abolished 1994

Kweichow — see GUIZHOU

Kweilin — see GUILIN

Kyo·ga *or* **Kio·ga** \kē-'ō-gə\ lake *cen* Uganda N of Lake Victoria traversed by the Victoria Nile *area* 1000 *sq mi* (2600 *sq km*)

Kyo·to \kē-'ō-(ˌ)tō\ city Japan in W *cen* Honshu NNE of Osaka; formerly (794–1869) **☀** of Japan *pop* 1,461,140

Kyr·gyz·stan \ˌkir-gi-'stan, -'stän; 'kir-gi-,\ independent country W *cen* Asia; a constituent republic (**Kir·giz Republic** *or* **Kir·ghiz Republic** \(,\)kir-'gēz\ *or* **Kir·ghi·zia** \kir-'gē-zh(ē-)ə, -zē-ə\) of the U.S.S.R. 1936–91; **☀** Bishkek *area* 76,100 *sq mi* (197,860 *sq km*), *pop* 4,291,000

Kyu·shu \kē-'ü-(ˌ)shü\ island S Japan S of W end of Honshu *area* 16,240 *sq mi* (42,224 *sq km*) *pop* 13,296,054

Labe — see ELBE

Lab·ra·dor \'la-brə-ˌdor\ **1** peninsula E Canada bet. Hudson Bay & the Atlantic; divided bet. Que. & Nfld. **2** the section of the peninsula belonging to Nfld. *area* 101,881 *sq mi* (264,891 *sq km*) — **Lab·ra·dor·ean** *or* **Lab·ra·dor·ian** \ˌla-brə-'dor-ē-ən, -'dor-\ *adj or n*

Labrador Sea arm of the Atlantic bet. Labrador & Greenland

La·bu·an \lə-'bü-ən\ island Malaysia off W coast of Sabah *pop* 14,904

La Ca·na·da–Flint·ridge \ˌlä-kə-'nyä-də-'flint-(ˌ)rij\ city SW Calif. NW of Pasadena *pop* 19,378

Lac·ca·dive Islands \'la-kə-ˌdēv, -ˌdïv\ *or* **Can·na·nore Islands** \'ka-nə-ˌnōr\ islands India in Arabian Sea N of Maldive Islands

Lacedaemon — see SPARTA — **Lac·e·dae·mo·nian** \ˌla-sə-di-'mō-nē-ən, -nyən\ *adj or n*

La·cey \'lä-sē\ city W Wash. E of Olympia *pop* 19,279

La Chaux–de–Fonds \lä-ˌshō-də-'fōⁿ\ commune W Switzerland in Neuchâtel canton in Jura Mountains WNW of Bern *pop* 36,107

La·chine \lə-'shēn\ town Canada in S Que. above the **Lachine Rapids** on St. Lawrence River SW of Montreal *pop* 35,266

La·chish \'lä-kish\ ancient city S Palestine W of Hebron

Lach·lan \'lä-klən\ river 800 *mi* (1287 *km*) SE Australia in *cen* New South Wales flowing W into the Murrumbidgee

Lack·a·wan·na \ˌla-kə-'wä-nə\ city W N.Y. *pop* 20,585

La·co·nia \lə-'kō-nē-ə, -nyə\ ancient country S Greece in SE Peloponnisos bordering on the Aegean & the Mediterranean **☀** Sparta — **La·co·ni·an** \-nē-ən, -nyən\ *adj or n*

Laconia, Gulf of inlet of the Mediterranean on S coast of Greece in Peloponnisos bet. Capes Matapan & Malea

La Co·ru·ña \ˌlä-kə-'rü-nyə\ **1** province NW Spain in Galicia bordering on the Atlantic *area* 3051 *sq mi* (7933 *sq km*), *pop* 1,068,088 **2** *or* **Co·run·na** \kə-'rə-nə\ commune & port, its **☀** *pop* 231,721

La Crosse \lə-'kros\ city W Wis. *pop* 51,003

La·dakh \lə-'däk\ district N India in E Kashmir on border of Tibet **☀** Leh *area* 45,762 *sq mi* (118,981 *sq km*) — **La·dakhi** \-'dä-kē\ *adj or n*

Lad·o·ga, Lake \'lä-də-gə, 'lä-\ lake W Russia in Europe near St. Petersburg *area* 7000 *sq mi* (18,200 *sq km*); largest in Europe

La·dy·smith \'lä-dē-ˌsmith\ city E Republic of South Africa in W Natal *pop* 28,920

Lae \'lä-ˌä\ city Papua New Guinea on Huon Gulf *pop* 61,617

La·fay·ette \ˌla-fē-'et, ˌlä-\ **1** city W Calif. E of Berkeley *pop* 23,501 **2** city W *cen* Ind. *pop* 43,764 **3** city S La. *pop* 94,440

La·gash \'lä-ˌgash\ ancient city of Sumer bet. the Euphrates & the Tigris at modern village of Telloh \te-'lō\ in S Iraq

Lagoa Dos Patos — see PATOS (Lagoa dos)

La·gos \'lä-ˌgäs, -ˌgōs\ city & port, former **☀** of Nigeria on an offshore island in Bight of Benin & on mainland opposite the island *pop* 1,060,848

La Gou·lette \ˌlä-gù-'let\ city N Tunisia on Bay of Tunis; port for Tunis *pop* 41,912

La Grange \lə-'grānj\ city W Ga. *pop* 25,597

La Granja — see SAN ILDEFONSO

La Guai·ra \lə-'gwī-rə\ city N Venezuela on the Caribbean; port for Caracas *pop* 20,344

La·gu·na Beach \lə-'gü-nə\ city SW Calif. SE of Long Beach *pop* 23,170

Laguna Madre — see MADRE (Laguna)

La·gu·na Ni·guel \lä-'gü-nə-nē-'gel\ city Calif. *pop* 44,400

La Habana — see HAVANA

La Ha·bra \lə-'hä-brə\ city SW Calif. SE of Los Angeles *pop* 51,266

La Hague, Cape \lə-'häg, -'häg\ *or* **F Cap de la Hague** \käp-də-là-ˈäg\ headland NW France at tip of Cotentin Peninsula

Lake Hav·a·su City \'ha-və-ˌsü\ city W Ariz. *pop* 24,363

La Hogue \lə-'hōg\ roadstead NW France in English Channel off E coast of Cotentin Peninsula

La·hore \lə-'hōr, -'hor\ city Pakistan in E Punjab province near the Ravi *pop* 2,922,000

Lah·ti \'lä-tē\ city S Finland NNE of Helsinki *pop* 93,132

La Jol·la \lə-'hoi-ə\ a NW section of San Diego, Calif.

Lake Charles \'chär(-ə)lz\ city SW La. *pop* 70,580

Lake Clark National Park \'klärk\ reservation S *cen* Alaska WSW of Anchorage

Lake District area NW England in S Cumbria & NW Lancashire containing many lakes & peaks

Lake Jack·son \'jak-sən\ city SE Tex. *pop* 22,776

Lake·land \'läk-lənd\ city *cen* Fla. E of Tampa *pop* 70,576

Lake Os·we·go \-ä-'swē-(ˌ)gō\ city NW Oreg. S of Portland *pop* 30,576

Lake·ville \'läk-ˌvil\ village SE Minn. SE of Minneapolis *pop* 24,854

Lake·wood \'läk-ˌwud\ **1** city SW Calif. NE of Long Beach *pop* 73,557 **2** city *cen* Colo. W of Denver *pop* 126,481 **3** city NE Ohio on Lake Erie W of Cleveland *pop* 59,718

Lake Worth \'worth\ city SE Fla. on Lake Worth (lagoon) S of W. Palm Beach *pop* 28,564

Lak·shad·weep \lək-'shä-dwēp, ˌlək-shə-'dwēp\ *or formerly* **Lac·ca·dive, Min·i·coy, and Amin·di·vi Islands** \'la-kə-ˌdēv, -ˌdïv; 'mi-ni-ˌkoi; ˌə-mən-'dē-vē\ union territory India comprising the Laccadive group **☀** Kavaratti *area* 11 *sq mi* (29 *sq km*), *pop* 40,237

La Li·nea \lä-'lē-nē-ə\ commune SW Spain on Bay of Algeciras *pop* 51,021

La Man·cha \lə-'män-chə, -'man-\ region S *cen* Spain in S New Castile — **Man·che·gan** \man-'chē-gən, män-'chä-\ *adj or n*

La Mau·ri·cie National Park \lä-ˌmor-ē-'sē\ reservation SE Canada in S Quebec

Lam·ba·ré·né \ˌläm-bə-'rä-nē, -rə-'nä\ city W Gabon *pop* 17,770

Lam·beth \'lam-bəth, -ˌbeth\ borough of S Greater London, England *pop* 256,200

La Me·sa \lə-'mā-sə\ city SW Calif. NE of San Diego *pop* 52,931

La·mia \lə-'mē-ə\ city E *cen* Greece NW of Thermopylae *pop* 43,898

La Mi·ra·da \ˌlä-mə-'rä-də\ city SW Calif. SE of Los Angeles *pop* 40,452

Lam·mer·muir \'la-mər-ˌmyur\ *or* **Lam·mer·moor** \-ˌmur\ hills SE Scotland in Lothian & Borders regions

Lam·pe·du·sa \ˌlam-pə-'dü-sə, -zə\ island Italy in the Pelagians

La·nai \lə-'nï, lä-\ island Hawaii W of Maui *area* 141 *sq mi* (367 *sq km*)

Lan·ark \'la-nərk\ *or* **Lan·ark·shire** \-ˌshir, -shər\ former county S *cen* Scotland; chief city Glasgow **2** burgh *cen* Scotland in Strathclyde SE of Glasgow *pop* 9778

Lan·ca·shire \'laŋ-kə-ˌshir, -shər\ *or* **Lan·cas·ter** \'laŋ-kəs-tər\ county NW England bordering on Irish Sea **☀** Preston *area* 1174 *sq mi* (3052 *sq km*), *pop* 1,382,200

Lan·cas·ter \'laŋ-kəs-tər; 'lan-ˌkas-tər, 'laŋ-\ **1** city SW Calif. NE of Los Angeles *pop* 97,291 **2** city S *cen* Ohio SE of Columbus *pop* 34,507 **3** city SE Pa. *pop* 55,551 **4** city NE Tex. S of Dallas *pop* 22,117 **5** city NW England in Lancashire *pop* 46,321 — **Lan·cas·tri·an** \'kas-trē-ən, lan-\ *adj or n*

Landes \'läⁿ(n)d\ coastal region SW France on Bay of Biscay bet. Gironde estuary & the Adour

Land's End \'lan(d)z-'end\ cape SW England at SW tip of Cornwall; extreme W point of England, at 5°41′W

Lang·dale Pikes \'laŋ-ˌdäl\ two mountain peaks NW England in Cumbria in Lake District

Lang·ley \'laŋ-lē\ city Canada in B.C. ESE of Vancouver *pop* 66,040

Lan·gue·doc \ˌlaŋ-gə-'däk, ˌläⁿg-'dok\ region & former province S France extending from Auvergne to the Mediterranean

Lanka — see CEYLON

\ə\ abut \ᵊ\ kitten, F table \ər\ further \a\ ash \ā\ ace \ä\ mop, mar \aù\ out \ch\ chin \e\ bet \ē\ easy \g\ go \i\ hit \ï\ ice \j\ job \ŋ\ sing \ō\ go \ò\ law \òi\ boy \th\ thin \t̲h̲\ the \ü\ loot \ù\ foot \y\ yet \zh\ vision \à, k̲, ⁿ, œ, œ̄, ue, uē, ᵊ\ *see* Guide to Pronunciation

Lan·sing \'lan(t)-siŋ\ **1** village NE Ill. SSE of Chicago *pop* 28,086 **2** city S Mich., its ✳ *pop* 127,321

Lan·tao \'län-'daù\ island Hong Kong colony W of Hong Kong Is. *area* 58 *sq mi* (151 *sq km*)

La·nús \lə-'nüs\ city E Argentina S of Buenos Aires *pop* 465,891

Lan·zhou *or* **Lan–chou** \'län-'jō\ city N *cen* China ✳ of Gansu *pop* 1,500,000

La·od·i·cea \(,)lā-,ä-də-'sē-ə\ **1** ancient city W *cen* Asia Minor in Phrygia **2** — see LATAKIA — **La·od·i·ce·an** \-'sē-ən\ *adj or n*

Laoighis \'läsh, 'lēsh\ *or* **Leix** \'läsh, 'lēsh\ *or formerly* **Queen's** county *cen* Ireland in Leinster ✳ Portlaoighise *area* 664 *sq mi* (1726 *sq km*), *pop* 52,325

Laon \'lä\ commune N France NE of Paris *pop* 27,420

Laos \'laùs, 'läs\ country SE Asia; a republic, until 1975 a kingdom; formerly a state of French Indochina; ✳ Vientiane *area* 91,482 *sq mi* (237,853 *sq km*), *pop* 4,104,000

La Pal·ma \lə-'päl-mə\ island Spain in Canary Islands; chief town Santa Cruz de la Palma *area* 280 *sq mi* (728 *sq km*)

La Paz \lə-'päz, -'päs, -'paz\ **1** city, administrative ✳ of Bolivia E of Lake Titicaca at altitude of 11,910 *ft* (3630 *m*), *pop* 635,283 **2** town W Mexico ✳ of Baja California Sur on **La Paz Bay** (inlet of Gulf of California) *pop* 46,011

Lap·land \'lap-,land, -lənd\ region N Europe above the arctic circle in N Norway, N Sweden, N Finland, & Kola Peninsula of Russia — **Lap·land·er** \-,lan-dər, -lən-\ *n*

La Pla·ta \lə-'plä-tə\ city E Argentina SE of Buenos Aires *pop* 454,884

La Plata Peak \lə-'pla-tə, -'plä-\ mountain 14,336 *ft* (4370 *m*) *cen* Colo. in Sawatch Mountains

La Porte \lə-'pōrt, -'pȯrt\ **1** city N Ind. *pop* 21,507 **2** city SE Tex. on Galveston Bay *pop* 27,910

Lap·tev Sea \'lap-,tef, -,tev\ *or formerly* **Nor·den·skjöld Sea** \'nȯr-dᵊn-,shȯld, -,shùld, -,shēld\ arm of Arctic Ocean Russia bet. Taimyr Peninsula & New Siberian Islands

La Pu·en·te \lä-'pwen-tē\ city SW Calif. ESE of Los Angeles *pop* 36,955

L'Aqui·la \'lä-kwi-lə, 'lä-\ commune *cen* Italy NE of Rome ✳ of Abruzzi *pop* 67,348

Lar·a·mie \'lar-ə-mē\ **1** river 200 *mi* (322 *km*) N Colo. & SE Wyo. flowing N & NE into N. Platte River **2** city SE Wyo. *pop* 26,687

Larch \'lärch\ river 270 *mi* (434 *km*) Canada in W Que. flowing NE to unite with the Caniapiskau forming Koksoak River

La·re·do \lə-'rā-(,)dō\ city S Tex. on Rio Grande *pop* 122,899

Lar·go \'lär-(,)gō\ town W Fla. S of Clearwater *pop* 65,674

La Rio·ja \,lä-rē-'ō-hä\ *or the* **Rioja** region N Spain along the upper Ebro

La·ris·sa \lə-'ri-sə\ city N *cen* Greece in E Thessaly *pop* 113,426

Lar·i·stan \,lar-ə-'stan\ region S Iran bordering on Persian Gulf

Larne \'lärn\ district NE Northern Ireland, established 1974 *area* 131 *sq mi* (341 *sq km*), *pop* 28,929

La Ro·chelle \,lä-rō-'shel\ city & port W France *pop* 72,936

Lar·vik \'lär-vik\ town & port SE Norway *pop* 8133

La·Salle \lə-'sal\ town Canada in S Que. on the St. Lawrence *pop* 73,804

Las·caux \la-'skō\ cave SW *cen* France near town of Montignac

Las Cru·ces \läs-'krü-səs\ city S N.Mex. *pop* 62,126

La Se·re·na \,lä-sə-'rā-nə\ city N *cen* Chile *pop* 83,283

Lashkar — see GWALIOR

Las Pal·mas \läs-'päl-məs\ **1** province Spain comprising the E Canary Islands *area* 1279 *sq mi* (3325 *sq km*), *pop* 767,912 **2** city & port, its ✳, in NE Grand Canary Is. *pop* 360,098

La Spe·zia \lä-'spet-sē-ə\ city & port NW Italy in Liguria *pop* 104,511

Las·sen Peak \'la-sᵊn\ volcano 10,457 *ft* (3187 *m*) N Calif. at S end of Cascade Range; central feature of **Lassen Volcanic National Park**

Las Ve·gas \läs-'vā-gəs\ city SE corner of Nev. *pop* 258,295

Lat·a·kia \,la-tə-'kē-ə\ *or anc* **La·od·i·cea** \(,)lä-,ä-də-'sē-ə\ city & port, its chief town, on the Mediterranean *pop* 196,791

La·ti·na \lə-'tē-nə\ commune *cen* Italy *pop* 101,936

Latin America **1** Spanish America & Brazil **2** all of the Americas S of the U.S. — **Latin–American** *adj* — **Latin American** *n*

Latin Quarter section of Paris, France, S of the Seine frequented by students & artists

La·tium \'lā-sh(ē-)əm\ *or It* **La·zio** \'lät-sē-,ō\ region *cen* Italy bordering on Tyrrhenian Sea & traversed by the Tiber ✳ Rome *pop* 5,170,672

Lat·via \'lat-vē-ə\ independent country N *cen* Europe bordering on the Baltic; an independent republic 1918–40, a constituent republic (**Latvian Republic** \'lat-vē-ən\) of the U.S.S.R. 1940–91; ✳ Riga *area* 25,200 *sq mi* (65,520 *sq km*), *pop* 2,681,000

Lau·der·dale Lakes \'lȯ-dər-,dāl\ city SE Fla. *pop* 27,341

Lau·der·hill \'lȯ-dər-,hil\ city SE Fla. *pop* 49,708

Laun·ces·ton \'lȯn(t)-səs-tən, 'län(t)-\ city & port Australia in N Tasmania *pop* (with suburbs) 66,286

Lau·ra·sia \lȯ-'rä-zhə, -shə\ hypothetical land area believed to have once connected the landmasses of the northern hemisphere except for the Indian subcontinent

Lau·rel \'lȯr-əl, 'lär-\ town S Md. NNE of Washington, D.C. *pop* 19,438

Lau·ren·tian Hills \lȯ-'ren(t)-shən\ hills Canada in S Que. N of the St. Lawrence On S edge of Canadian Shield

Laurentian Shield — see CANADIAN SHIELD

Lau·ri·um \'lȯr-ē-əm, 'lär-\ mountain SE Greece at SE tip of Attica

Lau·sanne \lō-'zän, -'zan\ commune W Switzerland ✳ of Vaud canton on Lake of Geneva *pop* 124,897

Lausitz — see LUSATIA

Lava Beds National Monument reservation N Calif. SE of Lower Klamath Lake

La·val \lə-'val\ town Canada in S Que. NW of Montreal *pop* 314,398

La Vendée — see VENDÉE

La Verne \lə-'vərn\ city SW Calif. E of Los Angeles *pop* 30,897

Lawn·dale \'lȯn-,dāl, 'län-\ city SW Calif. SSW of Los Angeles *pop* 27,331

Law·rence \'lȯr-ən(t)s, 'lär-\ **1** town *cen* Ind. NE of Indianapolis *pop* 26,763 **2** city NE Kans. WSW of Kansas City *pop* 65,608 **3** city NE corner of Mass. *pop* 70,207

Law·ton \'lȯ-tᵊn\ city SW Okla. *pop* 80,561

Lay·san \'lī-,sän\ island Hawaii in the Leewards NW of Niihau

Lay·ton \'lā-tᵊn\ city N Utah N of Salt Lake City *pop* 41,784

League City \'lēg\ city SE Tex. *pop* 30,159

Leam·ing·ton \'le-miŋ-tən\ *or* **Royal Leamington Spa** borough S *cen* England in Warwickshire *pop* 44,989

Leav·en·worth \'le-vən-,wərth\ city NE Kans. on Missouri River NW of Kansas City *pop* 38,495

Lea·wood \'lē-,wùd\ city E Kans. S of Kansas City *pop* 19,693

Leb·a·non **1** \'le-bə-nən\ city SE *cen* Pa. E of Harrisburg *pop* 24,800 **2** \-nən, -,nän\ country SW Asia bordering on the Mediterranean; a republic since 1944, formerly (1920–44) a French mandate ✳ Beirut *area* 4105 *sq mi* (10,673 *sq km*), *pop* 2,707,000 — **Leb·a·nese** \,le-bə-'nēz, -'nēs\ *adj or n*

Lebanon Mountains *or anc* **Lib·a·nus** \'li-bə-nəs\ mountains Lebanon running parallel to coast W of Bekaa Valley

Lebda — see HOMS

Le Bour·get \lə-,bùr-'zhā\ commune N France, NE suburb of Paris

Lec·ce \'lā-chē, 'le-, -(,)chā\ commune SE Italy in Apulia *pop* 101,957

Lec·co \'lā-(,)kō, 'le-\ commune N Italy in Lombardy on SE arm (**Lake Lecco**) of Lake Como *pop* 47,174

Lech \'lek, 'lek\ river 177 *mi* (285 *km*) Austria & Germany flowing from Vorarlberg N into the Danube

Le·do \'lē-(,)dō, 'lā-\ town NE India in NE Assam

Leeds \'lēdz\ city N England in W. Yorkshire *pop* 448,528

Lee's Summit \'lēz\ city W Mo. SE of Kansas City *pop* 46,418

Leeu·war·den \'lā-,vär-dᵊn\ commune N Netherlands ✳ of Friesland *pop* 85,058

Lee·ward Islands \'lē-wərd\ **1** island chain *cen* Pacific extending 1250 *mi* (2012 *km*) WNW from main islands of the Hawaiian group; includes Nihoa, Necker, Laysan, Midway, & Kure islands **2** *or F* **Iles sous le Vent** \ēl-sü-lə-vän\ islands S Pacific, W group of the Society Islands *pop* 22,232 **3** islands West Indies in the N Lesser Antilles extending from Virgin Islands (on N) to Dominica (on S) **4** former colony Brit. West Indies in the Leewards including Antigua, St. Kitts= Nevis, & Montserrat

Leg·horn \'leg-,hȯrn, 'le-,gȯrn\ *or It* **Li·vor·no** \lē-'vȯr-(,)nō\ commune & port *cen* Italy in Tuscany on Tyrrhenian Sea *pop* 171,346

Leg·ni·ca \leg-'nēt-sə\ city SW Poland *pop* 104,196

Leh \'lā\ town India in E Kashmir on the Indus ✳ of Ladakh

Le Ha·vre \lə-'hävrᵊ, -'häv\ *or* **Havre** *or formerly* **Le Havre–de–Grâce** \-də-'gräs\ city & port N France on English Channel on N side of Seine estuary *pop* 216,917

Le·high \'lē-,hī\ river 100 *mi* (161 *km*) E Pa. flowing SW & SE into Delaware River

Leh·man Caves \'lē-mən\ limestone caverns E Nev. on E slope of Wheeler Peak in Great Basin National Park

Leices·ter \'les-tər\ city *cen* England ✳ of Leicestershire *pop* 279,791

Leices·ter·shire \'les-tər-,shir, -shər\ *or* **Leicester** \'les-tər\ county *cen* England ✳ Leicester *area* 986 *sq mi* (2564 *sq km*), *pop* 857,700

Lei·den *or* **Ley·den** \'lī-dᵊn, *D usu* 'lā-yə\ city W Netherlands in S. Holland on a branch of the lower Rhine *pop* 103,678

Leie — see LYS

Lei·ne \'lī-nə\ river 119 *mi* (192 *km*) *cen* Germany

Lein·ster \'len(t)-stər\ province E Ireland *area* 7580 *sq mi* (19,708 *sq km*), *pop* 1,860,037

Leip·zig \'līp-sig, -sik\ city E Germany in Saxony *pop* 561,867

Lei·ria \lā-'rē-ə\ town W *cen* Portugal SSW of Coimbra

Leith \'lēth\ port section of Edinburgh, Scotland, on Firth of Forth

Lei·tha \'lī-(,)tä\ river 112 *mi* (180 *km*) E Austria & NW Hungary flowing SE into the Raba

Lei·trim \'lē-trəm\ county NW Ireland in Connacht ✳ Carrick on Shannon *area* 589 *sq mi* (1531 *sq km*), *pop* 25,297

Leix — see LAOIGHIS

Lei·xões \lā-'shōⁱsh\ town NW Portugal on the Atlantic; port for Porto

Lei·zhou *or* **Lei–chou** \'lā-'jō\ *or* **Lui–chow** \lə-'wē-'jō\ peninsula SE China in Guangdong bet. S. China Sea & Gulf of Tonkin

Lek \'lek\ river 40 *mi* (64 *km*) Netherlands flowing W into the Atlantic; the N branch of the lower Rhine

Lely·stad \'lā-lə-,stät\ commune *cen* Netherlands ✳ of Flevoland

Le Maine — see MAINE

Leman, Lake — see GENEVA (Lake of)

Le Mans \lə-'mäⁿ\ city NW France on the Sarthe *pop* 150,289

Le Marche — see MARCHES

Lemberg — see LVOV

Lem·nos \'lem-,näs, -nəs\ *or NGk* **Lím·nos** \'lēm-,nȯs\ island Greece in the Aegean ESE of Chalcidice peninsula; chief town Kástron *area* 175 *sq mi* (455 *sq km*)

Lemon Grove city S Calif. E of San Diego *pop* 23,984

Le·na \'lē-nə, 'lā-\ river 3000 *mi* (4828 *km*) E Russia in Asia flowing from mountains W of Lake Baikal NE & N into Laptev Sea through wide delta

Le·nexa \lə-'nek-sə\ city E Kans. SW of Kansas City *pop* 34,034

Leningrad — see SAINT PETERSBURG **2** — **Len·in·grad·er** \'le-nən-,gra-dər, -,grä-\ *n*

Le·nin Peak \'le-nən, 'lā-, -,nēn\ mountain 23,405 *ft* (7134 *m*) on border bet. Kyrgyzstan & Tajikistan; highest in Trans Alai Range

Lens \'läⁿs\ city N France SW of Lille *pop* 39,973

Leom·in·ster \'le-mən-stər\ city *cen* Mass. N of Worcester *pop* 38,145

Le·ón \lā-'ōn\ **1** *or* **León de los Al·da·mas** \də-lōs-,al-'dä-məs\ city *cen* Mexico in Guanajuato *pop* 453,976 **2** city W Nicaragua *pop* 90,897 **3** region & ancient kingdom NW Spain W of Old Castile **4** province NW Spain in N León region *area* 5936 *sq mi* (15,434 *sq km*), *pop* 491,911 **5** city, its ✳ *pop* 127,095

Le·o·ne, Mon·te \,mōn-tē-lā-'ō-nē\ mountain 11,657 *ft* (3553 *m*) on border bet. Switzerland & Italy SW of Simplon Pass; highest in Lepontine Alps

Le·o·pold II, Lake \'lē-ə-,pōld, 'lā-\ lake 90 *mi* (145 *km*) long W Zaire

Léopoldville — see KINSHASA

Lepanto, Gulf of — see CORINTH

Le·pon·tine Alps \li-'pän-,tīn, 'le-pən-\ range of *cen* Alps on border bet. Switzerland & Italy — see LEONE (Monte)

Lep·tis Mag·na \\,lep-təs-'mag-nə\ ancient seaport N Africa near present-day Homs

Lé·ri·da \'lā-rə-də, 'ler-ə-\ **1** province NE Spain in NW Catalonia *area* 4690 *sq mi* (12,194 *sq km*), *pop* 340,167 **2** commune, its * *pop* 106,814

Ler·wick \'lər-(,)wik, 'ler-\ burgh & port N Scotland * of Shetland on Mainland Is. *pop* 7223

Les Ey·zies \,lāz-ā-'zē\ commune SW *cen* France SE of Périgueux

Le·so·tho \lə-'sō-(,)tō, -'sü-(,)tü\ *or formerly* **Ba·su·to·land** \bə-'sü-tə-,land\ country S Africa surrounded by Republic of South Africa; a constitutional monarchy, in the Commonwealth of Nations * Maseru *area* 11,716 *sq mi* (30,462 *sq km*), *pop* 1,528,000

Lesser Antilles islands in the W. Indies including Virgin, Leeward, & Windward Islands, Trinidad, Barbados, Tobago, & islands in the S Caribbean N of Venezuela

Lesser Armenia region S Turkey corresponding to ancient Cilicia

Lesser Slave Lake \'slāv\ lake Canada in *cen* Alta. draining through the **Lesser Slave River** to Athabasca River *area* 461 *sq mi* (1199 *sq km*)

Lesser Sunda Islands — see SUNDA ISLANDS

Lés·vos \'lez-,vòs\ *or* **Les·bos** \'lez-,bäs, -bəs\ island Greece in the Aegean off NW Turkey *area* 623 *sq mi* (1620 *sq km*) *pop* 103,700

Leth·bridge \'leth-(,)brij\ city Canada in S Alta. *pop* 60,974

Le·ti·cia \lə-'tē-sē-ə\ town SE Colombia on the Amazon

Leuc·tra \'lük-trə\ ancient village Greece in Boeotia SW of Thebes

Leuven — see LOUVAIN

Le·val·lois–Per·ret \lə-,val-'wä-pə-'rā\ commune N France on the Seine, NW suburb of Paris *pop* 52,460

Le·vant \lə-'vant\ the countries bordering on the E Mediterranean — **Le·van·tine** \'le-vən-,tīn, -,tēn, lə-'van-\ *adj or n*

Levant States — see SYRIA

Le·ven, Loch \'lē-vən\ **1** inlet of Loch Linnhe W Scotland in Highland region **2** lake 4 *mi* (6.4 *km*) long E Scotland SSE of Perth

Le·ver·ku·sen \'lā-vər-,kü-zªn\ city W Germany on the Rhine SE of Düsseldorf *pop* 160,825

Lé·vis–Lau·zon \'lē-vəs-lō-'zōⁿ, lā-'vē-\ town Canada in S Que. *pop* 39,452

Lev·kás \lef-'käs\ island Greece in the Ionians at entrance to Ambracian Gulf *area* 111 *sq mi* (289 *sq km*)

Lew·es \'lü-əs\ **1** the upper Yukon River S of its junction with the Pelly **2** borough S England * of E. Sussex on Ouse River S of London

Lewis and Clark Cavern \'lü-əs-ən(d)-'klärk\ *or* **Mor·ri·son Cave** \'mòr-ə-sən, 'mär-\ cavern *cen* Mont. WNW of Bozeman

Lewis and Clark Lake 30 *mi* (48 *km*) long SE S.Dak. & NE Nebr. formed by Gavins Point Dam

Lew·i·sham \'lü-ə-shəm\ borough of SE Greater London, England *pop* 238,600

Lew·is·ton \'lü-əs-tən\ **1** city NW Idaho on Wash. border *pop* 28,082 **2** city SW Maine on the Androscoggin opposite Auburn *pop* 39,757

Lew·is·ville \'lü-əs-,vil, -vəl\ city N Tex. *pop* 46,521

Lewis with Har·ris \'lü-əs-with-'har-əs, -wəth-\ island NW Scotland in the Outer Hebrides divided administratively into **Lewis** (in the N; chief town & port Stornoway) & **Harris** (in the S); largest of the Hebrides, in Western Isles regional division *area* 770 *sq mi* (2002 *sq km*)

Lex·ing·ton \'lek-siŋ-tən\ town NE Mass. NW of Boston *pop* 28,974

Lexington–Fay·ette \-'fā-'et, -'fā-ət\ city N *cen* Kentucky ESE of Frankfort *pop* 225,366

Leyden — see LEIDEN

Ley·te \'lā-tē\ island Philippines in the Visayans W of **Leyte Gulf** (inlet of the Pacific); chief town Tacloban *area* 2785 *sq mi* (7241 *sq km*)

Ley·ton \'lā-tⁿn\ former municipal borough SE England in Essex, now part of Waltham Forest

Lha·sa \'läs-ə, 'la-\ city SW China * of Tibet *pop* 175,000

Lho·tse \'lōt-,sā, 'hlòt-\ mountain 27,923 *ft* (8511 *m*) in Mt. Everest massif S of Mt. Everest; 4th highest in the world

Lian·yun·gang \lē-'än-'yün-'gäŋ\ *or* **Lien–yün–kang** \le-'ən-'yün-'gäŋ\ *or formerly* **Tung·hai** \'duŋ-'hī\ city E China in N Jiangsu *pop* 210,000

Liao \lē-'aú\ river 700 *mi* (1126 *km*) NE China flowing into Gulf of Liaodong

Liao·dong *or* **Liao·tung** \lē-'aú-'dúŋ\ peninsula NE China in S Liaoning bet. Korea Bay & **Gulf of Liaodong** (arm of Bo Hai)

Liao·ning \lē-'aú-'niŋ\ *or formerly* **Feng·tien** \'fəŋ-tē-'en\ province NE China in S Manchuria * Shenyang *area* 58,301 *sq mi* (151,583 *sq km*), *pop* 35,721,693

Liao·si \lē-'aú-'shē\ former province (1948–54) NE China in S Manchuria bordering on Gulf of Liaodong * Chin-chou

Liao·yang \lē-'aú-'yäŋ\ city NE China in *cen* Liaoning NE of Anshan *pop* 200,000

Liao·yuan \lē-'aú-yü-'än\ city NE China in W Jilin S of Changchun on the Liao *pop* 177,000

Li·ard \lē-ərd\ river 755 *mi* (1215 *km*) W Canada flowing from Stikine Mountains in Yukon Territory E & N into Mackenzie River

Libanus — see LEBANON MOUNTAINS

Li·be·rec \'li-bə-,rets\ city N Czech Republic in N Bohemia *pop* 104,158

Li·be·ria \lī-'bir-ē-ə\ country W Africa, a republic * Monrovia *area* 43,000 *sq mi* (111,800 *sq km*), *pop* 1,503,368 — **Li·be·ri·an** \-ē-ən\ *adj or n*

Lib·er·ty \'li-bər-tē\ city NW Mo. NNE of Kansas City *pop* 20,459

Liberty Island *or formerly* **Bed·loe's Island** \'bed-,lōz\ island SE N.Y. in Upper New York Bay; comprises **Statue of Liberty National Monument**

Lib·er·ty·ville \'li-bər-tē-,vil, -vəl\ city NE Ill. *pop* 19,174

Li·bre·ville \'lē-brə-,vil, -,vē(ə)l\ city & port * of Gabon at mouth of Gabon River *pop* 105,080

Lib·ya \'li-bē-ə\ **1** the part of Africa N of the Sahara bet. Egypt & Syrtis Major (Gulf of Sidra) — an ancient name **2** N Africa W of Egypt — an ancient name **3** country N Africa bordering on the Mediterranean: a colony of Italy 1912–43, an independent kingdom 1951–69, a republic since 1969 * Tripoli *area* 679,358 *sq mi* (1,766,331 *sq km*), *pop* 3,224,000

Lib·y·an Desert \'li-bē-ən\ desert N Africa W of the Nile in Libya, Egypt, & Sudan

Lich·field \'lich-,fēld\ city W *cen* England in Staffordshire *pop* 25,600

Lick·ing \'li-kiŋ\ river 350 *mi* (563 *km*) NE Ky. flowing NW into Ohio river

Li·di·ce \'li-də(t)-sē, -,sä\ village W *cen* Czech Republic in W *cen* Bohemia

Li·do \'lē-(,)dō\ island Italy in the Adriatic separating Lagoon of Venice & Gulf of Venice

Liech·ten·stein \'lik-tən-,shtīn, -,stīn\ country W Europe bet. Switzerland & Austria bordering on the Rhine; a principality * Vaduz *area* 62 *sq mi* (161 *sq km*), *pop* 28,877 — **Liech·ten·stein·er** \-,shtī-nər, -,stī-\ n

Li·ège \lē-'ezh, -'āzh\ *or Flem* **Luik** \'līk, 'lœœk\ **1** province E Belgium *area* 1525 *sq mi* (3965 *sq km*), *pop* 999,646 **2** city, its * *pop* 194,596

Lie·pa·ja \lē-'e-pə-yə, -'e-pä-yə\ *or G* **Li·bau** \'lē-,baú\ city & port W Latvia on the Baltic *pop* 108,000

Lif·fey \'li-fē\ river 50 *mi* (80 *km*) E Ireland flowing into Dublin Bay

Lif·ford \'li-fərd\ town NW Ireland (republic) in Ulster * of county Donegal *pop* 1478

Li·gu·ria \lə-'gyúr-ē-ə\ region NW Italy bordering on Ligurian Sea * Genoa *pop* 1,727,212 — **Li·gu·ri·an** \-ē-ən\ *adj or n*

Ligurian Sea arm of the Mediterranean N of Corsica

Li·ka·si \li-'kä-sē\ *or formerly* **Ja·dot·ville** \,zha-dō-'vē(ə)l, zha-'dō-,vil\ city SE Zaire in SE Shaba *pop* 146,394

Lille \'lē(ə)l\ *or formerly* **Lisle** \'lē(ə)l, 'lī(ə)l\ city N France; medieval * of Flanders *pop* 171,010

Li·long·we \li-'lòŋ-(,)wā\ city * of Malawi *pop* 102,924

Li·ma **1** \'lī-mə\ city NW Ohio *pop* 45,549 **2** \'lē-mə\ city * of Peru, on the Rímac *pop* 3,968,972

Lim·a·vady \,li-mə-'va-dē\ district N Northern Ireland, established 1974 *area* 226 *sq mi* (588 *sq km*), *pop* 26,270

Li·may \lē-'mī\ river 250 *mi* (402 *km*) W Argentina flowing out of Lake Nahuel Huapí & joining the Neuquén forming Negro River

Lim·burg \'lim-,bərg\ **1** region W Europe E of the Meuse including parts of present Limburg province, Netherlands, & Limburg province, Belgium **2** province NE Belgium * Hasselt *area* 929 *sq mi* (2415 *sq km*), *pop* 750,435 **3** province SE Netherlands * Maastricht *area* 851 *sq mi* (2213 *sq km*), *pop* 1,080,309

Lime·house \'līm-,haús\ district E London, England, in Tower Hamlets on N bank of Thames River

Lim·er·ick \'li-mə-rik, 'lim-rik\ **1** county SW Ireland in Munster *area* 1037 *sq mi* (2696 *sq km*), *pop* 161,856 **2** city & county borough & port, its *, on the Shannon *pop* 52,040

Límnos — see LEMNOS

Li·moges \lē-'mōzh, li-\ city SW *cen* France *pop* 136,059

Li·món \li-'mòn\ *or* **Puer·to Limón** \'pwer-tō\ city & port E Costa Rica on the Caribbean *pop* 29,621

Li·mou·sin \,lē-mü-'zaⁿ\ region & former province S *cen* France W of Auvergne * Limoges

Lim·po·po \lim-'pō-(,)pō\ *or* **Croc·o·dile** \'krä-kə-,dīl\ river 1000 *mi* (1609 *km*) S Africa flowing from Northern Transvaal, Republic of South Africa, into Indian Ocean in Mozambique

Li·na·res \li-'när-əs\ commune S Spain N of Jaén *pop* 45,330

Lin·coln **1** \'liŋ-kən\ city SE Nebr., its * *pop* 191,972 **2** city E England * of Lincolnshire *pop* 76,660

Lincoln Park city SE Mich. SW of Detroit *pop* 41,832

Lin·coln·shire \'liŋ-kən-,shir, -shər\ *or* **Lincoln** county E England * Lincoln *area* 2272 *sq mi* (5907 *sq km*), *pop* 547,700

Lin·den \'lin-dən\ city NE N.J. SSW of Elizabeth *pop* 36,701

Lin·den·hurst \'lin-dən-,hərst\ village SE N.Y. in *cen* Long Is. *pop* 26,879

Lin·des·nes \'lin-dəs-,nās\ cape Norway at S tip on North Sea

Lindisfarne — see HOLY

Lind·sey, Parts of \'lin(d)-zē\ district & former administrative county E England in N Lincolnshire * Lincoln *area* 1520 *sq mi* (3952 *sq km*)

Line Islands \'līn\ islands Kiribati in *cen* Pacific S of Hawaii formerly divided bet. the U.S. (Kingman Reef & Palmyra) & Great Britain (Teraina, Tabuaeran, & Kiritimati) *pop* 5400

Lin·ga·yen Gulf \,liŋ-gə-'yen\ inlet of S. China Sea Philippines in NW Luzon

Linguetta, Cape — see GJUHEZES (Cape)

Lin·kö·ping \'lin-,shə(r)-piŋ\ city SE Sweden *pop* 120,562

Lin·lith·gow \lin-'lith-(,)gō\ **1** *or* **Lin·lith·gow·shire** \-,shir, -shər\ — see WEST LOTHIAN **2** burgh SE Scotland in Lothian region W of Edinburgh *pop* 9524

Linn·he, Loch \'li-nē\ inlet of the Atlantic on W coast of Scotland extending NE from head of Firth of Lorne

Linz \'lints, 'linz\ city N Austria on the Danube *pop* 202,855

Li·ons, Gulf of \'lī-ənz\ *or F* **Golfe du Lion** \gólf-dᵫ-lyōⁿ\ arm of the Mediterranean on S coast of France

Lip·a·ri \'li-pə-rē\ *or anc* **Lip·a·ra** \'li-pə-rə\ island, chief of the Lipari Islands

Lipari Islands *or It* **Iso·le Eo·lie** \'ē-zə-,lā-ä-'ò-lē-,ā\ islands Italy in SE Tyrrhenian Sea off NE Sicily *area* 45 *sq mi* (117 *sq km*) — see STROMBOLI

Li·petsk \'lē-,petsk\ city SW *cen* Russia in Europe N of Voronezh *pop* 396,000

Lip·pe \'li-pə\ **1** river 150 *mi* (241 *km*) W Germany flowing from Teutoburger Wald W into the Rhine **2** former principality & state W Germany bet. Teutoburger Wald & the Weser * Detmold

Li·ri \'lir-ē\ river 100 *mi* (161 *km*) *cen* Italy flowing into Gulf of Gaeta

Lis·bon \'liz-bən\ *or Pg* **Lis·boa** \lēzh-'vō-ə\ city & port * of Portugal on Tagus estuary *pop* 807,167 — **Lis·bo·an** \liz-'bō-ən\ n

Lis·burn \'liz-(,)bərn\ district E Northern Ireland, established 1974 *area* 171 *sq mi* (445 *sq km*), *pop* 82,091

Lis·burne, Cape \'liz-(,)bərn\ cape NW Alaska projecting into Arctic Ocean near W end of Brooks Range

---

\ə\ abut \ªʼ\ kitten, F table \ər\ further \a\ ash \ā\ ace \ä\ mop, mar
\aú\ out \ch\ chin \e\ bet \ē\ easy \g\ go \i\ hit \ī\ ice \j\ job
\ŋ\ sing \ō\ go \ò\ law \òi\ boy \th\ thin \t̲h̲\ the \ü\ loot \ú\ foot
\y\ yet \zh\ vision \ä, k̲, ⁿ, œ, œ̄, ᵫ, ᵫ̄, ʸ\ *see* Guide to Pronunciation

Li·sieux \lēz-'yə(r), -'yœ\ city NW France E of Caen *pop* 24,972
Lisle \'līl\ village NE Ill. *pop* 19,512
Li·ta·ni \li-'tä-nē\ river 90 *mi* (144 *km*) S Lebanon flowing into Mediterranean
Lith·u·a·nia \,li-thə-'wā-nē-ə, ,li-thyə-, -nyə\ *or Lith* **Lie·tu·va** \lē-,e-tù-'vä\ country N *cen* Europe bordering on the Baltic; remnant of a medieval principality extending from Baltic Sea to Black Sea; a republic 1918–40, a constituent republic (**Lithuanian Republic**) of the U.S.S.R. 1940–91; ✱ Vilnius *area* 31,200 *sq mi* (81,120 *sq km*), *pop* 3,690,000
Little Abaco — see ABACO
Little Bighorn river 80 *mi* (129 *km*) N Wyo. & S Mont. flowing N into Bighorn River
Little Colorado river 300 *mi* (483 *km*) NE Ariz. flowing NW into Colorado River
Little Diomede — see DIOMEDE ISLANDS
Little Inagua — see INAGUA
Little Kabylia — see KABYLIA
Little Karroo — see KARROO
Little Minch — see MINCH
Little Missouri river 560 *mi* (901 *km*) W U.S. flowing from NE Wyo. N into Missouri River in W N.Dak.
Little Namaqualand — see NAMAQUALAND
Lit·tle Rock \'li-t'l-,räk\ city ✱ of Ark. on Arkansas River *pop* 175,795
Little Saint Ber·nard \,sānt-bər-'närd\ mountain pass 7177 *ft* (2188 *m*) over Savoy Alps bet. France & Italy S of Mont Blanc
Lit·tle·ton \'li-t'l-tən\ town N *cen* Colo. S of Denver *pop* 33,685
Little Walachia — see OLTENIA
Liu·zhou *or* **Liu-chow** *or* **Liu–chou** \lē-'ü-'jō\ city S China in *cen* Guangxi Zhuangzu *pop* 190,000
Liv·er·more \'li-vər-,mōr, -,mȯr\ city W Calif. SE of Oakland *pop* 56,741
Liv·er·pool \'li-vər-,pül\ city & port NW England in Merseyside on Mersey estuary *pop* 510,306 — **Liv·er·pud·li·an** \,li-vər-'pəd-lē-ən\ *adj or n*
Liv·ing·stone \'li-viŋ-stən\ city S Zambia on the Zambezi *pop* 71,987
Livingstone Falls rapids in lower Congo River W equatorial Africa below Malebo Pool; a series of cascades dropping *ab* 900 *ft* (273 *m*) in 220 *mi* (352 *km*)
Li·vo·nia \lə-'vō-nē-ə, -nyə\ 1 region *cen* Europe bordering on the Baltic in Latvia & Estonia 2 city SE Mich. W of Detroit *pop* 100,850 — **Li·vo·ni·an** \-nē-ən, -nyən\ *adj or n*
Livorno — see LEGHORN
Lizard Head *or* **Lizard Point** headland SW England in S Cornwall at S tip of **The Lizard** (peninsula projecting into English Channel); extreme S point of Great Britain, at 49°57'30"N, 5°12'W
Lju·blja·na \lē-,ü-blē-'ä-nə\ city *cen* Slovenia, its ✱ *pop* 169,064
Llan·ber·is \lan-'ber-əs, hlan-\ village NW Wales in Gwynedd near Snowdon at entrance to **Pass of Llanberis** (1169 *ft or* 354 *m*)
Llan·drin·dod Wells \lan-'drin-,dȯd, hlan-\ town E Wales ✱ of Powys
Llan·dud·no \lan-'did-(,)nō, hlan-, -'dəd-\ town NW Wales on coast of Gwynedd *pop* 18,991
Lla·nel·li *or* **Lla·nel·ly** \hla-'ne-hlē; la-'ne-lē, hla-\ borough & port S Wales in Dyfed *pop* 24,079
Llan·gef·ni \lan-'gev-nē, hlan-\ town NW Wales in Gwynedd on Anglesey Is. *pop* 4265
Lla·no Es·ta·ca·do \'la-(,)nō-,es-tə-'kä-(,)dō, 'lä-, 'yä-\ *or* **Staked Plain** \'stāk(t)-\ plateau region SE N.Mex. & NW Tex.
Llu·llai·lla·co \,yü-,yī-'yä-(,)kō\ volcano 22,057 *ft* (6723 *m*) N Chile in Andes on Argentina border SE of Antofagasta
Lo·an·ge \lō-'aŋ-gə\ *or Pg* **Lu·an·gue** \lü-'aŋ-gə\ river 425 *mi* (684 *km*) NE Angola & SW Congo flowing N into Kasai River
Lo·bi·to \lō-'bē-(,)tō\ city & port W Angola *pop* 59,528
Lo·bos, Point \'lō-(,)bōs\ 1 promontory Calif. in San Francisco on S side of entrance to the Golden Gate 2 promontory Calif. on the Pacific SW of Monterey
Lo·car·no \lō-'kär-(,)nō\ commune SE *cen* Switzerland
Loch·gilp·head \läk-'gilp-,hed, läk-\ burgh W Scotland on Loch Fyne
Lock·port \'läk-,pōrt, -,pȯrt\ city N N.Y. NE of Buffalo *pop* 24,426
Lo·cris \'lō-krəs, 'lä-\ region of ancient Greece N of Gulf of Corinth — **Lo·cri·an** \-krē-ən\ *adj or n*
Lod \'lōd\ *or* **Lyd·da** \'li-də\ city *cen* Israel *pop* 30,500
Lo·di 1 \'lō-,dī\ city *cen* Calif. SSE of Sacramento *pop* 51,874 2 \'lō-,dī\ borough NE N.J. SE of Paterson *pop* 22,355 3 \'lō-(,)dē\ commune N Italy in Lombardy SE of Milan *pop* 42,770
Lodz \'lüj, 'lädz\ city *cen* Poland WSW of Warsaw *pop* 851,690
Lo·fo·ten \'lō-,fō-t'n\ island group Norway off NW coast SW of Vesterålen *area* 475 *sq mi* (1235 *sq km*)
Lo·gan \'lō-gən\ city N Utah *pop* 32,762
Logan, Mount mountain 19,850 *ft* (6050 *m*) Canada in SW Yukon Territory; highest in St. Elias & Coast ranges & in Canada & 2d highest in N. America
Lo·gro·ño \lə-'grō-(,)nyō\ 1 province N Spain in NE Old Castile *area* 1946 *sq mi* (5060 *sq km*), *pop* 241,957 2 commune, its ✱, on the Ebro *pop* 109,536
Loire \lə-'wär, lwär\ river 625 *mi* (1006 *km*) *cen* France flowing from the Massif Central NW & W into Bay of Biscay
Lol·land \'lä-lənd\ island Denmark in the Baltic S of Sjælland *area* 477 *sq mi* (1240 *sq km*), *pop* 73,564
Lo·ma·mi \lō-'mä-mē\ river 900 *mi* (1448 *km*) *cen* Zaire flowing N into Congo River
Lo·mas \'lō-,mäs\ *or* **Lomas de Za·mo·ra** \,-mäz-də-zə-'mōr-ə, -'mȯr-\ city E Argentina SW of Buenos Aires *pop* 508,620
Lom·bard \'läm-,bärd\ village NE Ill. W of Chicago *pop* 39,408
Lom·bar·dy \'läm-bər-dē, -,bär- *also* 'ləm-\ *or It* **Lom·bar·dia** \,läm-bər-'dē-ə, ,lȯm-\ region N Italy chiefly N of the Po ✱ Milan *pop* 8,911,995
Lom·blen \'läm-,blen\ island Indonesia in the Lesser Sundas E of Flores *area* 468 *sq mi* (1217 *sq km*)
Lom·bok \'läm-,bäk\ island Indonesia in the Lesser Sundas E of Bali; chief town Mataram *area* 1825 *sq mi* (4745 *sq km*), *pop* 1,300,234
Lo·mé \lō-'mā\ city & port ✱ of Togo *pop* 229,400
Lo·mi·ta \lō-'mē-tə\ city SW Calif. S of Los Angeles *pop* 19,382

Lo·mond, Ben \ben-'lō-mənd\ mountain 3192 *ft* (973 *m*) S *cen* Scotland on E side of Loch Lomond
Lomond, Loch lake 24 *mi* (39 *km*) long S *cen* Scotland in Strathclyde & Central regions; largest in Scotland
Lom·poc \'läm-,pōk\ city SW Calif. W of Santa Barbara *pop* 37,649
Lon·don \'lən-dən\ 1 city Canada in SE Ont. on Thames River *pop* 303,165 2 city & port SE England formerly constituting an administrative county ✱ of United Kingdom; comprises City of London & 12 inner boroughs of Greater London *pop* 2,395,200 3 *or* **City of London** *or anc* **Lon·din·i·um** \län-'di-nē-əm, ,lən-\ city within Greater London, England on Thames River *area* 675 *acres* (270 *hectares*) 4 GREATER LONDON — **Lon·don·er** \-də-nər\ *n*
Lon·don·der·ry 1 \'lən-dən-,der-ē\ town SE N.H. NE of Nashua *pop* 19,781 2 — see DERRY 3 \,lən-dən-'der-ē, 'lən-dən-,\ traditional county N Northern Ireland
Long Beach 1 city & port SW Calif. S of Los Angeles *pop* 429,433 2 city SE N.Y. on island S of Long Is. *pop* 33,510
Long Branch city E *cen* N.J. on the Atlantic *pop* 28,658
Long·ford \'lȯŋ-fərd\ 1 county E *cen* Ireland in Leinster *area* 403 *sq mi* (1048 *sq km*), *pop* 30,293 2 urban district, its ✱ *pop* 6457
Long Island island 118 *mi* (190 *km*) long SE N.Y. S of Conn. *area* 1401 *sq mi* (3643 *sq km*)
Long Island City section of New York City in NW Queens
Long Island Sound inlet of the Atlantic bet. Conn. & Long Is.
Long·mont \'lȯŋ-,mänt\ city N Colo. N of Denver *pop* 51,555
Longs Peak \'lȯŋz\ mountain 14,255 *ft* (4345 *m*) N *cen* Colo. in Front Range in Rocky Mountain National Park
Lon·gueuil \lȯŋ-'gā(ə)l\ town Canada in S Que. E of Montreal *pop* 129,874
Long·view \'lȯŋ-,vyü\ 1 city NE Tex. *pop* 70,311 2 city SW Wash. on Columbia River *pop* 31,499
Long Xuy·en \laủŋ-'swē-ən\ city S Vietnam in SW Cochin China on S side of Mekong delta
Lookout, Cape cape E N.C. on the Atlantic SW of Cape Hatteras
Lookout Mountain ridge 2126 *ft* (648 *m*) SE Tenn., NW Ga., & NE Ala. near Chattanooga, Tenn.
Lo·rain \lə-'rān, lō-\ city N Ohio on Lake Erie W of Cleveland *pop* 71,245
Lor·ca \'lȯr-kə\ commune SE Spain W of Murcia *pop* 60,609
Lord Howe Island \lȯrd-'haủ\ island Australia in Tasman Sea ENE of Sydney belonging to New South Wales *area* 5 *sq mi* (13 *sq km*)
Lo·re·to \lə-'rā-(,)tō, -'re-\ commune *cen* Italy in the Marches S of Ancona
Lo·ri·ent \,lȯr-ē-'äⁿ\ commune & port NW France in Brittany on Bay of Biscay *pop* 68,655
Lorne, Firth of \'lȯrn\ *or* **Firth of Lorn** strait W Scotland bet. E Mull Is. & mainland
Lor·raine \lə-'rān, lȯ-\ *or G* **Lo·thring·en** \'lō-triŋ-ən\ region & former duchy NE France around the upper Moselle & the Meuse; remnant (**Upper Lorraine**) of medieval kingdom of **Lo·tha·rin·gia** \,lō-thə-'rinj(ē)ə\ including also territory to N (**Lower Lorraine**) bet. the Rhine & the Scheldt — see ALSACE-LORRAINE
Los Al·tos \lȯs-'al-(,)tōs\ city W Calif. SSE of Palo Alto *pop* 26,303
Los An·ge·les \lȯs-'an-jə-ləs *also* -,lēz, *sometimes* -'aŋ-g(ə-)ləs *or* -gə-,lēz\ city & port SW Calif. on the Pacific *pop* 3,485,398 — **Los An·ge·le·no** \-,an-jə-'lē-(,)nō *also* -,aŋ-gə-'lē-\ *n*
Los An·ge·les \lȯs-'äŋ-hā-,läs\ city S *cen* Chile
Los Gat·os \lȯs-'ga-(,)tōs\ city W Calif. S of San José *pop* 27,357
Lot \'lät, 'lȯt\ river 300 *mi* (483 *km*) S France flowing W into the Garonne
Lo·thi·an \'lō-thē-ən\ region S Scotland bordering on Firth of Forth, established 1975 ✱ Edinburgh *area* 678 *sq mi* (1763 *sq km*), *pop* 735,892; formerly divided into three counties (the **Lothians**): East Lothian, Midlothian, & West Lothian
Lough·bor·ough \'ləf-,bə-rə, -,bə-rə, -b(ə-)rə\ borough *cen* England in Leicestershire S of Nottingham *pop* 47,647
Lou·ise, Lake \-'ēz\ lake W Canada in SW Alta. in Banff National Park
Lou·i·si·ade Archipelago \lü-,ē-zē-'äd, -'ad\ island group in Solomon Sea SE of New Guinea; belongs to Papua New Guinea *pop* 14,599
Lou·i·si·ana \lù-,ē-zē-'a-nə, ,lü-ə-zē-, ,lüzē-\ state S U.S. ✱ Baton Rouge *area* 48,523 *sq mi* (126,160 *sq km*), *pop* 4,219,973 — **Lou·i·si·an·an** \-'a-nən\ *adj or n* — **Lou·i·si·an·i·an** \-,a-nē-ən, -'a-nyən\ *adj or n*
Louisiana Purchase region W *cen* U.S. bet. Mississippi River & the Rockies purchased 1803 from France *area* 885,000 *sq mi* (2,301,000 *sq km*)
Lou·is·ville \'lü-i-,vil, -vəl\ city N Ky. on Ohio River *pop* 269,063
Loup \'lüp\ river 290 *mi* (467 *km*) with longest headstream (the Middle Loup) E *cen* Nebr. flowing E into Platte River
Lourdes \'lürd(z)\ commune SW France on the Gave de Pau SSW of Tarbes *pop* 17,685
Lourenço Marques — see MAPUTO
Louth \'laủth\ county E Ireland in Leinster bordering on Irish Sea ✱ Dundalk *area* 317 *sq mi* (824 *sq km*), *pop* 90,707
Lou·vain \lü-'vaⁿ\ *or Flem* **Leu·ven** \'lœ(r)-və(n), 'lœ-\ city *cen* Belgium in Brabant E of Brussels *pop* 85,018
Love·land \'ləv-lənd\ city N Colo. N of Denver *pop* 37,352
Loveland Pass mountain pass N *cen* Colo. in Front Range of Rocky Mountains
Low Countries region W Europe bordering on North Sea & comprising modern Belgium, Luxembourg, & the Netherlands
Low·ell \'lō-əl\ city NE Mass. NW of Boston *pop* 103,439
Lower Canada the province of Canada 1791–1841 corresponding to modern Que. — see UPPER CANADA
Lower 48 the continental states of the U.S. excluding Alaska
Lower Klamath Lake lake N Calif. on Oreg. border SSE of Upper Klamath Lake (in Oreg.)
Lower Peninsula S part of Mich., S of Straits of Mackinac
Lower Saxony *or G* **Nie·der·sach·sen** \,nē-dər-'zäk-sən\ state of Germany & formerly of W. Germany bordering on North Sea ✱ Hannover *area* 18,289 *sq mi* (47,551 *sq km*), *pop* 7,256,386 — see SAXONY
Lowes·toft \'lō-stəf(t), -,stȯft\ borough & port E England in E. Suffolk on North Sea *pop* 55,231

Low·lands \'lō-lən(d)z, -,lan(d)z\ the *cen* & E part of Scotland lying bet. the Highlands & the Southern Uplands

Loyalty Islands islands SW Pacific E of New Caledonia; a dependency of New Caledonia *area* 800 *sq mi* (2080 *sq km*), *pop* 12,248

Lu·a·la·ba \,lü-ə-'lä-bə\ river 400 *mi* (640 *km*) SE Zaire flowing N to join the **Lu·a·pu·la** \-'pü-lə\ (outlet of Lake Bangweulu) forming Congo River

Lu·an·da \lü-'an-də\ city & port ✳ of Angola *pop* 475,328

Luang Pra·bang \,lü-,äŋ-prə-'bäŋ\ city NW Laos on the Mekong NNW of Vientiane *pop* 44,244

Luangue — see LOANGE

Lub·bock \'lə-bək\ city NW Tex. *pop* 186,206

Lü·beck \'lü-,bek, 'lūē-\ city & port N Germany NE of Hamburg *pop* 220,588

Lu·blin \'lü-blən, -,blēn\ city E Poland SE of Warsaw *pop* 349,672

Lu·bum·ba·shi \,lü-büm-'bä-shē\ *or formerly* **Elis·a·beth·ville** \i-'li-zə-bəth-,vil\ city SE Zaire in SE Shaba *pop* 588,307

Lucania — see BASILICATA

Lu·ca·nia, Mount \lü-'kä-nē-ə, -nyə\ mountain 17,147 *ft* (5226 *m*) Canada in SW Yukon Territory in St. Elias Range N of Mt. Logan

Luc·ca \'lü-kə\ commune *cen* Italy in Tuscany NW of Florence *pop* 86,676

Lu·cerne \lü-'sərn\ *or G* **Lu·zern** \lüt-'sern\ **1** canton *cen* Switzerland *area* 579 *sq mi* (1505 *sq km*), *pop* 316,210 **2** commune, its ✳, on Vierwaldstätter See *pop* 59,932

Lucerne, Lake of — see VIERWALDSTÄTTER SEE

Luchow — see HEFEI

Luck·now \'lək-,naú\ city N India ESE of Delhi ✳ of Uttar Pradesh *pop* 1,006,538

Lü·da *or* **Lü·ta** \'lü-'dä, 'lūē-\ *or* **Dai·ren** \'dī-'ren\ city NE China in S Liaoning on Liaodong Peninsula

Lü·de·ritz \'lü-də-rəts\ town & port SW Namibia

Lu·dhi·a·na \,lü-dē-'ä-nə\ city NW India in Punjab SE of Amritsar *pop* 606,250

Lud·wigs·burg \'lüd-vigz-,búrg, 'lüt-viks-,búrk\ city SW Germany in Baden-Württemberg N of Stuttgart *pop* 81,589

Lud·wigs·ha·fen \,lüd-vigz-'hä-fən, ,lüt-viks-\ city SW Germany on the Rhine opposite Mannheim *pop* 159,399

Luf·kin \'ləf-kən\ city E Tex. NNE of Houston *pop* 30,206

Lu·ga·no \lü-'gä-(,)nō\ commune S Switzerland in Ticino canton on Lake Lugano

Lugano, Lake lake on border bet. Switzerland & Italy E of Lake Maggiore *area* 19 *sq mi* (49 *sq km*)

Lu·gansk \lü-'gän(t)sk\ *or alternately since 1935* **Vo·ro·shi·lov·grad** \,vór-ə-'shē-ləf-,grad, ,vär-, -ləv-, -,grad\ city E Ukraine in Donets basin *pop* 463,000

Lu·go \'lü-(,)gō\ **1** province NW Spain in NE Galicia on Bay of Biscay *area* 3814 *sq mi* (9916 *sq km*), *pop* 384,365 **2** commune, its ✳ *pop* 71,299

Luichow — see LEIZHOU

Luik — see LIÈGE

Lu·lea \'lü-lä-,ō\ city & port N Sweden near head of Gulf of Bothnia *pop* 66,834

Lu·le·bur·gaz \,lü-lə-búr-'gäz\ city *cen* Turkey in Europe

Luluabourg — see KANANGA

Lund \'lúnd, 'lənd\ city SW Sweden NE of Malmö *pop* 86,412

Lun·dy Island \'lən-dē\ island SW England at mouth of Bristol Channel off coast of Devon *area* 2 *sq mi* (5.2 *sq km*)

Lü·ne·burg \'lü-nə-,búrg, 'lūē-nə-,búrk\ city N Germany SE of Hamburg & NE of **Lüneburg Heath** *or G* **Lü·ne·bur·ger Hei·de** \-,búr-gər,-hī-də\ (tract of moorland 50 *mi or* 80 *km* long) *pop* 62,225

Lü·nen \'lü-nən, 'lūē-\ city W Germany S of Münster *pop* 85,872

Lu·nen·burg \'lü-nən-,bərg\ town Canada in S N.S. *pop* 25,720

Lu·né·ville \'lü-nə-,vil, lūē-nə-'vēl\ city NE France on the Meurthe SE of Nancy *pop* 22,438

Lungki — see ZHANGZHOU

Luo·yang \lə-'wō-'yäŋ\ *or* **Lo·yang** \'lō-'yäŋ\ city E China in N Henan in the Huang basin *pop* 171,200

Lu·ray Caverns \'lü-,rā, lü-'\ caverns N Va. in Blue Ridge Mountains

Lu·ri·stan \'lúr-ə-,stan, -,stän\ region W Iran; chief town Burujird

Lu·sa·ka \lü-'sä-kə\ city ✳ of Zambia *pop* 538,469

Lu·sa·tia \lü-'sä-sh(ē-)ə\ *or G* **Lau·sitz** \'laú-(,)zits\ region E Germany NW of Silesia E of the Elbe

Lusitania — see PORTUGAL — **Lu·si·ta·ni·an** \,lü-sə-'tā-nē-ən, -nyən\ *adj or n*

Lutetia — see PARIS

Lu·ton \'lü-t²n\ borough SE *cen* England in SE Bedfordshire *pop* 164,049

Lüt·zen \'lüt-sən, 'lúet-\ town E Germany in Saxony SW of Leipzig

Lux·em·bourg *or* **Lux·em·burg** \'lək-səm-,bərg, 'lúk-səm-,búrg\ **1** province SE Belgium ✳ Arlon *area* 1705 *sq mi* (4433 *sq km*), *pop* 232,813 **2** country W Europe bet. Belgium, France, & Germany; a grand duchy *area* 999 *sq mi* (2597 *sq km*), *pop* 364,606 **3** city, its ✳ *pop* 79,596 — **Lux·em·bourg·er** *or* **Lux·em·burg·er** \-,bər-gər, -,búr-\ *n* — **Lux·em·bourg·i·an** *or* **Lux·em·burg·i·an** \,lək-səm-'bər-gē-ən, ,lúk-səm-'búr-\ *adj*

Lux·or \'lək-,sór, 'lúk-\ *or Ar* **El Uq·sor** \el-'úk-,súr\ city S Egypt on the Nile on S part of site of ancient Thebes *pop* 92,748

Lu·zon \lü-'zän\ island N Philippines, chief island of the group *area* 40,420 *sq mi* (105,092 *sq km*), *pop* 16,669,724

Lvov \lə-'vóf, -'vóv\ *or Pol* **Lwów** \lə-'vúf, -'vúv\ *or G* **Lem·berg** \'lem-,bərg, -,berk\ city W Ukraine *pop* 238,600

Lyallpur — see FAISALABAD

Ly·ca·bet·tus *or Gk* **Ly·ka·bet·tos** \,li-kə-'be-təs, ,lī-\ mountain 909 *ft* (277 *m*) in NE part of Athens, Greece

Ly·ca·o·nia \,li-kā-'ō-nē-ə, -nyə\ ancient region & Roman province SE *cen* Asia Minor N of Cilicia

Ly·cia \'li-sh(ē-)ə\ ancient region & Roman province SW Asia Minor on coast SE of Caria

Lydda — see LOD

Lyd·ia \'li-dē-ə\ ancient country W Asia Minor bordering on the Aegean ✳ Sardis

Lyn·brook \'lin-,brúk\ village SE N.Y. on Long Is. *pop* 19,208

Lynch·burg \'linch-,bərg\ city S *cen* Va. on James River *pop* 66,049

Lynn \'lin\ **1** city NE Mass. NE of Boston *pop* 81,245 **2** *or* **Lynn Regis** — see KING'S LYNN

Lynn Canal narrow inlet of the Pacific 80 *mi* (129 *km*) long SE Alaska extending N from Juneau

Lynn·wood \'lin-,wúd\ city W Wash. N of Seattle *pop* 28,695

Lyn·wood \'lin-,wúd\ city SW Calif. S of Los Angeles *pop* 61,945

Ly·on·nais *or* **Ly·o·nais** \,lē-ə-'nä\ former province SE *cen* France NE of Auvergne & W of the Saône & the Rhône ✳ Lyons

Ly·ons \lē-'ōⁿ, 'lī-ənz\ *or* **Lyon** \lyōⁿ\ *or anc* **Lug·du·num** \lúg-'dü-nəm, ,ləg-\ city SE *cen* France at confluence of the Saône & the Rhône *pop* 462,841

Lys \'lēs\ *or* **Leie** \'lī-ə\ river 120 *mi* (193 *km*) France & Belgium flowing NE into the Scheldt

Lyt·tel·ton \'li-t²l-tən\ borough New Zealand on South Is.; port for Christchurch, on **Port Lyttelton** (inlet) *pop* 3184

Maarianhamina — see MARIEHAMN

Maas — see MEUSE

Maas·tricht *or* **Maes·tricht** \'mä-,strikt, -,strikt; mä-'\ commune SE Netherlands on the Meuse ✳ of Limburg *pop* 112,598

Ma·cao *or* **Ma·cau** \mə-'kaú\ **1** island SE China in Guangdong in Xi delta W of Hong Kong **2** Portuguese overseas territory comprising peninsula on SE Macao Is. & adjacent islands *area* 6 *sq mi* (16 *sq km*), *pop* 452,300 **3** city & port, its ✳ *pop* 161,252 — **Mac·a·nese** \,mä-kə-'nēz, -'nēs\ *n*

Ma·ca·pá \,mä-kə-'pä\ city & port N Brazil ✳ of Amapá *pop* 137,698

Macassar — see MAKASSAR — **Ma·cas·sar·ese** \mə-,ka-sə-'rēz, -'rēs\ *n*

Mac·cles·field \'ma-kəlz-,fēld\ borough W England in E Cheshire SSE of Manchester *pop* 46,832

Mac·don·nell Ranges \mək-'dä-n²l\ series of mountain ridges *cen* Australia in S Northern Territory; highest point Mt. Ziel 4955 *ft* (1510 *m*)

Mac·e·do·nia \,ma-sə-'dō-nē-ə, -nyə\ **1** region S Europe in Balkan Peninsula in NE Greece, the former Yugoslav section of Macedonia, & SW Bulgaria including territory of ancient kingdom of Macedonia (*or* **Mac·e·don** \'ma-sə-dən, -,dän\ ✳ Pella) **2** country S *cen* Balkan Peninsula; a federated republic of Yugoslavia 1946–92 ✳ Skopje *area* 10,229 *sq mi* (26,595 *sq km*), *pop* 1,623,598

Ma·ceió \,ma-sā-'ō\ city NE Brazil ✳ of Alagoas *pop* 400,041

Mac·gil·li·cud·dy's Reeks \mə-'gi-lə-,kə-dēz-'rēks\ mountain range SW Ireland in County Kerry — see CARRANTUOHILL

Ma·ches·ney Park \mə-'chez-nē\ village N Ill. N of Rockford *pop* 19,033

Ma·chi·da \mə-'chē-də, 'mä-chi-,dä\ city Japan on Honshu *pop* 349,030

Ma·chi·li·pat·nam \,mə-chə-lə-'pət-nəm\ *or* **Ban·dar** \'bən-dər\ city & port SE India in E Andhra Pradesh SW of Kakinada *pop* 138,525

Ma·chu Pic·chu \,mä-(,)chü-'pē-(,)chü\ site S Peru of ancient Inca city on a mountain NW of Cuzco

Macias Nguema Biyogo — see BIOKO

Mac·ken·zie \mə-'ken-zē\ **1** river 1120 *mi* (1802 *km*) NW Canada flowing from Great Slave Lake NW into Beaufort Sea; sometimes considered to include the Finlay, Peace, & Slave rivers (total length 2635 *mi or* 4216 *km*) **2** former district Canada in W Northwest Territories in basin of Mackenzie River

Mackenzie Mountains mountain range NW Canada in the Rockies in Yukon Territory & W Northwest Territories

Mack·i·nac \'ma-kə-,nò, -,nak\ *or formerly* **Mich·i·li·mack·i·nac** \,mi-shə-lē-\ island N Mich. in Straits of Mackinac

Mackinac, Straits of channel N Mich. connecting Lake Huron & Lake Michigan; 4 *mi* (6.4 *km*) wide at narrowest point

Ma·comb \mə-'kōm\ city W Ill. SW of Peoria *pop* 19,952

Ma·con \'mä-kən\ city *cen* Ga. on the Ocmulgee *pop* 106,612

Mâ·con \mä-'kōⁿ\ city E France *pop* 39,130

Mac·quar·ie \mə-'kwär-ē\ river 750 *mi* (1200 *km*) SE Australia in E *cen* New South Wales flowing NNW to Darling River

Mac·tan \mäk-'tän\ island S *cen* Philippines off E coast of Cebu

Mad·a·gas·car \,ma-də-'gas-kər, -,kär\ island W Indian Ocean off SE Africa; formerly a French territory; became (1958) a republic of the French Community as the **Mal·a·gasy Republic** \,ma-lə-'ga-sē\ *or F* **Ré·pu·blique Mal·gache** \,rä-pūē-blēk-mal-'gash\ *or since 1975* **Dem·ocratic Republic of Madagascar** ✳ Antananarivo *area* 226,657 *sq mi* (589,308 *sq km*), *pop* 9,985,000 — **Mad·a·gas·can** \,ma-də-'gas-kən\ *adj or n*

Ma·dei·ra \mə-'dir-ə, -'der-ə\ **1** river 2100 *mi* (3380 *km*) W Brazil formed at Bolivian border by confluence of the Mamoré & the Beni & flowing NE to the Amazon **2** islands N Atlantic N of the Canaries belonging to Portugal ✳ Funchal *area* 302 *sq mi* (785 *sq km*), *pop* 257,822 **3** island, chief of group *area* 285 *sq mi* (741 *sq km*) — **Ma·dei·ran** \-'dir-ən, -'der-\ *adj or n*

Ma·de·ra \mə-'der-ə\ city S *cen* Calif. NW of Fresno *pop* 29,281

Ma·dhya Bha·rat \,mä-dyə-'bär-ət\ former state *cen* India; a union of 20 states including Gwalior, Indore, & Malwa formed 1948; became part of Madhya Pradesh 1956

Madhya Pra·desh \-prə-'desh, -'däsh\ state *cen* India ✳ Bhopal *area* 171,201 *sq mi* (445,123 *sq km*), *pop* 52,131,717 — see CENTRAL PROVINCES AND BERAR, MADHYA BHARAT

Ma·di·nat ash Sha'b \mə-'dē-,nə-tash-'shab\ city S Yemen; formerly a national ✳ of People's Democratic Republic of Yemen & (as **Al It·ti·had** \al-,i-tə-'had\) ✳ of Federation of South Arabia

Mad·i·son \'ma-də-sən\ **1** river 180 *mi* (290 *km*) SW Mont. — see THREE FORKS **2** city S Wis., its ✳ *pop* 191,262

Madison Heights city SE Mich. N of Detroit *pop* 32,196

Ma·dras \mə-'dras, -'dräs\ **1** — see TAMIL NADU **2** city & port S India ✳ of Tamil Nadu *pop* 4,276,635 — **Ma·drasi** \-'dra-sē, -'drä-\ *n*

\ə\ abut \ᵊ\ kitten, F table \ər\ further \a\ ash \ā\ ace \ä\ mop, mar
\aú\ out \ch\ chin \e\ bet \ē\ easy \g\ go \i\ hit \ī\ ice \j\ job
\ŋ\ sing \ō\ go \ó\ law \ói\ boy \th\ thin \t͟h\ the \ü\ loot \ú\ foot
\y\ yet \zh\ vision \á, k̲, ⁿ, œ, œ̄, ue, ūē, ᵞ\ see Guide to Pronunciation

Ma·dre, La·gu·na \lə-ˌgü-nə-ˈmä-drä\ inlet of Gulf of Mexico S Tex. bet. Padre Is. & mainland

Ma·dre de Dios \ˈmä-drā-(ˌ)dā-dē-ˈōs\ river 900 mi (1448 km) rising in SE Peru & flowing E into the Beni in Brazil

Ma·drid \mə-ˈdrid\ 1 province cen Spain in NW New Castile area 3084 sq mi (8018 sq km), pop 5,024,549 2 city, its ✳ & ✳ of Spain pop 3,158,818 — **Mad·ri·le·nian** \ˌma-drə-ˈlē-nē-ən, -dri-, -nyən\ adj or n — **Ma·dri·le·ño** \ˌmä-drə-ˈlā-(ˌ)nyō, -dri-\ n

Ma·du·ra or D **Ma·doe·ra** \mə-ˈdūr-ə\ island Indonesia off coast of NE Java area (with adjacent islands) 2113 sq mi (5494 sq km), pop 1,858,131 — **Ma·du·rese** \ˌma-də-ˈrēz, ˌma-jə-, -ˈrēs\ adj or n

Ma·du·rai \ˈmä-də-ˌrī\ city S India in S Tamil Nadu pop 904,362

Maeander — see MENDERES

Ma·fia \ˈmä-fē-ə, ˈma-\ island Tanzania in Indian Ocean S of Zanzibar area 170 sq mi (442 sq km), pop 16,748

Maf·i·king or **Maf·e·king** \ˈma-fə-kiŋ\ town N Republic of South Africa in North West province pop 6515

Ma·ga·dan \ˌmä-gə-ˈdan, -ˈdän\ city & port E Russia in Asia on N shore of Sea of Okhotsk pop 121,000

Magallanes — see PUNTA ARENAS

Mag·da·la \ˈmag-də-lə\ 1 ancient city N Palestine on W shore of Sea of Galilee N of Tiberias 2 town N cen Ethiopia

Mag·da·le·na \ˌmag-də-ˈlā-nə, -ˈlē-\ river 1000 mi (1609 km) Colombia flowing N into the Caribbean

Mag·da·len Islands \ˈmag-də-lən\ or F **Îles de la Ma·de·leine** \ēl-də-lä-mád-len, -mä-də-len\ islands Canada in Que. in Gulf of Saint Lawrence bet. Newfoundland & P.E.I. area 102 sq mi (265 sq km), pop 13,991

Mag·de·burg \ˈmäg-də-ˌbùrk, ˈmag-də-ˌbərg\ city cen Germany on the Elbe WSW of Berlin pop 289,292

Ma·gel·lan, Strait of \mə-ˈje-lən, chiefly Brit -ˈge-\ strait 370 mi (595 km) long at S end of S. America bet. mainland & Tierra del Fuego (Archipelago)

Magerøy — see NORTH CAPE

Mag·gio·re, Lake \ma-ˈjōr-ē, -ˈjor-\ lake 40 mi (64 km) long N Italy & S Switzerland traversed by Ticino River

Magh·er·a·felt \ˈmär-ə-ˌfelt, ˈma-kə-rə-ˌfelt\ district cen Northern Ireland, established 1974 area 221 sq mi (575 sq km), pop 30,825

Ma·ghrib or **Ma·ghrib** \ˈmä-grəb\ 1 NW Africa &, at time of the Moorish occupation, Spain; now considered as including Morocco, Algeria, Tunisia, & sometimes Libya 2 or **El Ma·ghreb al Aq·sa** \el-ˈmä-grəb-äl-ˈäk-sä\ MOROCCO — **Ma·ghre·bi** or **Ma·ghri·bi** \ˈmä-grə-bē\ adj or n — **Ma·ghreb·i·an** \mə-ˈgre-bē-ən\ or **Ma·ghrib·i·an** \-ˈgri-\ adj or n

Mag·na Grae·cia \ˌmag-nə-ˈgrē-shə\ the ancient Greek colonies in S Italian peninsula including Tarentum, Sybaris, Crotona, Heraclea, & Neapolis

Mag·ne·sia \mag-ˈnē-shə, -zhə\ 1 city & port NE Greece pop 77,907 2 — see MANISA

Mag·ni·to·gorsk \mag-ˈnē-tə-ˌgorsk\ city W Russia in Asia on Ural River pop 406,000

Magyarorszag — see HUNGARY

Ma·hal·la el Ku·bra \mə-ˌha-lə-el-ˈkü-brə\ city N Egypt in Nile delta NE of Tanta pop 292,114

Ma·ha·na·di \mə-ˈhä-nə-dē\ river 512 mi (1331 km) E India flowing into Bay of Bengal in Orissa through several mouths

Ma·ha·rash·tra \ˌmä-hə-ˈräsh-trə\ 1 region W cen India S of the Narbada; the original home of the Marathas 2 state W India bordering on Arabian Sea formed 1960 from SE part of former Bombay state ✳ Bombay area 118,717 sq mi (308,664 sq km), pop 62,093,898

Ma·hé \mä-ˈhā\ 1 island in Indian Ocean, chief of the Seychelles group pop 61,183 2 or formerly **May·ya·li** \mī-ˈyä-lē\ city SW India in N Kerala; a settlement of French India until 1954 pop 8972

Ma·hón \mə-ˈhon, mä-ˈon\ or **Port Ma·hon** \mə-ˈhon\ city & port Spain on Minorca Is. pop 17,802

Ma·hone Bay \mə-ˈhon\ inlet of the Atlantic E Canada in S N.S.

Maid·en·head \ˈmä-dᵊn-ˌhed\ borough S England in Berkshire on Thames River W of London pop 49,038

Maid·stone \ˈmād-stən, -ˌstōn\ borough SE England ✳ of Kent on the Medway ESE of London pop 72,311

Mai·kop \mī-ˈkop\ city S Russia in Europe ✳ of Adygea pop 111,000

Main \ˈmīn, ˈmän\ river 305 mi (491 km) S cen Germany rising in N Bavaria in the Fichtelgebirge & flowing W into the Rhine

Maine \ˈmān\ 1 state NE U.S. ✳ Augusta area 33,215 sq mi (86,359 sq km), pop 1,227,928 2 or **Le Maine** \lə-ˈmän, -ˈmen\ region & former province NW France S of Normandy ✳ Le Mans 3 — see MAYENNE

Main·er \ˈmā-nər\ n

Main·land \ˈmān-ˌland, -lənd\ 1 HONSHU 2 island N Scotland, largest of the Orkneys 3 island N Scotland, largest of the Shetlands

Mainz \ˈmīnts\ or F **Ma·yence** \mä-ˈyäⁿs\ city SW cen Germany on the Rhine ✳ of Rhineland-Palatinate pop 187,392

Mait·land \ˈmāt-lənd\ city SE Australia in E New South Wales pop 43,247

Ma·jor·ca \mä-ˈjor-kə, mə-, -ˈyor-\ or Sp **Ma·llor·ca** \mä-ˈyor-kə\ island Spain, largest of the Balearic Islands; chief city Palma area 1405 sq mi (3653 sq km) — **Ma·jor·can** \-ˈjor-kən, -ˈyor-\ adj or n

Ma·jun·ga \mə-ˈjəŋ-gə\ or **Ma·ha·jan·ga** \ˌmə-hə-ˈjəŋ-gə\ city & port NW Madagascar pop 65,864

Ma·ju·ro \mə-ˈjür-(ˌ)ō\ island (atoll) W Pacific in Marshall Islands; contains ✳ of the group

Ma·ka·lu \ˈma-kə-ˌlü\ mountain 27,824 ft (8481 m) in the Himalayas in NE Nepal SE of Mt. Everest; 5th highest in world

Ma·kas·sar \mə-ˈka-sər\ — see UJUNG PANDANG — **Ma·kas·sa·rese** \mə-ˌka-sə-ˈrēz, -ˈrēs\ n

Makassar Strait or **Ma·kas·ar** or **Ma·cas·sar** strait Indonesia bet. E Borneo & Sulawesi

Ma·ke·yev·ka \mə-ˈkā-yəf-kə\ city E Ukraine in Donets Basin NE of Donetsk pop 393,000

Ma·kga·di·kga·di \mä-ˌkä-dē-ˈkä-dē\ large salt basin NE Botswana

Ma·khach·ka·la \ˌmä-ˌkäch-kə-ˈlä\ or formerly **Pe·trovsk** \pə-ˈtrofsk\ city SE Russia in Europe on the Caspian ✳ of Dagestan pop 251,000

Ma·kin \ˈmä-kən, ˈma-\ or **Bu·ta·ri·ta·ri** \bü-ˌtär-ē-ˈtär-ē\ island (atoll) W Pacific at N end of Kiribati area 4 sq mi (10 sq km), pop 2714

Mal·a·bar Coast \ˈma-lə-ˌbär\ region SW India on Arabian Sea in Karnataka & Kerala states

Ma·la·bo \mä-ˈlä-(ˌ)bō\ or formerly **San·ta Is·a·bel** \ˌsan-tə-ˈi-zə-ˌbel\ city ✳ of Equatorial Guinea on Bioko Is. pop 37,237

Malacca — see MELAKA — **Ma·lac·can** \-kən\ adj

Ma·lac·ca, Strait of \mə-ˈla-kə, -ˈla-\ channel 500 mi (805 km) long bet. S Malay Peninsula & island of Sumatra

Má·la·ga \ˈma-lə-gə, ˈmä-\ 1 province S Spain in Andalusia area 2812 sq mi (7311 sq km), pop 958,967 2 city & port, its ✳, NE of Gibraltar pop 502,232

Malagasy Republic — see MADAGASCAR

Ma·lai·ta \mə-ˈlä-tə\ island SW Pacific in the SE Solomons NE of Guadalcanal area 2500 sq mi (6500 sq km), pop 50,661

Ma·lang \mə-ˈläŋ\ city Indonesia in E Java S of Surabaja pop 695,618

Mä·lar·en \ˈmä-ˌlär-ən\ lake SE Sweden extending from Baltic Sea 70 mi (113 km) inland

Ma·la·tya \ˌmä-lə-ˈtyä\ or anc **Mel·i·te·ne** \ˌme-lə-ˈtē-nē\ city E Turkey NE of Gaziantep pop 184,390

Ma·la·wi \mə-ˈlä-wē, -ˈlaü-ē\ or formerly **Ny·asa·land** \nī-ˈa-sə-ˌland, nē-\ country SE Africa bordering on Lake Malawi; formerly a Brit. protectorate; independent member of the Commonwealth of Nations since 1964; a republic since 1966 ✳ Lilongwe area 37,374 sq mi (97,172 sq km), pop 5,547,460 — **Ma·la·wi·an** \-ən\ adj or n

Malawi, Lake or **Lake Ny·asa** \nī-ˈa-sə, nē-\ lake SE Africa in Great Rift valley in Malawi, Mozambique, & Tanzania

Ma·laya \mə-ˈlā-ə, mä-\ 1 MALAY PENINSULA 2 BRITISH MALAYA 3 or **Federation of Malaya** former country SE Asia; a Brit. dominion 1957–63, since 1963 a territory (now called **Peninsular Malaysia**) of Malaysia ✳ Kuala Lumpur area 50,690 sq mi (131,794 sq km)

Ma·lay Archipelago \mə-ˈlā, ˈmā-(ˌ)lā\ archipelago SE Asia including Sumatra, Java, Borneo, Sulawesi, Moluccas, & Timor; usu. considered as including also the Philippines & sometimes New Guinea

Malay Peninsula peninsula 700 mi (1126 km) long SE Asia divided bet. Thailand & Malaysia

Ma·lay·sia \mə-ˈlā-zh(ē-)ə, -sh(ē-)ə\ 1 MALAY ARCHIPELAGO 2 or **Federation of Malaysia** country SE Asia, a union of Malaya, Sabah (N. Borneo), Sarawak, & (until 1965) Singapore; a limited constitutional monarchy in the Commonwealth of Nations ✳ Kuala Lumpur area 128,703 sq mi (334,628 sq km), pop 13,700,000 — **Ma·lay·sian** \mə-ˈlā-zhən, -shən\ adj or n

Malay Sea sea SE Asia surrounding the Malay Archipelago

Mal·den \ˈmol-dən\ 1 city E Mass. N of Boston pop 53,884 2 island cen Pacific, one of the Line Islands

Mal·dive Islands \ˈmol-ˌdēv, -ˌdīv- also ˈmal-, -div\ islands in Indian Ocean S of the Laccadives; a sultanate under Brit. protection until 1965; now an independent member of the Commonwealth of Nations as **Republic of Maldives** ✳ Male area 115 sq mi (299 sq km), pop 143,046 — **Mal·div·i·an** \mol-ˈdi-vē-ən, mal-\ adj or n

Ma·le \ˈmä-lē\ island (atoll), ✳ of the Maldives

Ma·lea, Cape \mə-ˈlē-ə\ cape S Greece at extremity of E peninsula of the Peloponnisos

Ma·le·bo Pool \mä-ˈlä-ˌbō\ or **Stanley Pool** expansion of Congo River ab 20 mi (32 km) long 300 mi (483 km) above its mouth bet. Congo & Zaire

Mal·e·ku·la or **Mal·a·ku·la** \ˌma-lə-ˈkü-lə\ island SW Pacific in Vanuatu area 781 sq mi (2023 sq km), pop 19,289

Malgache, République — see MADAGASCAR

Mal·heur Lake \mal-ˈhùr\ lake SE Oreg. in Harney Basin

Ma·li \ˈmä-lē, ˈma-\ 1 federation 1959–60 of Senegal & Sudanese Republic 2 or formerly **Sudanese Republic** country W Africa in W Sahara & Sudan regions; a republic; before 1958 constituted **French Sudan** (a territory of France); ✳ Bamako area 461,389 sq mi (1,199,611 sq km), pop 6,524,650 — **Ma·li·an** \-lē-ən\ adj or n

Malines — see MECHLIN

Mal·in Head \ˈma-lən\ cape Ireland (republic) in county Donegal; northernmost tip of Ireland

Mal·mé·dy \ˌmal-mə-ˈdē\ commune E Belgium SE of Liège; formerly in Germany, transferred (with Eupen) to Belgium 1919 pop 10,291

Malmö \ˈmal-ˌmœ, -(ˌ)mō\ city & port SW Sweden on Øresund opposite Copenhagen, Denmark pop 232,908

Mal·ta \ˈmol-tə\ or anc **Mel·i·ta** \ˈme-lə-tə\ 1 or **Mal·tese Islands** \mol-ˈtēz, -ˈtēs\ group of islands in the Mediterranean S of Sicily; a dominion of the Commonwealth of Nations since 1964 ✳ Valletta area 122 sq mi (317 sq km), pop 354,949 2 island, chief of the group area 95 sq mi (247 sq km)

Maluku — see MOLUCCAS

Mal·vern Hills \ˈmo(l)-vərn\ hills W England in Hereford and Worcester

Malvinas, Islas — see FALKLAND ISLANDS

Mam·be·ra·mo \ˌmam-bə-ˈrä-(ˌ)mō\ river 500 mi (805 km) W. New Guinea flowing NW into the Pacific

Mam·moth Cave \ˈma-məth\ limestone caverns SW cen Kentucky in **Mammoth Cave National Park**

Ma·mo·ré \ˌmä-mə-ˈrā\ river 1200 mi (1931 km) Bolivia flowing N to unite with the Beni on Brazilian border forming Madeira River

Man, Isle of \ˈman\ or anc **Mo·na·pia** \mə-ˈnä-pē-ə\ or **Mo·na** \ˈmō-nə\ island British Isles in Irish Sea; a possession of the Brit. Crown; has own legislature & laws ✳ Douglas area 221 sq mi (575 sq km), pop 60,496 — **Manx·man** \ˈmaŋks-mən\ n

Ma·na·do \mə-ˈnä-(ˌ)dō\ city & port Indonesia on NE Sulawesi Is. on Celebes Sea pop 318,796

Ma·na·gua \mə-ˈnä-gwə\ city ✳ of Nicaragua on Lake Managua pop 552,900

Managua, Lake lake 38 mi (61 km) long W Nicaragua draining S to Lake Nicaragua

Ma·na·ma \mə-ˈna-mə\ city ✳ of Bahrain pop 108,684

Ma·nas·sas \mə-ˈna-səs\ city NE Va. pop 27,957

Ma·naus \mə-ˈnaüs\ city W Brazil ✳ of Amazonas on Negro River 12 mi (19 km) from its junction with the Amazon pop 634,659

Mancha, La — see LA MANCHA

Manche, La — see ENGLISH CHANNEL

Man·ches·ter \ˈman-ˌches-tər, -chəs-tər\ 1 town cen Conn. E of Hartford pop 51,618 2 city S N.H. on the Merrimack pop 99,567 3 city

NW England ENE of Liverpool *pop* 448,934 — see GREATER MANCHES-TER — **Man·cu·ni·an** \man-'kyü-nē-ən, -nyən\ *adj or n*
Man·chu·kuo \'man-'chü-'kwō, man-'chü-\ former country (1931–45) E Asia in Manchuria & E Inner Mongolia ✲ Changchun
Man·chu·ria \man-'chúr-ē-ə\ region NE China S of the Amur including Heilongjiang, Jilin, & Liaoning provinces & part of Inner Mongolia — **Man·chu·ri·an** \-ē-ən\ *adj or n*
Man·da·lay \,man-də-'lā\ city *cen* Myanmar *pop* 453,000
Man·ga·ia \män-'gī-ə, -'ī-ə\ island S Pacific in SE Cook Islands; completely encircled by reef *area* 25 *sq mi* (65 *sq km*)
Man·ga·lore \'maŋ-gə-,lōr, -,lór\ city S India in Karnataka on Malabar coast W of Bangalore *pop* 305,513
Man·ga·re·va \,mäŋ-gə-'rä-və, ,mäŋ-ə-\ island S Pacific, chief of the Gambier Islands *area* 7 *sq mi* (18 *sq km*)
Man·hat·tan \man-'ha-t⁹n, mən-\ **1** city NE *cen* Kans. on Kansas River *pop* 37,712 **2** island 13 *mi* (21 *km*) long SE N.Y. on New York Bay **3** borough of New York City comprising Manhattan Is., several small adjacent islands, & a small area (Marble Hill) on mainland *pop* 1,487,536 — **Man·hat·tan·ite** \-,īt\ *n*
Manhattan Beach city SW Calif. SW of Los Angeles *pop* 32,063
Ma·ni·hi·ki \,mä-nə-'hē-kē\ island, chief of the Northern Cook Islands; an atoll *pop* 408
Manihiki Islands — see NORTHERN COOK ISLANDS
Ma·ni·la \mə-'ni-lə\ city & port ✲ of the Philippines on W coast of Luzon on **Manila Bay** (inlet of S. China Sea) *metropolitan area pop* 7,832,000
Man·i·pur \,ma-nə-'púr, ,mə-\ **1** river 210 *mi* (338 *km*) NE India & W Myanmar flowing into the Chindwin **2** state NE India bet. Assam & Myanmar ✲ Imphal *area* 8628 *sq mi* (22,433 *sq km*)
Ma·ni·sa *or* **Ma·nis·sa** \,mä-nə-'sä\ *or anc* **Mag·ne·sia** \mag-'nē-shə, -zhə\ city W Turkey NE of Izmir *pop* 93,970
Man·i·to·ba \,ma-nə-'tō-bə\ province S *cen* Canada ✲ Winnipeg *area* 251,000 *sq mi* (652,600 *sq km*), *pop* 1,091,942 — **Man·i·to·ban** \-bən\ *adj or n*
Manitoba, Lake lake 120 *mi* (193 *km*) long Canada in S Man. *area* 1817 *sq mi* (4724 *sq km*)
Man·i·tou·lin Island \,ma-nə-'tü-lən\ island 80 *mi* (129 *km*) long Canada in Ont. in Lake Huron *area* 1068 *sq mi* (2777 *sq km*)
Man·i·to·woc \'ma-nə-tə-,wäk\ city E Wis. *pop* 32,520
Ma·ni·za·les \,ma-nə-'zä-ləs, -'za-\ city W *cen* Colombia in Cauca valley *pop* 267,543
Man·ka·to \man-'kā-(,)tō\ city S Minn. *pop* 31,477
Man·nar, Gulf of \mə-'när\ inlet of Indian Ocean bet. Sri Lanka & S tip of India S of Palk Strait
Mann·heim \'man-,hīm, 'män-\ city SW Germany at confluence of the Rhine & the Neckar *pop* 304,303
Mans·field \'man(t)s-,fēld, 'manz-\ **1** town *cen* Conn. *pop* 21,103 **2** city N *cen* Ohio *pop* 50,627 **3** borough N *cen* England in Nottinghamshire N of Nottingham *pop* 58,949
Mansfield, Mount mountain 4393 *ft* (1339 *m*) N Vt.; highest in Green Mountains & in state
Man·su·ra \man-'súr-ə\ *or* **El Mansûra** \,el-\ city N Egypt in Nile delta *pop* 212,300
Man·te·ca \man-'tē-kə\ city *cen* Calif. S of Stockton *pop* 40,773
Man·tua \'man-chə-wə, 'manch-wə, 'man-tə-wə\ *or* **Man·to·va** \'män-tə-və\ commune N Italy in Lombardy WSW of Venice *pop* 54,808 — **Man·tu·an** \'man-chə-wən, 'manch-wən, 'man-tə-wən\ *adj or n*
Ma·nua Islands \mə-'nü-ə\ islands SW Pacific in American Samoa E of Tutuila *area* 22 *sq mi* (57 *sq km*)
Ma·nus \'mä-nəs\ island SW Pacific in Admiralty Islands; largest of group *area* 600 *sq mi* (1560 *sq km*)
Man·za·la, Lake \man-'zä-lə\ *or anc* **Ta·nis** \'tā-nəs\ lagoon N Egypt in Nile delta W of N entrance of Suez Canal
Man·za·nil·lo \,man-zə-'nē-(,)ō, ,män-sə-\ **1** city & port E Cuba on the Caribbean *pop* 124,537 **2** city & port SW Mexico in Colima *pop* 29,347
Mao·ke Mountains \'maú-kā\ *or formerly* **Snow Mountains** \'snō\ mountains W. Irian, Indonesia, include Sudirman & Djajawidjaja ranges — see DJADJA (Mount)
Maple Grove city SE *cen* Minn. *pop* 38,736
Maple Heights city NE Ohio SE of Cleveland *pop* 27,089
Maple Ridge municipality Canada in SW B.C. E of Vancouver *pop* 48,422
Ma·ple·wood \'mā-pəl-,wúd\ village SE Minn. *pop* 30,954
Ma·pu·to \mä-'pü-(,)tō\ *or formerly* **Lou·ren·ço Mar·ques** \lə-'ren(t)-(,)sō-,mär-'kes, -'mär-kəs, -'märk(s)\ city & port ✲ of Mozambique on Delagoa Bay *pop* 755,300
Ma·quo·ke·ta \mə-'kō-kə-tə\ river 150 *mi* (241 *km*) E Iowa flowing SE into Mississippi River
Mar·a·cai·bo \,mar-ə-'kī-(,)bō\ city NW Venezuela on channel bet. Lake Maracaibo & Gulf of Venezuela *pop* 1,249,670
Maracaibo, Lake the S extension of Gulf of Venezuela in NW Venezuela *area* 6300 *sq mi* (16,380 *sq km*)
Maracanda — see SAMARKAND
Ma·ra·cay \,mar-ə-'kī\ city N Venezuela WSW of Caracas *pop* 354,196
Marais des Cygnes \,mer-ə-'zēn, -'sēn\ river 150 *mi* (241 *km*) E Kans. & W Mo. flowing into the Osage
Ma·ra·nhão \,mar-ə-'nyaú\ state NE Brazil bordering on the Atlantic ✲ São Luís *area* 133,674 *sq mi* (347,552 *sq km*), *pop* 4,097,231
Ma·ra·ñón \,mar-ə-'nyōn\ river 800 *mi* (1287 *km*) N Peru flowing from the Andes NNW & E to join the Ucayali forming the Amazon
Ma·raş *or* **Ma·rash** \mə-'räsh\ city S *cen* Turkey *pop* 63,284
Mar·a·thon \'mar-ə-,thän\ **1** plain E Greece in Attica NE of Athens on the Aegean **2** ancient town on the plain
Marble Canyon canyon of Colorado River N Ariz. just above the Grand Canyon, sometimes considered its upper portion
Mar·ble·head \'mär-bəl-,hed, ,mär-bəl-'\ town E Mass. *pop* 19,971
Mar·burg \'mär-,búrk, -,bərg\ city W *cen* Germany in Hesse N of Frankfurt am Main *pop* 76,419
Marche \'märsh\ region & former province *cen* France NW of Auvergne
March·es \'mär-chəz\ *or* **Le Mar·che** \lä-'mär-(,)kā\ region *cen* Italy on the Adriatic NW of Abruzzi ✲ Ancona *pop* 1,430,726

Mar·cus Island \'mär-kəs\ island W Pacific E of the Bonin Islands, belonging to Japan; occupied 1945–68 by U.S. *area* 1 *sq mi* (2.6 *sq km*)
Mar·cy, Mount \'mär-sē\ mountain 5344 *ft* (1629 *m*) NE N.Y.; highest in Adirondack Mountains & in state
Mar del Pla·ta \,mär-del-'plä-tə\ city & port E Argentina SSE of Buenos Aires *pop* 407,024
Mare Island \'mar, 'mer\ island W Calif. in San Pablo Bay
Ma·rem·ma \mə-'re-mə\ low-lying district W Italy on Tyrrhenian coast in SW Tuscany; formerly swampland
Ma·ren·go \mə-'reŋ-(,)gō\ village NW Italy in SE Piedmont
Mar·e·o·tis, Lake \,mar-ē-'ō-təs\ *or Ar* **Mar·yût** \mər-'yüt\ lake N Egypt in Nile delta; Alexandria is situated bet. it & the Mediterranean
Ma·reth \'mär-əth, 'mar-\ town SE Tunisia SSE of Gabes
Mar·ga·ri·ta \,mär-gə-'rē-tə\ island N Venezuela in the Caribbean, chief of the **Nue·va Es·par·ta** \,nü-,ä-və-ə-'spär-tə\ group; chief town & port Porlamar *area* 444 *sq mi* (1154 *sq km*)
Mar·gate \'mär-,gāt\ **1** city SE Fla. *pop* 42,985 **2** \-,gāt, -gət\ borough SE England in Kent on coast of Isle of Thanet *pop* 53,280
Mar·i·ana Islands \,mar-ē-'a-nə, ,mer-\ *or formerly* **La·drone Islands** \lə-'drōn\ islands W Pacific S of Bonin Islands; comprise commonwealth of Northern Mariana Islands & Guam
Ma·ri·a·nao \,mär-ē-ə-'naú\ city W Cuba, W suburb of Havana *pop* 127,563
Ma·ri·án·ské Láz·ně \'mär-ē-,än(t)-skə-'läz-nə\ *or G* **Ma·ri·en·bad** \mə-'rē-ən-,bad, -,bät; 'mär-ē-ən-, 'mer-\ town W Czech Republic in NW Bohemia NE of Plzeň
Mar·i·as \mə-'rī-əs, -əz\ river 250 *mi* (402 *km*) NW Mont. flowing SE to Missouri River
Marias Pass mountain pass 5213 *ft* (1589 *m*) NW Mont. in Lewis Range at SE corner of Glacier National Park
Ma·ri·bor \'mär-i-,bór\ city NE Slovenia *pop* 97,167
Ma·rie Byrd Land \mə-,rē-'bərd\ region W Antarctica E of Ross Ice Shelf & Ross Sea
Ma·rie Ga·lante \mə-,rē-gə-'länt\ island E W. Indies in the Leewards; a dependency of Guadeloupe *area* 60 *sq mi* (156 *sq km*), *pop* 15,912
Ma·rie·hamn \mə-,rē-'hä-mən\ *or* **Maa·rian·ha·mi·na** \'mär-yän-,hä-mə-,nä\ seaport SW Finland ✲ of Ahvenanmaa *pop* 10,067
Mar·i·et·ta \,mar-ē-'e-tə, ,mer-\ city NW Ga. NW of Atlanta *pop* 44,129
Ma·ri·na \mə-'rē-nə\ city W Calif. on Monterey Bay *pop* 26,436
Ma·rin·du·que \,mar-ən-'dü-(,)kā, ,mär-\ island Philippines in Sibuyan Sea S of Luzon; chief town Boac *area* 355 *sq mi* (923 *sq km*), *pop* 173,715
Mar·i·on \'mer-ē-ən, 'mar-\ **1** city N *cen* Ind. *pop* 32,618 **2** city E Iowa NE of Cedar Rapids *pop* 20,403 **3** city *cen* Ohio *pop* 34,075
Ma·ri Republic \'mär-ē\ autonomous republic E *cen* Russia in Europe ✲ Ioshkar Ola *area* 8900 *sq mi* (23,140 *sq km*), *pop* 685,000
Maritime Alps section of the W Alps SE France & NW Italy extending to the Mediterranean; highest point Punta Argentera 10,817 *ft* (3297 *m*)
Maritime Provinces *or* **Maritimes** the Canadian provinces of N.B., N.S., P.E.I. & sometimes thought to include Nfld. — see ATLANTIC PROVINCES
Maritime Territory *or Russ* **Pri·mor·ye** \prē-'mór-yə\ territory E Russia in Asia bordering on Sea of Japan ✲ Vladivostok *area* 64,900 *sq mi* (168,740 *sq km*), *pop* 1,722,000
Ma·ri·tsa \mə-'rēt-sə\ *or NGk* **Ev·ros** \'ev-,rós\ *or Turk* **Me·riç** \mə-'rēch\ river 320 *mi* (515 *km*) S Europe flowing from W Rhodope Mountains in S Bulgaria E & S through Thrace into the Aegean
Ma·ri·u·pol \,mar-ē-'ü-,pól\ *or 1949–1989* **Zhda·nov** \zhə-'dä-nəf, 'shtä-\ city E Ukraine *pop* 417,000
Mark·ham \'mär-kəm\ **1** town Canada in SE Ont. NE of Toronto *pop* 153,811 **2** river 200 *mi* (322 *km*) Papua New Guinea flowing S & SE into Solomon Sea
Markham, Mount mountain 14,275 *ft* (4351 *m*) Antarctica W of Ross Ice Shelf
Marl \'märl\ city W Germany in the Ruhr *pop* 89,082
Marl·bor·ough *or* **Marl·boro** \'märl-,bər-ə, 'mól-, -,bə-rə, -b(ə-)rə\ city E Mass. E of Worcester *pop* 31,813
Mar·ma·ra, Sea of \'mär-mə-rə\ *or anc* **Pro·pon·tis** \prə-'pän-təs\ sea NW Turkey connected with Black Sea by the Bosporus & with Aegean Sea by the Dardanelles *area* 4250 *sq mi* (11,050 *sq km*)
Mar·mo·la·da \,mär-mə-'lä-də\ mountain 10,965 *ft* (3342 *m*) NE Italy; highest in the Dolomites
Marne \'märn\ river 325 *mi* (523 *km*) NE France flowing W into the Seine
Ma·ro·ni \mə-'rō-nē\ *or D* **Ma·ro·wij·ne** \'mär-ō-,vī-nə\ river 420 *mi* (676 *km*) on border bet. Suriname & French Guiana flowing N into the Atlantic
Maros — see MURES
Mar·que·sas Islands \mär-'kā-zəz, -zəs, -,səz, -səs\ *or F* **Îles Marquises** \,ē(∂)l-mär-'kēz\ islands S Pacific N of Tuamotu Archipelago in French Polynesia ✲ Hakapehi (on Nuku Hiva) *area* 480 *sq mi* (1248 *sq km*), *pop* 7358
Mar·quette \mär-'ket\ city NW Mich. in Upper Peninsula on Lake Superior *pop* 21,977
Mar·ra·kech *or* **Mar·ra·kesh** \mə-'rä-kesh, 'mar-ə-, mə-'rä-kish\ *or formerly* **Mo·roc·co** \mə-'rä-(,)kō\ city *cen* Morocco in foothills of the Grand Atlas *pop* 439,728
Mar·sa·la \mär-'sä-lə\ city & port Italy on W coast of Sicily S of Trapani *pop* 80,869
Mar·seilles \mär-'sā, -'sā(ə)lz\ *or* **Mar·seille** \mär-'sā\ *or anc* **Mas·sil·ia** \mə-'si-lē-ə\ city & port SE France on Gulf of Lions *pop* 908,600 — **Mar·seil·lais** \,mär-sā-'yä(z), -sə-\ \-sā-'lā(z)\ *n*
Mar·shall \'mär-shəl\ city NE Tex. *pop* 23,682
Marshall Islands islands W Pacific ✲ Majuro; part of former Trust Territory of the Pacific Islands; internally self-governing since 1980 — **Mar·shall·ese** \,mär-shə-'lēz, -'lēs\ *adj or n*

\ə\ abut \ᵊ\ kitten, F table \ər\ further \a\ ash \ā\ ace \ä\ mop, mar
\aú\ out \ch\ chin \e\ bet \ē\ easy \g\ go \i\ hit \ī\ ice \j\ job
\ŋ\ sing \ō\ go \ò\ law \ói\ boy \th\ thin \ṯh\ the \ü\ loot \ú\ foot
\y\ yet \zh\ vision \à, k̲, ⁿ, œ, œ̄, ᴜe, ūe, ᵊ\ see Guide to Pronunciation

Mar·shall·town \'mär-shəl-ˌtaún\ city cen Iowa pop 25,178

Marsh·field \'märsh-ˌfēld\ **1** town E Mass. N of Plymouth pop 21,531 **2** city N cen Wis. pop 19,291

Mar·ston Moor \'mär-stən\ locality N England in N. Yorkshire W of York

Mar·ta·ban, Gulf of \ˌmär-tə-'ban, -'bän\ arm of Andaman Sea S Myanmar

Mar·tha's Vineyard \'mär-thəz\ island 20 mi (32 km) long SE Mass. in the Atlantic off SW coast of Cape Cod WNW of Nantucket — **Vine·yard·er** \'vin-yər-dər\ n

Mar·ti·nez \mär-'tē-nəs\ city W Calif. NE of Oakland pop 31,808

Mar·ti·nique \ˌmär-t°n-'ēk\ island W. Indies in the Windwards; department of France ✻ Fort-de-France area 385 sq mi (1001 sq km), pop 326,717 — **Mar·ti·ni·can** \-'ē-kən\ adj or n — **Mar·ti·ni·quais** \-ˌtē-ni-'kä\ adj

Marwar — see JODHPUR

Mary·land \'mer-ə-lənd\ state E U.S. ✻ Annapolis area 10,577 sq mi (27,500 sq km), pop 4,781,468 — **Mary·land·er** \-lən-dər, -ˌlan-\ n

Maryland Heights city E Mo. W of St. Louis pop 25,407

Mary·le·bone \'mar-(ə-)lə-bən, 'mar-i-bən\ or **Saint Marylebone** former metropolitan borough NW cen London, England; now part of Westminster

Mary·ville \'mer-ē-ˌvil, 'mar-ē-, 'mä-rē-, -vəl\ city E Tenn. pop 19,208

Ma·sa·da \mə-'sä-də\ fortress town of ancient Palestine, site in SE Israel W of Dead Sea

Ma·san \'mä-ˌsän\ or formerly **Ma·sam·po** \'mä-ˌsäm-ˌpō\ city & port SE S. Korea on an inlet of Korea Strait E of Pusan pop 448,746

Mas·ba·te \mäz-'bä-tē, mäs-\ island cen Philippines in the Visayans NE of Panay area 1571 sq mi (4085 sq km)

Mas·ca·rene Islands \ˌmas-kə-'rēn\ islands W Indian Ocean E of Madagascar including Mauritius, Réunion, and Rodrigues

Mas·couche \ma-'skǘsh\ town Canada in S Que. N of Montreal pop 25,828

Mas·e·ru \'ma-sə-ˌrü\ city ✻ of Lesotho pop 71,500

Mash·had \'mash-ˌad\ or **Me·shed** \mə-'shed\ city NE Iran pop 1,463,508

Ma·son City \'mä-s°n\ city N Iowa pop 29,040

Mason–Dix·on line \-'dik-sən\ the boundary line from the SW corner of Del. N to Pa. & W to approximately the SW corner of Pa. & often considered the boundary bet. the N & S states

Mas·sa·chu·setts \ˌma-sə-'chü-səts, ˌmas-'chü-, -zəts\ state NE U.S. ✻ Boston area 8257 sq mi (21,468 sq km), pop 6,016,425

Massachusetts Bay inlet of the Atlantic E Mass.

Mas·sa·nut·ten Mountain \ˌma-sə-'nə-t°n\ ridge N Va. in Blue Ridge Mountains

Mas·sa·wa \mə-'sä-wə, -'saú-ə\ city & port Eritrea on an inlet of Red Sea pop 18,490

Mas·sif Cen·tral \ma-'sēf-(ˌ)sen-'träl, -(ˌ)sän-\ plateau cen France rising sharply just W of the Rhône-Saône valley & sloping N to the Paris basin & W to the basin of Aquitaine

Mas·sil·lon \'ma-sə-lən, -ˌlän\ city NE Ohio pop 31,007

Mas·sive, Mount \'ma-siv\ mountain 14,421 ft (4396 m), cen Colo. in Sawatch Range N of Mt. Elbert

Ma·su·ria \mə-'zúr-ē-ə, -'súr-\ or G **Ma·su·ren** \mə-'zúr-ən\ region NE Poland SE of Gulf of Gdansk; formerly in E. Prussia, Germany — **Ma·su·ri·an** \mə-'zúr-ē-ən, -'súr-\ adj

Mat·a·be·le·land \ˌma-tə-'bē-lē-ˌland, -'bā-lā-\ region SW Zimbabwe bet. the Limpopo & the Zambezi; chief town Bulawayo

Ma·ta·di \mə-'tä-dē\ town & port W Zaire pop 140,475

Mat·a·gor·da Bay \ˌma-tə-'gór-də\ inlet of Gulf of Mexico 30 mi (48 km) long SE Tex.

Mat·a·mo·ros \ˌma-tə-'mòr-əs, -'mòr-\ city NE Mexico in Tamaulipas on Rio Grande opposite Brownsville, Tex. pop 182,887

Mat·a·nus·ka \ˌma-tə-'nüs-kə\ river 90 mi (145 km) S Alaska flowing SW to head of Cook Inlet

Ma·tan·zas \mə-'tan-zəs\ city & port W Cuba on Straits of Florida E of Havana pop 109,747

Matapan — see TAÍNARON

Ma·thu·ra \'mə-tə-rə\ or **Mut·tra** \'mə-trə\ city N India in W Uttar Pradesh NW of Agra pop 160,995

Mat·lock \'mat-ˌläk\ town N England ✻ of Derbyshire pop 20,610

Ma·to Gros·so or formerly **Mat·to Gros·so** \ˌma-tə-'grō-(ˌ)sō, -(ˌ)sü\ **1** state SW Brazil ✻ Cuiabá area 475,504 sq mi (1,236,310 sq km), pop 1,169,812   **2** plateau region in E cen Mato Grosso state

Ma·to Gros·so do Sul \dō-'sül, -dü-\ state SW Brazil ✻ Campo Grande area 140,219 sq mi (350,548 sq km), pop 1,401,151

Mato Tepee — see DEVILS TOWER

Ma·trûh \mə-'trü\ or **Mer·sa Matrûh** \(ˌ)mər-'sä\ town NW Egypt

Mats·qui \'mat-skwē\ municipality Canada in SW B.C. SE of Vancouver pop 68,064

Mat·su \'mät-'sü, 'mat-, -(ˌ)sü\ island off SE China in Formosa Strait; administered by Taiwan pop 11,002

Mat·su·do \mät-'sü-(ˌ)dō\ city Japan on Honshu, a suburb of Tokyo pop 456,211

Mat·su·shi·ma \ˌmät-sü-'shē-mə, mät-'sü-shi-mə\ group of over 200 islets Japan off N Honshu NE of Sendai

Mat·su·ya·ma \ˌmät-sə-'yä-mə\ city & port Japan in W Shikoku pop 443,317

Mat·tag·a·mi \mə-'ta-gə-mē\ river 275 mi (442 km) Canada in E Ont.

Mat·ta·po·ni \ˌma-tə-pə-'nī\ river 125 mi (201 km) E Va.

Mat·ter·horn \'ma-tər-ˌhórn, 'mä-\ or F **Mont Cer·vin** \ˌmō°-ser-'va°\ mountain 14,690 ft (4478 m) in Pennine Alps on border bet. Switzerland & Italy

Ma·tu·rín \ˌmä-tə-'rēn\ city NE Venezuela pop 206,654

Maui \'maú-ē\ island Hawaii NW of Hawaii (island) area 728 sq mi (1893 sq km)

Mau·mee \'mò-'mē\ river 175 mi (282 km) NE Ind. & NW Ohio flowing NE into Lake Erie at Toledo

Mau·na Kea \ˌmaú-nə-'kā-ə, ˌmò-nə-\ extinct volcano 13,796 ft (4205 m) Hawaii in N cen Hawaii (island)

Mauna Loa \-'lō-ə\ volcano 13,680 ft (4170 m) Hawaii in S cen Hawaii (island) in Hawaii Volcanoes National Park — see KILAUEA

Maures, Monts des \ˌmō°-dā-'mòr, -'mòr\ mountains SE France along the Riviera SW of Fréjus

Mau·re·ta·nia or **Mau·ri·ta·nia** \ˌmòr-ə-'tā-nē-ə, ˌmär-, -nyə\ ancient country N Africa W of Numidia in modern Morocco & W Algeria — **Mau·re·ta·ni·an** or **Mau·ri·ta·ni·an** \-nē-ən, -nyən\ adj or n

Mauritania or F **Mau·ri·ta·nie** \ˌmò-rē-tä-nē\ country NW Africa bordering on the Atlantic N of Senegal River; a republic within the French Community, formerly a territory ✻ Nouakchott area ab 432,000 sq mi (1,123,200 sq km), pop 1,419,939 — **Mau·ri·ta·ni·an** \ˌmòr-ə-'tā-nē-ən, ˌmär-, -nyən\ adj or n

Mau·ri·ti·us \mò-'ri-sh(ē-)əs\ island in Indian Ocean in cen Mascarenes; constitutes with Rodrigues & other dependencies a dominion of the Commonwealth of Nations ✻ Port Louis area 720 sq mi (1872 sq km), pop 993,000 — **Mau·ri·tian** \-'ri-shən\ adj or n

May, Cape \'mā\ cape S N.J. at entrance to Delaware Bay

May·a·gua·na \ˌmī-ə-'gwä-nə\ island in the SE Bahamas NNE of Great Inagua Is. area 96 sq mi (250 sq km)

Ma·ya·güez \ˌmī-ə-'gwez, -'gwes\ city & port W Puerto Rico pop 100,371

Ma·ya·pán \ˌmī-ə-'pän\ ruined city ✻ of the Mayas SE Mexico in Yucatán SSE of Mérida

Mayence — see MAINZ

Ma·yenne \mä-'yen\ river 125 mi (201 km) NW France uniting with the Sarthe to form the **Maine** \'mān, 'men\ (8 mi or 13 km long, flowing into the Loire)

May·fair \'mā-ˌfar, -ˌfer\ district of W London, England, in Westminster borough

May·field Heights \'mā-ˌfēld\ city NE Ohio E of Cleveland pop 19,847

May·nooth \mā-'nüth\ town E Ireland in County Kildare pop 4768

Mayo **1** \'mī-(ˌ)ō\ river 250 mi (402 km) NW Mexico in Sonora flowing SW into Gulf of California   **2** \'mä-(ˌ)ō\ county NW Ireland in Connacht ✻ Castlebar area 2084 sq mi (5418 sq km), pop 110,696

Ma·yon \mä-'yōn\ volcano 7943 ft (2421 m) Philippines in SE Luzon

Ma·yotte \mä-'yät, -'yòt\ island of the Comoro group; a French dependency area 144 sq mi (374 sq km) pop 90,000 — see COMORO ISLANDS

May·wood \'mā-ˌwúd\ **1** city SW Calif. W of Whittier pop 27,850   **2** village NE Ill. W of Chicago pop 27,139

Mayyali — see MAHÉ

Mazaca — see KAYSERI

Ma·za·tlán \ˌmä-zət-'län, -sət-\ city & port W Mexico in Sinaloa on the Pacific pop 147,010

Mba·ba·ne \em-bä-'bä-nä\ town ✻ of Swaziland pop 23,109

Mban·da·ka \em-ˌbän-'dä-kə\ or formerly **Co·quil·hat·ville** \ˌkō-kē-'at-ˌvil\ city W Zaire on Congo River pop 137,484

Mbi·ni \em-'bē-nē\ or formerly **Rio Mu·ni** \ˌrē-ō-'mü-nē\ mainland portion of Equatorial Guinea bordering on Gulf of Guinea ✻ Bata area 10,040 sq mi (26,104 sq km)

Mbomou — see BOMU

Mbu·ji–Ma·yi \em-ˌbü-jē-'mī-ˌyē\ or formerly **Ba·kwan·ga** \bə-'kwän-gə\ city S Zaire pop 285,470

Mc·Al·len \mə-'ka-lən\ city S Tex. WNW of Brownsville pop 84,021

Mc·Kees·port \mə-'kēz-ˌpòrt, -ˌpórt\ city SW Pa. S of Pittsburgh pop 26,016

Mc·Kin·ley, Mount \mə-'kin-lē\ or **De·na·li** \də-'nä-lē\ mountain 20,320 ft (6194 m) cen Alaska in Alaska Range; highest in U.S. & N. America; in **Denali National Park**

Mc·Kin·ney \mə-'ki-nē\ city NE Tex. N of Dallas pop 21,283

M'·Clure Strait \mə-'klùr\ channel N Canada bet. Banks Is. & Melville Is. opening on the W into Arctic Ocean

Mc·Mur·do Sound \mək-'mər-dō\ inlet of W Ross Sea Antarctica bet. Ross Is. & coast of Victoria Land

Mead, Lake \'mēd\ reservoir NW Ariz. & SE Nev. formed by Hoover Dam in Colorado River

Mearns, The — see KINCARDINE

Meath \'mēth, 'meth\ county E Ireland in NE Leinster ✻ Trim area 903 sq mi (2348 sq km), pop 105,540

Meaux \'mō\ commune N France ENE of Paris pop 41,831

Mec·ca \'me-kə\ city Saudi Arabia ✻ of Hejaz pop 366,801 — **Mec·can** \-kən\ adj or n

Mech·lin \'me-klən\ or Flem **Me·che·len** \'me-kə-lə(n)\ or F **Ma·lines** \mə-'lēn\ commune N Belgium pop 75,313

Meck·len·burg \'me-klən-ˌbərg, -ˌbúrg\ region NE Germany SE of Jutland Peninsula & E of the Elbe; in 18th & 19th centuries divided into duchies of **Mecklenburg–Schwe·rin** \-shvä-'rēn\ & **Mecklenburg–Stre·litz** \-'shträ-ləts, 'strä-\ which became grand duchies 1815 & states of Weimar Republic 1919

Me·dan \mā-'dän\ city Indonesia in NE Sumatra pop 1,730,752

Me·del·lín \ˌme-d°l-'ēn, ˌmā-thə-'yēn\ city NW Colombia NW of Bogotá pop 1,163,862

Med·ford \'med-fərd\ **1** city E Mass. N of Boston pop 57,407   **2** city SW Oreg. pop 46,951

Me·dia \'mē-dē-ə\ ancient country & province of Persian Empire SW Asia in NW modern Iran — **Me·di·an** \-dē-ən\ adj or n

Media Atropatene — see AZERBAIJAN

Medicine Bow \-ˌbō\ river 120 mi (193 km) S Wyo. flowing into N. Platte River

Medicine Bow Mountains mountains N Colo. & S Wyo. in the Rockies; highest **Medicine Bow Peak** (in Wyo.) 12,013 ft (3662 m)

Medicine Hat city Canada in SE Alta. pop 43,625

Me·di·na **1** \mə-'dī-nə\ city N Ohio WNW of Akron pop 19,231   **2** \mə-'dē-nə\ city W Saudi Arabia pop 198,186

Mediolanum — see MILAN

Med·i·ter·ra·nean Sea \ˌme-də-tə-'rā-nē-ən, -nyən\ sea 2330 mi (3750 km) long bet. Europe & Africa connecting with the Atlantic through Strait of Gibraltar & with Red Sea through Suez Canal

Mé·doc \mā-'däk, -'dòk\ district SW France N of Bordeaux

Med·way \'med-ˌwā\ river 60 mi (97 km) SE England in Kent flowing NE into Thames River

Mee·rut \'mä-rət, 'mir-ət\ city N India in NW Uttar Pradesh NE of Delhi pop 538,461

Meg·a·ra \'me-gə-rə\ or NGk **Mé·ga·ra** \'mä-gä-rä\ city & port Greece on Saronic Gulf W of Athens pop 17,294; chief town of ancient Megaris & Gulf of Corinth) — **Me·gar·i·an** \mə-'gar-ē-ən, me-, -'ger-\ adj or n

Me·gha·la·ya \‚mā-gə-'lā-ə\ state NE India ✻ Shillong *area* 8666 *sq mi* (22,532 *sq km*), *pop* 1,327,824

Megh·na \'meg-nə\ the lower course of the Surma, India

Me·gid·do \mi-'gi-(‚)dō\ ancient city N Palestine N of Samaria

Meis·sen \'mī-s°n\ city E Germany NW of Dresden *pop* 43,561

Méjico — see MEXICO

Mek·nes \mek-'nes\ city N Morocco WSW of Fez; former ✻ of Morocco *pop* 248,369

Me·kong \'mā-'koŋ, -'käŋ; 'mā-‚\ river 2600 *mi* (4184 *km*) SE Asia flowing from Qinghai (China) S & SE into S. China Sea in S Vietnam

Mel·aka *or* Ma·lac·ca \me-'la-kə, -'lä-\ 1 state Malaysia on W coast of Peninsular Malaysia *area* 633 *sq mi* (1646 *sq km*), *pop* 453,153 2 city, its ✻ *pop* 250,635

Mel·a·ne·sia \‚me-lə-'nē-zhə, -shə\ the islands in the Pacific NE of Australia & S of Micronesia including Bismarck Archipelago, the Solomons, Vanuatu, New Caledonia, & the Fijis

Mel·bourne \'mel-bərn\ 1 city E Fla. SSW of Cape Canaveral *pop* 59,646 2 city & port SE Australia ✻ of Victoria on Port Phillip Bay *metropolitan area pop* 2,645,484 — Mel·bour·ni·an *or* Mel·bur·ni·an \mel-'bər-nē-ən\ *n*

Me·li·lla \mə-'lē-yə\ city & port NE Morocco on coast NE of Fez; a Spanish presidio *pop* 60,843

Melita — see MALTA

Melitene — see MALATYA

Me·li·to·pol \‚me-lə-'tȯ-pəl\ city S Ukraine near Sea of Azov *pop* 137,000

Melos — see MÍLOS

Mel·rose \'mel-‚rōz\ city E Mass. N of Boston *pop* 28,150

Melrose Park village NE Ill. W of Chicago *pop* 20,859

Mel·ville, Lake \'mel-‚vil\ lake Canada in Nfld. in Labrador; the inner basin of Hamilton Inlet *area* 1133 *sq mi* (2946 *sq km*)

Melville Island island Canada in N Northwest Territories in Parry Islands *area* 16,141 *sq mi* (41,967 *sq km*)

Melville Peninsula peninsula Canada in E Northwest Territories bet. Foxe Basin & an arm of Gulf of Boothia

Memel — see KLAIPEDA

Mem·phis \'mem(p)-fəs\ 1 city SW Tenn. on Mississippi River *pop* 610,337 2 ancient city N Egypt on the Nile S of modern Cairo; once ✻ of Egypt — Mem·phi·an \-fē-ən\ *adj or n* — Mem·phite \'mem-‚fīt\ *adj or n*

Mem·phre·ma·gog, Lake \‚mem(p)-fri-'mā-‚gäg\ lake 30 *mi* (48 *km*) long on border bet. Canada & the U.S. in Que. & Vt.

Men·ai Strait \'me-‚nī\ strait 14 *mi* (22 *km*) long N Wales bet. Anglesey Is. & mainland

Me Nam — see CHAO PHRAYA

Men·den·hall \'men-dən-‚hȯl\ glacier SE Alaska N of Juneau

Men·de·res \‚men-də-'res\ 1 *or anc* Mae·an·der \mē-'an-dər\ river 240 *mi* (386 *km*) W Turkey in Asia flowing SW & W into the Aegean 2 *or anc* Sca·man·der \skə-'man-dər\ river 60 *mi* (96 *km*) NW Turkey in Asia flowing from Mt. Ida W & NW across the plain of ancient Troy into the Dardanelles

Men·dip \'men-‚dip, -dəp\ hills SW England in NE Somerset; highest Blackdown 1068 *ft* (326 *m*)

Men·do·ci·no, Cape \‚men-də-'sē-(‚)nō\ headland NW Calif. SSW of Eureka; extreme W point of Calif., at 124°8'W

Men·do·ta, Lake \men-'dō-tə\ lake 6 *mi* (9.6 *km*) long S Wis. NW of Madison

Men·do·za \men-'dō-zə\ city W Argentina SE of Aconcagua *pop* 109,122

Men·lo Park \'men-(‚)lō\ city W Calif. SE of San Francisco *pop* 28,040

Me·nom·i·nee \mə-'nä-mə-nē\ river 125 *mi* (201 *km*) NE Wis. flowing SE on Mich.-Wis. border into Green Bay

Menominee Range iron-rich mountain range NE Wis. & NW Mich. in Upper Peninsula

Me·nom·o·nee Falls \mə-'nä-mə-nē\ village SE Wis. *pop* 26,840

Menorca — see MINORCA

Men·ton \mäⁿ-'tōⁿ\ *or It* Men·to·ne \men-'tō-nē\ city SE France on the Mediterranean ENE of Nice *pop* 24,736

Men·tor \'men-tər\ city NE Ohio NE of Cleveland *pop* 47,358

Men·zel–Bour·gui·ba \men-‚zel-bür-'gē-bə\ *or formerly* Fer·ry·ville \'fer-ē-‚vil\ city N Tunisia on Lake Bizerte *pop* 42,111

Me·ra·no \mə-'rä-(‚)nō\ commune N Italy in Trentino-Alto Adige NW of Bolzano *pop* 33,601

Mer·ced \mər-'sed\ 1 river 150 *mi* (241 *km*) *cen* Calif. flowing W through Yosemite Valley into the San Joaquin 2 city *cen* Calif. in San Joaquin valley *pop* 56,216

Mer·cer Island \'mər-sər\ city W Wash. E of Seattle *pop* 20,816

Mer·cia \'mər-sh(ē-)ə\ ancient English Anglian kingdom *cen* England; one of kingdoms in the Anglo-Saxon heptarchy

Mer·gent·heim \'mer-gənt-‚hīm\ *or* Bad Mergentheim \‚bät-\ town S Germany in Baden-Württemberg NNE of Stuttgart

Meriç — see MARITSA

Mé·ri·da \'mer-ə-də\ 1 city SE Mexico ✻ of Yucatán *pop* 233,912 2 city W Venezuela SE of Lake Maracaibo *pop* 170,902

Mer·i·den \'mer-ə-d°n\ city S Conn. S of Hartford *pop* 59,479

Me·rid·i·an \mə-'ri-dē-ən\ city E cen Miss. *pop* 41,036

Merín — see MIRIM (Lake)

Mer·i·on·eth \‚mer-ē-'ä-nəth\ *or* Mer·i·on·eth·shire \-‚shir, -shər\ former county NW Wales ✻ Dolgellau

Mer·oë \'mer-ō-(‚)ē\ ancient city, site in N *cen* Sudan on the Nile — Mero·ite \'mer-ō-‚īt\ *n* — Mero·it·ic \‚mer-ō-'i-tik\ *adj*

Meroë, Isle of ancient region E Sudan bet. the Nile & Blue Nile rivers & the Atbara

Mersa Matrûh — see MATRÛH

Mer·sey \'mər-zē\ river 70 *mi* (113 *km*) NW England flowing NW & W into Irish Sea through a large estuary

Mer·sey·side \'mər-zē-‚sīd\ metropolitan county NW England ✻ Liverpool *area* 250 *sq mi* (650 *sq km*), *pop* 1,524,700

Mer·sin \mer-'sēn\ city & port S Turkey on the Mediterranean WSW of Adana *pop* 215,300

Mer·thyr Tyd·fil \'mər-thər-'tid-‚vil\ borough SE Wales in Mid Glamorgan *pop* 53,843

Mer·ton \'mər-t°n\ borough of SW Greater London, England *pop* 168,100

Me·ru \'mā-(‚)rü\ mountain 14,979 *ft* (4566 *m*) NE Tanzania

Me·sa \'mā-sə\ city SW cen Ariz. E of Phoenix *pop* 288,091

Me·sa·bi Range \mə-'sä-bē\ range of hills NE Minn. NW of Duluth containing large deposits of iron

Me·sa Verde National Park \'mā-sə-'vərd, -'vər-dē\ reservation SW Colo. containing prehistoric cliff dwellings

Me·se·ta \mā-'sä-tə\ the central plateau of Spain

Meshed — see MASHHAD

Me·so·amer·i·ca \‚me-zō-ə-'mer-i-kə, ‚mē-, -sō-\ region of S N. America that was occupied during pre-Columbian times — Me·so·amer·i·can \-kən\ *adj*

Mes·o·po·ta·mia \‚me-s(ə)pə-'tä-mē-ə, -myə\ 1 region SW Asia bet. the Tigris & the Euphrates extending from the mountains of E Asia Minor to the Persian Gulf 2 the entire Tigris-Euphrates valley — Mes·o·po·ta·mian \-mē-ən, -myən\ *adj or n*

Mes·quite \mə-'skēt, mē-\ city NE Tex. E of Dallas *pop* 101,484

Mes·se·ne *or NGk* Mes·si·ni \mə-'sē-nē\ town S Greece in SW Peloponnisos, ancient ✻ of Messenia

Mes·se·nia \mə-'sē-nē-ə, -nyə\ region S Greece in SW Peloponnisos bordering on Ionian Sea

Messenia, Gulf of inlet of the Mediterranean S Greece on S coast of Peloponnisos

Mes·si·na \mə-'sē-nə\ *or anc* Mes·sa·na \mə-'sä-nə\ *or* Zan·cle \'zaŋ-(‚)klē\ city & port Italy in NE Sicily *pop* 273,570

Messina, Strait of channel bet. S Italy & NE Sicily

Mes·ta \me-'stä\ *or Gk* Nés·tos \'nes-‚täs, -‚tȯs\ river 130 *mi* (209 *km*) SW Bulgaria & NE Greece flowing from W end of Rhodope Mountains SE into the Aegean

Me·ta \'mā-tə\ river 685 *mi* (1102 *km*) NE Colombia flowing into the Orinoco on Venezuela-Colombia boundary

Met·air·ie \'me-tə-rē\ population center SE La. *pop* 149,428

Me·tau·ro \mə-'taur-(‚)ō\ *or anc* Me·tau·rus \-'tȯr-əs\ river 70 *mi* (113 *km*) E cen Italy flowing E into the Adriatic

Me·thu·en \mə-'thü-ən, -'thyü-\ town NE Mass. *pop* 39,990

Metz \'mets, F mes\ city NE France on the Moselle *pop* 110,939

Meurthe \'mərt, 'mœrt\ river 100 *mi* (161 *km*) NE France flowing NW from Vosges Mountains to the Moselle

Meuse \'myüz, 'mə(r)z, 'mœz\ *or D* Maas \'mäs\ river 575 *mi* (925 *km*) W Europe flowing from NE France through S Belgium into North Sea in the Netherlands

Mewar — see UDAIPUR

Mex·i·cali \‚mek-si-'ka-lē\ city NW Mexico ✻ of Baja California state on Mexico-Calif. border *pop* 281,333

Mex·i·co \'mek-si-‚kō\ *or Sp* Mé·ji·co \'me-hē-(‚)kō\ *or MexSp* Mé·xi·co \'me-hē-(‚)kō\ 1 country S N. America S of the U.S.; a republic ✻ Mexico *area* 761,830 *sq mi* (1,980,758 *sq km*), *pop* 67,395,826 2 state S *cen* Mexico ✻ Toluca 8267 *sq mi* (21,494 *sq km*), *pop* 7,545,692 3 *or* Mexico City city ✻ of Mexico (republic) in Federal District (area surrounded on three sides by state of Mexico) *district pop* 9,373,353 — see TENOCHTITLÁN

Mexico, Gulf of inlet of the Atlantic on SE coast of N. America

Mé·zenc \mā-'zaŋk\ mountain 5755 *ft* (1754 *m*) S France; highest in the Cévennes

Mez·zo·gior·no \‚met-sō-'jȯr-(‚)nō, ‚med-zō-\ the Italian peninsula S of *ab* the latitude of Rome

Mfumbiro — see VIRUNGA

Mi·ami \mī-'a-mē, -'a-mə\ city & port SE Fla. on Biscayne Bay *pop* 358,548 — Mi·ami·an \-mē-ən\ *n*

Miami Beach city SE Fla. *pop* 92,639

Mich·i·gan \'mi-shi-gən\ state N U.S. in Great Lakes region including an upper (NW) & a lower (SE) peninsula ✻ Lansing *area* 58,216 *sq mi* (151,362 *sq km*), *pop* 9,295,297 — Mich·i·gan·der \‚mi-shi-'gan-dər\ *n* — Mich·i·gan·ite \'mi-shi-gə-‚nīt\ *n*

Michigan, Lake lake N cen U.S.; one of the Great Lakes *area* 22,400 *sq mi* (58,240 *sq km*)

Michigan City city N Ind. on Lake Michigan *pop* 33,822

Michilimackinac — see MACKINAC

Mi·cho·a·cán \‚mē-chō-ä-'kän\ state SW Mexico bordering on the Pacific ✻ Morelia *area* 23,200 *sq mi* (60,320 *sq km*), *pop* 3,048,704

Mi·cro·ne·sia \‚mī-krə-'nē-zhə, -shə\ the islands of the W Pacific E of the Philippines & N of Melanesia including the Caroline, Kiribati, Mariana, & Marshall groups

Micronesia, Federated States of islands W Pacific in the Carolines comprising Kusaie, Pohnpei, Truk, & Yap; part of former Trust Territory of the Pacific Islands; internally self-governing since 1986

Mid·del·burg \'mi-d°l-‚bərg\ city SW Netherlands on Walcheren Is. ✻ of Zeeland *pop* 38,697

Middle Congo former French territory W *cen* Africa — see CONGO, FRENCH EQUATORIAL AFRICA

Middle East *or* Mid·east \‚mid-'ēst\ the countries of SW Asia & N Africa — usu. considered as including the countries extending from Libya on the W to Afghanistan on the E — Middle Eastern *or* Mideast·ern \‚mid-'ē-stərn\ *adj* — Middle Easterner *n*

Mid·dles·brough \'mi-d°lz-brə\ town N England ✻ of Cleveland on Tees River *pop* 149,770

Mid·dle·sex \'mi-d°l-‚seks\ former county SE England, now absorbed in Greater London

Mid·dle·town \'mi-d°l-‚taun\ 1 city cen Conn. S of Hartford *pop* 42,762 2 city SE N.Y. *pop* 24,160 3 city SW Ohio SW of Dayton *pop* 46,022 4 town S R.I. N of Newport *pop* 19,460

\ə\ abut \ᵊ\ kitten, F table \ər\ further \a\ ash \ā\ ace \ä\ mop, mar
\au̇\ out \ch\ chin \e\ bet \ē\ easy \g\ go \i\ hit \ī\ ice \j\ job
\ŋ\ sing \ō\ go \ȯ\ law \ȯi\ boy \th\ thin \t̲h̲\ the \ü\ loot \u̇\ foot
\y\ yet \zh\ vision \á, k̲, ⁿ, œ, œ̄, ᵫ, ᵫ̄, ᵊ\ *see* Guide to Pronunciation

Mid Gla·mor·gan \'mid-glə-'mȯr-gən\ county SE Wales area 393 sq mi (1022 sq km), pop 537,000

Mi·di \mē-'dē\ the south of France

Mid·i·an \'mi-dē-ən\ ancient region NW Arabia E of Gulf of 'Aqaba

Mid·land \'mid-lənd\ **1** city cen Mich. NW of Saginaw pop 38,053 **2** city W Tex. NE of Odessa pop 89,443

Mid·lands \'mid-lən(d)z\ the central counties of England usu. considered as comprising Bedfordshire, Buckinghamshire, Cambridgeshire, Derbyshire, Leicestershire, Lincolnshire, Northamptonshire, Nottinghamshire, Oxfordshire, Staffordshire, Warwickshire, W. Midlands, & part of Hereford and Worcester

Mid·lo·thi·an \mid-'lō-thē-ən\ or earlier **Ed·in·burgh** \'e-d°n-,bər-ə, -,bə-rə, -b(ə-)rə\ or **Ed·in·burgh·shire** \-,shir, -shər\ former county SE Scotland ✳ Edinburgh — see LOTHIAN

Mid·way \'mid-,wā\ islands (atoll) cen Pacific 1300 mi (2092 km) WNW of Honolulu, Hawaii, belonging to the U.S., in Hawaiian group but not incorporated in state of Hawaii area 2 sq mi (5.2 sq km)

Mid·west \,mid-'west\ or **Middle West** region N cen U.S. including area around Great Lakes & in upper Mississippi valley from Ohio & sometimes Ky. on the E to N.Dak., S.Dak., Nebr., & Kans. on the W — **Mid·west·ern** \,mid-'wes-tərn\ or **Middle Western** adj — **Mid·west·ern·er** \,mid-'wes-tə(r)-nər\ or **Middle Westerner** n

Midwest City city cen Okla. E of Oklahoma City pop 52,267

Mie·res \mē-'er-əs\ commune NW Spain in Oviedo province pop 64,552

Míkonos — see MYKONOS

Mi·lan \mə-'lan, -'län\ or It **Mi·la·no** \mi-'lä-(,)nō\ or anc **Me·dio·la·num** \,me-dē-ō-'lä-nəm\ commune N Italy ✳ of Lombardy pop 1,449,403 — **Mil·a·nese** \,mi-lə-'nēz, -'nēs\ adj or n

Mi·laz·zo \mi-'lät-(,)sō\ or anc **My·lae** \'mī-(,)lē\ city & port Italy in NE Sicily W of Messina pop 32,101

Mi·le·tus \mī-'lē-təs, mə-\ ancient city on W coast of Asia Minor in Caria near mouth of Maeander River

Mil·ford \'mil-fərd\ **1** city S Conn. on Long Island Sound pop 49,938 **2** town E Mass. SE of Worcester pop 25,355

Milford Haven town & port SW Wales in Dyfed on Milford Haven (inlet of St. George's Channel) pop 13,934

Milk \'milk\ river 625 mi (1006 km) Canada & U.S. in Alta. & Mont. flowing SE into Missouri River

Mill·brae \'mil-,brā\ city W Calif. on San Francisco Bay S of San Francisco pop 20,412

Mille Lacs \'mil(l)-'lak(s)\ lake 20 mi (32 km) long E cen Minn.

Mill·ville \'mil-,vil\ city S N.J. pop 25,992

Mí·los or **Me·los** \'mē-,läs, -,lȯs\ island Greece in SW Cyclades area 57 sq mi (148 sq km)

Mil·pi·tas \mil-'pē-təs\ city W Calif. N of San José pop 50,686

Mil·ton \'mil-t°n\ **1** town E Mass. S of Boston pop 25,725 **2** town Canada in SE Ont. SW of Toronto pop 32,075

Mil·wau·kee \mil-'wȯ-kē\ city & port SE Wis. on Lake Michigan pop 628,088 — **Mil·wau·kee·an** \-kē-ən\ n

Min \'min\ **1** river 350 mi (563 km) cen China in Szechwan flowing SE into the Chang **2** river 250 mi (402 km) SE China in Fujian flowing SE into E. China Sea

Mi·nas Basin \'mī-nəs\ landlocked bay E Canada in cen N.S.; the NE extension of Bay of Fundy; connected with it by **Minas Channel**

Mi·nas de Rio·tin·to \'mē-nəs-(,)dā-,rē-ə-'tin-(,)tō\ commune SW Spain in Huelva province NE of Huelva

Mi·nas Ge·rais \,mē-nə(s)-zhə-'rīs\ state E Brazil ✳ Belo Horizonte area 226,179 sq mi (588,065 sq km), pop 13,651,852

Minch \'minch\ channel NW Scotland comprising **North Minch** & **Little Minch** bet. Outer Hebrides & NW coast of Scotland

Min·cio \'mēn-(,)chō, 'min-chē-,ō\ or anc **Min·cius** \'min(t)-sh(ē-)əs, -sē-əs\ river 115 mi (185 km) N Italy issuing from Lake Garda & emptying into the Po

Min·da·nao \,min-də-'nä-,ō, -'naŭ\ island S Philippines area (including adjacent islands) 36,537 sq mi (94,996 sq km), pop 7,292,691

Mindanao Sea sea S Philippines N of Mindanao

Min·do·ro \min-'dȯr-(,)ō, -'dȯr-\ island cen Philippines SW of Luzon area 3759 sq mi (9773 sq km), pop 473,940

Minhow — see FUZHOU

Min·i·coy \'mi-ni-,kȯi\ island India, southernmost of the Laccadives

Min·ne·ap·o·lis \,mi-nē-'a-p(ə-)ləs\ city SE Minn. on Mississippi River pop 368,383 — **Min·ne·a·pol·i·tan** \-,a-pə-'lä-t°n\ n

Min·ne·so·ta \,mi-nə-'sō-tə\ **1** river 332 mi (534 km) S Minn. flowing from Big Stone Lake to Mississippi River **2** state N U.S. ✳ St. Paul area 84,068 sq mi (218,577 sq km), pop 4,375,099 — **Min·ne·so·tan** \-'sō-t°n\ adj or n

Min·ne·ton·ka \,mi-nə-'tän-kə\ city SE Minn. E of **Lake Minnetonka** (12 mi or 19 km long) pop 48,370

Minni — see ARMENIA

Mi·nor·ca \mə-'nȯr-kə\ or Sp **Me·nor·ca** \mā-\ island Spain in the Balearic Islands ENE of Majorca; chief city Mahón area 264 sq mi (686 sq km) — **Mi·nor·can** \mə-'nȯr-kən\ adj or n

Mi·not \'mī-,nät, -nət\ city NW cen N.Dak. pop 34,544

Minsk \'min(t)sk\ city ✳ of Belarus pop 1,589,000

Min·yā, Al \al-'mi-nyə\ or **El Minya** \el-\ city cen Egypt on the Nile pop 146,366

Minya Konka — see GONGGA

Mi·que·lon \'mi-kə-,län, ,mē-kə-'lōⁿ\ island off S coast of Newfoundland, Canada, belonging to France — see SAINT PIERRE

Mir·a·mar \'mir-ə-,mär\ city SE Fla. pop 40,663

Mi·rim, Lake \mə-'rim\ or Sp **Me·rín** \mā-'rēn\ lake 108 mi (174 km) long on boundary bet. Brazil & Uruguay near Atlantic coast

Mir·za·pur \'mir-zə-,pŭr\ city N India in SE Uttar Pradesh on the Ganges SW of Banaras pop 128,179

Mi·se·num \mī-'sē-nəm\ ancient port & naval station S Italy at NW corner of Bay of Naples

Mish·a·wa·ka \,mi-shə-'wȯ-kə, -'wä-\ city N Ind. pop 42,608

Mis·kolc \'mish-,kōlts\ city NE Hungary NE of Budapest pop 207,300

Misr — see EGYPT

Mis·sion \'mi-shən\ **1** city S Tex. pop 28,653 **2** municipality Canada in SW B.C. pop 26,202

Missionary Ridge mountain SE Tenn. & NW Ga. SE of Chattanooga

Mission Vie·jo \vē-'ā-(,)hō\ city SW Calif. SE of Santa Ana pop 72,820

Mis·sis·sau·ga \,mi-sə-'sȯ-gə\ city Canada in S Ont. SW of Toronto pop 463,388

Mis·sis·sip·pi \,mi-sə-'si-pē, ,mis-'si-pē\ **1** river 2470 mi (3975 km) cen U.S. flowing from N cen Minn. to Gulf of Mexico — see ITASCA (Lake) **2** river 105 mi (169 km) Canada in SE Ont. flowing NE & N into Ottawa River **3** state S U.S. ✳ Jackson area 47,716 sq mi (124,062 sq km), pop 2,573,216

Mississippi Sound inlet of Gulf of Mexico E of Lake Pontchartrain

Mis·sou·la \mə-'zü-lə\ city W Mont. pop 42,918

Mis·sou·ri \mə-'zŭr-ē, -'zŭr-ə\ **1** river 2700 mi (4345 km) W U.S. flowing from SW Mont. into Mississippi River in E Mo. — see THREE FORKS **2** state cen U.S. ✳ Jefferson City area 69,686 sq mi (181,184 sq km), pop 5,117,073 — **Mis·sou·ri·an** \-'zŭr-ē-ən\ adj or n

Missouri City city SE Tex. pop 36,176

Mis·tas·si·ni \,mis-tə-'sē-nē\ **1** lake Canada in S cen Que. draining W to James Bay area 840 sq mi (2184 sq km) **2** river 185 mi (298 km) Canada in S Que. flowing S into Lake Saint John

Mis·ti, El \el-'mēs-tē, -'mis-\ dormant volcano 19,101 ft (5822 m) S Peru

Mitch·am \'mi-chəm\ former municipal borough S England in Surrey, now part of Merton

Mitch·ell, Mount \'mi-chəl\ mountain 6684 ft (2037 m) W N.C. in Black Mountains of the Blue Ridge Mountains; highest point in U.S. E of Mississippi River

Mix·co \'mēs-(,)kō\ city S cen Guatemala, a suburb of Guatemala City

Miyajima — see ITSUKUSHIMA

Mi·ya·za·ki \,mē-,yä-'zä-kē, mē-'yä-zə-(,)kē\ city & port Japan in Kyushu on SE coast pop 287,367

Mi·zo·ram \mi-'zȯr-əm\ state NE India area 8142 sq mi (21,169 sq km), pop 487,774

Mma·ba·tho \mä-'bä-(,)tō\ town N Republic of South Africa near Botswana border; formerly ✳ of Bophuthatswana

Mo·ab \'mō-,ab\ region Jordan E of Dead Sea; in biblical times a kingdom bet. Edom & the country of the Amorites

Mo·bile \mō-'bē(ə)l, 'mō-,bēl\ **1** river 38 mi (61 km) long SW Ala. formed by Alabama & Tombigbee rivers & flowing S into **Mobile Bay** (inlet of Gulf of Mexico) **2** city & port SW Ala. pop 196,278

Moçambique — see MOZAMBIQUE

Mocâmedes — see NAMIBE

Mo·cha \'mō-kə\ or Ar **Mu·khā** \mü-'kä\ town & port SW Yemen on the Red Sea

Mod·der \'mä-dər\ river 180 mi (290 km) Republic of South Africa in Orange Free State; a tributary of the Vaal

Mo·de·na \'mȯd-°n-ə, 'mō-, -d°n-,ä\ or anc **Mu·ti·na** \'myü-t°n-ə\ commune N Italy in Emilia SW of Venice pop 176,857 — **Mod·e·nese** \,mȯ-d°n-'ēz, ,mō-, -'ēs\ n

Mo·des·to \mə-'des-(,)tō\ city cen Calif. on the Tuolumne pop 164,730

Moe·sia \'mē-sh(ē-)ə\ ancient country & Roman province SE Europe in modern Serbia & Bulgaria S of the Danube from the Drina to Black Sea

Mog·a·di·shu \,mä-gə-'di-(,)shü, ,mȯ-, -'dē-\ or **Mog·a·di·scio** \-(,)shō\ city & port ✳ of Somalia on Indian Ocean pop 349,245

Mogador — see ESSAOUIRA

Mo·gi·lev \'mä-gə-,lef, -,lev\ city E Belarus on the Dnieper pop 202,000

Mo·go·llon Mountains \,mə-gə-'yōn, ,mō-\ mountains SW N.Mex.; highest Whitewater Baldy 10,892 ft (3320 m)

Mo·hacs \'mō-,hach, -,häch\ town S Hungary pop 21,385

Mo·hawk \'mō-,hȯk\ river 148 mi (238 km) E cen N.Y. flowing E into Hudson River

Mo·hen·jo–Da·ro \mō-,hen-(,)jō-'där-(,)ō\ prehistoric city Pakistan in Indus valley NE of modern Karachi

Mo·ja·ve Desert or **Mo·ha·ve Desert** \mə-'hä-vē, mō-\ desert S Calif. SE of S end of the Sierra Nevada

Mo·ji \'mō-(,)jē\ former city Japan in N Kyushu on Shimonoseki Strait — see KITAKYUSHU

Mok·po \'mäk-(,)pō\ city & port SW S. Korea on Yellow Sea SW of Kwangju pop 236,085

Mold \'mōld\ town NE Wales in Clwyd

Mol·da·via \mäl-'dā-vē-ə, -vyə\ **1** region Europe in NE Romania & Moldova bet. the Carpathians & Transylvanian Alps on the W & the Dniester on the E **2** — see MOLDOVA — **Mol·da·vian** \-vē-ən, -vyən\ adj or n

Mol·do·va \mäl-'dō-və, mȯl-\ independent country in E Moldavia region; formerly **Moldavian Republic** or **Moldavia**) a constituent republic of the U.S.S.R.; ✳ Chişinău area 13,100 sq mi (34,060 sq km), pop 4,341,000

Mo·len·beek \'mō-lən-,bāk\ or **Sint–Jans–Molenbeek** \sint-'yän(t)s-\ or **Molenbeek–Saint–Jean** \-saⁿ-'zhäⁿ\ commune cen Belgium in Brabant W of Brussels pop 68,759

Mo·line \mō-'lēn\ city NW Ill. on Mississippi River pop 43,202

Mo·li·se \'mō-li-,zā\ region cen Italy bet. the Apennines & the Adriatic S of Abruzzi ✳ Campobasso pop 335,348 — see ABRUZZI

Mo·lo·kai \,mä-lə-'kī, ,mō-\ island cen Hawaii area 259 sq mi (673 sq km)

Mo·lo·po \mə-'lō-(,)pō\ river 600 mi (966 km) S Africa flowing W along border bet. Botswana & Republic of South Africa & thence S into Orange River; now usu. dry

Molotov — see PERM

Mo·luc·cas \mə-'lə-kəz\ or Indonesian **Ma·lu·ku** \mə-'lü-(,)kü\ islands Indonesia in Malay Archipelago bet. Sulawesi & New Guinea area 32,300 sq mi (83,980 sq km), pop 995,000 — see HALMAHERA — **Mo·luc·ca** \mə-'lə-kə\ or **Mo·luc·can** \-kən\ adj

Mom·ba·sa \mäm-'bä-sə\ **1** island Kenya on coast N of Pemba **2** city & port on Mombasa Is. & adjacent mainland pop 341,148

Mona 1 — see ANGLESEY **2** or **Monapia** — see MAN (Isle of)

Mo·na·co \'mä-nə-,kō also mə-'nä-(,)kō\ **1** country S Europe on the Mediterranean coast of France; a principality area 368 acres (147 hectares), pop 27,063 **2** commune, its ✳ — **Mo·na·can** \'mä-nə-kən, mə-'nä-kən\ adj or n — **Mon·e·gasque** \,mä-ni-'gask\ adj or n

Mo·nad·nock, Mount \mə-'nad-,näk\ mountain 3166 ft (965 m) SW N.H.

Mon·a·ghan \'mä-nə-hən, -ˌhan\ **1** county NE Ireland (republic) in Ulster *area* 498 *sq mi* (1295 *sq km*), *pop* 51,262 **2** urban district, its ✳ *pop* 6075

Mo·na Passage \'mō-nə\ strait West Indies bet. Hispaniola & Puerto Rico connecting the Caribbean & the Atlantic

Monastir — see BITOLA

Mön·chen·glad·bach \ˌmə(r)n-kən-'glät-ˌbäk, ˌmœn-kən-'glät-ˌbäk\ *or formerly* **Mün·chen—Glad·bach** \ˌm(y)ün-kən-, ˌmœn-kən-\ city W Germany W of Düsseldorf *pop* 258,424

Monc·ton \'məŋk-tən\ city Canada in E N.B. *pop* 57,010

Mon·go·lia \män-'gōl-yə, mäŋ-, -'gō-lē-ə\ **1** region E Asia E of Altai mountains; includes Gobi Desert **2** *or* **Outer Mongolia** country E Asia comprising major portion of Mongolia region; a republic ✳ Ulan Bator *area* 580,158 *sq mi* (1,508,411 *sq km*), *pop* 1,594,800 **3** INNER MONGOLIA

Mon·he·gan \män-'hē-gən\ island Maine E of Portland

Mon·mouth \'män-məth, 'mən-\ *or* **Mon·mouth·shire** \-ˌshir, -shər\ former county SE Wales, often regarded as part of England ✳ Newport

Mo·noc·a·cy \mə-'nä-kə-sē\ river 60 *mi* (96 *km*) S Pa. & N Md. flowing S into the Potomac

Mo·no Lake \'mō-(ˌ)nō\ saline lake 14 *mi* (22 *km*) long E Calif.

Mo·non·ga·he·la \mə-ˌnän-gə-'hē-lə, -ˌnäŋ-gə-, -'hā-lə\ river 128 *mi* (206 *km*) N W.Va. & SW Pa. flowing N to unite with Allegheny River at Pittsburgh forming Ohio River

Mon·roe \(ˌ)mən-'rō\ **1** city N La. *pop* 54,909 **2** city SE Mich. SSW of Detroit on Lake Erie *pop* 22,902

Mon·roe·ville \(ˌ)mən-'rō-ˌvil\ borough SW Pa. E of Pittsburgh *pop* 29,169

Mon·ro·via \(ˌ)mən-'rō-vē-ə\ **1** city SW Calif. E of Pasadena *pop* 35,761 **2** city & port ✳ of Liberia, on the Atlantic *pop* 243,243

Mons \'mōⁿs\ *or Flem* **Ber·gen** \'ber-kə(n)\ commune SW Belgium ✳ of Hainaut *pop* 91,726

Mon·ta·na \män-'ta-nə\ state NW U.S. ✳ Helena *area* 147,138 *sq mi* (382,559 *sq km*), *pop* 799,065 — **Mon·tan·an** \-nən\ *adj or n*

Mont·au·ban \ˌmän-tō-'bän, mōⁿ-tō-'bäⁿ\ city SW France on the Tarn N of Toulouse *pop* 35,344

Mon·tauk Point \'män-ˌtȯk\ headland SE N.Y. at E tip of Long Is.

Mont Blanc \mōⁿ-'bläⁿ\ mountain peak 15,771 *ft* (4807 *m*) SE France on Italian border in Savoy Alps; highest of the Alps

Mont Blanc Tunnel tunnel 7½ *mi* (12 *km*) long France & Italy under Mont Blanc

Mont·clair \mänt-'klar, -'kler\ city SW Calif. E of Los Angeles *pop* 28,434

Mon·te Al·bán \ˌmän-tē-äl-'bän, ˌmōn-tä-\ ruined city of the Zapotecs S Mexico in Oaxaca state SW of Oaxaca

Mon·te·bel·lo \ˌmän-ti-'be-(ˌ)lō\ city SW Calif. *pop* 59,564

Mon·te Car·lo \ˌmän-ti-'kär-(ˌ)lō\ commune Monaco *pop* 13,154

Mon·te·go Bay \män-'tē-(ˌ)gō\ city & port NW Jamaica on Montego Bay (inlet of the Caribbean) *pop* 42,800

Mon·te·ne·gro \ˌmän-tə-'nē-(ˌ)grō, -'nä-, -'ne-\ federated republic S Yugoslavia on the Adriatic; formerly a kingdom (✳ Cetinje) ✳ Podgorica *area* 5343 *sq mi* (13,892 *sq km*), *pop* 530,361 — **Mon·te·ne·grin** \-grən\ *adj or n*

Mon·te·rey \ˌmän-tə-'rā\ city W Calif. on peninsula at S end of **Monterey Bay** (inlet of the Pacific) *pop* 31,954

Monterey Park city SW Calif. E of Los Angeles *pop* 60,738

Mon·ter·rey \ˌmän-tə-'rā\ city NE Mexico ✳ of Nuevo León *pop* 830,336

Mon·te·vi·deo \ˌmän-tə-və-'dā-(ˌ)ō, -'vi-dē-ˌō\ city & port ✳ of Uruguay on N shore of Río de la Plata *pop* 1,260,753

Mon·te·zu·ma Castle National Monument \ˌmän-tə-'zü-mə\ reservation *cen* Ariz. containing prehistoric cliff dwellings

Mont·gom·ery \(ˌ)mən(t)-'gə-mə-rē, män(t)-, -'gä-; -'gəm-rē, -'gäm-\ **1** city ✳ of Ala. on Alabama River *pop* 187,106 **2** *or* **Mont·gom·ery·shire** \-ˌshir, -shər\ former county E Wales ✳ Welshpool

Mont·mar·tre \mōⁿ-'märtrᵊ\ section of Paris, France, on a hill in N *cen* part of the city

Mont·mo·ren·cy \ˌmänt-mə-'ren(t)-sē, mōⁿ-mȯ-'räⁿ-sē\ commune N France, N suburb of Paris *pop* 20,927

Mont·mo·ren·cy Falls \ˌmänt-mə-'ren(t)-sē\ waterfall 270 *ft* (82 *m*) Canada in S Que. NE of Quebec (city) in **Montmorency River** (60 *mi* or 96 *km* flowing S into St. Lawrence River)

Mont·par·nasse \mōⁿ-(ˌ)pär-'näs, -'nas\ section of Paris, France, in S *cen* part of the city — **Mont·par·nas·sian** \-'na-shən, -'na-sē-ən\ *adj*

Mont·pe·lier \mänt-'pēl-yər, -'pil-\ city ✳ of Vt. *pop* 8247

Mont·pel·lier \mōⁿ-'pel-yā\ city S France WNW of Marseilles *pop* 178,136

Mon·tre·al \ˌmän-trē-'ȯl, ˌmən-\ *or* **Mont·ré·al** \mōⁿ-rā-'äl\ city & port Canada in S Que. on **Montreal Island** (32 *mi* or 51 *km* long, in St. Lawrence River) *pop* 1,017,666 — **Mon·tre·al·er** \ˌmän-trē-'ȯ-lər, ˌmən-\ *n*

Montreal North *or* **Montréal—Nord** \-nȯr\ town Canada in S Que. on Montreal Is. *pop* 85,516

Mon·treuil \mōⁿ-'trœi\ *or* **Montreuil—sous—Bois** \-ˌsü-'bwä\ commune N France, E suburb of Paris *pop* 96,684

Mont—Roy·al \mōⁿ-rwä-'yäl\ *or* **Mount Roy·al** \maunt-'rȯi(-ə)l\ height 769 *ft* (234 *m*) in Montreal, Que.

Mont—Saint—Mi·chel \mōⁿ-saⁿ-mē-'shel\ small island NW France in Gulf of St-Malo

Mont·ser·rat \ˌmän(t)-sə-'rat\ island Brit. West Indies in the Leewards SW of Antigua ✳ Plymouth *area* 40 *sq mi* (104 *sq km*), *pop* 11,606

Monument Valley region NE Ariz. & SE Utah containing red sandstone buttes, mesas, & arches

Mon·za \'mōnt-sə, 'män-sə\ commune N Italy in Lombardy SE of Milan *pop* 123,073

Moore \'mu̇r\ city *cen* Okla. S of Oklahoma City *pop* 40,318

Mo·o·réa \ˌmō-ə-'rā-ə\ island S Pacific in Society Islands NW of Tahiti *area* 51 *sq mi* (133 *sq km*)

Moor·head \'mu̇r-ˌhed, 'mȯr-, 'mu̇r-\ city W Minn. on Red River opposite Fargo, N.Dak. *pop* 32,295

Moor·park \'mȯr-ˌpärk, 'mȯr-\ city SW Calif. W of Los Angeles *pop* 25,494

Moose \'müs\ river 50 *mi* (80 *km*) Canada in NE Ont. flowing NE into James Bay; estuary of Abitibi, Mattagami, & other rivers

Moose·head Lake \'müs-ˌhed\ lake 35 *mi* (56 *km*) long NW *cen* Maine

Moose Jaw city Canada in S Sask. W of Regina *pop* 33,593

Mo·rad·a·bad \mə-'rä-də-ˌbäd, -'ra-də-ˌbad\ city N India in NW Uttar Pradesh ENE of Delhi *pop* 347,983

Mo·ra·tu·wa \mə-'rä-tə-wə\ city W Sri Lanka on Indian Ocean S of Colombo *pop* 166,000

Mo·ra·va \'mȯr-ə-və\ **1** river 180 *mi* (290 *km*), *cen* Europe flowing S from E Czech Republic & forming part of the borders bet. the Czech Republic & Slovakia and Austria & Slovakia before entering the Danube **2** river 134 *mi* (216 *km*) Serbia flowing N into the Danube

Mo·ra·via \mə-'rä-vē-ə\ *or* **Mo·ra·va** \'mȯr-ə-və\ region E Czech Republic S of Silesia traversed by Morava River; once an independent kingdom, later under shifting jurisdictions; chief city Brno

Mo·ra·vi·an Gate \mə-'rä-vē-ən\ mountain pass *cen* Europe bet. Sudety & Carpathian mountains

Moravska Ostrava — see OSTRAVA

Mor·ay \'mər-ē\ *or* **Mor·ay·shire** \-ˌshir, -shər\ *or* **El·gin** \'el-gən\ *or* **El·gin·shire** \-ˌshir, -shər\ former county NE Scotland bordering on North Sea ✳ Elgin

Moray Firth inlet of North Sea N Scotland

Mor·do·vi·an Republic \(ˌ)mȯr-'dō-vē-ən\ *or* **Mord·vin·i·an Republic** \(ˌ)mȯrd-'vi-nē-ən\ *or* **Mor·do·via** \(ˌ)mȯr-'dō-vē-ə\ autonomous republic *cen* Russia in Europe S & W of the middle Volga ✳ Saransk *area* 10,100 *sq mi* (26,260 *sq km*), *pop* 1,030,000 — **Mordvinian** *n*

Mo·reau \'mȯr-(ˌ)ō, 'mȯr-\ river 250 *mi* (402 *km*) NW S.Dak. flowing E into Missouri River

More·cambe and Hey·sham \'mȯr-kəm-ən(d)-'hē-shəm, 'mȯr-\ borough NW England in N Lancashire on **Morecambe Bay** (inlet of Irish Sea) *pop* 41,187

Mo·re·lia \mə-'räl-yə, mō-'rel-\ city SW Mexico ✳ of Michoacán *pop* 209,507

Mo·re·los \mə-'rā-ləs, mō-'re-lōs\ state S *cen* Mexico ✳ Cuernavaca *area* 1916 *sq mi* (4982 *sq km*), *pop* 931,675

Mo·re·no Valley \mə-'rē-(ˌ)nō\ city S Calif. E of Riverside *pop* 118,779

More·ton Bay \'mȯr-tᵊn, 'mȯr-\ inlet of the Pacific Australia in SE Queensland at mouth of Brisbane River

Mor·gan Hill \'mȯr-gən\ city W Calif. SE of San Jose *pop* 23,928

Mor·gan·town \'mȯr-gən-ˌtaun\ city N W.Va. *pop* 25,879

Mo·ri·ah \mə-'rī-ə\ hill *cen* Palestine in E part of Jerusalem

Mo·roc·co \mə-'rä-(ˌ)kō\ **1** country NW Africa bordering on the Atlantic & the Mediterranean; a kingdom ✳ Rabat, summer ✳ Tangier *area ab* 240,881 *sq mi* (626,291 *sq km*), *pop* 21,392,000; formerly (1911—56) divided into **French Morocco** (protectorate ✳ Rabat), **Spanish Morocco** (protectorate ✳ Tetuán), **Southern Morocco** (Spanish protectorate, chief town Cabo Yubi), & the **International Zone** of Tangier **2** — see MARRAKECH — **Mo·roc·can** \-kən\ *adj or n*

Mo·ro Gulf \'mȯr-(ˌ)ō, 'mȯr-\ arm of Celebes Sea S Philippines off SW coast of Mindanao

Mo·ro·ni \mȯ-'rō-nē\ city ✳ of Comoro Islands *pop* 23,432

Mor·ris Jes·up, Cape \'mȯr-əs-'je-səp, 'mär-\ headland N Greenland in Peary Land on Arctic Ocean; is world's northernmost dry land

Morrison, Mount — see YÜ SHAN

Morrison Cave — see LEWIS AND CLARK CAVERN

Mor·ris·town \'mȯr-əs-ˌtaun, 'mär-\ city E Tenn. ENE of Knoxville *pop* 21,385

Mor·ton Grove \'mȯr-tᵊn\ village NE Ill. W of Evanston *pop* 22,408

Mos·cow \'mäs-(ˌ)kō, -ˌkau\ *or Russ* **Mos·kva** \mäsk-'vä\ **1** river 315 *mi* (507 *km*) W *cen* Russia in Europe flowing E into Oka River **2** city ✳ of Russia & formerly of U.S.S.R. & of Soviet Russia on Moscow River *pop* 8,769,000 — see MUSCOVY

Mo·selle \mō-'zel\ *or G* **Mo·sel** \'mō-zəl\ river 320 *mi* (515 *km*) E France & W Germany flowing from Vosges Mountains into the Rhine at Koblenz

Mosquito Coast *or* **Mos·qui·tia** \mə-'skē-tē-ə\ region Central America bordering on the Caribbean in E Honduras & E Nicaragua

Mos·sel Bay \'mȯ-səl\ city & port S Republic of South Africa in S Cape of Good Hope on Mossel Bay (inlet of Indian Ocean) *pop* 17,574

Moss Point city SE Miss. E of Gulfport *pop* 17,837

Mos·tag·a·nem \mə-'sta-gə-ˌnem\ city & port NW Algeria *pop* 101,600

Mo·sul \mō-'sül, 'mō-səl\ city N Iraq on the Tigris *pop* 264,146

Moth·er·well and Wish·aw \mə-thər-,wel-ən-'wi-,shō, -wəl-\ burgh *cen* Scotland in Strathclyde SE of Glasgow *pop* 73,116

Moul·mein \mül-'mān, mōl-, -'min\ city S Myanmar on Gulf of Martaban at mouth of the Salween *pop* 171,977

Mound City Group National Monument reservation S Ohio N of Chillicothe containing prehistoric mounds

Mountain Brook city *cen* Ala. E of Birmingham *pop* 19,810

Mountain View city W Calif. NW of San Jose *pop* 67,460

Mount Des·ert Island \də-'zȯrt, 'de-zərt\ island S Maine in the Atlantic E of Penobscot Bay *area* 100 *sq mi* (260 *sq km*)

Mount·lake Terrace \maunt-,läk\ city W Wash. N of Seattle *pop* 19,320

Mount Pearl town Canada in Nfld. *pop* 23,689

Mount Pleasant **1** city *cen* Mich. NW of Saginaw *pop* 23,285 **2** town SE S.C. on the coast *pop* 30,108

Mount Pros·pect \'prä-,spekt\ village NE Ill. *pop* 53,170

Mount Rainier National Park — see RAINIER (Mount)

Mount Rev·el·stoke National Park \'re-vəl-,stōk\ reservation Canada in SE B.C. on a plateau including Mt. Revelstoke W of Selkirk Mountains

Mount Royal — see MONT-ROYAL

Mount Saint Helens National Volcanic Monument — see SAINT HELENS (Mount)

\ə\ abut \ᵊ\ kitten, F table \ər\ further \a\ ash \ā\ ace \ä\ mop, mar \au̇\ out \ch\ chin \e\ bet \ē\ easy \g\ go \i\ hit \ī\ ice \j\ job \ŋ\ sing \ō\ go \ȯ\ law \ȯi\ boy \th\ thin \t͟h\ the \ü\ loot \u̇\ foot \y\ yet \zh\ vision \à, k̲, ⁿ, œ, œ̄, ᴜᴇ, ᵫ, ʸ\ *see* Guide to Pronunciation

Mount Ver·non \'vər-nən\ city SE N.Y. N of New York City *pop* 67,153

Mourne \'mōrn, 'mȯrn\ district S Northern Ireland, established 1974 *area* 345 *sq mi* (897 *sq km*), *pop* 72,243

Mourne Mountains mountains SE Northern Ireland

Moyle \'mȯi(ə)l\ district N Northern Ireland, established 1974 *area* 191 *sq mi* (497 *sq km*), *pop* 14,252

Mo·zam·bique \,mō-zəm-'bēk\ *or Pg* **Mo·çam·bi·que** \,mü-səm-'bē-kə\ **1** channel 950 *mi* (1529 *km*) long SE Africa bet. Madagascar & Mozambique **2** *or formerly* **Portuguese East Africa** country SE Africa bordering on Mozambique Channel; a republic, until 1975 a dependency of Portugal ✳ Maputo *area* 297,654 *sq mi* (773,900 *sq km*), *pop* 11,673,725 — **Mo·zam·bi·can** \,mō-zəm-'bē-kən\ *adj or n*

Mtwa·ra \em-'twär-ə\ city & port Tanzania in SE mainland

Mu·dan·jiang *or* **Mu–tan–chiang** *or* **Mu-tan-kiang** \'mü-'dän-jē-'äŋ\ city NE China in S Heilongjiang on the **Mudan River** (310 *mi* or 496 *km* flowing NE into Songhua River) *pop* 251,000

Mu·gu, Point \mə-'gü\ cape SW Calif. W of Los Angeles

Muir Woods National Monument \'myür\ reservation N Calif. NW of San Francisco containing a redwood grove

Mui·zen·berg \'mī-z'n-,bərg\ town Republic of South Africa on False Bay, SSE suburb of Cape Town

Mu·kal·la \mü-'ka-lə\ city & port Yemen on Gulf of Aden; chief town of the Hadhramaut

Mukden — see SHENYANG

Mukhā — see MOCHA

Mül·heim \'mül-,hīm, 'myül-, 'mūēl-\ *or* **Mülheim an der Ruhr** \än-də(r)-'rür\ city W Germany on Ruhr River *pop* 181,279

Mul·house \mə-'lüz\ commune NE France in Alsace *pop* 116,494

Mull \'məl\ island W Scotland in the Inner Hebrides *area* 351 *sq mi* (913 *sq km*), *pop* 1499

Mul·lin·gar \,mə-lən-'gär\ town N *cen* Ireland ✳ of Westmeath *pop* 8077

Mul·tan \múl-'tän\ city NE Pakistan SW of Lahore *pop* 742,000

Mult·no·mah Falls \,mȯlt-'nō-mə\ waterfall 620 *ft* (189 *m*) NW Oreg. E of Portland in a tributary of Columbia River

München–Gladbach — see MÖNCHENGLADBACH

Mun·cie \'mən(t)-sē\ city E *cen* Ind. *pop* 71,035

Mun·de·lein \'mən-də-,līn\ village NE Ill. NW of Chicago *pop* 21,215

Mu·nich \'myü-nik\ *or G* **München** \'muen-ken\ city S Germany ✳ of Bavaria on the Isar *pop* 1,298,941

Mun·ster \'mən(t)-stər\ **1** town NW Ind. SW of Hammond *pop* 19,949 **2** province S Ireland *area* 9317 *sq mi* (24,224 *sq km*), *pop* 1,008,443

Mün·ster \'mən(t)-stər, 'mún(t)-, 'muen-\ city W Germany; formerly ✳ of Westphalia *pop* 203,300

Mun·te·nia \,mən-'te-nē-ə, mün-'te-nē-ə\ *or* **Greater Walachia** region SE Romania in E part of Walachia

Mur \'mür\ *or* **Mu·ra** \'mür-ə\ river 230 *mi* (370 *km*) Austria, NE Slovenia, & N tip of Croatia flowing into the Drava

Mu·rat \'mü-rät\ *or anc* **Ar·sa·ni·as** \är-'sā-nē-əs\ river 380 *mi* (612 *km*) E Turkey flowing WSW into the Euphrates

Mur·chi·son \'mər-chə-sən\ river 400 *mi* (644 *km*) Australia in W Western Australia flowing W into Indian Ocean

Murchison Falls — see KABALEGA FALLS

Mur·cia \'mü-,resh\ *or* **Mur·shē·ə**\ **1** region & ancient kingdom SE Spain bordering on the Mediterranean **2** province SE Spain bordering on the Mediterranean *area* 4453 *sq mi* (11,578 *sq km*), *pop* 922,866 **3** commune, its ✳ & ✳ of ancient kingdom of Murcia *pop* 284,585

Mu·res \'mü-,resh\ *or Hung* **Ma·ros** \'mȯr-,ōsh\ river 400 *mi* (644 *km*), *cen* Romania & E Hungary flowing W into the Tisza

Mur·frees·boro \'mər-f(r)ēz-,bər-ə, -,bə-rə\ city *cen* Tenn. *pop* 44,922

Mur·mansk \mur-'man(t)sk, -'män(t)sk\ city & port NW Russia in Europe on an inlet of Barents Sea *pop* 381,000

Mur·ray \'mər-ē, 'mə-rē\ **1** city N Utah *pop* 31,282 **2** river 1200 *mi* (1931 *km*) SE Australia flowing from near Mt. Kosciusko in E Victoria W into Indian Ocean in S.E. Australia

Mur·rum·bidg·ee \,mər-əm-'bi-jē, ,mə-rəm-\ river 1000 *mi* (1609 *km*) SE Australia in New South Wales flowing W into Murray River

Murviedro — see SAGUNTO

Mu·sa, Ge·bel \,je-bəl-'mü-sə\ mountain group NE Egypt in S Sinai peninsula — see HOREB, KATHERINA (Gebel)

Mu·sa, Je·bel \,je-bəl-'mü-səs\ *or anc* **Ab·i·la** *or* **Ab·y·la** \'a-bə-lə\ mountain 2775 *ft* (846 *m*) N Morocco opposite Rock of Gibraltar — see PILLARS OF HERCULES

Mus·cat \'məs-,kat, -kət\ town & port ✳ of Oman on Gulf of Oman *pop* 250,000

Muscat and Oman — see OMAN

Mus·ca·tine \,məs-kə-'tēn\ city E *cen* Iowa *pop* 22,881

Mus·co·vy \'məs-kə-vē\ **1** the principality of Moscow (founded 1295) which in 15th century came to dominate Russia **2** RUSSIA — a former name

Mus·ke·gon \mə-'skē-gən\ **1** river 200 *mi* (322 *km*) W *cen* Mich. flowing SW into Lake Michigan **2** city & port SW Mich. *pop* 40,283

Mus·kin·gum \mə-'skiŋ-(g)əm\ river 120 *mi* (193 *km*) E Ohio flowing SSE into Ohio River

Mus·ko·gee \(,)mə-'skō-gē\ city E Okla. *pop* 37,708

Mus·ko·ka, Lake \mə-'skō-kə\ lake Canada in SE Ont. E of Georgian Bay & N of Lake Simcoe *area* 54 *sq mi* (140 *sq km*)

Mus·sel·shell \'mə-səl-,shel\ river 300 *mi* (483 *km*) *cen* Mont. flowing E & N into Missouri River

Mutina — see MODENA

Mu·tsu Bay \'müt-(,)sü\ inlet N Japan on NE Honshu on Tsugaru Strait

Muttra — see MATHURA

Muz·tag \müs-'tä(g), məz-\ *or* **Ulugh Muz·tagh** \,ü-lə-müs-'tä(g), -məz-\ mountain 25,340 *ft* (7724 *m*) W China in S Xinjiang Uygur; highest in Kunlun Mountains

Mwe·ru \mə-'wer-(,)ü\ lake 80 *mi* (129 *km*) long on border bet. Zaire & Zambia SW of Lake Tanganyika

Myan·mar \'myän-,mär\ *or* **Myan·ma** \-,mä\ *or formerly* **Bur·ma** \'bər-mə\ country SE Asia on Bay of Bengal; a federal republic ✳ Yangon *area* 261,789 *sq mi* (680,651 *sq km*), *pop* 35,313,905

Myc·a·le \'mi-kə-(,)lē\ promontory W Turkey opposite Samos Is.

My·ce·nae \mī-'sē-(,)nē\ ancient city S Greece in NE Peloponnisos

Mykolayiv — see NIKOLAYEV

Myk·o·nos \'mi-kə-,nōs\ *or NGk* **Mí·ko·nos** \'mē-kō-,nòs\ island Greece in the Aegean in NE Cyclades *area* 35 *sq mi* (91 *sq km*)

Mylae — see MILAZZO

My·men·singh \,mī-mən-'siŋ\ city N Bangladesh *pop* 182,153

My·ra \'mī-rə\ ancient city S Asia Minor on coast of Lycia

Myr·tle Beach \'mər-t'l\ city E S.C. on the Atlantic *pop* 24,848

My·sia \'mi-sh(ē-)ə\ ancient country NW Asia Minor bordering on the Propontis — **My·sian** \-sh(ē-)ən\ *adj or n*

My·sore \mī-'sȯr, -'sòr\ **1** — see KARNATAKA **2** city S India in S Karnataka *pop* 476,446

Mys·tic \'mis-tik\ river E Mass. flowing SE into Boston harbor

Naas \'nās\ urban district E Ireland in Leinster ✳ of Kildare *pop* 10,017

Nab·a·taea *or* **Nab·a·tea** \,na-bə-'tē-ə\ ancient Arab kingdom SE of Palestine — **Nab·a·tae·an** *or* **Nab·a·te·an** \-'tē-ən\ *adj or n*

Na·be·rezh·nye Chel·ny \,nä-bə-'rezh-nə-'chel-nē, -'rezh-nyə-\ city E Russia in Europe in Tatar Republic *pop* 301,000

Nab·lus \'na-bləs, 'nä-\ *or anc* **She·chem** \'she-kəm, -,kem\ *or* **Ne·ap·o·lis** \nē-'a-pə-ləs\ city *cen* Palestine in Samaria; now in W Jordan *pop* 44,223

Nac·og·do·ches \,na-kə-'dō-chəz, -chəs\ city E Tex. *pop* 30,872

Na·fūd, An \,an-nə-'füd\ *or* **Ne·fud** \nə-'füd\ desert N Saudi Arabia in N Nejd

Na·ga Hills \'nä-gə\ hills E India & N Myanmar SE of the Brahmaputra; highest Saramati 12,553 *ft* (3826 *m*)

Na·ga·land \'nä-gə-,land\ state E India N of Manipur in Naga Hills ✳ Kohima *area* 6336 *sq mi* (16,474 *sq km*), *pop* 773,231

Na·ga·no \nä-'gä-(,)nō\ city Japan on Honshu *pop* 347,036

Na·ga·sa·ki \,nä-gə-'sä-kē, ,na-gə-'sä-kē\ city & port Japan in W Kyushu on E. China Sea *pop* 444,616

Na·gor·no–Ka·ra·bakh \nə-,gȯr-(,)nō-'kär-ə-,bäk\ autonomous oblast SW Azerbaijan ✳ Stepanakert *area* 1700 *sq mi* (4420 *sq km*), *pop* 149,000

Na·go·ya \nə-'gȯi-ə, 'nä-gō-(,)yä\ city Japan in S *cen* Honshu *pop* 2,154,664

Nag·pur \'näg-,pùr\ city E *cen* India in NE Maharashtra *pop* 1,297,977

Na·ha \'nä-(,)hä\ city & port Ryukyu Islands in SW Okinawa Is. ✳ of Okinawa *pop* 304,896

Na·han·ni National Park \nä-'hä-nē\ reservation W Canada in SW Northwest Territories

Na·huel Hua·pí \nä-'wel-wä-'pē\ lake SW Argentina in the Andes in **Nahuel Huapí National Park**

Nairn \'narn, 'nern\ **1** *or* **Nairn·shire** \-,shir, -shər\ former county NE Scotland **2** burgh, its ✳, on Moray Firth *pop* 7721

Nai·ro·bi \nī-'rō-bē\ city S *cen* Kenya, its ✳ *pop* 827,775

Najd — see NEJD — **Najdi** \'naj-dē, 'nazh-\ *adj or n*

Na·khi·che·van Autonomous Region \,nä-ki-chə-'vän\ **1** enclave of Azerbaijan separated from the rest of Azerbaijan by Armenia *area* 2100 *sq mi* (5460 *sq km*), *pop* 202,000 **2** city, its ✳, on the Araks *pop* 33,000

Nak·tong \'näk-,tȯŋ\ river 260 *mi* (418 *km*) S & E S. Korea flowing S & E into Korea Strait near Pusan

Na·ma·qua·land \nə-'mä-kwə-,land\ *or* **Na·ma·land** \'nä-mə-\ region SW Africa; divided by Orange River into **Great Namaqualand** (in Namibia) & **Little Namaqualand** (in Northern Cape province, Republic of South Africa, chief town Springbok)

Na·mi·be \nä-'mē-bə\ *or formerly* **Mo·çâ·me·des** \mə-'sä-mə-dish\ town & port SW Angola

Na·mib·ia \nə-'mi-bē-ə\ *or formerly* **South–West Africa** *or 1884–1919* **German Southwest Africa** country SW Africa on the Atlantic; until 1990 a territory administered by South Africa which captured it from Germany in World War I ✳ Windhoek *area* 318,099 *sq mi* (827,057 *sq km*), *pop* 1,184,000 — **Na·mib·ian** \-bē-ən, -byən\ *adj or n*

Nam·pa \'nam-pə\ city SW Idaho W of Boise *pop* 28,365

Nam·po \'nam-(,)pō, 'näm-\ *or formerly* **Chin·nam·po** \'chē(n)-,näm-(,)pō\ city & port SW N. Korea SW of Pyongyang *pop* 130,000

Na·mur \nə-'mür, -'myür\ **1** province S Belgium *area* 1413 *sq mi* (3674 *sq km*) **2** commune, its ✳ *pop* 103,443

Nan \'nän\ river 350 *mi* (563 *km*) N Thailand flowing S to join the Ping forming the Chao Phraya

Na·nai·mo \nə-'nī-(,)mō\ city Canada in B.C. on SE Vancouver Is. *pop* 60,129

Nan·chang \'nän-'chäŋ\ city SE China ✳ of Jiangxi on the Gan SW of Poyang Lake *pop* 520,000

Nan·chong \'nän-'chȯŋ\ *or* **Nan·chung** \-'chùŋ\ city *cen* China in E *cen* Szechwan *pop* 206,000

Nan·cy \'nan(t)-sē, 'nän-'sē\ city NE France on the Meurthe *pop* 106,906

Nan·da De·vi \,nän-də-'dā-vē\ mountain 25,645 *ft* (7816 *m*) N India in the Himalayas in Uttar Pradesh

Nan·di *or* **Na·di** \'nän-(,)dē\ village Fiji on W Viti Levu Is.

Nan·ga Par·bat \,nəŋ-gə-'pər-bət\ mountain 26,660 *ft* (8126 *m*) NW Kashmir in the W Himalayas

Nan·jing \'nän-'jiŋ\ *or* **Nan·king** \'nan-'kiŋ, 'nän-\ city E China on the Chang ✳ of Jiangsu & (1928–37 & 1946–49) ✳ of China *pop* 1,419,000

Nan Ling \'nän-'liŋ\ mountain system SE China roughly separating Guangdong & Guangxi Zhuangzu from Hunan & Guizhou

Nan·ning \'nän-'niŋ\ *or formerly* **Yung·ning** \'yùŋ-'niŋ\ city S China ✳ of Guangxi Zhuangzu on the You *pop* 600,000

Nan·terre \nä⁼(n)-'ter\ commune N France W of Paris *pop* 94,441

Nantes \'nant(s), 'nänt\ city W France on the Loire *pop* 252,537

Nan·ti·coke \'nan-ti-,kōk\ city Canada in SE Ont. *pop* 22,727

Nan·tong \'nän-'tȯŋ\ *or* **Nan·tung** \-'tùŋ\ city & port E China in SE Jiangsu on Chang estuary NW of Shanghai *pop* 240,000

Nan·tuck·et \nan-'tə-kət\ island Mass. S of Cape Cod on **Nantucket Sound** (inlet of the Atlantic) *pop* 6012 — **Nan·tuck·et·er** \-kə-tər\ *n*

Napa \'na-pə\ city W Calif. N of Vallejo *pop* 61,842

Na·per·ville \'nā-pər-,vil\ city NE Ill. W of Chicago *pop* 85,351

Na·pi·er \'nā-pē-ər\ borough & port New Zealand in E North Is. on Hawke Bay *pop* 48,314

Na·ples \'nā-pəlz\ **1** city SW Fla. *pop* 19,505 **2** *or It* **Na·po·li** \'nä-pə-lē\ *or anc* **Ne·ap·o·lis** \nē-'a-pə-ləs\ city & port S Italy on **Bay of Naples** (inlet of Tyrrhenian Sea) ✳ of Campania *pop* 1,204,149

Na·po \'nä-(,)pō\ river 550 *mi* (885 *km*) NW S. America rising near Mt. Cotopaxi in *cen* Ecuador & flowing E & SE into the Amazon

Na·ra \'när-ə\ city Japan in W *cen* Honshu E of Osaka; an early ✳ of Japan *pop* 349,356

Nar·bonne \när-'bän, -'bən\ city S France *pop* 36,525

Na·rew \'när-,ef, -,ev\ *or Russ* **Na·rev** \nar-'yóf, -'yòv\ river 285 *mi* (459 *km*) NE Poland flowing W & SW into Bug River

Nar·ma·da \nər-'mə-də\ river 800 *mi* (1287 *km*) *cen* India flowing W bet. Vindhya Mountains & Satpura Range into Gulf of Cambay

Nar·ra·gan·sett Bay \,nar-ə-'gan(t)-sət\ inlet of the Atlantic SE R.I.

Nar·vik \'när-vik\ town & port N Norway *pop* 19,326

Nash·ua \'na-shə-wə *also* -,wä\ city S N.H. *pop* 79,662

Nash·ville \'nash-,vil, -vəl\ city N *cen* Tenn., its ✳ *pop* 488,374

Nas·sau **1** \'na-,só\ city & port ✳ of the Bahamas on New Providence Is. *pop* 101,182 **2** \'na-,sò, *G* 'nä-,saú\ region Germany N & E of the Rhine; chief city Wiesbaden **3** — see SUDIRMAN

Nasser, Lake — see ASWĀN

Na·tal \nə-'tal, -'täl\ **1** city & port NE Brazil ✳ of Rio Grande do Norte *pop* 416,906 **2** province E Republic of South Africa bet. Drakensberg Mountains & Indian Ocean *area* 35,320 *sq mi* (91,479 *sq km*), *pop* 8,549,000

Natch·ez \'na-chəz\ city SW Miss. on Mississippi River *pop* 19,460

Natchez Trace pioneer road bet. Natchez, Miss., & Nashville, Tenn., used in the early 19th century

Na·tick \'nā-tik\ town E Mass. W of Boston *pop* 30,510

National City city SW Calif. S of San Diego *pop* 54,249

Native States — see INDIAN STATES

Natural Bridges National Monument reservation SE Utah

Nau·cra·tis \'nó-krə-təs\ ancient Greek city N Egypt in Nile delta

Nau·ga·tuck \'nó-gə-,tək\ borough SW *cen* Conn. *pop* 30,625

Nau·plia \'nó-plē-ə\ *or NGk* **Náv·pli·on** \'näf-plē-,ón\ town & port S Greece in E Peloponnisos near head of Gulf of Argolis *pop* 11,453

Nauplia, Gulf of — see ARGOLIS (Gulf of)

Na·u·ru \nä-'ü-(,)rü\ *or formerly* **Pleas·ant Island** \'ple-z²nt\ island (atoll) W Pacific 26 *mi* (42 *km*) S of the equator; formerly a joint Brit., New Zealand, & Australian trust territory; since 1968 an independent republic *area* 8 *sq mi* (21 *sq km*), *pop* 7254 — **Na·u·ru·an** \-'ü-rə-wən\ *adj or n*

Na·va·jo National Monument \'na-ə-,hō-, 'nä-\ reservation N Ariz. SW of Monument Valley near Utah boundary containing cliff dwellings

Na·varre \nə-'vär\ *or Sp* **Na·var·ra** \nə-'vär-ə\ **1** region & former kingdom N Spain & SW France in W Pyrenees **2** province N Spain ✳ Pamplona *area* 4055 *sq mi* (10,543 *sq km*), *pop* 497,223

Nav·e·sink, Highlands of \'na-və-,siŋk, 'ne-və(r)-\ *or* **Navesink Highlands** range of hills E N.J. from near Sandy Hook to Raritan Bay

Navigators Islands — see SAMOA

Náv·pak·tos \'näf-,päk-tós\ town & port Greece on N shore of strait connecting Gulf of Corinth & Patraïkós Kólpos

Nax·os \'nak-səs, -,säs\ **1** *or NGk* **Ná·xos** \'näk-,sós\ island Greece, largest of the Cyclades *area* 171 *sq mi* (445 *sq km*) **2** oldest Greek colony in Sicily; ruins SW of Taormina

Na·ya·rit \,nī-ə-'rēt\ state W Mexico bordering on the Pacific ✳ Tepic *area* 10,444 *sq mi* (27,154 *sq km*), *pop* 730,024

Naz·a·reth \'na-zə-rəth, 'naz-rəth\ city N Israel in Galilee SE of Haifa *pop* 33,300

Naze, The \'nāz\ headland SE England on E coast of Essex

Na·zil·li \nä-zə-'lē\ city SW Turkey SE of Izmir

N'Dja·me·na \,en-jə-'mä-nə, -'mē-\ *or formerly* **Fort–La·my** \,fòr-lə-'mē\ city on the Chari ✳ of Chad *pop* 179,000

Neagh, Lough \'nā\ lake *cen* Northern Ireland *area* 153 *sq km*); largest in British Isles

Neapolis **1** — see NABLUS **2** — see NAPLES

Near Islands \'nir\ islands SW Alaska at W end of the Aleutians — see ATTU

Near East **1** the Ottoman Empire at its greatest extent — a former usage **2** the countries of SW Asia & NE Africa — **Near Eastern** *adj*

Ne·bo, Mount \'nē-(,)bō\ mountain 2631 *ft* (802 *m*) Palestine in Jordan E of N end of Dead Sea

Ne·bras·ka \nə-'bras-kə\ state *cen* U.S. ✳ Lincoln *area* 77,227 *sq mi* (200,790 *sq km*), *pop* 1,578,385 — **Ne·bras·kan** \-kən\ *adj or n*

Ne·chako \ni-'cha-(,)kō\ river 287 *mi* (462 *km*) Canada in *cen* B.C. flowing N & E into the Fraser

Ne·ches \'na-chəz\ river 280 *mi* (451 *km*) E Tex. flowing S & SE into Sabine Lake

Neck·ar \'ne-kər, -,kär\ river 246 *mi* (396 *km*) SW Germany rising in the Black Forest & flowing N & W into the Rhine

Neck·er \'ne-kər\ island Hawaii in Leewards NW of Niihau Island

Need·ham \'nē-dəm\ town E Mass. WSW of Boston *pop* 27,557

Nee·nah \'nē-nə\ city E Wis. on Lake Winnebago *pop* 23,219

Nefud — see NAFŪD, AN

Neg·ev \'ne-,gev\ *or* **Neg·eb** \-,geb\ region S Israel, a triangular wedge of desert touching Gulf of 'Aqaba in S

Ne·gri Sem·bi·lan \'ne-grē-səm-'bē-lən\ state Malaysia in Peninsular Malaysia on Strait of Malacca ✳ Seremban *area* 2550 *sq mi* (6630 *sq km*), *pop* 563,955

Ne·gro \'nā-(,)grō, 'ne-\ **1** river 630 *mi* (1014 *km*) S *cen* Argentina flowing E into the Atlantic **2** river 1400 *mi* (2253 *km*) E Colombia & N Brazil flowing into the Amazon **3** river 290 *mi* (467 *km*) *cen* Uruguay flowing SW into Uruguay River

Ne·gros \'nā-(,)grōs, 'ne-\ island S *cen* Philippines in the Visayans SE of Panay Is. *area* 4905 *sq mi* (12,753 *sq km*)

Nei·jiang *or* **Nei–chiang** \'nā-jē-'äŋ\ city *cen* China in S *cen* Szechwan SE of Chengdu *pop* 180,000

Nei Monggol — see INNER MONGOLIA

Neis·se \'nī-sə\ **1** *or* **Lau·sitz·er Neisse** \'laú-zət-sər-\ river 140 *mi* (225 *km*) N Europe flowing from N Czech Republic N into the Oder **2** — see NYSA

Nejd \'nejd, 'nezhd\ *or* **Najd** \'najd, 'nazhd\ region *cen* & E Saudi Arabia; a viceroyalty ✳ Riyadh *area* 447,000 *sq mi* (1,162,200 *sq km*), *pop* 1,200,000 — **Nejdi** \'nej-dē, 'nezh-\ *adj or n*

Nel·son \'nel-sən\ **1** river 400 *mi* (644 *km*) Canada in Man. flowing from N end of Lake Winnipeg to Hudson Bay **2** city & port New Zealand on N coast of South Is. *pop* 33,304

Ne·man \'ne-mən\ *or* **Ne·mu·nas** \'na-mə-,näs\ river 500 *mi* (805 *km*) *cen* Europe flowing from *cen* Belarus N & W through Lithuania & along border with exclave of Russia into Kurland Gulf

Ne·mea \'nē-mē-ə\ valley & town Greece in NE Peloponnisos W of Corinth — **Ne·me·an** \'nē-mē-ən, ni-'mē-\ *adj*

Ne·o·sho \nē-'ō-(,)shō, -shə\ *or in Okla* **Grand** river 460 *mi* (740 *km*) SE Kans. & NE Okla. flowing SE & S into Arkansas River; now largely submerged in dam-created lakes and reservoirs in its lower course

Ne·pal \nə-'pól, nä-, -'päl *also* nə-'pal\ country Asia on NE border of India in the Himalayas; a kingdom ✳ Kathmandu *area* 54,000 *sq mi* (140,400 *sq km*), *pop* 15,020,451 — **Nep·a·lese** \,ne-pə-'lēz, -'lēs\ *adj or n*

Ne·pe·an \'nē-pē-ən\ city Canada in SE Ont. SW of Ottawa *pop* 107,627

Ness, Loch \'nes\ lake 23 *mi* (37 *km*) long NW Scotland in Highland region

Néstos — see MESTA

Neth·er·lands \'ne-thər-lən(d)z\ **1** LOW COUNTRIES — an historical usage **2** *or* **Hol·land** \'hä-lənd\ *or D* **Ne·der·land** \'nā-dər-,länt\ country NW Europe on North Sea; a kingdom, official ✳ Amsterdam, de facto ✳ The Hague *area* 15,785 *sq mi* (41,041 *sq km*), *pop* 15,009,000 — **Neth·er·land** \'ne-thər-lənd\ *adj* — **Neth·er·land·er** \-,lan-dər, -lən-\ *n* — **Neth·er·land·ic** \-,lan-dik\ *adj* — **Neth·er·land·ish** \-,lan-dish, -lən-\ *adj*

Netherlands Antilles Dutch overseas territory, W. Indies comprising Bonaire, Curaçao, Saba, St. Eustatius, & S part of St. Martin ✳ Willemstad (on Curaçao) *area* 403 *sq mi* (1048 *sq km*), *pop* 190,566

Netherlands East Indies — see INDONESIA

Netherlands Guiana — see SURINAME

Netherlands New Guinea — see WEST IRIAN

Netherlands Timor — see TIMOR

Néthou, Pic de — see ANETO (Pico de)

Net·tu·no \ne-'tü-(,)nō\ commune Italy on Tyrrhenian Sea SSE of Rome adjoining Anzio *pop* 34,653

Neu·châ·tel \,nü-shə-'tel, ,nyü-, ,nə(r)-, ,nōē-\ *or G* **Neu·en·burg** \'nòi-ən-,bərg, -,bürk\ **1** canton W Switzerland in Jura Mountains *area* 312 *sq mi* (811 *sq km*), *pop* 159,543 **2** commune, its ✳, on **Lake of Neuchâtel** (*area* 84 *sq mi or* 218 *sq km*), *pop* 32,757

Neuil·ly–sur–Seine \,nə(r)-,yē-,sür-'sän, -'sen\ commune N France NW of Paris near the Bois de Boulogne *pop* 65,941

Neu·mün·ster \nòi-'mœn-stər\ city N Germany SSW of Kiel *pop* 80,145

Neu·quén \nyü-'kän, neú-\ river 375 *mi* (604 *km*) W Argentina flowing from the Andes E to join the Limay forming Negro River

Neuse \'nüs, 'nyüs\ river 260 *mi* (418 *km*) E *cen* N.C. flowing SE into Pamlico Sound

Neuss \'nòis\ city W Germany W of Düsseldorf *pop* 149,334

Neus·tria \'nü-strē-ə, 'nyü-\ **1** the western part of the dominions of the Franks after the conquest by Clovis in 511, comprising the NW part of modern France bet. the Meuse, the Loire, & the Atlantic **2** a name for Normandy used after 912 — **Neus·tri·an** \-ən\ *adj or n*

Ne·va \'nē-və, 'nā-\ river 40 *mi* (64 *km*) W Russia in Europe flowing from Lake Ladoga to Gulf of Finland at St. Petersburg

Ne·va·da \nə-'va-də, -'vä-\ state W U.S. ✳ Carson City *area* 110,540 *sq mi* (287,404 *sq km*), *pop* 1,201,833 — **Ne·va·dan** \-'va-d²n, -'vä-\ *or* **Ne·va·di·an** \-'va-dē-ən, -'vä-\ *adj or n*

Ne·vers \nə-'ver\ city *cen* France SE of Orléans *pop* 45,122

Ne·ves \'nā-vəs\ city SE Brazil on Guanabara Bay *pop* 53,052

Ne·vis \'nē-vəs\ island Brit. West Indies, part of St. Kitts-Nevis, in the Leewards; chief town Charlestown *area* 50 *sq mi* (130 *sq km*) — **Ne·vis·i·an** \nə-'vi-zh(ē-)ən\ *adj*

New Albany city S Ind. on Ohio River *pop* 36,322

New Amsterdam town founded 1625 on Manhattan Is. by the Dutch; renamed New York 1664 by the British

New·ark \'nü-ərk, 'nyü-; 'nu̇(-ə)rk, 'nyu̇(-ə)rk\ *esp 2 & 4* 'nü-,ärk, 'nyü-\ **1** city W Calif. SE of San Francisco *pop* 37,861 **2** city NE Del. W of Wilmington *pop* 25,098 **3** city & port NE N.J. on **Newark Bay** (W extension of Upper New York Bay) *pop* 275,221 **4** city *cen* Ohio *pop* 44,389

New Bedford city & port SE Mass. on W side of Buzzards Bay *pop* 99,922

New Ber·lin \'bər-lən\ city SE Wis. W of Milwaukee *pop* 33,592

New Braun·fels \'braún-fəlz\ city SE *cen* Tex. *pop* 27,334

New Brighton village SE Minn. N of St. Paul *pop* 22,207

New Britain **1** city *cen* Conn. *pop* 75,491 **2** island Bismarck Archipelago; largest of group *area* 14,000 *sq mi* (36,400 *sq km*), *pop* 198,456

New Brunswick **1** city N *cen* N.J. *pop* 41,711 **2** province SE Canada bordering on Gulf of Saint Lawrence & Bay of Fundy ✳ Fredericton *area* 27,985 *sq mi* (72,761 *sq km*), *pop* 723,900

New·burgh \'nü-,bərg, 'nyü-\ city SE N.Y. on Hudson River S of Poughkeepsie *pop* 26,454

New Caledonia island SW Pacific SW of Vanuatu; with nearby islands, constitutes an overseas department of France ✳ Nouméa *area* 8548 *sq mi* (22,225 *sq km*), *pop* 164,173

New Castile — see CASTILE

New·cas·tle \'nü-,ka-səl, 'nyü-, *3 is locally* nü-', nyü-'\ **1** city & port SE Australia in E New South Wales at mouth of Hunter River *metropolitan area pop* 255,787 **2** town Canada in SE Ont. ENE of Toronto *pop* 49,479 **3** *or in full* **Newcastle upon Tyne** \'tīn\ city & port N England ✳ of Tyne and Wear *pop* 192,454 **4** *or in full* **Newcastle under Lyme** \'līm\ borough W *cen* England in Staffordshire *pop* 72,853

New Cas·tle \'nü-,ka-səl, 'nyü-\ city W Pa. ESE of Youngstown, Ohio *pop* 28,334

\ə\ abut \'ə\ kitten, F table \ər\ further \a\ ash \ā\ ace \ä\ mop, mar \aú\ out \ch\ chin \e\ bet \ē\ easy \g\ go \i\ hit \ī\ ice \j\ job \ŋ\ sing \ō\ go \ò\ law \òi\ boy \th\ thin \t̲h\ the \ü\ loot \ú\ foot \y\ yet \zh\ vision \ä, k̲, ⁿ, œ, œ̄, ᵫ, ᵫ̄, ᵊ\ *see* Guide to Pronunciation

New Delhi city ✳ of India in Delhi Territory S of city of (old) Delhi *pop* 324,283

New England 1 the NE U.S. comprising the states of Maine, N.H., Vt., Mass., R.I., & Conn. 2 region SE Australia in NE New South Wales; in area of **New England Range** (part of Great Dividing Range) — **New En·gland·er** \'iŋ-glən-dər *also* ,'iŋ-lən-\ *n* — **New En·glandy** \-dē\ *adj*

New Forest forested area S England in Hampshire bet. the Avon & Southampton Water; once a royal hunting ground

New·found·land \'nü-fən(d)-lənd, 'nyü-, -,land; ,nü-fən(d)-'land, ,nyü-\ 1 island Canada in the Atlantic E of Gulf of Saint Lawrence *area* 42,734 *sq mi* (111,108 *sq km*) 2 province E Canada comprising Newfoundland (island) & part of Labrador ✳ St. John's *area* 154,734 *sq mi* (402,308 *sq km*), *pop* 568,474 — **New·found·land·er** \-lən-dər, -,lan-; -'lan-dər\ *n*

New France the possessions of France in N. America before 1763

New Georgia 1 island group W Pacific in *cen* Solomon Islands 2 island 50 *mi* (80 *km*) long, chief island of the group

New Gra·na·da \,grə-'nä-də\ Spanish viceroyalty in NW S. America 1717–1819 comprising area included in modern Panama, Colombia, Venezuela, & Ecuador

New Guinea 1 island in Malay Archipelago N of E Australia divided bet. W. Irian on W & Papua New Guinea on E *area* 306,600 *sq mi* (797,160 *sq km*) 2 the NE portion of the island of New Guinea with the Bismarck Archipelago, Bougainville, Buka, & adjacent small islands; part of Papua New Guinea — see NORTH-EAST NEW GUINEA — **New Guin·ean** \'gi-nē-ən\ *adj or n*

New·ham \'nü-əm, 'nyü-\ borough of E Greater London, England *pop* 214,700

New Hamp·shire \'ham(p)-shər, -,shir\ state NE U.S. ✳ Concord *area* 9304 *sq mi* (24,190 *sq km*), *pop* 1,109,252 — **New Hamp·shire·man** \-mən\ *n* — **New Hamp·shire·ite** \-,īt\ *n*

New Ha·ven \'hā-vən\ city & port S Conn. *pop* 130,474 — **New Ha·ven·er** \'hā-və-nər, 'hāv-nər\ *n*

New Hebrides — see VANUATU

New Hope \'nü-,hōp, 'nyü-\ village E Minn. N of Minneapolis *pop* 21,853

New Iberia city S La. SE of Lafayette *pop* 31,828

New·ing·ton \'nü-iŋ-tən, 'nyü-\ town *cen* Conn. SW of Hartford *pop* 29,208

New Ireland island W Pacific in Bismarck Archipelago N of New Britain ✳ Kavieng *area* 3340 *sq mi* (8684 *sq km*), *pop* (with adjacent islands) 48,774

New Jer·sey \'jər-zē *also* -jəi-\ state E U.S. ✳ Trenton *area* 7836 *sq mi* (20,374 *sq km*), *pop* 7,730,188 — **New Jer·sey·an** \-ən\ *n* — **New Jer·sey·ite** \-,īt\ *n*

New London city & port SE Conn. on Long Island Sound at mouth of Thames River *pop* 28,540

New·mar·ket \'nü-,mär-kət, 'nyü-\ 1 town Canada in SE Ont. N of Toronto *pop* 45,474 2 town E England in Suffolk *pop* 16,235

New Mex·i·co \'mek-si-,kō\ state SW U.S. ✳ Santa Fe *area* 121,666 *sq mi* (316,332 *sq km*), *pop* 1,515,069 — **New Mex·i·can** \-si-kən\ *adj or n*

New Milford city W Conn. *pop* 23,629

New Neth·er·land \'ne-thər-lənd\ Dutch colony in N. America 1613–64 occupying lands bordering on Hudson River & later also on lower Delaware River ✳ New Amsterdam

New Or·leans \'ȯr-lē-ənz, 'ȯr-lənz, 'ȯrl-yənz, (,)ȯr-'lēnz\ city & port SE La. bet. Lake Pontchartrain & Mississippi River *pop* 496,938 — **New Or·lea·nian** \(,)ȯr-'lē-nyən, -nē-ən\ *n*

New·port \'nü-,pȯrt, 'nyü-, -pȯrt\ 1 city & port SE R.I. on Narragansett Bay *pop* 28,227 2 borough S England ✳ of Isle of Wight *pop* 23,570 3 borough SE Wales in Gwent WNW of Bristol *pop* 105,374 — **New·port·er** \-,pȯr-tər, -pȯr-\ *n*

Newport Beach city SW Calif. SE of Long Beach *pop* 66,643

New·port News \'nü-,pȯrt-'nüz, 'nyü-,pȯrt-'nyüz, -pȯrt-, -pərt-\ city & port SE Va. on James River & Hampton Roads *pop* 170,045

New Providence island in NW *cen* Bahamas E of Andros; site of Nassau *area* 58 *sq mi* (151 *sq km*)

New Quebec region Canada in N Que. N of the Eastmain bet. Hudson Bay & Labrador — see UNGAVA

New Quebec Crater *or* **Chubb Crater** \'chəb\ lake-filled meteoric crater Canada in N Que., in N Ungava Peninsula; 3 *mi* (4.8 *km*) in diameter

New Ro·chelle \,nŭr-ə-'shel, ,nyŭr-\ city SE N.Y. on Long Island Sound E of Mount Vernon *pop* 67,265

New Siberian Islands islands NE Russia in Asia in Arctic Ocean bet. Laptev & E. Siberian seas *area* 11,000 *sq mi* (28,600 *sq km*)

New South Wales state SE Australia bordering on the Pacific ✳ Sydney *area* 309,432 *sq mi* (804,523 *sq km*), *pop* 5,126,217

New Spain Spanish viceroyalty 1521–1821 including territory now in SW U.S., Mexico, Central America N of Panama, much of the West Indies, & the Philippines ✳ Mexico City

New Sweden Swedish colony in N. America 1638–55 bordering on W bank of Delaware River from modern Trenton, N.J., to its mouth

New Territories Hong Kong exclusive of Hong Kong Is. & Kowloon Peninsula

New·ton \'nü-t³n, 'nyü-\ city E Mass. W of Boston *pop* 82,585

New·town \'nü-,taùn, 'nyü-\ town SW Conn. E of Danbury *pop* 20,779

New·town·ab·bey \,nü-t³n-'a-bē, ,nyü-\ district E Northern Ireland, established 1974 *area* 58 *sq mi* (151 *sq km*), *pop* 71,631

New·town Saint Bos·wells \'nü-,taùn-sənt-'bäz-wəlz, 'nyü-, -sānt-\ village S Scotland W of Kelso ✳ of Borders region

New West·min·ster \wes(t)-'min(t)-stər\ city Canada in SW B.C. on the Fraser ESE of Vancouver *pop* 43,585

New Windsor — see WINDSOR

New York 1 state NE U.S. ✳ Albany *area* 49,576 *sq mi* (121,898 *sq km*), *pop* 17,990,456 2 *or* **New York City** city & port SE N.Y. at mouth of Hudson River; includes boroughs of Bronx, Brooklyn, Manhattan, Queens, & Staten Is. *pop* 7,322,564 3 the borough of Manhattan in New York City — **New York·er** \-'yȯr-kər\ *n*

New York Bay inlet of the Atlantic SE N.Y. & NE N.J. at mouth of Hudson River forming harbor of metropolitan New York & consisting of **Upper New York Bay** & **Lower New York Bay** connected by the **Narrows** (strait separating Staten Is. & Long Is.)

New York State Barge Canal — see ERIE

New Zea·land \'zē-lənd\ country SW Pacific ESE of Australia comprising chiefly North Is. & South Is.; a dominion of the Commonwealth of Nations ✳ Wellington *area* 103,736 *sq mi* (269,714 *sq km*), *pop* 3,175,737 — **New Zea·land·er** \-lən-dər\ *n*

Ngaliema, Mount — see STANLEY (Mount)

Nga·mi, Lake \eŋ-'gä-mē\ marshy depression NW Botswana N of Kalahari Desert; formerly a large lake

Ngau·ru·hoe \eŋ-gaù-rə-'hō-ē\ volcano 7515 *ft* (2291 *m*) New Zealand in *cen* North Is. in Tongariro National Park

Ni·ag·a·ra Falls \(,)nī-'a-g(ə-)rə\ 1 waterfalls on border bet. N.Y. & Ont. in the **Niagara River** (36 *mi* or 58 *km* flowing from Lake Erie N into Lake Ontario); divided by Goat Is. into Horseshoe, or Canadian, Falls (158 *ft* or 48 *m* high, 3010 *ft* or 917 *m* wide at crest) & American Falls (167 *ft* or 51 *m* high, 1060 *ft* or 323 *m* wide) 2 city W N.Y. at the falls *pop* 61,840 3 city Canada in SE Ont. *pop* 75,399

Nia·mey \nē-'ä-(,)mā, nyä-'mā\ city ✳ of Niger *pop* 225,314

Ni·as \'nē-,äs\ island Indonesia in Indian Ocean off W coast of Sumatra *area* 1569 *sq mi* (4079 *sq km*), *pop* 314,829 — **Ni·as·san** \'nē-ə-sən\ *n*

Ni·caea \nī-'sē-ə\ *or* **Nice** \'nīs\ ancient city of Byzantine Empire, site at modern village of Iznik in NW Turkey in Asia at E end of Iznik Lake — **Ni·cae·an** \nī-'sē-ən\ *adj*

Nic·a·ra·gua \,ni-kə-'rä-gwə\ 1 lake 100 *mi* (161 *km*) long S Nicaragua 2 country Central America bordering on the Pacific & the Caribbean; a republic ✳ Managua *area* 57,143 *sq mi* (148,572 *sq km*), *pop* 2,824,000 — **Nic·a·ra·guan** \-'rä-gwən\ *adj or n*

Nice \'nēs\ *or anc* **Ni·caea** \nī-'sē-ə\ city & port SE France on the Mediterranean *pop* 331,002

Nic·o·bar Islands \'ni-kə-,bär\ islands India in Indian Ocean S of Andaman Islands *area* 635 *sq mi* (1651 *sq km*), *pop* 14,563 — see ANDAMAN AND NICOBAR

Nicomedia — see IZMIT

Ni·cop·o·lis \nə-'kä-pə-ləs, nī-\ ancient city NW Greece in Epirus

Nic·o·sia \,ni-kə-'sē-ə\ city ✳ Cyprus, its ✳ *pop* 168,800

Niedersachsen — see LOWER SAXONY

Nieuw·poort *or* **Nieu·port** \'nü-,pȯrt, 'nyü-, -,pȯrt, *F* nyœ-'pȯr\ commune NW Belgium in W. Flanders on the Yser *pop* 9572

Ni·ger \'nī-jər, nē-'zher\ 1 river 2600 *mi* (4184 *km*) W Africa flowing from Fouta Djallon NE, SE, & S into Gulf of Guinea 2 country W Africa; a republic, until 1958 a territory of French West Africa ✳ Niamey *area* 458,874 *sq mi* (1,193,072 *sq km*), *pop* 5,098,427 — **Ni·ger·ois** \,nē-zhər-'wä, -zher-\ *n*

Ni·ge·ria \nī-'jir-ē-ə\ country W Africa bordering on Gulf of Guinea; a republic within the Commonwealth of Nations, formerly a colony & protectorate ✳ Abuja *area* 356,669 *sq mi* (927,339 *sq km*), *pop* 86,126,000 — **Ni·ge·ri·an** \-ē-ən\ *adj or n*

Nihon — see JAPAN

Nii·ga·ta \nē-'gä-tə, 'nē-gə-,tä\ city & port Japan in N Honshu on Sea of Japan *pop* 486,087

Nii·hau \'nē-,haù\ island Hawaii WSW of Kauai *area* 72 *sq mi* (187 *sq km*)

Nij·me·gen \'nī-,mā-gən, 'nä-, -,kə(n)\ commune E Netherlands in Gelderland on the Waal S of Arnhem *pop* 147,150

Ni·ko·la·yev \,ni-kə-'lī-əf\ *or* **My·ko·la·yiv** \,mē-kə-'lī-əf\ city & port S Ukraine *pop* 440,000

Ni·ko·pol \'nē-kə-,pól, 'nyē-\ city E *cen* Ukraine on the Dnieper *pop* 125,000

Nile \'nī(ə)l\ river 4037 *mi* (6497 *km*) E Africa flowing from Lake Victoria in Uganda N into the Mediterranean in Egypt; in various sections called specifically: **Vic·to·ria Nile** \vik-'tōr-ē-ə, -'tȯr-\ *or* **Som·er·set Nile** \'sə-mər-sət, -,set\ bet. Lake Victoria & Lake Albert; **Al·bert Nile** \'al-bərt\ bet. Lake Albert & Lake No; & **White Nile** from Lake No to Khartoum — see BLUE NILE

Niles \'nī(ə)lz\ 1 village NE Ill. NW of Chicago *pop* 28,284 2 city NE Ohio SE of Warren *pop* 21,128

Nil·gi·ri Hills \'nil-gə-rē\ hills S India in W Tamil Nadu; highest point Mt. Dodabetta 8640 *ft* (2633 *m*)

Nîmes \'nēm\ city S France NE of Montpellier *pop* 123,914

Nimrud — see CALAH

Nin·e·veh \'ni-nə-və\ *or* **L Ni·nus** \'nī-nəs\ ancient city ✳ of Assyria; ruins in Iraq on the Tigris opposite Mosul

Ning·bo *or* **Ning·po** \'niŋ-'bō\ *or formerly* **Ning·hsien** \'niŋ-shē-'en\ city E China in N Zhejiang ESE of Hangzhou *pop* 280,000

Ninghsia, Ningsia — see YINCHUAN

Ning·xia Hui·zu \'niŋ-shē-'ä-'hwēd-'zü\ *or* **Ning·sia Hui** \'niŋ-shē-'ä-'hwē\ region N China; formerly a province ✳ Yinchuan *area* 30,039 *sq mi* (78,101 *sq km*)

Ni·o·brara \,nī-ə-'brar-ə, -'brer-\ river 431 *mi* (694 *km*) E Wyo. & N Nebr. flowing E into Missouri River

Niort \nē-'ȯr\ city W France ENE of La Rochelle *pop* 59,297

Nip·i·gon, Lake \'ni-pə-,gän\ lake Canada in W Ont. N of Lake Superior *area* 1870 *sq mi* (4862 *sq km*)

Nip·is·sing, Lake \'ni-pə-siŋ\ lake Canada in SE Ont. NE of Georgian Bay *area* 330 *sq mi* (858 *sq km*)

Nippon — see JAPAN

Nip·pur \ni-'pŭr\ ancient city of Sumer SSE of Babylon

Nis *or* **Nish** \'nish, 'nēsh\ city E Yugoslavia in E Serbia *pop* 128,231

Ni·shi·no·mi·ya \nī-sho-'nō-mē-,yä\ city Japan in *cen* Honshu on Osaka Bay E of Kobe *pop* 426,919

Ni·te·rói \,nē-tə-'rói\ city SE Brazil on Guanabara Bay opposite Rio de Janeiro *pop* 400,140

Ni·tra \'ni-trə\ city W Slovakia *pop* 90,665

Ni·u·a·foo \nē-'ü-ə-,fō\ island SW *cen* Pacific in the N Tongas *pop* 599

Ni·ue \nē-'ü-(,)ā\ island *cen* Pacific; a self-governing territory of New Zealand *area* 100 *sq mi* (260 *sq km*), *pop* 2244 — **Ni·ue·an** \nyü-'wā-ən, 'nyü-,wä-\ *n*

Ni·velles \nē-'vel\ commune *cen* Belgium *pop* 23,217

Ni·ver·nais \,nē-vər-'nā\ region & former province *cen* France E of the upper Loire ✳ Nevers

Nizh·ni Nov·go·rod \,nizh-nē-'näv-gə-,räd, -'nòv-gə-rət\ *or 1932–89* **Gor'·kiy** *or* **Gor·ki** \'gòr-kē\ city *cen* Russia in Europe at confluence of Oka & Volga rivers *pop* 1,344,000

Nizh·ni Ta·gil \,nizh-nē-tə-'gil\ city W Russia in Asia on E slope of the Urals *pop* 398,000

No, Lake \'nō\ lake S *cen* Sudan where Bahr el Jebel & Bahr el Ghazal join to form the White Nile *area* 40 *sq mi* (104 *sq km*)

No·gal·es \nō-'ga-ləs, -'gä-\ 1 city S Ariz. on Mexican border *pop* 19,489 2 city NW Mexico in Sonora *pop* 14,254

Nome, Cape \'nōm\ cape W Alaska on S side of Seward Peninsula

Noot·ka Sound \'nùt-kə, 'nút-\ inlet of the Pacific Canada in SW B.C. on W coast of Vancouver Is.

Nor·co \'nòr-(,)kō, 'nòr-\ city SE Calif. W of Palm Springs *pop* 23,302

Nordenskjöld Sea — see LAPTEV SEA

Nord·kyn, Cape \'nòr-kən, 'nòr-; 'nür-kụen\ cape NE Norway on Barents Sea E of N. Cape; northernmost point of European mainland, at 71°8′N

Nor·folk \'nòr-fək, *US also* -,fòk\ 1 city NE Nebr. *pop* 21,476 2 city & port SE Va. on Elizabeth River S of Hampton Roads *pop* 261,229 3 county E England bordering on North Sea ✳ Norwich *area* 2067 *sq mi* (5374 *sq km*), *pop* 619,500

Norfolk Broads — see BROADS

Norfolk Island island S Pacific bet. New Caledonia & New Zealand; administered by Australia *area* 13 *sq mi* (34 *sq km*), *pop* 1912

Norge — see NORWAY

Nor·i·cum \'nòr-i-kəm, 'när-\ ancient country & Roman province S *cen* Europe S of the Danube in modern Austria & S Germany

No·rilsk \nò-'rēlsk\ city N Russia in Asia, N of arctic circle near mouth of the Yenisey *pop* 180,000

Nor·mal \'nòr-məl\ town *cen* Ill. N of Bloomington *pop* 40,023

Nor·man \'nòr-mən\ city *cen* Okla. on Canadian River *pop* 80,071

Nor·man·dy \'nòr-mən-dē\ *or F* **Nor·man·die** \nòr-mäⁿ-dē\ region & former province NW France NE of Brittany ✳ Rouen

Nor·ris·town \'nòr-əs-,taún, 'när-\ borough SE Pa. *pop* 30,749

Norr·kö·ping \'nòr-,shə(r)-piŋ\ city & port SE Sweden SW of Stockholm at head of an inlet of the Baltic *pop* 119,921

North·al·ler·ton \nòr-'tha-lər-tᵊn\ town N England ✳ of N. Yorkshire

North America continent of the western hemisphere NW of S. America bounded by Atlantic, Arctic, & Pacific oceans *area* 9,385,000 *sq mi* (24,401,000 *sq km*) — **North American** *adj or n*

North·amp·ton \nòr-'tham(p)-tən, nòrth-'ham(p)-\ 1 city W *cen* Mass. on Connecticut River N of Holyoke *pop* 29,289 2 borough *cen* England ✳ of Northamptonshire *pop* 145,421

North·amp·ton·shire \-,shir, -shər\ *or* **Northampton** county *cen* England ✳ Northampton *area* 914 *sq mi* (2376 *sq km*), *pop* 532,400

North Andover town NE Mass. E of Lawrence *pop* 22,792

North Atlantic — see ATLANTIC OCEAN

North At·tle·bor·ough *or* **North At·tle·boro** \'a-tᵊl-,bər-ə, -,bə-rə\ town SE Mass. *pop* 25,038

North Bay \'nòrth-,bā\ city Canada in SE Ont. *pop* 55,405

North Borneo — see SABAH

North Brabant *or D* **Noord–Bra·bant** \,nòrt-'brä-,bänt\ province S Netherlands ✳ 's Hertogenbosch *area* 1965 *sq mi* (5109 *sq km*), *pop* 2,093,929

North·brook \'nòrth-,brùk\ village NE Ill. NW of Chicago *pop* 32,308

North Canadian river 760 *mi* (1223 *km*) S *cen* U.S. flowing ESE from NE N.Mex. into Canadian River in E Okla. — see BEAVER

North Cape 1 cape New Zealand at N tip of North Is. 2 cape NE Norway on **Ma·ger·öy** \,mä-gə-'rəi\ island (*area* 111 *sq mi or* 289 *sq km*) at 71°10′20″N 3 — see HORN

North Car·o·li·na \,kar'(-ə)-'lī-nə\ state E U.S. ✳ Raleigh *area* 52,586 *sq mi* (136,724 *sq km*), *pop* 6,628,637 — **North Car·o·lin·ian** \-'li-nē-ən, -'li-nyən\ *adj or n*

North Cas·cades National Park \kas-'kādz, 'kas-\ reservation N *cen* Wash. on Canadian border

North Channel strait bet. NE Ireland & SW Scotland connecting Irish Sea & the Atlantic

North Charleston city SE S.C. *pop* 70,218

North Chicago city NE Ill. S of Waukegan *pop* 34,978

North Da·ko·ta \də-'kō-tə\ state NW *cen* U.S. ✳ Bismarck *area* 70,665 *sq mi* (183,729 *sq km*), *pop* 638,800 — **North Da·ko·tan** \-'kō-tᵊn\ *adj or n*

North Down district E Northern Ireland, established 1974 *area* 28 *sq mi* (73 *sq km*), *pop* 63,849

North Downs hills S England chiefly in Kent & Surrey

North East Frontier Agency — see ARUNACHAL PRADESH

North–East New Guinea the NE part of mainland Papua New Guinea

Northern Cape province W Republic of South Africa *area* 140,305 *sq mi* (363,390 *sq km*), *pop* 763,900

Northern Cir·cars \(,)sər-'kärz\ historic name for the coast region of E India now in E Andhra Pradesh

Northern Cook Islands \'kùk\ *or* **Ma·ni·hi·ki Islands** \,mä-nə-'hē-kē\ islands S *cen* Pacific N of Cook Islands; belong to New Zealand

Northern Dvi·na \də-,vē-'nä\ *or Russ* **Se·ver·na·ya Dvina** \'se-vər-nə-yə\ river 1100 *mi* (1770 *km*) N Russia in Europe flowing NW into White Sea

Northern Ireland country NE Ireland; a division of the United Kingdom of Great Britain and Northern Ireland ✳ Belfast *area* 5461 *sq mi* (14,199 *sq km*), *pop* 1,543,000 — see ULSTER

Northern Karroo — see KARROO

Northern Kingdom — see ISRAEL

Northern Mar·i·ana Islands \,mar-ē-'a-nə, ,mer-\ islands W Pacific; in Trust Territory of the Pacific Islands 1947–76 & a U.S. commonwealth since 1986; *area* 184 *sq mi* (478 *sq km*), *pop* 16,780

Northern Rhodesia — see ZAMBIA

Northern Sporades — see SPORADES

Northern Territory territory *cen* & N Australia bordering on Arafura Sea ✳ Darwin *area* 523,620 *sq mi* (1,361,412 *sq km*), *pop* 123,324

Northern Transvaal province N Republic of South Africa *area* 46,180 *sq mi* (119,606 *sq km*), *pop* 5,120,600

Northern Yukon National Park reservation NW Canada

North Frisian — see FRISIAN ISLANDS

North·glenn \'nòrth-,glen\ city N *cen* Colo. NE of Denver *pop* 27,195

North Ha·ven \'nòrth-,hā-vən\ town S Conn. *pop* 22,247

North Holland *or D* **Noord–Hol·land** \,nòrt-'hò-,länt\ province NW Netherlands ✳ Haarlem *area* 1163 *sq mi* (3024 *sq km*), *pop* 2,308,590

North Island island N New Zealand *area* 44,280 *sq mi* (115,128 *sq km*), *pop* 1,956,411

North Kings·town \'kiŋ-stən\ town S R.I. *pop* 23,786

North Korea — see KOREA — **North Korean** *adj or n*

North Las Vegas city SE Nev. *pop* 47,707

North Lau·der·dale \'lò-dər-,däl\ city SE Fla. *pop* 26,506

North Little Rock city *cen* Ark. *pop* 61,741

North Miami city SE Fla. *pop* 49,998

North Miami Beach city SE Fla. *pop* 35,359

North Minch — see MINCH

North Olm·sted \'òm-,sted\ city NE Ohio *pop* 34,204

North Os·se·tian Republic \ä-'sē-shən\ autonomous republic SE Russia in Europe on the N slopes of Caucasus Mountains ✳ Vladikavkaz *area* 3500 *sq mi* (9100 *sq km*)

North Pacific — see PACIFIC OCEAN

North Platte 1 river 618 *mi* (994 *km*) W U.S. flowing from N Colo. N & E through Wyo. into Nebr. to unite with the S. Platte forming Platte River 2 city SW *cen* Nebr. *pop* 22,605

North Providence town NE R.I. *pop* 32,090

North Rhine–Westphalia *or G* **Nord·rhein–West·fa·len** \'nòrt-,rīn-,vest-'fä-lən\ state of Germany & formerly of W. Germany formed 1946 by union of former Westphalia province, Lippe state, & N Rhine Province ✳ Düsseldorf *area* 13,107 *sq mi* (34,078 *sq km*), *pop* 17,058,193

North Rich·land Hills \'rich-lən(d)\ town N Tex. *pop* 45,895

North Ridge·ville \'rij-,vil\ village N Ohio *pop* 21,564

North Riding — see YORK

North River estuary of Hudson River bet. SE N.Y. & NE N.J.

North Roy·al·ton \'ròi(-ə)l-tən\ city N Ohio *pop* 23,197

North Saskatchewan — see SASKATCHEWAN

North Sea arm of the Atlantic 600 *mi* (966 *km*) long & 350 *mi* (563 *km*) wide E of Great Britain

North Slope region N Alaska bet. Brooks Range & Arctic Ocean

North Tonawanda city W N.Y. N of Buffalo *pop* 34,989

North Truchas Peak — see TRUCHAS PEAK

North·um·ber·land \nòr-'thəm-bər-lənd\ county N England ✳ Newcastle upon Tyne *area* 1943 *sq mi* (5052 *sq km*), *pop* 301,100

Northumberland Strait strait 180 *mi* (290 *km*) long Canada in Gulf of Saint Lawrence bet. P.E.I. & the mainland

North·um·bria \nòr-'thəm-brē-ə\ ancient country Great Britain bet. the Humber & Firth of Forth; one of kingdoms in Anglo-Saxon heptarchy

North Vancouver city Canada in SW B.C. *pop* 38,436

North Vietnam — see VIETNAM

North West province N Republic of South Africa *area* 45,834 *sq mi* (118,710 *sq km*), *pop* 3,506,800

North–West Frontier Province province of Pakistan & formerly of Brit. India on Afghanistan border ✳ Peshawar *pop* 10,885,000

Northwest Passage a passage by sea bet. the Atlantic & the Pacific along the N coast of N. America

Northwest Territories territory N Canada comprising the arctic islands, the mainland N 60° bet. Yukon Territory & Hudson Bay, & the islands in Hudson Bay; ✳ Yellowknife *area* 1,253,438 *sq mi* (3,258,939 *sq km*), *pop* 57,649

North York city Canada in SE Ont. N of Toronto *pop* 562,564

North Yorkshire county N England ✳ Northallerton *area* 3211 *sq mi* (8349 *sq km*), *pop* 673,900

Nor·ton Shores \'nòr-tᵊn\ city W Mich. S of Muskegon *pop* 21,755

Norton Sound arm of Bering Sea W Alaska bet. Seward Peninsula & the mouths of Yukon River

Nor·walk \'nòr-,wòk\ 1 city SW Calif. SE of Los Angeles *pop* 94,279 2 city SW Conn. on Long Island Sound *pop* 78,331

Nor·way \'nòr-,wā\ *or Norw* **Nor·ge** \'nòr-gə\ country N Europe in Scandinavia bordering on Atlantic & Arctic oceans; a kingdom ✳ Oslo *area* 119,085 *sq mi* (309,621 *sq km*), *pop* 4,233,116

Nor·we·gian Sea \nòr-'wē-jən\ arm of the N Atlantic W of Norway

Nor·wich 1 \'nòr-(,)wich; 'nòr-ich, 'när-\ city SE Conn. *pop* 37,391 2 \'när-ij, -ich\ city E England ✳ of Norfolk *pop* 121,688

Nor·wood \'nòr-,wùd\ 1 town E Mass. SW of Boston *pop* 28,700 2 city SW Ohio within city of Cincinnati *pop* 23,674

Not·ta·way \'nä-tə-,wā\ river 400 *mi* (644 *km*) Canada in SW Que. flowing NW into James Bay

Not·ting·ham \'nä-tiŋ-əm, *US also* -,ham\ borough N *cen* England ✳ of Nottinghamshire *pop* 271,080

Not·ting·ham·shire \'nä-tiŋ-əm-,shir, -shər, *US also* -,ham-\ *or* **Nottingham** *or* **Notts** \'näts\ county N *cen* England ✳ Nottingham *area* 836 *sq mi* (2174 *sq km*), *pop* 991,900

Nouak·chott \nù-'äk-,shät\ city ✳ of Mauritania near coast in SW *pop* 134,986

Nou·méa \nü-'mā-ə\ city & port ✳ of New Caledonia *pop* 65,110

No·va Igua·çu \,nō-və-ē-gwə-'sü\ city SE Brazil in Rio de Janeiro state NW of Rio de Janeiro *pop* 1,094,650

Nova Lisboa — see HUAMBO

No·va·ra \nō-'vär-ə\ commune NW Italy in Piedmont *pop* 103,088

No·va Sco·tia \,nō-və-'skō-shə\ province SE Canada comprising a peninsula (375 *mi or* 600 *km* long) & Cape Breton Is. ✳ Halifax *area* 21,103 *sq mi* (54,868 *sq km*), *pop* 899,942 — see ACADIA — **No·va Scotian** \-shən\ *adj or n*

No·va·to \nō-'vä-(,)tō\ city W Calif. N of San Francisco *pop* 47,585

No·va·ya Zem·lya \,nō-və-yə-,zem-lē-'ä\ two islands NE Russia in Europe in Arctic Ocean bet. Barents Sea & Kara Sea *area* 36,000 *sq mi* (93,600 *sq km*), *pop* 400

\ə\ abut \'ə\ kitten, F table \ər\ further \a\ ash \ā\ ace \ä\ mop, mar
\aú\ out \ch\ chin \e\ bet \ē\ easy \g\ go \i\ hit \ī\ ice \j\ job
\ŋ\ sing \ō\ go \ò\ law \òi\ boy \th\ thin \t̲h̲\ the \ü\ loot \ú\ foot
\y\ yet \zh\ vision \á, k̲, ⁿ, œ, œ̄, ụe, ū̄e, ᵊ\ see Guide to Pronunciation

Nov·go·rod \'näv-gə-ˌräd, 'nȯv-gə-rət\ **1** medieval principality E Europe extending from Lake Peipus & Lithuania to the Urals **2** city W Russia in Europe *pop* 128,000

No·vi \'nō-ˌvī\ village SE Mich. NW of Detroit *pop* 32,998

No·vi Sad \ˌnō-vē-'säd\ city N Yugoslavia on the Danube; chief city of Vojvodina *pop* 162,000

No·vo·kuz·netsk \ˌnō-(ˌ)vō-kùz-'netsk, ˌnō-və-\ *or formerly* **Sta·linsk** \'stä-lin(t)sk, 'sta-; 'stäl-yin(t)sk\ city S Russia in Asia at S end of Kuznetsk Basin *pop* 499,000

No·vo·si·birsk \ˌnō-(ˌ)vō-sə-'birsk, ˌnō-və-\ *or formerly* **No·vo·ni·ko·la·evsk** \-ˌni-kə-'lī-əfsk\ city S Russia in Asia on the Ob *pop* 1,221,000

Nu·bia \'nü-bē-ə, 'nyü-\ region & ancient kingdom NE Africa along the Nile in S Egypt & N Sudan

Nu·bi·an Desert \'nü-bē-ən, 'nyü-\ desert NE Sudan E of the Nile

Nu·e·ces \nü-'ā-səs, nyü-\ river 338 *mi* (544 *km*) S Tex. flowing S & SE into Nueces Bay at head of Corpus Christi Bay

Nueva Esparta — see MARGARITA

Nue·vo La·re·do \ˌnü-ˌā-(ˌ)vō-lə-'rā-(ˌ)dō\ city N Mexico in Tamaulipas on Rio Grande opposite Laredo, Tex. *pop* 175,750

Nuevo Le·ón \lā-'ōn\ state N Mexico in the Sierra Madre Oriental ✳ Monterrey *area* 25,134 *sq mi* (65,348 *sq km*), *pop* 2,463,298

Nu·ku·'a·lo·fa \ˌnü-kü-ä-'lō-fə\ town ✳ of Tonga on Tongatapu Is. *pop* 21,383

Nu·ku Hi·va \ˌnü-kə-'hē-və\ island S Pacific in the Marquesas; largest in group *area* 186 *sq mi* (484 *sq km*), *pop* 2100; chief town Hakapehi

Null·ar·bor Plain \'nə-lə-ˌbȯr\ treeless plain SW Australia in Western Australia & S. Australia bordering on Great Australian Bight

Num·foor \'nüm-ˌfȯr, -ˌfȯr\ island W. Irian in W Schouten Islands *area* 28 *sq mi* (73 *sq km*)

Nu·mid·ia \nü-'mi-dē-ə, nyü-\ ancient country N Africa E of Mauretania in modern Algeria; chief city Hippo — **Nu·mid·i·an** \-dē-ən\ *adj or n*

Nun·ea·ton \ˌnə-'nē-tⁿn\ borough *cen* England in Warwickshire E of Birmingham *pop* 71,530

Nu·ni·vak \'nü-nə-ˌvak\ island 50 *mi* (80 *km*) long W Alaska in Bering Sea

Nu·rem·berg \'nùr-əm-ˌbərg, 'nyùr-\ *or G* **Nürn·berg** \'nuern-ˌberk\ city S Germany in N *cen* Bavaria *pop* 484,403

Nu·ri·stan \ˌnùr-i-'stan, -'stän\ *or formerly* **Kaf·iri·stan** \ˌka-fə-ri-'stan, -'stän\ district E Afghanistan S of the Hindu Kush ✳ Puchal

Nyasa, Lake — see MALAWI (Lake)

Nyasaland — see MALAWI

Nyir·a·gon·go \nē-ˌir-ə-'gōn-(ˌ)gō, -'gän-, ˌnyir-\ volcano *ab* 11,400 *ft* (3475 *m*) E Zaire in Virunga Mountains NE of Lake Kivu

Nyi·regy·ha·za \'nē-ˌrej-hä-zō\ city NE Hungary *pop* 120,600

Nysa \'ni-sə\ *or* **Neis·se** \'nī-sə\ river 120 *mi* (193 *km*) SW Poland flowing NE into the Oder

Oa·he Reservoir \ō-'ä-(ˌ)hē\ reservoir *ab* 225 *mi* (362 *km*) long N S.Dak. & S N.Dak. formed in Missouri River by **Oahe Dam**

Oa·hu \ō-'ä-(ˌ)hü\ island Hawaii, site of Honolulu *area* 589 *sq mi* (1531 *sq km*)

Oak Creek city SE Wis. *pop* 19,513

Oak Forest village NE Ill. S of Chicago *pop* 26,203

Oak·ham \'ō-kəm\ town E *cen* England in E Leicestershire; ✳ of former county of Rutlandshire *pop* 7996

Oak·land \'ō-klənd\ city & port W Calif. on San Francisco Bay opposite San Francisco *pop* 372,242

Oakland Park city SE Fla. N of Fort Lauderdale *pop* 26,326

Oak Lawn village NE Ill. SW of Chicago *pop* 56,182

Oak Park **1** village NE Ill. W of Chicago *pop* 53,648 **2** city SE Mich. N of Detroit *pop* 30,462

Oak Ridge city E Tenn. W of Knoxville *pop* 27,310

Oak·ville \'ōk-ˌvil\ town Canada in SE Ont. SW of Toronto *pop* 114,670

Oa·xa·ca \wə-'hä-kə\ **1** state SE Mexico bordering on the Pacific *area* 36,371 *sq mi* (94,565 *sq km*), *pop* 2,518,157 **2** city, its ✳ *pop* 116,826 — **Oa·xa·can** \-kən\ *adj*

Ob \'äb, 'ōb\ river 2500 *mi* (4023 *km*) W Russia in Asia flowing NW & N into **Gulf of Ob** (inlet of Arctic Ocean 500 *mi or* 800 *km* long)

Ober·am·mer·gau \ˌō-bər-'ä-mər-ˌgaú\ town S Germany in Bavaria SSW of Munich *pop* 4906

Ober·hau·sen \'ō-bər-ˌhaú-zⁿn\ city W Germany in the Ruhr WNW of Essen *pop* 228,947

Oberland — see BERNER ALPEN

Oberpfalz — see PALATINATE

Obwald *or* **Obwalden** — see UNTERWALDEN

Oca·la \ō-'ka-lə\ city N *cen* Fla. S of Gainesville *pop* 42,045

Oce·a·nia \ˌō-shē-'a-nē-ə, -'ä-\ the lands of the *cen* & S Pacific including Micronesia, Melanesia, Polynesia (including New Zealand), often Australia, & sometimes the Malay Archipelago — **Oce·a·ni·an** \-nē-ən\ *adj or n*

Ocean Island **1** island W Pacific ESE of Nauru Is.; belongs to Kiribati *area* 2 *sq mi* (5.2 *sq km*), *pop* 2314 **2** — see KURE ISLAND

Ocean·side \'ō-shən-ˌsīd\ city SW Calif. NNW of San Diego *pop* 128,398

Oc·mul·gee \ōk-'məl-gē\ river 255 *mi* (410 *km*) *cen* Ga. flowing SE to join the **Oco·nee** \ō-'kō-nē\ (250 *mi or* 402 *km*) forming the Altamaha

Ocmulgee National Monument reservation *cen* Ga. at Macon containing American Indian mounds & other remains

Ocra·coke Island \'ō-krə-ˌkōk\ island off *cen* N.C. coast bet. Pamlico Sound & the Atlantic — see CROATAN

Oden·se \'ō-dⁿn-sə, 'ú-ən-zə\ city Denmark in N Fyn Is. *pop* 174,948

Oder \'ō-dər\ *or* **Odra** \'ō-drä\ river 563 *mi* (906 *km*) *cen* Europe rising in the mountains of Silesia, Czech Republic & flowing N to join Neisse River & thence N into the Baltic Sea

Odes·sa \ō-'de-sə\ **1** city W Tex. *pop* 89,699 **2** city & port S Ukraine on Black Sea *pop* 892,000

Oea — see TRIPOLI

Oe·ta \'ē-tə\ mountains *cen* Greece, E spur of Pindus Mountains; highest point 7060 *ft* (2152 *m*)

Of·fa·ly \'ȯ-fə-lē, 'ä-\ *or formerly* **King's** county *cen* Ireland in Leinster ✳ Tullamore *area* 771 *sq mi* (2005 *sq km*), *pop* 58,448

Of·fen·bach \'ȯ-fən-ˌbäk, -ˌbäk\ city SW Germany on Main River E of Frankfurt am Main *pop* 110,993

Oga·den \ō-'gä-ˌdän\ plateau region SE Ethiopia

Ogasawara Islands — see BONIN ISLANDS

Og·bo·mo·sho \ˌäg-bə-'mō-(ˌ)shō\ city W Nigeria *pop* 514,400

Og·den \'ȯg-dən, 'äg-\ city N Utah *pop* 63,909

Ogee·chee \ō-'gē-chē\ river 250 *mi* (402 *km*) E Ga. flowing SE into the Atlantic

Ohio \ō-'hī-(ˌ)ō, ə-, -ə\ **1** river 981 *mi* (1579 *km*) E U.S. flowing from junction of Allegheny & Monongahela rivers in W Pa. into Mississippi River **2** state E *cen* U.S. ✳ Columbus *area* 41,222 *sq mi* (107,177 *sq km*), *pop* 10,847,115 — **Ohio·an** \-'hī-ō-ən\ *n*

Ohře — see EGER

Oirot — see GORNO-ALTAI

Oise \'wäz\ river 186 *mi* (299 *km*) N France flowing SW into the Seine

Oi·ta \'ȯi-ˌtä, ō-'ē-tə\ city & port Japan in NE Kyushu *pop* 408,502

Ojos del Sa·la·do \ˌō-(ˌ)hōz-del-sə-'lä-(ˌ)dō\ mountain 22,539 *ft* (6870 *m*) NW Argentina in the Andes W of Tucumán

Oka \ō-'kä\ **1** river 530 *mi* (853 *km*) S *cen* Russia in Asia flowing N from the Sayan Mountains into the Angara **2** river 950 *mi* (1529 *km*) *cen* Russia in Europe flowing into the Volga

Oka·nog·an *or in Canada* **Oka·na·gan** \ˌō-kə-'nä-gən\ river 300 *mi* (483 *km*) U.S. & Canada flowing from **Okanagan Lake** (70 *mi or* 112 *km* long, in SE B.C.) into Columbia River in NE Wash.

Oka·van·go \ˌō-kə-'vaŋ-(ˌ)gō\ *or Pg* **Cu·ban·go** \kü-'vän(ŋ)-(ˌ)gü\ river 1000 *mi* (1609 *km*) SW *cen* Africa rising in *cen* Angola & flowing S & E to empty into **Okavango Swamps** (great marsh area N of Lake Ngami in NW Botswana)

Oka·ya·ma \ˌō-kə-'yä-mə\ city & port Japan in W Honshu on Inland Sea *pop* 593,742

Oka·za·ki \ˌō-kə-'zä-kē, ō-'kä-zə-kē\ city Japan in S *cen* Honshu SE of Nagoya *pop* 306,821

Okee·cho·bee, Lake \ˌō-kə-'chō-bē\ lake 37 *mi* (60 *km*) long S *cen* Fla.

Oke·fe·no·kee \ˌō-kə-fə-'nō-kē, ˌō-kē- *also* 'ōk-fə-ˌnōk\ swamp 40 *mi* (64 *km*) long SE Ga. & NE Fla.

Okhotsk, Sea of \ō-'kätsk, ä-'kȯtsk\ inlet of the Pacific E Russia in Asia W of Kamchatka peninsula & Kuril Islands

Oki Archipelago \'ō-(ˌ)kē\ archipelago Japan in Sea of Japan off SW Honshu

Oki·na·wa \ˌō-kə-'nä-wə, -'naú-ə\ **1** island group Japan in *cen* Ryukyu Islands ✳ Naha; occupied by the U.S. 1945–1972 **2** island in the group; largest in the Ryukyus *area* 579 *sq mi* (1505 *sq km*) — **Oki·na·wan** \-'nä-wən, -'naú-ən\ *adj or n*

Okla·ho·ma \ˌō-klə-'hō-mə\ state S *cen* U.S. ✳ Oklahoma City *area* 69,919 *sq mi* (181,789 *sq km*), *pop* 3,145,585 — **Okla·ho·man** \-mən\ *adj or n*

Oklahoma City city ✳ of Okla. on the N. Canadian *pop* 444,719

Oland \'ə(r)-ˌländ, 'œ-\ island Sweden in Baltic Sea off SE coast; chief town Borgholm *area* 519 *sq mi* (1349 *sq km*)

Ola·the \ō-'lā-thə\ city NE Kans. SW of Kansas City *pop* 63,352

Old Castile — see CASTILE

Ol·den·burg \'ōl-dən-ˌbȯrg, -ˌbùrk\ **1** former state NW Germany bordering on North Sea **2** city NW Germany W of Bremen *pop* 136,764

Old·ham \'ōl-dəm\ borough NW England in Greater Manchester *pop* 95,467

Old Point Comfort cape SE Va. on N shore of Hampton Roads

Old Sar·um \'sar-əm, 'ser-\ *or anc* **Sor·bi·o·du·num** \ˌsȯr-bē-ə-'dü-nəm, -'dyü-\ ancient city S England in Wiltshire N of Salisbury

Ol·du·vai Gorge \'ōl-də-ˌvī\ canyon Tanzania in N mainland SE of Serengeti Plain; fossil beds

Olek·ma \ō-'lek-mə\ river 700 *mi* (1126 *km*) E Russia in Asia rising in Yablonovy Mountains & flowing N into the Lena

Ole·nek \ˌä-lə-'nyȯk\ river 1325 *mi* (2132 *km*) N Russia in Asia flowing NE into Laptev Sea W of the Lena

Ol·i·fants \'ä-lə-fən(t)s\ river 350 *mi* (563 *km*) S Africa in Republic of South Africa & Mozambique flowing into the Limpopo

Olives, Mount of *or* **Ol·i·vet** \'ä-lə-ˌvet, ˌä-lə-'\ mountain ridge 2680 *ft* (817 *m*) W Jordan running N & S on E side of Jerusalem

Olo·mouc \'ȯ-lə-ˌmōts\ *or G* **Ol·mütz** \'ȯl-ˌmüts, -ˌmyüts, -ˌmuets\ city E Czech Republic in *cen* Moravia *pop* 106,595

Olsz·tyn \'ȯl-shtən\ *or G* **Al·len·stein** \'ä-lən-ˌshtīn, 'ä-, -ˌstīn\ city N Poland NNW of Warsaw *pop* 161,238

Olt \'ōlt\ river 308 *mi* (496 *km*) S Romania flowing S through the Transylvanian Alps into the Danube

Ol·te·nia \äl-'te-nē-ə\ *or* **Little Walachia** region S Romania W of the Olt; the W division of Walachia

Olym·pia \ə-'lim-pē-ə, ō-\ **1** city ✳ of Wash. on Puget Sound *pop* 33,840 **2** plain S Greece in NW Peloponnisos along the Alpheus — **Olym·pi·an** \-pē-ən\ *adj or n* — **Olym·pic** \-pik\ *adj*

Olympic Mountains mountains NW Wash. in *cen* Olympic Peninsula — see OLYMPUS (Mount)

Olympic National Park reservation NW Wash. including part of Olympic Mountains & strip of land along coast to the W

Olympic Peninsula peninsula NW Wash. W of Puget Sound

Olym·pus \ə-'lim-pəs\ **1** massif NE Greece in Thessaly near coast of Gulf of Salonika; highest point 9550 *ft* (2911 *m*)

Olympus, Mount **1** mountain 7965 *ft* (2428 *m*) NW Wash.; highest in Olympic Mountains **2** — see ULU DAG

Olyn·thus \ō-'lin(t)-thəs\ ancient city NE Greece in Macedonia on Chalcidice Peninsula

Om \'ȯm\ river 450 *mi* (724 *km*) SW Russia in Asia flowing into the Irtysh

Omagh \'ō-mə, -(ˌ)mä\ **1** district W Northern Ireland, established 1974 *area* 436 *sq mi* (1134 *sq km*), *pop* 41,159 **2** town W Northern Ireland in *cen* Omagh district *pop* 14,627

Oma·ha \'ō-mə-ˌhȯ, -ˌhä\ city E Nebr. on Missouri River *pop* 335,795

Oman \ō-'män, -'man\ *or formerly* **Muscat and Oman** country SW Asia in SE Arabia bordering on Arabian Sea; a sultanate ✳ Muscat *area* 82,000 *sq mi* (213,200 *sq km*), *pop* 2,000,000 — **Omani** \ō-'mä-nē, -'ma-\ *adj or n*

Oman, Gulf of arm of Arabian Sea bet. Oman & SE Iran

Om·dur·man \ˌäm-dər-'man, -'män\ city *cen* Sudan on the Nile opposite Khartoum & Khartoum North *pop* 299,000

Omi·ya \'ō-mē-,yä, ō-'mē-ə\ city Japan on Honshu, a suburb of Tokyo *pop* 403,779

Omo·lon \,ä-mə-'lȯn\ river 600 *mi* (966 *km*) E Russia in Asia flowing from the Kolyma Range N into Kolyma River

Omsk \'ȯm(p)sk, 'äm(p)sk\ city SW Russia in Asia at confluence of the Irtysh & the Om *pop* 1,014,000

Omu·ra \'ō-mu̇-,rä, ō-'mu̇r-ə\ city & port Japan in NW Kyushu on **Omura Bay** (inlet of E. China Sea) NNE of Nagasaki

One·ga, Lake \ō-'ne-gə\ lake NW Russia in Europe in S Karelian Republic *area* 3764 *sq mi* (9786 *sq km*)

Onei·da Lake \ō-'nī-də\ lake *ab* 22 *mi* (35 *km*) long *cen* N.Y. NE of Syracuse

On·tar·io \än-'ter-ē-,ō, -'tar-\ **1** city SW Calif. NW of Riverside *pop* 133,179 **2** province E Canada bet. Great Lakes & Hudson Bay ✳ Toronto *area* 363,282 *sq mi* (944,533 *sq km*), *pop* 10,084,885 — **On·tar·i·an** \-ē-ən\ *adj or n*

Ontario, Lake lake U.S. & Canada in N.Y. & Ont.; easternmost of the Great Lakes *area* 7540 *sq mi* (19,604 *sq km*)

Ope·li·ka \,ō-pə-'lī-kə\ city E Alabama *pop* 22,122

Opo·le \ō-'pȯ-lə\ *or G* **Op·peln** \'ȯ-pəln\ city SW Poland on the Oder *pop* 127,653

Oporto — see PORTO

Oquirrh Mountains \'ō-kər\ mountain range N *cen* Utah S of Great Salt Lake; highest point *ab* 11,000 *ft* (3353 *m*)

Ora·dea \ō-'rä-dē-ə\ city NW Romania in Transylvania near Hungarian border *pop* 225,416

Oran \ȯ-'rän\ city & port NW Algeria *pop* 491,900

Or·ange \'är-inj, 'är(-ə)nj, 'ȯr-inj, 'ȯr(-ə)nj\ **1** city SW Calif. N of Santa Ana *pop* 110,658 **2** city E Tex. E of Beaumont on the Sabine *pop* 19,381 **3** river 1300 *mi* (2092 *km*) S Africa flowing from the Drakensbergs in Lesotho W into the Atlantic

Orange \ȯ-'räzh\ city SE France N of Avignon *pop* 19,847

Or·ange Free State \'är-inj, 'är(-ə)nj, 'ȯr-inj, 'ȯr(-ə)nj\ *or* **Oran·je Vry·staat** \ō-,rän-yə-'frȯi-,stät\ province E *cen* Republic of South Africa bet. Orange & Vaal rivers *area* 49,647 *sq mi* (129,082 *sq km*), *pop* 1,988,293

Orasul Stalin — see BRASOV

Ordzhonikidze — see VLADIKAVKAZ

Öre·bro \,ər-ə-'brü\ city S *cen* Sweden *pop* 120,353

Or·e·gon \'ȯr-i-gən, 'är-, *chiefly by outsiders* -,gän\ **1** the Columbia River — an old name used esp. prior to discovery of mouth & renaming of river (1791) by Capt. Robert Gray **2** state NW U.S. ✳ Salem *area* 96,981 *sq mi* (252,151 *sq km*), *pop* 2,842,321 — **Or·e·go·nian** \,ȯr-i-'gō-nē-ən, ,är-, -nyən\ *adj or n*

Oregon Caves limestone caverns SW Oreg. SW of Medford in **Oregon Caves National Monument**

Oregon Country region W N. America bet. Pacific coast & the Rockies and bet. N Calif. & Alaska — so called *ab* 1818–46

Oregon Trail pioneer route to the Pacific Northwest *ab* 2000 *mi* (3219 *km*) long from vicinity of Independence, Mo., to Fort Vancouver, Wash.; used esp. 1842–60

Orel \ȯ-'rel, ȯr-'yȯl\ city Russia in Europe SSW of Moscow

Orem \'ȯr-əm, 'ȯr-\ city N *cen* Utah N of Provo *pop* 67,561

Oren·burg \'ȯr-ən-,bərg, 'ȯr-, -,bu̇rg\ *or formerly* **Chka·lov** \chə-'kä-ləf\ city SE Russia in Europe on Ural River *pop* 459,000

Oren·se \ȯ-'ren(t)-(,)sā\ **1** province NW Spain *area* 2694 *sq mi* (7004 *sq km*), *pop* 413,627 **2** city, its ✳ *pop* 86,951

Øre·sund \'ər-ə-,sȯn\ strait bet. Sjælland Is., Denmark, & S Sweden connecting Kattegat with Baltic Sea

Organ Pipe Cactus National Monument reservation S Ariz. on Mexican border

Oril·lia \ȯ-'ril-yə\ city Canada in SE Ont. on Lake Simcoe *pop* 25,925

Ori·no·co \,ȯr-ə-'nō-(,)kō, ,ȯr-\ river 1600 *mi* (2575 *km*) Venezuela flowing from Brazilian border to Colombia border & thence into the Atlantic through wide delta

Oris·sa \ȯ-'ri-sə\ state E India bordering on Bay of Bengal ✳ Bhubaneswar *area* 60,136 *sq mi* (156,354 *sq km*), *pop* 26,272,064

Ori·za·ba \,ȯr-ə-'zä-bə, ,ȯr-, -'sä-\ **1** — see CITLALTEPETL **2** city E Mexico in Veracruz state *pop* 105,150

Or·khon \'ȯr-,kän\ river 450 *mi* (724 *km*) N Mongolia flowing NE from N edge of the Gobi into the Selenga

Ork·ney Islands \'ȯrk-nē\ islands N Scotland constituting a region ✳ Kirkwall (on Mainland Is.) *area* 376 *sq mi* (978 *sq km*), *pop* 18,906 — **Ork·ney·an** \'ȯrk-nē-ən, ȯrk-'\ *adj or n*

Or·lan·do \ȯr-'lan-(,)dō\ city E *cen* Fla. NE of Tampa *pop* 164,693

Or·land Park \'ȯr-lənd\ village NE Ill. SW of Chicago *pop* 35,720

Or·lé·a·nais \,ȯr-lē-ə-'nā\ region & former province N *cen* France ✳ Orléans

Or·lé·ans \,ȯr-lā-'äⁿ\ commune N *cen* France *pop* 88,503

Or·ly \ȯr-'lē, 'ȯr-lē\ commune France, SSE suburb of Paris

Or·moc Bay \ȯr-'mäk\ inlet of Camotes Sea Philippines in NW Leyte Is.

Or·mond Beach \'ȯr-mənd\ city E Fla. *pop* 29,721

Ormuz — see HORMUZ

Orne \'ȯrn\ river 95 *mi* (153 *km*) NW France flowing N into Bay of the Seine

Oron·tes \ȯ-'rän-(,)tēz\ river 246 *mi* (396 *km*) Syria & Turkey rising in Lebanon in the Bekaa & flowing into the Mediterranean

Or·ping·ton \'ȯr-piŋ-tən\ former urban district SE England in Kent, now part of Bromley

Or·re·fors \,ȯr-ə-'fȯrz, -'fȯrsh\ town SE Sweden NW of Kalmar

Orsk \'ȯrsk\ city SE Russia in Europe on Ural River S of Magnitogorsk *pop* 247,000

Or·te·gal, Cape \,ȯr-ti-'gäl\ cape NW Spain

Ort·les \'ȯrt-,läs\ *or G* **Ort·ler** \-lər\ mountain range of E Alps N Italy bet. Venezia Tridentina & Lombardy; highest peak Ortles 12,792 *ft* (3899 *m*)

Oru·ro \ȯ-'rur-(,)ō\ city W Bolivia *pop* 124,213

Or·vie·to \,ȯr-vē-'ā-(,)tō, -'e-\ *or anc* **Vel·su·na** \vel-'sü-nə\ *or* **Vol·sin·ii** \väl-'si-nē-,ī\ commune *cen* Italy WNW of Terni *pop* 21,695

Osage \ō-'sāj, 'ō-,\ river E Kans. & Mo. flowing E into Missouri River; now partly submerged in Lake of the Ozarks

Osa·ka \ō-'sä-kə, 'ō-sä-,kä\ city & port Japan in S Honshu on **Osaka Bay** (inlet of the Pacific) *pop* 2,623,831

Osh·a·wa \'ä-shə-wə, -,wä, -,wȯ\ city Canada in SE Ont. on Lake Ontario ENE of Toronto *pop* 129,344

Osh·kosh \'äsh-,käsh\ city E Wis. on Lake Winnebago *pop* 55,006

Osi·jek \'ō-sē-,yek\ city E Croatia in Slavonia *pop* 94,989

Os·lo \'äz-(,)lō, 'äs-\ *or formerly* **Chris·ti·a·nia** *or* **Kris·ti·a·nia** \,kris-chē-'a-nē-ə, ,krish-chē-, ,kris-tē-, -'ä-\ city ✳ of Norway at N end of **Oslo Fjord** (inlet of the Skagerrak) *pop* 458,364

Os·na·brück \'äz-nə-,brük\ city NW Germany in Lower Saxony *pop* 157,367

Osor·no \ō-'sȯr-(,)nō\ volcano 8727 *ft* (2644 *m*) S *cen* Chile in lake district

Os·sa, Mount \'ä-sə\ mountain 6490 *ft* (1967 *m*) NE Greece in E Thessaly

Os·se·tia \ä-'sē-sh(ē-)ə\ region SE Russia in Europe in *cen* Caucasus — see NORTH OSSETIAN REPUBLIC, SOUTH OSSETIAN

Os·si·ning \'ä-sⁿn-iŋ, 'äs-niŋ\ village SE N.Y. *pop* 22,582

Ost·end \ä-'stend, 'ä-,\ *or Flem* **Oost·en·de** \ō-'sten-də\ *or F* **Os·tende** \ȯ-'stäⁿd\ city & port NW Belgium *pop* 68,500

Österreich — see AUSTRIA

Os·tia \'äs-tē-ə\ town *cen* Italy at mouth of the Tiber E of site of ancient town of the same name which was the port for Rome

Ostrasia — see AUSTRASIA

Ostra·va \'ȯs-trə-və\ *or formerly* **Mo·rav·ska Ostrava** \'mȯr-əf-skə\ city *cen* E Czech Republic in Moravia *pop* 331,241

Osu·mi Islands \'ō-sə-(,)mē, ō-'sü-mē\ island group Japan in N Ryukyus

Os·we·go \ä-'swē-(,)gō\ city N N.Y. on Lake Ontario *pop* 19,195

Oś·wię·cim \,ȯsh-vē-'ent-səm\ *or* **Ausch·witz** \'au̇sh-,vits\ commune S Poland W of Kraków; site of Nazi concentration camp during World War II

Ota·go Harbor \ō-'tä-gō\ inlet of the Pacific S New Zealand on E coast of South Is.; Dunedin is situated on it

Otran·to \ō-'tran-(,)tō, 'ō-trən-,tō\ commune & port S Italy on coast at SE tip of Apulia

Otranto, Strait of strait bet. SE Italy & W Albania

Ot·ta·wa \'ä-tə-wə, -,wä, -,wȯ\ **1** river 696 *mi* (1120 *km*) E Canada in SE Ont. & S Que. flowing E into St. Lawrence River **2** city ✳ of Canada in SE Ont. *pop* 313,987

Ot·to·man Empire \'ä-tə-mən\ former Turkish sultanate (✳ Constantinople) in SE Europe, W Asia, & N Africa including at greatest extent Turkey, Syria, Mesopotamia, Palestine, Arabia, Egypt, Barbary States, Balkans, & parts of Russia & Hungary

Ot·tum·wa \ə-'təm-wə, ō-'təm-\ city SE Iowa *pop* 24,488

Oua·chi·ta \'wä-shə-,tȯ\ river 605 *mi* (974 *km*) SW Ark. & E La. flowing into Black River

Ouachita Mountains mountains W Ark. & SE Okla. S of Arkansas River

Oua·ga·dou·gou \,wä-gə-'dü-(,)gü\ city *cen* Burkina Faso, its ✳ *pop* 366,000

Ouar·gla \'wȯr-glə, 'wär-, -,glä\ town & oasis Algeria in the Sahara *pop* 77,400

Oubangui — see UBANGI

Oubangui–Chari — see UBANGI-SHARI

Ou·den·aar·de \,au̇-dⁿ-'är-də, ,ō-\ *or F* **Au·de·narde** \,ō-dⁿ-'ärd\ commune Belgium in E Flanders on the Scheldt *pop* 27,162

Oudh \'au̇d\ region N India in E *cen* Uttar Pradesh ✳ Lucknow

Oudts·hoorn \'ōts-,hȯrn\ city S Republic of South Africa in Western Cape province E of Cape Town *pop* 26,907

Oues·sant, Ile d' \,ēl-dwe-'säⁿ\ *or* **Ush·ant** \'ə-shənt\ island NW France off tip of Brittany *pop* 1814

Ouj·da \üzh-'dä\ city NE Morocco near Algerian border *pop* 260,082

Ou·lu \'au̇-(,)lü, 'ō-\ *or Sw* **Ulea·borg** \'ü-lā-ō-,bȯr-ē\ city N *cen* Finland on Gulf of Bothnia *pop* 100,281

Ou·ro Prê·to \,ō-(,)rü-'prā-(,)tü\ city E Brazil in Minas Gerais *pop* 53,434

Ouse \'üz\ **1** *or* **Great Ouse** river 160 *mi* (257 *km*) *cen* & E England flowing into The Wash **2** river 57 *mi* (92 *km*) NE England flowing SE to unite with Trent River forming the Humber

Outer Banks chain of sand islands & peninsulas along N.C. coast

Outer Hebrides — see HEBRIDES

Outer Mongolia — see MONGOLIA — **Outer Mongolian** *adj or n*

Out Islands islands of the Bahamas group excepting New Providence

Ou·tre·mont \'ü-trə-,mänt, *F* ü-trə-mōⁿ\ town Canada in S Que. on Montreal Is. *pop* 22,935

Ova·lle \ō-'vï-,ā, -'vä-,yä\ city N *cen* Chile

Over·ijs·sel \,ō-və-'rī-səl\ province E Netherlands ✳ Zwolle *area* 1318 *sq mi* (3427 *sq km*), *pop* 1,038,341

Over·land Park \'ō-vər-lənd\ city NE Kans. S of Kansas City *pop* 111,790

Ovie·do \,ō-vē-'ā-(,)thō, ,ō-'vyä-\ **1** province NW Spain on Bay of Biscay *area* 4025 *sq mi* (10,465 *sq km*), *pop* 1,140,239 — see ASTURIAS **2** city ✳ of Oviedo province *pop* 184,473

Owas·co Lake \ō-'wäs-(,)kō\ lake 11 *mi* (18 *km*) long *cen* N.Y.; one of the Finger Lakes

Owa·ton·na \,ō-wə-'tä-nə\ city SE Minn. *pop* 19,386

Ow·en Falls \'ō-ən\ former waterfall E Africa in Uganda in the Nile N of Lake Victoria; now submerged in water behind **Owen Falls Dam**

Ow·ens \'ō-ənz\ river E Calif. formerly flowing into Owens Lake (now dry), now supplying water to city of Los Angeles by way of Los Angeles Aqueduct

Ow·ens·boro \'ō-ənz-,bər-ə, -,bə-rə\ city NW Ky. *pop* 53,549

Owen Sound city Canada in SE Ont. on Georgian Bay *pop* 21,674

Owen Stan·ley Range \'stan-lē\ mountain range E New Guinea; highest peak Mt. Victoria 13,363 *ft* (4073 *m*)

Owy·hee \ō-'wī-(,)(h)ē\ river 250 *mi* (402 *km*) SW Idaho & SE Oreg. flowing N into Snake River

---

\ə\ abut   \ⁿ\ kitten, F table   \ər\ further   \a\ ash   \ā\ ace   \ä\ mop, mar
\au̇\ out   \ch\ chin   \e\ bet   \ē\ easy   \g\ go   \i\ hit   \ī\ ice   \j\ job
\ŋ\ sing   \ō\ go   \ȯ\ law   \ȯi\ boy   \th\ thin   \t̲h̲\ the   \ü\ loot   \u̇\ foot
\y\ yet   \zh\ vision   \ä, k̲, ⁿ, œ, œ̄, ᵫ, ᵫ̄, ᵜ\ *see* Guide to Pronunciation

Ox·ford \'äks-fərd\ or ML **Ox·o·nia** \äk-'sō-nē-ə\ city S cen England ✳ of Oxfordshire pop 98,521 — **Ox·ford·ian** \äks-'fȯr-dē-ən, -'fȯr-\ adj or n

Ox·ford·shire \'äks-fərd-,shir, -shər\ or Oxford county S cen England ✳ Oxford area 1009 sq mi (2623 sq km), pop 455,200

Ox·nard \'äks-,närd\ city S Calif. SE of Santa Barbara pop 142,216

Oxus — see AMU DARYA

Oxy·rhyn·chus \,äk-si-'riŋ-kəs\ or Ar El Bah·na·sa \el-'ba-nə-sə\ archaeological site Egypt N of Al Minyā & S of El Faiyûm

Ozark Plateau \'ō-,zärk\ or Ozark Mountains eroded tableland region 1500–2500 ft (457–762 m) high cen U.S. N of Arkansas River in N Ark., S Mo., & NE Okla. with E extension in S Ill. — **Ozark·er** \'ō-,zär-kər\ n — **Ozark·ian** \ō-'zär-kē-ən\ adj or n

Ozarks, Lake of the \'ō-,zärks\ reservoir 130 mi (209 km) long cen Mo. formed in Osage River by Bagnell Dam

Pa·chu·ca \pə-'chü-kə\ city cen Mexico ✳ of Hidalgo pop 83,892

Pa·cif·i·ca \pə-'si-fi-kə\ city W Calif. S of San Francisco on the Pacific pop 37,670

Pa·cif·ic Islands, Trust Territory of the \pə-'si-fik\ former trust territory in association with U.S. comprising the Carolines & the Marshalls; with the Marianas (except Guam) constituted a Japanese mandate 1919–45

Pacific Ocean ocean extending from the arctic circle to the antarctic regions & from W N. America & W S. America to E Asia & Australia area 69,375,000 sq mi (180,375,000 sq km); often divided into **North Pacific Ocean & South Pacific Ocean**

Pacific Rim the countries bordering on or located in the Pacific Ocean — used esp. of the rapidly developing Asian countries on the Pacific

Pacific Rim National Park reservation SW Canada in Vancouver Island

Pac·to·lus \pak-'tō-ləs\ river Asia Minor in ancient Lydia flowing into the Hermus (modern Gediz) near Sardis

Pa·dang \pə-'däŋ\ city & port Indonesia in W Sumatra pop 631,543

Pad·ding·ton \'pa-diŋ-tən\ former metropolitan borough NW London, England, now part of Westminster

Pa·dre Island \'pä-drē, 'pa-\ island 100 mi (161 km) long S Tex. bet. Laguna Madre & Gulf of Mexico

Pad·ua \'pa-jə-wə, 'pa-də-wə\ or It Pa·do·va \'pä-də-,vä\ commune NE Italy W of Venice pop 220,358 — **Pad·u·an** \'pa-jə-wən, 'pa-də-\ adj or n

Pa·du·cah \pə-'dü-kə, -'dyü-\ city W Ky. on Ohio River pop 27,256

Padus — see PO

Paes·tum \'pes-təm, 'pēs-\ or earlier Po·sei·do·nia \,pä-,sī-'dō-nē-ə, ,pō-\ ancient city S Italy in W Lucania on Gulf of Salerno (ancient **Bay of Paestum**)

Pa·go Pa·go \,päŋ-ō-(,)päŋ-(,)gō, ,päŋ-(,)gō-'päŋ-(,)gō\ town & port ✳ of American Samoa on Tutuila Is.

Pa·hang \pə-'haŋ\ state E Malaysia (federation) bordering on S. China Sea ✳ Kuala Lipis area 13,873 sq mi (36,070 sq km), pop 770,644

Painted Desert region NE Ariz. E of the Little Colorado

Pais·ley \'pāz-lē\ burgh SW Scotland in Strathclyde pop 84,789

Pa·kan·ba·ru \,pä-kən-'bär-ü\ or Pe·kan·ba·ru \,pā-\ city Indonesia in cen Sumatra pop 398,694

Pa·ki·stan \'pa-ki-,stan, ,pä-ki-'stän\ country S Asia orig. comprising an E division & a W division; a dominion 1947–56, an Islamic republic since 1956, & a member of the Commonwealth of Nations 1956–72; formed from parts of former Brit. India; ✳ Islamabad area 310,403 sq mi (807,048 sq km), pop 83,782,000 — see EAST PAKISTAN, WEST PAKISTAN — **Pa·ki·stani** \,pa-ki-'sta-nē, ,pä-ki-'stä-\ adj or n

Pa·lat·i·nate \pə-'la-t'n-ət\ or G Pfalz \'(p)fälts\ either of two districts SW Germany once ruled by counts palatine of the Holy Roman Empire: **Rhenish Palatinate** or **Rhine Palatinate** or G **Rhein·pfalz** \'rīn-,(p)fälts\ (on the Rhine E of Saarland) & **Upper Palatinate** or G **Ober·pfalz** \'ō-bər-,(p)fälts\ (on the Danube around Regensburg) — see RHINELAND-PALATINATE

Pal·a·tine \'pa-lə-,tīn\ **1** hill in Rome, Italy, one of seven on which the ancient city was built — see AVENTINE **2** village NE Ill. NW of Chicago pop 39,253

Palau — see BELAU — **Pa·lau·an** \pə-'laü-ən\ n

Pa·la·wan \pə-'lä-wən, -,wän\ island 278 mi (445 km) long W Philippines W of the Visayans area 4550 sq mi (11,830 sq km), pop (with adjacent islands) 232,322

Pa·lem·bang \,pä-ləm-'bäŋ\ city & port Indonesia in SE Sumatra pop 1,141,036

Pa·len·cia \pə-'len(t)-sh(ē-)ə, -sē-ə\ **1** province N Spain area 3256 sq mi (8466 sq km), pop 165,215 **2** city, its ✳, NNE of Valladolid pop 66,496

Pa·len·que \pə-'leŋ-(,)kā\ ruined Mayan city S Mexico in N Chiapas SW of modern town of Palenque

Pa·ler·mo \pə-'lər-(,)mō, -'ler-\ or anc Pan·or·mus \pa-'nȯr-məs\ or **Pan·hor·mus** \pan-'hȯr-\ city & port Italy ✳ of Sicily pop 731,418 — **Pa·ler·mi·tan** \pə-'lər-mə-t'n, -'ler-\ adj or n

Pal·es·tine \'pa-lə-,stīn\ or L Pal·aes·ti·na \,pa-lə-'stē-nə, -'stī-\ **1** ancient region SW Asia bordering on E coast of the Mediterranean & extending E of Jordan River **2** former country bordering on the Mediterranean on W & Dead Sea on E; a part of the Ottoman Empire 1516–1917, a Brit. mandate 1923–48; now divided bet. Israel & Jordan — **Pal·es·tin·ian** \,pa-lə-'sti-nē-ən, -nyən\ adj or n

Pal·i·sades \,pa-lə-'sādz\ line of cliffs 15 mi (24 km) long SE N.Y. & NE N.J. on W bank of Hudson River

Palk Strait \'pȯ(l)k\ strait 40 mi (64 km) wide bet. N Sri Lanka & SE India connecting Gulf of Mannar & Bay of Bengal

Pal·ma \'päl-mə\ or Palma de Ma·llor·ca \də-mä-'yȯr-kə\ commune & port Spain ✳ of Baleares province on Majorca pop 310,421

Pal·mas, Cape \'päl-məs\ cape Liberia on extreme SE coast

Palm Bay city E Fla. pop 62,632

Palm Beach Gardens city SE Fla. pop 22,965

Palm·dale \'päl(l)m-,dāl\ city SW Calif. NE of Los Angeles pop 68,842

Palm Desert city SW Calif ESE of Riverside pop 23,252

Palmer Archipelago, Palmer Peninsula — see ANTARCTIC ARCHIPELAGO, ANTARCTIC PENINSULA

Palm·er Land \'pä-mər, 'päl-mər\ the S section of Antarctic Peninsula

Palm·er·ston \'pä-mər-stən, 'päl-mər-\ island (atoll) cen Pacific NW of Rarotonga Is.; belongs to New Zealand area 1 sq mi (2.6 sq km)

Palmerston North city New Zealand on S North Is. NE of Wellington pop 60,105

Palm Springs city SW Calif. E of Los Angeles pop 40,181

Pal·my·ra \pal-'mī-rə\ or bib Tad·mor \'tad-,mȯr\ or Ta·mar \'tā-,mär, -mər\ ancient city Syria on N edge of Syrian Desert NE of Damascus — **Pal·my·rene** \,pal-mə-'rēn, -mī-\ adj or n

Palmyra Island island cen Pacific in Line Islands area 1 sq mi (2.6 sq km)

Palo Al·to \,pa-lō-'al-(,)tō\ city W Calif. SE of San Francisco on San Francisco Bay pop 55,900

Pal·o·mar, Mount \'pa-lə-,mär\ mountain 6140 ft (1871 m) S Calif. NNE of San Diego

Pa·los \'pä-,lōs\ or Pa·los de la Fron·te·ra \-,lōz-dā-lə-,frən-'ter-ə\ town & former port SW Spain SE of Huelva

Pa·louse \pə-'lüs\ **1** river 150 mi (241 km) NW Idaho & SE Wash. flowing W & S into Snake River **2** fertile hilly region E Wash. & NW Idaho N of Snake & Clearwater rivers

Pa·mirs \pə-'mirz\ or Pa·mir \-'mir\ mountain region cen Asia in Tajikistan & on borders of Xinjiang Uygur, Kashmir, & Afghanistan from which radiate Tian Shan to N, Kunlun & Karakoram to E, & Hindu Kush to W; has many peaks over 20,000 ft (6096 m)

Pam·li·co \'pam-li-,kō\ river E N.C., estuary of Tar River, flowing E into **Pamlico Sound** (inlet of the Atlantic bet. the mainland & offshore islands)

Pam·pa \'pam-pə\ city NW Tex. ENE of Amarillo pop 19,959

Pam·phyl·ia \pam-'fi-lē-ə\ ancient district & Roman province S Asia Minor on coast S of Pisidia — **Pam·phyl·i·an** \-lē-ən\ adj or n

Pam·plo·na \pam-'plō-nə\ or formerly Pam·pe·lu·na \,pam-pə-'lü-nə\ city N Spain ✳ of Navarra province & once ✳ of Navarre kingdom pop 177,906

Pan·a·ji \'pə-nə-jē\ town & port W India ✳ of Goa & formerly ✳ of Portuguese India pop 34,953

Pan·a·ma or Sp Pa·na·má \'pa-nə-,mä, -,mȯ, ,pa-nə-'; ,pä-nə-'mä\ **1** country S Central America; a republic; before 1903 part of Colombia area (including Canal Zone) 29,129 sq mi (75,735 sq km), pop 2,315,047 **2** or Panama City city & port, its ✳, on Gulf of Panama pop 411,549 **3** ship canal 51 mi (82 km) cen Panama connecting the Atlantic (Caribbean Sea) & the Pacific (Gulf of Panama) — **Pan·a·ma·ni·an** \,pa-nə-'mä-nē-ən\ adj or n

Panama, Gulf of inlet of the Pacific on S coast of Panama

Panama, Isthmus of or formerly Isthmus of Dar·i·en \,dar-ē-'en, ,der-, ,där-\ isthmus Central America connecting N. America & S. America & comprised in Panama (republic)

Panama Canal Zone — see CANAL ZONE

Panama City **1** city & port NW Fla. on Gulf of Mexico pop 34,378 **2** — see PANAMA

Pan·a·mint Mountains \'pa-nə-,mint, -mənt\ mountains E Calif. W of Death Valley — see TELESCOPE PEAK

Pa·nay \pə-'nī\ island Philippines in the Visayans; chief town Iloilo area 4446 sq mi (11,560 sq km)

Pan·gaea \pan-'jē-ə\ hypothetical land area believed to have once connected the landmasses of the southern hemisphere with those of the northern hemisphere — see GONDWANALAND, LAURASIA

Pang–fou — see BENGBU

Pa·ni·pat \'pä-ni-,pət\ city NW India in SE Haryana state pop 137,953

Panjab — see PUNJAB

Panj·nad \,pənj-'näd\ river 50 mi (80 km) Pakistan, the combined stream of the Chenab & the Sutlej, flowing SW into the Indus

Pan·kow \'päŋ-(,)kō\ NE suburb of Berlin, Germany; formerly seat of E. German government

Pan·mun·jom \,pän-,mùn-'jəm\ village on N. Korea—S. Korea border SE of Kaesong

Pan·no·nia \pə-'nō-nē-ə\ Roman province SE Europe including territory W of the Danube now in Hungary & adjacent parts of Croatia & Vojvodina

Pantar — see ALOR

Pan·tel·le·ria \,pan-,te-lə-'rē-ə\ island Italy in the Mediterranean bet. Sicily & Tunisia

Pá·nu·co \'pä-nü\ river 240 mi (386 km) cen Mexico flowing from Hidalgo state NE into Gulf of Mexico

Pao–chi — see BAOJI

Pão de Açú·car \,paù(n)-dē-ə-'sü-kər\ or Sugarloaf Mountain peak 1296 ft (395 m) SE Brazil in city of Rio de Janeiro on W side of entrance to Guanabara Bay

Paoking — see SHAOYANG

Paoting — see BAODING

Pao–t'ou — see BAOTOU

Papal States — see STATES OF THE CHURCH

Pa·pee·te \,pä-pē-'ā-tē; ,pä-'pē-tē, pə-'pē-\ commune & port Society Islands on Tahiti ✳ of French Polynesia pop 23,555

Paph·la·go·nia \,paf-lə-'gō-nē-ə, -nyə\ ancient country & Roman province N Asia Minor bordering on Black Sea — **Paph·la·go·nian** \-nē-ən, -nyən\ adj or n

Pa·phos \'pā-,fäs\ town SW Cyprus on coast 10 mi (16 km) WNW of site of ancient city of Paphos pop 27,800

Pa–Pien — see BABIAN

Pa·pua \'pa-pyə-wə, 'pä-pə-wə\ the SE portion of the island of New Guinea; part of Papua New Guinea

Papua, Gulf of arm of Coral Sea SE New Guinea

Papua New Guinea country comprising territories of Papua & New Guinea; independent from 1975, formerly a U.N. trust territory administered by Australia ✳ Port Moresby area 182,700 sq mi (475,020 sq km), pop 3,010,727 — **Papua New Guinean** adj or n

Pa·rá \pə-'rä\ **1** river 200 mi (322 km) N Brazil, the E mouth of the Amazon **2** state N Brazil S of the Amazon ✳ Belém area 470,752 sq mi (1,223,955 sq km), pop 3,507,312 **3** — see BELÉM

Par·a·dise \'par-ə-,dīs, -,dīz\ **1** town N Calif. N of Sacramento pop 25,408 **2** population center Nev. pop 124,682

Par·a·guay \'par-ə-,gwī, -,gwä\ **1** river 1500 mi (2414 km) cen S. America flowing from Mato Grosso plateau in Brazil S into Paraná River in Paraguay **2** country cen S. America traversed by Paraguay river; a republic ✳ Asunción area 157,006 sq mi (408,216 sq km), pop 3,026,165 — **Par·a·guay·an** \,par-ə-'gwī-ən, -'gwä-\ adj or n

Pa·ra·i·ba \,par-ə-'ē-bə\ **1** or Paraíba do Nor·te \də-'nȯr-tē\ river

240 *mi* (386 *km*) NE Brazil flowing E into the Atlantic **2** *or* **Paraíba do Sul** \'sül\ river 660 *mi* (1062 *km*) SE Brazil flowing NE into the Atlantic **3** state NE Brazil bordering on the Atlantic ✻ João Pessoa *area* 21,591 *sq mi* (56,137 *sq km*), *pop* 2,810,032

Par·a·mar·i·bo \,par-ə-'mar-ə-,bō\ city & port ✻ of Suriname on Suriname River *pop* 110,867

Par·a·mount \'par-ə-,maùnt\ city SW Calif. N of Long Beach *pop* 47,669

Pa·ram·us \pə-'ra-məs\ borough NE N.J. *pop* 25,067

Pa·ra·ná \,par-ə-'nä\ **1** *or in upper course* **Al·to Paraná**\'al-(,)tō\ river 2040 *mi* (3283 *km*) cen S. America flowing from junction of Rio Grande & Paraíba River in Brazil SSW into the Río de la Plata in Argentina **2** state S Brazil E of Paraná River ✻ Curitiba *area* 82,741 *sq mi* (215,127 *sq km*), *pop* 7,749,752 **3** city NE Argentina on Paraná River *pop* 159,581

Pa·ra·na·i·ba *or formerly* **Pa·ra·na·hi·ba** \,par-ə-nə-'ē-bə\ river 530 *mi* (853 *km*) S Brazil flowing SW to unite with the Rio Grande forming Paraná River

Par·du·bi·ce \'pär-də-,bit-sə\ city cen Czech Republic in Bohemia on the Elbe E of Prague *pop* 91,855

Pa·ria Peninsula \'pär-ē-ə\ peninsula NE Venezuela

Paria, Gulf of inlet of the Atlantic bet. Trinidad & Venezuela

Pa·ri·cu·tín \pə-,rē-kü-'tēn\ volcano 7451 *ft* (2271 *m*) SW Mexico in NW Michoacán; first eruption 1943

Parida, La — see BOLÍVAR (Cerro)

Par·is \'par-əs\ **1** city NE Tex. *pop* 24,699 **2** *or anc* **Lu·te·tia** \lü-'tē-sh(ē-)ə\ city ✻ of France on the Seine *pop* 2,299,830 — **Pa·ri·sian** \pə-'ri·zhən, -'rē-\ *adj or n*

Par·kers·burg \'pär-kərz-,bərg\ city NW W.Va. *pop* 33,862

Park Forest village NE Ill. S of Chicago *pop* 24,656

Park Ridge city NE Ill. NW of Chicago *pop* 36,175

Par·ma \'pär-mə\ **1** city NE Ohio S of Cleveland *pop* 87,876 **2** commune N Italy in Emilia-Romagna *pop* 174,341

Parma Heights city NE Ohio S of Cleveland *pop* 21,448

Par·na·i·ba *or formerly* **Par·na·hy·ba** \,pär-nə-'ē-bə\ river 900 *mi* (1448 *km*) NE Brazil flowing NE into the Atlantic

Par·nas·sus \pär-'na-səs\ *or NGk* **Par·nas·sós** \,pär-nä-'sòs\ mountain 8061 *ft* (2457 *m*), cen Greece N of Gulf of Corinth

Par·os \'par-,äs, 'per-\ *or NGk* **Pá·ros** \'pär-,ós\ island Greece in cen Cyclades W of Naxos *area* 81 *sq mi* (211 *sq km*)

Par·ra·mat·ta \,par-ə-'ma-tə\ city SE Australia, W suburb of Sydney, on **Parramatta River** (estuary, W arm of Port Jackson) *pop* 130,943

Par·ris Island \'par-əs\ island S S.C. in Port Royal Sound

Par·ry Islands \'par-ē\ islands Canada in N Northwest Territories in Arctic Ocean N of Victoria Is.

Parsnip — see FINLAY

Par·thia \'pär-thē-ə\ ancient country SW Asia in NE modern Iran

Pas·a·de·na \,pa-sə-'dē-nə\ **1** city SW Calif. E of Glendale *pop* 131,591 **2** city SE Tex. E of Houston *pop* 119,363 — **Pas·a·de·nan** \-nən\ *n*

Pa·sar·ga·dae \pə-'sär-gə-,dē\ city of ancient Persia built by Cyrus the Great; ruins NE of site of later Persepolis

Pa·say \'pä-,sī\ municipality Philippines in Luzon on Manila Bay S of Manila *pop* 287,770

Pas·ca·gou·la \,pas-kə-'gü-lə\ city & port SE Miss. *pop* 25,899

Pas·co \'pas-(,)kō\ city SE Wash. *pop* 20,337

Pasco, Cerro de — see CERRO DE PASCO

Pascua, Isla de — see EASTER

Pas de Calais — see DOVER (Strait of)

Pa·sig \'pä-sig\ river 12 *mi* (19 *km*) Philippines in Luzon flowing from the Laguna de Bay through Manila into Manila Bay

Pas·sa·ic \pə-'sā-ik\ **1** river 100 *mi* (161 *km*) NE N.J. flowing into Newark Bay **2** city NE N.J. SSE of Paterson *pop* 58,041

Pas·sa·ma·quod·dy Bay \,pa-sə-mə-'kwä-dē\ inlet of Bay of Fundy bet. E Maine & SW N.B. at mouth of St. Croix River

Pas·se·ro, Cape \'pä-sə-,rō, 'pa-\ headland Italy at SE tip of Sicily

Pas·sy \'sē\ section of Paris, France, on right bank of the Seine near the Bois de Boulogne

Pas·ta·za \pə-'stä-zə, -sə\ river 400 *mi* (644 *km*) Ecuador & Peru flowing S into the Marañón

Pat·a·go·nia \,pa-tə-'gō-nyə, -nē-ə\ region S. America in S Argentina & S Chile bet. the Andes & the Atlantic S of *ab* 40° S lat.; sometimes considered as including Tierra del Fuego — **Pat·a·go·nian** \-nyən, -nē-ən\ *adj or n*

Pa·tan \'pä-,tən\ city E cen Nepal adjoining Kathmandu *pop* 48,577

Pa·tap·sco \pə-'tap-(,)skō, -si-,kō\ river 80 *mi* (129 *km*) N cen Md. flowing SE into Chesapeake Bay

Pat·er·son \'pa-tər-sən\ city NE N.J. N of Newark *pop* 140,891

Pa·ti·a·la \,pə-tē-'ä-lə\ **1** former state NW India, now part of Punjab state **2** city, its ✻, SW of Simla *pop* 205,849

Pat·mos \'pat-məs, 'pät-,mòs\ island Greece in the NW Dodecanese

Pat·na \'pət-nə\ city NE India on the Ganges, winter ✻ of Bihar

Pa·tos, La·goa dos \la-,gō-ə-dəs-'pa-təs, -(,)tüs\ lagoon 124 *mi* (200 *km*) long S Brazil in Rio Grande do Sul

Pa·trai·kós Kól·pos \,pä-trä-ē-'kòs-'kòl-,pòs\ *or* **Gulf of Pa·tras** \pə-'tras, pa-trəs\ inlet of Ionian Sea W Greece W of Gulf of Corinth

Pa·tras \pə-'tras, 'pa-trəs\ *or NGk* **Pa·trai** \pä-'tre\ *or anc* **Pa·trae** \'pä-(,)trē\ city & port W Greece in N Peloponnisos on Patraïkós Kólpos *pop* 155,180

Patrimony of St. Peter — see ROME (Duchy of)

Pa·tux·ent \pə-'tək-sənt\ river 100 *mi* (161 *km*) cen Md. flowing S & SE into Chesapeake Bay

Pau \'pō\ **1** *or F* **Gave de Pau** \gàv-də-pō\ river 100 *mi* (161 *km*) SW France rising in the Pyrenees SW of Pau & flowing to the Adour — see GAVARNIE **2** commune SW France on Pau River *pop* 81,560

Pa·via \pə-'vē-ə\ commune N Italy S of Milan *pop* 80,653

Pav·lof, Mount \'pav-,lòf\ volcano 8261 *ft* (2518 *m*) SW Alaska on SW Alaska Peninsula in Aleutian Range

Paw·tuck·et \pò-'tə-kət, pò-\ city NE R.I. *pop* 72,644

Pay·san·dú \,pī-,sän-'dü\ city & port W Uruguay *pop* 62,412

Pea·body \'pē-,bä-dē, -bə-dē\ city NE Mass. N of Lynn *pop* 47,039

Peace \'pēs\ river 945 *mi* (1521 *km*) W Canada flowing E & NE in N B.C. & N Alta. into Slave River — see FINLAY

Peach·tree City \'pēch-,trē\ city NW cen Ga. SSW of Atlanta *pop* 19,027

Pearl \'pər(-)l\ **1** river 490 *mi* (788 *km*) S Miss. flowing S into Gulf of Mexico **2** city S cen Miss. *pop* 19,588 **3** — see ZHU

Pearl City city Hawaii in S Oahu *pop* 30,993

Pearl Harbor inlet Hawaii on S coast of Oahu W of Honolulu; site of U.S. Navy base

Pea·ry Land \'pir-ē\ region N Greenland on Arctic Ocean

Pe·chen·ga \'pe-chən-gə\ *or Finn* **Pet·sa·mo** \'pet-sə-,mō\ town & port NW Russia in Europe on inlet of Barents Sea in district that belonged to Finland 1920–44 *pop* 3500

Pe·cho·ra \pə-'chòr-ə, -'chòr-\ river 1125 *mi* (1811 *km*) NE Russia in Europe flowing N into Barents Sea

Pe·cos \'pā-kəs\ river 735 *mi* (1183 *km*) E N.Mex. & W Tex. flowing SE into the Rio Grande

Pecos National Monument archaeological site N cen N.Mex. SE of Santa Fe containing Indian villages & a Spanish mission

Pécs \'pāch\ city S Hungary W of the Danube *pop* 179,000

Ped·er·nal·es \,pər-d'n-'a-ləs\ river 150 *mi* (241 *km*) cen Tex. flowing E into Colorado River

Pee·bles \'pē-bəlz\ **1** *or* **Pee·bles·shire** \'pē-bəl-,shir, -shər\ *or* **Tweed·dale** \'twēd-,dāl\ former county SE Scotland including upper course of the Tweed **2** burgh SE Scotland in Borders region

Pee Dee \'pē-,dē\ river 233 *mi* (375 *km*) N.C. & S.C. flowing SE into Winyah Bay — see YADKIN

Peeks·kill \'pēk-,skil\ city SE N.Y. N of Yonkers *pop* 19,536

Peel \'pē(ə)l\ river 425 *mi* (684 *km*) NW Canada rising in W Yukon Territory & flowing E & N into the Mackenzie

Pee·ne \'pā-nə\ river 70 *mi* (113 *km*) NE Germany flowing E through Pomerania and forming **Peene Estuary** which flows N–S bet. Stettiner Haff and the Baltic

Pee·ne·mün·de \,pā-nə-'mün-də, -'myün-, -'mʉen-\ village NE Germany on island at mouth of Peene Estuary

Pei·pus \'pī-pəs\ *or Estonian* **Peip·si** \'pāp-sē\ *or Russ* **Chud·skoe** \chüt-'skò-yə, -'skòi-(y)ə\ lake Europe, bet. Estonia & Russia *area* 1357 *sq mi* (3528 *sq km*)

Pekanbaru — see PAKANBARU

Pe·kin \'pē-kən, -,kin\ city N cen Ill. SSW of Peoria *pop* 32,254

Peking — see BEIJING

Pe·la·gian Islands \pə-'lā-j(ē-)ən\ islands Italy in the Mediterranean S of Sicily bet. Malta & Tunisia

Pe·lée, Mount \pə-'lā\ volcano French West Indies in N Martinique; erupted 1902

Pelee, Point — see POINT PELEE NATIONAL PARK

Pe·lee Island \'pē-lē\ island SE Canada in W Lake Erie SW of Point Pelee, Ont. *area* 18 *sq mi* (47 *sq km*) *pop* 272

Pel·e·liu \,pe-lə-'lē-(,)ü\ island W Pacific at S end of Belau Islands

Pe·li·on \'pē-lē-ən\ *or NGk* **Pi·lion** \'pēl-,yòn\ mountain 5089 *ft* (1551 *m*) NE Greece in E Thessaly SE of Mt. Ossa

Pel·la \'pe-lə\ ancient city NE Greece, ancient ✻ of Macedonia

Pel·ly \'pe-lē\ river 330 *mi* (531 *km*) NW Canada in Yukon Territory flowing W into Yukon River

Pel·o·pon·ni·sos \,pe-lə-'pò-nē-,sòs\ *or* **Pel·o·pon·ne·sus** \,pe-lə-pə-'nē-səs\ *or* **Pel·o·pon·nese** \'pe-lə-pə-,nēz, -,nēs, ,pe-lə-pə-'\ peninsula forming S part of mainland of Greece — **Pel·o·pon·ne·sian** \,pə-lə-pə-'nē-zhən, -shən\ *adj or n*

Pe·lo·tas \pə-'lō-təs\ city S Brazil in SE Rio Grande do Sul at S end of Lagoa dos Patos *pop* 260,190

Pem·ba \'pem-bə\ island Tanzania in Indian Ocean N of island of Zanzibar *pop* 207,919

Pem·broke \'pem-,brùk, *US also* -,brōk\ *or* **Pem·broke·shire** \-,shir, -shər\ former county SW Wales ✻ Haverfordwest

Pem·broke Pines \'pem-,brōk\ city SE Fla. *pop* 65,452

Pe·nang \pə-'naŋ\ **1** island SE Asia at N end of Strait of Malacca *area* 108 *sq mi* (281 *sq km*) **2** state Malaysia (federation) comprising Penang Island & mainland opposite: until 1948 one of the Straits Settlements ✻ George Town *area* 400 *sq mi* (1040 *sq km*), *pop* 911,586 **3** — see GEORGE TOWN

Pen·del·i·kón \,pen-de-li-'kòn\ mountain 3638 *ft* (1109 *m*) E Greece in Attica NE of Athens

Pend Oreille \,pän-də-'rā\ river 100 *mi* (161 *km*) N Idaho & NE Wash. flowing from **Pend Oreille Lake** (35 *mi* or 56 *km* long, in Idaho) W & N into Columbia River in B.C.

Penedos de São Pedro e São Paulo — see SAINT PAUL'S ROCKS

Pe·ne·us \pə-'nē-əs\ *or NGk* **Pi·niós** \pē-'nyòs\ *or formerly* **Sa·lam·bria** \sə-'lam-brē-ə\ river 125 *mi* (201 *km*) N Greece in Thessaly flowing E into Gulf of Salonika

P'eng·hu \'pəŋ-'hü\ *or* **Pes·ca·do·res** \,pes-kə-'dòr-ēz, -'dòr-, -əs\ islands E China in Formosa Strait, attached to Taiwan; chief town Makung (on P'eng-hu, chief island) *area* 49 *sq mi* (127 *sq km*)

Pengpu — see BENGBU

Peninsular Malaysia — see MALAYA

Pen·nine Alps \'pe-,nīn\ section of Alps on border bet. Switzerland & Italy NE of Graian Alps — see ROSA (Monte)

Pennine Chain mountains N England extending from Scotland border to Derbyshire & Staffordshire; highest Cross Fell 2930 *ft* (893 *m*)

Penn·syl·va·nia \,pen(t)-səl-'vā-nyə, -nē-ə\ state NE U.S. ✻ Harrisburg *area* 45,333 *sq mi* (117,866 *sq km*), *pop* 11,881,643

Pe·nob·scot \pə-'näb-skət, -skət\ river 101 *mi* (162 *km*) cen Maine flowing S into **Penobscot Bay** (inlet of the Atlantic)

Pen·rhyn \'pen-'rin, 'pen-,\ *or* **Ton·ga·re·va** \,täŋ-(g)ə-'rā-və\ island S Pacific in the Manihiki Islands

Pen·sa·co·la \,pen(t)-sə-'kō-lə\ city & port NW Fla. on **Pensacola Bay** (inlet of Gulf of Mexico) *pop* 58,165

Pen·tap·o·lis \pen-'ta-pə-ləs\ any one of several groups of five ancient cities in Italy, Asia Minor, & Cyrenaica

---

\ə\ abut \'ə\ kitten, F table \ər\ further \a\ ash \ā\ ace \ä\ mop, mar \aù\ out \ch\ chin \e\ bet \ē\ easy \g\ go \i\ hit \ī\ ice \j\ job \ŋ\ sing \ō\ go \ò\ law \òi\ boy \th\ thin \t̠h̠\ the \ü\ loot \ù\ foot \y\ yet \zh\ vision \á, k̠, ⁿ, œ, œ̄, ʉe, ʉē, ᵊ\ *see* Guide to Pronunciation

Pen·te·cost \'pen-ti-ˌkȯst, -'käst\ island SW Pacific in Vanuatu *pop* 11,336

Pen·tic·ton \pen-'tik-tən\ city Canada in S B.C. *pop* 27,258

Pent·land Firth \'pent-lənd\ channel bet. Orkneys & mainland of Scotland

Pentland Hills hills S Scotland in Borders, Lothian, & Strathclyde regions; highest peak Scald Law 1898 *ft* (578 *m*)

Pen·za \'pen-zə\ city S *cen* Russia in Europe W of Kuibyshev *pop* 374,000

Pen·zance \pen-'zan(t)s, pən-\ borough & port SW England in Cornwall on English Channel *pop* 19,521

Pen·zhin·ska·ya Bay \pen-'zhin(t)-skə-yə, 'pen-ˌzhin(t)-\ *or* **Pen·zhi·na Bay** \'pen-zhə-nə\ arm of Sea of Okhotsk, E Russia in Asia bet. Kamchatka Peninsula & mainland

People's Democratic Republic of Yemen — see YEMEN

People's Republic of China China exclusive of Taiwan

Pe·o·ria \pē-'ȯr-ē-ə, -'ȯr-\ **1** town SW *cen* Ariz. *pop* 50,618 **2** city N *cen* Ill. on Illinois River *pop* 113,504

Pep·in, Lake \'pi-pən, 'pe-\ expansion of upper Mississippi River 34 *mi* (55 *km*) long bet. SE Minn. & W Wis.

Pera — see BEYOGLU

Pe·raea *or* **Pe·rea** \pə-'rē-ə\ ancient region of Palestine E of Jordan River

Pe·rak \'per-ə, 'pir-ə, 'per-ˌak\ state Malaysia in W Peninsular Malaysia on Strait of Malacca ✻ Kuala Kangsar *area* 7980 *sq mi* (20,748 *sq km*), *pop* 1,762,288

Per·di·do \pər-'dē-(ˌ)dō\ river 60 *mi* (96 *km*) rising in SE Ala. & flowing S into Gulf of Mexico forming part of Ala.-Fla. boundary

Per·ga \'pər-gə\ ancient city S Asia Minor in Pamphylia

Per·ga·mum \'pər-gə-məm\ *or* **Per·ga·mus** \-məs\ *or* **Per·ga·mos** \-məs, -ˌmäs\ **1** ancient Greek kingdom covering most of Asia Minor; at its height 263–133 B.C. **2** *or modern* **Ber·ga·ma** \bər-'gä-mə\ city W Turkey NNE of Izmir ✻ of ancient Pergamum

Pé·ri·gord \ˌper-ə-'gȯr\ old division of N Guienne in SW France ✻ Périgueux

Pé·ri·gueux \ˌper-ə-'gə(r), pā-rē-'gœ\ commune SW France NE of Bordeaux *pop* 34,779

Pe·rim \pə-'rim, -'rēm\ island in Bab el Mandeb strait at entrance to Red Sea; belongs to Yemen

Per·lis \'per-ləs\ state Malaysia bordering on Thailand & Andaman sea ✻ Kangar *area* 310 *sq mi* (806 *sq km*), *pop* 147,726

Perm \'pərm, 'perm\ *or formerly* **Mo·lo·tov** \'mä-lə-ˌtȯf, 'mȯ-, 'mō-, -ˌtȯv\ city E Russia in Europe *pop* 901,000

Per·nam·bu·co \ˌpər-nəm-'bü-(ˌ)kō, -'byü-; ˌper-nəm-'bü-(ˌ)kü\ **1** state NE Brazil ✻ Recife *area* 38,315 *sq mi* (99,619 *sq km*), *pop* 6,242,933 **2** — see RECIFE

Per·nik \'per-nik\ *or formerly* **Di·mi·tro·vo** \də-'mē-trə-ˌvō\ city W Bulgaria S of Sofia *pop* 87,432

Per·pi·gnan \ˌper-pē-nyäⁿ\ city S France SE of Toulouse near Mediterranean coast *pop* 101,198

Per·ris \'per-əs\ city SE Calif. *pop* 21,460

Per·sep·o·lis \pər-'se-pə-ləs\ city of ancient Persia, site in SW Iran NE of Shiraz

Persia — see IRAN

Persian Gulf arm of Arabian Sea bet. SW Iran & Arabia

Persian Gulf States Kuwait, Bahrain, Qatar, & United Arab Emirates

Per·sis \'pər-səs\ ancient region SW Iran

Perth \'pərth\ **1** city ✻ of Western Australia on Swan River *metropolitan area pop* 895,710 — see FREMANTLE **2** *or* **Perth·shire** \-ˌshir, -shər\ former county *cen* Scotland **3** burgh *cen* Scotland *pop* 41,998

Perth Am·boy \ˌpərth-'am-ˌbȯi\ city & port NE N.J. on Raritan Bay at mouth of Raritan River *pop* 41,967

Pe·ru \pə-'rü\ country W S. America; a republic ✻ Lima 482,257 *sq mi* (1,253,868 *sq km*), *pop* 17,031,221 — **Pe·ru·vi·an** \-'rü-vē-ən\ *adj or n*

Pe·ru·gia \pə-'rü-j(ē-)ə, pā-\ commune *cen* Italy bet. Lake Trasimeno & the Tiber ✻ of Umbria *pop* 149,261

Pe·sa·ro \'pā-zə-ˌrō\ commune & port *cen* Italy on the Adriatic NW of Ancona *pop* 90,325

Pe·sca·ra \pe-'skär-ə\ commune & port *cen* Italy on the Adriatic *pop* 128,695

Pe·sha·war \pə-'shä-wər, -'shaủ-(ə)r\ city N Pakistan ESE of Khyber pass *pop* 555,000

Pe·tah Tiq·wa \ˌpe-tə(k)-'tik-(ˌ)vä, ˌpä-\ city W Israel *pop* 112,000

Pet·a·lu·ma \ˌpe-t'l-'ü-mə\ city W Calif. N of San Francisco *pop* 43,184

Pe·ta·re \pe-'tär-(ˌ)ä\ city N Venezuela, a SE suburb of Caracas *pop* 338,417

Pe·ter·bor·ough \'pē-tər-ˌbər-ə, -ˌbə-rə, -b(ə-)rə\ **1** city Canada in SE Ont. *pop* 68,371 **2** borough E *cen* England *pop* 88,346

Peterborough, Soke of \'sōk\ former administrative county E *cen* England in Northamptonshire; later part of Huntingdonshire & since 1974 in Cambridgeshire

Pe·ters·burg \'pē-tərz-ˌbərg\ **1** city SE Va. *pop* 38,386 **2** SAINT PETERSBURG

Pet·it·co·di·ac \ˌpe-tē-'kō-dē-ˌak\ river 60 *mi* (96 *km*) SE Canada in SE N.B. flowing to head of Bay of Fundy

Pe·ti·tot \'pe-ti-ˌtō\ river 295 *mi* (475 *km*) W *cen* Canada flowing W into the Liard

Pe·tra \'pē-trə, 'pe-\ ancient city of NW Arabia on slope of Mt. Hor, site now in SW Jordan; ✻ of the Edomites & Nabataeans

Petrified Forest National Park reservation E Ariz. in Painted Desert containing natural exhibit of petrified wood

Pe·tro·dvo·rets \ˌpe-trəd-və-'rets\ *or formerly* **Pe·ter·hof** \'pē-tər-ˌhȯf, -ˌhäf\ town W Russia in Europe W of St. Petersburg

Petrograd — see SAINT PETERSBURG

Pet·ro·pav·lovsk \ˌpe-trə-'pav-ˌlȯfsk, -'päv-\ city N Kazakhstan *pop* 173,000

Petropavlovsk–Kam·chat·ski \-kam-'chat-skē, -'chät-\ city & port E Russia in Asia on Kamchatka peninsula *pop* 154,000

Pe·tró·po·lis \pə-'trä-pə-ləs\ city SE Brazil in Rio de Janeiro state *pop* 241,884

Petrovsk — see MAKHACHKALA

Pet·ro·za·vodsk \ˌpe-trə-zə-'vätsk\ city NW Russia in Europe ✻ of Karelian Republic on Lake Onega *pop* 216,000

Petsamo — see PECHENGA

Pfalz — see PALATINATE

Pforz·heim \'(p)fȯrts-ˌhīm\ city SW Germany SE of Karlsruhe *pop* 106,500

Phar·os \'far-ˌäs, 'fer-\ peninsula N Egypt in city of Alexandria; formerly an island

Pharr \'fär\ city S Tex. E of McAllen *pop* 32,921

Phar·sa·lus \fär-'sā-ləs\ *or modern* **Phar·sa·la** \'fär-sə-lə\ *or NGk* **Fár·sa·la** \'fär-\ town NE Greece in E Thessaly in ancient district of Phar·sa·lia \fär-'sāl-yə, -'sā-lē-ə\

Phe·nix City \'fē-niks\ city E Ala. *pop* 25,312

Phe·rae \'fir-ē\ ancient town SE Thessaly

Phil·a·del·phia \ˌfi-lə-'del-fyə, -fē-ə\ **1** city & port SE Pa. on Delaware River *pop* 1,585,577 **2** — see ALASEHIR **3** — see AMMAN — **Phil·a·del·phian** \-fyən, -fē-ən\ *adj or n*

Phi·lae \'fī-(ˌ)lē\ former island S Egypt in the Nile above Aswân; now submerged

Philippeville — see SKIKDA

Phi·lip·pi \'fi-lə-ˌpī, fə-'li-ˌpī\ ancient town NE Greece in N *cen* Macedonia — **Phi·lip·pi·an** \fə-'li-pē-ən\ *adj or n*

Phil·ip·pine Islands \ˌfi-lə-'pēn, 'fi-lə-ˌ\ islands of the Malay Archipelago NE of Borneo — see PHILIPPINES

Phil·ip·pines \-'pēnz, -ˌpēnz\ *or Sp* **Re·pú·bli·ca de Fi·li·pi·nas** \re-'pü-blē-kä-thä-ˌfē-lē-'pē-(ˌ)näs\ *or Pilipino* **Re·pu·bli·ka ng Pi·li·pi·nas** \-näŋ-pē-lē-'pē-(ˌ)näs\ country E Asia comprising the Philippine Islands; a republic; once a Spanish possession & (1898–1945) a U.S. possession ✻ Manila *land area* 114,830 *sq mi* (298,558 *sq km*), *pop* 60,476,856 — **Philippine** *adj*

Philippine Sea sea comprising the waters of the W Pacific E of & adjacent to the Philippine Islands

Philippopolis — see PLOVDIV

Phi·lis·tia \fə-'lis-tē-ə\ ancient country SW Palestine on the coast; the land of the Philistines

Phnom Penh \(pə-)'näm-'pen, (pə-)'nȯm-\ city ✻ of Cambodia, on the Mekong *pop* 300,000

Pho·caea \fō-'sē-ə\ ancient city of Asia Minor on Aegean Sea in N Ionia — **Pho·cae·an** \-ən\ *adj or n*

Pho·cis \'fō-səs\ region *cen* Greece N of Gulf of Corinth

Phoe·ni·cia *or* **Phe·ni·cia** \fi-'ni-sh(ē-)ə, -'nē-\ *or* **Phe·ni·ce** \-'nī-sē\ ancient country SW Asia at E end of the Mediterranean in modern Syria & Lebanon

Phoe·nix \'fē-niks\ city ✻ of Ariz. on Salt River *pop* 983,403

Phoenix Islands islands *cen* Pacific belonging to Kiribati

Phry·gia \'fri-j(ē-)ə\ ancient country W *cen* Asia Minor divided *ab* 400 B.C. into **Greater Phrygia** (the inland region) & **Lesser Phrygia** (region along the Hellespont)

Pia·cen·za \pyä-'chen(t)-sə, ˌpē-ə-\ *or anc* **Pla·cen·tia** \plə-'sen(t)-sh(ē-)ə\ commune N Italy on the Po SE of Milan *pop* 104,023

Pi·auí *or formerly* **Pi·au·hy** \pyaủ-'ē, pē-ə-aủ-\ state NE Brazil bordering on the Atlantic E of Parnaíba River ✻ Teresina *area* 94,819 *sq mi* (246,529 *sq km*), *pop* 2,188,150

Pia·ve \'pyä-(ˌ)vä, pē-'ä-\ river 137 *mi* (220 *km*) NE Italy flowing S & SE into the Adriatic

Pic·ar·dy \'pi-kər-dē\ *or F* **Pi·car·die** \pē-kär-dē\ region & former province N France bordering on English Channel N of Normandy ✻ Amiens — **Pi·card** \'pi-ˌkärd, -kərd; pi-'kärd\ *adj or n*

Pi·ce·num \pī-'sē-nəm\ district of ancient Italy on the Adriatic SE of Umbria

Pick·er·ing \'pi-k(ə-)riŋ\ town Canada in SE Ont. *pop* 68,631

Pi·co Ri·ve·ra \ˌpē-(ˌ)kō-rə-'vir-ə\ city SW Calif. *pop* 59,177

Pied·mont \'pēd-ˌmänt\ **1** upland region E U.S. lying E of the Appalachian Mountains bet. SE N.Y. & *cen* Ala. **2** *or It* **Pie·mon·te** \pyä-'mōn-(ˌ)tā\ region NW Italy bordering on France & Switzerland W of Lombardy ✻ Turin *pop* 4,357,559 — **Pied·mon·tese** \ˌpēd-mən-'tēz, -(ˌ)män-, -'tēs\ *adj or n*

Pie·dras Ne·gras \ˌpyä-drəs-'nā-grəs, pē-ˌä-\ city N Mexico in Coahuila on the Rio Grande opposite Eagle Pass, Tex. *pop* 65,883

Pi·er·ia \pī-'ir-ē-ə, -'er-\ ancient region NE Greece in Macedonia N of Thessaly

Pierre \'pir\ city ✻ of S.Dak. on Missouri River *pop* 12,906

Pierre·fonds \ˌpē-ˌer-'fōⁿ, ˌpyer-\ town Canada in S Que. W of Montreal *pop* 48,735

Pie·ter·mar·itz·burg \ˌpē-tər-'mar-əts-ˌbərg\ city E Republic of South Africa in S *cen* Natal *pop* 128,598

Pigs, Bay of — see COCHINOS (Bahia de)

Pikes Peak \'pīks\ mountain 14,110 *ft* (4301 *m*) E *cen* Colo. at S end of Front Range

Pik Pobedy — see POBEDA PEAK

Pi·la·tus \pi-'lä-təs\ mountain 6983 *ft* (2128 *m*) *cen* Switzerland in Unterwalden SW of Lucerne

Pil·co·ma·yo \ˌpil-kə-'mī-(ˌ)ō\ river 1000 *mi* (1609 *km*) S *cen* S. America rising in Bolivia & flowing SE on Argentina-Paraguay boundary into Paraguay River

Pilion — see PELION

Pillars of Her·cu·les \'hər-kyə-ˌlēz\ the two promontories at E end of Strait of Gibraltar: Rock of Gibraltar (in Europe) & Jebel Musa (in Africa)

Pi·los \'pē-ˌlȯs\ town & port SW Greece in SW Peloponnisos

Pim·li·co \'pim-li-ˌkō\ district of W London, England, in SW Westminster

Pinang — see GEORGE TOWN

Pi·nar del Río \pi-ˌnär-del-'rē-(ˌ)ō\ city & port W Cuba *pop* 148,112

Pi·na·tu·bo, Mount \ˌpē-nə-'tü-(ˌ)bō\ volcano N Philippines on Luzon

Pin·dus Mountains \'pin-dəs\ mountains N Greece bet. Epirus & Thessaly; highest point over 7500 *ft* (2286 *m*)

Pine Bluff \'pīn-'bləf, -ˌbləf\ city SE *cen* Ark. *pop* 57,140

Pi·nel·las Park \pī-'ne-ləs\ city W Fla. NW of St. Petersburg *pop* 43,426

Pinellas Peninsula peninsula W Fla. W of Tampa Bay

Pines, Isle of 1 — see YOUTH (Isle of) **2** — see ILE DES PINS

Ping \'piŋ\ river 360 *mi* (579 *km*) W Thailand flowing SSE to join Nan River forming the Chao Phraya

Piniós — see PENEUS

Pinkiang — see HARBIN

Pinnacles National Monument reservation W *cen* Calif. in Coast Range SSE of Hollister

Pinsk \'pin(t)sk\ city SW Belarus *pop* 73,000

Pinsk Marshes — see PRIPET

Pio·tr·ków   Try·bu·nal·ski \'pyò-tər-,küf-,tri-bù-'näl-skē, pē-'ò-, -,kùv-\ commune *cen* Poland SSE of Lodz *pop* 80,529

Pipe Spring National Monument reservation NW Ariz. on Kaibab plateau containing old Mormon fort

Pipe·stone National Monument \'pīp-,stōn\ reservation SW Minn. containing quarry once used by Indians

Piq·ua \'pi-(,)kwä, -kwə\ city W Ohio N of Dayton *pop* 20,612

Pi·rai·évs \,pē-re-'efs\ *or* **Pi·rae·us** \pī-'rē-əs, pi-'rä-\ city E Greece on Saronic Gulf; port of Athens *pop* 169,622

Pirineos — see PYRENEES

Pir·ma·sens \,pir-mə-'zen(t)s\ city SW Germany near French border E of Saarbrücken *pop* 49,615

Pir·na \'pir-nə\ city E Germany SE of Dresden *pop* 48,001

Pi·sa \'pē-zə, *It* -sä\ commune W *cen* Italy in Tuscany on the Arno *pop* 102,150 — **Pi·san** \'pē-z°n\ *adj or n*

Pis·cat·a·qua \pi-'ska-tə-,kwò\ river 12 *mi* (19 *km*) Maine & N.H. formed by junction of Cocheco & Salmon Falls rivers & flowing SE on Maine-N.H. boundary into the Atlantic

Pi·sid·ia \pə-'si-dē-ə, pī-\ ancient country S Asia Minor N of Pamphylia — **Pi·sid·i·an** \-dē-ən\ *adj*

Pi·sto·ia \pi-'stòi-ə, -'stō-yə\ commune *cen* Italy NW of Florence *pop* 89,972

Pit \'pit\ river 280 *mi* (451 *km*) N Calif. flowing SW into the Sacramento

Pit·cairn Island \'pit-,karn, -,kern\ island S Pacific SE of Tuamotu Archipelago; a Brit. colony, with several smaller islands *pop* 62

Pi·tes·ti \pi-'tesht, -'tesh-tē\ city S *cen* Romania *pop* 162,395

Pitts·burg \'pits-,bərg\ city W Calif. NE of Oakland on San Joaquin River *pop* 47,564

Pitts·burgh \'pits-,bərg\ city SW Pa. at confluence of the Allegheny & the Monongahela where they form the Ohio *pop* 369,879 — **Pitts·burgh·er** \-,bər-gər\ *n*

Pitts·field \'pits-,fēld\ city W Mass. *pop* 48,622

Piz Bernina — see BERNINA

Pla·cen·tia \plə-'sen(t)-shə\ city SW Calif. *pop* 41,259

Placentia Bay inlet of the Atlantic E Canada in SE Newfoundland

Plac·id, Lake \'pla-səd\ lake 5 *mi* (8 *km*) long NE N.Y. in the Adirondacks

Plain·field \'plān-,fēld\ city NE N.J. *pop* 46,567

Plains of Abra·ham \'ā-brə-,ham\ plateau Canada in W part of city of Quebec

Plain·view \'plān-,vyü\ city NW Tex. N of Lubbock *pop* 21,700

Pla·no \'plä-(,)nō\ city N Tex. N of Dallas *pop* 128,713

Plantation city SE Fla. W of Fort Lauderdale *pop* 66,692

Plant City \'plant\ city W *cen* Fla. E of Tampa *pop* 22,754

Plas·sey \'pla-sē\ village NE India in W. Bengal N of Calcutta

Pla·ta, Río de la \,rē-ō-(,)de-lə-'plä-tə\ *or* **River Plate** \'plāt\ estuary of Paraná & Uruguay rivers S. America bet. Uruguay & Argentina; 225 *mi* (362 *km*) long

Pla·taea \plə-'tē-ə\ *or* **Pla·tae·ae** \-'tē-,ē\ ancient city Greece in SE Boeotia S of Thebes — **Pla·tae·an** \-'tē-ən\ *adj or n*

Platte \'plat\ **1** river 310 *mi* (499 *km*) *cen* Nebr. formed by junction of the N. Platte & S. Platte & flowing E into the Missouri **2** river 300 *mi* (483 *km*) SW Iowa & NW Mo. flowing into the Missouri

Plattensee — see BALATON (Lake)

Platts·burgh *or* **Platts·burg** \'plats-,bərg\ city NE N.Y. on Lake Champlain *pop* 21,255

Plau·en \'plau-ən\ *or* **Plauen im Vogt·land** \im-'fōkt-,länt\ city E Germany on the Weisse Elster *pop* 78,632

Pleasant — see NAURU

Pleasant Hill city W Calif. ENE of Oakland *pop* 31,585

Pleas·an·ton \'ple-z°n-tən\ city W Calif. SE of Oakland *pop* 50,553

Plenty, Bay of inlet of the S. Pacific N New Zealand on NE coast of North Is.

Ple·ven \'ple-vən\ city NW Bulgaria *pop* 107,567

Plock \'plòtsk\ commune NE *cen* Poland *pop* 121,996

Plo·iesti *or* **Plo·esti** \plò-'yesht, -'yesh-tē\ city SE *cen* Romania *pop* 247,502

Plov·div \'plòv-,dif, -,div\ *or* **Gk** **Phil·ip·pop·o·lis** \,fi-lə-'pä-pə-lis\ city S Bulgaria on the Maritsa N of the Rhodope Mountains *pop* 299,638

Plum \'pləm\ city SW Pa. *pop* 25,609

Plym·outh \'pli-məth\ **1** town SE Mass. *pop* 45,608 **2** village SE Minn. NW of Minneapolis *pop* 50,889 **3** city & port SW England in Devon *pop* 243,895

Plzeň \'pəl-,zen, --ze-nyə\ city W Czech Republic in Bohemia WSW of Prague *pop* 174,676

Po \'pō\ *or anc* **Pa·dus** \'pä-dəs\ river 418 *mi* (673 *km*) N Italy flowing from slopes of Mt. Viso E into the Adriatic through several mouths

Po·be·da Peak \pō-'be-də, pə-, -'bye-\ *or Russ* **Pik Po·be·dy** \,pēk-pə-'bye-dē, -'be-dē\ mountain 24,406 *ft* (7439 *m*) E Kyrgyzstan; highest in Tian Shan

Po·ca·tel·lo \,pō-kə-'te-(,)lō, -lə\ city SE Idaho *pop* 46,080

Po·co·no Mountains \'pō-kə-,nō\ mountains E Pa. NW of Kittatinny Mountain; highest point *ab* 1600 *ft* (488 *m*)

Pod·go·ri·ca *or* **Pod·go·ri·tsa** \'päd-gə-,rēt-sə\ *or* *1946–92* **Ti·to·grad** \'tē-(,)tō-,grad, -,gräd\ city S Yugoslavia * of Montenegro *pop* 54,509

Po·do·lia \pə-'dō-lē-ə, -'dòl-yə\ *or Russ* **Po·dolsk** \pə-'dòlsk\ region W Ukraine N of middle Dniester River

Po·dolsk \pə-'dòlsk\ city W *cen* Russia in Europe S of Moscow *pop* 169,000

Po Hai — see BO HAI

Pohn·pei \'pōn-,pā\ *or* **Po·na·pe** \'pō-nə-,pā\ island E Carolines, part of Federated States of Micronesia

Pointe–à–Pi·tre \,pwan-tə-'pētr°\ city & port French West Indies in Guadeloupe on Grande-Terre *pop* 25,312

Pointe–Claire \'pòint-'klar, pwant-, -'kler\ town Canada in S Que. on St. Lawrence River SW of Montreal *pop* 27,647

Pointe–Noire \,pwant-'nwär\ city & port SW Congo on the Atlantic; formerly * of Middle Congo *pop* 135,000

Point Pe·lee National Park \pòint-'pē-lē\ reservation Canada in SE Ont. on **Point Pelee** (cape projecting into Lake Erie)

Poi·tiers *or formerly* **Poic·tiers** \pwä-'tyä, 'pwä-tē-,ā\ city W *cen* France SW of Tours *pop* 78,739

Poi·tou \pwä-'tü\ region & former province W France SE of Brittany * Poitiers

Po·land \'pō-lənd\ *or* **Pol** **Pol·ska** \'pól-skä\ country E *cen* Europe bordering on Baltic Sea; in medieval period a kingdom, at one time extending to the lower Dnieper; partitioned 1772, 1793, 1795 among Russia, Prussia, & Austria; again a kindgom 1815–30; lost autonomy 1830–1918; since 1918 a republic * Warsaw *area* 120,355 *sq mi* (312,923 *sq km*), *pop* 38,038,400

Polish Corridor strip of land N Europe in Poland that bet. World War I & World War II separated E. Prussia from main part of Germany; area was before 1919 part of Germany

Pol·ta·va \pəl-'tä-və\ city *cen* Ukraine on Vorskla River WSW of Kharkov *pop* 220,000

Poltoratsk — see ASHKHABAD

Poly·ne·sia \,pä-lə-'nē-zhə, -shə\ the islands of the *cen* & S Pacific including Hawaii, the Line, Phoenix, Tonga, Cook, & Samoa islands, Tuvalu, Easter Is., French Polynesia, & often New Zealand

Pom·er·a·nia \,pä-mə-'rā-nē-ə, -nyə\ *or G* **Pom·mern** \'pò-mərn\ *or Pol* **Po·mo·rze** \pò-'mó-zhe\ **1** region N Europe on Baltic Sea; formerly in Germany, now mostly in Poland **2** former province of Prussia

Pom·er·e·lia \,pä-mə-'rē-lē-ə, -'rēl-yə\ *or G* **Pom·me·rel·len** \,pò-mə-'re-lən\ region E Europe on the Baltic W of the Vistula & E of Pomerania; orig. part of Pomerania

Po·mo·na \pə-'mō-nə\ city SW Calif. E of Los Angeles *pop* 131,723

Pom·pa·no Beach \'päm-pə-,nō, 'pəm-\ city SE Fla. on the Atlantic N of Fort Lauderdale *pop* 72,411

Pom·pe·ii \päm-'pā, -'pā-,ē\ ancient city S Italy SE of Naples destroyed A.D. 79 by eruption of Mt. Vesuvius — **Pom·pe·ian** *or* **Pompei·ian** \-'pā-ən\ *adj or n*

Pon·ca City \'päŋ-kə\ city N Okla. on Arkansas River *pop* 26,359

Pon·ce \'pòn(t)-(,)sä\ city & port S Puerto Rico *pop* 187,749

Pon·di·cher·ry \,pän-də-'cher-ē, -'sher-\ *or F* **Pon·di·ché·ry** \pōⁿ-dē-shä-rē\ **1** union territory SE India SSW of Madras constituted by Tamil Nadu; a settlement of French India before 1954, *area* 112 *sq mi* (291 *sq km*), *pop* 604,136 **2** city & port, its * *pop* 251,471

Pon·ta Del·ga·da \,pän-tə-del-'gä-də, -'ga-\ city & port Azores on São Miguel Is. *pop* 21,187

Pont·char·train, Lake \'pänt-shər-,trän, ,pänt-shər-'\ lake SE La. E of the Mississippi & N of New Orleans *area* 600 *sq mi* (1560 *sq km*)

Pon·te·fract \'pän-ti-,frakt, *formerly also* 'pəm(p)-frat, 'päm(p)-\ borough N England in W. Yorkshire, SE of Leeds *pop* 31,971

Pon·te·ve·dra \,pän-tə-'vā-drə\ **1** province NW Spain in SW Galicia on the Atlantic *area* 1695 *sq mi* (4407 *sq km*), *pop* 915,152 **2** commune & port, its *, NW of Vigo *pop* 68,645

Pon·ti·ac \'pän-tē-,ak\ city SE Mich. NW of Detroit *pop* 71,166

Pon·ti·a·nak \,pän-tē-'ä-,näk\ city Indonesia on SW coast of Borneo *pop* 398,357

Pon·tine Islands \'pän-,tīn, -,tēn\ islands Italy in Tyrrhenian Sea W of Naples; chief islands **Pon·za** \'pònt-sə\ & **Pon·ti·ne** \pōn-'tē-nä\

Pontine Marshes district *cen* Italy in SW Latium, separated from sea by low sand hills that prevent natural drainage; now reclaimed

Pon·tus \'pän-təs\ **1** country ancient NE Asia Minor; a kingdom 4th century B.C. to 66 B.C., later a Roman province **2** *or* **Pontus Euxinus** — see BLACK SEA

Pon·ty·pool \,pän-tə-'pül\ town SE Wales in Gwent *pop* 36,761

Pon·ty·pridd \,pän-tə-'prēth\ town SE Wales in Mid Glamorgan *pop* 32,992

Poole \'pül\ borough S England in Dorset on English Channel *pop* 118,922

Poo·na \'pü-nə\ city W India in Maharashtra ESE of Bombay *pop* 1,685,300

Po·o·pó, Lake \,pō-ə-'pō, (,)pò-'pō\ lake 60 *mi* (96 *km*) long W *cen* Bolivia S of Lake Titicaca at altitude of 12,000 *ft* (3658 *m*)

Pop·lar \'pä-plər\ former metropolitan borough E London, England, on N bank of the Thames, now part of Tower Hamlets

Po·po·ca·te·petl \,pō-pə-'ka-tə-,pet°l, ,pä-kə-'; -,ka-tə-'; -kə-'tä-,pe-\ volcano 17,887 *ft* (5452 *m*) SE *cen* Mexico in Puebla

Porcupine river 590 *mi* (950 *km*) in N Yukon Territory & NE Alaska flowing N & W into the Yukon

Po·ri \'pòr-ē\ city & port SW Finland *pop* 76,456

Pork·ka·la Peninsula \'pòr-kə-lə, -,lä\ peninsula S Finland W of Helsinki

Por·la·mar \,pòr-lə-'mär\ city & port NE Venezuela on Margarita Is.

Port Ad·e·laide \'a-d°l-,ād\ city SE S. Australia on Gulf of St. Vincent at mouth of Torrens River; port for Adelaide *pop* 35,407

Por·tage \'pòr-tij, 'pòr-\ **1** city NW Ind. E of Gary *pop* 29,060 **2** city SW Mich. S of Kalamazoo *pop* 41,042

Port Ar·thur \'är-thər\ **1** city & port SE Tex. on Sabine Lake *pop* 58,724 **2** — see THUNDER BAY **3** — see LÜ-SHUN

Port–au–Prince \,pòrt-ō-'prin(t)s, ,pòrt-, -pärⁿ(t)ō-'praⁿs\ city & port * of Haiti on SE shore of Gulf of Gonâve *pop* 763,188

Port Blair \'blar, 'bler\ town & port India on S. Andaman Is. * of Andaman and Nicobar union territory

Port Ches·ter \'pòrt-,ches-tər, 'pòrt-\ village SE N.Y. NE of New Rochelle on Long Island Sound *pop* 24,728

Port Co·quit·lam \kō-'kwit-ləm\ city Canada in SW B.C. E of Vancouver *pop* 36,773

Port Eliz·a·beth \i-'li-zə-bəth\ city & port S Republic of South Africa in S Eastern Cape province on Algoa Bay *pop* 468,797

Por·ter·ville \'pòr-tər-,vil, 'pòr-\ city S *cen* Calif. *pop* 29,563

\ə\ abut \ⁿ\ kitten, F table \ər\ further \a\ ash \ā\ ace \ä\ mop, mar \aú\ out \ch\ chin \e\ bet \ē\ easy \g\ go \i\ hit \ī\ ice \j\ job \ŋ\ sing \ō\ go \ò\ law \òi\ boy \th\ thin \th\ the \ü\ loot \ú\ foot \y\ yet \zh\ vision \á, k̲, ⁿ, œ, œ̄, ue, ūe, ʸ\ see Guide to Pronunciation

Port Ev·er·glades \'e-vər-ˌglädz\ seaport SE Fla. on the Atlantic S of Fort Lauderdale

Port Hed·land \'hed-lənd\ port Western Australia

Port Hue·ne·me \wī-'nē-mē\ city S Calif. near Oxnard *pop* 20,319

Port Hu·ron \'hyùr-ən, 'yùr-, -ˌän\ city E Mich. on Lake Huron & St. Clair River *pop* 33,694

Port Jack·son \'jak-sən\ inlet of S Pacific SE Australia in New South Wales; the harbor of Sydney

Port·land \'pōrt-lənd, 'pòrt-\ **1** city & port SW Maine on Casco Bay *pop* 64,358 **2** city & port NW Oreg. at confluence of Columbia & Willamette rivers *pop* 437,319

Portland Canal inlet of the Pacific *ab* 80 *mi* (129 *km*) long Canada & U.S. bet. B.C. & SE tip of Alaska

Port·laoigh·i·se \pōrt-'lā-ə-shə, pòrt-, -'lē-\ town *cen* Ireland ✱ of County Laoighis *pop* 3773

Port Lou·is \'lü-əs, 'lü-ē\ city & port ✱ of Mauritius *pop* 148,389

Port Lyautey — see KENITRA

Port Mahon — see MAHÓN

Port Mores·by \'mòrz-bē, 'mòrz-\ city & port SE New Guinea in Papua ✱ of Papua New Guinea *pop* 123,624

Por·to \'pōr-ˌtü, 'pòr-\ *or* **Opor·to** \ō-'pōr-ˌ,tü, -'pòr-\ city & port NW Portugal on the Douro *pop* 327,368 — see LEIXÕES

Pôr·to Ale·gre \ˌpòr-ˌtü-ə-'le-grə, ˌpòr-\ city & port S Brazil ✱ of Rio Grande do Sul state at N end of Lagoa dos Patos *pop* 1,300,000

Por·to·be·lo \ˌpōr-tə-'be-ˌ,lō, ˌpòr-\ town & port Panama on Caribbean coast; the great emporium of S. American trade in 17th & 18th centuries

Port of Spain city & port ✱ of Trinidad and Tobago, on NW Trinidad Is. *pop* 50,878

Por·to–No·vo \ˌpōr-tə-'nō-ˌ,vō, ˌpòr-\ city & port ✱ of Benin *pop* 192,000

Port Or·ange \'är-inj, 'är-(ə)nj, 'òr-inj, 'òr-(ə)nj\ city E Fla. *pop* 35,317

Porto Rico — see PUERTO RICO

Port Phil·lip Bay \'fi-ləp\ inlet of Bass Strait SE Australia in Victoria; the harbor of Melbourne

Port Roy·al \'roi-(ə)l\ town Jamaica at entrance to Kingston Harbor; early ✱ of Jamaica, destroyed by earthquakes 1692 & 1907 & partly engulfed by the sea

Port Royal Sound inlet of the Atlantic S S.C.

Port Said \sä-'ēd, 'sīd\ city & port NE Egypt on the Mediterranean at N end of Suez Canal *pop* 262,760

Port Saint Lu·cie \-ˌsänt-'lü-sē\ city E Fla. *pop* 55,866

Ports·mouth \'pōrts-məth, 'pòrts-\ **1** city & port SE N.H. on the Atlantic *pop* 25,925 **2** city S Ohio at junction of Ohio & Scioto Rivers *pop* 22,676 **3** city & port SE Va. on Elizabeth River opposite Norfolk *pop* 103,907 **4** city S England in Hampshire on **Port·sea** \'pōrt-sē, 'pòrt-\ (island in English Channel) *pop* 179,419

Port Stanley — see STANLEY

Port Sudan city & port NE Sudan on Red Sea *pop* 100,700

Por·tu·gal \'pōr-chi-gəl, 'pòr-\ *or anc* **Lu·si·ta·nia** \ˌlü-sə-'tā-nē-ə, -nyə\ country SW Europe in W Iberian Peninsula bordering on the Atlantic; a kingdom before 1910; now a republic ✱ Lisbon *area* (not including Azores & Madeira) 34,240 *sq mi* (89,024 *sq km*), *pop* 9,784,200

Portuguese East Africa — see MOZAMBIQUE

Portuguese Guinea — see GUINEA-BISSAU

Portuguese India former Portuguese possessions on W coast of India peninsula, annexed 1962 by India; comprised territory of Goa & districts of Daman & Diu

Portuguese Timor — see TIMOR

Portuguese West Africa — see ANGOLA

Port–Vi·la \pōrt-'vē-lə, pòrt-\ *or* **Vila** town & port ✱ of Vanuatu in SW Efate Is. *pop* 18,905

Porz am Rhein \ˌpòrts-äm-'rīn\ city W Germany ESE suburb of Cologne *pop* 76,762

Poseidonia — see PAESTUM

Potch·ef·stroom \'pä-chəf-ˌstrōm\ city NE Republic of South Africa in E North West province SW of Johannesburg *pop* 51,800

Po·to·mac \pə-'tō-mək, -mik\ river 287 *mi* (462 *km*) E U.S. flowing from W.Va. into Chesapeake Bay & forming S boundary of Md.

Po·to·sí \ˌpō-tə-'sē\ city S Bolivia *pop* 77,397

Pots·dam \'päts-ˌdam\ city NE Germany SW of Berlin *pop* 132,005

Potts·town \'päts-ˌtaün\ borough SE Pa. ESE of Reading *pop* 21,831

Pough·keep·sie \pə-'kip-sē, pō-\ city SE N.Y. *pop* 28,844

Po·way \'pō-(ˌ)wä\ city S Calif., a suburb of San Diego *pop* 43,516

Pow·der \'paù-dər\ **1** river 150 *mi* (241 *km*) E Oreg. flowing into the Snake **2** river 375 *mi* (604 *km*) N Wyo. & SE Mont. flowing N into the Yellowstone

Powell, Lake — see GLEN CANYON DAM

Pow·ys \'pō-əs\ county E *cen* Wales ✱ Llandrindod Wells *area* 1960 *sq mi* (5096 *sq km*), *pop* 111,300

Po·yang \'pō-'yäŋ\ lake 90 *mi* (145 *km*) long E China in N Jiangxi

Poz·nan \'pòz-ˌnan, 'pòz-, -ˌnän, -ˌnä-nyə\ *or G* **Po·sen** \'pō-zˌn\ city W *cen* Poland on the Warta *pop* 588,715

Poz·zuo·li \pòt-'swò-lē\ *or anc* **Pu·te·o·li** \pyü-'tē-ə-ˌlī, pü-\ commune & port S Italy in Campania W of Naples

Prague \'präg\ *or Czech* **Pra·ha** \'prä-(ˌ)hä\ city ✱ of Czech Republic & formerly of Czechoslovakia in Bohemia on Vltava River *pop* 1,214,772

Praia \'prī-ə\ town ✱ of Cape Verde on São Tiago Is. *pop* 37,480

Prairie Provinces the Canadian provinces of Man., Sask., & Alta.

Prairie Village city NE Kans. S of Kansas City *pop* 23,186

Pra·to \'prä-ˌtō\ commune *cen* Italy in Tuscany *pop* 165,888

Pratt·ville \'prat-ˌvil, -vəl\ city *cen* Ala. NW of Montgomery *pop* 19,587

Pres·cott \'pres-kət, -ˌkät\ city *cen* Ariz. *pop* 26,455

Presque Isle \presk-'ī(ə)l\ peninsula NW Pa. in Lake Erie forming **Presque Isle Bay** (harbor of Erie, Pa.)

Pressburg — see BRATISLAVA

Pres·ton \'pres-tən\ **1** former town, Ont., Canada — see CAMBRIDGE **2** borough NW England NNW of Liverpool ✱ of Lancashire *pop* 86,913

Prest·wich \'prest-(ˌ)wich\ borough NW England in Greater Manchester NNW of Manchester *pop* 31,198

Prest·wick \'prest-(ˌ)wik\ burgh SW Scotland in Strathclyde N of Ayr *pop* 13,532

Pre·to·ria \pri-'tōr-ē-ə, -'tòr-\ city, administrative ✱ of Republic of South Africa & formerly ✱ of Transvaal *pop* 303,684

Pretoria–Witwatersrand–Vereeniging province *cen* NE Republic of South Africa *area* 7243 *sq mi* (18,759 *sq km*), *pop* 6,847,000

Prib·i·lof Islands \'pri-bə-ˌlòf\ islands Alaska in Bering Sea

Prich·ard \'pri-chərd\ city SW Ala. N of Mobile *pop* 34,311

Primorye — see MARITIME TERRITORY

Prince Al·bert \'al-bərt\ city Canada in *cen* Sask. *pop* 34,181

Prince Albert National Park reservation Canada in *cen* Sask. in watershed area

Prince Ed·ward Island \'ed-wərd\ island SE Canada in Gulf of Saint Lawrence off E N.B. & N N.S.; a province ✱ Charlottetown *area* 2184 *sq mi* (5678 *sq km*), *pop* 129,765

Prince Edward Island National Park reservation Canada on N coast of P.E.I.

Prince George \'jòrj\ city Canada in E *cen* B.C. *pop* 69,653

Prince of Wales, Cape \'wā(ə)lz\ cape Alaska at W tip of Seward Peninsula; most westerly point of mainland of N. America, at 168°W

Prince of Wales Island 1 island SE Alaska, largest in Alexander Archipelago *area* 1500 *sq mi* (3900 *sq km*) **2** island N Canada bet. Victoria Is. & Somerset Is. *area* 12,830 *sq mi* (33,358 *sq km*)

Prince Ru·pert's Land \'rü-pərts\ historical region N & W Canada comprising drainage basin of Hudson Bay granted 1670 by King Charles II to Hudson's Bay Company; purchased 1869 by the Dominion

Prince Wil·liam Sound \'wil-yəm\ inlet of Gulf of Alaska S Alaska E of Kenai Peninsula

Prín·ci·pe Island \'prin(t)-sə-pə\ island W Africa in Gulf of Guinea N of São Tomé *area* 58 *sq mi* (151 *sq km*) — see SÃO TOMÉ

Prip·et \'pri-ˌpet, -pət\ *or Russ* **Pri·pyat** \'pri-pyət\ river 500 *mi* (805 *km*) E *cen* Europe in NW Ukraine & S Belarus flowing E through the **Pripet, *or* Pinsk, Marshes** to the Dnieper

Pro·gre·so \prə-'gre-(ˌ)sō\ city SE Mexico on Yucatán peninsula; port for Mérida *pop* 22,100

Pro·ko·pyevsk \prə-'kò-pyəfsk\ city S Russia in Asia at S end of Kuznetsk Basin NW of Novokuznetsk *pop* 275,000

Propontis — see MARMARA (Sea of)

Pro·vence \prə-'vän(t)s, prō-'vän(t)s\ region & former province SE France bordering on the Mediterranean ✱ Aix-en-Provence

Prov·i·dence \'prä-və-dən(t)s, -ˌden(t)s\ city & port N R.I., its ✱ *pop* 160,728

Pro·vo \'prō-(ˌ)vō\ city N *cen* Utah on Utah Lake *pop* 86,835

Prud·hoe Bay \'prü-(ˌ)dō, 'prə-; 'prüd-(ˌ)hō, 'prəd-\ inlet of Beaufort sea N Alaska

Prus·sia \'prə-shə\ *or G* **Preus·sen** \'pròi-sᵊn\ **1** historical region N Germany bordering on Baltic Sea **2** former kingdom & state of Germany ✱ Berlin — see EAST PRUSSIA. WEST PRUSSIA — **Prus·sian** \'prə-shən\ *adj or n*

Prut \'prüt\ river 500 *mi* (805 *km*) E Europe flowing from the Carpathians SSE into the Danube; forming the Romanian boundary (World War II to 1991) with the U.S.S.R. & (since 1991) with Moldova & Ukraine

Pskov \pə-'skòf, -'skòv\ city W Russia in Europe near **Lake Pskov** (S arm of Peipus Lake) *pop* 127,000

Ptol·e·ma·is \ˌtä-lə-'mā-əs\ **1** ancient town in upper Egypt on left bank of the Nile NW of Thebes **2** ancient town in Cyrenaica NW of Barca; site at modern village of Tolmeta **3** — see ACRE

Pu·chon \'pü-ˌchòn\ city NW S. Korea *pop* 456,292

Pueb·la \'pwe-blə\ **1** state SE *cen* Mexico *area* 13,124 *sq mi* (34,122 *sq km*), *pop* 3,279,960 **2** *or* **Puebla de Za·ra·go·za** \dä-ˌzar-ə-'gō-zə, -ˌsär-ə-'gō-sə\ city, its ✱ SE of Mexico (City) *pop* 521,885

Pueb·lo \'pwe-ˌblō\ city *cen* Colo. on the Arkansas *pop* 98,640

Puer·to Bar·rios \ˌpwer-tō-'bär-ē-ˌōs\ city & port E Guatemala on Gulf of Honduras *pop* 46,782

Puerto La Cruz \lə-'krüz, -'krüs\ city NE Venezuela NE of Barcelona *pop* 155,731

Puerto Limón — see LIMÓN

Puerto Montt \'mònt\ city & port S *cen* Chile *pop* 84,410

Puer·to Ri·co \ˌpwer-tə-'rē-(ˌ)kō, ˌpōr-, ˌpòr-\ *or formerly* **Por·to Rico** \ˌpōr-tə-, ˌpòr-\ island W. Indies E of Hispaniola; a self-governing commonwealth in union with the U.S. ✱ San Juan *area* 3435 *sq mi* (8931 *sq km*), *pop* 3,522,037 — **Puerto Ri·can** \'rē-kən\ *adj or n*

Pu·get Sound \ˌpyü-jət\ arm of the Pacific extending 80 *mi* (129 *km*) S into W Wash. from E end of Strait of Juan de Fuca

Puglia *or* **Le Puglie** — see APULIA

Pu·ka·pu·ka \ˌpü-kə-'pü-kə\ *or* **Dan·ger Islands** \'dān-jər\ atoll *cen* Pacific N of Cook Islands; chief island Pukapuka; administered with Cook Islands by New Zealand

Pu·la \'pü-lə\ city & port W Croatia at tip of Istrian Peninsula *pop* 45,000

Pul·ko·vo \'pül-kə-və, -ˌvō\ village W Russia in Europe S of St. Petersburg

Pull·man \'pül-mən\ city SE Wash. *pop* 23,478

Pu·log, Mount \'pü-ˌlòg\ mountain 9606 *ft* (2928 *m*) Philippines in N Luzon S end of Cordillera Central; highest in Luzon

Pu·na de Ata·ca·ma \ˌpü-nə-də-ə-'kä-mə, -ˌä-tə-\ high plateau region NW Argentina NW of San Miguel de Tucumán

Pun·jab *or* **Pan·jab** \ˌpən-'jäb, -'jab, 'pən-ˌ\ **1** region NW Indian subcontinent in Pakistan & NW India occupying valleys of the Indus & its five tributaries; formerly a province of Brit. India ✱ Lahore **2** *or* **East Punjab** former state NW India in E Punjab divided 1966 into two states of Punjabi Suba & Haryana **3** *or formerly* **West Punjab** province NE Pakistan ✱ Lahore **4** *or* **Pun·jabi Su·ba** \ˌpən-'jä-bē-'sü-bə, -'ja-\ state NW India formed from N part of former state of Punjab ✱ Chandigarh *area* 19,495 *sq mi* (50,687 *sq km*), *pop* 16,669,755

Punt \'pünt\ ancient Egyptian name for a part of Africa not certainly identified, probably Somaliland

Pun·ta Are·nas \ˌpün-tə-ə-'rä-nəs\ *or formerly* **Ma·ga·lla·nes** \ˌmä-gə-'yä-nəs\ city & port S Chile on Strait of Magellan *pop* 95,332

Punta del Es·te \del-'es-tē\ town S Uruguay E of Montevideo *pop* 5272

Pu·ra·cé \ˌpür-ə-'sä\ volcano 15,604 *ft* (4756 *m*) SW *cen* Colombia

Pur·beck, Isle of \\'pər-ˌbek\\ peninsula region S England in Dorset extending E into English Channel

Pur·ga·toire \\'pər-gə-ˌtwär, ˌpi-kə-ˌtwir\\ river 190 *mi* (306 *km*) SE Colo. flowing into the Arkansas

Pu·ri \\'pur-ē\\ city & port E India in SE Orissa on Bay of Bengal *pop* 101,089

Pu·rus \\pə-'rüs\\ river 2000 *mi* (3219 *km*) NW *cen* S. America rising in the Andes in SE Peru & flowing NE into the Amazon in Brazil

Pu·san \\'pü-ˌsän\\ city & port SE S. Korea on Korea Strait *pop* 3,514,798

Push·kin \\'push-kən\\ *or formerly* **Tsar·skoe Se·lo** \\'(t)sär-skə-yə-sə-'lò\\ *or* **Det·skoe Selo** \\'dyet-skə-yə-\\ city W Russia in Europe S of St. Petersburg *pop* 73,000

Puteoli — *see* POZZUOLI

Put–in–Bay \\'pút-ˌin-'bā\\ inlet of Lake Erie in Ohio on S. Bass Is. N of Sandusky Bay; site of **Perry's Victory and International Peace Memorial National Monument**

Pu·tu·ma·yo \\ˌpü-tə-'mī-(ˌ)ò\\ *or (in Brazil)* **Içá** \\ē-'sä\\ river 980 *mi* (1577 *km*) NW S. America flowing from SW Colombia into the Amazon in NW Brazil

Puy·al·lup \\pyü-'a-ləp\\ city W *cen* Wash. *pop* 23,875

Puy de Dôme — *see* DÔME (Puy de)

Puy de Sancy — *see* SANCY (Puy de)

Pya·ti·gorsk \\pē-ˌa-ti-'gòrsk\\ city S Russia in Europe in N Caucasus SE of Stravropol *pop* 130,000

Pyd·na \\'pid-nə\\ ancient town Macedonia on W shore of Gulf of Salonika

Pyong·yang \\pē-'òŋ-ˌyäŋ, pē-'əŋ-, -ˌyaŋ\\ city ✳ of N. Korea on the Taedong *pop* 1,250,000

Pyramid Lake lake 30 *mi* (48 *km*) long NW Nev. NE of Reno

Pyr·e·nees \\'pir-ə-ˌnēz\\ *or F* **Py·ré·nées** \\pē-rā-nā\\ *or Sp* **Pi·ri·ne·os** \\ˌpē-rē-'nā-(ˌ)òs\\ mountains along French-Spanish border from Bay of Biscay to Gulf of Lions — *see* ANETO (Pico de) — **Pyr·e·ne·an** \\ˌpir-ə-'nē-ən\\ *adj or n*

Qaraghandy — *see* KARAGANDA

Qa·tar \\'kä-tər, 'gä-, 'gə-; kə-'tär\\ country E Arabia on peninsula projecting into Persian Gulf; an independent emirate ✳ Doha *area* 6000 *sq mi* (15,600 *sq km*), *pop* 369,079 — **Qa·tari** \\kə-'tär-ē, gə-\\ *adj or n*

Qat·ta·ra Depression \\kə-'tär-ə\\ region NW Egypt, a low area 40 *mi* (64 *km*) from coast; lowest point 440 *ft* (134 *m*) below sea level

Qaz·vin *or* **Kaz·vin** \\kaz-'vēn\\ city NW Iran S of Elburz Mountains & NW of Tehran *pop* 248,591

Qe·na \\'ke-nə, 'kā-\\ city S Egypt N of Luxor *pop* 93,680

Qeshm \\'ke-shəm\\ island S Iran in Strait of Hormuz *pop* 15,000

Qing·dao \\'chiŋ-'daù\\ *or* **Tsing·tao** \\'tsiŋ-'daù\\ city & port E China in E Shandong on Jiaozhou Bay *pop* 1,900,000

Qing·hai \\'chiŋ-'hī\\ *or* **Ko·ko Nor** \\ˌkō-(ˌ)kō-'nòr\\ *or* **Ch'ing Hai** \\'chiŋ-'hī\\ low saline lake W *cen* China in NE Qinghai province at altitude of *ab* 10,000 *ft* (3048 *m*) *area* 2300 *sq mi* (5980 *sq km*) 2 *or* **Tsing·hai** \\'chiŋ-'hī\\ province W China ✳ Xining *area* 278,378 *sq mi* (723,783 *sq km*), *pop* 3,895,706

Qin·huang·dao *or* **Ch'in–huang–tao** *or* **Chin·wang·tao** \\'chin-'hwäŋ-'daù, -'wäŋ-\\ city & port NE China in NE Hebei *pop* 210,000

Qiong·zhou \\chē-'óŋ-'jó\\ *or* **Hai·nan Strait** \\'hī-'nän\\ *or* **Ch'iung·chou** \\chē-'ùŋ-'jó\\ strait bet. Hainan Is. & Leizhou Peninsula connecting Gulf of Tonkin with S. China Sea

Qi·qi·har \\'chē-'chē-'här\\ *or* **Ch'i–ch'i–ha–erh** \\'chē-'chē-'hä-'ər\\ *or* **Tsi·tsi·har** \\'(t)sēt-sē-ˌhär, 'chē-chē-\\ city NE China in W Heilongjiang *pop* 1,500,000

Qi·shon \\'kē-ˌshòn, kē-'\\ river 50 *mi* (80 *km*) N Israel flowing NW through Plain of Esdraelon to the Mediterranean

Qom \\'kùm\\ city NW *cen* Iran *pop* 543,139

Quad Cities \\'kwäd\\ the cities of Davenport, Iowa, Moline, Ill., Rock Island, Ill., & Bettendorf, Iowa

Quan·zhou *or* **Ch'üan–chou** *or* **Chuan·chow** \\chə-'wän-jō\\ city SE China in SE Fujian on Formosa Strait *pop* 110,000

Qu'Ap·pelle \\kwə-'pel\\ river 270 *mi* (434 *km*) Canada in S Sask. flowing E into the Assiniboine

Quathlamba — *see* DRAKENSBERG

Que·bec \\kwi-'bek, ki-\\ *or* **Qué·bec** \\kā-'bek\\ 1 province E Canada extending from Hudson Bay to Gaspé Peninsula *area* 523,860 *sq mi* (1,362,036 *sq km*), *pop* 6,895,963 2 city & port, its ✳, on the St. Lawrence *pop* 167,517 — **Que·bec·er** *or* **Que·beck·er** \\kwi-'bek-ər, ki-\\ *n*

Queen·bor·ough–in–Shep·pey \\'kwēn-ˌbər-ə-in-'she-pē, -ˌbə-rə-, -b(ə-)rə-\\ borough SE England in Kent at mouth of the Thames *pop* 33,362

Queen Char·lotte Islands \\'shär-lət\\ islands Canada in W B.C. in Pacific Ocean *area* 3970 *sq mi* (10,322 *sq km*)

Queen Charlotte Sound sound S of Queen Charlotte Islands

Queen Eliz·a·beth Islands \\i-'li-zə-bəth\\ islands N Canada N of water passage extending from M'Clure Strait to Lancaster Sound; include Parry, Sverdrup, Devon, & Ellesmere islands

Queen Maud Land \\'mòd\\ section of Antarctica on the Atlantic

Queens \\'kwēnz\\ borough of New York City on Long Is. E of Brooklyn *pop* 1,951,598

Queen's — *see* LAOIGHIS

Queens·land \\'kwēnz-ˌland, -lənd\\ state NE Australia ✳ Brisbane *area* 670,500 *sq mi* (1,743,300 *sq km*), *pop* 2,295,123 — **Queens·land·er** \\-ˌlan-dər, -ˌlən-\\ *n*

Queenstown — *see* COBH

Quelpart — *see* CHEJU

Que·moy \\ki-'mòi, kwi-; 'kwē-\\ island SE China in Formosa Strait 15 *mi* (24 *km*) E of Amoy; garrisoned by Taiwan since 1950 *pop* 60,544

Que·ré·ta·ro \\kə-'re-tə-ˌrò\\ 1 state *cen* Mexico *area* 4432 *sq mi* (11,523 *sq km*), *pop* 726,054 2 city, its ✳ *pop* 140,379

Quet·ta \\'kwe-tə\\ city Pakistan in N Baluchistan *pop* 285,000

Que·zal·te·nan·go \\ke(t)-ˌsäl-tə-'nän-(ˌ)gò\\ city SW Guatemala *pop* 72,745

Que·zon City \\'kā-ˌsòn\\ city Philippines in Luzon NE of Manila; former (1948–76) official ✳ of the Philippines *pop* 1,165,865

Quil·mes \\'kē(ə)l-ˌmäs, -ˌmes\\ city E Argentina SE of Buenos Aires *pop* 445,662

Quim·per \\kaⁿ(m)-'per\\ commune NW France W of Rennes near Bay of Biscay *pop* 50,856

Qui·nault \\kwi-'nòlt\\ river 65 *mi* (105 *km*) W Wash. flowing to the Pacific

Quin·cy 1 \\'kwin(t)-sē\\ city W Ill. on the Mississippi *pop* 39,681 2 \\'kwin-zē\\ city E Mass. SE of Boston *pop* 84,985

Quin·ta·na Roo \\kēn-ˌtä-nə-'rò\\ state SE Mexico in E Yucatán ✳ Chetumal *area* 19,438 *sq mi* (50,539 *sq km*), *pop* 209,858

Quin·te, Bay of \\'kwin-tē\\ inlet of Lake Ontario in Canada in SE Ont.; connected with Georgian Bay by Trent Canal

Quir·i·nal \\'kwir-ə-n²l\\ hill in Rome, Italy, one of seven on which the ancient city was built — *see* AVENTINE

Qui·to \\'kē-(ˌ)tò\\ city ✳ of Ecuador *pop* 599,828

Qum·ran \\kùm-'rän\\ *or* **Khir·bat Qumran** \\kir-ˌbät\\ site Palestine in NW Jordan on Wadi Qumran near NW shore of Dead Sea of an Essene community (*ab* 100 B.C. – A.D. 68) near a series of caves in which the Dead Sea Scrolls were found

Quoddy Bay PASSAMAQUODDY BAY

Qüqon — *see* KOKAND

Ra·ba \\'rä-bə\\ river 160 *mi* (257 *km*) SE Austria & W Hungary flowing E & NE into the Danube

Ra·bat \\rə-'bät\\ city ✳ of Morocco on Atlantic coast *pop* 518,616

Ra·baul \\rə-'baù(ə)l\\ city Bismarck Archipelago at E end of New Britain; formerly ✳ of Territory of New Guinea *pop* 14,973

Rabbah, Rabbath — *see* AMMAN

Race, Cape \\'räs\\ headland, SE point of Newfoundland, Canada

Ra·ci·bórz \\ˌrät-'sē-ˌbùsh\\ *or G* **Ra·ti·bor** \\'rä-tə-ˌbòr\\ city SW Poland in Silesia on the Oder

Ra·cine \\rə-'sēn, rä-\\ city SE Wis. S of Milwaukee *pop* 84,298

Rad·cliff \\'rad-ˌklif\\ city *cen* Ky. *pop* 19,772

Rad·nor \\'rad-nər, -ˌnòr\\ *or* **Rad·nor·shire** \\-ˌshir, -shər\\ former county E Wales ✳ Llandrindod Wells

Ra·dom \\'rä-ˌdòm\\ commune Poland NE of Kielce *pop* 226,317

Raetia — *see* RHAETIA — **Rae·tian** \\'rē-shən\\ *adj or n*

Rages — *see* RHAGES

Ra·gu·sa \\rə-'gü-zə\\ commune Italy in SE Sicily *pop* 68,850

Rah·way \\'rò-ˌwä\\ city NE N.J. SW of Elizabeth *pop* 25,325

Rainbow Bridge National Monument reservation S Utah near Ariz. boundary containing **Rainbow Bridge** (large natural bridge)

Rai·nier, Mount \\rə-'nir, rā-\\ *or formerly* **Mount Ta·co·ma** \\tə-'kō-mə\\ mountain 14,410 *ft* (4392 *m*) W *cen* Wash., highest in the Cascade Range & in Wash.; in **Mount Rainier National Park**

Rainy \\'rā-nē\\ river 80 *mi* (129 *km*) on Canada-U.S. boundary bet. Ont. & Minn. flowing from Rainy Lake into Lake of the Woods

Rainy Lake lake Canada & U.S. bet. Ont. & Minn. *area* 366 *sq mi* (952 *sq km*)

Rai·pur \\'rī-ˌpùr\\ city E India in SE Madhya Pradesh E of Nagpur *pop* 338,973

Rai·sin \\'rä-z²n\\ river 150 *mi* (241 *km*) SE Mich. flowing into Lake Erie

Ra·jah·mun·dry \\ˌrä-jə-'mùn-drē\\ city E India in E Andhra Pradesh on Godavari River W of Kakinada *pop* 267,749

Ra·jas·than \\ˌrä-jə-ˌstän\\ state NW India bordering on Pakistan ✳ Jaipur *area* 132,077 *sq mi* (343,340 *sq km*), *pop* 34,102,912

Raj·kot \\'räj-ˌkōt\\ 1 former state W India in N *cen* Kathiawar Peninsula 2 city, its ✳, now in Gujarat *pop* 444,156

Raj·pu·ta·na \\ˌräj-pə-'tä-nə\\ *or* **Rajasthan** region NW India bordering on Pakistan & including part of Thar Desert

Ra·leigh \\'rò-lē, 'rä-lē\\ city E *cen* N.C., its ✳ *pop* 207,951

Ra·lik \\'rä-lik\\ the W chain of the Marshall Islands

Ram·a·po Mountains \\'ra-mə-ˌpō\\ mountains of the Appalachians N N.J. & S N.Y.; highest point 1164 *ft* (355 *m*)

Ra·mat Gan \\rə-ˌmät-'gän, ˌrä-mät-\\ city W Israel E of Tel Aviv *pop* 120,900

Ram·bouil·let \\ˌräⁿ-bü-yä\\ town N France SW of Paris *pop* 18,446

Ram·gan·ga \\ˌräm-'gəŋ-gə\\ river 370 *mi* (595 *km*) N India in Uttar Pradesh flowing S into the Ganges

Ram·pur \\'räm-ˌpùr\\ 1 former state N India NW of Bareilly, now in Uttar Pradesh 2 city, its ✳, ENE of Delhi *pop* 203,491

Rams·gate \\'ramz-ˌgät, -gət\\ borough SE England in Kent on North Sea N of Dover *pop* 39,642

Ran·ca·gua \\rän-'kä-gwə, räŋ-\\ city *cen* Chile *pop* 139,925

Ran·chi \\'rän-chē\\ city E India in Bihar NW of Calcutta *pop* 500,593

Ran·cho Cu·ca·mon·ga \\'ran-(ˌ)chō-ˌkü-kə-'məŋ-gə, 'rän-, -'mäŋ-\\ city SW Calif. NW of Riverside *pop* 101,409

Rancho Pal·os Ver·des \\ˌpa-ləs-'vər-dēz\\ city SW Calif. on coast S of Torrance *pop* 41,659

Rand \\'rand, 'ränd\\ WITWATERSRAND

Ran·ders \\'rä-nərs\\ city & port NE Denmark *pop* 61,137

Ran·dolph \\'ran-ˌdälf\\ town E Mass. S of Boston *pop* 30,093

Range·ley Lakes \\'ränj-lē\\ chain of lakes W Maine & N N.H.

Ran·goon \\ran-'gün, raŋ-\\ 1 *or* **Yangon** river 185 *mi* (298 *km*) S Myanmar, the E outlet of the Irrawaddy 2 — *see* YANGON

Ran·noch, Loch \\'rä-nək, -nək\\ lake 9 *mi* (14 *km*) long *cen* Scotland

Rann of Kutch — *see* KUTCH (Rann of)

Ra·pa \\'rä-pə\\ island S Pacific in SE Tubuai group *area* 15 *sq mi* (39 *sq km*) *pop* 516

Ra·pal·lo \\rə-'pä-(ˌ)lō\\ commune NW Italy in Liguria ESE of Genoa on Gulf of Rapallo (inlet of Ligurian Sea) *pop* 29,790

Rapa Nui — *see* EASTER

Rap·i·dan \\ˌra-pə-'dan\\ river 70 *mi* (113 *km*) N Va. rising in Blue Ridge Mountains & flowing E into the Rappahannock

Rap·id City \\'ra-pəd\\ city W S.Dak. in Black Hills *pop* 54,523

Rap·pa·han·nock \\ˌra-pə-'ha-nək\\ river 185 *mi* (298 *km*) NE Va. flowing into Chesapeake Bay

Rap·ti \\'räp-tē\\ river 400 *mi* (644 *km*) Nepal & N India flowing SE into the Gogra

Rar·i·tan \\'rar-ə-t²n\\ river 75 *mi* (121 *km*) N *cen* N.J. flowing E into **Raritan Bay** (inlet of the Atlantic S of Staten Is., N.Y.)

\\ə\\ abut \\²\\ kitten, F table \\ər\\ further \\a\\ ash \\ā\\ ace \\ä\\ mop, mar \\aú\\ out \\ch\\ chin \\e\\ bet \\ē\\ easy \\g\\ go \\i\\ hit \\ī\\ ice \\j\\ job \\ŋ\\ sing \\ō\\ go \\ò\\ law \\òi\\ boy \\th\\ thin \\t̲h̲\\ the \\ü\\ loot \\ù\\ foot \\y\\ yet \\zh\\ vision \\à, k̲, ⁿ, œ, œ̄, ue, u̇e, ᵞ\\ see Guide to Pronunciation

Rar·o·ton·ga \ˌrar-ə-'täŋ-gə, -'täŋ-ə\ island S Pacific in SW part of Cook Islands; site of Avarua, ✳ of the group *pop* 9826

Ras al Khai·mah \ˌräs-al-'kī-mə, -'kī-\ sheikhdom, member of United Arab Emirates

Ras Da·shan \ˌräs-də-'shän\ mountain 15,158 *ft* (4260 *m*) N Ethiopia NE of Lake Tana; highest in Ethiopia

Ras el Tib — see BON (Cape)

Rashid — see ROSETTA

Rasht \'rasht\ city NW Iran near the Caspian *pop* 2,900,897

Ra·tak \'rä-ˌtäk\ the E chain of the Marshall Islands

Rat Islands \'rat\ islands SW Alaska in W Aleutians — see AMCHITKA, KISKA

Ra·ton \ra-'tōn, rə-, -'tün; *usu* -'tōn *in N Mex*, -'tün *in Colo*\ pass 7834 *ft* (2388 *m*) SE Colo. just N of Colo.-N.Mex. border in **Raton Range** (E spur of Sangre de Cristo Mountains)

Ra·ven·na \rə-'ve-nə\ commune N Italy NE of Florence *pop* 136,166

Ra·vi \'rä-vē\ *or anc* **Hy·dra·o·tes** \ˌhī-drə-'ō-(ˌ)tēz\ river 450 *mi* (724 *km*) N India flowing SW to the Chenab & forming part of boundary bet. E. Punjab (India) & W. Punjab (Pakistan)

Ra·wal·pin·di \ˌrä-wəl-'pin-dē, raůl-, rȯl-\ city NE Pakistan NNW of Lahore *pop* 966,000

Ray·town \'rā-ˌtaůn\ city W Mo. SE of Kansas City *pop* 30,601

Read·ing \'re-diŋ\ **1** town E Mass. N of Boston *pop* 22,539 **2** city SE Pa. on the Schuylkill *pop* 78,380 **3** borough S England ✳ of Berkshire *pop* 123,731

Re·bild \'rā-ˌbil\ village N Denmark in N Jutland S of Ålborg in **Re·bild Hills** (site of **Rebild National Park**)

Re·ci·fe \rə-'sē-fə\ *or formerly* **Per·nam·bu·co** \ˌpər-nəm-'bü-(ˌ)kō, -'byü-; ˌper-nəm-'bü-(ˌ)kü\ city & port NE Brazil ✳ of Pernambuco state *municipal area pop* 1,300,000

Reck·ling·hau·sen \ˌre-kliŋ-'hau-z°n\ city W Germany SW of Münster *pop* 119,418

Red \'red\ **1** river 1018 *mi* (1638 *km*) flowing E on Okla.-Tex. boundary & into the Atchafalaya & Mississippi in La. **2** river 310 *mi* (499 *km*) N cen U.S. & S cen Canada flowing N on Minn.-N.Dak. boundary & into Lake Winnipeg in Man. **3** — see ARCTIC RED **4** *or* **Hong** \'hȯŋ\ *or (in China)* **Yuan** \yü-'än\ river 500 *mi* (805 *km*) SE Asia rising in cen Yunnan, China, & flowing SE across N Vietnam into Gulf of Tonkin

Red·bridge \'red-(ˌ)brij\ borough of NE Greater London, England *pop* 229,800

Red Deer **1** river 385 *mi* (620 *km*) Canada in S Alta. flowing E & SE into the S. Saskatchewan **2** city Canada in S cen Alta. S of Edmonton *pop* 58,134

Red·ding \'re-diŋ\ city N Calif. *pop* 66,462

Red Lake lake 38 *mi* (61 *km*) long N Minn. divided into **Upper Red Lake** & **Lower Red Lake**; drained by **Red Lake River** (135 *mi or* 216 *km* flowing W into Red Lake River)

Red·lands \'red-lən(d)z\ city S Calif. SE of San Bernardino *pop* 60,394

Red·mond \'red-mənd\ city W cen Wash. NE of Seattle *pop* 35,800

Re·don·do Beach \ri-'dän-dō\ city SW Calif. *pop* 60,167

Red Sea sea 1450 *mi* (2334 *km*) long bet. Arabia & NE Africa

Red Volta river 200 *mi* (322 *km*) S Burkina Faso & N Ghana flowing into Lake Volta

Red·wood City \'red-ˌwůd\ city W Calif. SE of San Francisco *pop* 66,072

Redwood National Park reservation NW Calif.; groves of redwoods

Reel·foot \'rē(ə)l-ˌfut\ lake NW Tenn. near the Mississippi

Re·gens·burg \'rā-gənz-ˌbȯrg, -gəns-ˌbürk\ city SE Germany in Bavaria on the Danube NNE of Munich *pop* 132,604

Reg·gane \re-'gän, -'gan\ oasis cen Algeria in Tanezrouft SSE of Béchar

Reg·gio \'re-(ˌ)jō, -jē-(ˌ)ō\ **1** *or* **Reggio di Ca·la·bria** \dē-kə-'lä-brē-ə\ *or* **Reggio Calabria** *or anc* **Rhe·gi·um** \'rē-jē-əm\ commune & port S Italy on Strait of Messina *pop* 178,620 **2** *or* **Reggio nel·l'Emi·lia** \ˌne-lə-'mēl-yə\ *or* **Reggio Emilia** commune N Italy in Emilia-Romagna NW of Bologna *pop* 130,825

Re·gi·na \ri-'jī-nə\ city Canada ✳ of Sask. *pop* 179,178

Reims *or* **Rheims** \'rēmz, *F* raⁿs\ city NE France ENE of Paris *pop* 177,320

Reindeer Lake lake Canada on Man.-Sask. border *area* 2444 *sq mi* (6354 *sq km*)

Re·ma·gen \'rā-ˌmä-gən\ town W Germany on W bank of the Rhine NW of Koblenz

Rem·scheid \'rem-ˌshīt\ city W Germany in N. Rhine-Westphalia ESE of Düsseldorf *pop* 129,082

Ren·do·va \ren-'dō-və\ island W Pacific in cen Solomon Islands off SW cen coast of New Georgia Is.

Ren·frew \'ren-ˌfrü\ *or* **Ren·frew·shire** \-ˌshir, -shər\ former county SW Scotland ✳ Paisley

Rennes \'ren\ city NW France N of Nantes *pop* 194,094

Re·no \'rē-(ˌ)nō\ city W Nev. NNE of Lake Tahoe *pop* 133,850

Ren·ton \'ren-t°n\ city W Wash. SE of Seattle *pop* 41,688

Re·pen·ti·gny \rə-ˌpän-tē-'nyē\ town Canada in S Que. N of Montreal *pop* 49,630

Republican river 445 *mi* (716 *km*) Nebr. & Kans. rising in E Colo. & flowing E to unite with the Smoky Hill forming Kansas River

Re·thondes \rə-'tōⁿd\ village N France E of Compiègne

Ré·union \rē-'yü-nyən, ˌrā-ue-'nyōⁿ\ island W Indian Ocean in the W Mascarenes ✳ St.-Denis; an overseas department of France *area* 970 *sq mi* (2522 *sq km*) *pop* 476,675

Reut·ling·en \'rȯit-liŋ-ən\ city S Germany in Baden-Württemberg S of Stuttgart *pop* 95,456

Revel — see TALLINN

Re·vere \ri-'vir\ city E Mass. NE of Boston *pop* 42,786

Re·vil·la Gi·ge·do \ri-ˌvē-yə-hi-'hā-(ˌ)thō\ islands Mexico in the Pacific SW of S end of Baja California

Re·vil·la·gi·ge·do Island \ri-ˌvi-lə-gə-'gē-(ˌ)dō\ island SE Alaska in SE Alexander Archipelago S of Prince of Wales Is.

Reyes, Point \'rāz\ cape W Calif. at S extremity of peninsula extending into the Pacific NW of Golden Gate

Reyk·ja·vik \'rā-kyə-ˌvik, -ˌvēk\ city & port ✳ of Iceland *pop* 97,648

Reyn·olds·burg \'re-n°l(d)z-ˌbərg\ village cen Ohio *pop* 25,748

Rey·no·sa \rā-'nō-sə\ city NE Mexico in Tamaulipas on the Rio Grande *pop* 181,646

Re·zāi·yeh \rə-'zī-yə\ **1** *or* **Lake Ur·mia** \'ur-mē-ə\ shallow saline lake NW Iran **2** — see URMIA

Rhae·tia *or* **Rae·tia** \'rē-sh(ē-)ə\ ancient Roman province cen Europe S of the Danube including most of modern Tirol & Vorarlberg region of Austria & Graubünden canton of E Switzerland — **Rhae·tian** \-shən\ *adj or n*

Rhaetian Alps section of Alps E Switzerland in E Graubünden — see BERNINA

Rha·ges \'rā-jəz\ *or* **Rha·gae** \-(ˌ)jē\ *or bib* **Ra·ges** \'rā-jəz\ city of ancient Media; ruins at modern village of **Rai** \'rī\ S of Tehran, Iran

Rhein·fall \'rīn-ˌfäl\ waterfall in the Rhine N Switzerland 370 *ft* (113 *m*) wide, with two principal falls 50 *ft* (15 *m*) & 60 *ft* (18 *m*) high

Rheinpfalz — see PALATINATE

Rhenish Palatinate *or* **Rhine Palatinate** — see PALATINATE

Rheydt \'rīt\ city W Germany S of Mönchengladbach *pop* 100,300

Rhine \'rīn\ *or G* **Rhein** \'rīn\ *or F* **Rhin** \raⁿ\ *or D* **Rijn** \'rīn\ river 820 *mi* (1320 *km*) W Europe flowing from SE Switzerland to North Sea in the Netherlands; forms W boundary of Liechtenstein & Austria & SW boundary of Germany — **Rhe·nish** \'re-nish, 'rē-\ *adj*

Rhine·land \'rīn-ˌland, -lənd\ *or G* **Rhein·land** \'rīn-ˌjänt\ **1** the part of Germany W of the Rhine **2** RHINE PROVINCE — **Rhine·land·er** \'rīn-ˌlan-dər, -lən-\ *n*

Rhineland–Palatinate *or G* **Rheinland–Pfalz** \'(p)fälts\ state of Germany & formerly of W. Germany chiefly W of the Rhine ✳ Mainz *area* 7654 *sq mi* (19,900 *sq km*), *pop* 3,642,482

Rhine Province *or* **Rhenish Prussia** former province of Prussia, Germany, bordering on Belgium ✳ Koblenz

Rhode Is·land \rōd-'ī-lənd\ **1** *or officially* **Rhode Island and Providence Plantations** state NE U.S. ✳ Providence *area* 1214 *sq mi* (3156 *sq km*), *pop* 1,003,464 **2** — see AQUIDNECK — **Rhode Islander** *n*

Rhodes \'rōdz\ *or NGk* **Ró·dhos** \'rȯ-thós\ **1** island Greece in the SE Aegean, chief island of the Dodecanese *area* 545 *sq mi* (1417 *sq km*) *pop* 103,295 **2** city, its ✳ *pop* 43,619 — **Rho·di·an** \'rō-dē-ən\ *adj or n*

Rho·de·sia \rō-'dē-zh(ē-)ə\ **1** region cen S Africa S of Zaire comprising Zambia & Zimbabwe; contains rich archaeological findings **2** — see ZIMBABWE 2 — **Rho·de·sian** \-zh(ē-)ən\ *adj or n*

Rhodesia and Nyasaland, Federation of former country S Africa comprising S. Rhodesia, N. Rhodesia, & Nyasaland; a federal state within the Commonwealth; dissolved 1963

Rhod·o·pe \'rä-də-(ˌ)pē, rō-'dō-pē\ mountains S Bulgaria & NE Greece; highest Musala 9596 *ft* (2925 *m*)

Rhon·dda \'rän-də, '(h)rän-thə\ borough SE Wales in Mid Glamorgan *pop* 81,725

Rhône \'rōn\ river 500 *mi* (805 *km*) Switzerland & France rising in the Alps and flowing through Lake of Geneva into Gulf of Lions inlet of the Mediterranean

Rhyl \'ril\ town & port NE Wales in Clwyd at mouth of the Clwyd *pop* 22,714

Ri·al·to \rē-'al-(ˌ)tō\ **1** city SW Calif. W of San Bernardino *pop* 72,388 **2** island & district of Venice, Italy

Ri·au Archipelago *or formerly* **Ri·ouw Archipelago** \'rē-ˌaů\ archipelago Indonesia S of Singapore; chief island Bintan *area* 2279 *sq mi* (5925 *sq km*), *pop* 278,966

Ri·bei·rão Prê·to \ˌrē-bə-'raůⁿ-'prä-(ˌ)tü\ city SE Brazil in N cen São Paulo state *pop* 318,375

Rich·ard·son \'ri-chərd-sən\ city NE Tex. N of Dallas *pop* 74,840

Rich·e·lieu \'ri-shə-ˌlü, rē-shə-lyue\ river 210 *mi* (338 *km*) Canada in S Que. flowing N from Lake Champlain to head of Lake St. Peter in the St. Lawrence

Rich·field \'rich-ˌfēld\ village SE Minn.; a S suburb of Minneapolis *pop* 35,710

Rich·land \'rich-lənd\ city SE Wash. at confluence of Yakima & Columbia rivers *pop* 32,315

Rich·mond \'rich-mənd\ **1** city W Calif. NNW of Oakland on San Francisco Bay *pop* 87,425 **2** city E Ind. *pop* 38,705 **3** city cen Ky. *pop* 21,155 **4** borough of New York City — see STATEN ISLAND **5** city ✳ of Va. on the James *pop* 203,056 **6** city Canada in SW B.C. S of Vancouver *pop* 126,624 **7** *or in full* **Richmond upon Thames** royal borough of SW Greater London, England *pop* 163,000 — **Rich·mond·er** \-mən-dər\ *n*

Richmond Hill town Canada in SE Ont. N of Toronto *pop* 80,142

Ri·deau Canal \ri-'dō\ canal system Canada 126 *mi* (203 *km*) long in SE Ont. connecting Lake Ontario & Ottawa River & including **Rideau Lake** (20 *mi or* 32 *km* long) & **Rideau River** (flowing into the Ottawa)

Ridge·crest \'rij-ˌkrest\ city S Calif. NE of Bakersfield *pop* 27,725

Ridge·field \'rij-ˌfēld\ town SW Conn. NW of Norwalk *pop* 20,919

Ridge·wood \'rij-ˌwůd\ village NE N.J. NNE of Paterson *pop* 24,152

Rid·ing Mountain National Park \'rī-diŋ\ reservation Canada in SW Man.; has game preserve

Rif — see ER RIF

Rift Valley GREAT RIFT VALLEY

Ri·ga \'rē-gə\ city & port ✳ of Latvia at S extremity of the Gulf of Riga *pop* 915,000

Riga, Gulf of inlet of Baltic Sea bordering on Estonia & Latvia

Ri·je·ka *or* **Ri·e·ka** \rē-'ye-kə\ *or It* **Fiu·me** \'fyü-(ˌ)mā, fē-'ü-\ city & port W Croatia *pop* 128,883

Rijs·wijk \'rīs-ˌvīk\ commune SW Netherlands *pop* 50,514

Rí·mac \'rē-ˌmäk\ river 80 *mi* (129 *km*) W Peru flowing SW through Lima into the Pacific

Ri·mi·ni \'ri-mə-(ˌ)nē, 'rē-\ *or anc* **Arim·i·num** \ə-'ri-mə-nəm\ commune & port N Italy on the Adriatic ESE of Ravenna *pop* 130,638

Ri·mou·ski \ri-'müs-kē\ town Canada in E Que. on Gaspé Peninsula *pop* 30,873

Ring of Fire belt of volcanoes & frequent seismic activity nearly encircling the Pacific

Rio \'rē-(ˌ)ō\ RIO DE JANEIRO

Rio Bran·co \ˌrē-(ˌ)ō-'braŋ-(ˌ)kō, ˌrē-(ˌ)ü-'braŋ-(ˌ)kü\ **1** — see BRANCO **2** city W Brazil, ✳ of Acre *municipal area pop* 117,113

Rio de Ja·nei·ro \\'rē-(,)ō-dā-zhə-'ner-(,)ō, -dē-, -də-, -jə-'ner-, -'nir-\\ **1** state SE Brazil *area* 16,832 *sq mi* (43,763 *sq km*), *pop* 11,489,797 **2** city, its ✱ & port on Guanabara Bay; former ✱ of Brazil *pop* 6,100,000

Río de la Plata — see PLATA (Río de la)

Rio de Oro \\,rē-(,)ō-dē-'ōr-(,)ō, -'ór-\\ territory NW Africa comprising the S zone of Western Sahara

Rio Grande **1** \\,rē-(,)ō-'grand, -'gran-dē *also* ,rī-ō-'grand\\ *or MexSp* **Río Bra·vo** \\,rē-(,)ō-'brä-(,)vō\\ river 1885 *mi* (3034 *km*) SW U.S. forming part of Mexico-U.S. boundary & flowing from San Juan Mountains in SW Colo. to Gulf of Mexico **2** *or* **Rio Gran·de do Sul** \\,rē-ō-'gran-də-də-'sül, -'gran-dē-\\ city S Brazil in Rio Grande do Sul state W of entrance to Lagoa dos Patos *pop* 146,214 **3** \\,rē-(,)ō-'grän-dä, -dē\\ town NE Puerto Rico *pop* 45,648 **4** — see GRANDE (Rio)

Rio Grande de Cagayan — see CAGAYAN

Rio Gran·de do Nor·te \\,rē-(,)ü-,gran-də-də-'nòr-tə, -'gran-dē-\\ state NE Brazil ✱ Natal *area* 20,236 *sq mi* (52,614 *sq km*), *pop* 1,933,126

Rio Grande do Sul \\-'sül\\ state SE Brazil bordering on Uruguay ✱ Pôrto Alegre *area* 100,150 *sq mi* (260,390 *sq km*), *pop* 7,942,722

Rioja, the — see LA RIOJA

Rio Muni — see MBINI

Rio Pie·dras \\,rē-(,)ō-'pyä-drəs, -pē-'ä-\\ former city, since 1951 part of San Juan, Puerto Rico

Rio Ran·cho \\,rē-(,)ō-'ran-(,)chō, -'rän-\\ city *cen* N.Mex., a N suburb of Albuquerque *pop* 32,505

Rip·on Falls \\'ri-pən, -,pän\\ former waterfall in the Victoria Nile N of Lake Victoria; submerged by Owen Falls Dam

Riv·er·side \\'ri-vər-,sīd\\ city S Calif. *pop* 226,505

Riv·i·era \\,ri-vē-'er-ə\\ coast region SE France & NW Italy bordering on the Mediterranean — see CÔTE D'AZUR

Riviera Beach \\\\ city SE Fla. N of W. Palm Beach *pop* 27,639

Ri·yadh \\rē-'yäd\\ city ✱ of the Nejd & of Saudi Arabia *pop* 666,840

Rju·kan \\rē-'ü-,kän\\ town S Norway W of Oslo near **Rjukan Falls** (waterfall 780 *ft or* 238 *m*)

Ro·a·noke \\'rō-(ə-),nōk\\ **1** river 380 *mi* (612 *km*) S Va. & NE N.C. flowing E & SE into Albemarle Sound **2** city W *cen* Va. *pop* 96,397

Roanoke Island island N.C. S of entrance to Albemarle Sound

Rob·erts, Point \\'rä-bərts\\ cape NW Wash., tip of a peninsula extending S into Strait of Georgia from B.C. & separated from U.S. mainland by Boundary Bay

Rob·son, Mount \\'räb-sən\\ mountain 12,972 *ft* (3954 *m*) W Canada in E B.C.; highest in Canadian Rockies

Ro·ca, Cape \\'rō-kə\\ *or Pg* **Ca·bo da Ro·ca** \\,kä-bü-thə-'rò-kə\\ cape Portugal; westernmost point of continental Europe, at 9°30'W

Roch·dale \\'räch-,dāl\\ borough NW England in Greater Manchester NNE of Manchester *pop* 92,704

Roche·fort \\rōsh-'fòr, 'rōsh-fərt\\ *or* **Rochefort—sur—Mer** \\-,sür-'mer\\ city W France SSE of La Rochelle *pop* 27,264

Roch·es·ter \\'rä-chəs-tər, -,ches-tər\\ **1** city SE Minn. *pop* 70,745 **2** city SE N.H. *pop* 26,630 **3** city W N.Y. on the Genesee *pop* 231,636 **4** city SE England in Kent *pop* 52,505

Rochester Hills city SE Mich. *pop* 61,766

Rock \\'räk\\ river 300 *mi* (483 *km*) S Wis. & N Ill. flowing S & SW into the Mississippi at Rock Island

Rock·all \\'rä-,kòl\\ islet N Atlantic NW of Ireland, at 57°36'N, 13°41'W

Rock·ford \\'räk-fərd\\ city N Ill. NW of Chicago *pop* 139,426

Rock·hamp·ton \\räk-'ham(p)-tən, rä-'kam(p)-\\ city & port E Australia in E Queensland on Fitzroy River *pop* 54,362

Rock Hill city N.S.C. SSW of Charlotte, N.C. *pop* 41,643

Rock Island city NW Ill. on the Mississippi *pop* 40,552

Rock·lin \\'rä-klin, -klən\\ city E Calif. NE of Sacramento *pop* 19,033

Rock Springs city SW Wyo. near Utah border *pop* 19,050

Rock·ville \\'räk-,vil, -vəl\\ city SW Md. *pop* 44,835

Rockville Centre village SE N.Y. in W *cen* Long Is. *pop* 24,727

Rocky Mount \\'rä-kē\\ city NE *cen* N.C. *pop* 48,997

Rocky Mountain National Park reservation N Colo.

Rocky Mountains *or* **Rock·ies** \\'rä-kēz\\ mountains W N. America extending from N Alaska SE to N.Mex. — see ELBERT (Mount), ROBSON (Mount)

Rocky River city NE Ohio on Lake Erie W of Cleveland *pop* 20,410

Ró·dhos — see RHODES

Ro·dri·gues *or* **Ro·dri·guez** \\rō-'drē-gəs\\ island Indian Ocean in the Mascarenes; a dependency of Mauritius; chief town Port Mathurin *area* 40 *sq mi* (104 *sq km*), *pop* 18,335

Rog·ers \\'rä-jərz\\ city NW Ark. *pop* 24,692

Rogers Pass mountain pass Canada in SE B.C. in Selkirk Mountains

Rogue \\'rōg\\ river 220 *mi* (354 *km*) SW Oreg. rising in Crater Lake National Park & flowing W & SW into the Pacific

Ro·hil·khand \\'rō-,hil-,kənd\\ *or* **Ba·reil·ly** \\bə-'rā-lē\\ region N India in Uttar Pradesh; chief city Bareilly

Rohn·ert Park \\'rō-nərt\\ city W Calif. S of Santa Rosa *pop* 36,326

Rolling Meadows city NE Ill. NW of Chicago *pop* 22,591

Ro·ma·gna \\rō-'mä-nyə\\ district N Italy on the Adriatic comprising the E part of Emilia-Romagna region

Roman Campagna — see CAMPAGNA DI ROMA

Ro·ma·nia \\rü-'mā-nē-ə, rō-, -nyə\\ *or* **Ru·ma·nia** \\rü-\\ country SE Europe bordering on Black Sea ✱ Bucharest *area* 91,934 *sq mi* (239,028 *sq km*), *pop* 21,559,910

Rom·blon \\räm-'blòn\\ **1** islands Philippines in N Visayan Islands in Sibuyan Sea *area* 512 *sq mi* (1331 *sq km*) **2** island in the group

Rome \\'rōm\\ **1** city W Ga. NW of Atlanta *pop* 30,326 **2** city E *cen* N.Y. NW of Utica *pop* 44,350 **3** *or* **It Ro·ma** \\'rō-mä\\ *or anc* **Ro·ma** \\'rō-mə\\ city ✱ of Italy on the Tiber *pop* 2,803,931 **4** the Roman Empire

Rome, Duchy of division of Byzantine Empire 6th to 8th century *cen* Italy comprising most of modern Latium; later a province of the States of the Church called **Patrimony of Saint Pe·ter** \\'pē-tər\\

Rom·ford \\'räm(p)-fərd, 'rəm(p)-\\ former municipal borough SE England in Essex, now part of Havering

Rom·u·lus \\'rä-myə-ləs\\ city SE Mich. *pop* 22,897

Ron·ces·val·les \\,rōn(t)-səs-'vī-əs\\ *or F* **Ron·ce·vaux** \\rōⁿs-vō, rōⁿ-sə-\\ commune N Spain 5 *mi* (8 *km*) from French boundary in the Pyrenees near **Pass of Roncesvalles**

Ron·dô·nia \\rōⁿ(n)-'dō-nyə\\ *or formerly* **Gua·po·ré** \\,gwä-pə-'rä\\ state W Brazil ✱ Porto Velho *area* 96,986 *sq mi* (252,164 *sq km*), *pop* 503,125

Rong·er·ik \\'räŋ-ə-,rik, 'ròŋ-\\ island W *cen* Pacific in the Marshalls in Ratak chain E of Bikini

Ron·ne Ice Shelf \\'rò-nə, 'rə-nə\\ area of shelf ice Antarctica in Weddell Sea

Roo·de·poort \\'rō-də-,pòrt, 'rō-i-,pòrt, -,pòrt\\ city Republic of South Africa in Pretoria-Witwatersrand-Vereeniging W of Johannesburg *metropolitan pop* 141,764

Roo·se·velt \\'rō-zə-,velt, -vəlt *also* -'rü-\\ river 200 *mi* (322 *km*) W *cen* Brazil flowing from W Mato Grosso state N into the Aripuanã

Ro·rai·ma \\rō-'rī-mə\\ mountain 9094 *ft* (2772 *m*) N S. America in Serra Pacaraima on boundary bet. Venezuela, Guyana, & Brazil; has flat top

Ror·schach \\'ròr-,shäk, 'ròr-, -,shäk\\ commune NE Switzerland on S shore of Lake Constance *pop* 9878

Ro·sa, Mon·te \\,mòn-tē-'rō-zə\\ mountain 15,203 *ft* (4634 *m*) on Swiss-Italian border; highest in Pennine Alps

Ro·sa·rio \\rō-'zär-ē-,ō, -'sär-\\ city E *cen* Argentina on the Paraná *pop* 591,428

Ros·com·mon \\räs-'kä-mən\\ **1** county *cen* Ireland in Connacht *area* 951 *sq mi* (2473 *sq km*), *pop* 51,876 **2** town, its ✱ *pop* 1363

Rose, Mount \\'rōz\\ mountain 10,788 *ft* (3285 *m*) W Nev. in Carson Range SW of Reno

Ro·seau \\rō-'zō\\ seaport ✱ of Dominica *pop* 10,157

Ro·selle \\rō-'zel\\ **1** city NE Ill. *pop* 20,819 **2** borough NE N.J. W of Elizabeth *pop* 20,314

Rose·mead \\'rōz-,mēd\\ city SW Calif. E of Los Angeles *pop* 51,638

Ro·sen·berg \\'rō-z'n-,bərg\\ city SE Tex. *pop* 20,183

Ro·set·ta \\rō-'ze-tə\\ *or* **Ra·shid** \\rä-'shēd\\ *or anc* **Bol·bi·ti·ne** \\,bäl-bə-'tī-nē\\ **1** river 146 *mi* (235 *km*) N Egypt forming W branch of the Nile in its delta **2** city N Egypt on the Rosetta *pop* 36,711

Rose·ville \\'rōz-,vil\\ **1** city Calif. NE of Sacramento *pop* 44,685 **2** city SE Mich. NE of Detroit *pop* 51,412 **3** village SE Minn. N of St. Paul *pop* 33,485

Ross and Crom·ar·ty \\'ròs-ən(d)-'krä-mər-tē\\ former county N Scotland ✱ Dingwall

Rossbodenhorn — see FLETSCHHORN

Ross Dependency section of Antarctica lying bet. 160°E and 150°W long.; claimed by New Zealand

Ross Ice Shelf area of shelf ice Antarctica in S Ross Sea

Ross Sea arm of S Pacific extending into Antarctica E of Victoria Land

Ros·tock \\'räs-,täk, 'ròs-,tòk\\ city & port NE Germany on Warnow River near the Baltic coast *pop* 234,475

Ros·tov \\rä-'stòf, -'stòv\\ *or* **Rostov—on—Don** \\-,òn-'dän, -,än-\\ city S Russia in Europe on the Don *pop* 789,000

Ros·well \\'räz-,wel, -wəl\\ **1** city NW *cen* Ga. N of Atlanta *pop* 47,923 **2** city SE N.Mex. *pop* 44,654

Ro·ta \\'rō-tə\\ **1** island W Pacific at S end of the Marianas *area* 35 *sq mi* (91 *sq km*) **2** town & port SW Spain on the Atlantic NW of Cádiz

Roth·er·ham \\'rä-thə-rəm\\ borough N England in S. Yorkshire NE of Sheffield *pop* 81,988

Rothe·say \\'räth-sē\\ royal burgh SW Scotland on island of Bute in Strathclyde *pop* 5408

Ro·to·rua \\,rō-tə-'rü-ə\\ city New Zealand in N *cen* North Is. *pop* 38,157

Rot·ter·dam \\'rä-tər-,dam, -,däm\\ city & port SW Netherlands on the Nieuwe Maas *pop* 558,814 — **Rot·ter·dam·mer** \\-,da-mər, -,dä-\\ *n*

Ro·tu·ma \\rō-'tü-mə\\ island SW Pacific N of Fiji Islands *area* 14 *sq mi* (36 *sq km*); belongs to Fiji

Rou·baix \\rü-'bā\\ city N France NE of Lille *pop* 109,473

Rou·en \\rü-'äⁿ(n)\\ city & port N France on the Seine *pop* 113,536

Round Rock town *cen* Tex. N of Austin *pop* 30,923

Rous·sil·lon \\,rü-sē-'yōⁿ\\ region & former province S France bordering on the Pyrenees & the Mediterranean ✱ Perpignan

Rou·yn—No·ran·da \\'rü-ən-nə-'ran-də, rü-'aⁿ-\\ town central Canada in SW Que. *pop* 26,448

Row·lett \\'raü-lət\\ city NE Tex., a suburb of Dallas *pop* 23,260

Rox·burgh \\'räks-,bər-ə, -,bə-rə, -b(ə-)rə\\ *or* **Rox·burgh·shire** \\-,shir, -shər\\ former county SE Scotland ✱ Jedburgh

Roy \\'ròi\\ city NE Utah SW of Ogden *pop* 24,603

Royal Gorge section of the canyon of Arkansas River S *cen* Colo.

Royal Leamington Spa — see LEAMINGTON

Royal Oak city SE Mich. N of Detroit *pop* 65,410

Royal Tun·bridge Wells \\'tən-brij\\ borough SE England in Kent *pop* 44,506

Ruad — see ARWAD

Ru·an·da—Urun·di \\rü-'än-də-ü-'rün-dē\\ *or* **Belgian East Africa** former country E *cen* Africa bordering on Lake Tanganyika & comprising two districts, **Ruanda** (✱ Kigali) & **Urundi** (✱ Usumbura), administered by Belgium under League of Nations mandate 1919–45 & under U.N. trusteeship 1946–62 ✱ Usumbura — see BURUNDI, RWANDA

Ru·a·pe·hu \\,rü-ə-'pā-(,)hü\\ volcano 9175 *ft* (2796 *m*) New Zealand; highest peak in North Is., in Tongariro National Park

Rub' al Kha·li \\,rüb-al-'kä-lē, *Ar* -'kä\\ desert region S Arabia extending from Nejd S to Hadhramaut *area* 300,000 *sq mi* (780,000 *sq km*)

Ru·bi·con \\'rü-bi-,kän\\ river 15 *mi* (24 *km*) N *cen* Italy flowing E into the Adriatic

Ru·da Slas·ka \\,rü-də-'shlòⁿ-skə\\ commune S Poland *pop* 169,789

Ru·dolf, Lake \\'rü-,dälf\\ *or* **Lake Tur·ka·na** \\(,)tər-'ka-nə\\ lake N Kenya in Great Rift Valley *area* 3500 *sq mi* (9100 *sq km*)

Ru·fisque \\rü-'fēsk\\ city & port W Senegal *pop* 47,000

Rug·by \\'rəg-bē\\ borough *cen* England in Warwick on the Avon *pop* 59,564

Rü·gen \\'rü-gən, 'rūē-\\ island NE Germany in Baltic Sea off coast of Pomerania *area* 374 *sq mi* (972 *sq km*); chief town Bergen

Ruhr \\'rür\\ **1** river 144 *mi* (232 *km*) W Germany flowing NW & W to the Rhine **2** industrial district in valley of the Ruhr

---

\\ə\\ abut \\ᵊ\\ kitten, F table \\ər\\ further \\a\\ ash \\ā\\ ace \\ä\\ mop, mar \\aú\\ out \\ch\\ chin \\e\\ bet \\ē\\ easy \\g\\ go \\i\\ hit \\ī\\ ice \\j\\ job \\ŋ\\ sing \\ō\\ go \\ò\\ law \\òi\\ boy \\th\\ thin \\th\\ the \\ü\\ loot \\ú\\ foot \\y\\ yet \\zh\\ vision \\à, k̲, ⁿ, œ, œ̄, ᵫ, ūē, ᵊ\\ see Guide to Pronunciation

Ruis·lip North·wood \'rīs-ləp-'nȯrth-,wu̇d\ former urban district S England in Middlesex, now part of Hillingdon

Ru·me·lia or **Rou·me·lia** \rü-'mēl-yə, -'mē-lē-ə\ a division of the old Ottoman Empire including Albania, Macedonia, & Thrace

Run·ny·mede \'rə-nē-,mēd\ meadow S England in Surrey at Egham on S bank of the Thames

Ru·pert \'rü-pərt\ river 380 mi (612 km) Canada in W Que. flowing W into James Bay

Rupert's Land PRINCE RUPERT'S LAND

Ru·se \'rü-(,)sä\ or Turk **Rus·chuk** \rüs-'chük\ city NE Bulgaria on the Danube S of Bucharest pop 159,578

Rush·more, Mount \'rəsh-,mōr, -,mȯr\ mountain 5600 ft (1707 m) W S.Dak. in Black Hills on which are carved faces of presidents Washington, Jefferson, Lincoln, Theodore Roosevelt; a national memorial

Rus·sell Cave National Monument \'rə-səl\ reservation NE Ala. including cavern where remains of early pre-Columbian humans have been found

Rus·sell·ville \'rə-səl,vil\ city NW cen Ark. pop 21,260

Rus·sia \'rə-shə\ or Russ **Ros·si·ya** \rä-'sē-yə\ **1** former empire E Europe & N Asia coextensive (except for Finland & Kars region) with the U.S.S.R. ✳ St. Petersburg **2** the U.S.S.R. **3** independent country in E Europe & N Asia bordering on Arctic & Pacific oceans & on Baltic & Black seas; a constituent republic (**Russian Republic** or **Soviet Russia**) of the U.S.S.R. 1922–91 ✳ Moscow area 6,501,500 sq mi (16,903,900 sq km), pop 147,386,000

Russian Turkestan region formerly comprising the republics of Soviet Central Asia

Rus·ton \'rəs-tən\ city N La. pop 20,027

Ru·the·nia \rü-'thē-nyə, -nē-ə\ or **Carpathian Ruthenia** or **Za·kar·pat·ska·ya** \,zä-kər-'pät-ska-yə\ region W Ukraine S of the Carpathian Mountains; part of Hungary before 1918 & 1939–45; a province of Czechoslovakia 1918–38 ✳ Uzhgorod — **Ru·thene** \-'thēn\ n — **Ru·the·nian** \-'thē-nyən, -nē-ən\ adj or n

Rut·land \'rət-lənd\ or **Rut·land·shire** \-,shir, -shər\ former county E cen England ✳ Oakham

Ru·vu·ma or Pg **Ro·vu·ma** \rü-'vü-mə\ river 400 mi (644 km) SE Africa rising in S Tanganyika & flowing E into Indian Ocean

Ru·wen·zo·ri \,rü-ən-'zȯr-ē, -'zȯr-\ mountain group E cen Africa bet. Lake Albert & Lake Edward, on boundary bet. Uganda & Zaire — see STANLEY (Mount)

Rwan·da \rü-'än-də\ or formerly **Ru·an·da** country E cen Africa; a republic ✳ Kigali area 10,166 sq mi (26,432 sq km), pop 4,819,317 — see RUANDA-URUNDI — **Rwan·dan** \-dən\ adj or n — **Rwan·dese** \rü-,än-'dēz, -'dēs\ adj or n

Rya·zan \,rē-ə-'zan, -'zän\ city W cen Russia in Europe on Oka River SE of Moscow pop 351,000

Ry·binsk \'ri-bən(t)sk\ or 1946–57 **Shcher·ba·kov** \,sh(ch)er-bə-'kȯf, -'kȯv\ or 1984–89 **An·dro·pov** \an-'drō-,pȯf, -,pȯv\ city W cen Russia in Europe

Ryb·nik \'rib-nik\ commune S Poland pop 142,588

Rye \'rī\ borough SE England in E. Sussex pop 4293

Ryu·kyu Islands \rē-'yü-(,)kyü, -(,)kü\ islands W Pacific extending bet. Kyushu, Japan, & Taiwan; belonged to Japan 1895–1945; occupied by U.S. 1945; returned to Japan in 1953 (N islands) and 1972 (S islands) area 1803 sq mi (4688 sq km) — see AMAMI, OKINAWA, OSUMI ISLANDS, SAKISHIMA ISLANDS, TOKARA ISLANDS — **Ryu·kyu·an** \-,kyü-ən, -,kü\ adj or n

Rze·szow \'zhe-,shüf\ commune SE Poland pop 150,754

Saa·le \'zä-lə, 'sä-\ river 226 mi (364 km) E cen Germany rising in NE Bavaria in the Fichtelgebirge & flowing N into the Elbe

Saan·ich \'sa-nich\ municipality Canada in B.C. on SE Vancouver Is. N of Victoria pop 95,577

Saar \'sär, 'zär\ **1** or F **Sarre** \sär\ river 84 mi (135 km) Europe flowing from Vosges Mountains in France N to the Moselle in W Germany **2** or **Saar·land** \'sär-,land, 'zär-\ region W Europe in basin of Saar River bet. France & Germany; once part of Lorraine, became part of Germany in 19th century; administered by League of Nations 1919–35; became a state of Germany 1935; came under control of France after World War II; to W. Germany by a plebiscite Jan. 1, 1957, as a state (**Saarland**) ✳ Saarbrücken area 898 sq mi (2335 sq km), pop 1,066,299

Saar·brück·en \zär-'brü-kən, sär-, -'bru̇e-\ city SW Germany ✳ of Saarland pop 193,554

Saa·re·maa — see SAREMA

Sa·ba **1** \'sä-bə, 'sä-bə\ island SE W. Indies in Leeward Islands; part of Netherlands Antilles ✳ The Bottom area 5 sq mi (13 sq km), pop 1119 **2** — see SHEBA

Sa·ba·dell \,sa-bə-'del, ,sä-\ commune NE Spain NW of Barcelona pop 186,123

Sa·bah \'sä-bə\ or formerly **North Borneo** state Malaysia in NE Borneo, formerly a Brit. colony ✳ Kota Kinabalu area 29,388 sq mi (76,409 sq km), pop 1,002,608

Sa·bar·ma·ti \,sä-bər-'mə-tē\ river 200 mi (322 km) W India flowing S into head of Gulf of Cambay

Sa·bi \'sä-bē\ or in Mozambique **Sa·ve** \'sä-və\ river 400 mi (644 km) SE Africa rising in cen Zimbabwe & flowing E across S Mozambique to Indian Ocean

Sa·bine \sä-'bēn\ river 380 mi (612 km) E Tex. & W La. flowing SE through **Sabine Lake** (15 mi or 24 km long) & **Sabine Pass** (channel) into Gulf of Mexico

Sa·ble, Cape \'sä-bəl\ **1** cape at SW tip of Fla., southernmost point of U.S. mainland, at ab 25°7'N **2** headland E Canada on an islet S of **Cape Sable Island** (7 mi or 11 km long, at S end of N.S.)

Sable Island island Canada 20 mi (32 km) long in the Atlantic SE of Cape Canso; belongs to N.S.

Sab·ra·tha \'sa-brə-thə\ or anc **Sab·ra·ta** \-tə\ town Libya on the coast WNW of Tripoli pop 30,836

Sachsen — see SAXONY

Sa·co \'sȯ-(,)kō\ river 104 mi (167 km) E N.H. & SW Maine flowing SE into the Atlantic

Sac·ra·men·to \,sa-krə-'men-(,)tō\ **1** river 382 mi (615 km) N Calif. flowing S into Suisun Bay **2** city ✳ of Calif. on Sacramento River NE of San Francisco pop 369,365

Sacramento Mountains mountains S N.Mex. — see GUADALUPE MOUNTAINS, SIERRA BLANCA PEAK

Sa·fed Koh \sə-,fed-'kō\ mountain range E Afghanistan on Pakistan border; a S extension of the Hindu Kush

Sa·fi \'sa-fē\ city & port W Morocco SW of Casablanca pop 129,113

Sa·ga·mi Sea \sə-'gä-mē\ inlet of the Pacific Japan in cen Honshu SW of Tokyo Bay

Sa·ga·mi·ha·ra \sə-,gä-mē-'här-ə\ city Japan on Honshu pop 531,562

Saghalien — see SAKHALIN

Sag·i·naw \'sa-gə-,nȯ\ city E cen Mich. NNW of Flint pop 69,512

Saginaw Bay inlet of Lake Huron in E Mich.

Sa·gres \'sä-grish\ village SW Portugal E of Cape Saint Vincent

Sa·gua·ro National Monument \sə-'wär-ə, -'gwär-, -(,)ō\ reservation SE Ariz. E of Tucson

Sag·ue·nay \'sa-gə-,nā, ,sa-gə-'\ river 125 mi (201 km) Canada in S Que. flowing from Lake Saint John E into the St. Lawrence

Sa·guia el Ham·ra \sə-,gē-ə-el-'ham-rə\ territory NW Africa, the N zone of Western Sahara

Sa·gun·to \sə-'gün-(,)tō\ or formerly **Mur·vie·dro** \,mu̇r-vē-'ä-(,)drō\ commune E Spain NNE of Valencia pop 17,052

Sa·ha·ra \sə-'har-ə, -'her-, -'här-\ desert region N Africa N of the Sudan region extending from the Atlantic coast to Red Sea or, as sometimes considered, to the Nile — **Sa·ha·ran** \-ən\ adj

Sa·ha·ran·pur \sə-'här-ən-,pu̇r\ city N India in NW Uttar Pradesh NNE of Delhi pop 294,391

Sa·hel \'sä-hil, sə-'hil\ the semidesert S fringe of the Sahara that stretches from Mauritania to Chad — **Sa·hel·ian** \sə-'hil-yən\ adj

Saida — see SIDON

Saigon — see HO CHI MINH CITY — **Sai·gon·ese** \,sī-gə-'nēz, -'nēs\ adj or n

Sai·maa \'sī-,mä\ group of lakes SE Finland of which **Lake Saimaa** is the largest

Saint Al·bans \'ȯl-bənz\ borough SE England in Hertfordshire pop 50,888

Saint Al·bert \'al-bərt\ city Canada in cen Alta. pop 42,146

Saint Bar·thé·le·my \san-bär-tä-lə-mē\ island French West Indies in department of Guadeloupe; chief town Gustavia pop 2351

Saint Bernard — see GREAT SAINT BERNARD, LITTLE SAINT BERNARD

Saint–Bru·no–de–Mon·tar·ville \sänt-'brü-,nō-də-'män-tər-,vil, sȯnt-, ,san-brü-'nō-də-,mōⁿ-tär-'vēl\ town Canada in S Que. E of Montreal pop 23,849

Saint Cath·a·rines \'ka-th(ə-)rənz\ city Canada in SE Ont. NW of Niagara Falls on Welland Ship Canal pop 129,300

Saint Charles \'chär(-ə)lz\ **1** city NE Ill. pop 22,501 **2** city E Mo. on the Missouri pop 54,555

Saint Clair, Lake \'klar, 'kler\ lake SE Mich. & SE Ont. area 460 sq mi (1196 sq km), connected by **Saint Clair River** (40 mi or 64 km) with Lake Huron & draining through Detroit River into Lake Erie

Saint Clair Shores city SE Mich. NE of Detroit pop 68,107

Saint–Cloud \sänt-'klau̇d, sȯnt-; san-'klü\ commune France, WSW suburb of Paris pop 28,052

Saint Cloud \'klau̇d\ city cen Minn. on the Mississippi pop 48,812

Saint Croix \sänt-'krȯi, sȯnt-\ **1** river 75 mi (121 km) Canada & U.S. bet. N.B. & Maine **2** river 164 mi (264 km) NW Wis. & E Minn. flowing into the Mississippi **3** or **San·ta Cruz** \,san-tə-'krüz\ island W. Indies, largest of the Virgin Islands of the U.S. area 80 sq mi (208 sq km) pop 50,139; chief town Christiansted

Saint Croix Island International Historic Site reservation E Maine on Canada border on island in Saint Croix River

Saint–Cyr–l'Ecole \san-'sir-lä-'kəl\ commune N France W of Versailles pop 17,795

Saint–De·nis \,san(t)-də-'nē\ **1** commune N France NNE of Paris pop 95,808 **2** commune ✳ of Réunion Is. pop 94,104

Sainte–Foy \sänt-'fȯi, sȯnt-; san̄t-fwä, san-tə-\ town Canada in SE Que. SW of Quebec city pop 71,133

Saint Eli·as, Mount \i-'lī-əs\ mountain 18,008 ft (5489 m) on Alaska= Canada boundary in St. Elias Range

Saint Elias Range mountain range of the Coast Ranges SW Yukon Territory & E Alaska — see LOGAN (Mount)

Sainte–Thé·rèse \,sänt-tə-'räz, ,san̄t-tä-'rez\ town Canada in S Que. pop 24,158

Saint–Étienne \san-tā-tyen\ city SE cen France pop 218,289

Saint–Eus·tache \,san-tyü-'stash\ town Canada in S Que. pop 37,278

Saint Eu·sta·ti·us \,sänt-yü-'stä-sh(ē-)əs\ or **Sta·tia** \'stä-shə\ island W. Indies in Netherlands Antilles NW of St. Kitts area 7 sq mi (18 sq km) pop 1715

Saint Fran·cis \sänt-'fran(t)-səs, sȯnt-\ **1** river 425 mi (684 km) SE Mo. & E Ark. flowing S into the Mississippi **2** or **Saint Fran·cois** \san-frän-swä\ river 165 mi (266 km) Canada in S Que. flowing NW into the St. Lawrence

Saint Francis, Lake expansion of St. Lawrence River Canada above Valleyfield, Que.

Saint Gall \sänt-'gȯl, sȯnt-; san-'gäl\ or G **Sankt Gal·len** \zän̄kt-'gä-lən\ **1** canton NE Switzerland area 800 sq mi (2080 sq km), pop 416,578 **2** commune, its ✳ pop 73,889

Saint George \'jȯrj\ city SW corner of Utah pop 28,502

Saint George's \'jȯr-jəz\ town ✳ of Grenada pop 29,400

Saint George's Channel strait British Isles bet. SW Wales & Ireland

Saint–Ger·main \,san-zhər-'maⁿ\ or **Saint–Ger·main–en–Laye** \-,maⁿ-,än̄-'lā\ commune N France WNW of Paris pop 35,351

Saint–Gilles \saⁿ-'zhē(ə)l\ or Flem **Sint–Gil·lis** \sint-'gi-ləs, -'ki-\ commune cen Belgium near Brussels pop 42,684

Saint Gott·hard \sänt-'gä-tərd, sȯnt-, 'gät-hərd, san-gō-'tär\ **1** mountains Switzerland in Lepontine Alps bet. Uri & Ticino cantons **2** mountain pass 6935 ft (2114 m) in St. Gotthard Range

Saint He·le·na \sänt-'l-'ē-nə, ,sänt-hə-'lē-\ island S Atlantic; a Brit. colony ✳ Jamestown area 47 sq mi (122 sq km), pop 5644

Saint Hel·ens \sänt-'he-lənz, sȯnt-\ borough NW England in Merseyside ENE of Liverpool pop 98,769

Saint Helens, Mount volcanic peak 8364 ft (2534 m) SW Wash. in Cascades; in **Mount Saint Helens National Volcanic Monument**

Saint Hel·ier \'hel-yər\ town Channel Islands ✳ of Jersey pop 28,135

Saint–Hu·bert \sänt-'hyü-bərt, sȯnt-; ,san-yü-'ber\ town Canada in S Que. E of Montreal pop 74,027

Saint–Hy·a·cinthe \sänt-'hī-ə-(,)sin(t)th, sənt-; ,sant-yə-'sant\ town Canada in S Que. E of Montreal *pop* 39,292

Saint–Jean–Cap–Fer·rat \saⁿ-'zhäⁿ-,kap-fə-'rä\ commune SE France on coast E of Nice

Saint–Jean–de–Luz \saⁿ-,zhäⁿ-də-'lüz, -'lüēz\ town SW France on Bay of Biscay SW of Biarritz *pop* 10,921

Saint–Jean–sur–Ri·che·lieu \säⁿ-'zhäⁿ-sür-'ri-shə-,lü, -,rē-shə-'lyœ\ town Canada in S Que. SE of Montreal *pop* 37,607

Saint–Jé·rôme \,saⁿ-zhä-'rōm, ,sänt-jə-'rōm\ town Canada in S Que. NW of Montreal *pop* 23,384

Saint John \sänt-'jän, sənt-\ 1 river 450 *mi* (724 *km*) NE U.S. & SE Canada flowing from N Maine into Bay of Fundy in N.B. 2 city & port Canada in S N.B. at mouth of the St. John *pop* 74,969

Saint John, Lake or **Lac Saint–Jean** \läk-saⁿ-zhäⁿ\ lake Canada in S Que. draining through the Saguenay to the St. Lawrence *area* 350 *sq mi* (910 *sq km*)

Saint John Island island W. Indies, one of the Virgin Islands of the U.S. *area* 20 *sq mi* (52 *sq km*), *pop* 3504

Saint Johns \sänt-'jänz, sənt-\ 1 river 276 *mi* (444 *km*) NE Fla. flowing N & E into the Atlantic 2 town Brit. West Indies ✳ of Antigua on Antigua Is. *pop* 24,359

Saint John's \sänt-'jänz, sənt-\ city & port Canada ✳ of Nfld. *pop* 95,770

Saint Jo·seph \'jō-zəf *also* -səf\ city NW Mo. *pop* 71,852

Saint Kitts \'kits\ or **Saint Chris·to·pher** \'kris-tə-fər\ island Brit. West Indies in the Leewards; chief town Basseterre *area* 68 *sq mi* (177 *sq km*); with Nevis, forms independent state of **Saint Kitts–Nevis** (✳ Basseterre *area* 152 *sq mi* or 395 *sq km*, *pop* 44,404) — **Kit·ti·tian** \kə-'ti-shən\ n

Saint–Lau·rent \,saⁿ-lô-'rän, ,sant-lô-'rent\ town Canada in S Que. on Montreal Is. *pop* 72,402

Saint Law·rence \sänt-'lôr-ən(t)s, sənt-, -'lär-\ river 760 *mi* (1223 *km*) E Canada in Ont. & Que. bordering on the U.S. in N.Y., flowing from Lake Ontario NE into the Atlantic, & forming at its mouth a wide bay (the **Gulf of Saint Lawrence**)

Saint Lawrence, Lake expansion of St. Lawrence River Canada & U.S. WSW of Cornwall, Ont.

Saint Lawrence Island island 95 *mi* (153 *km*) long W Alaska in N Bering Sea

Saint Lawrence Islands National Park reservation SE Canada in SE Ont.

Saint Lawrence Seaway waterway Canada & U.S. in & along the St. Lawrence River bet. Lake Ontario & Montreal

Saint–Lé·o·nard \,saⁿ-,lā-ə-'när; sänt-'le-nərd, sənt-\ town Canada in S Que. N of Montreal *pop* 73,120

Saint–Lô \sänt-'lō, sənt-; saⁿ-lō\ commune NW France *pop* 21,670

Saint–Lou·is \,saⁿ-lü-'ē\ 1 city & port Senegal on island at mouth of Senegal River; formerly ✳ of Senegal *pop* 88,404 2 city & port Réunion

Saint Lou·is \sänt-'lü-əs, sənt-\ 1 river 220 *mi* (354 *km*) NE Minn. flowing to W tip of Lake Superior 2 city E Mo. on the Mississippi *pop* 396,685 — **Saint Lou·i·san** \'lü-ə-sən\ n — **Saint Lou·i·sian** \'lü-ə-zhən, -shən\ n

Saint Lou·is, Lake \sänt-'lü-ē, sənt-\ expansion of St. Lawrence River Canada above Lachine Rapids

Saint Lou·is Park \'lü-əs\ city SE Minn. *pop* 43,787

Saint Lu·cia \sänt-'lü-shə, sənt-\ island Brit. West Indies in the Windwards S of Martinique; an independent member of the Commonwealth of Nations since 1979 ✳ Castries *area* 233 *sq mi* (606 *sq km*), *pop* 148,183

Saint–Ma·lo \,saⁿ-mə-'lō\ city & port NW France in Brittany on island in Gulf of Saint-Malo *pop* 43,277

Saint–Malo, Gulf of arm of English Channel NW France bet. Cotentin Peninsula & Brittany

Saint Mar·tin \sänt-'mär-tᵊn, sənt-\ or D **Sint Maar·ten** \sint-\ island W. Indies in the N Leewards; divided bet. France & Netherlands *area* 33 *sq mi* (86 *sq km*)

Saint Marylebone — see MARYLEBONE

Saint Mar·ys \'mer-ēz, 'mar-ēz, 'mā-rēz\ 1 river 175 *mi* (282 *km*) on Fla.-Ga. border flowing from Okefenokee Swamp to the Atlantic 2 river 63 *mi* (101 *km*) bet. Canada & U.S. in Ont. & Upper Peninsula of Mich. flowing from Lake Superior into Lake Huron; descends 20 *ft* (6.1 *m*) in a mile at **Saint Marys Falls** — see SAULT SAINTE MARIE CANALS

Saint–Maur–des–Fos·sés \,saⁿ-,môr-dā-fô-'sā\ commune N France SE of Paris on the Marne *pop* 80,797

Saint Mau·rice \sänt-'môr-əs, sənt-, -'mär-; ,saⁿ-mə-'rēs\ river 325 *mi* (523 *km*) Canada in S Que. flowing S into the St. Lawrence

Saint–Mi·hiel \saⁿ-mē-yel\ town NE France on the Meuse *pop* 5544

Saint Mo·ritz \sänt-mə-'rits, saⁿ-mə-\ or G **Sankt Mo·ritz** \,zäŋkt-mə-'rits\ town E Switzerland in Graubünden canton SSE of Chur *pop* 5900

Saint–Na·zaire \,saⁿ-nə-'zar, -'zer\ commune & port NW France at mouth of the Loire *pop* 65,228

Sain·tonge \saⁿ-tōⁿzh\ region & former province of France on Bay of Biscay N of the Gironde ✳ Saintes

Saint–Ouen \saⁿ-twäⁿ\ commune France, N suburb of Paris *pop* 43,569

Saint Pan·cras \sänt-'paŋ-krəs, sənt-\ former metropolitan borough NW London, England, now part of Camden

Saint Paul \'pȯl\ city E Minn., its ✳ *pop* 272,235 — **Saint Paul·ite** \'pȯ-,līt\ n

Saint Paul's Rocks or Pg **Pe·ne·dos de São Pe·dro e São Pau·lo** \pə-'nä-thüs-thə-,saüⁿ(m)-'pāth-rü-ä-,saüⁿ(m)-'paü-lü\ rocky islets in the Atlantic 600 *mi* (966 *km*) NE of Natal, Brazil; belong to Brazil

Saint Pe·ter, Lake \'pē-tərz\ expansion of St. Lawrence River Canada bet. Sorel & Trois-Rivières, Que.

Saint Pe·ters \'pē-tərz\ city E Mo. WNW of St. Louis *pop* 45,779

Saint Pe·ters·burg \'pē-tərz-,bərg\ 1 city W Fla. on Pinellas Peninsula SW of Tampa *pop* 238,629 2 or 1914–24 **Pet·ro·grad** \'pe-trə-,grad, -,gräd\ or 1924–91 **Len·in·grad** \'le-nən-,grad, -,gräd\ city W Russia in Europe, at E end of Gulf of Finland; ✳ of Russian Empire 1712–1917, *pop* 3,513,000

Saint Pierre and Mi·que·lon \saⁿ-'pyer-ən(d)-,mē-kə-'lōⁿ\ French islands in the Atlantic off S Newfoundland ✳ St. Pierre, *area* 93 *sq mi* (242 *sq km*), *pop* 6051

Saint–Quen·tin \sänt-'kwen-tᵊn, sənt-, F saⁿ-kän-taⁿ\ commune N France on the Somme NW of Laon *pop* 69,956

Saint Si·mons Island \sänt-'sī-mənz, sənt-\ island SE Ga. in the Atlantic

Saint Thom·as \'tä-məs\ 1 island W. Indies, one of the Virgin Islands of the U.S. *area* 32 *sq mi* (83 *sq km*) 2 — see CHARLOTTE AMALIE 3 city Canada in SE Ont. S of London *pop* 29,990

Saint–Tro·pez \,saⁿ-trô-'pā\ commune SE France on the Mediterranean SW of Cannes *pop* 4484

Saint Vin·cent \sänt-'vin(t)-sənt, sənt-\ island Brit. West Indies in *cen* Windwards; with N Grenadines became independent 1979 as **Saint Vincent and the Grenadines** ✳ Kingstown *area* 150 *sq mi* (390 *sq km*), *pop* 124,000

Saint Vincent, Cape or Pg **Ca·bo de São Vi·cen·te** \'kä-bü-thə-,saü-vē-'sän(n)-tə\ cape SW Portugal

Saint Vincent, Gulf inlet of Indian Ocean Australia in S. Australia E of Yorke Peninsula

Sai·pan \sī-'pan, -'pän, 'sī-,\ island W Pacific in S *cen* Marianas *area* 70 *sq mi* (182 *sq km*), *pop* 7967 — **Sai·pa·nese** \,sī-pə-'nēz, -'nēs\ *adj or n*

Sa·is \'sā-əs\ ancient city Egypt in Nile delta

Sa·ja·ma \sə-'hä-mə\ mountain 21,391 *ft* (6520 *m*) W Bolivia near Chilean boundary

Sa·kai \(,)sä-'kī\ city Japan in S Honshu on Osaka Bay *pop* 807,859

Sak·a·ka·wea, Lake \,sa-kə-kə-'wē-ə\ reservoir 140 *mi* (225 *km*) long W N.Dak. formed in the Missouri by the Garrison Dam

Sa·kar·ya \sä-'kär-yə\ river 300 *mi* (483 *km*) NW Turkey in Asia flowing into the Black Sea E of the Bosporus

Sa·kha·lin \'sa-kə-,lēn, -,lən; ,sa-kə-'lēn\ or *formerly* **Sa·gha·lien** \'sa-gə-,lēn, ,sa-gə-'\ or Jp **Ka·ra·fu·to** \kə-'rä-fə-,tō\ island SE Russia in Asia in Sea of Okhotsk N of Hokkaido; formerly (1905–45) divided bet. Russia & Japan *area* 24,560 *sq mi* (63,856 *sq km*)

Sa·ki·shi·ma Islands \,sä-ki-'shē-mə, sä-'ki-shə-mə\ island group Japan in S Ryukyus off E coast of N Taiwan; occupied 1945–72 by the U.S. *area* 343 *sq mi* (892 *sq km*)

Sakkara — see SAQQĀRA

Sa·kon·net River \sə-'kä-nət\ inlet of the Atlantic SE R.I., E of Aquidneck Is.

Sal·a·ber·ry–de–Val·ley·field \'sa-lə-,ber-ē-də-'va-lē-,fēld\ or **Valleyfield** town Canada in S Que. SW of Montreal *pop* 27,598

Sa·la·do \sə-'lä-(,)dō\ 1 or *in upper course* **Ju·ra·men·to** \,hür-ə-'men-(,)tō\ river 1120 *mi* (1802 *km*) N Argentina flowing from the Andes SE into the Paraná 2 or *in upper course* **Des·agua·de·ro** \,dä-,sä-gwə-'der-(,)ō\ river 850 *mi* (1368 *km*) W *cen* Argentina flowing S into the Colorado

Salajar — see SELAJAR

Sal·a·man·ca \,sa-lə-'maŋ-kə, sä-lə-'mäŋ-\ 1 province W Spain *area* 4829 *sq mi* (12,555 *sq km*), *pop* 319,137 2 commune, its ✳, WNW of Madrid *pop* 153,981

Sal·a·maua \,sa-lə-'maü-ə\ town Papua New Guinea on Huon Gulf

Salambria — see PENEUS

Sal·a·mis \'sa-lə-məs\ 1 ancient city Cyprus on E coast 2 island Greece in Saronic Gulf off Attica

Sal·da·nha Bay \sal-'da-nyə\ inlet of the Atlantic on W coast of Western Cape province, Republic of South Africa

Sa·lé \sa-'lā\ or *formerly* **Sal·lee** \'sa-lē\ city & port NW Morocco, N suburb of Rabat *pop* 289,391

Sa·lem \'sā-ləm\ 1 city & port NE Mass. NE of Lynn *pop* 38,091 2 town SE N.H. E of Nashua *pop* 25,746 3 city ✳ of Oreg. on Willamette river *pop* 107,786 4 town W *cen* Va. WNW of Roanoke *pop* 23,756 5 city S India in N Tamil Nadu SW of Madras *pop* 515,021

Sa·ler·no \sə-'lər-(,)nō, -'ler-\ commune & port S Italy on **Gulf of Salerno** (inlet of Tyrrhenian Sea) ESE of Naples *pop* 152,159 — **Sa·ler·ni·tan** \-'lər-nə-tən, -'ler-\ *adj or n*

Sal·ford \'sȯl-fərd\ urban area NW England in Greater Manchester *pop* 98,024

Sa·li·na \sə-'lī-nə\ city *cen* Kans. on Smoky Hill River *pop* 42,303

Sa·li·nas \sə-'lē-nəs\ 1 river 150 *mi* (241 *km*) W Calif. flowing NW into Monterey Bay 2 city W Calif. near Monterey Bay *pop* 108,777

Salinas National Monument reservation *cen* N. Mex. containing archaeological ruins

Salis·bury \'sȯlz-,ber-ē, -b(ə-)rē, US also 'salz-\ 1 city SE Md. *pop* 20,592 2 city W *cen* N.C. SSW of Winston-Salem *pop* 23,087 3 — see HARARE 4 city & borough S England in Wiltshire on the Avon *pop* 35,355

Salisbury Plain plateau S England in Wiltshire NW of Salisbury

Salm·on \'sa-mən\ river 420 *mi* (676 *km*) *cen* Idaho flowing into Snake River

Salmon River Mountains mountains *cen* Idaho; many peaks over 9000 *ft* (2743 *m*)

Salonika — see THESSALONÍKI

Salonika, Gulf of — see THERMAĪKÓS KÓLPOS

Sal·op \'sa-ləp\ or *formerly* **Shrop·shire** \'shräp-,shir, -shər\ 1 county W England bordering on Wales ✳ Shrewsbury *area* 1347 *sq mi* (3502 *sq km*), *pop* 382,100 2 — see SHREWSBURY — **Sa·lo·pi·an** \sə-'lō-pē-ən\ *adj or n*

Salt \'sȯlt\ 1 river 200 *mi* (322 *km*) Ariz. flowing W into the Gila 2 river 100 *mi* (161 *km*) N *cen* Ky. flowing into Ohio River 3 river 200 *mi* (322 *km*) NE Mo. flowing SE into Mississippi River

Sal·ta \'säl-tə\ city NW Argentina *pop* 260,323

Sal·ti·llo \säl-'tē-(,)yō, sal-\ city NE Mexico ✳ of Coahuila *pop* 200,712

Salt Lake City city N Utah, its ✳ *pop* 159,936

Sal·to \'säl-(,)tō\ city & port NW Uruguay on Uruguay River *pop* 74,881

\ə\ abut \ᵊ\ kitten, F table \ər\ further \a\ ash \ā\ ace \ä\ mop, mar \aů\ out \ch\ chin \e\ bet \ē\ easy \g\ go \i\ hit \ī\ ice \j\ job \ŋ\ sing \ō\ go \ȯ\ law \ȯi\ boy \th\ thin \ṯẖ\ the \ü\ loot \ů\ foot \y\ yet \zh\ vision \à, k̲, ⁿ, œ, œ̄, ᵫ, ūē, ᵊ\ *see* Guide to Pronunciation

Sal·ton Sea \'sȯl-t°n\ saline lake *ab* 235 *ft* (72 *m*) below sea level SE Calif. at N end of Imperial Valley formed by diversion of water from Colorado River into depression called **Salton Sink**

Salt sea — see DEAD SEA

Sa·lu·da \sǝ-'lü-dǝ\ river 200 *mi* (322 *km*) W *cen* S.C. flowing SE to unite with Broad River forming the Congaree

Sal·va·dor \'sal-vǝ-ˌdȯr, ˌsal-vǝ-'\ **1** EL SALVADOR **2** *or formerly* **São Salvador** \saủⁿ-\ *or* **Ba·hia** \bǝ-'ē-ǝ\ port NE Brazil ✻ of Bahia *pop* 2,000,000 — **Sal·va·do·ran** \ˌsal-vǝ-'dȯr-ǝn, -'dōr-\ *adj or n* — **Sal·va·do·re·an** *or* **Sal·va·do·ri·an** \-ē-ǝn\ *adj or n*

Sal·ween \'sal-ˌwēn\ river 1750 *mi* (2816 *km*) SE Asia flowing from Tibet S into Gulf of Martaban in Myanmar

Salz·burg \'sȯlz-ˌbǝrg, 'sälz-, 'salz-, 'sōlts-, -ˌbừrg, *G* 'zälts-ˌbừrk\ city W Austria ESE of Munich, Germany *pop* 143,971

Salz·git·ter \'zälts-ˌgi-tǝr\ *or formerly* **Wa·ten·stedt–Salzgitter** \'vä-t°n-ˌshtet, -ˌstet\ city N *cen* Germany SW of Brunswick *pop* 113,600

Salz·kam·mer·gut \'zälts-ˌkä-mǝr-ˌgüt\ district N Austria E of Salzburg; chief town Bad Ischl

Samanala — see ADAM'S PEAK

Sa·mar \'sä-ˌmär\ island *cen* Philippines in the Visayans N of Leyte *area* 5050 *sq mi* (13,130 *sq km*)

Sa·ma·ra \sǝ-'mär-ǝ\ *or* 1935–91 **Kuy·by·shev** \'kwē-bǝ-ˌshef, 'kü-ē-bǝ-, -ˌshev\ city E Russia in Europe in valley of the Volga *pop* 1,047,000

Sa·mar·ia \sǝ-'mer-ē-ǝ, -'mar-\ **1** district of ancient Palestine W of the Jordan bet. Galilee & Judaea **2** city, its ✻ & ✻ of the Northern Kingdom (Israel); rebuilt by Herod the Great & renamed **Se·bas·te** \sǝ-'bas-tē\; site in Jordan at modern village of Sebastye

Sam·a·rin·da \ˌsa-mǝ-'rin-dǝ\ city Indonesia in E Borneo *pop* 407,339

Sam·ar·kand \'sa-mǝr-ˌkand\ *or anc* **Mar·a·can·da** \ˌmar-ǝ-'kan-dǝ\ city E Uzbekistan *pop* 477,000

Sam·ni·um \'sam-nē-ǝm\ ancient country *cen* Italy E & SE of Latium

Sa·moa \sǝ-'mō-ǝ\ *or formerly* **Navigators Islands** islands SW *cen* Pacific N of Tonga Islands; divided at long. 171°W into American, or Eastern, Samoa & Western Samoa *area* 1209 *sq mi* (3143 *sq km*)

Sa·mos \'sā-ˌmäs, 'sä-ˌmȯs\ island Greece in the Aegean off coast of Turkey N of the Dodecanese *area* 171 *sq mi* (445 *sq km*) *pop* 41,850 — **Sa·mi·an** \'sā-mē-ǝn\ *adj or n*

Sam·o·thrace \'sa-mǝ-ˌthrās\ *or NGk* **Sa·mo·thrá·ke** \ˌsä-mō-'thrä-kē\ island Greece in the NE Aegean — **Sam·o·thra·cian** \ˌsa-mǝ-'thrā-shǝn\ *adj or n*

Sam·sun \säm-'sün\ city & port N Turkey on Black Sea NW of Ankara *pop* 107,510

San·'a \sa-'nä, 'sa-ˌnä\ city S Arabia ✻ of Yemen & formerly ✻ of Yemen Arab Republic *pop* 125,093

Sa·nan·daj \ˌsä-nǝn-'däj\ city NW Iran *pop* 204,537

San An·dre·as Fault \ˌsan-an-'drā-ǝs\ zone of faults Calif. extending from N coast toward head of Gulf of California

San An·ge·lo \san-'an-jǝ-ˌlō\ city W *cen* Tex. *pop* 84,474

San An·to·nio \ˌsan-ǝn-'tō-nē-ˌō\ **1** river 200 *mi* (322 *km*) S Tex. flowing SE into Gulf of Mexico **2** city S Tex. on San Antonio River *pop* 935,933 — **San An·to·ni·an** \-nē-ǝn\ *n*

San Be·ni·to \ˌsan-bǝ-'nē-(ˌ)tō\ city S Tex. NW of Brownsville *pop* 20,125

San Ber·nar·di·no \ˌsan-ˌbǝr-nǝ(r)-'dē-(ˌ)nō\ city SW Calif. E of Los Angeles *pop* 164,164

San Bernardino Mountains mountains S Calif. S of Mojave Desert; highest **San Gor·go·nio Mountain** \ˌsan-gȯr-'gō-nē-(ˌ)ō\ 11,502 *ft* (3506 *m*)

San Bru·no \san-'brü-(ˌ)nō\ city W Calif. S of San Francisco *pop* 38,961

San Buenaventura — see VENTURA

San Car·los \san-'kär-lǝs\ city W Calif. SE of San Francisco *pop* 26,167

San Carlos de Bariloche — see BARILOCHE

San Cle·men·te \san-klǝ-'men-tē\ city W Calif. NW of San Diego *pop* 41,100

San Clemente Island island S Calif., southernmost of Channel Islands

San Cris·to·bal \san-kri-'stō-bǝl\ island W Pacific in SE Solomons

San Cris·tó·bal \san-kri-'stō-bǝl\ **1** *or* **Chatham Island** island Ecuador in the Galápagos *pop* 1404 **2** city W Venezuela SSW of Lake Maracaibo *pop* 220,675

Sanc·ti Spí·ri·tus \ˌsäŋk-tē-'spir-ǝ-ˌtüs\ city W *cen* Cuba SE of Santa Clara *pop* 103,116

San·cy, Puy de \ˌpwē-dǝ-ˌsäⁿ-'sē\ mountain 6188 *ft* (1886 *m*) S *cen* France; highest in the Monts Dore & Auvergne Mountains

San·da·kan \san-'dä-kǝn\ city & port Malaysia in Sabah on Sulu Sea; former ✻ of N. Borneo *pop* 118,417

Sand·hurst \'sand-ˌhǝrst\ village S England in E Berkshire SE of Reading *pop* 6445

San·dia Mountains \san-'dē-ǝ\ mountains N *cen* N.Mex. E of Albuquerque; highest **Sandia Crest** 10,678 *ft* (3255 *m*)

San Di·e·go \ˌsan-dē-'ā-(ˌ)gō\ city & port SW Calif. on **San Diego Bay** (inlet of the Pacific) *pop* 1,110,549 — **San Di·e·gan** \-gǝn\ *adj or n*

San Di·mas \san-'dē-mǝs\ city SW Calif. NW of Pomona *pop* 32,397

San Domingo 1 — see HISPANIOLA **2** — see DOMINICAN REPUBLIC **3** — see SANTO DOMINGO

San·dring·ham \'san-driŋ-ǝm\ village E England in NW Norfolk

San·dus·ky \san-'dǝs-kē, sǝn-\ **1** river 150 *mi* (241 *km*) N Ohio flowing N into Lake Erie **2** city N Ohio at entrance to **Sandusky Bay** (inlet of Lake Erie) *pop* 29,764

Sand·wich \'san(d)-(ˌ)wich\ borough SE England in Kent on Stour River *pop* 4227

Sandwich Islands — see HAWAII

Sandy \'san-dē\ city N Utah S of Salt Lake City *pop* 75,058

Sandy Hook peninsula E N.J. extending N toward New York Bay

San Fer·nan·do \ˌsan-fǝr-'nan-(ˌ)dō\ **1** valley S Calif. NW of Los Angeles; partly within Los Angeles city limits **2** city SW Calif. in San Fernando Valley *pop* 22,580

San·ford \'san-fǝrd\ **1** city NE Fla. *pop* 32,387 **2** town SW Maine *pop* 20,463

Sanford, Mount mountain 16,237 *ft* (4949 *m*) S Alaska at W end of Wrangell Mountains

San Fran·cis·co \ˌsan-frǝn-'sis-(ˌ)kō\ city & port W Calif. on **San Francisco Bay** & the Pacific *pop* 723,959 — **San Fran·cis·can** \-kǝn\ *adj or n*

San Francisco Peaks mountain N *cen* Ariz. N of Flagstaff; includes three peaks: Mt. Humphreys 12,633 *ft* (3851 *m*), highest point in the state; Mt. Agassiz 12,340 *ft* (3761 *m*); & Mt. Fremont 11,940 *ft* (3639 *m*)

San Ga·bri·el \san-'gā-brē-ǝl\ city SW Calif. S of Pasadena *pop* 37,120

San Gabriel Mountains mountains S Calif. SW of Mojave Desert & NE of Los Angeles; highest San Antonio Peak 10,080 *ft* (3072 *m*)

San·ga·mon \'saŋ-gǝ-mǝn\ river 225 *mi* (362 *km*) *cen* Ill. flowing SW & W into Illinois River

San·gay \säŋ-'gī\ volcano 17,159 *ft* (5230 *m*) SE *cen* Ecuador

San·gi·he Islands \ˌsäŋ-gē-'ā\ *or* **San·gi Islands** \'säŋ-gē\ islands Indonesia NE of Sulawesi *area* 134 *sq mi* (348 *sq km*), *pop* 194,253; largest of the group **Sangihe** *or* **Sangi**

San Gi·mi·gna·no \ˌsän-jē-mē-'nyä-(ˌ)nō\ commune *cen* Italy NW of Siena

San·gre de Cris·to Mountains \ˌsaŋ-grē-dǝ-'kris-(ˌ)tō\ mountains S Colo. & N N.Mex. in Rocky Mountains — see BLANCA PEAK

San·i·bel Island \'sa-nǝ-bǝl, -ˌbel\ island SW Fla. SW of Fort Myers

San Il·de·fon·so \ˌsan-ˌil-dǝ-'fän(t)-(ˌ)sō\ *or* **La Gran·ja** \lǝ-'grän-(ˌ)hä\ commune *cen* Spain SE of Segovia

San Isi·dro \ˌsan-ǝ-'sē-(ˌ)drō\ city E Argentina *pop* 287,048

San Ja·cin·to \ˌsan-jǝ-'sin-tǝ, -hǝ-'sin-\ river 100 *mi* (161 *km*) SE Tex. flowing S into Galveston Bay

San Joa·quin \ˌsan-wä-'kēn, -wȯ-\ river 350 *mi* (563 *km*) *cen* Calif. flowing from the Sierra Nevada SW & then NW into Sacramento River

San Jo·se \ˌsan-ǝ-'zā\ *also* ˌsan-(h)ō-'zā\ city W Calif. SSE of San Francisco *pop* 782,248

San Jo·sé \ˌsan-ǝ-'zā, ˌsan-(h)ō-'zā\ city *cen* Costa Rica, its ✻ *pop* 203,148

San Juan \san-'wän, -'hwän\ **1** river 360 *mi* (579 *km*) SW Colo., NW N.Mex., & SE Utah flowing W into Colorado River **2** city & port NE Puerto Rico, its ✻ *pop* 437,745 **3** city W Argentina N of Mendoza *pop* 106,564 — **San Jua·ne·ro** \ˌsan-wä-'ner-(ˌ)ō, -'hwä-\ *n*

San Juan Cap·is·tra·no \ˌka-pǝ-'strä-(ˌ)nō\ city SW Calif. SE of Los Angeles *pop* 26,183

San Juan Hill hill E Cuba near Santiago de Cuba

San Juan Islands islands NW Wash. bet. Vancouver Is. & the mainland

San Juan Mountains mountains SW Colo. in the Rocky Mountains — see UNCOMPAHGRE PEAK

Sankt An·ton am Arl·berg \zäŋkt-'än-ˌtōn-äm-'är(-ǝ)l-ˌbǝrg, -ˌberk\ village W Austria in Tirol W of Innsbruck

Sankt Gallen — see SAINT GALL

Sankt Moritz — see SAINT MORITZ

San Le·an·dro \ˌsan-lē-'an-(ˌ)drō\ city W Calif. SE of Oakland *pop* 68,223

San Lo·ren·zo \ˌsan-lǝ-'ren-(ˌ)zō\ city S Paraguay E of Asunción

San Lu·cas, Cape \san-'lü-kǝs\ headland NW Mexico, the S extremity of Baja California

San Lu·is \san-'lü-ǝs\ valley S Colo. & N N.Mex. along the upper Rio Grande bet. the San Juan & Sangre de Cristo mountains

San Lu·is Obis·po \san-ˌlü-ǝs-ǝ-'bis-(ˌ)pō\ city W Calif. NW of Santa Barbara *pop* 41,958

San Lu·is Po·to·sí \ˌsän-lü-ˌēs-ˌpō-tǝ-'sē\ **1** state *cen* Mexico *area* 24,415 *sq mi* (63,479 *sq km*), *pop* 1,670,637 **2** city, its ✻, NE of León *pop* 274,320

San Mar·cos \san-'mär-kǝs\ **1** city SW Calif. NNW of San Diego *pop* 38,974 **2** city S Tex. NE of San Antonio *pop* 28,743

San Ma·ri·no \ˌsan-mǝ-'rē-(ˌ)nō\ **1** country S Europe on Italian peninsula SSW of Rimini; a republic *area* 24 *sq mi* (62 *sq km*), *pop* 19,149 **2** town, its ✻ — **Sam·mar·i·nese** \ˌsa(m)-ˌmar-ǝ-'nēz, -'nēs\ *n* — **San Mar·i·nese** \ˌsan-ˌmar-\ *adj or n*

San Mar·tín \ˌsan-mär-'tēn\ *or* **Ge·ne·ral San Martín** \ˌhä-nǝ-'räl\ city E Argentina, NW suburb of Buenos Aires *pop* 384,306

San Ma·teo \ˌsan-mǝ-'tā-(ˌ)ō\ city W Calif. SSE of San Francisco *pop* 85,486

San Mi·guel de Tu·cu·mán \ˌsan-mi-'gel-dǝ-ˌtü-kǝ-'män\ *or* **Tucumán** city NW Argentina at foot of E ranges of the Andes *pop* 271,546

San Pab·lo \san-'pa-(ˌ)blō\ city W Calif. N of Oakland on **San Pablo Bay** (N extension of San Francisco Bay) *pop* 25,158

San Pe·dro Channel \san-'pē-(ˌ)drō, -'pä-\ channel SW Calif. bet. Santa Catalina Is. & the mainland

San Pe·dro Su·la \san-'pā-(ˌ)drō-'sü-lǝ\ city NW Honduras *pop* 300,400

San Ra·fael \ˌsan-rǝ-'fel\ city W Calif. N of San Francisco on San Pablo Bay *pop* 48,404

San Ra·mon \ˌsan-rǝ-'mōn\ city W Calif. E of Oakland *pop* 35,303

San Re·mo \san-'rä-(ˌ)mō, sän-'rē-\ city & port NW Italy in Liguria near French border *pop* 59,635

San Sal·va·dor \san-'sal-vǝ-ˌdȯr\ **1** island *cen* Bahama Islands *area* 60 *sq mi* (156 *sq km*) **2** city W *cen* El Salvador, its ✻ *pop* 349,333

San Se·bas·tián \ˌsan-si-'bas-chǝn, ˌsän-ˌse-bäs-'chän\ city & port N Spain ✻ of Guipúzcoa on Bay of Biscay *pop* 172,303

San Stefano — see YESILKOY

San·ta Ana \ˌsan-tǝ-'a-nǝ\ **1** city SW Calif. ESE of Long Beach *pop* 293,742 **2** city NW El Salvador NW of San Salvador *pop* 168,047

Santa Bar·ba·ra \ˌbär-b(ǝ-)rǝ\ city S Calif. *pop* 85,571

Santa Barbara Channel channel SW Calif. bet. the N Channel Islands & mainland

Santa Barbara Islands — see CHANNEL ISLANDS

Santa Catalina — see CATALINA

San·ta Ca·ta·ri·na \ˌsan-tǝ-ˌka-tǝ-'rē-nǝ\ state S Brazil bordering on the Atlantic ✻ Florianópolis *area* 31,118 *sq mi* (80,907 *sq km*), *pop* 3,687,652

Santa Clara \'klar-ǝ, 'kler-\ **1** city W Calif. NW of San Jose *pop* 93,613 **2** city W *cen* Cuba *pop* 189,092

San·ta Cla·ri·ta \klǝ-'rē-tǝ\ city SW Calif. *pop* 110,642

Santa Cruz \'krüz\ **1** island SW Calif. in NW Channel Islands **2** city W Calif. S of San Jose on Monterey Bay *pop* 49,040 **3** — see SAINT CROIX **4** river 250 *mi* (402 *km*) S Argentina flowing E into the Atlantic **5** city E Bolivia *pop* 254,682

Santa Cruz de Te·ne·ri·fe \də-,te-nə-'rē-(,)fā, -'ref, -'rif\ **1** province Spain comprising W Canary Islands *area* 1528 *sq mi* (3973 *sq km*), *pop* 762,503 **2** city & port, its ✳, on NE Tenerife Is. *pop* 185,899

Santa Cruz Islands islands SW Pacific in SE Solomons N of Vanuatu, chief island Ndeni; until 1978 administratively attached to Brit. Solomon Islands *area* 380 *sq mi* (988 *sq km*)

San·ta Fe \,san-tə-'fā\ **1** city ✳ of N.Mex. *pop* 55,859 **2** city *cen* Argentina on Salado River *pop* 287,240 — **Santa Fe-an** \'fā-ən\ *n*

Santa Fe Trail pioneer route to the Southwest used esp. 1821–80 from vicinity of Kansas City, Mo., to Santa Fe, N.Mex.

San·ta Is·a·bel \,san-tə-'i-zə-,bel\ **1** island W Pacific in the E *cen* Solomons NE of Guadalcanal *area* 1500 *sq mi* (3900 *sq km*) **2** — see MALABO

Santa Ma·ria \mə-'rē-ə\ city W Calif. NW of Santa Barbara *pop* 61,284

Santa Ma·ría \mə-'rē-ə\ volcano 12,362 *ft* (3768 *m*) W Guatemala

Santa Mar·ta \'mär-tə\ city & port N Colombia on the Caribbean E of Barranquilla *pop* 137,474

Santa Mon·i·ca \'mä-ni-kə\ city SW Calif. adjacent to Los Angeles on **Santa Monica Bay** (inlet of the Pacific) *pop* 86,905

San·tan·der \,sän-,tän-'der, ,san-,tan-\ **1** province N Spain in N Old Castile bordering on Bay of Biscay *area* 2108 *sq mi* (5481 *sq km*), *pop* 507,489 **2** city & port, its ✳, on Bay of Biscay *pop* 179,694

San·ta Pau·la \,san-tə-'pȯ-lə\ city SW Calif. NW of Los Angeles *pop* 25,062

San·ta·rém \,san-tə-'rem\ city N Brazil in W Pará at confluence of the Tapajoz & the Amazon *pop* 192,203

San·ta Ro·sa \,san-tə-'rō-zə\ city W Calif. N of San Francisco *pop* 113,313

Santa Rosa Island island SW Calif. in NW Channel Islands

San·tee \,san-'tē, 'san-,\ river 143 *mi* (230 *km*) S.C. flowing SE into the Atlantic — see CONGAREE **2** city S Calif., a suburb of San Diego *pop* 52,902

San·ti·a·go \,san-tē-'ä-(,)gō, ,sän-\ **1** city *cen* Chile, its ✳ *metropolitan area pop* 3,902,356 **2** *or* **Santiago de los Ca·ba·lle·ros** \də-lȯs-,kä-bə-'yȯs\ city N *cen* Dominican Republic *pop* 382,244 **3** *or* **Santiago de Com·pos·te·la** \də-,käm-pə-'ste-lə, -,kȯm-\ commune NW Spain *pop* 70,893 — **San·ti·a·gan** \,san-tē-'ä-gən, ,sän-\ *n*

Santiago de Cu·ba \də-'kyü-bə\ city & port SE Cuba *pop* 403,604

Santiago del Es·te·ro \(,)del-ə-'ster-(,)ō\ city N Argentina SE of San Miguel de Tucumán *pop* 148,357

San·to Do·min·go \,san-tə-də-'miŋ,(,)gō\ **1** *or* **Santo Domingo de Guz·mán** \də-güs-'män\ *or formerly* **Tru·ji·llo** \trü-'hē,(,)yō\ *or* **Ciu·dad Trujillo** \,sē-ü-'thä(th), sē-ü-'dad\ city & port ✳ of Dominican Republic on Caribbean Sea *pop* 654,757 **2** — see HISPANIOLA **3** — see DOMINICAN REPUBLIC — **San·to Do·min·gan** \,san-tə-də-'miŋ-gən\ *adj or n*

San·to·rin \,san-tə-'rēn, -'rin\ *or NGk* **San·to·rí·ni** \-'rē-nē\ *or* **Thí·ra** \'thir-ə\ *or anc* **The·ra** \'thir-ə\ island Greece in S Cyclades *area* 30 *sq mi* (78 *sq km*)

San·tos \'san-təs\ city & port SE Brazil in SE São Paulo state SSE of São Paulo on an island in a tidal inlet *pop* 416,784

San·tur·ce \,sän-'túr-(,)sā\ a NE section of San Juan, Puerto Rico

São Fran·cis·co \,saúⁿ(m)-fran-'sis-(,)kō\ river 1800 *mi* (2897 *km*) E Brazil flowing from S *cen* Minas Gerais NE & E into the Atlantic

São Luís \,saú-lü-'ēs\ city & port NE Brazil ✳ of Maranhão state on Maranhão Is. *pop* 449,877

São Ma·nuel \,saúⁿ-mən-'wel\ river 600 *mi* (966 *km*), *cen* Brazil flowing NW to join the Juruena forming the Tapajoz

São Mi·guel \,saúⁿ-mi-'gel\ island Portugal in E Azores; chief town Ponta Delgada *area* 297 *sq mi* (772 *sq km*)

Saône \'sōn\ river 275 *mi* (442 *km*) E France flowing SSW into the Rhône

São Pau·lo \saúⁿ(m)-'paú-(,)lü, -(,)lō\ **1** state SE Brazil *area* 95,459 *sq mi* (248,193 *sq km*), *pop* 25,375,199 **2** city, its ✳ *pop* 10,900,000

São Ro·que, Cabo de \saúⁿ-'rȯ-kə\ headland NE Brazil N of Natal

São Salvador — see SALVADOR

São Tia·go \,saúⁿ(n)-tē-'ä-(,)gü, -(,)gō\ island Cape Verde Islands, largest of the group; chief town Praia *area* 359 *sq mi* (933 *sq km*)

São To·mé \,saúⁿ(n)-tə-'mā\ island W Africa in Gulf of Guinea; with Principe Is., forms the republic (until 1975 a Portuguese territory) of **São Tomé and Principe** (✳ São Tomé *area* 377 *sq mi* or 980 *sq km*, *pop* 89,000)

São Vicente, Cabo de — see SAINT VINCENT (Cape)

Sap·po·ro \'sä-pə-,rō; sə-'pōr-(,)ō, -'pȯr-\ city Japan on W Hokkaido *pop* 1,671,765

Saq·qâ·ra *or* **Saq·qā·rah** *or* **Sak·ka·ra** \sə-'kär-ə\ village N Egypt SW of ruins of Memphis

Sarabat — see GEDIZ

Saragossa — see ZARAGOZA

Sa·ra·je·vo \,sar-ə-'yā-(,)vō, ,sär-ə-; 'sär-ə-ye-,vō\ city SE *cen* Bosnia and Herzegovina, its ✳ *pop* 223,000

Sar·a·nac \'sar-ə-,nak\ river 100 *mi* (161 *km*) NE N.Y. flowing NE from **Saranac Lakes** (three lakes in the Adirondacks: Upper Saranac, Middle Saranac, & Lower Saranac) into Lake Champlain

Sa·ransk \sə-'rän(t)sk, -'ran(t)sk\ city *cen* Russia in Europe ✳ of Mordvinian Republic *pop* 190,000

Sar·a·so·ta \,sar-ə-'sō-tə\ city W Fla. S of Tampa *pop* 50,961

Sar·a·to·ga \,sar-ə-'tō-gə\ city W Calif. SW of San Jose *pop* 28,061

Saratoga Lake lake 7 *mi* (11 *km*) long E N.Y. S of Lake George

Saratoga Springs *or* **Saratoga** city NE N.Y. *pop* 25,001

Sa·ra·tov \sə-'rä-təf\ city *cen* Russia in Europe on a reservoir of the Volga *pop* 758,000

Sa·ra·wak \sə-'rä-(,)wä(k), -,wak\ state Malaysia in N Borneo, formerly a Brit. colony ✳ Kuching *area* 47,000 *sq mi* (122,200 *sq km*), *pop* 1,294,753

Sardica — see SOFIA

Sar·din·ia \sär-'di-nē-ə, -'di-nyə\ *or It* **Sar·de·gna** \sär-'dā-nyə\ island Italy S of Corsica; with surrounding smaller islands, constitutes a region of Italy ✳ Cagliari *area* 9283 *sq mi* (24,136 *sq km*), *pop* 1,657,562

Sar·dis \'sär-dəs\ *or* **Sar·des** \(,)dēz\ ancient city W Asia Minor ✳ of ancient kingdom of Lydia; site E of Izmir — **Sar·di·an** \'sär-dē-ən\ *adj or n*

Sa·re·ma *or Estonian* **Saa·re·maa** \'sär-ə-,mä\ island Estonia at mouth of Gulf of Riga *area* 1010 *sq mi* (2626 *sq km*)

Sa·re·ra Bay \sə-'rer-ə\ *or formerly* **Geel·vink Bay** \'gā(ə)l-(,)viŋk, 'kā(ə)l-\ inlet Indonesia in N W. Irian

Sar·gas·so Sea \sär-'ga-(,)sō\ tract of comparatively still water N Atlantic lying chiefly bet. 25° & 35°N & 40° & 70°W

Sark \'särk\ island in the English Channel, one of the Channel Islands; a dependency of Guernsey *area* 2 *sq mi* (5.2 *sq km*) — **Sark·ese** \,sär-'kēz, -'kēs\ *n*

Sar·ma·tia \sär-'mā-sh(ē-)ə\ ancient region E Europe in modern Poland & Russia bet. the Vistula & the Volga — **Sar·ma·tian** \-shən\ *adj or n*

Sar·nia–Clear·wa·ter \'sär-nē-ə-'klir-,wȯ-tər, -,wä-\ city Canada in SE Ont. on St. Clair River opposite Port Huron, Mich. *pop* 74,376

Sa·ron·ic Gulf \sə-'rä-nik\ inlet of the Aegean SE Greece bet. Attica & the Peloponnisos

Sa·ros, Gulf of \'sar-,äs, 'ser-\ inlet of the Aegean SW Turkey in Europe N of Gallipoli Peninsula

Sarre — see SAAR

Sarthe \'särt\ river 175 *mi* (282 *km*) NW France flowing S to unite with the Mayenne forming Maine River

Sarum OLD SARUM

Sa·se·bo \'sä-sə-,bō\ city & port Japan in NW Kyushu on an inlet of E. China Sea *pop* 244,693

Sas·katch·e·wan \sə-'ska-chə-wən, sa-, -,wän\ **1** river 340 *mi* (547 *km*) S *cen* Canada formed by confluence in *cen* Sask. of two branches rising in the Rockies in Alta., the **North Saskatchewan** (760 *mi or* 1216 *km*) & the **South Saskatchewan** (865 *mi or* 1384 *km*), & flowing E into Lake Winnipeg **2** province SW Canada ✳ Regina *area* 237,975 *sq mi* (618,735 *sq km*), *pop* 988,928 — **Sas·katch·e·wan·ian** \-,ska-chə-'wä-nē-ən\ *adj or n*

Sas·ka·toon \,sas-kə-'tün\ city Canada in *cen* Sask. on S. Saskatchewan River *pop* 186,058

Sas·sa·ri \'sä-sə-(,)rē\ commune Italy in NW Sardinia *pop* 119,717

Sa·til·la \sə-'ti-lə\ river 220 *mi* (354 *km*) SE Ga. flowing E into the Atlantic

Sat·pu·ra Range \'sät-pə-rə\ range of hills W *cen* India bet. the Narmada & the Tapti

Sa·tu-Ma·re \,sä-(,)tü-'mär-(,)ä\ city NW Romania in Transylvania on the Somes *pop* 136,881

Sau·di Arabia \'saú-dē, 'sȯ-dē, sä-'ü-dē\ country SW Asia occupying most of Arabian Peninsula; a kingdom, comprising former kingdoms of Nejd & Hejaz & principality of Asir ✳ Riyadh *area* 870,000 *sq mi* (2,262,000 *sq km*), *pop* 12,000,000 — **Saudi** *adj or n* — **Saudi Arabian** *adj or n*

Sau·gus \'sȯ-gəs\ town NE Mass. W of Lynn *pop* 25,549

Sault Sainte Ma·rie \'sü-(,)sänt-mə-'rē\ city Canada in Ont., across the St. Marys River from Michigan *pop* 81,476

Sault Sainte Marie Canals *or* **Soo Canals** \'sü\ three ship canals, two in the U.S. & one in Canada, at rapids in St. Marys River connecting Lake Superior & Lake Huron

Sau·mur \sō-'múr, -'myúr, -'mūer\ commune NW France on the Loire SE of Angers *pop* 30,984

Sau·rash·tra \saú-'räsh-trə\ former state (1948–56) W India on Kathiawar peninsula; in Bombay state 1956–60 & since 1960 in Gujarat

Sa·va \'sä-və\ river 450 *mi* (724 *km*) flowing from Italian border E through Slovenia, into Croatia, along Croatia-Bosnia and Herzegovina border, & into Yugoslavia where it flows into the Danube at Belgrade

Sa·vaii \sə-'vī-,ē\ island SW *cen* Pacific, largest in Samoa, in W. Samoa

Sa·van·nah \sə-'va-nə\ **1** river 314 *mi* (505 *km*) E Ga. flowing SE to the Atlantic & forming Ga.-S.C. boundary **2** city & port E Ga. at mouth of Savannah River *pop* 137,560

Save — see SABI

Sa·vo \'sä-(,)vō\ island W Pacific in SE Solomons N of W Guadalcanal

Sa·vo·na \sə-'vō-nə\ commune & port NW Italy SW of Genoa *pop* 69,806

Sa·voy \sə-'vȯi\ *or F* **Sa·voie** \sá-vwä\ *or It* **Sa·vo·ia** \sä-'vȯ-yä\ region SE France in Savoy Alps SW of Switzerland & bordering on Italy; duchy 1416–1720, part of kingdom of Sardinia 1720–1860; became part of France 1860 — **Sa·voy·ard** \sə-'vȯi-,ärd, ,sa-,vȯi-'ärd, ,sa-,vwä-'yär(d)\ *adj or n*

Savoy Alps section of W Alps SE France — see MONT BLANC

Sa·watch Range \sə-'wäch, 'sȯ-wȯsh\ mountain range *cen* Colo. in Rocky Mountains — see ELBERT (Mount)

Saxe \'saks\ SAXONY — its French form, used in English chiefly in names of former duchies in Thuringia: **Saxe–Al·ten·burg** \-'äl-t²n-,búrg\, **Saxe–Co·burg** \-'kō-,bərg\, **Saxe–Go·tha** \-'gō-tə, -thə\, **Saxe–Mei·ning·en** \-'mī-niŋ-ən\, & **Saxe–Wei·mar–Ei·se·nach** \-'vī-,mär-'ī-z²n-,äk, -,äk\

Sax·o·ny \'sak-s(ə-)nē\ *or G* **Sach·sen** \'zäk-sən\ **1** region & former duchy NW Germany S of Jutland peninsula between the Elbe & the Rhine — see LOWER SAXONY **2** region & former state E Germany N of the Erzgebirge — see SAXE

Sa·yan Mountains \sə-'yän\ mountains S Russia in Asia on border of Tuva N of Altai Mountains

Sayre·ville \'sar-, vil\ borough E *cen* N.J. *pop* 34,986

Sa·zan \'sä-,zän\ *or It* **Sa·se·no** \sə-'zä-(,)nō, sä-\ island Albania in N Strait of Otranto

Sca·fell \skȯ-'fel\ mountain 3162 *ft* (964 *m*) NW England in Cumbrians SW of Keswick; second highest peak in England

Scafell Pike mountain 3210 *ft* (978 *m*) NW England in Cumbria NE of Scafell; highest in the Cumbrians & in England

Scamander — see MENDERES

Scan·di·na·via \,skan-də-'nä-vē-ə, -vyə\ **1** peninsula N Europe occupied by Norway & Sweden **2** Denmark, Norway, Sweden, & sometimes also Iceland, the Faeroe Islands, & Finland

Scapa Flow \,ska-pə-'flō\ sea basin N Scotland in the Orkneys

---

\ə\ abut \ᵊ\ kitten, F table \ər\ further \a\ ash \ā\ ace \ä\ mop, mar \aú\ out \ch\ chin \e\ bet \ē\ easy \g\ go \i\ hit \ī\ ice \j\ job \ŋ\ sing \ō\ go \ȯ\ law \ȯi\ boy \th\ thin \t͟h\ the \ü\ loot \ú\ foot \y\ yet \zh\ vision \à, k̟, ⁿ, œ, œ̄, ᴜe, ūe, ᵊ\ *see* Guide to Pronunciation

Scar·bor·ough \'skär-,bər-ə, -,bə-rə, -b(ə-)rə\ **1** city Canada in SE Ont. near Toronto *pop* 524,598 **2** borough & port NE England in N. Yorkshire *pop* 43,103

Schaer·beek *or* **Schaar·beek** \'skär-,bāk, 'skar-\ commune *cen* Belgium, NE suburb of Brussels *pop* 102,702

Schaff·hau·sen \shäf-'haů-z⁸n\ **1** canton N Switzerland bordering on SW Germany *area* 114 *sq mi* (296 *sq km*), *pop* 71,210 **2** commune, its ✳ *pop* 34,101

Schaum·burg \'shäm-(,)bərg\ village NE Ill. NW of Chicago *pop* 68,586

Schaum·burg–Lip·pe \'shaům-,bùrk-'li-pə\ state of Germany 1918–33 in NW bet. Westphalia & Hannover

Scheldt \'skelt\ *or* **Schel·de** \'skel-də\ *or F* **Es·caut** \e-skō\ river 270 *mi* (434 *km*) W Europe flowing from N France through Belgium into North Sea in Netherlands

Sche·nec·ta·dy \skə-'nek-tə-dē\ city E N.Y. *pop* 65,566

Scher·er·ville \'shir-ər-,vil\ town NW Ind. *pop* 19,926

Sche·ve·ning·en \'skā-və-,niŋ-ə(n), 'skā-\ town SW Netherlands on North Sea W of The Hague

Schie·dam \skē-'däm, skē-\ commune SW Netherlands *pop* 71,281

Schles·wig \'shles-(,)wig, 'sles-, -(,)vik\ **1** *or Dan* **Sles·vig** \'slis-vē\ region N Germany & S Denmark in S Jutland Peninsula **2** city N Germany *pop ab* 29,798

Schleswig–Hol·stein \-'hōl-,stīn, -,shtīn\ state of Germany & formerly of W. Germany consisting of Holstein & part of Schleswig ✳ Kiel *area* 6052 *sq mi* (15,735 *sq km*), *pop* 2,611,285

Scho·field Barracks \'skō-,fēld\ city Hawaii in *cen* Oahu *pop* 19,597

Schou·ten Islands \'skaů-t⁸n\ islands Indonesia in N W. Irian at mouth of Sarera Bay *area* 1230 *sq mi* (3198 *sq km*)

Schuyl·kill \'skü-k⁸l\ river 131 *mi* (211 *km*) SE Pa. flowing SE into Delaware River at Philadelphia

Schwaben — see SWABIA

Schwarzwald — see BLACK FOREST

Schwein·furt \'shvīn-,fùrt\ city S *cen* Germany on Main River *pop* 52,445

Schweiz — see SWITZERLAND

Schwe·rin \shvā-'rēn\ city N Germany E of Hamburg *pop* 122,179

Schwyz \'shvēts\ **1** canton E *cen* Switzerland *area* 351 *sq mi* (913 *sq km*), *pop* 108,576 **2** town, its ✳, E of Lucerne *pop* 12,596

Scil·ly, Isles of \'si-lē\ island group SW England off Land's End comprising 140 islands ✳ Hugh Town (on St. Mary's, largest island) *area* 6 *sq mi* (16 *sq km*), *pop* 2428 — see CORNWALL AND ISLES OF SCILLY — **Scil·lo·ni·an** \si-'lō-nē-ən\ *adj or n*

Sci·o·to \sī-'ō-tə\ river 237 *mi* (381 *km*) Ohio flowing S into Ohio River

Scone \'skün\ locality E Scotland NE of Perth *pop* 3713

Sco·pus, Mount \'skō-pəs\ mountain Palestine in W Jordan in small area belonging to Israel

Scores·by Sound \'skòrz-bē, 'skòrz-\ inlet of Norwegian Sea E Greenland N of 70°N

Sco·tia Sea \'skō-shə\ part of the S Atlantic SE of Falkland Islands, W of S. Sandwich Islands, & N of S. Orkney Islands

Scot·land \'skät-lənd\ *or L* **Cal·e·do·nia** \,ka-lə-'dō-nyə, -nē-ə\ ML **Sco·tia** \'skō-shə\ country N Great Britain; a division of United Kingdom of Great Britain and Northern Ireland ✳ Edinburgh *area* 29,794 *sq mi* (77,464 *sq km*), *pop* 5,116,000

Scotts Bluff National Monument \'skäts\ reservation W Nebr. on N. Platte River including **Scotts Bluff** (high butte that was a landmark on the Oregon Trail)

Scotts·dale \'skäts-,dāl\ city SW *cen* Ariz. E of Phoenix *pop* 130,069

Scran·ton \'skran-t⁸n\ city NE Pa. *pop* 81,805

Scun·thorpe \'skən-,thòrp\ borough E England in Humberside WSW of Hull *pop* 66,353

Scu·ta·ri, Lake \'skü-tə-rē\ *or* **Ska·dar·sko Je·ze·ro** \skä-'där-(,)skō-'yä-zə-(,)rō\ lake NW Albania & S Yugoslavia in Montenegro *area* 130 *sq mi* (338 *sq km*)

Scyth·ia \'si-thē-ə, -thē-\ the country of the ancient Scythians comprising parts of Europe & Asia in regions N & NE of Black Sea & E of Aral Sea

Sea Islands islands SE U.S. in the Atlantic off coast of S.C., Ga., & Fla. bet. mouths of Santee & St. Johns rivers

Seal Beach city SW Calif. SE of Los Angeles *pop* 25,098

Sea·side \'sē-,sīd\ city W Calif. on Monterey Bay *pop* 38,901

Se·at·tle \sē-'a-t⁸l\ city & port W Wash. bet. Puget Sound & Lake Washington *pop* 516,259 — **Se·at·tle·ite** \-t⁸l-,īt\ *n*

Se·ba·go Lake \sə-'bā-(,)gō\ lake 13 *mi* (21 *km*) long SW Maine

Sebaste *or* **Sebastia** — see SIVAS   **2** — see SAMARIA

Se·cun·der·a·bad \si-'kən-də-rə-,bad, -,bäd\ city S *cen* India in Andhra Pradesh, NE suburb of Hyderabad *pop* 345,052

Se·da·lia \sə-'dāl-yə\ city W *cen* Mo. *pop* 19,800

Se·dan \si-'dan, F sə-däⁿ\ city NE France on the Meuse NE of Reims *pop* 23,867

Sedge·moor \'sej-,mùr, -,mōr, -,mòr\ tract of moorland SW England in *cen* Somerset

Se·dom \sə-'dōm\ town Israel near S end of Dead Sea

Se·go·via \sä-'gō-vyə, sə-, -vē-ə\ **1** — see COCO **2** province N *cen* Spain in Old Castile *area* 2635 *sq mi* (6851 *sq km*), *pop* 132,467 **3** commune, its ✳, NW of Madrid *pop* 53,366

Seim — see SEYM

Seine \'sān, 'sen\ river 480 *mi* (772 *km*) N France flowing NW into Bay of the Seine (inlet of English Channel)

Se·la·jar *or* **Sa·la·jar** \sə-'lä-,yär\ *or* **Ka·bia** \'kä-bē-ə\ island Indonesia off SW Sulawesi *area* 256 *sq mi* (666 *sq km*), *pop* 87,278

Se·lang·or \sə-'laŋ-ər, -,òr\ state *cen* Malaysia (federation) on Strait of Malacca ✳ Shah Alam *area* 3072 *sq mi* (7987 *sq km*), *pop* 1,467,441

Se·lat Sun·da \sə-'lät-'sün-də, -'sün-\ strait bet. Java & Sumatra

Sel·en·ga \,se-lən-'gä\ river 750 *mi* (1207 *km*) N *cen* Asia rising in W Mongolia & flowing to Lake Baikal

Se·leu·cia \sə-'lü-sh(ē-)ə\ **1** *or* **Seleucia Tra·che·o·tis** \,trä-kē-'ō-təs\ ancient city SE Asia Minor in Cilicia NW of Tarsus **2** ancient city, chief city of the Seleucid Empire; ruins now in Iraq on the Tigris SSE of Baghdad **3** *or* **Seleucia Pi·er·ia** \pī-'ir-ē-ə, -'er-\ ancient city Asia Minor N of mouth of the Orontes; port for Antioch

Sel·kirk \'sel-,kərk\ **1** *or* **Sel·kirk·shire** \-,shir, -shər\ former county SE Scotland **2** burgh *cen* Borders region SE of Edinburgh *pop* 5417

Selkirk Mountains mountains SW Canada in SE B.C. W of the Rockies; highest Mt. Sir Sandford 11,590 *ft* (3533 *m*)

Sel·ma \'sel-mə\ city *cen* Ala. W of Montgomery *pop* 23,755

Se·ma·rang \sə-'mär-,äŋ\ city & port Indonesia in *cen* Java on N coast *pop* 1,250,971

Sem·i·nole, Lake \'se-mə-,nōl\ reservoir SW Ga. & NW Fla. formed by confluence of Chattahoochee & Flint rivers & emptying by the Apalachicola

Sem·i·pa·la·tinsk \,se-mi-pə-'lä-,tin(t)sk\ city NE Kazakhstan on the Irtysh *pop* 283,000

Sen·dai \(,)sen-'dī\ city Japan in NE Honshu *pop* 918,378

Sen·e·ca Lake \'se-ni-kə\ lake 35 *mi* (56 *km*) long W *cen* N.Y.; one of the Finger Lakes

Sen·e·gal \,se-ni-'gòl, -'gäl, 'se-ni-,\ **1** river 1050 *mi* (1690 *km*) W Africa flowing from Fouta Djallon NW & W into the Atlantic **2** country W Africa on the Atlantic; a republic of the French Community, formerly a territory of French West Africa ✳ Dakar *area* 81,081 *sq mi* (210,811 *sq km*), *pop* 5,811,000 — **Sen·e·ga·lese** \,se-ni-gə-'lēz, -'lēs\ *adj or n*

Sen·e·gam·bia \,se-nə-'gam-bē-ə\ **1** region W Africa around Senegal & Gambia rivers **2** confederation of Senegal & Gambia; formed 1982 — **Sen·e·gam·bi·an** \-ən\ *adj or n*

Sen·lac \'sen-,lak\ hill SE England in Sussex NW of Hastings

Sen·lis \sän-lēs\ commune N France NNE of Paris *pop* 13,481

Sen·nar *or* **Sen·naar** \sə-'när\ region E Sudan chiefly bet. White Nile & Blue Nile rivers; an ancient kingdom

Sens \säⁿs\ city NE *cen* France WSW of Troyes *pop* 25,621

Seoul \'sōl\ city NW S. Korea on Han River; formerly ✳ of Korea, since 1948 ✳ of S. Korea *pop* 9,639,110

Se·pik \'sä-pik\ river 600 *mi* (966 *km*) N Papua New Guinea

Sept–Iles \se-'tē(ə)l\ *or* **Seven Islands** town Canada in E Que. at the mouth of St. Lawrence River *pop* 24,848

Se·quoia National Park \si-'kwòi-ə\ reservation SE *cen* Calif.; includes Mt. Whitney

Seram — see CERAM

Ser·bia \'sər-bē-ə\ *or formerly* **Ser·via** \-vē-ə\ federated republic *cen* Yugoslavia traversed by Morava River; once a kingdom ✳ Belgrade *area* 34,080 *sq mi* (88,608 *sq km*), *pop* 11,596,572

Serbs, Croats, and Slovenes, Kingdom of the — see YUGOSLAVIA

Serdica — see SOFIA

Serendib — see CEYLON

Ser·en·geti Plain \,ser-ən-'ge-tē\ area N Tanzania including **Serengeti National Park** (wild game reserve)

Ser·gi·pe \sər-'zhē-pə\ state NE Brazil ✳ Aracajú *area* 8321 *sq mi* (21,635 *sq km*), *pop* 1,156,642

Se·rin·ga·pa·tam \sə-,riŋ-gə-pə-'tam\ town S India N of city of Mysore

Se·rowe \sə-'rō-ē\ city E Botswana *pop* 15,723

Ser·ra da Es·tre·la \,se-rə-(,)dä-e-'stre-lə\ mountain range Portugal; highest point Malhão da Estrela (highest in Portugal) 6532 *ft* (1991 *m*)

Serra do Mar \də-'mär\ mountain range S Brazil along coast; highest point 7323 *ft* (2232 *m*)

Ser·rai \'ser-(,)ī\ city N Greece *pop* 50,875

Serra Pa·ca·rai·ma \,pa-kə-'rī-mə\ *or* **Si·er·ra Pacaraima** \sē-,er-ə\ mountain range N S. America in SE Venezuela, N Brazil, & W Guyana — see RORAIMA

Ser·ra Pa·ri·ma \,ser-ə-pə-'rē-mə\ mountain range N S. America on Venezuela-Brazil border SW of Serra Pacaraima; source of the Orinoco; highest peak *ab* 8000 *ft* (2438 *m*)

Ser·re·kun·da *or* **Se·re·kun·da** \,sä-rä-'kùn-də\ city W Gambia *pop* 68,824

Ses·tos \'ses-təs\ ruined town Turkey in Europe on the Dardanelles (Hellespont) at narrowest point

Ses·to San Gio·van·ni \'ses-tō-,san-jō-'vä-nē, -,sän-\ commune N Italy *pop* 89,517

Sète \'set\ *or formerly* **Cette** \'set\ commune & port S France SSW of Montpellier *pop* 39,075

Se·te Que·das \,sä-tə-'kä-dəsh\ *or* **Guai·rá Falls** \'gwī-(,)rä\ former cataract in Alto Paraná River on Brazil-Paraguay boundary; now submerged in reservoir formed by Itaipu dam

Sé·tif \sā-'tēf\ commune NE Algeria *pop* 144,200

Se·tú·bal \sə-'tü-bäl\ city & port SW Portugal *pop* 77,885

Se·van \sə-'vän\ lake N Armenia *area* 540 *sq mi* (1404 *sq km*)

Se·vas·to·pol \sə-'vas-tə-,pòl, -,pól, -pəl; ,se-və-'stō-pəl, -'stō-\ *or formerly* **Se·bas·to·pol** \-'bas-\ city & port SW Crimea *pop* 301,000

Sev·ern \'se-vərn\ **1** inlet (**Severn River**) of Chesapeake Bay, in Md., on which Annapolis is situated **2** river 610 *mi* (982 *km*) Canada in NW Ont. flowing NE into Hudson Bay **3** river 210 *mi* (338 *km*) Great Britain flowing from E cen Wales into Bristol Channel in England

Severnaya Dvina — see NORTHERN DVINA

Se·ver·na·ya Zem·lya \'se-vər-nə-yə-,zem-lē-'ä\ islands N Russia in Asia N of Taimyr Peninsula in Arctic Ocean bet. Kara & Laptev seas *area* 14,300 *sq mi* (37,180 *sq km*)

Se·vier \sə-'vir\ river 280 *mi* (451 *km*) SW *cen* Utah flowing into **Se·vier Lake** (25 *mi* or 40 *km* long; saline)

Se·ville \sə-'vil\ *or Sp* **Se·vi·lla** \sā-'vē-(,)yä\ **1** province SW Spain *area* 5428 *sq mi* (14,113 *sq km*), *pop* 1,397,554 **2** city, its ✳, on the Guadalquiver *pop* 645,817

Sè·vres \'sevr\ commune N France SW of Paris *pop* 21,100

Sew·ard Peninsula \'sü-ərd\ peninsula 180 *mi* (290 *km*) long & 130 *mi* (209 *km*) wide W Alaska projecting into Bering Sea bet. Kotzebue & Norton sounds — see PRINCE OF WALES (Cape)

Sey·chelles \sā-'shel(z)\ island group W Indian Ocean NE of Madagascar; formerly a Brit. colony, a republic in the Commonwealth of Nations since 1976 ✳ Victoria (on Mahé Is.) *area* 178 *sq mi* (462 *sq km*), *pop* 68,598

Sey·han \sā-'hän\ **1** *or* **Sei·hun** \-'hün\ river 300 *mi* (483 *km*) Turkey flowing SSW into the Mediterranean **2** — see ADANA

Seym *or* **Seim** \'säm\ river 435 *mi* (700 *km*) N Ukraine & Russia in Europe flowing W into the Desna

Sfax \'sfaks\ city & port Tunisia on Gulf of Gabes *pop* 171,297
's Gravenhage — see HAGUE (The)
Shaan·xi \'shän-'shē\ *or* **Shen·si** \'shen-'sē, 'shən-'shē\ province N *cen* China bordering on the Huang ✻ Xi'an *area* 75,598 *sq mi* (196,555 *sq km*), *pop* 28,904,423
Sha·ba \'shä-bə\ *or formerly* **Ka·tan·ga** \kə-'täŋ-gə, -'taŋ-\ region SE Zaire; chief city Lubumbashi
Shah·ja·han·pur \,shä-jə-'hän-,pùr\ city N India in *cen* Uttar Pradesh NNW of Kanpur *pop* 205,325
Shah·pur \'shä-'pùr\ ancient city SW Iran W of Shiraz
Shak·er Heights \'shā-kər\ city NE Ohio E of Cleveland *pop* 30,831
Shakh·ty \'shäk-tē, 'shak-\ *or formerly* **Ale·ksan·drovsk Gru·shev·ski** \,a-lik-'san-drəfsk-grü-'shef-skē, ,e-, -lig-'zan-, -'shev-\ city S Russia in Europe NE of Rostov *pop* 209,000
Shan·dong \'shän-'dòŋ\ province E China including Shandong Peninsula ✻ Jinan *area* 59,189 *sq mi* (153,891 *sq km*), *pop* 74,419,054
Shandong Peninsula *or* **Shan·tung Peninsula** \'shan-'təŋ, 'shän-'dùŋ\ peninsula E China projecting ENE bet. Yellow Sea & Bo Hai
Shang·hai \shaŋ-'hī\ municipality & port E China on the Huangpu near the Chang estuary *pop* 11,859,748
Shang·qiu *or* **Shang–ch'iu** \'shäŋ-chē-'ü\ *or* **Shang·kiu** \-jē-'ü\ city E China in E Henan *pop* 165,000
Shan·non \'sha-nən\ river 240 *mi* (386 *km*) W Ireland flowing S & W into the Atlantic
Shan State \'shän, 'shan\ *or formerly* **Federated Shan States** province E Myanmar comprising a mountainous region (the **Shan Hills**) ✻ Taunggyi *pop* 3,178,000
Shan·tou \'shän-'tō\ *or* **Swa·tow** \'swä-'taù\ city & port SE China in E Guangdong on S. China Sea *pop* 250,000
Shan·xi \'shän-'shē\ *or* **Shan·si** \-'sē, -'shē\ province N China bordering on the Huang ✻ Taiyuan *area* 60,656 *sq mi* (157,706 *sq km*), *pop* 25,291,389
Shao·xing *or* **Shao–hsing** \'shaù-'shiŋ\ city E China in N Zhejiang SE of Hangzhou *pop* 160,000
Shao·yang \'shaù-'yäŋ\ *or formerly* **Pao·king** \'baù-'chiŋ\ city SE China in *cen* Hunan W of Hengyang *pop* 170,000
Shari — see CHARI
Shar·ja \'shär-jə\ sheikhdom, member of the United Arab Emirates
Shark Bay inlet of Indian Ocean 150 *mi* (241 *km*) long W Western Australia, at *ab* 25°S
Shar·on, Plain of \'shar-ən, 'sher-\ region Israel on coast bet. Mt. Carmel & Jaffa
Sha·shi \'shä-'shē\ *or* **Sha–shih** \-'shir, -'shē\ *or* **Sha·si** \-'shē\ city E *cen* China in S Hubei on the Chang *pop* 120,000
Shas·ta, Mount \'shas-tə\ mountain 14,162 *ft* (4316 *m*) N Calif. in Cascade Range; an isolated volcanic cone
Shatt al Ar·ab \,shät-al-'ar-əb\ river 120 *mi* (193 *km*) SE Iraq formed by the Tigris & the Euphrates & flowing SE into Persian Gulf
Shaw·an·gunk Mountains \'shäŋ-gəm, shə-'wän-(,)gəŋk\ mountain ridge SE N.Y.; part of Kittatinny Mountain
Shaw·nee \shò-'nē, 'shò-; shä-'nē, 'shä-\ **1** city NE Kans. S of Kansas City *pop* 37,993 **2** city *cen* Okla. *pop* 26,017
Shcherbakov — see RYBINSK
She·ba \'shē-bə\ *or* **Sa·ba** \'sä-bə\ ancient country S Arabia, probably Yemen
She·boy·gan \shi-'bòi-gən\ city & port E Wis. *pop* 49,676
Shechem — see NABLUS
Sheer·ness \shir-'nes\ former urban district & port SE England in Kent at mouth of Thames River; now part of Queenborough-in-Sheppey
Shef·field \'she-,fēld\ city N England in S. Yorkshire *pop* 477,142
Shel·i·kof \'she-li-,kòf\ strait S Alaska bet. Alaska Peninsula & islands of Kodiak & Afognak
Shel·ton \'shel-tᵊn\ city SW Conn. *pop* 35,418
Shen·an·do·ah \,she-nən-'dō-ə, sha-nə(n)-'dō-ə\ river 55 *mi* (88 *km*) N Va. flowing NE bet. Allegheny & Blue Ridge Mountains across NE tip of W.Va. & into the Potomac; forms **Shenandoah Valley**
Shenandoah National Park reservation N Va. in Blue Ridge Mountains
Shensi — see SHAANXI
Shen·yang \'shən-'yäŋ\ *or* **Muk·den** \'mùk-dən, 'mək-; mùk-'den\ *or formerly* **Feng·tien** \'fəŋ-tē-'en\ city NE China ✻ of Liaoning; chief city of Manchuria *pop* 4,012,000
Sher·brooke \'shər-,brùk\ town E Canada in S Que. *pop* 76,429
Sher·man \'shər-mən\ city NE Tex. N of Dallas *pop* 31,601
's Her·to·gen·bosch \,ser-,tō-gən-'bòs, -kən-\ city S Netherlands ✻ of N. Brabant *pop* 81,471
Sher·wood Forest \'shər-,wùd- *also* 'sher-\ ancient royal forest *cen* England chiefly in Nottinghamshire
Shet·land \'shet-lənd\ **1** islands N Scotland NE of the Orkneys **2** *or* **Zet·land** \'zet-\ region comprising the Shetlands ✻ Lerwick (on Mainland Is.) *area* 550 *sq mi* (1430 *sq km*), *pop* 26,716 — **Shet·land·er** \'shet-lən-dər\ *n*
Shey·enne \shī-'an, -'en\ river 325 *mi* (523 *km*) SE *cen* N.Dak. flowing into Red River
Shi·bîn el Kôm \shi-,bēn-el-'kōm\ city N Egypt *pop* 100,000
Shigatse — see XIGAZÊ
Shi·jia·zhuang *or* **Shih–chia–chuang** *or* **Shih·kia·chwang** \'shir-jē-'äj-'wäŋ, 'shē-jē-\ city NE China ✻ of Hebei *pop* 1,500,000
Shi·kar·pur \shi-'kär-,pùr\ city S *cen* Pakistan in Sind *pop* 88,000
Shi·ko·ku \shi-'kō-(,)kü\ island S Japan E of Kyushu *area* 7246 *sq mi* (18,840 *sq km*) *pop* 3,195,106
Shil·ka \'shil-kə\ river 300 *mi* (483 *km*) SE Russia in Asia flowing NE to unite with the Argun forming the Amur
Shil·long \shi-'lòŋ\ city NE India ✻ of Meghalaya *pop* 173,064
Shi·loh \'shī-(,)lō\ **1** locality SW Tenn., site of Civil War battle **2** ancient village Palestine W of Jordan River on slope of Mt. Ephraim
Shi·mi·zu \shi-'mē-(,)zü, 'shē-mi-,zü\ city & port Japan in *cen* Honshu on Suruga Bay; port for Shizuoka *pop* 241,524
Shi·mo·da \shi-'mō-də, -,dä\ city & port Japan in S Honshu SW of Yokohama on Sagami Sea *pop* 30,081
Shi·mo·no·se·ki \,shi-mə-nō-'se-kē\ *or formerly* **Ba·kan** \'bä-,kän\ city & port Japan in SW Honshu on Shimonoseki Strait *pop* 262,643

Shimonoseki Strait strait Japan bet. Honshu & Kyushu connecting Inland Sea & Korea Strait
Shi·nar \'shī-nər, -,när\ a country known to the early Hebrews as a plain in Babylonia; prob. Sumer
Ship Rock isolated mountain 7178 *ft* (2188 *m*) N.Mex. in NW corner
Shi·raz \shi-'räz\ city SW *cen* Iran *pop* 848,289
Shi·re \'shē-(,)rā, 'shir-ē\ river 370 *mi* (595 *km*) S Malawi & *cen* Mozambique flowing from Lake Malawi S into the Zambezi
Shi·shal·din \shi-'shal-dən\ volcano 9387 *ft* (2861 *m*) SW Alaska on Unimak Is.; highest in Aleutian Range
Shi·zu·o·ka \,shi-zə-'wō-kə, ,shē-zə-'ō-kə\ city Japan in *cen* Honshu near Suruga Bay SW of Shimizu *pop* 472,199
Shko·dër \'shkō-dər\ city NW Albania *pop* 64,700
Sho·la·pur \'shō-lə-,pùr\ city W India in SE Maharashtra SE of Bombay *pop* 514,461
Shore·ditch \'shòr-,dich, 'shòr-\ former metropolitan borough N *cen* London, England; now part of Hackney
Shore·view \'shòr-,vyü, 'shòr-\ city E Minn. *pop* 24,587
Short·land Islands \'shòrt-lənd\ islands W Pacific in the Solomons off S end of Bougainville
Sho·sho·ne \shə-'shō-nē, shə-'shōn\ river 120 *mi* (193 *km*) NW Wyo. flowing NE into Bighorn River
Shoshone Falls waterfall 210 *ft* (64 *m*) S Idaho in Snake River
Shreve·port \'shrēv-,pòrt, -,pòrt, *esp South* 'srēv-\ city NW La. on Red River *pop* 198,525
Shrews·bury 1 \'sh(r)üz-,ber-ē, -b(ə-)rē\ town E Mass. E of Worcester *pop* 24,146 **2** *Brit often* 'shrōz-\ *or* **Sal·op** \'sa-ləp\ borough W England ✻ of Salop *pop* 59,826
Shropshire — see SALOP
Shu·ma·gin \'shü-mə-gən\ islands SW Alaska S of Alaska Peninsula; largest Unga
Shushan — see SUSA
Shymkent — see CHIMKENT
Si — see XI
Si·al·kot \sē-'äl-,kōt\ city NE Pakistan NNE of Lahore *pop* 308,000
Siam — see THAILAND
Si·am, Gulf of \sī-'am\ *or* **Gulf of Thailand** arm of S. China Sea bet. Indochina & Malay Peninsula
Sian — see XI'AN
Siang — see YOU
Siangtan — see XIANGTAN
Si·be·ria \sī-'bir-ē-ə\ region N Asia in Russia extending from the Urals to the Pacific; roughly coextensive with Russia in Asia — **Si·be·ri·an** \-ən\ *adj or n*
Si·biu \sē-'byü\ city W *cen* Romania in Transylvania *pop* 184,036
Si·bu·yan Sea \,sē-bü-'yän\ body of water *cen* Philippines bounded by Mindoro, S Luzon, & the Visayan Islands
Sic·i·ly \'si-s(ə-)lē\ *or It* **Si·ci·lia** \sē-'chēl-yä\ *or anc* **Si·cil·ia** \sə-'sil-yə\ *or* **Tri·nac·ria** \trī-'na-krē-ə, trī-\ island S Italy in the Mediterranean; a region ✻ Palermo *area* 9926 *sq mi* (25,808 *sq km*), *pop* 5,172,785 — **Si·cil·ian** \sə-'sil-yən\ *adj or n*
Si·cy·on \'si-shē-,än, 'si-sē-\ *or* **Gk** **Sik·y·on** \'si-kē-\ ancient city S Greece in NE Peloponnisos NW of Corinth
Si·di Bar·râ·ni \,sē-dē-bə-'rä-nē\ village NW Egypt on coast
Si·di–bel–Ab·bès \-,bel-ə-'bes\ commune NW Algeria *pop* 116,000
Si·don \'sī-dᵊn\ *or* **Ar Sai·da** \'sī-də\ city & port SW Lebanon; a chief city of ancient Phoenicia — **Si·do·ni·an** \sī-'dō-nē-ən\ *adj or n*
Sid·ra, Gulf of \'si-drə\ *or* **Gulf of Sir·te** \'sir-tə\ *or anc* **Syr·tis Major** \'sər-təs\ inlet of the Mediterranean on coast of Libya
Sie·ben·ge·bir·ge \'zē-bən-gə-,bir-gə\ hills W Germany on right bank of the Rhine SSE of Bonn — see DRACHENFELS
Si·ena *or* **Si·en·na** \sē-'e-nə\ commune *cen* Italy in Tuscany *pop* 58,278 — **Si·en·ese** *or* **Si·en·nese** \,sē-ə-'nēz, -'nēs\ *adj or n*
Si·er·ra Blan·ca Peak \sē-,er-ə-'blaŋ-kə\ mountain 12,003 *ft* (3658 *m*) S *cen* N.Mex. in Sierra Blanca range of the Sacramento Mountains
Sierra de Cór·do·ba \də-'kòr-də-bə, -və\ mountain range *cen* Argentina chiefly in Córdoba province; highest peak Cerro Champaquí 9350 *ft* (2850 *m*)
Sierra de Gre·dos \də-'grā-(,)dōs\ mountain range W *cen* Spain, SW extension of Sierra de Guadarrama; highest peak Plaza de Almanzor 8504 *ft* (2592 *m*)
Sierra de Gua·dar·ra·ma \də-,gwä-də-'rä-mə\ mountain range *cen* Spain; highest peak Pico de Peñalara 7972 *ft* (2430 *m*)
Sier·ra Le·one \sē-,er-ə-lē-'ōn, ,sir-ə-, lē-'ō-nē\ country W Africa on the Atlantic; a dominion of the Commonwealth of Nations ✻ Freetown *area* 27,925 *sq mi* (72,605 *sq km*), *pop* 2,735,159 — **Sierra Le·on·ean** \-'ō-nē-ən\ *adj or n*
Si·er·ra Ma·dre del Sur \sē-,er-ə-'mä-drā-del-'sùr\ mountain range S Mexico along Pacific coast in Guerrero & Oaxaca
Sierra Madre Oc·ci·den·tal \,äk-sə-den-'täl\ mountain range NW Mexico parallel to the Pacific coast
Sierra Madre Ori·en·tal \,òr-ē-,en-'täl, ,òr-\ mountain range E Mexico parallel to coast of Gulf of Mexico
Sierra Mo·re·na \mə-'rā-nə\ mountain range SW Spain bet. the Guadiana & the Guadalquivir; highest peak Estrella 4339 *ft* (1322 *m*)
Sierra Ne·va·da \nə-'va-də, -'vä-\ **1** mountain range E Calif. — see WHITNEY (Mount) **2** mountain range S Spain; highest peak Mulhacén 11,411 *ft* (3478 *m*)
Sierra Nevada de Mérida — see CORDILLERA MÉRIDA
Sierra Nevada de San·ta Mar·ta \də-,san-tə-'mär-tə\ mountain range N Colombia on Caribbean coast; highest peak 19,030 *ft* (5800 *m*)
Sierra Pacaraima — see SERRA PACARAIMA
Sierra Vis·ta \'vis-tə\ city SE Ariz. *pop* 32,983
Si·kang \'shē-'käŋ\ former province S China ✻ Yaan
Si·kho·te Alin \sē-kə-,tä-ə-'lēn\ mountain range SE Russia in Asia in Maritime Territory; highest point 6575 *ft* (2004 *m*)
Sik·kim \'si-kəm, -,kim\ former country SE Asia on S slope of the

\ə\ abut \ᵊ\ kitten, F table \ər\ further \a\ ash \ā\ ace \ä\ mop, mar
\aù\ out \ch\ chin \e\ bet \ē\ easy \g\ go \i\ hit \ī\ ice \j\ job
\ŋ\ sing \ō\ go \ò\ law \òi\ boy \th\ thin \t͟h\ the \ü\ loot \ù\ foot
\y\ yet \zh\ vision \ä, k̲, ⁿ, œ, œ̄, ᵫ, ᵫ̄, ᶉ\ see Guide to Pronunciation

Himalayas bet. Nepal & Bhutan; since 1975 a state of India ✳ Gangtok *area* 2818 *sq mi* (7327 *sq km*), *pop* 315,682 — **Sik·kim·ese** \ˌsi-kə-ˈmēz, -ˈmēs\ *adj or n*

Si·le·sia \sī-ˈlē-zh(ē-)ə, sə-, -sh(ē-)ə\ region E *cen* Europe in valley of the upper Oder bordering on Sudety Mountains; formerly chiefly in Germany, now chiefly in E Czech Republic & SW Poland — **Si·le·sian** \-zh(ē-)ən, -sh(ē-)ən\ *adj or n*

Simbirsk — see ULYANOVSK

Sim·coe, Lake \ˈsim-(ˌ)kō\ lake E Canada in SE Ont. SE of Georgian Bay *area* 280 *sq mi* (728 *sq km*)

Sim·fe·ro·pol \ˌsim(p)-fə-ˈrò-pəl, -ˈrō-\ city in the Crimea *pop* 250,000

Si·mi Valley \sē-ˈmē\ city SW Calif. W of Los Angeles *pop* 100,217

Sim·la \ˈsim-lə\ city N India N of Delhi ✳ of Himachal Pradesh & former summer ✳ of India *pop* 55,368

Si·mons·town \ˈsī-mənz-ˌtaùn\ town & port SW Republic of South Africa in Western Cape province on False Bay S of Cape Town

Sim·plon Pass \ˈsim-ˌplän\ mountain pass 6589 *ft* (2008 *m*) in Lepontine Alps bet. Switzerland & Italy in Valais & Piedmont

Simplon Tunnel tunnel *ab* 12 *mi* (19 *km*) long through Monte Leone near Simplon Pass

Sims·bury \ˈsimz-ˌber-ē, -b(ə-)rē\ town N Conn. *pop* 22,023

Si·nai \ˈsī-ˌnī *also* -nē-ˌī\ peninsula extension of continent of Asia NE Egypt bet. Red Sea & the Mediterranean — **Si·na·it·ic** \ˌsī-nē-ˈi-tik\ *adj*

Sinai, Mount — see HOREB

Si·na·loa \ˌsē-nə-ˈlō-ə, si-\ state W Mexico bordering on Gulf of California ✳ Culiacán *area* 22,580 *sq mi* (58,708 *sq km*), *pop* 1,880,098

Sind \ˈsind\ province S Pakistan in lower Indus valley ✳ Karachi

Sin·ga·pore \ˈsiŋ-ə-ˌpòr, -ˌpór *also* ˈsiŋ-gə-\ **1** island Malay Archipelago in S. China Sea off S end of Malay Peninsula; formerly a Brit. crown colony, from 1963 to 1965 a state of Malaysia (federation), an independent republic in the Commonwealth of Nations since 1965, *area* 225 *sq mi* (585 *sq km*), *pop* 2,413,945 **2** city & port, its ✳, on Singapore Strait *pop* 206,500 — **Sin·ga·por·ean** \ˌsiŋ-ə-ˈpòr-ē-ən, -ˈpòr- *also* ˈsiŋ-gə-\ *adj or n*

Singapore Strait channel SE Asia bet. Singapore Is. & Riau Archipelago connecting Strait of Malacca & S. China Sea

Sining — see XINING

Sinkiang Uighur — see XINJIANG UYGUR

Si·nop \sə-ˈnòp\ *or anc* **Si·no·pe** \-ˈnò-pē\ town & port N Turkey on peninsula in Black Sea NW of Ankara *pop* 18,381

Sinsiang — see XINXIANG

Sint–Gillis — see SAINT-GILLES

Sint–Jans–Molenbeek — see MOLENBEEK

Sint Maarten — see SAINT MARTIN

Sin·tra *or* **Cin·tra** \ˈsēn-trə\ city W Portugal NW of Lisbon *pop* 224,763

Sin·ui·ju \ˈshi-nē-ˌjü\ city W N. Korea on the Yalu opposite Antung, China *pop* 165,000

Sion **1** \sē-ˈòⁿ\ *or G* **Sit·ten** \ˈzi-tⁿn, ˈsi-\ commune SW *cen* Switzerland ✳ of Valais *pop* 24,727 **2** — see ZION

Sioux City \ˈsü\ city NW Iowa on Missouri River *pop* 80,505

Sioux Falls city SE S.Dak. on the Big Sioux *pop* 100,814

Si·ping \ˈsē-ˈpiŋ\ *or* **Ssu–p'ing** \ˈsü-ˈpiŋ\ *or formerly* **Sze·ping·kai** \ˈsù-ˈpiŋ-ˈgī\ city NE China in Jilin SW of Changchun *pop* 150,000

Sip·par \si-ˈpär\ ancient city of Babylonia on the Euphrates SSW of modern Baghdad; Sargon's capital

Siracusa — see SYRACUSE

Si·ret \si-ˈret\ river 270 *mi* (434 *km*) E Romania flowing from the Carpathians SE into the Danube

Sí·ros \ˈsē-ˌrós\ island Greece in the Cyclades S of Andros

Sis·ki·you Mountains \ˈsis-ki-ˌyü\ mountains N Calif. & SW Oreg., a range of Klamath Mountains; highest Mt. Ashland (in Oreg.) 7530 *ft* (2295 *m*)

Sit·tang \ˈsi-ˌtäŋ\ river 350 *mi* (563 *km*) E *cen* Myanmar flowing S into Gulf of Martaban

Sit·twe \ˈsi-ˌtwä\ *or formerly* **Ak·yab** \a-ˈkyab\ city & port W Myanmar; chief town of Arakan coast *pop* 42,329

Si·vas \si-ˈväs\ *or anc* **Se·bas·te** \sə-ˈbas-tē\ *or* **Se·bas·tia** \sə-ˈbas-ch(ē-)ə, -tē-ə\ city E *cen* Turkey on the upper Kizil Irmak *pop* 173,831

Si·wa \ˈsē-wə\ *or anc* **Am·mo·ni·um** \ə-ˈmō-nē-əm\ oasis & town NW Egypt W of Qattara Depression *pop* 4999

Si·wa·lik Range \si-ˈwä-lik\ foothills of the Himalayas N India extending SE from N Punjab into Uttar Pradesh

Sjæl·land \ˈshe-ˌlän\ island, largest of islands of Denmark; site of Copenhagen *area* 2709 *sq mi* (7043 *sq km*) *pop* 1,971,946

Skadarsko Jezero — see SCUTARI (Lake)

Skag·er·rak \ˈska-gə-ˌrak\ arm of the North Sea bet. Norway & Denmark

Skag·it \ˈska-jət\ river 200 *mi* (322 *km*) SW B.C. & NW Wash. flowing S & W into Puget Sound

Skan·e·at·e·les Lake \ˌska-nē-ˈat-ləs, ˌski-nē-\ lake 16 *mi* (26 *km*) long *cen* N.Y. SW of Syracuse; one of the Finger Lakes

Skaw, The \ˈskö\ *or* **Ska·gens Od·de** \ˈskä-gənz-ˌò-də\ cape Denmark at N extremity of Jutland

Skee·na \ˈskē-nə\ river 360 *mi* (579 *km*) Canada in W B.C. flowing S & W into Hecate Strait

Skid·daw \ˈski-ˌdò\ mountain 3054 *ft* (931 *m*) NW England in NW *cen* Cumbria

Skik·da \ˈskik-(ˌ)dä\ *or formerly* **Phi·lippe·ville** \ˈfi-ləp-ˌvil, fi-ˌlēp-ˈvē(ə)l\ city & port NE Algeria N of Constantine *pop* 107,700

Skí·ros \ˈskē-ˌrós\ island Greece in the Northern Sporades E of Évvoia

Sko·kie \ˈskō-kē\ village NE Ill. N of Chicago *pop* 59,432

Skop·je \ˈskò-ˌpyä\ city ✳ of Macedonia on the Vardar *pop* 308,117

Skunk river 264 *mi* (425 *km*) SE Iowa flowing SE into Mississippi River

Skye \ˈskī\ island Scotland, one of the Inner Hebrides *area* 670 *sq mi* (1742 *sq km*)

Slave \ˈslāv\ river 258 *mi* (415 *km*) Canada flowing from W end of Lake Athabasca N into Great Slave Lake

Slave Coast region W Africa bordering on Bight of Benin bet. Benin & Volta rivers

Slav·kov \ˈsläf-ˌkóf, ˈsläv-ˌkòv\ *or* **Aus·ter·litz** \ˈò-stər-ˌlits, ˈaù-stər-\ town SE Czech Republic ESE of Brno

Sla·vo·nia \slə-ˈvō-nē-ə, -nyə\ region E Croatia bet. the Sava, the Drava, & the Danube — **Sla·vo·ni·an** \-nē-ən, -nyən\ *adj or n*

Slea·ford \ˈslē-fərd\ town E England in SW Lincolnshire SSE of Lincoln

Slesvig — see SCHLESWIG

Sli·dell \sli-ˈdel\ town SE La. NE of New Orleans *pop* 24,124

Slide Mountain \ˈslīd\ mountain 4204 *ft* (1281 *m*) SE N.Y. W of Kingston; highest in the Catskills

Sli·go \ˈslī-(ˌ)gō\ **1** county N Ireland (republic) in N Connacht *area* 694 *sq mi* (1804 *sq km*), *pop* 54,736 **2** municipal borough & port, its ✳, on Sligo Bay (inlet of Atlantic Ocean) *pop* 17,259

Slough \ˈslaù\ borough SE *cen* England in Berkshire *pop* 87,005

Slo·va·kia \slō-ˈvä-kē-ə, -ˈva-\ *or* **Slo·ven·sko** \ˈslò-ven-ˌskó\ country *cen* Europe; a constituent republic of Czechoslovakia 1918–92 ✳ Bratislava *area* 18,925 *sq mi* (49,510 *sq km*), *pop* 4,991,168

Slo·ve·nia \slō-ˈvē-nē-ə, -nyə\ country S Europe N & W of Croatia; a federated republic of Yugoslavia 1946–91 ✳ Ljubljana *area* 7708 *sq mi* (20,041 *sq km*), *pop* 1,697,068

Smith·field \ˈsmith-ˌfēld\ city N R.I. NW of Providence *pop* 19,163

Smoky Hill river 540 *mi* (869 *km*) *cen* Kans. flowing E to unite with Republican River forming the Kansas River

Smo·lensk \smō-ˈlen(t)sk\ city W Russia in Europe on the upper Dnieper WSW of Moscow *pop* 276,000

Smyr·na \ˈsmər-nə\ **1** town NW Ga. NW of Atlanta *pop* 30,981 **2** — see IZMIR

Snake \ˈsnāk\ river 1038 *mi* (1670 *km*) NW U.S. flowing from NW Wyo. across S Idaho & into Columbia River in Wash.

Snake Range mountain range E Nevada

Sno·qual·mie Falls \snō-ˈkwäl-mē\ waterfall 268 *ft* (82 *m*) W *cen* Wash. in **Snoqualmie River** 70 *mi* (118 *km*)

Snoqualmie Pass mountain pass 3004 *ft* (916 *m*) W *cen* Wash. in Cascade Range SE of Seattle

Snow — see MAOKE

Snow·don \ˈsnō-dⁿn\ massif 3560 *ft* (1085 *m*) NW Wales in Gwynedd; highest point in Wales

Snow·do·nia \snō-ˈdō-nē-ə, -nyə\ mountain region NW Wales centering around Snowdon

Snowy river 240 *mi* (386 *km*) SE Australia flowing from Snowy Mountains to the Pacific in SE Victoria

Snowy Mountains mountains SE Australia in SE New South Wales

So·bat \ˈsō-ˌbat\ river 460 *mi* (740 *km*) W Ethiopia & SE Sudan flowing W into White Nile River

Soča — see ISONZO

So·chi \ˈsō-chē\ city & port S Russia in Europe on NE coast of Black Sea *pop* 224,000

So·ci·e·ty Islands \sə-ˈsī-ə-tē\ *or F* **Îles de la So·cié·té** \ēl-də-lä-sò-syā-tā\ islands S Pacific belonging to France ✳ Papeete (on Tahiti) *area* 650 *sq mi* (1690 *sq km*), *pop* 162,573

So·cor·ro \sə-ˈkòr-(ˌ)ō\ town Tex., a S suburb of El Paso *pop* 22,995

So·co·tra \sə-ˈkō-trə\ island Indian Ocean E of Gulf of Aden in Yemen ✳ Tamrida (Hadibu) *area* 1400 *sq mi* (3640 *sq km*), *pop* 8000

Sö·der·täl·je \ˌsə(r)-dər-ˈtel-yə, ˌsœ-\ town SE Sweden, a suburb of Stockholm *pop* 81,460

Sod·om \ˈsä-dəm\ city of ancient Palestine in plain of Jordan River

So·fia \ˈsō-fē-ə, ˈsò-, ˈsō-\ *or Bulg* **So·fi·ya** \ˈsò-fē-ə\ *or anc* **Ser·di·ca** \ˈsər-di-kə\ *or* **Sar·di·ca** \ˈsär-\ city W Bulgaria, its ✳ *pop* 967,214

Sog·di·a·na \ˌsäg-dē-ˈa-nə, -ˈä-nə, -ˈā-nə\ province of ancient Persian Empire bet. the Jaxartes (Syr Darya) & Oxus (Amu Darya) ✳ Maracanda (Samarkand)

Sog·ne Fjord \ˈsòŋ-nə\ inlet of Norwegian Sea SW Norway; longest fjord in Norway

So·hâg \sō-ˈhäj\ city *cen* Egypt on the Nile SE of Asyût *pop* 85,300

So·ho \ˈsō-ˌhō\ district of *cen* London, England, in Westminster

Sois·sons \swä-ˈsōⁿ\ commune N France NW of Paris *pop* 29,694

So·lent, The \ˈsō-lənt\ channel S England bet. Isle of Wight & the mainland

So·li·hull \ˌsō-li-ˈhəl\ borough *cen* England in W. Midlands SE of Birmingham *pop* 111,541

So·li·mões \ˌsü-lē-ˈmòiⁿsh\ the upper Amazon, Brazil, from Peruvian border to the mouth of Negro River

So·ling·en \ˈzō-liŋ-ən, ˈsō-\ city W Germany in the Ruhr ESE of Düsseldorf *pop* 166,085

Sol·na \ˈsòl-ˌnä\ city E Sweden, N suburb of Stockholm *pop* 50,441

Solo — see SURAKARTA

Sol·o·mon Islands \ˈsä-lə-mən\ islands W Pacific E of New Guinea divided bet. Papua New Guinea & the independent country (formerly a Brit. protectorate) of the Solomon Islands (✳ Honiara) *area* 16,120 *sq mi* (41,912 *sq km*), *pop* 249,000

Solomon Sea arm of Coral Sea W of Solomon Islands

So·lo·thurn \ˈzō-lə-ˌtúrn, ˈsō-\ *or F* **So·leure** \sō-ˈlœr, -ˈlœr\ **1** canton NW Switzerland *area* 306 *sq mi* (796 *sq km*), *pop* 223,803 **2** commune, its ✳, on the Aare *pop* 15,531

Sol·way Firth \ˈsäl-ˌwā\ inlet of Irish Sea in Great Britain on boundary bet. England & Scotland

So·ma·lia \sō-ˈmä-lē-ə, sə-, -ˈmäl-yə\ country E Africa bordering on Gulf of Aden & Indian Ocean; formed 1960 by union of Brit. Somaliland & Italian Somaliland ✳ Mogadishu *area* 262,000 *sq mi* (681,200 *sq km*), *pop* 4,760,000 — **So·ma·lian** \-lē-ən, -ˈmäl-yən\ *adj or n*

So·ma·li·land \sō-ˈmä-lē-ˌland, sə-\ region E Africa comprising Somalia, Djibouti, & the Ogaden region of E Ethiopia

Som·er·set \ˈsə-mər-ˌset, -sət\ *or* **Som·er·set·shire** \-ˌshir, -shər\ county SW England ✳ Taunton *area* 1620 *sq mi* (4212 *sq km*), *pop* 428,900

Somerset Island island N Canada in Northwest Territories N of Boothia Peninsula *area* 9370 *sq mi* (24,362 *sq km*)

Somerset Nile — see NILE

Som·er·ville \ˈsə-mər-ˌvil\ city E Mass. N of Cambridge *pop* 76,210

So·mes \sō-ˈmesh\ *or* **Hung Sza·mos** \ˈsò-ˌmösh\ river 200 *mi* (322 *km*) NE Hungary & NW Romania flowing NW into the Tisza

Somme \ˈsäm, ˈsòm\ river 147 *mi* (236 *km*) N France flowing NW into the English Channel

Song·hua \ˈsòŋ-ˈhwä\ *or* **Sun·ga·ri** \ˈsùŋ-gə-rē\ river 800 *mi* (1287 *km*) NE China in E Manchuria flowing from N. Korea border NW & NE into the Amur; dammed in upper part to form Songhua Reservoir

Song·nam \'soṅ-'näm\ city NW S. Korea *pop* 447,692

So·no·ra \sə-'nōr-ə, -'nȯr-\ **1** river 300 *mi* (483 *km*) NW Mexico flowing SW into upper Gulf of California **2** state NW Mexico bordering on U.S. & Gulf of California ✻ Hermosillo *area* 70,477 *sq mi* (183,240 *sq km*), *pop* 1,498,931 — **So·no·ran** \-ən\ *adj or n*

Sonoran Desert *or* **Sonora Desert** desert SW U.S. & NW Mexico in S Ariz., SE Calif., & N Sonora

Soo Canals — *see* SAULT SAINTE MARIE CANALS

Soochow — *see* SUZHOU

Sop·ron \'shō-,prōn\ city W Hungary *pop* 57,500

Sorata — *see* ILLAMPU

Sorbiodunum — *see* OLD SARUM

So·ria \'sȯr-ē-ə, 'sȯr-\ **1** province N *cen* Spain *area* 3983 *sq mi* (10,356 *sq km*), *pop* 88,772 **2** commune, its ✻, W of Zaragoza *pop* 30,558

So·ro·ca·ba \,sȯr-ə-'ka-bə, ,sȯr-, -'kä-\ city SE Brazil in SE São Paulo state *pop* 269,880

Sor·ren·to \sə-'ren-(,)tō\ *or anc* Sur·ren·tum \sə-'ren-təm\ commune & port S Italy on S side of Bay of Naples

Sos·no·wiec \sä-'snō-,vyets\ *or* Sos·no·wi·ce \,sȯs-nə-'vēt-sə\ city SW Poland NE of Katowice *pop* 259,269

Sou·fri·ère \,sü-frē-'er\ **1** volcano 4813 *ft* (1467 *m*) French West Indies in S Basse-Terre, Guadeloupe **2** volcano 4048 *ft* (1234 *m*) Brit. West Indies on St. Vincent Is.

Sou·ris \'sùr-əs\ river 450 *mi* (724 *km*) Canada & U.S. flowing from SE Sask. SE into N.Dak. & N into the Assiniboine in SW Man.

Sousse \'süs\ *or anc* Had·ru·me·tum \,ha-drə-'mē-təm\ city & port NE Tunisia *pop* 69,530

South Africa, Republic of country S Africa S of the Limpopo, Molopo, & Orange rivers bordering on Atlantic & Indian oceans; a republic, until 1961 (as **Union of South Africa**) a Brit. dominion; administrative ✻ Pretoria, legislative ✻ Cape Town, judicial ✻ Bloemfontein *area* 472,359 *sq mi* (1,228,133 *sq km*), *pop* 30,193,000

Sou·thall \'saù-,thȯl\ former municipal borough S England in Middlesex, now part of Ealing

South America continent of the western hemisphere lying bet. the Atlantic & Pacific oceans SE of N. America & chiefly S of the equator *area* 7,035,357 *sq mi* (18,291,928 *sq km*) — **South American** *adj or n*

South·amp·ton \saù-'tham(p)-tən, saùth-'ham(p)-\ city & port S England in Hampshire on **Southampton Water** (estuary of Test River) *pop* 204,406

Southampton Island island N Canada in Northwest Territories, bet. Hudson Bay & Foxe Channel *area* 15,700 *sq mi* (40,820 *sq km*)

South Arabia, Federation of former Brit. protectorate comprising crown colony of Aden & numerous semi-independent Arab sultanates & emirates; made part of People's Democratic Republic of Yemen 1967

South Atlantic — *see* ATLANTIC OCEAN

South Australia state S Australia ✻ Adelaide *area* 380,070 *sq mi* (988,182 *sq km*), *pop* 1,285,033

South Bend \'bend\ city N Ind. NW of Fort Wayne *pop* 105,511

South Canadian — *see* CANADIAN

South Cape — *see* KA LAE

South Car·o·li·na \,kar-(ə)-'lī-nə\ state SE U.S. ✻ Columbia *area* 31,055 *sq mi* (80,743 *sq km*), *pop* 3,486,703 — **South Car·o·lin·ian** \-'li-nē-ən, -'li-nyən\ *adj or n*

South China Sea part of W Pacific enclosed by SE China, Taiwan, Philippines, Indochina, Malaya, & Borneo

South Da·ko·ta \də-'kō-tə\ state NW *cen* U.S. ✻ Pierre *area* 77,047 *sq mi* (200,322 *sq km*), *pop* 696,004 — **South Da·ko·tan** \-'kō-t'n\ *adj or n*

South Downs hills S England chiefly in Sussex

South El Monte city SW Calif. SE of Los Angeles *pop* 20,850

South·end on Sea \,saù-,thend-,ȯn-'sē, -,än-\ borough SE England in Essex at mouth of Thames estuary *pop* 156,683

Southern Alps mountain range New Zealand in W South Is. extending almost the length of the island — *see* COOK (Mount)

Southern Morocco — *see* MOROCCO

Southern Ocean the Antarctic Ocean

Southern Rhodesia — *see* ZIMBABWE

Southern Up·lands \'əp-lən(d)z, -,lan(d)z\ elevated moorland region S Scotland extending from English border to a line joining Girvan & Dunbar

Southern Yemen — *see* YEMEN

South Euclid city NE Ohio E of Cleveland *pop* 23,866

South·field \'saùth-,fēld\ city SE Mich. NW of Detroit *pop* 75,728

South·gate \'saùth-,gāt\ city SE Mich. S of Detroit *pop* 30,771

South Gate \,gāt\ city SW Calif. SE of Los Angeles *pop* 86,284

South Georgia island S Atlantic E of Tierra del Fuego in Falkland Islands Dependencies *area* 1450 *sq mi* (3770 *sq km*)

South Glamorgan county SE Wales ✻ Cardiff *area* 161 *sq mi* (419 *sq km*), *pop* 390,400

South Holland 1 village NE Ill. S of Chicago *pop* 22,105 **2** *or D* **Zuid–Hol·land** \zīt-'hȯ-,länt\ province SW Netherlands ✻ Rotterdam *area* 1212 *sq mi* (3151 *sq km*), *pop* 3,130,426

South·ing·ton \'sə-thin-tən\ town W *cen* Conn. *pop* 38,518

South Island island S New Zealand *area* 58,092 *sq mi* (151,039 *sq km*), *pop* 798,681

South Kings·town \'kiṅ-stən, 'kiṅz-,taùn\ town S R.I. *pop* 24,631

South Korea — *see* KOREA

South Lake Tahoe city E Calif. on Lake Tahoe *pop* 21,586

South Milwaukee city SE Wis. on Lake Michigan *pop* 20,958

South Mountain ridge S Pa. & W Md. at N end of Blue Ridge

South Na·han·ni \nə-'ha-nē\ river 350 *mi* (563 *km*) Canada in SW Northwest Territories flowing SE into the Liard

South Orkney Islands islands S Atlantic SE of the Falklands in Falkland Islands Dependencies *area* 400 *sq mi* (1040 *sq km*)

South Os·se·tia \ä-'sē-shə\ autonomous region N Georgia ✻ Tskhinvali *area* 1500 *sq mi* (3900 *sq km*), *pop* 100,000

South Pacific — *see* PACIFIC OCEAN

South Pasadena city SW Calif. *pop* 23,936

South Pass broad level valley SW *cen* Wyo. crossing Continental Divide

South Plainfield borough NE N.J. SW of Elizabeth *pop* 20,489

South Platte river 424 *mi* (682 *km*) Colo. & Nebr. flowing E to join N. Platte River forming the Platte River

South·port \'saùth-,pȯrt, -,pȯrt\ borough NW England in Merseyside on coast N of Liverpool *pop* 89,745

South Portland city SW Maine *pop* 23,163

South Saint Paul city SE Minn. on Mississippi River *pop* 20,197

South Sandwich Islands islands S Atlantic SE of S. Georgia Is. in Falkland Islands Dependencies *area* 120 *sq mi* (312 *sq km*)

South San Francisco city W Calif. *pop* 54,312

South Saskatchewan — *see* SASKATCHEWAN

South Seas the areas of the Atlantic, Indian, & Pacific oceans in the southern hemisphere, esp. the S Pacific

South Shetland Islands islands S Atlantic SE of Cape Horn off tip of Antarctic Peninsula in Falkland Islands Dependencies

South Shields \'shē(ə)l(d)z\ borough N England in Tyne and Wear at mouth of the Tyne E of Newcastle *pop* 87,203

South Tirol — *see* ALTO ADIGE

South Vietnam — *see* VIETNAM

South·wark \'sə-thərk, 'saùth-wərk\ borough of S London, England *pop* 221,300

South–West Africa — *see* NAMIBIA

South Windsor town N Conn. NE of Hartford *pop* 22,090

South Yemen SOUTHERN YEMEN — **South Ye·me·ni** \ye-mə-nē\ *adj*

South Yorkshire metropolitan county N England ✻ Barnsley *area* 602 *sq mi* (1565 *sq km*), *pop* 1,315,100

So·vetsk \sə-'vyetsk\ *or G* Til·sit \'til-sət, -zət\ city W Russia in Europe on the Neman *pop* 36,000

So·vet·ska·ya Ga·van \sə-'vyet-skə-yə-'gä-vən, -'gä-və-nyə\ city & port SE Russia in Asia on Tatar Strait *pop* 26,000

Soviet Central Asia the portion of *cen* Asia formerly belonging to the U.S.S.R. & comprising the Kirghiz, Tadzhik, Turkmen, & Uzbek republics & sometimes Kazakhstan

Soviet Russia 1 — *see* RUSSIA **2** the U.S.S.R.

Soviet Union — *see* UNION OF SOVIET SOCIALIST REPUBLICS

So·we·to \sə-'wā-tō, -'we-, -tü\ township NE Republic of South Africa in Pretoria-Witwatersrand-Vereeniging adjoining SW Johannesburg; a black residential complex

Spa \'spä\ town E Belgium SE of Liège *pop* 10,140

Spain \'spān\ *or Sp* Es·pa·ña \i-'spä-nyä\ country SW Europe in the Iberian Peninsula; a kingdom ✻ Madrid *area* 193,144 *sq mi* (502,174 *sq km*), *pop* 37,746,260

Span·dau \'shpän-,daù, 'spän-\ a W section of Berlin, Germany

Spanish America 1 the Spanish-speaking countries of the Americas **2** the parts of America settled & formerly governed by the Spanish

Spanish Guinea former Spanish colony W Africa bordering on Gulf of Guinea including Río Muni (Mbini), Fernando Po (Bioko) & other islands — *see* EQUATORIAL GUINEA

Spanish Main \'mān\ **1** the mainland of Spanish America esp. along N coast of S. America **2** the Caribbean Sea & adjacent waters esp. at the time when region was infested with pirates

Spanish Morocco — *see* MOROCCO

Spanish Peaks two mountains (**East Spanish Peak** 12,683 *ft or* 3866 *m* & **West Spanish Peak** 13,623 *ft or* 4152 *m*) S Colo.

Spanish Sahara former Spanish possessions Río de Oro & Saguia el Hamra — *see* WESTERN SAHARA

Spanish Town town SE *cen* Jamaica W of Kingston; former ✻ of Jamaica

Sparks \'spärks\ city W Nev. E of Reno *pop* 53,367

Spar·ta \'spär-tə\ *or* Lac·e·dae·mon \,la-sə-'dē-mən\ ancient city S Greece in Peloponnisos ✻ of Laconia

Spar·tan·burg \'spär-t'n-,bərg\ city NW S.C. *pop* 43,467

Spen·cer Gulf \'spen(t)-sər\ inlet of Indian Ocean SE S. Australia

Spey \'spā\ river 110 *mi* (177 *km*) NE Scotland flowing into Moray Firth

Spey·er \'shpī(-ə)r, 'spī(-ə)r\ *or* Spires \'spīrz\ city SW Germany on W bank of the Rhine SW of Heidelberg *pop* 43,864

Spezia, La — *see* LA SPEZIA

Spits·ber·gen \'spits-,bər-gən\ group of islands in Arctic Ocean N of Norway; belongs to Norway *area* 24,280 *sq mi* (63,128 *sq km*) — *see* SVALBARD

Split \'split\ city & port S Croatia on Dalmatian coast *pop* 150,739

Spo·kane \spō-'kan\ **1** river 120 *mi* (193 *km*) N Idaho & E Wash. flowing from Coeur d'Alene Lake W into Columbia River **2** city E Wash. at Spokane Falls in Spokane River *pop* 177,196

Spo·le·to \spə-'lā-(,)tō, -'lē-\ commune *cen* Italy SE of Perugia *pop* 37,885

Spor·a·des \'spȯr-ə-,dēz, 'spär-\ two island groups Greece in the Aegean: the **Northern Sporades** (chief island Skíros, N of Evvoia & E of Thessaly) & the **Southern Sporades** (chiefly Samos, Icaria, & the Dodecanese, off SW Turkey)

Sprat·ly Islands \'sprat-lē\ islands *cen* S. China Sea SE of Cam Ranh Bay, Vietnam; claimed by several countries

Spree \'shprā, 'sprā\ river 220 *mi* (354 *km*) E Germany flowing N into the Havel

Spree·wald \-,vält\ marshy district E Germany in Spree valley

Spring·dale \'spriṅ-,dāl\ city NW Ark. *pop* 29,941

Spring·field \'spriṅ-,fēld\ **1** city ✻ of Ill. on the Sangamon *pop* 105,227 **2** city SW Mass. on Connecticut River *pop* 156,983 **3** city SW Mo. *pop* 140,494 **4** city W *cen* Ohio NE of Dayton *pop* 70,487 **5** city W Oreg. on the Willamette E of Eugene *pop* 44,683

Springs \'spriṅz\ city NE Republic of South Africa in Pretoria= Witwatersrand-Vereeniging *pop* 142,812

Spring Valley village SE N.Y. N of New York City *pop* 21,802

Spuy·ten Duy·vil Creek \,spī-t'n-'dī-vəl\ channel New York City N of Manhattan Is. connecting Hudson & Harlem rivers

Sri Lan·ka \(,)srē-'läṅ-kə, (,)shrē-, -'laṅ\ *or formerly* Cey·lon \si-'län, sā-\ country coextensive with island of Ceylon; an independent republic in the Commonwealth of Nations ✻ Colombo *area* 25,332 *sq mi*

\ə\ abut \'ə\ kitten, F table \ər\ further \a\ ash \ā\ ace \ä\ mop, mar \aù\ out \ch\ chin \e\ bet \ē\ easy \g\ go \i\ hit \ī\ ice \j\ job \ṅ\ sing \ō\ go \ȯ\ law \ȯi\ boy \th\ thin \t͟h\ the \ü\ loot \ù\ foot \y\ yet \zh\ vision \à, k̲, ⁿ, œ, œ̄, ʊe, ǖ, ᵊ\ *see* Guide to Pronunciation

(65,863 *sq km*), *pop* 14,850,001 — **Sri Lan·kan** \-'län-kən, -'laŋ-\ *adj or n*

Sri·na·gar \sri-'nə-gər\ city India, summer ✻ of Jammu and Kashmir, in W Kashmir on the Jhelum NNE of Lahore *pop* 423,253

Ssu–p'ing — see SIPING

Staf·fa \'sta-fə\ islet W Scotland in the Inner Hebrides W of Mull — see FINGAL'S CAVE

Staf·ford \'sta-fərd\ borough W *cen* England ✻ of Staffordshire *pop* 55,497

Staf·ford·shire \'sta-fərd-,shir, -shər\ *or* **Stafford** county W *cen* England ✻ Stafford *area* 1049 *sq mi* (2727 *sq km*), *pop* 1,015,700

Staked Plain — see LLANO ESTACADO

Sta·kha·nov \stə-'kä-nəf, -'kä-\ *or formerly* **Ka·di·yev·ka** \kə-'dē-yəf-kə\ city E Ukraine *pop* 108,000

Stalin **1** — see BRASOV **2** — see DONETSK **3** — see VARNA

Stalinabad — see DUSHANBE

Stalingrad — see VOLGOGRAD

Stalino — see DONETSK

Stalinsk — see NOVOKUZNETSK

Stam·boul *or* **Stam·bul** \stam-'bül, stäm-\ **1** the older part of Istanbul S of the Golden Horn **2** ISTANBUL

Stam·ford \'stam(p)-fərd\ city SW Conn. *pop* 108,056

Stanislav — see IVANO-FRANKOVSK

Stan·ley \'stan-lē\ *or* **Port Stanley** town ✻ of the Falklands

Stanley, Mount *or in Zaire* **Mount Nga·lie·ma** \eŋ-gäl-'yā-mə\ mountain with two peaks (higher Margherita Peak 16,763 *ft or* 5109 *m*) E cen Africa; highest of Ruwenzori

Stanley Falls — see BOYOMA FALLS

Stanley Pool — see MALEBO POOL

Stanleyville — see KISANGANI

Stan·o·voi \,sta-nə-'vȯi\ mountain range SE Russia in Asia N of the Amur; highest point 8143 *ft* (2482 *m*)

Stan·ton \'stan-t°n\ city SW Calif. SE of Los Angeles *pop* 30,491

Sta·ra Za·go·ra \,stär-ə-zə-'gȯr-ə, -'gȯr-\ city *cen* Bulgaria *pop* 122,200

State College borough *cen* Pa. NE of Altoona *pop* 38,923

Stat·en Island \'sta-t°n\ **1** island SE N.Y. SW of mouth of Hudson River **2** *or formerly* **Rich·mond** \'rich-mənd\ borough of New York City including Staten Is. *pop* 378,977

States of the Church *or* **Papal States** temporal domain of the popes in *cen* Italy 755–1870

Statia — see SAINT EUSTATIUS

Statue of Liberty National Monument — see LIBERTY ISLAND

Staun·ton \'stan-t°n\ city NW *cen* Va. *pop* 24,461

Sta·van·ger \stə-'väŋ-ər, -'vaŋ-\ city & port SW Norway *pop* 97,570

Stav·ro·pol \sta-'vrȯ-pəl, -'vrō-\ **1** territory S Russia in Europe N of the Caucasus *area* 29,600 *sq mi* (76,960 *sq km*), *pop* 2,306,000 **2** city, its ✻ *pop* 198,000 **3** — see TOL'YATTI

Ste·bark \'ste(n)m-,bärk\ *or G* **Tan·nen·berg** \'ta-nən-,bərg, 'tä-nən-,berk\ village NE Poland SW of Olsztyn

Steens Mountain \'stēnz\ mountain mass SE Oreg.; highest point 9354 *ft* (2851 *m*)

Stel·len·bosch \'ste-lən-,bäs, -,bäsh, *Afrik* ,ste-ləm-'bȯs\ city SW Republic of South Africa in SW Western Cape province *pop* 29,955

Step·ney \'step-nē\ former metropolitan borough E London, England, on N bank of Thames River, now part of Tower Hamlets

Ster·ling Heights \'stər-liŋ\ city SE Mich. N of Detroit *pop* 117,810

Steu·ben·ville \'stü-bən-,vil, 'styü-\ city E Ohio *pop* 22,125

Ste·vens Point \'stē-vənz\ city *cen* Wis. *pop* 23,006

Stew·art \'stü-ərt, 'stü(-ə)rt, 'styü-ərt, 'styü(-ə)rt\ river 320 *mi* (515 *km*) Canada in *cen* Yukon Territory flowing W into Yukon River

Stewart Island island New Zealand S of South Is. *area* 670 *sq mi* (1742 *sq km*)

Sti·kine \sti-'kēn\ river 335 *mi* (539 *km*) Canada & Alaska flowing from **Stikine Mountains** (in B.C. & Yukon Territory) into the Pacific

Still·wa·ter \'stil-,wȯ-tər, -,wä-\ city N *cen* Okla. *pop* 36,676

Stir·ling \'stər-liŋ\ **1** *or* **Stir·ling·shire** \-,shir, -shər\ former county *cen* Scotland **2** burgh *cen* Scotland ✻ of Central region *pop* 38,638

Stock·holm \'stäk-,hō(l)m\ city ✻ of Sweden on Mälaren Lake *pop* 672,187 — **Stock·holm·er** \-,hō(l)-mər\ *n*

Stock·port \'stäk-,pȯrt, -,pȯrt\ borough NW England in Greater Manchester S of Manchester *pop* 136,496

Stock·ton \'stäk-tən\ city *cen* Calif. on the San Joaquin *pop* 210,943

Stockton–on–Tees \-'tēz\ borough N England in Cleveland *pop* 81,274

Stoke New·ing·ton \stōk-'nü-iŋ-tən, -'nyü-\ former metropolitan borough N London, England, now part of Hackney

Stoke on Trent \'stōk-,ȯn-'trent, -,än-\ city W England in Staffordshire *pop* 252,351

Stone·ham \'stō-nəm, 'stȯn-,ham\ town E Mass. *pop* 22,203

Stone·ha·ven \stōn-'hā-vən, stän-'hi\ burgh & port E Scotland in Grampian region *pop* 7885

Stone·henge \'stōn-,henj, (,)stōn-'\ assemblage of megaliths S England in Wiltshire on Salisbury Plain erected by prehistoric peoples

Stone Mountain mountain 1686 *ft* (514 *m*) NW *cen* Ga. E of Atlanta

Stones \'stōnz\ river 60 *mi* (96 *km*) *cen* Tenn. flowing NW into Cumberland River

Ston·ey Creek \'stō-nē\ city Canada in SE Ont. *pop* 49,968

Stor·mont \'stȯr-mənt\ E suburb of Belfast, Northern Ireland; site of Parliament House

Stor·no·way \'stȯr-nə-,wā\ burgh NW Scotland in Lewis ✻ of Western Isles region *pop* 8660

Stough·ton \'stō-t°n\ town E Mass. NW of Brockton *pop* 26,777

Stour **1** \'stu̇r\ river 60 *mi* (96 *km*) SE England flowing E bet. Essex & Suffolk into the North Sea **2** \'stȧu̇r, 'stu̇r\ river 55 *mi* (88 *km*) S England in Dorset & Hampshire flowing SE into Avon River **3** \'stu̇r *also* 'stȧu̇r\ river 40 *mi* (64 *km*) SE England in Kent flowing NE into the North Sea **4** \'stȧu̇r, 'stȯr\ river 20 *mi* (32 *km*) *cen* England in Oxfordshire & Warwickshire flowing NW into Avon River **5** *same as* 4\ river 20 *mi* (32 *km*) W *cen* England in Staffordshire & Hereford and Worcester flowing S into Severn River

Stour·bridge \'stȧu̇r-(,)brij, 'stȯr-\ borough W England in W. Midlands W of Birmingham *pop* 54,661

Stow \'stō\ city NE Ohio NE of Akron *pop* 27,702

Stra·bane \strə-'ban\ district W Northern Ireland, established 1974 *area* 336 *sq mi* (874 *sq km*), *pop* 35,028

Straits Settlements former country SE Asia bordering on Strait of Malacca & comprising Singapore Is., Penang, & Malacca; now divided bet. Singapore (republic) & Malaysia (federation) *area* 1242 *sq mi* (3229 *sq km*)

Stral·sund \'shträl-,zu̇nt, 'sträl-, -,su̇nt\ city & port NE Germany on the Baltic opposite Rügen Is. *pop* 75,070

Stras·bourg \'sträs-,bu̇rg, 'sträz-, -,bȯrg\ *or G* **Strass·burg** \'shträs-,bu̇rk\ city NE France on Ill River *pop* 251,520

Strat·ford \'strat-fərd\ **1** town SW Conn. *pop* 49,389 **2** city Canada in SE Ont. W of Kitchener *pop* 27,666

Stratford–upon–Avon \-'ā-vən, -'a-\ borough *cen* England in Warwickshire SSE of Birmingham *pop* 20,858

Strath·clyde \strath-'klīd\ **1** Celtic kingdom of 6th to 11th centuries S Scotland & NW England ✻ Dumbarton; its S part called **Cum·bria** \'kəm-brē-ə\ **2** region SW Scotland, established 1975; ✻ Glasgow *area* 5348 *sq mi* (13,905 *sq km*), *pop* 2,397,827

Strath·more \strath-'mȯr, -'mȯr\ great valley of E *cen* Scotland S of the Grampians

Stream·wood \'strēm-,wu̇d\ village NE Ill. E of Elgin *pop* 30,987

Stre·sa \'strā-zə\ town NW Italy in Piedmont on Lake Maggiore

Stret·ford \'stret-fərd\ borough NW England in Greater Manchester SW of Manchester *pop* 47,600

Stri·món, Gulf of \strē-'mȯn\ *or* **Stri·mon·i·kós Kól·pos** \strē-,mȯ-nē-'kȯs-'kȯl-pȯs\ *or* **Stry·mon·ic Gulf** \strī-'mä-nik\ inlet of the Aegean NE Greece NE of Chalcidice peninsula

Strom·bo·li \'sträm-bə-(,)lē\ *or anc* **Stron·gy·le** \'strän-jə-,lē\ **1** island Italy in Lipari Islands **2** volcano 3038 *ft* (926 *m*) on the island

Strom·lo, Mount \'sträm-(,)lō\ hill 2500 *ft* (758 *m*) SE Australia in Australian Capital Territory W of Canberra

Strongs·ville \'strȯŋz-,vil\ city NE Ohio SW of Cleveland *pop* 35,308

Stry·mon \'strī-,män\ *or NGk* **Stri·món** \strē-'mȯn\ *or Bulg* **Stru·ma** \'strü-mə\ river 225 *mi* (362 *km*) W Bulgaria & NE Greece flowing SE into Gulf of Strimón

Stutt·gart \'shtu̇t-,gärt, 'stu̇t-, 'stət-\ city SW Germany ✻ of Baden-Württemberg on the Neckar *pop* 580,648

Styr \'stir\ river 300 *mi* (483 *km*) NW Ukraine flowing N into the Pripet in the Pripet Marshes

Styr·ia \'stir-ē-ə\ *or Ger* **Stei·er·mark** \'shtī(-ə)r-,märk, 'stī(-ə)r-\ region *cen* & SE Austria; chief city Graz — **Styr·i·an** \'stir-ē-ən\ *adj or n*

Sua·kin \'swä-kən\ town & port NE Sudan on Red Sea

Su·bic \'sü-bik\ town Philippines in W Luzon at head of **Subic Bay** (inlet of S. China Sea NW of Bataan peninsula) *pop* 30,340

Su·bo·ti·ca \'sü-bə-,tēt-sə\ city N Yugoslavia in N Vojvodina near Hungarian border *pop* 88,787

Süchow **1** — see XUZHOU **2** — see YIBIN

Su·cre \'sü-(,)krā\ city, constitutional ✻ of Bolivia, SE of La Paz *pop* 63,625

Su·dan \sü-'dan, -'dän\ **1** region N Africa bet. the Atlantic & the upper Nile S of the Sahara including basins of Lake Chad & Niger River & the upper Nile **2** country NE Africa S of Egypt; a republic, until 1956 a territory (**Anglo–Egyptian Sudan**) under joint Brit. & Egyptian rule ✻ Khartoum *area* 967,500 *sq mi* (2,515,500 *sq km*), *pop* 20,564,364 — **Su·da·nese** \,sü-d°n-'ēz, -'ēs\ *adj or n*

Sudanese Republic — see MALI

Sud·bury \'səd-,ber-ē, -,b(ə-)rē\ city Canada in SE Ont. N of Georgian Bay *pop* 92,884

Sudd \'səd\ swamp region S Sudan drained by White Nile River

Su·de·ten·land \sü-'dā-t°n-,land, -,länt\ region N Czech Republic in Sudety Mountains

Su·de·ty *Czech* 'sü-de-tē, *Polish* sü-'de-tē\ *or* **Su·de·ten** \sü-'dā-t°n\ mountains *cen* Europe W of the Carpathians bet. Czech Republic & Poland — **Sudeten** *adj or n*

Su·dir·man Range \sü-'dir-mən\ *or formerly* **Nas·sau Range** \'na-,sȯ\ mountain range *cen* W. Irian — see DJAJA (Mount)

Su·ez \sü-'ez, 'sü-,ez, *chiefly Brit* 'sü-iz\ city & port NE Egypt at S end of Suez Canal on **Gulf of Suez** (arm of Red Sea) *pop* 193,282

Suez, Isthmus of isthmus NE Egypt bet. Mediterranean & Red seas connecting Africa & Asia

Suez Canal canal 92 *mi* (148 *km*) long NE Egypt traversing Isthmus of Suez

Suf·folk \'sə-fək, *US also* -,fȯk\ **1** city SE Va. W of Chesapeake *pop* 52,141 **2** county E England bordering on North Sea ✻ Ipswich *area* 1462 *sq mi* (3800 *sq km*), *pop* 604,900; formerly divided into administrative counties of **East Suffolk** (✻ Ipswich) & **West Suffolk** (✻ Bury St. Edmunds)

Suffolk Broads — see BROADS

Sugar Land city SE Tex. W of Houston *pop* 24,529

Sugarloaf Mountain — see PÃO DE AÇÚCAR

Suisse — see SWITZERLAND

Sui·sun Bay \sə-'sün\ the E extension of San Pablo Bay *cen* Calif.

Sui·sun City \sə-'sün\ city *cen* Calif. SW of Sacramento *pop* 22,686

Su·i·ta \sü-'ē-tə\ city Japan on Honshu *pop* 345,187

Sukarnapura — see DJAJAPURA

Su·khu·mi \'sü-kə-mē, sü-'kü-mē\ city & port NW Georgia ✻ of Abkhaz Republic on Black Sea *pop* 102,000

Suk·kur \'sü-kər\ city Pakistan in N Sind on the Indus *pop* 193,000

Su·la·we·si \,sü-lə-'wä-sē\ *or* **Ce·le·bes** \'se-lə-,bēz, sə-'lē-bēz\ island Indonesia E of Borneo ✻ Ujung Pandang *area* 69,255 *sq mi* (180,063 *sq km*), *pop* 8,925,000

Sul·grave \'səl-,grāv\ village England in S Northamptonshire

Sul·phur \'səl-fər\ city SW La. *pop* 20,125

Su·lu Archipelago \'sü-(,)lü\ archipelago SW Philippines SW of Mindanao

Sulu Sea sea W Philippines N of Celebes Sea

Su·ma·tra \sü-'mä-trə\ island W Indonesia S of Malay Peninsula *area* 166,789 *sq mi* (433,651 *sq km*) — **Su·ma·tran** \-trən\ *adj or n*

Sum·ba \'süm-bə\ island Indonesia in the Lesser Sundas *area* 4306 *sq mi* (11,196 *sq km*), *pop* 251,126

Sum·ba·wa \süm-'bä-wə\ island Indonesia in the Lesser Sundas *area* 5693 *sq mi* (14,802 *sq km*), *pop* 195,554

Su·mer \'sü-mər\ the S division of ancient Babylonia — see AKKAD, SHINAR
Sum·ga·it \,süm-gä-'ēt\ city & port Azerbaijan on the Caspian NW of Baku *pop* 124,000
Sum·mer·ville \'sə-mər-,vil\ town SE S.C. NW of Charleston *pop* 22,519
Sum·mit \'sə-mət\ city NE N.J. W of Newark *pop* 19,757
Sum·ter \'səm(p)-tər\ city E *cen* S.C. E of Columbia *pop* 41,943
Sun·belt \'sən-,belt\ region S & SW U.S.
Sun·da Islands \'sün-də, 'sən-\ islands Malay Archipelago comprising the **Greater Sunda Islands** (Sumatra, Java, Borneo, Sulawesi, & adjacent islands) & the **Lesser Sunda Islands** (extending E from Bali to Timor); with exception of N Borneo, belongs to Indonesia
Sunda Strait SELAT SUNDA
Sun·der·land \'sən-dər-lənd\ borough N England in Tyne and Wear on North Sea *pop* 196,152
Sunds·vall \'sən(t)s-,väl, 'sùn(t)s-\ city & port E Sweden on Gulf of Bothnia *pop* 93,404
Sungari — see SONGHUA
Sun·ny·vale \'sə-nē-,väl\ city W Calif. WNW of San Jose *pop* 117,229
Sun·rise \'sən-,rīz\ city SE Fla. *pop* 64,407
Sunset Crater volcanic crater N *cen* Ariz. in **Sunset Crater National Monument**
Suomi — see FINLAND
Su·pe·ri·or \su̇-'pir-ē-ər\ city & port NW Wis. on Lake Superior *pop* 27,134
Superior, Lake lake U.S. & Canada; largest, northernmost, & westernmost of the Great Lakes *area* 31,820 *sq mi* (82,732 *sq km*)
Superstition Mountains range S *cen* Ariz. E of Phoenix
Sur \'sùr\ *or* **Tyre** \'tīr\ *or* **Tyr** \'tir\ town S Lebanon on the coast; ancient ✳ of Phoenicia
Sur, Point \'sȯr\ promontory Calif. on the Pacific SSW of Monterey — see BIG SUR
Su·ra·ba·ja *or* **Su·ra·ba·ya** \,sùr-ə-'bī-ə\ city & port Indonesia in NE Java on **Surabaya Strait** (bet. Java & W end of Madura) *pop* 2,483,871
Su·ra·kar·ta \,sùr-ə-'kär-tə\ *or* **So·lo** \'sō-(,)lō\ city Indonesia in *cen* Java *pop* 504,176
Su·rat \'sùr-ət, sə-'rat\ city W India in SE Gujarat *pop* 912,568
Sur·bi·ton \'sər-bə-tᵊn\ former municipal borough S England in Surrey WSW of London, now part of Kingston upon Thames
Su·ri·ba·chi, Mount \,sùr-ə-'bä-chē\ volcano 548 *ft* (167 *m*) in the Volcano Islands at S end of Iwo Jima
Su·ri·na·me \,sùr-ə-'nä-mə\ **1** *or formerly* **Dutch Guiana** *or* **Netherlands Guiana** country N S. America bet. Guyana & French Guiana; a republic, until 1975 territory of the Netherlands ✳ Paramaribo *area* 55,142 *sq mi* (143,369 *sq km*), *pop* 403,000 **2** river 400 *mi* (644 *km*) N Suriname flowing N into the Atlantic — **Su·ri·nam·er** \'sùr-ə-,nä-mər, ,sùr-ə-'nä-\ *n* — **Su·ri·nam·ese** \,sùr-ə-nə-'mēz, -'mēs\ *adj or n*
Sur·ma \'sùr-mə\ river 560 *mi* (901 *km*) NE India (subcontinent) in Manipur & Bangladesh — see MEGHNA
Surrentum — see SORRENTO
Sur·rey \'sər-ē, 'sə-rē\ **1** county SE England S of London ✳ Kingston upon Thames *area* 648 *sq mi* (1,678 *sq km*), *pop* 1,014,800 **2** municipality Canada in SW B.C. SE of Vancouver *pop* 245,173
Surts·ey \'sərt-,sā, 'sùrt-\ island Iceland off S coast *area* 1 *sq mi* (2.6 *sq km*); formed 1963 by volcanic eruption
Su·ru·ga Bay \'sùr-ə-gə\ inlet of the Pacific Japan on coast of SE Honshu W of Sagami Sea
Su·sa \'sü-zə\ *or bib* **Shu·shan** \'shü-shən, -,shan\ ancient city ✳ of Elam; ruins in SW Iran
Susiana — see ELAM
Sus·que·han·na \,səs-kwə-'ha-nə\ river 444 *mi* (714 *km*) E U.S. flowing from *cen* N.Y. S through Pa. & into Chesapeake Bay in N Md.
Sus·sex \'sə-siks, *US also* -,seks\ former county SE England bordering on English Channel; one of kingdoms in Anglo-Saxon heptarchy — see EAST SUSSEX, WEST SUSSEX
Suth·er·land \'sə-thər-lənd\ *or* **Suth·er·land·shire** \-lən(d)-,shir, -,shər\ former county N Scotland ✳ Dornoch
Sutherland Falls waterfall 1904 *ft* (580 *m*) New Zealand in SW South Is.
Sut·lej \'sət-,lej\ river 900 *mi* (1448 *km*) N India (subcontinent) flowing from Tibet W & SW through the Punjab to join the Chenab
Sut·ton \'sə-tᵊn\ borough of S Greater London, England *pop* 169,900
Sutton Cold·field \'kōl(d)-,fēld\ borough *cen* England in W. Midlands NE of Birmingham *pop* 86,494
Sutton-in-Ash·field \-'ash-,fēld\ town N *cen* England in Nottinghamshire N of Nottingham *pop* 41,270
Su·va \'sü-və\ city & port ✳ of Fiji, on Viti Levu Is. *pop* 63,628
Su·wał·ki \sü-'väl-kē\ **1** district NE Poland **2** city in the district
Su·wan·nee \sə-'wä-nē, 'swä-\ river 240 *mi* (386 *km*) SE Ga. & N Fla. flowing SW into Gulf of Mexico
Su·won \'sü-,wän\ city NW S. Korea S of Seoul *pop* 430,752
Su·zhou \'sü-'jō\ *or* **Soo·chow** \'jō, -'chaù\ *or formerly* **Wu·hsien** \'wü-shē-'en\ city E China in SE Jiangsu W of Shanghai *pop* 630,000
Sval·bard \'sväl-,bär\ islands in the Arctic Ocean including Spitsbergen, Bear Is., & other small islands *area* 25,000 *sq mi* (65,000 *sq km*); under Norwegian administration
Sverdlovsk — see YEKATERINBURG
Sver·drup Islands \'sver-drəp\ islands N Canada W of Ellesmere Is. including Axel Heiberg, Ellef Ringnes, & Amund Ringnes Islands
Swa·bia \'swä-bē-ə\ *or* **G Schwa·ben** \'shvä-bən\ region and medieval county SW Germany chiefly in area comprising modern Baden-Wurttemberg & W Bavaria — **Swa·bi·an** \'swä-bē-ən\ *adj or n*
Swan \'swän\ *or in its upper course* **Av·on** \'a-vən\ river 150 *mi* (241 *km*) SW Western Australia flowing W into Indian Ocean
Swan Islands two islands in the Caribbean NE of Honduras
Swan·sea \'swän-zē *also* -,sē\ city & port SE Wales ✳ of W. Glamorgan *pop* 167,796
Swat \'swät\ river 400 *mi* (644 *km*) Pakistan flowing into Kabul River
Swatow — see SHANTOU
Swa·zi·land \'swä-zē-,land\ country SE Africa N of Natal bet. Eastern Transvaal & Mozambique; a former Brit. protectorate, an independent

kingdom since 1968 ✳ Mbabane *area* 6705 *sq mi* (17,433 *sq km*), *pop* 494,534
Swe·den \'swē-dᵊn\ *or* **Sw Sve·ri·ge** \'sve-rē-yə\ country N Europe on Scandinavian peninsula W of Baltic Sea; a kingdom ✳ Stockholm *area* 173,349 *sq mi* (450,707 *sq km*), *pop* 8,208,544
Swin·don \'swin-dən\ borough S England in NE Wiltshire *pop* 91,136
Swi·no·ujś·cie \,shvē-nō-'üish-(,)chä\ city & port NW Poland on N coast of Uznam (Usedom) Is. NNW of Szczecin *pop* 48,292
Swin·ton and Pen·dle·bury \'swin-tᵊn-ən-'pen-dᵊl-,ber-ē, -b(ə-)rē\ borough NW England in Greater Manchester NW of Manchester *pop* 39,621
Swit·zer·land \'swit-sər-lənd\ *or* **F Suisse** \swᵉēs\ *or* **G Schweiz** \'shvīts\ *or* **It Sviz·ze·ra** \'zvēt-tsä-rä\ *or* **L Hel·ve·tia** \hel-'vē-sh(ē-)ə\ country W Europe in the Alps; a federal republic ✳ Bern *area* 15,940 *sq mi* (41,444 *sq km*), *pop* 6,723,042
Syb·a·ris \'si-bə-rəs\ ancient Greek city S Italy on Gulf of Tarentum; destroyed 510 B.C.
Syd·ney \'sid-nē\ **1** city & port SE Australia on Port Jackson ✳ of New South Wales *metropolitan area* 2,989,070 **2** city Canada in NE N.S. on Cape Breton Is. *pop* 26,063 — **Syd·ney·ite** \-,īt\ *n* — **Syd·ney·sid·er** \-,sī-dər\ *n*
Syene — see ASWĀN
Sylt \'zilt, 'silt\ island NW Germany, chief of the N. Frisian Islands *area* 36 *sq mi* (94 *sq km*)
Syr·a·cuse \'sir-ə-,kyüs, -,kyüz\ **1** city *cen* N.Y. near Oneida Lake *pop* 163,860 **2** *or* **It Si·ra·cu·sa** \,sē-rə-'kü-zə\ *or anc* **Syr·a·cu·sae** \,sir-ə-'kyü-(,)sē, -(,)zē\ city & port Italy in SE Sicily *pop* 124,606 — **Syr·a·cu·san** \,sir-ə-'kyü-sᵊn, -'kyü-\ *adj or n*
Syr Dar·ya \,sir-'där-yə\ *or anc* **Jax·ar·tes** \jak-'sär-(,)tēz\ river 1500 *mi* (2414 *km*) Kyrgyzstan & S Kazakhstan flowing from Tian Shan W & NW into Lake Aral
Syr·ia \'sir-ē-ə\ **1** ancient region SW Asia bordering on the Mediterranean & covering modern Syria, Lebanon, Israel, & Jordan **2** former French mandate (1920–44) comprising the **Le·vant States** \lə-'vant\ (Syria, Lebanon, Latakia, & Jebel ed Druz), administrative ✳ Beirut, legislative ✳ Damascus **3** country SW Asia bordering on the Mediterranean; a republic 1944–58 & since 1961; a province of United Arab Republic 1958–61 ✳ Damascus *area* 72,234 *sq mi* (187,808 *sq km*), *pop* 9,171,622 — **Syr·i·an** \'sir-ē-ən\ *adj or n*
Syrian Desert desert W Asia bet. Mediterranean coast & the Euphrates covering N Saudi Arabia, NE Jordan, SE Syria, & W Iraq
Syrtis Major — see SIDRA (Gulf of)
Syrtis Minor — see GABÈS (Gulf of)
Szamos — see SOMES
Szcze·cin \'shche-,chēn\ city & port NW Poland *pop* 412,058
Sze·chwan \'sech-'wän, 'sesh-\ *or* **Si·chuan** \'sēch-'wän\ province SW China ✳ Chengdu *area* 219,691 *sq mi* (571,197 *sq km*), *pop* 99,713,310
Sze·ged \'se-,ged\ city S Hungary *pop* 184,000
Sze·kes·fe·her·var \'sā-,kesh-,fe-ər-,vär\ city W *cen* Hungary *pop* 111,200
Szepingkai — see SIPING
Szol·nok \'sōl-,nōk\ city E *cen* Hungary *pop* 82,900
Szom·bat·hely \'sōm-,bót-,hā\ city W Hungary *pop* 87,700
Ta·bas·co \tə-'bas-(,)kō\ state SE Mexico on the Caribbean SW of Yucatán Peninsula ✳ Villahermosa *area* 9782 *sq mi* (25,433 *sq km*), *pop* 1,149,756
Ta·blas \'tä-bläs\ island *cen* Philippines in Romblon group
Table Bay harbor of Cape Town, Republic of South Africa
Table Mountain mountain 3563 *ft* (1086 *m*) Republic of South Africa S of Cape Town
Ta·bor, Mount \'tā-bər, -,bór\ mountain 1929 *ft* (588 *m*) N Palestine E of Nazareth
Ta·bo·ra \tə-'bōr-ə, -'bór-\ city W *cen* Tanzania *pop* 67,392
Ta·briz \tə-'brēz\ *or anc* **Tau·ris** \'tór-əs\ city NW Iran in Azerbaijan *pop* 971,482
Ta·bu·a·er·an \,tə-,bü-ə-'er-ən\ *or formerly* **Fan·ning Island** \'fa-niŋ\ island *cen* Pacific in the Line Islands *area* 15 *sq mi* (39 *sq km*), *pop* 376
Ta·bun Bog·do \,tä,-bün-'bóg-(,)dō\ mountain 15,266 *ft* (4653 *m*) W Mongolia; highest in Altai Mountains
Tac·na \'tak-nə\ city S Peru near Chilean border *pop* 97,108; in region (**Tacna–Ari·ca** \-ə-'rē-kə\) occupied 1884–1930 by Chile & now divided bet. Chile & Peru
Ta·co·ma \tə-'kō-mə\ city & port W Wash. on Puget Sound S of Seattle *pop* 176,664
Tacoma, Mount — see RAINIER (Mount)
Ta·con·ic Range \tə-'kä-nik\ mountains along N part of Conn.-N.Y. boundary, entire Mass.-N.Y. boundary & in SW Vt.; highest Mt. Equinox (in Vt.) 3816 *ft* (1163 *m*)
Ta·djou·ra, Gulf of \tə-'jür-ə\ inlet of Gulf of Aden in E Djibouti
Tadmor — see PALMYRA
Tae·dong \ta-'dúŋ\ river 200 *mi* (322 *km*) *cen* N. Korea flowing SW into Korea Bay
Tae·gu \ta-'gü, tī-\ city SE S. Korea NNW of Pusan *pop* 2,029,853
Tae·jon \ta-'jön, tī-\ city *cen* S. Korea NW of Taegu *pop* 866,148
Ta·gan·rog \'ta-gən-,räg\ city S Russia in Europe on **Gulf of Taganrog** (NE arm of Sea of Azov) *pop* 276,000
Ta·gus \'tä-gəs\ *or* **Sp Ta·jo** \'tä-(,)hō\ *or* **Pg Te·jo** \'tā-(,)zhü\ river 566 *mi* (911 *km*) Spain & Portugal flowing W into the Atlantic
Ta·hi·ti \tə-'hē-tē\ island S Pacific in Windward group of the Society Islands; chief town Papeete *area* 402 *sq mi* (1045 *sq km*), *pop* 131,309
Ta·hoe, Lake \'tä-,hō\ lake 22 *mi* (35 *km*) long on Calif.-Nev. boundary
Tai·chung \'tī-'chùŋ\ city W Taiwan *pop* 607,238
Tai Hu \'tī-'hü\ lake 40 *mi* (64 *km*) long & 35 *mi* (56 *km*) wide E China in Jiangsu

\ə\ abut \ᵊ\ kitten, F table \ər\ further \a\ ash \ā\ ace \ä\ mop, mar \aù\ out \ch\ chin \e\ bet \ē\ easy \g\ go \i\ hit \ī\ ice \j\ job \ŋ\ sing \ō\ go \ó\ law \ói\ boy \th\ thin \th\ the \ü\ loot \ù\ foot \y\ yet \zh\ vision \á, k̠, ⁿ, œ, œ̄, ü, ǖ, ʸ\ see Guide to Pronunciation

Tai·myr Peninsula or **Tai·mir Peninsula** \tī-'mir\ peninsula N Russia in Asia bet. the Yenisey & the Khatanga — see CHELYUSKIN (Cape)

Tai·na·ron \'tī-nän\ city SW Taiwan pop 594,739

Tai·na·ron \tä-nə-ˌrȯn\ or **Mat·a·pan** \ˌma-tə-'pan\ cape S Greece at S tip of Peloponnisos bet. Gulfs of Laconia & Messenia

Tai·pei \'tī-'pā, -'bā\ city ✳ of (Nationalist) Republic of China, on Taiwan pop 2,270,983

Tai Shan \'tī-'shän\ mountain 5069 ft (1545 m) E China in W Shandong

Tai·wan \'tī-'wän\ or **For·mo·sa** \fȯr-'mō-sə, fər-, -zə\ island China off SE coast E of Fujian; belonged to Japan 1895–1945; since 1949 seat of (Nationalist) Republic of China (✳ Taipei) area 13,900 sq mi (36,140 sq km) — **Tai·wan·ese** \ˌtī-wə-'nēz, -'nēs\ adj or n

Tai·yu·an \'tī-yü-'än\ or formerly **Yang·ku** \'yäŋ-'kü\ city N China ✳ of Shanxi pop 1,053,000

Tai·zhou or **T'ai–chou** \'tī-jō\ city E China in cen Jiangsu

Ta·jik·i·stan \tä-ˌji-ki-'stan, tə-, -ˌjē, -'stän; -'ji-ki-, -'jē\ country W cen Asia bordering on China & Afghanistan; a constituent republic (**Ta·dzhik Republic** \tä-'jik, tə-, -'jēk\ or **Ta·dzhik·i·stan** \same as TA-JIKISTAN\) of the U.S.S.R. 1929–91 ✳ Dushanbe area 54,900 sq mi (142,740 sq km), pop 5,112,000

Ta·ju·mul·co \ˌtä-hü-'mül-(ˌ)kō\ mountain 13,845 ft (4220 m) W Guatemala; highest in Central America

Ta·ka·mat·su \ˌtä-kä-'mät-(ˌ)sü, tä-'kä-mət-sü\ city & port Japan in NE Shikoku on Inland Sea pop 329,695

Ta·kat·su·ki \tä-'kät-sü-(ˌ)kē\ city Japan in S Honshu pop 359,867

Tak·ka·kaw \'ta-kə-ˌkȯ\ waterfall 1650 ft (503 m) Canada in SE B.C. in Yoho National Park; highest in Canada

Ta·kla·ma·kan or **Ta·kla Ma·kan** \ˌtä-klə-mə-'kän\ desert W China in cen Xinjiang Uygur bet. Tian Shan & Kunlun mountains

Ta·la·ud Islands \'tä-ˌlä-ˌüd\ or **Ta·laur Islands** \-ˌlä-ˌu̇r\ islands Indonesia NE of Sulawesi area 494 sq mi (1284 sq km), pop 194,253

Tal·ca \'täl-kə\ city cen Chile S of Santiago pop 128,544

Tal·ca·hua·no \ˌtal-kə-'hwä-(ˌ)nō, -'hwä-\ city & port S cen Chile NW of Concepción pop 202,368

Tal·la·has·see \ˌta-lə-'ha-sē\ city ✳ of Fla. pop 124,773

Tal·la·hatch·ie \ˌta-lə-'ha-chē\ river 301 mi (484 km) N Miss. flowing SW

Tal·la·poo·sa \ˌta-lə-'pü-sə\ river 268 mi (431 km) NW Ga. & E Ala. flowing SW to join the Coosa forming Alabama River

Tal·linn \'ta-lən, 'tä-\ or formerly **Re·vel** \'rā-vəl\ city & port ✳ of Estonia pop 482,000

Ta·ma·le \tə-'mä-lē\ town N Ghana pop 135,952

Tam·al·pais, Mount \ˌta-məl-'pī-əs\ mountain 2604 ft (794 m) W Calif. NW of San Francisco

Ta·man \tə-'män\ peninsula S Russia in Europe in Ciscaucasia bet. Sea of Azov & Black Sea

Tam·an·ras·set \ˌta-mən-'ra-sət\ wadi & oasis SE Algeria

Ta·mar \'tä-mär\ **1** river 40 mi (64 km) Australia in N Tasmania flowing N to Bass Strait **2** river 60 mi (96 km) SW England flowing SE from NW Devon into English Channel **3** — see PALMYRA

Tam·a·rac \'ta-mə-ˌrak\ city SE Fla. pop 44,822

Tamatave — see TOAMASINA

Ta·mau·li·pas \ˌtä-ˌmau̇-'lē-pəs, tə-\ state NE Mexico bordering on Gulf of Mexico ✳ Ciudad Victoria area 30,731 sq mi (79,901 sq km), pop 1,924,934

Tam·bo·ra \täm-'bōr-ə, -'bȯr-\ volcano 9350 ft (2850 m) Indonesia on Sumbawa Is.

Tam·bov \täm-'bȯf, -'bȯv\ city S cen Russia in Europe SE of Moscow pop 270,000

Tam·il Na·du \ˌta-məl-'nä-(ˌ)dü, ˌtä-\ or formerly **Madras** state SE India bordering on Bay of Bengal ✳ Madras area 50,110 sq mi (130,286 sq km), pop 48,297,456

Tamiş — see TIMIŞ

Tam·pa \'tam-pə\ city W Fla. on **Tampa Bay** (inlet of Gulf of Mexico) pop 280,015 — **Tam·pan** \-pən\ adj or n

Tam·pi·co \tam-'pē-(ˌ)kō\ city & port E Mexico in S Tamaulipas on the Pánuco 7 mi (11 km) from its mouth pop 212,188

Ta·na, Lake \'tä-nə\ **1** lake NW Ethiopia; source of Blue Nile River area 1418 sq mi (3687 sq km) **2** river 500 mi (805 km) E Africa in Kenya flowing into Indian Ocean

Ta·na·gra \'ta-nə-grə, tə-'nä-grə\ village E cen Greece E of Thebes; an important town of ancient Boeotia

Tan·a·na \'ta-nə-ˌnȯ\ river 475 mi (764 km) E & cen Alaska flowing NW into Yukon River

Tananarive, Tananarivo — see ANTANANARIVO

Tan·ez·rouft \ˌta-nəz-'rüft\ extremely arid region of W Sahara in SW Algeria & N Mali

Tan·ga \'taŋ-gə\ city & port Tanzania on NE mainland pop 103,409

Tan·gan·yi·ka \ˌtaŋ-gə-'nyē-kə, ˌtan-gə-, -'nē-\ former country E Africa bet. Lake Tanganyika & Indian Ocean; administered by Britain 1920–61; became an independent member of the Commonwealth of Nations 1961 ✳ Dar es Salaam; since 1964 united with Zanzibar as Tanzania — see GERMAN EAST AFRICA — **Tan·gan·yi·kan** \-kən\ adj or n

Tanganyika, Lake lake E Africa in Great Rift Valley bet. Zaire & Tanzania area 12,700 sq mi (33,020 sq km)

Tan·gier \tan-'jir\ or **Tan·giers** \-'jirz\ **1** city & port N Morocco on Strait of Gibraltar; summer ✳ of Morocco pop 187,894 **2** the International Zone of Tangier — see MOROCCO — **Tan·ger·ine** \ˌtan-jə-'rēn\ adj or n

Tang·shan \'däŋ-'shän, 'täŋ-\ city NE China in E Hebei pop 1,200,000

Ta·nim·bar Islands \tə-'nim-ˌbär, -ˌä\ islands Indonesia in SE Moluccas ENE of Timor pop 50,000

Ta·nis \'tä-nəs\ or bib **Zo·an** \'zō-ˌan\ ancient city N Egypt in E Nile delta near Lake Tanis

Tanis, Lake — see MANZALA (Lake)

Tan·na \'tä-nə\ island SW Pacific in Vanuatu pop 19,825

Tannenberg — see STĘBARK

Tan·ta \'tän-tə\ city N Egypt in cen Nile delta pop 283,240

Tan–tung — see DANDONG

Tan·za·nia \ˌtan-zə-'nē-ə, ˌtän-\ republic E Africa formed 1964 by union of Tanganyika & Zanzibar ✳ Dar es Salaam area 362,844 sq mi (943,394 sq km), pop 17,527,564 — **Tan·za·ni·an** \-'nē-ən\ adj or n

Taor·mi·na \ˌtau̇r-'mē-nə\ or anc **Tau·ro·me·ni·um** \ˌtȯr-ə-'mē-nē-əm\ commune Italy in NE Sicily

Ta·pa·joz \ˌta-pə-'zhȯs, ˌtä-\ river 500 mi (805 km) N Brazil flowing NE into the Amazon — see JURUENA

Tap·pan Zee \ˌta-pən-'zē\ expansion of Hudson River SE N.Y.

Taprobane — see CEYLON

Tap·ti \'täp-tē\ river 436 mi (702 km) W India S of Satpura Range flowing W into Gulf of Cambay

Ta·qua·ri \ˌta-kwə-'rē\ river 450 mi (724 km) S cen Brazil rising in S cen Mato Grosso & flowing WSW into Paraguay River

Tar \'tär\ river 215 mi (346 km) NE N.C. — see PAMLICO

Tara \'tar-ə\ village Ireland in County Meath NW of Dublin near **Hill of Tara** (seat of ancient Irish kings)

Tarabulus — see TRIPOLI

Taranaki — see EGMONT (Mount)

Ta·ran·to \'tär-ən-ˌtō, tə-'ran-(ˌ)tō\ or anc **Ta·ren·tum** \tə-'ren-təm\ city & port SE Italy on **Gulf of Taranto** (inlet of Ionian Sea) pop 244,512

Ta·ra·wa \tə-'rä-wə, 'tar-ə-ˌwä\ island cen Pacific ✳ of Kiribati area 8 sq mi (21 sq km), pop 20,203

Tarbes \'tärb\ city SW France ESE of Pau pop 54,286

Ta·ri·fa, Cape \tä-'rē-fə, 'tä-\ cape S Spain; southernmost point of continental Europe, at 36°01'N

Ta·rim \'dä-'rēm, 'tä-\ river 1250 mi (2012 km) W China in Xinjiang Uygur in the Taklimakan flowing E & SE into Yuli (marshy depression)

Tar·lac \'tär-ˌläk\ city Philippines in cen Luzon pop 688,457

Tarn \'tärn\ river 233 mi (375 km) S France flowing W into the Garonne

Tar·nów \'tär-ˌnüf\ city S Poland E of Kraków pop 120,385

Tar·qui·nia \tär-'kwē-nyə, -'kwi-, -nē-ə\ or formerly **Cor·ne·to** \kȯr-'nä-(ˌ)tō\ or anc **Tar·quin·ii** \tär-'kwi-nē-ˌī\ town cen Italy in N Latium NW of Viterbo

Tar·ra·go·na \ˌtar-ə-'gō-nə\ **1** province NE Spain on the Mediterranean area 2505 sq mi (6513 sq km), pop 537,617 **2** commune & port, its ✳, SW of Barcelona pop 132,164

Tar·ra·sa \tə-'rä-sə\ commune NE Spain NNW of Barcelona pop 155,614

Tar·shish \'tär-(ˌ)shish\ ancient maritime country referred to in the Bible, by some located in S Spain & identified with Tartessus

Tar·sus \'tär-səs\ city S Turkey near the Cilician Gates ✳ of ancient Cilicia pop 57,035

Tar·tes·sus or **Tar·tes·sos** \tär-'te-səs\ ancient kingdom on SW coast of Spanish peninsula — see TARSHISH

Tar·tu \'tär-(ˌ)tü\ or G **Dor·pat** \'dȯr-ˌpät\ city E Estonia W of Lake Peipus pop 105,000

Tash·kent \tash-'kent, täsh-\ city E of the Syr Darya ✳ of Uzbekistan pop 2,073,000

Tas·man, Mount \'taz-mən\ mountain 11,475 ft (3498 m) New Zealand in South Is. in Southern Alps NE of Mt. Cook

Tas·ma·nia \taz-'mā-nē-ə, -nyə\ or formerly **Van Die·men's Land** \van-ˌdē-mənz\ island SE Australia S of Victoria; a state ✳ Hobart area 26,215 sq mi (68,159 sq km), pop 418,957 — **Tas·ma·ni·an** \taz-'mā-nē-ən, -nyən\ adj or n

Tasman Sea the part of the S Pacific bet. SE Australia & W New Zealand

Ta·ta·ban·ya \'tȯ-tȯ-ˌbä-(ˌ)nyȯ\ city NW Hungary pop 75,300

Ta·tar Republic \'tä-tər\ autonomous republic E cen Russia in Europe ✳ Kazan area 26,100 sq mi (67,860 sq km), pop 3,131,000

Tatar Strait strait bet. Sakhalin Is. & mainland of Asia

Ta·ta·ry \'tä-tə-rē\ or **Tar·ta·ry** \'tär-\ an indefinite historical region in Asia & Europe extending from coast of Sea of Japan to the Dnieper

Ta·try \'tä-trē\ or **Ta·tra** \'tä-trə\ mountain group N Slovakia & S Poland in cen Carpathian Mountains — see GERLACHOVKA

Tatung — see DATONG

Tau·ghan·nock Falls \tə-'ga-nək\ waterfall 215 ft (66 m) S cen N.Y. NW of Ithaca

Taung·gyi \'tau̇n-jē\ town E Myanmar ✳ of Shan State pop 8652

Taun·ton \'tȯn-t³n, 'tän-, 'tau̇n-\ city SE Mass. pop 49,832

Tau·nus \'tau̇-nəs\ mountain range SW cen Germany E of the Rhine & N of lower Main River; highest peak Grosser Feldberg 2887 ft (880 m)

Tauric Chersonese — see CHERSONESE

Tauris — see TABRIZ

Tau·rus Mountains \'tȯr-əs\ or Turk **To·ros Mountains** \tȯ-'rȯs\ mountains S Turkey parallel to Mediterranean coast; highest Ala Dag 12,251 ft (3734 m)

Tax·co \'täs-(ˌ)kō\ or **Taxco de Alar·cón** \thä-ˌä-ˌlär-'kȯn\ city S Mexico in Guerrero SSW of Mexico City pop 27,089

Tay \'tā\ river 120 mi (193 km) E cen Scotland flowing into North Sea through **Loch Tay** and **Firth of Tay**

Tay·lor \'tā-lər\ city SE Mich. SW of Detroit pop 70,811

Tay·side \'tā-ˌsīd\ region E cen Scotland, established 1975 ✳ Dundee area 2928 sq mi (7613 sq km), pop 391,529

Tbi·li·si \tə-'bē-lə-sē, tə-bə-'lē-sē\ or **Tif·lis** \'ti-fləs, tə-'flēs\ city ✳ of Republic of Georgia on the Kura pop 1,260,000

Tchad — see CHAD

Teche, Bayou \'tesh\ stream 175 mi (282 km) S La. flowing SE into the Atchafalaya

Tees \'tēz\ river 70 mi (113 km) N England flowing E into North Sea

Tees·side \'tē(z)-ˌsīd\ former county borough (1968–74) N England; since 1974 part of Cleveland

Te·gu·ci·gal·pa \tə-ˌgü-sə-'gal-pə, -'gäl-\ city ✳ of Honduras district pop 608,100

Te·hach·a·pi Mountains \ti-'ha-chə-pē\ mountains SE Calif. N of Mojave Desert running E–W bet. S end of Sierra Nevada & the Coast Ranges; highest Double Mountain 7988 ft (2435 m); at E end is **Te·hachapi Pass** 3793 ft (1156 m)

Teh·ran or **Te·he·ran** \ˌtä-(ə-)'ran, te-'ran, -'rän\ city ✳ of Iran at foot of S slope of Elburz Mountains pop 6,042,584

Teh·ri \'tä-rē\ or **Tehri Garh·wal** \(ˌ)gər-'wäl\ district N India in NW Uttar Pradesh on Tibet border; chief town Tehri

Te·huan·te·pec, Isthmus of \tə-'wän-tə-,pek\ the narrowest section of Mexico, bet. **Gulf of Tehuantepec** (on Pacific side) & Bay of Campeche; 130 *mi* (209 *km*) wide at narrowest point

Tejo — see TAGUS

Te·jon Pass \tē-'hōn\ pass 4183 *ft* (1275 *m*) SW Calif. in Tehachapi Mountains NW of Los Angeles

Tel·a·nai·pura \,te-lə-'ni-,pur-ə\ *or formerly* **Djam·bi** *or* **Jam·bi** \'jäm-bē\ city & port Indonesia in SE *cen* Sumatra *pop* 340,066

Tel Aviv \,tel-ə-'vēv\ city W Israel on the Mediterranean *pop* 386,612 — see JAFFA \ **Tel Avi·van** \-'vē-vən\ *n*

Tel el Amar·na \'tel-,el-ə-'mär-nə\ locality *cen* Egypt on E bank of the Nile NW of Asyût; site of ruins

Tel·e·mark \'te-lə-,märk\ mountain region SW Norway

Telescope Peak mountain 11,045 *ft* (3366 *m*) E Calif., highest in Panamint Mountains

Te·ma \'tā-mə\ city & port Ghana E of Accra *pop* 100,052

Te·mec·u·la \tə-'me·kyü-lə\ city S Calif. bet. Riverside & San Diego *pop* 27,099

Tem·pe \tem-'pē\ city S *cen* Ariz. SE of Phoenix *pop* 141,865

Tempe, Vale of \'tem-pē\ *or NGk* **Tém·bi** \'tem-bē\ valley in NE Thessaly bet. Mounts Olympus & Ossa

Tem·ple \'tem-pəl\ city NE *cen* Tex. SSW of Waco *pop* 46,109

Temple City city SW Calif. SE of Pasadena *pop* 31,100

Te·mu·co \tā-'mü-(,)kō\ city S *cen* Chile *pop* 157,634

Tenedos — see BOZCAADA

Te·ne·ri·fe \,te-nə-'rē-(,)fä, -'rēf, -'rif\ *or formerly* **Ten·er·iffe** \,te-nə-'rif, -'rēf\ island Spain, largest of the Canary Islands; chief town Santa Cruz de Tenerife *area* 782 *sq mi* (2033 *sq km*)

Ten·nes·see \,te-nə-'sē, 'te-nə-,\ **1** river 652 *mi* (1049 *km*) E U.S., in Tenn., Ala., & Ky. flowing into Ohio River **2** state SE *cen* U.S. ✳ Nashville *area* 42,244 *sq mi* (109,434 *sq km*), *pop* 4,877,185 — **Ten·nes·se·an** *or* **Ten·nes·see·an** \,te-nə-'sē-ən\ *adj or n*

Tennessee–Tom·big·bee Waterway \-täm-'big-bē\ waterway 234 *mi* (374 *km*) long from Tennessee River on Tenn.-Miss. border to Tombigbee River in W *cen* Ala.

Te·noch·ti·tlán \tā-,nōch-tēt-'län\ name for Mexico City when it was capital of the Aztec Empire

Ten·sas \'ten-,sò\ river 250 *mi* (402 *km*) NE La. uniting with Ouachita River to form Black River

Ten·saw \'ten-,sò\ river 40 *mi* (64 *km*) SW Ala. formed by Tombigbee & Alabama rivers & flowing S into Mobile Bay

Te·o·ti·hua·cán \,tā-ō-,tē-wə-'kän\ city S *cen* Mexico in Mexico state NE of Mexico City; once ✳ of the Toltecs *pop* 2238

Te·pic \tā-'pēk\ city W Mexico ✳ of Nayarit *pop* 108,924

Te·quen·da·ma Falls \,tā-kən-'dä-mə\ waterfall 475 *ft* (145 *m*) *cen* Colombia S of Bogotá

Te·rai·na \te-'rī-nə\ *or formerly* **Washington Island** island *cen* Pacific in the Line Islands *pop* 437

Ter·cei·ra \tər-'ser-ə, -'sir-\ island *cen* Azores *area* 233 *sq mi* (606 *sq km*)

Termonde — see DENDERMONDE

Ter·na·te \tər-'nä-(,)tä\ **1** island Indonesia in N Moluccas off W Halmahera *pop* 33,964 **2** city & port, chief city on Ternate *pop* 24,287

Ter·ni \'ter-nē\ commune *cen* Italy NNE of Rome *pop* 110,020

Ter·ra·ci·na \,ter-ə-'chē-nə\ city & port *cen* Italy in Latium SE of Pontine Marshes *pop* 39,393

Ter·ra No·va National Park \,ter-ə-'nō-və\ reservation E Canada in E Newfoundland (island)

Terre·bonne \'ter-ə-,bän, ter-'bòn\ town Canada in Que. N of Montreal *pop* 39,678

Ter·re Haute \,ter-ə-'hòt *also* -'hət, *rapid* ter-'hòt, -'hət\ city W Ind. on the Wabash *pop* 57,483

Te·ruel \,ter-ə-'wel\ **1** province E Spain in S Aragon *area* 5720 *sq mi* (14,872 *sq km*), *pop* 133,068 **2** commune, its ✳, S of Zaragoza *pop* 25,532

Teschen — see CIESZYN

Tessin — see TICINO

Te·thys \'tē-thəs\ hypothetical sea believed to have extended into E Pangaea & later to have separated Laurasia to the N & Gondwanaland to the S with the Mediterranean being a remnant of it — **Te·thy·an** \-thē-ən\ *adj*

Te·ton Range \'tē-,tän, 'tē-t²n\ mountain range NW Wyo. — see GRAND TETON

Té·touan \tā-'twän\ *or Sp* **Te·tuán** \te-'twän\ city & port N Morocco on the Mediterranean *pop* 139,105

Teu·to·burg Forest \'tü-tə-,bərg, 'tyü-\ *or G* **Teu·to·bur·ger Wald** \'tòi-tə-,bùr-gər-,vält\ range of forested hills W Germany in region bet. Ems & Weser rivers; highest point 1530 *ft* (466 *m*)

Tewkes·bury \'tüks-,ber-ē, 'tyüks-, 'tùks-, -b(ə-)rē\ city SW *cen* England in Gloucestershire on Avon & Severn rivers *pop* 9554

Tewks·bury \'tüks-,ber-ē, 'tyüks-, 'tùks-, -b(ə-)rē\ town NE Mass. *pop* 27,266

Tex·ar·kana \,tek-sər-'ka-nə, -sär-\ **1** city SW Ark. *pop* 22,631 **2** city NE Tex. adjacent to Texarkana, Ark. *pop* 31,656

Tex·as \'tek-səs, -siz\ state S U.S. ✳ Austin *area* 267,339 *sq mi* (695,081 *sq km*), *pop* 16,986,510 — **Tex·an** \-sən\ *adj or n*

Texas City city & port SE Tex. on Galveston Bay *pop* 40,822

Tex·co·co \tes-'kō-(,)kō\ city *cen* Mexico in Mexico state E of Mexico City *pop* 18,044

Thai·land \'tī-,land, -lənd\ *or formerly* **Si·am** \sī-'am\ country SE Asia on Gulf of Siam; a kingdom ✳ Bangkok *area* 198,247 *sq mi* (515,442 *sq km*), *pop* 44,278,000 — **Thai·land·er** \-,lan-dər, -lən-\ *n*

Thailand, Gulf of — see SIAM (Gulf of)

Thames \'temz, 'thämz, 'tämz\ river 15 *mi* (24 *km*) SE Conn., an estuary flowing S into Long Island Sound **2** \'temz\ river 135 *mi* (217 *km*) Canada in SE Ont. flowing S & SW into Lake St. Clair **3** \'temz\ river 209 *mi* (336 *km*) S England flowing from the Cotswolds in Gloucestershire E into the North Sea — see ISIS

Than·et, Isle of \'tha-nət\ tract of land SE England in NE Kent cut off from mainland by arms of Stour River *area* 42 *sq mi* (109 *sq km*)

Thar Desert \'tär\ *or* **Great Indian Desert** desert S Asia in Pakistan & India bet. Aravalli Range & the Indus

Thá·sos \'thä-,sòs\ island Greece in the N Aegean E of Chalcidice Peninsula *area* 152 *sq mi* (395 *sq km*)

The·ba·id \thi-'bā-əd, 'thē-bā-,id\ ancient district surrounding Thebes in Egypt or in Greece

Thebes \'thēbz\ **1** *or anc* **The·bae** \'thē-(,)bē\ *or* **Di·os·po·lis** \dī-'äs-pə-ləs\ ancient city S Egypt on the Nile S of modern Qena — see KARNAK, LUXOR **2** ancient city E Greece in Boeotia NNW of Athens — **The·ban** \'thē-bən\ *adj or n*

The Colony city N Tex. *pop* 22,113

The Hague — see HAGUE (The)

The·lon \'thē-,län\ river *ab* 550 *mi* (885 *km*) N Canada in E Northwest Territories flowing NE to Baker Lake

Theodore Roosevelt National Park \'thē-ə-,dōr, -,dòr, -dər\ reservation W N.Dak. comprising three areas in badland region on the Little Missouri

Thera — see SANTORIN

Ther·ma·i·kós Kól·pos \ther-,mä-ē-'kòs-'kòl-(,)pòs\ *or* **Gulf of Sa·lo·ni·ka** \sə-'lä-ni-kə\ arm of Aegean Sea N Greece W of Chalcidice

Ther·mop·y·lae \(,)thər-'mä-pə-(,)lē\ locality E Greece bet. Mt. Oeta & Gulf of Lamia; once a narrow pass along the coast, now a rocky plain 6 *mi* (9.6 *km*) from the sea

Thes·sa·lo·ni·ki \,the-sə-lə-'nē-kē\ *or formerly* **Sa·lo·ni·ka** \sə-'lä-ni-kə\ *or anc* **Thes·sa·lo·ni·ca** \,the-sə-'lä-ni-kə, -lə-'nē-kə\ city & port N Greece in Macedonia *pop* 402,443

Thes·sa·ly \'the-sə-lē\ *or Gk* **Thes·sa·lía** \,the-sə-'lē-ə\ region E Greece bet. Pindus Mountains & the Aegean — **Thes·sa·lian** \the-'sā-lē-ən, -'sāl-yən\ *adj or n*

Thim·bu \'thim-(,)bü\ city W *cen* Bhutan, its ✳

Thíra — see SANTORIN

Tho·hoy·an·dou \tō-,hòi-an-'dü\ town NE Republic of South Africa; formerly ✳ of Venda

Thomp·son \'täm(p)-sən\ river 304 *mi* (489 *km*) Canada in S B.C. flowing S (as the **North Thompson**) & thence W & SW into the Fraser; joined by a branch, the **South Thompson**

Thorn·ton \'thòrn-t²n\ city NE *cen* Colo. N of Denver *pop* 55,031

Thors·havn *or* **Tórs·havn** \'tòrs-,haùn, tòrs-'\ town & port ✳ of the Faeroe Islands, on Strömö Is. *pop* 11,618

Thousand Islands island group Canada & U.S. in St. Lawrence River in Ont. & N.Y.

Thousand Oaks city SW Calif. W of Los Angeles *pop* 104,352

Thrace \'thrās\ region SE Europe in Balkan Peninsula N of the Aegean; as ancient country (**Thra·ce** \'thrā-(,)sē\ *or* **Thra·cia** \'thrā-sh(ē-)ə\), extended to the Danube; modern remnant divided bet. Greece (**Western Thrace**) & Turkey (**Eastern Thrace**, constituting Turkey in Europe) — **Thra·cian** \'thrā-shən\ *adj or n*

Thracian Chersonese — see CHERSONESE

Three Forks locality SW Mont. where Missouri River is formed by confluence of Gallatin, Jefferson, & Madison rivers *pop* 1203

Three Rivers TROIS-RIVIÈRES

Thu·le \'tü-lē\ settlement & district NW Greenland N of Cape York

Thun \'tün\ commune E *cen* Switzerland *pop* 37,817

Thunder Bay city & port Canada in SW Ont. on Lake Superior, formed 1970 by consolidation of Fort William & Port Arthur *pop* 113,946

Thun·er See \'tü-nər-,zā\ *or* **Lake of Thun** \'tün\ lake 10 *mi* (16 *km*) long *cen* Switzerland; an expansion of Aare River

Thur·gau \'tùr-,gaù\ *or F* **Thur·go·vie** \tūer-gò-vē\ canton NE Switzerland ✳ Frauenfeld *area* 397 *sq mi* (1032 *sq km*), *pop* 201,773

Thu·rin·gia \thù-'rin-j(ē-)ə, thyù-\ *or G* **Thü·ring·en** \'tüe-riŋ-ən\ region *cen* Germany including the **Thu·rin·gian Forest** \thù-'rin-j(ē-)ən, thyù-\ *or G* **Thü·ring·er Wald** \'tüe-riŋ-ər-,vält\ (wooded mountain range bet. the upper Werra & the Czech border)

Thur·rock \'thər-ək, 'thə-rək\ former urban district SE England in Essex

Thursday Island island NE Australia off N Queensland in Torres Strait

Thyatira — see AKHISAR

Ti·a·hua·na·co \,tē-ə-wə-'nä-(,)kō\ locality W Bolivia near SE end of Lake Titicaca; site of prehistoric ruins

Tian·jin \tē-'än-'jin\ *or* **Tien·tsin** \tē-'en(t)-'sin, 'tin(t)-\ municipality & port NE China SE of Beijing *pop* 7,764,141

Tian Shan \tē-'än-'shän\ *or* **Tien Shan** \tē-'en-\ mountain system *cen* Asia extending from the Pamirs NE into Xinjiang Uygur — see POBEDA PEAK

Ti·ber \'tī-bər\ *or It* **Te·ve·re** \'tā-vā-rā\ river 224 *mi* (360 *km*) *cen* Italy flowing through Rome into Tyrrhenian Sea

Ti·be·ri·as \tī-'bir-ē-əs\ city N Palestine in Galilee on W shore of Sea of Galilee; now in NE Israel *pop* 23,900

Tiberias, Sea of — see GALILEE (Sea of)

Ti·bes·ti Mountains \tə-'bes-tē\ mountains N *cen* Africa in the Sahara in NW Chad; highest Emi Koussi 11,204 *ft* (3415 *m*)

Ti·bet \tə-'bet\ *or* **Xi·zang** \'shēd-'zäŋ\ region SW China on high plateau (average altitude 16,000 *ft or* 4877 *m*) N of the Himalayas ✳ Lhasa *area* 471,660 *sq mi* (1,226,316 *sq km*), *pop* 1,892,393

Ti·bu·rón \,tē-bə-'ròn\ island 34 *mi* (55 *km*) long NW Mexico in Gulf of California off coast of Sonora

Ti·ci·no \ti-'chē-(,)nō\ **1** river 154 *mi* (248 *km*) Switzerland & Italy flowing from slopes of St. Gotthard Range SE & SW through Lake Maggiore into the Po **2** *or F* **Tes·sin** \te-sa²\ canton S Switzerland bordering on Italy ✳ Bellinzona *area* 1085 *sq mi* (2821 *sq km*), *pop* 286,537 — **Ti·ci·nese** \,ti-chə-'nēz, -'nēs\ *adj or n*

Tientsin — see TIANJIN

Tier·ra del Fue·go \tē-'er-ə-(,)del-fù-'ā-(,)gō, -'fwä-, -fyù-'ā-\ **1** archipelago off S S. America S of Strait of Magellan; in Argentina & Chile *area* 27,600 *sq mi* (71,760 *sq km*) **2** chief island of the archipelago; divided bet. Chile and Argentina *area* 18,530 *sq mi* (48,178 *sq km*)

Tiflis — see TBILISI

\ə\ abut \²\ kitten, F table \ər\ further \a\ ash \ā\ ace \ä\ mop, mar \aù\ out \ch\ chin \e\ bet \ē\ easy \g\ go \i\ hit \ī\ ice \j\ job \ŋ\ sing \ō\ go \ò\ law \òi\ boy \th\ thin \t̲h̲\ the \ü\ loot \ù\ foot \y\ yet \zh\ vision \ä, k̲, ⁿ, œ, œ̄, ᵾe, ᵾē, ᵾ\ *see* Guide to Pronunciation

Ti·gard \'tī-gərd\ city NW Oreg. SSW of Portland *pop* 29,344
Ti·gre 1 \'tē-(ˌ)grā\ city E Argentina, NW suburb of Buenos Aires, on islands in Paraná delta *pop* 199,366 2 \ti-'grä, 'ti-(ˌ)grä\ region N Ethiopia bordering on Eritrea — **Ti·gre·an** \ti-'grā-ən\ *adj or n*
Ti·gris \'tī-grəs\ river 1150 *mi* (1851 *km*) Iraq & SE Turkey flowing SSE & uniting with the Euphrates to form the Shatt-al-Arab
Ti·jua·na \ˌtē-ə-'wä-nə, tē-\ city NW Mexico on U.S. border in Baja California *pop* 335,125
Ti·kal \ti-'käl\ ancient Mayan city N Guatemala
Til·burg \'til-ˌbərg\ commune S Netherlands SE of Rotterdam *pop* 153,889
Til·bury \'til-b(ə-)rē, *US also* -ˌber-ē\ town & port SE England in Essex on Thames River E of London
Til·la·mook Bay \'ti-lə-ˌmək, -ˌmuk\ inlet of the Pacific NW Oreg.
Tilsit — see SOVETSK
Ti·ma·ga·mi, Lake \tə-'mä-gə-mē\ lake Canada in Ont. N of Lake Nipissing
Timbuktu — see TOMBOUCTOU
Tim·gad \'tim-ˌgad\ ancient Roman city NE Algeria
Ti·miş *or* **Ta·miš** \'tē-mish\ *or* \'tä-mish\ river 270 *mi* (434 *km*) Romania & Yugoslavia flowing W & S into the Danube downstream from Belgrade
Ti·mi·soa·ra \ˌtē-mi-'shwär-ə\ city W Romania *pop* 333,365
Tim·mins \'ti-mənz\ city Canada in E Ont. N of Sudbury *pop* 47,461
Ti·mor \'tē-ˌmor, tē-'\ 1 island E Indonesia in Lesser Sunda Islands *area* 13,094 *sq mi* (34,044 *sq km*), *pop* 3,000,000; W part (formerly **Netherlands Timor**) belonged to the Dutch until 1946, E part (formerly **Portuguese Timor**) to Portugal until 1975 2 sea bet. Timor Is. & Australia — **Ti·mor·ese** \(ˌ)tē-ˌmō-'rēz, -'rēs\ *adj or n*
Tim·pa·no·gos, Mount \ˌtim-pə-'nō-gəs\ mountain 12,008 *ft* (3660 *m*) N *cen* Utah N of Provo; highest in Wasatch Range
Timpanogos Cave National Monument series of limestone caverns N *cen* Utah on N slope of Mt. Timpanogos
Ti·ni·an \ti-nē-'an\ island W Pacific in the S Marianas
Tin·ley Park \'tin-lē\ city NE Ill. *pop* 37,121
Ti·nos \'tē-ˌnos\ island Greece in N Cyclades SE of Andros
Tin·tag·el Head \tin-'ta-jəl\ headland SW England in NW Cornwall
Tip·pe·ca·noe \ˌti-pē-kə-'nü\ river 200 *mi* (322 *km*) N Ind. flowing SW into the Wabash
Tip·per·ary \ˌti-pə-'rer-ē\ 1 county S Ireland in Munster ✳ Clonmel *area* 1643 *sq mi* (4272 *sq km*), *pop* 132,620 2 urban district in SW County Tipperary *pop* 5033
Ti·ra·në *or* **Ti·ra·na** \ti-'rä-nə\ city *cen* Albania, its ✳ *pop* 190,200
Tir·gu—Mu·res \ˌtir-(ˌ)gü-'mü-ˌresh\ city NE *cen* Romania ESE of Cluj-Napoca *pop* 164,781
Ti·rich Mir \ˌtir-ich-'mir\ mountain 25,230 *ft* (7690 *m*) Pakistan on Afghan border; highest in the Hindu Kush
Ti·rol *or* **Ty·rol** \tə-'rōl; 'tī-ˌrōl, ti-'\ *or It* **Ti·ro·lo** \tē-'rō-(ˌ)lō\ region Europe in E Alps chiefly in Austria; the section S of Brenner Pass has belonged since 1919 to Italy — **Ti·ro·le·an** \tə-'rō-lē-ən, tī-; ˌtir-ə-', ˌtī-rə-'\ *adj or n* — **Ti·ro·lese** \ˌtir-ə-'lēz, ˌti-rə-, -'lēs\ *adj or n*
Ti·ruch·chi·rap·pal·li *or* **Ti·ru·chi·ra·pal·li** \ˌtir-ə-chə-'rä-pə-lē\ city S India in *cen* Tamil Nadu *pop* 607,815
Ti·ryns \'tir-ənz, 'ti-rənz\ city of pre-Homeric Greece; ruins in E Peloponniss SE of Argos
Ti·sza \'ti-ˌsȯ\ river 800 *mi* (1287 *km*) E Europe flowing from the Carpathians in W Ukraine W & SW into the Danube
Ti·ti·ca·ca, Lake \ˌti-ti-'kä-kə\ lake on Peru-Bolivia boundary at altitude of 12,500 *ft* (3810 *m*), *area* 3200 *sq mi* (8320 *sq km*)
Titograd — see PODGORICA
Ti·tus·ville \'tī-təs-ˌvil, -vəl\ city E Fla. E of Orlando *pop* 39,394
Tiv·o·li \'ti-və-lē\ *or anc* **Ti·bur** \'tī-bər\ commune *cen* Italy in Latium ENE of Rome *pop* 54,352
Tji·la·tjap \chi-'lä-ˌchäp\ city & port Indonesia in S Java ESE of Bandung *pop* 55,333
Tjir·e·bon \ˌchir-ə-'bȯn\ *or* **Cher·i·bon** \ˌcher-ə-\ city Indonesia in W Java on N coast E of Djakarta *pop* 223,776
Tlax·ca·la \tlä-'skä-lə\ 1 state *cen* Mexico *area* 1555 *sq mi* (4043 *sq km*), *pop* 547,261 2 city, its ✳, E of Mexico City *pop* 21,421
Tlem·cen \tlem-'sen\ *or* **Ti·lim·sen** \tə-lim-'sen\ city NW Algeria *pop* 109,400
Toa Al·ta \ˌtō-ə-'äl-tə\ town NE *cen* Puerto Rico *pop* 44,101
Toa Ba·ja \-'bä-(ˌ)hä\ town NE *cen* Puerto Rico W of San Juan *pop* 89,454
To·a·ma·si·na \ˌtō-ə-mə-'sē-nə\ *or* **Ta·ma·tave** \ˌtä-mə-'täv, ˌtä-\ city & port E coast of Madagascar *pop* 77,395
To·ba·go \tə-'bä-(ˌ)gō\ island SE W. Indies, a territory of Trinidad and Tobago; chief town Scarborough *area* 116 *sq mi* (302 *sq km*), *pop* 50,282 — **To·ba·go·ni·an** \ˌtō-bə-'gō-nē-ən, -nyən\ *n*
To·bol \tə-'bȯl\ river 800 *mi* (1287 *km*) N Kazakhstan & SW Russia in Asia flowing from SE foothills of the Urals NNE into the Irtysh
To·bruk \tō-'brük, 'tō-\ city & port NE Libya *pop* 34,200
To·can·tins \ˌtō-kən-'tēnz, ˌtü-kən-'tēns\ river 1700 *mi* (2736 *km*) E *cen* & NE Brazil rising in S *cen* Goiás & flowing N into Pará River
To·go \'tō-(ˌ)gō\ republic W Africa on Bight of Benin ✳ Lomé *area* 21,893 *sq mi* (56,922 *sq km*), *pop* 2,703,000 — **To·go·lese** \ˌtō-gə-'lez, -'lēs\ *adj or n*
To·go·land \'tō-(ˌ)gō-ˌland\ region W Africa on Gulf of Guinea bet. Benin & Ghana; until 1919 a German protectorate, then divided into two trust territories: **British Togoland** (in W; since 1957 part of Ghana) & **French Togo** (in E; since 1958 Togo) — **To·go·land·er** \'tō-(ˌ)gō-ˌlan-dər\ *n*
To·ho·pe·kal·i·ga Lake \ˌtō-hō-pi-'ka-li-gə\ lake S Fla. S of Orlando
To·ka·ra Islands \tō-'kär-ə\ island group Japan in N Ryukyus
To·ke·lau Islands \'tō-kə-ˌlaů\ islands *cen* Pacific N of Samoa belonging to New Zealand *pop* 1690 — **To·ke·lau·an** \ˌtō-kə-'laů-ən\ *n*
To·ko·ro·za·wa \ˌtō-kə-'rō-zə-(ˌ)wä\ city Japan on Honshu, a suburb of Tokyo *pop* 303,047
To·ku·shi·ma \ˌtō-kə-'shē-mə\ city & port Japan on E coast of Shikoku Is. *pop* 263,336
To·kyo \'tō-kē-ˌō\ *or formerly* **Edo** \'e-(ˌ)dō\ *or* **Ye·do** \'ye-(ˌ)dō\ city ✳ of Japan in SE Honshu on **Tokyo Bay** (inlet of the Pacific) *pop* 11,854,987 — **To·kyo·ite** \'tō-kē-(ˌ)ō-ˌīt\ *n*
To·le·do \tə-'lē-(ˌ)dō, -'lē-də, *for 2 & 3 also* -'lā-\ 1 city & port NW Ohio on the Maumee River *pop* 332,943 2 province *cen* Spain in W

New Castile *area* 5919 *sq mi* (15,389 *sq km*), *pop* 445,326 3 commune, its ✳ *pop* 60,133 — **To·le·dan** \-'lē-dᵊn\ *adj or n* — **To·le·do·an** \-'lē-dō-ən\ *adj or n*
To·li·ma \tə-'lē-mə\ dormant volcano W *cen* Colombia 17,110 *ft* (5215 *m*)
To·lu·ca \tə-'lü-kə\ *or* **Toluca de Ler·do** \də-'ler-(ˌ)dō\ city *cen* Mexico ✳ of Mexico state *pop* 220,195
Toluca, Ne·va·do de \nə-'vä-dō-(ˌ)dā-\ extinct volcano 15,016 *ft* (4577 *m*) S *cen* Mexico in Mexico state
Tol'·yat·ti *or* **To·gliat·ti** \tȯl-'yä-tē\ *or formerly* **Stav·ro·pol** \stav-'rȯ-pəl, -'rō-\ city SE *cen* Russia in Europe NW of Samara *pop* 251,000
Tom \'täm, 'tȯm\ river 450 *mi* (724 *km*) S Russia in Asia rising in NW Altai Mountains & flowing into the Ob
Tom·big·bee \täm-'big-bē\ river 300 *mi* (483 *km*) NE Miss. & W Ala. flowing S to Mobile & Tensaw rivers
Tom·bouc·tou \tōⁿ-bük-tü\ *or* **Tim·buk·tu** \ˌtim-ˌbak-'tü, tim-'bak-(ˌ)tü\ town W Africa in Mali near Niger River *pop* 20,483
Tomsk \'täm(p)sk, 'tȯm(p)sk\ city S *cen* Russia in Asia on Tom River near its junction with the Ob *pop* 339,000
Ton·ga \'täŋ-gə, 'täŋ-ə\ islands SW Pacific E of Fiji; a kingdom in the Commonwealth of Nations ✳ Nukualofa *area* 270 *sq mi* (702 *sq km*), *pop* 94,649
Tongareva — see PENRHYN
Ton·ga·ri·ro \ˌtäŋ-gə-'rir-(ˌ)ō, ˌtäŋ-ə-\ volcano 6516 *ft* (1986 *m*) New Zealand in *cen* North Is. in Tongariro National Park
Tong·hua \'tȯŋ-'hwä, -'wä\ *or* **T'ung·hua** *or* **Tung·hwa** \'tůŋ-\ city NE China in S Jilin *pop* 158,000
Tongue \'təŋ\ river 240 *mi* (386 *km*) N Wyo. & S Mont. flowing N into Yellowstone River
Ton·kin \'täŋ-kən; 'tän-'kin, 'täŋ-\ *or* **Tong·king** \'täŋ-'kiŋ\ region N Indochina bordering on China, since 1946 forming N part of Vietnam; chief city Hanoi — **Ton·kin·ese** \ˌtäŋ-kə-'nēz, ˌtän-, -'nēs\ *or* **Tong·king·ese** \ˌtäŋ-kiŋ-'ēz, -'ēs\ *adj or n*
Tonkin, Gulf of arm of S. China Sea E of N Vietnam
Ton·le Sap \ˌtän-ˌlā-'sap\ *or* **F Grand Lac** \grän-'läk\ lake 87 *mi* (140 *km*) long SW Indochina in W Cambodia
Ton·to National Monument \'tän-(ˌ)tō\ reservation S *cen* Ariz. E of Phoenix containing cliff-dweller ruins
Too·woom·ba \tə-'wům-bə\ city E Australia in SE Queensland *pop* 71,362
To·pe·ka \tə-'pē-kə\ city ✳ of Kans. on Kansas River *pop* 119,883
To·po·lo·bam·po \tə-ˌpō-lə-'bäm-(ˌ)pō\ town & port NW Mexico in Sinaloa on Gulf of California
Tor·bay \(ˌ)tȯr-'bā\ former county borough SW England in Devonshire on **Tor Bay** (inlet of English Channel); included Brixham, Paignton, & Torquay
Tor·cel·lo \tȯr-'che-(ˌ)lō\ island Italy in Lagoon of Venice
Tor·de·si·llas \ˌtȯr-də-'sē-yəs, -'sēl-yəs\ village NW Spain SW of Valladolid
Torino — see TURIN
Tor·ne \'tȯr-nə\ *or Finn* **Tor·nio** \'tȯr-nē-ˌō\ river 250 *mi* (400 *km*) NE Sweden flowing S, forming part of Finnish-Swedish border, to head of Gulf of Bothnia
To·ron·to \tə-'rän-(ˌ)tō, -'rän-tə\ city & port Canada ✳ of Ont. on Lake Ontario *pop* 635,395 — **To·ron·to·ni·an** \tə-ˌrän-'tō-nē-ən; ˌtȯr-ən-, ˌtär-ən-\ *adj or n*
Toros — see TAURUS
Tor·rance \'tȯr-ən(t)s, 'tär-\ city SW Calif. SSW of Los Angeles *pop* 133,107
Tor·re An·nun·zi·a·ta \ˌtȯr-ē-ə-ˌnün(t)-sē-'ä-tə, ˌtȯr-ā-\ commune S Italy on Bay of Naples SE of Naples *pop* 56,471
Torre de Cerredo — see CERREDO
Tor·re del Gre·co \ˌtȯr-ē-del-'gre-(ˌ)kō, ˌtȯr-ā-, -'grä-\ commune S Italy on Bay of Naples *pop* 103,577
Tor·rens, Lake \'tȯr-ənz\ salt lake Australia in E S. Australia N of Spencer Gulf; 25 *ft* (8 *m*) below sea level
Tor·re·ón \ˌtȯr-ē-'ōn\ city N Mexico in Coahuila *pop* 257,045
Tor·res Strait \'tȯr-əs\ strait 80 *mi* (129 *km*) wide bet. island of New Guinea & N tip of Cape York Peninsula, Australia
Tor·res Ve·dras \ˌtȯr-əs-'vā-drəs\ town W Portugal N of Lisbon
Tor·ring·ton \'tȯr-iŋ-tən, 'tär-\ city NW Conn. *pop* 33,687
Tórshavn — see THORSHAVN
Tor·to·la \tȯr-'tō-lə\ island Brit. West Indies, chief of the Brit. Virgin Islands; site of Road Town *area* 24 *sq mi* (62 *sq km*), *pop* 9730
Tor·tu·ga \tȯr-'tü-gə\ island Haiti off N coast *area* 70 *sq mi* (182 *sq km*); a resort of pirates in 17th century *pop* 13,723
To·ruń \'tȯr-ˌün, -ˌü-nyə\ city N Poland on the Vistula *pop* 200,822
Toscana — see TUSCANY
Tot·ten·ham \'tä-tᵊn-əm, 'tät-nəm\ former municipal borough SE England in Middlesex, now part of Haringey
Toub·kal, Je·bel \je-bəl-tüb-'käl\ mountain 13,665 *ft* (4165 *m*) W *cen* Morocco; highest in Atlas Mountains
Toug·gourt \tə-'gürt\ town & oasis NE Algeria S of Biskra *pop* 75,600
Tou·lon \tü-lōⁿ\ commune & port SE France on the Mediterranean *pop* 180,508
Tou·louse \tù-'lüz\ city SW France on the Garonne *pop* 373,796
Tou·raine \tù-'rān, -'ren\ region & former province NW *cen* France ✳ Tours
Tourane — see DA NANG
Tour·coing \tür-'kwaⁿ\ city N France NE of Lille *pop* 102,092
Tour·nai *or* **Tour·nay** \tür-'nā\ *or Flem* **Door·nik** \'dōr-nik, 'dȯr-\ commune SW Belgium on the Scheldt *pop* 67,732
Tours \'tür\ city NW *cen* France *pop* 139,560
Tower Hamlets borough of E Greater London, England *pop* 146,300
Towns·ville \'taůnz-ˌvil, -vəl\ city & port NE Australia in NE Queensland *pop* 96,230
To·ya·ma \tō-'yä-mə\ city Japan in *cen* Honshu near **Toyama Bay** (inlet of Sea of Japan) *pop* 321,259
To·yo·ha·shi \ˌtȯi-ə-'hä-shē\ city Japan in S Honshu SE of Nagoya *pop* 337,988
To·yo·na·ka \ˌtȯi-ə-'nä-kə\ city Japan on Honshu *pop* 409,843
To·yo·ta \tȯi-'ō-tə\ city Japan on Honshu *pop* 332,336
Trab·zon \trab-'zän\ *or* **Treb·i·zond** \'tre-bə-ˌzänd\ *or anc* **Trap·e·zus** \'tra-pi-zəs\ city & port NE Turkey on Black Sea *pop* 107,412

Tra·cy \'trā-sē\ city cen Calif. SSW of Stockton pop 33,558

Tra·fal·gar, Cape \trə-'fal-gər, Sp ,trä-fäl-'gär\ cape SW Spain SE of Cádiz at W end of Strait of Gibraltar

Tra·lee \trə-'lē\ urban district & port SW Ireland ✻ of Kerry pop 17,109

Trans Alai \,tran(t)s-ə-'lī, ,tranz\ mountain range Kyrgyzstan & Tajikistan in NW Pamirs — see LENIN PEAK

Transalpine Gaul the part of Gaul included chiefly in modern France & Belgium

Transcaucasia — see CAUCASUS — **Trans·cau·ca·sian** \,tran(t)s-kò-'kā-zhən, -'ka-\ adj or n

Transjordan — see JORDAN — **Trans·jor·da·ni·an** \,tran(t)s-jór-'dā-nē-ən, ,tranz-\ adj or n

Trans·kei \(,)tran(t)s-'kī\ former black enclave in the Republic of South Africa ✻ Umtata; granted independence 1976; abolished 1994 — **Trans·kei·an** \-ən\ adj or n

Trans·vaal \tran(t)s-'väl, tranz-\ former province NE Republic of South Africa bet. the Vaal & the Limpopo; in 19th century a Boer republic (**South African Republic**) ✻ Pretoria area 110,450 sq mi (287,170 sq km)

Tran·syl·va·nia or Romanian **Tran·sil·va·nia** \,tran(t)-səl-'vā-nyə, -nē-ə\ region W Romania bounded on the N, E, & S by the Carpathians & the Transylvanian Alps; part of Hungary 1867–1918 — **Tran·syl·va·nian** \-nyən, -nē-ən\ adj or n

Transylvanian Alps a S extension of the Carpathian Mountains in cen Romania

Tra·pa·ni \'trä-pə-nē\ commune & port Italy at NW tip of Sicily pop 72,837

Tra·si·me·no, Lake \,tra-zə-'me-(,)nō, ,trä-zə-'mā-\ lake 10 mi (16 km) wide cen Italy W of Perugia

Trav·an·core \'tra-vən-,kōr, -,kór\ region & former state SW India on Malabar coast extending N from Cape Comorin; included (1949–56) in former **Travancore and Co·chin** \'kō-chən\ state (✻ Trivandrum) — see KERALA

Trav·erse, Lake \'tra-vərs\ lake NE S.Dak. & W Minn.; drained by the Bois de Sioux (headstream of Red River)

Treb·bia \'tre-bē-ə\ or anc **Tre·bia** \'trē-bē-ə\ river 71 mi (114 km) NW Italy flowing N into the Po

Treb·i·zond \'tre-bə-,zänd\ 1 — see TRABZON 2 Greek empire 1204–1461, an offshoot of Byzantine Empire; at greatest extent included Georgia, Crimea, & S coast of Black Sea E of the Sakarya

Trem·blant, Mont \,mōⁿ-trä⁻'bläⁿ\ mountain 3150 ft (960 m) Canada in S Que. in Laurentian Hills NW of Montreal

Treng·ga·nu \treŋ-'gä-(,)nü\ state Malaysia in NE Peninsular Malaysia on S. China Sea ✻ Kuala Trengganu area 5050 sq mi (13,130 sq km)

Trent \'trent\ 1 river 150 mi (241 km) Canada in SE Ont. flowing from Kawartha Lakes through Rice Lake into Lake Ontario (Bay of Quinte) 2 river 170 mi (274 km) cen England flowing NNE & uniting with Ouse River to form the Humber

Trent Canal or **Trent–Sev·ern Canal** \-'se-vərn\ canal system Canada 224 mi (360 km) long in SE Ont. connecting Lake Huron (Georgian Bay) with Lake Ontario (Bay of Quinte)

Tren·ti·no \tren-'tē-(,)nō\ district N Italy in S Tirol; with Alto Adige, forms **Trentino–Alto Adige** region ✻ Trento area 6327 sq mi or 16,450 sq km, pop 886,679)

Tren·to \'tren-(,)tō\ commune N Italy pop 101,416

Tren·ton \'tren-tⁿn\ 1 city SE Mich. on Detroit River pop 20,586 2 city ✻ of N.J. on Delaware River pop 88,675

Tre·vi·so \trā-'vē-(,)zō\ commune NE Italy NW of Venice pop 84,066

Trier \'trir\ city W Germany on the Moselle near Luxembourg border pop 104,100

Tri·este \trē-'est, -'es-tē\ or Serbo-Croatian **Trst** \'tərst\ city & port NE Italy ✻ of Friuli-Venezia Giulia, on **Gulf of Trieste** (inlet at head of the Adriatic NW of the Istrian Peninsula) pop 263,908; once belonged to Austria; part of Italy 1919–47; in 1947 made with surrounding territory the **Free Territory of Trieste** under administration of the United Nations; city with N part of Free Territory returned to Italy 1953, S part of territory having previously been absorbed into Yugoslavia — **Tri·es·tine** \trē-'es-tən, -,tēn\ adj

Trik·ka·la \'tri-kə-lə, 'trē-\ city cen Greece pop 48,810

Trim \'trim\ urban district E Ireland ✻ of County Meath pop 1967

Trinacria — see SICILY — **Tri·nac·ri·an** \trə-'na-krē-ən, trī-\ adj

Trin·co·ma·lee \,triŋ-kō-mə-'lē, triŋ-'kə-mə-lē\ city & port NE Sri Lanka on Bay of Bengal pop 49,000

Trin·i·dad \'tri-nə-,dad\ island SE W. Indies off coast of NE Venezuela pop 1,184,106; with Tobago, a dominion (**Trinidad and Tobago**) of the Commonwealth of Nations since 1962; formerly a Brit. colony ✻ Port of Spain area 1864 sq mi (4846 sq km), pop 1,234,388 — **Trin·i·da·di·an** \,tri-nə-'dä-dē-ən, -'da-\ adj or n

Trin·i·ty \'tri-nə-tē\ river 360 mi (579 km) E Tex. flowing SE into Galveston Bay

Trip·o·li \'tri-pə-lē\ 1 or Ar **Ta·rā·bu·lus** \tə-'rä-bə-ləs\ or anc **Trip·o·lis** \'tri-pə-ləs\ city & port NW Lebanon NNE of Beirut pop 127,611 2 or Ar **Tarābulus** or anc **Oea** \'ē-ə\ city & port NW Libya, a ✻ of Libya pop 247,365 3 Tripolitania when it was one of the Barbary States — see **Tri·pol·i·tan** \tri-'pä-lə-tən\ adj or n

Tri·po·li·ta·nia \,tri-,pä-lə-'tā-nyə, tri-pə-lə-\ or anc **Trip·o·lis** \'tri-pə-ləs\ region & former province NW Libya bordering on the Mediterranean — **Tri·po·li·ta·nian** \,tri-,pä-lə-'tā-nyən, ,tri-pə-lə-\ adj or n

Tri·pu·ra \'tri-pə-rə\ state E India bet. Bangladesh & Assam ✻ Agartala area 4032 sq mi (10,483 sq km), pop 2,060,189

Tris·tan da Cu·nha \,tris-tən-də-'kü-nə, -nyə\ island S Atlantic, chief of the Tristan da Cunha Islands attached to Brit. colony of St. Helena area 42 sq mi (109 sq km), pop 251; volcanic eruptions 1961

Tri·van·drum \tri-'van-drəm\ city & port S India NW of Cape Comorin ✻ of Kerala pop 519,766

Tro·as \'trō-,as\ 1 or **Tro·ad** \-,ad\ territory surrounding the ancient city of Troy in NW Mysia, Asia Minor 2 ancient city of Mysia S of site of Troy — **Tro·ad·ic** \trō-'a-dik\ adj

Tro·bri·and \'trō-brē-,änd, -,and\ islands SW Pacific in Solomon Sea; attached to Papua New Guinea area 170 sq mi (442 sq km) — **Tro·bri·and·er** \'trō-brē-'än-dər, -'an-\ n

Trois–Ri·vières \,t(r)wä-ri-'vyer\ town Canada in S Que. NE of Montreal on N bank of St. Lawrence River pop 49,426

Trom·sö \'träm-,sö, -,sə(r)\ city & port N Norway pop 50,548

Trond·heim \'trän-,hām\ city & port cen Norway on **Trondheim Fjord** (80 mi or 128 km long) pop 137,346

Tros·sachs \'trä-səks, -,saks\ valley cen Scotland bet. Loch Katrine & Loch Achray

Trou·ville \trü-'vē(ə)l\ or **Trouville–sur–Mer** \-(,)sùr-'mer\ town & port N France on English Channel S of Le Havre pop 5718

Trow·bridge \'trō-(,)brij\ town S England ✻ of Wiltshire pop 22,984

Troy \'trói\ 1 city SE Mich. N of Detroit pop 72,884 2 city E N.Y. on Hudson River NNE of Albany pop 54,269 3 city W Ohio pop 19,478 4 or **Il·i·um** \'i-lē-əm\ or **Il·i·on** \'i-lē-,än, -lē-ən\ or **Troia** \'trói-ə, 'trō-yə\ or **Tro·ja** \'trō-jə, -yə\ ancient city NW Asia Minor in Troas SW of the Dardanelles

Troyes \'t(r)wä\ city NE France SE of Paris pop 71,600

Tru·chas Peak \'trü-chəs\ or **North Truchas Peak** mountain 13,110 ft (3996 m) N N.Mex. in Sangre de Cristo Mountains NE of Santa Fe; highest of three peaks forming **Truchas Peaks**

Trucial Oman, Trucial States — see UNITED ARAB EMIRATES

Truck·ee \'trə-kē\ river 120 mi (193 km) E Calif. & W Nev. flowing from Lake Tahoe into Pyramid Lake

Tru·ji·llo \trü-'hē-(,)yō\ 1 city NW Peru NW of Lima pop 193,528 2 — see SANTO DOMINGO

Trujillo Al·to \'äl-(,)tō\ town NE cen Puerto Rico pop 61,120

Truk Islands \'trək, 'trúk\ islands cen Carolines, part of Federated States of Micronesia

Trum·bull \'trəm-bəl\ town SW Conn. N of Bridgeport pop 32,016

Tru·ro \'trúr-(,)ō\ city & borough SW England, a ✻ of Cornwall and Isles of Scilly pop 16,277

Tsang·po \'(t)säŋ-'pò\ the upper Brahmaputra in Tibet

Tsaritsyn — see VOLGOGRAD

Tsarskoe Selo — see PUSHKIN

Tsinan — see JINAN

Tsinghai — see QINGHAI

Tsingtao — see QINGDAO

Tsitsihar — see QIQIHAR

Tskhin·va·li \'(t)skin-və-lē\ town N Republic of Georgia NW of Tbilisi ✻ of S. Ossetian autonomous oblast pop 30,000

Tsu·ga·ru Strait \'(t)sü-gə-,rü\ strait Japan bet. Honshu & Hokkaido

Tsu·shi·ma \'(t)sü-'shē-mə\ islands Japan in Korea Strait separated from Kyushu and Honshu by **Tsushima Strait** (the SE part of Korea Strait) area 271 sq mi (705 sq km)

Tu·a·mo·tu Archipelago \,tü-ə-'mō-(,)tü\ archipelago S Pacific E of Society Islands; belongs to France area 330 sq mi (858 sq km) pop 11,754

Tü·bing·en \'tü-biŋ-ən, 'tyü-, 'tūē-\ city SW Germany on the Neckar S of Stuttgart pop 73,132

Tu·buai Islands \tü-'bwä-ē\ or **Aus·tral Islands** \'òs-trəl, 'äs-\ islands S Pacific S of Tahiti belonging to France area 115 sq mi (299 sq km), pop 6509

Tuc·son \tü-'sän, 'tü-,\ city SE Ariz. pop 405,390 — **Tuc·son·an** \'tü-,sä-nən\ n

Tucumán — see SAN MIGUEL DE TUCUMÁN

Tu·ge·la \tü-'gä-lə\ river 300 mi (483 km) E Republic of South Africa in cen Natal flowing E to Indian Ocean; near its source on Mont Aux Sources are the **Tugela Falls** (3110 ft or 948 m)

Tu·la \'tü-lə\ 1 or **Tula de Allen·de** \(,)dä-ä-'yen-dä\ city cen Mexico in SW Hidalgo N of Mexico City; ancient ✻ of the Toltecs pop 36,460 2 city SW cen Russia in Europe S of Moscow on a tributary of Oka River pop 462,000

Tu·la·gi \tü-'lä-gē\ island S Pacific in S cen Solomons

Tu·lare \tü-'lar(-ē), -'ler(-ē)\ city S cen Calif. S of Fresno pop 33,249

Tulare Lake former lake S cen Calif. S of Hanford; drained for farmland

Tul·la·more \,tə-lə-'mōr, -'mór\ urban district cen Ireland ✻ of county Offaly pop 8484

Tul·sa \'təl-sə\ city NE Okla. on Arkansas River pop 367,302 — **Tul·san** \-sən\ n

Tu·ma·ca·co·ri National Monument \,tü-mə-'kä-kə-rē\ historic site S Ariz. S of Tucson; contains remains of Franciscan mission

Tu·men \'tü-'mən\ river 320 mi (354 km) E Asia on border bet. N. Korea, China, & Russia flowing NE & SE into Sea of Japan

Tu·muc–Hu·mac Mountains \tə-,mük-ə-'mäk\ or Pg **Se·rra Tumu·cu·maque** \'se-rə-tə-,mü-kə-'mäk\ range of low mountains NE Brazil on Suriname–French Guiana boundary

Tunbridge Wells ROYAL TUNBRIDGE WELLS

T'ung–hua — see TONGHUA

Tun·gus·ka \tùŋ-'gü-skə, tən-\ any of three rivers in cen Russia in Asia, tributaries of the Yenisey: **Lower Tunguska, Stony Tunguska**, & **Upper Tunguska** (lower course of the Angara)

Tu·nis \'tü-nəs, 'tyü-\ 1 city ✻ of Tunisia near site of ancient Carthage pop 550,404 2 TUNISIA — used esp. of the former Barbary State

Tu·ni·sia \tü-'nē-zh(ē-)ə, tyü-, -'ni-\ country N Africa bordering on the Mediterranean; formerly one of the Barbary States; a French protectorate 1881–1956, a monarchy 1956–57, & a republic since 1957 ✻ Tunis area 48,300 sq mi (125,580 sq km), pop 6,966,173 — **Tu·ni·sian** \-zh(ē-)ən\ adj or n

Tu·ol·um·ne \tü-'ä-lə-mē\ river 155 mi (249 km) cen Calif. flowing W from Yosemite National Park into the San Joaquin

Tu·pe·lo \'tü-pə-,lō, 'tyü-\ city NE Miss. pop 30,685

Tu·pun·ga·to \,tü-pəŋ-'gä-(,)tō\ mountain 22,310 ft (6800 m) in the Andes on Argentina–Chile boundary ENE of Santiago, Chile

Tu·rin \'túr-ən, 'tyúr-; tü-'rin, tyü-\ or It **To·ri·no** \tō-'rē-(,)nō\ commune NW Italy on the Po ✻ of Piedmont pop 1,002,863 — **Tu·rin·ese** \,túr-ə-'nēz, ,tyúr-, -'nēs\ adj or n

Turkana, Lake — see RUDOLF, LAKE

Tur·key \'tər-kē\ country W Asia & SE Europe bet. Mediterranean & Black seas; formerly center of an empire (✻ Constantinople), since

---

\ə\ abut \ᵊ\ kitten, F table \ər\ further \a\ ash \ā\ ace \ä\ mop, mar \aú\ out \ch\ chin \e\ bet \ē\ easy \g\ go \i\ hit \ī\ ice \j\ job \ŋ\ sing \ō\ go \ò\ law \òi\ boy \th\ thin \t͟h\ the \ü\ loot \ù\ foot \y\ yet \zh\ vision \á, k̲, ⁿ, œ, œ̄, ᵫ, ūē, ᵊ\ see Guide to Pronunciation

1923 a republic ✳ Ankara area 301,302 sq mi (783,385 sq km), pop 50,664,458 — see OTTOMAN EMPIRE

Tur·ki·stan or **Tur·ke·stan** \ˌtər-kə-'stan, -'stän; 'tər-kə-ˌ\ region cen Asia bet. Iran & Siberia; now divided bet. Turkmenistan, Uzbekistan, Tajikistan, Kyrgyzstan, Kazakhstan, China, & Afghanistan — see CHINESE TURKESTAN, RUSSIAN TURKESTAN

Turk·men·i·stan \(ˌ)tərk-ˌme-nə-'stan, -'stän; (ˌ)tərk-'me-nə-ˌ\ country cen Asia bordering on Afghanistan, Iran, & the Caspian Sea; a constituent republic (**Turk·men Republic** \'tərk-mən\) of the U.S.S.R. 1925–91 ✳ Ashkhabad area 187,200 sq mi (486,720 sq km), pop 3,534,000 — **Turk·man** \'tərk-mən\ n, pl **Turk·men** \-mən\ — **Turkmen** adj — **Turk·me·ni·an** \ˌtərk-'mē-nē-ən\ adj

Turks and Cai·cos \'tərks-ən(d)-'kā-kəs\ two groups of islands (Turks Islands & Caicos Islands) Brit. West Indies at SE end of the Bahamas; a Brit. colony; seat of government on **Grand Turk** (7 mi or 11 km long) area 166 sq mi (432 sq km), pop 12,350

Tur·ku \'tur-(ˌ)kü\ city & port SW Finland pop 159,469

Tur·lock \'tər-ˌläk\ city cen Calif. SE of Modesto pop 42,198

Tur·mero \tür-'mer-(ˌ)ō\ city N Venezuela SE of Maracay pop 174,280

Turn·hout \'türn-ˌhaut, tür-'nüt\ commune N Belgium pop 37,874

Tur·tle Bay \'tər-tᵊl\ section of New York City in E cen Manhattan on East River; site of United Nations headquarters

Tus·ca·loo·sa \ˌtəs-kə-'lü-sə\ city W cen Ala. on Black Warrior River SW of Birmingham pop 77,759

Tus·ca·ny \'təs-kə-nē\ or It **To·sca·na** \tō-'skä-nə\ region NW cen Italy bordering on Ligurian & Tyrrhenian seas ✳ Florence area 8861 sq mi (23,039 sq km), pop 3,560,582

Tus·cu·lum \'təs-kyə-ləm, -kə-\ ancient town Italy in Latium SE of Rome

Tus·tin \'təs-tən\ city SW Calif. E of Santa Ana pop 50,689

Tu·tu·i·la \ˌtü-tə-'wē-lə\ island, chief of American Samoa group area 52 sq mi (135 sq km) — **Tu·tu·i·lan** \-lən\ adj or n

Tu·va Republic \'tü-və\ autonomous republic S Russia in Asia N of Mongolia area 65,810 sq mi (171,106 sq km)

Tu·va·lu \tü-'vä-(ˌ)lü, -'vär-(ˌ)ü\ or formerly **El·lice Islands** \'e-ləs\ islands W Pacific N of Fiji; a Brit. territory 1976–78; became an independent member of the Commonwealth of Nations 1978 ✳ Funafuti area 9 sq mi (23 sq km), pop 7300 — see GILBERT AND ELLICE

Tux·tla \'tüst-lə\ or **Tuxtla Gu·tiér·rez** \gü-'tyer-əs\ city SE Mexico ✳ of Chiapas pop 66,851

Tu·zi·goot National Monument \'tü-zi-ˌgüt\ reservation cen Ariz. SW of Flagstaff containing ruins of prehistoric pueblo

Tver — see KALININ

Tweed \'twēd\ river 96 mi (154 km) SE Scotland & NE England flowing E into North Sea

Tweeddale — see PEEBLES

Twick·en·ham \'twi-kə-nəm, 'twik-nəm\ former municipal borough SE England in Middlesex, now part of Richmond upon Thames

Twin Cities the cities of Minneapolis & St. Paul, Minn.

Twin Falls city S Idaho SW of Twin Falls (waterfall 125 ft or 38 m in Snake River) pop 27,591

Two Sic·i·lies \'si-s(ə-)lēz\ former kingdom consisting of Sicily & S Italy

Ty·chy \'ti-kē, -ke\ town S Poland pop 189,874

Ty·ler \'tī-lər\ city E Tex. ESE of Dallas pop 75,450

Tyn·dall, Mount \'tin-dᵊl\ 1 mountain 14,025 ft (4275 m) S cen Calif. in Sierra Nevada NW of Mt. Whitney 2 mountain 8280 ft (2524 m) New Zealand in cen South Is. in Southern Alps

Tyne \'tīn\ river 35 mi (56 km) N England flowing E into North Sea

Tyne and Wear \'wir\ metropolitan county N England ✳ Newcastle upon Tyne area 208 sq mi (541 sq km), pop 1,161,100

Tyne·mouth \'tīn-ˌmauth, -məth\ borough N England in Tyne and Wear on North Sea at mouth of the Tyne pop 60,022

Tyr, Tyre — see SUR — **Tyr·i·an** \'tir-ē-ən\ adj or n

Ty·ree, Mount \tī-'rē\ mountain 16,290 ft (4965 m) W Antarctica in Ellsworth Mountains NW of Vinson Massif

Tyrol — see TIROL — **Ty·ro·le·an** \tə-'rō-lē-ən, tī-; tir-ə-', ˌtī-rə-ˌ\ adj or n — **Ty·ro·lese** \ˌtir-ə-'lēz, ˌti-rə-, -'lēs\ adj or n

Ty·rone \ti-'rōn\ former county W cen Northern Ireland ✳ Omagh area 1218 sq mi (3167 sq km)

Tyr·rhe·ni·an Sea \tə-'rē-nē-ən\ the part of the Mediterranean W of Italy, N of Sicily, & E of Sardinia & Corsica

Tyu·men \tyü-'men\ city W Russia in Asia on the **Tu·ra** \tü-'rä\ (a tributary of the Tobol) pop 359,000

Tzu–kung — see ZIGONG

Tzu–po — see ZIBO

Uap — see YAP

Uau·pés \wau-'pes\ or Sp **Vau·pés** \vau\ river 700 mi (1126 km) Colombia & Brazil flowing ESE into Negro River

Uban·gi \ü-'baŋ-(g)ē, yü-\ or F **Ou·ban·gui** \ü-bäⁿ-gē\ river 700 mi (1126 km) W cen Africa on NW border of Zaire flowing W & S into Congo River — see UELE

Ubangi–Sha·ri \-'shär-ē\ or F **Oubangui–Cha·ri** \-shä-rē\ former French territory N cen Africa — see CENTRAL AFRICAN REPUBLIC

Uca·ya·li \ˌü-kə-'yä-lē\ river 1200 mi (1931 km) cen & N Peru flowing N to unite with the Marañón forming the Amazon

Uc·cle \'ükl², 'ēkl²\ or Flem **Uk·kel** \'ə-kəl, 'œ-\ commune cen Belgium pop 73,721

Udai·pur \ü-'dī-ˌpur\ 1 or **Me·war** \mā-'wär\ former state NW India, now part of Rajasthan state 2 city, its ✳, pop 229,762

Udi·ne \'ü-di-ˌnā\ commune NE Italy NE of Venice in Friuli-Venezia Giulia region pop 98,872

Ud·murt Republic \'üd-ˌmurt, üd-'murt\ autonomous republic E Russia in Europe in the foothills of the Urals ✳ Izhevsk area 16,200 sq mi (42,120 sq km), pop 1,417,000

Ue·le \'we-lē\ river 700 mi (1126 km) cen Africa flowing W in N Zaire to unite with the Bomu forming Ubangi River

Ufa \ü-'fä\ 1 river 430 mi (692 km) E Russia in Europe in S Urals flowing NW & SW into the Belaya 2 city E Russia in Europe ✳ of Bashkir Republic pop 969,000

Ugan·da \ü-'gan-də, yü-, -'gän-\ republic E Africa N of Lake Victoria; member of the Commonwealth of Nations ✳ Kampala area 93,981 sq mi (244,351 sq km), pop 12,630,076 — **Ugan·dan** \-dən\ adj or n

Uga·rit \ü-'gär-it, yü-\ ancient city, Syria on Mediterranean coast

Uin·ta Mountains \yü-'in-tə\ mountain range NE Utah — see KINGS PEAK

Uj·jain \'ü-ˌjīn\ city NW cen India in W Madhya Pradesh NNW of Indore pop 281,878

Ujung Pan·dang \ü-ˌjuŋ-(ˌ)pän-'däŋ\ or formerly **Ma·kas·sar** \mə-'ka-sər\ city & port Indonesia in SW Sulawesi pop 944,685

Ukraine \yü-'krān, 'yü-, also yü-'krīn\ or **the Ukraine** country E Europe on N coast of Black Sea; a constituent republic of the U.S.S.R. 1923–91 ✳ Kiev area 222,600 sq mi (578,760 sq km), pop 51,704,000

Ulan Ba·tor \ˌü-ˌlän-'bä-ˌtór\ or formerly **Ur·ga** \'ür-gə\ city N cen Mongolia (republic), its ✳ pop 418,700

Ulan–Ude \ˌü-ˌlän-ü-'dā\ or formerly **Verkh·ne·u·dinsk** \ˌverk-nə-'ü-ˌdin(t)sk\ city E Russia in Asia ✳ of Buryat Republic on the Selenga pop 300,000

Uleåborg — see OULU

Ulls·wa·ter \'əlz-ˌwó-tər, -ˌwä-\ lake 7 mi (11 km) long NW England in Cumbria

Ulm \'ulm\ city S Germany in E Baden-Württemberg pop 100,671

Ul·san \'ül-'sän\ city SE S. Korea pop 551,014

Ul·ster \'əl-stər\ 1 region N Ireland (island) comprising Northern Ireland & N Ireland (republic); ancient kingdom, later a province comprising nine counties, three of which in 1921 joined Irish Free State (now Ireland) while the rest remained with United Kingdom 2 province N Ireland (republic) comprising counties Cavan, Donegal, & Monaghan area 3093 sq mi (8042 sq km) pop 232,012 3 Northern Ireland comprising counties Antrim, Armagh, Down, Fermanagh, Londonderry, & Tyrone ✳ Belfast — **Ul·ster·ite** \-stə-ˌrīt\ n — **Ul·ster·man** \-stər-mən\ n

Ulu Dag \ˌü-lü-'dä(g)\ or anc **Mount Olym·pus** \ə-'lim-pəs, ō-\ mountain 8343 ft (2543 m) NW Turkey in Asia SE of Bursa

Ulugh Muztagh — see MUZTAG

Ul·ya·novsk \ül-'yä-nəfsk\ or formerly **Sim·birsk** \sim-'birsk\ city SE cen Russia in Europe on the Volga pop 464,000

Uma·til·la \ˌyü-mə-'ti-lə\ river 80 mi (129 km) NE Oreg. flowing W & N into Columbia River

Um·bria \'əm-brē-ə\ region cen Italy in the Apennines ✳ Perugia pop 820,316

Umeå \'ü-mā-(ˌ)ō\ city & port N Sweden on Gulf of Bothnia pop 90,004

Umm al Qai·wain \'üm-al-kī-'wīn\ sheikhdom, member of United Arab Emirates

Um·nak \'üm-ˌnak\ island SW Alaska in Fox Islands

Ump·qua \'əm(p)-ˌkwó\ river 200 mi (322 km) SW Oreg. flowing into the Pacific

Um·ta·ta \üm-'tä-tə\ city ✳ of Transkei

Un·alas·ka \ˌə-nə-'las-kə\ island SW Alaska in Fox Islands

Unalaska Bay bay SW Alaska on N coast of Unalaska Is.

Un·com·pah·gre Peak \ˌən-kəm-'pä-grē\ mountain 14,309 ft (4361 m) SW Colo.; highest in San Juan Mountains

Uncompahgre Plateau tableland W Colo. SW of the Gunnison

Un·ga·va \ˌən-'ga-və\ region Canada N of the Eastmain & W of Labrador including Ungava Peninsula, divided 1927 bet. Que. & Nfld. — see NEW QUEBEC

Ungava Bay inlet of Hudson Strait Canada in N Que.

Ungava Peninsula peninsula Canada in N Que. bet. Hudson Bay & Ungava Bay

Uni·mak \'yü-nə-ˌmak\ island SW Alaska in Fox Islands

Union City 1 city W Calif. S of Oakland pop 53,762 2 city NE N.J. N of Jersey City pop 58,012

Union of South Africa — see SOUTH AFRICA (Republic of)

Union of Soviet Socialist Republics or **Soviet Union** country 1922–91 E Europe & N Asia bordering on the Arctic & Pacific oceans & Baltic & Black seas; a union of 15 constituent republics ✳ Moscow area 8,662,400 sq mi (22,522,240 sq km), pop 286,717,000

United Arab Emirates or formerly **Tru·cial States** \'trü-shəl\ or **Trucial Oman** \ō-'män, -'man\ country NE Arabia on Persian Gulf between Qatar & Oman; a republic composed of seven sheikdoms (Abu Dhabi, Ajman, Dubai, Fujaira, Ras al Khaimah, Sharja, & Umm al Qaiwain) formerly under Brit. protection ✳ Abu Dhabi area 32,000 sq mi (83,200 sq km), pop 1,700,000

United Arab Republic former name (1961–71) of republic of Egypt & previously (1958–61) of union of Egypt & Syria

United Kingdom 1 or **United Kingdom of Great Britain and Northern Ireland** country W Europe in British Isles comprising Great Britain & Northern Ireland ✳ London area 89,034 sq mi (231,488 sq km), pop 55,671,000 2 or **United Kingdom of Great Britain and Ireland** country 1801–1921 comprising Great Britain & Ireland

United Nations political organization established 1945; headquarters in New York City in E cen Manhattan overlooking East River — see TURTLE BAY

United Provinces or **United Provinces of Agra and Oudh** former province N India formed 1902 ✳ Allahabad; as Uttar Pradesh, became a state of India (republic) 1950

United States of America or **United States** \yu-ˌnī-təd-'stāts, esp Southern 'yü-\ country N. America bordering on Atlantic, Pacific, & Arctic oceans; a federal republic ✳ Washington area 3,615,123 sq mi (9,399,320 sq km), pop 249,632,692

University City city E Mo. WNW of St. Louis pop 40,087

University Park city NE Tex. within city of Dallas pop 22,259

Un·ter·wal·den \'ün-tər-ˌväl-dən\ former canton cen Switzerland, now divided into two cantons (formerly half cantons): **Nid·wal·den** \'nēt-ˌväl-dən\ or F **Nid·wald** \nēd-väld\ (✳ Stans area 112 sq mi or 291 sq km, pop 32,323) & **Ob·wal·den** \'óp-ˌväl-dən\ or F **Ob·wald** \ób-väld\ (✳ Sarnen area 183 sq mi or 476 sq km, pop 28,831)

Up·land \'əp-lənd\ city SW Calif. W of San Bernardino pop 63,374

Upo·lu \ü-'pō-(ˌ)lü\ island S Pacific in Western Samoa

Upper Adige — see ALTO ADIGE

Upper Arlington city cen Ohio W of Columbus pop 34,128

Upper Canada the Canadian province 1791–1841 corresponding to modern Ont. — see LOWER CANADA

Upper Karroo — see KARROO

Upper Klamath Lake lake 30 mi (48 km) long S Oreg. SSE of Crater Lake National Park drained by Klamath River — see LOWER KLAMATH LAKE

Upper Palatinate — see PALATINATE
Upper Peninsula the N part of Mich. bet. Lakes Superior & Michigan
Upper Volta — see BURKINA FASO — **Upper Vol·tan** \'väl-t°n, 'vōl-, 'vōl-\ *adj or n*
Upp·sa·la \'ŭp-,sä-lə, 'ŭp-, -lä\ city E Sweden NNW of Stockholm *pop* 164,754
Ur \'ər, 'ŭr\ city of ancient Sumer; site in S Iraq NW of Basra
Ural \'yŭr-əl\ river 1400 *mi* (2253 *km*) Russia & Kazakhstan rising at S end of Ural Mountains & flowing S into the Caspian
Ural Mountains mountain system Russia & Kazakhstan extending from Kara Sea to steppes N of Aral Sea; usu. considered the dividing line bet. Asia & Europe; highest Narodnaya 6214 *ft* (1894 *m*)
Uralsk \yŭ-'ralsk\ city W Kazakhstan on Ural River *pop* 167,000
Ura·ri·coe·ra \ŭ-,rär-i-'kwer-ə\ river 360 *mi* (579 *km*) N Brazil, a headstream of the Branco
Ura·wa \ŭ-'rä-wə\ city Japan in Honshu N of Tokyo *pop* 418,267
Ur·ba·na \,ər-'ba-nə\ city E cen Ill. *pop* 36,344
Ur·ban·dale \'ər-bən-,dāl\ city S cen Iowa *pop* 23,500
Ur·bi·no \ŭr-'bē-(,)nō\ commune cen Italy
Ur·fa \ŭr-'fä\ or anc **Edes·sa** \i-'de-sə\ city SE Turkey *pop* 148,434
Urga — see ULAN BATOR
Uri \'ŭr-ē\ canton cen Switzerland S of Vierwaldstätter See ✻ Altdorf *area* 415 *sq mi* (1079 *sq km*), *pop* 34,042
Ur·mia, Lake — see REZĀIYEH
Ur·mia \'ŭr-mē-ə\ or formerly **Re·zāi·yeh** \rə-'zī-yə\ city NW Iran *pop* 300,746
Uru·bam·ba \,ŭr-ə-'bäm-bə\ river 450 *mi* (724 *km*) cen Peru flowing NNW to unite with the Apurímac forming the Ucayali
Uru·guay \'ŭr-ə-,gwī, 'yŭr-; 'yŭr-ə-,gwä\ 1 river 980 *mi* (1577 *km*) SE S. America rising in Brazil & flowing into the Río de la Plata 2 or **Re·pú·bli·ca Ori·en·tal del Uru·guay** \re-'pü-bli-(,)kä-,ōr-ē-,en-'täl-del-,ŭr-ə-'gwī, -,ōr-ē-,en-\ country SE S. America bet. the lower Uruguay & the Atlantic; a republic ✻ Montevideo *area* 72,172 *sq mi* (187,647 *sq km*), *pop* 2,788,429 — see BANDA ORIENTAL — **Uru·guay·an** \,ŭr-ə-'gwī-ən, ,yŭr-; ,yŭr-ə-'gwä-\ *adj or n*
Ürüm·qi \'ŭE-'rŭEm-'chē\ or **Urum·chi** \ŭ-'rŭm-chē, ,ŭr-əm-'\ or **Wu·lu—mu—ch'i** \'wŭ-'lŭ-'mŭ-'chē\ city NW China ✻ of Xinjiang Uygur on N side of Tian Shan *pop* 320,000
Urundi — see BURUNDI
Ushant — see OUESSANT, ÎLE D'
Us·hua·ia \ŭ-'swī-ə\ town S Argentina on S coast of Tierra del Fuego Is., at 54°48'S; southernmost city in the world *pop* 10,998
Usk \'əsk\ river 60 *mi* (96 *km*) S Wales & W England flowing E & S into Severn estuary
Üs·kü·dar \,üs-kə-'där\ suburb of Istanbul, Turkey, on Asian side of the Bosporus
Us·pa·lla·ta Pass \,üs-pə-'yä-tə, -'zhä-\ or **La Cum·bre** \lə-'küm-(,)brä\ mountain pass (12,572 *ft or* 3832 *m*) & tunnel S S. America in the Andes bet. Mendoza, Argentina & Santiago, Chile
Us·su·ri \ŭ-'sŭr-ē\ river 450 *mi* (724 *km*) E Asia on border bet. Russia & China flowing N into the Amur
Usti nad La·bem \'üs-tē-'näd-lä-,bem\ city NW Czech Republic in N Bohemia on the Elbe *pop* 106,345
Ustinov — see IZHEVSK
Usumbura — see BUJUMBURA
Utah \'yü-,tō, -,tä\ state W U.S. ✻ Salt Lake City *area* 84,916 *sq mi* (220,782 *sq km*), *pop* 1,722,850 — **Utah·an** \-,tò(-ə)n, -,tä(-ə)n\ *adj or n* — **Utahn** \-,tò(-ə)n, -,tä(-ə)n\ *n*
Utah Lake lake 30 *mi* (48 *km*) long N cen Utah drained by Jordan River
Uti·ca \'yü-ti-kə\ 1 city E cen N.Y. on Mohawk River *pop* 68,637 2 ancient city N Africa on Mediterranean coast NW of Carthage
Utrecht \'yü-,trekt, 'ū-,trekt\ 1 province cen Netherlands S of the IJsselmeer *area* 535 *sq mi* (1391 *sq km*), *pop* 922,821 2 city, its ✻ *pop* 231,600
Utsu·no·mi·ya \,üt-sə-'nō-mē-ə\ city Japan in cen Honshu N of Tokyo *pop* 426,809
Ut·tar Pra·desh \,ŭ-tər-prə-'desh, -'däsh\ state N India bordering on Tibet & Nepal ✻ Lucknow *area* 113,409 *sq mi* (294,863 *sq km*), *pop* 110,358,019 — see UNITED PROVINCES
Ux·bridge \'əks-(,)brij\ former municipal borough SE England in Middlesex, now part of Hillingdon
Ux·mal \üsh-'mäl, üs-\ site of ancient Maya city SE Mexico in W Yucatán
Uz·bek·i·stan \(,)ŭz-,be-ki-'stan, ,əz-, -'stän; 'be-ki-,\ country W cen Asia E of the Amu Darya; a constituent republic (**Uz·bek Republic** \'ŭz-,bek, 'əz-, üz-'\) of the U.S.S.R. 1924–91 ✻ Tashkent *area* 171,070 *sq mi* (444,782 *sq km*), *pop* 19,906,000
Vaal \'väl\ river 700 *mi* (1126 *km*) Republic of South Africa rising in Eastern Transvaal & flowing W into Orange River in Northern Cape province
Vaa·sa or Sw **Va·sa** \'vä-sə\ city & port W Finland *pop* 53,364
Vaca·ville \'vä-kə-,vil\ city W Calif. SW of Sacramento *pop* 71,479
Va·duz \vä-'düts\ commune ✻ of Liechtenstein on the upper Rhine
Vah \'vä(k)\ or Hung **Vag** \'väg\ river 210 *mi* (338 *km*) W Slovakia rising in Tatry Mountains & flowing W & S into the Danube
Va·lais \va-'lā\ or G **Wal·lis** \'vä-ləs\ canton SW cen Switzerland bordering on France & Italy ✻ Sion *area* 2026 *sq mi* (5268 *sq km*), *pop* 249,473
Val·dai Hills \väl-'dī\ hills W Russia in Europe SE of Lake Ilmen; highest point 1053 *ft* (321 *m*)
Val·di·via \väl-'dē-vē-ə\ city & port S cen Chile *pop* 100,046
Val d'Or \'val-'dòr\ town Canada in SW Que. *pop* 23,842
Val·dos·ta \val-'däs-tə\ city S Ga. *pop* 39,806
Va·lence \va-'lä°s\ commune SE France S of Lyons *pop* 67,101
Va·len·cia \və-'len(t)-sh(ē-)ə, -se-ə\ 1 region & ancient kingdom E Spain bet. Andalusia & Catalonia 2 province E Spain *area* 4150 *sq mi* (10,790 *sq km*), *pop* 2,112,921 3 commune & port on the Mediterranean, its ✻ *pop* 744,748 4 city N Venezuela WSW of Caracas *pop* 903,621
Va·len·ci·ennes \və-,len(t)-sē-'en(z)\ city N France *pop* 41,976
Va·len·tia or **Va·len·cia** \və-'len(t)-sh(ē-)ə\ island SW Ireland in County Kerry in the Atlantic S of entrance to Dingle Bay

Val·la·do·lid \,va-lə-də-'lid, ,vä-yə-də-, -'lē(d)\ 1 province NW cen Spain *area* 2922 *sq mi* (7597 *sq km*), *pop* 488,373 2 commune, its ✻, NNW of Madrid *pop* 320,293
Val·lau·ris \,va-lō-'rēs\ village SE France NE of Cannes
Val·le·cas \vä-'yā-kəs\ commune cen Spain, SE suburb of Madrid
Val·le d'Ao·sta \,vä-lā-dä-'ōs-tə\ or **Val d'Ao·sta** \,väl-dä-\ autonomous region NW Italy bordering on France & Switzerland NW of Piedmont ✻ Aosta *area* 1260 *sq mi* (3276 *sq km*), *pop* 115,270
Val·le·jo \və-'lā-(,)ō\ city W Calif. on San Pablo Bay *pop* 109,199
Val·let·ta or **Va·let·ta** \və-'le-tə\ city & port ✻ of Malta *pop* 9210
Valley East town Canada in S Ont. N of Sudbury *pop* 21,939
Valleyfield — see SALABERRY-DE-VALLEYFIELD
Valley of Ten Thousand Smokes volcanic region SW Alaska in Katmai National Monument
Valley Stream village SE N.Y. on Long Is. *pop* 33,946
Va·lois \'val-,wä, val-'\ medieval county & duchy N France in NE Île-de-France ✻ Crépy-en-Valois
Valona — see VLORË
Val·pa·rai·so 1 \,val-pə-'rā-(,)zō\ city NW Ind. SE of Gary *pop* 24,414 2 \-'rī-(,)zō, -'rä-\ or Sp **Val·pa·ra·í·so** \,väl-pä-rä-'ē-sō\ city & port cen Chile WNW of Santiago *pop* 265,718
Van \'van\ salt lake E Turkey in Armenia *area* 1425 *sq mi* (3705 *sq km*)
Van·cou·ver \van-'kü-vər\ 1 city SW Wash. on Columbia River opposite Portland, Oreg. *pop* 46,380 2 city & port Canada in SW B.C. on Burrard Inlet *pop* 471,844 — **Van·cou·ver·ite** \-və-,rīt\ *n*
Vancouver, Mount mountain 15,700 *ft* (4785 *m*) on Alaska-Yukon boundary in St. Elias Range
Vancouver Island island W Canada in B.C. off SW coast; chief city Victoria *area* 12,408 *sq mi* (32,261 *sq km*)
Van Die·men Gulf \van-'dē-mən\ inlet of Arafura Sea N Australia in N Northern Territory
Van Diemen's Land — see TASMANIA
Vä·nern \'ve-nərn\ lake SW Sweden *area* 2141 *sq mi* (5567 *sq km*)
Van·taa \'vän-(,)tä\ town S Finland N of Helsinki *pop* 152,262
Va·nua Le·vu \və-,nü-ə-'le-(,)vü\ island S Pacific in the Fijis NE of Viti Levu *area* 2128 *sq mi* (5533 *sq km*)
Van·u·a·tu \,van-,wä-'tü, ,vän- also -wä-(,)tü\ or formerly **New Heb·ri·des** \'he-brə-,dēz\ islands SW Pacific NE of New Caledonia & W of Fiji; formerly under joint Brit. & French administration, a republic since 1980 ✻ Vila (on Efate) *area* 5700 *sq mi* (14,820 *sq km*), *pop* 142,419
Varanasi — see BANARAS
Var·dar \'vär-,där\ river 200 *mi* (322 *km*) Macedonia (country) & N Greece flowing S into Thermaïkós Kólpos
Va·re·se \və-'rā-sä\ commune N Italy NW of Milan *pop* 88,018
Var·na \'vär-nə\ or formerly **Sta·lin** \'stä-lən, 'sta-, -,lēn\ city & port E Bulgaria on Black Sea *pop* 252,525
Väs·ter·ås \,ves-tə-'ròs\ city E Sweden on Mälaren Lake NW of Stockholm *pop* 118,386
Vaté — see EFATE
Vat·i·can City \'va-ti-kən\ or It **Cit·tà del Va·ti·ca·no** \chēt-'tä-del-,vä-tē-'kä-nō\ independent papal state within commune of Rome, Italy; created Feb. 11, 1929 *area* 109 *acres* (43 *hectares*), *pop* 771
Vät·tern \'ve-tərn\ lake S Sweden *area* 733 *sq mi* (1906 *sq km*)
Vaud \'vō\ or G **Waadt** \'vät\ canton W Switzerland N of Lake of Geneva ✻ Lausanne *area* 1256 *sq mi* (3266 *sq km*), *pop* 576,319
Vaughan \'vòn, 'vän\ city Canada in SE Ont. N of Toronto *pop* 111,359
Vaupés — see UAUPÉS
Vegas LAS VEGAS
Ve·ga Ba·ja \'vä-gə-'bä-(,)hä\ town N Puerto Rico *pop* 55,997
Ve·ii \'vē-,ī, 'vā-\ ancient city of Etruria in cen Italy NNW of Rome
Vej·le \'vī-lə\ city & port Denmark *pop* 50,879
Vel·bert \'fel-bərt\ city W Germany in N. Rhine-Westphalia in Ruhr valley NE of Düsseldorf *pop* 93,056
Vel·la La·vel·la \'ve-lə-lə-'ve-lə\ island SW Pacific in cen Solomons
Vel·lore \və-'lōr, ve-, -'lòr\ city SE India in N Tamil Nadu WSW of Madras *pop* 246,937
Vel·sen \'vel-sən, -zən\ commune W Netherlands; outer port for Amsterdam *pop* 59,191
Velsuna — see ORVIETO
Vence \väs\ commune SE France W of Nice *pop* 7332
Ven·da \'ven-də\ former black enclave in the Republic of South Africa ✻ Thohoyandou; granted independence 1979; abolished 1994
Ven·dée \vä°(n)-'dä\ or **La Vendée** \lä-\ region W France bordering on Bay of Biscay S of Brittany
Ven·dôme \vä°(n)-'dōm\ town N cen France WSW of Orléans
Ve·ne·tia \və-'nē-sh(ē-)ə\ or It **Ve·ne·zia** \və-'net-sē-ə\ 1 area NE Italy, W Slovenia, & W Croatia including territory bet. the lower Po & the Alps 2 VENEZIA EUGANEA — **Ve·ne·tian** \-'nē-shən\ adj
Ve·ne·to \'ve-nə-,tō, 'vā-\ region NE Italy comprising most of Venezia Euganea ✻ Venice *area* 7092 *sq mi* (18,439 *sq km*), *pop* 4,385,023
Ve·ne·zia Eu·ga·nea \və-'net-sē-ə-,eü-'gä-nē-ə\ the S portion of Venetia
Venezia Giu·lia \'jül-yə\ the E portion of Venetia including Julian Alps & Istria; now mainly in Slovenia & Croatia
Venezia Tri·den·ti·na \,trē-,den-'tē-nə\ the NW portion of Venetia N of Lake Garda; included in Trentino-Alto Adige region
Ven·e·zu·e·la \,ve-nə-'zwā-lə, -zə-'wä- also -zwē- or -zə-'wē-\ country N S. America; a republic ✻ Caracas *area* 352,141 *sq mi* (915,567 *sq km*), *pop* 18,105,265 — **Ven·e·zu·e·lan** \-lən\ adj or n
Venezuela, Gulf of inlet of the Caribbean NW Venezuela N of Lake Maracaibo
Ven·iam·i·nof Crater \ve-'nya-mə-,nòf\ volcano 8225 *ft* (2507 *m*) SW Alaska on cen Alaska Peninsula in Aleutian Range
Ven·ice \'ve-nəs\ or It **Ve·ne·zia** \və-'net-sē-ə\ or L **Ve·ne·tia** \və-'nē-sh(ē-)ə\ city & port NE Italy ✻ of Veneto, on islands in **Lagoon of**

\ə\ abut \ə, kitten, F table \ər\ further \a\ ash \ā\ ace \ä\ mop, mar
\au̇\ out \ch\ chin \e\ bet \ē\ easy \g\ go \i\ hit \ī\ ice \j\ job
\ŋ\ sing \ō\ go \ò\ law \ói\ boy \th\ thin \t̸h\ the \ü\ loot \u̇\ foot
\y\ yet \zh\ vision \ä, k̲, ⁿ, œ, œ̄, ᵫ, ᵫ̄, ᵞ\ see Guide to Pronunciation

Venice (inlet of Gulf of Venice) *pop* 320,990 — **Ve·ne·tian** \və-'nē-shən\ *adj or n*

Venice, Gulf of arm of the Adriatic bet. Po delta & Istria

Ven·lo *or formerly* **Ven·loo** \'ven-(,)lō\ commune SE Netherlands on Maas River near German border *pop* 62,564

Ven·ta \'ven-tə\ river 200 *mi* (322 *km*) in Lithuania & Latvia flowing into the Baltic

Ven·ti·mi·glia \,ven-ti-'mēl-yə\ commune NW Italy on Ligurian Sea W of San Remo near Menton, France *pop* 25,649

Vents·pils \'vent,spils, -,spilz\ *or G* **Win·dau** \'vin,daů\ city & port Latvia at mouth of the Venta *pop* 37,000

Ven·tu·ra \ven-'túr-ə, -'tyúr-\ *or officially* **San Buen·a·ven·tu·ra** \(,)san-,bwe-nə-,ven-\ city & port SW Calif. on Santa Barbara Channel ESE of Santa Barbara *pop* 29,996

Ve·nue, Ben \,ben-və-'nü, -'nyü\ mountain 2393 *ft* (729 *m*) *cen* Scotland S of Loch Katrine

Ve·ra·cruz \,ver-ə-'krüz, -'krüs\ **1** state E Mexico * Jalapa *area* 27,736 *sq mi* (72,114 *sq km*), *pop* 5,264,611 **2** *or* **Vera Cruz Lla·ve** \'yä-(,)vā\ city & port E Mexico in Veracruz state on Gulf of Mexico *pop* 242,351

Ver·cel·li \ver-'che-lē, (,)vər-\ commune NW Italy *pop* 50,313

Verde, Cape \'vərd\ *or* **Cap Vert** \kap-'vərt\ *or* **Cape Vert** \'vərt\ promontory W Africa in Senegal; westernmost point in Africa at 17°30' W

Ver·di·gris \'vər-də-grəs\ river 280 *mi* (451 *km*) SE Kans. & NE Okla. flowing into Arkansas River

Ver·dun \(,)vər-'dən, ver-\ **1** town Canada in S Que. on Montreal Is. *pop* 61,307 **2** *or* **Verdun–sur–Meuse** \-,sür-\ city NE France on the Meuse ESE of Reims *pop* 22,889

Ver·ee·ni·ging \fə-'rā-nə-giŋ, -nə-kəŋ\ city NE Republic of South Africa in Pretoria-Witwatersrand-Vereeniging on the Vaal S of Johannesburg *pop* 94,500

Verkhneudinsk — SEE ULAN-UDE

Ver·mont \vər-'mänt\ state NE U.S. * Montpelier *area* 9609 *sq mi* (24,983 *sq km*), *pop* 562,758 — **Ver·mont·er** \-'mänt-ər\ *n*

Ver·non \'vər-nən\ **1** town N *cen* Conn. NE of Hartford *pop* 29,841 **2** city Canada in S B.C. *pop* 23,514

Vernyi — SEE ALMA-ATA

Vé·roia \'ver-yə\ *or anc* **Be·rea** *or* **Be·roea** \bə-'rē-ə\ town NE Greece in Macedonia W of Thessaloníki

Ve·ro·na \və-'rō-nə\ commune NE Italy on the Adige *pop* 258,476 —
Ver·o·nese \,ver-ə-'nēz, -'nēs\ *adj or n*

Ver·sailles \(,)vər-'sī, ver-\ city N France, WSW suburb of Paris *pop* 93,359

Ver·viers \ver-'vyā\ commune E Belgium E of Liège *pop* 53,482

Ves·ta·via Hills \ve-'stā-vē-ə\ city *cen* Ala. S of Birmingham *pop* 19,749

Ves·ter·ål·en \'ves-tə-,rò-lən\ island group Norway off NW coast NE of Lofoten island group

Ve·su·vi·us \və-'sü-vē-əs\ *or It* **Ve·su·vio** \vä-'sü-vyō, -'zü-\ volcano 4190 *ft* (1277 *m*) Italy in Campania on Bay of Naples

Vet·lu·ga \vet-'lü-gə\ river 500 *mi* (805 *km*) *cen* Russia in Europe flowing S into the Volga

Ve·vey \və-'vā\ commune W Switzerland in Vaud on NE shore of Lake Geneva *pop* 16,139

Viatka — SEE VYATKA

Vi·cen·te Ló·pez \və-'sen-tē-'lō-,pez, -,pes\ city E Argentina, N suburb of Buenos Aires, on Río de la Plata *pop* 289,815

Vi·cen·za \vi-'chen(t)-sə\ commune NE Italy W of Venice *pop* 109,109

Vi·chu·ga \vi-'chü-gə\ city *cen* Russia in Europe NE of Moscow *pop* 53,000

Vichy \'vi-shē, 'vē-\ commune *cen* France on the Allier *pop* 32,107

Vicks·burg \'viks-,bərg\ city W Miss. *pop* 20,908

Vic·to·ria \vik-'tòr-ē-ə, -'tòr-\ **1** city SE Tex. on Guadalupe River *pop* 55,076 **2** city Canada * of B.C. on SE Vancouver Is. *pop* 71,228 **3** river 350 *mi* (563 *km*) Australia in NW Northern Territory flowing N & NW to Timor Sea **4** state SE Australia * Melbourne *area* 87,884 *sq mi* (228,498 *sq km*), *pop* 3,832,443 **5** *or* **Hong Kong** \'häŋ-,käŋ, -'käŋ; 'hòŋ-,kòŋ, -'kòŋ\ city & port * of Hong Kong colony on NW Hong Kong Is. *pop* 1,026,870 — **Vic·to·ri·an** \vik-'tòr-ē-ən, -'tòr-\ *adj or n*

Victoria, Lake lake E Africa in Tanzania, Kenya, & Uganda *area* 26,200 *sq mi* (68,120 *sq km*)

Victoria Falls waterfall 200 to 350 *ft* (61 to 107 *m*) high & 5580 *ft* (1701 *m*) wide S Africa in the Zambezi on border bet. Zambia & Zimbabwe

Victoria Island island N Canada SE of Banks Is. *area* 81,930 *sq mi* (213,018 *sq km*)

Victoria Land region E Antarctica S of New Zealand on W shore of Ross Sea & Ross Ice Shelf

Victoria Nile — SEE NILE

Vic·tor·ville \'vik-tər-,vil\ city SE Calif. N of San Bernardino *pop* 40,674

Vied·ma \'vyäd-mä\ town S *cen* Argentina *pop* 24,338

Vi·en·na \vē-'e-nə\ *or G* **Wien** \'vēn\ city * of Austria on the Danube *pop* 1,533,176 — **Vi·en·nese** \,vē-ə-'nēz, -'nēs\ *adj or n*

Vi·enne \vē-'en\ **1** river 217 *mi* (349 *km*) SW *cen* France flowing NW into the Loire **2** city SE France on the Rhône *pop* 25,981

Vien·tiane \(,)vyen-'tyän\ city * of Laos, near Thailand border *pop* 132,253

Vie·ques \vē-'ā-kəs\ island W. Indies off E Puerto Rico, belonging to Puerto Rico; chief town Isabel Segunda

Vier·wald·stät·ter See \fir-'vält-,shte-tər-,zā, -,ste-\ *or* **Lake of Lucerne** \lü-'sərn\ lake 24 *mi* (39 *km*) long *cen* Switzerland *area* 44 *sq mi* (114 *sq km*)

Viet·nam \vē-'et-'näm, vyet-, ,vē-ət-, vēt-, -'nam\ country SE Asia in Indochina; state, including Tonkin & N Annam, set up 1945–46; with S Annam & Cochin China, an associated state of French Union 1950–54; after civil war, divided 1954–75 at 17th parallel into republics of **North Vietnam** (* Hanoi) & **South Vietnam** (* Saigon) reunited 1975 (* Hanoi) *area* 127,207 *sq mi* (330,738 *sq km*), *pop* 52,741,766

Vi·go \'vē-(,)gō\ city & port NW Spain on Vigo Bay (inlet of the Atlantic) *pop* 261,331

Viipuri — SEE VYBORG

Vi·ja·ya·na·gar \,vi-jə-yə-'nə-gər\ *or* **Bi·ja·na·gar** \,bi-jə-'nə-\ Hindu kingdom (1336–1565) S India S of the Krishna

Vi·ja·ya·wa·da \,vi-jə-yə-'wä-də\ *or formerly* **Bez·wa·da** \be-'zwä-də\ city SE India in E Andhra Pradesh on the Krishna, at head of its delta *pop* 544,958

Vila — SEE PORT-VILA

Villa Cisneros — see DAKHLA

Vi·lla·her·mo·sa \,vē-yə-,er-'mō-sə\ city SE Mexico * of Tabasco state *pop* 78,034

Vil·la Park \'vi-lə\ village NE Ill. W of Chicago *pop* 22,253

Ville·franche \,vēl-'fräⁿsh, ,vē-lə-\ **1** *or* **Villefranche–sur–Mer** \-,sür-'mer\ commune & port SE France E of Nice *pop* 6600 **2** *or* **Villefranche–sur–Saône** \-'sōn\ commune E *cen* France NNW of Lyons *pop* 8100

Vil·leur·banne \(,)vē-,yər-'ban, -'bän\ commune E France, E suburb of Lyons *pop* 115,913

Vil·ni·us \'vil-nē-əs\ city * of Lithuania *pop* 582,000

Vi·lyui \vil-'yü-ē\ river 1500 *mi* (2414 *km*) *cen* Russia in Asia flowing E into the Lena

Vim·i·nal \'vi-mə-n²l\ hill in Rome, Italy, one of seven upon which the ancient city was built — see AVENTINE

Vi·my Ridge \'vē-mē, vi-'mē\ ridge near Vimy commune N France N of Arras

Vi·ña del Mar \'vē-nyə-(,)del-'mär\ city & port *cen* Chile E of Valparaiso *pop* 249,977

Vin·cennes \(,)vin-'senz; *for 2, F* vaⁿ-'sen\ **1** city SW Ind. *pop* 19,859 **2** commune N France, E suburb of Paris *pop* 44,256

Vin·dhya Mountains \'vin-dyə, -dē-ə\ mountain range N *cen* India N of & parallel to the Narmada River

Vindhya Pra·desh \prə-'desh, -'dāsh\ former state NE *cen* India * Rewa; became (1956) part of Madhya Pradesh

Vine·land \'vīn-lənd\ city S N.J. *pop* 54,780

Vin·land \'vin-land\ a portion of the coast of N. America visited & so called by Norse voyagers *ab* A.D. 1000; perhaps N tip of Newfoundland

Vin·ni·tsa \'vi-nət-sə\ city W *cen* Ukraine *pop* 211,000

Vin·son Massif \'vin(t)-sən\ mountain 16,864 *ft* (5140 *m*) W Antarctica S of Ellsworth Land in Ellsworth Mountains; highest in Antarctica

Vir·gin \'vər-jən\ river 200 *mi* (322 *km*) SW Utah & SE Nev. flowing to Lake Mead

Vir·gin·ia \vər-'ji-nyə, -'ji-nē-ə\ state E U.S. * Richmond *area* 40,817 *sq mi* (106,124 *sq km*), *pop* 6,187,358 — **Vir·gin·ian** \-nyən, -nē-ən\ *adj or n*

Virginia Beach city SE Va. on the Atlantic *pop* 393,069

Virginia Capes Cape Charles & Cape Henry in Va. forming entrance to Chesapeake Bay

Virgin Islands group of islands W. Indies E of Puerto Rico — see BRITISH VIRGIN ISLANDS, VIRGIN ISLANDS OF THE UNITED STATES

Virgin Islands National Park reservation W. Indies in Virgin Islands of the U.S. on St. John Is.

Virgin Islands of the United States the W islands of the Virgin Islands group including St. Croix, St. John, & St. Thomas; a territory * Charlotte Amalie (on St. Thomas Is.) *area* 132 *sq mi* (343 *sq km*), *pop* 101,809 — see DANISH WEST INDIES

Vi·run·ga \və-'rün-gə\ *or* **Mfum·bi·ro** \em-'füm-bə-,rō\ volcanic mountain range E *cen* Africa in E Zaire, SW Uganda & NW Rwanda N of Lake Kivu; highest peak Karisimbi 14,780 *ft* (4505 *m*)

Vi·sa·lia \vī-'sāl-yə\ city S *cen* Calif. SE of Fresno *pop* 75,636

Vi·sa·yan Islands \və-'sī-ən\ *or* **Bi·sa·yas** \bə-'sī-əz\ islands *cen* Philippines bet. Luzon & Mindanao — see BOHOL, CEBU, LEYTE, MASBATE, NEGROS, PANAY, ROMBLON, SAMAR

Vis·by \'viz-bē\ city & port Sweden on Gotland Is. in the Baltic *pop* 19,319

Vish·a·kha·pat·nam \vi-,shä-kə-'pət-nəm\ *or* **Vi·sa·kha·pat·nam** \vi-,sä-\ city & port E India in NE Andhra Pradesh *pop* 594,259

Vi·so \'vē-(,)zō\ mountain 12,602 *ft* (3841 *m*) NW Italy in Piedmont SW of Turin near French border; highest in Cottian Alps

Vis·ta \'vis-tə\ city SW Calif. N of San Diego *pop* 71,872

Vis·tu·la \'vis-chə-lə, 'vish-chə-, 'vis-tə-\ *or Pol* **Wis·ła** \'vē-(,)slä\ river 630 *mi* (1014 *km*) Poland flowing N from the Carpathians into Gulf of Gdansk

Vistula Lagoon FRISCHES HAFF

Vi·tebsk \'vē-,tepsk, -,tebsk, və-'\ city NE Belarus on Dvina River *pop* 231,000

Vi·ter·bo \vi-'ter-(,)bō\ commune *cen* Italy in Latium *pop* 59,798

Vi·ti Le·vu \,vē-tē-'le-(,)vü\ island SW Pacific, largest of the Fiji group *area* 4053 *sq mi* (10,538 *sq km*)

Vi·tim \və-'tēm\ river 1100 *mi* (1770 *km*) S Russia in Asia flowing NE & N into the Lena

Vi·to·ria \vi-'tòr-ē-ə, -'tòr-\ city N Spain * of Álava province SSE of Bilbao *pop* 189,533

Vi·tó·ria \vi-'tòr-ē-ə, -'tòr-\ city & port E Brazil * of Espírito Santo state on Espírito Santo Is. *pop* 207,560

Vi·try–sur–Seine \vi-,trē-,sùr-'sän, -'sen\ commune N France, SSE suburb of Paris *pop* 87,119

Viz·ca·ya \vis-'kī-ä\ *or* **Bis·ca·ya** \bis-\ *or* **Bis·cay** \'bis-,kā, -kē\ province N Spain on Bay of Biscay; one of the Basque Provinces * Bilbao *area* 836 *sq mi* (2174 *sq km*), *pop* 1,280,018

Vlaanderen — SEE FLANDERS

Vlaar·ding·en \'vlär-diŋ-ə(n)\ commune & port SW Netherlands W of Rotterdam *pop* 77,069

Vlad·i·kav·kaz \,vla-də-,käf-'käz, -,kaf-'kaz\ *or* 1932–43 & 1955–91 **Or·dzha·ni·kid·ze** \,òr-jä-nə-'kid-zə\ *or* 1944–54 **Dzau·dzhi·kau** \(d)zaů-'jē-,kaů\ city S Russia in Europe *pop* 279,000

Vla·di·mir \'vla-də-,mir, vlə-'dē-,mir\ city *cen* Russia in Europe on the Klyazma E of Moscow *pop* 234,000

Vlad·i·vos·tok \,vla-də-və-'stäk, -'väs-,täk\ city & port SE Russia in Asia * of Maritime Territory *pop* 442,000

Vlis·sing·en \'vli-siŋ-ə(n)\ *or* **Flush·ing** \'flə-shiŋ\ city & port SW Netherlands on Walcheren Is. *pop* 46,379

Vlo·rë \'vlòr-ə, 'vlòr-\ *or* **Va·lo·na** \və-'lō-nə\ *or formerly* **Av·lo·na** \av-'lō-nə\ city & port S Albania *pop* 56,400

Vlta·va \'vəl-tə-və\ river 270 *mi* (434 *km*) W Czech Republic in Bohemia flowing N into the Elbe

Vodena — see EDESSA
Vogelkop — see DOBERAI
Voiotía — see BOEOTIA
Voj·vo·di·na \'vói-və-ˌdē-nə, -di-ˌnä\ autonomous region N Yugoslavia N of the Danube; chief city Novi Sad area 8683 sq mi (22,576 sq km), pop 1,950,268
Volcano Islands or Jp **Ka·zan Ret·to** \ˌkä-ˌzän-'re-(ˌ)tō\ islands W Pacific S of Bonin Islands; belong to Japan; under U.S. control 1945–68 area 11 sq mi (29 sq km) — see IWO JIMA
Vo·len·dam \'vō-lən-ˌdam, ˌvō-lən-'däm\ village NW Netherlands on IJsselmeer SE of Edam pop 10,123
Vol·ga \'väl-gə, 'vȯl-, 'vōl-\ river 2325 mi (3742 km) Russia in Europe rising in Valdai Hills & flowing into the Caspian
Vol·go·grad \'väl-gə-ˌgrad, 'vȯl-, 'vōl-, -ˌgräd\ or formerly **Sta·lin·grad** \'stä-lən-ˌgrad, 'sta-, -ˌgräd\ or **Tsa·ri·tsyn** \(t)sə-'rēt-sən\ city S Russia in Europe on the Volga pop 929,000
Vo·log·da \'vȯ-ləg-də\ city cen Russia in Europe NNE of Moscow pop 237,000
Vo·los \'vō-ˌläs\ or NGk **Vó·los** \'vȯ-ˌlȯs\ city & port E Greece on Gulf of Volos (inlet of the Aegean)
Volsinii — see ORVIETO
Vol·ta \'vȯl-tə, 'vȯl-, 'vōl-\ river ab 100 mi (161 km) W Africa flowing from **Lake Volta** (reservoir area 3275 sq mi or 8515 sq km receiving the **Black Volta & White Volta**) in N cen Ghana & flowing S into Bight of Benin — see RED VOLTA
Vol·ta Re·don·da \'väl-tə-ri-'dän-də, 'vōl-, 'vȯl-\ city E Brazil on Paraíba River NW of city of Rio de Janeiro pop 183,917
Vol·tur·no \väl-'túr-(ˌ)nō, vōl-, vȯl-\ river 110 mi (177 km) S cen Italy flowing from the Apennines SE & SW into Gulf of Gaeta
Vor·arl·berg \'fȯr-ˌärl-ˌbərg, 'fȯr-, -ˌberk\ province W Austria W of Tirol on boundary with Switzerland ✻ Bregenz pop 305,615
Vo·ro·nezh \və-'rȯ-nish\ city S cen Russia in Europe near Don River pop 783,000
Voroshilovgrad — see LUGANSK
Vosges \'vōzh\ mountains NE France on W side of Rhine valley; highest Ballon de Guebwiller 4672 ft (1424 m)
Voy·a·geurs National Park \ˌvói-ə-'zhȯrz\ reservation N Minn. on Canadian border S of Rainy Lake
Vrangelya — see WRANGEL
Vyat·ka or **Viat·ka** \vē-'ät-kə\ **1** river 800 mi (1287 km) E cen Russia in Europe flowing into the Kama **2** — see KIROV
Vy·borg \'vē-ˌbȯrg\ or Finn **Vii·pu·ri** \'vē-pə-rē\ city & port W Russia in Europe on arm of Gulf of Finland; belonged to Finland 1917–40 pop 76,000
Vy·cheg·da \'vi-chig-də\ river 700 mi (1120 km) NE cen Russia in Europe flowing W to the Northern Dvina
Waadt — see VAUD
Waal \'väl\ river Netherlands, the S branch of the lower Rhine
Wa·bash \'wȯ-ˌbash\ river 475 mi (764 km) Ind. & Ill. flowing into Ohio River
Wa·co \'wā-(ˌ)kō\ city NE cen Tex. on the Brazos pop 103,590
Wad·den Zee \ˌväd-ə°n-'zā\ inlet of North Sea N Netherlands bet. W. Frisian Islands & IJsselmeer
Wad·ding·ton, Mount \'wä-diŋ-tən\ mountain 13,260 ft (4042 m) W Canada in SW B.C. in Coast mountains; highest in the province
Wad Me·da·ni \ˌwäd-'me-d°n-ē\ city cen Sudan on the Blue Nile pop 106,715
Wa·gram \'vä-ˌgräm\ village Austria NE of Vienna
Wai·a·le·a·le \wī-ˌä-lā-'ä-lā\ mountain 5080 ft (1548 m) Hawaii in cen Kauai
Wai·ka·to \wī-'kä-(ˌ)tō\ river 220 mi (354 km) New Zealand in NW North Is. flowing NW into Tasman Sea
Wai·ki·ki \ˌwī-ki-'kē\ resort section of Honolulu, Hawaii NW of Diamond Head on **Waikiki Beach**
Wai·mea Canyon \wī-'mā-ə\ gorge Hawaii on SW coast of Kauai
Wai·pa·hu \wī-'pä-(ˌ)hü\ city Hawaii in W Oahu pop 31,435
Wai·ta·ki \wī-'tä-kē\ river 135 mi (217 km) New Zealand in SE cen South Is. flowing ESE into the Pacific
Wa·ka·ya·ma \ˌwä-kə-'yä-mə\ city & port Japan in SW Honshu on Inland Sea pop 396,554
Wake Island \'wāk\ island N Pacific N of Marshall Islands belonging to the U.S.
Wake·field \'wāk-ˌfēld\ **1** town E Mass. N of Boston pop 24,825 **2** city & borough N England ✻ of W. Yorkshire pop 60,540
Wa·la·chia or **Wal·la·chia** \wä-'lä-kē-ə\ region S Romania bet. the Transylvanian Alps & the Danube; includes Muntenia & Oltenia; chief city Bucharest — **Wa·la·chi·an** or **Wal·la·chi·an** \-ən\ adj or n
Wał·brzych \'välb-ˌzhik, -ˌzhik\ city SW Poland pop 141,139
Wal·deck \'väl-ˌdek\ former county, principality, & state of Germany bet. Westphalia & Hesse-Nassau ✻ Arolsen
Wal·den Pond \'wȯl-dən\ pond NE Mass. S of Concord
Wales \'wā(ə)lz\ or W **Cym·ru** \'kəm-ˌrē\ or ML **Cam·bria** \'kam-brē-ə\ principality SW Great Britain; a division of the United Kingdom of Great Britain and Northern Ireland ✻ Cardiff area 7469 sq mi (19,419 sq km), pop 2,790,462
Wal·la·sey \'wä-lə-sē\ borough NW England in Merseyside on coast W of Liverpool pop 90,057
Wal·la Wal·la \ˌwä-lə-'wä-lə, 'wä-lə-\ city SE Wash. pop 26,478
Wal·ling·ford \'wä-liŋ-fərd\ town S Conn. NNE of New Haven pop 40,822
Wallis — see VALAIS
Wal·lis Islands \'wä-ləs\ islands SW Pacific NE of Fiji Islands; with Futuna Islands, constitute a French overseas territory (**Wallis and Futuna Islands** pop 8546)
Wal·lops Island \'wä-ləps\ island E Va. in the Atlantic SW of Chincoteague Bay
Wal·lowa Mountains \wä-'laú-ə\ mountains NE Oreg. E of Blue Mountains; highest Sacajawea Peak 9833 ft (2997 m)
Walnut city SW Calif. E of Los Angeles pop 29,105
Walnut Canyon National Monument reservation N cen Ariz. ESE of Flagstaff containing cliff dwellings
Walnut Creek city W Calif. E of Berkeley pop 60,569
Wal·pole \'wȯl-ˌpōl, 'wäl-\ town E Mass. SW of Boston pop 20,212

Wal·sall \'wȯl-ˌsȯl, -səl\ borough W cen England in W. Midlands NNW of Birmingham pop 178,909
Wal·tham \'wȯl-ˌtham, chiefly by outsiders -thəm\ city E Mass. W of Boston pop 57,878
Wal·tham Forest \'wȯl-thəm\ borough of NE Greater London, England pop 217,400
Wal·tham·stow \'wȯl-thəm-ˌstō\ former municipal borough SE England in Essex, now part of Waltham Forest
Wal·vis Bay \'wȯl-vəs\ town & port W Namibia on Walvis Bay (inlet) W of Windhoek; formerly an exclave of Republic of South Africa forming a district area (of district) 374 sq mi (972 sq km)
Wands·worth \'wän(d)z-(ˌ)wərth\ borough of SW Greater London, England pop 265,200
Wang·a·nui \ˌwäŋ-gə-'nü-ē, ˌwäŋ-ə-\ **1** river 150 mi (241 km) New Zealand in SW cen North Is., flowing into Tasman Sea **2** city & port New Zealand in North Is. on Tasman Sea pop 37,012
Wan·ne-Eick·el \'vä-nə-'ī-kəl\ city W Germany in the Ruhr N of Bochum pop 100,300
Wan·stead and Wood·ford \'wän-stəd-°n-'wûd-fərd\ former municipal borough S England in Essex, now part of Redbridge
Wap·si·pin·i·con \ˌwäp-si-'pi-ni-kən\ river 225 mi (362 km) SE Minn. & E Iowa flowing SE into Mississippi River
Wa·ran·gal \wə-'rəŋ-gəl\ city S cen India in N Andhra Pradesh NE of Hyderabad pop 336,018
War·bur·ton Creek \'wȯr-(ˌ)bər-t°n\ river 275 mi (442 km) Australia in NE S. Australia flowing SW into Lake Eyre
Ware·ham \'war-əm, 'wer-, -ˌham\ city SE Mass. ENE of New Bedford pop 19,232
War·ley \'wȯr-lē\ town W cen England, a NW suburb of Birmingham pop 152,455
War·ner Rob·ins \'wȯr-nər-'rä-bənz\ city cen Ga. pop 43,726
War·ren \'wȯr-ən, 'wär-\ **1** city SE Mich. N of Detroit pop 144,864 **2** city NE Ohio NW of Youngstown pop 50,793
War·ring·ton \'wȯr-iŋ-tən, 'wär-\ borough NW England in Cheshire on the Mersey E of Liverpool pop 57,389
War·saw \'wȯr-ˌsȯ\ or Pol **War·sza·wa** \vär-'shä-və\ city ✻ of Poland on the Vistula pop 1,655,063
War·ta \'vär-tə\ or G **War·the** \'vär-tə\ river 445 mi (716 km) Poland flowing NW & W into the Oder
War·wick \'wär-ik, US also 'wȯr-ik, 'wȯr-(ˌ)wik\ **1** city cen R.I. S of Providence on Narragansett Bay pop 85,427 **2** borough cen England ✻ of Warwickshire pop 21,936
War·wick·shire \'wär-ik-ˌshir, -shər, US also 'wȯr-ik-, 'wȯr-(ˌ)wik-\ or **Warwick** county cen England ✻ Warwick area 765 sq mi (1989 sq km), pop 474,500
Wa·satch Range \'wȯ-ˌsach\ mountain range SE Idaho & N & cen Utah — see TIMPANOGOS (Mount)
Wash, The \'wȯsh, 'wäsh\ inlet of North Sea E England bet. Norfolk & Lincoln
Wash·ing·ton \'wȯsh-iŋ-tən, 'wä-, chiefly Midland also 'wȯr-shiŋ- or 'wär-shiŋ-\ **1** state NW U.S. ✻ Olympia area 68,192 sq mi (177,299 sq km), pop 4,866,692 **2** city ✻ of the U.S., coextensive with District of Columbia pop 609,909 **3** — see TERAINA — **Wash·ing·to·nian** \ˌwȯ-shiŋ-'tō-nē-ən, ˌwä-, -nyən\ adj or n
Washington, Lake lake 20 mi (32 km) long W Wash. E of Seattle
Washington, Mount mountain 6288 ft (1916 m) N N.H.; highest in White Mountains
Wash·i·ta \'wä-shə-ˌtò, 'wȯ-\ river 500 mi (805 km) NW Tex. & SW Okla. flowing SE into Red River
Wa·tau·ga \wä-'tȯ-gə\ **1** river 60 mi (96 km) NW N.C. & NE Tenn. flowing into S fork of the Holston **2** town N Tex. pop 20,009
Watenstedt–Salzgitter — see SALZGITTER
Wa·ter·bury \'wȯ-tə(r)-ˌber-ē, 'wä-\ city W cen Conn. pop 108,961
Wa·ter·ee \'wȯ-tə-ˌrē, 'wä-\ river S.C., lower course of the Catawba — see CONGAREE
Wa·ter·ford \'wȯ-tər-fərd, 'wä-\ **1** county S Ireland in Munster area 710 sq mi (1846 sq km), pop 91,608 **2** city & port, its ✻ pop 40,345
Wa·ter·loo \ˌwȯ-tər-'lü, 'wä-; 'wȯ-tər-ˌlü, 'wä-\ **1** city NE cen Iowa pop 66,467 **2** town cen Belgium S of Brussels pop 27,860 **3** city Canada in SE Ont. W of Kitchener pop 71,181
Wa·ter·ton–Glacier International Peace Park \'wȯ-tər-t°n, 'wä-\ reservation comprising **Glacier National Park** (reservation NW Mont.) & **Waterton Lakes National Park** (reservation Canada in Rocky Mountains in S Alta.)
Wa·ter·town \'wȯ-tər-ˌtaún, 'wä-\ **1** town SW Conn. NW of Waterbury pop 20,456 **2** town E Mass. W of Boston pop 33,284 **3** city N cen N.Y. SE of Kingston, Ont. pop 29,429 **4** city SE Wis. pop 19,142
Wat·ford \'wä-fərd\ borough SE England in Hertfordshire NW of London pop 78,117
Wat·son·ville \'wät-sən-ˌvil\ city W Calif. pop 31,099
Wat·ten·scheid \'vä-t°n-ˌshīt\ city W Germany E of Essen pop 80,527
Watts \'wäts\ section of Los Angeles, Calif. S of the downtown district
Wau·ke·gan \wȯ-'kē-gən\ city NE Ill. N of Chicago pop 69,392
Wau·ke·sha \'wȯ-kə-ˌshȯ\ city SE Wis. pop 56,958
Wau·sau \'wȯ-ˌsȯ, -sə\ city N cen Wis. pop 37,060
Wau·wa·to·sa \ˌwȯ-wə-'tō-sə\ city SE Wis. pop 49,366
Wayne \'wān\ village SE Mich. SW of Detroit pop 19,899
Wa·zir·i·stan \wə-ˌzir-i-'stan, -'stän\ region W Pakistan on border of Afghanistan NE of Baluchistan
Weald \'wē(ə)ld\ region SE England in Kent, Surrey, & Sussex, bet. N. Downs & S. Downs; once heavily forested
Wear \'wir\ river 67 mi (108 km) N England flowing into North Sea at Sunderland
Web·ster Groves \'web-stər\ city E Mo. pop 22,987
Wed·dell Sea \wə-'del, 'we-d°l\ arm of the S Atlantic E of Antarctic Peninsula

---

\ə\ abut \ᵊ\ kitten, F table \ər\ further \a\ ash \ā\ ace \ä\ mop, mar
\aú\ out \ch\ chin \e\ bet \ē\ easy \g\ go \i\ hit \ī\ ice \j\ job
\ŋ\ sing \ō\ go \ó\ law \ói\ boy \th\ thin \t̷h\ the \ü\ loot \ú\ foot
\y\ yet \zh\ vision \ȧ, k̫, ⁿ, œ, œ̄, ᵫ, ᵬ, ʸ\ see Guide to Pronunciation

Wei \\'wā\ river 400 *mi* (644 *km*) N *cen* China flowing E to join the Huang

Wei·fang \\'wā-'fän\ city E China in E *cen* Shandong *pop* 190,000

Wei·hai \\'wā-'hi\ *or formerly* **Wei·hai·wei** \\,wā-,hi-'wā\ city & port E China in NE Shandong on Yellow Sea *pop* 175,000

Wei·mar \\'vī-,mär, 'wī-\ city E *cen* Germany E of Erfurt *pop* 64,000

Weimar Republic the German republic 1919–33

Weir·ton \\'wir-t²n\ city N W.Va. on Ohio River *pop* 22,124

Wel·land \\'we-lənd\ city Canada in SE Ont. SW of Niagara Falls *pop* 47,914

Welland Ship Canal canal 28 *mi* (45 *km*) Canada in SE Ont. connecting Lake Erie & Lake Ontario

Welles·ley \\'welz-lē\ town E Mass. WSW of Boston *pop* 26,615

Wel·ling·ton \\'we-liŋ-tən\ city & port ✳ of New Zealand in SW North Is. on Port Nicholson (Wellington Harbor) on Cook Strait *pop* 135,688

Wells \\'welz\ city & borough SW England in Somerset *pop* 8374

Welsh·pool \\'welsh-,pül\ town E Wales in Powys *pop* 7317

Wel·wyn Garden City \\'we-lən\ urban district SE England in Hertfordshire N of London *pop* 40,369

Wem·bley \\'wem-blē\ former municipal borough SE England in Middlesex, now part of Brent

We·natch·ee \\wə-'na-chē\ city *cen* Wash. *pop* 21,756

Wen·zhou *or* **Wen·chow** *or* **Wen–chou** \\'wən-'jō\ city & port E China in S Zhejiang on E. China Sea *pop* 210,000

Wer·ra \\'ver-ə\ river 180 *mi* (290 *km*), *cen* Germany flowing N

We·ser \\'vā-zər\ river 280 *mi* (451 *km*) *cen* & NW Germany flowing into North Sea

Wes·la·co \\'wes-li,kō\ city S Tex. W of Harlingen *pop* 21,877

Wes·sex \\'we-siks\ ancient Anglian kingdom S England ✳ Winchester; one of kingdoms in Anglo-Saxon heptarchy

West Al·lis \\'a-ləs\ city SE Wis. *pop* 63,221

West Antarctica — see ANTARCTICA

West Bank area Palestine W of Jordan River; occupied by Israel since 1967 — **West Bank·er** \\'baŋ-kər\ *n*

West Bend \\'bend\ city SE Wis. NNW of Milwaukee *pop* 23,916

West Bengal state E India comprising the W third of former Bengal province ✳ Calcutta *area* 33,945 *sq mi* (88,257 *sq km*), *pop* 54,485,560

West Beskids — see BESKIDS

West Brom·wich \\'brä-mich\ borough W *cen* England in W. Midlands NW of Birmingham *pop* 154,930

West Co·vi·na \\kō-'vē-nə\ city SW Calif. *pop* 96,086

West Des Moines city S *cen* Iowa *pop* 31,702

Wes·ter·ly \\'wes-tər-lē\ town SW R.I. *pop* 21,605

Western — see HEBRIDES

Western Australia state W Australia on Indian Ocean ✳ Perth *area* 975,920 *sq mi* (2,537,392 *sq km*), *pop* 1,273,624

Western Cape province SW Republic of South Africa *area* 49,955 *sq mi* (129,383 *sq km*), *pop* 3,620,200

Western Ghats \\'gäts, 'gots, 'gots\ chain of mountains SW India extending SSE parallel to coast from mouth of the Tapti to Cape Comorin; highest Anai Mudi 8842 *ft* (2695 *m*) — see EASTERN GHATS

Western Isles **1** the Outer Hebrides, constituting since 1975 a region of W Scotland ✳ Stornoway *area* 1120 *sq mi* (2912 *sq km*), *pop* 31,766 **2** — used unofficially for the entire Hebrides group

Western Reserve tract of land NE Ohio on S shore of Lake Erie; part of W lands of Conn., ceded 1800 *area ab* 5470 *sq mi* (14,222 *sq km*)

Western Sahara *or* **Spanish Sahara** former Spanish possessions Río de Oro & Saguia el Hamra in NW Africa, divided 1975 bet. Mauritania, which gave up its claim in Aug. 1979, & Morocco, which subsequently occupied the entire territory

Western Samoa group of islands of Samoa W of 171°W; until 1962 a territory administered by New Zealand; became an independent member of the Commonwealth of Nations 1962 ✳ Apia (on Upolu Is.) *area* 1133 *sq mi* (2946 *sq km*), *pop* 156,349

Western Thrace — see THRACE

Wes·ter·ville \\'wes-tər-,vil, -vəl\ city *cen* Ohio *pop* 30,269

West·field \\'wes(t)-,fēld\ **1** city SW Mass. WNW of Springfield *pop* 38,372 **2** town NE N.J. WSW of Elizabeth *pop* 28,870

West Flanders province NW Belgium bordering on North Sea ✳ Bruges *area* 1248 *sq mi* (3245 *sq km*), *pop* 1,106,829

West Frisian — see FRISIAN ISLANDS

West Germany — see GERMANY

West Glamorgan county SE Wales ✳ Swansea *area* 315 *sq mi* (819 *sq km*), *pop* 369,700

West Ham \\'ham\ former county borough SE England in Essex, now part of Newham

West Hartford town *cen* Conn. *pop* 60,110

West Ha·ven \\'west-,hā-vən\ city S Conn. *pop* 54,021

West Hollywood city SW Calif. *pop* 36,118

West Indies **1** the islands lying bet. SE N. America & N S. America bordering the Caribbean & comprising the Greater Antilles, Lesser Antilles, & Bahamas **2** *or* **West Indies Federation** former country including all of the Brit. West Indies except the Bahamas & the Brit. Virgin Islands; established 1958, dissolved 1961 — **West Indian** *adj or n*

West Indies Associated States the self-governing states of Antigua, Dominica, St. Kitts-Nevis, St. Lucia, & St. Vincent, associated with United Kingdom in foreign relations & defense

West Iri·an \\,ir-ē-'än\ *or* **Irian Ja·ya** \\'jä-yə, 'jī-ə\ *or formerly* **Netherlands New Guinea** *or* **Dutch New Guinea** territory of Indonesia comprising the W half of New Guinea & adjacent islands; belonged to the Netherlands until 1963 ✳ Djajapura *area* 164,159 *sq mi* (426,813 *sq km*), *pop* 1,173,875

West Jordan city N *cen* Utah *pop* 42,892

West Lafayette city W *cen* Ind. *pop* 25,907

West·lake \\'west-,lāk\ city N Ohio W of Cleveland *pop* 27,018

West·land \\'west(t)-lənd\ city SE Mich. W of Detroit *pop* 84,724

West Lo·thi·an \\'lō-thē-ən\ *or earlier* **Lin·lith·gow** \\lin-'lith-(,)gō\ *or* **Lin·lith·gow·shire** \\-,shir, -shər\ former county SE Scotland bordering on Firth of Forth ✳ Linlithgow — see LOTHIAN

West Malaysia the peninsular part of Malaysia — see MALAYA 3

West·meath \\(,)wes(t)-'mēth, -'mēth\ county E *cen* Ireland in Leinster ✳ Mullingar *area* 681 *sq mi* (1771 *sq km*), *pop* 61,882

West Memphis city E Ark. on Mississippi River *pop* 28,259

West Midlands metropolitan county W *cen* England ✳ Birmingham *area* 347 *sq mi* (902 *sq km*), *pop* 2,674,000

West Miff·lin \\'mi-flən\ borough SW Pa. SE of Pittsburgh *pop* 23,644

West·min·ster \\'wes(t)-,min(t)-stər\ **1** city SW Calif. E of Long Beach *pop* 78,118 **2** city N Colo. NW of Denver *pop* 74,625 **3** borough of W *cen* Greater London, England *pop* 194,900

West·mont \\'wes(t)-,mänt\ city NE Ill. *pop* 21,228

West·mor·land \\'wes(t)-mər-lənd, *US also* wes(t)-'mȯr- *or* -'mȯr-\ former county NW England ✳ Kendal

West New York town NE N.J. on Hudson River *pop* 38,125

Wes·ton–su·per–Mare \\'wes-tən-,sü-pər-'mar, -'mer\ borough SW England in Avon on Bristol Channel *pop* 57,980

West Pakistan the former W division of Pakistan, now coextensive with Pakistan

West Palm Beach city SE Fla. on Lake Worth inlet *pop* 67,643

West·pha·lia \\wes(t)-'fāl-yə, -'fā-lē-ə\ *or G* **West·fa·len** \\,vest-'fä-lən\ region W Germany bordering on the Netherlands E of the Rhine; includes Ruhr valley; a province of Prussia 1816–1945 ✳ Münster — see NORTH RHINE-WESTPHALIA — **West·pha·lian** \\wes(t)-'fāl-yən, -'fā-lē-ən\ *adj or n*

West·port \\'wes(t)-,pȯrt, -,pȯrt\ town SW Conn. *pop* 24,410

West Prussia region N Europe bordering on the Baltic bet. Pomerania & E. Prussia; since 1945 in Poland

West Punjab — see PUNJAB

West Quod·dy Head \\'kwä-dē\ cape NE Maine at entrance to Passamaquoddy Bay

Wes·tra·lia \\we-'sträl-yə, -'strä-lē-ə\ WESTERN AUSTRALIA

West Riding — see YORK

West Sacramento city Calif. *pop* 28,898

West Saint Paul city SE Minn. S of St. Paul *pop* 19,248

West Spitsbergen island in Arctic Ocean, largest of the Spitsbergen group *area* 14,600 *sq mi* (37,960 *sq km*) — see SVALBARD

West Springfield town SW Mass. on Connecticut River *pop* 27,537

West Suffolk — see SUFFOLK

West Sus·sex \\'sə-siks, *US also* -,seks\ county S England ✳ Chichester *area* 769 *sq mi* (1999 *sq km*), *pop* 666,000

West Valley City city N Utah bordering Salt Lake City on the S *pop* 86,976

West Vancouver municipality Canada in SW B.C. N of Vancouver *pop* 38,783

West Virginia state E U.S. ✳ Charleston *area* 24,181 *sq mi* (62,871 *sq km*), *pop* 1,793,477 — **West Virginian** *adj or n*

West Warwick town *cen* R.I. *pop* 29,268

West Yorkshire metropolitan county NW England ✳ Wakefield *area* 787 *sq mi* (2046 *sq km*), *pop* 2,065,400

Weth·ers·field \\'we-thərz-,fēld\ town *cen* Conn. *pop* 25,651

Wex·ford \\'weks-fərd\ **1** county SE Ireland in Leinster *area* 908 *sq mi* (2361 *sq km*), *pop* 102,045 **2** municipal borough & port, its ✳ *pop* 10,336

Wey·mouth \\'wā-məth\ town E Mass. SE of Boston *pop* 54,063

Whales, Bay of inlet of Ross Sea Antarctica in Ross Ice Shelf

Whangpoo — see HUANGPU

Whea·ton \\'hwē-t²n, 'wē-\ city NE Ill. W of Chicago *pop* 51,464

Wheat Ridge city N *cen* Colo. W of Denver *pop* 29,419

Whee·ler Peak \\'hwē-lər, 'wē-\ **1** mountain 13,063 *ft* (3982 *m*) E Nev. in Snake Range **2** mountain 13,161 *ft* (4011 *m*) N N.Mex. in Sangre de Cristo Mountains; highest in the state

Whee·ling \\'hwē-liŋ, 'wē-\ **1** village NE Ill. NNE of Chicago *pop* 29,911 **2** city N W.Va. on Ohio River *pop* 34,882

Whid·bey Island \\'hwid-bē, 'wid-\ island 40 *mi* (64 *km*) long NW Wash. at N end of Puget Sound E of Admiralty Inlet

Whit·by \\'hwit-bē, 'wit-\ town Canada in S Ont. *pop* 61,281

White **1** river 690 *mi* (1110 *km*) N Ark. & SW Mo. flowing SE into Mississippi River **2** river 160 *mi* (257 *km*) NW Colo. & E Utah flowing W into Green River **3** river 50 *mi* (80 *km*) SW Ind. flowing W into the Wabash **4** river 325 *mi* (523 *km*) S S.Dak. flowing E into Missouri River **5** river 75 *mi* (121 *km*) NW Tex.

White Bear Lake city E Minn. NE of St. Paul *pop* 24,704

White·chap·el \\'hwīt-,cha-pəl, 'wit-\ district of E London, England, N of Thames River in Tower Hamlets

White·friars \\'hwit-,frī(-ə)rz, 'wit-\ district of *cen* London, England, on Thames River

White·hall \\-,hȯl\ city *cen* Ohio, E suburb of Columbus *pop* 20,572

White·horse \\'hwit-,hȯrs, 'wit-\ city NW Canada ✳ of Yukon Territory on upper Yukon River *pop* 17,925

White Mountains **1** mountains E Calif. & SE Nev. **2** mountains N N.H. in the Appalachians — see WASHINGTON (Mount)

White Nile — see NILE

White Pass mountain pass 2885 *ft* (879 *m*) SE Alaska N of Skagway

White Plains city SE N.Y. NE of Yonkers *pop* 48,718

White Sands National Monument reservation S N.Mex. SW of Alamogordo comprising an area of gypsum sand dunes

White Sea *or Russ* **Be·lo·ye Mo·re** \\'bye-lə-yə-'mȯr-yə, 'be-lə-\ inlet of Barents Sea NW Russia in Europe enclosed on the N by Kola Peninsula

White Volta — see VOLTA

Whit·ney, Mount \\'hwit-nē, 'wit-\ mountain 14,494 *ft* (4418 *m*) SE *cen* Calif. in Sierra Nevada in Sequoia National Park; highest in the U.S. outside of Alaska

Whit·ti·er \\'hwi-tē-ər, 'wi-\ city SW Calif. SE of Los Angeles *pop* 77,671

Wich·i·ta \\'wi-chə-,tȯ\ **1** city S *cen* Kans. on Arkansas River *pop* 304,011 **2** river 230 *mi* (370 *km*) N Tex. flowing ENE into Red River

Wichita Falls city N Tex. on Wichita River *pop* 96,259

Wichita Mountains mountains SW Okla.; highest Mt. Scott 2464 *ft* (751 *m*)

Wick·low \\'wi-(,)klō\ **1** county E Ireland in Leinster *area* 782 *sq mi* (2033 *sq km*), *pop* 97,293 **2** urban district & port, its ✳, SSE of Dublin *pop* 5304

Wicklow Mountains mountains Ireland along E coast; highest Lugnaquilla 3039 *ft* (926 *m*)

Wien — see VIENNA

Wies·ba·den \\'vēs-,bä-d²n\ city SW *cen* Germany on the Rhine W of Frankfurt am Main ✳ of Hesse *pop* 274,464

Wig·an \'wi-gən\ borough NW England in Greater Manchester W of Manchester *pop* 79,535

Wight, Isle of \'wīt\ island S England in English Channel constituting **Isle of Wight** county (✻ Newport *area* 147 *sq mi or* 382 *sq km, pop* 116,300)

Wig·town \'wig-tən, -,taùn\ *or* **Wig·town·shire** \-,shir, -shər\ former county SW Scotland ✻ Wigtown

Wilderness Road trail from SW Va. to *cen* Ky. through Cumberland Gap blazed to site of Boonesborough by Daniel Boone 1775 & later extended to falls of the Ohio at Louisville

Wil·helms·ha·ven \,vil-,helmz-'hä-fən, 'vi-ləmz-,\ city & port NW Germany NW of Bremen *pop* 99,230

Wilkes–Barre \'wilks-,bar-ə, -,bar-ē, -,bar\ city NE Pa. on the Susquehanna SW of Scranton *pop* 47,523

Wilkes Land \'wilks\ coast region E Antarctica extending along Indian Ocean S of Australia

Wil·kins·burg \'wil-kənz-,bərg\ borough SW Pa. *pop* 21,080

Wil·lam·ette \wə-'la-mət\ river 190 *mi* (306 *km*) NW Oreg. flowing N into Columbia River

Wil·la·pa Bay \'wi-lə-,pò, -,pä\ inlet of the Pacific SW Wash.

Wil·lem·stad \'vi-ləm-,stät\ city ✻ of Netherlands Antilles on Curaçao Is. *pop* 43,547

Willes·den \'wilz-dən\ former municipal borough SE England in Middlesex, now part of Brent

Wil·liams·burg \'wil-yəmz-,bərg\ city SE Va. NNW of Newport News; ✻ of Virginia 1699–1780; site of large-scale restoration (Colonial Williamsburg) *pop* 11,530

Wil·liam·son, Mount \'wil-yəm-sən\ mountain 14,375 *ft* (4382 *m*) SE *cen* Calif. in Sierra Nevada NNW of Mt. Whitney

Wil·liams·port \'wil-yəmz-,pōrt, -,pòrt\ city N *cen* Pa. on W branch of the Susquehanna *pop* 31,933

Wil·lough·by \'wi-lə-bē\ city NE Ohio NE of Cleveland *pop* 20,510

Wil·mette \wil-'met\ village NE Ill. N of Chicago *pop* 26,690

Wil·ming·ton \'wil-miŋ-tən\ **1** city & port N Del. *pop* 71,529 **2** city & port SE N.C. *pop* 55,530

Wil·son \'wil-sən\ city E *cen* N.C. E of Raleigh *pop* 36,930

Wilson, Mount mountain 5710 *ft* (1740 *m*) SW Calif. NE of Pasadena

Wilt·shire \'wilt-,shir, -shər\ county S England ✻ Trowbridge *area* 1345 *sq mi* (3497 *sq km*), *pop* 521,300

Wim·ble·don \'wim-bəl-dən\ former municipal borough SE England in Surrey, now part of Merton

Win·ches·ter \'win-,ches-tər, -chəs-tər\ **1** town E Mass. NW of Boston *pop* 20,267 **2** city N Va. *pop* 21,947 **3** city & borough S England ✻ of Hampshire *pop* 30,642

Wind \'wind\ river W *cen* Wyo., the upper course of Bighorn River

Windau — see VENTSPILS

Wind Cave limestone cavern SW S. Dak. in Black Hills in **Wind Cave National Park**

Win·der·mere \'win-də(r)-,mir\ lake 10 *mi* (16 *km*) long NW England in Cumbria; largest in England

Wind·ham \'win-dəm\ town E *cen* Conn. *pop* 22,039

Wind·hoek \'vint-,húk\ city ✻ of Namibia *pop* 36,051

Wind River Canyon gorge of Bighorn River W *cen* Wyo.

Wind River Range mountain range W *cen* Wyo. — see GANNETT PEAK

Wind·sor \'win-zər\ **1** town N *cen* Conn. N of Hartford *pop* 27,817 **2** city Canada in SE Ont. on Detroit River opposite Detroit, Mich. *pop* 191,435 **3** *or* **New Windsor** royal borough S England in Berkshire on Thames River W of London *pop* 30,065

Wind·ward Islands \'win(d)-wərd\ **1** islands W. Indies in the S Lesser Antilles extending S from Martinique but not including Barbados, Tobago, or Trinidad **2** former colony Brit. West Indies comprising territories of St. Lucia, St. Vincent, & Grenada in the Windward group & Dominica in the Leewards **3** *or* *F* **Iles du Vent** \ēl-dǖe-vän\ islands S Pacific, E group of the Society Islands, including Tahiti *pop* 140,341

Windward Passage channel bet. Cuba & Hispaniola

Win·ne·ba·go, Lake \,wi-nə-'bā-(,)gō\ lake 30 *mi* (48 *km*) long E Wis.

Win·ni·peg \'wi-nə-,peg\ **1** river 200 *mi* (322 *km*) Canada in W Ont. & SE Man. flowing from Lake of the Woods to Lake Winnipeg **2** city Canada ✻ of Man. *pop* 616,790 — **Win·ni·peg·ger** \-,pe-gər\ *n*

Winnipeg, Lake lake 275 *mi* (442 *km*) long Canada in S *cen* Man. drained by Nelson River *area* 9460 *sq mi* (24,596 *sq km*)

Win·ni·pe·go·sis, Lake \,wi-nə-pə-'gō-səs\ lake Canada in W Man. W of Lake Winnipeg *area* 2086 *sq mi* (5424 *sq km*)

Win·ni·pe·sau·kee, Lake \,wi-nə-pə-'sò-kē\ lake *cen* N.H. *area* 71 *sq mi* (185 *sq km*)

Wi·no·na \wə-'nō-nə\ city SE Minn. *pop* 25,399

Wi·noo·ski \wə-'nüs-kē\ river 100 *mi* (161 *km*) N *cen* Vt. flowing into Lake Champlain

Win·ston-Sa·lem \,win(t)-stən-'sā-ləm\ city N N.C. *pop* 143,485

Winter Haven city *cen* Fla. E of Lakeland *pop* 24,725

Winter Park city E Fla. N of Orlando *pop* 22,242

Winter Springs city E *cen* Fla. N of Orlando *pop* 22,151

Win·ter·thur \'vin-tər-,tür\ commune N Switzerland in Zurich canton NE of Zurich *pop* 85,882

Win·yah Bay \'win-,yó\ inlet of the Atlantic E S.C.

Wis·con·sin \wis-'kän(t)-sən\ **1** river 430 *mi* (692 *km*) *cen* Wis. flowing S & W into Mississippi River **2** state N *cen* U.S. ✻ Madison *area* 56,164 *sq mi* (146,026 *sq km*), *pop* 4,891,769 — **Wis·con·sin·ite** \-sə-,nīt\ *n*

Wisconsin Dells — see DELLS OF THE WISCONSIN

Wisła — see VISTULA

Wis·mar \'vis-,mär, 'wiz-,mär\ city & port N Germany *pop* 57,586

Wis·sa·hick·on Creek \,wi-sə-'hi-kən\ stream SE Pa. flowing into the Schuylkill at Philadelphia

With·la·coo·chee \,with-lə-'kü-chē\ **1** river 110 *mi* (177 *km*) S Ga. & NW Fla. flowing SE into the Suwannee **2** river 120 *mi* (193 *km*) NW *cen* Fla. flowing NW into Gulf of Mexico

Wit·ten \'vi-t⁵n\ city W Germany SW of Dortmund *pop* 105,876

Wit·ten·berg \'wi-t⁵n-,bərg, 'vi-t⁵n-,berk\ city E *cen* Germany E of Dessau *pop* 54,094

Wit·wa·ters·rand \'wit-,wò-tərz-,rand, -,wä-, -,ränd, -,ränt\ ridge of auriferous rock 62 *mi* (100 *km*) long & 23 *mi* (37 *km*) wide NE Repub-

lic of South Africa in Pretoria-Witwatersrand-Vereeniging and North West provinces

Wło·cła·wek \vlòt-'slä-,vek\ commune N *cen* Poland on the Vistula *pop* 120,823

Wo·burn \'wü-bərn, 'wō-\ city E Mass. NW of Boston *pop* 35,943

Wo·dzi·sław Ślą·ski \vó-'jē-släf-'shlòⁿ-skē\ town S Poland *pop* 111,329

Wolds, The \'wōl(d)z\ chalk hills NE England in N. Yorkshire, Humberside, & N Lincolnshire

Wolfs·burg \'wùlfs-,bərg, 'vòlfs-,bùrk\ city N *cen* Germany *pop* 125,935

Wol·lon·gong \'wù-lən-,gän, -,gòŋ\ city SE Australia in E New South Wales S of Sydney *metropolitan area pop* 206,803

Wol·ver·hamp·ton \,wùl-vər-'ham(p)-tən\ borough W *cen* England in W. Midlands NW of Birmingham *pop* 252,447

Won·san \'wən-,sän\ city & port N. Korea on E coast *pop* 215,000

Wood Buffalo National Park reservation W Canada in N Alta. & S Northwest Territories

Wood·bury \'wùd-,ber-ē, -,bə-rē\ city E Minn., a suburb of St. Paul *pop* 20,075

Wood Green former municipal borough SE England in Middlesex, now part of Haringey

Wood·land \'wùd-lənd\ city W Calif. NW of Sacramento *pop* 39,802

Wood·lark \'wùd-,lärk\ island W Pacific in Solomon Sea off SE end of New Guinea; attached to Papua New Guinea *area* 400 *sq mi* (1040 *sq km*)

Wood·ridge \'wùd-(,)rij\ city NE Ill. *pop* 26,256

Woods, Lake of the lake S Canada & N U.S. in Ont., Man., & Minn. SE of Lake Winnipeg *area* 1485 *sq mi* (3861 *sq km*)

Wood·stock \'wùd-,stäk\ city Canada in SE Ont. *pop* 30,075

Wool·wich \'wù-lij, -lich\ former metropolitan borough E London, England, now part of Greenwich

Woom·era \'wù-mə-rə\ town S. Australia W of Lake Torrens

Woon·sock·et \wün-'sä-kət, 'wùn-,\ city N R.I. *pop* 43,877

Woos·ter \'wùs-tər\ city N *cen* Ohio SW of Akron *pop* 22,191

Worces·ter \'wùs-tər\ **1** city E *cen* Mass. W of Boston *pop* 169,759 **2** *or* **Worces·ter·shire** \-tə(r)-,shir, -shər\ former county W *cen* England — see HEREFORD AND WORCESTER **3** city, ✻ of Hereford and Worcester *pop* 73,445

Worms \'wərmz, 'vòrm(p)s\ city SW Germany on the Rhine NNW of Mannheim *pop* 73,603

Worth, Lake \'wərth\ inlet (lagoon) of the Atlantic SE Fla.

Wor·thing \'wər-thiŋ\ borough S England in W. Sussex on English Channel *pop* 91,668

Wound·ed Knee \,wün-dəd-'nē\ locality SW S. Dakota; site of 1890 massacre of American Indians by U.S. troops

Wran·gel \'raŋ-gəl\ *or Russ* **Vran·ge·lya** \'vrän-gəl-yə\ island in Arctic Ocean off NE coast of Russia in Asia

Wran·gell, Cape cape on Attu Is. in Aleutians

Wran·gell, Mount active volcano 14,163 *ft* (4317 *m*) S Alaska in Wrangell Mountains NW of Mt. Blackburn

Wrangell Mountains mountain range S Alaska NW of St. Elias Range — see BLACKBURN (Mount)

Wrangell–Saint Eli·as National Park \-sänt-i-'lī-əs\ reservation S *cen* Alaska; largest park in the world covering 12,318,000 *acres* (4,927,200 *hectares*)

Wrath, Cape \'rath, *Sc* 'ròth *or* 'räth\ extreme NW point of Scotland, at 58°35′N

Wrex·ham \'rek-səm\ borough NE Wales in Clwyd *pop* 40,272

Wro·cław \'vròt-,släf, -,släv\ *or G* **Bres·lau** \'bres-,laù, 'brez-\ city SW Poland, chief city of Silesia *pop* 642,334

Wu \'wü\ river 500 *mi* (805 *km*) *cen* China rising in W Guizhou & flowing through Szechwan into the Chang

Wu·chang \'wü-'chäŋ\ former city E *cen* China — see WUHAN

Wu·han \'wü-'hän\ city E *cen* China ✻ of Hubei at junction of Han & Chang rivers; formed from the former separate cities of Hankow, Hanyang, & Wuchang *pop* 4,250,000

Wuhsien — see SUZHOU

Wu·hu \'wü-'hü\ city E China in E Anhui *pop* 300,000

Wu·lu·mu·ch'i — see ÜRÜMQI

Wu·pat·ki National Monument \wü-'pat-kē\ reservation N Ariz. NNE of Flagstaff containing prehistoric Indian dwellings

Wup·per·tal \'vù-pər-,täl\ city W Germany in Ruhr valley ENE of Düsseldorf *pop* 393,381

Würt·tem·berg \'wər-təm-,bərg, 'wùr-; 'vùer-təm-,berk\ region SW Germany bet. Baden & Bavaria; chief city Stuttgart; once a duchy, kingdom 1813–1918, state 1918–45; divided 1945–51, S part being joined to Hohenzollern forming **Württemberg–Hohenzollern** state & N part to N Baden forming **Württemberg–Baden** state; since 1951 part of Baden-Württemberg state

Würz·burg \'wərts-,bərg, 'wùrts-; 'vuerts-,bùrk\ city S Germany on Main River in N Bavaria NW of Nuremberg *pop* 128,652

Wu·xi *or* **Wu·hsi** *or* **Wu·sih** \'wü-'shē\ city E China in S Jiangsu NW of Suzhou

Wu·zhou *or* **Wu·chou** *or* **Wu·chow** \'wü-'jō\ city S China in E Guangxi Zhuangzu at junction of the Gui & the Xi *pop* 120,000

Wy·an·dotte \'wī-ən-,dät *also* 'win-\ city SE Mich. *pop* 30,938

Wye \'wī\ river 130 *mi* (209 *km*) E Wales & W England flowing into Severn River

Wy·o·ming \wī-'ō-miŋ\ **1** state NW U.S. ✻ Cheyenne *area* 97,914 *sq mi* (254,576 *sq km*), *pop* 453,588 **2** valley NE Pa. along the Susquehanna **3** city SW Mich. *pop* 63,891 — **Wy·o·ming·ite** \-miŋ-,īt\ *n*

Xan·thus \'zan(t)-thəs\ city of ancient Lycia; its site near mouth of Koca River in SW Turkey

Xe·nia \'zē-nyə, -nē-ə\ city SW *cen* Ohio *pop* 24,664

Xeres — see JEREZ

\ə\ abut \'ə\ kitten, F table \ər\ further \a\ ash \ā\ ace \ä\ mop, mar \aú\ out \ch\ chin \e\ bet \ē\ easy \g\ go \i\ hit \ī\ ice \j\ job \ŋ\ sing \ō\ go \ò\ law \òi\ boy \th\ thin \t̲h̲\ the \ü\ loot \ù\ foot \y\ yet \zh\ vision \ä, k̲, ⁿ, œ, œ̄, ue, ū̄e, ᵊ\ *see* Guide to Pronunciation

Xi or **Hsi** or **Si** \'shē\ river 300 mi (483 km) SE China in Guangxi Zhuangzu & Guangdong flowing E into S. China Sea

Xia·men or **Hsia-men** \shē-'ä-'mən\ or **Amoy** \ä-'mȯi, a-, ə-\ city & port SE China in S Fujian on two islands pop 308,000

Xi'·an or **Si·an** \'shē-'än\ or formerly **Chang·an** \'chän-'än\ city E cen China ✳ of Shaanxi on the Wei pop 1,900,000

Xiang or **Hsiang** \shē-'äŋ\ river 350 mi (560 km) SE cen China flowing from N Guangxi Zhuangzu N into Hunan

Xiang·tan or **Hsiang–t'an** or **Siang-tan** \shē-'äŋ-'tän\ city SE China in E Hunan on the Xiang S of Changsha pop 281,523

Xi-ga-zê \'shē-'gäd-ze\ or **Shi-ga-tse** \shi-'gät-sə\ or **Jih-k'a-tse** \'zhir-'käd-zə\ town W China in SE Tibet on the Tsangpo W of Lhasa

Xin-gu \shēŋ-'gü\ river 1300 mi (2092 km) cen & N Brazil rising on Mato Grosso plateau & flowing N into the Amazon near its mouth

Xi-ning or **Si-ning** or **Hsi–Ning** \'shē-'niŋ\ city NW China ✳ of Qinghai pop 300,000

Xin-jiang Uy-gur or **Sin-kiang Ui-ghur** \'shin-jē-'äŋ-'wē-gər\ region W China bet. the Kunlun & Altai mountains; formerly a province ✳ Ürümqi area 635,829 sq mi (1,653,154 sq km), pop 13,081,681

Xin-xiang or **Hsin–hsiang** or **Sin-siang** \'shin-shē-'äŋ\ city E China in N Henan N of Zhengzhou pop 203,000

Xizang — see TIBET

Xo-chi-mil-co \,sō-chi-'mēl(,)-kō, ,sō-shi-, -'mil-\ city S cen Mexico, SE suburb of Mexico City pop 116,493

Xuan-hua or **Hsüan–hua** \shü-'än-'hwä, -'wä\ city NE China in NW Hebei NW of Beijing pop 114,000

Xu-zhou \'shü-'jō\ or **Hsü–chou** or **Sü-chow** \'shü-'jō, 'sü-; 'sü-'chaü\ city E China in NW Jiangsu pop 1,500,000

Ya-blo-no-vy Mountains or **Ya-blo-no-vyy Mountains** \,yä-blə-nə-'vē\ mountain range S Russia in Asia

Yacarana — see JAVARI

Yad-kin \'yad-kən\ river 202 mi (325 km) cen N.C., the upper course of the Pee Dee

Yafo — see JAFFA

Ya-ha-ta \yə-'hä-tə\ or **Ya-wa-ta** \-'wä-\ former city Japan in N Kyushu — see KITAKYUSHU

Yak-i-ma \'ya-kə-,mȯ\ **1** river 200 mi (322 km) S Wash. flowing SE into Columbia River **2** city SE cen Wash. pop 54,827

Yak-u-tat Bay \'ya-kə-,tat\ inlet of the Pacific SE Alaska

Ya-kut Republic \yə-'küt\ autonomous republic E cen Russia in Asia ✳ Yakutsk area 1,182,300 sq mi (3,073,980 sq km), pop 664,000

Ya-kutsk \yä-'kütsk\ city E cen Russia in Asia pop 152,000

Ya-long or **Ya-lung** \'yä-'lüŋ\ river 725 mi (1167 km) SW China in W Szechwan flowing S into the Chang

Yal-ta \'yȯl-tə\ city & port on S coast of Crimea pop 57,000

Ya-lu \'yä-(,)lü\ river 300 mi (483 km) SE Manchuria & NW N. Korea flowing N, W, & SW into Korea Bay

Ya-mal \yə-'mäl\ peninsula NW Russia in Asia at N end of Ural Mountains bet. Gulf of Ob & Kara Sea

Ya-mous-sou-kro \,yä-mə-'sü-krō\ town cen Ivory Coast

Yam-pa \'yam-pə\ river 200 mi (322 km) NW Colo. flowing W into Green River in Dinosaur National Monument

Ya-na \'yä-nə\ river 750 mi (1207 km) N Russia in Asia flowing N into Laptev Sea

Yan'·an \'yä-'nän\ or **Yen-an** \'ye-'nän\ city NE cen China in cen Shaanxi pop 45,000

Yangku — see TAIYUAN

Yan-gon \,yän-'gōn\ **1** — see RANGOON 1 **2** or formerly **Rangoon** city & port ✳ of Myanmar on Rangoon River 21 mi (34 km) from its mouth pop 1,717,649

Yang-quan or **Yang-chüan** \'yäŋ-chù-'än\ city N China in E Shanxi E of Taiyuan pop 200,000

Yangtze — see CHANG

Yang-zhou or **Yang–chou** or **Yang-chow** \'yäŋ-'jō\ city E China in SW Jiangsu NE of Nanjing pop 160,000

Yan-tai \'yän-'tī\ or **Yen–t'ai** \'yən-\ or **Che-foo** \'jə-'fü\ city & port E China in NE Shandong on Shandong Peninsula on Bo Hai pop 140,000

Yao \'yaü\ city Japan on Honshu, a suburb of Osaka pop 277,724

Yaoun-dé or **Yaun-de** \yaün-'dā\ city S cen Cameroon, its ✳ pop 435,892

Yap \'yap, 'yäp\ or **Uap** \'wäp\ islands W Carolines, part of Federated States of Micronesia — **Yap-ese** \yä-'pēz, ya-, -'pēs\ adj

Ya-quí \yä-'kē\ river 420 mi (676 km) NW Mexico in Sonora flowing SW into Gulf of California

Yar-kand \yär-'kand\ river 500 mi (805 km) Kashmir & China flowing from Karakoram Range N & W to join the Hotan in Xinjiang Uygur forming the Tarim

Yar-mouth \'yär-məth\ **1** city SE Mass. E of Barnstable pop 21,174 **2** or **Great Yarmouth** borough & port E England in Norfolk on North Sea pop 50,152

Ya-ro-slavl \,yär-ə-'slä-vəl\ city cen Russia in Europe on the Volga NE of Moscow pop 597,000

Yau-co \'yaü-,kō\ town SW Puerto Rico pop 42,058

Yavarí — see JAVARI

Yazd \'yazd\ or **Yezd** \'yezd\ city cen Iran pop 230,483

Yaz-oo \'ya-zü, 'ya-(,)zü\ river 188 mi (302 km) Miss. flowing SW into Mississippi River

Yedo — see TOKYO

Ye-gor'-yevsk \yə-'gȯr-yəfsk, -əfsk\ city W cen Russia in Europe SE of Moscow pop 65,000

Ye-ka-te-rin-burg \yi-'ka-tə-rən-,bərg, yi-,kä-tə-rən-'bu̇rk\ or 1924–91 **Sverd-lovsk** \sverd-'lȯfsk\ city W Russia in Asia in cen Ural Mountains pop 1,026,000

Yellow — see HUANG

Yel-low-knife \'ye-lō-,nīf\ city Canada ✳ of Northwest Territories on Great Slave Lake pop 15,179

Yellow Sea inlet of E. China Sea bet. N China, N. Korea, & S. Korea

Yel-low-stone \'ye-lō-,stōn\ river 671 mi (1080 km) NW Wyo. & S & E Mont. flowing N through **Yellowstone Lake** (area 140 sq mi or 364 sq km) & **Grand Canyon of the Yellowstone** in Yellowstone National Park & NE into Missouri River in NW N.Dak. near Mont. border

Yellowstone Falls two waterfalls NW Wyo. in Yellowstone River at head of Grand Canyon of the Yellowstone; upper fall 109 ft (33 m), lower fall 308 ft (94 m)

Yellowstone National Park reservation NW Wyo., E Idaho, & S Mont. including plateau region notable for numerous geysers & hot springs

Ye-men \'ye-mən\ country S Arabia bordering on Red Sea & Gulf of Aden; a republic formed 1990 by merger of **Yemen Arab Republic** (✳ San'a) with **People's Democratic Republic of Yemen** or **Southern Yemen** (✳ Aden) ✳ San'a area 186,074 sq mi (483,792 sq km), pop 7,395,893 — **Ye-me-ni** \'ye-mə-nē\ adj or n — **Ye-men-ite** \-mə-,nīt\ n or adj

Yen-i-sey \,ye-nə-'sā\ river ab 2300 mi (3701 km) Russia in Asia flowing N into Arctic Ocean

Yen–t'ai — see YANTAI

Ye-re-van \,yer-ə-'vän\ city ✳ of Armenia pop 1,199,000

Ye-ru-pa-ja, Mount \,yer-ə-'pä-(,)hä\ mountain 21,765 ft (6634 m) W cen Peru

Ye-sil Ir-mak \,ye-'shē(ə)l-ir-'mäk\ river ab 250 mi (402 km) N Turkey in Asia flowing N into Black Sea

Ye-sil-koy \,ye-(,)shēl-'kȯi\ or formerly **San Ste-fa-no** \san-'ste-fə-,nō\ town Turkey in Europe on Sea of Marmara W of Istanbul

Ye-vrey-ska-ya \yi-'vrä-skə-yə\ or **Jewish Autonomous Region** autonomous oblast E Russia in Asia, bordering on the Amur ✳ Birobidzhan area 14,085 sq mi (36,621 sq km), pop 173,000

Yezo — see HOKKAIDO

Yi-bin \'yē-'bēn\ or **I–pin** \'ē-'bēn, -'pin\ or formerly **Sü-chow** \'shü-jō, 'sü-; 'sü-'chaü\ city cen China in S Szechwan pop 190,000

Yi-chang \'yē-'chäŋ\ or **I–ch'ang** \'ē-'chäŋ\ city cen China in W Hubei pop 110,000

Yin-chuan \'yin-chü-'än\ or formerly **Ning-sia** or **Ning-hsia** \'niŋ-shē-'ä\ city N China ✳ of Ningxia Huizu on the Huang pop 91,000

Ying-kou \'yiŋ-'kō\ or **Ying-kow** \'yiŋ-'kaü, -'kō\ city & port NE China in cen Liaoning on Gulf of Liaodong pop 161,000

Yi-ning \'yē-'niŋ\ or **Gul-ja** \'gül-(,)jä\ or **Kul-dja** \'kül-(,)jä\ city W China in NW Xinjiang Uygur pop 85,000

Yog-ya-kar-ta \,yō-gyə-'kär-tə\ or **Jog-ja-kar-ta** \,jōg-yə-\ or **Djok-ja-kar-ta** \,jō-kyə-\ city Indonesia in S Java pop 412,392

Yo-ho National Park \'yō-(,)hō\ reservation W Canada in SE B.C. on Alta. border

Yo-ko-ha-ma \,yō-kə-'hä-mə\ city & port Japan in SE Honshu on Tokyo Bay S of Tokyo pop 3,220,350

Yo-ko-su-ka \yō-kō-s(ə-)kə\ city & port Japan in Honshu W of entrance to Tokyo Bay pop 433,361

Yon-kers \'yäŋ-kərz\ city N.Y. N of New York City pop 188,082

Yonne \'yän, 'yȯn\ river 120 mi (193 km) NE cen France flowing NNW into the Seine

Yor-ba Lin-da \,yȯr-bə-'lin-də, ,yȯr-\ city SW Calif. SE of Los Angeles pop 52,422

York \'yȯrk\ **1** city SE Pa. SE of Harrisburg pop 42,192 **2** city Canada in SE Ont. near Toronto pop 140,525 **3** or **York-shire** \-,shir, -shər\ former county N England bordering on North Sea comprising city of York & (former) administrative counties of **East Rid-ing** \'rī-diŋ\ (✳ Beverley), **North Riding** (✳ Northallerton), & **West Riding** (✳ Wakefield) — see HUMBERSIDE, NORTH YORKSHIRE, SOUTH YORKSHIRE, WEST YORKSHIRE **4** or anc **Ebo-ra-cum** \i-'bȯr-ə-kəm, -'bär-\ city N England in N. Yorkshire on Ouse River pop 99,787

York, Cape — see CAPE YORK PENINSULA

Yorke Peninsula \'yȯrk\ peninsula Australia in SE S. Australia bet. Spencer Gulf and Gulf of St. Vincent

York River estuary 40 mi (64 km) E Va. flowing SE into Chesapeake Bay

Yo-sem-i-te Falls \yō-'se-mə-tē\ waterfall E cen Calif. descending from rim of Yosemite Valley in two falls (upper fall 1430 ft or 436 m, lower fall 320 ft or 98 m connected by a cascade)

Yosemite Valley glaciated valley of Merced River E cen Calif. on W slope of Sierra Nevada in **Yosemite National Park**

Yo-su \'yō-(,)sü\ city & port S S. Korea on Korea Strait pop 171,933

You or **Yü** \'yü\ or **Siang** \shē-'äŋ\ river 400 mi (644 km) SE China in Yunnan & Guangxi Zhuangzu flowing E

Yough-io-ghe-ny \,yä-kə-'gā-nē, ,yȯ-hə-, -'ge-nē\ river 135 mi (217 km) NE W.Va., NW Md., & SW Pa. flowing N & NW into the Monongahela

Youngs-town \'yəŋz-,taün\ city NE Ohio E of Akron pop 95,732

Youth, Isle of or formerly **Isle of Pines** island W Cuba in the Caribbean area 1180 sq mi (3068 sq km)

Ypres — see IEPER

Yp-si-lan-ti \,ip-sə-'lan-tē\ city SE Mich. pop 24,846

Yser \ē-'zer\ river 55 mi (88 km) France & Belgium flowing into North Sea

Ysyk–Köl — see ISSYK KUL

Yu-an \yü-'än\ **1** river 500 mi (805 km) SE cen China flowing from Guizhou N to NE Hunan **2** — see RED

Yu-ba City \'yü-bə\ city N Calif. N of Sacramento pop 27,437

Yu-cai-pa \yü-'kī-pə\ city S Calif. E of Riverside pop 32,824

Yu-ca-tán \,yü-kə-'tan, -'tän\ **1** peninsula SE Mexico & N Central America including Belize & part of Guatemala **2** state SE Mexico at N end of Yucatán peninsula ✳ Mérida area 23,926 sq mi (62,208 sq km), pop 1,034,648 — **Yu-ca-te-can** \-'te-kən\ adj

Yucatán Channel channel bet. Yucatán & W end of Cuba

Yuc-ca House National Monument \'yə-kə\ reservation SW Colo.; contains prehistoric ruins

Yu-go-sla-via or **Ju-go-sla-via** \,yü-gō-'slä-vē-ə, ,yü-gə-\ country S Europe on Balkan Peninsula comprising Serbia, Montenegro, Vojvodina, & Kosovo; together with Slovenia, Croatia, Bosnia and Herzegovina, & Macedonia established 1918 as a kingdom (**Kingdom of the Serbs, Croats, and Slovenes**), became a federal republic 1945; ✳ Belgrade area 49,376 sq mi (83,445 sq km), pop 13,747,377 — **Yu-go-slav** \-,släv, -,slav; 'yü-gō-,\ or **Yu-go-sla-vi-an** \,yü-gō-'slä-vē-ən, -gə-\ adj or n

Yu-kon \'yü-,kän\ **1** city cen Okla. pop 20,935 **2** river 1979 mi (3185 km) Yukon Territory & Alaska flowing NW & SW into Bering Sea — see LEWES **3** or **Yukon Territory** territory NW Canada bet. Alaska &

B.C. bordering on Arctic Ocean ✳ Whitehorse *area* 205,346 *sq mi* (533,900 *sq km*), *pop* 27,797

Yu·ma \'yü-mə\ city SW Ariz. on Colorado River *pop* 54,923

Yungki — see JILIN

Yungning — see NANNING

Yun·nan \yü-'nän\ **1** province SW China bordering on Indochina & Myanmar ✳ Kunming *area* 168,417 *sq mi* (437,884 *sq km*), *pop* 32,553,817 **2** *or* **Yunnanfu** — see KUNMING — **Yun·nan·ese** \ˌyü-nə-'nēz, -'nēs\ *adj or n*

Yun·que, El \el-'yün-(ˌ)kā\ mountain 3494 *ft* (1065 *m*) E Puerto Rico

Yü Shan \'yü-'shän\ *or* **Hsin·kao** \'shin-'kaù\ *or* **Mount Mor·ri·son** \'mȯr-ə-sən, 'mär-\ mountain 13,113 *ft* (3997 *m*) *cen* Taiwan; highest on island

Yuzovka — see DONETSK

Yver·don \ē-ver-dōⁿ\ commune W Switzerland N of Lausanne *pop* 20,802

Zaan·dam \'zän-ˌdäm\ commune W Netherlands *pop* 129,341

Zab·rze \'zäb-(ˌ)zhä\ *or* G **Hin·den·burg** \'hin-dən-bərg, -ˌbùrk\ city SW Poland in Silesia *pop* 203,367

Za·ca·te·cas \ˌzä-kə-'tā-kəs, ˌsä-kə-, -'te-\ **1** state N *cen* Mexico *area* 28,122 *sq mi* (73,117 *sq km*), *pop* 1,145,327 **2** city, its ✳ *pop* 56,829

Za·dar \'zä-ˌdär\ *or* It **Za·ra** \'zär-ə\ city & port Croatia; held by Italy 1920–47 *pop* 43,588

Zag·a·zig \'za-gə-ˌzig\ *or* **Az Za·qā·zīq** \ˌaz-zə-ˌkä-'zēk\ city N Egypt NNE of Cairo *pop* 202,637

Za·greb \'zä-ˌgreb\ city ✳ of Croatia *pop* 561,773

Zag·ros Mountains \'za-grəs, -ˌgrōs\ mountains W & S Iran bordering on Turkey, Iraq, & Persian Gulf; highest over 14,000 *ft* (4267 *m*)

Za·he·dan \ˌzä-hi-'dän\ city E Iran *pop* 281,923

Zaire \zä-'ir\ **1** river in Africa — see CONGO **2** *or formerly* **Congo** *or* **Democratic Republic of the Congo** *or earlier* **Belgian Congo** country *cen* Africa comprising most of Congo River basin E of lower Congo River; a republic ✳ Kinshasa *area* 893,000 *sq mi* (2,321,800 *sq km*), *pop* 30,261,000 — **Zair·ean** *or* **Zair·ian** \zä-'ir-ē-ən\ *adj or n*

Zakarpatskaya — see RUTHENIA

Zá·kin·thos \'zä-kēn-ˌthōs\ *or* **Zan·te** \'zan-tē\ *or anc* **Za·cyn·thus** \zə-'sin(t)-thəs\ **1** island N Greece, one of the Ionian Islands, SSE of Cephalonia *area* 156 *sq mi* (406 *sq km*) *pop* 32,746 **2** its chief town *pop* 10,205

Za·ma \'zä-mə, 'zä-\ ancient town N Africa SW of Carthage

Zam·be·zi *or* **Zam·be·si** \zam-'bē-zē\ river 1650 *mi* (2655 *km*) SE Africa flowing from NW Zambia into Mozambique Channel

Zam·bia \'zam-bē-ə\ *or formerly* **Northern Rhodesia** country S Africa; formerly a Brit. protectorate; independent republic within the Commonwealth of Nations since 1964 ✳ Lusaka *area* 290,410 *sq mi* (755,066 *sq km*), *pop* 5,679,808 — **Zam·bi·an** \'zam-bē-ən\ *adj or n*

Zam·bo·an·ga \ˌzam-bō-'äŋ-gə\ city & port Philippines on SW coast of Mindanao *pop* 176,800

Za·mo·ra \zə-'mȯr-ə, -'mȯr-\ **1** province NW Spain in *cen* León *area* 4097 *sq mi* (10,652 *sq km*), *pop* 201,869 **2** city, its ✳ *pop* 54,299

Zancle — see MESSINA

Zanes·ville \'zānz-ˌvil\ city E *cen* Ohio *pop* 26,778

Zan·jan \zan-'jän\ city NW Iran *pop* 215,261

Zan·zi·bar \'zan-zə-ˌbär\ **1** island E Africa off NE Tanzania mainland *area* 640 *sq mi* (1664 *sq km*), *pop* 122,004; formerly a sultanate, with Pemba & adjacent islands forming a Brit. protectorate; became independent 1963; united 1964 with Tanganyika to form Tanzania **2** city & port ✳ of Zanzibar & formerly of protectorate *pop* 110,669 — **Zan·zi·bari** \ˌzan-zə-'bär-ē\ *n or adj*

Za·po·rozh'·ye \ˌzä-pə-'rȯ-zhə\ *or formerly* **Ale·ksan·drovsk** \ˌa-lik-'san-drəfsk, ˌe-, -lig-'zan-\ city SE Ukraine *pop* 658,000

Za·ra·go·za \ˌzar-ə-'gō-zə\ *or* **Sar·a·gos·sa** \ˌsar-ə-'gä-sə\ **1** province NE Spain in W Aragon *area* 6726 *sq mi* (17,488 *sq km*), *pop* 828,692 **2** city, its ✳, on the Ebro *pop* 571,855

Zee·brug·ge \'zā-ˌbrə-gə, -ˌbrù-\ town NW Belgium; port for Bruges

Zee·land \'zē-lənd, 'zā-; 'zā-ˌlänt\ province SW Netherlands ✳ Middelburg *area* 1040 *sq mi* (2704 *sq km*), *pop* 354,816

Zeist \'zīst\ commune *cen* Netherlands E of Utrecht *pop* 61,332

Zem·po·al·te·pec \ˌzem-pō-'äl-tə-ˌpek\ *or* **Zem·po·al·te·petl** \-ˌäl-'tä-ˌpe-t'l, -ˌäl-tə-\ mountain 11,138 *ft* (3395 *m*) SE Mexico in Oaxaca

Zer·matt \(t)ser-'mät\ village SW *cen* Switzerland in Valais in Pennine Alps NE of the Matterhorn

Zetland — see SHETLAND

Zhang·jia·kou \'jäŋ-jē-'ä-'kō\ *or* **Ch'ang–chia–k'ou** \'chäŋ-jē-'ä-'kō\ *or* **Kal·gan** \'kal-'gan\ city NE China in NW Hebei NW of Beijing *pop* 229,300

Zhang·zhou *or* **Chang–chou** \'jäŋ-'jō\ *or* **Chang·chow** *same or* 'chaŋ-'chaù\ *or formerly* **Lung·ki** \'lùŋ-kē\ city SE China in S Fujian

Zhda·nov — see MARIUPOL

Zhe·jiang *or* **Che·kiang** \'jə-jē-'äŋ\ province E China bordering on E. China Sea ✳ Hangzhou *area* 39,305 *sq mi* (102,193 *sq km*), *pop* 38,884,603

Zheng·zhou *or* **Cheng–chou** *or* **Cheng·chow** \'jəŋ-'jō\ city NE *cen* China ✳ of Henan on the Huang *pop* 766,000

Zhen·jiang *or* **Chen–chiang** \'jən-jē-'äŋ\ *or* **Chin·kiang** \'jin-jē-'äŋ\ city & port E China in NW *cen* Jiangsu *pop* 190,000

Zhi·to·mir \zhi-'tȯ-ˌmir\ city W Ukraine *pop* 161,000

Zhou·shan *or* **Chou–shan** \'jō-'shän\ archipelago E China in E. China Sea at entrance to Hangzhou Bay

Zhu \'jü\ *or* **Chu** \'jü, 'chü\ *or* **Pearl** river SE China SE of Guangzhou

Zhu·zhou *or* **Chu–chou** *or* **Chu·chow** \'jü-'jō\ city SE China in E Hunan *pop* 285,780

Zi·bo *or* **Tzu–po** \'(d)zə-'bō\ city E China in *cen* Shandong *pop* 806,000

Zie·lo·na Go·ra \zhe-'lȯ-nə-'gùr-ə\ city W *cen* Poland *pop* 113,322

Zi·gong *or* **Tzu–kung** *or* **Tze·kung** \'(d)zə-'gùŋ\ city S *cen* China in S *cen* Szechwan *pop* 280,000

Zi·li·na \'zhi-lə-ˌnä\ city N Slovakia *pop* 97,254

Zim·ba·bwe \zim-'bä-bwē, -(ˌ)bwä\ **1** archaeological site NE Zimbabwe (country) **2** *or formerly* **Southern Rhodesia** *or* 1970–79 **Rhodesia** country S Africa S of the Zambezi; a self-governing Brit. colony which declared itself a republic 1970; adopted majority rule 1979 ✳ Harare *area* 150,333 *sq mi* (390,866 *sq km*), *pop* 7,550,000 — **Zim·ba·bwe·an** \-ən\ *adj or n*

Zinovievsk — see KIROVOGRAD

Zi·on \'zī-ən\ city NE Ill. N of Waukegan *pop* 19,775

Zi·on \'zī-ən\ *or* **Si·on** \'sī-\ **1** the stronghold of Jerusalem conquered by David **2** JERUSALEM **3** ISRAEL

Zion, Mount hill E Jerusalem, Israel; occupied in ancient times by the Jewish Temple

Zi·on National Park \'zī-ən\ reservation SW Utah centering around Zion Canyon of Virgin River

Zi·pan·gu \zə-'paŋ-(ˌ)gü\ the name for Japan used by Marco Polo

Zi·pa·qui·rá \ˌsē-pə-ki-'rä\ town *cen* Colombia N of Bogotá

Zla·to·ust \ˌzlä-tə-'üst\ city W Russia in Asia in the S Urals *pop* 181,000

Zoan — see TANIS

Zom·ba \'zäm-bə\ city SE Malawi S of Lake Malawi *pop* 21,000

Zon·gul·dak \ˌzȯŋ-gəl-'däk\ city & port NW Turkey *pop* 108,661

Zug \'(t)sük, 'züg\ *or* F **Zoug** \'züg\ **1** canton N *cen* Switzerland *area* 92 *sq mi* (239 *sq km*), *pop* 84,742 **2** commune, its ✳, on Lake of Zug *pop* 21,752

Zug, Lake of lake N *cen* Switzerland in Zug & Schwyz cantons N of Vierwaldstätter See *area* 15 *sq mi* (39 *sq km*)

Zug·spit·ze \'(t)sük-ˌshpit-sə, 'züg-, -ˌspit-\ mountain 9721 *ft* (2963 *m*) S Germany; highest in Bavarian Alps & in Germany

Zui·der Zee \ˌzī-dər-'zä, -'zē\ former inlet of North Sea N Netherlands — see IJSSELMEER

Zuidholland — see SOUTH HOLLAND

Zu·lu·land \'zü-(ˌ)lü-ˌland\ territory E Republic of South Africa in NE Natal bordering on Indian Ocean N of the Tugela *area* 10,427 *sq mi* (27,110 *sq km*), *pop* 570,160

Zu·rich \'zùr-ik\ *or* G **Zü·rich** \'tsüē-rik\ **1** canton N Switzerland *area* 665 *sq mi* (1729 *sq km*), *pop* 1,152,769 **2** city, its ✳, at NW end of Lake of Zurich *pop* 347,021 — **Zü·rich·er** \-i-kər, -ri-kər\ *n*

Zurich, Lake of lake 25 *mi* (40 *km*) long N *cen* Switzerland

Zut·phen \'zət-fən\ commune E Netherlands on the IJssel *pop* 31,495

Zwick·au \'tsfi-ˌkaù, 'zwi-\ city E Germany S of Leipzig *pop* 121,787

Zwol·le \'zvȯ-lə, 'zwȯ-\ city E Netherlands ✳ of Overijssel *pop* 86,388

\ə\ abut \ᵊ\ kitten, F table \ər\ further \a\ ash \ā\ ace \ä\ mop, mar
\aù\ out \ch\ chin \e\ bet \ē\ easy \g\ go \i\ hit \ī\ ice \j\ job
\ŋ\ sing \ō\ go \ȯ\ law \ȯi\ boy \th\ thin \t͟h\ the \ü\ loot \ù\ foot
\y\ yet \zh\ vision \à, k̲, ⁿ, œ, œ̄, ùe, ūē, ᵞ\ see Guide to Pronunciation

Signs and Symbols

Astronomy

SUN, GREATER PLANETS, ETC.

⊙	the sun; Sunday
☽, ☾, or ☽	the moon; Monday
●	new moon
☽, ☽, ☽,)	first quarter
○ or ☽	full moon
☾, ☽, ☾, (	last quarter
☿	Mercury; Wednesday
♀	Venus; Friday
⊕, ⊖, or ♁	the earth
♂	Mars; Tuesday
♃	Jupiter; Thursday
♄ or ♄	Saturn; Saturday
♁, ♅, or ♅	Uranus
♆, ♆, or ♆	Neptune

♇	Pluto
☄	comet
✳ or ✵	fixed star

ASPECTS AND NODES

☌	conjunction—indicating that the bodies have the same longitude, or right ascension
☐	quadrature—indicating a difference of 90° in longitude, or right ascension
△	trine—indicating a difference of 120° in longitude, or right ascension
☍	opposition—indicating a difference of 180° in longitude, or right ascension; as, ☍ ♆ ⊙ opposition of Neptune to the sun
☊	ascending node
☋	descending node

Biology

○	an individual, specif., a female—used chiefly in inheritance charts
☐	an individual, specif., a male—used chiefly in inheritance charts
♀	female
♂ or ♂	male

×	crossed with; hybrid
+	wild type
F_1	offspring of the first generation
F_2	offspring of the second generation
F_3, F_4, F_5	offspring of the third, fourth, fifth, etc., generation

Business and Finance

a/c	account ⟨in a/c with⟩
@	at; each ⟨4 apples @ 5¢ = 20¢⟩
P	principal; present value
i,r	rate of interest
n	number of periods (as of interest) and esp. years
/ or ℔	per
c/o	care of
#	number if it precedes a numeral ⟨track #3⟩; pounds if it follows ⟨a 5 # sack of sugar⟩
℔	pound; pounds

%	percent
‰	per thousand
$	dollars
¢	cents
£	pounds
/	shillings
	(for other currency symbols see MONEY table)
©	copyrighted
®	registered trademark

Chemistry

+ signifies "plus", "and", "together with", and is used between the symbols of substances brought together for, or produced by, a reaction; placed to the right of a symbol above the line it signifies a unit charge of positive electricity: Ca++ denotes the ion of calcium, which carries two positive charges; the plus sign is used also to indicate a dextrorotatory compound [as (+) tartaric acid]

— signifies a unit charge of negative electricity when placed to the right of a symbol above the line: Cl⁻ denotes a chlorine ion carrying a negative charge; the minus sign is used to indicate a levorotatory compound [as (−) quinine]; it is also used to indicate the removal of a part from a compound (as − CO_2)

— signifies a single bond and is used between the symbols of elements or groups which unite to form a compound: H—Cl for HCl, H—O—H for H_2O

· is used to separate parts of a compound regarded as loosely joined (as $CuSO_4 \cdot 5H_2O$); the centered dot is also used to denote the presence of a single unpaired electron (as H·)

○ or ◎ denotes the benzene ring

1531

$=$ indicates a double bond; placed to the right of a symbol above the line, it signifies two unit charges of negative electricity (as $SO_4^=$, the negative ion of sulfuric acid, carrying two negative charges)

$\equiv$ signifies a triple bond or a triple negative charge

$:$ is used to indicate an unshared pair of electrons (as in $: NH_3$); is sometimes used to indicate a double bond (as in $CH_2:CH_2$)

$(\ )$ marks groups within a compound [as in $C_6H_4(CH_3)_2$, the formula for xylene which contains two methyl groups (CH_3)]

$\frown$ or $\smile$ join attached atoms or groups in structural formulas for cyclic compounds, as that for glucose

$$\overbrace{}^{O}$$
$$CH_2OHCH(CHOH)_3CHOH$$

$=$ give or form

$\rightarrow$ gives, leads to, or is converted to

$\rightleftarrows$ forms and is formed from, is in equilibrium with

$\downarrow$ indicates precipitation of the substance

$\uparrow$ indicates that the substance passes off as a gas

$\equiv$ is equivalent—used in statements to show how much of one substance will react with a given quantity of another so as to leave no excess of either

1-, 2-, etc.   used initially in names, referring to the positions of substituting groups, attached to the first, etc., of the numbered atoms of the parent compound

H   enthalpy

^{2}H *also* H^2 deuterium

^{3}H *also* H^3 tritium

M   metal

R   organic group, alkyl or aryl group

S   entropy

X   halogen atom

Z   atomic number
(for element symbols see ELEMENT table)

$'$ is used to distinguish between different substituents of the same kind (as R', R'', R''' to indicate different organic groups)

Mathematics

$+$ plus; positive $\langle a+b=c \rangle$—used also to indicate omitted figures or an approximation

$-$ minus; negative

$\pm$ plus or minus $\langle$the square root of $4a^2$ is $+2a\rangle$

$\times$ multiplied by; times $\langle 6\times 4 = 24\rangle$—also indicated by placing a dot between the factors $\langle 6{\cdot}4 = 24\rangle$ or by writing the factors one after the other, often enclosed in parentheses, without explicitly indicating multiplication $\langle (4)(5)(3) = 60 \rangle$ $\langle -4abc\rangle$

$\div$ or $:$ divided by $\langle 24\div 6 = 4\rangle$—also indicated by writing the divisor under the dividend with a line between $\langle \frac{24}{6}=4\rangle$ or by writing the divisor after the dividend with an oblique line between $\langle 3/8\rangle$

E   times 10 raised to an indicated exponent $\langle 4.52E5 = 4.52 \times 10^5\rangle$—used esp. in calculator and computer displays

$=$ equals $\langle 6+2=8\rangle$

$\neq$ or $\pm$ is not equal to

$>$ is greater than $\langle 6>5\rangle$

$<$ is less than $\langle 3<4\rangle$

$\geqq$ or $\geq$ is greater than or equal to

$\leqq$ or $\leq$ is less than or equal to

$\not>$ is not greater than

$\not<$ is not less than

$\approx$ is approximately equal to

$\equiv$ is identical with

$\sim$ is similar to; the negation of; the negative of

$\cong$ is congruent to

$\propto$ varies directly as; is proportional to

$:$ is to; the ratio of

$\therefore$ therefore

∞ infinity

$\angle$ angle; the angle $\langle \angle ABC\rangle$

$\llcorner$ right angle $\langle \llcorner ABC\rangle$

$\perp$ the perpendicular; is perpendicular to $\langle AB \perp CD\rangle$

$\|$ parallel; is parallel to $\langle AB \| CD\rangle$

$\odot$ or $\circ$ circle

$\frown$ arc of a circle

$\triangle$ triangle

$\square$ square

$\square$ rectangle

$\sqrt{\ }$ or $\sqrt{}$ root—used without a figure to indicate a square root (as in $\sqrt{4} =2$) or with an index above the sign to indicate a higher degree (as in $\sqrt[3]{}$, $\sqrt[7]{}$); also denoted by a fractional index at the right of a number whose denominator expresses the degree of the root $\langle 3^{1/3} = \sqrt[3]{3}\rangle$

$(\ )$ parentheses

$[\ ]$ brackets $\Big\}$ indicate that the quantities enclosed by them are to be taken together

$\{\ \}$ braces

$-$ (above the quantities) vinculum

Δ the operation of finding the difference between two nearby values of a variable (as y) or of a function (as f) for two values of its independent variable (as x) differing by a small nonzero amount (as h) $\langle \Delta y = y_2 - y_1\rangle$ $\langle \Delta f(x) = f(x+h) - f(x)\rangle$

$\int$ integral; integral of $\langle \int 2x dx = x^2 + C\rangle$

$\int_b^a$ the integral taken from the value b to the value a of the variable

$\dfrac{df(x)}{dx}$ the derivative of the function f(x) with respect to x

$\dfrac{\partial f(x,y)}{\partial x}$ the partial derivative of the function f(x,y) with respect to x

δ_j^i Kronecker delta

s standard deviation of a sample taken from a population

σ standard deviation of a population

Σ sum; summation $\langle \sum_{i=1}^{n} x_i = x_1 + x_2 + \ldots + x_n\rangle$

$\bar{x}$ arithmetic mean of a sample of a variable x

μ (1) micrometer (2) arithmetic mean of a population

μ_2 or σ^2 variance

X^2 chi-square

P the probability of obtaining a result as great as or greater than the observed result in a statistical test if the null hypothesis is true

r correlation coefficient

$E(x)$ expected value of the random variable x

π pi; the number 3.14159265+; the ratio of the circumference of a circle to its diameter

Π product $\langle \prod_{i=1}^{n} x_i = (x_1)(x_2)\ldots(x_n)\rangle$

$!$ factorial $\langle n\, ! = n(n\text{-}1)(n\text{-}2).\,.\,.1\rangle$

e or ϵ (1) the number 2.7182818+; the base of the natural system of logarithms (2) the eccentricity of a conic section

i the positive square root of minus one $\sqrt{-1}$

n an unspecified number (as an exponent) esp. when integral

$^\circ$ degree $\langle 60^\circ\rangle$

$'$ minute; foot $\langle 30'\rangle$—used also to distinguish between different values of the same variable or between different variables (as a', a'', a''', usually read a prime, a double prime, a triple prime) or between the first and higher derivatives of a function (as f', f'' or $f'(x)$, $f''(x)$ for the first and second derivatives of f or $f(x)$)

$''$ second; inch ⟨30$''$⟩

$^{0, 1, 2, 3}$, etc.   —used as exponents placed above and at the right of an expression to indicate that it is raised to a power whose degree is indicated by the figure ⟨a^0 equals 1⟩ ⟨a^1 equals a⟩ ⟨a^2 is the square of a⟩

$^{-1, -2, -3}$, etc.   —used as exponents placed above and at the right of an expression to indicate that the reciprocal of the expression is raised to the power whose degree is indicated by the figure ⟨a^{-1} equals $1/a$⟩ ⟨a^{-2} equals $1/a^2$⟩

$\sin^{-1}x$ arc sine of x
$\cos^{-1}x$ arc cosine of x
$\tan^{-1}x$ arc tangent of x
f function
f^{-1} the inverse of the function f
$|z|$ the absolute value of z
$[a_{ij}]$ matrix with element a_{ij} in the i th row and jth column
$|a_{ij}|$ determinant of a square matrix with elements a_{ij}
$||A||$ or $||x||$ norm of the matrix A or the vector x

A^{-1} inverse of the matrix A
A^T transpose of the matrix A
$\oplus$ an operation in a mathematical system (as a group or ring) with $A \oplus B$ indicating the sum of the two elements A and B
$\otimes$ an operation in a mathematical system (as a group or ring) with $A \otimes B$ indicating the product of the two elements A and B
$[x]$ the greatest integer not greater than x
(a,b) the open interval $a < x < b$
$[a,b]$ the closed interval $a \leqq x \leqq b$
$\aleph_0$ aleph-null
ω the ordinal number of the positive integers
$\ni$ or :   such that ⟨choose a and $b \ni a + b = 6$⟩
$\exists$ there exists ⟨$\exists\ a \ni a + 2 = 4$⟩
$\forall$ for every, for all ⟨$\forall\ a \ni a$ is a real number, $a^2 \geq 0$⟩
$\cup$ union of two sets
$\cap$ intersection of two sets
$\subset$ is included in, is a subset of
$\supset$ contains as a subset
$\in$ or ϵ is an element of
$\notin$ is not an element of
Λ or 0   empty set, null set
or ϕ or { }

Medicine

$\overline{A}\overline{A}$, $\overline{A}$, or $\overline{aa}$ ana; of each
℞   take—used on prescriptions; prescription; treatment
☣   poison

APOTHECARIES' MEASURES

℥   ounce
f℥   fluid ounce
f ℨ   fluid dram
min or ♏   minim

APOTHECARIES' WEIGHTS

℔   pound
℥   ounce (as ℥ i or ℥ j, one ounce; ℥ ss, half an ounce; ℥ iss or ℥ jss, one ounce and a half; ℥ ij, two ounces)
ℨ   dram
℈   scruple

Miscellaneous

&   and
&c   et cetera; and so forth
"or"   ditto marks
/   diagonal or slant or solidus or virgule; used to mean "or" (as in *and/or*), "and/or" (as in *dead/wounded*), "per" (as in *feet/second*), indicates end of a line of verse; separates the figures of a date (4/4/73)
☞   index or fist
<   derived from ⎫
>   whence derived ⎬ used in
+   and ⎭ linguistics
*   hypothetical, ungrammatical
†   died—used esp. in genealogies
✝   cross (for variations see CROSS illustration)
☧   monogram from Greek XP signifying Christ
卐   swastika
✡   Magen David

☥   ankh
♈   versicle
℟   response
✶   —used in Roman Catholic and Anglican service books to divide each verse of a psalm, indicating where the response begins
✠ or +   —used in some service books to indicate where the sign of the cross is to be made; also used by certain Roman Catholic and Anglican prelates as a sign of the cross preceding their signatures
LXX   Septuagint
f/ or f: relative aperture of a photographic lens
☮   civil defense
⊕   peace
Ⓤ or Ⓚ   kosher certification
x   by ⟨3×5 cards⟩

Physics

α alpha particle
β beta particle, beta ray
γ gamma, photon, surface tension
ϵ permittivity

η efficiency, viscosity
λ wavelength
μ micro-, permeability
ν frequency, neutrino

ρ density, resistivity
σ conductivity, cross section, surface tension
φ luminous flux, magnetic flux
Ω ohm
B magnetic induction, magnetic field
c speed of light
e electron, electronic charge
E electric field, energy, illumination, modulus of elasticity, potential difference
h Planck's constant
H magnetic field strength
J angular momentum

L inductance, self-inductance
n index of refraction, neutron
p momentum of a particle, proton
S entropy
T absolute temperature, period
V electrical potential
W work
X power of magnification, reactance
Y admittance
Z impedance

Reference marks

* asterisk *or* star
† dagger
‡ double dagger
§ section *or* numbered clause

|| parallels
¶ *or* ⁋ paragraph

Stamps and stamp collecting

★ *or* * unused
★★ *or* ** unused with original gum intact and never mounted with a stamp hinge
⊙ *or* ○ *or* 0 used

⊞ block of four
✉ entire cover or card

Weather

Barometer, changes of:
⟋ Rising, then falling
╱ Rising, then steady; or rising, then rising more slowly
╱ Rising steadily, or unsteadily
✓ Falling or steady, then rising; or rising, then rising more quickly
— Steady, same as 3 hours ago
╲ Falling, then rising, same or lower than 3 hours ago
╲ Falling, then steady; or falling, than falling more slowly
╲ Falling steadily, or unsteadily
⋀ Steady or rising, then falling; or falling, then falling more quickly

◎ calm
○ clear
◐ cloudy (partly)
● cloudy (completely overcast)
⊹ drifting or blowing snow
, drizzle

≡ fog
∿ freezing rain
⌃⌃⌃⌃ front, cold
▬▬ warm
▬⌃▬ occluded
⌄⌃⌄ stationary
)(funnel clouds
∞ haze
⬤ hurricane
♉ tropical storm
⟷ ice needles
● rain
✳ rain and snow
⩔ rime
� sandstorm or dust storm
▽ shower(s)
▽̇ shower of rain
⍬ shower of hail
△ sleet
✳ snow
⍐ thunderstorm
⌇ visibility reduced by smoke

A Handbook of Style

Punctuation

The English writing system uses punctuation marks to separate groups of words for meaning and emphasis; to convey an idea of the variations of pitch, volume, pauses, and intonations of speech; and to help avoid contextual ambiguity. The use of the standard English punctuation marks is discussed in the following pages; examples are provided to illustrate the general rules.

' Apostrophe

1. Indicates the possessive case of nouns and indefinite pronouns. The possessive case of almost all singular nouns may be formed by adding 's. Traditionally, however, only the apostrophe is added when the s would not be pronounced in normal speech. The possessive case of plural nouns ending in s or in an \s\ or \z\ sound is generally formed by adding an apostrophe only; the possessive of irregular plurals is formed by adding 's.

> her mother-in-law's car
>
> anyone's guess
>
> the boy's mother
>
> the boys' mothers
>
> Degas's drawings
>
> Knox's products
>
> Aristophanes' play
>
> for righteousness' sake
>
> the Stephenses' house
>
> children's laughter

2. Marks omission of letters in contracted words.

> didn't
>
> o'clock
>
> hang 'em up

3. Marks omission of digits in numbers.

> class of '83

4. Is often used to form plurals of letters, figures, punctuated abbreviations, symbols, and words referred to as words.

> Dot your *i*'s and cross your *t*'s.
>
> His *1*'s and his *7*'s looked alike.
>
> Two of the junior faculty have Ph.D's.
>
> She has trouble pronouncing her *the*'s.

[ ] Brackets

1. Set off interpolated editorial matter within quoted material.

> He wrote, "I ain't [sic] going."
>
> Vaulting ambition, which o'erleaps itself
> And falls on the other [side].
> —Shakespeare

2. Function as parentheses within parentheses.

> Bowman Act (22 Stat., ch. 4, § [or sec.] 4, p. 50)

3. Set off phonetic symbols and transcriptions.

> [t] in British *duty*
>
> the word is pronounced ['ek-sə-jənt]

: Colon

1. Introduces a clause or phrase that explains, illustrates, amplifies, or restates what has gone before.

> The sentence was poorly constructed: it lacked both unity and coherence.

2. Directs attention to an appositive.

> He had only one pleasure: eating.

3. Introduces a series.

> Three abstained: England, France, and Belgium.

4. Introduces lengthy quoted material set off from the rest of a text by indentation but not by quotation marks.

> I quote from the text of Chapter One:

5. Separates elements in page references, in bibliographical and biblical citations, and in set formulas used to express ratios and time.

Journal of the American Medical Association 48:356

Stendhal, *Love* (New York: Penguin, 1975)

John 4:10   a ratio of 3:5   8:30 a.m.

6. Separates titles and subtitles (as of books).

   Battle Cry of Freedom: The Era of the Civil War

7. Follows the salutation in formal correspondence.

   Dear Sir or Madam:

   Ladies and Gentlemen:

8. Punctuates headings in memorandums and formal correspondence.

   TO: VIA:

   SUBJECT: REFERENCE:

Comma   ,

1. Separates main clauses joined by a coordinating conjunction (such as *and, but, or, nor,* or *for*), and sometimes short parallel clauses not joined by conjunctions.

   She knew very little about him, and he volunteered nothing.

   I came, I saw, I conquered.

2. Sets off an adverbial clause or a long adverbial phrase that precedes or interrupts the main clause.

   When she discovered the answer, she reported it to us.

   The report, after being read aloud, was put up for consideration.

3. Sets off transitional words and expressions (such as *on the contrary, on the other hand*), conjunctive adverbs (such as *consequently, furthermore, however*), and expressions that introduce an illustration or example (such as *namely, for example*).

   My partner, on the other hand, remains unconvinced.

   The regent's whim, however, threw the negotiations into chaos.

   She responded as completely as she could; that is, she answered each of the individual questions specifically.

4. Sets off contrasting and opposing expressions within sentences.

   The cost is not $65.00, but $56.65.

   He changed his style, not his ethics.

5. Separates words, phrases, or clauses in series. (Many omit the comma before the conjunction introducing the last item in a series when no ambiguity results.)

   He was young, eager, and restless.

   It requires one to travel constantly, to have no private life, and to live on almost nothing.

   Be sure to pack a flashlight, a sweater and an extra pair of socks.

6. Separates coordinate adjectives modifying a noun. However, a comma is not used between two adjectives when the first modifies the combination of the second adjective and the word or phrase it modifies.

   The harsh, damp, piercing wind cut through his jacket.

   a low common denominator

7. Sets off parenthetical elements such as nonrestrictive clauses and phrases.

   Our guide, who wore a blue beret, was an experienced traveler.

   We visited Gettysburg, site of the famous battle.

   The book's author, Marie Jones, was an accomplished athlete.

8. Introduces a direct quotation, terminates a direct quotation that is neither a question nor an exclamation, and sets off split quotations. The comma is not used with quotations that are tightly integrated into the sentences in which they appear (e.g., as subject or predicate nominatives) or those that do not represent actual dialogue.

   Mary said, "I am leaving."

   "I am leaving," Mary said.

   "I am leaving," Mary said with determination, "even if you want me to stay."

   "The computer is down" was the reply she feared.

   The fact that he said he was about to "faint from hunger" doesn't mean he actually fainted.

9. Sets off words in direct address, absolute phrases, and mild interjections.

   You may go, John, if you wish.

   I fear their encounter, his temper being what it is.

   Ah, that's my idea of an excellent dinner.

10. Separates a tag question from the rest of the sentence.

    It's a fine day, isn't it?

11. Indicates the omission of a word or words used in a parallel construction earlier in the sentence. When the meaning of the sentence is quite clear without the comma, the comma is omitted.

    Common stocks are preferred by some investors; bonds, by others.

    He was in love with her and she with him.

12. Is used to avoid ambiguity that might arise from adjacent words.

    To Mary, Jane was someone special.

13. Is used to divide digits in numbers into groups of three; however, it is generally not used in pagination, in dates, or in street numbers, and sometimes not used in numbers with four digits.

    Smithville, pop. 100,000

    4,550 cars

    but

    page 1411   4507 Main St.

    3600 rpm   the year 1983

14. Punctuates an inverted name.

> Morton, William A.

15. Separates a surname from a following title or degree and often from the words "Junior" and "Senior"and their abbreviations.

> Sandra H. Cobb, Vice President
>
> Jesse Ginsburg, D.D.M.

16. Sets off geographical names (such as state or country from city), elements of dates, and addresses. When just the month and the year are given in a date, the comma is usually omitted.

> Shreveport, Louisiana, is the site of a large air base.
>
> On Sunday, June 23, 1940, he was wounded.
>
> Number 10 Downing Street, London, is a famous address.
>
> She began her career in April 1993 at a modest salary.

17. Follows the salutation in informal correspondence, and follows the complimentary close of a letter.

> Dear Mark,
>
> Affectionately,
>
> Very truly yours,

— Dash

1. Usually marks an abrupt change or break in the continuity of a sentence.

> When in 1960 the stockpile was sold off—indeed, dumped as surplus—natural rubber sales were hard hit.—Barry Commoner

2. Is sometimes used in place of commas or parentheses when special emphasis is required.

> The presentations—and especially the one by Ms. Dow—impressed the audience.

3. Introduces a statement that explains, summarizes, or expands on what precedes it.

> Oil, steel, and wheat—these are the sinews of industrialization.
>
> The motion was then tabled—that is, removed indefinitely from consideration.

4. Often precedes the attribution of a quotation.

> My foot is on my native heath. . . .—Sir Walter Scott

5. Sets off an interrupting clause or phrase. The dash takes the place of a comma that would ordinarily set off the clause, but an exclamation point or question mark is retained.

> If we don't succeed—and the critics say we won't—then the whole project is in jeopardy.
>
> They are demanding that everything—even the marshland!—be transferred to the new trust.
>
> Your question—it was *your* question, wasn't it, Mr. Jones?—just can't be answered.

. . . . Ellipsis (or Suspension Points)

1. Indicates the omission of one or more words within a quoted passage. When four dots are used, the ellipsis indicates the omission of one or more sentences within the passage or the omission of words at the end of a sentence. The first or the last of the four dots is a period.

> In the little world in which children have their existence, . . . there is nothing so finely perceived and so finely felt as injustice.—Charles Dickens
>
> Security is mostly a superstition. . . . Avoiding danger is no safer in the long run than outright exposure. . . . Life is either a daring adventure or nothing.—Helen Keller

2. Usually indicates omission of one or more lines of poetry when ellipsis is extended the length of the line.

> I think that I shall never see
> A poem lovely as a tree
> . . . .
> Poems are made by fools like me,
> But only God can make a tree.
> —Joyce Kilmer

3. Indicates halting speech or an unfinished sentence in dialogue.

> "I'd like to . . . that is . . . if you don't mind. . . ."

! Exclamation Point

1. Ends an emphatic phrase or sentence.

> Get out of here!
>
> Her notorious ostentation—she flew her friends to Bangkok for her birthday parties!—was feasted on by the popular press.

2. Ends an emphatic interjection.

> Encore!
>
> All of this proves—at long last!—that we were right from the start.

- Hyphen

The hyphen is often used between parts of a compound. The styling of such words varies; when in doubt, see the entry in the dictionary at its own place or in a list of undefined words at an individual prefix. For unentered compounds, advice will be found in *Merriam-Webster's Standard American Style Manual* or a comparable guide.

1. Is often used between a prefix and root, especially whenever the root is capitalized, when two identical vowels come together, or when the resulting word could be confused with another identically spelled word.

> pre-Renaissance   co-opted

anti-inflationary

re-cover a sofa

but

recover from an illness

2. Is used in some compounds, especially those containing prepositions.

president-elect   sister-in-law

good-for-nothing   over-the-counter

falling-out   write-off

3. Is often used in compound modifiers in attributive position.

traveling in a fast-moving van

She has gray-green eyes.

a come-as-you-are party

4. Suspends the first element of a hyphenated compound or a prefix (hyphenated or not) when the second element or base word is part of a following hyphenated compound or derived form.

a six- or eight-cylinder engine

pre- and postadolescent trauma

5. Marks division of a word at the end of a line.

sion of his life   The ruling pas-

6. Is used in writing out compound numbers between 21 and 99.

thirty-four

one hundred thirty-eight

7. Is often used between the numerator and the denominator in writing out fractions, especially when they are used as modifiers. However, fractions used as nouns are often written as open compounds, especially when either the numerator or the denominator already contains a hyphen.

a two-thirds majority of the vote

three fifths of her paycheck

one seventy-second of an inch

8. Serves as an equivalent of *through* or (*up*) *to and including* when used between indicators of range such as numbers and dates. (In typeset material the longer en dash is used.)

pages 40–98

the years 1980–89

9. Serves as the equivalent of *to, and,* or *versus* in indicating linkage or opposition. (In typeset material the longer en dash is used.)

the New York–Paris flight

the Hardy–Weinberg law

the Lincoln–Douglas Debates

The final score was 7–2.

Hyphen, Double   ⸗

Is used at the end-of-line division of a hyphenated compound to indicate that the compound is hyphenated and not closed.

self⸗ [end of line] seeker

but

self- [end of line] same

Parentheses   ( )

1. Enclose words, numbers, phrases, or clauses that provide examples, explanations, or supplementary material that does not essentially alter the meaning of the sentence.

Three old destroyers (all now out of commission) will be scrapped.

He has followed the fortunes of the modern renaissance (*al-Nahdad*) in the Arabic-speaking world.

2. Enclose numerals that confirm a written number in a text.

Delivery will be made in thirty (30) days.

3. Enclose numbers or letters in a series.

We must set forth (1) our long-term goals, (2) our immediate objectives, and (3) the means at our disposal.

4. Enclose abbreviations that follow their spelled-out forms or spelled-out forms that follow their abbreviations.

a ruling by the Federal Communications Commission (FCC)

the manufacture and disposal of PVC (polyvinyl chloride)

5. Indicate alternative terms.

Please indicate the lecture(s) you would like to attend.

6. Enclose publication data in footnotes and endnotes.

Marguerite Yourcenar, *The Dark Brain of Piranesi and Other Essays* (New York: Farrar, Straus and Giroux, 1985), p. 9.

7. Are used with other punctuation marks in the following ways:

If the parenthetic expression is an independent sentence standing alone, its first word is capitalized and a period is included *inside* the last parenthesis. However, if the parenthetic expression, even if it could stand alone as a sentence, occurs within a sentence, it is uncapitalized and has no sentence period but may have an exclamation point, a question mark, a period for an abbreviation, or quotation marks within the closing parenthesis.

The discussion was held in the boardroom. (The results are still confidential.)

Although we liked the restaurant (their Italian food was the best), we seldom went there.

After waiting in line for an hour (why do we do these things?), we finally left.

Years ago, someone (I wish I could remember who!) told me about it.

What was once informally known as A.B.D. status is now often recognized by the degree of Master of Philosophy (M. Phil.).

He was depressed ("I must resign") and refused to do anything.

No punctuation mark should be placed directly before parenthetical material in a sentence; if a break is required, punctuation should be placed *after* the final parenthesis.

I'll get back to you tomorrow (Friday), when I have more details.

.   Period

1. Ends sentences or sentence fragments that are neither interrogatory nor exclamatory.

Not bad.

Give it your best.

I gave it my best.

He asked if she had given it her best.

2. Follows some abbreviations and contractions.

Dr.   A.D.   ibid.   i.e.

Jr.   etc.   cont.

3. Is normally used with an individual's initials.

F. Scott Fitzgerald

T. S. Eliot

4. Is used after numerals and letters in vertical enumerations and outlines.

Required skills are:
1. Shorthand
2. Typing
3. Transcription
I. Objectives
 A. Economy
  1. low initial cost
  2. low maintenance cost
 B. Ease of operation

?   Question Mark

1. Ends a direct question.

How did she do it?

"How did she do it?" he asked.

2. Ends a question that is part of a larger sentence, but not an indirect question.

How did she do it? was the question on each person's mind.

He wondered, Will it work?

He wondered whether it would work.

3. Indicates the writer's ignorance or uncertainty.

Geoffrey Chaucer, English poet (1342?–1400)

"   "   Quotation Marks, Double

1. Enclose direct quotations but not indirect quotations.

She said, "I am leaving."

She said that she was leaving.

2. Enclose words or phrases borrowed from others, words used in a special way, and words of marked informality when introduced into formal writing.

Much of the population in the hellish future he envisions is addicted to "derms," patches that deliver potent drug doses instantaneously through the skin.

He called himself "emperor," but he was really just a dictator.

He was arrested for smuggling "smack."

3. Enclose titles of poems, short stories, articles, lectures, chapters of books, short musical compositions, and radio and TV programs.

Robert Frost's "After Apple-Picking"

Cynthia Ozick's "Rosa"

The third chapter of *Treasure Island* is entitled "The Black Spot."

"All the Things You Are"

Debussy's "Clair de lune"

NBC's "Today Show"

4. Are used with other punctuation marks in the following ways:

The period and the comma fall *within* the quotation marks.

"I am leaving," she said.

It was unclear how she maintained such an estate on "a small annuity."

The colon and semicolon fall *outside* the quotation marks.

There was only one thing to do when he said "I may not run": promise him a large campaign contribution.

He spoke of his "little cottage in the country"; he might better have called it a mansion.

The dash, the question mark, and the exclamation point fall *within* the quotation marks when they refer to the quoted matter only; they fall *outside* when they refer to the whole sentence.

"I can't see how—" he started to say.

He asked, "When did she leave?"

What is the meaning of "the open door"?

The sergeant shouted "Halt!"

Save us from his "mercy"!

5.   Are not used with *yes* or *no* except in direct discourse.

She said yes to all our requests.

6.   Are not used with lengthy quotations set off from the text.

He took the title for his biography of Thoreau from a passage in *Walden*:

I long ago lost a hound, a bay horse, and a turtle-dove, and am still on their trail. . . . I have met one or two who had heard the hound, and the tramp of the horse, and even seen the dove disappear behind a cloud, and they seemed as anxious to recover them as if they had lost them themselves.

However, the title *A Hound, a Bay Horse, and a Turtle-Dove* probably puzzled some readers.

Quotation Marks, Single   ' '

1.   Enclose a quotation within a quotation in American usage. When both single and double quotation marks occur at the end of a sentence, the period typically falls within *both* sets of marks.

The witness said, "I distinctly heard him say, 'Don't be late,' and then heard the door close."

The witness said, "I distinctly heard him say, 'Don't be late.'"

2.   Are sometimes used in place of double quotation marks, especially in British usage. In this case a quotation within a quotation is set off by double quotation marks.

The witness said, 'I distinctly heard him say, "Don't be late," and then heard the door close.'

Semicolon   ;

1.   Links independent clauses not joined by a coordinating conjunction.

Some people have the ability to write well; others do not.

2.   Links clauses joined by a conjunctive adverb (such as *consequently, furthermore, however*).

Speeding is illegal; furthermore, it is very dangerous.

3.   Often occurs before expressions that introduce expansions or series (such as *for example, for instance, that is, e.g.,* or *i.e.*).

As a manager she tried to do the best job she could; that is, to keep her project on schedule and under budget.

4.   Separates phrases that contain commas.

The country's resources consist of large ore deposits; lumber, waterpower, and fertile soils; and a strong, rugged people.

Send copies to our offices in Portland, Maine; Springfield, Illinois; and Savannah, Georgia.

5.   Is placed outside quotation marks and parentheses.

They again demanded "complete autonomy"; the demand was again rejected.

Virgule (or Slash)   /

1.   Separates alternatives.

high-heat and/or high-speed applications

. . . sit hour after hour . . . and finally year after year in a catatonic/frenzied trance rewriting the Bible —William Saroyan

2.   Replaces the word *to* or *and* between related terms that are compounded.

the fiscal year 1983/1984

in the May/June issue

3.   Divides run-in lines of poetry.

Say, sages, what's the charm on earth/Can turn death's dart aside?—Robert Burns

4.   Divides elements in dates and divides numerators and denominators in fractions.

offer expires 5/19/94

Fifteen and 44/100 dollars

5.   Often represents *per* or *to* when used with units of measure or to indicate the terms of a ratio.

9 ft/sec

risk/reward trade-off

6.   Sets off phonemes and phonemic transcription.

/b/ as in *but*

Capitalization

Capitals are used for two broad purposes in English: they mark a beginning (as of a sentence) and they signal a proper noun, pronoun, or adjective. The following principles, each with examples, describe the most common uses of capital letters.

Beginnings

1. The first word of a sentence or sentence fragment is capitalized.

> The play lasted nearly three hours.
>
> How are you feeling?
>
> Bravo!

2. The first word of a sentence contained within parentheses is capitalized if it does not occur within another sentence. The first word of a parenthetical sentence within another sentence is not capitalized.

> The discussion was held in the boardroom. (The results are still confidential.)
>
> Although we liked the restaurant (their Italian food was the best), we seldom ate there.
>
> After waiting in line for an hour (why do we do these things?), we finally left.

3. The first word of a direct quotation is capitalized. However, if the quotation is interrupted in the middle of a sentence, the second part does not begin with a capital. When a quotation, whether a sentence fragment or a complete sentence, is syntactically dependent on the sentence in which it occurs, the quotation does not begin with a capital.

> The President said, "We have rejected this report entirely."
>
> "We have rejected this report entirely," the President said, "and we will not comment on it further."
>
> The President made it clear that "there is no room for compromise."

4. The first word of a sentence within a sentence is usually capitalized when it represents a direct question, a motto or aphorism, or spoken or unspoken dialogue. The first word following a colon may be either lowercased or capitalized if it introduces a complete sentence. While the former is more usual, the latter is common when the sentence is fairly lengthy and distinctly separate from the preceding clause.

> The question, as Disraeli said, is this: Is man an ape or an angel?
>
> My first thought was, How can I avoid this assignment?
>
> The advantage of this particular system is clear: it's inexpensive.
>
> The situation is critical: This company cannot hope to recoup the fourth-quarter losses that were sustained in five operating divisions.

5. The first word of a line of poetry is traditionally capitalized; however, in much twentieth-century poetry the line beginnings are lowercased.

> The best lack all conviction, while the worst
> Are full of passionate intensity.
> —W. B. Yeats

6. The first words of run-in enumerations that form complete sentences are capitalized, as are usually the first words of vertical lists and enumerations. However, enumerations of words or phrases run in with the introductory text are generally lowercased.

> Do the following tasks at the end of the day:
> 1. Clear your desktop of papers. 2. Cover office machines. 3. Straighten the contents of your desk drawers, cabinets, and bookcases.
>
> This is the agenda:
> Call to order
> Roll call
> Minutes of the previous meeting
> Treasurer's report
>
> On the agenda will be (1) call to order, (2) roll call, (3) minutes of the previous meeting, (4) treasurer's report. . . .

7. The first word in an outline heading is capitalized.

> I. Editorial tasks
> II. Production responsibilities
>   A. Cost estimates
>   B. Bids

8. The first word of the salutation of a letter and the first word of a complimentary close are capitalized.

> Dear Mary,
>
> Ladies and Gentlemen:
>
> Sincerely yours,

Proper Nouns, Pronouns, and Adjectives

Capitals are used with almost all proper nouns—that is, nouns that name particular persons, places, or things (including abstract entities), distinguishing them from others of the same class—and proper adjectives—that is, adjectives that take their meaning from what is named by the proper noun. The essential distinction in the use of capitals and lowercase letters at the beginnings of words lies in this individualizing significance of capitals as against the generalizing significance of lowercase. The following subject headings are in alphabetical order.

ARMED FORCES

1.   Branches and units of the armed forces are capitalized, as are easily recognized short forms of full branch and unit designations. However, the words *army, navy,* etc., are lowercased when used in their plural forms or when they are not part of an official title.

> United States Army
>
> a contract with the Army
>
> Corps of Engineers
>
> a bridge built by the Engineers
>
> allied armies

AWARDS

2.   Names of awards and prizes are capitalized.

> the Nobel Prize in Chemistry
>
> Distinguished Service Cross
>
> Academy Award

DERIVATIVES OF PROPER NAMES

3.   Derivatives of proper names are capitalized when used in their primary sense. However, if the derived term has taken on a specialized meaning, it is usually not capitalized.

> Roman customs
>
> Shakespearean comedies
>
> Edwardian era
>
> > *but*
>
> quixotic
>
> herculean
>
> bohemian tastes

GEOGRAPHICAL REFERENCES

4.   Divisions of the earth's surface and names of distinct areas, regions, places, or districts are capitalized, as are most derivative adjectives and some derivative nouns and verbs.

> The Eastern Hemisphere
>
> Midwest
>
> Tropic of Cancer
>
> Springfield, Massachusetts
>
> the Middle Eastern situation
>
> an Americanism
>
> > *but*
>
> french fries
>
> a japan finish
>
> manila envelope

5.   Popular names of localities are capitalized.

> the Corn Belt   the Loop
>
> The Big Apple   the Gold Coast
>
> the Pacific Rim

6.   Words designating global, national, regional, or local political divisions are capitalized when they are essential elements of specific names. However, they are usually lowercased when they precede a proper name or stand alone. (In legal documents, these words are often capitalized regardless of position.)

> the British Empire   Washington State
>
> New York City   Ward 1
>
> > *but*
>
> the fall of the empire   the state of Washington
>
> the city of New York   fires in three wards

7.   Generic geographical terms (such as *lake, mountain, river, valley*) are capitalized if they are part of a specific proper name.

> Hudson Bay   Long Island
>
> Niagara Falls   Crater Lake
>
> the Shenandoah Valley

8.   Generic terms preceding names are usually capitalized.

> Lakes Michigan and Superior
>
> Mounts Whitney and Rainier

9.   Generic terms following names are usually lowercased, as are singular or plural generic terms that are used descriptively or alone.

> the Himalaya and Andes mountains
>
> the Atlantic coast of Labrador
>
> the Hudson valley
>
> the river valley
>
> the valley

10.   Compass points are capitalized when they refer to a geographical region or when they are part of a street name, but they are lowercased when they refer to simple direction.

> up North
>
> back East
>
> the Northwest
>
> West Columbus Avenue
>
> Park Avenue South
>
> > *but*
>
> west of the Rockies
>
> the east coast of Florida

11.   Adjectives derived from compass points and nouns designating the inhabitants of some geographical regions are capitalized. When in doubt, see the entry in the dictionary.

> a Southern accent
>
> Northerners

12.   Terms designating public places are capitalized if they are part of a proper name.

> Brooklyn Bridge
>
> Lincoln Park
>
> the St. Regis Hotel
>
> Independence Hall
>
> > *but*

Wisconsin and Connecticut avenues

the Plaza and St. Regis hotels

GOVERNMENTAL AND JUDICIAL BODIES

13. Full names of legislative, deliberative, executive, and administrative bodies are capitalized, as are short forms of these names. However, nonspecific noun and adjective references to them are usually lowercased.

the U.S. House of Representatives

the House

the Federal Bureau of Investigation

but

both houses of Congress

a federal agency

14. Names of international courts, the U.S. Supreme Court, and other higher courts are capitalized. However, names of city and county courts are usually lowercased.

The International Court of Arbitration

the Supreme Court of the United States

the Supreme Court

the United States Court of Appeals for the Second Circuit

the Michigan Court of Appeals

Lawton municipal court

Newark night court

HISTORICAL PERIODS AND EVENTS

15. Names of congresses, councils, and expositions are capitalized.

the Yalta Conference

the Republican National Convention

16. Names of historical events, some historical periods, and some cultural periods and movements are capitalized. When in doubt, consult the entry in the dictionary, especially for periods.

the Boston Tea Party

the Renaissance

Prohibition

the Augustan Age

the Enlightenment

but

the space age

neoclassicism

17. Numerical designations of historical time periods are capitalized when they are part of a proper name; otherwise they are lowercased.

the Third Reich

the Roaring Twenties

but

the eighteenth century

the eighties

18. Names of treaties, laws, and acts are capitalized.

Treaty of Versailles

The Clean Air Act of 1990

ORGANIZATIONS

19. Names of firms, corporations, schools, and organizations and their members are capitalized. However, common nouns occurring after the names of two or more organizations are lowercased. The word *the* at the beginning of such names is only capitalized when the full legal name is used.

Thunder's Mouth Press

University of Wisconsin

European Community

Rotary International

Kiwanians

American and United airlines

20. Words such as *group, division, department, office,* or *agency* that designate a corporate and organizational unit are capitalized only when used with its specific name.

in the Editorial Department of Merriam-Webster

but

a notice to all department heads

PEOPLE

21. Names of persons are capitalized. However, the capitalization of particles such as *de, della, der, du, l', la, ten,* and *van* varies widely, especially in names of people in English-speaking countries.

Noah Webster

W.E.B. Du Bois

Daphne du Maurier

Wernher von Braun

Anthony Van Dyck

22. Titles preceding the name of a person and epithets used instead of a name are capitalized. However, titles following a name or used alone are usually lowercased.

President Roosevelt

Professor Kaiser

Queen Elizabeth

Old Hickory

the Iron Chancellor

but

Henry VIII, king of England

23. Corporate titles are capitalized when used with an individual's name; otherwise, they are lowercased.

Lisa Dominguez, Vice President

The sales manager called me.

24. Words of family relationship preceding or used in place of a person's name are capitalized; however, these words are lowercased if they are part of a noun phrase used in place of a name.

Cousin Julia

I know when Mother's birthday is.

but

I know when my mother's birthday is.

25. Words designating peoples, nationalities, religious groups, tribes, races, and languages are capitalized. Other terms used to refer to groups of people are often lowercased. Designations based on color are usually lowercased.

Canadians	Iroquois
Ibo	African-American
Latin	Indo-European
highlander (an inhabitant of a highland)	
Highlander (an inhabitant of the Highlands of Scotland)	
black	white

PERSONIFICATIONS

26. Personifications are capitalized.

> She dwells with Beauty—Beauty that must die;
> And Joy, whose hand is ever at his lips
> Bidding adieu.
> —John Keats

obey the commands of Nature

PRONOUNS

27. The pronoun I is capitalized. For pronouns referring to the Deity, see rule 29 below.

. . . no one but I myself had yet printed any of my work.—Paul Bowles

RELIGIOUS TERMS

28. Words designating the Deity are capitalized.

An anthropomorphic, vengeful Jehovah became a spiritual, benevolent Supreme Being.—A.R. Katz

29. Personal pronouns referring to the Deity are usually capitalized, even when they closely follow their antecedent. However, many writers never capitalize such pronouns.

> All Thy works, O Lord, shall bless Thee.
> —*Oxford American Hymnal*

> God's in his heaven—
> All's right with the world!
> —Robert Browning

30. Traditional designations of revered persons, such as prophets, apostles, and saints, are often capitalized.

our Lady

the Prophet

the Lawgiver

31. Names of religions, creeds and confessions, denominations, and religious orders are capitalized, as is the word *Church* when used as part of a proper name.

Judaism

Apostles' Creed

the Thirty-nine Articles of the Church of England

Society of Jesus

Hunt Memorial Church

but

the local Baptist church

32. Names for the Bible or parts, versions, or editions of it and names of other sacred books are capitalized but not itali-cized. Adjectives derived from the names of sacred books are irregularly capitalized or lowercased; when in doubt, see the entry in the dictionary.

Authorized Version	New English Bible
Old Testament	Pentateuch
Apocrypha	Gospel of Saint Mark
Talmud	Koran
biblical	Koranic

SCIENTIFIC TERMS

33. Names of planets and their satellites, asteroids, stars, constellations and groups of stars, and other unique celestial objects are capitalized. However, the words *sun, earth,* and *moon* are usually lowercased unless they occur with other astronomical names.

Venus	Ganymede
Sirius	the Pleiades
the Milky Way	
enjoying the beauty of the moon	
probes heading for the Moon and Mars	

34. New Latin genus names in zoology and botany are capitalized; the second term in binomial scientific names, identifying the species, is not.

a cabbage butterfly (*Pieris rapae*)

a common buttercup (*Ranunculus acris*)

35. New Latin names of all groups above genus in zoology and botany (such as class or family) are capitalized; however, their derivative adjectives and nouns are not.

Gastropoda	*but*	gastropod
Mantidae	*but*	mantid

36. Names of geological eras, periods, epochs, and strata and names of prehistoric divisions are capitalized.

Silurian period	Pleistocene epoch
Age of Reptiles	Neolithic age

SEASONS, MONTHS, DAYS

37. Names of months, days of the week, and holidays and holy days are capitalized.

January	Ramadan
Tuesday	Thanksgiving
Yom Kippur	Easter

38. Names of seasons are not capitalized except when personified.

last spring

the sweet breath of Spring

TITLES OF PRINTED MATTER AND WORKS OF ART

39. Words in titles are capitalized, with the exception of internal conjunctions, prepositions, and articles. In some publications, prepositions of five or more letters are capitalized also.

Of Mice and Men

"The Man Who Would Be King"

"To His Coy Mistress"

Slouching Towards Bethlehem

40. Capitalization of the titles of movies, plays, paintings, sculpture, and musical compositions follow similar conventions. For more details, see the Italicization section below.

41. Major sections of books, long articles, or reports are capitalized when they are referred to within the same material.

> See the Appendix for further information.

> The Introduction explains the scope of this book.

> discussed later in Chapter 4

42. Nouns used with numbers or letters to designate major reference headings are capitalized. Nouns designating minor elements are typically lowercased.

Volume V   Table 3
page 101   note 10

TRADEMARKS

43. Registered trademarks and service marks are capitalized.

Express Mail   Orlon

Kleenex   Walkman

VEHICLES

44. Names of ships, aircraft, and spacecraft are capitalized.

> *Titanic*

> Lindbergh's *Spirit of St. Louis*

> *Apollo 13*

Italicization

The following are usually italicized in print and underlined in manuscript and typescript.

1.   Words and passages that are to be emphasized.

> This was their fatal error: there *was* no cache of supplies in the now-abandoned depot.

2.   Titles of books, magazines, newspapers, plays, long poems, movies, paintings, sculpture, and long musical compositions (but not musical compositions identified by the name of their genre).

> Dickens's *Bleak House*
>
> *National Geographic*
>
> *Christian Science Monitor*
>
> Shakespeare's *Othello*
>
> Eliot's *The Waste Land*
>
> the movie *Back to the Future*
>
> Gainsborough's *Blue Boy*
>
> Mozart's *Don Giovanni*
>
> > *but*
>
> Schubert's Sonata in B-flat Major, D. 960

NOTE: In the plurals of such italicized titles, the *s* or *es* endings are usually in roman type.

> hidden under a stack of *New Yorker*s

3.   Names of ships, aircraft, and spacecraft.

> *Titanic*
>
> Lindbergh's *Spirit of St. Louis*
>
> *Apollo 13*

4.   Words, letters, and figures when referred to as such.

> The *g* in *align* is silent.
>
> The first *2* and the last *0* are barely legible.

5.   Unfamiliar words when first introduced and defined in a text.

> Heart failure is often accompanied by *edema,* an accumulation of fluid which tends to produce swelling of the lower extremities.

6.   Foreign words and phrases that have not been naturalized in English. In general, any word entered in the main A–Z vocabulary of this dictionary need not be italicized.

> *c'est la vie*
>
> *aere perennius*
>
> *che sarà, sarà*
>
> *sans peur et sans reproche*
>
> > *but*
>
> pasta   ad hoc   ex officio

7.   New Latin scientific names of genera, species, subspecies, races, and varieties (but not groups of higher rank, such as phyla, classes, or orders) in botanical or zoological names.

> a thick-shelled American clam *(Mercenaria mercenaria)*
>
> a mallard *(Anas platyrhynchos)*
>
> > *but*
>
> the family Hominidae

8.   Case titles in legal citations, both in full and shortened form; "v." for "versus" is set in either roman or italic.

> *Jones* v. *Ohio*
>
> *Smith et al* v. *Jones*
>
> the *Jones* case
>
> *Jones*

Documentation of Sources

Writers and editors use various methods to indicate the source of a quotation or piece of information borrowed from another work. In works published for the general public and traditionally in scholarly works in the humanities, footnotes or endnotes have been preferred. In this system, sequential numbers within the text refer the reader to notes at the bottom of the page or at the end of the article, chapter, or book; these notes contain full bibliographical information on the works cited. In scholarly works in the social and natural sciences, and increasingly in the humanities as well, parenthetical references within the text refer the reader to an alphabetically arranged list of sources at the end of the work. The system of footnotes or endnotes is the more flexible, in that it allows for commentary on the work or subject and can also be used for brief peripheral discussions not tied to any specific work. However, style manuals tend to encourage the use of parenthetical references in addition to or instead of footnotes or endnotes, since for most kinds of material they are efficient and convenient for both writer and reader. In a carefully documented work, a bibliography or list of sources normally follows the entire text (including any endnotes) regardless of which system is used.

Though different publishers and journals have adopted slightly varying styles, the following examples illustrate standard styles for references, notes, and bibliographic entries. For more extensive treatment than can be provided here, *Merriam-Webster's Standard American Style Manual, The Chicago Manual of Style, The MLA Style Manual,* or the *Publication Manual of the American Psychological Association* may be consulted.

Footnotes and Endnotes

Footnotes and endnotes are indicated by superscript Arabic numerals placed immediately after the material to be documented. The numbering is consecutive throughout an article or monograph; in a book, it usually starts over with each new chapter or section. Footnotes appear at the bottom of the page; endnotes, which take the same form as footnotes, are gathered at the end of the article, chapter, or book. Endnotes are generally preferred over footnotes by writers and publishers because they are easier to handle when preparing both manuscript and printed pages, though they can be less convenient for the reader. All of the examples shown reflect humanities citation style. All of the cited works appear again in the Lists of Sources section below.

Books

One author
[1]Elizabeth Bishop, *The Complete Poems: 1927–1979* (New York: Farrar, Straus & Giroux, 1983), 46.

Two or more authors
[2]Bert Holldobler and Edward O. Wilson, *The Ants* (Cambridge, Mass.: Belknap–Harvard Univ. Press, 1990), 119.

[3]Randolph Quirk et al., *A Comprehensive Grammar of the English Language* (London: Longman, 1985), 135.

Edition and/or translation
[4]Arthur S. Banks, ed., *Political Handbook of the World: 1992* (Binghamton, N.Y.: CSA Publications, 1992), 293–95.

[5]Simone de Beauvoir, *The Second Sex,* trans. and ed. H. M. Parshley (New York: Knopf, 1953; Random House, 1974), 446.

Second or later edition
[6]Albert C. Baugh and Thomas Cable, *A History of the English Language,* 3d ed. (Englewood Cliffs, N.J.: Prentice Hall, 1978), 14.

Article in a collection or festschrift
[7]Ernst Mayr, "Processes of Speciation in Animals," in *Mechanisms of Speciation,* ed. C. Barigozzi (New York: Alan R. Liss, 1982), 1–3.

Work in two or more volumes
[8]Ronald M. Nowak, *Walker's Mammals of the World,* 5th ed. (Baltimore: Johns Hopkins Univ. Press, 1991), 2:661.

Corporate author	[9]Commission on the Humanities, *The Humanities in American Life* (Berkeley: Univ. of California Press, 1980), 46.
Book lacking publication data	[10]*Photographic View Album of Cambridge* [England], n.p., n.d., n.pag.
Subsequent reference	[11]Baugh and Cable, 18–19.

Articles

Journal paginated consecutively throughout annual volume	[12]Stephen Jay Gould and Niles Eldredge, "Punctuated Equilibria: The Tempo and Mode of Evolution Reconsidered," *Paleobiology* 3 (1977): 121.
Journal paginated consecutively only within each issue	[13]Roseann Duenas Gonzalez, "Teaching Mexican American Students to Write: Capitalizing on the Culture," *English Journal* 71.7 (Nov. 1982): 22–24.
Monthly magazine	[14]John Lukacs, "The End of the Twentieth Century," *Harper's,* Jan. 1993: 40.
Weekly magazine	[15]Richard Preston, "A Reporter at Large: Crisis in the Hot Zone," *New Yorker,* 26 Oct. 1992: 58.
Newspaper	[16]William J. Broad, "Big Science Squeezes Small-Scale Researchers," *New York Times,* 29 Dec. 1992: C1.
Signed review	[17]George Steiner, review of *Oeuvres en Prose Complètes, Tome 3,* by Charles Péguy, *Times Literary Supplement,* 25 Dec. 1992: 3.

Parenthetical References

Parenthetical references are highly abbreviated bibliographical citations that appear within the text itself, enclosed in parentheses. Such references direct the reader to a detailed bibliography or list of sources at the end of the work, often removing the need for footnotes or endnotes. The parenthetical references usually include only the author's last name and a page reference. (In the social and natural sciences, the year of publication is included after the author's name, and the page number is often omitted.) Any element of the reference that is clear from the context may be omitted. To distinguish among cited works published by the same author, the author's name may be followed by the specific work's title, which is usually shortened. (If the author-date system is being used, a lowercase letter can be added after the year—e.g., 1992a, 1992b—to distinguish between works published in the same year.) Each of the following references is keyed to an entry in the Lists of Sources section below.

Humanities style	(Quirk et al., 135) (Baugh and Cable, *History,* 14) (Commission on the Humanities, 46)
Sciences style	(Mayr 1982, 1–3) (Nowak 1991, 2:661) (Gould and Eldredge 1977)

Lists of Sources

A bibliography or list of sources in alphabetical order usually appears at the end of the work. The following lists of cited works illustrate standard styles employed in, respectively, the humanities and the social and natural sciences. The principal differences between the two styles are these. In the sciences, (1) an initial is generally used instead of the author's first name, (2) the date is placed directly after the author's name, (3) all words in titles are lowercased except the first word and the first word of any subtitle as well as proper nouns and adjectives, and (4) article titles are not set off by quotation marks. (In some scientific publications, book and journal titles are not italicized.)

Humanities style

Baugh, Albert C., and Thomas Cable. *A History of the English Language.* 3d ed. Englewood Cliffs, N.J.: Prentice Hall, 1978.

Beauvoir, Simone de. *The Second Sex.* Trans. and ed. H. M. Parshley. New York: Alfred A. Knopf, 1953. Reprint. New York: Random House, 1974.

Bishop, Elizabeth. *The Complete Poems: 1927–1979.* New York: Farrar, Straus & Giroux, 1983.

Commission on the Humanities. *The Humanities in American Life.* Berkeley: University of California Press, 1980.

Gonzalez, Roseann Duenas. "Teaching Mexican American Students to Write: Capitalizing on the Culture." *English Journal* 71.7 (November 1982): 22–24.

Lukacs, John. "The End of the Twentieth Century." *Harper's,* January 1993: 39–58.

Photographic View Album of Cambridge [England]. N.d., n.p., n. pag.

Quirk, Randolph, Sidney Greenbaum, Geoffrey Leech, and Jan Svartvik. *A Comprehensive Grammar of the English Language.* London: Longman, 1985.

Steiner, George. Review of *Oeuvres en Prose Complètes, Tome 3,* by Charles Péguy. *Times Literary Supplement,* 25 December 1992: 3–4.

Sciences style

Banks, A. S., ed. 1992. *Political handbook of the world: 1992.* Binghamton, N.Y.: CSA Publications.

Broad, W. J. 1992. Big science squeezes small-scale researchers. *New York Times,* 29 Dec.: C1+.

Gould, S. J., and N. Eldredge. 1977. Punctuated equilibria: The tempo and mode of evolution reconsidered. *Paleobiology* 3: 115–151.

Holldobler, B., and E. O. Wilson. 1990. *The ants.* Cambridge, Mass.: Belknap–Harvard Univ. Press.

Mayr, E. 1982. Processes of speciation in animals. In C. Barigozzi, ed., *Mechanisms of speciation.* New York: Alan R. Liss: 1–19.

Nowak, R.M. 1991. *Walker's mammals of the world.* 5th ed. 2 vols. Baltimore: Johns Hopkins Univ. Press.

Preston, R. 1992. A reporter at large: Crisis in the hot zone. *New Yorker,* 26 Oct.: 58–81.

Forms of Address

Since the relationship between correspondents affects the form of address used in letters, no rigid guidelines can be set down for all occasions; however, the following examples show a generally accepted form. When two or more salutations are shown for the same entry, the more formal comes first. In general, male and female names are used alternately. For any given entry, the form of address for the opposite sex can be easily determined. The female equivalent of "Sir" is "Madam" (or "Madame" when the addressee is foreign). The female equivalent of "Mr." when it immediately precedes a name is "Ms." (or "Mrs." or "Miss" if either is known to be preferred by the addressee). The male equivalent of "Madam" standing alone is "Sir." When "Madam" precedes another title, the male equivalent is "Mr." The male equivalent of "Ms." is "Mr."

Addressee	Form of Address	Salutation

Clerical and Religious Orders

Addressee	Form of Address	Salutation
abbot	The Right Reverend John R. Smith, O.S.B. Abbot of ——	Right Reverend and dear Father: Dear Father Abbot: Dear Father:
archbishop	The Most Reverend Archbishop of —— *or* The Most Reverend John R. Smith Archbishop of ——	Your Excellency: (same) Dear Archbishop Smith:
bishop, Catholic	The Most Reverend John R. Smith Bishop of ——	Most Reverend Sir: Your Excellency: Dear Bishop Smith:
bishop, Episcopal	The Right Reverend John R. Smith Bishop of ——	Right Reverend Sir: Dear Bishop Smith:
bishop, Protestant (excluding Episcopal)	The Reverend John R. Smith *or* Bishop John R. Smith	Reverend Sir: Dear Bishop Smith:
brotherhood, Catholic, member of	Brother James, S.J.	Dear Brother James:
brotherhood, Catholic, superior of	Brother Michael, S.J., Superior	Dear Brother Michael:
cardinal	His Eminence John Cardinal Smith	Your Eminence: Dear Cardinal Smith:
clergy, Protestant	The Reverend Amelia R. Smith *or with a doctorate* The Reverend Dr. Amelia R. Smith *or* The Reverend Amelia R. Smith, D.D.	Dear Ms. Smith: *or* Dear Dr. Smith:

Addressee   Form of Address   Salutation

Addressee	Form of Address	Salutation
monsignor	The Reverend Monsignor John R. Smith *or* The Rev. Msgr. John R. Smith	Reverend and dear Monsignor Smith: Dear Monsignor Smith:
patriarch (of an Eastern church)	His Beatitude the Patriarch of ——	Most Reverend Lord: Your Beatitude:
pope	His Holiness Pope —— *or* His Holiness the Pope	Your Holiness: Most Holy Father:
priest	The Reverend John R. Smith *or* The Reverend Father Smith	Reverend Father: Dear Father Smith: Dear Father:
rabbi	Rabbi Amelia R. Smith *or with a doctorate* Rabbi Amelia R. Smith, D.D.	Dear Rabbi Smith: *or* Dear Dr. Smith:
sisterhood, member of	Sister Mary Angelica, S.C.	Dear Sister Mary Angelica: Dear Sister:
sisterhood, superior of	The Reverend Mother Superior, S.C., Superior	Reverend Mother: Dear Reverend Mother:

College and University Officials

Addressee	Form of Address	Salutation
chancellor	Dr. Amelia R. Smith Chancellor	Dear Dr. Smith:
dean	Dean John R. Smith	Dear Dean Smith: Dear Dr. Smith:
president	President Amelia R. Smith *or* Dr. Amelia R. Smith	Dear President Smith: *or* Dear Dr. Smith:
professor, assistant or associate	Mr. John R. Smith Assistant/Associate Professor of —— *or with a doctorate* Dr. John R. Smith Assistant/Associate Professor of ——	Dear Professor Smith: Dear Mr. Smith: *or* Dear Dr. Smith:
professor, full	Professor Amelia R. Smith *or* Dr. Amelia R. Smith	Dear Professor Smith: *or* Dear Dr. Smith:

Diplomats and Consular Officers

Addressee	Form of Address	Salutation
ambassador, American	The Honorable John R. Smith American Ambassador *or if in Canada or Latin America* The Ambassador of the United States of America	Sir: Dear Mr. Ambassador:

Addressee	Form of Address	Salutation
ambassador, foreign	Her Excellency Amelia R. Smith Ambassador of ——	Excellency: Dear Madame Ambassador:
chargé d'affaires, American	John R. Smith, Esq. American Chargé d'Affaires *or if in Canada or Latin America* The United States Chargé d'Affaires	Sir: Dear Mr. Smith:
chargé d'affaires, foreign	Ms. Amelia R. Smith Chargé d'Affaires of ——	Madame: Dear Ms. Smith:
consul, American	The American Consul *or if in Canada or Latin America* The Consul of the United States of America	Sir: Dear Sir:
	or if individual name is known John R. Smith, Esq. American Consul *or if in Canada or Latin America* John R. Smith, Esq. Consul of the United States of America	Sir: Dear Mr. Smith:

consul, foreign	The Consul of ——
	   or if individual name is known
	The Honorable Amelia R. Smith
	—— Consul
	   or
	Consul of ——
		Sir:
		
		Madame:
		Dear Ms. Smith:

secretary-general, U.N.	His Excellency John R. Smith Secretary-General of the United Nations	Excellency: Dear Mr. Secretary-General:

Foreign Heads of State or Government

Addressee	Form of Address	Salutation
premier	Her Excellency Amelia R. Smith Premier of ——	Excellency: Dear Madame Premier:
president	His Excellency John R. Smith President of ——	Excellency: Dear Mr. President:
prime minister	Her Excellency Amelia R. Smith Prime Minister of ——	Excellency: Dear Madame Prime Minister:

Government Officials, Federal

Addressee	Form of Address	Salutation
attorney general	The Honorable John R. Smith Attorney General	Sir: Dear Mr. Attorney General:
cabinet officer (other than attorney general)	The Secretary of —— *or* The Honorable Amelia R. Smith Secretary of ——	Madam: Dear Madam Secretary: Dear Ms. Smith:

Addressee   Form of Address   Salutation

Addressee	Form of Address	Salutation
chair of a committee or subcommittee, U.S. Congress	The Honorable John R. Smith Chairman, Committee on — United States Senate/House of Representatives	Dear Mr. Chairman: Dear Senator/Representative Smith:
commissioner	The Honorable Amelia R. Smith Commissioner	Dear Madam Commissioner: Dear Ms. Smith:
director of an agency	The Honorable John R. Smith Director	Dear Mr. Smith:
judge	The Honorable Amelia R. Smith Judge of the United States District Court of the —— District of ——	Madam: Dear Judge Smith:
president	The President The White House *or* The Honorable John R. Smith President of the United States The White House	Mr. President: Dear Mr. President:
representative, U.S. Congress	The Honorable Amelia R. Smith United States House of Representatives *or for local address* The Honorable Amelia R. Smith Representative in Congress	Madam: Dear Representative Smith: Dear Ms. Smith:
senator, U.S. Senate	The Honorable John R. Smith United States Senator	Sir: Dear Senator Smith:
speaker, U.S. House of Representatives	The Honorable Speaker of the House of Representatives *or* The Honorable Amelia R. Smith Speaker of the House of Representatives	Madam: Dear Madam Speaker: Dear Ms. Smith:
supreme court, associate justice	Mr. Justice Smith The Supreme Court of the United States	Sir: Dear Justice Smith:
supreme court, chief justice	The Chief Justice of the United States The Supreme Court of the United States *or* The Chief Justice The Supreme Court	Madam: Dear Madam Chief Justice:
vice president	The Vice President of the United States United States Senate *or* The Honorable John R. Smith Vice President of the United States	Sir: Dear Mr. Vice President:

Government Officials, State and Local

alderman	— see COUNCIL MEMBER	
assemblyman	— see REPRESENTATIVE, STATE	

Addressee	Form of Address	Salutation
attorney, city (state's)	The Honorable Amelia R. Smith	Dear Ms. Smith:
clerk of a court	John R. Smith, Esq. Clerk of the Court of ——	Dear Mr. Smith:
council member	The Honorable Amelia R. Smith Councilwoman *or* Councilwoman Amelia R. Smith	Dear Ms. Smith: Dear Councilwoman Smith:
county clerk	The Honorable John R. Smith Clerk of —— County	Dear Mr. Smith:
county treasurer	—— see COUNTY CLERK	
delegate	—— see REPRESENTATIVE, STATE	
governor	The Honorable Amelia R. Smith Governor of —— *or in some states* Her Excellency, the Governor of ——	Madam: Dear Governor Smith:
judge, state or local court	The Honorable John R. Smith Judge of the —— Court	Dear Judge Smith:
lieutenant governor	The Honorable Lieutenant Governor of —— *or* The Honorable Amelia R. Smith Lieutenant Governor of ——	Madam: Dear Ms. Smith:
mayor	The Honorable John R. Smith Mayor of ——	Sir: Dear Mayor Smith:
representative, state	The Honorable Amelia R. Smith House of Representatives	Madam: Dear Ms. Smith:
secretary of state	The Honorable Secretary of State of —— *or* The Honorable John R. Smith Secretary of State of ——	Sir: Dear Mr. Secretary:
selectman	—— see COUNCIL MEMBER	
senate, state, president of	The Honorable Amelia R. Smith President of the Senate of the State of ——	Madam: Dear Senator Smith: Dear Ms. Smith:
senator, state	The Honorable John R. Smith The Senate of ——	Sir: Dear Senator Smith: Dear Mr. Smith
speaker, state assembly (house of delegates, house of representatives)	The Honorable Amelia R. Smith Speaker of ——	Madam: Dear Ms. Smith:

Addressee   Form of Address   Salutation

supreme court, state, associate justice	The Honorable John R. Smith Associate Justice of the Supreme Court of ——	Sir: Dear Justice Smith:
supreme court, state, chief justice	The Honorable Amelia R. Smith Chief Justice of the Supreme Court of ——	Madam: Dear Madam Chief Justice:

Military Personnel

The first entry below describes the appropriate form of address for any member of the armed forces. The central column of the subsequent entries shows only the special rank abbreviations used by the different service branches. In actual practice, salutations will differ according to degree of formality. The most formal will often employ the addressee's full title (as shown in the left column). The salutations listed below generally represent a level of formality between the highly formal and the familiar.

all ranks	*full or abbreviated rank* + *full name* + *comma* + *abbreviation for branch of service* (USA, USN, USAF, USMC, USCG) *Example:* First Lieutenant John R. Smith, USAF *or* 1LT John R. Smith, USAF	Dear Lieutenant Smith:
Admiral	*Navy, Coast Guard:* ADM	Dear Admiral Smith:
Fleet Admiral	*Navy:* FADM	(same)
Rear Admiral	*Navy, Coast Guard:* RADM	(same)
Vice Admiral	*Navy, Coast Guard:* VADM	(same)
Airman	*Air Force:* Amn	Dear Airman Smith:
Airman First Class	*Air Force:* A1C	(same)
Airman Basic	*Air Force:* AB	(same)
Captain	*Army:* CPT; *Navy, Coast Guard:* CAPT; *Air Force, Marine Corps:* Capt	Dear Captain Smith:
Colonel	*Army:* COL; *Air Force, Marine Corps:* Col	Dear Colonel Smith:
Lieutenant Colonel	*Army:* LTC; *Air Force, Marine Corps:* LtCol	(same)
Commander	*Navy, Coast Guard:* CDR	Dear Commander Smith:
Lieutenant Commander	*Navy, Coast Guard:* LCDR	(same)
Corporal	*Army:* CPL; *Marine Corps:* Cpl	Dear Corporal Smith:
Lance Corporal	*Marine Corps:* LCpl	(same)
Ensign	*Navy, Coast Guard:* ENS	Dear Ensign Smith:

Addressee	Form of Address	Salutation
General	*Army:* GEN; *Air Force, Marine Corps:* Gen	Dear General Smith:
Lieutenant General	*Army:* LTG; *Air Force, Marine Corps:* LtGen	(same)
Major General	*Army:* MG; *Air Force, Marine Corps:* MajGen	(same)
Brigadier General	*Army:* BG; *Air Force:* BGen; *Marine Corps:* BrigGen	(same)
Lieutenant	*Navy, Coast Guard:* LT	Dear Lieutenant Smith:
First Lieutenant	*Army:* 1LT; *Air Force, Marine Corps:* 1stLt	(same)
Second Lieutenant	*Army:* 2LT; *Air Force, Marine Corps:* 2ndLt	(same)
Lieutenant Junior Grade	*Navy, Coast Guard:* LTJG	Dear Mr./Ms. Smith:
Major	*Army:* MAJ; *Air Force, Marine Corps:* Maj	Dear Major Smith:
Petty Officer (1st, 2nd, 3rd Class)	*Navy, Coast Guard:* PO1, PO2, PO3	Dear Petty Officer Smith:
Chief Petty Officer	*Navy, Coast Guard:* CPO	Dear Chief Smith:
Master Chief Petty Officer	*Navy, Coast Guard:* MCPO	Dear Master Chief Smith:
Senior Chief Petty Officer	*Navy, Coast Guard:* SCPO	Dear Senior Chief Smith:
Private	*Army:* PVT; *Marine Corps:* Pvt	Dear Private Smith:
Private First Class	*Army, Marine Corps:* PFC	(same)
Seaman	*Navy, Coast Guard:* Seaman	Dear Seaman Smith:
Seaman Apprentice	*Navy, Coast Guard:* SA	(same)
Seaman Recruit	*Navy, Coast Guard:* SR	(same)
Sergeant	*Army:* SGT; *Air Force, Marine Corps:* Sgt	Dear Sergeant Smith:
Sergeant Major	*Army:* SGM; *Marine Corps:* SgtMaj	Dear Sergeant Major Smith:
Sergeant Major of the Army	*Army:* SMA	(same)
Sergeant Major of the Marine Corps	*Marine Corps:* SgtMaj	(same)
Command Sergeant Major	*Army:* CSM	(same)
Master Sergeant	*Army:* MSG; *Air Force, Marine Corps:* MSgt	Dear Sergeant Smith
Chief Master Sergeant	*Air Force:* CMSgt	(same)

Addressee	Form of Address	Salutation
Chief Master Sergeant of the Air Force	*Air Force:* CMSAF	(same)
Sergeant First Class	*Army:* SFC	(same)
First Sergeant	*Army:* 1SG; *Marine Corps:* 1stSgt	(same)
Staff Sergeant	*Army:* SSG; *Air Force, Marine Corps:* SSgt	(same)
Technical Sergeant	*Air Force:* TSgt	(same)
Gunnery Sergeant	*Marine Corps:* GySgt	(same)
Master Gunnery Sergeant	*Marine Corps:* MGySgt	(same)
Specialist	*Army:* SPC	Dear Specialist Smith:
Warrant Officer	*Army:* WO1, WO2; *Navy:* WO-1; *Air Force, Marine Corps:* WO	Dear Warrant Officer Smith:
Chief Warrant Officer	*Army:* CW2, CW3, CW4, CW5; *Navy, Coast Guard, Air Force:* CWO-2, CWO-3, CWO-4; *Marine Corps:* CWO2, CWO3, CWO4	Dear Chief Warrant Officer Smith:

Miscellaneous Professional Ranks and Titles

attorney	Mr. John R. Smith Attorney-at-Law *or* John R. Smith, Esq.	Dear Mr. Smith:
certified public accountant	Amelia R. Smith, C.P.A.	Dear Ms. Smith:
dentist	John R. Smith, D.D.S. (*or* D.M.D.) (office address) *or* Dr. John R. Smith (home address)	Dear Dr. Smith:
physician	Amelia R. Smith, M.D. (office address) *or* Dr. Amelia R. Smith (home address)	Dear Dr. Smith:
veterinarian	John R. Smith, D.V.M. (office address) *or* Dr. John R. Smith (home address)	Dear Dr. Smith:

Index